Merriam-Webster's
Encyclopedia
of
Literature

Merriam-Webster's
Encyclopedia
of
Literature

Merriam-Webster, Incorporated, Publishers
Springfield, Massachusetts

A GENUINE MERRIAM-WEBSTER

The name *Webster* alone is no guarantee of excellence. It is used by a number of publishers and may serve mainly to mislead an unwary buyer.

Merriam-Webster™ is the name you should look for when you consider the purchase of dictionaries or other fine reference books. It carries the reputation of a company that has been publishing since 1831 and is your assurance of quality and authority.

Library of Congress Cataloging-in-Publication Data
Main entry under title:

Merriam-Webster's encyclopedia of literature.
     p.   cm.
   ISBN 0-87779-042-6
   1. Literature—Dictionaries.   I. Merriam-Webster, Inc.
  PN41.M42   1995
  803—dc20   94-42741
                                       CIP

Made in the United States of America

2345HC979695

Contents

Preface

It is through the naming of objects, the telling of stories, and the singing of songs that we know ourselves and others. Whether trickster tales or nursery rhymes are the first things we remember hearing, we have learned how to live our lives by means of narrative—the stories our mothers told us, the books our brothers and sisters read to us (and the volumes we chose to read to them), the holy books and textbooks we memorized as children and still recall with perfect clarity. By these means we develop—however weakly or strongly—our moral natures; we discover who we are and who we are not, what we would give anything to be and precisely what we would be willing to sacrifice to gain that prize. We need stories and songs to live fully.

Reference books are one of the most efficient means we have of organizing what we know. The most useful reference book on literature will help us find biographical data on the greatest writers of all places and all periods and on less-well-known contemporary writers, too. It will remind us of the plots of favorite folktales as well as inform us of the significance of an epic novel. It will introduce us to major literary characters, explain the meaning of a literary term, and describe the significance of a literary style or movement. It will permit us to quickly review a mode of criticism and tell us precisely what the adjectival form of an author's name is meant to convey. If, in addition, it includes an etymology and gives us a clue about how to pronounce the subject at hand, then we have a satisfying book, a true companion.

It is at this sort of comprehensive coverage of the literatures of the world that the present work aims. *Merriam-Webster's Encyclopedia of Literature* merges the lexical work for which Merriam-Webster dictionaries have long been known—defining, pronunciation, and etymology—with the extensive and varied yet rigorously edited and verified information that typifies *Encyclopædia Britannica*. The editorial staff of this volume includes members of both organizations. Together they have created a singular—and they hope singularly useful—product.

Those Merriam-Webster editors who helped produce this volume include James L. Rader, who prepared the etymologies; Brian M. Sietsema, who prepared the pronunciations; Joanne M. Despres, Madeline L. Novak, and Stephen J. Perrault, who reviewed the final copy; and Gloria J. Afflitto, Jennifer N. Cislo, Ruth W. Gaines, Jennifer S. Goss, Maria A. Sansalone, and Katherine C. Sietsema, who provided production assistance. Encyclopædia Britannica staff members who were instrumental in the project include editors Mary Rose McCudden and Anita Wolff; members of the Encyclopædia Britannica production staff, particularly Ellen Finkelstein, Ann Belaski, and Maria Ottolino; picture editor Amy G. Segelbaum; page makeup operator Griselda Cháidez; and Marilyn Barton and Stephanie Green of production control. Additional services were provided by Vincent Star and Stephen Bosco in computer services; Melvin Stagner, Mimi Srodon, Sylvia Wallace, and Marsha Mackenzie, who helped in production planning; Terry Passaro and Shantha Uddin, who provided library assistance; and Velia Palomar and Sandra Langeneckert, who helped with administrative details.

Many others helped in writing, compiling, editing, copyediting, proofreading, and other stages of production. Their additional support was invaluable. They are (in alphabetical order): Zachary M. Baker, Michael Born, Jr., James P. Carnes, Mary W. Cornog, Dennis Flaherty, David W. Foster, Amanda E. Fuller, Lisa Grayson, Dale H. Hoiberg, Lisa Jacobson, Sharon Johnson, Graziano E. Krätli, John Krom, Jr., Robert Lewis, John Litweiler, the late Adam G. Liu, John Mathews, Tom Michael, Frederick C. Mish, Stephanie Motz, Frank Nipp, Fukiko Ogisu, Paula Peterson, Diana M. Pitstick, Kenneth Pletcher, Naomi Polonsky, Robert Rauch, Cindy Rutz, Marco Sampaolo, Fran Sherman, Beverly Sorkin, Christine Sullivan, Amy Tikkanen, Judith West, Lee Anne Wiggins, and Janice M. Wolff.

The plan for this book was conceived by Robert McHenry, Editor in Chief of Encyclopædia Britannica, and John M. Morse, Executive Editor of Merriam-Webster. The plan was refined and improved through the review and comments of Mark A. Stevens, Senior Editor, General Reference of Merriam-Webster, and Joseph J. Esposito, President and Publisher of Encyclopædia Britannica North America, who provided generous support and guidance throughout the project.

Kathleen Kuiper
Editor

Explanatory Notes

This book contains entries for authors, works, literary landmarks, literary and critical terms, mythological and folkloric figures, fictional characters, literary movements and prizes, and other miscellaneous matters. For the most part the presentation of information in these entries requires little explanation, but the following notes will assist the reader.

Entry names.

1. *Boldface entry selection.* In general, biographical entries are listed under the family name, when there is one. Exceptions to the family-name rule are pseudonyms, some non-English-language names, and subjects lacking family names or better known by what we would now call their prenames. Writers who are better known to readers by the pseudonym under which they published are found at the pseudonym. Thus, the writer Eric Blair, better known to readers by his pseudonym, is listed under **Orwell**, George. Writers who are better known by prename are so listed. Dante Alighieri and Michelangelo di Buonarroti Simoni, for example, are listed at **Dante** and **Michelangelo**, respectively. Subjects lacking family names, including those whose surnames are not family names, are generally entered at the given names by which they are known in English. Christine de Pisan is entered at **Christine**.

2. *Non-English-language names.* In virtually all cases, vernacular usage has governed spelling. For languages not written in the Roman alphabet, the following conventions have been adopted:

Russian and other nonromanized languages have been transcribed using the systems followed in the *Encyclopædia Britannica.*

Chinese names (except for persons identified with the Nationalist movement or regime) are romanized and alphabetized under the Pinyin rather than Wades-Giles system, but cross-references are consistently provided at the Wade-Giles version.

In Japanese and Korean names, with few exceptions, the distinction between family and personal names is observed. (Note that in those languages normal name order places the family name first; hence in this dictionary no comma appears between family and personal name as it does in an inverted English name—as, for example, Ōe Kenzaburō). Hungarian names, which also follow family-personal name order, are, on the other hand, treated as English names and the comma is used.

Alphabetization.

Alphabetization is letter-by-letter, not word-by-word. Thus **belles lettres** falls between **Bellerophon** and **Bell for Adano**. The order of entries is determined by ordinary rules of alphabetization applied to the boldface entry names and by the following additional rules:

Diacritical marks, marks of punctuation, and spaces within the boldface names are ignored, as are roman numerals.

Names beginning with M', Mac, or Mc are alphabetized according to their spelling.

Titles of works.

For ease of use, titles of works that are given individual treatment are usually entered at a conventional shortened form of the title, often a character's name (as **Humphry Clinker**), with the full title following in parentheses (*in full* The Expedition of Humphry Clinker). In general, non-English-language works are entered at their English-language titles (as in **Human Comedy** rather than **Comédie humaine**). In virtually all cases, titles are not inverted. **Book of the Dun Cow** is entered at Book.

Cross-references.

Cross-references are indicated by small capitals. Because a one-volume work of this type affords the reader easy access to any entry, cross-references have been used sparingly—except for Wades-Giles transliterations of Chinese names (which in this book have been entered at their Pinyin spelling). Biographies of writers known for their participation in a particular movement or their use of a particular style will mention those details, but often will not contain a cross-reference to the movement or style. It is assumed that the reader who desires more information about the movement or style will look at that entry without the editor's direction. Cross-references in this book are employed chiefly to lead the reader to further information on his or her subject of immediate inquiry. Although the book enters the article **Harlem Renaissance** and the movement is mentioned in the Zora Neale **Hurston** entry, Harlem Renaissance—because it gives no new information on Hurston—is not mentioned in small capitals in the Hurston entry.

Dates in text.

In general, dates following the titles of works indicate the date of first publication. The date following mention of a foreign-language title is the year in which the book was first published in the original language. The dates following play titles should be assumed to refer to the dates of original publication unless otherwise indicated. The Edward **Albee** entry, for example, lists *Who's Afraid of Virginia Woolf?* (1962) and *Three Tall Women* (produced 1991).

Translations in text.

For non-English-language works, the date of publication is usually followed by a translation (if the title is not an obvious cognate or a proper name) in roman type. Translations that appear within quotation marks are approximate renderings. Italicized titles within parentheses indicate that the work has been published in English. In the Czesław **Miłosz** entry, for example, one of his untranslated volumes is treated in this manner: *Poemat o czasie zastygłym* ("Poem of Frozen Time"). A collection of Miłosz's essays that has been translated into English is treated in the following manner: *Zniewolony umysł* (1953; *The Captive Mind*). In this example, 1953 indicates the date of publication of the original Polish text and *The Captive Mind* is the English-language version. Of course, the title of the English-language version may not be a literal rendering of the original title.

Etymologies.

Etymologies in this book are meant to provide historical and philological background for the terminology of literary studies. The book provides etymologies for common nouns, such as names of genres, verse forms, and movements, and for some proper nouns, such as schools of criticism. However, for most proper nouns, such as personal or geographical names or titles of works, etymologies have not been given. Etymologies are also not provided for terms whose literary significance depends on a more general sense of a word (for example, **icon**), or for terms that are obviously compounds or derivatives of words or word-forming elements with unspecialized senses (for example, **flashback** and **naturalism**). Ordinarily, etymologies are enclosed in square brackets and placed after the pronunciation and before the body of the entry. In some entries the origin of the word is discussed in the text, and there a bracketed etymology will be lacking unless it provides additional data. In general, intermediate languages, remoter ancestors, and the philological detail appropriate to a dictionary of etymology have been omitted in this book, unless such information is relevant to the literary use of a term.

Pronunciation.

This book provides pronunciation respellings for most entry words. All personal and geographical names are given phonetic transcriptions when they constitute an entry or occur in a title; respellings are given also for literary terms that appear in boldface entries. The only entry words without respellings are familiar words and connectives which appear in compounds or titles, such as the "and" in **Pelléas and Mélisande**, the first two words of the entry **Waiting for Godot**, or the title of the play **Peace**. The pronunciation for these words may be found in *Merriam-Webster's Collegiate Dictionary, Tenth Edition*. Common nouns which do not have entries in the latter dictionary are given pronunciations here, as at the entry for **The Deerslayer**. Names that appear in titles in the genitive case are respelled in pronunciation in the nominative case, as at **Grimm's Fairy Tales**, unless the proper name is always found in the genitive, as is the case for the entry **Harper's Magazine**.

Pronunciation respellings are also included for most pseudonyms, original names, alternative spellings, irregular plurals, and for some unusual first names, as for Ayn **Rand**. These sorts of names are not given pronunciations, however, when they are simple transpositions of the elements of the entry name:

Ngugi wa Thiong'o \ŋ-'gū-gē-wä-'thyòŋ-gō \, *original name* James Thiong'o Ngugi

When two or more variant spellings of a name have the same pronunciation, the respelling is placed after the last spelling with that pronunciation:

Frigg \'frig\, *also called* Friia, Frija \'frē-ə \, *or* Frea \frā-ə \

Prefixes like *d'*, *de*, *van*, and *von* are included in pronunciation respellings only if the surname is typically cited with the prefix, as for Joost van den **Vondel**, but not for Eduard von **Bauernfeld**. Arabic names are transcribed only in their shorter, familiar form, not in the full patronymic form:

Ibn Jubayr \,ib-ən-zhū-'bīr \, *in full* Abū al-Ḥusayn Muḥammad ibn Aḥmad ibn Jubayr

Names of fictional characters, such as **Tom Sawyer**, are transcribed in full; unlike real people they are more likely to be referred to by their first or full name.

Names from English literature are transcribed in a composite dialect which approximates the speech of the majority of Americans. British names are shown with variants from the Received Pronunciation of British English where this dialect differs noticeably from American speech. Names from ancient and classical literature are sometimes fully anglicized and other times are transcribed in a reconstructed classical pronunciation, according to the prevailing usage in modern English. Foreign language names are respelled in their native pronunciation and are generally rendered in the standard dialect of the language in question with allowances made for regional variation, as between Castilian and Latin-American Spanish. A variant labeled *Angl* is added for names with familiar anglicizations, as for Friedrich **Nietzsche**, and for exceptionally difficult foreign names. Additional notes on anglicized pronunciation are found in the following Guide to Pronunciation.

For the names of living authors, every effort has been made to secure the author's own pronunciation. When our research shows that an author's pronunciation of his or her name differs from common usage, the author's pronunciation is listed first, and the descriptor *commonly* precedes the more familiar pronunciation:

Brontë \'brän-tē, *commonly* 'brän-tā \, Charlotte

The pronunciations in this book are informed by the scholarship of many people. James L. Rader provided information for Russian and Polish names, as did Karen L. Wilkinson for Spanish names, Amy West for Old Norse names, and Jill J. Cooney and Joanne M. Despres for French names. Katherine C. Sietsema gave assistance with names from classical literature. Ralph Emerson contributed significantly for names of British and American authors. A scholarly debt is owed also to the following consultants (in alphabetical order):

Mansur G. Abdullah, Dina Amin, Sujata Banerjee, Kim Bechari, Elie Birnbaum, Ahmed Birsel, Henri Boyi, Karen Cunliffe, Vincent Dowling, John Fox, Amelia R. Gintautas, Sylvia Gon, Bernadette Goovaerts, Thomas Hagrup, David Hasenfratz, Donald Herdeck, Carmen-Maria Hetrea, Dale H. Hoiberg, John Huehnergard, Lloyd Hustvedt, Richard Impola, Kyria Kalavratsou, Marita Karlische, Graziano E. Krätli, Joan Mandry, Nouran Menugian, Fred Mudawwer, Fukiko Ogisu, Ruth Ohayan, Graham Pointon, Kathy Prisender, Gerald Rasmussen, Fred C. Robinson, Leo Schelbert, George Schoolfield, Adam Stern, Ryo Suganame, Paul Nadim Tarazi, Naomi Tutu, Maria Tymoczko, Shantha Uddin, Jurgen Van de Leur, Aleksandar Vlajkovic.

Guide to Pronunciation

The following paragraphs set out the value of the pronunciation symbols in English and other languages. Symbols which are not letters of the English alphabet are listed first. Sounds discussed in the following paragraphs are also rendered in symbols from the International Phonetic Alphabet (IPA) where appropriate.

\ \ Pronunciation respellings are printed between reversed virgules. Pronunciation symbols are printed in roman type, and language labels, descriptors, and remarks are printed in italics.

\'‚\ A high-set stress mark precedes a syllable with primary (strongest) stress; a low-set mark precedes a syllable with secondary (medium) stress. Stress in English words is manifested especially as a change in intonation; in other languages stress may be realized as a marked jump in pitch (up or down), increased energy, or lengthening of syllables. Some languages, such as French, show few distinctions between stressed and unstressed syllables except in phrases. Chinese, Vietnamese, and to a lesser extent Swedish and Norwegian distinguish words by differing pitches of syllables. Japanese words are spoken with intonational contours that are very unlike English stress. These various prosodic features are approximated by renderings in terms of English stress. A respelling system that could precisely encode prosody in these languages would exceed the needs of most English-speaking readers of a reference book of this nature.

\-\ Hyphens are used in respellings to separate syllables. The placement of these hyphens is based on phonetic and orthographic criteria and may not match the phonological syllabication of a given language.

\‚;\ Pronunciation variants are separated by commas; groups of related variants are separated by semicolons.

\ʻ\ is a sound of Arabic and Persian that is pronounced much like \h \ with simultaneous vibration of the vocal cords (IPA [ʕ]). It may be omitted in anglicized pronunciations of these names.

\ə\ is a neutral vowel found in unstressed syllables in English as in anoint, collide, data (IPA [ə]).

\'ə, ‚ə\ as in cut, conundrum (IPA [ʌ]). In English such syllables have some degree of stress; in respellings of Russian names \‚ə\ denotes this vowel with no stress.

\ə̇\ is a high, unrounded, centralized vowel as in Russian bylo 'was (neut.)', Turkish kız 'girl', Chinese shih 'lion,' and Japanese netsuke 'netsuke' (IPA [ɨ, ɪ, ɯ]). This is not a distinctive vowel of English, but it may be heard as a variant of the unstressed vowels \i\ and \ə\, as in the last syllables of biologist and matches. In anglicized pronunciations \ə̇\ may be replaced in Turkish names by \i\, and in Chinese and Russian names by \i\ or \ē\; the vowel may be dropped entirely in anglicizations of Japanese names.

\a\ as in rap, cat, sand, lamb (IPA [æ]). This vowel may be reduced to \ə\ in unstressed syllables.

\ā\ as in way, paid, late, eight. In English pronunciation this symbol stands for a diphthong (IPA [ei, eɪ]), whereas in most other languages this symbol should be understood as a short or long monophthong of the front mid-high vowel (IPA [e, e:]). In anglicized pronunciations the English diphthong may be substituted.

\ä\ as in opt, cod, mach (IPA [ɑ]). The low, back, unrounded vowel of American English is often pronounced with some lip-rounding in British English when the vowel is spelled with the letter o (IPA [ɒ]). This vowel may be reduced to \ə\ in unstressed syllables, but only \ä\ is shown in this book.

\å\ as in French chat 'cat,' table 'table' (IPA [a]). This sound is found in some Eastern dialects of American English, as in the pronunciation of car in the speech of some Bostonians; it is also the initial element of the diphthong \ī\ in words like wide or tribe. The sound \å\ can be characterized as a vowel produced with the tongue in a position midway between that of \a\ and \ä\, or as the vowel \ə\ produced with the jaws somewhat further apart. In Arabic the vowel \å\ may be fronted somewhat to \a\ or even \e\ when it occurs as a short vowel in closed syllables. In anglicized pronunciations of Scandinavian names \å\ may be replaced by \ä\; in French names it may be anglicized as \ä\ or \a\; in Arabic names it may be replaced by \a\.

\ar\ as in air, care, laird (IPA [ær]). In some American dialects this may also be pronounced with a mid-low initial element as \er\ (IPA [ɛr]).

\au̇\ as in out, loud, tout, cow (IPA [aʊ, au]).

\b\ as in bat, able, rib (IPA [b]). This symbol is also used to transcribe a sound in names from India which appears in English spelling as bh and which in the original language is a voiced aspirate (IPA [bʰ]).

\ḅ\ as in the "soft" b or v of Spanish hablar 'speak' or Avila 'Avila' (IPA [β]). This sound is a voiced bilabial fricative, formed by setting the mouth in the position for \b\ but separating the lips just enough to allow the passage of breath as with \v\. The sound \ḅ\ may be anglicized as \v\.

\ch\ as in chair, reach, catcher (IPA [tʃ]).

\d\ as in day, red, ladder (IPA [d]). This symbol is also used to transcribe a sound in names from India which appears in English spelling as dh and which in the original language is a voiced aspirate (IPA [dʰ]). (See also the section on \t\ below.)

\e\ as in egg, bed, bet (IPA [ɛ]). This symbol is also used sometimes to transcribe the short monophthongal front mid-high vowel found in some European languages (IPA [e]). This vowel may be reduced to \ə\ in unstressed syllables, but only \e\ is shown in this book.

\ˈē, ‚ē\ as in **eat**, r**ee**d, fl**ee**t, p**ea** (IPA [i, i:]). This sound may be diphthongized in some dialects of English, but it is always a monophthong in other European languages.

\ē\ as in penn**y**, gen**ie** (IPA [i, ɪ]). In some dialects of American and British English the unstressed \ē\ is pronounced as a vowel similar to \i\.

\ei\ as in Dutch **ei**eren 'eggs,' d**ij**k 'dike' (IPA [ɛi]). This sound is a diphthong formed of a sequence of the vowels \e\ and \ē\. It may be anglicized as \ā\ or as \ī\.

\f\ as in **f**ine, cha**ff**, o**ff**ice (IPA [f]).

\g\ as in **g**ate, ra**g**, ea**g**le (IPA [g]). This symbol is also used to transcribe a sound in names from India which appears in English spelling as gh and which in the original language is a voiced aspirate (IPA [gʰ]).

\ḡ\ as in Spanish la**g**o 'lake' (IPA [ɣ]). This sound is a voiced velar fricative, produced by setting the mouth in the position for \g\ but separating the tongue from the hard palate just enough to allow the passage of breath as with the sound \ḵ\. The sound \ḡ\ may be anglicized as \g\.

\h\ as in **h**ot, a**h**oy (IPA [h]). This sound appears only at the beginning of syllables in English; in Arabic and Persian names this sound may also be found at the end of a syllable.

\hl\ as in Welsh **ll**aw 'hand' or Icelandic **hl**aup 'slide' (IPA [ɬ]). This sound is a voiceless \l\: it can be approximated by producing \h\ while holding the mouth in the position for \l\. The sound \hl\ may be anglicized as \l\.

\hr\ as in Welsh **rh**ad 'free' or Icelandic **hr**aun 'lava' (IPA [r̥]). This sound is a voiceless consonantal \r\: it can be approximated by producing \h\ while holding the mouth in the position for \r\. The sound \hr\ may be anglicized as \r\.

\hw\ as in **wh**eat, **wh**en (IPA [w̥]). In some dialects of English this sound is replaced by \w\.

\i\ as in **i**ll, h**i**p, b**i**d (IPA [ɪ]). This vowel may be reduced to \ə\ in unstressed syllables, but only \i\ is shown in this book.

\ī\ as in **ai**sle, fr**y**, wh**i**te, w**i**de (IPA [ai, aɪ, ɑi, ɑɪ]).

\j\ as in **j**ump, fu**dg**e, bu**dg**et (IPA [dʒ]).

\k\ as in **k**ick, ba**k**er, s**c**am, as**k** (IPA [k]). This symbol is used also to respell the voiceless uvular stop of Arabic and Persian (IPA [q]) which appears in English spellings as the letter q. For the latter sound the tongue is brought in contact with the soft palate rather than the hard palate.

\ḵ\ as in lo**ch**, Ba**ch**, German Bu**ch** (IPA [x]), and German i**ch** 'I' (IPA [ç]). This sound is a voiceless velar or palatal fricative, produced by setting the mouth in the position for \k\ but separating the tongue from the hard palate just enough to allow the passage of breath. Some English speakers produce this sound in imitation of a cat's hissing or of static over a radio set. The symbol \ḵ\ is used also to respell the voiceless pharyngeal fricative of

Arabic and Persian (IPA [ħ]) which appears in English spellings as the letter ḥ. In European names \ḵ\ may be anglicized as \k\; in Arabic and Persian names it may be anglicized as \h\.

\l\ as in **l**ap, pa**l**, a**ll**ey (IPA [l, ɬ]). In some contexts this sound may be heard as a syllabic consonant (IPA [l̩]), which in this book is respelled as the syllable \-əl\, as at the **Tower of Babel** \ˈbab-əl, ˈbab-\. When this sound falls at the end of a syllable in French pronunciations it is heard as a voiceless \l\ (IPA [l̥]), as in **cénacle** \sā-ˈnåkl\. The latter sound often disappears entirely in French pronunciations, and it may be anglicized as the syllable \-lə\ or by omitting the \l\ sound entirely.

\m\ as in **m**ake, ja**m**, ha**mm**er (IPA [m]). In some contexts this sound may be heard as a syllabic consonant (IPA [m̩]), which in this book is respelled as the syllable \-əm\, as at **Bottom** \ˈbät-əm\.

\n\ as in **n**ow, wi**n**, ba**nn**er (IPA [n]). In some contexts this sound may be heard as a syllabic consonant (IPA [n̩]), which in this book is respelled as the syllable \-ən\, as at Bruce **Catton** \ˈkat-ən\. In Japanese names this symbol is used at the end of syllables to represent the uvular nasal sound in that language.

\ⁿ\ is used to show nasalization of the preceding vowel, as in French **en** \äⁿ\ 'in'.

\ŋ\ as in ri**ng**, si**ng**er, go**ng** (IPA [ŋ]). In English this sound appears only at the end of a syllable, but in non-European languages it may occur at the beginning of a syllable followed either by a vowel or another consonant. In these contexts \ŋ\ may be anglicized as \əŋg\.

\ō\ as in **o**ak, b**oa**t, t**oe**, g**o** (IPA [o, o:, ou]). This sound is a diphthong in most dialects of English, but it is always a monophthong in other European languages. In the Received Pronunciation of British English the diphthong is \əu̇\ (IPA [əʊ]), where the initial element is a central mid vowel. The symbol \ō\ is used also to respell the low or low-mid, back, rounded vowel of Greek (IPA [ɒ, ɔ]) which appears in English spelling as the letter o or ō.

\ȯ\ as in **h**awk, b**aw**l, c**au**ght, **ou**ght, Ut**ah** (IPA [ɔ]). In some dialects of American English this sound is replaced by \ä\. The symbol \ȯ\ is used to respell the low, back, rounded vowel of Hungarian (IPA [ɒ]) which is spelled as the letter a without an acute accent. The vowel \ȯ\ may be reduced to \ə\ in unstressed syllables, but only \ȯ\ is shown in this book.

\œ\ as in French n**eu**f 'new' and German K**ö**pfe 'heads' (IPA [œ]). This vowel can be approximated by producing the vowel \e\ while rounding the lips as if pronouncing the vowel \ȯ\. The sound \œ\ may be anglicized as \ər\.

\œ̄\ as in French d**eu**x 'two' and German L**ö**hne 'wages' (IPA [ø]). This vowel can be approximated by producing the vowel \ā\ while rounding the lips as if pronouncing the vowel \ō\. The sound \œ̄\ may be anglicized as \ûr\ with a very light \r\ sound.

\œ̄œ̄\ as in Dutch t**ui**n 'yard' (IPA [œy, øy]). This vowel can be approximated by producing the vowel \ī\ while rounding the lips as if pronouncing the vowel \ü\. The sound \œ̄œ̄\ may be anglicized as \ī\.

\ȯi\ as in **oy**ster, t**oy**, f**oi**l (IPA [ɔɪ, ɔi]).

\ȯr\   as in **core**, **born**, **oar** (IPA [ɔr]). In some American dialects this may also be pronounced with a mid-high initial element \ōr\ (IPA [or]) in many words.

\p\   as in **pet**, **tip**, **upper** (IPA [p]).

\r\   as in **rut**, **tar**, **error**, **cart**. What is transcribed here as \r\ in reality represents several distinct sounds. As an English consonant \r\ is produced with the tongue tip slightly behind the teethridge (IPA [ɹ]). As a semivowel in words like *cart* and *fore* \r\ appears as retroflexion of the tongue tip in some dialects and as a transitional vowel like \ə\ in the so-called "R-dropping" dialects of American and British English.

   In other languages \r\ represents a stronger consonant, such as a trill or tap of the tongue tip against the teethridge (IPA [r, ɾ]) or a trill of the back of the tongue against the soft palate (IPA [ʀ]). When \r\ falls at the end of a syllable in French pronunciations it is sometimes heard as a devoiced uvular fricative (IPA [χ]), as in **belles lettres** \bel-'letr\. The latter sound often disappears entirely in French pronunciations, and it may be anglicized as the syllable \-rə\ or by omitting the \r\ sound entirely. The \r\ sounds of Danish, German, Portuguese, and Spanish also vary according to phonetic context, but all may be anglicized with the \r\ of English.

\s\   as in **sink**, **bass**, **lasso**, **city** (IPA [s]).

\sh\   as in **shin**, **lash**, **pressure** (IPA [ʃ]).

\t\   as in **top**, **pat**, **later** (IPA [t]). In some contexts, as when a stressed or unstressed vowel precedes and an unstressed vowel follows, the sound represented in English spelling by *t* or *tt* is pronounced in most American speech as a voiced flap produced by tapping the tongue tip against the teethridge (IPA [ɾ]). In similar contexts the sound represented by *d* or *dd* has the same pronunciation.

\th\   as in **third**, **bath**, **Kathy** (IPA [θ]).

\th̲\   as in **this**, **other**, **bathe** (IPA [ð]).

\ü\   as in **ooze**, **blue**, **noon** (IPA [u, uː, uʊ]). This sound is a diphthong in most dialects of English, but it is always a monophthong in other European languages.

\u̇\   as in **wool**, **took**, **should**, **put** (IPA [ʊ]).

\œ\   as in German *Bünde* 'unions,' *füllen* 'to fill' (IPA [ʏ]). This vowel can be approximated by producing the vowel \i\ while rounding the lips as if pronouncing the vowel \u̇\. The sound \œ\ may be anglicized as \yu̇\ or \u̇\.

\œ̄\   as in German *kühl* 'cool' and French *vue* 'view' (IPA [y]). This vowel can be approximated by producing the vowel \ē\ while rounding the lips as if pronouncing the vowel \ü\. The sound \œ̄\ may be anglicized as \yü\ or \u̇\.

\ūy\   as in Welsh *gwyl* 'festival' (IPA [ʉɪ]). This diphthong does not occur in English. It is produced as a sequence of the vowels \ü\ and \i\. This vowel may be anglicized as \ȯi\.

\v\   as in **veer**, **rove**, **ever** (IPA [v]).

\w\   as in **well**, **awash** (IPA [w]).

\y\   as in **youth**, **yet**, **lawyer** (IPA [j]). In some languages the consonant \y\ may occur after a vowel in the same syllable, as in French *famille* \fä-'mēy\ 'family.' The pronunciation of \y\ in these contexts is the same as at the beginning of a syllable in English.

\ʸ\   is used to show palatalization of a preceding consonant, as in French *campagne* \kä^n-'pȧnʸ\ 'country' and Russian *perestroika* \pʸi-rʸi-'strȯi-kə\ 'restructuring' (IPA [ʲ]). A palatalized consonant is produced with the body of the tongue raised as if in the position to pronounce \y\. In anglicized pronunciations \ʸ\ may be sounded as the consonantal \y\ of English when it falls in the middle of a syllable or as \-yə\ at the end of French words. In anglicizations of Russian and other Slavic names it may be omitted entirely.

\z\   as in **zoo**, **haze**, **razor** (IPA [z]).

\zh\   as in **pleasure**, **decision** (IPA [ʒ]).

Pronunciation Symbols

For more information *see* Guide to Pronunciation

ə .... in anoint, collide, data

'ə, ˌə .... cut, conundrum

ə̇ .... biologist, matches

a .... rap, cat, sand, lamb

ā .... way, paid, late, eight

ä .... opt, cod, mach

à .... French *chat*, *table*

ar .... air, care, laird

aù .... out, loud, tout, cow

b .... bat, able, rib

ḅ .... Spanish *hablar*, *Avila*

ch .... chair, reach, catcher

d .... day, red, ladder

e .... egg, bed, bet

'ē, ˌē .... eat, reed, fleet, pea

ē .... penny, genie

ei .... Dutch *eieren*, *dijk*

f .... fine, chaff, office

g .... gate, rag, eagle

ḡ .... Spanish *lago*

h .... hot, ahoy

hl .... Welsh *llaw*, Icelandic *hlaup*

hr .... Welsh *rhad*, Icelandic *hraun*

hw .... wheat, when

i .... ill, hip, bid

ī .... aisle, fry, white, wide

j .... jump, fudge, budget

k .... kick, baker, scam, ask

ḵ .... loch, Bach, German *Buch*

l .... lap, pal, alley

m .... make, jam, hammer

n .... now, win, banner

ⁿ .... shows that a preceding vowel is nasalized, as in French *en* \äⁿ\

ŋ .... ring, singer, gong

ō .... oak, boat, toe, go

ȯ .... hawk, bawl, caught, ought, Utah

œ .... French *neuf*, German *Köpfe*

œ̄ .... French *deux*, German *Löhne*

œ̄œ̄ .... Dutch *tuin*

ȯi .... oyster, toy, foil

ȯr .... core, born, oar

p .... pet, tip, upper

r .... rut, tar, error, cart

s .... sink, bass, lasso

sh .... shin, lash, pressure

t .... top, pat, later

th .... third, bath, Kathy

t̲h̲ .... this, other, bathe

ü .... ooze, blue, noon

u̇ .... wool, took, should

ue .... German *Bünde*, *füllen*

u̅e̅ .... German *kühl*, French *vue*

üy .... Welsh *gwyl*

v .... veer, rove, ever

w .... well, awash

y .... youth, yet, lawyer

ʸ .... shows palatalization of a preceding consonant, as in French *campagne* \käⁿ-'pàⁿʸ\

z .... zoo, haze, razor

zh .... pleasure, decision

ʻ .... indicates a consonant that is pronounced like \h\ with vibration of the vocal cords

\\ .... reversed virgules used to mark the beginning and end of a phonetic respelling

ˈ .... mark preceding a syllable with primary stress: boa \'bō-ə\

ˌ .... mark preceding a syllable with secondary stress: beeline \'bē-ˌlīn\

- .... mark indicating syllable divisions

A

Aakjær \\'ô-,ker\\, Jeppe (b. Sept. 10, 1866, Aakjær, Den.—d. April 22, 1930, Jenle) Poet and novelist, leading exponent of Danish regional literature and of the literature of social consciousness.

Aakjær grew up in the Jutland farming area and so was well aware of the harsh conditions endured by farm laborers. His early novels deal primarily with this theme. As a young man he went to study in Copenhagen, earning his living as a proofreader and later as a journalist. *Vredens børn, et tyendes saga* (1904; "Children of Wrath: A Hired Man's Saga"), which is considered to be his most powerful novel, was a strong plea for the betterment of the farm laborer's lot. It initiated much public discussion and helped bring about some minimal reforms. He is best-known, however, for his poems, especially those collected in *Fri felt* (1905; "Free Fields") and *Rugens sange* (1906; "Songs of the Rye").

Aaron \\'ar-ən\\ (fl. *c.* 14th century BC) The traditional founder and head of the Jewish priesthood, who, with his brother Moses, led the Israelites out of Egypt. The figure of Aaron is built up from several sources of tradition. In the Talmud and Midrash he is seen as the leading personality at the side of Moses. The sign that he was God's choice for high priest was the blossoming of his walking stick, or rod.

Aaron's Rod Novel by D.H. LAWRENCE, published in 1922. Lawrence constructed a parallel between the power that was miraculously manifested in the blossoming rod wielded by the biblical figure Aaron and the effect of the flute played by the protagonist of the novel, Aaron Sisson.

Sisson is an amateur flutist who works in a coal mine. He abandons his wife and the life he has known to travel and seek new adventures, making his living as a flutist. While he is in Florence, Italy, his flute is shattered during political riots.

Abaddon \\ə-'bad-ən\\ The angel of the bottomless pit, referred to in the Book of Revelations. John Milton extended the meaning of the term to include the pit (*i.e.*, the abyss of hell) itself in his poem *Paradise Regained*.

Abasıyanık \\,ȧb-ä-'sȯ-yän-ȯk\\, Sait Faik (b. Nov. 23, 1906, Adapazarı, Ottoman Empire [now in Turkey]—d. May 11, 1954, Istanbul) Short-story writer, a major figure in modern Turkish literature.

Educated in Constantinople (now Istanbul) and Bursa, he lived in France from 1931 to 1935. On his return to Turkey, he began to publish his short stories in *Varlık* ("Existence"), the nation's leading avant-garde periodical. Abasıyanık's stories were written in a style new to Turkish literature. Despite their formlessness and lack of a conventional story line, they conveyed in a single, compelling episode a wide range of human emotions. In 1936 Abasıyanık published his first volume of short stories, *Semaver* ("The Samovar"). A dozen others followed, including *Lüzumsuz adam* (1948; "The Useless Man"), *Kumpanya* (1951; "The Company"), and *Alemdağda var bir yılan* (1953; "There's a Snake at Alem Mountain"). He also wrote an experimental novel.

Abbaye group \\ä-'bā\\ A short-lived cooperative community of French writers and artists who promoted new works and who lived together in a house called L'Abbaye, in a Paris suburb, from 1906 to 1907. The group included the writers Charles Vildrac and Georges Duhamel. The house was a center of artistic activity, and other writers and artists, including Jules Romains, were associated with the group (though they were not inhabitants of the house). The Abbaye artists supported themselves by selling books that they printed on their own printing press. One of the works published by the group was the influential *La Vie unanime* (1908) by Romains. The Abbaye community was portrayed by Duhamel in his novel *Le Désert de Bièvres* (1937). *See also* UNANIMISME.

Abbey \\'ab-ē\\, Edward (b. Jan. 29, 1927, Home, Pa., U.S.—d. March 14, 1989, Oracle, Ariz.) American writer whose works, set primarily in the southwestern United States, reflect an uncompromising environmentalist philosophy.

The son of a Pennsylvania farmer, Abbey earned bachelor's and master's degrees at the University of New Mexico in the 1950s. He subsequently worked as a park ranger and fire lookout for the National Park Service in the Southwest. Central to this experience was the perspective it afforded on the human presence in the environment. Abbey observed both the remnants of ancient Indian cultures and the encroachment of consumer civilization. His book *Desert Solitaire* (1968) is an extended meditation on the sublime and forbidding wilderness of southeastern Utah and the human incursions upon it. This work, along with the novel *The Monkey Wrench Gang* (1975), which recounts the exploits of a band of guerrilla environmentalists, became virtual handbooks of the environmental movement. The strain of cynicism that runs through much of Abbey's writing is leavened by a bracing prose style and mischievous wit. His numerous other works include *The Brave Cowboy* (1958), *Slickrock* (1971), *Abbey's Road* (1979), and *The Fool's Progress* (1988). *Hayduke Lives!*, a sequel to *The Monkey Wrench Gang*, was published posthumously in 1990.

Abbey Theatre \\'ab-ē\\ Dublin theater that was established in 1904. It grew out of the Irish Literary Theatre, founded in 1899 by William Butler YEATS and Isabella Augusta, Lady GREGORY, and was devoted to fostering Irish poetic drama. In 1902 the Irish Literary Theatre was taken over by the Irish National Dramatic Society, which had been formed to present Irish actors in Irish plays. In 1903 this became the Irish National Theatre Society, with which many leading figures of the IRISH LITERARY RENAISSANCE were closely associated. The quality of its productions was quickly recognized, and in 1904 an Englishwoman, Annie Horniman, a friend of Yeats, paid for the conversion of an old theater in Abbey Street, Dublin, into the Abbey Theatre. The Abbey opened in December 1904 with a bill of plays by Yeats, Lady Gregory, and John Millington SYNGE (who joined the other two as codirector).

In 1924, the Abbey became the first state-subsidized theater in the English-speaking world. The emergence of playwright Sean O'CASEY also stimulated new interest in the theater. Although the Abbey has broadened its repertoire in recent decades, it continues to rely primarily on Irish plays.

Abbott \'ab-ət\, Jacob (b. Nov. 14, 1803, Hallowell, Maine, U.S.—d. Oct. 31, 1879, Farmington, Maine) American clergyman, teacher, and writer, best known as a writer of children's books.

Abbott attended Bowdoin College and studied at Andover Newton Theological School. He taught at Amherst College, moving in 1829 to Boston, where he founded and was the first principal of the Mount Vernon School, a secondary school for girls. Abbott was sole author of 180 books and coauthor or editor of 31 others, notably the 28-volume, instructive "Rollo" series. Although now they are chiefly noted for their picture of 19th-century rural American life, Abbott intended them to entertain, to edify, to make children think, and to help them learn to read. Abbott also wrote 22 volumes of biographical histories and the *Franconia Stories* (10 vol.).

Abdülhak Hamid Tarhan *see* TARHAN.

Abdulla \ab-'dəl-ə\, Muhammed Said (b. April 25, 1918, Zanzibar, Tanz.) Tanzanian novelist generally regarded as the father of Swahili popular literature.

After completing his formal education, Abdulla worked as an inspector in the Colonial Health Department. A decade later, he took up journalism, and in 1948 he was made editor of the newspaper *Zanzibari*. For the next decade he also served as assistant editor on several magazines.

Abdulla's first success with fiction occurred when his "Mzimu wa Watu wa Kale" ("Shrine of the Ancestors") won a prize. It was published as a novel in 1960. In this work, Abdulla introduced his detective hero, Bwana Msa, and the other characters who recur in many of his subsequent novels, including *Kisima cha Giningi* (1968; "The Well of Giningi"); *Duniani Kuna Watu* (1973; "In the World There Are People"); *Siri ya Sifuri* (1974; "The Secret of the Zero"); *Mke Mmoja Waume Watatu* (1975; "One Wife, Three Husbands"); and *Mwana wa Yungi Hulewa* (1976; "The Devil's Child Grows Up").

Abdullah bin Abdul Kadir \ab-'dəl-ə-bin-'äb-dəl-'kä-dir\ (b. 1796, Malacca, Malaya—d. 1854, Jiddah, Turkish Arabia [now in Saudi Arabia]) Malayan writer who transformed Malay literature by the introduction of realism. He is considered to be the father of modern Malay literature.

Of mixed Arab (Yemeni) and Tamil descent and Malayo-Muslim culture, Abdullah was born and grew up in a Malacca that was newly British, and he spent most of his life interpreting Malay society to Westerners and vice versa. Styled *munshi* (teacher) from an early age, in recognition of his teaching Malay to Indian soldiers of the Malacca garrison (and later to a whole generation of British and American missionaries, officials, and businessmen), he rapidly became an indispensable functionary in the fledgling Straits Settlements. He was copyist and Malay scribe for Sir Stamford Raffles and, from 1815, was translator of the Gospels and other texts into Malay for the London Missionary Society in Malacca.

Hikayat Abdullah (1849; "Abdullah's Story") is his much-translated autobiography. Its chief distinction—beyond the vivid picture it gives of his life and times—is its radical departure from traditional Malay literary style. In contrast to the largely court literature of the past, the *Hikayat Abdullah* provided a lively and colloquial descriptive account of events and people with a freshness and immediacy hitherto unknown.

abecedarius \ˌā-bē-sē-'där-ē-əs\ [Late Latin, alphabetical, from the names of the letters *a, b, c, d*] A type of ACROSTIC in which the first letter of each line of a poem or the first letter of the first word of each stanza taken in order forms the alphabet. Examples of these are some of the Psalms (in Hebrew), such as Psalms 25 and 34, where successive verses begin with the letters of the Hebrew alphabet in order.

Abe \'äb-ā\ Kōbō, *byname of* Abe Kimifusa (b. March 7, 1924, Tokyo, Japan—d. Jan. 22, 1993, Tokyo) Japanese novelist and playwright noted for his avant-garde techniques and his use of bizarre and allegorical situations to examine the isolation of the individual.

Abe grew up in Mukden (now Shenyang) in Japanese-occupied Manchuria, where his father, a physician, taught medicine. In 1941 Abe went to Japan, and in 1943 he began studying medicine at the University of Tokyo but returned to Manchuria before the end of World War II. Repatriated to Japan, he graduated from medical school in 1948 but never practiced. In 1947 he published *Mumei shishū* ("Poems of an Unknown Poet") at his own expense. The critical acceptance of his novel *Owarishi michi no shirube ni* (1948; "The Road Sign at the End of the Street") established his reputation.

Among Abe's important novels are *Suna no onna* (1962; THE WOMAN IN THE DUNES), *Daiyon kampyōki* (1959; *Inter Ice Age 4*), *Tanin no kao* (1964; *The Face of Another*), *Moetsukita chizu* (1967; *The Ruined Map*), *Hako otoko* (1973; THE BOX MAN), and *Mikkai* (1977; *Secret Rendezvous*). Of his many plays, which met with great success in Japan, *Tomodachi* (1967; *Friends*) and a few others have been performed in English. He directed his own theater company in Tokyo.

Abel \'ā-bəl\ In the Old Testament, second son of Adam and Eve, who was slain by his older brother, CAIN (Genesis 4:1–16). According to Genesis, Abel, a shepherd, offered the Lord the firstborn of his flock. The Lord respected Abel's sacrifice but did not respect that offered by Cain. In a jealous rage, Cain murdered Abel. Because his brother's innocent blood had put a curse on him, Cain then became a fugitive.

The characters of Cain and Abel appear in some form in several works of literature, including works by Samuel Taylor Coleridge, Lord Byron, William Blake, Miguel de Unamuno, and John Steinbeck.

Abelard \ˈa-bā-ˈlärd, *Angl* 'ab-ə-ˌlärd\, Peter, *also called* Pierre Abélard *or* Pierre Abailard, *Latin* Petrus Abaelardus *or* Petrus Abeilardus (b. 1079, Le Pallet, near Nantes, Brittany [now in France]—d. April 21, 1142, Priory of Saint-Marcel, near Chalon-sur-Saône, Burgundy [now in France]) French theologian and philosopher best known in literature for his poetry and for his celebrated love affair with HÉLOÏSE.

Hired to tutor the gifted Héloïse, Abelard fell in love with her. A child was born to them and they married secretly, but Héloïse's vengeful relatives had Abelard castrated and the couple took up separate religious lives. After Héloïse became head of a new foundation of nuns called the Paraclete, Abelard became abbot of the new community and provided it with a rule and with a justification of the nun's way of life; in this he emphasized the virtue of literary study. In the early 1130s he and Héloïse composed a collection of their own love letters and religious correspondence. In three of his most original literary works, his relationship with Héloïse is a prominent feature. The *Hymnarius Paraclitensis*, for example, features six *planctus* ("laments")—meditations on guilt and suffering—set in the mouths of biblical personages.

Of Abelard's philosophical works, *Sic et non* (completed *c.* 1136; "Yes and No") is the most notable. Abelard's autobiographical work, the *Historia calamitatum* (written *c.* 1136; *The Story of My Misfortunes*), recounts the story of his love affair and its theological consequences.

Abe Lincoln in Illinois \'ab-'liŋ-kən ... ˌil-ə-'nȯi, -'nȯiz\ Drama in 12 scenes by Robert E. SHERWOOD, produced in 1938 and published in 1939.

The play, which in 1939 was awarded the Pulitzer Prize for drama, concerns Lincoln's life and career—from his early, unsuccessful days as a postmaster in New Salem, Ill., through his initial forays into local politics, his relationship with Mary Todd, and his debates with Stephen Douglas, and culminates with his election to the presidency and imminent departure for Washington, D.C., 30 years later.

Abell \\'äb-əl, 'ab-\\, Kjeld (b. Aug. 25, 1901, Ribe, Den.— d. March 5, 1961, Copenhagen) Danish dramatist and social critic, best known outside Denmark for two plays, *Melodien der blev væk* (1935; English adaptation, *The Melody That Got Lost*) and *Anna Sophie Hedvig* (1939), which defends the use of force by the oppressed against the oppressor.

Abell studied political science but afterward began a career as a stage designer in Paris. He then went on to become Denmark's most unconventional man of the theater, not only as an original dramatist but also as a stage designer who made full use of the technical apparatus of the theater to achieve new and striking scenic effects, as in *Daga paa en Sky* (1947; "Days on a Cloud") and *Skrige* (1961; "The Scream").

Abenteuerroman \\'ä-ben-ˌtȯi-ər-rō-ˌmän\\ [German, literally, adventure novel] German form of the PICARESQUE NOVEL. The *Abenteuerroman* is an entertaining story of the adventures of the hero, but there is also often a serious aspect to the story. An example is the 17th-century *Der Abentheurliche Simplicissimus* (*Adventurous Simplicissimus*) by H.J.C. von Grimmelshausen. *Compare* BILDUNGSROMAN.

Abercrombie \\'ab-ər-ˌkrəm-bē, *in U.S. commonly* -ˌkräm-\\, Lascelles \\'las-əlz\\ (b. Jan. 9, 1881, Ashton upon Mersey, Cheshire, Eng.—d. Oct. 27, 1938, London) Poet and critic associated with GEORGIAN POETRY.

Abercrombie was educated at Malvern College, Worcestershire, and Owens College, Manchester, and then became a journalist and began to write poetry. His first book, *Interludes and Poems* (1908), was followed by *Mary and the Bramble* (1910), a dramatic poem (*Deborah*), *Emblems of Love* (1912), and the prose work *Speculative Dialogues* (1913). These were marked by lyric power, lucidity, love of natural beauty, and mysticism. Abercrombie also contributed poetry to *Georgian Poetry*. After World War I, he was appointed to the first lectureship in poetry at the University of Liverpool. His critical works include *An Essay Towards a Theory of Art* (1922) and *Poetry, Its Music and Meaning* (1932).

Abhijñānaśakuntala \\ə-ˌbi-'gyä-nə-'shä-kün-ˌtəl-ə\\ ("The Recognition of Śakuntalā") Drama by KĀLIDĀSA composed about the 5th century AD that is generally considered to be the greatest Indian literary work of any period.

Taken from legend, the work tells of the seduction of the nymph Śakuntalā by King Duṣyanta, his rejection of the girl and his child, and their subsequent reunion in heaven. The epic myth is important because the child that is born is Bharata, eponymous ancestor of the Indian nation (Bhāratavarṣa, "Subcontinent of Bharata"). Kālidāsa remakes the story into a love idyll whose characters represent a pristine aristocratic ideal: the girl, sentimental, selfless, alive to little but the delicacies of nature, and the king, first servant of the dharma (religious and social law and duties), protector of the social order, resolute hero, yet tender and suffering agonies over his lost love. The plot and characters are made believable by a change Kālidāsa has wrought in the story: Duṣyanta is not responsible for the lovers' separation; he acts only under a delusion caused by a sage's curse. As in all of Kālidāsa's works, the beauty of nature is depicted with a precise elegance of metaphor.

Abish \\'ab-ish\\, Walter (b. Dec. 24, 1931, Vienna, Austria) American writer of experimental novels and short stories whose fiction took as its subject language itself.

Abish spent his childhood in Shanghai, China, where his family were refugees from Nazi-occupied Europe. In 1949 they moved to Israel, where Abish served in the army and developed strong interests in architecture and writing. He moved to the United States in 1957 and became a citizen in 1960. From 1975 Abish taught at several eastern colleges and universities.

In *Alphabetical Africa* (1974), the first of the 52 chapters (twice 26) consists solely of words beginning with "A," the second chapter adds words beginning with "B," and so forth through the alphabet and back again. *Minds Meet* (1975) contains short stories in which language is used symbolically rather than to relay specific information. *In the Future Perfect* (1977) features experimental short stories in which words are juxtaposed in unusual patterns. *How German Is It/Wie Deutsch ist es* (1980), often considered Abish's best work, is a multilayered novel about postwar Germany and its past. Other works include a collection of poems, *Duel Site* (1970); *99: The New Meaning* (1990), a group of narratives; and the novel *Eclipse Fever* (1993).

ab ovo \\ab-'ō-vō\\ A Latin phrase meaning literally "from the egg" that alludes to the practice of beginning a poetic narrative at the earliest possible chronological point. The Latin poet and critic Horace notes approvingly (in *Ars poetica*) that Homer does not begin a tale of the Trojan war with the twin egg from which Helen was born but rather in the middle of events. *Compare* IN MEDIAS RES.

abozzo \\ə-'bȯt-sō\\ [Italian] A rough sketch or draft (as of a poem).

Abraham \\'ā-brə-ˌham\\ or **Avraham** \\'äv-rə-ˌhäm\\, *also called* Abram \\'ā-brəm\\ *or* Avram \\'äv-ˌräm\\ (fl. early 2nd millennium BC) First of the Hebrew patriarchs and a figure revered by Judaism, Christianity, and Islām. According to the biblical book of Genesis, Abraham left Ur, in Mesopotamia, because God called him to found a new nation in an undesignated land that he later learned was Canaan. He obeyed unquestioningly the commands of God, from whom he received repeated promises and a covenant that his "seed" would inherit the land.

Abraham figures in several later works of literature, including *Piers Plowman*, many medieval religious dramas, and Margaret Laurence's *The Stone Angel*.

Abraham ben Meir ibn Ezra *see* Abraham ben Meir IBN EZRA.

Abraham Lincoln: The War Years \\'ā-brə-ˌham-'liŋ-kən\\ Four-volume biography by Carl SANDBURG, published in 1939. It was awarded the 1940 Pulitzer Prize for history.

After the success of his 1926 biography, *Abraham Lincoln: The Prairie Years*, Sandburg turned to Lincoln's life after 1861, devoting 11 years to research and writing. The biography is informed not only by the author's journalistic style but also by his unwavering admiration for Franklin D. Roosevelt's liberal New Deal politics. Sandburg believed that both presidents were representative of the voice of the American people, and in many respects the biography expresses his faith in the workings of democracy through the office of a compassionate, gifted leader.

Abrahams \\'ā-brə-ˌhamz\\, Peter (Henry) (b. March 19, 1919, Vrededorp, near Johannesburg, S.Af.) Expatriate South African writer noted for his eloquence in charting the complex issues of the nonwhites' struggle in his native land for a voice and for dignity.

Abrahams left South Africa at the age of 20, first settling in Britain and then in Jamaica. He became editor of the *West Indian Economist* and took charge of the daily radio news network, West Indian News, until 1964, when he devoted himself full-time to writing.

Although he lived in Jamaica from 1956, most of his work remained rooted in his South African experiences. In one of his early novels, *Mine Boy* (1946), he tells of a country youth thrown into the alien and oppressive culture of a large South African industrial city, and his semiautobiographical *Tell Freedom: Memories of Africa* (1954; rev. ed., 1970) deals with his own struggles in the slums of Johannesburg. The widely translated novel *The Path of Thunder* (1948) depicts a young "mixed" couple who love under the menacing shadow of enforced segregation. *Wild Conquest* (1950) follows the great northern trek of the Boers, and *A Night of Their Own* (1965) sets forth the plight of the Indian in South Africa. Abrahams' other books include *A Wreath for Udomo* (1956; rev. ed., 1971), *This Island Now* (1966; rev. ed., 1971), and *The View from Coyaba* (1985).

Abramov \,ə-'brä-məf\, Fyodor (Aleksandrovich) (b. Feb. 29, 1920, Verkola, Russian S.F.S.R., U.S.S.R.—d. May 14, 1983, Leningrad [St. Petersburg]) Russian writer, academic, and literary critic whose work focused on the difficulties and discrimination faced by Russian peasants.

Of peasant ancestry, Abramov studied at Leningrad State University, interrupting his studies to serve as a soldier in World War II. In 1951 he finished his studies at the university, then taught there until 1960, when he became a full-time writer.

His essay *Lyudi kolkhoznoy derevni v poslevoyennoy proze* (1954; "People in the Kolkhoz Village in Postwar Prose"), which took issue with the official, idealized portrayal of life in communal Soviet villages, was condemned by the Writers Union. In a subsequent essay, which led to his expulsion from the editorial staff of the journal *Neva*, Abramov urged rescinding the law that denied peasants internal passports; he also favored allotting to the peasantry larger shares of the profits of their labors. His first novel, *Bratya i syostri* (1958; "Brothers and Sisters"), dealt with the deprivations and harsh life experienced by northern Russian villagers during World War II. Two sequels were *Dve zimy i tri leta* (1968; *Two Winters and Three Summers*) and *Puti—pereputya* (1973; "Paths and Crossroads"). This saga of peasant life was collected under the title *Pryasliny* (1974; "The Pryaslins"), concluding with a fourth novel, *Dom* (1978; "The House").

Abrams \'ā-brəmz\, M.H., *in full* Meyer Howard (b. July 23, 1912, Long Branch, N.J., U.S.) American literary critic known for his analysis of the Romantic period in English literature.

Following his graduation from Harvard in 1934, Abrams studied for a year at the University of Cambridge before returning to his alma mater for master's and doctoral degrees. He joined the faculty of Cornell University, Ithaca, N.Y., in 1945, becoming professor emeritus in 1983.

Abrams wrote his first book, *The Milk of Paradise: The Effects of Opium Visions on the Works of De Quincey, Crabbe, Francis Thompson, and Coleridge* (1934), while an undergraduate. With his second work, *The Mirror and the Lamp: Romantic Theory and the Critical Tradition* (1953), he joined the front rank of scholars of Romantic literature. The book's title denotes the two metaphors by which Abrams characterized 18th- and 19th-century English literature, respectively—the former as a cool, intellectual reflection of outward reality and the latter as an illumination shed by artists upon their inner and outer worlds. His later work *Natural Supernaturalism* (1971) explores a broader reach of the Romantic sensibility, including its religious implications and its influence on modern literature. Critical essays by Abrams were collected in *The Correspondent Breeze* (1984) and *Doing Things with Texts* (1989).

Abrantès *see* JUNOT.

abridged edition A version of a work that has been shortened or condensed by the omission of words, presumably without sacrifice of the principal meaning. When it is done for purposes of censorship, abridgment is known as bowdlerization (*see* BOWDLERIZE).

Absalom \'ab-sə-ləm\ (fl. *c.* 1020 BC, Palestine) Third and favorite son of David, king of Israel and Judah. The picture of Absalom presented in II Samuel 13–19 suggests that he was the Alcibiades of the Old Testament, alike in his personal attractiveness, his lawless insolence, and his tragic fate. He is first mentioned as murdering his half brother Amnon, David's eldest son, in revenge for the rape of his full sister Tamar. For this deed he was driven into banishment, but he was eventually restored to favor through the good offices of Joab. Later, when some uncertainty seems to have arisen as to the succession, Absalom organized a revolt. He was eventually killed by Joab.

Later literature that deals with aspects of Absalom's life includes John Dryden's *Absalom and Achitophel* and Alan Paton's *Cry, the Beloved Country*.

Absalom, Absalom! Novel by William FAULKNER, published in 1936.

The principal narrative, set in 19th-century Mississippi, concerns the efforts of Thomas Sutpen to transcend his lowly origins by establishing and maintaining a slave-driven empire— "Sutpen's Hundred"—on the frontier. Sutpen's consuming notion of racial superiority undermines his closest relationships and proves his undoing. By the novel's end his plantation is in ruins and his only living heir is a mentally deficient great-grandson of mixed blood.

Bracketing this mythic story is the struggle of Quentin Compson, a young Mississippian at Harvard decades later (and the grandson of a Sutpen acquaintance), to come to terms with the story's implications for his native region. Criticized by contemporary critics for its turgid style and convoluted, redundant narration, the book later came to be considered one of the finest in American literature.

Absalom and Achitophel \'ab-sə-ləm . . . ə-'kit-ə-,fel\ Verse satire by John DRYDEN published in 1681. The poem, which is written in heroic couplets, is about a contemporary episode in which anti-Catholics, notably the Earl of Shaftesbury, sought to bar James, Duke of York, a Roman Catholic convert and brother to King Charles II, from the line of succession in favor of the king's illegitimate (but Protestant) son, the Duke of Monmouth. Dryden based his work on an Old Testament incident recorded in II Samuel 13–19; these chapters relate the story of King David's favorite son Absalom and his false friend Achitophel (Ahithophel), who persuades Absalom to revolt against his father. In his poem, Dryden assigns each figure in the crisis a biblical name, *e.g.*, Absalom (Monmouth), Achitophel (Shaftesbury), and David (Charles II). Despite the strong anti-Catholic tenor of the times, Dryden's clear and persuasive dissection of the intriguers' motives helped to preserve the Duke of York's position.

A second part of the poem, largely composed by Nahum Tate but containing 200 lines by Dryden that were directed at his literary rivals Thomas Shadwell and Elkanah Settle, was published in 1682.

Abse \'ab-zē\, Dannie (b. Sept. 22, 1923, Cardiff, Wales) British poet, playwright, essayist, and novelist, known for the characteristically Welsh voice and sensibility of his poetry.

Abse was reared in Cardiff. He trained as a physician and qualified as a doctor in 1950. From 1949 to 1954 he edited a literary magazine, *Poetry and Poverty*, and from 1951 to 1955 he served in the Royal Air Force. Thereafter he worked part-time as a physician at a London clinic while pursuing a freelance writing career.

Best known for his poetry, Abse wrote his first book of verse, *After Every Green Thing* (1948), in a declamatory style. *Walking under Water* (1952) followed. He established his mature voice and his reputation with *Tenants of the House* (1957), in which he addressed moral and political concerns with parables. *Poems, Golders Green* (1962) explored the poet's outsider identities. With this volume, Abse's work became increasingly personal, a trend continued in *A Small Desperation* (1968) and the acclaimed *Funland* (1973), a nine-part extended allegory on the quest for meaning in a madhouse world. *Way Out in the Centre* (1981; U.S. title, *One-Legged on Ice*) further explored, with his characteristic dark wit, Abse's life as a doctor. *White Coat, Purple Coat: Collected Poems, 1948–1988* was published in 1989 and *Remembrance of Crimes Past* in 1990.

The most noted of Abse's novels is *Ash on a Young Man's Sleeve* (1954). *There Was a Young Man from Cardiff* (1991) is a sequel. His theatrical works include *The Dogs of Pavlov* (1973) and *Pythagoras* (1979).

absolute \ˈab-sə-ˌlüt, ˌab-sə-ˈlüt\ Being self-sufficient and free of external references or relationships. In criticism, an absolutist believes that there are inviolable standards by which a work of art should be judged and that there are certain basic and immutable values that determine worth.

Absolute, Sir Anthony and Captain Jack \sər-ˈanth-ə-nē-ˌab-sə-ˈlüt . . . ˈkap-tən-ˈjak\ Fictional characters, father and son protagonists of Richard Brinsley Sheridan's comic play THE RIVALS. Sir Anthony is a wealthy aristocrat whose son, Captain Jack, masquerades as the penniless Ensign Beverley in order to court Lydia Languish, who has romantic notions of marrying a poor man.

abstract \ˈab-ˌstrakt\ A summary of points (as of a written work) usually presented in skeletal form; also, something that summarizes or concentrates the essentials of a larger thing or several things.

abstract poem Term coined by the English poet Edith Sitwell to describe a poem in which the words are chosen for their aural quality rather than specifically for their sense or meaning. An example from "Popular Song" in Sitwell's *Façade* follows:

> The red retriever-haired satyr
> Can whine and tease her and flatter,
> But Lily O'Grady,
> Silly and shady,
> In the deep shade is a lazy lady;
> Now Pompey's dead, Homer's read,
> Heliogabalus lost his head,
> And shade is on the brightest wing,
> And dust forbids the bird to sing.

absurdism \əb-ˈsər-ˌdiz-əm, -ˈzər-\ A philosophy based on the belief that humans exist in an irrational and meaningless universe and that the search for order brings one into conflict with that universe. *See also* THEATER OF THE ABSURD.

Abū al-ʿAtāhiyah \ä-ˈbül-ä-ˈtä-hē-yə, *Arabic* ʾä-ˈtä-\, *original name* Abū Isḥāq Ismāʿīl ibn al-Qāsim ibn Suwayd ibn Kaysān (b. 748, al-Kūfah or ʿAyn at-Tamr, Iraq—d. 825/826, Baghdad) First Arab poet of note to break with the conventions established by the pre-Islāmic poets of the desert and to adopt a simpler and freer language of the village.

Abū al-ʿAtāhiyah ("Father of Craziness") came from a family of *mawlās*, poor non-Arabs who were clients (*i.e.*, paid for the protection) of the ʿAnaza Arab tribe. The family's poverty prevented Abū al-ʿAtāhiyah from receiving a formal education,

which may account for his subsequently original and untraditional poetic style. He began to write ghazels (lyric poems) during his early years in al-Kūfah; they later gained him notoriety as well as the favor of the noted caliph Hārūn ar-Rashīd. Abū al-ʿAtāhiyah's fame, however, rested on the ascetic poems of his later years, the *Zuhdīyāt*, collected in 1071 by the Spanish scholar Ibn ʿAbd al-Barr. The *Zuhdīyāt* gave vent to his feelings of social resentment in verses depicting the leveling of the rich and powerful by the horrors of death. These found an enthusiastic following among the masses.

Abū al-Faraj al-Iṣbahānī \ä-ˈbül-fä-ˈräzh-äl-ˌis-bä-ˈhä-ˌnē\, *in full* Abū al-Faraj ʿAlī ibn al-Ḥusayn al-Qurashī al-Iṣbahānī, *also called* al-Iṣfahānī \äl-ˌis-fä-ˈhä-ˌnē\ (b. 897, Isfahan [Iran]—d. Nov. 20, 967, Baghdad, Iraq) Literary scholar who composed an encyclopedic and fundamental work on Arabic song, composers, poets, and musicians.

Abū al-Faraj was a descendant of Marwān II, the last Umayyad caliph of Syria. He spent most of his life in Baghdad, where from 945 he enjoyed the patronage of the Būyid emirs. *Kitāb al-aghānī* ("The Book of Songs"), his major work, contains songs, biographical details (or data), and much information concerning the life and customs of the early Arabs and of the Muslim Arabs of the Umayyad period (661–750) and the subsequent ʿAbbāsid period (which lasted from 750 to 1258).

Abū al-Fidāʾ \ä-ˈbül-ˈfē-ˌdä\, *in full* Abū al-Fidāʾ Ismāʿīl ibn ʿAlī al-Mālik al-Muʾayyad ʿImad ad-Dīn, *also called* Abulfeda \ä-ˈbül-ˈfē-dä\ (b. Nov. 1273, Damascus [now in Syria]—d. Oct. 27, 1331, Ḥamāh) Historian, geographer, and man of letters who became a local sultan under the Mamlūk Empire.

Abū al-Fidāʾ was a descendant of Ayyūb, the father of Saladin, founder of the Sunnite Muslim Ayyūbid dynasty (late 12th and early 13th centuries) that had been supplanted by the Mamlūks in Egypt and elsewhere before his birth. In 1285 he accompanied his father and his cousin to Mamlūk sieges of Crusader strongholds. Abū al-Fidāʾ served the Mamlūk governor of Ḥamāh until he was made first governor of Ḥamāh (1310), then prince for life (1312). In 1320, after making a pilgrimage to Mecca with the Mamlūk sultan al-Nāṣir Muḥammad, he was given the title al-Malik al-Muʾayyad and the rank of sultan.

Abū al-Fidāʾ was a patron of scholars and a scholar himself. His two major works were a history, *Mukhtaṣar tāʾrīkh al-bashar* ("Brief History of Man"), spanning pre-Islāmic and Islāmic periods to 1329; and a geography, *Taqwīm al-buldān* (1321; "Locating the Lands"). Both works are compilations of other authors, arranged and added to by Abū al-Fidāʾ, rather than original treatises. Popular in their day in the Middle East, they were much used by 18th- and 19th-century European Orientalists before earlier sources became available.

Abu ʾl-Faḍl ʿAllāmī \ä-ˈbül-ˈfäd-əl-ä-ˈlä-ˌmē, *Arabic* ʾä-ˈlä-\, Abu ʾl-Faḍl *also spelled* Abu-l-Faẓl \ä-ˈbül-ˈfäth-əl\ (b. Jan. 14, 1551, Āgra, India—d. Aug. 22, 1602) Historian, military commander, secretary, and theologian to the Mughal emperor Akbar.

Abu ʾl-Faḍl ʿAllāmī studied with his father, a distinguished scholar, and after teaching in his father's school was presented to Akbar in 1574. Appointed a military commander in the Deccan in 1599, he distinguished himself both as a soldier and as an administrator. He was called back to court during a rebellion of Akbar's son Salīm (afterward the emperor Jahāngīr) but, at Salīm's instigation, was stopped en route and assassinated.

Abu ʾl-Faḍl's major literary achievement was a history of Akbar and his ancestors, *Akbar-nāmeh* (*The Akbarnāma of Abu-l-Faẓl*), concluded by the *Āīn-e Akbarī* (Eng. trans., *ʿAin-i-Ākbari of Abul Fazl-i-ʿĀllami*), which includes a manual of government operations—ranging from the jewel office and elephant stables to tax collection—and an account of Hindu culture and sciences.

Abu Madi \á-bù-'mä-dē\, Iliya (b. *c.* 1889, al-Muḥaydithah, Lebanon—d. Nov. 23, 1957, New York, N.Y., U.S.) Arab poet and journalist noted as one of the chief poets of the *mahgar* (Arab emigration to America).

When he was 11 years old, Abu Madi moved with his family from their mountain village in Lebanon to Alexandria, Egypt. He published his first collection of poetry in Alexandria in 1911. The following year he immigrated to the United States, settling in Cincinnati, Ohio, where he worked with his brother. In 1916 he moved to New York City and began editing several Arabic newspapers and magazines. In 1929 he started his own bimonthly magazine, *As-Samīr* ("The Companion"), which he expanded into a daily newspaper in 1936 and continued to publish until his death.

Abu Madi published a collection of poetry in 1916 and a second, *Al-Jadāwil* ("Streams"), in 1927. *Al-Khamā'il* (1946; "Thickets") was printed in Beirut, as was the posthumous *Tibr wa-turāb* (1960; "Gold and Dust"). His poetry was popular because of his expressive and natural use of language and his mastery of the traditional patterns of Arabic poetry.

Abū Nuwās \á-,bū-nù-'wäs\, *also spelled* Abū Nu'ās \nū-'äs\, *in full* Abū Nuwās al-Ḥasan ibn Hāni' al-Ḥakamī (b. *c.* 747–762, Ahvāz [Iran]—d. *c.* 813–815, Baghdad [now in Iraq]) Important poet of the early 'Abbāsid period (750–835).

Of mixed Arab and Persian heritage, Abū Nuwās studied in Basra and al-Kūfah, first under the poet Wālibah ibn al-Ḥubāb, later under Khalaf al-Aḥmar. Abū Nuwās' initial appearance at the 'Abbāsid court in Baghdad met with little success; his alliance with the Barmakids, the 'Abbāsid viziers, forced him to seek refuge in Egypt when the Barmakid dynasty collapsed. On his return to Baghdad, however, his panegyrics earned the favor of the caliphs Hārūn ar-Rashīd and al-Amīn, and he enjoyed great success in the 'Abbāsid court until his death.

The language of Abū Nuwās' formal odes (qasidas) is based on the old Arab traditions; his themes, however, are drawn from urban life, not the desert. He is particularly renowned for his poems on wine and pederasty. His verse is laced with humor and irony, reflecting the genial yet cynical outlook he had developed by spending much of his life in pursuit of pleasure.

Abū Rīshah \á-,bū-'rē-shá\, 'Umar (b. April 10, 1910, 'Akko, Palestine [now in Israel]—d. July 15, 1990, Riyadh, Saudi Arabia) Syrian poet and diplomat who is noted for his early poetry, which broke with the traditions of Arab classicism.

Abū Rīshah attended the University of Damascus in Syria, the American University in Beirut, Lebanon, and the University of Manchester, England. He was an early contributor to the influential Egyptian literary journal *Apollo*, and from 1940 he worked as a librarian in Aleppo, Syria. In 1949 his increasingly political poems attracted the attention of the new military government, and for many years he served in various diplomatic posts, including ambassadorships to Brazil, Argentina, India, and the United States. After his retirement he settled in Saudi Arabia. Abū Rīshah published verse dramas and several volumes of poetry in Arabic, as well as one volume that was translated into English as *Roving Along*.

Abū Tammām \á-,bū-tám-'mäm\, *in full* Abū Tammām Ḥabib ibn Aws (b. 804, near Damascus [now in Syria]—d. *c.* 845, Mosul, Iraq) Poet and editor of an anthology of early Arabic poems known as the ḤAMĀSAH.

Abū Tammām changed his Christian surname and invented for himself an Arab genealogy. In his youth he worked in Damascus as a weaver's assistant but on going to Egypt be-

gan to study poetry. By the time of the caliph al-Mu'taṣim (reigned 833–842), he had established a small reputation. This was greatly enlarged through his association with al-Mu'taṣim's court, where he became the most acclaimed panegyrist of his day. He traveled to Armenia and Nīshāpūr [Iran], and on his return journey, he began compiling his *Ḥamāsah*. Abū Tammām's divan, or collection of poems, generally deals with contemporary events of historical significance.

abyss \ə-'bis, a-; 'ab-is\ [Greek *ábyssos,* from *ábyssos* (adjective) bottomless] The bottomless gulf, pit, or chaos of the old cosmogonies. The term can also have any of three specific meanings: **1.** A confined subterranean body of water that according to the Old Testament was once an ocean surrounding the earth. **2.** The infernal regions, including the abode of the dead and of the evil powers and the place where the wicked are punished. **3.** The formless chaos out of which the earth and the heavens were created.

academese \ə-,kad-ə-'mēz, -'mēs; ,ak-əd-ə-\ A style of writing held to be characteristic of those in academic life. The term is generally pejorative, implying jargon-filled writing.

academic \,ak-ə-'dem-ik\ *or* **academical** \-mi-kəl\ Conforming to the traditions or rules of a school, as of literature or art, or an official academy. Conventional or formalistic.

academic drama Any play written and performed at schools and colleges in England in the early 16th century. *See also* SCHOOL DRAMA.

Académie Française \á-kä-dā-,mē-frä^n-'sez\ French literary academy, established by the French first minister Cardinal de Richelieu in 1634 and incorporated in 1635, and existing, except for an interruption during the era of the French Revolution, to the present day. Its original purpose was to maintain standards of literary taste and to establish the literary language. Its membership is limited to 40. Though it has often acted as a conservative body, opposed to innovations in literary content and form, its membership has included most of the great names of French literature—*e.g.*, Pierre Corneille, Jean Racine, Voltaire, Chateaubriand, Victor Hugo, Joseph-Ernest Renan, and Henri Bergson. In 1980 Marguerite Yourcenar became the first woman to be elected to the academy.

academy \ə-'kad-ə-mē\ [Greek *Akādēmeia, Akadēmía* a public grove and gymnasium near Athens where Plato taught, a derivative of *Akádēmos,* a legendary Attic hero after whom the grove and gymnasium were named] A society of learned individuals organized to advance art, science, literature, music, or some other cultural or intellectual area of endeavor.

At the close of the European Middle Ages, academies began to be formed in Italy, first for the study of classical and then of Italian literature. One of the earliest was the Platonic Academy, founded in Florence in 1442. Literary academies sprang up all over Italy in the 16th and 17th centuries; the most famous of these was the Crusca Academy.

The Académie Française, which would become Europe's best-known literary academy, began in 1635. The Royal Spanish Academy was founded in 1713 to preserve the Spanish language, and it published a landmark Spanish dictionary for that purpose.

Academies of science began to appear in the 16th century, and academies of fine arts, music, social sciences, medicine, mining, and agriculture were formed from the 18th century on. Most European countries now have at least one academy or learned society that is sponsored by or otherwise connected with the state.

The United States, like Great Britain, Canada, and other English-speaking countries, has no state-established academies of science or literature, a fact reflective of English beliefs that culture should basically be a matter for private initiative. The first learned society in what would become the United States was founded by Benjamin Franklin in 1743 and called the American Philosophical Society. The rival American Academy of Arts and Sciences was founded in 1779, and the National Academy of Sciences was founded in Washington, D.C., in 1863.

acatalectic \ˌā-ˌkat-ə-ˈlek-tik\ [Greek *akatálēktos*, literally, not stopping] In prosody, metrically complete (*i.e.*, not falling short of the expected number of syllables in the last foot). It is the opposite of *catalexis*, the suppression or absence of the final syllable of a line.

Accademia della Crusca   *see* CRUSCA ACADEMY.

Accademia dell'Arcadia   *see* Academy of ARCADIA.

accent \ˈak-ˌsent, -sənt\ [Latin *accentus* variation in pitch, intonation, from *ad* to, toward + *cantus* song; a calque of Greek *prosōidía*] In prosody, rhythmically significant stress on the syllables of a verse, usually at regular intervals. The word *accent* is often used interchangeably with *stress*, though some prosodists use *accent* to mean the emphasis that is determined by the normal meaning of the words while *stress* is used to mean metrical emphasis. *Compare* STRESS.

Accent (*in full* Accent: A Quarterly of New Literature) Literary magazine published from 1940 to 1960 at the University of Illinois. Founded by Kerker Quinn and Charles Shattuck, the journal evolved from an earlier version called *Direction* that Quinn put out in his undergraduate days. *Accent* published some of the best examples of contemporary writing by both new and established authors, including Wallace Stevens, Katherine Anne Porter, William Gass, James T. Farrell, Eudora Welty, Thomas Mann, Bertolt Brecht, and Richard Wright.

accentual-syllabic verse In prosody, the metrical system that is most commonly used in English poetry. It is based on both the number of stresses, or accents, and the number of syllables in each line of verse. A line of iambic pentameter verse, for example, consists of five feet, each of which is an iamb (an unstressed followed by a stressed syllable). Although accentual-syllabic verse is very strictly measured, variations in both accent placement and number of syllables are often allowed. *See also* METER.

accentual verse \ak-ˈsen-chü-wəl\ In prosody, a metrical system based only on the number of stresses or accented syllables in a line of verse. In accentual verse the total number of syllables in a line can vary as long as there are the prescribed number of accents. This system is used in Germanic poetry, including Old English and Old Norse, as well as in some English verse. The poem "What if a Much of a Which of a Wind," by E.E. Cummings, is an example of accentual verse. In the following lines from the poem the number of accents is constant at four while the number of syllables per line varies from seven to ten:

> what if a much of a which of a wind
> gives the truth to summer's lie;
> bloodies with dizzying leaves the sun
> and yanks immortal stars awry?
> Blow king to beggar and queen to seem
> (blow friend to fiend: blow space to time)
> —when skies are hanged and oceans drowned,
> the single secret will still be man

See also METER.

accismus \ak-ˈsiz-məs\ [Greek *akkismós* prudery, a derivative of *akkízesthai* to feign ignorance] A form of irony in which a person feigns indifference to, or pretends to refuse, something he or she desires. The fox's dismissal of the grapes in the Ae-

sop fable of the fox and the grapes is an example of accismus. A classic example is that of Caesar's initial refusal to accept the crown, a circumstance reported by one of the conspirators in William Shakespeare's *Julius Caesar.*

Accius \ˈak-shē-əs\ or **Attius** \ˈat-ē-əs\, Lucius (b. 170 BC, Pisaurum, Umbria [Italy]—d. *c.* 86 BC) One of the greatest of the Roman tragic poets, in the view of his contemporaries. His plays (more than 40 titles are known, and about 700 lines survive) were mostly free translations from Greek tragedy, many from Euripides, with violent plots, flamboyant characterizations, and forceful rhetoric.

Accius also wrote several scholarly treatises: the *Didascalica,* a work on the history of Greek and Latin poetry, Greek and Roman theater, and other literary subjects; and *Annales,* which seems to have dealt with aspects of the calendar.

Account of My Hut, An Poetic diary by KAMO Chōmei, written in Japanese in 1212 as *Hōjōki.* It is admired as a classic literary and philosophical work.

An Account of My Hut (the title is sometimes translated as *The Ten Foot Square Hut*) relates the musings of a Buddhist who renounces the world to live a life of meditation and refined solitude in a small mountain hut. The work reflects the author's belief in the transience of life and includes brief regrets on the fickleness of the world as well as descriptions of natural disasters and internecine conflicts involving the Minamoto and Taira families in the late 12th century. Reflecting the Buddhist teaching that desiring nothing is the way to transcend the pain of life, the work describes the author's retreat to smaller and smaller living quarters. Even then he realizes that his love for his tiny hut compromises his renunciation of all material things.

acephalous \ā-ˈsef-ə-ləs, ə-\ [Greek *aképhalos* headless, from *a-* not + *kephalē* head] *see* HEADLESS.

Acestes \ə-ˈses-tēz\ In Greek mythology, legendary king of Segesta (Greek: Egesta) in Sicily. His mother, Egesta, had been sent from Troy by her parents to save her from being devoured by a sea serpent. Going to Sicily she met the river god Crimisus, by whom she became the mother of Acestes.

Acestes appears notably in Virgil's *Aeneid,* offering hospitality to Aeneas when he lands in Sicily. Virgil uses Acestes to emphasize the mythological connection of Sicily with Troy; in Greek legend Aeneas, whose descendants founded Rome, traveled no farther than Sicily. In the *Aeneid* Acestes brings the funeral games of Anchises, Aeneas' father, to a climax by shooting into the air an arrow that becomes a comet, a sign of Anchises' eternal life.

Acevedo Díaz \ˌäs-ā-ˈbā-ᵺō-ˈᵺē-äs\, Eduardo (b. April 20, 1851, Villa de la Unión, Uruguay—d. June 18, 1924, Buenos Aires, Arg.) Writer and politician who is considered to be Uruguay's first novelist.

Acevedo Díaz attended the University of Montevideo, where he first became active in politics. He took part in the Revolución Blanca (1870–72) and the Revolución Tricolor (1885), supporting the cause of the Blancos, a nationalist, rurally oriented political party. Often credited with being the founder of *gauchismo* (a literary movement that emphasized the role of the gaucho in Spanish-American history), Acevedo Díaz did most of his writing while in exile in Argentina. His first novel, *Brenda* (1886), was followed by a popular trilogy of historical novels concerned with the Uruguayan wars for independence (from about 1808 to the late 1820s): *Ismael* (1888), *Nativa* (1890), and *Grito de gloria* (1893; "The Battle Cry of Glory"). *Soledad* (1894; "Solitude") was his masterpiece.

Acharnians \ə-ˈkär-nē-ənz\ (*Greek* Acharneis) Earliest of the extant comedies of ARISTOPHANES, produced in 425 BC.

It is a forthright attack on the folly of war. Its farmer-hero, Dicaeopolis, is tired of the Peloponnesian War and therefore secures a private peace treaty with the Spartans for himself in spite of the violent opposition of a chorus of embittered and bellicose old charcoal burners of Acharnae. Dicaeopolis takes advantage of his private treaty to trade with the allies of the Spartans. The Athenian commander Lamachus tries to stop him, but by the end of the play Lamachus slumps wounded and dejected while Dicaeopolis enjoys a peacetime life of food, wine, and sex.

Achebe \ä-'chä-bä\, Chinua, *in full* Albert Chinualumogu Achebe (b. Nov. 16, 1930, Ogidi, Nigeria)   Prominent Igbo (Ibo) novelist acclaimed for his unsentimental depictions of the social and psychological disorientation accompanying the imposition of Western customs and values upon traditional African society. His particular concern was with emergent Africa at its moments of crisis.

Educated in English at the University of Ibadan, Achebe taught for a short time before joining the staff of the Nigerian Broadcasting Corporation in Lagos. In 1967 he cofounded a publishing company at Enugu with the poet Christopher Okigbo. He was later appointed research fellow at the University of Nigeria and then became professor of English, a position he held until 1981 (professor emeritus from 1985).

Both THINGS FALL APART (1958), Achebe's first novel, and *Arrow of God* (1964) concern traditional Igbo life as it clashes with colonial powers in the form of missionaries and colonial government. *No Longer at Ease* (1960), *A Man of the People* (1966), and *Anthills of the Savannah* (1988) deal with corruption and other aspects of postcolonial African life. Achebe also published collections of short stories, poetry, essays, and several books for juvenile readers. His novels have been translated into many languages.

Acheron \'ak-ə-rän\   River in Thesprotía in Epirus, Greece, that was thought in ancient times to go to Hades because it flowed through dark gorges and went underground in several places; an oracle of the dead was located on its bank. In Greek mythology Acheron is a river in Hades, and the name sometimes refers to the lower world generally. Several other rivers in Greece are also called Acheron, which traditionally means "river of woe."

Achilles \ə-'kil-ēz\   In Greek mythology, son of the mortal Peleus, king of the Myrmidons, and the Nereid Thetis. He was the bravest, handsomest, and greatest warrior of the army of Agamemnon in the Trojan War. One of the non-Homeric tales of his childhood relates that Thetis dipped Achilles in the waters of the River Styx, by which he became invulnerable, except for the part of his heel by which she held him—the proverbial "Achilles' heel."

The later mythographers related that Peleus, having received an oracle that his son would die fighting at TROY, sent Achilles to the court of Lycomedes on Scyros, where he was dressed as a girl and kept among the king's daughters (one of whom, Deïdamia, bore his son Neoptolemus). After the soothsayer Calchas warned that Troy could not be taken without Achilles, the Greeks searched for him and found him.

Homer's epic the ILIAD tells the story of Achilles' subsequent part in the Trojan War, including his slaying of Hector, son of the Trojan king Priam. The poet Arctinus in his *Aethiopis* (now lost) took up the story of the *Iliad* and related that Achilles, having slain the Ethiopian king Memnon and the Amazon queen Penthesilea, was himself slain by Priam's son Paris, whose arrow was guided by Apollo.

Achilles Tatius \ə-'kil-ēz-'tā-shē-əs\ (fl. 2nd century AD, Alexandria, Egypt)   Teacher of rhetoric and author of *Leu-

cippe and Cleitophon, one of the Greek prose romances that influenced the development of the novel centuries later.

Nothing certain is known of Achilles' life. The romance, a typical adventure story of love triumphant over innumerable obstacles is related in the first person by Cleitophon himself, whom Achilles claims to have met in Sidon. The work's style is typical of Atticism, with its extreme purity of diction, short unconnected sentences, parallel clauses, detailed descriptions, and frequent declamations and disquisitions, often in antithetical form—*e.g.*, on love for women and pederasty. Achilles shows uncommon ingenuity in inventing coups de theatre (Leucippe apparently dies three times but always reappears), but his characterization is poor, and plot is relegated to the background by irrelevant interruptions. The romance was admired by Byzantine critics and was widely translated in the Renaissance.

Achitophel   *see* ABSALOM AND ACHITOPHEL.

Achterberg \'äk-tər-ˌberk\, Gerrit (b. May 20, 1905, Langbroek, Neth.—d. Jan. 17, 1962, Oud-Leusden)   Dutch poet whose use of surreal language and imagery influenced a generation of poets known as the Experimentalists.

In his first commercially published volume of poetry, *Afvaart* (1931; "Departure"), Achterberg introduced a theme that permeates his oeuvre: the magical power of language, notably his belief that poetry could revitalize the beloved. He often used apostrophe to address this beloved, which represented such things as a lover, God, death, beauty, poetry, and the absolute. His second volume of verse, *Eiland der ziel* (1939; "Island of the Soul"), treated the theme with optimism, but the tone of his next book, *Dead End* (1940), was one of disappointment.

A four-volume anthology, *Cryptogamen* (1946–61; "Cryptogamia"), which was translated into many languages, includes *Eiland der ziel* and *Sneeuwwitje* (1949; "Snow White"). Some of Achterberg's other works were *Stof* (1946; "Stuff"), *Hoonte* (1949; "Insulted"), *Voorbij de laatste stad* (1955; "Past the Last City"), and *Verzamelde gedichten* (1963; "Collected Verses").

Acis \'ā-sis\   In the Greek mythology of Ovid, the son of Faunus (Pan) and the nymph Symaethis. Acis was a handsome shepherd of Sicily and the lover of the Nereid Galatea. His rival, Polyphemus the Cyclops, surprised them together and crushed Acis with a rock. His blood, gushing forth from beneath the rock, was metamorphosed by Galatea into a river bearing his name (Acis or Acinius—the modern river Jaci). Ovid is the only extant source for the tale.

Acker \'ak-ər\, Kathy (b. 1948)   American novelist whose writing style and subject matter reflect the so-called punk sensibility that emerged in youth culture in the 1970s.

Acker studied classics at Brandeis University and the University of California at San Diego. Her early employment ranged from clerical work to performing in pornographic films. In 1972 she began publishing willfully crude, disjointed prose that drew heavily from her personal experience and constituted a literary analog to contemporary developments in music, fashion, and the visual arts. From the outset, Acker blatantly lifted material from other writers, manipulating it for her own often unsettling purposes. In the early novel *The Childlike Life of the Black Tarantula* (1973), this process of appropriation is central to the narrator's quest for identity. The book's themes of alienation and objectified sexuality recur in such later novels as *Great Expectations* (1982), *Don Quixote* (1986), and *Empire of the Senseless* (1988). In 1993 *My Mother: Demonology*, which consists of seven love stories, was published.

Ackerley \'ak-ər-lē\, J.R., *in full* Joe Randolph (b. Nov. 4, 1896, Herne Hill, Kent, Eng.—d. June 4, 1967, Putney, near

London)   British novelist, dramatist, poet, and magazine editor known for his eccentricity.

Ackerley's education was interrupted by his service in World War I, during which he was captured and imprisoned for eight months in Germany. Following the war, he graduated from Magdalene College, Cambridge, in 1921. He examined his wartime experiences in the play *The Prisoners of War* (1925). A five-month position as private secretary to an Indian maharaja in 1923 provided the material for his humorous *Hindoo Holiday: An Indian Journal* (1932).

Ackerley joined the British Broadcasting Corporation in 1928; from 1935 to 1959 he was the literary editor of *Listener*, the company's weekly magazine. Although he published very little himself while at the BBC, he forged close relationships with many of London's literati, most notably with E.M. Forster. But, according to Ackerley, his most prized relationship was with his Alsatian dog; he wrote tenderly of this platonic love affair in *My Dog Tulip* (1956). Drawing largely on personal experience, the comic novel *We Think the World of You* (1960) is the strange tale of a man's love for a friend's dog. Ackerley's autobiography, *My Father and Myself* (published posthumously, 1968), describes the remarkable double life of his father, a prosperous banana importer who secretly maintained two families in separate locations. Ackerley's correspondence was published as *The Ackerley Letters* (1975).

Ackerman \ 'ak-ər-mən \, Diane, *original surname* Fink \ 'fiŋk \ (b. Oct. 7, 1948, Waukegan, Ill., U.S.)   American writer whose works often reflected her interest in natural science.

Ackerman was educated at Pennsylvania State University (B.A., 1970) and Cornell University, Ithaca, N.Y. (M.F.A., 1973; M.A., 1976; Ph.D., 1978). From 1980 to 1983 she taught English at the University of Pittsburgh and from 1984 to 1986 directed the writers' program and was writer-in-residence at Washington University, St. Louis, Mo. From 1988 she was a staff writer at *The New Yorker* magazine.

Ackerman's memoir *On Extended Wings* (1985) was adapted for the stage in 1987. Her later books include *A Natural History of the Senses* (1990), *The Moon By Whale Light, and Other Adventures Among Bats, Penguins, Crocodilians, and Whales* (1991), and *A Natural History of Love* (1994).

Ackerman considered such matters as amino acids, viruses, quasars, and corpuscles to be as much in the realm of poetic experience as anything else in the universe. Her published poetry includes *The Planets: A Cosmic Pastoral* (1976), *Wife of Light* (1978), *Lady Faustus* (1983), and *Jaguar of Sweet Laughter: New and Selected Poems* (1991). Ackerman wrote a series of nine radio programs for the Canadian Broadcasting Corporation under the title "Ideas into the Universe" (1975). She also wrote *Twilight of the Tenderfoot: A Western Memoir* (1980) and the play *Reverse Thunder* (1988).

Ackermann \ 'äk-ər-,män \, Louise-Victorine, *original surname* Choquet \ shô-'kä \ (b. Nov. 30, 1813, Paris, Fr.—d. Aug. 2, 1890, Nice)   French poet who is best-known for her works of deep pessimism. Educated by her father in the philosophy of the Encyclopédistes, she traveled to Berlin in 1838 to study German and there married (1843) Paul Ackermann, an Alsatian philologist. Two years later her husband died, and she went to live with her sister at Nice. There she wrote *Contes en vers* (1855; "Stories in Verse") and *Contes et poésies* (1862; "Stories and Poetry"), but her real reputation rests on the *Poésies, premières poésies, poésies philosophiques* (1874; "Poetry, First Poetry, Philosophical Poetry"), a volume of somber and powerful verse, expressing her revolt against human suffering.

Ackroyd \ 'ak-,ròid \, Peter (b. Oct. 5, 1949, London, Eng.)   British novelist, critic, biographer, and scholar whose techni-

cally innovative novels presented an unconventional view of history.

Ackroyd graduated from Cambridge University (M.A., 1971) and then attended Yale University for two years. In 1973 he returned to England and worked as an editor for *The Spectator*. In 1986 he became the principal book reviewer for the London *Times*.

Ackroyd published several books, including two collections of absurdist poetry, a study of transvestism, and a biography, *Ezra Pound and His World* (1980; revised as *Ezra Pound*, 1987), before turning to fiction. His first novel, *The Great Fire of London* (1982), was followed by *The Last Testament of Oscar Wilde* (1983), *Hawksmoor* (1985; winner of the Prix Goncourt and the Whitbread prize), *Chatterton* (1987), *First Light* (1989), *English Music* (1992), and *The House of Doctor Dee* (1993). Ackroyd's later biographies include *T.S. Eliot: A Life* (1984) and *Dickens* (1990).

Acmeist \ 'ak-mē-ist \, *Russian* Akmeist \ ,ək-mē-'ēst \, *plural* Akmeisty \ -'ēs-tē \ [Russian *akmeist,* from Greek *akmē* highest point, acme]   Member of a small group of early 20th-century Russian poets reacting against what they considered to be the vagueness and affectations of Symbolism. The Acmeist movement was formed by the poets Sergey Gorodetsky and Nikolay S. GUMILYOV. They reasserted the poet as craftsman and used language freshly and with intensity. Centered in St. Petersburg, the Acmeists were associated with the review *Apollon* (1909–17). In 1912 they founded the Guild of Poets, whose most outstanding members were Anna AKHMATOVA and Osip MANDELSHTAM. Because of their preoccupation with form and their aloofness, the Acmeists were regarded with suspicion by the Soviet regime. Gumilyov was executed in 1921 for his alleged activities in an anti-Soviet conspiracy. Akhmatova was silenced during the most productive years of her life, and Mandelshtam died en route to a labor camp.

Acontius \ ə-'kän-shē-əs, -shəs \   In Greek legend, a beautiful youth of the island of Chios. During the festival of Artemis at Delos, Acontius saw and fell in love with Cydippe, a girl of a rich and noble family. He wrote on an apple the words "I swear to wed Acontius" and threw it at her feet. She picked it up and mechanically read the words aloud, thus binding herself by an oath. The goddess Artemis witnessed the oath and subsequently, when Cydippe ignored the oath and became betrothed to another, caused her to fall ill. After this happened several times, Cydippe's father went to the Delphic oracle to discover the reason for Cydippe's illnesses. When the situation was explained to him, he arranged for Cydippe to marry Acontius.

Acquainted with the Night   Novel by Heinrich BÖLL, published in German in 1953 as *Und sagte kein einziges Wort* ("And Said Not a Single Word").

One of Böll's best-known works, the novel is set in Germany just after World War II. It examines the marriage of Fred and Käthe Bogner, who alternately narrate the work. Their marriage suffers from stresses caused by poverty and the acute postwar shortages of food and shelter. Fred abuses their children; the couple separate. Among the institutions Böll satirizes is the Roman Catholic church. At the work's end, Käthe is pregnant and the couple are somewhat tentatively reunited.

acronym \ 'ak-rə-,nim \ [Greek *ákros* outermost, at the tip + *ónyma* name]   A word formed from the initial letter or letters of each of the successive parts or major parts of a compound term, such as RADAR from *ra*dio *d*etecting *a*nd *r*anging or SONAR from *so*und *na*vigation ranging.

acrostic \ ə-'kròs-tik \ [Greek *akrostichís,* from *ákros* outermost + *stíchos* line, verse]   **1.** Short verse composition, so constructed that one or more sets of letters (such as the initial, middle, or final letters of the lines), taken consecutively, form words. An acrostic in which the initial letters form the alphabet is an ABECEDARIUS.

The word *acrostic* was first applied to the prophecies of the Erythraean Sibyl, which were written on leaves and arranged so that the initial letters of the leaves always formed a word. Acrostics were common among the Greeks of the Alexandrine period, and many of the arguments of the plays of the Latin writers Ennius and Plautus were written in acrostic verses that spelled out the titles of the plays. Medieval monks were also fond of acrostics, as were the poets of the Middle High German and Italian Renaissance periods.

2. A type of word puzzle utilizing the acrostic principle. A popular form is double acrostics, puzzles constructed so that not only the initial letters of the lines but in some cases also the middle or last letters form words. In the United States, a Double Crostic puzzle, devised by Elizabeth Kingsley for *The Saturday Review* in 1934, had an acrostic in the answers to the clues giving the author and title of a literary work; the letters, keyed by number to blanks like those of a crossword puzzle, spelled out a quotation.

act \ˈakt\ [Latin *actus,* literally, action, activity]   One of the principal divisions of a theatrical work.

Actaeon \ak-ˈtē-ən\   In Greek mythology, son of the god Aristaeus and Autonoë (daughter of Cadmus, the founder of Thebes in Boeotia); he was a Boeotian hero and hunter. According to Ovid's *Metamorphoses,* Actaeon accidentally saw the goddess Artemis while she was bathing; for this reason he was changed by her into a stag and was pursued and killed by his own 50 hounds. In another version, he offended Artemis by boasting that his skill as a hunter surpassed hers. The story was well known in antiquity, and several of the tragic poets presented it on the stage (*e.g.,* Aeschylus' lost *Toxotides,* "The Archeresses").

action \ˈak-shən\ [translation of Greek *práxis* (in Aristotle's *Poetics*)]   **1.** A real or imaginary event or series of events forming the subject of a play, poem, or other composition.   **2.** The unfolding of the events of a drama or work of fiction, also called the PLOT.

Acuña \ä-ˈkūn-yä\, Rosario de, *surname in full* Acuña y Villanueva de la Iglesia \ē-,vēl-yä-ˈnwä-vä-thä-lä-ē-ˈgläs-yä\, *pseudonym* Remigio Andrés Delafón \,thä-lä-ˈfȯn\ (b. 1851, Madrid, Spain—d. 1923, Gijón)   Spanish playwright, essayist, and short-story writer known for her controversial liberal views.

Little is known of Acuña's early life. One of Spain's few women playwrights, she was considered radical for her willingness to address such issues as religious fanaticism, atheism, illegitimacy, civil marriage (and the possibility of divorce, anathema in Roman Catholic Spain), and reform of the criminal justice system.

Acuña is best known for her verse drama *Rienzi el tribuno* (produced 1876; "Rienzi the Tribune"); the tragedy describes the futile efforts of the 14th-century Roman tribune Cola di Rienzo to restore the greatness of ancient Rome. In *Amor a la patria* (1877; "Love of Country"), which celebrates peasants' resistance to Napoleon, the playwright contrasts the noble heroism of women with the venality of the male characters. Her other verse dramas include *El padre Juan* (1891), which caused a scandal with its attack on hypocritical clergy, and *La voz de la patria* (1893; "The Voice of the Nation").

Acuña's collections of poetry include *Ecos del alma* (1876; "Echoes from the Soul"), *Morirse a tiempo* (1880; "To Die on Time"), and *Sentir y pensar* (1884; "Feeling and Thought"). She

also wrote works that contributed to efforts to liberalize social policy. *El crimen de la calle de Fuencarral; odia el delito y compadece al delincuente* (1880?; "The Crime of Fuencarral Street: Hate the Crime and Pity the Criminal"), based on a sensational murder case, was a then-radical call for understanding the social roots of crime.

Ada (*in full* Ada; or, Ardor: A Family Chronicle) \ˈä-də\   Novel by Vladimir NABOKOV, written in English and published in 1969. In its prodigious length and with the family tree on its frontispiece the book recalls the great 19th-century novels of the author's native Russia, but *Ada* boldly turns its predecessors on their heads. For his rich, sweeping saga of the Veen-Durmanov clan, Nabokov invented an incestuous pair of "cousins" (actually siblings, Van and Ada), a hybrid country (Amerussia), a familiar but strange planet (Antiterra), and a dimension of malleable time. The novel follows the lovers from their childhood idylls through impassioned estrangements and reunions to a tenderly shared old age. The work's rich narrative style incorporates untranslated foreign phrases, esoteric data, and countless literary allusions.

adab \ˈä-dȧb\ [Arabic]   Islāmic concept that became a literary genre distinguished by its broad humanitarian concerns; it developed during the height of ʿAbbāsid culture in the 9th century and continued to be of importance through the Muslim Middle Ages.

The original sense of the word was simply "norm of conduct," or "custom," derived in ancient Arabia from ancestors revered as models. As such practice was deemed praiseworthy in the medieval Muslim world, *adab* acquired a further connotation of good breeding, courtesy, and urbanity.

Parallel to and growing out of this expanded social meaning of *adab* there appeared an intellectual aspect. *Adab* came to connote the knowledge of poetry, oratory, ancient Arab tribal history, rhetoric, grammar, philology, and non-Arab civilizations that qualified an individual to be called well-bred, or *adīb.* The vast and erudite *adab* literature was concerned with human achievements and was written in an expressive and flexible style that was rich in vocabulary and idiom. The best-known writers of *adab* include the 9th-century essayist al-Jāḥiz of Basra and his 11th-century follower Abū Hayyān at-Tawḥīdī; the 9th-century Kūfan critic, philologist, and theologian Ibn Qutaybah; and the 11th-century poet al-Maʿarrī.

As the golden age of the ʿAbbāsids declined, however, the boundaries of *adab* narrowed into belles lettres: poetry, elegant prose, anecdotal writing (*maqāmah*). In the modern Arab world, *adab* signifies literature.

adage \ˈad-ij\ [Latin *adagium* proverb]   A saying, often in metaphorical form, that embodies a common observation, such as "If the shoe fits, wear it," "Out of the frying pan, into the fire," or "Early to bed, early to rise, makes a man healthy, wealthy, and wise." The scholar Erasmus published a well-known collection of adages as *Adagia* in 1508. *See also* PROVERB.

Adam \ȧ-ˈdäⁿ\, Paul (b. Dec. 7, 1862, Paris, Fr.—d. Jan. 1, 1920, Paris)   Author whose early works exemplify the naturalist and Symbolist schools and who later won considerable reputation for his historical and sociological novels. Publication of his first naturalist novel, *Chair molle* (1885; "Soft Flesh"), led to his being prosecuted; his second, *Le Thé chez Miranda* (1886; "Tea at Miranda's"), written with Jean Moréas, is an early example of Symbolism. In 1899, with *La Force,* he began a series of novels depicting French life during the period 1800–30; the last, *Au soleil de Juillet,* appeared in 1903. He traveled widely and wrote two books on his American journeys, *Vues d'Amérique* (1906) and *Le Trust* (1910). His autobiography, in the form of a novel, *Jeunesse et amours de Manuel Héricourt*, appeared in 1913.

Adam and Eve \'ad-əm . . . 'ēv\ In Judeo-Christian and Islāmic traditions, the original humans, parents of the human race.

The Bible offers two accounts of their creation. In the first, which stems from the 5th or 6th century BC (Genesis 1:1–2:4), God on the sixth day of Creation fashioned humans "in his own image" as both "male and female." According to the second and lengthier narrative of the 10th century BC (Genesis 2:5–7, 2:15–4:1, 4:25), God created Adam when the earth was still void, forming him from the earth's dust and breathing "into his nostrils the breath of life." God then gave Adam the primeval Garden of Eden to tend but commanded him, on penalty of death, not to eat of the fruit of the "tree of knowledge of good and evil." Subsequently God created other animals but, finding these insufficient to help Adam and keep him company, God put Adam to sleep, took a rib from him, and with it created a new companion, Eve. The two were innocent until Eve yielded to the temptations of the serpent and Adam joined her in eating the forbidden fruit. For their transgression, God cast Adam and Eve out of the Garden. Their first children were CAIN and ABEL.

In the Qur'ānic version of the story of Adam and Eve, Allah created Adam from clay but exalted him with such knowledge that the angels were commanded to prostrate themselves before him. All did so except the angel Iblīs (Satan), who subsequently tempted both Adam and Eve to eat of the forbidden fruit. Allah drove them from the paradisal Garden and doomed their progeny to live as enemies; but, being merciful, Allah offered Adam and his progeny eternal guidance if they would follow only him, not Satan.

The story of Adam and Eve has been treated by several authors, notably John Milton (*Paradise Lost*) and Friedrich Klopstock (*Der Messias*). Many important literary themes have arisen from the story of Adam and Eve, including the loss of innocence and the fall from grace, the garden as a symbol of innocence, the apple as a symbol of temptation, the evilness of the serpent, and the "mark of Cain." *See also* LILITH.

Adam Bede \'ad-əm-'bēd\ Novel written by George ELIOT, published in three volumes in 1859. The title character, a carpenter, is in love with a woman who bears a child by another man. Although Bede tries to help her, he eventually loses her but finds happiness with Dinah Morris, a Methodist preacher.

Adam Bede was Eliot's first long novel. Its masterly realism—evident, for example, in the recording of Derbyshire dialect—brought to English fiction the same truthful observation of minute detail that John Ruskin was commending in the Pre-Raphaelites. But what was new in this work of English fiction was the combination of deep human sympathy and rigorous moral judgment.

Adam de la Halle \à-'dän-də-là-'àl\, *byname* Adam le Bossu *or* Adam the Hunchback (b. *c.* 1250, Arras, Fr.—d. *c.* 1306, Naples [Italy]) Poet, musician, and innovator of the earliest French secular theater. His *Jeu de la feuillée* ("Play of the Greensward") is a satirical fantasy based on his own life, written to amuse his friends in Arras upon his departure for Paris to pursue his studies. As court poet and musician to the Comte d'Artois, he visited Naples and became famous for his polyphony as well as his topical productions, considered the predecessors of comic opera. His other works include *Jeu de Robin et de Marion* and *Jeu du pélérin* ("Play of the Pilgrim").

Adamic \ə-'däm-ich, *Angl* 'ad-ə-mik, ə-'dam-ik\, Louis (b. March 23, 1899, Blato, Slovenia, Austria-Hungary—d. Sept. 4, 1951, near Riegelsville, N.J., U.S.) Novelist and journalist

who wrote about the experiences of American minorities, especially immigrants, in the early 1900s.

Adamic immigrated to the United States from Carniola (now in Slovenia) at age 14 and was naturalized in 1918. He wrote about what he called the failure of the American melting pot in *Laughing in the Jungle* (1932). He returned to Slovenia on a Guggenheim Fellowship and used that journey as the basis for *The Native's Return* (1934). Two successful sequels, *Grandsons* (1935) and *Cradle of Life* (1936), were followed by publication of his first novel, *The House in Antigua* (1937). His next book, *My America* (1938), a mixture of memoir and social philosophy, outlines his dream of a unified American people.

An intensely political man, Adamic suffered greatly because of the fragmentation of what was then unified Yugoslavia. He eventually committed suicide.

Adamnán *see* THE VISION OF ADAMNÁN.

Adamov \ə-'dä-məf\, Arthur (b. Aug. 23, 1908, Kislovodsk, Russia—d. March 16, 1970, Paris, Fr.) Avant-garde writer, a founder and one of the most important playwrights of the THEATER OF THE ABSURD.

In 1912 Adamov's wealthy Armenian family left Russia and settled in Freudenstadt, Ger. He was subsequently educated in Geneva, Mainz, and Paris, where his family settled in 1924 and where he began associating with Surrealist groups. He edited a periodical, *Discontinuité*, and wrote poetry. In 1938 he suffered a nervous breakdown, later writing *L'Aveu* (1938–43; "The Confession"), an autobiography that revealed his tortured conscience and portrayed a terrifying sense of alienation.

Strongly influenced by the Swedish dramatist August Strindberg—with whose own mental crisis Adamov identified—and by Franz Kafka, he began writing plays in 1947. His first play, *La Parodie*, features a handless clock that looms eerily over characters who are constantly questioning one another about time. In *L'Invasion*, he attempted to depict the human situation realistically. His third play, *La Grande et La Petite Manoeuvre*, reveals the influence of Antonin Artaud, theoretician of the Theater of Cruelty.

Le Professeur Taranne (performed 1953) is about a university professor unable to live up to his public role. In his best-known play, *Le Ping-pong* (performed 1955), the powerful central image is that of a pinball machine to which the characters surrender themselves in a never-ending, aimless game of chance, perfectly illustrating the futility of action and the human tendency to adhere to false objectives. Adamov's later plays (*Paolo Paoli*, 1957; *Le Printemps 71*, 1961; *La Politique des restes*, 1963) embodied radical political statements, though his interest in dramatic experimentation continued. Finally concluding that life was not absurd but merely difficult, he committed suicide.

Adams \'ad-əmz\, Abigail, *original surname* Smith \'smith\ (b. Nov. 11 [Nov. 22, New Style], 1744, Weymouth, Mass.—d. Oct. 28, 1818, Quincy, Mass., U.S.) Prolific letter writer whose correspondence gives an intimate and vivid portrayal of life in the young American republic.

Although her formal education was meager, Abigail Smith was an avid reader of history. Several enforced separations from her husband, John Adams—including a 10-year period when he was at the Continental Congress in Philadelphia—prompted streams of letters, and the development of Mrs. Adams' genius as a correspondent. Her artless spontaneity brings the times to life with a charming blend of comments on minutiae of the day with observations on the momentous events of the Revolutionary period.

Following the peace treaty of 1783, Mrs. Adams joined her husband abroad in Paris, The Hague, and London. Her letters to friends and family at home again provide a colorful commentary on manners and customs, and her correspondence continued when they returned to the United States. Successive printings of Mrs. Adams' letters (1840, 1876, 1947, 1963, 1977) periodically revived public appreciation of her contribution to the original source material of the early American period.

Adams \'ad-əmz\, **Charles Follen** (b. April 21, 1842, Dorchester, Mass., U.S.—d. March 8, 1918, Roxbury, Mass.) American regional poet, best known for his humorous Pennsylvania German dialect poems.

As a teenager, Adams was employed by a dry-goods firm. After serving in the army during the American Civil War, he returned to Boston, where he established himself as a "dealer in dry and fancy goods." In 1872 he began writing humorous verses for periodicals and newspapers in a Pennsylvania German dialect. Collections of his verse are *Leedle Yawcob Strauss, and Other Poems* (1877) and *Dialect Ballads* (1888). His complete poetical writings, *Yawcob Strauss, and Other Poems*, with illustrations by "Boz," were published in 1910.

Adams \'ad-əmz\, **Douglas (Noël)** (b. March 11, 1952, Cambridge, Eng.) British comic writer whose works satirized contemporary life using a luckless protagonist who deals ineptly with societal forces beyond his control. Adams was best known for the mock science-fiction series known collectively as *The Hitchhiker's Guide to the Galaxy*.

Adams received both a B.A. and an M.A. in English literature from Cambridge University. He was an editor for the television series *Dr. Who* and wrote scripts for the British Broadcasting Corporation from 1978 to 1980.

The Hitchhiker's Guide series includes *The Restaurant at the End of the Universe* (1980), *Life, the Universe and Everything* (1982), *So Long, and Thanks for All the Fish* (1985), *More Than Complete Hitchhiker's Guide* (1990), and *Mostly Harmless* (1992). Adams satirized the detective story genre with *Dirk Gently's Holistic Detective Agency* (1987) and *The Long Dark Tea-Time of the Soul* (1988). Other works include *The Meaning of Liff* (with John Lloyd; 1983), and *The Utterly Utterly Merry Comic Relief Christmas Book* (coeditor, with Peter Fincham; 1986).

Adams \'ad-əmz\, **Franklin Pierce**, *byname* F.P.A. (b. Nov. 15, 1881, Chicago, Ill., U.S.—d. March 23, 1960, New York, N.Y.) American newspaper columnist, translator, poet, and radio personality whose humorous syndicated column earned him the reputation of godfather of the contemporary newspaper column.

Adams' newspaper career began in 1903, with the *Chicago Journal.* The next year he went to New York, where he wrote for several newspapers. His column "The Conning Tower" appeared in the *Herald Tribune* and several other New York newspapers from 1913 to 1937, with two major interruptions: during the years of World War I, when Adams wrote a column for *Stars and Stripes*, and from 1923 to 1931, when he worked for the New York *World* until it ceased publication. Witty and well-written, his columns consisted of informal yet careful critiques of the contemporary U.S. scene. His Saturday columns imitated the language and style of Samuel Pepys' diary, and Adams is credited with a renewal of interest in Pepys. Reprints were collected in *The Diary of Our Own Samuel Pepys* (1935).

Adams' poetry is light and conventionally rhymed. It is collected in 10 volumes, beginning with *Tobogganning on Parnassus* (1911); the final volume, *The Melancholy Lute* (1936), is Adams' selection from 30 years of his writing. In 1938 Adams became one of the panel of experts on the radio show "Information, Please."

Adams \'ad-əmz\, **Henry (Brooks)** (b. Feb. 16, 1838, Boston, Mass., U.S.—d. March 27, 1918, Washington, D.C.) Ameri-

can historian, man of letters, and author of one of the outstanding autobiographies of Western literature, THE EDUCATION OF HENRY ADAMS (1918).

Library of Congress

Adams was the great-grandson of John Adams and the grandson of John Quincy Adams, both presidents of the United States. He graduated from Harvard in 1858 and embarked upon a grand tour of Europe. In 1861 he went to London with his father (who had been appointed U.S. minister to England), and acted as his private secretary until 1868.

Returning to the United States, Adams traveled to Washington, D.C., as a newspaper correspondent for *The Nation* and other leading journals. He wrote numerous essays exposing political corruption and continued his reformist activities as editor of the *North American Review* (1870–76). But after the failure of Horace Greeley's campaign for the presidency, Adams grew disillusioned. His anonymously published novel *Democracy, an American Novel* (1880) reflected his loss of faith in Americans.

In 1870 Adams was appointed professor of medieval history at Harvard, where he was the first American to employ the seminar—as contrasted with the lecture—method in teaching history. In 1877 he resigned and soon completed two biographies, *The Life of Albert Gallatin* (1879) and *John Randolph* (1882). His study of American democracy culminated in his nine-volume *History of the United States of America* (1889–91), a scholarly work that received immediate acclaim. In 1884 Adams wrote another novel, *Esther*, which he published under a pseudonym. The following year his wife of 13 years, Marian Hooper (known as Clover), committed suicide.

From the 1870s until his last years, intellectuals gravitated to his home to discuss art, science, politics, and literature. His closest friends were the geologist Clarence King and the diplomat John Hay. Adams and King were inseparable. Their letters remain a rich source of information on everything from gossip to the most current trends of thought.

On several trips to France, Adams examined medieval Christendom, and in MONT-SAINT-MICHEL AND CHARTRES (1913) he described the medieval worldview as reflected in its cathedrals. *The Education of Henry Adams*, a companion volume to *Chartres*, remains Adams' best-known work and one of the most distinguished of all autobiographies. In 1908 Adams edited the letters and diary of his friend John Hay, secretary of state from 1898 to 1905. His last book, *The Life of George Cabot Lodge*, was published in 1911.

Adams \'ad-əmz\, **Léonie (Fuller)** (b. Dec. 9, 1899, Brooklyn, N.Y., U.S.—d. June 27, 1988, New Milford, Conn.) American lyrical poet and educator whose verse interprets emotions and nature with an almost mystical vision.

After graduating from Barnard College (A.B., 1922), she became editor of *The Measure*, a literary publication, in 1924. She was persuaded to publish a volume of poetry, *Those Not Elect*, in 1925. She spent two years (1928–30) in France, and her second collection of poetry, *High Falcon & Other Poems*, was published during that period. She began to teach the writing of poetry in New York City and in 1932 edited *Lyrics of François Villon*. She published rarely after 1933, but she lectured at various American colleges and universities over the years and served as poetry consultant for the Library of Congress (1948–49). Her *Poems, a Selection* (1954) won the Bollingen Prize for Poetry in 1955.

Adams \ˈad-əmz\, Samuel Hopkins (b. Jan. 26, 1871, Dunkirk, N.Y., U.S.—d. Nov. 15, 1958, Beaufort, S.C.)   American journalist and author of more than 50 books of fiction, biography, and exposé.

Adams graduated from Hamilton College in 1891 and worked for the *New York Sun* until 1900. From 1901 to 1905 he was associated in various capacities with McClure's syndicate and *McClure's Magazine*. One of the so-called muckrakers of the period, Adams contributed to *Collier's, the National Weekly* in 1905 a series of articles exposing quack patent medicines, followed by *The Great American Fraud* (1906), which furthered the passage of the Pure Food and Drug Act in 1906. In articles appearing in 1915–16 in the *New York Tribune*, he exposed dishonorable practices in advertising. The novel *Revelry* (1926) and a biography of Warren G. Harding, *Incredible Era* (1939), set forth the scandals of the Harding administration. Adams also wrote biographies of Daniel Webster (*The Godlike Daniel*, 1930) and Alexander Woollcott (1945).

Adams \ˈad-əmz\, William Taylor, *pseudonym* Oliver Optic \ˈäp-tik\ (b. July 30, 1822, Medway, Mass., U.S.—d. March 27, 1897, Boston, Mass.)   American teacher and author best known for his children's magazine and the series of adventure books that he wrote under his pseudonym.

Although he never graduated from college, Adams was a teacher and principal in Boston elementary schools for more than 20 years. Under the pen name Oliver Optic, he wrote stories for boys, and in 1865 he resigned his position as a principal to pursue his writing full-time. Soon after that he began *Oliver Optic's Magazine for Boys and Girls* (1867–75), which enjoyed great popularity.

Adams was a prolific writer, producing about a thousand magazine and newspaper stories and well over a hundred full-length books. His books are written in series and take young heroes through exotic and educational adventures. His characters travel much and are athletic and patriotic, and the stories are laced with a strong moral. A significant rival for the readership attracted by Horatio Alger, Adams, too, wrote on the level of the dime novel; libraries occasionally banned his books because of their sensationalism.

Adams, Nick \ˈnik-ˈad-əmz\   Fictional character, protagonist of early semiautobiographical short stories by Ernest HEMINGWAY. Adams first appears in *In Our Time* (1925), a collection of 15 stories, including coming-of-age experiences in the woods of the Upper Peninsula of Michigan. The character also appears, at various stages of his life, in the short-story collection *Men Without Women* (1927).

Adams, Parson \ˈpär-sən-ˈad-əmz\   Fictional character, the protagonist's traveling companion in the picaresque novel JOSEPH ANDREWS by Henry Fielding. Parson Adams is an erudite but guileless man who expects the best of everyone and is frequently the victim of deceit.

adaptation \ˌad-ap-ˈtā-shən\   Something that is adapted; especially, a composition rewritten into a new form, such as a novel reworked as a film script.

ad captandum or **ad captandum vulgus** \ˌad-ˌkap-ˈtan-dəm-ˈvəl-gəs\ [Latin, for pleasing the crowd]   Designed to attract or please the crowd. An argument in drama, verse, or rhetoric that is directed chiefly to the emotions is often called an argument *ad captandum*.

Adcock \ˈad-ˌkäk\, Fleur, *in full* Kareen Fleur Adcock (b. Feb. 10, 1934, Papakura, New Zealand)   New Zealand-born British poet known for her tranquil domestic lyrics intercut with flashes of irony and glimpses of the fantastic and the macabre.

Adcock received her early education in England and later earned degrees at Wellington Girls' College and Victoria University of Wellington. She served as lecturer and librarian at a number of New Zealand institutions before immigrating to England in 1963. Her first collection of poetry, *The Eye of the Hurricane*, appeared the following year. In this and subsequent volumes, including *Tigers* (1967), *High Tide in the Garden* (1971), *The Incident Book* (1986), and *Time Zones* (1991), Adcock brought a measured, classical detachment to bear upon the vagaries of emotional experience. *The Inner Harbour* (1979) is generally cited as her most artistically successful work.

Addams, Frankie \ˈfraŋ-kē-ˈad-əmz\   Fictional character, the protagonist of Carson McCullers' novel THE MEMBER OF THE WEDDING. Frankie is a lonely 12-year-old tomboy who feels the need for human connection. She particularly longs to be a member of her brother Jarvis' wedding and to accompany him on his honeymoon. Though this plan is thwarted, by the end of the novel she is more comfortable with herself.

Addison \ˈad-ə-sən\, Joseph (b. May 1, 1672, Milston, Wiltshire, Eng.—d. June 17, 1719, London)   English essayist, poet, and dramatist, who, with Richard STEELE, was a leading contributor to and guiding spirit of the periodicals THE TATLER and THE SPECTATOR.

Oil painting by Michael Dahl, 1719
National Portrait Gallery, London

After grammar school, Addison was enrolled at the age of 14 in the Charterhouse in London. There he began a lifelong friendship with Steele. Both went on to the University of Oxford, where Addison matriculated at Queen's College and later won election to Magdalen College. In 1695 *A Poem to His Majesty* (William III) brought favorable notice and he was given a treasury grant to travel and to prepare for government service.

Upon his return to London following his European tour (1699–1704), Addison renewed his friendship with members of the Kit-Cat Club, an association of prominent Whig leaders and literary figures of the day. The Whig success in the election of May 1705 brought Addison an appointment as under secretary to the secretary of state for southern affairs, a position of considerable importance. During this period he began to see much of Steele, helping him write *The Tender Husband* (1705), for which he also provided a prologue; when the play was published it carried a dedication to Addison in honor of "an inviolable friendship." Addison also assisted Steele with substantial loans and the appointment as editor of the official London *Gazette* and he frequently supplied him with material for the paper.

In 1708 Addison was elected to Parliament for Lostwithiel in Cornwall and later in the same year was made secretary to the Earl of Wharton, the new lord lieutenant of Ireland. It was during his two years as Irish secretary that his friend Steele began publishing *The Tatler*, and from Ireland he began contributing to the new periodical. When the Whigs lost power in 1710, Addison easily retained his seat in the Commons but was without employment. He continued contributing to *The Tatler*, which Steele finally brought to a close on Jan. 2, 1711. Two months later the friends started *The Spectator*.

With the death of Queen Anne and the accession of George I in 1714, Addison's political fortunes rose. Ill health, however, prevented his taking a very active part in government affairs, and he resigned as secretary of state in 1718, after just a year. Meanwhile, he had married the dowager Countess of Warwick, and he spent the remaining years of his life in comparative affluence at Holland House in Kensington. The dispute over Lord Sunderland's bill for restricting the peerage, in which Addison and Steele took opposing sides, unfortunately estranged the two friends during the last year of Addison's life. He was buried in Westminster Abbey.

Ade \'ād\, George (b. Feb. 9, 1866, Kentland, Ind., U.S.—d. May 16, 1944, Brook, Ind.)   American playwright and humorist known for his *Fables in Slang*.

After graduating from Purdue University, Ade joined the staff of the *Chicago Record* newspaper from 1890 to 1900. Characters introduced in his widely acclaimed editorial-page column, "Stories of the Streets and of the Town," became the subjects of his early books, *Artie* (1896), *Pink Marsh* (1897), and *Doc Horne* (1899). His greatest recognition came with *Fables in Slang* (1899), a national best-seller that was followed by a weekly syndicated fable and by 11 other books of fables. The fables, which contained only a little slang, were, rather, examples of the vernacular.

In 1902 Ade's light opera *The Sultan of Sulu* began a long run in New York, followed by such successful comedies as *The County Chairman* (1903) and *The College Widow* (1904). He was recognized as one of the most successful playwrights of his time. He also wrote many motion-picture scripts and, during the Prohibition era, what many called one of his most amusing books, *The Old Time Saloon* (1931).

Adelphi, The \ə-'del-fē\, *also called* (1927–30) The New Adelphi.   British literary journal founded by John Middleton Murry in 1923. The publication was more a periodical manifesto than a literary magazine. Originally dedicated to promoting the work and views of the novelist D.H. Lawrence, and of the editor himself, *The Adelphi* (from the Greek word for "brothers") attempted to reach readers beyond the traditional upper-class literary circle of the time, although this effort met with little success. In fact, Murry's radical politics, coupled with a disdain for religion as manifested in Lawrence's

published declaration that "Jesus was a failure," alienated the general readers Murry had hoped to attract. While the periodical published the work of W.H. Auden, T.S. Eliot, George Orwell, and W.B. Yeats, it is best known as the repository of its founder's controversial commentary on religious, political, and cultural life.

Adenet le Roi \ȧd-'nȧ-lə-'rwä\, *also called* Roi Adam, Li Rois Adenes, Adan le Ménestrel, *or* Adam Rex Menestrallus (b. *c.* 1240—d. *c.* 1300)   French trouvère (poet-musician), interesting for the detailed documentary evidence that his poems provide about his career as a household minstrel.

He received his training in the court of Henry III, duke of Brabant, at Louvain; after his patron's death in 1261, his fortunes wavered until in 1268 or 1269 he entered the service of Guy of Dampierre, heir to the county of Flanders, as principal minstrel (whence his title *roi*—*i.e.*, "king of minstrels"). Adenet accompanied Guy in 1270–71 on the Tunisian crusade, and his poems contain many precise references to their return journey through Sicily and Italy. Of his written work, three chansons de geste and a romance, all considered to be rather pallid and unoriginal, are preserved.

Adler \'ad-lər\, Renata (b. Oct. 19, 1938, Milan, Italy)   Italian-born American journalist, experimental novelist, and film critic best known for her analytical essays and reviews.

Adler was educated at Bryn Mawr College (Pa.), the Sorbonne, and Harvard University. From 1962 to 1968 and from 1970 to 1982 she was a staff writer-reporter for *The New Yorker*. Essays and reviews she wrote there were collected and published as *Toward a Radical Middle: Fourteen Pieces of Reporting and Criticism* (1969). From her controversial single-year tenure as film critic for the *New York Times* came a collection of reviews that was published as *A Year in the Dark: Journal of a Film Critic, 1968–69* (1970). Adler then turned to writing short stories, some of which were published under the pseudonym Brett Daniels.

Adler reworked previously published short fiction into *Speedboat* (1976), her first novel. Set mainly in New York City, *Speedboat* consists mainly of a series of disparate sketches and vignettes. Like *Speedboat*, Adler's second novel, *Pitch Dark* (1983), is episodic and nonlinear; critical response to both was mixed.

Adler also wrote the nonfiction work *Reckless Disregard* (1986), an investigation into libel suits brought by American and Israeli generals against major American news organizations. In 1988 she published *Politics and Media*, a collection of essays.

Admetus \ad-'mē-təs\   In Greek mythology, son of Pheres, king of Pherae in Thessaly. Admetus sued for the hand of Alcestis, the most beautiful of the daughters of Pelias, king of Iolcos in Thessaly, who in turn required him to harness a lion and a boar to a chariot. The god Apollo yoked the pair for Admetus, who thus obtained Alcestis. Finding that Admetus was soon to die, Apollo persuaded the Fates to prolong his life, on the condition that someone could be found to die in his place. Alcestis consented, but she was rescued by Heracles, who successfully wrestled with Death at the grave. The death and resurrection of Alcestis form the subject of many ancient reliefs and vase paintings, as well as of the *Alcestis* of Euripides.

Adolphe \ȧ-'dȯlf\   Novel by Benjamin CONSTANT, published in 1816. Written in a lucid classical style, *Adolphe* describes in minute analytical detail a young man's passion for a woman older than himself. A forerunner of the modern psychological novel, it is a thinly disguised account of the end of Constant's passionate 14-year relationship with Madame de Staël, a well-known (and married) woman of letters.

Adonais \,ad-ō-'nā-is\   Pastoral elegy by Percy Bysshe SHEL-
LEY, written and published in 1821 to commemorate the death
of John Keats earlier that year.

Referring to Adonis, the handsome young man of Greek
mythology who was killed by a wild boar, the title was probably taken from Bion's *Lament for Adonis*, which Shelley had
translated into English. Written in 55 Spenserian stanzas, the
poem is ranked with John Milton's "Lycidas" for its purity of
classical form. In it the poet mourns the death of the fair Adonais but ends by placing him among the immortals, declaring
that, while "We decay/Like corpses in a charnel," the creative
spirit of Adonais, "like a star,/Beacons from the abode where
the Eternal are."

Adonias Filho \à-dō-'nē-əs-'fèl-yü\, *in full* Adonias Aguiar
Filho (b. Nov. 27, 1915, Itajuípe, Braz.—d. Aug. 2, 1990, Ilhéus)   Novelist, essayist, journalist, and literary critic whose
works of fiction embrace both regionalism and existentialism.

Adonias Filho's literary career began in the early 1930s under
the aegis of the Neo-Catholic writers' group of Rio de Janeiro.
Until the late 1940s his writing consisted chiefly of journalism
and translations of English-language fiction, notably the works
of Graham Greene, Virginia Woolf, and William Faulkner.

For a time in the 1950s Adonias Filho served as director
of the National Book Institute and worked in the National
Theatrical Service. He subsequently became director of the
National Library and was elected to the Brazilian Academy of
Letters in 1965. In 1972 he was elected president of the Brazil-
ian Press Association.

He began writing fiction in the 1940s, taking a psychological approach to characterization. His book *Os servos da morte*
(1946; "The Servants of Death"), was the first of three novels depicting life in the cacao-growing region of northeastern
Brazil. *Memórias de Lázaro* (1952; *Memories of Lazarus*) and *O
forte* (1965; "The Fortress") completed the trilogy. His other
novels include *Corpo vivo* (1962; "Living Body") and *Noite sem
madrugada* (1983; "Night Without Dawn").

Adonic \ə-'dän-ik\ *or* **Adonian** \ə-'dō-nē-ən\ [Late Greek
Adŏnion an Adonic verse, a derivative of *Adŏnis* Adonis]   In
classical prosody, having a meter consisting of a dactyl (− ∪ ∪)
followed by a spondee (− −). It is found in dactylic contexts,
and especially in aeolic and sapphic verse.

Adonis \ə-'dän-is, -'dōn-\   In Greek mythology, a youth of
remarkable beauty, the favorite of the goddess Aphrodite
(Venus). Traditionally, he was the son of the Syrian king Theias
by his daughter Smyrna (Myrrha).

Aphrodite was charmed by the beauty of the infant Adonis
and put him in a box and handed him over to the care of Persephone, the queen of the underworld, who afterward refused
to give him up. An appeal was made to Zeus, who decided
that Adonis should spend a third of the year with Persephone
and a third with Aphrodite, the remaining third being at his
own disposal. William Shakespeare's poem *Venus and Adonis*,
taken from Ovid's *Metamorphoses*, relates the story of Venus'
attempted seduction of Adonis while he was hunting. When he
demurred, she warned him that he would be killed if he continued his boar hunt the next day and implored him to meet her
instead. The next day, to her abiding grief, she indeed found
him dead, killed by the wild boar he was chasing. Numerous
other variants of the legend exist.

The name Adonis is believed to be of Phoenician origin (from
'adōn, "lord"). Adonis himself is identified with the Babylonian
fertility god Tammuz and is generally viewed by modern scholars as a vegetation spirit, whose death and rebirth represented
the cycle of nature.

Adonis   *see* SA'ID.

Adorno \ä-'dòr-nō\, Theodor (Wiesengrund) (b. Sept. 11,
1903, Frankfurt am Main, Ger.—d. Aug. 6, 1969, Visp, Switz.)
German philosopher noted in literary circles for his influence
on the Frankfurt school, a neo-Marxist body of scholars who
attempted to define a dialectical "critical theory" of society.

Musical training and a degree in philosophy from the liberal Johann Wolfgang Goethe University (1924) influenced
Adorno's early writings, which emphasized aesthetic development as important to historical evolution and the search for
truth. After teaching two years at the University of Frankfurt,
Adorno, who was Jewish, immigrated to England in 1934 to escape Nazism. He lived in the United States from 1938 to 1948
and returned to the University of Frankfurt in 1949.

Adorno's notable essays on literature discuss such classical
writers as J.W. von Goethe and Friedrich Hölderlin as well
as the modernist writers who were his chief literary focus.
His best-known collections of essays on literature is the four-
volume *Noten zur Literatur* (1958–74; *Notes to Literature*).

Adūnīs   *see* SA'ID.

Adventures of Augie March, The \'òg-ē-'märch\   Novel
by Saul BELLOW, published in 1953. It is a picaresque story
of a poor Jewish youth from Chicago, his progress, sometimes
highly comic, through the world of the 20th century, and his
attempts to make sense of it. *The Adventures of Augie March*
won the National Book Award in 1954.

Adverse, Anthony \'anth-ə-nē-'ad-,vərs\   Fictional character, hero of the historical novel ANTHONY ADVERSE by Hervey Allen. Adverse is an illegitimate but well-born child, the
heir to his wealthy grandfather, under whom he apprentices.

Ady \'òd-ē\, Endre (b. Nov. 22, 1877, Érmindszent, Hung.,
Austria-Hungary [now Ady Endre, Rom.]—d. Jan. 27, 1919,
Budapest, Hung.)   One of the greatest Hungarian lyric poets.
Particularly notable are his love poems, which are striking in
their originality and their mystical approach to physical love.

Ady studied law for a time, but from 1900 until his death
he worked as a journalist. In 1903 he published his first significant volume of poetry, *Még egyszer*. With his next book, *Uj
versek* (1906; "New Poems"), he burst into Hungarian literary
life. His poems were revolutionary in form, language, and content; his unconventional though splendid language shocked the
public. After a stay as a journalist in Paris Ady had come to see
Hungary as narrow and materialistic, and in the early poems he
expressed the scorn and hostility that he felt toward his country. Ady became the target of onslaughts that soon developed
into a political struggle in which he was supported by left-wing
radicals, who hailed him as a prophet, and abused by right-
wing nationalists.

In his later work, Ady was less insulting toward his fellow
citizens. His understanding of the country, of its social and
political ills, and of the sufferings that had been inflicted by
World War I inspired him to find new means of expressing pain
and anger. By the time he died of alcoholism, he had published
10 volumes of poetry in 12 years, as well as short stories and
countless articles.

adynaton \ə-'dī-nə-,tän\ [Greek *adýnaton*, neuter of *adýnatos*
impossible]   A kind of hyperbole in which the exaggeration is
so great that it refers to an impossibility, as in the following
lines from Andrew Marvell's "To His Coy Mistress":

> Thou by the Indian Ganges' side
> Shouldst rubies find; I by the tide
> Of Humber would complain. I would
> Love you ten years before the flood
> And you should, if you please, refuse
> Till the conversion of the Jews.

Æ \'ā-'ē\, *pseudonym of* George William Russell \'rəs-əl\ (b. April 10, 1867, Lurgan, County Armagh, Ire.—d. July 17, 1935, Bournemouth, Hampshire, Eng.) Irish poet and mystic, a leading figure in the IRISH LITERARY RENAISSANCE of the late 19th and early 20th centuries. Russell took his pseudonym from a proofreader's query about his earlier pseudonym, "Æon."

Russell attended the Metropolitan School of Art, Dublin, where he met the poet William Butler Yeats. Eventually he became editor of the periodicals *The Irish Homestead* (1904–23) and *The Irish Statesman* (1923–30). In 1894 he published the first of many books of verse, *Homeward: Songs by the Way*. His first volume of *Collected Poems* appeared in 1913 and a second in 1926. Other collections followed. Russell maintained a lifelong interest in theosophy, the origins of religion, and mystical experience. *The Candle of Vision* (1918) is the best guide to his religious beliefs.

At the turn of the century, Russell was considered by many to be the equal of W.B. Yeats; yet he did not grow and develop. He was prolific and versatile, but many critics found him facile, vague, and monotonous, with "rather too much of the Celtic Twilight" in his work.

Aeacus \'ē-ə-kəs\ In Greek mythology, son of Zeus and Aegina, the daughter of the river god Asopus. His mother was carried off by Zeus to the island of Oenone, which was afterward called by her name. Aeacus was celebrated for justice and in Attic tradition became a judge of the dead, together with Minos and Rhadamanthus.

Aegaeon *see* BRIAREUS.

Aegeus \'ē-jūs, -jē-əs, *in Shakespeare's work* ē-'jē-əs\ In Greek mythology, the father of THESEUS and king of Athens. Aegeus drowned himself in the sea when he mistakenly believed his son to be dead. The sea was thereafter called the Aegean.

Ægir \'ag-ir, 'ē-jir\ *also called* Oegir \'e-gir, -yir\ Norse god of the sea, husband of Ran. He fathered nine daughters whose names indicate that they were personifications of the waves.

aegis or **egis** \'ē-jis\ *plural* aegises *or* egises [Greek *aigís*, probably a derivative of *aig-, aíx* goat] In Greek mythology, a shield or breastplate forged by Hephaestus and emblematic of majesty. It was originally associated chiefly with Zeus but later, bordered with serpents and set with a Gorgon's head, it was associated mainly with Athena, who adopted it for ordinary dress. Occasionally, another god (*e.g.*, Apollo in the *Iliad*) used it to provoke terror. In later myth the aegis was described as a goatskin cloak, although as early as Homer the aegis was something more than the ordinary goatskin cloak, for it was decorated with golden tassels.

Aelfric \'al-frik, -frich\ (fl. *c.* 955–*c.* 1010, Eynsham, Oxfordshire, Eng.) Anglo-Saxon prose writer, considered the greatest of his time. He wrote both to instruct the monks and to spread the learning of the 10th-century monastic revival. His *Catholic Homilies*, written in 990–992, provided orthodox sermons based on the writings of the Church Fathers. Aelfric also wrote a Latin grammar and *Lives of the Saints*.

Aelian \'ē-lē-ən\, *original name* Claudius Aelianus (b. *c.* 170, Praeneste, near Rome [Italy]—d. *c.* 235) Roman author and teacher of rhetoric, who spoke and wrote so fluently in Greek—in which language his works were written—that he was nicknamed "Honey-tongued."

Aelian was an admirer and student of the writings of Plato, Aristotle, Isocrates, Plutarch, Homer, and others, and his own works preserve many excerpts from earlier writers. Aelian is chiefly remembered for his *On the Nature of Animals*, curious stories of birds and other animals often in the form of anecdotes, folklore, or fables that pointed a moral. This work set a pattern that continued in bestiaries and medical treatises throughout the European Middle Ages. His *Various History* related anecdotes of men and customs and miraculous events. Fragments of other works survive.

Aelius Stilo *see* STILO PRAECONINUS.

Aeneas \ē-'nē-əs\ Mythical hero of Troy and Rome, son of the goddess Aphrodite and Anchises. Aeneas was a member of the royal line of Troy and a cousin of Hector. He played a prominent part in the Trojan War, being second only to Hector in ability. Homer implies that Aeneas did not like his subordinate position, and from that suggestion arose a later tradition that Aeneas helped to betray Troy to the Greeks. The more common version, however, made Aeneas the leader of the Trojan survivors after Troy was taken by the Greeks.

The association of Homeric heroes with Italy and Sicily goes back to the 8th century BC, and the Greek colonies founded in those regions in the 8th and 9th centuries BC frequently claimed descent from leaders in the Trojan War. As Rome expanded over Italy and the Mediterranean, its patriotic writers began to construct a mythical tradition that would at once dignify their land with antiquity and satisfy a lingering animosity toward Greek cultural superiority. Aeneas, as a Trojan, represented an enemy of the Greeks; because tradition had him alive and free after the war, he was peculiarly fit for the part assigned him—that of the founder of Roman greatness.

It was Virgil who assimilated the various strands of legend related to Aeneas and gave them the form they have possessed ever since. The family of Julius Caesar, including Virgil's patron Augustus, claimed descent from Aeneas, whose son Ascanius was also called Iulus. Incorporating these different traditions, Virgil created his masterpiece, the *Aeneid*, the Latin epic poem whose hero symbolized not only the course and aim of Roman history but also the career and policy of Augustus himself. In the journeying of Aeneas from Troy westward to Sicily, Carthage, and finally to the mouth of the Tiber in Italy, Virgil portrayed the qualities by which he felt Rome had been built: persistence, self-denial, and obedience to the gods.

The death of Aeneas is described by Dionysius of Halicarnassus. After he had fallen in battle against the Rutuli, his body could not be found, and he was thereafter worshiped as a local god, *Juppiter indiges*, as Livy reports.

Aeneid \ē-'nē-id\ Latin epic poem written about 29–19 BC by VIRGIL. Composed in hexameters, about 60 lines of which were left unfinished at his death, the *Aeneid* incorporates the various legends of Aeneas and makes him the founder of Roman greatness. The work is organized into 12 books that relate the story of the legendary founding of Lavinium (parent town of Alba Longa and of Rome). The town was founded by Aeneas, who had been informed as he left the burning ruins of Troy that it was his fate to found a new city with a glorious destiny in the West.

In Book I Aeneas, journeying to his fated destination, encounters foul weather and is forced to land his fleet on the Libyan coast. There he is welcomed by the widowed Dido, queen of Carthage. Books II and III contain Aeneas' account (told to Dido) of events both natural and supernatural that have led him to her shore. In Book IV Dido confesses her love for Aeneas, who (though he regrets his fate) is then forced by the gods to set sail again. She prepares to kill herself. The Trojans, in Book V, journey to Sicily, where they engage in a series of competitions to commemorate the anniversary of the death of Aeneas' father, Anchises. They then set sail again. Book VI is the account of Aeneas' journey to the underworld and Elysium, where he meets the ghosts of Dido and Anchises, among others. In this book the destiny of Rome is revealed. Books

VII through XII relate the fate of the Trojans as they reach the Tiber and are received by Latinus, the king of the region. Other Latins (encouraged by the gods) resent the arrival of the Trojans and the projected marriage alliance between Aeneas and Lavinia, Latinus' daughter; notable among the resentful are Latinus' wife and Turnus, leader of a local tribe known as the Rutuli and heretofore Lavinia's favored suitor. War breaks out, but the Trojans, with the help of the Etruscans, prevail and Turnus is killed. As fated, Aeneas marries Lavinia and founds Lavinium.

Homer is Virgil's model. The story of Aeneas' journey, recounted in the first six books, is patterned after the *Odyssey*, with many imitative passages and even direct translations, while the description of the war in the last six books abounds with incidents modeled after those in the *Iliad*. More basically, however, Virgil made use of another model, Rome's own national legend about the war fought under Romulus against the Sabines. This legend preserves, in a historical disguise, an original Indo-European myth about a primitive conflict between the gods of sovereignty and war and the gods of fecundity, ending with the unification of the two divine races. In Virgil's development of this theme, Aeneas and the Etruscans can be seen as representing the gods of sovereignty and war, and the Latins as representing the gods of fecundity.

aeolic \ē-'äl-ik\ [Greek *Aiolikós,* literally, of the Aeolians, a people of ancient Greece] Of or relating to a group of meters used in Greek lyric poetry. "Aeolic" alludes to the poets Sappho and Alcaeus, of the Aeolian island of Lesbos, who first used these meters. Aeolic meters, such as the glyconic, typically are formed around a choriamb ($- \cup \cup -$), which may be preceded or followed (or both) by a variety of other metrical units to create a wide variety of metrical sequences. (For example, choriambic dimeter has the form $- \cup \cup - | \cup - \cup -$; glyconic takes the form $\cup \cup | - \cup \cup - | \cup -$.) *See also* POLYSCHEMATIST.

Aeolus \'ē-ə-ləs\ In Greek mythology, mythical king of Magnesia in Thessaly, the son of Hellen (the eponymous ancestor of the true Greeks, or Hellenes) and father of Sisyphus. Aeolus' daughter Canace and son Macareus committed incest and then took their own lives. Their story provided the subject of Euripides' lost *Aeolus*.

Aeolus \'ē-ə-ləs\ In the works of Homer, controller of the winds and ruler of the floating island of Aeolia. In the *Odyssey* he gave Odysseus a favorable wind and a bag in which the unfavorable winds were confined. Odysseus' companions opened the bag; the winds escaped and drove them back to the island. Although he appears as a human in Homer, Aeolus later was described as a minor god.

aepyornis \,ē-pē-'ȯr-nəs\ [New Latin, from Greek *aipýs* high + *órnis* bird] *see* ROC.

Aeschylus \'es-kə-ləs, 'ēs-\ (b. 525/524 BC, Eleusis?—d. 456/455 BC, Gela, Sicily) First of classical Athens' great tragic dramatists, who lifted the art of tragedy from a choral and largely static recitation to fully developed drama. He added a second actor to the dramatic performance, developed the ensuing possibilities of dialogue, and thus enabled tragic drama to become the presentation of action. He was also the first known writer to express in dramatic form the vision of life that is recognized as tragic.

Aeschylus was wounded at Marathon (490 BC), where Athens defeated the invading Persians, and again fought against the Persians when they invaded Greece in 480. He was also a notable participant in Athens' major dramatic competition, the Great Dionysia. Aeschylus is recorded as having participated

in this competition, probably for the first time, in 499 BC. He won his first victory in 484 BC, and 12 years later his earliest extant work, PERSIANS, was performed.

About this time, Aeschylus is said to have visited the court of Hieron I at Syracuse, Sicily. Aeschylus' later career is a record of sustained dramatic success, though he is said to have suffered one memorable defeat, at the hands of the novice Sophocles during the Dionysian festival of 468 BC. For the following festival, Aeschylus produced an Oedipus trilogy (of which the third play, SEVEN AGAINST THEBES, survives). After producing his masterpiece, the ORESTEIA trilogy, in 458, Aeschylus went to Sicily again, where he died at the age of 69.

Aeschylus' plays are of lasting literary value in their majestic and compelling lyrical language, in the intricate architecture of their plots, and in their universal themes. His language in both dialogue and choral lyric is marked by force, majesty, and emotional intensity. He makes bold use of compound epithets, metaphors, and figurative turns of speech that are firmly linked to the dramatic action. Aeschylus deploys throughout a play or trilogy of plays several leading motifs that are often associated with a particular word or group of words. In the *Oresteia*, for example, such themes as wrath, mastery, persuasion, and the contrasts of light and darkness, of dirge and triumphal song, run throughout the trilogy. Of the approximately 90 plays that Aeschylus wrote, about 80 titles are known. Only seven tragedies (*Persians, Seven Against Thebes,* SUPPLIANTS, the *Oresteia* trilogy, and PROMETHEUS BOUND) have survived entire.

Aesculapius *see* ASCLEPIUS.

Æsir or **Aesir** \'ā-zir, 'a-, -sir\ [Old Norse *Æsir,* plural of *áss* god] In Scandinavian mythology, either of two main groups of deities, four of whom were common to the Germanic nations: Odin, chief of the Æsir; Frigg, Odin's wife; Tyr, god of war; and Thor, whose name was the Teutonic word for thunder. Some of the other important Æsir were Balder, Jǫrd, Heimdall, and Loki. *Compare* VANIR.

Aesop \'ē-säp, 'ā-\ The supposed author of a collection of Greek fables, almost certainly a legendary figure. Various attempts were made in ancient times to establish him as an actual personage. Herodotus in the 5th century BC said that he had lived in the 6th century and that he was a slave, and Plutarch in the 1st century AD made him adviser to Croesus, the 6th-century-BC king of Lydia. One tradition holds that he came from Thrace, while a later one styles him a Phrygian. An Egyptian biography of the 1st century AD places him on the island of Samos as a slave who gained his freedom from his master, thence going to Babylon as riddle solver to King Lycurgus, and, finally, meeting his death at Delphi. The probability is that Aesop was no more than a name invented to provide an author for fables centering on beasts, so that "a story of Aesop" became synonymous with "fable."

The Western fable tradition begins effectively with those tales attributed to Aesop, but before that time the Greek poet Hesiod (8th century BC) recounted the "Aesop" fable of the hawk and the nightingale, while fragments of similar tales survive in Archilochus, a 7th-century-BC warrior-poet.

Modern editions list approximately 200 "Aesop" fables, but there is no way of knowing who invented which tales or what their original occasions might have been. Aesop had already receded into legend when Demetrius of Phaleron, a rhetorician, compiled an edition of Aesop's fables in the 4th century BC. A versified Latin collection made by Phaedrus, a freed slave in the house of the Roman emperor Augustus, included fables invented by the poet, along with the traditional favorites, which he retold with many elaborations and considerable grace. A similar extension of range marks the work of the Hellenized Roman Babrius, writing in the 2nd century AD. Phaedrus' treatment of the fables also influenced later writers, notably the 17th-century French poet and fabulist Jean de LA FONTAINE. *See also* FABLE.

aesthete \\'es-,thēt, 'ēs-\\ One professing devotion to the beautiful, especially in art. The word (usually capitalized) was applied in particular to a group of English writers and artists of the late 19th century whose belief in the doctrine of Aestheticism was manifested in dandyism and affectation. This group included Oscar Wilde, Aubrey Beardsley, Arthur Symons, and Ernest Dowson.

aesthetic distance The frame of reference that an artist creates by the use of technical devices in and around the work of art to differentiate it psychologically from reality. German playwright Bertolt Brecht built his dramatic theory known in English as the alienation effect to accomplish aesthetic distance.

Aestheticism \\es-'thet-ə-,siz-əm, ēs-\\ Late 19th-century European arts movement that centered on the doctrine that art exists for the sake of its beauty alone.

The movement began in reaction to prevailing utilitarian social philosophies and to what was perceived as the ugliness and philistinism of the industrial age. Its philosophical foundations were laid in the 18th century by Immanuel Kant, who postulated the autonomy of aesthetic standards, setting them apart from considerations of morality, utility, or pleasure. This idea was amplified by J.W. von Goethe, J.L. Tieck, and others in Germany and by Samuel Taylor Coleridge and Thomas Carlyle in England. It was popularized in France by Madame de Staël, Théophile Gautier, and the philosopher Victor Cousin, who coined the phrase *l'art pour l'art* ("art for art's sake") in 1818.

In England, the artists of the Pre-Raphaelite Brotherhood, from 1848, had sown the seeds of Aestheticism, and the work of Dante Gabriel Rossetti, Edward Burne-Jones, and Algernon Charles Swinburne exemplified it in expressing a yearning for ideal beauty through conscious medievalism. The attitudes of the movement were also represented in the writings of Oscar Wilde and Walter Pater and the illustrations of Aubrey Beardsley in the periodical *The Yellow Book*.

Contemporary critics of Aestheticism included William Morris and John Ruskin and, in Russia, Leo Tolstoy, who questioned the value of art divorced from morality. The movement shared certain affinities with the French Symbolist movement and was a precursor of Art Nouveau. *See also* DECADENT; SYMBOLIST MOVEMENT.

Aethra \\'ēth-rə\\ In Greek mythology, daughter of King Pittheus of Troezen, who married her to Aegeus, king of Athens. She became mother of Theseus by Aegeus or by Poseidon, who had ravished her in Troezen. (The two versions may reflect the ancient confusion of Aegeus with the sea god—*e.g.*, the Aegean Sea.)

Later she guarded Helen after Helen was stolen from Sparta by Theseus; in retribution Aethra was carried to Sparta by the Dioscuri to be Helen's slave, thereafter following her to Troy. Freed after the 10-year war, Aethra later killed herself in grief over her son's death.

Afanasyev \\,ə-,fə-'nȧ-shyif\\, Aleksandr Nikolayevich (b. July 11 [July 23, New Style], 1826, Boguchar, Voronezh province, Russia—d. Sept. 23 [Oct. 5], 1871, Moscow) Historian and scholar of Russian folklore known for his compilation of Russian folktales.

Afanasyev studied law at Moscow University. His early work included a study of Russian satirical journals of the late 18th century and commentaries on contemporary Russian literature.

During the period 1866–69 he brought out his *Poeticheskiye vozzreniya slavyan na prirodu* (*The Slav's Poetical Views of Nature*) in three volumes, which provided the first synthesis of the theories of the Mythological school, a 19th-century Romantic literary movement that drew its inspiration from folklore.

Afanasyev is best remembered for his *Narodnyye russkiye skazki* ("Russian Popular Fairy Tales"), compiled between 1855 and 1864 and including more than 600 tales. His *Narodnyye russkiye legendy* ("Russian Popular Legends") was banned until 1914, and his *Lyubimyye skazki* ("Beloved Fairy Tales") collection, which included children's stories satirizing landowners and members of the clergy, was originally published anonymously in Geneva.

affective fallacy In literary criticism, the error of judging a work on the basis of its effect on the reader. The notion of affective fallacy was described by the proponents of New Criticism as a direct challenge to impressionistic critics who argued that the reader's response to a poem is the ultimate indication of its value.

Those who support the affective criterion for judging poetry cite its long and respectable history, beginning with Aristotle's dictum that the purpose of tragedy is to evoke "terror and pity," and many modern critics continue to assert that emotional communication and response cannot be separated from the evaluation of a poem. *See also* NEW CRITICISM.

afreet *also spelled* afrit, afrite, efreet, ifrit \\ə-'frēt, *in poetry often* 'af-,rēt, 'ef-, 'if-\\ [Arabic *'ifrīt*] In Islāmic mythology, a class of infernal jinn (spirits below the level of angels and devils) noted for their strength and cunning. An afreet is an enormous winged creature of smoke, either male or female, who lives underground and frequents ruins. As with the jinn, afreets may be either believers or unbelievers, good or evil, but they are most often depicted as wicked and ruthless beings.

The rare appearance of the term *'ifrīt* (feminine *'ifrītah*) in the Qur'ān (the sacred scripture of Islām) and in Ḥadīth (eyewitness narratives recounting Muḥammad's words, actions, or approbations) is always in the phrase "the afreet of the jinn" and probably means "rebellious." The word subsequently came to refer to an entire class of formidable, rebellious beings, but, in the confused world of chthonic (underworld) spirits, it was difficult to differentiate one from another. The afreet thus became virtually indistinguishable from the *mārid*, also a wicked and rebellious demon. *See also* JINNI.

After Many a Summer Dies the Swan A comedic novel written by Aldous HUXLEY. Published in 1939 under the title *After Many a Summer*, the novel was republished under its current title later in the same year.

Written soon after Huxley left England and settled in California, the novel is Huxley's examination of American culture, particularly what he saw as its narcissism, superficiality, and obsession with youth. The title is a line from Alfred, Lord Tennyson's poem "Tithonus," about a figure from Greek mythology to whom Zeus gave eternal life but not eternal youth. In Huxley's novel, California millionaire Jo Stoyte learns of an English nobleman who discovered a way to vastly extend the human life span. Stoyte travels to England and finds the nobleman still alive, but he has devolved into an apelike creature. Stoyte decides to extend his life regardless of the consequences.

afterpiece \\'af-tər-,pēs\\ Supplementary entertainment presented after full-length plays in 18th-century England. Afterpieces usually took the form of a short comedy, farce, or pantomime and were intended to lighten the solemnity of Neoclassical drama and make the bill more attractive to audiences. Long theater programs that included interludes of music, song, and dance developed in the first 20 years of the 18th century, promoted primarily by John Rich at Lincoln's Inn Fields in order to compete with the Drury Lane. The addition of afterpieces to the regular program may also have been an attempt to attract working citizens, who often missed the early opening production and paid a reduced charge to be admitted later, usually at the end of the third act of a five-act play.

Before 1747, afterpieces were generally presented with old plays, but after that date, almost all new plays were accompanied by afterpieces as well. Although farce and pantomime were the most popular forms of afterpiece—the latter usually integrating classical themes with commedia dell'arte characters—other kinds of afterpiece occasionally were performed. These included processions, burlettas (comic operas popular in England in the second half of the 18th century) or burlesques, and ballad operas, which gained popularity after the success of John Gay's *Beggar's Opera* in 1728.

After the Fall A play in two acts by Arthur MILLER, produced and published in 1964.

The play presents retrospectively a series of encounters that have occurred over a 25-year span between the protagonist, Quentin, a lawyer about the age of 50, and his intimate associates. His first wife, Louise, accuses him of failing to acknowledge her personhood. A friend from his days as a Communist Party member appears now as an informer before congressional investigators. Another former "fellow traveler" commits suicide before Quentin has the opportunity to defend him. The second act traces the downward course of Maggie, Quentin's second wife, from popular entertainer to bitter neurotic to suicide. As the play ends, Quentin appears poised to marry Holga, whose struggle against Nazism in Germany embodies his own desire to confront evil. Thematic issues of ethical ambiguity and personal integrity help to unify the work's somewhat disjointed dramatic structure.

Against the Grain Novel by Joris-Karl HUYSMANS, published in French as *À rebours* in 1884. It was also translated as *Against Nature*.

In both its style and its subject, the work epitomizes the decadence of late 19th-century French elite culture. The protagonist, Des Esseintes, exhibits the debilitating symptoms of neurasthenia, a generalized psychosomatic disorder that came into vogue during that period. The condition necessitates his temporary retirement from Paris to his country estate at Fontenay, where he sets his course "against the grain" of ordinary life. Cloistered in luxury, Des Esseintes contrives a regimen of exquisite sensualism. Unchecked indulgence only deepens his malaise, however, prompting his doctor to order him back to Paris. The story ends there, with an appeal by Des Esseintes for pity from a God he only vaguely believes in. Although the author intended the work for a select group of readers, it has become a sourcebook on fin-de-siècle aestheticism.

Agamemnon \ˌag-ə-'mem-ˌnän\ In Greek legend, king of Mycenae or Argos. He was the son (or grandson) of the Mycenaean king Atreus and his wife Aërope and was the brother of Menelaus. After Atreus is murdered by his own nephew Aegisthus (son of Thyestes), Agamemnon and Menelaus take refuge with Tyndareus, king of Sparta, whose daughters, Clytemnestra and Helen, they respectively marry. By Clytemnestra, Agamemnon has a son, Orestes, and three daughters, Iphigeneia (Iphianassa), Electra (Laodice), and Chrysothemis. Menelaus succeeds Tyndareus, while Agamemnon recovers his father's kingdom.

After Paris (Alexandros), son of King Priam of Troy, carries off Helen, Agamemnon calls on the princes of the country to unite in a war of revenge against the Trojans. He himself furnishes 100 ships and is chosen commander in chief of the combined forces. The fleet assembles at the port of Aulis in Boeotia but is prevented from sailing by calms or contrary winds sent by the goddess Artemis because Agamemnon has in some way offended her. To appease the wrath of Artemis, Agamemnon sacrifices his own daughter Iphigeneia.

On his return from Troy, Agamemnon lands in Argolis, where Aegisthus, who in the interval had seduced Clytemnestra, treacherously carries out his murder. The Greek poet Aeschylus—in his play *Agamemnon*—attributed the murder to Clytemnestra alone. Agamemnon's murder is avenged by Orestes (aided by Electra), who returns to slay both Clytemnestra and her paramour.

Agamemnon may have been a historical character, the overlord of the Mycenaean or Achaean states of the Greek mainland.

Agamemnon \ˌag-ə-'mem-ˌnän\ The first drama in the trilogy known as the ORESTEIA by Aeschylus.

Agate \'ā-gət, 'ag-ət\, James Evershed (b. Sept. 9, 1877, Pendleton, Lancashire, Eng.—d. June 6, 1947, London) Drama critic for the London *Sunday Times* (1923–47), book reviewer, novelist, essayist, diarist, and raconteur. He is remembered for his wit and perverse yet lovable personality, for the sparkle and fundamental seriousness of his dramatic criticism, and for his racy, entertaining diary, called, characteristically, *Ego*, 9 vol. (1935–49).

Educated at the Giggleswick and Manchester grammar schools, Agate went to London to become a journalist, working as drama critic for several papers. During World War I he served as an army officer. Between 1917, when, as he said, he "stormed London" with a lively account of an uneventful war, and 1949, 44 volumes of his writings were published, not counting the nine volumes of *Ego*. His works included drama, book, and film reviews as well as essays, novels, and surveys of the contemporary theater for 1923–26 and 1944–45. He was perhaps one of the last of a long line of English dramatic critics to take for granted his position as arbiter of taste and was also one of the last outstanding journalists of a great age of English journalism.

Agathias \ə-'gā-thē-əs, ə-'gath-ē-əs\ (b. *c.* 536, Myrina, Aeolis, Asia Minor—d. *c.* 582) Byzantine poet and author of a history covering part of Justinian I's reign.

After studying law at Alexandria, he completed his training at Constantinople and practiced in the courts as an advocate. He wrote a number of short love poems in epic meter, called *Daphniaca*, and compiled an anthology of epigrams by earlier and contemporary poets, including his own. About 100 epigrams by Agathias have been preserved in the *Greek Anthology*. After the death of Justinian I (565), Agathias began a history of his own times. This unfinished work in five books stands as the chief authority for the period 552–558.

Agathon \'ag-ə-ˌthän\ (b. *c.* 445 BC—d. *c.* 400 BC, Macedonia) An Athenian tragic poet and playwright who is credited with two innovations in Greek drama. His first victory at the festival of the Great Dionysia, in which plays were presented and judged, was gained in 416 BC. Plato makes the event of Agathon's victory the occasion for his dialogue *Symposium*, and the banquet at Agathon's house is the setting of the dialogue. Aristotle, in the *Poetics*, ascribes to Agathon two innovations: one of his plays (possibly *The Flower*) contains characters invented by Agathon rather than set characters derived from the stock of Greek mythology; and Agathon changed the traditional function of the choral lyrics so that they became musical interludes in the action of the play instead of offering comment upon it. Aristophanes parodies Agathon in his play *Women at the Thesmophoria*, but in another of his plays, *Frogs*, calls him "a good [*agathos*] poet sorely missed by his friends." Agathon spent his last years at the court of Archelaus of Macedonia. Only some 40 lines of his writing are extant.

Agave \ə-'gä-vē\ In Greek mythology, the daughter of Cadmus and Harmonia and the mother of Pentheus. When Agave slandered her sister Semele, Semele's son Dionysus retaliated by causing Agave to go mad and kill Pentheus with her own hands. The story is told in the play the BACCHAE by Euripides.

Agee \'ā-jē\, James (b. Nov. 27, 1909, Knoxville, Tenn., U.S.—d. May 16, 1955, New York, N.Y.) American poet, novelist, and one of the most influential American film critics in the 1930s and '40s.

Agee grew up in Tennessee's Cumberland Mountain area, attended Harvard University, and wrote for *Fortune* and *Time* after he graduated in 1932. *Permit Me Voyage*, a volume of poems, appeared in 1934. For a proposed article in *Fortune*, Agee and the photographer Walker Evans lived for about six weeks among poverty-stricken sharecroppers in Alabama in 1936. The article never appeared, but the material they gathered became the lyrical LET US NOW PRAISE FAMOUS MEN (1941).

From 1948 until his death, Agee worked mainly as a film scriptwriter, notably for *The African Queen* (1951) and *The Night of the Hunter* (1955). The novel A DEATH IN THE FAMILY (1957) and his novella *The Morning Watch* (1951), on the religious experiences of a 12-year-old boy, are both autobiographical.

Age of Anxiety, The Poem by W.H. AUDEN, published in 1947. Described as a "baroque eclogue," the poem was the last of Auden's long poems; it won the Pulitzer Prize for poetry in 1948.

The poem highlights human isolation, a condition magnified by the lack of tradition or religious belief in the modern age. The setting is nighttime at a bar in New York City, where four strangers—three men and one woman—meet, talk, and drink. The carousing ends in the woman's apartment. Two men leave, and the third disappoints her by passing out from too much liquor.

After exploring the spiritual emptiness, the loneliness, and the anxiety-ridden purposelessness of these characters' lives, the poem ends at dawn on the streets of the city.

Age of Innocence, The Novel by Edith WHARTON, published in 1920. The work presents a picture of upper-class New York society in the late 19th century. The story is presented as a kind of anthropological study of this society through references to the families and their activities as tribal. In the story Newland Archer, though engaged to May Welland, a beautiful and proper fellow member of elite society, is attracted to Ellen Olenska, a former member of their circle who has been living in Europe but who has left her husband under mysterious circumstances and returned to her family's New York milieu. May prevails by subtly adhering to the conventions of that world. The novel was awarded a Pulitzer Prize.

agitprop \'aj-it-,präp\ Political propaganda promulgated chiefly in literature, drama, music, or art.

Agitprop or *agitpropotdel* was a shortening of the Russian *agitatsionno-propagandistsky otdel* ("agitation-propaganda section"), a department of the Central Committee, or a local committee, of the Communist Party in the Soviet Union in the years after the Bolshevik Revolution of 1917. The word is used in English to describe the work of such departments, and by extension any work, especially in the theater, that aims to educate and indoctrinate the public. It typically has a negative connotation, reflecting in part Western distaste for overt use of drama and other arts to achieve political goals.

The twin strategies of agitation and propaganda were originally elaborated by the Russian Marxist theorist Georgy Plekhanov, who defined propaganda as the promulgation of a number of ideas to an individual or small group, and agitation as the promulgation of a single idea to a large mass of people. Expanding on these notions in the pamphlet *Chto delat?* (1902; *What Is to Be Done?*), V.I. Lenin stated that the propagandist, whose primary medium was print, explained the cause of social inequities such as unemployment or hunger, while the agitator, whose primary medium was the spoken word, seized on emotional aspects of these issues to arouse his audience's indignation.

Aglauros \ə-'glȯr-əs\ In Greek mythology, eldest daughter of the Athenian king Cecrops; she died with her sisters by leaping in fear from the Acropolis after seeing the infant Erechthonius, a human with a serpent's tail. The Roman poet Ovid, however, related that Aglauros was turned to stone by the god Mercury in retribution for her attempt to frustrate his abduction of Herse, Aglauros' youngest sister.

Agnes Grey \'ag-nəs-'grā\ Novel by Anne BRONTË, published in 1847. The strongly autobiographical narrative concerns the travails of Agnes Grey, a rector's daughter, in her service as governess, first to the unruly Bloomfield children and then with the callous Murrays. Agnes's sole consolations in this dreary life are the natural environment and her blossoming relationship with Weston, the local curate, whom she eventually marries.

Agnon \ˌäg-'nōn\, S.Y.\'shī\, *pseudonym of* Shmuel Yosef Halevi Czaczkes (b. July 17, 1888, Buczacz, Galicia, Austria-Hungary [now Buchach, Ukraine]—d. Feb. 17, 1970, Reḥovot, Israel) Israeli writer, one of the greatest modern Hebrew novelists and short-story writers. In 1966 he and Nelly Sachs shared the Nobel Prize for Literature.

Born of a family of Polish Jewish merchants, rabbis, and scholars, he at first wrote in Yiddish and Hebrew, under his own name and various pseudonyms; but, soon after settling in Palestine in 1907, he took the surname Agnon and chose Hebrew as the language in which to write.

Agnon's real literary debut was made with *Agunot* (1908; "Forsaken Wives"), his first "Palestinian" story. His first major work was the novel *Hakhnasat kalah*, 2 vol. (1919; *The Bridal Canopy*). Its hero, Reb Yudel Hasid, is the embodiment of every wandering, drifting Jew in the ghettos of the tsarist and Austro-Hungarian empires. His second novel, *Ore'aḥ Nata' Lalun* (1938; *A Guest for the Night*), describes the material and moral decay of European Jewry after World War I. His third and perhaps greatest novel, *'Tmol shilshom* (1945; "The Day Before Yesterday"), examines the problem facing the westernized Jew who immigrates to Israel.

Agnon's works all underwent innumerable revisions, as is shown by two widely different versions of his collected works, one in 11 volumes (*Kol sipurav shel Sh.Y. Agnon*, vol. i–vi, Berlin, 1931–35; vii–xi, Jerusalem and Tel Aviv, 1939–52) and one in 8 volumes (Tel Aviv, 1953–62).

Agnon edited an anthology of folktales inspired by the High Holidays of the Jewish year, *Yamim nora'im* (1938; *Days of Awe*), and a selection of famous rabbinic texts, *Sefer, sofer, vesipur* (1938). He also wrote an autobiographical sketch that was published in 1958.

agon \'ag-ˌän, ä-'gōn\ *plural* agons *or* agones \ ə-'gō-ˌnēz\ [Greek *agōn* gathering, assembly, contest, a derivative of *ágein* to lead, bring] **1.** A contest or conflict; specifically, the dramatic conflict between the chief characters in a Greek play. In particular, in Attic comedy, debate or contest between two characters, constituting one of several formal conventions of

OLD COMEDY. **2.** The struggle between protagonist and antagonist in a literary work.

agonist \'ag-ə-nist\ [Greek *agōnistés* contestant, combatant] A leading character (such as the PROTAGONIST or ANTAGONIST) in a literary work.

Agoult \ā-'gü\, Marie de Flavigny, Countess (comtesse) d', *original name in full* Marie-Catherine-Sophie de Flavigny, *pseudonym* Daniel Stern \'stern\ (b. Dec. 31, 1805, Frankfurt am Main [now in Germany]—d. March 5, 1876, Paris, Fr.) Writer famous for her position in Parisian society in the 1840s and for her liaison with the composer Franz Liszt.

De Flavigny was the daughter of the émigré Count de Flavigny. In 1827 she married Colonel Charles d'Agoult, 20 years her senior. Meeting Liszt, she decided in 1834 to run away with him. Their relationship lasted till 1839, and their separation became permanent in 1844. Their daughter Cosima was the second wife of the composer Richard Wagner.

Returning to Paris in 1839, Mme d'Agoult began her career as a writer and in 1846 published a largely autobiographical novel, *Nélida*. She was a close friend of George Sand, whose views on morals, politics, and society she shared and in whose house she had lived for a time with Liszt. She also became the leader of a salon. Her other writings include *Lettres républicaines* (1848); *Histoire de la révolution de 1848* (1850–53); a play, *Jeanne d'Arc* (1857); a dialogue, *Dante et Goethe* (1866); and *Mes Souvenirs 1806–1833* (1877), supplemented by *Mémoires, 1833–1854* (1927).

Aguecheek, Sir Andrew \sər-'an-,drü-'ā-gyü-,chēk\ Character in William Shakespeare's TWELFTH NIGHT, a ludicrous knight whose hopeless pursuit of Olivia subjects him to numerous indignities.

Aguilar \'ag-ē-,lär, *Angl* ə-'gwil-ər\, Grace (b. June 2, 1816, London, Eng.—d. Sept. 16, 1847, Frankfurt am Main [Germany]) Poet, novelist, and writer on Jewish history and religion, best known for her sentimental novels of domestic life, especially for *Home Influence* (1847) and *The Mother's Recompense* (1851). Aguilar was the daughter of Sephardic Jews. She was tutored in the classics at home and (even in adulthood) was not permitted to move outside of her family circle. Before becoming known as a novelist, she gained a considerable reputation as an educator about Jewish culture for an English-speaking public. Within the bounds of a painfully circumscribed life, Aguilar managed to write 12 books. *Home Influence* was the only novel published during her lifetime.

Agustín \,äg-ü-'stēn\, José, *surname in full* Agustín Ramírez \rä-'mē-rās\ (b. Aug. 19, 1944, Acapulco, Guerrero, Mex.) Mexican novelist whose prolific writings, reflecting an urban sensibility and the modern culture of youth, highlighted urban violence and decay.

Agustín was educated at National Autonomous University of Mexico and at Centro Mexicano de Escritores. He was a leader of Onda, a youth movement sympathetic to rock music and drug culture. His fiction reflected his involvement in Onda.

His first novel, *La tumba* (1964; "The Tomb"), published when he was 20, is told from a teenager's viewpoint. Subsequent works included the prizewinning play *Círculo vicioso* (1974; "Vicious Circle") and the award-winning novel *Ciudades desiertas* (1982; "Deserted Cities"). In 1985 Agustín published an autobiography, *El rock de la cárcel* ("Jailhouse Rock"); a collection of essays, *La nueva música clásica* ("The New Classical Music"); and the novels *Ahí viene la plaga* ("Here Comes the Plague") and *Furor matutino* ("Morning Fury"). The novel *Cerca del fuego* (1986; "Near the Fire") was a mordantly humorous indictment of life in Mexico City.

Agustini \,äg-ü-'stē-nē\, Delmira (b. Oct. 24, 1886, Montevideo, Uruguay—d. July 6, 1914, Montevideo) Modernist poet considered to be one of the most important poets of South America. She was the first woman to deal boldly with the themes of sensuality and passion.

Agustini was a child prodigy born into a scholarly family. Her fame spread rapidly throughout the Spanish-speaking world with the publication of her first two volumes of poetry, *El libro blanco* (1907; "The White Book"), and *Cantos de la mañana* (1910; "Morning Songs"). Her third book, *Los cálices vacíos* ("Empty Chalices"), was published in 1913. Her life ended tragically when she was murdered by her estranged husband. Two later collections were published in 1924—*El rosario del Eros* ("Eros' Rosary") and *Los astros del abismo* ("The Stars of the Abyss")—and there have been several editions of her complete works. A collection of her letters was published in 1969.

Ahab \'ā-,hab\ or **Achab** \'ā-,kab\ (reigned *c.* 874–*c.* 853 BC) Seventh king of the northern kingdom of Israel, according to the Old Testament, and son of King Omri. The story of Ahab is related in the First Book of Kings. Ahab's reign was generally peaceful, and by an alliance (through lineal intermarriage) with the southern kingdom of Judah he withstood the Assyrians. His wife JEZEBEL aroused strong opposition, especially from the prophet Elijah, by her worship of the Canaanite god Baal.

Ahab, Captain \'ā-,hab\ Fictional character, a one-legged captain of the whaling vessel *Pequod* in the novel MOBY-DICK, by Herman Melville. From the time that his leg is bitten off by the huge white whale called Moby-Dick, Captain Ahab monomaniacally pursues his elusive nemesis.

Aḥad Ha'am \ä-'ḳäd-hä-'äm\, *original name* Asher Ginzberg \'gʸins-bʸirg\ (b. Aug. 18, 1856, Skvira, near Kiev, Ukraine, Russian Empire—d. Jan. 2, 1927, Tel Aviv, Palestine [now Tel Aviv–Yafo, Israel]) Zionist leader and writer whose concepts of Hebrew culture significantly influenced early Jewish settlement in Palestine and whose lucid and precise writing style made him a major force in Hebrew literature.

Reared in Russia in a rigidly Orthodox Jewish family, Aḥad Ha'am mastered rabbinic literature but soon was attracted to the rationalist school of medieval Jewish philosophy and to the writings of the Haskala ("Enlightenment"), a liberal Jewish movement that attempted to integrate Judaism with modern Western thought. At the age of 22, he went to Odessa, the center of the Jewish nationalist movement known as Ḥibbat Zion ("Love of Zion"). After joining the movement, he published his first essay, "Lo ze ha-derekh" (1889; "This Is Not the Way"), which emphasized the spiritual basis of Zionism.

Aḥad Ha'am made two visits to Palestine. From 1896 to 1903 he was editor of the periodical *Ha-Shiloʾaḥ*, in which he criticized the political Zionism of Theodor Herzl, the foremost Jewish nationalist leader of the time. Remaining outside the Zionist organization, Aḥad Ha'am asserted that a Jewish state would be the end result of a Jewish spiritual renaissance rather than the beginning. He called for a renaissance of Hebrew-language culture, and to that end he urged the creation of a Jewish national homeland in Palestine as the model for Jewish life in the Diaspora (*i.e.*, the settlements of Jews outside Palestine).

Aḥad Ha'am's last years were spent in Palestine, editing his *Iggerot Aḥad Ha'am*, 6 vol. (1923–25; "Letters of Aḥad Ha'am"). Further letters and his memoirs were published in *Aḥad Ha'am: Pirqe zikhronot we-iggerot* (1931; "Collected Memoirs and Letters"). His essays comprise four volumes (1895, 1903, 1904, and 1913).

Ahlin \ä-'lēn\, Lars \'lärsh\ (b. April 4, 1915, Sundsvall, Swed.) Influential Swedish novelist of the mid-20th century.

Ahlin's first novel, *Tåbb med manifestet* (1943; "Tåbb with the Manifesto"), contains many of the central ideas of his writings. In it, a young unemployed worker finds communist ideology unsatisfactory, rejects the notion of social rather than individual value, and reaches a better understanding of himself and the world through a secularized Lutheran theology in which people are judged according to their deeds. The search for grace through love, usually experienced with humiliation and suffering, is traced in a number of subsequent novels, of which *Min död är min* (1945; "My Death Is My Own"), *Kanelbiten* (1953; "The Cinnamon Girl"), and *Natt i marknadstältet* (1957; "Night in the Market Tent") are the best known. His most experimental work is *Om* (1946; "If, About, Around"). Ahlin published several more books in the 1980s, including an autobiographical novel, *Sjätte munnen* (1985; "The Sixth Mouth").

Ahmed Haşim \äh-'met-'häsh-im\ (b. 1884, Baghdad [now in Iraq]—d. June 4, 1933, Istanbul, Tur.)   Writer who is an outstanding representative of the Symbolist movement in Turkish literature.

Haşim developed his knowledge of French literature and his fondness for poetry at Galatasaray Lycée in Constantinople (now Istanbul). After briefly studying law, he worked for the government tobacco offices. Later he served as a government translator. After military service in World War I, he worked for the Ottoman Public Debt Administration and then held various teaching positions. In 1924 and 1928 he made trips to Paris during which he met leading French literary figures.

Haşim's early poetry was written in classical Ottoman style, but, after his study of the poetry of Charles Baudelaire and the Symbolist poetry of Arthur Rimbaud, Stéphane Mallarmé, and others, his poetic style changed. In 1909 he joined the Fecr-i âti ("Dawn of the Future") literary circle but gradually drew apart from this group and developed his own style. Following the French masters, Haşim worked to develop the Turkish Symbolist movement. His poetry at times seems intentionally obscure; nevertheless, he creates images and moods of great beauty and sensitivity. Among his most famous poetry collections are *Göl saatleri* (1921; "Hours by the Lake") and *Piyale* (1926; "The Wine Cup").

Ahmedî \,äh-med-'ē\, *in full* Taceddin İbrahim bin Hızır Ahmedî (b. 1334/35, Kütahya?, Anatolia [now Turkey]—d. 1412, Amasya, Ottoman Empire)   One of the greatest poets of 14th-century Anatolia.

As a young man, Ahmedî studied with the famous scholar Akmal ad-Din (al-Babarti) in Cairo. He then went to Kütahya, in Anatolia, and wrote for the ruler Amīr Süleyman (1367–86). Later he went to the court of the Ottoman sultan Bayezid I (1389–1403), and, at the Battle of Ankara, in which the Ottomans suffered a drastic defeat, Ahmedî apparently met the victor, the world conqueror Timur, and wrote a qasida (ode) for him.

At the death of Sultan Bayezid, Ahmedî presented the monarch's son Süleyman Çelebi with panegyrics and one of his best-known works, the *İskendernâme* ("The Book of Alexander"), a work that he had dedicated originally to Amīr Süleyman of the house of Germiyan in Kütahya but that he revised and added to for many years. Modeled after the work of the great Persian poet Neẓāmī (died 1209), Ahmedî's poem comprises some 8,000 rhymed couplets (*maṣnawī*) in which he uses the legend of Alexander as a framework for discourses on theology, philosophy, and history. The last part is regarded as an important early source for Ottoman history because the poet apparently based it on a very early chronicle that is no longer extant.

At the death of Süleyman in 1411, Ahmedî wrote panegyrics for the new Ottoman sultan, Mehmet Çelebi I (died 1421), un-

til his own death. In addition to the *İskendernâme*, Ahmedî wrote a divan, or collection of poems; many *maṣnawī*; a poem, *Cemşid ü Hurşid*; and a didactic work, *Tervihü'l-ervah* ("The Comfort of the Spirit").

Ahmed Paşa \äh-'met-pä-'shä\, *also called* Ahmed Paşa Bursali (b. Edirne, Ottoman Empire [now in Turkey]—d. 1496/ 97, Bursa)   One of the most important figures in 15th-century Turkish literature.

Ahmed Paşa received a classical Islāmic education and was appointed as a teacher in the madrasah (religious college) in the city of Bursa. In 1451 he became judge of the city of Edirne. He had a career of government service, though it was interrupted by many years in virtual exile in Bursa.

Principally a panegyrist, Ahmed Paşa wrote mainly qasida (odes) and ghazels (lyrics) and is considered the first master of classical poetry in Ottoman literature. The melodious poems in his divan, or collection of poems, had a strong influence on later Ottoman classical poets, securing for him an important place in Turkish literary history.

Ahmed Yesevi \äh-'met-,yes-e-'vē\ *or* **Aḥmad Yasawī** \äh-'mäd-,yäs-ä-'vē\, Yesevi *also spelled* Yasavī (b. second half of the 11th century, Sayrām [now in Kazakhstan]—d. 1166, Yasī, Turkistan [now Turkmenistan])   Turkish poet and Ṣūfī (Muslim mystic) who influenced the development of mystical orders throughout the Turkish-speaking world.

Very little is known about Ahmed Yesevi's life. The family moved to Yasī (hence his name), and there he began his mystical teaching. He is said to have gone to Bukhara to study with famous mystics, but to have finally returned to Yasī. The extant work attributed to the poet is the *Divan-ı hikmet* ("Book of Wisdom"), containing poems on mystical themes. Scholars believe that the work is probably not his. It is felt, however, that the poems in the *Divan* are similar in style and sentiment to what he wrote. Legends about his life were spread throughout the Turkish Islāmic world, and he developed a tremendous following. The conqueror Timur in 1397/98 erected over the poet's grave a magnificent mausoleum to which pilgrims came, revering Ahmed Yesevi as a saint.

Ahmed Yesevi wrote poetry for the people; he is also credited with having influenced the development of mystical folk literature in Turkey.

Aho \'ä-hō\, Juhani, *pseudonym of* Johannes Brofeldt \'brü-,felt\ (b. Sept. 11, 1861, Lapinlahti, Finland, Russian Empire—d. Aug. 8, 1921, Helsinki, Fin.)   Novelist and short-story writer who helped introduce modernism into Finnish literature.

Brofeldt studied at Helsinki University, worked as a journalist, and was an active member of the liberal group Nuori Suomi ("Young Finland"). His early realistic stories and novels humorously describe life in the Finnish backwoods he knew so well. His novel *Rautatie* (1884; "The Railway"), the story of an elderly couple's first railway trip, is a Finnish classic. Influenced by contemporary Norwegian and French writers—Henrik Ibsen, Bjørnstjerne Martinius Bjørnson, Guy de Maupassant, and particularly Alphonse Daudet—he described the life of the educated classes in *Papin tytär* (1885; "The Parson's Daughter") and *Papin rouva* (1893; "The Parson's Wife").

In the 1890s Aho was drawn toward romantic nationalism: the long novel *Panu* (1897) dealt with the struggle between paganism and Christianity in 17th-century Finland, and *Kevät ja takatalvi* (1906; "Spring and the Untimely Return of Winter"), with the national awakening of the 19th century. His soundest romantic work, *Juha* (1911), is the story of the unhappy marriage. Aho's short stories, *Lastuja*, 8 series (1891–1921; "Chips"), have been most enduring; they are concerned with peasant life, fishing, and the wildlife of the lakelands. In these, as in his reminiscences of childhood, *Muistatko—?* (1920; "Do You Remember?"), Aho displays a quiet lyricism.

Ah, Wilderness! Comedy in four acts by Eugene O'NEILL, published and first performed in 1933. Perhaps the most atypical of the author's works, the play presents a sentimental tale of youthful indiscretion in a turn-of-the-century New England town. Richard, adolescent son of the local newspaper publisher, Nat Miller, exhibits the wayward tendencies of his maternal uncle, Sid Davis. Forbidden to court the neighbor girl, Muriel, by her father, Richard goes on a bender and falls under the influence of Belle, whom he tries to impress but whose worldly ways frighten him. It is the dissolute Sid who handles the situation upon the prodigal's drunken return, and with the aid of warmhearted Nat and the forgiving Muriel everything is put to right. The play has since become a staple of the community-theater repertoire.

Aicard \ä-'kàr\, Jean, *in full* François-Victor-Jean (b. Feb. 4, 1848, Toulon, Fr.—d. May 13, 1921, Paris) French poet, novelist, and dramatist best known for his poems of the Provence region.

As a young man, Aicard studied law but abandoned it to devote himself to literature. His first book of poetry, *Jeunes croyances* (1867; "Beliefs of a Youth"), showed the influence of the Romantic poet Alphonse de Lamartine and was well received. He went to Paris after the Franco-Prussian War and published *Les Rebellions et les apaisements* (1871; "Rebellions and Reassurances"). *Poèmes de Provence*, a sensitive evocation of the Provençal scene, followed in 1874; two years later *La Chanson de l'enfant* ("Child's Song") was published. Of his 14 plays the most successful was *Le Père Lebonnard* ("Father Lebonnard"), first performed in 1889. Most of his novels, the best of which is *Maurin des maures* (1908; "Maurin of the Moors"), are also based on Provençal life. He became a member of the Académie Française in 1909.

Aichinger \'īk-iŋ-ər\, Ilse (b. Nov. 1, 1921, Vienna, Austria) Austrian poet and prose writer whose work, often dreamlike, surreal, and presented in the form of parables, reflected her preoccupation with the Nazi persecution of the Jews during World War II.

Aichinger's education was interrupted by World War II when, because she was half-Jewish, she was refused entrance to medical school. Although she eventually did begin medical school in 1947, she left to concentrate on writing. Her only novel, *Die grössere Hoffnung* ("The Greater Hope"; Eng. trans., *Herod's Children*), was published in 1948.

In addition to her novel, Aichinger's works include *Rede unter dem Galgen* (1951; "Speech Under the Gallows"; Eng. trans., *The Bound Man and Other Stories*); *Knöpfe* (1953; "Buttons"), a radio play in which workers in a button factory slowly turn into the products they make; *Plätze und Strassen* (1954; "Squares and Streets"), a series of meditations on places in Vienna; *Zu keiner Stunde* (1957; "Never at Any Time"), a collection of surreal dialogues; and the short-story collection *Schlechte Wörter* (1976; "Inferior Words"), in which language is sometimes seen as a bar to communication.

Aidoo \'ä-,dü\, Ama Ata, *in full* Christina Ama Ata Aidoo (b. March 23, 1942, Abeadzi Kyiakor, near Saltpond, Gold Coast [now Ghana]) Ghanaian writer whose work emphasized the paradoxical nature of the modern African woman's role.

Aidoo first published poetry while at the University of Ghana (B.A., 1964). She won early recognition with a problem play, *The Dilemma of a Ghost* (1965), in which a Ghanaian student returning home brings back his African-American wife to the traditional culture and the extended family he now finds restrictive. Their dilemma reflects Aidoo's characteristic concern

with the "been-to" (African educated abroad), voiced again in her semiautobiographical experimental first novel, *Our Sister Killjoy; or, Reflections from a Black-Eyed Squint* (1966). Aidoo taught for many years in the United States and Kenya.

No Sweetness Here (1970), a collection of short stories, and *Anowa* (1970), another problem play, are concerned with Western influences on the role of women and on the individual in a communal society. Aidoo rejected the argument that Western education emancipates African women. She published little between 1970 and 1985, when *Someone Talking to Sometime*, a collection of poetry, appeared. Later titles include *The Eagle and the Chickens* (1986; a collection of children's stories), *Birds and Other Poems* (1987) and the novel *Changes: A Love Story* (1991).

Aiken \'ā-kən\, Conrad Potter (b. Aug. 5, 1889, Savannah, Ga., U.S.—d. Aug. 17, 1973, Savannah) Poet, short-story writer, novelist, and critic whose works, influenced by early psychoanalytic theory, are concerned largely with the human need for self-awareness.

Aiken himself confronted considerable childhood trauma caused by finding the bodies of his parents after his father had killed his mother and committed suicide. Educated at private schools and at Harvard, where he was a friend and contemporary of T.S. Eliot (whose poetry was to influence his own), Aiken divided his life almost equally between England and the United States until 1947, when he settled in Massachusetts. He played a significant role in introducing American poets to the British.

After three early collections of verse, he wrote five "symphonies" between 1915 and 1920 in an effort to create poetry that would resemble music in its ability to express several levels of meaning simultaneously. Then came a period of narrative poems, volumes of lyrics and meditations, and, after World War II, a return to musical form but with richer philosophical and psychological overtones. The best of his poetry is contained in *Collected Poems* (1953), including a long sequence "Preludes to Definition," which some critics consider his masterwork, and the frequently anthologized "Morning Song of Senlin."

Most of his fiction was written in the 1920s and '30s. Generally more successful than his novels of this period were his short stories, notably "Strange Moonlight" from *Bring! Bring!* (1925) and "Silent Snow, Secret Snow" and "Mr. Arcularis" from *Among the Lost People* (1934). *The Short Stories of Conrad Aiken* was published in 1950 and his autobiography, *Ushant*, in 1952.

Aiken \'ā-kən\, Joan (Delano) (b. Sept. 4, 1924, Rye, Sussex, Eng.) Prolific British author of fantasy, adventure, horror, and suspense tales for both juvenile and adult readers. Perhaps best known as inventor of a genre called the "unhistorical romance," Aiken wrote tales that combined humor and action with traditional mythic and fairy tale elements. Many of these works were set in an invented historical era during the imagined reign of James III of England, who was known as the Old Pretender.

Aiken was the daughter of the poet Conrad Aiken. While still a student, she had two poems published in *The Abinger Chronicle*, a prestigious little magazine. As an adult she wrote radio scripts and some short stories. In 1955 she became an editor for the literary magazine *Argosy*. Her first books, *All You've Ever Wanted* (1953) and *More Than You Bargained For* (1955), were short-story collections.

The Wolves of Willoughby Chase (1962) was Aiken's first novel to combine elements of history, horror, and adventure. It was the first of some 60 short-story collections and novels for children. Her many books of adult fiction, beginning with *The Silence of Herondale* (1964), also were categorized as terror, suspense, and mystery stories. Aiken also wrote *The Way to Write for Children* (1982).

Aimard \e-'mår\, Gustave, *pseudonym of* Olivier Gloux \'glü\ (b. Sept. 13, 1818, Paris, Fr.—d. June 20, 1883, Paris)   Popular novelist who wrote adventure stories about life on the American frontier and in Mexico.

At the age of 12 Aimard went to sea as a ship's boy and subsequently witnessed local wars and conspiracies in Turkey, the Caucasus, and South America. After taking part in the Revolution of 1848 in Paris, he traveled to North America in 1854. In 1870 he fought in the siege of Paris during the Franco-Prussian war.

Many of his adventure romances appeared serially in newspapers. Among the most popular of his 43 books, some of which were translated into English, were *Les Trappeurs de l'Arkansas* (1858; "The Trappers of Arkansas"), *Les Bohèmes de la mer* (1865; "The Gypsies of the Sea"), and *Par mer et par terre* (1879; "By Sea and by Land").

Ainsworth \'ānz-wərth\, William Harrison (b. Feb. 4, 1805, Manchester, Lancashire, Eng.—d. Jan. 3, 1882, Reigate, Surrey)   English author of popular historical romances.

Ainsworth initially studied law but abandoned it for literature. His first success came with the novel *Rookwood* (1834), featuring the highwayman Dick Turpin as its main character. This book was followed by many other historical novels, 39 in all, the best known of which are *The Tower of London* (1840), *Old St. Paul's, a Tale of the Plague and the Fire of London* (1841), *Windsor Castle: An Historical Romance* (1843), and *The Lancashire Witches* (1849).

Ainsworth became editor of *Bentley's Miscellany* in 1839, and he owned that periodical from 1854 to 1868. He was also editor at various times of *The New Monthly Magazine* and his own *Ainsworth's Magazine*. His novels made him a wealthy man, but his ventures as an editor and publisher were generally unsuccessful. His novels excel in accurately and vividly conveying the pageantry and bustle of history, but they lack coherence of plot and subtlety of characterization.

Ai Qing or **Ai Ch'ing** \'ī-'chiŋ\, *pseudonym of* Jiang Haiqing (b. March 27, 1910, Jinhua, Zhejiang province, China)   Chinese poet who was committed to the doctrines of Mao Zedong.

The son of a well-to-do landowner, Ai Qing was encouraged to learn Western languages. He studied painting in Paris from 1928 to 1932, and he developed an appreciation for Western literature. Imprisoned for his radical political activities, he began to write poetry under his pen name. He published his first book of poetry in 1939. It reflected his concern for the common people of China and his agreement with the literary teachings of Mao. He published a number of additional volumes in the 1940s. His poetry grew nationalistic and folk-oriented and became an increasingly effective instrument for propaganda. From 1949 to 1953 Ai Qing worked on the editorial staff of the magazine *Renmin wenxue* ("People's Literature"). He served on various cultural committees until he was officially censured in 1957.

Ai Qing remained silent for 21 years and was interned in labor camps in Heilongjiang and Xinjiang. He began publishing again in 1978. *Selected Poems of Ai Qing* was published in 1982.

Air-Conditioned Nightmare, The   Nonfiction account of Henry MILLER's travels through the United States, published in 1945. Miller undertook these travels in 1940 and 1941 after returning from a lengthy stay in Europe. Miller comments, mostly negatively, on America's physical landscape as well as on the mood and spirit of the American people. Among other things, he contrasts the ideals of the original founders with contemporary Americans' love of making money. Miller com-

mented further on these themes in the sequel *Remember to Remember* (1947).

aisling \'ash-liŋ\ *plural* aislings *or* aislingi \ash-'liŋ-ē\ [Irish, vision, description of a vision]   In Irish literature, a poetical or dramatic description or representation of a vision. THE VISION OF ADAMNÁN is one of the best-known examples. In the 18th century the aisling became popular as a means of expressing support for the restoration of the Roman Catholic Stuart line to the throne.

Aistis \'ă-ē-stəs\, Jonas, *also called* Jonas Kossu-Aleksandravičius, *or* Jonas Kuosa-Aleksandriškis, *pseudonym of* Jonas Aleksandravičius \ă-lek-,sän-'drä-vē-,chūs\ (b. July 7, 1904, Kampiškės, near Kaunas, Lithuania, Russian Empire—d. June 13, 1973, Washington, D.C., U.S.)   Poet whose lyrics are considered among the best in Lithuanian literature and who was the first modern Lithuanian poet to turn to personal expression.

Aistis studied at the University of Kaunas and the University of Grenoble in France. Because of the Soviet occupation, he did not return to Lithuania but went in 1946 to the United States, where, in 1958, he joined the staff of the Library of Congress, Washington, D.C.

Aistis' early collections of verse, including his fourth collection, *Užgesę chimeros akys* (1937; "The Dead Eyes of the Chimera"), contain his finest work. His patriotic verse, written in exile, was not as successful as his earlier work. Aistis edited several collections of poetry, among them *Lietuvių poezijos antologija* (1950; "Anthology of Lithuanian Poetry"). *Poezija* (1961; "Poetry") contains his collected poems to that time. Three collections of his essays also have been published.

aition \'ī-tē-,än\ *plural* aitia \-tē-ə\ *or* aitions [Greek *aítion* cause]   A tale devised to explain the origin of a religious observance.

Aitmatov   *see* AYTMATOV.

Ajax \'ā-,jaks\, *Greek* Aias, *byname* Ajax the Greater.   In Greek mythology, son of Telamon, king of Salamis, described in the *Iliad* as being of great stature and colossal frame, second only to the Greek hero Achilles in strength and bravery. He engaged Hector (the chief Trojan warrior) in single combat and, with the aid of the goddess Athena, rescued the body of Achilles from the hands of the Trojans. He competed with the Greek hero Odysseus for the armor of Achilles but lost, which so enraged him that it caused his death. According to a later story Ajax' disappointment drove him mad. On coming to his senses he slew himself with the sword that he had received as a present from Hector.

Among the authors who have examined the character of Ajax are Aeschylus, Sophocles, Ovid, Pieter Corneliszoon Hooft, James Shirley, André Gide, and Joseph Brodsky.

Ajax \'ā-,jaks\ (Latin), *Greek* Aias, *byname* Ajax the Lesser.   In Greek legend, son of Oileus, king of Locris. In spite of his small stature, he held his own among the other heroes before Troy; but he was also boastful, arrogant, and quarrelsome. For his crime of dragging King Priam's daughter Cassandra from the statue of the goddess Athena and violating her, he barely escaped being stoned to death by his Greek allies. Voyaging homeward, his ship was wrecked, but Ajax was saved. Then, boasting of his escape, he was cast by Poseidon into the sea and drowned.

Ajax \'ā-,jaks\ (*Greek* Aias mastigophoros)   Drama by SOPHOCLES, constructed around the hero of the Trojan War whose pride causes his downfall. The date of the play is uncertain, but it is generally regarded as his earliest extant play.

The plot centers on Ajax' anger at being passed over for the prize of valor (the dead Achilles' armor). In his rage, Ajax attempts to assassinate Odysseus and the contest's judges—the Greek commanders Agamemnon and Menelaus—but he is frustrated by the intervention of the goddess Athena. He cannot bear his humiliation and throws himself on his own sword. Agamemnon and Menelaus order that Ajax' corpse be left unburied as punishment, but Odysseus persuades the commanders to grant Ajax an honorable burial. In the end Odysseus is revealed as the only one with the wisdom to both recognize and accept the changeability of human fortune.

Akenside \'ā-kən-ˌsīd\, Mark (b. Nov. 9, 1721, Newcastle upon Tyne, Northumberland, Eng.—d. June 23, 1770, London) British poet and physician, best known for his poem *The Pleasures of Imagination*, an eclectic philosophical essay.

Akenside attended the University of Edinburgh, intending to become a minister but instead studying medicine. His first poem, "The Virtuoso," in imitation of the Elizabethan poet Edmund Spenser, appeared in 1737. *The Pleasures of Imagination* first appeared in three books in 1744. A fourth book was added later, and the whole poem was extensively revised, finally appearing posthumously in *The Poems of Mark Akenside, M.D.* (1772). Written in blank verse derived from Milton's, it was modeled on the Roman poets Virgil (the *Georgics*) and Horace (the *Epistles*). Later adopting the ode as his favorite poetic form, Akenside was more than willing to consider himself the English Pindar, one of several aspects of his character that was satirized in Tobias Smollett's novel *The Adventures of Peregrine Pickle*, in which Akenside appears as the physician in scenes set on the European continent. In 1745 Akenside published *Odes on Several Subjects* and in 1746 "Hymn to the Naiads" and "To the Evening Star." He was eventually made physician to the queen.

Akhmadulina \ˌək-ˌmə-'dū-lē-nə\, Bella, *in full* Izabella Akhatovna Akhmadulina (b. April 10, 1937, Moscow, Russia, U.S.S.R.) Russian-language poet of Tatar and Italian descent, a distinctive voice in post-Stalinist Soviet literature.

Akhmadulina completed her education at the Gorky Literary Institute in 1960 and then traveled in Central Asia. She was eventually admitted to the Soviet Writers' Union, although her uncompromisingly individualistic work elicited official criticism and she often experienced some difficulty in getting it published. Like her fellow poet Yevgeny Yevtushenko, to whom she was married during the 1950s, she drew large audiences at readings of her work.

Her first collection, *Struna* ("The Harp String"), appeared in 1962. The long poem *"Moya rodoslovnaya"* (1964; "My Family Tree"), the title of which alludes to a poem by Aleksandr Pushkin from 1830, is marked by experimentation in both theme and technique. The creative act was a recurring theme in her work. Subsequent volumes include *Uroki muzyki* (1969; "Music Lessons"), *Stikhi* (1975; "Poems"), and *Taina* (1983; "Secret"). Akhmadulina also published translations of poetry from Georgian and other languages.

Akhmatova \ˌək-'mä-tə-və\, Anna, *pseudonym of* Anna Andreyevna Gorenko (b. June 11 [June 23, New Style], 1889, Bolshoy Fontan, near Odessa, Ukraine, Russian Empire—d. March 5, 1966, Domodedovo, near Moscow) One of the greatest Russian poets.

Akhmatova at 21 became a member of the Acmeist group of poets, whose leader, Nikolay Gumilyov, she married in 1910 but divorced in 1918. Her first collections, *Vecher* (1912; "Evening") and especially *Chyotki* (1914; "Rosary"), brought her fame. While exemplifying the best kind of personal or even confessional poetry, they achieve a universal appeal deriving from their artistic and emotional integrity. Akhmatova's principal motif is love.

Later she included civic, patriotic, and religious motifs, as in the collections *Belaya staya* (1917; "The White Flock"), *Podorozhnik* (1921; "Plantain"), and *Anno Domini MCMXXI* (1922), but this did not prevent official Soviet critics from condemning her poetry for its narrow preoccupation with love and God. The execution in 1921 of her former husband, Gumilyov, on charges of participation in an anti-Soviet conspiracy further complicated her position. In 1923 she entered a period of almost complete poetic silence and literary ostracism, and no volume of her poetry was published in the Soviet Union until 1940. In that year several of her poems were published in the literary monthly *Zvezda* ("The Star"), and a volume of selections from her earlier work appeared under the title *Iz shesti knig* ("From Six Books"). A few months later, however, it was abruptly withdrawn from sale and libraries.

In August 1946 she was harshly denounced for her "eroticism, mysticism, and political indifference." She was expelled from the Union of Soviet Writers; an unreleased book of her poems, already in print, was destroyed; and none of her work appeared in print for three years.

Then, in 1950, a number of her poems eulogizing Joseph Stalin and Soviet communism were printed in several issues of the illustrated weekly magazine *Ogonyok* ("The Little Light") under the title *Iz tsikla "Slava miru"* ("From the Cycle 'Glory to Peace' "). This uncharacteristic capitulation was motivated by Akhmatova's desire to win the freedom of her son, Lev Gumilyov, who had been arrested in 1949 and exiled to Siberia. The tone of these poems is far different from the moving and universalized lyrical cycle, *Rekviem* ("Requiem"), composed between 1935 and 1940 and occasioned by Akhmatova's grief over an earlier arrest and imprisonment of her son in 1937.

Following Stalin's death, Akhmatova was slowly rehabilitated, and a slim volume of her lyrics and translations was published in 1958. After 1958, a number of editions of her works were published in the Soviet Union. Akhmatova's longest work, *Poema bez geroya* ("Poem Without a Hero"), is widely regarded as one of the great poems of the 20th century. It combines symbolism, allegory, and autobiography, and skillfully weaves the themes of time, poetry, suffering, and affirmation around the central tragedy of a young poet's suicide.

Akhmatova executed a number of superb translations of the works of other poets, including Victor Hugo, Rabindranath Tagore, Giacomo Leopardi, and various Armenian and Korean poets. She also wrote sensitive personal memoirs on Symbolist writer Aleksandr Blok, the artist Amedeo Modigliani, and fellow Acmeist Osip Mandelshtam. A two-volume edition of Akhmatova's collected works was published in Moscow in 1986, and *The Complete Poems of Anna Akhmatova*, also in two volumes, appeared in 1990.

Akhtal, al- \ˌäl-'äḳ-tål\, *in full* Ghiyāth ibn Ghawth ibn aṣ-Ṣalt al-Akhṭal (b. *c.* 640, al-Ḥīrah, Mesopotamia, or the Syrian Desert—d. 710) Poet of the Umayyad period (661–750) who is esteemed for his perfection of Arabic poetic form in the old Bedouin tradition.

Al-Akhṭal ("The Loquacious") was a favorite panegyrist and friend of the Umayyad caliph Yazīd I and his generals Ziyād ibn Abīhī and al-Ḥajjāj. He continued as court poet to the caliph ʿAbd al-Malik but fell into disfavor under Walīd I.

The poets Jarīr, al-Farazdaq, and al-Akhṭal form a famous trio in early Arabic literary history. Because they closely resembled one another in style and vocabulary, their relative superiority was much disputed.

Aksakov \ˌək-'sä-kəf\, Sergey Timofeyevich (b. Sept. 20 [Oct. 1, New Style], 1791, Ufa, Russia—d. April 30 [May 12], 1859, Moscow) Novelist noted for his realistic and humorous narratives and for his introduction of a new genre, a cross between the memoir and the novel, into Russian literature.

Aksakov was educated at the newly founded university in Kazan. He became a translator in the legislative commission of the civil service, served in the militia in the struggle against Napoleon in 1812, and in 1816 retired to the family estate. After a decade as a country squire, he returned to the civil service in Moscow and became literary censor, inspector, and, later, director of the college of land surveying. He retired again in 1839.

Before 1834, when his successful *Buran* ("Blizzard") was published, Aksakov's writings were undistinguished. But then he was inspired—by his love of rural Russia in the days of serfdom, by his Slavophile sons, and by his admiration of the novelist Nikolay Gogol—to set down the story of his grandfather, his parents, and his own childhood, transposed into realistic fiction. This effort resulted in three books that have become classics: *Semeynaya khronika* (1856; *The Family Chronicle*), *Vospominaniya* (1856; "Reminiscences"; *A Russian Schoolboy*), and *Detskie gody Bagrova-vnuka* (1858; *Childhood Years of Grandson Bagrov*). Aksakov unfolds his chronicles objectively in an unaffected style and simple language. Their interest lies in the illusion of reality and intimacy created by his vivid remembrance of his own and his forebears' past. These works, blending personal reminiscence with the techniques of the novelist, brought Aksakov fame. The finest book of the trilogy, *The Family Chronicle*, also shows a remarkable understanding of family psychology.

Also of interest are Aksakov's books on shooting, fishing, and butterfly collecting and his recollections of Gogol.

Aksyonov or **Aksenov** \ˌək-ˈsyȯn-əf\, Vasily Pavlovich (b. Aug. 20, 1932, Kazan, Russia, U.S.S.R.) Russian novelist and short-story writer, one of the leading literary spokesmen for the generation of Soviets who reached maturity after World War II.

The son of parents who spent many years in Soviet prisons, Aksyonov was raised in a state home and graduated from medical school in 1956. After working a few years as a doctor, he turned to writing, and in the cultural thaw of the late 1950s and early '60s he published a number of short stories and novels. His novels *Kollegi* (1960; *Colleagues*), *Zvezdnyi bilet* (1961; *A Ticket to the Stars*), and *Apel'siny iz Morokko* (1963; "Oranges From Morocco") are fast-moving narratives dealing with youthful rebels and misfits in Soviet society. Aksyonov excels in reproducing the racy slang and jargon of characters who are attracted to Western culture even though they share the collectivist ideals of the previous generation.

Aksyonov began incorporating stronger elements of fantasy, satire, and parody in such later novels as *Zatovarennaia bochkotara* (1968; *Surplussed Barrelware*) and *Ostrov Krym* (1981; *The Island of Crimea*). His independent spirit had incurred the disfavor of the Soviet authorities beginning in the late 1960s. In 1980 he was forced into exile, but his citizenship was restored by decree in 1990. One of his most important later novels was *Ozhog* (1980; *The Burn*), an anarchic blend of memory, fantasy, and realistic narrative in which the author tries to sum up Russian intellectuals' spiritual responses to their homeland.

Akutagawa \ˌä-ˈkü-tä-ˌgä-wä\ Ryūnosuke, *pseudonym* Chōkō-dō Shujin *or* Gaki \ˈgäk-ē\ (b. March 1, 1892, Tokyo, Japan—d. July 24, 1927, Tokyo) Prolific Japanese writer of stories, plays, and poetry, noted for his stylistic virtuosity.

Akutagawa began his literary career while attending Tokyo Imperial University. The publication in 1915 of his short story RASHŌMON led to his introduction to Natsume Sōseki, the outstanding Japanese novelist of the day. With Sōseki's encouragement he began to write a series of stories derived largely

from 12th- and 13th-century collections of Japanese tales but retold in the light of modern psychology in a highly individual style. Many of his stories have a feverish intensity that is well-suited to their often macabre themes.

In 1922 he turned toward autobiographical fiction, but Akutagawa's stories of modern life lack the exotic and sometimes lurid glow of the older tales, perhaps accounting for their comparative unpopularity. His last important work, "Kappa" (1927), although a satirical fable about elflike creatures (*kappa*), is written in the mirthless vein of his last period and reflects his depressed state at the time. His suicide came as a shock to the literary world. Akutagawa is one of the most widely translated of all Japanese writers, and a number of his stories have been made into films.

Akutagawa Prize \ˌä-ˌkü-tä-ˈgä-wä\ Japanese literary prize awarded semiannually for the best serious work of fiction by a promising new Japanese writer. Called in Japanese the Akutagawa Ryūnosuke Shō, it is generally considered, along with the Naoki Prize, Japan's most prestigious and sought-after literary award. Short stories or novellas win the prize more frequently than do full-length novels.

The Akutagawa Prize was established in 1935 by the writer Kikuchi Kan to honor the memory of his friend and colleague, Akutagawa Ryūnosuke, an esteemed writer who had committed suicide in 1927.

Alabaster \ˈal-ə-ˌbäs-tər, -ˌbas-\, William (b. 1567, Hadleigh, Suffolk, Eng.—d. early April 1640, Little Shelford, Cambridgeshire) English poet, mystic, and scholar in Latin and Hebrew, author of a Latin tragedy, *Roxana* (1597, published 1632).

Alabaster was educated at the University of Cambridge and in 1596 accompanied the Earl of Essex's expedition to Cádiz, Spain, as chaplain but became a Roman Catholic in 1597, consequently suffering intermittent imprisonment. When visiting Rome in 1609, he was denounced to the Inquisition because of his mystical writings. After much wavering he reverted to Anglicanism and became the king's chaplain in 1618. He also wrote an unfinished Latin epic, *Elisaeis*, glorifying Elizabeth I, as well as occasional poems, spiritual sonnets, mystically inclined prose works, and biblical commentaries.

Aladdin \ə-ˈlad-in\ *Arabic* ʿAlāʾ ad-Dīn. Hero of one of the best-known stories in THE THOUSAND AND ONE NIGHTS. The son of a deceased Chinese tailor and his poor wife, Aladdin is a lazy, careless boy who meets an African magician claiming to be his uncle. The magician brings Aladdin to the mouth of a cave and bids him enter and bring out a wonderful lamp that is inside, giving him a magic ring for his safety in the meantime. Aladdin goes in and returns with the lamp but refuses to hand it over to the magician until he is safely out of the cave. The magician thereupon shuts him inside the cave with the lamp and departs. Wringing his hands in dismay in the dark, Aladdin finds that he can summon up powerful jinn, or genies, by rubbing the ring. He returns home and soon finds that rubbing the lamp also produces genies. These supernatural spirits grant him his every wish, and Aladdin eventually becomes immensely wealthy, builds a wonderful jeweled palace, and marries the beautiful daughter of the sultan. He lives in longtime marital happiness, succeeds the sultan, and reigns for many years, "leaving behind him a long line of kings."

Alain *pseudonym of* Émile-Auguste CHARTIER.

Alain de Lille \ä-leⁿ-də-ˈlēl\, *Latin* Alanus de Insulis \ə-ˈlä-nəs-dē-ˈin-sȯl-is\ (b. *c.* 1128, probably Lille, Flanders [now Lille, Fr.]—d. 1202, Cîteaux, Fr.) Theologian and poet so celebrated for his varied learning that he was known as "the universal doctor." He studied and taught at Paris, lived for some time at Montpellier, and later joined the Cistercian monastic order in Cîteaux.

As a theologian, Alain adopted an eclectic scholasticism composed of rationalism and mysticism. He wrote many theological treatises, including an argument against heresy and a collection of proverbs on moral conduct. He is noted in the history of medieval Latin literature for two poems: *De planctu Naturae* (*Plaint of Nature*), a clever satire on human vices, and *Anticlaudianus*, a lengthy allegory concerning the creation and perfection of the human soul.

Alain-Fournier \á-‚leⁿ-für-'nyă\, *pseudonym of* Henri-Alban Fournier (b. Oct. 3, 1886, La Chapelle-d'Angillon, Cher, Fr.— reported missing in action Sept. 22, 1914, in the vicinity of Épargues, near Verdun) French writer whose only completed novel, *Le Grand Meaulnes* (1913; *The Lost Domain*), is a modern classic. Based on his happy childhood in a remote village in central France, it reflects his longing for a lost world of delight. The hero, an idealistic but forceful schoolboy, runs away and at a children's party in a decrepit country house meets a beautiful girl—whose prototype Alain-Fournier had met in 1905. The rest of the novel describes his search for her and for the house and the mood of wonderment he knew there. Its outstanding quality is evocation of an atmosphere of otherworldly nostalgia, against a realistically observed rural background. Other works, mainly published posthumously, include a correspondence (2 vol., 1948) with the critic Jacques Rivière, his brother-in-law.

Alarcón \ál-ár-'kòn\, Pedro Antonio de, *surname in full* Alarcón y Ariza \ē-ä-'rē-thä\ (b. March 10, 1833, Guadix, Spain— d. July 10, 1891, Valdemoro) Writer remembered for his novel *El sombrero de tres picos* (1874; *The Three-Cornered Hat*).

Alarcón had achieved a considerable reputation as a journalist and poet when his play *El hijo pródigo* ("The Prodigal Son") was hissed off the stage in 1857. The failure so exasperated him that he enlisted as a volunteer in the Moroccan campaign of 1859–60. The expedition provided the material for his eyewitness account *Diario de un testigo de la guerra de África* (1859; "Diary of a Witness of the African War"), a masterpiece of description. On his return Alarcón became editor of the anticlerical periodical *El Látigo*, but in the years 1868–74 he ruined his political reputation by rapid changes of position. His literary reputation, however, steadily increased. *El sombrero de tres picos*, a short novel inspired by a popular ballad, is a masterpiece of the genre known as *costumbrismo*. Manuel de Falla based his ballet of the same title on the story. Alarcón's other major novels were *El final de Norma* (1855; *The Last Act of Norma*), *El escándalo* (1875; "The Scandal"), and *El niño de la bola* (1880; "The Lucky Kid").

Alarcón y Mendoza, Juan Ruiz de *see* RUIZ DE ALARCÓN.

À la recherche du temps perdu \à-làr-‚shersh-dǖ-tän-per-'dǖ\ *see* REMEMBRANCE OF THINGS PAST.

alarums and excursions \ə-'lar-əmz, -'lär- . . . ik-'skər-zhənz\ Martial sounds and the movement of soldiers across the stage— used as a stage direction in Elizabethan drama.

Alas \ä-'läs\, Leopoldo, *surname in full* Alas y Ureña \ē-ü-'rän-yä\, *byname* Clarín \klä-'rēn\ (b. April 25, 1852, Zamora, Spain—d. June 13, 1901, Oviedo) Novelist and the most influential literary critic of Spain in the late 19th century. His biting and often bellicose articles made him the nation's most feared critical voice.

After studying law in Madrid, Alas went to the University of Oviedo in 1870, received his degree, and took a position in the university as professor, a post he held until his death. His

early novels, *La regenta* (1884–85; "The Regent's Wife") and *Su único hijo* (1890; *His Only Son*), are considered two of the greatest Spanish naturalistic novels of the century. These books mercilessly depicted the provincial society of Vetusta, an imaginary town modeled upon Oviedo. Alas' short stories, as collected in *Cuentos morales* (1896; *The Moral Tales*) and *El gallo de Sócrates* (1900; "Socrates' Rooster"), are considered inferior to his novels.

Alastor \ə-'las-tər\ Any of certain avenging deities or spirits, especially in Greek antiquity. The term is associated with Nemesis, the goddess of divine retribution who signified the gods' disapproval of human presumption. Percy Bysshe Shelley's poem *Alastor; or, The Spirit of Solitude* (1816) was a visionary work in which he warned idealists (like himself) not to abandon "sweet human love" and social improvement for the vain pursuit of evanescent dreams.

'Alavī \'a-la-‚vē, *Persian* "a-\, Buzurg, Buzurg *also spelled* Bozorg (b. Feb. 2, 1904, Tehrān, Iran) One of the leading prose writers of 20th-century Persian literature.

Educated in Iran, 'Alavi was sent to Berlin in 1922, where he learned German and translated a number of German works into Persian. Upon returning to Iran, he taught, wrote, and translated. He also became involved with a group of Iranian socialists. He was imprisoned with them (1937–41) and while in jail wrote *Panjāh va sih nafar* ("Fifty-Three People"), describing the members of the socialist group and their ordeal in prison, and also a short-story collection, *Varaq-pārahā-yē zendān* ("Notes from Prison").

After World War II, 'Alavi published another collection of stories, *Nāmah'hā* (1952; "Letters"). After the fall of the Iranian prime minister Mohammed Mosaddeq in 1954, 'Alavi left Iran and took a post as visiting professor at Humboldt University in East Germany.

'Alavi is best known for his short-story collection *Chamadān* ("Baggage"), in which he exhibits the strong influence of Freudian psychology, and for his novel *Chashmhāyash* (*Her Eyes*), an extremely controversial work about a revolutionary leader and the upper-class woman who loves him. In addition to translating many works from German into Persian, 'Alavi wrote a number of works on Iran and Persian literature in German.

alba \'äl-bä\ [Old Provençal, literally, dawn] A Provençal song of lament for lovers parting at dawn or of a watchman's warning to lovers at dawn. Albas were sung by the 11th and 12th-century troubadours. Some sources consider it an early form of an aubade, though unlike the alba, an aubade is usually a celebration of the dawn. The minnesingers, German counterparts of the troubadours, also used the form, calling it *Tagelied*.

Albee \'òl-bē\, Edward (Franklin) (b. March 12, 1928, Virginia, U.S.) American dramatist and theatrical producer, best known for WHO'S AFRAID OF VIRGINIA WOOLF? (1962), which examined illusion and reality with slashing insight and witty dialogue in its gruesome portrayal of married life.

Albee was an adopted child, and he grew up in New York City and nearby Westchester County. He was educated at Choate School (graduated 1946) and Trinity College, Hartford, Conn. (1946–47). He began writing plays in the late 1950s. Among his early one-act plays, THE ZOO STORY, THE AMERICAN DREAM, and THE SANDBOX (all published 1959) were the most successful; they established Albee as an astute critic of American values and of human interaction. Many critics, however, consider his first full-length play, *Who's Afraid of Virginia Woolf?* (film, 1966), to be his most important work. It was followed by a number of full-length works—including *Tiny Alice* (1964), A DELICATE BALANCE (1966; winner of a Pulitzer Prize), SEASCAPE (1975; winner of a Pulitzer Prize), and *The*

Man Who Had Three Arms (1982). His play *Three Tall Women* (produced 1991) won him a third Pulitzer.

Alberich \'ăl-bə-‚riḳ\ Fictional character, a dwarf in various German legends, notably the Middle High German epic poem *Nibelungenlied* ("Song of the Nibelungs").

In the *Nibelungenlied*, Alberich owns the cloak of darkness which magically renders its wearer invisible. Alberich is forced to give up the cloak when he is defeated by Siegfried. Later in the poem, Alberich aids Siegfried in his courtship of Brünhild. Alberich is a minor character in the *Dietrichsage* ("Dietrich legend"), which became fused with the Nibelung saga.

In *Ortnit*, another Middle High German epic, the dwarf Alberich uses his magical powers to help Ortnit, the king of Lombardy, to woo and marry the daughter of a heathen king.

Alberti \äl-'ber-tē\, Rafael (b. Dec. 16, 1902, Puerto de Santa María, Spain) Spanish writer of Italian-Irish ancestry who is regarded as one of the major Spanish poets of the 20th century.

Alberti enjoyed some success as a painter before 1923, when he began publishing poems in magazines. His first book of poetry, the playful *Marinero en tierra* (1925; "Sailor on Land"), recalled the sea of his native Cádiz region and won a national prize. A member of the so-called Generation of 1927, Alberti revealed Góngorist influence in the work published in that period, *El alba del alhelí* (1927; "The Dawn of the Wallflower") and *Cal y canto* (1928; "Quicklime and Song"). With his next book, however, the somewhat Surrealist *Sobre los ángeles* (1929; *Concerning the Angels*), Alberti established himself as a mature and individual voice.

Alberti fought for the Republic in the Spanish Civil War and afterward fled to Argentina. In 1941 he published a collection of poems, *Entre el clavel y la espada* ("Between the Carnation and the Sword"), and in 1942 his autobiography, *La arboleda perdida* (*The Lost Grove*), and a book about the Civil War, *De un momento a otro* ("From One Moment to Another"). He published a collection of poems inspired by painting, *A la pintura* (1945; "On Painting"), and collections on maritime themes, such as *Pleamar* (1944; "High Tide"). He lived in Italy from 1961 to 1977, when he returned to Spain.

Albertine \ȧl-ber-'tēn\, *in full* Albertine Simonet \sē-mō-'ne\ Fictional character, the mistress of Marcel, narrator of *À la recherche du temps perdu* (REMEMBRANCE OF THINGS PAST) by Marcel Proust. She appears in several volumes of the seven-part novel, notably *À l'ombre des jeunes filles en fleurs* (*Within a Budding Grove*), *Sodome et Gomorrhe* (*Cities of the Plain*), and *La Prisonnière* (*The Captive*).

Albinovanus Pedo \al-‚bin-ə-'vä-nəs-'pē-dō\ (fl. early 1st century AD) Roman poet who wrote a *Theseid*, referred to in a letter from his friend the poet Ovid; epigrams that are commended by the Latin poet Martial; and an epic poem on the military exploits of the Roman general Germanicus Caesar, the emperor Tiberius' adopted son, under whom Pedo probably served. This epic may have been used as a source by the Roman historian Tacitus. All that remains of Pedo's works is a beautiful fragment, preserved in the *Suasoriae* of Seneca the Elder, that describes the voyage of Germanicus (AD 16) through the Ems River to the Northern Ocean.

Alcaeus \al-'sē-əs\ or **Alkaios** \al-'kī-əs\ (b. *c.* 620 BC, Mytilene, Lesbos—d. *c.* 580 BC) Greek lyric poet whose work was highly esteemed in the ancient world. A collection of Alcaeus' surviving poems in 10 books (now lost) was made in the 2nd century BC, and he was a favorite model of the Roman lyric poet Horace, who adapted from him his own alcaic stanza.

The surviving fragments and quotations from Alcaeus' work may be classed in four groups: hymns in honor of gods and heroes, love poetry, drinking songs, and political poems. Many of the fragments reflect the vigor of the poet's involvement in the life of Mytilene.

After years of political unrest, some measure of stability had come to Mytilene through the acquisition of power by Pittacus. He had a reputation for mildness and was rated one of the Seven Sages of Greece. Alcaeus fought beside Pittacus against the Athenians, but Pittacus betrayed Alcaeus, whose respect turned into hatred. Several fragments reveal the bitterness of his attack. He derides Pittacus for his appearance, his stinginess, his intemperance, and his commonness.

Other fragments of Alcaeus' work picture everyday life in 6th-century Mytilene. He writes of ships and rivers, of wine and banquets, of a girls' beauty contest, of a flock of widgeon in flight, and of the flowers that herald the spring. He conveys what can well be believed to have been the spirit and the values of the city-states of the Aegean, as, for example, when he declares that real greatness lies: "Not in well-fashioned houses, nor in walls, canals, and dockyards, but in men who use whatever Fortune sends them."

alcaic \al-'kā-ik\ Classical Greek poetic stanza composed of four lines of varied metrical feet, with five long syllables in each of the first two lines, four in the third and fourth lines, and an unaccented syllable at the beginning of the first three lines (anacrusis). The Greek alcaic stanza is scanned:

$$\cup \mid - \cup \mid - \underline{\cup} \mid - \cup \cup \mid - \cup \mid -$$
$$\cup \mid - \cup \mid - \underline{\cup} \mid - \cup \cup \mid - \cup \mid -$$
$$\underline{\cup} \mid - \cup \mid - \underline{\cup} \mid - \cup \mid - \underline{\cup}$$
$$- \cup \cup \mid - \cup \cup \mid - \cup \mid - \underline{\cup}.$$

Named for and perhaps invented by the poet Alcaeus, the alcaic became an important Latin verse form, especially in the *Odes* of Horace. Variations on the traditional alcaic include the use of a long initial syllable and of a spondee ($--$) in the first complete foot of the first three lines.

Alcaics were adapted to English and French verse during the Renaissance and later appeared in works such as Alfred, Lord Tennyson's "Milton."

Alceste \ȧl-'sest\ Title character of Molière's comedy LE MISANTHROPE. Alceste's disgust with the superficialities and deceits of his fellows, culminating in his withdrawal from society, provides the play's mild dramatic conflict.

Alcestis \al-'ses-tis\ In Greek mythology, daughter of Pelias and wife of Admetus, an Argonaut and the king of Pherae. Alcestis has served in Western literature as the model wife, for when her husband was about to die she alone of all his kith and kin agreed to die in his place. She was brought back from the underworld by Heracles. Euripides tells the story in his *Alcestis*, and his characterization of Admetus as selfish was much imitated.

Later writers who treated the theme include William Morris, Robert Browning, John Milton, Rainer Maria Rilke, Geoffrey Chaucer, and T.S. Eliot (*The Cocktail Party*). Alcestis' sacrifice has also been the subject of several operas.

Alcestis \al-'ses-tis\ (*Greek* Alkēstis) Drama by EURIPIDES, performed in 438 BC. Though tragic in form, the play ends happily. It took the place of the satyr play that usually ended the series of three tragedies that were produced for festival competition.

The story concerns the imminent death of King Admetus, who is advised that he will be allowed to live if he can find someone willing to die in his place. Alcestis, his wife, gives up her life before she recognizes that the fact and manner of her dying will blight his life. Admetus' old friend Heracles appears just in time to rescue Alcestis from the clutches of Death and restore her to her relieved husband.

Alchemist, The   Comedy in five acts by Ben JONSON, performed in 1610 and published in 1612. The play concerns the turmoil of deception that ensues when Lovewit leaves his London house in the care of his scheming servant, Face. With the aid of a fraudulent alchemist named Subtle and his companion, Dol Common, Face sets about dispensing spurious charms and services to a steady stream of dupes. These include the intemperate knight Sir Epicure Mammon, the pretentious Puritans Ananias and Tribulation Wholesome, the ambitious tobacconist Abel Drugger, the gamester law clerk Dapper, and the parvenu Kastril with his widowed sister, Pliant. The shrewd gambler Surly nearly exposes the sham, but the gullible parties reject his accusations. When Lovewit reappears without warning, Subtle and Dol flee the scene, leaving Face to make peace by arranging the marriage of his master to the beautiful and wealthy Dame Pliant.

Alcinous \al-'sin-ō-es\   In Greek mythology, king of the Phaeacians (on the legendary island of Scheria) and grandson of the god Poseidon. In the *Odyssey* he entertains Odysseus, who has been cast by a storm on the shore of the island. In the legend of Jason and the Argonauts, Alcinous lives on the island of Drepane, where he gives shelter to Jason and Medea in their flight from Colchis.

Alciphron \'al-sə-,frän\ (fl. 2nd or 3rd century AD, Athens)   Rhetorician who wrote a collection of fictitious letters, a form of literature popular in his day. More than 100 of the letters have survived. The background of them all is the Athens of the 4th century BC, and the imaginary writers are farmers, fishermen, and courtesans. The material of the letters is largely derived from the writers of the so-called New Comedy.

Alcithoë \al-'sith-ō-ē\   In Greek legend, the daughter of Minyas of Orchomenus, in Boeotia. She and her sisters once refused to participate in Dionysian festivities, remaining at home spinning and weaving. Late in the day Dionysian music clangs about them, the house is filled with fire and smoke, and the sisters are metamorphosed into bats and birds. According to Plutarch, the sisters, driven mad for their impiety, cast lots to determine which one of their children they will eat. In retribution their female descendants were pursued at the Agrionia (an annual festival) by the priest of Dionysus, who was permitted to kill the one he caught.

Alcmaeon or **Alcmeon** \alk-'mē-ən\   In Greek legend, the son of the seer Amphiaraus and his wife Eriphyle. Sworn to avenge his father's death with the Seven Against Thebes, Alcmaeon kills his treacherous mother and as punishment is driven mad by the Furies. He is purified by King Phegeus of Arcadia, whose daughter Arsinoë he marries. He settles at the mouth of the Achelous River and, forgetting his wife, marries the daughter of the river god. He is then slain by Phegeus and his sons. Alcmaeon's story was the subject of the modern parody "A Fragment of a Greek Tragedy," by A.E. Housman.

Alcman or **Alkman** \'alk-mən\ (fl. late 7th century BC, Sparta, Greece)   Greek poet, the first known writer of Dorian choral lyrics. His work survives in fragments, the longest being a *parthenion* (a choir song for girls) discovered in a 1st-century papyrus in Egypt in 1855. In the *Suda* lexicon, an encyclopedic dictionary of the 10th or 11th century AD, Alcman is described as a man "of an extremely amorous disposition and the inventor of love poems." He was clearly a learned man, and his verse is full of geographic detail. One fragment, telling of the sleeping world at the end of the day, is almost unique in Greek poetry for its sympathy with nature.

Alcman's light, gay manner, so different from the later Spartan style, gave rise to the tradition that he was not a native Spartan. He is thought by some to have come from Sardis in Lydia, but this is uncertain.

Alcmanian \alk-'mä-nē-ən\   In poetry, a metrical line named for the Greek poet Alcman. It consists of four dactyls and is scanned: $-\cup\cup\mid-\cup\cup\mid-\cup\cup\mid-\cup\cup.$

Alcmene \alk-'mē-nē\   In Greek mythology, a mortal princess, the granddaughter of Perseus and Andromeda and the mother of Heracles by Zeus, who disguised himself as her husband Amphitryon and seduced her. *See* AMPHITRYON.

Alcott \'ȯl-kət, *in U.S. commonly* 'al-, -,kät\, Bronson, *in full* Amos Bronson Alcott (b. Nov. 29, 1799, Wolcott, Conn., U.S.—d. March 4, 1888, Concord, Mass.)   American philosopher, teacher, reformer, and member of the New England Transcendentalist group.

The self-educated son of a poor farmer, Alcott traveled in the South as a peddler before establishing a series of schools for children. His aim as an educator was to stimulate thought and "awaken the soul." His innovations were not widely accepted, however, and before he was 40 he was forced to close his last school, the famous Temple School in Boston. In 1842 with money from Ralph Waldo Emerson he visited England, where a similar school founded near London was named Alcott House in his honor. He returned from England with a kindred spirit, the mystic Charles Lane, and together they founded a short-lived utopian community, Fruitlands, in Massachusetts. Always poor or in debt, Alcott was not financially secure until his second daughter, Louisa May Alcott, established herself as a writer.

Alcott \'ȯl-kət, *in U.S. commonly* 'al-, -,kät\, Louisa May (b. Nov. 29, 1832, Germantown, Pa., U.S.—d. March 6, 1888, Boston, Mass.)   American author known for her children's books, especially LITTLE WOMEN.

E.B. Inc.

Alcott spent most of her life in Boston and Concord, Mass., where she grew up in the company of Ralph Waldo Emerson, Theodore Parker, and Henry David Thoreau. She soon came to

understand that her Transcendentalist father was too impractical to provide for his wife and four daughters; after the failure of Fruitlands, a utopian community that he had founded,
Louisa's lifelong concern for the welfare of her family began.
In order to earn money she taught briefly, worked as a domestic, and finally began to write, producing potboilers at first, and
eventually more serious works. An ardent abolitionist, Alcott
volunteered as a nurse during the American Civil War. She contracted typhoid from unsanitary hospital conditions, however,
and was sent home. She was never completely well again, but
the publication of her letters in book form, *Hospital Sketches*
(1863), brought her the first taste of fame.

Alcott's stories then began to appear in *The Atlantic Monthly*
(now *The Atlantic*). She wrote the autobiographical *Little
Women* (1868–69) under the pressure of serious financial need.
The book was an immediate success, and in 1869 Alcott was
able to write in her journal: "Paid up all the debts . . . thank
the Lord!" Other books for which Alcott drew from her early
experiences included *An Old-Fashioned Girl* (1870); *Aunt Jo's
Scrap Bag*, 6 vol. (1872–82); *Little Men: Life at Plumfield with
Jo's Boys* (1871); *Eight Cousins* (1875); and *Jo's Boys and How
They Turned Out* (1886).

Exhausted and in constant pain, she spent the last years of
her life shadowed by the deaths of her mother and her youngest
sister, May, who left behind a little daughter for Alcott to rear.

Aldanov \,əl-'då-nəf\, Mark, *pseudonym of* Mark Aleksandrovich Landau (b. Oct. 26 [Nov. 7, New Style], 1889, Kiev,
Ukraine, Russian Empire—d. Feb. 25, 1957, Nice, Fr.)   Russian émigré writer best known for work bitterly critical of the
Soviet system.

In 1919 Aldanov emigrated to France, which he left for the
United States in 1941. He wrote an essay on Lenin (1921);
Deux Révolutions (1921; "Two Revolutions"), a work com-
paring the Russian and French revolutions; and many novels.
Most of Aldanov's works were translated into English, includ-
ing a tetralogy on revolutionary France, *Myslitel* (1923–25; *The
Thinker*); an anti-Soviet satire, *Nachalo kontsa* (1939; *The Fifth
Seal*); and *Istoki* (1947; *Before the Deluge*), a picture of Europe
in the 1870s.

Aldecoa \,äl-dā-'kō-ä\, Ignacio (b. July 11, 1925, Vitoria,
Spain—d. Nov. 15, 1969, Madrid)   Spanish novelist whose
work is noted for its local color and careful composition.

Aldecoa studied at the University of Madrid, became a newspaper writer, and from 1947 to 1956 was a broadcaster for
the radio station Voice of the Falange. He published essays on
politics, several collections of short stories, and two books of
poems, *Todavía la vida* (1947; "Life Goes On") and *Libro de las
algas* (1949; "Book of Algae"), before his first novels, *El ful-
gor y la sangre* (1954; "The Brightness and the Blood") and *Con
el viento solano* (1956; "With the East Wind"). Aldecoa wrote
about ordinary workers, their hopes, their fears, and the tendency of their lives toward monotony.

Aldhelm \'äld-,helm\ (*c.* 639–709)   West Saxon abbot of
Malmesbury, the most learned teacher of 7th-century Wessex, a pioneer in the art of Latin verse among the Anglo-
Saxons, and the author of numerous extant writings in Latin
verse and prose.

Aldhelm was trained in Latin and in Celtic-Irish scholarship
by Malmesbury's Irish founder and went on to study at the
famous school at Canterbury, where he was exposed to continental influences. About 675 he became abbot of Malmesbury,
where he remained, carrying on a threefold career, as monk and
priest, as encourager of learning, and as Latin poet. In 705 he
was consecrated bishop of Sherborne. He was also a popular
vernacular poet, though none of his Old English verse survives.

Metrical science was Aldhelm's special preoccupation, and
his most famous work is a treatise on metrics sent to his friend
Aldfrith, king of Northumbria (685–704). It includes as examples 100 *aenigmata* (riddles) of Aldhelm's own invention in
Latin hexameters.

Aldington \'öl-diŋ-tən\, Richard, *original name* Edward God-
free Aldington (b. July 8, 1892, Hampshire, Eng.—d. July
27, 1962, Sury-en-Vaus, Fr.)   Prolific writer and editor who
served as one of the self-appointed guardians of European letters during the first half of the 20th century.

Educated at Dover College and London University, he early
attracted attention through his volumes of Imagist verse. In
1913 he married Hilda DOOLITTLE (divorced 1938), an American Imagist poet. He served in France during World War I,
thereafter continuing to write and to review French literature
for the *Times Literary Supplement*. Aldington's best and best-
known novel, *Death of a Hero* (1929), to which *All Men Are
Enemies* (1933) was a sequel, reflected the disillusionment of
a generation that had fought through World War I. His later
works include the novel *The Colonel's Daughter* (1931) and two
long poems, *A Dream in the Luxembourg* (1930) and *A Fool i'
the Forest* (1925), as well as translations from French, Italian,
and ancient Greek and Latin poets. He also wrote a book of
reminiscences, *Life for Life's Sake* (1941).

Aldiss \'öl-dis\, Brian Wilson (b. Aug. 18, 1925, East Dereham, Norfolk, Eng.)   Prolific English author, chiefly of science fiction, whose novels and short stories display considerable range in style.

Aldiss served with the British Army (1943–47), part of the
time in the Royal Corps of Signals, then was a bookseller until
1956. Noted for his many works of science fiction, Aldiss was
also an influential anthologist of science fiction. His own collections include *Best Science Fiction Stories of Brian W. Aldiss*
(1965) and *A Brian Aldiss Omnibus* (1969 and 1971). Outstanding individual volumes of stories include *Hothouse* (1962) and
The Saliva Tree (1966). His notable departures from science
fiction were the semiautobiographical *The Hand-Reared Boy*
(1970) and *A Soldier Erect* (1971). Later fiction includes *A Rude
Awakening* (1978); *Life in the West* (1980); *Moreau's Other Island* (1980; U.S. title, *An Island Called Moreau*); the *Helliconia
Trilogy*, consisting of *Helliconia Spring* (1982), *Helliconia Summer* (1983), and *Helliconia Winter* (1985); *Forgotten Life* (1988);
and *Remembrance Day* (1993). His autobiography, *Bury My
Heart at W.H. Smith's*, was published in 1990.

Aldrich \'öl-drich, -drij\, Thomas Bailey (b. Nov. 11, 1836,
Portsmouth, N.H., U.S.—d. March 19, 1907, Boston, Mass.)
Poet, short-story writer, and editor whose use of the surprise
ending influenced the development of the short story in America. He drew upon his childhood experiences in New Hampshire in his popular classic THE STORY OF A BAD BOY (1870).

Aldrich left school at 13 to work as a merchant's clerk in
New York City and soon began to contribute to various newspapers and magazines. After publication of his first book of
verse, *The Bells* (1855), he became junior literary critic on the
New York Evening Mirror and later an editor of the *Home Journal*. From 1881 to 1890 he was editor of *The Atlantic Monthly*
(now *The Atlantic*).

His poems, which reflect the cultural atmosphere of New
England and his frequent European tours, were published in
such volumes as *Cloth of Gold* (1874), *Flower and Thorn* (1877),
Mercedes and Later Lyrics (1884), and *Windham Towers* (1890).
His best-known prose is *Marjorie Daw and Other People* (1873),
a collection of short stories.

Aleardi \,äl-ā-'är-dē\, Aleardo, Count (Conte), *original name*
Gaetano Aleardi (b. Nov. 4, 1812, Verona, Austrian Empire

[now in Italy]—d. July 17, 1878, Verona)   Poet, patriot, and political figure, an archetype of the 19th-century Italian poet-patriots. His love poems and passionate diatribes against the Austrian government brought him renown.

Brought up in Verona (which was then controlled by Austria), Aleardi studied law at the University of Padua. His love lyrics, *Le lettere a Maria* (1846; "The Letters to Maria"), were eagerly read. But when he returned to Verona, he was prevented by the Austrian government from practicing law, and he wrote a series of bitterly anti-Austrian poems, notably *Le città italiane marinare e commercianti* (1856; "The Maritime and Commercial Italian Cities"), *Il tre fiumi* (1857; "The Three Rivers"), and *I sette soldati* (1861; "The Seven Soldiers"). He also edited, with the poet Giovanni Prati, an outspoken journal, *Il Caffè Pedrocchi*. The Austrians imprisoned him twice (1852 and 1859) and finally sent him into exile. When the Austrians were expelled in 1866, he returned to Verona and remained in public life until his death.

Alecsandri \ˌäl-ek-ˌsän-'drē\, Vasile (b. June 14, 1821, Bacău, Moldavia [now in Romania]—d. Aug. 22, 1890, Mircesti, Rom.)   Lyric poet and dramatist, the first collector of Romanian popular songs and a leader of the movement for the union of the Romanian principalities.

Alecsandri was educated at Iaşi and subsequently in Paris (1834–39). He published his first collection of folk songs in 1844 and was also active in the Romanian revolutionary cause.

His lyrical poems, *Doine şi lăcrimioare*, were published in Paris in 1853, and during 1852–53 he published two volumes of ballads and songs. In 1868–75 he published his descriptive poems of landscapes, entitled *Pasteluri*. As a playwright he created Romanian social comedy, but his most important contributions to the theater were his poetic dramas: *Despot Vodă* (1879), *Fântâna Blanduziei* (1883; "Blanduzia's Fountain"), and *Ovidiu* (1885; "Ovid"). In later life Alecsandri played an important part in his country's affairs.

Alegría \ˌäl-ä-'grē-ä\, Ciro (b. Nov. 4, 1909, Saltimbanca, Peru—d. Feb. 17, 1967, Lima)   Peruvian novelist who wrote about the lives of the Peruvian Indians.

Educated at the National College of San Juan, Alegría acquired a firsthand knowledge of Indian life in his native province of Huamachuco; this first appeared in his novel *La serpiente de oro* (1935; *The Golden Serpent*), which portrays the diverse human life to be found along the Marañón River in Peru. *Los perros hambrientos* (1938; "The Hungry Dogs") describes the difficulties faced by the sheepherding Indians of the Peruvian highlands. The novel that is generally considered Alegría's masterpiece is *El mundo es ancho y ajeno* (1941; *Broad and Alien Is the World*). It depicts in epic manner the struggles of an Indian tribe to survive in the Peruvian highlands in the face of land-hungry white men. A collection of short fiction (*Duelo de caballeros* [1963]) and *Novelas completas* (1963) were his last works.

In 1930 Alegría joined a militantly pro-Indian organization and became an agitator for social reform. He was twice jailed, in 1931 and 1933, for illegal political activity and was exiled to Chile in 1934. From 1941 to 1948 Alegría lived in the United States, but in 1948 he returned to Peru.

Alegría \ˌä-lä-'grē-ä\, Claribel (b. May 12, 1924, Estelí, Nicaragua)   Poet, essayist, and journalist who was a major voice in the literature of contemporary Central America. Noted for her *testimonio* (testament) concerning the Sandinista revolution in Nicaragua, she was best known in the United States for the bilingual edition of her volume of poetry, *Flores del volcán/Flowers from the Volcano* (1982), translated by the poet Carolyn Forché.

Alegría spent her childhood in exile in El Salvador and considered herself Salvadoran. A graduate of George Washington University, she lived in the United States, Mexico, Chile, Uruguay, and Majorca before returning to Nicaragua in 1979. She collaborated with her husband, writer Darwin Flakoll, on such works as *Nuevas voces de Norteamérica* (1962; *New Voices of Hispanic America*; coeditor and cotranslator), *Cenizas de Izalco* (1966; *Ashes of Izalco*; coauthor), and *No me agarran viva* (1983; *They Won't Take Me Alive*; coauthor).

La mujer del río/Woman of the River (1989), with parallel English and Spanish poetry texts, and *Fuga de Canto Grande* (1992; *Fugues*) were among more than a dozen published volumes of her poetry. Alegría won the Cuban-sponsored Casa de las Américas prize in 1978 for *Sobrevivo* (1978; "I Survive"). Her fiction, which contains much sociopolitical commentary, includes *El detén* (1977; *The Talisman*), *Albúm familiar* (1982; *Family Album*), *Pueblo de Dios y de Mandinga* (1985; *Village of God and the Devil*), all three novellas published in English in *Family Album*; and *Luisa en el país de la realidad* (1987; *Luisa in Realityland*). She also wrote *Tres cuentos* (1958; "Three Stories") and other works for children.

Aleichem   *see* SHOLEM ALEICHEM.

Aleixandre \ˌäl-ä-'sän-drä\, Vicente (b. April 26, 1898, Seville, Spain—d. Dec. 14, 1984, Madrid)   Spanish poet and member of the Generation of 1927 who received the Nobel Prize for Literature in 1977. He was strongly influenced by the Surrealist technique of poetic composition.

Aleixandre studied law and business management and from 1920 to 1922 taught commercial law. He became seriously ill in 1925 and during his convalescence wrote his first poems. He remained in Spain during the Spanish Civil War although his poetry was banned from 1936 to 1944. In 1949 Aleixandre was elected to the Spanish Royal Academy.

Aleixandre's first major book, *La destrucción o el amor* (1935; "Destruction or Love"), was awarded the National Prize for Literature. In this work he explored the theme of human identification with the physical cosmos. A greater emphasis upon human life is found in *Historia del corazón* (1954; "History of the Heart") and *En un vasto dominio* (1962; "In a Vast Domain"), works that deal with time, death, and human solidarity. Aleixandre's later poetry is of a metaphysical nature; he explores death, knowledge, and experience in *Poemas de la consumación* (1968; "Poems of Consummation") and *Diálogos del conocimiento* (1974; "Dialogues of Insight").

In addition to writing poetry of great originality and depth, Aleixandre published the notable prose work *Los encuentros* (1958; "The Meetings"), a book of fond sketches of his fellow writers.

Alemán \ˌäl-ä-'män\, Mateo (baptized Sept. 28, 1547, Seville, Spain—d. *c.* 1614, Mexico)   Novelist, a master stylist best known for his picaresque novel GUZMÁN DE ALFARACHE (1599; a second part, 1604; *The Spanish Rogue*).

Descended from Jews who had been forcibly converted to Roman Catholicism, Alemán expressed many aspects of the experiences and feelings of the New Christians in 16th-century Spain. His most important literary work, *Guzmán de Alfarache*, which brought him fame throughout Europe but little profit, is one of the earliest picaresque novels. The first part ran through many editions, almost all pirated; even before he could finish the second part, a spurious sequel had appeared. Alemán's life, in many ways like that of his protagonist, Guzmán, was afflicted with severe economic and personal reverses. He was the son of a prison doctor and studied medicine at Salamanca and Alcalá for four years after graduating from the University of Seville in 1564, but he never practiced. In 1580 he was imprisoned for debt. Only after he immigrated to Mexico in 1608 did his fortunes become settled and his life stable.

Alencar \á-le^n-'kår\, José de, *in full* José Martiniano de Alencar (b. May 1, 1829, Mecejana, Braz.—d. Dec. 12, 1877, Rio de Janeiro)   Journalist, novelist, and playwright whose novel *O Guarani* (1857; "The Guarani Indian") initiated the vogue of the Brazilian INDIANISTA NOVEL (romantic tales of indigenous life). *O Guarani* depicts the platonic love affair of Perí, a noble savage, and Ceci, the daughter of a wealthy landowner.

Alencar's next most popular novel, *Iracema* (1865), deals with the love of a beautiful Indian maiden for a Portuguese soldier. In *O gaúcho* (1870; "The Gaucho") and *O sertanejo* (1876; "The Backlander"), Alencar treats life in Brazil's frontier lands. In novels such as *Lucíola* (1862), *Diva* (1864), and *Senhora* (1875), he laid the foundation for Brazilian psychological fiction. Alencar, who is considered the father of Brazilian fictional writing, also cultivated the historical novel in such works as *As minas de prata* (1862; "The Silver Mines").

Alencar also was a lawyer, a deputy in the legislature, and minister of justice (1868–70).

Alexander III \,al-ig-'zan-dər\, *byname* Alexander the Great *or* Alexander of Macedonia \,mas-ə-'dō-nē-ə\ (b. 356 BC, Pella, Macedonia [now in Greece]—d. June 13, 323, Babylon [now in Iraq])   Son of Philip II and king of Macedonia from 336 to 323 BC. One of the greatest generals in history, he overthrew the Persian empire, carried Macedonian arms to India, and laid the foundations for the Hellenistic world of territorial kingdoms. In the process he became a legendary hero.

The legend of Alexander inspired writers down through the ages, from Plutarch (who wrote of him in *Parallel Lives*) and Ferdowsī (in the *Shāh-nāmeh*) to John Lyly, Pedro Calderón de la Barca, Jean Racine, Jakob Wassermann, and many others.

Alexander \,al-ig-'zan-dər\, Meena (b. Feb. 17, 1951, Allahabad, India)   Indian poet and teacher whose works reflect her multicultural life in India, The Sudan, and the United States.

Educated at the University of Khartoum in The Sudan and at the University of Nottingham in England, Alexander held a number of teaching positions in India, France, and elsewhere. She lived in the United States from 1979.

The subjects explored in her writing include language, memory, and the significance of place. Her poetry collections include *The Bird's Bright Ring* (1976), *I Root My Name* (1977), *Without Place* (1978), *Stone Roots* (1980), *House of a Thousand Doors* (1988), and *The Storm: A Poem in Five Parts* (1989). She also wrote a semiautobiographical novel, *Nampally Road* (1991), and a memoir, *Fault Lines* (1993).

Alexander Aetolus \,al-ig-'zan-dər-ē-'tō-ləs\ (fl. *c.* 280 BC) Greek poet of Pleuron, in Aetolia. He was appointed by Ptolemy II Philadelphus, Macedonian king of Egypt, to arrange and catalog the tragedies in the library at Alexandria. Nothing remains of his own tragedies except the title of one play, *Astragalistae* ("The Dice Players"). A few fragments of his shorter writings are extant, including a brief appreciation of Euripides. The titles of Alexander's other works are known only because they were quoted by other writers.

Alexander romance \,al-ig-'zan-dər\   Any of a body of legends about the career of Alexander the Great, told and retold with varying emphasis and purpose by succeeding ages and civilizations.

The chief source of all Alexander romance literature was a folk epic written in Greek by a Hellenized Egyptian in Alexandria during the 2nd century AD. Surviving translations and copies make its reconstruction possible. It portrayed Alexander as a national messianic hero, the natural son of an Egyptian

wizard-king by the wife of Philip II of Macedon. Magic and marvels played a subsidiary part in the epic—in the story of Alexander's birth, for example, and in his meeting with the Amazons in India. In later romances, however, marvels and exotic anecdotes predominated and gradually eclipsed the historical personality. Minor episodes in the original were filled out, often through "letters" supposedly written by or to Alexander, and an independent legend about his capture of the wild peoples of Gog and Magog was incorporated into several vernacular texts. In the 11th century a Middle Irish Alexander romance appeared, and about 1100, the Middle High German *Annolied*. During the 12th century, Alexander appeared as a pattern of knightly chivalry in a succession of great poems.

The Arabs, expanding Syrian versions of the legend, passed them on to the many peoples with whom they came in contact. Through them, the Persian poets, notably Neẓāmī in the 12th century, gave the stories new form. Alexander romance literature declined in the late 12th century, and, with the revival of classical scholarship during the Renaissance, historical accounts displaced it entirely.

Alexandrian \,al-ig-'zan-drē-ən\   **1.** Of, relating to, or resembling the Alexandrian school, the school of Greek literature, especially poetry, that flourished in Alexandria during the 4th century BC.   **2.** In reference to a writer or literary work, overly recondite, derivative, or artificial. Also, concerned primarily with the technical perfection of language or literary form.

Alexandria Quartet, The \,al-ig-'zan-drē-ə\   Series of four novels by Lawrence DURRELL. The lush and sensuous tetralogy, which consists of *Justine* (1957), *Balthazar* (1958), *Mountolive* (1958), and *Clea* (1960), is set in Alexandria, Egypt, during the 1940s. Three of the books are written in the first person, *Mountolive* in the third. The first three volumes describe, from different viewpoints, a series of events in Alexandria before World War II; the fourth carries the story forward into the war years. The events of the narrative are mostly seen through the eyes of one L.G. Darley, who observes the interactions of his lovers, friends, and acquaintances in Alexandria.

In *Justine*, Darley attempts to recover from and understand his recently ended affair with Justine Hosnani. Reviewing various papers and examining his memories, he reads the events of his recent past in romantic terms. *Balthazar*, named for Darley's friend, a doctor and mystic, reinterprets Darley's views from a philosophical and intellectual point of view. The third novel is a straightforward narrative of events, and *Clea*, volume four, reveals Darley healing, maturing, and becoming capable of loving Clea Montis, a painter and the woman for whom he was destined.

alexandrine \,al-ig-'zan-,drēn, -drən, -,drīn\ [French *alexandrin* of or pertaining to the alexandrine, from Middle French] A line of 12 syllables with a caesura, or pause, after the sixth syllable and with major stresses on the sixth and on the last syllable and one secondary accent in each half line. Because six syllables is a normal breath group and the secondary stresses can be on any other syllables in the line, the alexandrine is a flexible form, adaptable to a wide range of subjects. Its structural metrical principle is stress according to sense. It is the most popular measure in French poetry.

The name alexandrine is probably derived from the early use of the verse in the French *Roman d'Alexandre*, a collection of romances compiled in the 12th century about the adventures of Alexander the Great. Revived in the 16th century by the poets of La Pléiade, especially Pierre de Ronsard, the alexandrine became, in the following century, the preeminent French verse form for dramatic and narrative poetry and reached its highest development in the classical tragedies of Pierre Corneille and

Jean Racine. In the late 19th century, a loosening of structure occurred, notably in the work of Paul Verlaine; poets often wrote a modified alexandrine, a three-part line known as *vers romantique*, or *trimètre*.

In English versification, the alexandrine, also called iambic hexameter, contains six primary accents rather than the two major and two secondary accents of the French. Though it was introduced to England in the 16th century and was adapted to German and Dutch poetry in the 17th century, its use outside France has been limited.

Alexis \ə-'lek-sis\ (b. *c.* 375 BC, Thurii, Lucania [now in Italy]—d. *c.* 275 BC) One of Athens' foremost writers of Middle and New Comedy. He apparently lived most of his long life in Athens. According to Plutarch, he lived to the age of 106 and died while on the stage. Alexis is said to have written 245 plays, of which only 1,000 lines survive.

Alexis \ə-'lek-sis\, Willibald, *pseudonym of* Georg Wilhelm Heinrich Häring (b. June 29, 1798, Breslau, Silesia, Prussia [now Wrocław, Pol.]—d. Dec. 16, 1871, Arnstadt, Ger.) German writer and critic best known for his historical novels about Brandenburg and Prussia.

Alexis grew up in Berlin. He studied law at Berlin and Breslau but abandoned his legal career for writing after the success of his literary hoax *Walladmor* (1824), a parody of Sir Walter Scott published as "freely translated from the English of Walter Scott." The joke, detrimental to Alexis' literary reputation, was repeated in the more ambitious and original novel *Schloss Avalon* (1827; "Avalon Castle"). He traveled widely in Europe and recounted his experiences in travel books, among them *Herbstreise durch Skandinavien* (1828; "Autumn Journey Through Scandinavia").

With *Cabanis* (1832), a story of the age of Frederick the Great, Alexis embarked on a cycle of novels intended to bring to light forgotten but significant periods of Prussian history. However, the tone of his writing is uneven—passages of effective realistic description alternate with others in which romantic mysticism predominates—and his stories, poems, and dramas are largely derivative. From 1842 until 1860 he edited, almost singlehandedly, a remarkable collection of famous lawsuits, *Der neue Pitaval* ("The New Pitaval").

Alfieri \äl-'fyer-ē\, Vittorio, Count (conte) (b. Jan. 16, 1749, Asti, Piedmont [Italy]—d. Oct. 8, 1803, Florence) Italian tragic poet whose predominant theme was the overthrow of tyranny. Through his lyrics and dramas he helped to revive the national spirit of Italy.

Educated at the Military Academy of Turin, Alfieri became an ensign. A distaste for military life led him to obtain leave to travel. In England he found the political liberty that became his ideal, and in France the literature that influenced him most profoundly. He studied Voltaire, Jean-Jacques Rousseau, and, above all, Montesquieu. Alfieri settled in Turin in 1772 and resigned his commission the following year. To divert himself, he wrote *Cleopatra*, a tragedy performed with great success in 1775. Thereupon Alfieri decided to devote himself to literature. By 1782 he had written 14 tragedies as well as many poems (including four odes in the series *L'America libera* [*America the Free*], on American independence, to which a fifth ode was added in 1783) and a prose treatise on tyranny, *Della tirannide* (1777; *Of Tyranny*).

Alfieri's genius was essentially dramatic. His rough, forthright, and concise style was chosen deliberately, so that he could persuade the oppressed and the resigned to accept his political ideas and inspire them to heroic deeds. Nearly always, his tragedies present the struggle between a champion of liberty and a tyrant. Of the 19 tragedies that he approved for publication in a Paris edition of his works of 1787–89, the best are *Filippo*, in which Philip II of Spain is presented as the tyrant; *Antigone*; *Oreste*; and, above all, *Mirra* and *Saul*. *Saul*, his masterpiece, is often considered the most powerful drama in the Italian theater.

Alfieri's autobiography, published posthumously as *Vita di Vittorio Alfieri scritta da esso* (1804; *The Life of Vittorio Alfieri Written by Himself*), is his chief work in prose. He also wrote sonnets, comedies, satires, and epigrams.

Alger \'al-jər\, Horatio, Jr. (b. Jan. 13, 1832, Chelsea, Mass., U.S.—d. July 18, 1899, Natick, Mass.) One of the most popular late 19th-century American authors and perhaps the most socially influential American writer of his generation.

Alger was the son of a Unitarian minister. The young Alger showed an interest in writing, and at Harvard University he distinguished himself in the classics and graduated with Phi Beta Kappa honors in 1852. After leaving Harvard, Alger worked as a schoolteacher and contributed to magazines. In 1857 he enrolled in the Harvard Divinity School, from which he took his degree in 1860.

In 1864 Alger was ordained and accepted the pulpit of a church in Brewster, Mass., but was forced to leave in 1866 following allegations of sexual activities with local boys. In that year he moved to New York City, and with the publication and sensational success of RAGGED DICK (1868), the story of a poor shoeshine boy who rises to wealth, Alger found the vein in which he was to write more than 100 volumes.

In a steady succession of books that are almost alike except for the names of their characters, he preached that by honesty, cheerful perseverance, and hard work, the poor but virtuous lad would have his just reward—though the reward was almost always precipitated by a stroke of good luck. Alger's most popular books were the Ragged Dick, Luck and Pluck, and Tattered Tom series. His books sold more than 20,000,000 copies despite the fact that their plots, characterizations, and dialogue were consistently and even outrageously bad.

Algernon \'al-jər-nən, -,nän\ Fictional character, a witty man-about-town in Oscar Wilde's play THE IMPORTANCE OF BEING EARNEST. Algernon Moncrieff, known as Algy, is the nephew of Lady Bracknell. He pretends to be the brother of his friend Jack Worthing so that he may meet Cecily, Jack's ward.

Algonquin Round Table \al-'gän-kwən, -'gäŋ-\, *also called* The Round Table. Informal group of American literary men and women who met daily for lunch on weekdays at a large round table in the Algonquin Hotel in New York City during the 1920s and '30s. The Algonquin Round Table began meeting in 1919, and within a few years its participants included many of the best-known writers, journalists, and artists in New York City. Among them were Dorothy Parker, Alexander Woollcott, Heywood Broun, Robert Benchley, Robert Sherwood, George S. Kaufman, Franklin P. Adams, Marc Connelly, Harold Ross, Harpo Marx, Edna Ferber, and Russel Crouse. The Round Table became celebrated in the 1920s for its members' lively, witty conversation and urbane sophistication. After 1925, many of them were closely associated with *The New Yorker*, whose editorial offices were established on the same block. The last meeting of the Round Table took place in 1943.

Algren \'ôl-grən\, Nelson, *original name* Nelson Ahlgren Abraham \'ā-brə-,ham\ (b. March 28, 1909, Detroit, Mich., U.S.—d. May 9, 1981, Sag Harbor, N.Y.) Writer whose novels of the poor are lifted from routine naturalism by his vision of their pride, humor, and unquenchable yearnings. He also captures with uncommon skill the mood of the city's underside.

The son of a machinist, Algren grew up in Chicago, where his parents moved when he was three. He worked his way through the University of Illinois, graduating in journalism in the depth of the Depression. He held a variety of jobs. During this period he edited a periodical, *The New Anvil*, with the prole-

tarian writer Jack Conroy. *Somebody in Boots* (1935), his first novel, relates the driftings during the Depression of a young, poor white Texan who ends up among the down-and-outs of Chicago. *Never Come Morning* (1942) tells of a Polish petty criminal who dreams of escaping from his squalid Northwest Side Chicago environment by becoming a prize-fighter. Algren served as a U.S. Army med-

Library of Congress

ical corpsman during World War II, then published the short-story collection *The Neon Wilderness* (1947), which contains some of his best writing.

Algren's first popular success was THE MAN WITH THE GOLDEN ARM (1949; film, 1956), which won the National Book Award. Its hero is Frankie Machine, whose golden arm as a poker dealer is threatened by shakiness connected with his drug addiction. In A WALK ON THE WILD SIDE (1956; film, 1962) Algren returned to the 1930s in a picaresque novel of New Orleans bohemian life.

His nonfiction includes the prose poem *Chicago, City on the Make* (1951) and sketches collected as *Who Lost an American?* (1963) and *Notes from a Sea Diary: Hemingway All the Way* (1965).

Ali \\'ä-lē\\, Ahmed (b. July 1, 1910, Delhi, India) Pakistani author whose novels and short stories examine Islāmic culture and tradition in Hindu-dominated India. Proficient in both English and Urdu, Ali was also an accomplished translator and literary critic.

Ali was educated at Aligarh Muslim University (1925–27) and at Lucknow University (B.A., 1930; M.A., 1931). In addition to pursuing a career as a writer, he was a professor, diplomat, and businessman. In 1932 he helped publish *Angaray* ("Burning Coals"), an anthology of short stories written in Urdu that was immediately banned for its bitter critique of middle-class Muslim values. Subsequently, in 1936, he became a founder of the All-India Progressive Writers' Association, which promoted innovation in Urdu literature. His influential short fiction, which filled several volumes, was characterized by its sense of realism and social awareness and its use of stream of consciousness.

Ali earned international acclaim with the publication of his first novel, *Twilight in Delhi* (1940), which was written in English. It nostalgically chronicles the passing of the traditional Muslim aristocracy in light of encroaching British colonialism in the early 20th century. His second novel, *Ocean of Night* (1964), examines the cultural rift in India that preceded the creation of India and Pakistan in 1947. Like *Ocean of Night*, *Of Rats and Diplomats* (1985) was written decades before its publication. It is a satirical novel about a diplomat whose rat-like tail is the physical manifestation of his moral dissolution. Other notable works include *Purple Gold Mountain* (1960), a volume of verse, and *The Prison-House* (1985), a collection of short stories.

Ali Baba \\ˌäl-ē-'bä-bə, ˌal-\\ *Arabic* 'Alī Bābā \\"ä-ˌlē-'bä-ˌbä\\ Fictional character, the hero of "Ali Baba and the Forty Thieves," one of the best-known stories in THE THOUSAND AND ONE NIGHTS. Ali Baba is a poor woodcutter who secretly watches as 40 thieves hide their booty in a cave, the door to which can be opened only by the verbal command of "Open, Sesame!" He later uses this magic phrase, steals riches from the cave, and lives a prosperous life.

Alice \\'al-is\\ Fictional character, the strong-willed, curious, fanciful young English girl who is the protagonist of Lewis Carroll's ALICE'S ADVENTURES IN WONDERLAND, its sequel THROUGH THE LOOKING-GLASS, and several occasional poems. Invented during a story-telling session, the character was based on Alice Liddell, who was the daughter of the dean of Christ Church, the college at which Carroll taught.

Alice Adams \\'al-is-'ad-əmz\\ Novel by Booth TARKINGTON, published in 1921. The story of the disintegration of a lower middle-class family in a small Midwestern town, *Alice Adams* was awarded the Pulitzer Prize for best novel in 1922.

A social climber, the title character is ashamed of her unsuccessful family. Hoping to attract a wealthy husband, she lies about her background, but she is found out and is shunned by those whom she sought to attract. At the novel's end, she knows her chances for happiness and a successful marriage are bleak, but she remains unbowed.

Alice's Adventures in Wonderland \\'al-is\\ Novel by Lewis CARROLL, published in 1865. *Alice* is one of the best-known and most popular works of English-language fiction. It was notably illustrated by John Tenniel.

The story centers on Alice, a young girl who falls asleep in a meadow and dreams that she follows a White Rabbit down a rabbit hole. She has many wondrous, often bizarre adventures with thoroughly illogical and very strange creatures. Often changing size unexpectedly (she grows as tall as a house and shrinks to three inches), Alice encounters such characters as the March Hare, the Cheshire Cat, the Duchess, the Mad Hatter, the Mock Turtle, and the Red Queen. Carroll also wrote a sequel, THROUGH THE LOOKING-GLASS, and both books are sometimes referred to as *Alice in Wonderland*.

alienation effect or **a-effect** \\'ā-i-ˌfekt\\, *also called* distancing effect, *German* Verfremdungseffekt \\fer-'frem-dů̇ṇks-e-ˌfekt\\ *or* V-Effekt \\'faů̇-e-ˌfekt\\ Idea central to the dramatic theory of the German dramatist-director Bertolt Brecht. It involves the use of techniques designed to distance the audience from the action of the play and to provoke the audience's awareness that it is watching a performance.

Examples of such techniques include explanatory captions or illustrations projected on a screen; actors disengaging themselves from the scene to summarize, lecture, or sing songs; and stage designs that, by exposing the lights and ropes, keep the spectators aware of being in a theater.

Aliger \\ˌə-lʲi-'gʸer\\, Margarita Iosifovna (b. Sept. 24 [Oct. 7, New Style], 1915, Odessa, Ukraine, Russian Empire) Russian poet, journalist, and Soviet propagandist.

Aliger was a committed communist from an early age. She studied writing in Moscow from 1934 to 1937 at what later became the Gorky Literary Institute. In the late 1930s she wrote prose sketches and verse diaries of her tour of Soviet Central Asia. "Zoya" (1942), a narrative poem about a martyred Soviet female partisan, won the State Prize of the U.S.S.R. in 1943.

After World War II Aliger traveled in South America, from which she reported in verse and prose; she was in Chile during the Allende regime of 1970–73. Much of her poetry repeated Soviet political jargon and catch-phrases. Collections include *God rozhdeniya* (1938; "Year of Birth"), *Kamni i travy* (1940; Stones and Grasses"), *Leninskiye gory* (1953; "The Lenin Hills"), and *Neskolko shagov* (1962; "A Few Paces"). Her later publications include *Tropinka vo rzhi* (1980; "A Path in the Rye"), a collection of essays; and *Chetvert veka* (1981; "A Quarter of a Century"), a book of poetry.

allegory \'al-ə-ˌgȯr-ē\ [Greek *allēgoría*, a derivative of *allē-goreîn* to speak figuratively, from *állos* other + *-ēgorein* to speak]   A more or less symbolic fictional narrative that conveys a secondary meaning (or meanings) not explicitly set forth in the literal narrative. It encompasses such forms as fable, parable, and apologue and may involve either a literary or an interpretative process.

Literary allegories typically express situations, events, or abstract ideas in terms of material objects, persons, and actions or interactions. Such early writers as Plato, Cicero, Apuleius, and Augustine made use of allegory, but it became especially popular in sustained narratives of the Middle Ages. Probably the most influential allegory of that period is the *Roman de la Rose* (*Romance of the Rose*). The poem, a DREAM VISION, illustrates the allegorical technique of personification (in which a fictional character—in this case, for example, The Lover—transparently represents a concept or a type). As in most allegories, the action of the narrative "stands for" something not explicitly stated. The Lover's eventual plucking of the crimson rose represents his conquest of his lady. Other notable examples of personification allegory are John Bunyan's *The Pilgrim's Progress* and the medieval morality play *Everyman*. Their straightforward embodiments of aspects of human nature and abstract concepts, through such characters as Knowledge, Beauty, Strength, and Death in *Everyman* and such places as Vanity Fair and the Slough of Despond in *The Pilgrim's Progress*, are typical examples of the techniques of personification allegory.

Another variant is the symbolic allegory, in which a character or material thing is not merely a transparent vehicle for an idea, but rather has a recognizable identity or a narrative autonomy apart from the message it conveys. In Dante's *Divine Comedy*, for example, the character Virgil represents both the historical author of *The Aeneid* and the human faculty of reason, the character Beatrice both the historical woman of Dante's acquaintance and the concept of divine revelation. Ranging from the simple fable to the complex, multi-layered narrative, the symbolic allegory has frequently been used to represent political and historical situations and has long been popular as a vehicle for satire. In the verse satire *Absalom and Achitophel*, for example, John Dryden relates in heroic couplets a scriptural story that is a thinly veiled portrait of the politicians involved in an attempt to alter the succession to the English throne. A modern example of political allegory is George Orwell's *Animal Farm* (1945), which, under the guise of a fable about domestic animals who take over a farm from their human oppressor, expresses the author's disillusionment with the outcome of the Bolshevik Revolution and shows how one tyrannical system of government in Russia was merely replaced by another.

Allegory may involve an interpretive process that is separate from the creative process; that is, the term allegory can refer to a specific method of reading a text, in which characters and narrative or descriptive details are taken by the reader as an elaborate metaphor for something outside the literal story. For example, the early Church Fathers sometimes used a threefold (later fourfold) method of interpreting texts, encompassing literal, moral, and spiritual meanings. One variety of such allegorical interpretation is the typological reading of the Old Testament, in which characters and events are seen as foreshadowing specific characters and events in the New Testament. *See also* FABLE; PARABLE.

Allen \'al-ən\, Hervey, *in full* William Hervey Allen, Jr. (b. Dec. 8, 1889, Pittsburgh, Pa., U.S.—d. Dec. 28, 1949, Coconut Grove, Fla.)   American poet, biographer, and novelist who had a great impact on popular literature with his historical novel ANTHONY ADVERSE.

Allen's first published work was a book of poetry, *Ballads of the Border* (1916). During the 1920s he established a reputation as a poet, publishing several more volumes of verse. He had been wounded in World War I, and his novel *Toward the Flame* (1926) came out of his wartime experience. That same year his authoritative biography *Israfel: The Life and Times of Edgar Allan Poe* was published.

In 1933, after five years of work, Allen published *Anthony Adverse*, which was a huge success. The book's considerable length and its undisguised passages about sex introduced a new standard for popular fiction. Allen's later novels were less successful.

Allen \'al-ən\, Walter (Ernest) (b. Feb. 23, 1911, Birmingham, Eng.)   British novelist and critic best known for the breadth and accessibility of his criticism.

Allen graduated from the University of Birmingham (B.A., 1932) and taught until 1945, when he became a literary editor for the *New Statesman*.

Early in his career Allen published a rapid succession of novels, beginning with *Innocence Is Drowned* (1938). These dealt affectingly with contemporary English working-class life, a subject that he refracted through the memory of an aging radical in what is perhaps his best novel, *All in a Lifetime* (1959; U.S. title, *Threescore and Ten*). In 1986, after a 27-year hiatus from fiction, Allen published *Get Out Early*, the story of a cynical rake and his redemption. A memoir of Allen's encounters with the leading writers of the day, *As I Walked down New Grub Street*, appeared in 1982. His other works of nonfiction included *The English Novel: A Short Critical History* (1954), *Tradition and Dream: The English and American Novel from the Twenties to Our Time* (1964), and *The Short Story in English* (1981).

Allende \ä-'yen-dä, äl-\, Isabel (b. Aug. 2, 1942, Lima, Peru)   Chilean writer in the magic realist tradition who is considered one of the first successful woman novelists in Latin America.

Allende worked as a journalist in Chile until she was forced to flee to Venezuela after the assassination (1973) of her uncle, Chilean president Salvador Allende Gossens. In Venezuela she did odd jobs for several years. A letter to her grandfather evolved into her first novel, *La casa de los espíritus* (1982; *The House of the Spirits*). This was followed by the novels *De amor y de sombra* (1984; *Of Love and Shadows*), *Eva Luna* (1987), and *El plan infinito* (1991; *The Infinite Plan*) and a collection of stories entitled *Cuentos de Eva Luna* (1990; *The Stories of Eva Luna*).

Allende wrote in the magic realist tradition. Her works combine that tradition, however, with a portrayal of the political realities of South America. Her novels reflect her personal experiences with those realities and examine the role of women in Latin America. *El plan infinito*, however, was set in the United States, and its leading character was male.

Allingham \'al-iŋ-əm\, Margery Louise (b. May 20, 1904, London, Eng.—d. June 30, 1966, Colchester, Essex)   British detective-story writer of unusual subtlety, wit, and imaginative power who created the bland, bespectacled, keen-witted detective Albert CAMPION.

Allingham published her first story at the age of 8. Her first novel, *Blackkerchief Dick*, was published in 1923 when she was 19, and her first detective story, *The White Cottage Mystery*, appeared in serial form in 1927 in the *Daily Express* and in book form in 1928.

The Campion series began with several ingenious, popular thrillers. A series of more tightly constructed intellectual problem stories, beginning with *Death of a Ghost* (1934) and including *Flowers for the Judge* (1936), *The Fashion in Shrouds* (1938), and *Traitor's Purse* (1941), gained Allingham critical esteem. With the novels *Coroner's Pidgin* (1945; U.S. title, *Pearls Before Swine*); *More Work for the Undertaker* (1948); *Tiger in the Smoke* (1952), which revealed her psychological insight and her power to create an atmosphere of pervasive, mindless evil; and *The China Governess* (1962), she helped develop the detective story as a serious literary genre.

alliteration \ə-ˌlit-ə-'rā-shən \, *also called* head rhyme [Latin *ad* to, toward + *littera* letter; probably modeled on Latin *oblitteratio, obliteratio* effacement, obliteration, falsely taken to be a derivative of *littera*] In prosody, the repetition of consonant sounds in two or more neighboring words or syllables. In the most common form of alliteration, the initial sounds are the same, thus the alternate name head rhyme. As a poetic device, alliteration is often discussed with assonance and consonance.

Alliteration is found in many common phrases, such as "pretty as a picture" and "dead as a doornail." In its simplest form, it reinforces one or two consonantal sounds, as in this line from William Shakespeare's Sonnet XII:

When I do count the clock that tells the time

A more complex pattern of alliteration is created when consonants both at the beginning of words and at the beginning of stressed syllables within words are repeated, as in the following line from Percy Bysshe Shelley's "Stanzas Written in Dejection Near Naples":

The City's voice itself is soft like Solitude's

Compare ASSONANCE; CONSONANCE.

alliterative prose \ə-'lit-ər-ə-tiv \ Prose that uses alliteration and some of the techniques of alliterative verse. Notable examples are from Old English and Middle English, including works by the Anglo-Saxon writer Aelfric and the so-called Katherine Group of five Middle English devotional works.

alliterative verse Early, usually unrhymed verse of the Germanic languages in which alliteration, the repetition of consonant sounds at the beginning of words or stressed syllables, is a basic structural principle rather than an occasional embellishment. Although alliteration is a common device in almost all poetry, the only Indo-European languages that used it as a governing principle, along with strict rules of accent and quantity, were Old Norse, Old English, Old Saxon, and Old High German. The Germanic alliterative line consists of two hemistichs (half lines) separated by a caesura (pause). There are one or two alliterating letters in the first half line preceding the medial caesura; these also alliterate with the first stressed syllable in the second half line. Alliteration falls on accented syllables; unaccented syllables are not effective, even if they begin with the alliterating letter.

The introduction of rhyme, derived from medieval Latin hymns, contributed to the decline of alliterative verse. In Low German, pure alliterative verse is not known to have survived after 900; and, in Old High German, rhymed verse was by that time already replacing it. In England, alliteration as a strict structural principle is not found after 1066 (the date of the Norman Conquest of Britain) except in the western part of the country. Although alliteration continued to be an important element, the alliterative line became freer: the second half line often contained more than one alliterating word, and other formalistic restrictions were gradually disregarded.

England experienced a period known as the Alliterative Revival in the late 14th century, when a series of alliterative poems appeared. These verses were freer in form than earlier alliterative verse, and such works as *Piers Plowman*, *Sir Gawayne and the Grene Knight*, and *Pearl* use end rhyme extensively. The last alliterative poem in English is usually held to be "Scottish Fielde," which deals with the Battle of Flodden in 1513.

Later Norse poets (after 900) also combined many forms of rhyme and assonance with alliteration in a variety of stanzaic forms. After 1000, Old Norse alliterative verse became practically confined to the Icelanders, among whom it continues to exist. In Celtic poetry, alliteration was from the earliest times an important, but subordinate, principle. In Welsh poetry, it gave rise to the verse form known as CYNGHANEDD.

All My Sons Drama in three acts by Arthur MILLER, performed and published in 1947.

All My Sons was considered Miller's first significant play. With an underlying theme of guilt and responsibility, the drama centers on Joe Keller, a manufacturer of substandard and defective war materials, whose faulty airplane parts cause the death of his son and other fliers during World War II.

alloeostropha \ˌal-ē-'äs-trə-fə \ [Greek *alloióstrophos* having irregular strophes, from *alloîos* of another sort + *strophḗ* strophe] Irregular strophes or stanzas. The term was used by John Milton to describe the irregular stanzas or strophes of the choric odes in his *Samson Agonistes*.

allonym \'al-ə-ˌnim \ [French *allonyme,* from Greek *állos* other + *ónyma* name] 1. A name that is assumed by an author but that actually belongs to another person. 2. A work published under the name of a person other than the author.

All Quiet on the Western Front Novel by Erich Maria REMARQUE, published in 1929 as *Im Westen nichts Neues*. An antiwar novel set during World War I, it was written after the war and reflects the disillusionment of the period. The book is an account of a young man's experiences in battle and of his short career as a soldier. It details the daily routine of soldiers who seem to have no past or future apart from their life in the trenches. Its title, the language of routine communiqués, is typical of its cool, terse style, which records the daily horrors of war in laconic understatement. Its casual amorality was in shocking contrast to patriotic rhetoric. The book was an immediate international success.

All's Well That Ends Well Comedy in five acts by William SHAKESPEARE, produced about 1602–03 and published in the First Folio of 1623. The principal source of the plot is a tale in Giovanni Boccaccio's *Decameron*.

The play concerns the efforts of Helena, daughter of a renowned physician, to make Bertram, the count of Rousillon, her husband. When Bertram is summoned by the gravely ill king of France, Helena follows and administers a cure that had been provided by her father. In return, the king invites her to select a husband, her choice being the evasive Bertram. He concedes to the royal imperative but promptly flees to Tuscany. By letter Bertram informs Helena that he may not be considered her husband until she has taken the ring from his finger and conceived a child by him. Disguised as a pilgrim, Helena follows Bertram to Florence only to discover that he has been courting the daughter of her hostess. Helena spreads a rumor of her own death and has a rendezvous with Bertram in the daughter's stead. In exchange for his ring, she gives him one that the king has given her. When Bertram returns to Rousillon, where the king is visiting the countess, the royal guest recognizes the ring and suspects foul play. Helena then appears to explain her machinations and claim her rightful spouse.

All the King's Men Novel by Robert Penn WARREN, published in 1946. The story concerns the rise and fall of Willie

Stark, a character modeled on Huey Long, the governor of Louisiana during the time frame of the novel (late 1920s to early 1930s). The book won the Pulitzer Prize in 1947.

Stark comes from a poor background, becomes a lawyer, and is elected governor. A self-styled man of the people, he soon learns to use such tactics as bribery and intimidation to assure passage of his populist programs such as the building of new rural roads and hospitals. These methods account for his power, but at the same time are responsible for his downfall.

allusion \ə-'lü-zhən\ [Late Latin *allusio* play on words, game, a derivative of Latin *alludere* to play around, refer to mockingly, from *ad* to + *ludere* to play] In literature, an implied or indirect reference to a person, event, thing, or a part of another text. Allusion is distinguished from such devices as direct quote and imitation or parody. Most are based on the assumption that there is a body of knowledge that is shared by the author and the reader and that therefore the reader will understand the author's referent. Allusions to biblical figures and figures from classical mythology are common in Western literature for this reason.

Allworthy, Squire \'ol-,wər-the\ Fictional character, a kind-hearted widower who acts as a surrogate father to the foundling in Henry Fielding's novel TOM JONES. Squire Allworthy initially is misled into believing ill of Tom but in the end his good nature wins out, and he brings about a happy ending to the story.

Almagest \'al-mə-jest\ [Medieval Latin *Almagesti,* from Arabic *al-majusţ,* from Greek *megístē* (*sýntaxis*) greatest (composition)] Astronomical encyclopedia compiled about AD 140 by PTOLEMY. The word *almagest* was derived from the Arabic name for Ptolemy's work, and in the Middle Ages the use of the word was broadened to refer to any great treatise on a branch of knowledge. Ptolemy's *Almagest* is divided into 13 books, each of which deals with certain astronomical concepts pertaining to stars and to objects in the solar system. It is the major source of knowledge about the work of Hipparchus, most probably the greatest astronomer of antiquity.

almanac \'ol-mə-,nak, 'al-\ [Medieval Latin *almanach,* from Spanish Arabic *al-manākh* the calendar] Book or table containing such items as a calendar of the days, weeks, and months of the year; a register of ecclesiastical festivals and saints' days; and a record of various astronomical phenomena, often with weather prognostications and seasonal suggestions for farmers.

Almanacs have appeared in one form or another since the beginnings of astronomy. The first printed almanac appeared in the mid-15th century, and in 1533 the French writer François Rabelais published his *Pantagrueline Prognostication,* a parody of the astrological predictions of the almanacs that were exercising a growing hold on the Renaissance mind.

The first standard almanacs were issued at Oxford. The most famous of these early English almanacs was the *Vox Stellarum* of Francis Moore, the first number of which was completed in July 1700 and contained predictions for 1701.

The first American almanacs were printed in Cambridge, Mass., under the supervision of Harvard College. Benjamin Franklin (under the nom de plume Richard Saunders) began his *Poor Richard's* almanacs, the most famous of American almanacs, in Philadelphia in 1733.

The 18th-century almanac was the forerunner of the modern magazine. It enabled the farmer to tell the time of day and to estimate the proper season for various farm chores. It also furnished much instructive and entertaining incidental information and was greatly appreciated where reading matter was scarce. A particular popular version was the *Farmer's Almanac,* later called *Old Farmer's Almanac.*

Almaviva, Count \,äl-mə-'vē-və\ Character in two plays, THE BARBER OF SEVILLE and THE MARRIAGE OF FIGARO, by Pierre-Augustin Beaumarchais. Almaviva is introduced in *The Barber of Seville* as a young count in love with the heroine, Rosine. With the help of the barber Figaro, he cleverly outwits Rosine's guardian and wins Rosine's hand in marriage. In *The Marriage of Figaro* Almaviva is a philandering husband who tries to seduce Figaro's fiancée Suzanne.

Almeida \äl-'mā-də\, José Américo de (b. Jan. 10, 1887, Paraíba, Braz.—d. March 10, 1980, Rio de Janeiro) Novelist who was the first of a generation of important Brazilian regional writers. His fiction presents a predominantly socioeconomic interpretation of life in Brazil's northeastern region, the most impoverished and drought-stricken part of the country, and is filled with local color and appeals for just treatment of the poor.

Almeida's literary career was paralleled by a career in politics. He served in the first Cabinet of President Getúlio Vargas as minister of public works and transportation (1930–34) and was governor of the state of Paraíba (1951–54).

The problems endemic to the Brazilian northeast, including banditry in the arid backlands and the poverty and ignorance of the sugarcane workers in the more fertile coastal zone, are the focus of Almeida's novels. These include *A bagaceira* (1928; *Trash*), his best-known work; *O boqueirão* (1935; "Canyon"); and *Coiteiros* (1935; "Bandit-hiders"). *See also* NORTHEASTERN SCHOOL.

Almeida, José Valentim Fialho de *see* FIALHO DE ALMEIDA.

Almeida \äl-'mā-də\, Manuel Antônio de (b. Nov. 17, 1831, Magé, Rio de Janeiro, Braz.—d. Nov. 28, 1861, at sea off Brazilian coast) Author of what is now considered to have been the first great novel in Brazilian literature, *Memórias de um sargento de milícias* (anonymously in parts, 1853; as a novel, 1854–55; *Memoirs of a Militia Sergeant*), his only fictional work. Its realism was not only far in advance of the Romanticism of his Brazilian contemporaries but several years in advance of European naturalism. It attracted little critical or popular attention until it was rediscovered by the Modernists in the 20th century.

Almeida studied art and, later, medicine, but his education was frequently interrupted for lack of money, and he supported himself as a translator and journalist. He died in a shipwreck while on a newspaper assignment.

Memoirs mirrors life in early 19th-century Rio de Janeiro. Written in an intimate, colloquial style, it offers a vivid glimpse of customs, personalities, and court intrigues, as viewed by the character Leonardo, a young man of slight social standing who seeks adventure wherever he can find it—among beggars, society women, priests, or sailors.

Almeida de Portugal \äl-'mā-də-dē-,por-tü-'gäl\, Leonor de, Marquesa de Alorna, *pseudonym* Alcipe *or* Alcippe (b. 1750, Lisbon, Port.—d. 1839, Lisbon) Portuguese poet whose work formed a bridge between the literary periods of ARCÁDIA and Romanticism in Portugal. Her influential verse, translations, and letters were collected in the six-volume *Obras poéticas* (1844).

When her grandmother was executed for political reasons in 1758, Almeida de Portugal was detained along with her mother and sister in the convent of Chelas until 1777. She was tutored by Francisco Manuel do Nascimento, who gave her the Arcadian name Alcipe. After founding a political group called the Society of the Rose in 1803, she was exiled to London until 1814. Upon her return to Lisbon, she inherited the title of Marquesa de Alorna and founded a literary salon. Her diverse writings were concerned with such idealistic themes as political liberty and scientific progress. Among the authors she translated or paraphrased were Homer, Horace, Alexander Pope, Oliver Goldsmith, and Alphonse de Lamartine.

Almqvist or **Almquist** \'älm-,kvĕst\, Carl Jonas Love (b. Nov. 28, 1793, Ed, near Stockholm, Swed.—d. Sept. 26, 1866, Bremen, Bremen [Germany]) Writer whose complex personality, extravagant imagination, and vast literary output greatly influenced the development of Swedish literature.

After studying at Uppsala, Almqvist worked in the civil service in Stockholm and later went to western Sweden to farm. In 1825 he returned to Stockholm, and from 1829 to 1841 was principal of an experimental secondary school.

Most of his works, including prose and verse, were collected in a series called *Törnrosens bok* ("The Book of the Wild Rose"; 13 vol., 1832–40; vol. 14, 1851; 2nd series, 1839–50). Particularly important was *Drottningens juvelsmycke* (1834; "The Queen's Diadem"), a historical novel whose heroine, the mysterious, androgynous Tintomara, is Almqvist's most fascinating character and a central symbol in his creative writings. *Det går an* (1838; *Sara Videbeck*) is a brilliant presentation of Almqvist's unconventional views about love and marriage. Publication of the book essentially ruined Almqvist's life. Forced to quit his job, he began a downhill slide. In 1851 he fled to the United States after being accused of fraud and the attempted murder of a moneylender. He traveled in the United States until 1865, when he returned, ill and poverty-stricken, to Europe.

Almqvist is considered to be one of the major figures of Swedish literature. His method of treating moral and social issues is a clear foreshadowing of playwright August Strindberg's style.

Aloadae \ə-'lō-ə-dē\ or **Aloidae** \,al-ō-'ī-dē\ In Greek legend, the twin sons of Iphimedia, the wife of Aloeus, by the god Poseidon. Named Otus and Ephialtes, the Aloadae were of extraordinary strength and stature. The Aloadae attacked the Olympian gods and tried to storm heaven itself, but Apollo destroyed them before they reached manhood. In a later myth, when they sought Artemis and Hera in marriage, Artemis appeared between them in the shape of a stag; they tried to kill the stag but ended up killing each other.

a lo divino \,ä-lō-dē-'bē-nō\ A Spanish phrase meaning literally "in the sacred style" or "in sacred terms" that in Spanish literature alludes to the recasting of a secular work as a religious work, or more generally to a treatment of a secular theme in religious terms through the use of allegory, symbolism, and metaphor. Adaptations *a lo divino* were popular during the 16th and 17th centuries.

Alonso \ä-'lôn-sō\, Dámaso (b. Oct. 22, 1898, Madrid, Spain—d. Jan. 24, 1990, Madrid) Spanish poet, literary critic, and scholar, a member of the Generation of 1927.

Educated at the University of Madrid, Alonso taught from 1923 to 1968 in Spain, Germany, Britain, and the United States. His first volume of poems, *Poemas puros* (1921; "Pure Poems"), were imagist, emphasizing economy of expression, but his later poetry evolved into a freer, more complex style, especially in his most famous poetical works, *Oscura noticia* (1944; "Dark Message") and *Hijos de la ira* (1944; *Children of Wrath*). *Poemas escogidos* ("Selected Poetry") appeared in 1969. In 1978 Alonso was awarded Spain's highest literary honor, the Miguel de Cervantes prize.

As a critic, he helped revive the reputation of the 17th-century Baroque poet Luis de Góngora with his edition of Góngora's *Soledades* (1927; "Solitudes") and his essay *La lengua poética de Góngora* (1935; "The Poetic Language of Góngora") and other later works. His criticism is best seen in *Poesía española* (1950; 5th edition, 1966; "Spanish Poetry").

Alós \ä-'lōs\, Concha (b. May 24, 1922, Valencia, Spain) Spanish prose writer, best known for her Neorealistic, often existentialist works deploring social injustice, especially the institutionally sanctioned victimization of women.

Alós and her family fled to Murcia during the Spanish Civil War. She was educated in Palma, Majorca, as a teacher, and for 10 years she taught school in Majorcan villages. After settling in Barcelona in 1960, Alós began writing. She achieved national recognition in 1964, when *Las hogueras* ("Bonfires"), her third novel, received a literary award.

Among Alós' other works were *Los enanos* (1962; "The Dwarfs"), set in a dingy rooming house populated with characters from all walks of life; *Los cien pájaros* (1963; "The Hundred Birds"), about a young woman who rejects traditional Spanish mores and chooses to live independently; and *El caballo rojo* (1966; "The Red Horse"), a semiautobiographical account of Alós' family's experience as refugees during the Spanish Civil War. *El rey de gatos (Narraciones antropófagas)* (1972; "King of Cats, Cannibalistic Tales") is a collection of short stories. Her later novels include *Os habla Electra* (1975; "Electra Speaking"), *Argeo ha muerto, supongo* (1982; "Argeo Has Died, I Suppose"), and *El asesino de los sueños* (1986; "The Assassin of Dreams").

alphabet rhyme \'al-fə-,bet\ Mnemonic verse or song used to help children learn an alphabet; such devices appear in almost every alphabetic language. One of the early English favorites is a cumulative rhyme to which there is a printed reference as early as 1671. It often appeared in 18th-century chapbooks under the imposing name *The Tragical Death of A, Apple Pye Who was Cut in Pieces and Eat by Twenty-Five Gentlemen with whom All Little People Ought to be Very well acquainted*. It begins:

> A was an apple-pie;
> B bit it,
> C cut it,
> D dealt it, etc.

Another, known as "Tom Thumb's Alphabet," enjoyed continuous popularity. The earliest printed record of it dates to roughly 1712. In its most familiar version, the rhyme begins:

> A was an archer, who shot at a frog.
> B was a butcher, and had a great dog.

Lines such as "D was a drunkard, and had a red face" or "Y was a youth, that did not love school" were later considered to have a harmful effect on children; they were replaced by the widely taught alphabet rhyme of the 17th-century *New-England Primer*, which combined moral messages with the learning of letters:

> In Adam's fall
> We sinned all.

A simplified version of English alphabet rhyme that is popular today is one in which the alphabet is sung to the tune of "Twinkle, Twinkle, Little Star."

Also Sprach Zarathustra \'äl-zō-'shpräk-,tsä-rä-'tùs-trä\ *see* THUS SPOKE ZARATHUSTRA.

altar poem *see* PATTERN POETRY.

Aluko \ä-'lü-kō\, T.M., *in full* Timothy Mofolorunso (b. June 14, 1918, Ilesha, Nigeria) Nigerian writer whose short stories and novels deal with social change in modern Africa.

A civil engineer and town planner by profession, Aluko was educated in Nigeria and England and held positions as director of public works for western Nigeria and faculty member at the University of Lagos.

Aluko's first published works were short stories. *One Man, One Wife* (1959), a satirical novel about the conflict of Christian and Yoruba ethics, relates the disillusionment of a village community with the tenets of missionary Christianity. A second novel, *One Man, One Matchet* (1964), humorously presents the clash of an inexperienced district officer with an unscrupulous politician. *Kinsman and Foreman* (1966) is a penetrating study of an idealistic young engineer's battle against the corrupt practices of his highly respected public works foreman, who is also his uncle. Later novels include *Chief the Honourable Minister* (1970), *His Worshipful Majesty* (1973), *Wrong Ones in the Dock* (1982), and *A State of Our Own* (1986). Aluko's economy of style, graceful prose, and gentle irony brought him critical acclaim.

Āḷvār \'äl-ˌvär, 'al-\ [Tamil *ārvār,* a derivative of *ār-* to sink, be immersed]   Any of a group of South Indian mystics who in the 7th to 10th century wandered from temple to temple singing ecstatic hymns in adoration of the Hindu god Vishnu. The songs of the Āḷvārs rank among the world's greatest devotional literature. Among the followers of the Hindu god Śiva, the counterpart of the Āḷvārs were the Nāyaṇārs.

The name Āḷvār means, in the Tamil language in which they sang, "one who is immersed in meditation of God." Their bhakti (religious devotion) was of an intensely passionate kind; they compared the soul to a woman who yearns for her lord's love.

The hymns of the Āḷvārs, entitled *Nālāyira Prabandham* ("Collection of 4,000 Songs"), were gathered in the 10th century by Nāthamuni, a leader of the Śrīvaiṣṇava sect.

Alvarez \al-'vär-ez\, A., *in full* Alfred (b. Aug. 5, 1929, London, Eng.)   British novelist, essayist, and critic whose works explore the interaction of public and private forces that shape personality and behavior.

Although Alvarez' family enjoyed economic and cultural advantages, both of his parents attempted suicide during his childhood. He entered Corpus Christi College at Oxford, where he founded the Critical Society. Alvarez later pursued his critical interests as a visiting fellow at Princeton (1953–54) and elsewhere.

After publishing two books of criticism and several assessments of contemporary authors in a variety of periodicals, Alvarez turned to his own creative writing in 1966. His first collection of poetry, *Lost,* appeared two years later, followed by *Apparition* (1971) and *Autumn to Autumn, and Selected Poems, 1953–1976* (1978). His novels include *Hers* (1974), a bleak portrait of a loveless marriage; *Hunt* (1978), in which the protagonist becomes entangled in the life of a woman he discovers unconscious on Hampstead Heath; and *Day of Atonement* (1991), a psychological thriller.

Álvarez Quintero \ˌäl-bä-räth-ken-'tä-rō\, Serafín and Joaquín (respectively b. March 26, 1871, Utrera, Seville, Spain—d. April 12, 1938, Madrid; b. Jan. 20, 1873, Utrera—d. June 14, 1944, Madrid)   Brothers who collaborated in writing almost 200 dramas depicting the life, manners, and speech of Andalusia. Their work was quite popular in Spain during the early 20th century and greatly added to the revival of the Spanish theater. Their dramas are notable for lively dialogue. Among their better-known plays are *Los galeotes* (1900; "The Galley Slaves"), *El amor que pasa* (1904; "The Love That Passes"), and *Malvaloca* (1912). Their complete works were published in *Obras completas,* 7 vol. (1953–54).

Alvaro \äl-'vä-rō\, Corrado (b. April 15, 1895, San Luca, Italy—d. June 11, 1956, Rome)   Italian novelist and journalist whose works investigated the pressures of life in the 20th century.

Alvaro began his writing career in 1916, working on daily newspapers in Bologna and in Milan. Military service in World War I temporarily interrupted his studies at the University of Milan. After graduation he worked for several journals, including the antifascist weekly *Il Mondo.*

Alvaro's first novel, *L'uomo nel labirinto* (1926; "Man in the Labyrinth"), explores the growth of fascism in Italy in the 1920s. *Gente in Aspromonte* (1930; *Revolt in Aspromonte*) examines the exploitation of rural peasants by greedy landowners in Calabria. Inspired by a trip to the Soviet Union in 1934, *L'uomo è forte* (1938; *Man is Strong*) is a defense of the individual against totalitarianism. Alvaro's other novels include *Vent'anni* (1930; "Twenty Years"), *Itinerario italiano* (1933; "Italian Route"), *L'età breve* (1946; "The Brief Era"), and *Tutto è accaduto* (1961; "All Has Happened"). He also published a verse collection, *Poesie grigioverdi* (1917; "Green-Gray Poems"); a play entitled *La lunga notte di Medea* (1949; "The Long Night of Medea"); and two memoirs, *Quasi una vita* (1950; "Almost a Life") and *Ultimo diario* (1959; "Final Diary").

Alving, Helen and Oswald \'hel-en-'äl-viṇ . . . 'ôs-ˌväl\   Fictional characters, mother and son, in Henrik Ibsen's drama *Gengangere* (GHOSTS). Both characters continue to be affected by the dissolute behavior of Captain Alving, Mrs. Alving's husband and Oswald's father, long after the captain's death.

Amadi \ä-mä-'dē\, Elechi (b. May 12, 1934, Aluu, near Port Harcourt, Nigeria)   Nigerian novelist and playwright, best known for works that explore the role of the supernatural in Nigerian village life.

Amadi, an Ijo (Ijaw) who wrote in English, was educated at Government College, Umuahia, and University College, Ibadan, in physics and mathematics. He served in the Nigerian army, taught, and worked for the Ministry of Information in Rivers State.

Amadi was best known for his historical trilogy about traditional life in rural Nigeria: *The Concubine* (1966), *The Great Ponds* (1969), and *The Slave* (1978). These novels concern human destiny and the extent to which it can be changed; the relationship between people and their gods is the central issue explored. He was a keen observer of details of daily life and religious rituals, which he unobtrusively described in his dramatic stories. Similar emphases are found in his verse play, *Isiburu* (1973), about a champion wrestler who is ultimately defeated by the supernatural power of his enemy. His other plays include *Peppersoup and the Road to Ibadan* (1977), two plays published jointly, and *Damer of Johannesburg* (1978). A later novel, *Estrangement* (1986), was set during the Nigerian civil war of 1967–70.

Amadi's works of nonfiction include *Sunset in Biafra* (1973), which recounts his experiences as a soldier and civilian during the Biafran conflict, and *Ethics in Nigerian Culture* (1982).

Amadís of Gaul \ˌäm-ä-'thēs . . . 'gôl\, *Spanish* Amadís de Gaula \thä-'gaü-lä\   Prose romance of chivalry, possibly Portuguese in origin. The first known version of this work, dating from 1508, was written in Spanish by Garci Ordóñez (or Rodríguez) de Montalvo, who claimed to have "corrected and emended" corrupt originals. Internal evidence suggests that the *Amadís* had been in circulation since the early 14th century or even the late 13th. In Montalvo's version, Amadís was the most handsome, upright, and valiant of knights. The story of his incredible feats of arms, in which he is never defeated, was interwoven with that of his love for Oriana, daughter of Lisuarte, king of England.

Many characters in the *Amadís* were based on figures from Celtic romance, and the work was very like Arthurian legend in spirit. It differed, however, from the Arthurian cycle in several important respects. Whereas earlier romance had reflected a feudal society, the *Amadís* invested the monarchy with an authority that heralds the advent of absolutism. And Amadís himself was more idealized than such earlier heroes as Lancelot and Tristan.

In the 16th century a number of sequels and feeble imitations appeared, the fashion being given its deathblow by parody early in the 17th century in Miguel de Cervantes' novel *Don Quixote* (though Cervantes held the original in high esteem). The first English adaptation of the *Amadís* appeared in 1567; one of the best English translations is an abridged version by the poet Robert Southey, first published in 1803.

Amado \ä-'mä-dü\, Jorge (b. Aug. 10, 1912, Ferradas, near Ilhéus, Braz.)   Novelist internationally known for his stories of life in the Brazilian northeast.

Born and reared on a cacao plantation, Amado was educated at the Jesuit college and another school in Salvador. He published his first novel at the age of 20. Three of his early works deal with the cacao plantations, emphasizing the exploitation and the misery of those who pick the beans. The best of these works, *Terras do sem fim* (1942; *The Violent Land*), about the struggle of rival planters for some cacao groves, has the primitive grandeur of a folk saga.

Amado's literary career parallels a career in radical politics that won him election to the Constituent Assembly in 1946. He was imprisoned as early as 1935 and periodically exiled for his leftist activities, and many of his books were banned in Brazil and Portugal. He continued to produce novels with facility, most of them picaresque, ribald tales of Bahian city life, especially that of the racially mixed lower classes. *Gabriela, cravo e canela* (1958; *Gabriela, Clove and Cinnamon*) and *Dona Flor e seus dois maridos* (1966; *Dona Flor and Her Two Husbands*; film, 1978) both preserve Amado's political attitude in their satire. His later works include *Tenda dos milagres* (1969; *Tent of Miracles*), *Tieta do agreste* (1977; *Tieta, the Goat Girl*), *Tocaia grande* (1984; *Show Down*), and *Sumiço da santa* (1993; *The War of the Saints*).

a maiore or **a majore** \ˌä-mä-'yō-rē, -rä\ [Latin, from the larger]   Of or relating to an IONIC foot beginning with two long syllables.

Amalthaea or **Amalthea** \ˌam-əl-'thē-ə\   In Greek (originally Cretan) mythology, the foster mother of Zeus. She is sometimes represented as the goat that suckled the infant god in a cave in Crete, sometimes as a nymph who fed him the milk of a goat. This goat having broken off one of its horns, Amalthaea filled the horn with flowers and fruits and presented it to Zeus, who, according to one version, placed it, together with the goat, among the stars.

Amaryllis \ˌam-ə-'ril-is\   In Roman literature, a name given to a stock female character, a natural, pretty young woman who was usually a shepherdess. Amaryllis is mentioned in classical pastoral poetry and in later works, such as Thomas Campion's "I Care Not for These Ladies" (1601) and John Milton's "Lycidas" (1638).

Amaterasu \ˌäm-ä-tä-'räs-ˌü\, *in full* Amaterasu Ōmikami ("Great Divinity Illuminating Heaven")   In Japanese mythology, the celestial sun goddess from whom the Japanese imperial family claims descent, and an important Shintō deity. She was born from the left eye of her father, Izanagi, who placed her in charge of *Takamagahara* ("High Celestial Plain"), the abode of all the *kami* (divinities). One of her brothers, the storm god Susanoo, was sent to rule the sea plain. Before going, Susanoo went to take leave of his sister. As an act of good faith, they produced children together, she by chewing and spitting out pieces of the sword he gave her, and he by doing the same with her jewels. Susanoo then began to behave very rudely—he

broke down the divisions in the rice fields, defiled his sister's dwelling place, and finally threw a flayed horse into her weaving hall. Indignant, Amaterasu withdrew in protest into a cave, and darkness fell upon the world.

The other gods conferred on how to lure the sun goddess out. They collected cocks, whose crowing precedes the dawn, and hung a mirror on a tree in front of the cave. The goddess AMENOUZUME began a dance in which she partially disrobed herself, which so delighted the assembled gods that they roared with laughter. Amaterasu became curious how the gods could make merry while the world was plunged into darkness and was told that outside the cave there was a deity more illustrious than she. She peeped out, saw her reflection in the mirror, heard the cocks crow, and was thus drawn out from the cave.

Amazon \'am-ə-zän\   In Greek mythology, one of a race or nation of female warriors usually associated with Scythia or Asia Minor with whom the ancient Greeks of mythology repeatedly warred.

The story of the Amazons probably originated as a variant of a tale recurrent in many cultures, that of a distant land organized oppositely from one's own. The ascribed habitat of the Amazons necessarily became more remote as Greek geographic knowledge developed. The tribe is mentioned in Virgil, in Herodotus' *History*, and in other early sources.

Subsidiary tales about the Amazons began to accumulate. They were popularly said to have removed one breast the better to release their bowstrings. Other tales explained why a whole nation of women did not die out in a generation. The most common explanation was that the Amazons mated with men of another people and kept the resulting female children, while the male children were killed, maimed, or sent away to their fathers.

The legendary ninth Labor of Heracles (Hercules) was the taking of the girdle of Hippolyte (Hippolyta), queen of the Amazons. He succeeded, but Hippolyte was killed. In another tale, Theseus attacked the Amazons either with Heracles or independently. The Amazons in turn invaded Attica but were finally defeated, and at some point Theseus married an Amazon queen, Antiope (Hippolyte's sister). Another notable queen of the Amazons was Penthesilea, who was killed while helping to defend Troy.

A 20th-century retelling of Amazon narratives may be found within Marian Zimmer Bradley's *The Firebrand*, a popular account of the Trojan War.

Ambassadors, The   Novel by Henry JAMES, published in 1903. The "eye" of the story, Lambert Strether, is a Massachusetts editor engaged to the widowed Mrs. Newsome. Disturbed by reports concerning her son Chadwick's love life in Paris, Mrs. Newsome presses Strether to engineer the young man's return to his mother's sphere of influence. The Chad that Strether finds is, to his mind, an improvement over the former one, although the nature of his relationship with Marie de Vionnet, a few years his senior, and her young daughter Jeanne remains indeterminate. Strether's "investigations" proceed slowly with the aid of Miss Gostrey, an expatriate friend of the Vionnets. By the time the impatient Mrs. Newsome sends the Pococks (her daughter, son-in-law, and his sister Mamie, Chad's fiancée) as reinforcements, her son has voiced compliance, but Strether has now fallen under the Vionnets' spell. His discovery of Chad and Marie's affair is considered one of the sublime revelations in American literature. The Pococks eventually defer to Chad regarding the direction of his own future. He heeds Strether's advice to remain in Paris.

ambiguity \ˌam-bə-'gyü-ə-tē\   Use of words that allow alternative interpretations. In factual, explanatory prose, ambiguity is considered an error in reasoning or diction; in literary prose or poetry, it often functions to increase the richness and subtlety of language and to imbue it with a complexity that expands the literal meaning of the original statement. William Empson's classic *Seven Types of Ambiguity* (1930; rev. ed., 1947 and 1953) remains a useful treatment of the subject.

Ambler \'am-blər\, Eric (b. June 28, 1909, London, Eng.) Author widely regarded as one of the most distinguished writers of stories of espionage and of crime.

After studying engineering at London University, Ambler turned to literature and established his reputation with *The Dark Frontier* (1936), *Uncommon Danger* (1937; U.S. title, *Background to Danger*), *Epitaph for a Spy* (1938), *Cause for Alarm* (1938), *The Mask of Dimitrios* (1939; U.S. title, *A Coffin for Dimitrios*), and *Journey into Fear* (1940). Following service in World War II, Ambler wrote screenplays. With Charles Roda he wrote a series of novels under the joint pseudonym Eliot Reed. His first postwar book under his own name was *Judgment on Deltchev* (1951). *The Night-Comers* (1956; U.S. title, *State of Siege*) describes the fear engendered by a revolution in Southeast Asia. In a two-novel series, *The Light of Day* (1962) and *Dirty Story* (1967), he chronicled the life of a battered soldier of fortune who has been involved in shady deals in Istanbul, Athens, and central Africa. Later works include *The Levanter* (1972), *Doctor Frigo* (1974), *Send No More Roses* (1977; U.S. title, *The Siege of the Villa Lipp*), and *The Care of Time* (1981). Ambler's autobiography, *Here Lies*, was published in 1985.

Ambrose d'Évreux \än-'brwäz-dä-'vrœ\ (fl. *c.* 1190) Norman poet and chronicler, who accompanied Richard I of England as a minstrel on the Third Crusade. Nothing more is known of him than that he was probably a native of Évreux and was a noncombatant making the pilgrimage to Jerusalem. His account of the crusade is preserved in the *Estoire de la guerre sainte* ("History of the Holy War"), a poem of more than 12,000 lines extant in an Anglo-Norman manuscript; but the *Estoire* is only an adaptation of Ambrose's work. The original poem was used by Richard, a canon of Holy Trinity, London, as the source for his *Itinerarium Regis Ricardi* ("Concerning the Expedition of King Richard"). The *Estoire* has not much literary merit, but it is a valuable historical source.

ambrosia \am-'brō-zhə, -zhē-ə\ [Greek *ambrosia,* from feminine of *ambrosíos* immortal, divine] **1.** The food of the Greek and Roman gods. *Compare* NECTAR. **2.** The ointment or perfume of the gods.

Amenouzume \'äm-en-ō-,ü-zü-mä\, *in full* Amenouzume no Mikoto. In Japanese mythology, the celestial goddess who performed a spontaneous dance enticing the sun goddess Amaterasu out of the cave in which she had secluded herself and had thus deprived the world of light. In popular mythology, as the embodiment of the female principle, Amenouzume is often associated with SARUDAHIKO, who represents male sexuality.

American, The Novel by Henry JAMES, published serially in 1876 in *The Atlantic Monthly* and in book form a year later, and produced as a four-act play in 1891. *The American* is the story of a self-made American millionaire, Christopher Newman, whose guilelessness and forthrightness contrast him with a family of arrogant and cunning French aristocrats, the Bellegardes, whose daughter he unsuccessfully seeks to marry.

In 1868 Newman travels to Paris to submerge himself in European culture and to find himself a wife. He courts Claire de Cintré, an aristocratic young widow, but he is deemed socially unacceptable by Claire's older brother and by her mother. Newman befriends Claire's younger brother, Valentin, who, on his deathbed, tells Newman how he can blackmail the family

into approving the marriage with Claire, who has since joined a convent. Newman decides not to carry out his threat of blackmail, which nevertheless had failed to sway the Bellegardes' uncompromising allegiance to social class and family tradition.

American Academy of Arts and Letters *also called* (1904–92) The American Academy and Institute of Arts and Letters, *original name* National Institute of Arts and Letters. Organization founded 1898 whose stated purpose is to "foster, assist and sustain an interest" in literature, art, and music. The New York-based academy has 250 members.

The academy was the inspiration of H. Holbrook Curtis, a medical doctor, and Simeon E. Baldwin, a judge. After they had organized the original 250 members, they decided (perhaps with an eye to the Académie Française's 40 "Immortals") that they had not been exclusive enough; they renamed the 250-member body an institute and from among its members were elected the academy—an elite membership of 50. The first seven members, who were elected to the academy in 1904, were the writers William Dean Howells, Mark Twain, and Edmund C. Stedman, sculptor Augustus Saint-Gaudens, painter John LaFarge, composer Edward MacDowell, and historian-statesman John Hay. The first female member of the institute was Julia Ward Howe (author of "The Battle Hymn of the Republic"), who was elected to the institute in 1907 and to the academy in 1908. She was followed by Edith Wharton in 1926. In 1992 members voted to return to a single form of membership of 250, and the merger was announced in 1993. Membership in the academy is for life. One member, Wilhelm Diederich, was expelled in 1947 for using official stationery to write anti-Semitic letters.

Committees of the organization award to selected struggling artists any of several annual monetary gifts, including the Mildred and Harold Strauss Livings (to two distinguished prose writers for a period of five consecutive years).

American Buffalo Two-act play by David MAMET, produced in 1975 and published in 1976. With sparse action and vivid dialogue, it examines mistrust and dishonesty among the conspirators in an aborted burglary.

Don Dubrow, the owner of a junk shop where the action takes place, decides to steal a customer's coin collection when he feels that he has been bested in a transaction involving a buffalo nickel. He enlists the help of a young junkie named Bobby, but is convinced by a manipulative friend that Bobby is incompetent. Unable to trust either, Don invites a third person to join him. Bobby becomes a scapegoat as the burglary plot unravels and tensions build into suspicion, anger, and violence.

American Dream, The One-act drama by Edward ALBEE, published in 1959 (with *The Zoo Story*) and first produced in 1961. This brief absurdist drama established the playwright as an astute, acerbic critic of American values.

The American Dream addresses issues of childlessness and adoption. The play's central figures, Mommy and Daddy, represent banal American life. Clubwoman Mrs. Barker visits and Grandma reminds her of an earlier visit, when she brought an infant. This child did not turn out as Mommy and Daddy expected and so was abused by them until it died. When a handsome but emotionless young man—the American Dream—later arrives, Grandma suggests Mommy and Daddy adopt him, since his emptiness seems what they desire.

American Mercury \'mer-kyə-rē\ American monthly literary magazine known for its often satiric commentary on American life, politics, and customs. It was founded in 1924 by H.L. Mencken and George Jean Nathan.

Under the editorship of Mencken, the periodical fast gained a reputation for Mencken's vitriolic articles directed at the

American public (the "booboisie") and for Nathan's excellent theatrical criticism. Its fiction and other articles were the work of the most distinguished American authors and often the sharpest satiric minds of the day. Later, the magazine developed a militant anticommunist stand and a strident right-wing tone.

American Notes Nonfiction book written by Charles DICKENS, published in 1842. It is an account of his first visit to the United States, a five-month tour (January–June 1842) that led him to criticize the vulgarity and meanness he found there. Although he was a vocal critic of Britain's institutions, he had expected more from "the republic of my imagination" than he found in democratic America. Dickens protested the absence of copyright protection and made a vigorous attack on slavery. He continued his criticism of the United States in *Martin Chuzzlewit* (1844).

American Poetry Review, The Literary periodical founded in 1972 in Philadelphia by Stephen Berg and Stephen Parker. Issued bimonthly in a newspaper tabloid format, *The APR* sought a mass-market readership for its high-quality contributors and content. *The APR* offered an eclectic collection of serious poetry and prose by outstanding English-language writers and critics as well as works in translation from Europe, the Middle East, Africa, Latin America, and Asia. Contributors included Richard Wilbur, David Ignatow, Allen Ginsberg, Denise Levertov, Tess Gallagher, Adrienne Rich, Marge Piercy, May Swenson, William Stafford, Ntozake Shange, John Updike, Isaac Bashevis Singer, Vladimir Nabokov, Elie Wiesel, Octavio Paz, Czesław Miłosz, and Roland Barthes.

American Renaissance *also called* New England Renaissance. Period from the 1830s roughly until the end of the American Civil War in which American literature, in the wake of the Romantic movement, came of age as an expression of a national spirit.

The literary scene of the period was dominated by a group of New England writers, the BRAHMINS, notably Henry Wadsworth Longfellow, Oliver Wendell Holmes, and James Russell Lowell. They were aristocrats, steeped in foreign culture, active as professors at Harvard College, and interested in creating an American literature based on foreign models. Longfellow adapted European methods of storytelling and versifying to narrative poems dealing with American history; Holmes, in his occasional poems and his "Breakfast Table" series (1858–91), brought touches of urbanity and jocosity to polite literature; and Lowell put much of his homeland's outlook and values into verse, especially in his satirical *Biglow Papers* (1848–67).

One of the most important influences in the period was that of TRANSCENDENTALISM. This movement, centered in the village of Concord, Mass., and including among its members Ralph Waldo Emerson, Henry David Thoreau, Bronson Alcott, George Ripley, and Margaret Fuller, contributed to the founding of a new national culture based on native elements. The Transcendentalists advocated reforms in church, state, and society, fostering the rise of Free Religion and the abolition movement and the formation of various utopian communities, such as Brook Farm. The abolition movement was also bolstered by other New England writers, including the Quaker poet John Greenleaf Whittier and the novelist Harriet Beecher Stowe.

Apart from the Transcendentalists, there emerged during this period great imaginative writers—Nathaniel Hawthorne, Herman Melville, and Walt Whitman—whose novels and poetry left a permanent imprint on American literature. Contemporary with these writers but outside the New England circle was the Southern genius Edgar Allan Poe, who later in the century had a strong impact on European literature.

American Tragedy, An Novel by Theodore DREISER, published in 1925. It is a complex and compassionate account of the life and death of a young antihero named Clyde GRIFFITHS. The novel begins with Clyde's blighted background, recounts his path to success, and culminates in his apprehension, trial, and execution for murder. The book was called by one influential critic "the worst-written great novel in the world," but its questionable grammar and style are transcended by its narrative power. Dreiser's intricate speculations on the extent of Clyde's guilt are countered by his searing indictment of materialism and the American dream of success.

Amerika \ä-ˈmä-rē-kä\ Unfinished novel by Franz KAFKA, written between 1912 and 1914 and prepared for publication by Max Brod in 1927, three years after the author's death. The manuscript was entitled *Der Verschollene* ("The Lost One"). Kafka had published the first chapter separately under the title *Der Heizer* ("The Stoker") in 1913.

The narrative concerns the efforts of young Karl Rossmann, newly arrived in America, to find his place in an enigmatic and hostile society. The account of his expulsion from his parents' household in Prague following an affair with the family cook exhibits the surreal distortion of memory that characterizes much of Kafka's best work. The narration becomes increasingly conventional, however, in the later sections recounting Karl's exploitation. The novel breaks off just as the protagonist has seemingly found his niche with the traveling Oklahoma Theater.

Amhurst \ˈam-ərst\, Nicholas (b. Oct. 16, 1697, Marden, Kent, Eng.—d. April 12, 1742, Twickenham, Middlesex) Satirical poet, political pamphleteer on behalf of the Whigs, and editor of *The Craftsman*, a political journal of unprecedented popularity.

Expelled from the University of Oxford in 1719, Amhurst settled in London and began a series of satirical papers entitled *Terrae Filius* ("Son of the Land"). *The Craftsman*, founded in 1726, published articles by Tories as well as by Whigs. In 1737 Amhurst published in it a letter purporting to come from Colley Cibber, then poet laureate, attacking the new (censorship) act for licensing plays; for this "suspected libel," Amhurst and the printer of the journal were imprisoned. After release he was forgotten and passed the rest of his life in obscurity and poverty.

Amichai \ˌä-mi-ˈkī\, Yehuda (b. May 3, 1924, Würzburg, Ger.) Israeli writer who is best known for his poetry.

Amichai and his Orthodox Jewish family immigrated to Palestine in 1936; he lived in Jerusalem and attended the Hebrew University. He served in the British army during World War II but later fought the British as a guerrilla prior to the formation of Israel.

Amichai's poetry reflects his total commitment to the state of Israel, and from his first collection, *Akhshav u-ve-yamim aherim* (1955; "Now and in Other Days"), he employed biblical images and Jewish history. He also compared modern times with ancient, heroic ages and sought to expand biblical language in order to encompass contemporary phenomena. In the 1970s he introduced sexuality as a subject in his poems. The English-language collection *The Selected Poetry of Yehuda Amichai* (1986) contains translated selections from his many Hebrew volumes. Apart from short stories and two plays, Amichai wrote novels, of which the best known is *Lo meachshav, lo mi-kan* (1963; *Not of This Time, Not of This Place*), about the quest for identity of a Jewish immigrant to Israel. *Gam ha-ˈegrof hayah paˈam yad petuḥah* (1989; *Even a Fist Was Once an Open Palm with Fingers*) is a selection of his poetry in translation.

Amiel \ȧm-'yel\, Henri Frédéric (b. Sept. 27, 1821, Geneva, Switz.—d. May 11, 1881, Geneva) Swiss writer known for his *Journal intime*, a widely translated masterpiece of self-analysis. Despite apparent success as professor of aesthetics and later of philosophy at Geneva, Amiel felt himself a failure. Driven inward, he lived in his *Journal*, which he kept from 1847 until his death. First published in part as *Fragments d'un journal intime* (1883–84; later enlarged editions; definitive edition, 1939–48), it reveals a sensitive man of great intellectual ability, struggling for values against the skepticism of the age.

Amiles *see* AMIS AND AMILES.

ʿĀmilī, al- \ȧl-'ä-mē-,lē, *Arabic* -"ä-\, Bahāʾ ad-Dīn Muḥammad ibn Ḥusayn, *also called* Shaykh Bahāʾī \'shāḵ-bȧ-'hä-,ē, 'shīḵ\ (b. March 20, 1546, Baalbek, Syria—d. Aug. 20, 1622, Iran) Poet, theologian, mathematician, jurist, and astronomer who was a major figure in the cultural revival of Iran during the Ṣafavid dynasty (1502–1736).

Al-ʿĀmilī was the son of a Shīʿite theologian. After his family left Syria in 1559 to escape persecution by the Ottoman Turks, he lived in Herāt (now in Afghanistan) and Eṣfahān (Isfahan), Iran. He attached himself to the court of ʿAbbās I the Great, serving for many years as the chief judge of Eṣfahān.

In his poetry al-ʿĀmilī expounded complex mystical doctrines in simple and unadorned verse. His best-known poem, *Nān u-ḥalwā* ("Bread and Sweets"), describes the experiences of an itinerant holy man who may well be al-ʿĀmilī himself on the Mecca pilgrimage. *Kashkūl* ("The Beggar's Bowl"), containing both stories and verses, was translated widely.

His major work of astronomy is *Tashrīhuʾl-aflāk* ("Anatomy of the Heavens"). Al-ʿĀmilī also revived mathematical sciences in Iran and is noted for his *Khulāṣat al-ḥisāb* ("The Essentials of Arithmetic").

a minore \ä-mi-'nō-rē, mī-, -rä\ [Latin, from the lesser] In prosody, of or relating to an IONIC foot beginning with two short syllables.

Amīr Khosrow \'a-,mēr-'ḵȯs-,rō\ (b. 1253, Patiāli, Uttar Pradesh [India]—d. 1325, Delhi) Poet and historian, considered one of India's greatest Persian-language poets.

Amīr Khosrow for his entire life enjoyed the patronage of the Muslim rulers of Delhi. Sometimes known as "the parrot of India," Amīr Khosrow wrote numerous works, among them five divans, which were compiled at different periods in his life, and his *Khamsah* ("Pentalogy"), a group of five long idylls in emulation of the *Khamseh* of the celebrated Persian poet Neẓāmī (c. 1141–1209). Amīr Khosrow's pentalogy deals with general themes famous in Islāmic literature. In addition to his poetry, he is known for a number of prose works, including the *Khazāʾin al-futūḥ* ("The Treasure-Chambers of the Victories"), also known by the title *Tārīkh-e ʿAlāʾī* ("The History of ʿAla"). Two historical poems for which he is well known are *Nuh Sipihr* ("The Nine Heavens") and the *Tughluq-nāmah* ("The Book of Tughluq").

Amis \'ā-mis\, Kingsley, *in full* Sir Kingsley Amis (b. April 16, 1922, London, Eng.) Novelist, poet, critic, and teacher who created in his first novel, *Lucky Jim* (1954; film, 1957), a comic figure who became a household word in Great Britain in the 1950s. Amis was generally grouped among the ANGRY YOUNG MEN, though he denied the affiliation. He was the father of writer Martin Amis.

Amis was educated at St. John's College, Oxford (B.A., 1949), with an interruption during World War II for service in the Royal Corps of Signals. During his 12 years as a lecturer in English at the University College of Swansea in Wales, he began publishing poetry and fiction.

Amis' poetry is not particularly distinguished. *Lucky Jim*, however, was an immediate hit, and Amis' later novels continued to strike a chord with many readers. His apparent lack of sympathy with his characters and his sharply satirical rendering of well-turned dialogue were enhanced by his own curmudgeonly persona. He wrote more than 40 books, including some 20 novels, many volumes of poetry, and several collections of essays; particularly notable are the novels *That Uncertain Feeling* (1955; film, *Only Two Can Play*), *The Green Man* (1969), *Jake's Thing* (1978), and *The Old Devils* (1986), which won the Booker Prize. In 1990 Amis was knighted. In 1991 he published an entertaining but mostly nasty collection of anecdotes about his contemporaries and (usually former) friends, entitled *Memoirs*.

Amis \'ā-mis\, Martin (b. Aug. 25, 1949, Oxford, Eng.) Writer and critic who is known for his fascination with the grotesque as well as his inventive literary style.

The son of writer Kingsley Amis, Martin Amis was educated at Exeter College, Oxford. After graduating in 1971 he worked for the *Times Literary Supplement* (1972–75) and the *New Statesman* (1975–79) before becoming a full-time writer. His novels include *The Rachel Papers* (1973), *Dead Babies* (1975), *Success* (1978), *Money: A Suicide Note* (1984), and *London Fields* (1989). His works are full of inventive word play as they satirize the horrors of modern urban life and depict the often brutal way individuals treat each other. In his novel *Time's Arrow* (1991), Amis relates in reverse chronology the life of a German doctor who participated in his profession's notorious atrocities during the Nazi era.

Amis and Amiles \ȧ-'mē . . . ȧ-'mēl\ Chief characters in an Old French metrical romance based on an older and widespread legend of friendship and sacrifice. In its simplest form the story tells of the knights Amis and Amiles and of their lifelong devotion to one another.

The tale, probably of Oriental origin, was introduced to the West by way of Byzantium and found its way into French literature through Latin (hence the characters' names: "Amicus" and "Amelius" in Latin). It became attached to the web of Charlemagne legends in the late 12th-century chanson de geste of *Amis et Amiles*, a poem that contains passages of great beauty, and later versions appeared in most European languages. The first version of the story in English was *Amis and Amiloun*, composed in the Midlands dialect toward the end of the 13th century.

Ammers-Küller \vän-'äm-ȧrs-'kᵫl-ȧr\, Jo van, *in full* Johanna van Ammers-Küller (b. Aug. 13, 1884, Noordeloos, Neth.—d. Jan. 23, 1966, Bakel) Dutch writer best known for her historical novels.

Van Ammers-Küller began her writing career as a playwright. Her first successful novels, *Het huis der vreugden* (1922; *The House of Joy*) and *Jenny Huysten* (1923; *Jenny Huysten's Career*), deal with life in and around the theater and draw on her experiences as a dramatist in London from 1912 to 1921. Her most successful novel, *De opstandigen* (1925; *The Rebel Generation*), presents the struggle of three generations of women in the Coornvelt family for equality with men and against the strictures of their Calvinist environment.

The family saga was a form that particularly suited van Ammers-Küller, and she wrote several more historical novels. Her pro-German stand during World War II contributed to the waning of her popularity after the war.

Ammianus Marcellinus \,am-ē-'ä-nȧs-,mär-sȧ-'lī-nȧs\ (b. *c.* 330, Antioch, Syria [now Antakya, Tur.]—d. 395, Rome [Italy]) Last major Roman historian, whose work continued the history of the later Roman Empire to 378.

Born of a noble Greek family, Ammianus served in the army of Constantius II in Gaul and Persia. He eventually settled in Rome, where he wrote his Latin history of the Roman Empire from the accession of Nerva to the death of Valens, thus continuing the work of Tacitus.

This history, *Rerum gestarum libri* ("The Chronicles of Events"), consisted of 31 books, of which only the last 18, covering the years 353–378, survive. It is a clear, comprehensive account of events by a writer of soldierly qualities, independent judgment, and wide reading. Drawing upon his own experience, Ammianus presents vivid pictures of the empire's economic and social problems. A pagan who was religiously tolerant, he took a detached view of the intellectual trends of the day. His judgment in political affairs was limited only by his own straightforward attitude. He used the regular techniques of later Roman historiography—rhetoric in his speeches, ethnographical digressions in descriptions and characterizations, along with literary allusion, overabundant metaphor, and much verbal ornament. In conscious imitation of Tacitus, he wrote with vivid and striking dramatic power.

Ammons \'am-ənz\, A.R., *in full* Archie Randolph (Feb. 18, 1926, Whiteville, N.C., U.S.) American poet, one of the leading late 20th-century exponents of the Transcendentalist tradition.

A 1949 graduate of Wake Forest College (now University), Ammons worked as an elementary school principal and as a glass company executive before turning his full attention to literature. From 1964 he taught creative writing at Cornell University. In his first collection of poems, *Ommateum: With Doxology* (1955), Ammons wrote about nature and the self, themes that remained the central focus of his work. Subsequent books, such as *Expressions of Sea Level* (1963), *Tape for the Turn of the Year* (1965; composed on adding-machine tape), and *Uplands* (1970), continued the poet's investigation into the relationship between the knowable and the unknowable. Ammons' style is both cerebral and conversational, embodying the often lofty meditations of one well-rooted in the mundane. Among the clearest influences on his work were Robert Frost, Wallace Stevens, and William Carlos Williams. His later work—notably *A Coast of Trees* (1981), which won a National Book Critics Circle Award, and *Sumerian Vistas* (1988)—exhibit a mature command of imagery and ideas, balancing the scientific approach to the universe with a subjective, even romantic one. *Garbage* (1993), Ammons' book-length poem, received a National Book Award in 1993.

amoebean verse \,am-ē-'bē-ən, ,am-i-\ [Greek *amoibaîos* interchanging, reciprocating] Poetry written in the form of a dialogue between two speakers. *Compare* STICHOMYTHIA. An example is the English popular ballad *Lord Randal*, which begins:

> "O where ha' you been, Lord Randal, my son?
> And where ha' you been, my handsome young man?"
> "I ha' been at the greenwood; mother, mak my bed soon,
> For I'm wearied wi' huntin', and fain wad lie down."

amorist \'am-ər-ist\ or **amourist** \'am-ər-ist, ə-'mùr-\ [Latin *amor* or French *amour* love] One who writes about romantic love.

Amoroso Lima \à-mō-'rō-zō-'lē-mə\, Alceu, *pseudonym* Tristão de Athayde \à-'tïj-ē\ (b. Dec. 11, 1893, Rio de Janeiro, Braz.—d. Aug. 15, 1983, Rio de Janeiro) Essayist, philosopher, and literary critic, a leading champion of the cause of intellectual freedom in Brazil. He was also an enthusiastic supporter of Modernismo, a Brazilian cultural movement of the 1920s, and, after his conversion to Roman Catholicism in 1928, a leader in the Neo-Catholic intellectual movement.

Amoroso Lima's multifaceted career included positions as professor of sociology, law, and literature, university president, literary critic for the *Jornal do Brasil* and numerous other periodicals, and director of the Cultural Division of the Pan American Union in Washington, D.C. (1951–53). He was elected to the Brazilian Academy of Letters (1935) and was a founder of the Agir Publishing House (1944). *Tristão de Athayde: Teoria, crítica e história literária* (1980; "Tristão de Athayde: Theory, Criticism, and Literary History") is a representative collection of Amoroso Lima's works on the art of literature, the role of the critic, and critical theory.

Amory \'ā-mə-rē\, Thomas (b. 1691?—d. Nov. 25, 1788, London?, Eng.) British writer of Irish descent, best known for his extravagant "autobiography," *The Life of John Buncle*, 2 vol. (1756 and 1766), in which the hero marries seven wives in succession, each wife embodying one of Amory's ideals of womanhood. Rich, racy, and eccentric, his works contain something of the spirit of Charles Dickens and François Rabelais.

A staunch Unitarian and a student of medicine, geology, and antiquities, he filled his writings with information on these and other subjects. He is thought to have lived in Dublin and later at Westminster.

Amos \'ā-məs\ (fl. 8th century BC) The first Hebrew prophet to have a biblical book named for him. He accurately foretold the destruction of the northern kingdom of Israel, and, as a prophet of doom, anticipated later Old Testament prophets.

Little is known of Amos' life. Under the impact of powerful visions of divine destruction of the Hebrews in such natural disasters as a swarm of locusts and fire, Amos traveled from Judah to the neighboring kingdom of Israel, where he began to preach. He fiercely castigated corruption and social injustice among Israel's pagan neighbors, Israel itself, and Judah; he asserted God's absolute sovereignty over mortals; and he predicted the imminent destruction of Israel and Judah. After preaching at Bethel, a famous shrine under the special protection of Israel's king Jeroboam II, Amos was ordered to leave the country. Thereafter his fate is unknown.

From his book in the Hebrew scriptures, Amos emerges as a thoughtful, probably well-traveled man of fierce integrity, who possessed a poet's gift for homely but forceful imagery and rhythmic language.

amour courtois [French] *see* COURTLY LOVE.

Ampère \äⁿ-'per\, Jean-Jacques(-Antoine) (b. Aug. 12, 1800, Lyon, Fr.—d. March 27, 1864, Pau) French historian and philologist who initiated important studies of the diverse cultural origins of western European languages and mythology.

The son of the distinguished scientist André-Marie Ampère, Jean-Jacques Ampère in 1826 made his first journey to Germany. On the basis of his study of Scandinavian mythology, Ampère was named to a chair in the history of foreign literature at the Sorbonne in Paris in 1830; three years later he became a professor at the Collège de France, where he did the research for his major philological works, *Histoire littéraire de la France avant le douzième siècle*, 3 vol. (1839–40; "History of French Literature Before the 12th Century"), and *Histoire de la formation de la langue française* (1841; "History of the Development of the French Language"). Enamored of the famous beauty and hostess Madame de Récamier, who was much older than he, Ampère was a habitué of her salon. In 1848 he was elected to the Académie Française. Ampère's major historical work is *L'Histoire romaine à Rome*, 4 vol. (1861–64; "Roman History in Rome"); his other works include *De l'histoire de la poésie* (1830; "On the History of Poetry") and *Promenade en Amérique: États-Unis, Cuba et Mexique* (1855; "Travels in America: The United States, Cuba, and Mexico").

amphibology \,am-fə-'bäl-ə-jē\ or **amphiboly** \am-'fib-ə-lē\ [Greek *amphibolía* ambiguity, a derivative of *amphíbolos* doubtful, ambiguous] A sentence or phrase susceptible of more than one interpretation, such as "Nothing is good enough for you."

amphibrach \'am-fə-,brak\ [Greek *amphíbrachys*, literally, short at both ends, from *amphi-* around, on both sides + *brachýs* short] In prosody, a three-syllable foot consisting in quantitative verse of a long syllable between two short syllables or in accentual verse of a stressed syllable between two unstressed syllables. An example of the amphibrach is:

ŭ ´ ŭ
ămázemĕnt.

The inverse of this meter is the amphimacer.

amphigory \'am-fi-,gȯr-ē, am-'fig-ə-rē\ or **amphigouri** \,äⁿ-fē-gü-'rē\ *plural* amphigories *or* amphigouris [French *amphigouri*] A nonsense verse or parody (such as those written by Edward Lear and Lewis Carroll) or any composition that appears to have meaning, but proves to have none (such as Algernon Swinburne's "Nephelidia").

amphimacer \am-'fim-ə-sər\ [Greek *amphímakros*, from *amphí* on both sides of, around + *makrós* long] Outmoded term once interchangeable with CRETIC.

Amphion and Zethus \am-'fī-ən . . . 'zē-thəs\ In Greek mythology, the twin sons of Zeus by Antiope. When children, they were left to die on Mount Cithaeron but were found and brought up by a shepherd. Amphion became a great singer and musician, Zethus a hunter and herdsman.

amphisbaena \,am-fəs-'bē-nə\ [Greek *amphísbaina*, from *amphís* on both sides + *-baina* one who walks] A legendary serpent having a head at each end and being capable of moving in either direction. The amphisbaena is mentioned by Pliny the Elder, by Brunetto Latini in his *Tesoretto*, and by Sir Thomas Browne, who doubted the existence of such a creature.

Amphitrite \,am-fə-'trī-tē\ In Greek mythology, the goddess of the sea, wife of the god Poseidon, and one of the 50 (or 100) daughters (the Nereids) of Nereus and Doris (the daughter of Oceanus). Poseidon chose Amphitrite from among her sisters as the Nereids performed a dance on the isle of Naxos. Refusing his offer of marriage, she fled to Atlas, from whom she was retrieved by a dolphin sent by Poseidon. Amphitrite then returned, becoming Poseidon's wife; he rewarded the dolphin by making it a constellation.

Amphitryon \am-'fit-rē-ən\ In Greek mythology, the son of Alcaeus, king of Tiryns. Having accidentally killed his uncle Electryon, king of Mycenae, Amphitryon fled with Alcmene, Electryon's daughter, to Thebes, where he was cleansed from the guilt by Creon, king of Thebes.

In one of the legends concerning Amphitryon, he is rebuffed by Alcmene until he manages to avenge the deaths of her brothers. The more famous portion of the myth concerns Amphitryon's wife. When Amphitryon was once absent at war, Alcmene became pregnant by Zeus disguised as her husband; she became pregnant again by her real husband upon his return. Of these unions were born twin boys, of whom Iphicles was the son of Amphitryon, Heracles the son of Zeus. A number of ancient dramatists presented the theme, notably Plautus, whose comedy *Amphitruo* still survives.

amplification \,am-pli-fi-'kā-shən\ [Latin *amplificatio* (translation of Greek *aúxēsis*), a derivative of *amplificare* to enlarge upon, emphasize, literally, to enlarge] A rhetorical device or figure of speech that extends or enlarges a statement or idea. The subject of amplification was a matter of concern for many of the ancient rhetoricians, including Aristotle, Quintilian, and Cicero. Well-suited to epic and tragic forms, amplification is a standard device in much great literature.

'Amr ibn Kulthūm \'äm-ər-,ib-ən-kùl-'thüm, *Arabic* "äm-\ (fl. 6th century) Pre-Islāmic Arab poet included among the seven poets of the celebrated anthology of pre-Islāmic verse *Al-Mu'allaqāt*.

Little is known of 'Amr ibn Kulthūm's life. He became chief of the tribe of Taghlib in Mesopotamia at an early age and according to tradition killed 'Amr ibn Hind, the Arab king of al-Ḥīrah, about 568.

'Amr ibn Kulthūm lived to a very advanced age and was highly respected for his noble character and for a poem, allegedly his, praising a Taghlib victory over the Bakr tribe. 'Amr ibn Kulthūm's qasida (ode) as it appears in *Al-Mu'allaqāt* was probably altered by a later poet. It violently attacks 'Amr ibn Hind for an insult addressed to the poet's mother.

Amrouche \äm-'rüsh\, Jean (b. Feb. 7, 1906, Ighil Ali, Alg.—d. April 16, 1962, Paris, Fr.) Foremost poet of the earliest generation of French-speaking North African writers.

Amrouche immigrated with his family to Tunisia when still quite young. He completed his studies in Tunis and Paris. As a young man, Amrouche published *Cendres* (1934; "Cinders") and *Étoile secrète* (1937; "Secret Star"), the most significant volumes of Algerian poetry ever written in French. Taking inspiration from his Berber roots as well as from modern European post-Symbolism, Amrouche testifies to the purity of his origins, evoking the quest for a lost homeland and the sense of ancestral nobility. A lyricist of the first order, he produced verses of eloquent and fluid beauty. Later works included a translation into French of Berber lyrics and an essay, "L'Éternel Jugurtha" (1946), that stands as the definitive statement on the Maghrebian identity torn by the complexes of acculturation and alienation.

Amrouche \äm-'rüsh\, Marguerite Taos, *original name* Marie-Louise Amrouche, *also called* Marguerite Taos (b. March 4, 1913, Tunis [now in Tunisia]—d. April 2, 1976, Saint-Michel-l'Observatoire, Fr.) Kabyle singer and writer.

Amrouche was born after the family had moved from Algeria to Tunisia to escape persecution following their conversion to Roman Catholicism. Despite this exile, both she and her brother Jean returned to Algeria for extended visits. Through her mother's influence she became interested in the rich oral traditions of the Kabyle Berber people. In 1934 she attended school in Tunis, and in the following year she went to France to study. Starting in 1936, with Jean and her mother, Amrouche collected and began to interpret Kabyle songs.

Amrouche's first novel, *Jacinthe noire* (1947; "Black Hyacinth"), is one of the earliest ever published in French by a North African woman writer. It recounts the story of an "uncivilized" young Tunisian girl who is sent to a French pension for studies. Differences in life-style, attitudes, and experiences set her apart, limning the novel's themes of exile, prejudice, and rupture. A second novel, *Rue des tambourins* (1960; "Street of the Tabors"), describes the protagonist's sense of marginality and owes a great deal to its author's recollections of her childhood in Tunis.

Amyot \äm-'yō\, Jacques (b. Oct. 30, 1513, Melun, near Paris, Fr.—d. Feb. 6, 1593, Auxerre) Bishop and classical scholar famous for his translation of Plutarch's *Parallel Lives* (*Les Vies des hommes illustres Grecs et Romains*, 1559), which became a major influence in shaping the Renaissance concept of the tragic hero.

Amyot was educated at Paris University and at Bourges, where he became professor of Latin and Greek and translated

Heliodorus' *Aethiopica*. For this Francis I gave him the abbey of Bellozane and commissioned him to complete his translation of Plutarch's *Lives*. He went to Rome to study the Vatican text of Plutarch. On his return to France he was appointed tutor to the sons of Henry II. Both favored him on accession, making him grand almoner and, in 1570, bishop of Auxerre. Amyot translated seven books of the *Bibliotheca historica* of Diodorus Siculus in 1554, the *Daphnis and Chloe* of Longus in 1559, and the *Moralia* of Plutarch in 1572, as well as the *Lives*.

Amyot's *Vies* was an important contribution to the development of Renaissance humanism in France and England. Moreover, Amyot supplied his readers with a sense of identification with the past and the writers of many generations with characters and situations to build upon. He also gave the French an example of simple and pure style. The work was translated into English by Sir Thomas North (1579), whose rendition was the source for William Shakespeare's Roman plays.

Anabasis \ə-'nab-ə-sis\ (*in full* Anabasis Kyrou; "Upcountry March")   Prose narrative account by XENOPHON of the experiences of the Greek mercenary soldiers who fought for Cyrus in his unsuccessful attempt to seize the Persian throne from his brother, Artaxerxes II. It contains a famous account of the mercenaries' long trek ("the march of the 10,000") from near Babylon to the Euxine (Black Sea). Xenophon, who had accompanied the force in a private capacity, was largely responsible for their successful retreat through his resourcefulness and courage.

anachronism \ə-'nak-rə-,niz-əm\ [Medieval Greek *anachronismós,* from Greek *aná* back + *chrónos* time]   Neglect or falsification, intentional or not, of chronological relation. It is most frequently found in works of imagination that rest on a historical basis, in which appear details borrowed from a later age; *e.g.,* a clock in William Shakespeare's *Julius Caesar*.

Anachronisms abound in early literature. With the development of modern realism, the progress of archaeological research, and the scientific approach to history, unconscious anachronism became an offense. On the other hand, a writer may deliberately introduce anachronisms to achieve a burlesque, satirical, or other desired effect; such intentional use effectively points up contrasts between the past and the present. Thus Mark Twain in his satirical novel *A Connecticut Yankee in King Arthur's Court* used anachronism to contrast homespun American ingenuity with the superstitious ineptitude of a chivalric monarchy.

anaclasis \ə-'nak-lə-sis\ *plural* anaclases \-,sēz\ [Greek *anáklasis* act of bending back, reflection]   In Greek prosody, an exchange of place between a short syllable and a preceding long one that is frequent in ionic rhythms.

anacoluthon \,an-ə-kə-'lü-,thän\ [Late Latin, from Greek, neuter of *anakólouthos* inconsistent, anomalous]   Syntactical inconsistency or incoherence within a sentence; especially, a shift in an unfinished sentence from one syntactic construction to another (as in "you really ought—well, do it your own way").

Anacreon or **Anakreon** \ə-'nak-rē-ən\ (b. *c.* 582 BC, Teos, Ionia—d. *c.* 485)   Last great lyric poet of Asian Greece. Only fragments of his poetry have survived. He spent much of his life at the court of Polycrates of Samos; later he lived at Athens, writing mostly under the patronage of Hipparchus.

Though Anacreon may well have written serious poems, those that were quoted by later writers are chiefly in praise of love and wine. He disliked the excessive and the unrefined, however, and his treatment of these subjects is unusually formal. His sentiments and style were widely imitated, and the anacreontic meter in poetry was named for him.

Later writers influenced by Anacreon include the 16th-century French poet Pierre de Ronsard and the 19th-century Italian Giacomo Leopardi.

anacreontic \ə-,nak-rē-'än-tik\   **1.** In Greek prosody, one of the aeolic meters used for lyric poetry. It originated with Anacreon. The basic unit of anacreontic verse was scanned as: ∪ ∪ − ∪ − ∪ − −.   **2.** A poem in imitation of or in the manner of Anacreon; especially, a drinking song or light lyric. The best-known examples in English are those of Abraham Cowley and Thomas Moore.

anacrusis \,an-ə-'krü-sis\ *plural* anacruses \-,sēz\, *also called* arsis \'är-sis\ [Greek *anákrousis* act of pushing back, beginning of a tune]   In classical prosody, the up (or weak) beat, one or more syllables at the beginning of a line of poetry that are not regarded as a part of the metrical pattern of that line. Some scholars do not acknowledge this phenomenon.

anadiplosis \,an-ə-di-'plō-sis\ *plural* anadiploses \-,sēz\ [Greek *anadíplōsis,* literally, doubling, repetition]   A device in which the last word or phrase of one clause, sentence, or line is repeated at the beginning of the next. An example is the phrase that is repeated between stanzas one and two of John Keats's poem "The Eve of St. Agnes":

> Numb were the beadsman's fingers, while he told
> His rosary, and while his frosted breath,
> Like pious incense from a censer old,
> Seem'd taking flight for heaven, without a death,
> Past the sweet Virgin's picture, while his prayer he saith.
>
> His prayer he saith, this patient, holy man:

anagnorisis \,an-əg-'nòr-ə-sis\ [Greek *anagnôrisis,* literally, recognition]   In a literary work, the startling discovery that produces a change from ignorance to knowledge. Anagnorisis is discussed by Aristotle in the *Poetics* as an essential part of the plot of a tragedy, although it occurs in comedy, epic, and, at a later date, in the novel as well.

Anagnorisis usually involves revelation of the true identity of persons previously unknown, as when a father recognizes a stranger as his son, or vice versa. One of the finest examples occurs in Sophocles' *Oedipus the King* when a messenger reveals to Oedipus his true birth and Oedipus then recognizes his wife Jocasta as his mother, the man he slew at the crossroads as his father, and himself as the unnatural sinner who brought misfortune on Thebes. This recognition is the more artistically satisfying because it is accompanied by a PERIPETEIA ("reversal"), the shift in fortune from good to bad that moves on to the tragic catastrophe. An anagnorisis is not always accompanied by a peripeteia. In the *Odyssey,* for example, when Alcinous, ruler of Phaeacia, has his minstrel entertain a shipwrecked stranger with songs of the Trojan War, the stranger begins to weep and reveals himself as none other than Odysseus. Aristotle discusses several kinds of anagnorisis employed by dramatists. The simplest kind, used, as he says, "from poverty of wit," is recognition by scars, birthmarks, or tokens. More interesting are those that arise naturally from incidents of the plot.

anagram \'an-ə-,gram\ [Greek *anagrammatismós,* a derivative of *anagrammatízein* to transpose letters so as to form an anagram, from *aná* up + *grámma* letter]   A word or phrase made by transposing the letters of another word or phrase, such as *calm* and *clam*. The construction of anagrams is of great antiquity. Their invention is often ascribed without authority to the Jews, probably because the later Hebrew writers, particularly the Kabbalists, were fond of them, asserting that "secret mysteries are woven in the numbers of letters." Anagrams were known to the Greeks and Romans and were popular throughout Europe during the Middle Ages. Some scientists of the 17th century—Galileo, Christiaan Huygens, and Robert Hooke, for example—embodied their discoveries in anagrams, while they were engaged in further verification, to keep others from claiming the credit.

Analects   *see* LUN YÜ.

analects \'an-ə-ˌlekts\ [Greek *análekta,* neuter plural of *análektos,* verbal adjective of *analégein* to gather up, collect] Selected miscellaneous written passages.

analogue or **analog** \'an-ə-ˌlȯg, -ˌläg\ [French *analogue,* from Greek *análogon,* neuter of *análogos* having a relationship, proportional] Something that is analogous or similar to something else. In literature the word refers to a story for which there is a counterpart or another version in other literatures. Several of the stories in Geoffrey Chaucer's *The Canterbury Tales* are versions of earlier tales that can be found in such sources as Giovanni Boccaccio's *Decameron* and John Gower's *Confessio amantis.* The French medieval beast fable *Roman de Renart* has analogues in several languages.

analytical bibliography   *see* CRITICAL BIBLIOGRAPHY.

anamnesis \ˌan-am-'nē-sis\ [Greek *anámnēsis,* a derivative of *anamnéiskesthai* to recall, remember] A recalling to mind, or reminiscence. Anamnesis is often used as a narrative technique in fiction and poetry as well as in memoirs and autobiographies. A notable example is Marcel Proust's *Remembrance of Things Past.*

Anand \'än-ənd\, Mulk Raj (b. Dec. 12, 1905, Peshāwar, India)   Prominent Indian author of novels, short stories, and critical essays in English known for his realistic and sympathetic portrayal of the poor in India.

Anand graduated with honors in 1924 from Punjab University, Lahore, and pursued additional studies at the University of Cambridge and at University College, London. While in Europe, he became active in India's struggle for independence and shortly thereafter wrote a series of books on diverse aspects of South Asian culture, including *Persian Painting* (1930), *Curries and Other Indian Dishes* (1932), *The Hindu View of Art* (1933), *The Indian Theatre* (1950), and *Seven Little-Known Birds of the Inner Eye* (1978).

Anand first gained wide recognition for his novels *Untouchable* (1935) and *Coolie* (1936), both of which examined the problems of poverty in Indian society. In 1945 he returned to Bombay to campaign for national reforms. Among his other major works are *The Village* (1939), *The Sword and the Sickle* (1942), and *The Big Heart* (1945; rev. ed., 1980). Anand wrote several other novels and collections of short stories and edited numerous magazines and journals. Parts of a projected seven-volume autobiographical novel (vol. 1. 1951; vol. 2, 1968; vol. 3, 1976; vol. 4, 1984) also were published.

Ananke \ə-'naŋ-kē\   In post-Homeric Greek literature, a personification of compelling necessity or ultimate fate to which even the gods must yield.

Ananke is particularly prominent in the mystic cult of Orphism, but is definitely known to emerge into a cult only at Corinth. Because of her unalterable nature it was pointless to render to her offerings or sacrifice—"Nothing is stronger than dread Necessity" was a Greek byword.

In literature Ananke is associated with the nymph Adrasteia, the Moirai (or Fates, of whom she was the mother, according to Plato in the *Republic*), and similar deities.

anapest \'an-ə-ˌpest\ or **anapaest** \'an-ə-ˌpēst\ [Greek *anápaistos,* literally, struck back (i.e., the reverse of a dactyl)]   In verse, a metrical foot of three syllables, the first two being unstressed and the last being stressed (as in Edgar Allen Poe's

" 'Tis the vault of thy lost Ulalume!") or the first two being short and the last being long (as in classical prosody).

First found in early Spartan marching songs, anapestic meters were widely used in Greek and Latin dramatic verse, especially for the entrance and exit of the chorus. (The classical anapest is scanned ∪ ∪ – ∪ ∪ –.) Lines composed primarily of anapestic feet, often with an additional unstressed syllable at the end of the first line, are much rarer in English verse. Because of its jog-trot rhythm, pure anapestic meter was originally used only in light or popular English verse, but after the 18th century it appeared in serious poetry. Byron used it effectively to convey a sense of excitement and galloping in "The Destruction of Sennacherib":

The Assyr|ian came down|like a wolf | on the fold.

And his co|horts were gleam|ing in pur|ple and gold.

In Algernon Charles Swinburne's "By the North Sea," however, anapestic trimeter conveys a more subdued effect:

And his hand | is not wea|ry of giv|ing.

And the thirst | of her heart|is not fed.

anaphora \ə-'naf-ə-rə\ [Late Greek *anaphorá,* from Greek, the act of carrying back]   Repetition of a word or words at the beginning of two or more successive clauses or verses especially for rhetorical or poetic effect.

An example of anaphora is the well-known passage from the Old Testament (Ecclesiastes 3:1–2) that begins:

> For everything there is a season, and a time
>   for every matter under heaven:
> a time to be born, and a time to die;
> a time to plant, and a time to pluck up
>   what is planted; . . .

Anaphora (sometimes called epanaphora) is used most effectively for emphasis in argumentative prose and sermons and in poetry, as in these lines from Shakespeare's *Hamlet:* "to die, to sleep / To sleep—perchance to dream."

anastrophe \ə-'nas-trə-fē\ [Greek *anastrophé,* literally, turning back, upsetting]   The deliberate inversion of the usual syntactical order of words for rhetorical effect. An example is the locution "I kid you not."

anatomy \ə-'nat-ə-mē\ [Greek *anatomḗ* dissection]   A separating or dividing into parts for detailed examination, or an analysis. In literature the word has been applied to several well-known examinations of general topics, notably John Lyly's *Euphues: The Anatomy of Wit* and Robert Burton's *Anatomy of Melancholy.* The literary critic Northrop Frye, in his book *Anatomy of Criticism,* narrowed the definition of the word in literature to mean a work resembling a Menippean satire, or one in which a mass of information was brought to bear on the subject being satirized, usually a particular attitude or type of behavior.

Anatomy of Criticism: Four Essays   Work of literary criticism by Northrop FRYE, published in 1957 and generally considered the author's most important work. In his introduction, Frye explains that his initial intention to examine the poetry of Edmund Spenser had given way in the process to a broader survey of the ordering principles of literary theory. The four essays address modes, symbols, myths, and genres, corresponding respectively to what Frye sees as the historical, ethical, archetypal, and rhetorical dimensions of literary expression. In his view, the task of evaluating a particular poem or novel falls to the reviewer, while the critic brings to light those aspects of a work that situate it within the body of literature.

Anatomy of Melancholy (*in full* Anatomy of Melancholy, What it is; with all the Kindes, Causes, Symptomes, Prognostickes and Several Cures of it: In Three Maine Partitions With Their Several Sections, Members, and Subsections, Philosophically, Medicinally, Historically Opened and Cut up, by Democritus Junior)   Exposition by Robert BURTON, published in 1621 and expanded and altered in five subsequent editions (1624, 1628, 1632, 1638, 1651/52).

In the first part of the treatise, Burton defines the "inbred malady" of melancholy, discusses its causes, and sets down the symptoms. The second part is devoted to its cure. Love melancholy is the subject of the first three sections of the third part. A master of narrative, Burton includes as examples most of the world's great love stories, again showing a modern approach to psychological problems. The fourth section deals with religious melancholy, and on the cure of despair he rises to heights of wisdom and of meditation.

Burton's lively, colloquial style is as individual as his subject matter. It is imaginative and eloquent, full of classical allusions and Latin tags that testify to his love of curious and out-of-the-way information as well as to his erudition. He is a master of lists and catalogs, but their sonorous roll is often broken by his humorous asides.

Anaya \ä-'nī-ə\, Rudolfo A., *in full* Alfonso (b. Oct. 30, 1937, Pastura, New Mexico, U.S.)   American novelist and educator whose fiction expressed his Mexican-American heritage, the tradition of folklore and oral storytelling in Spanish, and the Jungian mythic perspective.

Anaya graduated from the University of New Mexico and worked as a public school teacher from 1963 to 1970. He then became director of counseling at the University of Albuquerque. From 1974 he taught at the University of New Mexico.

Bless Me, Ultima (1972), Anaya's acclaimed first novel, concerns a young boy growing up in New Mexico in the late 1940s. *Heart of Aztlán* (1976) follows a family's move from rural to urban surroundings and confronts some of the problems of Chicano laborers. In *Tortuga* (1979), a boy encased in a body cast stays at a hospital for paralyzed children. These three novels make up a trilogy about Hispanic children in the United States. The novel *The Legend of La Llorona* (1984) is about La Malinche, an Indian slave who became the consort of the conquistador Hernán Cortés. Anaya's other works include *The Adventures of Juan Chicaspatas* (1985) and his nonfiction *A Chicano in China* (1986).

Ancaeus \an-'sē-əs\   In Greek mythology, the son of Zeus or Poseidon and king of the Leleges of Samos. In accounts of the Argonautic expedition, Ancaeus became helmsman of the *Argo* after the death of Tiphys. Traditionally, while planting a vineyard, he was told by a seer that he would never drink of its wine. When the grapes were ripe, he squeezed the juice into a cup and, raising it to his lips, mocked the seer, who retorted with the words "There is many a slip between cup and the lip." At that moment it was announced that a wild boar was ravaging the land. Ancaeus set down the cup, leaving the wine untasted, hurried out, and was killed by the boar.

anceps \'än-,cheps, 'an-,seps\ [Latin, equivocal, literally, facing in opposite directions]   In classical prosody, a syllable in a metrical pattern that is of indeterminate length or duration, that is, one that can be either long or short. In scansion, anceps is indicated by the symbol ⌣ or ✕.

Anchieta \äⁿ-'shet-ə\, José de (b. March 19, 1534, Canary Islands—d. June 9, 1597, Espírito Santo, Braz.)   Portuguese Jesuit acclaimed as a poet, dramatist, and scholar who is considered one of the founders of the national literature of Brazil.

Anchieta was educated in Portugal and entered the Society of Jesus in 1551. He arrived in Brazil on July 13, 1553, in what is now the province of Bahia. In 1554 he went to São Paulo, a new Jesuit settlement in the interior, where he played a major role in Jesuit efforts to convert the Indians. He also attempted to protect the Indians from the institution of slavery, which was developing in the growing plantation economy.

Anchieta's most famous literary work was the Latin mystic poem *De beata virgine dei matre Maria* ("The Blessed Virgin Mary"). He also wrote and staged religious plays in the Brazilian wilderness, many of which have been lost. In addition, he wrote many letters describing the Indians' way of life, customs, folklore, and diseases, as well as the flora and fauna of Brazil.

Anchises \an-'kī-sēz, aŋ-\   In Greek legend, member of the junior branch of the royal family of Troy; he was king of Dardanus on Mount Ida. There the goddess Aphrodite met him and, enamored of his beauty, bore him Aeneas. For revealing the name of the child's mother, Anchises was killed or struck blind by lightning. In later legend and in Virgil's *Aeneid*, he was conveyed out of Troy on the shoulders of his son Aeneas, whose descendants founded Rome, and he died in Sicily.

ancients and moderns   Subject of a celebrated literary dispute that raged in France and England in the 17th century. The "ancients" maintained that the classical literature of Greece and Rome offered the only models for literary excellence; the "moderns" challenged the supremacy of the classical writers. The rise of modern science tempted some French intellectuals to assume that, if Descartes had surpassed ancient science, it might be possible to surpass other ancient arts. The first attacks on the ancients came from Cartesian circles in defense of some heroic poems by Jean Desmarets de Saint-Sorlin that were based on Christian rather than classical mythology. The dispute broke into a storm with the publication of Nicolas Boileau's *L'Art poétique* (1674), defining the case for the ancients and upholding the classical traditions of poetry. From then on, the quarrel became personal and vehement. Among the chief supporters of the moderns were Charles Perrault and Bernard de Fontenelle. Supporters of the ancients were Jean de La Fontaine and Jean de La Bruyère.

In England the quarrel continued until well into the first decade of the 18th century. Eventually two main issues emerged: whether literature progressed from antiquity to the present as science did, and whether, if there was progress, it was linear or cyclical. These matters were seriously and vehemently discussed. Jonathan Swift satirized the conflict in his *Tale of a Tub* (1704) and, more importantly, in *The Battle of the Books* (1704). In 1726 Swift was to make an even more devastating attack in *Gulliver's Travels*, Book III, "The Voyage to Laputa."

Ancrene Wisse \'aŋ-krə-nə-'wis-ə\ ("Guide for Anchoresses") *also called* Ancrene Riwle \'rū-lə\ ("Rule for Anchoresses")   Anonymous work written in the early 13th century for the guidance of women recluses outside the regular orders. It may have been intended specifically for a group of women sequestered near Limebrook in Herefordshire.

Translated from English into French and Latin, the manual remained popular until the 16th century. It is notable for its humanity, practicality, and insight into human nature but even more for its brilliant style. Like the other prose of its time, it uses alliteration as ornament, but its author was influenced by contemporary fashions in preaching, which had originated in the universities, rather than by vernacular traditions. With its richly figurative language, rhetorically crafted sentences, and carefully logical divisions and subdivisions, it achieved linguistic effects that were remarkable for the English language of the time. *Ancrene Wisse* is often associated with the Katherine Group, a collection of devotional works also written near Herefordshire.

Andersen \ˈän-ər-sən, *Angl* ˈan-dər-sən \, Hans Christian (b. April 2, 1805, Odense, near Copenhagen, Den.—d.

E.B. Inc.

Aug. 4, 1875, Copenhagen) Danish writer whose natural storytelling abilities and great imaginative power combined with universal elements of folk legend to produce a body of fairy tales appreciated in many cultures.

Andersen was eventually admitted to the University of Copenhagen in 1828. The next year he produced what is considered his first important literary work, *Fodrejse fra Holmens Kanal til Østpynten af Amager i aarene*

1828 og 1829 (1829; "A Walk from Holmen's Canal to the East Point of the Island of Amager in the Years 1828 and 1829"), a fantastic tale in the style of the German Romantic writer E.T.A. Hoffmann. This work was an immediate success. He then turned to playwriting. After two unsuccessful attempts, he achieved recognition for *Mulatten* (1840; "The Mulatto"), a play portraying the evils of slavery. The theater was not to become Andersen's field, however, and for a long time he was regarded primarily as a novelist. Most of his novels are autobiographical; among the best known are *Improvisatoren* (1835; *The Improviser*), *O.T.* (1836), and *Kun en spillemand* (1837; *Only a Fiddler*).

Andersen's first book of tales, *Eventyr, fortalte for børn* (1835; "Tales, Told for Children"), included such stories as "The Tinderbox," "Little Claus and Big Claus," and "The Princess and the Pea." Two further installments of stories made up the first volume of *Eventyr* (1837); a second volume was completed in 1842, and to these was added *Billedbog uden Billeder* (1840; *A Picture-book Without Pictures*). New collections appeared in 1843, 1847, and 1852. The genre was expanded in *Nye eventyr og historier* (1858–72; "New Fairy Tales and Stories").

These collections broke new ground in both style and content. A true innovator in his method of telling tales, Andersen employed the idioms and constructions of the spoken language. While some of his tales reveal an optimistic belief in the ultimate triumph of goodness and beauty (*e.g.*, "The Snow Queen"), others are deeply pessimistic and end unhappily. Part of what makes some of the tales so compelling is Andersen's identification with the unfortunate and the outcast.

From 1840 to 1857 Andersen traveled throughout Europe, Asia Minor, and Africa, and his impressions are recorded in a number of travel books (notably *En digters bazar* [1842; *A Poet's Bazaar*], *I Sverrig* [1851; *Pictures of Sweden*], and *I Spanien* [1863; *In Spain*]). His diaries and thousands of his letters are extant.

Andersen \ˈän-ər-sən \, Tryggve (b. Sept. 27, 1866, Ringsaker, Nor.—d. April 10, 1920, Gran) Novelist and short-story writer of the Neoromantic movement in Norway who depicted the conflict between bureaucratic and peasant cultures.

Educated at the University of Kristiania, Andersen made his living as an office worker. In his youth he became fascinated

with German Romanticism, especially as seen in the fantastic tales of E.T.A. Hoffmann. In his main work, *I cancelliraadens dage* (1897; *In the Days of the Counsellor*), a group of short stories tied together by a central figure, Andersen portrayed the world of rural civil servants in Norway. His novel *Mot kvæld* (1900; "Toward Evening") dealt with middle-class narrow-mindedness. He also published four volumes of short stories. His diary of a sea voyage after the death of his wife and a son in 1902, *Dagbog fra en sjøreise* ("Journal of a Sea Voyage"), was published in 1923.

Anderson \ˈan-dər-sən \, Margaret (Caroline) (b. Nov. 24, 1886?, Indianapolis, Ind., U.S.—d. Oct. 18, 1973, Le Cannet, Fr.) Founder and editor of the LITTLE REVIEW magazine, in which she introduced works by many of the best-known American and English writers of the 20th century.

Raised in a conventional Midwestern home and educated at Western College for Women, Oxford, Ohio, Anderson renounced the "bourgeois" values of her background at an early age and moved to Chicago. There she joined the staff of *The Dial*, a literary review. In 1914 she founded the *Little Review*, a magazine that reflected her interest in avant-garde art, philosophy, feminism, and psychoanalysis, among other subjects. Ezra Pound, whom she engaged as her European editor, attracted expatriate American and European writers to the magazine. For six months in 1914, after her financial backers abandoned the *Little Review*, she lost her home and offices and camped with family and staff members on the shores of Lake Michigan.

When Anderson began serializing James Joyce's *Ulysses* in the *Little Review* in 1918, the U.S. Post Office seized and burned four issues of the magazine and then convicted Anderson and the associate editor, Jane Heap, on obscenity charges; each was fined $50. Nevertheless Anderson continued to publish for another 11 years. Among her subsequent writings were her three-volume autobiography, consisting of *My Thirty Years' War* (1930), *The Fiery Fountains* (1951), and *The Strange Necessity* (1962).

Anderson \ˈan-dər-sən \, Maxwell (b. Dec. 15, 1888, Atlantic, Pa., U.S.—d. Feb. 28, 1959, Stamford, Conn.) American playwright who attempted to popularize verse tragedy.

Anderson was educated at the University of North Dakota and Stanford University. He collaborated with Laurence Stallings in the comedy *What Price Glory?* (1924), his first hit, a realistically ribald and profane view of World War I. He then composed two ambitious historical dramas in verse—*Elizabeth the Queen* (1930) and *Mary of Scotland* (1933)—and his humorous Pulitzer Prize-winning prose satire, *Both Your Houses* (1933), an attack on venality in the U.S. Congress. He reached the peak of his career with *Winterset* (1935), a poetic drama inspired by the Sacco and Vanzetti case of the 1920s and set in the urban slums. Collaborating with the German refugee composer Kurt Weill (1900–50), Anderson also wrote for the musical theater a play based on early New York history, *Knickerbocker Holiday* (1938), and *Lost in the Stars* (1949), a dramatization of Alan Paton's South African novel *Cry, the Beloved Country*.

Anderson \ˈan-dər-sən \, Patrick John MacAllister (b. Aug. 4, 1915, Ashtead, Surrey, Eng.—d. March 17, 1979, Halstead, Essex) English-born Canadian poet whose writings are characterized by a rapid juxtaposition of contrasting images.

Educated at Oxford and Columbia universities, Anderson settled in Montreal and taught at McGill University from 1940 to 1950. He was instrumental in establishing the literary magazine *Preview*; he also wrote sensuous descriptions of nature that revitalized traditional lyrical praise of the Canadian landscape. The collections *A Tent for April* (1945) and *The White Centre* (1946) were followed by *The Colour as Naked* (1953), the autobiographical *Search Me* (1957), and his study *Over the Alps: Reflections on Travel and Travel Writing* (1969). Anderson's last published work was *Return to Canada: Selected Poems* (1977).

Anderson \\'an-dər-sən\\, Poul (William) (b. Nov. 25, 1926, Bristol, Pa., U.S.)   Prolific American writer of science fiction and fantasy often praised for his scrupulous attention to scientific detail.

Anderson published his first science-fiction story while an undergraduate at the University of Minnesota and became a freelance writer following his graduation with a degree in physics in 1948. He published his first novel, *Vault of the Ages*, in 1952 and thereafter worked at the rate of several books per year. A number of his works concern the "future history" of what he calls the Technic Civilization, an age of human history lasting from the years 2100 to 7100. Much of the sociological, political, and economic content of these books, such as *Agent of the Terran Empire* (1965), derives from patterns associated with the European Age of Exploration. In *Tau Zero* (1970), considered by some to be his best work, Anderson turns from the broad canvas of future history to the confines of a spaceship, the speed of which is approaching the speed of light. Inside, the travelers experience time as they have always known it while witnessing through the portholes the collapse and rebirth of the universe.

Anderson's interest in Scandinavian languages and literatures informs many of his fantasy novels. *The Merman's Children* (1979), for example, portrays the plight of a surviving species of mermen within human society, a theme found in medieval Danish balladry.

Anderson \\'an-dər-sən\\, Regina M., *married name* Andrews \\'an-,drüz\\, *pseudonym* Ursala (Ursula) Trelling \\'trel-iŋ\\ (b. May 21, 1901, Chicago, Ill., U.S.)   Librarian, playwright, and patron of the arts whose New York City home was a salon for Harlem Renaissance writers and artists.

Anderson attended several colleges and worked as a librarian in the New York Public Library System, for which she produced lecture and drama series and arts exhibitions, from the early 1920s to 1967. The Harlem apartment she shared with two other women became an important meeting place for African-American artists and intellectuals in the early 1920s. In 1924 Anderson helped organize a dinner at the Civic Club, attended by such notable authors as W.E.B. Du Bois, Jean Toomer, Countee Cullen, and Langston Hughes, that helped launch the Harlem Renaissance. Later that year she helped Du Bois found the Krigwa Players, a company of black actors performing plays by black authors; it was based at the 135th Street Public Library, where Anderson worked.

The Krigwa Players evolved into the Negro Experimental Theatre (also known as the Harlem Experimental Theatre), which in 1931 produced Anderson's one-act play *Climbing Jacob's Ladder*, about a lynching that happened while people prayed in church. The next year the theater produced her one-act play *Underground*, about the Underground Railroad. Both plays were written under her pseudonym. The Negro Experimental Theatre served as an inspiration to little theater groups around the country, and it was especially influential in the encouragement of serious black theater and of black playwrights. Anderson also coedited the *Chronology of African-Americans in New York, 1621–1966* (1971; with Ethel Ray Nance).

Anderson \\'an-dər-sən\\, Sherwood (b. Sept. 13, 1876, Camden, Ohio, U.S.—d. March 8, 1941, Colón, Pan.)   Author who strongly influenced American short-story writing between World Wars I and II. His prose style, based on everyday speech and derived from the experimental writing of Gertrude Stein, was markedly influential on Ernest Hemingway.

Anderson held a variety of jobs while writing fiction in his spare time. Eventually he began to earn enough from his published work to quit the business world. Encouraged by several literary men, he began to contribute experimental verse and short fiction to little magazines. His first novels, *Windy McPherson's Son* (1916; rev. ed., 1921) and *Marching Men* (1917), were written while he was still a manufacturer. *Winesburg, Ohio* (1919) was his first mature book and made his reputation. Its related short sketches and tales are told by a newspaper reporter-narrator who is as emotionally limited in some ways as the people he describes. His novels include *Many Marriages* (1923), which stresses the need for sexual fulfillment; *Dark Laughter* (1925), which values the "primitive" over the civilized; and *Beyond Desire* (1932), a novel of Southern textile mill labor struggles. His best work is generally thought to be in his short stories, collected in *The Triumph of the Egg* (1921), *Horses and Men* (1923), *Death in the Woods* (1933), and the previously mentioned *Winesburg, Ohio*.

Andersson \\'än-dər-,shòn\\, Dan, *byname of* Daniel Andersson (b. April 6, 1888, Skattlösbergett, Swed.—d. Sept. 20, 1920, Stockholm)   Swedish writer of working-class literature who became one of the few popular Swedish poets.

Born to a poor family, Andersson was a woodsman and charcoal burner before he became a temperance lecturer. His first two published volumes were *Kolarhistorier* (1914; "Charcoal Burner's Tales") and *Kolvaktarens visor* (1915; "Charcoal Watcher's Songs"; a selection was translated into English in *Charcoal Burner's Ballad & Other Poems*, 1943). He published one more book of poems during his lifetime, *Svarta ballader* (1917; "Black Ballads"), and two autobiographical novels, *De tre hemlösa* (1918; "The Three Homeless Ones") and *David Ramms arv* (1919; "David Ramm's Heritage"). A considerable part of his verse and prose was published after his death in *Efterskörd* (1929; "Late Harvest") and *Tryck och Otrycke* (1942; "Printed and Unprinted").

And Quiet Flows the Don \\'dän\\   First part of the novel *Tikhy Don* by Mikhail SHOLOKHOV. The Russian novel was published between 1928 and 1940; the English translation of the first part appeared in 1934. *The Don Flows Home to the Sea*, part two of the original novel, was published in English translation in 1940.

Set in the Don River basin of southwestern Russia at the end of the czarist period, the novel traces the progress of the Cossack Gregor Melekhov from youthful lover to Red Army soldier and finally to Cossack nationalist. War—in the form of both international conflict and civil revolution—provides the epic backdrop for the narrative and determines its tone of moral ambiguity.

Andrade \\äⁿ-'dräj-ē\\, Eugénio de, *pseudonym of* José Fontinhas \\fōⁿ-'tēⁿ-yásh\\ (b. Jan. 19, 1923, Povoa da Atalia, Port.)   Portuguese poet who, influenced by Surrealism, used concrete images that included earth, water, and the human body to explore such themes as love, nature, and death. His work was widely translated.

Andrade, who began publishing poetry as a teenager, worked as a civil servant in Porto from 1950 to 1983. His first major verse collection was *As Mãos e os frutos* (1948; "Hands and Fruit"). *Branco no branco* (1984; *White on White*) examines the joys and sorrows of remembrance. His other verse collections include *Adolescente* (1942; "Adolescent"), *Coração do dia* (1958; "The Heart of Day"), *Obscuro domínio* (1971; "Dark Dominion"), *Memória doutro rio* (1978; *Memory of Another River*), and *O outro nome da terra* (1988; "The Former Name of the Earth"), as well as the Portuguese- and English-language volume *Inhabited Heart* (1985).

Andrade \ä\u207fn-'dräj-ē\, Jorge, *in full* Aluísio Jorge Andrade Franco \'fräŋ-kü\ (b. April 21, 1922, Barretos, Braz.—d. March 13, 1984, São Paulo)   One of the most powerful playwrights to surface in the Brazilian theatrical renewal of the mid-20th century.

After staging *O faqueiro de prata* ("The Silver Cutlery") and *O telescópio* ("The Telescope") in 1954, Andrade gained considerable public attention in 1955 with his play *A moratória* ("The Moratorium"). *Pedreira das almas* (1958; "Quarry of the Souls") and *Rasto atrás* (1967; "The Road Back") are the most dramatic of his plays. Among his favorite staging techniques was the use of a two-level stage to depict two time periods within the lives of the same group of protagonists.

Andrade's works reflect the rural-to-urban population shift in southern Brazil, the rise and fall of the one-crop coffee economy, and the drama of individuals trying to come to terms with themselves, their backgrounds, and their changing environment. In *Vereda da salvação* (1965; "The Path of Salvation") he vividly depicted the delirium of a group of religious mystics and their destruction at the hands of the authorities. In 1970 Andrade won the Molière Prize for the three-play cycle *Marta, A árvore* ("The Tree"), and *O relógio* ("The Watch").

Andrade \ä\u207fn-'dräj-ē\, Mário de, *in full* Mário Raul de Morais Andrade (b. Oct. 9, 1893, São Paulo, Braz.—d. Feb. 25, 1945, São Paulo)   Writer whose chief importance was his introduction of a highly individual prose style that attempted to reflect colloquial Brazilian speech rather than "correct" Portuguese. He was also important in Modernismo, Brazil's modernist movement.

Andrade helped organize what proved to be a key event in the future artistic life of Brazil, the Semana de Arte Moderna ("Week of Modern Art"), held in São Paulo in February 1922. His own contribution, a reading of poems drawn from his *Paulicéia desvairada* (1922; *Hallucinated City*), has since been recognized as one of the more significant events in modern Brazilian poetry.

Andrade headed the Department of Culture of São Paulo from 1935 until his death, organizing research into Brazilian folklore and folk music. His own novels reflect his concern for folk themes; *Macunaíma* (1928) is written in his highly idiomatic style in an attempt to recreate actual Brazilian speech. Andrade's complete poems were collected and published posthumously in *Poesías completas* (1955). These, together with his critical writings, continue to influence the arts in Brazil.

Andrade \ä\u207fn-'dräj-ē\, Oswald de, *in full* José Oswald de Sousa Andrade (b. Jan. 11, 1890, São Paulo, Braz.—d. Oct. 22, 1954, São Paulo)   Poet, playwright, and novelist, social agitator and revolutionary, one of the leaders of Brazil's Modernismo movement in the arts.

Born into a wealthy and aristocratic family, Andrade traveled extensively in Europe during his youth and there became aware of avant-garde literary trends in Paris and Italy. After his return to São Paulo, where he received his degree in law in 1919, he and Mário de Andrade (no relation) helped organize the Semana de Arte Moderna ("Week of Modern Art") at São Paulo in 1922, to introduce Modernismo to the public.

Andrade focused specifically on the nationalistic aspects of Modernismo in his literary manifesto *Pau-Brasil* (1925; "Brazil Wood"). He called for a return to what he saw as the primitive spontaneity of expression of the indigenous Brazilians, emphasizing the need for modern Brazil to become aware of its own heritage. To this end, he founded the literary movement known as Antropofagia ("Cannibalism"), a splinter group of Modernismo, which, although short-lived, proved influential in its emphasis on folklore and native themes.

In the years after his death, his novels, especially *Memórias sentimentais de João Miramar* (1924; "Sentimental Memoirs of João Miramar"), came to be appreciated as much for their originality of style as for their broader significance.

André le Chapelain \ä\u207f-drä-lə-shảp-'la\u207f\, *Latin* Andreas Capellanus \an-'drä-əs-,kap-ə-'lä-nəs\ (fl. 12th century)   French writer on the art of courtly love, best known for his three-volume treatise *Liber de arte honeste amandi et reprobatione inhonesti amoris* (*c.* 1185; "Book of the Art of Loving Nobly and the Reprobation of Dishonorable Love"). He is thought to have been a chaplain at the court of Marie, Countess of Champagne, daughter of Eleanor of Aquitaine. André wrote the *Liber* at Marie's request. The document twice was translated into French during the 13th century; Guillaume de Lorris drew upon it for the *Roman de la Rose*. The *Liber* codifies the whole doctrine of courtly love, detailing virtually all the elements of the cult.

Andrea da Barberino \än-'drä-ä-dä-,bär-bä-'rē-nō\ (b. *c.* 1370, Barberino di Val d'Elsa, near Florence [Italy]—d. *c.* 1432, Florence)   Ballad singer, prose writer, and compiler of epic tales.

The material for Andrea's prose compilation of Charlemagne legends, *I reali di Francia* (1491; "The Royalty of France"), was drawn for the most part from earlier Italian versions. His epic tale *Guerrin meschino* (1473) is largely of Andrea's own creation. It follows the fortunes of the slave-born hero Guerrino, who emerges strong and unshaken from a multitude of fantastic adventures and dangers to discover his royal parentage, secure his parents' release from prison, marry a Persian princess, and live happily until his death.

Andrea also compiled (and himself recited) such romances as *Aspramonte, Storie Narbonesi* (published 1873–82) and *La storia di Ugone* and *La discesa di Guerrino all'inferno* (both published in 1882).

Andrea del Sarto \an-'drä-ə-del-'sär-tō\   Poem by Robert BROWNING, published in the collection *Men and Women* (1855).

The work is written as a dramatic monologue delivered by the painter Andrea del Sarto (1486–1531) to his beloved and unfaithful wife, Lucrezia. Browning based the poem on the treatment of the artist's marriage in Giorgio Vasari's *The Lives of the Painters.* As explained by Vasari and implied in the poem, it is the painter's willing and tolerant devotion to Lucrezia that limits his dedication to art and thus keeps him from the first rank of creative geniuses.

Andreas Capellanus   *see* ANDRÉ le Chapelain.

Andreas-Salomé \än-'drä-äs-'zä-lō-,mä\, Lou, *original surname* Salomé (b. Feb. 12, 1861, St. Petersburg, Russia—d. Feb. 5, 1937, Göttingen, Ger.)   German writer remembered for her friendships with the great men of her day. Beloved of Friedrich Nietzsche in 1882, she rejected his proposal of marriage and later married an Orientalist, F.C. Andreas. In 1897 she met the poet Rainer Maria Rilke, who was 14 years younger than she and who fell in love with her; she became one of the formative influences on his life. In 1911 she became associated with the Vienna circle of psychoanalysts and was a friend and disciple of Sigmund Freud.

Besides novels, her works include *Friedrich Nietzsche in seinen Werken* (1894; "Friedrich Nietzsche in His Works"), *Rainer Maria Rilke* (1928), and *Mein Dank an Freud* (1931; "My Thanks to Freud"). Her correspondence with Rilke was published in 1952.

Andreev   *see* ANDREYEV.

Andreini \än-drä-'ē-nē\, Giovambattista (b. Feb. 9, 1579?, Florence [Italy]—d. June 7/8, 1654, Reggio nell'Emilia, Sicily)

Actor of commedia dell'arte and son of Francesco and Isabella Andreini. Giovambattista was also author of the play *Adamo* ("Adam"), which, it has been claimed, suggested the idea of *Paradise Lost* to John Milton.

Andreini began his stage career with the Compagnia dei Gelosi founded by his parents, but about 1601 he formed his own troupe, the Compagnia dei Fedeli, and toured Italy until 1613. He performed throughout Europe nearly until his death. His writings include several ecclesiastical dramas, some religious poems, and a number of comedies.

Andreini \,än-drä-'ē-nē\, Isabella, *original surname* Canali \kä-'nä-lē\ (b. 1562, Padua, Republic of Venice [Italy]—d. July 10, 1604, Lyons, Fr.) Celebrated muse and the leading lady of the Compagnia dei Gelosi, most famous of the early commedia dell'arte companies.

Together with her husband Francesco and others, she cofounded the Gelosi troupe, with which she toured Italy and France until her death. A brilliant and beautiful woman, she was the subject of adoring verse by both French and Italian poets. Isabella was herself a minor poet and author of a pastoral play, *Mirtilla*. Her son Giovambattista was a commedia dell'arte actor and a prolific author.

Andrew of Wyntoun *see* WYNTOUN.

Andrews, Joseph \'jō-səf-'an-,drüz, -zəf\ Fictional character, hero of Henry Fielding's novel JOSEPH ANDREWS. Joseph is an agreeable young man whose innocence and naïveté expose the affectations of those he meets on his journey.

Andrews, Pamela \'pam-ə-lə-'an-,drüz\ Fictional character, the virtuous, long-suffering heroine of PAMELA by Samuel Richardson.

Andreyev or **Andreev** \,ən-'drʸā-yəf\, Leonid Nikolayevich (b. Aug. 9 [Aug. 21, New Style], 1871, Oryol, Russia—d. Sept. 12, 1919, Kuokkala, Fin.) Novelist whose best work is notable for its strong evocation of a mood of despair and absolute pessimism.

At the age of 20 Andreyev entered St. Petersburg University; after several attempts at suicide, he transferred to the University of Moscow, becoming a barrister and then a law and crime reporter and publishing his first stories in newspapers and periodicals. Encouraged by Maksim Gorky, Andreyev wrote a number of stories that received wide attention. Among his best tales are *Gubernator* (1905; *His Excellency the Governor*) and *Rasskaz o semi poveshennykh* (1908; *The Seven That Were Hanged*).

His fame as a novelist declined rapidly as his works became increasingly bizarre and sensational. He began a career as a dramatist in 1905. His most successful plays—*Zhizn cheloveka* (1907; *The Life of Man*) and *Tot, kto poluchayet poshchyochiny* (1916; *He Who Gets Slapped*)—were allegorical dramas, but he also attempted to write realistic comedy.

During World War I, Andreyev became editor of a government-inspired newspaper, and his writing became predominantly patriotic. A fervent antirevolutionary, Andreyev moved to Finland after the Bolsheviks came to power; his last work, *S.O.S.* (1919), was an appeal to the Allies to save Russia.

Andrić \'än-drēch\, Ivo (b. Oct. 10, 1892, Dolac, near Travnik, Bosnia—d. March 13, 1975, Belgrade, Yugos.) Writer of Serbo-Croatian novels and short stories who was awarded the Nobel Prize for Literature in 1961.

Andrić established his reputation with *Ex Ponto* (1918), a contemplative, lyrical prose work written during his internment for nationalistic political activities during World War I. Collections of his short stories were published at intervals from 1920 onward.

Following World War I, he entered the Yugoslavian diplomatic service. Of his three novels, written during the Second World War, two—*Travnička hronika* (1945; *Bosnian Story* or *The Days of the Consuls*) and *Na Drini ćuprija* (1945; *The Bridge on the Drina*)—are concerned with the history of Bosnia.

Andrić's works reveal his deterministic philosophy and his sense of compassion and are written objectively and soberly, in language of great beauty and purity. Other translations of Andrić's works include *The Damned Yard* (1992) and *Conversation with Goya* (1992).

Andrieux \än-drē-'œ̄\, François(-Guillaume-Jean-Stanislas) (b. May 6, 1759, Strasbourg, Fr.—d. May 9, 1833, Paris) French lawyer and comic dramatist who met with considerable success in both his literary and political activities.

Andrieux achieved his first great literary success with *Les Étourdis* (1787; "The Scatterbrained") and wrote a number of popular narrative poems. As a professor at the Collège de France (1814), he was reputedly so ardent a defender of the classical tradition against the rising influence of Romanticism that he advised the young Honoré de Balzac to choose any profession other than the writing of plays. Andrieux became permanent secretary to the Académie Française in 1829 and spent his last years working on the 1835 edition of the *Dictionnaire de l'Académie*.

Androcles \'an-drō-,klēz\ or **Androclus** \'an-drō-kləs\ Roman slave who allegedly lived about the time of the emperor Tiberius or Caligula and who became the hero of a story by Aulus Gellius. The story, taken originally from a work by Apion and also found in Aelian's *De natura animalium*, tells that Androcles had taken refuge from the cruelties of his master in a cave in Africa, when a lion entered the cave and showed him his swollen paw, from which Androcles extracted a large thorn. Later, the grateful animal recognized him when Androcles had been captured and thrown to the wild beasts in the circus and, instead of attacking him, began to caress him; he was then set free.

Androcles and the Lion \'an-drō-,klēz\ Drama consisting of a prologue and two acts by George Bernard SHAW, performed in Berlin in 1912 and published in 1916. Using the story of Androcles, Shaw examines true and false religious exaltation, combining the traditions of miracle play and Christmas pantomime into a philosophical farce about early Christianity; the play's central theme, recurrent in Shaw, is that one must have something worth dying for—an end outside oneself—to make life worth living.

Andromache \an-'dräm-ə-kē\ In Greek legend, the daughter of Eëtion (prince of Thebe in Mysia) and wife of Hector (son of King Priam of Troy). All her relations perished in or shortly after the taking of Troy by the Greek warrior Neoptolemus, the son of Achilles. When the captives were allotted, Andromache fell to Neoptolemus, by whom she is said to have borne three sons. Neoptolemus was slain at Delphi, and he left Andromache and the rule of Epirus to Helenus, the brother of Hector. After the death of Helenus, Andromache returned to Asia Minor with her youngest son, Pergamus.

Writers who treated the myth include Jean Racine, William Congreve, Gilbert Murray, and Gabriele D'Annunzio.

Andromache \an-'dräm-ə-kē\ Drama by EURIPIDES, performed about 426 BC. Set in the aftermath of the Trojan War, the play has an exciting beginning marked by strong anti-Spartan feeling. Most of the original characters disappear, however, and interest is soon dissipated.

Andromeda \an-'dräm-ə-də\ In Greek mythology, beautiful daughter of King Cepheus and Queen Cassiope of Joppa in Palestine (called Ethiopia) and wife of Perseus. Cassiope offended the Nereids by boasting that Andromeda was more beautiful than they, so in revenge Poseidon sent a sea monster to devastate Cepheus' kingdom. Since only Andromeda's sacrifice would appease the gods, she was chained to a rock and left to be devoured by the monster. Perseus flew by on the winged horse Pegasus, fell in love with Andromeda, and asked Cepheus for her hand. Cepheus agreed, and Perseus slew the monster. At their marriage feast, however, Andromeda's uncle, Phineus, to whom she had originally been promised, tried to claim her. Perseus turned him to stone with Medusa's head.

Andrzejewski \ăn-je-'yef-sk⁽ʸ⁾ē\, Jerzy (b. Aug. 19, 1909, Warsaw, Pol.—d. April 19/20, 1983, Warsaw) Polish novelist, short-story writer, and political dissident.

Andrzejewski studied at the University of Warsaw and became a contributor to a conservative literary weekly, *Prosto z mostu* ("Straight from the Shoulder"). He admired the French Catholic writers François Mauriac and Georges Bernanos, and his novels *Drogi nieuniknione* (1936: "Unavoidable Ways") and *Ład serca* (1938; "Heart's Harmony") show their influence. During World War II Andrzejewski remained in Warsaw and was active in the resistance.

He was elected president of the Polish Writers' Union in 1949, and he wrote a few books in the Socialist Realist vein. After 1956, however, he became one of the principal critics of literature written in the service of the state. Many of his writings published in Poland in the late 1950s and '60s contained veiled criticisms of the government, and for several years he was forbidden to publish.

Andrzejewski is probably best known for his satiric *Popiół i diament* (1948; *Ashes and Diamonds*; film, 1961), generally considered his finest novel, in which he presented the tragic situation of young Polish nationalists in conflict with idealistic communists in the time immediately after World War II.

anecdote \'an-ik-ˌdōt\ [French, minor incident, anecdote, from Late Greek *Anékdota* (plural), title of the Byzantine historian Procopius' private history of Justinian's court, literally, unpublished things, from Greek *anékdotos* unpublished] A usually short narrative of an interesting, amusing, or biographical incident.

Aneirin or **Aneurin** \ə-'nī-rin, *Welsh* ä-'nəi-rĕn\ (fl. 6th century AD) One of five poets renowned among the Welsh in the 6th century, according to Nennius in his *Historia Britonum* (written *c.* 800). (The other poets are Taliesin, Talhaearn Tad Awen, Blwchbardd, and Cian, whose works are unknown.) Aneirin's reputation rests on a single work, *Y Gododdin*, considered the earliest extant Welsh work, though preserved only in a manuscript known as *The Book of Aneirin*, which dates from about 1250. The language of the poem is direct for the most part, although simile and metaphor are skillfully used, and alliteration and internal rhyme abound. The poem praises the courage and prowess of Aneirin's contemporaries in the army of Mynyddawg Mwynfawr ("Mynyddawg the Wealthy") of Caereidyn (near Edinburgh) and consists of a series of sharp characterizations of each hero in the ill-starred expedition of the war band of 300 men sent by Mynyddawg Mwynfawr to recapture the old Roman stronghold of Catraeth (Catterick in North Yorkshire, Eng.) from the Saxons of Deira.

angel \'ān-jəl\ [Greek *ángelos,* literally, messenger] In several religions—including Zoroastrianism, Judaism, Christianity, and Islām—any of numerous benevolent spiritual beings, powers, or principles that mediate between the realm of the sacred and the profane realm of time, space, and cause and effect. Comparable beings in Eastern religions include the Hindu avatars and the Buddhist bodhisattvas.

Functioning as messengers or servants of the deity or as guardians of individuals or nations, angels were variously classified into ranks or hierarchies. In postbiblical Judaism—especially in apocalyptic literature, which describes God's dramatic intervention in history—seven angels, sometimes called archangels, lead the "heavenly hosts": Uriel (leader of the heavenly hosts and guardian of *sheol*, the underworld); Raphael (guardian of human spirits); Raguel (avenger of God against the world of lights); Michael (guardian of Israel); Sariel (avenger of the spirits); Gabriel (ruler of paradise, the seraphim, and the cherubim); and Remiel, also called Jeremiel (guardian of the souls in *sheol*). In rabbinic literature, angels are classified into two basic groupings, higher and lower. Included among the higher group are the cherubim and seraphim, winged guardians of God's throne or chariot, and the *ofannim*, all of which are noted in the Old Testament.

Christianity developed a hierarchy of angels based on the Judaic tradition. In addition to angels, archangels, seraphim, and cherubim, five other spiritual angelic groups—named in the letters of Paul in the New Testament—were accepted in the church by the 4th century: virtues, powers, principalities, dominions, and thrones.

Inheriting concepts of angelology from Judaism and Christianity, Islām also developed a hierarchy of angels, listed here in descending order: the four throne bearers of Allāh (*ḥamalat al-'arsh*); the cherubim (*karūbiyūn*), who praise Allāh; four archangels (Jibrīl, or Gabriel, the revealer; Mīkāl, or Michael, the provider; 'Izrā'īl, the angel of death; and Isrāfīl, the angel of the Last Judgment); and lesser angels, such as the *ḥafaẓah*, or guardian angels.

Angelica \ăn-'jel-ē-kä\ Fictional character who is beloved by Orlando (Roland) in two epic Italian poems, Matteo Maria Boiardo's *Orlando innamorato* (1483; *Roland in Love*) and Ludovico Ariosto's ORLANDO FURIOSO (1516; *Mad Roland*).

Angelica, daughter of the king of Cathay, is a beautiful young woman with whom many men, including the hero, Orlando, fall in love. She is the cause of many duels. When she runs away, Orlando attempts to find her. Eventually, she falls in love with and marries Medoro, a Saracen knight. Orlando's loss of Angelica causes him to go mad.

Angelou \'an-jə-ˌlō, *commonly* -ˌlü\, Maya (Annie), *original name* Marguerite Johnson \'jän-sən\ (b. April 4, 1928, St. Louis, Mo., U.S.) African-American poet whose several volumes of autobiography explore the themes of economic, racial, and sexual oppression.

Raped at the age of eight by her mother's boyfriend, Angelou went through an extended period of muteness. Her early life is the focus of Angelou's first autobiographical work, *I Know Why the Caged Bird Sings* (1970). Her subsequent volumes include *Gather Together in My Name* (1974), *The Heart of a Woman* (1981), and *All God's Children Need Traveling Shoes* (1986). Angelou's poetry, collected in such volumes as *Just Give Me a Cool Drink of Water 'fore I Diiie* (1971) and *And Still I Rise* (1978), draws heavily on her personal history but employs the points of view of various personae. In 1981 she received a lifetime appointment as Reynolds Professor of American Studies at Wake Forest University, Winston-Salem, N.C. Among numerous other honors was her invitation to compose and deliver a poem for the inauguration of President Bill Clinton in 1993.

Angilbert \'aŋ-gil-bərt\ (b. *c.* 740, Aachen, kingdom of the Franks [now in Germany]—d. Feb. 18, 814, Centula, Picardy [now in France]) Frankish poet and prelate at the court of Charlemagne.

Of noble parentage, Angilbert was educated at the palace school at Aachen under Alcuin and was closely connected with the court and the imperial family. He was made abbot of Centula (Saint-Riquier), Picardy, in 794. Angilbert's Latin poems show the culture and tastes of a man of the world. A fragment of an epic probably written by him describes life at the palace and a meeting between Charlemagne and Pope Leo III; this work earned him the nickname of "Homer" from Alcuin. His shorter poems show skill in versification and present a picture of the imperial circle.

Angiolieri \‚än-jō-'lyer-ē\, Cecco (b. *c.* 1260, Siena [Italy]—d. *c.* 1312)   Poet who was an early master of Italian comic verse.

It is known that Angiolieri married, had children, did military service, was exiled for a time, sometimes had trouble with the law, and was a womanizer, drinker, and gambler. Some critics consider him to have been an irascible man, for his sonnets pour contempt upon his parents, his wife, his former mistress, and such contemporary poets as Dante and Guido Cavalcanti. Other critics, however, attribute his subject matter and attitude to the medieval European goliard tradition, whose followers were writers of ribald and disrespectful verse. Whatever his motives, his poetry is enlivened by considerable poetic skill, vivid language, and a keen sense of the incongruities of life.

Angiolieri's works were collected in *Sonetti burleschi e realistici dei primi due secoli* (1920; "Comic and Realistic Sonnets of the First Two Centuries") and in *Il canzoniere* (1946; "The Collection of Sonnets"). A translation, *The Sonnets of a Handsome and Well-Mannered Rogue*, appeared in 1970.

Anglistics \aŋ-'glis-tiks\   The study of the English language or of literature composed in English.

Angria and Gondal \'aŋ-grē-ə ... 'gän-däl\   Elaborate imaginary kingdoms that were invented by Charlotte, Branwell, Emily, and Anne Brontë during their childhood play and that continued to influence their adult writings. The two kingdoms evolved from the stories inspired by a box of wooden soldiers.

In 1834 Charlotte and Branwell collaborated in the elaborate invention of the kingdom of Angria. Several editions of Charlotte's Angria stories were published after her death, and two of Branwell's stories were published as *The Hand of the Arch-Sinner* in 1993. The kingdom of Gondal was invented by Emily and Anne after Charlotte and Branwell had created Angria. Although no prose excerpts on Gondal survive, Gondal was the setting for many of Emily's poems, such as "Remembrance" and "The Prisoner." The names and initials she appended to her verse—such as A.G.A., J. Brenzaida, and R. Alcona—stood for characters from the world of Gondal.

angry young man   One of a group of young British writers of the mid-20th century whose works express the bitterness of the lower classes toward the established sociopolitical system and toward the mediocrity and hypocrisy of the middle and upper classes.

The trend that was evident in John Wain's novel *Hurry on Down* (1953) and in *Lucky Jim* (1954) by Kingsley Amis was crystallized in 1956 in the play *Look Back in Anger*, which became the representative work of the movement. When the play's 26-year-old author John Osborne was described in print as an "angry young man," the label was extended to all his contemporaries who expressed a rage at the persistence of class distinctions, a pride in their lower-class mannerisms, and a dislike for anything highbrow or "phoney." Among the other writers embraced in the term are the novelists John Braine and Alan Sillitoe and the playwrights Bernard Kops and Arnold Wesker. A dominant literary force in the '50s, the movement had faded by the early 1960s.

Angstrom, Harry \'har-ē-'aŋ-strəm\   Fictional character, the protagonist of four novels by John Updike—RABBIT, RUN and its sequels. The character, whose nickname is Rabbit, is an ordinary middle-class man lost in the sterility of the modern world.

Anhava \'än-há-vá\, Tuomas (b. June 5, 1927, Helsinki, Fin.)   Finnish modernist poet and translator.

Anhava had a fanatical concern for *le mot propre* and a great theoretical interest in the aesthetics of modern poetry. His *Runoja* (1953; "Poems") has as its central theme alienation and a search for a transcendence of everyday reality. The images in the technically difficult poems of *36 runoja* (1958; "36 Poems") are strongly reminiscent of the Japanese and Chinese poetry Anhava translated during the same period. He also employed the simplification and compression of Asian epigrams in *Runoja 1961* and *Kuudes kirja* (1966; "The Sixth Book"). Later works include *Runot 1951–1966* (1967) and *Valitut runot* (1976; "Selected Poems"). Anhava's perfectionism had a great influence on younger Finnish poets.

Animal Farm   Anti-utopian satire by George ORWELL, published in 1945. One of Orwell's finest works, it is a political fable based on the events of Russia's Bolshevik revolution and the betrayal of the cause by Joseph Stalin. The book concerns a group of barnyard animals who overthrow and chase off their exploitative human masters and set up an egalitarian society of their own. Eventually the animals' intelligent and power-loving leaders, the pigs, subvert the revolution and form a dictatorship even more oppressive and heartless than that of their former human masters.

anisometric \‚an-‚ī-sō-'met-rik\   Of verse, not having equal or corresponding poetic meters. An anisometric stanza is one composed of lines of unequal metrical length, as in William Wordsworth's "Ode: Intimations of Immortality," which begins:

> There was a time when meadow, grove, and stream,
> The earth, and every common sight,
>   To me did seem
>   Appareled in celestial light,
> The glory and the freshness of a dream.

Compare ISOMETRIC.

Anius \'an-ē-əs\   In Greek mythology, the son of the god Apollo and of Rhoeo, a descendant of the god Dionysus. His mother, when pregnant, had been placed in a chest and cast into the sea by her father; floating to the island of Delos, she gave birth to Anius, who became a seer and a priest of Apollo. Anius' three daughters, Oeno, Spermo, and Elais—that is, wine, seed grain, and oil—were granted by Dionysus the gift of bringing these three crops to fruition. They supplied both the Greek expedition on its way to Troy and Aeneas in his flight from Troy to Italy.

Anna Comnena \'an-ə-käm-'nē-nə\ (b. Dec. 1, 1083—d. after 1148)   Byzantine historian and daughter of the emperor Alexius I Comnenus. She is remembered for her *Alexiad*, a history of the life and reign of her father, which became a valuable source as a pro-Byzantine account of the early Crusades.

Anna received a remarkable education. She married the leader of Bryennium, Nicephorus Bryennius (1097), and joined her mother, the empress Irene, in a vain effort to persuade her father, during his last illness, to disinherit his son, John II Comnenus, in favor of Nicephorus. Later conspiring to depose her brother after his accession to the throne (1118), Anna was, however, unable to obtain the support of her husband; the plot was discovered, and she forfeited her property. She then retired to a convent, where she wrote the *Alexiad*.

Written in Greek, the *Alexiad* provides a picture of religious and intellectual activities within the empire, reflecting the

Byzantine conception of the imperial office. It also contains a vivid description of the Frankish barbarians—as the Crusaders appeared in the eyes of the civilized Byzantines. For example, Anna gives a careful account of the Crusaders' armor. She recounts that Alexius exhorted his archers to shoot at the Franks' horses rather than their riders, whose armor rendered them almost invulnerable. The shields that she describes are similar to those depicted in the Bayeux Tapestry. Later scholars note that the work suffers from a defective chronology and from glorification of Alexius I.

Annabel Lee \'an-ə-ˌbel-'lē\ Lyric poem by Edgar Allan POE, published in the *New York Tribune* on Oct. 9, 1849, two days after his death. Thought to be written in memory of his young wife and cousin, Virginia, who died in 1847, the poem expresses one of Poe's recurrent themes—the death of a young, beautiful, and dearly beloved woman.

Anna Christie \'an-ə-'kris-tē\ Four-act play by Eugene O'NEILL, produced in 1921 and published in 1922, during which year it was also awarded the Pulitzer Prize.

The title character, long separated from her bargemaster father, is reunited with him in adulthood. Not realizing that she has become a prostitute, her sentimental father comes to blows with a seaman who has been smitten by her. When Anna reveals her sordid past, both men abandon her, go their separate ways, get drunk, and unwittingly sign on for the same distant voyage. At the play's end, Anna has agreed to wait for their return.

Anna Karenina \ˌän-ə-kä-'ren-yin-ə, *Russian* 'än-nə-ˌkə-'rʸen-yi-nə\ Novel by Leo TOLSTOY, published in installments between 1875 and 1877 and considered one of the pinnacles of world literature.

The narrative centers on the adulterous affair between Anna, wife of Aleksey Karenin, and Count Vronsky, a young bachelor. Karenin's discovery of the liaison arouses only his concern for his own public image. Anna promises discretion for the sake of her husband and young son but eventually becomes pregnant by Vronsky. After the child is born, Anna and the child accompany Vronsky first to Italy, then to his Russian estate. She begins making furtive trips to see her older child and grows increasingly bitter toward Vronsky, eventually regarding him as unfaithful. In desperation she goes to the train station, purchases a ticket, and then impulsively throws herself in front of the incoming train. A parallel love story, involving the difficult courtship and fulfilling marriage of Kitty and Levin, provides rich counterpoint to the tragedy and is thought to reflect Tolstoy's own marital experience.

There is an inevitability about the tragic fate that hangs over the adulterous love of Anna and Vronsky. "Vengeance is mine, I will repay" is the leitmotiv of the story. Anna pays not so much because she transgresses the moral code but because she refuses to observe the proprieties customarily exacted in such liaisons by the hypocritical high society to which she belongs.

Annales \ä-'näl-ās\ Epic poem written by Quintus ENNIUS that is a history of Rome from the time of Aeneas to the 2nd century BC. Only some 600 lines survive. The fragment mixes legendary origins and eyewitness accounts of contemporary history. Though the work is not balanced—Ennius almost ignored the First Punic War and became more detailed as he added books about his own time—its great merit is evident in his nobility of ethos as well as his nobility of language.

Anna of the Five Towns \'an-ə\ Novel by Arnold BENNETT, published in 1902. It was the first in a series of novels set in the Potteries, Bennett's native region of northern Staffordshire. The book details the constrictions of provincial life among the self-made business classes.

Anna and her half-sister Agnes grow up unloved by their strict father, Ephraim Tellwright, a wealthy miser and a rigid Methodist. Anna dutifully allows her father to manage her inheritance, a fortune that attracts a marriage proposal from Henry Mynors, a religion teacher with business acumen. The engaged couple plan to live in the former home of Titus Price, Ephraim's delinquent tenant who committed suicide. Long accustomed to being dominated by her father and her fiancé, Anna is tragically unable to act on her long-suppressed love for Price's timid son Willie, who kills himself in despair.

annotation \ˌan-ō-'tā-shən\ A note added to a text by way of comment or explanation. Such a note can be added by the author or by the editor.

annual \'an-yü-wəl\ A publication that appears yearly. Examples include yearbooks and almanacs. In the early to mid-19th century a number of annual books under such titles as *The Gift* and *The Token* were published in the United States and England. They included poetry, stories, essays, and lavish illustrations by the foremost writers and illustrators of the day and were intended as giftbooks.

anonymuncule \ə-ˌnän-i-'məŋ-ˌkyül\ [blend of *anonymous* and *homuncule* little man, from Latin *homunculus*] An insignificant or petty anonymous writer.

Another Country Novel by James BALDWIN, published in 1962. The novel is renowned for its graphic portrayal of bisexuality and interracial relations. Shortly after the action begins, Rufus Scott, a black jazz musician, commits suicide, impelling his friends to search for the meaning of his death and, consequently, for a deeper understanding of their own identities. Employing a loose, episodic structure, this work traces the affairs—heterosexual and homosexual as well as interracial—among Scott's friends. In its language and structure, the novel is a departure from Baldwin's earlier work.

Anouilh \ä-'nüy\, Jean(-Marie-Lucien-Pierre) (b. June 23, 1910, Bordeaux, Fr.—d. Oct. 3, 1987, Lausanne, Switz.) Playwright who became one of the strongest personalities of the French theater and achieved an international reputation as a skillful exponent of the well-crafted play. Anouilh's characteristic techniques include the play within the play, flashbacks and flash-forwards, and the exchange of roles.

Anouilh's first mounted play was *L'Hermine* (performed 1932; *The Ermine*), and success came in 1937 with *Le Voyageur sans bagage* (*Traveller Without Luggage*). *Le Bal des voleurs* (1938; *Thieves' Carnival*) confirmed his comic gifts. His plays *Antigone* (1944), *L'Alouette* (1953; *The Lark*), and *Becket ou l'honneur de Dieu* (1959; *Becket, or, The Honor of God*) were considered his greatest achievements. Anouilh rejected both naturalism and realism in favor of what has been called "theatricalism," the return of poetry and imagination to the stage. He exhibited great technical versatility, moving readily from the stylized use of Greek myth, to the rewriting of history, to the *comédie-ballet*, to the modern comedy of character. In the early plays he poses the question of how far the individual must compromise with truth to obtain happiness. Some of his characters accept the inevitable; some live lies; and others, such as Antigone, reject any compromise. His later work showed a lasting fascination with theatrical reality and illusion and an increased preoccupation with the absurdities of the human condition.

Ansky or **An-ski** \'än-skē\, S., *pseudonym of* Solomon Zanvel Rappoport \'rap-ə-ˌpȯrt\ (b. 1863, Vitebsk, Russia [now Vitsebsk, Belarus]—d. Nov. 8, 1920, Warsaw, Poland) Russian Jewish writer and folklorist best known for his play *Der Dibek* (written 1914; performed 1920; published 1921; THE DYBBUK).

Ansky was educated in a Ḥasidic environment and as a young man was attracted to the Jewish Enlightenment (Haskala) and to the populist doctrines of the Narodniki, a group of socialist revolutionaries. For a time he worked among the peasants and contributed articles to the Narodnik journal. His first novel, written in Yiddish, was published in 1884.

Compelled to leave Russia in 1892, he settled in Paris. In 1905 he was permitted to return to St. Petersburg. He joined the Socialist Revolutionary Party, ideological heir of the Narodniki, and continued to write articles, folktales, and short stories on Jewish life.

In 1911 Ansky organized an ethnographic expedition to gather Jewish folklore, songs, melodies, manuscripts, and books. His fieldwork was interrupted by the outbreak of World War I. During this period he produced his most famous work, the classic Yiddish drama *Der Dibek*. The play, which drew on Jewish mystical folklore, was widely translated and performed, most notably in the celebrated Moscow production of the Hebrew company Habima.

Anstey \'an-stē\, Christopher (b. Oct. 31, 1724, Brinkley, Cambridgeshire, Eng.—d. Aug. 3, 1805, Bath, Somerset) Poet whose epistolary novel in verse, *The New Bath Guide*, went through more than 30 editions between 1766 and 1830.

After an education at Eton and at King's College, Cambridge, Anstey in 1754 inherited an independent income; and in 1770 he settled permanently at Bath, a fashionable spa of the 18th century. *The New Bath Guide; or, Memoirs of the B—r—d Family* (1766) satirizes various aspects of Bath life. Much of the poem's charm arises from Anstey's mastery of versification, but the element of parody, together with the simple caricature and occasional accurate delineation of scenes well known to 18th-century readers, helps to explain the poem's popularity.

Antaeus \an-'tē-əs\ In Greek mythology, a giant of Libya, the son of the sea god Poseidon and the Earth goddess Gaea. Antaeus compelled all strangers who were passing through the country to wrestle with him. Whenever he touched the earth (his mother), his strength was renewed, so that even if thrown to the ground, he was invincible. Heracles, in combat with him, discovered the source of his strength and, lifting him up from earth, crushed him to death.

Antaeus \an-'tē-əs\ Literary magazine founded by Paul Bowles and Daniel Halperin in 1970. It was first published in Tangier, Morocco; by its third issue (1971) Ecco Press, with offices in Tangier, London, and New York, was its publisher. Its contributing editors included William Burroughs, John Hawkes, W.S. Merwin, Muriel Rukeyser, and Tennessee Williams. Issues of the magazine often focused on particular genres or subdivisions of literature such as poetry and poetics, translation, British poetry, autobiography, and contemporary fiction. Occasionally it published long critical works, plays, and novellas. It also frequently published interviews and exchanges between leading international figures in the arts.

antagonist \an-'tag-ə-nist\ [Greek *antagōnístēs* opponent, rival, from *anti-* against + *agōnístēs* contestant] The principal opponent or foil of the main character in a drama or narrative. The main character is referred to as the PROTAGONIST.

antanaclasis \ˌan-tə-'nak-lə-sis\ [Greek *antanáklasis,* literally, reflection, echo] A word used in two or more of its possible meanings, as in the final two lines of Robert Frost's "Stopping by Woods on a Snowy Evening":

> The woods are lovely, dark, and deep,
> But I have promises to keep,
> And miles to go before I sleep,
> And miles to go before I sleep.

The first use of "sleep" refers to nocturnal rest, the second to death.

'Antar *see* ROMANCE OF 'ANTAR.

antepirrhema \ant-ˌep-ə-'rē-mə\ In ancient Greek Old Comedy, a continuation of an EPIRRHEMA following an antistrophe.

anthology \an-'thäl-ə-jē\ [Medieval Greek *anthología,* literally, gathering of flowers] A selection of literary, musical, or artistic works or parts of works.

One of the first major anthologies of literature was the *Anthologia Hellēnikē* ("Greek Anthology"), a renowned collection of Greek prose and poetry. The authors represented date from about 700 BC to AD 1000 and were edited variously from the 1st to the 11th centuries. Another early anthology was the *Shi jing* ("Classic of Poetry"), a collection of Chinese poetry compiled by Confucius (551–479 BC).

The first anthologies of English literature appeared in the 16th century. Among these was *Songes and Sonettes, Written by the Ryght Honorable Lorde Henry Howard Late Earle of Surrey and Other* (1557; usually known as *Tottel's Miscellany*), which first made lyric poetry available to the public. Later influential anthologies include Thomas Percy's *Reliques of Ancient English Poetry* (1765); *Des Knaben Wunderhorn* (1805–08; "The Boy's Magic Horn"), an anthology of German folk songs compiled by Clemens Brentano and Achim von Arnim; Arthur Quiller-Couch's *The Oxford Book of English Verse 1250–1900* (1900); and Francis J. Child's *The English and Scottish Popular Ballads* (1882–98).

Anthony \'an-thə-nē\, Katharine (Susan) (b. Nov. 27, 1877, Roseville, Ark., U.S.—d. Nov. 20, 1965, New York, N.Y.) American biographer who is best known for *The Lambs* (1945), a controversial study of the British writers Charles and Mary Lamb.

Anthony was deeply interested in psychiatry. Eventually this interest came to shape her approach to biography, and her books centered increasingly on the psychological development and motivation of her subjects. Some of these works include *Margaret Fuller, A Psychological Biography* (1920); *Catherine the Great* (1925); *Louisa May Alcott* (1938); *Dolly Madison, Her Life and Times* (1949); and *Susan B. Anthony, Her Personal History and Her Era* (1954). Anthony's readers were scandalized by *The Lambs,* subtitled *A Story of Pre-Victorian England,* in which she theorized that incestuous feelings within the Lamb family were reflected in the lives and literary collaborations of Charles Lamb and his sister, Mary.

Anthony, Marc *see* Mark ANTONY.

Anthony \'anth-ə-nē, 'ant-\, Michael (b. Feb. 10, 1932, Mayaro, Trinidad and Tobago) West Indian author of novels, short stories, and travelogues about domestic life in his homeland of Trinidad. Written in a sparse style, his works were often coming-of-age stories featuring young protagonists from his native village of Mayaro.

In the mid-1950s Anthony left Trinidad to live in England, where he began his career as a writer. He returned to Trinidad in 1970 to work as an editor and diplomat. His first novel, *The Games Were Coming* (1963), is the story of Leon, an ascetic young bicyclist who neglects the annual carnival in order to train for an upcoming race. His other novels include *The Year in San Fernando* (1965; rev. ed., 1970), *Green Days by the River* (1967), *King of the Masquerade* (1974), *Streets of Conflict* (1976), and *All that Glitters* (1981). Among his collections of short fiction are *Michael Anthony's Tales for Young and Old* (1967), *Cricket in the Road* (1973), *Sandra Street and Other Stories* (1973), *Folk Tales and Fantasies* (1976), and *The Chief-*

tain's Carnival and Other Stories (1993). He also wrote several histories and travel books on Trinidad.

Anthony Adverse \\'anth-ə-nē-'ad-,vərs\\ Historical novel by Hervey ALLEN, published in 1933. A rambling work set in Europe, Africa, and the Americas during the Napoleonic era, *Anthony Adverse* relates the many adventures of the eponymous hero. These include slave trading in Africa, his experiences as a plantation owner in New Orleans, and his imprisonment and eventual death in Mexico.

antibacchius \\,an-tē-bə-'kī-əs, ,an-tī-\\ *plural* antibacchii \\-bə-'kī-,ī\\ A metrical foot of three syllables. In classical, particularly Latin, prosody, the first two syllables are long and the last is short (— — ◡); this foot is not used in itself as the basis for any rhythm, but rather as a variant of the bacchius. In accentual or modern prosody, the first two syllables have either primary or intermediate stress and the last is unstressed. A modern antibacchius is scanned ′ ′ ◡. *Compare* BACCHIUS.

Antic Hay Novel by Aldous HUXLEY, published in 1923. A satire of post–World War I London intellectuals, the work follows Theodore Gumbril, Jr., the protagonist, and his bohemian friends as they drift aimlessly through their lives in search of happiness. Huxley's witty and allusive narrative style is a strong counterpoint to his nihilistic vision of humanity.

Antichrist \\'an-,tī-,krīst, 'an-tē-\\ In Christianity, the chief enemy of Christ. The earliest mention of the name Antichrist, which was probably coined in Christian eschatological literature (concerned with the end of time), is in the letters of St. John (I John 2: 18, 22; II John 7), although the figure does appear in Paul's second letter to the Thessalonians as "the lawless one." The conception of a mighty ruler who will appear at the end of time and whose essence will be enmity of God, however, is older and was taken over by Christianity from Judaism, which in turn had been influenced by Iranian and Babylonian myths of the battle of God and the devil at the end of time.

anticlimax \\,an-tē-'klī-,maks, ,an-,tī-\\ A figure of speech that consists of the usually sudden transition in discourse from a significant idea to a trivial or ludicrous idea. Alexander Pope's *The Rape of the Lock* uses anticlimax liberally; an example is "Here thou, great Anna, whom three realms obey,/Dost sometimes counsel take, and sometimes tea."

Antigone \\an-'tig-ə-nē\\ In Greek legend, the daughter born of the unwittingly incestuous union of OEDIPUS and his mother, Jocasta. After her father blinded himself upon discovering that Jocasta was his mother and that, also unwittingly, he had slain his father, Antigone and her sister Ismene serve as Oedipus' guides, leading him from Thebes into exile until his death near Athens. Returning to Thebes, they attempt to reconcile their brothers, Eteocles and Polyneices, who are battling over the throne of Thebes. Both brothers are killed, and their uncle Creon becomes king. After performing an elaborate funeral service for Eteocles, Creon forbids the burial of the corpse of Polyneices, declaring him to have been a traitor. Antigone, moved by love, loyalty, and humanity, defies Creon and secretly buries Polyneices. Creon orders her execution for that act. According to Sophocles' version, Antigone is immured in a cave, where she hangs herself. In Euripides' version of the story, Antigone escapes and is reunited with Haemon, Creon's son and her beloved.

The story of loyalty to family versus duty to the state is but one of the elements of this story that has intrigued writers through the ages. George Steiner's *Antigones* (1984) is a discussion of the many versions that have been written.

Antigone \\an-'tig-ə-nē\\ Drama by SOPHOCLES, possibly performed in 442 or 441 BC. It examines the conflicting obligations of civic duties versus personal loyalties and religious mores.

Antigone concerns that part of the Oedipus story that occurs after Eteocles and Polyneices have killed each other over the succession to the throne of Thebes. Antigone's uncle Creon succeeds to the throne and decrees that anyone who buries the dishonored Polyneices will face capital punishment. Antigone, however, obeys her instincts of love and loyalty and defies the orders of her uncle, willing to face the consequences of her act of humanity. Believing that civic duty outweighs family ties, Creon refuses to commute Antigone's death sentence. By the time he is finally persuaded to free Antigone, she has killed herself. The discovery of her body prompts Creon's son, Haemon, to kill himself out of love and sympathy for the dead Antigone, and Creon's wife, Eurydice, then kills herself out of grief over these tragic events. At the play's end Creon is left desolate and broken.

antihero \\'an-tē-,hir-ō, 'an-,tī-, -,hē-rō\\, *also called* nonhero \\,nän-'hir-ō, -'hē-rō\\ A protagonist of a drama or narrative who is notably lacking in heroic qualities. This type of character has appeared in literature since the time of the Greek dramatists and can be found in the literary works of all nations. Examples include the title characters of Miguel de Cervantes' *Don Quixote* (Part I, 1605; Part II, 1615) and Henry Fielding's *Tom Jones* (1749). Some examples of the modern, postwar antihero, as defined by the "angry young man" generation of writers, include Joe Lampton, in John Braine's *Room at the Top* (1957), and Arthur Seaton, in Alan Sillitoe's *Saturday Night and Sunday Morning* (1958). *See also* PROTAGONIST.

antiheroine \\,an-,tī-'her-ə-win, ,an-tē-, -'hir-\\ A female antihero.

Antilochus \\an-'til-ə-kəs\\ In Greek mythology, the son of Nestor, king of Pylos. One of the Greek suitors of Helen of Troy, he accompanied his father to the Trojan War and distinguished himself as acting commander of the Pylians.

Antimachus \\an-'tim-ə-kəs\\ of Colophon \\'käl-ə-,fän\\ (fl. *c.* 410 BC) Greek poet and scholar who wrote a lengthy epic entitled *Thebais*, an account of the expedition of the Seven Against Thebes. His work was greatly admired in antiquity, and his pedantic style made him the model of the learned Alexandrian epic poets. His work survives chiefly in the quotations cited by later writers to illustrate obscure words and minute mythological detail.

antimetabole \\,an-,tī-mə-'tab-ə-lē, ,an-tē-\\ [Greek *antimetabolē*, from *anti-* counter-, opposite + *metabolē* change] A type of chiasmus in which the repetition of two or more words in reverse order in successive clauses, as in Quintilian: "non ut edam vivo sed ut vivam edo" ("I do not live to eat but eat to live").

Antin \\'ant-ən\\, David (b. Feb. 1, 1932, New York, N.Y., U.S.) American poet, translator, and art critic who championed primitive art and poetry and the use of clichés and pop vernacular. He became perhaps best known for his improvisational "talk poems," first published in *Talking* (1972).

Antin was educated at the City College of New York (B.A., 1955) and New York University (M.A., 1966). He first worked as an editor, translator, and researcher. He was curator of the Institute of Contemporary Art (1967) in Boston and from 1968 taught visual arts at the University of California at San Diego.

His poetry collections include *Definitions* (1967), *Code of Flag Behavior* (1968), *After the War (A Long Novel with Few Words)* (1973), *Talking at the Boundaries* (1976), and *Tuning* (1984). Antin improvised his talk poems in public places, tape-recording his performances. Considering the resulting poems to be "adapted notations" of his performances, he later published those he thought had merit. His subsequent works include *Selected Poems: 1963–73* (1991) and *What It Means to Be Avant Garde* (1993).

Antin \'an-tən\, Mary (b. 1881, Polotsk, Russia—d. May 15, 1949, Suffern, N.Y., U.S.) Author of the autobiographical *Promised Land* and other books on immigrant life in the United States.

Antin immigrated to the United States in 1894 and attended Teachers College of Columbia University and Barnard College, New York City, 1901–04. She wrote (in Yiddish) about her voyage to the United States in her first book, *From Polotsk to Boston* (Eng. trans., 1899). Her widely acclaimed *The Promised Land* (1912) narrates the experiences of European Jews and the contrast with Jewish immigrant experience in the United States. After its publication she toured the United States as a lecturer. Her third book on immigrants, *They Who Knock at Our Gates*, was published in 1914.

Antinous \an-'tin-ə-wəs\ Fictional character, Penelope's most arrogant suitor in the *Odyssey*, Homer's epic poem of ancient Greece. Antinous throws a stool at the disguised Odysseus, who has returned after two decades of absence. After Odysseus reveals his identity he kills Antinous.

antinovel \'an-tē-,näv-əl, 'an-tī-\ [translation of French *anti-roman*] Type of avant-garde novel that marks a radical departure from the conventions of the traditional novel in that it is a work of the fictional imagination which ignores such traditional elements or properties as plot, dialogue, and human interest. In their efforts to overcome literary habits and to challenge the expectations of their readers, authors of such works deliberately frustrate conventional literary expectations, avoiding any intrusion of the author's personality, preferences, or values.

The term *antinovel* was first used by Jean-Paul Sartre in an introduction to *Portrait d'un inconnu* (1948; *Portrait of a Man Unknown*) by Nathalie Sarraute. It has also been applied to works by Claude Simon, Alain Robbe-Grillet, and Michel Butor and therefore is usually associated with the French NOUVEAU ROMAN of the 1950s and '60s. Though the word is of recent coinage, this approach to novel writing is at least as old as the work of Laurence Sterne. Works of the same period as the *nouveau roman* but in other languages, such as *Mutmassungen über Jakob* (1959; *Speculations About Jakob*) by the German novelist Uwe Johnson and *Connecting Door* (1962) by the British author Rayner Heppenstall, also contain many of the characteristics of the antinovel—vaguely identified characters, casual arrangement of events, and ambiguity of meaning.

Antiope \an-'tī-ō-pē\ In Greek mythology, the mother, by the god Zeus, of the twins Amphion and Zethus. According to one account, her beauty attracted Zeus, who assumed the form of a satyr and raped her. Eventually she bore Amphion and Zethus, who were brought up by herdsmen.

Antiope was also the name of a daughter of Ares, the god of war, and a queen of the Amazons, a race of warrior women.

Antiphanes \an-'tif-ə-,nēz\ (fl. early 4th century BC, Athens) Together with Alexis, the principal representative of the writers of the Middle Comedy at Athens. In this genre, which succeeded the Old Comedy of Aristophanes, scurrility gave place to parody and to criticism of literature and philosophy. Only fragments of Antiphanes' writing survive, though the titles of 134 plays by him are known.

Antiphon \'an-ti-,fän\ (fl *c.* 480–411 BC, Athens) Orator and statesman, the earliest Athenian known to have taken up rhetoric as a profession. He was a logographer and a writer of speeches for other men to deliver in their defense in court.

As a politician Antiphon was the prime mover in the antidemocratic revolution of the Four Hundred, an oligarchic council set up in 411 BC in an attempt to seize the Athenian government in the midst of war. When the regime of the Four Hundred fell, he defended himself in a speech the ancient Greek historian Thucydides described as the greatest ever made by a man on trial for his life. Nevertheless, the defense was unsuccessful and Antiphon was executed for treason.

Fifteen of Antiphon's compositions survive, of which three, "On the Murder of Herodes," "On the Choreutes," and "Against a Stepmother," were actually delivered in court. The remaining 12 speeches are arranged in three sets of four known as tetralogies, which were composed as exercises for the instruction of students. Each tetralogy consists of two speeches apiece for the defense and the prosecution in a homicide case.

Antiphon's language was dignified and free of the personal abuse that characterizes many of the later orators.

antiphrasis \an-'tif-rə-sis\ *plural* antiphrases \-,sēz\ [Greek *antíphrasis* the substitution of words with positive meaning for those with negative associations, from *anti-* against, opposite + *phrásis* way of speaking, diction] The usually ironic or humorous use of words in senses opposite to the generally accepted meanings (as in "this giant of three feet four inches").

antispast \'an-tē-,spast\ [Greek *antíspastos,* literally, drawn in the contrary direction] In classical prosody, the sequence ∪ — — ∪ is not itself used as the basis for any rhythm. In modern, accentual prosody, a metrical foot or system of four syllables in which an iamb (one unstressed and one stressed syllable) is followed by a trochee (one stressed and one unstressed syllable), scanned ∪ ′ ′ ∪.

antistrophe \an-'tis-trə-fē\ In Greek lyric odes, the second part of the traditional three-part structure. The antistrophe followed the strophe and preceded the epode. In the choral odes of Greek drama each of these parts corresponded to a specific movement of the chorus as it performed that part. During the strophe the chorus moved from right to left on the stage; during the antistrophe they reversed their movement.

antithesis \an-'tith-ə-sis\ [Greek *antíthesis,* literally, opposition] A rhetorical device in which irreconcilable opposites or strongly contrasting ideas are placed in sharp juxtaposition and sustained tension, as in the phrase "they promised freedom and provided slavery."

The opposing clauses, phrases, or sentences are often roughly equal in length and balanced in parallel grammatical structures, as in the following from Abraham Lincoln's "Gettysburg Address":

The world will little note nor long remember what we say here,
but it can never forget what they did here.

anti-utopia \'an-,tī-yū-'tō-pē-ə, 'an-tē-\ A literary work describing an imaginary place where people lead dehumanized and often fearful lives. *See also* UTOPIA.

Antoninus, Brother *see* EVERSON.

António \än-'tōn-yü\, Mário, *in full* Mário António Fernandes de Oliveira \fer-'nän-des-dē-ō-lē-'vā-rü\ (b. April 5, 1934, Maquela do Zombo, Angola) Scholar, short-story writer, and poet whose works focus alternately on Angolan and Portuguese cultures. A poet of personal love and social protest in his early years, António in his later poems frequently presents verbal portraits of moods, places, and experiences.

António completed his primary and secondary studies in Luanda. After spending 11 years as a public civil servant in the Angolan capital, he moved to Lisbon in 1963.

António argued in his essays that Portuguese colonialism produced a creole, or mixed, culture in Angola in which European and African attitudes, values, and perspectives were shared by whites and blacks, as well as mulattos. He was a prolific contributor to journals and magazines in Angola and Portugal. His principal volumes of poetry include *Amor: poesias* (1960; "Love: Poems"), *100 Poemas* (1963), and *Rosto de Europa* (1968; "Face of Europe"). By the mid-1980s he was the author of more than 20 works in Portuguese, including poems, several collections of stories, cultural and literary essays on 19th- and 20th-century Angola, and translations.

Antonio \än-'tōn-yō\, Nicolás (b. July 28/31, 1617, Seville, Spain—d. April 13, 1684, Madrid) First systematic historian of Spanish literature. His *Bibliotheca hispana* appeared in two parts (*Nova*, 1672; *Vetus*, 1696). The first is a vast bibliography of Peninsular and Spanish colonial writers after 1500, with critical evaluations. The second, a history of Peninsular literature from the reign of Augustus (*c.* 27 BC to AD 14) to 1500, marks the emergence of modern bibliography and the transformation of literary history into a scholarly discipline. A second edition (1788; vol. 1 of the *Nova* dated 1783), with additions from Antonio's manuscripts, is still consulted.

antonomasia \an-,tän-ə-'mā-zhē-ə\ [Greek *antonomasía*, a derivative of *antonomázein* to call by a new name, from *anti*- against, in place of + *onomázein* to name] A figure of speech in which some defining word or phrase is substituted for a person's proper name (for example, "the Bard of Avon" for William Shakespeare). In fiction, the practice of giving to a character a proper name that defines or suggests a leading quality of that character (such as Squire *Allworthy*, Doctor *Sawbones*) is also called antonomasia.

Antony, Mark \'märk-'an-tə-nē\, *also spelled* Marc Anthony, *Latin* Marcus Antonius (b. 82/81 BC—d. August, 30 BC, Alexandria) Roman general under Julius Caesar and later triumvir (43–30 BC) who, with Cleopatra, queen of Egypt, was defeated by Octavian (the future emperor Augustus) in the last of the civil wars that destroyed the Roman Republic.

Antony was written of in such works as Plutarch's *Parallel Lives*, William Shakespeare's *Antony and Cleopatra*, and John Dryden's *All for Love*.

Antony and Cleopatra \'an-tə-nē . . . ,klē-ə-'pat-rə, -'pät-\ Tragedy in five acts by William SHAKESPEARE, produced about 1607 and published in the First Folio, 1623; it is considered one of Shakespeare's richest and most moving works. The principal source of the play is Sir Thomas North's 1579 English version of Plutarch's *Lives*.

The story concerns Mark Antony, Roman military leader and triumvir, who is desperately in love with Cleopatra, queen of Egypt and former mistress of Julius Caesar. Summoned to Rome upon the death of his wife, Fulvia, who had openly antagonized Octavius, Antony heals the residual political rift by marrying his fellow triumvir's sister, Octavia. Word of the event enrages Cleopatra. Renewed contention with Octavius, however, sends Antony back to his lover's arms. When the rivalry erupts into warfare, Cleopatra accompanies Antony to the Battle of Actium, where her presence proves controversial. She heads back to Egypt, and Antony follows, pursued by Octavius. At Alexandria, Octavius eventually defeats Antony. Cleopatra sends a false report of her suicide, which prompts him to wound himself mortally. Carried by one of the queen's messengers to her hiding place, he dies in her arms. Rather than submit to Roman conquest, the grieving Cleopatra arranges to have a poisonous snake delivered to her in a basket of figs.

Antrobus, Mr. and Mrs. \'an-trə-bəs, an-'trō-bəs\ Protagonists of Thornton Wilder's THE SKIN OF OUR TEETH. They are Adam and Eve as well as Everyperson figures.

Anvarī \än-'vä-,rē\, *pseudonym of* Awḥad ad-Dīn ʿAlī ibn Vāḥid ad-Dīn Muḥammad Khāvarānī \'aü-ḳad-ád-'dēn-'ä-lē-,ib-ən-'wä-,ḳēd-ád-'dēn-mù-'ḳàm-mád-,ḳà-và-'rä-,nē\, *also called* Awḥad ad-Dīn Muḥammad ibn Muḥammad *or* Awḥad ad-Dīn ʿAlī ibn Maḥmūd \,mák-'mūd\ (b. *c.* 1126, Abivard, Turkistan [now in Turkmenistan]—d. *c.* 1189, Balkh, Khorāsān [now in Afghanistan]) Poet considered one of the greatest panegyrists of Persian literature. He wrote with great technical skill, erudition, and a strong satirical wit.

Anvarī's work is replete with extremely erudite and obscure allusions, making his poems difficult to understand without some accompanying commentary. He was a prolific writer who especially excelled in the art of the qasida (ode) and ghazel (lyric). His odes display great formal virtuosity, while his comparatively simple lyrics are noted for their tenderness and charm. In his divan, or collected poems, are 632 pages of qasidas and ghazels, robāʿīs (quatrains), qiṭʿahs (shorter poems), and maśnawīs (couplets). Of his life relatively little is known. Rather early in his career he certainly served as court poet of Sultan Sanjar of the great Seljuq dynasty (11th to 13th century). Later he composed biting and satirical works sharply criticizing all aspects of the social order. His longest poem is a lament on the devastation wrought in Khorāsān (in northeastern Persia) in 1153 by invading Oğuz tribesmen. *Dīvan-i Anvarī* ("The Collected Poems of Anvarī"), edited by Saʿid Nafīsī, was published in 1959.

Anyte \ă-'nē-tā\ (fl. early 3rd century BC, Tegea, Arcadia) Greek poet of the Peloponnese who was highly esteemed in antiquity. So well respected was she that in the nucleus of the Greek Anthology—the well-known *Stephanos* ("Garland"), a collection compiled by Meleager (early 1st century)—the "lilies of Anyte" are the first poems to be entwined in the "wreath of poets." Anyte's fame persisted, and Antipater of Thessalonica, writing during the reign of Augustus (27 BC–AD 14), called her "a woman Homer" and placed her in a list of nine female lyric poets. Of 24 extant epigrams assigned to her, 20 are believed to be genuine. Her dedications for fountains and to the nymphs of the springs show the feeling for a quiet landscape that is so often illustrated in the Greek Anthology. Anyte also wrote epitaphs, perhaps literary rather than for actual use, on various animals. She gives no suggestion of herself in her poems and never employs the theme of love. Her love of nature and interest in animals mark her as typical of the early years of the Hellenistic period.

Anzengruber \'änt-sən-,grü-bər\, Ludwig (b. Nov. 29, 1839, Vienna [Austria]—d. Dec. 10, 1889, Vienna) Viennese playwright and novelist who won acclaim for his realistic plays depicting peasant life.

After working for a time as an actor, Anzengruber published an anticlerical drama, *Der Pfarrer von Kirchfeld* (1870; "The Pastor of Kirchfeld"), which was a great success. Except for the melancholy *Der Meineidbauer* (1872; "The Farmer Forsworn"), most of his plays were gay and witty comedies set among the people of small towns; they included *Die Kreuzelschreiber* (1872; "The Cross Makers"), *Der G'wissenswurm* (1874; "The Worm of Conscience"), and *Doppelselbstmord* (1876; "Double Suicide"). He wrote a problem play, *Das vierte Gebot* (1878; "The Fourth Commandment"), and also the novels *Der Schandfleck* (1877, rev. ed., 1884; "The Stain") and *Der Sternsteinhof* (1884; "The Sternstein Farm"), as well as other tales of village life.

Aonian \ā-'ō-nē-ən\ Of or relating to the district of ancient Greece called Aonia or to the Muses, the Greek goddesses who presided over various branches of learning and the arts and whose home was in Aonia on Mount Helicon.

aphaeresis or **apheresis** \ə-'fer-ə-sis\ [Greek *aphaíresis*, literally, taking away, removal] The loss of one or more sounds or letters at the beginning of a word (such as in *round* for *around* or *coon* for *raccoon*). Compare APOCOPE.

aphorism \'af-ə-ˌriz-əm\ [Greek *aphorismós* distinction, determination, pithy statement, a derivative of *aphorízein* to mark off, distinguish, determine] **1.** A concise statement of a principle. **2.** A terse formulation of any generally accepted truth or sentiment conveyed in a pithy, memorable statement. It is a synonym for ADAGE.

Aphorisms have been used especially in dealing with subjects for which principles and methodology developed relatively late—for example, art, agriculture, medicine, jurisprudence, and politics. The term was first used in the *Aphorisms* of Hippocrates, a long series of propositions concerning the symptoms and diagnosis of disease and the art of healing and medicine. The first aphorism, which serves as a kind of introduction to the book, runs as follows: "Life is short, Art long, Occasion sudden and dangerous, Experience deceitful, and Judgment difficult. Neither is it sufficient that the physician be ready to act what is necessary to be done by him, but the sick, and the attendants and all outward necessaries must be lightly prepared and fitted for the business."

The word gradually came to be used for the principles of other fields and finally for any statement generally accepted as true, so that it is now roughly synonymous with maxim.

Aphrodite \ˌaf-rō-'dī-tē\ Ancient Greek goddess of sexual love and beauty, identified by the Romans with VENUS. Because the Greek word *aphros* means "foam," the legend arose that Aphrodite was born from the white foam produced by the severed genitals of Uranus (Heaven) after his son Cronus had thrown them into the sea. Aphrodite was, in fact, widely worshiped as a goddess of the sea and of seafaring; she was also honored as a goddess of war, especially at Sparta, Thebes, Cyprus, and other places. Aphrodite was, however, primarily a goddess of love and fertility and even occasionally presided over marriage. Although prostitutes considered Aphrodite their patron, her public cult was generally solemn and even austere.

According to Homer, she was the daughter of Zeus and Dione, his consort at Dodona. In the *Odyssey*, Aphrodite was mismatched with Hephaestus, the lame smith god, and she consequently spent her time philandering with the handsome god of war, Ares (by whom she became the mother of Harmonia). Of Aphrodite's mortal lovers, the most important were the Trojan shepherd Anchises, by whom she bore Aeneas, and the handsome youth Adonis.

Aphrodite's close association with Eros, the Graces, and the Horae emphasized her role as a promoter of fertility. She was universally honored as Genetrix, the creative element in the world. Among her symbols were the dove, pomegranate, swan, and myrtle.

apocalyptic literature \ə-ˌpäk-ə-'lip-tik\ Literature that expounds a prophetic revelation and especially that predicts the destruction of the world.

The term is sometimes applied specifically to a literary genre that flourished from about 200 BC to about AD 200, especially in Judaism and Christianity. Written primarily to give hope to religious groups undergoing persecution or cultural upheaval, apocalyptic works described in cryptic language interpreted by believers the sudden, dramatic intervention of God in history on behalf of the faithful elect. They further detailed the cataclysmic events that would accompany or herald God's dramatic intervention in human affairs—such as a temporary rule of the world by Satan, signs in the heavens, persecutions, wars, famines, and plagues.

Although writers of these texts also examined the present to determine whether or not current afflictions were fulfillments of past apocalyptic prophecies, they generally concentrated on the future—the overthrow of evil, the coming of a messianic figure, and the establishment of the Kingdom of God and of eternal peace and righteousness.

The Book of Daniel in the Old Testament and the Revelation to John in the New Testament represent apocalyptic writing, and several intertestamental books contain apocalyptic themes. These themes were revived in modern literature; in poetry, notably that of William Blake; in novels such as Mary Shelley's *The Last Man*; and in many works of science fiction.

apocope \ə-'päk-ə-pē\ [Greek *apokopḗ*, literally, the act of cutting off, a derivative of *apokóptein* to cut off] The loss of one or more sounds or letters at the end of a word (as in *sing* from Old English *singen*).

apocrypha \ə-'päk-rə-fə\ [Late Greek *apókryphos* secret, uncanonical, from Greek, hidden] **1.** *usually capitalized also called* deuterocanonical. Quasi-scriptural writings that are of doubtful authorship and authority but that are accepted as part of the canon, or approved list, of the books of some versions of the Bible, specifically the Septuagint and the Vulgate. These books are excluded from the Jewish and Protestant canons. **2.** Writings or statements of doubtful or spurious authorship. The word is used to refer to works that are attributed to an author but not accepted as part of the author's canon.

Apollinaire \à-ˌpȯl-ē-'ner\, Guillaume, *pseudonym of* Guillelmus (or Wilhelm) Apollinaris de Kostrowitzky \də-kȯs-trō-vēt-'skē\ (b. Aug. 26, 1880, Rome?—d. Nov. 9, 1918, Paris, Fr.) Poet who in his short life took part in all the avant-garde movements that flourished in French literary and artistic circles at the beginning of the 20th century.

Apollinaire kept his origins secret, and his early history (including the identity of his father) was a matter of much conjecture. Sources differ as to his original name. He went at the age of 20 to Paris, where he led a bohemian life. By frequenting cafés patronized by other literary men, he soon became well known as a writer. He also made friends with some young painters and applied himself to the task of defining the principles of a Cubist aesthetic in literature as well as painting. His *Peintures cubistes* (*Cubist Painters*) appeared in 1913.

His first volume, *L'Enchanteur pourrissant* (1909; "The Rotting Magician"), is a strange dialogue in poetic prose between the magician Merlin and the nymph Viviane. In the following year a collection of vivid stories, some whimsical and some wildly fantastic, appeared under the title *L'Hérésiarque et Cie* (1910; "The Heresiarch and Co."). Then came *Le Bestiaire* (1911), in mannered quatrains. But his poetic masterpiece was *Alcools* (1913; Eng. trans., 1964). In these poems he relived all his experiences and expressed them sometimes in alexandrines and regular stanzas, sometimes in short unrhymed lines, and always without punctuation.

In 1914 Apollinaire enlisted in the infantry and became a second lieutenant; he received a head wound in 1916. Discharged, he returned to Paris and published a symbolic story, *Le Poète assassiné* (1916; *The Poet Assassinated*), and more significantly, a new collection of poems, CALLIGRAMMES (1918). His play *Les Mamelles de Tirésias* ("The Breasts of Tiresias") was staged in 1917, the year before he died. He called it Surrealist, using the term for what is believed to be the first time.

In his poetry Apollinaire made daring, even outrageous, technical experiments. More generally, Apollinaire set out to create an effect of surprise or even astonishment by means of unusual verbal associations and, because of this, is often considered the herald of Surrealism. *See also* PATTERN POETRY.

Apollo \ə-'päl-ō\ *byname* Phoebus \'fē-bəs\ In Greek mythology, the most widely revered and influential of all the Greek gods. Though his original nature is obscure, from the time of Homer onward he was the god of divine distance, who sent or threatened from afar; who made humans aware of their guilt and purified them of it; who presided over religious law and the constitutions of cities; who communicated through prophets and oracles his knowledge of the future and the will of his father, Zeus. Even the gods feared him, and only his father and his mother, Leto, could endure his presence. Distance, death, terror, and awe were summed up in his symbolic bow; a gentler side of his nature, however, was shown in his other attribute, the lyre, which proclaimed the joy of communion with Olympus (the home of the gods) through music, poetry, and dance. In humbler circles he was also a god of crops and herds, primarily as a divine bulwark against wild animals and disease, as his epithet Alexikakos ("Averter of Evil") indicates. His forename Phoebus means "bright" or "pure," and the view became current that he was connected with the sun. *See also* HELIOS.

Among Apollo's other epithets was Nomios ("Herdsman"), probably in reference to his reputed service to King Admetus of Pherae in the lowly capacities of groom and herdsman as penance for slaying Zeus's armorers, the Cyclopes. He was also called Lyceius, presumably because he protected the flocks from wolves (*lykoi*); because herdsmen and shepherds beguiled the hours with music, scholars have argued that this was Apollo's original role.

According to tradition, Apollo and his twin, Artemis, were born on the isle of Delos. From there Apollo went to Pytho (Delphi), where he slew Python, the dragon that guarded the area. He established his oracle by taking on the guise of a dolphin, leaping aboard a Cretan ship, and forcing the crew to serve him. Thus Pytho was renamed Delphi after the dolphin (*delphis*).

Although Apollo had many love affairs, they were mostly unfortunate: Daphne, in her efforts to escape him, was changed into a laurel, his sacred shrub; Coronis (mother of Asclepius) was shot by Apollo's twin, Artemis, when she proved unfaithful; and Cassandra (daughter of King Priam of Troy) rejected his advances and was punished by being made to utter true prophecies that no one believed.

In Italy Apollo was introduced at an early date and was primarily concerned, as in Greece, with healing and prophecy.

Apollon \ə-,pə-'lôn\ ("Apollo") Leading Russian monthly magazine published from 1909 to 1917 in St. Petersburg. Founded by Sergey Makovsky, an art historian, and Nikolay Gumilyov, a poet, *Apollon* was dedicated to contemporary art, sculpture, poetry, and literature. Initially, the journal was associated with the Acmeist group of Russian poets, of which Gumilyov was a member. Because of this association, in its early years the magazine contained much analysis of Russian modernist literature. By 1912, however, it was primarily an art publication, featuring excellent reproductions as well as reviews of foreign and domestic avant-garde art.

Apollonian \,ap-ə-'lō-nē-ən\ or **Apollonic** \,ap-ə-'län-ik\ or **Apollonistic** \ə-,päl-ə-'nis-tik\ Of, relating to, or resembling the god Apollo. Friedrich Nietzsche used the term in his book *The Birth of Tragedy* to describe one of the two opposing tendencies or elements in Greek tragedy. According to Nietzsche, the Apollonian attributes are reason, culture, harmony, and restraint. These are opposed to the Dionysian characteristics of excess, irrationality, lack of discipline, and unbridled passion. The Apollonian and Dionysian coalesce to create the tragic story, with the Apollonian tendency represented by the dialogue and the Dionysian by the dithyrambic choruses.

Apollonius \,ap-ə-'lō-nē-əs\ of Rhodes \'rōdz\ (b. *c.* 295 BC), Greek poet and grammarian who wrote the *Argonautica*.

The two lives contained in one manuscript of the *Argonautica* say that Apollonius was a pupil of Callimachus; that he gave a recitation of the *Argonautica* at Alexandria; and that when this proved a failure he retired to Rhodes. Both lives say that the *Argonautica* was well received in Rhodes, and the second cites a report that Apollonius returned to Alexandria and was appointed chief librarian. Another work has him succeed Eratosthenes in this post. But in a list of Alexandrian librarians on a late 2nd-century AD papyrus, Apollonius succeeds Zenodotus and precedes Eratosthenes. If this evidence is accepted it may be conjectured that Apollonius became a librarian about 260 BC and continued as such until about 247, when he fell out of favor under the new king, Ptolemy Euergetes, and retired to Rhodes.

In the *Argonautica*, an epic in four books on the voyage of the Argonauts, Apollonius adapted the language of Homer to the needs of a romantic epic with considerable success; in recounting Medea's love for Jason, he shows a capacity for sympathetic analysis not found in earlier Greek literature. Apollonius often holds the reader by his fresh handling of old episodes, his suggestive similes, and his admirable descriptions of nature.

Besides the *Argonautica*, Apollonius wrote epigrams and poems on the foundations (*Ktiseis*) of cities, most of which are lost. As a grammarian, he is credited with a work "against Zenodotus" and commentaries on several Greek poets.

Apollonius of Tyre \,ap-ə-'lō-nē-əs . . . 'tīr\ Chief personage in a medieval Latin romance of unknown authorship, which may be assumed to derive from a lost Greek original. The story enjoyed long and widespread popularity in European literature, and versions of it exist in almost every European language. It tells of the separation of Apollonius from his wife and daughter and his ultimate reunion with them after many travels.

The Greek original on which this story is thought to be based probably dates from the 3rd century AD. The Latin version is first mentioned in the second half of the 6th century. The most widespread versions in the Middle Ages include one by Godfrey of Viterbo in his *Pantheon*, a late 12th-century verse rendering that treated the story as authentic history, and one contained in the *Gesta Romanorum*, a 14th-century collection of folktales. An Anglo-Saxon translation (the first English vernacular version) was made in the 11th century, and the poet John Gower used the tale as an example of the seventh deadly sin (sloth) in his late 14th-century poem *Confessio amantis*. William Shakespeare used the story as the basis of his play *Pericles*.

apologue \'ap-ə-,lôg\ [Greek *apólogos*, from *apó* from, off + *lógos* word] An allegorical narrative (such as a beast fable) that is usually intended to convey a moral.

apology \ə-'päl-ə-jē\ [Greek *apología* speech in defense, from *apó* off, from + *lógos* word, speech] Autobiographical form in which a defense is the framework for a discussion by the author of his personal beliefs and viewpoints. An early example dating from the 4th century BC is Plato's *Apology*, in which Socrates answers the charges of his accusers by giving a brief history of his life and his moral commitment. Among the famous apologies of Western literature are *Apologie de Raimond Sebond* (1580), an essay by Montaigne, who uses a defense of the beliefs of a 15th-century Spaniard as a pretext for presenting his own views on the futility of reason; *An Apology for the Life of Mr. Colley Cibber, Comedian* (1740), in which the 18th-century English actor-manager answers his critic Alexander Pope with a summary of the achievements of his long career; and *Apologia pro Vita Sua* (1864; later retitled *History of My Religious Opinions*), in which John Henry Newman examines the religious principles that inspired his conversion to the Roman Catholic church.

aposiopesis \\,ap-ō-,sī-ō-'pē-sis\ [Greek *aposiōpēsis,* literally, the act of falling silent] In rhetoric, a speaker's deliberate failure to complete a sentence. Aposiopesis usually indicates speechless rage or exasperation, as in "Why, you . . . ," and sometimes implies vague threats, as in "Why, I'll . . . ." The listener is expected to complete the sentence in his mind. In ancient Greek rhetoric, the aposiopesis occasionally takes the form of a pause before a change of subject or a digression.

Apostle \ə-'päs-əl\ [Greek *apóstolos* messenger, ambassador, a derivative of *apostéllein* to send off, dispatch] Any of the 12 disciples chosen by Jesus Christ; the term is sometimes also applied to others, especially Paul, the missionary and theologian who was converted to Christianity a few years after the death of Jesus. The list of the Twelve is given with some variation in Mark 3, Matthew 10, and Luke 6 as: Peter; James and John, the sons of Zebedee; Andrew; Philip; Bartholomew; Matthew; Thomas; James, the son of Alphaeus; Thaddaeus or Judas, the son of James; Simon the Cananaean, or the Zealot; and Judas Iscariot.

apostrophe \ə-'päs-trə-fē\ [Greek *apostrophé,* literally, a turning away] A rhetorical device by which a speaker turns from the audience as a whole to address a single person or thing. For example, in William Shakespeare's *Julius Caesar,* Mark Antony addresses the corpse of Caesar in the speech that begins:

> O, pardon me, thou bleeding piece of earth,
> That I am meek and gentle with these butchers!
> Thou art the ruins of the noblest man
> That ever lived in the tide of times.
> Woe to the hand that shed this costly blood!

apothegm or **apophthegm** \'ap-ə-,them\ [Greek *apóphthegma,* a derivative of *apophthéngesthai* to speak out, speak one's opinion] A short, pithy, and instructive saying or formulation; an aphorism.

apparatus criticus \,ap-ə-'rat-əs-'krit-ə-kəs, ,ap-ə-'rā-təs-\ [New Latin, critical apparatus] Supplementary data (including such additional materials as variant readings) that are provided as part of an edition of a text to be used as a basis for critical study.

Appelfeld \'äp-əl-,feld\, Aharon *or* Aron (b. Feb. 16, 1932, Cernăuţi, Romania [now Chernivtsi, Ukraine]) Novelist and short-story writer who was best known for his Hebrew-language allegorical novels of the Holocaust.

At age 8 Appelfeld and his parents were captured by Nazi troops. His mother was killed and Aharon and his father were sent to a labor camp. Appelfeld eventually escaped and for two years roamed rural Ukraine, hiding and constantly on the move. He immigrated to Palestine in 1947. He served two years in the Israeli army, during which time he resumed his formal education, which had ended after the first grade. He later studied philosophy at Hebrew University and taught Hebrew literature at Israeli universities. Although Appelfeld's works in English translation dealt primarily with the Holocaust, his writings covered a wider range of subject matter.

Appelfeld's fiction includes *Bagai ha-poreh* (1963; *In the Wilderness*), *Badenheim, 'ir nofesh* (1979; *Badenheim 1939*), *Ha-Ketonet veha-pasim* (1983; *Tzili: The Story of a Life*), *Bartfus ben ha-almavet* (1988; *The Immortal Bartfuss*), *Katerinah* (1989; *Katerina*), *Mesilat barzel* (1991; "The Railway"), and *Unto the Soul* (1994). *Beyond Despair: Three Lectures and a Conversation with Philip Roth* was published in 1994.

Apple \'ap-əl\, Max (Isaac) (b. Oct. 22, 1941, Grand Rapids, Mich., U.S.) American writer known for the comic intelligence of his stories, which chronicle pop culture and other aspects of American life.

Educated at the University of Michigan (B.A., 1963; Ph.D., 1970), Apple taught at Reed College, Portland, Ore., from 1970 to 1971 and at Rice University, Houston, Tex., from 1972.

Apple's satire is distinguished by its gentle spoofing. His cast of characters often includes a mix of historical figures and fictional creations, as in *The Oranging of America* (1976), with its stories about materialism that feature such historical figures as C.W. Post, Howard Johnson, and Norman Mailer. In *Zip: A Novel of the Left and the Right* (1978), brief appearances are made by J. Edgar Hoover, Fidel Castro, and Jane Fonda. His later works include *Free Agents* (1984), *The Propheteers* (1987), and *Roommates: My Grandfather's Story* (1994).

apprenticeship novel Biographical novel that concentrates on an individual's youth and his social and moral initiation into adulthood. The term derives from J.W. von Goethe's *Wilhelm Meisters Lehrjahre* (1795–96; *Wilhelm Meister's Apprenticeship*). It became a subgenre of the novel in German literature, where it is called BILDUNGSROMAN. Examples of the form in English include Charles Dickens' *David Copperfield* (1850) and Thomas Wolfe's *Look Homeward, Angel* (1929).

aptronym \'ap-trō-nim\ A name that fits some aspect of a character, as in Mr. Talkative and Mr. Worldly Wiseman in John Bunyan's *The Pilgrim's Progress,* or Mrs. Malaprop in Richard Brinsley Sheridan's play *The Rivals.* The term *aptronym* was allegedly coined by the American newspaper columnist Franklin P. Adams, by an anagrammatic reordering of the first letters of *patronym* (to suggest *apt*).

Apuleius \,ap-ú-'lē-əs\, Lucius (b. *c.* 124, Madauros, Byzacium [now M'Daourouch, Alg.]—d. probably after 170) Platonic philosopher, rhetorician, and author remembered for THE GOLDEN ASS, a prose narrative that was long influential.

Apuleius was educated at Carthage and Athens. Intellectually versatile and acquainted with works of both Latin and Greek writers, he taught rhetoric in Rome before returning to Africa to marry a rich widow, Aemilia Pudentilla. To meet her family's charge that he had practiced magic to win her affection, he wrote the *Apologia* ("Defense"), the major source for his biography. After he was acquitted, he lived in Carthage.

Apuleius' *The Golden Ass* is an account of the ribald adventures of a young man (supposed to resemble the author) who is changed into an ass. In addition to its many notable episodes, it contains the most complete version of the tale of Cupid and Psyche.

His philosophical treatises included three books on Plato, two of which survive: *De Platone et eius dogmate* ("On Plato and His Teaching") and *De Deo Socratis* ("On the God of Socrates"), which expounds the Platonic notion of demons, beneficent creatures intermediate between gods and mortals. His *De mundo* ("On the World") adapts a treatise incorrectly attributed to Aristotle. The noted *Asclepius* (a Latin translation of a lost Greek Hermetic dialogue) has been wrongly attributed to him.

'Aqqād, al- \,äl-,äk-'käd, *Arabic* -,'äk-\, 'Abbās Maḥmūd (b. June 28, 1889, Aswān, Egypt—d. March 12, 1964, Cairo) Egyptian journalist, poet, and literary critic who was an innovator of 20th-century Arabic poetry and criticism.

Born in modest circumstances, al-'Aqqād continued his education through reading when his formal schooling was cut short. An outspoken political commentator, he was imprisoned for some months in 1930–31 for remarks opposing the government. In 1942, with the advance of German troops, al-'Aqqād sought refuge in the Sudan as a precaution against German reprisals for his attacks on Adolf Hitler.

Al-'Aqqād's literary works include poems; a novel, *Sarāh* (1938), based on one of his own romances; and critiques of classical and modern Arabic authors. His essays show the influence of 19th-century English essay writers, particularly Thomas Carlyle. His other works include studies of the Qur'ān and of political and social philosophy and biographies of various Muslim leaders.

arabesque \,ar-ə-'besk\ [French, intricate ornament, from Italian *arabesco,* literally, ornament in the style of the Arabs] A contrived intricate pattern of verbal expression, so called by analogy with a decorative style in which flower, fruit, and sometimes animal outlines appear in elaborate patterns of interlaced lines. That these designs can sometimes suggest fantastic creatures may have given rise to another sense of the term, denoting a tale of wonder or of the supernatural. Nikolay Gogol used this sense of the word in his *Arabeski* (1835; *Arabesques*) five years before Edgar Allan Poe collected some of his tales under the title *Tales of the Grotesque and Arabesque.*

Arabian Nights' Entertainment, The   *see* THE THOUSAND AND ONE NIGHTS.

Arabic literary renaissance *Arabic* An-Naḥdah al-Adabīyah. Nineteenth-century movement aimed at creating a modern Arabic literature, inspired by contacts with the West and a renewed interest in the great classical Arabic literature.

After the Napoleonic invasion of Egypt (1798) and the subsequent establishment of an autonomous and Western-minded ruling dynasty there, many Syrian and Lebanese writers sought out the freer environment of Egypt, making it the center of the renaissance. Under the impact of the dismemberment of the Ottoman Empire after World War I and the coming of independence following World War II, the revival spread to other Arab countries.

The novel and drama, forms new to Arabic literature, were developed largely under the influence of the European works that became available in the 19th century in Arabic translation. Other genres, such as the short story, new verse forms, and the essay, owed much to Western models but had roots in classical Arabic literature.

That the renaissance succeeded in altering the direction of Arabic literature is probably attributable to two factors. The emergence of an Arabic press made writing a realistic livelihood and forced writers to abandon the traditional, ornate style of past centuries in favor of a simpler and more direct style that would appeal to a wider reading public. The spread and modernization of education further served to provide a body of readers receptive to new styles and ideas.

Arachne \ə-'rak-nē\ ("Spider") In Greek mythology, the daughter of Idmon of Colophon in Lydia, a dyer in purple.

Arachne was a weaver who acquired such skill in her art that she ventured to challenge Athena. The goddess wove a tapestry depicting the gods in majesty, while that of Arachne showed their amorous adventures. Enraged at the perfection of her rival's work (or, alternatively, offended by its subject matter), Athena tore it to pieces, and in despair Arachne hanged herself. But the goddess out of pity loosened the rope, which became a cobweb; Arachne herself was changed into a spider, whence the name of the zoological class to which spiders belong, Arachnida. Ovid's *Metamorphoses* is the chief source of the myth.

Aragon \á-rá-'gōⁿ\, Louis, *original surname* Andrieux \áⁿ-drē-'yœ\ (b. Oct. 3, 1897, Paris, Fr.—d. Dec. 24, 1982, Paris) Poet, novelist, and essayist who was a political activist and spokesman for communism.

Through the Surrealist poet André Breton, Aragon was introduced to avant-garde movements such as Dadaism; and

together with Philippe Soupault, he and Breton founded the Surrealist review *Littérature* (1919). Aragon's first collections of poems, *Feu de joie* (1920; "Bonfire") and *Le Mouvement perpétuel* (1925; "Perpetual Motion"), were followed by a novel, *Le Paysan de Paris* (1926; *The Nightwalker*). In 1927 his search for an ideology led him to the Communist Party, with which he was identified thereafter, as he came to exercise a continuing authority over its literary and artistic expression. In 1928 he met Elsa Triolet (the Russian-born sister-in-law of the poet Vladimir Mayakovsky), who became his wife and his inspiration.

In 1930 Aragon visited the Soviet Union, and in 1933 his political commitment resulted in a break with the Surrealists. The four volumes of his long novel series, *Le Monde réel* (1933–44; "The Real World"), describe in historical perspective the class struggle of the proletariat toward social revolution. Aragon continued to employ traditional Socialist Realism in another long novel, *Les Communistes* (6 vol., 1949–51), a bleak chronicle of the party from 1939 to 1940. His next three novels—*La Semaine sainte* (1958; *Holy Week*), *La Mise à mort* (1965; "The Moment of Truth"), and *Blanche ou l'oubli* (1967; "Blanche, or Forgetfulness")—became a veiled autobiography, laced with pleas for the Communist Party.

The poems of *Le Crève-coeur* (1941; "The Heartbreak") and *La Diane française* (1945) express Aragon's ardent patriotism, and those of *Les Yeux d'Elsa* (1942; "Elsa's Eyes") and *Le Fou d'Elsa* (1963; "Elsa's Madman") contain a deep expression of love for his wife. From 1953 to 1972 Aragon served as editor of the communist weekly of arts and literature *Les Lettres françaises.*

Aramis \'ar-ə-mis, *French* ár-â-'mēs\ Fictional character, one of the swashbuckling heroes of THE THREE MUSKETEERS by Alexandre Dumas *père.* With the other two musketeers, Athos and Porthos, Aramis fights against various enemies, notably Cardinal Richelieu, during the reigns of the French kings Louis XIII and Louis XIV.

Arany \'ör-ònʸ\, János (b. March 2, 1817, Nagyszalonta, Hung.—d. Oct. 22, 1882, Budapest) The greatest Hungarian epic poet.

Arany went to school in Debrecen but abandoned his studies to join a group of strolling players. He made his real advent on the literary scene in 1847 with his popular epic *Toldi,* which was received with enthusiasm by a public craving a national literature of quality in a language all could grasp.

In 1848 Arany took part in the Hungarian revolution and for a short period edited a government newspaper for peasants. With the crushing of the revolution he took up teaching. In 1858 he was elected a member of the Hungarian Academy. He moved then from Nagykőrös to Pest, where he edited a literary periodical, the *Szépirodalmi Figyelő* (later the *Koszorú*).

Arany's main epic work is the trilogy *Toldi* (1847), *Toldi szerelme* (1848–79; "Toldi's Love"), and *Toldi estéje* (1854; "Toldi's Evening"). Its hero, a youth of great physical strength, is taken from a verse chronicle written by Péter Ilosvai Selymes in the 16th century. Set in the 14th century, the first part of the trilogy tells the adventures of Toldi in reaching the royal court; the second part, of his tragic love; and the third, of his conflicts with the king and his death. Though only a fragment, another epic poem, *Bolond Istók* (1850; "Stephen the Fool"), a strange mixture of humor and bitterness, is valuable for Arany's rare moments of self-revelation. Arany started work on a Hun trilogy, connected with Hungarian prehistory, but finished only the first part of it, *Buda halála* (1864; *The Death of King Buda*).

The poems of his two great lyrical periods are fraught with melancholy. The earlier poems, written in the 1850s, are deeply colored by the loss of his friend Sándor Petőfi and by Arany's despair for the Hungarian nation and for himself. The *Ős-zikék*, his beautiful swan song, written just before his death, poignantly reflects Arany's sense of unfulfillment and isolation.

Āraṇyaka \ā-'rən-yə-kə\ (Sanskrit: "Book of the Forest") Any of a number of texts that constitute a later development of the Brāhmaṇas, or expositions of the Vedas, which were composed in India about 900–700 BC. The Āraṇyakas are distinguished from the Brāhmaṇas in that they may contain information on secret rites to be carried out only by certain persons and they often include philosophic speculation about the internal, meditative meaning of the sacrifice, as contrasted to its actual, outward performance. *Compare* BRĀHMAṆA; UPANISHAD. *See also* VEDA.

Arason \'är-ä-ˌsòn\, Jón (b. 1484, Eyjafjördur, Ice.—d. Nov. 7, 1550, Skálholt) Poet and last Roman Catholic bishop in Iceland, remembered as a national as well as a religious hero.

The son of poor parents, he rose quickly to eminence in the church and was consecrated bishop of Hólar, the northern diocese of Iceland, in 1522. He administered his diocese prosperously until Christian III of Denmark began to impose Lutheranism on all his subjects. The two Icelandic bishops, Jón in the north and Ögmundr in the south, protested in 1537. Ögmundr was deported by the Danes in 1541, but Jón continued his resistance. He captured the Lutheran bishop Marteinn and occupied his see from 1549 to 1550 but was soon afterward taken by the king's agents and beheaded with two of his sons. Jón was the author of splendid religious and satirical poetry; he brought the first printing press to Iceland. His life was the subject of novels and plays by later Icelandic writers.

Aratus \ə-'rä-təs\ (fl. *c.* 315–*c.* 245 BC, Macedonia [Greece]) Greek poet of Soli in Cilicia, best remembered for his poem on astronomy, *Phaenomena*.

Aratus resided at the courts of Antigonus II Gonatas, king of Macedonia, and Antiochus I of Syria. The *Phaenomena*, a didactic poem in hexameters, is his only complete extant work. Lines 1–757 versify a prose work on astronomy by Eudoxus of Cnidus (*c.* 390–*c.* 340), while lines 758–1154 treat of weather signs and seem clearly indebted to an earlier meteorological work. The poem became immediately popular and provoked many commentaries, the most important of which is by Hipparchus (c. 150 BC) and is still extant. The *Phaenomena* enjoyed a high reputation among the Romans. Cicero, Caesar Germanicus, and Avienus translated it; the two last versions and fragments of Cicero's rendition survive. One verse from the opening invocation to Zeus has become famous because it was quoted by Paul in the Bible (Acts 17:28).

Arber \'är-bər\, Edward (b. Dec. 4, 1836, London, Eng.—d. Nov. 23, 1912, London) Scholar whose editing, and publication at reasonable prices, of Elizabethan and Restoration texts first made detailed study of them possible for the ordinary student.

An Admiralty clerk, Arber studied literature and entered academic life, serving as professor of English at Birmingham from 1881 to 1894. His editions of many texts remain the only ones easily accessible. Among them are his *English Reprints*, 30 vol. (1868–71), which began with a sixpenny edition of John Milton's *Areopagitica*. Later series include the important *English Garner*, 8 vol. (1877–96), and *The English Scholar's Library of Old and Modern Works*, 16 vol. (1878–84).

Arbuthnot \är-'bəth-nət, *commonly* 'är-bəth-ˌnät\, John (b. April 1667, Inverbervie, Kincardine, Scot.—d. Feb. 27, 1735, London, Eng.) Scottish mathematician, physician, and occasional writer, remembered as a founding member of the famous Scriblerus Club, which aimed to ridicule bad literature and false learning.

After taking a medical degree in 1696 at St. Andrews, Arbuthnot became a Fellow of the Royal Society in 1704 and was one of Queen Anne's physicians from 1705 until her death. Though he published mathematical and other scientific works, his fame rests on his reputation as a wit and on his satirical writings. One of his most important satires was an allegory dealing with the political jockeying of the British, French, Spanish, and Dutch that led to the Treaty of Utrecht (1713). Published in five pamphlets in 1712, it was collected (1727) under the composite title *Law Is a Bottom-less Pit; or, The History of John Bull* in Jonathon Swift and Alexander Pope's three-volume *Miscellanies in Prose and Verse*. This collection established and popularized for the first time the character JOHN BULL, who was to become the permanent symbol of England in cartoon and literature.

The other satire in which Arbuthnot had an important share was the *Memoirs of Martinus Scriblerus*, a mocking exposure of pedantry, first published in the 1741 edition of Pope's works, but largely written as early as 1713–14 by the members of the Scriblerus Club. The other members of the club acknowledged Arbuthnot as the chief contributor and guiding spirit of the work.

Arcadia \är-'kā-dē-ə\ or **Arcady** \'är-kə-dē\ *plural* Arcadias *or* Arcadies. An idealized region or scene of simple pleasure, rustic innocence, and uninterrupted quiet. The word was derived from the name of a pastoral region of ancient Greece that was represented as a rural paradise in Greek and Roman bucolic poetry. It was later used in the same sense in the literature of the Renaissance by such writers as the Italian poet Jacopo Sannazzaro and England's Sir Philip Sidney.

arcádia \är-'käj-ə\ Any of the 18th-century Portuguese literary societies that attempted to revive Portuguese poetry by urging a return to classicism. They were modeled after the Academy of Arcadia, established in Rome in 1690 as an arbiter of Italian literary taste.

In 1756 António Dinis da Cruz e Silva established with others the Arcádia Lusitana, its first aim being the uprooting of *gongorismo*, a style studded with Baroque conceits and Spanish influence in general. Other prominent Arcadians included Pedro António Correia Garção, an accomplished devotee of the Latin classical poet Horace, and Tomás Antônio Gonzaga, who is known for a collection of pastoral love lyrics written under the pseudonym Dirceu.

Cruz e Silva was sent to Brazil as a judge in 1776; there he helped stimulate Brazilian interest in the Arcadian movement, which flourished among the so-called Minas school of poets, including José Basílio da Gama and José de Santa Rita Durão.

In 1790 the New Arcadia was established. Its two most distinguished members were the rival poets Manuel Maria Barbosa du Bocage, who is now remembered for a few outstanding sonnets, and José Agostinho de Macedo, known for his experiments with the epic form.

Arcadia, Academy of \är-'kā-dē-ä\, *Italian* Accademia dell'Arcadia \ˌäk-ä-'dä-myä-del-är-'käd-yä\ Italian literary academy that was founded in Rome in 1690 to combat Marinism, the dominant Italian poetic style of the 17th century. The Arcadians sought a more natural, simple poetic style based on the classics and particularly on Greek and Roman pastoral poetry.

The Academy of Arcadia was inspired by Queen Christina of Sweden, who, having given up her throne, gathered a literary circle in Rome. After Christina's death in 1689, her friends founded the academy to give their meetings permanence. They named the academy for Arcadia, a pastoral region of ancient Greece, and assumed Greek names themselves.

Although most Arcadian poetry was rather pale and imitative, the academy had two outstanding writers in the 17th and 18th centuries: Paolo Rolli, who was particularly skilled in *canzonetti*, and Pietro Metastasio, one of the greatest lyricists and librettists in Italian literature. Gabriello Chiabrera, who experimented with metrical forms, was also an Arcadian, as were Gabriele Rossetti (the father of the English poets Dante Gabriel and Christina Rossetti) and Pope Leo XIII, an accomplished poet who wrote a poem for the academy's 200th anniversary.

The Academy of Arcadia was an important influence in the simplification of Italian poetry and inspired the establishment in Italy of many Arcadian colonies that did not have a specifically literary purpose but sought a return to a pastoral existence.

In 1925 the academy was made an academic and historical institute and was renamed the Accademia Letteraria Italiana.

archaic \är-'kā-ik\ [Greek *archaïkós* old-fashioned] Of a writer or literary work, characterized by the intentional use of old-fashioned language.

archangel \'är-ˌkān-jəl\ [Greek *archángelos*] Any of several chiefs, rulers, or princes of angels in the hierarchy of angels of the major world religions, especially Judaism, Christianity, and Islām, and of certain religions, such as Gnosticism, that combine the beliefs and practices of more than one established religion. The four best-known archangels, Michael, Gabriel, Uriel, and Raphael, figure in various works of literature, notably in John Milton's epic poem *Paradise Lost. See also* ANGEL.

Archer \'är-chər\, William (b. Sept. 23, 1856, Perth, Scot.— d. Dec. 27, 1924, London, Eng.) Drama critic whose translations introduced Henrik Ibsen to the British public.

While studying law at Edinburgh, Archer began his journalistic career on the *Edinburgh Evening News*. He later moved to London and became a drama critic. In 1884 he joined the *World*; his reviews for it and other periodicals were collected in *The Theatrical 'World' of 1893-1897*, 5 vol. (1894–98).

The translations of Ibsen that were to make Archer famous began with *Pillars of Society* (1880), the first of the plays produced in England. Later translations included *A Doll's House* (1889), *Ibsen's Prose Dramas*, 5 vol. (1890–91), *Peer Gynt* (1892), *The Master Builder* (1893), and the *Collected Works*, 12 vol. (1906–12). His own play *The Green Goddess* (1921) was extremely successful. Of his other dramatic works, four were posthumously published.

Archer, Isabel \'iz-ə-ˌbel-'är-chər\ Title character of the novel THE PORTRAIT OF A LADY by Henry James. A penniless young American, Isabel ventures to England in pursuit of cultural broadening and attracts the attention of numerous suitors. Her decision to marry the reclusive aesthete Gilbert Osmond eventually forces her to assess the relative merits of her own tendencies and deeper convictions.

Archer, Lew \'lü-'är-chər\ Fictional private investigator featured in the hard-boiled detective novels of Ross MACDONALD. Archer made his first appearance in *The Moving Target* (1949). In this and subsequent books, including *The Galton Case* (1959), *The Goodbye Look* (1969), and *The Underground Man* (1971), the no-frills P.I. unravels intricate webs of deception and violence among the wealthy of southern California. Behind his austere, streetwise exterior Archer is a man of deep introspection and personal integrity who avoids the entanglements of the world he dissects.

archetypal criticism \ˌär-kə-'tī-pəl\ A form of literary criticism that is concerned with the discovery and analysis of the original pattern or model for themes, motifs, and characters in poetry and prose.

This approach to literature is based on the idea that narratives are structured in accordance with an underlying archetypal model: the specific plot and characters are important insofar as they allude to a traditional plot or figure or to patterns that have recurred with wide implications in human history. An archetypal critic, for example, on examining Katherine Anne Porter's story "Flowering Judas," would note that it echoes and ironically inverts the traditional Christian legend of Judas Iscariot.

Archetypal criticism was effectively founded with the publication of the multivolume work *The Golden Bough* by British anthropologist and folklorist J.G. Frazer. The theories of the psychologist Carl Jung also contributed to the underlying principles of such criticism. Other important works on the subject are *Archetypal Patterns in Poetry* (1934) by Maud Bodkin and Northrop Frye's *Anatomy of Criticism* (1957).

archetype \'är-kə-ˌtīp\ [Greek *archétypon* original pattern] A primordial image, character, or pattern of circumstances that recurs throughout literature and thought consistently enough to be considered universal. The term was adopted by literary critics from the writings of the psychologist Carl Jung, who formulated a theory of the collective unconscious. For Jung, the varieties of human experience have somehow been genetically coded and transferred to successive generations. Originating in pre-logical thought, these primordial image patterns and situations evoke startlingly similar feelings in both reader and author.

The laurel and olive branches, the snake, whale, eagle, and vulture all are archetypal symbols. An example of an archetypal theme in literature is that of initiation, the passage from innocence to experience; archetypal characters that recur in literature include the blood brother, rebel, wise grandparent, generous thief, and prostitute with a heart of gold.

archilochean \ˌär-kə-'lō-kē-ən\ In classical poetry, one of several different verse forms ascribed to the Greek poet Archilochus, including the greater archilochean (a line composed of a dactylic tetrapody followed by a trochaic tripody) and the lesser archilochean (a dactylic tripody catalectic). This line was the chief component of a larger metrical unit called the archilochean strophe. In its most frequent form this strophe consisted of six lines: a dactylic hexameter followed by a lesser archilochean, another dactylic hexameter followed by an iambelegus, and a greater archilochean followed by an iambic trimeter catalectic.

Archilochus or **Archilochos** \är-'kil-ə-kəs\ (b. 675?, Paros [Greece]—d. 635?) Greek poet and soldier who is sometimes considered to be the best Greek poet after Homer.

Archilochus was the illegitimate son of a noble father. This would probably have made little difference to his social status had he not been spurned as a suitor by a certain Neobule. Perhaps as a result of this rebuff Archilochus went to live in Thasos, where he seems to have become a soldier of fortune, later serving in Thrace and other places and composing his poetry as he served. It is noteworthy that, unlike the writers who came before him, Archilochus saw no glory in war.

A master of iambic meter, Archilochus was much admired by later poets, particularly Horace. The popularity and influence of his poetry in later times testify to the universality, as well as to the force and originality, of his genius. He is especially memorable for his controlled, yet personal voice—a distinct departure from other surviving ancient Greek poetry, which is generally more formulaic and heroic.

arch-poet \ˌärch-'pō-ət\ A chief poet.

Archy and Mehitabel \'är-chē . . . mə-'hit-ə-,bel\ Collection of humorous stories by Don MARQUIS, originally published from 1916 in Marquis's newspaper columns "The Sun Dial" in the New York *Evening Sun* and "The Lantern" in the New York *Herald Tribune* and published in book form in 1927. The stories center on Archy, a philosophical cockroach who types messages to the author in lowercase letters (being unable to activate the shift mechanism), and Mehitabel, a free-spirited alley cat whose motto is "toujours gai." After initial publication, the work and its sequels were usually published without capital letters.

Archy and Mehitabel consists mostly of free-verse poems on such concerns of Archy's as transmigration of souls, social injustice, life in New York City, and death. Sequels included *Archys Life of Mehitabel* (1933) and *Archy Does His Part* (1935), both of which were included in *the lives and times of archy and mehitabel* (1940; illustrated by George Herriman), a posthumously published compendium of the previous books.

Arciniegas \,är-sē-'nyä-gäs, -gäh\, Germán (b. Dec. 6, 1900, Bogotá, Colom.) Colombian historian, essayist, diplomat, and statesman whose long career in journalism and public service strongly influenced Colombia's cultural development in the 20th century. As an educator and diplomat he played an important role in disseminating information about Latin-American history and culture.

Arciniegas became a prominent figure in public life soon after his graduation from the law school of the National University of Colombia in Bogotá in 1924. He contributed essays to several newspapers and magazines, founding the review *Universidad* ("University") in Bogotá in 1928 and becoming editor of the newspaper *El tiempo* ("The Times") there in 1939. Also active in education, he served as Colombian minister of education (1941–42 and 1945–46) and taught at several universities in the United States, including Columbia University (1947–57).

Arciniegas published numerous volumes—such as *Biografía del Caribe* (1945; *Caribbean, Sea of the New World*) and *El continente de siete colores* (1965; *Latin America: A Cultural History*)—on diverse aspects of Latin-American culture and history that reveal his original perceptions as well as his encyclopedic knowledge.

In his 50s Arciniegas turned to a diplomatic career. In 1959 he was appointed Colombian ambassador to Italy; later he also served in Israel, Venezuela, and Vatican City.

Arden \'är-dən\, John (b. Oct. 26, 1930, Barnsley, Yorkshire, Eng.) One of the most important of the British playwrights to emerge in the mid-20th century; his plays mix poetry and songs with colloquial speech in a boldly theatrical manner and involve strong conflicts purposely left unresolved.

Arden grew up in the industrial town of Barnsley, whose personality he captured in his play *The Workhouse Donkey* (1963). He studied architecture at the University of Cambridge and at Edinburgh College of Art, where fellow students performed his comedy *All Fall Down* (1955), about the construction of a railway. His first play to be produced professionally was a radio drama, *The Life of Man* (1956), about the fatal voyage of a boat captained by a madman. *The Waters of Babylon* (1957), a play with a roguish central character, revealed the moral ambiguity that was to trouble critics and audiences of his later dramas. His next two plays, *Live Like Pigs* (1958) and *Serjeant Musgrave's Dance* (1959), also caused controversy.

In 1960 his play *The Happy Haven*, a sardonic farce about an old people's home, was produced in London. *Armstrong's Last Goodnight* (1964), written in lowland Scots vernacular, dramatized the struggle between a courtier and a freebooter, pointing up resemblances between the play's 16th-century Scottish set-

ting and the contemporary Congo. *Left-Handed Liberty* (1965), written on the occasion of the 750th anniversary of the signing of Magna Carta, characteristically dwells on the failure of the document to achieve liberty. Arden's later plays include *The True History of Squire Jonathan and His Unfortunate Treasure* (1968); *The Island of the Mighty* (1972), written with his wife Margaretta D'Arcy; *The Non-Stop Connolly Show* (1975); *Vandaleur's Folly* (1978); and *The Little Gray Home in the West* (1982).

Arden, Enoch \'ē-nək-'är-dən\ Fictional character, protagonist of Alfred, Lord Tennyson's narrative poem ENOCH ARDEN.

À rebours \á-rə-'bür\ *see* AGAINST THE GRAIN.

Arenas \ä-'rā-näs\, Reinaldo (b. July 16, 1943, Holguín, Oriente, Cuba—d. Dec. 7, 1990, New York, N.Y., U.S.) Cuban-born writer of extraordinary and unconventional novels who fled persecution and immigrated to the United States.

As a teenager Arenas joined the revolution that brought Fidel Castro to power in 1959. He moved to Havana in 1961 and became a researcher in the José Martí National Library (1963–68) and a journalist and editor for the literary magazine *La Gaceta de Cuba* (1968–74).

His first novel, the award-winning *Celestino antes del alba* (1967; *Singing From the Well*), was the only one of his novels to be published in Cuba. His second and best-known novel, *El mundo alucinante* (1969; *Hallucinations: Being an Account of the Life and Adventures of Friar Servando Teresa de Mier*; also published as *The Ill-Fated Peregrinations of Fray Servando*), was smuggled out of the country and first published in French. During the 1970s, Arenas was imprisoned for his writings and open homosexuality.

In 1980 Arenas escaped to the United States. There he finally published *Otra vez el mar* (1982; *Farewell to the Sea*), the manuscript of which had been confiscated by the Cuban government. His other novels include *La vieja Rosa* (1980; *Old Rosa*); *La loma del ángel* (1987; *Graveyard of the Angels*); and *El portero* (1988; *The Doorman*). Suffering from AIDS, Arenas committed suicide in 1990. Some of his posthumously published works are *Viaje a La Habana: novela en tres viajes* (1990; "Journey to Havana: A Novel in Three Trips") and *Antes que anochezca: autobiografía* (1992; *Before Night Falls*).

Areopagitica \,ar-ē-ō-pə-'jit-i-kə\ (*in full* Areopagitica: A Speech of Mr John Milton for the Liberty of Unlicenc'd Printing, to the Parliament of England) Pamphlet by John MILTON, published in 1644 to protest an order issued by Parliament the previous year requiring government approval and licensing of all published books. Four earlier pamphlets by the author concerning divorce had met with official disfavor and suppressive measures.

The title of the work derives from "Areopagus" ("Hill of Ares"), the name of the site from which the high court of Athens administered its jurisdiction and imposed a general censorship. In a prose style that draws heavily on Greek models, Milton argues that to mandate licensing is to follow the example of the detested Papacy. He defends the free circulation of ideas as essential to moral and intellectual development. Furthermore, he asserts, to attempt to preclude falsehood is to underestimate the power of truth.

Ares \'ā-rēz, 'ar-ēz\ In Greek mythology, god of war or, more properly, the spirit of battle. Unlike his Roman counterpart, MARS, he was never very popular, and his worship was not extensive in Greece, where he represented the distasteful aspects of brutal warfare and slaughter. From at least the time of Homer, who established him as the son of Zeus and his consort

Hera, Ares was one of the Olympian deities; neither his fellow gods nor even his parents, however, were fond of him.

The mythology surrounding the figure of Ares is not extensive. He was associated with Aphrodite from earliest times. Occasionally, Aphrodite was Ares' legitimate wife, and by her he fathered Deimos, Phobos, and Harmonia. By Aglauros, the daughter of Cecrops, he was the father of Alcippe. He was the sire of at least two of Heracles' adversaries: Cycnus and Diomedes of Thrace.

aretalogy \\,ar-ə-'tal-ə-jē\ [Greek *aretalogía* celebration of miraculous deeds, from *aretaí* miraculous deeds, wonders + *légein* to say, speak] A narrative of the miraculous deeds of a god or hero.

Arethusa \\,ar-i-'thü-sə\ In Greek mythology, a nymph who gave her name to springs in Elis and on the island of Ortygia, near Syracuse.

The standard version of the legend holds that the river god Alpheus fell in love with Arethusa, who was in the retinue of Artemis. Arethusa fled to Ortygia, where she was changed into a spring. Alpheus, however, made his way beneath the sea and united his waters with those of the spring. According to Ovid's *Metamorphoses*, Arethusa, while bathing in the Alpheus River, was seen and pursued by the river god in human form. Artemis changed her into a spring that, flowing underground, emerged at Ortygia. In an earlier form of the legend, it was Artemis, not Arethusa, who was the object of the river god's affections.

Aretino \\,ä-rä-'tē-nō\, Pietro (b. April 20, 1492, Arezzo, Republic of Florence [Italy]—d. Oct. 21, 1556, Venice) Italian poet, prose writer, and dramatist celebrated throughout Europe in his time for his bold and insolent literary attacks on the powerful. His fiery letters and dialogues are of great biographical and topical interest.

Although Aretino was the son of an Arezzo shoemaker, he later pretended to be the bastard son of a nobleman and derived his adopted name ("the Aretine") from that of his native city (his real name is unknown). He lived for a while in Perugia before moving to Rome in 1517, where he wrote a series of viciously satirical lampoons supporting the candidacy of Giulio de' Medici for the papacy (Giulio became Pope Clement VII in 1523). Aretino was finally forced to leave Rome because of his general notoriety and his 1524 collection of *Sonetti lussuriosi* ("Lewd Sonnets"). From Rome he went to Venice, where he formed a friendship with the painter Titian and became the object of great adulation.

Among Aretino's many works, the most characteristic are his satirical attacks, often amounting to blackmail, on the powerful. He grew wealthy on gifts from kings and nobles who feared his satire and coveted the fame accruing from his adulation. His six volumes of letters (published 1537–57) show his power and cynicism and give ample justification for the name he gave himself, "*flagello dei principe*" ("scourge of princes"). Aretino was particularly vicious in his attacks on Romans because they had forced him to flee to Venice. In his *Ragionamenti* (1534–36; modern edition, 1914; "Discussions"), Roman prostitutes reveal to each other the moral failings of many important men of their city.

Only Aretino's dramas were relatively free of such venomous assaults. His five comedies are acutely perceived pictures of lower-class life, free from the conventions that burdened other contemporary dramas. He also wrote a tragedy, *Orazia* (published 1546; "The Horatii"), which has been judged by some the best Italian tragedy of the 16th century.

Arévalo Martínez \\,ä-rä-ḇä-lō-mär-'tē-näs\, Rafael (b. July 25, 1884, Quezaltenango, Guat.—d. June 13, 1975, Guatemala City) Guatemalan novelist and short-story writer whose work is considered one of the most important precursors of modern Latin-American fiction.

Arévalo Martínez was appointed director of the Guatemalan National Library in 1926, a post he held until 1946. A short-story writer of marked ability, he introduced a new form known as the "psychozoological" tale, the most famous of which, "El hombre que parecía un caballo" (1915; "The Man Who Looked Like a Horse"), deals with the conflict between spiritual and animal natures. As a novelist, Arévalo Martinez attempted to explore social problems and problems of the human personality without resorting to realism. He became one of the foremost writers of what has been called magic realism. His best-known novels are *La oficina de paz en Orolandia* (1925; "The Office of Peace in Orolandia"), *El mundo de los Maharachías* (1938; "The World of the Maharachías"), and *Viaje a Ipanda* (1939; "Voyage to Ipanda"). *Hondura* (1946) is an autobiographical novel.

Argens \\är-'zhäⁿ\, Jean-Baptiste de Boyer, Marquis d' (b. June 27, 1703, Aix-en-Provence, Fr.—d. Jan. 12, 1771, Toulon) French writer who helped disseminate the skeptical ideas of the Enlightenment by addressing his writings on philosophy, religion, and history to a popular readership.

Of an aristocratic Roman Catholic family, Argens led a life of dissipation in his youth. He joined the army and then eloped to Spain; at one time he attempted suicide. He spent 25 years in the court of Frederick the Great as chamberlain, producing 18 volumes of letters published as *Correspondance philosophique*. His *Lettres juives* (1738; "Jewish Letters"), *Lettres cabalistiques* (1741; "Cabalistic Letters"), and *Lettres chinoises* (1739–40; "Chinese Letters") are patterned after Montesquieu's satirical *Lettres persanes* ("Persian Letters"), which had been published in 1722.

Arghezi \\är-'gä-zē\, Tudor, *pseudonym of* Ion N. Theodorescu \\,tä-ō-dō-'resh-kü\ (b. May 21, 1880, Bucharest, Rom.—d. July 14, 1967, Bucharest) Romanian poet, novelist, and essayist whose creation of a new lyric poetry led to his recognition as one of the foremost writers in Romania.

Arghezi, who left home at age 11, first published a poem at age 14. In 1899 he took holy orders in a monastery in Cernica but soon renounced them. After traveling through Europe, he resettled in Bucharest in 1910. A pacifist during World War I, he was jailed in 1918 for contributing to a pro-German newspaper.

Arghezi's reputation was established with his first poetry collection, *Cuvinte potrivite* (1927; "Suitable Words"), which contained works on religious anguish and sympathy for peasants that were characterized by violent imagery and innovative prosody. In 1930 he published two novels detailing troublesome periods in his life: *Icoane de lemn* ("Wooden Icons"), about his disillusioning experience as a monk, and *Poarta neagră* ("Black Gate"), about his imprisonment.

Other notable works published in the 1930s included the dystopian satire *Tablete din ţara de Kuty* (1933; "Tablets from the Land of Kuty"), the bitter prose essays of 1935–36, and his poetic celebrations of nature and childhood: *Cartea cu jucării* (1931; "Book of Toys"), *Cărticică de seară* (1935; "Booklet for the Evening"), and *Hore* (1939; "Round Dances"). His career as a poet and a polemicist flourished during this period, but he was again imprisoned during World War II. After the war his failure to embrace Socialist Realism brought him into conflict with the communist regime. His later writings, which reflected his attempt to adapt to the new standards, lacked his former vigor. They included *1907* (1955) and *Cîntare omului* (1956; "Hymn to Mankind"). *Selected Poems of Tudor Arghezi* was published in 1976.

Argive \\'är-jīv, -ˌgīv\ Of or relating to the Achaeon city of Argos or the surrounding territory of Argolis. In translations of Homer, *Argive* has the broader meaning "Greek."

Argonaut \\'är-gə-ˌnȯt\ [Greek *Argonaútēs,* from *Argṓ* + *naútēs* sailor] In Greek mythology, one of the band of 50 legendary heroes who sailed with JASON on the ship *Argo* in quest of the GOLDEN FLEECE.

Jason, having undertaken the quest of the fleece, called upon the noblest heroes of Greece to take part in the expedition. According to the original story, the crew consisted of the chief members of Jason's own race, the Minyans; later, other and better-known heroes, such as Heracles, were added to their number. After many adventures, the Argonauts finally reached Colchis, where they found that the king, Aëtes (Aeetes), would not give up the fleece until Jason performed several tasks. After these were accomplished, Aëtes still refused to give it over. Aëtes' daughter, the sorceress Medea, who had fallen in love with Jason, helped him steal the fleece and fled with him. Various accounts are given of their homeward course; eventually the *Argo* reached Iolcos and was placed in a grove sacred to Poseidon in the Isthmus of Corinth.

The story of the expedition of the Argonauts was known at least as early as Homer, and the wandering of Odysseus may have been partly founded on it.

Arguedas \\är-'gwä-ᵗhäs, -ᵗhäh\, Alcides (b. July 15, 1879, La Paz, Bol.—d. May 8, 1946, Chulumani) Bolivian novelist, journalist, sociologist, historian, and diplomat whose sociological and historical studies and critically acclaimed realistic novels were among the first to focus attention on the social and economic problems of the South American Indian.

Arguedas studied sociology in Paris and pursued a career in government. He represented Bolivia in London, Paris, Colombia, and Venezuela and was a leader of Bolivia's Liberal Party. Throughout his public career he explored in his writing the plight of the Indians, sympathetically portraying their manners and customs and documenting the social and economic forces that had brought about their exploitation and decline.

Though noted for such sociological studies as *Pueblo enfermo* (1909; "Dying Pueblo") and for his *Historia general de Bolivia* (1922; "General History of Bolivia"), Arguedas is best remembered for his novels about the Indians, especially *Raza de bronce* (1919; "Race of Bronze"), an epic portrayal of the travels of a group of Bolivian Indians, ending with their extermination by white men.

Arguedas \\är-'gwä-ᵗhäs, -ᵗhäh\, José María (b. Jan. 18, 1911, Andahuaylas, Peru—d. Nov. 28, 1969, Lima) Peruvian novelist, short-story writer, and ethnologist whose writings capture the contrasts and tensions between white and Indian cultures.

Arguedas was the son of a white traveling judge and a Quechua Indian. Though his mother died when he was only three years old, Arguedas learned to speak Quechua before he learned Spanish. As a youth he studied Quechua music and customs in addition to absorbing the dominant Spanish culture. He attended the University of San Marcos in Lima, worked in the post office, and taught at the National University in Sicuani. After holding a series of administrative positions, he began teaching Peruvian regional cultures at the University of San Marcos in 1959. He also served as the director of the House of Culture (1963–64) and later of the National Museum of History (1964–69).

Agua (1935; "Water"), a collection of three stories, contrasts the violence and injustice of the white world with the peaceful and orderly existence of the exploited but passive Indians. *Yawar fiesta* (1941; "Bloody Feast") treats in detail the ritual of a primitive bullfight symbolizing the social struggle of the Indians against Spanish values. Arguedas' masterpiece is the autobiographical novel *Los ríos profundos* (1958; *Deep Rivers*). His later works include the novel *El sexto* (1961; "The Sixth One"); *Todas las sangres* (1964; "All the Races"); and an unfinished novel, *El zorro de arriba y el zorro de abajo* (1971; "The Fox from Above and the Fox from Below"), the writing of which was prescribed to him by his psychiatrist. In it Arguedas methodically and passionately discusses the events leading to his final day—he committed suicide in a deserted classroom in Lima.

argument \\'är-gyə-mənt\ [Latin *argumentum*] **1.** A form of rhetorical expression that is intended to convince or persuade. **2.** An abstract or summary of a literary work. **3.** The subject matter or central idea of a literary work.

Argus Panoptes \\'är-gəs-pan-'äp-tēz\ (Greek: "All Seeing") Figure in Greek mythology described variously as the son of Inachus, Agenor, or Arestor or as an aboriginal hero (autochthon). His surname derives from the hundred eyes reported to appear in his head or all over his body. Argus was appointed by the goddess Hera to watch the cow into which Io (Hera's priestess) had been transformed. While doing so he was slain by Hermes, and his eyes were transferred by Hera to the tail of the peacock. This Argus often has been confused with the legendary son of Niobe who gave his name to the city of Argos.

Ariadne \\ˌar-ē-'ad-nē\ In Greek mythology, daughter of Pasiphae and the Cretan king Minos. She fell in love with the Athenian hero Theseus and gave him the means (variously a thread, a piece of yarn, or glittering jewels) by which to retrace his path and escape the Labyrinth after he slew the Minotaur, a beast half bull and half man that Minos kept in the Labyrinth. Here the legends diverge: she was abandoned by Theseus and hanged herself; Theseus carried her to Naxos and left her there to die or to marry the god Dionysus; or she died in childbirth on Cyprus.

Ancient Greek poets and artists liked to portray Ariadne asleep on the shore of Naxos while Dionysus gazes at her with love and admiration. Ariadne's story was later taken up by European artists, writers, and composers, including Richard Strauss in his well-known opera *Ariadne auf Naxos* (1912; *Ariadne on Naxos*).

Aribau \\ˌä-rē-'baṷ\, Buenaventura Carles (b. Nov. 4, 1798, Barcelona, Spain—d. Sept. 17, 1862, Barcelona) Economist and author whose poem *Oda a la patria* (1832; "Ode to the Fatherland") marked the renaissance of Catalan literature in the 19th century in Spain.

Animated by a deep patriotism, Aribau's work is marked by the early Romanticist concern with history. He was one of the editors of *El europeo* and *El vapor,* two of the most important periodicals of the Romantic movement. His *Oda a la patria,* upon which his fame rests, was a defense of regional feeling, written in the vernacular of Catalan, which attempted to unite contemporary intellectual trends with native tradition. Aribau also edited, along with Manuel de Rivadeneyra, the first four volumes of the famous *Biblioteca de autores españoles* ("Library of Spanish Authors"), a monumental attempt to bring together all the important literature of Spain.

Ariel \\'ar-ē-əl\ The "airy spirit" in THE TEMPEST by William Shakespeare. The witch Sycorax, who formerly ruled the island on which the play is set, had imprisoned the recalcitrant Ariel in a pine tree. The exiled duke Prospero, now in charge, releases him and magically engages his services in thwarting Prospero's enemies, cultivating romance for his daughter, Miranda, and regaining his dukedom. After completing these tasks, Ariel is set free. The name Ariel, connoting the creative imagination, appears in the titles of works by a number of subsequent poets, including T.S. Eliot and Sylvia Plath.

Ariel \ˈar-ē-əl\ Collection of poetry by Sylvia PLATH, published posthumously in 1965. Most of the poems were written during the last five months of the author's life, which ended by suicide in 1963. Although the poems range in subject from pastoral chores ("The Bee Meeting") to medical trauma ("Tulips"), each contributes to an impression of the inevitability of the author's self-destruction. The collection contains "Daddy," one of Plath's best-known poems.

Arimasp \ˈar-ə-ˌmasp\ or **Arimaspian** \ˌar-ə-ˈmas-pē-ən\ plural Arimasps or Arimaspians also Arimaspi \-ˈmas-ˌpī, -pē\ Member of a mythical race of one-eyed men of Scythia. They are represented as in constant battle with griffins (creatures part eagle, part lion) for gold that the griffins guarded.

Arion \ə-ˈrī-ən\ Semilegendary poet and musician of Methymna in Lesbos, who is said to have given literary form to the dithyramb (a choral poem or chant performed at the festival of Dionysus). None of his works survives, and only one story about his life is known.

After a successful performing tour of Sicily and Magna Graecia, Arion sailed for home. The sight of the treasure he carried roused the cupidity of the sailors, who resolved to kill him and seize his wealth. Arion, as a last favor, begged permission to sing a song. The sailors consented, and the poet, standing on the deck of the ship, sang a dirge accompanied by his lyre. He then threw himself overboard; but he was miraculously borne up in safety by a dolphin, which had been charmed by the music. Arion's lyre and the dolphin became the constellations Lyra and Delphinus.

Ariosto \ˌär-ē-ˈōs-tō\, Ludovico (b. Sept. 8, 1474, Reggio Emilia, Duchy of Modena [Italy]—d. July 6, 1533, Ferrara) Italian poet remembered primarily for his epic poem ORLANDO FURIOSO. His plays, which are themselves minor works, were the first of those imitations of Latin comedy in the vernacular that came to characterize European domestic comedy.

Ariosto studied law, unwillingly, at Ferrara from 1489 to 1494, thereafter devoting himself to literary studies until 1499. His father died in 1500, and Ludovico, as the eldest son, had to provide for his four brothers and five sisters. In 1502 he became commander of the citadel of Canossa and in 1503 entered the service of Cardinal Ippolito d'Este, son of Duke Ercole I. After several years in the service of the cardinal and of the cardinal's brother Alfonso, Ariosto returned to Ferrara in about 1512. In 1518 Ariosto again entered the personal service of Duke Alfonso, and financial necessity forced him to accept a remote government post in 1522. By 1525, however, Ariosto had managed to save enough money to return to Ferrara for good.

In about 1505 Ariosto had begun writing *Orlando furioso*, an original continuation of Matteo Maria Boiardo's *Orlando innamorato*. He continued to revise and refine it for the rest of his life. The first edition was published in Venice in 1516.

During the period from 1517 to 1525, Ariosto composed his seven satires (titled *Satire*), modeled after the *Sermones* (satires) of Horace. The first is a noble assertion of the dignity and

Woodcut after a drawing by Titian from the third edition of *Orlando furioso*, 1532

Copyright British Museum; photograph, J.R. Freeman & Co. Ltd.

independence of the writer; the second criticizes ecclesiastical corruption; the third moralizes on the need to refrain from ambition; the fourth deals with marriage; the fifth and sixth describe his personal feelings at being kept away from his family by his masters' selfishness; the seventh (addressed to poet and scholar Pietro Bembo) points out the vices of humanists and reveals his sorrow at not having been allowed to complete his literary education in his youth.

Arishima \ä-ˈrē-shē-mä\ Takeo (b. March 4, 1878, Tokyo, Japan—d. June 9, 1923, Karuizawa) Novelist known in his country as "the man of love" for his humanitarian idealism.

Arishima was the eldest son of a talented and aristocratic family; his younger brothers included the painter Arishima Ikuma and the novelist Satomi Ton. He attended Sapporo Agricultural School (now Hokkaido University), noted in the late 19th century as a center of modern thought. There he was awakened to the plight of the lower classes. Arishima had studied English from childhood, and, after graduating in 1896, he went to the United States, where he spent three years at Harvard University.

After returning to Japan, he taught school in Sapporo and Kyōto; but in 1910 he joined his brothers and their friends Shiga Naoya and Mushanokōji Saneatsu in publishing the journal *Shirakaba* ("White Birch"), which was dedicated to disseminating humanistic and benevolent ideals. Arishima seems to have struggled deeply with the conflicts inherent in his position as a wealthy aristocrat and his ideal of universal love. His novel *Kain no matsuei* (1917; *Descendants of Cain*), dealing with the miserable condition of tenant farmers, attracted little attention, but he soon received recognition with the novel *Aru onna* (1919; *A Certain Woman*). In 1922 he published *Sengen hitotsu* ("A Manifesto"), in which he expressed his despairing conviction that only the laboring classes could help themselves and that there was nothing he as a bourgeois ideologist could do for them. That year he distributed his land and farms in Hokkaido among the tenants; the following year he committed suicide with his mistress at a mountain retreat.

Aristaeus \ˌar-is-ˈtē-əs\ Greek divinity whose worship was widespread but concerning whom myths are somewhat obscure. His name is derived from the Greek *aristos*, meaning "best." According to the generally accepted account, Aristaeus, son of Apollo and the nymph Cyrene, was born in Libya but later went to Thebes, where he received instruction from the Muses in the arts of healing and prophecy and became the son-in-law of Cadmus and the father of Actaeon. After traveling extensively, Aristaeus reached Thrace, where he finally disappeared near Mount Haemus.

aristarch \ˈar-əs-ˌtärk\ A severe critic. The term is derived from the name of the Greek grammarian and critic Aristarchus, who was known for his harsh judgments.

Aristarchus \ˌar-ə-ˈstär-kəs\ of Samothrace \ˈsam-ə-ˌthrās\ (b. c. 217 BC—d. 145 BC, Cyprus) Greek critic and grammarian, noted for his contribution to Homeric studies.

Aristarchus settled in Alexandria, where he was a pupil of Aristophanes of Byzantium and, about 153 BC, became chief librarian there. Later he withdrew to Cyprus. He founded a school of philologists, called Aristarcheans, which long flourished in Alexandria and afterward at Rome. Cicero and Horace regarded him as the supreme critic. His works fall into three categories: (1) two editions of the text of Homer and editions of Hesiod, Pindar, Archilochus, Alcaeus, and Anacreon; (2) numerous commentaries on these poets and on Aeschylus, Sophocles, Aristophanes, and Herodotus; (3) critical brochures, especially on Homeric problems.

aristophanean \ə-ˌris-tō-'fan-ē-ən\ In classical prosody, an aeolic meter that scans as — ∪ ∪ — | ∪ — — . It frequently follows a similar line that is a syllable longer: — ∪ ∪ — | ∪ — ∪ — . The name of the meter alludes to its use by the comic dramatist Aristophanes.

Aristophanes \ˌar-ə-'stäf-ə-ˌnēz\ (b. c. 450 BC—d. c. 388 BC) The greatest comic dramatist of ancient Greece, and the one whose works have been preserved in the greatest quantity. He is the only extant representative of OLD COMEDY, that is, of the phase of comic dramaturgy in which chorus, mime, and burlesque still played a considerable part and which was characterized by fantasy, merciless invective and outrageous satire, unabashedly licentious humor, and a marked freedom of political criticism.

Little is known about the life of Aristophanes, and most of the established facts come from references in his own plays. The son of Philippus, Aristophanes was an Athenian citizen. He began his career as a comic dramatist in 427 BC, and he is thought to have written about 40 plays in all.

A large part of Aristophanes' work reflects the social, literary, and philosophical life of Athens itself; its themes are inspired by the great Peloponnesian War (431–404 BC). Only 11 plays by him survive intact: ACHARNIANS, CLOUDS, WASPS, PEACE, BIRDS, LYSISTRATA, WOMEN AT THE THESMOPHORIA, FROGS, *Knights*, WOMEN AT THE ECCLESIA, and *Wealth*. The early comedy *Babylonians* is extant only in fragments. Two posthumous comedies, *Aiolosikon* (probably a skit on Euripides' *Aeolus*) and *Kokalos* (also, presumably, a mythological burlesque), were produced in or about the year of his death by his son, Araros.

Aristophanes' dramatic activity covered the end of the period of Old Comedy and the start of the so-called Middle Comedy, with most of his surviving plays belonging to the period of Old Comedy. His plays are still produced on the 20th-century stage in numerous translations that attempt to make the playwright's puns, witticisms, and topical allusions accessible to modern audiences.

Aristophanes' appeal lies in the wittiness of his dialogue, in his generally good-humored though occasionally malevolent satire, in the brilliance of his parody, and in the ingenuity and inventiveness of his comic scenes.

Aristophanes \ˌar-ə-'stäf-ə-ˌnēz\ of Byzantium \bi-'zan-tē-əm, -shē-əm, -shəm\ (b. c. 257 BC—d. 180 BC, Alexandria) Greek literary critic and grammarian who, after early study under leading scholars in Alexandria, was chief librarian there about 195 BC.

Aristophanes was the producer of a text of Homer and also edited Hesiod (*Theogony*), Alcaeus, Pindar, Euripides, Aristophanes, and perhaps Anacreon. Many of the *Arguments* prefixed to Greek tragedies and comedies in manuscript are ascribed to Aristophanes, and he revised and continued the *Pinakes* of Callimachus, a biographical history of Greek literature. As a lexicographer he compiled collections of archaic and unusual words, technical terms, and proverbs.

As a grammarian Aristophanes founded a school and wrote a treatise that laid down rules for Greek declensions, among other things. In editing the work of lyric and dramatic poets he introduced innovations in metrical analysis and textual criticism that were widely adopted by later scholars. These include a system of accentuation, the arrangement of lyrical texts according to metrical colons, and a system of critical signs to mark varying sorts of textual irregularities.

Aristophanes also was responsible for arranging Plato's dialogues in trilogies, and he is generally credited with the foundation of the so-called Alexandrian Canon, a selection in each genre of literary works that contemporaries considered to be models of excellence.

Aristotle \'ar-is-ˌtät-əl\ *Greek* Aristoteles \ˌar-is-'tät-ə-ˌlēz\ (b. 384 BC, Stagira, Chalcidice [Greece]—d. 322, Chalcis, Euboea) Ancient Greek philosopher, scientist, and organizer of research, one of the two greatest intellectual figures produced by the Greeks (the other being Plato). He surveyed the whole field of human knowledge as it was known in the Mediterranean world in his day; and his writings long influenced Western and Muslim thought.

The son of the court physician to the king of Macedonia, Aristotle was probably introduced to Greek medicine and biology at an early age. Following the death of his father, he was sent in 367 to the Athenian Academy of Plato, with which he was associated for 20 years. On Plato's death in 348/347 he left Athens and traveled for 12 years, establishing new academies at Assus and at Mytilene. For about three years he lived in Pella, the capital of Macedonia, where he tutored the future Alexander the Great. He retired to his paternal property at Stagira about 339. In 335 he returned to Athens and opened the Lyceum, an institution to rival the Academy. For the next 12 years he organized it as a center for speculation and research in every department of inquiry. On the death of Alexander in 323, an anti-Macedonian agitation broke out in Athens, and Aristotle withdrew to Chalcis, north of Athens, where he died the following year.

In the field of literature, Aristotle is best known for his *Peri poiētikēs* (POETICS), a work in which he treats the difference between tragedy and comedy, argues for the value of imitation (*mimēsis*) and the benefit of catharsis (*katharsis*), and presents a number of arguments that had a great influence on Western drama and literature through the ages.

Ari Thorgilsson \'är-ē-'thȯr-gil-sȯn\ the Learned (b. c. 1067—d. Nov. 9, 1148) Icelandic chieftain, priest, and historian whose *Íslendingabók* (*Libellus Islandorum; The Book of the Icelanders*) is the first history of Iceland written in the vernacular. Composed before 1133 and covering the period from the settlement of Iceland up to 1120, it includes information on the settlement of Greenland and Vinland. Ari is also believed to have written much of the original version of *Landnámabók* (*The Book of the Settlement of Iceland*), a work listing the genealogies and histories of noble Icelandic settlers. It served as a source for many of the 12th-century Icelanders' sagas.

Ariyoshi \ä-rē-'yō-shē\ Sawako (b. Jan. 20, 1931, Wakayama, Japan—d. Aug. 30, 1984, Tokyo) Japanese novelist, short-story writer, and playwright who reached a popular audience with serialized novels of social realism that chronicled domestic life in Japan.

Ariyoshi studied literature and theater at the Tokyo Women's Christian College from 1949 to 1952. After graduation she joined the staff of a publishing company, contributed to literary journals, worked for a theatrical dance troupe, and began publishing short stories, as well as scripts for stage, television, and radio.

Ariyoshi's first major novel, *Kinokawa* (1959; *The River Ki*), chronicles three generations of aristocratic women in the 20th century. *Hanaoka Seishū no tsuma* (1967; *The Doctor's Wife*), perhaps her best-known work, concerns the brave wife and domineering mother of Dr. Hanaoka Seishū, a 19th-century surgeon who pioneered the surgical use of anesthesia. Her novels examined such social issues as racism, in *Hishoku* (1967; "Without Color"); ageism, in *Kōkotso no hito* (1972; *The Twilight Years*); and environmental pollution, in *Fukugō osen* (1975; "The Compound Pollution"). She also wrote several short stories, the historical novel *Kazu no miyasama otome*

(1978; "Her Highness Princess Kazu"), and the travelogue *Chūgoku repōto* (1979; "China Report").

Arjuna \'är-jü-nə\ One of the five Pāṇḍava brothers who are the heroes of the Indian epic the MAHĀBHĀRATA ("Great Epic of the Bharata Dynasty"). Arjuna's hesitation before a battle became the occasion for his friend and charioteer, the god Krishna, to deliver a discourse on duty, or the right course of human action. These verses, which are in the form of a quasi-dialogue between Krishna and Arjuna, are collectively known as the BHAGAVADGĪTĀ, which is the most celebrated religious text of India.

Arland \är-'läⁿ\, Marcel (b. July 5, 1899, Varennes-sur-Amance, Fr.—d. Jan 12, 1986, Brinville, near Fountainebleau) French writer who first achieved wide literary recognition in 1929 when his novel *L'Ordre* gained him the prestigious Prix Goncourt.

Arland received his *baccalauréat* in 1918 and attended classes at the Sorbonne, where he earned a *licence-ès-lettres* (equivalent to a B.A.) before giving up his formal studies. In the early 1920s he and André Maurois were partners in the launching of two literary reviews, *Aventure* and *Dés*, and in 1925 Arland began a long association with *La Nouvelle Revue Française* (*NRF*).

Arland termed some of his novels *récits* (after Gide). His wide-ranging output included such *récits* as *Terres étrangères* (1923; "Foreign Lands") and *Zélie dans le désert* (1944; "Zélie in the Desert"); such short stories as "L'Eau et le feu" (1956; "Water and Fire") and "À perdre haleine" (1960; "Out of Breath"); and numerous collections of essays and critical studies, among them *Marivaux* (1949) and *La Grâce d'écrire* (1955; "The Gift of Writing"). *Lumière du soir* (1983; "Evening Light") was the last work published in his lifetime. Arland was elected to the Académie Française in 1968.

Arlecchino Stock theatrical character in Italian COMMEDIA DELL'ARTE. *See* HARLEQUIN.

Arlen \'är-lən\, Michael, *original name* Dikran Kouyoumdjian \kü-'yüm-jē-ən\ (b. Nov. 16, 1895, Ruse, Bulg.—d. June 23, 1956, New York, N.Y., U.S.) Author whose fiction reflects the brittle gaiety and underlying cynicism and disillusionment of fashionable post-World War I London society.

The son of an Armenian merchant, Arlen was brought up in England, where his father had fled to avoid Turkish persecution. By 1916 he was living in London and writing articles for periodicals and journals. He took the name Michael Arlen in 1922, when he became a British subject, and wrote two books of short stories before his first novel, *"Piracy"* (1922), was published. His best-known work, *The Green Hat* (1924), was a phenomenal popular success. A witty, sophisticated, but fundamentally sentimental novel about the "bright young things" of Mayfair (London's most fashionable and romantic district of the period), the novel made him famous almost overnight in Great Britain and the United States.

After 1928, when he married the Countess Atalanta Mercati, Arlen lived mainly in the south of France. Though he was for a time much celebrated, Arlen never repeated the popular success of *The Green Hat*. He wrote a screenplay, *The Heavenly Body* (1944), and a number of books, including *Man's Mortality* (1933) and the thriller *The Flying Dutchman* (1939), before retiring to New York City in 1945.

Arlt \'ärlt\, Roberto (b. April 2, 1900, Buenos Aires, Arg.—d. July 26, 1942, Buenos Aires) Novelist, short-story writer, dramatist, and journalist who pioneered the novel of the absurd in Argentinian literature.

A first-generation descendant of German immigrants, Arlt felt alienated from Argentine society. The world of his nov-

els *El juguete rabioso* (1926; "The Rabid Toy"), *Los siete locos* (1929; *The Seven Madmen*), *Los lanzallamas* (1931; "The Flame Throwers"), and *El amor brujo* (1932; "False Love") is grotesque and nightmarish and is filled with anguished, half-insane characters who are in revolt against society. His *Aguafuertes porteñas* (1950; "Etchings from the Port") and *Nuevas aguafuertes porteñas* (1960), orginally published as articles in *El Mundo*, are picaresque sketches of the people of Buenos Aires that show great psychological perception and intense irony. Among Arlt's plays, *Trescientos millones* (1932; "Three Hundred Million") and *Saverio el cruel* (1951; "Saverio the Cruel") stand out. Arlt's complete fictional works were published in 1963.

Armageddon \är-mə-'ged-ən\ The site or time of a final conclusive battle between the forces of good and evil. The scene of the battle is described in the New Testament, Revelation to John, chapter 16: 14–16.

Armah \'är-,mä\, Ayi Kwei (b. 1939, Takoradi, Gold Coast [now Ghana]) Ghanaian novelist whose work deals with corruption and materialism in contemporary Africa.

Armah was educated in local mission schools and at Achimota College before going to the United States in 1959 to complete his secondary education at Groton School and his bachelor's degree at Harvard University. He thereafter worked as a scriptwriter, translator, and English teacher in Paris, Tanzania, Lesotho, Senegal, and the United States, among other places.

In his first novel, *The Beautyful Ones Are Not Yet Born* (1968), Armah shows his deep concern for greed and political corruption in a newly independent African nation. In his second novel, *Fragments* (1970), a young Ghanaian returns home after living in the United States and is disillusioned by the Western-inspired materialism and moral decay he sees around him. The theme of return and disillusionment continues in *Why Are We So Blest?* (1972), but with a somewhat wider scope. In *Two Thousand Seasons* (1973) Armah borrows language from African dirges and praise songs to produce a chronicle of the African past. *The Healers* (1978) is a novel set in the early 19th century. Many of his literary essays were an attempt to come to grips with his role as an English-language African writer.

Arms and the Man Romantic comedy in three acts by George Bernard SHAW, produced in 1894 and published in 1898. The play is set in the Petkoff household in Bulgaria and satirizes romantic ideas concerning war and heroism. A battle-weary officer, a Swiss mercenary fighting for the Serbian army, takes refuge in Raina Petkoff's bedchamber, where she agrees to hide him from the authorities. In response to his matter-of-fact account of the war, in which he debunks her fiancé Sergius' heroism, Raina at first ridicules the intruder's cowardliness but ultimately appreciates his honesty. Some time later, after the war is over, the officer, Captain Bluntschli, returns. By the end of the play, Sergius has promised himself to the maidservant Louka, whose fiancé, the manservant Nicola, willingly forgoes his claim to her, and Raina has become engaged to Bluntschli, who has just inherited a number of Swiss hotels.

Arnaut or **Arnaud** Daniel \är-'nō-dän-yel\ (b. Ribérac? [France]; fl. 1180–1200) Celebrated Provençal poet, troubadour, and master of the *trobar clus*, a poetic style composed of complex metrics, intricate rhymes, and words chosen more for their sound than for their meaning.

A nobleman by birth, Arnaut was a highly regarded traveling troubadour. He is credited with inventing the sestina, a lyrical form of six unrhymed six-line stanzas with an elaborate scheme of word repetition. His skill with language was admired by Petrarch and in the 20th century by Ezra Pound and T.S. Eliot. He had his greatest influence, however, on Dante, who imitated him and gave him a prominent place in the *Purgatorio* section of his *The Divine Comedy* as a model for the vernacular poet. Arnaut's speech in Provençal is the only non-Italian passage in the *The Divine Comedy*.

Arnaut de Mareuil \är-'nō-də-mȧ-'rœy\ (b. Mareuil-sur-Belle, Périgord [France]; fl. 1170–1200) Perigordian troubadour who is credited with having introduced into Provençal poetry the amatory epistle (*salut d'amour*) and the short didactic poem (*ensenhamen*).

Little is known of Arnaut's life. His early poems were dedicated to his patroness, Adelaide, the daughter of Raymond V, count of Toulouse, and wife of Roger II, Viscount of Béziers. Later Arnaut was at the court of William VIII, Count of Montpellier. Most of his extant work is passionate love poetry that combines conventional courtly love imagery (extravagant praise of his lady's beauty, despair at her cruel indifference) with unexpectedly delicate sentiment.

Arndt \'ärnt\, Ernst Moritz (b. Dec. 26, 1769, Schoritz bei Gartz, Rügen, Swed.—d. Jan. 29, 1860, Bonn [Germany]) Prose writer, poet, and patriot who expressed German national awakening during the Napoleonic era.

Arndt was educated at Stralsund, Greifswald, and Jena and qualified for the Lutheran ministry. At the age of 28 he rejected his clerical career and for 18 months traveled through Europe. On his return to Germany the sight of ruined castles along the banks of the Rhine River moved him to bitterness against the French who had destroyed them.

In 1800 Arndt settled in Greifswald as assistant lecturer in history and in 1803 published *Germanien und Europa*, in which he proclaimed his views on French aggression. In 1806 Arndt was appointed to the chair of history at the University of Greifswald and published the first part of his *Geist der Zeit* (*Spirit of the Times*), in which he called on his countrymen to shake off the French yoke. To escape the vengeance of Napoleon, he took refuge in Sweden, from where he continued to communicate his patriotic ideals to his countrymen in pamphlets, poems, and songs.

Arndt returned to Germany in 1809. In 1812 Arndt was summoned to St. Petersburg to assist in the organization of the final struggle against France. When, after the peace, the University of Bonn was founded in 1818, Arndt was appointed to the chair of modern history. In this year appeared the fourth part of his *Geist der Zeit*, in which he criticized the reactionary policy of the German powers. The boldness of his demands for reform offended the Prussian government, and in the summer of 1819 he was arrested. He was soon set free but was not allowed to return to teaching until 1840.

Not all of Arndt's lyrical poems were inspired by political ideas; many of the *Gedichte* (1804–18; complete edition, 1860; "Poems") are religious poems of great beauty. Other important works include his autobiography, *Erinnerungen aus dem äusseren Leben* (1840; "Recollections from the External Life"), and *Meine Wanderungen und Wandelungen mit dem Reichsfreiherrn Heinrich Karl Friedrich von Stein* (1858; "My Travels and Saunterings with the Baron Heinrich Karl Friedrich von Stein").

Arngrímur or **Arngrímur** the Learned   *see* JÓNSSON.

Arniches \är-'nēch-es\, Carlos, *surname in full* Arniches y Barrera \ē-bȧr-'rer-ȧ\ (b. Oct. 11, 1866, Alicante, Spain—d. April 16, 1943, Madrid) Popular Spanish dramatist of the early 20th century, best known for works in the *género chico* ("lesser genre"), the one-act zarzuela (musical comedy), and the one-act *sainete* (sketch). These plays were based upon direct observation of the customs and speech of the working-class people of Madrid. He wrote some 270 of them and was considered a master of the genre, along with the Álvarez Quintero brothers.

Arnim \'är-nim\, Achim von, *byname of* Karl Joachim Friedrich Ludwig von Arnim (b. Jan. 26, 1781, Berlin [Germany]—d. Jan. 21, 1831, Wiepersdorf, Brandenburg) Folklorist, dramatist, poet, and story writer whose collection of folk poetry was a major contribution to German Romanticism.

While a student at the University of Heidelberg, Arnim published jointly with Clemens Brentano a remarkable collection of folk poetry, DES KNABEN WUNDERHORN; the title derives from the opening poem, which tells of a youth who brings the empress a magic horn. The first volume (published 1805, dated 1806) was dedicated to J.W. von Goethe, who reviewed it appreciatively, though others criticized it as unscholarly. The collection was completed in 1808.

Arnim's numerous plays, poems, and novels are forgotten, but a few of his short stories—all strangely compounded of realism and fantasy—occupy an important place in German prose fiction.

Arnim \'är-nim\, Bettina von, *byname of* Elisabeth Katharina Ludovica Magdalena von Arnim, *original surname* Brentano (b. April 4, 1785, Frankfurt am Main [Germany]—d. Jan. 20, 1859, Berlin) One of the outstanding figures in modern German literature who is memorable not only for the works she produced but also for the personality they reflect.

Copyright British Museum; photograph, J.R. Freeman & Co. Ltd.

Bettina von Arnim was unconventional to the point of eccentricity: wayward, yet a loyal wife (she married Achim von Arnim in 1811) and a devoted mother to her seven children; susceptible and passionate, but jealous of her personal freedom; capable of enthusiastic devotion to others, yet absorbed in a cult of her own personality, which verged on narcissism. Her three best-known works are rearranged and retouched records of her correspondence with J.W. von Goethe (*Goethes Briefwechsel mit einem Kinde*, 1835; *Goethe's Correspondence with a Child*), with Karoline von Günderode (*Die Günderode*, 1840), and with her brother Clemens BRENTANO (*Clemens Brentanos Frühlingskranz*, 1844; "Clemens Brentano's Spring Garland"). The result of her editing is a peculiar blend of documentation and fiction, written in a brilliantly vivid, uninhibited style.

She stated her political views, which were sympathetic to the underprivileged, in two books written for the special benefit of the king of Prussia, Frederick William IV: *Dies Buch gehört dem König* (1843; "This Book Belongs to the King") and *Gespräche mit Dämonen* (1852; "Conversations with Demons"). Von Arnim was also a gifted sculptor and musician. In the diversity of her talents and interests, she exhibited the universality that has been regarded as the hallmark of the German Romantic spirit.

Árni Magnússon   *see* Árni MAGNÚSSON.

Arnold \'är-nəld\, Edwin, *in full* Sir Edwin Arnold (b. June 10, 1832, Gravesend, Kent, Eng.—d. March 24, 1904, London) Poet and scholar, best known as the author of *The Light of Asia* (1879), an epic poem that tells, in elaborate language, of the life and teachings of the Buddha. From 1873 Arnold was chief editor of *The Daily Telegraph* of London. Before joining the

Telegraph, he had been principal of the British government college at Poona (Pune), India. He was knighted in 1888.

Arnold \\'är-nəld\\, Matthew (b. Dec. 24, 1822, Laleham, Middlesex, Eng.—d. April 15, 1888, Liverpool) English Victorian poet and literary and

Library of Congress

social critic who is considered a quintessential Victorian writer in his philosophy, his taste, and his manner of expression.

Arnold attended Balliol College, Oxford, and in 1851 became inspector of schools, a position that he held until within two years of his death. In 1849 he published his first volume of verse, which contained the title poem THE STRAYED REVELLER and THE FORSAKEN MERMAN. His second volume, published in 1852, contained the title poem EMPEDOCLES ON ETNA and, like the first, gave the author as simply "A." In 1853 he published *Poems* under his full name; this book contained a well-known preface that foreshadowed his later criticism in its insistence upon the classic virtues of unity, impersonality, universality, and architectonic power and upon the value of the classical masterpieces as models for "an age of spiritual discomfort." After 1867, though there were further editions, Arnold wrote little additional verse.

Not much of his verse meets his own criteria. Occasionally he rises, as in SOHRAB AND RUSTUM, to epic severity and impersonality; to lofty meditation, as in DOVER BEACH; and to sustained magnificence and richness, as in THE SCHOLAR GIPSY and THYRSIS—where he masterfully sustains an intricate stanza form.

In 1857 Arnold was elected to the Oxford chair of poetry, which he held for 10 years. In this position he wrote some of his most memorable lectures, later published as criticism, including "On the Modern Element in Literature," *On Translating Homer* (1861), and the lectures *On the Study of Celtic Literature* (1867). Some of Arnold's leading ideas and phrases were early put into currency in *Essays in Criticism* (First Series, 1865; Second Series, 1888) and CULTURE AND ANARCHY (1869). An important later essay was "The Study of Poetry," originally published as the general introduction to T.H. Ward's anthology *The English Poets* (1880), which contains many of the ideas for which Arnold is best remembered. In an age of crumbling creeds, he thought that poetry would replace religion; more and more, readers would "turn to poetry to interpret life for us, to console us, to sustain us." For that reason readers had to understand how to distinguish the best poetry from the inferior.

Lastly Arnold turned to religion, the constant preoccupation and true center of his whole life, and wrote *St. Paul and Protestantism* (1870), *Literature and Dogma* (1873), *God and the Bible* (1875), and *Last Essays on Church and Religion* (1877).

Around the World in Eighty Days Travel adventure novel by Jules VERNE, published serially in 1872 in *Le Temps* as *Le Tour du monde en quatre-vingt jours* and in book form in 1873.

The lively narrative recounts the journey undertaken by sedentary London gentleman Phileas Fogg and his valet, Passepartout, in order to win a wager with Fogg's fellow club members. Pursued by Fix, a private detective who believes Fogg to be a bank robber, the pair cross three continents and two oceans on trains, steamers, an elephant, and a sail-sledge. Delays and death-defying exploits abound. Assorted companions join the party, including the Hindu widow Aouda, whom Fogg rescues from ritual immolation. Back in London, having met the deadline, convinced Fix of his innocence, and collected the payment, he returns to his former life unchanged but for having Aouda as his bride.

Arrabal \\,är-rä-'ḅäl\\, Fernando (b. Aug. 11, 1932, Melilla, Spanish Morocco) Spanish-born French absurdist playwright, novelist, and filmmaker. Arrabal's dramatic and fictional world is often violent, cruel, and pornographic.

Arrabal worked as a clerk in a paper company, then studied law at the University of Madrid. He turned to writing in the early 1950s, and in 1955 he went to study drama in Paris, where he remained. The first volume of his plays was published in 1958, and the 1959 production of *Pique-nique en campagne* ("Picnic on the Battlefield"), an antiwar satire, brought him to the attention of the French avant-garde. Arrabal's most important play of this early period is probably *Le Cimitière des voitures* (1958; *Automobile Graveyard*), a parody of the Christ story.

After the mid-1960s, Arrabal's plays became increasingly formal and ritualistic, evolving into what Arrabal called Théâtre Panique ("Panic Theater"). Among the plays of this highly productive period are *L'Architecte et l'empereur d'Assyrie* (1967; *The Architect and the Emperor of Assyria*) and *Et ils passèrent des menottes aux fleurs* (1969; *And They Put Handcuffs on the Flowers*), which, with its theme of freedom from oppression, was inspired by the author's imprisonment while on a journey to Spain in 1967.

Arrabal's first novel, *Baal Babylone* (1959; *Baal Babylon*), dealt with his nightmarish childhood in fascist Spain; in 1970 he adapted it into the screenplay ¡*Viva la muerte!* ("Long Live Death!") and directed its filming in Tunisia.

Arrowsmith \\'ar-ō-,smith\\ Novel by Sinclair LEWIS, published in 1925. The author declined to accept a Pulitzer Prize for the work because he had not been awarded the prize for his *Main Street* in 1921.

The narrative concerns the personal and professional travails of Martin Arrowsmith, a Midwestern physician. Disheartened successively by rural practice, the state of public health care, and the elitism of an urban clinic, Martin accepts a research position at an institute in New York that leads him, along with his wife, Leora, a nurse, to an epidemic-ravaged island. Leora dies there, and Martin abandons his scientific principles in order to make an experimental serum more widely available. Returning to the institute, he marries a wealthy widow and finds her social demands a distraction. In a final move—and in realization of his ambitions—he leaves institutional medicine, as well as his wife, and sets up his own laboratory on a New England farm.

Ars Amatoria \\'ärz-,am-ə-'tȯr-ē-ə\\ ("Art of Love") Latin poem by OVID, published about 1 BC. *Ars Amatoria* comprises three books of mock-didactic elegiacs on the art of seduction and intrigue. One of the author's best-known works, it contributed to his downfall in AD 8 on allegations of immorality. The work, which presents a fascinating portrait of the sophisticated and hedonistic Roman aristocracy, attained wide popularity in its day. The message of this brilliant treatise was essentially subversive to the official program of moral reforms then being promoted by Augustus, and it cannot have been well received by those who were seriously committed to the goals and aspirations of Augustanism.

arsis \\'är-sis\\ *plural* **arses** \\-,sēz\\ [Greek *ársis,* act of raising or lifting, raising of the foot in beating time] **1.** The lighter or shorter part of a poetic foot especially in quantitative verse.

2. The accented or longer part of a poetic foot especially in accentual verse. Compare THESIS.

The Latin meaning, in which *arsis* refers to the accented part of the foot, has been retained in modern prosody.

Ars Poetica \'ärz-pō-'et-i-kə\ ("Art of Poetry") Work by HORACE, written about 19–18 BC for Piso and his sons and originally known as *Epistula ad Pisones* (*Epistle to the Pisos*). The work is an urbane, unsystematic amplification of Aristotle's discussion of the decorum or internal propriety of each literary genre, which at Horace's time included lyric, pastoral, satire, elegy, and epigram, as well as Aristotle's epic, tragedy, and comedy. For example, *Ars Poetica* elevates the Greek tradition of using narration to relate offstage events into a dictum forbidding such events as Medea's butchering of her boys from being performed on stage.

Written, like Horace's other epistles of this period, in a loose conversational frame, *Ars Poetica* consists of 476 lines containing nearly 30 maxims for young poets. The work was prized by Neoclassicists of the 17th and 18th centuries not only for its rules but also for its humor, common sense, and appeal to educated taste.

ars poetica \'ärz-pō-'et-i-kə\ *plural* ars poeticas. Any treatise that, in the manner of Horace's *Ars Poetica*, authoritatively sets down principles of poetic composition.

Artaud \är-'tō\, Antonin (b. Sept. 4, 1896, Marseille, Fr.—d. March 4, 1948, Ivry-sur-Seine) French dramatist, poet, actor, and theoretician of the Surrealist movement who attempted to replace the "bourgeois" classical theater with his THEATER OF CRUELTY, a primitive ceremonial experience intended to liberate the human subconscious and reveal human nature.

Artaud's parents were partly Levantine Greek, and he was much affected by this background, especially in his fascination with mysticism. Lifelong mental disorders forced him repeatedly into asylums. After studying acting in Paris, he made his debut in Aurélien-Marie Lugné-Poe's Dadaist-Surrealist Théâtre de l'Oeuvre. Artaud also wrote two volumes of Surrealist verse, *L'Ombilic des limbes* (1925; "Umbilical Limbo") and *Le Pèse-nerfs* (1925; *Nerve Scales*), but he broke with the Surrealists when their leader, the poet André Breton, pronounced their allegiance to communism.

Artaud's *Manifeste du théâtre de la cruauté* (1932; "Manifesto of the Theater of Cruelty") and *Le Théâtre et son double* (1938; *The Theatre and Its Double*) call for a communion between actor and audience in a magic exorcism; gestures, sounds, unusual scenery, and lighting combine to form a language, superior to words, that can be used to subvert thought and logic and to shock the spectator into seeing the world's corruption.

Artaud's own works, less important than his theories, were failures. *Les Cenci*, performed in Paris in 1935, proved an experiment too bold for its time. His vision, however, was a major influence on the plays of Jean Genet, Eugène Ionesco, Samuel Beckett, and others and on the entire movement away from the dominant role of language and rationalism in contemporary theater. His other works include *Van Gogh, le suicidé de la société* (1947), *Héliogabale, ou l'anarchiste couronné* (1934; "Heliogabalus, or the Crowned Anarchist"), and *Les Tarahumaras* (1955; *Peyote Dance*), a collection of texts written between 1936 and 1948 about his travels in Mexico.

arte mayor \'är-tä-mä-'yōr\ [Spanish, short for *versos* (*coplas*) *de arte mayor,* literally, verses of greater art] Spanish verse form consisting of eight-syllable lines, later changed to 12 syllables, usually arranged in eight-line stanzas with a rhyme scheme of *abbaacca.* The form originated in the late 13th to the early 14th century and was used for most serious poetry in the 15th century. It fell out of general use by the 16th century.

arte menor \'är-tä-mä-'nōr\ [Spanish, short for *versos de arte menor,* literally, verses of lesser art] In Spanish poetry, a line of two to eight syllables and usually only one accent, most often on the penultimate syllable. Because of the general nature of the form, it has been used for many different types of poetry, from traditional verse narratives to popular songs.

Artemis \'är-tə-mis\ In Greek mythology, the goddess of wild animals, the hunt, and vegetation, and of chastity and childbirth; she was identified by the Romans with DIANA. Artemis was the daughter of Zeus and Leto and the twin sister of Apollo.

While the mythological roles of other prominent Olympians evolved in the works of the poets, the lore of Artemis developed primarily from cult. Dances of maidens representing tree nymphs (dryads) were especially common in Artemis' worship as goddess of the tree cult, a role especially popular in the Peloponnese. Outside the Peloponnese, Artemis' most familiar form was that of Mistress of Animals. Poets and artists usually pictured her with the stag or hunting dog, but the cults showed considerable variety. The frequent stories of the love affairs of Artemis' nymphs are supposed by some to have originally been told of the goddess herself. The poets after Homer, however, stressed Artemis' chastity and her delight in the hunt, dancing and music, shadowy groves, and the cities of just men. The wrath of Artemis was proverbial, for to it myth attributed wild nature's hostility to humans.

art for art's sake A slogan translated from the French *l'art pour l'art,* which was coined in the early 19th century by the French philosopher Victor Cousin. The phrase expresses the belief held by many writers and artists, especially those associated with Aestheticism, that art needs no justification, that it need serve no political, didactic, or other end. *See also* AESTHETICISM.

Artful Dodger, The Fictional character in Charles Dickens' novel OLIVER TWIST. The Artful Dodger, whose real name is Jack Dawkins, is a precocious, streetwise boy who introduces the protagonist Oliver to the thief Fagin and his gang of children, who work as thieves and pickpockets.

Arthur \'är-thər\ Legendary British king who appears in a cycle of medieval romances (known as the Matter of Britain) as the sovereign of a knightly fellowship of the ROUND TABLE. It is not certain how or where these legends originated or whether the figure Arthur was based on a historical person.

Assumptions that a historical Arthur led Welsh resistance to the West Saxon advance from the middle Thames are based on a conflation of two early chroniclers, Gildas and Nennius, and on the *Annales Cambriae* ("Cambrian Annals") of the late 10th century. The 9th-century *Historia Brittonum* ("History of the Britons") of Nennius records 12 battles fought by Arthur against the Saxons, culminating in a victory at Mons Badonicus. The Arthurian section of this work, however, is from an undetermined source, possibly a poetic text. The *Annales Cambriae* also mention Arthur's victory at Mons Badonicus (516) and record the Battle of Camlann (537), "in which Arthur and Medraut fell." Gildas' *De excidio et conquestu Britanniae* (mid-6th century; "The Fall and Conquest of Britain") implies that Mons Badonicus was fought in about 500 but does not connect it with Arthur.

Another speculative view, put forward by R.G. Collingwood (*Roman Britain and the English Settlements,* 1936), is that Arthur was a professional soldier, serving the British kings and commanding a cavalry force trained on Roman lines, which he moved from place to place to meet the Saxon threat.

In any case, early Welsh literature quickly made Arthur into a king of wonders and marvels. The 12th-century prose romance

CULHWCH AND OLWEN associated him with other heroes, and this conception of a heroic band with Arthur at its head doubtless laid the groundwork for the idea of Arthur's court.

Arthurian legend \ăr-'thûr-ē-ən\   The body of stories and medieval romances, known as the Matter of Britain, centering on the legendary king Arthur. The stories chronicled Arthur's birth, the adventures of his knights, and the adulterous love between his knight Sir Lancelot and his queen, Guinevere. This liaison and the largely unsuccessful quest for the Holy Grail (the vessel used by Christ at the Last Supper) brought about the dissolution of the knightly fellowship, the death of Arthur, and the destruction of his kingdom.

Stories about Arthur and his court had been popular in Wales before the 11th century; they won fame in Europe partly through the *Historia regum Britanniae*, a pseudo-chronicle written between 1135 and 1139 by GEOFFREY of Monmouth. The *Historia* celebrates a glorious and triumphant king who defeated a Roman army in eastern France but was mortally wounded in battle during a rebellion at home led by his nephew Mordred. Later writers in the chronicle tradition, notably WACE of Jersey and LAYAMON, filled out certain details, especially in connection with Arthur's knightly fellowship.

The literary development of Arthurian legend flourished early in France, where Breton storytellers had orally transmitted the heroic accounts that their Briton ancestors had carried with them into France. Drawing from such Celtic material, CHRÉTIEN de Troyes in the late 12th century made Arthur the ruler of a realm of marvels in five romances of adventure. Chrétien's *Perceval* is the first extant Arthurian romance to treat the theme of the Grail.

Prose romances of the 13th century began to explore two major themes: the winning of the Grail and the love story of Lancelot and Guinevere. An early prose romance centering on Lancelot seems to have become the kernel of the Prose *Lancelot*, a section of the cyclic work known as the Vulgate cycle (*c.* 1210–30). Another branch of the Vulgate cycle was based on a very early 13th-century verse romance, *Merlin*, by ROBERT de Boron, that had told of Arthur's birth and childhood and his winning of the crown by drawing a magic sword from a stone. The writers of the Vulgate cycle (thought to be a group of Cistercian monks) turned this into prose, adding a pseudo-historical narrative dealing with Arthur's military exploits. A final branch of the Vulgate cycle contained an account of Arthur's Roman campaign and war with Mordred, to which was added a story of Lancelot's renewed adultery with Guinevere and the disastrous war between Lancelot and Sir Gawain that ensued. A later prose romance, known as the post-Vulgate Grail romance (*c.* 1240), combined Arthurian legend with material from the Tristan romance.

The legend told in the Vulgate cycle and post-Vulgate romance was transmitted to English-speaking readers in Thomas Malory's late 15th-century prose work *Le Morte Darthur*. The legend remained alive during the 17th century, though interest in it was by then confined to England. Of merely antiquarian interest during the 18th century, it again figured in literature during Victorian times, notably in Alfred, Lord Tennyson's *Idylls of the King* and, in quite a different vein, in Mark Twain's *A Connecticut Yankee in King Arthur's Court*. The Arthurian legend continued to be retold in the 20th century by writers such as Edwin Arlington Robinson, who wrote an Arthurian trilogy, and T.H. White, who wrote a series of novels collected as *The Once and Future King* (1958). A later treatment is Marion Zimmer Bradley's *The Mists of Avalon* (1982).

Art of Fiction, The   Critical essay by Henry JAMES, published in 1884 in *Longman's Magazine*. It was written as a rebuttal to "Fiction as One of the Fine Arts," a lecture given by Sir Walter Besant in 1884, and is a manifesto of literary realism that decries the popular demand for novels that are saturated with sentimentality or pessimism. It was published separately in 1885.

In *The Art of Fiction*, James disagrees with Besant's assertions that plot is more important than characterization, that fiction must have a "conscious moral purpose," and that experience and observation outweigh imagination as creative tools. James argues against these restrictive rules for writing fiction, responding that "no good novel will ever proceed from a superficial mind."

Art of Love   *see* ARS AMATORIA.

Artsybashev \‚ər-tsə-'bä-shəf\, Mikhail Petrovich (b. Oct. 24 [Nov. 5, New Style], 1878, Kharkov province [now Kharkiv *oblast*], Ukraine, Russian Empire—d. March 3, 1927, Warsaw [Poland])   Russian prose writer whose works were noted for their extreme pessimism, violence, and eroticism.

Artsybashev first published his material in newspapers as a teenager. His short stories were first published in 1901. With the failure of the Russian Revolution of 1905, Artsybashev joined in expressing the pessimism and cynicism that overtook the Russian literary world. The publication of his novel *Sanin* (1907) brought him widespread fame. In this novel, the antihero Sanin adopts a life-style of selfish and cynical hedonism in response to society's insoluble problems.

Conservative critics condemned Artsybashev for immorality, and progressive critics found little intrinsic literary merit in his books. He nonetheless enjoyed great popularity for a time. His later works were less controversial. Opposed to the Bolshevik revolution, Artsybashev immigrated to Poland, where he worked on an anti-Soviet journal. He was attacked by the Soviet critics, and *Sanin* and his other works were proscribed.

Arzamas society \‚ər-‚zə-'mäs\   Russian literary circle (flourished 1815–18) formed for the semi-serious purpose of ridiculing the conservative "Lovers of the Russian Word," who wished to keep the modern Russian language firmly tied to Old Church Slavonic. They took the name Arzamas from a small city in east-central Russia; it was the setting of a work by Dmitry Bludov that satirized the language conservatives.

The Arzamas circle supported the work begun by Nikolay KARAMZIN, who advocated the stylistic revision of written Russian. The members of Arzamas included the poets Vasily A. Zhukovsky, Konstantin Batyushkov, the young Aleksandr Pushkin, and many others. Though their Arzamas activities were limited to composing burlesques of the archaic Slavonic style, it was their adoption of the new style in their subsequent serious works that permanently influenced the formation of the modern Russian literary language.

Asbjørnsen \'äs-byœrn-sen\, Peter Christen and **Moe** \'mō\, Jørgen Engebretsen (respectively b. Jan. 15, 1812, Christiania [now Oslo], Nor.—d. Jan. 5, 1885, Kristiania; b. April 22, 1813, Hole, Nor.—d. March 27, 1882, Kristiansand)   Collectors of Norwegian folklore. Their NORSKE FOLKEEVENTYR (*Norwegian Folk Tales*) is a landmark in Norwegian literature. Closely united in their lives and work, they are rarely named separately. They met as youths in 1827 and became "blood brothers."

Asbjørnsen, the son of a glazier, became a private tutor in eastern Norway at the age of 20. There he began to collect folktales. Moe, the son of a rich and highly educated farmer, graduated with a degree in theology from King Frederick's University, Christiania, in 1839. He, too, became a tutor and spent holidays collecting folklore in southern Norway. Meanwhile, Asbjørnsen became a naturalist, and, while making investigations along the fjords, he added to his collection of tales.

The two men decided to pool their materials and publish them jointly.

At the time, the Norwegian literary style was too like that of Denmark to be suitable for national folklore, while the various dialects used in oral storytelling were too local. Asbjørnsen and Moe solved the problem of style by adopting the Grimm brothers' principle of using simple language in place of the various dialects, yet maintaining the traditional form of the folktales. Some of the first tales appeared as early as 1837 in *Nor*; others were published as *Norske folkeeventyr* in 1841. Enlarged and illustrated collections appeared in 1842, 1843, and 1844. The whole was published with critical notes in 1852. Accepted in Europe as a major contribution to comparative mythology, *Norske folkeeventyr* was widely translated. In Norway it provided a stylistic model that substantially influenced the development of Bokmål, the literary language of modern Norway.

Asbjørnsen later published a collection of fairy tales, *Norske huldreeventyr og folkesagn* (1845–48; *Norwegian Fairy Tales and Folk Legends*), and a translation of Darwin's *Origin of Species* (1860). Moe's *Digte* (1850; "Poems") placed him among the finest Norwegian romantic poets. His *I brønden og i tærnet* (1851; "In the Well and the Pond") is a Norwegian children's classic. In 1853 after experiencing a religious crisis, he was ordained and in 1875 became bishop of Kristiansand.

Ascanius \as-'kä-nē-əs\ In Roman legend, son of the hero Aeneas and traditional founder of Alba Longa, probably the site of the modern Castel Gandolfo, near Rome. There are several versions of his story, not all of which agree on when he lived. Those set earlier cite the Trojan Creusa as his mother. They relate that, after the fall of Troy, Ascanius and Aeneas escaped to Italy, where Aeneas subsequently founded Lavinium, the parent city of Alba Longa and Rome. Ascanius became king of Lavinium after his father's death. Thirty years after Lavinium was built, Ascanius founded Alba Longa and ruled it until he died.

In the Roman historian Livy's account, however, Ascanius was born after the founding of Lavinium and was the son of Aeneas and Lavinia, a daughter of King Latinus. Ascanius was also called Iulus, and through him by that name the gens Julia (including the family of Julius Caesar) traced its descent.

ascending rhythm *see* RISING RHYTHM.

Ascent of the F6, The \ˌef-'siks\ Poetic drama by W.H. AUDEN and Christopher ISHERWOOD, published in 1936 and performed in 1937.

F6 is an unconquered mountain in the Himalayan range. An experienced and renowned climber named Michael Ransom leads an expedition of fellow Britons up the slope of F6 in competition with a group of climbers from a different (unnamed) country. En route, all Ransom's climbers perish; Ransom dies when he reaches the peak, after realizing that his accession to other people's ambitions has contributed to his destruction.

Asch or **Ash** \'äsh, *Angl* 'ash\, Sholem, Sholem *also spelled* Shalom *or* Sholom (b. Nov. 1, 1880, Kutno, Poland, Russian Empire—d. Aug. 10, 1957, London, Eng.) Polish-born American novelist and playwright, one of the most widely known writers in modern Yiddish literature.

Asch was educated at Kutno's Hebrew school. In 1899 he went to Warsaw, and in 1900 published his highly praised first story—written, as was a cycle that followed, in Hebrew. On the advice of the Yiddish writer and leader I.L. Peretz, he subsequently decided to write only in Yiddish, and with *Dos Shtetl* (1904; *The Little Town*) he began a career outstanding for both output and impact.

Asch's work falls into three periods. In his first, he describes the tragicomedy of life in small eastern European Jewish vil-

lages. To this period belong the novels *Kidesh hashem* (1919) and *Motke ganef* (1916; *Mottke the Thief*) and the play *Got fun nekome* (1907; *The God of Vengeance*). To the American period (he visited the United States in 1910, returned in 1914, and was naturalized in 1920) belong *Onkl Mozes* (1918; *Uncle Moses*), *Khayim Lederers tsurikkumen* (1927; *Chaim Lederer's Return*), and *Toyt urteyl* (1926; *Judge Not*). These novels describe the cultural and economic conflicts experienced by eastern European Jewish immigrants in America. In his last, most controversial period he attempted to unite Judaism and Christianity through emphasis upon their historical and theological-ethical connections.

Aschenbach, Gustave von \'gus-ˌtäv-ə-fòn-'äsh-ən-ˌbäk\ Fictional character in Thomas Mann's novel DEATH IN VENICE. Aschenbach is a well-respected middle-aged German writer whose life is as disciplined and coldly intellectual as his writing. While on holiday in Venice he falls in love with Tadzio, a beautiful 14-year-old boy, and his obsession with the boy leads to his own deterioration and eventual death.

asclepiad \ə-'sklē-pē-əd, -ˌad\ [Greek *Asklēpiádeios*] A Greek lyric verse later used by Latin poets such as Catullus, Horace, and Seneca. The asclepiad consisted of an aeolic nucleus, a choriamb to which were added more choriambs and iambic or trochaic elements at the end of each line. A version with four choriambs is known as the *greater asclepiad*, a version with three choriambs, the *lesser choriamb*. The form was named for the 3rd-century-BC Greek poet Asclepiades.

Asclepius \as-'klē-pē-əs\ *Greek* Asklepios, *Latin* Aesculapius \ˌes-kyu-'lā-pē-əs, ˌēs-\ Greco-Roman god of medicine, the son of Apollo and the nymph Coronis. The centaur Chiron taught him the art of healing, but Zeus, afraid that he might render all humans immortal, slew him with a thunderbolt. Homer, in the *Iliad*, mentions him only as a skillful physician; in later times, however, he was honored as a hero and eventually worshiped as a god. Because it was supposed that Asclepius effected cures of the sick in dreams, the practice of sleeping in his temples became common. Asclepius was frequently represented standing, dressed in a long cloak, with bare breast; his usual attribute was a staff with a serpent coiled around it. This staff is the original symbol of medicine.

Asgard \'az-ˌgärd, 'as-\ or **Ásgard** \'aùs-ˌgärd\ In Norse mythology, the dwelling place of the gods, comparable to the Greek Mount Olympus.

Ásgrímsson \'aùs-ˌgrēm-sòn\, Eysteinn (b. *c.* 1310—d. March 14, 1361, Helgisetr Monastery, Nor.) Icelandic monk, author of *Lilja* ("The Lily"), the finest religious poem produced in pre-Reformation Iceland.

Records of Ásgrímsson's life are scant. In 1343 he was imprisoned, probably for thrashing his abbot and perhaps for a breach of chastity as well. In 1349 he was made an official of the Skálholt bishopric and attended the bishop on a mission to Norway from 1355 to 1357. After that, he was inspector of the Skálholt bishopric until excommunicated in 1360, when he returned to Norway, dying shortly thereafter.

Lilja is a survey of Christian history from the Creation to the Last Judgment, followed by 25 stanzas on contrition and a prayer to the Virgin Mary. By abandoning the circumlocutions of the skaldic poets, Ásgrímsson created a rapid, vivid narrative that remained the most popular of the Icelandic religious poems until the appearance of the Lutheran Passion hymns of Hallgrímur Pétursson in the 17th century.

Ash *see* ASCH.

A'shā, al- \ˌäl-'ä-shä, *Arabic* -''ä-\, *in full* Maymūn ibn Qays al-A'shā (b. before 570, Durnā, Arabia—d. *c.* 625, Durnā) Pre-

Islāmic poet whose qasida (ode) is included by the critic Abū 'Ubaydah (d. 825) in the celebrated *Mu'allaqāt*, a collection of seven pre-Islāmic qasidas.

Al-A'shā spent his youth in travels through Mesopotamia, Syria, Arabia, and Ethiopia. He continued to travel, even after becoming blind, particularly along the western coast of the Arabian Peninsula. It was then that he turned to the writing of panegyrics as a means of support. His style, reliant on sound effects and full-bodied foreign words, tends to be artificial.

Ashbery \'ash-ber-ē\, John (b. July 28, 1927, Rochester, N.Y., U.S.)   American poet noted for the elegance, originality, and obscurity of his poetry.

Ashbery graduated from Harvard University in 1949 and received a master's degree from Columbia University (N.Y.) in 1951. After working as a copywriter in New York City (1951–55), he worked as an art critic in Paris until 1965. Returning to New York, he served as executive editor of *Art News* from 1965 to 1972 and then took a teaching post at Brooklyn College.

Ashbery's first published book, *Turandot and Other Poems* (1953), was followed by *Some Trees* (1956), *The Tennis Court Oath* (1962), *Rivers and Mountains* (1966), and *The Double Dream of Spring* (1970). His collection entitled *Self-Portrait in a Convex Mirror* (1975) won several awards, including the Pulitzer Prize for poetry. His subsequent poetry volumes include *Houseboat Days* (1977), *A Wave* (1984), *April Galleons* (1987), and *Flow Chart* (1991).

Ashbery's poetry was initially greeted with puzzlement and even hostility owing to its extreme difficulty. His poems are characterized by arresting images and exquisite rhythms, an intricate form, and sudden shifts in tone and subject that produce curious effects of fragmentation and obscurity.

Ashley, Lady Brett \'bret-'ash-lē\   Fictional character, one of the principal characters of Ernest Hemingway's novel THE SUN ALSO RISES. An expatriate Englishwoman in Paris during the 1920s, she is typical of the Lost Generation of men and women whose lives have no focus or meaning and who therefore wander aimlessly from one party to another.

Ashton-Warner \,ash-tən-'wär-nər\, Sylvia (Constance) *married name* Henderson \'hen-dər-sən\ (b. Dec. 17, 1908, Stratford, N.Z.—d. April 28, 1984, Tauranga)   New Zealand educator and writer of fiction, nonfiction, and poetry. Most of her writing, both fiction and nonfiction, draws heavily upon her efforts to establish peace and communication between the two different cultures of the British and the native Maori.

Ashton-Warner's novels (*Spinster*, 1958; *Incense to Idols*, 1960; *Bell Call*, 1964; *Greenstone*, 1966; and *Three*, 1970) met with favorable critical response, and several of them became best-sellers. Her works of autobiographical nonfiction (*Teacher*, 1963; *Myself*, 1967; *Spearpoint: "Teacher" in America*, 1972; and *I Passed This Way*, 1979), however, did not fare as well critically or commercially. She also wrote several short stories and poems.

Ashvaghosa   *see* AŚVAGHOṢA.

Ash Wednesday   Long poem by T.S. ELIOT, first published as *Ash-Wednesday* in 1930; three of the poem's six sections had previously been published separately. Published after Eliot's confirmation in the Church of England (1927), *Ash Wednesday* expresses the pangs and the strain involved in the acceptance of religious belief and religious discipline.

The first section introduces the irony of the modern man whose intellectual dithering prevents him from achieving spiritual renewal. The second section is an allegory about rebirth, based on a prophecy by Ezekiel, with a famous image of devouring leopards. The following two sections discuss spiritual

journeys such as the one described in Dante's *Purgatorio*. In the fifth section, Eliot plays on the many religious and philosophical connotations of the word "word." The final section details the tension between meditation and distraction.

Asiaticism \,ā-zhē-'at-ə-,siz-əm, ,ā-shē-\   A literary style characterized by excessive ornamentation or emotionalism.

As I Crossed a Bridge of Dreams   Translation of the early Japanese classic SARASHINA NIKKI.

aside \ə-'sīd\   An actor's speech heard by the audience but supposedly not by other characters.

Aşık Paşa or **'Āshiq Pasha** \ä-'sɔk-pä-'shä\, *in full* Alâeddin Ali Aşik Paşa (b. *c.* 1272—d. 1333, Kırşehir, Seljuq empire [now in Turkey])   Poet who was one of the most important figures in early Turkish literature.

Very little about his life is known. A wealthy and respected figure in his community, he apparently was also a very religious sheikh (mystic leader: hence his name, Aşık, which means lover, given to an ecstatic mystic; *i.e.*, a lover of God).

His most famous work is the *Gharībnāmeh*, a long didactic, mystical poem written in more than 11,000 *masnawī*s (rhymed couplets) and divided into 10 chapters, each with 10 subsections. Each of the chapters is associated with a subject in relation to its number. For example, the fifth chapter deals with the five senses; the seventh, with the seven planets; and so on. It presents many moral precepts supported by examples and quotations from the holy book of Islām, the Qur'ān, and the Ḥadīth (the sayings of the Prophet Muḥammad). Although the work is not considered great poetry, it is important as representing a staunch orthodox Muslim point of view during a period when a great number of heterodox Muslim sects flourished in Anatolia. In addition, it is an interesting document from a linguistic standpoint, because it is one of the earliest examples of an Ottoman Turkish work, written at a time when Turkish was beginning to emerge as a literary language in Anatolia.

The *Faqrnāmeh* ("The Book of Poverty") is also attributed to the poet. Introduced by the famous Ḥadīth "poverty is my pride," this poem of 160 rhymed couplets deals with poverty and humility, the ideal ethic of the Muslim mystic.

As I Lay Dying   Novel by William FAULKNER, published in 1930. It is one of the many novels that Faulkner set in the fictional Yoknapatawpha County, Miss. The story unfolds by means of fragmented and intercut narration by each of the characters. These include Addie Bundren; her husband, Anse; their sons, Cash, Darl, and Vardaman, and daughter, Dewey Dell; and Addie's illegitimate son, Jewel. Addie watches from her deathbed as Cash builds her coffin. Upon her death, the family, under the direction of small-minded and ineffectual Anse, endeavors for once to respect Addie's wishes and transport her to her hometown for burial. The rest of the novel is an account of the family's journey and of the fates of the individual members of the family.

Asimov \'az-i-,mòf\, Isaac (b. Jan. 2, 1920, Petrovichi, Russia—April 6, 1992, New York, N.Y., U.S.)   American author and biochemist, a highly successful and prolific writer of science fiction and of science books for lay readers. He published more than 300 volumes.

Asimov was taken to the United States at the age of three. He grew up in Brooklyn, N.Y., graduating from Columbia University in 1939 and taking a Ph.D. there in 1948. He then joined the faculty of Boston University, with which he was associated thereafter.

He began contributing stories to science-fiction magazines in 1939 and in 1950 published his first book, *Pebble in the Sky*. His trilogy, *Foundation*, *Foundation and Empire*, and *Sec-*

ond Foundation (1951–53), which recounts the collapse of an empire in the universe of the future, won a Hugo Award in science fiction. Other novels and collections of stories include *I, Robot* (1950), *The Stars Like Dust* (1951), *The Currents of Space* (1952), *The Caves of Steel* (1954), *The Naked Sun* (1957), *Earth Is Room Enough* (1957), *Foundation's Edge* (1982), *The Robots of Dawn* (1983), *Prelude to Foundation* (1988), and the posthumously published *Forward the Foundation* (1993). His "Nightfall" (1941) is thought by many to be the finest science-fiction short story ever written. Asimov's books on various topics in science are written with lucidity and humor. These include *The Chemicals of Life* (1954), *Inside the Atom* (1956), *The Human Brain* (1964), and *Views of the Universe* (1981).

Asimov also wrote two volumes of autobiography: *In Memory Yet Green: The Autobiography of Isaac Asimov, 1920–1954* (1979) and *In Joy Still Felt: The Autobiography of Isaac Asimov, 1954–1978* (1980).

Askr and Embla \ˈäs-kər . . . ˈem-blä\   In Norse mythology, the first man and first woman, respectively, parents of the human race. They were created from tree trunks found on the seashore by three gods—Odin and his two brothers, Vili and Ve (some sources name the gods Odin, Hoenir, and Lodur). From each creator Askr and Embla received a gift: Odin gave them breath, or life, Vili gave them understanding, and Ve gave them their senses and outward appearance.

Aslan \ˈaz-ˌlan, ˈäz-ˌlän\   Fictional character, a wise and noble lion in THE CHRONICLES OF NARNIA series of children's fantasy books by C.S. Lewis. Aslan is the powerful and loving protector of Narnia, a fictional land he created with his musical voice. A symbol of Jesus Christ, he enlists children from the real world in his battle against evil, sacrifices himself and is resurrected, and returns to lead his chosen followers into heaven after bringing Narnia to an apocalyptic end.

Aṣmaʿī, al- \ˌäl-äs-ˈmä-ˌē, *Arabic* -ˌˈē\, *in full* Abū Saʿīd ʿAbd al-Malik ibn Qurayb al-Aṣmaʿī (b. *c.* 740, Basra, Iraq—d. 828, Basra)   Noted scholar and anthologist who was one of the three leading members of the Basra school of Arabic philology.

A gifted student of Abū ʿAmr ibn al-ʿAlāʾ (the founder of the Basra school), al-Aṣmaʿī joined the court of the caliph Hārūn ar-Rashīd in Baghdad. Renowned for his piety and plain living, he was a tutor to the caliph's son and a favorite of the viziers.

Al-Aṣmaʿī possessed an outstanding knowledge of the classical Arabic language. On the basis of the principles that he laid down, most of the existing divans, or collections of the pre-Islāmic Arab poets, were prepared by his disciples. He also wrote an anthology, *Al-Aṣmaʿīyāt*, displaying a marked preference for elegiac and devotional poetry. His method and his critical concern for authentic tradition are considered remarkable for his time. Some 15 monographs written by al-Aṣmaʿī, mainly on the animals, plants, customs, and grammatical forms in some way related to pre-Islāmic Arabic poetry, are extant, generally in recensions made by his students.

Asnyk \ˈäs-nik\, Adam (b. Sept. 11, 1838, Kalisz, Pol., Russian Empire—d. Aug. 2, 1897, Kraków, Austria-Hungary [now in Poland])   Polish poet whose works reflect his interest in revolutionary politics.

A disciple of the Polish Romantic poets, Asnyk published his first poetic volume, *Poezje* ("Poems"), in 1869; it was followed by three others. In 1883–94 he published a cycle of 30 sonnets, *Nad głębiami* ("Over the Depths"), in which the struggle for survival is shown not as the law of the jungle but as a mutual interdependence and cooperation among human communities. Asnyk felt that Poland, although deprived of independence and politically dead, would be reborn sooner or later because it refused to commit "spiritual suicide."

Asnyk also wrote comedies of manners, such as *Gałązka heliotropu* (1869; "A Sprig of Heliotrope"), and historical tragedies.

Aspects of the Novel   Collection of literary lectures by E.M. FORSTER, published in 1927. For the purposes of his study, Forster defines the novel as "any fictitious prose work over 50,000 words." The seven aspects offered for discussion are the story, people, plot, fantasy, prophecy, pattern, and rhythm. The author compares the form and texture of the novel to those of a symphony. As for subject, he expects the work "to reveal the hidden life at its source." Human nature, he concludes, is the novelist's necessary preoccupation.

Aspenström \ˈäs-pen-ˌstrœm\, Werner, *in full* Karl Werner Aspenström (b. Nov. 13, 1918, Norrbärke, Swed.)   Swedish lyrical poet and essayist.

Aspenström's images are characterized by intensity and a rare lyrical quality. In the cycle *Snölegend* (1949; "Snow Legend"), *Litania* (1952; "Litany"), and *Hundarna* (1954; "The Dogs"), the poet treats his metaphysical and social concerns in a symbolic form. Aspenström also wrote a number of poetic dramas. He re-created the world of his childhood in *Bäcken* (1958; "The Brook"), a series of short stories. He wrote several collections of essays on current issues, including *Sommar* (1968; "Summer") and *Skäl* (1970; "Arguments"). He was elected to the Swedish Academy in 1981.

Aspern Papers, The \ˈas-pərn\   Novelette by Henry JAMES, published in 1888, first in *The Atlantic Monthly* (March–May) and then in the collection *The Aspern Papers, Louisa Pallant, The Modern Warning*.

In "The Aspern Papers," an unnamed American editor rents a room in Venice in the home of Juliana Bordereau, the elderly mistress of Jeffrey Aspern, a deceased Romantic poet, in order to procure from her the poet's papers. Bordereau, a stingy, domineering woman, lives with her timid, middle-aged niece, Tina. (The niece was named Tita until James revised the text in 1908.) The manipulative editor, obsessed with possessing the Aspern papers, exhibits progressively unscrupulous behavior, such as assuming an alias, making false romantic overtures to Tina, and attempting burglary. When Bordereau dies, Tina offers the editor the coveted documents on the condition that he marry her. He initially refuses but returns to negotiate, only to find that Tina, in a display of newfound dignity, has burned the papers.

The novelette was inspired by an actual incident involving Claire Clairmont, once the mistress of Lord Byron.

Assistant, The   Novel by Bernard MALAMUD, published in 1957. Set in Brooklyn, the novel portrays the complex relationship that develops between Morris Bober, a worn-out Jewish grocer, and Frank Alpine, a young Italian-American who first robs Morris and then comes to his aid after wounding him. In the course of the novel, Frank becomes Morris's assistant, falls in love with his high-minded daughter, Helen, and challenges the old man's expectations of life. Morris pursues various schemes for unburdening himself of the store. Religious differences undermine Frank's amorous intentions, and Morris fires him for petty theft. After Morris's death, Frank comes back to revive the store and converts to Judaism.

assonance \ˈas-ə-nəns\ [Latin *assonare* to make a sound in accompaniment, respond] **1.** Resemblance of sound in words or syllables, such as the sound of *i* in *ring* and *hit*.   **2.** Relatively close juxtaposition of similar sounds, especially of vowels.   **3.** *also called* vowel rhyme.   In prosody, repetition of stressed vowel sounds within words with different end consonants, as in the phrase "quite like." In this sense, assonance is to be distinguished from regular rhyme, in which initial consonants differ but both vowel and end-consonant sounds are identical, as in the phrase "quite right."

As a poetic device, internal assonance is usually combined with ALLITERATION (repetition of initial consonant sounds) and CONSONANCE (repetition of end or medial consonant sounds) to enrich the texture of the poetic line. Sometimes two or more vowel sounds are repeated, as in the opening lines of Percy Bysshe Shelley's "The Indian Serenade":

> I arise from dreams of thee
> In the first sweet sleep of night

Assonance at the end of a line, producing an impure, or off, rhyme, is found in *La Chanson de Roland* and most French verses composed before the introduction of pure rhyme into French verse in the 12th century. Assonance remains a feature of Spanish and Portuguese poetry. In English verse, it is frequently found in the traditional ballads, where its use may have been careless or unavoidable. Otherwise, it was rarely used in English as a deliberate technique until the late 19th and 20th centuries, when it appears in the works of Gerard Manley Hopkins and Wilfred Owen. Their use of assonance instead of end rhyme was often adopted by such poets as W.H. Auden, Stephen Spender, and Dylan Thomas.

Astarte \as-'tär-tē\ *also spelled* Ashtart \'ash-,tärt\ Great goddess of the ancient Middle East and chief deity of Tyre, Sidon, and Elath, important Mediterranean seaports. Astarte, a goddess of love and war, was worshiped as Astarte in Egypt and Ugarit and among the Hittites, as well as in Canaan. Her Akkadian counterpart was Ishtar. Later she became assimilated with the Egyptian deities Isis and Hathor (a goddess of the sky and of women), and in the Greco-Roman world with Aphrodite, Artemis, and Juno, all aspects of the Great Mother.

Astarte, as Ashtoreth, is also mentioned in the Bible. According to the Old Testament, King Solomon, married to foreign wives, "went after Ashtoreth the goddess of the Sidonians" (I Kings 11:5). Later the cult places to Ashtoreth were destroyed by Josiah. Astarte/Ashtoreth is the Queen of Heaven to whom the Canaanites had burned incense and poured libations (Jeremiah 44).

Hebrew scholars now feel that the name Ashtoreth is a deliberate conflation of the Greek name Astarte and the Hebrew word *boshet*, "shame," indicating the Hebrew contempt for her cult. Ashtaroth, the plural form of the goddess's name in Hebrew, became a general term denoting goddesses and paganism.

Aṣṭchāp \'äsh-tə-,chāp\ [Sanskrit *aṣṭā* eight + Hindi *chāp* seal] Group of 16th-century Hindi poets, four of whom were disciples of the Vaishnava leader Vallabha, and four of his son and successor, Viṭṭhala. The greatest of the group was Sūrdās, a blind singer whose descriptions of the exploits of the child-god Krishna are the highlights of his collection of poetry called the *Sūrsāgar*, a work that is deeply loved throughout the Hindi-speaking areas of northern India. It is particularly rich in its details of daily life and in its sensitive depiction of human emotion, especially the parent's for the child and the maiden's for her lover.

Astley \'ast-lē\, Thea (Beatrice May) (b. Aug. 25, 1925, Brisbane, Queensland, Australia) Australian author who in her fiction examined, usually satirically, the lives of morally and intellectually isolated people in her native country.

Astley graduated from the University of Queensland in 1947 and taught in Queensland and New South Wales and at Macquarie University in Sydney. Drawing her subject from personal experience, her first two novels, *Girl with a Monkey* (1958) and *A Descant for Gossips* (1960), are ironic portrayals of philistine small-town life. In *The Well Dressed Explorer* (1962) and *The*

Acolyte (1972) Astley focused on individuals rather than on the larger community as the targets of her satire. With *A Kindness Cup* (1974) and *An Item from the Late News* (1982), however, Astley returned to the subject of the brutality of small-town Australian life. Later novels included *Reaching Tin River* (1990) and *Slow Natives* (1993). Astley has also written poetry, and *Hunting the Wild Pineapple* (1979) is a collection of her short stories.

Astraea \as-'trē-ə\ In classical mythology, the goddess of justice. In Greece she was the daughter of Zeus and Themis who, in the Golden Age of Greece, disseminated justice and virtue among all people. She often symbolized innocence or purity. Astraea returned to heaven and became the constellation Virgo after people turned to wickedness.

Astrophel and Stella \'as-trə-,fel . . . 'stel-ə\ An Elizabethan sonnet sequence of 108 sonnets, interspersed with 11 songs, by Sir Philip SIDNEY, written in 1582 and published posthumously in 1591. The work is often considered the finest Elizabethan sonnet cycle after William Shakespeare's sonnets.

The cycle tells the story of Stella ("star"), beloved by Astrophel ("star lover" or "beloved of a star," a play on Sidney's name), who loves poetry almost as much as he loves her. He details his passionate feelings for Stella, his struggles with conflicting emotions, and his final decision to abandon his pursuit of her in favor of a life of public service. In observance of contemporary poetic conventions, Sidney discourses in the sonnets on reason and passion, wit and will.

The publication of "Astrophel and Stella" generated a vogue for the sonnet sequence, and among the English poets who responded was Edmund Spenser, who also wrote the elegy "Astrophel" after his friend Sidney's death in 1586.

astrophic \,ā-'strōf-ik, -'sträf-\ 1. Of stanzas or stanzaic structure, arranged in series without regular repetition of stanzaic units. The term can also refer to stanzas that are irregular in arrangement. 2. Not arranged or divided into strophes or stanzas.

Asturias \äs-'tūr-yäs, -yäh\, Miguel Ángel (b. Oct. 19, 1899, Guatemala City, Guat.—d. June 9, 1974, Madrid, Spain) Guatemalan poet, novelist, diplomat, and winner of the Nobel Prize for Literature in 1967. His writings combine the mysticism of the Maya with an epic impulse toward social protest.

In 1923, after receiving his degree in law from the University of San Carlos of Guatemala, Asturias settled in Paris, where he studied ethnology at the Sorbonne and became a militant Surrealist under the influence of the French poet and literary theorist André Breton. His first major work, *Leyendas de Guatemala* (1930; "Legends of Guatemala"), describing the life and culture of the Maya before the arrival of the Spanish, brought him critical acclaim in France as well as at home. On his return to Guatemala, Asturias founded and edited *El diario del aire*, a radio magazine. During these years he published several volumes of poetry, beginning with *Sonetos* (1936; "Sonnets"). In 1946 he embarked upon a diplomatic career, continuing to write while serving in several countries in Central and South America.

It was during this period that Asturias' talent and influence as a novelist emerged, beginning with *El señor presidente* (1946; *The President*), an impassioned denunciation of the Guatemalan dictator Manuel Estrada Cabrera. In *Hombres de maíz* (1949; *Men of Maize*), the novel generally considered his masterpiece, Asturias depicts the seemingly irreversible wretchedness of the Indian peasant. Another aspect of that misery—the exploitation of Indians on the banana plantations—appears in the epic trilogy comprising the novels *Viento fuerte* (1950; *The Cyclone*), *El papa verde* (1954; *The Green Pope*), and *Los ojos de los enterrados* (1960; *The Eyes of the Interred*).

Astyanax \as-'tī-ə-naks\ *also called* Scamandrius \skə-'man-drē-əs\ In Greek legend, the son of the Trojan prince Hector and his wife Andromache. After the fall of Troy he was killed when the Greek warrior Neoptolemus hurled him from the battlements of the city. According to medieval legend, however, he survived the war, established the kingdom of Messina in Sicily, and founded the line from which Charlemagne was descended.

asura \'əs-ú-rə\ [Sanskrit *asuraḥ* evil spirit, demon, (originally) lord, a derivative of *asuḥ* life, vital energy] In Hindu mythology, a class of titans or demons, the enemies of the gods and mortals. In the earlier Vedic age the asuras and their counterparts, the devas, were both considered classes of gods, but gradually the two groups came to oppose each other. This development was reversed in Persia (Iran); there *ahura* (the etymological equivalent of asura) came to mean the supreme god and the *daeva*s (corresponding to devas) became demons. In Hindu mythology, the asuras and the devas together churned the milky ocean in order to extract from it the *amṛta*, the elixir of immortality. Strife arose over the possession of the *amṛta*, a conflict that is never ending. *Compare* DEVA.

Aśvaghoṣa or **Ashvaghosa** \ˌāsh-və-'gō-shə, -sə\ (b. AD 80?, Ayodhyā, India—d. 150?, Peshāwar) Philosopher and poet who is considered India's greatest poet before Kālidāsa (5th century) and the father of Sanskrit drama; he popularized the style of Sanskrit poetry known as KAVYA.

Aśvaghoṣa was born a Brahman. Legend obscures the man, but it is known that he was an outspoken opponent of Buddhism until, after a heated debate with a noted Buddhist scholar on the relative merits of the Vedāntic (Hindu) religion and the middle path (Buddhism), he accepted Buddhism and became a disciple of his erstwhile opponent.

Aśvaghosa's fame lay largely in his ability to explain the intricate concepts of Mahāyāna (Greater Vehicle) Buddhism. Among the works attributed to him are the *Mahāyāna-śraddhotpāda-śāstra* ("The Awakening of Faith in the Mahāyāna"), the *Buddhacarita* ("Life of the Buddha") in verse, and the *Mahālaṅkara* ("Book of Glory").

The original *Buddhacarita*, rediscovered in 1892, had been known from Tibetan and Chinese translations. The Sanskrit text is fragmentary, breaking off in the 14th canto with the enlightenment of the Buddha, while the other versions take the story through the Buddha's Nirvāṇa. Though intended to instruct the reader to turn away from the sensuous life and follow the Buddha's path, the work is most appealing in its descriptions of that very life. This effect is even more apparent in the *Saundarānanda* ("Of Sundarī and Nanda"), which recounts a well-known story of how the Buddha converted his half-brother Nanda to the monastic life of austerity. In his mastery of the intricacies of prosody and the subtleties of grammar and vocabulary, Aśvaghoṣa was clearly the forerunner of the Hindu *mahākāvya* ("great poem") authors.

asynartetic \ˌā-ˌsin-är-'tet-ik\ [Greek *asynártētos*, literally, disconnected] Of a line of verse, containing different or unconnected rhythmic units, as in the first two lines of one of John Donne's sonnets:

> ′ ∪ ∪ ′ , ′ ∪ ′ ∪ ′
> Batter my heart, three-personed God; for You
> ∪ ′ ∪ ′ , ′ ∪ ∪ ′ ∪ ′
> As yet but knock, breathe, shine, and seek to mend;

The term can be applied more specifically to a line in which the two parts that are separated by the caesura have different rhythms or to a line with a diaeresis or hiatus at the caesura so that a quasi independence of the two members is effected.

asyndeton \ə-'sin-də-ˌtän, ˌā-\ [Greek *asýndeton*, from neuter of *asýndetos* without conjunctions, literally, unconnected] Omission of the conjunctions that ordinarily join coordinate words or clauses, as in the phrase "I came, I saw, I conquered" or in Matthew Arnold's poem *The Scholar Gipsy*:

> Thou hast not lived, why should'st thou perish, so?
> Thou hadst *one* aim, *one* business, *one* desire;
> Else wert thou long since numbered with the dead!

As You Like It Five-act comedy by William SHAKESPEARE, written and performed about 1599 and first published in the Folio of 1623. Shakespeare based the play on *Rosalynde* (1590), a prose romance by Thomas Lodge. The play has two principal settings: the court that Frederick has usurped from his brother, the rightful Duke, and the Forest of Arden, where the Duke and his followers (including the disgruntled Lord Jaques and the jester Touchstone) are living. Rosalind, the Duke's daughter, who is still at court, falls in love with Orlando. The latter's hateful brother, Oliver, causes him to flee to Arden also. Frederick, upon learning that Orlando's father was the Duke's friend, banishes Rosalind. She assumes the guise of a young man (Ganymede) and pursues Orlando, promising him a cure for lovesickness by means of a feigned courtship. Oliver appears at the forest court intending to kill Orlando, but the latter saves his brother from a lioness and elicits his remorse. Oliver then falls in love with Celia, Rosalind's disguised cousin who has accompanied her. Revelation of the girls' true identities precipitates a mass wedding ceremony. Word arrives that Frederick has repented, and the Duke's exile ends.

The play is considered to be one of Shakespeare's "great" or "middle" comedies. Like *Two Gentlemen of Verona*, *Love's Labours Lost*, and *A Midsummer Night's Dream*, it contains a journey to a natural environment, where the constraints of everyday life are released and the characters are free to remake themselves, untrammeled by society's forms.

Atala \à-tà-'là\ Novel by François-Auguste-René CHATEAUBRIAND, published in French as *Atala, ou les amours de deux savages dans le désert* in 1801. It was revised and reissued with *René* in 1805. A portion of an unfinished epic about American Indians, the work tells the story of a Christian girl who has taken a vow to remain a virgin but who falls in love with a Natchez Indian. Torn between love and religion, she poisons herself to keep from breaking her vow.

Atalanta \ˌat-ə-'lan-tə\ In Greek mythology, a renowned and swift-footed huntress, probably a parallel and less important form of the goddess ARTEMIS. Her complex legend includes the following incidents: at her father's instance she was left to die at birth but was suckled by a she-bear; she took part in the Calydonian boar hunt; she offered to marry anyone who could outrun her—but those whom she overtook she speared. In one race Hippomenes (or Milanion) was given three of the golden apples of the HESPERIDES by the goddess Aphrodite; when he dropped them, Atalanta stopped to pick them up and so lost the race. Their son was Parthenopaeus, who later was one of the Seven against Thebes after the death of King Oedipus. She and her husband, proving ungrateful to Aphrodite, were led to profane a shrine, for which they were turned into lions.

Atalantis *see* ATLANTIS.

Ate \'ā-tē, 'ä-\ Greek mythological figure who induced rash and ruinous actions by both gods and mortals. She made Zeus take a hasty oath that resulted in the Greek hero Heracles becoming subject to Eurystheus, ruler of Mycenae. Zeus thereupon cast Ate out of Olympus, after which she remained on earth, working evil and mischief. She was followed by the Litai (meaning "Prayers"), the old and crippled daughters of Zeus, who repaired the harm done by her.

Athamas \'ath-ə-məs\   In Greek mythology, king of the prehistoric Minyans in the ancient Boeotian city of Orchomenus. His first wife was Nephele, a cloud goddess. Later Athamas became enamored of Ino, the daughter of Cadmus, and neglected Nephele, who disappeared in anger. Athamas and Ino also incurred the wrath of the goddess Hera because Ino had nursed the god Dionysus. Athamas (some sources say both Athamas and Ino) was driven mad by Hera, and Athamas (or both) killed one of his sons, Learchus; Ino, perhaps to escape Athamas or perhaps because she herself was mad, threw herself into the sea with her other son, Melicertes. Both were afterward worshiped as marine divinities—Ino as Leucothea, Melicertes as Palaemon.

Athena \ə-'thē-nə\ or **Athene** \ə-'thē-nē\   In Greek mythology, the city protectress, goddess of war, handicraft, and practical reason or wisdom, identified by the Romans with Minerva. Athena was probably a pre-Hellenic goddess later accepted by the Greeks. Hesiod, in the *Theogony*, told how Athena, having no known mother, sprang from Zeus's forehead, and Pindar added that Hephaestus struck open Zeus's head with an ax.

Athena was thought to have had neither consort nor offspring. She may not have been described as a virgin originally, but virginity was attributed to her very early and was the basis for the interpretation of her epithets Pallas and Parthenos (both meaning "the virgin"). As a war goddess Athena could not be dominated by other goddesses, such as Aphrodite, and as a palace goddess she could not be violated.

In Homer's *Iliad*, Athena, as a war goddess, inspired and fought alongside the Greek heroes; her aid was synonymous with military prowess. Also in the *Iliad*, Zeus specifically assigned the sphere of war to Ares and Athena. Athena's moral and military superiority to Ares derived in part from the fact that she represented the intellectual and civilized side of war and the virtues of justice and skill, whereas Ares represented mere blood lust. In the *Iliad*, Athena was the divine form of the heroic, martial ideal: she personified excellence in close combat, victory, and glory. The qualities that led to victory were found on the aegis, or breastplate, that Athena wore when she entered battle: fear, strife, defense, and assault. Athena appears in Homer's *Odyssey* as the tutelary deity of Odysseus, and myths from later sources portray her similarly as helper of Perseus and Heracles (Hercules). As the guardian of the welfare of kings, Athena became the goddess of good counsel, prudent restraint, and practical insight, as well as of war.

Athena later became the goddess of crafts and skilled peacetime pursuits in general. She was particularly known as the patroness of spinning and weaving. She ultimately became allegorized to personify wisdom and righteousness.

Athenaeum, The \ˌath-ə-'nē-əm\   Influential literary and critical journal, founded in London by James S. Buckingham. A successor to a general monthly magazine of the same name (published 1807–09), *The Athenaeum* appeared weekly from Jan. 2, 1828, until Feb. 11, 1921, when it merged with *The Nation*. Published for the next 10 years as *The Nation and Athenaeum*, the journal was absorbed in 1931 by *The New Statesman*.

Subtitled "A Journal of Literature, Science, the Fine Arts, Music, and the Drama," *The Athenaeum* sought to be considered the literary and intellectual forum through which the best contemporary intellectuals, poets, and writers could present their ideas. Among contributors in the 19th century were Robert Browning, Thomas Carlyle, Thomas Hood, Charles Lamb, and Walter Pater. Twentieth-century contributors included T.S. Eliot, Robert Graves, Thomas Hardy, Katherine Mansfield, John Middleton Murry (also editor, 1919–21), and Virginia Woolf.

Athenaeus \ˌath-ə-'nē-əs\ (fl. *c.* AD 200; b. Naukratis, Egypt)   Greek grammarian and author of *Deipnosophistai* ("The Gastronomers"), a work set forth as an aristocratic symposium, in which a number of learned men, some bearing the names of real persons, such as Galen, meet at a banquet and discuss food and other subjects. It is in 15 books, of which 10 have survived in their entirety, the others in summary form. The value of the work lies partly in the great number of quotations from lost works of antiquity that it preserves, nearly 800 writers being cited, and partly in the variety of unusual information it affords on all aspects of life in the ancient Greco-Roman world.

Atherton \'ath-ər-tən\, Gertrude Franklin, *original surname* Horn \'hȯrn\ (b. Oct. 30, 1857, San Francisco, Calif., U.S.—d. June 14, 1948, San Francisco)   American novelist who was noted as an author of fictional biography and history.

Atherton began her prolific writing career to escape the restrictions of a stifling marriage. Her first work, *The Randolphs of Redwoods* (*c.* 1882), was published anonymously in *The Argonaut* (republished 1899 as a book, *A Daughter of the Vine*). It was based on a local story of a well-bred girl turned alcoholic, and its publication offended her husband's prominent family.

After her husband's death Atherton traveled extensively, and the information she thus accumulated lent vividness to her writing. Her work generally drew mixed reviews, with the notable exception of *The Conqueror* (1902), a novelized account of the life of Alexander Hamilton. Her controversial novel *Black Oxen* (1923), the story of a woman revitalized by hormone treatments and based on Atherton's own experience, was her biggest popular success. Atherton wrote more than 40 novels and many nonfiction works. Her work is uneven in quality, but it displays a talent for vivid description.

athetesis \ˌath-ə-'tē-sis\ *plural* atheteses \-ˌsēz\ [Greek *athétēsis*, literally, abolition, annulling]   In literary criticism, the rejecting or marking of a passage (in a poem, for example) as spurious.

Athos \'ath-äs, 'äth-, -ȯs, *French* à-'tȯs\   Fictional character, one of the swashbuckling heroes of THE THREE MUSKETEERS by Alexandre Dumas *père*. The other two musketeers are his friends Porthos and Aramis, who join him in fighting various enemies during the reigns of the French kings Louis XIII and Louis XIV.

Atlantic, The, *also called* (1857–1932, 1971–81) The Atlantic Monthly.   Monthly journal of literature and opinion, founded in 1857 by Moses Dresser Phillips and published in Boston. One of the oldest and most respected of American reviews, *The Atlantic Monthly* has long been noted for the quality of its contents. Its long line of distinguished editors and authors included James Russell Lowell, Ralph Waldo Emerson, Henry Wadsworth Longfellow, and Oliver Wendell Holmes.

In the early 1920s, *The Atlantic Monthly* expanded its scope to political affairs, featuring articles by such figures as Theodore Roosevelt, Woodrow Wilson, and Booker T. Washington. The high quality of its literature and its literary criticism have preserved the magazine's reputation as a lively literary periodical with a moderate worldview.

Atlantis \at-'lan-tis\ or **Atalantis** \ˌat-ə-'lan-tis\, *also called* Atlantica \at-'lan-ti-kə\   A legendary island in the Atlantic Ocean, lying west of the Straits of Gibraltar, that was supposedly swallowed up by the sea as a result of earthquakes. The principal sources for the legend are two of Plato's dialogues, *Timaeus* and *Critias*.

The story of Atlantis, if Plato did not invent it, may echo ancient Egyptian records of a volcanic eruption on the island of Thera about 1500 BC. The legend has been a popular subject in literature, where Atlantis is often portrayed as a lost utopian world. Among those who have written on Atlantis are Francis Bacon, Daniel Defoe, P.B. Shelley, Jules Verne, Ignatius Donnelly, Paul Valéry, Hilda Doolittle, W.H. Auden, Louis Dudek, and James Merrill.

Atlas \\'at-ləs\\ In Greek mythology, son of the Titan Iapetus and the nymph Clymene (or Asia) and brother of Prometheus (creator of mortals). In the works of Homer, Atlas seems to have been a marine creation who supported the pillars that held heaven and earth apart. Later the name of Atlas was transferred to a range of mountains in northwestern Africa, and he was represented as the king of that district. According to the legend, Perseus, as punishment for Atlas' inhospitality, turned him into a rocky mountain by showing him the Gorgon's head, the sight of which turned mortals to stone. The Greek poet Hesiod portrayed Atlas as one of the Titans who took part in their war against Zeus, for which offense he was condemned to hold the heavens aloft.

Atlas Shrugged Novel by Ayn RAND, published in 1957. The book's female protagonist, Dagny Taggart, struggles to manage a transcontinental railroad amid the pressures and restrictions of massive bureaucracy. Her antagonistic reaction to a libertarian group seeking an end to government regulation is later echoed and modified in her encounter with a utopian community, Galt's Gulch, whose members regard self-determination rather than collective responsibility as the highest ideal. The novel contains the most complete presentation of Rand's personal philosophy, known as objectivism, in fictional form.

Atli *see* ATTILA.

Atli, Lay of *see* LAY OF ATLI.

atmosphere \\'at-mə-,sfir\\ The overall aesthetic effect of a work of art, or a dominant mood or emotional effect or appeal.

Atreus \\'ā-,trūs, 'ā-trē-əs\\ In Greek legend, the son of Pelops of Mycenae and his wife Hippodamia. Atreus was the elder brother of Thyestes and was the king of Mycenae. The story of his family—the House of Atreus—is virtually unrivaled in antiquity for complexity and corruption.

A curse said to have been pronounced by Myrtilus, a rival who died by Pelops' hand, plagued the descendants of Pelops. His sons Alcathous, Atreus, and Thyestes set upon a bloody course with the murder of their stepbrother Chrysippus, the son of Pelops' union with a nymph. After the crime the three brothers fled their native city of Pisa; Alcathous went to Megara, and Atreus and Thyestes stopped at Mycenae, where Atreus became king. But Thyestes either contested Atreus' right to rule or seduced Atreus' wife, Aërope, and thus was driven from Mycenae. To avenge himself, Thyestes sent Pleisthenes (Atreus' son, whom Thyestes had brought up as his own) to kill Atreus, but the boy was himself slain, unrecognized by his father.

When Atreus learned the identity of the boy, he recalled Thyestes to Mycenae in apparent reconciliation. At a banquet Atreus served Thyestes the flesh of Thyestes' own son (or sons), whom Atreus had slain in vengeance for the death of Pleisthenes. Thyestes fled in horror to Sicyon; there he impregnated his own daughter Pelopia in the hope of raising one more son to avenge himself. Atreus subsequently married Pelopia, and she afterward bore Aegisthus. Atreus believed this child to be his own, but Aegisthus was in fact the son of Thyestes.

Later, Agamemnon and Menelaus—sons of Atreus and Aërope—found Thyestes and imprisoned him at Mycenae.

Aegisthus was sent to murder Thyestes, but each recognized the other because of the sword that Pelopia had taken from her father and given to her son. Father and son slew Atreus, seized the throne, and drove Agamemnon and Menelaus out of the country.

ʿAṭṭār \\,ät-'tär, *Arabic* ,'ät-\\, Farīd od-Dīn (Moḥammad ebn Ebrāhīm), *also called* Farīd od-Dīn Abū Ḥamīd Moḥammad \\fä-'rēd-ȯd-'dēn-ä-'bü-ḵä-'mēd-mů-'ḵäm-mäd\\ (b. *c.* 1142?, Nīshāpūr [now in Iran]—d. *c.* 1220, Mecca [now in Saudi Arabia]) Persian poet who was one of the greatest Muslim mystical writers and thinkers, composing at least 45,000 distichs (couplets) and many brilliant prose works.

As a young man, ʿAṭṭār traveled widely, visiting Egypt, Syria, Arabia, India, and Central Asia. He finally settled in his native town, Nīshāpūr, in northeastern Persia, where he spent many years collecting the verses and sayings of famous Ṣūfīs (Muslim mystics). There is much controversy among scholars concerning the exact details of his life and death as well as the authenticity of many of the literary works attributed to him.

The greatest of his works is the well-known *Manṭeq al-ṭeyr* (*The Conference of the Birds*), an allegorical poem describing the quest of the birds (*i.e.*, Ṣūfīs) for the mythical Sīmorgh, or Phoenix, whom they wish to make their king (*i.e.*, God). Other important works of this prolific poet include the *Elāhī-nāma* (*The Ilahī-nāma or Book of God*) and the *Moṣībat-nāma* ("Book of Affliction"), both of which are mystical allegories similar in structure and form to *Manṭeq al-ṭeyr*; the *Dīvān* ("Collected Poems"); and the famous prose work *Tadhkerat al-Awlīyā*', an invaluable source of information on the early Ṣūfīs (abridged Eng. trans., *Muslim Saints and Mystics*). ʿAṭṭār's ideas, literary themes, and style strongly influenced Persian and other Islamic literatures.

Atterbom \\'ät-ter-,bům\\, Per Daniel Amadeus (b. Jan. 19, 1790, Åsbo, Swed.—d. July 21, 1855, Stockholm) Poet and literary historian who was a leader in the Swedish Romantic movement. While a student at Uppsala he founded, with some friends, the society Musis Amici (1807; renamed Auroraförbundet, 1808). Publishing in the group's periodical, *Phosphorus*, and in *Svensk Literatur Tidning* ("Swedish Literary News"), he became the leading poet and essayist of the new school of Swedish writers.

His greatest poetic work is the fairy-tale play *Lycksalighetens ö*, 2 vol. (1824–27; "The Isle of the Blessed"), which, on the literal level, deals with King Astolf, who deserts his northern kingdom for the temptations of sensual beauty, and, on the symbolic level, with the beguiling power of imagination in the history of poetry. Other works are *Blommorna* (1812; "The Flowers"), a cycle of poems envisioning eternal life beyond death; the unfinished *Fågel blå* (1814; "The Blue Bird"); and the six-volume *Svenska siare och skalder* (1841–55; "Swedish Prophets and Poets"), a six-volume work distinguished for its style and erudition that earned Atterbom the rank of Sweden's first great literary historian. It reflects his mature appreciation for the writings he had attacked in his youth.

atticism \\'at-ə-,siz-əm\\ A witty or well-turned phrase. The word refers to the characteristic literary style of Attic Greek, which was simple yet refined and elegant.

Atticus \\'at-i-kəs\\, Titus Pomponius (b. 109 BC, Rome—d. 32 BC) Roman *eques* ("knight"), Epicurean, and patron of letters, best remembered for his connection with Cicero, with whom he was educated. Born Titus Pomponius, he was given the name Atticus because of his long residence in Athens (88–65 BC) and his intimate acquaintance with Greek literature and language; he assumed the name of Quintus Caecilius Pomponianus when his rich uncle, Quintus Caecilius, died in 58.

Pomponius moved to Athens in 88 in order to escape the civil war. He lived quietly, devoting himself to study and business interests, and on his return to Rome he kept aloof from political life. His most intimate friend was Cicero, whose correspondence with him extended over many years.

None of Atticus' writings is extant, although he wrote a history, in Greek, of Cicero's consulship, a Roman history down to 54 BC, and genealogical works. His most important work was an edition of the letters addressed to him by Cicero.

Attila \\'at-əl-ə, ə-'til-ə \\, *byname* Flagellum Dei \\fla-'jel-ùm-'dā-ₑē \\ (Latin: "Scourge of God"), *also called* Etzel \\'et-səl \\, Atli \\'ät-lē \\, *or* Attila the Hun (d. 453) King of the Huns from 434 to 453 (ruling jointly with his elder brother Bleda until 445). He was one of the greatest of the barbarian rulers who assailed the Roman Empire, invading the southern Balkan provinces and Greece and then Gaul and Italy. In legend he appears under the name Etzel in the *Nibelungenlied* and under the name Atli in the Icelanders' sagas.

Attis \\'at-is \\, *also spelled* Atys. Mythical consort of the Great Mother of the Gods. Like the Great Mother, Attis was probably indigenous to Asia Minor, adopted by the invading Phrygians and blended by them with a mythical character of their own. According to the Phrygian tale, Attis was a beautiful youth born of Nana, the daughter of the river Sangarius, and the hermaphroditic Agdistis. Having become enamored of Attis, Agdistis struck him with frenzy as he was about to be married, with the result that Attis castrated himself and died. Agdistis in repentance prevailed upon Zeus to grant that the body of the youth should never decay or waste. Other versions also exist, but they all retain the essential etiological feature, the self-castration.

Attis was fundamentally a vegetation god, and in his self-mutilation, death, and resurrection he represents the fruits of the earth, which die in winter only to rise again in the spring.

Attius *see* ACCIUS.

Atwood \\'at-‚wùd \\, Margaret (Eleanor) (b. Nov. 18, 1939, Ottawa, Ont., Can.) Canadian poet, novelist, and critic, noted for her Canadian nationalism and her feminism.

Atwood attended the University of Toronto (B.A., 1961) and Radcliffe College, Cambridge, Mass. (M.A., 1962), continuing her studies at Harvard University (1962–63, 1965–67). She later taught literature at several Canadian universities.

Atwood was a published poet at age 19; her first book of poetry, *Double Persephone*, was published in 1961. Another early collection, *The Circle Game* (1964, revised in 1966), received the Canadian Governor General's Award for Poetry in 1966. In these and other early poetic works, Atwood pondered human behavior, celebrated the natural world, and condemned materialism. One of her many later volumes of poetry, *Power Politics* (1971), examined the use and meaning of power in personal relationships.

Atwood also wrote a number of novels, beginning with *The Edible Woman* (1969), an early feminist treatise. With mordant wit, she used her novels to examine aspects of a woman's role and her shifting relationship to the world and the individuals around her. Her later novels include *Surfacing* (1972), *Lady Oracle* (1976), *Life Before Man* (1979), *Bodily Harm* (1981), *The Handmaid's Tale* (1985; winner of the Governor General's Award for Fiction in 1986), *Cat's Eye* (1988), and *The Robber Bride* (1993). She also wrote short fiction (such as that in *Bluebeard's Egg* [1983]), critical prose (such as that in *Survival* [1972] and *Second Words* [1982]), and children's books.

aubade \\ō-'bäd \\ [French, ultimately from Old Provençal *albada*, a derivative of *alba* dawn] *also called* dawn song **1.** A song or poem greeting the dawn. **2.** A morning love song, or, more specifically, a song or poem of lovers parting at daybreak. *See also* ALBA; TAGELIED.

Aubignac \\ō-bē-'nyȧk \\, François Hédelin, abbé d' (b. Aug. 4, 1604, Paris, Fr.—d. July 25, 1676, Nemours) Playwright, critic, and associate of the statesman Cardinal de Richelieu who influenced French 17th-century writing and encouraged dramatic standards based on the classics.

Although trained as an advocate, Aubignac soon turned to the Roman Catholic church (1628) and was named tutor to Richelieu's nephew. Encouraged by the cardinal, he wrote several prose tragedies, three of which survive: *Cyminde* (1642), *La Pucelle d'Orléans* (1642; "The Maid of Orleans"), and *Zénobie* (1647). His polemical writings include four critical essays on the plays of Pierre Corneille and several other critical commentaries.

His major work, *La Pratique du théâtre* (1657; *The Whole Art of the Stage*), was commissioned by Richelieu and is based on the idea that the action on stage must have credibility (*vraisemblance*) in the eyes of the audience. Aubignac proposed, among other things, that the whole play should take place as close as possible in time to the crisis, that audiences should not be asked to imagine changes of scene or character, and that the number of actors be restricted so there is no confusion. Although it reached a limited audience, the *Pratique* was probably a force in the formation of French Classical taste as put into practice by Corneille and Jean Racine.

Aubigné \\dō-bē-'nyä \\, Théodore-Agrippa d' (b. Feb. 8, 1552, Pons, Fr.—d. April 29, 1630, Geneva [Switz.]) Major late 16th-century poet and renowned Huguenot captain, polemicist, and historian of his own times. After studies in Paris, Orléans, Geneva, and Lyon, he joined the Huguenot forces and served throughout the Wars of Religion on the battlefield and in the council chamber. He later became estranged from his Huguenot brethren and in 1620 moved to Geneva, where he remained until his death.

Among Aubigné's prose works, his commentary on life and manners ranges widely in the *Adventures du baron de Faeneste* (1617). The *Histoire universelle* is a history of the period from 1553 to 1602, with an appendix to cover the death of Henry IV (1610); an unfinished supplement was meant to bring the story up to 1622. It contains much lively writing and eyewitness accounts of many events.

Aubigné's major poem in seven cantos, the *Tragiques*, begun in 1577 (published 1616), celebrates the justice of God; it shows sectarian bias and is uneven in quality, but these flaws are offset by many passages of great poetic power. Modern research on Baroque literature has awakened interest in Aubigné's youthful love poetry, collected in *Printemps* (1570–73, unpublished). In these poems the stock characters and phraseology, modeled on Petrarch, are transmuted into a highly personal style full of tragic resonances by Aubigné's characteristic vehemence of passion and force of imagination.

Aubrey \\'ò-brē \\, John (b. March 12, 1626, Easton Piercy, Wiltshire, Eng.—d. June 1697, Oxford) Antiquarian and writer, best known for his vivid, intimate, and sometimes acid biographical sketches of his contemporaries. Educated at Oxford at Trinity College, he studied law in London at the Middle Temple. He early displayed his interest in antiquities by calling attention to the prehistoric stones at Avebury, Wiltshire. He was elected a fellow of the Royal Society in 1663.

In 1667 Aubrey met the historian and antiquarian Anthony à Wood and began gathering materials for Wood's projected *Athenae Oxonienses*, a vast biographical dictionary of Oxford writers and ecclesiastics. He also continued gathering antiquities. His *Miscellanies* (1696), a collection of stories of apparitions and curiosities, was the only work that appeared during his lifetime.

His biographies first appeared as *Lives of Eminent Men* (1813). The definitive presentation of Aubrey's biographical manuscripts, however, is *Brief Lives* (2 vol., 1898; edited by Andrew Clark). Though not biographies in the strict sense of the word, Aubrey's *Lives*, based on observation and gossip, are profiles graced by picturesque and revealing detail that have found favor with later generations.

Aucassin et Nicolette \ō-kȧ-'sä-nä-nē-kō-'let\ Early 13th-century French *chantefable* (a story told in alternating sections of verse and prose, the former sung, the latter recited) preserved in a single manuscript in France's Bibliothèque Nationale. Aucassin, "endowed with all good qualities," is the son of the Count of Beaucaire and falls in love with Nicolette, a captive Saracen turned Christian. The lovers are imprisoned but manage to escape and after many vicissitudes (including flight, capture, and shipwreck) are able to marry. This theme was also treated in the romance of FLOIRE ET BLANCHEFLOR, with which *Aucassin et Nicolette* is thought to share common Moorish and Greco-Byzantine sources.

The author of the *chantefable* may have been a professional minstrel from northeastern France, in whose dialect the work was written. The author mocks both epic and romance by portraying Nicolette as full of resourcefulness, while Aucassin is merely a lovesick swain, lacking initiative, unfilial in his attitude toward his parents, needing to be bribed to do his duty as a knight, and defending his heritage absentmindedly until faced with death. He also prefers hell with Nicolette and a merry company of sinners to heaven with ill-clad priests and the lame. The work was sufficiently esteemed to be plagiarized in *Clarisse et Florent*, a continuation of the 13th-century chanson de geste *Huon de Bordeaux*.

Auchincloss \'ȯk-in-ˌklȯs\, Louis (Stanton) (b. Sept. 27, 1917, Lawrence, N.Y., U.S.) American novelist, short-story writer, and critic best known for his novels of manners set in the world of contemporary upper-class New York City.

Auchincloss studied at Yale University from 1935 to 1939 and graduated from the University of Virginia Law School in 1941. He was admitted to the New York State bar that same year and began a legal career that would last until 1986.

For his first novel, *The Indifferent Children* (1947), Auchincloss used the pseudonym Andrew Lee, but by 1950 he was publishing stories under his own name. Noted for his stylistic clarity and skill at characterization, he became the prolific chronicler of life in the rarefied world of corporate boardrooms and brownstone mansions. His interests as a novelist privy to this world lay not so much in the excesses and intrigues of its inhabitants as in their formative influences and personal limitations.

Several of his best novels, including *The House of Five Talents* (1960) and *Portrait in Brownstone* (1962), examine family relationships over a period of decades. Others, notably *The Rector of Justin* (1964) and *Diary of a Yuppie* (1987), are studies of a single character, often from many points of view. Auchincloss frequently employed thematic or geographic linkage in his collections of short stories. *Tales of Manhattan* (1967) and *Skinny Island* (1987), for example, comprise tales set in Manhattan. In addition to his fiction, Auchincloss published critical works on Edith Wharton and Henry James, among other writers.

Auden \'ȯd-ən\, W.H., *in full* Wystan Hugh (b. Feb. 21, 1907, York, Yorkshire, Eng.—d. Sept. 29, 1973, Vienna, Austria) English-born poet and man of letters who achieved early fame in the 1930s.

Auden grew up in an Anglo-Catholic and scientific rather than literary atmosphere. His education followed the standard pattern for children of the middle and upper classes. In 1924 his

Horst Tappe

first poem was published in *Public School Verse*. The following year he entered the University of Oxford (Christ Church), where he exerted a strong influence on such other literary intellectuals as C. Day-Lewis, Louis Mac-Neice, and Stephen Spender, who printed by hand the first collection of Auden's poems in 1928. Upon graduating from Oxford in 1928, Auden lived for a year in Berlin, then spent the next five years working as a schoolmaster in Scotland and England.

In his *Collected Shorter Poems 1927–1957* (1966), Auden divides his career into four periods. The first extended from 1927 through *The Orators* of 1932. This period is best exemplified by the "charade" *Paid on Both Sides*, which helped establish Auden's reputation in 1930. During this time he also collaborated with Christopher Isherwood on three verse dramas, including THE ASCENT OF F6.

In his second period, 1933–38, Auden was the hero of the left. While pointing up the evils of capitalist society, he also warned of the rise of totalitarianism. In *Look, Stranger!* (1936; U.S. title, *On This Island*), his verse became more open in texture and accessible to a larger public. To this period also belong a group of experimental and noncommercial plays; some commentaries for documentary films, including a classic of that genre, *Night Mail* (1936); numerous essays and book reviews; and travel literature.

Auden's third period, 1939–46, reflected decisive changes in his life and in his religious and intellectual perspective. *Another Time* (1940) contains some of his best songs and topical verse, including MUSÉE DES BEAUX ARTS and SEPTEMBER 1, 1939. *The Double Man* (1941; U.K. title, *New Year Letter*) embodies his position on the verge of commitment to Christianity. The beliefs and attitudes that are basic to all of Auden's work after 1940 are defined in three long poems: religious in the Christmas oratorio *For the Time Being* (1944); aesthetic in the same volume's *The Sea and the Mirror*; and social-psychological in THE AGE OF ANXIETY (1947), the "baroque eclogue" that won Auden the Pulitzer Prize in 1948. Auden wrote no long poems after that.

In the fourth period, which began in 1948, Auden produced the collections *The Shield of Achilles* (1955), HOMAGE TO CLIO (1960), *About the House* (1965), and *City Without Walls* (1969). With Chester Kallman, an American poet who lived with him for more than 20 years, he also wrote opera librettos, notably *The Rake's Progress* (1951), for Igor Stravinsky; *Elegy for Young Lovers* (1961) and *The Bassarids* (1966), for Hans Werner Henze; and *Love's Labour's Lost* for Nicolas Nabokov. Auden also wrote criticism, worked as an editor, and translated poetry, notably *The Collected Poems of St. John Perse* (1972).

Audiberti \ō-dē-ber-'tē\, Jacques (b. March 25, 1899, Antibes, Fr.—d. July 10, 1965, Paris) French playwright, poet, and novelist whose extravagance of language and rhythm shows the influence of Symbolism and Surrealism.

Audiberti began his writing career as a journalist, moving to Paris in 1925 to write for *Le Journal* and *Le Petit Parisien*. Influenced by the theories of Antonin Artaud, he wrote his plays as an examination of the conflict between paganism and Christianity and of the presence of evil in daily life.

Among Audiberti's best-known plays are *Quoat-Quoat* (1946), which concerns a young passenger on a French ship bound for Mexico who chooses to accept death rather than loss of identity; *Le Mal court* (1947; "Evil Is in the Air"), which takes place in an 18th-century fairy-tale setting; and *La Hobereaute* (1956; "The Falcon"), an attack on religion. His verse collections include *Race des hommes* (1937; "The Race of Men") and *Des tonnes de semence* (1941; "Tons of Seed"). He also wrote 15 novels.

Auerbach \'aů-ər-ˌbäk\, Berthold (b. Feb. 28, 1812, Nordstetten, near Horb, Württemberg [Germany]—d. Feb. 8, 1882, Cannes, Fr.)   German novelist noted chiefly for his tales of village life.

Auerbach prepared for the rabbinate, but, estranged from Jewish orthodoxy by the study of the Dutch philosopher Benedict de Spinoza, he turned instead to literature. Spinoza's life formed the basis of his first novel (1837); a translation of Spinoza's works followed in 1841. In 1843 Auerbach began publishing the *Schwarzwälder Dorfgeschichten* (*Black Forest Village Stories*), and later produced novels on the same subject, among them *Barfüssele* (1856; *Little Barefoot*) and *Edelweiss* (1861). These fanciful studies of rural life found a wide public and many imitators.

Auerbach \'aů-ər-ˌbäk\, Erich (b. Nov. 9, 1892, Berlin, Ger.—d. Oct. 13, 1957, Wallingford, Conn., U.S.)   Educator and scholar of Romance literatures and languages.

After earning a doctorate in philology at the University of Greifswald, Germany, in 1921, Auerbach served as librarian of the Prussian State Library. From 1927 to 1947 he was professor of Romance philology at the University of Marburg in Germany and at the Turkish State University in Istanbul. He joined the faculty of Yale University in 1947.

His foremost work was *Mimesis: Dargestellte Wirklichkeit in der abendländischen Literatur* (1946; *Mimesis: The Representation of Reality in Western Literature*), which presents the development of Western literature in terms of the historical qualities of each era.

Augeas or **Augeias** or **Augias** \'ô-jē-əs, ô-'jē-əs\   In Greek legend, a king of the Epeians in Elis and a son of the sun god Helios. He possessed an immense wealth of herds, and King Eurystheus imposed upon the Greek hero HERACLES the task of clearing out all of Augeas' stables unaided in one day. Heracles did so by turning the Alpheus River through them.

Augelmir   *see* AURGELMIR.

Augier \ozh-'yā\, Émile, *in full* Guillaume-Victor-Émile Augier (b. Sept. 17, 1820, Valence, Fr.—d. Oct. 25, 1889, Croissy-sur-Seine)   Popular dramatist who wrote comedies extolling the virtues of middle-class life under the Second Empire and who, with Alexandre Dumas *fils* and Victorien Sardou, dominated the French stage.

Didactic in purpose, Augier's verse play *Gabrielle* (1849) attacks the Romantic belief in the divine right of passion, while his *Le Mariage d'Olympe* (1855; "The Marriage of Olympia") opposes the idea of the rehabilitation of a prostitute by love, as expressed in Dumas's *La Dame aux Camélias* ("The Lady of the Camellias"). An unbending moralist and a champion of the institution of marriage, Augier satirized adultery in *Les Lionnes pauvres* (1858; "The Poor Lionesses") and saw in greed the root of evil. His best-known play, *Le Gendre de Monsieur Poirier* (1854; "Monsieur Poirier's Son-in-Law"), written in collaboration with Jules Sandeau, advocated fusion of the new prosperous middle class and the dispossessed nobility.

Augustan Age \ô-'gəs-tən\   One of the most illustrious periods in Latin literary history, from approximately 43 BC to AD 18; together with the preceding CICERONIAN PERIOD, it forms the Golden Age of Latin literature. Marked by civil peace and prosperity, the age reached its highest literary expression in poetry, producing a polished and sophisticated verse generally addressed to a patron or to the emperor Augustus and dealing with themes of patriotism, love, and nature. One decade alone, 29 to 19 BC, saw the publication of Virgil's *Georgics* and the completion of the *Aeneid*; the appearance of Horace's *Odes*, Books I–III, and *Epistles,* Book I; the elegies (Books I–III) of Sextus Propertius; and Books I–II of the elegies of Tibullus. Also during those 10 years, Livy began his monumental history of Rome, and another historian, Pollio, was writing his important but lost history of recent events. Ovid was the last great writer of the Golden Age; his death in exile in AD 17 marked the close of the period.

By extension, the name Augustan Age also is applied to a "classical" period in the literature of any nation, especially to the 18th century in England and, less frequently, to the 17th century in France. Some critics prefer to limit the English Augustan Age to a period covered by the reign of Queen Anne (1702–14), when writers such as Alexander Pope, Joseph Addison, Sir Richard Steele, John Gay, and Matthew Prior flourished. Others, however, would extend it backward to include John Dryden and forward to take in Samuel Johnson.

Augustan History \ô-'gəs-tən\, *Latin* Historia Augusta.   A collection of biographies of the Roman emperors (Augusti) from Hadrian to Numerian (117–284), an important source for the history of the Roman Empire.

The work is incomplete in its surviving form (it probably originally began with one of Hadrian's predecessors, Nerva or Trajan), and its original title is unknown. Its authorship and date of composition are also matters of argument. The names of six authors of the early 4th century are given in the manuscript itself, but some scholars regard these as spurious and believe that the *History* was written in the late 4th century. Its point of view is consciously pagan, and the author or authors may have been trying to counteract the growing dominance of Christianity.

The first part of the work, from Hadrian to Caracalla, is thought to be based on reliable sources and is of great historical value; the remainder is considered to be generally less reliable.

Augustine \'ȯg-əs-ˌtēn, ȯ-'gəs-tin\, Saint, *also called* Saint Augustine of Hippo \'hip-ō\, Augustine *also spelled* Augustin, *original Latin name* Aurelius Augustinus \ȯ-'rē-lē-əs-ˌȯg-əs-'tī-nəs\ (b. Nov. 13, AD 354, Tagaste, Numidia [now in Algeria]—d. Aug. 28, 430, Hippo Regius [near modern Annaba, Alg.])   Bishop of Hippo in Roman Africa from 396 to 430 and the major Christian theologian of the early Western church. His best-known works are *Confessiones* (THE CONFESSIONS) and his masterpiece *De civitate Dei* (THE CITY OF GOD).

Augustine recounted the story of his restless youth and his conversion in *The Confessions*. Though his mother, Monica, was a devout Christian, Augustine was not baptized in infancy. As a 19-year-old student at Carthage he read a treatise of Cicero that directed him to philosophy. At the age of about 28, he went to Rome and then to Milan, where he met the bishop Ambrose. He was converted to Christianity in 386 and was baptized by Ambrose in 387.

Augustine returned to Africa, was ordained a priest in 391, and became bishop of Hippo in 396. He served as pastor, teacher, preacher, and civil judge. He wrote extensively, especially in controversy with heretical groups (the Manichaeans, Donatists, and Pelagians) and in commentary on the scriptures.

August 1914 Historical novel by Aleksandr SOLZHENIT-
SYN, published as *Avgust chetyrnadtsatogo* in Paris in 1971. An
enlarged version, nearly double in size, was published in 1983.
The novel treats Germany's crushing victory over Russia in
their initial military engagement of World War I, the Battle
of Tannenberg. The action takes place in the course of three
days. The book's combination of epic sweep and brief time-
span necessitated broad, efficient characterization, an effect
that Solzhenitsyn attempts to achieve by means of frequent literary allusions and often biting irony.

Aukrust \'eŭ-krŭst\, Olav (b. Jan. 21, 1883, Gudbrandsdalen, Nor.—d. Nov. 3, 1929, Gudbrandsdalen) Regional
poet whose verse contributed to the development of Nynorsk
(an amalgam of rural Norwegian dialects) as a literary language.

Aukrust was a teacher and later headmaster at a folk high
school. As a young man he was an eager student of the language
spoken in the countryside and received a government stipend to
study Gudbrandsdalen dialects, in which all his verse is written.
He drew inspiration from the folk legend, natural surroundings, and peasant life of his native area. As a result, although
he wrote about matters of universal interest, he remained a
poet of that region. The mystical poem *Himmelvarden* (1916;
"Cairn of Heaven") is considered his most important work.

Aulnoy or **Aunoy** \dō-'nwä\, Marie-Catherine Le Jumel de
Barneville, Countess (comtesse) d' (b. 1650/51, near Honfleur,
Fr.—d. Jan. 14, 1705, Paris) Writer of fairy tales and of novels
of court intrigue, whose personal intrigues were commensurate
with those described in her books.

Shortly after her marriage as a young girl in 1666, Marie
d'Aulnoy conspired with her mother and their two lovers to
lodge a false accusation of high treason against Marie's husband, a middle-aged financier. When the plot miscarried, she
was forced to spend the next 15 years out of the country.
She returned to Paris and began her literary career in 1685.
Her best remembered works are *Contes de fées* (1697; "Fairy
Tales") and *Les Contes nouveaux ou les fées à la mode* (1698;
"New Tales, or the Fancy of the Fairies"), written in the manner of the great fairy tales of Charles Perrault but laced with her
own sardonic touch. Her pseudo-historical novels, which were
immensely popular throughout Europe, included *Hippolyte,
comte de Douglas* (1690; *Hippolitus, Earl of Douglas*), *Mémoires
de la cour d'Espagne* (1690; *Memoirs from the Court of Spain*),
and *Relation du voyage d'Espagne* (1691; *Travels into Spain*). An
English-language translation of her works, including the fairy
tales, was published in four volumes in 1707. The fairy tales
were frequently reprinted.

Aunt Julia and the Scriptwriter \'jŭ-lē-ə\ Comic novel by
Mario VARGAS LLOSA, published as *La tía Julia y el escribidor*
in 1977. Vargas Llosa uses counterpoint, paradox, and satire to
explore the creative process of writing and its relation to the
daily lives of writers.

One half of the story is an autobiographical account of an
aspiring writer named Marito Varguitas, who falls in love with
Julia, the divorced sister-in-law of his Uncle Lucho. Marito's
success at writing and romance contrasts with the fortunes of
Pedro Camacho, the protagonist of the other half of the story,
who is a devoted but declining author of radio soap operas.

Aunt Polly \'päl-ē\ Fictional character, Tom Sawyer's aunt
and guardian in Mark Twain's TOM SAWYER.

Aunt Polly is a kindhearted, rather simple old woman who
takes her responsibility for Tom and his half-brother Sid very
seriously. Employing whacks on the head with her thimble, frequent scoldings, and quoting of Scripture, Aunt Polly tries, unsuccessfully, to force Tom to abandon his high-spirited ways.

aureate \'ȯr-ē-ət, -ˌāt\ [Middle English *aureat* golden, splendid, probably coined on the basis of Latin *auratus* gilded and
aureus golden] Marked by a style that is affected, pompous,
and heavily ornamental, that uses rhetorical flourishes excessively, and that often employs interlarded foreign words and
phrases. The style is often associated with the 15th-century
French, English, and Scottish writers.

Aurgelmir \'aŭr-gəl-ˌmir\ or **Augelmir** \'aŭ-\, *also called*
Ymir \'im-ir\ In Norse mythology, the first being, a giant
who was created from the drops of water that formed when the
ice of Niflheim met the heat of Muspelheim. Aurgelmir was the
father of all the giants; a male and a female grew under his arm,
and his legs produced a six-headed son. A cow, Audumbla,
nourished him with her milk. Audumbla was herself nourished
by licking salty, rime-covered stones. She licked the stones into
the shape of a man; this was Buri, who became the grandfather
of the great god Odin and his brothers. These gods later killed
Aurgelmir and put his body in the void, Ginnungagap. They
fashioned the earth from his flesh, the seas and lakes from his
blood, mountains from his bones, stones from his teeth, the
sky from his skull, and clouds from his brain. His eyelashes (or
eyebrows) became the fence surrounding Midgard, or Middle
Earth, the home of humans.

Aurora \ə-'rȯr-ə\ In Roman mythology, the personification
of the dawn, a counterpart to the Greek EOS. In Latin writings
such as those of Virgil, the word *aurora* was used for the east.

Aurora Leigh \ə-'rȯr-ə-'lē\ Novel in blank verse by Elizabeth
Barrett BROWNING, published in 1857.

The first-person narrative, which comprises some 11,000
lines, tells of the heroine's childhood and youth in Italy and
England, her self-education in her father's hidden library, and
her successful pursuit of a literary career. Initially resisting a
marriage proposal by the philanthropist Romney Leigh, Aurora
later surrenders her independence and weds her faithful suitor,
whose own idealism has also since been tempered by experience. Aurora's career, Romney's social theories, and a melodramatic subplot concerning forced prostitution elicit the author's
vivid observations on the importance of poetry, the individual's responsibility to society, and the victimization of women.
Although it was a great popular success, *Aurora Leigh* was not
admired by critics.

Ausonian \ȯ-'sō-nē-ən\ Pertaining to Ausonia, a name used
in ancient Greek and Latin verse for Italy. On the classical
model, *Ausonian* has been used in English as a poetic substitute
for "Italian."

Ausonius \ȯ-'sō-nē-əs\, Decimus Magnus (b. *c.* 310, Burdigala, Gaul [now Bordeaux, France]—d. *c.* 395, Burdigala)
Latin poet and rhetorician interesting chiefly for his preoccupation with the provincial scene of his native Gaul.

Ausonius taught in the famous schools of Burdigala, first as
a grammarian and then as a rhetorician. He also tutored the future emperor Gratian, who, on his accession, elevated Ausonius
to the prefecture of Africa, Italy, and Gaul and to the consulship in 379. After Gratian's murder in 383, Ausonius returned
to his estates on the Garonne River to read and write. His last
years were saddened by the action of his favorite and most outstanding pupil, Paulinus of Nola (later bishop and saint), who
deserted literature for a life of Christian retirement. Ausonius'
pleading, pained letters to Paulinus continued until his death.

An incorrigible trifler, Ausonius left few works of any consequence. A characteristic piece of trifling is the *Technopaegnion*
("A Game of Art"), a set of poems in which each line ends in
a monosyllable. Ausonius produced the useful autobiographical *Praefatiunculae* ("Prefaces"); *Eclogae*, mnemonic verses on

astronomy and astrology; *Ordo nobilium urbium* ("Order of Noble Cities"); *Ludus septem sapientum* ("Play of the Seven Sages"), a forerunner of the morality play; and many epigrams. His sentimental fondness for old ties is seen in *Parentalia*, a series of poems on deceased relatives, and *Professores Burdigalenses*, on the professors of Burdigala; these are delightful portraits that give a valuable picture of provincial Gallic life.

Austen \'ȯs-tən, 'äs-\, Jane (b. Dec. 16, 1775, Steventon, Hampshire, Eng.—d. July 18, 1817, Winchester, Hampshire) English writer who first gave the novel its distinctly modern character through her treatment of ordinary people in everyday life.

Detail of a pencil and watercolor portrait by Cassandra Austen, *c.* 1810
National Portrait Gallery, London

Austen was the daughter of a rector, the second daughter and seventh child in a family of eight. Her closest companion was her elder sister, Cassandra. The girls had only about five years of formal education; thereafter, their education continued at home. A lively and affectionate family circle and a network of widespread friends and family provided a stimulating context for her writing. It was the world of minor landed gentry and the country clergy that she was to use in her novels.

Her earliest-known writings date from about 1787. They include plays, verses, short novels, and other prose and are mainly parodies, notably of sentimental fiction. About 1793–94 she wrote a more serious work, *Lady Susan*, a short epistolary novel that was a portrait of a woman bent on the exercise of her own powerful mind and personality to the point of social self-destruction.

In 1801 Austen's father retired to Bath with his wife and daughters. For eight years the family experienced a succession of temporary lodgings or visits to relatives, in Bath, London, Clifton, Warwickshire, and finally Southampton, where they lived after the death of Austen's father in 1805 until 1809. Although the manuscript of "Susan" (*Northanger Abbey*) was sold in 1803 to the publisher Richard Crosby, it did not appear. In 1804 Austen began *The Watsons* but soon abandoned it.

Eventually, in 1809, Austen moved with her mother and sister to a large cottage in the village of Chawton. This renewed Austen, and she began to prepare SENSE AND SENSIBILITY and PRIDE AND PREJUDICE for publication. In November 1811 *Sense and Sensibility* was published anonymously, to good reviews. *Pride and Prejudice* was published in January 1813 and MANSFIELD PARK in 1814. By then Austen was an established and widely read (though anonymous) author. Between January 1814 and March 1815 she wrote EMMA, which appeared in December 1815. PERSUASION (written August 1815–August 1816) was published posthumously, with NORTHANGER ABBEY, in December 1817. It was only after Austen's death that her brother Henry made her authorship public.

In January 1817, Austen began what was to be her last work, *Sanditon* (so named by the family). It was finally put aside on March 18. This may have been a race against time, for her health had been in decline since early 1816. She supposed that she was suffering from bile, but the symptoms make it seem likely that she had developed Addison's disease.

In the six novels, published between 1811 and 1817, Austen revealed the possibilities of "domestic" literature. Her concentration on character and personality and on the tensions between her heroines and their society makes her works more closely related to the modern world than to the traditions of the 18th century. This modernity, together with the wit, realism, and timelessness of her prose style, helps to explain her continuing appeal.

Auster \'ȯs-tər\, Paul (b. Feb. 3, 1947, Newark, N.J., U.S.) American novelist, essayist, translator, and poet whose complex mystery novels are often concerned with the search for identity and personal meaning.

After graduating from Columbia University, Auster moved to France, where he began translating the works of French writers and publishing his own work in American journals. He gained renown for a series of experimental detective stories published collectively as *The New York Trilogy* (1987). It comprises *City of Glass* (1985), about a crime novelist who becomes entangled in a mystery that causes him to assume various identities; *Ghosts* (1986), about a private eye known as Blue who is investigating a man named Black for a client named White; and *The Locked Room* (1986), the story of an author who, while researching the life of a missing writer for a biography, gradually assumes the identity of that writer.

Other books that feature protagonists who are obsessed with chronicling someone else's life are the novels *Moon Palace* (1989) and *Leviathan* (1992). *The Invention of Solitude* (1982) is both a memoir about the death of his father and a meditation on the act of writing. Auster's other writings include the verse volumes *Unearth* (1974) and *Wall Writing* (1976), the essay collections *White Spaces* (1980) and *The Art of Hunger* (1982), and the novels *The Music of Chance* (1990) and *Mr. Vertigo* (1994).

Austin \'ȯs-tən, 'äs-\, Alfred (b. May 30, 1835, Leeds, Yorkshire, Eng.—d. June 2, 1913, Ashford, Kent) Successor to Alfred, Lord Tennyson as poet laureate. Although Austin could write simply in praise of the English and Italian countryside and could claim to represent popular feeling, he lacked the gift of transforming it into true poetry.

Before his official appointment, Austin studied law and was called to the bar, tried to enter politics, and practiced journalism.

Austin \'ȯs-tən, 'äs-\, Mary, *original surname* Hunter \'hən-tər\ (b. Sept. 9, 1868, Carlinville, Ill., U.S.—d. Aug. 13, 1934, Santa Fe, N.M.) Novelist and essayist who wrote on Native American culture and social problems.

Austin graduated from Blackburn College, Carlinville, Ill., in 1888, taught for a time, and then moved to California, where she became the friend and chronicler of nearby Native Americans. Her first book, *The Land of Little Rain* (1903), a description of desert life in the West, won her immediate fame, and was followed by two collections of short stories, *The Basket Woman* (1904) and *Lost Borders* (1909), and a play, *The Arrow Maker* (1911).

A prolific writer, she published 32 volumes and about 200 articles in her lifetime. Her "problem" novels include *A Woman of Genius* (1912). In her essays she discussed such issues as socialism and feminism.

author \'ȯ-thər\ [ultimately from Latin *auctor* authorizer, responsible agent, originator, maker] One who is the source of some form of intellectual or creative work; especially, one who composes a book, article, poem, play, or other literary work intended for publication. Usually a distinction is made between an author and others (such as a compiler, an editor, or a translator) who assemble, organize, or manipulate literary materials.

authorcraft \\'ȯ-thər-,kraft\\   Skill in or practice of authorship.

authoress \\'ȯ-thər-əs, 'ȯ-thrəs\\   A female author—now usually replaced by *author*.

authorship \\'ȯ-thər-,ship\\   1. The profession of writing.   2. The source (as the author) of a piece of writing, music, or art.   3. The state or act of writing, creating, or causing.

autobiography \\,ȯt-ō-bī-'ag-rə-fē, -bē-\\   The biography of oneself narrated by oneself. Autobiographical works can take many forms, from the intimate writings made during life that were not necessarily intended for publication (including letters, diaries, journals, memoirs, and reminiscences), to the formal autobiography.

There are but few and scattered examples of autobiographical literature in antiquity and the Middle Ages. Generally speaking, autobiography began with the Renaissance in the 15th century. One of the first examples was written in England by a woman named Margery Kempe.

There are roughly four different kinds of autobiography: thematic, religious, intellectual, and fictionalized. The first grouping includes books with such diverse purposes as *The Americanization of Edward Bok* (1920) and Adolf Hitler's *Mein Kampf* (1925, 1927). Religious autobiography claims a number of great works, ranging from *The Confessions* of St. Augustine in the Middle Ages to the autobiographical chapters of Thomas Carlyle's *Sartor Resartus* and Cardinal John Newman's beautifully wrought *Apologia* in the 19th century. That century and the early 20th saw the creation of several intellectual autobiographies, including the severely analytical *Autobiography* of the philosopher John S. Mill and *The Education of Henry Adams*. Finally, somewhat analogous to the novel as biography is the autobiography thinly disguised as, or transformed into, the novel. This group includes such works as Samuel Butler's *The Way of All Flesh* (1903), James Joyce's *A Portrait of the Artist as a Young Man* (1916), George Santayana's *The Last Puritan* (1935), and the novels of Thomas Wolfe.

Autobiography of Alice B. Toklas, The \\'al-is-'bē-'tō-kləs\\ Autobiography by Gertrude STEIN, written as if it were the autobiography of her lifelong companion, Alice B. Toklas. Published in 1933, the work ostensibly contains Toklas' first-person account not of her own life, but of Stein's, written from Toklas's viewpoint and replete with Toklas' sensibilities, observations, and mannerisms. *The Autobiography* was originally published in an abridged version in *The Atlantic Monthly* magazine.

The book describes the life that Toklas and Stein lead in Paris, including their at-homes with such artists, literary lions, and intellectuals as Pablo Picasso, Ernest Hemingway, Henri Matisse, and Georges Braque. While Stein exchanges ideas with men of genius, Toklas sits with their wives. Its droll premise, masterful execution, and witty insights concerning the writers and artists then living in France make clear Stein's ability to write for a general public.

Autobiography of an Ex-Colored Man, The   Novel by James Weldon JOHNSON, published in 1912. This fictional autobiography, originally issued anonymously in order to suggest authenticity, explores the intricacies of racial identity through the eventful life of its mixed-race (and unnamed) narrator.

Born in Georgia, the narrator tells of his childhood in Connecticut, where his mulatto mother, aided by monthly checks from the boy's white father, is able to provide a secure and cultured environment. Learning of his black heritage only by accident, the narrator experiences the first of several identity shifts that will eventually find him opting for membership in white society. Throughout the work, Johnson employs charac-

ters, locales, incidents, and motifs from his own life, but the narrator is less a conscious self-portrait than a representative of the author's own ambivalence.

Autobiography of Malcolm X, The \\'mal-kəm-'eks\\   Biography, published in 1965, of the American black militant religious leader and activist who was born Malcolm Little. Written by Alex HALEY, who had conducted extensive audiotaped interviews with Malcolm X just before his assassination in 1965, the book gained renown as a classic work on black American experience.

The *Autobiography* recounts the life of Malcolm X from his traumatic childhood plagued by racism to his years as a drug dealer and pimp, his conversion to the Black Muslim sect (Nation of Islam) while in prison for burglary, his subsequent years of militant activism, and the turn late in his life to more orthodox Islām.

Autobiography of Miss Jane Pittman, The \\'jān-'pit-mən\\ Novel by Ernest J. GAINES, published in 1971. Set in rural southern Louisiana, the novel spans 100 years of American history—from the early 1860s to the onset of the civil rights movement in the 1960s—in following the life of the elderly Jane Pittman, who witnessed those years.

A child at the end of the Civil War, Jane survives a massacre by former Confederate soldiers. She serves as a steadying influence for several black men who work hard to achieve dignity and economic as well as political equality. After the death of her husband, Joe Pittman, Jane becomes a committed Christian and a spiritual guide in her community. Spurred on by the violent death of a young community leader, Jane finally confronts a plantation owner who represents the white power structure to which she has always been subservient.

autochthon \\ȯ-'täk-thän\\ *plural* autochthons *or* autochthones \\ȯ-'täk-thə-,nēz\\ [Greek *autóchthōn*, from *auto-* self-, together with + *chthṓn* earth]   One supposed to have risen or sprung from the ground of the region he or she inhabits. The term may be meant literally, as in myth, or figuratively, as in reference to a writer always and only associated with a particular region.

Auto-da-Fé \\,aůt-ō-də-'fā, ,ȯt-\\   Novel by Elias CANETTI, published in 1935 in German as *Die Blendung* ("The Deception"). The translation into English that was published as *Auto-da-Fé* (also published as *The Tower of Babel*) was done in cooperation with Canetti.

Originally planned as the first in a series of eight novels examining mad visionaries, the book deals with the dangers inherent in believing that rigid, dissociated intellectualism and detached, dogmatic scholarship can prevail over evil, chaos, and destruction.

Set in Vienna and Paris, the novel tells the story of Peter Kien, an internationally respected scholar of Chinese studies who maintains a personal library of 25,000 volumes. After dreaming that the books are burned, Peter marries his housekeeper Therese, believing that she will preserve his beloved library should disaster befall him. Therese throws him out of his book-filled apartment, however, and Peter, now homeless, enters the grotesque underworld of the city. Delusional, he fluctuates between horrifying hallucinations and an unspeakable reality. Peter's disintegration finally leads him to set fire to his precious books and to await his own death in the ensuing inferno.

Autolycus \\ȯ-'täl-ə-kəs\\   In Greek mythology, the father of Anticleia, who was the mother of the hero Odysseus. Later ancient authors made Autolycus the son of the god Hermes. He was believed to live at the foot of Mount Parnassus and was famous as a thief and swindler. On one occasion Sisyphus (the son of Aeolus), during a visit to Autolycus, recognized his stolen cattle. It is said that on this occasion Sisyphus seduced Autolycus' daughter Anticleia and that hence Odysseus was really the son of Sisyphus, not of Laertes (whom Anticleia afterward married).

automatic writing   Writing produced without conscious intention and sometimes without awareness, as if of telepathic or spiritualistic origin. The phenomenon may occur when the subject is in an alert waking state or in a hypnotic trance. What is produced may be unrelated words, fragments of poetry, epithets, puns, obscenities, or well-organized fantasies. During the late 19th century, at the height of popular interest in the phenomenon, inspiration for automatic writing was generally attributed to external or supernatural forces. Since the advent, around 1900, of theories of personality that postulate unconscious (or subconscious) as well as conscious motivation, the inspiration for automatic writing has been assumed to be completely internal. Automatic writing was employed by many of the Surrealist writers (notably the French poet Robert Desnos), who considered the unconscious mind to be the wellspring of imagination.

auto sacramental \ *Spanish* 'aủ-tō-ˌsäk-rä-men-'tăl, *Portuguese* 'aủ-tū-sȧ-krȧ-'men-tȧl, -taủ \ [Spanish, literally, sacramental play] *plural* autos sacramentales.   A short play on a sacred or biblical subject, similar to a miracle or morality play. The genre reached its height in the 17th century with *autos* written by the Spanish playwright Pedro CALDERÓN DE LA BARCA. Performed out of doors as part of the Corpus Christi feast day celebrations, *autos* were short allegorical plays in verse dealing with some aspect of the mystery of the Holy Eucharist, which the feast of Corpus Christi solemnly celebrated. They derived from tableaus that had been part of the procession accompanying the Eucharist as it was carried through the streets at Corpus Christi. The tableaus became animated, then developed a dramatic form, and finally were detached from the Eucharistic procession to form one of their own. Mounted on carts, they were pulled to selected places in the municipality, and the actors presented their *autos*, one after another, much as the scriptural plays of the Netherlands and northern England had been presented on pageant wagons during the Middle Ages. Expenses for these superbly set and dressed *autos* were paid by the municipality.

These little plays had begun to appear in the late 16th century, but they were at first rough and primitive, a rustic form of pious entertainment. Important names in the development of the *autos* into works of polished art were a bookseller from Valencia, Juan de Timoneda, and the playwrights Jose de Valdivielso (c. 1560–1638) and his contemporary Lope de Vega. It was Calderón, however, who seized the opportunity allegory offered for covering a wide range of nonsacramental subjects, and he took the *auto* form to new heights of artistic achievement.

Accused of displaying irreverence toward the sacrament during the 18th century, their performance was in 1765 prohibited by royal decree. Some 20th-century poets have imitated their form and have written secularized versions of the old *autos*.

autotelism \ˌȯt-ō-'tel-ˌiz-əm, -'tĕl- \ [Greek *autotelḗs* complete in itself]   The belief that a work of art, especially a work of literature, is an end in itself or provides its own justification and does not exist to serve a moral or didactic purpose. It was adopted by proponents of New Criticism and is similar to the "art for art's sake" doctrine of the AESTHETICISM movement of the late 19th century.

Avalon \'av-ə-län\   Island to which Britain's legendary king Arthur was conveyed for the healing of his wounds after his fi-

nal battle. It is first mentioned in the 12th century in Geoffrey of Monmouth's *Historia regum Britanniae*. It was ruled by the enchantress MORGAN le Fay and her eight sisters, all of them skilled in the healing arts.

Avalon has been identified with Glastonbury in Somerset; this theory may be connected with Celtic legends about an "isle of glass" inhabited by deceased heroes, or it may perhaps represent an attempt by the monks of Glastonbury to exploit the ARTHURIAN LEGEND for the benefit of their own community.

avant-garde \ˌä-ˌvän-'gärd, ˌa-, -ˌvänt-; ə-ˌvänt- \ [French, vanguard]   An intelligentsia that develops new or experimental concepts, especially in the arts.

Avicebron *also called* Avencebrol   *see* IBN GABIROL.

Avison \'av-i-sən\, Margaret (b. April 23, 1918, Galt, Ont., Can.)   Canadian poet who revealed the progress of an interior spiritual journey in her three successive volumes of poetry.

The daughter of a Methodist minister, Avison attended the University of Toronto (B.A., 1940; M.A., 1964) and worked as a librarian, editor, lecturer, and social worker at church missions in Toronto. Her poems began to appear in magazines as early as 1939. She began writing the poems of *Winter Sun* (1960), her first collection, in 1956, while living in Chicago as a Guggenheim fellow. The introspective poems of this collection are concerned with belief and moral knowledge, and for the most part they are written in free verse.

In the early 1960s Avison experienced a religious awakening that confirmed her Christian beliefs, an experience she told about in the title poem of her second collection, *The Dumbfounding* (1966). Less introspective and more direct, these poems recall 17th-century Metaphysical poetry, as they present images of spiritual vitality in everyday life. Many of her poems in *Sunblue* (1978) are based on biblical stories; the poems further investigate her Christian beliefs, and she takes nature as a metaphor for spiritual realities. In 1991 she published a fourth collection, *Selected Poems*.

Awakening, The   Novel by Kate CHOPIN, published in 1899. When first published, the novel was considered controversial because of its frank treatment of both adulterous love between a married woman, Edna Pontellier, and an unmarried younger man, Robert LeGrun, and the subject of female sexuality.

Awangarda   Krakowska   \ä-vän-'gär-dä-krȧ-'kȯf-skȧ\ Avant-garde Polish literary movement launched at Kraków in 1922 that led to a regeneration of poetic technique and a renewed interest in Polish folklore and pre-17th-century Polish literature. Influenced by revolutionary trends in poetry, particularly Futurism, in France, Italy, and Spain, the Awangarda movement opposed the emphasis on lyricism and the anti-intellectualism of the contemporary SKAMANDER group. Associated with the Awangarda were Julian Przyboś, Adam Ważyk, and Józef Czechowicz.

awdl \'aủd-əl\ *plural* awdlau \'aủd-ˌlī\ [Welsh, song, ode]   In Welsh verse, a long ode characterized by alliterative verse and internal rhyme. By the 13th century the awdl had developed into the intricate system of consonant and vowel correspondence, or consonant correspondence and internal rhyme, called CYNGHANEDD. Twenty-four strict bardic meters were available to the poet; only four bardic meters are still commonly used. The *awdl* was, by the 15th century, the vehicle for many outstanding Welsh poems. It remains the predominant form in the annual national eisteddfod (bard and minstrel competition), where since 1887 a wooden chair (the chair is the Welsh bard's highest honor) has been awarded to the writer of the winning *awdl*. Despite the criticism advanced by some that the form is obsolete, *awdlau* of high poetic merit are still occasionally written.

Awkward Age, The Novel by Henry JAMES, published in 1899. Written mostly in dialogue with limited narrative explanation, *The Awkward Age* is the story of Nanda Brookenham, a young society woman whose attempts at marriage are foiled by various members of her mother's social circle.

Nanda's manipulative mother, Fernanda, is the hostess of a fashionable London salon. The two women both appear to love Gustavus Vanderbank, a young government employee, who becomes alienated from them. Nanda is befriended by the elderly Mr. Longdon, who once courted her grandmother, and by the young Mr. Mitchett, who unhappily marries Little Aggie, a naive young woman steered into the marriage by her conniving aunt, the Duchess.

Awoonor \ˌä-ˈwü-ˌnȯ, -ˌnȯr\, Kofi (Nyidevu), *original name* George Kofi Awoonor Williams \ˈwil-yəmz\ (b. March 13, 1935, Weta, Gold Coast [now Ghana]) Ghanaian novelist and poet whose verse has been widely translated and anthologized.

Awoonor studied at the University College of Ghana, University College, London, and the State University of New York at Stony Brook. In addition to teaching at the University of Ghana, he served as an editor of the literary journal *Okyeame* and as an associate editor of *Transition*. During the early 1970s he taught at the State University of New York at Stony Brook. He returned to Ghana in 1975 to teach but was arrested on political charges. His sentence was remitted in 1976, and he resumed teaching until 1982. From 1984 to 1988 he was Ghana's ambassador to Brazil and from 1988, to Cuba.

Awoonor's poetry often treats the subjects of Christianity, exile, and death. Each poem in *Rediscovery and Other Poems* (1964) records a single moment in a larger pattern of recognition and rediscovery. Subsequent volumes of poetry include *Night of My Blood* (1971), *Ride Me, Memory* (1973), *The House by the Sea* (1978), and *The Latin American and Caribbean Notebook* (1992). His collected poems (through 1985) were published in *Until the Morning After* (1987).

Awoonor sought to incorporate African vernacular traditions—notably the dirge song tradition of the Ewe people—into modern poetic form. Besides verse he published a novel, *This Earth, My Brother* (1971), and two short plays. *The Breast of the Earth: A Survey of the History, Culture, and Literature of Africa South of the Sahara* appeared in 1975 and *Comes the Voyager at Last: A Tale of Return to Africa* in 1992.

Axël \äk-ˈsel, *Angl* ˈak-səl, ˈäk-\ Dramatic prose poem by Auguste, Count de VILLIERS DE L'ISLE-ADAM, published in 1890.

Wagnerian in theme and scope, *Axël* combines symbolism and occult themes. Axël, the lord of a German castle, kills a relative who attempts to uncover the secret of a mysterious treasure buried in his home and is himself attacked by the young novice Sara just after she works the charm to reveal the gold and jewels hidden in the vault. Overcome by passion, the two remain below, Sara dreaming of a world of fortune, Axël contending that nothing in life can equal their moment of joyful expectation. During the night, both drink poison from a jeweled cup found among the treasure.

Axel's Castle \äk-ˈsel, *Angl* ˈak-səl, ˈäk-\ Book of critical essays by Edmund WILSON, published in 1931. Subtitled "A Study in the Imaginative Literature of 1870–1930," the book traced the origins of specific trends in contemporary literature, which, Wilson held, was largely concerned with Symbolism and its relationship to naturalism.

Wilson followed his introductory essay on Symbolism with essays that trace the development of these trends in the works of W.B. Yeats, Paul Valéry, T.S. Eliot, Marcel Proust, James Joyce, Gertrude Stein, and Arthur Rimbaud and Auguste Villiers de l'Isle-Adam.

Ayala \ä-ˈyä-lä\, Francisco (b. March 16, 1906, Granada, Spain) Spanish writer and scholar whose works reflected his interest in issues of sociology.

Ayala received a law degree from the University of Madrid in 1929, having published several works, including the novel *Tragicomedia de un hombre sin espíritu* (1925; "Tragicomedy of a Man Without Spirit") and the short-story collection *El boxeador y un ángel* (1929; "The Boxer and an Angel"). Two years after obtaining a doctoral degree in law from the University of Madrid in 1931, he joined that university's faculty. He went into exile during the Spanish Civil War (1936–39). In 1949 he published a book of short stories, *Los usurpadores*, in which he examined the innate immorality of one person subjugating another to his will. *La cabeza del cordero* (1949; *The Lamb's Head*) is a collection of short stories on similar themes, this time centering on the Spanish Civil War.

The collapse of moral order and the hopelessness of human relations in society were themes in Ayala's two long pessimistic and satirical novels, *Muertes de perro* (1958; *Death as a Way of Life*) and *El fondo del vaso* (1962; "The Bottom of the Glass"). Other works include the collection *El jardín de las delicias* (1971; "Garden of Delights"), later expanded and reissued as *El tiempo y yo, o, el mundo a la espalda* (1992; "Time and I, or The World on Your Back"), and *El jardín de las malicias* (1988; "Garden of Malice"). Ayala was elected to the Spanish Academy in 1987.

Ayckbourn \ˈak-ˌbȯrn\, Alan (b. April 12, 1939, London, Eng.) Successful and prolific British playwright, whose works—mostly farces and comedies—deal with marital and class conflicts and point up the fears and weaknesses of the English lower-middle class.

At age 15 Ayckbourn acted in school productions of William Shakespeare, and he began his professional acting career with the Stephen Joseph Company in Scarborough. When Ayckbourn wanted better roles to play, Joseph told him to write a part for himself in a play that the company would mount if it had merit. Ayckbourn produced his earliest plays in 1959–61 under the pseudonym Roland Allen.

His plays include *Relatively Speaking* (1968), *Mixed Doubles: An Entertainment on Marriage* (1970), *How the Other Half Loves* (1971), the trilogy *The Norman Conquests* (1973), *Absurd Person Singular* (1974), *Intimate Exchanges* (1985), *Mr. A's Amazing Maze Plays* (1989), *Body Language* (1990), and *Invisible Friends* (1991).

Ayesha \ˈīsh-ə, ä-ˈē-shə\ Fictional character, the supernatural white queen of a vanished African city in the romantic novel SHE by H. Rider Haggard. Ayesha ("She-Who-Must-Be-Obeyed") is a beautiful and majestic woman with supernatural powers who spends centuries waiting for the reincarnation of a lover from past ages.

John Mortimer, in his *Rumpole of the Bailey* series of books, has Rumpole refer habitually to his wife as "She-Who-Must-Be-Obeyed."

Aying or **A-ying** \ä-ˈyiŋ\, *pseudonym of* Qian Xingcun \ˈchyän-ˈshiŋ-ˈtsün\ (b. Feb. 6, 1900, Wuhu, Anhui province, China—d. June 17, 1977) Chinese critic and historian of modern Chinese literature who made great contributions to the record of modern culture in China. His other pseudonyms include Qian Qianwu, Zhang Ruoying, Ruan Wuming, Ying Sun, and Wei Ruhui.

Qian joined the Chinese Communist Party in 1926. After 1927 he began to advocate proletariat revolutionary literature in several volumes of essays on Chinese writers that were compiled in several volumes. He also published the short-story collections *Gemingde gushi* ("Revolutionary Stories"), *Yizhong* ("Potter's Field"), and *Malusha*; the novelette *Yitiao bianhen* ("Scar Left by a Whip"); the poetry collections *Eren yu jiying* ("Starving Man and Hungry Hawks") and *Huangdu* ("The Wasteland"); and the narrative poem "Baofengyude" ("Eve of the Hurricane").

Qian was elected as a member of the standing committee of the League of Left-wing Writers in 1930. During this time, he began gathering and studying materials on the literature of modern times and the Ming and Qing dynasties. His published works in these fields include *Xiandai Zhongguo nüzuojia* (1931; "Women Writers in Modern China"), *Xiandai Zhongguo wenxuelun* (1933; "Modern Chinese Literature"), *Zhongguo xinwentan milu* (1933; "The Secret Records of New Literary Circles of China"), *Yehhang ji* (1935; "Night Navigation"), and *Xiaoshuo xiantan* (1936; "Chats on the Novel").

After the Sino-Japanese War, he was appointed the principal of the College of Literature of the Middle China Construction University. His later literary criticism includes *WanQing xiqu xiaoshuo mu* (1954; "A Catalog of Operas and Novels of the Late Qing Dynasty"), *WanQing wenyi baokan shulüe* (1958; "An Outline of Literary and Artistic Newspapers and Magazines of the Late Qing Dynasty"), *Xiaoshuo ertan* (1958; "Two Talks on the Novel"), *WanQing wenxue congchao*, 9 vol. (1960–62; "Notes on the Literature of the Late Qing Dynasty"), and *Xiaoshuo santan* (1979; "Three Talks on the Novel").

Aymé \e-'mä\, Marcel (b. March 29, 1902, Joigny, Fr.—d. Oct. 14, 1967, Paris) Novelist, essayist, and playwright whose extravagant creations were long dismissed as minor works but who belatedly was recognized as a master of light irony and storytelling.

Aymé grew up in a rural farm community of the kind his works depict. After a short-lived attempt at a career in journalism, he began writing fiction. His first novels, *Brûlebois* (1926) and *La Table-aux-crevés* (1929; *The Hollow Field*), are comedies on country life. The broad Gallic wit of *La Jument verte* (1933; *The Green Mare*) continues in his next novels, *La Vouivre* (1943; *The Fable and the Flesh*) and *Le Chemin des écoliers* (1946; *The Transient Hour*). In these works the universe of Aymé takes shape. Through the familiar sites of town and field, strange denizens roam unquestioned, side by side with normal beings who, in turn, often act in absurd ways. This counterpoint of fantasy and reality finds its perfect format in such short stories as "Le Nain" (1934; "The Dwarf") and "Le Passe-muraille" (1943; "The Man Who Could Pass Through Walls"). *Les Contes du chat perché*, which appeared in three series in 1939, 1950, and 1958, delighted a vast public with its talking farm animals, including an ox that goes to school and a pig that thinks it is a peacock. Selections were published in English as *The Wonderful Farm* (1951).

Aymé made a late debut in the theater with *Lucienne et le boucher* (1947; "Lucienne and the Butcher"). *Clérambard* (1950) begins with St. Francis of Assisi appearing to a country squire. The initial absurdity is developed with rigorous logic in the manner of the Theater of the Absurd. Though Aymé's theatrical works are often cruel and heavy-handed, the wit, wisdom, and morality of his short stories place them in the tradition of the fables of La Fontaine and the fairy tales of Charles Perrault.

Ayrer \'ī-rər\, Jakob (b. March? 1543, Franconia [now part of Germany]—d. March 26, 1605, Nürnberg) Dramatist who incorporated elements of Elizabethan plays (*e.g.*, spectacular stage effects, violent action, histrionic bombast, the stock figure of the clown) into his own plays, particularly his *Fast-*

nachtsspiele, the farces performed at Shrovetide (the three days preceding Ash Wednesday).

A lawyer by profession, Ayrer spent his last 12 years as a city council member and imperial notary in Nürnberg, where he witnessed the plays of the English acting troupes that toured Germany in the late 16th and early 17th centuries. Although not as talented as his master, Hans Sachs, Ayrer was very prolific. He wrote more than 100 comedies, tragedies, historical dramas, *Fastnachtsspiele*, and *Singspiele*. The last—vaudeville plays in which strophic texts are sung to traditional tunes—is a genre he first popularized, and it represents his greatest artistic achievement. Sixty-six of his plays are preserved in his *Opus Theatricum* (1618; "Works of the Theatre").

Aytmatov or **Aitmatov** \,īt-'mȧ-təf\, Chingiz (b. Dec. 12, 1928, Sheker, Kirgiziya, U.S.S.R. [now Kyrgyzstan]) Author, translator, and journalist who began his literary career in 1952 and in 1959 became a *Pravda* correspondent in Kirgiziya.

He achieved major literary recognition with his collection of short stories, *Povesti gor i stepey* (1963; *Tales of Mountains and Steppes*), for which he was awarded the Lenin Prize in 1963. His most important works include *Trudnaya pereprava* (1956; "A Difficult Passage"), *Litsom k litsu* (1957; "Face to Face"), *Proshchay, Gulsary!* (1967; *Farewell, Gulsary!*), *Pervy uchitel* (1967; "The First Teacher"), and *Bely parokhod* (1972; *The White Ship*).

Although Aytmatov composed in both Russian and Kyrgyz, most of his early works were originally written in the latter language. His major themes were love and friendship, the trials and heroism of wartime, and the emancipation of Kyrgyz youth from restrictive custom and tradition. In 1967 Aytmatov became a member of the Executive Board of the Writers' Union of the U.S.S.R., and he was awarded the Soviet state prize for literature in 1968. His later novels, written originally in Russian, include *I dolshe veka dlitsya den* (1980; *The Day Lasts More Than a Hundred Years*) and *Plakha* (1986; *The Place of the Skull*).

Ayton or **Aytoun** \'ā-tən\, Sir Robert (b. 1570, Kinaldy, Fife, Scot.—d. c. Feb. 28, 1638, London, Eng.) One of the earliest Scottish poets to use standard (King's) English as a literary medium.

Educated at the University of St. Andrews, Ayton came into favor at court for a Latin panegyric on the accession of James VI to the English throne. He was knighted in 1612 and subsequently held various lucrative offices, including that of private secretary to the queens of James I and Charles I. Although Ayton also wrote poems in Latin, Greek, and French and enjoyed a considerable literary reputation, he never considered himself a poet. A poem, "Old Long Syne," that is ascribed to Ayton may have been the inspiration for the famous "Auld Lang Syne" by Robert Burns.

Aytoun \'ā-tən\, William Edmondstoune (b. June 21, 1813, Edinburgh, Scot.—d. Aug. 4, 1865, Elgin, Moray) Poet famous for parodies and light verse that greatly influenced the style of later Scottish humorous satire.

Aytoun was educated at the University of Edinburgh and in Germany, and in 1840 was called to the Scottish bar. That same year he first collaborated with Theodore Martin in a series of humorous and satirical papers for *Blackwood's Edinburgh Magazine*, later published as the *Bon Gaultier Ballads* (1845); these include Aytoun's parodies "The Queen in France," based on "Sir Patrick Spens," and "The Massacre of the Macpherson," both of which were models for later writers, especially for W.S. Gilbert in the *Bab Ballads* (1869).

Aytoun joined the staff of *Blackwood's* in 1844, contributing political as well as miscellaneous articles. He was appointed professor of rhetoric and belles lettres at Edinburgh in 1845. Four years later he published *Lays of the Scottish Cavaliers,* a set of Jacobite ballads that achieved wide popularity. In 1854, reverting to light verse, he published *Firmiliam, or the Student of Badajoz, a Spasmodic Tragedy,* in which the writings of the Spasmodic school were brilliantly ridiculed. His two-volume *The Ballads of Scotland* was published in 1858.

Azevedo \ä-ze-'vä-dü\, Aluízio *or* Aluísio (b. April 14, 1857, São Luís, Maranhão, Braz.—d. Jan. 21, 1913, Buenos Aires, Arg.)   Novelist who set the pattern for the naturalistic novel in Brazil and whose work anticipated later novels of social protest.

Azevedo studied at the school of fine arts of Rio de Janeiro and became a journalist. His works, modeled on the naturalistic novels of Émile Zola and imbued with antislavery, anticlerical, and antibourgeois sentiments, closely document aspects of Brazilian life of his day. His first success, *O mulato* (1881; "The Mulatto"), deals with racial prejudice. Two other memorable novels, *Casa de pensão* (1884; "The Boarding House") and *O cortiço* (1890; *A Brazilian Tenement*), provide detailed and highly critical accounts of the emergent middle-class society of Rio de Janeiro. Azevedo abandoned his literary career at 37 and entered the diplomatic service.

Aziz, Dr. \ä-'zēz\   Fictional character, a humble Islāmic surgeon in A PASSAGE TO INDIA by E.M. Forster. Aziz represents the native Indian community in conflict with the British ruling class. The central event of the novel is his trial for the alleged rape of a visiting Englishwoman, Adela Quested.

Azorín, \ä-thō-'rēn\, *pseudonym of* José Martínez Ruiz \mär-'tē-nāth-rü-'ēth\ (b. June 8/11, 1873, Monóvar, Spain—d. March 2, 1967, Madrid)   Novelist, essayist, and the foremost Spanish literary critic of his day. He was one of a group of writers who were engaged at the turn of the 20th century in a concerted attempt to revitalize Spanish life and letters. Azorín was the first to identify this group as the GENERATION OF '98.

Azorín studied law at Valencia, Granada, and Salamanca, but later he went to Madrid to be a journalist, only to find that his outspokenness closed most doors. He then wrote a trilogy of novels, *La voluntad* (1902; "Volition"), *Antonio Azorín*

(1903), and *Las confesiones de un pequeño filósofo* (1904; "The Confessions of a Minor Philosopher"), which are actually little more than impressionistic essays written in dialogue. His book *El alma castellana* (1900; "The Castilian Soul") and his essay collections *La ruta de Don Quijote* (1905; "The Route of Don Quixote") and *Una hora de España 1560–1590* (1924; *An Hour of Spain*) carefully and subtly reconstruct the spirit of Spanish life. Azorín's literary criticism, such as *Al margen de los clásicos* (1915; "Marginal Notes to the Classics"), helped to arouse a new enthusiasm for the Spanish classics.

Azorín edited the periodical *Revista de Occidente* ("Magazine of the West") from 1923 to 1936. He spent the period of the Spanish Civil War in Paris, writing for the Argentine newspaper *La Nación,* but he returned to Madrid in 1949.

Azrael \'az-rā-el\   The angel of death in Jewish and Islāmic thought who watches over the dying and separates the soul from the body.

Azuela \ä-'swä-lä\, Mariano (b. Jan. 1, 1873, Lagos de Moreno, Mex.—d. March 1, 1952, Mexico City)   Writer whose 20 novels chronicle the Mexican revolution.

Azuela received an M.D. degree in Guadalajara in 1899 and practiced medicine, first in his native town and after 1916 in Mexico City. His best-known work, *Los de abajo* (1916; *The Under Dogs*), depicting the horrors of the revolution, was written at the campfire during forced marches while he served as army doctor with Pancho Villa in 1915. Forced to flee across the border to El Paso, Texas, he first published the novel as a newspaper serial (October–December 1915). It received little notice until it was rediscovered in 1924. It widely influenced other Mexican novelists of social protest.

Returning to Mexico City in 1916, Azuela, disillusioned with the revolutionary struggle, wrote novels critical of the new regime: *Las moscas* (1918) and *Los caciques* (1917; together translated as *Two Novels of Mexico: The Flies. The Bosses*) and *Las tribulaciones de una familia decente* (1918; *The Trials of a Respectable Family*). In his later works—including *La malhora* (1923; "The Evil Hour"), *El desquite* (1925; "Revenge"), and *La luciérnaga* (1932; *The Firefly*)—he experimented with several stylistic devices.

B

Ba \'bä\, Oumar (b. 1914, French West Africa [Mauritania])   African historian and poet whose works dealt chiefly with the Fulani (Peul) peoples of the Senegal River region.

Ba was educated in France and subsequently held several academic and administrative positions. Using various approaches (oral tradition, linguistics, and comparative sociology), Ba presented the first scientific account of an early Fulani presence in the region of the Senegal River (now encompassing parts of the republics of Mauritania and Senegal). His book *Le Fouta Toro au carrefour des cultures* (1977; "The Futa Toro at the Crossroads of Cultures") was dedicated to Léopold Senghor, poet and statesman of Negritude, with whom Ba shared a concern about the development of the French language as a means of unification.

Ba's poetry is closely linked with Fulani oral and written lyrics and ballads. *Poèmes peuls modernes* (1965; "Modern Peul Poems"), *Dialogue; ou, D'une rive à l'autre* (1966; "Dialogue; or, From One Bank to the Other"), and *Paroles plaisantes au coeur et à l'oreille* (1977; "Words Pleasant to the Heart and Ear") are probably his most widely read works. Ba also published several distinguished works in the Fulani language, a dictionary of Mande words in Fulani, and several dictionaries of expressions in Fulani.

Baal \'bāl, 'bäl\ *plural* baalim.   Any of several Canaanite or Phoenician local deities. Among the Canaanites, Baal was apparently considered a fertility deity and one of the most important gods in the pantheon. In his capacity as the universal god of fertility, Baal was called Prince, Lord of the Earth. He was also called the Lord of Rain and Dew, the two forms of moisture that were indispensable for fertile soil in Canaan. In Ugaritic and Old Testament Hebrew, Baal's epithet as the storm god was He Who Rides on the Clouds. In Phoenician he was called Baal Shamen, Lord of the Heavens.

The worship of Baal was popular in Egypt from the later New Kingdom from approximately 1400 BC to 1075 BC. Through the influence of the Aramaeans, who borrowed the Babylonian pronunciation Bel, the god ultimately became known as the Greek Belos, identified with Zeus.

In the formative stages of Israel's history, the presence of Baal names did not necessarily mean apostasy or even syncretism; indeed, Baal epithets freely applied to the God of the Israelites. What made the very name Baal anathema to the Israelites was the program of Jezebel, in the 9th century BC, to introduce into Israel her Phoenician cult of Baal in opposition to the official worship of Yahweh (I Kings 18). By the time of the prophet Hosea (mid-8th century BC) the antagonism to Baalism was so strong that the use of the term Baal was often replaced by the contemptuous *boshet* ("shame").

Babalola \,bä-bä-'lō-lä\, S. Adeboye, *in full* Solomon Adeboye Babalola (b. Dec. 17, 1926, Nigeria)   Poet and scholar known for his illuminating study of Yoruba *ìjálá* (a form of oral poetry) and his translations of numerous folk tales.

Babalola received his education in Nigeria, Ghana, and Cambridge, Eng., and earned a Ph.D. at the University of London. On his return to Nigeria he held positions as lecturer at the Institute of African Studies, University of Ife; principal of Igbobi College, Lagos; and professor of African languages and literatures at the University of Lagos. His *Content and Form of Yoruba Ijala* (1966) provides both a critical introduction to this vernacular poetic form and an annotated anthology of *ìjálá* poems, with English translations.

Babar \bä-'bär\   Fictional character, a sartorially splendid elephant who is the hero of illustrated story books for young children by the French writer and illustrator Jean de Brunhoff (1899–1937). Babar and his queen, Celeste, rule a peaceful forest kingdom. The first Babar book, *L'Histoire de Babar, le petit éléphant* (1931; *The Story of Babar, the Little Elephant*), describes how he runs away to town when his mother is shot by hunters; eventually he returns to the forest and is crowned king. Other books in the series are *Le Roi Babar* (1933; *Babar the King*); *ABC de Babar* (1934; *Babar's ABC*); *Le Voyage de Babar* (1932; *The Travels of Babar*), and *Babar et le Père Noël* (1941; *Babar and Father Christmas*), the last two published posthumously. The author's son, Laurent de Brunhoff, continued the Babar series after his father's death.

Bābā Ṭāher \'bȯ-,bȯ-'tȯ-,her\, *byname* 'Aryān *also spelled* Oryan *or* Uryan \'ȯr-,yȯn, *Persian* "ȯr-\ (b. *c.* 1000, Luristan or Hamadan, Iran—d. after 1055, Hamadan)   One of the most revered early poets in Persian literature.

Little is known of his life. He probably lived in Hamadan. His nickname, 'Aryān ("The Naked"), suggests that he was a wandering dervish, or mystic. Legend tells that the poet, an illiterate woodcutter, attended lectures at a religious college, where he was ridiculed by the scholars and students because of his lack of education and sophistication. After experiencing a vision, he returned to the school and spoke of what he had seen, astounding those present with his wisdom. His poetry is written in a dialect of Persian, and he is most famous for his *dobaytī* (double distichs), exhibiting in melodious language a sincerity and spirituality with profound philosophical undertones. Bābā Ṭāher is highly revered by Iranians, who erected a magnificent mausoleum for him in Hamadan. Many of his poems have been translated into English.

Babbitt \'bab-ət\   Novel by Sinclair LEWIS, published in 1922. The novel's scathing indictment of middle-class Ameri-

can values made Babbittry a synonym for adherence to a conformist, materialistic, anti-intellectual way of life.

In the novel, George F. Babbitt is a prosperous real-estate broker in the Midwestern town of Zenith. He is a pillar of his community, a civic booster, and a believer in achieving success for its own sake. When his best friend is arrested for shooting his own wife, Babbitt begins to question and rebel against some of the values that he has always upheld. But Babbitt's rebellion is brief because he lacks inner strength.

Babbitt \'bab-ət\, Irving (b. Aug. 2, 1865, Dayton, Ohio, U.S.—d. July 15, 1933, Cambridge, Mass.)   American critic and teacher, leader of the movement in literary criticism known as NEW HUMANISM, or Neohumanism.

Babbitt was educated at Harvard University and at the Sorbonne and taught at Harvard from 1894 until his death. A vigorous teacher, lecturer, and essayist, Babbitt was the unrestrained foe of Romanticism and its offshoots, realism and naturalism; instead, he championed the classical virtues of restraint and moderation. His early followers included T.S. Eliot and George Santayana, who later criticized him; his major opponent was H.L. Mencken.

Babbitt extended his views beyond literary criticism: *Literature and the American College* (1908) calls for a return to the study of classical literatures; *The New Laokoön* (1910) deplores the confusion in the arts created by Romanticism; *Rousseau and Romanticism* (1919) criticizes the effects of Jean-Jacques Rousseau's thought in the 20th century; *On Being Creative* (1932) compares the Romantic concept of spontaneity adversely with classic theories of imitation.

Babel   *see* TOWER OF BABEL.

Babel \'bä-byilʸ\, Isaak Emmanuilovich (b. July 1 [July 13, New Style], 1894, Odessa, Ukraine, Russian Empire—d. March 17, 1941, Siberia, U.S.S.R.)   Short-story writer noted for his war stories and Odessa tales. He was considered an innovator in the early Soviet period and enjoyed a brilliant reputation in the early 1930s.

Born into a Jewish family, Babel grew up in an atmosphere of persecution that is reflected in the sensitivity, pessimism, and morbidity of his stories. His first works, later included in his *Odesskiye rasskazy* ("Odessa Tales"), were published in 1916 in a monthly edited by Maksim Gorky. On Gorky's advice, Babel decided to see the world. Perhaps his most significant experience in the next seven years was as a soldier in the war with Poland. Out of that campaign came the stories in *Konarmiya* (1926; *Red Cavalry*).

The "Odessa Tales" were published in collected book form in 1931. This cycle of realistic and humorous sketches of the Moldavanka—the ghetto suburb of Odessa—vividly portrays the life-style and jargon of a group of Jewish bandits and gangsters, led by their "king," the legendary Benya Krik.

Babel wrote other short stories, as well as two plays (*Zakat*, 1928; *Mariya*, 1935). In the early 1930s his literary reputation in the Soviet Union was high, but, under increasing Stalinist cultural regimentation, his writing was found incompatible with official literary doctrine. After the mid-1930s Babel lived in silence and obscurity. In May 1939 Babel was arrested, and he died in a prison camp in Siberia.

Babette's Feast \bä-'bet\   Short story by Isak DINESEN, published serially in the *Ladies' Home Journal* (1950), and later collected in the volume *Anecdotes of Destiny* (1958). It was also published in Danish in 1958. The tale concerns a French refugee whose artistic sensuality contrasts with the puritanical ethos of her new home in Norway.

Fleeing the Commune of Paris in 1871, Babette arrives in a small Norwegian town, where she is taken in as a servant in the home of Martine and Philippa, two elderly daughters of the town's late minister who maintain the austere lifestyle of their father's sect. When Babette wins the French lottery, she spends the fortune to lovingly prepare a magnificent French feast for the sisters and their friends.

Babits \'bȯb-ēch\, Mihály (b. Nov. 26, 1883, Szekszárd, Hung., Austria-Hungary—d. Aug. 4, 1941, Budapest) Poet, novelist, essayist, and translator who played an important role in the literary life of his country.

Babits studied at the University of Budapest, and his first volume of poetry was published in 1909. He taught in provincial secondary schools until forced to resign during World War I because of his pacifist views. Thereafter, he devoted all his energies to literature. He belonged to the literary circle that included Endre Ady, Zsigmond Móricz, and Dezső Kosztolányi, whose works were published in the periodical *Nyugat* ("The West"; founded 1908), one of the most important critical reviews in Hungarian literary history. Babits became its editor in 1929.

Babits' verse is intellectual and difficult to understand, but his prose is more accessible. Among his novels, *Halálfiai* (1927; "The Children of Death"), a sympathetic portrayal of the decaying middle class, is outstanding. His translations included plays of Sophocles, Dante's *Divine Comedy*, medieval Latin hymns, and works by William Shakespeare and J.W. von Goethe.

Babi Yar \'bä-bē-'yär, *Russian* 'bȧ-bʸē-'yȧr\ (*in full* Babi Yar: A Document in the Form of a Novel) Prose work by Anatoly KUZNETSOV, published serially as *Babi Yar* in 1966. This first edition, issued in the Soviet Union, was heavily censored. A complete, authorized edition, restoring censored portions and including further additions to the text by the author, was published under the pseudonym A. Anatoli in both Russian and English in 1970.

An account of the horrors that the author witnessed during the brutal Nazi occupation of Kiev from 1941 to 1944, the work is a scathing condemnation of both Nazi and Soviet policies toward the Ukraine in that period. The book is notable for its detached humor and ironical overtones. Its title is taken from Baby Yar, a ravine in Kiev where the Nazis killed and buried the bodies of more than 100,000 local inhabitants.

Babrius \'bā-brē-əs\, *in full* Valerius Babrius (fl. probably 2nd century AD) Author of one of the oldest surviving collections of fables. Little is known of the author. His fables are for the most part versions of the stock stories associated with the name of Aesop; however, Babrius rendered them into the scazon, or choliambic, meter.

Most of the Babrius fables are beast stories typical of the genre. In language and style they are very simple, but their satirical element suggests that the stories are the product of sophisticated urban society.

Bacchae \'bak-,ē, -,ī\ *also called* Bacchants \bə-'kants, -'känts; 'bak-ənts, 'bäk-\ (*Greek plural* Bakchai) Drama produced about 406 BC by EURIPIDES. It is regarded by many as his masterpiece.

In *Bacchae* the god Dionysus arrives in Greece from Asia intending to introduce his orgiastic worship there. He is disguised as a charismatic young Asian holy man and is accompanied by his women votaries, who make up the play's chorus. He expects to be accepted first in Thebes, but the Thebans reject his divinity and refuse to worship him, and the city's young king, Pentheus, tries to arrest him. In the end Dionysus drives Pentheus insane and leads him to the mountains, where Pentheus' own mother, Agave, and the women of Thebes in a bacchic frenzy tear him to pieces.

bacchante \bə-'kant, -'känt; bə-'kan-tē, -'kän-tē\ [Latin *bacchantes* (plural), from present participle of *bacchari* to celebrate the rites of Bacchus], *also called* maenad *or* Thyiad. A priestess or female follower of DIONYSUS (Bacchus), the nature god of fruitfulness and vegetation who is especially identified with wine and ecstasy.

According to tradition, Pentheus, king of Thebes, was torn to pieces by the bacchantes when he attempted to spy on their activities, while the Athenians were punished with impotence for dishonoring Dionysus' cult. The women abandoned their families and took to the hills, wearing fawn skins and crowns of ivy and shouting a ritual cry. Waving *thyrsoi* (fennel wands bound with vine leaves and tipped with ivy), they danced by torchlight to the rhythm of the flute and the tympanum. While they were under the god's inspiration, the bacchantes were believed to possess occult powers, the ability to charm snakes and suckle animals, as well as preternatural strength that enabled them to tear living victims to pieces before indulging in a ritual feast (*omophagia*).

Bacchelli \bäk-'kel-lē\, Riccardo (b. April 19, 1891, Bologna, Italy—d. Oct. 8, 1985, Monza) Italian poet, playwright, literary critic, and novelist chiefly known as a master of the historical novel.

Bacchelli attended the University of Bologna but left without a degree in 1912. He published a notable volume of poetry, *Poemi lirici* ("Lyric Poems"), in 1914, when he began service in World War I as an artillery officer. After the war, he contributed to the Roman literary periodical *La Ronda*, where he derided contemporary avant-garde writers, holding up as models the Renaissance masters and such writers as Giacomo Leopardi and Alessandro Manzoni. Somewhat later he was drama critic for the Milanese review *La fiera letteraria*.

Bacchelli's strongest works are historical novels. His first outstanding novel, *Il diavolo al pontelungo* (1927; *The Devil at the Long Bridge*), concerns an attempted socialist revolution in Italy, and his masterpiece, with the general title *Il mulino del Po* (1938–40; Eng. trans., vols. 1 and 2, THE MILL ON THE PO, vol. 3, *Nothing New Under the Sun*), is among the finest Italian works of that genre. Of Bacchelli's later historical novels, *I tre schiavi di Giulio Cesare* (1958; "The Three Slaves of Julius Caesar") is also notable. Among his critical works are *Confessioni letterarie* (1932; "Literary Declarations") and *Leopardi e Manzoni* (1960), a later work on two literary figures he greatly admired.

bacchius \ba-'kī-əs\ *plural* bacchii \-'kī-,ī\ [Greek *Bakcheîos*, from *Bakcheîos* (adjective) of Bacchus] A metrical foot of three syllables. In classical prosody the first is short and the others long (∪ — —). In accentual or modern prosody, the first syllable is unstressed and the other two have either primary or intermediate stress. A modern bacchius is scanned ∪ ′ ′. *Compare* ANTIBACCHIUS.

Bacchus *see* DIONYSUS.

Bacchylides \bə-'kil-ə-,dēz\ (fl. 5th century BC) Greek lyric poet of the Aegean island of Ceos, nephew of the poet Simonides and a younger contemporary of the Boeotian poet Pindar, whom he rivaled in the composition of the epinicion form of ode. Little was known of Bacchylides' work until the discovery in Egypt of papyrus fragments that reached the British Museum in 1896 and were published in the following year. Of the 21 poems wholly or partially restored, 14 are epinicion odes and the remainder are dithyrambs. Other fragments include passages from encomiums (songs in honor of distinguished men) and paeans (hymns in honor of the gods).

A firm date is provided by Ode 5, an epinicion written to celebrate the victory of Hieron I, ruler of Syracuse, in the horse race at the Olympian games of 476 BC. The poem implies that Bacchylides had already visited Syracuse before this date as a guest of Hieron, whose later victories in the Pythian horse race of 470 and the Olympian chariot race of 468 he celebrated in Odes 4 and 3, respectively. This brought him into direct competition with Pindar, who also celebrated two of these victories in *Olympian i* and *Pythian i*, and Pindar's uncomplimentary remarks about rival poets have been taken as referring to Bacchylides and Simonides. Bacchylides' style excels in narrative and in clarity of expression.

Bacheller \'bach-ə-lər\, Irving (Addison) (b. Sept. 26, 1859, Pierpont, N.Y., U.S.—d. Feb. 24, 1950, White Plains, N.Y.) Journalist and novelist whose books, generally set in upper New York state, are humorous and full of penetrating character delineations.

Bacheller began his career as a journalist. In 1883 in Brooklyn, N.Y., he founded the first modern newspaper syndicate and through its services distributed fiction by such writers as Joseph Conrad, Rudyard Kipling, and Stephen Crane, as well as nonfiction material. From 1898 to 1900 he was editor of the *New York World*.

Bacheller's novel *Eben Holden: A Tale of the North Country* (1900) sold more than 1,000,000 copies. It gives an authentic picture of 19th-century farm life and character in upper New York state. *D'ri and I* (1901), a novel about the Battle of Lake Erie in the War of 1812, was also popular. Bacheller's own favorites were *The Light in the Clearing* (1917) and *A Man for the Ages: A Story of the Builders of Democracy* (1919), the latter a story of Abraham Lincoln. *Opinions of a Cheerful Yankee* (1926); *Coming up the Road, Memories of a North Country Boyhood* (1928); and *From Stores of Memory* (1938) were autobiographical.

Bachmann \'bäk-män\, Ingeborg (b. June 25, 1926, Klagenfurt, Austria—d. Oct. 17, 1973, Rome, Italy) Austrian author whose somber, surreal writings often dealt with women in failed love relationships, the role of art in life, and the pain of self-examination.

Bachmann began her literary career in earnest in 1952 when she read her poetry before the avant-garde Gruppe 47. She produced two volumes of verse, *Die gestundete Zeit* (1953; "Borrowed Time"), about the urgency of time, and *Anrufung des Grossen Bären* (1956; "Invocation of the Great Bear"), featuring poems of fantasy and mythology. Of her several radio plays, the best known is *Der gute Gott von Manhattan* (1958; "The Good God of Manhattan").

Following Bachmann's landmark lectures on literature at the University of Frankfurt in 1959–60, she shifted her focus from poetry to fiction. She also wrote the libretti for the Hans Werner Henze operas *Der Prinz von Homburg* (1960) and *Der junge Lord* (1965). Among her other writings are *Das dreissigste Jahr* (1961; *The Thirtieth Year*), a collection of short stories, and the lyrical novel *Malina* (1971; *Malina*).

Bacon \'bā-kən\, Francis, Viscount Saint Albans (or Alban), Baron of Verulam \'ver-yu̇-ləm, 'ver-ù-\, *also called* (1603–18) Sir Francis Bacon (b. Jan. 22, 1561, York House, London, Eng.—d. April 9, 1626, London) Philosopher and man of letters whose ESSAYS (1597) and other writings mark him as a master of English prose.

Bacon became a barrister in 1582 and a member of Parliament in 1584, but he had little success in gaining political power until 1591, when Robert Devereux, 2nd Earl of Essex and a favorite of Queen Elizabeth, became his patron. By 1600, however, Bacon was the queen's learned counsel in the trial of Essex, and in 1601 he drew up a report denouncing Essex as a traitor.

With the accession of James I in 1603, Bacon sought anew to gain influence. He was appointed lord chancellor and Baron Verulam in 1618; in 1620/21 he was created Viscount St. Albans. Between 1608 and 1620 he prepared at least 12 drafts of his most celebrated work, the *Novum Organum*, in which he presented his scientific method; he developed his *Instauratio Magna*, a plan to reorganize the sciences; and he wrote several minor philosophical works.

Bacon fell from power in 1621 after being charged with bribery. Cut off from many of his favorite pastimes and from consultation with his physician and excluded from Parliament, Bacon offered his literary skills to the service of the king, writing among other works a digest of the laws, a history of Great Britain, and biographies of Tudor monarchs. Two of six planned natural histories were composed—*Historia Ventorum* ("History of the Winds") appeared in 1622 and *Historia Vitae et Mortis* ("History of Life and Death") in the following year. His collection of essays, enlarged as *Essays* in 1612, was again enlarged in 1625 for the third edition.

Baggesen \'båg-ə-sən, *German* 'bäg-ə-zən\, Jens (Immanuel) (b. Feb. 15, 1764, Korsør, Den.—d. Oct. 3, 1826, Hamburg [Germany]) Leading Danish literary figure in the transition between Neoclassicism and Romanticism.

In 1782 Baggesen went to Copenhagen to study theology. His first book of poems, *Comiske fortællinger* (1785; "Comical Tales"), was highly successful. Later, after his libretto for the first Danish opera, *Holger Danske*, received adverse criticism, mainly because of its supposed lack of nationalism, Baggesen traveled through Germany, Switzerland, and France. The journey became the basis of his most important book, the imaginative prose work *Labyrinten* (1792–93; "The Labyrinth"), a "sentimental journey" reminiscent of the work of the 18th-century English novelist Laurence Sterne. Baggesen was variously a Germanophile, a great admirer of Jean-Jacques Rousseau, an ardent supporter of the French Revolution, a disciple of Immanuel Kant, and a Romanticist and early admirer of Denmark's foremost Romantic poet, Adam Oehlenschläger. Late in life he vigorously opposed Romanticism, carrying on a seven-year feud with Oehlenschläger.

Baggins, Bilbo and Frodo \'bil-bō-'bag-inz . . . 'frō-dō\ Fictional characters from the novels of J.R.R. Tolkien. Both characters are hobbits, mythical beings who are characterized as small in stature, good-natured, and inordinately fond of creature comforts. Bilbo, the hero of THE HOBBIT, accompanies a group of dwarfs on an expedition to recover their stolen treasure. Bilbo's nephew and adopted heir, Frodo, is the hero of Tolkien's trilogy THE LORD OF THE RINGS, which traces the adventures of Frodo and other creatures as they attempt to triumph over the powers of darkness. Both characters find in themselves unexpected stores of courage and fortitude.

Bagnold \'bag-nōld\, Enid, *married name* Lady Jones \'jōnz\ (b. Oct. 27, 1889, Rochester, Kent, Eng.—d. March 31, 1981, London) Novelist and playwright who was known for her broad range of subject and style.

The daughter of an army officer, Bagnold spent her early childhood in Jamaica and attended schools in England and France. She served with the British women's services during World War I, describing this experience in her two earliest books, *A Diary Without Dates* (1917) and *The Happy Foreigner* (1920).

Bagnold's best-known work is the novel *National Velvet* (1935; film, 1944), which tells the story of an ambitious 14-year-old girl who rides to victory in Great Britain's Grand National steeplechase on a horse bought for only £10. Two quite different novels are *The Squire* (1938; also published as *The*

Door of Life), which conveys the mood of expectancy in a household awaiting the birth of a child, and *The Loved and Envied* (1951), a study of a woman facing the approach of old age. As a playwright, Bagnold achieved great success with *The Chalk Garden* (1955; film, 1964). *Enid Bagnold's Autobiography (from 1889)* was published in 1969.

Bagritsky \ˌbə-'gryēts-kyē\, Eduard Georgiyevich, *pseudonym of* Eduard Georgiyevich Dzyubin *or* Dziubin \'dyzyŭ-byin\ (b. Oct. 22 [Nov. 3, New Style], 1895, Odessa, Ukraine, Russian Empire—d. Feb. 16, 1934, Moscow, Russia, U.S.S.R.)   Soviet poet known for his revolutionary verses and for carrying on the Romantic tradition in the Soviet period.

Bagritsky enthusiastically welcomed the Revolution of 1917, fighting with the Red Army during the Civil War and writing propaganda poetry. The rigors of war left him in ill health, and he turned to writing as a full-time career. His first poems were in imitation of the Acmeists, a Russian literary group that advocated a concrete, individualistic realism, stressing visual vividness, emotional intensity, and verbal freshness. Before long, however, he began writing in a style of his own, publishing *Duma pro Opanasa* (1926; "The Lay of Opanas"), a skillful poetic narrative set during the revolution with a Ukrainian peasant named Opanas as its hero. Although his later works expressed accord with the aims of the Soviet regime, Bagritsky nevertheless retained his Romantic style. Bagritsky's poetry exhibits great metrical variety and reveals influences from classicism to Modernism; but his works have in common a positive, optimistic attitude toward the world.

Bagutta Prize \bä-'gŭt-tä\   Italian literary prize that is awarded annually to the author of the best book of the year. Established in 1927, it is named after the Milan trattoria in which the award ceremony is held. The prize recognizes authors in several genres.

Bahā' ad-Dīn Zuhayr \bä-'hä-ȧd-'dēn-zủ-'hīr\, *in full* Abū al-Faḍl Zuhayr ibn Muḥammad al-Muhallabī (b. Feb. 28, 1186, Mecca, Arabia [now in Saudi Arabia]—d. Nov. 2, 1258, Cairo, Egypt)   Arab poet attached to the branch of the Ayyūbid dynasty (a Sunnite Muslim dynasty of the late 12th and early 13th centuries) centered in Cairo.

Bahā' ad-Dīn Zuhayr studied at Qūṣ, a center of trade and scholarship in Upper Egypt, and eventually moved to Cairo. There he entered the service of the Ayyūbid prince aṣ-Ṣāliḥ Ayyūb. He became vizier in 1240, when aṣ-Ṣāliḥ Ayyūb was brought to power in Egypt, but the poet fell from favor in the last year of the sultan's life.

Bahā' ad-Dīn Zuhayr's divan (collection of poems) was published in an Arabic edition with an English translation, *The Poetical Works of Behā-ed-Dīn Zoheir*, 2 vol. (1876–77). Among his poems are qasidas (odes) of praise and other poems about love and friendship.

Bahār \bä-'här\, Muḥammad Taqī (b. 1885, Mashhad, Iran—d. April 22, 1951, Tehrān)   One of the greatest poets of early 20th-century Iran.

Bahār succeeded his father, Sabūrī, as court poet of the reigning monarch, Moẓaffar od-Dīn Shāh. Gradually, however, Bahār broke away from the court and became a sympathizer with the revolutionary movement in the country. As editor of a liberal democratic newspaper called *Now bahār* ("The New Spring"), he wrote in praise of the new Iranian constitution. He led an active political life as a deputy of the Iranian parliament and became head of a literary group called *Dānishkadeh* ("The Place of Knowledge"). The group published a journal in which Bahār expressed his conservative literary tastes, upholding the classical style against that of the avant-garde poets. He retired from politics in 1921 and devoted himself mainly to

teaching and cultural projects. His poetry, although written in essentially classical Persian style, was unique in its expression of modern social ideas and criticism of the government, often in biting satire. He also wrote many essays, a novel, and treatises on the works of great Persian poets and historians.

Bahr \'bär\, Hermann (b. July 19, 1863, Linz, Austrian Empire—d. Jan. 15, 1934, Munich, Ger.)   Austrian author and playwright who championed (successively) naturalism, Romanticism, and Symbolism.

After studying at Austrian and German universities, he settled in Vienna, where he worked on a number of newspapers. His early critical works *Zur Kritik der Moderne* (1890; "On Criticism of Modernity") and *Die Überwindung des Naturalismus* (1891; "Overcoming Naturalism") illustrate the first phase of his career, in which he attempted to reconcile naturalism with Romanticism. In 1907 he published *Wien*, a remarkable essay on the soul of Vienna. Bahr later became a champion of mysticism and Symbolism. His comedies, including *Wienerinnen* (1900; "Viennese Women"), *Der Krampus* (1901), and *Das Konzert* (1909), are superficially amusing.

In 1903 Bahr was appointed director of the Deutsches Theater, Berlin. His novel *Himmelfahrt* (1916; "The Ascension") represented the staunchly Roman Catholic school of thought. His later critical works, which show his interest in the social effect of creative art, include *Dialog vom Marsyas* (1904; "Dialogue on Marsyas") and *Expressionismus* (1914).

Baïf \bä-'ēf\, Jean-Antoine de (b. 1532, Venice [Italy]—d. October 1589, Paris, Fr.)   Most learned of the seven French poets who constituted the group known as La Pléiade.

Baïf received a classical education and in 1547 went with Pierre de Ronsard to study under Jean Dorat at the Collège de Coqueret, Paris, where they planned, with Joachim du Bellay, to transform French poetry by imitating the ancients and the Italians. To this program Baïf contributed two collections of Petrarchan sonnets and Epicurean lyrics, *Les Amours de Méline* (1552) and *L'Amour de Francine* (1555). In 1567 *Le Brave, ou Taillebras*, Baïf's lively adaptation of Plautus' *Miles gloriosus*, was played at court and published.

Baïf—who was the illegitimate son of Lazare de Baïf, humanist and diplomat—enjoyed royal favor and received pensions and benefices from Charles IX and Henry III. His *Euvres en rime* (1573; "Works in Rhyme") reveal great familiarity with Greek (especially Alexandrian), Latin, neo-Latin, and Italian models. His verse translations include Terence's *Eunuchus* and Sophocles' *Antigone*.

Baïf was a versatile, inventive poet and experimenter. His metrical inventions included the *vers baïfin*, a verse of 15 syllables. His theories were exemplified in *Etrénes de poezie fransoèze en vers mezurés* (1574; "Gifts of French Poetry in Quantitative Verse") and in his little songs, *Chansonnettes mesurées* (1586), with music by Jacques Mauduit. Baïf's *Mimes, enseignements et proverbes* (1576; "Mimes, Lessons, and Proverbs") is considered to be his most original work.

baihua or **pai-hua** \'bī-'hwä\ [Chinese *báihuà*]   In Chinese literature, vernacular style of Chinese that was adopted as a written language in a movement to revitalize the classical Chinese literary language and make literature more accessible to the average citizen. Started in 1917 by the philosopher and historian Hu Shi, the *baihua* literary movement succeeded in making *baihua* the language of textbooks, periodicals, newspapers, and public documents, as well as producing a flood of new literature in the vernacular. By 1922 the government had proclaimed *baihua* the national language. Traditionally considered inferior to *guwen*, *baihua* had long been studiously avoided for creative writing. *Compare* GUWEN.

Bailey \'bā-lē\, Paul, *original name* Peter Harry Bailey (b. Feb. 16, 1937, London, Eng.) English writer of brief, intense novels.

Bailey worked at a number of jobs before beginning a writing career. His first novel was *At the Jerusalem* (1967), the story of a lonely elderly woman attempting to survive in a retirement home. In *Trespasses* (1970) the protagonist is cited by his wife as the reason for her suicide and, broken by events, is committed to a mental institution. Bailey further examined alienation and breakdown in *A Distant Likeness* (1973) and *Old Soldiers* (1980). His considerably longer *Gabriel's Lament* (1986) is a tragicomic recounting of more than four decades in a family's life. Bailey's plays include an adaptation of Fyodor Dostoyevsky's novel *Crime and Punishment* (produced 1978). Among his later writings are the autobiography *An Immaculate Mistake: Scenes from Childhood and Beyond* (1990) and the novel *Sugar Cane* (1993). He also wrote a biography of novelist Henry Green.

Bailey \'bā-lē\, Philip James (b. April 22, 1816, Nottingham, Nottinghamshire, Eng.—d. Sept. 6, 1902, Nottingham) English poet notable for his *Festus* (1839), a version of the Faust legend. Containing 50 scenes of blank-verse dialogue, about 22,000 lines in all, it was first published anonymously.

Bailey's father, who himself published both prose and verse, owned and edited from 1845 to 1852 the *Nottingham Mercury*. The young Bailey moved in 1835 to London and entered Lincoln's Inn. Without making serious practice of the law, he settled at Basford (in Nottingham) and for three years was occupied with the composition of *Festus*. He was associated with the Spasmodic school, poets whose aesthetic, based on Romantic ideas of association and intuition, rejected the restraint of literary form.

Baillie \'bā-lē\, Lady Grizel, *original surname* Hume (b. Dec. 25, 1665, Redbraes Castle, Berwickshire, Scot.—d. Dec. 6, 1746, Berwickshire) Scottish poet remembered for her simple and sorrowful songs.

The eldest daughter of Sir Patrick Hume, later earl of Marchmont, she carried letters from her father to the imprisoned Scottish conspirator Robert Baillie of Jerviswood, whose son George she later married. Although she wrote several songs, only two are extant: "The ewe-buchtin's bonnie" and the well-known "And werena my heart licht I wad dee."

Baillie \'bā-lē\, Joanna (b. Sept. 11, 1762, Hamilton, Lanark, Scot.—d. Feb. 23, 1851, Hampstead, London, Eng.) Poet and prolific dramatist whose plays, mainly in verse, were highly praised at a time when serious drama was in decline. Her three-volume *Plays on the Passions* (1798–1812) brought her fame but has long been forgotten. She is remembered, rather, as the friend of her countryman Sir Walter Scott and for a handful of lyrics in *Fugitive Verses* (1790), her first published work, that catch the authentic note of Lowland Scots folk song.

Bailly, Harry \'bā-lē\ Bailly *also spelled* Bailey. Fictional character, the genial and outspoken host of the Tabard Inn who accompanies the group of pilgrims to Canterbury in Geoffrey Chaucer's THE CANTERBURY TALES. Bailly suggests the storytelling competition that is the frame for *The Canterbury Tales*.

Bainbridge \'bān-ˌbrij\, Beryl (Margaret) (b. Nov. 21, 1933, Liverpool, Eng.) English novelist known for her psychologically astute portrayals of lower-middle-class English life.

Bainbridge acted in various repertory theaters for many years before she published her first novel. Her work often presents in a comical yet macabre manner the destructiveness latent in ordinary situations. In *A Weekend with Claud* (1967), the titular hero is a predatory, violent man. *Another Part of the Wood*

(1968) concerns a child's death resulting from adult neglect. *Harriet Said* (1972) deals with two teenage girls who seduce a man and murder his wife. Other novels in this vein are *The Bottle Factory Outing* (1974), *Sweet William* (1975), *A Quiet Life* (1976), and *Injury Time* (1977). *Winter Garden* (1980) is a mystery about an English artist who disappears on a visit to the Soviet Union. Later novels include *An Awfully Big Adventure* (1989) and *The Birthday Boys* (1991).

Bajazet \bä-zhä-'zā\ A tragedy in five acts by Jean RACINE, performed in 1672 and published the same year. The play, considered one of Racine's noble tragedies, was supposedly based on an actual incident that occurred in Turkey in the 1630s.

The drama opens with the grand vizier Acomat worried about his position at the court and planning to use Bajazet in a plot to supplant Bajazet's brother Sultan Amurath. The plot also involves Amurath's favorite mistress, Roxane, and (inadvertently) Bajazet's love, Atalide. In the end Bajazet and Roxane are killed by order of Amurath. Atalide kills herself when she learns of Bajazet's death, and Acomat flees.

Ba Jin or **Pa Chin** \'bä-'jěn, -'jin\, *pseudonym of* Li Feigan \'lē-'fä-'kän\ (b. Nov. 25, 1904, Chengdu, Sichuan province, China) Chinese anarchist writer whose novels and short stories achieved widespread popularity in the 1930s and '40s. The pen name Ba Jin was formed from the Chinese equivalents of the first and last syllables, respectively, of Bakunin and Kropotkin, two Russian anarchists whom Li admired.

Born to a wealthy family, Li received a traditional Confucian education as well as training in modern foreign languages and literatures. His first novel, *Miewang* (1929; "Extinction"), met with great success. During the next four years he published seven novels, most of them dealing with social concerns and attacking the traditional family system. Best known of these was the novel *Jia* (*The Family*), the first volume of an autobiographical trilogy collectively titled *Jiliu* ("Torrent"). The trilogy was completed in 1940 with the publication of *Chun* and *Qiu* ("Spring" and "Autumn"). In these and other novels—such as *Qiyuan* (1944; "Pleasure Garden") and *Hanye* (1947; *Cold Nights*)—the influence of foreign writers, notably Ivan Turgenev and Émile Zola, is apparent.

Ba Jin's work was frequently attacked by the communists. After the establishment of the People's Republic of China in 1949, he was elected to important literary and cultural organizations, but he never fully adapted to the new society. During the Cultural Revolution (1966–76), he was labeled a counterrevolutionary and sharply criticized, but he was rehabilitated in 1977.

Baker \'bā-kər\, Carlos (Heard) (b. May 5, 1909, Biddeford, Maine, U.S.—d. April 18, 1987, Princeton, N.J.) American teacher, novelist, and critic known for his definitive biographies of Ernest Hemingway and Percy Bysshe Shelley.

Baker taught at Princeton University from 1951. His book *Shelley's Major Poetry: The Fabric of a Vision* (1948) dwells on Shelley's inner self as visible in his poetry and largely ignores the exterior circumstances of the poet's life. His widely acclaimed *Hemingway: The Writer as Artist* (1952), regarded as one of the definitive works on the writer, provides a portrait of an artist and his generation and a critique of Hemingway's novels in moral and aesthetic terms. Baker's *Ernest Hemingway: A Life Story* (1969) is an authoritative biography of the writer.

Baker \'bā-kər\, George Pierce (b. April 4, 1866, Providence, R.I., U.S.—d. Jan. 6, 1935, New York, N.Y.) Teacher of some of the most notable American dramatists, among them Eugene O'Neill, Philip Barry, Sidney Howard, and S.N. Behrman. The critic John Mason Brown and the novelists John Dos Passos and Thomas Wolfe also studied under Baker, who appears as

Professor Hatcher in Wolfe's autobiographical novel *Of Time and the River*.

Baker, who graduated from Harvard University in 1887, remained there to teach. In 1905 he started his class for playwrights, 47 Workshop (named after its course number), the first of its kind to be part of a university curriculum. He concerned himself not only with writing but also with stage design, lighting, costuming, and dramatic criticism. Baker's annual lecture tours introduced many Americans to European ideas of theater art. His university productions pioneered advanced staging techniques in the United States.

From 1925 until he retired in 1933, Baker was professor of the history and technique of drama at Yale University, founding a drama department there and directing the university theater. Of his writings, the best known are *The Development of Shakespeare as a Dramatist* (1907) and *Dramatic Technique* (1919).

Baker \'bā-kər\, Houston A., Jr., *in full* Houston Alfred Baker, Jr. (b. March 22, 1943, Louisville, Ky., U.S.)   African-American educator and critic who proposed new standards, based on African-American culture and values, for the interpretation and evaluation of literature.

Baker attended Howard University (B.A, 1965), the University of Edinburgh, and the University of California at Los Angeles (M.A., 1966; Ph.D., 1968) and taught at Yale and Cornell universities, Haverford College, and the University of Virginia. From 1974 to 1977 he directed the Afro-American studies program at the University of Pennsylvania. Besides editing collections of poetry and essays, he wrote the studies *Long Black Song* (1972), *Singers of Daybreak* (1974), *The Journey Back* (1980), and *Modernism and the Harlem Renaissance* (1987).

The works of Frederick Douglass, W.E.B. Du Bois, Booker T. Washington, Richard Wright, and Ralph Ellison figure prominently in Baker's studies.

Baker \'bā-kər\, Ray Stannard, *pseudonym* David Grayson \'grā-sən\ (b. April 17, 1870, Lansing, Mich., U.S.—d. July 12, 1946, Amherst, Mass.)   American journalist, popular essayist, literary crusader for the League of Nations, and authorized biographer of Woodrow Wilson.

A reporter for the *Chicago Record* from 1892 to 1898, Baker became associated with *Outlook*, *McClure's*, and other magazines. In 1906 he helped establish and edit the "muckraker" *American Magazine*. He explored the situation of black Americans in *Following the Color Line* (1908), a field report on race relations in America. As David Grayson he published *Adventures in Contentment* (1907), the first of his several collections of widely read essays. From 1910, when he first met Woodrow Wilson, Baker became an increasingly fervent admirer. At Wilson's request, Baker served as head of the American Press Bureau at the Paris Peace Conference (1919–20), where the two were in close and constant association. Despite prolonged ill health, Baker wrote *Woodrow Wilson: Life and Letters*, 8 vol. (1927–39). He was awarded the Pulitzer Prize for the work in 1940.

Baker \'bā-kər\, Richard, *in full* Sir Richard Baker (b. *c.* 1568—d. Feb. 18, 1645, London, Eng.)   British writer and author of *A Chronicle of the Kings of England*.

Baker was educated at Hart Hall, Oxford, studied law in London, and traveled abroad. A member of Parliament in 1593 and 1597, he was knighted in 1603. Encumbered by the debts of his wife's family, Baker was reported a crown debtor in 1625 and his property was seized. He was imprisoned in the Fleet Prison about 1635 and remained there, devoting himself to literary work, until his death.

The best known of his works, which included translations from Cato (1636), *Meditations on the Lord's Prayer* (1637), and

a series of meditations on the Psalms (1639), was his *Chronicle of the Kings of England* (1643). This, though of small historical value, was often referred to by Joseph Addison and Richard Steele in their essays written some 70 years later.

Baker \'bā-kər\, Russell (Wayne) (b. Aug. 14, 1925, Loudoun county, Va., U.S.)   American newspaper columnist, author, humorist, and political satirist, who used good-natured humor to comment slyly and trenchantly on a wide range of social and political matters.

After graduating from Johns Hopkins University in 1947, Baker worked as a journalist for the *Baltimore Sun* (1947–54). He also wrote a lively weekly column, "From a Window on Fleet Street." At the Washington bureau of the *New York Times* (1954–62), he covered the White House, the State Department, and the Congress. In the early 1960s he began writing the "Observer" column on the paper's editorial page. In this syndicated humor column he initially concentrated on political satire. Moving to New York City in 1974, he found other subjects to skewer, and in 1979 he won the Pulitzer Prize for commentary. His topics included tax reform, Norman Rockwell, inflation, and fear.

Baker's *Growing Up* (1982), which recalled his peripatetic childhood, won the 1983 Pulitzer Prize for autobiography. A sequel, *The Good Times*, was published in 1989. Other works include *American in Washington* (1961), *No Cause for Panic* (1964), *Poor Russell's Almanac* (1972), and other collections of his columns. In 1993 he succeeded Alistair Cooke as host of the television program *Masterpiece Theatre*.

Baker Street Irregulars \'bā-kər\   Fictional street urchins, a gang of boys who appear in three of the Sherlock Holmes mystery stories written by Sir Arthur Conan Doyle. Named for the street on which Holmes resides, the boys' absolute allegiance and streetwise canniness make them ideal for occasional errand running or discreet snooping.

In New York City, in 1933, a group of devotees of Sherlock Holmes founded a fan club they called the Baker Street Irregulars. They published *The Baker Street Journal*, devoted entirely to Holmesiana, footnoted scholarship about the detective, and minute dissection of his cases. *See also* Sir Arthur Conan DOYLE; Sherlock HOLMES.

Bakhtin \bək-'tʸēn\, Mikhail (Mikhailovich) (b. Nov. 5 [Nov. 17, New Style], 1895, Orel, Russia—d. March 7, 1975, Moscow)   Russian literary theorist and philosopher of language whose wide-ranging ideas significantly influenced Western thinking in cultural history, linguistics, literary theory, and aesthetics.

After graduating from St. Petersburg University in 1918, Bakhtin taught for a time, then moved to Vitebsk [now Vitsebsk, Belarus] and began to write and develop his critical theories. Because of Stalinist censorship, however, he often published works under the names of friends. These early works included *Formalny metod v literaturovedeni* (1928; *The Formal Method in Literary Scholarship*), an attack on the Formalists' view of history; *Freydizm* (1927; *Freudianism*); and *Marksizm i filosofiya yazyka* (1929; *Marxism and the Philosophy of Language*). Despite his precautions, Bakhtin was arrested in 1929 and was exiled to Kazakhstan. From 1945 to 1961 he taught at the Mordovian Teachers Training College.

Bakhtin is especially known for his work on the Russian writer Fyodor Dostoyevsky, *Problemy tvorchestva Dostoyevskogo* (1929; 2nd ed., 1963, retitled *Problemy poetiki Dostoyevskogo*; *Problems of Dostoevsky's Poetics*), which he published under his own name just before he was arrested. It expresses his belief in a mutual relation between meaning and context, involving the author, the work, and the reader, each constantly affecting and influencing the others, and the whole influenced by existing political and social forces. Bakhtin further developed this theory of polyphony, or "dialogics," in *Voprosy literatury i estetiki* (1975; *The Dialogic Imagination*), in which he postulated that language evolves dynamically and is affected by the culture that produces it as it helps to shape that culture.

Bakî or **Bāqî** \,bäk-'ē\, *in full* Mahmud Abdülbakî (b. 1526, Constantinople [now Istanbul, Tur.]—d. April 7, 1600, Constantinople)   One of the greatest lyric poets of the classical period of Ottoman Turkish literature.

After an apprenticeship as a saddler, Bakî studied Islāmic law. He also began to write poetry. In 1555 he submitted a qasida (ode) to the Ottoman sultan, Süleyman I, thereby gaining an entrée into court circles. At Süleyman's death he wrote his masterpiece, an elegy on the sultan that combines grandeur of style with sincere feeling. Later Bakî resumed his religious career. He wrote several religious treatises, but his *Divan* ("Collected Poems") is considered his most important work. He is especially known for his ghazels (lyrics), in which he laments the ephemeral nature of youth, happiness, and prosperity and urges the reader to enjoy the pleasures of love and wine while it is possible to do so. His mastery of form expresses itself in perfect versification, a meticulous choice of words, and a skillful use of onomatopoeic effect.

Balaam \'bā-ləm\   A non-Israelite prophet described in the Old Testament (Numbers 22–24) as a diviner. He is importuned by Balak, the king of Moab, to place a malediction on the people of Israel, who are camped ominously on the plains of Moab. For this he is to be handsomely rewarded. Balaam states that he will utter only what his god Yahweh inspires, but he is willing to accompany the Moabite messengers to Balak. He is met en route by an angel of Yahweh, who is recognized only by Balaam's ass, which refuses to continue. Three times Balaam beats the beast; when the animal actually speaks to him, Balaam finally sees the angel, who commands him to bless Israel. Despite pressure from Balak, Balaam remains faithful to Yahweh and blesses the people of Israel. In later literature, however, Balaam is held up as an example of one who apostasized for the sake of material gain.

Balaguer \,bä-lä-'ger\, Victor, *surname in full* Balaguer i Cirera \ē-thē-'rer-ä\ (b. Dec. 11, 1824, Barcelona, Spain—d. Jan. 14, 1901, Madrid)   Catalan writer and Spanish politician and historian who helped revive Catalan literature.

Balaguer's first dramatic essay, *Pépin el Jorobado; o, el hijo de Carlomagno* (1838; "Pepin the Hunchbacked; or, The Son of Charlemagne"), was staged in Barcelona when he was 14. At 19 he was publicly "crowned" after the production of his second play, *Don Enrique el Dadivoso* (1843; "Don Henry the Bountiful"); several other Romantic historical plays followed. In 1843 he became a leader of the Liberal Party in Barcelona and promoted the growth of Catalonian nationalism. In 1857 he wrote his first poem in Catalan and thereafter adopted the sometime pseudonym of Trovador de Montserrat ("Troubadour of Montserrat"). He moved to Madrid and eventually rose to the position of senator in the Spanish legislature.

His historical works include the *Historia de Cataluña y de la Corona de Aragón* (1860–63; "History of Catalonia and of the Crown of Aragon") and *Historia política y literaria de los trovadores* (1878–79; "Political and Literary History of the Troubadours").

balance \'bal-əns\   The juxtaposition in writing of syntactically parallel constructions containing similar, contrasting, or opposing ideas (such as the statement "To err is human; to forgive, divine").

Balassi \'bòl-ò-,shē\ or **Balassa** \-,shò\, Bálint (b. Oct. 20, 1554, Zólyom, Hung.—d. May 30, 1594, Esztergom)   The outstanding Hungarian lyric poet of his time.

Balassi was born into one of the richest Protestant families of the country and lived an adventurous life, fighting against the Turks and against his own relatives, who sought to despoil him of his heritage. At first his poetry was conventional, but his powerful personality soon found original expression. He wrote vividly about the beauties of the countryside and the rough pleasures of warfare. His love poems show genuine feeling. Balassi was the inventor of a stanza form that was copied by later poets. His conversion to Roman Catholicism led to a religious poetry in which he exhibited a strong spirituality. He died of wounds received during the siege of Esztergom.

Balbuena \bäl-'bwä-nä\, Bernardo de (b. 1568, Valdepeñas, Spain—d. Oct. 11, 1627, San Juan, P.R.)   Poet and first bishop of Puerto Rico whose poetic descriptions of the New World earned him an important position among the greatest poets of colonial America.

Balbuena, taken to Mexico as a child, studied there and in Spain. When he returned to the New World he held minor church offices in Jamaica (1608) and eventually became bishop of Puerto Rico (1620), remaining there until his death. He is best remembered for two epic poems, LA GRANDEZA MEXICANA (1604; "The Grandeur of Mexico") and *El Bernardo o la victoria de Roncesvalles* (1624; "Bernardo; or, The Victory at Roncesvalles"), and for a collection of eclogues, *El siglo de oro en las selvas de Erífile* (1608; "The Golden Age in the Jungles of Erífile"). Much of his work was lost when his library was destroyed by the Dutch in the attack on San Juan in 1625.

Balchin \'bòl-chin\, Nigel (Marlin) (b. Dec. 3, 1908, Wiltshire, Eng.—d. March 17, 1970, London)   Novelist who achieved popularity with his fictional psychological studies.

After studying at the University of Cambridge, Balchin divided his time between research work in science and industry (as an industrial psychologist) and writing. During World War II he was deputy scientific adviser to the Army Council.

In *The Small Back Room* (1943), his best-known novel, he describes the conversation, behavior, and intrigues for position and power of the "backroom boys" with whom he worked during the war. Almost as successful is *Mine Own Executioner* (1945), a study of a psychiatrist unable to cure his own neuroses. The problems of the psychologically and physically disabled recur in the novels *A Sort of Traitors* (1949), whose protagonist is a former pilot now missing both arms, and *The Fall of a Sparrow* (1955), which explores the mental processes of a psychopath.

Balcony, The   Play by Jean GENET, produced and published in 1956 as *Le Balcon*.

Influenced by the Theater of Cruelty, *The Balcony* contains nine scenes, eight of which are set inside the Grand Balcony bordello. The brothel is a repository of illusion in a contemporary European city aflame with revolution. After the city's royal palace and rulers are destroyed, the bordello's costumed patrons impersonate the leaders of the city. As the masqueraders warm to their roles, they convince even the revolutionaries that the illusion created in the bordello is preferable to reality.

Balder or **Baldr** \'bòl-dər, 'bäl-\   In Norse mythology, the beautiful and innocent son of Odin and his wife, Frigg, and a favorite of the gods.

Most legends about Balder concern his death. When he had dreams foreboding his death, Frigg took oaths from all creatures, as well as from fire, water, metals, trees, stones, and illnesses, not to harm Balder. Only the mistletoe was thought too young and slender to take the oath. Icelandic stories tell how the gods amused themselves by throwing objects at him, knowing that he was immune from harm. Deceived by the trickster Loki, the blind god Hǫd hurled a branch of mistletoe as a shaft through Balder's body and killed him. The gods sent an emissary to Hel, goddess of death, who agreed to release Balder if all things would weep for him. All did, except a giantess, who was none other than Loki in disguise. There is another version of the story, to which allusion is made in a west Norse poem entitled *Baldrs draumar* ("Dreams of Baldr"). According to this version, Hǫd alone is responsible for Balder's death.

The Danish historian Saxo presents Balder as a vicious and lustful demigod. He and Hǫd were rivals for the hand of Nanna, said in west Norse sources to be Balder's wife. After many adventures, Hǫd pierced Balder with a sword.

Later works on the subject of Balder include Johannes Ewald's tragedy of erotic passion *Balders død* (1774; *The Death of Balder*) and Matthew Arnold's poem "Balder Dead" (1855).

Bald Soprano, The Drama in 11 scenes by Eugène IONESCO, who called it an "antiplay." It was first produced in 1950 and published in 1954 as *La Cantatrice chauve*; the title is also translated *The Bald Prima Donna*. The play, an important example of the Theater of the Absurd, consists mainly of a series of meaningless conversations between two couples that eventually deteriorate into babbling.

Baldwin \'bȯl-dwǝn\, James (Arthur) (b. Aug. 2, 1924, New York, N.Y., U.S.—d. Dec. 1, 1987, Saint-Paul, Fr.) American

UPI/Bettmann Archive

essayist, novelist, and playwright noted for his eloquence and passion on the subject of race in America.

Baldwin grew up in poverty in Harlem in New York City. From 14 to 16 he was active during out-of-school hours as a preacher in a small revivalist church, a period he wrote about in his semiautobiographical first and finest novel, GO TELL IT ON THE MOUNTAIN (1953), and in his play about a woman evangelist, *The Amen Corner* (performed 1965).

After graduation from high school, he began a restless period of ill-paid jobs, self-study, and literary apprenticeship in New York City. He left in 1948 for Paris, where he lived for the next eight years and wrote a collection of essays, *Notes of a Native Son* (1955), and his second novel, GIOVANNI'S ROOM (1956), which concerns an American in Paris torn between his love for a man and his love for a woman. From 1969, Baldwin commuted between the south of France, New York, and New England.

In 1957 Baldwin became an active participant in the U.S. civil-rights struggle. A book of essays, *Nobody Knows My Name* (1961), explores black-white relations in the United States. This theme also was central to his novel ANOTHER COUNTRY (1962), which examines sexual as well as racial issues. The separatist Black Muslim (Nation of Islam) group and other aspects of the civil-rights struggle are the subject of THE FIRE NEXT TIME (1963). Baldwin also wrote a bitter play about racist oppression, BLUES FOR MISTER CHARLIE (produced 1964). Though Baldwin continued to write until his death, none of his later works achieved the popular and critical success of his early work.

Bale \'bāl\, John (b. Nov. 21, 1495, Cove, Suffolk, Eng.—d. November 1563, Canterbury, Kent) Bishop, controversial Protestant author, and dramatist whose *Kynge Johan* is asserted to have been the first English history play. He also wrote the first rudimentary history of English literature.

Bale was educated at a Carmelite convent in Norwich and at Cambridge. He was the prior of several Carmelite convents but became a Protestant and at some date (probably 1533) left his order, married, and became rector of Thorndon, Suffolk. Frequently attacked and once imprisoned for his religious views, he took refuge on the European continent from 1540 to 1548 and from 1553 to 1558. In 1560 he was appointed to the staff of Canterbury Cathedral.

Bale's voluminous writings are characterized by a fiercely partisan spirit, crude but vigorous satire, and frequent scurrility. His plays, only five of which survive, are thought to belong to the early 1530s. They employ the old forms of miracle and morality play as vehicles of Protestant propaganda. His most ambitious effort took the form of three biographical catalogs of English writers: the *Illustrium majoris Britanniae scriptorum* (1548; "Of Great Britain's Illustrious Writers"); the revised and much-expanded *Scriptorum illustrium majoris Britanniae catalogus* (1557–59; reprinted 1977; "Catalog of Great Britain's Illustrious Writers"); and the autograph notebook, first published in 1902 as *Index Britanniae Scriptorum Quos Collegit J. Baleus* ("Index of Britain's Writers Collected by J. Bale").

Balfour, David \'dā-vid-'bal-fǝr, -,fȯr\ Fictional character, hero of two novels by Robert Louis Stevenson, KIDNAPPED and *Catriona* (U.S. title, *David Balfour*), both set in Scotland in the middle 1700s.

Balkan Trilogy, The Series of three novels by Olivia MANNING, first published together posthumously in 1981. Consisting of *The Great Fortune* (1960), *The Spoilt City* (1962), and *Friends and Heroes* (1965), the trilogy is a semiautobiographical account of a British couple living in the Balkans during World War II. The complex narrative, composed of several different voices, is noted for its vivid historicity.

In *The Great Fortune*, newlyweds Guy and Harriet Pringle encounter an increasingly fascist environment in Bucharest, Romania, in 1939. Guy is a gregarious university lecturer whose liberal views contrast with those of his reserved wife. Clarence Lawson is a colleague of Guy who worships him and finds Harriet attractive. In *The Spoilt City*, Harriet faces marital problems and befriends Sasha Drucker, a Romanian army deserter, and Prince Yakimov, a Russian émigré. Just before the arrival of German troops in Bucharest, Guy sends Harriet to Greece, where they are reunited in *Friends and Heroes*. Guy acquires a teaching post and becomes involved in communist politics. By the end of the novel, the Pringles repair their marriage and flee to Cairo, where their story is continued in *The Levant Trilogy*.

Ball \'bȯl\, Hugo (b. Feb. 22, 1886, Pirmasens, Ger.—d. Sept. 14, 1927, St. Abbondio, Switz.) Writer, actor, and dramatist who is known for an early critical biography of German novelist Hermann Hesse.

Ball studied at the universities of Munich and Heidelberg (1906–07) and went to Berlin in 1910 to become an actor. He was a founder of the Dada movement in art. A staunch pacifist, he left Germany during World War I and moved to neutral Switzerland in 1916. His more important works included *Kritik der deutschen Intelligenz* (1919; "Critique of German Intelligence") and *Die Flucht aus der Zeit* (1927; "The Flight from Time").

ballad \'bal-ǝd\ [Old French *balade,* from Old Provençal *ballada* dance, song sung while dancing, a derivative of *ballar* to dance] A form of short narrative folk song, the distinctive style of which crystallized in Europe during the late Middle Ages. The ballad has been preserved as a musical and literary form up to modern times. It was originally part of the oral tradition, and the oral form has been preserved as the folk ballad, while a written, literary ballad evolved from that tradition.

Typically, the folk ballad (or standard ballad) tells a compact tale in a style that achieves bold, sensational effects through deliberate starkness and abruptness. Despite a rigid economy of narrative, it employs a variety of devices to prolong highly charged moments in the story and to thicken the emotional atmosphere, the most common being a frequent repetition of some key word, line, or phrase.

The ballad genre in its present form can scarcely have existed before about 1100. The oldest ballad in Francis J. Child's definitive compilation, *The English and Scottish Popular Ballads* (1882–98), dates from 1300.

Unlike the strictly impersonal folk ballad, the literary ballad calls attention to itself and to its composer. Early ballads of this sort were the work of professional entertainers employed in wealthy households from the Middle Ages until the 17th century, and many of these pieces glorify noble families. The modern literary ballad recalls in its rhythmic and narrative elements the traditions of folk balladry. Among the well-known poets who have written their own literary ballads are Sir Walter Scott, Samuel Taylor Coleridge, John Keats, and Heinrich Heine.

ballade \bə-'läd, ba-\ [Middle French *balade*, literally, ballad] One of several *formes fixes* ("fixed forms") in French lyric poetry and song, cultivated particularly in the 14th and 15th centuries. (*Compare* RONDEAU; VIRELAI.) Strictly, the ballade consists of three stanzas and a shortened final dedicatory stanza. All the stanzas have the same rhyme scheme and the same final line, which thus forms a refrain. Different forms have been used for the ballade stanza, but the most common is eight lines with a rhyme scheme of *ababbcbc* for the first three stanzas and four lines rhyming *bcbc* for the final dedicatory stanza. The last stanza is called the prince (because that is usually its first word) or the envoi. The *chant royale* is similar to the ballade but has five main stanzas.

The general shape of the ballade is present in the poetry of many ages and regions, but in its purest form the ballade is found only in France and England. The immediate precursors of the ballade can be found in the monophonic songs of the troubadours (poet-musicians using the Provençal language) and the trouvères (the northern counterparts of the troubadours). The history of the polyphonic ballade begins with Guillaume de Machaut, the leading French poet and composer of the 14th century.

The ballade was the most expansive of the *formes fixes*. The texts more often contained elaborate symbolism and classical references than did those of the other *formes fixes*. Later in the 14th century, the ballade was used for the most solemn and formal songs: the celebration of special patrons, the commemoration of magnificent occasions, the declarations of love in the highest style.

In the 15th century the form became less popular. Later in the century, musical ballades were rare except in the work of English composers. The form gradually disappeared among the poets, too, only to reappear spasmodically in the work of later writers as a conscious archaism.

ballade royal \bə-'läd-'rói-əl, bȧ-'läd-rwä-'yȧl\ *plural* ballade royals [Middle French, royal ballade] A ballade written in rhyme royal stanzas (stanzas of seven 10-syllable lines rhyming *ababbcc*).

ballad meter The meter common in English ballads consisting chiefly of iambic lines of seven accents, each arranged

in rhymed pairs and usually printed as the four-line BALLAD STANZA. *See also* COMMON METER.

balladmonger \'bal-əd-,mäŋ-gər, -,məŋ-gər\ A poor or inferior poet.

Ballad of Reading Gaol, The \'red-iŋ-'jäl\ Poem by Oscar WILDE, published in 1898. This long ballad, Wilde's last published work, is an eloquent plea for reform of prison conditions. It was inspired by the two years Wilde spent in the jail in Reading, Eng., after being convicted of sodomy.

Ballad of the Sad Café, The Long novella by Carson MCCULLERS, the title work in a collection of short stories, published in 1951. Peopled with bizarre and grotesque characters, the novella has a folkloric quality and is considered one of the author's best works.

Amelia Evans, a tall and lonely woman, falls passionately in love with her cousin Lymon, a malevolent dwarf. Amelia opens a café that serves as a much-needed social outlet for their tiny Southern town. Lymon falls in love with Amelia's estranged husband, Marvin Macy, who has just been released from prison. Lymon and Macy overpower Amelia physically and wreck her café, after which they disappear together, leaving Amelia and the townspeople without hope.

ballad revival Late 18th- and early 19th-century movement within English and German literary circles that was characterized by a renewal of interest in folk poetry. In reality the ballad revival was a rediscovery and new appreciation of the merits of popular poetry.

The trend that began in England in 1711 with the publication of Joseph Addison's *Spectator* papers cautiously defending "the darling Songs of the common People" crystallized in 1765 with the publication of Thomas Percy's *Reliques of Ancient English Poetry*, a collection of English and Scottish traditional ballads. The *Reliques* and a flood of subsequent collections, including Sir Walter Scott's three-volume *Minstrelsy of the Scottish Border* (1802–03), had great impact and provided the English Romantic poets with an alternative to outworn Neoclassical models as a source of inspiration. The folk ballad came to have an almost mystical distinction in Germany. The collection of lyrical and narrative folk songs entitled *Des Knaben Wunderhorn* (1805–08; "The Boy's Magic Horn"), edited by Clemens Brentano and Achim von Arnim, was the dominant influence on German poetry throughout the 19th century.

ballad stanza A verse stanza common in English ballads that consists of two lines in ballad meter, usually printed as a four-line stanza with a rhyme scheme of *abcb*, as in *The Wife of Usher's Well*, which begins:

> There lived a wife at Usher's Well,
> And a wealthy wife was she;
> She had three stout and stalwart sons,
> And sent them o'er the sea.

Ballantyne \'bal-ən-,tīn\, R.M., *in full* Robert Michael (b. April 24, 1825, Edinburgh, Scot.—d. Feb. 8, 1894, Rome, Italy) Scottish author chiefly famous for his adventure story *The Coral Island* (1858). This and all of Ballantyne's stories were written from personal experience. The heroes of his books are models of self-reliance and moral uprightness. *Snowflakes and Sunbeams; or, The Young Fur Traders* (1856) is a boys' adventure story based on his experiences with the Hudson's Bay Company. Annoyed by a mistake he had made in *The Coral Island* through lack of firsthand knowledge of the setting, he afterward traveled widely to research the backgrounds of his stories.

Ballard \'bal-ərd, -ˌärd\, J.G., *in full* James Graham (b. Nov. 15, 1930, Shanghai, China) British author of science fiction set in ecologically unbalanced landscapes caused by decadent technological excess.

The son of a British business executive based in China, Ballard spent four years of his boyhood in a Japanese prison camp near Shanghai during World War II. This experience was recounted in his largely autobiographical novel *Empire of the Sun* (1984; film, 1987). The devastated city and nearby countryside also provided settings for several of his apocalyptic novels. He attended King's College, Cambridge, but left without a degree. His first short stories appeared in the 1950s. Beginning in the 1960s, Ballard wrote longer works, including the well-known *The Drowned World* (1962), *The Wind from Nowhere* (1962), *The Burning World* (1964), and *The Crystal World* (1966).

With the gory images of his surreal short stories in *The Atrocity Exhibition* (1970; also published as *Love and Napalm: Export U.S.A.*), Ballard began writing of dehumanized sex and technology at their most extreme. His novels *Crash* (1973), *Concrete Island* (1974), and *High Rise* (1975) depict 20th-century middle-class people devolving into savagery. Contrasting with this apocalyptic vision of the future were his almost wistful short stories about the decadent technological utopia Vermilion Sands; these were collected in *Vermilion Sands* (1971). Later works include the short-story collection *War Fever* (1990) and the novel *The Kindness of Women* (1991).

Balthasar \bal-'thaz-ər, -'thäz-, *in Shakespeare's work* ˌbal-thə-'zär\ Legendary figure, said to be one of the MAGI.

Balzac \bȧl-'zȧk, *Angl* 'bȯl-ˌzak, 'bal-,\, Honoré de, *original name* Honoré Balssa \bȧl-'sȧ\ (b. May 20, 1799, Tours, Fr.—d. Aug. 18, 1850, Paris) French writer who produced a vast collection of novels and short stories collectively called *La Comédie humaine* (THE HUMAN COMEDY). He is generally considered to be the creator of realism in the novel and one of the greatest fiction writers of all time.

J.E. Bulloz

Balzac attended school at Vendôme and Paris and then, beginning at about age 16, spent three years as a lawyer's clerk. During this time he worked at a literary career, writing several unsuccessful plays and a variety of novels—gothic, humorous, historical—under composite pseudonyms. When these failed, he tried a business career, which nearly led to bankruptcy and left him with huge debts. From then on his life was to be one of mounting debts and almost incessant toil.

In 1829 were issued *Les Chouans*, the first novel he published under his own name, and *La Physiologie du mariage* (*The Physiology of Marriage*), a satire on cuckoldry. These two works brought Balzac to the brink of success, and the six stories in his *Scènes de la vie privée* (1830; SCENES FROM PRIVATE LIFE) further increased his reputation.

Balzac henceforth spent much time in Paris, frequenting some of the best-known Parisian salons. He was avid for fame, fortune, and love but was above all conscious of his own ge-

nius, which he pursued in phenomenal bouts of work—14 to 16 hours at a time spent writing.

From 1832 to 1835, Balzac produced more than 20 works, including the novels *Le Médecin de campagne* (1833; THE COUNTRY DOCTOR), EUGÉNIE GRANDET (1833), *L'Illustre Gaudissart* (1833; *The Illustrious Gaudissart*), and LE PÈRE GORIOT (1835), one of his masterpieces. Between 1836 and 1839, he wrote *Le Cabinet des antiques* (1839); the first two parts of another masterpiece, *Illusions perdues* (1837–43; *Lost Illusions*); *César Birotteau* (1837); and *La Maison Nucingen* (1838; *The Firm of Nucingen*). Between 1832 and 1837 he also published three sets of Rabelaisian *Contes drolatiques* (DROLL STORIES). In all these varied works Balzac emerged as the supreme observer and chronicler of contemporary French society.

By 1834 he had developed his great plan to group his individual novels so that they would comprehend the whole of contemporary society in a diverse but unified series of books, and by 1840 he had hit upon a Dantesque title for the whole: *La Comédie humaine*, which eventually totaled roughly 90 novels and novellas.

Balzac produced many notable works during the early and mid-1840s. These included the masterpieces *Une Ténébreuse Affaire* (1841; *A Shady Business*), *La Rabouilleuse* (1841–42; *The Black Sheep*), *Ursule Mirouët* (1841), and one of his greatest works, *Splendeurs et misères des courtisanes* (1843–47; A HARLOT HIGH AND LOW). Balzac's last two masterpieces were *La Cousine Bette* (1846; COUSIN BETTE) and *Le Cousin Pons* (1847; COUSIN PONS).

Balzac \bȧl-'zȧk, *Angl* 'bȯl-ˌzak, 'bal-,\, Jean-Louis Guez de (b. 1597, probably in Balzac, near Angoulême, Fr.—d. Feb. 18, 1654, Balzac) Man of letters and critic, an original member of the Académie Française; he was influential in the development of classical French prose.

Balzac hoped for a political career, but when his hopes were dashed he retired to his country house, from which he maintained relations with Parisian literary circles, chiefly by letter. Elected to the Académie Française in 1634, he rarely attended its sessions. His reputation, high in his lifetime, declined rapidly after his death. Balzac's published works included *Le Prince* (1631), a political treatise, and *Le Socrate chrétien* (1652), a synthesis of Stoic and Christian ethics. Far more influential, however, were the *Lettres*, short dissertations on political, moral, and literary matters, which appeared in numerous editions and were continually expanded from 1624.

Bambara \bäm-'bar-ə\, Toni Cade, *original name* Toni Cade (b. March 25, 1939, New York, N.Y., U.S.) American writer, civil-rights activist, and teacher who wrote about the concerns of the African-American community.

Bambara (a surname she adopted in 1970) was educated at Queens College and City College of the City University of New York. She was a frequent lecturer and teacher at universities and a political activist.

Bambara's fiction, which was set in the rural South as well as the urban North, was written in black street dialect and presented sharply drawn characters whom she portrayed with affection. She published the short-story collections *Gorilla, My Love* (1972) and *The Sea Birds Are Still Alive* (1977), as well as the novels *The Salt Eaters* (1980) and *If Blessing Comes* (1987). She edited and contributed to *The Black Woman: An Anthology* (1970) and to *Tales and Stories for Black Folks* (1971).

Bambi \'bam-bē, *German* 'bäm-bē\ (*in full* Bambi: A Life in the Woods) Novel by Felix SALTEN, published in 1923 as *Bambi: Eine Lebensgeschichte aus dem Walde*. The story is an enduring children's classic as well as an allegory for adults.

It is a realistic, although anthropomorphized, account of a deer from his birth to his final role as a wise and tough old denizen of the forest, struggling to survive against his chief enemy, man the hunter. The close parallel between the fawn becoming a stag and a child becoming an adult gives the book its moral overtone.

Bāṇa \'bän-ə\, *also called* **Bāṇabhaṭṭa** \,bän-ə-'bət-tə\ (fl. first half of 7th century)   One of the greatest masters of Sanskrit prose, famed principally for his chronicle, *Harṣacarita* ("Deeds of Harṣa"), depicting the court and times of the Buddhist emperor Harṣa (reigned *c.* 606–647) of northern India.

Bāṇa gave some autobiographical account of himself in the early chapters of the *Harṣacarita*. He was born into an illustrious family of Brahmans. Orphaned at 14, for some years he traveled adventurously with a group of colorful friends (including his two half brothers by a lower-caste woman, a snake doctor, a goldsmith, a gambler, and a musician). After returning home and marrying, he was called to the court of Harṣa. He was treated coolly at first by the emperor, perhaps because of some gossip about his wayward youth, but in time he won the emperor's high regard.

Bāṇa's biography of Harṣa provides valuable information about the period, though with some obvious exaggeration in the emperor's favor. Written in the ornate kavya style, which involves lengthy constructions, elaborate descriptions, and poetic devices, the work has great vitality and a wealth of keenly observed detail. Bāṇa's second great work, the prose romance *Kādambarī*, describes the affairs of two sets of lovers through a series of incarnations. Both works were left unfinished; the second was completed by the author's son, Bhūṣaṇabhaṭṭa.

Bandeira \bă\ⁿ-'dā-rə\, Manuel, *in full* Manuel Carneiro de Sousa Bandeira Filho \'fē-lyū\ (b. April 19, 1886, Recife, Braz.—d. Oct. 13, 1968, Rio de Janeiro)   Poet who was one of the principal figures in the Brazilian literary movement known as MODERNISMO.

Bandeira was educated in Rio de Janeiro and São Paulo. He taught literature at the College of Pedro II in Rio de Janeiro and became a professor at the University of Brazil. His first two books of verse, *A cinza das horas* (1917; "Ashes of the Hours") and *Carnaval* (1919; "Carnival"), show the influence of late Symbolist and Parnassian poetry, but some of the poems in his next collection, *O ritmo dissoluto* (1924; "Dissolute Rhythm"), display the sensibility of the emerging Modernismo movement. Bandeira's next collection, *Libertinagem* (1930; "Libertinism"), clearly displays the transition to Modernismo in its use of free verse, colloquial language, unconventional syntax, and themes based on Brazilian folklore. Bandeira's subsequent books, *Estrêla da manhã* (1936; "Morning Star"), *Estrêla da tarde* (1963; "Evening Star"), and *Estrêla da vida inteira* (1965; "Whole Life Star"), consolidated his reputation as one of the leading Brazilian poets.

In addition to writing poetry, he was also a translator, critic, anthologist, and literary historian. His reputation as a poet diminished somewhat after his death.

Bandello \bän-'dāl-lō\, Matteo (b. 1485, Castelnuovo Scrivia, duchy of Milan [Italy]—d. 1561, Agen, Fr.)   Italian writer whose *Novelle* ("stories") started a new trend in 16th-century narrative literature and had a wide influence.

A monk, diplomat, and soldier as well as a writer, Bandello was educated at Milan and the University of Pavia. After the material for his *Novelle* was destroyed in the Spanish attack on Milan (1522), he fled to France. In 1550 he was made bishop of Agen and spent the remainder of his life in France.

Bandello's stories were published in four volumes between the years 1554 and 1573. They contain a total of 214 short stories, or tales. These are frequently daring or sensual in the manner of Boccaccio's *Decameron*, and they provide valuable insights into the social intrigues of Renaissance Italy.

Bandello's stories were translated into both French and English in the 1560s and '70s, with the English translators adding a severe moral tone to the tales. The stories provided the themes for several important Elizabethan plays, notably William Shakespeare's *Romeo and Juliet*, *Much Ado About Nothing*, and *Twelfth Night* and John Webster's *The Duchess of Malfi*. Bandello's influence can also be discerned in French and Spanish literature.

Bang \'băṅ\, Herman (b. April 21, 1857, island of Als, Den.—d. Jan. 29, 1912, Ogden, Utah, U.S.)   Novelist who was one of Denmark's most important representatives of literary Impressionism.

Bang's first novel, *Håblose slaegter* (1880; "Hopeless Generations"), was confiscated as immoral for its depiction of the life of a decadent homosexual writer. Although he also wrote plays, poetry, short stories, and criticism, Bang is best known for his novels, including *Ludvigsbakke* (1896; *Ida Brandt*) and *De uden faedreland* (1906; *Denied a Country*). The work he did from 1886 to 1890—including a collection of short stories, *Stille existenser* (1886; "Quiet Existences"), and the novels *Stuk* (1887; "Stucco") and *Tine* (1889)—is considered to be his best. He died while on a lecture tour of the United States.

Banim \'ban-əm\, John and Michael (respectively b. April 3, 1798, County Kilkenny, Ire.—d. Aug. 13, 1842, County Kilkenny; b. Aug. 5, 1796, County Kilkenny—d. Aug. 30, 1874, Booterstown, near Dublin)   Brothers who collaborated on novels and stories depicting Irish peasant life.

John taught drawing, then moved to Dublin, where he worked as a journalist. After his blank verse tragedy *Damon and Pythias* was produced at Covent Garden in London (1821), he moved to London and continued to work as a journalist. In 1825 there appeared *Tales, by the O'Hara Family*, written in collaboration with Michael. All three *Tales*—two by John, *The Fetches* and *John Doe*, and one by Michael, *Crohoore of the Bill Hook*—are remarkable for their melodramatic invention and were immediately successful, John being dubbed "the Scott of Ireland." The next year John wrote *The Boyne Water*, a novel about the Jacobite wars in Ireland. In 1826 a second series of *Tales* appeared, containing *The Nowlans*, a story of passion, guilt, and religious fervor displaying a degree of insight that makes it possibly John's best work.

Despite a painful spinal malady, John continued to produce novels. Ill health eventually led to poverty, however, and in 1835 he returned to Kilkenny, where he lived on a government pension. *Father Connell* (1835), the Banims' last collaboration, was almost entirely by Michael, who continued to write after John's death.

Banks \'baṅks\, Russell (b. March 28, 1940, Newton, Mass.)   American novelist known for his portrayals of the interior lives of characters at odds with economic and social forces.

Banks was educated at Colgate University, Hamilton, N.Y., and the University of North Carolina. From 1966 he was associated with Lillabulero Press, initially as editor and publisher. The press issued his first novel, *Waiting to Freeze*, in 1967. Other early works included *Snow* (1975), *Family Life* (1975), and a collection of stories entitled *The New World* (1978). The novel *Hamilton Stark* (1978) was notable for its vividly rendered hardscrabble New Hampshire setting. The story collection *Trailerpark* (1981) explores the same locale. Banks's interest in the Caribbean, which led to his residence in Jamaica for an interval, shaped two of his novels, *The Book of Jamaica* (1980) and *Continental Drift* (1985), the latter being generally considered his best work. Later novels include *Affliction* (1989) and *The Sweet Hereafter* (1991).

Bannatyne \'ban-ə-,tīn\, George (b. 1545, Newtyle, Angus, Scot.—d. 1608?) Compiler of an important collection of Scottish poetry from the 15th and 16th centuries, the golden age of Scottish literature.

A prosperous Edinburgh merchant, he compiled his anthology of verse, known as the *Bannatyne Manuscript*, while living in isolation during a plague in 1568. This anthology contains many of the most familiar poems of the courtly poets known as makaris, or Scottish Chaucerians; it also preserves work by such poets as Alexander Scott who otherwise would be virtually unknown. It influenced the 18th-century Scottish revival, when Allan Ramsay reprinted a number of the poems (though often in altered form) in his *Ever Green* (1724).

banns \'banz\ [plural of *bann*, originally a spelling variant of *ban* proclamation, prohibition] *obsolete* The proclamation or prologue of a play.

Banquo \'baŋ-kwō\ Fictional character, one of the Scottish generals who with the title character serves King Duncan in William Shakespeare's MACBETH. At the outset of the play Banquo, in Macbeth's company, is informed by three witches that he will beget kings. Later in the play, the memory of this prophecy prompts the ambitious Macbeth to hire killers who manage to assassinate Banquo but allow his son Fleance to escape.

banshee or **banshie** \'ban-shē, ban-'shē\ [Irish *bean sídhe* and Scottish Gaelic *bean sìth*, literally, woman of a fairy mound] A female spirit in Gaelic folklore that warns a family of the approaching death of a family member by her presense and especially by wailing (called keening) unseen under the windows of the house a night or two before the time of the death she foretells. The Welsh counterpart, the *gwrach y Rhibyn* ("witch of Rhibyn"), visited only families of old Welsh stock.

Banti \'bän-tē\, Anna, *pseudonym of* Lucia Longhi Lopresti \lō-'pres-tē\ (b. 1895, Florence, Italy—d. 1985, Ronchi) Italian biographer, critic, and author of fiction about women's struggles for equal opportunity.

Banti earned a degree in art and became literary editor of the arts journal *Paragone*. Her early fiction, including short stories and the novel *Sette lune* (1941; "Seven Moons"), introduced the subject she would return to often—the low and lonely position of intelligent Italian women. In 1947 she published her most noted work, the novel *Artemisia*, based on the life of the 17th-century painter Artemisia Gentileschi. Other works include a short-story collection *Le donne muoiono* (1951; "The Women Die") and the novels *La monaca di Sciangai* (1957; "The Nun of Shanghai"), *Noi credevamo* (1967; "We Believed"), and *La camicia bruciata* (1973; "The Burned Shirt"). Besides biographies of such artists as Fra Angelico, Diego Velázquez, and Claude Monet, Banti wrote the play *Corte Savella* (1960; "Savella Court") and translated novels by William Makepeace Thackeray and Virginia Woolf into Italian.

Banville \bäⁿ-'vēl\, Théodore de, *in full* Étienne-Claude-Jean-Baptiste-Théodore-Faullain de Banville (b. March 14, 1823, Moulins, Fr.—d. March 13, 1891, Paris) French poet of the mid-19th century who was a late disciple of the Romantics, a leader of the Parnassian movement, and an influence on the Symbolists. His first book of verse, *Les Cariatides* (1842), owed much to the style and manner of Victor Hugo. His *Petit Traité de poésie française* (1872; "Little Treatise on French Poetry") shows his interest in the technicalities of versification, of which he became a master. Banville experimented with various fixed forms that had been neglected since the mid-16th century—

e.g., the ballade and the rondeau. His best-known collection is *Les Odes funambulesques* (1857; "Fantastic Odes").

Barabbas \'bä-rä-bəs\ Novel by Pär LAGERKVIST, published in Swedish in 1950. It is a psychological study of the spiritual journey of Barabbas, the criminal in the New Testament who was offered to the mob in place of Jesus but was spared from execution. The widely translated work was noted for its economical writing style, and it brought Lagerkvist international fame. He adapted *Barabbas* into a two-act play in 1953.

Barahona de Soto \,bä-rä-'ō-nä-thä-'sō-tō\, Luis (b. 1548?, Lucena, Spain—d. 1595) Spanish poet who is best remembered for his *Primera parte de la Angélica* (1586; "The First Part of the Angelica"), more commonly known as *Las lágrimas de Angélica* ("The Tears of Angelica"), a continuation of the Angelica and Medoro episode in Ludovico Ariosto's *Orlando furioso*. The fame that the *Angélica* received was in part attributable to Barahona's friendship with Miguel de Cervantes, who lavishly praised it in his *Don Quixote*.

Baraka \bə-'räk-ə\, Amiri, *also called* Imamu Amiri Baraka, *original name* (until 1968) (Everett) LeRoi Jones \'jōnz\ (b. Oct. 7, 1934, Newark, N.J., U.S.) Playwright, poet, novelist, and essayist who wrote of the experiences and anger of African-Americans with an affirmation of black life.

A graduate of Howard University, Baraka published his first major collection of poetry, *Preface to a Twenty Volume Suicide Note*, in 1961, followed by THE DEAD LECTURER (1964), *Black Art* (1966), and *Black Magic* (1969). His later collections included *It's Nation Time* (1970), *Spirit Reach* (1972), *Hard Facts* (1977), and *AM/TRAK* (1979). His poems reflected an interest in music that is also evident in the many books he wrote on the subject.

In 1964 Baraka's play DUTCHMAN appeared off-Broadway and won critical acclaim. Later that year his plays THE SLAVE and *The Toilet* were also produced. Baraka wrote many other plays in addition to an autobiographical novel, *The System of Dante's Hell* (1965); a collection of short stories, *Tales* (1967); several collections of essays, including *Home: Social Essays* (1966), *Black Music* (1967), and *Daggers and Javelins* (1984); and *The Autobiography of LeRoi Jones/Amiri Baraka* (1984).

Baraka founded the Black Arts Repertory Theatre in Harlem in 1965. In 1968 he founded the Black Community Development and Defense Organization, a Muslim group committed to affirming black culture and to gaining political power for blacks. He taught at several American universities.

Baranauskas \,bä-rä-'naus-käs\, Antanas (b. Jan. 17, 1835, Anykščiai, Lithuania, Russian Empire—d. Nov. 26, 1902, Seinai) Roman Catholic bishop and poet who wrote one of the greatest works in Lithuanian literature, *Anykščių šilelis* (1858–59; *The Forest of Anykščiai*). The 342-line poem is written in East High Lithuanian dialect. It describes the former beauty of a pine grove near his village and its despoliation under the Russians, symbolizing Lithuania under the czarist regime.

Baratynsky or **Boratynsky** \bə-rə-'tən-skʸē\, Yevgeny Abramovich (b. Feb 19 [March 2, New Style], 1800, Mara, Russia—d. June 29 [June 11], 1844, Naples [Italy]) Foremost Russian philosophical poet. Baratynsky's early romantic lyrics are strongly personal, dreamy, and disenchanted. His narrative poems *Eda* (1826), *Bal* (1828; "The Ball"), and *Nalozhnitsa* (1831; "The Concubine"; rewritten as *Tsyganka*, "The Gypsy Girl," 1842) treat the emotions analytically. The poem *Na smert Gyote* (1832; "On the Death of Goethe") is one of his masterpieces. Tragic pessimism dominates his later poetry, which is mainly on philosophical and aesthetic themes. Modern critics value his thought more highly than did his contemporaries.

Barbauld \bär-'bō, 'bär-,bȯld\, Anna Laetitia, *original surname* Aikin \'ăk-ən\ (b. June 20, 1743, Kibworth Harcourt, Leicestershire, Eng.—d. March 9, 1825, Stoke Newington, near London)   British writer, poet, and editor, whose best writings are on political and social themes. Her poetry belongs essentially in the tradition of 18th-century meditative verse. Although she is probably best known for her hymn "Life! I Know Not What Thou Art," her most important poems included "Corsica" (1768) and "The Invitation" (1773). She edited William Collins' *Poetical Works* (1794) as well as *The British Novelists*, 50 vol. (1810).

Barbeitos \bär-'bā-tüsh\, Arlindo (do Carmo Pires) (b. Dec. 24, 1940, Angola)   Angolan poet, many of whose works, written in Portuguese, portray in a subtle manner the struggle of his people for independence as well as the essential harmony between man and nature.

Barbeitos studied in West Germany and then taught at several bases of the Popular Movement for the Liberation of Angola during the country's struggle for independence. His poetry, which was collected in such volumes as *Angola Angolê Angolema* (1976) and *Nzoji* (1979; "Dream"), is noted for its density of thought, tenderness of tone, and simplicity of style. In 1985 he published *O rio: estorias de regresso* ("The River: Tales of Return").

Barber of Seville, The \sə-'vil, se-'vēl\   Four-act farcical drama by Pierre-Augustin BEAUMARCHAIS, performed and published in 1775 as *Le Barbier de Séville; ou, la precaution inutile* ("The Barber of Seville; or, The Useless Precaution"). It was the basis of the 1816 opera *Il barbiere di Siviglia* by Gioacchino Rossini. The play achieved great popularity for its ingeniously constructed plot and lively wit.

Rosine (known as Rosina in the opera), the ward of Dr. Bartholo, is kept locked in her room by Bartholo because he plans to marry her, though she despises him. Young Count Almaviva loves her from afar and uses various disguises, including one as Alonzo, a substitute music teacher, in his attempts to win her. Bartholo's roguish barber Figaro is part of the plot against him. Though in love with "Alonzo," Rosine is convinced by the suspicious Bartholo that Alonzo intends to steal her away and sell her to a wicked count. Disappointed, she agrees to wed Bartholo that very night. All of Figaro's ingenuity is required to substitute Count Almaviva for Bartholo at the wedding ceremony.

Barbey d'Aurevilly \bär-bā-dȯr-ə-vē-'yē\, Jules-Amédée (b. Nov. 2, 1808, Saint-Sauveur-le-Vicomte, Fr.—d. April 23, 1889, Paris)   French novelist and influential critic.

Barbey d'Aurevilly established himself in Paris in 1837 and began to earn a precarious living by writing for periodicals. He was appointed, in 1868, to alternate with Charles-Augustin Sainte-Beuve as literary critic for *Le Constitutionnel*, and on Sainte-Beuve's death in 1869 he became sole critic. Thenceforward his reputation grew, and he became known as Le Connétable des Lettres ("The Constable of Literature"). Though he was often arbitrary, vehement, and intensely personal in his criticism, especially of Émile Zola and the naturalistic school, many of his verdicts have stood the test of time; he early recognized the attainments of Honoré de Balzac, Stendhal, and Charles Baudelaire.

Most of his own novels are tales of terror in which morbid passions are acted out in bizarre crimes. Two of his best works are *Le Chevalier des Touches* (1864), about the rebellion of the Chouans (bands of Norman outlaws) against the French Republic, and *Un Prêtre marié* (1865; "A Married Priest"). *Les Diaboliques* (1874; *Weird Women*), a collection of six short stories, is often considered his masterpiece.

Barbosa \bär-'bō-sə\, Jorge (Vera-Cruz) (b. May 25, 1902, Praia, São Tiago, Cape Verde Islands—d. Jan. 6, 1971, Cova da Piedade)   African poet who expressed in Portuguese the cultural isolation and the tragic nature of life on the drought-stricken Cape Verde Islands.

He was one of the three founders of the literary journal *Claridade* ("Clarity") in the 1930s, which marked the beginning of modern Cape Verdean literature. His poetry was published as *Arquipélago* (1935), *Ambiente* (1941; "The Circle"), and *Caderno de um ilhéu* (1956; "An Islander's Notebook").

Barbour or **Barbere** or **Barbier** \'bär-bər\, John (b. 1325?—d. March 13, 1395, Aberdeen, Aberdeenshire, Scot.)   Author of a Scottish national epic known as *The Bruce*, the first major work of Scottish literature.

Records show that Barbour became archdeacon of Aberdeen while still a young man and studied at Oxford and in France. He completed *The Actes and Life of the Most Victorious Conqueror, Robert Bruce King of Scotland*, a metrical historical romance in 20 books, in 1376. The background of *The Bruce* is the political history of the Scottish struggle for independence, from the death of Alexander III in 1286 to the death of Douglas and the burial of Bruce's heart in 1332. The story emphasizes the chivalry and idealism of the Scottish heroes and exhorts their successors to emulate "thair nobill elderis." But the poem's central event, the Battle of Bannockburn of 1314, was still within the memory of his contemporaries, and *The Bruce* remains a harshly realistic depiction of recent history in the style of the chansons de geste rather than a romance of chivalry.

Barbusse \bär-'bŒs\, Henri (b. May 17, 1873, Asnières, Fr.—d. Aug. 30, 1935, Moscow, Russia, U.S.S.R.)   Novelist and member of an important group of French writers who span the period 1910 to 1939, mingling war memories with moral and political meditations.

Barbusse started as a neo-Symbolist poet, with *Pleureuses* (1895; "Mourners"), and continued as a neonaturalistic novelist, with *L'Enfer* (1908; *The Inferno*). He volunteered for the infantry in 1914, was twice cited for gallantry, and in 1917 was discharged because of his wounds. Barbusse's *Le Feu; journal d'une escouade* (1916; *Under Fire*), a firsthand witness of the life of French soldiers in World War I, was awarded the Prix Goncourt. Experience in war led Barbusse to become a pacifist, then a militant communist and a member of international peace organizations. After *Clarté* (1919; *Light*), his works acquired a definite political orientation.

barcarole or **barcarolle** \'bär-kə-,rōl\ [Italian dialect (Venice) *barcarola* gondolier's song, ultimately a derivative of *barca* boat]   A Venetian boat song characterized by the alternation of a strong and weak beat that suggests a rowing rhythm; or more generally, any poem or song connected with boats or water and whose sound suggests the movement of water.

Barchester Towers \'bär-chəs-tər, -,ches-\   Novel by Anthony TROLLOPE, published in three volumes in 1857. A satirical comedy, it is the second of the author's series of six BARSETSHIRE NOVELS and is considered to be his funniest.

Set in Barchester, a cathedral town in the west of England, the novel opens with the political appointment of Dr. Proudie as the new bishop of Barchester. This event sets up the main conflict of the novel—the traditional (represented by the High Church forces, led by Archdeacon Grantly) versus the new (represented by the Low Church newcomers, led by Mrs. Proudie and, initially, her protégé, the ambitious Mr. Obadiah Slope). Both forces contend for the newly vacant post of warden of Hiram's Hospital. A major subplot concerns Slope's unsuccessful attempts to marry into money.

Barclay \'bär-klē, -,klā\, Alexander (b. *c.* 1476—d. June 10, 1552, Croydon, Surrey, Eng.)   Poet who won contemporary fame chiefly for his adaptation of a popular German satire, *Das Narrenschiff* by Sebastian Brant, which he called *The Shyp of Folys of the Worlde* (first printed 1509). Barclay also wrote the first formal eclogues in English, filled with entertaining pictures of rural life.

Barclay \'bär-klē, -,klā\, John (b. Jan. 28, 1582, Pont-à-Mousson, near Nancy, Fr.—d. Aug. 15, 1621, Rome [Italy])   Scottish satirist and poet whose *Argenis* (1621), a long poem of romantic adventure, greatly influenced the development of the romance in the 17th century.

Barclay was a well-traveled cosmopolitan man of letters. His *Euphormionis Lusinini Satyricon* (1603–07; *Euphormio's Satyricon*), a severe social satire filled with villains and rogues, contributed to the later development of the picaresque novel. Barclay's most celebrated work was the *Argenis*, an outstanding example of modern Latin verse. It was reprinted more than 50 times during the 17th century, and literary figures such as William Cowper, Samuel Taylor Coleridge, Richard Crashaw, and Jean-Jacques Rousseau were familiar with it.

bard \'bärd\ [Middle English (Scots), from Scottish Gaelic and Irish]   A poet, especially one who writes impassioned, lyrical, or epic verse.

Bards were originally Celtic composers of eulogy and satire, or more generally, tribal poet-singers gifted in composing and reciting verses on heroes and their deeds. In Gaul the institution gradually disappeared, whereas in Ireland and Wales it survived. The Irish bard through chanting preserved a tradition of poetic eulogy. In Wales, where the word *bardd* has always been used for poet, the bardic order was codified into distinct grades in the 10th century. Despite a decline of the order toward the end of the European Middle Ages, the Welsh tradition persisted and is celebrated in the annual National Eisteddfod, an assembly of poets and musicians.

Bard of Avon, The \'av-ən, *commonly* 'äv-ən, -,än\, *also called* The Bard.   A byname of William SHAKESPEARE.

bardolater \bär-'däl-ə-tər\ or **bardolatrist** \bär-'däl-ə-trist\ [*Bard* (*of Avon*), nickname of Shakespeare + id*olater*]   One who idolizes William Shakespeare.

Bardolph \'bär-,dälf\   Fictional character, one of the comic sidekicks of Falstaff in William Shakespeare's two-part HENRY IV and THE MERRY WIVES OF WINDSOR.

Baren or **Pa Jen** \'bä-'rən, 'zhən\, *pseudonym of* Wang Renshu \'wäŋ-'rən-'shūᴇ\ (b. 1901, Fenghua, Zhejiang province, China—d. 1972)   Chinese prose writer and critic who was the first Chinese literary theorist to promote the Marxist point of view.

In 1920 Wang completed his studies and began his career as a teacher. In 1923 he started publishing novels and poems in *Xiaoshuo yuebao* ("Short Story Monthly") and became a member of the Literary Research Association. A year later he joined the Chinese Communist Party and in 1930 the League of Leftist Writers.

At the outbreak of the Sino-Japanese War in 1937, Wang remained in Shanghai and took part in anti-Japanese propaganda, edited various journals and the complete works of Lu Xun, and established the Social Sciences Institute. After the establishment of the People's Republic of China in 1949, he was appointed as the Chinese ambassador to Indonesia, and subsequently, as director of the Publishing House of People's Literature. In 1960 he was criticized for his article "Lun renqing" ("On Human Feelings"), and he died as the result of persecution during the Cultural Revolution (1966–76).

Baren produced several collections of short stories—including *Powu* (1928; "The Dilapidated House") and *Xun* (1928; "Sacrifice"), but he is better known for such novels as *Agui liulang ji* (1928; "Agui Roaming"), *Sixianshang* (1928; "On the Verge of Death"), and *Zhengjang* (1936; "The Badge"). His novel *Mangxiucai zaofan ji* (1984; "The Record of Rebellion of the Boorish Scholar") was published posthumously.

Baren's subject matter—chiefly the lives of peasants—gradually broadened, but his writing style did not develop. One exception is his well-crafted novel *Zhengjang*, which portrays the corrupt lives of bureaucrats in the Kuomintang government. In addition to the above-mentioned works, Baren wrote plays and literary criticism, including *Lun Lu Xunde zawen* (1940; "On Lu Xun's Essays") and *Cong Sulian zuopinzhong kan Sulianren* (1955; "Seeing Soviet People Through Soviet Literature").

Barghest or **Barguest** or **Bargest** \'bär-gest\ [origin unknown]   In folklore of northern England (especially Yorkshire), a monstrous goblin dog, with huge teeth and claws, that appears only at night. It was believed that those who saw one clearly would die soon after, while those who caught only a glimpse of the beast would live on, but only for some months. The Demon of Tidworth, the Black Dog of Winchester, the Padfoot of Wakefield, and the Barghest of Burnley are all related apparitions. Their Welsh counterparts were red-eyed Gwyllgi, the Dog of Darkness, and Cwn Annwn, the Dogs of Hell. In Lancashire the monster was called Trash, Skriker, or Striker; in East Anglia the dog had only one eye and was known as Black Shuck, or Shock. The Manchester Barghest was said to be headless. The Barghest appears in Charlotte Bronte's *Jane Eyre*, in which the title character recalls hearing tales of a creature called Gytrash—"a North-of-England spirit . . . in the form of horse, mule, or large dog."

Baring \'bar-iŋ, 'ber-\, Maurice (b. April 27, 1874, London, Eng.—d. Dec. 14, 1945, Beauly, Inverness, Scot.)   Journalist and man of letters.

The fourth son of the 1st Baron Revelstoke, the young Baring joined the diplomatic service and in 1904 he became a journalist and reported on the Russo-Japanese War in Manchuria; later he was a correspondent in Russia and Constantinople (Istanbul). He published novels, including *C* (1924), *Cat's Cradle* (1925), and *Daphne Adeane* (1926), as well as poems, parodies, and essays. He was also a distinguished Russian scholar, translator, and anthologist.

Barker \'bär-kər\, George, *in full* George Granville Barker (b. Feb. 26, 1913, Loughton, Essex, Eng.—d. Oct. 27, 1991, Itteringham, Norfolk)   English poet mostly concerned with the elemental forces of life. He became popular in the 1940s, about the same time as the poet Dylan Thomas, who voiced similar themes but whose reputation overshadowed Barker's.

Barker taught in Japan, the United States, and England from 1939 to 1974. His first novel, *Alanna Autumnal*, and *Thirty Preliminary Poems* appeared in 1933. Two of his important long poems are *Calamiterror* (1937), which was inspired by the Spanish Civil War, and *The True Confession of George Barker* (1950; rev. ed., 1957). His later poems include *Villa Stellar* (1978) and *Anno Domini* (1983). Barker's *Collected Poems* was published in 1987.

Barker \'bär-kər\, Lady Mary Anne, *original surname* Stewart \'stū-ərt, 'styū-\, *also called* Lady Broome \'brüm\ (b. 1831, Spanish Town, Jam.—d. March 6, 1911, London, Eng.)   Writer best known for her book *Station Life in New Zealand* (1870), a lively account of life in colonial New Zealand.

Stewart was educated in England. With her second husband, Frederick Napier Broome, she embarked for New Zealand. After three years there, the couple sold their sheep farm and returned to England. Barker's *Station Life*, which sold well, was followed by other books written in London.

In 1875 she joined her husband, who had been appointed colonial secretary of Natal (now in South Africa), later accompanying him to Mauritius, Western Australia, Barbados, and Trinidad and writing of these experiences. Broome was knighted in 1884, and Barker published the last of her 22 books, *Colonial Memories* (1904), as Lady Broome.

Barkis, Mr. \'bär-kis\ Fictional character, a stagecoach driver in the novel DAVID COPPERFIELD by Charles Dickens. Barkis is persistent in his courtship of Clara Peggotty, Copperfield's childhood nurse, and is known for the hopeful, often repeated phrase "Barkis is willin'."

Barleycorn, John \'jän-'bär-lē-ˌkȯrn\ Fictional humorous personification of alcohol, first appearing about 1620. John Barleycorn was a figure in British and American folklore. British sources often refer to the character as Sir John Barleycorn, as in a 17th-century pamphlet, *The Arraigning and Indicting of Sir John Barleycorn, Knight*, and in a ballad found in *The English Dancing Master* (1651). The Scottish poet Robert Burns reworked folk material for his poem "John Barleycorn" (1787).

Barlow \'bär-lō\, Joel (b. March 24, 1754, Redding, Connecticut Colony [U.S.]—d. Dec. 24, 1812, Zarnowiec, Pol.) Writer and poet primarily remembered for the mock-heroic poem *The Hasty Pudding* (1796).

Barlow was a chaplain for three years in the Revolutionary Army. In July 1784 he established a weekly paper, the *American Mercury*, at Hartford, Conn. He was a member of the group of young writers known as the Hartford (or Connecticut) wits, whose patriotism led them to attempt to create a national literature. Barlow's *Vision of Columbus* (1787), a poetic paean to America in nine books, brought the author immediate fame.

In 1788 Barlow went to France, where he lived periodically for the next 17 years. He returned to the United States in 1805 and lived there until 1811, when he became U.S. plenipotentiary to France.

In addition to religious verse and political writings, Barlow published an enlarged edition of his *Vision of Columbus* entitled *The Columbiad* (1807). His literary reputation now rests primarily on *The Hasty Pudding*, a pleasant and humorous mock epic inspired by homesickness for New England and containing vivid descriptions of rural scenes.

Barnaby Rudge \'bär-nə-bē-'rəj\ (*in full* Barnaby Rudge: A Tale of the Riots of 'Eighty) Historical novel by Charles DICKENS, published in 1841. *Barnaby Rudge* was Dickens' first attempt at a historical novel. It is set in the late 18th century and presents with great vigor and understanding (and some ambivalence of attitude) the spectacle of large-scale mob violence.

In a case of mistaken identification, Barnaby Rudge, the mentally retarded son of a murderer, is arrested as a leader of a mob of anti-Catholic rioters. Subsequently jailed and sentenced to death, he is pardoned at the scaffold.

Barnard \'bär-nərd, -närd\, Lady Anne, *original surname* Lindsay (b. Dec. 8, 1750, Balcarres House, Fifeshire, Scot.—d. May 6, 1825, London, Eng.) Author of the popular ballad "Auld Robin Gray" (1771).

In 1763 she married Sir Andrew Barnard and accompanied him to the Cape of Good Hope when he became colonial secretary there in 1797. Her journals, published as *Lady Anne Barnard at the Cape, 1797–1802* (1924), are a valuable source of information about the English occupation of the Cape during that period. When the Cape was ceded to Holland (1802), she and her husband settled permanently in London. "Auld Robin Gray," written to the music of an old song, was first published

anonymously; in 1823 she confided its authorship to her friend Sir Walter Scott, who in 1825 prepared an edition of the ballad.

Barnes \'bärnz\, Barnabe (b. 1569?, Yorkshire, Eng.—d. 1609) Elizabethan poet and author of *Parthenophil and Parthenophe*.

Barnes attended Brasenose College, Oxford; in 1591 he joined the expedition to Normandy led by the Earl of Essex. On his return he published *Parthenophil and Parthenophe* (1593), containing sonnets, madrigals, elegies, and odes, on which his literary reputation rests. His other works include *A Divine Century of Spiritual Sonnets* (1595), *Four Books of Offices* (1606), in prose, and two plays, *The Battle of Hexham* (now lost) and the anti-Roman Catholic *The Devil's Charter* (1607).

Barnes \'bärnz\, Djuna (b. June 12, 1892, Cornwall-on-Hudson, N.Y., U.S.—d. June 18?, 1982, New York, N.Y.) Avant-garde American writer who was a well-known figure in the Parisian literary scene of the 1920s and '30s.

Barnes attended the Pratt Institute and Art Students League and worked as an artist and journalist. She published an eccentric chapbook entitled *The Book of Repulsive Women: 8 Rhythms and 5 Drawings* in 1915; four years later three of her plays were produced by the Provincetown Players. She went to Paris in 1920 where she interviewed expatriate writers and artists for several magazines, and soon herself became an established figure. She wrote and illustrated a collection of plays, short stories, and poems titled *A Book* (1923; expanded as *A Night Among the Horses*, 1929; revised as *Spillway*, 1962); *Ladies Almanack* (1928); and the novel *Ryder* (1928), which Barnes called the story of "a female *Tom Jones*." Her second novel, *Nightwood* (1936), is her masterpiece, about the doomed homosexual and heterosexual loves of five extraordinary, even grotesque, people. Barnes also wrote a verse drama, *The Antiphon* (1958).

Barnes \'bärnz\, Julian (Patrick), *pseudonyms* Edward Pygge \'pig\ *and* Dan Kavanagh \'kav-ə-nə\ (b. Jan. 19, 1946, Leicester, Eng.) Popular British television critic and author of inventive and intellectual novels about obsessed characters curious about the past.

Barnes attended Magdalen College, Oxford, and began contributing reviews to the *Times Literary Supplement* in the 1970s. Meanwhile he began publishing thriller fiction under his Kavanagh pseudonym. These thrillers—which include *Duffy* (1980), *Fiddle City* (1981), *Putting the Boot In* (1985), and *Going to the Dogs* (1987)—feature a man named Duffy, a bisexual ex-cop turned private detective.

The first novel published under Barnes' own name was *Metroland* (1980). Jealous obsession moves the protagonist of *Before She Met Me* (1982) to exhaustively research his new wife's past. *Flaubert's Parrot* (1984) is a humorous mixture of biography, fiction, and literary criticism, as a scholar becomes obsessed with Flaubert. Barnes's later novels include *Staring at the Sun* (1986), *A History of the World in 10½ Chapters* (1989), *Talking It Over* (1991), and *The Porcupine* (1992).

Barnes \'bärnz\, William (b. Feb. 22, 1801, Bagber, near Sturminster Newton, Dorsetshire, Eng.—d. Oct. 7, 1886, Winterbourne Came, Dorsetshire) English dialect poet whose work depicted the life of rural southwestern England. He was a gifted philologist, and his linguistic theories as well as his poetry influenced Thomas Hardy and Gerard Manley Hopkins.

Barnes was ordained a priest in 1848. His first Dorset dialect poems were published in the Dorset *County Chronicle* (1833–34). His many books included an Anglo-Saxon primer, *An Outline of English Speech-Craft* (1878), and *Poems of Rural Life in Common English* (1868). His poems appeared in *Poems of Rural Life, in the Dorset Dialect* (two series: 1844, 1862) and *Hwomely Rhymes* (1859).

Barnes, Jake \\'jāk-'bärnz\\ Fictional character, the narrator of Ernest Hemingway's novel THE SUN ALSO RISES. An expatriate American living in Paris in the 1920s, Jake works as a newspaper correspondent. A wound suffered in the war has rendered him impotent and unable to consummate his love for Lady Brett Ashley, an English war widow. Although Jake is a typical manly Hemingway hero in his mastery of trout fishing and his appreciation of bullfighting, his physical flaw makes him a more rounded character than most of the Hemingway heroes that followed.

Barney \\'bär-nē\\, Natalie (Clifford) (b. Oct. 31, 1876, Dayton, Ohio, U.S.—d. Feb. 2, 1972, Paris, Fr.) Literary figure and writer who was noted for her international salon, her friendships with several writers, and her unabashed lesbianism.

At the age of 21, Barney inherited a fortune and determined to spend the rest of her life in Paris. In 1909 she established herself at 20 Rue Jacob, which for more than 60 years was the site of her well-attended Friday salon. Most French, American, and British writers of note were included in her circle. She was celebrated in several contemporary works, including Djuna Barnes' *Ladies Almanack*, Radclyffe Hall's *The Well of Loneliness*, and Renée Vivien's *Une Femme m'apparut* (*A Woman Appeared to Me*). The aging Rémy de Gourmont fell in love with Barney and produced two volumes concerning their platonic relationship: *Lettres à l'Amazone* (1914) and *Lettres intimes à l'Amazone* (posthumously published in 1927). Barney's own writing—eight slight volumes that include *Quelques Portraits: Sonnets de Femmes* (1900), *Pensées d'une Amazone* (1920; "Thoughts of an Amazon"), and *Souvenirs indiscrets* (1960)—is usually considered negligible.

Baroja \\bä-'rō-ḵä\\, Pío, *surname in full* Baroja y Nessi \\ē-'nes-ē\\ (b. Dec. 28, 1872, San Sebastián, Spain—d. Oct. 30, 1956, Madrid) Basque writer who was considered to be the foremost Spanish novelist of his time.

As a member of the Generation of '98, Baroja revolted against the stultifying aspects of Spanish life. His first two books were a collection of short stories, *Vidas sombrías* (1900; "Somber Lives"), and a novel, *La casa de Aizgorri* (1900; *The House of the Aizgorri*). He wrote 11 trilogies dealing with contemporary social problems, the best known of which, *La lucha por la vida* (1904; *The Struggle for Life*), portrays misery and squalor in the poor sections of Madrid. Of the almost 100 novels he wrote, the most ambitious project was *Memorias de un hombre de acción* (1913–28; "Memoirs of a Man of Action"), a series of 14 novels and 8 volumes of shorter narratives dealing with a 19th-century insurgent and his era. One of Baroja's best novels is *Zalacaín el aventurero* (1909).

Because of his anti-Christian views, his stubborn insistence on nonconformity, and a somewhat pessimistic attitude, Baroja's novels never achieved great popularity. His terse and unadorned style, which relied heavily upon understatement, is said to have had a great influence on Ernest Hemingway.

Baron Munchausen \\'mən-ˌchaůz-ən, 'mŭn-\\ Fictional character created by R.E. Raspe, based on the real-life German storyteller Karl Friedrich Hieronymus, Baron (Freiherr) von MÜNCHHAUSEN.

Baroque \\bə-'rōk, ba-, -'räk, -'rȯk\\ [French, probably from Middle French *barroque* irregularly shaped (of a pearl), from Portuguese *barroco* irregularly shaped pearl] A style of literary composition prevalent in most Western countries from the late 16th century to the early 18th century and marked typically by complexity and elaborateness of form and by the use of bizarre, calculatedly ingenious, and sometimes intentionally ambiguous imagery. *Compare* EUPHUISM.

Barrack-Room Ballads Collected poems by Rudyard KIPLING, published in 1892 and subsequently republished in expanded form. Included were such well-known, previously published verses as "Danny Deever," "Gunga Din," and "Mandalay." The book was a popular success and made Kipling a power among contemporary poets.

Many of the poems are rendered in a Cockney dialect. They all concern the British enlisted man, the soldier who defends the British Empire but is scorned because of his low birth.

Barrès \\bä-'res\\, Maurice, *in full* Auguste-Maurice Barrès (b. Aug. 19, 1862, Charmes-sur-Moselle, Fr.—d. Dec. 5, 1923, Paris) Writer and politician whose individualism and fervent nationalism strongly influenced his generation.

Barrès went to Paris to study law but instead turned to literature, publishing essays critical of the historians Hippolyte Taine and Ernest Renan, the spiritual mentors of his day. He then embarked on a solitary project of self-analysis through a rigorous method described in the trilogy *Le Culte du moi* ("The Cult of the Ego"). The work comprises *Sous l'oeil des Barbares* (1888; "Under the Eyes of the Barbarians"), *Un Homme libre* (1889; "A Free Man"), and *Le Jardin de Bérénice* (1891; "The Garden of Berenice").

At 27 he embarked on a tumultuous political career, adopting an increasingly intransigent nationalism. This stage was minutely reported in a new trilogy, *Le Roman de l'énergie nationale* ("The Novel of National Energy"), made up of *Les Déracinés* (1897; "The Uprooted"), *L'Appel au soldat* (1900; "The Call to the Soldier"), and *Leurs figures* (1902; "Their Figures"). His series entitled "Les Bastions de l'Est" became grist for the propaganda mill of World War I.

At times, however, the artist may be found to supersede the politician in Barrès' writing. His travels in Spain, Italy, Greece, and Asia inspired *Du sang, de la volupté et de la mort* (1894; "Of Blood, Pleasure, and Death") and *Un Jardin sur l'Oronte* (1922; "A Garden on the Orontes"). He was elected to the Académie Française in 1906.

Barrie \\'bar-ē\\, James M., *in full* Sir James Matthew, Baronet Barrie (b. May 9, 1860, Kirriemuir, Angus, Scot.—d. June 19, 1937, London, Eng.) Dramatist and novelist who is best known as the creator of Peter Pan, the boy who refused to grow up.

Barrie studied at the University of Edinburgh and spent two years on the Nottingham *Journal* before settling in London as a freelance writer in 1885. His first successful book, *Auld Licht Idylls* (1888), contained sketches of life in Kirriemuir, as did the stories in *A Window in Thrums* (1889). THE LITTLE MINISTER (1891), a highly sentimental novel in the same style, was a best-seller, and after its dramatization in 1897, Barrie wrote mostly for the theater. Most of his early works are marked by quaint Scottish dialect, whimsical humor and comic clowning, pathos, and sentimentality.

When the play PETER PAN was first produced in 1904, it added a new character to the mythology of the English-speaking world in the figure of Peter Pan. Its theme of heroic boyhood triumphant over the seedy, middle-aged pirate Captain Hook has proven to have a lasting appeal.

Barrie was created a baronet in 1913 and awarded the Order of Merit in 1922. He became president of the Society of Authors in 1928 and chancellor of Edinburgh University in 1930.

Most of Barrie's stage triumphs are marred by ephemeral whimsy, but at least six of his plays—*Quality Street* (produced 1901), *The Admirable Crichton* (produced 1902), *What Every Woman Knows* (produced 1908), *The Twelve-Pound Look* (produced 1910), *The Will* (produced 1913), and *Dear Brutus* (produced 1917)—are of high quality.

Barrios \'băr-yōs, -yōh\, Eduardo (b. Oct. 25, 1884, Valparaíso, Chile—d. Sept. 13, 1963, Santiago) Writer best known for his psychological novels.

Barrios began his literary career under the influence of Émile Zola with a collection of naturalistic stories, *Del natural* (1907; "In the Naturalistic Style"). His later novels, which established his reputation, include *El niño que enloqueció de amor* (1915; "The Love-Crazed Boy"), a fictionalized diary of a boy obsessed with love for one of his mother's friends; *Un perdido* (1918; "A Down-and-Outer"); and *El hermano asno* (1922; *Brother Asno*), about a mentally disturbed monk who attacks a girl in order to be despised by those who consider him a living saint. Barrios' most successful work was *Gran señor y rajadiablos* (1948; "Grand Gentleman and Big Rascal"), which portrays life on a Chilean farm.

His other works include a series of autobiographical sketches entitled *Páginas de un pobre diablo* (1923; "Pages from a Poor Devil") and the novels *Tamarugal* (1944) and *Los hombres del hombre* (1950; "Men Within Man").

Barry \'bar-ē\, Philip (b. June 18, 1896, Rochester, N.Y., U.S.—d. Dec. 3, 1949, New York, N.Y.) American dramatist best known for his comedies of life and manners among the socially privileged.

Barry was educated at Yale and in 1919 entered George Pierce Baker's 47 Workshop at Harvard. His *A Punch for Judy* was produced by the workshop in 1920. *You and I*, also written while Barry was a student, played 170 performances on Broadway in 1923. Over the next 20 years, a succession of plays included such comedies as *Paris Bound* (1927), *Holiday* (1928), *The Animal Kingdom* (1932), and *The Philadelphia Story* (1939). They are characterized by witty and graceful dialogue and humorous contrasts of character or situation.

Barry's thoughtful approach to life is apparent in *White Wings* (1926), a fantasy considered by some critics Barry's best play; *John* (1927), a drama about John the Baptist; *Hotel Universe* (1930); *Here Come the Clowns* (1938), an allegory of good and evil; and his final play, *Second Threshold* (1951).

Barry Lyndon \'bar-ē-'lin-dən\ (*in full* The Memoirs of Barry Lyndon, Esquire) Historical novel by William Makepeace THACKERAY, first published in *Fraser's Magazine* in 1844 as *The Luck of Barry Lyndon: A Romance of the Last Century*. The book was published in two volumes in 1852–53, and it was revised ("with admissions") as *The Memoirs of Barry Lyndon, Esq.* in 1856.

The novel concerns the life and times of the title character and narrator, a roguish Irishman. The fast-flowing satirical narrative reveals a man dedicated to success and good fortune. Born Redmond Barry, he leaves his homeland after shooting a man in a duel. He becomes a soldier of fortune and later works as a professional gambler. Remade as a man of fashion, he courts a wealthy widow, marries her, and assumes her aristocratic name of Lyndon. He mistreats both her and her son and spends and gambles away her money, but eventually she extricates herself from the alliance. By the novel's end he is in jail, cared for by his mother.

Barsetshire novels \'bar-sət-shir\ A series of six connected novels by Anthony TROLLOPE set in the fictional west England county of Barset.

Trollope prided himself on the scope and detail with which he imagined the geography, history, and social structure of his fictional county. Nevertheless, character interested him more than description, and many characters appear in more than one Barset novel. The Reverend Septimus Harding, whose moral dilemma is the central story of THE WARDEN (1855), reappears amid the ecclesiastical disputes of BARCHESTER TOWERS (1857). The kindly title character of *Doctor Thorne* (1858) weds a wealthy patent medicine heiress in *Framley Parsonage* (1861), a novel largely concerned with the financial scrapes of young vicar Mark Robarts. Many characters from preceding novels, including Lily Dale, whose broken engagement is the principal story of *The Small House at Allington* (1864), reappear in THE LAST CHRONICLE OF BARSET (1867). Of his 47 novels, Trollope considered *The Last Chronicle* his finest.

Barstow \'bar-,stō\, Stan, *in full* Stanley Barstow (b. June 28, 1928, Horbury, Yorkshire, Eng.) English novelist and short-story writer who achieved success with his first book, *A Kind of Loving* (1960; film, 1962; stage play, 1970).

Barstow grew up in a working-class environment and was employed in the engineering industry until 1962. He became associated with a group of young British writers (including Alan Sillitoe, John Braine, and others) who achieved immediate success in the 1950s and '60s with their unsentimental depiction of working-class life. His later novels include *The Watchers on the Shore* (1966), *A Raging Calm* (1968), *A Season with Eros* (1971), *The Right True End* (1976), *A Brother's Tale* (1980), and *Just You Wait and See* (1986).

Bart, Lily \'lil-ē-'bärt\ Fictional character, a beautiful, impoverished woman in Edith Wharton's novel THE HOUSE OF MIRTH. Tenuously associated with the upper-class New York society of the turn of the century, Lily lives by the values she has been taught since childhood: marry for money and social position. Her life slowly falls apart, however, as she is unable or unwilling to take advantage of the opportunities offered to her by society.

Bartas \bar-'tás\, Guillaume de Salluste, Seigneur du (b. 1544, Montfort, near Auch, Fr.—d. July 1590, Coudons) Author of *La Semaine* (1578; "The Week"), an influential poem about the creation of the world.

Du Bartas was an ardent Huguenot and a trusted counselor of Henry of Navarre. His aim was to employ the new poetic techniques introduced by La Pléiade for the presentation of distinctively Protestant views. He was himself dissatisfied with his first biblical epic, *Judith* (1574), but on the publication of *La Semaine*, du Bartas was hailed as a major poet. The poem, however, was ungainly and its didactic intent obvious, and it did not remain popular in largely Roman Catholic France. Indeed, the poem—as translated in *Devine Weekes and Workes* by Josuah Sylvester—made a more lasting impression in England; Sir Philip Sidney, Edmund Spenser, and John Milton were among those influenced by it.

Barth \'bärth\, John, *in full* John Simmons Barth, Jr. (b. May 27, 1930, Cambridge, Md., U.S.) American writer best known for novels that combine philosophical depth with biting satire and boisterous, often bawdy humor.

Barth studied at Johns Hopkins University in Baltimore and taught at various universities, including Johns Hopkins. His first two novels, *The Floating Opera* (1956) and *The End of the Road* (1958), describe characters burdened by a sense of futility. THE SOT-WEED FACTOR (1960) is a picaresque tale that burlesques the early history of Maryland, and GILES GOAT-BOY (1966) is a bizarre tale of the career of a mythical hero and religious prophet. His work *Lost in the Funhouse* (1968) consists of short experimental pieces interspersed with stories based on his childhood. It was followed by *Chimera* (1972), a volume of three novellas, and *Letters* (1979), an experimental novel. The novels *Sabbatical* (1982) and *The Tidewater Tales* (1987) are more traditional narratives.

Barthélemy \bar-tāl-'mē\, Jean-Jacques (b. Jan. 20, 1716, Cassis, Fr.—d. April 30, 1795, Paris) French archaeologist and author whose novel about ancient Greece was one of the most widely read books in 19th-century France.

In 1744 Barthélemy became assistant to the keeper of the royal collection of medals, and he succeeded the keeper in 1753. In 1755 he accompanied the French ambassador, the Count de Stainville (later the Duke de Choiseul), to Italy, where he spent three years in archaeological research.

Barthélemy wrote several technical works on archaeology, but his fame rests on *Voyage du jeune Anacharsis en Grèce, dans le milieu du quatrième siècle avant l'ère vulgaire* (1788; *Travels of Anacharsis the Younger in Greece During the Middle of the Fourth Century Before the Christian Era*), a rambling account of a young Scythian's journey through Greece. This well-documented introduction to Hellenic culture rekindled interest in Greece and was read by many generations of French schoolchildren. Barthélemy was elected to the Académie Française in 1789.

Barthelme \'bärt-əl-me\, Donald (b. April 7, 1931, Philadelphia, Pa., U.S.—d. July 23, 1989, Houston, Texas) American short-story writer known for modernist "collages" that were marked by melancholy gaiety.

A one-time journalist, Barthelme was managing editor of *Location*, an art and literature review, and director, from 1961 to 1962, of the Contemporary Arts Museum in Houston, Texas. In 1964 he published his first collection of short stories, *Come Back, Dr. Caligari*. His first novel, *Snow White* (1967), initially was published in *The New Yorker*. Other collections of stories include *City Life* (1970), *Sadness* (1972), *Sixty Stories* (1981), and *Overnight to Many Distant Cities* (1983). He wrote three additional novels: *The Dead Father* (1975), *Paradise* (1986), and *The King* (1990).

Barthelme \'bärt-əl-me\, Frederick (b. Oct. 10, 1943, Houston, Texas, U.S.) American writer of short stories and novels featuring characters who are shaped by the impersonal suburban environments in which they live.

Brother of writer Donald Barthelme, Frederick attended Tulane University, the University of Houston, and Johns Hopkins University. *Rangoon*, a collection of his surreal short fiction, drawings, and photographs, was published in 1970. This was soon followed by his novel *War & War* (1971). With the short stories of *Moon Deluxe* (1983), written in the present tense and almost all in the first person, he attracted wide notice. The protagonist of his humorous novel *Second Marriage* (1984) is a man whose wife kicks him out of their home in order to make room for his first wife. His subsequent works include the short-story collection *Chroma* (1987) and the novels *Two Against One* (1988), *Natural Selection* (1990), and *Breakers* (1993).

Barthes \'bärt\, Roland (Gérard) (b. Nov. 12, 1915, Cherbourg, Fr.—d. March 26, 1980, Paris) French social and literary critic whose writings on semiotics, the formal study of symbols and signs pioneered by Ferdinand de Saussure, helped establish structuralism as one of the leading intellectual movements of the 20th century.

Barthes studied at the University of Paris. After working (1952–59) at the Centre National de la Recherche Scientifique, he was appointed to the École Pratique des Hautes Études. In 1976 he became the first person to hold the chair of literary semiology at the Collège de France.

His first book, *Le Degré zéro de l'écriture* (1953; *Writing Degree Zero*), examined the arbitrariness of the constructs of language. In subsequent books—including *Mythologies* (1957), *Essais critiques* (1964; *Critical Essays*), and *La Tour Eiffel* (1964; *The Eiffel Tower and Other Mythologies*)—he applied the same critical apparatus to the "mythologies" (*i.e.*, the hidden assumptions) behind popular cultural phenomena. His *Sur*

Racine (1963; *On Racine*) set off a literary furor in France, pitting Barthes against traditional academics who thought the "new criticism," viewing texts as a system of signs, was desecrating the classics. Even more radical was *S/Z* (1970), in which Barthes stressed the active role of the reader in constructing a narrative based on textual "cues."

By the 1970s Barthes' theories had become extremely influential not only in France but throughout Europe and in the United States. Barthes' last two, very personal books established his late-blooming reputation as a stylist and writer. He published an "antiautobiography," *Roland Barthes par Roland Barthes* (1975; *Roland Barthes by Roland Barthes*), and *Fragments d'un discours amoureux* (1977; *A Lover's Discourse*), an account of a painful love affair. Several posthumous collections of his writings have been published, including *A Barthes Reader* (1982) and *Incidents* (1987). The latter volume revealed Barthes's homosexuality, which he had not publicly acknowledged.

Bartleby the Scrivener \'bärt-əl-,be\ (*in full* Bartleby the Scrivener: A Story of Wall Street) Short story by Herman MELVILLE, published anonymously in 1853 in *Putnam's Monthly Magazine*. It was collected in his 1856 volume *The Piazza Tales*.

Melville wrote "Bartleby" at a time when his career seemed to be in ruins, and the story reflects his pessimism. The narrator, a successful Wall Street lawyer, hires a scrivener named Bartleby to copy legal documents. Though Bartleby is initially a hard worker, one day, when asked to proofread, he responds, "I would prefer not to." As time progresses, Bartleby increasingly "prefers not to" do anything asked of him. Eventually he dies of self-neglect, refusing offers of help, while jailed for vagrancy.

Barzaz-Breiz \'bär-,zäz-'bräz\ (*in full* Barzaz-Breiz: Chants populaires de la Bretagne; "Breton Bardic Poems: Popular Songs of Brittany") A collection of folk songs and ballads purported to be survivals from ancient Breton folklore. The collection was made, supposedly from the oral literature of Breton peasants, by Théodore Hersart de La Villemarqué and was published in 1839. It was later demonstrated that *Barzaz-Breiz* was not an anthology of Breton folk poetry but rather a mixture of old poems, chiefly love songs and ballads, that were rearranged by the editor or others; modern poems made to look medieval; and spurious poems about such romance figures as Merlin and Nominoë. Nevertheless, *Barzaz-Breiz* was extremely influential: the historical poems exalting the Bretons' traditional struggle against oppression revived Breton pride in their language and heritage; it also led to the reawakening of Breton writers and stimulated further study of Breton folklore.

Bashkirtseff \,bəsh-'kyer-tsəf\, Marie, *original name* Mariya Konstantinovna Bashkirtseva \-tsə-və\ (b. Jan. 12 [Jan. 24, New Style], 1859?, Gavrontsy, Poltava, Ukraine, Russian Empire—d. Oct. 19 [Oct. 31], 1884, Paris, Fr.) Russian émigré best known for her sensitive and candid autobiography in French, *Journal de Marie Bashkirtseff, avec un portrait*, 2 vol. (1887; *Journal of Marie Bashkirtseff*).

The daughter of Russian nobility, she spent a peripatetic childhood with her mother in Germany and on the Riviera until they settled in Paris. Her earliest artistic inclination, toward a singing career, was succeeded by an interest in art. She studied painting at the Robert-Fleury studio in Paris and exhibited in the 1880 Salon. Just before her 24th birthday, she died of tuberculosis. Her diary, begun when she was 12, offers a frank picture of her artistic and emotional development and a strikingly modern psychological self-portrait of a young, gifted mind in the process of growth.

Bashō \\,bäsh-'ō\\, *in full* Matsuo Bashō, *pseudonym of* Matsuo Munefusa \\'mät-sū-ō-'mū-nä-,fū-sä\\ (b. 1644, Ueno, Iga province, Japan—d. Nov. 28, 1694, Ōsaka) Considered the greatest of the Japanese haiku poets.

Interested in haiku from an early age, Bashō at first put his literary interests aside and entered the service of a local feudal lord. After his lord's death in 1666, however,

Detail of an India ink portrait by Morikawa Kyoroku
International Society for Educational Information, Inc.

Bashō abandoned his samurai (warrior) status to devote himself to poetry. Moving to the capital city of Edo (now Tokyo), he gradually acquired a reputation as a poet and critic. In 1679 he wrote his first verse in the "new style," in which he attempted to go beyond the stale dependence on form and ephemeral allusions to current gossip that had been characteristic of haiku. Following the Zen philosophy he studied, Bashō attempted to compress the meaning of the world into the simple pattern of his poetry, disclosing hidden hopes in small things and showing the interdependence of all objects.

In 1684 Bashō made the first of many journeys that figure so importantly in his work. *Oku no hosomichi* (1694; THE NARROW ROAD TO THE DEEP NORTH), describing his visit to northern Japan, is one of the loveliest works of Japanese literature. On his travels Bashō also met local poets and competed with them in composing the linked verse (*renga*), an art in which he so excelled that some critics believe his *renga* were his finest work.

Living a life that was in true accord with the gentle spirit of his poetry, Bashō maintained an austere, simple hermitage. On occasion he withdrew from society altogether, retiring to Fukagawa, site of his Bashō-an ("Cottage of the Plantain Tree"), a simple hut from which the poet derived his pen name.

Basile \\bä-'sē-lä\\, Giambattista (b. *c.* 1575, Naples [Italy]—d. Feb. 23, 1632, Giugliano, Campania) Neapolitan soldier, public official, poet, and writer. His short-story collection *Lo cunto de li cunti* was one of the earliest such collections based on folktales and served as an important source both for later fairy-tale writers, such as Charles Perrault in France and the Brothers Grimm in Germany, and for the Italian commedia dell'arte dramatist Carlo Gozzi.

Basile was a soldier as a young man and began a career in government after moving to Naples in 1608. He later was part of the Mantuan court of Ferdinando Gonzaga, and then moved on to become governor, successively, of several small Italian states.

Basile was most at home in Naples, and during his career he collected fairy tales and folktales, setting them down in a lively Neapolitan style. *Lo cunto de li cunti* (1634; "The Story of Stories"; *The Pentamerone*) was published posthumously under the anagrammatic pseudonym Gian Alesio Abbattutis and referred to by its first editor as *Il pentamerone* because of the similarity of its framework to that of Boccaccio's *Decameron*.

In *Lo cunto de li cunti*, a prince and his wife are entertained for five days by 10 women who tell them 50 stories, among which are the familiar tales of Puss in Boots, Rapunzel, Cinderella, and Beauty and the Beast.

Basile also wrote Italian and Spanish verse. *Le muse napolitane* (1635) was a series of satirical verse dialogues on Neapolitan mores.

basilisk \\'bas-ə-lisk, 'baz-\\ [Greek *basilískos*, literally, little king, diminutive of *basileús* king; so called traditionally from a white spot on its head likened to a crown] A legendary reptile that is hatched from the egg of a seven-year-old cock and that has a fatal breath and glance. *Compare* COCKATRICE.

basis \\'bā-sis\\ *plural* bases \\-,sēz\\ [Greek *básis* metrical unit, measured movement, literally, the act of stepping, step] **1.** A step in a march or dance; the lifting and lowering of the foot, or arsis plus thesis. **2.** Two syllables or the first foot in some ancient verse that serve to introduce the line or stanza and often admit more variation from the norm of the line than appears in subsequent feet.

Bassani \\bäs-'sä-nē\\, Giorgio (b. March 4, 1916, Bologna, Italy) Italian author and editor noted for his novels and stories examining individual lives played out against the background of modern history.

The collection *Cinque storie ferraresi* (1956; U.K. title, *Prospect of Ferrara*; U.S. title, *Five Stories of Ferrara*; reissued as *Dentro le mura*, 1973; "Inside the Wall"), in which five novellas describe the growth of fascism and anti-Semitism, brought Bassani his first commercial success. The Ferrara setting recurs in two novels, *Il giardino dei Finzi-Contini* (1962; *The Garden of the Finzi-Continis*) and *L'airone* (1968; *The Heron*). He also wrote *L'odore del fieno* (1972; *The Smell of Hay*) and several collections of poetry, including *Rolls Royce and Other Poems* (1982), which contains selections in English and Italian from earlier collections.

Bataille \\bȧ-'täy\\, Georges (b. Sept. 10, 1897, Billom, Fr.—d. July 9, 1962, Paris) French librarian and writer whose essays, novels, and poetry express his fascination with eroticism, mysticism, and the irrational.

After training as an archivist, he worked as a librarian and medieval specialist at the Bibliothèque Nationale in Paris and became keeper of the Orléans library. He also edited scholarly journals and in 1946 founded the influential literary review *Critique*.

His first novel, on sexual excess, was published under a pseudonym, Lord Auch; it appeared in 1928 as *Histoire de l'oeil* (*The Story of the Eye*). As Pierre Angélique, another pseudonym, he wrote *Madame Edwarda* (1937). *Le Coupable* (1944; "The Guilty One") was the first major literary work published under his own name. *La Littérature et le mal* (1957; *Literature and Evil*) and *L'Érotisme* (1957; *Eroticism*) followed. A novel, *Ma Mère* (*My Mother*), was published in 1966.

Bataille \\bȧ-'täy\\, Henry, *in full* Félix-Henry Bataille (b. April 4, 1872, Nîmes, Fr.—d. March 2, 1922, Rueil-Malmaison) French dramatist whose luxuriant plays of passionate love and stifling social conventions were extremely popular at the beginning of the 20th century.

After several false starts Bataille's successful career began with *L'Enchantement* (1900), followed by such works as *Maman Colibri* (1904) and *La Femme nue* (1908; "The Nude Woman"), considered by many his best play. Although his art evolved toward the theater of ideas and social drama, as in *La Chair humaine* (1922; "Human Flesh"), his later works were less successful. The combination of exaggerated language and social messages soon dated his plays.

Bate \\'bāt\\, W. Jackson, *in full* Walter Jackson Bate (b. May 23, 1918, Mankato, Minn., U.S.) American author and literary biographer known for his studies of the English writers John Keats and Samuel Johnson.

Educated at Harvard University, Bate taught history and literature there from 1946. In 1945 the Modern Language Association published Bate's *Stylistic Development of Keats*. His *John Keats* (1963) was awarded the Pulitzer Prize for biography in 1964. *Samuel Johnson* (1977) won the acclaim of scholars and critics and was awarded the 1978 Pulitzer Prize and the National Book Award. Bate's other works include *From Classic to Romantic* (1946), *The Achievement of Samuel Johnson* (1955), and *Coleridge* (1968).

Bates \'bāts\, H.E., *in full* Herbert Ernest (b. May 16, 1905, Rushden, Northamptonshire, Eng.—d. Jan. 29, 1974, Canterbury, Kent) English novelist and short-story writer of high reputation and wide popularity.

Bates sharpened his skill as a reporter while a provincial journalist. He became known as a writer about the countryside and the life of the agricultural laborer with *The Poacher* (1935), *A House of Women* (1936), *My Uncle Silas* (1940), and *The Beauty of the Dead and Other Stories* (1941).

Commissioned as a writer for the Royal Air Force in 1941, as "Flying Officer X" Bates gained great popularity with *The Greatest People in the World* (1942) and *How Sleep the Brave* (1943), collections of stories that convey the feel of flying in wartime. Under his own name he wrote *Fair Stood the Wind for France* (1944), about a British bomber crew forced down in occupied France, and *The Purple Plain* (1946) and *The Jacaranda Tree* (1948), both set in Burma during the Japanese invasion. His later fiction includes *The Nature of Love* (1954), *A Moment in Time* (1964), *The Triple Echo* (1970), and the short-story collection *Colonel Julian* (1955). His autobiographical *The Vanished World* (1969) and *The Blossoming World* (1971) are also notable.

Bates \'bāts\, Katharine Lee (b. Aug. 12, 1859, Falmouth, Mass., U.S.—d. March 28, 1929, Wellesley, Mass.) Author and educator who wrote the text of the national hymn "America the Beautiful." Bates was educated at Wellesley College, Wellesley, Mass., where she taught from 1885 to 1925. Among her many works are *The College Beautiful and Other Poems* (1887), *English Religious Drama* (1893), and *The Pilgrim Ship* (1926). Her *America the Beautiful and Other Poems* was published in 1911.

bathos \'bā-thäs, -thōs\ [Greek *bāthos* depth] The unsuccessful, and therefore ludicrous, attempt to portray pathos in art, *i.e.*, to evoke pity, sympathy, or sorrow. The term was first used in this sense by Alexander Pope in his treatise *Peri Bathous; or, The Art of Sinking in Poetry* (1728). Bathos may result from an inappropriately dignified treatment of the commonplace, the use of elevated language and imagery to describe trivial subject matter, or greatly exaggerated pathos (emotion provoked by genuine suffering). It can also be seen as an unintentional anticlimax.

Bathsheba \bath-'shē-bə, 'bath-shib-ə\ or **Bethsabee** \beth-'sā-bē-ē\ Old Testament figure, the wife of Uriah the Hittite and later of King David, and by the latter mother of King Solomon. She was a beautiful woman and was seduced by David. When she became pregnant, David had Uriah killed and married her. The child conceived during their affair died, but Bathsheba later gave birth to Solomon.

Batsányi \'bòt-,shän-yē\, János (b. May 9, 1763, Tapolca, Hung.—d. May 12, 1845, Linz, Austria) Hungary's leading political poet during the French Revolutionary and Napoleonic periods in Europe.

Batsányi became the editor of *Magyar Museum* and emerged as an eloquent advocate of social progress and Enlightenment ideals in Hungary. He wrote political poetry as well as lyric poems, among which are many fine elegies. He was an ardent supporter of the French Revolution, an event that inspired his most famous political poem, *A franciaországi változásokra* (1789; "On the Changes in France"). After being imprisoned in Hungary for a year, he moved in 1796 to Vienna, where he married the Austrian poet Gabriella Baumberg. He supported Napoleon and finally settled in Paris, where he was seized by the Austrians after Napoleon's fall. He was thenceforth interned in the Austrian city of Linz for the remaining 30 years of his life and played little further role in Hungarian literature.

Batter My Heart Sonnet by John DONNE, one of the 19 "Holy Sonnets," or "Divine Meditations," originally published in 1633 in the first edition of *Songs and Sonnets*. Written in direct address to God and employing violent and sexual imagery, it is one of Donne's most dramatic devotional lyrics. The poet asks for help to overcome his religious ambivalence and to wholly accept divine grace.

Battle of Brunanburh, The \'brü-nən-bərg\, Brunanburh *also spelled* Brunnanburh. Old English poem of 73 lines included in several manuscripts of the Anglo-Saxon Chronicle under the year 937. It relates the victory of the Saxon king Athelstan over the allied Norse, Scots, and Strathclyde Briton invaders under the leadership of Olaf Guthfrithson, king of Dublin and claimant to the throne of York. The poem is basically the victors' bitter taunt of the defeated. It counts the dead kings and earls on the battlefield and pictures the Norsemen slinking home while their dead sons are being devoured by ravens and wolves.

Battle of Maldon, The \'mȯl-dən, 'mäl-\ Old English heroic poem describing a historical skirmish between East Saxons and Viking (mainly Norwegian) raiders in 991. It is a 325-line fragment, its beginning and ending both lost. The poem is remarkable for its vivid, dramatic combat scenes and for its expression of the Germanic ethos of loyalty to a leader. As it survives, the work opens with the war parties aligned on either side of a stream (the present River Blackwater near Maldon, Essex). When the Vikings cannot advance because of their poor position, the English commander Earl Byrhtnoth recklessly allows them safe conduct across the stream, and the battle follows. In spite of Byrhtnoth's supreme feats of courage, he is finally slain. In panic some of the English warriors desert. The names of the deserters are carefully recorded in the poem along with the names and genealogies of the loyal retainers who stand fast to avenge Byrhtnoth's death.

battle piece A work (such as a painting, musical composition, or poem) concerned with or descriptive of a battle.

Batyushkov or **Batiushkov** \'bä-t'ùsh-kəf\, Konstantin Nikolayevich (b. May 18 [May 29, New Style], 1787, Vologda, Russia—d. July 7 [July 19], 1855, Vologda) Russian elegiac poet noted for his sensual and melodious verses.

Batyushkov studied the classics and learned French and Italian, languages that were to have an important influence on his style of writing. He served in the army during the campaigns of 1813–14 against Napoleon. Afterward, he became a prominent member of the literary group known as the Arzamas society.

Batyushkov's literary output was not large—a few elegies and lyrics and some free translations of amorous epigrams from the Greek—but his verses are unique in their Italianate quality, producing a musical sweetness. His collected works appeared in 1817, and shortly afterward he ceased writing.

Baucis *see* PHILEMON AND BAUCIS.

Baudelaire \bōd-'ler\, Charles(-Pierre) (b. April 9, 1821, Paris, Fr.—d. Aug. 31, 1867, Paris) One of the greatest French poets of the 19th century.

Baudelaire was sent away to school. He passed his *baccalauréat* examinations in 1839 and announced his intention to live by writing. He enrolled as a law student, remaining at the École de Droit, nominally at least, until 1840. It was probably at this time that he became addicted to opium and hashish and contracted syphilis, from which he was to die.

On attaining his majority in April 1842, he spent his money recklessly on fine clothes and on rich furnishings. By 1844 Baudelaire had formed an association with Jeanne Duval, a woman of mixed race who inspired his first cycle of love poems, "Black Venus," which are among the finest erotic poems in the French language.

Bibliothèque Nationale, Paris

During those early years of leisure and freedom from anxiety, Baudelaire composed many—perhaps most—of the poems that were to form part of LES FLEURS DU MAL (*The Flowers of Evil*), his sole collection.

When within two years he had run through half his inheritance, the remainder was placed in a trust, from which he received a monthly income. He remained heavily in debt and from this point on was to know only straitened means and eventually real poverty.

He became a professional writer. His first published works were reviews of the Salon shows of 1845 and 1846, and some of his poems were printed in avant-garde journals. In 1847 he published his only novel, the autobiographical *La Fanfarlo*. Baudelaire's mature period began with his discovery early in 1852 of the writings of Edgar Allan Poe. From 1852 to 1865 he was occupied in translating Poe and in writing critical articles on him. The translations are, at their best, classics of French prose.

In 1852 Baudelaire took up with Apollonie-Aglaé Sabatier, a well-known beauty who was the inspiration of his cycle of the "White Venus." In 1854 he renewed an association with the actress Marie Daubrun, who inspired the cycle of the "Green-Eyed Venus." In many of the poems in these two cycles he reaches the highest peak of his art.

In June 1857 *Les Fleurs du mal* was published. All those involved—author, publisher, and printer—were prosecuted, found guilty of obscenity and blasphemy, and fined, and for several generations *Les Fleurs du mal* remained a byword for depravity, morbidity, and obscenity.

The remaining years of Baudelaire's life were darkened by a growing sense of failure, disillusionment, and despair. Although some of his finest works were written in these years, few were published in book form. In 1862 Baudelaire's financial difficulties became desperate. To escape his creditors, he went on a lecture tour in Belgium in 1864. It proved a failure. In February 1866, while he was still in Belgium, at Namur, Baudelaire became seriously ill. Taken back to Paris, he died there in his mother's arms in August 1867. He died unrecognized, with many of his writings still unpublished and those that had been published out of print. By the 20th century he had become widely recognized as one of the great French poets of the 19th century.

Baudissin \'baů-dis-ən\, Wolf Heinrich (Friedrich Karl), Count (Graf) von (b. Jan. 30, 1789, Copenhagen, Den.—d. April 4, 1878, Dresden, Ger.)   Man of letters who with Ludwig Tieck's daughter Dorothea was responsible for many translations of William Shakespeare and thus contributed to the development of German Romanticism.

Baudissin served in the diplomatic corps and traveled in Italy, France, and Greece. In 1827 he settled in Dresden, where he spent the rest of his life. The works he translated include those of Shakespeare and other Elizabethan dramatists (*Ben Jonson und seine Schule*, 2 vol., 1836; "Ben Jonson and His School"), Molière, several Italian plays, and the Middle High German epic *Iwein*.

Bauernfeld \'baů-ərn-,felt\, Eduard von (b. Jan. 13, 1802, Vienna [Austria]—d. Aug. 9, 1890, Vienna)   Dramatist who dominated the Vienna Burgtheater for 50 years with his politically oriented drawing room comedies.

Bauernfeld studied at the University of Vienna before turning to the theater. His comedies offer witty portrayals of Viennese society; cleverly plotted and elegant in language, they also deal with the acute social and political questions of the day. His most successful works include *Das Liebes-Protokoll* (1834; "The Love-Protocol"), *Die Bekenntnisse* (1834; "The Confession"), *Bürgerlich und romantisch* (1835; "Bourgeois and Romantic"), *Grossjährig* (1846; "Adult"), *Krisen* (1852; "Crises"), and *Aus der Gesellschaft* (1867; "From Society").

Baum \'bäm, 'bȯm\, L. Frank, *in full* Lyman (b. May 15, 1856, Chittenango, N.Y., U.S.—d. May 6, 1919, Hollywood, Calif.)   American writer known for his series of books for children about the imaginary Land of OZ.

Baum began his career as a journalist. His first book, *Father Goose* (1899), was a commercial success, and he followed it the next year with the even more popular *Wonderful Wizard of Oz*. Baum wrote 13 more Oz books, and the series was continued by another author after his death.

Baum \'bäm, 'bȯm\, Vicki, *original name* Hedwig Baum (b. Jan. 24, 1888, Vienna, Austria-Hungary [now in Austria]—d. Aug. 29, 1960, Hollywood, Calif., U.S.)   Novelist whose *Menschen im Hotel* (1929; "People at the Hotel"; *Grand Hotel*) became a best-seller and was adapted as an Academy Award-winning film in 1932.

By the time that Baum took a job at the magazine *Berliner Illustrierte Zeitung*, she had already finished *Menschen im Hotel*, and it first appeared serially in the magazine. It achieved immediate success in Germany. She rewrote it as a play, and it was a great success in translation as *Grand Hotel* on Broadway. She moved to the United States, becoming a screenwriter in Hollywood in 1932, and in 1938 she became an American citizen.

Her later novels include *Men Never Know* (1935), *Shanghai '37* (1939), *Grand Opera* (1942), *Hotel Berlin '43* (1944), *Mortgage on Life* (1946), *Danger from Deer* (1951), *The Mustard Seed* (1953), *Written on Water* (1956), and *Theme for Ballet* (1958).

Baumbach \'baům-,bäk\, Rudolf (b. Sept. 28, 1840, Kranichfeld, Thuringia [Germany]—d. Sept. 21, 1905, Meiningen, Ger.)   German writer of popular student drinking songs and of narrative verse.

Baumbach was a poet of the vagabond school and wrote many excellent drinking songs in imitation of J. Viktor von Scheffel, such as "Die Lindenwirtin" ("The Linden Hostess"), which endeared him to the German student world. His real strength, however, lay in narrative verse, especially concerning the scenery and life of his native Thuringia. Among his best-known works are *Frau Holde* (1880), *Spielmannslieder* (1882; "Songs of a Troubadour"), and *Von der Landstrasse* (1882; "On the Highway").

Baxter \'bak-stər\, James Keir (b. June 29, 1926, Dunedin, N.Z.—d. Oct. 22, 1972, Auckland)   Poet who was a central figure among New Zealand writers after World War II.

Educated in New Zealand and England, Baxter published his first book of verse, *Beyond the Palisade* (1944), when he was just 18. It was followed by *Blow, Wind of Fruitfulness* (1948). *Recent Trends in New Zealand Poetry* (1951), Baxter's first critical work, offers judgments that reveal a maturity beyond his years. His later verse collections, including *The Fallen House* (1953), the satirical *Iron Breadboard* (1957), *In Fires of No Return* (1958), and *Pig Island Letters* (1966), use Christian and classical mythology to examine the place of religion in society.

Baylebridge \'bāl-ˌbrij\, William, *pseudonym of* Charles William Blocksidge \'blăk-ˌsij\ (b. Dec. 12, 1883, Brisbane, Queen., Australia—d. May 7, 1942, Sydney)   Poet and short-story writer considered a leading Australian author in his day.

Baylebridge was educated in Brisbane, then at the age of 25 went to England, where he published his first booklet of verse, *Songs o' the South* (1908). He also traveled to France and Egypt, returning to Australia in 1919 and publishing more than 20 books and booklets of verse in private, limited editions.

His work leans heavily on Elizabethan and German models. The best-known volumes of his verse are *Love Redeemed* (1934) and *This Vital Flesh* (1939); some excellent short stories about World War I were collected in his *Anzac Muster* (1921).

Bazán   *see* PARDO BAZÁN.

Bazarov, Yevgeny \yiv-ˈgʸe-nʸē-bə-ˈzà-rəf, *Angl* yev-ˈgen-ē-bə-ˈzär-ôf\   Fictional character, a young physician whose actions and philosophy are the focus of the novel FATHERS AND SONS by Ivan Turgenev. Bazarov is rude, sarcastic, and strident in his profession of faith in nothing but science. He calls himself a nihilist and rejects all traditional institutions and forms of authority.

Bazin \bả-ˈzanⁿ\, Hervé, *pseudonym of* Jean-Pierre-Marie Hervé-Bazin \er-ˌvå-bả-ˈzanⁿ\ (b. April 17, 1911, Angers, Fr.)   Poet, novelist, and short-story writer who revitalized naturalism in postwar French fiction. (He was the great-nephew of the Roman Catholic novelist by the same name.)

After solid academic training, years of family conflict, and financial and professional failure, Bazin, a rebel and bohemian approaching middle age, finally achieved literary fame in 1948 with the autobiographical *Vipère au poing* (*Viper in the Fist*). His rebellious nature is also evident in *La Tête contre les murs* (1949; *Head Against the Wall*), a novel about penal institutions and the judicial system that supports them, and in a second autobiographical novel, *La Mort du petit cheval* (1950; "The Death of a Small Horse"). Having exorcised his youthful demons, Bazin became something of a moralist. He discovered paternal love (*Au nom du fils*, 1960; *In the Name of the Son*), spiritual fortitude (*Lève-toi et marche*, 1952; *Constance*), and conjugal responsibility (*Le Matrimoine*, 1967). Later works include the novels *Madam Ex* (1975; "Madam X") and *Un Feu devore un autre feu* (1978; "A Fire Devours Another Fire") and the books of verse *Traits* (1976) and *Ce que je crois* (1977; "What I Believe").

Bazin \bả-ˈzanⁿ\, René(-François-Nicolas-Marie) (b. Dec. 26, 1853, Angers, Fr.—d. July 20, 1932, Paris)   Influential French novelist of provincial life who was strongly traditionalist in outlook and was considered among the pantheon of French Roman Catholic writers of his day.

Bazin taught at the Catholic University at Angers. His early works presented an extremely idealistic view of peasant life, but after travels in Spain and Italy, begun in 1893, his views were altered. *La Terre qui meurt* (1899; "The Dying Earth") deals poignantly with the theme of emigration. *Les Oberlé* (1901) depicts the Germanization of Alsace-Lorraine through the divided loyalties within the Oberlé family. *Donatienne* (1903) is

an account of the fortunes of a young Breton couple. *Le Blé qui lève* (1907; "The Rising Wheat") portrays the corrupting influence of trade unionism on woodcutters.

Beach \'bēch\, Sylvia (b. March 14, 1887, Baltimore, Md., U.S.—d. Oct. 5, 1962, Paris, Fr.)   Bookshop operator who became important in the literary life of Paris, particularly in the 1920s, when her shop was a gathering place for expatriate writers.

The daughter of a Presbyterian minister, Beach developed at 14 a lifelong love of France when her father held a pastorate in Paris among American students. In 1919 she opened her shop, Shakespeare and Company, which included a lending library, on the Left Bank in Paris. Perhaps her most heroic service to literature was her publication in 1922 of James Joyce's *Ulysses* after it had been turned down by several other publishers because of its explicit sexual content. Her shop was closed in 1941, not to reopen, and she was interned for seven months by the occupying Germans. She wrote about her shop and its literary life in *Shakespeare and Company* (1959).

Beach of Falesá, The \ˌfä-lä-ˈsä\   Long story by Robert Louis STEVENSON, first published as "Uma" in 1892 and collected in *Island Nights' Entertainments* (1893). An adventure romance fused with realism, it depicts a man's struggle to maintain his decency in the face of uncivilized hostility.

John Wiltshire, the story's narrator and protagonist, is a white trader on the exotic island of Falesá in the South Seas. He is befriended by Case, a fellow trader who persuades him to marry the native Uma. When Wiltshire does so, the natives ostracize the couple. Gradually Wiltshire learns that Case has subdued the natives by manipulating their fears of the supernatural. Wiltshire exposes Case as a fraud and kills him in self-defense.

Bear, The   Novelette by William FAULKNER, early versions of which first appeared as "Lion" in *Harper's Magazine* of December 1935 and as "The Bear" in *Saturday Evening Post* in 1942, before it was published as one of the chapters in the novel GO DOWN, MOSES. Critical interpretations of the story vary depending upon whether it is judged as an independent work or as a chapter in the larger novel.

"The Bear," set in the late 19th century, is a hunting story told from the perspective of Isaac ("Ike") McCaslin, a young man from an old family in Yoknapatawpha county. In the first three parts of the novelette, Ike trains under the expert tracker Sam Fathers and hunts down the legendary bear Old Ben. The fourth part (omitted in some publications) comprises a long, convoluted dialogue between Ike and his cousin Carothers ("Cass") Edmonds, in which Ike repudiates his inheritance after he discovers incest and miscegenation in the family history. The final part concerns Ike's affinity for nature and his dismay at its gradual destruction.

bearwalker \'bar-ˌwôk-ər\   A powerful and malevolent person believed able to assume the shape of a bear or other animal. *Compare* WEREWOLF.

beast epic   A long verse narrative with climactic epic construction comprising beast tales, or stories of animals represented as acting with human feelings and motives. Although individual episodes may be drawn from fables, the beast epic differs from the fable not only in length but also in putting less emphasis on a moral. Instead it provides a satiric commentary on human society.

The earliest European beast epics were written in Latin, but vernacular epics in French, German, and Dutch existed in the late Middle Ages. Among the most famous are the 10th- and 11th-century cycles in which the hero is Reynard the Fox. The cycle includes the tale of the Fox and Chanticleer the Cock, the basis of "The Nun's Priest's Tale" in Geoffrey Chaucer's *The Canterbury Tales*.

beast fable   A prose or verse fable or short story that usually has a moral. In beast fables, animal characters are represented as acting with human feelings and motives. Among the best-known examples in Western literature are those attributed to the legendary Greek author Aesop. The best-known Asian collection of beast fables is the *Pañca-tantra* of India.

beast god   A deity represented wholly or partly in animal form, such as the Greek god Pan.

Beast in the Jungle, The   Short story by Henry JAMES that first appeared in *The Better Sort* (1903). Despite its sluggish pace, implausible dialogue, and excessively ornate style, it is a suspenseful story of despair, with powerful images of fire, ice, and hunting.

"The Beast in the Jungle" concerns John Marcher, a neurotic egoist obsessed with the lurking feeling that something incredible is to happen to him. This impending fate has a predatory quality, like "a crouching beast in the jungle." Consumed with anticipation and dread, Marcher is unable to reciprocate the love of his long-suffering companion, May Bartram. She comes to see his fate but is unable to make him understand it before she dies. While visiting her grave one year later, Marcher suddenly realizes that his terrible fate was precisely his inability to comprehend her love for him.

beast tale   A prose or verse narrative similar to the beast fable in that it portrays animal characters acting as humans, but unlike the fable in that it usually lacks a moral. Joel Chandler Harris' *Uncle Remus: His Songs and His Sayings* (1880) derived many episodes from beast tales carried to the United States by African slaves. *Animal Farm* (1945), an anti-utopian satire by George Orwell, is a modern adaptation of the beast tale.

beat \\'bēt\\   A metrical or rhythmic stress in poetry or music. The word can also refer to the overall rhythmic effect of these stresses.

Beat movement \\'bēt\\   American social and literary movement originating in the 1950s and centered in the bohemian artists' communities of San Francisco's North Beach, southern California's Venice West, and New York City's Greenwich Village. Its adherents, self-styled as "beat" (originally meaning "weary," but later also connoting a musical sense, a "beatific" spirituality, and other meanings) and derisively called "beatniks," expressed their alienation from conventional, or "square," society by adopting an almost uniform style of seedy dress, "cool"—detached, ironic—manners, and "hip" vocabulary borrowed from jazz musicians. Generally apolitical and indifferent to social problems, they advocated personal release, purification, and illumination through the heightened sensory awareness that might be induced by drugs, jazz, sex, or the disciplines of Zen Buddhism.

Beat poets—including Gregory CORSO, Lawrence FERLINGHETTI, Allen GINSBERG, Gary SNYDER, and Philip WHALEN—sought to liberate poetry from academic preciosity and bring it "back to the streets." Their verse was frequently chaotic and liberally sprinkled with obscenities but was sometimes, as in the case of Ginsberg's *Howl* (1956), ruggedly powerful and moving. Ginsberg and other major figures of the movement, such as the novelist Jack KEROUAC, advocated a type of free, unstructured composition in which the writer put down thoughts and feelings without plan or revision—to convey the immediacy of experience—an approach that led to the production of much undisciplined and incoherent verbiage on the part of their imitators. By about 1960, the Beat movement

had paved the way for acceptance of other unorthodox and previously ignored writers, such as the BLACK MOUNTAIN POETS and the novelist William BURROUGHS.

Beatrice \\,bā-ā-'trē-chā, *Angl* 'bē-ə-trəs\\   The woman to whom the great Italian poet Dante dedicated most of his poetry and almost all of his life, from his first sight of her at the age of nine ("from that time forward, Love quite governed my soul") through his glorification of her in *La divina commedia* (*The Divine Comedy*), completed 40 years later, to his death in 1321.

Beatrice is usually identified as Beatrice Portinari, the daughter of a noble Florentine family, who married Simone de' Bardi and died at the age of 24 on June 8, 1290. Dante first wrote of his relationship with her in *La vita nuova* (c. 1293; *The New Life*). But the supreme expression of his love for Beatrice is found in *La divina commedia*; there she acts as Dante's intercessor in the *Inferno*, his goal in traveling through *Purgatorio*, and his guide through *Paradiso*.

Beatrijs \\'bā-ə-,treis, *Angl* 'bā-ə-,tris, 'bē-\\   Lyrical narrative containing a noted medieval European Mary legend. The oldest extant *Beatrijs* manuscript dates from 1374, although it is thought to be taken from an earlier collection, *Dialogue miraculorum* (c. 1200) by Caesarius of Heisterbach. An anonymous text written in an East Flemish dialect, it is the simple courtly tale of a nun who flees from her convent to marry a man she has loved from childhood. After fathering two children, he deserts her; she is forced into a life of sin, but remorse eventually drives her back to the convent, where she discovers that she was not missed because the Virgin Mary had taken her place.

Beattie \\'bē-tē\\, Ann (b. Sept. 8, 1947, Washington, D.C., U.S.)   American writer of short stories and novels whose characters, having come of age in the 1960s, often have difficulties adjusting to the cultural values of later generations.

Beattie graduated from the American University in Washington, D.C., in 1969 and received a Master of Arts degree from the University of Connecticut in 1970. She had short stories published in *The New Yorker* and other literary magazines beginning in the early 1970s. Her first collection of stories, *Distortions*, and her first novel, *Chilly Scenes of Winter*, were both published in 1976.

Beattie's characters are usually passive, alienated people who cannot extricate themselves from unsatisfying careers and lives. In detached, unemotional prose Beattie chronicles their unfulfilling lives and catalogues their possessions and favorite songs. There is little examination of motivation, and historical background is usually absent.

Later collections of her stories include *Secrets and Surprises* (1978), *The Burning House* (1982), and *Where You'll Find Me and Other Stories* (1986). Novels include *Falling in Place* (1980) and *Picturing Will* (1989).

Beattie \\'bā-tē, *commonly* 'bē-\\, James (b. Nov. 5, 1735, Laurencekirk, Kincardine, Scot.—d. Aug. 18, 1803, Aberdeen)   Scottish poet and essayist, whose once-popular poem *The Minstrel* was one of the earliest works of the Romantic movement.

Beattie graduated from Marischal College, Aberdeen, and became professor of moral philosophy there. At the age of 25, he published *Original Poems and Translations* (1760), which already showed a Romantic attitude toward nature. He achieved fame with his *Essay on the Nature and Immutability of Truth, in Opposition to Sophistry and Scepticism* (1770), a vigorous defense of orthodoxy against the rationalism of David Hume. The next year he published the first part of *The Minstrel*, a poem in Spenserian stanza tracing the development of a poet's mind under the influence of nature. The second part was published in 1774. Although its setting is artificial and its moralizing tedious, the poem reflects the author's gentleness and sensitivity to natural beauty. To his generation it was a revelation, influencing Robert Burns, Sir Walter Scott, and Lord Byron.

Beauchemin \bōsh-e-'maⁿ\, Nérée (b. Feb. 20, 1850, Yamachiche, Que., Can.—d. June 29, 1931, Trois-Rivières, Que.) French-Canadian poet and physician, one of the leading regionalist poets of Quebec.

A traditionalist noted for his perfection of poetic form, Beauchemin drew on the religion and culture of Quebec and on a love of the Canadian landscape for his material. He published only two collections of poems, *Les Floraisons matutinales* (1897; "The Morning Efflorescence") and *Patrie intime* (1928; "Intimate Birthplace").

Beau Geste \'bō-'zhest\ Novel about the French Foreign Legion by Percival C. Wren, published in 1924.

The title character, whose given name is Michael, and his brothers, Digby and John, have joined the French Foreign Legion after being falsely accused of a crime. They meet many trials together in North Africa, facing a sadistic commanding officer and fierce Arab troops. Beau and Digby die honorably in battle.

Beaumarchais \bō-mår-'she, *Angl* ,bō-mär-'shä\, Pierre-Augustin Caron de (b. Jan. 24, 1732, Paris, Fr.—d. May 18, 1799, Paris) French author of two outstanding comedies of intrigue that still retain their freshness, *Le Barbier de Séville* (1775; THE BARBER OF SEVILLE) and *Le Mariage de Figaro* (1784; THE MARRIAGE OF FIGARO).

Although Beaumarchais did not invent the type character of the scheming valet (who appears in comedy as far back as Roman times), his Figaro, hero of both plays, became the highest expression of the type. The valet's resourcefulness and cunning were portrayed by Beaumarchais with a definite class-conscious sympathy.

Beaumarchais's life rivals his work as a drama of controversy, adventure, and intrigue. The son of a watchmaker, he invented an escapement mechanism, and the question of its patent led to the first of many legal actions. For his defense in these suits he wrote a series of brilliant polemics (*Mémoires*) that established his reputation, though he was only partly successful at law. His other activities included being sent on secret royal missions to England and elsewhere by both Louis XV and Louis XVI, buying arms for the American revolutionaries, and bringing out the first complete edition of the works of Voltaire.

Beaumont \'bō-mənt, -mänt, *perhaps originally* 'bē-mənt *or* 'bā-\, Francis (b. *c.* 1585, Grace-Dieu, Leicestershire, Eng.—d. March 6, 1616, London) English Jacobean poet and playwright who collaborated with John FLETCHER on comedies and tragedies between about 1606 and 1613.

Beaumont entered Broadgates Hall (later Pembroke College), Oxford, in 1597. He left the university without a degree. In November 1600, he entered London's Inner Temple, though he had little enthusiasm for legal studies.

In 1602 the poem *Salmacis and Hermaphroditus*, generally attributed to Beaumont, was published. At the age of 23 he prefixed some verses to Ben Jonson's *Volpone* (1607) in honor of his "dear friend" the author. John Fletcher contributed verses to the same volume, and by about this time the two were collaborating on plays for the Children of the Queen's Revels. Their collaboration was to last for some seven years. In 1613 Beaumont married an heiress and retired from the theater.

As a playwright, Beaumont remains a shadowy figure whose contributions to drama are not as clear as Fletcher's. Of the 54 plays with which their names or the names of their other collaborators are associated, one or two were written by Beaumont alone and only 9 or 10 were written by Beaumont and Fletcher in collaboration. Beaumont's hand also probably appears in three other plays written together with Fletcher and Philip Massinger.

Beaumont's *The Knight of the Burning Pestle* parodies a then-popular kind of play—sprawling, episodic, with sentimental lovers and chivalric adventures. It opens with The Citizen and his Wife taking their places on the stage to watch "The London Merchant"—itself a satire on the work of a contemporary playwright, Thomas Dekker. Beaumont satirizes bourgeois naiveté about art by having Citizen and Wife interrupt, advise, and insist that their apprentice should take a leading part.

In the three masterpieces of the Beaumont and Fletcher collaboration—*The Maides Tragedy*, PHILASTER, and *A King and No King*—Beaumont is assumed to have had the controlling hand, since the plays manifest a firmer structure than Fletcher's single or collaborative efforts. Attempts to disentangle the various shares of Beaumont and Fletcher in any given work are complicated by the fact that Beaumont sometimes revised scenes by Fletcher, and Fletcher edited some of Beaumont's work.

Beaumont \'bō-mənt, -mänt, *perhaps originally* 'bē-mənt *or* 'bā-\, Sir John, 1st Baronet (b. 1583, Grace-Dieu?, Leicestershire, Eng.—d. April 1627, London?) English poet who cultivated literary "order" and precision, together with natural simplicity of style. He wrote a drama for James I, *The Theatre of Apollo* (1625); a poem about the Battle of Bosworth Field (fought in 1485) and other poems to James I and Charles I; and elegies on the poet's friends and relatives, published posthumously. Beaumont was an elder brother of the dramatist Francis Beaumont.

Beautiful and Damned, The Novel by F. Scott FITZGERALD, published in 1922. Fitzgerald's second novel, it concerns a handsome young married couple who choose to wait for an expected inheritance rather than involve themselves in productive, meaningful lives.

Anthony Patch pursues and wins the beautiful and sought-after Gloria Gilbert. He decides that they can survive on his limited income until he comes into a large fortune he stands to inherit from his grandfather. Through the ensuing years, their lives deteriorate into mindless alcoholic ennui. Anthony's grandfather makes a surprise appearance at one of their wild parties and, in disgust, disinherits him. After his grandfather's death, Anthony institutes a lawsuit that takes years to settle. Although the Patches eventually win, by then Anthony's spirit is broken, he and Gloria have grown apart, and they care about nothing.

Beauty and the Beast A fairy tale, first collected in Gianfrancesco Straparòla's *Le piacevoli notti* (1550–53; *The Nights of Straparola*) and made popular by Charles Perrault's collection *Contes de ma mère l'oye* (1697; *Tales of Mother Goose*). It is the story of a beautiful young woman whose love for an enchanted beast frees him from an evil spell and allows him to turn back into a handsome prince.

Beauvoir \bō-'vwär\, Simone de, *in full* Simone Lucie-Ernestine-Marie-Bertrand de Beauvoir (b. Jan. 9, 1908, Paris, Fr.—d. April 14, 1986, Paris) French writer and feminist known primarily for her treatise *Le Deuxième Sexe*, 2 vol. (1949; *The Second Sex*), a scholarly and passionate plea for the abolition of what she called the myth of the "eternal feminine." It became a classic of feminist literature during the 1960s.

Schooled in private institutions, de Beauvoir attended the Sorbonne, where, in 1929, she met Jean-Paul SARTRE, beginning a lifelong association with him. She taught at a number of schools (1931–43) before turning to writing for her livelihood. In 1945 she and Sartre founded and began editing *Les Temps modernes*, a monthly review.

Her novels expound the major existential themes, demonstrating her conception of the writer's commitment to the times. *L'Invitée* (1943; *She Came To Stay*) describes the subtle destruction of the relationship of a couple brought about by a young girl's prolonged stay in their home. Of

Archive Photos

her other works of fiction, perhaps the best known is *Les Mandarins* (1954; THE MANDARINS), for which she won the Prix Goncourt. She also wrote four books of philosophy, including *Pour une morale de l'ambiguité* (1947; *The Ethics of Ambiguity*); travel books on China (*La Longue Marche: Essai sur la Chine* [1957]; *The Long March*) and the United States (*L'Amérique au jour de jour* [1948]; *America Day by Day*); and a number of essays.

Several volumes of her work are devoted to autobiography. These include *Mémoires d'une jeune fille rangée* (1958; MEMOIRS OF A DUTIFUL DAUGHTER), *La Force de l'âge* (1960; *The Prime of Life*), *La Force des choses* (1963; *Force of Circumstance*), and *Tout compte fait* (1972; *All Said and Done*). This body of work, beyond its personal interest, constitutes a clear and telling portrait of French intellectual life from the 1930s to the 1970s.

De Beauvoir was concerned with the issue of aging, which she addressed in *Une Mort très douce* (1964; *A Very Easy Death*), on her mother's death in a hospital, and in *La Vieillesse* (1970; *Old Age*), a bitter reflection on society's indifference to the elderly. In 1981 she wrote *La Cérémonie des adieux* (*Adieux: A Farewell to Sartre*), a painful account of Sartre's last years.

Beaux' Stratagem, The   Five-act comedy by George FARQUHAR, produced and published in 1707. Farquhar finished the play on his deathbed and died on the night of its third performance.

The story concerns Archer and Aimwell, two penniless antic rakes from London who decide that one of them must wed a wealthy lady. Aimwell therefore courts Dorinda, the daughter of wealthy Lady Bountiful; meanwhile Archer, who is posing as Aimwell's servant, and Lady Bountiful's daughter-in-law, Mrs. Sullen, fall in love. In the course of events, Aimwell and Archer manage to foil robbers, thereby becoming heroes. Eventually Aimwell inherits the family estate, Mrs. Sullen separates from her brutish drunkard of a husband, and the play ends happily.

In addition to its lively comedy, *The Beaux' Stratagem* presents a bold argument for divorce, which is voiced by Mrs. Sullen. Lady Bountiful's name became a byword for a rich, generous, and somewhat credulous philanthropist.

Beaver \'bē-vər\, Bruce (Victor) (b. Feb. 14, 1928, Manly, N.S.W., Australia)   Australian poet, novelist, and journalist noted for his experimental forms and courageous self-examination, both of which made him one of the major forces in Australian poetry during the 1960s and '70s.

At the age of 17 Beaver underwent the first of several periods of psychiatric treatment for manic depression. He worked at a variety of jobs before becoming a full-time freelance writer in 1964. While contributing reviews to Australian and New Zealand periodicals, he wrote the novels *The Hot Spring* (1965) and *You Can't Come Back* (1966).

In 1966, convinced that he would soon be insane, Beaver hastily wrote his first major collection of poems, *Letters to Live*

Poets (1969). It was, he said, an attempt at a "spiritual, intellectual, and emotional autobiography." His later collections included *Lauds and Plaints* (1974), *Odes and Days* (1975), *Death's Directives* (1978), and *As It Was* (1979).

Bebey \be-'bā\, Francis (b. July 15, 1929, Douala, Cameroon)   Cameroonian writer, guitarist, and composer of international reputation.

Trained at the Sorbonne and New York University, Bebey first became known as a musician. By 1967 he had made several recordings and had performed in New York City and Paris as well as in Africa. His first novel, *Le Fils d'Agatha Moudio* (1967; *Agatha Moudio's Son*), won the Grand Prix Littéraire de l'Afrique Noire, and in 1968 *Embarras & Cie: Nouvelles et poèmes* (nine short stories and poems) was published. His later works include *La Poupée Ashanti* (1973; *The Ashanti Doll*) and *Le Roi Albert d'Effidi* (1974; *King Albert*).

Bebey claimed that his wide experience as a radio broadcaster affected the style of his stories, which he directed toward hearers rather than readers. He also wrote a book on broadcasting in Africa and two books on African music.

Becher \'bek-ər\, Johannes Robert (b. May 22, 1891, Munich, Ger.—d. Oct. 11, 1958, Berlin)   Poet and critic, editor, and government official who was an important advocate of revolutionary social reform in Germany during the 1920s.

Becher studied medicine, literature, and philosophy and, in 1918, joined the German Communist Party. He was already an established commentator on the social and artistic scene and a leader of the movement to transform German society through a revolution of the proletariat. Involved in the Expressionist school that dominated German writing in the period 1910–20, he wrote romantic, emotionally complex poetry that mirrored both his personal turmoil and his visions of a new social order.

Though elected to the German Reichstag in 1933, Becher was forced into exile with the advent of Nazi power and went to Moscow, where he edited a German-language newspaper (1935–45). Returning to Germany in 1945, he was made president of the Association for the Democratic Rebirth of Germany. In 1954 he became East German minister of culture. Becher's diaries in the decade 1945–55 give intimate insights into his artistic and political conflicts.

Becket \'bek-it\, Saint Thomas, *also called* Thomas à Becket *or* Thomas of London (b. *c.* 1118, Cheapside, London, Eng.—d. Dec. 29, 1170, Canterbury, Kent)   Chancellor of England from 1155 to 1162 and archbishop of Canterbury from 1162 to 1170 during the reign of King Henry II. His long quarrel with Henry ended with Becket's murder in Canterbury cathedral.

His relationship with Henry II and his murder have featured in or been the subject of a number of works of literature, notably T.S. Eliot's *Murder in the Cathedral* (1935).

Beckett \'bek-ət\, Samuel (Barclay) (b. April 13?, 1906, Foxrock, County Dublin, Ire.—d. Dec. 22, 1989, Paris, Fr.)   Author, critic, and playwright who in 1969 won the Nobel Prize for Literature. He wrote in both French and English and is perhaps best known for his preoccupation with essential issues of the human condition—existence and communication.

Beckett graduated from Trinity College, Dublin (B.A., 1927), and became a reader in English at the École Normale Supérieure in Paris in 1928. There he met James Joyce and joined his circle. Publications from this period included the short-story collection *More Pricks Than Kicks* (1934), the novel MURPHY (1938), and two volumes of poetry, *Whoroscope* (1930) and *Echo's Bones* (1935). In 1937 Beckett settled permanently in Paris. He joined an underground resistance group in 1941, and in 1942 he went into hiding and eventually moved to the unoccupied zone of France. He returned to Paris in 1945.

During his years in hiding, Beckett completed the novel WATT (1953). Between 1946 and 1949 he produced the major prose narrative trilogy consisting of MOLLOY (1951), *Malone meurt* (1951; MALONE DIES), and *L'Innommable* (1953; THE UNNAMABLE); the plays *En attendant Godot* (1952; WAITING FOR GODOT) and the unpublished and unproduced three-act *Eleutheria*; and a number of stories.

Gisèle Freund

Beckett's writing, full of allusions to literature, philosophy, and theology, reveals his immense learning. Although he wrote chiefly of the ultimate mystery and despair of human existence, he was essentially a comic writer, evoking laughter with his perception of humans as pompous, self-important, and preoccupied with illusory ambitions and futile desires. He often placed characters in extreme situations that enabled him to examine the essence of human experience.

Many of Beckett's plays—including *Fin de partie* (1957; ENDGAME), KRAPP'S LAST TAPE (1959), and *Happy Days* (1961)—take place on a level of nearly complete abstraction, with few characters and minimal sets. His later works also tended toward extreme concentration and brevity, an attempt to pare his writing to absolute essentials. *Come and Go* (1967), a playlet, or "dramaticule," as he called it, contains only 121 words. The prose fragment "Lessness" consists of but 60 sentences, each of which occurs twice. His series *Acts Without Words* is exactly what the title denotes, and one of his last plays, *Rockaby*, lasts only 15 minutes.

Beckford \'bek-fərd\, William (b. Sept. 29, 1760, London, Eng.—d. May 2, 1844, Bath, Somerset) Eccentric English dilettante, author of the gothic novel VATHEK (1786). He also is renowned for having built Fonthill Abbey, the most sensational building of the English Gothic Revival.

Beckford was the only legitimate son of William Beckford the Elder, twice lord mayor of London, and was the heir to a vast fortune, which he inherited in 1770, upon the death of his father. After a period of travel and study in Europe, Beckford returned to England, where he later married Lady Margaret Gordon and served in Parliament. In early 1782 he wrote the story of the caliph Vathek. Completed in outline in three days and two nights, the tale was originally written in French. Though all agree that it is uneven and stylistically uncertain, the strength of its final image has sustained Beckford's reputation for more than two centuries.

In the autumn of 1784, scandal broke when Beckford was charged with sexual misconduct with a young boy. Though Beckford's guilt was never proved, in mid-1785 he, with his wife and baby daughter, was forced into exile. In May 1786, in Switzerland, his wife died after giving birth to a second daughter.

From 1796, after his return to England, Beckford devoted his energies to his Gothic "abbey" at Fonthill. He lived there as a recluse, collecting curios, costly furnishings, and works of art. His extravagances forced him to sell his estate in 1822. Beckford's literary reputation rests solely on *Vathek*. Among

Beckford's other published works are accounts of his travels, two parodies of Gothic and sentimental novels, and a journal, *Life at Fonthill, 1807–22*.

Becque \'bek\, Henry-François (b. April 18, 1837, Neuilly, Fr.—d. May 12, 1899, Paris) Dramatist and critic whose loosely structured plays, based on character and motivation rather than on closely knit plots, provided a healthy challenge to the "well-made plays" (as formulated by Eugène Scribe) that held the stage in his day. Although Becque disliked literary theory and refused identification with any school, he has been remembered as a forerunner of the naturalist movement.

Les Corbeaux (1882; *The Vultures*), Becque's masterpiece, describes a bitter struggle for an inheritance. The unvaried egotism of the characters and the realistic dialogue were unfavorably received, except by naturalistic critics, and the play had only three performances. *La Parisienne* (1885; *Parisienne*) scandalized the public by its treatment of the story of a married woman and her two lovers. Its importance, like that of *Les Corbeaux*, was not recognized until a decade after its appearance.

Bécquer \'bek-er\, Gustavo Adolfo, *original name* Gustavo Adolfo Domínguez Bastida \dō-'mēn-gäth-bäs-'tē-thä\ (b. Feb. 17, 1836, Seville, Spain—d. Dec. 22, 1870, Madrid) Poet and author of the late Romantic period who is considered one of the first modern Spanish poets.

Bécquer moved to Madrid at 17 in pursuit of a literary career and from 1861 to 1868 contributed to the newspaper *El Contemporáneo*. His major literary production consists of nearly 100 *Rimas*, a series of about 20 *Leyendas* ("Legends") in prose, and the literary essays *Cartas desde mi celda* ("Letters From My Cell"), written from the monastery of Veruela in 1864. Although many of his poems and prose works were published individually in *El Contemporáneo*, they did not appear in book form until after his death. His *Rimas*, probably his best-known works, are sensitive, restrained, and deeply subjective. Bécquer's poetry explores themes of love—particularly disillusionment and loneliness—and the mysteries of life and poetry.

The prose pieces, *Leyendas*, are characterized by medieval settings, supernatural characters such as nymphs, and a mysterious, dreamlike atmosphere. Written in a lyrical style, the narratives are based upon the themes of love, death, and the world beyond.

Beddoes \'bed-ōz\, Thomas Lovell (b. June 30, 1803, Clifton, Somerset, Eng.—d. Jan. 26, 1849, Basel, Switz.) Poet best known for his haunting dramatic poem *Death's Jest-Book; or, The Fool's Tragedy*.

The son of a distinguished scientist, Beddoes seems early to have acquired, from his father's dissections and speculations on anatomy and the soul, an obsession with death that was to dominate his life and work. In 1820 he went to Oxford University, where he wrote his first considerable work, *The Bride's Tragedy* (1822), based on the story of a murder committed by an undergraduate. In 1825 he went to Göttingen, Ger., to study anatomy and medicine. There he continued work on *Death's Jest-Book*, which he described as an example of "the florid Gothic" and in which he aimed to use gothic material to discuss the problems of mortality and immortality. Friends who read the first version advised revision, and Beddoes' acceptance of their advice hindered his poetic development: for the rest of his life he was unable to escape from the work or to complete it, and it was eventually published posthumously in 1850.

After trouble with the university authorities, Beddoes left Göttingen, moved to Würzburg (where he received his medical degree), and there involved himself in radical politics. More trouble caused him to leave Germany for Zürich. In 1840 he had to flee from Switzerland, probably for political reasons, and he never afterward settled in one place for long. He visited England for the last time in 1846–47. Two years later he committed suicide.

Bede \ˈbēd\ the Venerable, Bede *also spelled* Baeda *or* Beda \ˈbē-də\ (b. 672/673, traditionally Monkton in Jarrow, Northumbria [England]—d. May 25, 735, Jarrow) Anglo-Saxon theologian, historian, and chronologist, best known today for his *Historia ecclesiastica gentis Anglorum* ("Ecclesiastical History of the English People"), a source vital to the history of the conversion to Christianity of the Anglo-Saxon tribes. His method of dating events from the time of the incarnation, or Christ's birth—*i.e.*, AD—came into general use through the popularity of the *Historia ecclesiastica* and the two works on chronology.

Nothing is known of Bede's parentage. At the age of seven he was taken to the Monastery of St. Peter, founded at Wearmouth (near Sunderland, Durham) by Abbot Benedict Biscop, to whose care he was entrusted. By 685 he was moved to Biscop's newer Monastery of St. Paul at Jarrow. Bede was ordained deacon when 19 years old and priest when 30.

Bede's earliest works included treatises on spelling, hymns, figures of speech, verse, and epigrams. His first treatise on chronology, *De temporibus* ("On Times"), with a brief chronicle attached, was written in 703. In 725 he completed a greatly amplified version, *De temporum ratione* ("On the Reckoning of Time"), with a much longer chronicle. Both these books were mainly concerned with the reckoning of Easter. His earliest biblical commentary was probably that on the Revelation to John (703?–709).

In 731/732 Bede completed his *Historia ecclesiastica*. Divided into five books, it recorded events in Britain from the raids by Julius Caesar (55–54 BC) to the arrival in Kent (AD 597) of St. Augustine. For his sources he claimed the authority of ancient letters, the "traditions of our forefathers," and his own knowledge of contemporary events. It remains an indispensable source for some of the facts and much of the feel of early Anglo-Saxon history.

Bede, Adam \ˈad-əm-ˈbēd\ Fictional character, an honest and respectable carpenter who is the protagonist of ADAM BEDE by George Eliot.

Bédier \bād-ˈyā\ (Charles-Marie-) Joseph (b. Jan. 28, 1864, Paris, Fr.—d. Aug. 29, 1938, Le Grand-Serre) Scholar whose work on the Tristram (Tristan) and Isolde epic and the Roland epic made invaluable contributions to the study of medieval French literature.

Le Roman de Tristan et Iseult (1900) established Bédier's reputation as a writer, and his scholarship was fully expressed in his critical edition of *Le Roman de Tristan* (1902–05) by the Anglo-Norman poet Thomas. He proved that the earliest Tristan poem was the product of an individual genius, not of popular tradition. He was appointed to the Collège de France in 1903.

Les Légendes épiques, 4 vol. (1908–13), presents his theory on the origins of the old French epic poems, the chansons de geste. He marshals convincing evidence that they were originally composed by the troubadours on themes provided by monks traveling on the pilgrimage routes. In 1922 he published a critical edition of *La Chanson de Roland*. He was elected to the Académie Française in 1921.

Bedlam \ˈbed-ləm\ *byname of* Bethlehem Royal Hospital \ˈbeth-li-ˌhem; -lē-əm, -həm\ The first asylum for the insane in England. The word *bedlam* came to be used generally for all insane asylums and then colloquially for an uproar.

Bedny \ˈbʸed-nē\, Demyan, *byname of* Yefim Alekseyevich Pridvorov \prʸi-ˈdvȯ-rəf\ (b. April 1 [April 13, New Style],

1883, Gubovka, Ukraine, Russian Empire—d. May 25, 1945, Barvikha, near Moscow, U.S.S.R.) Soviet poet known both for his verses glorifying the Revolution of 1917 and for his satirical fables.

The natural son of a grand duke, Pridvorov began contributing to the socialist press before the revolution, adopting the name Demyan Bedny ("Damyan the Poor"). In 1912 his satires started to appear. His style was influenced by the 19th-century Russian fabulist Ivan Krylov; his verses often took the form of popular songs and "factory couplets" (a kind of workers' slogan or cheer). Between 1917 and 1930 Bedny was highly popular with the general public, and V.I. Lenin, while noting the crudeness of Bedny's songs, lauded their propaganda value.

In 1936 Bedny composed a new libretto for the comic opera *Bogatyri* ("Heroes") by Aleksandr Borodin; his verse text, in the spirit of the original music, satirized Russian history and its epic heroes. Although Bedny had been a longtime favorite of Joseph Stalin, the dictator personally berated him for his cynicism and lack of respect. In 1938 he was expelled from the Communist Party. Even the patriotic verses he wrote during World War II, which were extremely popular among the soldiers, did not help him regain his former status. Only in the 1960s was official approval of Bedny's works restored.

bedside \ˈbed-ˌsīd\ Suitable for reading in bed especially in short segments. Sometimes the word is used to mean light and entertaining.

bedtime story A simple story for young children, usually about animals, which are often portrayed anthropomorphically.

Beerbohm \ˈbir-ˌbōm, -bəm\, Sir Max, *original name* Henry Maximilian Beerbohm (b. Aug. 24, 1872, London, Eng.—d. May 20, 1956, Rapallo, Italy) English caricaturist, writer, and dandy, whose sophisticated drawings and parodies were unique in capturing, usually without malice, whatever was pretentious, affected, or absurd in his famous and fashionable contemporaries.

A younger half brother of the actor-producer Sir Herbert Beerbohm Tree, Beerbohm was accustomed to fashionable society from his boyhood. While still an undergraduate at Merton College, Oxford, he published witty essays in the periodical *The Yellow Book*. His first literary collection, *The Works of Max Beerbohm*, and his first book of drawings, *Caricatures of Twenty-five Gentlemen*, appeared in 1896. In 1898 he succeeded George Bernard Shaw as drama critic of the *Saturday Review*. His charming fable *The Happy Hypocrite* appeared in 1897 and his only novel, *Zuleika Dobson*, a burlesque of

E.B. Inc.

Oxford life, in 1911. *The Christmas Garland* (1912) is a group of Christmas stories that mirror the stylistic foibles of a number of well-known writers, notably Henry James. His collection of stories, *Seven Men* (1919), is considered a masterpiece. As a parodist, he is frequently held to be unsurpassed.

In 1910 Beerbohm married the actress Florence Kahn, and they settled in Rapallo, Italy, where, except for a return to England during World Wars I and II, they made their home for the rest of their lives. He attracted to Rapallo a constant stream of distinguished visitors who found in him a living archive of amusing anecdotes of the literary, artistic, and social circles of late Victorian and Edwardian England. He was knighted in 1939. After his wife's death in 1951, Beerbohm lived with his secretary-companion, Elizabeth Jungmann, whom he married shortly before he died.

Beets \\'bāts\\, Nicolaas (b. Sept. 13, 1814, Haarlem, Neth.—d. March 13, 1903, Utrecht)   Pastor and writer whose *Camera obscura* is a classic of Dutch literature.

As a student at Leiden, Beets was influenced by reading Byron and was one of the first Dutch authors to write Romantic poetry. His poems included *José* (1834), *Kuser* (1835), and *Guy de Vlaming* (1837). While still at Leiden, he also wrote the sketches, tales, and essays collected as *Camera obscura* (edited under the pseudonym Hildebrand, 1839; 4th definitive edition, 1854). These works continued the Dutch tradition of presenting domestic scenes realistically but combined with it a whimsical humor. Beets was ordained in 1839 and held pastorates at Heemstede (1840–53) and Utrecht (1854–74). He was professor at the State University of Utrecht from 1874 to 1884.

Before the Dawn   Historical novel by SHIMAZAKI Tōson, published serially as *Yoake mae* in the journal *Chūō koron* ("Central Review") from 1929 to 1935 and printed in book form in 1935. It details the effects of Westernization on a rural Japanese community in the second half of the 19th century. Despite its stylistic simplicity and undeveloped characterizations, it is considered a modern masterpiece for its impressive scope.

The novel traces the life of Aoyama Hanzō from 1853 to 1886. Hanzō (who was based on Shimazaki's father) eagerly welcomes the transfer of power from the military Tokugawa shogunate to the Meiji emperor. However, his idealism gives way to disillusionment as he is alienated by the old peasants and misled by the new bureaucrats. A tragic hero, he is convinced that the cause of pure patriotism has been betrayed by the modernizers; he dies alone and insane.

Beggar's Opera, The   A ballad opera in three acts by John GAY, performed at Lincoln's Inn Fields Theatre, London, in 1728 and published in the same year. The work combines comedy and political satire in prose interspersed with songs set to contemporary and traditional English, Irish, Scottish, and French tunes. In it, Gay portrays the lives of a group of thieves and prostitutes in 18th-century London. The action centers on Peachum, a fence for stolen goods; Polly, his daughter; and Macheath, a highwayman. Gay caricatures the government, fashionable society, marriage, and Italian operatic style.

Bertolt Brecht and Kurt Weill based their ballad opera *Die Dreigroschenoper* (1928; *The Threepenny Opera*) on Gay's work.

beginning rhyme   Rhyme at the beginning of successive lines of verse. Lines 3 and 4 of Robert Herrick's "To Daffodils" demonstrate beginning rhyme:

> As yet the early-rising sun
> Has not attained his noon.

The term is also used as a synonym for ALLITERATION.

Behan \\'bē-ən\\, Brendan (Francis) (b. Feb. 9, 1923, Dublin, Ire.—d. March 20, 1964, Dublin)   Irish author noted for his earthy satire and powerful political commentary.

Behan was reared in a family active in revolutionary and left-wing anti-British causes. At the age of eight he began what became a lifelong battle with alcoholism. After leaving school in 1937, he learned the house-painter's trade while concurrently working in the Irish Republican Army as a courier.

Behan was arrested in England while on a sabotage mission and sentenced (February 1940) to three years in a reform

school. He wrote an autobiographical account of this detention in BORSTAL BOY (1958). He was deported to Dublin in 1942 and was soon involved in a shooting incident in which a policeman was wounded; he was sentenced to 14 years. He served at Mountjoy Prison, Dublin, the setting of his first play, THE QUARE FELLOW (1954), and later at the Curragh Military Camp, County Kildare, from which he was released under a general amnesty in 1946. While imprisoned, he perfected his Irish, the language he used for his delicately sensitive poetry and for *An Giall* (produced 1957), the initial version of his second play, THE HOSTAGE (produced 1958).

In 1948 Behan went to Paris to write. Returning to Dublin in 1950, he wrote short stories and scripts for Radio Telefís Éireann and sang on a continuing program, *Ballad Maker's Saturday Night*. In 1953 he began a column about Dublin in the *Irish Press*, later collected in *Hold Your Hour and Have Another* (1963), with illustrations by his wife.

Behan's last works were *Brendan Behan's Island* (1962), a book of anecdotes; *The Scarperer* (1964), a novel about a smuggling adventure, first published serially in the *Irish Press*; *Brendan Behan's New York* (1964); and *Confessions of an Irish Rebel* (1965), further memoirs.

Behn \\'bän, 'ben\\, Aphra (b. July 1640, probably Harbledown, Kent, Eng.—d. April 16, 1689, London)   English dramatist, novelist, and poet, the first Englishwoman known to earn her living by writing. Her novel OROONOKO (1688; reprinted

1933), the story of an enslaved African prince whom Behn knew in South America, influenced the development of the English novel. Her poems, although not generally considered to be equal in merit to her fiction, have perhaps been underestimated.

Her origin remains a mystery; an unidentified child named Aphra traveled with a couple named Amis to Surinam (Dutch Guiana), then an English possession. Back in England

by 1658, she married a merchant named Behn, who died in the mid-1660s. She was employed by Charles II in secret service in the Netherlands. Unrewarded and briefly imprisoned for debt, she began to write to support herself.

In 1671 Behn's first play, *The Forc'd Marriage*, was produced; her witty and vivacious comedies, such as THE ROVER (two parts, produced 1677 and 1681), were highly successful. Toward the end of her life she wrote many popular novels. Her charm and generosity won her a wide circle of friends, and her relative freedom as a professional writer made her the object of some scandal.

Behrman \\'ber-mən\\, S.N., *in full* Samuel Nathaniel (b. June 9, 1893, Worcester, Mass., U.S.—d. Sept. 9, 1973, New York, N.Y.)   American short-story writer and playwright best known for popular Broadway plays that commented on volatile and usually complicated contemporary moral issues. Behrman wrote about the wealthy, intellectual sector of society, and he is notable for endowing his characters with eloquence and intelligence.

As a young man, Behrman contributed to several leading newspapers and magazines, including *New Republic* and *The New Yorker,* and studied drama at Harvard and Columbia University, N.Y. His play *The Second Man* (1927) was the first in a string of successes that included *Meteor* (1929), *Brief Moment* (1931), and *Biography* (1932). He tackled the subject of fascism in *Rain from Heaven* (1934). Criticized for not making his personal viewpoint known, but instead letting his characters speak for him, Behrman wrote *No Time for Comedy* (1939), in which the protagonist, an author of light comedy, criticizes himself for his failure to address effectively serious contemporary problems.

Behrman wrote more than two dozen comedies during his 40-year career, and nearly every one of them was a hit. He also wrote many short stories, two biographies, and a number of screenplays.

Bei Dao or **Pei-tao** \\'bā-'daù\\, *pseudonym of* Zhao Zhenkai \\'jaù-'jən-'kī\\ (b. Aug. 2, 1949, Beijing, China) Chinese poet and writer of fiction whose works were published underground for most of his career. He was one of the originators of *menglongshi,* or "shadows poetry," which used metaphor and cryptic language to avoid directly discussing contemporary political and social issues. In the 1970s he was considered the poetic voice of the pro-democracy faction of his generation.

The eruption of the Cultural Revolution in 1966 interrupted Zhao's formal education. He began to write as a substitute for active political involvement and as a means of protest against contemporary official literature. "Bei Dao" ("North Island") was one of several *noms de plume* he adopted in the 1970s. His poetry gradually gained a hearing in official publications but was considered difficult and arcane. *Bei Dao shi xuan* ("Bei Dao's Collected Poems") was published in 1986 and in an English translation as *The August Sleepwalker* in 1988. In 1989, when the Tiananmen Square uprising occurred, Zhao was in Berlin. He did not return to China but traveled throughout the West, gaining an international audience for his poetry, which began to reflect his profound sorrow at separation from his family and homeland. His later works include two bilingual editions, *Old Snow* (1991) and *Forms of Distance* (1994). He also wrote short stories, many of which were collected in *Bo dong* (1985; *Waves*).

Belch, Sir Toby \\sər-'tō-bē-'belch\\ Fictional character, the boisterous uncle of the heroine Olivia in William Shakespeare's comedy TWELFTH NIGHT. His alcohol-induced wit provides much of the humor for the play's subplot, the conspiracy to turn Olivia against Malvolio, her pompous steward.

Belial \\'bē-lē-əl, 'bēl-yəl\\ Fictional character, a fallen angel in John Milton's PARADISE LOST who tries to persuade the others to be more discreet so that their unacceptable behavior is less conspicuous. The Hebrew word *bĕlīya'al,* apparently with the literal meaning "worthlessness," was used in Old Testament epithets for the wicked and impious, such as "sons of Belial." In later traditions it was taken as a proper name, a byname for Satan.

Belinsky \\bʲi-'lʲẽn-skʲẽ\\, Vissarion Grigoryevich (b. May 30 [June 11, New Style], 1811, Viapori, Russian Empire—d. May 26 [June 7], 1848, St. Petersburg) Eminent Russian literary critic, often called the father of the Russian radical intelligentsia.

After being expelled from Moscow University in 1832, Belinsky earned his living as a journalist. His first substantial critical articles were part of a series that he wrote for the journal *Teleskop* ("Telescope") beginning in 1834. These were called "Literaturnye mechtaniya" ("Literary Dreams"), and they reflected the idealism of the German philosopher F.W.J. von

Schelling. Belinsky later wrote for the *Moskovsky nablyudatel* ("Moscow Observer") and the St. Petersburg *Otechestvennyye zapiski* ("Notes of the Fatherland"). Most of his last essays were written for the review *Sovremennik* ("The Contemporary").

In St. Petersburg Belinsky was a member of a group of progressive writers and journalists that included Ivan Goncharov and Ivan Turgenev. Through his involvement with that group and his essays in the "Notes of the Fatherland" he helped shape the literary and social views of other Russian intellectuals. By this time he had moved from the idealism of his early essays to a Hegelian view that art and the history of a nation are closely connected. Belinsky believed that Russian literature had to progress beyond the native form of Russian folk poetry to help the still embryonic Russian nation to develop into a mature, civilized society.

As a critic Belinsky reviewed the works of many contemporary writers, including Turgenev, Aleksandr Pushkin, Mikhail Lermontov, Fyodor Dostoyevsky, and particularly Nikolay Gogol. He laid the foundation for much of modern Russian literary criticism in his belief that Russian literature should be an honest reflection of Russian reality and that art should be judged for its social as well as its aesthetic qualities.

Bell \\'bel\\, Josephine, *pseudonym of* Doris Bell Ball \\'bȯl\\, *original surname* Collier \\'kȧl-yər\\ (b. Dec. 8, 1897, Manchester, Eng.—d. April 24, 1987) English physician and novelist best known for her numerous detective novels, in which poison and unusual methods of murder are prominent.

She was educated at Newnham College, Cambridge (1916–19), and University College Hospital, London, and was a practicing physician from 1922 to 1954. In 1937 her first novel, *Murder in Hospital,* was published, featuring David Wintringham, M.D., a fictional doctor-detective. Dozens of other mysteries followed. She also wrote many non-detective novels, short stories, radio plays, and some nonfiction pieces, such as *Crime in Our Time* (1962), all under her pseudonym.

Later works include the historical novel *A Question of Loyalties* (1974), *A Pigeon Among the Cats* (1974), and *Such a Nice Client* (1977; also published as *Stroke of Death*).

Bell, The Irish literary magazine, founded in October 1940 by Sean O'FAOLAIN, its editor until 1946. From its first issue, which included works by such writers as Frank O'Connor, Elizabeth Bowen, Jack B. Yeats, Flann O'Brien, and O'Faolain, *The Bell* published stories, poetry, essays, and book and theater reviews by Ireland's most celebrated modern writers.

The Bell was, during World War II, Ireland's sole organ of political liberalism and was particularly critical of the wartime censorship of books. Peadar O'Donnell became editor in 1946, guiding *The Bell* toward an increasingly radical political stance that gradually alienated its Irish reading public. Publication ended with issue 131, in December 1954.

Bellamy \\'bel-ə-mē\\, Edward (b. March 26, 1850, Chicopee Falls, Mass., U.S.—d. May 22, 1898, Chicopee Falls) American writer known chiefly for his utopian novel *Looking Backward, 2000–1887.*

Bellamy first became aware of the plight of the urban poor at 18 while studying in Germany. He studied law and was admitted to the bar in 1871, but he soon turned to journalism, first as an associate editor for the *Springfield Union* (Massachusetts) and then as an editorial writer for the *New York Evening Post.*

In *Looking Backward* (1888), set in Boston in the year 2000, he described the United States under an ideal socialist system that featured cooperation, brotherhood, and an industry geared to human need. Bellamy became an active propagandist for the nationalization of public services, and his ideas encouraged the foundation of nationalist clubs. Political groups inspired by Bellamy's works also appeared in Europe. Bellamy's sequel to *Looking Backward*, entitled *Equality* (1897), was less successful. Additional writings were published in *Edward Bellamy Speaks Again!* (1937) and as *Talks on Nationalism* (1938).

Bellay \bā-'le\, Joachim du (b. *c.* 1522, Liré, Fr.—d. Jan. 1, 1560, Paris) French poet, leader with Pierre de Ronsard of the literary group known as LA PLÉIADE. Du Bellay was the author of the La Pléiade's manifesto, *La Défense et illustration de la langue française* (1549; *The Defence and Illustration of the French Language*), in which he asserted that the French language could be enriched through study and imitation of the Greek and Roman classics and works of the Italian Renaissance.

Du Bellay studied law and the humanities in Poitiers and Paris, and in 1549–50 his first sonnets, inspired by those of the Italian poet Petrarch, were published. In 1553 he went with his cousin Jean du Bellay, a prominent cardinal and diplomat, on a mission to Rome. By this time he had started to write on religious themes, but his experience of court life in the Vatican seems to have disillusioned him. He turned instead to meditations on the vanished glories of ancient Rome in the *Antiquités de Rome* and to melancholy satire in his finest work, the *Regrets* (both published after his return to France in 1558).

Du Bellay had a sincere affection for his country and determined that it should have a literature to rival that of any other nation. He introduced new literary forms into French, with the first book of odes and the first of love sonnets in the language. Abroad, he influenced the English lyric poets of the 16th century, and some of his work was translated by Edmund Spenser.

Belleau \bā-'lō\, Rémy (b. 1528, Nogent-le-Rotrou, near Chartres, Fr.—d. March 6, 1577, Paris) Renaissance scholar and poet who wrote highly polished portraits known as miniatures. He was a member of the group called La Pléiade, a literary circle that sought to enrich French literature by reviving classical tradition.

A contemporary of the poet Pierre de Ronsard at the Collège de Cocqueret, Belleau at first gained the patronage of the Abbé Chretophle de Choiseul and later of Charles IX and Henry III, who made him secretary of the king's chamber. From about 1563 he lived at Joinville as tutor and counselor to the Guises, a powerful Catholic family. This life inspired Belleau to write *La Bergerie* (1565–72; "The Shepherd's Song"), a collection of pastoral odes, sonnets, hymns, and amorous verse. Belleau's detailed descriptions of nature and works of art earned him a reputation as a miniaturist in poetry. His other poetic works included didactic verse; *Les Amours et nouveaux échanges des pierres précieuses* (1576), a commentary on exotic stones and their inherent secret virtues written in the tradition of the medieval lapidaries; and *La Reconnue* (1577; "The Rediscovered Daughter"), a comedy in verse based on Plautus' *Casina*. His erudite translations of Anacreon's *Odes* (1556) won him the seventh seat or "star" in the constellation of La Pléiade.

Bellecour \bel-'kür\, *original name* Jean-Claude-Gilles Colson \kōl-'sōⁿ\ (b. Jan. 16, 1725, Paris, Fr.—d. Nov. 19, 1778, Paris) Playwright who was also was one of the leading comic actors of the Comédie-Française.

The son of a portraitist, Bellecour was a painter in his youth while concurrently appearing in various amateur theatrical productions. His success on stage caused him to set aside painting and become an actor. After playing in the provinces, he made his debut at the Comédie-Française on Dec. 21, 1750, as Achilles in Jean Racine's *Iphigénie*. Bellecour established his reputation, however, in comic roles. He wrote a successful play, *Les Fausses Apparences* ("The False Appearances"), in 1761.

Belle Dame sans Merci, La \lä-bel-dåm-sän-mer-'se\ ("The Lovely Lady Without Pity") Poem by John KEATS, first published in the May 10, 1820, issue of the *Indicator*. The poem describes the encounter between a knight and a mysterious elfin beauty who ultimately abandons him. It is written in the style of a folk ballad, with the first three stanzas a query to the knight and the remaining nine stanzas the knight's reply. The poem is sometimes seen as a counterpart to Keats' "The Eve of St. Agnes," which represents an idyllic view of love that contrasts with the dark view expressed in "La Belle Dame." Keats took his title from a medieval poem with the same name by the French poet Alain Chartier.

Bellenden \'bel-ən-dən\, John, Bellenden *also spelled* Ballenden, Ballentyne, Ballantyne, *or* Bannatyne (fl. 1533–87) Scottish writer whose translation of Hector Boece's *Scotorum historiae* made accessible the first account of Macbeth's meeting with the witches. The book had a profound influence on Scottish national feeling.

Educated at the universities of St. Andrews (Scotland) and Paris, Bellenden was in the service of James V as clerk of accounts and translated the *Historiae*, which appeared in Paris in 1526, at his request. Bellenden's translation was published in 1536 as *The History and Chronicles of Scotland*, prefaced by an original poem entitled *A Proheme to the Cosmographe* that was later reprinted separately under the various titles of *Vertue and Vyce* and *An Allegory of Virtue and Delyte*. Written in a fluent and vivid style, the *History* is one of the earliest pieces of literary Scottish prose extant. Also at the king's request, Bellenden translated the first five books of Livy's *Roman History*, prefacing them with *The Proheme of the History*, another original poem. It was not publicly printed until 1822.

Bellerophon \bə-'ler-ə-,fän\, *also called* Bellerophontes \bə-,ler-ə-'fän-,tēz\ Hero of Greek legend. In the *Iliad* he was the son of Glaucus, who was the son of Sisyphus of Ephyre (traditionally Corinth). Anteia (or Stheneboea), wife of Proetus, the king of Argos, loved him; when her overtures were rejected, she falsely accused him to her husband. Proetus then sent Bellerophon to the king of Lycia with a message that he was to be slain. The king, repeatedly unsuccessful in his assassination attempts, finally recognized Bellerophon as more than human and married him to his daughter.

Later authors added that, while still at Corinth, Bellerophon tamed the winged horse PEGASUS with a bridle given to him by Athena and that he used Pegasus to fight the Chimera and afterward to punish Anteia. He supposedly earned the wrath of the gods by trying to fly up to heaven and was thrown from Pegasus.

belles lettres \,bel-'let, -'let-rə, *French* bel-'letr *with* r *as a uvular trill*\ [French *belles-lettres,* literally, beautiful letters] Literature that is an end in itself and is not practical or purely informative. The term can refer generally to poetry, fiction, drama, etc., or more specifically to light, entertaining, sophisticated literature. It is also often used to refer to literary studies, particularly essays.

Bell for Adano, A \ä-'dän-ō\ Novel by John HERSEY, published in 1944 and awarded a Pulitzer Prize in 1945.

The novel's action takes place during World War II after the occupation of Sicily by Allied forces. Major Victor Joppolo, an American army officer of Italian descent, is part of the Allied military government ruling the town of Adano. In his attempts to reform the town and bring democracy to the people by treating them with respect and decency, Joppolo comes into conflict with his commanding officer, a hard-nosed general who eventually has Joppolo transferred because of his refusal to follow orders. Joppolo's concern for the town is epitomized by his efforts to replace a bell that the fascists had melted down to use for ammunition.

Belli \'bel-lē\, Carlos Germán (b. Sept. 15, 1927, Lima, Peru) Peruvian poet, translator, and journalist who was noted for his unique blend of precise classical expression and contemporary themes.

Belli was the son of Italian immigrants. His first works, *Poemas* (1958) and *Dentro & fuera* (1960; "Inside and Out"), are surrealist in tone but exhibit many of the characteristics that he honed in his later poems. Influenced by the modernism of Rubén Darío and then by the rigid forms, stylistic peculiarities, and unusual syntax of the masters of the Spanish Golden Age, Belli began to produce his characteristic poetry. Bemoaning his fate as a frustrated, powerless modern poet forced to work at a mundane job, Belli created a number of pseudoclassical figures to whom he addressed his complaints; these included Fisco, the god of income, and Hada Cibernética ("The Cybernetic Fairy"), who represents technological advances that would relieve humans of their drudgery. Though Belli's outlook was unremittingly nihilistic, his unusual form of expression made his poetry both personal and highly original. Among his many collections were *¡Oh Hada Cibernética!* (1961; "Oh Cybernetic Fairy"), *El pie sobre el cuello* (1964; "The Foot on the Neck"), *Por el monte abajo* (1966; "Through the Woods Below"), *Sextinas y otros poemas* (1970; "Sestinas and Other Poems"), *Canciones y otros poemas* (1982; "Songs and Other Poems"), *El buen mudar* (1987; "The Good Move"), and *En el restante tiempo terrenal* (1988; "In the Remaining Terrestrial Time").

Belli \'bäl-lē\, Giuseppe Gioacchino (b. Sept. 10, 1791, Rome [Italy]—d. Dec. 21, 1863, Rome) Poet whose satirical sonnets present a vivid picture of life in papal Rome in the early 19th century.

Belli was a clerical worker until, in 1816, marriage to a rich widow enabled him to devote his time to travel and poetry. After the death of his wife in 1837 he went to work for the papal bureaucracy as a means of supporting his son.

His more than 2,000 sonnets in Roman dialect contrast with his conformist way of life. Composed mainly during 1830–39, they seem to have provided an outlet for his repressed feelings. Although he also wrote conventional poems, his originality lies in the sonnets, which express his revolt against literary tradition, the academic mentality, and the social injustices of the papal system. The ritualism of the church and the accepted principles of commonplace morality were also objects of his derision. However, his anticlerical views were jolted by the violence that he witnessed during the Revolution of 1848 and the formation of the Roman republic of 1849. He stopped writing satiric verses and burned many of his sonnets.

Belli's greatest gift was for observing and describing the people of Rome, which he did with the range of a major novelist. An edition of Belli's sonnets appeared in three volumes in 1952. An English translation of 46 of the sonnets appeared in 1960 and 1974.

Bell Jar, The Novel by Sylvia PLATH, first published in January 1963 under the pseudonym Victoria Lucas, and later published under her real name. Plath committed suicide one month after the publication of *The Bell Jar*, her only novel. This thinly veiled autobiography details the life of Esther Greenwood, a college woman who struggles through a mental breakdown in the 1950s. Plath examines coming of age in a hypocritical world in this painfully introspective novel, which is noted for its symbolic use of bottles and jars and black and white colors and its symbols of imprisonment and death.

Bellman \'bel-ˌmȧn\, Carl Michael (b. Feb. 4, 1740, Stockholm, Swed.—d. Feb. 11, 1795, Stockholm) Outstanding poet-musician of 18th-century Sweden, whose songs have remained popular in Scandinavia, though he is little known elsewhere.

The son of a wealthy civil servant, Bellman studied at Uppsala University and entered government service. In early youth he published religious and satirical works and translations from German and French. By the 1760s, his drinking songs and biblical parodies were being sung throughout Scandinavia, circulated by word of mouth, handwritten copies, and printed sheets.

About 1765, Bellman began producing a cycle of songs, *Fredmans epistlar* (1790), the title alluding to the Pauline Epistles, which were parodied in the early songs. The 82 songs in the final collection reflect Bellman's poetic and personal development. The feeling for nature and vivid characterizations make it unique in Swedish poetry. It was followed in 1791 by *Fredmans sånger*, also a varied collection, but containing mainly drinking songs. *Bacchi tempel* (1783), a poem in alexandrines, also contained some songs and engravings. Bellman's other works, including plays and occasional poems, were published posthumously.

Bello \'bā-yō, 'bäl-\, Andrés (b. Nov. 29, 1781, Caracas [Venez.]—d. Oct. 15, 1865, Santiago, Chile) Poet and scholar, regarded as the intellectual father of South America.

At the University of Venezuela in Caracas, Bello studied philosophy, jurisprudence, and medicine. Acquaintance with the German naturalist and traveler Alexander von Humboldt led to the interest in geography so apparent in his later writings. He was a friend and teacher of the South American liberator, Simón Bolívar, with whom he was sent to London in 1810 on a political mission for the Venezuelan revolutionary junta. Bello elected to stay there for 19 years, acting as secretary to the legations of Chile and Colombia.

Bello's position in literature was secured by his *Silvas americanas*, two poems that convey the majestic impression of the South American landscape. These were published in London (1826–27) and were originally projected as part of a long, never-finished epic poem, *América*. The second of the two, *Silva a la agricultura de la zona tórrida*, is a poetic description of the products of tropical America, extolling the virtues of country life in a manner reminiscent of Virgil. It is one of the best-known poems in 19th-century Spanish-American letters.

In 1829 Bello accepted a post in the Chilean Ministry of Foreign Affairs. He was named senator of his adopted country and founded the University of Chile (1843), of which he was rector until his death.

Bello's prose works deal with such varied subjects as law, philosophy, literary criticism, and philology. Of the last, the most important is his *Gramática de la lengua castellana* (1847; "Grammar of the Spanish Language"), long the leading authority in its field.

Belloc \'bel-ȯk\, Hilaire, *in full* Joseph-Pierre Hilaire Belloc (b. July 27, 1870, La Celle-Saint-Cloud, Fr.—d. July 16, 1953, Guildford, Surrey, Eng.) French-born poet, historian, and essayist who was among the most versatile English writers of the first quarter of the 20th century. He is most remembered for his light verse, particularly for children, and for the lucidity and easy grace of his essays.

Belloc was educated at the Oratory School, Birmingham, and then worked as a journalist. After French military service, he studied at Balliol College, Oxford, graduating with honors in 1895. He became a naturalized British subject in 1902 and served as a member of Parliament from 1906 to 1910.

Verses and Sonnets (1895) and *The Bad Child's Book of Beasts* (1896) launched Belloc on his literary career. *Cautionary Tales*, which parodied some Victorian pomposities, appeared in 1907. His *Danton* (1899) and *Robespierre* (1901) displayed his lively historical sense and powerful prose style. *Lambkin's Remains* (1900) and *Mr. Burden* (1904) showed his mastery of satire and irony. In *The Path to Rome* (1902) he interspersed an account of a pilgrimage on foot from Toul to Rome with comments on Europe and its history. Belloc's deep Roman Catholic faith colored all his writings, most explicitly such historical works as *Europe and the Faith* (1920), *History of England*, 4 vol. (1925–31), and a series of biographies that included *James II* (1928) and *Wolsey* (1930).

Among Belloc's volumes of lighter verse are *The Modern Traveller* (1898) and the *Heroic Poem in Praise of Wine* (1932). He also wrote a number of satirical novels, which were illustrated by his friend, the novelist G.K. Chesterton.

Bellow \'bel-ō\, Saul (b. June 10, 1915, Lachine, near Montreal, Que., Can.)   American novelist whose characterizations of the modern urban dweller, disaffected by society but not destroyed in spirit, earned him the Nobel Prize for Literature in 1976. Brought up in a Jewish household and fluent in Yiddish, he was representative of the Jewish-American writers whose works became central to American literature after World War II.

Bellow's parents emigrated in 1913 from Russia to Montreal. When he was nine they moved to Chicago. He attended the University of Chicago and Northwestern University, from which he graduated (B.S.) in 1937, and afterward combined writing with a teaching career at various universities.

He won a reputation among a small group of readers with his first two novels, *Dangling Man* (1944) and *The Victim* (1947). THE ADVENTURES OF AUGIE MARCH (1953) brought wider acclaim. In this novel Bellow employed for the first time a loose, breezy style in conscious revolt against the preoccupation of writers of that time with perfection of form. HENDERSON THE RAIN KING (1959) continued the picaresque approach in its tale of an eccentric American millionaire on a quest in Africa. SEIZE THE DAY (1956), a novella, deals with a man who is a failure in a society where the only success is success. He also wrote a volume of short stories, *Mosby's Memoirs* (1968), and *To Jerusalem and Back* (1976), a nonfiction account of trip to Israel.

In his later novels and novellas—HERZOG (1964; National Book Award, 1965), MR. SAMMLER'S PLANET (1970; National Book Award, 1971), HUMBOLDT'S GIFT (1975; Pulitzer Prize, 1976), *The Dean's December* (1982), *More Die of Heartbreak* (1987), *A Theft* (1989), and *The Bellarosa Connection* (1989)—Bellow perfected the combination of cultural sophistication and the wisdom of the streets that constitutes his greatest originality.

Bells, The   Poem by Edgar Allan POE, published posthumously in the magazine *Sartain's Union* (November 1849). This incantatory poem examines bell sounds as symbols of four milestones of human experience—childhood, youth, maturity, and death.

Composed of four stanzas of increasing length, "The Bells" is a showcase of onomatopoeia, alliteration, repetition, and assonance. The first stanza, a study of merry sleigh bells, is followed by a depiction of joyous wedding bells. The third stanza is a cacophony of roaring alarm bells, while the final stanza dwells upon the sullen, rhythmic tolling of funeral bells.

Beloved \bə-'ləv-əd\   Novel by Toni MORRISON, published in 1987, and winner of the 1988 Pulitzer Prize for fiction. The work examines the destructive legacy of slavery, as it chronicles the life of a black woman named Sethe, following her from her pre-Civil War life as a slave in Kentucky to her life in Cincin-

nati, Ohio, in 1873; she is a free woman but is held prisoner by memories of the trauma of her life as a slave. During her escape Sethe gives birth to her fourth child, whom she kills rather than return to slavery. It is the spirit of this child, called Beloved, that returns to Sethe in her new life.

Bely \'bʲel-ē\, Andrey, *pseudonym of* Boris Nikolayevich Bugayev *or* Bugaev \bŭ-'gä-yəf\ (b. Oct. 14 [Oct. 26, New Style], 1880, Moscow, Russian Empire—d. Jan. 7, 1934, Moscow, U.S.S.R.)   Leading theorist and poet of Russian Symbolism, a literary school deriving from the modernist movement in western European art and literature and indigenous Eastern Orthodox spirituality, expressing mystical and abstract ideals through allegories from life and nature.

Bely was reared in an academic environment as the son of a mathematics professor. In 1901 he completed his first major work, *Severnaya simfoniya* (1902; "The Northern Symphony"), a prose poem that represented an attempt to combine prose, poetry, music, and even, in part, painting. Three more "symphonies" in this new literary form followed. By repeatedly using irregular meter (the "lame foot"), he introduced into Russian poetry the formalistic revolution that was brought to fruition by his aesthetic colleague Aleksandr Blok.

Bely's first three books of verse, *Zoloto v lazuri* (1904; "Gold in Azure"), *Pepel* (1909; "Ashes"), and *Urna* (1909; "Urn"), are, like Blok's, diaries in poetry. In 1909 Bely completed his first novel, *Serebryany golub* (1910; *The Silver Dove*). His most celebrated composition, *Peterburg* (published serially 1913–14; *St. Petersburg*), is regarded as a baroque extension of his earlier "symphonies." In 1913 he became an adherent of the Austrian social philosopher Rudolf Steiner and joined his anthroposophical colony in Basel, Switz. While in Switzerland Bely began writing his *Kotik Letayev* (1922; *Kotik Letaev*), a short autobiographical novel suggestive of the style of James Joyce. Bely returned to Moscow in 1916, and, like other Symbolists, he at first greeted the 1917 Bolshevik revolution ecstatically. His brief poem "Khristos voskrese" (1918; "Christ Has Prevailed") lauded the messianic promise of Russian socialism; however, after Blok's death and the execution by the Soviets of his literary colleagues, the dispirited Bely went abroad, although he returned to the Soviet Union in 1923.

Bembo \'bem-bō\, Pietro (b. May 20, 1470, Venice [Italy]—d. Jan. 18, 1547, Rome)   Renaissance cardinal who wrote one of the earliest Italian grammars and assisted in establishing the Italian literary language.

Of an aristocratic family, Bembo in 1513 became secretary to Pope Leo X in Rome. On Leo's death (1521), he retired to Padua. He accepted the office of historiographer of Venice in 1529 and was appointed librarian of St. Mark's Cathedral. Created a cardinal in 1539, Bembo returned to Rome, devoting himself to theology and classical history.

Bembo wrote Latin lyric poetry of formal excellence and then turned to the vernacular, modeling his poetry on that of Petrarch. His way of making direct imitations of Petrarch was widely influential and became known as *bembismo*. A collected edition of his Italian poems, *Rime*, appeared in 1530. His other vernacular works include *Gli Asolani* (1505), a history of Venice, and *Prose della volgar lingua* (1525; "Discussions of the Vernacular Language"). In *Prose*, Bembo codified Italian orthography and grammar, essential for the establishment of a standard language, and recommended 14th-century Tuscan as the model for Italian literary language.

Benavente y Martínez \,bā-nä-'bän-tā-ē-mär-'tē-näth\, Jacinto (b. Aug. 12, 1866, Madrid, Spain—d. July 14, 1954, Madrid)   One of the foremost Spanish dramatists of the 20th century and winner of the Nobel Prize for Literature in 1922.

The extent to which Benavente broadened the scope of the theater is shown by the range of his plays, *e.g., Los intereses creados* (1907; *The Bonds of Interest*), his most celebrated work, based on the Italian commedia dell'arte; *Los malhechores del bien* (performed 1905; *The Evil Doers of Good*); *La noche del sábado* (performed 1903; *Saturday Night*); and *La malquerida* (1913; "The Passion Flower"), a rural tragedy with the theme of incest. *Señora Ama* (1908), said to be his own favorite play, is an idyllic comedy set among the people of Castile.

In 1928 his play *Para el cielo y los altares* ("Toward Heaven and the Altars"), prophesying the fall of the Spanish monarchy, was banned by the government. In 1941 he reestablished himself in public favor with *Lo increíble* ("The Incredible"). His extraordinary productivity as a dramatist (he wrote more than 150 plays) recalled Spain's Golden Age and the prolific writer Lope de Vega. With the exception, however, of the harsh tragedy *La infanzona* (1948; "The Ancient Noblewoman"), and *El lebrel del cielo* (1952), inspired by Francis Thompson's poem "Hound of Heaven," Benavente's later works did not add much to his fame.

Benchley \'bench-lē\, Robert (Charles) (b. Sept. 15, 1889, Worcester, Mass., U.S.—d. Nov. 21, 1945, New York City) American drama critic, actor, and humorist noted for his motion-picture short subjects and humorous essays.

A graduate of Harvard University (1912), Benchley joined the staff of *Life* magazine in 1920 as drama critic. He was a regular member of the Algonquin Round Table. His monologue "The Treasurer's Report," delivered as a skit in an amateur revue in 1922, was the basis for one of the first all-talking short subjects. He subsequently wrote and acted in 46 shorts, his *How to Sleep* winning an Academy Award in 1935.

Benchley's essays were illustrated by Gluyas Williams' caricatures and collected in more than ten books, including *My Ten Years in a Quandary, and How They Grew* (1936) and *Benchley Beside Himself* (1943). His writing is characterized by its warmth and the non sequitur quality of its humor; his satire, although sharp, was never cruel. Benchley was drama critic for *The New Yorker* (1929–40), for which he also wrote "The Wayward Press" column under the pseudonym Guy Fawkes. *The Benchley Roundup* (1954) was a selection from his writings edited by his son Nathaniel, who also wrote his biography (1955).

Benda \ben-'dä\, Julien (b. Dec. 26, 1867, Paris, Fr.—d. June 7, 1956, Fontenay-aux-Roses, near Paris) French novelist and philosopher who was a leader of the anti-Romantic movement in French criticism and a persistent defender of reason and intellect against the philosophical intuitionism of Henri Bergson.

Benda graduated from the University of Paris in 1894. Among his first published works were articles on the Dreyfus affair issued in 1898. Literary renown came with the publication of his first novel, *L'Ordination* (1911; *The Yoke of Pity*). His lifelong assault on the philosophy of Bergson began with *Le Bergsonisme* in 1912. In his most important work, *La Trahison des clercs* (1927; U.S. title, *The Treason of the Intellectuals*; U.K. title, *The Great Betrayal*), Benda denounced as moral traitors those who betray truth and justice for racial and political considerations. The evolution of his thought can be traced in two autobiographical works: *La Jeunesse d'un clerc* (1937; "The Youth of an Intellectual") and *Un Régulier dans le siècle* (1938; "A Regulator in His Century").

Bend in the River, A   Novel by V.S. NAIPAUL, published in 1979. Reminiscent of Joseph Conrad's *Heart of Darkness*, *A Bend in the River* chronicles both an internal journey and a physical trek into the heart of Africa as it explores the themes of personal exile and political and individual corruption. It expresses Naipaul's skepticism about the ability of newly decolonized nations to forge independent and politically viable identities.

The narrator, Salim, a Muslim Indian merchant, opens a store in a sleepy small town at a bend in the river (ostensibly the Congo River). The town's inhabitants include a Belgian priest, a witch and her son Ferdinand, and a white intellectual named Raymond and his elegant wife Yvette. The president of the new country is a demagogue called the Big Man who hires Raymond as his speechwriter. Salim loses control of his store to the commercially inexperienced Citizen Theotime, who hires Salim to manage it. Gradually the town's veneer of civilization cracks, and chaos and corruption reign.

Bendis \'ben-dis\   Thracian goddess of warfare and the hunt, in whom the Greeks recognized a figure similar to their own Artemis. At the outbreak of the Peloponnesian War, the Athenians allowed the founding of a sanctuary for the goddess and shortly afterward created a state festival for her. The first celebration, held on the 19th of Thargelion (May–June), 429 BC, provided the dramatic setting for Plato's *Republic*.

Bend Sinister   Novel by Vladimir NABOKOV, published in 1947. It is the second novel the Russian-born author wrote in English. It tells the story of Adam Krug, a philosopher who disregards his country's totalitarian regime until his son David is killed by the forces he has attempted to ignore.

Benedetti \,bā-nā-'det-ē\, Mario (b. Sept. 14, 1920, Paso de Los Toros, Tacuarembó, Uru.)   Latin-American novelist, short-story writer, poet, and essayist.

Most of Benedetti's early life was spent in Montevideo, Uru. His first book of short stories, *Esta mañana* ("This Morning"), was published in 1949 and his first novel, *Quién de nosotros* ("Who of Us"), in 1953. On three different occasions from 1954 to 1960 Benedetti directed one of Uruguay's foremost weekly journals, *Marcha*. His simple and colloquial *Poemas de la oficina* (1956; "Office Poems") was an instant success.

With the publication of *Montevideanos* (1959), tragicomical tales of everyday city life, he won recognition as one of Uruguay's most perceptive writers. Other novels include *La tregua* (1960; *The Truce*) and *Gracias por el fuego* (1965; "Thanks for the Fire"). *El país de la cola de paja* (1960; "The Country with the Tail of Straw") is a collection of essays on the decline of Uruguay.

From 1967 to 1971 Benedetti lived in Cuba, where he was a member of Cuba's official international cultural organization. His impressions of Cuban life appeared in *Cuaderno cubano* (1969; "Cuban Notebook"). *El cumpleaños de Juan Ángel* (1971; "The Birthday of Juan Angel"), an autobiographical novella, tells of the author's crisis of political consciousness. He returned to Uruguay in 1971 to help establish a leftist coalition, but with the military takeover in 1973 Benedetti returned to his post in Cuba. *Con y sin nostalgia* (1977; "With and Without Nostalgia") is a collection of short stories about violence and exile.

Benedictsson \,ben-e-'dikt-sȯn\, Victoria, *byname* Ernst Ahlgren \'äl-,grän\ (b. March 6, 1850, Skåne, Swed.—d. July 21, 1888, Copenhagen, Den.)   Writer noted for her natural and unpretentious stories of Swedish folk life and her novels dealing with social issues.

Having grown up in a home marred by marital discord, Benedictsson married, at an early age, a widower much older than herself. Her marriage was also unhappy. After an illness that left her crippled, she turned to literature and in 1884 published a collection of stories of rural life in her native province, *Från Skåne* ("From Skåne"). It was followed by a novel, *Pengar* (1885; "Money"), a critical view of a society that confers status and security on women only through marriage, and another, somewhat contradictory novel, *Fru Marianne* (1887; "Mrs. Marianne"), in which a doll wife outgrows her early romantic notions and finds fulfillment in sharing work and responsibilities with her husband.

Benedictsson's success acquainted her with the brilliant and influential critic Georg Brandes. She fell deeply in love with him, but he did not return her feeling. Her posthumously published letters and diaries, describing her thwarted love and the desperation that drove her to suicide, rank with those of August Strindberg in the frankness of their self-revelation.

Benediktsson \'ben-e-,dikt-sòn\, Einar (b. Oct. 31, 1864, Ellidhavatn, Ice.—d. Jan. 14, 1940, Herdísarvík) Author considered by some to be the greatest Icelandic poet of the 20th century.

Son of a leader of the Icelandic independence movement, Benediktsson received a law degree at Copenhagen in 1892 and briefly edited a newspaper, *Dagskrá* (1896–98), advocating the cause of Icelandic independence. His five volumes of Symbolist verse—*Sögur og kvaedi* (1897; "Stories and Poems"), *Hafblik* (1906; "Smooth Seas"), *Hrannir* (1913; "Waves"), *Vogar* (1921; "Billows"), *Hvammar* (1930; "Grass Hollows")—show a masterful command of the language and exemplify his patriotism, mysticism, and love of nature, as well as the influence of his extensive travels. Benediktsson also translated Ibsen's *Peer Gynt* into Icelandic. A selection of his poems was translated into English as *Harp of the North* (1955).

Benet \'ben-et\, Juan, *surname in full* Benet Goita \'gói-tä\ (b. Oct. 7, 1927, Madrid, Spain—d. Jan. 5, 1993, Madrid) Spanish writer noted for his intricate novels and experimental prose style.

Benet lived with his family outside Spain during the Civil War (1936–39). After returning to Spain, he studied civil engineering and earned an advanced degree in 1954.

In 1961 he published a volume of short stories, *Nunca llegarás a nada* ("You'll Never Amount to Anything"). His first novel—*Volverás a Región* (1967; *Return to Región*)—stirred considerable interest in Spain because of its tantalizing effects. There are frequent changes in viewpoint, and many of the passages are open to conflicting interpretation. It constitutes a trilogy with *Una meditación* (1969; *A Meditation*) and *Un viaje de invierno* (1972; "A Winter Journey"). His later works include *En el estado* (1977; "In the State"), *Saúl ante Samuel* (1980; "Saul Before Samuel"), *En la penumbra* (1982; "In the Penumbra"), *Herrumbrosas lanzas* (1983; "Rusty Lances"), and *El caballero de Sajonia* (1991; "The Knight of Saxony"). Benet also wrote plays and critical essays.

Benét \bə-'nä\, Stephen Vincent (b. July 22, 1898, Bethlehem, Pa., U.S.—d. March 13, 1943, New York, N.Y.) Poet, novelist, and writer of short stories, best known for JOHN BROWN'S BODY (1928), a long narrative poem on the Civil War.

Benét published his first book at the age of 17. Civilian service during World War I interrupted his education at Yale. He received his M.A. degree after the war, submitting his third volume of poems instead of a thesis.

After publishing the much-admired *Ballad of William Sycamore 1790–1880* (1923), three novels, and a number of short stories, he went to France, where he wrote *John Brown's Body*. Dramatized by Charles Laughton in 1953, it was performed across the United States.

Library of Congress

A Book of Americans (1933), poems written with his wife, the former Rosemary Carr, brought many historical characters to life for American schoolchildren. Benét's preoccupation with historical themes was also the basis for *Western Star*, an ambitious story of America left uncompleted at the time of his death. Book I, complete in itself, was published posthumously. Benét's best-known short story, THE DEVIL AND DANIEL WEBSTER (1937), was the basis for a play, an opera by Douglas Moore, and a motion picture.

Bengtsson \'benkt-sòn\, Frans Gunnar (b. Oct. 4, 1894, Tossjö, Swed.—d. Dec. 19, 1954, Stockholm) Poet, biographer, novelist, and writer of numerous informal essays, a genre that he virtually introduced to Swedish literature and that brought him his greatest success.

Despite the dilatory pursuit of his studies at the University of Lund, Bengtsson eventually managed to acquire considerable erudition, which he used to good effect in his poetry and prose. His two extended prose works are a biography of Charles XII, 2 vol. (1935–36), and the novel *Röde Orm*, 2 vol. (1941, 1945; *The Long Ships*), both of which are written in an ornate and colorfully romantic style. Bengtsson's broad knowledge of history and mastery of a rich but informal prose style were used most effectively in his essays. These whimsical investigations of literary and historical curiosities were published in five volumes during 1929–55. An English translation of Bengtsson's essays was published in 1950 as *A Walk to an Ant Hill and Other Essays*.

Ben-Hur \,ben-'hər\ Historical novel by Lewis WALLACE, published in 1880 and widely translated. It depicts the oppressive Roman occupation of ancient Palestine and the origins of Christianity.

The Jew Judah Ben-Hur is wrongly accused by his former friend, the Roman Messala, of attempting to kill a Roman official. He is sent to be a slave and his mother and sister are imprisoned. Years later he returns, wins a chariot race against Messala, and is reunited with his now leprous mother and sister. Mother and daughter are cured on the day of the Crucifixion, and the family is converted to Christianity.

Benito Cereno \bə-'nē-tō-sə-'rä-nō\ Short story by Herman MELVILLE, published in *Putnam's Monthly Magazine* in 1855 and later included in the collection *The Piazza Tales* (1856). It is a chilling story narrated by Amasa Delano, the captain of a seal-hunting ship who encounters off the coast of Chile a slave ship whose human cargo has revolted. Although it takes Delano some time to unravel the situation, eventually he saves the title character, who is the captain of the slaver, and his remaining crew, and the leaders of the insurrection are slaughtered.

Benivieni \bä-nē-'vyä-nē\, Girolamo (b. 1453, Florence [Italy]—d. 1542, Florence) Poet whose versification of the philosopher Marsilio Ficino's translation of Plato's *Symposium* influenced writers during the Renaissance and after.

As a member of the Florentine Medici circle, Benivieni was well acquainted with the Renaissance humanists Ficino, Giovanni Pico della Mirandola, and Politian (Angelo Poliziano). Ficino translated the *Symposium* in about 1474 with his own commentary, which Benivieni summarized in the canzone "De lo amore celeste" ("Of Heavenly Love"), and this in turn became the subject of an extensive commentary by Pico della Mirandola. Benivieni eventually fell under the spell of the fiery religious reformer Girolamo Savonarola. After his conversion, Benivieni rewrote some of his sensual poetry, translated a treatise of Savonarola's into Italian (*Della semplicità della vita cristiana*; "On the Simplicity of the Christian Life"), and wrote religious poetry.

Benjamin \\'ben-yä-ˌmēn, *Angl* 'ben-jə-mən\\, Walter (b. July 15, 1892, Berlin, Ger.—d. Sept. 26, 1940, near Port-Bou, Fr.) Man of letters and aesthetician, now considered to have been the most important German literary critic in the first half of the 20th century.

Born into a prosperous Jewish family, Benjamin studied philosophy in Berlin, Freiburg im Breisgau, Munich, and Bern. He settled in Berlin in 1920 and worked thereafter as a literary critic and translator. Benjamin left Germany in 1933 upon the Nazis' rise to power and eventually settled in Paris, where he continued to write essays and reviews for literary journals. Fleeing from Nazi-occupied France in 1940, Benjamin committed suicide when he was told he would be turned over to the Gestapo.

The posthumous publication of Benjamin's essays won him a growing reputation later in the 20th century. His philosophical reflections on literature mix social criticism and linguistic analysis with historical nostalgia while communicating an underlying sense of pathos and pessimism. Benjamin's independence and originality are evident in the extended essay *Goethes Wahlverwandtschaften* (1924–25; "Goethe's Elective Affinities"); his doctoral thesis, *Ursprung des deutschen Trauerspiels* (1928; *The Origin of German Tragic Drama*), which was rejected by the University of Frankfurt; and the essays collected in *Illuminationen* (1961; *Illuminations*).

Ben Jelloun \\ben-'zhel-ūn\\, Tahar (b. Dec. 21, 1944, Fès, Mor.) Moroccan poet, novelist, and dramatist.

Ben Jelloun began his studies in philosophy and later earned a doctorate in social psychology. He taught and was a contributor to a number of magazines and newspapers, including *Souffles, Intégral, Les Lettres Nouvelles*, and *Le Monde*.

Ben Jelloun's first collection of poetry, *Hommes sous linceul de silence* (1971; "Men Under the Shroud of Silence"), was followed by *Cicatrices du soleil* (1972; "Scars of the Sun"). *Harrouda* (1973), a bildungsroman set in Fès and Tangier, was followed by two more poetry collections, *Le Discours du chameau* (1974; "The Discourse of the Camel") and *Grains de peau* (1974; "Particles of Skin").

Les Amandiers sont morts de leurs blessures (1976; "The Almond Trees Are Dead from Their Wounds") is a book of poems and stories. In 1976 *Chronique d'une solitude* ("Chronicle of Loneliness"), a play about the misery of the North African immigrant worker, reappeared as a novel, *La Réclusion solitaire* ("Solitary Confinement"). A third novel, *Moha le fou, Moha le sage* (1978; "Moha the Fool, Moha the Wise"), is a satire of the modern North African state. *À l'insu du souvenir* (1980; "Unknown to Memory"), a later collection of poetry, and "L'Écrivain public" (1983; "The Public Writer"), an essay on the intellectual in the Third World, displayed his conviction that his art must express the struggle for political, economic, and social freedom. Ben Jelloun's later works include *L'enfant de sable* (1985; *The Sand Child*), *La Nuit sacrée* (1987; *The Sacred Night*), *Jour de silence à Tanger* (1990; *Silent Day in Tangier*), *Les Yeux baissés* (1991; *With Downcast Eyes*), and *La remontée des cendres* (1991; "The Removal of Ashes").

Benn \\'ben\\, Gottfried (b. May 2, 1886, Mansfeld, Ger.—d. July 7, 1956, Berlin) German poet and essayist considered one of the most influential German writers of the mid-20th century.

The son of a Lutheran clergyman, Benn studied theology at the University of Marburg, then transferred to the academy there for military-medical instruction and became a specialist in venereal and skin diseases. He took medical jobs on cruise ships and as a German officer in World War I was made medical supervisor of jail inmates and prostitutes in occupied Brussels.

Degeneracy and medical aspects of decay are important allusions in his early poems. His first and third collections of verse were fittingly titled *Morgue und andere Gedichte* (1912; "Morgue and Other Poems") and *Fleisch* (1917; "Flesh"). Because of his Expressionism and despite his right-wing political views, the Nazi regime penalized him both as a writer and as a physician. To escape harassment, he rejoined the army.

Benn regained literary attention with *Statische Gedichte* (1948; "Static Poems") and the simultaneous reappearance of his old poems. His gradual loss of cynicism is reflected in the autobiography *Doppelleben* (1950; "Double Life"). A broad selection of his poetry and prose in English translation was published under the title *Primal Vision* (1961).

Bennet family \\'ben-ət\\ Fictional characters in Jane Austen's novel PRIDE AND PREJUDICE. Mr. Bennet is an intelligent but eccentric and sarcastic man who does not care for society's conventions and mocks his wife's obsession with finding suitable husbands for her daughters. Mrs. Bennet is a woman of little sense and much self-pity. The oldest daughter, Jane, is sweet-tempered and modest and is her sister Elizabeth's confidant and friend. Elizabeth, the heroine of the novel, is intelligent and high-spirited. She shares her father's distaste for the conventional views of society as to the importance of wealth and rank. The third daughter, Mary, is plain, bookish, and pompous. Lydia and Kitty, the two youngest, are flighty and immature young girls.

Bennett \\'ben-ət\\, Arnold, *in full* Enoch Arnold Bennett (b. May 27, 1867, Hanley, Staffordshire, Eng.—d. March 27, 1931, London) British novelist, playwright, critic, and essayist whose major works form an important link between the English novel and the mainstream of European realism.

Arnold was educated at the Middle School, Newcastle-under-Lyme. In 1889 he moved to London, working as a clerk, and soon began writing popular serial fiction and editing a women's magazine. After the publication of his first novel, *A Man from the North* (1898), he became a full-time writer.

Bennett learned his craft from intensive study of the French realist novelists, especially Gustave Flaubert and Honoré de Balzac. Bennett's literary criticism was of such high caliber that had he never written fiction he would rank as an important writer. He was less successful in his plays, although *Milestones* (1912; written with Edward Knoblock) and *The Great Adventure* (1913), adapted from his novel *Buried Alive* (1908), both had long runs and have been revived.

Bennett is best known for his highly detailed novels of the "Five Towns"—the Potteries in his native Staffordshire. His major novels—ANNA OF THE FIVE TOWNS (1902), THE OLD WIVES' TALE (1908), and the three novels that make up THE CLAYHANGER FAMILY (1925)—have their setting there. The novel *Riceyman Steps* (1923) is set in a lower-middle-class district of London.

Bennett \\'ben-it\\, Gwendolyn B. (b. July 8, 1902, Giddings, Tex., U.S.—d. May 30, 1981, Reading, Pa.) African-American poet, essayist, short-story writer, and artist who was a vital figure in the Harlem Renaissance.

Bennett, the daughter of teachers, grew up on a Nevada Indian reservation, in Washington, D.C., and in Brooklyn, N.Y. She attended Columbia University and Pratt Institute, then studied art in Paris in 1925–26. She wrote articles and created covers for *The Crisis* and *Opportunity* magazines. Her close friendships with fellow Harlem-based writers resulted in her becoming an *Opportunity* editor and writing its popular literary news column (1926–28). Most of her published work, including two short stories, appeared in 1923–28, and though it is often anthologized, it has not been collected. Her ballads, odes, sonnets, and protest poems are notable for their visual imagery; the best known is the sensual "To a Dark Girl."

Benoît de Sainte-Maure or **Benoît** de Sainte-More \bən-'wȧ-də-sanᵊ-'môr\ (fl. 12th century, probably from Sainte-Maure, near Poitiers, Fr.) Author of an Old French poem in about 30,000 octosyllabic couplets, the *Roman de Troie*. Benoît's poem, a travesty of the story told in Homer's *Iliad*, is an immense baroque tapestry of Greek lore and fable. His is the first version of the Troilus and Cressida story. It was translated by R.K. Gordon as *The Story of Troilus* (1934).

Benserade \banˢ-'rȧd\, Isaac de (b. either 1612, Normandy, Fr., or 1613, Paris—d. Oct. 20, 1691, Paris) Minor but brilliant French literary light of the courts of Louis XIII and Louis XIV. Benserade's romantic verses attracted attention, and he was repeatedly called on to write libretti for royal ballets, a function he discharged with a wit verging on impertinence. He composed 224 rondeaux as supplementary text to an illustrated version of Ovid's *Metamorphoses* published in 1676 as *Metamorphoses d'Ovide en rondeaux*.

Benson \'ben-sən\, E.F., *in full* Edward Frederic (b. July 24, 1867, Wellington College, Berkshire, Eng.—d. Feb. 29, 1940, London) Writer of fiction, reminiscences, and biographies, of which the best remembered are his arch, satirical novels and his urbane autobiographical studies of Edwardian and Georgian society.

Benson was educated at Cambridge. After graduation he worked in Athens for the British School of Archaeology and later in Egypt for the Society for the Promotion of Hellenic Studies. In 1893 he published *Dodo*, a novel that attracted wide attention. It was followed by other successful novels—such as *Mrs. Ames* (1912), *Queen Lucia* (1920), *Miss Mapp* (1922), and *Lucia in London* (1927)—and books on a wide range of subjects, including biographies of Queen Victoria, William Gladstone, and William II of Germany. Benson's reminiscences include *As We Were* (1930), *As We Are* (1932), and *Final Edition* (1940).

Bentley \'bent-lē\, E.C., *in full* Edmund Clerihew (b. July 10, 1875, London, Eng.—d. March 30, 1956, London) British journalist and man of letters who is remembered as the inventor of the CLERIHEW and as the author of *Trent's Last Case* (1913), a classic detective story.

After attending St. Paul's School in London and the University of Oxford, Bentley studied law. He soon abandoned the law, however, for journalism.

The light verse quatrain known as the clerihew was introduced in *Biography for Beginners*, by "E. Clerihew" (1905), and was immediately popular and soon widely imitated. Several other collections followed, including *Clerihews Complete* (1951). Bentley wrote *Trent's Last Case* in exasperation at the infallibility of Sherlock Holmes, and the book has been said to mark the end of the Holmes era in detective fiction. Two decades later, Bentley revived the character in *Trent's Own Case* (1936; with Warner Allen) and in *Trent Intervenes* (1938), a collection of short stories.

Bentley \'bent-lē\, Eric (Russell) (b. Sept. 14, 1916, Bolton, Lancashire, Eng.) Critic, translator, and stage director responsible for introducing the works of many European playwrights to the United States and known for his original, literate reviews of theater and critical works on drama.

Bentley studied at the University of Oxford and Yale University. His Ph.D. dissertation from Yale (1941) was expanded into the book *A Century of Hero Worship* (1944; reissued as *The Cult of the Superman*, 1969). From 1948 to 1951 Bentley directed plays in numerous European cities, including Dublin, Zürich,

Munich, and Padua. He also translated Bertolt Brecht's plays into English and contributed reports on European theater to *Theatre Arts* and the *Kenyon Review* in the United States. From 1974 to 1982 he was professor of theater at the State University of New York (Buffalo), and from 1982 he taught at the University of Maryland (College Park).

Bentley's criticism is noteworthy for covering practical, aesthetic, and philosophical aspects of theater, and it stems from a belief that art must rescue humanity from meaninglessness. His *The Life of the Drama* (1964) has been hailed as one of the best general books on the theater ever written. Other books include *The Playwright as Thinker* (1946; U.K. title, *The Modern Theatre*), *In Search of Theater* (1953), *The Theory of the Modern Theatre* (1968, rev. ed., 1976), *Brecht Commentaries* (1981), and *Thinking About the Playwright* (1987).

Bentley \'bent-lē\, Richard (b. Jan. 27, 1662, Oulton, Yorkshire, Eng.—d. July 14, 1742, Cambridge, Cambridgeshire) British clergyman, one of the great figures in the history of classical scholarship, who combined wide learning with critical acuteness.

Bentley was educated at St. John's College, Cambridge. Bentley's skill in textual emendation and his knowledge of ancient meter were strikingly displayed in the short treatise *Epistola ad Joannem Millium* (1691). Bentley was appointed Boyle lecturer at Oxford in 1692, and in 1694 he became keeper of the Royal Library and fellow of the Royal Society. In 1699 he published his *Dissertation upon the Epistles of Phalaris*, in which he brought all his learning and critical powers to bear in proof of the epistles' spuriousness.

In 1700 Bentley was chosen master of Trinity College, Cambridge, and in 1717 he became regius professor of divinity. He published a critical appendix to John Davies' edition of Cicero's *Tusculan Disputations* in 1709, and he published editions of Horace (1711), Terence (1726), and Marcus Manilius (1739). He made an important contribution through his discovery that a sound (represented by the letter digamma in transcriptions of some Greek dialects) was present in certain Homeric Greek words though not represented by any letter when the words were written.

Beowulf \'bā-ə-ˌwu̇lf\ A heroic poem, the highest achievement of Old English literature and the earliest European vernacular epic. Preserved in a single manuscript dated roughly to 1000, it deals with events of the early 6th century and is believed to have been composed between 700 and 750.

The first part of the two-part poem is set in Denmark, in Heorot, the mead hall of King Hrothgar. For 12 years Heorot has been ravaged by nightly visits from Grendel, an evil monster who carries off Hrothgar's warriors and devours them. Beowulf, who is a prince of the Geats of southern Sweden, arrives and offers to rid Heorot of its monster. That night, when Grendel arrives, he grapples with Beowulf, whose powerful grip he cannot escape. In his desperation Grendel wrenches himself free, leaving his arm in Beowulf's grip, and departs mortally wounded. The following night, Grendel's mother avenges her son, killing one of Hrothgar's men. In the morning Beowulf seeks her out and kills her. Enriched with honors and princely gifts, he returns home to King Hygelac of the Geats.

The second part of the poem passes rapidly over King Hygelac's subsequent death in a battle, the death of his son, and Beowulf's succession to the kingship and his peaceful 50-year rule. When a fire-breathing dragon ravages his land, the aging Beowulf engages it. He kills the dragon but is mortally wounded. The poem ends with his funeral rites and a lament.

Beowulf belongs metrically, stylistically, and thematically to the inherited Germanic heroic tradition. The ethical values are manifestly the Germanic code of loyalty to chief and tribe and vengeance to enemies. Yet the poem is so infused with a Christian spirit that it lacks the grim fatality of many of the Eddic lays or the Icelanders' sagas.

Béranger \bā-rän-'zhä\, Pierre-Jean de (b. Aug. 19, 1780, Paris, Fr.—d. July 16, 1857, Paris) French poet and writer of popular songs, celebrated for his liberal and humanitarian views.

Béranger was active in his father's business enterprises until they failed. He then found work as a clerk at the University of Paris (1809). After the downfall of Napoleon, he composed songs and poems highly critical of the government set up under the restored Bourbon monarchy. They brought him immediate fame through their expression of popular feeling, but they led to dismissal from his post (1821) and three months' imprisonment. He became an influential and respected figure in his own lifetime and was eventually able to live on the proceeds of his works.

Béranger's best-known poems are "Le Roi d'Yvetot" ("The King of Yvetot"), "Le Dieu des pauvres gens" ("The God of the Poor People"), "Le Sacre de Charles le Simple" ("The Coronation of Charles the Simple"), "La Grand-Mère" ("The Grandmother"), and "Le Vieux Sergent" ("The Old Sergeant").

Berberova \bʸir-'bʸer-ə-və\, Nina (Nikolayevna) (b. Aug. 8, 1901, St. Petersburg, Russia—d. Sept. 26, 1993, Philadelphia, Pa., U.S.) Russian-born emigré writer, biographer, editor, and translator, known for her exploration of the plight of exiles.

Berberova left the Soviet Union in 1922 and lived in Germany, Czechoslovakia, and Italy as part of Maksim Gorky's entourage before settling in Paris in 1925. While living in Europe she served as coeditor of the literary journal *Novy Dom* (1926; "New House") and as literary editor of the weekly *Russkaya Mysl* (1948–50; "Russian Thought"). Although she wrote four novels, including *Po.sledneye i pervoye* (1929; "The Last and the First") and *Povelitelnitsa* (1932; "Female Sovereign"), she was more successful as a writer of short stories and novellas. Her cycle of stories entitled "Biyankurskiye prazdniki" ("Billancourt Holidays") was published serially in 1928–40 in *Posledniye novosti* and was published in the U.S.S.R. in 1989. Another collection of stories was *Oblegcheniye uchasti* (1949; "The Easing of Fate"). She also wrote poetry and biographies.

Berberova moved to the United States in 1950 and later became a citizen. Her teaching career included positions as lecturer at Yale University (1958–63) and professor of literature at Princeton University (1963–71). Her autobiography *The Italics Are Mine* (1969) appeared in English first, then Russian. *The Tattered Cloak* (1991) is a collection, translated into English, of some of her early short stories. She also translated works of Romain Rolland, Constantine Cavafy, and T.S. Eliot into Russian, and of Fyodor Dostoyevsky into French.

Berceo \ber-'thä-ō\, Gonzalo de (b. c. 1198, Berceo, Spain—d. c. 1264) The first author of verse in Castilian Spanish whose name is known. His works combined classical rhetorical style, popular poetic form, and the exhortative style of the sermon.

Berceo's subjects were religious, and he wrote in Castilian, a dialect that was then considered inferior to Galician-Portuguese, in order to bring religious learning to the common people. Among his works were *Vida de San Millán* (c. 1234; "Life of Saint Millán"), *Vida de Santa Oria* (c. 1265; "Life of Saint Oria"), *Milagros de Nuestra Señora* (c. 1245–60; "Miracles of Our Lady"), and *Sacrificio de la misa* (c. 1237; "Sacrifice of the Mass").

Berdichevsky \,ber-di-'chef-skē\, Micah Joseph, *pseudonym* Micah Joseph bin Gorion \bin-'gòr-ē-ən\ (b. Aug. 19, 1865, Medzhibozh, Russia [now Medzhybizh, Ukraine]—d. Nov. 18, 1921, Berlin, Ger.) Author of works in Hebrew, German, and

Yiddish; his impassioned writings bear poignant witness to the "rent in the heart" of 19th-century Jews torn between tradition and assimilation.

Berdichevsky was the son of a rabbi of a Ḥasidic sect that stressed devoutness and joy in the service of God rather than adherence to the formal works of Jewish tradition. He studied for a time at Volozhin seminary and then entered the University of Breslau (now Wrocław, Pol.) at the age of 25. In these years the inner struggle between his upbringing and his desire for spiritual liberation was intensified. He spent the last 10 years of his life in Berlin, recreating with insight and poetic appreciation portions of the Aggadah, Jewish writings dealing with legends and folklore. He published part of them in Hebrew as *Me-Otsar ha-agadah* (1913–14; "From the Treasures of the Aggadah"). His stories, collected in volumes such as *Me-Ḥuts liteḥum* (1922–23; "Out of the Pale") and *Ben ha-homot* ("Between the Walls"), all deal with the travails of Jewish life.

Berdichevsky's essays, collected posthumously in nine volumes in 1922, include *Bi-sede sefer* ("In the Field of Literature"), *Ba-derekh* ("On the Way"), and *Maḥshavot ve-torot* ("Reflections and Teachings"). They variously contain literary criticism, polemics against the dead hand of Jewish tradition, and idealizations of Ḥasidism.

Bérénice \bā-rā-'nēs\ Tragic drama in five acts by Jean RACINE, performed in 1670 and published in 1671. It is loosely based upon events following the death of the Roman emperor Vespasian in the 1st century AD.

Bérénice is the story of a love triangle; Titus, who is to become the new emperor, and his friend Antiochus, king of Commagene, are both in love with Bérénice, the queen of Palestine. Events conspire against them, and at the play's end the three go their separate ways.

Berent \'ber-ent\, Wacław (b. Sept. 28, 1873, Warsaw, Pol.—d. Nov. 22, 1940, Warsaw) Novelist, a member of the Young Poland movement, which emphasized the expression of feeling and imagination in literature.

Berent's first novel, *Fachowiec* (1895; "The Expert"), composed while he was a student of biology at the University of Zürich, describes, in a realistic style, a student who leaves school to become a common laborer. Berent later studied biology in Munich and while there wrote his best-known and most characteristic work, *Próchno* (1903; "Rotten Wood"), a caustic portrait of late 19th-century artistic and intellectual life in Berlin. *Żywe kamienie* (1918; "Live Stones"), intended to be a poetic vision of the European Middle Ages, is long and elaborate and was not well received. His last novel, *Nurt* (1934; "The Current"), is an impressionistic and anecdotal biography of Polish personalities of the late 18th and early 19th centuries.

Bergbom \'berʸ-,bûm\, Kaarlo (b. Oct. 2, 1843, Vyborg, Russia—d. Jan. 17, 1906, Helsinki, Fin.) Activist in the struggle to enhance Finnish-language institutions, and founder-director of the first stable Finnish-language theater, the Finnish National Theatre. Bergbom directed the first performance of Aleksis Kivi's one-act biblical drama *Lea* (1869), the event cited as the beginning of professional theater in the Finnish language.

In 1872 Bergbom founded the Finnish National Theatre as a touring troupe. During the first year of its existence, the National Theatre performed 36 plays, of which only 13, all singleact, were native works; by its 20th season the ratio was reversed, two-thirds of the plays being Finnish and including the premieres of six full-length Finnish plays. Bergbom also produced notable Finnish versions of works by foreign authors, among them the first Finnish-language productions of William Shakespeare (*Romeo and Juliet*, 1881) and J.W. von Goethe (*Faust*, 1885).

Berger \'bər-gər\, John (Peter) (b. Nov. 5, 1926, London, Eng.)   British art critic, novelist, poet, translator, and screenwriter whose writings reflect his Marxist convictions.

Berger was educated at the Central and Chelsea schools of art and served in the British army during World War II. He later worked as a painter and a teacher of art and served as the art critic for the *New Statesman*. His first novel, *A Painter of Our Time* (1958), explores the relationship between politics and culture in the context of the London art world. *G* (1972), probably the best known of his novels, is an experimental work that portrays the influence of historical events on a Don Juan figure. Berger's later fiction includes the trilogy *Into Their Labours*, which consists of *Pig Earth* (1979), *Once in Europa* (1987), and *Lilac and Flag* (1990).

Berger's nonfiction includes *A Fortunate Man* (1967), about a doctor in rural England, and *A Seventh Man* (1975), about Europe's migrant workers, both of which features Jean Mohr's photographs. His books of art criticism include *The Success and Failure of Picasso* (1965); *Art and Revolution: Ernst Neizvestny and the Role of the Artist in the U.S.S.R.* (1969); and the book with which he is most often associated, *Ways of Seeing* (1972). A later collection of critical pieces is *Keeping a Rendezvous* (1991).

Berger \'bər-gər\, Thomas (Louis) (b. July 20, 1924, Cincinnati, Ohio, U.S.)   American novelist whose darkly comic fiction probed and satirized the American experience.

Berger graduated from the University of Cincinnati in 1948. His first novel, *Crazy in Berlin* (1958), inaugurated a tetralogy about Carlo Reinhart, who in the first novel is an adolescent American soldier in Germany. His story is continued in *Reinhart in Love* (1962), *Vital Parts* (1970), and *Reinhart's Women* (1981). In *Little Big Man* (1964; film, 1970), the only white survivor of the Battle of the Little Big Horn, the 111-year-old Jack Crabb, tells his life story.

Berger's other novels include *Killing Time* (1967), *Regiment of Women* (1973), *Who Is Teddy Villanova?* (1977), *Arthur Rex: A Legendary Novel* (1978), *Neighbors* (1980), *The Houseguest* (1988), *Changing the Past* (1989), and *Orrie's Story* (1990).

Bergerac, Cyrano de   *see* CYRANO DE BERGERAC.

Bergman \'ber-mån, *Angl* 'bərg-mən\, Bo Hjalmar (b. Oct. 6, 1869, Stockholm, Swed.—d. Nov. 17, 1967, Stockholm) Swedish lyrical poet whose early pessimistic and deterministic view of life gave way to a militant humanism; his simplicity and clarity of style greatly influenced 20th-century Swedish poetry.

Bergman began writing while an official of the Swedish post office. *Marionetterna* (1903; "Marionettes"), his first volume of poetry, was an expression of melancholy passivity, but each of the ensuing volumes increasingly attacked political developments in Europe. This was particularly true of his last three volumes of verse: *Trots allt* (1931; "In Spite of Everything"), *Gamla gudar* (1939; "Old Gods"), and *Riket* (1944; "The Kingdom"). Bergman's prose works include five volumes of short stories, five novels, five monographs, and autobiographical fragments.

Bergman \'ber-mån, *Angl* 'bərg-mən\, Hjalmar Fredrik Elgérus (b. Nov. 19, 1883, Örebro, Swed.—d. Jan. 1, 1931, Berlin, Ger.)   Swedish dramatist, novelist, and short-story writer who was intensely interested in psychological complexities.

As a young teen Bergman accompanied his father on business trips to the mining region that would become the setting for many of his works. He studied briefly at Uppsala University. His first play, *Maria, Jesu moder* (1905; "Mary, Mother of Jesus"), shows an original approach to the psychology of Christ and the Virgin Mary. His other early plays reveal the influence of Henrik Ibsen. His most original contribution to drama was *Marionettspel* (1917; "Plays of Marionettes"), re-

flecting the same pessimism as his later novels. His first popular novel, *Hans Nåds testamente* (1910; "His Grace's Will"), was set in the Bergslagen mining district. A collection of short stories, *Amourer* (1910), mostly set in Italy, displays his subtle understanding of the irrational as a decisive factor in human behavior. Bergman produced a series of novels and long short stories, starting with *Vi Bookar, Krokar och Rothar* (1912) and ending with *En döds memoarer* (1918; "Memoirs of One Dead"). These were mainly concerned with Bergslagen, from early times, and with the fortunes and complicated feuds of certain families and characters. With the comic novel *Markurells i Wadköping* (1919; *God's Orchid*), Bergman at last captured the notice of the wider public. Bergman followed this with other successes, including *Farmor och vår Herre* (1921; *Thy Rod and Thy Staff*), *Chefen Fru Ingeborg* (1924; *The Head of the Firm*), and *Clownen Jac* (1930; "The Clown Jac").

His play *Swedenhielms* (1925) is among the few existing successful Swedish comedies, and his dramatization of *Markurells* also has remained popular. Four of his plays (*Markurells of Wadkoping, The Baron's Will, Swedenhielms,* and *Mr. Sleeman Is Coming*) were published in English translation in 1968.

Bergson \berk-'sȯn, *Angl* 'berg-sən\, Henri(-Louis) (b. Oct. 18, 1859, Paris, Fr.—d. Jan. 4, 1941, Paris)   French philosopher, the first to elaborate what came to be called a process philosophy, which rejected static values in favor of values of motion, change, and evolution. He was also a master literary stylist, of both academic and popular appeal, and was awarded the Nobel Prize for Literature in 1927.

Bergson's first publication was his doctoral dissertation, *Essai sur les données immédiates de la conscience* (1889; *Time and Free Will: An Essay on the Immediate Data of Consciousness*), which is primarily an attempt to establish the notion of duration, or lived time, as opposed to science's spatialized conception of time measured by a clock.

His subsequent publications included *Matière et mémoire: Essai sur la relation du corps à l'esprit* (1896; *Matter and Memory*) and *L'Évolution créatrice* (1907; *Creative Evolution*), his most famous book, in which he proposed that the whole evolutionary process should be seen as the endurance of an *élan vital* ("vital impulse") that is continually developing and generating new forms. Twenty-five years elapsed before Bergson published another major work, *Les Deux Sources de la morale et de la religion* (1932; *The Two Sources of Morality and Religion*).

Bergson's other works include *Le Rire: Essai sur la signifi- cance du comique* (1900; *Laughter: An Essay on the Meaning of the Comic*) and *Introduction à la metaphysique* (1903; *An Introduction to Metaphysics*).

Berlin Alexanderplatz \ber-'lēn-,ä-lek-'sän-dər-,pläts, *Angl* bər-'lin\   Novel by Alfred DÖBLIN, published in 1929. It appeared in English under the original title and as *Alexanderplatz, Berlin*. It tells the story of Franz Biberkopf, a Berlin proletarian who tries to rehabilitate himself after his release from jail but undergoes a series of vicissitudes, many of them violent and squalid, before he can finally attain a normal life. The book is notable for its interior monologue (in colloquial language and Berlin slang) and somewhat cinematic technique.

Berliner Ensemble \ber-'lē-nər, *Angl* bər-'lin-ər\   Theatrical company founded in 1949 in East Berlin by the German playwright and poet Bertolt BRECHT as a branch of the Deutsches Theater. Originally designed as a touring company, the ensemble was composed primarily of younger members of the Deutsches Theater. The company devoted itself to works written or adapted by Brecht. In 1954 the Berliner Ensemble moved to the Theater am Schiffbauerdamm, where it was established as an independent state theater.

Several tours through Europe, including two visits to Paris in the mid-1950s, brought the Berliner Ensemble international fame and high critical esteem.

Berlin Stories, The \bər-'lin, *German* ber-'lēn\   Collection of two previously published novels written by Christopher ISHERWOOD, published in 1946. Set in pre–World War II Germany, the semiautobiographical work consists of *Mr. Norris Changes Trains* (1935; U.S. title, *The Last of Mr. Norris*) and *Goodbye to Berlin* (1939).

The Berlin Stories merge fact and fiction and contain ostensibly objective, frequently comic tales of marginal characters who live shabby and tenuous existences as expatriates in Berlin; the threat of the political horrors to come serves as subtext. In *Goodbye to Berlin* the character Isherwood uses the phrase "I am a camera with its shutter open" to claim that he is simply a passive recorder of events. The two novels that comprise *The Berlin Stories* made Isherwood's literary reputation; they later became the basis for the play *I Am a Camera* (1951; film, 1955) and the musical *Cabaret* (1966; film, 1972).

Bernanos \ber-nȧ-'nōs\, Georges (b. Feb. 20, 1888, Paris, Fr.—d. July 5, 1948, Neuilly-sur-Seine)   Novelist and polemical writer whose masterpiece, THE DIARY OF A COUNTRY PRIEST, established him as one of the most original and independent Roman Catholic writers of his time.

Bernanos began life as a Royalist journalist and later worked as an inspector for an insurance company. He was a man of humor and humanity who abhorred materialism and compromise with evil. His vehement sincerity is seen in his political pamphlets *La Grande Peur des bien-pensants* (1931; "The Great Fear of Right-Thinking People"), a polemic on the materialism of the middle classes, and *Les Grands Cimetières sous la lune* (1938; *A Diary of My Times*), a fierce attack on fascist excesses during the Spanish Civil War and on the church dignitaries who supported them.

Bernanos' first novel was *Sous le soleil de Satan* (1926; *The Star of Satan*). In 1936 he published *Journal d'un curé de campagne* (*The Diary of a Country Priest*), a story of a young priest's war against sin. Other notable works include *La Joie* (1929; *Joy*), *Nouvelle Histoire de Mouchette* (1937; *Mouchette*), and *Monsieur Ouine* (1943; *The Open Mind*).

Political events increasingly troubled Bernanos. In July 1938 he went into self-imposed exile in Brazil. His broadcast messages and *Lettre aux Anglais* (1942; *Plea for Liberty*) influenced his compatriots during World War II. A return to France in 1945 brought disillusionment with his country's lack of spiritual renewal, and he lived thereafter in Tunis until he returned to France suffering from a fatal illness. Shortly before his death, Bernanos completed DIALOGUES DES CARMÉLITES, a film script telling the story of 16 nuns martyred during the French Revolution.

Bernard \ber-'nȧr\, Jean-Jacques (b. July 30, 1888, Enghien-les-Bains, Fr.—d. Sept. 12, 1972, Paris)   French playwright and chief representative of what became known as *l'école du silence* ("the school of silence") or, as some critics called it, the "art of the unexpressed," in which the dialogue does not express the characters' real attitudes. As in *Martine* (1922), perhaps the best example of his work, emotions are implied in gestures, facial expressions, fragments of speech, and silence.

The son of the dramatist Tristan Bernard, he began writing plays before World War I. Unconscious jealousy is the theme of *Le Feu qui reprend mal* (1921; *The Sulky Fire*) and *Le Printemps des autres* (1924; *The Springtime of Others*). In *L'Âme en peine* (1926; *The Unquiet Spirit*), two characters who never meet feel an inexplicable disquiet whenever they are near one another. Among his later plays are the more conventional *À la recherche des coeurs* (1931; "In Search of Hearts") and *Jeanne de Pantin* (1933).

Bernard's nondramatic writings include *Le Camp de la mort lente* (1944; *The Camp of Slow Death*), a description of the German concentration camp at Compiègne, in which he, as a Jew, was interned, and *Mon ami le théâtre* (1958).

Bernard \ber-'nȧr\, Tristan, *pseudonym of* Paul Bernard (b. Sept. 7, 1866, Besançon, Fr.—d. Dec. 7, 1947, Paris)   French playwright, novelist, journalist, and lawyer. His works were characterized by a tone of light cynicism, a cross fire of lively dialogue, and a keen insight into the foibles of the bourgeoisie. Among his most successful plays were *L'Anglais tel qu'on le parle* (1899; "English As It Is Spoken"), *Triplepatte* (1905, written in collaboration with André Godfernaux and adapted by Clyde Fitch as *Toddles*), and *Monsieur Codomat* (1907). He also wrote several humorous novels: *Les Mémoires d'un jeune homme rangé* (1899; "Memoirs of a Proper Young Man") and *La Féerie bourgeoise* (1924; "The Bourgeois Fairyland").

Bernard de Ventadour \ber-nȧr-də-väⁿ-tȧ-'dür\, *also called* Bernart de Ventadorn \ber-nȧr-də-väⁿ-tȧ-'dȯrn\ (b. Limousin province, Aquitaine [now in France]—d. 1195?, Dalon)   Troubadour whose poetry is considered among the finest in the Provençal language. Bernard is known to have traveled in England. He lived at the court of Eleanor of Aquitaine and at the court at Toulouse, in later life retiring to the abbey of Dalon. His short love lyrics, 45 of which survive, convey emotional power with remarkable delicacy, lyricism, and simplicity.

Bernardin de Saint-Pierre \ber-nȧr-daⁿ-də-saⁿ-'pyer\, Jacques-Henri (b. Jan. 19, 1737, Le Havre, Fr.—d. Jan. 21, 1814, Éragny)   French writer who is best remembered for *Paul et Virginie*, a pastoral of innocent love.

Bernardin's army service on the island of Mauritius provided him with material for his first book, *Voyage à l'Île de France* (1773). The work brought him to the attention of Jean-Jacques Rousseau, whose friendship did much to mold the views expressed in Bernardin's *Études de la nature* (1784). To the third edition of *Études* (1788) he appended *Paul et Virginie*, the story of two island children whose love for each other, begun in their infancy, thrives in an unspoiled natural setting but ends tragically when civilization interferes. In *La Chaumière indienne* (1790), a traveler finds wisdom in the cottage of an Indian outcaste. Cultural primitivism, which Bernardin was one of the first to celebrate, became one of the central ideas of the Romantic movement.

Berners \'bər-nərz\, Lord, *in full* John Bourchier \'baủ-chər\, 2nd Baron Berners (b. 1467, Tharfield, Hertfordshire, Eng.—d. March 16, 1532/33, Calais?, Fr.)   English writer and statesman who is best known for his simple, fresh, and energetic translation (vol. 1, 1523; vol 2, 1525) from the French of Jean Froissart's *Chroniques*.

Berners was a frontline participant in the political and military conflicts of his age. His translation of the French romance *The Boke Huon de Bordeuxe*, which introduced Oberon, king of the fairies, into English literature, is almost as successful as his translation of Froissart. Near the end of his life he translated into English prose two of the newly fashionable courtesy books: *The Castell of Love* by Diego de San Pedro and *The Golden Boke of Marcus Aurelius* by Antonio de Guevara.

Bernhard \'bern-,härt\, Thomas (b. Sept. 11 or Feb. 9/10, 1931, Cloister Heerland, Neth.—d. Feb. 12, 1989, Gmunden, Austria)   Austrian writer who examined death, social injustice, and human misery in his deeply pessimistic novels.

Bernhard was born in a Dutch convent, where his unwed Austrian mother had retreated to give birth. In his youth Bernhard survived a life-threatening coma and three years of repeated hospitalizations in tuberculosis sanatoriums, but, after recovering his health, he studied in Salzburg and Vienna.

He published several collections of poetry in the late 1950s but received little notice until the publication of his first novel, *Frost* (1963). In such novels as *Verstörung* (1967; "Derangement"; *Gargoyles*), *Das Kalkwerk* (1970; *The Lime Works*), and *Korrektur* (1975; *Correction*), he combined a complex narrative structure with an increasingly misanthropic philosophy. His novel *Holzfällen* (1984; *Woodcutters*) was seized by police for allegedly criticizing a public figure. Even before its premier in November 1988, Bernhard's last play, *Heldenplatz* (1988; "Heroes' Square"), a bleak indictment of anti-Semitism in contemporary Austria, provoked violent protests. His other plays include *Ein Fest für Boris* (1968; *A Party for Boris*), *Die Jagdgesellschaft* (1974; *The Hunting Party*), *Die Macht der Gewohnheit* (1974; *The Force of Habit*), and *Der Schein trügt* (1983; *Appearances Are Deceiving*). Bernhard's memoirs were translated in *Gathering Evidence* (1985), a compilation of five works published in German between 1975 and 1982.

Berni \'ber-nē\, Francesco (b. 1497/98, Lamporecchio, Tuscany [Italy]—d. May 26, 1535, Florence) Tuscan poet and translator who produced a Tuscan version of Matteo Boiardo's epic poem *Orlando innamorato*. He is also noted for his distinctive style of Italian burlesque, which was called *bernesco* and imitated by many poets.

Berni's agile translation of *Orlando innamorato* was for a long time preferred to the original, which had been written in the Ferrarese dialect. His *La Catrina* (1567), a lively rustic farce, was also highly regarded, though his fame rests squarely on his burlesque poetry. Some poems are savagely satirical, especially those directed toward his contemporaries the poet Pietro Aretino and Popes Adrian VI and Clement VII. Berni's most masterly works, however, are rollicking expansions on trivial subjects (such as peaches, thistles, and a friend's shorn beard), which mock the lofty tone of contemporary Petrarchan verse.

Bernstein \bern-'sten\, Henry(-Léon-Gustave-Charles) (b. Jan. 20, 1876, Paris, Fr.—d. Nov. 27, 1953, Paris) French playwright, initially popular for a series of sensational melodramas, who later turned to more serious themes and experimented with new forms.

Son of a Jewish banker, Bernstein attended the University of Cambridge and later inherited a fortune. His first play, *Le Marché* ("The Market"), was produced in 1900 at the Théâtre-Libre in Paris. A comedy, *Frère Jacques* (1904; "Brother Jacques"), written with Pierre Véber, increased his reputation. His *La Rafale* (1905; "The Whirlwind"), *La Griffe* (1906; "The Claw"), and *Samson* (1907), quick-moving and violent, emphasized character study. *Israël* (1908; "Israel") and *Après moi* (1911; "After Me") denounced anti-Semitism in France; riots followed the premiere of *Après moi* and forced its closing.

In *Le Secret* (1913; *The Secret*), he stressed unconscious motivation. The influences of Sigmund Freud and Luigi Pirandello, the innovative Italian playwright, are obvious in *La Galerie des glaces* (1924; "The Gallery of Mirrors") and other plays written in the 1920s. Bernstein copied film techniques in *Mélo* (1929) and those of the novel in *Le Voyage* (1937). In 1940 his anti-Nazi *Elvire* was produced; it played in Paris until the city fell to the Germans. Bernstein escaped to the United States, but after the war, he returned to Paris and continued writing plays until a year before his death.

Berrigan \'ber-i-gən\, Daniel (b. May 9, 1921, Virginia, Minn., U.S.) Roman Catholic priest whose poems and essays reflected his deep commitment to social, political, and economic change in American society.

Berrigan grew up in Syracuse, N.Y., and taught at a preparatory school in New Jersey before being ordained a Roman Catholic priest in 1952. He later served in various ministries and taught or lectured at a series of colleges, including Cornell and Yale universities. Berrigan's political activism was closely linked to his vision of the responsibilities of Christianity. His poetry was a vehicle for social protest, yet it retained its artistic integrity.

Influenced by his brother Philip (also a priest), Berrigan became active in the antiwar movement during the Vietnam War period. His one-act play *The Trial of the Catonsville Nine* (1970) is a courtroom drama based on his conviction in a federal court for destroying draft records taken from a Maryland draft board. Some of his most eloquent poetry was published in *Prison Poems* (1973).

We Die Before We Live: Talking with the Very Ill (1980) was based on his experiences working in a cancer ward. In 1987 he published his autobiography, *To Dwell in Peace*, and in 1988 selections of his work were collected in *Daniel Berrigan: Poetry, Drama, Prose*.

Berry \'ber-ē\, Wendell (Erdman) (b. Aug. 5, 1934, Port Royal, Ky., U.S.) American author whose nature poetry, novels of America's rural past, and essays on ecological responsibility grew from his experiences as a farmer.

Berry was educated at the University of Kentucky (B.A., 1956; M.A., 1957). He later taught at Stanford and New York universities and spent a year in Italy. In 1964 he returned to the University of Kentucky to teach and settled on a farm near his birthplace. He left the university in 1977 to concentrate on writing and farming.

Berry's poetry, from his first collection, *The Broken Ground* (1964), to *Sabbaths* (1987), revealed a steadily growing concern with the abuse of the land and with the need to restore the balance of nature. The theme of human responsibility to the earth was also present in his novels, including *The Memory of Old Jack* (1974). Among Berry's nonfiction prose works, *The Hidden Wound* (1970; reprinted 1989) explored racism while *The Unsettling of America* (1977) discussed the late 20th-century crises of culture and morality. His essays in *The Long-Legged House* (1969), *The Unforeseen Wilderness: An Essay on Kentucky's Red River Gorge* (1971), *The Gift of Good Land* (1981), *Standing by Words* (1985), *Home Economics* (1987), *What Are People For?* (1990), and *Sex, Economy, Freedom, and Community* (1993) expanded on his themes of ecology and human responsibility.

Berryman \'ber-ē-mən\, John (b. Oct. 25, 1914, McAlester, Okla., U.S.—d. Jan. 7, 1972, Minneapolis, Minn.) American poet noted for his confessional poetry laced with humor.

Berryman graduated from Columbia University, where he was influenced by his teacher, the poet Mark Van Doren. After study at the University of Cambridge in 1938, he returned to the U.S. to teach at Wayne State University, Detroit, beginning a career that included posts at Harvard, Princeton, and the University of Minnesota.

Five Young American Poets (1940) contained 20 of his poems. Two volumes of poetry—*Poems* (1942) and *The Dispossessed* (1948)—followed. A richly erotic autobiographical sequence about a love affair, *Berryman's Sonnets*, appeared in 1967. He also wrote short fiction: "The Lovers" appeared in *The Best American Short Stories of 1946*, and his story "The Imaginary Jew" (1945) is often anthologized.

HOMAGE TO MISTRESS BRADSTREET (1956) was one of Berryman's first experimental poems. His new technical daring was also evident in 77 DREAM SONGS (1964), augmented to form a sequence of 385 "Dream Songs" by *His Toy, His Dream,*

His Rest (1968). The confessional nature of much of Berryman's poetry continued in *Love & Fame* (1970).

Berryman committed suicide by jumping from a bridge onto the ice of the Mississippi River. *Recovery*, an account of his struggle against alcoholism, was published in 1973.

berserker \bər-'sər-kər, -'zər-; 'bər-ˌsər-kər, -ˌzər-\ [Old Norse *berserkr,* from *ber-* (akin to *bera* female bear, *bjǫrn* bear) + *serkr* shirt] In premedieval and medieval Norse and Germanic history and folklore, a member of unruly warrior gangs that worshiped Odin, the supreme Norse deity, and attached themselves to royal and noble courts as bodyguards and shock troops. The berserkers raped and murdered at will (thus going "berserk"), and indeed in the Norse sagas they were often portrayed as villains.

Bertaut \ber-'tō\, Jean de Caen (b. 1552, Donnay?, Fr.—d. June 8, 1611, Séez, Normandy [France]) French poet notable as a writer of polished light verse.

As a young man Bertaut was tutor to the children of a noble family and accompanied them to court. There he wrote lyric and elegiac poetry that shows the influence of Pierre de Ronsard and Philippe Desportes. In his later work he turned to religious themes and paraphrases of the psalms. His poems are collected in two works: *Recueil des oeuvres poetiques* (1601; "Collection of Poetic Works") and *Recueil de quelques vers amoureux* (1602; "Collection of Some Amorous Verse").

Bertolucci \ˌber-tō-'lüt-chē\, Attilio (b. Nov. 18, 1911, San Lazzaro Parmense, near Parma, Italy) Italian poet, literary critic, and translator.

At age 18 Bertolucci published *Sirio* (1929; "Sirius"), a volume of 27 poems set in his native region of Italy. After attending the University of Parma (1931–35) and Bologna University (1935–38), he began teaching and contributing to such journals as *Circoli, Letteratura,* and *Corrente.* In 1951 Bertolucci moved to Rome and published *La capanna indiana* (1951; revised and enlarged, 1955, 1973; "The Indian Hut"), which discusses his struggle for peace and privacy in a turbulent world. *La camera da letto* (1984; enlarged, 1988; "The Bedroom") is a long autobiographical poem about his family history. Bertolucci's other books of poetry include *Fuochi in novembre* (1934; "Fires in November"), *Viaggio d'inverno* (1971; "Winter Voyage"), and the bilingual collection *Selected Poems* (1993). He translated works by Honoré de Balzac, Charles Baudelaire, Thomas Love Peacock, D.H. Lawrence, and Thomas Hardy.

Bertram family \'bər-trəm\ Fictional characters, the wealthy aunt, uncle, and four cousins with whom the protagonist, Fanny Price, is sent to live in Jane Austen's novel MANSFIELD PARK.

Bertran de Born \ber-träⁿ-də-'bȯrn\, Viscount (vicomte) de Hautefort (b. *c.* 1140, Viscounty of Limoges, Fr.—d. 1212–15, Abbey of Dalon) French soldier and celebrated medieval troubadour.

The lord of vast domains, Bertran twice warred with his brother Constantin for sole possession of the family heritage. Their liege lord, Richard the Lion-Heart, initially favored Constantin. Later, however, Bertran and Richard were reconciled, and Bertran abetted Richard and his brothers in their rebellions against their father, Henry II of England. After Richard became king of England (1189), Bertran accompanied him on the crusade to Palestine. After returning to France, he wrote violently militant poetry, encouraging Richard in his wars with Philip II of France.

In addition to his militaristic poetry, Bertran produced some of the most serene and beautiful poetry in Provençal literature, 45 fragments of which are extant. He is represented in

Dante's *Inferno,* in which he carries his severed head before him like a lantern and is compared with the biblical Achitophel (Ahithophel), who also incited a royal son (Absalom) against his father (David).

Bertrand \ber-'träⁿ\, Louis, *in full* Louis-Jacques-Napoléon Bertrand, *also called* Aloysius Bertrand (b. April 20, 1807, Ceva, Piedmont [Italy]—d. April 29, 1841, Paris, Fr.) Writer whose *Gaspard de la nuit* ("Gaspard of the Night") introduced the prose poem into French literature and was a source of inspiration to the Symbolist poets.

After his family settled in Dijon, Fr., in 1815, Bertrand developed a consuming interest in the ancient Burgundian capital, joining the Société d'Études and collecting historical material, some of which he used in early poems published under the title *Volupté* ("Voluptuousness"). He wrote for local newspapers, and for three years after the Revolution of 1830, he edited the revolutionary *Le Patriote de la Côte d'Or.*

Published posthumously in 1842, *Gaspard de la nuit,* which deals with medieval Dijon, at first aroused slight interest; but, discovered a few years later by the poets Charles Baudelaire and Stéphane Mallarmé, it secured for its author a place in literary history.

Berwiński \ber-'vēn^y-sk^yē\, Ryszard Wincenty (b. Feb. 28, 1819, Polwica, Posen, Prussia [now in Poland]—d. Nov. 9, 1879, Constantinople, Ottoman Empire [now Istanbul, Tur.]) Polish poet and writer whose collection *Poezje* (1844; "Poems") marked him as a social radical.

In his *Studia o literaturze ludowej* (1854; "Studies on Folk Literature"), Berwiński took an international view of folk traditions, stressing their universality and challenging nationalist interpretations popular at the time. A committed and unsentimental revolutionary, he was twice imprisoned, first by the Austrians and later by the Prussians. The Revolution of 1848 freed him, and he became a Polish deputy to the Prussian Parliament, a post he left to travel to the Crimea. There he aided a Polish poet, Adam Mickiewicz, in organizing a Polish armed force. After the war the Prussians refused to let him return home; he continued his work in Constantinople, a lonely and forgotten man.

Berzsenyi \'ber-zhen-yē\, Dániel (b. May 7, 1776, Egyházashetye, Hung.—d. Feb. 24, 1836, Nikla) Poet who first successfully introduced classical meters and themes in Hungarian poetry.

Berzsenyi was a country squire who lived far from any town and was for many years unconnected with any literary circle. His activity as a poet was discovered by chance, and he became known through the efforts of Ferenc Kazinczy, a leading advocate of reform in Hungarian prosody. His only volume of poetry was published in 1813. The influence of Latin poetry, particularly that of Horace, is noticeable not only in the form of his poems but also in his vocabulary, his choice of subjects, and his philosophy. In 1817 Ferenc Kölcsey, another Hungarian poet of the period, made an unduly severe judgment on Berzsenyi's work. Deeply hurt, Berzsenyi thereafter virtually ceased to write poetry.

Besant \bi-'zant\, Sir Walter (b. Aug. 14, 1836, Portsmouth, Hampshire, Eng.—d. June 9, 1901, London) Novelist and philanthropist whose descriptions of London's East End helped set in motion several movements to aid the poor.

From 1861 to 1867 Besant taught at the Royal College, Mauritius. In 1871 he began a literary collaboration with James Rice, editor of *Once a Week,* which lasted until Rice's death in 1882. Together they produced 14 novels.

In 1882 Besant published his first independent novel, *All Sorts and Conditions of Men,* based on his impressions of the

East London slums, which he saw as joyless rather than vicious. The "Palace of Delights" that he projected in his book became a reality in 1887, when the People's Palace was founded on Mile End Road, London, in an attempt to provide opportunities for education and amusement to the poor of the area. His book *Children of Gibeon* (1886) also described slum life.

Besant wrote 32 novels in the 19 years after Rice's death. He also wrote biographies, including *Rabelais* (1879); critical and topographical studies, notably about London; and an autobiography (1902). He helped to found the Society of Authors in 1884 and edited its journal until his death.

Bessa Luís \,bes-ă-'lwĕs\, Maria Agustina (b. Oct. 15, 1922, Vila Meã, Port.) Novelist and short-story writer whose fiction incorporated surrealistic elements.

Of the more than a dozen novels Bessa Luís had published by the late 20th century, the best known was *A sibila* (1954; "The Sybil"), in which the boundary between physical, psychological, and ironic reality is tenuous and the characters gain an almost mythic quality. In Bessa Luís' fiction, notions of time and space become vague, and planes of reality flow together, dimming the sense of a logical order of events. Other well-known novels by Bessa Luís include *Os incuráveis* (1956; "The Incurables"), *A muralha* (1957; "The Stone Wall"), *O susto* (1958; "The Fright"), *O manto* (1961; "The Mantle"), and *O sermão de fogo* (1963; "The Sermon of Fire").

Bessa Victor \'bes-ă-'vĕ-tŏr\, Geraldo, Victor *also spelled* Vítor (b. Jan. 20, 1917, São Paulo de Luanda, Angola) Angolan lyric poet and scholar whose work expresses the dream of racial harmony and the need to recapture the innocence of childhood.

Bessa Victor's poetry included *Ecos dispersos* (1941; "Scattered Echoes"), *Ao som das marimbas* (1943; "To the Sound of the Marimbas"), *Mucanda* (1946), *Debaixo do céu* (1949; "Under the Sky"), *Cubata abandonada* (1958; "The Abandoned Hut"), and *Monandengue* (1973; "Child"). He was noted for the musicality of his verse and his capacity to see the best in both African and European civilizations.

In addition to poetry, he wrote short stories that were collected in *Sanzala sem Batuque* (1967; "The Slave House with Gaiety"), as well as books on Kimbundu proverbs, Angolan history, and African literary themes.

Besserungsstück \'bes-ər-uŋk-,shtɯek\ [German, literally, improvement play] A genre of play popular in Vienna in the early 19th century. A form of *Volksstück*, a play written in local dialect for popular audiences, the *Besserungsstück* was concerned with the improvement in or remedy of some fault of the main character.

Bester \'bes-tər\, Alfred (b. Dec. 18, 1913, New York, N.Y., U.S.—d. Oct. 20?, 1987, Doylestown, Pa.) Innovative American writer of science fiction whose output was small but highly influential.

Bester attended the University of Pennsylvania (B.A., 1935). From 1939 to 1942 he published 14 short stories in science-fiction magazines, including "Hell Is Forever" (1942), which in its fast pacing and obsessive characters anticipated the style of his major novels. He then wrote scenarios for superhero comic books and scripts for radio and television, and he created English-language librettos for operas by Giuseppe Verdi and Modest Moussorgsky. His first novel was the satirical, non-science-fiction work *Who He?* (1953).

Bester's first major work, the novel *The Demolished Man* (1953), was followed by *Tiger! Tiger!* (1955; U.S. title, *The Stars My Destination*). Bester's fiction often employed narrative techniques—such as interior monologue—that were new to science fiction. He published several short-story collections, including

Starburst (1958) and *The Dark Side of the Earth* (1964). Later works included *The Computer Connection* (1975; also published as *Extro*), followed by *Golem*[100] (1980) and *The Deceivers* (1982), all of which were experimental and thus less accessible than his early work.

bestiary \'bes-chē-,er-ē, 'bēs-\ [Medieval Latin *bestiarium*, a derivative of Latin *bestia* beast] A medieval European work in verse or prose, often illustrated, that consisted of a collection of stories, each based on a description of certain qualities of the subject, usually an animal or a plant. The stories were allegories, used for moral and religious instruction and admonition.

The numerous manuscripts of medieval bestiaries ultimately are derived from the Greek *Physiologus*, a text compiled by an unknown author before the middle of the 2nd century AD. It consists of stories based on the "facts" of natural science as accepted by someone called Physiologus (Latin: "Naturalist") and on the compiler's own religious ideas.

The *Physiologus* consists of 48 sections, each dealing with one creature, plant, or other subject and each linked to a biblical text. The stories may derive from popular fables about animals and plants. Many attributes that have become traditionally associated with real or mythical creatures derive from the bestiaries: *e.g.*, the phoenix's burning itself to be born again, the parental love of the pelican, and the hedgehog's collecting its stores for the winter with its prickles.

Translations of the *Physiologus* were made from Latin into Anglo-Saxon before 1000. The only surviving Middle English *Bestiary* dates from the 13th century. It, and other lost Middle English and Anglo-Norman versions, influenced the development of the beast fable. Early translations into Flemish and German influenced the satirical BEAST EPIC. Bestiaries were popular in France and the Low Countries (Belgium, the Netherlands, and Luxembourg) in the 13th century. An Italian translation of the *Physiologus*, known as the *Bestiario toscano*, was made in the 13th century.

best-seller \'best-'sel-ər\ Book that, for a time, leads all others of its kind in sales, a designation that serves as an index of popular literary taste and judgment.

The best-seller list was initiated in 1895, when *Bookman*, an American magazine of literature and criticism, began publication. Its list was compiled from reports of sales at bookstores throughout the country. Similar lists began to appear in other literary magazines and in metropolitan newspapers. In the United States, the lists most commonly considered authoritative are those published in *Publishers Weekly* and *The New York Times*. The practice spread from the United States; the British list generally considered most authoritative is that of *The Sunday Times* (London), reprinted in *Bookseller*. In the compilation of such lists, the works of William Shakespeare, the Bible, and direct-mail and book-club sales are excluded.

Beti \bā-'tē\, Mongo, *also called* Erza Boto \bō-'tō\, *pseudonyms of* Alexandre Biyidi \bē-yē-'dē\ (b. June 30, 1932, Mbalmayo, Camer.) Cameroonian novelist and political essayist whose works advocated the removal of all vestiges of colonialism.

Beti's first important novel, *Le Pauvre Christ de Bomba* (1956; *The Poor Christ of Bomba*), satirizes the destructive influence of missionary activities in Cameroon. This was followed by *Mission terminée* (1957; U.K. title, *Mission to Kala*; U.S. title, *Mission Accomplished*), which attacks French colonial policy.

After some 15 years of silence, Beti produced *Main basse sur le Cameroun* (1972; "Rape of Cameroon"), which was immediately banned in France and in Africa. Two years later a pair of novels appeared, *Perpétue et l'habitude du malheur* (1974; *Perpetua and the Habit of Unhappiness*) and *Remember Ruben*

(1974). *Remember Ruben* and its sequel, *La Ruine presque cocasse d'un polichinelle* (1979; "The Nearly Comical Ruin of a Puppet"), chronicle the fortunes of several revolutionaries who fight against and defeat a French-backed regime in their newly independent country. Some of Beti's later works, including *Les Deux Mères de Guillaume Ismaël Dzewatama, futur camionneur* (1982; "The Two Mothers of Guillaume Ismaël Dzewatama, Future Truck Driver"), concern mixed marriage.

In 1978 Beti launched *Peuples Noirs/Peuples Africains* ("Black Peoples/African Peoples"), a political and cultural bimonthly periodical devoted to the exposure and defeat of neocolonialism in Africa. Beti settled in France before Cameroon achieved independence in 1960.

Betjeman \'bech-ə-mən\, Sir John (b. Aug. 28, 1906, London, Eng.—d. May 19, 1984, Trebetherick, Cornwall)   British poet known for his nostalgia for the near past, his exact sense of place, and his precise rendering of social nuance, which made him widely read at a time when much of what he wrote about was vanishing.

The son of a prosperous businessman, Betjeman grew up in a London suburb, where T.S. Eliot was one of his teachers. He later studied at Magdalen College, Oxford. The years from early childhood until he left Oxford were detailed in *Summoned by Bells* (1960), blank verse interspersed with lyrics.

Betjeman's first book of verse, *Mount Zion*, appeared in 1933. Four more volumes of poetry appeared before the publication of *Collected Poems* (1958). Later collections include *High and Low* (1966), *A Nip in the Air* (1974), *Church Poems* (1981), and *Uncollected Poems* (1982).

Betjeman's prose works include several guidebooks to English counties; *First and Last Loves* (1952), essays on places and buildings; *The English Town in the Last Hundred Years* (1956); and *English Churches* (1964; with Basil Clarke). He was knighted in 1969, and in 1972 he succeeded C. Day-Lewis as poet laureate of England.

Betrayed by Rita Hayworth \'rē-tə-'hā-wərth\   First novel by Manuel PUIG, published as *La traición de Rita Hayworth* in 1968. This semiautobiographical novel is largely plotless. It examines the psychosocial influence of motion pictures on an ordinary town in the Pampas of Argentina. The book focuses primarily on the first 15 years in the life of Toto Casals, from 1933 to 1948. He becomes obsessed with the films that he regularly attends with his mother. Like others in the community, Toto escapes into the artificial world of popular culture, accepting and absorbing its social norms. He is, however, troubled about sexuality, particularly his own latent homosexuality.

Betrothed, The   *see* I PROMESSI SPOSI.

Betti \'bāt-tē\, Ugo (b. Feb. 4, 1892, Camerino, Italy—d. June 9, 1953, Rome)   Italian playwright who achieved an international reputation in the first half of the 20th century.

Educated for the law, Betti fought in World War I and while imprisoned (1917–18) by the Germans wrote a volume of poems, *Il re pensieroso* (1922; "The Thoughtful King"). After the war he became a magistrate in Rome in 1920, rose to a judgeship in 1930, and became librarian at the Ministry of Justice in 1944. His legal career was interspersed with the writing of two more volumes of poetry, three books of short stories, a novel, much miscellaneous writing, and, most important, 26 plays.

His first play, *La padrona* (1927; "The Landlady"), drew mixed reactions, but later successful plays included *Frana allo scalo Nord* (1933; *Landslide*), the story of a natural disaster and collective guilt; *Delitto all'Isola delle Capre* (1950; *Crime on Goat Island*), a violent tragedy of love and revenge; *La regina e gli insorte* (1951; *The Queen and the Rebels*), a strong argument for compassion and self-sacrifice; and *La fuggitiva* (1953;

The Fugitive), a story presenting legal courts as a symbol of world salvation.

Bezruč \'bez-,rǔch\, Petr, *pseudonym of* Vladimir Vašek \'vă-,shek\ (b. Sept. 15, 1867, Opava, Silesia, Austria-Hungary [now in Czech Republic]—d. Feb. 17, 1958, Kostelec, Czech.)   One of the finest and most individual Czech poets.

Bezruč studied in Prague and served as a postal official in Moravia until his retirement in 1927. His literary reputation rests on a remarkable series of poems written during 1899–1900 and published in the periodical *Čas* between 1899 and 1903. The subject of almost all these poems is the people of Czech Silesia, whom Bezruč saw as a dying race, doomed to denationalization at the hands of German industrialists and Polish priests. From this local theme he created a poetry of national and, indeed, universal validity. The 32 poems of the Silesian issue of *Čas* (1903) had swelled to 88 by the last edition of the collected *Slezske pisne* (1956; "Silesian Songs").

Bezukhov, Pierre \'pyer-b'i-'zū-ḳəf\ Bezukhov *also spelled* Bezuhov.   Fictional character, a good-natured young idealist in Leo Tolstoy's epic novel WAR AND PEACE. Pierre matures over the course of the story through his involvement in a series of well-intentioned but often misguided attempts to change the world and the course of his own life.

Bhagavadgītā \,băg-ə-,văd-'gē-tə, 'bəg-ə-,vəd-'gē-,tä\ (Sanskrit: "Song of the Lord")   One of the greatest and most beautiful of the Hindu scriptures. It forms part of Book VI of the Indian epic the MAHĀBHĀRATA ("Great Epic of the Bharata Dynasty") and is written in the form of a dialogue between the warrior Prince Arjuna and his friend and charioteer, Krishna, who is also an earthly incarnation of the god Vishnu. The *Bhagavadgītā* is of a later date than the major parts of the *Mahābhārata* and was probably written in the 1st or 2nd century AD. The poem consists of 700 Sanskrit verses divided into 18 chapters.

The dialogue takes place on the field of battle, just as the great war between the Pāṇḍavas and the Kauravas is about to begin. The two armies stand opposing each other, and, on seeing many of his friends and kinsmen among those lined up on the other side, Prince Arjuna hesitates. He considers whether it would not be better to throw down his arms and allow himself to be slain rather than to engage in a just, but cruel, war. Krishna points out to him that the higher way is the dispassionate discharge of his duty, performed with faith in God. The *Bhagavadgītā* goes far beyond the ethical question with which it begins, to consider broadly the nature of God and the means by which mortals can know him.

Bhāgavata-Purāṇa \,băg-ə-'vət-ə-pu̇-'rän-ə\ (Sanskrit: "Ancient Stories of the Lord")   The most celebrated text of a variety of Hindu sacred literature in Sanskrit known as the Purāṇas, and the specific text that is held sacred by the Bhāgavata sect. Scholars are in general agreement that the *Bhāgavata-Purāṇa* was probably composed about the 10th century, somewhere in the Tamil country of South India. It is made up of some 18,000 stanzas divided into 12 books; but it is book 10, which deals with Krishna's childhood and his years spent among the cowherds of Vṛndāvana, that accounts for its immense popularity with Vaiṣṇavas (worshipers of Vishnu; Krishna is an incarnation of Vishnu) throughout India. The attempts on Krishna's life made by his wicked uncle Kaṃsa, the childhood pranks he played on his foster mother Yaśodā, his love for the *gopī*s (the wives and daughters of the cowherds), and their passionate abandonment to him are treated with endearing charm and grace, even while infused with deep religious significance. The *Bhāgavata-Purāṇa* prompted an enormous body of related vernacular literature. *See also* PURĀṆA.

bhakti poetry \\'bək-tē\ In Indian literature, poetry inspired by or reflecting bhakti (religious devotion), a mystical Hindu movement that emphasizes the intense emotional attachment and love of a devotee toward a personal god. The way of bhakti (bhakti-marga) is contrasted with other means of achieving salvation, such as knowledge (jnana-marga), ritual and good works (karma-marga), and ascetic disciplines of the body; it is claimed by its supporters to be a superior way, as well as one open to all, regardless of sex or caste.

An emotional attraction toward a personal god began to be expressed in the early 7th century. It was furthered by the Indian epics—the *Mahābhārata* and the *Rāmāyaṇa*—and by the *Purāṇa*s, encyclopedic texts that recount legends of the various incarnations and appearances of the deities, their genealogies, and the devotional practices accorded them.

The fervor of the 7th–10th-century hymnists of South India, the Ālvārs and the Nāyaṇārs, which were known as bhakti sects also traveled north, until in time bhakti became an extremely popular part of Hindu religious life.

Bharatendu *see* HARISHCHANDRA.

Bhārati \\'bär-ə-tē\, Subrahmanya C., *also spelled* Subramaṇia C. Bhārati (b. Dec. 11, 1882, Ettaiyapuram, Madras presidency, India—d. Sept. 12, 1921, Madras) Outstanding Indian writer of the nationalist period who is regarded as the father of the modern Tamil style.

The son of a learned Brahman, Bhārati became a Tamil scholar at an early age. He received little formal education, however, and in 1904 moved to Madras. There he translated English into Tamil for several magazines and later joined the Tamil daily newspaper *Swadesamitran*. This exposure to political affairs led to his involvement in the extremist wing of the Indian National Congress party, and, as a result, he was forced to live in exile from 1910 to 1919. During this time Bhārati's nationalistic poems and essays were popular successes. Upon his return to India in 1919 he was briefly imprisoned. He was killed by a temple elephant in Madras.

Bhārati's best-known works include *Kaṇṇan Pāṭṭu* (1917; *Songs to Krishna*), *Panchali Sapatham* (1912; *Panchali's Vow*), and *Kuyil Pāṭṭu* (1912; *Kuyil's Song*). Many of his English works were collected in *Agni and Other Poems and Translations* and *Essays and Other Prose Fragments* (both 1937).

Bhāravi \\'bä-rə-vē\ (fl. 6th century AD) Sanskrit poet, author of *Kirātārjunīya* ("Arjuna and the Mountain Man"), one of the classical Sanskrit epics classified as a *mahākāvya* ("great poem"). His verse is characterized by elevated expression and intricate structure.

Bhāravi probably lived in southern India. His *Kirātārjunīya* was based on an episode from the third *parvan*, or section, of the Sanskrit epic *Mahābhārata*. The poet describes in 18 cantos the Pāṇḍava prince Arjuna's encounter and ensuing combat with a *kirāta*, or wild mountaineer, who in the end proves to be the god Śiva. For his valor and penitence, Śiva awards the ascetic hero a coveted weapon of the Pāśupata Hindu sect.

Bhāsa \\'bäs-ə\ (fl. 2nd or 3rd century AD, India) The earliest known Sanskrit dramatist, whose plays were known only by the allusions of ancient Sanskrit dramatists until the manuscripts were found early in the 20th century.

In 1912 an Indian scholar discovered and published the texts of 13 of Bhāsa's dramas. His best work, *Svapnavāsavadattā* ("The Dream of Vāsavadattā"), depicts a king losing and then regaining his kingdom from a usurper. The majority of his plays are ingenious variations on themes of heroism and romantic love borrowed from India's two great epics, the *Rāmāyaṇa* and the *Mahābhārata*. Bhāsa deviated from the accepted dramaturgy of the time by portraying battle scenes and killings on the stage. His influence is seen in the works of the great 5th-century dramatist Kālidāsa, who consciously imitated and improved upon some of Bhāsa's literary motifs.

Bhaṭṭi \\'bət-tē\ (fl. 6th or 7th century AD) Sanskrit poet and grammarian, author of the influential *Bhaṭṭikāvya*, which is sometimes classified among the model *mahākāvya*s ("great poems"), or classical epics.

Bhaṭṭi lived in the ancient Indian city of Valabhī, writing under the patronage of one of four kings named Śrīdharasena. He is said to have taught Sanskrit to the princes of the court. His *Bhaṭṭikāvya*, comprising a total of 22 cantos and 1,650 verses, recounts the story of Rāma and Sītā based on the Sanskrit epic *Rāmāyaṇa*. At the same time it illustrates the principal rules of Sanskrit grammar and poetics codified by the grammarian Pāṇini. The first four cantos discuss miscellaneous rules; the next six cantos treat the primary rules; the following four cantos illustrate poetic techniques; and the remaining nine cantos cover the use of moods and tenses.

Bhavabhūti \\,bə-və-'bü-tē\ (fl. AD 700) Indian dramatist and poet, whose plays, written in Sanskrit, are noted for their suspense and vivid characterization.

A Brahman of Vidarbha (the part of central India later called Berār), Bhavabhūti passed his literary life chiefly at the court of Yaśovarman of Kanauj. He is best known as the author of three plays: *Mahāvīracarita* ("Exploits of the Great Hero"), which gives in seven acts the main incidents in the *Rāmāyaṇa* up to the defeat of Rāvaṇa and the coronation of Rāma; *Mālatī Mādhava* ("Mālatī and Mādhava"), a domestic drama in 10 acts abounding in stirring, though sometimes improbable, incidents; and *Uttararāmacarita* ("The Later Deeds of Rāma"), which continues the story of Rāma from his coronation to the banishment of Sītā and their final reunion. This last play shows Bhavabhūti at the height of his power in characterization and in presenting suspense and climax.

Bhêly-Quénum \bä-lē-kä-'nṳ̄ᵉⁿ\, Olympe (b. Sept. 26, 1928, Donukpa, Dahomey [now Benin]) Beninese French-language novelist, journalist, and short-story writer.

Bhêly-Quénum earned degrees in literature and in diplomacy from the Sorbonne in France. He taught school, worked at several foreign-service posts, and was a journalist for the United Nations Educational, Scientific and Cultural Organization (UNESCO). He also edited the journals *La Vie Africaine* (1962–65) and *L'Afrique Actuelle* (1965–68).

Bhêly-Quénum's major works include the novels *Un Piège sans fin* (1960; *Snares Without End*), in which a man's life is ruined when he is unjustly accused of adultery; *Le Chant du lac* (1965; "The Song of the Lake"), which illustrates the modern conflict between educated Africans and their superstitious compatriots; and *L'Initié* (1979; "The Initiate"), the protagonist of which is a French-trained doctor who is also an initiate of a faith-healing cult. *Liaison d'une été* (1968; "Summer Affair"), a collection of short stories, introduces his major theme of the supernatural. Bhêly-Quénum's novels and stories are for the most part violent episodes tied together by powerful narrative flow.

Bialik \\'byä-lik\, Ḥayyim Naḥman (b. Jan. 9, 1873, Rady, Volhynia, Ukraine, Russian Empire—d. July 4, 1934, Vienna, Austria) Leading Hebrew poet whose verse helped make modern Hebrew a flexible medium of poetic expression.

Bialik was brought up by his rigidly pious, learned grandfather. After an intensive education in the Jewish classics, he attended for a short time the Jewish academy in Volozhin (now Valozhyn, Belarus). In 1891 he went to Odessa, then the center of Jewish modernism, where he struck up a friendship with the Jewish author Aḥad Ha'am, who encouraged his writing.

The following year, Bialik moved to Zhitomir (now Zhytomyr, Ukraine) and married. He worked unsuccessfully as a lumber merchant, then taught for a few years in a Hebrew school. His first long poem, "Ha-Matmid" ("The Talmud Student"), published in the periodical *Ha-Shiloaḥ* (edited by Aḥad Ha'am), established Bialik's reputation as the outstanding Hebrew poet of his time.

Bialik returned to Odessa as a teacher and continued to write both poems and fiction. Such poems as "Be-'Ir he-haregah" ("In the City of Slaughter"), concerning the pogrom in Kishinyov (now Chişinău, Moldova), are powerful indictments of both cruelty and passivity. Other poems include a fragment of an epic, "Mete midbar" ("The Dead of the Desert"), and "Ha-Berekhah" ("The Pool").

Bialik translated into Hebrew *Don Quixote, Wilhelm Tell,* and the Yiddish play *Der Dibek.* He was a cofounder of the publishing firm Devir and edited *Sefer ha-agadah* (1907/08–1910/11; *The Book of Legends*), a collection of traditional Jewish homilies and legends. He also edited the poems of the great medieval poet and philosopher Ibn Gabirol and began a popular modern commentary on the Mishna.

Bianciardi \byän-'chär-dē\, Luciano (b. 1922, Grosseto, Italy—d. 1971, Milan)   Italian writer whose works are a skeptical examination of post-World War II Italy.

After graduating from the University of Pisa, Bianciardi taught high school in Grosseto for two years and then moved to Milan and to Rapallo, where he contributed to magazines and worked as a translator and publishing consultant. His disenchantment with the economic and political climate of postwar Italy reached its zenith with the novel *La vita agra* (1962; *It's a Hard Life*), in which the protagonist gradually abandons his revolutionary notions, worn down by the triviality of government bureaucracy and everyday urban life. His other works include *Il lavoro culturale* (1957; "Cultural Work"), *L'integrazione* (1960; "Integration"), *La battaglia soda* (1964; "The Soda-Water Battle"), and *Aprire il fuoco* (1969; "Setting the Fire").

Bian Zhilin or **Pien Chih-lin** \'byän-'jə-'lin, -'lĕn\ (b. Dec. 8, 1910, Haimen, Jiangsu province, China)   Chinese poet and translator especially noted for his highly evocative poetry.

Bian Zhilin left home to attend the university in Beijing in the early 1930s. There he met Western-educated poets Xu Zhimo and Wen Yiduo and became familiar with such poets as T.S. Eliot and the French Symbolists. Bian's first volume of poetry, *Sanqiu cao* (1933; "Leaves of Three Autumns"), contains verses filled with the melancholy and despair then prevalent among Chinese youth. His second work, entitled *Yumu ji* (1935; "Fish Eyes Collection"), is divided into five sections, mostly by order of composition. *Hanyuan ji* (1936; "The Han Garden Collection"), which Bian compiled, also contains the work of He Qifang and Li Guangtian. *Shinian shicao* (1942; "Poems of Ten Years") was an edition intended to represent the author's best work. He published little original poetry thereafter, concentrating instead on translations, notably a verse translation of *Hamlet*.

Bibaud \bē-'bō\, Michel (b. Jan. 19, 1782, Côte des Neiges, near Montreal [now in Quebec, Can.]—d. Aug. 3, 1857, Montreal)   Author of French Canada's first volume of poetry and of the first substantial history of Canada.

Educated at the Collège Saint-Raphaël, he became a teacher and journalist. Bibaud edited periodicals, of which *La Bibliothèque canadienne*, containing his own historical writing, was the best known. His first historical work, *Histoire du Canada, sous la domination française* (1837), covers the period from the founding of Canada to 1731; a second volume (1844) brings the story to 1830. (A third volume, treating events from 1830 to 1837, was published by his son.) Bibaud's volume of didactic poetry, *Épîtres, satires, chansons, épigrammes, et autres pièces de vers* (1830), contains four satires on ignorance, avarice, laziness, and envy.

Bible \'bī-bəl\   The sacred scriptures of Judaism and Christianity. The Christian Bible consists of the Old Testament and the New Testament, with the Roman Catholic and Eastern Orthodox versions of the Old Testament being slightly larger because of their acceptance of certain books and parts of books considered apocryphal by Protestants. The Jewish Bible includes only the books known to Protestants as the Old Testament.

The Jewish scriptures are divided into three parts: the TORAH ("Law"), or Pentateuch; the NEVI'IM ("Prophets"); and the KETUVIM ("Writings"), or Hagiographa. The Pentateuch, together with the book of Joshua (hence the name Hexateuch) can be seen as the account of how Israel became a nation and of how it came to possess the Promised Land. The Nevi'im continue the story of Israel in the Promised Land, describing the establishment and development of the monarchy and presenting the messages of the prophets to the people. The Ketuvim include the books of Job and Ecclesiastes, the poetical works, and some additional historical books.

In the Apocrypha of the Old Testament, various types of literature are represented; the purpose for including the books of the Apocrypha seems to have been to fill in some of the gaps left by the indisputably canonical books and to carry the history of Israel to the 2nd century BC.

The Christian scriptures include the New Testament, which contains a variety of early Christian literature. The four Gospels deal with the life, the person, and the teachings of Jesus. The Book of Acts carries the story of Christianity from the Resurrection of Jesus to the end of the career of Paul. The Letters, or Epistles, are correspondence by various leaders of the early Christian church to the early Christian congregations. The Book of Revelation (the Apocalypse) is the only canonical representative of a large genre of apocalyptic literature that appeared in the early Christian movement.

The Jewish Bible was originally written almost entirely in Hebrew, with a few short elements in Aramaic. The New Testament books were probably all first written or recorded in Greek, though some may have been first written in Aramaic. By the mid-3rd century BC, Greek was the dominant language, and Jewish scholars eventually translated the Hebrew canon into that language, in a version known as the Septuagint. About 405 Saint Jerome completed translating a Latin version begun and based in part on the Septuagint; this version, the Vulgate, despite corruption introduced by copyists, became the standard of Christianity for more than a thousand years.

Notable translations in English include the unsurpassed King James (Authorized) Version (1611), the English Revised Version (1881–85), the Revised Standard [American] Version (1946–57), the New English Bible (1970), the [Catholic] Confraternity Version (1952–61; later issued as the New American Bible, 1970), and the Jerusalem Bible (1966).

bibliography \ˌbib-lē-'äg-rə-fē\ [Greek *bibliographía* the copying of books, from *biblíon* book + *gráphein* to write] **1.** The history, identification, or description of writings or publications. **2.** A list often with descriptive or critical notes of writings relating to a particular subject, period, or author. In a closely related use, the word can also refer to a list of works written by an author or printed by a publishing house. **3.** The works or a list of the works referred to in a text or consulted by the author in its production. *See also* CRITICAL BIBLIOGRAPHY; DESCRIPTIVE BIBLIOGRAPHY.

bibliotics \,bib-lē-'ă-tiks\ [Greek *biblíon* book + the English suffix *-otics* (probably modeled on *semiotics* the study of signs)] The scientific study of handwriting, documents, and writing materials especially to determine authenticity or authorship.

Bichsel \'bik-səl\, Peter (b. March 24, 1935, Lucerne, Switz.) Swiss short-story writer, journalist, and novelist noted for his simple, self-conscious writing style.

Bichsel graduated from a teachers college in 1955 and, after briefly serving in the military, taught elementary school until 1968, when he became a full-time writer. Gruppe 47, a group of avant-garde German-language writers, gave him their annual award in 1965 for his *Eigentlich möchte Frau Blum den Milchmann kennenlernen* (1964; *And Really Frau Blum Would Very Much Like to Meet the Milkman*), a collection of vignettes of characters who speculate on mundane things.

Bichsel's success continued with *Die Jahreszeiten* (1967; "The Seasons"), a novel about a writer's frustrations. *Kindergeschichten* (1969; *There Is No Such Place as America*; also published as *Stories for Children*) is a volume of short stories about skepticism and miscommunication. *Der Busant: Von Trinkern, Polizisten und der schönen Magelone* (1985; "The Magpie: Of Drinkers, Policemen and the Beautiful Magelone") profiles eccentric characters. His magazine columns, many harshly critical of the Swiss government, were collected in several volumes.

Bickerstaff, Isaac Pseudonym of Sir Richard STEELE.

Bickerstaffe \'bik-ər-,staf\, Isaac (b. *c.* 1735, Ireland—d. *c.* 1812) Irish playwright whose farces and comic operas were popular in the late 18th century. There is no apparent connection between his name and the pseudonym earlier adopted by Jonathan Swift and also used by Joseph Addison and Richard Steele for *The Tatler*.

Bickerstaffe is said to have been a page to the lord lieutenant of Ireland and then an officer in the royal marines. His first theatrical success, *Love in a Village* (1762), was followed by many others, including *The Maid of the Mill* (based on Samuel Richardson's *Pamela*), *The Padlock*, and *The Hypocrite*. A frank plagiarist, he depended for his success on lively lyrics and sparkling dialogue. In 1772 he was forced into exile by allegations of sodomy, then a capital offense. He lived in poverty for many years, probably in France.

Bidart \bi-'därt\, Frank (b. 1939, California) American poet whose introspective verse, notably dramatic monologues by troubled characters, dealt with personal guilt, family life, and madness. His unconventional punctuation and typography gave his colloquial and economical style an added emphasis.

Bidart graduated from the University of California and later studied at Harvard University. His first volume of verse was *Golden State* (1973). It contains "Golden State," an autobiographical account of a father-and-son relationship, and "Herbert White," the lurid musings of a psychopathic pedophile. *The Book of the Body* (1977) features the dramatic monologues of an amputee and of a suicidal anorexic.

Critical acclaim attended Bidart's publication of *The Sacrifice* (1983), a collection of five long poems about guilt. *In the Western Night: Collected Poems 1965–90* was published in 1990.

Bierce \'birs\, Ambrose (Gwinnett) (b. June 24, 1842, Meigs county, Ohio, U.S.—d. 1914, Mexico?) American newspaperman, wit, satirist, and author of sardonic short stories based on themes of death and horror.

Reared in Indiana, Bierce became printer's devil (apprentice) on a local paper after about a year of high school. In 1861 he enlisted in the army and fought in a number of American Civil War battles. Seriously wounded in 1864, he served until 1865.

Library of Congress

Resettling in San Francisco, Bierce began contributing to periodicals, particularly the *News Letter*, of which he became editor in 1868. He was soon the literary arbiter of the West Coast. "The Haunted Valley" (1871) was his first story. From 1872 to 1875 he lived in England, where he wrote for London magazines, edited the *Lantern*, and published three books: *The Fiend's Delight* (1872), *Nuggets and Dust Panned Out in California* (1872), and *Cobwebs from an Empty Skull* (1874).

In 1877 he became associate editor of the San Francisco *Argonaut* but left it in 1879–80 for an unsuccessful try at mining in the Dakota Territory. Thereafter he was editor of the San Francisco *Wasp* for five years. In 1887 he joined the staff of the *San Francisco Examiner*, for which he wrote the "Prattler" column. In 1896 Bierce moved to Washington, D.C., and there continued newspaper and magazine writing. In 1913 he went to Mexico, then in the middle of a revolution led by Pancho Villa. His end is a mystery, but a reasonable conjecture is that he was killed in the siege of Ojinaga in January 1914.

As a newspaper columnist, Bierce specialized in attacks on frauds of all sorts. His principal books were *Tales of Soldiers and Civilians* (1891; revised as *In the Midst of Life*), which included some of his finest stories, such as AN OCCURRENCE AT OWL CREEK BRIDGE, "The Eyes of the Panther," and "The Boarded Window"; *Can Such Things Be?* (1893), which included "The Damned Thing" and "Moxon's Master"; and THE DEVIL'S DICTIONARY (originally published in 1906 as *The Cynic's Word Book*), a volume of ironic, even bitter, definitions, which has been often reprinted.

biform \'bī-,fôrm\ [Latin *biformis*] Having or appearing in two dissimilar guises. The term is used of characters in classical mythology that appeared to mortals in other than their customary bodily form. Zeus, for example, often took other forms; he appeared to Leda as a swan and to Europa in the form of a white bull.

Big Brother Fictional character, the dictator of the totalitarian empire of Oceania in the novel NINETEEN EIGHTY-FOUR by George Orwell. Though Big Brother does not appear directly in the story, his presence permeates Oceania's bleak society. Ubiquitous posters displaying his photograph feature the slogan "Big Brother Is Watching You"; hidden devices in every room enable his Thought Police to monitor the activities of all citizens. Oceania's constant, vicious wars; its propagandistic language (Newspeak); and its Anti-Sex League are the most blatant manifestations of his control.

Orwell's satiric portrait of Big Brother anticipated with alarming accuracy the characteristics of a number of real-life 20th-century despots. The term Big Brother has come to signify government control of and intrusion into individual lives. *See also* NEWSPEAK.

Big Daddy Fictional character, a wealthy plantation owner who confronts some painful truths with his son Brick in the play CAT ON A HOT TIN ROOF by Tennessee Williams.

Biggers, \'big-ərz\, Earl Derr (b. Aug. 26, 1884, Warren, Ohio, U.S.—d. April 5, 1933, Pasadena, Calif.)   American novelist and journalist best remembered for the popular literary creation Charlie CHAN. A wise Chinese-American detective on the Honolulu police force, Charlie Chan is the protagonist of a series of mystery detective novels that spawned popular feature films, radio dramas, and comic strips.

Biggers attended Harvard University (B.A., 1907) and became a journalist for the Boston *Traveler*. His successful mystery novel *Seven Keys to Baldpate* (1913) was adapted into a well-received play and a film. The six novels that feature Chan were all initially serialized in *The Saturday Evening Post*.

Biglow Papers \'big-lō\   Satirical poetry in Yankee dialect by James Russell LOWELL. The first series of *Biglow Papers* was published in *The Boston Courier* newspaper in 1846–48 and collected in book form in 1848. The second series was published in *The Atlantic Monthly* during the American Civil War and collected in a book published in 1867.

Lowell opposed the Mexican War, regarding it as an attempt to extend slavery. The first series of poems expressed his opposition to the war, using the voice of rustic poet Hosea Biglow. Birdofredum Sawin, one of Lowell's most inspired inventions, is a Massachusetts wastrel who reports on the war in several letters. He loses an arm, a leg, and an eye in the fighting. The radical fires in Lowell had cooled somewhat by the time he issued the second series of *Biglow Papers*, which contain less effective satire of the wartime South.

Bilderdijk \'bil-dər-,deik, *Angl* -,dīk\, Willem (b. Sept. 7, 1756, Amsterdam, Neth.—d. Dec. 18, 1831, Haarlem)   Dutch poet who had considerable influence on the intellectual and social life of the Netherlands.

Born of a strongly Calvinist and monarchist family, Bilderdijk had a crippled foot and spent a precocious childhood among books. After studying law at Leiden, he practiced as an advocate at The Hague until 1795, when he was forced into exile for his refusal to take the oath of allegiance to the republic established by the French. In 1806 he returned to the Netherlands.

Although much of his prolific output was in the dry, rhetorical style of previous generations, he occasionally produced a poetic diction and ideas on poetry that were totally new to the Dutch. With his passionate Gothic-style verse rendering (1803) of the 18th-century ballads of Ossian, Bilderdijk set the scene for early 19th-century Romantic nostalgia. In his poem *De kunst der poëzij* (1809; "The Art of Poetry") he maintained the importance of feeling in the writing of poetry, a principle that he introduced to the Netherlands. Bilderdijk's profusely religious poems inspired a number of theologian-poets throughout the 19th century. The work for which he is best remembered is the unfinished epic poem *De ondergang der eerste wareld* (1810; "The Destruction of the First World"), which dramatically portrays the primordial struggle between Cain's son and the progeny of Cain's daughters.

bildungsroman \'bil-,dùnz-rō-,män, *German* -,dùns-\ *plural* bildungsromane \-rō-,män-ə\ *or* bildungsromans [German, literally, novel of formation]   A class of novel in German literature that deals with the formative years of the main character.

The folklore tale of the dunce who goes out into the world seeking adventure and learns wisdom the hard way was raised to literary heights in Wolfram von Eschenbach's medieval epic *Parzival* and in Hans Grimmelshausen's picaresque tale *Der Abentheurliche Simplicissimus* (1669; "The Adventurous Simplicissimus"). The first novelistic development of this theme was J.W. von Goethe's *Wilhelm Meisters Lehrjahre* (1795–96; *Wilhelm Meister's Apprenticeship*), and it remains the classic example of the type. The bildungsroman ends on a positive note. If the grandiose dreams of the hero's youth are over, so are many foolish mistakes and painful disappointments, and a life of usefulness lies ahead.

A common variation of the bildungsroman is the KÜNSTLERROMAN, a novel that deals with the formative years of an artist. Other variations are the *Erziehungsroman* ("novel of upbringing") and the *Entwicklungsroman* ("novel of character development"), although the differences are slight.

Billetdoux \bĕ-ye-'dü\, François (b. Sept. 7, 1927, Paris, Fr.—d. Nov. 26, 1991, Paris)   French playwright whose works, linked with the avant-garde theater, examine human relationships and find them doomed to failure.

Billetdoux studied at the Charles Dullin School of Dramatic Art and the Institut des Hautes Études Cinématographiques. *Tchin-Tchin* (1959; *Chin-Chin*), his first play to win popular acclaim, traces the decline into alcoholism of a couple brought together by the infidelity of their spouses. In *Le Comportement des époux Bredbury* (1960; "The Behavior of the Bredbury Couple"), a wife attempts to sell her husband in the classified pages of a newspaper. Other plays include *Il faut passer par les nuages* (1964; "You Must Pass Through the Clouds"), and *Comment va le monde, môssieu? Il tourne, môssieu!* (1964; "How is the World, Mister? It's Turning, Mister!"). After several years of working on other projects, Billetdoux returned to writing for the stage with *Reveille-toi, Philadelphie* (1988; "Wake Up, Philadelphia"), for which he won a Molière, France's top theater award.

Billiards at Half-Past Nine   Novel by Heinrich BÖLL, first published in German as *Billard um halbzehn* in 1959. In its searing examination of the moral crises of postwar Germany, the novel resembles Böll's other fiction; its interior monologues and flashbacks, however, make it his most complex work.

The novel examines the lives of three generations of architects and their responses to the Nazi regime and its aftermath. The present-day action takes place on the 80th birthday of patriarch Heinrich Fähmel, who built St. Anthony's Abbey. At the end of World War II, his son Robert destroyed the abbey to protest the church's complicity with the Nazis; Robert's son, Joseph, is serving his apprenticeship by helping to restore St. Anthony's. All three characters confront their relationship to building and destruction, as well as their personal and historical past. By the novel's end, the three are reconciled and share a birthday cake in the shape of the abbey.

Billings \'bil-iŋz\, Josh, *pseudonym of* Henry Wheeler Shaw \'shô\ (b. April 21, 1818, Lanesboro, Mass., U.S.—d. Oct. 14, 1885, Monterey, Calif.)   American humorist whose philosophical comments in plain language were widely popular after the American Civil War through his newspaper pieces, books, and comic lectures. He employed the misspellings, fractured grammar, and hopeless logic then current among comic writers. His special contributions were his rustic aphorisms and droll delineations of animal life.

Expelled from Hamilton College, Clinton, N.Y., because of a prank, he spent some years in the West and Midwest before settling in Poughkeepsie, N.Y., in 1858 as an auctioneer and land dealer. He began writing when he was 45, but became successful only when he adopted the misspelling vogue. His "Essa on the Muel" made him famous, and after joining the *New York Weekly* in 1867 he became a national idol. Some of his best work is in the 10-year series *Josh Billings' Farmer's Allminax*, which he started in 1869 as a burlesque of *The Old Farmer's Almanac*. His other books were hasty collections of his newspaper writings, the most comprehensive being *Everybody's Friend* (1874).

Billy Budd, Foretopman \\'bil-ē-'bəd\ *also called* Billy Budd, Sailor.   Novel by Herman MELVILLE, written in 1891 and left unfinished at his death. It was first published in 1924, and the definitive edition was issued in 1962.

Provoked by a false charge, the sailor Billy Budd accidentally kills John Claggert, the satanic master-at-arms. In a time of threatened mutiny, he is hanged, and he goes willingly to his fate.

Melville's story is particularly noted for its powerful symbolic characterizations—with, for example, Billy Budd as both innocent (Adam) and Christ figure—and for its sympathetic treatment of the ambivalence of Captain Vere toward Billy's death.

Binchy \\'bin-chē\, Maeve (b. May 28, 1940, Dublin, Ire.) Irish journalist and author of best-selling novels and short stories about small-town Irish life.

Educated at University College, Dublin (B.A., 1960), Binchy taught school in Dublin from 1961 to 1968. In 1968 she began her career as a reporter for the daily newspaper *Irish Times*. Her earliest short stories, republished collectively as *London Transports* in 1983, were closely observed portraits of the struggles of contemporary women.

Binchy's first novel, *Light a Penny Candle* (1982), is about the friendship of two young women through two decades. Her second novel, *Echoes* (1985), tells of the struggle of an impoverished young woman to escape a narrow-minded, cruel resort town. A third best-seller, *Firefly Summer* (1987), concerns an Irish-American who is forced to reconsider his misconceptions about Ireland when he goes there to live. Binchy also wrote the short-story collections *Maeve Binchy's Dublin Four* (1982) and *The Lilac Bus* (1984), the novels *Silver Wedding* (1988) and *Circle of Friends* (1991), and several plays for the stage and television.

Bing Xin or **Ping Hsin** \\'biŋ-'shēn, 'shin\, *pseudonym of* Xie Wanying \\'shye-'wän-'yiŋ\ (b. Oct. 5, 1900, Minhou, Fujian province, China)   Chinese writer of gentle, melancholy stories and poems that enjoyed great popularity.

Bing Xin studied the Chinese classics and began writing traditional Chinese stories as a child, but her conversion to Christianity and her attendance at an American school in Beijing soon were reflected in a didactic and Western influence in her writing. The short stories and poems that she published during her years at Yanjing University in Beijing—lyrical pieces about childhood and nature—won her instant fame and a grant to study at Wellesley College in the United States, where she received an M.A. degree in 1926. *Bing Xin shiji* ("Collected Poems of Bing Xin") was published in 1933.

Bing Xin's collection of stories entitled *Gugu* ("The Paternal Aunt") was published in 1932 and one entitled *Donger guniang* ("Miss Danger") in 1935. She continued to write throughout the 1940s and '50s, producing such works as *Guanyu nüren* (1943; "About Women") and *Shisui xiaocha* (1964; "Miscellaneous Essays"). Bing Xin wrote little after the early 1960s, but she became active in cultural affairs under the communist government, especially in children's literature.

Binkis \\'biŋ-kis\, Kazys (b. Nov. 4, 1893, Gudeliai, Lithuania, Russian Empire—d. April 27, 1942, Kaunas, Lithuanian S.S.R.) Poet who led the "Four Winds" literary movement, which introduced Futurism into Lithuania.

From 1920 to 1923 Binkis studied literature and philosophy in Berlin, where he became acquainted with the newest trends in western European literature. The poems he wrote during his connection with the "Four Winds" movement, published in *Šimtas pavasarių* (1926; "One Hundred Springs"), caused a sensation because of their break with traditional forms. His best

work, however, is contained in his first collection of verse, *Eilėraščiai* (1920; "Poems").

In 1927 Binkis turned from Futuristic poetry to humorous pieces in verse, with themes drawn from Lithuanian country life. They were published in provincial newspapers and became immensely popular. He also wrote a number of successful children's books, edited several anthologies of poetry, and wrote two successful plays: *Atžalynas* (1938; "The Younger Generation") and *Generalinė repeticija* (1958; "General Rehearsal").

Binyon \\'bin-yən\, Laurence, *in full* Robert Laurence Binyon (b. April 10, 1869, Lancaster, Lancashire, Eng.—d. March 10, 1943, Reading, Berkshire)   English poet, dramatist, and art historian, a pioneer in the European study of Eastern painting.

Binyon attended Trinity College, Oxford, where he won the Newdigate Prize for his poem *Persephone* (1890). He combined his lifelong interests—books and painting—when in 1893 he began work at the British Museum, London. His first book on Oriental art was *Painting in the Far East* (1908), which is still a classic. His later books on art included *The Flight of the Dragon* (1911) and *The Spirit of Man in Asian Art* (1935).

World War I inspired Binyon's poem "For the Fallen" (1914), which won immediate recognition as the expression of the feelings of a disillusioned generation. It was set to music by Sir Edward Elgar. *Collected Poems* appeared in 1931. Binyon was also concerned with the revival of verse drama; his works in that form include *Attila* (1907), *Arthur* (1923), and *The Young King* (1934).

biocritical \\,bī-ō-'krit-i-kəl\ [*bio*graphical + *critical*]   Of, relating to, or being a study of the life and work of someone (such as a writer).

Biographia Literaria \\,bī-ō-'graf-ē-ə-,lit-ə-'rar-ē-ə\ (*in full* Biographia Literaria; or Biographical Sketches of My Literary Life and Opinions)   Work by Samuel Taylor COLERIDGE, published in two volumes in 1817. Another edition of the work, to which Coleridge's daughter Sara appended notes and supplementary biographical material, was published in 1847.

The first volume of the book recounts the author's friendship with poets Robert Southey and William Wordsworth. Coleridge goes on to describe the influences on his philosophical development, from his early teachers to such philosophers as Immanuel Kant, Johann Fichte, and Friedrich von Schelling. This section includes his well-known discussion of the difference between fancy and imagination. In the second volume Coleridge concentrates on literary criticism and proposes theories about the creative process and the historical sources of the elements of poetry.

Biographia Literaria was the most important work of literary criticism of the English Romantic period, combining philosophy and literary criticism in a new way, and it was lastingly influential.

biography \\bī-'äg-rə-fē, bē-\ [Late Greek *biographía,* from Greek *bíos* life + *gráphein* to write]   Form of nonfictional literature, the subject of which is the life of an individual. In general, the form is considered to include autobiography, in which the author recounts his or her own history.

The earliest biographical writing probably consisted of funeral speeches and inscriptions, usually praising the life and example of the deceased. From this evolved the laudatory and exemplary biography with its associated problems of uncritical or distorted interpretation of available evidence. Such lives are still found, but they have produced their own antithesis in the denunciatory or debunking biography of which Lytton Strachey's *Eminent Victorians* (1918) is a famous modern example.

The origins of modern biography as a distinct genre lie with Plutarch's moralizing lives of prominent Greeks and Romans and Suetonius' gossipy lives of the Caesars, which quote documentary sources. While kings and leaders attracted biographical attention as a part of the general historical record of their times, few lives of common individuals were considered for themselves until the 16th century. In England in the 17th century, William Roper's life of Thomas More is an important example, and Izaak Walton and John Aubrey also produced brief biographies of writers and eminent persons. But the major developments of English biography came in the 18th century with Samuel Johnson's critical *Lives of the English Poets* and James Boswell's massive *Life of Johnson*, which combines detailed records of conversation and behavior with considerable psychological insight. This provided the model for exhaustive, monumental 19th-century biographies such as A.P. Stanley's *Life of Arnold* and John Morley's *Gladstone*. Thomas Carlyle's conviction that history was the history of great men demonstrated the general belief of the time that biographical writing was an important method of understanding society and its institutions. In modern times, impatience with Victorian reticence and deference and the development of psychoanalysis have sometimes led to a more penetrating and comprehensive understanding of the biographical subject. Leon Edel's massive *Henry James* is a good example. Another modern development has been the group biography of a family or small body of close associates, such as Rebecca Fraser's *The Brontës*.

Biographical and autobiographical writing can easily pass into fiction when rational inference or conjecture pass over into imaginative reconstruction or frank invention or when the biographical subject itself is wholly or partly imaginary.

Bion \ˈbī-ən\ (fl. 100 BC; b. Smyrna, Lydia, Asia Minor)   Minor Greek bucolic poet. The *Lament for Bion*, written by an Italian pupil of the poet, suggests that he lived in Sicily. The 17 surviving fragments of Bion's *Bucolica*, mostly concerned with love, strike a playful, sometimes sententious note. Since the Renaissance Bion has also been credited with the *Lament for Adonis*, whose overheated and highly colored emotionalism may reflect the cult of Adonis, which was popular in the poet's homeland.

Bioy Casares \bē-ˈȯi-kä-ˈsä-räs, -räh\, Adolfo, *pseudonyms* Javier Miranda \mē-ˈrän-dä\ *and* Martin Sacastru \sä-ˈkäs-trü, -ˈkäh-\ (b. Sept. 15, 1914, Buenos Aires, Arg.)   Argentine writer and editor, known for his use of magic realism in both his own work and in his collaborations with Jorge Luis Borges.

Born into a wealthy family, Bioy Casares was encouraged in his writing by his father, who helped him publish his first book in 1929. In 1932 he met Borges, a meeting that resulted in lifelong friendship and literary collaboration. Bioy Casares published several books before 1940, including many collections of short stories, but he did not win wide notice until the publication of his novel *La invención de Morel* (1940; *The Invention of Morel*). A carefully constructed and fantastical work, it concerns a fugitive (the narrator) who has fallen in love and strives to establish contact with a woman who is eventually revealed to be only an image created by a movie projector. The novel *Plan de evasión* (1945; *A Plan for Escape*) and the six short stories of *La trama celeste* (1948; "The Celestial Plot," translated in *The Invention of Morel*) further explore imaginary worlds.

In the novel *El sueño de los héroes* (1954; *The Dream of Heroes*), Bioy Casares examines the meaning of love and the significance of dreams and memory to future actions. The novel *Diario de la guerra del cerdo* (1969; *Diary of the War of the Pig*) combines science fiction and political satire.

Other works include the short-story collections *El gran serafín* (1967; "The Great Seraphim"), *Historias de amor* (1972; "Love Stories"), and *Historias fantásticas* (1972; "Fantastic Stories"), as well as the novels *Dormir al sol* (1973; *Asleep in the Sun*) and *La aventura de un fotógrafo en La Plata* (1985; *The Adventure of a Photographer in La Plata*).

In their collaborative efforts, Borges and Bioy Casares often employed the pseudonyms Honorio Bustos Domecq, B. Suarez Lynch, and B. Lynch Davis. Together they published *Seis problemas para Don Isidro Parodi* (1942; *Six Problems for Don Isidro Parodi*) and *Crónicas de Bustos Domecq* (1967; *Chronicles of Bustos Domecq*), both of which satirize a variety of Argentine personalities. The two also edited a two-volume book of gaucho poetry (*Poesía gauchesca*, 1955), *Los mejores cuentos policiales* (1943; "The Greatest Detective Stories"), and other works. Bioy Casares collaborated with his wife, the poet Silvina Ocampo, and Borges to edit *Antología de la literatura fantástica* (1940; "Anthology of Fantastic Literature") and *Antología poética argentina* (1941; "Anthology of Argentine Poetry").

In 1990 Bioy Casares was awarded the Cervantes Prize for Literature, the highest honor in Hispanic letters.

Bird \ˈbərd\, Robert Montgomery (b. Feb. 5, 1806, New Castle, Del., U.S.—d. Jan. 23, 1854, Philadelphia, Pa.)   Novelist and dramatist whose work epitomizes the nascent American literature of the first half of the 19th century. Although immensely popular in his day, his writings are principally of interest in the 20th century to the literary historian.

Bird graduated with a medical degree from the University of Pennsylvania in 1827 but practiced for only a year. He wrote poetry, some of it published in periodicals, and several unproduced plays. His first drama to be staged was *The Gladiator* (1831), which dealt with a slave revolt in the Rome of 73 BC and by implication attacked the institution of slavery in the United States. Other plays included *Oralloossa* (1832), a romantic tragedy of Peru at the time of the Spanish conquest, and *The Broker of Bogota* (1834), a domestic drama set in 18th-century Colombia and considered his best by many critics.

Bird then turned to writing novels, beginning with *Calavar* (1834), a tale of the Spanish conquistadors in Mexico, and its sequel, *The Infidel* (1835). His remaining novels were frontier stories, the most popular of which was *Nick of the Woods* (1837).

Unable to make a living from his writing, Bird taught briefly at Pennsylvania Medical College in Philadelphia and tried his hand at farming. At the time of his death he was literary editor and part owner of a newspaper, the Philadelphia *North American*.

Birds (*Greek* Ornithes)   Drama by ARISTOPHANES, produced in 414 BC. Some critics regard *Birds* as a pure fantasy, but others see it as a political satire on the imperialistic dreams that had led the Athenians to undertake their ill-fated expedition of 415 BC to conquer Syracuse in Sicily. Peisthetaerus ("Trusty") is so disgusted with his city's bureaucracy that he persuades the birds to join him in building a new city to be suspended between heaven and earth; it is named Nephelokokkygia and is the original Cloud-cuckoo-land. The city is built, and Peisthetaerus and his bird comrades must then fend off the undesirable humans who want to join them in their new Utopia. He and the birds finally even starve the Olympian gods into cooperating with them. *Birds* is Aristophanes' most fantastical play, but its escapist mood possibly echoes the dramatist's sense of Athens' impending decline.

Birkin, Rupert \ˈrü-pərt-ˈbər-kin\   Fictional character, a sickly introspective school inspector in the novel WOMEN IN LOVE by D.H. Lawrence. Birkin, based on Lawrence himself, struggles to understand and act upon his desires. His relationship with his lover Ursula Brangwen is full of conflicts, for in his drive toward self-awareness he seeks an unsentimental partnership of equals, whereas her interests are more practical and physical. He is also contrasted with the strong-willed Gerald Crich.

Birney \\'bər-nē\\, Earle, *in full* Alfred Earle Birney (b. May 13, 1904, Calgary, Alta. [Canada]) Writer and educator whose contributions to Canadian letters reveal a deep and abiding love of language.

Birney received a Ph.D. from the University of Toronto, and his first collection of poetry, *David and Other Poems* (1942), was published during his tenure there. After serving in the army, he held a number of teaching and editorial positions.

Birney's other verse collections include *Now Is Time* (1945), *The Strait of Anian* (1948), and *Near False Creek Mouth* (1964). Most of his later poems are experimental. His verse drama, *Trial of a City* (1952; later revised as a stage play, *The Damnation of Vancouver*), is an indictment of modern Vancouver by heroes from Vancouver's past. Birney also wrote two novels: *Turvey* (1949), a picaresque novel of World War II, and *Down the Long Table* (1955), which is semiautobiographical. Also an essayist and critic, he edited *Twentieth-Century Canadian Poetry* (1953). His *Collected Poems* appeared in 1975. Later works include collections of verse and several radio plays.

Birthday Party, The Drama in three acts by Harold PINTER, produced in 1958 and published in 1959. Pinter's first full-length play established his trademark "comedy of menace," in which a character is suddenly threatened by the vague horrors at large in the outside world. The action takes place entirely in a shabby rooming house where Stanley, a lazy young boarder, is shaken out of his false sense of security by the arrival of two mysterious men who proceed to "punish" him for crimes that remain unrevealed. A birthday party staged by Stanley's landlady soon turns into an exhibition of violence and terror. Pinter's comic vision of paranoia and isolation is reinforced by his use of dialogue, including frequent pauses, disjointed conversations, and non sequiturs.

Birth of Tragedy, The (*in full* The Birth of Tragedy from the Spirit of Music) Book by German philosopher Friedrich NIETZSCHE, first published in 1872 as *Die Geburt der Tragödie aus dem Geiste der Musik*. A speculative rather than exegetical work, *The Birth of Tragedy* examines the origins and development of poetry, specifically Greek tragedy. Nietzsche argues that Greek tragedy arose out of the fusion of what he termed Apollonian and Dionysian elements—the former representing measure, restraint, harmony, and the latter unbridled passion—and that Socratic rationalism and optimism spelled the death of Greek tragedy. The final part of the book is a rhapsody on the rebirth of tragedy from the spirit of Wagner's music. Greeted by stony silence at first, the book became the object of heated controversy for those who mistook it for a conventional work of classical scholarship. It remains a classic in the history of aesthetics.

Bīrūnī, al- \\,al-'bē-,rū-,nē\\, *in full* Abū ar-Rayḥān Muḥammad ibn Aḥmad al-Bīrūnī (b. September 973, Khwārezm, Khorāsān [now in Turkmenistan]—d. Dec. 13, 1048, Ghazna, Ghaznavid Afghanistan [now Ghaznī, Afg.]) Persian scholar and scientist, one of the most learned men of his age and an outstanding intellectual figure.

Possessing a profound and original mind, al-Bīrūnī was conversant with Turkish, Persian, Sanskrit, Hebrew, and Syriac in addition to the Arabic in which he wrote. He applied his talents in many fields of knowledge, excelling particularly in astronomy, mathematics, chronology, physics, medicine, and history. He corresponded with the great philosopher Avicenna. Some time after 1017 he went to India and made a comprehensive study of its culture.

Al-Bīrūnī's most famous works are *Āthār al-bāqīyah* (*Chronology of Ancient Nations*); *At-Tafhīm* ("Elements of Astrology"); *Al-Qānūn al-Mas'ūdī* ("The Mas'ūdī Canon"), a major work on astronomy that he dedicated to Sultan Mas'ūd of Ghazna; and *Tā'rīkh al-Hind* ("A History of India").

Bishop \\'bish-əp\\, Elizabeth (b. Feb. 8, 1911, Worcester, Mass., U.S.—d. Oct. 6, 1979, Boston, Mass.) American poet known for her polished, witty descriptive verse. Her work appeared in *The New Yorker* and other magazines.

After graduating from Vassar College in 1934, Bishop traveled often, living for a time in Key West, Fla., and Mexico. During most of the 1950s and '60s she lived in Petrópolis, near the city of Rio de Janeiro, Braz., later dividing her time between Petrópolis and San Francisco. Her first book of poems, NORTH & SOUTH (1946), which contrasts her New England origins and her love of hot climates, was reprinted (1955) with additions as *North & South: A Cold Spring*. Bishop's *The Complete Poems* was published in 1969, and her GEOGRAPHY III appeared in 1976. She taught writing at Harvard University from 1970 to 1977. Posthumously published volumes include *The Complete Poems, 1927–1979* (1983) and *The Collected Prose* (1984). Bishop wrote a travel book, *Brazil* (1962), and translated from the Portuguese Alice Brant's Brazilian classic *The Diary of Helena Morley* (1957). She also edited and translated *An Anthology of Twentieth-Century Brazilian Poetry* (1972).

Bishop \\'bish-əp\\, John Peale (b. May 21, 1892, Charles Town, W.Va., U.S.—d. April 4, 1944, Hyannis, Mass.) American poet, novelist, and critic, and a close associate of American expatriate writers in Paris in the 1920s.

At Princeton University Bishop formed lifelong friendships with Edmund Wilson, the future critic, and with the novelist F. Scott Fitzgerald, who depicted Bishop as the highbrow writer Tom D'Invilliers in *This Side of Paradise*. Bishop published his first volume of verse, *Green Fruit*, in 1917. After military service in World War I, he was an editor at *Vanity Fair* magazine in New York City from 1920 to 1922. He married into wealth and traveled throughout Europe. From 1926 to 1933 he lived in France and acquired a deep admiration for French culture. His collection of stories about his native South, *Many Thousands Gone* (1931), was followed with a volume of poetry, *Now with His Love* (1933). *Act of Darkness*, a novel tracing the coming of age of a young man, and *Minute Particulars*, a collection of verse, both appeared in 1935. He became chief poetry reviewer for *The Nation* magazine in 1940. That year he published perhaps his finest poem, "The Hours," an elegy on the death of Fitzgerald. His *Collected Poems* and *Collected Essays* were published in 1948.

Bishop Blougram's Apology \\'blō-grəm, 'blaù-, 'blä-\\ Long poem by Robert BROWNING, published in the two-volume collection *Men and Women* (1855).

The poem contains conversations between Bishop Blougram and Gigadibs, a journalist he considers a hack. The two men argue about the nature of reality and the nature of faith. Neither man succeeds at his original intent: the journalist cannot pry from the prelate information that might be personally embarrassing, and the bishop is unsuccessful in demoralizing the journalist. At the end of the poem, it is disclosed that Gigadibs has become a convert to Christianity and will begin a new life in Australia.

Bishop Orders His Tomb at St. Praxed's Church, The \\'prak-sed\\ Poem considered to be the first blank verse dramatic monologue in English, by Robert BROWNING, published in the collection *Dramatic Romances and Lyrics* (1845).

The poem is a character study of a powerful, worldly prince of the Roman Catholic church at the time of the Renaissance.

The dying bishop is surrounded by his "nephews," who are really his illegitimate sons. The prelate asks that his funeral be more elaborate than that of his rival in life and love, Fra Gandolf. He also seeks the intercession of St. Praxed on behalf of his sons, to assure them a successful future.

Bissell \'bis-əl\, Richard (Pike) (b. June 27, 1913, Dubuque, Iowa, U.S.—d. May 4, 1977, Dubuque) American novelist and playwright whose works provide fresh and witty images of Midwestern speech and folkways.

Bissell graduated from Harvard. From his experiences as a river pilot came the novels *A Stretch on the River* (1950) and *The Monongahela* (1952). His first successful novel was *7 1/2 Cents* (1953; U.K. title, *A Gross of Pyjamas*), based on his experiences as a supervisor in a pajama factory in Dubuque. In collaboration with George Abbott, he turned *7 1/2 Cents* into a musical, *The Pajama Game* (1954; film, 1957), which had a long run on Broadway. From his experiences in the theater he produced a novel, *Say, Darling* (1957), which he then wrote as a musical under the same title (1958), in collaboration with his wife, Marian Bissell, and Abe Burrows. Among his later books are the novels *Good Bye, Ava* (1960), *Still Circling Moose Jaw* (1965), and *New Light on 1776 and All That* (1975).

Biton and Cleobis \'bī-tən ... 'klē-ə-bis\, Biton *also spelled* Bito \'bī-tō\ In Greek legend, the sons of Cydippe, priestess of Hera at Argos, noted for their filial devotion and for their athletic prowess and strength. During an Argive festival honoring Hera, Cydippe was called to the temple. When her ox team could not be found, the brothers took up the yoke of the ceremonial wagon and conveyed her there themselves.

Cydippe begged the goddess to grant them, as a reward for their piety, whatever was best for mortal men. They feasted and slept that night in the temple, waiting to take their mother home on the following day, but they never awakened.

Bjørneboe \'byœr-nə-,bō\, Jens (Ingvald) (b. Oct. 9, 1920, Kristiansand, Nor.—d. May 9, 1976, Veierland) Norwegian novelist, dramatist, essayist, and poet whose work was generally inspired by a sense of outrage at the misuse of power.

Bjørneboe began his literary career with three collections of verse, *Dikt* (1951; "Poems"), *Ariadne* (1953), and *Den store by* (1958; "The Big City"), all notable for their restraint and classical formality. He then turned to fiction, writing several novels before producing the trilogy for which he is best known: *Frihetens øyeblikk* (1966; *Moment of Freedom*), *Kruttårnet* (1969; "The Gun Powder Tower"), and *Stillheten* (1973; "The Silence"). These trace "bestiality's history," *i.e.*, recount instances of increasing violence on the part of the state against the powerless. His last novel, *Haiene* (1974; *The Sharks*), an allegorical sea novel, is also considered to be one of his strongest works.

Bjørneboe's plays show the influence of Bertolt Brecht. His satirical musical *Til lykke med dagen* (1965; "Happy Birthday") criticizes the Norwegian prison system, *Fugleelskerne* (1966; "The Bird Lovers") concerns the conflict between culpability and money, and *Amputasjon* (1970; "Amputation") parodies authority and its absolute standards for conformity.

Bjørneboe also was widely read as an essayist and journalist. His important essay collections include *Politi og anarki* (1972; "Police and Anarchy") and the posthumously published *Om Brecht* (1977; "On Brecht").

Bjørnson \'byœrn-sòn\, Bjørnstjerne Martinius (b. Dec. 8, 1832, Kvikne, Nor.—d. April 26, 1910, Paris, Fr.) Norwegian writer, editor, and theater director, and one of the most prominent public figures of his day. He is generally known, together with Henrik Ibsen, Alexander Kielland, and Jonas Lie, as one of "the four great ones" of 19th-century Norwegian literature,

and he won the Nobel Prize for Literature in 1903. His poem "Ja, vi elsker dette landet" ("Yes, We Love This Land Forever") is the Norwegian national anthem.

Bjørnson grew up in the small farming community of Romsdalen, which later became the scene of his country novels. From

Library of Congress

the start his writing was marked by clearly didactic intent; he sought to stimulate national pride in Norway's history and achievements and to instill ideals. He drew inspiration from the sagas of Norway and his personal knowledge of contemporary rural life. His early writings included the tales *Synnøve solbakken* (1857; *Trust and Trial*), *Arne* (1858), and *En glad gut* (1860; *The Happy Boy*), the one-act historical play *Mellem slagene* (1857; "Between the Battles"), and the play *Halte-Hulda* (1858; "Lame Hulda").

In 1857–59 he was Ibsen's successor as artistic director at the Bergen Theater and later director of the Christiania Theater. He also became the editor of the *Bergenposten* and the newspaper *Norsk Folkeblad*. In 1870 the first edition of his *Digte og sange* (*Poems and Songs*) and the epic poem *Arnljot Gelline* appeared. Bjørnson's political battles and literary feuds took up so much of his time that he left Norway in order to write. The two dramas that brought him an international reputation were thus written in self-imposed exile: *En fallit* (1875; *The Bankrupt*) and *Redaktøren* (1875; *The Editor*).

His later works include the novels *Det flager i byen og på havnen* (1884; *The Heritage of the Kurts*), which deals critically with Christianity and attacks the belief in miracles, and *På Guds veje* (1889; *In God's Way*), which deals with social change and suggests that such change must begin in the schools. His later dramas include *Over ævne I og II* (1883 and 1895; *Beyond Our Power* and *Beyond Human Might*), as well as *Paul Lange og Tora Parsberg* (1898), which is concerned with the theme of political intolerance.

black aesthetic movement *also called* black arts movement. Period of artistic and literary development among black Americans in the 1960s and early '70s. Based on the cultural politics of black nationalism, the movement sought to create a populist art form to promote the idea of black separatism. Many adherents viewed the artist as an activist responsible for the formation of racially separate publishing houses, theater troupes, and study groups. The literature of the movement, generally written in black English vernacular and confrontational in tone, addressed such issues as interracial tension, sociopolitical awareness, and the relevance of African history and culture to blacks in the United States.

Leading theorists of the black aesthetic movement included Houston A. Baker, Jr.; Henry Louis GATES, Jr.; Addison Gayle, Jr., editor of the anthology *The Black Aesthetic* (1971); Hoyt W. Fuller, editor of the journal *Negro Digest* (which became *Black World* in 1970); and LeRoi Jones and Larry Neal, editors of *Black Fire: An Anthology of Afro-American Writing* (1968). Jones, later known as Amiri BARAKA, wrote the critically acclaimed play *Dutchman* (1964) and founded the Black Arts

Repertory Theatre in Harlem (1965). Haki R. MADHUBUTI, known as Don L. Lee until 1973, became one of the movement's most popular writers with the publication of *Think Black* (1967) and *Black Pride* (1968). Characterized by an acute self-awareness, the movement produced such autobiographical works as *The Autobiography of Malcolm X* (1965) by Alex Haley, *Soul On Ice* (1968) by Eldridge Cleaver, and *Angela Davis: An Autobiography* (1974). Other notable writers were Toni Morrison, Ishmael Reed, Ntozake Shange, Sonia Sanchez, Alice Walker, and June Jordan.

Black Beauty (*in full* Black Beauty: The Autobiography of a Horse)   The only novel by Anna SEWELL and the first major animal story in children's literature. The author wrote it "to induce kindness, sympathy and an understanding treatment of horses"; it was published in 1877, shortly before Sewell's death.

Black Beauty, a handsome horse of the era before automobiles, narrates the story himself. Well-born, well-bred, and initially owned by kind masters, he is sold to successively crueler owners. Eventually he collapses from overwork and ill treatment, but in the end he is sold to another kind owner and recovers. Sewell's careful observation and extensive descriptions of equine behavior lend verisimilitude to the novel.

Black Boy   Autobiography by Richard WRIGHT, published in 1945 and considered to be one of his finest works. The book is sometimes considered a fictionalized autobiography or an autobiographical novel because of its use of novelistic techniques. *Black Boy* describes vividly Wright's often harsh, hardscrabble boyhood and youth in rural Mississippi and in Memphis, Tenn. When the work was first published, many white critics viewed *Black Boy* primarily as an attack on racist Southern white society. From the 1960s the work came to be understood as the story of Wright's coming of age and development as a writer whose race, though a primary component of his life, was but one of many that formed him as an artist.

Blackburn \'blak-bərn\, Thomas (b. Feb. 10, 1916, Hensingham, Cumberland, Eng.—d. Aug. 13, 1977, Wales)   English poet and critic noted for his technically skilled but often haunted personal examination.

The son of a clergyman, Blackburn was educated at the University of Durham. In his autobiographical novel, *A Clip of Steel* (1969), he depicts a childhood tormented by a tense and repressive father, his own breakdown in his early twenties, and his psychoanalysis.

Blackburn's first notable volume of verse was *The Holy Stone* (1954). Later verse includes *A Smell of Burning* (1961), *A Breathing Space* (1964), *The Fourth Man* (1971), *Selected Poems* (1976), and *Post Mortem* (1977). His collection *Bread for the Winter Birds* (1980) was published posthumously. Among his prose works are *Robert Browning* (1967); a survey of modern poets, *The Price of an Eye* (1961); a musical drama, *The Judas Tree* (1965; with composer Peter Dickinson); and the novel *The Feast of the Wolf* (1971).

Black Cat, The   Short story by Edgar Allan POE, first published in the *Saturday Evening Post* in August 1843 and included in the collection *Tales by Edgar Allen Poe* (1845). The story's narrator is an animal lover who, as he descends into alcoholism and perverse violence, begins mistreating his wife and his black cat Pluto. When Pluto attacks him in self-defense one night, he seizes the cat in a fury, cuts out one of its eyes, and hangs it. That night a fire destroys his house, leaving him in dire poverty. He later adopts a one-eyed black cat that he finds at a low-life tavern, but after he nearly trips on the cat, he attempts to kill it, too. When his wife intervenes he kills her instead and calmly conceals her in a wall. In the end the black cat reveals the narrator's crime to the police.

Black Elk Speaks   Subtitled *Being the Life Story of a Holy Man of the Oglala Sioux as Told to John G. Neihardt (Flaming Rainbow)*, the work is the autobiography of Black Elk. It was dictated by Black Elk in Sioux, translated into English by his son Ben Black Elk, written by John G. Neihardt, and published in 1932. The work became a major source of information about 19th-century Plains Indian culture.

Black Elk, a member of the Oglala Lakota branch of the Sioux nation, tells of his boyhood participation in battles with the U.S. Army, his becoming a medicine man, and his joining Buffalo Bill's Wild West Show in 1886. Upon his return from a European tour, he found his tribe living on the bleak Pine Ridge reservation in South Dakota, starving, diseased, and hopeless, and with many fellow Sioux he joined the Ghost Dance movement. The book concludes with a description of the infamous massacre at Wounded Knee.

Blackfriars Theatre \'blak-,frī-ərz\   Either of two separate London theaters, the second famed as the winter quarters (after 1608) of the King's Men, the company of actors for whom William Shakespeare served as chief playwright.

black humor [translation of French *humour noir*]   Humor marked by the use of morbid, ironic, or grotesquely comic episodes that ridicule human folly. A comic work that employs black humor is a black comedy.

Although the French Surrealist André Breton published his *Anthologie de l'humour noir* ("Anthology of Black Humor," frequently enlarged and reprinted) in 1940, the term did not come into common use until the 1960s. Among the best-known novelists to employ black humor were Nathanael West, Vladimir Nabokov, and Joseph Heller. An outstanding example of black comedy is Heller's *Catch-22* (1961). Other novelists who mined the same vein included Kurt Vonnegut, particularly in *Slaughterhouse Five* (1969); Thomas Pynchon, in *V* (1963) and *Gravity's Rainbow* (1973); and Bruce Jay Friedman in *Stern* (1962). The term black comedy also was applied to a number of playwrights in the THEATER OF THE ABSURD, especially to Eugène Ionesco.

Antecedents to black comedy include the comedies of Aristophanes (5th–4th century BC), François Rabelais's *Pantagruel* (1532), Jonathan Swift's "A Modest Proposal" (1729), and Voltaire's *Candide* (1759).

Black Mischief   Satiric novel by Evelyn WAUGH, published in 1932. The book skewers attempts to impose European customs and beliefs upon so-called primitive peoples.

The story is set in the fictional empire of Azania, an island off the coast of Africa. Upon the death of the emperor of Azania, rule is assumed by his grandson Seth, a recent graduate of Oxford who is eager to modernize his country. Seth's ideas are a muddle of fashionable notions and philosophies, and each of his new programs fails. Ultimately the country relapses into barbarism and cannibalism.

Black Monk, The   Short story by Anton CHEKHOV, first published in Russian as "Chorny monakh" in 1894. Chekhov's final philosophical short story, "The Black Monk" concerns Kovrin, a mediocre scientist who has grandiose hallucinations in which a black-robed monk convinces him that he possesses superhuman abilities and is destined to lead humanity to everlasting life and eternal truth. The spell is broken when the black monk fails to define "eternal truth" to Kovrin's satisfaction and disappears forever. Disappointed, Kovrin abandons his wife and family, wanders off in search of his lost illusions, and finally dies in his fruitless search.

Blackmore \'blak-,mȯr\, Richard Doddridge (b. June 7, 1825, Longworth, Berkshire, Eng.—d. Jan. 20, 1900, Teddington)

English Victorian novelist whose LORNA DOONE (1869) won a secure place among English historical romances.

After attending Exeter College, Oxford, Blackmore was called to the bar but withdrew because of ill health. He taught classics for five years, then, upon receiving a legacy, bought property and settled down to fruit growing and novel writing. After publishing some poems, Blackmore produced *Clara Vaughan*, a first and fairly successful novel, in 1864 and *Cradock Nowell* in 1866. *Lorna Doone* was his third published work. Its popularity grew slowly, until the qualities of this imaginative and exciting tale of Exmoor eventually brought it fame. Blackmore wrote 14 novels in all.

Blackmore \'blak-,mȯr\, Sir Richard (b. 1654, Corsham, Wiltshire, Eng.—d. 1729, Boxted, Essex)   English writer and physician to King William III (who knighted him in 1697 for professional services) and Queen Anne. Though he regarded poetry as merely a pastime, he wrote four epics in 10 or more books, *Prince Arthur* (1695), *King Arthur* (1697), *Eliza* (1705), and *Alfred* (1723).

To each poem Blackmore wrote a preface censuring the lewdness and impiety of modern wits, a subject also treated in his verse *Satyr Against Wit* (1700). These and other writings in prose provoked retorts from Alexander Pope and his friends and earned Blackmore his reputation as "father of the Bathos, and indeed the Homer of it."

Black Mountain poets   A loosely associated group of poets that formed an important part of the advance guard of American poetry in the 1950s. They published innovative yet disciplined poetry in the *Black Mountain Review* (1954–57), which became a leading forum of experimental verse. The group grew up around the poets Robert Creeley, Robert Duncan, and Charles Olson while they were teaching at Black Mountain College in North Carolina.

Turning away from the poetic tradition espoused by T.S. Eliot, the Black Mountain poets emulated the freer style of William Carlos Williams. Charles Olson's essay *Projective Verse* (1950) became their manifesto. Olson emphasized the creative process, in which the poet's energy is transferred through the poem to the reader. Inherent in this new poetry was the reliance upon decidedly American conversational language.

Much of the group's early work was published in the magazine *Origin* (1951–56). Dissatisfied with the lack of critical material in that magazine, Creeley and Olson established the *Black Mountain Review*. It featured the work of Williams and Duncan, as well as Paul Blackburn, Denise Levertov, Gary Snyder, and many others who later helped shape poetry in America.

Black Orpheus \'ȯr-,fyüs, -fē-əs\   Literary journal founded in 1957 in Lagos, Nigeria, to encourage the production and discussion of contemporary African writing. The journal was founded by Ulli Beier, a German teaching at the University of Ibadan, and published by the Nigerian Ministry of Education. *Black Orpheus* published articles about African literature, music, sculpture, and other art forms. Although it underwent major changes in editorial leadership and aesthetic and political philosophy, it always held to its initial purpose of encouraging contemporary African writing in the English language. Also included in its statement of purpose was the publication in English translation of works by African writers in French, Portuguese, and Spanish. Works by black American and West Indian authors also appeared, as did examples of literature from the African oral tradition. In time the journal published works from virtually all areas of Africa.

black theater   In the United States, dramatic movement encompassing plays written by, for, and about blacks. The minstrel shows of the early 19th century are believed by some to be the roots of black theater, but initially they were written by whites, acted by whites in blackface, and performed for white audiences. After the American Civil War, blacks began to perform in minstrel shows, and by the turn of the century they were producing black musicals, many of which were written, produced, and acted entirely by blacks. The first known play by an American black was James Brown's *King Shotaway* (1823). William Wells Brown's *Escape; or, A Leap for Freedom* (1858) was the first black play published, but the first real success of a black dramatist was Angelina W. Grimké's *Rachel* (1916).

Black theater flourished during the HARLEM RENAISSANCE of the 1920s and '30s. Experimental groups and black theater companies emerged in Chicago, New York City, and Washington, D.C. Garland Anderson's play *Appearances* (1925) was the first play of black authorship to be produced on Broadway, but black theater did not experience a Broadway hit until Langston Hughes's *Mulatto* (1935) won wide acclaim. In the late 1930s, black community theaters began to appear, and by 1940 black theater was firmly grounded in the American Negro Theater and the Negro Playwrights' Company.

After World War II black theater grew more progressive, more radical, and more militant, seeking to establish a mythology and symbolism apart from white culture. Councils were organized to abolish racial stereotypes in theater and to integrate black playwrights into the mainstream. Lorraine Hansberry's *A Raisin in the Sun* (1959) and other successful black plays of the 1950s portrayed the difficulty blacks had in maintaining an identity in a society that degraded them.

The 1960s saw the emergence of a new black theater, angrier and more defiant than its predecessors, with LeRoi Jones (later Amiri Baraka) as its strongest proponent. He established the Black Arts Repertory Theatre in Harlem in 1965 and inspired playwright Ed Bullins and others seeking to create a strong "black aesthetic" in American theater. Another playwright of this era was Ntozake Shange.

In the 1970s several black musicals were widely produced. In the early 1980s Charles Fuller's *A Soldier's Play* won a Pulitzer Prize, an award later given also to the powerful and prolific dramatist August Wilson.

Black Thunder   Historical novel by Arna BONTEMPS, published in 1936. One of Bontemps' most popular works, this tale of a doomed early 19th-century slave revolt in Virginia was noted for its detailed portrait of a slave community and its skillful use of dialect. Virtually unnoticed when it was first published, a second printing in 1968 attracted much critical attention.

Blackwell \'blak-,wel, -wəl\, John, *pseudonym* Alun \'al-in\ (b. 1797, Mold, Flintshire, Wales—d. May 19, 1841, Cardigan, Cardiganshire)   Poet and prose writer, regarded as the father of the modern Welsh secular lyric.

While an apprentice shoemaker, Blackwell began attending meetings of the Cymreigyddion, an organization of Welshmen in London dedicated to preserving ancient Welsh literature, and he participated in eisteddfod (arts festival) competitions. With financial help from friends he attended the University of Oxford, graduating in 1828, in which year his elegy to Bishop Heber won the prize at the Denbigh eisteddfod.

Blackwood \'blak-,wu̇d\, Algernon Henry (b. March 14, 1869, Shooters Hill, Kent, Eng.—d. Dec. 10, 1951, London)   British writer of tales of mystery and the supernatural.

After working at a variety of jobs in Canada, Alaska, and New York City, Blackwood returned to England in 1899. Seven years later he published his first book of short stories, *The Empty House* (1906), and became a full-time fiction writer. His later collections include *John Silence* (1908), stories about a detective sensitive to extrasensory phenomena, and *Tales of the Uncanny and Supernatural* (1949), 22 stories selected from his nine other books of short stories.

Blackwood \'blak-,wùd\, Caroline (Maureen), *in full* Lady Caroline Hamilton-Temple-Blackwood \'ham-il-tən-'tem-pəl\ (b. July 16, 1931, Northern Ireland)   Writer of psychological fiction who is noted for using physical and emotional deformity as a central element.

A descendant of the 18th-century dramatist Richard Brinsley Sheridan, Blackwood lived in Northern Ireland until she was 17. Her first book, *For All I Found There* (1973), is a collection of short stories and nonfiction, including reminiscences of life in Northern Ireland. Her next work of note, the novel *The Stepdaughter* (1976), concerns an isolated woman's obsession with and disapproval of her obese stepdaughter. The stingy misanthropic title character of *Great Granny Webster* (1977) lives out her miserable life in a crumbling mansion much like Blackwood's childhood home. *The Fate of Mary Rose* (1981) uses the form of a mystery to examine distorted, loveless lives. Blackwood's other works include the short stories of *Goodnight Sweet Ladies* (1983) and the novels *Corrigan* (1984) and *On the Perimeter* (1984).

Blackwood's Magazine \'blak-,wùdz\   Monthly publication that was an important literary force in 19th-century England. William Blackwood, Scottish founder of the publishing firm William Blackwood and Sons, Ltd., launched the *Edinburgh Monthly Magazine* in April 1817 as a Tory counterpart to the Whig-inclined *Edinburgh Review*. His magazine was retitled *Blackwood's Edinburgh Magazine* in October 1817 and was styled simply *Blackwood's Magazine* from 1906 until it ceased publication in 1980.

In its first year of publication writers John Gibson Lockhart, James Hogg, and John Wilson quickly made *Blackwood's* notorious throughout England with their biblical parody "Translations from an Ancient Chaldee Manuscript." Libel suits filed by victims of its satires also helped to make *Blackwood's* famous. Unlike its competitors, *Blackwood's* published short fiction and serialized novels; Thomas De Quincey, George Eliot, Joseph Conrad, and Alfred Noyes were among its contributors. It declined in influence, however, during the 20th century.

Blair \'blar\, Robert (b. 1699, Edinburgh, Scot.—d. Feb. 4, 1746, Athelstaneford, East Lothian)   Scottish poet remembered for a single poem, *The Grave*, which was influential in giving rise to the GRAVEYARD SCHOOL of poetry.

The Grave (1743), a long, uneven poem in blank verse, is a reflection on human mortality in mortuary imagery. Though it appeared a year after Edward Young's *Night Thoughts*, it is apparently uninfluenced by that work. It nonetheless reflects the general tendency of the graveyard poets to exploit sensibility and pathos. *The Grave* has none of the oppressive self-pity or pretentiousness of *Night Thoughts*. Its blend of Scottish ghoulishness and brisk sermonizing is presented in Shakespearean rhythms with a certain natural cheerfulness. William Blake made 12 illustrations that appeared in the 1808 edition.

Blais \'ble\, Marie-Claire (b. Oct. 5, 1939, Quebec, Que., Can.)   French-Canadian novelist and poet known for reporting the bleak inner reality and grinding poverty of characters born without hope, their empty lives often played out against a featureless, unnamed landscape.

In two early dreamlike novels, *La Belle Bête* (1959; *Mad Shadows*) and *Tête blanche* (1960), Blais stakes out her territory—lower-class people doomed to unrelieved sorrow and oppression. She moves her characters into a recognizably Canadian world in the novels *Une Saison dans la vie d'Emmanuel* (1965; *A Season in the Life of Emmanuel*); *Manuscrits de Pauline*

Archange (1968) and *Vivre! Vivre!* (1969), published together as *The Manuscripts of Pauline Archange* in English in 1970; *Un Joualonais sa joualonie* (1973; *St. Lawrence Blues*); and *Le Sourd dans la ville* (1979; *Deaf to the City*). She also published collections of poetry and several plays. Blais studied at Laval University, Quebec, and was made a Companion of the Order of Canada. In 1966 the French awarded her the Prix Médicis.

Blake \'blāk\, George (b. Oct. 28, 1893, Greenock, Renfrewshire, Scot.—d. Aug. 29, 1961, Glasgow)   Scottish journalist and novelist best known for his novels about Clydeside shipbuilders.

Blake worked as a journalist and in a publishing house before becoming a full-time writer. Among his many novels are *Vagabond Papers* (1922), *The Shipbuilders* (1935), and *David and Joanna* (1936) and the semiautobiographical work *Down to the Sea* (1937).

Blake \'blāk\, Nicholas   Pseudonym under which poet C. DAY-LEWIS published his detective novels.

Blake \'blāk\, William (b. Nov. 28, 1757, London, Eng.—d. Aug. 12, 1827, London)   English poet, painter, engraver, and

Brown Brothers

visionary mystic whose hand-illustrated series of lyrical and epic poems form one of the most strikingly original and independent bodies of work in the Western cultural tradition. Ignored by the public of his day, he is now regarded as one of the earliest and greatest figures of Romanticism.

Blake grew up in London and from 1772 to 1779 he was apprenticed to an engraver, thereafter entering the Royal Academy as an engraving student. His first volume of poetry, *Poetical Sketches. By W.B.* (1783), contains several verses remarkable for their freshness, purity of vision, and lyric intensity.

In 1784 Blake started a print shop in London. He developed "illuminated printing," a special technique of relief etching in which each page of the book was printed in monochrome from an engraved plate containing both text and illustration. Blake and his wife then usually colored the pages with watercolor or printed them in color.

The first examples of Blake's new printing method were two small tracts, *There is No Natural Religion* and *All Religions are One*, engraved about 1788. In an astonishing outburst of creative activity, Blake immediately followed these with his first masterworks, *Songs of Innocence* and *The Book of Thel* (both engraved 1789), *The French Revolution* (1791), *The Marriage of Heaven and Hell* and *Visions of the Daughters of Albion* (both engraved 1793), and SONGS OF INNOCENCE AND OF EXPERIENCE (1794).

After 1793 Blake's poetry appeared in the so-called prophetic books: *America, A Prophecy* (1793), *Europe, A Prophecy* (1794), *The Book of Urizen* (1794), and *The Book of Ahania*, *The Book of Los*, and *The Song of Los* (all 1795). In these works Blake elaborated a series of cosmic myths and epics through which he set forth a complex and intricate philosophical scheme.

In 1804–08 Blake engraved *Milton*, a comparatively brief epic that deals with a contest between the hero (Milton) and Satan. *Jerusalem*, Blake's third major epic and his longest poem, is also the most richly decorated of Blake's illuminated books; only a few of its 100 plates are without illustration.

The most notable poetry Blake wrote after *Jerusalem* is to be found in *The Everlasting Gospel* (1818?), a fragmentary and unfinished work containing a challenging reinterpretation of the character and teaching of Christ. Blake's last years were devoted mainly to pictorial art, and in these years he produced some of his most technically assured designs. In 1821 painter John Linnell commissioned him to make a series of 22 watercolors inspired by the Book of Job; these include some of his best-known pictures. Linnell also commissioned Blake's designs for Dante's *Divine Comedy*. Work on these watercolors was begun in 1825, but the commission was unfinished at his death. *See also* THE TYGER; URIZEN.

Blake, Sexton \'seks-tən-'blāk\   Fictional character, a popular detective hero of English boys' fiction since 1893. Approximately 200 authors have contributed Sexton Blake stories to a variety of magazines, newspapers, and novellas. The first Blake story was "The Missing Millionaire," by Hal Meredith (Harry Blyth); it was published in *Halfpenny Marvel* (1893).

Blake, who has rooms in Baker Street, relies more on his great physical strength and endurance than on his intellectual abilities. He is aided in his detecting by a boy named Tinker. Among the many criminal adversaries whom Blake defeats are Mademoiselle Yvonne, Dr. Huxton Rymer, Prince Wu Ling, and Waldo the Wonder Man.

Blanche, Anthony \'anth-ə-nē-'blanch\   Fictional character in the novel BRIDESHEAD REVISITED by Evelyn Waugh. A homosexual friend of Sebastian Marchmain, Blanche is an intellectual and an aesthete whose astute critical faculties fascinate and impress his Oxford classmates.

Blanco-Fombona \'blän-kō-fŏm-'bō-nä\, Rufino (b. June 17, 1874, Caracas, Venez.—d. Oct. 17, 1944, Buenos Aires, Arg.) Venezuelan literary historian and man of letters who played a major role in bringing the works of Latin-American writers to world attention.

Jailed during the early years of the dictatorship (1908–35) of Juan Vicente Gómez, Blanco-Fombono fled to Europe, where he established *Editorial América* in Madrid (1914), which presented Latin-American writers to the European literary world. A prolific author, he wrote poetry, short stories, novels, and essays.

Of his vast output, however, his literary essays are considered his best work, and two of his critical works, *El modernismo y los poetas modernistas* (1929; "Modernism and the Modernist Poets") and *Camino de imperfección, diario de mi vida (1906–1913)* (1929; "Road of Imperfection, Diary of My Life 1906–1913"), are considered standard works on Modernismo. Other important works include *Letras y letrados de Hispano-américa* (1908; "Letters and the Learned in Latin America") and *Grandes escritores de América* (1919; "Great Writers of America").

Blandiana \blän-'dyä-nä\, Ana, *pseudonym of* Otilia Valeria Coman Rusan (b. March 25, 1942, Timişoara, Rom.) Romanian lyric poet, essayist, and translator who is considered one of her generation's most significant literary voices.

A graduate of the University of Cluj, Blandiana was the poetry editor of two journals and a librarian at the Institute of Fine Arts, Bucharest, before becoming a freelance writer and poet. Because of her dissident poetry, her work was banned in the mid-1980s.

Her well-received first book, *Persoana întîa plural* (1964; "First-Person Plural"), was a collection of exuberant confessional poems. Through metaphoric reference to nature, she sought a spiritual connection to the natural world's cycles in such later collections as *A treia taină* (1969; "The Third Sacrament") and *Somnul din somn* (1977; "The Sleep within the Sleep"). Her poetry from the 1980s, for example, that in *Stea*

de pradă (1985; "Star of Prey"), was more somber and less optimistic. *The Hour of Sand: Selected Poems 1969–1989*, a translation of selections of her poetry, was published in 1990. She also published several novels and volumes of political and social criticism.

blank verse   Unrhymed verse, specifically unrhymed iambic pentameter, the preeminent dramatic and narrative verse form in English. It is also the standard form for dramatic verse in Italian and German.

Adapted from unrhymed Greek and Latin heroic verse, blank verse was introduced in 16th-century Italy along with other classical meters. The Italian humanist Francesco Maria Molza attempted the writing of consecutive unrhymed verse in 1514 in his translation of Virgil's *Aeneid*. Other experiments in 16th-century Italy were the tragedy *Sofonisba* (written 1514–15) by Gian Giorgio Trissino and the didactic poem *Le api* (1539) by Giovanni Rucellai. Rucellai was the first to use the term *versi sciolti*, which was translated into English as "blank verse." It soon became the standard meter of Italian Renaissance drama.

Henry Howard, Earl of Surrey, introduced the meter, along with the sonnet and other Italian humanist verse forms, to England in the early 16th century. Thomas Sackville and Thomas Norton used blank verse for the first English tragic drama, *Gorboduc* (first performed 1561), and Christopher Marlowe developed its musical qualities and emotional power in *Tamburlaine*, *Doctor Faustus*, and *Edward II*. William Shakespeare transformed the line and the instrument of blank verse into the vehicle for the greatest English dramatic poetry. In his early plays, he combined it with prose and a 10-syllable rhymed couplet; he later employed a blank verse dependent on stress rather than on syllabic length.

After a period of debasement, blank verse was restored to its former grandeur by John Milton in *Paradise Lost* (1667) and many later writers also used blank verse. The form's extreme flexibility can be seen in its range from the high tragedy of Shakespeare to the low-keyed, conversational tone of Robert Frost in *A Masque of Reason* (1945).

Blank verse was established in German drama by Gotthold Lessing's *Nathan der Weise* (1779). Examples of its use are found in the writings of J.W. von Goethe, Friedrich von Schiller, and Gerhart Hauptmann. It was also used extensively in Swedish, Russian, and Polish dramatic verse. *Compare* FREE VERSE.

Blasco Ibáñez \'bläs-kō-ē-'bän-yäth\, Vicente (b. Jan. 29, 1867, Valencia, Spain—d. Jan. 28, 1928, Menton, Fr.) Spanish writer and politician who achieved world renown for his novels dealing with World War I. He was associated with the Generation of '98.

At the age of 18, while studying law and contributing articles to political journals, Blasco Ibáñez wrote an antimonarchist poem for which he was sent to prison—the first of many such punishments for his political beliefs. He founded the republican journal *El Pueblo* in 1891 and was first elected to the Cortes (parliament) in 1901, to which he was returned seven times before he voluntarily exiled himself in 1923 and settled on the French Riviera because of his opposition to the military dictatorship.

Blasco Ibáñez' early work was composed mainly of regional novels such as *Flor de Mayo* (1895; *Mayflower*) and *Cañas y barro* (1902; *Reeds and Mud*). Later novels, such as *La bodega* (1905; *The Fruit of the Vine*), are held to have suffered from a heavy ideological treatment of serious social problems. More popular novels—*La maja desnuda* (1906; *Woman Triumphant*), *Sangre y arena* (1908; *Blood and Sand*), *Los cuatro jinetes del Apocalipsis* (1916; *The Four Horsemen of the Apocalypse*), and others—brought him fame but cost him critical approval because of their sensational nature.

blason \blä-'sōⁿ\ [French, from Middle French, eulogy, reproach, literally, coat of arms] A type of catalog verse in which something is either praised or blamed through a detailed listing of its faults or attributes. The word is normally used more specifically to refer to a type of verse in which aspects of the beloved's appearance are enumerated. This type of *blason* was said to have been invented by the French poet Clément Marot in 1536.

Bleak House Novel by Charles DICKENS, published serially in 1852–53 and in book form in 1853. Considered by some critics to be the author's best work, *Bleak House* is the story of several generations of the Jarndyce family who wait in vain to inherit money from a disputed fortune in the settlement of the lawsuit of *Jarndyce* v. *Jarndyce*. It is pointedly critical of England's Court of Chancery, in which cases could drag on through decades of convoluted legal maneuvering.

Blessington \'bles-iŋ-tən\, Marguerite Gardiner, Countess of, *original surname* Power (b. Sept. 1, 1789, Knockbrit, County Tipperary, Ire.—d. June 4, 1849, Paris, Fr.) Irish writer chiefly remembered for her *Conversations of Lord Byron* and for her London salon.

After a disastrous first marriage, the widowed Power married Charles Gardiner, Viscount Mountjoy and Earl of Blessington. She formed a brilliant salon and began to write essays and sketches of London life. In 1822 the Blessingtons went abroad. They spent two months in Genoa with Byron and lived in Italy and then in France until the earl's death in May 1829. Their extravagant tastes had drained his fortune, and the countess, returning to London, began to support herself by writing. Her journals furnished material for the popular *Conversations of Lord Byron* (1834), *The Idler in Italy* (1839), and *The Idler in France* (1841). She also wrote several novels and edited two annuals, *The Book of Beauty* and *The Keepsake*, to which she contributed.

Blest Gana \'blest-'gän-ä\, Alberto (b. May 4, 1830, Santiago, Chile—d. Nov. 9/11, 1920, Paris, Fr.) Novelist who was the father of the Chilean social novel.

While studying military engineering in France, Blest Gana came under the influence of the French realists, especially Honoré de Balzac. He returned to Chile in 1852 and taught mathematics in military academies. The fame he achieved through his literary work led to political appointments, and Blest Gana spent the last 50 years of his life serving as Chile's ambassador to England and France.

His early novels, such as *La aritmética en el amor* (1860; "Arithmetic in Love") and *Martín Rivas* (1862), realistically depict the middle and upper classes of Santiago, but character and plot suffer from the author's heavy-handed moralism. After a period of more than 30 years, during which he published no new works, he wrote what are considered to be his best novels, among them *Durante la Reconquista* (1897; "During the Reconquest") and *Los transplantados* (1904; "The Uprooted").

Blicher \'blē-kər\, Steen Steensen (b. Oct. 11, 1782, Vium, Jutland, Den.—d. March 26, 1848, Spentrup, Jutland) Danish poet and short-story writer who portrayed the people of Jutland with humor and irony and with a realism well in advance of his time.

An unhappily married, impoverished country parson, Blicher wrote poetry that expressed both humor and a melancholy acceptance of life. In the "Prelude" to *Trækfuglene* (1838; "Birds of Passage"), his finest collection of poems, he presents a self-portrait of a caged bird longing for freedom.

Blicher's fame rests primarily on his short stories and short novels. His best-known work is the novella *Brudstykker af en landsbydegns dagbog* (1824; "Fragments of the Journal of a Parish Clerk").

Bligh \'blī\, William (b. Sept. 9, 1754, County of Cornwall, Eng.—d. Dec. 7, 1817, London) English admiral who commanded HMS *Bounty* at the time of the celebrated mutiny on that ship (1789). The incident was the basis of the novel MUTINY ON THE BOUNTY by American authors Charles Nordhoff and James Norman Hall.

Bligh's character has been variously interpreted. He does not seem to have been unduly tyrannical, but his abusive tongue and his overbearing manner made him unpopular as a commander.

Blithedale Romance, The \'blīth-,dāl\ Minor novel by Nathaniel HAWTHORNE, published in 1852. The novel, about a group of people living in an experimental community, was based in part on Hawthorne's disillusionment with the Brook Farm utopian community near Boston in the 1840s.

Blithe Spirit Farce by Noël COWARD, produced and published in 1941. Often regarded as Coward's best work, this play about a man whose domestic life is disturbed by the jealous ghost of his first wife shows Coward's humor at its ripest. The combination of drawing-room comedy and ghost story enhances Coward's usual subject of people whose lifestyles defy conventional morality.

Bloch \'blôk\, Jean-Richard (b. May 25, 1884, Paris, Fr.—d. March 15, 1947, Paris) French essayist, novelist, and playwright active in the cause of socialism.

In 1910 Bloch started *L'Effort libre*, a "review of revolutionary civilization." His essay *Naissance d'une culture* (1936; "Birth of a Culture") called for an art that would associate the democratic tradition with a proletarian culture. The stories in *Lévy* (1912) included penetrating studies of Jewish psychology, and his Balzacian novel . . . *et Cie* (1918; . . . *& Co.*) dealt with a family of Jewish cloth manufacturers. His plays included a modern legend, *Le Dernier Empereur* (1926; "The Last Emperor"), and a popular fairy play, *Dix filles dans un pré* (1926; "Ten Girls in a Meadow"). Bloch, one of the writers associated with the Marxist review *Clarté*, spent most of World War II in Moscow.

Blok \'blôk\, Aleksandr Aleksandrovich (b. Nov. 16 [Nov. 28, New Style], 1880, St. Petersburg, Russia—d. Aug. 7, 1921, Petrograd [St. Petersburg]) Poet and dramatist who was the principal representative of Russian Symbolism.

Imbued with the early 19th-century Romantic poetry of Aleksandr Pushkin and the apocalyptic philosophy of the poet and mystic Vladimir Solovyov (1853–1900), Blok developed their concepts into an original poetic expression by a creative use of rhythmic innovations. For Blok, sound was paramount, and musicality is the primary characteristic of his verse.

His first collection of poems, the cycle *Stikhi o prekrasnoy dame* (1904; "Verses About the Lady Beautiful"), portrays his initial phase of Platonic idealism, personifying divine wisdom (Greek *sophia*) as the feminine world soul. But by 1904 Blok's romantic expectation of otherworldly fulfillment had been transformed into a concern for the human suffering surrounding him. Thus, to the consternation of his earlier admirers, in his next collections of poems, *Gorod* (1901–08; "The City") and *Snezhnaya maska* (1907; "Mask of Snow"), he sublimated his religious themes to images of sordid urban culture and transfigured his mystical woman into the "unknown courtesan." Blok later rejected what he termed the sterile intellectualism of the bourgeois Symbolists and embraced the Bolshevik movement as the change essential for the redemption of the Russian people. He felt doubly betrayed, however, first by the desertion of his literary colleagues and then by the Bolsheviks, who scorned his work and aesthetic aspirations.

His late poems are testaments of his alternate moods of hope and despair. The unfinished narrative poem *Vozmezdiye* (1910–21; "Retribution") reveals his disillusionment with the new regime, while *Rodina* (1907–16; "Homeland") and *Skify* (1918; *The Scythians*) exalt Russia's messianic role in the new world order.

Blok's preeminent work of impressionistic verse was his final composition, the enigmatic ballad *Dvenadtsat* (1918; *The Twelve*), which was written amid the chaos of the Revolution of 1917. The poem, notable for its mood-creating sounds, polyphonic rhythms, and harsh, slangy language, describes the march of a disreputable Red Army band, looting and killing, through a fierce blizzard during the 1917–18 St. Petersburg uprising, with a Christ figure at their head.

Blondel \blôⁿ-'del\ de Nesle \də-'nel\ (fl. late 12th century) Early lyric poet-musician, or trouvère, of northern France.

Nothing is known about Blondel outside of his poetry. He was probably from Nesle, in Picardy; but the name Blondel may be a nickname, and it is uncertain how many of the 25 songs attributed to him are actually his. His poetry is conventional in its complaints to an unknown lady. Blondel's popularity is apparent in the widespread use by contemporaries of his melodies, which are extant in various manuscripts.

blood \'bləd\ *British* A lurid work of fiction; especially a cheap and ill-written book of adventure or crime. The word is a short form of *blood-and-thunder book*.

bloodcurdler \'bləd-,kərd-ə-lər\ A gruesome, melodramatic theatrical or literary production.

Blood Wedding Folk tragedy in three acts by Federico GARCÍA LORCA, published and produced in 1933 as *Bodas de sangre*. *Blood Wedding* is the first play in Lorca's dramatic trilogy; the other two plays are *Yerma* and *The House of Bernarda Alba*. The protagonists of *Blood Wedding* are ordinary women confronting their own passionate natures and rebelling against the constraints of Spanish society. The unnamed bride in *Blood Wedding* runs away from her wedding reception with her former suitor, Leonardo, who is married. Death, in the person of a beggar, leads the frustrated bridegrooom to the guilty couple. The men kill each other, leaving Leonardo's wife, the bridegroom's mother, and the bride to bewail their losses.

Bloom \'blüm\, Allan (David) (b. Sept. 14, 1930, Indianapolis, Ind., U.S.—d. Oct. 7, 1992, Chicago, Ill.) American philosopher and writer best remembered for his provocative best-seller *The Closing of the American Mind: How Higher Education Has Failed Democracy and Impoverished the Souls of Today's Students* (1987).

Bloom received a Ph.D. from the University of Chicago, where he became a devotee of the Western classics. He taught at the University of Chicago and Yale and Cornell universities, and was on the faculties of several foreign universities. He published such well-received works as *Shakespeare's Politics* (1964), a collection of essays, and a translation of Plato's *Republic* (1968). He returned to the University of Chicago in 1979. In *The Closing of the American Mind*, Bloom argued that universities no longer taught students how to think and that students were unconcerned about the lessons of the past or about examining ideas in a historical context. His blistering critique blamed misguided curriculum, rock music, television, and academic elitism for the spiritual impoverishment of students.

Bloom \'blüm\, Harold (b. July 11, 1930, New York, N.Y., U.S.) American literary critic known for his innovative inter-

pretations of literary history and of the creation of literature.

Bloom attended Cornell and Yale universities and began teaching at Yale in 1955. His early books, *The Visionary Company: A Reading of English Romantic Poetry* (1961, rev. ed., 1971) and *The Ringers in the Tower: Studies in Romantic Tradition* (1971), explored the Romantic tradition and its influence on such poets as A.R. Ammons and Allen Ginsburg.

In *The Anxiety of Influence* (1973) and *A Map of Misreading* (1975), Bloom proposed one of his most original theories: that poetry results from poets deliberately misreading the works that influence them. *Figures of Capable Imagination* (1976) expands upon this theme. His most controversial work appeared in his commentary on *The Book of J*, published (1990) with David Rosenberg's translations of selected sections of the Pentateuch. Bloom speculated that the earliest known texts of the Bible were written by a woman who lived during the time of David and Solomon and that the texts were literary rather than religious ones on which later rewriters imposed beliefs of patriarchal Judaism.

Bloom, Leopold \'lē-ə-,pōld-'blüm\ Fictional character, the Odysseus figure whose wanderings through Dublin during one 24-hour period on June 16, 1904, form the central action of James Joyce's ULYSSES.

Bloom, Molly \'mäl-ē-'blüm\ One of the three central characters in the novel ULYSSES by James Joyce. The unfaithful wife of Leopold Bloom, Molly makes a derisively mocking parallel to Penelope, the faithful wife of Odysseus (Ulysses) in Homer's *Odyssey*.

Bloomfield \'blüm-,fēld\, Robert (b. Dec. 3, 1766, Honington, Suffolk, Eng.—d. Aug. 9, 1823, Shefford, Bedfordshire) Shoemaker and poet who achieved brief fame with poems describing the English countryside.

His first poem, *The Farmer's Boy* (1800), written after he had left the countryside to become a London shoemaker, owed its popularity to its blend of late 18th-century pastoralism with an early Romantic feeling for nature. The works that followed, from *Rural Tales, Ballads, and Songs* (1802) to *The Banks of Wye* (1811), were almost equally successful.

Bloomsbury group \'blümz-bə-rē, -,ber-ē\ Name given to a coterie of English writers, philosophers, and artists who frequently met between about 1907 and 1930 at the houses of Clive and Vanessa Bell and of Vanessa's brother and sister Adrian and Virginia Stephen (later Virginia Woolf) in the Bloomsbury district of London, the area around the British Museum. They discussed aesthetic and philosophical questions in a spirit of agnosticism and were strongly influenced by G.E. Moore's *Principia Ethica* (1903) and by A.N. Whitehead's and Bertrand Russell's *Principia Mathematica* (1910–13), in the light of which they searched for definitions of the good, the true, and the beautiful and questioned accepted ideas with a "comprehensive irreverence" for all kinds of sham.

The Bloomsbury group included the novelist E.M. Forster, the biographer Lytton Strachey, the art critic Clive Bell, the painters Vanessa Bell and Duncan Grant, the economist John Maynard Keynes, the Fabian writer Leonard Woolf, and the novelist and critic Virginia Woolf. The group survived World War I but by the early 1930s had ceased to exist in its original form.

Bloy \'blwả\, Léon (b. July 11, 1846, Périgueux, Fr.—d. Nov. 2, 1917, Bourg-la-Reine) French novelist, critic, and polemicist, a fervent Roman Catholic convert who preached spiritual revival through suffering and poverty.

As spiritual mentor to a group of friends that included writer Joris-Karl Huysmans, philosopher Jacques Maritain, and painter Georges Rouault, Bloy influenced their reconciliation with the Catholic church. Bloy's autobiographical novels, *Le Désespéré* (1886) and *La Femme pauvre* (1897; *The Woman who Was Poor*), express his mystical conception of woman as the Holy Spirit and of love as a devouring fire. The eight volumes of his *Journal* (written 1892–1917; complete edition published 1939) reveal him as a crusader of the absolute, launching onslaughts against lukewarm Christians. A number of volumes of his letters have also been published.

Bluebeard \'blü-,bird\   Murderous husband in the story "La Barbe bleue" in Charles Perrault's collection of fairy tales, *Contes de ma mère l'oye* (1697; *Tales of Mother Goose*). In Perrault's story Bluebeard goes on a journey, leaving the keys to his castle with his new wife. He tells her not to go into one particular room, but she becomes curious and when she opens the door to the room she finds the skeletons of Bluebeard's former wives. Bluebeard returns, discovers her disobedience, and is about to kill her when her brothers arrive to rescue her.

Illustration by Gustave Doré
Copyright British Museum

Similar stories exist in European, African, and Eastern folklore. Perrault's version probably derived from Brittany and may have been based on the career of the 15th-century marshal of France Gilles de Rais and that of Comorre the Cursed, a 6th-century Breton chief, each of whom committed crimes similar to those in the Bluebeard stories.

Blue Bird, The   Play for children by Maurice MAETERLINCK, published as *L'Oiseau bleu* in 1908. In a fairy-tale-like setting, Tyltyl and Mytyl, the son and daughter of a poor woodcutter, are sent out by the Fairy Bérylune to search the world for the Blue Bird of Happiness. After many adventures, they find it in their own backyard.

blue flower, the   A mystic symbol of longing. The *lichtblaue Blume* first appeared in a dream to the hero of Novalis' frag-

mentary novel *Heinrich von Ofterdingen* (1802), who associates it with the woman he loves but never possesses. The blue flower became a widely recognized symbol among the Romantics.

Blue Hotel, The   Short story by Stephen CRANE, published serially in *Collier's Weekly* (Nov. 26–Dec. 3, 1898), and then in the collection *The Monster and Other Stories* (1899). Combining symbolic imagery with naturalistic detail, it is an existential tale about human vanities and delusions.

As the story opens, three visitors find shelter from a blizzard at Pat Scully's hotel in Fort Romper, Neb.: a nervous New Yorker known as the Swede, a rambunctious Westerner named Bill, and a reserved Easterner called Mr. Blanc. The Swede becomes increasingly drunk, defensive, and reckless. He beats Scully's son, Johnnie, in a fight after accusing him of cheating at cards. When the Swede accosts a patron of a bar, he is stabbed and killed. The story ends ambiguously at a point several months later, when timid Mr. Blanc confesses to Bill that he feels somewhat responsible for the Swede's death because he failed to act when he saw that Johnnie was indeed cheating at cards.

Blues for Mister Charlie \'chär-lē\   Tragedy in three acts by James BALDWIN, produced and published in 1964. A denunciation of racial bigotry and hatred, the play was based on a murder trial that took place in Mississippi in 1955. "Mister Charlie" is a slang term for a white man.

The story concerns Richard Henry, a black man who returns to the Southern town of his birth to begin a new life and recover from drug addiction. Lyle Britten, a white bigot who kills him for "not knowing his place," is acquitted by an all-white jury. Racism scars both black and white members of the community who attempt to intervene.

blues stanza   Three-line stanza form associated originally with blues music developed by African-Americans. It is used to express a melancholy feeling or a complaint and involves frequent repetition, especially in the first two lines.

Bluest Eye, The   First novel by Toni MORRISON, published in 1970. This tragic study of a black adolescent girl's struggle to achieve white ideals of beauty and her consequent descent into madness was acclaimed as an eloquent indictment of some of the more subtle forms of racism in American society. Pecola Breedlove longs to have "the bluest eye" and thus to be acceptable to her family, schoolmates, and neighbors, all of whom have convinced her that she is ugly.

Bluestocking \'blü-,stäk-iŋ\   Any of a group of ladies who in mid-18th-century England held "conversations" to which they invited men of letters and members of the aristocracy with literary interests. The word has come to be applied derisively to a woman who affects literary or learned interests. The term probably originated when Mrs. Elizabeth Vesey invited the learned Benjamin Stillingfleet to one of her parties; he declined because he lacked appropriate dress, whereupon she told him to come "in his blue stockings"—the ordinary worsted stockings he was wearing at the time. He did so, and Bluestocking (or Bas Bleu) society became a nickname for the group.

The group was never a society in any formal sense. Mrs. Vesey and Mrs. Elizabeth Montagu became leaders of the literary ladies. Others included Madame d'Arblay (the diarist and novelist better known as Fanny Burney), Mrs. Frances Boscawen, Mrs. Hester Chapone, Mrs. Elizabeth Carter, Mrs. Mary Delany, and Miss Hannah More, whose poem "The Bas Bleu, or, Conversation" (1786) supplies valuable inside information about them. Guests included Samuel Johnson, James Boswell, David Garrick, George Lyttleton, and Horace Walpole.

Blue-Stockings, The   Comedy in five acts by MOLIÈRE, produced and published in 1672 as *Les Femmes savantes*. The play is sometimes translated as *The Learned Ladies*.

The central character, Chrysale, is a sensible man cowed by his masterful and learned wife. His sister and eldest daughter have also taken up the pseudointellectual fashion. The wife insists that her youngest daughter marry Trissotin, a pompous twit admired by the three. An honest and honorable suitor wins the daughter's hand, however, after Trissotin abandons his suit, mistakenly believing that the family has lost its fortune. Thus Chrysale quietly triumphs over the domineering learned ladies.

Despite the title, the play is less a satire on intellectual women than on didactic poseurs and their shallow followers. Trissotin was said to be a thinly veiled jab at the 17th-century abbé Cotin.

Blunden \'blən-dən\, Edmund Charles (b. Nov. 1, 1896, London, Eng.—d. Jan. 20, 1974, Long Melford, Suffolk)   Poet, critic, scholar, and man of letters, whose verses in the traditional mode are known for their rich and knowledgeable expression of rural English life.

Blunden's *Undertones of War* (1928), a moving account of World War I, established his international reputation. The war interrupted his studies at Oxford, but he returned in 1919, moving the following year to London as associate editor of *The Athenaeum*.

Blunden taught in Japan throughout most of the 1920s and returned there in the late 1940s, after teaching at Oxford and serving on the staff of *The Times Literary Supplement*. His poetry is collected in *The Poems of Edmund Blunden, 1914–1930* (1930) and *Poems 1930–1940* (1940). *Poems of Many Years* appeared in 1957.

Blunt \'blənt\, Wilfrid Scawen (b. Aug. 17, 1840, Petworth House, Sussex, Eng.—d. Sept. 12, 1922, Newbuildings, Sussex)   English writer and poet best known for his expression of anti-imperialism based on sympathy for small or oppressed nations.

Blunt entered diplomatic service in 1858 but retired after his marriage to Lady Anne Noel in 1869. With his wife he traveled frequently in North Africa, Asia Minor, and Arabia. Blunt became known as an ardent sympathizer with Muslim aspirations, and in *The Future of Islam* (1882) he directed attention to the forces that produced the movements of Pan-Islamism and Mahdism. *Ideas About India* (1885) was the result of two visits to that country, which confirmed his view of colonialism as exploitation. His best-known volume of verse, *Love Sonnets of Proteus* (1881), reveals his real merits as an emotional poet. Blunt published a complete edition of his poetical works in 1914 and the two-volume *My Diaries* (1919, 1920).

blurb \'blərb\   A short publicity notice (as on a book jacket). It is generally accepted that the word was coined by the American humorist Gelett Burgess.

Bly \'blī\, Robert (Elwood) (b. Dec. 23, 1926, Madison, Minn., U.S.)   American poet, translator, editor, and author.

Bly studied at St. Olaf College, Northfield, Minn.; Harvard University; and the University of Iowa. In 1958 he cofounded the magazine *The Fifties* (its name changed with the decades), which published other important young poets and Bly's own translations and serene nature poems. In 1966 Bly was a founder of American Writers Against the Vietnam War, and when his collection *The Light Around the Body* won a 1968 National Book Award he donated his prize money to the Resistance, a draft resisters' organization. His later poems and "prose poems," including those in *Sleepers Joining Hands* (1973) and *This Tree Will Be Here for a Thousand Years* (1979), returned to personal and pastoral themes. Throughout Bly's career he translated the work of many poets, ranging from German, Scandinavian, Spanish, and Latin-American writers to the 15th-century Indian mystic Kabīr.

His poems of *The Man in the Black Coat Turns* (1981) explore themes of male grief and the father-son connection. These were among the concerns of his best-selling *Iron John: A Book About Men* (1990), which drew upon myth, legend, folklore, fairy tales, and Jungian psychology.

boasting poem   Type of poem common in oral literature in which a character brags about personal exploits or great deeds. It can also be part of a longer written work, as in the Old English poem *Beowulf*. The *farsa* of the African Oromo people is a form of boasting poem.

bob and wheel \'bäb . . . 'hwēl, 'wēl\   In alliterative verse, a group of typically five rhymed lines following a section of unrhymed lines, often at the end of a strophe. The bob is the first line in the group and is shorter than the rest; the wheel is the quatrain that follows the bob.

Bobbsey Twins \'bäb-zē\   Fictional characters, two sets of fraternal twins—the older pair named Bert and Nan, the younger Freddie and Flossie—who are featured in an extended series of children's books by American author Laura Lee Hope (a collective pseudonym for many writers, including Harriet S. Adams). The characters made their first appearance in *The Bobbsey Twins; or, Merry Days Indoors and Out* (1904). A second series—the "New Bobbsey Twins"—was started in 1987.

Bocage \bu̇-'käj-ē\, Manuel Maria Barbosa du (b. Sept. 15, 1765, Setúbal, Port.—d. Dec. 21, 1805, Lisbon)   Portuguese neoclassical lyric poet who dissipated his energies in a stormy life.

At the Royal Navy Academy in Lisbon, Bocage devoted his time to love affairs, poetry, and bohemianism. In 1786 he was sent to India, but he deserted to Macau, returning to Lisbon in 1790. He then joined the New Arcadia, a literary society with vaguely egalitarian and libertarian sympathies, but his satires on his fellow members resulted in his expulsion.

In 1797 Bocage was accused of propagating republicanism and atheism and was imprisoned. During his imprisonment he undertook translations of Virgil and Ovid. After his release, these translations and those of such authors as Torquato Tasso, Jean-Jacques Rousseau, Jean Racine, and Voltaire provided him with a livelihood during the few remaining years of his life.

Bocage employed various verse forms, but he is at his best in the sonnet. His intensely personal accent, frequent violence of expression, and self-dramatizing obsession with fate and death anticipate Romanticism. His collected poems were published as *Rimas*, 3 vol. (1791, 1799, 1804).

Boccaccio \bōk-'kät-chō, *Angl* bō-'kä-chē-ō, -chō\, Giovanni (b. 1313, Paris, Fr.,—d. Dec. 21, 1375, Certaldo, Tuscany [Italy])   Italian poet and scholar, best remembered as the author of the DECAMERON.

Boccaccio passed his early childhood rather unhappily in Florence; he was sent not later than 1328 to Naples to learn business. He also studied canon law and mixed with the learned men of the court and came to know the work of Petrarch. About 1340 Boccaccio was recalled to Florence.

From Naples Boccaccio had brought a store of literary work already completed, including the short poem "La caccia di Diana" ("Diana's Hunt"), the prose work *Il filocolo* (c. 1336; "The Love Afflicted") in five books, and *Il filostrato* (c. 1338; "The Love Struck"), a poem in octava rima telling the story of Troilus and Criseida. From 1341 to 1345 Boccaccio worked on *Il ninfale d'Ameto* ("Ameto's Story of the Nymphs"), in prose and terza rima; *L'amorosa visione* (1342–43; "The Amorous Vision"), a mediocre allegorical poem of 50 short cantos in terza rima; the prose *Elegia di Madonna Fiammetta* (1343–44); and the ottava rima poem *Il ninfale fiesolano* (perhaps 1344–45; "Tale of the Fiesole Nymph").

Detail of a fresco by Andrea del Castagno; in the Cenacolo di Sant' Apollonia, Florence
Alinari/Art Resource, New York

Boccaccio probably composed the *Decameron* in the years 1349–53. In the broad sweep of its range and its alternately tragic and comic views of life, it is rightly regarded as his masterpiece. Stylistically, it is the most perfect example of Italian classical prose, and its influence on Renaissance literature throughout Europe was enormous.

Boccaccio's first meeting with Petrarch, in Florence in 1350, helped to bring about decisive change in Boccaccio's literary activity. After the *Decameron*, he wrote very little in Italian. Turning instead to Latin, he devoted himself to humanist scholarship rather than to imaginative or poetic creation. His encyclopedic *De genealogia deorum gentilium* ("On the Genealogy of the Gods of the Gentiles"), medieval in structure but humanist in spirit, was probably begun in 1350. His *Bucolicum carmen* (1351–66), a series of allegorical eclogues on contemporary events, follows classical models. His other Latin works include DE CLARIS MULIERIBUS (1360–74; *Concerning Famous Women*) and *De casibus virorum illustrium* (1355–74; "On the Fates of Famous Men").

Boccaccio's *Vita di Dante Alighieri* or *Trattatello in laude di Dante* (1354–55; "Little Tractate in Praise of Dante") show his devotion to Dante's memory. In 1373 he began public readings of Dante's *La divina commedia*. A revised text of the commentary that he gave with these readings is still extant but breaks off in the 17th canto of the *Inferno*, at the point he had reached when, early in 1374, ill health and criticism made him lose heart. He retired to the Tuscan town of Certaldo.

Boccalini \bōk-kä-'lē-nē\, Traiano (b. 1556, Loreto, Papal States [Italy]—d. Nov. 29, 1613, Venice) Prose satirist and anti-Spanish political writer, influential in the Europe of his time for a widely circulated satire, *Ragguagli di Parnaso* (1612–13; "Reports from Parnassus").

Boccalini was educated for the law and spent many years in Rome in papal service (1584–1612), becoming acquainted with a number of eminent men of his day. His political experience is mirrored particularly in *Ragguagli di Parnaso*, a light and fantastic satire on the actions and writings of his contemporaries, written in the form of 201 ironical newsletters in which the wise men of all centuries, presided over by Apollo, discuss art, literature, and politics. Another series appeared in *Pietra del paragone politico* (posthumously published, 1614; "Political Touchstones"), a vigorous denunciation of the Spanish domination of Europe.

A weightier work was *Commentari sopra Cornelio Tacito* (first published 1677; "Comments upon Cornelius Tacitus"), a discussion of politics and government, offering Machiavellian advice to princes.

Bodel \bȯ-'del\, Jehan *or* Jean (b. *c.* 1167, Arras, Artois [France]—d. 1210, Arras) Jongleur, epic poet, author of fabliaux, and dramatist, whose LE JEU DE SAINT NICOLAS ("Play of St. Nicholas") was the first miracle play in French.

Bodel probably held public office in Arras and certainly belonged to one of its *puys*, or literary confraternities. He planned to go on the Fourth Crusade but, stricken with leprosy, was admitted to a lazar house, where he died. He wrote five pastourelles (four in 1190–94; one in 1199), nine fabliaux (1190–97), *La Chanson des Saisnes* (before 1200; "Song of the Saxons"), *Le Jeu de Saint Nicolas* (performed *c.* 1200), and *Les Congés* (1202; "Leave-Takings"), his poignant farewell to his friends. Of these works Bodel's *Le Jeu* had the most lasting importance. It was one of the first of the miracle plays to be written in vernacular verse.

Bodenheim \'bō-dən-,hīm\, Maxwell, *original surname* Bodenheimer \'bō-dən-,hī-mər\ (b. May 26, 1893, Hermanville, Miss., U.S.—d. Feb. 6, 1954, New York, N.Y.) Poet who contributed to the development of the modernist movement in American poetry but is probably best known as a personality in literary bohemia.

Bodenheim appeared in Chicago in about 1913, during the period of the Chicago literary renaissance. He wrote plays with Ben Hecht and helped him edit the short-lived *Chicago Literary Times* (1923–24). Later they conducted a much-publicized feud, featuring each other as characters in their novels.

Bodenheim's poems were first published in *Poetry* magazine in 1914; his earliest collection was *Minna and Myself* (1918). Several other volumes of poetry followed, his *Selected Poems, 1914–44* appearing in 1946. In these works he employed many of the striking visual techniques of the Imagists.

Bodenheim settled in New York's Greenwich Village in the late 1920s. His novels and poetry appeared regularly during that decade and the next, but increasing dissipation had reduced him to peddling his poems in bars when he and his third wife were murdered by a former mental patient in their lodgings. His unfinished autobiography, *My Life and Loves in Greenwich Village*, appeared in 1954, shortly after his death. Among the better of his largely forgotten novels are *Blackguard* (1923), *Crazy Man* (1924), *Georgie May* (1928), *Sixty Seconds* (1929), and *Naked on Roller Skates* (1931).

Bodenstedt \'bō-dən-,shtet\, Friedrich Martin von (b. April 22, 1819, Peine, Hanover [Germany]—d. April 18, 1892, Wiesbaden, Ger.) German writer, translator, and critic whose poetry was very popular during his lifetime.

As a young man Bodenstedt obtained an appointment as head of a school in Tiflis (now Tbilisi, Georgia), where he made a study of Persian literature. His *Die Lieder des Mirza Schaffy* (1851; *The Songs of Mirza Schaffy*), a collection of poems written in an Oriental style, was instantly successful. In 1854 he became a professor at the University of Munich. During this period he made numerous translations from Russian authors, notably Aleksandr Pushkin, Ivan Turgenev, and Mikhail Lermontov. After 1858 he devoted his attention primarily to William Shakespeare. He collaborated with others in a translation of Shakespeare's works (1866–72), and he himself translated the sonnets. Among his other works are *Tausend und ein Tag im Orient* (1849–50; "One Thousand and One Days in the Orient") and *Shakespeares Zeitgenossen und ihre Werke* (1858–60; "Shakespeare's Contemporaries and Their Work").

bodice ripper   A historical or gothic romance typically featuring scenes in which the heroine is subjected to sexual violence.

Bodmer \\'bŏd-mər\\, Johann Jakob (b. July 19, 1698, Greifensee, Switz.—d. Jan. 2, 1783, near Zürich)   Historian and critical writer who contributed to the development of an original German literature in Switzerland.

Bodmer served as professor of Helvetian history in Zürich from 1725 until 1775, and from 1737 he was a member of the Grosser Rat (cantonal legislature). From 1721 to 1723 he published, in conjunction with others, *Die Discourse der Mahlern* ("The Discourses of the Painters"), a weekly journal after the model of *The Spectator*. His most important writings are the treatises *Von dem Einfluss und Gebrauche der Einbildungs-Kraft* (1727; "On the Influence and Use of the Imagination"), *Critische Abhandlung von dem Wunderbaren in der Poesie* (1740; "Critical Treatment of the Fantastic in Poetry"), and *Critische Betrachtungen über die Poetischen Gemälde der Dichter* (1741; "Critical Observations about the Poetic Paintings of the Poets"). Bodmer also engaged in studies of William Shakespeare, Torquato Tasso, Dante, and Miguel de Cervantes; translated Homer (in hexameters); and espoused the causes of Montesquieu and Jean-Jacques Rousseau—thus playing a part as a precursor of Johann Gottfried von Herder.

Bogan \\'bō-gan\\, Louise (b. Aug. 11, 1897, Livermore Falls, Maine, U.S.—d. Feb. 4, 1970, New York, N.Y.)   Poet and literary critic whose verse resembles that of the English Metaphysical poets in its restrained, intellectual style and use of traditional techniques while remaining essentially modern, both personal and immediate.

Bogan's poems first appeared in the *New Republic. Body of This Death* was published in 1923. She later wrote verse and literary criticism for the magazines *The New Yorker, Poetry: A Magazine of Verse, The Atlantic Monthly,* and *The Nation.* Her *Collected Poems 1923–1953* (1954) received the Bollingen Prize in Poetry. As a critic Bogan became known for fairness and generosity, and she focused on the strengths of authors in such works as the survey *Achievement in American Poetry 1900–1950* (1951) and *Selected Criticism: Prose, Poetry* (1955). Her other works include *The Sleeping Fury* (1937), *The Blue Estuaries: Poems 1923–1968* (1968), and *A Poet's Alphabet* (1970).

bogatyr \\bə-gə-'tŏrʸ, *Angl* ‚bō-gə-'tir\\ *plural* bogatyrs *or* bogatyri \\bə-gə-tə̇-'rʸē, *Angl* ‚bō-gə-'tir-ē\\ [Russian *bogatyr'* hero, warrior]   One of a group of heroes of the Russian folk epics known as byliny. The duty of the bogatyrs was to protect the Russian land against foreign invaders, especially the Tatars. The most prominent of the bogatyrs was ILYA of Murom, about whom Nikolay Karamzin wrote the poem "Ilya Muromets" (1795). *See also* BYLINA.

Bogusławski \\bŏ-gü-'swȧf-skʸē\\, Wojciech (b. April 9, 1757, Poznań, Pol.—d. July 23, 1829, Warsaw)   Actor, director, and leading playwright of the Polish Enlightenment. Considered by many to be the father of the Polish theater, he wrote more than 80 plays, mostly comedies adapted from writers of western Europe, and greatly raised the status of the acting profession. His best-known and most popular original play is *Cud mniemany, czyli, Krakowiacy i górale* (1794; "The Pretended Miracle, or Krakovians and Highlanders"), a patriotic comic opera based on national folklore.

Bohomolec \\bŏ-ķŏ-'mŏ-lets\\, Franciszek (b. Jan. 29, 1720, near Vitebsk, Pol.—d. April 24, 1784, Warsaw)   Jesuit priest, editor, and linguist who was also a prominent dramatist of the Enlightenment in Poland.

Bohomolec taught in Warsaw and began to adapt comedies of Carlo Goldoni and Molière for performance by his pupils. His early works satirized the ignorance and folly of the Polish aristocracy. He wrote a number of other plays for a wider public; these include *Małżeństwo z kalendarza* (1766; "Marriage by the Calendar"), which ridicules ignorance and superstition and is usually considered his best work, and *Czary* (1774; "Sorcery"), also satirizing superstition. For the last 20 years of his life Bohomolec edited the magazine *The Monitor*, one of the first modern periodicals in Poland.

Boiardo \\bō-'yär-dō\\, Matteo Maria, Count (Conte) di Scandiano (b. May 1440/41, Scandiano, Papal States [Italy]—d. Dec. 19, 1494, Reggio nell'Emilia)   Poet whose *Orlando innamorato* combined elements of both Arthurian and Carolingian romance and gave new life to the chivalrous epic.

Boiardo wrote numerous works, both in Latin and Italian. Of the Italian works, the *Amorum libri tres* (1499; "Three Books on Love") is personal and spontaneous, written at a time when most love poetry was a conventional exercise. *Orlando innamorato,* begun about 1476, was intended to consist of three parts, but only the first two (published 1483) and part of the third were completed at the time of the poet's death. Although the poem did not achieve popularity, Boiardo breathed an intimate, personal strain into the stereotype of the epic that future generations emulated and expanded.

Boie \\'bŏi-ə\\, Heinrich Christian (b. July 19, 1744, Meldorf, Holstein [Ger.]—d. March 3, 1806, Meldorf)   German poet and editor, chiefly noted as a founder of literary periodicals.

Boie founded the literary journal *Deutsches Museum* (1776; in 1789 renamed *Neues Deutsches Museum*). In 1776 he began a career in government concurrent with his literary activities. He served in various local posts, finally as provincial governor of the rural district of Süderdithmarschen.

Boileau \\bwȧ-'lō\\, Nicolas, *surname in full* Boileau-Despréaux \\-dā-prā-'ō\\ (b. Nov. 1, 1636, Paris, Fr.—d. March 13, 1711, Paris)   Poet and leading literary critic who upheld classical standards in both French and English literature.

Boileau was encouraged to take up literary work by his brother Gilles Boileau, who was already established as a man of letters. He began by writing satires (*c.* 1658) attacking well-known public figures, which were published in 1666. The following year he wrote one of the most successful of mock-heroic epics, *Le Lutrin,* dealing with a quarrel of two ecclesiastical dignitaries over where to place a lectern in a chapel. The first four cantos were published in 1674, the remaining two in 1683.

In 1674 he published *L'Art poétique,* a didactic treatise in verse setting out rules for the composition of poetry in the classical tradition. It is valued today for the insight it provides into the literary controversies of the period. Boileau himself became involved in one such controversy in 1692, when the literary world found itself divided between the so-called Ancients and Moderns. Seeing women as supporters of the Moderns, Boileau wrote his antifeminist satire *Contre les femmes* ("Against Women," published as *Satire X*, 1694), followed notably by *Sur l'amour de Dieu* ("On the Love of God," published as *Épître XII*, 1698).

Boileau also translated the classical treatise *On the Sublime*, attributed to Longinus. Ironically, it became one of the key sources of the aesthetics of Romanticism.

Boisrobert \bwȧ-rȯ-'ber\, François Le Métel \lə-mā-'tel\, Seigneur de (b. 1589, Caen, Fr.—d. March 30, 1662, Paris) Prolific dramatist, irreligious churchman, and practical benefactor of the French world of letters who was a founding member of the Académie Française.

A Norman Huguenot lawyer's son, Boisrobert became a Roman Catholic in the 1620s and began to take holy orders. His wit and effrontery won him the favor of Cardinal de Richelieu, and he was given a canonry at Rouen (1634) and an abbacy in Burgundy (1638). Meanwhile, he had published a paraphrase of the Psalms (1627); a novel, *Histoire indienne d'Anaxandre et d'Orazie* (1627; "Indian History of Anaxander and Orazia"); and a tragicomedy, *Pyrandre et Zysimène* (1633); as well as anthologies of poems eulogizing King Louis XIII and Richelieu (1634–35). He used his influence with Richelieu not only to procure subsidies for other writers but also to promote the establishment of the Académie Française.

Bojer \'bȯi-yer\, Johan (b. March 6, 1872, Orkesdalsøren, near Trondheim, Nor.—d. July 3, 1959, Oslo) Norwegian novelist, internationally popular in the 1920s because his works dramatized topical problems of the day. He is best remembered in his own country for novels depicting folk life in the fishing and farming communities of the Lofoten Islands, among them *Den siste viking* (1921; *Last of the Vikings*) and *Folk ved sjøen* (1929; *Folk by the Sea*), perhaps his finest work. Both of these works are epic in conception and contain remarkable passages of description.

Bojer's reputation in the English-speaking world was established with *Den store hunger* (1916; *The Great Hunger*). He also wrote an ambitious novel about America's Norwegian immigrants, *Vor egen stamme* (1924; *The Emigrants*).

Bo Juyi or **Po Chü-i** \'bwȯ-'jüē-'ē, 'bī\ (b. 772, Xinzheng, Shaanxi province, China—d. 846, Luoyang [now Henan], Henan province) Chinese poet of the Tang dynasty (618–907) who used his elegantly simple verse to protest the social evils of his day.

Bo Juyi began composing poetry at the age of five. At the age of 28 he took an examination for the bureaucracy and was given a minor post at the palace library, as was another successful examination candidate and poet, Yuan Zhen. Their friendship became perhaps the most famous in Chinese history. In 807 Bo became a member of the prestigious Hanlin Academy in Changan, the capital, and rose steadily in official life except for his temporary banishment in 814 to a minor post at Jiujiang, the cause for which remains unclear.

Bo was the informal leader of a group of poets who rejected the courtly style of the time and believed that every literary work should have a fitting moral and a well-defined social purpose. He considered his most important work to be his satirical ballads and social-protest poems, which usually took the form of free verse based on old folk ballads, or "new *yuefu*," as he entitled a series of 50 of these poems.

Bokenam \'bäk-ə-nəm\, Osbern, Bokenam *also spelled* Bokenham (b. Oct. 6, 1392?, Norfolk, Eng.—d. 1447?) English poet, best known as the author of *Legends of Holy Women*, a series of 13 legends of 12 saints. The 10,000-line work

is written mainly in seven- or eight-line decasyllabic stanzas. The prologues are more lively and interesting than the legends themselves, which are closely translated from Latin originals.

Little is known of Bokenam's life. A student of the devotional poet John Lydgate, he was probably inspired by Geoffrey Chaucer's poem *Legend of Good Women*.

Bokmål or **Bokmaal** \'bŭk-ˌmȯl, 'bȯk-\, *also called* Riksmål \'riks-ˌmȯl\ A literary form of Norwegian developed by the gradual reform of written Danish in conformity to Norwegian usage. Bokmål means in Norwegian "book language" and Riksmål approximately "official language" (literally, "language of the kingdom"). *Compare* NYNORSK.

Boland \'bō-lənd\, Eavan (Aisling) (b. Sept. 24, 1944, Dublin, Ire.) Irish poet and literary critic whose expressive verse explores familiar domestic themes and examines both the isolation and the fellowship of being a woman, wife, and mother.

Boland graduated with honors from Trinity College, Cambridge, and became a freelance lecturer and journalist, notably as a critic for *The Irish Times*. After publishing the amateurish pamphlet *23 Poems* (1962), she wrote *New Territory* (1967), a full-length book of 22 poems about Irish mythology, the creativity of artists, and her own identity.

Introducing Eavan Boland (1981), her first volume of verse published outside Ireland, reprinted both *The War Horse* (1975), with its controlled, conventionally styled poems about suburban life and political tension, and *In Her Own Image* (1980), featuring terse poetic narratives about women. The poems of *Night Feed* (1982) link her spiritual maturation to her entry into motherhood. *The Journey* (1983; expanded as *The Journey and Other Poems*, 1987) is a further examination of the poet's development. Boland's other books of poetry include *Selected Poems* (1989), *Outside History* (1990), and *In a Time of Violence* (1994). She also wrote *A Kind of Scar* (1989), a prose study of female Irish poets.

Boldrewood \'bōl-dər-ˌwŭd\, Rolf, *pseudonym of* Thomas Alexander Browne \'braŭn\ (b. Aug. 6, 1826, London, Eng.—d. March 11, 1915, Melbourne, Vic., Australia) Romantic novelist best known for his *Robbery Under Arms* (1888) and *A Miner's Right* (1890), both exciting and realistic portrayals of pioneer life in Australia. Boldrewood first wrote short stories, then composed his memoirs (*Old Melbourne Memories*, 1884), and finally wrote some 20 novels between 1878 and 1906.

Boldwood, William \'wil-yəm-'bōld-ˌwŭd\ Fictional character, a farmer whose passionate love for Bathsheba Everdene is his undoing in the novel FAR FROM THE MADDING CROWD by Thomas Hardy.

Bolkonsky family \ˌbəl-'kȯn-skʸē\ Principal characters of the novel WAR AND PEACE by Leo Tolstoy. The elderly and dictatorial Prince Nikolay Bolkonsky is father of Prince Andrey and Princess Marya.

Böll \'bœl\, Heinrich (Theodor) (b. Dec. 21, 1917, Cologne, Ger.—d. July 16, 1985, near Bonn) German writer, winner of the Nobel Prize for Literature in 1972. Böll's ironic novels on the travails of German life during and after World War II capture the changing psychology of the German nation.

Böll graduated from high school in 1937 and later served six years as a private and corporal in the German army. His wartime experiences were central to the art of a writer who remembered the "frightful fate of being a soldier and having to wish that the war might be lost."

Böll's first stories were published in 1947. In his first novels, *Der Zug war pünktlich* (1949; *The Train Was on Time*) and *Wo warst du, Adam?* (1951; *Adam, Where Art Thou?*), he describes the grimness and despair of soldiers' lives. The uneasiness of reality is explored in *Das Brot der frühen Jahre* (1955; *The Bread of Our Early Years*) and in *Billard um halb zehn* (1959; BILLIARDS AT HALF-PAST NINE). The popular *Ansichten eines Clowns* (1963; THE CLOWN) traces the deterioration of the protagonist.

Böll's other writings include *Und sagte kein einziges Wort* (1953; ACQUAINTED WITH THE NIGHT) and *Ende einer Dienstfahrt* (1966; *End of a Mission*). In his longest novel, *Gruppenbild mit Dame* (1971; GROUP PORTRAIT WITH LADY), Böll presented a panorama of German life from the world wars to the 1970s. *Die verlorene Ehre der Katharina Blum* (1974; THE LOST HONOR OF KATHARINA BLUM) attacked modern journalistic ethics as well as the values of contemporary Germany. *Was soll aus dem Jungen bloss werden?, oder, Irgendwas mit Büchern* (1981; *What's to Become of the Boy?, or Something to Do with Books*) is a memoir of the period 1933–37.

Bollingen Prize \ˈbō-liŋ-ən\ Award for achievement in American poetry, originally conferred by the Library of Congress with funds established in 1948 by the philanthropist Paul Mellon. An admirer of the psychoanalyst Carl Jung, Mellon named the prize after the Swiss town where Jung spent his summers. In 1949 the first award was made for *The Pisan Cantos* to Ezra Pound, who was then under indictment for treason for his World War II broadcasts from Italy, which were anti-Semitic and pro-fascist. A bitter controversy ensued in the press, and the Library of Congress was requested by a congressional committee to disassociate itself from the award. In 1950 the award was transferred to the Yale University Library, under the auspices of which it has since been administered. Originally annual, it became biennial in 1964. In 1961 the Bollingen Foundation also established a prize for translation.

Bolshoi Theatre \ˌbōl-ˈshȯi, ˈbōl-ˌshȯi\ *Russian* Bolshoy Teatr \ˌbȯlʸ-ˈshȯi-tē-ˈät-ər\ Leading theater company for ballet and opera in Russia. The original group, made up of several smaller troupes, was organized in Moscow in the mid-1770s. In 1780 the first permanent theater building in Moscow was opened as the company's home, but it burned in 1805. A year later the Bolshoi Theatre was made a government institution, and a new building was opened in 1825. By the end of the 19th century the Bolshoi's opera and ballet productions of Russian and other European works were influencing the performing arts throughout the Western world. The company was kept intact during the Revolution of 1917, both world wars, and the dissolution of the Soviet Union in 1991.

Bolt \ˈbōlt\, Robert (Oxton) (b. Aug. 15, 1924, Manchester, Eng.—d. Feb. 20, 1995, near Petersfield, Hampshire) English dramatist best known for his third play, *A Man for All Seasons* (1960; film, 1966), a study of Sir Thomas More.

The most successful of Bolt's other plays were *Flowering Cherry* (1957), a Chekhovian study of failure and self-deception, and *Vivat! Vivat! Regina!* (1970), popular both in London and in New York. Bolt also enjoyed much prestige as scriptwriter for such films as *Lawrence of Arabia* (1962); *Doctor Zhivago* (1965); *Ryan's Daughter* (1970); *Lady Caroline Lamb* (1972), which he also directed; *The Bounty* (1984); and *The Mission* (1986).

Bolton or **Boulton** \ˈbōlt-ən\, Edmund (b. 1575?—d. 1633?) English historian, antiquarian, and poet whose lyrics are among the best in the miscellany *Englands Helicon* (1600), a widely known anthology of late 16th-century lyric and pastoral poetry.

Bolton was educated at Cambridge and the Inner Temple, London. He obtained a minor position at court but was barred from public office because of his Roman Catholicism; he then tried to support himself by writing. His most considerable works are the history *Nero Caesar* (1624) and *Hypercritica*, a

treatise on the writing of history in which he reviews contemporary authors.

Bolton \ˈbōlt-ən\, Guy (Reginald) (b. Nov. 23, 1884, Broxbourne, Hertfordshire, Eng.—d. Sept. 5, 1979, London) American playwright and librettist perhaps best known for his witty and articulate librettos, on which he collaborated with such notables as P.G. Wodehouse, George Middleton, and Fred Thompson.

Bolton's first play appeared on Broadway in 1911. With his collaborators, he turned out scripts that were enhanced with music by composers such as Jerome Kern, George Gershwin, and Cole Porter. Among his finer works are *Oh, Boy!* (1917; with Wodehouse, music by Kern), *Sally* (1920; with music by Kern), *Lady, Be Good!* (1924; with Thompson, music by George and Ira Gershwin), *Oh, Kay!* (1926; with Wodehouse, music by the Gershwins and Howard Dietz), and *Anything Goes* (1934; with Wodehouse, Howard Lindsay, and Russel Crouse, music by Porter).

Bombal \bȯm-ˈbäl\, María Luisa (b. June 8, 1910, Viña del Mar, near Valparaíso, Chile—d. May 6, 1980, Santiago) Chilean novelist and short-story writer whose innovative narratives feature heroines who create fantasy worlds in order to escape unfulfilling love relationships and restricted social roles. Her surreal narrative style influenced later proponents of magic realism.

Bombal's first novel, *La última niebla* ("The Final Mist"), which she later revised and translated as *The House of Mist*, appeared in a limited edition in 1934 before its official publication date of 1935. It details a loveless marriage between a man who clings to the memory of his first wife and a woman who takes a mysterious blind lover who may or may not be a hallucination. Later editions of the book also contained three short stories: "El árbol" ("The Tree"), "Las islas nuevas" ("The New Islands"), and "Lo secreto" ("The Unknown"). Witnessing her own funeral, the deceased protagonist of the novel *La amortajada* (1938; *The Shrouded Woman*) contemplates her failed love affairs.

bombast \ˈbäm-ˌbast\ Pretentious, inflated speech or writing. The now obsolete literal sense of the word was "cotton padding."

Bond, James \ˈjāmz-ˈbänd\ Fictional character, an intelligent, heroic, resourceful, libidinous spy and enforcer of international law for the British secret service in a series of books—beginning with *Casino Royale* (1953)—by Ian FLEMING. Bond, known also as "Agent 007," is the consummate loner, yet he is ever loyal to the service and especially to his boss, "M."

Boner \ˈbō-nər\, Ulrich, *pseudonym* Ulrich Bonerius \bō-ˈner-ē-əs\ (fl. 1324–49) Swiss writer and Dominican monk whose collection of fables in verse was the first book to be printed in the German language (Bamberg, 1461).

Boner compiled and translated his collection of fables for Johann von Ringgenberg, his Bernese patron. The form that Boner used was referred to as *bîschaft* or *bîspel* ("examples"), and each of the tales includes a moral. Written in Middle High German, the collection was probably completed about 1350.

The fables were entitled *Der Edelstein* ("The Precious Stone"), because precious stones were said to cast a spell and Boner hoped that his tales would do the same. Although he named only two of his sources—Aesop's *Fables* and the fables of Flavius Avianus (a 4th-century Latin writer)—it is clear that he also drew on other material.

Bonjour tristesse \bōⁿ-zhür-très-ˈtes\ ("Hello Sadness") Novel by Françoise SAGAN, published in French in 1954. The story of a jealous, sophisticated 17-year-old girl whose meddling in her father's impending remarriage leads to tragic consequences, it was written with "classical" restraint and a tone of cynical disillusionment. The book showed the persistence of traditional form during a period of experimentation in French fiction.

Bonstetten \German 'bòn-,shtet-ən; French bòn-stä-'teⁿ\, Karl Viktor von or Charles Victor de (b. Sept. 3, 1745, Bern, Switz.—d. Feb. 3, 1832, Geneva) Swiss writer (in both French and German) of wide cosmopolitan interests and outlook.

Bonstetten's charm and worldly temperament made him an outstanding member of the international elite and are revealed in his wide correspondence and in various books, forerunners of modern comparative studies of national characteristics. The best is his excellent work *L'Homme du Midi et l'homme du nord; ou, l'influence des climats* (1824; "The Man of the Midi and the Man of the North; or, The Influence of Climates").

Bontempelli \,bòn-tem-'päl-lē\, Massimo (b. May 12, 1878, Como, Italy—d. July 21, 1960, Rome) Italian poet, novelist, dramatist, and literary critic whose magic realism developed from Futurism.

Bontempelli wrote some traditional poetry, later adopted the antitraditional, anarchic literary doctrine of the Futurists, and ultimately developed his own point of view, expressed particularly in his review *900* (founded 1926), which sought a middle ground between the extremes of traditionalism and the literary avant-garde.

La vita intensa (1920; "The Intense Life"), a Futuristic novel, was followed by more independent works, such as *Gente nel tempo* (1937; "People in Time") and *Giro del sole* (1941; "Revolution of the Sun"). His *L'amante fedele* (1953; "The Faithful Lover"), a collection of surrealistic stories, won Italy's highest literary award, the Strega Prize.

Bontempelli's best dramas are *Siepe a nord-ovest* (published 1919, performed 1923; "Barrier to the Northwest") and *Nostra dea* (performed 1925; "Our Goddess"). A particularly striking play is *La guardia alla luna* (performed 1916; "Watching for the Moon"), the story of a woman who blames the moon for her child's death and climbs a mountain to try to kill it.

Notable among Bontempelli's critical works are *L'avventura novecentista* (1939; "The 20th-Century Adventure") and *Introduzioni e discorsi* (1945; "Introductions and Discourses"), which treats the work of many major 19th- and 20th-century Italian writers.

Bontemps \bän-'täm\, Arna (Wendell) (b. Oct. 13, 1902, Alexandria, La., U.S.—d. June 4, 1973, Nashville, Tenn.) American writer who depicted the lives and struggles of black Americans.

Bontemps's poetry began to appear in the influential black magazines *Opportunity* and *Crisis* in the mid-1920s. His first novel, *God Sends Sunday* (1931), is considered the final work of the Harlem Renaissance. In collaboration with the poet Countee Cullen, the novel was dramatized as *St. Louis Woman* (1946). Bontemps' next two novels were about slave revolts— in Virginia in BLACK THUNDER (1936) and in Haiti in DRUMS AT DUSK (1939).

Bontemps's nonfiction works, many for younger readers, include *The Story of the Negro* (1948; 4th ed., 1964); *Chariot in the Sky* (1951); *Frederick Douglass: Slave-Fighter-Freeman* (1959); *One Hundred Years of Negro Freedom* (1961); and *Famous Negro Athletes* (1964). Among the anthologies he edited are *The Poetry of the Negro* (1949) and *The Book of Negro Folklore* (1958), both with Langston Hughes; *American Negro Poetry* (1963); and *Great Slave Narratives* (1969).

Bonvesin da la Riva \'bòn-vä-zēn-dä-lä-'rē-vä\ (b. c. 1240, Milan [Italy]—d. c. 1315, Milan) Italian teacher, moralist, and poet, whose most important work, the vernacular poetry of *Libro delle tre scritture* (1274; "Book of the Three Writings"), describes in three sections the pains of hell, the joys of heaven, and the passion of Christ.

A member of the Humiliati (Umiliati), a Milanese monastic order, Bonvesin taught grammar and wrote a great many moralistic and religious works in Latin and in the vernacular. Among his more interesting works are the Latin *De quinquaginta curialitatibus ad mensam* ("Concerning Fifty Gentilities for the Table"), which provides valuable information about the social mores and etiquette of his time, and *De magnalibus urbis Mediolani* ("Concerning the Great Works of the City of Milan").

Boojum \'bū-jəm\ Fictional character in THE HUNTING OF THE SNARK, a narrative nonsense poem by Lewis Carroll. In the poem, the elusive Snark turns out to be a mysterious monster called a Boojum.

book \'bůk\ [Old English *bōc*] **1.** A set of written sheets of skin or paper or tablets of wood or ivory. **2.** A set of written, printed, or blank sheets bound together into a volume. **3.** A long written or printed literary composition. **4.** A major division of a treatise or literary work. **5.** A libretto or the script of a play.

The papyrus roll of ancient Egypt is more nearly the direct ancestor of the modern book than is the clay tablet of the ancient Sumerians, Babylonians, Assyrians, and Hittites; examples of both date to about 3000 BC. The Chinese, somewhat later, independently created an extensive scholarship based on books. Primitive Chinese books were made of wood or bamboo strips bound together with cords. In AD 175, Confucian texts began to be carved into stone tablets and preserved by rubbings. Lampblack ink was introduced in China in AD 400 and printing from wooden blocks in the 6th century.

The Greeks adopted the papyrus roll and passed it on to the Romans. The parchment or vellum codex, which had superseded the papyrus roll by AD 400, was a revolutionary change in the form of the book. The advantages of the codex were that its series of pages enabled the reader to open to any point in the text, that both sides of the leaf could carry information, and that longer texts could be bound in a single volume. The medieval parchment or vellum leaves were prepared from the skins of animals. By the 15th century paper manuscripts were common. In medieval Europe, monasteries characteristically had libraries and scriptoria, places in which scribes copied books. The manuscript books produced there were the models for the first printed books.

The spread of printing was rapid in the second half of the 15th century. The availability of books and the increasing speed with which ideas and information could be disseminated made possible a revolution in thought and scholarship. Technical achievements, such as the development of offset printing, improved many aspects of book culture, but for sheer efficiency of storage and retrieval and rapidity of dissemination, the book was challenged in the mid to late 20th century by developments in electronic media.

Booker Prize \'bůk-ər\, *formerly* Booker McConnell Prize \mə-'kän-əl\ Prestigious British award given annually to a full-length novel; those eligible include English-language writers from the United Kingdom, the Commonwealth countries, the Republic of Ireland, and South Africa. Booker McConnell, a multinational company, established the award in 1968 to provide a counterpart to the Prix Goncourt in France. Well-known winners include V.S. Naipaul, Salman Rushdie, Nadine Gordimer, Ruth Prawer Jhabvala, Iris Murdoch, J.M. Coetzee, A.S. Byatt, Kingsley Amis, Penelope Lively, Ben Okri, Michael Ondaatje, and Barry Unsworth.

In 1992 the first Booker Russian Novel Prize was awarded, to Mark Kharitonov for "Lines of Fate."

Book of Deer, The \'dir\ Illuminated manuscript written in Latin, probably in the 9th century, at a monastery founded by St. Columba at Deer Abbey (now Deer district, Grampian Region, Scot.) and containing 12th-century additions in Latin and an early form of Scottish Gaelic. The Book of Deer includes the whole of the New Testament Gospel of St. John and parts of the other three Gospels, an early version of the Apostles' Creed, and a later charter granted to the monks by King David I of Scotland. The illuminations—capitals, borders, and pictures of the Evangelists—resemble those in earlier Irish Gospels.

The 12th-century Gaelic memorandums (the earliest extant Gaelic written in Scotland) provide information on a little-known period of Scottish history—the end of the Celtic period. They give details of clan organization, land divisions, and monastic land tenure and an account of the monastery's foundation.

Book of Job, The \'jōb\ A book of Hebrew scripture that is often counted among the masterpieces of world literature. It is part of the third section of the biblical canon known as the Ketuvim ("Writings"). The Book of Job may be divided into two sections of prose narrative, dating to before the 6th century BC, and intervening poetic disputation, dating to between the 4th and 6th century BC.

Job is a prosperous man of outstanding piety. Satan acts as an agent provocateur to test whether Job's piety is rooted merely in his prosperity. But faced with the sudden loss of his possessions, his children, and finally his own health, Job refuses to curse God. Three of his friends then arrive to comfort him, and at this point the poetic dialogue begins. The poetic discourses—which probe the meaning of Job's sufferings and the manner in which he should respond—consist of three cycles of speeches that contain Job's disputes with his three friends and his conversations with God. Job proclaims his innocence and the injustice of his suffering, while his friends argue that Job is being punished for his sins. Job, convinced of his own faithfulness and righteousness, speaks to God and settles this question, though the problem of undeserved suffering remains unresolved.

Book of Laughter and Forgetting, The Novel by Milan KUNDERA, written in Czech as *Kniha smíchu a zapomnění* but originally published in French as *Le Livre du rire et de l'oubli* (1979). The political situation in Czechoslovakia, where history and memory are manipulated to suit those in power, becomes a symbol for all of contemporary European culture.

The novel is written in seven parts with an interwoven structure that the author likened to polyphonic music. The repetition of incidents, characters, and themes provides *The Book of Laughter and Forgetting* with its formal shape. Memories, which the characters want to keep or to forget, are a recurring subject, as is laughter, which is as often ironic as joyous.

Book of Leinster, The \'len-star\ *Irish* An Leabhar Laighneach. Compilation of Irish verse and prose from older manuscripts and oral tradition and from 12th- and 13th-century religious and secular sources. It was tentatively identified in 1907 and definitively in 1954 as the *Lebar na Núachongbála* ("The Book of Noughval"), thought lost; thus it is not the book formerly known as *The Book of Leinster* or *The Book of Glendalough* and by various Irish titles.

Written about 1160 and completed sometime between 1201 and 1224, it contains historical and genealogical poems, mainly on Leinster kings and heroes; mythological and historical accounts of invasions and battles; descriptive prose and verse topographical lists giving the history and etymology of nearly 200 place-names; treatises on bardic and Greek meters; Latin hymns; a version of the hero tale *The Cattle Raid of Cooley*; and the oldest version of *The Tragic Death of the Sons of Usnech* (the legend of Deirdre). *See also* DEIRDRE.

Book of Songs, The Collection of verse by Heinrich HEINE, published as *Buch der Lieder* in 1827. Containing all his poetry to the time of publication, it features bittersweet, self-ironic verses about unrequited love that employ Romantic sensibilities but are at the same time suspicious of them.

The Book of Songs is divided into five sections, or cycles: "Junge Leiden" ("Young Sorrows"), "Lyrisches Intermezzo" ("Lyrical Intermezzo"), "Die Heimkehr" ("Homecoming"), "Aus der Harzreise" ("From the Harz Journey"), and "Die Nordsee" ("The North Sea"). Among its most notable verses are the balladic "Die Loreley" ("Loreley"), the patriotic "Die Grenadiere" ("The Grenadiers"), and the evocative "Der Tod, das ist die kühle Nacht" ("Death, It is the Cool Night").

Book of the City of Ladies, The Prose work by CHRISTINE de Pisan, published in 1405 as *Le Livre de la cité des dames*. Written in praise of women and as a defense of their capabilities and virtues, the work is a significant feminist argument against the misogynist male writing of the day. It was based in part on Giovanni Boccaccio's *De claris mulieribus* (1360–74; *Concerning Famous Women*).

The Book of the City of Ladies has a three-part structure. The first section introduces the three Virtues—Reason, Rectitude, and Justice—with whom the author communes. Christine then tells the stories of 11 ladies of political and military accomplishment, 18 ladies of learning and skill, and four ladies of prudence. The second section includes ladies who exemplify virtuous conduct, and the third section includes discussions of various holy women.

Of 25 extant manuscripts, the Harley 4431 manuscript is believed to represent the author's intended final form; it may have been corrected in her own hand.

Book of the Dead (*more accurately* Book of Going Forth By Day) Collection of ancient Egyptian mortuary texts made up of spells or magic formulas; copies of the work were placed in tombs to protect and aid the deceased in the afterlife.

Probably compiled and reedited during the 16th century BC, the collection included Coffin Texts dating to approximately 2100 BC, Pyramid Texts dating to approximately 2350 BC, and other writings. Later compilations included hymns to Re, the sun god. Many copies of the book have been found in Egyptian tombs, but none contains all of the roughly 200 known chapters. The collection was given the title *Book of the Dead* by Richard Lepsius, a German Egyptologist who published the first collection of the texts in 1842. *See also* COFFIN TEXTS; PYRAMID TEXTS.

Book of the Dean of Lismore, The \'liz-,mòr\ Miscellany of Scottish and Irish poetry, the oldest collection of Gaelic poetry extant in Scotland. It was compiled between 1512 and 1526, chiefly by Sir James MacGregor, the dean of Lismore (now in Argyll and Bute district, Strathclyde region), and his brother Duncan.

The manuscript, preserved in the National Library of Scotland, begins with a fragmentary Latin genealogy of MacGregor chiefs and contains the *Chronicle of Fortingall* to 1579 and a Latin list of Scottish kings to 1542. It concludes with a series of heroic tales and ballads from both the Ulster cycle and Fenian cycle of Irish legend, and it also contains miscellaneous poems by 44 Scottish and 21 Irish authors. The poems are written in literary Gaelic.

Book of the Dun Cow, The *Irish* Lebor na h-Uidre *or* Leabhar na h-Uidhri. Oldest surviving miscellaneous manuscript in Irish literature, so called because the original vellum upon which it was written was supposedly made from the hide of the famous cow of St. Ciarán of Clonmacnoise. Compiled about 1100 by learned Irish monks at the monastery of Clonmacnoise from older manuscripts and oral tradition, the book is a collection of factual material and legends that date mainly from the 8th and 9th centuries; it is interspersed with religious texts. It contains a partial text of *The Cattle Raid of Cooley,* as well as other descriptions of the conflict between Ulster and Connaught. Among many other works, the book includes a poem praising St. Columba, credited to Dallan Forgaill.

Boone \\'bün\\, Daniel (b. *c.* Nov. 2, 1734, Berks County, Pa.—d. *c.* Sept. 26, 1820, St. Charles, Mo., U.S.)   Early American frontiersman and legendary hero who helped blaze a trail through Cumberland Gap, a notch in the Appalachian Mountains near the juncture of Virginia, Tennessee, and Kentucky.

Boone had little formal schooling but learned to read and write. As a youth he moved with his family to the North Carolina frontier. Most of his life was spent as a wandering hunter and trapper.

In 1775 Boone and 28 others were hired to blaze a trail through the Cumberland Gap. Despite Indian attacks, the party built the Wilderness Road, which ran from eastern Virginia into the interior of Kentucky and beyond and became the main route to the region then known as the West. It helped make possible the immediate opening of the first settlements in Kentucky.

A legendary hero even at the time of his death, his fame spread worldwide when in 1823 Lord Byron devoted seven stanzas to him in "Don Juan."

Booth \\'büth\\, Wayne C., *in full* Clayson (b. Feb. 22, 1921, American Fork, Utah, U.S.)   American critic and teacher associated with the Chicago school of literary criticism.

Booth attended Brigham Young University, Salt Lake City, Utah (B.A., 1944). He became devoted to Neo-Aristotelian critical methods while studying with R.S. Crane at the University of Chicago (M.A., 1947; Ph.D., 1950). He taught at Haverford College, Haverford, Pa., and Earlham College, Richmond, Ind., and then at the University of Chicago until his retirement in 1992.

In his influential first book, *The Rhetoric of Fiction* (1961; rev. ed., 1983), Booth argued that as a technique rhetoric can enhance communication between author and reader, not merely manipulate the reader's response, and he also offered a critical methodology. In addition to further works of criticism, Booth cofounded (1974) and coedited from 1974 to 1985 the quarterly *Critical Inquiry.* His other books include *Now Don't Try to Reason with Me: Essays and Ironies for a Credulous Age* (1970), *A Rhetoric of Irony* (1974), and *Critical Understanding: The Powers and Limits of Pluralism* (1979).

Boratynsky   *see* BARATYNSKY.

Borchert \\'bȯr-ḵərt\\, Wolfgang (b. May 20, 1921, Hamburg, Ger.—d. Nov. 20, 1947, Basel, Switz.)   Playwright and short-story writer who gave voice to the anguish of the German soldier after World War II.

As young man Borchert wrote several plays and a large number of poems, but he was determined to be an actor. In 1941 he was drafted into the army. The rigors of his army service resulted in jaundice, frostbite, malnutrition, and progressive liver degeneration. He spent much of his military career in jail, accused of self-mutilation (he lost a finger). Borchert returned to Hamburg after the war, but ill health forced him to leave an acting troupe he had cofounded. He began writing short stories

in January 1946 and, though bedridden, produced most of the body of his work in the remaining two years of his life. He died the day before his most famous work, the play *Draussen vor der Tür* (1947; "Outside the Door"; *The Man Outside*), was first staged. It presents a wounded ex-prisoner's attempt to discover a reason to keep on living.

Many of Borchert's stories, first collected in *Die Hundeblume: Erzählungen aus unseren Tagen* (1947; "The Dandelions: Tales of Our Days"), are based on personal experience. The heroes of his stories, who are victims and often in pain, seek meaning but find death and ruin.

border ballad   Type of spirited heroic ballad celebrating the raids, feuds, seductions, and elopements on the lawless border between England and Scotland in the 15th and 16th centuries. Among the better-known border ballads are "Johnny Cock," "Jock o' the Side," "Hobie Noble," and "The Bonny Earl of Murray." Most are concerned with the personal retributions of the outlaws and robber clans who maintained their own grim code on the border. *See also* CORONACH.

Boreas \\'bȯr-ē-əs\\   In Greek mythology, the personification of the north wind. He carried off the beautiful Oreithyia, a daughter of Erechtheus, king of Athens; they lived in Thrace as king and queen of the winds and had two sons, Calais and Zetes.

Borel \\bȯ-'rel\\, Jacques (b. Dec. 17, 1925, Paris, Fr.)   French writer, translator, and critic.

Borel graduated from the Sorbonne in 1949, and for several years he was an English teacher at various lycées in France (1952–67) and a visiting professor at colleges and universities in the United States (1966–83). His principal novel, *L'Adoration* (1965; *The Bond*), which won the Prix Goncourt, was a semiautobiographical account of a son's relationship to a widowed mother. The work reflected the influence of James Joyce and Marcel Proust in its extensive use of details of events and thoughts. It was followed by a sequel, *Le Retour* (1970; "The Return"), and by other novels, books of poetry, and critical writings. Borel also edited the complete works of Paul Verlaine (1959–62) and translated poems by Joyce (1967).

Borel \\bȯ-'rel\\, Petrus, *pseudonym of* Joseph-Pierre Borel, *also called* Borel d'Hauterive (b. June 29, 1809, Lyon, Fr.—d. July 1859, Mostaganem, Alg.)   French poet, novelist, and critic who played a leading role in the Romantic movement.

Borel was trained as an architect but turned to literature and became one of the most eccentric young writers of the 1830s, assuming the name of "Lycanthrope" ("Wolf-Man"). He became a leader of the group of daring writers known as Les Bousingos, among whom were Gérard de Nerval and Théophile Gautier. With the revival of interest in classical style, he fell into poverty; however, he was able to obtain a post in the colonization of Algeria. Because of his proud and touchy nature, he was dismissed in 1855, and he spent the rest of his life in a Gothic mansion in Mostaganem as a ragged eccentric. His works, redolent of horror and melodrama, include *Rhapsodies* (1832), the short stories of *Champavert, contes immoraux* (1833; "Champavert, Immoral Stories"), and *Madame Putiphar* (1839), with a verse prologue that foreshadows the poet Charles Baudelaire's spiritual style.

Borgen \\'bȯr-gen\\, Johan (Collet Müller) (b. April 28, 1902, Kristiania [now Oslo], Nor.—d. Oct. 16, 1979, Hvaler)   Norwegian novelist, short-story writer, dramatist, and essayist, one of Norway's most important and versatile 20th-century writers.

His principal work was a novel trilogy: *Lillelord* (1955), *De mørke kilder* (1956; "The Dark Springs"), and *Vi har ham nå* (1957; "Now We Have Him"), all three translated into English under the title *Lillelord* (1982). In these novels Borgen gives a picture of upper-middle-class life in Norway from 1917 through World War II.

Borgen began his career as a short-story writer with the collection *Mot mørket* (1925; "Toward the Dark") and continued to do some of his best work in that genre; other collections were *Noveller om kjaerlighet* (1952; "Love Stories") and *Noveller i utvalg* (1961; "Selected Short Stories"). He won the Nordic Council's literary prize for the collection of short stories *Nye noveller. Frydenberg* (1965; "New Stories. Frydenberg").

In his later, more experimental novels, Borgen continued to create works exploring alienation and identity: *Jeg* (1959; "I"); *Blåtind* (1964; "Blue Mountain"); and *Den røde tåken* (1967; *The Red Fog*). Borgen also wrote plays, and over a long career he developed a mastery of the short, witty essay. From 1954 to 1959, he was editor of the literary journal *Vinduet*.

Borges \'bòr-ˌgăs, -ˌgäh\, Jorge Luis (b. Aug. 24, 1899, Buenos Aires, Arg.—d. June 14, 1986, Geneva, Switz.)   Argentine

Bettmann Archive

poet, essayist, and short-story writer whose works have become classics of 20th-century world literature.

Borges' family included British ancestry, and he learned English before Spanish. In 1914 he moved with his family to Geneva, where he learned French and German and received his B.A. from the Collège de Genève. The family spent a year on Majorca and a year in Spain. In 1921 Borges returned to Buenos Aires, where he began to write of the city's beauty in poems—such as those of *Fervor de Buenos Aires, poemas* (1923)—that imaginatively reconstructed its past and present. During this decade of his career, he wrote several volumes of essays and poems and founded three literary journals.

During his next phase Borges gradually began to create pure fiction. At first he preferred to retell the lives of more or less infamous men, as in the sketches of his *Historia universal de la infamia* (1935; *A Universal History of Infamy*). In 1938 Borges suffered a severe head wound and subsequent blood poisoning, which left him near death, bereft of speech, and fearing for his sanity. This experience appears to have freed in him the deepest forces of creativity. In the next eight years he produced his best fantastic stories, those later collected in the series of *Ficciones* ("Fictions") and the volume of English translations entitled *The Aleph and Other Stories, 1933–69*. During this time, he and another writer, Adolfo Bioy Casares, jointly wrote detective stories under the pseudonym Honorio Bustos Domecq; these were published in 1942 as *Seis problemas para Don Isidro*

Parodi (*Six Problems for Don Isidro Parodi*). The works of this period revealed for the first time Borges' entire dreamworld, an ironical or paradoxical version of the real one, with its own language and systems of symbols. A collection of essays, *Otras inquisiciones (1937–1952)* (1952; *Other Inquisitions, 1937–1952*) revealed him at his analytical best.

In 1955 Borges became director of the Argentine national library, an honorary position, and also professor of English and American literature at the University of Buenos Aires. By this time, he had become totally blind. The works that date from this late period, such as *El hacedor* (1960; "The Doer," Eng. trans. *Dreamtigers*) and *El libro de los seres imaginarios* (1967; *The Book of Imaginary Beings*), almost erase the distinctions between the genres of prose and poetry. Later collections of stories included *El informe de Brodie* (1970; *Dr. Brodie's Report*) and *El libro de arena* (1975; *The Book of Sand*).

Boris Godunov \ˌbə-'rʸēs-gə-dù-'nòf, *Angl* 'bòr-is-'gùd-ə-ˌnòf\ Historical drama in 23 scenes by Russian poet and playwright Aleksandr PUSHKIN, written in 1824–25, published in 1831, and considered one of the most important plays of the early 19th century. Its theme is the tragic guilt and inexorable fate of a great hero, Boris Fyodorovich Godunov, who reigned as czar from 1598 to 1605. Pushkin's masterly development of the dramatic action on two planes—one political and historical, the other psychological—is set against a background of turbulent events and ruthless ambitions.

Boron or **Borron**, Robert de   *see* ROBERT de Boron.

Borowski \bò-'ròf-skʸē\, Tadeusz (b. Nov. 12, 1922, Zhitomir, Ukrainian S.S.R. [now Zhytomyr, Ukraine]—d. July 3, 1951, Warsaw, Pol.)   Polish fiction writer and poet.

In German-occupied Warsaw, Borowski illegally published a collection of poems entitled *Gdziekolwiek ziemia* (1942; "Wherever the Land"). During 1943–45 he was an inmate of the German concentration camps at Auschwitz (Oświęcim) and Dachau. After the war he published in Munich a volume entitled *Imiona nurtu* (1945; "The Names of the Undercurrent").

In Poland under communist rule, Borowski in 1948 turned to publishing prose. Two series of stories, *Pożegnanie z Marią* ("Farewell to Maria") and *Kamienny świat* ("World of Stone"), deal mainly with life in Nazi concentration camps and explore the depths of human depravity and degradation.

Borrow \'băr-ō, 'bòr-\, George (Henry) (b. July 5, 1803, East Dereham, Norfolk, Eng.—d. July 26, 1881, Oulton Broad) English traveler and linguist and one of the most imaginative prose writers of the 19th century.

Borrow, the son of a professional soldier, led a wandering childhood as his father's regiment was moved around the British Isles; these peregrinations inspired memorable passages in his masterpiece, *Lavengro* (1851). Between 1815 and 1818 he attended grammar school at Norwich, and it was here that he began to acquire a smattering of many languages. Borrow's adventures, including many contacts with Gypsies, provided some of the background for *Lavengro* and *The Romany Rye* (1857), both of which were based on his own experiences, although they mixed fact with fiction. *Romantic Ballads* (1826) was translated from the Danish. In Spain he found his literary homeland, whence came the raw materials for *The Zincali: An Account of the Gypsies in Spain* (1841) and for his brilliantly picturesque yet highly informative travel book *The Bible in Spain* (published 1842; title page date 1843).

Borrowers, The   Race of tiny people in *The Borrowers* series of novels for children by British author Mary NORTON. Secretive and resourceful, the Borrowers live concealed in the houses of full-sized human beings, subsisting on bits of food and cleverly using odds and ends that they "borrow" and fashion into clothing, tools, and furnishings.

Borstal Boy \\'bȯrs-təl\\   Autobiographical work by Brendan BEHAN, published in 1958. The book portrays the author's early rebelliousness, his involvement with the Irish Republican cause, and his subsequent incarceration for two years in an English Borstal, or reformatory, at age 16. Interspersed with tales of brutality are anecdotes about dramatic and musical pastimes and Behan's gardening and handicraft activities. The book is notable for capturing the immediacy of conversation among the inmates.

Boscán \\bȯs-'kän\\, Juan, *original name* Joan Boscà i Almogàver \\bȯs-'kä-ē-ˌäl-mō-'gä-ber\\ (b. *c.* 1490, Barcelona, Aragon [Spain]—d. Sept. 21, 1542, Barcelona)   Catalan poet who wrote exclusively in Castilian and adapted the Italian hendecasyllable (11-syllable line) to that language.

Though a minor poet, Boscán is of major historical importance because of his naturalizing of Italian meters and verse forms, an experiment that induced one of the greatest of all Spanish poets, Boscán's friend Garcilaso de la Vega, to follow his example. Their works appeared together posthumously in 1543.

In 1534 Boscán published a translation of Baldassare Castiglione's *Il cortegiano* (*The Courtier*). His prose was greatly superior to his verse, and *El Cortesano* is not only one of the influential books of the Spanish Renaissance but a work of art in its own right.

Bosman \\'bōs-ˌmän, *Angl* 'bȯs-mən\\, Herman Charles (b. Feb. 5, 1905, Kuils River, near Cape Town, S.Af.—d. Oct. 14, 1951, Edendale)   South African writer who is noted for his short stories depicting rural Afrikaner character and life.

The son of Afrikaner parents, Bosman took a degree in education at the University of Witwatersrand, Johannesburg. His teaching post was at remote Groot Marico in northwestern Transvaal. The experience proved to be highly significant to Bosman's writing.

His teaching at Marico was terminated abruptly when, home on a visit, he shot and killed his stepbrother. Although he was sentenced to death, his sentence was commuted to 10 years, of which he actually served four. The earliest of his stories featuring the Afrikaner Oom Schalk Lourens were written in prison, and later Bosman wrote *Cold Stone Jug* (1949), a collection of sardonic, comic prison sketches.

His stories were first collected in *Mafeking Road* (1947). The rest were posthumously published in *Unto Dust* (1963), *Jurie Steyn's Post Office* (1971), and *A Bekkersdal Marathon* (1971). Bosman also wrote several books of poems and two complete novels, *Jacaranda in the Night* (1947) and *Willemsdorp* (1977). *Bosman at His Best* (1965) and *The Collected Works of Herman Charles Bosman* (1981) were edited by Lionel Abrahams.

Boston \\'bȯs-tən\\, Lucy, *original name* Lucy Maria Wood \\'wu̇d\\ (b. Dec. 10, 1892, Southport, Lancashire, Eng.—d. May 25, 1990, Hemingford Grey, Cambridgeshire)   English writer whose 12th-century country house inspired her to write a series of children's books that centered on its fictional counterpart.

Wood served at a military hospital in France during World War I and married Harold Boston, a cousin and flying corps officer, in 1917. The marriage ended after 18 years, and she left England to study painting in Austria. With the outbreak of World War II, she returned to England and purchased the Manor House (built about 1120) near Cambridge.

With her son Peter, she slowly restored the decaying house and gardens with a passion that she likened to falling in love. In 1954 she published *Yew Hall* and *The Children of Green Knowe*,

the first of six books set in a fictional version of Manor House; its successors included *The Chimneys of Green Knowe* (1958), *A Stranger at Green Knowe* (1961), and *The Stones of Green Knowe* (1976). Her other works include *The Sea Egg* (1967), *The House That Grew* (1969), and two autobiographies, *Memory in a House* (1973) and *Perverse and Foolish* (1979).

Bostonians, The \\bȯs-'tō-nē-ənz\\   Satirical novel by Henry JAMES, published serially in *Century Illustrated Magazine* in 1885–86 and in book form in three volumes in 1886. It was one of the earliest American novels to deal—even obliquely—with lesbianism.

Olive Chancellor, a Boston feminist in the 1870s, thinks she has found a kindred spirit in Verena Tarrant, a beautiful young woman who, though passive and indecisive, is a spellbinding orator for women's rights. Olive vies for Verena's attention and affections with Basil Ransom, a gracious but reactionary Confederate army veteran. Verena marries Basil and leaves Boston.

The Bostonians is based on Alphonse Daudet's novel *L'Évangéliste* (1883); James transposed the work to Boston and to the milieu of the rising feminist movement.

Boswell \\'bäz-wəl, -ˌwel\\, James (b. Oct. 29, 1740, Edinburgh, Scot.—d. May 19, 1795, London, Eng.)   Scottish friend and biographer of Samuel Johnson, known for his two-volume THE LIFE OF SAMUEL JOHNSON, LL.D. (1791). The 20th-century publication of Boswell's journals showed him to have been also one of the world's greatest diarists.

Boswell was the son of a noted jurist, Lord Auchinleck. From 1753 to 1758 he went through the arts course at the University of Edinburgh and then began to study law. Sent to the University of Glasgow, he ran away to London; thereafter, from 1760 to 1762, Boswell studied law at home under strict supervision. When he came of age, he was allowed to go to London to seek a commission in the foot guards. Anticipating great happiness, he began, in the autumn of 1762, the journal that was to be the central expression of his genius. Boswell's second London visit lasted from November 1762 to August 1763. On May 16, 1763, he was introduced to Samuel Johnson, and soon a great friendship was initiated.

Convinced that his scheme to join the guards was not practicable, Boswell capitulated to his father and consented to become a lawyer. He spent a winter studying civil law at Utrecht and then traveled to Berlin and Switzerland. He also made a six weeks' tour of the island of Corsica to interview the heroic Corsican chieftain Pasquale de Paoli, who was then engaged in establishing his country's independence from Genoa.

Back in Scotland, Boswell was admitted to the Faculty of Advocates and for 17 years practiced law at Edinburgh. His cher-

Detail of an oil painting from the studio of Sir Joshua Reynolds, 1786

National Portrait Gallery, London

ished trips to London were by no means annual and until 1784 were always made during vacations.

In February 1768 Boswell published *An Account of Corsica, The Journal of a Tour to That Island; and Memoirs of Pascal Paoli*. France had unmasked its intention of annexing the island, and because people were greedy for information about Corsica and Paoli, the book made Boswell famous. In 1773 Boswell was elected to The Club, the brilliant circle that Sir Joshua Reynolds had formed around Dr. Johnson, and later in the year Johnson made with him the famous tour of the Hebrides.

Between 1777 and 1783 he published in *The London Magazine* a series of 70 essays, entitled *The Hypochondriack*. Boswell succeeded his father as laird of Auchinleck in 1782. Johnson died on Dec. 13, 1784, and Boswell decided to take his time in writing Johnson's biography and to publish his journal of the Hebridean tour as a first installment. THE JOURNAL OF A TOUR TO THE HEBRIDES appeared in 1785.

In 1786 Boswell was called to the English bar from the Inner Temple and moved to London, but thereafter he had almost no legal practice. His principal business was writing the *Life*, which he worked at irregularly but with anxious attention. It was published in May 1791. Contemporary criticism set the pattern of acclaim for the work and derision for its author. Boswell took intense pleasure in his literary fame but ultimately felt himself to be a failure. He saw the second edition of the *Life* through the press (July 1793) and was at work on the third when he died in 1795.

Bottom \\'bät-əm\\ Fictional character, one of the "mechanicals" in William Shakespeare's comedy A MIDSUMMER NIGHT'S DREAM whose low-comedy antics contrast with the machinations of the aristocratic lovers. A weaver, Bottom leads a group of tradesmen in a performance of the tragedy of *Pyramus and Thisbe*.

Boucicault \\'bü-sē-ˌkō\\, Dion, *original name* Dionysius Lardner Boursiquot \\'bür-sē-ˌkō\\ (b. Dec. 26, 1820/22, Dublin, Ire.—d. Sept. 18, 1890, New York, N.Y., U.S.) Irish-born American playwright and actor who exerted a major influence on the form and content of American drama.

Boucicault began acting in 1837. His second play, *London Assurance* (1841), which foreshadowed the modern social drama, was a huge success. Other notable early plays were *Old Heads and Young Hearts* (1844) and *The Corsican Brothers* (1852). In 1853 Boucicault and his second wife, Agnes Robertson, arrived in New York City, where his plays and adaptations were long popular. He led a movement of playwrights that in 1856 produced the first copyright law for drama in the United States. His play *The Poor of New York* had a long run at Wallack's Theatre in 1857 and was adapted for presentation elsewhere (as, for example, *The Poor of Liverpool*). *The Octoroon; or, Life in Louisiana* (1859) caused a sensation with its implied attack on slavery.

Boucicault and his wife joined Laura Keene's theater in 1860 and began a series of his popular Irish plays—*The Colleen Bawn* (1860), *Arrah-na-Pogue* (1864), *The O'Dowd* (1873), and *The Shaughraun* (1874). Returning to London in 1862, he provided Joseph Jefferson with a successful adaptation of *Rip Van Winkle* (1865). About 150 plays are credited to Boucicault, who, as both writer and actor, raised the stage Irishman from caricature to character.

Boudjedra \\büj-ə-'drä\\, Rachid (b. Sept. 5, 1941, Aïn Beïda, Alg.) Prolific and revolutionary Algerian writer whose first novel, *La Répudiation* (1969; "The Repudiation"), was a frontal assault on Muslim traditionalism in contemporary Algeria. He was hailed as the leader of a new movement of experimental fiction.

Boudjedra was given a traditional Muslim upbringing in Algeria and Tunisia, then continued his education in Spain, in Algeria, and in Paris at the Sorbonne. He later taught philosophy in Paris and at Rabat, Mor., and worked for the Algerian Bureau of Cinematography.

La Répudiation drew upon Boudjedra's difficult youth. He rejected conventional values and the complacency of the established powers in newly independent Algeria, and his unortho-

dox sexual fury and lyrical savagery defied traditional morality. Boudjedra's next novel, *L'Insolation* (1972; "Sunstroke"), mingles dreams with reality. *Topographie idéale pour une agression caractérisée* (1975; "Ideal Topography for a Specific Aggression") takes as its protagonist an illiterate Berber peasant drawn to the city by the prospect of work. In *L'Escargot entêté* (1977; "The Stubborn Snail"), a petty bureaucrat exposes his mediocre life and values, symbolizing the incompleteness of the Algerian revolution. With *Les 1001 Années de la nostalgie* (1979; "1,001 Years of Nostalgia"), a Saharan village is confronted with the newest symbol of contemporary cultural imperialism, an American film company. Later works include *Le Démantèlement* (1982; "The Dismantling"); *Greffe* (1984; "Graft"), a collection of poems; and *Le Désordre des choses* (1991; "The Disorder of Things").

Boufflers \\bü-'fler\\, Stanislas-Jean, Chevalier de (b. May 31, 1738, Nancy, Fr.—d. Jan. 18, 1815, Paris) French writer, soldier, and academician remembered chiefly for the picaresque romance *Aline, reine de Golconde* (1761; "Aline, Queen of Golconde").

While studying theology at Saint-Sulpice in Paris, Boufflers wrote his masterwork, *Aline*, a charming tale of a milkmaid who, after a series of improper adventures, becomes queen of Golconda. The story won its author immediate fame but caused his expulsion from Saint-Sulpice.

Boufflers then joined the Knights of Malta. For the next 24 years he fought in campaigns in Europe, with frequent returns to the salons of Paris, where he established a reputation for wit. After serving as governor of the new French colony of Senegal, he returned to France and won election to the Académie Française (1788). Boufflers immigrated to Germany in 1791, but in 1800 he returned to Paris and supervised the edition of his complete works (1803).

Boule de Suif \\bül-də-'swᵉf\\ Short story by Guy de MAUPASSANT, originally published in *Les Soirées de Médan* (1880), an anthology of stories of the Franco-Prussian War.

Boule de Suif ("Ball of Fat") is the nickname given to a well-known prostitute who finds herself traveling in a coach with conventionally respectable people through Prussian-occupied France during wartime. The travelers are detained by a Prussian officer who will not allow the coach to proceed until Boule de Suif gives herself to him, which she refuses on principle to do. Ironies abound in the story, contrasting Boule de Suif's authentic principles and generosity with her bourgeois fellow passengers' shallow platitudes and cold-heartedness.

Boulle \\'bül\\, Pierre(-François-Marie-Louis) (b. Feb. 20, 1912, Avignon, Fr.—d. Jan. 30, 1994, Paris) French novelist who successfully combined adventure and psychology in works dealing largely with his experiences in Southeast Asia.

Boulle spent eight years in Asia as a planter and soldier. He is best known for his novel *Le Pont de la rivière Kwaï* (1952; *The Bridge over the River Kwai*; film, 1957). An ambiguous moral fable, it presents virtue gradually shading into vice—or, at least, absurdity—in its portrayal of a British officer in a Japanese prisoner-of-war camp whose self-discipline and work ethic compel him to complete a bridge for the enemy.

From the legends of the Orient, Boulle created *Le Bourreau* (1954; U.S. title, *The Executioner*; U.K. title, *The Chinese Executioner*), philosophical tales in the manner of Voltaire. Departing from the Asian setting, he turned to a literature of the fantastic in *Contes de l'absurde* (1953; "Stories of the Absurd") and to science fiction in *La Planète des singes* (1963; *Planet of the Apes*; film, 1968) and $E = mc^2$ (1957). Later works include *Les Oreilles de jungle* (1972; *Ears of the Jungle*), *Les Vertus de l'enfer* (1974; *The Virtues of Hell*), *Le Bon Léviathan* (1978; *The Good*

Leviathan), *Miroitements* (1982; *Mirrors of the Sun*), *La Baleine des Malovines* (1983; U.S. title, *The Whale of the Victoria Cross*; U.K. title, *The Falklands Whale*), *Pour l'amour de l'art* (1985; "For the Love of Art"), *Le Professeur Mortimer* (1988), and *À nous deux, Satan!* (1992).

Bounderby, Josiah \jō-'sī-ə-'baùn-dər-bē, jō-'zī-\ Fictional character, a wealthy businessman in Charles Dickens' novel HARD TIMES. Bounderby uses everyone around him to further his own interests and keeps the existence of his mother a secret as he perpetuates the myth that he began life as an orphan who had to struggle to survive and to establish himself in life.

Bouraoui \bü-rä-'wē\, Hédi (André) (b. July 16, 1932, Sfax, Tunisia) Tunisian poet and scholar whose creative and critical works seek to illuminate the human condition and transcend cultural boundaries.

Bouraoui specialized in English literature at the University of Toulouse in France and then, in the United States, received degrees in English and American literature at Indiana University and in Romance studies at Cornell University. He later taught at York University, Toronto, and became a Canadian citizen in 1971.

His scholarly publications include the two-volume *Créaculture* (1971), essays on comparative culture, and *Structure intentionnelle du 'Grand Meaulnes': vers le poème romancé* (1976; "Intentional Structure of 'Grand Meaulnes': Toward the Poetic Novel"), a book of literary criticism on Alain-Fournier. Bouraoui also published several volumes of French poetry: *Musocktail* (1966), *Tremblé* (1969; "Wavy"), *Éclate module* (1972; "Modulated Explosion"), *Vésuviade* (1976), *Vers et l'envers* (1982; "Verse and the Reverse"), *Arc-en-terre* (1991), and *Émigressence* (1992).

Bourboune \bür-'bün\, Mourad (b. Jan. 23, 1938, Jijel, Alg.) Algerian novelist who criticized the oppressiveness of newly independent Algeria as well as its religious traditionalism.

Bourboune's first novel, *Le Mont des genêts* (1962; "The Mountain of Broom"), describes the collapse of the old order and the coming of a new age beginning with the insurrection of Nov. 1, 1954, the event that precipitated the Algerian war for independence. In *Le Muezzin* (1968) the protagonist is an atheistic muezzin (the caller to daily prayers) whose sacrilegious violence acts to delineate and exorcise the sham and hypocrisy of the Algerian government since independence.

Bourchier, John *see* BERNERS.

Bourdet \bür-'de\, Édouard (b. 1887, Saint-Germain-en-Laye, Fr.—d. Jan. 17, 1945, Paris) French dramatist noted for his satirical and psychological analyses of contemporary social problems.

Bourdet's first plays, *Le Rubicon* (1910) and *L'Homme enchaîné* (1923; "The Man Enchained"), were not successful. His reputation was secured, however, by *La Prisonnière* (1926; *The Captive*), a psychological study of the sufferings of a sexually maladjusted woman. With *Vient de paraître* (1928; "Just Appeared"), a satire on the literary world, Bourdet established a formula for the series of satirical comedies that he produced between the world wars. Notable plays in the series are *Le Sexe faible* (1931; "The Weaker Sex"; *The Sex Fable*) and *Les Temps difficiles* (1934; "The Difficult Times"). His later plays include *Hyménée* (1941; "Hymen") and *Père* (1943; "Father").

Bourgeois Gentleman, The Comedy in five acts by Molière, gently satirizing the pretensions of the social climber whose affectations are absurd to everyone but himself. It was first performed as *Le Bourgeois Gentilhomme* in 1670 with music by Jean-Baptiste Lully and was published in 1671. It has also been translated into English as *The Prodigious Snob*.

The would-be gentleman is Monsieur Jourdain, a wealthy tradesman who hires tutors in music, dancing, fencing, and philosophy and patronizes a fashionable tailor in order to acquire gentlemanly polish. Molière makes the character as delightful as he is fatuous, as genuine as his is naïve; his folly is embedded in an expansive disposition.

Bourget \bür-'zhe\, Paul(-Charles-Joseph) (b. Sept. 2, 1852, Amiens, Fr.—d. Dec. 25, 1935, Paris) Novelist and critic, a molder of opinion among French conservative intellectuals in the period before World War I.

Bourget began his career as a poet, and several of his poems were set to music by Claude Debussy. Encouraged and deeply influenced by the critic Hippolyte Taine, he published a series of brilliant essays tracing the sources of contemporary pessimism to the works of Stendhal, Gustave Flaubert, Charles Baudelaire, Taine, and Ernest Renan. His early novels, such as *Cruelle Énigme* (1885), *Un Crime d'amour* (1886), and *André Cornélis* (1887), were psychological studies in the naturalistic tradition.

Bourget's most important novel, *Le Disciple* (1889), heralded a marked change in his intellectual position. Prefaced by an appeal to youth to abide by traditional morality rather than modern scientific theory, the novel portrays the pernicious influence of a highly respected positivist philosopher and teacher (who strongly resembles Taine) on a young man. Bourget converted to Roman Catholicism in 1901. His later novels, such as *L'Étape* (1902) and *Un Divorce* (1904), are increasingly didactic theses in support of the church, traditionalism, nationalism, and monarchy.

Bourne \'bùrn, *commonly* 'bòrn\, Randolph Silliman (b. May 30, 1886, Bloomfield, N.J., U.S.—d. Dec. 22, 1918, New York, N.Y.) American literary critic and essayist whose polemical articles made him a spokesman for young radicals on the eve of World War I.

Bourne held a variety of odd jobs before winning a scholarship (at age 23) to Columbia University. That same year his *Youth and Life* appeared, essays asserting that the youth of his day would sweep away much that was antiquated and unworthy in American life. After a year in Europe, resulting in 1914 in "Impressions of Europe: 1913–14," he turned his attention to the progressive educational theories of the pragmatist philosopher John Dewey, who had been his teacher at Columbia. The outcome was two books: *The Gary Schools* (1916) and *Education and Living* (1917).

Bourne's early death was brought on by influenza during the epidemic of 1918–19. He left incomplete a group of writings analyzing culture, power, and the modern state, some of which were collected and edited by Olaf Hansen in *The Radical Will: Randolph Bourne, Selected Writings, 1911–1918* (1977). Two posthumous volumes of Bourne's essays appeared: *Untimely Papers* (1919) and *The History of a Literary Radical and Other Essays* (1920).

Boursault \bür-'sō\, Edme (b. October 1638, Mussy l'Évêque, Fr.—d. Sept. 15, 1701, Paris) French man of letters, active in the literary world of mid-17th-century Paris.

Boursault composed plays, many of which became highly successful, and light verse that appeared in the collection *Délices de la poésie galante* (1663; "Delights of Gallant Poetry"). His first play was *Le Portrait du peintre ou la contre-critique de l'école des femmes* (1663; "The Portrait of the Painter; or the Countercriticism of the School for Wives"), an attack on Molière, who was provoked to reply in his play *L'Impromptu de Versailles*.

In 1667 he published a reply to Nicolas Boileau's celebrated satires with a *Satire des satires*; this was later recast as a play, the public performance of which seems to have been prevented by Boileau.

Boursault also wrote novels, including some pseudo-historical works, and his *Lettres* went through several editions.

Bousoño \bō-'sōn-yō\, Carlos (b. May 9, 1923, Boal, Spain) Spanish poet and critic, a leading theorist of Hispanic literature.

In 1945 Bousoño published his first volume of poetry, *Subida al amor* ("Ascent to Love"), which deals with struggles for religious faith. His second book, *Primavera de la muerte* (1946; "Springtime of Death"), takes up themes of death, love, and the value of life.

His later works include *Noche del sentido* (1957; "Night of Feeling"), which brings together romantic views and religious ideas, *Invasión de la realidad* (1962; "Invasion of Reality"), *Oda en la ceniza* (1967; "Ode on the Ashes"), *Selección de mis versos* (1980), and *Metáfora del desafuero* (1988; "Metaphor of Violence").

From an early age he found a mentor in the poet Vicente Aleixandre, and in 1950 Bousoño published *La poesía de Vicente Aleixandre*. Bousoño's *Teoría de la expresión poética* (1952; rev. ed., 1966; "Theory of Poetic Expression") analyzes poetic devices and seeks general rules and a scientific basis for the study of poetry. It is his major critical work and received the Spanish Academy's Fastenrath Prize. He also wrote books on irrationalism (*El irracionalismo poético*, 1977), Surrealism (*Superrealismo poético y simbolización*, 1979), and Romanticism (*Epocas literarias y evolución*, 1981) as part of his comprehensive study of poetry.

boustrophedon \ˌbüs-trə-'fē-ˌdän, -dən\ [Greek *boustrophēdón*, literally, turning like oxen (in plowing)] The writing of alternate lines in opposite directions, one line from left to right and the next from right to left. Some Etruscan texts are written in boustrophedon style, as are some Greek ones of about the 6th century BC.

Boutens \'baù-tənz\, Pieter Cornelis (b. Feb. 20, 1870, Middelburg, Neth.—d. March 14, 1943, The Hague) Dutch poet, mystic, and classical scholar who evolved a very personal and sometimes esoteric style and influenced a number of other poets.

Boutens' mysticism, or divine revelation, was achieved by linking the soul with the spirit of immortal beauty through complete introspection, or contemplation of the inner life. The immense spiritual solitude he came to experience is exquisitely expressed in the poem "Ik sloot de blinkevenstren van mijn ziel" ("I Closed the Shining Windows of My Soul"), from *Verzen* (1898).

Boutens' later volumes, from *Stemmen* (1907; "Voices") to *Lentemaan* (1916; "Spring Moon"), symbolically treat the themes of solitude, pain, and death with a mastery of form and rhythm. His popular *Beatrijs* (1908), a narrative poem of child-like simplicity, tells of a nun who went to her lover "from May to May" but always returned to continue the life of the spirit. Boutens also was noted for his translations of Homer, Sophocles, J.W. von Goethe, and others.

bouts-rimés \ˌbü-ˌrē-'mā, -'māz\ [French, literally, rhymed ends] Rhyming words or syllables to which verses are to be written; or the literary game of making verses from a list of rhyming words supplied by another person. The game, which requires that the rhymes follow a given order and that the result make some sense, is said to have been invented by the minor French poet Dulot in the early 17th century. Its wide popularity inspired at least one notable tour de force, an extended satirical poem by the French poet Jean-François Sarasin, entitled *Dulot vaincu* (1654; "Dulot Defeated"). The fad was revived in the 19th century when Alexandre Dumas (*père*) invited French po-

ets and versifiers to try their skill with given sets of rhymes and published the results in 1865.

In 19th-century England, John Keats is said to have produced his charming poem "On the Grasshopper and Cricket" (1816) in a bouts-rimés competition with his friend Leigh Hunt, and Dante Gabriel Rossetti and his brother William tested their ingenuity by filling in verses from bouts-rimés. Most of William's poems in the Pre-Raphaelite magazine *The Germ* were bouts-rimés experiments. *See also* CRAMBO.

Bovary, Emma \em-à-bō-và-'rē, *Angl* 'em-ə-'bō-və-rē\ Fictional character, heroine of the novel MADAME BOVARY by Gustave Flaubert.

Bowdler \'baùd-lər, *commonly* 'bōd-\, Thomas (b. July 11, 1754, Ashley, near Bath, Somerset, Eng.—d. Feb. 24, 1825, Rhydding, near Swansea, Glamorganshire, Wales) English doctor of medicine, philanthropist, and man of letters known for his *Family Shakspeare* (1818), in which, by expurgation and paraphrase, he aimed to provide an edition of the plays suitable for a father to read aloud to his family without fear of offending their susceptibilities or corrupting their minds. The first edition, the title of which was spelled *The Family Shakespeare* (1807), contained a selection of 20 plays that probably were expurgated by Bowdler's sister, Harriet.

Although criticized for tampering with Shakespeare's text, Bowdler deserves a certain amount of credit for making the plays well known to a wide audience. The word bowdlerize was current by the mid-1830s as a synonym for expurgate, and it is now used in a pejorative sense. It remains his most lasting memorial.

Bowen \'bō-ən\, Catherine (Shober), *original surname* Drinker \'driŋ-kər\ (b. Jan. 1, 1897, Haverford, Pa., U.S.—d. Nov. 1, 1973, Haverford) American historical biographer known for her partly fictionalized biographies. After attending the Peabody Institute and the Juilliard School of Music, she became interested in writing. Not surprisingly, her earliest works were inspired by the lives of musicians.

Her biography of the Elizabethan jurist Sir Edward Coke, *The Lion and the Throne* (1957), won her the National Book Award in 1958. Her many other books include *Beloved Friend* (1937), about the relationship between Tchaikovsky and Nadezhda von Meck; *Yankee from Olympus: Justice Holmes and His Family* (1944); *John Adams and the American Revolution* (1950); and *Miracle at Philadelphia: The Story of the Constitutional Convention, May to September 1787* (1966).

Bowen \'bō-ən\, Elizabeth (Dorothea Cole) (b. June 7, 1899, Dublin, Ire.—d. Feb. 22, 1973, London, Eng.) British novelist and short-story writer who employed a finely wrought prose style in fiction frequently detailing uneasy and unfulfilling relationships among the upper middle class. THE DEATH OF THE HEART (1938), the title of one of her most highly praised novels, might have served for most of them.

Bowen was born of the Anglo-Irish gentry and spent her early childhood in Dublin, as related in her autobiographical fragment *Seven Winters* (1942), and at the family house she later inherited at Kildorrery, County Cork. The history of the house is recounted in *Bowen's Court* (1942), and it is the scene of her novel *The Last September* (1929).

Bowen began writing short stories at 20. Her first collection,

Culver Pictures

Encounters, appeared in 1923. It was followed in 1927 by *The Hotel*, which contains a typical Bowen heroine—a girl attempting to cope with a life for which she is unprepared. THE HOUSE IN PARIS, another of Bowen's highly praised novels, was published in 1935.

Her novel set in wartime London, THE HEAT OF THE DAY (1949), is among her most significant works. The war also forms the basis for one of her collections of short stories, *The Demon Lover* (1945; U.S. title, *Ivy Gripped the Steps*). Her essays appear in *Collected Impressions* (1950) and *Afterthought* (1962). Bowen's last book, *Pictures and Conversations* (1975), is an introspective, partly autobiographical collection of essays and articles.

Bowen \'bō-ən\, John Griffith (b. Nov. 5, 1924, Calcutta, India)   British playwright and novelist noted for exploding popular assumptions by his examination of the complexity and ambivalence of human motives and behavior.

After graduation from Oxford, Bowen went to Ohio State University, U.S., for a year's study. While in the United States, he was revolted by the investigations of Senator Joseph McCarthy. That experience inspired his first novel, *The Truth Will Not Help Us* (1956), about an unjust trial of three Englishmen in Scotland in 1705 for piracy. Back in England, Bowen worked in journalism and advertising and was a consultant on television drama for Associated Television (1960–67). *The Essay Prize* (1962) is a collection of his own television plays with an essay on writing for television. His novel *After the Rain* (1958), about survivors from a worldwide flood, was adapted as a play in 1966. Among his other plays are *I Love You, Mrs. Patterson* (1964); *Little Boxes* (1968); *The Disorderly Women* (1969), a modern version of the Bacchae legend; *The Corsican Brothers* (1970), a play with music based on the story by Alexandre Dumas *père*; *Florence Nightingale* (1975); *Spot the Lady* (1981); and *The Oak Tree Tea-Room Siege* (1990). Later novels by Bowen include *Storyboard* (1960), *The McGuffin* (1984), and *The Girls: A Story of Village Life* (1986).

Bowles \'bōlz\, Jane (Sydney), *original surname* Auer \'aù-ər\ (b. Feb. 22, 1917, New York, N.Y., U.S.—d. May 4, 1973, Malaga, Spain)   American author whose reputation rests on a small body of highly individualistic work that enjoyed an underground reputation even when it was no longer in print.

Auer married composer-author Paul Bowles in 1938. They lived in Costa Rica, France, Mexico, and the United States, where she began writing her only published novel, *Two Serious Ladies* (1943). The couple settled in Tangier, Morocco, in 1952. In December 1953 her play *In the Summer House* was staged in New York. In addition to the novel and the play, she also published seven short stories.

Bowles deliberately constructed *Two Serious Ladies* without a plot. Its title characters, one sinful and victimized, the other virtuous and domineering, meet only twice; their lives are presented alternately, in a style praised for its wit. Her short stories and play also contrast domineering and weak women. Her *Collected Works* was published in 1966; it was expanded after her death and published as *My Sister's Hand in Mine* (1978).

Bowles \'bōlz\, Paul (Frederick) (b. Dec. 30, 1910, New York, N.Y., U.S.)   American-born composer, translator, and author of novels and short stories in which violent events and psychological collapse are recounted in a detached and elegant style. His protagonists are often Europeans or Americans who are maimed by their contact with powerful traditional cultures.

Bowles began publishing Surrealist poetry in the magazine *transition* at the age of 16. He studied musical composition under Aaron Copland and composed music for more than 30 theatrical productions and films. He became a member of

the loose society of literary expatriates in Europe and North Africa. In Tangier, Morocco, his most potent source of inspiration, he wrote his first novel, THE SHELTERING SKY (1948), a harsh tale of death, rape, and sexual obsession.

His later novels include *Let It Come Down* (1952), *The Spider's House* (1955), and *Up Above the World* (1966). Bowles' *Collected Stories, 1939–1976* (1979) and his subsequent short-story collections, which include *Midnight Mass* (1981) and *Call at Corazón* (1988), also depict human depravity amid exotic settings. Bowles recorded Moroccan folk music for the U.S. Library of Congress, wrote travel essays, translated works from several European and Middle Eastern languages into English, and recorded and translated oral tales from Maghrebi Arabic into English. *Without Stopping* (1972) and *Two Years Beside the Strait: Tangier Journal 1987–1989* (1990; U.S. title, *Days*) are autobiographical.

Bowles \'bōlz\, William Lisle (b. Sept. 24, 1762, Kings Sutton, Northamptonshire, Eng.—d. April 7, 1850, Salisbury, Wiltshire)   English poet, critic, and clergyman, noted for his *Fourteen Sonnets* (1789), which expresses the thoughts and feelings inspired in a mind of delicate sensibility by the contemplation of natural scenes.

Bowles was educated at Trinity College, Oxford, and became an Anglican priest in 1792. His *Fourteen Sonnets* was enthusiastically received by and influenced the theory and practice of the early Romantic poets, particularly Samuel Taylor Coleridge.

As a critic, Bowles is remembered for his assertion that natural objects and basic passions are intrinsically more poetic than are artificial products or mannered feelings. This attitude may have influenced his annotated 1806 edition of the works of Alexander Pope, in which, under a mask of judicial impartiality, Bowles attacked Pope's moral character and poetic principles. So began the pamphlet war known as the "Pope–Bowles controversy," in which Pope's chief defenders were Thomas Campbell and Lord Byron; Byron's characterization of Bowles as "the maudlin prince of mournful sonneteers" is perhaps the only memorable remnant of this seven-year-long (1819–26) public argument.

Bowles, Sally \'sal-ē-'bōlz\   Fictional character, the eccentric heroine of Christopher Isherwood's novella *Sally Bowles* (1937) and of his collected stories *Goodbye to Berlin* (1939). Sally Bowles is a young, iconoclastic, minimally talented English nightclub singer in the Berlin of the Weimar Republic period (1919–33).

Isherwood's tales about Sally Bowles and her acquaintances became the basis for John Van Druten's play *I Am a Camera* (1951; film, 1955). Fred Ebb and John Kander turned this material into the much-acclaimed stage musical *Cabaret* (1966; film, 1972).

Boxer \'bäk-sər\   Fictional character, an old, noble cart horse in George Orwell's allegorical novel ANIMAL FARM. His unquestioning acceptance of the commands of the other animals and his willingness to work ever harder are exploited by the leaders of the revolution in the farmyard.

Box Man, The   Avant-garde satiric novel by ABE Kōbō, published in Japanese in 1973 as *Hako otoko*.

A bizarre commentary on contemporary society, *The Box Man* concerns a man who relinquishes normal life to live in a "waterproof room," a cardboard box that he wears on his back. Like a medieval Buddhist monk, the man observes society's goings-on but disdains any interaction with the world he has abandoned as a mad place.

Boyd \'bòid\, Martin à Beckett, *pseudonym* Martin Mills \'milz\ (b. June 10, 1893, Lucerne, Switz.—d. June 3, 1972,

Rome, Italy)   Anglo-Australian novelist best known for *The Montforts* (1928), a novel noted for its vigorous and humorous characterizations.

Boyd spent his childhood in Victoria, Australia. He was educated in Melbourne and then traveled to England, where he served during World War I. His first three novels were published under the pen name Martin Mills; thereafter he used his real name. *The Montforts*, his only completely Australian novel, is the saga of several generations of an English family that immigrated to Victoria during pioneer days. *The Picnic* (1937) and *Lucinda Brayford* (1946) portray Australian characters but are set almost entirely in England. He wrote two volumes of memoirs: *A Single Flame* (1939), largely concerned with his youth and war experiences, and the well-received *Day of My Delight* (1965).

Boye \'bȯ-yə\, Karin (Maria) (b. Oct. 26, 1900, Göteborg, Swed.—d. April 24, 1941, Alingsås)   Poet, novelist, and short-story writer who is considered to be one of the leading poets of Swedish modernism.

Boye became a leading figure in the socialist movement inspired by the French novelist Henri Barbusse and cofounded and wrote for *Spektrum*, a review examining psychoanalytical theory and modernist literary views. Her five collections of poems—beginning with *Moln* (1922; "Clouds") and ending with the posthumously published *De sju dödssynderna* (1942; "The Seven Deadly Sins")—show the evolution of her outlook and style from the simple expression of a middle-class girl's dreams and a young radical's eager acceptance of life to bolder images, wider perspectives, and feeling for the problems of humanity. She also wrote a number of short stories and four short novels. Among her novels are *Kris* (1934; "Crisis"), based on her struggle to accept her own lesbianism, and *Kallocain* (1940), which describes the insupportable oppression of a totalitarian society of the future.

Boyle \'bȯil\, Kay (b. Feb. 19, 1902, St. Paul, Minn., U.S.—d. Dec. 27, 1992, Mill Valley, Calif.)   American novelist, poet, essayist, and short-story writer noted for her elegant style.

Boyle studied architecture and music and, after meeting and marrying a French student, moved with him to France in 1923, living there and in England and Austria until returning to the United States in 1941. From 1946 to 1953 she served as a foreign correspondent in France and West Germany for *The New Yorker*. She later taught at several colleges and universities in the United States.

Boyle wrote two award-winning short stories, "The White Horses of Vienna" (1935) and "Defeat" (1941). Among her more notable novels are *Plagued by the Nightingale* (1931), *Monday Night* (1938), and *Generation Without Farewell* (1960). Her major short-story collections include *The White Horses of Vienna and Other Stories* (1936), *The Smoking Mountain: Stories of Postwar Germany* (1951), and *Fifty Stories* (1980). Two critically acclaimed verse collections are *Testament for My Students and Other Poems* (1970) and *This Is Not a Letter and Other Poems* (1985). Boyle's early works center on the conflicts and disappointments that individuals encounter in their search for romantic love. Her later fiction usually deals with the need for an individual's commitment to wider political or social causes as a prerequisite to attaining self-knowledge and fulfillment. *Words That Must Somehow Be Said: Selected Essays of Kay Boyle, 1927–1984*, was published in 1985.

Boylesve \bwȧ-'lev\, René, *pseudonym of* René-Marie-Auguste Tardiveau \tȧr-dē-'vȯ\ (b. April 14, 1867, La Haye-Descartes, Fr.—d. Jan. 14, 1926, Paris)   French novelist noted for his social histories set in the Touraine region of west-central France.

Boylesve was educated in Poitiers, Tours, and Paris. It was under his mother's maiden name that he wrote his first novel, *Le Médecin des dames de Néans* (1894; "The Doctor of the Ladies of Néans"), which anticipated Marcel Proust in style. Other books followed, including the powerful series known as the *romans tourangeaux* ("novels of Touraine")—*Mademoiselle Cloque* (1899), *La Becquée* (1901; *Daily Bread*), *L'Enfant à la balustrade* (1903; *The Child at the Balustrade*), *La Jeune Fille bien élevée* (1909; "The Well Brought-Up Girl"), and others. In these works, notable for their studies of provincial personality and for their richly detailed style, Boylesve utilized a characteristic irony to chronicle the triumph of conventional values over artistic and spiritual aspirations. He was elected to the Académie Française in 1918.

Boz \'bäz\   Pseudonym used by Charles DICKENS for his early stories and essays. In 1833 Dickens began contributing stories and descriptive essays to magazines and newspapers; they attracted favorable attention and were reprinted as *Sketches by "Boz"* (February 1836). Dickens took the pen name of Boz from a corruption of "Moses," the nickname he had bestowed on his youngest brother, Augustus.

Dickens' articles published by the *Morning Chronicle* were signed "Boz." "Boz" was also the pseudonym under which Dickens wrote *The Pickwick Papers*, which was first published serially in 1836–37.

Braak \ter-'bräk\, Menno ter (b. Jan. 26, 1902, Eibergen, Neth.—d. May 14, 1940, The Hague)   Dutch critic whose cutting intellect earned him the title of the "conscience of Dutch literature."

In 1932 ter Braak founded, with Edgar du Perron, the magazine *Forum*, which called for a rejection of contemporary aestheticism (with its emphasis on elegance and form) and a return to sincerity and substance in content. His main literary essay is *Het carnaval der burgers* (1930; "The Carnival of Citizens"). His mistrust of political and religious dogma is especially evident in *Politicus zonder partij* (1934; "Politician Without a Party") and in *Van oude en nieuwe Christenen* (1937; "Concerning Old and New Christians").

Ter Braak's views made him an opponent of Nazism, and when the Germans invaded The Netherlands he committed suicide.

Braaten \'brȯt-en\, Oskar (b. Nov. 25, 1881, Kristiania [now Oslo], Nor.—d. July 17, 1939, Oslo)   Norwegian novelist and dramatist who first brought the life of the factory worker to readers and theatergoers.

Braaten was a journalist, editor, and assistant director of the Norwegian Theater in Oslo. His works depict childhood and youth in the tenement houses of the east side of Oslo, where he grew up. He gained great popular success with the play *Den store barnedåpen* (1925; "The Big Baptism"). His two most widely read novels are *Ulvehiet* (1919; "The Wolf's Lair") and *Matilde* (1920).

Brackenridge \'brak-ən-ˌrij\, Hugh Henry (b. 1748, Kintyre, near Campbeltown, Argyll, Scot.—d. June 25, 1816, Carlisle, Pa., U.S.)   Author of *Modern Chivalry* (1792–1805; final revision, 1819), the first novel portraying frontier life in the United States after the Revolutionary War.

Brackenridge was educated at Princeton, and later he joined George Washington's army as a chaplain. He published two verse dramas on Revolutionary themes, *The Battle of Bunkers-Hill* (1776) and *The Death of General Montgomery at the Siege of Quebec* (1777), and *Six Political Discourses Founded on the Scripture* (1778). In an attempt to promote a national American literature, he established and edited *The United States Magazine* in 1779, but it failed within the year.

Brackenridge became a lawyer and settled in the frontier village of Pittsburgh in 1781, where he helped start *The Pittsburgh Gazette*, the first newspaper in what was then the Far West. After he was elected to the Pennsylvania Assembly in 1786, he obtained funds to found the academy that became the University of Pittsburgh. In 1795 he published *Incidents of the Insurrection in the Western Parts of Pennsylvania in the Year 1794*.

Bracknell, Lady Augusta \'lă-dē-ȯ-'gəs-tə-'brak-,nel\   Fictional character, the mother of Gwendolen Fairfax in Oscar Wilde's THE IMPORTANCE OF BEING EARNEST.

An imposing dowager, Lady Bracknell is the embodiment of upper-class conventional Victorian respectability. She vehemently disapproves of the romance between her daughter Gwendolen and Jack Worthing, the protagonist of the play and a supposed orphan. Several turns in the plot eventually reveal that Jack is the son of Lady Bracknell's late sister and a perfectly acceptable suitor for Gwendolen.

Bradamante \,brä-dä-'män-tä\   Fictional character, a female Christian knight in ORLANDO FURIOSO by Ludovico Ariosto. Her chaotic romance with the Saracen knight Ruggiero is a major element of the plot.

Bradamante is a skilled warrior who survives many dangers in pursuit of her beloved Ruggiero. Even though Ruggiero is baptized a Christian, her parents demand that she marry the noble Leo. She decides to wed whoever withstands her in battle—a challenge that only Ruggiero meets. Their union originates the ancestral line of the Este family, the author's patrons.

Bradbury \'brad-bə-rē, -,ber-ē\, Malcolm (Stanley) (b. Sept. 7, 1932, Sheffield, Eng.)   British novelist and critic who is best known for his satirical first novel, *Eating People Is Wrong* (1959).

Bradbury studied at the universities of Leicester, London, and Manchester. After traveling in the United States on a fellowship, he taught at the University of Hull, then at Birmingham and at East Anglia. His less successful second novel, *Stepping Westward* (1965), leans heavily on his experience on an American university campus.

Beginning with *The History Man* (1975), also an academic novel, Bradbury's works became more technically innovative as well as harsher in tone. His later novels include *Rates of Exchange* (1983), *Why Come to Slaka?* (1986), *Cuts* (1987), and *Doctor Criminale* (1992). Bradbury also wrote several books and essays of criticism and literary history.

Bradbury \'brad-bər-ē, -,ber-ē\, Ray (Douglas) (b. Aug. 22, 1920, Waukegan, Ill., U.S.)   American author best known for highly imaginative science-fiction stories and novels that blend social criticism with an awareness of the hazards of runaway technology.

Bradbury's first book of short stories, *Dark Carnival* (1947), was followed by *The Martian Chronicles* (1950; film, 1966), generally considered a science-fiction classic. Bradbury's other important short-story collections include *The Illustrated Man* (1951), *The Golden Apples of the Sun* (1953), *The October Country* (1955), *A Medicine for Melancholy* (1959), *The Machineries of Joy* (1964), and *I Sing the Body Electric!* (1969). His novels include *Fahrenheit 451* (1953), *Dandelion Wine* (1957), *Something Wicked This Way Comes* (1962), and *Death Is a Lonely Business* (1985). He wrote stage plays and several screenplays, including *Moby Dick* (1956; with John Huston). From the 1970s Bradbury wrote poetry, children's stories, and crime fiction.

Braddon \'brad-ən\, Mary Elizabeth, *married name* Maxwell \'maks-,wel, -wəl\ (b. Oct. 4, 1837, London, Eng.—d. Feb. 4, 1915, Richmond, Surrey)   English novelist whose *Lady Audley's Secret* (1862) was a sensational and financial success.

Braddon produced her first novel, *The Trail of the Serpent*, in 1861. In the same year appeared *Garibaldi and Other Poems*, a volume of spirited verse. In 1862 her reputation as a novelist was made by the success of *Lady Audley's Secret*. A three-volume novel, it told a lurid story of crime in high society.

Braddon published more than 70 novels, among them *Dead Men's Shoes* (1876), *Vixen* (1879), *Asphodel* (1881), *London Pride* (1896), and *The Green Curtain* (1911). Her sons W.B. Maxwell and Gerald Maxwell also became novelists.

Bradford \'brad-fərd\, Roark (Whitney Wickliffe) (b. Aug. 21, 1896, Lauderdale county, Tenn., U.S.—d. Nov. 13, 1948, New Orleans, La.)   American novelist and short-story writer whose works of fiction and folklore were based on his contacts with American blacks.

Bradford had little formal education. He began work as a reporter in 1920 and became reacquainted with the musicians, preachers, and storytellers familiar from his youth on a plantation. These encounters spurred him to write a series of stories for the New York *World*. When collected, the stories became his popular first book, *Ol' Man Adam an' His Chillun* (1928), which consisted of biblical stories as related by unlettered blacks. The stories were adapted by Marc Connelly into the play *Green Pastures*, which won a Pulitzer Prize in 1930. Bradford also wrote novels that showed American blacks in historical perspective, such as *This Side of Jordan* (1929), about the arrival of machines on the plantations.

Bradley \'brad-lē\, A.C., *in full* Andrew Cecil (b. March 26, 1851, Cheltenham, Gloucestershire, Eng.—d. Sept. 2, 1935, London)   Literary critic and preeminent Shakespearean scholar of the late 19th and early 20th centuries.

Bradley attended Oxford University and held professorships at the University of Liverpool, the University of Glasgow, and Oxford. His *Shakespearean Tragedy* (1904), praised not only for its penetrating analysis but also for its lucid prose style, is recognized as a classic of modern Shakespeare criticism. Bradley also published *Oxford Lectures on Poetry* (1909) and *A Miscellany* (1929), in which appears a well-known commentary on Alfred, Lord Tennyson's *In Memoriam*.

Bradstreet \'brad-,strēt\, Anne, *original surname* Dudley \'dəd-lē\ (b. *c.* 1612, Northampton?, Northamptonshire, Eng.—d. Sept. 16, 1672, Andover, Massachusetts Bay Colony [U.S.])   One of the first poets to write English verse in the American colonies. She won critical acceptance in the 20th century, particularly for her sequence of religious poems, "Contemplations," written for her family and not published until the mid-19th century.

Dudley married Simon Bradstreet when she was 16, and two years later they sailed with other Puritans to settle on Massachusetts Bay. She wrote her poems while rearing eight children. Her brother-in-law, without her knowledge, took her poems to England, where they were published as *The Tenth Muse Lately Sprung Up in America* (1650). The first American edition of this work was published in revised and expanded form as *Several Poems Compiled with Great Variety of Wit and Learning* (1678).

Her later poems, written for her family, show her spiritual growth as she came fully to accept the Puritan creed. She also wrote more personal poems about such subjects as her thoughts before childbirth and her response to the death of a grandchild. Her prose works include "Meditations," a collection of succinct and pithy aphorisms.

Braga \'brä-gə\, Rubem (b. Jan. 12, 1913, Cachoeiro de Itapemirim, Braz.)   Brazilian journalist and author, best known for his numerous volumes of *crônica*s, short prose sketches integrating elements of essay and fiction.

Braga worked as a journalist and foreign correspondent and served as Brazilian ambassador to Morocco. In his *crônicas*, he reflected the joy of living and a sense of benevolent humor. His best-known collections include *O conde e o passarinho* (1936; "The Count and the Little Bird"), *O homem rouco* (1949; "The Hoarse Man"), *A borboleta amarela* (1956; "The Yellow Butterfly"), *Ai de Ti, Copacabana!* (1960; "Woe to You, Copacabana!"), *Livro de versos* (1980; "Book of Verses"), and *Crônicas do Espírito Santo* (1984; "Sketches of the Holy Spirit").

Braga \ˈbrä-gə\, Teófilo, *in full* Joaquim Teófilo Fernandes Braga (b. Feb. 24, 1843, Ponta Delgada, Azores, Port.—d. Jan. 28, 1924, Lisbon) Poet, critic, and statesman who was the first to attempt a complete history of Portuguese literature.

Braga wrote profusely on literary, social, historical, and political subjects and produced some verse. He also published several books on Portuguese folklore and collections of early songs and ballads.

Braga's investigations ranged widely over the history of Portuguese literature, but the valuable material he accumulated is often obscured by digressions and theorizings that have lost much of their validity. Among his historical works are *História do Romantismo em Portugal* (1880; "History of Romanticism in Portugal"), *História da literatura portuguesa*, 14 vol. (1869–72; "History of Portuguese Literature"), and studies of the Romantic poetry of the Viscount de Almeida Garrett and of the 18th-century Portuguese poets.

Brahm \ˈbräm\, Otto (b. Feb. 5, 1856, Hamburg [Germany]—d. Nov. 28, 1912, Berlin) German literary critic and man of the theater whose realistic staging exerted considerable influence on 20th-century theater.

In 1889 Brahm helped establish and then directed the theater company Freie Bühne, and in 1890 he founded the periodical of the same name (later *Neue Deutsche Rundschau*); the Freie Bühne was modeled after André Antoine's celebrated naturalistic Théâtre-Libre in Paris.

The Freie Bühne failed after two seasons, but Brahm later directed the Deutsches Theater in Berlin. His productions attempted the exact reproduction of reality and were a stimulus to existing German realism. Brahm's works of criticism consist of a monograph on Heinrich von Kleist, an unfinished book on Friedrich von Schiller and a collection of theatrical criticism published posthumously.

Brahmā \ˈbrä-mä\ One of the major gods of Hinduism during the late Vedic period of India. With the rise of sectarian worship, Brahmā was gradually eclipsed by Vishnu and Śiva. Brahmā (a masculine form not to be confused with Brahman, a neuter noun, which denotes the supreme power, or ultimate reality, of the universe) is associated with the Vedic creator god Prajāpati, whose identity he came to assume. Brahmā is said to have been born from a golden egg and in turn to have created the earth and all things on it. Later sectarian myths describe him as having come forth from a lotus that issued from Vishnu's navel.

In classical times an attempt to synthesize the diverging sectarian traditions is evident in the doctrine of Trimurti, which considers Vishnu, Śiva, and Brahmā as three forms of the supreme, unmanifested deity. By the 7th century, when the Smārtas initiated their worship of five deities, omitting Brahmā, he had lost all claims as a supreme deity. Today there is no cult or sect that exclusively worships Brahmā.

Brāhmaṇa \ˈbrä-mə-nə\ Any of a number of prose commentaries attached to the Vedas, the most ancient Hindu sacred literature.

The Brāhmaṇas belong to the period 900–700 BC, when the sacred hymns were gathered into Saṃhitās ("collections").

They represent a digest of accumulated teachings, illustrated by myth and legend, on various matters of ritual and on hidden meanings of the sacred texts. They are the oldest extant sources for the history of Vedic ritual.

Of the Brāhmaṇas handed down by the followers of the Rigveda (Ṛgveda), two have been preserved: the *Aitareya Brāhmaṇa* and the *Kauṣītaki* (or *Śāṅkhayāna*) *Brāhmaṇa*. Appended to the Brāhmaṇas are chapters written in similar language and style, but with a more philosophic content. These later works, called Āraṇyakas, served as a link between the Brāhmaṇas and the Upanishads. *Compare* ĀRAṆYAKA; UPANISHAD. *See also* VEDA.

Brahmin \ˈbräm-ən\ Member of any of several New England families of aristocratic and cultural pretensions, from which came some of the most distinguished American literati of the 19th century. Originally a humorous reference to the Brahmans, the highest caste of Hindu society, the term came to be applied to a number of prominent New England writers, including Oliver Wendell Holmes, Henry Wadsworth Longfellow, and James Russell Lowell. All three were educated in Europe and became associated with Harvard University.

Assuming the role of arbiters of literary taste, the Brahmins made Boston the literary capital of America in their day. Though they espoused democratic ideals, they remained aesthetically conservative. In an age that brought forth the masterpieces of Ralph Waldo Emerson, Henry David Thoreau, Nathaniel Hawthorne, Herman Melville, Walt Whitman, Edgar Allan Poe, and Mark Twain, they advocated a genteel, rational humanism, quite out of step with their brilliant contemporaries. Nevertheless, the Brahmins exerted the main influence on American literary taste until the 1890s.

Braine \ˈbrān\, John (Gerard) (b. April 13, 1922, Bradford, Yorkshire, Eng.—d. Oct. 28, 1987, London) British novelist, one of the so-called angry young men, whose *Room at the Top* (1957; film, 1958) typified the concerns of a generation of post-World War II British writers.

Braine was working as a librarian when *Room at the Top* appeared. Its protagonist, a young working-class man, marries the daughter of a wealthy businessman. None of Braine's later novels approached it in critical or popular success, although *Waiting for Sheila* (1976) and *Stay with Me Till Morning* (1970) were both adapted for television.

Bramble, Matthew \ˈmath-yü-ˈbram-bəl\ Fictional character, the irritable protagonist of Tobias Smollett's epistolary novel HUMPHRY CLINKER.

Brand \ˈbränd, ˈbrän\ Dramatic poem written in 1866 by Henrik IBSEN. Its central figure is a dynamic rural pastor who undertakes his religious calling with a blazing sincerity that transcends not only all forms of compromise but all traces of human sympathy and warmth as well. Brand's God demands of him all or nothing, and Brand makes that same demand of others. Both moral hero and monster, Brand is torn by the anguish that his moral program demands he inflict on his family. He never hesitates, never stoops to the level of the petty compromisers and spiritual sluggards around him. Yet in the last scene, when Brand stands alone before his God, a thundering voice from on high repudiates Brand's moral stance, and he is crushed in an avalanche. *Brand* is both a denunciation of small-mindedness and a tragedy of the spirit that would transcend it.

Brandes \ˈbrän-dəs\, Georg (Morris Cohen) (b. Feb. 4, 1842, Copenhagen, Den.—d. Feb. 19, 1927, Copenhagen) Danish critic and scholar who, from 1870 through the turn of the century, exerted an enormous influence on the Scandinavian literary world.

In 1871 Brandes began a series of lectures at the University of Copenhagen, published as *Hovedstrømninger i det 19de aarhundredes litteratur*, 6 vol. (1872–90; *Main Currents in 19th Century Literature*), which catalyzed the breakthrough to realism in Danish literature. He called for writers to reject the fantasy and abstract idealism of late Romanticism and instead to work in the service of progressive ideas and the reform of modern society. Brandes befriended and championed such important writers as Bjørnstjerne Bjørnson, Henrik Ibsen, Jens Peter Jacobsen, Jonas Lie, Alexander Kielland, and August Strindberg, and he became a principal leader of the naturalistic movement in Scandinavian literature. Though Brandes gained a following among the Copenhagen liberal intelligentsia, he was strongly opposed by conservative countrymen.

Brandes wrote many scholarly studies illustrating his radical ideas, including monographs on the Danish religious philosopher Søren Kierkegaard, the German socialist leader Ferdinand Lassalle, and the Scandinavian playwright Ludvig Holberg. Notable among his critical works are *Det moderne gjennembruds mænd* (1883; "Men of the Modern Breakthrough"; *i.e.*, his own followers) and *Danske digtere* (1877; "Danish Poets").

Brandes later developed a philosophy of aristocratic radicalism, expressed in *Aristokratisk radikalisme* (1889) and in biographies of William Shakespeare, J.W. von Goethe, Voltaire, Julius Caesar, and Michelangelo. He always remained a controversial figure, never failing to denounce what he saw as tyranny or reaction; such works as *Sagnet om Jesus* (1925; *Jesus, a Myth*) made him many enemies.

Brandon, Colonel \ˈbran-dən\ Fictional character, the calm, quiet, and practical man who falls in love with and eventually wins the love of Marianne Dashwood in Jane Austen's novel SENSE AND SENSIBILITY.

Brandstetter, Dave \ˈdāv-ˈbrand-ˌstet-ər\ Fictional character, the homosexual detective featured in a series of crime novels by Joseph HANSEN. Brandstetter, a middle-aged insurance investigator from Southern California, is a savvy, sympathetic detective whose homosexuality is integral but unobtrusive.

Brandys \ˈbrän-dis\, Kazimierz (b. Oct. 27, 1916, Łódź, Poland, Russian Empire) Polish novelist and essayist.

Brandys' first novel was *Drewniany koń* (1946; "The Wooden Horse"), in which he related the ordeal of the Polish intelligentsia under the Nazi terror. In a more ambitious, four-volume epic novel, *Między wojnami* (1948–53; "Between the Wars"), he described the experiences of a generation of Polish intellectuals before, during, and after World War II.

Brandys began to voice mild criticism of communist ideology in the novellas *Obrona Grenady* (1956; "Defense of Grenada") and *Matka Królów* (1957; "Mother Królów"; *Sons and Comrades*). In his *Listy do Pani Z.*, 3 vol. (1957–61; *Letters to Mrs. Z*), as well as in a volume of short stories, *Romantyczność* (1960; "Romanticism"), he analyzed the moral and psychological transformations of contemporary Poland. Later works include *Wariacje pocztowe* (1972; "The Postal Variations"), *Nierzeczywistość* (1978; *A Question of Reality*), and *Rondo* (1982).

In the late 1970s Brandys helped found the underground journal *Zapis* ("The Record"), in which he published the essays on life in Warsaw that were eventually part of his multivolume series of memoirs entitled *Miesiące* (1980– ; "Months"). Volume one was translated into English as *A Warsaw Diary 1978–1981* (1983) and an abridged version of volume three as *Paris, New York: 1982–1984* (1988).

Brangwen, Gudrun \ˈgŭd-ˌrūn-ˈbraŋ-gwən\ Fictional character, a woman of artistic and modernist temperament in the novel WOMEN IN LOVE by D.H. Lawrence. Her ruinous passion for destructive Gerald Crich is set in contrast with the

richly rewarding relationship between her sister Ursula and Rupert Birkin.

Brangwen, Ursula \ˈər-sə-lə-ˈbraŋ-gwən\ A principal character of two novels, THE RAINBOW and WOMEN IN LOVE, by D.H. Lawrence. In *The Rainbow* Ursula is a schoolteacher who is in love with Anton, the son of a Polish emigré. He proves to be too conventional for Ursula, and at the end of the novel she is alone. In *Women in Love* Ursula's relationship with and eventual marriage to Rupert Birkin is contrasted with her sister Gudrun's destructive love affair with Gerald Crich.

Branner \ˈbrän-ər\, Hans Christian (b. June 23, 1903, Ordrup, near Copenhagen, Den.—d. April 24, 1966, Copenhagen) Leading Danish novelist of the post-World War II period whose themes are the moral and emotional tensions accompanying power and fear.

Branner's collection of short stories, *Om lidt er vi borte* (1939; "In a Little While We Are Gone"), was his first work to attract attention. *Historien om Børge* (1942; *The Story of Börge*) is an account of a child's everyday life, and Branner's interest in psychoanalytic psychology is evident in his short novel *Rytteren* (1949; *The Riding Master*) and his play *Søskende* (1952; *The Judge*). *Two Minutes of Silence* (1966) has the same title as an earlier collection of stories, *To minutters stilhed* (1944), but consists of 16 translated stories selected by Branner before his death.

Brant \ˈbränt\, Sebastian (b. 1458?, Strassburg, Ger. [now Strasbourg, Fr.]—d. May 10, 1521, Strassburg) Satirical poet best known for his DAS NARRENSCHIFF (1494; *The Ship of Fools*), the most famous German literary work of the 15th century.

Brant's writings are varied, encompassing works on law, religion, politics, and, especially, morals. His chief work, however, is *Das Narrenschiff*, a story of fools on a ship bound for a fool's paradise. It ridicules all the vices of the age and is the most famous of the satiric or didactic works in German literature of the period. An immediate success, the work was widely translated and gave rise to a whole school of FOOL'S LITERATURE.

Brantôme \bräⁿ-ˈtōm\, Pierre de, *in full* Pierre de Bourdeille, Abbé et Seigneur de Brantôme (b. *c.* 1540, Périgord, Fr.—d. July 15, 1614, France) Soldier and chronicler, author of a valuable and informative account of his own life and times.

Brantôme's adventurous career as a courtier and soldier took him to Italy, Spain, Portugal, and the British Isles. In later years, a severe incapacity resulting from a fall from a horse provided him with the leisure to write.

Brantôme's works were published posthumously as *Mémoires de Messire Pierre de Bourdeilles* (1665–66; "Memoirs of Pierre de Bourdeille"). Characterized by frankness and naïveté, they consist mainly of accounts of battles or tales of chivalry. Though he is not generally considered a reliable historian, his bold, capricious character well equipped him to be a chronicler of the 16th century.

Brathwait \ˈbrath-ˌwāt\, Richard (b. 1588, Kendal, Westmorland, Eng.—d. May 4, 1673, Catterick, Yorkshire) English poet best known for the lively *Barnabees Journal* (1638), which was written in Latin rhymed verse under the pseudonym Corymbaeus and contained amusing topographical information and unflagging gaiety.

After education at Oxford and Cambridge universities, Brathwait went to London to practice law but instead wrote plays and pastoral poetry of little merit. He later retired to Westmorland as a country gentleman, writing *The English Gentleman* (1630) and *The English Gentlewoman* (1631), books on social conduct of interest to the social historian.

Brathwaite \\'brath-ˌwāt\\, Kamau, *original name* Lawson Edward Brathwaite, *also published as* Edward Brathwaite *and* Edward Kamau Brathwaite (b. May 11, 1930, Bridgetown, Barbados) Barbadian author whose works examine the African and indigenous roots of Caribbean culture.

Brathwaite taught at the University of the West Indies at Kingston, Jamaica. Brathwaite first published his poetry in the 1950s in England and the West Indies. His collections *Rights of Passage* (1967), *Masks* (1968), and *Islands* (1969) brought him international recognition. These volumes, later published together as *The Arrivants* (1973), record a West Indian's search for cultural identity. Another trilogy, including *Mother Poem* (1977), *Sun Poem* (1982), and *X/Self* (1987), also examines the issues of identity. In addition to several collections of poetry, notably *Barabajan Poems, 1492–1992* (1994), Brathwaite produced a number of cultural, historical, and literary studies, among them *Folk Culture of the Slaves in Jamaica* (1970; rev. ed., 1981), *History of the Voice: The Development of Nation Language in Anglophone and Caribbean Poetry* (1984), and *Roots* (1986).

Braun \\'braún\\, Volker (b. May 7, 1939, Dresden, Ger.) Prolific Marxist author whose plays, fiction, and poetry revealed deep divisions in socialist East Germany.

Braun studied at Leipzig University. He then wrote and produced plays for the Berliner Ensemble, Berlin; City Theater, Leipzig; and Deutsches Theater, Berlin. His plays examine the alienation of workers, the threat of political and economic stasis, and the failure of leadership. His characters Kunze and Hinze, a party hack and his chauffeur, occur in the play *Hinze und Kunze* (1972; earlier produced as *Hans Faust*), in the story collection *Berichte von Hinze und Kunze* (1983; "An Account of Hinze and Kunze"), and in the novel *Hinze-Kunze-Roman* (1985; "Hinze-Kunze Novel"). Braun examined the role of women in East German factories in the plays *Tinka* (1975) and *Schmitten* (1981). The early years of the Soviet Union are the subject of his plays *Lenins Tod* (produced 1983; "Lenin's Death") and *T.* (1989).

Brautigan \\'braút-i-gən\\, Richard (Gary) (b. Jan. 30, 1933, Tacoma, Wash., U.S.—d. September?, 1984, Bolinas, Calif.) American writer of pastoral, whimsical, often surreal works popular among 1960s and '70s counterculture readers.

Brautigan's humorous first novel, *A Confederate General from Big Sur*, was published in 1964. His second novel, *Trout Fishing in America* (1967), a commentary on the state of nature in contemporary America, sold two million copies, and its title was adopted as the name of several American communes.

Brautigan's novels feature passive protagonists whose innocence shields them from the moral consequences of their actions. His later novels include *In Watermelon Sugar* (1968), *The Abortion: An Historical Romance, 1966* (1971), *The Hawkline Monster: A Gothic Western* (1974), and *The Tokyo-Montana Express* (1979). Brautigan also published a short-story collection, *Revenge of the Lawn: Stories, 1962–1970* (1971), and several poetry collections before his suicide in 1984.

Brave New World Novel by Aldous HUXLEY, published in 1932. The book presents a nightmarish vision of a future society.

The novel depicts a scientifically balanced, efficiently controlled state that allows for no personal emotions or individual responses; art and beauty are considered disruptive, and *mother* and *father* are forbidden terms (everyone belongs to everyone). Into this world is introduced John the Savage, who was abandoned with his mother in a primitive outpost by a former Director of (human) Hatcheries. John is a thinking, feeling individual who has read William Shakespeare, witnessed primitive

religious rituals, and known loneliness. When his mother dies of an overdose of the brave new world's feel-good drug, John swells a violent revolt. He engages in a dialogue with the World Controller, is harassed as a freak of the accepted social order, and, finally despairing, kills himself.

Brazdžionis \\ˌbräz-'jō-nis\\, Bernardas, *pseudonym* Vytė Nemunėlis \\'vē-tä-ˌnem-ū-'nä-lis\\ (b. Feb. 14, 1907, Stebeikėliai, Lithuania, Russian Empire) Leading Lithuanian poet, editor, critic, and—under his pseudonym—author of popular children's books.

While studying at the University of Kaunas, Brazdžionis showed his originality with a collection of verse entitled *Amžinas žydas* (1931; "The Eternal Jew"). In 1940 he was appointed director of the Maironis Museum of Literature, Kaunas. He moved to the United States in 1949, where he worked as the editor of world literature for *Lietuvių enciklopedija* ("Lithuanian Encyclopedia") and editor of the Lithuanian cultural magazine *Lietuvių dienos* ("Lithuanian Days").

Although the form of Brazdžionis' poetry is largely traditional, his poetic language is not: word order is broken up, words and sounds repeated. Brazdžionis' earlier poetry, written in Lithuania, has biblical themes; after Lithuania lost its independence during World War II, patriotic and humanistic themes became dominant.

Brazdžionis' verse for children is among the best and most popular in Lithuanian literature. He also edited several anthologies of Lithuanian literature.

break \\'brāk\\ **1.** Discontinuity in the flow or tone of a composition. A notable change of subject matter, attitude, or treatment. **2.** A pause or interruption (as a caesura or diaeresis) within or at the end of a verse.

Brecht \\'breḵt\\, Bertolt, *original name* Eugen Berthold Friedrich Brecht (b. Feb. 10, 1898, Augsburg, Ger.—d. Aug. 14, 1956, East Berlin, E.Ger.) German poet, playwright, and theatrical reformer who developed the drama as a social and ideological forum.

Mary Evans Picture Library

Until 1924 Brecht lived in Bavaria, studied medicine, and served in an army hospital. During this period he wrote several works: his first play, *Baal* (produced 1923); his first success, *Trommeln in der Nacht* (produced 1922; *Drums in the Night*); the poems and songs collected as *Hauspostille* (1927; *A Manual of Piety*); and his first professional production, *Leben Eduards des Zweiten von England* (1924; after Christopher Marlowe's *Edward II*; written with L. Feuchtwanger).

In Berlin (1924–33) Brecht worked briefly for the directors Max Reinhardt and Erwin Piscator, but mainly with his own group of associates. With the composer Kurt Weill he wrote the satirical, successful ballad opera *Die Dreigroschenoper* (produced 1928; THE THREEPENNY OPERA; after John Gay's *The Beggar's Opera*) and the opera *Aufstieg und Fall der Stadt Mahagonny* (produced 1930; *Rise and Fall of the City of Mahagonny*; see MAHAGONNY). In these years he developed his theory of EPIC THEATER and an austere form of irregular verse. He also became a Marxist.

In 1933 he went into exile, first in Scandinavia and then in the United States. In Germany his books were burned and his citizenship was withdrawn. Between 1937 and 1941 he wrote most of his great plays, his major theoretical essays and dialogues, and many of the poems collected as *Svendborger Gedichte* (1939). Notable among the plays of these years are *Mutter Courage und ihre Kinder* (produced 1941; MOTHER COURAGE AND HER CHILDREN); *Leben des Galilei* (produced 1943; *The Life of Galileo*); *Der gute Mensch von Sezuan* (produced 1943; THE GOOD WOMAN OF SETZUAN); *Der aufhaltsame Aufstieg des Arturo Ui* (produced 1958; *The Resistible Rise of Arturo Ui*); *Herr Puntila und sein Knecht Matti* (produced 1943; *Herr Puntila and His Man Matti*); and THE CAUCASIAN CHALK CIRCLE (first produced in English, 1948; *Der kaukasische Kreidekreis*).

Brecht left the United States in 1947. He spent a year in Zürich, working mainly on an adaptation of Friedrich Hölderlin's translation of Sophocles' *Antigone* (produced 1948) and on his most important theoretical work, the *Kleines Organon für das Theater* (1949; "A Little Organum for the Theater"). The essence of his theory of drama, as revealed in this work, is the idea that a truly Marxist drama must avoid the Aristotelian premise that the audience should be made to believe that what they are witnessing is happening here and now. Epic theater, as defined by Brecht, is based on detachment, on the *Verfremdungs-Effekt* (alienation, or distancing, effect), which reminds the spectator that what is being presented is a demonstration of human behavior in scientific spirit rather than an illusion of reality.

In 1949 Brecht went to Berlin to help stage *Mutter Courage und ihre Kinder* at Reinhardt's old Deutsches Theater. This led to formation of Brecht's own company, the BERLINER ENSEMBLE, and to his permanent return to Berlin.

Bredero \'brä-də-ˌrō\, Gerbrand Adriaenszoon (b. March 16, 1585, Amsterdam [Neth.]—d. Aug. 23, 1618, Amsterdam)   Poet and playwright who wrote folk songs, farces, and comedies on cosmopolitan Dutch life. The conflict between Bredero's experiences of the medieval, full-blooded life of the backstreets of Amsterdam and the sophistication of the Renaissance intelligentsia is most evident in his earliest poetry, collected in *Groot Liedt-Boeck* (1622; "Great Songbook"). The work contains humorous poems, amorous songs and sonnets, and devotional poetry.

In addition to three tragicomedies based on Spanish romances, Bredero wrote three farces that mark the zenith of this medieval genre: *Klucht van de Koe* (1612; "Farce of the Cow"), *Klucht van den Molenaar* (1613; "Farce of the Miller"), and *Klucht van Symen sonder Soetigheyd* (1612 or 1613; "Farce of Symen Without Kindness"). Day-to-day existence in the burgeoning metropolis of Amsterdam provided material for two comedies: *Het Moortje* (1615; "The Little Moorish Girl") and *Spaanschen Brabander* (1617; "The Spanish Brabanter").

Bregendahl \'brī-ən-ˌdel\, Marie (b. Nov. 6, 1867, Fly, Den.—d. July 22, 1940, Copenhagen)   Danish writer of regional literature who portrayed the life of the inhabitants of rural areas with sympathy and a deep understanding. Bregendahl's father was a farmer in the Viborg district, and she lived most of her life in that area, making it the milieu of her books. She started to write rather late in life, publishing her first stories in 1902. Her best-known novel is *En dødsnat* (1912; *A Night of Death*). *Billeder af Sødalsfolkenes liv*, 8 vol. (1914–23; "Pictures from the Life of the People of Sodal"), however, is considered her main contribution to Danish literature.

Breitinger \'brī-tiŋ-ər\, Johann Jakob (b. March 1, 1701, Zürich, Switz.—d. Dec. 13, 1776, Zürich)   Swiss-German writer, one of the most influential 18th-century literary critics in the German-speaking world.

Breitinger studied theology and became professor at the Collegium Carolinum, lecturing on Hebrew, Greek, Latin, logic, and rhetoric. Under the inspiration of *The Spectator* papers of

England's Joseph Addison and Richard Steele, he also founded and wrote essays for the weekly *Discourse*. The most important of his many publications was the *Critische Dichtkunst* (1740), in which he attacked the narrowly rationalist poetic theory of Johann Christoph Gottsched. Breitinger stressed the place of the imagination in poetry; fired the German-speaking public with enthusiasm for Homer; and spread the ideas of John Locke, Lord Shaftesbury, and Alexander Pope. He was visited by J.W. von Goethe, and his pupils included the writer Johann Kaspar Lavater and the writer and educator Johann Heinrich Pestalozzi.

Bremer \'brä-mer\, Fredrika (b. Aug. 17, 1801, Åbo, Swedish Finland [now Turku, Fin.]—d. Dec. 31, 1865, Årsta, near Stockholm, Swed.)   Writer, reformer, and champion of women's rights who introduced the domestic novel into Swedish literature.

Bremer's private means enabled her to devote her life to social work, travel, and writing. Her quiet domestic novels, such as *Familjen H.* (1831; *The H——— Family*), *Grannarna* (1837; *The Neighbours*), and *Hemmet* (1839; *The Home*), were popular at home and abroad. Bremer visited the United States, where she was welcomed in New England as a kindred spirit for her antislavery sentiments. She met Ralph Waldo Emerson, Henry Wadsworth Longfellow, and Nathaniel Hawthorne and wrote about her impressions in *Hemmen i den nya verlden*, 3 vol. (1853–54; *The Homes of the New World, America of the Fifties*). The later novels *Hertha* (1856) and *Fader och dotter* (1858; *Father and Daughter*) deal with the social effects of the assertion of women's rights.

Bremer Beiträger \'brä-mər-'bī-ˌtreg-ər\   Group of mid-18th-century German writers, among them Johann Elias Schlegel, who objected to the restrictive, Neoclassical principles laid down in 1730 by Johann Christoph Gottsched, according to which "good" literature was to be produced and judged. They demanded room for the play of genius and inspiration. Their organ was the *Bremer Beiträge* (1745–48).

Brennan \'bren-ən\, Christopher (John) (b. Nov. 1, 1870, Sydney, Australia—d. Oct. 5, 1932, Sydney)   Poet and scholar whose highly personal verse was never popular with the Australian public but was highly regarded by critics for its vitality and sincerity.

Brennan was educated in the classics at the University of Sydney. His verse shows the influence of Greek and Latin poets. While in Germany on a traveling scholarship, he became interested in the Symbolists. He later taught at the University of Sydney for several years.

In 1897 *XXI Poems: Towards the Source* was published in an edition of only 200 copies. *Poems* (1914) was followed by *A Chant of Doom* (1915). A collected edition of his poetry appeared in 1958.

Brentano \bren-'tä-nō\, Clemens (b. Sept. 9, 1778, Ehrenbreitstein, near Koblenz [Germany]—d. July 28, 1842, Aschaffenburg, Bavaria)   Poet, novelist, and dramatist, one of the founders of the Heidelberg Romantic school, which emphasized German folklore and history.

As a student in Jena, Brentano became acquainted with Friedrich von Schlegel and Ludwig Tieck, the leaders of the earlier phase of Romanticism. Giving up his studies, he traveled throughout Germany. In Heidelberg he met Achim von Arnim, with whom he published the collection of German folk songs DES KNABEN WUNDERHORN (1805–08), which became an important inspiration to later German lyric poets.

Among Brentano's most successful works are his fairy tales, particularly *Gockel, Hinkel and Gackeleia* (1838). His well-known "Geschichte vom braven Kasperl und dem schönen

Annerl" (1817; "The Story of the Just Casper and Fair Annie") is a brilliantly executed short story in which themes from German folklore are used. His other major works include the dramas *Ponce de Leon* (1801) and *Die Gründung Prags* (1815; "The Foundation of Prague") and the novel *Godwi* (1801–02).

Clemens Brentano; detail of an etching by Ludwig Grimm, 1837
Staatsbibliothek, Berlin

Brer Rabbit \'brə-'rab-ət, 'brər-, 'brer-\ Trickster figure originating in African folklore and transmitted by African slaves to America. Brer, or Brother, Rabbit was popularized in the United States in the stories of Joel Chandler Harris (1848–1908). The character's adventures embody an idea considered to be a universal creation among oppressed peoples—that a small, weak, but ingenious force can overcome a larger, stronger, but dull-witted power. Brer Rabbit continually outsmarts his bigger animal associates, Brer Fox, Brer Wolf, and Brer Bear. *See also* TRICKSTER TALE.

Breton \brə-'tō^n\, André (b. Feb. 18, 1896, Tinchebray, Fr.—d. Sept. 28, 1966, Paris) French poet, essayist, critic, and editor, chief promoter and one of the founders of the Surrealist movement.

Influenced by psychiatry and Symbolist poetry, Breton joined the Dadaists and cofounded the review *Littérature*; in its pages appeared "Les Champs magnétiques" (1920; "Magnetic Fields"), the first example of the Surrealist technique of automatic writing. In 1924, Breton's *Manifeste du surréalisme* provided a definition of SURREALISM. His own novels, which explore mental disorders and dreams, included *Nadja* (1928), *L'Immaculée Conception* (1930), *Les Vases communicants* (1932; "The Communicating Vessels"), and *L'Amour fou* (1937; "Mad Love"). Breton also wrote theoretical and critical works, including *Les Pas perdus* (1924; "The Lost Steps"), *Légitime Défense* (1926; "Legitimate Defense"), *Le Surréalisme et le peinture* (1926; "Surrealism and Painting"), *Qu'est-ce que le surréalisme?* (1934; *What is Surrealism?*), and *La Clé des champs* (1953; "The Key to the Fields").

In the 1930s Breton joined the French Communist Party. He later broke with the party but remained committed to Marxism. With Leon Trotsky in Mexico he founded the Fédération de l'Art Revolutionnaire Independant in 1938. During the German occupation of France, Breton escaped to the United States. In 1946 Breton returned to France. His *Poèmes* appeared in 1948 and *Selected Poems* in 1969.

Breton \'bret-ən\, Nicholas (b. 1553?—d. 1625?) Prolific English writer of religious and pastoral poems, satires, dialogues, and essays.

At the end of the 16th century Breton was accounted one of the best lyrical poets, but he outlived his reputation. His satires are rather mild and general; more successful are the descriptions of simple country pleasures, whether in the pastoral poetry of *The Passionate Shepheard* (1604) or in the prose descriptions of the months and the hours in his *Fantasticks* (1604?). Breton also wrote two character books, *The Good and the Badde* (1616) and *Characters Upon Essaies* (1615), which contain brief sketches describing a dominant virtue or vice.

Bretón de los Herreros \brā-'tōn-dā-lōs-er-'rer-ōs\, Manuel (b. Dec. 19, 1796, Quel, Spain—d. Nov. 8, 1873, Madrid) Spanish poet and one of the most important and prolific comic playwrights of his era.

Bretón de los Herreros served in the army from 1812 to 1822. He held various governmental positions throughout his life and was director of the national library from 1847. *A la vejez, viruelas* ("In Old Age, Chickenpox"), his first play, was produced in 1824 and brought him immediate success. Of the almost 180 plays he produced during his lifetime, including translations from French and German playwrights and adaptations of earlier Spanish dramatists, he is chiefly noted for his comedies, mostly written in verse, dealing with the day-to-day life of the Spanish middle class.

Breton lay \'bret-ən\ *Middle English* lai Breton.   A short medieval French narrative poem usually based upon Celtic legends.

The form is so called because Breton professional storytellers supposedly recited similar poems, though none are extant. The Breton lay is typically a short, rhymed romance recounting a love story; it includes supernatural, mythological, chivalric, and fairy-tale elements. Derived from the late 12th-century French lays of Marie de France, it was adapted into English in the late 13th century and became very popular. The few extant English Breton lays include *Sir Gowther* (*c.* 1400); the incomplete, early 14th-century *Lai le Freine*; *Sir Orfeo*, a recasting of the Orpheus and Eurydice story; the 14th-century *Sir Launfal*, or *Launfalus Miles*, by Thomas Chestre; *Sir Emare*, of the late 14th or early 15th century, on the theme of the constant wife; and the 15th-century *Sir Landeval*. Some of Geoffrey Chaucer's *Canterbury Tales* are derived from Breton lays. *See also* LAY.

brevis brevians \'brev-is-'brev-ē-ˌanz\ [New Latin, literally, short (syllable) shortening (the following syllable)]   In classical prosody, especially that of Latin comedy, the tendency to make a long syllable short when it follows a short syllable and is adjacent to an accented syllable.

brevis in longo \'brev-is-in-'lŏŋ-gō\ [New Latin, short for *syllaba brevis in elemento longo* short syllable in a long element]   In classical prosody, the presence of a short syllable in the final position in a line of verse where there is normally a long syllable.

brevity \'brev-i-tē\   A short piece (as of writing, music).

Breytenbach \'breit-ən-ˌbäḵ, *Angl* 'brīt-, -ˌbäk\, Breyten, *pseudonym* Jan Blom \'blŏm\ (b. Sept. 16, 1939, Bonnievale, S.Af.)   Exiled South African writer who was a leading Afrikaner poet and critic of apartheid.

Breytenbach attended the University of Cape Town but left school at age 20 for travel in Europe. In 1961 he settled in Paris. His first book of poetry, *Die ysterkoei moet sweet* ("The Iron Cow Must Sweat"), and a book of prose pieces, *Katastrofes*, were published in 1964. Several books of poetry followed, and they were highly acclaimed in South Africa. On a return visit to South Africa in 1975 Breytenbach was arrested as a terrorist and jailed for seven years. While incarcerated, he continued to write; *'n Seisoen in die Paradys* (*A Season in Paradise*) was published in 1976, and *Mouroir: Bespieelende notas van 'n roman* (*Mouroir: Mirrornotes of a Novel*) in 1983. In 1982 Breytenbach was freed and allowed to leave South Africa. *The True Confessions of an Albino Terrorist* (1984), his account of his arrest and detention, cemented his international reputation.

Březina \'brzhez-ē-nə\, Otakar, *pseudonym of* Václav Jebavý \'yä-bá-vē\ (b. Sept. 13, 1868, Počátky, Bohemia, Austria-Hungary [now in Czech Republic]—d. March 25, 1929, Jaroměřice, Czech.)   Poet who had a considerable influence on the development of 20th-century Czech poetry.

Březina spent most of his life as a schoolmaster in Moravia, isolated from the political and literary movements that influenced the work of many of his contemporaries. His lasting poetical achievement is contained in a lyrical cycle of five books: *Tajemné dálky* (1895; "The Mysterious Distances"), *Svítání na západě* (1896; "Dawn in the West"), *Větry od pólů* (1897; "Polar Winds"), *Stavitelé chrámu* (1899; "Builders of the Temple"), and *Ruce* (1901; "Hands"). Earlier poems, written under a different pseudonym, are of less account.

Briareus \brī-'ar-ē-əs\ In Greek mythology, one of three 100-armed, 50-headed Hecatoncheires (from the Greek words for "hundred" and "hands"), the sons of the deities Uranus and Gaea. The gods called him Briareus; mortals called him Aegaeon. According to one legend, Briareus and his brothers successfully aided Zeus against the attack by the Titans. Another account made Briareus an opponent of Zeus and one of the assailants of Olympus. According to that account, after Briareus was defeated he was buried under Mount Etna. Still another tradition made him a giant of the sea, an enemy of Poseidon, and the inventor of warships.

Bricriu's Feast \'brik-,rüz-'fēst\ *Middle Irish* Fled Bricrenn \'flā-'brik-rən\ In early Irish literature, a comic, rowdy account of rivalry among Ulster warriors. One of the longest hero tales of the ULSTER CYCLE, it dates from the 8th century and is preserved in *The Book of the Dun Cow* (*c.* 1100). Bricriu, the trickster, promises the hero's portion of his feast to three different champions, Lóegaire Buadach, Conall Cernach, and Cú Chulainn. A violent dispute over precedence ensues, which leads to a series of contests. One night a giant carrying an ax challenges the knights of Ulster to behead him in exchange for a chance to behead them in turn. On successive nights, Conall and Lóegaire behead the giant, who each time replaces his head and leaves but comes back to take his turn only to find that the warriors have departed. At last Cú Chulainn beheads the giant and, when the giant returns, places his own head on the block, true to his bargain. The giant, really the wizard Cú Roi in disguise, proclaims Cú Chulainn the first hero of Ulster.

Bride Comes to Yellow Sky, The Short story by Stephen CRANE, published in *The Open Boat and Other Stories* in London and a smaller collection, *The Open Boat and Other Tales of Adventure*, in New York in 1898.

Set at the end of the 19th century in a town called Yellow Sky, the story concerns the marshal, Jack Potter, and his unnamed bride and the effect their marriage has on the town. The drunken, belligerent Scratchy Wilson, a cowboy who represents the Old West, tries to effect a showdown with Jack, his nemesis. When Jack refuses to fight, responding to the cowpoke's taunts with "I'm married," Scratchy leaves without fighting, bewildered that the old rules have changed.

Bridel \brē-'del\, Philippe-Sirice (b. Nov. 20, 1757, Begnins, Switz.—d. May 20, 1845, Montreux) Man of letters, known as *le doyen* Bridel, who encouraged the development of an indigenous Swiss literature and helped to bring French-speaking and German-speaking Swiss together in politics as well as in literature and science.

While serving as a pastor at Basel, Château-d'Oex, and Montreux, Bridel devoted most of his attention to literature, linguistics, natural science, and Swiss history. His poetry is less important than his philological work, *Glossaire du patois de la Suisse romande* (posthumously published, 1866; "Glossary of the Patois of French Switzerland"), and two series of his miscellaneous writings: *Étrennes helvétiennes* (1783–87; "Helvetic Gifts") and *Conservateur suisse* (1813–31; "Swiss Conservator").

Bride of the Innisfallen, The \'in-is-,fäl-ən\ Collection of short stories by Eudora WELTY, published in 1955. The seven stories, focused largely on female characters, elaborate upon tenuous relationships of the heart in a difficult world and upon the importance of place; they share a more experimental, allusive style than the rest of her work.

Brideshead Revisited \'brīdz-,hed\ Satirical novel by Evelyn WAUGH, published in 1945. According to Waugh, a convert to Roman Catholicism, the novel was intended to show "the operation of divine grace" in the affairs of a particular group of people. This is revealed through the story of the wealthy Roman Catholic Marchmain family as told by Charles Ryder, a friend of the family. Despite the seeming indifference to, or outright repudiation of, the church by various members of the family, particularly Lord Marchmain, his daughter Julia, and his son Sebastian, by the end of the novel each has shown some sign of acceptance of the faith.

bridge \'brij\ A passage, section, or scene in a literary or dramatic work serving as a transition between two other more significant passages, sections, or scenes.

Bridge of San Luis Rey, The \,sän-lü-,ēs-'rā\ Pulitzer prize-winning novel by Thornton WILDER, published in 1927. Wilder's career was established with this book, in which he first made use of historical subject matter as a background for his interwoven themes of the search for justice, the possibility of altruism, and the role of Christianity in human relationships.

The plot centers on five travelers in 18th-century Peru who are killed when a bridge across a canyon collapses; a priest interprets the story of each victim in an attempt to explain the workings of divine providence.

Bridges \'brij-əz\, Robert (Seymour) (b. Oct. 23, 1844, Walmer, Kent, Eng.—d. April 21, 1930, Boar's Hill, Oxford) English poet noted for his technical mastery of prosody and for his sponsorship of the poetry of his friend Gerard Manley Hopkins.

Bridges attended Eton College and then Oxford, where he met Hopkins. His edition of Hopkins' poetry that appeared in 1916 rescued it from obscurity.

Although Bridges published several long poems and poetic dramas, his reputation rests upon the lyrics collected in *Shorter Poems* (1890, 1894). *New Verse* (1925) contains experiments using a meter based on syllables rather than accents. He used this form for the long philosophical poem *The Testament of Beauty*, published on his 85th birthday. Bridges was poet laureate from 1913 until his death.

Bridie \'brī-dē\, James, *pseudonym of* Osborne Henry Mavor \'māv-ər\ (b. Jan. 3, 1888, Glasgow, Scot.—d. Jan. 29, 1951, Edinburgh) Playwright whose popular, witty comedies were significant in the revival of the Scottish drama during the 1930s.

Bridie's first play, *The Sunlight Sonata* (1928), written under the pseudonym of Mary Henderson, was staged by the Scottish National Players. Three years later he achieved success with his London production of *The Anatomist* (1931), based on a well-known criminal case. Considered distinctively Scottish in their unexpected twists of fancy and thought-provoking content, his plays include *Jonah and the Whale* (1932); *A Sleeping Clergyman* (1933); *Marriage Is No Joke* (1934); *Colonel Wotherspoon* (1934); *The King of Nowhere* (1938); *One Way of Living* (1939), an autobiographical drama; *Mr. Bolfry* (1943); *Dr. Angelus* (1947); and *The Queen's Comedy* (1950).

Briefroman \'brēf-rō-,män\ [German, literally, letter novel] An epistolary novel, in which the text consists solely of letters written by one or more of the characters. Examples include J.W. von Goethe's *Die Leiden des jungen Werthers* (1774) and

Sophie von La Roche's *Geschichte des Fräuleins von Sternheim* (1771). *See* EPISTOLARY NOVEL.

Brieux \brē-'œ̄\, Eugène (b. Jan. 19, 1858, Paris, Fr.—d. Dec. 6, 1932, Nice) French dramatist and one of the leading exponents of the realistic drama, whose somewhat didactic works attacked the social evils of his day. Brieux's works formed part of the repertory of the famed Théâtre-Libre of André Antoine, which had a far-reaching effect on the spread of the new naturalistic style. Brieux was hailed by critics in his day, but his reputation has since declined. His principal works were *Blanchette* (1892), the story of a peasant girl educated above her station, and *La Robe rouge* (1900; *The Red Robe*), an attack on the magistracy. In 1901 he caused a scandal by tackling the subject of venereal disease in *Les Avariés* (*Damaged Goods*).

Brighella \brē-'gäl-lä\ Stock character of the Italian COMMEDIA DELL'ARTE; a roguish, quick-witted, opportunistic, and sometimes lascivious and cruel figure. Originally one of the comic servants, or zanni, of the commedia, Brighella was a jack-of-all-trades whose loyalty as a soldier, hangman's varlet, assassin, or gentleman's valet could be easily bought. Because of his somewhat sentimental view of love, though, the young lovers could trust him.

In the 16th and 17th centuries the role of Brighella was gradually reduced to that of an unreliable valet. By the 18th century he was scarcely more than a flunky dressed in the livery of the period and locale.

Brighton Rock \'brīt-ən\ Novel of sin and redemption by Graham GREENE, published in 1938.

The novel presents the story of Pinkie Brown, a chilling, utterly evil 17-year-old gang leader who marries the plodding Rose in order to insure her silence about his crimes. Both Pinkie and Rose were reared as Roman Catholics, and that background continues to inform their thoughts, if not their actions. In the end Pinkie dies while attempting to kill Rose; later, a priest tells Rose that her love for Pinkie may have saved her, as the mercy of God may have saved Pinkie.

Brink \'briŋk\, André Philippus (b. May 29, 1935, Vrede, S.Af.) Writer whose novels often criticized the South African government.

Brink was one of a new generation of Afrikaans writers known as the Sestigers ("Sixtyers," or writers of the 1960s), whose declared aim was "to broaden the rather too parochial limits of Afrikaner fiction." His early novels *Lobola vir die lewe* (1962; "The Price of Living") and *Die Ambassadeur* (1963; *The Ambassador*) were essentially apolitical, but his novels increasingly presented evidence of the disintegration of human values that occurs under apartheid. *Kennis van die aand* (1973; *Looking on Darkness*), *'N Oomblik in die wind* (1975; *An Instant in the Wind*), and *Rumours of Rain* (1978) used the sexual relationship between a black man and a white woman to show the destructiveness of racial hatred. His later works include *A Dry White Season* (1979), in which a white liberal investigates the death of a black activist in police custody; *A Chain of Voices* (1982); *States of Emergency* (1988); and *An Act of Terror* (1991). Brink's works were well received abroad, but some were banned in South Africa.

Brink \ten-'briŋk\, Bernhard ten (b. Jan. 12, 1841, Amsterdam, Neth.—d. Jan. 29, 1892, Strassburg, Ger. [now Strasbourg, Fr.]) Scholar whose research stimulated a revival of British and German study of Geoffrey Chaucer's works.

Brink taught at the University of Marburg and was professor of English at the University of Strassburg. Besides his critical editions of the *Prologue* to the *Canterbury Tales* and the *Compleynte to Pité*, he published *Chaucer: Studien zur Geschichte*

seiner Entwicklung und zur Chronologie seiner Schriften (1870; "Chaucer: Studies in the History of His Development and on the Chronology of His Writings") and *Chaucers Sprache und Verskunst* (1884; *The Language and Metre of Chaucer*). His *Beowulf-Untersuchungen* (1888; "Beowulf Researches") was an important contribution to Anglo-Saxon studies. His best-known work was *Geschichte der englischen Literatur*, 2 vol. (1877–93; *History of English Literature*).

Brinker, Hans \'häns-'briŋ-kər\ Title character of Mary Mapes Dodge's HANS BRINKER.

Brinnin \'brin-in\, John Malcolm (b. Sept. 13, 1916, Halifax, N.S., Can.) American poet, editor, and social historian, also known for his biographies of other poets.

Brinnin's first volume of poetry, *The Garden Is Political* (1942), was highly praised. Subsequent collections, which increasingly displayed his interest in and experiments with form, included *The Lincoln Lyrics* (1942), *No Arch, No Triumph* (1945), *The Sorrows of Cold Stone: Poems 1940–1950* (1951), and *Skin Diving in the Virgins* (1970); his *Selected Poems* was published in 1963.

Brinnin accompanied Dylan Thomas on his tours of America in the early 1950s, and after Thomas' death he wrote *Dylan Thomas in America* (1955). He also wrote *William Carlos Williams* (1963), the memoirs collected in *Sextet: T.S. Eliot & Truman Capote & Others* (1981), and *Truman Capote* (1986). Among the books he edited were three anthologies of 20th-century American and British poetry. Brinnin also wrote three histories of North Atlantic steamships.

Briscoe, Lily \'lil-ē-'bris-kō\ Fictional character, a painter in the novel TO THE LIGHTHOUSE by Virginia Woolf. She represents Woolf's ideal artist, who mingles "masculine" rationality with "feminine" sympathy.

Briseis \brī-'sē-is\ Fictional character, the slave-concubine of Achilles in the *Iliad*, the epic poem on the Trojan War attributed to the ancient Greek poet Homer. The Greek chieftain Agamemnon, forced to return his war prize Chryseis to her father, retaliates by appropriating Briseis. This action precipitates the feud between Achilles and Agamemnon that occupies a large part of the story of the *Iliad*.

Britannicus \brē-tä-nē-'kūes\ A tragedy in verse in five acts by Jean RACINE, performed in French in 1669 and published the following year.

The play, a political drama, is set in imperial Rome. It centers upon the machinations of the emperor Nero, who, though he has been placed on the throne by his mother Agrippina (Agrippine), fears his half brother Britannicus as a rival for the throne.

Britannicus is considered to be one of Racine's noble tragedies. Its plot is said to have been derived from the writings of the Roman historian Tacitus.

British Theatre Association *formerly* (until 1973) British Drama League. Organization created in 1919 for the encouragement of the art of the theater, both for its own sake and as a means of intelligent recreation among all classes of the community. The work of the association has been mainly among amateur groups though its members have also urged the establishment of a national theater policy. Its library is one of the principal theatrical collections of the world. The journal *Drama* was founded by the association in July 1919.

Britomartis \,brit-ō-'mär-tis\ Cretan goddess sometimes identified with the Greek Artemis. According to legend, Britomartis was a daughter of Zeus and lived in Crete; she was a huntress and a virgin. Minos, king of Crete, fell in love with her and pursued her for nine months until she, in desperation, leapt from a high cliff into the sea. She was caught in fishermen's nets and hauled to safety. For her chastity she was rewarded by Artemis with immortality.

broadside \'bròd-ˌsīd\ 1. A sizable sheet of paper printed usually on one side only. 2. Something (especially a broadside ballad) printed on a broadside usually for general sale or distribution.

broadside ballad A descriptive or narrative verse or song, commonly in a simple ballad form, on a popular theme, and sung or recited in public places or printed on broadsides for sale in the streets.

Broadside ballads appeared shortly after the invention of printing in the 15th century and were hawked in the streets, fairs, and marketplaces of Europe into the 19th century. Typical broadsides included hack-written topical ballads on recent crimes, executions, or disasters. Many ballads passed into the oral tradition from broadside origins. Although older texts were often "beautified" by the addition of flowery, sentimental, or moralizing language, broadsides also preserved versions of traditional ballads that might otherwise have disappeared from popular tradition. *See also* GOOD-NIGHT.

Brobdingnag \'bräb-diŋ-ˌnag\ An imaginary country created by Jonathan Swift in GULLIVER'S TRAVELS. The people of Brobdingnag were giants.

Broch \'bròk\, Hermann (b. Nov. 1, 1886, Vienna, Austria-Hungary—d. May 30, 1951, New Haven, Conn., U.S.) German writer who achieved international recognition for his multidimensional novels, in which he used innovative literary techniques to present a wide range of human experience.

Broch's first major work was the trilogy *Die Schlafwandler* (1931–32; THE SLEEPWALKERS), which traces the disintegration of European society between 1888 and 1918. Paralleling the historical process, the novel moves from a subtle parody of 19th-century realism through expressionism to a juxtaposition of many different forms, including poetry, drama, narrative, and essay. *Der Versucher* (1953; THE SPELL) exemplifies Broch's theory of mass hysteria in the portrayal of a Hitlerian stranger's domination of a mountain village.

One of Broch's later works, *Der Tod des Vergil* (1945; THE DEATH OF VIRGIL), presents the last 18 hours of Virgil's life, in which he reflects on his times—an age of transition that Broch considered similar to his own. His other works include *Die unbekannte Grösse* (1933; *The Unknown Quantity*), *Die Schuldlosen* (1950; "The Innocents"), and numerous essays, letters, and reviews.

Brockes \'bròk-əs\, Barthold Heinrich (b. Sept. 22, 1680, Hamburg [Germany]—d. Jan. 16, 1747, Ritzebüttel, Hanover) Poet whose works were among the most popular and influential expressions of the early Enlightenment in Germany.

Brockes was a member of the Hamburg senate and a magistrate in Ritzebüttel. Influenced by the 18th-century British poets James Thomson and Alexander Pope, whose works he translated, he wrote poetry, such as *Irdisches Vergnügen in Gott* (1721–48; "Earthly Pleasure in God"), in which natural phenomena are seen as aspects of God's perfectly ordered universe. One of the first modern poets to treat nature as a principal subject, he was the forerunner of the new poetic attitude toward nature in German literature that culminated in the works of Heinrich von Kleist and the Swiss anatomist and physiologist Albrecht von Haller.

Brod \'bròt\, Max (b. May 27, 1884, Prague, Bohemia, Austria-Hungary [now in Czech Republic]—d. Dec. 20, 1968, Tel Aviv, Israel) Czech-born, German-language novelist and essayist known primarily as the editor of the major works of Franz KAFKA.

Brod studied law at the University of Prague, and in 1902 he met Kafka and formed a friendship with him that was to last until Kafka's death. Kafka had instructed Brod to destroy his unpublished manuscripts after his death, but Brod instead edited and published the materials in the 1930s. Of Brod's own numerous novels, which blend fantasy, mysticism, and eroticism, his most famous work is a historical novel, *Tycho Brahes Weg zu Gott* (1916; *The Redemption of Tycho Brahe*). Brod also wrote essays on modern Zionism. In addition, he wrote *Franz Kafka, eine Biographie* (1937; *Franz Kafka: A Biography*) and also edited Kafka's diaries and letters.

Brodkey \'bräd-kē\, Harold (Roy), *original surname* Weintraub \'wīn-ˌtròb\ (b. Oct. 25, 1930, Staunton, Ill., U.S.) American novelist and short-story writer whose near-autobiographical fiction avoids plot, instead concentrating upon careful, close description of feeling.

Brodkey attended Harvard University and soon began publishing short stories in magazines. His first collection, *First Love and Other Sorrows* (1957), contained stories of youthful romance and marriage, using incidents from his own life. It was about this time that he began writing an autobiographical novel which was to occupy him for most of the next 30 years. The novel, *The Runaway Soul*, was finally published in 1991 to mixed reviews. Excerpts from it were published earlier as *Women and Angels* (1985). Wiley Silenowicz, the protagonist of *The Runaway Soul*, is also featured in 12 of the 18 tales in *Stories in an Almost Classical Mode* (1988).

Brodsky \'bròd-skē, *Angl* 'bròd-skē, 'bräd-\, Joseph, *original name* Iosip Aleksandrovich Brodsky (b. May 24, 1940, Leningrad [now St. Petersburg], Russia, U.S.S.R.) Russian-born poet who was awarded the Nobel Prize for Literature in 1987 for his lyric and elegiac poems.

Brodsky's early poetry had begun to earn him a reputation in the Leningrad literary scene when his independent spirit and his irregular work record led to his being sentenced to five years of hard labor for "social parasitism." The sentence was commuted in 1965 after prominent Soviet literary figures protested. Exiled from the Soviet Union in 1972, Brodsky lived thereafter in the United States. He was a poet-in-residence and visiting professor at several universities. He served as poet laureate of the United States in 1991–92.

Brodsky's poetry treats in a powerful, meditative fashion the universal concerns of life, death, and the meaning of existence. His earlier works include *Stikhotvoreniya i poemy* (1965; "Verses and Poems") and *Ostanovka v pustyne* (1970; "A Halt in the Wasteland"); these and other works were translated by George L. Kline in *Selected Poems* (1973). His important later works include the poetry collections *A Part of Speech* (1980), *History of the Twentieth Century* (1986), and *To Urania* (1988) and the essays collected in *Less Than One* (1986).

broken-backed line A line truncated in the middle. The term is used especially of John Lydgate's poetry, many lines of which have nine syllables and appear to lack an unstressed syllable at the medial break or caesura.

broken rhyme 1. Rhyme in which one of the rhyming elements is actually two words (*i.e.*, "gutteral" with "sputter all"). 2. Rhyme involving division of a word by the break between two lines in order to end a line with a rhyme provided by the first part of the word, as in the second stanza of Gerard Manley Hopkins's untitled poem that begins "No worst, there is none. Pitched past pitch of grief":

> My cries heave, herds-long; huddle in a main, a chief-
> woe, world-sorrow; on an age-old anvil wince and sing—
> Then lull, then leave off. Fury had shrieked 'No lingering! Let me be fell: force I must be brief'.

Brome \\'brüm, 'brōm\\, Alexander (b. 1620—d. June 30, 1666, London, Eng.)   Royalist poet who wrote drinking songs and satirical verses against the Rump Parliament in England. (The Rump is the name historians have given to what remained of the Long Parliament following the expulsion of two-thirds of its members in 1648.) Brome was also the author of a comedy, *The Cunning Lovers* (1654), and edited two volumes of plays by Richard Brome (no relation) and a translation of Horace. His *Songs and Other Poems* (1661), the work for which he was most noted, was a collection of songs, ballads, epistles, elegies, and epitaphs.

Brome \\'brüm, 'brōm\\, Richard (d. *c.* 1652)   English dramatist generally deemed the most considerable of the minor Jacobean playwrights.

He was originally Ben Jonson's servant and probably acted as his secretary. The relationship developed into friendship, and Jonson wrote a sonnet to Brome which was prefixed to Brome's *Northern Lasse* (published 1632).

Filled with pictures of contemporary London and its life, Brome's comedies are of historical value and interest. *The Northern Lasse* made his reputation as a dramatist and was the most popular of his plays, although the later play *A Jovial Crew* (1652) is considered to be his best work.

Bromfield \\'bräm-,fēld\\, Louis (b. Dec. 27, 1896, Mansfield, Ohio, U.S.—d. March 18, 1956, Columbus, Ohio)   American novelist and essayist.

Bromfield was decorated for his service in the French army, which he joined at the outbreak of World War I. He went on to serve as a critic for several periodicals, including the *Bookman* and *Time* magazine. In 1923 he moved to France and began to concentrate on writing fiction. During these expatriate years, he produced his most highly acclaimed novels, including *The Green Bay Tree* (1924), *Possession* (1925), *Early Autumn* (1926; Pulitzer Prize), and *A Good Woman* (1927).

With the onset of World War II, Bromfield returned to the United States, where he wrote *Wild Is the River* (1941), *Until the Day Break* (1942), *Mrs. Parkington* (1943), and *What Became of Anna Bolton* (1944).

Broniewski \\brȯ-'nʸef-skʸē\\, Władysław (b. Dec. 17, 1897, Płock, Kingdom of Poland, Russian Empire—d. Feb. 10, 1962, Warsaw, Pol.)   Polish poet of exceptional emotional power and impact.

Broniewski joined the antitsarist Polish legions in 1915, and later, when Poland's independence was restored, he enlisted in the new national army and fought in the Russo-Polish War of 1919–20. Later he began to write revolutionary poems espousing the cause of the working class. His first volume, *Wiatraki* (1925; "The Windmills"), was followed by *Dymy nad miastem* (1927; "Smoke over the City") and *Komuna Paryska* (1929; "Paris Commune"). Upon the outbreak of World War II he fled to the Soviet Union, where he was arrested and sent to a forced-labor camp. Liberated in 1941, he joined the Polish army and spent the remaining war years in Jerusalem, where he published *Bagnet na broń* (1943; "Bayonet On"). In 1945 he arrived in London, where he wrote *Drzewo rozpaczające* ("The Despairing Tree"). He then returned to Poland, where he was acclaimed by the communists as a prodigal son. New collections of verse followed, including *Słowo o Stalinie* (1949; "The Word on Stalin") and *Anka* (1956).

Brontë \\'brän-tē, *commonly* 'brän-tä\\, Anne, *pseudonym* Acton Bell (b. Jan. 17, 1820, Thornton, Yorkshire, Eng.—d. May 28, 1849, Scarborough, Yorkshire)   English poet and novelist, author of AGNES GREY (1847) and THE TENANT OF WILDFELL HALL (1848), which are generally considered lesser than the novels of her two sisters, Charlotte and Emily Brontë.

Anne was the youngest of six children of Patrick and Maria Brontë. She took a position as governess briefly in 1839 and then again for four years, 1841–45, with the Robinsons, the family of a clergyman.

In 1846 Anne contributed 21 poems to *Poems by Currer, Ellis and Acton Bell*, a joint work with Charlotte and Emily. Her first novel, *Agnes Grey*, about the life of a governess, was published together with Emily's *Wuthering Heights* in December 1847. The reception to these volumes, associated in the public mind with the immense popularity of Charlotte's *Jane Eyre* (October 1847), led to quick publication of Anne's second novel, *The Tenant of Wildfell Hall*, an unsoftened picture of a young man's debauchery and degradation. Published in three volumes in June 1848, it sold well. She fell ill with tuberculosis toward the end of the year and died the following May.

Brontë \\'brän-tē, *commonly* 'brän-tä\\, Charlotte, *married name* Nicholls \\'nik-əlz\\, *pseudonym* Currer Bell \\'kər-ər-'bel\\

Detail of a chalk drawing by George Richmond, 1850
National Portrait Gallery, London

(b. April 21, 1816, Thornton, Yorkshire, Eng.—d. March 31, 1855, Haworth, Yorkshire)   English writer noted for the novel JANE EYRE (1847), a powerful narrative of a woman in conflict with her natural desires and social condition.

Brontë was the daughter of an Anglican clergyman who moved with his wife and six small children to Haworth amid the Yorkshire moors in 1820. Soon after, Mrs. Brontë and the two eldest children died, and Charlotte, Emily, Anne, and Branwell were left to the care of their father and an aunt, Elizabeth Branwell.

In 1824 Charlotte and Emily attended Clergy Daughters' School at Cowan Bridge in Lancashire where the fees were low, the food unappealing, and the discipline harsh. They returned home in June 1825. In 1831 Charlotte was sent to school at Roe Head, near Huddersfield, where she stayed a year and made lasting friendships. In 1832 she came home to teach her sisters, but in 1835 she returned to Roe Head as a teacher. The work was uncongenial to her and she fell into ill health and melancholia, and in the summer of 1838 she resigned her position. In 1842, with a view toward opening a school together, Charlotte and Emily went to Brussels as pupils to improve their qualifications in French and acquire some German. The talent displayed by both brought them to the notice of the headmaster, Constantin Héger, to whom Charlotte developed a romantic attachment.

In 1844 Charlotte attempted to start a school in the Haworth parsonage, but no pupils were registered. In the autumn of 1845 she and Emily and Anne gathered verses for the publication of the volume *Poems by Currer, Ellis and Acton Bell* (1846). The pseudonyms were assumed to preserve secrecy and avoid the special treatment they believed reviewers accorded to women. The book was issued at their own expense. It received few reviews and only two copies were sold. Nevertheless, their venture into publishing had encouraged them to try to place the novels they had written. Charlotte failed to place THE PROFESSOR (published posthumously 1857), but when in 1847 Smith, Elder and Company showed some interest in publishing something else by her, she completed and submitted *Jane Eyre* at once. It was accepted, published less than eight weeks later, and had an immediate success. Within 19 months of the novel's publication, Charlotte's three remaining siblings had died. She completed SHIRLEY in the empty parsonage, and it appeared in October 1849. VILLETTE was published in 1853. In 1854 she married her father's curate, Arthur Bell Nicholls. Her subsequent pregnancy, however, was accompanied by an exhausting and soon fatal illness.

Brontë \'brän-tē, *commonly* 'brän-tā\, Emily (Jane), *pseudonym* Ellis Bell \'bel\ (b. July 30, 1818, Thornton, Yorkshire, Eng.—d. Dec. 19, 1848, Haworth, Yorkshire) English novelist and poet who produced but one novel, WUTHERING

Detail of an oil painting by Branwell Brontë, 1833
National Portrait Gallery, London

HEIGHTS (1847), a highly imaginative story of passion and hatred set on the Yorkshire moors. Emily was perhaps the greatest writer of the three Brontë sisters.

Her father, Patrick Brontë, an Irishman, held a number of curacies before becoming the rector of Haworth in 1820. After the death of their mother in 1821, the six Brontë children were left very much to themselves in the bleak moorland rectory (though an aunt, Elizabeth Branwell, did move in to help out). Most of the children's time was spent in reading and in composition. The two oldest, Maria and Elizabeth, died in 1825. In 1835, when Charlotte secured a teaching position at Miss Wooler's school at Roe Head, Emily accompanied her as a pupil but suffered from homesickness and remained only three months. In 1838 Emily spent six exhausting months as a teacher in Miss Patchett's school at Law Hill, near Halifax, and then resigned.

To facilitate their plan to keep a school for girls at Haworth, in February 1842 Emily and Charlotte went to Brussels to learn foreign languages and school management at the Pension Héger. In October, however, when her aunt died, Emily returned permanently to Haworth.

In 1845 Charlotte came across some poems by Emily, and this led to the discovery that all three sisters—Charlotte, Emily, and Anne—had written verse. A year later they published jointly a volume of verse, *Poems by Currer, Ellis and Acton Bell*; it contained 21 of Emily's poems, and a consensus of later critics believe that Emily's verse alone reveals true poetic genius. Only two copies of the book were sold.

By midsummer of 1847 Emily's *Wuthering Heights* and Anne's *Agnes Grey* had been accepted for joint publication, but publication of the two volumes was delayed until the appearance of their sister Charlotte's *Jane Eyre*, which was immediately and hugely successful. *Wuthering Heights*, when published

in December 1847, did not fare well; only later did it come to be considered one of the finest novels in the English language.

Soon after the publication of her novel, Emily's health began to fail rapidly and she soon succumbed to tuberculosis.

Bronx Primitive: Portraits in a Childhood \'bräŋks\ Memoir by Kate SIMON, published in 1982. It evokes working-class Jewish immigrant life in the Bronx during the early 20th century. *A Wider World: Portraits in an Adolescence* (1986) and *Etchings in an Hourglass* (1990) were later installments in Simon's autobiography.

Bronze Horseman, The Poem by Aleksandr PUSHKIN, published in 1837 as *Medny vsadnik*. It poses the problem of the "little man" whose happiness is destroyed by the great leader in pursuit of ambition.

Brooke \'brük\, Henry (b. *c.* 1703, County Cavan, Ire.—d. Oct. 10, 1783, Dublin) Irish novelist and dramatist, best known for *The Fool of Quality*, one of the outstanding English-language examples of the novel of sensibility—a novel in which the characters demonstrate a heightened emotional response to events around them.

After attending Trinity College, Dublin, Brooke went to London in 1724 to study law. In 1739 he wrote a celebrated drama, *Gustavus Vasa, the Deliverer of His Country*; its performance was forbidden because of the supposition that Sir Robert Walpole, the prime minister, was depicted in the part of the villain. Brooke returned to Ireland, and the play was printed and later performed in Dublin as *The Patriot*. Brooke's novel, *The Fool of Quality* (1765–70), is a rambling narrative centered on the education of an ideal nobleman. Its moral message recommended it to John Wesley, a founder of Methodism, who edited an abridged version in 1780, and, later, to the clergyman and author Charles Kingsley, who published it with an enthusiastic biographical preface in 1859.

Brooke \'brük\, Rupert (b. Aug. 3, 1887, Rugby, Warwickshire, Eng.—d. April 23, 1915, Skyros, Greece) English

Posthumous portrait drawing by J.H. Thomas
National Portrait Gallery, London

poet whose early death in World War I contributed to his idealized image in the interwar period. His best-known work is the sonnet sequence *1914* (1915).

Brooke was educated at King's College, Cambridge. In 1911 his volume entitled *Poems* was published. He spent a year wandering in North America and the South Seas. With the outbreak of the war he received a commission in the Royal Navy. After taking

part in a disastrous expedition to Antwerp that ended in a harrowing retreat, he died of septicemia on a hospital ship off Skyros and was buried on the island.

Brooke's wartime sonnets in *1914*, in particular the poem THE SOLDIER, brought him immediate fame. They express an idealism in the face of death that is in strong contrast to later poetry of trench warfare.

Brooke, Dorothea \,dôr-ə-'thē-ə-'brük\ Fictional character, the heroine of MIDDLEMARCH, George Eliot's acknowledged masterpiece. Dorothea's intelligence and idealism lead her to blindly marry Edward Casaubon, a middle-aged scholar she hopes to assist who proves both pompous and ineffectual. Her story parallels that of Tertius Lydgate, another thwarted idealist in Middlemarch who marries disastrously.

Brook Farm \'brùk \, *in full* The Brook Farm Institute of Agriculture and Education.   A utopian experiment in communal living that lasted from 1841 to 1847. The farm itself was located in West Roxbury, Mass., near Boston. It was organized and virtually directed by George Ripley, editor of *The Dial* (a critical literary monthly) and a leader in the Transcendental Club, an informal gathering of intellectuals of the Boston area.

Among the original shareholders in the project were Charles A. Dana and Nathaniel Hawthorne. Ralph Waldo Emerson, Bronson Alcott, Margaret Fuller, Elizabeth Peabody, and Orestes A. Brownson were among its interested visitors.

For a while the project seemed to prosper. But disaster struck when the members put all available funds into the construction of a large central building that burned to the ground as its completion was being celebrated. Though the colony struggled on for a while, the enterprise gradually failed; the land and buildings were sold in 1849.

Hawthorne's *The Blithedale Romance* (1852) is a fictional treatment of some aspects of the Brook Farm setting.

Brookner \'brùk-nər\, Anita (b. July 16, 1928, London, Eng.) English art historian and novelist known for her novels of lonely people, especially middle-aged women who feel they have been betrayed by literature into expecting more from life than they are able to achieve.

Brookner received a Ph.D. from the Courtauld Institute of Art in London and then held several teaching positions, including one year as the first woman Slade professor of art at Cambridge University. She wrote several books of art criticism during this time, including *Jacques-Louis David* (1967) and *The Genius of the Future: Studies in French Art Criticism* (1971). In the early 1980s she began to concentrate on writing fiction. Her novels include *A Start in Life* (1981; U.S. title, *The Debut*); *Providence* (1982); *Look at Me* (1983); *Hotel du Lac* (1984), winner of Britain's most prestigious literary award, the Booker Prize; *Latecomers* (1988); *Brief Lives* (1990); *A Closed Eye* (1991); and *Fraud* (1992).

Brooks \'brùks\, Cleanth (b. Oct. 16, 1906, Murray, Ky., U.S.—d. May 10, 1994, New Haven, Conn.)   American teacher and critic whose work was important in establishing the New Criticism, which stressed close reading and structural analysis of literature.

Brooks was educated at Vanderbilt University, Nashville, Tenn., and at Tulane University, New Orleans. From 1932 he taught at several universities, including Louisiana State University, Baton Rouge, and Yale University. From 1935 to 1942, with Charles W. Pipkin and poet and critic Robert Penn Warren, he edited *The Southern Review*, a journal that advanced the New Criticism, as did Brooks's critical works, *Modern Poetry and the Tradition* (1939) and *The Well-Wrought Urn* (1947). Authoritative college texts by Brooks, with others, reinforced the popularity of the New Criticism: *Understanding Poetry* (1938) and *Understanding Fiction* (1943), written with Warren, and *Understanding Drama* (1945), with Robert Heilman.

Brooks's later works include *Literary Criticism: A Short History* (1957; cowritten with William K. Wimsatt); *A Shaping Joy: Studies in the Writer's Craft* (1972); *The Language of the American South* (1985); and several books on William Faulkner.

Brooks \'brùks\, Gwendolyn (Elizabeth) (b. June 7, 1917, Topeka, Kan., U.S.)   American poet whose works deal with the everyday life of urban blacks. She was the first black poet to win the Pulitzer Prize (1949).

Brooks's first published collection, *A Street in Bronzeville* (1945), reveals her talent for making the ordinary life of her

neighbors extraordinary. *Annie Allen* (1949), for which she won the Pulitzer Prize, is a loosely connected series of poems related to a black girl growing up in Chicago. The same theme was used

for Brooks's novel *Maud Martha* (1953).

The Bean Eaters (1960) contains some of her best verse. Her *Selected Poems* (1963) was followed in 1968 by *In the Mecca*, half of which is a long narrative poem about people in the Mecca, a vast apartment building on the South Side of Chicago. Brooks also wrote a book for children, *Bronzeville Boys and Girls* (1956). The autobiographical *Report from Part One* (1972) was an assemblage

of personal memoirs, interviews, and letters. Later works include *Primer for Blacks* (1980), *Young Poets' Primer* (1981), *To Disembark* (1981), *The Near-Johannesburg Boy, and Other Poems* (1986), *Blacks* (1987), *Winnie* (1988), and *Children Coming Home* (1991).

Brooks \'brùks\, Van Wyck \van-'wīk, *commonly* -'wik\ (b. Feb. 16, 1886, Plainfield, N.J., U.S.—d. May 2, 1963, Bridgewater, Conn.)   American critic, biographer, and literary historian, whose *Finders and Makers* series traces American literary history in rich biographical detail from 1800 to 1915.

In 1908 Brooks published his first book, *The Wine of the Puritans*, in which he blamed the Puritan heritage for America's cultural shortcomings. He explored this theme more thoroughly in his first major work, *America's Coming-of-Age* (1915), with its thesis that the Puritan duality separating the spiritual from the material had resulted in a corresponding split in contemporary American culture between "highbrow" and "lowbrow."

Brooks's book *The Ordeal of Mark Twain* (1920; rev. ed., 1933) was a psychological study attempting to show that Twain had repressed his natural artistic bent for the sake of his Calvinist upbringing. In *The Pilgrimage of Henry James* (1925), Brooks argued that James's writing suffered because of his too-long separation from his native land. In *The Life of Emerson* (1932), Brooks depicted an American writer who he felt had successfully bridged the gap between art and life.

The *Finders and Makers* series began with *The Flowering of New England, 1815–1865* (1936), followed by *New England: Indian Summer, 1865–1915* (1940), *The World of Washington Irving* (1944), *The Times of Melville and Whitman* (1947), and *The Confident Years: 1885–1915* (1952).

Broom \'brüm\   Important international magazine of the arts, founded by Harold A. Loeb as a showcase for experimental writing, criticism, and graphic arts. The magazine was initially edited by Loeb and Alfred Kreymborg and published from November 1921 through January 1924. *Broom* published works by Guillaume Apollinaire, Malcolm Cowley, E.E. Cummings, Robert Graves, Luigi Pirandello, Jean Toomer, and William Carlos Williams, among others.

Broome \'brüm\, William (b. May 3, 1689, Haslington, Cheshire, Eng.—d. Nov. 16, 1745, Bath, Somerset)   British scholar and poet, best known as a collaborator with Alexander Pope and Elijah Fenton in a project to translate Homer's *Odyssey*. Broome also made translations of Anacreon, and his own *Poems on Several Occasions* was published in 1727.

Brophy \ˈbrō-fē\, Brigid (Antonia) (b. June 12, 1929, London, Eng.) English writer whose satiric, witty novels explore the psychology of sex and modern relationships.

The daughter of the novelist John Brophy, she began writing at an early age. Her first novel, *Hackenfeller's Ape*, was published in 1953. With the art historian Michael Levey (her husband) and the author and literary critic Charles Osborne, Brophy wrote the controversial *Fifty Works of English and American Literature We Could Do Without* (1967). Her other nonfiction includes critical portraits, a well-received collection of selected journalism, *Don't Never Forget* (1966), and a treatise, *Black Ship to Hell* (1962). *Flesh* (1962), *In Transit* (1969), *Pussy Owl: Superbeast* (1976), and *Palace Without Chairs* (1978), are among her other novels. Later nonfiction works include *The Prince and the Wild Geese* (1983), *Baroque 'n' Roll and Other Essays* (1987), and *Reads* (1989).

Brothers Karamazov, The \kə-ˌrä-'mä-zəf, *Angl* ˌkar-ə-'mä-zôf\ The final novel by Fyodor DOSTOYEVSKY, first published as *Bratya Karamazovy* in 1879–80, and generally considered to be his masterpiece. It is the story of Fyodor Karamazov and his sons Alyosha, Dmitry, and Ivan. It is also a story of patricide, into the sordid unfolding of which Dostoyevsky introduces a love-hate struggle with profound psychological and spiritual implications.

Throughout the whole novel there persists a search for faith, for God—the central idea of the work. The dramatization of Ivan's repudiation of God is concentrated in the famous "Legend of the Grand Inquisitor." A response to Ivan is contained in the preaching of the monk Zosima that the secret of universal harmony is not achieved by the mind but by the heart.

Brougham \ˈbrüm, ˈbrōm, ˈbrüm, ˈbrō-əm, ˈbrü-əm\, John (b. May 9, 1814, Dublin, Ire.—d. June 7, 1880, New York, N.Y., U.S.) Irish-born American author of more than 75 popular 19th-century plays, theater manager, and actor who excelled in eccentric comic roles.

Brougham made his acting debut in 1830, playing six parts in *Tom and Jerry*. A year later he wrote his first play, a burlesque, which was followed by a number of other works. In 1840 became manager of the Lyceum Theatre, writing *Life in the Clouds*, *Love's Livery*, *Enthusiasm*, *Tom Thumb the Second*, and *The Demon Gift* (with Mark Lemon). In 1842 Brougham went to the United States, managing theaters in New York City and writing a number of comedies and dramas until, in 1860, a trip to London led to a five-year stay in England. In 1865 he returned to the United States .

Brown \ˈbraůn\, Charles Brockden (b. Jan. 17, 1771, Philadelphia, Pa. [U.S.]—d. Feb. 22, 1810, Philadelphia) Writer known as the "father of the American novel." His gothic romances in American settings were the first in a tradition adapted by two of the greatest American authors, Edgar Allan Poe and Nathaniel Hawthorne.

Brown was apprenticed to a lawyer in 1787, but his strong interest in writing led him to help found a literary society. In 1793 he gave up the law entirely to pursue a literary career. His first novel, WIELAND (1798), a minor masterpiece in American fiction, shows the ease with which mental balance is lost when the test of common sense is not applied to strange experiences. Brown also wrote *Ormond* (1799), *Edgar Huntly* (1799), and *Arthur Mervyn* (1799–1800), as well as a number of less well-known novels and a book on the rights of women.

Brown \ˈbraůn\, George Mackay (b. Oct. 17, 1921, Stromness, Orkney Islands, Scot.) Author of poetry, plays, fiction, and children's books set in his native North Atlantic islands.

Educated at Newbattle Abbey College and the University of Edinburgh, Brown lived virtually all of his life in the Orkneys.

In his cycle of verse and prose entitled *Fishermen with Ploughs* (1971), he celebrated the traditional values and sense of community he experienced there.

His novels include *Greenvoe* (1972), *Magnus* (1973), and *Time in a Red Coat* (1984). His short stories were collected in more than 10 volumes, beginning with *A Calendar of Love* (1967). His noted children's tales include *The Two Fiddlers* (1974) and *Six Lives of Fankle the Cat* (1980), and he wrote plays for stage, radio, and television and adapted two of his stories into librettos for operas. His later works include *Three Plays* (1984), *Songs for St. Magnus Day* (1988), and *Rockpools and Daffodils: An Orcadian Diary 1979–1991* (1992).

Brown \ˈbraůn\, Sterling (Allen) (b. May 1, 1901, Washington, D.C., U.S.—d. Jan. 17, 1989, Washington, D.C.) Influential African-American teacher and literary critic whose poetry was rooted in folklore sources and black dialect.

Brown was educated at Williams College, Williamstown, Mass., and Harvard University. While teaching at several schools he began collecting folk songs and stories from blacks. In 1929 Brown began a 40-year teaching career at Howard University, and in 1932 his first volume of poetry, *Southern Road*, was published. Ballads, work songs, spirituals, and blues were primary influences on his work.

Though *Southern Road* was widely praised, Brown found no publisher for his second collection, *No Hiding Place*; it eventually was incorporated into his *Collected Poems* (1980). As critic, essayist, and *Opportunity* magazine columnist, he supported realistic writing and harshly attacked literature that distorted black life. In 1937 he published the pioneering studies *Negro Poetry and Drama* and *The Negro in American Fiction*, and in 1941 he was coeditor of *The Negro Caravan*, a major anthology of African-American writing.

Brown \ˈbraůn\, Thomas (b. 1663, Shifnal, Shropshire, Eng.—d. June 16, 1704, London) British satirist best known for his reputedly extemporaneous translation of Martial's 33rd epigram beginning "*Non amo te, Sabidi*." Brown entered Christ Church, Oxford, in 1678, but the irregularity of his life there brought him before Dr. John Fell, dean of Christ Church, who agreed to stay Brown's expulsion if he could translate the epigram on the spot. Brown's reply was:

> I do not love thee, Dr. Fell,
> The reason why I cannot tell;
> But this I know, and know full well,
> I do not love thee, Dr. Fell.

Brown later left Oxford without taking a degree and settled in London. He translated works from Latin and French and wrote many epigrams, lampoons, and satires. Under the pseudonym Dudly Tomkinson he wrote three satires on John Dryden. His prose *Amusements Serious and Comical, Calculated for the Meridian of London* (1700; modern edition, 1927) presents a vivid picture of the city and its inhabitants as seen by Grub Street writers.

Brown \ˈbraůn\, William Hill (b. November 1765, Boston, Mass. [U.S.]—d. Sept. 2, 1793, Murfreesboro, N.C.) Novelist and dramatist whose anonymously published *The Power of Sympathy, or the Triumph of Nature Founded in Truth* (1789) is considered the first American novel. An epistolary novel about tragic, incestuous love, it imitated the sentimental manner developed by Samuel Richardson.

Brown wrote the romantic tale "Harriot, or the Domestic Reconciliation" (1789), which was published in the first issue of *Massachusetts Magazine*, and the play *West Point Preserved* (published posthumously, 1797). He also wrote a series of verse fables, the comedy *Penelope*, essays, and a short second novel about incest and seduction, *Ira and Isabella* (1807).

Brown \\'braủn\\, William Wells (b. 1814?, near Lexington, Ky., U.S.—d. Nov. 6, 1884, Chelsea, Mass.) American writer who is considered to be the first African-American to publish a novel.

Born into slavery, Brown escaped in 1834 and adopted the name of a Quaker, Wells Brown, who aided him when he was a runaway. In 1847 his popular autobiography *Narrative of William W. Brown, A Fugitive Slave* was published. Having educated himself, Brown began lecturing on abolitionism and temperance reform. His antislavery lectures in Europe inspired *Three Years in Europe* (1852), which was expanded as *The American Fugitive in Europe* (1855).

Brown's only novel, CLOTEL (1853), tells the story of the daughters and granddaughters of President Thomas Jefferson and his slave Currer. His only published play was *The Escape; or, A Leap for Freedom* (1858). Brown's historical writings include *The Black Man* (1863), *The Negro in the American Rebellion* (1867), and *The Rising Son* (1873). His final book, *My Southern Home* (1880), contains miscellanea about slave life, abolitionism, and racism.

Brown, Father \\'braủn\\ Fictional character, a priest who is the protagonist of a series of detective stories by G.K. CHESTERTON. Father Brown appears clumsy and naive, with a face "as round and dull as a Norfolk dumpling." His appearance, however, disguises a clever mind, penetrating insight, a gift for careful observation, and a deep understanding of human evil. Father Brown first appeared in Chesterton's *The Innocence of Father Brown* (1911).

Brown, Tom \\'tăm-'braủn\\ Fictional character, hero of the popular English novel TOM BROWN'S SCHOOL DAYS and of its sequel, *Tom Brown at Oxford*, both by Thomas Hughes.

Browne \\'braủn\\, E. Martin, *in full* Elliott (b. Jan. 29, 1900, Zeals, Wiltshire, Eng.—d. April 27, 1980, London) British theatrical director and producer who was a major influence on poetic and religious drama and, for more than 25 years, the director chosen by T.S. Eliot for his plays. He first collaborated with Eliot in 1934 on a religious spectacle called *The Rock*. This led to Eliot's *Murder in the Cathedral* (1935), also directed by Browne, and to Eliot's four modern poetic dramas, in the writing of which he worked in consultation with the director.

During World War II Browne formed the Pilgrim Players and in the postwar years helped to encourage the revival of poetic drama, producing work by such new writers as Christopher Fry.

Browne \\'braủn\\, Sir Thomas (b. Oct. 19, 1605, London, Eng.—d. Oct. 19, 1682, Norwich, Norfolk) English physician and author, best known for his book of reflections, *Religio Medici*.

After studying at Winchester and Oxford, Browne became a doctor and settled in Norwich in 1637. Browne had earlier begun his parallel career as a writer with *Religio Medici*, a journal largely about the mysteries of God, nature, and man. In 1642 it was printed without his permission in London and had to be acknowledged, and so an authorized version was published in 1643. An immediate success in England, the book soon circulated widely in Europe as well.

From notebooks of miscellaneous jottings, Browne compiled his second and larger work, *Pseudodoxia Epidemica, or, Enquiries into Very many received Tenets, and commonly presumed truths* (1646), often known as *Browne's Vulgar Errors*. In 1658 he published his third book, two treatises on antiquarian subjects. A smaller work of great beauty and subtlety, entitled *A Letter to a Friend, Upon occasion of the Death of his Intimate Friend*, was published posthumously in 1690. Browne's fame brought him a knighthood in 1671.

Browne \\'braủn\\, William (b. 1591?, Tavistock, Devonshire, Eng.—d. 1645?) English poet, author of *Britannia's Pastorals* (1613–16) and other pastoral and miscellaneous verse.

Britannia's Pastorals, modeled on the work of the poet Edmund Spenser, is a long, discursive pastoral narrative interspersed with songs. Devoted to his country, and especially to his native Devonshire, he attempted to glorify them in pastoral verse of epic dignity.

Brownell \\braủ-'nel\\, W.C., *in full* William Crary (b. Aug. 30, 1851, New York, N.Y., U.S.—d. July 22, 1928, Williamstown, Mass.) Critic who sought to expand the scope of American literary criticism.

After graduating from Amherst College, Amherst, Mass., in 1871, Brownell worked as an editor and literary adviser. His first two books, *French Traits* (1889) and *French Art* (1892), established a new and high standard for the American critic, one that Brownell maintained for himself in his succeeding books: *Victorian Prose Masters* (1901), *American Prose Masters* (1909), *Criticism* (1914), *Standards* (1917), *The Genius of Style* (1924), and *Democratic Distinction in America* (1927).

Brown Girl, Brownstones First novel by Paule MARSHALL, originally published in 1959. Somewhat autobiographical, this groundbreaking work describes the coming of age of Selina Boyce, a Caribbean-American girl in New York City in the mid-20th century. Although the book did not gain widespread recognition until it was reprinted in 1981, it was initially noted for its expressive dialogue.

brownie \\'braủ-nē\\ [a derivative of *brown;* apparently so called from its supposed dusky color] A good-natured goblin believed to perform helpful services (such as threshing, churning, and sweeping) during the night.

The brownie of English and Scottish folklore is a small, industrious fairy believed to inhabit houses and barns. Rarely seen, it was often heard at night, cleaning and doing housework; it also sometimes mischievously rearranged rooms. The brownie would ride for the midwife, and in Cornwall it caused swarming bees to settle quickly.

A hostile, mischievous brownie, known as a boggart in Yorkshire and bogle in Scotland, is considered indistinguishable from the poltergeist.

The American Palmer Cox wrote and illustrated a series of highly popular children's books about brownies, beginning with *The Brownies, Their Book* (1887).

Browning \\'braủ-niŋ\\, Elizabeth Barrett (b. March 6, 1806, near Durham, Eng.—d. June 29, 1861, Florence [Italy]) English poet whose reputation rests chiefly upon her love poems, SONNETS FROM THE PORTUGUESE. Her husband was Robert Browning.

At the age of 15 Elizabeth fell seriously ill, probably as the result of a spinal injury, and her health was permanently affected. In 1836 her family moved to London, and she began to contribute to several periodicals. Her first collection, *The Seraphim and Other Poems*, appeared in 1838. After the death by drowning of her brother, Edward, she developed an almost morbid fear of meeting anyone apart from a small circle of intimates. In 1844 her second volume of poetry, *Poems*, was enthusiastically received. In 1845 she met the poet Robert Browning. Their courtship was kept a close secret from Elizabeth's despotic father, of whom she stood in some fear. They were married in 1846 and settled in Florence.

In 1850 Elizabeth's *Sonnets from the Portuguese*, which are a record of the Brownings' courtship and which had been written during that time, were published as part of a larger collection. During a visit to London, Elizabeth completed her most ambitious work, AURORA LEIGH (1857), a long blank-verse poem that did not impress most critics, though it was a huge popular success.

Browning \\'brau̇-niŋ\\, Robert (b. May 7, 1812, London, Eng.—d. Dec. 12, 1889, Venice, Italy)   Major English poet of

E.B. Inc.

the Victorian age, noted for his mastery of DRAMATIC MONO-LOGUE and psychological portraiture. He was married to poet Elizabeth Barrett Browning.

Browning's first published work was *Pauline: A Fragment of a Confession* (1833, anonymous), which embodied many of his own adolescent passions and anxieties. In 1835 he published *Paracelsus* and in 1840 SORDELLO.

Browning devoted his main energies for some years to verse drama, a form that he had already adopted for *Strafford* (1837). Between 1841 and 1846, in a series under the general title of *Bells and Pomegranates*, he published seven more plays in verse, including PIPPA PASSES (1841). The series also included the volume *Dramatic Lyrics*, in which such poems as MY LAST DUCHESS and THE PIED PIPER OF HAMELIN appeared.

In 1845 he met Elizabeth Barrett and they married in September 1846; a week later they left for Italy, where they remained for most of their married life. Browning produced comparatively little poetry during the next 15 years. The most notable production of these years was *Men and Women* (1855), a collection of 51 poems, including such dramatic lyrics as "Memorabilia," "Love Among the Ruins," and "A Toccata of Galuppi's" and the great monologues FRA LIPPO LIPPI, "How It Strikes a Contemporary," and BISHOP BLOUGRAM'S APOLOGY. Elizabeth Barrett Browning died in June 1861, and in the autumn Browning returned to London with his young son.

He published another collected edition in 1863, and with his next book of poems, *Dramatis Personae* (1864)—including "Abt Vogler," RABBI BEN EZRA, CALIBAN UPON SETEBOS, and "Mr. Sludge, 'The Medium' "—Browning at last won popular recognition. In 1868–69 he published his greatest work, THE RING AND THE BOOK, based on the proceedings in a murder trial in Rome in 1698. It was received with enthusiasm, and Browning was established as an important literary figure.

The best works of his last years were his long narrative or dramatic poems, often dealing with contemporary themes, such as *Prince Hohenstiel-Schwangau* (1871), *Fifine at the Fair* (1872), *Red Cotton Night-Cap Country* (1873), *The Inn Album* (1875). In addition to many collections of shorter poems, Browning published toward the end of his life two books of unusually personal origin—*La Saisiaz* (1878), at once an elegy for a friend and a meditation on mortality, and *Parleyings with Certain People of Importance in Their Day* (1887), in which he discussed books and ideas that had influenced him.

Browning influenced many modern poets, partly through his development of the dramatic monologue, with its emphasis on the psychology of the individual, and his use of stream of consciousness, but even more through his success in writing about the variety of modern life in language that owed nothing to convention.

Brú \\'brü\\, Hedin, *original name* Hans Jakob Jacobsen \\'yä-kȯp-sen\\ (b. Aug. 17, 1901, Skálevig, Faroe Islands, Den.—d. May 18, 1987, Tórshavn, Faroe Islands)   Faroese writer who helped to establish Faroese as a literary language.

At 14 Brú worked as a fisherman. He spent much of the 1920s studying agriculture in Denmark, and from 1928 he was an agricultural adviser to the Faroese government. His first two novels, *Longbrá* (1930; "Mirage") and *Fastatøkur* (1937; "Firm Grip"), dramatized the changing face of Faroese life as subsistence agriculture gave way to the fishing industry. A similar contrast between old and new was the main theme of his best work, *Fedgar á ferd* (1940; *The Old Man and His Sons*). Brú played a central role in cultural life as coeditor of the literary periodical *Vardin* and as a member of the Faroese Scientific Society and began to acquire an international reputation. He also produced Faroese versions of *Hamlet* and *The Tempest* and wrote a volume of memoirs.

Bruce \\'brüs\\, Michael (b. March 27, 1746, Kinnesswood, Kinross, Scot.—d. July 5, 1767, Kinnesswood)   Scottish poet whose works were allegedly stolen by the poet and divine John LOGAN, provoking a long-lasting controversy.

Bruce's finest poem is considered to be "Elegy Written in Spring" (1766). His reputation was spread, first through sympathy for his early death and second through the alleged theft by John Logan of several of his poems. In 1770 Logan edited *Poems, on Several Occasions*, which included works by Michael Bruce and in which the "Ode to the Cuckoo" appeared. In the preface he stated that "to make up a miscellany, some poems written by different authors are inserted." In a collection of his own poems in 1781, Logan printed an altered version of the "Ode to the Cuckoo" as his own.

Bruin \\'brw ͮē ͮn\\ or **Brun** \\'brü̇ē ͮn\\   A character in French folklore and in the *Roman de Renart*, a medieval collection of beast tales that satirized human society by bestowing human characteristics upon animals. In the *Roman de Renart*, Brun is a bear who is wedged into a honey-filled log by the hero, Reynard the Fox. The name of the character, ultimately from Middle Dutch *bruun* ("brown"), has come to be an appellation for any bear.

Brun \\'brün\\, Johan Nordahl (b. March 21, 1745, Byneset, Nor.—d. July 26, 1816, Bergen)   Poet, dramatist, bishop, and politician who wrote the first Norwegian national anthem.

Brun became a pastor in Bergen in 1774. His song "For Norge, kjæmpers fødeland" (1771; "For Norway, Land of Heroes") was banned until independence in 1814. The beginning and high point of his literary career was the drama *Zarine* (1772), which was followed in the same year by another patriotic tragedy, *Einer Tambeskielver*. His primary interest, however, lay in the church, and he became bishop of Bergen in 1804. He is remembered for his many hymns.

Brunhild or **Brünhild** or **Brynhild**, \\'brün-,hilt, -,hild, *German* 'brʊen-,hilt\\ *also called* Brunhilda *or* Brunhilde \\,brün-'hil-də, ,brün-, *German* ,brʊen-'hil-də\\   A beautiful Amazonlike princess in ancient Germanic heroic literature, known from Old Norse sources (the Eddic poems and the *Vǫlsunga saga*) and from the NIBELUNGENLIED in German. In the Eddic poems in which she appears, she plays the leading role; in the *Nibelungenlied*, her prominence is greatly reduced.

Common to both, and no doubt original, is the conception of Brunhild as the central figure of a story in which she vows to marry a man of the most outstanding qualities and only one who can surpass her in strength. One man, SIEGFRIED, is able to fulfill her conditions, but he woos and wins her not for himself but for another. When Brunhild discovers this deception, she exacts vengeance, which results in the death of Siegfried.

In some of the Norse sources, Brunhild has supernatural qualities and is described as a Valkyrie; it is still a matter of dispute whether these attributes are an accretion or whether their absence from the German version is an omission.

Brut \ˈbrüt\ Any of several medieval chronicles of Britain tracing the history and legend of the country from the time of the mythical Brutus, descendant of Aeneas and founder of Britain. The *Roman de Brut* (1155) by the Anglo-Norman author Wace was one such chronicle. Perhaps the outstanding adaptation of the story is Layamon's *Brut* (*c.* 1200), written in Middle English; it lent a distinctly Germanic and heroic flavor to the story and signaled the revival of English literature after the Norman Conquest of 1066. *See also* LAYAMON; WACE.

Brutus \ˈbrüt-əs\, Dennis (Vincent) (b. Nov. 28, 1924, Salisbury, Southern Rhodesia [now Harare, Zimbabwe]) Poet known for his powerful literature of protest.

For 14 years Brutus taught English and Afrikaans in South Africa. His outspoken protests against apartheid resulted in an 18-month term in prison, as well as his being banned from teaching, writing, publishing, attending social or political meetings, and other activities.

After leaving South Africa in 1966, Brutus made his home in England and then taught at the University of Denver and at Northwestern University, Evanston, Ill. In 1983, after a protracted legal struggle, he won the right to stay in the United States as a political refugee.

Brutus' first collection of poetry, *Sirens, Knuckles and Boots* (1963), was published in Nigeria while he was in prison. His verse, while political in nature, is highly developed and restrained. Even in *Letters to Martha and Other Poems from a South African Prison* (1968), which records his experiences of misery and loneliness as a political prisoner, Brutus exhibits artistic control and combines tenderness with anger. His later works include *A Simple Lust* (1973), *China Poems* (1975), *Stubborn Hope* (1978), *Salutes and Censures* (1982), and *Airs and Tributes* (1989).

Brutus \ˈbrü-təs\, Marcus Junius, *also called* Quintus Caepio Brutus (b. 85 BC—d. 42, near Philippi, Macedonia [now in Greece]) A leader of the conspirators who assassinated the Roman dictator Julius Caesar in March 44 BC. The son of Marcus Junius Brutus (d. 77), he acquired the alternative name Quintus Caepio through adoption by his uncle, Quintus Servilius Caepio.

Although Brutus was admired by his contemporaries for his dignity and idealism, he was extortionate and cruel in his financial dealings with provincials. William Shakespeare's portrayal of Brutus in the play *Julius Caesar* is flattering. A Stoic, Brutus wrote a number of philosophical treatises and other literary works, none of which has survived. Only two of the nine books of his correspondence with the famed orator Cicero are extant.

Bryant \ˈbrī-ənt\, William Cullen (b. Nov. 3, 1794, Cummington, Mass., U.S.—d. June 12, 1878, New York, N.Y.) Poet of nature, best remembered for THANATOPSIS, and editor for 50 years of the New York *Evening Post*.

Bryant at 16 entered the sophomore class of Williams College. He left without graduating, but he later studied law and at 21 was admitted to the bar. He spent nearly 10 years as an attorney, a calling for which he held a lifelong aversion. In 1825 he moved to New York City to become coeditor of the *New York Review*. He became an editor of the *Evening Post* in 1827; in 1829 he became editor in chief and part owner and continued in this position until his death.

The religious conservatism imposed on Bryant in childhood found expression in pious doggerel; the political conservatism of his father stimulated "The Embargo" (1808), in which the 13-year-old poet demanded the resignation of President Thomas Jefferson. But in "Thanatopsis," which he wrote when he was 17 and which made him famous when it was published in *The North American Review* in 1817, he rejected Puritan

dogma for deism; thereafter he was a Unitarian. Turning also from federalism, he joined the Democratic party and made the *Post* an organ of free trade, workers' rights, free speech, and abolition. As a man of letters, Bryant securely established himself at the age of 27 with *Poems* (1821), which included TO A WATERFOWL.

Bryher \ˈbrī-ər\, *byname of* Annie Winifred Ellerman \ˈel-ər-mən\ (b. Sept. 2, 1894, Margate, Kent, Eng.—d. Jan. 28, 1983, Vevey, Switz.) British novelist, poet, and critic, best known for her historical fiction, in which she vividly and accurately re-created ancient cultures in times of change, disorder, and conflict.

Bryher, the daughter of British shipping magnate Sir John Ellerman, traveled extensively with her parents. She took the name Bryher (from her favorite of the Isles of Scilly) when she began to write because she did not want the eminent family name to influence publishers or critics. She was closely associated for most of her life with the poet Hilda Doolittle.

Although Bryher wrote some poetry and nonfiction, it was her historical novels that brought her critical acclaim. These works include *Beowulf* (1948), *The Fourteenth of October* (1952), *The Player's Boy* (1953), and *Ruan* (1960), all set in Britain in various historical eras, and *The Roman Wall* (1954) and *The Coin of Carthage* (1963), which are set in the Roman Empire.

Brynhild *see* BRUNHILD.

Bryusov or **Briusov** \ˈbryü-səf\, Valery Yakovlevich (b. Dec. 1 [Dec. 13, New Style], 1873, Moscow, Russia—d. Oct. 9, 1924, Moscow, Russian S.F.S.R.) Poet, novelist, playwright, translator, and essayist who pioneered Russian modernism.

Bryusov became interested in French Symbolist poetry in the early 1890s. He first gained critical recognition when he published (with A.A. Lang) *Russkie simvolisty* (1894–95; "Russian Symbolists"), an anthology of original poems by Russian Symbolists as well as of translations of the French Symbolists. This work was an important landmark in the Russian modernist movement, and Bryusov eventually became the recognized leader of Russian Symbolism when he assumed the editorship of its leading critical journal, *Vesy* ("The Scales"), in 1904. The most important of the 10 volumes of Bryusov's original poetry published between 1895 and 1921 were *Tertia vigilia* (1900; "Third Vigil"), *Urbi et orbi* (1903; "To the City and the World"), and *Stephanos* (1906). As a poet Bryusov displayed great technical skill and erudition in his mystical and eroticized treatments of history and mythology, but his highly ornate and cerebral poetry also evinces qualities of coldness, detachment, and artificiality. His prose fiction includes the novels *Ognenny angel* (1908; *The Fiery Angel*) and *Altar pobedy* (1913; "Altar of Victory"). He broke with the Symbolist movement in 1910 and taught literature after the Revolution of 1917, holding teaching and publishing posts until his death. He is most notable for his work as a translator, critic, and essayist to improve modern poetry in Russia.

Brzozowski \bzhȯ-ˈzȯf-skʸē\, Stanisław (Leopold), *pseudonym* Adam Czepiel \ˈche-pyel\ (b. June 28, 1878, Maziarnia, near Chelm, Pol., Russian Empire—d. April 30, 1911, Florence, Italy) Polish critic, novelist, and playwright who is considered a major force in 20th-century Polish literature.

Brzozowski was educated in Russian schools in Lublin (now in Poland) and in Ukraine. He was a student leader at Warsaw University but was suspended for a year for his political activities. Blackmailed by the police for a youthful indiscretion, he was accused (evidently falsely) of being an agent of the secret police. He went to Galicia (then under Austrian rule) in 1905 but, having contracted tuberculosis in a Warsaw jail, moved to Italy for his health.

Brzozowski's first novel, *Płomienie* (1908; "Flames"), is a fictional account of the Russian revolutionary movements connected with the secret organization Zemlya i Volya ("Land and Freedom"). His novel *Sam wśród ludzi* (1911; "Alone Among Men") is the first volume of what was intended to be a series of examinations of "the philosophical and political transformation of European consciousness." A third novel was incomplete at his death.

Brzozowski's philosophy was a complex synthesis of philosophical and literary influences that included Romanticism, Marxism, and Roman Catholic modernism. His major philosophical achievement is his belief that the foundation of freedom lies in the power of human hands over nature. He uses this thesis in his incisive analyses of the connections between culture and society, perhaps best noted in his critical work *Legenda Młodej Polski* (1909; "The Legend of Young Poland").

Bucephalus \byü-'sef-ə-ləs\ A black horse that was the favorite steed of Alexander the Great (Alexander III), king of Macedonia.

Buchan \'bək-ən, *commonly* 'bək-\, John, 1st Baron Tweedsmuir \'twēdz-,myúr\ (b. Aug. 26, 1875, Perth, Perthshire, Scot.—d. Feb. 11, 1940, Montreal, Que., Can.) Statesman and writer best known for his swift-paced adventure stories.

Buchan was educated at the universities of Glasgow and Oxford, where he began to publish fiction and history. He was called to the bar in 1901 and worked on the staff of the high commissioner for South Africa in that country (1901–03), forming a lifelong attachment to the cause of empire. Back in London, he became a director of Nelson's, the publishers for whom he wrote *Prester John* (1910), a vivid, prophetic account of an African uprising. His *Thirty-Nine Steps* (1915) was the most popular of his series of secret-service thrillers and the first of many to feature Richard Hannay.

His biographies, *Montrose* (1928) and *Sir Walter Scott* (1932), are illuminated by compassionate understanding of Scottish history and literature. In 1935 Buchan was raised to the peerage and appointed governor-general of Canada, which was the setting for his novel *Sick Heart River* (1941; U.S. title, *Mountain Meadow*). His autobiography, *Memory Hold-the-Door*, was published in 1940.

Buchanan \bə-'kan-ən, *commonly* byü-\, George (b. February 1506, Killearn, Stirlingshire, Scot.—d. Sept. 29, 1582, Edinburgh) Scottish humanist, educator, and man of letters who was known as a scholar and a Latin poet.

After attending the University of Paris and the University of St. Andrews, Buchanan became a teacher in the Collège de Sainte-Barbe in Paris. Because of Buchanan's two bitter attacks on the Franciscans—*Somnium* (1535) and *Franciscanus et fratres* (1527)—he was jailed as a heretic. Buchanan escaped and later found diversion in translating Euripides' *Medea* and *Alcestis* into Latin and in writing original dramas—e.g., *Baptistes* (1534) and *Jephthes* (1578)—attacking tyranny. His paraphrase of the Psalms was long used for Latin instruction.

After serving as a tutor in France, during which time he wrote *De sphaera* (1555), a Latin poem in five books, and *Epithalamium* (1558), a poem on the marriage of Mary, Queen of Scots, to the French dauphin, he returned to Scotland in 1561. After the murder of her second husband, Lord Darnley, in 1567, he helped to prepare the case against Mary that resulted eventually in her execution. *De jure regni apud Scotos* (1579), the most important of his political writings, was a resolute argument, in dialogue form, for limited monarchy; *Rerum Scoticarum historia* (1582), which he was completing at the time of his death, traces the history of Scotland from the mythical Fergus.

Buchanan \byü-'kan-ən\, Robert Williams (b. Aug. 18, 1841, Caverswall, Staffordshire, Eng.—d. June 10, 1901, London) English poet, novelist, and playwright, chiefly remembered for his attacks on the Pre-Raphaelites.

London Poems (1866) established Buchanan as a poet. He followed his first novel, *The Shadow of the Sword* (1876), with a continuous stream of poems, novels, and melodramas, of which *Alone in London* (produced 1884) may be taken as typical. Buchanan's own forcefulness and moral fervor roused his contempt for Algernon Charles Swinburne, Dante Gabriel Rossetti, and other of the Pre-Raphaelite poets. His attacks culminated in an article entitled "The Fleshly School of Poetry," published pseudonymously in the *Contemporary Review*. *See also* FLESHLY SCHOOL OF POETRY.

Buchanan, Daisy and Tom \'dā-zē-byü-'kan-ən . . . 'täm\ Fictional characters, the wealthy and careless couple who help to bring about the tragic end of Jay Gatsby in F. Scott Fitzgerald's masterpiece THE GREAT GATSBY.

Büchner \'búk-nər\, Georg (b. Oct. 17, 1813, Goddelau, Hesse-Darmstadt [Ger.]—d. Feb. 19, 1837, Zürich, Switz.) German dramatist, a major forerunner of the German Expressionists of the early 20th century.

Büchner's three plays were clearly influenced in style by William Shakespeare and by the German Romantic Sturm und Drang movement. In content and form they were far ahead of their time. Their short, abrupt scenes combined extreme naturalism with visionary power. His first play, *Dantons Tod* (1835; "Danton's Death"), is a drama of the French Revolution that is suffused with deep pessimism. *Leonce und Lena* (1838), a satire on the nebulous nature of Romantic ideas, shows the influence of Alfred de Musset and Clemens Brentano. His last work, WOYZECK (published posthumously in 1879), which remained a fragment, anticipated the social drama of the 1890s with its compassion for the poor and oppressed. Except for *Dantons Tod* (which was not produced until 1902) and the fragment of a novel, *Lenz*, Büchner's writings were published only after his death.

Buck \'bək\, Pearl, *original surname* Sydenstricker \'sī-dən-,strik-ər\, *pseudonym* John Sedges \'sej-iz\ (b. June 26, 1892, Hillsboro, W.Va., U.S.—d. March 6, 1973, Danby, Vt.) American author noted for her novels of life in China and recipient of the Nobel Prize for Literature in 1938.

She spent her youth in China, where her parents were Presbyterian missionaries. She graduated from Randolph-Macon Woman's College, Lynchburg, Va., in 1914, then returned to China and later became a university teacher in Nanjing.

Her stories about Chinese life first appeared in American magazines in 1923, but it was not until 1931 that she reached a wide audience with THE GOOD EARTH, which described the struggle of a Chinese peasant and his slave wife to gain land and position. That novel was followed by *Sons* (1932) and *A House Divided* (1935); the trilogy was published as *The House of Earth* (1935).

She turned to biography with lives of her father, Absalom Sydenstricker, *Fighting Angel* (1936), and her mother, Caroline, *The Exile* (1936). Her later books include *Dragon Seed* (1942) and *Imperial Woman* (1956), novels; *The First Wife and Other Stories* (1933), *Far and Near* (1947), and *The Good Deed* (1969), short stories; *The Child Who Never Grew* (1950), concerning her retarded daughter; and an autobiography, *My Several Worlds* (1954). She also wrote five novels under her pseudonym, John Sedges.

Bucket, Inspector \'bək-it\ Fictional character, the detective who solves the mystery of the novel BLEAK HOUSE by Charles Dickens. For Dickens' 19th-century readers, Inspector

Bucket's colorless but skillful and decent methods became the standards by which to judge all policemen. He has been called the first important detective in English literature.

bucoliast \byū-'kō-lē-ast\   *obsolete*   A pastoral poet.

bucolic \byū-'käl-ik\ [Greek *bukolikós,* a derivative of *boukólos* cowherd]   Of or relating to shepherds or herdsmen, or typical of rural life. In literature the word refers to a type of pastoral writing that deals with rural life in a formal and fanciful style. *See also* PASTORAL.

bucolic diaeresis or **bucolic caesura**   see DIAERESIS.

Budd, Billy \'bil-ē-'bəd\   Fictional character, the protagonist of Herman Melville's novel BILLY BUDD, FORETOPMAN.

Buddenbrooks \'bùd-ən-ˌbrōks\   Novel by Thomas MANN, published in 1901 in two volumes in German as *Buddenbrooks, Verfall einer Familie* ("Buddenbrooks, The Decline of a Family"). Mann's first novel, it expressed the ambivalence of his feelings about the value of the life of the artist as opposed to ordinary, bourgeois life. The novel is the saga of the fall of the Buddenbrooks, a family of merchants, from the pinnacle of their material wealth in 1835 to their extinction in 1877.

Budgell \'bəj-əl\, Eustace (b. Aug. 19, 1686, St. Thomas, near Exeter, Eng.—d. May 4, 1737, London)   British writer who, apart from Joseph Addison and Richard Steele, was the principal contributor to *The Spectator.*

In 1710 his cousin Addison, who was then secretary to the lord lieutenant of Ireland, offered Budgell a clerkship; and until 1718 Budgell filled many posts with considerable ability. Meanwhile, after perhaps helping with *The Tatler,* he wrote for *The Spectator* and *The Guardian.* Budgell wrote libels against Sir Robert Walpole in the antigovernmental *Craftsman* and founded his own weekly, the *Bee* (1733–35), which ran to 100 numbers, many filled with vainglorious self-justification. Disliked by many, Budgell was criticized by Alexander Pope in the *Epistle to Dr. Arbuthnot* and in *The Dunciad.*

Buendía family \bwen-'dē-ä\   Fictional founders of Macondo, the South American town that is the setting of the novel *Cien años de soledad* (ONE HUNDRED YEARS OF SOLITUDE) by Gabriel García Márquez.

Buero Vallejo \'bwer-ō-bäl-'yä-ḵō\, Antonio (b. Sept. 29, 1916, Guadalajara, Spain)   Playwright considered the most important Spanish dramatist of the post-World War II generation.

During the Spanish Civil War (1936–39), Buero Vallejo served as a medical orderly in the Republican Army. After the war, he was imprisoned for more than six years by the Nationalists.

In 1949 he won national notice with his play *Historia de una escalera* (*The Story of a Stairway*), for which he was awarded the Lope de Vega Prize. His one-act play produced in the same year, *Las palabras en la arena* ("Words in the Sand"), won another Spanish literary award, as did many of the plays that followed. In *En la ardiente oscuridad* (first performed 1950; *In the Burning Darkness*), his second full-length play, a home for the blind stands as a metaphor for society. Other plays include *La tejedora de sueños* (1952; *The Dream Weaver*), *Irene; o, el tesoro* (1954; "Irene; or, The Treasure"), and *Hoy es fiesta* (1956; *Today's a Holiday*). Buero Vallejo's later works show the influence of Bertolt Brecht, whose works he translated.

His historical plays were carefully researched. They include *Un soñador para un pueblo* (1958; "A Dreamer for the Nation"), *Las meninas* (1960; "The Ladies-in-Waiting"), and *El concierto de San Ovidio* (1962; *The Concert at Saint Ovide*). *El tragaluz* (1967; *The Basement Window*) deals with the Civil War. Later works include *El sueño de la razón* (1970; *The Sleep of Rea-*

son), *La doble historia del Doctor Valmy* (1970; "The Double Life of Doctor Valmy"), *Los jueces en la noche* (1979; "Judges in the Night"), and *Lazaro en el laberinto* (1986; "Lazaro and the Labyrinth").

In 1986 Buero Vallejo became the first playwright to win the Cervantes Prize, Spain's foremost literary award.

Buffalo Bill \'bil\, *byname of* William Frederick Cody \'kō-dē\ (b. Feb. 26, 1846, Scott county, Iowa, U.S.—d. Jan. 10, 1917, Denver, Colo.)   Buffalo hunter, U.S. Army scout, and Indian fighter who dramatized the facts and flavor of the American West through fiction and melodrama. From 1883 his colorful Wild West exhibition became an international institution.

Cody early became an accomplished horse wrangler, hunter, and Indian fighter. He served in the American Civil War and worked for the U.S. Army as a civilian scout and dispatch bearer from 1866 to 1867. In 1867–68 he hunted buffalo to feed construction crews on the Union Pacific Railroad.

Cody was much in demand as a scout and guide during 1868–76, when the government was attempting to wipe out Indian resistance to settlement west of the Mississippi River. In all, Cody engaged in 16 Indian fights, including the much-publicized scalping (July 17, 1876) of the Cheyenne warrior Yellow Hair (erroneously translated Yellow Hand) in Sioux county, Neb. Such exploits provided choice material not only for newspaper reporters but also for dime novelists, who transformed the hard-riding, fast-shooting Cody into a Western folk hero. Among these early authors were Ned Buntline (pen name of E.Z.C. Judson) and Prentiss Ingraham.

Buḥturī, al- \al-'bùḵ-tù-ˌrē\, *in full* Abū 'Ubādah al-Walīd ibn 'Ubayd Allāh al-Buḥturī (b. 821, Manbij [now in Syria]—d. 897, Manbij)   Prominent poet of the 'Abbāsid period (750–1258).

Al-Buḥturī devoted his early poetry, written between the ages of 16 and 19, to his tribe, the Ṭayyi'. On a visit to Baghdad, in about 848, al-Buḥturī was introduced to the caliph, al-Mutawakkil, and thus launched a court career, notorious for its opportunism and greed. In 892 he went to Egypt as court poet to its ruler, but he later returned to his birthplace, where he died.

The majority of al-Buḥturī's poems were produced during his years as court poet and are panegyrics, poems of praise (usually addressed to a patron) that were famed for their finely conceived and detailed descriptions and their musicality of tone. Those written during the early part of his career are historically valuable for the allusions they make to contemporary events.

Bukhārī, al- \al-bù-'ḵä-ˌrē\, *in full* Abū 'Abd Allāh Muḥammad ibn Ismā'īl al-Bukhārī (b. July 19, 810, Bukhara, Central Asia [now in Uzbekistan]—d. Aug. 31, 870, Khartank, near Samarkand)   One of the greatest Muslim compilers and scholars of Ḥadīth (the sayings and acts of the Prophet Muḥammad). His chief work is accepted by Sunnite Muslims—*i.e.,* those following the majority tradition—as second only to the Qur'ān as both a source of religious law and a sacred work.

While still a child al-Bukhārī began learning by heart the utterances and actions of the Prophet. His travels in search of more information about them began with a pilgrimage to Mecca when he was 16. For 16 years he sought out informants, traveling from Cairo to Merv in Central Asia. From the approximately 600,000 traditions he gathered, he selected about 7,275 that he deemed completely reliable for his *Al-Jāmi' aṣ-Ṣaḥīḥ* ("The Authentic Collection"). As a preliminary to his *Ṣaḥīḥ,* al-Bukhārī wrote *At-Tā'rīkh al-kabīr* ("The Large History"), which contains biographies of the persons forming the chain of oral transmission and recollection of traditions back to the Prophet.

Bukowski \byū-'kaù-skē\, Charles (b. Aug. 16, 1920, Andernach, Ger.—d. March 9, 1994, San Pedro, Calif., U.S.) American author noted for his use of violent images and graphic language in poetry and fiction that depicted survival in a corrupt, blighted society.

Bukowski lived most of his life in Los Angeles. He briefly attended Los Angeles City College (1939–41) and worked at menial jobs while writing short stories, the first of which were published in the mid-1940s. In 1955 he began publishing poetry; beginning with *Flower, Fist and Bestial Wail* (1959), volumes of his poetry appeared almost annually. By 1963, the year he published *It Catches My Heart in Its Hands*—a collection of poetry about alcoholics, prostitutes, losing gamblers, and down-and-out people—Bukowski had a loyal following.

Bukowski's short stories were unsparingly realistic and most often comic. Collections of his stories include *Notes of a Dirty Old Man* (1969), taken from his underground newspaper column of that name, and *Erections, Ejaculations, Exhibitions, and General Tales of Ordinary Madness* (1972). His later works include the novels *Post Office* (1971) and *Factotum* (1975) and the screenplay (published 1984) for the 1987 motion picture *Barfly*, a semiautobiographical comedy about alcoholic lovers on skid row. The filming of *Barfly* was the subject of his novel *Hollywood* (1989).

Bulba, Taras \,tə-'rås-'bül'y-bə\ Fictional character, the protagonist of the story TARAS BULBA by Nikolay Gogol.

Bulgakov \bül-'gå-kəf\, Mikhail Afanasyevich (b. May 3 [May 15, New Style], 1891, Kiev, Ukraine, Russian Empire—d. March 10, 1940, Moscow, Russia, U.S.S.R.) Russian playwright, novelist, and short-story writer best known for his humor and penetrating satire.

Ardis Publishers

Bulgakov's first major work was the novel *Belaya gvardiya* (*The White Guard*), partially serialized in 1925 but not published in book form until 1969. It was met by a storm of official criticism for its lack of a communist hero. Bulgakov reworked it into a play, *Dni Turbinykh* ("The Days of the Turbins"), which was staged with great success in 1926 but was subsequently banned. In 1925 he published a book of satirical fantasies, *Dyavoliada* ("Deviltries"; *Diaboliad*), implicitly critical of Soviet society. This work, too, was officially denounced. In the same year he wrote *Sobachye serdtse* (THE HEART OF A DOG), a scathing comic satire on pseudoscience that was not openly published in the U.S.S.R. until 1987.

From 1925 to 1929 Bulgakov wrote and staged many plays, including dramatizations of his novels. Because of their realism and humor, Bulgakov's works enjoyed great popularity, but his trenchant criticism of Soviet mores was increasingly unacceptable to the authorities, and his work was censored. By 1930 he was, in effect, prohibited from publishing.

Bulgakov produced two more masterpieces during the 1930s. His unfinished *Teatralny roman* (1965; *Black Snow: A Theatrical Novel*) includes a merciless satire on Konstantin Stanislavsky and the backstage life of the Moscow Art Theater, where he had served as literary consultant in the early 1930s. His dazzling Gogolesque fantasy *Master i Margarita* (THE MASTER AND MARGARITA) was published in the Soviet Union only in 1966–67, and then in an egregiously censored form.

Bull \'bül\, Olaf (Jacob Martin Luther) (b. Nov. 10, 1883, Kristiania [now Oslo], Nor.—d. June 23, 1933, Oslo) One of the greatest Norwegian poets of his generation, often referred to as the Keats of Norway.

Bull's first volume, *Digte* (1909; "Poems"), immediately led to recognition. He was influenced by the French Symbolists and by the philosophy of Henri Bergson. Besides poetry, he wrote one detective story and collaborated on a play. Throughout his work, the reader is conscious of his forceful intellect, but not until his later poems, *De hundrede år* (1928; "The Hundred Years") and *Ignis ardens* (1932), did he become less esoteric and more involved with society.

Bull, John *see* JOHN BULL.

Bulletin \'bül-ə-tin\ Leading Australian literary journal founded in 1880 by J.F. Archibald and John Haynes. Based in Sydney, N.S.W., the *Bulletin* had its major success from 1886 to 1903 under Archibald's direction. Key elements in its success were its radical political position and its humor. Perhaps the most significant legacy of the journal was the emphasis on stories and poetry by Australian writers; this policy encouraged cultural nationalism and reflected unique Australian values. Over time the journal became increasingly conservative, and its writers and cartoonists often promulgated racist stereotypes; in 1908 "Australia for the White Man" became its slogan, and remained so until 1960. Declining sales led to a change in content, and after 1960 the *Bulletin* became a news magazine.

Bullins \'bül-inz\, Ed (b. July 2, 1935, Philadelphia, Pa., U.S.) American playwright, novelist, poet, and journalist who emerged as one of the leading and most prolific dramatists of black theater in the 1960s.

Bullins made his theatrical debut in August 1965 with the production of three one-act plays: *How Do You Do?*, *Dialect Determinism, or The Rally*, and *Clara's Ole Man*. His first full-length play, *In the Wine Time* (produced 1968), examines the scarcity of options available to the black urban poor. It was the first in a series of plays—called the Twentieth-Century Cycle—that centered on a group of young friends growing up in the 1950s. Other plays in the cycle were *The Corner* (produced 1968), *In New England Winter* (produced 1969), *The Duplex* (produced 1970), *The Fabulous Miss Marie* (produced 1971), *Home Boy* (produced 1976), and *Daddy* (produced 1977). In 1975 he received critical acclaim for *The Taking of Miss Janie*, a play about the failed alliance of an interracial group of political idealists in the 1960s. Sharing the tenets of the black aesthetic movement, his naturalistic plays incorporated elements of black nationalism, "street" lyricism, and interracial tension. His other notable works include the plays *Goin' A Buffalo* (produced 1968) and *Salaam, Huey Newton, Salaam* (produced 1991), as well as the short-story collection *The Hungered One* (1971) and the novel *The Reluctant Rapist* (1973).

Bulwer-Lytton \,bül-wər-'lit-ən\, Edward, *in full* Edward George Earle Bulwer-Lytton, 1st Baron Lytton of Knebworth \'neb-wərth\ (b. May 25, 1803, London, Eng.—d. Jan. 18, 1873, Torquay, Devonshire) British politician, poet, and critic, chiefly remembered as a prolific novelist.

The publication of *Pelham* (1828), the adventures of a dandy, inaugurated Bulwer-Lytton's career as a popular novelist. His political career began in 1831, when he entered Parliament as Liberal member for Lincoln. In 1841 he retired to protest the repeal of the Corn Laws. This, together with his friendship with Benjamin Disraeli, converted him into a Tory supporter, and in 1852 he returned to the House as Tory member for Hertfordshire.

Bulwer-Lytton followed *Pelham* with a series of historical novels, weighted with meticulous detail. In *Eugene Aram*, 3 vol.

(1832), he made use of current fascination with criminals and the underworld. The most notable of his historical novels were *The Last Days of Pompeii*, 3 vol. (1834), and *Harold, the Last of the Saxon Kings* (1848). He turned to realism and portrayal of English society in *The Caxtons*, 3 vol. (1849), and *My Novel* (1853). Bulwer-Lytton also published several volumes of poetry, a satirical novel in verse (containing an attack on Alfred, Lord Tennyson, the poet laureate), and an unsuccessful long epic, *King Arthur* (1848). He was created a peer in 1866.

Bulwer-Lytton \ˌbul-wər-ˈlit-ən\, Robert, *in full* Edward Robert Bulwer-Lytton, 1st Earl of Lytton, Viscount Knebworth \ˈneb-wərth\ of Knebworth, 2nd Baron Lytton of Knebworth, *pseudonym* Owen Meredith \ˈmer-ə-dith\ (b. Nov. 8, 1831, London, Eng.—d. Nov. 24, 1891, Paris, Fr.)   British diplomat and viceroy of India (1876–80) who also achieved, during his lifetime, a reputation as a poet.

Bulwer-Lytton, son of Edward Bulwer-Lytton, began his diplomatic career as an unpaid attaché to his uncle Sir Henry Bulwer, then minister at Washington, D.C. His first paid appointment was at Vienna (1858), and in 1874 he was appointed minister at Lisbon. He inherited his father's barony in 1873. From 1875 to 1880 he served as governor-general of India. He ended his career as British minister to France (1887–91).

To his contemporaries, Bulwer-Lytton was better known as a poet than as a diplomat or administrator. His first collections—a volume of verse narratives entitled *Clytemnestra . . . and Other Poems* (1855) and a volume of autobiographical lyrics entitled *The Wanderer* (1858)—were well received, as was *Lucile* (1860), a witty and romantic novel in verse. In 1883 he published a two-volume work entitled *The Life, Letters and Literary Remains of Edward Bulwer, Lord Lytton*.

Bumble, Mr. \ˈmis-tər-ˈbəm-bəl\   Fictional character in the novel OLIVER TWIST by Charles Dickens. Mr. Bumble is the cruel, pompous beadle of the poorhouse where the orphaned Oliver is raised. "Bumbledom," named after him, characterizes the meddlesome self-importance of the petty bureaucrat.

Bumppo, Natty \ˈnat-ē-ˈbəm-pō\   Fictional character, a mythic frontiersman and guide, the protagonist of James Fenimore Cooper's five novels of frontier life that are known collectively as THE LEATHER-STOCKING TALES. The character is known by various names throughout the series, including Leather-Stocking, Hawkeye, Pathfinder, and Deerslayer.

Bunbury \ˈbən-bər-ē\   A fictitious character invented by one of the main characters in Oscar Wilde's play THE IMPORTANCE OF BEING EARNEST.

In the play, Bunbury is the supposed invalid friend of Algernon Moncrieff. Bunbury's frequent acute attacks of ill health necessitate Algernon's leaving London to attend Bunbury at his country home. Algernon devises this ruse to avoid attending the insufferably dull dinner parties given by his aunt, Lady Bracknell.

Bunin \ˈbü-nʸin\, Ivan Alekseyevich (b. Oct. 10 [Oct. 22, New Style], 1870, Voronezh, Russia—d. Nov. 8, 1953, Paris, Fr.) Poet and novelist, the first Russian to receive the Nobel Prize for Literature (1933).

Bunin's first volume of verse was published in 1891. For his translation of Henry Wadsworth Longfellow's *Hiawatha* he was awarded a Pushkin prize in 1903 by the Russian Academy, which later elected him an honorary fellow (1909). He also translated Lord Byron's *Manfred* and *Cain*.

Bunin made his name as a short-story writer with such masterpieces as "Gospodin iz San-Frantsisko," the title piece in one of his collections (1916; *The Gentleman from San Francisco*). His last book of stories, *Tyomnyye allei* (*Dark Avenues*), was

published in 1943. His longer works include *Derevnya* (1910; *The Village*), *Mitina lyubov* (1925; *Mitya's Love*), the fictional autobiography *Zhizn Arsenyeva* (1930; "The Life of Arsenev"; *The Well of Days*) and its sequel, *Lika* (1939), and two volumes of memoirs, *Okayannyye dni* (1935; "The Cursed Days") and *Vospominaniya* (1950; *Memories and Portraits*). He also wrote books on Leo Tolstoy (*Osvobozhdeniye Tolstogo*, 1937; "Tolstoy's Liberation") and Anton Chekhov. The latter book, *O Chekhove* ("On Chekhov"), remained unfinished and was published posthumously (1955).

Bunner \ˈbən-ər\, Henry Cuyler (b. Aug. 3, 1855, Oswego, N.Y., U.S.—d. May 11, 1896, Nutley, N.J.)   Poet, novelist, and editor whose verse and fiction primarily depict the scenes and people of New York City.

Educated in New York City, Bunner served on the staff of the *Arcadian*. At 22 he became assistant editor and later editor of *Puck*, a position he held until his death. He developed *Puck* from a new, struggling comic weekly into a powerful social and political organ. Bunner's fiction, particularly *"Made in France"; French Tales Retold with a United States Twist* (1893), reflects the influence of Guy de Maupassant and other French writers.

Bunner published several novels, but these are considered inferior to his stories and sketches. As a playwright he is known chiefly for *Tower of Babel* (1883). Collections of his verse, which has been praised for its technical dexterity, playfulness, and smoothness of finish, include *Airs from Arcady and Elsewhere* (1884), *Rowen* (1892), and *Poems* (1896).

bunraku \ˈbun-rä-kü\ [Japanese]   Japanese traditional puppet theater in which nearly life-size dolls act out a chanted dramatic narrative, called *jōruri*, to the accompaniment of a small samisen (or *shamisen*; three-stringed Japanese lute). The term bunraku derives from the name of a troupe organized by puppet master Uemura Bunrakuken in the early 19th century; the term for puppetry is *ayatsuri*, and puppetry theater is more accurately rendered *ayatsuri jōruri*. Puppet theater reached its height in the 18th century with the plays of Chikamatsu Monzaemon. Its fortunes rose and fell with the quality of *jōruri* writers. *See also* JŌRURI.

Bunter \ˈbən-tər\   Fictional character, the perfect valet in the Lord Peter Wimsey mysteries of Dorothy L. SAYERS. A knowledgeable bibliophile, an expert photographer, and a superb brewer of coffee, Bunter is exquisitely attuned to Wimsey's tastes and affectations and is an able assistant during investigations.

Bunter, Billy \ˈbil-ē-ˈbən-tər\   Fictional character, a fat English schoolboy at Greyfriars School who, though an antihero, is the best-known character in a much-loved series of stories by Frank Richards (Charles Hamilton), published in the English boys' weekly paper the *Magnet* (1908–40) and in hardbound books (from after World War II until 1961). After the author's death in 1961, other writers sporadically contributed to the Billy Bunter canon.

Buntline, Ned   Pseudonym of E.Z.C. JUDSON.

Bunyan \ˈbən-yən\, John (b. November 1628, Elstow, Bedfordshire, Eng.—d. Aug. 31, 1688, London)   English minister and author who is best known for THE PILGRIM'S PROGRESS (Part I, 1678; Part II, 1684), the most characteristic expression of the Puritan religious outlook. Until the decline of religious faith and the increase of books of popular instruction in the 19th century, Bunyan, like the Bible, was found in every English home and was known to every ordinary reader.

Bunyan was brought up in the agricultural Midlands of England. When civil war broke out in 1644, he was mustered and sent to reinforce the garrison at Newport Pagnell. Bunyan's military service brought him in touch with the seething religious life of the left-wing sects within Oliver Cromwell's army.

Bunyan married in 1649. In the years following (1650–55), he was plunged into a period of spiritual crisis. He was aided in his recovery from the crisis by his association with the Bedford Separatist church. During 1655–60 his main activity was confrontation with the early Quakers, both in public debate and in his first printed works, *Some Gospel Truths Opened* (1656) and *A Vindication of Some Gospel Truths Opened* (1657), in which he protests against what seemed to him the dangerously blurred and self-centered mysticism of the Quakers.

The Restoration of Charles II brought to an end 20 years of comparative religious freedom. In November 1660, Bunyan was charged with holding a service not in conformity with those of the Church of England. He refused to give an assurance that he would not repeat the offense and was imprisoned in the county jail, where he remained for 12 years. Conditions were lenient enough for him to be let out at times to visit friends and family and to address meetings.

During this imprisonment Bunyan wrote and published his spiritual autobiography, GRACE ABOUNDING (1666). His release from prison came in March 1672 under Charles II's Declaration of Indulgence to the Nonconformists. When persecution was renewed he was again imprisoned, this time probably for no longer than six months.

Upon the publication of *The Pilgrim's Progress*, the allegory of Christian's journey to the Celestial City was instantly popular with all classes, though it was perhaps the last great expression of the folk tradition of the common people before the divisive effects of modern enlightened education began to be felt. Bunyan's next publication, *The Life and Death of Mr. Badman* (1680), gave insight into the problems of money and marriage at a time when the Puritans were beginning to find their social role as an urban middle class. He later wrote THE HOLY WAR (1682).

Bunyan published a large number of works in the last 10 years of his life. One of the most interesting of these is *A Book for Boys and Girls* (1686), with its vigorous poems commenting on emblematic pictures.

Bunyan, Paul \'bən-yən\ Giant lumberjack, mythical hero of the lumber camps in the United States, a symbol of bigness, strength, and vitality. The tales and anecdotes that form the Paul Bunyan legend are typical frontier tall tales.

A few anecdotes of Paul Bunyan recorded from oral folklore suggest that the character was known to lumbermen in Pennsylvania, Wisconsin, and the Northwest before the first Bunyan stories were published by James MacGillivray in "The Round River Drive" (*Detroit News-Tribune*, July 24, 1910). Within 15 years, through popularization by professional writers, Bunyan was transformed from an occupational folk figure into a national legend. Paul was introduced to a wider audience by W.B. Laughead, a Minnesota advertising man, in a series of pamphlets (1914–44) used to publicize the products of the Red River Lumber Company. These influenced Esther Shephard, who wrote of the mythic hero in *Paul Bunyan* (1924), and James Stevens in his *Paul Bunyan* (1925).

The lumberjack is the subject of poems by the Americans Robert Frost, Carl Sandburg, and Richard Wilbur and of an operetta by the Anglo-American poet W.H. Auden and the English composer Benjamin Britten.

bunyip \'bən-yip\ [Wemba (Australian Aboriginal language of Victoria) *banib*] In Australian Aboriginal folklore, a legendary monster said to inhabit the reedy swamps and lagoons of the interior of Australia. The bunyip purportedly made booming or roaring noises and was given to devouring human prey, especially women and children. The origin of the belief probably lies in the rare appearance of fugitive seals far upstream; the monster's alleged cry may be that of the Australian bittern, a marsh bird.

Bürger \'buer-gər\, Gottfried August (b. Dec. 31, 1747, Molmerswende bei Halberstadt, Brandenburg [Germany]—d. June 8, 1794, Göttingen, Hanover) One of the founders of German Romantic ballad literature whose style reflects the renewed interest in folk song in Europe during the late 1700s.

In Göttingen Bürger first came into contact with a group of Sturm und Drang poets known as the Göttinger Hain, who drew inspiration from folk ballads. In 1773 Bürger published the bizarre ballad "Lenore," a spectral romance in which a ghostly rider, posing as Lenore's dead lover, carries her away on a macabre night ride through an eerie landscape illuminated by flashes of lightning. It culminates in a revelation of the rider as Death itself—a skeleton with scythe and hourglass. The poem's use of refrain and its simple and naïve language, as well as its sensational theme, had a profound effect upon the subsequent development of Romanticism throughout Europe.

In addition to a number of Petrarchan sonnets, Bürger is also noted for his translations from the English, especially for his renderings of the influential collection of English and Scottish traditional ballads, Thomas Percy's *Reliques of Ancient English Poetry*.

Burgess \'bər-jəs\, Anthony, *also called* Joseph Kell \'kel\, *original name* John Anthony Burgess Wilson \'wil-sən\ (b. Feb. 25, 1917, Manchester, Eng.—d. Nov. 22, 1993, London) English novelist, critic, and man of letters, whose fictional explorations of modern dilemmas combine wit, moral earnestness, and a note of the bizarre.

Burgess taught in the extramural department of Birmingham University (1946–50), worked for the Ministry of Education (1948–50), and was English master at Banbury Grammar School (1950–54). He then served as education officer in Malaya and Borneo (1954–59), where he wrote three novels with a Malayan setting. Under the pseudonym Anthony Burgess he wrote the novels *The Wanting Seed* (1962), an anti-utopian view of an overpopulated world, and *Honey for the Bears* (1963). As Joseph Kell he wrote *One Hand Clapping* (1961) and *Inside Mr. Enderby* (1963).

A CLOCKWORK ORANGE (1962; film, 1971) made Burgess' reputation as a novelist of comic and mordant power. Other novels include *The Eve of Saint Venus* (1964) and *Enderby Outside* (1968). The latter is a part of a series of humorous novels centered on the lyric poet F.X. Enderby, whom many critics have seen as a spokesman for Burgess himself. His later works include the novels *Earthly Powers* (1980), *The End of the World News* (1983), *Any Old Iron* (1989), and *A Dead Man in Deptford* (1993). Burgess' novels are characterized by verbal inventiveness, erudition, and sharp social satire. He also wrote two volumes of autobiography, *Little Wilson and Big God* (1986) and *You've Had Your Time* (1990), literary criticism, and several biographies.

Burgess \'bər-jəs\, Gelett, *in full* Frank Gelett Burgess (b. Jan. 30, 1866, Boston, Mass., U.S.—d. Sept. 17, 1951, Carmel, Calif.) American humorist and illustrator best known for a single, early, whimsical quatrain:

> I never saw a purple cow,
> I never hope to see one;
> But I can tell you, anyhow,
> I'd rather see than be one.

In 1895 Burgess became the founding editor of *Lark*, a humor magazine, and in 1897 he began to publish books of his self-illustrated whimsical writings. Among his best-known works are *Goops and How to Be Them* (1900) and subsequent books on Goops (bad-mannered children). He is credited with adding several words to the English language, including *blurb*. Among his many other works are *Are You a Bromide?* (1906), *Why Men Hate Women* (1927), and *Look Eleven Years Younger* (1937).

Buried Child   Three-act tragedy by Sam SHEPARD, performed in 1978 and published in 1979. The play was awarded the 1979 Pulitzer Prize for drama.

Shepard had his first critical and commercial success with this corrosive study of American family life. The play, set on an Illinois farm, centers on the homecoming of Vince and his girlfriend, Shelly. Vince cherishes a romantic, bucolic vision of the home he left six years earlier, but the actual family turns out to be a collection of twisted grotesques.

Shepard considered the work to be part of a family trilogy with *Curse of the Starving Class* (1976) and *True West* (1981), both of which also portrayed destructive blood relationships.

Burke \'bərk\, Kenneth (Duva) (b. May 5, 1897, Pittsburgh, Pa., U.S.—d. Nov. 19, 1993, Andover, N.J.)   American literary critic best known for his psychologically based analyses of the nature of knowledge and his views of literature as "symbolic action," that is, a symbolic means by which the writer can act out personal psychic conflicts and tensions.

Burke wrote poems, a novel, and short stories and translated the works of many German writers into English. He was the music critic of the *Dial* (1927–29) and of *The Nation* (1934–36). He then turned to literary criticism, lecturing on this subject at the University of Chicago (1938; 1949–50). He also taught at Bennington College (Vermont) and several other schools throughout the United States.

Burke's chief aim as a literary critic was to use sociological, psychological, and anthropological concepts to integrate all human knowledge and experience into a workable system. Among his books are *Counter-Statement* (1931), *The Philosophy of Literary Form* (1941), *Permanence and Change: An Anatomy of Purpose* (1935), *Attitudes Toward History*, 2 vol. (1937), *A Grammar of Motives* (1945), *A Rhetoric of Motives* (1950), and *Language as Symbolic Action* (1966).

burlesque, \bər-'lesk\ [French, from the adjective *burlesque* mocking, burlesque in style, from Italian *burlesco*, a derivative of *burla* joke, harmless prank]   In literature, comic imitation of a serious literary or artistic form that relies on an extravagant incongruity between a subject and its treatment. Burlesque is closely related to parody, although burlesque is generally broader and coarser.

The long history of burlesque includes such early examples in Greece as *Batrachomyomachia* (*The Battle of the Frogs and Mice*), an anonymous burlesque of Homer, and the comedies of Aristophanes (5th–4th century BC). The long-winded medieval romance is satirized in Geoffrey Chaucer's 14th-century "The Tale of Sir Thopas"; the Charlemagne story and the whole theme of chivalry is mocked in the epic-style *Morgante* by Luigi Pulci. Italian burlesque of the 15th century attacked the concept of chivalry as a dying aristocratic notion lacking in common sense, and it thus anticipates Miguel de Cervantes' novel *Don Quixote*. The *Virgile travesty* (1648–53) of Paul Scarron is one of the best known of many burlesque or antiheroic epics on classical or even sacred themes.

English burlesque is chiefly dramatic, notable exceptions being Samuel Butler's satiric poem *Hudibras* (1663–78), an indictment of Puritan hypocrisy; the mock-heroic couplets of John Dryden and Alexander Pope; and the prose burlesques of Jonathan Swift and Henry Fielding. *The Rehearsal* (1671), a play by George Villiers, the 2nd Duke of Buckingham, mocks the Restoration drama of Dryden and Thomas Otway.

John Gay's *The Beggar's Opera* (1728), Henry Fielding's *Tom Thumb* (1730), Richard Brinsley Sheridan's *The Critic* (1779), and Henry Carey's "most tragical tragedy" *Chrononhotonthologos* (1734) are the outstanding survivals from an age when burlesque was cruelly satirical and often defamatory. Authors of Victorian burlesque—light entertainment with music and with plots frivolously modeled on those of history, literature, or classical mythology—included H.J. Byron, J.R. Planché, and W.S. Gilbert (before his partnership with Arthur Sullivan). Before the end of the 19th century, burlesque had largely yielded in popular favor to other forms.

Burnett \bər-'net, 'bər-nət\, Frances (Eliza) Hodgson, *original surname* Hodgson \'häj-sən\ (b. Nov. 24, 1849, Manchester, Eng.—d. Oct. 29, 1924, Plandome, N.Y., U.S.)   American playwright and author who wrote the popular novel LITTLE LORD FAUNTLEROY.

Burnett first gained recognition for *That Lass o' Lowrie's* (1877), a tale of the Lancashire, England, coal mines. Her novel *Through One Administration* (1883) had as its theme corruption in Washington, D.C. In addition to *Little Lord Fauntleroy* (1886), *Sara Crewe* (1888; dramatized as *A Little Princess* in 1905) and THE SECRET GARDEN (1911) were also written for children. *A Lady of Quality* (1896) has been considered the best of her other plays. These, like most of her 40-odd novels, stress sentimental, romantic themes.

Burney \'bər-nē\, Fanny, *original name* Frances, *married name* d'Arblay \'där-blā\ (b. June 13, 1752, King's Lynn, Norfolk, Eng.—d. Jan. 6, 1840, London)   English novelist and letter writer, author of EVELINA (1778), a landmark in the development of the novel of manners.

Fanny educated herself by omnivorous reading at home. Her first journal letters were lively accounts of the musical evenings at the Burneys' London house, where the elite among European performers entertained informally.

Her practice of observing and recording society led eventually to her novel *Evelina*. Published anonymously in 1778, the book took London by storm. When it was discovered that she was the author of *Evelina*, Burney's debut into literary society was launched. Burney's journals from this period have been prized for their vignettes of contemporary scenes and celebrities. Her next novel, the five-volume *Cecilia, or Memoirs of an Heiress* (1782), incorporated morally didactic themes with social satire into a more complex plot.

Burney's later publications include a potboiler, *Camilla: or, A Picture of Youth* (1796). An edition of her journals and letters in eight volumes was published in 1972–80.

Burns \'bərnz\, Robert (b. Jan. 25, 1759, Alloway, Ayrshire, Scot.—d. July 21, 1796, Dumfries, Dumfriesshire)   National poet of Scotland who wrote lyrics and songs in the Scottish dialect. He was also famous for his rebellion against orthodox religion and morality.

Burns was the son of a poor farmer. He received some formal schooling and read most of the important 18th-century English writers as well as William Shakespeare and John Milton. His knowledge of Scottish literature was confined mainly to orally transmitted folk songs and folk tales.

Though he wrote poetry for his own amusement and that of his friends, Burns was restless and dissatisfied. He won the reputation of being a dangerous rebel against orthodox religion, and when in 1786 he fell in love with Jean Armour, her father refused to permit their marriage. Burns's *Poems, Chiefly in the Scottish Dialect* (1786) met with immediate and overwhelming success.

On the publication of this volume, Burns had gone to Edinburgh, which unsettled him. After a number of amorous and other adventures there and several trips to other parts of Scotland, he settled in the summer of 1788 at a farm in Ellisland, Dumfriesshire. He found farming at Ellisland difficult, though he was helped by Armour, with whom he had been reconciled and whom he finally married in 1788.

Detail of an oil painting by Alexander Nasmyth

National Portrait Gallery, London

In Edinburgh Burns had met James Johnson, a keen collector of Scottish songs who was bringing out a series of volumes of songs and who enlisted Burns's help in finding, editing, improving, and rewriting items. Later, he became involved with a similar project for George Thomson. Johnson's *Scots Musical Museum* (1787–1803) and Thomson's *Select Collection of Original Scotish Airs for the Voice* (1793–1818) contain the bulk of Burns's songs. Burns spent the latter part of his life in assiduously collecting and writing songs to provide words for traditional Scottish airs. He regarded his work as service to Scotland and refused payment. The only poem he wrote after his Edinburgh visit that showed a hitherto unsuspected side of his poetic genius was *Tam o'Shanter*, a spirited narrative poem in skillfully handled eight-syllable couplets based on a folk legend.

That Burns has become the Scottish national poet is an indication of his continuing hold on the popular imagination. Among the songs for which he is best known are "Green Grow the Rashes, O," "John Anderson My Jo," "A Red, Red Rose," "Willie Brew'd a Peck o' Maut," and "Ye Banks and Braes o' Bonnie Doon."

Burns meter or **Burns stanza**   In poetry, a stanza often used by Robert Burns and other Scottish poets. The stanza consists of six lines rhyming *aaabab* of which the fourth and sixth are regularly iambic dimeters and the others iambic tetrameters, as in Burns's *Holy Willie's Prayer*:

> I bless and praise thy matchless might,
> Whan thousands thou hast left in night,
> That I am here afore thy sight,
> For gifts an' grace
> A burnin' an' a shinin' light,
> To a' this place.

Burnt Norton \\'bərnt-'nȯrt-ən\\   Poem by T.S. ELIOT, the first of the four poems that make up THE FOUR QUARTETS. "Burnt Norton" was published in *Collected Poems 1909–1935* (1936); it was published with the remaining three poems of the *The Four Quartets* in 1943.

Burnt Norton is a country house in the Cotswold Hills of Gloucestershire that Eliot visited in the summer of 1934. Set in the rose garden of the house, the poem addresses the pervasive theme of cyclical patterns in time. The opening lines, taken from a passage deleted from *Murder in the Cathedral* (1935), resonate with contradiction and ambiguity:

> Time present and time past
> Are both perhaps present in time future,
> And time future contained in time past.

Burnt-Out Case, A   Novel by Graham GREENE, published in 1961, that examines the possibility of redemption.

The story opens as Querry, a European who has lost the ability to connect with emotion or spirituality, arrives at a leprosarium in the Belgian Congo. His spiritual aridity is likened to a medical burnt-out case—a leper who is in remission but who has been eaten up by his disease. Querry is invigorated by his contact with the leprosarium and its inhabitants, and he begins to come to life. Parkinson, an opportunistic journalist, discovers that Querry is a distinguished architect with a lurid past and begins to write sensationalized newspaper articles about him. When Querry innocently consoles the wife of the manager of a local factory, he is shot dead by her husband.

Burroughs \\'bər-ōz\\, Edgar Rice (b. Sept. 1, 1875, Chicago, Ill., U.S.—d. March 19, 1950, Encino, Calif.)   American novelist whose TARZAN stories created a folk hero known around the world.

Burroughs began writing advertising copy and then turned to fiction. His first published piece, "Under the Moons of Mars," appeared in the adventure magazine *All-Story* in 1911 and was so successful that Burroughs began writing full-time. The first Tarzan story appeared in 1912, followed in 1914 by *Tarzan of the Apes*, the first of 25 such books about the son of an English nobleman abandoned in the African jungle during infancy and brought up by apes.

Burroughs continued to write other novels as well, ultimately publishing some 68 titles in all. During World War II he became a correspondent for the *Los Angeles Times* and, at age 66, was the oldest war correspondent covering the South Pacific.

Burroughs \\'bər-ōz\\, John (b. April 3, 1837, near Roxbury, N.Y., U.S.—d. March 29, 1921, en route from California to New York)   American essayist and naturalist who lived and wrote after the manner of Henry David Thoreau, studying and celebrating nature.

In his earlier years Burroughs worked as a teacher and a farmer and for nine years as a clerk in the U.S. Treasury Department in Washington, D.C. In 1867 he paid tribute to his friend Walt Whitman in the book *Notes on Walt Whitman as Poet and Person*. In 1871 *Wake-Robin*, the first of his books on birds, flowers, and rural scenes, was published. Two years later he moved to a farm in the Hudson River valley and, from various retreats, wrote for half a century on nature subjects. His chief books, in addition to *Wake-Robin*, are *Birds and Poets* (1877), *Locusts and Wild Honey* (1879), *Signs and Seasons* (1886), and *Ways of Nature* (1905). He also wrote a volume of poems, *Bird and Bough* (1906). *Winter Sunshine* (1875) and *Fresh Fields* (1884) are sketches of travel in England and France. His *Whitman: A Study* was published in 1896. Other collections of his essays are *Time and Change* (1912), *The Summit of the Years* (1913), *The Breath of Life* (1915), *Under the Apple Trees* (1916), and *Field and Study* (1919).

Burroughs \\'bər-ōz\\, William Seward (b. Feb. 5, 1914, St. Louis, Mo., U.S.)   American writer of experimental novels that evoke, in deliberately erratic prose, a nightmarish, sometimes wildly humorous world. His sexual explicitness (he was an avowed and outspoken homosexual) and the frankness with which he dealt with his own experiences as a drug addict won him a following among writers of the Beat Movement.

Burroughs grew up in comfortable circumstances, graduating from Harvard University in 1936. Becoming addicted to drugs—notably heroin—in New York City in 1944, he moved with his second wife to Mexico, where in 1951 he shot and killed her in an accident. Fleeing Mexico, he wandered through the Amazon region of South America, continuing his experiments with drugs. This period of his life was detailed in *The Yage Letters*, his correspondence with Allen Ginsberg written in 1953 but not published until 1963.

He used the pen name William Lee in his first published book, *Junkie: Confessions of an Unredeemed Drug Addict* (1953, abridged version; 1977, unexpurgated). *The Naked Lunch* (Paris, 1959; U.S. title, *Naked Lunch*, 1962; film, 1991) was completed after his treatment for drug addiction. The grotesqueness of the drug addict's world is vividly satirized in *The Naked Lunch*, which also is much preoccupied with homosexuality and police persecution. In the novels that followed—notably, *The Soft Machine* (1961), *The Ticket That Exploded* (1962), *Nova Express* (1964), *The Last Words of Dutch Schultz* (1970), *The Wild Boys* (1971), *Exterminator!* (1973), *Cities of the Red Night* (1981), *Place of Dead Roads* (1983), *Queer* (1985), and *The Western Lands* (1987)—Burroughs further experimented with the structure of the novel.

Burton \ˈbərt-ən\, Richard, *in full* Sir Richard Francis Burton (b. March 19, 1821, Torquay, Devonshire, Eng.—d. Oct. 20, 1890, Trieste, Austria-Hungary [now in Italy]) English scholar-explorer and Orientalist who published 43 volumes on his explorations and almost 30 volumes of translations, including an unexpurgated translation of *The Thousand and One Nights*.

Burton was reared in France and Italy and became fluent in French, Italian, and the Béarnais and Neapolitan dialects, as well as in Greek and Latin. Expelled from Oxford in 1842, he joined the army in India. Eventually in his travels over the world he learned 25 languages, with dialects bringing the number to 40.

In 1853, disguising himself as an Afghani Muslim, Burton went to Cairo, Suez, Medina, and the sacred city of Mecca. His *Pilgrimage to El-Medinah and Mecca* (1855–56) is a great adventure story and a classic commentary on Muslim life and manners. In 1854 he organized a new expedition to the equally forbidden East African city of Harar (Harer). He described his adventures in *First Footsteps in East Africa* (1856).

After two failed attempts to find the source of the White Nile, Burton entered the British Foreign Office in 1861. During three years as consul in Fernando Po, a Spanish island off the coast of West Africa, he wrote extensively on tribal rituals concerning birth, marriage, and death, as well as on fetishism, ritual murder, cannibalism, and bizarre sexual practices. He then spent four years as consul in Santos, Braz., where he wrote a book on the highlands of Brazil (1869) and translated *Vikram and the Vampire; or, Tales of Hindu Devilry* (1870).

In 1872 Burton reluctantly accepted the consulate at Trieste, where he stayed until his death, publishing an astonishing variety of books, none of which was successful. He emerged as a translator of extraordinary virtuosity. He translated and annotated six volumes of the works of the Portuguese poet-explorer Luís de Camões, a volume of Neapolitan Italian tales by Giambattista Basile, and Latin poems by Catullus. He risked prosecution and imprisonment to translate and print secretly the *Kama Sutra of Vatsyayana* (1883), *Ananga Ranga* (1885), and *The Perfumed Garden of the Cheikh Nefzaoui* (1886). He also published openly, but privately, the 16-volume edition of *The Thousand and One Nights* (1885–88), an unexpurgated translation so exceptional for its vigor and literary skill that it long frightened away all competitors.

Burton \ˈbərt-ən\, Robert (b. Feb. 8, 1577, Lindley, Leicestershire, Eng.—d. Jan. 25, 1640, Oxford) English scholar, writer, and Anglican clergyman whose ANATOMY OF MELANCHOLY is a masterpiece of style, a mine of curious information, and a valuable index to the philosophical and psychological ideas of the time.

Burton was educated at Oxford, elected a student (life fellow) of Christ Church in 1599, and lived there the rest of his life, becoming a bachelor of divinity in 1614 and vicar of St. Thomas' Church, Oxford, in 1616. His "silent, sedentary, solitary" life, as he himself describes it, lent his view of humanity an ironic detachment, but it certainly did not make it that of a scholar remote from reality: he is as informative on the pastimes of his day as on the ideas of the ancients, and as keen to recommend a rational diet as to relate human disorders to his own essentially Christian view of the universe.

Burton's first work was the Latin comedy *Philosophaster* (1606), a vivacious exposure of charlatanism that has affinities with Ben Jonson's *The Alchemist*. It was acted at Christ Church in 1618. The *Anatomy of Melancholy*, which first appeared in 1621, went through five subsequent editions (1624, 1628, 1632, 1638, and 1651), incorporating Burton's revisions and alterations. In its allusive richness and synthetic clarity, the book amounts to a virtual compendium of Jacobean scholarship.

Busch \ˈbůsh\, Frederick (Matthew) (b. Aug. 1, 1941, Brooklyn, N.Y., U.S.)   American critic, editor, novelist, and short-story writer whose work often examined aspects of family life from diverse points of view.

Busch graduated from Muhlenberg College, Allentown, Pa., in 1962 and received an M.A. in 1967 from Colgate University, Hamilton, N.Y., where he later served as Fairchild professor of literature.

In his second novel, *Manual Labor* (1974), a married couple grapple with the death of their unborn child. They reappear later in *Rounds* (1979), in which their lives are intertwined with those of a doctor and a psychologist. *Domestic Particulars: A Family Chronicle* (1976), a collection of interlinked short stories, catalogs in vivid detail the everyday lives of people caught up in often futile attempts to express love. *The Mutual Friend* (1978), which represented a departure for Busch in terms of subject matter, is an imaginative account of the last years of Charles Dickens as told by his friend George Dolby. In the novella *War Babies* (1989), Busch returned to the subject of family relationships with the story of a man who attempts to rid himself of feelings of guilt over his now-dead father's imprisonment for treason. *Harry and Catherine* (1990) examines the long and often unpleasant relationship of two lovers.

Būṣīrī, al- \ál-,bū-ˈsē-,rē\, *in full* Sharaf ad-Dīn Muḥammad ibn Saʿīd al-Būṣīrī aṣ-Ṣanhājī (b. *c.* 1212, Abūṣīr or Dilāṣ, Egypt—d. *c.* 1295, Alexandria)   Arabic poet of Berber descent who won fame for his poem *Al-Burdah* (*The Poem of the Scarf*).

In his poem al-Būṣīrī said that he had devoted his life to poetry. He also worked as a copyist, being known for his calligraphy. It was said that he wrote his famous poem in praise of the Prophet Muḥammad after being cured of partial paralysis when the Prophet appeared to him in a dream and wrapped him in a mantle. In the poem, al-Būṣīrī contrasts the shortcomings of his life with the miracles of Muḥammad. The poem has been much venerated by Muslims, and its verses have been used as text on amulets and in lamentations for the dead.

Busken Huet \ˈbůes-kən-ˈhůe-wet\, Conrad (b. Dec. 28?, 1826, The Hague, Neth.—d. June 1, 1886, Paris, Fr.)   The greatest and one of the liveliest Dutch literary critics of his time.

A descendant of an old French Protestant family, Busken Huet studied theology at Leiden and became pastor of the Walloon chapel at Haarlem but resigned because of his modernist views. He turned to literary criticism and from 1863 to 1865 was an editor of the influential literary magazine *De Gids* ("The Guide"). After many disappointments, he left The Netherlands for the Dutch East Indies (now Indonesia), where he worked as a journalist. For the last years of his life he lived in Paris.

As a critic, Busken Huet took the French dean of critics, Charles-Augustin Sainte-Beuve, and the Danish Georg Brandes as his guides and sought to bring Dutch literature into closer touch with other European cultures. He wrote brilliantly about the Dutch classics, the minor Dutch poets, and both the classic and modern literature of other countries. Busken Huet collected his most important critical writings in 25 volumes entitled *Litterarische fantasiën en kritieken* (1868–88; "Literary Fantasies and Criticisms"). His history of Dutch culture in the 17th century, *Het land van Rembrandt* (1882–84; "The Country of Rembrandt"), remains a classic.

buskin \'bəs-kin\ [probably modification of Middle French *brouzequin* kind of foot covering] A thick-soled boot worn by actors in ancient Greek tragedies. Because of the association the term has come to mean tragedy. It is contrasted with sock, which refers to the foot covering worn by actors in comedies.

Buson or **Yosa Buson** \yō-'sä-bü-'sȯn, -'sȯⁿ\, *original name* Taniguchi Buson (b. 1716, Kema, Settsu province, Japan—d. Jan. 17, 1784, Kyōto) One of the great haiku poets, also noted as a painter.

Buson came of a wealthy family but chose to leave it behind to pursue a career in the arts. He traveled extensively in northeastern Japan and studied haiku under several masters, among them Hayano Hajin, whom he eulogized in *Hokuju Rōsen o itamu* (1745; "Mourning for Hokuju Rōsen"). In 1751 he settled in Kyōto as a professional painter, remaining there for most of his life. He did, however, spend three years (1754–57) in Yosa, Tango province, a region noted for its scenic beauty. There he worked intensively to improve his technique in both poetry and painting. During this period he changed his surname from Taniguchi to Yosa. Buson's fame as a poet rose particularly after 1772. He urged a revival of the tradition of his great predecessor Matsuo Bashō but never reached the level of humanistic understanding attained by Bashō. Buson's poetry, perhaps reflecting his interest in painting, is ornate, sensuous, and rich in visual detail. Buson's interest in Chinese poetry is especially evident in three long poems that are irregular in form. His experimental poems have been called "Chinese poems in Japanese," and two of them contain passages in Chinese.

Bus Stop Romantic comedy in three acts by William INGE, performed and published in 1955. An expansion of *People in the Wind*, a one-act play, *Bus Stop* is set in a small town in Kansas. The story concerns the passengers of a cross-country bus who are stranded overnight by a blizzard and congregate in Grace's restaurant. The passengers include Cherie, a flighty blonde bar singer, cowboys Bo and Virgil, and a drunken doctor, and they are joined by the sheriff, the bus driver, and a waitress. The passengers devise entertainments for themselves, and the men vie for Cherie's attention. When Bo eventually confesses his love to Cherie and tells her she is his first girl, she agrees to go to Montana with him.

Bussy-Rabutin \bᵫ-,sē-rȧ-bᵫ-'taⁿ\, Roger de, *in full* Roger de Rabutin, Count (comte) de Bussy (b. April 13, 1618, Épiry, Fr.—d. April 9, 1693, Autun) French libertine who amused the nobility of his time with scandalous tales told in a light classical prose style; he was the cousin and confidant of the celebrated letter writer the Marquise de Sévigné.

During the civil wars of the Fronde (uprisings against the government of Cardinal Mazarin), Bussy-Rabutin served first the rebels, then the government. Although his raffish escapades got him into trouble, he was nevertheless allowed to buy the exalted rank of lieutenant colonel general of the light cavalry in 1653 and was elected to the Académie Française in 1665.

Then came his downfall with the unauthorized printing, in 1665, of *Histoire amoureuse des Gaules*, four scandalous and amusingly written tales about court ladies. After 13 months in prison he was exiled from Paris to his native Burgundy. His disgrace deepened when his enemies produced more libelous pamphlets dressed up as supplements to the *Histoire*. From exile, however, he conducted a voluminous correspondence, which was highly esteemed until the Marquise de Sévigné's correspondence set a new standard.

Butler \'bət-lər\, Alban (b. Oct. 24, 1710, Northampton, Northamptonshire, Eng.—d. May 15, 1773, Saint-Omer, Fr.) Roman Catholic priest and educator, renowned for his classic *Lives of the Saints*. Butler was educated at the English College in Douai, Fr., where he taught after ordination in 1734. In 1749 he returned to England but later became president of the English College at Saint-Omer.

Butler's monumental four-volume work *The Lives of the Fathers, Martyrs, and Other Principal Saints* (1756–59) was considered a sound, critical, and authoritative work. Containing more than 1,600 hagiographies, it went through many editions and was revised in the mid-20th century.

Butler \'bət-lər\, Guy, *in full* Frederick Guy Butler (b. Jan. 21, 1918, Cradock, Cape Province, S.Af.) South African poet and playwright, many of whose poems have extraordinary sensitivity and brilliant imagery.

Butler began writing during military service in North Africa and Europe (1940–45). After studying at Oxford, he joined the faculty of Rhodes University in Grahamstown, S.Af. He studied and edited diaries of colonial settlers and edited an influential broadsheet of contemporary poetry, *New Coin*, but he was also considerably involved in the theater. His first play, *The Dam* (1953), took a prize at the Van Riebeeck Festival, and subsequent verse drama included *The Dove Returns* (1956), *Take Root or Die* (1970), and *Cape Charade* (1968). *Stranger to Europe* (1952) contains some of Butler's first poetry. Other poetry volumes include *Selected Poems* (1975; rev. ed., 1989), *Songs and Ballads* (1978), and *Pilgrimage to Dias Cross* (1987). The two volumes of Butler's autobiography, *Karoo Morning* (1977) and *Bursting World* (1983), proceed from early memories of his family up to his war service. In 1989 he edited (with Jeff Opland) *The Magic Tree*, a collection of 119 narrative poems translated from several South African languages and chosen for their South African setting.

Butler \'bət-lər\, Octavia E., *in full* Estelle (b. June 22, 1947, Pasadena, Calif., U.S.) African-American author chiefly noted for her award-winning science-fiction novels about future societies and superhuman powers.

Encouraged by Harlan Ellison, Butler began her writing career in 1970. The first of her novels, *Patternmaster* (1976), was the beginning of her five-volume Patternist series about an elite group of mentally linked telepaths. Other novels in the series were *Mind of My Mind* (1977), *Survivor* (1978), *Wild Seed* (1980), and *Clay's Ark* (1984).

In *Kindred* (1979) a contemporary black woman is sent back in time to a pre-Civil War plantation, becomes a slave, and rescues her white, slave-owning ancestor. Butler's short story "Bloodchild" (1984), about human male slaves who incubate their alien masters' eggs, won several awards. Her later novels include the Xenogenesis trilogy—*Dawn: Xenogenesis* (1987), *Adulthood Rites* (1988), and *Imago* (1989)—and *The Parable of the Sower* (1993).

Butler \'bət-lər\, Samuel (baptized Feb. 8, 1612, Strensham, Worcestershire, Eng.—d. Sept. 25, 1680, London) Poet and satirist, famous as the author of HUDIBRAS, the most memorable burlesque poem in the English language and the first English satire to make a notable and successful attack on ideas rather than on personalities.

Butler, the son of a farmer, was educated at the King's school, Worcester. He afterward obtained employment in various households, including that of Sir Samuel Luke, a colonel in the Parliamentary army. In his service Butler undoubtedly had firsthand opportunity to study the motley collection of cranks, fanatics, and scoundrels who attached themselves to the Puritan army and whose antics were to form the subject of *Hudibras*, which was published in three parts between 1663 and 1678.

Butler's other works include "The Elephant in the Moon," mocking the solemnities of the newly founded Royal Society, and "Repartees between Puss and Cat at a Caterwalling," laughing at the absurdities of contemporary rhymed heroic tragedy. *Genuine Remains in Verse and Prose of Mr. Samuel Butler*, in two volumes (1759), was edited by Robert Thyer from Butler's papers and includes more than 100 brilliant prose "Characters" in the manner of Theophrastus.

Butler \'bət-lər\, Samuel (b. Dec. 4, 1835, Langar Rectory, Nottinghamshire, Eng.—d. June 18, 1902, London) English novelist, essayist, and critic whose satire EREWHON (1872) foreshadowed the collapse of the Victorian illusion of eternal progress. THE WAY OF ALL FLESH (1903), his autobiographical novel, is generally considered his masterpiece.

Butler went to St. John's College, Cambridge, and graduated in 1858. Soon thereafter he immigrated to New Zealand, where (with funds advanced by his father) he set up a sheep run in the Canterbury settlement.

After reading Charles Darwin's *Origin of Species* (1859), Butler became "one of Mr. Darwin's many enthusiastic admirers," and for the next 25 years he fixed his attention mainly on religion and evolution. To the New Zealand *Press* he contributed several articles on Darwinian topics; two of these—"Darwin Among the Machines" (1863) and "Lucubratio Ebria" (1865)—were incorporated into *Erewhon*.

Having doubled his capital in New Zealand, Butler returned to England in 1864. For a few years he studied painting at Heatherley's art school, and he exhibited occasionally at the Royal Academy. Later he tried his hand at musical composition, publishing *Gavottes, Minuets, Fugues and Other Short Pieces for the Piano* (1885); *Narcissus* (1888), a comic cantata in the style of George Frideric Handel; and *Ulysses: An Oratorio* (1904). His native wit and constitutional iconoclasm led him into such literary adventures as his attempt to prove that the *Odyssey* was written in Sicily by a woman (*The Authoress of the Odyssey*, 1897) and his new interpretation of William Shakespeare's sonnets (*Shakespeare's Sonnets Reconsidered, and in Part Rearranged*, 1899).

During his lifetime, Butler's literary reputation rested primarily on *Erewhon*. Although he made very little profit on the book, it was received by many as the best work of its kind since *Gulliver's Travels*—a satire on contemporary life and thought conveyed by the time-honored convention of travel in an imaginary country.

The Fair Haven (1873) is an ironical defense of Christianity. Many of his later works reflected Butler's suspicion that Darwin might prove to be a fraud. This suspicion dawned upon him while writing *Life and Habit* (1878) and envenomed the series of evolutionary books that followed: *Evolution, Old and New* (1879), *Unconscious Memory* (1880), and *Luck or Cunning* (1887).

Butler's *The Way of All Flesh* was published the year after his death. This largely autobiographical novel tells, with ruthless wit, realism, and lack of sentiment, the story of Butler's escape from the suffocating moral atmosphere of his home circle.

Butler, Rhett \'ret-'bət-lər\ Fictional character, the rakish third husband of Scarlett O'Hara in Margaret Mitchell's novel GONE WITH THE WIND. Though born a Southern gentle-

man, Butler consorts with Northerners during the American Civil War. He has a realistic view of the South's chances in the war, but, just before the South capitulates, he joins its hopeless cause.

Butor \bǖ-'tȯr\, Michel(-Marie-François) (b. Sept. 14, 1926, Mons-en-Baroeul, Fr.) French novelist and essayist who was one of the leading figures among exponents of the *nouveau roman* ("new novel"), the avant-garde French novel that emerged in the 1950s.

Butor studied at the Sorbonne. He taught in Manchester, Eng.; Thessaloníki, Greece; and Geneva, Switz. After an early experimental novel, *Passage de Milan* (1954; "Passage from Milan"), Butor won critical acclaim with *L'Emploi du temps* (1956; *Passing Time*), a complex evocation of his gloomy season in Manchester. With his third novel, *La Modification* (1957; U.K. title, *Second Thoughts*; U.S. title, *A Change of Heart*), Butor perfected his experimental technique.

Butor regarded the novel as a blend of philosophy and poetry. A feature common to all his novels is a rigid structure. *Passage de Milan* takes place in a single day in a tenement building, and in *La Modification* the setting is a journey in a compartment of the Paris-Rome express. *Degrés* (1960; *Degrees*), his fourth novel, imposes on the action the rigid pattern of a college timetable. His later fiction includes *Intervalle* (1973) and *Explorations* (1981; with verse). Outstanding among his nonfiction works are *Mobile* (1962), a prose rhapsody aiming to capture the spirit of the United States, and *Description de San Marco* (1963; *Description of San Marco*). Later works include *Portrait de l'artiste en jeune singe* (1967; "Portrait of the Artist as a Young Monkey"), *Boomerang* (1978), and *Improvisations sur Rimbaud* (1989). He also published several collections of poetry and essays.

Buysse \'bœœ-ɐ, *Angl* 'bīs-\, Cyriel (b. Sept. 21, 1859, Nevele, near Ghent, Belg.—d. July 25, 1932, Afsnee) Belgian novelist and playwright, one of the outstanding exponents of Flemish naturalism.

Buysse was given the usual French education thought suitable for the sons of well-to-do Flemings, but he decided to devote his energies to writing in Flemish. His first major novel, *Het recht van den sterkste* (1893; "The Right of the Strongest"), shows his powers as a realist in the tradition of Émile Zola and Guy de Maupassant. Its grim picture of the miserable life of the peasantry leads to some general reflections of man's inhumanity to man. Some of Buysse's later works, such as *Sursum corda* (1894) contain a more explicit socialist message.

Buysse fostered the development of Flemish literature and was one of the founders of the influential literary journal *Van nu en straks* ("Of Now and Later") in 1893. He also wrote a number of Flemish plays. In some—for example, *Het gezin Van Paemel* (1903; "The Van Paemel Family")—Buysse presents the struggles of the oppressed peasantry, as he does in his novels. But he also had considerable success in a lighter vein with such comedies as *De plaatsvervangende vrederechter* (1895; "The Substitute Magistrate").

Buzzati \büt-'tsä-tē\, Dino (b. Oct. 16, 1906, Belluno, Italy—d. Jan. 28, 1972, Rome) Italian journalist, dramatist, short-story writer, and novelist, internationally known for his fiction and plays.

Buzzati began his career on the Milan daily *Corriere della Sera* in 1928. His two novels of the mountains, written in the style of traditional realism, *Barnabò delle montagne* (1933; "Barnabus of the Mountains") and *Il segreto del bosco vecchio* (1935; "The Secret of the Ancient Wood"), introduced the Kafkaesque surrealism, symbolism, and absurdity that suffused all of his writing.

The novel generally considered Buzzati's finest, *Il deserto dei Tartari* (1940; *The Tartar Steppe*), is a powerful and ironic tale of garrison troops at a frontier military post, poised in expectancy for an enemy who never comes and unable to go forward or retreat.

His collections of tales include *Sessanta racconti* (1958; "Sixty Tales"), which included the previously published novellas *I sette messaggeri* (1942; "The Seven Messengers") and *Paura alla scala* (1949; "Terror on the Staircase"). Among his other novels are *Il grande ritratto* (1960; *Larger Than Life*), a science-fiction novel, and *Un amore* (1963; *A Love Affair*).

Of Buzzati's extremely popular plays (some of which were taken from his short stories), the most important is *Un caso clinico* (1953; "A Clinical Case"), a modern Kafkaesque horror story in which medical specialists and machinery destroy a perfectly healthy man. Buzzati's other plays include *Il mantello* (performed 1960; "The Overcoat") and *L'uomo che andrà in America* (1962; "The Man Who Will Go to America"). An English translation of some of his stories is *Catastrophe: The Strange Stories of Dino Buzzati* (1966). *Cronache terrestri* (1972; "Earthly Chronicles") and an autobiography (1973) were published posthumously.

Byatt \ˈbī-ət\, A.S., *in full* Antonia Susan, *original surname* Drabble \ˈdrab-əl\ (b. Aug. 24, 1936, Sheffield, Eng.)   English scholar, literary critic, and novelist known for her erudite works that featured academics or artists through whom she was able to examine and comment on the intellectual process.

The daughter of a judge, and the sister of the novelist Margaret Drabble, Byatt was educated at Cambridge University, Bryn Mawr College (Pa.), and Oxford University. She taught at University College, London, from 1972 to 1983, when she left to write full-time. Among her critical works was *Degrees of Freedom* (1965), the first full-length study of the British writer Iris Murdoch.

Despite publishing two novels, *The Shadow of a Sun* (1964) and *The Game* (1967), Byatt continued to be considered mainly a scholar and a critic until the publication of the highly acclaimed *The Virgin in the Garden* (1978). The novel is a complex story set in 1953, at the time of the coronation of Queen Elizabeth II. It was the first of a projected tetralogy that would chronicle the lives of three members of one family from the coronation to 1980. The second volume of the series, *Still Life* (1985), concentrated on the art of painting. *Possession* (1990), not part of the tetralogy, was part mystery and part romance, in which Byatt developed two related stories, one set in the 19th and one in the 20th century. Considered a brilliant example of postmodernist fiction, it was a popular success and was awarded the Booker Prize for 1990. In addition to her novels Byatt wrote *Sugar and Other Stories* (1987); *Passions of the Mind* (1991), a collection of essays; and *Angels & Insects* (1991), a pair of novellas.

bylina \bə-ˈlē-nə\ *plural* byliny \-nē\ *or* bylinas [Russian, adaptation of Old Russian *bylina,* a word occurring only in *The Song of Igor's Campaign* and taken to mean "tale of a past event"]   Traditional form of Old Russian and Russian heroic narrative poetry transmitted orally.

The term *bylina* came into use in the 1830s as a scholarly name for what is popularly called a *starina.* Although byliny originated about the 10th century during the Kievan period of Russian history, or possibly earlier, they were first written down about the 17th century. Byliny have been classified into several groupings or cycles, the largest of which deals with the golden age of Kiev in the 10th to 12th century. The byliny of this cycle center on the deeds of Prince Vladimir I and a group of heroes called the bogatyrs. One of the favorite heroes is the

independent peasant Ilya of Murom, who defended the Kievan Rus from the Tatar khans.

Other byliny may relate events from the reigns of Ivan the Terrible or Peter the Great, or deal with the Cossack rebels Stenka Razin and Yemelyan Ivanovich Pugachov. Taken together, byliny constitute a folk history in which facts and sympathies are often at variance with official history.

Byrd \ˈbərd\ of Westover \ˈwes-ˌtō-vər\, William (b. March 28, 1674, Virginia Colony [U.S.]—d. Aug. 26, 1744, Westover, Va.)   Virginia planter, satirist, and diarist who portrayed plantation life in colonial America.

His birthplace was the James River plantation home of his father, also named William Byrd, an Indian trader and slave importer. He studied law in the Middle Temple, London. After he was admitted to the bar in 1695, he returned to Virginia, but two years later was again in London as colonial agent. In 1705, after his father died, Byrd returned to Virginia to manage the large family estate. He spent the years 1715 to 1726 (except for a trip home in 1720–21) in England, part of the time as colonial agent. He then returned to the colony for the last time, to lead the busy life of a planter and a member of Virginia's ruling clique.

His diaries illuminate the domestic economy of the great plantations. His "History of the Dividing Line," a witty, satirical account of a 1728 survey of the North Carolina–Virginia boundary, is among the earliest colonial literary works. His accounts of similar expeditions, "A Journey to the Land of Eden" and "A Progress to the Mines," were published in *The Westover Manuscripts* (1841). He also kept a less literary but more revealing diary in shorthand, published as *The Secret Diary of William Byrd of Westover, 1709–12* (1941).

Byron \ˈbī-rən\, Lord, *in full* George Gordon Byron, 6th Baron Byron (b. Jan. 22, 1788, London, Eng.—d. April 19, 1824, Missolonghi [now Mesolóngian, Greece])   English Romantic poet and satirist whose poetry, personality, and many love affairs captured the imagination of Europe.

Byron had been born with a clubfoot and early developed an extreme sensitivity to his lameness. In 1805 Byron entered Trinity College, Cambridge, where he piled up debts at an alarming rate. His incipient bisexuality surfaced in a passionate but platonic love for a schoolmate.

In 1806 Byron had his early poems privately printed in a volume entitled *Fugitive Pieces.* His first published volume of poetry, HOURS OF IDLENESS (1807), was given a sarcastic review in *The Edinburgh Review,* and Byron retaliated in 1809 with a couplet satire, ENGLISH BARDS AND SCOTCH REVIEWERS, in which he attacked the contemporary literary scene.

In 1812 the first two cantos of CHILDE HAROLD'S PILGRIMAGE (1812–18) were published and Byron "woke to find himself famous." His fame and notoriety grew; each new publication quickly sold out and was heatedly discussed. Not only literature but fashion and art were influenced by Byron's unconventional style.

Detail of a portrait by Richard Westall, 1813

National Portrait Gallery, London

During the summer of 1813, Byron apparently entered into intimate relations with Augusta Leigh, his half sister. He then carried on a flirtation with Lady Frances Webster. The sense of mingled guilt and exultation these affairs aroused in Byron are reflected in the series of gloomy and remorseful Oriental verse tales he wrote at this time: *The Giaour* (1813), *The Bride of Abydos* (1813), *The Corsair* (1814), and *Lara* (1814).

Byron married Anne Isabella (Annabella) Milbanke in January 1815. From the start the marriage was doomed; in January 1816, after the birth of their daughter, Annabella left Byron, and the couple obtained a legal separation. Wounded by the general moral indignation directed at him, Byron went abroad in April 1816, never to return.

He settled in Geneva, near the residence of Percy Bysshe Shelley and Mary Godwin. There he wrote the third canto of *Childe Harold* and THE PRISONER OF CHILLON (1816). A visit to the Bernese Oberland provided the scenery for the Faustian poetic drama MANFRED (1817).

At the end of the summer the Shelley party left for England, where Mary Godwin's stepsister Claire Clairmont gave birth to Byron's daughter Allegra in January 1817. In October Byron again departed for Italy. Rome provided impressions that were recorded in a fourth canto of *Childe Harold*. He also

wrote *Beppo*, a poem in ottava rima that satirically contrasts Italian with English manners. In the light, mock-heroic style of *Beppo* Byron found the form in which he would write his greatest poem, DON JUAN (1819–24), a satire in the form of a picaresque verse tale.

A chance meeting with Countess Teresa Gamba Guiccioli energized Byron and changed the course of his life. He followed her to Ravenna, where he wrote *The Prophecy of Dante*; cantos III, IV, and V of *Don Juan*; and the poetic dramas *Marino Faliero, Sardanapalus, The Two Foscari*, and CAIN (all published in 1821). Byron followed Teresa to Pisa in 1821. He again became associated with Shelley, and in early summer of 1822 they all went to Leghorn (Livorno). The poet and essayist Leigh Hunt arrived from England to help edit the radical journal *The Liberal*. Despite the drowning of Shelley on July 8, the periodical went forward, and its first number contained *The Vision of Judgment*, Byron's satire on the poet Robert Southey.

In 1823 Byron agreed to act as agent of the London Committee, which had been formed to aid the Greeks' struggle for independence from the Turks. He left for Cephalonia and then sailed for Missolonghi. In April 1824 he contracted the fever from which he died. Deeply mourned, he became a symbol of disinterested patriotism and a Greek national hero.

Caballero \ˌkä-b̯äl-'yer-ō\, Fernán, *pseudonym of* Cecilia Böhl de Faber \'bœl-də-'fä-bər\ (b. Dec. 24, 1796, Morges, Switz.—d. April 7, 1877, Seville, Spain) Novelist famous for her defense of the traditional virtues of Spain—Roman Catholic, monarchist, moral, and rural—against the upsurge of 19th-century liberalism. Caballero's best-known novel, *La gaviota* (1849; *The Seagull*), is considered a precursor of the 19th-century Spanish realistic novel. It is also the first outstanding example of a novel influenced by *costumbrismo*, the literary movement that depicted in short prose sketches the rapidly changing customs of rural Spain.

caballine \'kab-ə-ˌlīn, -lin\ [Latin *fons caballinus*, literally, horse's spring, an epithet of Hippocrene] Of a fountain, imparting poetic inspiration. The source of this derivation is the ancient belief that the Muses' spring, Hippocrene (from Greek *hippos*, horse, and *krēnē*, fountain), came from a hoofprint of the winged horse Pegasus.

Cabell \'kab-əl\, James Branch (b. April 14, 1879, Richmond, Va., U.S.—d. May 5, 1958, Richmond) American writer known chiefly for his novel JURGEN (1919).

Cabell began writing fiction shortly after the turn of the century, but acclaim arrived only after a controversy developed over the morality of *Jurgen*. For a decade or more Cabell was extravagantly praised, especially for the attack in *Jurgen* on American orthodoxies and institutions, in a story replete with sexual symbolism. In the 1930s his mannered style and his philosophy of life and art lost favor.

Along with *Jurgen*, the 18-volume *Works* (1927–30) includes THE CREAM OF THE JEST (1917), *Beyond Life* (1919), *Figures of Earth* (1921), and *The High Place* (1923). Many of his

works were allegories, set in the mythical French province of Poictesme, through which Cabell commented on American life and demonstrated his skeptical view of human experience. In the 1940s he published three novels as well as *Let Me Lie* (1947), a collection of essays about Virginia. A volume of autobiographical essays, *Quiet Please*, was published in 1952.

Cabiri or **Cabeiri** \kə-'bī-rī, -rē\ A group of ancient Greek deities probably of Phrygian, possibly chthonic (*i.e.*, infernal), origin who were worshiped over much of Asia Minor, on the islands nearby, and in Macedonia and northern and central Greece. The Cabiri were promoters of fertility and protectors of seafarers.

The Cabiri are often identified with the Great Gods of Samothrace, where the mysteries (secret religious rites) attracted great attention and initiation was looked upon as a general safeguard against misfortune. The mysteries of Samothrace were second in repute only to the Eleusinian Mysteries. In the period after the death of Alexander the Great (323 BC), their cult reached its height of popularity.

Cable \'kā-bəl\, George Washington (b. Oct. 12, 1844, New Orleans, La., U.S.—d. Jan. 31, 1925, St. Petersburg, Fla.) American author and reformer. His first books—*Old Creole Days* (1879), a collection of stories, and *The Grandissimes* (1880), a novel—marked Creole New Orleans as his literary province and were widely praised. In these works he employed a realism new to Southern fiction.

Although Cable was the son of slaveholders and fought in the Confederate cavalry, he believed that slavery and the attempts to deny freed slaves full public rights were morally wrong. Thus, in his early fiction, his handling of caste and class and sanctioned oppression contained overtones of moral condemnation. In the face of violent abuse in the Southern press, he used essays and public lectures to urge the cause of black rights, and he published two collections of his social essays, *The Silent South* (1885) and *The Negro Question* (1888). In 1885 he settled in Northampton, Mass. He wrote novels, many of which were set in the South, until he was past 70; these later novels, though better constructed, were felt to lack the freshness and charm and also the force of moral conviction that characterized his early books.

Cabral de Melo Neto \kå-'braŭ-dē-'mel-ŭ-'net-ŭ\, João (b. Jan. 6, 1920, Recife, Braz.) Poet and diplomat, the leading Brazilian poet of his generation.

As a member of the foreign service from 1945, Cabral served in a consular capacity in Spain, the United Kingdom, France, and Switzerland. His literary career began in 1942 with the publication of the collection of poems *Pedra do sono* ("Stone of Sleep"). *O engenheiro* ("The Engineer"), published in 1945, gave rise to the epithet "Generation of '45" for the poets and other writers of the era who brought an increasing austerity to the Brazilian poetic style.

Cabral also published *O cão sem plumas* (1950; *The Dog Without Feathers*), *Duas águas* (1955; "Two Waters," including the poet's single most famous composition, "Morte e vida severina"), *Uma faca só lâmina* (1956; *A Knife All Blade*), *A educação pela pedra* (1966; "Education by Stone"), *A escola das facas* (1980; "The School of Knives"), *Auto do frade* (1983; "The Friar"), and *Agrestes* (1985; "Rough and Rude"). *Obra completa* and *Selected Poetry, 1937–1990* were published in 1994.

His early poetry has a Surrealistic and Cubistic quality, which he later abandoned in favor of a precise lucidity and spare, "arid" imagery inspired by the drought-stricken Brazilian northeast. Cabral de Melo Neto was elected to the Brazilian Academy of Letters in 1968.

Cabrera \kä-'b̦rä-rä\, Lydia (b. May 20, 1900, Havana, Cuba—d. September 19, 1991, Miami, Fla., U.S.) Cuban ethnologist and short-story writer noted for her collections of Afro-Cuban folklore.

As a child, Cabrera was told African folk legends by her black nanny and servants. In 1927 she went to Paris to study at L'Ecole du Louvre. There she wrote *Cuentos negros de Cuba* ("Black Tales from Cuba") and in 1936 first published it in a French translation. A collection of 22 mostly Yoruba folktales, the work has come to be considered a classic. Having returned to Cuba after 1938, Cabrera wrote the 28 folktales of *¿Por Qué?* (1948; "Why?"), which she gathered from ex-slaves and others. These stories are populated by personified animals and objects, supernatural beings, magic, and good and wicked Yoruba gods in distinctively Cuban landscapes and attitudes. Together with *Cuentos negros de Cuba*, *¿Por Que?* is considered a forerunner of the literary style known as magic realism. *El monte* (1954; "The Bush") is her noted study of Santería, an Afro-Caribbean religion. *Anagó: Vocabulario lucumí* (1957) studies the Lucumí language and its adaptation into Cuban Spanish. Cabrera was forced to flee Cuba during the revolution of 1959. Thereafter she lived in Spain and the United States.

Cabrera Infante \kä-'b̦rä-ēn-'fän-tä\, Guillermo (b. April 22, 1929, Gibara, Cuba) Cuban writer and critic best known for his brilliant novel *Tres tristes tigres* (1967; *Three Trapped Tigers*).

In 1947 Cabrera Infante began his association with *Bohemia*, a popular Cuban magazine. The following year he edited the magazine *Nueva Generación* and became the literary editor of *Bohemia*. In 1954, writing under a pseudonym, he served as the film critic for the magazine *Carteles*. He supported the revolutionary forces of Fidel Castro, and after the revolution he was named director of the Cuban Department of Culture. His first

major publication was a collection of short stories, *Así en la paz como en la guerra* (1960; "In Peace as in War"). Cabrera Infante later became disenchanted with the revolution, and he eventually settled in London and became a British subject.

Tres tristes tigres is full of puns, neologisms, and humorous word play. Set in the summer of 1958, the story is an account of the end of the chaotic era of Fulgencio Batista. *Vista del amanecer en el trópico* (1974; *View of Dawn in the Tropics*) is a collection of vignettes of Cuban history. In 1975 Cabrera Infante published *O*, a collection of essays and articles that treat various aspects of contemporary life with irony and satire. *Exorcismos de esti(l)o* (1976; "Exorcisms of Style," or, omitting the parenthetical *l*, "of Summer") is a series of short sketches, poems, and aphorisms. *Arcadia todas las noches* (1978; "Arcadia Every Night") is a collection of Cabrera Infante's critical writings on motion pictures. In 1979 he published the parody *La Habana para un infante difunto* (*Infante's Inferno*). *Holy Smoke*, his first book written in English, was published in 1985.

caccia \'kät-chä\ [Italian, literally, chase, hunt] Italian verse and musical form popular mainly in the mid-14th to mid-15th centuries. The caccia texts consisted of short, free-verse lyrics describing realistic, animated scenes such as the hunt or the market place, and horn calls, bird calls, shouts, and dialogue frequently enlivened the musical settings. Very few poems of this type have survived. The musical form consisted of two voices in strict canon at the unison (that is, in strict melodic initiation at the same pitch), and often of a noncanonic third part, composed of long notes that underlay the canonic voices, followed by a ritornello (short, recurrent instrumental passage).

The caccia is related in name to a 14th-century French genre, the chace, a setting of a text in three-part canon. The English catch, a type of round, may derive its name from caccia.

cacodaemon or **cacodemon** \,kak-ə-'dē-mən\ [Greek *kakodaímōn*, from *kakós* bad + *daímōn* spirit] An evil spirit, demon, or devil. Its counterpart, a good spirit, is called a EUDAEMON.

cacophony \kə-'käf-ə-nē, -'kòf-, -'kaf-\ [Greek *kakophōnía*, from *kakós* bad + *phōnḗ* sound] Harsh or discordant sound; specifically, harshness in the sound of words or phrases. It is opposite in meaning from EUPHONY. Cacophony is usually produced by combinations of words that require a staccato, explosive delivery. Used skillfully, intentional cacophony can vitalize the content of imagery. Three lines from Walt Whitman's "The Dalliance of the Eagles" illustrate cacophony:

> The clinching interlocking claws, a living, fierce, gyrating wheel,
> Four beating wings, two beaks, a swirling mass tight grappling,
> In tumbling turning clustering loops, straight downward falling

Cadalso y Vázquez or **Cadahlso y Vázquez** \kä-'thäl-sō-ē-'bäth-käth\, José de (b. Oct. 8, 1741, Cádiz, Spain—d. Feb. 27, 1782, Gibraltar) Spanish writer famous for his *Cartas marruecas* (1793; "Moroccan Letters"), in which a Moorish traveler in Spain makes penetrating criticisms of Spanish life.

Educated in Madrid, Cadalso y Vázquez traveled widely and, although he hated war, he enlisted in the army during the Seven Years' War. His prose satire *Los eruditos a la violeta* (1772; "Wise Men Without Learning"), directed against the pseudo-learned, was his most popular work. Although influenced by the classics, as seen in his neoclassical drama *Sancho García* (1771) and his anacreontic verse in *Ocios de mi juventud* (1773; "Diversions of My Youth"), Cadalso y Vázquez is considered a forerunner of Spanish Romanticism because of his *Noches lúgubres* (1789–90; "Somber Nights"), an autobiographical prose work inspired by the death of his love, the actress María Ignacia Ibáñez.

Cade \'kād\, Jack, *byname of* John Cade (b. Ireland—d. July 12, 1450, Heathfield, Sussex, Eng.)   Leader of a major rebellion (1450) against the government of King Henry VI of England. Although the uprising was suppressed, it contributed to the breakdown of royal authority that led to the Wars of the Roses (1455–85) between the houses of York and Lancaster.

William Shakespeare's *Henry VI, Part 2*, dramatizes Cade's story. Act 4, scene 2, of that play is the source of a statement often wrongly attributed to Cade: "The first thing we do, let's kill all the lawyers." (It is actually said to Cade by Dick the butcher.)

cadence \'kā-dəns\ [Medieval Latin *cadentia*, literally, falling motion]   **1.** A rhythmic sequence or flow of sounds in language; specifically, a particular rhythmic sequence distinctive of an individual author or literary composition.   **2.** The rising or falling order of strong, long, or stressed syllables and weak, short, or unstressed syllables. *Compare* ARSIS; IONIC; METER.   **3.** An unmetrical or irregular arrangement of stressed and unstressed syllables in prose or free verse that is based on natural stress groups.

Cadmus \'kad-məs\   In Greek mythology, the son of Phoenix or Agenor (king of Phoenicia) and brother of Europa. Europa was carried off by Zeus, and Cadmus was sent out to find her. Unsuccessful, he consulted the Delphic oracle, which ordered him to give up his quest, follow a cow, and build a town on the spot where she lay down. The cow guided him to Boeotia ("Cow Land"), where he founded the city of Thebes. Later, Cadmus sowed in the ground the teeth of a dragon he had killed. From these sprang a race of fierce, armed men, called Sparti, or Spartoi (meaning "The Sown Men"). Five of them assisted him to build the Cadmea, or citadel, of Thebes and became the founders of the noblest families of that city. Cadmus later took as his wife Harmonia, by whom he had five children. According to tradition Cadmus brought the alphabet to Greece.

Caecilius \sə-'sil-ē-əs, -'sil-yəs\, Statius \'stā-shē-əs, -shəs\ (b. *c.* 219 BC—d. 166 BC, Rome)   Roman comic poet ranked by the literary critic Volcatius Sedigitus at the head of all Roman writers of comedy. Information is too meager to justify any firm statement beyond saying that he was a writer of considerable moral power (a tribute paid by the poet Horace), that he admired and imitated the Greek playwright Menander, and that his work was less lively than that of his predecessor Plautus and less polished than that of his young contemporary Terence.

Little about his life is known for certain, though many writers refer to him. Of his comedies only 42 titles (most of them identical with titles of plays by Menander) and 280 lines or parts of lines have survived.

Caecilius \sə-'sil-ē-əs, -'sil-yəs\ of Calacte \kə-'lak-tē\ (fl. early 1st century AD; b. Calacte, Sicily)   One of the most important of the Greek rhetoricians and critics of the Augustan Age. Only fragments of his works are extant, among them *On the Style of the Ten Orators*; *On the Sublime*, which was attacked by the author known as Longinus (or Pseudo-Longinus) in a more famous work of the same title; *History of the Servile Wars*, on slave risings in Sicily; *On Rhetoric* and *Rhetorical Figures*; the *Alphabetical Selection of Phrases*, an Attic lexicon, mentioned in the later *Suda* lexicon as one of its authorities; and *Against the Phrygians*, probably an attack on the florid style of the Asiatic school of rhetoric.

Caedmon \'kad-mən\ (fl. 658–680)   First Old English Christian poet, whose fragmentary hymn to the creation remains a symbol of the adaptation of the aristocratic-heroic Anglo-Saxon verse tradition to the expression of Christian themes.

His story is known from Bede's *Ecclesiastical History of the English People*, which tells how Caedmon, an illiterate herdsman, retired from company one night in shame because he could not comply with the demand made of each guest to sing. Then in a dream a stranger appeared, commanding him to sing of "the beginning of things," and the herdsman found himself uttering "verses which he had never heard." When Caedmon awoke, he related his dream to the farm bailiff under whom he worked and was conducted by him to the monastery at Streaneshalch (now called Whitby). The abbess St. Hilda believed that Caedmon was divinely inspired and, to test his powers, proposed that he should render into verse a portion of sacred history, which the monks explained. By the following morning he had fulfilled the task. At the request of the abbess he became an inmate of the monastery. Throughout the remainder of his life his more learned brethren expounded Scripture to him, and all that he heard he reproduced in vernacular poetry. In spite of all the poetic renderings that Caedmon supposedly made, however, it is only the original dream hymn of nine historically precious, but poetically uninspired, lines that can be attributed to him with confidence. The hymn set the pattern for almost the whole art of Anglo-Saxon religious verse.

Caedmon manuscript or **Junius manuscript** \'jü-nē-əs\   Collection of Old English poetic scriptural paraphrases copied about 1000. Its history is uncertain prior to 1651, when it was given to the scholar Franciscus Junius by Archbishop James Ussher of Armagh; it is now housed in the Bodleian Library, University of Oxford. The collection was first published (as *Caedmon's Paraphrase*) in 1655.

The Caedmon manuscript of 5,019 lines contains the poems *Genesis*, *Exodus*, *Daniel*, and *Christ and Satan*, originally attributed to Caedmon because these subjects correspond roughly to the subjects described in Bede's *Ecclesiastical History of the English People* (731) as having been rendered by Caedmon into vernacular verse. Later studies make the attribution to Caedmon doubtful, because the poems seem to have been written at different periods and by more than one author.

Caeneus \'sē-nüs\   In Greek mythology, the son of Elatus, a Lapith. At the marriage of Pirithous, king of the Lapiths, the centaurs (creatures part man and part horse), who were guests, attacked the bride and other women. Caeneus joined in the ensuing battle and, because of his invulnerable body, killed five centaurs. In desperation the other centaurs combined against him, piling huge pine trees upon him until the accumulated weight forced him underground, never to appear again. This attack on Caeneus became a favorite theme of Greek art.

Caesar \'sē-zər\, Julius, *in full* Gaius Julius Caesar \'gā-əs-'jü-lē-əs, 'gī-əs\ (b. July 12/13, 100? BC, Rome [Italy]—d. March 15, 44 BC, Rome)   Celebrated Roman general and statesman, the conqueror of Gaul (58–50 BC), victor in the Roman civil war of 49–45 BC, and dictator (46–44 BC), who was launching a series of political and social reforms when he was assassinated by a group of nobles in the Senate House on the Ides of March.

A patrician by birth, Caesar held a series of increasingly important public offices. With Pompey and Crassus he formed the first triumvirate in 60, and he was elected consul in 59. Caesar conquered Gaul in a number of campaigns between 58 and 50; in 49, after being instructed by the Senate to lay down his command, he crossed the Rubicon, signifying the beginning of the Roman civil war. He waged campaigns on several fronts, aided Cleopatra of Egypt in 49, and acquired the title of dictator. He was assassinated by a group of senatorial conspirators led by Gaius Cassius Longinus and Marcus Junius Brutus.

Caesar's writings include *Commentarii de bello Gallico* (52–51 BC), on the Gallic War, and *Commentarii de bello civili* (45

BC), on the civil war. But he is perhaps best known as the inspiration for many popular works of Western literature, among them Jacques Grévin's *La Mort de César*, William Shakespeare's *Julius Caesar*, Voltaire's *La Mort de César*, and George Bernard Shaw's *Caesar and Cleopatra*.

Caesar and Cleopatra \'sē-zər..., klē-ə-'pat-rə, -'pät-\ Four-act play by George Bernard SHAW, written in 1898, published in 1901, and first produced in 1906.

Caesar and Cleopatra, considered Shaw's first great play, opens as Caesar's armies arrive in Egypt to conquer the ancient, divided land for Rome. Caesar meets the young Cleopatra crouching at night between the paws of a sphinx, where—having been driven from Alexandria—she is hiding. He returns her to the palace, reveals his identity, and compels her to abandon her girlishness and accept her position as coruler of Egypt (with Ptolemy Dionysus, her brother). *Caesar and Cleopatra* was extraordinarily successful, largely because of Shaw's talent for characterization.

caesura *or* **cesura** \si-'zyủr-ə, -'zhủr-ə\ *plural* caesuras *or* caesurae \-'zyủr-ē, -'zhủr-ē\ [Late Latin, literally, the act of cutting or felling; a calque of Greek *tomē* caesura, literally, cutting] **1.** In Greek and Latin prosody, a break in the flow of sound within a verse that is caused by ending a word within a foot (arma vi/rumque ca/no ‖ Tro/jae qui/ primus ab/oris). It is represented in scansion by the sign ‖. It is usually distinguished from DIAERESIS, in which the word ending and the foot ending coincide. In classical prosody, the caesura is strictly a metrical element, not an element of expression. **2.** In modern prosody, a pause within a poetic line that breaks the regularity of the metrical pattern. The caesura sometimes is used to emphasize the formal metrical construction of a line, but it more often introduces the cadence of natural speech patterns and habits of phrasing into the metrical scheme. The caesura may coincide with conventional punctuation marks, but does not necessarily do so.

In Germanic and Old English alliterative poetry, the caesura was a formal device dividing each line centrally into two half lines. In Romance and Neoclassical verse, the caesura occurs most frequently in the middle of the line (medial caesura), but in modern verse its place is flexible. There may be several caesuras within a single line.

Types of caesura that are differentiated in modern prosody are the *masculine caesura*, a caesura that follows a stressed or long syllable, and the *feminine caesura*, which follows an unstressed or short syllable. The feminine caesura is further divided into the epic caesura and the lyric caesura. An *epic caesura* is a feminine caesura that follows an extra unstressed syllable that has been inserted in accentual iambic meter. An epic caesura occurs in these lines from Shakespeare's Macbeth: "but how of Cawdor? ‖ The Thane of Cawdor lives." The *lyric caesura* is a feminine caesura that follows an unstressed syllable normally required by the meter. It can be seen in A.E. Housman's "they cease not fighting ‖ east and west."

Cahan \kə-'hän, 'kän\, Abraham (b. July 7, 1860, Vilna, Russian Empire [now Vilnius, Lithuania]—d. Aug. 31, 1951, New York, N.Y., U.S.) Journalist, reformer, and novelist who for more than 40 years served as editor of the New York Yiddish-language daily newspaper *Forverts*, known in English as the *Jewish Daily Forward*.

Himself an immigrant, Cahan arrived in the United States in 1882. While working in a cigar factory, he learned enough English in six years to lecture and write. In 1897 he helped found and joined the staff of the *Forverts*. He prompted the paper to become more outspoken politically, causing it to be regarded as one of the most important institutions upholding the interests of immigrants. Intensely political and bitterly anticommunist, Cahan was also active in organizing trade unions, particularly in the garment industries.

Cahan's fiction is largely unremarkable except for *The Rise of David Levinsky* (1917), one of the first books about the Jewish immigrant's experience. Critics agree that the value of the book is historical rather than literary; its strength lies chiefly in its vivid re-creation of life in New York City's Lower East Side. Cahan was more influential as a mentor than as an author, providing for young writers a Yiddish-language forum.

Cain \'kān\ (*in full* Cain: A Mystery) Romantic tragedy in three acts by Lord BYRON, published in 1821. The drama is an adaptation of the biblical story of Cain and Abel.

Byron's sympathetic treatment of the fratricidal Cain met with a hail of abuse, in part because the author obviously preferred Cain to his pious brother Abel, and because Lucifer appears as an intelligent, likable character. Cain was an ideal Byronic hero, absorbed in his own failings and in the injustices done to him by others and searching for truth and self.

Cain \'kān\ In the Old Testament, firstborn son of Adam and Eve, who murdered his brother ABEL (Genesis 4:1–16). Cain, a farmer, became enraged when God accepted the offering of his brother Abel, a shepherd, in preference to his own. He murdered Abel, and when asked where Abel was, Cain's reply (much quoted) was "I do not know; am I my brother's keeper?" As a result of his crime, Cain was banished by God from the settled country. Because he feared that in his exile he could be killed by anyone, God gave him a sign for his protection (the "mark of Cain") and a promise that if he were killed he would be avenged sevenfold.

Among writers who have treated the themes of the story of Cain are Dante, William Shakespeare, Herman Melville (in *Billy Budd*), Lord Byron, H.G. Wells, Joseph Conrad, Hermann Hesse, and John Steinbeck.

Cain \'kān\, James M., *in full* Mallahan (b. July 1, 1892, Annapolis, Md., U.S.—d. Oct. 27, 1977, University Park, Md.) Novelist whose violent, sexually obsessed, and relentlessly paced melodramas epitomized the hard-boiled fiction that flourished in the U.S. in the 1930s and '40s. Three of his novels—*The Postman Always Rings Twice* (1934), *Double Indemnity* (1936), and *Mildred Pierce* (1941)—were also made into classics of the American screen.

Cain's first novel, *The Postman Always Rings Twice*, was a spectacular success. Its sordid milieu, its characters who seek to gain their ends through violence, and its taut, fast-paced prose set the pattern for most of his later books. *Serenade* (1937) was daring for its period in its presentation of a bisexual hero. *Three of a Kind* (1943) contained the short novels *Sinful Woman*, *Double Indemnity*, and *The Embezzler*. His books continued to appear after World War II—among them *The Butterfly* (1947), *The Moth* (1948), *The Root of His Evil* (1954), *The Magician's Wife* (1965), and *Rainbow's End* (1975)—but none approached the success of his earlier works.

Caine \'kān\, Sir Hall, *in full* Sir Thomas Henry Hall Caine (b. May 14, 1853, Runcorn, Cheshire, Eng.—d. Aug. 31, 1931, Isle of Man) British writer known for his popular novels combining sentiment, moral fervor, local atmosphere, and strong characterization.

Caine was secretary to Dante Gabriel Rossetti from 1881 to Rossetti's death in 1882. His first novel, *The Shadow of a Crime*, was published in 1885. It was followed by several others—including *The Deemster* (1887), *The Manxman* (1894), *The External City* (1901), *The Woman Thou Gavest Me* (1913), and *The Woman of Knockaloe* (1923). Caine settled in the Isle of Man and sat from 1901 to 1908 in the House of Keys, the lower house of its legislature. He was knighted in 1918 for services as an Allied propagandist in the United States.

Caine Mutiny, The \'kān\   Novel by Herman WOUK, published in 1951. The novel was awarded the 1952 Pulitzer Prize for fiction.

The Caine Mutiny grew out of Wouk's experiences aboard a destroyer-minesweeper in the Pacific in World War II. The novel focuses on Willie Keith, a rich New Yorker assigned to the USS *Caine*, who gradually matures during the course of the book. But the work is best known for its portrayal of the neurotic Captain Queeg, who becomes obsessed with petty infractions at the expense of the safety of ship and crew. Cynical, intellectual Lieutenant Tom Keefer persuades loyal Lieutenant Steve Maryk that Queeg's bizarre behavior is endangering the ship; Maryk reluctantly relieves Queeg of command. Much of the book describes Maryk's court-martial and its aftermath. The unstable Queeg eventually breaks down completely.

Cakes and Ale (*in full* Cakes and Ale; or, The Skeleton in the Cupboard)   Comic novel by W. Somerset MAUGHAM, published in 1930.

The story is told by Willie Ashenden, who previously appeared in Maugham's short story collection *Ashenden*. A novelist, Ashenden is befriended by the ambitious, self-serving Alroy Kear, who has been commissioned to write an official biography of the famous novelist Edward Driffield. Kear believes that he must ignore the less than noble aspects of his subject's life in order to write a best-seller. Driffield's first wife, Rosie—vital, open-hearted, generous, but too amoral to fit into Kear's narrow understanding of human behavior—is the cupboard skeleton of the subtitle. She is contrasted with Driffield's hypocritical second wife, and the rather cold Driffield is contrasted with Rosie's warm, gentlemanly second husband.

The story satirizes London literary circles and has been widely considered a roman à clef with Maugham as Ashenden, Thomas Hardy as Driffield, and Hugh Walpole as Kear.

Calais and Zetes \'kal-ā-is . . . 'zē-tēz\   In Greek mythology, the winged twin sons of Boreas and Oreithyia. They were among the Argonauts, who helped Jason secure the Golden Fleece. On their arrival with the Argonauts at Salmydessus in Thrace, they liberated their sister Cleopatra, who had been thrown into prison by her husband, Phineus, the king of the country. According to another story, they delivered Phineus from harassment by the Harpies when he was old and blind. They were slain by Heracles near the island of Tenos. Calais traditionally founded Cales in Campania.

Calasso \kä-'läs-sō\, Roberto (b. 1941, Florence, Italy)   Italian editor, publisher, and writer whose book *Le nozze di Cadmo e Armonia* (1988; *The Marriage of Cadmus and Harmony*) achieved international critical and popular acclaim.

While a student at the University of Rome, where he received a degree in English literature, Calasso began working for Adelphi Edizioni, a publisher of classic and modern literature. He married novelist Fleur Jaeggy and became managing director and managing editor of Adelphi. His first novel, *L'impuro folle* (1974; "The Impure Madman"), is an emotive presentation of madness, written in lyrical styles from comic to epic and from arcane to popular. His second novel was *La rovina di Kasch* (1983; *The Ruins of Kasch*), a chaotic text built on an ancient African legend of the kingdom of Kasch and its decline after it abandons its traditional ritual sacrifice of the king. *Le nozze di Cadmo e Armonia*, his best-known work, retells classic Greek myths in an attempt to evoke the primal meanings they once conveyed—the absolute and arbitrary power of nature and existence as embodied in the gods.

Calchas \'kal-kes\   In Greek mythology, the son of Thestor (a priest of Apollo) and the most famous soothsayer among the Greeks at the time of the Trojan War. He foretold the duration of the siege, demanded the sacrifice of Iphigeneia, daughter of Agamemnon (king of Mycenae), and advised the construction of the wooden horse with which the Greeks finally took Troy. It had been predicted that he would die when he met his superior in divination; beaten by Mopsus in a trial of soothsaying, Calchas died of chagrin or committed suicide.

Caldecott Medal \'kal-də-ˌkät, *commonly* 'käl-\   Annual prize awarded "to the artist of the most distinguished American picture book for children." It was established in 1938 by Frederic G. Melcher, chairman of the board of the R.R. Bowker Publishing Company, and named for the 19th-century English illustrator Randolph Caldecott. It is presented at the annual conference of the American Library Association along with the Newbery Medal for children's literature.

Calderón de la Barca \ˌkäl-dā-'rōn-dā-lä-'b̪är-kä\, Pedro (b. Jan. 17, 1600, Madrid, Spain—d. May 25, 1681, Madrid)   Dramatist and poet who succeeded Lope de Vega as the leading Spanish playwright of the Golden Age.

Strained family relations apparently had a profound effect on the youthful Calderón, for several of his plays show

a preoccupation with the psychological and moral effects of family life. Destined for the church, Calderón attended the Universities of Alcalá and Salamanca. He abandoned an ecclesiastical career, and in 1623 he began to write plays for the court, rapidly becoming the leading member of the small group of dramatic poets whom King Philip IV gathered around him.

Calderón returned to his religious vocation after a hiatus of nearly 30 years. He was ordained in 1651

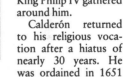
Biblioteca Nacional, Madrid

and, although he announced that he would write no more for the stage, the king insisted that he continue to contribute to the court theater.

The plays *El pintor de su deshonra* (c. 1645; *The Painter of His Dishonour*) and *La cisma de Inglaterra* (c. 1627; "The Schism of England") are masterly examples of Calderón's skillful technique, in which poetic imagery, characters, and action are subtly interconnected by dominant symbols that elucidate the significance of the theme. Among his best-known secular dramas are *El médico de su honra* (1635; *The Surgeon of His Honour*), *La vida es sueño* (1635; *Life a Dream*), *El alcalde de Zalamea* (c. 1640; *The Mayor of Zalamea*), and *La hija del aire* (1653; "The Daughter of the Air"), sometimes considered his masterpiece. Plays in which mythological themes predominate, with a more or less allegorical treatment, include *Eco y Narciso* (1661; "Echo and Narcissus"), *La estatua de Prometeo* (1669; "The Statue of Prometheus"), and *Fieras afemina amor* (1669; "Wild Beasts Are Tamed by Love").

In addition, Calderón produced a large body of work on religious themes. The most characteristic of these are stories of conversion and martyrdom, usually of the saints of the early church. One of the most beautiful is *El príncipe constante* (1629; *The Constant Prince*), which dramatizes the martyrdom of Prince Ferdinand of Portugal. *El mágico prodigioso* (1637; *The Wonder-Working Magician*) is a more complex religious play; *Los dos amantes del cielo* (1636; "The Two Lovers of Heaven") and *El José de las mujeres* (c. 1640; "The Female Joseph") are the most subtle and difficult.

Seventy-four *autos sacramentales* (morality plays), written for open-air performance on the Feast of Corpus Christi, are also extant. In them Calderón crystalized the tradition of the medieval morality play. His greatest achievement in this type of drama is to be found among those *autos* of his old age that dramatize the dogmas of the Fall and the Redemption, notably *La viña del Señor* (1674; "The Lord's Vineyard"), *La nave del mercader* (1674; "The Merchant's Ship"), *El nuevo hospicio de pobres* (1675; "The New Shelter for the Poor"), *El día mayor de los días* (1678; "The Greatest Day of Days"), and *El pastor fido* (1678; "The Faithful Shepherd").

Caldwell \\'kåld-wel\\, Erskine (b. Dec. 17, 1903, Coweta County, Ga., U.S.—d. April 11, 1987, Paradise Valley, Ariz.) American author whose unadorned novels and stories about the rural poor of the American South mix violence and sex in grotesque tragicomedy.

Caldwell's father was a home missionary who moved frequently from church to church, and Caldwell acquired a deep familiarity with the impoverished sharecroppers that his father ministered to. He attended Erskine College, Due West, S.C., and the University of Virginia but did not graduate.

Fame arrived with TOBACCO ROAD (1932), a highly controversial novel whose title grew to be a byword for rural squalor and degradation. A dramatization of *Tobacco Road* ran for seven and a half years in the 1930s and early '40s on the New York stage. Caldwell's reputation as a novelist largely rests on *Tobacco Road* and on *God's Little Acre* (1933), another best-selling novel featuring a cast of hopelessly poor and degenerate whites in the rural South. Among his other works are *Trouble in July* (1940); the episodic narrative *Georgia Boy* (1943), a well-told story of boyhood; the literary autobiography *Call It Experience* (1951); and *In Search of Bisco* (1965).

Caldwell provided the text and Margaret Bourke-White (later his wife) provided the photographs for a powerful documentary book about the rural South entitled *You Have Seen Their Faces* (1937). They collaborated on two more such picture-and-text books, one on Czechoslovakia and one on the Soviet Union.

Caliban \\'kal-ə-,ban\\ Fictional character, a feral, sullen, deformed creature in William Shakespeare's play THE TEMPEST. The son of a witch named Sycorax, Caliban is the sole inhabitant of his island (excluding the imprisoned Ariel) until Prospero and his infant daughter Miranda are cast ashore. Prospero makes the creature his servant and over the years teaches him to speak. Caliban has been seen by some as Shakespeare's negative representation of the natural human and by others as an example of native peoples suffering under imperialist oppression.

Caliban Upon Setebos \\'kal-ə-,ban . . . 'set-ə-,bäs\\ Dramatic monologue by Robert BROWNING, published in *Dramatis Personae* in 1864, constituting an inquiry into the nature of human relationships with God and with one another.

Caliban, the brutish, not-quite-human servant of Prospero in William Shakespeare's play *The Tempest*, reflects on the character of his god, Setebos, and ponders the reason Setebos created the world. Among Caliban's conclusions are that his god is an entity much like himself and that the world was created for his entertainment.

Caligula \\kə-'lig-yü-lə\\, *byname of* Gaius Caesar, *in full* Gaius Caesar Germanicus (b. Aug. 31, AD 12, Antium, Latium [now Anzio, Italy]—d. Jan. 24, 41, Rome) Roman emperor from 37 to 41, in succession to Tiberius. Accounts of his reign by ancient historians are so biased against him that the truth is almost impossible to ascertain.

Caligula was severely ill seven months after his accession; after this he restored treason trials, showed great cruelty, and engaged in wild, despotic caprice. In 38 he executed Naevius Sutorius Macro, prefect of the Praetorian Guard, to whose support he owed his accession, and Tiberius Gemellus, grandson of Tiberius, whom he had supplanted in the succession. He made pretensions to divinity and showed extravagant affection for his sisters, especially for Drusilla, who on her death (38) was consecrated Diva Drusilla, the first woman in Rome to be so honored. Some scholars thought that after his illness he was mad, but much evidence of this is suspect and some—*e.g.*, that he made his horse consul—is untrue. He may have suffered from epilepsy.

Caligula was a subject for both August Strindberg (*Historika miniatyrer*, 1905) and Albert Camus (*Caligula*, 1944).

Calisher \\'kal-ish-ər\\, Hortense (b. Dec. 20, 1911, New York, N.Y., U.S.) American writer of novels, novellas, and short stories, known for the elegant style and insightful rendering of characters in her short fiction, much of which was published originally in *The New Yorker*.

The daughter of a German immigrant father and an uprooted Southern mother, Calisher had a middle-class upbringing in New York City. She graduated from Barnard College in 1932 and later taught there.

Her short-story collections *In the Absence of Angels* (1951) and *The Collected Stories of Hortense Calisher* (1975), a compilation of previous collections featuring Calisher's alter ego, Hester Elkins, a Jewish child living in New York City with her extended family. The recipient of four O. Henry short-story awards, Calisher excelled in well-plotted, psychologically perceptive short fiction peopled by well-drawn characters.

Her collected fiction includes *Tale for the Mirror: A Novella and Other Stories* (1962), *Extreme Magic: A Novella and Other Stories* (1964), and *Saratoga, Hot* (1985). Her first novel, *False Entry* (1961), contains characters who are reintroduced in a radically different setting in *The New Yorkers* (1969), in which a 12-year-old girl kills her father's unfaithful wife. Other novels include *Queenie* (1971), *On Keeping Women* (1977), *Mysteries of Motion* (1983), *Age* (1987), and *In the Palace of the Movie King* (1993).

Callaghan \\'kal-ə-han\\, Morley (Edward) (b. Sept. 22, 1903, Toronto, Ont., Can.—d. Aug. 25, 1990, Toronto) Canadian novelist and short-story writer.

Callaghan attended the University of Toronto (B.A., 1925) and Osgoode Hall Law School (LL.B., 1928). He never practiced law, but he became a full-time writer in 1928 and won critical acclaim for his short stories collected in *A Native Argosy* (1929). Later collections of stories include *Morley Callaghan's Stories* (1959) and *No Man's Meat and The Enchanted Pimp* (1978).

The first of more than 10 novels, *Strange Fugitive* (1928) describes the destruction of a social misfit, a type that recurs in Callaghan's fiction. A second characteristic element in his later works is the emphasis on Christian love as an answer to social injustice, as in *Such Is My Beloved* (1934), *They Shall Inherit the Earth* (1935), *The Loved and the Lost* (1951), and *A Passion in Rome* (1961). He published little in the 1940s, turning his hand to playwriting and to work with the Canadian Broadcasting Company. Notable among his later works are *That Summer in*

Paris (1963), a memoir of Callaghan's days in Paris in 1929 and his friendship with F. Scott Fitzgerald and Ernest Hemingway, and *A Fine and Private Place* (1975), the story of an author who wants artistic recognition in his own country.

Calligrammes \kȧ-lē-'grȧm\ Collection of poetry by Guillaume APOLLINAIRE, published in French in 1918. The poems in the collection reflect Apollinaire's experiences as a soldier during World War I as well as his association with the Parisian art world. The collection is especially noted for a verse form in which the words of a poem are arranged so as to form a pattern suggesting the subject of the poem. *See also* PATTERN POETRY.

Callimachus \kə-'lim-ə-kəs\ (b. *c.* 305 BC, Cyrene, North Africa—d. *c.* 240) Greek poet and scholar, the most representative poet of the erudite and sophisticated Alexandrian school.

Callimachus migrated to Alexandria, where King Ptolemy II Philadelphus of Egypt gave him employment in the Library of Alexandria, the most important in the Hellenistic world. Of Callimachus' voluminous writings, only fragments survive, many of them discovered in the 20th century. His most famous poetical work is the *Aitia* (*Causes*), probably produced about 270. This work is a narrative elegy in four books, containing a medley of obscure tales from Greek mythology and history by which the author seeks to explain the legendary origin of obscure customs, festivals, and names. Of his elegies for special occasions, the best known is the *Lock of Berenice*, a polished piece of court poetry later freely adapted into Latin by Catullus.

Callimachus' other works include the *Iambi*, 13 short poems on occasional themes; the *Hecale*, a small-scale epic, or epyllion, which set a new poetic fashion for concise, miniaturistic detail; and the *Ibis*, a polemical poem that was directed against the poet's former pupil Apollonius of Rhodes, whose grand-scale epic *Argonautica* marked a rebellion against his master's canon of taste. In the *Hymns*, Callimachus adapted the traditional religious form of the Homeric Hymns to an original and purely literary use. The *Epigrams*, of which some 60 survive, treat a variety of personal themes with consummate artistry. Of his prolific prose works, certainly the most famous is the *Pinakes* ("Tablets") in 120 books. This work consists of an elaborate catalog of the authors of the works held in the Library of Alexandria.

Callinus \kə-'lī-nəs\ (fl. mid-7th century BC, Ephesus, Ionia, Asia Minor) Greek elegiac poet, the few surviving fragments of whose work reflect the troubled period when Asia Minor was invaded by the Cimmerians, a race originating in what was later southern Russia. The longest fragment is an appeal to young men to cast off their cowardly sloth and prepare to fight—and if necessary die—in defense of their country. While the poem's vocabulary and imagery are Homeric, the phrasing is sometimes fresh and original.

Calliope or **Kalliope** \kə-'lī-ə-pē\ In Greek mythology, foremost of the nine Muses, patron of epic poetry. At the behest of Zeus, she judged the dispute between the goddesses Aphrodite and Persephone over Adonis. In most accounts she and King Oeagrus of Thrace were the parents of Orpheus, the lyre-playing hero. She was also loved by the god Apollo, by whom she had two sons, Hymen and Ialemus. Other versions present her as the mother of Rhesus, king of Thrace and a victim of the Trojan War, or as the mother of Linus the musician, who was the inventor of melody and rhythm.

Call It Sleep Novel by Henry ROTH, published in 1934. It centers on the character and perceptions of a young boy, the son of Yiddish-speaking Jewish immigrants in a ghetto in New York City. Roth uses stream-of-consciousness techniques to trace the boy's psychological development and to explore his

perceptions of his family and of the larger world around him. The book powerfully evokes the terrors and anxieties the child experiences in his anguished relations with his father and realistically describes the squalid urban environment in which the family lives.

The novel was rediscovered in the late 1950s and early '60s and came to be viewed both as an important proletarian novel of the 1930s and as a classic of Jewish-American literature.

Call of the Wild, The Novel by Jack LONDON, published in 1903 and often considered to be his masterpiece. London's version of the classic quest story using a dog as the protagonist has sometimes been erroneously categorized as a children's novel.

Buck, who is shipped to the Klondike to be trained as a sled dog, eventually reverts to his primitive, wolflike ancestry. He then undertakes an almost mythical journey, abandoning the safety of his familiar world to encounter danger, adventure, and fantasy. When he is transformed into the legendary "Ghost Dog" of the Klondike, he has become a true hero.

Calvary \'kal-və-rē\, *also called* Golgotha \'gäl-gə-thə, gäl-'gäth-ə\ A skull-shaped hill in Jerusalem, site of the crucifixion of Jesus of Nazareth.

Calvino \kȧl-'vē-nō\, Italo (b. Oct. 15, 1923, Santiago de las Vegas, Cuba—d. Sept. 19, 1985, Siena, Italy) Italian journalist, short-story writer, and novelist, whose whimsical and imaginative fables made him one of the most important Italian fiction writers of the 20th century.

Jerry Bauer

Calvino left Cuba for Italy in his youth. He joined the Italian Resistance during World War II and after the war settled in Turin, obtaining his degree in literature from the University of Turin while working for the communist periodical *L'Unità* and for Einaudi publishing house. From 1959 to 1966 he edited, with Elio Vittorini, the left-wing magazine *Il Menabò di letteratura*.

Calvino's work in the Resistance inspired two of his early books of fiction, the Neorealistic novel *Il sentiero dei nidi di ragno* (1947; *The Path to the Nest of Spiders*) and the collection of stories entitled *Ultimo viene il corvo* (1949; *Adam, One Afternoon, and Other Stories*).

Calvino turned decisively to fantasy and allegory in the 1950s, producing the three fantastic tales—*Il visconte dimezzato* (1952; "The Cloven Viscount,"), *Il barone rampante* (1957; *The Baron in the Trees*), and *Il cavaliere inesistente* (1959; "The Nonexistent Knight")—that brought him international acclaim. His *Fiabe italiane* (1956; *Italian Folktales*) assembled a collection of traditional tales rendered in regional dialects. Among Calvino's later works of fantasy is *Le cosmicomiche* (1965; *Cosmicomics*), an engaging collection of stream-of-consciousness narratives that treat the creation and evolution of the universe. In the later novels *Le città invisibili* (1972; INVISIBLE CITIES), *Il castello dei destini incrociati* (1973; THE CASTLE OF CROSSED DESTINIES), and *Se una notte d'inverno un viaggiatore* (1979; IF ON A WINTER'S NIGHT A TRAVELER),

Calvino used playfully innovative structures and shifting viewpoints. His later *Una pietra sopra: Discorsi di letteratura e società* (1980; *The Uses of Literature*) is a collection of essays he wrote for *Il Menabò*.

Calvus \'kal-vəs\, Gaius Licinius Macer (b. 82 BC—d. *c.* 47 BC) Roman poet and orator who, as a poet, followed his friend Catullus in style and choice of subjects.

Calvus was a son of the chronicler Licinius Macer. As an orator he was the leader of a group who opposed the florid Asiatic school and took the simplest Attic orators as their model. Of his speeches, 21 are mentioned, the most famous being those delivered against the tribune Publius Vatinius. Only 20 meager fragments of his poetry survive.

Calypso \kə-'lip-sō\ In Greek mythology, the daughter of the Titan Atlas (or Oceanus or Nereus), a nymph of the mythical island of Ogygia. She entertained the Greek hero Odysseus for seven years but could not overcome his longing for home even by a promise of immortality. At last the god Hermes was sent by Zeus, to ask her to release Odysseus. According to later stories she bore Odysseus a son, Auson, and twins, Nausithous and Nausinous.

Cambridge critics \'kām-brij\ Group of critics who were a major influence in English literary studies from the mid-1920s and who established an intellectually rigorous school of critical standards in the field of literature.

The leaders of the group were I.A. Richards and F.R. Leavis of the University of Cambridge and Richards' pupil William Empson. C.K. Ogden, a writer and linguist, was associated with Richards in linguistic studies (*The Meaning of Meaning*, 1923) at Cambridge. These critics' treatment of literature was based upon a close examination of the literary text, as exemplified in two seminal books by Richards, *Principles of Literary Criticism* (1924) and *Practical Criticism* (1929), and upon their belief in a close relationship of literature to social issues. This view was part of a larger criticism of life, which was treated by Leavis in such books as *Culture and Environment* (1933) and *The Great Tradition* (1948), a work on the English novel. Leavis' quarterly *Scrutiny* (1932–53) was devoted to both aspects, and its contributors—among them L.C. Knights, Denys Thompson, and Leavis' wife, Q.D. Leavis (*Fiction and the Reading Public*, 1932)—made notable contributions to criticism. William Empson's *Seven Types of Ambiguity* (1930) and *The Structure of Complex Words* (1951) demonstrated the scope of criticism stemming from linguistic analysis. Cambridge criticism conformed to no special type, but its analytical bent, astringency, and disdain of merely appreciative writing sprang from its creators' formidable training and interests in philosophy, linguistics, psychology, and social sciences and from their immense reading in literature. *See also* NEW CRITICISM.

Camelot \'kam-ə-,lät\ In ARTHURIAN LEGEND, the seat of King Arthur's court. It is variously identified with Caerleon, Monmouthshire, in Wales, and, in England, with the following: Queen Camel, Somerset; the little town of Camelford, Cornwall; Winchester, Hampshire; and Cadbury Castle, South Cadbury, Somerset.

cameo \'kam-ē-,ō\ A usually brief literary or dramatic piece that brings into delicate or sharp relief the character of a person, place, or event.

Camilla \kə-'mil-ə\ In Roman mythology, legendary Volscian maiden who became a warrior and was a favorite of the goddess Diana. According to the Roman poet Virgil, her father, Metabus, was fleeing from his enemies with the infant Camilla when he encountered the Amisenus River. He fastened the child to a javelin, dedicated her to Diana, and hurled her

across the river. He then swam to the opposite bank, where he rejoined Camilla.

Living among shepherds and in the woods, Camilla became a skilled hunter and resolute warrior through her father's tutelage in the rustic arts. She became the leader of a band of warriors and fought in a battle against the Roman hero Aeneas. She was killed by Arruns, an Etruscan, as she was chasing a retreating soldier.

Camille \kä-'mēy\ Alternate name of the fictional character Marguerite Gautier, protagonist of *La Dame aux camélias* (1848; staged 1852) by Alexandre Dumas *fils*.

Camille made her way in life as a courtesan, and her byname referred to the camellias she carried as a signal of her availabil-

Illustration by Aubrey Beardsley

ity. After falling in love with a young man, Camille gives up her former way of life but selflessly returns to it (even knowing that she is mortally ill and that he is her last chance for happiness) rather than ruin his life by her association with him. Her protracted death scene has been much parodied.

The story is enduring; it was used by Giuseppe Verdi as the basis for his opera *La traviata* (1853), and Greta Garbo portrayed the character in a memorable film (*Camille*, 1936).

Camillo, Don \,dōn-kä-'mēl-lō\ Fictional character, a pugnacious Italian village priest whose confrontations with his equally belligerent adversary, the local communist mayor Peppone, formed the basis for a series of popular, humorous short stories by Italian author Giovanni Guareschi. The character also figured in a series of successful French-language films (1950s and '60s) starring the French comic actor Fernandel.

Don Camillo's exploits were first published in the Italian magazine *Candido* in the late 1940s. Collections of these short stories include *Mondo piccolo "Don Camillo"* (1948; *The Little World of Don Camillo*), *Mondo piccolo: "Don Camillo e il suo gregge"* (1953; *Don Camillo and His Flock*), *Don Camillo prende il diavolo per la coda* (1956; U.K. title, *Don Camillo Takes the Devil by the Tail*; U.S. title, *Don Camillo and the Devil*), *Il compagno Don Camillo* (1963; *Comrade Don Camillo*), and *Don Camillo e i giovani d'oggi* (1969; *Don Camillo Meets the Flower Children*).

Camões or **Camoëns** \kà-ˈmȯiⁿnsh\, Luís (Vaz) de, *surname also spelled* Camoens (b. *c.* 1524/25, Lisbon, Port.—d. June 10, 1580, Lisbon)   Portugal's great national poet, author of the epic poem *Os Lusíadas* (1572; THE LUSIADS), which describes Vasco da Gama's discovery of the sea route to India. Camões had a permanent and unparalleled impact on Portuguese and Brazilian literature alike.

Mary Evans Picture Library

Biographical information about Camões is scant. Research has shown him to have been a member of the impoverished old aristocracy. There is no evidence that Camões pursued regular studies, but few other European poets of that time achieved such a vast knowledge of both classical and contemporary culture and philosophy. In his youth he is supposed to have been in territories held by the Portuguese in Morocco. He also spent about 17 years in India.

Camões returned to Portugal in 1570, and his *Os Lusíadas* was published in Lisbon in early 1572. In July of that year he was granted a royal pension, probably in recompense for both his service in India and his having written *Os Lusíadas*.

The first edition of Camões' *Rimas* was published in 1595. The editor, Fernão Rodrigues Lobo Soropita, had exercised scrupulous care in collecting the poems from manuscript songbooks, but even so he could not avoid the inclusion of some apocryphal poems. Nevertheless, there are sufficient authentic poems to confirm Camões' position as Portugal's finest lyric poet. Drawing on his experiences during his long absence from Portugal, he wrote with deep sincerity and genuine feeling of his sense of "yearning fraught with loneliness" (*saudade-soledade*). This was a new and convincing undertone unique in Portuguese literature.

In his dramatic works Camões tried to combine national and classical tendencies. In his comedy *Anfitriões* (*Enfatriões*; "The Two Amphitryons"), an adaptation of Plautus' *Amphitryon*, he accentuated the comic aspect of the myth of Amphitryon; in the comedy *El-rei Seleuco* ("King Seleucas") he reduced the situation found in Plutarch (in which Seleucas' son wins his stepmother from his father) to pure farce; and in *Filodemo* he developed the *auto*, a kind of morality play, which Gil Vicente had earlier made popular. The editions of Camões' works in Portuguese and other languages number in the hundreds, and his bibliography is immense.

Campana \käm-ˈpä-nä\, Dino (b. Aug. 20, 1885, Marradi, Italy—d. March 1, 1932, Florence)   Innovative Italian lyric poet who is almost as well known for his tragic, flamboyant personality as for his controversial writings.

Campana began to show signs of mental instability in his early teens; although he studied chemistry intermittently at the University of Bologna, he failed to graduate. Thereafter he began a wandering life, traveling throughout Europe and Latin America. He held a variety of jobs and was sometimes jailed briefly or committed to mental institutions for extended periods. His only poetry collection, *Canti orfici* (1914; *Orphic Songs*), was noted for its emotional intensity. A strain of nihilism persists through the conflicting attitudes of his fragmentary poems; they alternate erratically between hallucination and reality, love and fear, Christian and pagan beliefs, at times achieving stunning clarity of expression. His *Lettere* (1958; "Letters"), written in 1916–18, reveal his decline into insanity and melancholia. In January 1918 he was committed to the mental institution where he lived for the rest of his life.

Campbell \ˈkam-bəl, *US also* ˈkam-əl\, John W., *in full* John Wood Campbell, Jr. (b. June 8, 1910, Newark, N.J., U.S.—d. July 11, 1971, Mountainside, N.J.)   American science-fiction writer, considered the father of modern science fiction.

Campbell began writing science fiction while in college. His first published story, "When the Atoms Failed" (1930), contained one of the earliest depictions of computers in science fiction.

Through the early 1930s Campbell wrote stories of outer space but also began writing a different kind of science fiction under the pseudonym of "Don A. Stuart" (derived from his wife's name, Dona Stuart). In these stories, technology was secondary to the development of characterization and mood. One such story is "Twilight" (1934), in which machines work on incessantly, long after humans are gone. These popular works prompted much imitation.

Campbell's influence on other science fiction writers continued when he turned his attention in 1937 to editing *Astounding Stories*, later titled *Astounding Science Fiction*, then *Analog*. The magazine's contributors, including Isaac Asimov and Robert A. Heinlein, dominated the field in the mid-20th century.

Campbell \ˈkam-bəl, *US also* ˈkam-əl\, Joseph (b. March 26, 1904, New York, N.Y., U.S.—d. Oct. 31, 1987, Honolulu)   Prolific American author and editor whose works on comparative mythology examined the universal functions of mythology in various human cultures and examined the mythic figure in a wide range of literatures.

A reader of American Indian folklore as a child, Campbell later revived his interest in the subject while working on a master's degree in English literature. Discovering that many themes in Arthurian legend resembled the basic motifs in American Indian folklore, he pursued the problem of mythological archetypes. In his essay "The Hero," in *Where the Two Came to Their Father* (1969), he compared the concept of the hero in American Indian mythology with that in the mythology of other peoples. *The Hero with a Thousand Faces* (1949) is another work examining the archetype of the hero. Campbell's major work is a vast study of world mythology, *The Masks of God*, 4 vol. (1959–67). Other books by Campbell include *Flight of the Wild Gander* (1969), a collection of his essays; *Myths to Live By* (1972); *The Mythic Image* (1975; with M.J. Abadie);

and *The Way of the Animal Powers*, vol. 1 (1983), a historical atlas of world mythology. He was also the editor of *Myths, Dreams, and Religion* (1971).

Campbell \'kam-bəl, *US also* 'kam-əl\, Roy, *in full* Ignatius Roy Dunnachie Campbell (b. Oct. 2, 1901, Durban, S.Af.—d. April 22, 1957, near Setúbal, Port.) Poet whose vigorous extrovert verse contrasted with the uneasy self-searching of the more prominent socially conscious English poets of the 1930s.

Campbell led an adventurous life—much of it in France, Spain, and Portugal—and followed a variety of occupations, including bullfighting. He fought with the Nationalists in the Spanish Civil War and during World War II served in East and North Africa until disabled. He settled in Portugal five years before his death in an automobile crash.

Campbell's first long poem, *The Flaming Terrapin* (1924), which won him immediate recognition, exalts the instinctive vital force that brings forth intelligent human effort out of apathy and disillusionment. *The Wayzgoose* (1928) is a satire on South African intellectuals; and *The Georgiad* (1931) is a savage attack on the Bloomsbury group in England. Campbell's lyrical works include *Adamastor* (1930), *Flowering Reeds* (1933), and *Talking Bronco* (1946). Campbell did brilliant translations of a number of Spanish, Portuguese, and French writers and wrote two autobiographical books, *Broken Record* (1934) and *Light on a Dark Horse* (1951).

Campbell \'kam-bəl, *US also* 'kam-əl\, Thomas (b. July 27, 1777, Glasgow, Scot.—d. June 15, 1844, Boulogne, Fr.) Scottish poet, remembered chiefly for his sentimental and martial lyrics.

Campbell went to Mull, an island of the Inner Hebrides, as a tutor in 1795 and two years later settled in Edinburgh to study law. His *The Pleasures of Hope* (1799), a traditional 18th-century survey of human affairs written in heroic couplets, went through four editions within a year. He also produced several stirring patriotic war songs—"Ye Mariners of England," "The Soldier's Dream," "Hohenlinden," and, in 1801, "The Battle of the Baltic." With others he launched a movement in 1825 to found the University of London for students excluded from Oxford or Cambridge by religious tests or lack of funds.

Campbell \'kam-bəl, *US also* 'kam-əl\, William Wilfred (b. June 1, 1861, Berlin, Canada West [now Ontario, Canada]—d. Jan. 1, 1918, near Ottawa) Canadian poet, best remembered for his first volume of poetry, *Lake Lyrics and Other Poems* (1889), which celebrates the scenery of the Lake Huron–Georgian Bay country near his home.

Campbell was educated at the University of Toronto, ordained (1885), and, upon retiring from the ministry (1891), employed by the civil service in Ottawa until his death. His works are informed by a missionary zeal for the culture of the British "race" and an interest in primitive mythology uncommon in his day. His other books of verse are *The Dread Voyage* (1893), *Beyond the Hills of Dream* (1889), *The Collected Poems* (1905), and *Sagas of Vaster Britain* (1914). Campbell's output includes verse plays, descriptive studies of Canadian life, and two historical novels. He edited an edition of *The Oxford Book of Canadian Verse* (1913). W.J. Sykes edited his *Poetical Works* (1923).

Campion or **Campian** \'kam-pē-ən\, Thomas (b. Feb. 12, 1567, London, Eng.—d. before March 1, 1620, London?) English poet, composer, musical and literary theorist, and physician, one of the outstanding songwriters of the brilliant English lutenist school of the late 16th and early 17th centuries.

Campion's first publication was five sets of verses appearing anonymously in the pirated 1591 edition of Philip Sidney's *Astrophel and Stella*. In 1595 his *Poemata* (Latin epigrams) appeared, followed in 1601 by *A Booke of Ayres* (written with Philip Rosseter), of which much of the musical accompaniment and verses were Campion's. He wrote a masque in 1607 and three more in 1613, the year his *Two Bookes of Ayres* probably appeared. *The Third and Fourth Booke of Ayres* came out in 1617, probably followed by a treatise (undated) on counterpoint.

Campion's lyric poetry and songs for lute accompaniment are his works of most lasting interest. In *Observations in the Art of English Poesie* (1602), he attacked the use of rhymed, accentual meters, insisting instead that timing and sound duration are the fundamental elements in verse structure.

Campion's originality as a lyric poet lies in his unusual treatment of the conventional Elizabethan subject matter. Rather than using visual imagery, he expresses the delights of the natural world in terms of sound, music, movement, or change. This approach and Campion's flowing but irregular verbal rhythms give freshness to hackneyed subjects and seem also to suggest an immediate personal experience of even the commonest feelings. *The Selected Songs*, edited by W.H. Auden, was published in 1972.

Campion, Albert \'al-bərt-'kam-pē-ən\ Fictional English detective, the upper-class protagonist of a series of mystery novels beginning with *The Crime at Black Dudley* (1929; U.S. title, *The Black Dudley Murder*) by Margery ALLINGHAM.

Campo \'käm-pō\, Estanislao del (b. Feb. 7, 1834, Buenos Aires, Arg.—d. Nov. 6, 1880, Buenos Aires) Argentine poet and journalist whose *Fausto* is one of the major works of gaucho poetry.

Campo descended from a patrician family and fought in defense of Buenos Aires against General Justo José de Urquiza's troops. He became a newspaperman, writing with harsh humor in support of liberal causes. He began writing romantic poetry in 1855. Two years later he published his gaucho poem "Décimas," written in the style of Hilario Ascasubi, who used the byname Aniceto the Rooster. Campo's major work was the 1,278-line *Fausto: Impresiones del gaucho Anastasio el Pollo en la representación de ésta ópera* (1866; "Faust: Impressions of the Gaucho Anastasio the Chicken on the Presentation of This Opera"; *Faust*).

Campo was inspired to retell the story of Charles Gounod's *Faust* in verse form, in the language of a rough-hewn gaucho whom he named Anastasio the Chicken. Parody, commentary on the opera's characters, vignettes of gaucho life, and a description of nature are all elements of Campo's poem. The result is earthy rural humor at the expense of the opera's cultured urban audiences.

Campoamor y Campoosorio \,käm-pō-ä-'mòr-ē-,käm-pō-ō-'sòr-yō\, Ramón de (b. Sept. 24, 1817, Navia, Spain—d. Feb. 12, 1901, Madrid) Spanish poet whose value lies in his expression of contemporary social attitudes.

After studying Latin and philosophy, Campoamor went to Madrid in 1838 to pursue a degree in medicine but turned to literature instead. Although his two early books, *Ternezas y floras* (1840; "Endearments and Flowers") and *Ayes del alma* (1842; "Laments of the Soul"), show the influence of the Spanish Romantic poet José Zorrilla y Moral, he broke away from Romanticism with his book *Doloras* (1845), simple verses of worldly wisdom, much like proverbs, that were claimed to herald a breakthrough into new poetic forms. Continuing his experimentation, he published *Pequeños poemas* (1871; "Little Poems") and *Humoradas* (1886; "Pleasant Jokes"). Most of his verse is now seen as little more than sentimental philosophy cloaked in a rhymed prose of affected simplicity.

Campos \'käm-püsh\, Haroldo de and Augusto de (respectively b. Aug. 19, 1929, São Paulo, Braz.; b. 1931, São Paulo)

Poets and literary critics, best known as the prime exponents of Brazilian concrete poetry movement in the 1950s.

Together with the poets Décio Pignatari and Ferreira Gullar, the Campos brothers produced the first exposition of concrete poetry in 1956 and published the avant-garde art and poetry magazines *Noigandres* and *Invenção*. The Campos brothers and Pignatari published *Teoria da poesia concreta* ("Theory of Concrete Poetry") in 1965. Haroldo and Augusto also translated into Portuguese works of Ezra Pound (1960), E.E. Cummings (1960), James Joyce (1962), Stéphane Mallarmé (1970), and Vladimir Mayakovsky (1967).

Haroldo de Campos published some of his essays in *Metalinguagem* (1967; "Metalanguage") and *A arte no horizonte do provável* (1969; "Art on the Horizon of the Probable"). Other critical works of Haroldo's include the books *Ideograma* (1977) and *Deus e o Diabo no Fausto de Goethe* (1981; "God and the Devil in Goethe's Faust") and several essays on the works of Oswald de Andrade, an earlier Brazilian poet. Haroldo wrote poetry of his own, including the prose poem *Galáxias* (1984; "Galaxies"). Some of his poetry was collected in *Os melhores poemas de Haroldo de Campos* (1992; "The Best Poems of Haroldo de Campos"). Augusto's poem collections include *Linguaviagem* (1967; "Languagetravel"), *Poemóbiles* (1974), *Caixa preta* (1975; "Black Box"), and *Ex poemas* (1985).

campus novel A novel set on a university campus, usually written by someone who is or was an academic. Examples include Kingsley Amis' *Lucky Jim* (1954), John Barth's *Giles Goat-Boy* (1966), and Robertson Davies' *The Rebel Angels* (1981).

Camus \kȧ-'mᵫ\, Albert (b. Nov. 7, 1913, Mondovi, French Algeria [now Drean, Alg.]—d. Jan. 4, 1960, near Sens, Fr.) French novelist, essayist, and playwright who addressed the isolation of the individual in an alien universe, the estrangement of the individual from himself, the problem of evil, and the inescapable finality of death, reflecting the anomie of the postwar intellectual. He received the 1957 Nobel Prize for Literature.

Camus grew up in a working-class district of Algiers. He won a scholarship to the Algiers *lycée* (high school) in 1923. A period of intellectual awakening followed, accompanied by great enthusiasm for sports; in 1930, however, he had the first of several severe attacks of tuberculosis. Supporting himself by a variety of jobs, he registered as a philosophy student at the University of Algiers. Camus obtained a degree from the university, but was prevented from pursuing a teaching career by another attack of tuberculosis.

Throughout the 1930s, Camus was a prominent figure among the young leftwing intellectuals of Algiers. He wrote, produced, adapted, and acted for a theater company dedicated to bringing outstanding plays to working-class audiences. Ironically, his plays are the least admired part of his literary output, although *Le Malentendu* (1944; *Cross Purpose*) and *Caligula* (1944) remain landmarks in the Theater of the Absurd. His other plays include *L'État de siege* (1948; *State of Siege*) and *Les*

H. Cartier-Bresson—Magnum

Justes (1950; *The Just Assassins*). Two of his most enduring contributions were his stage adaptations of William Faulkner's *Requiem for a Nun* (*Requiem pour une nonne*, 1956) and Fyodor Dostoyevsky's *The Possessed* (*Les Possédés*, 1959).

Camus's first published collection of essays, *L'Envers et l'endroit* (1937; "The Wrong Side and the Right Side"), described the physical setting of his early years and included portraits of his mother, grandmother, and uncle. A second collection of essays, *Noces* (1938; "Nuptials"), contained lyrical meditations on the Algerian countryside and presented natural beauty as a form of wealth that even the very poor can enjoy. Some of these essays were published in English in *Lyrical and Critical* (1967; also published as *Lyrical and Critical Essays*).

In the two years before the outbreak of World War II, Camus worked as a journalist with *Alger-Républicain*. He reviewed some of Jean-Paul Sartre's early literary work and wrote an important series of articles analyzing social conditions among the Muslims of the Kabylie region. These articles, reprinted in abridged form in *Actuelles III* (1958; earlier collections had appeared under the titles *Actuelles* and *Actuelles II* in 1950 and 1953), drew attention to many of the injustices that led to the outbreak of the Algerian War of Independence in 1954.

During the final years of the German occupation of France and the immediate postwar period, he was editor of the Parisian daily *Combat*, the successor to a Resistance news sheet he had run. He maintained an independent position based on his ideas of justice and truth and the belief that all political action must have a solid moral basis. Later, disillusioned, he severed his connection with *Combat*.

L'Étranger (U.S. title, THE STRANGER; U.K. title, *The Outsider*), a brilliant first novel begun before the war and published in 1942, was a study of 20th-century alienation. The same year saw the publication of the influential philosophical essay *Le Mythe de Sisyphe* (1942, revised and enlarged edition, 1945; THE MYTH OF SISYPHUS), in which Camus, with considerable sympathy, analyzed contemporary nihilism and the sense of the "absurd." His second novel, *La Peste* (1947; THE PLAGUE), addressed the same issues by depicting human dignity and camaraderie in the face of an epidemic. Camus's concept of the absurd evolved into an idea of moral and metaphysical "rebellion." He contrasted this latter ideal with political-historical revolution in a second long essay, *L'Homme révolté* (1951; THE REBEL). His other major literary works include the technically brilliant novel *La Chute* (1956; THE FALL) and a collection of short stories, *L'Exil et le royaume* (1957; *Exile and the Kingdom*).

Canaan \'kā-nən\ Area variously defined in historical and biblical literature, but always centered on Palestine. The Israelites occupied and conquered Palestine, or Canaan, beginning in the late 2nd millennium BC, or perhaps earlier; and the Bible justifies such occupation by identifying Canaan with the Promised Land, the land promised to the Israelites by God.

In many later references (including slave narratives and early Christian hymnody), Canaan has no earthly location; rather, it is an idealized home, a promised land, or a sweet land of rest.

Cancer Ward Novel by Aleksandr SOLZHENITSYN. Though banned in the Soviet Union, the work was published in 1968 by Italian and other European publishers in the Russian language as *Rakovy korpus*. It was also published in English translation in 1968.

Solzhenitsyn based *Cancer Ward* on his own hospitalization and successful treatment for supposedly terminal cancer during his forced exile in Kazakhstan in the mid-1950s. The novel's iconoclastic main character is Oleg Kostoglotov, like the author a recently released inmate of the brutal forced labor camps. His fellow patients in the provincial city hospital are a microcosm of Soviet society.

cancioneiro \Spanish ˌkän-thē-ō-'nä-rō, Portuguese ˌkäⁿn-syō-'nä-rū\ [Portuguese *cancioneiro*, from Spanish *cancionero*, a derivative of *canción* song] A Spanish or Portuguese collection of songs and poems, usually by several authors. The earliest examples of Portuguese-Galician poetry, composed from the 12th to the 14th century, were collected during the 14th and 15th centuries into three manuscript songbooks: the *Cancioneiro da Ajuda*, the *Cancioneiro da Vaticana*, and the *Cancioneiro de Colocci-Brancuti* (or *da Bíblioteca Nacional de Lisbōa*). The 2,000 poems in these books can be classified by content into three major categories: (1) the *cantigas de amigo*, laments of women for their lovers, dealing with sad partings, grief, and patient waiting and containing descriptions of nature that are permeated with *saudade* (the melancholy tone characteristic of Portuguese poetry); (2) the *cantigas de amor*, in which the pining lover is a man; and (3) the *cantigas de escárnio e maldizer*, ribald satires on contemporary themes. The collections also contain occasional religious songs extolling the miracles of the Virgin.

The later *Cancioneiro Geral* (1516), compiled by Garcia de Resende, contains nearly 1,000 *cantigas* in Portuguese and Castilian. Dealing with love and satiric themes, the verses are more intricate and sophisticated than those in the earlier collections and show evidence of Spanish and Italian influence.

Outstanding among the Spanish examples are the *Cancionero de Baena* (1445), a collection of 583 poems made by Juan Alfonso Baena that shows the influence of the Portuguese lyric but is more intellectual, using symbol, allegory, and classical allusion in the treatment of themes of high moral, philosophical, or political intent, and the *Cancionero general* (1511), a collection of late medieval lyrics made by Hernando del Castillo.

Candida \'kan-did-ə\ Drama in three acts by George Bernard SHAW, performed in 1897 and published the following year. Candida, the heroine, must choose between two men—James Morell, her popular clergyman husband, and Eugene Marchbanks, a gifted 18-year-old poet who adores her. Eventually Candida elects to remain with the man who needs her the most—her husband. Ostensibly a confident, secure man, Morell is actually weaker than Marchbanks, who, Candida realizes, has artistic vision and the capacity to forgo personal happiness for future creative achievement.

Caṇḍīdās or **Chandidas** \'chən-dē-ˌdäs, -ˌdäsh\ (fl. late 14th to early 15th century, Bengal, India) Bengali poet whose love songs addressed to the washerwoman Rāmī were popular in the medieval period. They were a source of inspiration to Vaiṣṇava and Sahajīyā religious movements that explored parallels between human and divine love.

The popularity of Caṇḍīdās' songs inspired much imitation, making it difficult to establish firmly the identity of the poet. The poems themselves claim that the author was a Brahman and a village priest who broke with tradition by openly declaring his love for the low-caste Rāmī. The lovers viewed their relationship as sacred, the closest possible analogy to the spiritual union of the divine lovers Rādhā and Krishna. Caṇḍīdās

refused to relinquish either his temple duties or his love for Rāmī, much to the chagrin of his family. A feast to placate the village Brahmans was prepared, but it was thrown into confusion by the unexpected appearance of Rāmī.

What happened afterward is obscured by legend. According to one version, Caṇḍīdās assumed the form of Vishnu. Another claims that he was dismissed as priest and fasted to death as a protest but came to life again on the funeral pyre. A third version (based on poems supposedly written by Rāmī) states that he was whipped to death, while tied to the back of an elephant, for having attracted the attention of a woman of high rank.

The poetry of Caṇḍīdās had a strong influence on later Bengali art, literature, and religious thought. In the *sahajīyā* (Sanskrit: "natural") movement of the 16th-century Sahajīya cult, religious experience was pursued through the senses, and the love of a man for the wife of another or for a woman of unsuitably low caste was praised above others for its intensity in the face of social disapproval.

Candide \kä⁻-'dēd, *Angl* kan-\ Satirical novel published in 1759 that is the best-known work by VOLTAIRE. It is a savage denunciation of metaphysical optimism—as espoused by the German philosopher Gottfried Wilhelm Leibniz—that reveals a world of horrors and folly.

In this philosophical fantasy, naive Candide sees and suffers such misfortune that he ultimately rejects the philosophy of his tutor Doctor Pangloss, who claims that "all is for the best in this best of all possible worlds." Candide and his companions—Pangloss, his beloved Cunegonde, and his servant Cacambo—

Line drawing by Paul Klee for a 1920 German edition of *Candide*

display an instinct for survival that provides them hope in an otherwise somber setting. When they all retire together to a simple life on a small farm, they discover that the secret of happiness is "to cultivate one's garden," a practical philosophy that excludes excessive idealism and nebulous metaphysics.

Cane \'kān\ Experimental novel by Jean TOOMER, published in 1923 and reprinted in 1967, about the black experience in the United States. This symbolic, poetic work comprises a variety of literary forms, including poems and short stories, and incorporates elements from both Southern black folk culture and the contemporary white avant-garde. Some literary critics associated the title with the Old Testament figure of Cain, the exiled son of Adam.

Cane is divided into three sections, the first focusing on the rural Southern past and sexuality. The characters in this section are unable to find success and are constantly frustrated by what life offers them. The second section deals with people moving from the agrarian South to the urban North and the spiritual quest of those who abandon their rural roots in hopes of finding a new life. The final section, "Kabnis," is a prose work that synthesizes the preceding sections. Kabnis is a black teacher and writer who struggles with the dilemma of race, with his ambivalent feelings about his African heritage and Southern enslavement, and with his difficulties in being a creative artist.

Canetti \kä-'net-tē\, Elias (b. July 25, 1905, Ruse, Bulg.—d. Aug. 13, 1994, Zurich, Switz.) Novelist and playwright whose works explore the emotions of crowds and the position of the individual at odds with the society around him. He was awarded the Nobel Prize for Literature in 1981.

Canetti was educated in Zürich, Switz., in Frankfurt, Ger., and at the University of Vienna. His interest in crowds crystallized after he witnessed street rioting over inflation in Frankfurt in the 1920s. A planned eight-novel saga of the madness he saw around him was reduced to *Die Blendung* (1935; AUTO-DA-FÉ or *The Tower of Babel*). Shortly before World War II, Canetti immigrated to England and devoted much of his time to research on the psychopathology of power. *Masse und Macht* (1960; *Crowds and Power*) is an outgrowth of that interest, as are Canetti's three plays, *Hochzeit* (1932; *The Wedding*), *Komödie der Eitelkeit* (1950; *Comedy of Vanity*), and *Die Befristeten* (1964; *Life-Terms*). The plays were published as *Dramen* in 1964. He also wrote *Die Provinz des Menschen: Aufzeichnungen 1942–1972* (1973; *The Human Province*) and *Das Geheimherz der Uhr: Aufzeichnungen 1973–1985* (1987; *The Secret Heart of the Clock*), both excerpts from his notebooks; *Der Ohrenzeuge: Fünfzig Charaktere* (1974; *Earwitness: Fifty Characters*); and three volumes of his autobiography.

Canfield, Dorothy.   Pen name of Dorothy Canfield FISHER.

Canitz \'kän-its\, Friedrich Rudolf, Baron (Freiherr) von (b. Nov. 27, 1654, Berlin [Germany]—d. Aug. 11, 1699, Berlin) One of a group of German court poets who prepared the way for the new ideas of the Enlightenment. His satires (*Nebenstunden unterschiedener Gedichte*; 1700) helped to introduce classical standards of taste and style into German literature. He was made a privy councillor by the elector Frederick III in 1697; the emperor Leopold I created him a baron of the empire.

caṅkam literature \'chäŋ-gäm\, caṅkam *also spelled* śaṅgam \'shäŋ-gäm\   The earliest writings in Tamil, thought to have been produced in three *caṅkam*s, or literary academies, in Madurai, India, from the 1st to the 4th century AD. The *Tolkāppiyam*, a book of grammar and rhetoric, was compiled along with eight anthologies (*Eṭṭuttokai*) of secular poetry: *Kuruntokai, Narriṇai, Akanāṉūru, Aiṅkurunūru, Kalittakai, Puranāṉūru, Patirruppattu*, and *Paripāṭal*. The poems are probably unique in early Indian literature, which is otherwise almost entirely religious. Two topics, love and the praise of kings and their deeds, predominate. Many of the verses, especially those written about noble deeds, display great freshness and vigor, and they are singularly free of the elaborate literary conceits of much other early and medieval literature of India. As largely secular works, they are also free of the complex mythical allusions that are characteristic of most Indian art forms. Among the rare instances of religious works in *caṅkam* writing, *Pattupāṭṭu* ("The Ten Long Poems") contains the earliest Indian poem of personal devotion to a god, and *Paripāṭal* contains poems about Vishnu, Śiva, and Murugaṉ.

Cankar \'tsäŋ-kär\, Ivan (b. May 10, 1876, Vrhnika, Carniola, Austria-Hungary [now in Slovenia]—d. Dec. 11, 1918, Ljubljana, Slovenia)   Slovene writer and patriot.

After a childhood spent in poverty, Cankar went to Vienna and soon began to earn his living by his writings, which made satirical attacks upon those who exploited the oppressed. He

returned to Slovenia in 1907. Cankar was a prolific writer of short stories, novels, articles, drama, and verse; he was also a political speaker and was imprisoned for his criticism of the Austrian regime. In spite of being colored by his championship of the oppressed, his work reveals an original style—simple yet eloquent, subtle, and melodious. Cankar's complete works were collected in 20 volumes (1925–36).

Cannery Row   Novel by John STEINBECK, published in 1945. Like most of Steinbeck's postwar work, *Cannery Row* is sentimental in tone while retaining the author's characteristic social criticism. Peopled by stereotypical good-natured bums and warm-hearted prostitutes living on the fringes of Monterey, Calif., the picaresque novel celebrates lowlifes who are poor but happy.

Cannibals and Missionaries   Novel of ideas that probes the psychology of terrorism, by Mary MCCARTHY, published in 1979.

The action of the novel begins when a plane carrying Americans bound for Iran is hijacked by terrorists. Some passengers are rich art collectors; others are politicians and activists planning to investigate allegations that Savak, the shah's secret police, is using torture against political dissidents. At first the terrorists intend to use the politicians and activists as hostages, but they soon realize that masterworks of art are of more value than any human being and decide to trade the art collectors for their artworks.

canon \'kan-ən\ [Greek *kanōn* rod, measuring line, rule, standard]   **1.** An authoritative list of books accepted as Holy Scripture.   **2.** The authoritative works of a writer.   **3.** A sanctioned or accepted group or body of related works.

Canonization, The   Poem by John DONNE, written in the 1590s and originally published in 1633 in the first edition of *Songs and Sonnets*. The poem's speaker uses sacred terms to attempt to prove that his love affair is an elevated bond that approaches saintliness. In the poem, Donne makes able use of paradox, ambiguity, and wordplay.

The five stanzas of the poem—which feature the rhyme scheme of *abbacccaa*—thematically correspond to the steps of Christian canonization. The speaker begins his defense with the words "For God's sake hold your tongue, and let me love." He then proceeds to justify the holiness of his love affair, concluding with the hope that his saintly relationship will become a model for others.

Canon's Yeoman's Tale, The   One of the 24 stories in THE CANTERBURY TALES by Geoffrey Chaucer.

A humorous description of a roguish canon and alchemist, as told by his assistant, the tale pokes fun both at alchemical "science" and at the clergy. After describing failed alchemical processes in detail, the Canon's Yeoman tells his tale of a canon who swindled a priest by selling him powders to transmute mercury into silver. The canon disappeared and was never caught.

cantar \kän-'tär\ [Spanish, song, poem set to music, a noun derivative of *cantar* to sing]   In Spanish literature, originally, the lyrics of a song. The word was later used for a number of different poetic forms. In modern times it has been used specifically for an octosyllabic quatrain in which assonance occurs in the even-numbered lines and the odd-numbered lines are unrhymed with the accent falling on the last syllable.

The *cantar de gesta* was a medieval narrative epic poem similar to the French chanson de geste though with somewhat longer lines arranged in irregular stanzas, each based on a single recurring rhyme. The *Cantar de mio Cid* is the most famous example. The *cantar de pandeiro* is a Galician folksong arranged in three-line stanzas.

Cantar de mio Cid \kän-'tär-<u>th</u>ä-'mē-ō-'the<u>th</u>\ ("Song of My Cid"), *also called* Poema de mio Cid \pō-'em-ä\ Spanish epic poem composed in the mid-12th to early 13th century. The poem is the earliest surviving monument of Spanish literature and is generally considered one of the great medieval epics and one of the masterpieces of Spanish literature.

Cantar de mio Cid tells part of the story of the 11th-century Castilian noble and military leader Rodrigo Díaz de Vivar (c. 1043–99), popularly known as The Cid, who became Spain's national hero. The original manuscript has been lost, and the earliest existing copy, called *Poema del Cid*, dates from 1307. The theme, with many additions and variations, inspired numerous writers in Spain and elsewhere and helped to fix the popular conception of the Spanish character. One of the better known Spanish works that treats the life of The Cid is Guillén de Castro y Bellvís' *Las mocedades del Cid* (c. 1618; "The Youth of the Cid"). But perhaps the best-known non-Spanish treatment is Pierre Corneille's verse tragedy *Le Cid* (1637), a landmark of French Neoclassical drama. *See also* THE CID.

Cantemir *see* KANTEMIR.

canterbury tale or **canterbury story** \'kan-tər-,ber-ē, -bə-rē\ 1. A cock-and-bull story, a yarn, or a fable. 2. A long, tedious tale. Both senses are derived from *The Canterbury Tales* of Geoffrey Chaucer.

Canterbury Tales, The \'kan-tər-,ber-ē, -bə-rē\ Frame story by Geoffrey CHAUCER, written in Middle English in 1387–1400.

The framing device for the collection of stories is a pilgrimage to the shrine of Thomas à Becket in Canterbury, Kent. The 30 pilgrims who undertake the journey gather at the Tabard Inn in Southwark. They agree to engage in a storytelling contest as they travel, and Harry Bailly, host of the Tabard, serves as master of ceremonies for the contest. Most of the pilgrims are introduced by vivid brief sketches in the "General Prologue." Interspersed between the 24 tales are short dramatic scenes (called links) presenting lively exchanges, usually involving the host and one or more of the pilgrims. Chaucer did not complete the full plan for his book: the return journey from Canterbury is not included, and some of the pilgrims do not tell stories. The use of a pilgrimage as the framing device enabled Chaucer to bring together people from many walks of life. The multiplicity of social types, as well as the device of the storytelling contest itself, allowed presentation of a highly varied collection of literary genres: religious legend, courtly romance, racy fabliau, saint's life, allegorical tale, beast fable, medieval sermon, alchemical account, and, at times, mixtures of these genres. The pilgrimage, which combined a fundamentally religious purpose with a spring vacation, made possible extended consideration of the relationship between the pleasures and vices of this world and the spiritual aspirations for the next.

The Canterbury Tales consists of the General Prologue, THE KNIGHT'S TALE, THE MILLER'S TALE, THE REEVE'S TALE, THE COOK'S TALE, THE MAN OF LAW'S TALE, THE WIFE OF BATH'S TALE, THE FRIAR'S TALE, THE SUMMONER'S TALE, THE CLERK'S TALE, THE MERCHANT'S TALE, THE SQUIRE'S TALE, THE FRANKLIN'S TALE, THE SECOND NUN'S TALE, THE CANON'S YEOMAN'S TALE, THE PHYSICIAN'S TALE, THE PARDONER'S TALE, THE SHIPMAN'S TALE, THE PRIORESS'S TALE, THE TALE OF SIR THOPAS, THE TALE OF MELIBEUS (in prose), THE MONK'S TALE, THE NUN'S PRIEST'S TALE, THE MANCIPLE'S TALE, and THE PARSON'S TALE (in prose), and ends with "Chaucer's Retraction." Not all the tales are complete; several contain their own prologues or epilogues.

Probably influenced by French syllable-counting in versification, Chaucer developed for *The Canterbury Tales* a line of 10 syllables with alternating accent and regular end rhyme—an ancestor of the heroic couplet.

Canth \'kȧnt\, Minna, *in full* Ulrika Wilhelmina Canth, *original surname* Johnsson \'yȯn-,sȯn\ (b. March 19, 1844, Tampere, Russian Finland—d. May 12, 1897, Kuopio) Novelist, dramatist, and late 19th-century leader of the revival of the Finnish vernacular and realist movement.

In her early short stories, *Novelleja ja kertomuksia* (1878; "Novellas and Short Stories"), Canth wrote somewhat idealistic descriptions of country life, but in later novels and plays she turned to the realistic treatment of urban social problems, as in *Työmiehen vaimo* (1885; "The Laborer's Wife") and *Sylvi* (1893). Among her best works are the short story "Kauppa-Lopo" (1889) and the play *Anna Liisa* (1895). As a dramatist she long ranked second only to the founder of Finnish drama, Aleksis Kivi, and as a personality she ranked among the most notable Finnish women.

canto \'kan-tō\ [Italian, act of singing, song, poem, division of a poem] One of the major divisions of an epic poem or other long narrative poem. As its etymology suggests, it probably originally indicated a portion of a poem that could be sung or chanted by a minstrel at one sitting. Though early oral epics, such as Homer's, are divided into discrete sections, the name canto was first adopted for these divisions by the Italian poets Dante, Matteo Maria Boiardo, and Ludovico Ariosto. The first long English poem to be divided into cantos was Edmund Spenser's *The Faerie Queene* (1590–1609).

Canto general \'kän-tō-,gä-nä-'räl\ ("General Song") An epic poem of Latin America by Pablo NERUDA, published in two volumes in 1950. Mixing communism with nationalistic pride, Neruda depicts Latin American history as a grand, continuous struggle against oppression.

Comprising more than 300 poems, *Canto general* is arranged into 15 sections, or cantos, that chronicle successive historical periods and follow the foibles of famous emperors, explorers, dictators, and freedom fighters. The opening poem, "Amor América" ("America, My Love"), is a lyrical ode to the continent as it existed before the arrival of Spaniards, when it was troubled only with wars between Indian tribes. Other notable individual poems in the epic include the Whitmanesque "Alturas de Macchu Picchu" (THE HEIGHTS OF MACCHU PICCHU) and the patriotic "Canto General de Chile" ("General Song of Chile").

Cantos, The Collection of poems by Ezra POUND, who began writing these philosophical reveries in 1915. The first were published in *Poetry* magazine in 1917; through the decades the writing of cantos gradually became Pound's major poetic occupation, and the last were published in 1968. The complete edition of *The Cantos* (1970) consists of 117 sections.

In his early cantos Pound offered personal, lyrical reactions to such writers as Homer, Ovid, Dante, and Rémy de Gourmont, as well as to sundry politicians and economists. The early verses include memories of his teenage trips to Europe. *The Pisan Cantos* (1948), written while Pound was incarcerated—first in a prison camp for war criminals and later in a hospital for the criminally insane—were among the most admired sections of the poem; they won a Bollingen Prize in 1949.

canvas or **canvass** \'kan-vəs\ The background, setting, or scope of a historical or fictional account or narrative. The metaphor, which is drawn from painting, seems to have originated in the 18th century.

Can You Forgive Her? Novel by Anthony TROLLOPE, published serially in 1864–65 and in two volumes in 1864–65. The work was the first of his PALLISER NOVELS, named for the character of Plantagenet Palliser, who is introduced in this novel. It tells the interwoven stories of two women, Alice Vavasor and Lady Glencora M'Cluskie, who struggle to come to terms with the choices available to them concerning marriage.

canzone \kan-'zō-nē, känt-'sō-nä\ or **canzona** \-nä\ [Italian, from Latin *cantio* song] **1.** A medieval Italian or Provençal lyric poem in stanzaic form. Masters of the form included Petrarch, Dante, Torquato Tasso, and Guido Cavalcanti. **2.** An elaborately constructed ode suited to musical setting.

Cao Yu or **Ts'ao Yü** \'chaú-'yŒ\, *pseudonym of* Wan Jiabao \'wän-'jyä-'baú\ (b. Sept. 24, 1910, Tianjin, Hubei province, China) Chinese playwright who was a pioneer in *huaju* ("speech drama"), a genre that was influenced by Western theater rather than traditional Chinese drama (which is usually sung).

Cao Yu was educated at Nankai University in Tianjin and Qinghua University in Beijing, where he studied contemporary Chinese literature and Western drama. Cao Yu taught in Baoding and Tianjin and at the National Institute of Dramatic Art in Nanjing. In 1934 his first play, *Leiyu* (*Thunderstorm*; adapted for film [1938] and as a dance-drama [1981]), was published. Cao Yu's next works were *Richu* (1936; *Sunrise*; adapted as an opera [1982] and for film [1938 and 1985]) and *Yuanye* (1937, rev. ed., 1982; *The Wilderness*), a story of love and revenge that clearly reflects the influence of American playwright Eugene O'Neill.

After the outbreak of the war against Japan, Cao Yu moved with the drama school to Chongqing and later to Jiang'an, where he wrote *Tuibian* (1940; "Metamorphosis"), a patriotic work, and *Beijingren* (1941; rev. ed., 1947; *Peking Man*), thought by many to be one of the masterpieces of modern Chinese drama. He also wrote a screenplay and historical plays.

Cao Zhan or **Ts'ao Chan** \'tsaú-'jän\, *also called* Cao Xueqin \'shŒ-'chin\ (b. 1715?, Jiangning, China—d. Feb. 12, 1763, Beijing) Author of *Hong lou meng* (translated in part as DREAM OF THE RED CHAMBER), generally considered China's greatest novel. A partly autobiographical work written in the vernacular, it describes in lingering detail the decline of the powerful Jia family and the ill-fated love between Baoyu and Lin Daiyu.

Cao Zhan was the grandson of Cao Yin, one of the most eminent and wealthy men of his time. In 1728, however, his family, which held the hereditary office of commissioner of imperial textiles in Nanjing, suffered the first of a series of reverses and moved to Beijing. By 1742 Cao's contemporaries reported him to be living in reduced circumstances and engaged on a work that could hardly be anything other than the *Dream*. The author had finished at least 80 chapters of the novel before his death. The work was completed by Gao Ê, about whom little is known.

Cao Zhi or **Ts'ao Chih** \'tsaú-'chi, 'chē\, *also called* Chen Si Wang \'chən-'sə-'wäŋ\ or Prince Si of Chen (b. 192, China—d. 232, China) One of China's greatest lyric poets.

Cao Zhi was born at the time his father, Cao Cao, was assuming command over the northern third of China, later known as the Wei kingdom. In a family of poets—the verses of Cao Cao and Cao Pei (Cao Zhi's older brother and bitter rival) were also widely known—Cao Zhi's talents quickly surpassed those of his father and brother. Indeed, Cao Cao was so impressed with Cao Zhi's poetic skill that he once considered making him crown prince instead of Cao Pei. Added to Cao Pei's resentment of Cao Zhi was the fact that as an adolescent Cao Zhi had been smitten with Lady Zhen, who later became the consort of his elder brother. Thus, when Cao Pei ascended the throne as Emperor Wen of Wei in 220, he took pains to make his younger brother's life as difficult as possible.

Cao Zhi's resulting frustration and misery is the subject of much of his poetry. Writing in the then-standard five-word line, Cao Zhi extended and strengthened its use to make it a flexible and yet precise vehicle for the expression of his wide-ranging emotions.

Čapek \'chá-pek\, Karel (b. Jan. 9, 1890, Malé Svatoňovice, Bohemia, Austria-Hungary [now in Czech Republic]—d. Dec. 25, 1938, Prague, Czech.) Internationally renowned Czech novelist, short-story writer, playwright, and essayist.

Čapek studied philosophy in Prague, Berlin, and Paris and in 1917 settled in Prague as a writer and journalist. From 1907 until well into the 1920s he wrote much of his work with his brother Josef, a painter and illustrator. His early short stories include *Zářivé hlubiny* (with Josef, 1916; "The Luminous Depths"), *Krakonošova zahrada* (with Josef, 1918; "The Garden of Krakonoš"), and *Trapné povídky* (1921; in *Money and Other Stories*). Čapek's "black utopias," works showing the dangers of technological progress, include the play R.U.R. (1920); the novel *Továrna na absoluto* (1922; *The Absolute at Large*); *Krakatit* (1924; *An Atomic Phantasy*); and *Válka s mloky* (1936; *The War with the Newts*).

In another vein, Čapek's comic fantasy *Ze života hmyzu* (with Josef, 1921; *The Insect Play*) satirizes human greed. The quest for justice inspired most of the stories in *Povídky z jedné kapsy* and *Povídky z druhé kapsy* (both 1929; published together as *Tales from Two Pockets*).

Čapek's most mature work includes a trilogy of novels that together present three aspects of knowledge, *Hordubal* (1933), *Povětroň* (1934; *Meteor*), and *Obyčejný život* (1934; *An Ordinary Life*). The realistic novel *První parta* (1937; *The First Rescue Party*) stressed the need for solidarity. His last plays were *Bílá nemoc* (1937; *Power and Glory*) and *Matka* (1938; *The Mother*).

Capella \kə-'pel-ə\, Martianus Minneus Felix (fl. late 4th and early 5th century AD) A native of North Africa and an advocate at Carthage whose introduction to the liberal arts, written in prose and verse, was of immense cultural influence down to the late Middle Ages.

Capella's major work was written perhaps about AD 400 and certainly before 439. Its overall title is not known. Manuscripts give the title *De nuptiis Philologiae et Mercurii* to the first two books and entitle the remaining seven *De arte grammatica*, *De arte dialectica*, *De arte rhetorica*, *De geometrica*, *De arithmetica*, *De astrologia*, and *De harmonia*.

Capgrave \'kap-ɡrāv\, John (b. April 21, 1393, Lynn, Norfolk, Eng.—d. Aug. 12, 1464, Lynn) English historian, theologian, and hagiographer whose *Life of St. Katharine* was vigorous in its verse form and dramatically energetic in its debate.

Capgrave became a priest, lectured in theology at the University of Oxford, and later joined an order of hermits. He made at least one journey to Rome, described in *Solace of Pilgrims* (1911).

Most of his theological works seem to have been compiled from other authors, or freely translated, and consist of biblical commentaries, lectures, sermons, treatises, and lives of saints. His unfinished *Chronicle of England* is of some interest and he wrote several lives of saints in English.

Capitano \käp-ē-'tä-nō\ Stock character of the Italian theatrical form known as the COMMEDIA DELL'ARTE. He was the prototype of the pretentious but cowardly military man. An unsympathetic character, he was originally a parody of the French and Spanish mercenaries who overran 16th-century Italy. His blustering claims to wealth and military and amatory successes were exploded, often by the roguish asides of his squire and confidant.

The character of Capitano had several different names that varied as different actors interpreted the role. In the late 16th century he was called Capitano Mattamoros ("Captain Death to the Moors") and later Capitano Spavento della Valle Inferno ("Captain Fearsome of Hell's Valley"). Other names include Scaramouche, Capitano Cocodrillo, and Capitano Rodomante.

Capote \kə-'pō-tē\, Truman, *original name* Truman Streckfus Persons \'pər-sənz\ (b. Sept. 30, 1924, New Orleans, La., U.S.—d. Aug. 25, 1984, Los Angeles, Calif.) American novelist, short-story writer, and playwright, whose early writing extended the Southern gothic tradition. He later developed a more journalistic approach, notably with *In Cold Blood* (1966; copyright 1965), an account of a multiple murder committed by two sociopaths, which he called a "nonfiction novel."

Capote's first novel, *Other Voices, Other Rooms* (1948), tells of a 13-year-old boy's search for his father and his own identity. Two years earlier he had won an O. Henry award for his story "Shut a Final Door." This and other tales were collected in *A Tree of Night* (1949). *The Grass Harp* (1951) is a story of nonconforming innocents who retire temporarily from life to a tree house. In 1954, with the composer Harold Arlen, Capote wrote *The House of Flowers*, a musical set in a West Indies bordello. He also wrote several screenplays. *Local Color* (1950) is a collection of travel sketches. Capote's travels accompanying a tour of *Porgy and Bess* in the Soviet Union resulted in *The Muses Are Heard* (1956). *Breakfast at Tiffany's* (1958; film, 1961) is a novella about a young, fey Manhattan prostitute.

His increasing preoccupation with journalism—as well as with celebrity—was reflected in *Observations* (1959; photographs by Richard Avedon). *The Dogs Bark* (1973) consists of collected essays and profiles, while *Music for Chameleons* (1980) includes both fiction and nonfiction. His novel *Answered Prayers* (published posthumously 1986) was left unfinished at his death.

Caproni \kä-'prō-nē\, Giorgio (b. Jan. 7, 1912, Livorno, Italy—d. Jan. 22, 1990, Rome) Italian poet whose work was largely collected in *Tutti le poesie* (1983; "All the Poems").

Caproni served in World War II, an experience recorded in *Giorni aperti* (1942; "Clear Days"). His first three volumes of verse were *Come un'allegoria* (1936; "Like an Allegory"), *Ballo a Fontanigorda* (1938, "Dance in Fontanigorda"), and *Finzioni* (1941; "Fictions"). In 1956 he published *Il passaggio di Enea* ("The Passage of Aeneas"), an existential look at the effects of the war. *Il seme del piangere* (1959; "The Seed of Crying") was a nostalgic volume of verse about his mother. Foremost among his later volumes of poetry were *Congedo del viaggiatore cerimonioso* (1965; "Departure of the Ceremonious Traveler"), *Il muro della terra* (1975; *The Wall of the Earth*), *Il franco cacciatore* (1982; "The Free Shooter"), and *Res amissa* (1991; "The Lost Thing").

Captains Courageous (*in full* Captains Courageous, A Story of the Grand Banks) Novel of maritime adventure by Rudyard KIPLING, published as a serial in *McClure's* magazine beginning in 1896 and in book form in 1897.

The action of the novel takes place on the *We're Here*, a small fishing boat whose crew members rescue the protagonist, Harvey Cheyne, when he is washed overboard from an ocean liner. The captain refuses to take him back to port and instead makes Harvey a member of the crew. The rest of the story focuses on Harvey's personal transformation from the arrogant, pampered son of a millionaire to an admirable young man who has learned the values of hard work, simple living, and self-reliance.

Capuana \kä-'pwä-nä\, Luigi (b. May 28, 1839, Mineo, Sicily [Italy]—d. Nov. 29, 1915, Catania) Critic and writer who was one of the earliest Italian advocates of realism.

Capuana worked as a drama critic for *La Nazione*, and taught for a time in Rome and at the University of Catania. He embraced the literary movement called verismo, exhibiting in both his criticism and his fiction a preference for naturalism and objectivity. In 1877 the first of his 15 volumes of short stories appeared and in 1879 his first novel, *Giacinta*, a psychological study of a wronged woman. Another important novel, *Il marchese di Roccaverdina* (1901; "The Marquis of Roccaverdina"), is a study of guilt. His best critical works are *Studi sulla letteratura contemporanea* (1880, 1882), essays on Balzac, Edmond and Jules Goncourt, Émile Zola, and Giovanni Verga, and *Gli "ismi" contemporanei* (1898; "Contemporary 'Isms' ").

Capulet and Montague families \'kap-yü-let, 'kap-ə-lət . . . 'män-tə-ˌgyü, 'mən-\ The two Veronese families whose blood feud brings about the deaths of the title characters in William Shakespeare's ROMEO AND JULIET, when Juliet (the daughter of Capulet) and Romeo (the son of Montague) fall in love.

Caragiale \ˌkä-rä-'jyä-lä\, Ion Luca (b. Jan. 30, 1852, Haimanale, Walachia, Ottoman Empire [now in Romania]—d. June 10, 1912, Berlin, Ger.) Playwright and prose writer whose comedies show the effects on Romanian urban society of the hasty introduction of a modern way of life. *Conul Leonida* (1879; "Mr. Leonida"), *O noapte furtunoasă* (1880; "A Stormy Night"), and *O scrisoare pierdută* (1884; "A Lost Letter") are among his most popular plays. With *Năpasta* (1890; "The False Accusation"), he created what has come to be known as the peasant drama. His short stories *O făclie de Paște* (1889; "An Easter Torch"), *Păcat* (1892; "The Sin"), and *Kir Ianulea* (1909) are considered among the best prose works in Romanian literature.

Cardarelli \ˌkär-dä-'rel-lē\, Vincenzo, *original name* Nazareno Cardarelli (b. May 1, 1887, Tarquinia, Italy—d. June 15, 1959, Rome) Italian poet, essayist, literary critic, and journalist.

Cardarelli worked in Rome and Florence for such literary periodicals as *La Voce*, *Il Marzocco*, *La Lirica*, and *Avanti!* In 1919 he helped found the literary journal *La Ronda* (1919–23), which supported classicism over the avant-garde movements of Futurism and Hermeticism.

Cardarelli was noted for his early verse—collected in *Poesie* (1936; enlarged 1942, 1948)—which was characterized by a nostalgic attention to nature, sorrow, and his homeland. His best-known prose includes *Il sole a picco* (1929; "The Sun Overhead"), *Il cielo sulle città* (1939; "The Sky over the Cities"), *Lettere non spedite* (1946; "Letters Never Sent"), *Villa Tarantola* (1948), and *Viaggio d'un poeta in Russia* (1954; "Voyage of a Poet in Russia").

Cardenal \ˌkär-thä-'näl\, Ernesto, *surname in full* Cardenal Martinez \mär-'tē-näs\ (b. Jan. 20, 1925, Granada, Nic.) Roman Catholic priest who is considered to be one of the most important Nicaraguan poets.

Cardenal studied at the University of Mexico and at Columbia University. While active in revolutionary politics in Nicaragua during the 1950s, he wrote *La hora O* (1960; *Zero Hour and Other Documentary Poems*), a masterpiece of protest poetry, and the ironic love lyrics and political poems of *Epigramas* (1961).

After studying with poet Thomas Merton, Cardenal became a priest in 1965. The tension between revolutionary political fervor and religious faith informs his poems in *Salmos* (1964; *The Psalms of Struggle and Liberation*) and *Oración por Marilyn Monroe y otros poemas* (1965; *Marilyn Monroe, and Other Poems*). After the overthrow of Nicaragua's dictatorship in 1979, Cardenal served as minister of culture in the Sandinista government. His later works of poetry include *Nueva Antología poética* (1978), *Vuelos de victoria* (1985; *Flights of Victory*), and *Cántico cósmico* (1989; *Cosmic Canticles*).

Carducci \kär-'düt-chē\, Giosuè (b. July 27, 1835, Val di Castello, near Lucca, Duchy of Lucca [Italy]—d. Feb. 16, 1907, Bologna, Italy) Italian poet, winner of the Nobel Prize for Literature in 1906, and one of the most influential literary figures of his age.

Library of Congress

Carducci studied at the University of Pisa and became professor of Italian literature at Bologna. He was made a senator for life in 1890.

In his youth Carducci was the center of a group of young men determined to overthrow the prevailing Romanticism and to return to classical models. His first books of poems were *Rime* (1857; later collected in *Juvenilia*) and *Levia gravia* (1868; "Light and Serious Poems"). The strength of his republican, anticlerical feeling is evident in his hymn to Satan, "Inno a Satana" (1863), and in *Giambi ed epodi* (1867–69; "Iambics and Epodes"). *Rime nuove* (*The New Lyrics*) and *Odi barbare* (*The Barbarian Odes*), which appeared in the 1880s, contain the best of Carducci's poetry. He adapted Latin prosody to Italian verse, and the *Odi barbare* are written in meters imitative of Horace and Virgil. Carducci has also been noted for his prose works on Italian literature.

Caretaker, The Three-act play by Harold PINTER, published and first produced in 1960. Pinter's second full-length play, it concerns the delicate balance between trust and betrayal in familial relationships.

The action of the play occurs in the flat of Aston and Mick, two brothers. Aston, who is slow-witted, befriends a wheedling, garrulous tramp named Davies. When Davies appears at the brothers' flat, Mick, who is the quicker of the brothers but is unstable, vies for Davies' friendship. Individually, both brothers offer Davies a role as caretaker. Finally realizing that the equilibrium they have established is in jeopardy, the brothers reject Davies and he leaves.

Carew \'kar-ē, *commonly* kə-'rū\, Richard (b. July 17, 1555, East Antony, Cornwall, Eng.—d. Nov. 6, 1620) English scholar and antiquary known especially for a history of Cornwall.

Entering Christ Church, Oxford, at age 11, Carew later spent three years studying law and subsequently traveled abroad. He entered Parliament in 1584, became high sheriff of Cornwall in 1586, and served as treasurer under the lord lieutenant.

In 1589 he began his *Survey of Cornwall* (1602; modern edition, 1953). He translated the first five cantos of Torquato Tasso's *Gerusalemme liberata*, as *Godfrey of Bulloigne, or the Recouverie of Hierusalem* (1594). His last work was *The Excellencie of the English Tongue* (1614).

Carew \'kar-ē, *commonly* kə-'rū\, Thomas (b. 1594/95, West Wickham, Kent, Eng.—d. March 22, 1639/40, London) English poet and first of the Cavalier song writers.

Educated at the University of Oxford and at the Middle Temple, London, Carew served in several embassies and received a court appointment. His brilliant circle of friends included the playwright Ben Jonson.

Carew's only masque, *Coelum Britannicum*, was performed by the king and his gentlemen in 1634 and published the same year. His poems, circulated in manuscript, were amatory lyrics or occasional poems addressed to members of the court circle. His elegy on John Donne, whose poems he greatly admired, was deemed the outstanding piece of poetic criticism of the age. Carew also translated a number of the Psalms. The definitive edition of his poems is *The Poems of Thomas Carew, with His Masque "Coelum Britannicum"* (1949).

Carey \'kar-ē\, Henry (b. *c.* 1687, England—d. Oct. 4, 1743, London) English poet, playwright, and musician chiefly remembered for his ballads, especially "Sally in Our Alley," which appeared in a collection of his best poems set to music, called *The Musical Century* (1737). Carey went to London (perhaps from Yorkshire) sometime before 1713, when his first book of poems was published. He studied music and began to work for the theater, often providing both words and music for a number of farces, burlesques, ballad operas, and interludes; of his theater work, the best is perhaps *The Honest Yorkshire-Man* (1735).

Carey \'kar-ē\, Peter (Philip) (b. May 7, 1943, Bacchus Marsh, Victoria, Australia) Australian writer known for use of the surreal in his stories.

Carey worked as an advertising copywriter and at various other odd jobs in Australia and England until 1988, when he became a full-time writer. His collections of short stories, *The Fat Man in History* (1974; U.K. title, *Exotic Pleasures*) and *War Crimes* (1979), exhibited many grotesque and macabre elements. His novels *Bliss* (1981), *Illywhacker* (1985), and *Oscar and Lucinda* (1988) were more realistic, though Carey used black humor throughout all three. The later novels were based on the history of Australia, especially its founding and early days. Carey received the 1988 Booker Prize for *Oscar and Lucinda*.

Carey, Philip \'fil-ip-'kar-ē\ Fictional character, a handicapped young medical student who is the protagonist of W. Somerset Maugham's novel OF HUMAN BONDAGE.

caricature \'kar-ə-kə-,chūr, -,chər, -,tyūr, -,tūr\ [Italian *caricatura* exaggeration, caricature, literally, the act of loading, a derivative of *caricare* to load, pile up, increase] A representation characterized by exaggeration. The effect is usually produced by means of deliberate oversimplification and often ludicrous distortion of characteristics.

Carleton \'kärl-tən\, William (b. Feb. 20, 1794, Prillisk, County Tyrone, Ire.—d. Jan. 30, 1869, Dublin) Prolific writer who realistically portrayed the life of the rural Irish.

Carleton was born the youngest of 14 children on a small farm. At first a village tutor, he published a two-volume collection of sketches, *Traits and Stories of the Irish Peasantry* (1830). The writings that followed—*e.g.*, *Tales of Ireland* (1834) and *Fardorougha the Miser* (1839)—deal with such rural problems as the land question (redistribution of agricultural land), secret patriotic societies, and the potato famine of the 1840s. His stories had wide appeal and were translated into French, German, and Italian.

Carlyle \kär-'līl, *commonly* 'kär-,līl\, Thomas (b. Dec. 4, 1795, Ecclefechan, Dumfriesshire, Scot.—d. Feb. 5, 1881, London, Eng.) Scottish historian and essayist who was a leading figure of the Victorian era.

The son of a mason and small farmer, Carlyle was brought up in a strict Calvinist household. He was educated at the University of Edinburgh. He studied German literature, J.W. von

Goethe in particular, and in 1824 he published *Wilhelm Meister's Apprenticeship*, a translation of Goethe's bildungsroman.

In 1826 Carlyle married Jane Welsh. In the early years of their marriage the Carlyles lived mostly in Scotland, where Carlyle contributed to *The Edinburgh Review* and worked on SARTOR

Detail of an oil painting by G.F. Watts, 1877

National Portrait Gallery, London

RESARTUS (1836), a fantastic hodgepodge of autobiography and German philosophy.

In 1834 Carlyle and his wife moved to London, where he began an ambitious historical work, the three-volume THE FRENCH REVOLUTION (1837). It soon won both serious acclaim and popular success.

In *Chartism* (1840), Carlyle appeared as a bitter opponent of conventional economic theory. ON HEROES, HERO-WORSHIP, AND THE HEROIC IN HISTORY (1841) showed his reverence for strength, particularly when combined with the conviction of a God-given mission. Choosing Oliver Cromwell as the greatest English example of his ideal man, Carlyle produced *Oliver Cromwell's Letters and Speeches; With Elucidations* (1845). His next important work was *Latter-Day Pamphlets* (1850). In 1857 he embarked on a massive study of another of his heroes, and *The History of Friedrich II of Prussia, Called Frederick the Great* appeared between 1858 and 1865.

The speech that he delivered at his installation as rector of Edinburgh University in April 1866 was an immediate success. It was published in 1866 under the title *On the Choice of Books*. Soon after this, his wife died suddenly in London. Carlyle never completely recovered from her death, and in his last years he wrote little. His *Reminiscences* was published in 1881, and his edition of his wife's letters appeared in 1883.

Carman \'kär-mən\, Bliss, *in full* William Bliss Carman (b. April 15, 1861, Fredericton, N.B. [Canada]—d. June 8, 1929, New Canaan, Conn., U.S.) Canadian regional poet of the Maritime Provinces and the New England region of the United States.

Carman was educated primarily at Fredericton Collegiate and at the University of New Brunswick in Fredericton. In 1890 he went to New York City and for two decades earned a living doing editorial work on various journals. Between 1893 and 1905 he published nearly 20 volumes of verse, including *Low Tide on Grand Pré* (1893); three series of *Songs from Vagabondia* (1894, 1896, 1901), written in collaboration with Richard Hovey, a poet whom he had met at Harvard; and *Sappho* (1904). He also wrote several prose works on nature, art, and the human personality.

carmen \'kär-mən\ *plural* carmina \-mə-nə\ [Latin, incantation, song, poem] A song, poem, or incantation. *See* POEM; INCANTATION.

Carmen \'kär-men\ Novella about Spanish Gypsy life by French author Prosper MÉRIMÉE, first published serially in 1845. Georges Bizet's opera *Carmen* is based on the story.

As a hot-blooded young corporal in the Spanish cavalry stationed near Seville, Don José is ordered to arrest Carmen, a young, flirtatious Gypsy woman, for assaulting a coworker.

Greatly charmed by her, José allows her to escape. He deserts the army, kills two men on Carmen's account, and takes up a life as a robber and smuggler. He is insanely jealous of Carmen, who is unfaithful to him, and when she refuses to change on his behalf, he kills her and surrenders himself to the authorities.

carmen figuratum [New Latin, shaped poem] *see* PATTERN POETRY.

Carmina Burana \'kär-mə-nə-bû-'rän-ə, kär-'mē-nə\ (*German Lieder aus Beuern*) Thirteenth-century manuscript that contains songs (the *Carmina Burana* proper) and six religious plays. The contents of the manuscript are attributed to goliards, the wandering scholars and students of western Europe during the 10th to the 13th centuries who were known for their songs and poems in praise of revelry. The collection is also called the Benediktbeuern manuscript, because it was found (in 1803) at the Benedictine monastery in Benediktbeuern (from which *burana* is derived), Bavaria. The songs, rhymed lyrics mainly in Latin with a few in German, vary in subject and style: there are drinking songs, love songs, religious poems, pastoral lyrics, and satires. Some of the poems were set to music by Carl Orff in his cantata *Carmina Burana* (1937). The plays, in Latin, include the only two known surviving complete texts of medieval Passion plays. These are the *Ludus breviter de Passione* ("Play in Brief of the Passion"), a prologue to a Resurrection play, and a longer text, probably amplified from a play on St. Mary Magdalene's life and the raising of Lazarus. *See also* GOLIARD.

Caro \'kä-rō\, Annibale (b. June 19, 1507, Civitanova Marche, Papal States [Italy]—d. Nov. 21, 1566, Rome) Roman lyric poet, satirist, and translator.

Secretary first to a monseigneur, then to a cardinal, Caro received benefices that freed him to write. His poetry, collected as *Rime* in 1569, and his satires are considered unimportant.

Caro's most outstanding works are his free and graceful *Lettere familiare* (1572–74; "Familiar Letters") and a translation of Virgil's *Aeneid* (1581). He also wrote one of the most original comedies of his time, *Straccioni* (completed 1544), and a version of Longus' *Daphnis and Chloe* called *Amori pastorali di Dafni e Cloe* ("The Pastoral Loves of Daphnis and Chloe").

Carossa \kä-'rô-sä\, Hans (b. Dec. 15, 1878, Tölz, Ger.—d. Sept. 12, 1956, Rittsteig, W.Ger.) Poet and novelist who contributed to the development of the German autobiographical novel.

Carossa was a physician who lived most of his life in Bavaria. His literary career began with a book of lyric poetry, *Stella Mystica* (1902; "Mystical Star"). His first novel, *Doktor Bürgers Ende* (1913; "The End of Doctor Bürger"; revised and republished in 1930 as *Die Schicksale Doktor Bürgers*, "The Fortunes of Doctor Bürger"), depicts a young doctor driven to despair by the suffering around him. *Rumänisches Tagebuch* (1924; *A Roumanian Diary*; republished in 1934 as *Tagebuch im Kriege*, "War Diary") is based on Carossa's observations as an army doctor during World War I; it was the first of his books to gain recognition outside Germany.

More directly autobiographical works are *Eine Kindheit* (1922; *A Childhood*), *Das Jahr der schönen Täuschungen einer Jugend* (1941; *The Year of Sweet Illusions*), *Verwandlungen einer Jugend* (1928; *Boyhood and Youth*), and *Ungleiche Welten* (1951; "Different Worlds"). Carossa's last and unfinished work was *Der Tag des jungen Arztes* (1955; "The Day of the Young Doctor").

carpe diem \'kär-pā-'dē-ˌem, -pē, 'dī-, -əm\ Latin phrase (meaning literally "pluck the day!"), used by the Roman poet Horace to express the idea that one should enjoy life while one can. The sentiment has been expressed in many literatures, especially in 16th- and 17th-century English poetry. Two of the best-known examples are in Robert Herrick's "To the Virgins, to Make Much of Time" and Andrew Marvell's "To His Coy Mistress."

Carpenter \\'kär-pən-tər\\, Edward (b. Aug. 29, 1844, Brighton, Sussex, Eng.—d. June 28, 1929, Guildford, Surrey) English writer identified with social reform and the late 19th-century arts and crafts movement.

Carpenter was educated at Cambridge and ordained in 1869. He became a traveling lecturer for the newly founded university extension movement. Carpenter's long, unrhymed poem *Towards Democracy* (1883; expanded 1905) shows the influence of Walt Whitman, whom he had met on a visit to the United States. His papers on social subjects (*England's Ideal*, 1887; *Civilization: Its Cause and Cure*, 1889, enlarged, 1921) were widely translated, as were his later works on the relation of art to life (*Angels' Wings*, 1898; *The Art of Creation*, 1904) and on relationships between the sexes (*Love's Coming-of-Age*, 1896; *The Intermediate Sex*, 1908). Carpenter also composed the well-known labor song "England Arise."

Carpentier \\,kär-pen-'tyär\\, Alejo, *surname in full* Carpentier y Valmont \\-ē-väl-'mōnt\\ (b. Dec. 26, 1904, Havana, Cuba—d. April 24, 1980, Paris, Fr.) The leading Cuban novelist of his generation and a major influence on Latin-American literature.

Carpentier studied at the University of Havana before becoming a journalist. In 1928 he fled to France to escape imprisonment for his opposition to the regime of Gerardo Machado. He became a frequent contributor to the journal *Révolution surréaliste*, but later rejected Surrealism. In 1933 he published the documentary novel *¡Ecué-Yamba-Ó!*, an account of Afro-Cuban life and culture. After returning to Cuba, Carpentier published the novel *El reino de este mundo* (1949; *The Kingdom of This World*), an imaginative evocation of the life of the early 19th-century Haitian leader Henri Christophe.

His masterpiece is considered to be *Los pasos perdidos* (1953; *The Lost Steps*), which defines Latin-American reality as coexistence between primeval myths and imposed Spanish civilization. His other works include *Guerra del tiempo* (1958; *War of Time*); *El siglo de las luces* (1962; *Explosion in a Cathedral*); *Tientos y diferencias* (1964; "Acts of Feeling and Differences"), a collection of essays on cultural and literary themes; *El recurso del método* (1974; *Reasons of State*), about the career of Machado; *Concierto barroco* (1974; "Baroque Concerto"); a history of Cuban music; and the librettos for several operas.

Carr \\'kär\\, Emily (b. Dec. 13, 1871, Victoria, B.C., Can.—d. March 2, 1945, Victoria) Painter and writer, regarded as a major Canadian artist for her paintings of western coast Indians and landscape.

While teaching art in Vancouver, B.C., Carr made frequent sketching trips to British Columbian Indian villages. After ill health ended her painting trips, she turned to writing, producing six autobiographical books that were enlivened by satiric character studies. Among them are *Klee Wyck* (1941), dealing with the Indians; *The House of All Sorts* (1944), describing her experiences as a boardinghouse owner and dog breeder in Victoria; *Growing Pains* (1946), an autobiography; and *Pause: A Sketch Book* (1953), telling of her stay in an English sanatorium.

Carr \\'kär\\, John Dickson, *pseudonyms* Carr Dickson, Carter Dickson \\'dik-sən\\, Roger Fairbairn \\'far-,bärn\\ (b. Nov. 30, 1906, Uniontown, Pa., U.S.—d. Feb. 27, 1977, Greenville, S.C.) American writer of detective fiction whose work is considered among the best in the genre.

Carr's first novel, *It Walks by Night* (1930), won favor that endured as Carr continued to create well-researched "locked-room" puzzles of historical England. Among his later works are

The Witch of the Low-Tide: An Edwardian Melodrama (1961), *Dark of the Moon* (1967), and *The Hungry Goblin* (1972). Fifty of his mysteries feature one of his three detectives—Henri Bencolin, Dr. Gideon Fell, and Sir Henry Merrivale.

Carr's other successful work include *The Life of Sir Arthur Conan Doyle* (1949) and *The Exploits of Sherlock Holmes* (1954), the further deeds of Doyle's famous sleuth cowritten by Carr and Doyle's youngest son, Adrian.

Carrasquilla \\,kär-räs-'kē-yä, -räh-, -'kēl-\\, Tomás (b. Jan. 17, 1858, Santo Domingo, Antioquia, Colom.—d. Dec. 19, 1940, Medellín) Colombian novelist and short-story writer who is best remembered for his realistic depiction of the people of his native Antioquia.

When civil war interrupted his study of law at Antioquia University, Carrasquilla began his long literary career with the publication of *Frutos de mi tierra* (1896; "Fruits of My Native Land"), a realistic novel critical of the hypocrisy of small-town life that immediately appealed to a wide audience. He continued to deal with regional subjects in his short stories and in such later novels as *El Padre Casafús* (1914; "Father Casafús") and *La Marquesa de Yolombó* (1928; "The Marchioness of Yolombó"). His blindness in later life forced him to dictate *Hace tiempos*, 3 vol. (1935–36; "Long Ago"), the work many critics consider his best.

Carraway, Nick \\'nik-'kar-ə-,wā\\ Fictional character, the compassionate young narrator of F. Scott Fitzgerald's THE GREAT GATSBY. As Jay Gatsby's neighbor, Carraway has ample opportunity to observe the unfortunate Gatsby pursue his version of the American dream.

Carrillo y Sotomayor \\kä-'rēl-yō-ē-,sō-tō-mä-'yȯr\\, Luis (b. 1583?, Córdoba, Spain—d. 1610, Puerto de Santo María) Spanish poet known as the chief exponent of *culteranismo*, which developed from the highly ornate and rhetorical style *gongorismo*, originated by the poet Luis de Góngora. In Carrillo's treatise on poetry, *Libro de la erudición poética* (mod. ed., 1946), he attempted to justify his methods.

Although his life was short and his output small, he wrote several fine poems. The ambitious *Fábula de Acis y Galatea* is his best-known work. His work was published in 1611 and reedited in 1613.

Carrió de la Vandera \\kär-'rē-ō-tha-lä-bạn-'der-ä\\, Alonso, *pseudonym* Concolorcorvo \\,kȯn-,kō-lōr-'kȯr-bō\\ (b. 1715, Gijón, Spain—d. 1778?) Spanish colonial administrator whose accounts of his travels from Buenos Aires to Lima are considered to be a precursor of the Spanish-American novel.

Carrió's *El lazarillo de ciegos caminantes* (1775; *El Lazarillo: A Guide for Inexperienced Travellers Between Buenos Aires and Lima*) was originally attributed to Don Calixto Bustamente, Carrió's Indian guide and traveling companion. Investigation revealed that Carrió had used a pseudonym to avoid punishment for having been critical of the Spanish regime. Critics have praised the book's clear and vibrant style, detailed descriptions, and satiric tone. Carrió's realistic observations of the life and customs of the *gauderios*, the cowboys of the Pampas, contrast sharply with the highly romanticized picture that was common among later writers.

Carrion Comfort Sonnet by Gerard Manley HOPKINS, written in the 1885 and published posthumously in 1918 in the collection *Poems of Gerard Manley Hopkins*. It is one of his "terrible sonnets," a series of six despairing poems about spiritual apathy, with an underlying sense of artistic frustration.

Carroll \\'kar-əl\\, Lewis, *pseudonym of* Charles Lutwidge Dodgson \\'däd-sən, *commonly* 'dȧj-\\ (b. Jan. 27, 1832, Daresbury, Cheshire, Eng.—d. Jan. 14, 1898, Guildford, Surrey)   English logician, mathematician, and novelist, especially remembered for ALICE'S ADVENTURES IN WONDERLAND (1865) and its sequel, THROUGH THE LOOKING-GLASS (1871).

Brown Brothers

His poem THE HUNTING OF THE SNARK (1876) is nonsense literature of the highest order.

Dodgson was the third child in a family of eleven born to Frances Jane Lutwidge and the Rev. Charles Dodgson, and he grew up in parsonages at Daresbury and at Croft in Yorkshire. From the first he showed great aptitude for inventing games. He was the chief author of the "Rectory Magazines," manuscript compilations to which all the family were expected to contribute and many of which were later published. Dodgson was educated at Christ Church, Oxford. He excelled in mathematical and classical studies, and after earning a bachelor of arts degree he was appointed lecturer (tutor) in mathematics, a post he resigned in 1881.

Although Dodgson suffered from a bad stammer, he was able to speak naturally and easily to children. Of the many children he entertained, those of Henry George Liddell, dean of Christ Church, held an especially high place in his affections. In 1862 Dodgson and a friend rowed the Liddell children up the Thames, picnicked on the bank, and returned late in the evening. During the picnic Dodgson was inspired to tell so much better a story than usual that Alice Liddell asked him to write it out for her.

Dodgson wrote down the story more or less as told and added to it several adventures that he had told on other occasions. He then gave it to Alice. When the novelist Henry Kingsley, while visiting the deanery, chanced to pick it up and read it, he urged Mrs. Liddell to persuade the author to publish it. Dodgson revised it for publication and commissioned John Tenniel, a *Punch* magazine cartoonist, to make illustrations to his specifications. The book was published as *Alice's Adventures in Wonderland* in 1865. By the following year Dodgson was already considering a sequel; the result was *Through the Looking-Glass.*

Dodgson's humorous and other verses were collected in 1869 as *Phantasmagoria and Other Poems* and later separated (with additions) as *Rhyme? and Reason?* (1883) and *Three Sunsets and Other Poems* (published posthumously, 1898). A later work, SYLVIE AND BRUNO (1889), and its sequel *Sylvie and Bruno Concluded* (1893), represent Carroll's attempt to recapture the spirit of *Alice.*

Carruth \kə-'rüth\, Hayden (b. Aug. 3, 1921, Waterbury, Conn., U.S.)   American poet and literary critic.

Carruth was educated at the University of North Carolina and the University of Chicago. He worked as an editor for several magazines, including *Poetry.* Much of Carruth's poetry is concerned with sanity and madness. During hospitalization for psychiatric illness and alcoholism in 1953, he began a long poem later published as *The Bloomingdale Papers* (1975). *Brothers, I Loved You All* (1978), considered his best work by some critics, uses imagery from jazz. Other volumes of collected poems include *North Winter* (1964), *For You* (1970), *Almanach du Printemps Vivarois* (1979), *Lighter Than Air Craft* (1985), and *Sonnets* (1989). Books of literary criticism include *After "The Stranger": Imaginary Dialogues with Camus* (1965) and *Effluences from the Sacred Caves: More Selected Essays and Reviews* (1983).

Carstone, Richard \'rich-ərd-'kär-,stōn\   Fictional character, the heir of John Jarndyce in Charles Dickens' BLEAK HOUSE.

Carter \'kär-tər\, Angela (Olive), *original surname* Stalker \'stök-ər\ (b. May 7, 1940, Eastbourne, Sussex, Eng.—d. Feb. 16, 1992, London)   British author who used motifs from mythology, legends, and fairy tales in her novels and short stories.

Carter worked as a journalist and later studied at the University of Bristol. She had moderate success with her novels *Shadow Dance* (1966; U.S. title, *Honeybuzzard*) and *The Magic Toyshop* (1967; film, 1986). Other novels include *Several Perceptions* (1968), *The Passion of New Eve* (1977), and *Wise Children* (1991). Her chief nonfiction work is *The Sadeian Woman: An Exercise in Cultural History* (1979). She also wrote radio plays, children's books, and essays.

Carter \'kär-tər\, Elizabeth (b. Dec. 16, 1717, Deal, Kent, Eng.—d. Feb. 19, 1806, London)   English poet, translator, and member of a famous group of literary Bluestockings who gathered around Mrs. Elizabeth Montagu.

Carter was the daughter of a learned cleric who taught her Latin, Greek, and Hebrew along with a wide range of other subjects. Her *Poems upon Particular Occasions* were published in 1738 and *Poems on Several Occasions* in 1762. It was her translations, however, that ensured her reputation. In 1749 she undertook her most considerable translation, *All the Works of Epictetus Which Are Now Extant,* published in 1758.

Carter, Nick \'nik-'kär-tər\   Fictional character, a detective who was created by John Russell Coryell in the story "The Old Detective's Pupil," published in 1886 in the *New York Weekly.* The character was further developed by Frederic Van Rensselaer Dey, who from 1892 (*The Piano Box Mystery*) to 1913 (*The Spider's Parlor*) wrote some 500 novellas featuring Carter. Many other authors, among them Johnston McCulley (creator of the character Zorro) and Martin Cruz Smith (author of *Gorky Park*), wrote Nick Carter stories and novellas, publishing them anonymously. The magazines *Nick Carter Detective Library* and *Nick Carter Weekly* chronicled the character's exploits.

In the early stories, Carter was all-American, youthful, idealistic, and a master of disguise. By the late 1960s the writers of the Nick Carter stories had drastically revised the character. Carter became identified as an author and was also the tough, violent protagonist (known as the "Killmaster") of a series of lurid paperback novels that included *The China Doll* (1964), *The Inca Death Squad* (1972), *Pleasure Island* (1981), and *The Caribbean Coup* (1984).

Cartland \'kärt-lənd\, Barbara (Hamilton), *married name* Mc-Corquodale \mə-'kȯr-kə-,dāl\ (b. July 9, 1901, EdgBaston, Birmingham, England)   English author of more than 550 books, mostly formulaic novels of romantic love set in the 19th century.

Cartland's first novel, *Jigsaw* (1925), was a popular success. She also wrote charity pageants, the play *Blood Money*, and two more novels during the 1920s. Her output of books grew steadily, averaging 23 a year from the mid-1970s; altogether, her works had sold 600 million copies by 1993. Her nonfiction includes five autobiographies and books of advice on health food, vitamins, and beauty. She also wrote film scripts for several of her novels.

Carton, Sydney \'sid-nē-'kärt-ən\ Fictional character, one of the protagonists of Charles Dickens' A TALE OF TWO CITIES, set in France and England before and during the French Revolution.

Carton first appears as a cynical drunkard who serves as a legal aide to a London barrister. He is secretly in love with Lucie Manette, whose French émigré husband, Charles Darnay, physically resembles Carton. This coincidence enables Carton to stand in for Darnay, who has been sentenced to die on the guillotine. By this act Carton gives meaning to his misspent life.

Cartwright \'kärt-,rīt\, William (b. September 1611, Northway, Gloucestershire, Eng.—d. Nov. 29, 1643, Oxford, Oxfordshire) Writer greatly admired in his day as a poet, scholar, wit, and author of plays in the comic tradition of Ben Jonson.

Educated at the University of Oxford, Cartwright wrote his plays before about 1635, when he took holy orders; one of them, *The Ordinary* (produced 1635?), subjected Puritans to amusing mockery. On the outbreak of the English Civil Wars in 1642 he joined the war council of Charles I (who wore black on Cartwright's funeral day). His plays, though popular in his day, have not withstood the test of time.

Carver \'kär-vər\, Raymond, *in full* Raymond Clevie Carver, Jr. (b. May 25, 1938, Clatskanie, Ore., U.S.—d. Aug. 2, 1988, Port Angeles, Wash.) American short-story writer noted for his spare, unadorned tales about the wrenching lives of working-class people.

The son of a sawmill worker, Carver married a year after finishing high school and supported his wife and two children by working as a janitor, gas-station attendant, and delivery boy. He became interested in writing after taking a creative-writing course and went on to study at Humboldt State College in Arcata, Calif.

Carver taught for several years in universities throughout the United States. In 1967 his story "Will You Please Be Quiet, Please?" was published to great critical acclaim. His first collection of short stories, *Put Yourself in My Shoes* (1974), was followed in 1976 by the highly successful *Will You Please Be Quiet, Please?*, which established his reputation. His later collections include *What We Talk About When We Talk About Love* (1981), *Cathedral* (1983), and *Where I'm Calling From* (1988). Carver is credited as a major force in the revitalization of the short story in the late 20th century.

Cary \'kar-ē\, Alice and Phoebe (respectively b. April 26, 1820, Mount Healthy, near Cincinnati, Ohio, U.S.—d. Feb. 12, 1871, New York, N.Y.; b. Sept. 4, 1824, Mount Healthy— d. July 31, 1871, Newport, R.I.) American writers and sisters whose work was both moralistic and idealistic.

Self-educated, the Cary sisters never married and wrote in unbroken companionship throughout their lives. After moving to New York City, they wrote to support themselves. Their poems were first collected in a volume entitled *Poems of Alice and Phoebe Cary* (1849). Alice, much the more voluminous writer of the two, also wrote prose sketches and novels, the best of which treat the difficult lives of the neighbors and friends of her girlhood. Phoebe published only two individual volumes of poems—*Poems and Parodies* (1854) and *Poems of Faith, Hope, and Love* (1868). She is perhaps best known as the author of the hymn "Nearer Home."

Cary \'kar-ē\, Joyce, *in full* Arthur Joyce Lunel Cary (b. Dec. 7, 1888, Londonderry, Ire.—d. March 29, 1957, Oxford, Eng.) English novelist who developed a trilogy form in which each volume is narrated by one of three protagonists.

Cary studied at Trinity College, Oxford. He joined the colonial service in 1914 and served in the Nigeria Regiment during World War I. Resolved to become a writer, Cary settled in Oxford in 1920. That year he published 10 short stories in the *Saturday Evening Post*, an American magazine. Study occupied the next several years, then in 1932 his first novel, *Aissa Saved*, appeared. It was followed by three more African novels—*An American Visitor* (1933), *The African Witch* (1936), and *Mister Johnson* (1939). Childhood was the theme of *A House of Children* (1941) and *Charley Is My Darling* (1940).

Cary's trilogy on art begins with the first-person narration of a woman, Sara Monday, in HERSELF SURPRISED (1941) and follows with that of two men in her life, the lawyer Tom Wilcher in TO BE A PILGRIM (1942) and the artist Gulley Jimson in THE HORSE'S MOUTH (1944), his best-known novel. He then wrote another trilogy—*A Prisoner of Grace* (1952), *Except the Lord* (1953), and *Not Honour More* (1955)—as well as the novel *The Captive and the Free* (1959). His short stories were collected in *Spring Song* (1960).

Casa \'kä-zä\, Giovanni Della (b. June 28, 1503, La Casa, Mugello, Tuscany [Italy]—d. Nov. 14, 1556, Montepulciano, Siena) Italian bishop, poet, and translator who is remembered chiefly for his popular and widely translated treatise on manners, *Galateo*.

Della Casa studied in Bologna, Florence, Padua, and Rome. Besides youthful satirical verse in the manner of Francesco Berni, Della Casa produced lyrical poems in a majestic style and several political works, such as *Orazioni politiche* (1707; "Political Discourses"), in which he expressed his sorrow for the calamities of Italy.

The work that brought Della Casa international renown, however, was his sane and witty *Galateo*, which was written between 1550 and 1555, first published with his *Rime* in 1558, and first translated into English by Robert Peterson in 1576. *Galateo* is more concerned with the details of correct behavior in polite society than with courtly etiquette.

Casal \kä-'säl\, Julián del (b. Nov. 7, 1863, Havana [Cuba]—d. Oct. 21, 1893, Havana) Poet who was one of the most important forerunners of the modernist movement in Latin America.

Casal's first volume of poetry, *Hojas al viento* (1890; "Leaves in the Wind"), shows the influence of the French Parnassian poets, especially Charles Baudelaire. Throughout his poetry, Casal expressed an almost compulsive preference for the artificial and man-made over the natural. A chronic invalid, he died of tuberculosis while preparing his third book, *Bustos y rimas* (1893; "Busts and Rhymes"), which was published shortly after his death.

Casanova \,kä-sä-'nō-vä, *Angl* ,kas-ə-'nō-və, ,kaz-\, Giovanni Giacomo, *byname* Jean-Jacques, Chevalier de Seingalt (b. April 2, 1725, Venice [Italy]—d. June 4, 1798, Dux, Bohemia [now Duchcov, Czech Republic]) Ecclesiastic, writer, soldier, spy, and diplomatist, chiefly remembered as the prince of Italian adventurers whose name became synonymous with "libertine." His autobiography is a splendid description of 18th-century society in the capitals of Europe.

Son of an actor, Casanova was expelled as a young man from the seminary of St. Cyprian for scandalous conduct and launched on a colorful, dissolute career. After a time in the service of a Roman Catholic cardinal, he was a violinist in Venice, joined the Masonic Order in Lyon, then traveled to Paris, Dresden, Prague, and Vienna. Back in Venice in 1755, Casanova was denounced as a magician and sentenced to five years in the Piombi, prisons under the roof of the Doges' Palace. On Oct. 31, 1756, he achieved a spectacular escape and made his way to Paris, where he introduced the lottery in 1757 and made a name for himself among the aristocracy.

Fleeing from his creditors in Paris in 1760, he assumed the name Chevalier de Seingalt (which he retained for the rest of his life) and traveled extensively across Europe. In Warsaw, a scandal followed by a duel forced him to flee, and he eventually sought refuge in Spain. Permitted to return to Venetian territory between 1774 and 1782, he acted as a spy for the Venetian inquisitors of state.

As versatile in his writing as he was in his career, Casanova wrote occasional verse, criticism, a translation of the *Iliad* (1775), and a satirical pamphlet on Venetian aristocracy, especially the powerful Grimani family. His most important work, however, is his vivid autobiography, first published after his death as *Mémoires de J. Casanova de Seingalt*, 12 vol. (1826–38). A definitive edition, based on the original manuscripts, was published in 1960–62 with the title *Histoire de ma vie* (*History of My Life*).

Casaubon, Edward \\'ed-wərd-kə-'sòb-ən\\ Fictional character, one of the main figures in George Eliot's masterpiece MIDDLEMARCH. Casaubon is a pompous and ineffectual middle-aged scholar who marries the heroine, Dorothea Brooke, because he needs an assistant for his work.

Cask of Amontillado, The Short story by Edgar Allan POE, first published in *Godey's Lady's Book* in November 1846. The narrator of this tale of horror is the aristocrat Montresor, who, having endured, as he claims, a thousand injuries at the hand of the connoisseur Fortunato, is finally driven by yet another insult to seek revenge. Amid the carnival celebrations Montresor encounters the drunken Fortunato and, on the pretext of seeking his judgment of a newly purchased cask of amontillado sherry, takes him to his palazzo.

While keeping up a conversation heavy with irony, Montresor leads Fortunato into the cellar to the deepest crypt. There Montresor chains the unlucky Fortunato in a small chamber and, brick by brick, walls him in.

Casper Alternate name for Gaspar, a legendary figure said to have been one of the MAGI.

Cassandra \\kə-'san-drə, -'sän-\\ In Greek mythology, the daughter of Priam, the last king of Troy, and his wife Hecuba. Cassandra was loved by the god Apollo, who promised to bestow on her the power of prophecy if she would comply with his desires. Cassandra accepted his proposal, received the gift, and then refused to hold up her part of the bargain. In revenge, Apollo modified his gift such that Cassandra's prophecies should never be believed. She accurately predicted such events as the fall of Troy and the death of Agamemnon, but her warnings went unheeded. In the distribution of the spoils after the capture of Troy, Cassandra fell to Agamemnon and was later murdered with him. She was worshiped, under the name of Alexandra, with Apollo.

Cassius \\'kash-yəs, 'kas-ē-əs\\ Fictional character in William Shakespeare's *Julius Caesar* who was the leader of the plot to assassinate Caesar. He was said by Caesar to have "a lean and hungry look."

Cassola \\käs-'sō-lä\\, Carlo (b. March 17, 1917, Rome, Italy—d. Jan. 29, 1987, Monte Carlo, Monaco) Italian Neorealist novelist who portrayed the landscapes and the ordinary people

of rural Tuscany in simple prose. His lack of action and emphasis on detail caused him to be regarded as a forerunner of the French nouveau roman, or antinovel.

After studying at the University of Rome, Cassola fought with the Resistance during World War II. The period formed the background of some of his best-known works, among them the short-story collection *Il taglio del bosco* (1955; "Timber Cutting") and the novel *Fausto e Anna* (1952; *Fausto and Anna*), both semiautobiographical. In 1960 Cassola won the Strega Prize for *La ragazza di Bube* (*Bebo's Girl*; film, 1964). These austere novels portray with sympathy and restraint individuals—especially women—whose lives are bleak and unfulfilled. Cassola's later concern with the environment and the threat of nuclear war was reflected in essays and in the novel *Il paradiso degli animali* (1979; "Animals' Paradise").

cast \\'kast\\ The set of characters in a narrative.

Castalia \\ka-'stā-lyə, -lē-ə\\ or **Castalie** \\'kas-tə-lē\\ A source of poetic inspiration. Castalia was the name of a nymph who threw herself into or was transformed into a spring to evade the pursuit of Apollo. The spring then was named Castalia for her, and it was a source of inspiration for Apollo and for the Muses. The Muses were sometimes called Castalides because of their association with the spring.

Castelo Branco \\käsh-'tel-ü-'bräⁿg-kü\\, Camilo (b. March 16, 1825, Lisbon, Port.—d. June 1, 1890, Seide) Portuguese novelist whose 58 novels range from Romantic melodramas to works of realism.

Born illegitimate into a family believed to have had a hereditary tendency to insanity, Castelo Branco was orphaned and brought up by relatives. He studied irregularly at Porto, first medicine and later for the priesthood, but eventually decided upon a literary career. For a time he wrote Gothic tales such as *Mysterios de Lisboa* (1854; "Mysteries of Lisbon") and *Livro negro do Padre Diniz* (1855; "Black Book of Father Dennis"), until he arrived at his mature style with *Onde está a felicidade?* (1856; "Where Is Happiness?") and *Vingança* (1858; "Revenge"). He engaged in a series of love affairs, culminating in his elopement with Ana Plácido, the wife of a Porto businessman. The two lovers were imprisoned for adultery (1861), during which time Castelo Branco wrote in two weeks his best-known work, *Amor de perdição* (1862; "Fatal Love"), the story of a love thwarted by family opposition that eventually leads the hero to crime and exile.

In 1864, after his release from prison and the death of Plácido's husband, Castelo Branco settled with her in the village of Seide, where he supported himself by writing unceasingly, producing indifferent verse, plays, works of erudition, polemical works, and novels of unequal merit—many written to order for publishers. In 1885 he was awarded the title of viscount of Correia Botelho for his writing. Despondent over his son's insanity and his own ill health and impending blindness, he committed suicide.

Though many of Castelo Branco's works are on the level of popular serials, others, such as *Amor de perdição*, *O romance d'um homem rico* (1861; "The Love Story of a Rich Man") and *O retrato de Ricardina* (1868; "Portrait of Ricardina"), have a tragic quality and are narrated with conciseness and vigor.

Castelvetro \\,käs-tāl-'vet-rō\\, Lodovico (b. c. 1505, Modena, Duchy of Modena [Italy]—d. Feb. 21, 1571, Chiavenna, Swiss Confederation) A dominant literary critic of the Italian Renaissance, particularly noted for his translation of and independently rendered conclusions from Aristotle's *Poetics*, in which he defended the dramatic unities of time, place, and action; he thereby helped set the critical norms for drama in the Renaissance and the French Neoclassical period.

Castelvetro was a law student in Bologna, Ferrara, and Padua, then began studies of literature in Siena. Eventually he returned to Modena and became prominent in literary circles and as a teacher of law. A quarrel with the poet Annibale Caro, initiated by Castelvetro's criticism of one of Caro's poems, erupted into a major literary feud that led in 1560 to Castelvetro's summons to Rome by the Inquisition, his subsequent flight from Italy, and his excommunication.

Castelvetro's work on the *Poetics* of Aristotle, called *La poetica di Aristotele vulgarizzata* ("Aristotle's *Poetics* Popularized"), was published in 1570. Though often erroneous in transmitting Aristotle's ideas, *La poetica* was extremely influential in the history of drama and of criticism. Castelvetro emphasized realism in drama, clarified the distinction between rhetoric and poetry, and defended poetry as a means of pleasure alone—as opposed to the earlier opinion that poetry should instruct as well as delight.

Casti \'käs-tē\, Giovanni Battista (b. Aug. 29, 1724, Acquapendente, Papal States [Italy]—d. Feb. 5, 1803, Paris, Fr.) Italian poet, satirist, and author of comic opera librettos, chiefly remembered for the verse satires *Poema tartaro* (1787; "Tartar Poem") and *Gli animali parlanti* (1802, "The Talking Animals"; *The Court and Parliament of Beasts*).

Casti took holy orders at the seminary of Montefiascone but soon abandoned the church to be a pleasure-seeking poet at the courts of Germany, Austria, and Russia. Between 1778 and 1802 he wrote his witty society verse *Novelle galanti* ("Amatory Tales"), first published in a critical edition in 1925. In 1778 Casti visited the court of Catherine the Great in St. Petersburg; his *Poema tartaro* mocked the adulation shown the empress. Returning to Vienna, he was named poet laureate in 1790. After a time in Italy, he settled in Paris, where he lived for the rest of his life. There he wrote his other major work, *Gli animali parlanti*, which personifies the European nations as animals in order to contrast the monarchical concept with the republican spirit generated by the French Revolution. In addition to his society verse and his satires, he wrote comic opera librettos to the music of Antonio Salieri and Giovanni Paisiello.

Castiglione \,käs-tēl-'yō-nä\, Baldassare (b. Dec. 6, 1478, Casatico, near Mantua [Italy]—d. Feb. 2, 1529, Toledo, Spain) Italian diplomat and courtier, whose *Il libro del cortegiano* (*The Book of the Courtier*) made him the arbiter of aristocratic manners during the Renaissance.

Educated in Milan, Castiglione learned the art of chivalry at the court of Ludovico Sforza and eventually entered the service of Guidobaldo da Montefeltro, duke of Urbino, in 1507. He remained at the court of Urbino until 1513, serving Guidobaldo's successor, Francesco Maria della Rovere.

In Urbino he met Pietro Bembo, Bernardo Bibbiena, Guiliano de' Medici, l'Unico Aretino (Bernardo Accolti), Ludovico di Canossa, and Ottaviano and Federico Fregóso, who became the interlocutors of his *Cortegiano*. There he also composed most of his minor works.

The *Cortegiano* (written 1513–18; published 1528), in dialogue form, deals with the perfect courtier, the noble lady, and the relationships between the courtier and the prince. One of the outstanding books of the century, it found immediate favor outside Italy and was translated into many languages. Sir Thomas Hoby's English version, *The Courtyer* (1561), was one of the most influential prose works of its day.

Castilho \kásh-'tēl-yū\, António Feliciano de (b. Jan. 28, 1800, Lisbon, Port.—d. June 18, 1875, Lisbon) Poet, a central figure in the Portuguese Romantic movement.

Blind from childhood, Castilho became a classical scholar and at the age of 16 published a series of poems, translations, and pedagogical works. During the early phase of his literary career, he published a series of poems in which he tried to assimilate current Romantic trends while continuing to be guided by a basically Neoclassical spirit.

With the publication of his *Obras completas* in 1837, Castilho became a literary figure in Lisbon. He was offered the directorship of an important journal, *O panorama*, and in 1838 he began to collaborate with Almeida Garrett, the leading Portuguese Romantic poet, in the revival of a national theater. His romantic narratives of the lives of Portuguese medieval heroes, *Quadros históricos de Portugal*, were begun in 1838, and in 1842 he took charge of the *Revista universal Lisbonense*, a major cultural review.

Castilho had never been a wholehearted Romantic, and after 1850 he made a gradual break from the movement. Scholarly rather than imaginative, he began to return to a genteel traditionalism that had much in common with the earlier generation of Portuguese arcadian poets. However, his lifeless style so dominated literary taste that it provoked a rebellion of the younger generation of writers. The initial attack against Castilho came from the young poet Antero de Quental, who wrote the pamphlet *Bom-senso e bom-gosto* (1865; "Good Sense and Good Taste") in reply to Castilho's criticism of certain younger writers. This riposte eventually dethroned Castilho as literary dictator.

Castillejo \,käs-tēl-'yä-ḳō\, Cristóbal de (b. 1490?, Ciudad Rodrigo, Spain—d. probably June 12, 1550, Vienna [Austria]) Poet who was the foremost critic of the Italianate innovations of the Spanish poet Garcilaso de la Vega and the Catalan poet Juan Boscán.

One of the last Spanish poets to use the medieval octosyllabic line exclusively, Castillejo ruthlessly attacked the new Italianate meters introduced by his contemporaries, writing *Contra los que dejan los metros castellanos y siguen los italianos* (c. 1540; "Against Those Who Abandon Castilian Meters for Italian Ones") in rhymed couplets. He is also known for his erotic poetry, *Sermón de amores* (1542), which was suppressed by the Inquisition, in part because of its lack of respect for sacred texts.

Castillo \käs-'tēl-yō\, Michel del, *in full* Michel-Xavier Janicot del Castillo (b. Aug. 2, 1933, Madrid, Spain) Spanish-born novelist writing in French, who became famous at age 24 for a short novel, *Tanguy* (1957; *Child of Our Time*). Though written as fiction, it is the story of his actual experiences as a political refugee and a prisoner in concentration camps; and, like *The Diary of Anne Frank*, it has the poignancy of a child's witness to cruel historical events.

Del Castillo fled Spain for France as a boy in 1939 with the exodus of refugees at the end of the Civil War. Shortly after, with his mother, who was a political radical, he was sent to Nazi concentration camps. *Tanguy* and *Le Colleur d'affiches* (1958; *The Disinherited*) deal with these traumatic experiences. They reflect his anguish at social injustice and his need for solace in fellow feeling.

Deeply attached to Spain, he returned to its strife-torn soil in *La Guitare* (1957; *The Guitar*) and in *Le Manège espagnol* (1960; *Through the Hoop*), a colorful but heavy-handed satire of religion. Later works include *Gerardo Laín* (1967; *The Seminarian*), *Le Silence des pierres* (1975; "The Silence of Stones"), *Les Cyprès meurent en Italie* (1979; "The Cypresses Die in Italy"), *La Nuit de décret* (1981; "The Night of the Decree"), and *Une Femme en soi* (1991; "A Woman Herself").

Castillo Solórzano \käs-'tēl-yō-sō-'lōr-thä-nō\, Alonso de (b. 1584, Tordesillas, Spain—d. c. 1648) Spanish writer best known for his short stories.

Castillo Solórzano's stories are usually of adventure, often treated with wit and sophistication. Many of his tales are strung together by an artifice or are arranged, in indirect imitation of Giovanni Boccaccio's *Decameron*, within a framework. Examples include *Jornadas alegres* (1626; "Gay Trips") and *Noches de placer* (1631; "Nights of Pleasure"). His picaresque novels make much of the female *pícara* ("rogue") as protagonist.

Castle, The Allegorical novel by Franz KAFKA, published posthumously in German as *Das Schloss* in 1926.

The setting of the novel is a village dominated by a castle. Time seems to have stopped in this wintry landscape, and nearly all the scenes occur in the dark. K., the otherwise nameless protagonist, arrives at the village claiming to be a land surveyor appointed by the castle authorities. His claim is rejected by the village officials, and the novel recounts K.'s efforts to gain recognition from an elusive authority. Arthur and Jeremiah introduce themselves to K. as his assistants but provide comic relief rather than genuine help. Klamm, a castle superior who is widely respected by the villagers, proves utterly inaccessible. K. aggressively challenges both the petty, arrogant officials and the villagers who accept their authority. All his stratagems fail. He makes love to the barmaid Frieda, a former mistress of Klamm. They plan to marry, but she leaves him when she discovers that he is merely using her.

The Castle is an unfinished novel. As Max Brod, Kafka's literary executor, observed, Kafka intended that K. should die exhausted by his efforts, but that on his deathbed he was to receive a permit to stay.

Castle of Crossed Destinies, The Semiotic fantasy novel by Italo CALVINO, published in Italian in 1973 as *Il castello dei destini incrociati*. It consists of a series of short tales gathered into two sections, "The Castle of Crossed Destinies" and "The Tavern of Crossed Destinies."

The novel concerns two groups of travelers through a forest, both of which have lost the power to speak as the result of traumatic events. One group is spending the night in a tavern, the other in a castle. In each place, the travelers tell the stories of their lives, using tarot cards instead of words. A narrator at each place interprets the cards for the reader, but since the tarot cards are subject to multiple interpretations, the stories the narrators offer are not necessarily the stories intended by the mute storytellers.

Castle of Otranto, The \ō-'trän-tō, *Angl* -'tran-\ Horror tale by Horace WALPOLE, published in 1765. The work is considered the first gothic novel in the English language; its supernatural happenings and mysterious ambiance were widely emulated in the genre.

Manfred is the tyrannical usurper of the princedom of Otranto. On the day his son Conrad is to marry Isabella, Conrad is found dead in the courtyard, crushed by a mammoth plumed helmet. Manfred decides to divorce his wife and marry Isabella in order to produce the heir he needs to retain control of the realm, but Isabella escapes to Father Jerome with the help of Theodore, a handsome young peasant. From a birthmark on Theodore's neck, Father Jerome discovers that the young man is really his natural son, born before he entered the priesthood, when he was the prince of Falconara. Later, the giant form of the martyred rightful prince Alfonso appears, proclaiming Theodore's right of succession, and then ascends to heaven. Manfred and his wife enter separate convents. Theodore marries Isabella and rules Otranto as prince.

Castle Rackrent \'rak-,rent\ (*in full* Castle Rackrent, an Hiberian Tale: Taken from Facts, and from the Manners of the Irish Squires, Before the Year 1782) Novel by Maria EDGEWORTH, published in 1800. The work satirizes the Irish land-lords of the late 18th and early 19th centuries. Noted for its insight into Irish regional life, the book chronicles three generations of the landed Rackrent family and was the model on which Sir Walter Scott based his historical novels.

Castor and Pollux \'kas-tər . . . 'päl-əks\ *see* DIOSCURI.

Castorp, Hans \'häns-'käs-tòrp\ Fictional character, a young German engineer who is the protagonist of the novel THE MAGIC MOUNTAIN by Thomas Mann.

Castro \'käs-trō\, Américo, *surname in full* Castro y Quesada \ē-kä-'sä-thä\ (b. May 4, 1885, Cantagallo, Braz.—d. July 25, 1972, Lloret de Mar, Spain) Spanish philologist and cultural historian who explored the cultural roots of Spain and Latin America.

Castro was born in Brazil of Spanish parents, who returned with him to Spain in 1890. He graduated from the University of Granada in 1904 and studied at the Sorbonne in Paris (1905–07). In 1910 he organized the Center for Historical Studies in Madrid, serving as the head of its department of lexicography. He remained at the center, even after becoming professor at the University of Madrid in 1915. Castro published several scholarly works, notably *Vida de Lope de Vega* (1919; "Life of Lope de Vega"), *Lengua, enseñanza y literatura* (1924; "Language, Teaching, and Literature"), and *El pensamiento de Cervantes* (1925; "The Thought of Cervantes"), and he also lectured abroad. He went to the United States when the Spanish Civil War broke out in 1936 and taught literature at the Universities of Wisconsin and Texas and at Princeton University, thereafter retiring from teaching.

Castro \'käsh-trō\, Eugénio de (b. March 4, 1869, Coimbra, Port.—d. Aug. 17, 1944, Coimbra) Leading Portuguese Symbolist and Decadent poet. His best-known collection of poetry, *Oaristos* (1890; "Intimate Chats"), launched Symbolism in Portugal. His Symbolism maintains the essential doctrines of the French theorists of the movement, in contrast with the nostalgic nationalism that characterized the poetry of his contemporaries in Portugal. Among his numerous published collections, the best known include *Horas* (1891; "Hours"), *Sagramor* (1895), *Salomé e outros poemas* (1896; "Salome and Other Poems"), *Saudades do Céu* (1899; "Longings for Heaven"), and *Constança* (1900).

Castro \'käs-trō\, Rosalía de (b. February 1837, Santiago de Compostela, Spain—d. July 15, 1885, Padrón, near Santiago) The foremost modern writer in the Galician language.

In 1858 Castro married the historian Manuel Murguía (1833–1923), a champion of the Galician Renaissance. Although Castro was the author of a number of novels, she is best known for her poetry, contained in *Cantares gallegos* (1863; "Galician Songs") and *Follas novas* (1880; "New Medleys"), both written in her own language, and *En las orillas del Sar* (1884; *Beside the River Sar*), written in Castilian. Part of her work expresses with sympathetic power the spirit of the Galician people—their gaiety, their wisdom and folklore, their resentment of Castilian domination, their love of their homeland, and the sorrows of poverty and emigration. About 1867, however, Castro began to write more personally, describing in verse her own deepest feelings. Her complete works appeared in 1973.

Castro Alves \'käsh-trū-'ȧl-vȧsh\, Antônio de (b. March 17, 1847, Muritiba, Braz.—d. July 6, 1871, Salvador) Romantic poet whose sympathy for the Brazilian abolitionist cause won him the name "poet of the slaves."

While still a student Castro Alves produced a play that brought him to the attention of José de Alencar and Joaquim Maria Machado, Brazilian literary leaders. His romantic image was heightened by his two-year affair with a well-known actress, by his extravagant behavior, and by the elevated style of his poetry. In 1868 he shot himself in the foot while hunting. He lived and wrote at a fever pitch while the wound worsened and gangrene developed. After his foot was amputated, tuberculosis set in, and he died at age 24.

Espumas flutuantes (1870; "Floating Foam"), the only collection published during his lifetime, contains some of his finest love lyrics. His dramatic poem *A cachoeira de Paulo Afonso* (1876; "The Paulo Afonso Falls") tells the story of a slave girl who is raped by her master's son. This and Castro Alves' other abolitionist poems were collected in a posthumous book, *Os escravos* (1883; "The Slaves").

Castro y Bellvís \\'käs-trō-ē-ḇelʸ-'ḇēs\\, Guillén de (b. 1569, Valencia, Spain—d. July 28, 1631, Madrid) The most important and representative of a group of Spanish dramatists that flourished in Valencia. He is remembered chiefly for his work *Las mocedades del Cid* (c. 1618; "The Youth of the Cid"), upon which the French playwright Pierre Corneille based his famous drama *Le Cid* (1637).

Las mocedades del Cid, written in two parts, was inspired by the ballad-legends of El Cid, and it effectively transferred the tragedy to the stage. Having himself married unhappily, Castro is considered the first playwright to have dealt with the seamier aspects of marriage, as in *Los mal casados de Valencia* ("The Unhappy Marriages of Valencia"). He also wrote several cloak-and-sword dramas. Attracted to the culture of Castile, he drew heavily upon the traditional ballads of the region, and three of his plays are based upon novels by Miguel de Cervantes. In all he wrote some 50 plays.

casual \\'kazh-ə-wəl\\ An essay written in a familiar, often humorous style. The word is usually associated with the style of essay that was cultivated at *The New Yorker* magazine.

catachresis \\,kat-ə-'krē-sis\\ [Greek *katáchrēsis*, a derivative of *katachrêsthai* to make use of, use up, misuse] Use of the wrong word for the context; specifically, use of a forced and especially paradoxical figure of speech (such as "blind mouths").

catalexis \\,kat-ə-'lek-sis\\, *plural* catalexes \\-,sēz\\ [Greek *katálēxis* final syllable, close of a rhetorical period, a derivative of *katalēgein* to leave off, stop] Omission of one or more syllables in the last foot of a line in metrical verse. Thus if the chief meter of a poem is iambic tetrameter and a line scans ∪ ′ | ∪ ′ | ∪ ′ | ∪ ′ | ∪ | , that line is catalectic. *Compare* HYPERMETRY.

catalog verse or **catalogue verse** \\'kat-ə-,lȯg, -,läg\\ Verse that presents a list of people, objects, or abstract qualities. The genealogical lists in the Bible and the lists of heroes in epics such as Homer's *Iliad* are types of catalog verse, as are more modern poems such as Gerard Manley Hopkins' "Pied Beauty," which begins:

> Glory be to God for dappled things—
>   For skies of couple-colour as a brinded cow;
>   For rose-moles all in stipple upon trout that swim;
> Fresh-firecoal chestnut-falls; finches' wings;
>   Landscape plotted and pieced—fold, fallow, and plough;
>   And áll trádes, their gear and tackle and trim.

catastasis \\kə-'tas-tə-sis\\, *plural* catastases \\-,sēz\\ [Greek *katástasis* settlement, state, condition] 1. The dramatic complication that immediately precedes the climax of a play. 2. The climax of a play. *Compare* CATASTROPHE; EPITASIS; PROTASIS.

catastrophe \\kə-'tas-trə-fē\\ [Greek *katastrophḗ* end of a tragedy, end, close, a derivative of *katastréphein* to turn down, overturn] The final action that completes the unraveling of the plot in a play, especially in a tragedy. Catastrophe is a synonym of DENOUEMENT. The term is sometimes applied to a similar action in a novel or story.

catch \\'kach, 'kech\\ In prosody, an extra unstressed syllable at the beginning of a line that should start with a stressed syllable in order to fit the meter.

Catch-22 Satirical novel by Joseph HELLER, first published in 1961. The plot of the novel centers on the antihero Captain John Yossarian, stationed at an airstrip on a Mediterranean island in World War II, and portrays his desperate attempts to stay alive. The "catch" in *Catch-22* involves a mysterious Air Force regulation which asserts that a man is considered insane if he willingly continues to fly dangerous combat missions, but that if he makes the necessary formal request to be relieved of such missions, the very act of making the request proves that he is sane and therefore ineligible to be relieved. The term catch-22 thereafter entered the English language with the meaning "a problematic situation for which the only solution is denied by a circumstance inherent in the problem" and later developed several additional senses.

In 1994 Heller published a sequel entitled *Closing Time*, which details the current lives of the characters established in *Catch-22*.

Catcher in the Rye Novel by J.D. SALINGER, published in 1951. The influential and widely acclaimed story details the two days in the life of 16-year-old Holden Caulfield after he has been expelled from prep school. Confused and disillusioned, he searches for truth and rails against the "phoniness" of the adult world. He ends up exhausted and emotionally ill, in a psychiatrist's office. After he recovers from his breakdown, Holden relates his experiences to the reader.

catharsis \\kə-'thär-sis\\ *plural* catharses \\-,sēz\\ The purification or purgation of the emotions (especially pity and fear) primarily through art. The term, derived from the medical term *katharsis* ("purgation" or "cleansing"), was used as a metaphor by Aristotle (*Poetics*) to describe the effects of true dramatic tragedy on the spectator. Aristotle states that the purpose of tragedy is to arouse "terror and pity" and thereby effect the catharsis of these emotions.

Aristotle's meaning has been the subject of critical debate over the centuries. The 18th-century German dramatist and literary critic Gotthold Lessing held that catharsis converts excess emotions into virtuous dispositions. Other critics saw tragedy as a moral lesson in which the fear and pity excited by the tragic hero's fate serve to warn the spectator not similarly to tempt providence. The interpretation generally accepted is that, through experiencing fear vicariously in a controlled situation, the spectator's own anxieties are directed outward, and, through sympathetic identification with the tragic protagonist, his insight and outlook are enlarged. Tragedy then has a healthful and humanizing effect on the spectator or reader.

Cather \\'kath-ər\\, Willa (Sibert \\'sī-bərt\\) (b. Dec. 7, 1873, Winchester, Va., U.S.—d. April 24, 1947, New York, N.Y.) American novelist noted for her portrayals of frontier life on the American plains.

In 1883 Cather moved with her family from Virginia to the Nebraska village of Red Cloud. There she grew up among the immigrants from Europe—Swedes, Bohemians, Russians, Germans—who were establishing homesteads on the Great Plains.

After graduating from the University of Nebraska in 1895, she obtained a position in Pittsburgh on a family magazine. Later she worked as copy editor and music and drama editor of the *Pittsburgh Leader*. She turned to teaching in 1901, and in 1903 she published her first book of verses, *April Twilights*. In

1905, after the publication of THE TROLL GARDEN, her first collection of short stories, she was appointed managing editor of *McClure's* (the New York muckraking monthly). She left in 1912 to devote herself wholly to writing novels.

Cather's first novel, *Alexander's Bridge* (1912), was an artificial story of cosmopolitan life. Under the influence of Sarah Orne Jewett's regionalism, she turned to her familiar Nebraska for material. With O PIONEERS! (1913) and MY ÁNTONIA (1918), which has frequently been judged her finest achievement, she found her characteristic themes—the spirit and courage of the frontier she had known in her youth. ONE OF OURS (1922), which won the Pulitzer Prize, and A LOST LADY (1923) mourned the passing of the pioneer spirit.

In her earlier SONG OF THE LARK (1915), as well as in the tales assembled in YOUTH AND THE BRIGHT MEDUSA (1920), including the much-anthologized PAUL'S CASE, and in *Lucy Gayheart* (1935), Cather reflected the other side of her experience—the struggle of a talent to emerge from the constricting life of the prairies and the stifling effects of small-town life.

A mature statement of both themes can be found in *Obscure Destinies* (1932). With success and middle age, however, Cather experienced a strong disillusionment, which was reflected in THE PROFESSOR'S HOUSE (1925) and her essays *Not Under Forty* (1936).

Her solution was to write of the pioneer spirit of another age, that of the French Catholic missionaries in the Southwest in DEATH COMES FOR THE ARCHBISHOP (1927) and of the French Canadians at Quebec in SHADOWS ON THE ROCK (1931). Her last novel, SAPPHIRA AND THE SLAVE GIRL (1940), marked a return to the Virginia of her ancestors.

Catherine \'kath-ə-rin\, Saint, *also called* Saint Catherine dei Ricci \dā-'rēt-chē\, *original name* Alessandra dei Ricci (b. April 23, 1522, Florence [Italy]—d. Feb. 2, 1590, Prato, Rep. of Florence) Italian Dominican mystic. At the age of 13 she entered the Dominican convent at Prato, serving as prioress from 1560 to 1590. Famous for her visions of the Passion and her stigmata, she was the author of letters (1912; edited by Sisto of Pisa) and other minor works.

Catherine \'kath-ə-rin\, Saint. In Christian legend, a young woman of Alexandria who spoke out against the Roman emperor's idolatry. She was said to have outreasoned 50 of the emperor's philosophers. A dedicated virgin, she spurned the emperor, who then tortured her on a wheel of fire (or a spiked wheel in some versions of the story). The wheel was struck by lightning and disintegrated, and she emerged from the ordeal unscathed. When she was later beheaded, it was discovered that milk flowed in her veins.

Her symbol is the wheel ("the Catherine wheel"), which figured prominently in medieval literature and art.

Cato \'kā-tō\, Publius Valerius (fl. 1st century BC) Roman poet and grammarian, the leader of the "new" school of poetry (*poetae novi*, as Cicero called its members). Its followers rejected the national epic and drama in favor of the short mytho-

logical epics (epyllia), elegies, and lyrics of the Alexandrian school. The compliments paid to Cato's verse by contemporary poets bear witness to his preeminence.

Nothing is known of Cato's grammatical treatises. Of his poems, two titles survive: the "Lydia" and the "Diana."

Cat on a Hot Tin Roof Play by Tennessee WILLIAMS, published and produced in 1955. It won a Pulitzer Prize. The play exposes the emotional lies governing relationships in the family of a wealthy Southern planter of humble origins. The patriarch, Big Daddy, is about to celebrate his 65th birthday. His two married sons, Gooper (Brother Man) and Brick, have returned for the occasion, the former with his pregnant wife and five children, the latter with his wife Margaret (Maggie). The interactions between Big Daddy, Brick, and Maggie form the substance of the play.

Catriona \kə-'trē-ō-nə\ Novel by Robert Louis Stevenson, published in 1893 as a sequel to his novel KIDNAPPED.

Cats \'käts\, Jacob *or* Jacobus (b. Nov. 10, 1577, Brouwershaven, Zeeland, Spanish Netherlands [now in The Netherlands]—d. Sept. 12, 1660, Zorgh-vliet, near The Hague) Dutch writer of emblem books and didactic verse whose place in the affections of his countrymen is shown by his nickname, "Father Cats."

Cats took his doctor's degree in law at Orléans and practiced at The Hague. He was primarily a writer of poetic emblem books, a type of literature popular in the 17th century that consisted of woodcuts or engravings accompanied by verses pointing a moral. He used this form to express the major ethical concerns of early Dutch Calvinists, especially those dealing with love and marriage. By being the first to combine emblem literature with love poetry, and by his skill as a storyteller, he achieved enormous popularity.

His first book, *Sinne- en minnebeelden* (1618; "Portraits of Morality and Love"), contained engravings with text in Dutch, Latin, and French. Each picture has a threefold interpretation, expressing what were for Cats the three elements of human life: love, society, and religion. Perhaps his most famous emblem book is *Spiegel van den ouden ende nieuwen tijdt* (1632; "Mirror of Old and New Times"), many quotations from which have become household sayings in The Netherlands. It is written in a more homely style than his earlier works, in popular rather than classical Dutch. Two other works—*Houwelyk* (1625; "Marriage") and *Trou-ringh* (1637; "Wedding Ring")—are rhymed dissertations on marriage and conjugal fidelity. In one of his last books, *Ouderdom, buyten-leven en hof-gedachten* (1655; "Old Age, Country Life, and Garden Thoughts"), Cats wrote movingly about old age.

Cat's Cradle Science-fiction novel by Kurt VONNEGUT, Jr., published in 1963. Notable for its black humor, it is considered one of the author's major early works.

The novel features two notable inventions: Bokononism, a religion of lies "that make you brave and kind and healthy and happy," and ice-nine, a type of ice that forms at any temperature up to 114.4 degrees and continues freezing all of the liquid it contacts in a kind of chain reaction. The story's two principal figures are Bokonon, the religion's founder, and Dr. Felix Hoenikker, inventor of ice-nine. The narrator, a journalist who calls himself Jonah, confronts the opposing forces of rationality and irrationality. The novel concludes with the inevitable end of the world caused by the release of ice-nine (as transmitted by a frozen body to the ocean).

Cattle of the Sun In Greek mythology, cattle that were sacred to the sun god Helios and that lived on the island of Thrinacia. They were tended by Helios' daughters, Lampetia and Phaëthusa. In the *Odyssey*, when Odysseus' crew begs him to stop there for rest, he relents and permits them to go ashore, provided they don't harm the sacred herds. Unfavorable winds detain them for so long that they run out of supplies and are forced to slay and eat some of the cattle. Odysseus is horrified at the sacrilege, and the men attempt to atone by preparing sacrifices. Fair weather eventually returns and the sailors resume their voyage. Soon, however, a violent storm arises and destroys the ship; all except Odysseus perish.

Cattle Raid of Cooley, The \'kü-lē\ *Irish* Táin Bó Cuáilnge.   Old Irish epic-like tale, the longest of the ULSTER CYCLE of hero tales dealing with the conflict between Ulster and Connaught over possession of the brown bull of Cooley. Composed in prose with verse passages in the 7th and 8th centuries, it is partially preserved in *The Book of the Dun Cow* (*c.* 1100) and is also found in *The Book of Leinster* (*c.* 1160) and *The Yellow Book of Lecan* (late 14th century). Although it contains passages of lively narrative and witty dialogue, it is not a coherent work of art, and its text has been marred by revisions and interpolations.

In the tale Medb (Maeve), warrior-queen of Connaught, disputes with her husband, Ailill, over their respective wealth. Because possession of the white-horned bull guarantees Ailill's superiority, Medb resolves to secure the even more famous brown bull of Cooley from the Ulstermen. Although Medb is warned by a prophetess of impending doom, the Connaught army proceeds to Ulster. The Ulster warriors are temporarily disabled by a curse, but CÚ CHULAINN, the youthful Ulster champion, is exempt from the curse and singlehandedly holds off the Connaughtmen. The climax of the fighting is a three-day combat between Cú Chulainn and Fer Díad, his friend and foster brother, who is in exile with the Connaught forces. Cú Chulainn is victorious, and, nearly dead from wounds and exhaustion, he is joined by the Ulster army, which routs the enemy. The brown bull, however, has been captured by Connaught and defeats Ailill's white-horned bull, after which peace is made.

Catton \'kat-ən\, Bruce, *in full* Charles Bruce Catton (b. Oct. 9, 1899, Petoskey, Mich., U.S.—d. Aug. 28, 1978, Frankfort, Mich.)   American journalist and historian, noted for his books on the American Civil War.

As a child living in a small town in Michigan, Catton was stimulated by reminiscences of the Civil War by local veterans. While he worked as a reporter for the *Boston American*, the *Cleveland News*, and the *Cleveland Plain Dealer* (1920–26), Catton continued his lifelong study of the Civil War period. In 1954 he joined the staff of *American Heritage* magazine and from 1959 was its senior editor.

A commission to write a centennial history of the Civil War evolved into Catton's celebrated trilogy on the Army of the Potomac: *Mr. Lincoln's Army* (1951), *Glory Road* (1952), and *A Stillness at Appomattox* (1953). The latter earned Catton both a Pulitzer Prize and the National Book Award in 1954. A second trilogy consisted of *The Coming Fury* (1961), *Terrible Swift Sword* (1963), and *Never Call Retreat* (1965).

Catton's brilliance as a historian lay in his ability to bring to historical narrative the immediacy of reportage. Other works by Catton include *The War Lords of Washington* (1948) and *U.S. Grant and the American Military Tradition* (1954).

Catullus \kə-'təl-əs\, Gaius Valerius (b. *c.* 84 BC, Verona, Cisalpine Gaul—d. *c.* 54 BC, Rome)   Roman poet whose expressions of love and hatred are generally considered the finest lyric poetry of ancient Rome.

No ancient biography of Catullus survives, and the certain facts of his life are scanty. On the evidence of four of his poems, Catullus was alive in 55–54 BC. The poet Ovid states that he died young. On his own evidence he was born at Verona in northern Italy and owned property at Sirmio (modern Sirmione) on Lake Garda, though he preferred to live in Rome.

Catullus' poetry records two emotional crises, the death of a brother and an intense and unhappy love affair, portrayed variously in 25 poems, with a woman named Clodia who was married and whom he calls Lesbia in the poems. His poems also record, directly or indirectly, a homosexual affair with a youth named Juventius.

The collection of Catullus' lyrics displays a versatility disproportionate to the slim size of the extant work. Most of the poems are written in assorted occasional-verse meters or in elegiac distich. Traditionally both forms had served for inscriptions and dedications and as verse of light occasions, satirical comment, and elegant sentiment. In some 37 instances Catullus uniquely converted these verse forms to serve as vehicles of feelings and observations expressed with great beauty and wit, on the one hand, or great passion, on the other. The conversational rhythms in particular, as he managed them for lyric purposes, achieved an immediacy that no other classic poet can rival.

Caucasian Chalk Circle, The   A play consisting of a prologue and five scenes by Bertolt BRECHT, first produced in English in 1948 and in German as *Der kaukasische Kreidekreis* in 1949. The work is based on the German writer Klabund's play *Der Kreidekreis* (1924), itself a translation and adaptation of a Chinese play from the Yuan dynasty (1206–1368).

Brecht's play is set within the context of a dispute over land claimed by two communes in the Soviet Union after World War II. The main action of the play consists of a parable that is performed to celebrate the decision in the dispute. The parable, set during a feudal insurrection in the 13th century, concerns the struggle of two women over the custody of a child. The dispute between the governor's wife, who abandoned the child, and the young servant who saved the child and cared for him is settled by an eccentric judge who places the child in a chalk circle and declares that whichever woman can pull him from the circle will be granted custody. When the servant, not wanting to harm the child, lets the governor's wife have him, she is awarded the child, having demonstrated greater love than the natural mother.

Caulfield, Holden \'hōld-ən-'kōl-,fēld\   Fictional character, the teenaged protagonist and narrator of J.D. Salinger's novel THE CATCHER IN THE RYE. Because he called attention to the hypocrisy and ambiguity of the adult world, Holden Caulfield was considered a paradigm of adolescent anguish for several generations of high school and college students.

causerie \,kōz-'rē, ,kō-zə-\ [French, literally, chat, conversation]   In literature, a short, informal essay, often on a literary topic. This sense of the word is derived from the title of a series of essays by the French author Charles-Augustin Sainte-Beuve, *Causeries du lundi.*

Causeries du lundi \kōz-'rē-dœ-lœⁿ-'dē\ ("Monday Chats") Series of informal essays by Charles-Augustin SAINTE-BEUVE. The 640 critical and biographical essays on literary topics and French and other European authors were published weekly in several Paris newspapers, on Mondays, from 1849 to 1869. The essays were collected in the 15-volume *Causeries du lundi* (1851–62) and the 13-volume *Nouveaux lundis* (1863–70).

Prodigious research went into each 3,000-word "chat." Sainte-Beuve, who wished his readers to have a well-rounded view of his subjects, provided extensive data on such matters as an author's character, family background, physical appearance, education, religion, love affairs, and friendships.

Cavafy \kə-'väf-ē\, Constantine, *pseudonym of* Konstantínos Pétrou Kaváfis \kä-'vä-fès\ (b. April 17, 1863, Alexandria, Egypt—d. April 29, 1933, Alexandria)   Greek poet who developed his own consciously individual style.

Dimitri Papadimos

Cavafy wrote much but was his own harshest critic, publishing only about 200 poems. His most important poetry was written after his 40th year, and with some justification he called himself a "poet of old age." A skeptic, he denied or ridiculed traditional Christian values, patriotism, and heterosexuality, though he was ill at ease with his own nonconformity. His language is a strange mixture of the refined and stilted Greek called Katharevusa, inherited from the Byzantines, and the Demotic, or spoken, tongue. The lyric treatment he gave to familiar historical themes made him popular and influential after his death. He is well known to English readers from the many references to his work in Lawrence Durrell's *Alexandria Quartet*. Cavafy's poems were first published without dates before World War II and reprinted in 1949.

Cavalcanti \kä-väl-'kän-tē\, Guido (b. *c.* 1255, Florence [Italy]—d. Aug. 27/28, 1300, Florence)   Italian poet who is considered, next to Dante, the most striking poet and personality in 13th-century Italian literature.

Born into an influential Florentine family, Cavalcanti studied with the philosopher and scholar Brunetto Latini. Cavalcanti's strong, temperamental, and brilliant personality and the poems that mirror it were admired by many contemporary poets. He left about 50 poems, many addressed to two women: Mandetta, whom he met in Toulouse in 1292, and Giovanna, whom he calls Primavera ("Springtime"). Cavalcanti's poems glow with the brilliance, grace, and directness of diction characteristic of the *dolce stil nuovo* ("sweet new style") at its best. Love is the poet's dominant theme, generally love that causes deep suffering.

Two of Cavalcanti's poems are canzone, a type of lyric derived from Provençal poetry, of which the most famous is "Donna mi prega" ("A Lady Asks Me"), a beautiful and complex philosophical analysis of love. His other poems are sonnets and ballate (ballads), the latter type usually considered his best. One of his best-known ballate was also one of his last: "Perch'io non spero di tornar giamai" ("Because I hope not ever to return").

Cavalcanti's poetry was first collected in 1527 and later in *Le rime de Guido Cavalcanti* (1902). Many poems were translated by Dante Gabriel Rossetti in *The Early Italian Poets* (1861; later retitled *Dante and His Circle*) and by Ezra Pound in *The Sonnets and Ballate of Guido Cavalcanti* (1912).

Cavalier poet \kav-ə-'lir\   Any of a group of English gentlemen poets who were Cavaliers (supporters of Charles I [1625–49] during the English Civil Wars, as opposed to the Roundheads, who supported Parliament). They counted the writing of polished and elegant lyrics as only one of their many accomplishments as soldiers, courtiers, gallants, and wits. The term embraces Richard Lovelace, Thomas Carew, Sir John Suckling, Edmund Waller, and Robert Herrick. Although Herrick, a clergyman, was detached from the court, his short, fluent, graceful lyrics on love and dalliance and his carpe diem ("seize the day") philosophy ("Gather ye rosebuds while ye may") are typical of the Cavalier style. Besides writing love lyrics, the Cav-

aliers sometimes wrote of war, honor, and their duty to the king. Sometimes they deftly combined all these themes, as in Richard Lovelace's well-known poem "To Lucasta, Going to the Wars," which ends,

> I could not love thee, dear, so much
> Loved I not honour more.

Cavalleria rusticana \kä-väl-lä-'rē-ä-rūs-tē-'kä-nä\ ("Rustic Chivalry")   Short story by Giovanni VERGA, written in verismo style and published in 1880. The author's adaptation of the story into a one-act tragedy (produced in 1884) was his greatest success as a playwright.

On his return to his village from army service, Turiddu Macca discovers that his sweetheart, Lola, is bethrothed to Alfio. Spitefully, Turiddu begins a flirtation with Santa, the daughter of his employer. Jealous of this new relationship, Lola takes Turiddu as a lover. Santa informs Alfio of Lola's infidelity. Alfio challenges Turiddu to a duel to the death, and Turiddu is killed.

The Italian composer Pietro Mascagni used this material as the basis for his one-act opera (1890) of the same name.

Cavendish \'kav-ən-dish\, George (b. 1500—d. 1561/62)   English courtier and writer who won a minor but lasting reputation through a single work, his *Life* of Cardinal Wolsey, a landmark in the development of English biography, an important document for the student of Tudor history, and a rare source of information on the character of the author himself. Cavendish applied to his subject methods of concrete observation in matters of behavior, gesture, and speech, so that in his shapely and unaffected narrative the figure of the cardinal emerges with an air of life.

About 1526 Cavendish entered Wolsey's service as a gentleman usher and remained loyal to him from the height of his power to his rapid fall under the disfavor of Henry VIII. After Wolsey's death in 1530 Cavendish left public employment and retired to Suffolk, where in 1557 he completed the *Life*.

The printing of the complete *Life* was obstructed during the reign of Elizabeth I, but it circulated freely in manuscript. In 1810 Christopher Wordsworth attempted to restore the original by issuing, in his *Ecclesiastical Biography*, a text based upon original manuscripts. In 1815 S.W. Singer published a more completely restored text.

Caxton \'kaks-tən\, William (b. *c.* 1422, Kent, Eng.—d. 1491, London)   The first English printer, who as a translator and publisher exerted an important influence on English literature.

Caxton was a prosperous, politically connected mercer living in Brugge (now in Belgium). By about 1470 his interests were turning to literature. In March 1469 he had begun to translate Raoul Le Fèvre's *Recueil des histoires de Troye*, which he finished in 1471. He lived in Cologne (now in Germany) from 1470 to the end of 1472, and there he learned printing. He set up a press in Brugge about 1474, and *The Recuyell of the Historyes of Troye*, the first book printed in English, was published there in 1475. Caxton's translation from the French of the allegory *The Game and Playe of the Chesse* was published in 1476. Toward the end of 1476 he returned to England and established his press at Westminster.

Although a pioneer of printing in England, Caxton showed no great typographical originality and produced no books of remarkable beauty. The first dated book printed in English, *Dictes and Sayenges of the Phylosophers*, appeared on Nov. 18, 1477. Caxton's wealthy patrons sometimes commissioned special books, but his varied output—including books of chivalric romance, conduct, morality, history, devotion and philosophy, and an encyclopedia, *The Myrrour of the Worlde* (1481), the first illustrated English book—shows that he catered also to a general public. He printed nearly all the English literature available to him in his time, including *The Canterbury Tales* (printed 1478? and 1484?) and other poems by Geoffrey Chaucer, John Gower's *Confessio amantis* (printed 1483), Sir Thomas Malory's *Le Morte Darthur* (printed 1485), and much of the work of John Lydgate. Caxton translated 24 books, some of them immensely long. By the time of his death, he had published about 100 items of various kinds.

Cayrol \ke-'rôl\, Jean(-Raphaël-Marie-Noël) (b. June 6, 1911, Bordeaux, Fr.) French poet, novelist, and essayist who stood at the frontiers of the *nouveau roman* ("new novel"), the avant-garde French novel that emerged in the 1950s.

In World War II Cayrol was deported to a concentration camp after participating in the Resistance, the experience that lies at the heart of his art. It inspired his first poems, *Poèmes de la nuit et du brouillard* (1946; "Poems of the Night and of the Fog"); his seminal essay *Lazare parmi nous* (1950; "Lazarus Among Us"); and his prizewinning trilogy of novels, *Je vivrai l'amour des autres* (1947–50; "I Will Live the Love of Others"). The figure of Lazarus (a biblical character who was raised from the dead) is a central image in Cayrol's work.

Cayrol was a prolific writer, producing fiction, poems, essays, and screenplays. He was elected to the Académie Goncourt in 1974. His novels include *L'Espace d'une nuit* (1954; *All in a Night*) and *Les Corps étrangers* (1959; *Foreign Bodies*), the only translated works to receive a considerable English audience. Other notable novels are *Le Froid du soleil* (1963; "The Chill of the Sun"); *Midi Minuit* (1966; "Midday Midnight"); *Je l'entends encore* (1967; "I Still Hear It"); a series of novels examining the characteristics of place, including *Histoire d'un prairie* (1969; "Story of a Prairie"), *Histoire d'un désert* (1972; "Story of a Desert"), *Histoire de la mer* (1973; "Story of the Sea"), *Histoire de la forêt* (1975; "Story of the Forest"), *Histoire une maison* (1976; "Story of a House"), and *Histoire du ciel* (1979; "Story of the Sky"); *Les Quatre Saisons* (1977; "The Four Seasons"); and *Exposés au soleil* (1980; "Exposed to the Sun"). He also wrote several volumes of *Poésie-Journal* (1969, 1977, 1980), a running record of his impressions, and several later volumes of poetry.

Cecchi \'chet-chē\, Emilio (b. July 14, 1884, Florence, Italy—d. Sept. 6, 1966, Rome) Italian essayist and critic noted for his writing style and for introducing a number of significant English and American writers to his Italian readers.

Cecchi attended the University of Florence and wrote articles for the influential review *La Voce*. He also wrote a number of short stories and the verses that were collected in *Inno* (1910; "Hymn") before becoming a book reviewer. In his *Storia della letteratura inglese nel secolo XIX* (1915; "History of 19th-Century English Literature") he used Thomas De Quincey and Charles Lamb as his critical models. In 1919 he cofounded the review *La Ronda*. His best-known works are two wide-ranging collections of newspaper essays, *Pesci rossi* (1920; "Goldfish") and *Corse al trotto* (1936; "Trotting Races"), which discuss with grace and considerable humor modern life and the future as well as literary topics. Among his later volumes are his travel writings of *Messico* (1932; "Mexico") and an attack on American attitudes, *America amara* (1939; "Bitter America").

Cecil \'sis-əl, commonly 'ses-\, Lord David, in full Lord Edward Christian David Gascoyne Cecil (b. April 9, 1902, London, Eng.—d. Jan. 1, 1986, Cranborne, Dorset) English biographer, literary critic, and educator, best known for his discerning, sympathetic, and elegantly written studies of many literary figures.

Lord Cecil was the younger son of the 4th marquess of Salisbury. Educated at Oxford, he was a fellow of Wadham College

(1924–30) and of New College (1939–69). He taught English literature at Oxford University from 1948 to 1969.

Among his subjects for biography were the poet William Cowper (*The Stricken Deer*, 1929), Jane Austen (1935), Lord Melbourne (*The Young Melbourne*, 1939), Thomas Hardy (*Hardy the Novelist*, 1943), the poet Thomas Gray (*Two Quiet Lives*, 1948), and the writer and caricaturist Sir Max Beerbohm (*Max*, 1964). *Library Looking-glass* (1975) is a personal anthology, tracing his intellectual history.

Cecilia \si-'sil-yə, -'sēl-\ or **Cecily** \'ses-ə-lē, 'sis-\, Saint (fl. 2nd or 3rd century, Rome) Patroness of music, one of the most famous Roman martyrs of the early church, and historically one of the most discussed. She is often represented in art playing the organ. Her legend is popular. John Dryden wrote "A Song for St. Cecilia's Day" (1687) and Alexander Pope "An Ode for Music on St. Cecilia's Day" (1713).

Cecrops \'sē-ˌkräps\ In Greek mythology, one of the sons of Gaea. The upper part of his body was human and the lower part was that of a snake. According to legend he was the first king of Attica in ancient Greece. He was said to have instituted the laws of marriage and property and a new form of worship. The introduction of bloodless sacrifice, the burial of the dead, and the invention of writing were also attributed to him. He acted as arbiter during the dispute between the deities Athena and Poseidon for the possession of Attica.

Ceiriog Pseudonym of John Ceiriog HUGHES.

Cela \'thā-lä\, Camilo José, surname in full Cela Trulock \'trü-lôk\ (b. May 11, 1916, Iria Flavia, Spain) Spanish writer who won the Nobel Prize for Literature in 1989. His literary works are characterized by experimentation and innovation in form and content. Cela is also credited by some critics with having established the narrative style known as *tremendismo*, a tendency to emphasize violence and grotesque imagery.

Cela attended the University of Madrid before and after the Spanish Civil War (1936–39), during which he served with Franco's army. His first novel, *La familia de Pascual Duarte* (1942; *The Family of Pascal Duarte*), established his European reputation. Traditional in form, it was both a popular and critical success. His second novel, *La colmena* (1951; *The Hive*), with its fragmented chronology and large cast of characters, is an innovative and perceptive story of postwar Madrid. Another of his better-known avant-garde novels, *San Camilo, 1936* (1969), presents one continuous stream of consciousness. His later novels include *Mazurca para dos muertos* (1983; "Mazurka for Two Dead People") and *Cristo versus Arizona* (1988; "Christ Versus Arizona").

Cela's acute powers of observation and skill in colorful description also are apparent in his travel books. The most noted of these are *Viaje a la Alcarría* (1948; *Journey to the Alcarría*), *Del Miño al Bidasoa* (1952; "From the Miño to the Bidasoa"), and *Judíos, moros y cristianos* (1956; "Jews, Moors, and Christians"). He retraced the itinerary of his first travel book for *Nuevo viaje a la Alcarría* (1986). Among his numerous short narratives are *Esas nubes que pasan* (1945; "The Passing Clouds") and the four works included in the collection *El molino de viento, y otras novelas cortas* (1956; "The Windmill and Other Short Fiction"). Cela also wrote essays, poetry, and memoirs and in his later years made frequent television appearances.

In 1955 he settled in Majorca, where he founded a well-respected literary review, *Papeles de son armadans* (1956–79), and published books in fine editions. He began in 1968 to publish his multivolume *Diccionario secreto* (vol. 11 was published in 1972), a compilation of "unprintable" but well-known words and phrases. Cela became a member of the Spanish Academy in 1957.

Celan \'tsä-,län\, Paul, *pseudonym of* Paul Antschel \'änt-shəl\ (b. Nov. 23, 1920, Cernăuți, Rom. [now Chernivtsi, Ukraine]—d. May 1, 1970, Paris, Fr.)   Poet who, though he never lived in Germany, gave post-World War II German literature one of its most powerful and regenerative voices. His style shows the influence of Surrealism.

When Romania came under virtual Nazi control in World War II, Celan, a Jew, was sent to a forced-labor camp and his parents were murdered. He moved to Vienna in 1947, where he published his first collection of poems, *Der Sand aus den Urnen* (1948; "The Sand from the Urns"). From the outset his poetry was marked by a phantasmagoric perception of the terrors and injuries of reality and by a sureness of imagery and prosody.

Settling in Paris in 1948, he lectured on language at the École Normale and translated French, Italian, and Russian poetry, as well as William Shakespeare, into German. His second volume of poems, *Mohn und Gedächtnis* (1952; "Poppy and Memory"), established his reputation in West Germany. Seven volumes of poetry followed, including *Lichtzwang* (1970; "Lightforce"). The fullest English translation of his work is *Speech-Grille and Selected Poems* (1971). He died by his own hand.

Celebrated Jumping Frog of Calaveras County, The
\,kal-ə-'ver-əs\   Short story by Mark TWAIN, first published in *The Saturday Press* in 1865.

The narrator of the story, who is searching for a Reverend Leonidas Smiley, visits the long-winded Simon Wheeler, a miner, in hopes of learning his whereabouts. Wheeler instead relates an elaborate story of a different man named Jim Smiley who was a compulsive and imaginative gambler and who once spent three months training a frog named Daniel Webster to jump and then won money by betting on the frog. The gambler, Wheeler reveals, was eventually duped by a quick-thinking stranger.

Celestial Railroad, The
Allegorical short story by Nathaniel HAWTHORNE, published in 1843 and included in his short-story collection *Mosses from an Old Manse* (1846).

Following the path of Christian in John Bunyan's *The Pilgrim's Progress*, the narrator travels from the City of Destruction to the Celestial City—not on foot as had the original pilgrim but as a passenger on the Celestial Railroad. Mr. Smooth-it-away, a friendly fellow traveler, comments contemptuously about the arduous trip the old-fashioned pilgrims had to undergo. At the journey's end, Mr. Smooth-it-away leaves the other passengers and divulges his true identity by breathing fire and brimstone. The narrator awakens and realizes, with great relief, that it has all been a dream.

Celestina, La
\lä-,thel-es-'tē-nä\   Spanish dialogue novel, generally considered the first masterpiece of Spanish prose and the greatest and most influential work of the early Renaissance in Spain.

Originally published in 16 acts as the *Comedia de Calisto y Melibea* (1499; "Comedy of Calisto and Melibea") and shortly thereafter in an expanded version with 21 acts as the *Tragicomedia de Calisto y Melibea* (1502), the work has been popularly known since shortly after its publication as *La Celestina* for its chief character, the bawd who serves as the go-between for the young lovers Calisto and Melibea. Celestina's deeply explored personality dominates the plot, ostensibly tragic, of the uncontrolled passion of the lovers, which ends in disaster after its consummation.

Authorship of the work, which was published anonymously, is generally attributed to Fernando de ROJAS, a converted Jewish lawyer about whom little else is known. Often considered the first European novel, *La Celestina* was profoundly influential in the development of European prose fiction and is valued by critics today as much for its greatness as literature as for its historical significance.

Céline
\sā-'lēn\, Louis-Ferdinand, *pseudonym of* Louis-Ferdinand Destouches \dā-'tüsh\ (b. May 27, 1894, Courbevoie, near Paris, Fr.—d. July 1, 1961, Meudon)   French writer and physician noted for his novels about the search for meaning in life.

Céline received his medical degree in 1924 and traveled extensively on medical missions for the League of Nations. In 1928 he opened a practice in a suburb of Paris, writing in his spare time. He became famous with his first novel, *Voyage au bout de la nuit* (1932; *Journey to the End of Night*), the story of a man's tortured and hopeless search for meaning, written in a vehement and disjointed style that marked its author as a major innovator of 20th-century French literature. There followed *Mort à crédit* (1936; *Death on the Installment Plan*), a similarly bleak portrayal of a world bereft of value, beauty, and decency.

Though a favorite of the left wing, Céline was disenchanted by a visit to the Soviet Union and said so in *Mea culpa* (1937). He later developed fanatically anti-Semitic sentiments, expressed in three notorious pamphlets: *Bagatelles pour un massacre* (1937; "Trifles for a Massacre"), *L'École des cadavres* (1938; "School for Corpses"), and *Les Beaux Draps* (1941; "The Fine Mess"). These works also excoriated the French.

At the outbreak of World War II, Céline enlisted in the ambulance service, but after the fall of France in 1940 he rejected both collaboration and resistance and returned instead to work at a dispensary at Bezons. Threatened by the Resistance as a collaborator during the Allied liberation of France, he fled to Denmark, where he was imprisoned because of the accusations. He was permitted to return to his homeland after France exonerated him in 1951. His last works—a trilogy composed of *D'un château l'autre* (1957; *Castle to Castle*), *Nord* (1960; *North*), and *Rigodon* (1969; *Rigadoon*)—depict World War II as seen from within Germany. Other works include *Guignol's Band* (1944), *Casse Pipe* (1949; "Shooting Gallery"), and *Entretiens avec le Professeur Y* (1955; "Conversations with Professor Y").

Celtic revival
also called Celtic Twilight.   Mystical element in the GAELIC REVIVAL and especially the IRISH LITERARY RENAISSANCE, Irish literary movements of the 19th century. Originating in Romanticism and sustained by Irish nationalism, Celtic revival literature was characterized by an emphasis on Irish myth and legend combined with a moody sense of gothic mystery, supernatural magic, and romantic melancholy.

Notable proponents of the Celtic revival were Æ (George Russell) and William Butler Yeats, who compiled a volume of folklore called *The Celtic Twilight* (1893; revised and enlarged 1902). Other authors who made use of the Celtic revival were Thomas Love Peacock, Alfred, Lord Tennyson, and Gerard Manley Hopkins. The movement faded with the development of realism in Irish literature at the turn of the century.

Celtis
\'tsel-tis\ *or* **Celtes** \-təs\, Conradus, *pseudonym of* Conrad Pickel \'pik-əl\ (b. Feb. 1, 1459, Wipfeld, near Würzburg [Germany]—d. Feb. 4, 1508, Vienna [Austria]) German scholar known as *Der Erzhumanist* ("The Archhumanist").

Celtis studied at Cologne and Heidelberg. He was crowned poet laureate by the Holy Roman emperor Frederick III at Nürnberg in 1487 (the first German to receive this honor). He studied mathematics and astronomy at Kraków and became professor of poetry and rhetoric in Ingolstadt in 1491. In 1497 Maximilian I appointed him professor in Vienna, where Celtis founded, on Italian models, a center for humanistic studies, the Sodalitas Danubiana.

Celtis rediscovered the manuscripts of Germany's first woman poet, the 10th-century nun Hrosvitha, and also the so-called Peutinger Table, a map of the Roman Empire. Among his scholarly works are editions of Tacitus' *Germania* (1500), Hrosvitha's plays (1501), and the 12th-century poem on Barbarossa, *Ligurinus* (1507).

The dominant theme of patriotism that partly inspired these editions is an important element in Celtis' works. Celtis' masques with music, *Ludus Dianae* (1501) and *Rhapsodia* (1505), were early forerunners of Baroque opera. His greatest work, however, is his lyric poetry—*Odes* (published posthumously, 1513), *Epigrams* (in manuscript until 1881), and especially *Amores* (1502), love poems of forthright sensuality and true lyrical intensity.

cénacle \'sen-ə-kəl, *French* sā-'nåkl\ [French, literally, the room where Christ and his apostles had the Last Supper, from Latin *cenaculum* upper story, dining room] A type of literary coterie formed around various early leaders of the Romantic movement in France, replacing the salon as a place for writers to read and discuss their works. An early cénacle formed around Victor Hugo after the founding of the short-lived but influential *La Muse française.* When the review ceased publication in 1824, the young contributors shifted to the salon of Charles Nodier, who was then librarian of the Arsenal Library, second of the great French libraries. The activities of this group, which included Hugo, Alphonse de Lamartine, Alfred de Vigny, and Alfred de Musset, are described in the *Mémoires* of Alexandre Dumas *père.* Three years later, Hugo and the critic Charles-Augustin Sainte-Beuve formed a cénacle at Hugo's house on the rue Notre-Dame-des-Champs, where other young writers, including Prosper Mérimée, Théophile Gautier, and Gérard de Nerval, joined the group. The entourage of Gautier, Nerval, and Petrus Borel, the more turbulent, bohemian Romantics, became known as the Petit Cénacle.

Cenci, The \'chen-chē\ Verse tragedy in five acts by Percy Bysshe SHELLEY, published in London in 1819 and first staged privately by the Shelley Society in 1886. Modeled after Shakespearean tragedy, it is noted for its powerful characters, evocative language, and moral ambiguities. It is based on an incident in Renaissance Rome.

The story centers on Count Francesco Cenci, who is notorious for his depravity. He gives a party at which, to the horror of his guests, he gleefully announces the deaths of two of his sons. Another victim of his cruelty is his daughter Beatrice, whom he has raped. Beatrice enlists the help of Orsino, a priest and Roman nobleman whom she had once hoped to marry. With the approval of the Cenci family, Orsino plots the murder of the count. When the other conspirators are found out, Orsino evades capture; the rest are tried and executed.

Cendrars \sän-'drår\, Blaise, *pseudonym of* Frédéric Sauser \sō-zā\ (b. Sept. 1, 1887, La Chaux-de-Fonds, Switz.—d. Jan. 21, 1961, Paris, Fr.) Writer in French whose powerful poetic style embraced techniques of Cubism, Dadaism, and Surrealism.

Cendrars left home in 1904. He worked in Russia as an apprentice watchmaker and was there during the Revolution of 1905. He traveled incessantly and after 1914 became involved in the movie industry in Italy, France, and the United States. For the remainder of his life he continued to travel and to work at a variety of jobs.

To Cendrars, poetry was action sealed into words by bold new devices. Much of his poetry consisted of a jumble of images, feelings, associations, and surprise effects conveyed in a halting, syncopated rhythm. Largely ignored by critics, Cendrars was at first noted chiefly for his poems *Les Pâques à New*

York (1912; "Easter in New York") and *La Prose du Transsibérien et de la petite Jehanne de France* (1913; "The Prose of the Trans-Siberian and of Little Jehanne of France"), both of which are combination travelogue and lament. Known during his lifetime for fictionalizing his past (*e.g.,* he sometimes claimed to have been born in Egypt), Cendrars wrote mostly semiautobiographical fiction. One such work of note is *Bourlinguer* (1948; *The Knockabout*), which glorifies the dangerous life.

Cen Shen or **Ts'en Shen** \'tsən-'shən\, *also called* Cen Jiazhou \'jyă-'jō\ (b. 715, Nanyang [Jiangling], China—d. 770, Chengdu, Sichuan province) One of the celebrated poets of the Tang dynasty (618–907).

Because of the decline of his aristocratic family, Cen Shen had to rely upon his literary skill to secure a government appointment through the examination system. During the 750s he held several assignments in the Central Asian outposts of the far-flung Tang empire until the eruption of the An Lushan Rebellion of 755 forced him to return to China. Having supported the loyalist cause, he succeeded to a number of provincial posts under the restoration until his retirement in 768.

A member of the second generation of High Tang poets, which included such masters as Li Bo and Du Fu, Cen Shen participated in the effort to reinvigorate the *lüshi,* or "regulated poem," through innovations in diction and meter. Contemporaries praised him for his craftsmanship, particularly his skill at creating unconventional metaphors and imaginative phrases. But he came to be best known as a "frontier poet" because he so frequently set his poems in exotic Central Asia.

censorship \'sen-sər-,ship\ The suppression or prohibition of anything that is considered objectionable or subversive of the common good.

In Christendom one of the most notable forms of censorship was the *Index librorum prohibitorum,* by which the Roman Catholic church for centuries policed the literature available to its followers. The struggle against censorship in the Anglo-American world began to take its modern form in the 17th and 18th centuries. Of special importance was John Milton's *Areopagitica* (1644), in which he argued against a government's right to license (or previously restrain) publication. Milton's definition of freedom of the press, however, did not preclude the condemnation of material after publication.

centaur \'sen-,tôr, -,tär\ [Greek *Kéntauros*] One of an ancient mythical Greek race, dwelling in the mountains of Thessaly and Arcadia, who were men with the bodies of horses and half-bestial natures.

Traditionally the centaurs were the offspring of Ixion, king of the neighboring Lapiths. They were best known for their fight (centauromachy) with the Lapiths, which resulted from their attempt to carry off the bride of Pirithous, son and successor of Ixion. After losing the battle, they were driven from Mount Pelion. In later Greek times they were often represented drawing the chariot of the wine god Dionysus or bound and ridden by Eros, the god of love, in allusion to their drunken and amorous habits. Their general character was that of wild, lawless, and inhospitable beings, the slaves of their animal passions. A notable exception was the centaur CHIRON, who instructed many of the Greek heroes and was renowned for his wisdom and his knowledge of medicine.

cento \'sen-,tō\, *plural* centones \sen-'tō-nēz\, centoes, *or* centos [Latin, patchwork quilt or curtain] An often poetic patchwork composition of words, phrases, or lines from other works. An early example is Decimus Magnus Ausonius' *Cento nuptialis,* a patchwork in which lines of Virgil are pieced together to form a shockingly explicit account of the consummation of a marriage. This type of composition, sometimes known as a collage or pastiche, is still written, some notable examples being works by practitioners of Dada and Surrealism.

Cephalus and Procris \'sef-ə-ləs . . . 'prō-kris\   In Greek mythology, legendary couple parted by a jealous god. Cephalus was a great hunter. His wife, Procris, was a favorite of Artemis, and received from her a dog, Laelaps ("Hurricane"), and a javelin that would never miss its mark. Procris gave Artemis' gifts to her husband. He was noticed by the goddess Eos (Dawn), and she became enamored of him and carried him off for a time. Rumor started that Procris had a rival, and one day she followed Cephalus and his dog to the hunt. She emerged suddenly from a thicket and was fatally wounded when Cephalus, who mistook her for his prey, hurled his magic javelin.

The story is discussed in later literature, notably in the play *Il rapimento di Cefalo* (1600) by Gabriello Chiabrera.

Cerberus \'sər-bə-rəs\   In Greek mythology, the watchdog who guarded the gate of the underworld. He had three heads, a snake's tail, and a row of serpent heads growing out of his back. The offspring of the monster Typhon and the half-woman, half-serpent Echidna, Cerberus had a number of siblings who were also monsters (including the many-headed Hydra and the fire-breathing monster Chimera). Cerberus lavished affection on new arrivals to the underworld, but his principal duty was to eat anyone who tried to escape. Another of his duties was to prevent living mortals from entering.

Cereno, Benito \bā-'nē-tō-sā-'rā-nō\   Fictional character, the protagonist of Herman Melville's short story BENITO CERENO.

Ceres \'sir-ēz, 'sē-rēz\   In Roman mythology, goddess of the growth of food plants, worshiped either alone or in association with the earth goddess Tellus. At an early date her cult was overlaid by that of DEMETER, who was widely worshiped in Sicily and Magna Graecia.

Cernuda \ther-'nü-thä\, Luis, *surname in full* Cernuda y Bidón \ē-bē-'thōn\ (b. Sept. 21, 1902, Seville, Spain—d. Nov. 5, 1963, Mexico City, Mex.)   Spanish poet, critic, and member of the Generation of 1927, whose work expresses the gulf between what is wished and what can be attained.

In 1925 Cernuda received a law degree from the University of Seville and published several poems. In 1927 his collection *Perfil del aire* ("Profile of the Wind") was published. Later collections of poems, notably *Los placeres prohibidos* (1931; "Forbidden Pleasures"), were influenced by Surrealism and indicate an increasing bitterness toward life, partially influenced by his facing his homosexuality. All of his poems were collected in *La realidad y el deseo* ("Reality and Desire"), which was frequently expanded and reissued.

A supporter of the Spanish Republic, Cernuda toured Britain for the government in 1938 and after its fall became a professor in Britain. From 1947 to 1952 he taught at Mount Holyoke College in the United States, and he settled in Mexico in 1952. He published criticism of earlier poets and collections of poems using classical and Mexican myths for reference. All of his poems appeared in the final edition of *Realidad y deseo*, published posthumously in 1964. An English-language anthology of his work, *The Poetry of Luis Cernuda*, was published in 1971 and *Selected Poems of Luis Cernuda* in 1977.

Cervantes \ther-'băn-täs, *Angl* sər-'văn-tēz, -'van-\, Miguel de, *surname in full* Cervantes Saavedra \ˌsä-ä-'bäth-rä\ (b. Sept. 29?, 1547, Alcalá de Henares, Spain—d. April 23, 1616, Madrid)   Spanish novelist, playwright, and poet, the creator of DON QUIXOTE (Part I, 1605; Part II, 1615) and the most important figure in Spanish literature.

After studying in Madrid, in 1569 Cervantes went to Italy, and in 1570 he became a soldier in a Spanish infantry regiment stationed in Naples. He took part in the decisive sea battle against the Turks at Lepanto (1571), during which he received a wound that permanently crippled his left hand. En route to Spain after his military service, he was captured by the Turks and, together with his brother Rodrigo, was sold into slavery in Algiers. He was ransomed five years later and returned to Spain.

The remainder of Cervantes' life stands in sharp contrast to this adventuresome decade. He was in chronic financial difficulties, and his tangled affairs led to several brushes with the law. An affair with a married woman produced his only child, Isabel de Saavedra, who was reared in her father's household. In 1584 he married Catalina de Salazar y Palacios, a woman 18 years his junior.

Cervantes produced his first book, the pastoral romance *La galatea*, in 1585. He claimed to have written some 20 or 30 plays from 1582 to 1587; two of these, *El trato de Argel* ("The Traffic of Algiers") and *La Numancia* ("Numantia"), survive. Unsuccessful as a playwright, he took a series of government positions that were both difficult and unsatisfying. Irregularities in his accounting landed him briefly in prison. He had some success writing poetry and began to write short stories.

The first part of *Don Quixote* (1605) was an immediate success. It quickly went into multiple editions both in Spain and abroad. Though it did not bring him riches, it put him in the front rank of men of letters. Among his subsequent works are a collection of 12 short stories, *Novelas ejemplares* (1613; "Exemplary Tales"), which Cervantes claimed to be the first written in Castilian. The second part of *Don Quixote* appeared in 1615. Cervantes turned again to drama with a collection of comedies, *Ocho comedias y ocho entremeses nuevos* (1615; "Eight Comedies and Eight New Interludes"). He achieved success with his last published work, the romance *Los trabaios de Persiles y Sigismunda, historia setentrional* (1617; "The Labors of Persiles and Sigismunda: A Northern Story").

Cervantes Prize \ther-'băn-täs, *Angl* sər-'văn-tēz, -'van-\, *in full* Premio de Literatura en Lengua Castellana Miguel de Cervantes.   Literary award established in 1976 by the Spanish Ministry of Culture. It is the most prestigious and remunerative award given for Spanish-language literature. The Cervantes Prize is presented to an author whose work as a whole is judged to have most enriched Spanish culture. The award of 10 million Spanish pesetas is given annually and cannot be divided.

Césaire \sā-'zer\, Aimé(-Fernand) (b. June 25, 1913, Basse-Pointe, Martinique)   French-speaking Martiniquais poet and playwright, cofounder with Léopold Sédar Senghor and Léon Damas of NEGRITUDE, an influential movement to restore the cultural identity of black Africans.

Césaire was educated in Paris, where he was active in the movement to restore black African cultural identity. In the early 1940s he returned to Martinique and engaged in political action supporting the decolonization of the French colonies of Africa. He became a deputy to the Constituent Assembly in 1946 and joined the Communist Party. He voiced his ardent rebellion in a language heavy with African imagery. In the fiery poems of *Cahier d'un retour au pays natal* (1939; *Return to My Native Land*) and *Soleil cou-coupé* (1948; "Sun's Slashed Throat"), he lashed out against the French oppressors.

Césaire later turned to the theater, discarding Negritude for black militancy. *La Tragédie du Roi Christophe* (1963; *The Tragedy of King Christophe*), a drama of decolonization in 19th-century Haiti, and *Une Saison au Congo* (1966; *A Season in the Congo*), an epic of the 1960 Congo rebellion and of the assassination of the Congolese political leader Patrice Lumumba, depict black power as forever doomed to failure. Later poetry collections include *Aimé Césaire: The Collected Poetry* (1983) and *Non-Vicious Circle: Twenty Poems* (1985).

Cesarotti \chä-zä-'rōt-tē\, Melchiorre (b. May 15, 1730, Padua, Republic of Venice [Italy]—d. Nov. 4, 1808, Selvazzano, near Padua)   Italian poet, essayist, translator, and literary critic who, by his essays and his translation of the purported poems of the legendary Gaelic bard Ossian, encouraged the development of Romanticism in Italy.

Educated in Padua, Cesarotti later taught at the University of Padua. His versified translation, from the English version of James Macpherson, of the Ossian poems (*Poesie di Ossian*, 1763–72) revived interest in nature poetry. Two important essays also encouraged would-be Romantic writers: *Saggio sulla filosofia del gusto* (1785; "Essay on the Philosophy of Taste") and *Saggio sulla filosofia delle lingue* (1785; "Essay on the Philosophy of Languages"), the latter demanding the freeing of literature from academic bonds.

As one of the Italian ambassadors who met Napoleon I in 1797 at Campo Formio, Cesarotti praised him in an epic poem called *Pronea* (1807; "Providence"). He also wrote miscellaneous verse, a prose version of the *Iliad*, and translations of Aeschylus, Demosthenes, Voltaire, and Thomas Gray's "An Elegy Written in a Country Church Yard."

Céspedes \'thäs-pä-<u>th</u>äs\, Gonzalo de, *surname in full* Céspedes y Meneses \ē-mā-'nā-sās\ (b. 1585?, Madrid, Spain—d. 1638)   Spanish writer of histories and short stories, best known for an early work, the romance *Poema trágico del español Gerardo, y desengaño del amor lascivo* (1615–18). This work was translated in 1622 by Leonard Digges as *Gerardo the Unfortunate Spaniard, or a Patterne for Lascivious Lovers* and was drawn upon by John Fletcher for two plays, *The Spanish Curate* (1622; with Philip Massinger) and *The Maid in the Mill* (1623; with William Rowley).

Céspedes ran into political difficulties upon the publication of his *Historia apologética de los sucessos del reyno de Aragón y su ciudad de Zaragoza, años de 1591 y 1592* (1622; "Apologetic History on Advent of the Kingdom of Aragon and Its City of Zaragosa, Years from 1591 to 1592"). It was confiscated, and Céspedes moved to Zaragoza and later to Lisbon. While in exile, he published *Historias peregrinas y exemplares* (1623; "Stories Foreign and Exemplary"), short stories that, despite an affected style, show considerable imagination and insight into character.

cesura   *see* CAESURA.

Cetina \thä-'tē-nä\, Gutierre de (b. 1520?, Seville, Spain—d. 1557?)   Spanish poet, author of "Ojos claros serenos" ("Clear, Serene Eyes"), one of the most frequently anthologized poems in the Spanish language.

Influenced by the poet Garcilaso de la Vega, Cetina drew heavily upon classical and Italian poetry for his sources, and he wrote extensively in Italianate meters. A considerable portion of his verse is freely translated from Petrarch, Ausiàs March, and others. His sonnets, marked by elegance and dextrous meter, are considered to be his finest work.

Cevdet Paşa \jev-'det-pä-'shä\, Ahmed (b. March 22, 1822, Lovča, Ottoman Empire [now Lovech, Bulg.]—d. May 25, 1895, Constantinople [now Istanbul, Tur.])   Statesman and historian who was an outstanding figure in 19th-century Turkish letters.

Born into an Ottoman family long active in government service, Cevdet Paşa received a classical Islāmic education and studied mathematics and Persian as well. Throughout his life he held a number of important government positions, including the post of minister of justice, in which position he supervised the official codification and consolidation of Ottoman law, known as the Mecelle.

Although he wrote poetry in his early years, Cevdet Paşa is mainly known for his historical works, among them his 12-volume *Tarih-ı Cevdet* ("Cevdet's Chronicle"), covering the period 1774 to 1826; the *Tezakir-i Cevdet* ("The Memoirs of Cevdet"), a collection of observations made on the events during his service as official court chronicler; and the *Marûzat* ("Observations"), written about the events from 1839 to 1876. Cevdet Paşa also wrote a number of Turkish grammars, including the *Kavaid-i Osmaniye* ("Ottoman Fundamentals"; in collaboration with Mehmed Fuad Paşa), as well as a simpler version, the *Kavaid-i Türkiye* ("Turkish Fundamentals").

Other works include his *Takvim-i edvar* ("The Calendar of the Ages"), which deals with the reform of the calendar, and, finally, his completion of the translation of the *Muqaddimah* ("Prologomena") to the historical work of the great 14th-century Arab historian Ibn Khaldūn.

Chaadayev or **Chaadaev** \,chə-,ə-'dá-yəf\, Pyotr Yakovlevich (b. May 27 [June 7, New Style], 1794, Moscow, Russian Empire—d. April 14 [April 26], 1856, Moscow)   Intellectual and writer whose ideas precipitated the controversy between Slavophiles and Westernizers.

Chaadayev traveled in Europe, afterward writing in French his *Lettres philosophiques* (1827–31; "Philosophical Letters"), which articulated a ruthless criticism of Russian history, culture, and the Orthodox religion and advocated assimilation of Russian culture with Roman Catholicism and western European culture. The first letter of this work was published in Russian translation in the review *Teleskop* ("Telescope") in 1836. The periodical was banned, and Chaadayev was declared insane and placed under medical supervision. He remained a source of inspiration for the young Westernizers.

Chacel \chä-'thel\, Rosa (b. June 3, 1898, Valladolid, Spain—d. July 27, 1994, Madrid)   One of the leading Spanish novelists of the mid-20th century who was also an accomplished essayist and poet.

Chacel taught at the Spanish Academy in Rome in the 1920s, where she wrote her first novel, *Estación, ida y vuelta* (1930; "Two-way Station"). After returning to Spain she wrote her sonnet collection *A la orilla de un pozo* (1936; "At the Well's Edge"). While living in South America, she published the novels *Memorias de Leticia Valle* (1945; *Memoirs of Leticia Valle*) and *La sinrazón* (1960; "Without Reason"). *Barrio de Maravillas* (1976; *The Maravillas District*), *Acrópolis* (1984), and *Ciencias naturales* (1988; "Natural Sciences") together comprise a trilogy about the growth and maturation of two girls. Among her later writings are essays, poetry, autobiographical works, and short stories.

Chadwick \'chad-wik\, H. Munro, *in full* Hector Munro Chadwick (b. Oct. 22, 1870, Thornhill Lees, Yorkshire, Eng.—d. Jan. 2, 1947, Cambridge, Cambridgeshire)   English philologist and historian who helped develop an integral approach to Old English studies.

Chadwick attended Clare College, Cambridge, and went on to teach there for many years. He began his career as a classical philologist but soon turned to the history and literature of Britain in the early Middle Ages. His early books were *Studies in Anglo-Saxon Institutions* (1905) and *The Origin of the English Nation* (1907). In *The Heroic Age* (1912) Chadwick began to develop a comparative method of the study of literature. By applying this method to Greek and Germanic heroic poetry, he developed the concept of the "Heroic Age" as a stage in the growth of civilization. In *The Growth of Literature*,

3 vol. (1932–40), Chadwick applied his method to other literary traditions.

chain of being   see GREAT CHAIN OF BEING.

Chalkhill \'chȯk-ˌhil, 'chȯ-kil\, John (b. *c.* 1595, possibly at Chalkhill House, Kingsbury, Middlesex, Eng.—d. April 8, 1642, Westminster) English poet whose *Thealma and Clearchus* was published posthumously in 1683 by Izaak Walton. He was identified in the third edition of Walton's *Compleat Angler* as the author of two songs that appeared there from the first edition (1653).

Because little was known of Chalkhill's life, it was often speculated that he never existed save as a nom de plume for Walton or another writer, but in 1958 the mystery was solved with the discovery of distinctive autograph manuscripts. The manuscripts include a number of previously unknown poems.

Chalmers \'chä-mərz, 'chal-mərz\, Alexander (b. March 29, 1759, Aberdeen, Scot.—d. Dec. 10, 1834, London, Eng.) Scottish editor and biographer best known for his *General Biographical Dictionary* (1812–17), a 32-volume revision of a work first published in 11 volumes (1761). His *Glossary to Shakespeare* (1797) was followed by *The Works of the English Poets from Chaucer to Cowper* (1810), a revised and expanded version of Dr. Johnson's *Lives of the Poets* (1779–81).

A prolific editor, Chalmers published *The British Essayists: With Prefaces Historical and Biographical* in 45 volumes (1817), as well as the works of the Scottish poet and philosopher James Beattie, the novelist Henry Fielding, the historian Edward Gibbon, and others.

Chambered Nautilus, The Poem by Oliver Wendell HOLMES, first published in the February 1858 issue of *The Atlantic Monthly* in his "Breakfast-Table" column. Written in five seven-line stanzas, the poem later appeared in collections of poems by Holmes. The poem takes as its central metaphor the sea creature of the title, which constructs its shell in an ever-widening coil of chambers.

Chamberlain's Men \'chăm-bər-lin\, *also called* The Lord Chamberlain's Men. An English theatrical company, the most important company of players in Elizabethan and Jacobean England. William Shakespeare was intimately connected with the company for most of his professional career as a dramatist.

The company's early history is somewhat complicated. A company known as Hunsdon's Men, whose patron was Henry Carey, 1st Lord Hunsdon, is traceable to 1564–67. Hunsdon took office as Lord Chamberlain in 1585, and another company (The Lord Chamberlain's Men) under his patronage is traceable to 1590. Two years later the theaters closed because of plague; when they reopened in 1594, a strong Lord Chamberlain's company emerged. After their patron's death in 1596, the company came under the protection of his son, the 2nd Lord Hunsdon, who himself became Lord Chamberlain in 1597. The company was known as The Lord Chamberlain's Men until the accession of James I in March 1603, when, by letters patent, it was taken under royal patronage and henceforth known as the King's Men.

The records of performances given at court show that it was by far the most favored of the theatrical companies. Although the company frequently toured outside of London, its base remained in London, from 1599 to 1608 at the Globe Theatre. Shakespeare was the company's principal dramatist (he also acted with them), but works by Ben Jonson, Thomas Dekker, and the partnership of Francis Beaumont and John Fletcher were also presented. The company ceased to exist when, at the outbreak of English Civil Wars in 1642, the theaters were closed and remained so until the Restoration 18 years later.

Chambers \'chăm-bərz\, Ephraim (b. *c.* 1680, Kendal, Westmorland, Eng.—d. May 15, 1740, London) British encyclopedist whose work formed a basis for the 18th-century French Encyclopédistes. The first edition of his CYCLOPAEDIA appeared in 1728, and its success led to Chambers' election to the Royal Society. The *Encyclopédie* of Denis Diderot began as a French translation of Chambers' work, though it eventually went far beyond the *Cyclopaedia*.

Chamfort \shäⁿ-'fȯr\, Sébastien-Roch Nicolas (b. April 1740/41, Clermont, Fr.—d. April 13, 1794, Paris) Playwright famous for his wit, whose maxims became popular bywords during the French Revolution.

Chamfort's comedies *La Jeune Indienne* (produced 1764; "The Young Indian Girl") and *Le Marchand de Smyrne* (produced 1770; "The Merchant of Smyrna") and a tragedy, *Mustapha et Zéangir* (produced 1776), established his reputation. *Eloge de Molière* (1769) won him entry into the Académie Française, but he later attacked academies with his *Discours sur les Académies* (1791).

In 1795 he wrote the revolutionary *Pensées, maximes et anecdotes*. Chamfort collaborated with the Count de Mirabeau on the newspaper *Mercure de France* and became secretary to the radical Jacobin Club. Many of his sayings, such as "War to the châteaus, peace to the cottages," became famous. Later, shocked by the excesses of the Reign of Terror, Chamfort joined the Moderates. Threatened with prison, he attempted suicide, eventually dying of the wounds.

Chamisso \fȯn-shä-'mis-ō\, Adelbert von, *original name* Louis-Charles-Adélaïde Chamisso de Boncourt \də-bōⁿ-'kür\ (b. Jan. 30, 1781, Château de Boncourt, Champagne, Fr.—d. Aug. 21, 1838, Berlin, Prussia [now in Germany]) One of the most gifted lyricists of the Berlin Romanticists and best remembered for the Faust-like fairy tale *Peter Schlemihls wundersame Geschichte* (1814; *Peter Schlemihl's Remarkable Story*).

When he was nine, Chamisso's family escaped the terrors of the French Revolution by taking refuge in Berlin. Chamisso published his first works in German in the *Berliner Musenalmanach*, which he coedited. In 1804 he founded the *Nordsternbund*, a society of Berlin Romanticists. In 1814 Chamisso published the peculiar tale of Peter Schlemihl. The story of a man who sold his shadow to the devil, it allegorized Chamisso's own political fate as a man without a country.

Chamisso's early poetry—as, for example, the cycle of poems *Frauen-Liebe und Leben* ("Woman's Love and Life"), set to music by Robert Schumann—depicted simple emotions with a sentimental naïveté. His narrative ballads and poems, such as "Vergeltung" ("Reward") and "Salas y Gomez," sometimes inclined to bizarre and mournful subjects. Many of his later, more realistic poems were patterned after the political lyrics of the French poet Pierre-Jean de Béranger, whose works Chamisso translated in 1838. Chamisso is considered by many critics to be the forerunner of the political poets of the 1840s.

Champfleury \shäⁿ-flœ̄-'rē\, *pseudonym of* Jules-François-Félix Husson \hü-'sōⁿ\ (b. Sept. 17, 1821, Laon, Fr.—d. Dec. 6, 1889, Sèvres) French novelist and journalist, theoretician of the realist movement, which he analyzed in *Le Réalisme* (1857). Although his reputation has declined, he was an influential figure in his day.

After an interrupted education, Champfleury went to Paris and lived a bohemian existence in a literary group that included the poet Charles Baudelaire. One of his best-known works is *Chien-Caillou* (1847), the story of an unhappy love affair. His massive output also included a history of caricature.

Chan, Charlie \'chär-lē-'chan\ Fictional character, a Chinese-American detective employed by the police force of

Honolulu. Chan is the protagonist of six novels—*The House Without a Key* (1925), *The Chinese Parrot* (1926), *Behind That Curtain* (1928), *The Black Camel* (1929), *Charlie Chan Carries On* (1930), and *Keeper of the Keys* (1932)—by the American writer Earl Derr BIGGERS. The character was based on Chang Apana, a real Honolulu police detective.

Chancellor, Olive \'ăl-iv-'chans-ə-lər\   Fictional character, a feminist social reformer in THE BOSTONIANS by Henry James. A woman of discrimination, taste, and intelligence, Chancellor gets caught up in the cause of women's suffrage and is subsequently consumed by her desire for political change. She is much taken with Verena Tarrant, a beautiful and spellbinding orator who becomes her protégé. Her archrival for the soul of Verena is her own cousin, Basil Ransom, a quintessential Southern gentleman who desires nothing more than a beautiful wife and a mother for his children.

Chandler \'chand-lər\, Raymond (Thornton) (b. July 23, 1888, Chicago, Ill., U.S.—d. March 26, 1959, La Jolla, Calif.) American author of detective fiction, creator of the private detective Philip MARLOWE. Set in the Los Angeles area, Chandler's novels and short stories are esteemed (especially by European critics) as outstanding examples of regional writing.

Chandler fought in World War I. After the war he returned to California, where he eventually turned to writing for a living. His first published short story appeared in the "pulp" magazine *Black Mask* in 1933. From 1943 he was a Hollywood screenwriter; *Double Indemnity* (1944), *The Blue Dahlia* (1946), and *Strangers on a Train* (1951), the latter written in collaboration with Czenzi Ormonde, are his best-known film scripts.

Chandler completed seven novels, all with Philip Marlowe as hero: *The Big Sleep* (1939), *Farewell, My Lovely* (1940), *The High Window* (1942), *The Lady in the Lake* (1943), *The Little Sister* (1949), *The Long Good-Bye* (1953), and *Playback* (1958). Among his numerous short-story collections are *Five Murderers* (1944) and *The Midnight Raymond Chandler* (1971).

Chang Chün-hsiang   *see* ZHANG JUNXIANG.

changeling \'chănj-liŋ\, *also called* elf child.   In European folk tradition, a deformed or weak-witted offspring of fairies or elves substituted by them surreptitiously for a comely human child.

According to legend, the abducted human children are given to the devil or used to strengthen fairy stock. The return of the original child may be effected by making the changeling laugh or by torturing it; this latter belief was responsible for numerous cases of actual child abuse. In the *Medieval Chronicles* by Ralph of Coggeshall and in other sources, the fairies are said expressly to prey upon children who have not been baptized.

changga [Korean, song, singing]   *see* PYŎLGOK.

Chang T'ien-i   *see* ZHANG TIANYI.

Chang Tzu-p'ing   *see* ZHANG ZIPING.

chanson \shăⁿ-'sŏⁿ\ [French, song]   French art song of the Middle Ages and the Renaissance. The chanson before 1500 is preserved mostly in large manuscript collections.

Dating back to the 12th century, the monophonic chanson reached its greatest popularity with the trouvères in the 13th century, and it occurs as late as the lays of the composer and poet Guillaume de Machaut in the 14th century. Only the melodies survive. The monophonic chansons show the development of intricate musical-poetic forms deriving from the songs of the troubadours, who were slightly earlier counterparts of the trouvères. These forms were eventually simplified to become the three *formes fixes* ("fixed forms") of the accompanied chanson. *See also* BALLADE; RONDEAU; VIRELAY.

chanson à personnages \shăⁿ-sŏⁿ-à-per-sŏ-'năzh\ [French, literally, song with characters]   Medieval French song in the form of a dialogue, often between a husband and a wife, a knight and a shepherdess, or lovers parting at dawn. Specific forms of such chansons include the pastourelle and the aubade.

chanson de geste \shăⁿsŏⁿ-də-'zhest\, *plural* chansons de geste *same*\ [French, literally, song of heroic deeds]   Any of several Old French epic poems that form the core of the Charlemagne legends.

More than 80 chansons de geste have survived in manuscripts dating from the 12th to 15th centuries, but they deal chiefly with events of the 8th and 9th centuries during the reigns of Charlemagne and his successors. In general, the poems contain a core of historical truth overlain with legendary accretions. A few poems have authors' names, but most are anonymous.

Chansons de geste are composed in lines of 10 or 12 syllables grouped into *laisses* (irregular stanzas) based on assonance or, later, rhyme. The poems' lengths range from approximately 1,500 to more than 18,000 lines. The fictional background of the chansons is the struggle of Christian France against an idolatrous "Muslim" enemy. The emperor Charlemagne is portrayed as the champion of Christendom. He is surrounded by his court of Twelve Noble Peers, among whom are Roland, Oliver, OGIER the Dane, and Archbishop Turpin.

A subordinate cycle of 24 poems concerns GUILLAUME d'Orange, a loyal and long-suffering supporter of Charlemagne's weak son, Louis the Pious. Another cycle deals with the wars of such powerful barons as DOON de Mayence, Girart de Roussillon, Ogier the Dane, and Raoul de Cambrai.

The earlier chansons are heroic in spirit and theme. After the 13th century, elements of romance and courtly love came to be introduced, and the austere early poems were supplemented by *enfances* (youthful exploits) of the heroes and fictitious adventures of their ancestors and descendants.

The masterpiece and probably the earliest of the chansons de geste is the CHANSON DE ROLAND. Appearing at the threshold of French epic literature, *Roland* was the formative influence on the rest of the chansons de geste. The chansons, in turn, spread throughout Europe. They strongly influenced Spanish heroic poetry such as the mid-12th-century Spanish epic CANTAR DE MIO CID ("Song of the Cid"). In Italy stories about Orlando and Rinaldo (Roland and Oliver) formed the basis for the Renaissance epics *Orlando innamorato* (Matteo Boiardo; 1483) and *Orlando furioso* (Ludovico Ariosto; 1532). In the 13th century the German poet Wolfram von Eschenbach based his epic *Willehalm* on Guillaume d'Orange, and the chansons were recorded in prose in the Icelandic *Karlamagnús saga*. Charlemagne legends were long staple subjects of romance.

Chanson de Roland, La \lă-shăⁿ-'sŏⁿ-də-rō-'läⁿ\ ("The Song of Roland")   Old French epic poem written about 1100 that is probably the earliest and certainly the masterpiece of the form known as chanson de geste. The poem's probable author was a Norman poet, Turold (Turoldus), whose name is introduced in the last line of the poem. The song deals with the historical Battle of Roncesvalles (Roncevaux) in 778. Though the encounter was actually a skirmish against the Basques, the poem transforms Roncesvalles into a heroic battle against Saracens.

The composition of the poem is firm and coherent, the style direct, sober, and, on occasion, stark. Placed in the foreground is the personality clash between the recklessly courageous Roland and his more prudent friend Oliver, which is also a conflict between divergent conceptions of feudal loyalty.

The poem opens as Charlemagne, having conquered all of Spain except Saragossa, sends the knight Ganelon, Roland's stepfather, to negotiate peace terms. Angry because Roland proposed him for the dangerous task, Ganelon plots with the Saracens to achieve his stepson's destruction and, on his return, ensures that Roland will command the rear guard of the army when it withdraws from Spain. As the army crosses the Pyrenees, the rear guard is surrounded at the pass of Roncesvalles by an overwhelming Saracen force.

Roland rejects his friend Oliver's advice to blow his horn and summon help from Charlemagne. On Roland's refusal, the hopeless battle is joined, and the flower of Frankish knighthood is reduced to a handful of men. The horn is finally sounded, too late to save them, but in time for Charlemagne to avenge his heroic vassals. The poem ends with the trial and execution of Ganelon.

chanson de toile \shäⁿ-sōⁿ-də-'twäl\ Early form of French lyric poetry dating from the beginning of the 12th century. The poems consisted of short monorhyme stanzas with a refrain. The Old French phrase *chançon de toile* (literally, "linen song") alluded to songs sung over needlework.

chansonnier \shäⁿ-sən-'yā\ [French, a derivative of *chanson* song] **1.** A writer or singer of chansons; especially, a cabaret singer. **2.** A collection of songs or of verses for singing.

chantefable \shäⁿt-'fäbl, *Angl* -'fäb-lə\ [French, from Old French (Picard dialect) *cantefable*, literally, (it) sings (and it) narrates] A medieval tale of adventure told in alternating sections of sung verse and recited prose. The word itself was used—and perhaps coined—by the anonymous author of the 13th-century French work *Aucassin et Nicolette* in its concluding lines: "No cantefable prent fin" ("Our *chantefable* is drawing to a close"). It is the sole surviving example of the genre.

Chanticleer or **Chantecler** or **Chauntecleer** \'chan-ti-,klir, 'chän-\ A character in several medieval beast tales, in which human society is satirized through the actions of animals endowed with human characteristics. Most famous of these works is a 13th-century collection called *Roman de Renart*, whose hero is REYNARD the Fox. The *Roman* includes the story of Reynard and Chantecler, a cock, a tale soon afterward retold in German, Dutch, and English versions. In *The Canterbury Tales*, Geoffrey Chaucer took it as the basis for "The Nun's Priest's Tale." The character appeared in later works as well, such as Edmond Rostand's verse drama *Chantecler* (1910), which is set in a barnyard and features a boastful rooster.

chant royal \shäⁿ-rwä-'yäl\, *plural* chants royaux \shäⁿ-rwä-'yō\ [French, literally, royal song] A fixed form of verse, an elaboration of the ballade that was developed by French poets of the 13th to 15th centuries.

The chant royal is composed of five stanzas, identical in arrangement, of 11 lines each, and of an envoi (a short, fixed final stanza) of 5 lines. All the stanzas are written on the five rhymes exhibited in the first stanza, the entire poem, therefore, consisting of 60 lines in the course of which five rhymes are repeated. The rhyme scheme is *ababccddede*.

Because of its length and the rigidity of its form, the chant royal was more suitable than the ballade for solemn themes, such as the exploits of a noble hero or the praise of the Virgin Mary. Like the ballade, the chant royal had variations. As the *serventois*, for example, a poem in honor of the Virgin Mary, the chant royal early acquired, then lost, a refrain. Other variations on the chant royal were the *amoureuse* ("love poem"), the *sotte amoureuse* ("playful love poem"), and the *sotte chanson* ("comic poem").

In Old French, the most admired chants royaux are those of Clément Marot; his *Chant royal chrétien* was well known. The 17th-century fabulist Jean de La Fontaine was the last exponent of the chant royal before its eclipse.

Known only in French literature during its development, the chant royal was introduced into England by Sir Edmund Gosse in his poem "The Praise of Dionysus" (1877). Since then, it has been adapted by a number of English-language poets, but its solemn or religious tone is a thing of the past. It is now largely used for *vers de société* (urbane, ironic poetry).

Chaos \'kā-,äs\ In early Greek cosmology, either the primeval emptiness of the universe before things came into being or the abyss of Tartarus, the underworld. Both concepts occur in the *Theogony* of Hesiod. In his system, first there was Chaos, then Gaea and Eros (Earth and Desire). The offspring of Chaos were Erebus (Darkness) and Nyx (Night). Nyx begat Aether, the bright upper air, and Day. Nyx later begat dark and dreadful aspects of the universe (*e.g.*, Dreams, Death, Strife, and Famine). This tied in with the other early notion that saw in Chaos the darkness of the underworld.

In the later cosmologies Chaos generally designated the original state of things, however conceived. The modern meaning of the word is derived from Ovid, who saw Chaos as the original disordered and formless mass, from which the maker of the Cosmos produced the ordered universe. This concept of Chaos was applied to the interpretation of the creation story in Genesis 1 (to which it is not native) by the early church fathers.

Chao Shu-li *see* ZHAO SHULI.

chapbook \'chap-,bůk\ A small, inexpensive stitched book or pamphlet formerly sold by itinerant dealers, or chapmen, in western Europe and in North America. Most chapbooks were 5½ by 4¼ inches (14 by 11 cm) in size and were made up of four pages (or multiples of four), illustrated with woodcuts. They contained tales of popular heroes, legend and folklore, jests, reports of notorious crimes, ballads, almanacs, nursery rhymes, school lessons, farces, biblical tales, dream lore, and other popular matter. The texts were mostly crude and anonymous, but they formed the major part of secular reading and now serve as a guide to the manners and morals of their times.

Many of the earliest English and German chapbooks derived from French examples, which began to appear at the end of the 15th century. The *Volksbücher* (a type of chapbook) began to flourish in Germany in the mid-16th century. When religious and other more serious tracts appeared, and as publication of inexpensive magazines developed in the early 19th century, chapbooks lost popularity and went into eclipse. With the rebirth of the small press in the late 20th century and the resurgence of letterpress use in fine printing, chapbooks began to reappear in specialty bookstores.

Chapelain \shȧ-'plaⁿ\, Jean (b. Dec. 4, 1595, Paris, Fr.—d. Feb. 22, 1674, Paris) French literary critic and poet who attempted to apply empirical standards to literary criticism.

Chapelain's approach was a challenge to others of his day who appealed in doctrinaire fashion to classical Greek authorities. His critical views were advanced primarily in short articles and monographs and in his voluminous correspondence. Chapelain's own poetic works are considered mediocre. He was instrumental in founding the Académie Française and his prestige in literary circles was great.

Chaplin \'chap-lən\, Sid, *in full* Sidney (b. Sept. 20, 1916, Shildon, Durham, Eng.—d. Jan. 11, 1986, Newcastle-upon-Tyne, Northumberland) British novelist and short-story writer noted for his depictions of working-class life.

The son of a coal miner, Chaplin began working in the mines at age 15 and continued to do so while obtaining an education from the Workers' Educational Association of the University of Durham and the Fircroft College for Working Men, Birmingham.

The Leaping Lad (1946; rev. ed., 1970), a collection of short stories about the Durham mining community, established Chaplin as a talented regional writer. Chaplin's subsequent works include the novels *The Thin Seam* (1950), *The Day of the Sardine* (1961), *The Watchers and the Watched* (1962), and *The Mines of Alabaster* (1971), and the short-story collections *On Christmas Day in the Morning* (1979) and *The Bachelor Uncle* (1980).

Chapman \'chap-mən \, George (b. 1559?, Hitchin, Hertfordshire, Eng.—d. May 12, 1634, London)   English poet and dramatist whose translation of Homer long remained the standard English version.

Chapman attended the University of Oxford but took no degree. His first work was *The Shadow of Night . . . Two Poeticall Hymnes* (1594), followed in 1595 by *Ovids Banquet of Sence*. The first books of his translation of the *Iliad* appeared in 1598. It was completed in 1611, and his version of the *Odyssey* appeared in 1616.

Euthymiae Raptus; or the Teares of Peace (1609) is Chapman's major poem, but his verse is not well known in the 20th century. Of his dramatic works, about a dozen plays survive, chief of which are his tragedies *Bussy d'Ambois* (1607), *The Conspiracie, and Tragedie of Charles Duke of Byron . . .* (1608), and *The Widdowes Teares* (1612).

Chapman \'chap-mən \, John Jay (b. March 2, 1862, New York, N.Y., U.S.—d. Nov. 4, 1933, Poughkeepsie, N.Y.) American poet, dramatist, and critic who attacked the get-rich-quick morality of the post-Civil War "Gilded Age."

Chapman attended Harvard Law School and practiced law for several years. At the same time, he became editor and publisher of the periodical *The Political Nursery* (1897–1901). His two books *Causes and Consequences* (1898) and *Practical Agitation* (1900) stressed his belief that individuals should take a moral stand on issues troubling the nation. His play *The Treason and Death of Benedict Arnold* appeared in 1910. In 1912, on the first anniversary of a lynching in Coatesville, Pa., Chapman made a speech, burning with indignation, that became a classic and was reprinted in his book of essays *Memories and Milestones* (1915).

Other works include a biography of William Lloyd Garrison (1913), collected *Songs and Poems* (1919), and volumes of criticism such as *Emerson, and Other Essays* (1898), *Greek Genius, and Other Essays* (1915), and *A Glance Toward Shakespeare* (1922).

Char \'shär \, René (b. June 14, 1907, L'Isle-sur-la-Sorgue, Fr.—d. Feb. 19, 1988, Paris)   French poet who began as a Surrealist and later wrote economical verse with moralistic overtones.

Char lived in Paris in the late 1920s, where he became friends with Surrealist writers and wrote poems about his native Provence. His most important early book of verse was *Le Marteau sans maître* (1934; "The Hammer Without a Master"). During World War II Char led a Resistance unit in the French Alps. After the war he published some of his finest poems in the collections *Seuls demeurent* (1945) and *Feuillets d'Hypnos* (1946; "Leaves of Hypnos"). The latter work, his poetic journal of the war years, reflects his anger at the brutality of war. Char's subsequent volumes include *Les Matinaux* (1950; "The Early Risers"), *Recherche de la base et du sommet* (1955; "Search for the Base and the Summit"), and *Commune présence* (1964; "Common Presence"). His *Oeuvres complètes* ("Complete Works") was published in 1983.

character \'kar-ik-tər \ [Greek *charaktḗr* stamp, mark, characteristic, character]   **1.** A descriptive, often satiric analysis (usually in the form of a short literary sketch) of a human virtue or vice or of a general type of human character. In 17th-century English and French literature, the quality of a particular place or thing may also be analyzed. A representative human (such as a busybody, an old man, a country bumpkin) usually is made to stand for the trait, quality, or type. *See also* CHARACTER WRITER.   **2.** Personality as represented or realized in fiction or drama.   **3.** One of the persons of a drama or novel.   **4.** Characterization, especially in fiction or drama.

characterization \,kar-ik-tə-rə-'zā-shən, -,rī- \   The representation in fiction or drama of human character or personality.

character study   **1.** Analysis or portrayal in literature of the traits of character of an individual.   **2.** A brief narrative or sketch devoted primarily to the examination of character.

character writer   Any of the writers who produced a type of character sketch that was popular in 17th-century England and France.

Their writings stemmed from a series of character sketches produced by the Greek philosopher and teacher Theophrastus (fl. *c.* 372 BC). These sketches may have been part of a larger work and probably were written with the intention of instructing and amusing his students of rhetoric. Theophrastus' technique was to define an undesirable personal quality (such as vanity or stinginess) and then to describe the characteristic speech and behavior of the person who exemplified it. His work was introduced to Europe during the Renaissance in an edition of 1529; admiring his wit and insight into human failings, a number of contemporary writers imitated his example. They included, in France, Jean de La Bruyère, and, in England, Joseph Hall, Sir Thomas Overbury, John Earle, and Samuel Butler.

charactonym \'kar-ik-tə-,nim \ [*charact*er + -*onym* (as in *toponym*)]   A name of a fictional character that suggests a distinctive trait of that character. Examples of charactonyms include Mistress Quickly and Caspar Milquetoast.

Charbonneau \shär-bȯ-'nō \, Jean (b. 1875, Montreal, Que., Can.—d. Oct. 25, 1960, Saint-Eustache)   French-Canadian poet who was the primary force behind the founding of the Montreal Literary School (1895), a group of Symbolists and Aesthetes who reacted against the traditional Canadian themes of patriotism and local color and, following the Parnassians, espoused the principle of art for art's sake. Charbonneau later wrote the only history of the school, *L'École littéraire de Montréal* (1935; "The Literary School of Montreal"). In 1912 Charbonneau wrote *Les Blessures* ("The Wounds"), the first of several volumes of poetry that dealt primarily with philosophical speculation and myth. *Sur la borne pensive* (1952; "On the Bounds of Thought") is characteristic of his mature style.

Charbonneau \shär-bȯ-'nō \, Robert (b. Feb. 3, 1911, Montreal, Que., Can.—d. June 26, 1967, Sainte-Jovite, Que.) French Canadian novelist and literary critic, well known for promoting the autonomy of Quebec literature.

During his teens Charbonneau joined Jeune Canada ("Young Canada"), a French nationalist organization, and in 1934 he cofounded *La Relève* (later called *La Nouvelle Relève*, "The New Relief"), a nationalist review of art, literature, and philosophy. Over the years, he also worked as a journalist on various French journals, newspapers, and Radio-Canada.

Charbonneau wrote five novels, the most noted being his first, *Ils posséderont la terre* (1941; "They Shall Possess the Earth"). He also published a collection of poems, *Petits poèmes retrouvés* (1945; "Little Poems Rediscovered"), critical essays and lectures, and radio plays.

Charge of the Light Brigade, The   A poem by Alfred, Lord TENNYSON, published in 1855. The poem commemorates the heroism of a brigade of British soldiers at the Battle of Balaklava (1854) in the Crimea. The 600 troops followed ambiguous orders to charge a heavily defended position though they knew they had little chance of survival.

Chariton \\'kar-i-ˌtän\\ (fl. not later than 2nd century AD, Aphrodisias, Caria, Asia Minor [now in southwestern Turkey]) Greek novelist, author of *Chaereas and Callirhoë*, the earliest fully extant romantic novel in Western literature. The complex but clearly narrated plot concerns a husband and wife whose love is tested by a series of fast-moving, perilous adventures in Sicily, Persia, and Egypt but ends in eventual happiness. Historical persons are introduced as characters but are treated with free invention.

Charles, Nick and Nora \\'nik-'chärlz ... 'nȯr-ə\\ Fictional characters, a husband-and-wife detective team, created by Dashiell Hammett in his mystery novel THE THIN MAN but probably best known from a popular series (1934–47) of six witty comedy-mystery films starring William Powell and Myrna Loy.

Nick and Nora Charles are an urbane, happily married couple who dote on their Airedale terrier, Asta. A former police detective, Nick has retired and the couple live quite well on Nora's inheritance. The sophisticated banter and the personal chemistry between the couple made the solving of crime somewhat secondary.

Charlotte's Web \\'shär-lət\\ Children's novel by E.B. WHITE, published in 1952, with illustrations by Garth Williams. One of the classics of children's literature, this widely read tale takes place on a farm in Maine and concerns a pig named Wilbur and his devoted friend Charlotte, the spider who manages to save his life by writing words in her web.

Charlus, Baron de \\də-shär-'lüe, -'lües\\ Fictional character, licentious homosexual in the novel series REMEMBRANCE OF THINGS PAST by Marcel Proust. First introduced in the second novel, *Within a Budding Grove* (1919), Baron Palamède de Charlus is a member of the influential Guermantes family. A symbol of decadent aristocracy, the baron has a cultured exterior that hides an inner depravity. His homosexuality both attracts and repels the narrator, Marcel. In the last book Baron de Charlus has become senile.

charm \\'chärm\\ [Old French *charme,* from Latin *carmen* ritual utterance, incantation, song] A practice or expression believed to have magic power, similar to an incantation or a spell. Charms are among the earliest examples of written literature. Among the charms written in Old English are those against a dwarf and against the theft of cattle.

Charon \\'kar-ən, -ˌän\\ In Greek mythology, the son of Erebus and Nyx (Night), whose duty it was to ferry over the Rivers Styx and Acheron those souls of the deceased who had received the rites of burial. In payment he received the coin that was placed in the mouth of the corpse. In Etruscan he was called Charun and appeared as a death demon, armed with a hammer. Eventually he came to be regarded as the image of death and of the world below. As such he survives as Charos, or Charontas, the angel of death in modern Greek folklore.

Charrière \\shär-'yer\\, Isabelle de, *original name* Isabella Agneta Elisabeth van Tuyll van Serooskerken \\vän-'ser-ūs-ˌkerk-ən\\, *bynames* Belle van Zuylen, Belle de Charrière, Zélide, Abbé de la Tour (b. Oct. 20, 1740, Zuilen, near Utrecht, Neth.—d. Dec. 27, 1805, Colombier, Switz.) Swiss novelist especially noted for her powerful and eloquent epistolary novels.

Influenced by Denis Diderot and Jean-Jacques Rousseau, Charrière expressed views critical of aristocratic privilege,

moral conventions (*Trois femmes,* 1797; "Three Women"), religious orthodoxy, and poverty (*Lettres trouvées sous la neige,* 1794; "Letters Found on the Snow"). She carried on a vast correspondence and wrote plays and music in addition to essays. She is best known, however, for her novels. The most important of these are *Lettres écrites de Lausanne* (1785; "Letters Written from Lausanne") and *Caliste, ou suite de lettres écrites de Lausanne* (1787; "Caliste, or the Sequel to Letters Written from Lausanne").

Charterhouse of Parma, The \\'pär-mə\\ Novel by STENDHAL, published in French as *La Chartreuse de Parme* in 1839. It is generally considered one of Stendhal's masterpieces, second only to *The Red and the Black,* and is remarkable for its highly sophisticated rendering of human psychology and its subtly drawn portraits.

The novel is set mainly in the court of Parma, Italy, in the early 19th century. It follows the fortunes of Fabrice del Dongo, a young aristocrat and ardent admirer of Napoleon. He fights at Waterloo and returns to Parma, where he joins the church for worldly advantage. In the course of the story he kills a rival, fathers a child, and eventually retires to the Carthusian monastery, or charterhouse, of Parma, where he dies.

Charteris \\'chär-tər-is\\, Leslie, *original name* Leslie Charles Bowyer Yin \\'yin\\ (b. May 12, 1907, Singapore—d. April 15, 1993, Windsor, Eng.) Author of highly popular mystery-adventure novels and creator of Simon Templar, better known as "the Saint" and sometimes called the "Robin Hood of modern crime."

Charteris briefly attended King's College, Cambridge, then worked as a merchant seaman. A U.S. resident from 1932, he was employed from 1933 as a Hollywood screenwriter, preparing scripts for eight "Saint" movies and several other films. From 1928 he published some 50 novels and collections of stories about "the Saint"; translations exist in at least 15 languages.

Chartier \\shär-'tyä\\, Alain (b. *c.* 1385, Bayeux, Normandy, Fr.—d. *c.* 1433, Avignon, Provence?) French poet and political writer whose didactic, elegant, and Latinate style was regarded as a model by succeeding generations of poets and prose writers.

Educated at the University of Paris, Chartier entered the royal service, acting as secretary and notary to both Charles VI and the dauphin, later Charles VII. His earliest-known poem, the *Livre des quatre dames* (1415 or 1416), is a discussion between four ladies who have lost their lovers at the Battle of Agincourt. The same dialogue technique is used in the prose *Quadrilogue invectif,* written in 1422.

Chartier's poems include *La Belle Dame sans merci, Le Lay de paix,* and *Le Bréviaire des nobles,* the first of which, a tale of unrequited love, is the best known and was translated into English in the 15th century.

Chartier \\shär-'tyä\\, Émile-Auguste, *pseudonym* Alain \\à-'leⁿ\\ (b. March 3, 1868, Mortagne, Fr.—d. June 2, 1951, Le Vésinet, near Paris) French philosopher whose work profoundly influenced several generations of readers.

While teaching in Rouen, Chartier began contributing articles to a newspaper under the general heading *Propos d'un Normand.* The literary quality of these articles soon attracted attention. In 1908 the first of a series of collections of his articles was published. Chartier enlisted in the army in World War I and wrote several books, including *Mars, ou la guerre jugée* (1921; *Mars; or, The Truth About War*), on the front line or in the dugouts.

His most important publications after the war were *Les Idées et les âges* (1927; "Ideas and Ages"), *Entretiens au bord de la mer* (1931; "Discussions by the Sea"), *Idées* (1932), *Les Dieux* (1934; "The Gods"), *Histoire de mes pensées* (1936; "Story of My Thoughts"), and *Les Aventures de coeur* (1945; "Adventures of the Heart"). In 1951 he became the first recipient of the Grand Prix National de Littérature.

Charybdis \kə-'rib-dis\ *see* SCYLLA AND CHARYBDIS.

Chase \'chās\, Mary Ellen (b. Feb. 24, 1887, Blue Hill, Maine, U.S.—d. July 28, 1973, Northampton, Mass.) American scholar and writer whose novels are largely concerned with the Maine seacoast and its inhabitants.

Three autobiographical works describe Chase's childhood in Maine: *A Goodly Heritage* (1932), *A Goodly Fellowship* (1939), and *The White Gate: Adventures in the Imagination of a Child* (1954). She obtained a Ph.D. in English from the University of Minnesota and also studied in England, which she wrote of in a book of essays, *This England* (1936).

Chase began her writing career with books for children such as *The Girl from the Big Horn Country* (1916) and *Mary Christmas* (1926). Her first novel, *Uplands* (1927), was followed by two of her most powerful novels: *Mary Peters* (1934) and *Silas Crockett* (1935). *Dawn in Lyonesse* (1938) is a retelling of the Tristan and Isolde story. She also wrote literary criticism, biblical studies, and essays.

chase literature Literature in which suspense is created by the action of pursuit.

chaser \'chā-sər\ A literary work or portion of a literary work that is of a light or mollifying nature in comparison with that which it follows or accompanies. The metaphor may stem from the practice of following the consumption of strong alcoholic drink with consumption of a less potent beverage or, occasionally, with food.

Chastellain or **Chastelain** \shȧs-tȧ-'leⁿ, shȧt-'leⁿ\, Georges (b. *c.* 1405 or *c.* 1415, Aalst, Brabant [now in Belgium]—d. 1475, Valenciennes, Burgundian Hainaut [now in France]) Burgundian chronicler and one of the leading court poets.

Chastellain served Philip the Good, Duke of Burgundy, as a soldier and later entered Philip's household. In 1455 he was appointed Burgundian historiographer. Only about one-third of his *Chronique des ducs de Bourgogne* has survived. The chronicle extends, with gaps, from 1419 to 1474. Its interest lies in its description and factual information and in its shrewd assessment of contemporary figures and motives. Chastellain's other work consists of political pieces, formal poems, ballades, works addressed to fellow writers, and didactic works and plays.

chasten \'chā-sən\ To prune a work of art or literature of excess, pretense, or falsity; to refine.

chastushka \chʸi-'stüsh-kə\ [Russian, a derivative of *chastyĭ* frequent, in quick succession; probably originally referring to the refrain of a song] A rhymed folk verse usually composed of four lines. The chastushka is traditional in form but often has political or topical content.

Chateaubriand \shȧ-tō-brē-'äⁿ\, François-Auguste-René, Viscount (vicomte) de (b. Sept. 4, 1768, Saint-Malo, Fr.—d. July 4, 1848, Paris) French author and diplomat, one of his country's first Romantic writers. He was the preeminent literary figure in the France of his day and had a profound influence on youth.

At the beginning of the French Revolution, Chateaubriand, a cavalry officer, refused to join the Royalists and sailed for the United States, where he traveled with fur traders and had firsthand acquaintance with Indians. After learning of Louis XVI's flight in June 1791, Chateaubriand returned to France, where he joined the Royalist army. Wounded at the siege of Thionville, he was discharged. He went to England in 1793

where he wrote *Essai sur les révolutions* (1797), an emotional survey of world history in which he drew parallels between ancient and modern revolutions.

In 1800 Chateaubriand returned to Paris, where he worked as a freelance journalist. A fragment of an unfinished Indian epic appeared as ATALA (1801) and was immediately successful. His treatise extolling Christianity, *Le Génie du christianisme* (1802; THE GENIUS OF CHRISTIANITY), won favor both with the Royalists and with Napoleon, who was restoring Roman Catholicism as the state religion.

Chateaubriand was first secretary to the embassy at Rome in 1803 and 1804. He spent the next years in literary work—including creation of the novel RENÉ (1805)—and in many love affairs. In 1811 he was elected to the Académie Française, and in 1815 he was created a viscount and a member of the House of Peers. His *Mémoires d'outre-tombe* (1849–50; THE MEMOIRS OF CHATEAUBRIAND), written for posthumous publication, are perhaps his most lasting monument.

Châtiments, Les \lä-shȧ-tē-'mäⁿ\ ("The Punishments") Collection of poems by Victor HUGO, published in 1853 and expanded in 1870. The book is divided into seven sections containing more than 100 odes, popular songs, narrative poems, and anthems in which Hugo denounces injustice and tyranny and rails against Louis-Napoleon (Napoleon III) and the abuses of the Second Empire. Composed in Brussels and Jersey during Hugo's first year of voluntary exile from France, the work is suffused with his horror and indignation, but ends with his commitment to progress and peace and his belief in freedom and brotherhood.

Chatterjee \'chat-ər-,jē\, Bankim Chandra, *original surname* Ҫaṭṭopādhyāy \,chȧṭ-tō-'päth-,yī\ (b. June 26/27, 1838, near Naihati, Bengal, India—d. April 8, 1894, Calcutta) Writer considered the greatest novelist of Bengali literature.

Chatterjee graduated from the University of Calcutta and served as a deputy magistrate in the Indian civil service for many years. In 1858 he published a volume of poems entitled *Lalita O Manas*. For a while he wrote in English, and his novel *Rajmohan's Wife* appeared serially in *Indian Field* in 1864. His first notable Bengali work was the novel *Durgeśnandinī* (1865; "Daughter of the Lord of the Fort"), and with it the Bengali novel was established. He followed it with *Kapālkuṇḍalā* (1866) and *Mṛṇālinī* (1869). *Baṅgadarśan*, Chatterjee's epoch-making newspaper, commenced publication in 1872, and in it some of his later novels were serialized. Among the novels that followed were *Biṣabṛkṣa* (1873; "The Poison Tree"); *Yugalāṅgurīya* (1874; "The Two Rings"); *Rajanī* (1877); *Kṛṣṇakānter Uil* (1878; "The Will of Krishnakanta"), which the author considered his greatest novel; *Rājsiṃha* (1881); *Ānandamaṭh* (1882; "Abode of Bliss"); and *Sītārām* (1887).

Chatterjee's novels are considered structurally faulty; however, to his contemporaries his voice was that of a prophet, and his valiant Hindu heroes aroused their patriotism and pride of race. The song "Bande Mātaram" ("Hail to thee, Mother")—from his novel *Ānandamaṭh*—later became the *mantra* ("hymn") and slogan of Hindu India in its struggle for independence.

Chatterton \'chat-ər-tən, shȧ-ter-'tôⁿ\ French prose drama in three acts by Alfred de VIGNY, performed and published in 1835. Considered Vigny's masterpiece, the play depicts a fictitious episode in the life of the 18th-century English poet Thomas Chatterton. It glorifies the noble anguish of a misunderstood artist and condemns a materialistic society in which there is no place for "nonproductive" art and artists.

Chatterton \'chat-ər-tən\, Thomas (b. Nov. 20, 1752, Bristol, Gloucestershire, Eng.—d. Aug. 24, 1770, London) Chief poet of the 18th-century "Gothic" literary revival and precursor of the Romantic movement.

At the age of 11, Chatterton inscribed an old parchment with a pastoral eclogue, "Elinoure and Juga," supposedly of the 15th century, that deceived its readers. Thereafter, he wrote other such poems, supposedly the works of a 15th-century monk of Bristol, Thomas Rowley, a fictitious character created by Chatterton. With all their shortcomings, these poems marked him as a poet of genius and an early Romantic pioneer.

In 1767 Chatterton was apprenticed to a Bristol attorney but spent most of his time on his own writing. By a mock suicide threat ("The Last Will and Testament of me, Thomas Chatterton of Bristol"), he forced his employer to release him from his contract and he set out for London. A lively burletta (comic opera), *The Revenge*, brought some money, but the death of a prospective patron quenched Chatterton's hopes. Though literally starving, he refused the food of friends and, on the night of Aug. 24, 1770, took arsenic in his Holborn garret and died. The aftermath was fame. He was praised and eulogized by, among others, Samuel Taylor Coleridge, William Wordsworth, John Keats, and Lord Byron.

Chatwin \ˈchat-win\, Bruce, *in full* Charles Bruce Chatwin (b. May 13, 1940, Sheffield, Yorkshire, Eng.—d. Jan 18, 1989, Nice, Fr.)   British writer who won international acclaim for books based on his nomadic life.

Chatwin studied archaeology at the University of Edinburgh. He worked for a time as a traveling correspondent for *The Sunday Times* (London). The book, *In Patagonia* (1977), based on his own travels, won awards in Britain and the United States. *The Viceroy of Ouidah* (1980; filmed as *Cobra Verde*, 1987) is a fictionalized biography of a Brazilian slave trader. His first novel, *On the Black Hill* (1982; film, 1988), won the Whitbread literary award. *The Songlines* (1987), Chatwin's most commercially successful work, was both a study of Australian Aboriginal creation myths and a philosophical reverie on the nature of nomads. His last novel was *Utz* (1988). *What Am I Doing Here?*, a collection of essays, was published posthumously.

Chaucer \ˈchȯ-sər\, Geoffrey (b. *c.* 1342/43, London?, Eng.—d. Oct. 25, 1400, London)   The outstanding English poet before William Shakespeare whose THE CANTERBURY TALES ranks as one of the greatest poetic works in English.

Chaucer was born into a middle-class family. Little is known of his education, but his works reveal a close familiarity with the important books of his time and of antiquity. In addition to English, he was doubtless fluent in French, and he had knowledge of Latin and Italian as well. In 1357 Chaucer was in the service of the Countess of Ulster and by 1359 in the army in France with Edward III, who ransomed him after he was captured at the siege of Reims. In 1367 he was appointed a court official, and for most of his lifetime he held a succession of diplomatic and government positions.

Chaucer's first important poem, *Book of the Duchesse* (1369/70), was a dream-vision elegy for Blanche, Duchess of Lancaster and the first wife of John of Gaunt, who had died of the plague. In the next decade Chaucer traveled in Flanders, France, and Italy on diplomatic missions and was appointed comptroller of the customs. His most important work of the next decade was the narrative poem *Hous of Fame*, also in dream-vision form. During the period 1380–90 he wrote works of a high order, including the love-vision poem THE PARLEMENT OF FOULES; a prose translation of Boethius' *Consolation of Philosophy*; his first great mature work, the romance TROILUS AND CRISEYDE; and his final dream-vision, LEGEND OF GOOD WOMEN.

Chaucer formed a close relationship with John of Gaunt's son the Earl of Derby, later Henry IV, during the 1390s, when

Portrait miniature painted after the poet's death (Harley Ms. 4866)

he also began his best-known work, the unfinished *The Canterbury Tales*. In December 1399 Chaucer leased a house in the garden of Westminster Abbey. He died within a year and was buried in the abbey, at the time a signal honor for a commoner.

Chayefsky \chä-ˈyef-skē\, Paddy, *original name* Sidney Chayefsky (b. Jan. 29, 1923, New York, N.Y., U.S.—d. Aug. 1, 1981, New York City)   American playwright and screenwriter.

Chayefsky worked as a printer's apprentice, then began writing radio adaptations and mystery dramas for television series. His first full-length television play was *Holiday Song* (1952). His greatest success was *Marty* (1953; film, 1955). Two other successful television plays were made into motion pictures—*The Bachelor Party* (1954; film, 1957) and *The Catered Affair* (1955; film, 1956). The television drama, *The Middle of the Night* (1954), was Chayefsky's first stage play (1956). His other stage plays include *The Tenth Man* (1959), *Gideon* (1961), *The Passion of Josef D.* (1964), and *The Latent Heterosexual* (published 1967; performed 1968). He also wrote film scripts and scenarios.

Cheever \ˈchē-vər\, John (b. May 27, 1912, Quincy, Mass., U.S.—d. June 18, 1982, Ossining, N.Y.)   American short-story writer and novelist whose work described, often through fantasy and ironic comedy, the life, manners, and morals of middle-class, suburban America. He is noted for his clear and elegant prose and his careful fashioning of incidents and anecdotes.

A master of the short story, Cheever worked from "the interrupted event," which he considered the prime source of short stories. His first published story appeared in *The New Republic* in 1930. His works also appeared in *The New Yorker*, *Collier's*, *Story*, and *The Atlantic*. Cheever's first collection of short stories, *The Way Some People Live* (1943), was followed by many others, including *The Enormous Radio and Other*

Archive Photos

Stories (1953) and *The Brigadier and the Golf Widow* (1964). The latter collection included the much anthologized story THE SWIMMER. *The Stories of John Cheever* (1978) won the Pulitzer Prize for fiction. Cheever's first novel, THE WAPSHOT CHRONICLE (1957), earned him the National Book Award. Later novels include *The Wapshot Scandal* (1964), *Falconer* (1977), and *Oh What a Paradise It Seems* (1982). *The Letters of John Cheever*, edited by his son Benjamin Cheever, was published in 1988, and *The Journals of John Cheever* in 1991.

chef d'oeuvre \shä-'dȫvr *with r as a uvular trill*, *Angl* -'dɔrv \, *plural* chefs d'oeuvre *same*\ [French *chef-d'oeuvre*, literally, leading work]   A masterpiece, especially in literature or art.

Chekhov \'chek̲-əf, *Angl* 'chek-ȯf, -ȯv \, Anton (Pavlovich) (b. Jan. 17 [Jan. 29, New Style], 1860, Taganrog, Russia—d. July 1/2 [July 14/15], 1904, Badenweiler, Ger.)   Russian playwright and master of the modern short story.

Chekhov graduated from Moscow University's medical faculty in 1884. By this time he was already the economic mainstay of his family through his earnings as a freelance journalist and pseudonymous writer of short comic sketches, a form he perfected. In 1888 the long story "Step" ("The Steppe") appeared in *Severny vestnik* ("Northern Herald"), the first time his work had been published by a leading literary review. Chekhov also wrote several profoundly tragic studies at this time, the most notable of which was "Skuchnaya istoriya" (1889; "A Dreary Story"), a penetrating study into the mind of an elderly and dying professor of medicine.

In early 1890 Chekhov journeyed to a remote island, Sakhalin, the site of an imperial Russian penal settlement. On his return he published *Ostrov Sakhalin* (1893–94; *The Island of Sakhalin*), which remains a classic of Russian penology. During the years just before and after his Sakhalin expedition, Chekhov continued his experiments as a dramatist. His *Leshy* (1889;

Library of Congress

The Wood-Demon) is a four-act play that he converted—largely by cutting—into *Dyadya Vanya* (1897; UNCLE VANYA), one of his greatest stage masterpieces. Other dramas of the period include several of the one-act farces known as vaudevilles, among them *Medved* (1888; *The Bear*), *Predlozheniye* (1889; *The Proposal*), *Svadba* (1889; *The Wedding*), and *Yubiley* (1891; *The Anniversary*).

In 1892 Chekhov bought a country estate in the village of Melikhovo. During the Melikhovo period Chekhov wrote his most effective short stories, including "Sosedi" (1892; "Neighbors"), "Chorny monakh" (1894; THE BLACK MONK), "Ubiystvo" (1895; "The Murder"), and "Ariadna" (1895; "Ariadne"). "Muzhiki" (1897; "Peasants") is a short sequence of brilliant sketches that created more stir in Russia than any other single work of Chekhov's, partly owing to his unsentimental view of the Russian peasantry. Though he had been attracted to Tolstoyan principles, such as the simple life and nonresistance to evil, Chekhov came to reject these doctrines. He illustrated his changed view in several stories, including "Palata No. 6" (1892; WARD NUMBER SIX). *Chayka* (1897; revised edition, 1904; THE SEAGULL) is Chekhov's only dramatic work dating with certainty from the Melikhovo period. His last two plays—*Tri sestry* (1901; THREE SISTERS) and *Vishnyovy sad* (1904; THE CHERRY ORCHARD)—were both written for the Moscow Art Theater.

Though already celebrated by the Russian literary public at the time of his death, Chekhov did not become internationally famous until the years after World War I, by which time his works had begun to be read in English translation.

Chelkash \chil-'kȧsh \   Short story by Maksim GORKY, published in Russian in 1895 in the St. Petersburg journal *Russkoye bogatstvo* ("Wealth of Russia"). Like many of Gorky's works, it is a profile of a free-spirited tramp, in this case a tough, brazen thief who prowls the Black Sea port of Odessa. Through his complex relationship with a meek, avaricious peasant boy named Gavrila, whom he uses as an accomplice in a robbery, his own nature is revealed.

Cheng Chen-to   *see* ZHENG ZHENDUO.

Chénier \shän-'yā \, André(-Marie) de (b. Oct. 30, 1762, Constantinople [now Istanbul, Tur.]—d. July 25, 1794, Paris, Fr.)   Poet and political journalist, generally considered the greatest French poet of the 18th century.

Chénier was educated at the Collège de Navarre, and, after an unsuccessful attempt at a military career, he accepted a post in the French embassy in London. The Revolutionary upheavals in France in 1789 brought him back to Paris, where he began to take an active part in political journalism, attacking the extremes both of monarchist reaction and of Revolutionary terror. In March 1794 he was arrested and imprisoned at Saint-Lazare, and four months later he was guillotined. In his works of the Revolutionary period, including a group of poems that he smuggled out of prison in a laundry basket, he passionately defended the ideals of liberty and justice. The *Iambes*, the last of which dates from very shortly before his execution, are a moving testimonial to the human spirit in the face of persecution.

When the first collected edition of Chénier's poetry appeared in 1819, it was universally acclaimed. The legend of his political struggle and heroic death was celebrated in Chateaubriand's work *Le Génie du christianisme* (1802; "The Genius of Christianity"), Charles-Augustin Sainte-Beuve's *Joseph Delorme* (1829), and Alfred de Vigny's *Stello* (1832).

Chénier \shän-'yā \, Marie-Joseph(-Blaise) de (b. April 28, 1764, Constantinople [now Istanbul, Tur.]—d. Jan. 10, 1811, Paris, Fr.)   Poet, dramatist, politician, and supporter of the French Revolution from its early stages.

The brother of the poet André de Chénier, Marie-Joseph attended the Collège de Navarre, then joined the regiment of Montmorency for two years. A member of the Convention and the Council of Five Hundred, he wrote patriotic songs and hymns such as the "Chant du départ" and the "Hymne à la liberté."

His tragedies, based on historical subjects, served as vehicles for his political ideals. They include *Charles IX* (1789) and *Henri VIII* (1791). After he expressed his disapproval of the Reign of Terror in *Caius Gracchus* (1792) and *Fénelon* (1793), his tragedies were censored. He was made a member of the Académie Française in 1803.

Chéri \shā-'rē\ Novel by COLETTE, published in 1920, about a love affair between Léa, a still-beautiful 49-year-old courtesan, and Chéri, a handsome but selfish young man 30 years her junior. It is an exquisite analysis of not only May-December romance but also age and sexuality. Colette also wrote a sequel, *La Fin de Chéri* (1926; *The Last of Chéri*).

Chernikhovsky *see* TCHERNICHOWSKY.

Cherry Orchard, The Drama in four acts written by Anton CHEKHOV as *Vishnyovy sad*. Chekhov's final play, it was first performed and published in 1904. Though Chekhov insisted that the play was "a comedy, in places even a farce," playgoers and readers often find a touch of tragedy in the decline of the charming Ranevskaya family.

Madame Ranevskaya, who has spent five years in Paris to escape grief over her young son's death, returns to her home in Russia ridden with debt. She is obliged to decide how to dispose of her family's estate, with its beautiful and famous cherry orchard. The coarse but wealthy merchant Ermolai Lopakhin suggests that Mme Ranevskaya develop the land on which the orchard sits. Eventually Lopakhin purchases the estate and proceeds with his plans for a housing development. As the unhappy Ranevskayas leave the estate, the sound of saws can be heard in the orchard.

Cheshire Cat \'chesh-ər\ Fictional character, a cat notable for its broad grin and its ability to disappear and reappear at will, in ALICE'S ADVENTURES IN WONDERLAND by Lewis Carroll. The phrase "grin like a Cheshire cat" predates Carroll's story, and its origin remains mysterious.

Chesnut \'ches-,nət\, Mary Boykin Miller (b. March 31, 1823, Pleasant Hill, S.C., U.S.—d. Nov. 22, 1886, Camden, S.C.) Author of *A Diary from Dixie*, an insightful view of Southern life and leadership during the American Civil War.

The daughter of a prominent South Carolina political leader, in 1840 Miller married James Chesnut, Jr., who later served as a U.S. senator from South Carolina until he resigned to take an important role in the secession movement and the Confederacy. Accompanying her husband, who was a staff officer, on his military missions during the Civil War, Chesnut began recording her views and observations on Feb. 15, 1861, and closed her diary on Aug. 2, 1865. *A Diary from Dixie* was not published until 1905, long after her death. Although not a day-by-day account, the diary is highly regarded by historians for its perceptive views of Confederate military and political leaders and for its insight into Southern society during the Civil War.

Chesnutt \'ches-,nət\, Charles Waddell (b. June 20, 1858, Cleveland, Ohio, U.S.—d. Nov. 15, 1932, Cleveland) The first important black American novelist.

Chesnutt was the son of free blacks who had left their native North Carolina prior to the American Civil War. Following the war his parents moved back to North Carolina. By the time Chesnutt was 25, he was married and was already a successful school principal, but he became so distressed about the treatment of blacks in the South that he moved his wife and children to Cleveland.

Between 1885 and 1905 Chesnutt published more than 50 tales, short stories, and essays, as well as two collections of short stories, a biography of the antislavery leader Frederick Douglass, and three novels. His "The Goophered Grapevine,"

the first work by a black accepted by *The Atlantic Monthly* (August 1887), was so subtle in its refutation of the romantic view of plantation life fostered by such writers as Thomas Nelson Page that most readers missed the irony. This and similarly authentic, psychologically realistic stories of folk life among North Carolina blacks were collected in THE CONJURE WOMAN (1899). *The Wife of His Youth and Other Stories of the Color Line* (1899) examines color prejudice among blacks as well as between the races in a manner reminiscent of George W. Cable. *The Colonel's Dream* (1905) deals trenchantly with problems of the freed slave.

Chesterfield \'ches-tər-,fēld\, Philip Dormer Stanhope, 4th Earl of (b. Sept. 22, 1694, London, Eng.—d. March 24, 1773, London) British statesman, diplomat, and wit, chiefly remembered as the author of *Letters to His Son* and *Letters to His Godson*—guides to manners, the art of pleasing, and the art of worldly success.

He succeeded to the earldom in 1726 and became ambassador to Holland in 1728. Returning to England in 1732, Chesterfield took up a parliamentary career for the next decade. He later served a short term as lord lieutenant of Ireland and a term as secretary of state before gradually retiring from public life because of increasing deafness.

Chesterfield was the patron of many struggling authors but had unfortunate relations with one of them, Samuel Johnson, who condemned him in a famous letter (1755) attacking patrons. Johnson further damaged Chesterfield's reputation when he described the *Letters* as teaching "the morals of a whore, and the manners of a dancing master." Charles Dickens later caricatured him as Sir John Chester in *Barnaby Rudge* (1841). The strongest charge against his philosophy is that it leads to concentration on worldly ends. But within this limitation his advice is shrewd and presented with wit and elegance.

Chester plays \'ches-tər\ A 14th-century cycle of 25 scriptural, or mystery, plays, performed at the prosperous city of Chester, in the north of England, during the Middle Ages. They are traditionally dated about 1325, but a date of about 1375 has also been suggested. They were presented on three successive days at Corpus Christi, a religious feast day that falls in summer. On the first day there was a performance of plays 1–9 (from the Fall of Lucifer, through key episodes in the Old Testament, up to the Nativity and the Adoration of the Wise Men); on the second day a performance of plays 10–18 (including the Flight into Egypt, Jesus' ministry, the Passion and Crucifixion, the Descent into Hell, and the arrival in paradise of the virtuous who had died before the Redemption had been achieved); and, finally, on the third day a performance of plays 19–25 (including the Resurrection, the Ascension, the Descent of the Holy Spirit, the coming of the Antichrist, and the Last Judgment).

The Chester plays are rich in content, yet tell the great story of human redemption more simply than the other surviving cycles of York, Wakefield, and "N-Town." The Chester cycle was published by the Early English Text Society (1892–1916). *See also* MYSTERY PLAY.

Chesterton \'ches-tər-tən\, G.K., *in full* Gilbert Keith (b. May 29, 1874, London, Eng.—d. June 14, 1936, Beaconsfield, Buckinghamshire) English critic and author of verse, essays, novels, and short stories, known also for his exuberant personality and rotund figure.

Chesterton's writings to 1910 were of three kinds. First, his social criticism, largely from his voluminous journalistic writings, was gathered in *The Defendant* (1901), *Twelve Types* (1902), and *Heretics* (1905). His second preoccupation was literary criticism. *Robert Browning* (1903), *Charles Dickens* (1906), and *Appreciations and Criticisms of the Works of Charles Dick-*

ens (1911), a collection of prefaces to the individual novels, are among his finest contributions to criticism. His *George Bernard Shaw* (1909) and *The Victorian Age in Literature* (1913)

Detail of chalk drawing by James Gunn, 1932
National Portrait Gallery, London

together with *William Blake* (1910) and the later monographs *William Cobbett* (1925) and *Robert Louis Stevenson* (1927) have a spontaneity that places them above the works of many academic critics.

Chesterton's third major concern was theology and religious argument. He was converted from Anglicanism to Roman Catholicism in 1922 and thereafter wrote several theologically oriented works.

In his verse Chesterton was a master of ballad forms, as shown in the stirring "Lepanto" (1911). He is seen at his happiest in such essays as "On Running After One's Hat" (1908) and "A Defence of Nonsense" (1901), in which he says that nonsense and faith are "the two supreme symbolic assertions of truth."

Many readers value Chesterton's fiction most highly. *The Napoleon of Notting Hill* (1904), a romance of civil war in suburban London, was followed by the loosely knit collection of short stories *The Club of Queer Trades* (1905) and the popular allegorical novel THE MAN WHO WAS THURSDAY (1908). But the most successful association of fiction with social judgment is in Chesterton's series on the priest-sleuth FATHER BROWN: *The Innocence of Father Brown* (1911), followed by *The Wisdom* . . . (1914), *The Incredulity* . . . (1926), *The Secret* . . . (1927), and *The Scandal of Father Brown* (1935). Chesterton's *Autobiography* was published in 1936.

Chettle \'chet-əl\, Henry (b. *c.* 1560—d. *c.* 1607) English dramatist, typical of the versatile, popular writers of the Elizabethan Age.

Chettle began his career as a printer. He prepared for posthumous publication *Greenes Groats-Worth of Witte* (1592), with its attack on William Shakespeare as an "upstart Crow," but offered Shakespeare compliments and an olive branch in his own *Kind-Harts Dreame* (1592), a topical satire framed in a

dream fable. His *Piers Plainnes Seaven Yeres Prentiship* (1595) is a picaresque romance. Between 1598 and 1603 he had a hand in 49 plays. Of these only five were published: *The Downfall of Robert, Earle of Huntington* (1601), a play mainly by Anthony Munday, revised by Chettle; *The Death of Robert, Earle of Huntington* (1601), written with Munday; *The Pleasant Comodie of Patient Grissill* (1603), with Thomas Dekker and William Haughton; the posthumously published *The Blind-Beggar Of Bednal-Green* (1659), with John Day; and the revenge play *The Tragedy of Hoffman* (1631), which is the only extant play attributed to Chettle alone.

cheville \shə-'vē\ [French, literally, peg] A redundant word or phrase used to fill out a sentence or verse.

Chiabrera \kē-ä-'brä-rä\, Gabriello (b. June 18, 1552, Savona [Italy]—d. Oct. 14, 1638, Savona) Poet who introduced new meters and a Hellenic style to Italian poetry.

Civic and diplomatic posts and the protection of several princes gave Chiabrera the leisure to write a prodigious amount of poetry in various forms: lyrics, narrative poems, eclogues, epitaphs, epics, tragedies, and satires. His canzones (lyrics derived from Provençal poetry) introduced stylistic innovations. His best works, however, are his graceful, musical canzonets. These are lighthearted compositions, apparently influenced by the 16th-century French Pléiade poets, in which he experiments with the introduction of 4-, 5-, 6-, 8-, and 9-syllable lines (rather than the 11- and 7-syllable lines of previous practice) and with varieties of syllabic stress. His work was imitated by the 18th-century Italian Arcadian poets and was admired by the 19th-century Romantic poet William Wordsworth, who translated some of his epitaphs.

chiasmus \kī-'az-məs, kē-\ [Greek *chiasmós,* literally, the act of placing crosswise, a derivative of *chiázein* to mark with an X (the letter chi), place crosswise] An inverted relationship between the syntactic elements of parallel phrases (as in Oliver Goldsmith's "to stop too fearful, and too faint to go").

Chicago \shi-'käg-ō, -'kôg-\ Poem by Carl SANDBURG, first published in *Poetry* magazine in March 1914 and later in the book *Chicago Poems* (1916). An ode to the city in which Sandburg lived, "Chicago" is perhaps his best-known poem. Reminiscent of the poetry of Walt Whitman, the work celebrates ordinary life with strong affirmation.

In "Chicago" Sandburg used apostrophe to describe the city, notably in the terse epithets of the opening and closing lines of the poem, where the city is personified with the qualities of its leading industries:

> Hog Butcher for the World,
> Tool Maker, Stacker of Wheat,
> Player with Railroads and the Nation's Freight Handler;
> Stormy, husky, brawling,
> City of the Big Shoulders

Chicago critics \shi-'käg-ō, -'kôg-\, *also called* The Chicago school. A group of pluralist, formalist American literary critics—including Richard McKeon, Elder Olson, R.S. Crane, and Norman Maclean—that exerted a significant influence in the development of modern American criticism. The group, associated from the 1940s with the University of Chicago, often were called "Aristotelian" or, more accurately, "Neo-Aristotelian" because of their concern with form and genre. Their approach emphasized an evaluation of the author's solutions to specific problems in the construction of a text.

One of the most complete discussions of the Chicago critics is found in *Critics and Criticism: Ancient and Modern* (1952), edited by Crane. A full exposition of the theoretical basis of the group's method is to be found in Crane's study *The Languages of Criticism and the Structure of Poetry* (1953). Wayne C. Booth, one of the younger Chicago critics, applied the group's principles to fiction in *The Rhetoric of Fiction* (1961) and expanded its theories in later works.

Chicago literary renaissance \shi-'käg-ō, -'kȯg-\ The flourishing of literary activity in Chicago during the period from approximately 1912 to 1925. The leading writers of this renaissance—Theodore DREISER, Sherwood ANDERSON, Edgar Lee MASTERS, and Carl SANDBURG—realistically depicted the contemporary urban environment, condemning the loss of traditional rural values in the increasingly industrialized and materialistic American society. They mourned the failure of the romantic promise that hard work would automatically bring material and spiritual rewards. Most of these writers were originally from small Midwestern towns and were deeply affected by the regional writing of the 1890s. The renaissance also encompassed the revitalization of journalism as a literary medium; writers such as Floyd Dell, Anderson, Dreiser, and Sandburg all were associated at one time with Chicago newspapers.

The Little Theatre, established in Chicago in 1912 by Maurice Browne, became an important outlet for the creative talents of young playwrights. The Little Room, a literary group that included both artists and patrons of the arts, encouraged literary activity. *The Dial* magazine, established in 1880, grew to be a respected literary organ. Henry Blake Fuller and Robert Herrick, who belonged to the genteel tradition, wrote several novels that foreshadowed the later realistic novels of Dreiser and Anderson. Hamlin Garland, already famous for novels on the bleakness of rural life in the Midwest, was associated briefly with the Little Room.

The appearance of Dreiser's naturalistic novel *Sister Carrie* (1900), Masters' collection of poetic epitaphs entitled *Spoon River Anthology* (1915), Sandburg's *Chicago Poems* (1916), and Anderson's *Winesburg, Ohio* (1919) marked the height of the Chicago renaissance. Two Chicago literary magazines—PO-ETRY: *A Magazine of Verse*, founded in 1912 by Harriet Monroe, and THE LITTLE REVIEW (1914–29), founded by Margaret Anderson—published exciting new verse by such local poets as Vachel Lindsay, Masters, and Sandburg. Dell, a journalist associated with the *Friday Literary Review* (1909–11), the weekly literary supplement to the *Chicago Evening Post,* was the center of a vital literary circle that included Dreiser, Sherwood Anderson, Margaret Anderson, and Monroe.

Ch'ien Chung-shu *see* QIAN ZHONGSHU.

Ch'i Ju-shan or **Qi Rushan** \'chē-'rü-'shän\ (b. Dec. 23, 1876, Gaoyang, Hebei province, China—d. March 18, 1962, Taiwan)   Playwright and scholar who revived interest in traditional Chinese drama.

Ch'i Ju-shan received a classical Chinese education, also studying traditional Chinese theater from childhood and learning European languages as a young man. Between 1908 and 1913 he traveled to Paris several times and managed to take in a great deal of European drama, which spurred his desire to restore traditional Chinese theater to its former place of importance.

On his return to China, Ch'i Ju-shan met Mei Lanfang, then emerging as one of China's greatest actors. The two combined talents, with Mei Lanfang executing the new dramas of Ch'i Ju-shan that were based on historical and legendary sources. The highly successful partnership culminated in 1930 when Ch'i Ju-shan accompanied Mei Lanfang on a tour of the United States. From 1931 until 1948 Ch'i Ju-shan spent most of his time compiling his lifelong research on Chinese drama. With friends he founded the Traditional Chinese Theater Association, which sponsored a school and a museum that published most of Ch'i Ju-shan's writings.

In 1948 the political situation in China forced Ch'i Ju-shan to go to Taiwan, where he continued his research on the theater until his death.

Chikamatsu Monzaemon \chē-'kä-mät-sù-mōn-'zä-ä-mōn\, *original name* Sugimori Nobumori \nō-bù-'mō-rē\ (b. 1653, Echizen [now in Fukui prefecture], Japan—d. Jan. 6, 1725, Ōsaka)   Japanese playwright, widely regarded as the greatest Japanese dramatist. He is credited with more than 100 plays, most of which were written for the bunraku (puppet theater). He was the first author of bunraku plays to write works that not only gave the puppet operator the opportunity to display his skill but also were of considerable literary merit. His works remained popular into the late 20th century.

Yotsugi Soga (1683; "The Soga Heir"), a bunraku play, is the first work that can be definitely attributed to Chikamatsu. The following year he wrote a kabuki play, and by 1693 he was writing plays almost exclusively for live theater. In 1703 he reestablished contact with the bunraku chanter Takemoto Gidayū, and in 1705 he moved from Kyōto to Ōsaka to be nearer to Gidayū's puppet theater, Takemotoza. He remained a writer for Takemotoza until his death.

Chikamatsu wrote mostly historical romances and domestic tragedies. The vast majority of the domestic tragedies were based on actual incidents, such as the then-popular trend of double suicide of lovers. Chikamatsu's most popular work was *Kokusenya kassen* (1715; *The Battles of Coxinga*), a historical melodrama that is based loosely on events in the life of the Chinese-Japanese adventurer who attempted to restore the Ming dynasty in China. Another famous work is *Shinjū ten no Amijima* (1720; DOUBLE SUICIDE AT AMIJIMA), which is still frequently performed.

Chilam Balam \chē-'läm-bä-'läm\ (*in full* Books of Chilam Balam)   Group of documents written in Yucatec Maya (with Spanish characters) during the 17th and 18th centuries. A principal source of knowledge of ancient Mayan custom, they contain myth, divination, prophecy, medical lore, calendrical information, and historical chronicles. Although originally there were probably many documents, only a few remain. Those of Chumayel, Tizimín, and Maní (towns where they were written) are particularly important for Mayan history. *Chilam balam* means "jaguar spokesman."

child *see* CHILDE.

Child \'chīld\, Francis J., *in full* James (b. Feb. 1, 1825, Boston, Mass., U.S.—d. Sept. 11, 1896, Boston)   American scholar and educator who studied, collected, and cataloged folk ballads.

Child graduated from Harvard University in 1846. After studying in Europe, he taught rhetoric, oratory, elocution, and English at Harvard. Child studied English drama and Germanic philology, the latter at Berlin and Göttingen, and assumed the general editorial supervision of a large collection of British poetry. He edited the poetic works of Edmund Spenser, 5 vol. (1855), and published an important treatise on Geoffrey Chaucer in the *Memoirs of the American Academy of Arts and Sciences* for 1863.

Child's largest undertaking grew out of an original collection of *English and Scottish Ballads*, 8 vol. (1857–58). He accumulated within the Harvard library one of the largest folklore collections in existence, studied manuscript rather than printed versions of old ballads, and investigated songs and stories in other languages that were related to the English and Scottish ballads. His final collection was published as *The English and Scottish Popular Ballads*, first in 10 parts (1882–98) and then in five quarto volumes, containing 305 ballads. Child's collection remains the authoritative treasury.

Child \'chīld\, Lydia Maria (Francis) (b. Feb. 11, 1802, Medford, Mass., U.S.—d. Oct. 20, 1880, Wayland, Mass.)   American author of influential antislavery works.

In the 1820s, Child taught, wrote historical novels, and founded a periodical for children, *Juvenile Miscellany* (1826). After meeting the abolitionist William Lloyd Garrison in 1831, she devoted her life to his cause. Child's best-known work, *An Appeal in Favor of That Class of Americans Called Africans* (1833), recounts the history of slavery and denounces the inequality of education and employment for blacks; it was the first such work published in book form. Although Child was ostracized socially and her magazine failed in 1834, she succeeded in inducing many people to join the abolitionist movement. Child's further abolitionist efforts included editing the *National Anti-Slavery Standard* (1841–43) and later transcribing the recollections of slaves who had been freed. In addition, her home was part of the Underground Railroad that aided escaping slaves.

Child's other work includes once-popular volumes of advice for women, such as *The Frugal Housewife* (1829), and books on behalf of Native Americans.

childe \'chīld\ [spelling variant of *child*] *archaic*   A youth of noble birth or a youth in training to be a knight. In literature the word is often used as a title, as in the character Childe Roland of Robert Browning's poem "Childe Roland to the Dark Tower Came" and Lord Byron's *Childe Harold's Pilgrimage*.

Childe Harold's Pilgrimage \'chīld-'har-əld\   Autobiographical poem in four cantos by Lord BYRON. Cantos I and II were published in 1812, Canto III in 1816, and Canto IV in 1818. Byron gained his first poetic fame with the publication of the first two cantos.

"Childe" is a title from medieval times, designating a young noble who is not yet knighted. Disillusioned with his aimless life devoted to pursuing pleasure, Childe Harold seeks distraction by going on a solitary pilgrimage to foreign lands. On each segment of the journey, Byron evokes associated historical events and people, such as the philosopher Jean-Jacques Rousseau and Napoleon before the Battle of Waterloo. In the fourth canto the imaginary pilgrim is replaced by the poet himself, speaking in the first person about Venice, Ferrara, Florence, and Rome and the artists and heros associated with those cities.

To Byron's literary public, the work offered a poetic travelogue of picturesque lands and gave vent to the prevailing moods of melancholy and disillusionment. The world-weary Childe Harold came to personify the so-called Byronic hero. The work also voiced with a frankness unprecedented in the literature of that time the disparity between romantic ideals and the realities of the world.

Children of Heracles \'her-ə-,klēz\ (*Greek* Hērakleidai)   Minor political play by EURIPIDES, performed in 430 BC. It concerns the Athenians' defense of the young children of the dead Heracles from the murderous King Eurystheus of Argos. The play is essentially a simple glorification of Athens.

children's company *also called* boys' company.   Any of a number of troupes of boy actors whose performances enjoyed great popularity in Elizabethan England. The young actors were drawn primarily from choir schools attached to the great chapels and cathedrals, where they received musical training and were taught to perform in religious dramas and classical Latin plays. By the time of Henry VIII, groups such as the Children of the Chapel and the Children of Paul's were often called upon to present plays and to take part in ceremonies and pageants at court. During the reign of Queen Elizabeth I,

these groups were formed into highly professional companies, usually consisting of from 8 to 12 boys, who gave public performances outside the court.

In the late 16th and early 17th centuries, these companies were so popular that they posed a serious threat to the professional men's companies. Children acted in the first Blackfriars Theatre (*c.* 1576–80), and in 1600 a syndicate representing the Children of the Chapel acquired a lease on the second Blackfriars Theatre, where the boys performed many important plays, including those of John Marston and Ben Jonson. By about 1610 the children's companies had greatly declined in popularity.

Children's Hour, The   Drama in three acts about the tragic repercussions of a schoolgirl's malicious gossip by Lillian HELLMAN, performed and published in 1934. Hellman based the plot on an actual case in 19th-century Edinburgh that was detailed in the essay "Closed Doors, or The Great Drumsheugh Case" in *Bad Companions* (1931) by William Roughead.

The story concerns an attempt by Mary Tilford, a student at a New England boarding school, to explain to her rich, indulgent grandmother why she has run away from school. Angry over her mild altercation with Karen Wright and Martha Dobie, the women who own and run the school, Mary says that she knows the women to be lesbians, and she successfully blackmails another student into corroborating her accusation. Dr. Joe Cardin, Karen's fiancé, exposes Mary as a liar, but the school is forced to close. After Karen and Martha lose a libel suit, Karen realizes that Cardin's trust in her is altered and ends their relationship. Martha confesses her self-doubt to Karen and commits suicide.

children's literature   The body of written works and accompanying illustrations produced to entertain or instruct young people. The genre encompasses a wide range of works, including acknowledged classics of world literature, picture books and easy-to-read stories written expressly for children, and fairy tales, lullabies, fables, folk songs, and other primarily orally transmitted materials.

Children's literature emerged as a distinct and independent form only in the second half of the 18th century. Its late development may be traced to low literacy rates, the prohibitive cost of bookmaking, and the general perception of children as simply diminutive or miniature adults.

One of the first printed works of children's literature was the Czech educator John Amos Comenius' *Orbis Sensualium Pictus* (1658; *The Visible World in Pictures*), a teaching device that was also the first picture book for children. It was the first such work to acknowledge that children are different from adults in many respects. The work considered to be the first novel written specifically for children is *The History of Little Goody Two-Shoes* (1765). One of the earliest and most enduring classics of children's literature is the collection of nursery rhymes known as *Mother Goose*, the first English edition of which appeared in 1781. Children's literature blossomed in the 19th century, particularly in England and the United States, into a rich and complex genre. It emerged in the 20th century as a major genre in the Germanic- and Romance-language countries of Europe, as well as in the Soviet Union. Folktales, myths, and legends—not particularly geared to children—make up the major portion of stories for children in most other cultures.

Childress \'chil-drəs\, Alice (b. Oct. 12, 1916, Charleston, S.C., U.S.—d. Aug. 14, 1994, New York, N.Y.)   African-American playwright, novelist, and actress, known for her realistic stories about the enduring optimism of black Americans.

Childress grew up in Harlem, New York City, where she studied drama with the American Negro Theatre in the 1940s.

There she wrote, directed, and starred in her first play, *Florence* (produced 1949), about a black woman who, after meeting an insensitive white actress in a railway station, comes to respect her daughter's attempts to pursue an acting career. *Trouble in Mind* (produced 1955; revised and published 1971), *Wedding Band* (produced 1966), *String* (produced 1969), and *Wine in the Wilderness* (produced 1969) all examine racial and social issues. Among Childress' plays that feature music are *Just a Little Simple* (produced 1950; based on Langston Hughes's *Simple Speaks His Mind*), *Gold Through the Trees* (produced 1952), *The African Garden* (produced 1971), *Gullah* (produced 1984; based on her 1977 play *Sea Island Song*), and *Moms* (produced 1987; about the life of comedienne Jackie "Moms" Mabley).

Childress was also a successful writer of children's literature. A HERO AIN'T NOTHIN' BUT A SANDWICH (1973) is a novel for adolescents about a teenage drug addict. Similarly, the novel *Rainbow Jordan* (1981) concerns the struggles of poor black urban youth. Her other novels include *A Short Walk* (1979), *Many Closets* (1987), and *Those Other People* (1989).

Child's Christmas in Wales, A \ˈwȯlz\   A prose recollection by Dylan THOMAS, published posthumously in 1955.

A Child's Christmas in Wales is a lyrical, minutely remembered evocation of the Christmas season, as perceived by a happy child. The work captures all aspects of the season: the weather, the village activities, the villagers, the sights and sounds, the purchasing and opening of gifts, and the preparation and enjoyment of food and drink for the holiday.

Child's Garden of Verses, A   Volume of 64 poems for children by Robert Louis STEVENSON, published in 1885. The collection was one of the most influential children's works in the 19th century, and its verses were widely imitated.

Originally planned for a volume to be called *Penny Whistles*, the poems were inspired by a children's book published in 1880. The verses, set in a Victorian environment of enclosed gardens and a separate nursery for young children apart from the adult household, are timeless in their appeal.

ch'i-lin   *see* QILIN.

Chillingworth, Roger \ˈraj-ər-ˈchil-iŋ-wərth\   Fictional character, the vengeful cuckolded physician husband of Hester Prynne, protagonist of Nathaniel Hawthorne's THE SCARLET LETTER.

Chimera or **Chimaera** \kī-ˈmir-ə, ki-\ [Greek *chímaira* young female goat, chimera]   In Greek mythology, a fire-breathing female monster resembling a lion in the forepart, a goat in the middle, and a dragon or serpent behind. She devastated Caria and Lycia until she was slain by Bellerophon.

The word *chimera* is now used generally to denote an illusion, figment of the imagination, or unrealizable dream.

Chingachgook \chin-ˈgäch-gu̇k, -ˈgach-\, *also called* John Monhegan \ˈjän-män-ˈhē-gən\ *or* Indian John.   Fictional character, a Mohican chief in four of the novels by James Fenimore Cooper known under the collective title THE LEATHERSTOCKING TALES. Chingachgook is a lifelong friend of Natty Bumppo, the white frontiersman and hero of the saga. Chingachgook and his son Uncas (who is the last of the Mohicans) frequently help defend the English settlers against hostile attacks by other native tribes and the French.

ching-hsi   *see* JINGXI.

Chin p'ing mei   *see* JIN PING MEI.

Chips, Mr. \ˈmis-tər-ˈchips\   Fictional character, a gentle and kindly English schoolteacher in the novel GOODBYE, MR. CHIPS by James Hilton. Mr. Chips was the nickname given to Arthur Chipping by his students.

Chiron \ˈkī-ˌrän\   In Greek mythology, one of the centaurs, the son of the god Cronus and the sea nymph Philyra. Chiron lived at the foot of Mount Pelion in Thessaly and was famous for his wisdom and knowledge of medicine. Many Greek heroes, including Heracles, Achilles, Jason, and Asclepius, were instructed by him. Accidentally pierced by a poisoned arrow shot by Heracles, he renounced his immortality in favor of Prometheus and was placed among the stars as the constellation Sagittarius.

Chocano \chō-ˈkä-nō, shō-\, José Santos (b. May 14, 1875, Lima, Peru—d. Dec. 13, 1934, Santiago, Chile)   Peruvian poet famous for his attempt to synthesize in poetry the history and culture of Latin America.

Imprisoned for his political beliefs before he was 20, an experience for which he bitterly attacked his opponents in his volume *Iras santas* (1895; "Holy Wrath"), Chocano joined the forces of the Mexican insurgent Pancho Villa. He remained an active revolutionary throughout his life, both his diplomatic missions and his intrigues taking him to most South and Central American countries. While living in exile in Santiago, Chile, he was murdered by a mentally disturbed friend.

Although Chocano experimented with a number of poetic styles, including Modernismo, his verse is essentially romantic in nature, expressing his deep love for the landscapes and cultures of Latin America. His major works include *Alma América* (1906; "American Soul"), *Fiat lux* (1908; "Let There be Light"), and *Primicias de oro de las Indias* (1934; "First Gold of the Indies").

Choerilus \ˈkē-rə-ləs, ˈker-ə-\ (fl. *c.* 510 BC, Athens [Greece])   One of the earliest recorded Athenian tragic poets, of whose work only one title and one disputed fragment remain. Choerilus is said to have produced his first play in about 523 BC and to have competed against the tragedian Aeschylus in about 498. Some sources credit him with 13 victories and with certain innovations in tragic masks and costumes.

Choerilus \ˈkē-rə-ləs, ker-ə-\ (fl. 5th century BC, Samos, Ionia [Greece])   Greek epic poet of the Aegean island of Samos, author of a lost verse chronicle, the *Persica*, probably relating the story of the Persian wars as narrated in prose by the historian Herodotus. According to the biographer Plutarch, Choerilus was later employed by the Spartan general Lysander to celebrate his exploits. Scanty extant fragments of his work include a lament for the decline of the epic tradition, of which he saw himself as a last representative.

chōka \ˈchō-kä\ [Japanese]   A form of waka (Japanese court poetry of the 6th to 14th century) consisting of alternating lines of five and seven syllables and ending with an extra line of seven syllables. The length is indefinite. *See also* WAKA.

choliamb \ˈkȯ-lē-ˌam, -ˌamb\ or **choliambus** \ˌkȯ-lē-ˈam-bəs\, *plural* choliambs *or* choliambi \ˌkȯ-lē-ˈam-ˌbī, -ˌbē\ [Greek *chōlíambos*, from *chōlós* lame + *íambos* iamb], *also called* scazon.   In classical prosody, an iambic trimeter verse of six feet or three metra having a spondee in the last foot. It scans as:
∪ – ∪ – | ∪ – ∪ – | ∪ – – .

Chopin \shō-ˈpan; ˈshō-pan, -pən\, Kate, *original name* Katherine O'Flaherty \ō-ˈflä-ər-tē, -ˈflar-\ (b. Feb. 8, 1851, St. Louis, Mo., U.S.—d. Aug. 22, 1904, St. Louis)   American author and local colorist known as an interpreter of New Orleans culture. There was a revival of interest in Chopin in the late 20th century because her concerns about the freedom of women foreshadowed later feminist literary themes.

Chopin lived in Louisiana after her marriage (1870) to Oscar Chopin; after his death she began to write about the Creole and Cajun people she had observed in the South. Her first novel, *At*

Fault (1890), was undistinguished, but she was later acclaimed for her finely crafted short stories, of which she wrote more than 100. Two of these stories, DÉSIRÉE'S BABY and "Madame Celestin's Divorce," continue to be widely anthologized.

In 1899 Chopin published THE AWAKENING, a realistic novel about the sexual and artistic awakening of a young mother who abandons her family and eventually commits suicide. This work, roundly condemned in its time, later received critical approval for the beauty of its writing and for its modern sensibility.

Her stories were collected in *Bayou Folk* (1894) and *A Night in Acadie* (1897).

Choquette \shō-'ket\, Robert Guy (b. April 22, 1905, Manchester, N.H., U.S.) American-born French-Canadian writer whose work was regarded as revolutionary and who influenced an entire younger generation of poets.

Choquette moved to Montreal at the age of eight. His first collection of poetry, *A travers les vents* (1925; "Through the Winds"), won him a reputation based on his disregard of syntax and his freedom of expression. Other books of poetry were *Metropolitan Museum* (1930), *Suite marine* (1953), *Oeuvres poétiques* (1956; "Poetic Works"), and *Poèmes choisis* (1970; "Select Poems").

La Pension Leblanc (1928), Choquette's first published novel, provided a foundation on which future television and radio series were to be based. A group of recognizable characters from his novels *Le Curé de village* (1936; "The Village Curate") and *Les Velder* (1941) peopled a radio series called *Le Curé de village*. Two other serials, *La Pension Velder* and *Métropole*, followed. Choquette also brought out a collection of prose sketches, *Le Fabuliste La Fontaine à Montréal* (1935; "The Fabulist La Fontaine in Montreal"), *Language and Religion* (1975), and *Moi, Pétrouchka* (1980), as well as a collection of both prose and poetry entitled *Le Choix de Robert Choquette dans l'oeuvre de Robert Choquette* (1981; "The Choice of Robert Choquette in the Work of Robert Choquette").

Choquette was elected to the French-Canadian Academy and Académie Ronsard (Paris), and he served as Canadian consul general to Bordeaux, France (1965–68), and Canadian ambassador to Argentina, Uruguay, and Paraguay (1968–70).

choral speaking Ensemble speaking by a group often using various voice combinations and contrasts to bring out the meaning or tonal beauty of a passage of poetry or prose.

choreion \'kȯr-ē-,än\ [Greek *choreîos,* from *choreîos* (adjective) of a chorus] In classical prosody, a trochee (— ∪). The term was originally used especially of the trochee or the iamb when resolved into the tribrach (a metrical foot of three short syllables).

choriamb \,kȯr-ē-'am, -'amb\ or **choriambus** \,kȯr-ē-'ambəs\, *plural* choriambi \-'am-,bī\ or choriambuses [Greek *choríambos,* from *choreîos* choreus + *íambos* iamb] In prosody, a metrical unit of four syllables. The choriamb was frequently used by the Greek poets Sappho and Alcaeus and by the Latin poet Horace. In classical prosody, a choriamb is scanned — ∪ ∪ —; it is sometimes used by itself to form a complete system but is more often found as the nucleus of a colon such as a glyconic or another aeolic pattern. The corresponding pattern of cadence in accentual prosody is scanned ′ ∪ ∪ ′. Its use as a sustained pattern is rare in modern poetry, but examples can be found, for example, in J.W. von Goethe's *Pandora* (which is written in choriambic dimeter) and in Algernon Charles Swinburne's *Choriambics.*

Choromański \kȯ-rȯ-'mȧyⁿ-skʸē\, Michał (b. June 22, 1904, Yelizavetgrad, Russian Empire [now Kirovohrad, Ukraine]—

d. May 24, 1972, Warsaw, Pol.) Polish novelist and playwright who plumbed the depths of the human psyche.

Although born of Polish parents, Choromański was educated in the Soviet Union, and when he returned to Poland in 1924, he began his literary activity as a translator of the work of Polish poets into Russian. His first success as a Polish novelist was *Zazdrość i medycyna* (1932; *Jealousy and Medicine*), which was remarkable for its clinical analysis of the jealousy and eroticism experienced by the participants in a love triangle. Another psychological study was his collection of essays and short stories entitled *Kobieta i mężczyzna* (1959; "Female and Male"). Choromański's tales show his strong interest in describing such psychopathological states as nymphomania and narcotic euphoria, which he treats in a macabre and ironic fashion. Later works include *Schodami w górę, schodami w dół* (1967; "Upstairs, Downstairs"), *W rzecz wstąpić* (1968; "To Get to the Heart of the Matter"), and *Słowacki wysp tropikalnych* (1969; "Słowacki of the Tropical Islands").

chorus \'kȯr-əs\ [Greek *chorós* dance, place for dancing, group of dancers and singers, chorus] In classical Greek drama, a group of actors who described and commented upon the main action of a play with song, dance, and recitation. Greek tragedy had its beginnings in choral performances, in which a group of 50 men danced and sang dithyrambs—lyric hymns in praise of the god Dionysus. Choral performances continued to dominate the early plays until the time of Aeschylus (5th–4th century BC), who added a second actor and reduced the chorus from 50 to 12 performers. Sophocles, who added a third actor, increased the chorus to 15 but reduced its role to one of commentary in most of his plays. The chorus in Greek comedy numbered 24, and its function was displaced eventually by interspersed songs. The distinction between the passivity of the chorus and the activity of the actors is central to the artistry of the Greek tragedies.

As the importance of the actors increased, the choral odes became fewer in number and tended to have less importance in the plot, until at last they became mere decorative interludes separating the acts. During the Renaissance the role of the chorus was revised. In the drama of Elizabethan England, for example, the name chorus designated a single person, often the speaker of the prologue and epilogue, as in Christopher Marlowe's *Doctor Faustus.* The use of the group chorus was revived in a number of modern plays, such as Eugene O'Neill's *Mourning Becomes Electra* (1931) and T.S. Eliot's *Murder in the Cathedral* (1935).

chosism \'shō-,ziz-əm\ [French *chosisme,* a derivative of *chose* thing] A literary style involving the detailed description of things, used particularly by such French authors as Michel Butor and Alain Robbe-Grillet and others associated with the *nouveau roman.*

Chou li *see* ZHOU LI.

Chou Tso-jen *see* ZHOU ZUOREN.

Chraïbi \'shrī-bē\, Driss (b. July 15, 1926, Mazagan [now El-Jadida], Mor.) Moroccan novelist, dramatist, and radio producer and commentator.

Chraïbi's first novel—*Le Passé simple* (1954; "Simple Past"), published shortly before the outbreak of hostilities in Algeria—is a powerful, bitter, ironic cry of revolt against oppressive traditionalism. *Les Boucs* (1955; *The Butts*) shifted the author's accusatory finger to the oppressed condition of many North Africans living in France. Chraïbi then turned to more allegorical political expression in *L'Âne* (1956; "The Donkey") and *La Foule* (1961; "The Crowd"). In *Un Ami viendra vous voir* (1966; "A Friend Is Coming to See You"), Chraïbi combines the themes of insanity, violence, and the oppression of women. Women's rights, in Europe as in North Africa, are also touched on in *Succession ouverte* (1962; *Heirs to the Past*), a sequel to his first novel, and in *La Civilisation, ma mère!* (1972; *Mother Comes of Age*). *Mort au Canada* (1975; "Death in Canada") is a study of passionate love. Other works include *Une Enquête au pays* (1981; *Flutes of Death*), *La mère du printemps* (1982; *Mother Spring*), *Naissance à l'aube* (1986; "Birth at Dawn"), and *L'Inspecteur Ali* (1991; "Inspector Ali").

Chrestien \kres-'tya^n\, Florent (b. Jan. 26, 1541, Orléans, Fr.—d. Oct. 3, 1596, Vendôme)   French satirist and Latin poet, known for his translations of Greek and Latin texts and as one of the authors of the *Satire Ménippée* (1593), a satirical pamphlet about the Holy League, an association of Roman Catholics during the French Wars of Religion.

The son of Guillaume Chrestien, an eminent physician and writer on physiology, he became a pupil of Henri Estienne, the Hellenist, at an early age. Later, he was appointed tutor to Henry of Navarre, afterward Henry IV of France, who made him his librarian.

Chrestien was the author of many good translations from the Greek into Latin verse—among others, of versions of the *Hero and Leander* attributed to Musaeus and of many epigrams from the *Anthology* of the 2nd century AD. His translations into French were less successful.

chrestomathy \kres-'täm-ə-thē\ [Greek *chrēstomátheia*, from *chrēstós* useful + *-matheia*, a derivative of *matheîn, manthánein* to learn]   A volume of selected passages or stories of an author.

Chrétien de Troyes \krā-'tya^n-də-'trwä\ (fl. 1165–80)   French poet, who is known as the author of five Arthurian romances: *Erec; Cligès; Lancelot, ou Le Chevalier de la charrette; Yvain, ou Le Chevalier au lion;* and *Perceval, ou Le Conte du Graal.* The non-Arthurian tale *Guillaume d'Angleterre,* based on the legend of St. Eustace, may also have been written by Chrétien.

Little is known of his life. His tales, written in the vernacular, followed the appearance in France of Wace's *Roman de Brut* (1155), a translation of Geoffrey of Monmouth's *Historia regum Britanniae,* which introduced Britain and the Arthurian legend to continental Europe. Chrétien's romances were imitated almost immediately by other French poets and were translated and adapted frequently as the romance continued to develop as a narrative form. *Erec,* for example, supplied some of the material for the 14th-century poem *Sir Gawayne and the Grene Knight.*

Chrétien's romances combine separate adventures into a *conjointure,* or well-knit story. *Erec* is the tale of the submissive wife who proves her love for her husband by disobeying his commands. *Cligès* relates the story of the victim of a marriage made under constraint who feigns death and wakens to a new and happy life with her lover. *Lancelot* is an exaggerated but perhaps parodic treatment of the lover who is servile to the god of love and to his imperious mistress Guinevere, who is the wife of his overlord Arthur. In *Yvain,* a brilliant extravaganza, Chrétien combines the theme of a widow's too hasty marriage to her husband's slayer with that of the new husband's fall from grace and final restoration to favor. *Perceval,* which Chrétien left unfinished, unites the religious theme of the Grail with fantastic adventure. *See also* ARTHURIAN LEGEND.

Christabel \'kris-tə-bel\   Unfinished gothic ballad by Samuel Taylor COLERIDGE, first published in *Christabel; Kubla Khan, A Vision; The Pains of Sleep* (1816). The first part of the poem was written in 1797, the second in 1800. In it Coleridge aimed to show how naked energy might be redeemed through contact with a spirit of innocent love.

Christabel is the innocent, virtuous daughter of Sir Leoline. While praying in the woods at night for her fiancé, she finds Geraldine, a lady in distress whom she takes home to her father's castle. Geraldine says that she is the daughter of Lord Roland de Vaux, once a friend of Sir Leoline before the two men quarreled, and claims to have been kidnapped. In truth, however, she is an evil supernatural creature disguised as Geraldine. Christabel penetrates her deception but is forced into silence by magic. When she finally speaks, Sir Leoline rejects her entreaty, and the narrative ends with Sir Leoline sending a message telling Lord Roland that his daughter is safe and offering reconciliation.

Christian \'kris-chən\, Barbara (b. Dec. 12, 1943, St. Thomas, U.S. Virgin Islands)   Caribbean-American educator and feminist critic who attempted to define an African-American feminist philosophy.

Educated at Marquette (B.A., 1963) and Columbia universities (M.A., 1964; Ph.D., 1970), Christian taught at the City College of the City University of New York (1965–72) and in the department of African-American studies of the University of California at Berkeley (from 1971).

Her published works include *Black Feminist Criticism: Perspectives on Black Women Writers* (1985), a work emphasizing literary, textual analysis of fiction by black women; *Black Women Novelists: The Development of a Tradition* (1980); and *Teaching Guide to Accompany Black Foremothers* (1980). She contributed to *Black Expression* (1969; edited by Addison Gayle) and to the journals *The Black Scholar* and *The Journal of Ethnic Studies.*

Christian, Fletcher \'flech-ər-'kris-chən\   Fictional character, a rebellious sailor in the novel MUTINY ON THE BOUNTY by James N. Hall and Charles B. Nordhoff. Angered by the tyranny of Captain Bligh, Fletcher Christian leads a mutiny and succeeds in taking control of the HMS *Bounty* after setting the captain adrift in a small boat.

Christie \'kris-tē\, Agatha, *in full* Dame Agatha Mary Clarissa Christie (b. Sept. 15, 1890, Torquay, Devon, Eng.—d. Jan. 12, 1976, Wallingford, Oxfordshire)   English detective novelist and playwright whose books have sold more than 100,-000,000 copies.

Christie began writing detective fiction while working as a nurse during World War I. Her first novel, *The Mysterious Affair at Styles* (1920), introduced Hercule POIROT, her eccentric and egotistic Belgian detective who reappeared in about 25 novels and many shorter stories before returning to Styles, where in *Curtain* (1975) he died. The elderly spinster Miss Jane MARPLE, her other principal detective figure, first appeared in *Murder at the Vicarage* (1930). Christie's first major recognition came with *The Murder of Roger Ackroyd* (1926), which was followed by some 75 novels that usually made best-seller lists and were serialized in popular magazines in England and the United States. Her books were also translated into some 100 languages. Her plays include *The Mousetrap* (1952), which set a world record for the longest continuous run at one theater (8,862 performances—more than 21 years—at the Ambassadors Theatre, London) and then moved to another theater, and *Witness for the Prosecution* (1953), which was adapted into a very successful film (1958). Other works by Christie that have been adapted for film include *Murder on the Orient Express* (1933; film, 1974) and *Death on the Nile* (1937; film, 1978).

She also wrote romantic novels, such as *Absent in the Spring* (1944), under the pseudonym Mary Westmacott. Her *Autobiography* (1977) appeared posthumously. She was created a Dame of the British Empire in 1971.

Christie, Anna \'an-ə-'kris-tē\ Fictional character, the protagonist of the play ANNA CHRISTIE by Eugene O'Neill.

Christine de Pisan *or* de Pizan \krēs-'tēn-də-pē-'zän\ (b. *c.* 1365, Venice [Italy]—d. *c.* 1431) Prolific and versatile French

Christine de Pisan presents her book to Isabeau of Baviere. Detail of an illuminated manuscript; in the British Library, London

Bridgeman/Art Resource, New York

poet and author whose diverse writings include numerous poems of courtly love and several works championing women.

Christine's Italian father was astrologer to Charles V, and she spent her childhood at the French court. At 15 she married Estienne de Castel, who became court secretary. Widowed after 10 years of marriage, she took up writing in order to support herself and her three young children. Her first poems were ballades of lost love written to the memory of her husband. These verses met with success, and she continued writing ballads, rondeaux, lays, and complaints in which she expressed her feelings with grace and sincerity. In all she wrote 10 volumes in verse, including *L'Épistre au Dieu d'amours* (written 1399; "Letter to the God of Loves"), in which she defended women against the satire of Jean de Meun in the *Roman de la Rose*.

Christine's prose works include *Le Livre de la cité des dames* (1405; THE BOOK OF THE CITY OF LADIES), in which she wrote of women known for their heroism and virtue, and *Le Livre des trois vertus* (1405; "Book of Three Virtues"), a sequel comprising a classification of women's roles in medieval society and a collection of moral instructions for women in the various social spheres. The story of her life, *L'Avision de Christine* (1405), told in an allegorical manner, was a reply to her detractors. At the request of the regent, Philip the Bold of Burgundy, Christine wrote the life of the deceased king—*Le Livre des fais et bonnes meurs du sage roy Charles V* (1404; "Book of the Deeds and Good Morals of the Wise King Charles V"), a firsthand picture of the king and his court. Her eight additional prose works reveal her remarkable breadth of knowledge.

Her last work, *Le Ditié de Jehanne d'Arc* (written in 1429), is a lyrical, joyous outburst inspired by the early victories of Joan of Arc; it is the only such French-language work written during Joan's lifetime.

Christmas Carol, A (*in full* A Christmas Carol, in Prose: Being a Ghost Story of Christmas) Short novel by Charles DICKENS, originally published in 1843. The story, suddenly conceived and written in a few weeks, is perhaps the outstanding Christmas myth of modern literature.

Through a series of spectral visions, the miserly Ebenezer Scrooge is allowed to review his life and to change its outcome. The Ghost of Christmas Past reveals vignettes of Scrooge's early life as a schoolboy, an apprentice, and a young man in love. The Ghost of Christmas Present reveals to Scrooge that joy has little to do with wealth; together they visit the homes of Bob Cratchit, Scrooge's much abused clerk, and of his generous nephew Fred, who has married for love. Finally the Ghost of Christmas Yet to Come allows Scrooge a vision of what his end will be like if he continues on his present course—he will die despised and unmourned. After witnessing these scenes Scrooge is a changed man. He immediately sets about mending his ways, becoming generous and thoughtful and thereby finding redemption and joy.

chronicle \'krän-i-kəl\ [Middle English *cronicle,* from Anglo-French, alteration of Old French *chronique,* from Late Latin *chronica,* from Greek *chroniká* annals, chronology, from neuter plural of *chronikós* of time, a derivative of *chrónos* time] A usually continuous historical account of events arranged in order of time without analysis or interpretation. Examples of such accounts date from Greek and Roman times, but the best-known examples were written or compiled in the Middle Ages and the Renaissance. Examples include the Anglo-Saxon Chronicle, Geoffrey of Monmouth's *Historia regum Britanniae* (*History of the Kings of Britain*), and Andrew of Wyntoun's *Orygynale Cronykil.*

chronicle play or **chronicle history** *also called* history play. A play with a theme from history, consisting usually of loosely connected episodes chronologically arranged. Chronicle plays often point to the past as a lesson for the present.

The genre is characterized by its assumption of a national consciousness in its audience. It has flourished in times of intensely nationalistic feeling, notably in England from the 1580s until the 1630s, when it fell out of fashion. Early chronicle plays had such titles as *The Famous Victories of Henry the Fifth, The Life and Death of Jacke Straw, The Troublesome Raigne of John King of England,* and *The True Tragedie of Richard III.* The genre came to maturity with the work of Christopher Marlowe (*Edward II*) and William Shakespeare (especially *Henry VI,* Parts 2 and 3).

Elizabethan dramatists drew their material from the wealth of chronicle writing for which the age is renowned, notably Edward Hall's *The Union of the Two Noble and Illustrate Famelies of Lancastre and York* and Raphael Holinshed's *Chronicles of England, Scotlande, and Irelande.* The genre was a natural development from the didactic MORALITY PLAY of the Middle Ages. In a forerunner of the chronicle play, John Bale's *Kynge Johan,* all the characters except the king himself are allegorical and have names such as Widow England, Sedition, and Private Wealth.

Chronicles of Narnia, The \'när-nē-ə\ Series of seven children's books by C.S. LEWIS, including *The Lion, the Witch, and the Wardrobe* (1950), *Prince Caspian* (1951), *The Voyage of the "Dawn Treader"* (1952), *The Silver Chair* (1953), *The Horse and His Boy* (1954), *The Magician's Nephew* (1955), and *The Last Battle* (1956).

Lewis wrote the works for his goddaughter Lucy Pevensie, who—with her siblings Susan, Edmund, and Peter—figures as a character in the series. Lucy first discovers Narnia when peering into an old wardrobe in the first volume; soon she and the three others are drawn into the wonderful land created by the lion Aslan. The kingdom's first years are told in *The Magician's Nephew*. Throughout the series Narnia is wracked by conflicts between good and evil—the latter notably personified by the White Witch (who brings perennial winter) and murderous warriors from neighboring Telmar. The series is considered a classic of fantasy literature.

Chrysoloras \krē-'sòl-ô-räs\, Manuel (b. *c.* 1353, Constantinople [now Istanbul, Tur.]—d. April 15, 1415, Konstanz [Germany]) Greek scholar who was a pioneer in reintroducing Greek literature to the West.

The Byzantine emperor Manuel II Palaeologus sent Chrysoloras to Italy to enlist aid against the invasion of the Ottoman Turks. From 1394 onward Chrysoloras traveled in Europe, and beginning in 1396, he accompanied Manuel II on his tour of the European countries. When the emperor returned to Constantinople in 1403, Chrysoloras remained in the West; he taught Greek at Florence, where he became well known as a translator of Homer and Plato. He was also active in trying to arrange for a general council to consider union of the Greek and Latin churches. He was on his way to the Council of Constance, having been chosen to represent the Greek church, when he died. He left the *Erotemata* ("Questions"), a Greek grammar based on the question-and-answer (Socratic) method; some letters; the *Syncrisis*, a comparison of old and new Rome; and a Latin translation of Plato's *Republic*.

chthonic \'thän-ik\ or **chthonian** \'thō-nē-ən\ [Greek *chthōn* earth] **1.** Of a divinity or a spirit, dwelling or reigning in the underworld; infernal. **2.** Relating to infernal deities or spirits; ghostly.

chuanqi or **ch'uan-ch'i** \'chwän-'chē\ [Chinese *chuánqí*] Form of traditional Chinese operatic drama that developed from the *nanxi* in the late 14th century. *Chuanqi* alternated with the *zaju* as the major form of Chinese drama until the 16th century, when *kunqu*, a particular style of *chuanqi*, began to dominate serious Chinese drama. The average *chuanqi* was characterized by 30 to 50 changes of scene; the frequent and free change of end rhymes in arias; singing parts that were probably more languorous than those of the *zaju* and were distributed among many actors (not just the hero and heroine); and plots often taken from popular accounts of historical figures or from contemporary life.

Chūbak \'chū-ˌbak\, Ṣādeq-i or Ṣādiq \'sò-dek\ (b. Aug. 5, 1916, Bushire, Iran) Author of short fiction, drama, and novels, one of the leading 20th-century Iranian writers. Chūbak's short stories are characterized by their intricacy, economy of detail, and concentration upon a single theme, causing some to compare them to Persian miniature paintings.

Chūbak grew up in Shīrāz, Iran, and graduated from the American College of Tehrān in 1937. His best-known works include *Khaymah-i shabbāzī* (1945; "Puppet Show"), a volume of short stories that is divided into 11 sections, each of which portrays an aspect of daily life; *Antarī kih lūṭiyash murda būd* (1949; "The Baboon Whose Master Was Dead"); the satirical play *Tūp-i lāstikī* (1962; *The Rubber Ball*); and two novels, *Tangsīr* (1963; *One Man and His Gun*) and *Sang-i ṣabūr* (1967; *The Patient Stone*). Chūbak also translated a number of works from English into Persian, including Lewis Carroll's *Alice's Adventures in Wonderland* and *Through the Looking-Glass*.

chüeh-chü *see* JUEJU.

Chu I-tsun *see* ZHU YIZUN.

Chukovsky \chù-'kòf-skʸē\, Korney Ivanovich, *pseudonym of* Nikolay Vasilyevich Korneychukov \kər-ˌnʸē-chù-'kòf\ (b. March 19 [March 31, New Style], 1882, St. Petersburg, Russian Empire—d. Oct. 28, 1969, Moscow, Russian S.F.S.R.) Russian literary critic, language theorist, translator, and author of children's books, often called the first modern Russian writer for children.

Chukovsky pursued a career in journalism, writing for an Odessa newspaper from 1901 to 1905. He subsequently (1905–08) edited the satirical journal *Signal* and began, with a book on Leonid Andreyev, a series of memoirs and analyses that would span three generations of Russian literary life. He translated works by English and American authors, notably Charles Dickens, Mark Twain, and Walt Whitman.

While his translations and criticism, particularly his lifelong study of the 19th-century poet Nikolay Nekrasov, were highly esteemed, Chukovsky's larger reputation rests on his writings for and about children. Many of his verse tales, including *Krokodil* (1917; "The Crocodile"), *Moydodyr* (1923; "Wash 'Em Clean"), and *Tarakanishche* (1923; "The Giant Roach"), are regarded as classics of the form; their clockwork rhythms and air of mischief and lightness in effect dispelled the plodding stodginess that had characterized earlier children's poetry. Adaptations of these tales for the theater, motion pictures, and even opera and ballet (Sergey Prokofiev produced several) remained popular throughout the 20th century.

Chung yung *see* ZHONG YONG.

Chunqiu or **Ch'un-ch'iu** \'chün-'chyù\ ("Spring and Autumn [Annals]") The first Chinese chronological history, said to be the traditional history of Lu, as revised by Confucius. It is one of the Five Classics (*Wu jing*) of Confucianism. The name, actually an abbreviation of "Spring, Summer, Autumn, Winter," derives from the old custom of dating events by season as well as by year. The work is a complete—though exceedingly sketchy—month by month account of significant events of the reigns of 12 rulers of Lu, Confucius' native state. The account begins in 722 BC and ends shortly before Confucius' death (479 BC). The book is said to pass moral judgment on events in subtle ways, as when Confucius deliberately omits the title of a degenerate ruler.

The fame of *Chunqiu* is mainly due to *Zuo zhuan*, a commentary (*zhuan*) by a scholar named Zuo whose dates and identity are even more uncertain than his name (probably Zuoqiu Ming, or Zuo Qiuming). Two other commentaries on *Chunqiu* further added to its fame. Like *Zuo zhuan*, *Gongyang zhuan* and *Guliang zhuan* carry the name of their authors. All three commentaries are listed among the alternative lists of the Nine, Twelve, and Thirteen Classics of Confucianism.

Churchill \'chər-chil\, Caryl (b. Sept. 3, 1938, London, Eng.) British playwright whose work frequently dealt with feminist issues, the abuses of power, and sexual politics.

When she was 10, Churchill and her family immigrated to Canada. She attended Oxford University and remained in England after receiving a B.A. in 1960. Her three earliest plays were performed by Oxford-based theatrical ensembles. During the 1960s and '70s, she wrote radio dramas and then television plays. *Owners* (1973), a play about the obsession with power, was her first major theater piece. During her tenure as resident dramatist at London's Royal Court Theatre, Churchill became associated with David Hare and Max Stafford-Clark's Joint Stock Company and with Monstrous Regiment, a feminist group. *Cloud Nine* (1979), a farce about sexual politics, was successful in the United States as well as in Britain, winning an Obie award in 1982 for best Off-Broadway play. *Top*

Girls (1982), which features a 1980s career woman dining with several women from history, examines the price a woman must pay to attain power in a male-dominated environment; it also received an Obie award. Her later plays include *Softcops* (1984), *Serious Money* (1987), *Icecream* (1989), *Mad Forest* (1990), and *The Skriker* (produced 1994).

Churchill \'chər-chil\, Charles (b. February 1731, London, Eng.—d. Nov. 4, 1764, Boulogne, Fr.) Poet noted for his lampoons and polemical satires written in heroic couplets.

Churchill won his fame in 1761 with *The Rosciad*, a satire on the London stage that spoke unfavorably of every prominent actor of the day except David Garrick. The brilliant and immediate success of this poem brought recognition and money to the bankrupt Churchill, and he launched himself on the town and indulged his profligate tastes.

In 1763 he published *The Prophecy of Famine*, the first of several political satires attacking the government. A quarrel with the artist Hogarth produced Churchill's *Epistle to William Hogarth* in June 1763. In 1764, when his friend John Wilkes (a champion of freedom of the press) was outlawed and in France, Churchill defended him in *The Duellist*. He traveled to Boulogne to join Wilkes but, weakened by disease and dissipation, fell ill and died there.

Churchill \'chər-chil\, Winston (b. Nov. 10, 1871, St. Louis, Mo., U.S.—d. March 12, 1947, Winter Park, Fla.) American author of historical novels of wide popularity.

Churchill graduated from the U.S. Naval Academy in 1894, and having private means, he soon devoted himself to writing. His first novel, *The Celebrity*, appeared in 1898. His next, *Richard Carvel* (1899), a novel of Revolutionary Maryland in which the hero serves as a naval officer under John Paul Jones, sold nearly one million copies. Then followed another great success, *The Crisis* (1901), a novel of the American Civil War, in which the heroine is a descendant of Richard Carvel, and *The Crossing* (1904), which tells of Kentucky pioneers during the American Revolution. His later work consisted chiefly of novels dealing with political, religious, or social problems.

Churchyard \'chər-chərd\, Thomas (b. *c.* 1520, Shrewsbury, Shropshire, Eng.—d. 1604, London) English writer who won brief fame through his occasional verse, pamphlets on wartime experiences, pageants for Queen Elizabeth I, and historical and antiquarian works—all reflecting aspects of a busy career. Churchyard's earliest work was *A Myrrour for Man* (about 1552), reflections on the estate of man. His prolific output included "The Legend of Shore's Wife," his most popular poem, and *The Worthiness of Wales* (1587), written in prose and verse.

After serving in the household of Henry Howard, Earl of Surrey, Churchyard became a mercenary, for 30 years fighting in almost every campaign in Scotland, Ireland, the Low Countries, and France under various banners. Later, at court, he devised pageants for Queen Elizabeth's progresses to Bristol (1574) and Norwich (1578), but when a passage in his *Generall rehearsall of warres* (1579) offended Elizabeth, Churchyard fled to Scotland. He was restored to favor about 1584.

churning of the milky ocean In Hindu mythology, one of the central events in the ever-continuing struggle between the *deva*s (gods) and the *asura*s (demons or titans). The *deva*s, who had become weakened as a result of a curse, invite the *asura*s to help them recover the elixir of immortality from the depths of the cosmic ocean.

Mt. Mandara (a spur of the world axis, Mt. Meru) is torn out to use as a churning stick and is steadied at the bottom of the ocean by Vishnu in his aspect as the tortoise Kūrma. The *asura*s hold the head of the *nāga* (serpent) Vāsuki, who was procured for a churning rope, and the *deva*s hold his tail. When

Vāsuki's head hits the rocks and he vomits forth poison that threatens to fall into the ocean and contaminate the elixir, Śiva takes the poison and holds it in his throat, a feat that turns his throat blue.

In the churning of the ocean many wonderful treasures that become the prototypes for their earthly and heavenly counterparts are brought up from the depths. They include Candra, the moon; the four-tusked elephant Airāvata, Indra's mount; Kāmadhenu, the cow of plenty; Madirā, the goddess of wine; the goddess Lakṣmī, who becomes the wife of Vishnu; and Dhanvantari, the physician of the gods, who rises from the waters carrying in his hands the supreme treasure, the elixir.

After further struggle, the *deva*s ultimately consume the elixir and are restored in strength.

Chūshingura \'chū-'shiŋ-gù-rā\ (*in full* Kanadehon Chūshingura; "Copybook of the Treasury of Loyal Retainers") Classic play cycle of the Japanese kabuki theater. The kabuki drama was adapted from an original written in about 1748 for the bunraku puppet theater by Takeda Izumo with Namiki Sōsuke (Senryū) and Miyoshi Shōraku. In 11 acts it dramatizes the incidents that took place from 1701 to 1703, when 47 *rōnin* (masterless samurai) waited two years before avenging themselves on a man who had forced their overlord to commit suicide. The cycle has been the basis of a number of popular films. An English translation of the puppet play by Donald Keene (*Chūshingura: The Treasury of Loyal Retainers*) was published in 1971.

Chu Yi-tsun *see* ZHU YIZUN.

Ch'ü Yüan *see* QU YUAN.

Chuzzlewit, Martin \'märt-ən-'chəz-əl-wit\ Fictional character, the protagonist of the novel MARTIN CHUZZLEWIT by Charles Dickens.

ci or **tz'u** \'chə\ [Chinese (Beijing dialect) *cí*] In Chinese poetry, song form characterized by lines of unequal length, with prescribed rhyme schemes and tonal patterns, each bearing the name of a musical air. The varying line lengths are comparable to the natural rhythm of speech and therefore easily understood when sung. First sung by ordinary people, they were popularized by professional women singers and attracted the attention of poets during the Tang dynasty (618–907). The *ci* served as a major vehicle for Song dynasty (960–1279) verse.

It was not, however, until the transitional period of the Five Dynasties (907–960), a time of division and strife, that *ci* became the major vehicle of lyrical expression. Of *ci* poets in this period, the greatest was Li Yu, last monarch of the Nan Tang (Southern Tang).

Ciardi \'chär-dē, 'chyär-\, John (Anthony) (b. June 24, 1916, Boston, Mass., U.S.—d. March 30, 1986, Edison, N.J.) American poet, critic, and translator who contributed to making poetry accessible to both adults and children.

Educated at Bates College (Lewiston, Maine), Tufts University (A.B., 1938), and the University of Michigan (M.A., 1939), Ciardi served in the U.S. Army Air Corps (1942–45) and then taught at universities until 1961. He served as poetry editor of the *Saturday Review* from 1956 to 1972. He felt that interaction between audience and author was crucial, and he generated continuous controversy with his critical reviews.

Ciardi's first volume of poetry, *Homeward to America*, appeared in 1940. His *How Does a Poem Mean?* (1960; rev. ed., with Miller Williams, 1975) found wide use as a poetry textbook in high schools and colleges. His other books of poetry include *Person to Person* (1964), *The Little That Is All* (1974), and *For Instance* (1979). He also wrote many books of prose and verse for children.

His translation of Dante's *Divine Comedy* was highly acclaimed. Rather than following Dante's rhyme scheme, Ciardi attempted to capture the feeling of the original in a tense and economical modern verse idiom.

His later works include two books written with Isaac Asimov: *Limericks, Too Gross* (1978) and *A Grossery of Limericks* (1981). Ciardi also wrote *A Browser's Dictionary and Native's Guide to the Unknown American Language* (1980) and *A Second Browser's Dictionary and Native's Guide to the Unknown American Language* (1983).

Cibber \'sib-ər\, Colley (b. Nov. 6, 1671, London, Eng.—d. Dec. 11, 1757, London) English actor, theater manager, playwright, and poet laureate of England, whose play *Love's Last Shift; or, The Fool in Fashion* (1696) is generally considered one of the first sentimental comedies, a form of drama that dominated the English stage for nearly a century. His autobiography, *An Apology for the Life of Mr. Colley Cibber* (1740), contains the best account of the theater of his day and is an invaluable study of the art of acting as it was practiced by his contemporaries.

Cibber began his acting career in 1690 at the Drury Lane Theatre, London. He wrote *Love's Last Shift* to provide himself with a role; the play established his reputation both as actor and as playwright. The playwright Sir John Vanbrugh honored it with a sequel, *The Relapse: or, Virtue in Danger* (1696). In 1700 Cibber produced his famous adaptation of William Shakespeare's *Richard III*, which held the stage as the preferred acting version of the play for more than 150 years. Cibber also wrote other comedies of manners, including *She wou'd, and She wou'd not* (1702) and *The Careless Husband* (1704).

By 1710 Cibber was one of a famous "triumvirate" of actor-managers under which Drury Lane Theatre conspicuously prospered. After the death of Queen Anne, he entered the political arena, writing and adapting plays (notably *The Non-Juror*, in 1717, from Molière's *Tartuffe*) in support of the Whig cause with a skill and energy that in 1730 led to his appointment as poet laureate. In 1728 Cibber completed *The Provok'd Husband*, a play left unfinished by Vanbrugh at his death in 1726. Cibber made his final stage appearance on Feb. 15, 1745, when he played in his own adaptation of Shakespeare's *King John*.

Cibber \'sib-ər\, Theophilus (b. Nov. 26, 1703—d. 1758, at sea) Actor and playwright, a figure of general disrepute in the English theater.

The son of Colley Cibber, he made his first appearance on the stage in 1721. He was a capable actor, but the plays he wrote are considered worthless. There is perhaps no contemporary reference to Cibber that does not set him down as a scoundrel. He traded dishonestly on his father's name and engaged in blackmail, shameless plagiarism, and scandalous lawsuits to obtain money. He died in a shipwreck while on his way to act in Dublin.

Cicero \'sis-ə-,rō\, Marcus Tullius, *English byname* Tully \'təl-ē\ (b. 106 BC, Arpinum, Latium [now Arpino, Italy]—d. Dec. 7, 43 BC, Formiae, Latium [now Formia]) Roman statesman, lawyer, scholar, and writer who vainly tried to uphold republican principles in the final civil wars that destroyed the republic of Rome. His writings include books of rhetoric, orations, philosophical and political treatises, and letters. He is remembered in modern times as the greatest Roman orator and innovator of what became known as Ciceronian rhetoric.

Cicero was the son of a wealthy family and was educated in Rome and in Greece. He quickly established a reputation as a brilliant lawyer. His public career began in 75 BC and in 63 he was elected consul. He plunged into the treacherous waters of Roman politics, rife with conspiracy and factionalism. His oratorical powers were successfully brought to bear against the

conspiracy of Catiline in 63 but by 58 he had been sent into exile. Forced into supporting the alliance of Julius Caesar, Crassus, and Pompey, he abandoned public life in 56.

In the next few years he completed the treatises *De oratore* (55; "On the Orator") and *De republica* (52; "On the State") and began the *De legibus* (52; "On Laws"). In 51 he was persuaded to leave Rome to govern the province of Cilicia, in south Asia Minor, for a year. By the time he returned to Rome, Pompey and Caesar were struggling for complete power. Works of this period included *Brutus* and *Orator*, in 46; *De finibus bonorum et malorum* ("On the Different Conceptions of the Chief Good and Evil"), in 45; and *Tusculanae disputationes* ("Discussions at Tusculum"), *De natura deorum* ("On the Nature of Gods"), and *De officiis* ("On [Moral] Duties"), finished after Caesar's murder, in 44.

Cicero's 14 Philippic orations (so called in imitation of Demosthenes' speeches against Philip II of Macedonia) were delivered in the turmoil after Caesar's death in an attempt to drive the Senate to declare war on Antony. Cicero had made an enemy of Caesar's adopted son Octavian, and, when the triumvirate of Octavian, Antony, and Lepidus was formed at the end of October 43, Cicero was executed.

From Cicero's correspondence between 67 and July 43 BC more than 900 letters survive. These constitute a primary historical source such as exists for no other part of the ancient world. Cicero is a minor but by no means negligible figure in the history of Latin poetry. His verse, surviving only in fragments, is technically important; he refined the hexameter and applied rhetorical devices to poetry.

Cicero's chief reputation is as an orator in politics and in the law courts, where he preferred appearing for the defense and generally spoke last because of his emotive powers. His rhetoric was a complex art form, and the ears of the audience were keenly attuned to these effects. Of the speeches, 58 have survived, some in an incomplete form.

Ciceronian period \,sis-ə-'rō-nē-ən\ The first great age of Latin literature, from approximately 70 to 43 BC; together with the following AUGUSTAN AGE, it forms the Golden Age of Latin literature. The political and literary scene was dominated by Cicero, a statesman, orator, poet, critic, and philosopher who perfected the Latin language as a literary medium, expressing abstract and complicated thoughts with clarity and creating the important quantitative prose rhythm. Cicero's influence on Latin prose was so great that subsequent prose—not only in Latin but in later vernacular languages up to the 19th century—was either a reaction against or a return to his style. Other outstanding figures of the Ciceronian period are Julius Caesar, notable for political oratory and vivid military narratives; Marcus Terentius Varro, who wrote on topics as varied as farming and the Latin language; and Sallust, who opposed Cicero's style and espoused one later imitated by Seneca, Tacitus, and Juvenal. Among Ciceronian poets are Catullus, the first master of the Latin love lyric, and Lucretius, the author of the long didactic poem *De rerum natura* (*On the Nature of Things*).

Cid, Le \lə-'sēd\ Five-act verse tragedy about the national hero of Spain by Pierre CORNEILLE, performed and published in 1637. It is regarded as the first classical tragedy of French theater and one of Corneille's finest plays.

Initially issued as a tragicomedy, *Le Cid* proved an immense popular success. It sparked a literary controversy, however, and the Académie Française issued a judgment that admitted the play's beauties but criticized it as dramatically implausible and morally defective. Cardinal de Richelieu used the judgment of the Académie as an excuse for suppressing public performances of the play. Corneille, indeed, had not observed the dramatic unities in *Le Cid*. He also rejected the discursive treatment of the subject given in his Spanish source, concentrating instead on a conflict between passionate love and family loyalty or honor, thus anticipating the so-called pure tragedy of Jean Racine.

Cid, The \\'sid\\, *Spanish* El Cid \el-'thēth, 'sēth\\, *also called* El Campeador \el-ˌkäm-pē-'äth-ôr\ ("The Champion"), *byname of* Rodrigo \rōth-'rē-g̱ō\, *or* Ruy, Díaz de Vivar \'rwē . . . 'thē-äth-thä-'ḇē-ḇär\ (b. *c.* 1043, Vivar, near Burgos, Castile [Spain]—d. July 10, 1099, Valencia) Castilian military leader and national hero. His popular name, El Cid (from Spanish Arabic *as-sīd*, "lord"), dates from his lifetime.

For authentic information on The Cid's life, historians relied mainly on a few contemporary documents, on the *Historia Roderici* (a reliable, private 12th-century Latin chronicle of The Cid's life), and on a detailed eyewitness account of his conquest of Valencia by the Arab historian Ibn 'Alqāmah. The Cid's biography presents special problems for the historian because he was speedily elevated to the status of national hero of Castile, and a complex heroic biography of him, in which legend played a dominant role, came into existence; the legend was magnified by the influence of the mid-12th- to early 13th-century epic poem of Castile, CANTAR DE MIO CID ("Song of My Cid"), and was further developed by such writers as Guillén de Castro y Belvís and Pierre Corneille.

cielito \ˌsē-e-'lē-tō, ˌthē-\ Poetic form associated with gaucho literature, consisting of an octosyllabic quatrain written in colloquial language and rhyming in the second and fourth lines. The Uruguayan poet Bartolomé Hidalgo was especially known for his poems in this form. The form takes its name from the frequent use of the word *cielito* (Spanish: "darling," literally "little heaven") in refrains.

Cilappatikāram \ˌsē-lə-pə-tē-'kä-rəm\ ("The Jewelled Anklet") The earliest epic Tamil poem in three books, written in the 5th-6th century AD by Iḷaṅkō Aṭikaḷ. Its plot is derived from a well-known story. It was published in English translation as *Shilappadikaram (The Ankle Bracelet)*.

The *Cilappatikāram* tells of the young merchant Kōvalaṇ's marriage to the virtuous Kaṇṇaki, his love for the courtesan Mātavi, and his consequent ruin and exile in Maturai, where he is unjustly executed after trying to sell his wife's anklet to a wicked goldsmith who had stolen the queen's similar anklet and charged Kōvalaṇ with the theft. The widow Kaṇṇaki comes to Maturai, proves Kōvalaṇ's innocence, then tears off one breast and throws it at the kingdom of Maturai, which goes up in flames. Such is the power of a faithful wife. The third book deals with a king's expedition to obtain Himalayan stone for an image of Kaṇṇaki, now a goddess of chastity.

The *Cilappatikāram* is a fine synthesis of mood poetry in the ancient Tamil *caṅkam* tradition and the rhetoric of Sanskrit poetry, including the dialogues of *Kalittokai* (poems of unrequited or mismatched love), chorus folk song, descriptions of city and village, lovingly technical accounts of dance and music, and strikingly dramatic scenes of love and tragic death. One of the great achievements of Tamil genius, the *Cilappatikāram* is a detailed poetic witness to Tamil culture, its varied religions, town plans and city types, the commingling of Greek, Arab, and Tamil peoples, and the arts of dance and music. An incomplete sequel by Cātaṇār entitled *Maṇimēkalai* (the heroine's name, meaning "girdle of gems") is the story of Mātavi's daughter and her struggle to overcome her passion for a princely lover and to find spiritual fulfillment.

Cimmerian \si-'mir-ē-ən\ One of a mythical people described by Homer as dwelling in a remote realm of mist and gloom.

Cinderella \ˌsin-də-'rel-ə\ Heroine of a European folktale, the theme of which appears in many stories worldwide. More than 500 versions of the story have been recorded in Europe alone. Its essential features are a youngest daughter who is mistreated by her jealous stepmother and elder stepsisters or a cruel father, intervention of a supernatural helper on her behalf, and the reversal of fortune brought about by a prince who falls in love with her and marries her. One of the oldest known literary renderings of the theme is a Chinese version recorded in the 9th century AD.

The familiar English version is a translation of Charles Perrault's "Cendrillon," which appeared in his influential collection of fairy tales, *Contes de ma mère l'oye* (1697; *Tales of Mother Goose*). The prince's recognition of the heroine by the token of a glass slipper is unique in Perrault.

Cinna \sē-'nà\ (*in full* Cinna, ou la clémence d'Auguste) Play in five acts by Pierre CORNEILLE, produced in 1641 and published in 1643. Subtitled "The Clemency of Augustus" and based on a passage in *De clementia* by Seneca the Younger, the Neoclassical tragedy recounts a plot to assassinate the Roman emperor Augustus and the mercy he shows to the conspirators after their arrest. It is noted for its elevated language and powerful characterizations.

Cinna \'sin-ə\, Gaius Helvius (fl. 1st century BC) Roman poet who wrote a mythological epic poem *Smyrna*. Cinna is also credited with having written a *Propempticon Pollionis*, a poem in the form of a "send-off" to his friend Asinius Pollio. In both these poems, the language of which was so obscure that they required special commentaries, his model appears to have been Parthenius of Nicaea, the Greek poet and teacher of Virgil.

Cino da Pistoia \'chē-nō-dä-pēs-'tôi-ä\, *original name* Cino dei Sighibuldi \ˌdä-ˌsē-gē-'bül-dē\ (b. *c.* 1270, Pistoia, near Florence [Italy]—d. 1336/37, Pistoia) Italian jurist, poet, and prose writer whose poetry, written in the *dolce stil nuovo* ("sweet new style"), was admired by Dante and was a great influence on Petrarch.

With the completion of his highly praised Latin commentary, *Lectura in Codicem* ("Studies on the Code"), on the first nine books of Justinian's Codex Constitutionum, Cino received his doctorate in law (1314) at the University of Bologna and then taught law at several universities. In 1334 he returned to Pistoia, where he spent the rest of his life.

One of the most prolific of the *dolce stil nuovo* poets, Cino is generally considered inferior to others of the school despite the fact that in *De vulgari eloquentia* ("Of Eloquence in the Vulgar Tongue") Dante calls him the best Italian love poet. Some of his poems are biographical, such as his canzone to Dante on the death of Beatrice. Most of them, however, have been praised for their gracefulness rather than for their content or emotional depth. Petrarch, who called Cino his master and wrote a poem mourning his death, used some of Cino's themes as starting points for his own verse.

Cinq-Mars \ˌseⁿk-'màrs\ Novel by Alfred de VIGNY, published in two volumes in 1826 as *Cinq-Mars; ou, une conjuration sous Louis XIII* (*Cinq-Mars; or, A Conspiracy Under Louis XIII*). It was the first significant historical novel in French.

The novel recreates the failed conspiracy against Cardinal Richelieu led by the Marquis de Cinq-Mars. Cinq-Mars, a favorite of Louis XIII, and his fellow aristocratic coconspirator, François de Thou, are beheaded after Cardinal Richelieu foils their plot to discredit him. *Cinq-Mars* illustrates the waning power of the 17th-century aristocracy and Richelieu's subversion of the French feudal system, which foreshadowed the inevitable downfall of the monarchy.

cinquain \'siŋ-ˌkān\ [Middle French, from *cinq* five + *-ain,* suffix forming nouns from numerals] A five-line stanza. An American poet, Adelaide Crapsey (1878–1914), applied the term in particular to a five-line verse form of specific meter that she developed. Analogous to the Japanese verse forms haiku and tanka, it has two syllables in its first and last lines and four, six, and eight in the intervening three lines and generally has an iambic cadence. An example is her poem "November Night":

> Listen..
> With faint dry sound
> Like steps of passing ghosts,
> the leaves, frost-crisp'd, break from the trees
> And fall.

cinquecento \ˌchēŋ-kwä-'chen-tō\ [Italian, literally, five hundred, short for *mille cinquecento* the year 1500] The 16th century; specifically, the 16th-century period in Italian literature and art.

Cinzio or **Cinthio**   *see* Giambattista GIRALDI.

Circe \'sər-sē\ In Greek legend, a sorceress, the daughter of Helios (the sun god), and the ocean nymph Perse. She was able by means of drugs and incantations to change humans into wolves, lions, and swine. The Greek hero Odysseus visited her island, Aeaea, with his companions, whom she changed into swine. But Odysseus, protected by the herb moly (a gift from Hermes), compelled her to restore them to their original shape. He stayed with her for one year before resuming his journey.

circular tale A factitious jocular narrative indefinitely repeated in which the last element leads to repetition of the first.

circumbendibus \ˌsər-kəm-'ben-di-bəs\ [Latin *circum* round about + English *bend* + Latin *-ibus,* ablative plural ending] An indirect or roundabout course, especially one taken in writing or speech.

circumlocution \ˌsər-kəm-lō-'kyü-shən\ [Latin *circumlocutio,* from *circum* around + *locutio* speech, expression; a calque of Greek *períphrasis*] **1.** *also called* PERIPHRASIS The use of an unnecessarily large number of words to express an idea. **2.** Evasion in speech.

Cisneros \sis-'ner-ōs\, Sandra (b. Dec. 20, 1954, Chicago, Ill., U.S.) Short-story writer and poet best known for her evocation of Mexican-American life in Chicago.

After graduating from Chicago's Loyola University (B.A., 1976), Cisneros attended the University of Iowa Writers' Workshop (M.F.A., 1978). There she developed what was to be the theme of most of her writing, her unique experiences as a Hispanic woman in a largely alien culture.

Cisneros' first book of fiction, *The House on Mango Street* (1983), was a collection of semiautobiographical prose-poems that recall a girlhood spent trying to be a creative writer in an antagonistic environment. *Woman Hollering Creek and Other Stories* (1991) contained tales of beleaguered girls and women who nonetheless feel that they have power over their destinies. Cisneros' volumes of poetry include *Bad Boys* (1980) and *The Rodrigo Poems* (1985). *My Wicked, Wicked Ways* (1987) collected 60 poems on subjects such as her hometown of Chicago, European travels, and sexual guilt.

citizen comedy A form of drama produced in the early 17th century in England. Such comedies were set in London and portrayed the everyday life of the middle classes. Examples include Ben Jonson's *Bartholomew Fair* (1614) and Thomas Middleton's *A Chaste Mayd in Cheape-side* (1630).

City of God, The Philosophical treatise vindicating Christianity written by the medieval philosopher Saint AUGUSTINE as *De civitate Dei* about AD 413–26. A masterpiece of Western culture, *The City of God* was written in response to pagan claims that the sack of Rome by barbarians in 410 was one of the consequences of the abolition of pagan worship by Christian emperors. St. Augustine responded by asserting, to the contrary, that Christianity saved the city from complete destruction and that Rome's fall was the result of internal moral decay. He further outlined his vision of two societies, that of the elect ("The City of God") and that of the damned ("The City of Man"). These "cities" are symbolic embodiments of the two spiritual powers—faith and unbelief—that have contended with each other since the fall of the angels. St. Augustine also developed his theological interpretation of human history, which he perceives as linear and predestined, beginning with creation and ending with the Second Coming of Christ.

The City of God was one of the most influential works of the Middle Ages. St. Augustine's famous theory that people need government because they are sinful served as a model for church-state relations in medieval times.

civic poetry A 19th-century Russian literary movement whose proponents held that poetry should serve social and civic purposes and that poets should be accepted as integral members of the community. The movement was led by Nikolay Alekseyevich Nekrasov, and many of its adherents were noted for their caustic satires against the government. Many of these poets wrote for liberal journals, notably *Sovremennik* ("The Contemporary"), under Nekrasov's editorship in 1846–66. The civic poets, most of whom came from the lower classes, emphasized the political possibilities of poetry and introduced the culture of the common people into the national verse. One of the most important of the civic poets was the Decembrist Kondraty Fyodorovich Ryleyev, who expressed abhorrence of czarist oppression and glorified death in the struggle against it. Other major civic poets included Nikolay Dobrolyubov, Ivan Nikitin, and Ivan Aksakov.

Civil Disobedience Essay by Henry David THOREAU, originally delivered as a lecture at the Concord Lyceum in January–February 1848 and published in the only issue of the magazine *Aesthetic Papers* in May 1849 as "Resistance to Civil Government"; it was retitled "Civil Disobedience" in the posthumous collection *A Yankee in Canada, with Anti-Slavery and Reform Papers* (1866).

The essay is a defense of the private, individual conscience against the expediency of the majority and as such it contains Thoreau's defiantly anarchistic views of government. To Thoreau, moral law is superior to civil law, even if a penalty ensues, because "under a government which imprisons any unjustly, the true place for a just man is also a prison." The essay remains an important treatise on American individualism.

Cixous \sē-'zü\, Hélène (b. June 5, 1937, Oran, Alg.) French feminist critic, novelist, and playwright.

Cixous's first language was German. She was reared in North Africa, a circumstance that, by her own account, gave her the undying desire to fight the violations of the human spirit wrought by power. In France during the 1960s she taught at the University of Bordeaux and at the Sorbonne. In 1968 she helped establish the innovative University of Paris VIII–Vincennes and assumed the professorship of English literature there. In 1969, the year her first novel, *Dedans* (*Inside*), was published, she helped found the literary review *Poetique*. During 1970–72 she issued her fiction trilogy *Le Troisième Corps* ("The Third Body"), *Les Commencements* ("Beginnings"), and *Neutre* ("Neuter").

In her essay collection *Prénoms de personne* (1974; "Nobody's Name") and in *La Jeune Née* (1975; *The Newly Born Woman*, coauthored by Catherine Clément), Cixous wrote about issues of sexual difference and about female experience in writing. In books such as *Le Livre de Promethea* (1983; *The Book of Promethea*), she reinterpreted myths and the mythic past and analyzed the representations of women in Western culture. *Portrait de Dora* (1976; *Portrait of Dora*) was the first of her plays to be produced. Her later works include the play *L'Indiade; ou, l'Inde de leurs rêves* (1987; "The Indiade; or, India of their Dreams"), collections of essays and lectures, and the novels *L'heure de Clarice Lispector* (1989; *Reading with Clarice Lispector*) and *L'Ange au secret* (1991).

Claes \'kläs\, Ernest (André Jozef) (b. Oct. 24, 1885, Zichem, Belg.—d. Sept. 2, 1968, Uccle)   Popular Flemish novelist and short-story writer who sometimes wrote in German. The novel that made his reputation, *De Witte* (1920; *Whitey*), is a regional novel about a playful, prankish youngster.

Claes's writings were varied in subject. Animals and children were treated in such works as *Herman Coene* (1925–30), *Kiki* (1925), and *Floere het fluwijn* (1950; "Floere the Polecat"). World War I was the topic of *Namen 1914* (1916). *De fanfare 'De Sint-Jans-vrienden'* (1924; "The Fanfare 'The Friends of St. John' ") and *Het leven en de dood van Victalis van Gille* (1951; "The Life and the Death of Victalis van Gille") describe village life and village folk. His tone was occasionally judgmental, as in *De vulgaire geschiedenis van Charelke Dop* (1924; "The Ignoble History of Charelke Dop"), a bitter tale of a war profiteer, and *Clementine* (1940), the story of a dishonest servant girl.

Claggert, John \'jän-'klag-ərt\   Fictional character, the sinister master-at-arms aboard the ship *Indomitable* in the novel BILLY BUDD, FORETOPMAN by Herman Melville.

Clampitt \'klam-pit\, Amy (b. June 15, 1920, New Providence, Iowa, U.S.—d. Sept. 10, 1994, Lenox, Mass.)   American poet whose work won critical acclaim for its evocation of the natural world.

After graduating from Grinnell College, Clampitt worked as a reference librarian and as an editor, publishing her first book of poetry, *Multitudes, Multitudes* (1973), at her own expense. Her first full-length collection was *The Kingfisher* (1983). It was especially noted for its use of elaborate syntax and vocabulary. *What the Light Was Like* (1985), also highly praised, contained several poems about death, including two elegies to her brother, who had died in 1981 and to whom the work was dedicated. Literary critics commented on the ease and certainty with which Clampitt employed literary allusions as well as references to nature and on her ornamented, sometimes eccentric style. Later collections include *Archaic Figure* (1987), *Westward* (1990), and *Silence Opens* (1994).

Clanvowe \'klan-,vō\, Sir Thomas (fl. *c.* 1400)   English courtier and poet, the reputed author of *The Cuckoo and the Nightingale*, long attributed to Geoffrey Chaucer. The poem is a traditional dialogue between the two birds about the power of love, with delicate and attractive descriptions of spring. It has a verse style that, though faulty at times, is Chaucerian in inspiration. *The Cuckoo and the Nightingale*, called in some manuscripts *The Book of Cupid, God of Love*, first appeared in William Thynne's edition of Chaucer in 1532, and it was not until W.W. Skeat's edition of Chaucer's works in 1894–97 that the poem was ascribed to Clanvowe, whose name appeared on the best of the extant manuscripts.

Clare \'klar\, John (b. July 13, 1793, Helpston, near Peterborough, Northamptonshire, Eng.—d. May 20, 1864, Northampton, Northamptonshire)   English peasant poet of the Romantic school.

Clare grew up in extreme poverty and began work as a herder at the age of seven. Though he had little access to books, he had a prodigious memory, and his poetic gift, which revealed itself early, was nourished by his parents' store of folk ballads. His early work was chiefly influenced by the Scottish poet James Thomson.

In 1820 his first book, *Poems Descriptive of Rural Life and Scenery*, was published and created a stir. Clare visited London, where he enjoyed a brief season of celebrity in fashionable circles. That same year he married Martha Turner, the daughter of a neighboring farmer and the "Patty of the Vale" of his verses. From then on he encountered increasing misfortune. His second volume of poems attracted little attention. His third, *The Shepherd's Calendar; with Village Stories, and Other Poems* (1827), though containing better poetry, met with the same fate. Poverty, the lack of patronage, and drink took their toll on his health. His last book, *The Rural Muse* (1835), though praised by critics, again sold poorly. Clare began to suffer from fears and delusions. In 1837, through the agency of his publisher, he was placed in a private asylum at High Beech, Epping, where he remained for four years. Improved in health and driven by homesickness, he escaped in July 1841. He walked the 80 miles to Northborough, penniless, eating grass by the roadside to stay his hunger. He left a moving account in prose of the extraordinary journey, addressed to his imaginary wife "Mary Clare." He was home about seven months, but at the end of 1841 he was certified insane. He spent the final 23 years of his life at St. Andrew's Asylum, Northampton, writing, with strangely unquenched lyric impulse, some of his best poetry. *Selected Poems and Prose*, edited by Eric Robinson and Geoffrey Summerfield, was published in 1966.

Clare, Angel \'än-jəl-'klar\   Fictional character, the idealistic husband of the title character in TESS OF THE D'URBERVILLES by Thomas Hardy. He is disillusioned by Tess's revelations to him, but he eventually comes to terms with his love for her.

Clarín   *see* Leopoldo ALAS.

Clarissa (*in full* Clarissa; or, The History of a Young Lady) \klə-'ris-ə\   Epistolary novel by Samuel RICHARDSON, published in 1747–48.

Richardson first presents the heroine, Clarissa Harlowe, when she is discovering the barely masked motives of her family, who want to force her into a loveless marriage to improve their fortunes. When Lovelace, a romantic who holds the code of the Harlowes in contempt, offers her protection, she runs off with him. She is physically attracted by if not actually in love with Lovelace, but she is to discover that he wants her only on his own terms and she refuses to marry him. In Lovelace's letters to his friend Belford, Richardson shows that what is driving him to conquest and finally to rape is really revenge for her family's insults and his sense of Clarissa's moral superiority. For Clarissa, however, accepting marriage as a convenience is no better than accepting the opportunistic moral code of her family. As the novel comes to its long-drawn-out close, she is removed from the world of both the Harlowes and the Lovelaces, and she dies true to herself to the end.

Clark \'klärk\, John Pepper, *pseudonym* J.P. Clark Bekederemo \,bä-kä-dä-'rä-mō\ (b. April 6, 1935, Kiagbodo, Nigeria)   Nigerian poet whose collection *A Reed in the Tide* (1965) was the first collection of poems by a black African to be published internationally. He also won note as a journalist, playwright, and scholar-critic who conducted research into traditional Ijo (Ijaw) myths and legends and wrote a number of essays on African poetry.

Clark graduated from the University of Ibadan in 1960 with honors in English. A year's study at Princeton University resulted in his *America, Their America* (1964), in which he attacks

American middle-class values, from capitalism to black American lifestyles. He later became a lecturer in English at the University of Lagos and coeditor of the distinguished literary journal *Black Orpheus.*

In *Poems* (1962) and *A Reed in the Tide*, each poem is the result of a single lyrical impulse, which is frequently inspired by a specific moment in the past. His *Casualties: Poems 1966–68* (1970) is concerned primarily with the Nigerian civil war. Other poetry collections include *A Decade of Tongues* (1981) and *State of the Union* (1985, as J.P. Clark Bekederemo).

Of his plays, the first three (published together under the title *Three Plays* in 1964) are tragedies in which individuals are unable to escape the doom brought about by an inexorable law of nature or society. *Song of a Goat* and *The Masquerade* are family tragedies, and *The Raft* is considered to be his finest piece of dramatic writing. The situation of four men helplessly adrift on a raft in the Niger River suggests both the human predicament and the dilemma of Nigeria in the modern world.

A more experimental work, *Ozidi* (1966), is a stage version of a traditional Ijo ritual play, which in a native village would take seven days to perform. Like Yoruba folk opera, it is alive with music, dancing, mime, and spectacle. Clark also produced a film, *The Ozidi of Atazi* (1972; with Francis Speed), and an English translation of this Ijo epic.

Clark \\'klärk\\, Walter van Tilburg (b. Aug. 3, 1909, East Orland, Maine, U.S.—d. Nov. 10, 1971, Reno, Nev.) American novelist and short-story writer whose works, set in the American West, used the familiar regional materials of the cowboy, outdoor, or frontier tale as a starting point for the exploration of philosophical issues.

Clark grew up in Reno, which forms the background for his novel *The City of Trembling Leaves* (1945), the story of a sensitive adolescent boy's development. His best-known work is THE OX-BOW INCIDENT (1940; film, 1943). The story of a lynching in 1885 of three innocent men, it conveys a powerful and dramatic insight into mob psychology. *The Track of the Cat* (1949), a tale of a hunt for a black panther during a blizzard, is also a moral parable. *The Watchful Gods* (1950) is a collection of short stories.

Clarke \\'klärk\\, Arthur C., *in full* Charles (b. Dec. 16, 1917, Minehead, Somerset, Eng.) English science-fiction writer, some of whose concepts have had remarkable real-life parallels, particularly in the development of satellite communications.

Interested in science from childhood, Clarke as a youth mapped the Moon with the aid of a telescope of his own construction. Lacking sufficient money for higher education, he worked as a government auditor. From 1941 to 1946 Clarke served in the Royal Air Force, becoming a radar instructor and technician. While in the service he published his first science-fiction stories.

After the war, Clarke earned a degree from King's College, London (B.Sc., 1948), with honors in physics and mathematics, and then became a prolific science-fiction writer, known especially for such novels as *Childhood's End* (1953), *Earthlight* (1955), *A Fall of Moondust* (1961), *Rendezvous with Rama* (1973), and *The Fountains of Paradise* (1979). Collections of essays and lectures include *Voices from the Sky* (1965), *The View from Serendip* (1977), *Ascent to Orbit: A Scientific Autobiography* (1984), and *Astounding Days: A Science Fictional Autobiography* (1989).

In the 1950s Clarke developed an interest in undersea exploration and moved to Ceylon (now Sri Lanka). He reported his underwater ventures in a succession of books, the first of which was *The Coast of Coral* (1956). In the 1960s Clarke collaborated with motion-picture director Stanley Kubrick in making the innovative science-fiction film *2001: A Space Odyssey* (1968), based on Clarke's short story "The Sentinel" (1951), subsequently developed into a novel (1968). A sequel novel, *2010: Odyssey Two* (1982), was made into a film in 1984. A further novel in the series was *2061: Odyssey Three* (1987).

Clarke \\'klärk\\, Charles Cowden and **Clarke**, Mary (Victoria) Cowden, *original surname* Novello (respectively b. Dec. 15, 1787, Enfield, Middlesex, Eng.—d. March 13, 1877, Genoa, Italy; b. June 22, 1809, London, Eng.—d. Jan. 12, 1898, Genoa) English editors and critics best known for their work on William Shakespeare.

Charles Clarke became a partner in music publishing with Alfred Novello, whose sister, Mary, he married in 1828. Six years later Clarke began his public lectures on Shakespeare and other dramatists and poets. Those published include *Shakespeare Characters; Chiefly Those Subordinate* (1863) and *Molière Characters* (1865). In 1863 he edited George Herbert's poems and in the next 14 years produced new editions of nearly all the English poets.

After Mary had compiled her *Shakespeare Concordance* (1845), the couple collaborated on an edition of Shakespeare (completed in 1868) and *The Shakespeare Key: Unlocking the Treasures of His Style* (1879). They were mainly interested in character study, and Mary's *Girlhood of Shakespeare's Heroines* appeared in 1851–52.

Clarke \\'klärk\\, Marcus (Andrew Hislop) (b. April 24, 1846, London, Eng.—d. Aug. 2, 1881, Melbourne, Vic., Australia) English-born Australian author known for his novel *His Natural Life* (1874; the phrase *For the Term of* was added to the title without authority after his death), the first novel regarded as an Australian classic.

At the age of 17 Clarke left England for Australia, where his uncle was a county court judge. By 1867, however, he was writing stories for *Australian Magazine* and working as a theater critic on the *Melbourne Argus*. Commissioned by the *Australian Journal* to write a serial about convict life, Clarke produced his masterwork, *His Natural Life*, the story of Rufus Dawes, a man falsely convicted of a crime who falls into the degradation of the convict world. It was written melodramatically in a style of almost garish realism. Clarke's numerous novels and tales were collected in *The Austral Edition of the Selected Works of Marcus Clarke* (1890).

classic \\'klas-ik\\ [French *classique,* from Latin *classicus* belonging to the highest of the five classes of Roman citizens] **1.** A literary work of ancient Greece or Rome. **2.** A work of enduring excellence or the author of such a work.

classicism \\'klas-ə-,siz-əm\\ **1.** The principles, historical tradition, aesthetic attitudes, or style of the literature of Greece and Rome in antiquity. In the context of the tradition, classicism refers either to the work produced in antiquity or to later works inspired by those of antiquity; NEOCLASSICISM always refers to the art produced later but inspired by antiquity. The terms are sometimes used interchangeably. **2.** Classical scholarship. **3.** Adherence to or practice of the virtues thought to be characteristic of classicism or to be universally and enduringly valid (such as formal elegance and correctness, simplicity, dignity, restraint, order, proportion). The term is often opposed to ROMANTICISM.

Periods of classicism in literature have generally coincided with the classical periods in the visual arts. In literature, for instance, the first major revival of classicism occurred during the Renaissance, when Cicero's prose was especially imitated. France in the 17th century developed a rich and diversified classicism in literature, as it did in the visual arts. The dramatists Pierre Corneille and Jean Racine, together with the philosophers Blaise Pascal and René Descartes, were particularly important. In England, classicism in literature arose later than in France and reached its zenith in the 18th-century writings of John Dryden and Alexander Pope. *Compare* AUGUSTAN AGE. G.E. Lessing, J.W. von Goethe, and Friedrich Schiller were major figures in the German classical literary movement. In the early 20th century, T.S. Eliot and proponents of New Criticism were sometimes considered classicists because they valued restraint and because they emphasized form and discipline.

Claudel \klō-'del\, Paul(-Louis-Charles-Marie) (b. Aug. 6, 1868, Villeneuve-sur-Fère, Fr.—d. Feb. 23, 1955, Paris) Poet, playwright, and essayist, a towering force in French literature of the first half of the 20th century, whose works derive their lyrical inspiration, their unity and scope, and their prophetic tone from his faith in God.

Claudel was born into a family of farmers and gentry. Becoming expert in economic affairs, he embarked in 1890 on a long and brilliant career in the foreign service. As he traveled the world, he slowly elaborated his theocentric conception of the universe and conceived his vocation: the revelation through lyrical and dramatic poetry of the grand design of creation. This idea was inspired in part by Claudel's conversion to Roman Catholicism when he was 18.

Claudel reached his largest audience through his Symbolist plays—works that powerfully synthesized all theatrical elements to evoke a unified mood, atmosphere, and leitmotif. His heroes are men of action—generals, conquerors, born masters of the earth—who display pride, greed, ambition, violence, and passion. But Claudel suggests a firm path to redemption.

In the early 1900s Claudel met a married Polish woman with whom he had a four-year relationship (which both then renounced). Although Claudel married a French woman, Reine Sainte-Marie-Perrin, in 1906, this episode of forbidden love became a major mythic element of his subsequent works, beginning with the searching autobiographical *Partage de midi* (1906; *Break of Noon*). *L'Annonce faite à Marie* (1912; *Tidings Brought to Mary*) is a medieval mystery in tone, in which Claudel expounds on woman's place in God's scheme. Woman, the daughter of Eve, temptress and source of evil, is also the child of Mary, the initiator of the search for salvation: such is the Doña Prouhèze of *Le Soulier de satin* (1929; THE SATIN SLIPPER), Claudel's masterpiece. The Spanish Catholic world of the Renaissance is the stage for this story of the pursuit of the unattainable (because she is married) Doña Prouhèze by the worldly, passionate, and predatory adventurer Rodrigue.

Claudel's other dramatic works include the historical trilogy *L'Otage* (1911; *The Hostage*), *Le Pain dur* (1918; *Crusts*), and *Le Père humilié* (1920; *The Humiliation of the Father*). He also wrote the libretto for the opera *Le Livre de Christophe Colomb* (1933; *The Book of Christopher Columbus*), with music by Darius Milhaud, and the oratorio *Jeanne d'arc au bûcher* (1939; "Joan of Arc at the Stakes"), with music by Arthur Honegger.

His best-known and most impressive lyrical works are the ambitious, confessional *Cinq grandes odes* (1910; *Five Great Odes*). He very early adopted the long, unscanned, usually unrhymed line; known as the *verset claudélien*, it is his distinctive contribution to French prosody.

Claudian \'klōd-ē-ən\, *in full* Claudius Claudianus (b. c. 370, Alexandria [Egypt]—d. c. 404, Rome [Italy]) The last important poet of the classical tradition.

Claudian showed his mastery of Latin in a poem celebrating the consulship (395) of Probinus and Olybrius. An epigram (*Deprecatio ad Hadrianum*) on his superior, the Greek Hadrianus, put him in jeopardy of losing his civil post; but, by assiduously praising Stilicho, minister of the Western emperor Flavius

Honorius, and denouncing his rivals at the court of Flavius Arcadius, he gained high rank.

Together with epistles, epigrams, and idylls, the Stilicho poems form part of the canon, in two books, known as *Claudianus major*. There are also invectives against ministers of Arcadius, two poems addressed to Serena (Stilicho's wife), two epithalamiums (nuptial poems), a delightful *De sene Veronensi* ("Old Man of Verona"), and *Gigantomachia* ("Battle of the Giants"). *Claudianus minor* contains the mythological epic *Raptus Proserpinae* ("The Rape of Proserpine"), on which Claudian's medieval fame largely depended.

Regarded during the Middle Ages in Europe as nearly the peer of Statius and Lucan, Claudian is faulted by modern critics for rhetoric too elaborate for his inferior themes, but his work is valuable as a historical source.

Claudine \klō-'dēn\ Fictional character, the heroine of a series of novels by COLETTE, originally published as the work of her then-husband, Henri Gauthier-Villars ("Willy"). The works include *Claudine à l'école* (1900; *Claudine at School*), *Claudine à Paris* (1901; *Claudine in Paris*), *Claudine en ménage* (1902; republished as *Claudine amoureuse*, translated as *The Indulgent Husband*), and *Claudine s'en va: Journal d'Annie* (1903; *The Innocent Wife*). The young Colette drew on her own experiences as a girl from the provinces and as a young married woman with a libertine husband to produce scenes from the life of the young ingénue. Both Claudine and the passive, domestic Annie, who narrates the fourth Claudine book, reappear in Colette's *La Retraite sentimentale* (1907; *Retreat from Love*), which was published under the name Colette Willy.

Claudius \'klȯd-ē-əs\, *in full* Tiberius Claudius Caesar Augustus Germanicus, *original name* (until AD 41) Tiberius Claudius Nero Germanicus (b. Aug. 1, 10 BC, Lugdunum, Gaul [now Lyon, Fr.]—d. Oct. 13, AD 54, Rome [Italy]) Roman emperor (AD 41–54), who extended Roman rule in North Africa and made Britain a province. He wrote Etruscan and Carthaginian histories (in Greek), an autobiography, and a historical treatise on the Roman alphabet, but none of his written works has survived.

Claudius' life was the subject of two novels by Robert Graves, *I, Claudius* (1934) and *Claudius, the God and His Wife Messalina* (1935).

Claudius \'klȯd-ē-əs\, Matthias (b. Aug. 15, 1740, Reinfeld, Holstein [Germany]—d. Jan. 21, 1815, Hamburg) German poet, most notable for *Der Mond ist aufgegangen* ("The Moon Has Risen") and editor of the important journal *Der Wandsbecker Bote*. Under Claudius' editorship (1771–75), *Der Wandsbecker Bote* was popular not only with the common people, for whose enlightenment it was designed, but also with the most important literary figures of the time. Among the journal's contributors were the philosopher Johann Gottfried von Herder, the poet Friedrich Klopstock, and the critic and dramatist Gotthold Ephraim Lessing; these three, along with Claudius, formed a circle that fought against the prevailing rationalist and classical spirit and sought to preserve a natural and Christian atmosphere in literature. Claudius' own poems have a naive, childlike, and devoutly Christian quality.

Claussen \'klȯs-sən\, Sophus Niels Christen (b. Sept. 12, 1865, Helletofte, Island of Langeland, Den.—d. April 11, 1931, Gentofte, near Copenhagen) Danish neo-Romantic poet of the 1890s who was influenced by the French Symbolists and who in turn greatly influenced Danish modernist poets of the 1940s, '50s, and 60s.

In spite of Claussen's close French literary connections, his humorous, romantic treatment of the myths of human existence in *Naturbørn* (1887; "Children of Nature") and *Pilefløjter*

(1899; "Willow Pipes") remains in the Danish tradition. His later work is darker and less playful, as the title of his collection *Djævlerier* (1904; "Demonisms") indicates. Claussen's antimaterialistic feelings reached their climax of expression in his last important collection, *Heroica* (1925).

Claussen published several travel books and lyrical prose tales of small-town life in Denmark. He also translated some of his favorite poets, including Percy Bysshe Shelley, Heinrich Heine, and Charles Baudelaire.

clausula \ˈklȯ-zhə-lə\ *plural* clausulae \-ˌlē\ [Latin, ending, close of a rhetorical period, a derivative of *claudere* to close] In Greek and Latin rhetoric, the rhythmic close to a sentence or clause, or a terminal cadence. The clausula is especially important in ancient and medieval Latin prose rhythm; most of the clausulae in Cicero's speeches, for example, follow a specific pattern and distinctly avoid certain types of rhythmic endings. The final words of a speech were an important element of its effectiveness.

Clavell \klə-ˈvel\, James (duMaresq) (b. Oct. 10, 1924, Sydney, N.S.W., Australia—d. Sept. 6, 1994, Vevey, Switz.) Author of popular action novels that portray Asian cultures. Initially a writer of screenplays, Clavell based his first novel, *King Rat* (1962), on his experiences as a prisoner of the Japanese during World War II. Struggles for power and wealth and, secondarily, sex and love occupy his fiction, as East and West and male and female clash. Other Clavell novels include *Tai-Pan* (1966) and *Noble House* (1981), set in historic and modern Hong Kong; *Shōgun* (1975), set in 17th-century Japan; *Whirlwind* (1986), set in Iran during its 1979 revolution; and *Gai-Jin* (1993), set in 19th-century Japan.

Clavijo y Fajardo \klä-ˈbē-ḵō-ē-fä-ˈkär-ᵗhō\, José (b. 1730, Lanzarote, Spain—d. 1806, Madrid) Spanish naturalist and man of letters known for his campaign against public performance of the Corpus Christi *autos sacramentales*, one-act, open-air dramas that portrayed the eucharistic mystery. From his position as editor of the literary periodical *El pensador*, Clavijo issued constant attacks against the performance of these plays, which had become little more than vulgar public spectacles. Because of his activity, the *autos* were banned in 1765. His love affair with Louise, sister of the French playwright P.-A. Caron de Beaumarchais, was dramatized by J.W. von Goethe in his tragedy *Clavigo*.

Largely educated in France, Clavijo translated works by Racine and Voltaire and the French naturalist Count de Buffon.

Clayhanger Family, The \ˈklā-ˌhaŋ-ər\ Trilogy of semi-autobiographical novels by Arnold BENNETT. The first and best-known book of the three is *Clayhanger* (1910); it was followed by *Hilda Lessways* (1911) and *These Twain* (1915). They were published together in 1925.

Set in the late 19th century in a drab potters' town in the industrial Midlands, *Clayhanger* begins the story of Edwin Clayhanger as he is attempting to take control of his life from his tyrannical and pragmatic father. Repressed and shy, he falls in love with Hilda Lessways, a forthright young woman who, despite her attraction to Edwin, marries another man. After many years he finds her living a broken, destitute life, her husband imprisoned for bigamy and her child thus considered illegitimate. In spite of all, Clayhanger still loves Hilda.

Hilda Lessways, told from Hilda's point of view, chronicles her early life. In *These Twain*, Clayhanger and Hilda are married. He adopts her son, and the couple attempt to adapt their very different temperaments and routines to each other.

Clean, Well-Lighted Place, A Much-anthologized short story by Ernest HEMINGWAY, first published in *Scribner's*

Magazine in March 1933 and later that year in the collection *Winner Take Nothing*. Late one night two waiters in a café wait for their last customer, an old man who has recently attempted suicide, to leave. The younger waiter, eager to get home to his wife, turns the old man out, but the older waiter is sympathetic to the human need for a clean, well-lighted place, an outpost in the darkness.

The story is a powerful existential statement about the insufficiency of religion as a source of comfort, and it contains an often cited version of the Lord's Prayer that substitutes the Spanish word *nada* ("nothing") for most of the prayer's nouns.

Cleland \ˈklel-ənd, ˈklē-lənd\, John (baptized Sept. 24, 1710, Kingston-upon-Thames, Surrey, Eng.—d. Jan. 23, 1789, London) English novelist, author of the notorious FANNY HILL (1748–49).

After serving as a consul at Smyrna and later as an agent of the British East India Company in Bombay, Cleland became a penniless wanderer. In such reduced circumstances, he wrote *Fanny Hill* for a fee of 20 guineas. An elegant, flowery work of pornography describing the activities of a London prostitute, this novel has enjoyed enormous popularity for more than two centuries as a classic of erotic literature. When originally published, it was immediately suppressed (an action later repeated many times), and Cleland was called before the Privy Council. He pleaded his extreme poverty and was not sentenced. Instead, Lord Granville, thinking him talented, secured him a yearly pension of £100 that he might put his gifts to better use. Thereafter, he became a journalist, playwright, and amateur philologist.

Clemens, Samuel Langhorne. Real name of Mark TWAIN.

Clemo \ˈklem-ō\, Jack, *original name* Reginald John Clemo (b. March 11, 1916, St. Austell, Cornwall, Eng.—d. July 25, 1994, Weymouth, Dorset) English poet whose physical sufferings—he became deaf in about 1936 and totally blind in 1955—greatly influenced his poetry.

The son of a Cornish clay worker, Clemo revealed in his early work a love for the scarred country in which he lived—farmland that had given way to the workings of a china-clay industry. He afterward began to write about his personal response to his religious conversion. In 1968 he married a Westmorland art teacher who inspired his later work, in which a theme of regeneration in apparently dead nature is strikingly apparent.

Clemo's major poetic collections are *The Clay Verge* (1951), *The Map of Clay* (1961), *Cactus on Carmel* (1967), *The Echoing Tip* (1971), *Broad Autumn* (1975), *Selected Poems* (1988), *Banner Poems* (1989), and *Approach to Murano* (1993). He also wrote novels, including *Wilding Graft* (1948) and *The Shadowed Bed* (1986), as well as several nonfiction works.

Clennam, Arthur \ˈär-thər-ˈklen-əm\ Fictional character, a middle-aged, kindly man who loves Amy Dorrit, the heroine of Charles Dickens' novel LITTLE DORRIT.

Cleobis *see* BITON AND CLEOBIS.

Cleopatra \ˌklē-ə-ˈpat-rə, -ˈpät-\, *in full* Cleopatra VII Thea Philopator ("Goddess Loving Her Father") (b. 69 BC—d. Aug. 30, 30 BC, Alexandria) Egyptian queen famous in history and drama, lover of Julius Caesar and later the wife of Mark Antony. She became queen on the death in 51 BC of her father, Ptolemy XII, ruling successively with her two brothers Ptolemy XIII (51–47) and Ptolemy XIV (47–44) and her son Ptolemy XV Caesar (44–30). After the Roman armies of Octavian (the future emperor Augustus) defeated their combined forces, Antony and Cleopatra committed suicide, and Egypt fell under Roman domination. Her ambition no less than her charm actively influenced Roman politics at a crucial period, and she came to represent, as did no other woman of antiquity, the prototype of the romantic femme fatale.

Ancient literature on Cleopatra is voluminous and mostly hostile. Later writers showed somewhat more sympathy. William Shakespeare was the first to present Cleopatra as the *grande amoureuse*, and it is a splendid characterization. Other writers who have been inspired by the story of Cleopatra include John Dryden (*All For Love; or The World Well Lost*, 1677) and George Bernard Shaw (*Caesar and Cleopatra*, 1901).

clerihew \\'kler-i-ˌhyü\\   A light verse quatrain in lines usually of varying length, rhyming *aabb*, and usually dealing with a person named in the initial rhyme.

This type of comic biographical verse form was invented by Edmund Clerihew Bentley, who introduced it in *Biography for Beginners* (1905) and continued in *More Biography* (1929) and *Baseless Biography* (1939). The humor of the form lies in its purposefully flat-footed inadequacy. It is written as a four-line verse of two rhyming couplets, the first line almost invariably ending with the name of the subject:

> After dinner, Erasmus
> Told Colet not to be "blas'mous"
> Which Colet, with some heat
> Requested him to repeat.

The number of accents in the line is irregular, and one line is usually extended to tease the ear. Another requisite of the successful clerihew is an awkward rhyme, as in Bentley's "Cervantes":

> The people of Spain think Cervantes
> Equal to half-a-dozen Dantes:
> An opinion resented most bitterly
> By the people of Italy.

Illustration by G.K. Chesterton of the "Cervantes" clerihew by E. Clerihew Bentley

Some of the best clerihews were written by Sir Francis Meynell, W.H. Auden, and Clifton Fadiman.

Clerk's Tale, The \\'klərk, *British* 'klärk\\   One of the 24 stories in THE CANTERBURY TALES by Geoffrey Chaucer.

Chaucer borrowed the story of Patient Griselda from Petrarch's Latin translation of Giovanni Boccaccio's *Decameron*. A marquis marries beautiful low-born Griselde (Griselda) after she agrees to obey his every whim; he then subjects her to a series of cruelties to test her love. He abducts their children, telling Griselde they must die. Years later, he asks her to leave, and later calls her back to decorate his chambers, supposedly for his new wife. Griselde amiably agrees, as she has patiently endured all her previous indignities. At last the marquis relents, proclaiming his love for Griselde; instead of a new wife, the young woman who arrives is Griselde's grown daughter, and both she and her brother are restored to their mother as a reward for her constancy.

Cleveland or **Cleiveland** \\'klēv-lənd\\, John (b. June 16, 1613, Loughborough, Leicestershire, Eng.—d. April 29, 1658, London)   The most popular British poet of his time and an influential satirist who later became the most commonly abused Metaphysical poet.

Educated at Cambridge, Cleveland became a fellow there before joining the Royalist army at Oxford in 1643. In 1645–46 he was judge advocate with the garrison at Newark until it surrendered to the Parliamentary forces. When Charles I put himself in the hands of the Scots' army and they turned him over to the Parliamentary forces, Cleveland excoriated the Scots in a satire they have never forgiven.

His poems first appeared in *The Character of a London Diurnal* (1647) and thereafter in some 20 collections in the next quarter century. From the time of John Dryden's deprecatory criticism of the Metaphysical poets, Cleveland has been a whipping boy for them, largely because his conceits are profuse and cosmetic rather than integral to his thought.

cliché or **cliche** \\klē-'shā, 'klē-ˌshā, kli-'\\ [French, literally, stereotype (in printing)]   **1.** A trite or stereotyped phrase or expression.   **2.** The idea expressed by a cliché.   **3.** A hackneyed theme, plot, or situation in fiction or drama.

cliff-hanger \\'klif-ˌhaŋ-ər\\   An adventure serial or melodrama; especially one presented in installments each of which ends in suspense.

Clifton \\'klif-tən\\, Lucille, *in full* Thelma Lucille Sayles Clifton (b. June 27, 1936, Depew, N.Y., U.S.)   American poet who employed black vernacular in her examinations of family relationships and life in the urban ghetto.

Clifton's work reflected her pride in being a woman, an African-American, and a poet. Her poetry collections include the ironically titled *Good Times* (1969); *Good News About the Earth* (1972); and *An Ordinary Woman* (1974). *Generations: A Memoir* (1976) is a prose piece celebrating her origins, and *Good Woman: Poems and a Memoir: 1969–1980* (1987) collects her previously published verse.

Clifton's many children's books, written with a young African-American audience in mind, include *All Us Come Cross the Water* (1973) and *My Friend Jacob* (1980). She also wrote a series of books chronicling the everyday adventures of a young black boy.

climax \\'klī-ˌmaks\\ [Greek *klîmax*, literally, ladder]   **1.** A figure of speech in which a number of phrases or sentences are arranged in ascending order of rhetorical forcefulness. The following passage from Herman Melville's *Moby Dick* is an example:

> All that most maddens and torments; all that stirs up the lees of things; all truth with malice in it; all that cracks the sinews and cakes the brain; all the subtle demonisms of life and thought; all evil, to crazy Ahab, were visibly personified and made practically assailable in Moby Dick.

2. The last and highest member of a rhetorical climax. **3.** The point of highest dramatic tension or a major turning point in the action of a play, story, or other literary composition. In the structure of a play the climax, or crisis, is the decisive moment, or turning point, at which the rising action of the play is reversed to falling action. In the influential pyramidal outline of five-act dramatic structure, advanced by the German playwright Gustav Freytag in *Die Technik des Dramas*, the climax, in the sense of crisis, occurs close to the conclusion of the third act. By the end of the 19th century, when the traditional five-act drama was abandoned in favor of the three-act, both the crisis and the emotional climax were placed close to the end of the play.

clinch \'klinch\ *archaic* A pun or play on words.

Clinker, Humphry \'həm-frē-'kliŋ-kər\ Fictional character, a poor, naive young man encountered by Matthew Bramble in the epistolary novel HUMPHRY CLINKER by Tobias Smollett.

Clio \'klī-ō, 'klē-\ In Greek mythology, one of the nine Muses, the patron of history.

cloak-and-dagger Dealing in intrigue and action of a romantic and melodramatic kind, usually with characters in a colorful historical setting and involving espionage, duels, pursuit, and rescue.

cloak-and-sword [translation of Spanish (*comedia de*) *capa y espada* cloak-and-sword comedy] Dealing in fictional or semifictional romance and adventure of the nobility in a period when swordplay and colorful elaborate dress were common.

The term specifically refers to a type of 17th-century Spanish play of upper middle-class manners and intrigue. The type was anticipated by the plays of Bartolomé de Torres Naharro, but its popularity was established by the inventive dramas of Lope de Vega and Tirso de Molina. The extremely complicated plots deal with the frustration of an idealized love by the conventional Spanish *pundonor* ("point of honor"). The affairs of the lady and her gallant are mirrored or parodied in the actions of the servants; the hero's valet (the *gracioso*) also supplies a commonsense commentary on the manners of his master. After many misunderstandings, duels, renunciations, and false alarms about honor, the plays usually end happily with several marriages.

Clockwork Orange, A Novel by Anthony BURGESS, published in 1962. Set in a dismal dystopia, it is the first-person account of a juvenile delinquent who undergoes state-sponsored psychological rehabilitation for his aberrant behavior. The novel satirizes extreme political systems that are based on opposing models of the perfectibility or incorrigibility of humanity. Written in a futuristic slang vocabulary invented by Burgess, in part by adaptation of Russian words, it was his most original and best-known work.

Alex, the protagonist, has a passion for classical music and is a member of a vicious teenage gang that commits random acts of brutality. Captured and imprisoned, he is transformed through behavioral conditioning into a model citizen, but his taming also leaves him defenseless. He ultimately reverts to his former behavior. The final chapter of the original British edition, in which Alex renounces his amoral past, was removed when the novel was first published in the United States.

Clodia \'klō-dē-ə\ (fl. 1st century BC) Profligate Roman beauty and sister of the demagogue Publius Clodius Pulcher. She was married in 63 BC to Quintus Metellus Celer and was suspected of responsibility for his death in 59 BC. She was mistress to the poet Catullus, who wrote of her as Lesbia, and was the most important influence in his life. Cicero defended her lover Marcus Caelius Rufus against a charge of attempting to poison her, painting a graphic picture of Clodia as a dangerous beauty.

Cloete \'klü-tē\, Stuart, *in full* Edward Fairly Stuart Graham Cloete (b. July 23, 1897, Paris, Fr.—d. March 19, 1976, Cape Town, S.Af.) South African novelist, essayist, and short-story writer known for his vivid narratives and characterizations in African settings.

Cloete's first novel, *Turning Wheels* (1937), expresses a negative view of Boer life and deals with interracial love affairs. It stimulated much discussion, being published during the centennial celebration of the Great Trek (mass emigration of Afrikaners from Cape Colony viewed as a central event in their history). Later works include *Rags of Glory* (1963) and *The Abductors* (1966). He also wrote poems, collected in *The Young Men and the Old* (1941), and a collection of biographies, *African Portraits* (1946). His autobiography, *A Victorian Son*, appeared in 1972.

Cloister and the Hearth, The Picaresque historical novel by Charles READE, published in 1861. Critically acclaimed as one of the greatest historical novels in English, *The Cloister and the Hearth* contains a meticulous recreation of 15th-century European life. Mingled with its cast of vividly drawn characters are various historical personages.

The plot concerns Gerard Eliason, a young Dutch artist who abandons thought of the priesthood when he falls in love with Margaret Brandt. Gerard's father opposes their engagement and arranges to have his son kidnapped. The young lovers find each other, but Gerard is soon forced to flee. While they are separated, Margaret gives birth to their son, of whose existence Gerard is unaware. Indeed, his enemies inform Gerard that Margaret is dead. Wild with grief, he eventually becomes a monk. Later, the lovers are reunited and Gerard meets his son. Bound by his vows of celibacy, Gerard simply lives near Margaret, and both lead pious, charitable lives. Eventually Margaret dies from the plague and Gerard dies soon after. Their son is revealed to be the illustrious scholar and theologian Erasmus.

close \'klōz\ The concluding passage, as of a speech or play.

closed couplet A rhymed couplet in which the sense is complete. *See* COUPLET.

closet drama A drama suited primarily for reading rather than production.

Examples of the genre include John Milton's *Samson Agonistes* (1671) and Thomas Hardy's *The Dynasts* (three parts, 1903–08). Closet drama is not to be confused with readers' theater, in which actors read or recite without decor before an audience.

Clotel \klō-'tel\ (*in full* Clotel; or, The President's Daughter: A Narrative of Slave Life in the United States) Novel by William Wells BROWN, first published in England in 1853. Brown revised it three times for publication in the United States—serially and in book form—each time changing the plot, the title, and the names of characters. The book was first published in the United States in 1864 as *Clotelle: A Tale of Southern States*. It was the first novel written by an African-American, but it was published in the United States after Harriet Wilson's *Our Nig*. It is a melodramatic tale of three generations of black women who struggle with the constrictions of slavery, miscegenation, and concubinage. Although criticized for its cluttered narrative and its stiff characters, the novel provides insight into the antebellum slave culture.

Cloud-cuckoo-land \,klaůd-'kü-kü-,land, -'ků-\, *Greek* Nephelokokkygia \,nef-ə-lō-,käk-'sij-ē-ə\ In Aristophanes' comedy BIRDS, an ideal city that is suspended between heaven and earth. By extension, the word Cloud-cuckoo-land has come to mean a realm of fantasy or of whimsical or foolish behavior.

Clouds (*Greek* Nephelai) Drama by **ARISTOPHANES**, produced in 423 BC. The play attacks "modern" education and morals as imparted and taught by the radical intellectuals known as the Sophists. The main victim of the play is the leading Athenian thinker and teacher Socrates, who is purposely (and unfairly) given many of the standard characteristics of the Sophists. In the play Socrates is consulted by an old rogue, Strepsiades ("Twisterson"), who wants to evade his debts. The instruction at Socrates' academy, the Phrontisterion ("Thinking Shop"), which consists of making a wrong argument sound right, enables Strepsiades' son to defend the beating of his own father. At the play's end the Phrontisterion is burned to the ground.

Clough \'kləf\, Arthur Hugh (b. Jan. 1, 1819, Liverpool, Eng.—d. Nov. 13, 1861, Florence, Italy) Poet whose work reflects the religious doubt of mid-19th-century England. He was a friend of Matthew Arnold and the subject of his commemorative elegy "Thyrsis."

While at Oxford, Clough had intended to become a clergyman, but his increasing religious skepticism caused him to leave the university. He became head of University Hall, London, in 1849, and in 1852, at the invitation of Ralph Waldo Emerson, he spent several months lecturing in Massachusetts. While on a visit to Italy he contracted malaria and died at age 42.

Clough's deeply critical and questioning attitude made him as doubtful of his own powers as he was about the spirit of his age, and he gave his contemporaries the impression of promise unfulfilled, especially since he left the bulk of his verse unpublished. Nonetheless, Clough's *Poems* (1862) proved so popular that they were reprinted 16 times within 40 years of his death. Among his works are *Bothie of Tober-na-Vuolich* (1848) and *Amours de Voyage* (1858), poems written in classical hexameters and dealing with romantic love, doubt, and social conflict. The long, incomplete poem *Dipsychus* most fully expresses Clough's doubts about the social and spiritual developments of his era.

The Poems of Arthur Hugh Clough (1974), edited by F.L. Mulhauser, is the standard edition of Clough's work.

clown \'klaůn\ [earlier "countryman, ill-mannered person," perhaps of Low German origin] Familiar comic character of pantomime and the circus, known by distinctive makeup and costume and ludicrous antics, whose purpose is to induce hearty laughter. The clown, unlike the traditional court jester, usually performs a set routine characterized by broad, graphic humor, absurd situations, and vigorous physical action.

The earliest ancestors of the clown flourished in ancient Greece—bald-headed, padded buffoons who performed as secondary figures in farces and mime. The clown emerged as a professional comic actor in the late Middle Ages, when traveling entertainers sought to imitate the antics of the court jesters and the amateur fool societies, such as the Enfants san Souci, who specialized in comic drama at festival times. The traveling companies of the Italian commedia dell'arte developed one of the most famous and durable clowns of all time, the Arlecchino, or **HARLEQUIN**, sometime in the latter half of the 16th century. The English clown was descended from the Vice character of the medieval mystery plays, a buffoon and prankster who could sometimes deceive even the Devil.

Clown, The Novel by Heinrich **BÖLL**, published in 1963 as *Ansichten eines Clowns*. Set in West Germany during the period of recovery following World War II, the novel examines the hypocrisy of contemporary German society in repressing memory of the historical past in order to concentrate on material reconstruction. In the book the figure of a clown (the narrator, Hans Schnier) represents the social conscience of the society. Through conversations the clown has with members of his family and others who represent various segments of the community, Böll presents his criticism of that world, especially of the institutions of the church and industry.

Club, The *also called* The Literary Club. A group of men who beginning in 1764 met regularly for supper and conversation. The Club was founded (at the suggestion of Joshua Reynolds), presided over, and frequently dominated by Samuel Johnson. Among the original members, besides Reynolds and Johnson, were Edmund Burke, Topham Beauclerk, Bennet Langton, and Oliver Goldsmith. Later additions included James Boswell, Edward Gibbon, Adam Smith, and David Garrick. The Club continued to meet for many years, with Sir Walter Scott and Alfred, Lord Tennyson among its later members.

Clurman \'klůr-mən\, Harold (b. Sept. 18, 1901, New York, N.Y., U.S.—d. Sept. 9, 1980, New York City) Influential American theatrical director and drama critic.

Clurman attended Columbia University in New York City, then the University of Paris, where he received a degree in letters in 1923. He made his stage debut the following year as an extra at the Greenwich Village Theatre in New York City. In 1931 Clurman became a founding member of the Group Theatre, an experimental company, for which he directed several plays, notably *Awake and Sing!* (1935) by Clifford Odets. Clurman's achievements as a director range over many categories of drama, including Carson McCullers' *A Member of the Wedding* (1950); Jean Giraudoux's drama of ideas *Tiger at the Gates* (1955); and Jean Anouilh's farce *Waltz of the Toreadors* (1957). He also directed Eugene O'Neill's *Touch of the Poet* (1957) and Arthur Miller's *Incident at Vichy* (1965). Clurman directed the Kumo Theatre Company of Japan in O'Neill's *Long Day's Journey into Night* (1965) and *The Iceman Cometh* (1968).

Clurman also became a drama critic, writing for *The New Republic* in 1948–52, then for *The Nation* from 1953 until his death. He also wrote *On Directing* (1972); *The Divine Pastime* (1974), theatrical essays; and his memoirs, *All People Are Famous* (1974).

Clytemnestra \ˌklī-təm-'nes-trə\ In Greek legend, a daughter of Leda and Tyndareus and wife of Agamemnon, commander of the Greek forces in the Trojan War. She took Aegisthus as her lover while Agamemnon was away at war. Upon his return, Clytemnestra and Aegisthus murdered Agamemnon. Clytemnestra was then killed by her son Orestes, with the help of his sister Electra, in revenge for his father's murder.

In Aeschylus's play *Agamemnon*, part of his Oresteia trilogy, Clytemnestra is driven to murder Agamemnon partly to avenge the death of her daughter Iphigeneia, whom Agamemnon had sacrificed for the sake of success in the war, partly by her adulterous love for Aegisthus, and partly as agent for the curse on Agamemnon's family, the House of Atreus. Clytemnestra's story is also told in plays by Sophocles and Euripides.

Cobb \'käb\, Irvin Shrewsbury (b. June 23, 1876, Paducah, Ky., U.S.—d. March 10, 1944, New York, N.Y.) American journalist and humorist.

Cobb was a staff writer for the *Evening World* and *Sunday World* in New York City. First through syndicated newspaper features and later in magazines, he became widely known for such articles as "Speaking of Operations," which in book form sold more than 500,000 copies, and for short stories.

Cobb's stories about shrewd and kindly Judge Priest first brought him fame. Some of them were collected in *Back Home* (1912) and *Old Judge Priest* (1916). He wrote many books and columns for journals, as well as plays and scenarios for motion pictures.

Cockaigne or **Cockayne** \kä-'kān, kə-\ [Middle English *Cokaygne*, from Old French *Cocagne*]   An imaginary land of extreme luxury and ease where physical comforts and pleasures are always immediately at hand.

References to Cockaigne are especially prominent in medieval European lore. These accounts describe rivers of wine, houses built of cake and barley sugar, streets paved with pastry, and shops that gratuitously give goods to everyone. Roast geese wander about inviting people to eat them, and buttered larks fall from the skies.

The origin of the word Cockaigne has been much disputed, but all versions tend to see it as adapted or derived from a word meaning "cake." An outstanding early Irish version of the legend is *Aislinge Meic Conglinne* (*The Vision of MacConglinne*), a parody of the traditional saint's vision in which a king possessed by a demon of gluttony is cured by a vision of the land of Cockaigne. A 13th-century French fabliau, *Cocagne*, was possibly intended to ridicule the idea of the mythical Avalon, the Island of the Blest. An English poem "The Land of Cockaygne" of about the same period satirizes monastic life. The name Lubberland displaced that of Cockaigne in the 17th century. The Big Rock Candy Mountain of American hobo folklore expresses the same idea.

cockatrice \'käk-ə-tris, -,trīs\ [Old French *cocatris* ichneumon, crocodile, cockatrice]   In Greek and Roman legend, a small serpent with deadly glance said to be hatched by a reptile from a cock's egg on a dunghill and often conceived of as having the head, wings, and legs of a cock and the tail of a serpent. Only the weasel, which secreted a venom deadly to the cockatrice, was safe from its powers. By the beginning of the 17th century, the cock was also believed to be an enemy of the creature, which would die shortly after hearing the cock crow. This legend caused travelers through regions allegedly infested by the serpent to travel with cocks. *Compare* BASILISK.

cockneyism \'käk-nē-,iz-əm\   The writing or the qualities of the writing of the 19th-century English authors John Keats, Percy Bysshe Shelley, William Hazlitt, and Leigh Hunt. The term was used disparagingly by some contemporaries, especially the Scottish critic John Lockhart, in reference to the fact that these writers lived in, or were natives of, London, as the term *cockney* was a derogatory term for Londoners in general.

Cocktail Party, The   Verse drama in three acts by T.S. ELIOT, produced in 1949 and published in 1950. Based on *Alcestis* by Euripides, it is a morality play presented as a comedy of manners. Eliot's most commercially successful play, it was more conventional and less poetic than his earlier dramatic works.

The marital problems of Edward and Lavinia Chamberlayne are of special interest to an unidentified guest at their dismal cocktail party. The guest is later identified as Sir Henry Harcourt-Reilly, a prescient psychiatrist who helps heal the Chamberlaynes' marriage. He also counsels Celia Coplestone, Edward's mistress and the main moral figure of the piece, to work out her salvation.

Cocteau \kôk-'tō\, Jean (b. July 5, 1889, Maisons-Laffitte, near Paris, Fr.—d. Oct. 11, 1963, Milly-la-Forêt, near Paris)   French writer and artist known for the wide variety of forms in which he worked, including poetry, fiction, ballet, motion pictures, and painting.

At 19 Cocteau published his first volume of poems, *La Lampe d'Aladin* ("Aladdin's Lamp"). During World War I, he served as an ambulance driver on the Belgian front, later the setting for his novel *Thomas l'imposteur* (1923). *Le Cap de Bonne-Espérance* (1919; "The Cape of Good Hope") was a volume of poems inspired by aviation.

Soon after the war, the writer Max Jacob introduced Cocteau to the future poet and novelist Raymond Radiguet. The 16-year-old Radiguet, who appeared to be a prodigy, advocated an aesthetic of simplicity and of classical clarity, qualities that would become characteristic of Cocteau's own work. An addiction to opium, brought on by Cocteau's grief over Radiguet's death in 1923, necessitated a period of cure and brought on a brief return to religious practice. During this period he produced some of his most important works.

In his long poem *L'Ange Heurtebise* (1925; "The Angel Heurtebise"), the poet engages in a violent combat with an angel that was to reappear continually in his works. His play *Orphée* (*Orpheus*), first performed in 1926, played a part in the resurrection of tragedy in contemporary theater. The novel *Les Enfants terribles* (1929; "The Incorrigible Children"; *Children of the Game*) is a study of the inviolability of the character of a brother and sister.

In 1930 Cocteau made his first film, *Le Sang d'un poète* (*The Blood of a Poet*), a commentary on his own private mythology. In 1934 he wrote what is usually thought to be his greatest play, *La Machine infernale* (*The Infernal Machine*). In the 1940s, Cocteau returned to filmmaking, first as a screenwriter and then also as a director of *La Belle et la bête* (1946; *Beauty and the Beast*) and *Orphée* (1950).

coda \'kō-də\   A concluding portion of a literary or dramatic work; usually, a portion or scene that rounds off or integrates preceding themes or ideas.

codex \'kō-,deks\ *plural* **codices** \'kōd-ə-,sēz, 'käd-\ [Latin *caudex, codex* tree trunk, book made originally of wooden tablets]   A manuscript book, especially of Scripture, early literature, or ancient mythological or historical annals.

The earliest type of manuscript in the form of a modern book (*i.e.*, a collection of pages stitched together along one side), the codex replaced the earlier rolls of papyrus and wax tablets. The codex had several advantages over the roll, or scroll. It could be opened at once to any point in the text, it enabled one to write on both sides of the leaf, and it could contain long texts.

The oldest extant Greek codex, said to date from the 4th century, is the Codex Sinaiticus, a biblical manuscript written in Greek. Also important is the Codex Alexandrinus, a Greek text of the Bible probably produced in the 5th century and now preserved in the British Library, London. The term codex aureus describes a volume that includes gold letters written on sheets that have been stained with a purple dye called murex. Existing examples of the codex aureus date from the 8th and 9th centuries.

In a completely separate development, codices also were made by pre-Columbian peoples of Mesoamerica after about AD 1000. These books contained pictographs and ideograms rather than written script. They dealt with the ritual calendar, divination, ceremonies, and speculations on the gods and the universe. Among these codices are the Vienna Codex, the Dresden Codex, the Codex Colombino, and the Codex Fejérváry-Mayer, all believed to have been produced before the Spanish conquest of the region. Certain collections of formulas or standards are also referred to as codices; for example, the Codex Alimentarius and the *British Pharmaceutical Codex*.

Codex Regius \'kō-,deks-'rej-ē-əs, 'rā-gē-ùs\   Norse manuscript that contains most of the *Sæmundar Edda*, commonly designated by scholars as the *Poetic Edda*, or *Elder Edda*. The manuscript dates from the second half of the 13th century and may be a copy of the original. It was acquired in the 17th century by Bishop Brynjólfur Sveinsson, who incorrectly attributed the work to Sæmundar the Learned and who in 1622 sent the manuscript to King Frederik III of Denmark. Although the codex is missing several pages, some of the lost poems were preserved in prose form in the *Vǫlsunga saga*.

Coetzee \kůt-'sē, -'siə\, J.M., *in full* John Michael (b. Feb. 9, 1940, Cape Town, S.Af.)   South African novelist, critic, and translator noted for his novels about the effects of apartheid.

Coetzee was educated at the University of Cape Town and the University of Texas. He taught English at the University of Cape Town, translated works from the Dutch, and wrote literary criticism.

Dusklands (1974), his first book, contains two short novellas, "The Vietnam Project" and "The Narrative of Jacobus Coetzee." *In the Heart of the Country* (1977; U.S. title, *From the Heart of the Country*) is the stream-of-consciousness narrative of a Boer madwoman, and *Waiting for the Barbarians* (1980) is a parable of South Africa. *Life and Times of Michael K* (1983), which won the Booker Prize, concerns the dilemma of a man of limited intelligence beset by conditions he can neither comprehend nor control during a civil war in an unnamed country. Later novels include *Foe* (1986) and *Age of Iron* (1990).

coffeehouse \'kòf-ē-,haùs, 'kàf-\   A place where coffee and other refreshments are sold. In 17th- and 18th-century England, coffeehouses became centers of political, social, literary, and eventually business influence. Vienna also had famous literary and theatrical cafés where artists and personalities held court. An excellent description of the importance of the coffeehouse in British political and literary life can be found in Thomas Babington Macaulay's *History of England*.

Coffin \'kòf-ən, 'kàf-\, Robert Peter Tristram (b. March 18, 1892, Brunswick, Maine, U.S.—d. Jan. 20, 1955, Portland, Maine)   American poet whose works were based on New England farm and seafaring life.

Coffin regarded poetry as a public function that should speak well of life so that people might find inspiration. *Strange Holiness* (1935) won the Pulitzer Prize for poetry in 1936; *Saltwater Farm* (1937) is a collection of poems about Maine.

Coffin also lectured widely and took part in numerous poetry workshops. He taught at Wells College in Aurora, N.Y., and at Bowdoin College in Brunswick, Maine, and was book and poetry editor for *Yankee* magazine. Coffin also wrote the novel *Red Sky in the Morning* (1935); *Kennebec* (1937), part of a historical series on American rivers; and *Maine Doings* (1950), informal essays on New England life.

Coffin Texts   A collection of ancient Egyptian funerary texts consisting of spells or magic formulas that were painted on the burial coffins dating from roughly 2100 BC. The Coffin Texts and the earlier Pyramid Texts from which they were derived were the primary sources of the Book of the Dead (literally translated "Book of Going Forth By Day"). These three collections represent the most extensive body of Egyptian religious literature available to modern scholars. *See also* BOOK OF THE DEAD; PYRAMID TEXTS.

Cohen \kò-'en\, Albert (b. Aug. 16, 1895, Corfu, Greece—d. Oct. 17, 1981, Geneva, Switz.)   Greek-born Swiss-Jewish novelist, journalist, and diplomat best known for a trilogy that concluded with the novel *Belle du Seigneur* (1968).

Cohen studied law in Geneva, became a Swiss citizen, and began a career as a writer and civil servant. In 1921 he published *Paroles juives* ("Jewish Words"), an examination of Judaism.

The title character of *Solal* (1930), Cohen's first novel, struggles to synthesize his Jewish upbringing with his role as an international diplomat. His story continues in *Mangeclous* (1938) and *Belle du Seigneur*. Among Cohen's other works were the one-act play *Ézéchiel* (1956) and the memoirs *Le Livre de ma mère* (1954; "Book of My Mother"), *Ô vous, frères humains* (1972; "O You, Brother Humans"), and *Carnets 1978* (1979; "Notebooks"). Much of his work appeared in the posthumous anthology *Oeuvres* (1993).

Cohen \'kō-ən\, Leonard (Norman) (b. Sept. 21, 1934, Montreal, Que., Can.)   Canadian novelist and lyric poet who became a popular singer of his original songs.

Cohen attended McGill University and Columbia University. His second and third poetry collections, *The Spice-Box of Earth* (1961) and *Flowers for Hitler* (1964), established his reputation as a lyrical love poet and also as a writer of surreal imagery. In his partly autobiographical first novel, *The Favorite Game* (1963), a youth discovers sexual freedom and his vocation as a poet. His second novel was *Beautiful Losers* (1966). His later works include the poetry collections *Death of a Lady's Man* (1977), *Book of Mercy* (1984), and *Stranger Music* (1993). After other singers had recorded songs by Cohen, he himself began a recording career in 1968.

Colby \'kōl-bē\, Frank Moore (b. Feb. 10, 1865, Washington, D.C., U.S.—d. March 3, 1925, New York, N.Y.)   American encyclopedia editor and essayist.

Early in his career Colby taught history and economics at Columbia University, Amherst (Mass.) College, and New York University. In 1898 he became editor of the *International Year Book* (later the *New International Year Book*). He was editor, with Daniel Colt Gilman and Harry Thurston Peck, of the *New International Encyclopedia* (1900–03) and helped supervise publication of the second edition.

Colby contributed to many magazines, including *Bookman, The New Republic*, and *Vanity Fair*, and his witty essays were widely read. After his death, his popularity rose with the publication of *The Colby Essays* (1926), edited by Clarence Day, Jr.

Cold Comfort Farm   Comic novel by Stella GIBBONS, published in 1932, a successful parody of regional and rural fiction by such early 20th-century English writers as Mary Webb and D.H. Lawrence. A popular and clever work, *Cold Comfort Farm* was awarded the Femina Vie Heureuse Prize in 1933.

When Flora Poste visits her relatives in Sussex, she encounters a collection of rustic eccentrics enmeshed in a web of violent emotions, despair, and scheming. She manages to set things right.

Colegate \'kōl-,gāt\, Isabel (Diana), *married name* Briggs \'brigz\ (b. Sept. 10, 1931, Lincolnshire, Eng.)   British author of novels about life among the upper classes in England during the 20th century.

Colgate's first novel was *The Blackmailer* (1958). Among her next novels were *A Man of Power* (1960), the partly autobiographical *The Great Occasion* (1962), and *Statues in a Garden* (1964). *The Orlando Trilogy* (1984), composed of *Orlando King* (1968), *Orlando at the Brazen Threshold* (1971), and *Agatha* (1973), is a modern retelling of the myth of Oedipus and Antigone. *The Shooting Party* (1980; film, 1985) is about a group of aristocrats and their help who are gathered for a weekend pheasant hunt. Colegate also wrote *News from the City of the Sun* (1979), *A Glimpse of Sion's Glory* (1985), *Deceits of Time* (1988), and *The Summer of the Royal Visit* (1991).

Coleridge \'kōl-rij, *commonly* 'kōl-ə-rij, 'käl-\, Samuel Taylor (b. Oct. 21, 1772, Ottery St. Mary, Devonshire, Eng.—d. July 25, 1834, Highgate, near London)   English lyrical poet, critic, and philosopher, whose LYRICAL BALLADS (1798), written with William Wordsworth, heralded the English Romantic movement.

Coleridge attended Jesus College, Cambridge. There, with the poet Robert Southey, he planned a utopian society to be established on the banks of the Susquehanna River in Pennsylvania. To this end Coleridge left Cambridge and set up with Southey as a public lecturer in Bristol. In 1795 Coleridge married, at Southey's urging, Sara Fricker, daughter of a local schoolmistress. Shortly afterward, Southey defected from the joint scheme, leaving Coleridge married to a woman whom he did not really love. His career never fully recovered from this blow. During the same year, Coleridge became acquainted with Wordsworth; together they entered upon one of the most influential creative periods of English literature. Coleridge worked on a new, informal mode of poetry in which he used a conversational tone

Detail of an oil painting by Washington Allston, 1814

National Portrait Gallery, London

and rhythm to unify a work. Several of these experiments, including FROST AT MIDNIGHT and THE RIME OF THE ANCIENT MARINER, were published in 1798 in *Lyrical Ballads*. CHRISTABEL and the poem fragment KUBLA KHAN, both composed during this period, were not published until 1816.

The tensions of Coleridge's marriage were exacerbated when he fell in love with Sara Hutchinson, the sister of Wordsworth's future wife, at the end of 1799. His health worsened and he grew increasingly dependent on opium. In 1802 Coleridge's domestic unhappiness gave rise to DEJECTION: AN ODE, and ultimately he separated from his wife. In 1810 Hutchinson fled to Wales.

The period immediately following was the darkest of Coleridge's life. The writings that survive from this period are redolent of unhappiness. He began to revive during the winter of 1811–12 when his course of lectures on William Shakespeare attracted a large audience. His psychological interpretations of the characters were new and exciting to his contemporaries.

In the end, Coleridge found consolation in his return to the Anglican church. The stability this affiliation gave him enabled him to produce large works again. He drew together a collection of his poems (published in 1817 as *Sibylline Leaves*) and wrote BIOGRAPHIA LITERARIA (1817), an influential work in which he outlined the evolution of his thought and developed an extended critique of Wordsworth's poems. A new dramatic piece, *Zapolya*, was also published in 1817. He was elected a fellow of the Royal Society of Literature in 1824.

Coleridge \\'kōl-rij, 'kō-lə-rij\\, Sara (b. Dec. 22, 1802, Keswick, Cumberland, Eng.—d. May 3, 1852, London)   English translator and author of children's verse, known primarily as the editor of the works of her father, Samuel Taylor Coleridge.

In 1829 Coleridge married her cousin, Henry Nelson Coleridge. For her children she wrote *Pretty Lessons in Verse for Good Children* (1834) and *Phantasmion* (1837), a fairy story with some delightful lyrics. When her husband died in 1843, she took up his unfinished task of editing her father's works and also made several contributions to Coleridgean studies. Notable among these were an "Essay on Rationalism," appended to the 5th edition of *Aids to Reflection* (1843), and a

supplement and exhaustive notes to the 2nd edition of *Biographia Literaria* (1847).

Colet \\kȯ-'le\\, Louise, *original name* Louise Revoil \\rəv-'wȧl\\ (b. Aug. 15, 1810, Aix-en-Provence, Fr.—d. March 9, 1876, Paris)   French poet and novelist, as noted for her friendships with leading men of letters as for her own work.

She married a musician, Hippolyte Colet, in 1834, and her Paris salon became a meeting place for literary lights, notably Gustave Flaubert, with whom she had a stormy eight-year liaison. Their estrangement was followed by her bitter novel *Lui* (1859; "Him"). Among her other intimates were the poets Alfred de Musset and Alfred de Vigny and the philosopher Victor Cousin. Her other novels include *La Jeunesse de Mirabeau* (1841; "Mirabeau's Youth") and *Les Coeurs brisés* (1843; "Broken Hearts"). Among her better-known works in verse are *Penserosa* (1840), *Ce qui est dans le coeur des femmes* (1852; "In Women's Hearts"), *Ce qu'on rêve en aimant* (1854; "What One Dreams in Love"), and *Le Poème de la femme* ("The Woman's Poem").

Colette \\kȯ-'let\\, *in full* Sidonie-Gabrielle Colette (b. Jan. 28, 1873, Saint-Sauveur-en-Puisaye, Burgundy, Fr.—d. Aug. 3, 1954, Paris)   Outstanding French writer of the first half of the 20th century, whose novels, largely concerned with the pleasures and pains of love, are remarkable for their exact sensory evocation of sounds, smells, tastes, textures, and colors.

Charles Leirens—Black Star

At age 20, Colette married writer and critic Henri Gauthier-Villars, who introduced her to the improprieties of the Parisian demimonde. He discovered her talent for writing and published the four CLAUDINE novels (1900–03), reminiscences of an uninhibited young heroine, under his pen name, Willy. Turning from the semiautobiographical adventures of a libertine ingénue, Colette wrote sensitively of animals, with whom she maintained a mischievous alliance against the disappointing world of men.

After her divorce in 1906, Colette became a music-hall performer. During this period she was associated with the Marquise de Belbeuf (Mathilde de Morny) for a number of years. Her attempts to achieve independence inspired her to write *La Vagabonde* (1910; *The Vagabond*) and *L'Envers du music-hall* (1913; *Music-Hall Sidelights*). She also contributed theater chronicles and short stories to the paper *Le Matin*.

All these works belong to what Colette called her years of apprenticeship (*Mes Apprentissages*, 1936; *My Apprenticeships*). After 1920 came the decade of her masterpieces. A first group revolves around slightly depraved youth of the post-World War I era, such as the tainted hero of CHÉRI (1920) and *La Fin de Chéri* (1926; *The Last of Chéri*)—with his older mistress and young wife—and the adolescents of *Le Blé en herbe* (1923; *The Ripening Seed*), whose story deals with the loss of innocence. In a second group, she looked back to the countryside of her enchanted childhood, as in *La Maison de Claudine* (1922; *My Mother's House*) and *Sido* (1930), which are poetic meditations on her childhood.

In 1935 Colette married Maurice Goudeket, who left his memoirs on their life together (*Près de Colette*, 1955; *Close to Colette*). Her later works were diverse in theme. In *Ces Plaisirs* (1932; "Those Pleasures," later published as *Le Pur et l'impur* [1941; *The Pure and the Impure*]) she examined aspects of female sexuality. *La Chatte* (1933; *The Cat*) and *Duo* (1934) are treatments of jealousy. GIGI (1944), the story of a girl reared by two elderly sisters to become a courtesan, was adapted for both stage and screen. Colette was made a member of the Belgian Royal Academy (1935) and France's Académie Goncourt (1945) and a grand officer of the Légion d'Honneur.

Colin Muset \kȯ-'laⁿ-mǖ-'ze\ (fl. 13th century)   French trouvère, a professional vielle player and jongleur, who performed in châteaus of the Upper Marne Valley between Langres and Joinville. Colin was a native of Lorraine; his poetry, skillfully written, praised the pleasures of wine and good living. He also wrote and sometimes parodied courtly poetry.

collation \kə-'lā-shən, kä-, kō-\ [Latin *collatio* placing together, comparison]   **1.** A comparison of manuscripts or editions of a text in order to determine the original version or the condition or authenticity of a particular copy. The term may also be used to refer to the conclusions drawn and recorded from such a comparison.   **2.** The bibliographical description of a book expressed in a formula in which information about size, signatures, and pagination is represented by symbols.

collectanea \ˌkä-lek-'tā-nē-ə\ [Latin, neuter plural of *collectaneus* collected]   Collected writings or literary items forming a collection.

collected edition   A uniform, usually complete edition of an author's work.

collective biography   A volume containing biographies of a number of people. The best-known classical example is Plutarch's *Parallel Lives* (*Bioi paralléloi*), which describes the characters and recounts the deeds of many prominent Greeks and Romans. A modern example is Phyllis Rose's *Parallel Lives*, a study of several Victorian couples. *See also* BIOGRAPHY.

collective unconscious   A form of the unconscious (that part of the mind containing memories and impulses of which the individual is not aware) common to humanity as a whole and originating in the inherited structure of the brain. The term was introduced in German as *collektive Unbewusstes* by psychiatrist Carl Jung. He distinguished the collective unconscious from the personal unconscious, which arises from the experience of the individual. According to Jung, the collective unconscious contains archetypes, or universal primordial images and ideas. Thus, ARCHETYPAL CRITICISM regularly identifies literary power with the presence of certain themes that run through the myths and beliefs of all cultures. *See also* ARCHETYPE.

Collett \ˌkȯ-'let\ Camilla, *original name* Jacobine Camilla Wergeland \'ver-gə-ˌlän\ (b. Jan. 23, 1813, Kristiansand, Nor.—d. March 6, 1895, Kristiania [now Oslo])   Novelist and passionate advocate of women's rights who wrote the first Norwegian novel dealing critically with the position of women. She had an immense influence on later writers such as Henrik Ibsen, Bjørnstjerne Bjørnson, Jonas Lie, and Alexander Kielland.

The sister of Norway's beloved national poet Henrik Wergeland, she married Peter Jonas Collett. After his death she wrote the novel for which she is most famous, *Amtmandens døttre* (1854–55; "The Governor's Daughter"), in which she attacked the existing inequality of the sexes. Her second novel, *I de lange nætter* (1862; "In the Long Nights"), dealt with reminiscences of her childhood. The rest of her works were dedicated to the emancipation of women.

Collier \'käl-ē-ər, *US also* 'käl-yər\, Jeremy (b. Sept. 23, 1650, Stow by Quy, Cambridgeshire, Eng.—d. April 26, 1726, London)   English bishop of the nonjurors (clergy who refused to take the oaths of allegiance to William III and Mary II in 1689) and the author of a celebrated attack on the immorality of the stage.

Collier attended Caius College, Cambridge, and was ordained a priest in 1677. He was made lecturer of Gray's Inn in 1685 but resigned at the Revolution of 1688. He was imprisoned twice for remaining loyal to James II and for a time lived under sentence of outlawry.

In his notorious *A Short View of the Immorality and Profaneness of the English Stage* (1698), Collier attacks William Wycherley, John Dryden, William Congreve, Sir John Vanbrugh, and Thomas D'Urfey. An ensuing pamphlet war lasted spasmodically until 1726.

Collins, Tom.   Pseudonym of Joseph FURPHY.

Collins \'käl-ənz\, Wilkie, *in full* William Wilkie Collins (b. Jan. 8, 1824, London, Eng.—d. Sept. 23, 1889, London)   Early master of the mystery story and the first English novelist to write in this genre.

After studying law at Lincoln's Inn, Collins was admitted to the bar in 1851 but proved to have little aptitude for the law. He worked, instead, on a historical novel. His first published work was a memoir to his father, a landscape painter, *Memoirs of the Life of William Collins, Esq., R.A.* (1848). His fiction followed shortly after: *Antonina; or, The Fall of Rome* (1850) and *Basil* (1852), a highly colored tale of seduction and vengeance with a contemporary middle-class setting and passages of uncompromising realism. In 1851 he began an association with Charles Dickens that exerted a formative influence on his career. Collins began contributing serials to Dickens' periodical *Household Words*, and his first major work, THE WOMAN IN WHITE (1860), appeared in Dickens' *All the Year Round*. Among his most successful subsequent books were *No Name* (1862), *Armadale* (1866), and THE MOONSTONE (1868).

Collins \'käl-ənz\, William (b. Dec. 25, 1721, Chichester, Sussex, Eng.—d. June 12, 1759, Chichester)   Pre-Romantic poet who is considered one of the finest English lyric poets of the 18th century.

Collins was educated at Winchester College and Magdalen College, Oxford. When only 17, he composed his four *Persian Eclogues* (1742; 2nd edition, *Oriental Eclogues*, 1757). In 1744 he published his verse *Epistle: Addrest to Sir Thomas Hanmer on his Edition of Shakespeare's Works*, containing his exquisite "Dirge from Cymbeline." He collaborated with his friend the poet Thomas Warton on a volume of odes, which appeared separately in 1746. Warton's collection was well received, but Collins' *Odes on Several Descriptive and Allegorical Subjects* was barely noticed. Though disappointed, he continued to perfect the style exemplified in his "Ode to Simplicity." In 1749 he wrote "Ode on the Popular Superstitions of the Highlands of Scotland," which anticipates many of the attitudes and interests of the Romantic poets.

Collodi \kōl-'lō-dē\, Carlo, *pseudonym of* Carlo Lorenzini \lō-ren-'tsē-nē\ (b. Nov. 24, 1826, Florence [Italy]—d. Oct. 26, 1890, Florence)   Italian author and journalist, best known as the creator of PINOCCHIO, the childlike puppet whose adventures have delighted children around the world.

As a young man Collodi joined a seminary. The Risorgimento—the movement for Italian national unification—usurped his calling, however, as he took to journalism in support of Italy in its struggle with Austria. With the founding of the Kingdom of Italy in 1861, Collodi ceased his journalistic and military activities and began writing for children.

The first chapter of *Pinocchio* appeared in the *Giornale dei bambini* ("Children's Magazine") in 1881 and was an immediate success. All of Collodi's works portray children in a realistic light, imbuing them with mischievous behavior with which youngsters easily identify.

Colloquy of the Old Men, The *Irish* Agallamh na Seanórach, *also called* Dialogue of the Ancients *or* Colloquy of the Ancients.   In Gaelic literature, the preeminent tale of the Fenian cycle of heroic tales. The "old men" are the Fenian poets Oisín (Ossian) and Caoilte, who, having survived the destruction of their comrades at the Battle of Gabhra, return to Ireland from the timeless Land of Youth (Tír na nÓg) to discover that they have been gone 300 years. They meet St. Patrick, who interrogates them about the deeds of the legendary Finn MacCumhaill (MacCool) and the heroes of the past. Caoilte travels with St. Patrick throughout Ireland, recounting the legends, history, and myths associated with each place they visit, while St. Patrick's scribe Brogan records the tales. This framework combines the traditional Irish *Dindshenchas* ("Lore of Places") with heroic legend and folklore.

The *Colloquy* was probably compiled from older sources and oral tradition by a single author in about 1200. Preserved in the 16th-century manuscript *The Book of the Dean of Lismore*, it is written in prose with verse passages that later gave rise to the Ossianic ballads. *See also* FENIAN CYCLE.

Colluthus \kəl-'yü-thəs\ of Lycopolis \lī-'kăp-ə-ləs\ (fl. *c.* AD 500)   Greek epic poet now represented by only one extant poem, *The Rape of Helen*. The poem, which was discovered in Calabria, Italy, is in imitation of Homer and Nonnus and tells the story of Paris and Helen from the wedding of Peleus and Thetis down to Helen's arrival at Troy. According to the *Suda* (or *Suidas*) lexicon (an encyclopedic dictionary of the 10th or 11th century), Colluthus was also the author of *Calydoniaca* (probably an account of the Calydonian boar hunt), *Persica* (an account of the Persian wars), and *Encomia* (laudatory poems in epic verse).

Colman \'kōl-mən\, George, the Elder (b. April 1732, Florence [Italy]—d. Aug. 14, 1794, London, Eng.)   A leading English comic dramatist of his day and an important theater manager who sought to revive the vigor of Elizabethan drama with adaptations of plays by Ben Jonson and the team of Francis Beaumont and John Fletcher.

Colman abandoned a legal career for literature and the theater, and his first play, *Polly Honeycombe* (1760), satirized the current craze for romantic novels. His next play, *The Jealous Wife* (1761), an adaptation of Henry Fielding's novel *Tom Jones*, was one of the best comedies of the age and held its place in the stock theatrical repertoire for nearly a century. Colman collaborated with the actor-manager David Garrick on *The Clandestine Marriage* (1766), a play blending sentiment with satire, which is still stage-worthy. In 1767 Colman bought a quarter share in Covent Garden Theatre, London, which he managed for seven years, during which time he appreciably raised the standard of acting and of drama. In 1776 he bought the Little Theatre in the Hay, Haymarket, London, a summer theater that reached the peak of its fame under his management.

Colman \'kōl-mən\, George, the Younger (b. Oct. 21, 1762, London, Eng.—d. Oct. 17, 1836, London)   English playwright, writer of scurrilous satiric verse, and prominent theater manager.

Dr. Pangloss, the elderly pedant in *The Heir at Law* (first performed 1797), is his only outstanding comic creation. But the comic opera *Two to One* (1784), his first success; the melodramas *The Battle of Hexham* (1789) and *The Iron Chest* (1796), the

latter based on William Godwin's novel *Caleb Williams* (1794); and *John Bull* (1803), his most popular comedy, long kept their place in the repertoire of the Little Theatre in the Hay, London, the management of which Colman took over from his father. When his father died in 1794, he bought the theater, though large debts forced him to sell part of his share in 1805 and the rest in 1820. As examiner (or censor) of plays from 1824 until his death, Colman aroused resentment owing to his narrow severity and petty tyranny.

colometry \kə-'läm-ə-trē\ [Medieval Greek *kōlometría,* from Greek *kôlon* part of a strophe + *-metria,* a derivative of *métron* measure]   A measurement or division (as of a manuscript) by colons (rhythmic units).

colon \'kō-lən\ *plural* colons *or* cola \'kō-lə\ [Greek *kôlon* limb, part of a strophe, clause of a sentence]   **1.** A rhythmic unit of an utterance; specifically, in Greek or Latin verse, a rhythmic measure of lyric meter ("lyric" in the sense of verse that is sung, rather than recited or chanted), with a recognizable recurring pattern. Also, the different parts that make up an asynarteton, a verse made up of two or more metrical units that follow each other without a pause, but are separated by diaeresis, the demanded or recommended ending of a word between two metra or feet.   **2.** In prose, a division (by sense or rhythm) of an utterance that is smaller and less independent than the sentence and larger and less dependent than the phrase.

Colonna \kō-'lōn-nä\, Vittoria (b. 1492, Marino, near Rome [Italy]—d. Feb. 25, 1547, Rome)   Italian poet, less important for her poetry than for her personality and her associations with famous contemporaries, particularly Michelangelo.

Of a noble family, Vittoria Colonna married Ferdinando Francesco d'Avalos, Marchese di Pescara, in 1509. When her husband died in 1525 she began a series of poems in his memory, the best modern edition of which is *Rime spirituali* (1882; *The "In Memoriam" of Italy: A Century of Sonnets from the Poems of Vittoria Colonna*). She also wrote much religious poetry, but her life has drawn more interest than her work.

Learned and intelligent, of a religious and emotional nature, Vittoria was much respected by the poet Ludovico Ariosto and was a close friend of other literary figures, including the poet Jacopo Sannazaro, the humanist Pietro Bembo, and the renowned author of the etiquette manual *Il cortegiano* (*The Courtier*), Baldassare Castiglione, as well as several contemporary religious reformers. Her most famous platonic association, however, was with Michelangelo, whom she met in Rome in 1538 and with whom she exchanged many letters and philosophical sonnets.

colophon \'käl-ə-,fän, -fən\ [Greek *kolophôn* summit, finishing touch]   An inscription placed at the end of a book or manuscript, usually with facts that relate to its production. These details might include the name of the printer and the date and place of printing. Colophons are found in some manuscripts and books made as long ago as the 6th century AD. In medieval and Renaissance manuscripts, a colophon was occasionally added by the scribe and provided facts such as his name and the date and place of his completion of the work, sometimes accompanied by an expression of pious thanks for the end of his task.

The printer's colophon grew from this practice; it often included such information as the title of the book, the date and place of printing, the name and house device of the printer, and a bit of self-advertisement. The first such printed colophon occurs in the Mainz Psalter produced by Johann Fust and Peter Schöffer in 1457.

Printed colophons soon became more elaborate, however, evolving into a means whereby the printer might praise the book at length and even insert a short essay upon its merits. Ultimately, by about 1480, part of the contents of the colophon was transferred to the blank cover page at the front of the book.

In most countries, the colophon appears on the page opposite the title page and consists of a one-sentence statement that the book was printed by a given printer at a given location. Fine editions often retain the former practice, including colophons stating the typeface, paper, and other production details on the last page. *Compare* EXPLICIT.

color \\'kəl-ər\\   **1.** *archaic* Rhetorical ornaments of language. Stylistic decorations, especially figures of speech. **2.** Vividness or variety of emotional effects of language (such as those of sound and image) in prose or poetry.

Color Purple, The   Novel by Alice WALKER, published in 1982. It won a Pulitzer Prize in 1983. A feminist novel about an abused and uneducated black woman's struggle for empowerment, the novel was praised for the depth of its female characters and for its eloquent use of black English vernacular.

Colum \\'käl-əm\\, Padraic (b. Dec. 8, 1881, Longford, County Longford, Ire.—d. Jan. 11, 1972, Enfield, Conn., U.S.)   Irish-born American poet whose lyrics capture the traditions and folklore of rural Ireland.

Influenced by the literary activity of the Celtic revival centered in Dublin at the turn of the century, Colum published the collection of poetry *Wild Earth* (1907). He cofounded *The Irish Review* in 1911, then three years later settled permanently in the United States. Colum's varied literary output includes volumes of poetry, *e.g., Dramatic Legends* (1922) and *Creatures* (1927); plays, such as *Broken Soil* (first performed 1903); novels; anthologies of folklore; and children's books. The reminiscence *Our Friend James Joyce* (1959) was written with his wife Mary (1887?–1957), a well-known literary critic.

columbiad \\kə-'ləm-bē-,ad\\ [New Latin *Columbia* United States + English *-ad* (as in *Iliad, Dunciad*)]   Any of certain epics recounting the European settlement and growth of the United States. It may have been derived from *La Colombiade, ou la foi portée au nouveau monde*, a poem by the French author Marie Anne Fiquet de Boccage. A relatively well-known example is *The Columbiad* (1807; an extensive revision of *The Vision of Columbus*, 1787), by Joel Barlow.

Columbine \\'käl-əm-,bīn\\ or **Colombina** \\,kō-lòm-'bē-nə\\   Stock theatrical character that originated about 1530 in Italian COMMEDIA DELL'ARTE as the saucy and adroit servant girl; her Italian name means "Little Dove." In French theater the character became a lady's maid and intrigant and assumed a variety of roles opposite Pantaloon (Pantalone), Harlequin (Arlecchino), and Pierrot (Pedrolino). In English comedies she was usually the daughter or ward of Pantaloon and in love with Harlequin. The soubrette of the 20th-century musical comedy is a version of the Columbine character.

Combe \\'küm, 'kōm\\, William (b. 1741, Bristol, Gloucestershire, Eng.—d. June 19, 1823, London)   Prolific English writer of miscellaneous prose and satirical verse whose poem *The Tour of Dr. Syntax in Search of the Picturesque* (1812) was one of the most popular books of early 19th-century England.

Combe was educated at Eton College. He was left a legacy by a wealthy London merchant, William Alexander, and used it to travel widely and to live in a princely manner. He fell heavily into debt and, after a varied career as private soldier, waiter, teacher, and cook, returned to London about 1771 and thereafter earned his living as a writer. Dr. Syntax was introduced in 1809 in *The Poetical Magazine*. Combe's first Dr. Syntax book and its successors, *The Second Tour of Dr. Syntax in Search of Consolation* (1820) and *The Third Tour . . . in Search of a Wife*

(1821), satirize the many 18th- and early 19th-century writers whose "Tours," "Travels," and "Journeys" were vehicles for sententious moralizing, uninspired raptures, and sentimental accounts of amorous adventures. The popularity of Combe's work owed much to the illustrations of Thomas Rowlandson. Combe and Rowlandson also collaborated on *The English Dance of Death* (1815), which contains some of Combe's best verse, and *The Dance of Life* (1816–17).

Come Back, Little Sheba \\'shē-bə\\   Drama in two acts by William INGE, published in 1949 and first performed in 1950.

The play centers on the frustrated lives of Doc and Lola. Trapped in a barren 20-year-old marriage, Doc drowns his disappointment in alcohol and fantasizes about Marie, their young boarder. Lola sublimates her pain over her empty life in pining for Sheba, her lost dog. When in a drunken outburst Doc wrecks their home and nearly kills Lola, the couple are forced to see their lives clearly and to realize their mutual dependence.

comedia \\kō-'mä<u>th</u>-yä\\ [Spanish, comedy]   A Spanish regular-verse drama or comedy. Specific forms included the *comedia de capa y espada*, a cloak-and-sword comedy of love and intrigue, and the *comedia de figurón*, a form in which the emphasis is placed on one particular character who is presented as an exaggerated personification of a vice or flaw. *See also* COMEDY.

Comedians, The   Novel concerning the need for courage in the face of evil by Graham GREENE, published in 1966.

The story is set in Haiti in the mid-1960s, during the regime of the brutal dictator François Duvalier. It is narrated by Brown, a ne'er-do-well who has inherited a failing hotel near the capital, Port-au-Prince; he is returning after an abortive attempt to flee a doomed love affair.

The Comedians is principally a novel of character. Each of the leading characters reveals a new facet of personality: a naive fool who was once a Vegetarian Party candidate for U.S. president proves to be compassionate and courageous; a lying, cowardly gunrunner dies a hero; a former Freedom Rider transcends her simple liberalism to save Brown's life when she confronts a brutal secret policeman.

Comédie-Française \\kō-mā-'dē-fräⁿ-'sez\\, *formally* Le Théâtre-Français, *also called* La Maison de Molière.   National theater of France and the world's longest established national theater. It is chiefly associated with the plays of MOLIÈRE.

After the death of Molière in 1673, his company of actors joined forces with a company playing at the Théâtre du Marais, the resulting company being known as the Théâtre Guénégaud. In 1680 the company that has survived as the Comédie-Française was founded when the Guénégaud company merged with that at the Hôtel de Bourgogne, to become the only professional French company then playing in Paris.

After the French Revolution, in 1791, one group within the company established separate headquarters at the present home of the Comédie-Française in what is now the Place de Théâtre-Français, while the more conservative group remained at the original site as the Théâtre de la Nation. In 1803 the Comédie-Française was again reconstituted, this time under Napoleon's administration. A decree issued by him while in Moscow in 1812 established the rules under which the Comédie-Française was to function.

Throughout its long history, the Comédie-Française has exercised a lasting influence on the development of French theater, arts, and letters. Although it remains a theater primarily rooted in past traditions, after the appointment of Pierre Dux as its head in 1970 the Comédie-Française also began to introduce the work of new playwrights, directors, and stage designers.

Comédie humaine, La   *see* THE HUMAN COMEDY.

Comédie-Italienne \kō-mā-'dē-ē-tȧl-'yen\   Troupe of Paris-based Italian actors of the Italian COMMEDIA DELL'ARTE. The Comédie-Italienne was established under Louis XIV's royal grant in 1680 and was given the name to distinguish the plays performed by Italian players from those performed by the Comédie-Française, the French national theater troupe.

Italian commedia dell'arte companies had appeared in France from the 16th century. In 1697 the Comédie-Italienne offended the king with their satire on his second wife; they were banished from France until 1716, after Louis's death.

Prior to their banishment, the Comédie-Italienne had increasingly interspersed French words, phrases, and sometimes whole scenes into productions. After the troupe received official sanction from Louis XIV to use French, the Comédie-Italienne became a new market for French dramatists. Allowed in 1716 to return to France, the Italian players increasingly performed French works by French dramatists, particularly those of Pierre Marivaux, and from that time only some of the spirit of the commedia dell'arte—foreign flavor and the ribaldry, drolleries, pantomime, as well as some of the characters—remained.

French actors began to replace the Italians. As tastes changed, Comédie-Italienne productions turned toward opéra-bouffe (comic opera). In 1801 the company merged with a former rival, the Théâtre Feydeau, to form the Opéra-Comique, and the Comédie-Italienne was dissolved.

comédie larmoyante \kō-mā-'dē-lȧr-mwȧ-'yäⁿt\ [French, literally, tearful comedy]   Eighteenth-century genre of French sentimental drama that formed a bridge between the decaying tradition of aristocratic Neoclassical tragedy and the rise of serious bourgeois drama. Such comedies made no pretense of being amusing; virtuous characters were subjected to distressing domestic crises, but even if the play ended unhappily, virtue was rewarded.

The form is best exemplified in the 40 or so verse plays of Pierre-Claude Nivelle de La Chaussée, such as *Le Préjugé à la mode* (1735; "Fashionable Prejudice"). The effect of the *comédie larmoyante* was to blur the distinctions between comedy and tragedy, drive both from the French stage, and form the basis for the DRAME BOURGEOIS, realistic contemporary comedy heralded by Denis Diderot's *Le Fils naturel* (1757; "The Natural Son"; *Dorval; or, The Test of Virtue*).

comedy \'käm-ə-dē\ [Greek *kōmōidía*, a derivative of *kōmōidós* singer in a revel, from *kômos* band of revelers, revel + -*oidos*, a derivative of *aeídein* to sing]   The genre of dramatic literature that deals with the light or the amusing or with the serious and profound in a light, familiar, or satirical manner. *Compare* TRAGEDY.

As a genre, comedy dates to the 5th century BC, when it was associated originally with the revels that were part of the worship of the Greek god Dionysus. The first period of ancient Greek comedy, known as OLD COMEDY, is represented by the plays of Aristophanes, most of which satirized public officials and events. A transitional period followed. NEW COMEDY, which came into vogue beginning about 320 BC, shifted the focus to ordinary citizens who were portrayed as stock characters. The plots, too, followed a formula, usually a story of young love, as seen in the works of Menander. These works were later adapted by the Romans Terence and Plautus, who produced almost the only other examples of comedy in classical literature. It was not until the end of the Middle Ages that comedy reappeared in literature in any lasting form.

The medieval meaning of the word *comedy* was simply a story with a happy ending. Thus some of Geoffrey Chaucer's tales are called comedies, and Dante used the term in that sense in the title of his poem *La divina commedia*. Modern usage combines this sense with that in which Renaissance scholars applied it to the ancient comedies.

Consideration of the form as it actually exists suggests that what might be regarded as different kinds of comedy derive fundamentally from differences in the attitude of authors toward their subjects. When an author's intention is to ridicule, satirical comedy emerges; when ridicule is turned on individuals, the result is the comedy of character; satire of social convention and within social convention creates the comedy of manners; social comedy concerns the structure of society itself; and satire of conventional thinking produces the comedy of ideas. Progress from troubles to the triumph of love in a happy outcome produces romantic comedy. The comedy of intrigue derives from a dominant intention of providing amusement and excitement with an intricate plot of reversals with artificial, contrived situations. Such is the comedy of Spain as seen in the works of such dramatists as Lope de Vega and Tirso de Molina. Where the author wants to exploit potentially serious issues merely sentimentally—without approaching the truly tragic aspects of the subject or examining its underlying significance—sentimental comedy results. Tragicomedy (or sometimes comitragedy) combines elements of the tragic and the comedic. In the 20th century, a mordant form of humor, so-called black humor (or black comedy), and absurdism reflected existentialist concerns. Musical comedy, in which true comedy is often subservient to broad farce and spectacular effects, has been popular in Great Britain and the United States since the late 19th century.

comedy drama   Serious drama with comedy interspersed.

comedy of character   Comedy in which the emphasis is on characterization rather than plot or lines. *Compare* COMEDY OF SITUATION.

Comedy of Errors, The   A five-act comedy by William SHAKESPEARE, first performed in 1592–93 and first published in the First Folio of 1623. The play, Shakespeare's shortest, was based on *Menaechmi* by Plautus.

Aegeon, a merchant of Syracuse, is arrested in Ephesus and, unable to pay the local ransom, is condemned to death. He tells the duke, Solinus, his sad tale: years earlier he and his wife had been shipwrecked with their infant sons, identical twins, and a pair of infant slaves, also identical twins. The parents, each with a son and a slave, were rescued but then permanently separated. Antipholus of Syracuse, the son raised by Aegeon, has for five years been seeking his mother and brother, and Aegeon has been seeking him. Aegeon's story wins from Solinus a day's respite to raise the ransom money.

Meanwhile, Antipholus of Syracuse and his slave Dromio have arrived in Ephesus, not knowing that his brother Antipholus of Ephesus and his brother's slave, also named Dromio, are already there. A series of misidentifications ensues. Antipholus of Syracuse is entertained by his brother's wife and woos her sister; he receives a gold chain meant for his brother and is chased by a goldsmith for nonpayment. He and his slave hide in a priory, where they observe Aegeon on his way to execution and recognize the priory's abbess as their mother Aemilia. The two separated families are reunited, and Antipholus of Ephesus pays his father's ransom.

comedy of humors   A dramatic genre most closely associated with the English playwright Ben JONSON from the late 16th century. The term derives from the Latin *humor* (more properly *umor*), meaning "fluid." Medieval and Renaissance medical theory held that the human body had a balance of four fluids, or humors: blood, phlegm, yellow bile (choler), and black bile (melancholy). Variant mixtures of these humors determined an individual's "complexion," or temperament, physical and intellectual qualities, and disposition.

Each of these complexions—sanguine, phlegmatic, choleric, and melancholic—had specific characteristics, so that the words carried much weight which they have since lost: the choleric man, for example, was not only quick to anger but also yellow-faced, lean, hairy, proud, ambitious, revengeful, and shrewd.

In his play *Every Man Out of his Humour* (1600), Jonson explains that the system of humors governing the body may by metaphor be applied to the general disposition, so that a peculiar quality may so possess one as to cause particular actions. Jonson's characters usually represent one humor and, thus unbalanced, are basically caricatures.

comedy of intrigue   A comedy of situation in which complicated conspiracies and stratagems dominate the plot.

The complex plots and subplots of comedies of intrigue are often based on ridiculous and contrived situations with large doses of farcical humor. In the hands of a master such as Molière, the comedy of intrigue often shades into a comedy of manners. Thus, *Le Médecin malgré lui* (1666; *The Doctor in Spite of Himself*), which begins as a farce based on the simple joke of mistaking the ne'er-do-well woodcutter Sganarelle for a doctor, gradually becomes a satire on learned pretension and bourgeois credulity as Sganarelle fulfills his role as a doctor with great success.

comedy of manners   Witty, cerebral form of drama that satirizes the manners and fashions of a particular social class or set.

A comedy of manners is concerned with social usage and the ability (or inability) of certain characters to meet social standards. Often the governing social standard is morally trivial but exacting. The plot of such a comedy, usually concerning an illicit love affair or similarly scandalous matter, is subordinate to the play's brittle atmosphere, witty dialogue, and pungent commentary on human foibles.

Usually written by sophisticated authors for members of their own coterie or social class, the comedy of manners has historically thrived in periods and societies that combined material prosperity and moral latitude. Such was the case in ancient Greece when Menander (c. 342–c. 292 BC) inaugurated NEW COMEDY, the forerunner of comedy of manners. Menander's graceful style, elaborate plots, and stock characters were imitated by the Roman poets Plautus (c. 254–184 BC) and Terence (c. 195–159 BC), whose comedies were widely known and copied during the Renaissance.

One of the greatest exponents of the comedy of manners was Molière, who satirized the hypocrisy and pretension of 17th-century French society in such plays as *L'École des femmes* (1663; *The School for Wives*) and *Le Misanthrope* (1667; *The Misanthrope*).

In England the comedy of manners had its great day during the Restoration period. Playwrights declared themselves against affected wit and acquired follies and satirized these qualities in caricature characters with label-like names such as Sir Fopling Flutter (in Sir George Etherege's *The Man of Mode*, 1676) and Tattle (in William Congreve's *The Old Bachelour*, 1693). The masterpieces of the genre were the witty, cynical, and epigrammatic plays of William Wycherley (*The Country-Wife*, 1675) and Congreve (*The Way of the World*, 1700). In the late 18th century Oliver Goldsmith (*She Stoops to Conquer*, 1773) and Richard Brinsley Sheridan (*The Rivals*, 1775; *The School for Scandal*, 1777) revived the form.

The tradition was carried on by the Anglo-Irish playwright Oscar Wilde in *Lady Windermere's Fan* (1893) and *The Impor-*

tance of Being Earnest (1899). In the 20th century the comedy of manners reappeared in the witty, sophisticated drawing-room plays of the British dramatists Noël Coward and W. Somerset Maugham and the Americans Philip Barry and S.N. Behrman.

comedy of situation   Comedy in which the comic effect depends chiefly upon the involvement of the main characters in a predicament or ludicrous complex of circumstances. *Compare* COMEDY OF CHARACTER.

Comici Confidènti \kō-'mē-chē-,kôn-fē-'dän-tē\   Either of two companies of the Italian commedia dell'arte that were instrumental in extending the reputation of this form of improvised theater throughout Europe. The first company, which performed in France and Spain as well as in Italy, was formed about 1574; early in the 17th century, with the demise of the Gelosi, the leading commedia company, Comici Confidènti became the favorite of the Mantuan court.

The second troupe traveled principally in Italy, and after its dissolution (c. 1621) a number of its actors became associated with the Comédie-Italienne in Paris.

comic relief or **comedy relief**   A release of emotional or other tension resulting from a comic episode or item interposed in the midst of serious or tragic elements (as in drama); also, something that causes such relief.

Comisso \kō-'mēs-sō\, Giovanni (b. Oct. 3, 1895, Treviso, Italy–d. Jan. 21, 1969, Treviso)   Italian author of letters and of lyrical and autobiographical novels.

Comisso lived with Gabriele D'Annunzio in Fiume, Italy (now Rijeka, Croatia), and operated a bookstore in Milan and an art dealership in Paris. While working for several major Italian newspapers, Comisso traveled extensively in Italy and abroad. He then collected and published his letters in groups: his letters from Paris in *Questa è Parigi* (1931; "This Is Paris"); from East Asia in *Amori d'Oriente* (1949; "Loves of the Orient"), *Giappone* (1954; "Japan"), and *Donne gentili* (1959; "Kind Women"); from Italy in *L'italiano errante per l'Italia* (1937; "An Italian Roaming Italy") and *Sicilia* (1953; "Sicily"); and from Europe in *Viaggi felici* (1949; "Happy Journeys") and *Approdo in Grecia* (1954; "Landing on Greece"). He also wrote several novels, including *Capricci italiani* (1952; "Italian Whims") and *Un gatto attraversa la strada* (1954; "A Cat Crossing the Street"), which was awarded the prestigious Strega prize.

comitragedy \,käm-i-'traj-ə-dē\   Tragedy with an element of comedy. *See also* TRAGICOMEDY.

comma \'käm-ə\ [Latin, from Greek *kómma* clause, literally, something cut off, a derivative of *kóptein* to cut off]   **1.** In Greek and Latin prosody or rhetoric, a short phrase or word group smaller than a colon; a fragment of a few words or metrical feet. **2.** *obsolete* A clause or short section of a treatise or argument.

commedia dell'arte \kōm-'mä-dyä-del-'lär-tä\ [Italian, comedy of art]   Italian theatrical form that flourished throughout Europe from the 16th through the 18th century. Outside of Italy, the form had its greatest success in France, where it became the COMÉDIE-ITALIENNE. In England, certain elements of commedia dell'arte were naturalized in the harlequinade in pantomime and in the Punch-and-Judy show, a puppet play involving the commedia dell'arte character PUNCH.

The commedia dell'arte emphasized ensemble acting; its improvisations were set in a firm framework of masks and stock situations, and its plots were frequently borrowed from the classical literary tradition of the commedia erudita, or literary drama.

Professional companies of actors arose in the 16th century; they experimented with forms suited to popular taste: vernacular dialects, plenty of comic action, and recognizable characters derived from the exaggeration or parody of regional or stock fictional types.

The first date certainly associated with an Italian commedia dell'arte troupe is 1545. The most famous early company was the GELOSI; others included the DESIOSI (formed 1595), the COMICI CONFIDÈNTI (1574–1621), and the UNITI (first mentioned 1574).

Each commedia dell'arte company had a stock of scenarios, commonplace books of soliloquies and witty exchanges, and about a dozen actors. Most players created their own masks to represent the standardized characters they played, or they developed masks already established. For an understanding of the commedia dell'arte, the mask is more important than the player.

A typical scenario involved a young couple's love being thwarted by their parents. The scenario used symmetrical pairs of characters: two elderly men, two lovers, two ZANNI (madcap servants), a maidservant, a soldier, and extras. The lovers, who played unmasked, were scarcely true commedia dell'arte characters. Another character without a mask was COLUMBINE, a saucy servant girl. PANTALOON was a Venetian merchant: serious, rarely consciously comic, and prone to long tirades and good advice. DOTTORE was, in origin, a Bolognese lawyer; gullible and lecherous, he spoke in a pedantic mixture of Italian and Latin. *See also* CAPITANO; HARLEQUIN; PIERROT; and SCARAMOUCHE.

Commedia dell'arte began to decline as the rich verbal humor of the regional dialects was lost on foreign audiences; physical comedy came to dominate the performance, and, as the comic business became routine, it lost its vitality. The characters became fixed and no longer reflected the conditions of real life, thus losing an important comic element. The efforts of such playwrights as Carlo Goldoni to reform Italian drama sealed the fate of the decaying commedia dell'arte. Goldoni borrowed from the older style to create a new, more realistic form of Italian comedy, and audiences greeted the new comedy with enthusiasm.

commedia erudita \kōm-'mā-dyä-ā-rü-'dē-tä\ [Italian, literally, erudite comedy]   Sixteenth-century Italian comedy played from a text written in Latin or Italian and based on the scholarly works of earlier Italian and ancient Roman authors. *Compare* COMMEDIA DELL'ARTE.

Because the language used in the commedia erudita was not easily comprehensible to the general public, the plays were performed for the nobility, usually by nonprofessional actors (*dilettanti*). Sources for commedia erudita included the comedies of the Roman dramatists Plautus and Terence and works of the 14th-century Italian humanist Giovanni Boccaccio. Other dramas were contributed by Ludovico Ariosto, considered the best writer of early Italian vernacular comedy and a principal figure in the establishment of this literary form; the philosopher-playwright Giambattista della Porta, author of a number of stinging satires; and Niccolò Machiavelli, whose *La mandragola* (first dated publication 1524; "The Mandrake") was one of the outstanding comedies of the century.

commentary \'käm-ən-,ter-ē\ [Latin *commentarius, commentarium* notebook, commentary]   **1.**   *usually plural*   An explanatory treatise.   **2.**   *usually plural*   A record of a set of events usually written by a participant and marked by less formality and elaborateness than a history.   **3.** A systematic series of explanations or interpretations of a text.

Commodianus \kə-,mō-dē-'ä-nəs\ (fl. between 3rd and 5th centuries AD)   Christian Latin poet, perhaps of African origin. His *Carmen apologeticum* ("Song with Narrative") expounds Christian doctrine, dealing with the Creation, God's revelation of himself, the Antichrist, and the end of the world. All but two of his *Instructiones*—80 poems in two books—are in acrostic form, undoubtedly because the technique was a useful mnemonic device. His verse has no poetic value and is of interest chiefly for its employment of vulgar Latin idiom at a period when the Romance languages were emerging from Latin.

common meter or **common measure**, *abbreviated* C.M., *also called* hymnal stanza.   A meter used in English ballads that is equivalent to ballad meter, though ballad meter is often less regular and more conversational than common meter. Whereas ballad meter usually has a variable number of unaccented syllables, common meter consists of regular iambic lines with an equal number of stressed and unstressed syllables. The song "Amazing Grace" by John Newton is an example of common meter, as can be seen in the following verse:

> Amazing grace! how sweet the sound.
> That saved a wretch like me!
> I once was lost, but now am found,
> Was blind, but now I see.

See also BALLAD METER.

common particular meter or **common particular measure**   A variation of ballad meter in which the four-stress lines are doubled to produce a stanza of six lines in tail-rhyme arrangement (*i.e.*, with short lines rhyming). The number of stresses in the lines is thus 4, 4, 3, 4, 4, 3.

commonplace \'käm-ən-,plās\ [translation of Latin *locus communis* passage of a speech not directly concerned with the issue at hand, general observation, translation of Greek *koinòs tópos*]   **1.**   *obsolete*   A passage of general significance that may be applied to particular cases.   **2.**   *obsolete*   The theme, topic, or text of a discourse.   **3.**   *archaic*   A striking or especially noticeable passage; usually, such a passage entered in a commonplace book.   **4.**   *obsolete*   A commonplace book.

commonplace book   A book of literary passages, cogent quotations, occasional thoughts, or other memorabilia.

Common Reader, The   Collection of essays by Virginia WOOLF, published in two series, the first in 1925 and the second in 1932. The title indicates Woolf's intention that her essays be read by the educated but non-scholarly "common reader," who examines books for personal enjoyment.

Woolf outlines her literary philosophy in the introductory essay to the first series, "The Common Reader," and in the concluding essay to the second series, "How Should One Read a Book?" The first series includes essays on Geoffrey Chaucer, Michel de Montaigne, Jane Austen, George Eliot, and Joseph Conrad, as well as discussions of the Greek language and the modern essay. The second series features essays on John Donne, Daniel Defoe, Dorothy Osborne, Mary Wollstonecraft, and Thomas Hardy, among others.

companion piece   A work (as of literature) that is associated with and complements another.

Company She Keeps, The   First novel by Mary MC-CARTHY. Originally published as six separate short stories, the novel appeared in 1942.

Protagonist Margaret Sargent, a young student at a women's college, "a princess among the trolls," is based upon the author herself. The stories are barely disguised and acutely observed accounts of the author's own years as a young New Yorker and describe the failure of a marriage, random love affairs, and a passing flirtation with Trotskyism. Margaret's search for personal identity and her need for honesty and for distinguishing appearance from reality are the themes of the stories.

complaint \kəm-'plānt\, *also called* plaint \'plānt\ A formerly popular variety of poem that laments or protests unrequited love or tells of personal misfortune, misery, or injustice. Works of this type include Rutebeuf's *La Complainte Rutebeuf* (late 13th century) and Pierre de Ronsard's "Complainte contre fortune" (1559).

Compleat Angler, The (*in full* The Compleat Angler; or, the Contemplative Man's Recreation) A pastoral discourse on the joys of fishing by Izaak WALTON, first published in 1653. A much enlarged edition appeared in 1655, and the last edition supervised by the author, published in 1676, included additional material by Charles Cotton. The complete book, including Cotton's additions, has been among the most often reprinted books in English literature.

The book opens on the first day of May, as three sportsmen—Auceps the fowler, Venator the hunter, and Piscator the fisherman—compare their favored pastimes while traveling through the English countryside along the River Lea. The discourse is enlivened by more than 40 songs and poems, country folklore, recipes, anecdotes, moral meditations, quotes from the Bible and from classic literature, and lore about fishing and waterways.

The Compleat Angler is based in part on 15th- and 16th-century fishing manuals, and the sections on fly fishing and the making of artificial flies are by Cotton.

complication \,käm-plə-'kā-shən\ A situation or a detail of character that enters into and complicates the main thread of a plot.

composition \,käm-pə-'zish-ən\ The construction of a literary work, especially with reference to its degree of success in meeting criteria of correctness, order, or proportion.

Compson family \'kämp-sən\ Fictional characters created by William FAULKNER in his novels about Yoknapatawpha County, Mississippi, including *Absalom, Absalom!*, *The Town*, and *The Mansion*. The Compsons are principal characters of *The Sound and the Fury* in particular, and in the 1940s Faulkner appended a family history to that novel.

Quentin MacLachlan Compson came from Scotland to America in the 18th century. Quentin's grandson Jason Lycurgus Compson acquired Mississippi land around which the town of Jefferson has grown. Successive generations produce Quentin II, a state governor, and Jason II, a Confederate general. With Jason III, a cynical, alcoholic lawyer, the decline of the Compson family becomes evident. His wife Caroline feels that in having married a Compson and given birth to a family of misfits she must be paying for some terrible sin. Their children are Quentin III, who commits suicide; Jason IV, a misanthropic and conniving bachelor; Benjy, an "idiot"; and Caddy, the promiscuous daughter. Caddy's illegitimate daughter Quentin is the last of the Compsons. Together the family represents the disintegration of the Old South.

Compton-Burnett \'kämp-tən-'bər-nit\, Dame Ivy (b. June 5, 1884, Pinner, Middlesex, Eng.—d. Aug. 27, 1969, London) English writer who developed a distinct form of novel; set almost entirely in dialogue, her works dissected personal relationships in the middle-class Edwardian household.

Pastors and Masters (1925), Compton-Burnett's second novel, was published 14 years after her first, and it introduced the style that was to make her name. In this book the struggle for power, which occupies so many of her characters, is brought to light through clipped, precise dialogue. She achieved her full stature with *Brothers and Sisters* (1929), about a willful woman who inadvertently marries her half brother. *Men and Wives* (1931) has at its center another determined woman, one whose tyranny drives her son to murder her. Murder again appears in *More Women Than Men* (1933). The tyrant is a father in *A House and Its Head* (1935). The range of Compton-Burnett's characterization is considerable. The butler Bullivant is the most memorable of the cast of *Manservant and Maidservant* (1947; U.S. title, *Bullivant and the Lambs*), while the children in *Two Worlds and Their Ways* (1949) are the most tellingly drawn. Compton-Burnett was created Dame of the British Empire in 1967.

Comus \'kō-məs\ Masque by John MILTON, presented on Sept. 29, 1634, before John Egerton, Earl of Bridgewater, at Ludlow Castle in Shropshire, and published anonymously in 1637. Milton wrote the text in honor of the Earl becoming lord president of Wales and the Marches at the suggestion of the composer Henry Lawes, who wrote the music for it. *Comus* is a masque against "masquing," contrasting a private heroism in chastity and virtue with the courtly round of revelry and pleasure. It was Milton's first dramatizing of his great theme, the conflict of good and evil.

The allegorical story centers on a virtuous Lady who becomes separated from her two brothers while traveling in the woods. The Lady encounters the evil sorcerer Comus, son of Bacchus and Circe, who imprisons her by magic in his palace. In debate the Lady rejects Comus' hedonistic philosophy and defends temperance and chastity. She is eventually freed by the two brothers, with the help of the Attendant Spirit and the river nymph Sabrina.

Conan the Barbarian \'kō-,nan, -nən\ A fictional hero of pulp novels, comic books, and films whose fantasy adventures take place in a prehistoric past. Conan is an adventurer-warrior from Cimmeria who lives in the Hyborian age, an era that supposedly follows the disappearance of the mythical continent of Atlantis. Conan was created by American writer Robert E. Howard and first appeared in short stories published in *Weird Tales* magazine in the early 1930s. Howard's single extended-length Conan tale, which was serialized (1935–36) as "The Hour of the Wolf," was published after his death as the first Conan novel, *Conan the Conqueror* (1950). Other previously serialized stories and unpublished story fragments were edited by various people and published as *The Sword of Conan* (1952), *The Coming of Conan* (1953), *King Conan* (1953), *Conan the Barbarian* (1954), and *Tales of Conan* (1955).

conceit \kən-'sēt\ An elaborate or strained metaphor. This sense of the word *conceit*, which originally meant "idea" or "concept," was influenced by Italian *concetto*, which from its original sense "concept" came to denote a fanciful metaphor. The Petrarchan conceit, especially popular with Renaissance writers of sonnets, is a hyperbolic comparison made generally by a suffering lover of his beautiful and cruel mistress to some physical object; *e.g.*, a tomb, the ocean, the sun. The metaphysical conceit, associated with the Metaphysical poets of the 17th century, is a more intricate and intellectual device. It sets up an analogy, usually between one entity's spiritual qualities and an object in the physical world, that sometimes controls the whole structure of the poem. For example, in the following stanzas from "A Valediction: Forbidding Mourning," John Donne compares two lovers' souls to a draftsman's compass:

> If they be two, they are two so
> As stiffe twin compasses are two,
> Thy soule the fixt foot, makes no show
> To move, but doth, if th'other doe.
>
> And though it in the center sit,
> Yet when the other far doth rome,
> It leanes, and hearkens after it,
> And growes erect, as that comes home.

Conceits often were so far-fetched as to become absurd, degenerating into strained ornamentation. With the advent of Romanticism they fell into disfavor along with other poetic artifices. In the late 19th century they were revived by the French Symbolists and are commonly found, although in brief and condensed form, in the works of such poets as Emily Dickinson, T.S. Eliot, and Ezra Pound.

conceptismo \,kōn-thep-'tēz-mō, -sep-\ or **conceptism** \'kän-,sep-,tiz-əm\ [Spanish *conceptismo*, a derivative of *concepto* concept, conceit, ingenious expression] In Spanish literature, an obscurely allusive style cultivated by essayists, especially satirists, in the 17th century. *Conceptismo* was characterized by the use of striking metaphors, either expressed concisely and epigrammatically or elaborated into lengthy conceits.

Concerned primarily with the stripping off of appearances in a witty manner, *conceptismo* found its best expression in the satirical essay. Its chief exponents were Francisco Gómez de Quevedo, who is generally considered the master satirist of his age, in *Sueños* (1627; *Dreams*), and Baltasar Gracián, the theoretician of *conceptismo*, who codified its stylistic precepts in *Agudeza y arte de ingenio* (1642; 2nd edition, 1648; "Subtlety and the Art of Genius"). *Compare* CULTERANISMO.

concetto \kən-'chet-ō\ *plural* concetti \-'chet-ē\ [Italian, notion, idea, literary conceit, from Late Latin *conceptus* thought, concept] A conceit, especially in literary style.

Conchubar or **Conchobar** *see* CONOR.

concinnity \kən-'sin-ə-tē\ [Latin *concinnitas,* a derivative of *concinnus* neatly arranged, elegant] Harmony or fitness in the adaptation of parts to a whole or to each other. The term is often used to mean studied elegance of design or arrangement and is used especially of literary style.

concision \kən-'sizh-ən\ The quality or state of being concise, used especially of literary style.

concordance \kən-'kòr-dəns, kän-\ [Medieval Latin *concordantiae* index containing parallel occurrences of a word or passage in Scripture, plural of *concordantia* agreement, harmony] An alphabetical index of the principal words in a book or the works of an author with their immediate contexts.

concrete poetry [translation of Portuguese *poesia concreta* or German *konkrete Dichtung*] Poetry in which the poet's intent is conveyed by graphic patterns of letters, words, or symbols rather than by the meaning of words in conventional arrangement. The writer of concrete poetry uses typeface and other typographical elements in such a way that chosen units—letter fragments, punctuation marks, graphemes (letters), morphemes (any meaningful linguistic unit), syllables, or words—and graphic spaces form an evocative picture. The origins of concrete poetry are roughly contemporary with those of *musique concrète*, an experimental technique of musical composition.

Max Bill and Eugen Gomringer were among the early practitioners of concrete poetry. The Vienna Group of Hans Carl Artmann, Gerhard Rühm, and Konrad Bayer also promoted concrete poetry, as did Ernst Jandl and Friederike Mayröcker. The movement drew inspiration from Dada, Surrealism, and other early 20th-century movements. Concrete poetry has an extreme visual bias and in this way is usually distinguished from PATTERN POETRY. It attempts to move away from a purely verbal concept of verse toward what its proponents call "verbivocovisual expression," incorporating geometric and graphic elements into the poetic act or process. It often cannot be read aloud to any effect, and its essence lies in its appearance on the page, not in the words or typographic units that form it. Concrete poetry is still produced in many countries. Notable

contemporary concrete poets include Haroldo de Campos and Augusto de Campos.

Condé \kòⁿ-'dā\, Maryse \mả-'rēs\, *original surname* Boucolon \bü-kò-'lòⁿ\ (b. Feb. 11, 1937, Pointe-à-Pitre, Guadeloupe) Guadeloupean author of epic historical fiction, much of it set in Africa.

Condé began writing at an early age and had already produced a novel by the time her parents sent her to study in France in 1953. While there she was introduced to the anticolonial Negritude movement and developed an idealistic and romantic fascination with Africa. In the 1960s she taught in Guinea and later in Ghana and Senegal.

Condé's experiences living abroad provided the background for her novel *Hérémakhonon* (1976; *Heremakhonon*), about a young black West Indian woman's quest for roots. *Une Saison à Rihata* (1981; *A Season in Rihata*) is also set in a late 20th-century African land. Her major work is the best-selling two-volume novel, *Ségou* (1984; *Segu*) and *Ségou II* (1985; *The Children of Segu*). Set in historic Ségou (now part of Mali), it portrays the violent effect of the slave trade, Islām, Christianity, and white colonization on a royal family from the late 18th to the mid-19th century. *Moi, Tituba, sorcière noire de Salem* (1986; *I, Tituba, Black Witch of Salem*) is based on the story of an American slave tried for witchcraft in Salem, Mass., in the 17th century. In 1986 Condé returned to live in Guadeloupe, where *La Vie scélérate* (1987; *Tree of Life*) is set. Condé also wrote the novel *La Colonie du nouveau monde* (1993; "The Colony of the New World") as well as several plays, children's books, and controversial essays on literature and politics.

Condell \kän-'del\, Henry (d. December 1627, London, Eng.) English actor who was apparently one of the chief movers in sponsoring and preparing the Shakespeare First Folio of 1623. He and John Heminge jointly signed the letters to the noble patrons and "the great variety of readers" that preface the volume.

Condell appeared in Ben Jonson's *Every Man in His Humour* in 1598. Thereafter he was regularly with William Shakespeare's company (Chamberlain's Men; after 1603, King's Men) and retired about 1623. His name and that of Heminge were linked with Shakespeare's for 30 years: they had been associates financially and were fellow actors in the Blackfriars and Globe theaters.

confection \kən-'fek-shən\ An artistic or literary work marked by artificiality or lack of sincerity; a work made up of unsuitable or incongruous elements that are combined without real unification or feeling of purpose.

Confederation group \kən-,fed-ə-'rā-shən\ Canadian English-language poets of the late 19th century whose work expressed the national consciousness inspired by the Confederation of 1867. Their transcendental and romantic view of the Canadian landscape dominated Canadian poetry until the 20th century. The Confederation group is also called the Maple Tree school because of the love characteristically shown for that dominant feature of the Canadian landscape. The group includes four poets: Charles G.D. Roberts, whose *Orion, and Other Poems* (1880) heralded the movement; Bliss Carman, who wrote lyric poems on nature, love, and the open road; Archibald Lampman, known for his vivid descriptions of nature; and Duncan Campbell Scott, who composed ballads and dramas of the northern Ontario wilderness.

Confessio amantis \kən-'fesh-ē-ō-ə-'man-tis, kän-'fes-ē-ō-ä-'män-tēs\ Late 14th-century poem by John GOWER. The *Confessio* (begun about 1386) runs to some 33,000 lines in octosyllabic couplets and takes the form of a collection of exemplary tales of love placed within the framework of a lover's confession to a priest of Venus. The priest, Genius, instructs the poet, Amans, in the art of both courtly and Christian love. The stories are chiefly adapted from classical and medieval sources and are told with a tenderness and the restrained narrative art that constitute Gower's main appeal today. Many classical myths (especially those deriving from Ovid's *Metamorphoses*) make the first of their numerous appearances in English literature in the *Confessio*.

confession \kən-'fesh-ən\   In literature, an autobiography, either real or fictitious, in which intimate and hidden details of the subject's life are revealed.

The first outstanding example of the genre, written about AD 400, was *The Confessions* of St. Augustine, a painstaking examination of Augustine's progress from youthful debauchery to conversion to Christianity and the triumph of the spirit over the flesh. Other notable examples include Thomas De Quincey's *Confessions of an English Opium-Eater* (1822), which reveals the writer's early life and his gradual addiction to drugs, and *Confessions* (1782–89), the intimate autobiography of Jean-Jacques Rousseau. André Gide used the form to great effect in such works as *Si le grain ne meurt* (1920 and 1924; *If It Die . . .*), an account of his life from birth to marriage.

Such 20th-century poets as John Berryman, Robert Lowell, Sylvia Plath, and Anne Sexton wrote poetry in the confessional vein, revealing intensely personal, often painful perceptions and feelings.

confessional \kən-'fesh-ə-nəl\   Of, relating to, or being intimately autobiographical writing or fiction.

Confessions, The   Spiritual self-examination by Saint AUGUSTINE, written in Latin as *Confessiones* about AD 400. The book tells of Augustine's restless youth and of the stormy spiritual voyage that had ended some 12 years before the writing in the haven of the Roman Catholic church. In reality, the work is not so much autobiography as an exploration of the philosophical and emotional development of an individual soul. *The Confessions* broke entirely fresh ground as literature, and the genre of autobiography owes many of its characteristics to Augustine.

Confessions of an English Opium-Eater   Autobiographical narrative by English author Thomas DE QUINCEY, first published in *The London Magazine* in two parts in 1821, then as a book, with an appendix, in 1822.

The avowed purpose of the first version of the *Confessions* was to warn the reader of the dangers of opium, and it combined the interest of a journalistic exposé of a social evil, told from an addict's point of view, with a somewhat contradictory and seductive picture of the subjective pleasures of drug addiction. The highly poetic and imaginative prose of the *Confessions* makes it one of the enduring stylistic masterpieces of English literature.

Athough De Quincey ends his narrative at a point at which he is drug-free, he remained an opium addict for the rest of his life. In 1856 he rewrote the *Confessions* and added descriptions of opium-inspired dreams that had already appeared in *Blackwood's Magazine* in about 1845 under the title *Suspiria de Profundis* ("Sighs from the Depths"). But his literary style in the revised version tends to be difficult, involved, and even verbose, and his additions and digressions dilute the artistic impact of the original.

Confessions of Nat Turner, The \'nat-'tər-nər\   Novel by William STYRON, published in 1967 and awarded the Pulitzer Prize for fiction in 1968. A fictional account of the Virginia slave revolt of 1831, the novel is narrated by the leader of the rebellion. Styron based *The Confessions of Nat Turner* on a

pamphlet of the same title published in Virginia shortly after the revolt, but he took many liberties in developing Turner's character. Styron's Turner is a man of moral depth and farseeing vision who is nevertheless a bitter, self-denying, sexually repressed man who cannot attain either physical or spiritual freedom. Not surprisingly, the book generated controversy, primarily among black critics who objected to the white author's attempt to speak in the voice of a black slave. These critics also accused Styron of falsifying historical facts and misrepresenting Turner himself, and in 1968 a book of essays appeared called *William Styron's Nat Turner: Ten Black Writers Respond*. Styron answered in his own defense and was supported by several eminent historians.

Confidence-Man, The (*in full* The Confidence-Man: His Masquerade)   Satirical allegory by Herman MELVILLE, published in 1857. The last novel to be published during Melville's lifetime, it reveals the author's pessimistic view of an America grown tawdry through greed, self-delusion, and lack of charity.

Set on a steamboat traveling on the Mississippi River, the work is an episodic series of vignettes of various passengers—some dupes, some tricksters—who represent a gullible American public that can be deceived by charlatans and by the lure of easy money.

conflate \kən-'flāt\   In literature, to combine two readings of a text into a composite whole. To produce a composite reading or text by conflation.

conflict \'kän-,flikt\   In drama or fiction, the opposition of persons or forces upon which the dramatic action depends.

Confucius \kən-'fyü-shəs\, *Chinese* Kongfuzi (K'ung-fu-tzu) \'kùŋ-'fü-'dzə\ *or* Kongzi (K'ung-tzu) \'kùŋ-'chyü\, *literary name* Zhongni \'jùŋ-'nē\ (b. 551 BC, Qufu, state of Lu [now in Shandong province, China]—d. 479, Lu)   China's most famous teacher, philosopher, and political theorist, whose ideas have influenced all civilizations of East Asia.

Although little reliable information exists about Confucius' early life, his family was probably of the impoverished nobility; he was orphaned at an early age and grew up poor. He was largely self-educated but apparently became the most learned man of his day.

Learning, however, was not his greatest interest. Confucius was deeply disturbed by the political and social conditions of his times. Unable to obtain an official position in which he could implement his ideas of reform, he spent the greater part of his life educating a group of disciples.

Confucius was not a religious leader in the ordinary sense, for his teaching was essentially a social ethic. Though his interest in books was secondary to his passion for reform, many of the ancient classics were attributed to his authorship and editorship. These books, interpreted in Confucian terms, formed the basic curriculum of Chinese education for more than 2,000 years.

Congreve \'kän-,grēv, 'käŋ-\, William (b. Jan. 24, 1670, Bardsey, near Leeds, Yorkshire, Eng.—d. Jan. 19, 1729, London)   English Neoclassical dramatist who shaped the English comedy of manners through his brilliant comic dialogue, his satirical portrayal of fashionable society, and his ironic scrutiny of the affectations of his age.

Congreve's father was an army officer stationed in Ireland. In April 1686 Congreve entered Trinity College, Dublin (M.A., 1696). In 1691 he was entered as a law student at the Middle Temple, but he was never a serious reader in law. In 1692 he published under the pseudonym Cleophil a light but skillful near-parody of fashionable romance, *Incognita: or, Love and Duty Reconcil'd*. He quickly became known among men of letters, had some verses printed in a miscellany of the same year, and became a protégé of John Dryden.

In March 1693 Congreve became famous with the production of his play *The Old Bachelour*. It ran for the then unprecedented length of two weeks. But his next play, *The Double-Dealer* (produced 1693), though considered far better, did not meet with the same success. *Love for Love*, his best acting play, almost repeated the success of his first. Performed in April 1695, it was the first production staged for the new theater in Lincoln's Inn Fields. Congreve became one of the managers of the new theater, promising to provide a new play every year.

Detail of an oil painting by Sir Godfrey Kneller, 1709

National Portrait Gallery, London

In 1695 he began to write his more public occasional verse, such as his pastoral on the death of Queen Mary II. Though he signally failed to carry out his promise of writing a play a year, he showed his good intentions with THE MOURNING BRIDE. This tragedy, produced early in 1697, swelled his reputation enormously and became his most popular play. No further dramatic work appeared until March 1700, when Congreve's masterpiece, THE WAY OF THE WORLD, was produced—with a brilliant cast—at Lincoln's Inn Fields; though it is now his only frequently revived piece, it was a failure with the audience. This was Congreve's last attempt to write a play, though he did not entirely desert the theater. He wrote librettos for two operas, and in 1704 he collaborated in translating Molière's *Monsieur de Pourceaugnac*.

He continued to write a considerable number of poems, some of the light social variety, some sound scholarly translations from Homer, Juvenal, Ovid, and Horace, as well as a number of Pindaric odes. The volume containing the odes also included his timely "Discourse on the Pindarique Ode" (1706).

Coningsby \'kō-niŋz-bē\ (*in full* Coningsby, or The New Generation)   Political novel by Benjamin DISRAELI, published in 1844. It is the first novel in Disraeli's trilogy completed by *Sybil* (1845) and *Tancred* (1847). *Coningsby* follows the fortunes of Harry Coningsby, the orphaned grandson of the Marquis of Monmouth. It also traces the waning of the Whigs and the Tories and the nascency of the Conservative party. Above all, *Coningsby* is a tribute to a political group called "Young England," which hoped for an alliance of the nobility and the common people.

Conjure Woman, The   The first collection of stories by Charles W. CHESNUTT. The seven stories began appearing in magazines in 1887 and were first collected in a book in 1899.

The narrator of *The Conjure Woman* is a white male Northerner living in the southern United States who passes along the stories told him by ex-slave Julius McAdoo. Unusual for dialect tales of the period, the stories give a realistic picture of the pre-Civil War South, including descriptions of penurious, brutish masters. Conjuration—magic effected by hoodoo practitioners—helps slaves to overcome difficulties; thus, spells are cast

and humans are transformed into birds and mammals in the course of these tales.

The relationships between the patronizing narrator, his wife, who sometimes glimpses the stories' deeper meanings, and the crafty, sometimes manipulative Uncle Julius—each of whom is subtly characterized—develop over the course of the book.

Connecticut Yankee in King Arthur's Court, A \kə-'net-i-kət\   Satirical novel by Mark TWAIN, published in 1889. It is the tale of a commonsensical Yankee who is carried back in time to Britain in the Dark Ages, and it celebrates homespun ingenuity and democratic values in contrast to the superstitious ineptitude of a feudal monarchy. Twain wrote it after reading Sir Thomas Malory's *Le Morte Darthur*.

Hank Morgan, a mechanic at a gun factory, is knocked unconscious and awakens in England in the year 528. He is captured and taken to Camelot, where he is put on exhibit before the knights of King Arthur's Round Table. He is condemned to death, but remembering having read of an eclipse on the day of his execution, he amazes the court by predicting the eclipse. It is decided that he is a sorcerer like Merlin, and he is made minister to the ineffectual king. In an effort to bring democratic principles and mechanical knowledge to the kingdom, he strings telephone wire, starts schools, trains mechanics, and teaches journalism. He also falls in love and marries.

But when Hank tries to better the lot of the peasants, he meets opposition from many quarters. He and Arthur, in disguise, travel among the miserable common folk, are taken captive and sold as slaves, and only at the last second are rescued by 500 knights on bicycles. Hank and his family briefly retire to the seaside. When they return they find the kingdom engulfed in civil war, Arthur killed, and Hank's innovations abandoned. Hank is wounded, and Merlin, pretending to nurse him, casts a spell that puts him to sleep until the 19th century.

Connell \'kän-əl\, Evan S., Jr., *in full* Evan Shelby (b. Aug. 17, 1924, Kansas City, Mo, U.S.)   Writer whose works explore philosophical and cultural facets of the American experience.

Connell's first published work, the critically acclaimed *The Anatomy Lesson and Other Stories* (1957), consists of stories set in various parts of the United States and incorporates subject matter ranging from the near-mythic to the mundane. *Mrs. Bridge* (1959), his first novel and the one with which subsequent works were often compared, dissects the life of a conventional upper middle-class Kansas City matron who lacks a sense of purpose and conforms blindly to what is expected of her. Ten years later Connell published *Mr. Bridge* (1969), which relates the same story from the point of view of the husband. *Son of the Morning Star: Custer and the Little Bighorn* (1984), which retells an almost legendary clash of personalities and cultures, was a critical as well as popular success. Among Connell's other works are the novels *The Diary of a Rapist* (1966), *The Connoisseur* (1974), and *The Alchymist's Journal* (1991) and a book-length poem, *Notes from a Bottle Found on the Beach at Carmel* (1963).

Connelly \'kän-ə-lē\, Marc, *byname of* Marcus Cook Connelly (b. Dec. 13, 1890, McKeesport, Pa., U.S.—d. Dec. 21, 1980, New York, N.Y.)   American playwright, journalist, teacher, actor, and director, best known for *Green Pastures* (a folk version of the Old Testament dramatized through the lives of blacks of the southern United States) and for the comedies that he wrote with George S. KAUFMAN.

Connelly worked as a reporter in Pittsburgh until 1917, when he joined the *Morning Telegraph* in New York City, covering theatrical news. He then began his collaboration with Kaufman. Their first successful play, *Dulcy* (1921), written as a vehicle for the actress Lynn Fontanne, was followed by *To the*

Ladies (1922), a vehicle for Helen Hayes. *Beggar on Horseback* (1924), in the style of German Expressionist drama, depicts the threat to art from a society dominated by bourgeois values.

While they collaborated in writing a satire on Hollywood, *Merton of the Movies* (1922), and two musicals, *Helen of Troy, New York* (1923) and *Be Yourself* (1924), Connelly and Kaufman were members of the Algonquin Round Table. Connelly described this phase of his career in *Voices Offstage: A Book of Memoirs* (1968).

Green Pastures, based on Roark Bradford's book *Ol' Man Adam an' His Chillun,* was first performed in 1930 and was extremely popular both on the stage and in its motion-picture version (1936), but when it was revived in 1951 it was criticized for perpetuating unacceptable stereotypes of blacks.

Connelly's last Broadway success, *The Farmer Takes a Wife* (1934; film, 1935), written with Frank Elser, was a comedy about life along the Erie Canal in the 19th century. From 1946 to 1950 he taught playwriting at Yale University. His novel *A Souvenir from Qam* was published in 1965.

Connolly \ˈkän-ə-lē\, Cyril (Vernon) (b. Sept. 10, 1903, Coventry, Warwickshire, Eng.—d. Nov. 26, 1974, London) English critic, novelist, and man of letters, founder and editor of *Horizon,* a magazine of contemporary literature that was a major influence in Britain in its time. As a critic he was personal and eclectic rather than systematic, but his idiosyncratic views were perceptive and conveyed with wit and grace.

In 1927 Connolly began a career of literary journalism as a contributor to the *New Statesman, The Sunday Times,* the *Observer,* and other periodicals. His only novel, *The Rock Pool,* about the headlong decline of a young Englishman in a Riviera art colony, appeared in 1936. His most noted books are his collections of essays—*Enemies of Promise* (1938), which contains an autobiographical section, and *The Condemned Playground* (1945)—and an assemblage of introspective jottings, *The Unquiet Grave* (1944). *Previous Convictions: Selected Writings of a Decade* was published in 1963, and *The Evening Colonnade,* a collection of essays, in 1975.

Connor \ˈkän-ər\, Ralph, *pseudonym of* Charles William Gordon \ˈgȯr-dən\ (b. Sept. 13, 1860, Indian Lands, Glengarry County, Ont., Can.—d. Oct. 31, 1937, Winnipeg, Man.) Canadian Presbyterian minister and writer of numerous popular novels that combine religious messages, wholesome sentiment, and adventure.

Ordained in 1890, Gordon became a missionary to mining and lumber camps in the Canadian Rocky Mountains. It was from this experience and memories of his Glengarry childhood that he derived the major background for his fiction. His first books, the missionary adventure tales *Black Rock* (1898) and its sequel, *The Sky Pilot* (1899), met with phenomenal success. His highest literary achievements are considered to be the books dealing with the pioneer traditions of his Ontario boyhood: *The Man from Glengarry* (1901) and *Glengarry School Days* (1902).

Conor \ˈkän-ər\, *also called* Conchubar *or* Conchobar \ˈkän-ü-ər, ˈkäŋk-ō-ər\, *in full* Conchobar mac Nessa \mək-ˈnes-ə\ Legendary king of Ulster in northern Ireland during its heroic age. Conor was said to have been born sometime in the 1st century BC, and he died in approximately 33 AD. Conflicting myths and folktales leave his paternity uncertain, but his mother was Nessa, whose husband, King Fergus mac Roich, Conor deposed. A wise, brave, powerful hero, Conor is featured in the tales of the ULSTER CYCLE as the uncle of Cú Chulainn, the greatest of the Ulster heroes. His love for the heroine DEIRDRE is the subject of another of the tales.

Conrad \ˈkän-ˌrad\, Joseph, *original name* Józef Teodor Konrad Korzeniowski \kȯ-zhe-ˈnʸȯf-skʸē\ (b. Dec. 3, 1857, Berdichev, Ukraine, Russian Empire [now Berdychiv, Ukraine]—d. Aug. 3, 1924, Canterbury, Kent, Eng.) Polish-born English novelist and short-story writer who is noted for the richness of his prose and his renderings of dangerous life at sea and in exotic places. His initial reputation as a masterful teller of colorful adventures of the sea grew as his deeply pessimistic vision of the complexity of the human struggle was revealed.

Library of Congress

Conrad's father, a poet and an ardent Polish patriot, was arrested in late 1861 and sent into exile in northern Russia. His wife and four-year-old son followed him there, and by 1869 both of Conrad's parents had died of tuberculosis. The boy was put in the care of his maternal uncle. In 1874 Conrad left for Marseille with the intention of going to sea. He joined the French merchant marine as an apprentice, voyaging first to the West Indies. Personalities and events from these experiences—and from all his subsequent voyages—found their place in his novels.

In 1878 Conrad signed on as a deckhand on a British freighter bound for Constantinople, the beginning of 16 years in the British merchant navy. He sailed to the Far East for the first time in 1881; his initial landing, on an island off Sumatra, took place only after a 13½-hour voyage in an open boat after his ship caught fire and had to be abandoned. In 1898 Conrad published an account of this experience, with only slight alterations, as the short story "Youth," a remarkable tale of a young officer's first command.

He then shipped to India. This voyage gave him material for his novel THE NIGGER OF THE "NARCISSUS" (1897), the story of a black sailor's deterioration and death aboard ship. In 1886 Conrad became a British subject and obtained his master mariner's certificate. A voyage to Java yielded the prototype for the heroic, unimaginative captain of the steamer *Nan Shan* in TYPHOON (1902). Conrad obtained his first command on the *Otago,* sailing from Bangkok, an experience out of which were to come his stories "The Shadow-Line" and "Falk."

Back in London in the summer of 1889, he began to write *Almayer's Folly.* The task was interrupted by his appointment to a four-month command of a Congo River steamboat. What he saw, did, and felt during this traumatic stay in the Congo is largely recorded in HEART OF DARKNESS (1902), perhaps his most famous but most enigmatic story. *See also* MARLOW. Conrad made several more voyages, but by 1894 his sea life was over. *Almayer's Folly* (1895), which was published under the name by which he is known, was followed in 1896 by *An Outcast of the Islands.*

Not until 1910, after he had written what are now considered his finest novels—LORD JIM (1900), NOSTROMO (1904), THE SECRET AGENT (1907), and *Under Western Eyes* (1911)—did Conrad's financial situation became relatively secure. His novel *Chance* was serialized in the *New York Herald* in 1912, and his novel *Victory* was published in 1915. Though hampered by rheumatism, Conrad continued to write for the remaining years of his life. He refused an offer of knighthood in 1924.

Conrart \kō̃-ˈrȧr\, Valentin (b. 1603, Paris, Fr.—d. Sept. 23, 1675, Paris) Man of letters and authority on grammar and style, known as the practical inaugurator of classicism in French literature through his leading role in the founding of the Académie Française.

Conrart was brought up in pious austerity and was never taught Latin or Greek, although he learned Italian and Spanish as soon as he was free of his father's tutelage. He bought himself an appointment as king's counselor-secretary in 1627, introduced himself into literary society, and began to build up a great library.

From around 1629, writers met every week in Conrart's house. This group was the nucleus of the Académie Française, which was formed in 1634–35, with Conrart himself appropriately nominated as its permanent secretary. Thereafter he made himself the "tyrant" of the French language, correcting the spelling, grammar, and word order in the manuscripts and printers' proofs of the works of many writers whose creative or imaginative genius was greater than his own.

Of Conrart's original writings, the only ones that have proved to be of lasting interest are his records of events in Paris during the Fronde (the insurrections against the government of Cardinal Mazarin), together with a few extended notes on persons of historical or literary significance.

Conroy \\'kän-ˌrȯi\\, Jack, *byname of* John Wesley Conroy, *pseudonym* Tim Brennan \\'bren-ən\\ *or* John Norcross \\'nȯr-ˌkrȯs\\ (b. Dec. 5, 1899, near Moberly, Mo., U.S.—d. Feb. 28, 1990, Moberly)   Leftist American writer best known for his contributions to "proletarian literature," fiction and nonfiction about the life of American workers during the early decades of the 20th century.

Conroy was a migratory worker in the 1920s. He first became known in 1933 with his critically acclaimed novel *The Disinherited.* This largely autobiographical book depicts the coming of age of a coal miner's son during the Great Depression. From 1931 to 1941 Conroy edited successively the magazines *Rebel Poet, Anvil,* and *New Anvil.* He included writings by Erskine Caldwell, Langston Hughes, and William Carlos Williams. Conroy later edited, with Curt Johnson, a collection of these works entitled *Writers in Revolt: The Anvil Anthology* (1973).

In 1938 Conroy began to work on the Federal Writers' Project of the Works Progress Administration (WPA). With Arna Bontemps, Conroy wrote a juvenile book, *The Fast-Sooner Hound* (1942), and *They Seek a City* (1945), a history of black migration and settlement with biographical data on important black figures. A revised and expanded version of the latter book, *Anyplace But Here* (1966), added background on contemporary events such as the Watts riots. A collection of works entitled *The Jack Conroy Reader* was published in 1980.

Conscience \\kȯⁿs-'yäⁿs\\, Hendrik (b. Dec. 3, 1812, Antwerp [Belgium]—d. Sept. 10, 1883, Brussels)   Belgian Romantic novelist who so dominated the birth and development of the Flemish novel that it was said he "taught his people to read."

After his mother's death in 1820, when he and his father went to live outside the town walls, Conscience discovered nature, which was to remain a constant solace and which inspired him to write the remarkable *Enige bladzijden uit het boek der natuur* (1846; "A Few Pages from the Book of Nature"). After spending several years as an assistant teacher, he enlisted in the army in 1831. About this time he was introduced to French Romanticism and began to write French verse, Flemish being considered too vulgar to be a literary medium. Demobilized in 1836, he entered the literary and artistic life of Antwerp. He was fascinated by his country's past and wrote in Flemish *In't wonderjaar* (1837; "In the Year of Miracles"), a series of 16th-century historical scenes. With *De leeuw van Vlaanderen* (1838;

The Lion of Flanders), he became not only the creator of the Flemish novel but also the author of one of the outstanding historical novels of European Romanticism.

After 1840 Conscience turned more and more to an idyllic realism and wrote novels and tales about urban and rural life. They include *Wat een moeder lijden kan* (1844; "What a Mother Can Suffer"), *Houten Clara* (1850; "Wooden Clara"), and *De arme edelman* (1851; *The Poor Gentleman*), as well as the village idylls *Blinde Rosa* (1850; *Blind Rosa*), *De Loteling* (1850; *The Conscript*), and *Rikke-tikke-tak* (first published serially, 1845; as a book, 1851; Eng. trans., *Ricketicketack*). At the same time he was publishing historical novels, for example *Jacob van Artevelde* (1849). By the mid-19th century, Conscience was at the height of his genius, and his works became widely known through translations. But his spendthrift manner of life and the burdens of an expensive household caused him to write prolifically, sometimes to the detriment of his style. Among the many books of this last period are *Het Goudland* (1862; "The Land of Gold"), the first Flemish adventure novel, and *De Kerels van Vlaanderen* (1871; "The Boys of Flanders"), a historical novel. The publication of his 100th book in 1881 led to unprecedented demonstrations in Brussels, and in 1883 a statue was erected in his honor in Antwerp.

consonance \\'kän-sə-nəns\\ [Latin *consonantia* concord, harmony], *also called* consonant-rhyme.   Recurrence or repetition of identical or similar consonants; specifically, the correspondence of end or intermediate consonants unaccompanied by like correspondence of vowels at the ends of two or more syllables, words, or other units of composition.

As a poetic device, consonance is often combined with assonance (the repetition of stressed vowel sounds within words with different end consonants) and alliteration (the repetition of initial consonant sounds). Consonance is also occasionally used as an off-rhyme, but it is most commonly found as an internal sound effect, as in William Shakespeare's song "The ousel co*ck* so bla*ck* of hue" or in "The curfew to*ll*s the kne*ll* of parting day" from Thomas Gray's "An Elegy Written in a Country Church Yard." *Compare* ALLITERATION; ASSONANCE.

Constant \\kȯⁿ-'stäⁿ\\, Benjamin, *in full* Henri-Benjamin Constant de Rebecque \\də-rə-'bek\\ (b. Oct. 25, 1767, Lausanne, Switz.—d. Dec. 8, 1830, Paris, Fr.)   Franco-Swiss novelist and political writer, the author of ADOLPHE (1816), a forerunner of the modern psychological novel.

In 1794 Constant began a relationship with Mme Germaine de STAËL, who had much to do with his decision to support the French Revolution. Their tumultuous and passionate relationship lasted until 1806. After the coup d'état of 18 Brumaire in 1799, he quickly became, like Mme de Staël, an opponent of the Bonapartist regime and followed her into exile in 1803. Constant was associated with the brothers Friedrich and August von Schlegel, the pioneers of German Romanticism, and with them he inspired Mme de Staël's book *De l'Allemagne* ("On Germany").

During his exile, Constant worked on his *De la religion considérée dans sa source, ses formes et ses développements,* 5 vol. (1824–31; "On Religion Considered in Its Source, Its Forms, and Its Developments"), a historical analysis of religious feeling. In it he revealed his inner self, as he also did in his intimate diaries and in *Adolphe,* the barely disguised account of his break with Mme de Staël in 1806. Nearly 150 years after the publication of *Adolphe,* another of Constant's autobiographical novels, *Cécile,* dealing with events between 1793 and 1808, was discovered. Constant's *Journaux intimes* ("Intimate Journals") were first published in their entirety in 1952, adding to the autobiographical picture of Constant provided by his *Cahier rouge* (1907; *The Red Notebook*).

In 1808 Constant secretly married Charlotte von Hardenberg. But his intellectual relationship with Mme de Staël and her circle remained unbroken. On his return to Paris after a short exile, Constant became one of the leaders of liberal journalism. He was elected a deputy in 1819. After the revolution of July 1830, he was appointed president of the council of state but died the same year.

Constant's complete works were published in 1957, and the first edition of *Cécile* appeared in 1951.

Contact Literary magazine founded in 1920 by American author Robert McAlmon, aided by poet William Carlos Williams. Devoted to avant-garde writing of the period, it led to McAlmon's important Contact Editions book-publishing enterprise.

Contact began in New York as a mimeographed magazine and relocated to Paris in 1921 following McAlmon's marriage to English author Bryher (Annie Winifred Ellerman). Four issues were published in 1920–21 and a fifth in 1923. Contributors included Kay Boyle, H.D., Marianne Moore, Ezra Pound, Wallace Stevens, and Glenway Wescott. Meanwhile, in 1922 McAlmon had himself published his short-story collection *A Hasty Bunch*. This, his contacts with fellow expatriate writers in Paris, and a large gift of money from his father-in-law led McAlmon to establish a book-publishing venture. Contact Editions books began to appear in 1923. Over the years McAlmon issued works by himself and Bryher; Williams' *Spring and All*; Ernest Hemingway's first book; *The Making of Americans* by Gertrude Stein; and *Contact Collection of Contemporary Writers*, an anthology including works by James Joyce and Ford Madox Ford. Nathanael West's novel *The Dream Life of Balso Snell* (1931) was the last Contact book. Williams and West revived *Contact* magazine for three issues in the United States in 1932, publishing prose by S.J. Perelman, James T. Farrell, and McAlmon and poetry by E.E. Cummings and Louis Zukofsky.

contamination \kən-ˌtam-ə-'nā-shən\ In manuscript tradition, a blending whereby a single manuscript contains readings belonging to different groups. In literature, a blending of legends or stories that results in new combinations of incident or in modifications of plot.

conte \'kōnt, 'kōⁿt\ *plural* contes *same or* 'kōnts\ [French, a derivative of *conter* to relate] **1.** A short tale especially of adventure. *Compare* SHORT STORY. **2.** A narrative that is somewhat shorter than the average novel but longer than a short story.

Contending Forces (*in full* Contending Forces: A Romance Illustrative of Negro Life North and South) Novel by Pauline HOPKINS, published in 1900.

The complicated plot of *Contending Forces* follows a mixed-race family from early 19th-century slavery in the West Indies and the southern United States to early 20th-century Massachusetts. The story centers on Will and his sister Dora as each works to improve the social and political situations faced by African-Americans. Their marriages to ideological opposites suggest Hopkins' hopes for reconciling the contrary philosophies of Booker T. Washington and W.E.B. Du Bois. Other characters are used to depict the horrors of rape, lynching, racism, and sexism. *Contending Forces* is especially notable as one of the earliest novels by an African-American woman.

conteur \kōn-'tər, kōⁿ-\ *plural* conteurs *same or* -'tərz\ [French, a derivative of *conter* to relate] A reciter or composer of contes. A storyteller.

context \'kän-ˌtekst\ [Latin *contextus* connection, structure, literally, the act of weaving together, a derivative of *contexere*

to weave together] **1.** *obsolete* A written composition. **2.** The parts of a discourse that surround a word or passage and can throw light on its meaning.

Continental Op \'äp\ Fictional character, one of the first hard-boiled detectives in fiction and the narrator of several 1920s crime stories by Dashiell HAMMETT. The Op is nameless and is described only as "fat and forty"; he is employed by the Continental Detective Agency in San Francisco. The Op appeared in stories published in the mid-1920s in *Black Mask* magazine, in those issued in the posthumous collections *The Big Knockover* (1966) and *The Continental Op* (1974), and in the novels *Red Harvest* (1929) and *The Dain Curse* (1929).

continuation \kən-ˌtin-yə-'wā-shən\ **1.** A book begun by one writer and continued by another; also, the portion of such a book that continues the original part. **2.** A work (such as a periodical or numbered monograph) that is issued in successive parts; also, one of the parts.

contraction \kən-'trak-shən\ In classical prosody, the substitution of one long syllable for two short ones, as when a spondee (− −) appears as a contracted form of the dactyl (− ◡ ◡). The word is contrasted with RESOLUTION. *See also* PROSODY; SCANSION.

convention \kən-'ven-chən\ An established technique, practice, or device in literature or the theater. Dramatic conventions include the willing suspension of disbelief, the use of stock characters, and the use of soliloquy.

conversation piece A piece of writing (such as a play) that depends for its effect chiefly upon the wit or excellent quality of its dialogue. The term is also used to describe a poem that has a light, informal tone despite its serious subject. Examples include Samuel Taylor Coleridge's "The Nightingale," William Wordsworth's "Tintern Abbey," and W.H. Auden's "September 1, 1939."

Conway \'kän-ˌwā\, Moncure Daniel (b. March 17, 1832, Stafford County, Va., U.S.—d. Nov. 15, 1907, Paris, Fr.) American clergyman, author, and vigorous abolitionist.

Conway was born of slaveholding parents. While serving in the Methodist ministry he was converted to Unitarianism, but because of his outspoken abolitionist views he was dismissed from his first Unitarian pastorate, in Washington, D.C., in 1856. He moved to Cincinnati, Ohio, and became active in abolitionist causes, even settling a colony of fugitive slaves at Yellow Springs, Ohio.

In 1862 he became coeditor in Boston of the *Commonwealth*, an antislavery paper. During the Civil War he went to England to lecture on behalf of the North. Conway contributed to journals in both England and the United States and wrote more than 70 books and pamphlets on a great variety of subjects. His scholarly works include *Life of Thomas Paine*, 2 vols. (1892), and *The Writings of Thomas Paine*, 4 vols. (1894–96). His *Autobiography* (1904) is valuable for sketches of important 19th-century figures.

Cook \'kŭk\, George Cram (b. Oct. 7, 1873, Davenport, Iowa, U.S.—d. Jan. 14, 1924, Delphi, Greece) American novelist, poet, and playwright who, with his wife, Susan GLASPELL, established the noncommercial Provincetown Players.

After completing his degree at Harvard, Cook studied at Heidelberg and the University of Geneva. He taught at the University of Iowa and at Stanford University and then worked as a small farmer.

The influence of Friedrich Nietzsche is reflected in Cook's first novel, *Roderick Taliaferro* (1903), a historical romance set in the Mexico of Emperor Maximilian. One of his workers, Floyd Dell, who later became a novelist, converted him to socialism (Cook appears as Tom Alden in Dell's *Moon-Calf* [1920]). In Cook's novel *The Chasm* (1911) his protagonist is torn between Nietzschean aristocratic individualism and socialist ideas; the latter eventually win.

Cook worked with Dell at the *Chicago Evening Post* and married the novelist and playwright Susan Glaspell. In 1915 they launched the Provincetown Players in Provincetown, Mass., initially to perform their jointly written one-act play *Suppressed Desires* (1915, published 1920), a satire on psychoanalysis. Cook continued with the group in New York City's Greenwich Village as the Playwrights' Theatre, performing plays written by American authors. From 1921, he lived in Greece, an experience that influenced his poems *Greek Coins* (1925) and his play *The Athenian Women* (1926).

Cooke \ˈkůk\, Alistair, *in full* Alfred Alistair Cooke (b. Nov. 20, 1908, Manchester, Eng.)   Anglo-American journalist and commentator best known for his lively and insightful interpretations of American history and culture.

Cooke graduated from Jesus College, University of Cambridge, and won a fellowship to study theater in the United States. Following a brief period as a scriptwriter in Hollywood, he returned to England to become a film critic for the British Broadcasting Corporation (BBC) and later served as London correspondent for the National Broadcasting Company (NBC) of the United States. From the late 1930s, Cooke reported and commented on American affairs for BBC radio and several major British newspapers. He became a U.S. citizen in 1941. His weekly radio program, *Letter from America*, commenced in 1946 and ran for three decades. The texts of these broadcasts were collected in *One Man's America* (1952) and *Talk About America* (1968).

Cooke's interpretation of the American experience culminated in his BBC-produced television series *America* (1972–73). *Alistair Cooke's America*, the book based on the award-winning program, was a best-seller in the United States. He wrote a number of additional works and also for nearly two decades served as the host of the BBC's dramatic television program *Masterpiece Theatre*.

Cook's Tale, The   An incomplete story in THE CANTERBURY TALES by Geoffrey Chaucer.

This 58-line fragment of a tale of "harlotrie," as the poet described it, tells of a womanizing, gambling apprentice cook who is dismissed from his job. He moves in with a fellow reveler and his wife, a shopkeeper by day and prostitute by night. Scholars are uncertain how Chaucer intended the story to end, and some manuscript versions of *The Canterbury Tales* omit this fragment altogether.

Cooper \ˈkůp-ər, ˈkůp-\, James Fenimore (b. Sept. 15, 1789, Burlington, N.J., U.S.—d. Sept. 14, 1851, Cooperstown, N.Y.)   First major American novelist, author of the novels of frontier adventure known as THE LEATHER-STOCKING TALES.

James was a year old when his father, a Federalist congressman, moved his family to the frontier settlement (now Cooperstown) that he had founded in upstate New York. Cooper attended Yale and was expelled during his junior year because of a prank. He then joined the navy but became financially independent upon his father's death in 1809.

For 10 years he led the life of a dilettante. His first fiction, reputedly written on a challenge from his wife, was *Precaution* (1820), a plodding imitation of Jane Austen's novels of English gentry manners. His second novel, *The Spy* (1821), was based on Sir Walter Scott's Waverley novels, but in his own narrative Cooper used an American Revolutionary War setting and introduced several distinctively American character types.

The book soon brought him international fame and a certain amount of wealth. The latter was very welcome, indeed necessary, since his father's estate had proved less ample than anybody had thought, and, with the deaths of his elder brothers, he had found himself responsible for the entire Cooper family.

The first of the renowned Leather-Stocking Tales, *The Pioneers* (1823), adhered to the successful formula of *The Spy*. No known prototype exists for the novel's principal character— the wilderness scout Natty Bumppo, alias Leather-Stocking. Public fascination with the character led Cooper to write a series of sequels in which the entire life of the frontier scout was gradually unfolded. *The Pioneers* was followed by *The Last of the Mohicans* (1826), *The Prairie* (1827), *The Pathfinder* (1840), and *The Deerslayer* (1841).

Cooper's fourth novel, THE PILOT (1823), inaugurated a series of popular and influential sea novels—especially *The Red Rover* (1827) and *The Sea Lions* (1849). As developed by Cooper, the genre became a powerful vehicle for spiritual as well as moral exploration. Cooper also wrote a meticulously researched, highly readable *History of the Navy of the United States of America* (1839).

Between 1822 and 1826 Cooper lived in New York City and participated in its intellectual life, founding the Bread and Cheese Club, which had many influential members. In the gentlemanly tradition of Thomas Jefferson and others, he attacked the oligarchical Whig Party, which opposed the egalitarian democracy of President Andrew Jackson. The lawsuits, conflict, and unrest provoked by his political stance were hard to bear, especially because he was writing more and earning less as the years went by. And though he wrote some of his best romances—such as *Satanstoe; or, The Littlepage Manuscripts* (1845)—during the last decade of his life, his profits from publishing had so diminished that he gained little benefit from his increased popularity. He was forced to go on writing for income, and some of his later novels, such as *Mercedes of Castile* (1840) and *Jack Tier* (1846–48), were mere hack work.

Cooper \ˈkůp-ər, ˈkůp-\, Thomas (b. March 20, 1805, Leicester, Leicestershire, Eng.—d. July 15, 1892, Lincoln, Lincolnshire)   English writer whose political epic *The Purgatory of Suicides* (1845) promulgated in verse the principles of Chartism, Britain's first specifically working-class national movement.

Cooper became a schoolmaster in 1827 and in 1829 a Methodist lay preacher. He worked for the newspaper *Leicestershire Mercury* until his support of Chartism led to his dismissal in 1841, and he then began to edit various Chartist weeklies. In 1842 he toured the potteries to urge support for a general strike. In 1843 he was convicted of sedition and spent two years in jail, where he wrote his verse epic. After 1856 most of his writings were in defense of Christianity, as his political enthusiasm declined after quarreling with Feargus O'Connor, a Chartist leader.

Coornhert \ˈkōrn-hert\, Dirck Volckertszoon (b. 1522, Amsterdam [Neth.]—d. Oct. 29, 1590, Gouda)   Dutch poet, translator, playwright, and moralist who was the first to set down humanist values in the vernacular. His clear, unpretentious prose style contrasted with that of the contemporary Rederijkers (rhetoricians) and served as a model to the great 17th-century Dutch writers. His book of songs *Liedekens* (1575) shows his determination to choose a form for the content and not vice versa.

Coornhert published Dutch translations of Cicero, Seneca, and Boethius. His translation of Homer's *Odyssey—De dolinghe van Ulysse* (1561)—was the first great work of the Dutch early Renaissance. It revealed powers of imagery and sensuous description that are largely absent from his original poetry.

Coornhert's dramas are allegorical and didactic: the *Comedie van Israël* (1575) attacks the worldly, hypocritical Netherlands of his time. His best-known prose work is the moralist tract *De wellevenskunste* (1586; "The Polite Art"), in which he holds that the true path can be found only through spiritual love.

Coover \'kū-vər\, Robert (Lowell) (b. Feb. 4, 1932, Charles City, Iowa, U.S.)   American writer of avant-garde fiction, plays, poetry, and essays whose use of experimental forms and techniques mixed reality and illusion.

Coover attended Southern Illinois University, Indiana University, and the University of Chicago. He taught at several universities, notably Brown University, Providence, R.I. His first novel, *The Origin of the Brunists* (1966), the most conventional of his fiction, tells of the rise and eventual disintegration of a religious cult. The protagonist of *The Universal Baseball Association, Inc.* (1968) creates an imaginary baseball league, in which fictitious players take charge of their own lives. The stories in *Pricksongs & Descants* (1969) were praised for their "verbal magic." *The Public Burning* (1976) was what Coover called a "factional account" of the trial and execution of Julius and Ethel Rosenberg; using Richard Nixon as the work's narrator, it satirized the national mood of the early 1950s. Among his other works are *Whatever Happened to Gloomy Gus of the Chicago Bears?* (1987) and *Pinocchio in Venice* (1991). Several of Coover's short stories were adapted for theatrical performance, including "The Baby Sitter" and "Spanking the Maid."

Cope \'kōp\, Jack, *byname of* Robert Knox Cope (b. June 3, 1913, Mooi River, Natal, S.Af.)   South African writer best known for his lucid short stories and novels about South African life.

Cope was a journalist in Durban and in London before he returned to South Africa to write fiction. *The Fair House* (1955), a family history centering on the Zulu revolt of 1902, was the first of a series of his novels that include *The Golden Oriole* (1958), *The Road to Ysterberg* (1959), *Albino* (1964), *The Dawn Comes Twice* (1969; belatedly banned in the late 1970s), *The Student of Zend* (1972), and *My Son Max* (1977). His short-story collections include *The Tame Ox* (1960), *The Man Who Doubted* (1967), and *Alley Cat* (1973). *Selected Stories* was published in 1986.

Cope's writing shows genuine insight into the varied classes, races, and individuals who populate his fiction. He founded and for many years edited the English-Afrikaans journal *Contrast* and edited and translated the works of many other writers. In 1982 Cope published *The Adversary Within: Dissident Writers in Afrikaans.*

Coppard \'käp-ərd\, A.E., *in full* Alfred Edgar (b. Jan. 4, 1878, Folkestone, Kent, Eng.—d. Jan. 13, 1957, London)   Writer who achieved fame with his short stories depicting the English rural scene and its characters.

Coppard's love for literature, painting, and music led him to abandon an office career for a cottage in the country. His first book of short stories, *Adam and Eve and Pinch Me*, was published when he was 43. His talent was recognized and other collections of stories followed, including *Fishmonger's Fiddle* (1925), which contained what is perhaps his best story, "The Higgler." The charm of his stories lay in his poetic feeling for the countryside and in his amusing and dramatic presentation of rustic characters.

Coppard's other works include several volumes of poems and a partial autobiography, *It's Me, O Lord*, which appeared after his death.

Coppée \kȯ-'pā\, François (b. Jan. 26, 1842, Paris, Fr.—d. May 23, 1908, Paris)   French Parnassian poet, known for his somewhat sentimental treatment of the life of the poor.

Coppée served as a clerk in the ministry of war and achieved success in 1869 with the play *Le Passant* ("The Passer-by"). His best-known and most characteristic collection of verse is *Les Humbles* (1872; "The Humble"). He was elected to the Académie Française in 1884. In 1898, after a serious illness, he was reconverted to Roman Catholicism; that same year he published *La Bonne Souffrance* ("The Good Suffering"), a novel arising from this experience.

Coppée's reputation has been diminished because of his involvement in nationalist and racist politics. He was active on behalf of the prosecution against the Jewish officer Alfred Dreyfus, whose trial on a charge of treason divided France. Coppée later helped to found the anti-Semitic Ligue de la Patrie Française ("French Fatherland League").

Copperfield, David \'dā-vid-'käp-ər-ˌfēld\   Fictional character, the young hero of Charles Dickens' most popular novel, the semiautobiographical DAVID COPPERFIELD.

coquecigrue \'käk-si-ˌgrü\ [French]   An imaginary creature regarded as an embodiment of absolute absurdity. François Rabelais in *Gargantua* uses the phrase *à la venue des cocquecigrues* to mean "never." Charles Kingsley in *The Water Babies* has the fairy Bedonebyasyoudid report that there are seven things he is forbidden to tell until "the coming of the Cocqcigrues."

Corbière \kȯr-'byer\, Tristan, *pseudonym of* Édouard Joachim Corbière (b. July 18, 1845, Coat-Congar, near Morlaix, Fr.—d. March 1, 1875, Morlaix)   French poet remarkable for his realistic pictures of seafaring life and for his innovative use of irony and slang and the rhythms of common speech, which contrasted sharply with the elevated lyricism of the French Romantics, whom he frequently parodied.

Corbière settled in Roscoff, where, apart from three years in Paris, he spent the rest of his life and wrote most of his only volume of poems, *Les Amours jaunes* (1873; "Yellow Loves"). His main themes are love, Paris, the sea, and his native province. He did not belong to any literary school and was almost unknown until Paul Verlaine included him in *Les Poètes maudits* (1884; rev. ed., 1888; "The Damned [or Maligned] Poets"). His influence is apparent in the poetry of his contemporary Jules Laforgue and in the early works of Ezra Pound and T.S. Eliot.

Cordelia \kȯr-'dēl-yə\   Fictional character, the king's youngest daughter in William Shakespeare's tragedy KING LEAR. Although Cordelia refuses to compete with her sisters Goneril and Regan in their false and extravagant professions of love and devotion to their father, it is only she who truly loves him.

Corelli \kə-'rel-ē\, Marie, *pseudonym of* Mary Mackay \mə-'kī, -'kā\ (b. 1855, London, Eng.—d. April 21, 1924, Stratford-upon-Avon, Warwick)   English author of 28 romantic melodramatic novels of immense popularity.

Her first book, *A Romance of Two Worlds* (1886), dealt with psychic experience—a theme in many of her later novels as well. Her earliest success was *Barabbas: A Dream of the World's Tragedy* (1893), in which her treatment of the Crucifixion was designed to appeal to popular taste. *The Sorrows of Satan* (1895), also a melodramatic treatment of a religious theme, had an even wider vogue, and the climax of her career was reached with *The Murder of Delicia* (1896).

Thereafter, she was frequently attacked by the more critical public for her sentimentality and poor taste.

Corineus \kə-'rin-ūs, 'kȯr-i-ˌnūs\   Legendary eponymous hero of Cornwall. According to Geoffrey of Monmouth's *Historia regum Britanniae* (1135–39), he was a Trojan warrior who accompanied Brutus the Trojan, the legendary founder of Britain, to England. Corineus killed Gogmagog (Goëmagot), the greatest of the giants inhabiting Cornwall, by hurling him from a cliff. A cliff near Totnes, Devon, is still called Giant's Leap.

Corinna or **Korinna** \kə-'rin-ə\ (fl. *c.* 500 BC?)   Greek lyric poet of Tanagra in Boeotia, traditionally considered a contemporary and rival of the lyric poet Pindar though some scholars have put her date as late as about 200 BC. Surviving fragments of her poetry, written in Boeotian dialect, include a song contest between the mountain gods Cithaeron and Helicon. Written in a simple style, her lyrics were mainly concerned with Boeotian mythology.

Corinthian \kə-'rin-thē-ən\   Elegant and ornate in style or manner, especially in literary style. The allusion is to the reputed elegance of the art of ancient Corinth.

Coriolanus \ˌkȯr-ē-ō-'lā-nəs, -'lä-\   The last of the so-called political tragedies by William SHAKESPEARE, produced in 1607–08 and published in the First Folio of 1623. The five-act play, based on the life of Gnaeus Marcius Coriolanus, a legendary Roman hero of the late 6th and early 5th centuries BC, is essentially an expansion of the Plutarchan biography. Though it is Elizabethan in structure, it is sharply classical in tone.

The action of the play follows Caius Marcius (afterwards Caius Marcius Coriolanus) through several phases of his career. He is shown as an arrogant young nobleman in peacetime, as a bloodstained and valiant warrior against the city of Corioli, and as a modest victor and candidate for consul. When he refuses to flatter the Roman citizens, for whom he feels contempt, or to show them his wounds to win their vote, they turn on him and banish him. Bitterly he joins forces with his enemy Tullus Aufidius, a Volscian, against Rome. Leading the enemy to the edge of the city, Coriolanus is ultimately persuaded by his mother to make peace with Rome, and in the end he is killed.

Coriolanus is in many ways unusual for Shakespearean drama: it has a single narrative line, its images are compact and sharply effective, and its most effective moments are characterized by understatement or silence.

Corippus \kə-'rip-əs\, Flavius Cresconius (fl. 6th century AD)   Important Latin epic poet and panegyrist.

Of African origin, Corippus migrated to Constantinople (now Istanbul, Tur.). His *Johannis*, an epic poem in eight books, treats the campaign conducted against the insurgent Mauretanians by John Troglita, the Byzantine commander, and is the principal source of knowledge of these events. The poem, written about 550, shows the tenacity of the classical tradition in Africa and the continuance of the poetic revival that took place under Vandal rule. *In laudem Justini*, the four books of which eulogize Justinian I's successor Justin II, was written after Corippus arrived in Constantinople. It is interesting for the account it gives of the death of Justinian and his successor's accession and of the embassy of the Avars.

corn \'kȯrn\   Something (such as writing, music, or acting) that is corny (mawkishly old-fashioned or tiresomely simple and sentimental).

Corn \'kȯrn\, Alfred, *in full* Alfred Dewitt Corn III (b. Aug. 14, 1943, Bainbridge, Ga., U.S.)   American poet whose mild-mannered, meditative lyrics belie a considerable sophistication.

Corn attended Emory University and Columbia University and taught at several universities. He earned critical acclaim for his first volume of verse, *All Roads at Once* (1976). The poems in *A Call in the Midst of the Crowd* (1978) are all about New York City, notably the lengthy title poem. *Notes from a Child of Paradise* (1984), one of Corn's best-known works, is a long semiautobiographical poem modeled after the *Paradiso* in Dante's *La divina commedia*. Other verse collections

include *The Various Light* (1980), *An Xmas Murder* (1987), *The West Door* (1988), and *Autobiographies* (1992). *The Pith Helmet* (1992) is a book of aphorisms.

Corneille \kȯr-'nāy; *Angl* -'nā, -'nāl\, Pierre (b. June 6, 1606, Rouen, Fr.—d. Oct. 1, 1684, Paris)   French poet and dramatist who is considered to be the creator of French classical tragedy.

Corneille's first play, written before he was 20, was an elegant and witty comedy, *Mélite*, performed in Paris in 1630. His next plays were the tragicomedy *Clitandre* (performed 1631) and a series of comedies that included *La Veuve* (performed 1632; *The Widow*), *La Suivante* (performed 1634; "The Maidservant"), and *La Place royale* (performed 1634).

Detail of an oil painting attributed to Charles Le Brun, 1647
Cliché Musées Nationaux, Paris

Support had been growing for a new approach to tragedy that aimed at "regularity" through observance of what were called the classical unities. Corneille responded by experimenting in the tragic form with *Médée* (performed 1635). He then wrote the tragicomedy LE CID (1637), which is now commonly regarded as the most significant play in the history of French drama.

Corneille followed this masterpiece with the Roman tragedy HORACE (1641); another, CINNA, was published in 1643. Taken as a group, *Le Cid, Horace, Cinna,* and POLYEUCTE (1643) are known as Corneille's classical tetralogy, and together they represent perhaps his finest body of work for the theater. Their arguments, presented elegantly, rhetorically, in the grand style, remain firm and sonorous. The alexandrine verse that he employed was used with astonishing flexibility.

The Roman plays were followed by more tragedies: *La Mort de Pompée* (performed 1644; *The Death of Pompey*); *Rodogune* (performed 1645), which was one of his greatest successes; *Théodore* (performed 1646), which was his first taste of failure; and *Héraclius* (performed 1647). In 1644 Corneille had successfully turned to comedy with *Le Menteur* (*The Liar*), the one outstanding French comedy that was produced before the plays of Molière.

In 1647 Corneille moved with his family to Paris and was at last admitted to the Académie Française, having twice previously been rejected on the grounds of nonresidence in the capital. He wrote the heroic comedy *Don Sanche d'Aragon* (performed 1650); the tragedy *Andromède* (performed 1650), a spectacular play in which stage machinery was very important; and the tragedy *Nicomède* (performed 1651) during 1648–53, the period of political upheaval and civil war known as the Fronde. In 1652 his play *Pertharite* seems to have been brutally received, and for the next eight years Corneille wrote nothing for the theater. In 1659 he presented *Oedipe*. For the next 14 years he wrote almost one play a year, including the tragedies *Sertorius* (performed 1662) and *Attila* (performed 1667), both of which contain violent and surprising incidents. Other late plays include the tragedies *La Toison d'or* (performed 1660; "The Golden Fleece"), *Othon* (performed 1664), *Agésilas* (performed 1666), and *Pulchérie* (performed 1672). In collaboration with Molière and Philippe Quinault he wrote *Psyché* (1671), a comedy that incorporated both music and ballet sequences. A year earlier, however, he had presented the tragedy *Tite et Bérénice*, in deliberate contest with a play on the same subject by Jean Racine. Its failure indicated the public's growing preference for the younger playwright.

Corneille's final play was the tragedy *Suréna* (performed 1674), which showed an uncharacteristic delicacy and sentimental appeal. After this he published nothing except for a few beautiful verses (1676) thanking King Louis XIV for ordering the revival of his plays.

Corneille \kȯr-'nāy; *Angl* -'nā, -'nȧl\, Thomas (b. Aug. 20, 1625, Rouen, Fr.—d. Dec. 8, 1709, Les Andelys) French dramatist, younger brother of the great French classical playwright Pierre Corneille and a highly successful dramatic poet in his own right, whose works helped to confirm the character of the French classical theater.

Between 1656 and 1678 Corneille put on no fewer than 16 tragedies, starting with *Timocrate* (1656), which was among the dramatic successes of the century. His best play is the tragedy *Ariane* (1672; *The Labyrinth*). He also experimented with comedy in the then-popular Spanish style (*Le Geôlier de soi-même* [1655; "His Own Jailer"]), with opera, and with lyric drama.

Corneille had an acute sense of timing and a flair for ingenious dramatic effects. One original contribution to the drama was the extended use in his later works of stage machinery in an attempt to enlarge the range of tragedy. Elected to the Académie Française in 1685, he helped to compile an encyclopedic dictionary.

Cornford \'kȯrn-fərd\, Frances Crofts, *original surname* Darwin \'där-win\ (b. March 30, 1886, Cambridge, Cambridgeshire, Eng.—d. Aug. 19, 1960, Cambridge) Poet perhaps known chiefly, and unfairly, for the sadly comic poem "To a Fat Lady Seen from a Train" ("O fat white woman whom nobody loves,/Why do you walk through the fields in gloves . . .").

A granddaughter of Charles Darwin, she was educated at home. Darwin's first book of poems, including the "Fat Lady" verse, was published in 1910. Later volumes include *Spring Morning* (1915), *Autumn Midnight* (1923), *Different Days* (1928), *Mountains and Molehills* (1934), and *Travelling Home* (1948). Her *Collected Poems* appeared in 1954, and she was awarded the Queen's Medal for Poetry in 1959. Many of her poems, often very short, express her deep love for Cambridge and its traditions.

Cornhill Magazine, The \,kȯrn-'hil\ Long-lived British literary periodical (1860–1975) that specialized in publishing novels in serial form and was renowned for its uniformly high literary quality. Its founder and first editor was William Makepeace Thackeray. It was the first literary magazine to achieve a circulation of 100,000. *The Cornhill Magazine* suspended publication from 1940 to 1943 during the height of World War II, resuming in January 1944.

Among the major novelists, poets, and critical writers whose work appeared in the periodical were George Eliot, Thomas Hardy, Alfred, Lord Tennyson, Robert Browning, Algernon Swinburne, John Ruskin, and Leslie Stephen, who also served as the magazine's editor (1871–82).

coronach \'kȯr-ə-nȧk, 'kär-\ [Scottish Gaelic *corronach* and Irish *corónach*] In Scottish and Irish tradition, choral lament or outcry for the dead; also, a funeral song sung or uttered by women. Though observers frequently reported hearing such songs in Ireland or in the Scottish Highlands, no such songs have been recorded. The Scottish border ballad "The Bonny

Earl of Murray" was supposedly composed in the tradition of the coronach. It begins:

> Ye Highlands, and ye Lawlands,
> Oh where have you been?
> They have slain the Earl of Murray,
> And they layd him on the green.

corpus \'kȯr-pəs\ *plural* corpora \'kȯr-pə-rə\ [Latin, body] The whole body or total amount of writings of a particular kind or on a particular subject (as the total production of a writer [*compare* OEUVRE] or the whole of the literature on a subject).

correct \kə-'rekt\ Of literary or artistic style, conforming to recognized conventions or an established mode.

correption \kə-'rep-shən\ [Latin *correptio* shortening of a vowel or syllable, a derivative of *corripere* to pronounce a syllable short, literally, to reduce, diminish] In classical prosody, the shortening of a final long vowel or diphthong when the next word begins with a vowel. The device occurs most often in the works of Homer.

corrupt \kə-'rəpt\ To alter from the original or correct form or version (as by error, omission, or addition).

Corso \'kȯr-sō\, Gregory (Nunzio) (b. March 26, 1930, New York, N.Y., U.S.) American poet, a leading member in the mid-1950s of the Beat movement.

At 17 Corso was sentenced to three years in Clinton Prison in Dannemora, N.Y., for theft. While there, he was introduced to literature. He met the poet Allen Ginsberg in Greenwich Village in 1950 and published his first volume of verse, *The Vestal Lady on Brattle*, in 1955. In 1956 Corso went to San Francisco, where Ginsberg was residing and the Beat movement was gaining momentum.

Corso's poems in the collection *Gasoline* (1958) use the rhythmic, incantatory style effective in spoken verse. In *The Happy Birthday of Death* (1960) he returned to an easier, conversational tone. *Long Live Man* (1962), *Selected Poems* (1962), *The Mutation of the Spirit* (1964), *Elegiac Feelings American* (1970), *Herald of the Autochthonic Spirit* (1981), *Mindfield* (1989), and other books of poetry followed. He also wrote plays and a novel.

Cortázar \kȯr-'tä-sär\, Julio, *pseudonym* Julio Denis \'dän-ēs\ (b. Aug. 26, 1914, Brussels, Belg.—d. Feb. 12, 1984, Paris, Fr.) Argentine novelist and short-story writer who combined existential questioning with experimental writing techniques in his works.

Cortázar was educated in Argentina, where he worked as a teacher and a translator. *Bestiario* (1951; "Bestiary"), his first short-story collection, was published the year he moved to Paris. He received French citizenship in 1981, though he kept his Argentine citizenship as well.

Another collection of short stories, *Final del juego* (1956; "End of the Game"), was followed by *Las armas secretas* (1958; "Secret Weapons"). Some of the stories were translated into English as *End of the Game, and Other Stories* (1967). The main character of "El perseguidor" ("The Pursuer"), one of the stories in *Las armas secretas*, embodies many of the traits of Cortázar's later characters. The metaphysical anguish that the protagonist feels in his search for artistic perfection and in his failure to come to grips with the passage of time, coupled with his rejection of 20th-century values, was among Cortázar's central preoccupations.

Cortázar's masterpiece, *Rayuela* (1963; HOPSCOTCH), is an open-ended novel; the reader is invited to rearrange the different parts of the novel according to a plan prescribed by the author. A series of playful and humorous stories written between 1952 and 1959 were published in *Historias de cronopios y de famas* (1962; *Cronopios and Famas*). His other works include *Todos los fuegos el fuego* (1966; *All Fires the Fire*) and *Libro de Manuel* (1973; *A Manual for Manuel*).

Cortez \kȯr-'tez\, Jayne (b. May 10, 1936, Arizona, U.S.) African-American poet especially noted for performing her own poetry, often accompanied by jazz.

Cortez was artistic director of the Watts Repertory Theatre Company from 1964 to 1970. Unfulfilled love, unromantic sex, and jazz greats from Bessie Smith to Cortez's ex-husband Ornette Coleman are subjects of her first collection of poems, *Pissstained Stairs and The Monkey Man's Wares* (1969). With the poems of *Festivals and Funerals* (1971) she turned to larger social issues, including the place of the artist in revolutionary politics. In *Scarifications* (1973) she confronted the Vietnam War and wrote with a newfound romanticism about a journey to Africa.

The frequent cruelty of Cortez's images and their startling juxtapositions often yield surrealistic effects. These elements and the rhythmic cadences of her lines enhance the impact of her poetry readings, as her recordings show, beginning with *Celebrations and Solitudes* (1975). Among her later works are *Coagulations: New and Selected Poems* (1984), *Everywhere Drums* (1990), and *Poetic Magnetic* (1991).

Corvo *see* ROLFE.

Cory, Richard \'rich-ərd-'kȯr-ē\ Fictional character, the subject of the poem RICHARD CORY by Edwin Arlington Robinson.

Corybant \'kȯr-ə-,bant, 'kär-\ *plural* Corybants *or* Corybantes \,kȯr-ə-'ban-tēz, ,kär-\ [Greek *Korybant-, Korýbas*] Any of the wild, half-demonic attendants of the Great Mother of the Gods, the ancient Oriental and Greco-Roman deity, who were said to accompany her with wild dances and music. The Corybants were often identified or confused with the Cretan Curetes (attendants of Zeus) and were distinguished only by their Asiatic origin and by the more pronouncedly orgiastic nature of their rites. Accounts of the origin of the Corybants vary, and their names and number differ from one authority to another. They apparently had a mystic cult, and a prominent feature of their ritual was a wild dance, which was claimed to have powers of healing mental disorder.

Corydon \'kȯr-i-dən\ Stock character, a rustic or lovesick youth. The name appears notably in Virgil's *Eclogues*, a collection of 10 unconnected pastoral poems composed between 42 and 37 BC. In the second eclogue, the shepherd Corydon bewails his unrequited love for the boy Alexis. In the seventh, Corydon and Thyrsis, two Arcadian herdsmen, engage in a singing match. The name Corydon was also used by French writer André Gide as the title of a Socratic dialogue that he wrote in defense of homosexuality.

Ćosić \'chō-sēch\, Dobrica (b. Dec. 29, 1921, Velika Drenova, Serbia) Serbian novelist, essayist, and politician who wrote historical novels about the tribulations of the Serbs.

After attending agricultural school, Ćosić served in World War II with the Yugoslav communists known as Partisans and afterwards became a member of the Central Committee of the Communist Party. As a result of his strong Serbian nationalism, the government expelled him in 1968. He openly rejoined politics in the 1990s, serving as president of Yugoslavia in 1992–93, following the secession of Croatia and Slovenia.

Ćosić examined the resistance movement and many other aspects of Serbian involvement in World War II in such novels as *Daleko je sunce* (1951; *Far Away Is the Sun*) and *Deobe*, 3 vol. (1961; "Divisions"). *Koreni* (1954; "Roots") chronicles the establishment of Serbian independence from the Ottoman

Empire in the 19th century. Another of his early novels was *Bajka* (1966; "A Fable"). Tracing characters introduced in *Koreni*, the four-volume epic *Vreme smrti* (1972–79; *This Land, This Time*) is set during World War I. Ćosić brought the story of Serbia into the mid-20th century with the trilogy entitled *Vreme zla* (1990–91; "A Time of Evil"), which consists of *Grešnik* (1985; "Sinner"), *Otpadnik* (1986; "Renegade"), and *Vernik* (1990; "Believer").

Costa \də-'kòs-tə\, Isaäc da (b. Jan. 14, 1798, Amsterdam, Neth.—d. April 28, 1860, Amsterdam) Dutch writer and poet, best known as a leading figure in the conservative Calvinist political and literary group called the Réveil movement.

Although poetry written in Latin by da Costa had been published earlier, it was his first Dutch-language poetry, *De lof der dichtkunst* (1813; "In Praise of Poetry"), that came to the attention of the influential poet Willem Bilderdijk. Under Bilderdijk's influence, da Costa, who was of Portuguese-Jewish descent, converted to Calvinism. Thereafter he was dedicated to the suppression of liberal and revolutionary thought.

He soon published *Bezwaren tegen den geest der eeuw* (1823; "Objections to the Spirit of the Age"), which attacked the moral climate of the times as expressed in the principles of the French Revolution. He settled in Amsterdam and began lecturing in theology and other subjects. From 1834 to 1840 da Costa served as editor of the *Nederlandsche stemmen*. Religious and political argument make up the bulk of da Costa's writing. He spent the later years of his life writing the biography of Bilderdijk and editing 15 volumes of Bilderdijk's poetry.

Costa Alegre \'kòsh-tä-'leg-rä\, Caetano da (b. April 26, 1864, São Tomé, Portuguese Africa [now in São Tomé and Príncipe]—d. April 18, 1890, Alcobaça, Port.) African poet who wrote in Portuguese about being black.

Costa Alegre was born into a Creole family and moved in 1882 to Portugal, where he enrolled in the Medical School of Lisbon. Before he could graduate, however, he died of tuberculosis at the age of 26. It was not until 1916 that his friend, the journalist Cruz Magalhães, collected and published Costa Alegre's poetry as *Versos*.

Color dominates the poetry of Costa Alegre. Rejected by a Portuguese woman whom he loved, he laments his blackness, yet he exalts black women. In one of his more famous poems, he confesses "My color is black/It stands for mourning and grief." He misses his island home and his African heritage. Time and again he expresses his racial alienation and his personal suffering, but at times he does so with ironic self-mockery. Technically, Costa Alegre's poetry is rooted in the Romantic mode that dominated much 19th-century Portuguese verse. He uses the sonnet form in such poems as "Aurora" and "Longe," and his personal, confessional style is far removed from traditional African oral poetry.

Costain \'käs-,tān\, Thomas Bertram (b. May 8, 1885, Brantford, Ont., Can.—d. Oct. 8, 1965, New York, N.Y., U.S.) Canadian-born American historical novelist.

A journalist for many years on Canadian newspapers and a *Saturday Evening Post* editor from 1920 to 1934, Costain was 57 when he published his first romance, *For My Great Folly* (1942), dealing with the 17th-century rivalry between England and Spain. An immediate success, it was followed almost yearly by historical adventure tales, the best known of which are *The Black Rose* (1945), whose medieval English hero ranges as far as Kublai Khan's China, and *The Silver Chalice* (1952), about the early Christians in Rome.

Coster \də-'kòs-tər\, Charles de, *in full* Charles-Théodore-Henri de Coster (b. Aug. 20, 1827, Munich, Bavaria [Germany]—d. May 17, 1879, Brussels, Belg.) Belgian novelist, writing in French, who stimulated Belgian national consciousness and prepared the ground for an original native literature.

De Coster lived most of his life in poverty and obscurity and took 10 years to write his masterpiece, *La Légende et les aventures héroïques, joyeuses, et glorieuses d'Ulenspiegel et de Lamme Goedzak au pays de Flandres et ailleurs* (1867; *The Glorious Adventures of Tyl Ulenspiegl*). Freely adapting the traditional tales of the folk heroes Till Eulenspiegel (Ulenspiegel) and Lamme, he set his story in the 16th century, at the height of the Inquisition; the hero's father is burned at the stake as a heretic, and Ulenspiegel swears an oath to avenge him. De Coster's characters combine heroic qualities with a typically Belgian realism. His literary style is highly colored and archaistic, being derived from François Rabelais, Michel de Montaigne, and 16th-century historical chroniclers. With its theme of resistance against oppression, the book has been called "the Bible of Flanders" and "the breviary of freedom." The contrast between *La Légende* and the traditional Belgian novels of the period is sharp and striking.

costumbrismo \,kôs-tûm-'brēz-mō\ [Spanish, a derivative of *costumbre* custom, manner] In Spanish literature, a movement that emphasized the depiction of the everyday manners and customs of a particular social or provincial milieu. Although the origins of *costumbrismo* go back to the Golden Age of Spanish literature in the 16th and 17th centuries, it grew into a major force in the literature of the first half of the 19th century, first in verse and then in prose sketches called *cuadros de costumbres* ("scenes of customs") that stressed detailed descriptions of typical regional characters and social conduct, often with a satirical or philosophical intent.

Among its early practitioners were Mariano José de Larra, who wrote about Madrid, and Serafín Estébanez Calderón, who wrote about Andalusia. Significant costumbrista writers of the last half of the 19th century included Fernán Caballero, Pedro Antonio de Alarcón, and José María de Pereda.

Costumbrismo's lasting importance lies in its influence on the development of the regional novel in Spain and Latin America.

Cotton \'kät-ən\, Charles (b. April 28, 1630, Beresford Hall, Staffordshire, Eng.—d. Feb. 16, 1687, London) English poet and country squire, chiefly remembered for his share in Izaak Walton's *The Compleat Angler*.

Cotton made a number of translations from the French, including, in 1685, the often-reprinted *Essays of Michael Seigneur de Montaigne*, Pierre Corneille's *Horace* (1671), and several historical and philosophical works. Following the French fashion, he wrote *Scarronides* (1664, 1665), which is a coarse burlesque of the *Aeneid*, books 1 and 4, and the *Burlesque upon Burlesque . . . Being some of Lucians Dialogues newly put into English fustian* (1675).

Cotton's name is most often associated with a section he added to the fifth edition of *The Compleat Angler* (1676); at Walton's suggestion he added material on fly-fishing. Cotton's own works include *The Compleat Gamester* (1674) and *The Planter's Manual* (1675).

Cotys \'kō-tis\ or **Cotytto** \kō-'tit-ō\ Thracian goddess worshiped with orgiastic rites, especially at night. Her worship was apparently adopted publicly in Corinth (c. 425 BC) and perhaps privately in Athens about the same time; it then included a baptismal ceremony. In literature she was compared with the Great Mother of the Gods (Cybele).

couch \'kaûch\ To place or compose in a specified kind of language. It means much the same as "to word" or "to phrase."

Counterfeiters, The Novel by André GIDE, published in French in 1926 as *Les Faux-Monnayeurs*. Constructed with a greater range and scope than his previous short fiction, *The Counterfeiters* is Gide's most complex and intricately plotted work. It is a novel within a novel, concerning the relatives and teachers of a group of schoolboys who are subjected to corrupting influences both in and out of the classroom. In a progression of unconnected scenes and events, the novel approximates the texture of daily life.

Schoolboys of diverse ages and dispositions attend the Pension Azaïs. Some are suspected of having attempted to circulate counterfeit coins. Édouard, an author writing a novel entitled *The Counterfeiters*, observes that if a counterfeit coin is thought to be authentic, it is accepted as valuable; if it is found to be counterfeit, it is perceived as worthless. Therefore, he concludes, value is wholly a matter of perception and has nothing to do with reality. The counterfeiters are thus representative of those who disguise themselves with false personalities, either in unconscious self-deception or through conscious, hypocritical conformity to convention.

counterpoint \'kaûn-tər-,pôint\ Any artistic arrangement or device using significant contrast or interplay of distinguishable elements; specifically, motions in dance juxtaposed rhythmically and visually against the music or against other motions by parts of the body or groups of dancers. The term was adapted by literary critics to denote metrical variation in poetry.

counterpoint rhythm Rhythm that includes so much metrical inversion that the prevailing cadence ceases at times to prevail and so that a complex rhythm results from the conjunction of the basic cadence with its inversion. The term was applied by Gerard Manley Hopkins particularly to the work of John Milton, whose choruses in *Samson Agonistes* were for Hopkins an excellent example of counterpoint rhythm. *See also* INVERSION; SUBSTITUTION.

counterturn \'kaûn-tər-,tərn\ [translation of Greek *antistrophē*] An unexpected turn or development in the action of a play, especially at the climax.

Countess Cathleen, The \kath-'lēn\ Verse drama by William Butler YEATS, published in 1892 and performed in 1899.

Like many of Yeats's plays, *The Countess Cathleen* was inspired by Irish folklore. In a time of famine, demons sent by Satan come to Ireland to buy the souls of the starving people. The saintly Cathleen disposes of her vast estates and wealth in order to feed the peasants, yet the demons thwart her at every turn; at last, she sacrifices her own soul to save those of the poor.

Count of Monte Cristo, The \'män-tē-'kris-tō\ Romantic novel by Alexandre DUMAS *père*, published in French as *Le Comte de Monte-Cristo* in 1844–45.

The hero of the novel, Edmond Dantès, is a young sailor who is unjustly accused of aiding the exiled Napoleon. As punishment he is sentenced to life imprisonment in a French island fortress. After 14 years, Dantès makes a daring escape by taking the place of a dead companion; he is sewn into a burial shroud and thrown into the sea. Having learned from his dead prison mate of a vast treasure on the island of Monte-Cristo, Dantès eventually makes his way there to uncover and claim it. Adopting the persona of the Count of Monte Cristo, Dantès becomes a powerful, shadowy figure who eventually avenges himself on those who wronged him.

Country Doctor, The Novel by Honoré de BALZAC, published in 1833 as *Le Médecin de campagne*. The novel was part of Balzac's monumental fictional undertaking, *La Comédie humaine* (*The Human Comedy*).

Dr. Benassis is a compassionate and conscientious physician who ministers to the psychological and spiritual as well as the physical needs of the villagers among whom he has chosen to practice medicine. He has been instrumental in transforming the once-impoverished community into a progressive and healthy town, and he is now also its elected mayor. To Genestas, a soldier at a nearby military garrison, Dr. Benassis relates stories of the transformation he has wrought and eventually imparts the secrets of his buried past. Genestas asks the doctor to care for his sickly 16-year-old adopted son. Later, in gratitude for his son's recovery, Genestas swears that he will settle in the village and carry on the doctor's good and noble work.

Country Girls Trilogy, The Three novels by Edna O'BRIEN that follow the lives of friends Kate and Baba from their school days and strict Roman Catholic upbringing in the Irish countryside to their disillusioned adulthood and failed marriages in London. The trilogy consists of *The Country Girls* (1960), *The Lonely Girl* (1962), and *Girls in Their Married Bliss* (1964). In 1986, the three novels with an epilogue were published in one volume as *The Country Girls Trilogy and Epilogue*. The trilogy concerns women enmeshed in their sexuality and almost inevitably destroyed by their dependence on men. Because of graphic sexual content and frank treatment of women's attitudes toward sexuality, the novels, and six of the author's subsequent works, were banned in Ireland.

Country of the Pointed Firs, The Collection of sketches about life in a fictional coastal village in Maine by Sarah Orne JEWETT; published in 1896, it is an acclaimed example of local color.

Highly regarded for its sympathetic yet unsentimental portrayal of the town of Dunnet Landing and its residents, this episodic book is narrated by a nameless summer visitor who relates the life stories of various inhabitants, capturing the idiomatic language, customs, mannerisms, and humor peculiar to Down-Easters. Among the villagers are the narrator's landlady, Mrs. Almira Todd, a widow of great inner strength; a former seaman, Captain Littlepage, who scorns modern ways; Mrs. Todd's gracious mother, Mrs. Blackett; Mrs. Todd's brother, William; and a former fisherman, Elijah Tilley, an old widower.

The book evokes both the isolation and the sense of community of this small, dying town, whose inhabitants live chiefly to preserve memory and affirm and maintain values of the past.

Country-Wife, The Comedy of manners in five acts by Restoration dramatist William WYCHERLEY, performed and published in 1675. It satirizes the sexual duplicity of the aristocracy during the reign of Charles II. Popular for its lively characters and its double entendres, the bawdy comedy was occasionally vilified for immorality.

The main plot concerns the activities of lusty Margery, a country woman whose jealous husband, Mr. Pinchwife, sequesters her at home to ensure her fidelity. At a rare outing to the theater she is noticed by Mr. Horner, a notorious rake who starts a false rumor that he is a eunuch in order to gain the confidence of suspicious husbands. Margery soon learns the art of deception, and lies, disguises, and conspiracies thicken the plot.

coup de theatre \ˌkü-də-tä-'ätr *with* r *as a uvular trill*\ *plural* coups de theatre \same\ [French *coup de théâtre*, literally, stroke of theater] **1.** A sudden sensational turn in a play; also, a sudden dramatic effect or turn of events. **2.** A theatrical success.

Couperus \kü-'pā-rəs\, Louis Marie Anne (b. June 10, 1863, The Hague, Neth.—d. July 16, 1923, De Steeg) One of the greatest Dutch novelists of the 1880s literary revival.

Couperus grew up in the Dutch East Indies, resided in Italy, and later traveled through Africa and East Asia, describing his journeys in a series of impressionistic newspaper sketches.

Couperus' novels show a rare versatility of style and genre, ranging from the French-influenced realism of his first and best-known work, *Eline Vere* (1889), dealing with contemporary life in The Hague, to the fin de siècle spirit of luxurious decadence in *Extaze* (1892; *Ecstasy*) and *De berg van licht* (1906; "The Mountain of Light"). He developed an interest in the occult and in Oriental attitudes toward fate, which provided themes for several of his novels, in particular, *Van oude menschen, de dingen, die voorbijgaan* (1906; *Old People and the Things That Pass*).

couplet \'kəp-lət\ [Middle French, a derivative of *couple* pair] Two successive lines of verse marked usually by rhythmic correspondence, rhyme, or the inclusion of a self-contained utterance. In classical prosody, the synonym *distich* is often preferred.

A couplet in which the sense is relatively independent is a *closed couplet*; a couplet that cannot stand alone is an *open couplet*. In a closed couplet, each of the two lines may be end-stopped (that is, both sense and meter end in a pause at a line's end); alternatively, the meaning of the first line may continue to the second (this is called *enjambment*).

Couplets are most frequently used as units of composition in long poems; but, since they lend themselves to pithy, epigrammatic statements, they are often composed as independent poems or function as parts of other verse forms. William Shakespeare concluded his sonnets with a couplet. In French narrative and dramatic poetry, the rhyming alexandrine (12-syllable line) is the dominant couplet form, and German and Dutch verse of the 17th and 18th centuries reflects the influence of the alexandrine couplet. The term *couplet* is also commonly substituted for *stanza* in French versification. A "square couplet," for example, is a stanza of eight lines, with each line composed of eight syllables. The preeminent English couplet is the *heroic couplet*, two rhyming lines of iambic pentameter with a caesura (pause), usually in the middle of each line. Couplets were also frequently introduced into the blank verse of Elizabethan and Jacobean drama for heightened dramatic emphasis at the conclusion of a long speech or in running dialogue, as in the following example from Shakespeare's *Richard II*:

> Think what you will, we seize into our hands
> His plate, his goods, his money, and his lands.

Courage, Mother \'məth-ər-'kər-ij\ Fictional character, the protagonist of the play MOTHER COURAGE AND HER CHILDREN by Bertolt Brecht.

Courteline \kür-tə-'lēn\, Georges, *pseudonym of* Georges-Victor-Marcel Moineau \mwä-'nō\ (b. June 25, 1858, Tours, Fr.—d. June 25, 1929, Paris) French writer and dramatist whose humorous work constitutes a brilliant social anatomy of the late 19th-century middle and lower-middle classes.

Courteline served in the military and worked in the government while publishing sketches and short stories. From 1891 he offered farces to the leading Parisian theaters and after 1894 he was able to devote himself entirely to literature.

Courteline's volumes of novels and short stories include *Les Gaîtés de l'escadron* (1886; dramatized 1895; "The High Spirits of the Squadron"), *Le Train de 8 h 47* (1888; "The 8:47 Train"), and *Messieurs les ronds-de-cuir* (1893; *The Bureaucrats*). He had many plays produced, notably the farces *Boubouroche* (1893), *La Paix chez soi* (1903; "The Peace at His Place"), and *La Conversion d'Alceste* (1905).

Courteline's works present a colorful and acutely observed picture of his day. He portrayed the life of the barrack room, the office, and of daily middle-class life with shrewdness and accuracy, though his powerful sense of humor often concealed an underlying bitterness.

courtesy literature \\'kər-tə-sē, 'kȯr-\\ Literature comprising courtesy books and similar pieces. Though it was essentially a book of etiquette, the typical courtesy book was in fact much more than a guide to manners. It concerned the establishment of a philosophy of life, a code of principles and ethical behavior by which to live.

The earliest courtesy literature was written in Italian and German in the 13th century. By the end of 17th century, much courtesy literature had begun to evolve into the literature of proper behavior and was designed more to produce the veneer of civility than to educate the whole person.

courtly love *French* amour courtois \\á-mür-kür-'twä\\ A late medieval, highly conventionalized code that prescribed the behavior and emotions of ladies and their lovers. *Amour courtois* also provided the theme of an extensive courtly medieval literature that began with the troubadour poetry of Aquitaine and Provence in southern France toward the end of the 11th century.

The courtly lover existed to serve his lady. His love was invariably adulterous, upper-class marriage at that time being usually the result of economic interest or the seal of a power alliance. The lover ultimately saw himself as serving the all-powerful god of love and worshiping his lady-saint. Faithlessness was the one mortal sin.

The Roman poet Ovid undoubtedly provided inspiration in the developing concept of courtly love. His *Ars Amatoria* (*The Art of Love*) had pictured the lover as the slave of passion—sighing, trembling, growing pale and sleepless, even dying for love. The Ovidian lover's adoration was calculated to win sensual rewards; the courtly lover, however, while displaying the same outward signs of passion, was usually willing to love his lady from afar.

The idea of courtly love spread swiftly across Europe, and a decisive influence in this transmission was Eleanor of Aquitaine, wife first to Louis VII of France and then to Henry II of England, who inspired some of the best poetry of Bernard de Ventadour, among the last and finest of troubadour poets. Eleanor's daughter Marie of Champagne encouraged the composition of Chrétien de Troyes's courtly romance *Lancelot, ou Le Chevalier de la charrette*. Soon afterward the doctrine of courtly love was "codified" in a three-book treatise by André le Chapelain. In the 13th century a long allegorical poem, the *Roman de la rose*, expressed the concept of a lover suspended between happiness and despair.

Courtly love soon pervaded the literatures of Europe. The German minnesinger lyrics and court epics such as Gottfried von Strassburg's *Tristan und Isolde* are evidence of its power. Italian poetry embodied the courtly ideals as early as the 12th century, and during the 14th century their essence was distilled in Petrarch's sonnets to Laura. But perhaps more significantly, Dante had earlier managed to fuse courtly love and mystical vision: his Beatrice was, in life, his earthly inspiration, and in *La divina commedia* she became his spiritual guide to the mysteries of Paradise. Courtly love was also a vital influential force on most medieval literature in England, but there it came to be adopted as part of the courtship ritual leading to marriage.

courtly makar or **courtly maker** *see* MAKAR.

courtyard theater Any temporary or permanent theater structure established in an inn's courtyard in England or a residential courtyard (*corrale*) in Spain. The first reference to the courtyard theater is from the mid-16th century. The size and shape of the stage varied, and in most theaters of this type the audiences stood. Because there was no roof, performances were always held in the afternoon and were frequently canceled because of inclement weather.

Cousin Bette \\'bet\\ Novel by Honoré de BALZAC, published in 1846 as *La Cousine Bette*. The novel, part of Balzac's epic series *La Comèdie humaine* (*The Human Comedy*), is considered one of his two final masterpieces. Thematically a testament to female vindictiveness, *Cousin Bette* recounts the story of Lisbeth Fischer, an embittered, unmarried peasant woman who hides her envy and hatred behind a mask of kindness as she attempts to ruin the Hulot family. She succeeds up to a point, but eventually the family regains its wealth through judicious and fortuitous marital and business connections. Bette herself, bitterly disappointed, sickens and dies.

Cousin Pons \\'pȯⁿs\\ Novel by Honoré de BALZAC, published in 1847 as *Le Cousin Pons*. One of the novels that makes up Balzac's series *La Comèdie humaine* (*The Human Comedy*), *Cousin Pons* is often paired with *La Cousine Bette* under the title *Les Parents pauvres* ("The Poor Relations"). One of the last and greatest of Balzac's novels of French urban society, the book tells the story of Sylvain Pons, a poor musician who is swindled by his wealthy relatives when they learn that his collection of art and antiques is worth a fortune. In contrast to his counterpart Cousin Bette, who seeks revenge against those who have humiliated her, Cousin Pons suffers passively as his health deteriorates and he eventually dies. Balzac shows how a person without means can be crushed by a society that has no values except material ones.

Cousins \\'kəz-ənz\\, Norman (b. June 24, 1912, Union Hill, N.J., U.S.—d. Nov. 30, 1990, Los Angeles, Calif.) American essayist and editor, long associated with the *Saturday Review*.

Cousins began his editorial career in 1934. From 1942 to 1972 he was editor of the *Saturday Review*; he introduced essays that drew a connection between literature and current events. He felt strongly that a unique potential for greatness existed in America, as he wrote in *The Good Inheritance: The Democratic Chance* (1942). Cousins wrote on a variety of subjects, including a biography of Albert Schweitzer and a book of reflections on humanity in the atomic age, *Modern Man Is Obsolete* (1945). In 1979 *Anatomy of an Illness* appeared; a book based on Cousins' own experience with a life-threatening illness, it explored the healing ability of the human mind. He also wrote *Human Options* (1981), *The Physician in Literature* (1982), and *The Pathology of Power* (1987).

Coutinho \\kü-'tēⁿn-yü\\, Afrânio (b. March 5, 1911, Salvador, Braz.) Journalist, essayist, and literary critic who was a staunch proponent of the "close reading" of literary texts for critical purposes. He was influential in introducing New Criticism to Brazil in the 1950s.

Throughout most of his life, Coutinho also carried on an active career teaching literature at the high school and university levels. He edited the Portuguese-language edition of *Reader's Digest* and the literary journal *Cadernos brasileiros*. Among his critical publications, the most widely known are *A filosofia de Machado de Assis* (1940; "The Philosophy of Machado de Assis"), a study of the influence of Pascal on the 19th-century Brazilian literary giant; *Aspectos da literatura barroca* (1951; "Aspects of Baroque Literature"); *Por uma crítica estética* (1953; "Toward Aesthetic Criticism"); *Da crítica e da nova crítica* (1957; "On Criticism and the New Criticism"); and *Conceito de literatura brasileira* (1960; "The Concept of Brazilian Literature"). He also organized and edited the four-volume *A literatura no Brasil* (1955–59; "Literature in Brazil") and the *Enciclopédia de literatura brasileira* (1990; "Encyclopedia of Brazilian Literature").

Coverley, Sir Roger de \\'räj-ər-də-'kəv-ər-lē\\ Fictional character, devised by Joseph Addison, who portrayed him as the ostensible author of papers and letters that were published in Addison and Richard Steele's influential periodical THE SPECTATOR. As imagined by Addison, Sir Roger was a baronet of Worcestershire and was meant to represent a typical landed country gentleman. He was also a member of the fictitious Spectator Club, and the de Coverley writings included entertaining vignettes of early 18th-century English life that were often considered *The Spectator*'s best feature.

Coward \'kaú-ərd\, Noël, *in full* Sir Noël Peirce Coward (b. Dec. 16, 1899, Teddington, near London, Eng.—d. March 26, 1973, St. Mary, Jamaica) British playwright, actor, and composer best known for highly polished comedies of manners.

Coward caught the brittle disillusion of the generation that emerged from World War I. His other style, sentimental but theatrically effective, was used for romantic, backward-glancing musicals and for plays constructed around patriotism or some other presumably serious theme. He performed almost every function in the theater—including producing, directing, dancing, and singing—and acted, wrote, and directed for films as well.

Coward appeared professionally as an actor from the age of 12. Between acting engagements he wrote such light comedies as *I'll Leave It to You* (1920) and *The Young Idea* (1923), but his reputation as a playwright was not established until the serious play *The Vortex* (1924), which was highly successful in London. HAY FEVER, the first of his durable comedies, appeared in 1925 in New York City and the next year in London. Coward ended the decade with his most popular musical play, *Bitter Sweet* (1929).

Another of his classic comedies, PRIVATE LIVES (1930), is often revived. It shares with DESIGN FOR LIVING (1933) a worldly milieu and characters unable to live with or without one another. His patriotic pageant of British history, *Cavalcade* (1931), traces an English family from the time of the Boer War through the end of World War I. Other successes included *Tonight at 8:30* (1936), a group of one-act dramas performed by Coward and Gertrude Lawrence, with whom he often played. He rewrote one of the short plays, STILL LIFE, as the film *Brief Encounter* (1946). *Present Laughter* (1939) and BLITHE SPIRIT (1941; film, 1945; musical version, *High Spirits*, 1964) are usually listed among his better comedies.

Coward's *Collected Short Stories* appeared in 1962, followed by a further selection, *Bon Voyage*, in 1967. Coward also wrote *Pomp and Circumstance* (1960), a light novel, and *Not Yet the Dodo* (1967), a collection of verse. His autobiography through 1931 appeared as *Present Indicative* (1937) and was extended through his wartime years in *Future Indefinite* (1954); a third volume, *Past Conditional*, was incomplete at his death. Among his more notable songs are "Mad Dogs and Englishmen," "I'll See You Again," "Some Day I'll Find You," "Poor Little Rich Girl," "Mad About the Boy," and "Marvellous Party."

Coward was knighted in 1970. He spent his last years chiefly in Switzerland and the Caribbean.

Cowl \'kaúl\ or **Cowles** \'kaúlz, 'kōlz\, Jane, *original name* Grace Bailey \'bā-lē\ (b. Dec. 14, 1883, Boston, Mass., U.S.—d. June 22, 1950, Santa Monica, Calif.) Highly successful American playwright and actress.

Cowl made her acting debut in New York City in 1903 at the theater of her mentor, David Belasco, in *Sweet Kitty Bellairs*. Among her many successful roles were Jeannine in *Lilac Time* (1917) and Moonyean Claire and Kathleen Dungannon in 1,170 performances of *Smilin' Through* (1919–22); both plays were written by Alan Langdon Martin (pseudonym for Cowl and her most frequent collaborator, Jane Murfin) and produced by her husband, Adolph Klauber, drama critic for the *New York Times*. Other successful plays she wrote include

Daybreak (1917) and *Information Please* (1918), with Murfin; *The Jealous Moon* (1928), with Theodore Charles; and *Hervey House* (1935), with Reginald Lawrence.

Cowley \'kaú-lē, 'kū-\, Abraham (b. 1618, London, Eng.—d. July 28, 1667, Chertsey) English poet and essayist who wrote poetry of a fanciful, decorous nature. He also adapted the Pindaric ode to English verse.

Cowley was educated at Westminster School and the University of Cambridge. He went abroad with the queen's court in 1645 and performed various Royalist missions until his return to England in 1656. In 1660 he retired to Chertsey and wrote sober, reflective essays reminiscent of Montaigne.

Cowley tended to use grossly elaborate, self-consciously poetic language that decorated, rather than expressed, his feelings. In *The Mistress* (1647, 1656) he exaggerated John Donne's "metaphysical wit"—jarring the reader's sensibilities by unexpectedly comparing quite different things—into what later tastes felt was fanciful poetic nonsense. His *Pindarique Odes* (1656) try to reproduce the Greek poet's enthusiastic manner through lines of uneven length and even more extravagant poetic conceits.

Cowley also wrote an unfinished epic, *Davideis* (1656). His stage comedy *The Guardian* (1641, revised 1661) introduced the fop Puny, who became a staple of Restoration comedy.

Cowley is often considered a transitional figure from the Metaphysical poets to the Augustan poets of the 18th century. Perhaps his most effective poem is the elegy on the death of Richard Crashaw.

Cowley \'kaú-lē\, Malcolm (b. Aug. 24, 1898, Belsano, Pa., U.S.—d. March 27, 1989, New Milford, Conn.) American literary critic and social historian who chronicled the writers of the Lost Generation of the 1920s and their successors. As literary editor of *The New Republic* from 1929 to 1944, with a generally leftist position on cultural questions, he played a significant part in many of the literary and political battles of the Depression years.

Cowley was educated at Harvard University and in France at the University of Montpellier. He helped to publish the little magazines *Secession* and *Broom* in Paris. His *Exile's Return: A Narrative of Ideas* (1934; rev. ed., *Exile's Return: A Literary Odyssey of the 1920's*, 1951) is an important social and literary history of the expatriate American writers of the period. Cowley revived the literary reputation of William Faulkner with his editing of the anthology *The Portable Faulkner* (1946).

Among Cowley's other works are *The Literary Situation* (1954), a study of the role of the American writer in society, and the collections of criticism and comment *Think Back on Us* (1967) and *A Many-Windowed House* (1970). The correspondence he exchanged with Faulkner appeared in 1966 in *The Faulkner-Cowley File: Letters and Memories, 1944–1962*. Among the many books he edited are *After the Genteel Tradition: American Writers Since 1910* (1937, reprinted 1964) and *Books That Changed Our Minds* (1939). *And I Worked at the Writer's Trade* (1976) combines literary history and autobiography.

Cowleyan ode \'kaú-lē-ən\ *see* IRREGULAR ODE.

Cowper \'kúp-ər, *commonly* 'kúp-, 'kaúp-\, William (b. Nov. 26, 1731, Great Berkhamstead, Hertfordshire, Eng.—d. April 25, 1800, East Dereham, Norfolk) One of the most widely read English poets of his day, whose most characteristic work, as in *The Task* or the melodious short lyric "The Poplar Trees," brought a new directness to 18th-century nature poetry.

Cowper, the son of an Anglican clergyman, studied law at Westminster School in London. He was called to the bar in 1754, and during this period he began to show signs of the mental instability that plagued him throughout his life. His father died in 1756, leaving little wealth, and Cowper's family used its influence to obtain two administrative posts for him in the House of Lords, which entailed a formal examination. This prospect so disturbed him that he attempted suicide and was confined for 18 months in an asylum, troubled by religious doubts and fears.

Religion, however, also provided the comfort of Cowper's convalescence, which he spent at Huntingdon, lodging with the Reverend Morley Unwin, his wife Mary, and their small family. In 1767 Morley Unwin was killed in a riding accident, and his family, with Cowper, took up residence at Olney, in Buckinghamshire. The curate there, John Newton, collaborated with Cowper on a book of religious verse, eventually published as *Olney Hymns* (1779).

In 1773 thoughts of marriage with Mary Unwin were ended by Cowper's relapse into near madness. He recovered the following year and produced six moral satires entitled "The Progress of Error" and the poems "Conversation" and "Retirement" during this time. Cowper's ballad "The Journey of John Gilpin" was sung throughout London after it was printed in 1783. His long, discursive poem *The Task*, written "to recommend rural ease and leisure," was an immediate success on its publication in 1785. Cowper began translating Homer, but his health suffered under the strain and he had occasional periods of mental illness. In 1795 he moved with Mary Unwin to live in Norfolk. When she died in December 1796, Cowper sank into despair from which he never emerged.

Robert Southey edited his writings in 15 volumes between 1835 and 1837. Cowper is considered one of the best letter writers in English, and some of his hymns, such as "God Moves in a Mysterious Way" and "Oh! For a Closer Walk with God," have become part of the folk heritage of Protestant England. *The Letters and Prose Writings* was published in two volumes in 1979–80.

Coyote \'kī-,ōt, kī-'ō-tē\   In the mythology and folklore of North American Indians of the Central Plains, California, and the Southwest, the chief animal of the prehuman animal age. His exploits as creator, culture hero, lover, magician, and trickster are celebrated in a vast cycle of oral tales. Among the tribes of the American West, he was predominantly a demiurge (independent creative force) or maker of fateful decisions. Among the Plains tribes, however, he was more often regarded as a culture hero, who secured such human necessities as fire and daylight or who originated human arts.

Although almost all tribes believed he possessed the power to transform beings and objects, they also attributed to Coyote certain negative character traits. In humorous tales he was often shown as a clever trickster who, nevertheless, was frequently bested by those who exploited his greed or turned his cunning against him.

Among tribes of eastern North America, Coyote was paralleled by the Great Hare, or Master Rabbit, whose adventures became a supplementary source for the Brer Rabbit folk tales of southern black Americans.

Cozzens \'kəz-ənz\, James Gould (b. Aug. 19, 1903, Chicago, Ill., U.S.—d. Aug. 9, 1978, Stuart, Fla.)   American novelist whose writings dealt with life in middle-class America.

Cozzens grew up on Staten Island, N.Y., graduated from the Kent (Conn.) School, and attended Harvard University. In a year of teaching in Cuba he accumulated background material for the short novels *Cockpit* (1928) and *The Son of Perdition* (1929). He gained critical attention in 1931 with his novella *S.S. San Pedro*. Thereafter he published increasingly complex novels, most of which focus on professional people.

In *The Last Adam* (1933) the protagonist is a doctor; *Men and Brethren* (1936) depicts the life of an Episcopalian minister; *The Just and the Unjust* (1942) and *By Love Possessed* (1957) are about lawyers; and *Guard of Honor* (1948) concerns air force officers and men. *Ask Me Tomorrow* (1940) is an autobiographical novel, and *Children and Others* (1964) is a short-story collection.

Cozzens' works reflect a philosophy of political and social conservatism. He received the Pulitzer Prize for fiction in 1949 for *Guard of Honor* and the Howells Medal of the American Academy of Arts and Letters in 1960 for *By Love Possessed*, his greatest popular success. His later works became increasingly convoluted in plot and style, especially his last novel, *Morning, Noon, and Night* (1968).

Crabbe \'krab\, George (b. Dec. 24, 1754, Aldeburgh, Suffolk, Eng.—d. Feb. 3, 1832, Trowbridge, Wiltshire)   English writer of verse tales memorable for their realistic details of everyday life. He is called the last of the Augustan poets because he followed John Dryden, Alexander Pope, and Samuel Johnson in using the heroic couplet.

Crabbe grew up in the impoverished seacoast village of Aldeburgh. In 1780 he left for London, where he demonstrated his full powers as a poet with *The Village* (1783). Written in part as a protest against Oliver Goldsmith's *Deserted Village* (1770), which Crabbe thought too sentimental and idyllic, the poem was his attempt to show the misery and degradation of rural poverty. This successful poem was followed by *The Newspaper* (1785), and after that Crabbe published nothing for the next 22 years. In 1807 he began to publish again, reprinting his poems, together with a new work, "The Parish Register," in which he used the register of births, deaths, and marriages to compassionately depict the life of a rural community. Other verse tales followed: *The Borough* (1810), *Tales in Verse* (1812), and *Tales of the Hall* (1819).

Crack-Up, The \'krak-,əp\   Essay by F. Scott FITZGERALD, published serially in *Esquire* magazine in 1936 and posthumously, in book form, in *The Crack-Up: With Other Uncollected Pieces, Note-Books, and Unpublished Letters* (1945). This confessional essay documents the spiritual and physical deterioration of Fitzgerald in the mid-1930s.

Craddock \'krad-ək\, Charles Egbert, *pseudonym of* Mary Noailles Murfree \'mər-,frē\ (b. Jan. 24, 1850, near Murfreesboro, Tenn., U.S.—d. July 31, 1922, Murfreesboro)   American writer who depicted Tennessee mountain life in her short stories. She is characterized as a local colorist (a writer who describes the features and peculiarities of a particular region and its inhabitants).

For her stories published in *Appleton's Journal* and *The Atlantic Monthly*, she utilized the pen name Charles Egbert Craddock, and her identity was not disclosed until after the publication of her first volume of short stories, *In the Tennessee Mountains* (1884). Most of her stories present the narrow, stern life of the mountaineers who were left behind in the advance of modern civilization.

cradle book   A book printed before 1501. *See* INCUNABULUM.

crambo \'kram-bō\ *plural* cramboes.   A game in which one player gives a word or line of verse to be matched in rhyme by other players. The word *crambo*, altered from the earlier *crambe*, apparently alludes to the proverbial Latin phrase *crambe repetita* ("dull repetition," literally, "repeated [*i.e.*, reserved] cabbage"). *Compare* BOUTS-RIMÉS.

Crane \'krān\, Hart, *in full* Harold Hart Crane (b. July 21, 1899, Garrettsville, Ohio, U.S.—d. April 27, 1932, at sea,

Caribbean Sea)   American poet who celebrated the richness of life in lyrics of visionary intensity. His most noted work, *The Bridge* (1930), was an attempt to create an epic myth of the American experience. As a coherent epic it has been deemed a failure, but many of its individual lyrics are judged to be among the best American poems of the 20th century.

Crane worked in a variety of jobs in New York City and Cleveland and, as his poetry began to be published in little magazines, eventually settled in New York in 1923. His first published book was *White Buildings* (1926). It contains his long poem "For the Marriage of Faustus and Helen," which he wrote as an answer to what he considered to be the cultural pessimism of *The Waste Land* by T.S. Eliot. In 1930 *The Bridge* was published. Inspired in part by the Brooklyn Bridge and standing for the human creative power uniting the present and the past, the poem has 15 parts and is unified by a structure modeled after that of a symphony.

Crane was granted a Guggenheim Fellowship and went to Mexico City, where he wrote "The Broken Tower" (1932). Despondent over the tensions of his life, on his way back to the United States he jumped from the ship into the Caribbean and was drowned.

Crane's *Collected Poems* appeared in 1933, and in 1966 *The Complete Poems and Selected Letters and Prose*, which incorporated some of his previously uncollected writings, was published.

Crane \ˈkrān\, R.S., *in full* Ronald Salmon Crane (b. Jan. 5, 1886, Tecumseh, Mich., U.S.—d. July 12, 1967, Chicago, Ill.) American literary critic who was a leading figure of the Neo-Aristotelian Chicago school. His landmark book, *The Languages of Criticism and the Structure of Poetry* (1953), formed the theoretical basis of the group. Although Crane was an outspoken opponent of New Criticism, he argued persuasively for a pluralism that values separate, even contradictory, critical schools.

Crane was educated at the University of Michigan and the University of Pennsylvania. He taught at Northwestern University, Evanston, Ill., and at the University of Chicago. In addition to publishing many journal articles, he edited the influential book *Critics and Criticism: Ancient and Modern* (1952). Much of his writing was collected in *The Idea of the Humanities and Other Essays Critical and Historical* (1967) and *Critical and Historical Principles of Literary History* (1971). *See also* CHICAGO CRITICS.

Crane \ˈkrān\, Stephen (b. Nov. 1, 1871, Newark, N.J., U.S.—d. June 5, 1900, Badenweiler, Baden, Ger.)   American author whose first novel was a milestone in the development of literary realism. He later became a proficient short-story writer.

Crane had finished only one full year of college before he moved to New York City, where he wrote his first book, *Maggie: A Girl of the Streets* (1893), a sympathetic, uncompromisingly realistic study of a slum girl's descent into prostitution and eventual suicide. At that time its subject was so shocking that Crane published it under a pseudonym and at his own expense. He struggled as a poor and unknown freelance journalist until he was befriended by Hamlin Garland and the influential critic William Dean Howells. Suddenly, in 1895, the publication of THE RED BADGE OF COURAGE, a subtle, impressionistic study of a young soldier, and of his first book of poems, *The Black Riders*, brought him international fame.

Crane traveled to Greece and then to Cuba as a war correspondent. His first attempt, in 1897, to report on the insurrection in Cuba ended in near disaster; the ship on which he was traveling sank, and Crane—reported drowned—finally rowed into shore in a dinghy with the captain, cook, and oiler.

The result was one of the world's great short stories, THE OPEN BOAT.

Crane then went to Greece to report the Greco-Turkish War for the New York *Journal*, and later to Cuba to report on the Spanish-American War, first for the New York *World* and then for the *Journal*. Afterwards he settled in Sussex, England. He died of tuberculosis that was compounded by the recurrent malarial fever he had caught in Cuba.

Crane's mastery of the short story was remarkable. He exploited youthful small-town experiences in *The Monster and Other Stories* (1899) and *Whilomville Stories* (1900); the Bowery in *George's Mother* (1896); an early trip to the Southwest and in Mexico in THE BLUE HOTEL and THE BRIDE COMES TO YELLOW SKY; the Civil War again in *The Little Regiment* (1896); and experiences as a war correspondent in *The Open Boat* (1898) and *Wounds in the Rain* (1900). His last poems are contained in the volume *War Is Kind* (1899).

Crane, Ichabod \ˈik-ə-ˌbăd-ˈkrän\   Fictional character, a lanky and unattractive schoolmaster who is the protagonist of Washington Irving's short story THE LEGEND OF SLEEPY HOLLOW. Ichabod Crane is quite poor, and his main interest is self-advancement. He attempts to further his cause by impressing the daughters of rich families with his learning. He is also very suggestible, however, and his belief in ghosts and other supernatural phenomena ultimately get the better of him.

Cranford \ˈkran-fərd\   Novel by Elizabeth Cleghorn GASKELL, published serially in Charles Dickens' magazine *Household Words* from 1851 to 1853 and in book form in 1853.

Basing her tales on the village in which she was reared, Gaskell produced a gently comic picture of life and manners in an English country village during the 1830s. The novel's narrator (a young woman who periodically visits Cranford) describes the small adventures in the lives of two middle-aged sisters in reduced circumstances who do their best to maintain their standards of propriety, decency, and kindness. Using an intimate, gossipy voice that never turns sentimental, Gaskell conveys the old-fashioned habits, subtle class distinctions, and genteel poverty of the townspeople. *Cranford* quickly became one of the author's best-loved works.

Crashaw \ˈkrash-ˌȯ\, Richard (b. *c.* 1613, London, Eng.—d. Aug. 21, 1649, Loreto [Italy])   English poet known for religious verse of vibrant stylistic ornamentation and brilliant wit.

The son of a Puritan minister, Crashaw was educated at Cambridge. In 1634 he published *Epigrammatum Sacrorum Liber* ("A Book of Sacred Epigrams"), a collection of Latin verse on scriptural subjects. He went to France in 1644 and became a Roman Catholic. He later went to Rome, where he eventually was appointed canon of the cathedral of Santa Casa (Holy House) at Loreto.

Cranshaw prepared the first edition of his *Steps to the Temple: Sacred Poems, with Other Delights of the Muses* for publication in 1646. His English religious poems, titled *Carmen Deo Nostro* ("Hymn to Our Lord"), were republished in Paris in 1652, including some of his finest lines, those appended to "The Flaming Heart," a poem on St. Teresa of Avila.

crasis \ˈkras-is\ *plural* crases \-ēz\ [Greek *krâsis,* literally, mixing, blending]   In classical Greek, the contraction of two vowels or diphthongs at the end of one word and the beginning of an immediately following word, as *kán* for *kaì án* or *houmós* for *ho emós.* Crasis is especially common in some lyric poetry and in Old Comedy. The term sometimes refers to word-internal contraction in Latin, as *nīl* from *nihil.*

Cratchit family \ˈkrach-it\   Fictional characters, an impoverished, hardworking, and warmhearted family in A CHRIST-

MAS CAROL by Charles Dickens. The family comprises Bob Cratchit, his wife, and their six children: Martha, Belinda, Peter, two smaller Cratchits (an unnamed girl and boy), and the crippled but ever-cheerful Tiny Tim.

Crates \'krā-tēz\ (fl. *c.* 449–*c.* 424 BC, Athens)   Actor and author of comedies who is regarded as the founder of Greek comedy proper. According to Aristotle's *Poetics*, Crates abandoned the traditional comedy of invective and introduced stories of a more general and nonpersonal nature with well-developed plots. He is said to have been the first to represent the drunkard on stage. Before turning to writing, he acted in the plays of Cratinus, a celebrated Athenian author of the Old Comedy.

Crates \'krā-tēz\ of Mallus \'mal-əs\, *also called* Crates of Pergamum \'pər-gə-məm\ (fl. early 2nd century BC)   Stoic philosopher from Mallus in Cilicia, primarily important as a grammarian. His chief work was a commentary on Homer. Leader of the literary school and head of the library of Pergamum, he was the principal representative of the allegorical theory of exegesis, maintaining that Homer intended to express scientific or philosophical truths in the form of poetry. About 170 BC he went to Rome as ambassador of Eumenes II, king of Pergamum; the lectures that he delivered there gave the first impulse to the study of grammar and criticism among the Romans.

Cratinus \krə-'tī-nəs\ (d. *c.* 420 BC)   Greek poet, regarded in antiquity as one of the three greatest writers, with Eupolis and Aristophanes, of the vigorous and satirical Athenian Old Comedy.

Only about 460 fragments survive of Cratinus' 27 known plays, the earliest of which was written not long after 450 BC. His comedies, like those of Aristophanes, seem to have been a mixture of parodied mythology and topical allusion. The Athenian war leader Pericles was a frequent target. In the *Putine* (*The Bottle*), which defeated Aristophanes' *Clouds* for the first prize at the Athenian dramatic contest in 423, Cratinus good-humoredly exploited his own drunkenness (caricatured the previous year in Aristophanes' *Knights*).

Craveirinha \krä-vā-'rēⁿn-yə\, José, *pseudonym of* José G. Vetrinha \ve-'trēⁿn-yə\ (b. May 28, 1922, Lourenço Marques, Portuguese East Africa [now Maputo, Mozambique])   Mozambican journalist, story writer, and poet.

Craveirinha was an ardent supporter of the anti-Portuguese group Frelimo during the colonial wars and was imprisoned in 1966. He was one of the pioneers of Negritude poetry in Mozambique, a poetry that concentrated on an examination of past African traditions and the emphatic reaffirmation of African values.

His poem "Grito Negro" ("Black City") is an outcry against colonialism that blends a sense of African rhythms with the nasal sounds of the Portuguese language. Craveirinha's literary works appeared in various anthologies and in such collections as *Chigubo* (1964), *Cantico a un dio di Catrane* (1966; "Canticle to a Catrane God"), *Karingana ua karingana* (1974; "Once Upon a Time"), *Cela I* (1980; "Cell I"), and *Maria* (1988). He also wrote for various journals.

Crawford \'krô-fərd\, F. Marion, *in full* Francis Marion Crawford (b. Aug. 2, 1854, Bagni di Lucca, Grand Duchy of Tuscany [Italy]—d. April 9, 1909, Sorrento, Italy)   Italian-American novelist noted for the vividness of his characterizations and settings.

In his youth Crawford lived in both Italy and America. He later chose to live in Italy, but remained a U.S. citizen. A stay in India provided the inspiration for *Mr. Isaacs* (1882), a tale of a diamond merchant whose sale of a unique stone brings protest

from Britain. This novel marked the beginning of Crawford's prosperous career. His best works are set in the Italy he loved. They include *Saracinesca* (1887), *Sant' Ilario* (1889), and *Don Orsino* (1892), part of a series about the effect of social change on an Italian family during the late 1800s.

Crawford \'krô-fərd\, Isabella Valancy (b. Dec. 25, 1850, Dublin, Ire.—d. Feb. 12, 1887, Toronto, Ont., Can.)   Major 19th-century Canadian poet. She is especially noted for her vivid descriptions of Canadian landscape.

The daughter of a physician who immigrated to Canada in 1858, Crawford spent most of her girlhood in the Kawartha Lakes district of Ontario. From 1875 until her death, she and her mother lived in Toronto, meagerly sustained by the sale of her stories and poems to newspapers and magazines.

The only book published during her lifetime (at her own expense) was *Old Spookses' Pass, Malcolm's Katie, and Other Poems* (1884). A later collection of her poems was published in 1905 and reprinted in 1972. Crawford's work was rediscovered in the 1970s. Among the works that have since been published are *Selected Stories of Isabella Valancy Crawford* (1975), *Fairy Tales of Isabella Valancy Crawford* (1977), *Hugh and Ion* (1977; an unfinished narrative poem), *The Halton Boys* (1979), and *Malcolm's Katie: A Love Story* (1987).

Crawford, Janie \'jā-nē-'krô-fərd\   Fictional character, the spirited protagonist of THEIR EYES WERE WATCHING GOD by Zora Neale Hurston. Janie's story is her search for identity through the few avenues open to a black woman in the 1920s and '30s. She finally reaches fulfillment with her third husband, who meets a tragic end.

Creacionismo \,krä-ä-syō-'nēz-mō, -thyō-\ [Spanish, a derivative of *creación* creation]   A short-lived experimental literary movement founded about 1916 in Paris by the Chilean poet Vicente HUIDOBRO.

For *Creacionistas*, the function of the poet was to create an autonomous, highly personal, imaginary world rather than to describe the world of nature. Creationist poets boldly juxtaposed images and metaphors and often used an original vocabulary, frequently combining words idiosyncratically or irrationally. The movement strongly influenced the generation of avant-garde poets in France, Spain, and Latin America—notably the Spanish poets Gerardo Diego and Juan Larrea—during the period immediately after World War I.

Cream of the Jest, The   Novel by James Branch CABELL, published in 1917 and revised in 1920. It is the 16th book of the 18-volume series called *The Works of James Branch Cabell* (1927–30), also known as *The Biography of the Life of Manuel*. The comic novel blends contemporary realism and historical romance.

create \krē-'āt, 'krē-,āt\   To produce a work of art or of dramatic interpretation along new or unconventional lines.

creation myth \krē-'ā-shən\ or **cosmogonic myth** \,käz-mə-'gän-ik\   A symbolic narrative of the beginning of the world as understood in a particular tradition and community. Many rituals may be thought of as dramatizations of the creation myth. In addition, a culture's modes of artistic expression—the gestures and dance of ritual and the imagery of the visual and verbal arts—find their models and meanings in the myths of creation.

The major cosmogonic myths include those that feature a supreme creator deity, those that describe the emergence of the world through various stages of development, and those that view the world as the offspring of primordial parents.

Creation Society *Chinese* Chuangzao she.   Chinese literary society founded in 1921 by Zhang Ziping, Guo Moruo, and a number of other Chinese writers studying in Japan. At first, the group advocated the idea of "art for art's sake"; the works produced by its members, notably Guo, Tian Han, and Yu Dafu, were influenced by Western Romanticism and were highly individualistic and subjective. In 1924, however, Guo, the society's leading figure, converted to Marxism. The Creation Society subsequently evolved into China's first Marxist literary society and began to advocate proletarian literature. *See also* LITERARY RESEARCH ASSOCIATION.

Crébillon \krä-bē-'yŏⁿ\, Claude-Prosper Jolyot, Sieur (Lord) de, *known as* Crébillon *fils* ("son") (b. Feb. 14, 1707, Paris, Fr.—d. April 12, 1777, Paris) French novelist whose works provide a lighthearted, licentious, and satirical view of 18th-century high society in France.

The son of an outstanding French dramatist, Prosper Jolyot de Crébillon, Crébillon *fils* spent all his life in Paris except for two periods of exile in the provinces as a result of satirical allusions in his novels. Of these novels, the best known are *L'Écumoire* (1735; *The Skimmer*), *Les Égarements du coeur et de l'esprit* (1736; *The Wayward Head and Heart*), and *Le Sopha, conte moral* (1742; *The Sofa; A Moral Tale*). Crébillon was also a founder, in 1729, of the Société du Caveau, named after a café in which he and his friends dined, where Crébillon earned a reputation as a wit and storyteller.

Crébillon \krä-bē-'yŏⁿ\, Prosper Jolyot, Sieur (Lord) de, *known as* Crébillon *père* ("father") (b. Jan. 13, 1674, Dijon, Fr.—d. June 17, 1762, Paris) French dramatist of some skill and originality who was considered in his day the rival of Voltaire.

Crébillon's masterpiece, the tragedy *Rhadamiste et Zénobie* (produced 1711), was followed by a run of failures, and in 1721 he retired from literary life. He returned, however, in 1726 with *Pyrrhus*, which was successful, and he wrote for another 20 years. He was elected to the Académie Française in 1731.

Crébillon's tragedies were modeled after those of the Roman tragic writer Seneca and, like them, bordered on melodrama. His specialty was horror: according to his preface to *Atrée et Thyeste* (1707), he aimed to move the audience to pity through terror.

Creeley \'krē-lē\, Robert (White) (b. May 21, 1926, Arlington, Mass., U.S.) American poet and founder of the BLACK MOUNTAIN POETS, a loose group associated during the 1950s with Black Mountain College in North Carolina.

Creeley attended Harvard University, spent a year in India and Burma, then lived on a farm in New Hampshire. He first began to publish his poems in small magazines. He lived in Europe in the early 1950s, and in Majorca, Spain, he started the Divers Press. In 1955, after graduating from Black Mountain College, he joined its faculty and was editor of the *Black Mountain Review* for its first three years. The *Review* published poems by Creeley, as well as works by other faculty members and poets.

In *For Love* (1962), Creeley emerged as a master technician. He followed this with other books of poetry, most notably *Pieces* (1968). Creeley taught poetry in several universities, including the State University of New York at Buffalo. His *Selected Poems* appeared in 1976. Later collections include *Later* (1979), *The Collected Poems of Robert Creeley 1945–1975* (1982), *Memory Gardens* (1986), and *Windows* (1990).

Cremation of Sam McGee, The \'sam-mə-'gē\ Ballad by Robert SERVICE, published in Canada in 1907 in *Songs of a Sourdough* (U.S. title, *The Spell of the Yukon, and Other Verses*). A popular success upon publication, this exaggerated folktale about a pair of a Yukon gold miners was reprinted 15 times in its first year.

In the ballad, set in the icy wilds of northwestern Canada, the title character dies after asking the narrator to cremate his body rather than bury it. After placing the body in a blazing furnace, the narrator takes a last look into the fire and hears McGee urge him to close the door before the heat escapes. The ballad has remained a favorite recitation piece because of its internal rhymes, driving rhythms, and macabre irony.

Crémazie \krā-mȧ-'zē\, Octave, *byname of* Claude-Joseph-Olivier Crémazie (b. April 16, 1827, Quebec [Canada]—d. Jan. 16, 1879, Le Havre, Fr.) Poet considered the father of French-Canadian poetry. His poems are characterized by a patriotic love of Canada and its landscape.

An 1860 Crémazie helped found the first literary school of Quebec and in 1861 began issuing the magazine *Les Soirées canadiennes* to preserve the folklore of French Canada. He published poems in the *Journal de Québec* from 1854.

Crémazie left Canada in 1862 for France, where he spent the rest of his life in great poverty under the assumed name of Jules Fontaine. In this period he wrote the pessimistic poem "Promenade des trois morts" ("Parade of Three Corpses"), which remained unfinished, and a journal, *Siège de Paris*, that gave an eyewitness account of the siege of 1870. His most famous patriotic poems were "Le Vieux Soldat canadien" (1855; "The Old Canadian Soldier"), celebrating a French naval ship to visit Quebec, and "Le Drapeau de Carillon" (1858; "The Flag of Carillon"), which almost became Canada's national anthem. *Oeuvres complètes* ("Complete Works") was published in 1882.

Crepuscolarismo \ˌkrā-pü-ˌskō-lä-'rēz-mō\ [Italian, a derivative of *crepuscolare* of the twilight, after *poeti crepuscolari* or *i crepuscolari,* the members of the group, literally, twilight poets] A movement of early 20th-century Italian poets whose work was characterized by disillusionment, nostalgia, a taste for simple things, and a direct, unadorned style. Like Futurism, a contemporaneous movement, Crepuscolarismo reflected the influence of European Decadence and was a reaction to the florid ornamental language of Gabriele D'Annunzio. It differed from the militant Futurist movement in its passivity, but both movements expressed the same spirit of desolation, and many *crepuscolari* later became *futuristi.*

The movement was named in a 1910 article, "Poesie crepuscolare," by the critic Giuseppe Borgese, who saw in their poetry the twilight of D'Annunzio's day. The main poets associated with it were Guido Gozzano, Fausto Maria Martini, Sergio Corazzini, Marino Moretti, and Aldo Palazzeschi; the last two poets later became notable writers of fiction. Though it died out in the second decade of the 20th century, Crepuscolarismo was an important influence in returning Italian poetry to simple language and simple subjects.

Crescent Moon Society *Chinese* Xinyue she \'shin-'yǖ-'shə\ Chinese literary society that was influential during the 1920s. An offshoot of the earlier Creation Society, this group of Chinese poets was led by the British-educated Xu Zhimo and the American-educated Wen Yiduo, both of whom created new forms based on Western models.

Cressida \'kres-i-də\, *also called* Criseyde *or* Criseide. In Greek mythology, the daughter of the seer Calchas, a Trojan who defected to the Greek side, and lover of Troilus. *See* TROILUS AND CRESSIDA.

cretic \'krē-tik\ [Greek *Krētikós,* from *Krētikós* (adjective) Cretan] In prosody, a three-syllable foot consisting in quantitative verse of a short syllable between two long syllables ($-\cup-$) or in accentual verse of an unstressed syllable between two stressed syllables ($'\cup'$). An example is the word *twenty-two.* The inverse of this meter is the amphibrach.

Creutz \'kröits\, Gustav Philip, Count (Greve) (b. May 1, 1731, Anjala, Swedish Finland—d. Oct. 30, 1785, Stockholm, Swed.)   Swedish poet whose light and graceful verse expressed the prevailing Rococo spirit and Epicurean philosophy of his time.

Creutz's literary output was small, and he is remembered mainly for two poems—his early "Sommar-qväde" (1756; "Summer Song") and the rather erotic "Daphne" (1762)—and for the pastoral narrative *Atis och Camilla* (1762). After the well-known poet Hedvig Charlotta Nordenflycht, with whom he had been closely associated, died in 1763, Creutz wrote nothing more of literary importance.

Crèvecoeur \krev-'kœr\, Michel-Guillaume-Saint-Jean de, *also called* Hector Saint John de Crèvecoeur *or (especially in America)* J. Hector St. John (b. Jan. 31, 1735, Caen, Fr.—d. Nov. 12, 1813, Sarcelles)   French-American author and naturalist whose work provided a broad picture of life in the New World.

After studying in Jesuit schools and spending four years as an officer and mapmaker in Canada, Crèvecoeur chose in 1759 to remain in the New World. He wandered the Great Lakes region, took out citizenship papers in New York in 1765, became a farmer in Orange county, and was married in 1769. Torn between the two factions in the American Revolution, Crèvecoeur languished for months in an English army prison in New York City before sailing for Europe in 1780, accompanied by one son. In London he arranged for the publication of 12 essays called *Letters from an American Farmer* (1782).

Within two years this book—charmingly written, optimistic, and timely—went through many editions. He was appointed French consul to three of the new American states. Before assuming his consular duties in 1784, Crèvecoeur translated and added to the original 12 essays in *Lettres d'un cultivateur américain*, 2 vol. (1784). When he returned to America, Crèvecoeur found his home burned, his wife dead, and his daughter and second son with strangers in Boston. Reunited with his children, he set about organizing a packet service between the United States and France. During a two-year furlough in Europe he brought out a larger, second edition of the French *Lettres*, 3 vol. (1790). Recalled from his consulship in 1790, Crèvecoeur wrote one other book on America, *Voyage dans la haute Pennsylvanie et dans l'État de New York*, 3 vol. (1801; *Travels in Upper Pennsylvania and New York*). He lived quietly in France and Germany until his death.

Crèvecoeur was for a while the most widely read commentator on America. His reputation was further increased in the 1920s when a bundle of his unpublished English essays was discovered in an attic in France. These were brought out as *Sketches of Eighteenth Century America, or More Letters from an American Farmer* (1925).

Crews \'krūz\, Frederick C., *in full* Campbell (b. Feb. 20, 1933, Philadelphia, Pa., U.S.)   American literary critic known for his use of psychoanalytic principles.

Crews attended Yale and Princeton universities, and from 1958 he taught at the University of California at Berkeley. He first attracted notice in academic circles with a controversial book of criticism, *The Sins of the Fathers: Hawthorne's Psychological Themes* (1966), in which he claimed that Nathaniel Hawthorne's work has little value unless read on a Freudian level. Crews was probably best known for his satirical send-up of literary criticism, *The Pooh Perplex: A Freshman Casebook* (1963), which contained parodies of scholarly journal articles. In *Out of My System: Psychoanalysis, Ideology, and Critical Method* (1975), Crews presented a witty defense of the psychoanalytic method while acknowledging its shortcomings. Crews

also edited several works, including *The Random House Handbook* (1974; 6th edition, 1992), a text on rhetoric and grammar. He also wrote *Skeptical Engagements* (1986) and *The Critics Bear It Away: American Fiction and the Academy* (1992).

crib \'krib\ [English argot *crib* to pilfer]   In literature, a key to an understanding of a literary work; especially, an explication of a work that follows the text line by line or page by page. *Compare* EXPLICATION DE TEXTE.

Crich, Gerald \'jer-əld-'krich\   Fictional character, a successful but emotionally destructive mine owner in the novel WOMEN IN LOVE by D.H. Lawrence. Crich's ill-fated love affair with Gudrun Brangwen contrasts with the deep and fruitful relationship of Rupert Birkin and Ursula Brangwen.

Crich is portrayed as domineering, soulless, and surrounded by death. At 30 he inherits his father's mine and sets about modernizing it into a profitable model of efficiency. His friendship with Birkin and his affair with Gudrun, however, are failures. In the end, despairing, he wanders off into the snow and dies.

Crichton \'krit-ən\, James (b. August 1560, Eliock House, Dumfries, Scot.—d. July 1582, Mantua, Mantua [Italy])   Orator, linguist, debater, man of letters, and scholar commonly called the "Admirable" Crichton. Many considered him to be a model of the cultured Scottish gentleman.

After graduating from the University of St. Andrews , Crichton went to Paris, where he seems to have distinguished himself at the Collège de Navarre. His first known activity in Europe was his oration of July 1579 in the ducal palace at Genoa. The next year he presented himself to the Venetian printer Aldus Manutius the Younger, who introduced him to leading local humanists.

At Padua in 1581 Crichton enhanced his reputation in two debates, and Manutius paid tribute to his successes in his dedication for his own edition of *Paradoxa* (1581) by Cicero. The next year Crichton entered the service of the Duke of Mantua but was slain there at the instigation, and probably at the hand, of the young prince Vincenzo Gonzaga, whose jealousy he had aroused.

Despite the achievements of his short life, the picture of Crichton painted by Sir Thomas Urquhart in *The Discovery of a Most Exquisite Jewel* (1652) is probably exaggerated. Published letters suggest that constant indebtedness was among several of Crichton's weaknesses. The term "admirable" was first applied to him in 1603 in John Johnston's *Heroes Scotici*, for his knowledge of philosophy, his memory, his linguistic skill, and his ability to debate.

Cricket on the Hearth, The (*in full* The Cricket on the Hearth: A Fairy Tale of Home)   Short tale written by Charles DICKENS as a Christmas book for 1845 but published in 1846.

The title creature is a sort of barometer of life at the home of John Peerybingle and his much younger wife Dot. When things go well, the cricket on the hearth chirps; it is silent when there is sorrow. Tackleton, a jealous old man, poisons John's mind about Dot, but the cricket through its supernatural powers restores John's confidence and all ends happily.

Crime and Punishment   Novel by Fyodor DOSTOYEVSKY, published in 1866 as *Prestupleniye i nakazaniye*. Dostoyevsky's first masterpiece, the novel is a psychological analysis of the poor student Raskolnikov, whose theory that humanitarian ends justify evil means leads him to murder a St. Petersburg pawnbroker. The act produces nightmarish guilt in Raskolnikov.

The narrative's feverish, compelling tone follows the twists and turns of Raskolnikov's emotions and elaborates his struggle with his conscience and his mounting sense of horror as he wanders the city's hot, crowded streets. In prison, Raskolnikov comes to the realization that happiness cannot be achieved by a reasoned plan of existence but must be earned by suffering. The novel's status as a masterpiece is chiefly a result of its narrative intensity and its moving depiction of the recovery of a man's diseased spirit.

crime novel Subgenre of the DETECTIVE NOVEL in which the focus of the work is on the environment and psychology of the criminal. Prominent writers of the genre include John Wainwright, Colin Watson, Nicholas Freeling, Ruth Rendell, Jessica Mann, Mickey Spillane, and Patricia Highsmith. Crime novels differ from police procedurals, which are written from the point of view of the criminal investigator.

Crimes of the Heart Drama in three acts by Beth HENLEY, produced in 1979 and published in 1982. It won the Pulitzer Prize in 1981.

Set in a small Mississippi town, the play examines the lives of three quirky sisters who have gathered at the home of the youngest. During the course of the work the sisters unearth grudges, criticize each other, reminisce about their family life, and attempt to understand their mother's suicide years earlier.

criollismo \,krē-ō-'yēz-mō, -ōl-\ [Spanish, a derivative of *criollo* person native to the Americas, Creole] Preoccupation in the arts and especially the literature of Latin America with native scenes and types; especially, nationalistic preoccupation with such matter. The gaucho literature of Argentina was a form of criollismo. Writers associated with the movement included Tomás Carrasquilla, Rufino Blanco Fombona, Benito Lynch, and Ricardo Güiraldes.

crisis \'krī-sis\ *plural* crises \-,sēz\ *or* crisises [Greek *krísis* decision, event, turning point] The decisive moment in the course of the action of a play or other work of fiction. *Compare* CLIMAX; RESOLUTION.

Crisis, The (*in full* The Crisis: A Record of the Darker Races) Monthly magazine published by the National Association for the Advancement of Colored People (NAACP). It was founded in 1910 and, for its first 24 years, edited by W.E.B. DU BOIS; by the end of its first decade it had achieved a monthly circulation of 100,000 copies. In its pages, Du Bois displayed the evolution of his thought from his early, hopeful insistence on racial justice to his resigned call for black separatism.

The Crisis was an important medium for the young black writers of the Harlem Renaissance, especially from 1919 to 1926, when Jessie Redmon Fauset was its literary editor. The writers she discovered or encouraged included the poets Arna Bontemps, Langston Hughes, and Countee Cullen and the novelist-poet Jean Toomer. After Fauset's departure *The Crisis* was unable to sustain its high literary standards.

Criterion, The English literary review published primarily as a quarterly magazine from 1922 to 1939. It was founded by T.S. Eliot, whose poem *The Waste Land* was published in the first issue.

The magazine was published briefly as *The Criterion, The New Criterion*, and *The Monthly Criterion* but reverted to its original title and to its quarterly schedule from September 1928 to January 1939, when it ceased publication.

Considered by some critics to reflect fascist leanings, *The Criterion* published poems, short fiction, essays, and reviews; among its contributors were W.H. Auden, Ezra Pound, and Stephen Spender. Works by European writers such as Marcel Proust and Jean Cocteau had their first publication in *The Criterion*.

critic \'krit-ik\ [Latin *criticus*, from Greek *kritikós*, from *kritikós* (adjective) discerning, critical, a derivative of *kritós*, verbal adjective of *krínein* to distinguish, judge] One who expresses a reasoned opinion on any matter especially involving a judgment of its value, truth, righteousness, beauty, or technique. Also, one who engages, often professionally, in the analysis, evaluation, or appreciation of works of art. *See also* CRITICISM.

Critic, The (*in full* The Critic, or a Tragedy Rehearsed) Burlesque drama in three acts by Richard Brinsley SHERIDAN, produced in 1779 and published in 1781.

A delightful satire on stage conventions, *The Critic* has always been thought much funnier than its model, *The Rehearsal* (1671) by George Villiers. It is the story of Puff, a literary public-relations man who has written a preposterous historical melodrama that embodies all the worst features of conventional verse dramas—among them bloated emotions, contrived plots, and absurd madness scenes. The critics of the title include the empty and pretentious poet Sir Fretful Plagiary and the petty, malicious critics Sneer and Dangle.

critical bibliography *or* **analytical bibliography** The systematic study and description of books as tangible objects.

The field of critical bibliography grew largely from the study of incunabula (books printed in the first 50 years after the invention of printing, *i.e.*, before 1501). The earliest printed books display the individual styles of their printers in such features as the type used, the typesetting, and the layout of the pages. These were used to deduce the order of individual books in a printer's total production and hence their approximate dates. For books lacking a printer's mark, these same stylistic variants were often used to attribute a book to a particular printer.

The two most significant studies in the development of critical bibliography are William Blades's *The Life and Typography of William Caxton* (1861–63), in which typographical details were used to arrange the publications of England's first printer in chronological order, and Henry Bradshaw's special study of 15th-century books printed in the Netherlands. Bradshaw's method was still more widely applied by Robert Proctor, who assigned the incunabula in the library of the British Museum (now part of the British Library) and the Bodleian Library at Oxford to countries and towns of origin and to particular printers. Proctor meticulously examined all the features of a book—paper, type, makeup, ornamentation, sewing, binding, manuscript notes, and marks of ownership—and, by publishing his descriptions of these books, firmly established this method of study, which was later applied to books by 16th- and 17th-century English authors. In one of the earliest examples of this method in action, the question of the priority between the two 1609 issues of William Shakespeare's *Troilus and Cressida* was resolved.

criticaster \'krit-i-,kas-tər\ An inferior or petty critic.

criticism \'krit-ə-,siz-əm\ 1. The art of evaluating or analyzing works of art or literature. *See* LITERARY CRITICISM. 2. The scientific investigation of literary documents (as the Bible) in regard to such matters as origin, text, composition, or history.

critique \kri-'tēk\ [French] An act of criticizing; especially, a critical examination or estimate of a thing or situation (as a work of art or literature) with a view to determining its nature and limitations or its conformity to standards.

Crockett \'kräk-ət\, Davy, *byname of* David Crockett (b. Aug. 17, 1786, eastern Tennessee, U.S.—d. March 6, 1836, San Antonio, Texas) American frontiersman and politician who became a legendary figure. His image as a rough backwoods legislator caught the popular imagination during his lifetime and continued to do so after his death.

Crockett had no formal schooling. As a young man, he made a name for himself fighting in the Creek War from 1813 to 1814. In 1821 he was elected to the Tennessee legislature, winning popularity through campaign speeches filled with yarns and homespun metaphors. Following a second term in the state legislature in 1823, he won a seat in the U.S. House of Representatives in 1827, 1829, and 1833. He then went to Texas, joined the American forces, and died with those who were slaughtered at the Alamo.

Contrary to his image as an eccentric but shrewd "b'ar-hunting" and Indian-fighting frontiersman, Crockett engaged in several business ventures and delivered his speeches in fairly conventional English. A series of Crockett almanacs, appearing from 1835 to 1856, developed the legend along the lines of Old World folk epics. His *Narrative*, an autobiography written in 1834 with Thomas Chilton, helped introduce a new style of vigorous writing into American literature.

Crockett \\'kräk-ət\\, Samuel Rutherford (b. Sept. 24, 1859, Little Duchrae, near New Galloway, Kirkcudbrightshire, Scot.—d. April 16, 1914, Tarascon, near Avignon, Fr.) Scottish novelist and a leader of the KAILYARD SCHOOL of writers, who depicted Scottish rural life in a sentimental fashion.

After graduating from Edinburgh University and studying for the ministry at New Colly, Edinburgh, Crockett became a minister. With the success of his novels *The Stickit Minister* (1893) and *The Lilac Sunbonnet* (1894), he abandoned the ministry for writing, following the vogue for novels in Scots dialect set by James M. Barrie. Crockett published more than 40 books, mainly novels.

Crofts \\'krôfts\\, Freeman Wills (b. June 1879, Dublin, Ire.—d. April 11, 1957, Worthing, Sussex, Eng.) Internationally popular Irish author of detective novels whose tight plots and exact and scrupulous attention to detail set new standards in detective-fiction plotting.

Educated in Belfast, Crofts was a railroad engineer in Northern Ireland from 1899 to 1929. During a long convalescence he wrote his first novel, *The Cask* (1920). Considered a classic of the detective genre, it was followed by more than 30 detective novels, most of which featured Inspector French of Scotland Yard.

Croker \\'krō-kər\\, John Wilson (b. Dec. 20, 1780, Galway, Ire.—d. Aug. 10, 1857, Hampton, Middlesex, Eng.) British politician and writer noted for his rigid Tory principles.

After graduating from Trinity College, Dublin, and studying law at Lincoln's Inn in London, Croker was called to the Irish bar in 1802. He entered Parliament in 1807 and from 1810 to 1830 was secretary of the Admiralty during the long Tory predominance. Strongly opposed to the Reform Bill of 1832, Croker resigned from Parliament when it was passed (though he continued thereafter his close contacts with Tory leaders). From about this period there began the lifelong antagonism between Croker and Lord Macaulay, a major champion of the Reform Bill and Whiggism.

From 1831 to 1854 Croker was one of the chief writers for *The Quarterly Review*, to which he contributed about 270 articles on a variety of subjects. His literary tastes were largely those of the 18th century, as may be seen from his severe criticism of John Keats's *Endymion*, Alfred, Lord Tennyson's *Poems* of 1832, and the first two volumes of Macaulay's *History of England* (1849). He edited the collected letters or memoirs of various 18th-century figures.

Croker \\'krō-kər\\, Thomas Crofton (b. Jan. 15, 1798, Cork, Ire.—d. Aug. 8, 1854, London, Eng.) Irish antiquary whose collections of songs and legends formed a storehouse for writers of the Irish Literary Renaissance.

Croker had little formal education but read widely. During rambles in southern Ireland from 1812 to 1816, he collected legends, folk songs, and keens (dirges for the dead), some of which he sent to the poet Thomas Moore, who acknowledged a debt to Croker in his *Irish Melodies*. This collection formed the basis of Croker's *Fairy Legends and Traditions of the South of Ireland* (1825–28), which was translated into German by the Brothers Grimm. After 1818 Croker lived in England, working as a clerk in the Admiralty until 1850. His later works include *Popular Songs of Ireland* (1839).

Croly \\'krō-lē\\, Herbert David (b. Jan. 23, 1869, New York, N.Y., U.S.—d. May 17, 1930, New York City) American author, editor, and political philosopher, founder of the magazine *The New Republic*.

The son of widely known journalists, Croly was educated at Harvard University and spent his early adult years editing or contributing to architectural journals. In 1914 he founded the liberal weekly *The New Republic*, "A Journal of Opinion." In its pages Croly attacked what he viewed as American complacency and argued that democratic institutions must constantly be revised to suit changing situations.

The most important of his books was the first, *The Promise of American Life* (1909), which treated social and political problems. It influenced both Presidents Theodore Roosevelt and Woodrow Wilson. In his last years, Croly turned his attention chiefly to philosophic and religious questions.

Crome Yellow \\'krōm-'yel-ō\\ First novel by Aldous HUXLEY, published in 1921. The book is a social satire of the British literati in the period following World War I.

Crome Yellow revolves around the hapless love affair of Denis Stone, a sensitive poet, and Anne Wimbush. Her uncle, Henry Wimbush, hosts a party at his country estate, Crome Yellow, that brings together a humorous coterie of characters.

Crommelynck \\'krôm-ə-,liŋk\\, Fernand (b. Nov. 19, 1885, Brussels, Belg.—d. March 17, 1970, Saint-Germaine-en-Laye, Fr.) Belgian playwright known for farces in which commonplace weaknesses are developed into monumental obsessions.

Crommelynck was trained as an actor. After some early successes in Belgium, such as in *Nous n'irons plus au bois* (1906; "We'll Go No More to the Woods"), Crommelynck won international honors with his play *Le Cocu magnifique* (*The Magnificent Cuckold*). Produced in Paris in 1920 and filmed in 1921, it has been revived many times and has retained its appeal. A penetrating study of sexual jealousy, it concerns a young husband's utter incapacity to calm his suspicions about his wife's fidelity. Eventually he drives her to resolve his uncertainty by betraying him.

Of his later plays, *Tripes d'or* (1926; "Gold in the Guts") is the most striking. As in *The Magnificent Cuckold*, Crommelynck combined farce and deep seriousness in his reinterpretation of the subject of avarice. In the play a miser can never bring himself to pay proper attention to the girl he says he loves. In *Une Femme qui a le coeur trop petit* (1934; "A Woman with Too Little Heart"), Crommelynck portrayed a perfect wife whose obsessive virtuousness and efficiency withers all love. With *Chaud et froid* (1934; "Hot and Cold"), Crommelynck returned to the theme of marital constancy.

Cronin \\'krō-nən\\, A.J., *in full* Archibald Joseph (b. July 19, 1896, Cardross, Dumbartonshire, Scot.—d. Jan. 6, 1981, Montreux, Switz.) Scottish novelist and physician who combined realism with social criticism in his works.

Cronin was educated at the University of Glasgow and served as a surgeon in the Royal Navy during World War I. He practiced in South Wales and then, as medical inspector of mines, investigated occupational diseases in the coal industry. He opened a medical practice in London in 1926 but quit because of ill health, using his leisure to write his first novel, *Hatter's Castle* (1931; film, 1941), the story

of a Scottish hatmaker obsessed with the idea of the possibility of his noble birth. The book was an immediate success in Britain.

Cronin's fourth novel, *The Stars Look Down* (1935; film, 1939), which chronicles various social injustices in a North England mining community, is a classic work of 20th-century British fiction. It was followed by

E.B. Inc.

The Citadel (1937; film, 1938), which showed how private physicians' greed can distort good medical practice. *The Keys of the Kingdom* (1942; film, 1944), about a Roman Catholic missionary in China, was one of his most popular books. Cronin's subsequent novels include *The Green Years* (1944; film, 1946), *Shannon's Way* (1948), *The Judas Tree* (1961), and *A Song of Sixpence* (1964). One of his more interesting late works is *A Thing of Beauty* (1956), a study of a gifted young painter who must break free of middle-class conventions to realize his potential.

Cronus or **Cronos** or **Kronos** \\'krō-nəs\\ In ancient Greek mythology, a male deity who was worshiped by the pre-Hellenic population of Greece but probably was not widely worshiped by the Greeks themselves; he was later identified with the Roman god Saturn. Cronus' functions were connected with agriculture.

In Greek mythology Cronus was the son of Uranus (Heaven) and Gaea (Earth), being the youngest of the 12 Titans. On the advice of his mother he castrated his father, thus separating Heaven from Earth. He then became the king of the Titans and took for his consort his sister Rhea; she bore by him Hestia, Demeter, Hera, Hades, and Poseidon, all of whom he swallowed because his own parents had warned that he would be overthrown by his own child. When his son Zeus was born, however, Rhea hid Zeus in Crete and tricked Cronus into swallowing a stone instead. Zeus grew up, forced Cronus to disgorge his brothers and sisters, waged war on Cronus, and was victorious.

Crosby \\'kròz-bē\\, Harry, *byname of* Henry Grew Crosby (b. June 4, 1898, Boston, Mass., U.S.—d. Dec. 10, 1929, New York, N.Y.) American poet who, as an expatriate in Paris in the 1920s, established the Black Sun Press.

Crosby was known for his bizarre behavior. After barely escaping death in World War I, he became morbid and rebellious. He settled in Paris in the early 1920s and soon joined the circle of literary expatriates. In 1927 he and his wife, Caresse Crosby (1892–1970), began to publish their own poetry under the imprint Editions Narcisse, later the Black Sun Press. The following year they started printing books by other writers, including Archibald MacLeish, D.H. Lawrence, and James Joyce, for which the press is best remembered.

In his poetry—which has little artistic merit—Crosby unconsciously traced literary tradition from 19th-century Romanticism, in *Sonnets for Caresse* (1925), to automatic writing, in *Sleeping Together* (1929), descriptions of his dreams. His

work includes poetry, such as *Chariot of the Sun* (1928); diaries, *Shadows of the Sun* (1928–30); and contributions to the avant-grade magazine *transition* that demonstrate his obsessive, mystical sun worship. Crosby took his own life in 1929.

Cross, Amanda. Pseudonym under which the scholar Carolyn HEILBRUN published a series of detective novels that feature English professor Kate Fansler.

Crossing Brooklyn Ferry \\'bruk-lin\\ Poem by Walt WHITMAN, published as "Sun-Down Poem" in the second edition of *Leaves of Grass* in 1856 and revised and retitled in later editions. It is a sensitive, detailed record of the poet's thoughts and observations about the continuity of nature and of brotherhood while aboard a ferry between Brooklyn and Manhattan. His panoramic description of the harbor includes rich images of sunlight on the water, the flight of seagulls, and the commerce of ships. Through the use of repetition, exclamation, and apostrophe, Whitman conveys his joyful belief in world solidarity.

Crossing the Bar Short poem by Alfred, Lord TENNYSON, written three years before he died and published in the collection *Demeter and Other Poems* (1889). Describing a ferry trip to the Isle of Wight, it concerns his imminent death and his hopes for an afterlife. Tennyson requested that it be printed as the final poem in all volumes of his verse.

Crothers \\'krəth-ərz\\, Rachel (b. Dec. 12, 1878, Bloomington, Ill., U.S.—d. July 5, 1958, Danbury, Conn.) American playwright whose works reflected the position of women in American society more accurately than any other dramatist of her time.

Crothers graduated from the Illinois State Normal School (now Illinois State University) in 1892 and then studied dramatic art in Boston and New York City and acted in New York City. Her career as a playwright began in 1906 with the success of her first full-length play, *The Three of Us*. For the next three decades, until *Susan and God* (1937), Broadway saw an average of one new Crothers play each year, the majority of them popular and critical successes, an achievement unequaled by any other American woman playwright.

Crothers chronicled, sometimes seriously, more often humorously, such timely problems as the double standard (*A Man's World*, 1909), trial marriage (*Young Wisdom*, 1914), the problems of the younger generation (*Nice People*, 1921), Freudianism (*Expressing Willie*, 1924), and divorce (*As Husbands Go*, 1931; *When Ladies Meet*, 1932). These and other successes were marked by simplicity of plot, happy endings, and expert dialogue, which featured shrewdly combined instruction and amusement. Her comedies always advocated rationality and moderation.

Crothers took full responsibility for the entire production of almost all her plays, casting and directing many of the leading stars of the contemporary stage. The best and most instructive statement of her dramatic theory is to be found in her essay "The Construction of a Play," collected in *The Art of Playwriting* (1928).

Crouchback, Guy \\'gī-,krauch-,bak\\ Fictional character, the protagonist of Evelyn Waugh's trilogy SWORD OF HONOUR. Crouchback is alienated from his Roman Catholic religion, his personal relationships, and the modern world in general. He believes that his wartime military service is a noble undertaking. The progress of his disillusionment and the honor he discovers within himself are the subject of the trilogy.

Crouse, Russel   *see* Howard LINDSAY and Russel Crouse.

Crucible, The A four-act play by Arthur MILLER, performed and published in 1953. Set in 1692 during the Salem witch trials, *The Crucible* is an examination of contemporary events in American politics during the era of fear and desire for conformity brought on by Senator Joseph McCarthy's sensational allegations of communist subversion in high places.

Crumley \\'krəm-lē\\, James (b. Oct. 12, 1939, Three Rivers, Texas, U.S.)   American writer of violent mystery novels featuring vivid characters and sordid settings.

Crumley attended Georgia Institute of Technology, Texas Arts and Industries University, and the Writers' Workshop at the University of Iowa. His experiences during service in the U.S. Army (1958–61) are reflected in his Vietnam War novel *One to Count Cadence* (1969). After 1969, apart from occasional pieces of journalism and the short stories collected in *The Muddy Fork and Other Things* (1991), he wrote only detective novels.

His down-and-out detectives, Milo Milodragovitch and C.W. Sughrue, and a number of other notable characters work in the fictional mountain city of Meriwether, Montana. Crumley's first detective novel, featuring Milodragovitch, was *The Wrong Case* (1975). Sughrue and an author with writer's block drink their way through the West while hunting a missing pornography actress in *The Last Good Kiss* (1978); Milodragovitch foils an anti-environmentalist conspiracy in *Dancing Bear* (1983); and Sughrue hunts the mother of a vile-tempered drug dealer in the especially violent *The Mexican Tree Duck* (1993). While the plots of Crumley's novels are conventional, the quality of his writing, his recurring comedy, and his emphasis on cataclysmic climaxes are distinctive.

Crusca Academy \\'krüs-kə\\ (Accademia della Crusca \\äk-kä-'dā-myä-del-lä-'krüs-kä\\; "Academy of the Chaff")   Italian literary academy founded in Florence in 1582 for the purpose of purifying Tuscan, the literary language of the Italian Renaissance. Partially through the efforts of its members, the Tuscan dialect, particularly as it had been employed by Petrarch and Boccaccio, became the model for Italian literature in the 16th and 17th centuries.

Founded by five members of the Florentine Academy, with the purpose of sifting the impure language (*crusca*, literally, "bran" or "chaff") from the pure, the Crusca Academy set itself up immediately as the arbiter of the literature of its time. Members of the academy became known as linguistic conservatives, and in 1612 they began publication of their official dictionary, *Vocabolario degli Accademici della Crusca*, which continues to be published. Though the academy was suppressed in the late 18th century, Napoleon reestablished it in 1808, and it gained autonomy in 1811.

In the early 20th century, legislation by the Italian government limited the academy to the publication of classical authors and linguistic documents and periodicals.

Crusoe, Robinson \\'räb-in-sən-'krü-ˌsō, -ˌzō\\   One of the best-known characters in world literature, a fictional English seaman who is shipwrecked on an island for 28 years. The eponymous hero of Daniel Defoe's novel ROBINSON CRUSOE, he is a self-reliant, God-fearing man who uses his practical intelligence and resourcefulness to survive.

crux \\'krəks\\ [Latin, cross, torture]   A puzzling, confusing, difficult, or unsolved problem, as for example a scholarly question about the literal meaning of a word or line in a work of literature.

Cruz \\'krüs\\, Sor Juana Inés de la, *original name* Juana Inés de Asbaje \\ē-'näs-<u>th</u>ä-äz-'bä-kä\\ (b. Nov. 12, 1651, San Miguel Nepantla, Mex.—d. April 17, 1695, Mexico City)   Poet, scholar, and nun, an outstanding lyric poet of Mexico's colonial period.

An intellectual prodigy, at eight she composed a *loa* (short dramatic poem) in honor of the Blessed Sacrament. At nine she went to live in Mexico City, where she studied Latin, mastering the language in 20 lessons.

In 1669 she entered the convent of San Jerónimo so that she could dedicate her life to learning. There she assembled a library of about 4,000 volumes, experimented in the sciences, and wrote poems and religious and secular plays. She was admonished for her nonreligious, intellectual activities by the bishop of Puebla, who wrote under the pseudonym of Sor Filotea. In her *Respuesta a Sor Filotea* ("Reply to Sister Philotea"), written March 1, 1691, Cruz defended her desire for broad knowledge. She became famous for the poem "Hombres necios que acusés" ("Foolish Men Who Accuse [Women]"). Two years later, however, she gave up all contact with the world and devoted her time exclusively to religious duties.

The three volumes of her works were printed in Spain: *Inundación castálida* (1689; "Flood from the Muses' Springs"), *Segundo volumen de las obras de Sóror Juana Inés de la Cruz* (1692; "Second Volume of the Works of Sister Juana Inés de la Cruz"), and *Fama y obras pósthumas de Fénix de México y Dézima Musa* (1700; "Fame and Posthumous Works of the Mexican Phoenix and Tenth Muse").

Cruz e Sousa \\'krüs-ē-'saü-sə\\, João da (b. Nov. 24, 1861, Desterro, Braz.—d. March 19, 1898, Sítio)   Poet who was the leading figure of the Symbolist movement in Brazil.

Cruz e Sousa was the son of freed slaves. His first poems were published in 1877, but his career gained momentum shortly after 1890, when he came in contact with the literary circle of Rio de Janeiro. His three best-known collections of poetry were published in the 1890s: *Broquéis* (1893; "Shields"), *Missal* (1893; a volume of poetic prose), and *Faróis* (1900; "Beacons").

Called the *Cisne Negro* ("Black Swan") by his contemporaries, he was the chief poet and luminary of the Symbolist movement. His poetry weds the technical principles of French Symbolism to themes drawn from his social concerns (chiefly abolition) and his own personal suffering. He was widely admired and emulated by younger poets of his own country, as well as those involved in the Modernismo movement in Latin America.

Cry, the Beloved Country   Novel by Alan PATON, published in 1948.

The novel relates the story of a black South African, Absalom Kumalo, who has murdered a white man. This situation is Paton's basis for examining aspects of guilt, both Kumalo's personal guilt and responsibility and the collective guilt of a society that creates such disparity in living conditions.

Csokonai Vitéz \\'chō-kō-ˌnō-ē-'vē-ˌtāz\\, Mihály (b. Nov. 17, 1773, Debrecen, Hung.—d. Jan. 28, 1805, Debrecen)   The outstanding poet of the Hungarian Enlightenment.

Csokonai's early sympathies with the revolutionary trends of his age made life difficult for him in the wave of reaction that accompanied Napoleon's invasion of Europe. Dismissed after a brief career as an assistant teacher at the Calvinist college in Debrecen, he became a wandering poet. For the sake of a wealthy girl (the "Lilla" of his poems), he tried to secure a permanent post, but by the time he had obtained such a position, in a small town, she had married. He returned to Debrecen poor and ill, and he died there without having seen his poems published.

Csokonai's prime interest was poetic form. He was one of the first Hungarian theorists of prosody and successfully adapted the rhymed metrics of western Europe to Hungarian verse forms. His poetry breathes the spirit of the Enlightenment. He was also a playwright and the author of the first Hungarian comic epic, *Dorottya* (1799), his most popular work.

Csoóri \'chō-ō-rē\, Sándor (b. Feb. 3, 1930, Zámoly, Hung.) Hungarian poet, essayist, and screenwriter who was considered one of the finest poets of his generation.

Born into a peasant family, Csoóri was chosen with other peasant children to receive a free education. In the late 1940s he began contributing to journals in Budapest and briefly attended the Lenin Institute. Initially political, his verse became more personal and surreal in the 1960s, beginning with *Menekülés a magányból* (1962; "Escape from Solitude"). His later collections include *Második születésem* (1967; "My Second Birth"), *A látogató emlékei* (1977; "The Memories of a Visitor"), and *Kezemben zöld ág* (1985; "In My Hand a Green Branch").

Among the collections of his sociopolitical essays about Eastern Europe are *Tudósítás a toronyból* (1963; "Report from the Tower"), *Készülődés a számadásra* (1987; "Preparation for the Reckoning"), and *Nappali hold* (1991; "Moon at Daylight"). He also wrote scripts for theater and film. English-language volumes of his poetry include *Wings of Knives and Nails* (1981), *Memory of Snow* (1983), *Barbarian Prayer* (1989), and *Selected Poems of Sándor Csoóri* (1992).

cubism \'kyü-ˌbiz-əm\ [French *cubisme*, a derivative of *cube* cube] A style of art that stresses abstract structure at the expense of the pictorial (or in writing, the narrative). Written attempts to produce cubist effects used bizarre associations and dissociations in imagery, the simultaneous evocation of several points of view toward the material, and other devices. One of the better-known practitioners of literary cubism was the writer Gertrude Stein, whose good friend Pablo Picasso had helped invent the cubist style. Stein's experiments in *Tender Buttons* (1914), while obscure and virtually impossible to decode, provide the occasional telling or evocative phrase.

Cú Chulainn \kü-'k̬əl-ən\, *also called* Cuchulain, Cuchulinn, or Cuchullin. The central character of the Ulster cycle in medieval Irish literature. He was the greatest of the Knights of the Red Branch, the warriors loyal to Conor (Conchobar mac Nessa), the reputed king of the Ulaids of northeastern Ireland at about the beginning of the 1st century BC. Cú Chulainn was of great size and masculine beauty and won distinction for his exploits while still a child. His prowess was increased by the gift of seven fingers on each hand, seven toes on each foot, and seven pupils in each eye. Favored by the gods and exempt from the curse of periodic feebleness laid upon the men of Ulster, he performed superhuman exploits and labors comparable to those of the Greek hero Achilles. In times of rage he took on the characteristics of the Scandinavian berserkers and would become monstrously deformed and uncontrollable. THE CATTLE RAID OF COOLEY records his single-handed defense of Ulster at the age of 17 against the forces of Medb (Maeve), queen of Connaught. According to the best-known legends, he was tricked by his enemies into an unfair fight and slain at the age of 27.

Cueva \'kwä-b̬ä\, Juan de la, *in full* Juan de la Cueva de Garoza \thä-lä-'kwä-b̬ä-thä-gä-'rō-thä\ (b. *c.* 1550, Seville [Spain]—d. *c.* 1610, Seville) Spanish dramatist and poet, one of the earliest Spanish writers to depart from classical forms and use national historical subjects.

Cueva differed from his contemporaries in having his plays published, thus transmitting to posterity intact examples of early, albeit mediocre, Spanish drama. Cueva's plays in the collection *Primera parte de las comedias y tragedias* (1583; "First Part of the Comedies and Tragedies"), including such works as *Tragedia de Ayax Telamón* ("Tragedy of Ajax Telamon") and *Tragedia de la muerte de Virginia* ("Tragedy of the Death of Virginia"), drew on Greco-Roman themes. Cueva was particularly skilled at adapting medieval Spanish legends and ballads;

his *Tragedia de los siete infantes de Lara* (1588; "Tragedy of the Seven Princes of Lara") and *La muerte del rey don Sancho* (1588; "The Death of King Don Sancho") were later used by Lope de Vega and the Romantic novelists, and his treatise on poetry, *Ejemplar poético* (1606), was an important antecedent of Vega's *Arte nuevo de hacer comedias* ("New Art of Writing Comedies"). Other important plays by Cueva include the mythological farces *El saco de Roma y muerte de Borbón* ("The Sacking of Rome and the Death of [the Duke of] Bourbon") and *El infamador* (1581; "The Slanderer").

Cuff, Sergeant \'kəf\ Fictional character, the detective in Wilkie Collins' THE MOONSTONE. Like Inspector Bucket in Charles Dickens' *Bleak House*, the character of Sergeant Cuff was based upon Inspector Jonathan Whicher, a Scotland Yard detective. Cuff's careful procedures—including a reconstruction of the jewel robbery and the assembling of suspects to explain the crime's solution—served as models for many subsequent detective stories.

Culhwch and Olwen \'kil-hu̬k̬ . . . 'ȯl-wen\, Culhwch *also spelled* Kulhwch, *Welsh* Culhweh as Olwen. Welsh prose romance (*c.* 1100), one of the earliest known that treats Arthurian subject matter. It is a lighthearted tale that skillfully incorporates themes from mythology, folk literature, and history. The earliest form of the story survives in an early 14th-century manuscript called *The White Book of Rhydderch*, and the first translation of the story into modern English was made by Lady Charlotte Guest from *The Red Book of Hergest* (*c.* 1375–1425) and was included in her translation of *Mabinogion*.

The story uses the folk formula of a stepmother's attempt to thwart her stepson. Culhwch, after refusing to marry the daughter of his stepmother, is told by her that he shall never wed until he wins Olwen, the daughter of the malevolent giant Yspadadden Penkawr. Because of a prophecy that if she marries he will die, Olwen's father first tries to kill Culhwch but then agrees to the marriage if Culhwch performs several perilous feats and brings him the 13 treasures he desires. Culhwch is aided in several of his adventures by his cousin Arthur and some of Arthur's men, including Kei (Sir Kay) and Gwalchmei (Sir Gawain). Culhwch returns to Yspadadden with only part of his goal accomplished, kills him, and marries Olwen.

Cullen \'kəl-ən\, Countee (Porter), Countee *also spelled* Countée \'kaùn-tē\ (b. May 30, 1903, Louisville, Ky.?, U.S.—d. Jan. 9, 1946, New York, N.Y.) American poet, one of the finest of the HARLEM RENAISSANCE.

Reared by a woman who was probably his paternal grandmother, at age 15 he was unofficially adopted by the Reverend F.A. Cullen, minister of Salem M.E. Church, one of Harlem's largest congregations. During young Cullen's schooling, academic honors came easily to him. He won a citywide poetry contest as a schoolboy and saw his winning stanzas widely reprinted. At New York University he continued to attract critical attention. Major American literary magazines accepted his poems regularly, and his first collection of poems, *Color* (1925)—which includes the powerful YET DO I MARVEL—was published to critical acclaim before he finished college. Cullen attended Harvard and worked as an assistant editor for *Opportunity* magazine. After publication of *The Black Christ and Other Poems* (1929), his reputation as a poet waned. From 1934 until the end of his life he taught in the New York City public schools.

Most notable among Cullen's other works are *Copper Sun* (1927), *The Ballad of the Brown Girl* (1928), and *The Medea and Some Poems* (1935).

culteranismo \ˌkül-ter-ä-'nēz-mō\ [Spanish] In Spanish literature, an esoteric style of writing that attempted to elevate poetic language and themes by re-Latinizing them, using classical allusions, vocabulary, syntax, and word order. The name *culterano* for a practitioner of this style is a derivative of *culto* ("cult"), which was perhaps modeled with a mixture of humor and disdain on *luterano* ("Lutheran").

Announced as a theory by Luis Carillo y Sotomayor in 1611 with his *Libro de la erudición poética* ("Book of Poetic Erudition"), *culteranismo* reached its height in the 17th century with the poetry of Luis de GÓNGORA. Góngora's complex imagery, unusual grammatical constructions, and obscure mythological allusions in *Soledades* (1613; "Solitudes") carried *culteranismo* to such extremes that *gongorismo* entered the language as a synonym for literary affectation. Lesser imitators of Góngora deliberately cultivated obscurity in their work, thus overshadowing the original aim of the style, which was to create a poetry that would be timeless and universally appealing.

After 300 years of almost universal ridicule, *culteranismo* was rediscovered by early 20th-century avant-garde poets in Spain as a fruitful method of poetic expression, and Góngora himself was reevaluated by modern critics as one of Spain's greatest poets.

Culture and Anarchy Major work of criticism by Matthew ARNOLD, published in 1869. In it Arnold contrasts culture, which he defines as "the study of perfection," with anarchy, the prevalent mood of England's then new democracy, which lacks standards and a sense of direction. Arnold classified English society into the Barbarians (with their lofty spirit, serenity, and distinguished manners and their inaccessibility to ideas), the Philistines (the stronghold of religious nonconformity, with plenty of energy and morality but insufficient "sweetness and light"), and the Populace (still raw and blind). He saw in the Philistines the key to culture; they were the most influential segment of society; their strength was the nation's strength, their crudeness its crudeness; it therefore was necessary to educate and humanize the Philistines. Arnold saw in the idea of "the State," and not in any one class of society, the true organ and repository of the nation's collective "best self." No summary can do justice to *Culture and Anarchy*, however; it is written with an inward poise, a serene detachment, and an infusion of subtle humor that make it a masterpiece of ridicule as well as a searching analysis of Victorian society. The same is true of its sequel, *Friendship's Garland* (1871).

culture myth A myth that accounts for the discovery of arts and sciences.

Cumalı \jŭ-mä-'lә\, Necati (b. 1921, Flórina, Greece) Turkish writer and translator whose notable contributions to his native literature included poetry, short fiction, essays, and plays. He was one of the best-known Turkish writers of the 20th century.

At the age of 18 Cumalı began publishing poetry. After graduating from Ankara University, he held a variety of jobs. In 1959 he became a professional writer. Cumalı's first book of poetry was *Kızılçullu yolu* (1943; "The Road to Kızılçullu"), and he wrote several more volumes of poetry before he began to publish fiction. His collected poetry was published under the title *Aç güneş* (1980; "Hungry Sun"), later enlarged and published as *Tufandan önce* (1983; "Before the Deluge"). His first published fiction was the short-story collection *Yalnız kadın* (1955; "Woman Alone"), and his first play, *Boş Beşik* (1949; "Empty Cradle"; film, 1952), is a retelling of the traditional story of an infant lost by nomads.

Cumalı's concerns were wide-ranging; he wrote of the hardships of rural life, of Turkish history and cultural traditions, and of urban life. One of his best-known stories is *Susuz Yaz* (1962; published as *Dry Summer* in *Modern Turkish Drama*; film, 1963), a tragedy of an unfaithful wife, her husband, and his two-faced brother. Later plays include *Nalınlar* (1962; "The Clogs") and *Derya Gülü* (1963; *Sea Rose*). Cumalı also translated poetry by Guillaume Apollinaire and Langston Hughes.

Cumberland \'kәm-bәr-lәnd\, Richard (b. Feb. 19, 1732, Cambridge, Cambridgeshire, Eng.—d. May 7, 1811, London) English dramatist and creator of sentimental plays who is perhaps best known today as the model for the character of Sir Fretful Plagiary in Richard Brinsley Sheridan's *The Critic; or a Tragedy Rehearsed*.

After leaving Trinity College, Cambridge, Cumberland held a series of government positions. His first success as a dramatist came with *The Brothers* (1769), a sentimental comedy whose plot is reminiscent of Henry Fielding's novel *Tom Jones,* and he continued to write prolifically. *The West Indian* (1771) held the stage throughout the rest of the 18th century. *The Fashionable Lover,* another sentimental comedy, achieved success in 1772.

Cumberland, however, hankered after the grand style. He regarded an early tragedy, *Tiberius in Capreae,* as his masterpiece but could not persuade management to produce it. His serious works were for the most part unsuccessful. Cumberland quarreled with many famous contemporaries, notably Sheridan and Oliver Goldsmith, both of whom were opposed to sentimentalism in drama.

Cummings \'kәm-iŋz\, Bruce Frederick, *pseudonym* Wilhelm Nero Pilate Barbellion \bär-'bel-yәn\ (b. Sept. 7, 1889, Barnstaple, Devon, Eng.—d. Oct. 22, 1919, Gerard's Cross, Buckinghamshire) English author of *The Journal of a Disappointed Man* (1919), extracts from diaries he kept between 1903 and 1917. It was immediately acclaimed upon its publication a few months before his death as a poignant revelation of the sense of failure and thwarted ambitions of a sensitive man.

Determined for a career as a naturalist, Cummings won a post at the British Museum of Natural History, which enabled him to abandon his journalism career, work that he found disagreeable. Posthumous books were *Enjoying Life and Other Literary Remains* (1919) and *A Last Diary* (1920).

Cummings \'kәm-iŋz\, E.E., *in full* Edward Estlin Cummings (b. Oct. 14, 1894, Cambridge, Mass., U.S.—d. Sept. 3, 1962, North Conway, N.H.) American poet and painter who first attracted attention, in an age of literary experimentation, for his eccentric punctuation and phrasing. The spirit of New England dissent and of Emersonian self-reliance underlies the urbanized Yankee colloquialism of Cummings' verse. The commonly held belief that Cummings had his name legally changed to lowercase letters only is erroneous.

Cummings graduated from Harvard. During World War I he served with an ambulance corps in France, where he was interned for a time in a detention camp because of his friendship with an American who had written letters home that the French censors thought critical of the war effort. This experience deepened his distrust of officialdom and was the basis for his first book, *The Enormous Room* (1922).

In the 1920s and '30s he divided his time between Paris, where he studied art, and New York City. His first book of verse was *Tulips and Chimneys* (1923), followed by *XLI Poems* (1925) and *&* (1925).

In 1927 his play *him* was produced by the Provincetown Players in New York City. During these years he exhibited his paintings and drawings, but they failed to attract as much critical interest as his writings. His experimental prose work *Eimi* (1933) recorded a visit to the Soviet Union that confirmed his repugnance for collectivism. He published his discussions as the Charles Eliot Norton lecturer on poetry at Harvard University under the title *i: six nonlectures* (1953).

In all Cummings wrote 12 volumes of verse, which are assembled in his two-volume *Complete Poems* (1968). His moods in these are alternately satirical and tough or tender and whimsical. His erotic poetry and love lyrics have a childlike candor and freshness.

Cunégonde \kœ-na̅-'gȯⁿd\ Fictional character who is the childhood friend, lover, and wife of the title character in Voltaire's satiric novel CANDIDE.

Cunha \'kün-yə\, Euclides Rodrigues Pimenta da (b. Jan. 20, 1866, Santa Rita do Rio Negro, Braz.—d. Aug. 15, 1909, Rio de Janeiro) Brazilian author of the classic historical narrative *Os sertões* (1902; *Rebellion in the Backlands*), the first written protest in behalf of the forgotten inhabitants of Brazil's frontier.

Originally a military engineer, Cunha left the army to become a civil engineer and later a journalist. As a reporter, he accompanied the army to Canudos, a village in the backlands of Bahia state, where the messianic Antônio Conselheiro ("the Counselor") and his followers had established their own "empire." Five successive government expeditions were required to subdue the rebels, who resisted to the last man. Cunha's eyewitness account of the drama of rebellion and reprisal has the vividness of a novel. Cunha perceived not only the particular event but also the larger significance of the inhospitable backlands and its rude inhabitants to the nation as a whole. In defiance of the common 19th-century pseudoscientific belief in the inferiority of mixed races (a theme that haunts Brazilian literature), he concludes with a strongly worded plea for assimilation.

Cunningham \'kən-iŋ-əm, *commonly* -iŋ-ˌham\, Allan (b. Dec. 7, 1784, Keir, Dumfriesshire, Scot.—d. Oct. 30, 1842, London, Eng.) Scottish poet, a member of the brilliant circle of contributors to the *London Magazine* in its heyday in the early 1820s.

Cunningham read the works of Sir Walter Scott, and, with the encouragement of Robert Burns (who was his father's friend), he himself began to write. After publishing some poems disguised as old ballads in *Remains of Nithsdale and Galloway Songs* (1810), he went to London, where he continued to write while working as a sculptor's assistant and as an editor. He collected and edited old ballads and stories, published as *Traditional Tales of the English and Scottish Peasantry* (1822) and *The Songs of Scotland, Ancient and Modern* (1825). His lyrical poems, though lacking the unselfconsciousness of the true ballad, are memorable for their rhythm and their verbal felicity. He also wrote *The Lives of the Most Eminent British Painters, Sculptors, and Architects*, 6 vol. (1829–33), and he edited *The Works of Robert Burns* (1834), prefacing it with a biography of Burns that contained much valuable new material.

Cunningham \'kən-iŋ-ˌham\, J.V., *in full* James Vincent (b. Aug. 23, 1911, Cumberland, Md., U.S.—d. March 30, 1985, Waltham, Mass.) American poet and antimodernist literary critic whose terse, epigrammatic verse is full of sorrow and wit.

Cunningham studied poetry with Yvor Winters at Stanford University. He taught at several universities before settling at Brandeis University in 1953. *The Helmsman* (1942) and *The Judge Is Fury* (1947) offer a mix of his early and mature poetry. In *The Quest of the Opal: A Commentary on "The Helmsman"* (1950) he explains why he came to reject the modernism of his early verse.

In the 1950s Cunningham wrote two volumes of epigrams, *Doctor Drink* (1950) and *Trivial, Vulgar and Exalted* (1957). *To What Strangers, What Welcome* (1964) is a sequence of short poems about his travels through the American West. Among Cunningham's other verse collections are *The Exclusions of a Rhyme* (1960), *Some Salt* (1967), and *The Collected Poems and*

Epigrams of J.V. Cunningham (1971). He also published *The Collected Essays of J.V. Cunningham* (1976).

Cupid \'kyü-pid\ Ancient Roman god of love in all its varieties, the counterpart of the Greek god EROS and the equivalent of Amor in Latin poetry. According to myth, Cupid was the son of Venus, the goddess of love; he usually appeared as a winged infant carrying a bow and a quiver of arrows, whose wounds inspired love or passion in his victims. He was sometimes portrayed wearing armor, perhaps to suggest ironic parallels between warfare and romance or to symbolize the invincibility of love.

Although sometimes portrayed as callous and careless, Cupid was generally viewed as beneficent, because he imparted happiness to couples both mortal and immortal. At the worst he was considered mischievous in his matchmaking; this mischief often was directed by his mother. In one tale, Venus' machinations backfired when she used Cupid in revenge on the mortal Psyche, only to have Cupid fall in love with her and make her his immortal wife. *See also* PSYCHE.

Curel \kœ-'rel\, François de (b. June 10, 1854, Metz, Fr.—d. April 26, 1928, Paris) French dramatist and novelist, one of the brightest lights of André Antoine's famous Théâtre-Libre, which was founded as a forum for original dramatic art.

Curel is noted for his austere dramas that show the working out of social, moral, or psychological conflicts: the destructiveness of an embittered woman in *L'Envers d'une sainte* (1892; *A False Saint*); the decadence of a noble family in *Les Fossiles* (1892; *The Fossils*); the impulses of love and revenge in *L'Invitée* (1893; "The Guest"); capital-labor relations in *Le Repas du lion* (1897; "The Lion's Meal"); and the cult of science at the expense of human value in *La Nouvelle Idole* (1895; "The New Idol"). Unlike the popular "thesis plays" of his time, which emphasized abstractions, Curel's dramas emphasized the characters' emotions and actions. After 1906 Curel abandoned writing for several years. When he resumed, his work was comic and ironic in tone. *L'Âme en folie* (1919; "The Soul Gone Mad"), his only popular success, was a comedy comparing human and animal emotions. He was elected to the Académie Française in 1918.

Curll \'kərl\, Edmund (b. 1675, England—d. Dec. 11, 1747, London) London bookseller remembered for his long quarrel with Alexander Pope.

Curll became a bookseller in 1705 and was set up in his own business by 1708. In 1716 he published *Court Poems* and suggested that Pope was one of the contributors. Pope, in an effort to suppress this publication, met Curll at a tavern, played a practical joke on him, and wrote the comic *A Full and True Account of a Horrid and Barbarous Revenge by Poison on the Body of Mr. Edmund Curll, Bookseller* (1716). Pope also satirized Curll in *The Dunciad* (1728). In 1716 and 1721 Curll was reprimanded at the bar of the House of Lords for his publications concerning its members and was convicted in 1725 and fined in 1728 for obscene publications. Indeed, his notoriety in this respect made "Curlicism" a synonym for literary indecency.

When Curll advertised his edition of *Mr. Pope's Literary Correspondence* (1735), Pope caused all the books to be seized. But the book was restored to Curll, and it has been proved that Pope deviously instigated Curll's publication of the letters in order to provide himself with an excuse for printing his own edition (1737). Curll's vast output included scores of standard biographies, histories, individual and collective literary works, and books of criticism.

Curnow \'kər-nō\, Allen, *in full* Thomas Allen Munro Curnow (b. June 17, 1911, Timaru, N.Z.) One of the major modern poets of New Zealand.

Curnow studied theology at the University of New Zealand. In 1933 his first book of poems, *Valley of Decision*, was published. During the 1930s and '40s Curnow worked as a journalist, and he taught English at the University of Auckland from 1951 to 1976.

Some of Curnow's early poems were inspired by a personal religious crisis. Other early poems tended towards political or social satire. As his work matured, Curnow's verse centered more on New Zealand, especially on its history; he sought the broader significance and universal metaphor in both personal and historical events.

Curnow's later collections include *A Small Room with Large Windows* (1962), *Trees, Effigies, Moving Objects* (1972), *You Will Know When You Get There: Poems 1979–81* (1982), and *Selected Poems, 1940–1989* (1990). He also wrote several plays and edited two books of poetry by New Zealand authors: *A Book of New Zealand Verse 1923–45* (1945; rev. ed., 1951) and *The Penguin Book of New Zealand Verse* (1960).

curtain-raiser \'kərt-ən-,rā-zər\   A short play, usually of one scene, that is presented before the main full-length drama.

curtal sonnet \'kər-təl\   A curtailed or contracted sonnet; specifically, a sonnet of 11 lines rhyming *abcabc dcbdc* or *abcabc dbcdc* with the last line a tail, or half a line. The term was used by Gerard Manley Hopkins to describe the form that he used in such poems as "Pied Beauty" and "Peace." *Curtal* is a now obsolete word meaning "shortened."

Curtis \'kər-təs\, George William (b. Feb. 24, 1824, Providence, R.I., U.S.—d. Aug. 31, 1892, Staten Island, N.Y.) American author, editor, and leader in civil-service reform.

Early in life Curtis spent two years at the Brook Farm community and school, later traveling in Europe, Egypt, and Palestine. In 1850 he joined the *New York Tribune*. As a result of his travels, he became a popular lecturer and published *Nile Notes of a Howadji* (1851) and *The Howadji in Syria* (1852). As an associate editor of *Putnam's Monthly Magazine* and author of "The Lounger" column in *Harper's Weekly* and "The Easy Chair" column in *Harper's Magazine*, he wrote prolifically. Many of his essays were collected, chiefly in *The Potiphar Papers* (1853), a satire on fashionable society, and *Prue and I* (1856).

In 1863 Curtis became political editor of *Harper's Weekly*, and from 1871 until his death he led the movement for civil-service reform.

Custom of the Country, The   A novel of manners by Edith WHARTON, published in 1913.

The Custom of the Country is the story of Undine Spragg, a young woman with social aspirations who convinces her nouveau riche parents to leave the Midwest and settle in New York. There she captures and marries a young man from New York's high society. This and each subsequent relationship she engineers prove unsatisfactory, chiefly because of her greed and great ambition.

cutback \'kət-,bak\   A shift from a chronological order in narration to events that took place earlier than those last presented. *Compare* FLASHBACK.

Cutpurse \'kət-,pərs\, Moll, *byname of* Mary *or* Moll Frith \,mäl-'frith\ (b. 1584?, London, Eng.—d. July 26, 1659, London)   The most notorious female member of 17th-century England's underworld.

London-born, she began her career as a pickpocket, or cutpurse, but after being caught four times, she assumed male attire and turned to highway robbery, until she was apprehended and jailed briefly at Newgate. She then achieved a safer and more profitable position in crime on opening a shop in Fleet Street, where for years she fenced stolen articles, receiving goods from thieves and catering to the privileged until she died a natural death, aged 74, of dropsy.

She was the subject of *The Roaring Girle* (performed 1604–10; published 1611), a play by Thomas Middleton and Thomas Dekker.

Cybele   *see* GREAT MOTHER OF THE GODS.

cyberpunk \'sīb-ər-,pəŋk\   A science-fiction subgenre comprising works characterized by countercultural antiheroes trapped in a dehumanized, high-tech future.

The word cyberpunk was coined by writer Bruce Bethke, who wrote a story with that title in 1982. He derived the term from the words *cybernetics*, the science of replacing human functions with computerized ones, and *punk*, the cacophonous music and nihilistic sensibility that developed in youth culture during the 1970s and '80s. Science-fiction editor Gardner Dozois is generally credited with popularizing the term.

The roots of cyberpunk extend past Bethke's tale to the technological fiction of the 1940s and '50s, to the writings of Samuel R. Delany and others who took up themes of alienation in a high-tech future, and to the criticism of Bruce Sterling, who in the 1970s called for science fiction that addressed the social and scientific concerns of the day. Not until the publication of William Gibson's 1984 novel *Neuromancer*, however, did cyberpunk take off as a movement within the genre. Other members of the cyberpunk school included Sterling, John Shirley, and Rudy Rucker.

cycle \'sī-kəl\ [Greek *kýklos,* literally, ring, circle]   **1.** A group or series of works (such as poems, plays, novels, or songs) that treat the same theme.   **2.** The complete series of poetic or prose narratives (usually of different authorship) that deal typically with the exploits of legendary heroes and heroines and their associates.

The term cyclic poems was first used in late classical times to refer to the independent poems that appeared after Homer to supplement his account of the Trojan War and the heroes' homecomings. Another classical Greek cycle is the "Theban" group, dealing with Oedipus and his descendants.

Medieval romance is classified into three major cycles: the Matter of Rome the great, the Matter of France, and the Matter of Britain. The Matter of Rome, a misnomer, refers to all tales derived from Latin classics. The Matter of France includes the stories of Charlemagne and his Twelve Noble Peers. The Matter of Britain refers to stories of King Arthur and his knights, the Tristram stories, and independent tales having an English background, such as *Guy of Warwick.*

Groups of mystery plays that were regularly performed in various towns in England were also known as cycles. (*See* CHESTER PLAYS; N-TOWN PLAYS; WAKEFIELD PLAYS; YORK PLAYS.)

The word cycle is also used for a series of poems, plays, or novels that are linked in theme, such as Émile Zola's Rougon-Macquart cycle of 20 novels (1871–93), which traces the history of a family.

cyclic poets   The post-Homeric poets who composed epics on the Trojan War and its heroes.

Cyclopaedia \,sī-klō-'pē-dē-ə\ (*in full* Cyclopaedia; or, An Universal Dictionary of Arts and Sciences)   A two-volume, alphabetically arranged encyclopedia compiled and edited by Ephraim CHAMBERS, published in 1728. The work treats the arts and sciences; names of persons or places are not included. The materials for seven additional volumes were published in two folio volumes in 1753 as a *Supplement* after having been reworked first by John Lewis Scott and then by John Hill following the death of Chambers.

Although Chambers declined an invitation in 1739 to publish a French edition of his *Cyclopaedia*, a projected French translation of the work became the starting point for *L'Encyclopédie*, the great 18th-century French encyclopaedia edited by the French philosopher and translator Denis Diderot and the French mathematician Jean d'Alembert.

Cyclops \'sī-,kläps\ *plural* Cyclopes \sī-'klō-pēz\ [Greek *Kýklōps*, from *kýklos* ring, circle, wheel + *ŏps* eye, face] In Greek mythology, one of a race of giants with a single eye in the middle of the forehead. In Homer the Cyclopes were cannibals, living a rude pastoral life in a distant land (traditionally Sicily); the *Odyssey* contains a well-known episode in which Odysseus escapes death by blinding the Cyclops Polyphemus. In Hesiod the Cyclopes were three sons of Uranus and Gaea—Arges, Brontes, and Steropes ("Bright," "Thunderer," "Lightener")—who forged the thunderbolts of Zeus.

Cyclops \'sī-,kläps\ (*Greek* Kyklōps) Satyr play by EURIPIDES, the only complete drama of its type that survives. The date of its first performance is unknown. The play's cowardly, lazy satyrs with their disgraceful old father Silenus are slaves of the man-eating one-eyed Cyclops Polyphemus in Sicily. Odysseus arrives, driven to Sicily by adverse weather, and eventually he succeeds (as in Homer's *Odyssey*) in blinding the Cyclops, thus enabling the captives to escape.

Cymbeline \'sim-bə-,lēn\ Comedy in five acts by William SHAKESPEARE, one of his later plays, first performed in 1609–10 and published in the First Folio of 1623.

Set in the pre-Christian Roman world, *Cymbeline* draws its main theme, that of a wager by a husband on his wife's fidelity, from Giovanni Boccaccio's *Decameron*. In the play Cymbeline, the king of Britain, decides that his daughter, Imogen, must marry his stepson. Imogen, however, is secretly married to Posthumus, who is banished when Cymbeline discovers the secret. Posthumus goes to Rome, where he meets Iachimo and makes a wager on Imogen's virtue. By trickery Iachimo obtains a token from Imogen that he uses to convince Posthumus of her infidelity. Posthumus sends a servant to kill Imogen, but the servant instead warns her of the plan and she disguises herself as a young boy and sets out for Rome. Losing her way in Wales, Imogen encounters Lord Belarius and her two brothers, whom she had believed dead (Belarius had kidnapped Cymbeline's sons in retribution for his unjust banishment). Posthumus (who has left Rome), Imogen, and her brothers are caught up in the advance of the Roman army, which has come to collect the tribute that Cymbeline has refused to pay to Rome. The forces clash and Cymbeline's army is victorious, largely because of the valor of Posthumus, Cymbeline's sons, and Belarius. A lengthy series of revelations and explanations ensues. Posthumus and Imogen are reunited, and Cymbeline is reconciled to them and to Belarius as well.

Cynddelw Brydydd Mawr \,kən-'thel-,ū-'brə-,dith-'maūr\ ("Cynddelw the Great Poet") (fl. 1155–1200) Outstanding Welsh poet of the 12th century, court bard to Madog ap Maredudd, prince of Powys (d. 1160), and then to Madog's enemy Owain Gwynedd, prince of Gwynedd (d. 1170). The approximately 50 extant poems ascribed to him are composed in the Welsh bardic tradition of deliberate archaism and include a small amount of religious verse and a large number of eulogies to the chief princes throughout Wales. Cynddelw seems, therefore, to have been the chief bard of all of Wales.

Cynewulf or **Cynwulf** or **Kynewulf** \'kin-ə-,wŭlf, 'kin-,wŭlf\ (fl. 8th or 9th century AD, Northumbria or Mercia [now in England]) Author of four Old English poems preserved in late 10th-century manuscripts. *Elene*, an account of the finding of

the True Cross by St. Helena, and *The Fates of the Apostles* are in the Vercelli Book. *The Ascension* (also called *Christ II*) is a lyrical version of a homily by Pope Gregory I that forms the second part of *Christ*, a trilogy by different authors. Both *The Ascension* and *Juliana*, a retelling of a Latin prose life of St. Juliana, are in the Exeter Book. An epilogue to each poem, asking for prayers for the author, contains runic characters representing the letters *c, y, n, (e), w, u, l, f*, which are thought to spell his name. A rhymed passage in the *Elene* proves that the author was from Northumbria or Mercia. Nothing is known of him outside his poems. The fact that all of his poems are based on Latin sources suggests that he may have been a learned cleric.

Although the poems do not have great power or originality, they are more than mere paraphrases. Imagery from everyday Old English life and from the Germanic epic tradition enlivens descriptions of battles and sea voyages. At the same time, the poet, a careful and skillful craftsman, consciously applies the principles of Latin rhetoric to achieve a clarity and orderly narrative progress that is quite unlike the confusion and circumlocution of the native English style.

Several poems not by Cynewulf are associated with him because of their subject matter. These include two lives of St. Guthlac and *Andreas*. Also in the "Cynewulf group" are several poems with Christ as their subject, of which the most important is "The Dream of the Rood."

cynghanedd \,kən-'hän-eth\ *plural* cynganeddion \,kən-ä-'neth-yŏn\ [Welsh, literally, consonance, harmony] In Welsh poetry, a strict, intricate system of alliteration and internal rhyme that is obligatory in the 24 strict meters of Welsh bardic verse.

Cynghanedd had developed by the 13th century from the prosodic devices of the early bards and was formally codified at the Caerwys Eisteddfod (assembly of bards) of 1524. The device thus became an obligatory adornment of poems in the strict (classical bardic) meters. There are four fundamental types of cynghanedd, but within these there are a number of refinements and variations. Characteristic of all but the simplest form is a rule of serial alliteration that requires the same consonants to occur in the same order in relation to the main stress in each half of a line, as in the following couplet:

Dwyn ei geiniog / dan gwynaw
d n g n d n g n

Rhoi angen un / rhewng y naw
rh ng n rh ng n

("He brings his penny home amid complaints and sets one person's need among the nine.")

cynocephalus \,sin-ō-'sef-ə-ləs, ,sī-nō-\ [Greek *Kynoképhaloi* (plural), from *kynoképhalos* dog-headed] One of a fabled race of dog-headed men alluded to in classical antiquity.

Cynthius *see* Giambattista GIRALDI.

Cynwulf *see* CYNEWULF.

Cyrano de Bergerac \'sir-ə-nō-də-'bər-zhə-,rak, *French* sē-rà-nō-də-ber-zhə-'ràk\ Verse drama in five acts by Edmond ROSTAND, performed in 1897 and published the following year.

Set in 17th-century Paris, the action revolves around the emotional problems of the noble, swashbuckling Cyrano, who, despite his many gifts, feels that no woman can ever love him because he has an enormous nose. Secretly in love with the lovely Roxane, Cyrano agrees to help his inarticulate rival, Christian, win her heart by allowing him to present Cyrano's love poems, speeches, and letters as his own work. Eventually Christian recognizes that Roxane loves him for Cyrano's qualities, not his own, and he asks Cyrano to confess his identity to Roxane; Christian then goes off to a battle that proves fatal. Cyrano remains silent about his own part in Roxane's courtship. As he is dying years later, he visits Roxane and recites one of the love letters. Roxane realizes that it is Cyrano she loves, and he dies content.

Cyrano de Bergerac was based only nominally on the 17th-century nobleman of the same name, known for his bold adventures and large nose.

Cyrano de Bergerac \sē-rȧ-'nō-də-ber-zhə-'rȧk\, Savinien (b. March 6, 1619, Paris, Fr.—d. July 28, 1655, Paris) French satirist and dramatist whose works combining political satire and science-fantasy inspired a number of later writers. He has been the basis of many romantic but unhistorical legends.

As a young man, Cyrano joined a company of guards and was wounded at the Siege of Arras in 1640. He gave up his military career in the following year to study under the philosopher and mathematician Pierre Gassendi. Under the influence of Gassendi's scientific theories and libertine philosophy, Cyrano wrote his two best-known works, *Histoire comique des états et empires de la lune* and *Histoire comique des états et empires du soleil* (*Voyages to the Moon and Sun*). These stories of imaginary journeys to the Moon and Sun, published posthumously in 1656 and 1662, satirize 17th-century religious and astronomical beliefs, which saw humanity and the Earth as the center of creation. Cyrano's plays include a tragedy, *La Mort d'Agrippine* (1654; "The Death of Agrippine"), which was suspected of blasphemy, and a comedy, *Le Pédant joué* (1654; "The Pedant Imitated"). As long as classicism was the established taste, *Le Pédant joué*, a colossal farce, was despised; but its liveliness appeals to modern readers as it did to Molière, who based two scenes of *Les Fourberies de Scapin* ("The Cheats of Scapin") on it.

Cyrano's *Lettres* show him to be a master of Baroque prose, marked by bold and original metaphors. His contemporaries regarded them as absurdly far-fetched, but they came to be esteemed in the 20th century as examples of the Baroque style.

Cyrene \sī-'rē-nē\ In Greek mythology, a nymph, daughter of Hypseus (king of the Lapiths) and Chlidanope (a Naiad). One day Cyrene wrestled a lion that had attacked her father's flocks. Apollo, who was watching, fell in love with her and carried her off from Mount Pelion, in Thessaly, to Libya. There he founded the city of Cyrene and made her its queen. Cyrene was the mother by Apollo of Aristaeus and Idmon the seer.

Cytherean \,sith-ə-'rē-ən\ Of or relating to the goddess Venus (or Aphrodite) or to the planet Venus. The word Cytherean is derived from the name of the island of Cythera, off the southern coast of Laconia in the Peloponnese.

cywydd \'kə-,with\ *plural* cywyddau \kə-'wə-,thī\ [Welsh] A Welsh verse form, a short ode in rhyming couplets (or occasionally triplets) using cynghanedd (a complex system of alliteration and internal rhyme). Especially, a verse that consists of couplets of seven-syllable lines with varying cynghanedd and terminal rhymes that fall alternately on accented and on unaccented syllables.

Developed in the 14th century in South Wales by Dafydd ap Gwilym, the cywydd shows affinities with forms used by the earlier *bardd teulu* ("bard of the [king's] war band"), the second grade in the Welsh bardic system, and with those of the French trouvère and jongleur. It was the leading Welsh verse form from the 14th to the early 17th century. It was revived, with other bardic forms, by the classical school of Welsh poets in the mid-18th century and again in the 19th century. It remains in use by those modern Welsh poets who prefer strict (*i.e.*, classical) forms to the free meters that are derived from Welsh folk song and from English verse.

Czechowicz \che-'ḳȯ-vēch\, Józef (b. March 15, 1903, Lublin, Poland, Russian Empire—d. Sept. 9, 1939, Lublin) Polish poet noted for his mixture of avant-garde technique with traditional lyricism and folk rhythms.

The son of a poor family, Czechowicz was educated at a teachers college. His style is ostentatiously modern and remarkable for its verbal economy, but his poems remain expressive because of their extensive use of metaphor. His first collection of poems, *Kamień* (1927; "Stone"), was followed by *Dzień jak codzień* (1930; "A Day Like Every Day"), *Ballada z tamtej strony* (1932; "A Ballad from Beyond"), *W błyskawicy* (1934; "In Lightning"), *Nic więcej* (1936; "Nothing More"), and *Nuta człowiecza* (1939; "A Human Note"). They are characterized by a tone of tenderness underlaid by anxiety and are filled with dreams and myths.

His work is also imbued with "catastrophism," the pervasive presentiments of a general conflagration and of his own death. Czechowicz, who had lived in Warsaw from 1930, was evacuated immediately after the German invasion of 1939 to his native Lublin but was killed there in a Luftwaffe bombardment. He is sometimes associated with Awangarda Krakowska, an avant-garde Polish literary movement based in Kraków.

Dąbrowska or **Dombrowska** \dȯⁿm-'brȯf-skȧ\, Maria, *original name* Marja Szumska \'shüm-skȧ\ (b. Oct. 6, 1889, Russów, near Kalisz, Poland, Russian Empire—d. May 19, 1965, Warsaw, Pol.) Polish author and literary critic who is especially known for her epic narrative *Noce i dnie*, 4 vol. (1932–34; "Nights and Days"), popularly and critically considered one of the best works of Polish prose.

Educated in Poland and Belgium and at the University of Lausanne in Switzerland, Dąbrowska lived in France and Britain before World War II. In 1909 she began to write articles for Polish newspapers on political and economic reform and on the cooperative movement. Her first short story, "Janek," was published in 1914. She published three collections of short stories during the 1920s, including *Ludzie stamtąd: Cykl opowieści* (1926; "Folks from Over Yonder: A Cycle of Tales"), inspired by her lifelong sympathy with the peasantry. A later volume of stories, *Gwiazda zaranna* (1955; "The Morning Star"), which contained the much-anthologized story "Na wsi wesele" ("A Village Wedding"), was published in English as *A Village Wedding* in 1957.

In 1932 Dąbrowska produced the first volume of her classic four-part novel *Noce i dnie*. Often compared to other acclaimed family sagas (such as Thomas Mann's *Buddenbrooks*), *Noce i dnie* relates the story of Bogumil and Barbara from courtship through their marriage and the birth of their children to old age and Bogumil's death (spanning the years 1863–1914). Dąbrowska's theme of the human potential for development within uncertain circumstances is subtly and profoundly wrought.

In addition to her masterwork and short stories, Dąbrowska also wrote two historical plays and a number of essays, including a series of critical essays on the Polish-born English author Joseph Conrad, *Szkice o Konradzie* (1959; "Essays on Conrad"), and she translated many foreign-language works, notably the diary of the 17th-century Englishman Samuel Pepys, into Polish.

She continued to be active in political and social issues throughout her life; after her death she was given a state funeral. *Przygody człowieka myślącego* ("Adventures of a Thinker"), a novel she left unfinished at her death, was published in 1970.

Dach \ˈdäk\, Simon (b. July 29, 1605, Memel, East Prussia [now in Lithuania]—d. April 15, 1659, Königsberg [now Kaliningrad, Russia]) Prussian poet who was best known as the leader of the 17th-century Königsberg circle of middle-class poets. The Königsberg circle is important in early Baroque literature for reflecting the stress and turmoil of the period of the Thirty Years' War.

Dach became a professor of poetry at the University of Königsberg in 1639. His occasional poetry, which commemorated the births, deaths, and marriages of the Königsberg bourgeoisie, is characterized by a sweet simplicity and musicality. He went beyond this conventional manner, however, in poems with elements from folk songs and in religious poetry.

Dacier \dȧs-ˈyā\, André (b. April 6, 1651, Castres, Fr.—d. Sept. 18, 1722, Paris) Classical scholar and translator who with his wife, Anne, was responsible for some of the famous Delphin series of editions of Latin classics.

Dacier studied at Saumur with the humanist Tanneguy Lefèbvre, whose daughter Anne he married in 1683. He was appointed keeper of the library of the Louvre and was elected to the Académie Française in 1695, becoming its permanent secretary in 1713. His pedantic, somewhat uninspired works include translations of Horace, Aristotle's *Poetics*, Plato's dialogues, Sophocles' *Oedipus* and *Electra*, and Plutarch's *Parallel Lives*. For the Delphin series, he translated works by Festus and Flaccus.

Dacier \dȧs-ˈyā\, Anne, *original surname* Lefèbvre \lə-ˈfevr\ (b. 1654, Preuilly-sur-Claise, Fr.—d. Aug. 17, 1720, Paris) Classical commentator, translator, and editor, famous throughout Europe for her translations of the *Iliad* and the *Odyssey* and for her work, with her husband, André Dacier, on the famous Delphin series of editions of Latin classics.

Anne Dacier was the daughter of a French humanist, Tanneguy Lefèbvre, who educated her and launched her in the field of classical studies. In 1683 she married one of her father's students, André Dacier (also engaged in classical studies and translations). Prior to her marriage, Dacier had already produced notable translations, and her translations in prose of the *Iliad* (1699) and the *Odyssey* (1708) brought her renown throughout Europe. It was partly through these translations that a literary dispute known since as the *querelle des anciens et des modernes* arose as a contest of the merits of classical as opposed to contemporary authors. One of her important works on the subject was *Des Causes de la corruption de goût* (1714; "Of the Causes of the Corruption of Taste").

dactyl \ˈdak-təl\ [Greek *dáktylos*, literally, finger; from the fact that the syllables of the metrical foot are three in number like the joints of the finger] In prosody, a metrical foot of three syllables, the first being stressed and the last two being unstressed (as in "take her up tenderly"). A falling cadence, the dactyl is scanned — ∪ ∪ (long, short, short) in classical prosody or ′ ∪ ∪ (stressed, unstressed, unstressed) in English prosody. The scansion may also be written 6oo. *Compare* ANAPEST.

Probably the oldest and most common meter in classical verse is the dactylic hexameter, the meter of Homer's *Iliad* and *Odyssey* and of other ancient epics. Dactylic meters are fairly rare in English verse, one difficulty being that the prolonged use of the dactyl tends to distort normal word accent, giving the lines a jerky movement. They appeared with regularity only after poets such as Robert Browning and Algernon Charles Swinburne successfully used the form in the 19th century. Dactylic rhythm produces a lilting movement as in the following example from Lord Byron's *Bride of Abydos*:

′ ∪ ∪ ′ ∪ ∪ ′ ∪ ∪ ′ ∪
Know ye the | land where the | cypress and | myrtle.

This line exhibits catalexis, the common variation of omitting an unstressed syllable at the end of a line.

dactylo-epitrite \ˌdak-tə-lō-ˈep-i-ˌtrīt\ In classical prosody, the metrical compound associated particularly with the poets Pindar and Bacchylides. It consists of various combinations of the hemiepes (— ∪ ∪ | — ∪ ∪ | —) and the cretic (— ∪ —), often linked by an anceps syllable.

Dada \ˈdä-dä\ or **Dadaism** \ˈdä-dä-ˌiz-əm\ [French, from *dada*, child's word for a horse] Nihilistic movement in the arts that flourished chiefly in France, Switzerland, and Germany from 1916 to about 1920 and that was based on principles of deliberate irrationality, anarchy, and cynicism and the rejection of laws of beauty and social organization.

The most widely accepted account of the movement's naming concerns a meeting held in 1916 at Hugo Ball's Cabaret (Café) Voltaire in Zürich, during which a paper knife inserted into a French–German dictionary pointed to the word *dada*; this word was seized upon by the group as appropriate for their anti-aesthetic creations and protest activities, which were engendered by disgust for bourgeois values and despair over World War I.

In the United States the movement was centered in New York at Alfred Stieglitz's gallery, "291," and at the studio of the Walter Arensbergs. Dada-like activities, arising independently but paralleling those in Zürich, were engaged in by such chiefly visual artists as Man Ray and Francis Picabia. Both through their art and through such publications as *The Blind Man*, *Rongwrong*, and *New York Dada*, the artists attempted to demolish current aesthetic standards. Traveling between the United States and Europe, Picabia became a link between the Dada groups in New York City, Zürich, and Paris; his Dada periodical, *291*, was published in Barcelona, New York City, Zürich, and Paris from 1917 through 1924.

In 1917 the Dada movement was transmitted to Berlin, where it took on a more political character. The Berlin artists, too, issued Dada publications: *Club Dada*, *Der Dada*, *Jedermann sein eigner Fussball* ("Everyman His Own Football"), and *Dada Almanach*.

In Paris Dada took on a literary emphasis under one of its founders, the poet Tristan TZARA. Most notable among Dada pamphlets and reviews was *Littérature* (published 1919–24), which contained writings by André Breton, Louis Aragon, Philippe Soupault, and Paul Éluard. After 1922, however, Dada faded and many Dadaists grew interested in SURREALISM.

Daddy \'dad-ē\ Poem by Sylvia PLATH, published posthumously in 1965 in the collection ARIEL. One of Plath's most famous poems, "Daddy" was completed during a brief prolific period of writing before her suicide in February 1963. In images that progress from domestic to demonic, the poem confronts a woman's conflicting feelings about her father's death when she was a child.

Dadié \dắd-'yắ\, Bernard Binlin (b. 1916, Assini, Côte d'Ivoire) Ivorian poet, dramatist, novelist, and administrator whose works have been inspired both by traditional themes from Africa's past and by a need to assert the modern African's desire for equality, dignity, and freedom.

Dadié received his higher education in Senegal, where his involvement in a folklore and drama movement first encouraged him to write plays. This interest continued when he returned to Côte d'Ivoire in 1947; it led to his work as teacher, writer, founder of a National Drama Studio, and eventually minister of culture (from 1961) for Côte d'Ivoire.

His first published work was a collection of poems, *Afrique debout* (1950; "Africa Upright"), followed by two volumes of stories, *Légendes africaines* (1954; "African Legends") and *Le Pagne noir* (1955; *The Black Cloth*). Dadié's love of Africa's oral traditions caused him to collect and publish several more volumes of legends, fables, folktales, and proverbs, which he felt provided the moral backbone of African society. The autobiographical novel *Climbié* (1956) re-creates the social milieu of colonial Côte d'Ivoire. *Un Nègre à Paris* (1959), his examination of Parisian society, is presented in epistolary form. Two later novels, *Patron de New York* (1964) and *La Ville où nul ne meurt* (1968; *The City Where No One Dies*), satirize American and Roman life and society. Between 1967 and 1970 he published another verse collection and several plays, including *Monsieur Thôgô-gnini* (1970). His later works include the novel *Commandant Taurcault et ses nègres* (1980; "Commander Taurcault and His Negroes") and *Les Contes de Koutou-As-Samala* (1982; "The Stories of Koutou-As-Samala"), a book of short stories.

Daedalus \'ded-ə-les, 'dēd-\ ("Skillfully Wrought") In Greek mythology, an architect and sculptor who was said to have built, among other things, the Labyrinth for King Minos of Crete. Daedalus later fell out of favor with Minos and was imprisoned. He fashioned wings of wax and feathers for himself and for his son Icarus and escaped to Sicily. Icarus, however, flew too near the Sun, and when his wings melted, he fell into the sea and drowned. The island on which his body was washed ashore was later named Icaria.

The Greeks of the historic age attributed to Daedalus buildings and statues whose origins were lost in the past. A phase of early Greek art, Daedalic sculpture, has been named for him.

Dafydd ab Edmwnd \'dăv-ith-,ăb-'ed-,mûnd\ (fl. *c.* 1450–97) Poet who authoritatively classified and defined the 24 Welsh bardic meters (announced at the Carmarthen eisteddfod, or poets' assembly, in 1451). A master of bardic forms, he wrote elegant and technically perfect love lyrics, eulogies, and elegies. His works are collected in *Gwaith Dafydd ab Edmwnd* (1914), edited by Thomas Roberts.

Dafydd ap Gwilym \'dăv-ith-,ăp-'gwil-im\ (b. *c.* 1320, probably at Brogynin, Cardiganshire, Wales—d. *c.* 1380, Strata Florida, Cardiganshire) Poet generally considered one of the greatest figures in Welsh literature. He introduced into a formalistic poetic tradition an authenticity, freshness, and naturalness hitherto unknown.

Little is known of Dafydd's life, except that he was a member of an aristocratic family from South Wales and that he visited Anglesey and Caernarvonshire. His *awdlau* (odes) and cywyd-dau (rhymed couplets) show that he was trained in the Welsh bardic art and connect him historically with the native "poets of the princes." His use of certain poetic conventions as well as of looser poetic constructions and vocabulary probably reflect the influence of the troubadours and wandering scholars. His outstanding poems are elaborate descriptions of the beauties of nature and of love.

Dafydd Nanmor \'dăv-ith-'năn-,môr\ (b. before 1440, Nanmor, Merioneth, Wales—d. *c.* 1480, Whitland, Carmarthenshire?) Welsh poet, master of the cywydd form (characterized by rhyming couplets), whose poems express his belief in tradition and aristocracy. Many of his poems reflect his support of the political aspirations of the Tudors; others are simple and sincere love poems. "Llio's Hair" and "Maiden's Elegy" are considered to be his finest cywyddau. *The Poetical Works of Dafydd Nanmor*, edited by Thomas Roberts and Ifor Williams, was published in 1923.

Dagerman \'dăg-ər-,măn\, Stig (b. Oct. 5, 1923, Älvkarleby, Swed.—d. Nov. 4, 1954, Enebyberg, near Stockholm) Swedish short-story writer, novelist, and playwright whose works were representative of the sense of existential anguish prevalent in the years following World War II.

Dagerman worked as an editor of a syndicalist newspaper. He was also associated with the literary magazines *40-tal* (1947–48) and *Prisma* (1948–50). He scored a critical success with his play *Den dödsdömde* (1948; "The Condemned"), which, together with his novels *Ormen* (1945; "The Serpent") and *De dömdas ö* (1946; *Island of the Doomed*), concerns the subject of terror and the need to face it directly in order to overcome it. All three are written in a highly expressionistic style. His novel *Bränt barn* (1948; *A Burnt Child*) is a psychological study of a young man's relationship with his father and the father's mistress. Dagerman's other writings include a collection of stories, *Nattens lekar* (1947; *The Games of Night*); *Tysk höst* (1947; *German Autumn*), a nonfiction work on postwar Germany; and the drama *I skuggan av Mart* (1949; "In Mart's Shadow"). His last book, the prose work *Tusen år hos Gud* (1954; "A Thousand Years with God"), was published posthumously, after Dagerman's suicide.

Dahl \'däl\, Roald (b. Sept. 13, 1916, Llandaff, Wales—d. Nov. 23, 1990, Oxford, Eng.) British writer popular for his ingenious, irreverent children's books and adult horror stories.

Dahl avoided a university education and joined an expedition to Newfoundland, Can. After working from 1937 to 1939 in Dar es Salaam, Tanganyika (now in Tanzania), he enlisted in the Royal Air Force when war broke out. He served with his squadron in Greece and then Syria before a stint as assistant air attaché in Washington, D.C., from 1942 to 1943. There the novelist C.S. Forester encouraged him to write about his most exciting RAF adventures, which were published by the *Saturday Evening Post*. Dahl's life was studded with tragedy: his father and sister died when he was three; he suffered brutal treatment in school; one of his children died of measles, and another was permanently injured as an infant; and his first wife, actress Patricia Neal, suffered a series of debilitating strokes.

Dahl's first book, *The Gremlins* (1943), was written for Walt Disney and later became a popular movie. He achieved bestseller status with *Someone Like You* (1953; rev. 1961), a collection of stories for adults, which was followed by *Kiss, Kiss* (1959). His children's book *James and the Giant Peach* (1961) was a popular success, as was *Charlie and the Chocolate Factory* (1964), which was made into the film *Willy Wonka and the Chocolate Factory* (1971). Dahl also wrote several scripts for films, among them *You Only Live Twice* (1967) and *Chitty Chitty Bang Bang* (1968).

Daisy Miller \'dā-zē-'mil-ər\ Novel by Henry JAMES, published in *Cornhill Magazine* in 1878 and published in book form in 1879.

The book's title character is a young American woman traveling in Europe with her mother. There she is courted by Frederick Forsyth Winterbourne, an American living abroad. In her innocence, Daisy is compromised by her friendship with an Italian man. Her behavior shocks Winterbourne and the other Americans living in Italy, and they shun her. Only after she dies does Winterbourne recognize that her actions reflected her spontaneous, genuine, and unaffected nature and that his suspicions of her were unwarranted. Like others of James's works, *Daisy Miller* uses the contrast between American innocence and European sophistication as a powerful tool with which to examine social conventions.

Dalin \dä-'lēn\, Olof von (b. Aug. 29, 1708, Vinberg, Swed.—d. Aug. 12, 1763, Stockholm) Writer and historian who wrote the first easily readable and popular Swedish works.

Dalin was educated at the University of Lund. He became the center of Swedish literary attention when he was discovered to be the author of the first literary periodical to appear in Sweden, the extremely popular *Then swänska Argus* (1732–34), which was modeled on Joseph Addison's *Tatler* and *Spectator*. This periodical helped introduce the ideas of the Enlightenment into Sweden, but its language and literary style were of even greater importance; it is regarded as ushering in the age of modern Swedish prose. Neither of Dalin's two dramatic works nor his rather ambitious epic poem, *Swenska friheten* (1742; "Swedish Liberty"), proved very successful. His best and most popular work is the allegory *Sagan om hästen* (1740; "The Tale About the Horse"), in which a horse represents the Swedish people and its masters represent the various Swedish kings. Of his folk ballads, which indirectly conveyed his political views, the best known is *Hattvisan* ("The Hat Ballad"). Dalin's great interest was history; he wrote three volumes of a lively *Svea rikes historia* (1747–62; "History of the Swedish Kingdom").

Dallan Forgaill \'dä-,län-'fòr-,gĭlʸ\ (fl. late 6th century AD) Chief Irish poet of his time, probably the author of the *Amra Choluim Chille*, or *Elegy of St. Columba*, one of the earliest Irish poems of any length.

Nothing certain is known of Dallan Forgaill's life. According to the preface to the *Elegy of St. Columba*, he met Columba in 575 at the assembly of Druim Cetta, where Columba successfully defended the fili (professional bards) against charges of demanding excessive payment. The poem was composed after Columba's death in 597 in the alliterative, accentual poetic form of the period, in stanzas of irregular length. It has survived in the language of later transcripts; its earliest extant copies are in *The Book of the Dun Cow* (c. 1100) and in the *Liber hymnorum*, a collection begun in 860 of Irish and Latin hymns. The obscure text is accompanied by extensive glosses and commentary.

Daly \'dā-lē\, Augustin, *in full* John Augustin Daly (b. July 20, 1838, Plymouth, N.C., U.S.—d. June 7, 1899, Paris, Fr.) American playwright and theatrical manager whose companies were major features of the New York and London stage.

Beginning in 1859, Daly was drama critic for several New York newspapers. *Leah the Forsaken*, adapted from a German play in 1862, was Daly's first success as a playwright. His first important original play, *Under the Gaslight* (1867), was popular for years. In 1869 he formed his own company and later developed such outstanding actresses as Fanny Davenport and Maude Adams. Daly's best play, *Horizon* (1871), drew heavily upon the Western-type characters of Bret Harte and gave impetus to the development of a drama based on American themes and characters rather than European models. *Divorce* (1871), another of his better plays, ran for 200 performances. After opening Daly's Theatre in New York City in 1879, with a company headed by John Drew and Ada Rehan, he confined himself to adaptations and management; in 1893 he opened Daly's Theatre in London.

Damastes *see* PROCRUSTES.

Damocles \'dam-ə-klēz\ (fl. 4th century BC) A courtier of Dionysius the Elder of Syracuse, Sicily (tyrant from 405 to 367 BC), known to history through the legend of the "Sword of Damocles."

According to the legend, when Damocles spoke in extravagant terms of his sovereign's happiness, Dionysius invited him to a sumptuous banquet and seated him beneath a naked sword that was suspended from the ceiling by a single thread. Thus did the tyrant demonstrate that the fortunes of those who hold power are as precarious as the predicament in which he had placed his guest. The story is related in Cicero's *Tusculanae disputationes*.

Damon and Pythias \'dā-mən . . . 'pith-ē-əs\ In Greek legend, a celebrated pair of friends who came to signify the willingness to sacrifice oneself for the sake of a friend. Versions of the tale differ, but in the best known of them, Damon, a Sicilian, pledges his life for that of his friend Pythias, who has been condemned to death by Dionysius of Syracuse. Dionysius is so moved by this ultimate act of friendship that he releases both men.

Dana \'dā-nə\, Richard Henry (b. Aug. 1, 1815, Cambridge, Mass., U.S.—d. Jan. 6, 1882, Rome, Italy) American lawyer and author of the popular autobiographical narrative *Two Years Before the Mast*.

Dana withdrew from Harvard College when measles weakened his eyesight, and he shipped to California as a sailor in August 1834 to regain his health. After voyaging among California's ports, he rounded Cape Horn, returned home in 1836, and reentered Harvard.

In 1840, the year of his admission to the bar, he published *Two Years Before the Mast*, a personal narrative presenting "the life of a common sailor at sea as it really is" and showing the abuses endured by his fellow sailors. In 1841 he published *The Seaman's Friend* (U.K. title, *The Seaman's Manual*), which became known as an authoritative guide to the legal rights and duties of seamen. Against vigorous opposition in Boston, Dana gave free legal aid to blacks captured under the Fugitive Slave Law. In 1863, while serving as U.S. attorney for Massachusetts, he won before the U.S. Supreme Court the case of the *Amy Warwick*, securing the right of Union forces to blockade Southern ports without giving the Confederate states an international status as belligerents.

His scholarly edition of Henry Wheaton's *Elements of International Law* (1866) precipitated a lawsuit by an earlier editor. The charges of plagiarism that resulted from the suit contributed to Dana's defeat in the congressional election of 1868 and caused the Senate to refuse his confirmation when President Ulysses S. Grant named him minister to Great Britain in 1876. Among Dana's other works are *To Cuba and Back* (1859) and the posthumously published *Speeches in Stirring Times* (1910) and *An Autobiographical Sketch* (1953).

Danaus \'dan-ā-əs\ In Greek legend, son of Belus, king of Egypt, and twin brother of Aegyptus. Driven out of Egypt by his brother, Danaus fled with his 50 daughters (the Danaïds) to Argos, where he became king. Soon thereafter the 50 sons of Aegyptus arrived in Argos, and Danaus was forced to consent to their marriage with his daughters; however, he commanded each daughter to slay her husband on the marriage night. They all obeyed except Hypermestra, who spared Lynceus. In punishment for their crime the Danaïds were condemned to the endless task of filling with water a vessel that had no bottom. (According to another story, Lynceus slew Danaus and his daughters and seized the throne of Argos.) The murder of the sons of Aegyptus by their wives is thought to represent the drying up of the rivers and springs of Argolis in summer.

dance of death *also called* danse macabre \'däns-mə-'käb, -'kä-brə, -'kä-bər\ *or* skeleton dance. Medieval allegorical concept of the all-conquering and equalizing power of death, expressed in the drama, poetry, music, and visual arts of western Europe mainly in the late Middle Ages. Strictly speaking, it is a literary or pictorial representation of a procession or dance of both living and dead figures, the living arranged in order of their rank, from pope and emperor to child, clerk, and hermit, and the dead leading them to the grave. The dance of death had its origins in late 13th- or early 14th-century poems that combined the essential ideas of the inevitability and the impartiality of death. The concept probably gained momentum in the late Middle Ages as a result of the obsession with death inspired by the Black Death in the mid-14th century and the devastation of the Hundred Years' War (1337–1453) between France and England.

The earliest known example of the fully developed dance of death concept was a series of paintings (1424–25) with explanatory verses painted on the walls of a building in the Cimetière des Innocents in Paris. The work was destroyed in 1699, but a reproduction can be seen in the woodcuts of the Paris printer Guy Marchant (1485), and the explanatory verses have been preserved in a translation by the English poet John Lydgate.

The proliferation of literary versions of the dance of death included a 15th-century Spanish masterpiece, the poem "La danza general de la muerte," which was inspired by the verses at the Innocents and by several German poems. Though depictions of the dance of death declined after the 16th century, much later literature, including works by Miguel de Cervantes, J.W. von Goethe, Robert Browning, Thomas Beddoes, Hugo von Hofmannsthal, August Strindberg, Federico García Lorca, and W.H. Auden, contains references to the theme.

Dance to the Music of Time, A Twelve-volume series of novels by Anthony POWELL, published from 1951 to 1975. The series—which includes *A Question of Upbringing* (1951), *A Buyer's Market* (1952), *The Acceptance World* (1955), *At Lady Molly's* (1957), *Casanova's Chinese Restaurant* (1960), *The Kindly Ones* (1962), *The Valley of Bones* (1964), *The Soldier's Art* (1966), *The Military Philosophers* (1968), *Books Do Furnish a Room* (1971), *Temporary Kings* (1973), and *Hearing Secret Harmonies* (1975)—traces events in the lives of a number of characters from Britain's upper classes and bohemia, following them from adolescence in the 1920s to senescence in the 1970s.

Powell found inspiration for the title and form of his opus in Nicolas Poussin's painting "A Dance to the Music of Time," which depicts the Four Seasons dancing to music played by Father Time. The novels focus on social behavior; all characters are dealt with objectively, as they would wish to appear to outside observers. Personality and motivation are revealed through minute and subtle analysis of disconnected incidents. Nicholas Jenkins, a nonparticipant who is secure in his own values, narrates much of the action of people obsessed with power, style, creativity, and public image.

Dancourt \dä⁼-'kür\, Florent Carton (b. Nov. 1, 1661, Fontainebleau, Fr.—d. Dec. 7, 1725, Courcelles-le-Roi, near Orléans) Actor and playwright who created the comedy of manners in the French theater.

In 1680 Dancourt married the actress Thérèse de La Thorillière. They debuted with the Comédie-Française in 1685, beginning an association that flourished for 33 years. Dancourt's skill as a comic actor and playwright gained him the favor of Louis XIV and established him as the successor to Molière.

Like Molière, Dancourt was an expert at portraying current social types, and his comedies ridiculed the decadence and social pretenses of the period. Written in prose, they were peopled by characters whose vices were made hilarious by Dancourt's witty, effortless dialogue and his ability to make the most of a comic situation. His best-known work, *Le Chevalier à la mode* (1687; "The Modish Cavalier"), deals with a fortune hunter's simultaneous courtship of three women. Other plays are *Les Bourgeoises à la mode* (1692; "The Fashionable Ladies") and *Les Bourgeoises de qualité* (1700; "The Ladies of Quality"), in which middle-class women ape the nobility; and *La Maison de campagne* (1688; "The Country House"), which makes fun of crude provincial manners.

Some of the more than 50 plays printed under Dancourt's name were collaborations with other writers.

Daṇḍin \'dən-,din\ (fl. late 6th and early 7th centuries, India) Indian Sanskrit writer of prose romances and expounder on poetics. Scholars attribute to him with certainty only two works: the *Daśakumāracarita*, translated in 1927 as *The Adventures of the Ten Princes*, and the *Kāvyādarśa* ("Mirror of Poetry").

The *Daśakumāracarita* tells of the vicissitudes of 10 princes in their pursuit of love and power. The work is imbued both with realistic portrayals of human vice and with magic, including the intervention of deities in human affairs. The *Kāvyādarśa* defines the ideals of style and sentiment appropriate to each genre of kavya (a type of courtly epic).

dandyism \'dan-dē-,iz-əm\ A literary and artistic style of the latter part of the 19th century marked by artificiality and excessive refinement.

Dangerous Liaisons Novel by Pierre Choderlos de LACLOS, first published in 1782 as *Les Liaisons dangereuses*. The work, also translated as *Dangerous Acquaintances*, is considered one of the earliest examples of the psychological novel.

Laclos' first novel, *Dangerous Liaisons* caused an immediate sensation. Written in epistolary form, it deals with the seducer Valmont and his accomplice, Madame de Merteuil, who surpasses him in decadence and evil. Both take unscrupulous delight in their victims' misery, their pleasure being proportional to the difficulty of the conquest. Mme de Merteuil, secretly seeking vengeance for Valmont's earlier rejection of her, arranges for Valmont's death at her current lover's hand. She is herself destroyed in the end: ostracized for her machinations, disfigured by smallpox, and left in financial ruin.

Daniel \'dan-yəl\ Biblical character, a wise and pious Jew who lived in the 6th century BC at the court of Nebuchadrezzar II (Nebuchadnezzar) during the period of the Babylonian exile. His visions were recorded in the Old Testament Book of Daniel.

With divine intervention, Daniel interpreted the meaning of the king's dreams of a great image, made of four metals, that was shattered by a stone cut supernaturally and of a tree reduced to a stump. To Belshazzar, Daniel interpreted the meaning of the Aramaic writing on a wall, "*mene, mene, tekel, upharsin*," as evidence of God's decision to destroy the city. In another instance, the king responded to the mob's envy of Daniel by throwing him into a den of hungry lions. Tradition has it that Daniel emerged unscathed on the seventh day.

Daniel \'dan-yəl\, Samuel (b. 1562?, Taunton, Somerset, Eng.—d. 1619, near Beckington) English contemplative poet, marked in both verse and prose by his philosophic sense of history.

Daniel entered Oxford in 1581. After publishing a translation in 1585 for his first patron, Sir Edward Dymoke, he secured a post with the English ambassador at Paris; he then traveled in Italy. After 1592 he returned to Dymoke's service and later became a tutor. In 1604 Queen Anne chose him to write a masque, *The Vision of the Twelve Goddesses*, in which she danced. She awarded him the right to license plays for the boy actors at the Blackfriars Theatre and a position as a groom, and later gentleman, of her privy chamber.

Edmund Spenser praised Daniel for his first book of poems, *Delia*, published with a romance, *The Complaint of Rosamond*, in 1592. Daniel published 50 sonnets in this book, and more were added in later editions. *The Civile Warres* (1595–1609), a verse history of the Wars of the Roses, influenced William Shakespeare's *Richard II* and *Henry IV*.

Daniel's finest poem is probably "Musophilus: Containing a Generall Defence of Learning," dedicated to Fulke Greville. His *Defence of Ryme*, a critical essay answering Thomas Campion's *Observations in the Art of English Poesie*, was published in 1603. Fame and honor are the subjects of "Ulisses and the Syren" (1605) and of *A Funerall Poeme upon the Earle of Devonshire* (1606). Daniel defended himself against a charge of sympathizing with the Earl of Essex in *The Tragedie of Philotas* (1605). His other masques include *The Queenes Arcadia* (1606), a pastoral tragicomedy in the Italian fashion, and *Tethys' Festival* (1610). Daniel's last pastoral was *Hymens Triumph* (1615). He also wrote *The Collection of the Historie of England* (1612–18) as far as the reign of Edward III.

Daniel \də-nʸi-'elʸ\, Yuly Markovich, *pseudonym* Nikolay Arzhak \ˌär-'zhàk\ (b. Nov. 15, 1925, Moscow, Russian S.F.S.R., U.S.S.R.—d. Dec. 30, 1988, Moscow)   Soviet poet and short-story writer who was convicted of anti-Soviet slander in a sensational 1966 trial that marked the beginning of a new era of literary repression in the Soviet Union.

Daniel served in the Soviet Army from 1943 to 1944, when he was seriously wounded. He graduated from Moscow Province Teachers Training College in 1951. Daniel then taught Russian literature from 1951 to 1957 and worked as a translator in an effort to create a unified body of literature from the languages of the various Soviet nationalities. During this time he smuggled several anti-Stalinist short stories to Paris, where they were published under the pseudonym Nikolay Arzhak as *Govorit Moskva* (1962; *This Is Moscow Speaking*). In the title story the Soviet government declares murder legal on "Public Murder Day"—a day that passes uneventfully, underscoring the apathy of the Soviet citizenry.

At Daniel and Andrey D. Sinyavsky's four-day joint trial, which was closed to the public, no evidence was allowed on their behalf; dozens of Soviet and Western writers protested the convictions. After serving five years of hard labor (1966–70), Daniel worked as a translator in Kaluga and Moscow and published a bilingual collection entitled *Tyuremnye stikhi/Prison Poems* (1971). In 1988 several of his poems were published in the Soviet Union for the first time.

Daniel \'dan-yəl\ the Pilgrim (Daniyl Palomnik), *also called* Daniel of Kiev \'kē-ˌef, -ˌev, -əf\ (Daniyl Kievsky) (fl. 12th century)   The earliest known Russian travel writer, whose account of his pilgrimage to the Holy Land is the earliest surviving record in Russian of such a trip.

Abbot of a Russian monastery, Daniel visited Palestine probably between 1106 and 1108. His narrative begins at Constantinople; from there he traveled along the west and south coasts of Asia Minor to Cyprus and the Holy Land. Despite his credulity and errors in topography and measurement, his description of Jerusalem, where he lived for more than a year, is detailed and accurate. His account of Easter services there sheds light on the liturgy and ritual of the time. Daniel made three excursions—to the Dead Sea, Hebron, and Damascus, where he claims to have accompanied Baldwin I, the king of the crusader state of Jerusalem. There are 76 manuscripts extant of his account, only five of which are dated earlier than 1500.

Daniel Deronda \'dan-yəl-də-'rän-də\   Novel by George ELIOT, published in eight parts in 1876. It is notable for its exposure of Victorian anti-Semitism. The novel builds on the contrast between Mirah Cohen, a poor Jewish girl, and the upper-class Gwendolen Harleth, who marries for money and regrets it. The less convincingly realized hero, Daniel, after discovering that he is Jewish, marries Mirah and departs for Palestine to establish a home for his people. The warm picture of the Cohen family evoked grateful praise from Jewish readers, but the best part of *Daniel Deronda* is the keen analysis of Gwendolen's character, which seems to many critics the peak of George Eliot's achievement.

D'Annunzio \dän-'nünt-sē-ō\, Gabriele (b. March 12, 1863, Pescara, Italy—d. March 1, 1938, Gardone Riviera, on Lake

Brown Brothers

Garda)   Italian poet, novelist, dramatist, short-story writer, journalist, military hero, and political leader, the leading writer of Italy in the late 19th and early 20th centuries.

D'Annunzio was educated at the University of Rome. When he was 16 his first poems, *Primo vere* (1879; "In Early Spring"), were published. The poems in *Canto novo* (1882; "New Song") had more individuality and were full of exuberance and passionate, sensuous descriptions. The autobiographical novel *Il piacere* (1898; *The Child of Pleasure*) introduced the first of D'Annunzio's many passionate Nietzschean-Superman heroes; another appeared in *L'innocente* (1892; *The Intruder*). D'Annunzio had already become famous by the time his best-known novel, *Il trionfo della morte* (1894; *The Triumph of Death*), appeared. It and his next major novel, *Le vergini delle rocce* (1896; *The Maidens of the Rocks*), featured viciously self-seeking and thoroughly amoral Nietzschean heroes.

D'Annunzio continued his prodigious literary production until World War I. His most important work in poetry was the lyrical collection *Laudi del cielo del mare della terra e degli eroi* (1899; "In Praise of Sky, Sea, Earth, and Heroes"). The third book in this poetic series, *Alcyone* (1904), a re-creation of the smells, tastes, sounds, and experiences of a Tuscan summer, is considered by many his greatest poetic work.

In 1894 D'Annunzio began a long liaison with the actress Eleonora Duse, and he wrote several plays for her, notably the tragedies *La Gioconda* (performed 1899) and *Francesca da Rimini* (performed 1901). He eventually broke off the relationship and exposed their intimacy in the erotic novel *Il fuoco* (1900; *The Flame of Life*). D'Annunzio's greatest play was *La figlia di Iorio* (performed 1904; *The Daughter of Jorio*), a powerful poetic drama of the fears and superstitions of Abruzzi peasants.

New plays and a novel followed, but these failed to finance D'Annunzio's extravagant lifestyle, and his indebtedness forced him to flee to France in 1910. When World War I broke out, he returned to Italy to passionately urge his country's entry into the war. After Italy declared war he plunged into the fighting himself.

In 1919 D'Annunzio and about 300 supporters, in defiance of the Treaty of Versailles, occupied the Dalmatian port of Fiume (Rijeka in present-day Croatia), which D'Annunzio believed rightly belonged to Italy. D'Annunzio ruled Fiume as dictator until December 1920, at which time Italian military forces compelled him to abdicate his rule. The port became Italian in 1924. D'Annunzio subsequently became an ardent fascist, but he exercised no further influence on Italian politics.

D'Annunzio's colorful life made him one of the most striking personalities of his day. His literary works are marked by their egocentric perspective, their fluent and melodious style, and an overriding emphasis on sensual gratification.

danse macabre   *see* DANCE OF DEATH.

Dante \\'dän-tā, *Angl* 'dän-,tā, 'dan-, -tē \\, *in full* Dante Alighieri \\,ä-lē-'gye-rē\\ (b. *c.* May 15–June 15, 1265, Florence [Italy]—d. Sept. 13/14, 1321, Ravenna)   The greatest Italian poet and

Library of Congress

one of the towering figures in western European literature. He is best known for the monumental epic poem *Commedia*, later named *La divina commedia* (*c.* 1310–14; THE DIVINE COMEDY), a profoundly Christian vision of human temporal and eternal destiny.

Most of what is known about Dante's life he told himself. Born of a Florentine family of noble ancestry, Dante grew up in Florence. By the time he was 18, as he himself says in LA VITA NUOVA (*c.* 1293; *The New Life*), he had already taught himself the art of making verse. He sent an early sonnet to the most famous poets of his day. Several of them responded, most significantly Guido Cavalcanti, and this was the beginning of their great friendship.

About 1285 Dante married Gemma Donati, to whom he had been betrothed since 1277, but his life was given its direction by his spiritual love for Beatrice Portinari (d. 1290), whom he first saw as a child when he himself was nine years old. She remained his ideal lady, the inspiration of his poetry and of his Christian devotion.

La vita nuova was the first of two collections of verse, the other being *Il convivio* (*c.* 1304–07; "The Banquet"). Each is a *prosimetrum*, that is, a work composed of verse and prose. In each case the prose is a framing device for binding together poems composed over about a 10-year period. In 1295 Dante became a member of the guild of physicians and apothecaries (to which philosophers could belong), which opened his way to public office, but he entered the public arena at a most perilous time. The city was divided into the Black Guelfs, led by Corso Donati, and White Guelfs, the party to which Dante belonged. When events led to the eventual ascendancy of the Black Guelfs (who had the pope's support), Dante and his associates were exiled. After 1302 Dante never saw Florence again. Sheltered by various Italian cities and princely rulers, he made his final home in Ravenna.

Difficult though they were, Dante's many years of exile were productive; during them he wrote *De vulgari eloquentia* (1304–07; *Concerning Vernacular Eloquence*), the first theoretical discussion and definition of the Italian literary language; *Il convivio*; and a Latin treatise, *De monarchia* (*c.* 1313; *On Monarchy*), a major tract of medieval political philosophy that sets forth his view of Christian polity. He also was sustained by work on *The Divine Comedy*, possibly begun before 1308 and completed just before his death in 1321.

The Divine Comedy is the story of a man's journey through Hell, Purgatory, and Paradise. He has two guides: Virgil, who leads him through the *Inferno* and *Purgatorio*, and Beatrice, who introduces him to *Paradiso*. Recognition and honor for the work were not long in coming: by the year 1400 no fewer than 12 commentaries devoted to detailed expositions of its meaning had appeared. Giovanni Boccaccio wrote a life of the poet and then in 1373–74 delivered the first public lectures on *The Divine Comedy*. Dante became known as the *divino poeta*, and in a splendid edition of his great poem published in Venice in 1555 the adjective *divine* was also applied to the poem's title. Thus, the work that Dante had entitled simply *Commedia* became *La divina commedia*.

Dantès, Edmond \\ed-'mȯⁿ-dän-'tās\\   Fictional character, the hero of the novel THE COUNT OF MONTE CRISTO by Alexandre Dumas *père*. When Dantès is imprisoned as a young sailor because of the treachery of four acquaintances, he spends the rest of his life plotting and then carrying out plans for revenge against his betrayers.

Dantiscus \\dan-'tis-kəs\\, Johannes, *original name* Jan Dantyszek \\dän-'tish-ek\\, *also called* Jan Flachsbinder \\'fläks-,bin-dər\\ (b. Oct. 31, 1485, Danzig [now Gdańsk, Pol.]—d. Oct. 27, 1548, Lidzbark Warmiński)   Polish author of incidental verse, love poetry, and panegyric (formal speeches of praise). He wrote in Latin and was among the first Renaissance humanist writers in Poland. Courtier to the Polish king Sigismund I, he accompanied the king to Vienna in 1515. Later in life he joined the Roman Catholic church, becoming bishop of Chełmno in 1530 and prince bishop of Warmiński in 1537.

Dantist \\'dan-tist, 'dän-\\   A Dante scholar.

Daode jing or **Tao-te ching** \\'daú-'də-'jiŋ\\ ("Classic of the Way of Power")   Classic of Chinese philosophical literature. The name was first used during the Han dynasty (206 BC–AD 220); it had previously been called *Laozi* in the belief that it was written by Laozi (Lao-tzu), but the problem of its authorship is still unresolved. The *Daode jing*, moreover, contains no references to other writings, persons, events, or places that might provide a clue for dating the composition. Scholarly opinions consequently range between the 8th and 3rd centuries BC.

The *Daode jing* presents a way of life intended to restore harmony and tranquillity to a kingdom racked by widespread disorders. It is critical of the unbridled wantonness of self-seeking rulers and is disdainful of social activism based on the type of abstract moralism and mechanical propriety characteristic of Confucian ethics. The Dao (Chinese *dao*, "way") of the *Daode jing* has received a wide variety of interpretations because of its elusiveness and mystical overtones and has been a basic concept in both philosophy and religion. In essence it consists of "nonaction" (*wuwei*), understood as no unnatural action, rather than complete passivity. It implies spontaneity, noninterference, letting things take their natural course: "Do nothing and everything is done." Chaos ceases, quarrels end, and self-righteous feuding disappears because the Dao is allowed to flow unchallenged and unchallenging.

The popularity of the *Daode jing* is reflected in the vast number of commentaries that have been written on it: more than 350 have been preserved in Chinese, about 250 in Japanese. Since 1900 more than 40 translations have appeared in English.

Daphne \\'daf-nē\\   In Greek mythology, the personification of the laurel (Greek *daphnē*), a tree whose leaves, formed into garlands, were particularly associated with Apollo. Traditionally, the special position of the laurel was connected with Apollo's love for Daphne, the beautiful daughter of a river god (probably Ladon). She rejected every lover, including Apollo. When the god pursued her, Daphne prayed to the Earth or to her father to rescue her, whereupon she was transformed into a laurel. Apollo appropriated the laurel for poets and, in Rome, for triumphs. Daphne was also loved by Leucippus, who was killed because of Apollo's jealousy.

Daphnis \\'daf-nis\\   Legendary hero of the shepherds of Sicily and the reputed inventor of bucolic poetry. According to tradition, Daphnis was the son of Hermes and a Sicilian nymph and was found by shepherds in a grove of laurels (Greek: *daphnē*). He later won the affection of a nymph, but, upon his proving unfaithful to her, she blinded him. Daphnis tried to console himself by playing the flute and singing shepherds' songs, but he soon died or was taken up to heaven by Hermes. According to Theocritus' version of the story, Daphnis offended Eros and Aphrodite and, in return, was smitten with unrequited love; he died, although Aphrodite, moved by compassion, tried unsuccessfully to save him.

Daphnis and Chloe \\'daf-nis . . . 'klō-ē\\   Work by LONGUS, written in the 2nd or 3rd century AD and considered the first pastoral prose romance. The work tells the story of two foundlings who are brought up by shepherds and who fall in love at an early age. They are soon kidnapped and separated, but after several adventures they are reunited. The novel was the inspiration for several later literary works, including such Elizabethan pastoral romances as Sir Philip Sidney's *Arcadia* (1590) and Thomas Lodge's *Rosalynde* (1590), the source book for William Shakespeare's *As You Like It*.

Da Ponte \\dä-'pōn-tā\\, Lorenzo, *original name* Emanuele Conegliano \\kō-nāl-'yä-nō\\ (b. March 10, 1749, Céneda, near Treviso, Veneto [Italy]—d. Aug. 17, 1838, New York, N.Y., U.S.)   Italian poet and librettist chiefly known for his collaboration with W.A. Mozart.

Born of a Jewish family, he was baptized in 1763 and later became a priest; his youthful libertinism and freethinking, however, led to his expulsion from the Venetian state in 1779. Taking up residence in Vienna, he became official poet to the court of Emperor Joseph II and in that capacity wrote successful libretti for numerous musicians. It was there in 1783 that Da Ponte made the acquaintance of Mozart and entered upon the finest period of his literary career. Three masterpieces appeared in rapid succession—*Le nozze di Figaro* (1786), *Don Giovanni* (1787), and *Così fan tutte* (1790). Da Ponte's enduring merit was his ability to infuse borrowed themes with new life and to interweave tragic and comic elements.

On Joseph II's death Da Ponte resumed his wanderings. After a period in London (1792–1805), he immigrated to the United States, settling finally in New York, where he taught Italian language and literature at Columbia College. His *Memorie*, 4 vol. (1823–27; *Memoirs of Lorenzo Da Ponte*), although mainly concerned with portraying the author as a victim of fate and enemies, is valuable for its portrait of early 19th-century America.

Daqīqī \\'dȧ-,kē-,kē\\, *in full* Abū Manṣūr Muḥammad ibn Aḥmad Daqīqī (d. *c.* 976–981, Ṭūs, Iran)   Persian poet who was one of the most important figures in early Persian literature.

Very little is known about Daqīqī's life. A panegyrist, he wrote poems praising various Sāmānid princes and much lyrical poetry, but he is remembered chiefly for an uncompleted epic dealing with the introduction of Zoroastrianism and the conflicts and exploits of mythical heroes from the Persian past. He paved the way for the great FERDOWSĪ, who included Daqīqī's verses in his own *Shāh-nāmeh* ("Book of Kings"). Although Daqīqī cannot be wholly credited with originating the meter and style that became dominant in Persian epic literature, he contributed a great deal to its creation.

Darcy, Fitzwilliam \\fits-'wil-yəm-'där-sē\\   Fictional character, the arrogant suitor of Elizabeth Bennet in the novel PRIDE AND PREJUDICE by Jane Austen. At first Elizabeth spurns him because of his extreme pride, but when Darcy and Elizabeth come to know one another, Darcy's haughtiness melts and his true character is revealed.

Dardanus \\'där-də-nəs\\   In Greek mythology, the founder of Dardania on the Hellespont. He was the ancestor of the Dardanians of the Troad and, through Aeneas, of the Romans.

According to tradition, Dardanus was the son of Zeus and the Pleiad Electra. After slaying his brother Iasion, Dardanus fled from Arcadia across the sea to Samothrace. When that island was inundated, he crossed over to the Troad, a region surrounding Troy in Asia Minor. There he was hospitably received by Teucer (ruler of Phrygia). He married Teucer's daughter Bateia and subsequently became the founder of the royal house of Troy.

Dares Phrygius \\'dar-ēz-'frij-ē-əs, 'dā-rēz\\   A Trojan priest of Hephaestus who appears as one of the characters in Homer's *Iliad* and is the reputed author of a lost pre-Homeric "eyewitness" account of the Trojan War. The *Daretis Phrygii de Excidio Trojae historia*, a Latin work purporting to be a translation of this account, probably dates from the 5th century AD. The influence of this pro-Trojan work in the Latin-speaking West from the fall of the Roman Empire to the Renaissance, a period when the works of Homer were known only by hearsay, was enormous. Together with the fictional account of Dictys Cretensis, Dares Phrygius' account was widely used as a source by medieval writers. *See also* TROY.

Darío \\dä-'rē-ō\\, Rubén, *pseudonym of* Félix Rubén García Sarmiento \\gär-'sē-ä-sär-'myen-tō\\ (b. Jan. 18, 1867, Metapa, Nic.—d. Feb. 6, 1916, León)   Influential Nicaraguan poet, journalist, and diplomat. As a leader of the literary movement known as MODERNISMO, which flourished in Latin America at the end of the 19th century, he revivified and modernized poetry in Spanish.

Precocious and prolific, from the age of 14 he signed the name Rubén Darío to his poems and stories. He left Nicaragua in 1886 and settled for a time in Chile, where in 1888 he published his first major work, *Azul* ("Blue"). This collection of short stories, descriptive sketches, and verse was an attempt to apply the tenets of French Parnassian poetry to Spanish writing.

After his return to Central America, Darío took up an appointment (1893) as Colombian consul in Buenos Aires, Arg. Young writers there hailed him as their leader, and the Modernismo movement was organized around him. Darío's next significant collection of poems, *Prosas profanas y otros poemas* (1896; "Profane Hymns and Other Poems"), treated its exotic scenes and personages in a manner influenced by the contemporary French Symbolist poets.

Darío went to Europe in 1898 as a correspondent for *La nación*. By this time, world events and his own advancing age had brought about a profound change in his outlook on life. He became vitally concerned with several political issues: the threat of North American imperialism, the future of Spanish America after Spain's defeat in the Spanish-American war of 1898, and the solidarity of Spanish-speaking peoples. The collection generally considered to be his masterpiece, *Cantos de vida y esperanza* (1905; "Songs of Life and Hope"), reflects these concerns and is the culmination of his technical experimentation and his artistic resourcefulness.

On the outbreak of World War I in 1914, Darío left Europe, physically ill and on the brink of poverty. He began a lecture tour of North America, but he developed pneumonia in New York and died shortly after his return to his homeland.

In addition to the three major collections on which his greatest fame rests and his journalistic work, Darío wrote approximately 100 short stories and tales, as well as several additional volumes of poetry and penetrating literary criticism.

Dark Lady   One of two individuals (the other was a young man, a "fair youth") who are the main subjects of William Shakespeare's sonnets. In Sonnet 144 the poet refers explicitly to "a woman colour'd ill," and scholars have since referred to her as the "Dark Lady." Most of the late sonnets (numbers 127 to 154) concern the poet's relationship to her. The poems suggest that this "worser spirit" was a mistress to both the poet and the young man. The true identity of the dark lady, which is still unknown, has fueled intense and continuing scholarly debate.

Darkness at Noon   Novel by Arthur KOESTLER, published in 1940. The action is set during Stalin's purge trials of the 1930s and concerns Nicholas Rubashov, an old-guard Bolshevik who at first denies, then confesses to, crimes that he has not committed. Reflecting Koestler's own disenchantment with communism, the plot examines the dilemma of an aging revolutionary who can no longer condone the excesses of a regime he helped establish. The book is a powerful examination of the moral danger inherent in a system that is willing to employ any means to an end.

Darley \'där-lē\, George (b. 1795, Dublin, Ire.—d. Nov. 23, 1846, London, Eng.)   Poet and critic praised by 20th-century writers for his intense evocation of a symbolic dreamworld in his unfinished lyrical epic *Nepenthe* (1835). Long regarded as unreadable, the epic came to be admired in the 20th century for its dream imagery, use of symbolism to reveal inner consciousness, and tumultuous metrical organization.

Darley became a freelance writer in London in 1821. A perceptive critic, he wrote for the literary *London Magazine* and other journals, meanwhile publishing a succession of failures. In his own day, Darley's greatest successes were his mathematical textbooks.

Darnay, Charles \'chärlz-där-'nā\   Fictional character, one of the protagonists of Charles Dickens' A TALE OF TWO CITIES. Darnay is a highly principled young French aristocrat (his real name is Charles St. Evrémonde) who is caught up in the events leading up to the French Revolution and is saved from the guillotine by Sydney Carton.

D'Artagnan \där-'tan-yən, *French* där-tä-'nyäⁿ\   A protagonist of THE THREE MUSKETEERS by Alexandre Dumas *père*. The character was based on a real person who served as a captain of the musketeers under Louis XIV, but Dumas' account of this young, impressionable, swashbuckling hero must be regarded as primarily fiction.

Dashwood family \'dash-ˌwúd\   Major characters in Jane Austen's novel SENSE AND SENSIBILITY. The widowed Mrs. Dashwood and her daughters Elinor and Marianne are impoverished by the death of Mr. Dashwood and by the selfishness and neglect of his heir, who is his son by his first wife. The Dashwood sisters represent opposite temperaments: Elinor, the older of the two, is "sensible," rational, and capable of exercising self-restraint, while Marianne, who shares her mother's temperament, is emotional and impulsive.

Dass \'däs\, Petter (b. 1647, Nord Herøy, near Alstahaug, Nor.—d. 1707, Alstahaug)   Norwegian poet who, in an age of pedantry and artifice, stands out among his contemporaries for the vivid freshness, everyday language, and common appeal of his works.

The son of a Scottish merchant who had settled in Bergen, Dass studied at Copenhagen. He was ordained in 1677 and became pastor of Alstahaug in northern Norway, where he remained for the rest of his life. Dass's poems were circulated in manuscript and memorized by the farmers, shepherds, and fishermen who were his parishioners. Only the poem *Den Nordske dale-viise* (1683; "The Norwegian Song of the Valley") was published during his lifetime. His sacred poems were collected after his death, but he is best known for *Nordlands trompet* (written 1678–1700; published 1739; *The Trumpet of Nordland*), a rhyming description of the natural features, people, and occupations of Nordland (in northern Norway).

Datta \'dət-ə\, Michael Madhusudan, *surname also spelled* Dutt \'dət\ (b. Jan. 25, 1824, Sāgardari, Bengal, India [now in Bangladesh]—d. June 29, 1873, Calcutta, India)   Poet and dramatist, the first great poet of modern Bengali literature.

Datta was educated at the Hindu College, Calcutta, the cultural home of the Western-educated Bengali middle class. His early compositions were in English, but they were unsuccessful, and he turned, reluctantly at first, to Bengali. His principal works, written mostly between 1858 and 1862, include prose drama, long narrative poems, and lyrics. His first play, *Sarmistha* (1858), based on an episode of the ancient Sanskrit epic the *Mahābhārata*, was well received. His poetical works are *Tilottamasambhab* (1860), a narrative poem on the story of Sunda and Upasunda; *Meghnadbadh* (1861), his most important composition, an epic on the *Rāmāyaṇa* theme; *Brajangana* (1861), a cycle of lyrics on the *Rādhā-Kṛṣṇa* theme; and *Birangana* (1862), a set of 21 epistolary poems on the model of Ovid's *Heroides*.

Datta experimented ceaselessly with diction and verse forms, and it was he who introduced *amitraksar* (a form of blank verse with run-on lines and varied caesuras), the Bengali sonnet (both Petrarchan and Shakespearean variants) and many original lyric stanzas.

Däubler \'dói-blər\, Theodor (b. Aug. 17, 1876, Trieste, Austria-Hungary [now in Italy]—d. June 14, 1934, Sankt Blasien, Ger.)   German poet whose extraordinary vitality, poetic vision, and optimism contrast sharply with the despair expressed by many writers of his time.

Däubler lived a wandering life, without settled income or occupation. He traveled widely in Europe, the Middle East, and Egypt and tapped many diverse sources of inspiration. His poetry owes much to classical as well as Romantic aesthetics, although he exercised his greatest influence through his early enthusiasm for Expressionism, as voiced in his essays "Der neue Standpunkt" (1916; "The New Point of View") and "Im Kampf um die moderne Kunst" (1918; "Joining the Battle for Modern Art"). His major work, *Das Nordlicht* (1910; rev. ed., 1921; "The Northern Lights"), an epic of more than 30,000 lines, is an original cosmic myth. Although his style is often considered to be somewhat cramped, Däubler's poetical works *Das Sternen Kind* (1916; "The Star Child") and *Die Treppe zum Nordlicht* (1920; "The Stairway to the Northern Lights") are remarkably free of this tendency. Other well-known works are *Der sternhelle Weg* (1915; "The Star-Lit Road"), *Päan und Dithyrambos* (1924; "Paeons and Dithyrambs"), and *Attische Sonette* (1924; "Greek Sonnets"). He also published tales and two novels.

Daudet \dō-'de\, Alphonse (b. May 13, 1840, Nîmes, Fr.—d. Dec. 16, 1897, Paris?)   French short-story writer and novelist, remembered chiefly for the humor and sentiment with which he portrayed the life and characters of southern France.

Daudet wrote his first poems and his first novel at the age of 14. In 1857 his parents lost all their money, and Daudet was unable to continue his schooling. At the end of the year he went to join his elder brother, Ernest, in Paris. He formed a liaison with a model, Marie Rieu, to whom he dedicated his only book of poems, *Les Amoureuses* (1858; "Women in Love"). His long and troubled relationship with her was to be reflected, much later, in his novel *Sapho* (1884; *Sappho*). He also contributed articles to newspapers, in particular to *Figaro*. In 1860 he met Frédéric Mistral, the leader of the 19th-century revival of Provençal language and literature, who awakened his enthusiasm for the life of the south of France. In the same year he obtained a secretarial post under the future Duke de Morny.

His health undermined by poverty and by the venereal disease that was eventually to cost him his life, Daudet spent the winter of 1861–62 in Algeria. One of the fruits of this visit was *Chapatin le tueur de lions* (1863; "Chapatin the Lion Killer"), whose lion-hunter hero can be seen as the first sketch of the author's future Tartarin. Daudet's first play, *La Dernière Idole*, made a great impact when it was produced in Paris in 1862. His full social life over the years 1863–65 (until Morny's death) provided him with the material that he analyzed mercilessly in *Le Nabab* (1877; *The Nabob*). In January 1867 he married Julia Allard, herself a writer of talent, who gave him great help in his subsequent work.

Daudet enlisted in the army during the Franco-Prussian War, but he fled from the terrors of the Paris Commune of 1871. This experience had a profound effect on his writing, as can be judged from his second volume of short stories, *Les Contes du lundi* (1873; *Monday Tales*). His *Les Aventures prodigieuses de Tartarin de Tarascon* (1872; *The New Don Quixote or the Wonderful Adventures of Tarascon*) was not well received. His play *L'Arlésienne* ("The Woman of Arles") was also a failure (although its 1885 revival was acclaimed). His next novel, *Fromont jeune et Risler aîné* (1874; *Fromont the Younger and Risler the Elder*), which won an award from the Académie Française, was a success, and for a few years he enjoyed prosperity and fame.

In his last years Daudet suffered from an agonizing ailment of the spinal cord caused by his venereal disease. *La Doulou* (not published until 1931; *Suffering, 1887–95*) represents his attempt to alleviate his pain by investigating it. His reminiscences are contained in *Trente ans de Paris* (1888; *Thirty Years of Paris and of My Literary Life*) and *Souvenirs d'un homme de lettres* (1888; *Recollections of a Literary Man*).

Daudet \dō-'de\, Léon, *in full* Alphonse-Marie-Léon Daudet (b. Nov. 16, 1867, Paris, Fr.—d. July 1, 1942, Saint-Rémy-de-Provence)   French journalist and novelist, the most virulent and courageous polemicist of his generation, whose reputation rests on his journalistic work and his vivid memoirs.

Son of the famous novelist Alphonse Daudet, Léon studied medicine before turning to journalism with contributions to *Le Figaro* and *Le Gaulois*. His first novel, *L'Astre noir* (1893; "The Black Planet"), was followed by a scathing indictment of the medical profession, *Les Morticoles* (1894; "The Sawbones"). His novel *Le Voyage de Shakespeare* (1896) was more successful than many that followed it.

In 1908 Daudet and Charles Maurras refashioned *L'Action française* into a daily paper of avowedly reactionary, nationalist, and royalist opinion. Daudet had published an antirepublican satire in 1901, and his contributions to *L'Action française* showed a similar satirical and Rabelaisian flavor.

Among Daudet's other works, the most important are *L'Avant-Guerre* (1913); *Le Monde des images* (1919), a stubbornly anti-Freudian work on psychology; and *Le Stupide XIXe Siècle* (1922; *The Stupid XIXth Century*). Daudet's six volumes of memoirs, *Souvenirs des milieux littéraires, politiques, artistiques, et médicaux* (1914–21; selections translated in *Memoirs of Léon Daudet*), are informative, vivid, and partisan.

Daurat   *see* DORAT.

Davenant or **D'Avenant** \'dav-ə-nənt\, Sir William (b. 1606, Oxford, Eng.—d. April 7, 1668, London)   English poet, playwright, and theater manager who was made poet laureate on the strength of such successes as the comedy *The Witts* (licensed 1634); the masques *The Temple of Love, Britannia Triumphans*, and *Luminalia*; and a volume of poems, *Madagascar* (published 1638).

William Shakespeare was apparently Davenant's godfather, and gossip held that the famous playwright may even have been his father. Davenant became a page in London in 1622 and later served a famous literary courtier, Fulke Greville, Lord Brooke. Meanwhile Davenant was writing revenge tragedies, such as *Albovine* (produced *c.* 1629), and tragicomedies, such as *The Colonel*. His engaging, reckless personality and his plays and occasional verses attracted the patronage of Queen Henrietta Maria. Davenant was appointed to the poet laureateship in 1638, after the death of Ben Jonson the previous year.

In 1641 Davenant risked his life in a bungled army plot, and the outbreak of the first phase of the English Civil Wars in 1642 nullified a royal patent he had secured to build a theater. A supporter of King Charles I, he was knighted by the king in 1643 for running supplies across the English Channel. Later, having joined the defeated and exiled Stuart court in Paris, he began his unfinished verse epic *Gondibert* (1651), a tale of chivalry in 1,700 quatrains. After the execution of Charles I, his queen sent Davenant to aid the Royalist cause in America. Davenant's ship was captured in the English Channel, however, and he was imprisoned in the Tower of London until 1654.

In 1656 Davenant made the first attempt to revive English drama, which had been banned under Oliver Cromwell, with *The First Day's Entertainment* (produced 1656), a work disguised under the title *Declamations and Musick*. In 1660, after the Restoration, he was granted a royal patent to establish new acting companies and founded the new Duke of York's Playhouse in Lincoln's Inn Fields. As manager, director, and playwright, he continued to produce, write, and adapt plays.

Davenport \'dav-ən-ˌpȯrt\, Guy, *in full* Guy Mattison Davenport, Jr. (b. Nov. 23, 1927, Anderson, S.C., U.S.)   American author and scholar, best known for his short, experimental fiction. He was also an illustrator, an essayist, a translator, and a critic.

Davenport's first, and best received, collection of short fiction, *Tatlin!* (1974), was heavily influenced by the works of the poet Ezra Pound. Davenport's other works include the collections *Da Vinci's Bicycle* (1979), *Eclogues* (1981), *Apples and Pears* (1984), and *A Table of Green Fields* (1993). These and other works reveal the author's great erudition; his writing is filled with literary, classical, and historical allusions conveyed by a variety of avant-garde techniques.

Originally published in various journals, the essays and reviews collected in *The Geography of the Imagination* (1981) cover a wide variety of subjects. *Cities on Hills: A Study of I–XXX of Ezra Pound's Cantos* (1983) and *A Balthus Notebook* (1989) are other works of criticism. Davenport made many translations, including *Sappho: Songs and Fragments* (1965), *Archilochos, Sappho, Alkman* (1980), and *Anakreon: The Extant Fragments* (1991). He also illustrated several books, including poet Hugh Kenner's *The Stoic Comedians* and his own *Apples and Pears.*

David \ˈdā-vid\ (b. Bethlehem, Judah—d. *c.* 962 BC, Jerusalem) Second of the Israelite kings, reigning from approximately 1000 BC to his death, who established a united kingdom throughout Israel, with Jerusalem as its capital. He was also a skilled musician and poet. In Jewish tradition he became the ideal king, the founder of an enduring dynasty around whose figure and reign clustered messianic expectations of the people of Israel. Because he was a symbol of fulfillment in the future, the New Testament writers emphasized that Jesus was of the lineage of David. He was also held in high esteem in the Islāmic tradition.

David began his career as an aide at the court of Saul, Israel's first king, and became a close friend of Saul's son and heir, Jonathan, and the husband of Saul's daughter Michal. Eventually David was proclaimed king of Judah, and soon of all Israel. He conquered Jerusalem and made it the capital of the united kingdom. Notable among his many children was Absalom, who launched a rebellion against the king and was killed by David's general. Other events in David's life include an adulterous relationship with Bathsheba and the murder of her husband Uriah.

The love of David and Jonathan, the relationship between David and Bathsheba, and David's great grief over the death of his son Absalom are the subjects of much later literature.

David Copperfield \ˈdā-vid-ˈkäp-ər-ˌfēld\ (*in full* The Personal History of David Copperfield) Novel by Charles DICKENS, published serially from 1849 to 1850 and in book form in 1850.

The book is perhaps most notable for its childhood chapters, "an enchanting vein which he had never quite found before and which he was never to find again," according to the critic Edmund Wilson. Largely for this reason and for its autobiographical interest, it has always been among his most popular novels and was Dickens' own "favorite child." It incorporates material from the autobiography he had recently begun but soon abandoned and is written in the first person, a new technique for him. Although Copperfield differs from his creator in many ways, Dickens uses many early personal experiences that had meant much to him—his own period of work in a factory while his father was jailed, his schooling and reading, his passion for Maria Beadnell (a woman much like Dora Spenlow), and (more cursorily) his emergence from parliamentary reporting into successful novel writing.

Davidescu \ˌdäv-ē-ˈdes-ˌkü\, Nicolae (b. 1888, Bucharest, Rom.—d. 1954) Romanian poet and novelist whose early poems, *Inscripţii* (1916), showed the influence of Charles Baudelaire. Among his prose works the novel *Zâna din fundul lacului* (1912; "The Fairy at the Bottom of the Lake") was an exercise in symbolism, and *Viora mută* (1928; "The Muted Violin"), in social psychology. In the epic *Cântecul omului* (1928-

37; "The Song of Man"), he aimed at re-creating world history. Two collections of his literary criticism were published posthumously, *Aspecte şi direcţii literare* (1975; "Literary Conventions and Directions") and *Poezii, teatru, proză* (1977; "Poetry, Drama, Prose").

Davidson \ˈdā-vid-sən\, Donald (Grady) (b. Aug. 18, 1893, Campbellsville, Tenn., U.S.—d. April 25, 1968, Nashville, Tenn.) American poet, essayist, and teacher who warned against technology as indicative of modern spiritual disorder and idealized the agrarian South and its traditions.

While attending Vanderbilt University (B.A., 1917; M.A., 1922) Davidson became one of the Fugitives, a group of Southern writers determined to conserve their region's distinctive literature and rural economy. They published a journal *The Fugitive* (1922–25) and contributed essays to the book *I'll Take My Stand* (1930). In time Davidson's fellow Fugitives—Robert Penn Warren, Allen Tate, and John Crowe Ransom among them—altered their views, but Davidson, who taught for many years at Vanderbilt, remained passionately devoted to his early ideals. In his verse collections, including *The Tall Men* (1927), *Lee in the Mountains, and Other Poems* (1938), and *Poems, 1922–1961* (1966), and in his prose, including *The Attack on Leviathan: Regionalism and Nationalism in the United States* (1938), *Why the Modern South Has a Great Literature* (1951), and *Still Rebels, Still Yankees, and Other Essays* (1957), he praised historic Southern heroes, defended racial segregation, and warned against the evils of industrialism, which he saw as the enemy of spiritual values. His two-volume *The Tennessee* (1946, 1948) is a history of the Tennessee River and its valley.

Davidson \ˈdā-vəd-sən\, John (b. April 11, 1857, Barrhead, Renfrewshire, Scot.—d. March 23, 1909, Penzance, Cornwall, Eng.) Scottish poet and playwright, a master of the narrative lyrical ballad.

Davidson wrote a number of blank-verse dramas that failed to win recognition. In 1890 he went to London, where he practiced journalism and wrote novels and short stories to earn a living. He finally established himself with *Fleet Street Eclogues* (1893), *Ballads and Songs* (1894), and a second series of eclogues (1896). A series of "Testaments," written toward the end of his life, were verse dramas incorporating scientific language. They expressed his idiosyncratic vision, which combined scientific materialism and romantic will that is also in evidence in the work of such writers as Thomas Carlyle and Friedrich Nietzsche.

Exhausted by his efforts to support his family and dependent relatives and increasingly frustrated by the public response to his work, he moved to Cornwall in 1908. In the following year he committed suicide.

Davidson's poetry varies widely in tone and execution; among his finer poems are "The Crystal Palace," "The Wasp," and "Snow."

Davie \ˈdā-vē\, Donald (Alfred) (b. July 17, 1922, Barnsley, Yorkshire, Eng.) British poet, critic, and teacher whose anti-Romantic attitude was influenced by Sir William Empson.

Davie graduated from Cambridge. He taught at Trinity College, Dublin (1950–57); the University of California, Berkeley (1957–58); and Cambridge (1958–64); and he was pro-vice-chancellor at the University of Essex from 1965 until his appointment as professor of English at Stanford University, Palo Alto, Calif., in 1968.

His poetry has been characterized as Neo-Augustan, austere, and elegant. *Brides of Reason* (1955) was followed by *Six Epistles to Eva Hesse* (1970), *Collected Poems 1950–70* (1972), *In the Stopping Train* (1977), and *To Scorch or Freeze: Poems About the Sacred* (1988). Among his critical works are *Purity of Diction* in *English Verse* (1952), *Ezra Pound: Poet as Sculptor* (1965), *The Poet in the Imaginary Museum* (1977; essays), and *Czesław Miłosz and the Insufficiency of Lyric* (1986).

Davies \'dā-vis, *US also* 'dā-vēz\, Sir John (b. April 1569, Tisbury, Wiltshire, Eng.—d. Dec. 8, 1626)   English poet and lawyer whose *Orchestra, or a Poem of Dancing* reveals a typically Elizabethan pleasure in the contemplation of the correspondence between the natural order and human activity.

Educated at Oxford, Davies was called to the bar in 1595. He was sent to Ireland as solicitor general and in 1606 was made attorney general for Ireland. Davies took an active part in the Protestant settlement of Ulster. He entered the Irish Parliament and was elected speaker; on his return to England he sat in the English Parliament of 1621. He was appointed lord chief justice in 1626 but died before he took office.

Much of Davies' early poetry consisted of epigrams. *Epigrammes and Elegies by J.D. and C.M.* (1590?) contained both Davies' work and unpublished work of Christopher Marlowe; it was one of the books the archbishop of Canterbury ordered burned in 1599. *Orchestra* (1596) is a poem in praise of dancing set against the background of Elizabethan cosmology and its theory of the harmony of the spheres. In *Nosce teipsum* (1599; "Know Thyself"), he gave a lucid account of his philosophy on the nature and immortality of the soul. In the same year he published *Hymnes of Astraea in Acrosticke Verse*, a series of poems in which the initials of the first lines form the words "Elisabetha Regina." A volume of his collected poems was published in 1622.

Davies \'dā-vis, *US also* 'dā-vēz\, Robertson, *in full* William Robertson Davies, *pseudonym* Samuel Marchbanks \'märch-,baŋks\ (b. Aug. 28, 1913, Thamesville, Ont., Can.)   Playwright and novelist probably best known for THE DEPTFORD TRILOGY, a series of novels (*Fifth Business* [1970], *The Manticore* [1972], and *World of Wonders* [1975]) that examine the intersecting lives of three men from the small Canadian town of Deptford.

Educated in England at Oxford, Davies had training in acting, directing, and stage management as a member of the Old Vic Repertory Company. He also edited the Peterborough *Examiner* (1942–63) and taught English at the University of Toronto (1960–81; emeritus thereafter). Davies wrote plays—such as *Eros at Breakfast* (1949), *At My Heart's Core* (1950), *A Jig for the Gypsy* (1954), and *A Masque of Mr. Punch* (1963)—novels, and nonfiction—*The Diary of Samuel Marchbanks* (1947), *A Voice From the Attic* (1960), and *Samuel Marchbanks' Almanack* (1967) before publishing his masterwork.

Known as a traditional (that is, nonexperimental) storyteller, Davies was a master of imaginative writing and wicked wit. Among his other notable works of fiction are his SALTERTON TRILOGY (*Tempest-Tost* [1951], *Leaven of Malice* [1954], and *A Mixture of Frailties* [1958]), THE REBEL ANGELS (1981), WHAT'S BRED IN THE BONE (1985), and THE LYRE OF ORPHEUS (1988). *Murther & Walking Spirits*, written from the perspective of a dead man, was published in 1991. His later nonfiction includes *The Mirror of Nature* (1983).

Davies \'dā-vis, *US also* 'dā-vēz\, William Henry (b. July 3, 1871, Newport, Monmouthshire, Wales—d. Sept. 26, 1940, Nailsworth, Gloucestershire, Eng.)   English poet whose lyrics have a force and simplicity uncharacteristic of most Georgian poetry.

After serving as apprentice to a picture framer, Davies had many adventures. He tramped through the United States, crossed the Atlantic many times on cattle boats, lost a foot while trying to jump a train headed for the Klondike region in Canada, and became a peddler and a street singer in En-

gland. After several years of this wandering life, he published his first volume of poetry, *The Soul's Destroyer, and Other Poems* (1905), while living in London. *The Autobiography of a Super-Tramp* (1907)—the best known of his prose works—appeared with a preface by George Bernard Shaw. His works of poetry include *Nature Poems and Others* (1908), *Forty New Poems* (1918), *Poems 1930–31* (1932), and *The Loneliest Mountain* (1939). The first collected edition appeared in 1916. Although his work achieved wide popularity, Davies lived the life of a recluse. His *Collected Poems* appeared in 1942.

Davies \'dā-vis, *US also* 'dā-vēz\ of Hereford \'her-ə-fərd\, John (b. *c.* 1565, Hereford, Herefordshire, Eng.—d. July 1618, London)   Poet and writing master whose chief work was *Microcosmos* (1603), a didactic religious treatise. The epigrams of his *Scourge of Folly* (*c.* 1611) contain current notices of his eminent contemporaries, including Ben Jonson and William Shakespeare.

He settled in Oxford, writing, besides other religious verse treatises, *Wittes Pilgrimage . . .* (*c.* 1610), containing love sonnets; *Humours Heav'n on Earth; With the Civile Warres of Death and Fortune* (1609), a description of plague; and *The Writing Schoole-Master* (16th edition, 1636), a popular writing manual.

Davis \'dā-vis\, H.L., *in full* Harold Lenoir (b. Oct. 18, 1896, Yoncalla, Ore., U.S.—d. Oct. 31, 1960, San Antonio, Texas)   American novelist and poet who wrote realistically about the West, rejecting the stereotype of the cowboy as hero.

Davis worked as a cowboy, a typesetter, and a surveyor among other jobs before being noticed for his writing. He first received recognition for his poems, which were written in imitation of the poetry of Detlev von Liliencron, a 19th-century German poet. Later Davis was encouraged by the critic H.L. Mencken to try prose, and the results appeared in *American Mercury*. In 1932 Davis went to Mexico on a Guggenheim Fellowship, and he stayed there to write *Honey in the Horn* (1935), which won a Pulitzer Prize in 1936. This novel secured Davis' reputation as a novelist of the West whose slow-moving books explore the magic of the landscape, while realistically examining the problems facing frontier men and women. Davis' later books include *Beulah Land* (1949) and *The Distant Music* (1957).

Davis \'dā-vis\, Richard Harding (b. April 18, 1864, Philadelphia, Pa., U.S.—d. April 11, 1916, Mount Kisco, N.Y.)   American author of romantic novels and short stories who was also the best-known reporter of his generation.

Davis studied at Lehigh and Johns Hopkins universities and then worked on various newspapers in Philadelphia and New York and wrote short stories. In 1890 he became managing editor of *Harper's Weekly*. On assignments for *Harper's*, he toured various parts of the globe, recording his impressions of the American West, Europe, and South America in a series of books from 1892 to 1896. He also acted as a war correspondent, reporting on fighting from the Greco-Turkish war of 1897 to World War I. His early collections of stories achieved immediate success, particularly *Gallegher and Other Stories* (1891), *Van Bibber and Others* (1892), and *Ranson's Folly* (1902). Many of his published works were illustrated by Charles Dana Gibson. He wrote seven popular novels published between 1897 and 1909. Several of his 25 plays were also very successful, notably *Ranson's Folly* (1904; a dramatization of his earlier work by the same name), *The Dictator* (1904), and *Miss Civilization* (1906).

Davis \'dā-vis\, Thomas Osborne (b. Oct. 14, 1814, Mallow, County Cork, Ire.—d. Sept. 16, 1845, Dublin)   Irish writer and politician who was the chief organizer and poet of the nationalistic Young Ireland movement.

A Protestant who resented the traditional identification of Irish nationalism with Roman Catholic interests, Davis evolved an ideal of uniting all creeds and classes in a vigorous national movement while at Trinity College, Dublin. In 1842 he cofounded the weekly *Nation*, which supported Daniel O'Connell's agitation for restoring an Irish parliament and which became the organ of the writers known as the Young Irelanders. Davis wrote patriotic verses such as "A Nation Once Again" and "The Battle of Fontenoy"; his writings virtually became the gospel of the Sinn Féin movement. His *Essays and Poems, with a Centenary Memoir, 1845–1945* appeared in 1945.

Davy Jones \'dā-vē-'jōnz\ The personification of the spirit of the sea, usually seen as a spirit malevolent to sailors. *Davy Jones' locker* is a common phrase for the bottom of the ocean, the grave of those who die at sea.

dawn song Any of several genres of song or poem greeting the dawn. *See* ALBA; AUBADE; TAGELIED.

Da xue or **Ta hsüeh** \'dä-'shᴜᴇ\ ("Great Learning") Brief Chinese text generally attributed to the ancient sage Confucius (551–479 BC) and his disciple Zengzi. For centuries the text existed only as a chapter of *Li ji* ("Collection of Rituals"), one of the Five Classics (WU JING) of Confucianism. It gained lasting renown when Zhu Xi, a 12th-century philosopher, published the text separately as one of the "Four Books" (SI SHU).

In his preface to *Da xue*, Zhu Xi explained that the treatise is a means to personal development. Each individual, he says, must cultivate benevolence (*ren*), righteousness (*yi*), propriety (*li*), and wisdom (*zhi*), but virtue will not be acquired in equal measure by all.

The text itself states that world peace is impossible unless a ruler first regulates his own country, but no ruler can do this without first setting his own household in order. This action in turn presupposes that he has oriented his personal life by rectifying his heart and acquiring sincerity. These virtues are the natural consequence of the expanded wisdom that results from investigating all things. *Da xue* thus views good government and world peace as inseparably bound up with a ruler's personal wisdom.

Day \'dā\, Clarence (Shepard) (b. Nov. 18, 1874, New York, N.Y., U.S.—d. Dec. 28, 1935, New York City) American writer whose greatest popular success was his autobiographical *Life with Father*.

Educated at St. Paul's School, Concord, N.H., and at Yale (A.B., 1896), Day joined his father's brokerage firm as a partner. He enlisted in the U.S. Navy the following year but was stricken by arthritis, which left him an invalid.

In 1920 Day published his first book, *This Simian World*, a collection of humorous essays and illustrations. This was followed by *The Crow's Nest* (1921) and *Thoughts Without Words* (1928). He achieved great success with *God and My Father* (1932), *Life with Father* (1935), and *Life with Mother* (1936). Drawn from his own family experiences, these were pleasant and gently satirical portraits of a late Victorian household dominated by a gruff, opinionated father and a warm, charming mother. Day was a frequent contributor to *The New Yorker* magazine. *Life with Father* was dramatized by Howard Lindsay and Russel Crouse in 1939.

Day \'dā\, John (b. 1574, Cawston, Norfolk, Eng.—d. 1640?) Minor Elizabethan dramatist whose verse allegory *The Parliament of Bees* shows unusual ingenuity and delicacy of imagination.

About 1598 Day became a playwright for the theater proprietor and manager Philip Henslowe. His first extant play is *The Blind-Beggar of Bednal-Green* (written in 1600, with Henry Chettle; published 1659). Among his other plays are *The Ile of Guls* (1606) and *Humour Out of Breath* (1608). Day's reputation rests mainly on *The Parliament of Bees*, which is traditionally dated 1607, although no edition earlier than that of 1641 exists. This exquisite masque, which is actually a series of pastoral eclogues, is about "the doings, the births, the wars, the wooings" of bees. The bees hold a parliament under Prorex, the "Master Bee," and grievances are presented against the bumblebee, the wasp, the drone, and other insects whom the author uses to represent various human types. The satirical allegory ends with a royal procession of the fairy king Oberon, who dispenses justice.

Day-Lewis \'dā-'lü-əs\, C., *in full* Cecil Day-Lewis (b. April 27, 1904, Ballintubbert, County Leix, Ire.—d. May 22, 1972, Hadley Wood, Hertfordshire, Eng.) One of the leading British poets of the 1930s; he turned from poetry of left-wing political statement in his early years to an individual lyricism expressed in more traditional forms.

The son of a clergyman, Day-Lewis was educated at the University of Oxford and taught school until 1935. His *Transitional Poem* (1929) had already attracted attention, and in the 1930s he was closely associated with W.H. Auden (whose style influenced his own) and other poets who sought a left-wing political solution to the ills of the day. Typical of his views at that time is the verse sequence *The Magnetic Mountain* (1933) and the critical study *A Hope for Poetry* (1934).

Day-Lewis was Clark lecturer at the University of Cambridge in 1946; his lectures there were published as *The Poetic Image* (1947). In 1952 he published his verse translation of Virgil's *Aeneid*, which was commissioned by the BBC. He also translated Virgil's *Georgics* (1940) and *Eclogues* (1963). He was professor of poetry at Oxford from 1951 to 1956. *The Buried Day* (1960), his autobiography, discusses his acceptance and later rejection of communism. *Collected Poems* appeared in 1954. Later volumes of verse include *The Room and Other Poems* (1965) and *The Whispering Roots* (1970). *The Complete Poems of C. Day-Lewis* was published in 1992.

At his death he was poet laureate, having succeeded John Masefield in 1968. Under the pseudonym of Nicholas Blake he also wrote detective novels, including *Minute for Murder* (1948) and *Whisper in the Gloom* (1954).

Day of the Locust, The Novel by Nathanael WEST about the savagery lurking beneath the Hollywood dream. Published in 1939, it is one of the most striking examples of the "Hollywood novel" in American fiction.

Tod Hackett, a set designer, becomes involved in the lives of several individuals who have been warped by their proximity to the artificial world of Hollywood. Hackett's completion of his painting "The Burning of Los Angeles" coincides with the explosion of the other characters' unfulfilled dreams in a conflagration of riot and murder.

Dazai Osamu \dä-'zī-ō-'sä-mù\, *pseudonym of* Tsushima Shūji \'shū-jē\ (b. June 19, 1909, Kanagi, Aomori prefecture, Japan—d. June 13, 1948, Tokyo) Japanese novelist who emerged at the end of World War II as the literary voice of his time. His dark, wry tone perfectly captured the confusion of postwar Japan, when traditional values were discredited.

Born in northern Japan, the sixth son of a wealthy landowner and politician, Dazai often made use of his background as material for his fiction. Although the dominant mood of much of his writing was gloomy, he was also famed for his humor, which sometimes approached farce. In his first collection of short stories, *Bannen* (1936; "The Twilight Years"), Dazai experimented with many styles and topics, but he was most drawn to the I novel, or *shishōsetsu*, form, and the persona of the author was thenceforth to be seen in the majority of his fictional characters.

Almost alone among Japanese writers, Dazai continued to produce works of real literary merit during the war years (1941–45). *Otogi zōshi* (1945; "Fairy Tales"), new versions of traditional tales, represented a triumph of his style and wit. *Tsugaru* (1944), perhaps his best work, was a deeply sympathetic memorial to his place of birth. The tone of his postwar works—*Shayō* (1947; THE SETTING SUN), *Biyon no tsuma* (1947; *Villon's Wife*), and *Ningen shikkaku* (1948; *No Longer Human*)—became increasingly despairing, reflecting the emotional crisis of the author. Dazai committed suicide in 1948, leaving uncompleted a novel ominously entitled *Goodbye*. Many of his works were later translated into English by Donald Keene.

Dead, The Short story by James Joyce, appearing in 1914 in his collection DUBLINERS. It is considered his best short work and a masterpiece of modern fiction.

The story takes place before, during, and after an evening Christmas party attended by Gabriel and Gretta Conroy and their friends and relatives. It leads gradually to Gabriel's late-night epiphany about his life and marriage when a tender song reminds Gretta of a boy who died of love for her.

Dead Lecturer, The Collection of verse by Amiri BARAKA, published in 1964 under the name LeRoi Jones. The collection marked a separation for Baraka from the style and literary philosophy of the Beats, with whom he had previously been associated. In the poem "Rhythm & Blues" he uses the structures of jazz and blues to forge a new, distinctly African-American voice. Poems such as "Black Dada Nihilismus" and "An Agony. As Now." reveal the anger and despair of a black man trapped in a white, middle-class society. The collection is notable for its strong imagery and lyrical treatment of violence.

Dead Souls Novel by Nikolay GOGOL, published in Russian as *Myortvye dushi* in 1842. Considered one of the world's finest satires, this picaresque work traces the adventures of the social-climbing Pavel Ivanovich Chichikov, a dismissed civil servant out to seek his fortune. It is admired not only for its enduring comic portraits but also for its sense of moral purpose.

In the Russia of the novel, landowners must pay taxes on dead serfs until a new census removes them from the tax rolls. Chichikov sets off to buy dead serfs—thus relieving their owners of a tax burden—and mortgaging them to acquire funds to create his own estate. He charms his way into the homes of several influential landowners and puts forth his strange proposal, but he neglects to tell them the real purpose behind his plan. Gogol draws on broad Russian character types for his portraits of landowners. These comic descriptions make up some of the finest scenes in the novel.

Eventually, rumors spread about Chichikov, and he is discovered and arrested. His crafty lawyer defends him by interweaving every scandal in the province with his client's deeds; the embarrassed officials offer to drop the entire matter if Chichikov leaves town, which he gladly does.

Deal in Wheat, A Short story by Frank NORRIS, first published serially in 1902 and then in the book *A Deal in Wheat and Other Stories of the New and Old West*, published posthumously in 1903. Employing the techniques of naturalism, the five-part story examines the business of wheat speculation at the Chicago Board of Trade at the turn of the 20th century. Norris was concurrently working on the unfinished trilogy *The Epic of Wheat*, comprising *The Octopus* (1901) and *The Pit* (1903).

The first episode of "A Deal in Wheat" features Sam Lewiston, who loses his Kansas farm as a result of low wheat prices. The middle three episodes detail the economic warfare of two wealthy speculators, Mr. Hornung of the bull market and Mr.

Truslow of the bear market. In the last episode Lewiston is denied free bread in Chicago because of high wheat prices.

De Amicis \dā-ä-'mē-chēs\, Edmondo (b. Oct. 31, 1846, Oneglia, Kingdom of Sardinia [now part of Italy]—d. March 11, 1908, Bordighera, Italy) Italian writer who is known for his popular travel books and children's stories.

Educated at the military academy at Modena, De Amicis was commissioned in the artillery. He wrote many sketches of military life for the army journal *L'Italia militare* and became its editor in 1867. His stories were collected in *La vita militare* (1868; *Military Life in Italy*), followed by the highly regarded *Novelle* (1872; "Short Stories"). His poetry was collected in *Poesie* (1880). His most important work is the sentimental children's story *Cuore* (1886; *The Heart of a Boy*), written in the form of a schoolboy's diary.

Death \'deth\, *also called* Grim Reaper \'grim-'rē-pər\ The destroyer of life personified and conventionally represented as a skeleton with a scythe. *See also* DANCE OF DEATH.

Death, Be Not Proud Sonnet by John DONNE, one of the 19 "Holy Sonnets," or "Divine Meditations," published in 1633 in the first edition of *Songs and Sonnets*. This devotional lyric directly addresses death, raging defiantly against its perceived haughtiness. The theme, seen throughout Donne's poetry, is that death is unable to corrupt the eternal soul.

In the opening octave, the poet debunks the belief that death is a victor, explaining that it cannot kill him; it can merely rest his weary body and free his soul to heaven. In the concluding sestet, the poet lambasts death's proud posturing, explaining that death cannot choose its victim but must rely on the whims of fate and human decision.

Death Comes for the Archbishop Novel by Willa CATHER, published in 1927. The novel is based on the lives of Bishop Jean Baptiste L'Amy and his vicar Father Joseph Machebeut and is considered emblematic of the author's moral and spiritual concerns.

Death Comes for the Archbishop traces the friendship and adventures of Bishop Jean Latour and vicar Father Joseph Vaillant as they organize the new Roman Catholic diocese of New Mexico. Latour is patrician, intellectual, introverted; Vaillant, practical, outgoing, sanguine. Friends since their childhood in France, the clerics triumph over corrupt Spanish priests, natural adversity, and the indifference of the Hopi and Navajo to establish their church and build a cathedral in the wilderness.

The novel, essentially a study of character, explores Latour's inner conflicts and his relationship with the land, which through the author's powerful description becomes an imposing character in its own right.

Death in the Family, A Novel by James AGEE about a family's reactions to the accidental death of the father. Published in 1957, the novel was praised as one of the best examples of American autobiographical fiction, and it won a Pulitzer Prize in 1958.

As told through the eyes of six-year-old Rufus Follet, the story emerges as an exploration of conflicts both among members of the family and in society. The differences between black and white, rich and poor, country life and city life, and, ultimately, life and death are richly depicted. Agee used contrasting narratives as a structural device to link the past and present; italicized passages describing the family's life before the fatal automobile accident are incorporated into the primary narrative of the crash and its immediate effects.

Death in Venice \'ven-is\ Novella by Thomas MANN, published in German as *Der Tod in Venedig* in 1912. A symbol-laden story of aestheticism and decadence, Mann's best-known novella exemplifies the author's regard for Sigmund Freud's writings on the unconscious.

Gustav von Aschenbach is a revered author whose work is known for its discipline and formal perfection. At his Venetian hotel he encounters the strikingly handsome young teenager Tadzio. Aschenbach is disturbed by his attraction to the boy, and although he watches Tadzio, he dare not speak to him. Despite warnings of a cholera epidemic Aschenbach stays in Venice; he sacrifices his dignity and well-being to the immediate experience of beauty as embodied by Tadzio. After exchanging a significant look with the boy on the day of Tadzio's scheduled departure, Aschenbach dies of cholera.

As in his other major works, Mann explores the role of the artist in society. The cerebral Aschenbach summons extraordinary discipline and endurance in his literary work, but his private desires overwhelm him.

Death of Artemio Cruz, The \är-'tä-mē-ō-'krŭz, *Spanish* är-'täm-yō-'krŭs\   Novel by Carlos FUENTES, published in Spanish as *La muerte de Artemio Cruz* in 1962. An imaginative portrait of an unscrupulous individual, the story also serves as commentary on Mexican society, most notably on the abuse of power—a theme that runs throughout Fuentes' work.

As the novel opens, Artemio Cruz, former revolutionary turned capitalist, lies on his deathbed. He drifts in and out of consciousness, and when he is conscious his mind wanders between past and present. The story reveals that Cruz became rich through treachery, bribery, corruption, and ruthlessness. As a young man he had been full of revolutionary ideals. Acts committed as a means of self-preservation soon developed into a way of life based on opportunism. A fully realized character, Cruz can also be seen as a symbol of Mexico's quest for wealth at the expense of moral values.

Death of a Salesman   A play in "two acts and a requiem" by Arthur MILLER, written in 1948 and produced in 1949. Miller won a Pulitzer Prize for the work, which he described as "the tragedy of a man who gave his life, or sold it" in pursuit of the American Dream.

After many years on the road as a traveling salesman, Willy Loman realizes he has been a failure as a father and husband. His sons, Happy and Biff, are not successful—on his terms (being "well-liked") or any others. His career fading, Willy escapes into reminiscences of an idealized past. In the play's climactic scene, Biff prepares to leave home, starts arguing with Willy, confesses that he has spent three months in jail, and mocks his father's belief in "a smile and a shoeshine." Willy, bitter and broken, his illusions shattered, commits suicide.

Death of Ivan Ilich, The \i-'vän-i-'lʸēch\   Novella by Leo TOLSTOY, published in Russian as *Smert Ivana Ilycha* in 1886, considered a masterpiece of psychological realism. (The name *Ilich* is also transliterated Ilitch, Ilych, or Ilyich.) Ivan Ilich's crisis is remarkably similar to that of Tolstoy himself as described in *A Confession* (1882).

The first section of the story portrays Ivan Ilich's colleagues and family after he has died, as they reflect on the significance of his death for their careers and fortunes. In the second section, Tolstoy reveals the life of the man whose death seems so trivial: "Ivan Ilich's life had been most simple and most ordinary and therefore most terrible." The perfect bureaucrat, Ivan Ilich treasures his orderly domestic and official routine. Diagnosed with an incurable illness, he at first denies the truth, but influenced by the simple acceptance of his servant Gerasim, Ivan Ilich comes to embrace the boy's belief that death is natural and not shameful. He comforts himself with happy memories of childhood and gradually realizes that he has ignored all

his inner yearnings as he tried to do what was expected of him. By the story's end he is at peace.

Death of the Heart, The   Novel by Elizabeth BOWEN, published in 1938. One of Bowen's best-known works, it demonstrates her debt to Henry James in the careful observation of detail and the theme of innocence darkened by experience. The novel is noted for its dexterous portrayal of an adolescent's stormy inner life. Its three sections—"The World," "The Flesh," and "The Devil"—refer to the baptismal rite in the Anglican Book of Common Prayer.

The novel is set chiefly in London in the period between the World Wars. Sixteen-year-old orphan Portia Quayne goes to live with her half brother Thomas and his wife Anna, both of whom are portrayed as urbane and empty. Bored and lonely, Portia falls in love with Eddie, one of Anna's friends; he does not return her love. Weeks later, Portia learns that Anna has been reading her diary. Thoroughly humiliated, Portia preposterously proposes marriage to a kindly family friend, who refuses her and encourages her to return to Thomas and Anna. In the end, Anna and Portia come to terms with each other, and Anna finally sympathizes with Portia's "frantic desire to be handled with feeling."

Death of the Hired Man, The   Narrative poem by Robert FROST, published in *North of Boston* in 1914. The poem, written in blank verse, consists of a conversation between the farmer Warren and his wife Mary about their former farmhand Silas, an elderly man who has come "home" to their farm to die. Silas' plight is poignantly presented, and the characterizations of home as "where, when you have to go there,/They have to take you in" and "Something you somehow haven't to deserve" are well known.

Death of Virgil, The \'vər-jəl, *German* ver-'gēl\   Novel by Hermann BROCH, published simultaneously in German (as *Der Tod des Vergil*) and in English in 1945. Best known of the author's works, the novel imaginatively recreates the last 18 hours of the poet Virgil's life as he is brought to Brundisium. Broch, an Austrian Jewish refugee from Hitler's Europe, concerns himself here and in his other works with the place of literature in a culture in crisis.

Written in rich poetic language and rhythmic sentences, the novel has four "symphonic" movements. In the first, the poet who had glorified Rome confronts its vile street life. Having decided that his writing, which excludes the ugly, is false and meaningless, Virgil in the novel's second part decides to burn the *Aeneid*. In the third part, the emperor Augustus convinces Virgil to turn over the manuscript for safekeeping in exchange for the freeing of his slaves. The fourth movement completes the first three as the moribund author manages to reconcile the opposites of life and death, beauty and ugliness. In what is considered to be one of the most remarkable passages in modern literature, Virgil has a dying vision of himself on a rapturous sea voyage.

Deaths and Entrances   Volume of verse by Dylan THOMAS, published in 1946. It demonstrated an affirmative and deepening harmony between Thomas and his Welsh environment. Using elemental and religious imagery, the poet looks with sympathy at the impact of World War II, particularly the bombing of London. The poetry is noted for its lyrical movement and is characterized by the rhythmic use of complex syllabic lines of variable lengths.

Two often-anthologized poems in the collection, FERN HILL and "Poem in October," are expressive, visionary, and mystical odes to innocence and childhood, based on adult recollections. Other poems include "The Conversation of Prayer," "A Winter's Tale," "Ceremony After a Fire Raid," "Vision and

Prayer," and "A Refusal to Mourn the Death, by Fire, of a Child in London."

débat \dā-'bă\ [French, literally, debate, altercation] **1.** A type of literary composition popular especially in medieval times in which two or more usually allegorical characters discuss or debate some subject, most often a question of love, morality, or politics, and then refer the question to a judge. Compare TENSON. **2.** An extended discussion, debate, or philosophical argument between two characters in a work of literature. George Bernard Shaw incorporated such discussions into several of his plays, including *Major Barbara*.

Deborah or **Debbora** \'deb-rə, -ə-rə\ Biblical character, the first notable judge of the tribal confederacy of Israel. Primarily a seer, poet, and interpreter of dreams, Deborah was known for her charismatic leadership, which, together with the military leadership of Barak, her commander, inspired the Israelites to military victory over the Canaanites.

The two narratives of her exploits are a prose account in Chapter 4 of Judges and the martial poem known as "The Song of Deborah" in Judges 5. The Canaanites, under the leadership of Jabin, king of a reestablished Hazor, and his general Sisera, had oppressed an apostate Israel. Deborah sends word to all the tribes to unite against the Canaanites, but only about half the tribes respond. The Israelites meet the Canaanites in the Valley of Jezreel near the river Kishon in open battle. A cloudburst occurs, causing the river to flood, thus limiting the maneuverability of the Canaanite chariots. General Sisera, seeing defeat for his forces, seeks refuge in the tent of a Kenite woman, Jael. A supporter of Israel's cause, Jael gives Sisera a drink of milk, possibly fermented, and he falls asleep "from weariness," whereupon she kills him, thus ending decisively the Canaanite threat. The victory song of Deborah in Chapter 5 is one of the oldest literary sections of the Old Testament. It is a hymn that incorporates the literary forms of a confession of faith, a praise of Yahweh's theophany (manifestation), an epic, a curse, a blessing, and a hymn of victory.

decadence \'dek-ə-dəns, di-'kā-\ A period of decline or deterioration of art or literature that follows an era of great achievement. Examples include the SILVER AGE of Latin literature, which began about AD 18 following the end of the Golden Age, and the Decadent movement at the end of the 19th century in France and England.

Decadent \'dek-ə-dənt, di-'kā-\ [French *décadent*, literally, person living in a decadent period] Any of several poets of the end of the 19th century, including the French Symbolist poets in particular and their contemporaries in England, the later generation of the Aesthetic movement. Both the Symbolists and the Aesthetes aspired to set literature and art free from all influences. They emphasized the idea of art for art's sake, seeing art as autonomous and opposed to nature as well as to the materialistic preoccupations of industrialized society. They therefore stressed the bizarre and the incongruous and artificial in their work as well as their personal lives. In both, the freedom of some members' morals helped to enlarge the connotation of the term, which is almost equivalent to fin de siècle.

Decadence was primarily associated with poetry, but its psychological basis is well illustrated in Joris-Karl Huysmans' novel *À rebours* (1884; *Against the Grain*) and the trilogy *Le Culte du moi* (1888–91) by Maurice Barrès. The impetus to Decadent poetry came partly from the study of Charles Baudelaire and partly from the works of Stéphane Mallarmé and Paul Verlaine.

In Verlaine's work two impressions predominate: that only the self is important, and that the function of poetry is to preserve moments of extreme sensation and unique impression. These were the features, together with experiments in form, on

which the younger generation of poets seized in the 1880s. The poetic movement found its best exponent in Jules LaForgue. The review *Le Décadent*, whose title consecrated a label originally coined by hostile critics, was founded in 1886.

In England the Decadents were the poets of the 1890s—Arthur Symons, Oscar Wilde, Ernest Dowson, and Lionel Johnson, who were members of the Rhymers' Club or contributors to the avant-garde journal *The Yellow Book*. Compare AESTHETICISM; SYMBOLIST MOVEMENT.

decadentismo \ˌdā-kä-dän-'tēz-mō\ or **Decadentism** [Italian, from French *décadentisme*, a derivative of *décadent* decadent] Italian artistic movement that derived its name but not all its characteristics from the French and English Decadents, who flourished in the last 10 years of the 19th century. Writers of the Italian movement, which did not have the cohesion usual in such cases, generally reacted against the tenets of positivism and the belief in scientific rationalism and the significance of society as a whole. They instead stressed instinct, the irrational, the subconscious, and the individual.

The writers of the movement—Antonio Fogazzaro, Giovanni Pascoli, Gabriele D'Annunzio, Italo Svevo, and Luigi Pirandello—differed greatly from each other in style and philosophical approach, but they all created highly subjective pictures of society and the world.

Decameron \di-'kam-ə-rən, -ˌrän\ Collection of tales by Giovanni BOCCACCIO, probably composed between 1349 and 1353. The work is regarded as a masterpiece of classical Italian prose. While romantic in tone and form, it breaks from medieval sensibility in its insistence on the human ability to overcome, even exploit, fortune.

The *Decameron* comprises a group of stories united by a frame story. As the frame narrative opens, 10 young people (seven women and three men) flee plague-stricken Florence to a delightful villa in nearby Fiesole. Each rules for a day and sets stipulations for the daily tales to be told by all participants, resulting in a collection of 100 pieces. Each day ends with a canzone (song), some of which represent Boccaccio's finest poetry.

Each daily collection of stories takes a different tone or theme. Day 1 consists of a witty discussion of human vices. On Day 2, fortune triumphs over its human playthings, but it is trounced by human will on Day 3. Day 4 is marked by tragic love stories. Day 5 brings happy endings to love that does not at first run smoothly. Wit and gaiety again reign on Day 6. Trickery, deceit, and often bawdy license run free on Days 7, 8, and 9. By Day 10, earlier themes are brought to a high pitch; the widely borrowed story "The Patient Griselda" closes the cycle of tales.

It is generally acknowledged that Boccaccio borrowed many of the stories from folklore and myth, but the exquisite writing and sophisticated structure of the work make clear that its author was no mere anthologist. His prose influenced many Renaissance writers, and his tales themselves have been borrowed for centuries.

decameter \də-'kam-ə-tər\ [Greek *dekámetron*, from *déka* ten + *métron* meter, measure] In prosody, a poetic line of 10 feet.

decastich \'dek-ə-ˌstik\ [Greek *déka* ten + *stíchos* line, verse] A poem or stanza of 10 lines.

decasyllable \'dek-ə-ˌsil-ə-bel\ In prosody, a line of verse having 10 syllables.

decency \'dē-sən-sē\ **1.** Literary decorum or its observance. **2.** The established conventions of literary decorum often with special reference to syntactical or grammatical propriety.

De claris mulieribus \dā-'klä-rēs-ˌmü-lē-'ä-rē-bús\, *also called* De mulieribus claris (*Concerning Famous Women*)

Work by Giovanni BOCCACCIO, written about 1360–74. One of the many Latin works the author produced after his meeting with Petrarch, *De claris mulieribus* contains the biographies of more than 100 notable women. In it Boccaccio decried the practice of sending women without vocation to nunneries. He intended the book to provide female readers with models of female lives fully lived.

Decline and Fall   First novel of Evelyn WAUGH, published in 1928, a social satire based on his own experiences as a teacher.

The protagonist, Paul Pennyfeather, accepts passively all that befalls him. Expelled for indecent behavior from Scone College, Oxford, he becomes a teacher. When taken up by Margot, a wealthy society woman, he undergoes a series of outrageous experiences. Because of Margot's involvement in the white slave trade, he suffers imprisonment, which he bears stoically. After Margot engineers his escape from prison, he returns to Scone College as a student of theology, pretending to be Paul Pennyfeather, a remote cousin of the more notorious man of the same name.

Decline and Fall of the Roman Empire, The (*in full* The History of the Decline and Fall of the Roman Empire)   Historical work by Edward GIBBON, published in six volumes between 1776 and 1788. A continuous narrative from the 2nd century AD to the fall of Constantinople in 1453, it is distinguished by its rigorous scholarship, its historical perspective, and its incomparable literary style.

The Decline and Fall is divided into two parts, equal in bulk but different in treatment. The first half covers about 300 years to the end of the empire in the West, about 480 AD; in the second half nearly 1,000 years are compressed. Gibbon viewed the Roman Empire as a single entity in undeviating decline from the ideals of political and intellectual freedom that had characterized the classical literature he had read. For him, the material decay of Rome was the effect and symbol of moral decadence.

deconstruction \,dē-kən-'strək-shən\   A method of literary criticism which assumes that language refers only to itself rather than to an extratextual reality and which asserts multiple conflicting interpretations of a text and bases such interpretations on the philosophical, political, or social implications of the use of language in the text rather than on the author's intention.

Deconstruction was initiated by French critic Jacques DERRIDA, who in a series of books published beginning in the late 1960s launched a major critique of traditional Western metaphysics. He introduced the words *déconstruire* ("to deconstruct") and *déconstruction* ("deconstruction") in *De la grammatologie* (1967). Like Sigmund Freud's psychological theories and Karl Marx's political theories, Derrida's deconstructive strategies, which expand on Ferdinand de Saussure's insistence on the arbitrariness of the verbal sign, have subsequently established themselves as an important part of postmodernism, especially in poststructural literary theory and text analysis.

The deconstruction of philosophy involves the questioning of the many hierarchical oppositions—such as cause and effect, presence and absence, speech ("phonocentrism") and writing—in order to expose the bias (the privileged terms) of those tacit assumptions on which Western metaphysics rest. Deconstruction takes apart the logic of language in which authors make their claims, a process that reveals how all texts undermine themselves in that every text includes unconscious "traces" of other positions exactly opposite to that which it sets out to uphold. Deconstruction undermines "logocentrism" (literally, a focus on the word, the original and originating word in relation to which other concepts such as truth, identity, and certainty can be validated; but understood more generally as a

belief in reason and rationality, the belief that meaning inheres in the world independently of any human attempt to represent it in words). It follows from this view that the "meaning" of a text bears only accidental relationship to the author's conscious intentions. One of the effects of deconstructive criticism has been a loosening of language from concepts and referents.

To many American scholars deconstruction seemed a logical step beyond NEW CRITICISM (with its strong emphasis on text), and it was readily accepted and enlarged upon at Yale University by such proponents as Paul de Man and J. Hillis Miller. *See also* POSTSTRUCTURALISM.

decorum \di-'kôr-əm\ [Latin (Cicero's translation of Greek *prépon*), neuter of *decorus* becoming, suitable, decent]   Literary and dramatic propriety especially as formulated and practiced by the Neoclassicists. The concept of literary propriety, in its simplest stage of development, was outlined by Aristotle. In later classical criticism, Horace maintained that, to retain its unity, a work of art must be consistent in every aspect: the subject or theme must be dealt with in the proper diction, meter, form, and tone. Characters, for example, should speak in a manner befitting their social position.

Dedalus, Stephen \'stēv-ən-'ded-ə-ləs, 'dēd-\   Fictional character, the protagonist of James Joyce's autobiographical novel A PORTRAIT OF THE ARTIST AS A YOUNG MAN and a central character in his novel ULYSSES. Joyce gave his hero the surname Dedalus after the mythic craftsman Daedalus.

In *A Portrait of the Artist*, set in Dublin in the late 19th century, Dedalus rebels against what he sees as the pervasive, repressive influence of the Roman Catholic church and the parochial and provincial attitudes of his family and of Ireland itself. He leaves Ireland for France in order to fulfill the artistic promise inherent in his name.

In *Ulysses* Dedalus is once more a searcher, this time for meaning. He symbolizes Telemachus, the son of Ulysses (Odysseus), here represented by Leopold Bloom, the universal man.

dedication \,ded-ə-'kā-shən\   A name and often a message prefixed to a literary, musical, or artistic production. Formerly, a dedication was used to testify to the artist's respect for a patron and often recommended the work to the patron's favor. Contemporary dedications usually express admiration or affection for a person or for a cause.

dedication copy   The copy of a book presented by its author to the person to whom it is dedicated.

Dedlock, Lady Honoria \hō-'nȯr-ē-ə-'ded-,läk\   Fictional character in the novel BLEAK HOUSE by Charles Dickens, a beautiful woman who harbors the secret that she bore an illegitimate daughter before her marriage to a wealthy baronet. Privilege and wealth have not fulfilled Lady Dedlock's expectations of life. When she learns her own past is in danger of being exposed, she runs away in shame and despair.

Deerbrook \'dir-,brůk\   The first and best-regarded novel by Harriet MARTINEAU, published in 1839.

The novel's plot centers on the Ibbotson sisters—beautiful, self-absorbed Hester and pragmatic, sensitive Margaret. They are rivals for the affections of Edward Hope, the village doctor, who is eventually forced by social pressure to choose Hester for his bride. Both his marriage and his practice are undermined by gossip and rumormongering.

A secondary character, governess Maria Young, is physically impaired and impoverished, as was the author herself. Society presents the governess with few options, and she is seen as the prototype of the single woman struggling with genteel poverty in the Victorian novel.

Deerslayer, The \'dir-ˌslā-ər\ (*in full* The Deerslayer; or, The First War-Path) The fifth of five novels in the series THE LEATHER-STOCKING TALES by James Fenimore COOPER, published in two volumes in 1841.

In *The Deerslayer*, Cooper returns to Natty Bumppo's youth at Lake Oswego, N.Y. (called Glimmerglass in the novel), in the 1740s, at the time of the French and Indian War. Known as "Deerslayer" among the Delaware Indians with whom he lives, young Bumppo and the giant Hurry Harry help the trapper Thomas Hutter to resist an attack by the Iroquois, who are allied with the French. The Iroquois capture Hutter and Hurry Harry; Bumppo and his friend, the Mohican chief Chingachgook, secure their release, but in an attempt to rescue Chingachgook's bride, Bumppo himself is captured. Hutter is killed. His daughter, Judith, confesses her love to Bumppo and manages to delay his execution until Chingachgook arrives with a troop of British soldiers to effect a rescue.

Defarge, Madame Thérèse \di-'färzh\ Fictional character in A TALE OF TWO CITIES, a novel by Charles Dickens set during the period of the French Revolution.

A symbol of vengefulness and revolutionary excess, Madame Defarge sits outside her Paris wine shop endlessly knitting a scarf that is—in effect—a list of those to be killed. Incorporated into the scarf's pattern are the names of hated aristocrats—including the St. Evrémondes, the family of Charles Darnay, a leading character.

Defence of Guenevere, The \'gwin-ə-vir\ (*in full* The Defence of Guenevere and Other Poems) Collection of poetry by William MORRIS, published in 1858.

The poems that make up the collection, many of which are dramatic monologues, fall into three groups. The first group consists of four poems of a cycle (never completed) on legends of King Arthur and his court. Accused of adultery, a crime punishable by death, Queen Guenevere presents her defense in the title poem. The ancient setting permitted Morris to discuss issues of love and sexual desire with a forthrightness uncommon in Victorian literature. A second group of poems, based on the 14th-century *Chroniques* of Jean Froissart, shows England's decline at the conclusion of the Hundred Years' War. The poems in the third group are highly evocative, yet their meanings are elusive.

Defence of Poesie, The \'pō-ə-zē, -sē\ Literary criticism by Sir Philip SIDNEY, written about 1582 and published posthumously in 1595. Another edition of the work, published the same year, is titled *An Apologie for Poetrie*. Considered the finest work of Elizabethan literary criticism, Sidney's elegant essay suggests that literature is a better teacher than history or philosophy, and it masterfully refutes Plato's infamous decision to ban poets from the state in his *Republic*.

Sidney composed his eloquent defense of imaginative literature against charges of time-wasting, prevarication, and allurement to vice. Writing before England's great age of poetry and drama, he thus finds English literature sadly wanting. He does, however, praise such works as Geoffrey Chaucer's *Troilus and Criseyde*, the anthology *The Mirror for Magistrates*, and Edmund Spenser's *The Shepheardes Calender*. While Sidney's ideas are not considered particularly original, the work did introduce the critical thought of continental Renaissance theorists to England.

Deffand \de-'fäⁿ\, Marie de Vichy-Chamrond, Marquise du (b. 1697, Château of Chamrond, Burgundy, Fr.—d. Sept. 23, 1780, Paris) Woman of letters and a leading figure in French society.

Marie de Vichy-Chamrond was born of a noble family, educated at a convent in Paris, and married at 21 to her kinsman Jean-Baptiste de La Lande, Marquis du Deffand, from whom she separated in 1722. She became the mistress of Philippe II, Duke d'Orléans, and was frequently seen at Sceaux, where the Duchess du Maine held court amid a brilliant company that included Fontenelle, the Marquise de Lambert, Voltaire, and Jean-François Hénault, president of the Parlement of Paris.

Mme du Deffand set up her own salon, but by 1754 she had lost her sight and engaged Julie de Lespinasse to help her in entertaining. The salon was broken up following the 1764 dismissal of Mlle de Lespinasse, who took with her many of its patrons.

The principal friendships of Mme du Deffand's later years were with the Duchess de Choiseul and Horace Walpole. Her letters to the duchess are full of life and have great charm. Those to Voltaire, extending over 43 years, contain great wit. Among her best letters are those to Walpole, 20 years her junior, for whom she had developed a passion. Her prose developed qualities of style and eloquence of which her earlier writings had given little promise, and her chronicle of events at court and at home form a fascinating and valuable document.

definitive \də-'fin-i-tiv\ Most authoritative, reliable, and complete. The word is used in reference to research, scholarship, or criticism, especially of a biographical or historical study, or of a text or edition of a literary work or author.

Defoe \di-'fō\, Daniel, *original surname* Foe \'fō\ (b. 1660, London, Eng.—d. April 24, 1731, London) English novelist, pamphleteer, and journalist, author of ROBINSON CRUSOE (1719) and MOLL FLANDERS (1722).

Although his Nonconformist father intended him for the ministry, Defoe by 1683 had set up as a merchant. He traveled widely and became an acute and intelligent economic theorist. He proved to be a staunch supporter of and leading pamphleteer for William of Orange. In 1701, in reply to attacks on the "foreign" king, Defoe published his eloquent and witty poem *The True-Born Englishman*.

Engraving by Michiel van der Gucht, after a portrait by J. Taverner, first half of the 18th century

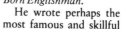

National Portrait Gallery, London

He wrote perhaps the most famous and skillful of all his pamphlets, "The Shortest-Way With The Dissenters" (1702), to discredit the High Churchmen, writing as if from their viewpoint but reducing their arguments to absurdity. The pamphlet had a huge sale, but Dissenters and High Churchmen alike took it seriously and were furious when the hoax was exposed. Defoe was arrested in May 1703 and prosecuted for seditious libel. Although miserably apprehensive of his punishment, Defoe had spirit enough to write the audacious "Hymn To The Pillory," which helped to turn the occasion into something of a triumph.

He was led back to Newgate Prison, where he remained while his business collapsed. He appealed to Robert Harley, 1st Earl of Oxford, who finally secured his release in return for his services as a pamphleteer and intelligence agent. Defoe paid several visits to Scotland, keeping Harley closely in touch with public opinion. These trips also provided material for the three volumes of his admirable and informative *Tour Through the Whole Island of Great Britain* (1724–26).

Perhaps Defoe's most remarkable achievement during Queen Anne's reign, however, was the periodical *Review*. He wrote this serious and forceful paper practically single-handedly from 1704 to 1713. It was, effectively, the main government organ, but Defoe also discussed other topics.

With George I's accession in 1714, the Tories (including Harley) fell from power. Defoe continued to write for the Whig government and to carry out intelligence work. At about this time he wrote the best known and most popular of his many didactic works, *The Family Instructor* (1715). He achieved literary immortality in 1719 when he turned his talents to an extended work of prose fiction and (drawing partly on the memoirs of voyagers and castaways such as Alexander Selkirk) produced *Robinson Crusoe*.

Here (as in his works of 1722, which included *Moll Flanders*, A JOURNAL OF THE PLAGUE YEAR, and *Colonel Jack*) Defoe displays his finest gift as a novelist—his insight into human nature. Although the men and women he writes about are all placed in unusual circumstances and are all, in one sense or another, solitaries, Defoe writes of them first as ordinary human beings. Writing always in the first person, Defoe enters into their minds and analyzes their motives. In 1724 he published his last major work of fiction, ROXANA, but he remained active and enterprising as a writer despite failing health.

DeForest \dǝ-'fȯr-ǝst\, John William (b. May 31, 1826, Humphreysville, Conn., U.S.—d. July 17, 1906, New Haven, Conn.)   American writer of realistic fiction, author of a major novel of the American Civil War—*Miss Ravenel's Conversion from Secession to Loyalty* (1867).

DeForest traveled in the Middle East from 1848 to 1849. He returned home to write a scholarly *History of the Indians in Connecticut* (1851) before setting out for Europe, where he lived from 1851 to 1854. Two travel books came out of these experiences abroad: *Oriental Acquaintance* (1856) and *European Acquaintance* (1858).

When the American Civil War broke out, DeForest organized a company of New Haven volunteers and served as captain in several Union campaigns. After the war, he was district commander of the Freedmen's Bureau in Greenville, S.C. (1866–67). His experiences in war and its aftermath were published posthumously as *A Volunteer's Adventures* (1946) and *A Union Officer in the Reconstruction* (1948).

In addition to *Miss Ravenel's Conversion*, DeForest wrote *Kate Beaumont* (1872), which depicts the social life in South Carolina before the war, and *The Bloody Chasm* (1881), its social life after the war. Two other novels, *Honest John Vane* (1875) and *Playing the Mischief* (1875), deal with corruption during the administration of President Ulysses S. Grant. His last novel, *A Lover's Revolt* (1898), is a romance of the American Revolution.

Dehmel \'dā-mǝl\, Richard (b. Nov. 18, 1863, Wendisch-Hermsdorf, Brandenburg, Prussia [Germany]—d. Feb. 8, 1920, Blankenese, near Hamburg)   German poet who exerted a major influence through his innovations in form and content.

Dehmel chose naturalistic social themes for his early works and was one of the first major poets to write about the misery of the working classes. Influenced by Friedrich Nietzsche, he extolled individualism and a life of uninhibited instincts and passion, but at the same time he felt drawn to self-sacrifice and the search for harmonious ethical ideas. In Dehmel's first collection of poems, *Erlösungen* (1891; "Redemptions"), the conflict is expressed in the opposition of unbridled sensuality and ascetic self-discipline. He came to view the sensual

relations between a man and a woman as the basis for a full development of the human personality and for a higher spiritual life. This is the theme of the cyclical epic poem *Zwei Menschen* (1903; "Two People"). This work and others are characterized by an ecstatic rhetoric that can be sensitive at its finest and sensational at its worst. Dehmel's treatment of sexual themes was not only passionate but, for the times, shockingly frank.

Dehmel volunteered for service in World War I but expressed his disillusionment in his last work, a war diary, *Zwischen Volk und Menschheit* (1919; "Between People and Humanity"). His other works include *Weib und Welt* (1896; "Woman and World"), *Die Verwandlungen der Venus* (1907; "The Transformations of Venus"), and *Schöne wilde Welt* (1913; "Beautiful, Wild World").

Deighton \'dāt-ǝn\, Len, *in full* Leonard Cyril Deighton (b. Feb. 18, 1929, Marylebone, London, Eng.)   English author best known for his light and droll spy stories. His light touch, combined with painstaking attention to detail, set his work apart from others of the genre.

Deighton was educated at St. Martin's School of Art, London, and the Royal College of Art. His first two spy novels, *The Ipcress File* (1962) and *Funeral in Berlin* (1964), established his reputation. He wrote a notable screenplay for the movie *Oh! What a Lovely War* (1969) and also contributed a weekly comic strip on cooking to *The Observer*. In the early 1980s he published his most ambitious espionage novels, the trilogy *Berlin Game* (1983), *Mexico Set*, and *London Match* (both 1985). *City of Gold* was published in 1992 and *Violent Ward* in 1993. Deighton also wrote military history, historical novels, and cookbooks.

Deirdre or **Deirdriu** \'dir-drē, -drǝ; 'dar-drǝ; *Irish* 'dʸärʸ-dʸrʸǝ \   In early Irish literature, the gentle and fair heroine of THE TRAGIC DEATH OF THE SONS OF USNECH (*Oidheadh Chloinne Uisneach*), the great love story of the Ulster cycle.

Dejection: An Ode   Autobiographical poem by Samuel Taylor COLERIDGE, published in 1802 in the *Morning Post*, a London daily newspaper.

When he wrote this poem, Coleridge was addicted to opium, was unhappy in his marriage, and had fallen in love with Sara Hutchinson. Intended originally as a letter in verse to Sara (who is referred to by the anagram "Asra"), it describes his complaints and fears with great emotional intensity. The poet is afraid that his poetic powers are waning and that he no longer responds intensely to nature. He reveals the disintegration of his marriage and the damaging effects of opium.

Deken \'dā-kǝn\, Aagje, *byname of* Agatha Deken (b. Dec. 10, 1741, Amstelveen, Neth.—d. Nov. 14, 1804, The Hague)   Writer and collaborator with Betje WOLFF on the first Dutch novel, *De historie van mejuffrouw Sara Burgerhart*, 2 vol. (1782; "The History of Miss Sara Burgerhart").

Deken had written a little-known volume of devotional poetry by the time she met Betje Wolff in 1776. The next year, following the death of Wolff's husband, the two set up house together and began collaborating on fiction. With their third book, *Sara Burgerhart*, they changed the direction of Dutch writing. They developed the epistolary technique that had been introduced by Samuel Richardson in England and produced a realistic novel that was free of sentimentality and unnatural motivations. Deken's chief contribution to the plot was her experience, as a girl, of orphanage life and domestic service.

Further though less notable collaborations in the epistolary style followed, including *De historie van den heer Willem Leevend*, 8 vol. (1784–85; "The History of Mr. William Leevend"), and *De historie van mejuffrouw Cornelia Wildschut*, 6 vol. (1793–94; "The History of Miss Cornelia Wildschut").

During the Prussian invasion of 1788, Deken and Wolff moved to Trévoux, Fr., where they lived for 10 years. Their book *Wandelingen door Bourgogne* (1789; "Strolling Through Burgundy") told of their impressions of the French countryside.

Although Deken wrote an additional four volumes of instructional verse, she is chiefly remembered for her association with Wolff.

Dekker \'dek-ər\, Thomas (b. *c.* 1572, London, Eng.—d. *c.* 1632) English dramatist and writer of prose pamphlets, memorable for his lively depictions of London life.

Few facts of Dekker's life are certain. First mentioned as a playwright in 1598, he wrote to support himself and had a hand in at least 42 plays. Dekker's ability to construct dramatic action was defective; in the dispute known as "the poets' war," or "the war of the theaters," he was satirized in Ben Jonson's *Poetaster* (produced 1601). This precipitated Dekker's own attack on Jonson in the play *Satiro-mastix* (produced 1601). Eleven more plays survive in which Dekker collaborated with such figures as Thomas Middleton, John Webster, Philip Massinger, John Ford, and William Rowley.

Of the five plays that are entirely Dekker's work, probably the best known are *The Shomakers Holiday* (1600) and *The Honest Whore, Part 2* (1630). These plays are typical of his work in their use of the moralistic tone of traditional drama, in the rush of their prose, in their boisterousness, in their colloquial speech, and in their mixture of realistic detail with a romanticized plot.

There is a similar vigor in his prose pamphlets, such as *The Wonderfull Yeare* (1603), about the plague; *The Belman of London* (1608), about roguery and crime; and *The Guls Horne-Booke* (1609), about London theaters.

de la Mare \,del-ə-'mar\, Walter (John) (b. April 25, 1873, Charlton, Kent, Eng.—d. June 22, 1956, Twickenham, Middlesex) British poet and novelist with an unusual power to evoke the ghostly, evanescent moments in life.

De la Mare was educated at St. Paul's School, London, and from 1890 to 1908 worked in the office of an oil company. From 1902, however, when his *Songs of Childhood* appeared under the pseudonym Walter Ramal, he devoted himself increasingly to writing. His first novel, *Henry Brocken*, was published in 1904 and his *Poems* in 1906. He wrote poems and short stories; novels, of which *Memoirs of a Midget* (1921) achieved the greatest poetic fantasy; a fairy play, *Crossings* (1921); and essays and literary studies. His anthology *Come Hither* (1923) is often held to be one of the best and most original in the language.

Collected Poems appeared in 1920, 1935, and 1942; *Collected Rhymes and Verses* in 1944; and *Collected Stories for Children* in 1947. Later poetry includes *The Burning Glass* (1945), *The Traveller* (1946), *Inward Companion* (1950), and *O Lovely England* (1953).

Deland \di-'land\, Margaret, *byname of* Margaretta Wade Deland, *original surname* Campbell \'kam-bəl, *US also* 'kam-əl\ (b. Feb. 23, 1857, Allegheny, Pa., U.S.—d. Jan. 13, 1945, Boston, Mass.) American writer who frequently portrayed small-town life.

In 1886 Deland published *The Old Garden*, a collection of poems. Her first novel, *John Ward, Preacher* (1888), dealt with religious and social questions after the manner of the British writer Mrs. Humphry Ward. Her most popular works were a nostalgic series of stories set in the fictional small town of Old Chester, which was based on the town of Manchester, Pa., where she was raised. These were collected in *Old Chester Tales* (1898), *Dr. Lavendar's People* (1903), *Around Old Chester*

(1915), and *New Friends in Old Chester* (1924). Among her other works were several "problem" novels dealing with such issues as divorce, feminism, and adultery. These include *The Awakening of Helena Richie* (1906), *The Iron Woman* (1911), *The Rising Tide* (1916), and *The Vehement Flame* (1922). She also wrote a volume of childhood memories, *If This Be I, As I Suppose It Be* (1935), and an autobiography, *Golden Yesterdays* (1941).

Delaney \di-'lā-nē\, Shelagh (b. Nov. 25, 1939, Salford, Lancashire, Eng.) British playwright who, at the age of 19, won critical acclaim and popular success with her first play, *A Taste of Honey* (1958; film, 1961).

Set in the bleak industrial area of Delaney's native country, the play blends humor and pathos in its vivid account of an illegitimate pregnancy. A second play, *The Lion in Love* (1961), was received less favorably. Delaney later produced a volume of short stories, *Sweetly Sings the Donkey* (1963), and she won wide praise in 1968 for her screenplay *Charlie Bubbles*. Her third play, *The House That Jack Built* (1977), was first produced for television. During the 1970s and '80s she wrote primarily for radio and television, although she also wrote a successful screenplay (1985; *Dance With a Stranger*).

Delany \də-'lā-nē\, Martin R., *in full* Robinson (b. May 6, 1812, Charles Town, Va. [now W.Va.], U.S.—d. Jan. 24, 1885, Xenia, Ohio) African-American writer and activist whose dedication to the cause of black nationalism in the pre-Civil War era marked him as a thinker ahead of his time.

Born to free parents, Delany was educated illegally during a period when black literacy was prohibited by law. He began the study of medicine in Philadelphia, where he first formed the Pan-Africanist views that confused and angered many of his contemporaries, including fellow blacks. From 1847 until 1849, he was a coeditor with Frederick Douglass of the antislavery newspaper *North Star*.

After the passage of the 1850 Fugitive Slave Act, by which the federal government undertook to help in the search for and return of runaway slaves, Delany wrote his most important work, *The Condition, Elevation, Emigration, and Destiny of the Colored People of the United States* (1852). He urged blacks to be self-reliant both financially and intellectually. *Blake; or, The Huts of America* (partially published 1859; full publication, 1861–62), his only novel, was one of the first novels by a black American to be published in the United States. It is a penetrating examination of slavery and its many ramifications. Although the book received little critical attention at the time of publication, it was revived in the 1960s and hailed as an early model for African-American consciousness and activism.

Delany \də-'lā-nē\, Samuel R., *in full* Samuel Ray Delany, Jr. (b. April 1, 1942, New York, N.Y., U.S.) African-American science-fiction novelist and critic whose highly imaginative works address racial and social issues, heroic quests, and the nature of language.

Delany's first novel, *The Jewels of Aptor*, was published in 1962. *Babel-17* (1966), which clinched his reputation, has an artist as the protagonist and explores the nature of language and its ability to give structure to experience. Similarly, *The Einstein Intersection* (1967) features an artist-outsider and addresses issues of cultural development and sexual identity. *Dhalgren* (1975), considered his most controversial novel, is the story of a young bisexual man searching for identity in a large, decaying city. The main character of *Triton* (1976) undergoes a sex-change operation, and in this novel the author examines bias against women and homosexuals.

Delany's Neveryon series (*Tales of Nevèrÿon* [1979]; *Neveryóna; or, The Tale of Signs and Cities* [1983]; *Flight from Nevèrÿon* [1985]; and *The Bridge of Lost Desire* [1987]) is set in a magical past at the beginning of civilization. His complex *Stars in My Pocket Like Grains of Sand* (1984) is regarded as a stylistic breakthrough for the author. He also wrote the novella "Time Considered as a Helix of Semi-Precious Stones" (1969) and the criticism *The Jewel-Hinged Jaw: Notes on the Language of Science Fiction* (1977). Delany has also written scripts for film, radio, and *Wonder Woman* comic books.

de la Roche \də-lə-'rȯsh, -'rōsh\, Mazo (b. Jan. 15, 1879, Newmarket, Ont., Can.—d. July 12, 1961, Toronto) Canadian author whose series of novels about the Whiteoak family of Jalna (their estate in Ontario) made her one of the most popular "family saga" novelists of her time.

De la Roche's first success, *Jalna* (1927), ended with the 100th birthday of Grandmother Adeline Whiteoak, a lusty character later celebrated in a long-running play, *Whiteoaks* (1936), and a film, *Jalna* (1935). Though not written in chronological order, the saga continues with 15 other books, covering 100 years of Whiteoak family history. De la Roche's other works include children's stories, travel books, drama, and an autobiography, *Ringing the Changes* (1957).

Delblanc \'däl-ˌblänk\, Sven (Axel Herman) (b. May 26, 1931, Swan River, Manitoba, Can.—d. December 1992, Uppsala, Swed.) Swedish novelist who was notable for his use of the intrusive narrator and for the incorporation of grotesque, visionary, and mythical elements in his work.

Delblanc taught at the University of Uppsala until the early 1970s, when he began to write full-time. His first novel, *Eremitkräftan* (1962; "The Hermit Crab"), was an allegorical exploration of the roles of freedom, love, and mysticism in human existence. He continued to pursue those themes in such novels as *Prästkappan* (1963; "The Cassock"), set in late 18th-century Germany, and *Kastrater* (1975; *The Castrati*), set in 18th-century Florence. A popular quartet of novels—*Åminne* (1970; "Memorial"), *Stenfågel* (1973; "Stone Bird"), *Vinteride* (1974; "Winter Lair"), and *Stadsporten* (1976; "The Town Gate")—is set in rural Sweden in the 1930s. A companion series written in the 1980s chronologically precedes the quartet and contains many autobiographical elements. In addition to fiction he wrote essays and plays and published two volumes of memoirs, *Livets ax* (1991; "The Staff of Life" or "Gleanings from Life") and *Agnar* (1992; "Chaff").

Deledda \dā-'läd-dä\, Grazia (b. Sept. 27, 1871, Nuoro, Sardinia, Italy—d. Aug. 15, 1936, Rome) Novelist who was influenced by the verismo ("realism") school in Italian literature. She was awarded the Nobel Prize for Literature in 1926.

With little formal schooling, Deledda wrote her first stories at age 17, based on sentimental treatment of folklore themes. With *Il vecchio della montagna* (1900; "The Old Man of the Mountain") she began to write about the tragic effects of temptation and sin among primitive human beings.

Among her notable works are *Dopo il divorzio* (1902; *After the Divorce*), *Elias Portolu* (1903), *Cenere* (1904; *Ashes*), and *La madre* (1920; *The Woman and the Priest*; U.S. title, *The Mother*). In these and others of her 40 some novels, Deledda often used Sardinia's landscape as a metaphor for the difficulties in her characters' lives. The ancient ways of Sardinia often conflict with modern mores, and her characters are forced to work out solutions to their moral issues. *Cosima*, an autobiographical novel, was published posthumously in 1937.

deliberative oratory According to Aristotle, a type of suasive speech designed to advise political assemblies. *Compare* EPIDEICTIC ORATORY; FORENSIC ORATORY.

Delicate Balance, A Drama in three acts by Edward ALBEE, published and produced in 1966. Winner of a Pulitzer Prize in 1967, the play, about a middle-aged couple's struggle to restore the "balance" of their routine after it has been threatened by intruding friends, is representative of the playwright's concerns with the hidden terrors of everyday life.

The drama is set in the living room of an upper-middle-class home in suburbia. Using a relatively simple story of a frightened couple who ask their friends for refuge, Albee examines illusion and loss in American families. Although the play was criticized for repeating the structure and thematic content of his *Who's Afraid of Virginia Woolf*, it stood as a dark comic portrait of modern angst.

Delilah \də-'lī-lə\ Biblical character, a Philistine woman who discovers the secret of Samson's strength and then betrays him. *See* SAMSON.

Delille \də-'lēl\, Jacques, *byname* Abbé Delille (b. June 22, 1738, Aigueperse, Fr.—d. May 1, 1813, Paris) Poet and classicist who enjoyed an impressive reputation in his day as the French Virgil.

Delille was a brilliant student and taught Latin poetry at the Collège de France. His reputation was established with a verse translation of Virgil's *Georgics* (1770). Delille entered the Académie Française at age 36, translating the *Aeneid* in 1804 and John Milton's *Paradise Lost* in 1805. His own rather artificial poetry celebrates and is dedicated to nature. His fame did not survive long after his death.

DeLillo \di-'lil-ō\, Don (b. Nov. 20, 1936, New York, N.Y., U.S.) Novelist whose postmodernist works portray the anomie of an America cosseted by material excess and stupefied by empty mass culture and politics.

DeLillo's first novel, *Americana* (1971), is the story of a network television executive in search of the "real" America. It was followed by *End Zone* (1972) and *Great Jones Street* (1973). *Ratner's Star* (1976) attracted critical attention with its baroque comic sense and verbal facility.

Beginning with *Players* (1977), DeLillo's vision turned darker and his characters became more willful in their destructiveness and ignorance. Critics found little to like in the novel's protagonists, but much to admire in DeLillo's elliptic prose. The thrillers *Running Dog* (1978) and *The Names* (1982) followed. *White Noise* (1985), which won the American Book Award for fiction, tells of a professor of Hitler Studies who is exposed to an "airborne toxic event"; he discovers that his wife is taking an experimental substance said to combat the fear of death, and he vows to obtain the drug for himself at any cost. In *Libra* (1988), DeLillo presents a fictional portrayal of Lee Harvey Oswald, the assassin of President John F. Kennedy. *Mao II* (1991) opens with a mass wedding officiated by cult leader Sun Myung Moon. It tells the story of a reclusive writer who becomes enmeshed in a world of political violence.

Dell \'del\, Floyd (b. June 28, 1887, Barry, Ill., U.S.—d. July 23, 1969, Bethesda, Md.) Novelist and radical journalist whose fiction examined the changing mores in sex and politics among American bohemians before and after World War I.

Moving to Chicago in 1908, Dell worked as a newspaperman and soon was a leader of the city's literary movement. From 1909 he edited the *Friday Literary Review* of the *Evening Post*, making it one of the most noted American literary supplements. As a critic, he furthered the careers of Sherwood Anderson and Theodore Dreiser.

A socialist from his youth, he moved to New York in 1914 and was associate editor of the left-wing *The Masses* until 1917. He was on the staff of its successor, *The Liberator*, from 1918 to 1924.

Dell's first and best novel, the largely autobiographical *Moon-Calf*, appeared in 1920, and its sequel, *The Briary-Bush*, in 1921. His other novels on life among the unconventional include *Janet March* (1923), *Runaway* (1925), and *Love in Greenwich Village* (1926). His nonfiction includes *Were You Ever a Child?* (1919), on child rearing; the biography *Upton Sinclair: A Study in Social Protest* (1927); *Love in the Machine Age* (1930), which presented his views on sex; and his autobiography, *Homecoming* (1933).

Della-Cruscan \,del-ə-'krüs-kən\   1. Of, relating to, or resembling the Italian Accademia della Crusca, which was founded in 1582 for the cultivation of the Italian language and literature, or the literary style it championed.   2. Of, relating to, or resembling a school of English writers of pretentious, affected, rhetorically ornate poetry in the late 18th century. The school was centered on Robert Merry, who belonged to the Italian academy, and was satirized by William Gifford in *The Baviad* (1791) and *The Maeviad* (1795).   3. Affectedly pedantic—used of writings or literary style.

Della Valle \,del-lä-'väl-lä\, Federico (b. *c.* 1560, Asti, Piedmont [Italy]—d. 1628, Milan)   Italian dramatist and poet recognized in the 20th century as a major literary figure.

Little is known of Della Valle's life at the Savoy court in Turin and in Milan, where in 1628 three of his tragedies were published. Written in 1591, the intensely lyrical *La reina di Scozia* ("The Queen of Scotland") centers on Mary Stuart's last hours, when, despite her longing to see again her native Scotland, she resigns herself to martyrdom. Against similar backgrounds of corrupt and ferocious courts, the biblical heroines of his other two tragedies, *Judit* ("Judith") and *Ester* ("Esther"), also fight uncompromisingly for their faith in a world where the only redemption is offered by God in heaven. Della Valle's tragic outlook further underlies his tragicomedy *Adelonda di Frigia* (1595; "Adelonda of Phrygia"), in which the heroine's ideals are contrasted with a barbarous reality.

Deloney \də-'lō-nē\, Thomas (b. 1543?, Norwich?, Eng.—d. 1600)   Writer of ballads, pamphlets, and prose stories that form the earliest English popular fiction.

Through his pamphlets, Deloney took part in religious controversy and was proscribed in London for alleged sedition. As an itinerant silk weaver and seller of topical ballads, Deloney collected material in the provinces for his prose stories. His "many pleasant songs and pretty poems to new notes" appeared as *The Garland of Good Will* (1593). His *Jacke of Newberie* (1597), *The Gentle Craft*, Parts I and II (1597–*c.* 1598), and *Thomas of Reading* (1599?) furnished plots for such dramatists as Thomas Dekker. *The Gentle Craft* is a collection of stories, each devoted to a particular craft, such as cloth making, shoe making, and weaving.

Though widely read, Deloney was dismissed as a mere ballad maker and purveyor of plebeian romance, and his literary merits went unrecognized until the 20th century.

Delphi \'del-,fī\   Seat of the most important ancient Greek temple and oracle of Apollo. It lay in the territory of Phocis on the steep lower slope of Mount Parnassus. Delphi was considered by the ancient Greeks to be the center of the world.

The prestige of the Delphic oracle was at its height by about 580 BC. The oracle was consulted on private matters and also on affairs of state, and its utterances often swayed national policy. With the spread of Christianity, the old pagan sanctuary of Delphi fell into decay. *See also* ORACLE.

Delphin \'del-fin\   Of or relating to the Delphin classics, an edition of the Latin classics prepared in the reign of Louis XIV of France. The name originated from a Latin inscription on the title page of the books, *in usum serenissimi Delphini* ("for the use of the most serene Dauphin").

Delta Wedding   Novel by Eudora WELTY, published in 1946. It was Welty's first full-length novel, presenting a comprehensive and insightful portrait of a Southern plantation family in 1923.

Set in the context of the wedding of one of the daughters, the novel explores the relationships among members of the Fairchild family, most of whom have been sheltered from any contact with the world outside the Mississippi Delta. Although they quarrel among themselves, they also unite against any threats to the family's status, honoring the belief in the family as a sacred and unchanging entity. Only Ellen Fairchild, who has married into the family, has a more worldly perspective; her clear-sightedness allows her to work toward family harmony without being defeated by the internal bickering.

de Man \də-'män\, Paul (b. Dec. 6, 1919, Antwerp, Bel.—d. Dec. 21, 1983, New Haven, Conn., U.S.)   Literary critic, one of the major proponents of the critical theory known as deconstruction.

De Man graduated from the University of Brussels in 1942 and immigrated to the United States in 1947. After attending Harvard University, he taught at Harvard, Cornell, and Johns Hopkins universities. In 1970 he joined the faculty at Yale University, where he remained until his death.

While at Yale, de Man wrote his groundbreaking book *Blindness and Insight: Essays in the Rhetoric of Contemporary Criticism* (1971). The essays contained in the book give de Man's deconstructive readings of works as well as his analysis of commentary on literature written by other philosophers, as in "Heidegger's Exigesis of Hölderlin." With the publication of the book Yale became the center for deconstructive literary criticism in the United States. De Man's later works include *Allegories of Reading: Figural Language in Rousseau, Nietzsche, Rilke, and Proust* (1979) and *The Rhetoric of Romanticism* (1984). His other works on the theory of deconstruction include *The Resistance to Theory* (1986; written with Harold Bloom, Jacques Derrida, Geoffrey Hartman, and J. Hillis Miller) and *Aesthetic Ideology* (1988).

De Man's involvement from 1940 to 1942 with *Le Soir*, a Belgian pro-Nazi newspaper, was revealed in the late 1980s. Writings from the newspaper, including one overtly anti-Semitic essay, were collected and published under the title *Wartime Journalism, 1939–1943* (1988).

Demeter \di-'mē-tər\   In Greek religion, daughter of the deities Cronus and Rhea, sister and consort of Zeus, and goddess of agriculture. Her name may mean either "grain mother" or "mother earth."

Demeter is rarely mentioned by Homer, nor is she included among the Olympian gods, but the roots of her legend are probably ancient. The legend centered on the story of her daughter PERSEPHONE, who was carried off by Hades, the god of the underworld. Demeter went in search of Persephone and, during her journey, revealed her secret rites to the people of Eleusis, who had hospitably received her. (*See also* ELEUSINIAN MYSTERIES.) Her distress at her daughter's disappearance was said to have diverted her attention from the harvest and caused a famine. In addition to Zeus, Demeter had a consort, Iasion, to whom she bore Plutus (god of abundance or wealth).

Demeter appeared most commonly as a grain goddess, but she also appeared as a goddess of health, birth, and marriage and as a divinity of the underworld. Her attributes were chiefly connected with her character as goddess of agriculture and vegetation—ears of corn, the mystic basket filled with flowers, corn, and fruit of all kinds. The pig was her favorite animal, and as a chthonian deity she was accompanied by a snake. The Romans identified Demeter with Ceres.

Demeter \di-'mē-tər\ English translation of *Die Versucher* by Hermann Broch, also known in English as THE SPELL.

demigod \'dem-ē-ˌgäd\ [translation of Latin *semideus*] A mythological divine or semidivine being (such as the offspring of a deity and a mortal) thought to possess less power than a god. One such demigod is Perseus. Compare HERO.

demigoddess \'dem-ē-ˌgäd-əs\ A female demigod.

De Mille \də-'mil\, James (b. Aug. 23, 1836, Saint John, N.B. [Canada]—d. Jan. 28, 1880, Halifax, N.S.) Canadian author of more than 30 novels with a wide range of appeal who is particularly noted for his wit and humor.

While a student at Acadia College, De Mille traveled extensively in Europe, and scenes of Italy became settings for many of his novels. After an unsuccessful venture as a bookseller, De Mille taught at Acadia College and Dalhousie University. De Mille's adult fiction includes thrillers, such as *The Cryptogram* (1871); comic adventures, such as *The Dodge Club; or, Italy in 1859* (1860); and historical romances, such as *A Tale of Rome in the First Century* (1867). He appealed to young readers with the "B.O.W.C." ("Brethren of the White Cross") series, the first popular boys' adventure stories produced in Canada. De Mille's most imaginative work is *A Strange Manuscript Found in a Copper Cylinder* (1888), set in a future time when humanity, devoid of inspiring ideas, rejects the drive for achievement and lapses into conformity.

Democratic Vistas Prose pamphlet by Walt WHITMAN, published in 1871. The work comprises three essays that outline the author's ideas about the role of democracy in establishing a new cultural foundation for America.

Writing a few years after the American Civil War, Whitman suggested that some notion of heroism and honor had been lost by Americans. He particularly criticized the materialism and the preoccupation with business he observed in society. The antidote, he felt, was a return to the Jeffersonian-Jacksonian brand of democracy and the cultivation of spiritual fellowship. Often criticized for its optimistic belief in progress and its naive dismissal of history as a factor in human development, the pamphlet remains an important supplement to Whitman's poetry as well as an example of his philosophy of government.

Demolder \də-mȯl-'der\, Eugène (b. Dec. 16, 1862, Brussels, Belg.—d. Oct. 8, 1919, Essonnes, Fr.) Belgian novelist and story writer, a member of the Jeune Belgique ("Young Belgium") literary renaissance of the late 19th century who wrote in French.

Demolder was trained to be a lawyer, and his memoirs, *Sous la robe* (1897; "Under the Robe"), provide a record of the professional and cultural life of a class that was in the forefront of Belgian literary reform. His novels, which are known for their evocation of atmosphere, may be regarded more as sequences of tableaux than as coherent narratives.

In early works, such as *La Légende d'Yperdamme* (1891), Demolder transposed stories from the Gospels into Flemish medieval settings whose scenes have been compared with the paintings of Pieter Bruegel. In *La Route d'emeraude* (1899; "The Emerald Road") Demolder provided rich graphic descriptions in his story of the life of a would-be painter in the Low Countries in the 17th century. His other important novel, *Le Jardinier de la Pompadour* (1904; "Madame de Pompadour's Gardener"), is set in France. His *L'Espagne en auto* (1906; "Spain by Auto") is one of the earliest narratives of automobile travel.

demon or **daemon** \'dē-mən\ [Greek *daímōn*] **1.** An evil spirit. A source or agent of evil, harm, distress, or ruin. **2.** In Greek mythology, a supernatural being whose nature is inter-mediate between that of a god and that of a mortal. Also used to mean an inferior divinity.

demythologize \ˌdē-mi-'thäl-ə-ˌjīz\ To divest a written work of mythological forms in order to uncover the meaning underlying such forms. Also, to separate the meaning of a writing from the mythological forms in which it is expressed. The term may also be used to refer to the interpretation of a work's mythological elements in order to uncover the meaning of the work.

Denham \'den-əm\, Sir John (b. 1615, Dublin, Ire.—d. March 10, 1669, London, Eng.) Poet who established topographical poetry, a leisurely meditative poem describing a particular landscape, as a new English genre.

Educated at the University of Oxford, Denham translated six books of the *Aeneid*, parts of which were later printed. He made his reputation with *The Sophy*, a blank-verse historical tragedy acted in 1641, and with *Cooper's Hill*, a poem published in 1642. A supporter of Charles II during the English Civil Wars, he was made a knight of the Bath and elected to the Royal Society after the Restoration in 1660. He served as a member of Parliament and was buried in Westminster Abbey.

Denham's poetry is essentially didactic. His strength lies in his thought, particularly his neatly turned expressions of ethical and moral truisms. Critics praised him for the development of the closed heroic couplet (a rhyming couplet that contains a complete idea). Denham greatly increased the popularity of that style with *Cooper's Hill*, a new type of descriptive landscape verse that was imitated by English poets for the next 100 years.

Dennie \'den-ē\, Joseph (b. Aug. 30, 1768, Boston, Mass. [U.S.]—d. Jan. 7, 1812, Philadelphia, Pa.) Essayist and editor who was a major American literary figure in the early 19th century.

Dennie graduated from Harvard and together with Royall Tyler formed a literary partnership; under the pseudonyms Colon and Spondee, they began contributing satirical pieces to local newspapers. Between 1792 and 1802 Dennie wrote his "Farrago" essays in various periodicals. He edited the newspaper *Farmer's Weekly Museum* from 1796 to 1798, contributing the series of graceful, moralizing "Lay Preacher" essays that established his literary reputation.

Dennie's pro-Federalist positions secured him an appointment as personal secretary to Secretary of State Timothy Pickering in 1799–1800. With Asbury Dickins, Dennie began in 1801 a politico-literary periodical called *The Port Folio*, which became the most distinguished literary weekly of its time in America. He contributed "Lay Preacher" essays and also commissioned work from other prominent writers. As the founder of the Tuesday Club, Dennie was the center of the aristocratic literary circle in Philadelphia and was for a time the leading literary arbiter in the country. He derided American rusticity and crudity and praised English literature, manners, and sophistication. He also advocated sound critical standards and encouraged talented younger writers, such as Washington Irving.

Dennis \'den-əs\, John (b. 1657, London, Eng.—d. Jan. 6, 1734, London) English critic and dramatist whose insistence upon the importance of passion in poetry led to a long quarrel with Alexander Pope.

At first Dennis wrote odes and plays, but, although a prolific dramatist, he was never very successful. The most important of his critical works were *The Usefulness of the Stage* (1698), *The Advancement and Reformation of Modern Poetry* (1701), *The Grounds of Criticism in Poetry* (1704), and *An Essay on the Genius and Writings of Shakespear* (1712). His basic contention was that literature, and especially drama, is comparable to religion in that its effect is to move minds by means of the emotions. What he looked for primarily in a work of art was passion and elevation rather than decorum and polish. His idol among English poets was John Milton.

Pope, who thought Dennis' work bombastic, included an adverse allusion to Dennis in *An Essay on Criticism.* Dennis replied with *Reflections Critical and Satyrical* (1711), which mixed criticism of Pope's poem with a vicious personal attack upon Pope. Their quarrel continued sporadically until Dennis' death.

Dennis \'den-əs\, Nigel (Forbes) (b. Jan. 16, 1912, Bletchingley, Surrey, Eng.—d. July 19, 1989, Hertfordshire)   English writer and critic who used absurd plots and witty repartee to satirize psychiatry, religion, and social behavior, most notably in the novel *Cards of Identity* (1955).

Traveling to the United States in 1934, Dennis worked for the National Board of Review of Motion Pictures in New York City from 1935 to 1936 and then as associate editor and book reviewer for *The New Republic.* He was employed as a staff book reviewer at *Time* magazine from 1940 to 1958. After his return to London in 1949, he wrote reviews for *Encounter* magazine (1960–63) and later served as joint editor from 1967 to 1970. His book reviews also appeared regularly in the *Sunday Telegraph* (1961–82).

In his first novel, *Boys and Girls Come Out to Play* (1949; U.S. title, *A Sea Change*), Dennis explored the Adlerian notion that each individual's personality adapts to fit its social context. Both *Cards of Identity* and *A House in Order* (1966) retained some of his original preoccupations with inauthentic modern existence. *The Making of Moo* (performed 1957), a satirical play on the psychological power of religious fervor, was published with the stage version of *Cards of Identity* as *Two Plays and a Preface* (1958). His knowledge of journalism sharpened the satire of *August for the People* (1961), a much-praised play about the power of the press. His nonfiction included a critical biography of Jonathan Swift.

denouement \,dā-nū-'mäⁿ, dä-'nū-,mäⁿ\ [French *dénouement*, literally, the action of untying]   The events following the climax of the plot. The final outcome, result, or unraveling of the main dramatic complication in a play or other work of literature.

Densuşianu \,den-sū-'shyä-,nū\, Ovid (b. Dec. 29, 1873, Făgăraş, Rom.—d. June 9, 1938, Bucharest)   Folklorist, philologist, and poet who introduced trends of European modernism into Romanian literature.

Educated at Iaşi and later in Berlin and Paris, Densuşianu taught at the University of Bucharest. Strongly influenced by Symbolism, he opposed the bucolic school of writing then popular in Romania. In 1905 he founded the opposition review *Viaţa nouă* ("New Times"), which he published for 20 years. In French he wrote *Histoire de la langue roumaine* (1901–14; "History of the Romanian Language"). In Romanian he wrote *Dicţionar general al limbii române* (1909; "A General Dictionary of the Romanian Tongue"), *Flori alese din cântecele poporului* (1920; "An Anthology of the Songs of the People"), the poetry collection *Raze pe lespezi* (1920; "Sunlight on the Paving Stones"), and *Literatura română modernă* (1920–33; "Modern Romanian Literature"). His poetry is published under the pseudonym Ervin.

Deor \'dā-,ôr\   Old English heroic poem of 42 lines preserved in the Exeter Book, one of the two surviving Old English poems to have a refrain. (The other is the fragmentary "Wulf and Eadwacer.") "Deor," also known as "Deor's Lament," is the complaint of a scop (minstrel), Deor, who was replaced at his court by another minstrel and deprived of his lands and his lord's benevolence. In the poem Deor recalls, in irregular stanzas, five examples of the sufferings of various figures from

Germanic legend. Each stanza ends with the refrain "That trouble passed; so can this." Though some scholars believe that the lament is merely a conventional pretext for introducing heroic legends, the mood of the poem remains intensely personal. *See also* EXETER BOOK.

De Profundis \,dē-prō-'fən-dis, *in classical Latin pronunciation* dā-prō-'fūn-dēs\ ("Out of the Depths")   Letter written from prison by Oscar WILDE. It was edited and published posthumously in 1905 as *De Profundis.* Its title—the first two words of Psalm 130, part of the Roman Catholic funeral service—was supplied by Wilde's friend and literary executor Robert Ross.

While imprisoned in Reading Gaol from 1895 to 1897 for homosexual practices, Wilde wrote an impassioned letter to his lover, Lord Alfred Douglas. In the first section of the letter, Wilde records his relationship with Douglas in merciless detail; he rails against his lover's selfishness and extravagance, accuses him of being the agent of Wilde's destruction, and turns a cold eye on his own behavior. The letter's tone changes from bitterness to resignation as Wilde acknowledges his own responsibility for his fate and extends a hopeful offer for a renewed, calmer friendship.

Deptford Trilogy, The \'det-fərd\   A series of three novels by Robertson DAVIES, consisting of *Fifth Business* (1970), *The Manticore* (1972), and *World of Wonders* (1975). Throughout the trilogy, Davies interweaves moral concerns and bits of arcane lore.

The novels trace the lives of three men from the small town of Deptford, Ont., connected and transformed by a single childhood event: Percy "Boy" Staunton throws a snowball containing a stone at Dunstable (later Dunstan) Ramsay. Ramsay dodges the snowball and it hits Mary Dempster, who gives birth prematurely to a son, Paul, and slides into dementia.

Fifth Business is an autobiographical letter written by Dunstan upon his retirement as headmaster of a boys' school; he has been tormented by guilt throughout his life. Boy Staunton lies at the bottom of Lake Ontario at the opening of *The Manticore*; the stone that hit Mrs. Dempster some 60 years earlier is found in his mouth. Much of the book describes the course of Jungian analysis undertaken by Boy's son David. *World of Wonders* tells the story of Paul Dempster. Kidnapped as a boy by a magician, he learns the trade and eventually becomes Magnus Eisengrim, one of the most successful acts on the European continent.

De Quincey \di-'kwin-sē\, Thomas (b. Aug. 15, 1785, Manchester, Lancashire, Eng.—d. Dec. 8, 1859, Edinburgh, Scot.)   English essayist and critic, best known for his CONFESSIONS OF AN ENGLISH OPIUM-EATER (1822).

De Quincey ran away at age 17 to Wales, then lived incognito in London. Reconciled to his family in 1803, he entered Worcester College, Oxford, where in 1804 he took his first opium to relieve the pain of facial neuralgia. By 1813 he had become an opium addict, keeping a decanter of laudanum by his elbow and steadily increasing the dose. He remained addicted to opium for the rest of his life.

In 1807 De Quincey, who was an early admirer of *Lyrical Ballads,* became a close associate of its authors, William Wordsworth and Samuel Taylor Coleridge. Though De Quincey wrote voluminously, he published almost nothing. His financial position as head of a large family went from bad to worse until the appearance of *Confessions* in *London Magazine* in 1821 made him famous.

Among his other autobiographical writings, the so-called *Lake Reminiscences* (first printed in *Tait's Magazine,* 1834–40), which deeply offended Wordsworth and the other Lake poets, remains of great interest, although it is highly subjective, not without malice, and unreliable in matters of detail. As a literary critic De Quincey is best known for his essay "On the Knocking at the Gate in *Macbeth*" (first printed in the *London Magazine*, October 1823), a brilliant piece of psychological insight and a classic of Shakespearean criticism.

Dermoût \der-'maùt\, Maria, *in full* Helena Antonia Maria Elisabeth Dermoût-Ingermann \'iŋ-ər-₁mån\ (b. June 15, 1888, Pekalongan, Java, Dutch East Indies [now in Indonesia]—d. June 27, 1962, Noordwijk, Neth.)   Dutch novelist and short-story writer known for her subtle and evocative portraits of colonial life in the Dutch East Indies.

Dermoût, who was the descendant of employees of the Dutch East India Company, spent most of her life on the islands. Her work was not published until she was in her 60s. Her first two novels, *Nog pas gisteren* (1951; *Yesterday*) and *De tienduizend dingen* (1955; *The Ten Thousand Things*), are fictionalized accounts of her youth. Although written in an economical style, the two novels are rich in details of island life as experienced by both the colonials and the native people. Among Dermoût's other books are three volumes of short stories—*De juwelen haarkam* (1956; "The Jeweled Haircomb"), *De sirenen* (1963; "The Sirens"), and *De kist; en enige verhalen* (1958; "The Wooden Box: A Unique Account")—and a book of sketches, *Spel van Tifagongs* (1954; "Tifagong's Play").

Deronda, Daniel   Title character of George Eliot's novel DANIEL DERONDA.

Derrida \de-rē-'då\, Jacques (b. July 15, 1930, El Biar, Alg.) French philosopher whose critique of Western philosophy encompasses literature, linguistics, and psychoanalysis.

Derrida studied at the École Normale Supérieure in Paris, where he later taught the history of philosophy. From 1960 to 1964 he taught at the Sorbonne. In 1967 Derrida published three influential works: *La Voix et le phénomène* (*Speech and Phenomena*), a study of Edmund Husserl, and two collections of essays, *L'Écriture et la différence* (*Writing and Difference*) and *De la grammatologie* (*Of Grammatology*). The works *Marges de la philosophie* (*Margins of Philosophy*), *Positions* (a series of interviews), and *La Dissémination* (*Dissemination*) were all published in 1972.

Derrida's thought is based on his disapproval of the search for some ultimate metaphysical certainty or source of meaning that has characterized most Western philosophy. In his works he offers a way of reading philosophic texts, called DECONSTRUCTION, that enables him to make explicit the metaphysical suppositions and a priori assumptions used even by those philosophers who are the most deeply critical of metaphysics. Derrida eschewed the holding of any philosophical doctrine and instead sought to analyze language in an attempt to provide a radically alternative perspective in which the basic notion of a philosophical thesis is called into question.

His later works include *Glas* (1974), *La Vérité en peinture* (1978; *The Truth in Painting*), *La Carte postale* (1980; *The Post Card*), *L'Oreille de l'autre* (1982; *The Ear of the Other*), and *Psyche: Inventions de l'autre* (1987; "Psyche: Inventions of the Other").

Derzhavin \dyir-'zhå-vyin\, Gavrila Romanovich (b. July 3 [July 14, New Style], 1743, Kazan province, Russia—d. July 8 [July 20], 1816, Zvanka, Novgorod province, Russia)   Russia's greatest and most original 18th-century poet, whose finest achievements lie in his lyrics and odes.

Derzhavin joined the army as a common soldier in 1762, was made an officer in 1772, and entered the civil service in 1777. His *Oda k Felitse* (1782; "Ode to Felicia"), addressed to Catherine the Great, gained her favor, and he was, for a time, her

private secretary. His liberal political inclinations finally put an end to his career in 1803.

Derzhavin preserved the grandeur and solemnity of the classical ode as practiced in Russia but made it less restrictive and more lyrical and personal in its tone and subject matter. He worked in many other poetic genres, and his poems express both lofty and idealistic moralism and his strongly sensual appreciation of life. His lyrics and odes include "Na smert knyazya Meshcherskogo" (1779; "On the Death of Prince Meshchersky"), *Bog* (1784; *Ode to the Deity*), and *Vodopad* (1794; "The Waterfall").

Desai \'då-₁sī, *commonly* dā-'sī\, Anita, *original surname* Mazumdar \'mȯ-zūm-₁där\ (b. June 24, 1937, Mussoorie, India)   English-language Indian novelist and author of children's books, considered India's premier imagist writer. She excelled in evoking character and mood through visual images ranging from the meteorological to the botanical.

Desai, who was the daughter of a German-Jewish mother and a Bengali father, addressed the theme of the suppression and oppression of Indian women in her first novel, *Cry, the Peacock* (1963), and in *Where Shall We Go This Summer?* (1975). *Fire on the Mountain* (1977) was criticized as relying too heavily on imagery at the expense of plot and characterization, but it was praised for its poetic symbolism and use of sounds. *Clear Light of Day* (1980), considered the author's most successful work, is a highly evocative portrait of two sisters caught in the lassitude of Indian life. As do most of her works, the novel reflects Desai's essentially tragic view of life. *Baumgartner's Bombay* (1988) explores German and Jewish identity in the context of a chaotic contemporary India. Desai also wrote short fiction for magazines and several children's books, including the popular *The Village by the Sea* (1982).

De Sanctis \dā-'säŋk-tēs\, Francesco (b. March 28, 1817, Morra Irpina, Kingdom of Naples [now in Italy]—d. Dec. 29, 1883, Naples)   Italian literary critic whose work remains invaluable for the understanding of Italian literature and culture.

De Sanctis took up the work of educational reform, becoming minister of education (1861–62) and, in 1871, professor of comparative literature at the University of Naples.

A scholar of literature and history, De Sanctis brought to his criticism a knowledge of philosophy, particularly Hegelian aesthetics. His essays on the Italian poets (*Saggi critici* ["Critical Essays"], 1866; *Nuovi saggi critici* ["New Critical Essays"], 1873) relate these poets to the society of their times. His masterpiece, *Storia della letteratura italiana* (1870–71; *History of Italian Literature*), is an illuminating account not only of Italian literature but also of the development of Italian society from the 13th to the 19th century.

Desbordes-Valmore \dā-'bȯrd-vål-'mȯr\, Marceline (b. June 30, 1786, Douai, Fr.—d. July 23, 1859, Paris)   French poet and woman of letters of the Romantic period.

Desbordes-Valmore turned to writing when illness threatened her stage voice as an actress at the Opéra-Comique and the Odéon. Her poetry—*Pauvres Fleurs* (1839; "Poor Flowers"), *Les Pleurs* (1833; "The Tears"), and *Bouquets et prières* (1843; "Bouquets and Prayers")—is poignant and elegiac. It treats religious themes, sadness, death, and the author's love for her daughters and her native Douai. Her prose work *L'Atelier d'un peintre* (1833; "A Painter's Studio") is autobiographical. The poet Charles Baudelaire esteemed her writing, and Paul Verlaine admitted his debt to her, giving her a place in his revised edition of *Les Poètes maudits* (1888; "The Damned [or Maligned] Poets").

descending rhythm   *see* FALLING RHYTHM.

Deschamps, Émile, *surname in full* Deschamps de Saint-Amand \dā-'shäⁿ-də-saⁿ-tȧ-'mäⁿ\ (b. Feb. 20, 1791, Bourges, Fr.—d. April 23, 1871, Versailles) French poet prominent in the development of Romanticism.

Deschamps's literary debut took place in 1818, when, with Henri de Latouche, he produced two plays. Five years later, with Victor Hugo, he founded *La Muse française,* the journal of the Romantic movement, and the preface to Deschamps's *Études françaises et étrangères* (1828) formed a manifesto of the movement. His translations into French of William Shakespeare's *Romeo and Juliet* (1839) and *Macbeth* (1844), though never performed, were also important. He wrote several librettos, notably that for Hector Berlioz's *Roméo et Juliette,* and his prose works include *Contes physiologiques* (1854) and *Réalités fantastiques* (1854).

Deschamps \dā-'shäⁿ\, Eustache, *byname* Morel \mȯ-'rel\ (b. *c.* 1346, Vertus, Fr.—d. *c.* 1406) Poet and author of *L'Art de dictier* (1392), the first treatise on French versification.

Deschamps was educated in Reims by the poet Guillaume de Machaut, who had a lasting influence on him. After law studies in Orléans, he held administrative and diplomatic posts under the kings Charles V and VI. His leisure was devoted to poetry, and he was immensely prolific, producing farces, traditional love poetry, and satires—notably a satire on women.

Deschamps's later poetry shows sympathy for the sufferings of the people during the Hundred Years' War and affection for his country. He influenced the English poet Geoffrey Chaucer, to whom he addressed a ballade.

descort \des-'kȯr\ [Old French & Old Provençal, literally, quarrel, discord] **1.** A synonym for LAI, a medieval Provençal lyric in which the stanzas are unlike. **2.** A poem in medieval Provençal literature with stanzas in different languages.

descriptive bibliography or **enumerative bibliography** Bibliography in which the primary purpose is to organize detailed information, item by item, culled from a mass of materials in a systematic way so that others can have access to useful information. In the earliest bibliographies, the organizing principle was simply that of compiling all the works of a given writer, either a writer's list of his own works (autobibliography) or a biographer's lists of his subjects' writings.

Early Western autobibliographies include those by the 2nd-century Greek physician Galen and by the Venerable Bede. With the invention of printing in the 15th century, books proliferated, and the organization of information about them became both more necessary and more practical. As early as 1545 the idea of a universal bibliography aroused the German-Swiss writer Conrad Gesner to compile his *Bibliotheca universalis* of all past and present writers. Part of his plan, completed in 1555, was to divide entries into categories of knowledge. His attempts at both universality and classification earned him the title "father of bibliography."

Among modern methods of classification are the Dewey Decimal Classification, the Library of Congress Classification, and the Universal Decimal Classification. In the last quarter of the 20th century, the widespread use of computers in processing such systematized information revived the possibility of creating a universal bibliography, including articles in periodicals.

Desdemona \ˌdez-də-'mō-nə\ Fictional character, the wife of Othello and the object of his unwarranted jealousy, in William Shakespeare's tragic drama OTHELLO. The daughter of a Venetian senator, Desdemona is greatly loved by Othello, an honored and heroic Moorish general in the service of Venice.

Deserted Village, The Pastoral elegy by Oliver GOLD-SMITH, published in 1770. Considered to be one of his major poems, it idealizes a rural way of life that was being destroyed by the displacement of agrarian villagers, the greed of landlords, and economic and political change. In response to the poem's perceived sentimentality, George Crabbe created a bleak view of the country poor in his poem *The Village* (1783).

Des Esseintes, Jean \zhäⁿ-dez-e-'säⁿt\ Fictional character, a reclusive aesthete in the novel AGAINST THE GRAIN by Joris-Karl Huysmans. The last in a depleted line of nobles, Des Esseintes is a wealthy effete who grows impotent from dissolution. At the age of 30, he abandons society to lead a life of experimental sensualism.

Deshoulières \dā-zül-'yer\, Antoinette du Ligier de la Garde (b. Jan. 1, 1638, Paris, Fr.—d. Feb. 17, 1694, Paris) French poet who, from 1672 until her death, presided over a salon that was a meeting place for the prominent literary figures of her day. She was also a leading member of the coterie that attacked Jean Racine's *Phèdre.*

Deshoulières's poems, the first of which were published in the *Mercure galant* in 1672, were appreciated throughout the 18th century, her idylls and eclogues being especially popular. Her early poems celebrate the simple joys of nature and mark the small and large events in the lives of French royalty. Her later poems describe her sufferings from old age, cancer, and poverty. In addition to poems, Deshoulières wrote an opera, *Zoroastre* (1680), and two tragedies, *Jules-Antoine* and *Genséric* (1680).

design \di-'zīn\ A conceptual outline or sketch according to which the elements of a literary or dramatic composition or series are arranged.

Design for Living Comedy in three acts by Noël COWARD, produced and published in 1933. Often compared to Coward's *Private Lives,* this worldly tale involving a painter, a playwright, and the woman they both love is notable for its portrait of characters who are unable to live by any conventional moral codes and who devise, through trial and error, a different way of life to suit them.

The play ends with the three characters bursting into laughter, a gesture that critics have interpreted in a variety of ways. Coward's theme of "moral relativism" and his three witty, disillusioned main characters shocked London producers, who at first refused to stage the play. His polished style and clipped dialogue accurately captured the spirit of post-World War I Europe. Along with Alfred Lunt and Lynn Fontanne, Coward himself acted in the play when it opened on Broadway.

Desiosi \ˌdā-sē-'ō-sē\ (*in full* Compagnia dei Desiosi) One of the Italian acting troupes performing commedia dell'arte (improvised popular comedy) in the late 16th and early 17th centuries.

Désirée's Baby \'dez-ə-ˌrā\ Short story by Kate CHOPIN, published in her collection *A Night in Acadie* in 1897. A widely acclaimed, frequently anthologized story, it is set in antebellum New Orleans and deals with slavery, the Southern social system, Creole culture, and the ambiguity of racial identity.

Désirée and her husband Armand are happily married. But when Désirée gives birth to a child who is obviously of mixed racial ancestry, Armand forces her and the child into exile and to a tragic end and becomes more brutal toward his slaves. Only when it is too late does Armand discover that it is he, and not Désirée, who is part black.

Desire Under the Elms Tragedy in three parts by Eugene O'NEILL, produced in 1924 and published in 1925. The last of O'Neill's naturalistic plays and the first in which he re-created the starkness of Greek tragedy, *Desire Under the Elms* draws from Euripides' *Hippolytus* and Jean Racine's *Phèdre,* both of which feature a father returning home with a new wife who falls in love with her stepson.

In this play Ephraim Cabot abandons his farm and his three sons, who hate him. The youngest son, Eben, buys out his brothers, who head off to California. Shortly after this, Ephraim returns with his young new wife, Abbie. Abbie becomes pregnant by Eben; she lets Ephraim believe that the child is his, but she later kills the infant when she sees it as an obstacle between herself and Eben. Eben, enraged, turns Abbie over to the sheriff, but not before he realizes his love for her and confesses his complicity.

One of O'Neill's most admired works, *Desire Under the Elms* invokes the playwright's own family conflicts and Freudian treatment of sexual themes. Although the play is now considered a classic of 20th-century American drama, it scandalized some early audiences for its treatment of infanticide, alcoholism, vengeance, and incest; the first Los Angeles cast was arrested for performing an obscene work.

Des Knaben Wunderhorn \des-'knäb-ən-'vůn-dər-,hȯrn\ ("The Boy's Magic Horn")   Anthology of German folk songs, subtitled *Alte deutsche Lieder* ("Old German Songs"), collected by the poet Clemens BRENTANO and the antiquarian Achim von ARNIM and published in 1805–08. The collection established its editors as leaders of the Romantic movement by reviving enthusiasm for the *Volkslied* ("folk song," or "peasant song") tradition in German lyric poetry. Reputedly genuine folk songs dating from the Middle Ages, many of the poems were, in fact, either anonymously composed by such 17th-century poets as Simon Dach and Hans Jacob Grimmelshausen or rewritten by Brentano and Arnim to improve what Arnim called "authentically historical discords." Nonetheless, the work was praised for preserving the language and meters of old German folk songs.

Desmarets de Saint-Sorlin \dä-må-rä-də-sᵃⁿ-sȯr-'laⁿ\, Jean (b. 1595, Paris, Fr.—d. Oct. 28, 1676, Paris)   French author, Christian polemicist, and political figure who was deeply involved in the long literary battle that has since been called the *querelle des anciens et des modernes*.

Desmarets had written a number of literary works before the publication of his popular romance *Ariane* (1632) finally gained for him entrance to Parisian literary circles. Flattery soon won him the favor of Cardinal de Richelieu, under whose patronage he held a succession of important government posts and wrote a number of tragedies and tragicomedies, the best of which was *Les Visionnaires* (1637).

A fervent Christian apologist, Desmarets also based his poetry on chiefly Christian themes rather than classical mythology, arguing that the true models for modern French literature were Romance legends and the Bible rather than classical Greek and Roman writers. Several of his works reflect this point of view, notably *La Comparaison de la langue et de la poésie française avec la grecque et la latine* (1670) and *Défense de la poésie et de la langue française* (1675). Desmarets was one of the original members and the first chancellor of the Académie Française. *See also* ANCIENTS AND MODERNS.

Desnos \dås-'nȯs\, Robert (b. July 4, 1900, Paris, Fr.—d. June 8, 1945, Theresienstadt concentration camp [now in Terezín, Czech Republic])   French poet who joined André Breton in the early Surrealist movement.

Desnos early became one of the foremost Surrealists because of his ability to fall into a hypnotic trance, under which he could recite his dreams, write, and draw. His rich texts from his early period appeared in the Surrealist review *Littérature* and in his book *La Liberté ou l'amour!* (1927; "Liberty or Love!"). Humor, tenderness, and eroticism pervade his works, in which

acrobatic verbal techniques never detract from the spontaneity of the inspiration. Dreams and reality merge in freely associated images in *Corps et biens* (1930; "Bodies and Goods").

In 1930 he broke from the doctrinaire Surrealist rigidity of Breton and for a decade wrote motion-picture and radio scripts, including the highly successful *Complainte de Fantomas* (1933; "Fantomas' Lament"). Later he abandoned Surrealistic verse for more traditional forms that made it easier to express his humanitarian sympathies. His works of this period include *Fortunes* (1942), *État de veille* (1943; "The Wakeful State"), and *Contrée* (1944; "Country"). Arrested for his activity in the Resistance, he was deported and died of typhus a few days after Theresienstadt was liberated. A collection that includes both his early Surrealist poems and his later works, *Domaine public* ("Public Domain"), appeared in 1953. *The Selected Poems of Robert Desnos* was published in 1991.

Des Périers \dā-pār-'yā\, Bonaventure (b. *c.* 1500, Arnay-le-duc, Fr.?—d. *c.* 1544, Lyon)   French storyteller and humanist who attained notoriety as a freethinker.

Des Périers assisted Pierre-Robert Olivétan and Jacques Lefèvre d'Étaples in the preparation of the vernacular version of the Old Testament and Étienne Dolet in the *Commentarii linguae Latinae*. Margaret of Angoulême, queen of Navarre, made him her valet de chambre in 1536. He acted as her secretary and transcribed her *Heptaméron*; some maintain that he in fact wrote the work.

Des Périers's *Cymbalum Mundi* (1538; *Cymbalum Mundi: Four Very Ancient Joyous and Facetious Dialogues*) is a brilliant and violent attack upon Christianity. The allegorical form of its four dialogues in imitation of the Greek rhetorician Lucian did not conceal its real meaning. It was suppressed (*c.* 1538) and made many bitter enemies for Des Périers.

His collected works, published in 1544, include his poems, the *Traité des quatre vertus cardinales après Sénèque* ("Treatise on the Four Cardinal Virtues After Seneca"), and a translation of Plato's *Lysis*. *Nouvelles Récréations et joyeux devis* (1558; *The Mirrour of Mirth and Pleasant Conceits*, or *Novel Pastimes and Merry Tales*), his best-regarded collection, contains stories and fables that are models of simple, direct narration in the vigorous, witty, and picturesque French of the 16th century.

Desportes \dā-'pȯrt\, Philippe (b. 1546, Chartres, Fr.—d. Oct. 5, 1606, Abbey of Bonport)   French courtier poet whose light, facile verse prepared the way for the new taste of the 17th century in France and whose sonnets served as models for the late Elizabethan poets. Desportes based his style on that of the Italians—chiefly Petrarch, Ludovico Ariosto, and Pietro Bembo.

About 1567 he displaced Pierre de Ronsard as the favorite poet of Henry, Duke of Anjou, whom he accompanied to Kraków when Henry was elected king of Poland in 1573. With the publication in 1573 of Desportes's *Premières Oeuvres* ("First Works"), he became Ronsard's rival. Desportes returned to France with Henry on the death of Charles IX in 1574. He wrote sonnets and elegies in graceful alexandrines for Henry III and others to present to their mistresses. In 1583 he received the livings of the abbeys of Tiron and Josaphat.

His *Dernières amours* (1583; "Last Loves"), also known as *Cléonice*, mark his farewell to secular verse. His translations of the Psalms (1591, 1598, 1603) were attacked by François de Malherbe and vigorously defended by the poet Mathurin Régnier, Desportes's nephew. Desportes's clear, harmonious style found ready acceptance by many English poets.

Desrosiers \dā-rōz-'yā\, Léo-Paul (b. April 11, 1896, Berthier, Que., Can.—d. April 20, 1967, Montreal)   French-Canadian writer best known for his historical novels.

In addition to writing fiction, Desrosiers worked as a journalist, an editor, and a librarian. Both *Âmes et paysages* (1922; "People and Landscapes"), a collection of stories, and his first novel, *Nord-Sud* (1931), are set in the Quebec countryside. *Les Engagés du Grand Portage* (1938; *The Making of Nicolas Montour*) depicts the cutthroat behavior exhibited by rival fur companies in the early 19th century. Desrosiers's *L'Ampoule d'or* (1951; "The Gold Phial") is considered a minor masterpiece for its poetic language and imagery. His philosophical trilogy—*Vous qui passez*, *Les Angoisses et les tourments*, and *Rafales sur les cimes* (1958–60; "You Who Pass," "Agony and Torment," and "Squalls on the Summit")—was less successful.

Destouches \dā-'tüsh\, Philippe Néricault (b. April 9, 1680, Tours, Fr.—d. July 4, 1754, Fortoiseau) Dramatist whose plays brought to the tradition of French classical comedy influences derived from the English Restoration theater.

After classical studies in Tours and Paris, Destouches entered the diplomatic service. He was posted to Switzerland and, in 1717, to London. There he became acquainted with English writers and developed an affection for Restoration drama. Following his return to Paris, he was successful with his comedy *Le Philosophe marié* (1727; *The Married Philosopher*), although his plays were too moralistic for many of his contemporaries. His masterpiece is *Le Glorieux* (1732; *The Conceited Count*), which examines the conflict between the nobility and the bourgeoisie.

detective story Type of popular literature dealing with the step-by-step investigation and solution of a crime, usually murder.

The traditional elements of the detective story are: (1) the seemingly perfect crime; (2) the wrongly accused suspect at whom circumstantial evidence points; (3) the bungling of dim-witted police; (4) the greater powers of observation and superior mind of the detective; and (5) the startling and unexpected denouement, in which the detective reveals how he or she has ascertained the identity of the culprit. Detective stories frequently operate on the principle that superficially convincing evidence is ultimately irrelevant.

The first detective story was "The Murders in the Rue Morgue" by Edgar Allan Poe, published in April 1841. The detective story soon expanded to novel length. The greatest of all fictional detectives, Sherlock Holmes, made his first appearance in Sir Arthur Conan Doyle's novel *A Study in Scarlet* (1887) and continued into the 20th century.

The early years of the 20th century produced a number of distinguished detective novels, among them Mary Roberts Rinehart's *The Circular Staircase* (1908) and G.K. Chesterton's *The Innocence of Father Brown* (1911). From 1920 on, the names of many fictional detectives became household words, including Hercule Poirot and Miss Marple (creations of Agatha Christie), Lord Peter Wimsey (created by Dorothy L. Sayers), Philo Vance (created by S.S. Van Dine), and Ellery Queen (created by Frederic Dannay and Manfred B. Lee).

The 1930s was the golden age of the detective novel, particularly as seen in the books of Dashiell Hammett, in whose work the character of the detective became as important as the "whodunit" aspect of ratiocination had been earlier. Successors to Hammett included Raymond Chandler, Ross Macdonald; and Mickey Spillane.

The introduction of the mass-produced paperback book in the late 1930s made the detective story readily accessible to a wide public. Among the writers who capitalized on this new market were Erle Stanley Gardner, Rex Stout, and Frances and Richard Lockridge. In France, Georges Simenon created Inspector Jules Maigret, one of the best-known detectives since Sherlock Holmes. Other detective-story writers included

Nicholas Blake (pseudonym of the poet C. Day-Lewis), Michael Innes, Ngaio Marsh, Josephine Tey, and John Dickson Carr. The 1980s and '90s saw a large number of female writers—notably Sara Paretsky and Sue Grafton—whose works often featured women sleuths.

The Mystery Writers of America, a professional organization founded in 1945 to elevate the standards of mystery writing, including the detective story, has exerted an important influence through its annual Edgar Allan Poe Awards for excellence. *See also* MYSTERY STORY; HARD-BOILED FICTION.

Deucalion \dü-'kā-lē-,än\ In Greek legend, the son of Prometheus (the creator of the human race), king of Phthia in Thessaly, and husband of Pyrrha; he was also the father of Hellen, the mythical ancestor of the Hellenic race.

When Zeus resolved to destroy all humans by a flood, Deucalion constructed an ark in which, according to one version, he and his wife rode out the flood and landed on Mount Parnassus. Offering sacrifice and inquiring how to renew the human race, they were ordered to cast behind them the bones of their mother. The couple correctly interpreted this to mean they should throw behind them the stones of the hillside ("mother earth"), and did so. Those stones thrown by Deucalion became men; those thrown by Pyrrha, women. *Compare* NOAH.

Deus \'deûsh\, João de, *in full* João de Deus Nogueira Ramos \nô-'gwä-rə-'räm-üsh\ (b. March 8, 1830, São Bartolomeu de Messines, Algarve, Port.—d. Jan. 11, 1896, Lisbon) Lyric poet who fashioned a simple, direct, and expressive language that revitalized Portuguese Romantic poetry. He was a major influence on Portuguese literature of the early 20th century.

Deus was an influential figure among the younger poets who were to break with the literary formalism of the period. Though his first collection of poems, *Flores do campo* (1868; "Wildflowers"), was well received, he was constantly in financial difficulties. His friends succeeded in having him elected to Parliament in 1869, but he renounced his office over a question of principle, a gesture that brought him great popularity but little material comfort. After his marriage he was forced to eke out a living by composing verses on commission for tradesmen and by doing menial jobs. During this period he devoted himself to developing a new method of teaching reading. His second volume of verse, *Fôlhas sôltas* ("Loose Leaves"), and his *Cartilha maternal* ("Maternal Primer") both appeared in 1876. His reading method was officially adopted in 1888, and he was appointed to introduce it. In 1893 his collected works were published as *Campo de flores* ("Field of Flowers"); in 1895 he was publicly proclaimed the greatest Portuguese poet of his generation.

deus ex machina \'dā-əs-,eks-'mak-i-nə, -'mäk-; -mə-'shē-nə\ [New Latin, literally, a god from a machine, translation of Greek *apò mēchanês theós* (Demosthenes) or *theòs ek mēchanês* (Menander)] A person or thing that appears or is introduced into a situation suddenly and unexpectedly and provides an artificial or contrived solution to an apparently insoluble difficulty.

The term was first used in ancient Greek and Roman drama, where it meant the timely appearance of a god to unravel and resolve the plot. The deus ex machina was named for the convention of having the god appear in the sky, an effect achieved by means of a crane (Greek: *mēchanē*). The dramatic device dates from the 5th century BC; a god appears in Sophocles' *Philoctetes* and in most of the plays of Euripides to solve a crisis by divine intervention.

Since ancient times, the phrase has also been applied to an unexpected savior, or to an improbable event that brings order out of chaos (for example, in a western film the arrival, in time to avert tragedy, of the U.S. cavalry).

Deutsch \\'dȯich\\, Babette (b. Sept. 22, 1895, New York, N.Y., U.S.—d. Nov. 13, 1982, New York, N.Y.) American poet, critic, translator, and novelist whose volumes of literary criticism, *Poetry in Our Time* (1952) and *Poetry Handbook* (1957), were standard English texts in American universities. With her husband, Avraham Yarmolinsky, Deutsch translated poetry from Russian and German, including *Two Centuries of Russian Verse* (1966).

Deutsch published poems in magazines such as the *North American Review* and the *New Republic* while still a student at Barnard College, New York City. She first attracted critical notice for her poetry with *Banners* (1919), whose title poem celebrated the beginning of the Russian Revolution of 1917. Her literary collaboration with Yarmolinsky produced several acclaimed translations, many of which were the first rendering into English of important works of European literature.

Deutsch's poetry collections include *Honey Out of the Rock* (1925), Imagist verse on marriage, motherhood, and the arts; *Fire for the Night* (1930); *One Part Love* (1939); and *Take Them, Stranger* (1944) and *Animal, Vegetable, Mineral* (1954), both of which contain antiwar poetry. Among her critical studies are a collection of essays on poetry and poets entitled *Potable Gold* (1929), *Heroes of the Kalevala, Finland's Saga* (1940), *Walt Whitman, Builder for America* (1941), and *The Reader's Shakespeare* (1946). Her novels include the semiautobiographical *A Brittle Heaven* (1926); *In Such a Night* (1927); *Mask of Silenus* (1933), a novel about the philosopher Socrates; and *Rogue's Legacy* (1942), about the poet François Villon.

deva \\'dä-və, 'dē-\\ [Sanskrit *devaḥ* god] In Hindu mythology, a class of divine powers, roughly divided on the basis of their identification with the forces of nature into sky, air, and earth divinities (*e.g.*, Varuṇa, Indra, Soma). They are considered to be subordinate to the one supreme being. During the Vedic period the gods were divided into two classes, the devas and the asuras. In India the devas came to be more powerful than the asuras, and the latter word eventually took on the meaning of demon. In Iran the reverse took place, and the *daeva*s (the etymological counterpart of *deva* in Avestan) were denounced as demons by Zoroaster. They still survive as such in the *dīv*s of Persian folklore, especially through Ferdowsī's 11th-century epic, *Shāh-nāmeh* ("Book of Kings"). *Compare* ASURA.

device \\də-'vīs\\ Something (such as a figure of speech or a special method of narration) designed to achieve a particular effect.

Devil and Daniel Webster, The \\'dan-yəl-'web-stər\\ Often-anthologized short story by Stephen Vincent BENÉT, published in 1937. Two years later it reappeared as a one-act folk opera by Benét and composer Douglas Moore.

Jabez Stone, a New Hampshire farmer, receives a decade of material wealth in return for selling his soul to the Devil—Mr. Scratch. When the Devil comes to claim Stone's soul, the farmer has the statesman and orator Daniel Webster argue his case at midnight before a jury of historic American villains. The Faust legend, gentle satire of New England eccentricities, patriotism, and faith in humanity's higher aspirations are all elements of this tall tale; Benét's prose style, colloquial yet flexible, is important to the story's success.

Devil and Tom Walker, The \\'täm-'wȯk-ər\\ Short story by Washington IRVING, published as part of the collection *Tales of a Traveller* in 1824. This all-but-forgotten tall tale is considered by some to be one of Irving's finest short stories. Set in Massachusetts, the plot is a retelling of the Faust legend,

with a Yankee twist. The story is especially notable for Irving's mastery of narrative technique.

Devil's Dictionary, The Satiric lexicon by Ambrose BIERCE, first compiled as *The Cynic's Word Book* in 1906 and reissued under the author's preferred title five years later. The barbed definitions that Bierce began publishing in the *Wasp*, a weekly journal he edited in San Francisco from 1881 to 1886, brought this 19th-century stock form to a new level of artistry. Employing a terse, aphoristic style, Bierce lampooned social, professional, and religious convention, as in his definitions for *bore*—"A person who talks when you wish him to listen"; *architect*—"One who drafts a plan of your house, and plans a draft of your money"; and *saint*—"A dead sinner revised and edited." Many of the entries include "authenticating" citations from spurious scholarly sources.

De Voto \\di-'vō-tō\\, Bernard (Augustine) (b. Jan. 11, 1897, Ogden, Utah, U.S.—d. Nov. 13, 1955, New York, N.Y.) American novelist, journalist, historian, and critic, best known for his works on American literature and the history of the western frontier.

After attending the University of Utah and Harvard University, De Voto taught at Northwestern University and Harvard before becoming editor of the *Saturday Review of Literature*. After two years he resigned and returned to Cambridge, Mass., where he lived during the remainder of his life. Although he wrote a number of novels, De Voto probably found his largest audience through his essays in the "Easy Chair" column for *Harper's Magazine*. His combination of sound scholarship and a vigorous, outspoken style made him one of the most widely read critics and historians of his day. His strong opinions and admitted prejudices for American life and culture put him at the center of many critical controversies.

Among the nonfiction works De Voto wrote are *Mark Twain's America* (1932); *Mark Twain at Work* (1942); *Across the Wide Missouri* (1948), for which he won a Pulitzer Prize; *The World of Fiction* (1950); *The Hour* (1951); and *The Course of Empire* (1952). He also edited several books, including *Mark Twain in Eruption* (1940) and *The Journals of Lewis and Clark* (1953). His novels include *The Crooked Mile* (1924) and *Mountain Time* (1947).

De Vries \\də-'vrēs\\, Peter (b. Feb. 27, 1910, Chicago, Ill., U.S.—d. Sept. 28, 1993, Norwalk, Conn.) American editor and novelist widely known as a satirist, linguist, and comic visionary.

De Vries, the son of Dutch immigrants, was reared in a Calvinist environment. He graduated from Calvin College in Grand Rapids, Mich. After several years as an editor for *Poetry* magazine in Chicago, he joined the editorial staff of *The New Yorker* and thereafter made his home in Westport, Conn.

De Vries' first novel, *But Who Wakes the Bugler?* (1940), was most notable for having been illustrated by the cartoonist Charles Addams. Although his next two novels were hardly noticed at all, his first book of short stories, *No But I Saw the Movie* (1952), won critical acclaim, and his subsequent novel, *The Tunnel of Love* (1954), became a best-seller and was successfully adapted both as a play and as a motion picture. Noted for being light on plot and filled with wit, puns, and sardonic humor, De Vries' novels were appreciated for their imaginative wordplay and ironic vision. Among his better novels are *Comfort Me with Apples* (1956), *The Tents of Wickedness* (1959), *Reuben, Reuben* (1964), *Madder Music* (1977), and *Slouching Towards Kalamazoo* (1983).

Deyssel \\vän-'deis-əl, *Angl* 'dīs-\\, Lodewijk van, *pseudonym of* Karel Joan Lodewijk Alberdingk Thijm \\'teim, *Angl* 'tīm\\ (b. Sept. 22, 1864, Amsterdam, Neth.—d. Jan. 26, 1952, Haarlem) Leading Dutch writer and critic of the late 19th and early 20th centuries.

The son of J.A. Alberdingk Thijm (who promoted a Roman Catholic cultural revival in The Netherlands), Deyssel joined the largely agnostic, individualistic group associated with the avant-garde literary magazine *De Nieuwe Gids* ("The New Guide"). His passionate critical writings were published as *Verzamelde opstellen*, 11 vol. (1894–1911; "Collected Essays"). An admirer of Émile Zola, Deyssel published the naturalistic novel *Een liefde* ("A Love Affair") in 1887. He later abandoned naturalism and wrote highly personal, impressionistic prose and clever, somewhat overwrought "prose-verses." A sensitive artist with great powers of observation, he was a powerful influence on Dutch literature.

Dhammapada \ˈdəm-ə-ˌpäd-ə\ ("Words of Doctrine," or "Way of Truth")   One of the best-known books of the Pāli Buddhist canon, an anthology of basic Buddhist teachings (primarily ethical teachings) in a simple, aphoristic style. As the second text in the *Khuddaka Nikāya* ("Short Collection") of the *Sutta Piṭaka* ("Basket of Discourse"), the *Dhammapada* contains 423 stanzas arranged in 26 chapters. It also appears in somewhat different versions in Prākrit, Sanskrit, and Chinese, and there are translations in other languages. More than half the verses are excerpted from other canonical texts and include many of the most famous Buddhist sayings; others come from the storehouse of pithy sayings drawn upon by much of Indian literature.

Dharma Bums, The   Autobiographical novel by Jack KEROUAC, published in 1958. The story's narrator, Raymond Smith, is based on Kerouac himself, and the poet-woodsman-Buddhist, Japhy Ryder, is a thinly disguised portrait of the poet Gary Synder. The book contains a number of other characters who are drawn from actual poets and writers.

The plot unfolds when Smith, who is suffering spiritual conflicts amid the emptiness of middle-class American life, meets Ryder, whom he immediately recognizes as a spiritual model. The novel tells of the growth of their friendship and Smith's groping toward personal understanding. Much of the story occurs on the American West Coast.

Dhlomo \ˈdlō-mō *or with aspirated* d\, R.R.R., *in full* Rolfus Reginald Raymond (b. 1901, Siyamu, Natal [South Africa]—d. 1971)   African novelist, journalist, and editor who wrote in Zulu and English. His *An African Tragedy* (1928) was the first novel in English by a Zulu writer.

Dhlomo earned a teacher's certificate from Adams College in South Africa. During this period he contributed sketches and moral tales to *The Sjambok, Ilanga lase Natal*, and *The Bantu World*. In 1942 he became editor of *The Bantu World* and then *Ilanga lase Natal*, for which he wrote a leading feature in English and numerous articles in Zulu.

An African Tragedy, a novel about the corrosive effects of the city on a pair of lovers from the country, is a Christian fable of sin and forgiveness. Dhlomo's major novels in Zulu—*UNomalanga kaNdengezi* (1934; "Nomalanga, Daughter of Ndengezi") and *Indlela yababi* (1946; "The Way of the Wicked")—paint portraits of Zulu life in Natal and Johannesburg, respectively. Many of his other Zulu works are semibiographical accounts of members of the Zulu dynasty.

diablerie \dē-ˈäb-lə-rē\ [French, literally, devilry, manifestations of the devil or of devils]   A representation in words or pictures of black magic or of dealings with the devil. Among the literary works that contain such representations are Nathaniel Hawthorne's "Young Goodman Brown" and Sylvia Townsend Warner's *Lolly Willowes*.

diaeresis or **dieresis** \dī-ˈer-ə-sis, -ˈir-\ *plural* diaereses *or* diereses \-ˌsēz\ [Greek *diaíresis*, literally, the act of dividing, division]   **1.** The resolution of one syllable into two, especially by separating the vowel elements of a diphthong and, by extension, two adjacent vowels, as in the word *coöperation*; it is also the mark placed over a vowel to indicate that it is pronounced as a separate syllable, as in *naïve* or *Brontë*.   **2.** In classical prosody, the break in a line of verse that occurs when the completion of a metrical foot coincides with the end of a word. A diaeresis after the fourth foot in a dactylic hexameter, especially common in pastoral poetry, is called a bucolic diaeresis or bucolic caesura. *Compare* CAESURA.

Dial, The   Quarterly journal published between July 1840 and April 1844 and associated with the New England Transcendentalist movement. Edited first by Margaret Fuller and later by Ralph Waldo Emerson, *The Dial* printed poems and essays by Emerson, Fuller, Henry David Thoreau, and Bronson Alcott, among others. Although the magazine often suffered from undeveloped material and a lack of consensus about its purpose, it was an important vehicle for Transcendental philosophy. *See also* TRANSCENDENTALISM.

Dial, The   Literary magazine founded in Chicago by Francis F. Browne and published from 1880 to 1929. It moved to New York City in 1918. Intended as a forum in which to carry on the tradition of the Transcendentalist journal of the same name, *The Dial* became famous for introducing some of the best new writing and artwork of the early 20th century. In its heyday it published works by Thomas Mann, T.S. Eliot, Sherwood Anderson, Djuna Barnes, D.H. Lawrence, and E.E. Cummings, among others. Line drawings by Henri de Toulouse-Lautrec, Pablo Picasso, and Marc Chagall also appeared in its pages. The prestigious succession of its editors included Conrad Aiken, Van Wyck Brooks, Scofield Thayer, and Marianne Moore.

dialectic \ˌdī-ə-ˈlek-tik\ [Greek *dialektikē* discussion and reasoning by dialogue, from feminine of *dialektikós*, adjective derivative of *diálektos* discussion, debate]   Any systematic reasoning, exposition, or argument, especially in literature, that juxtaposes opposed or contradictory ideas and usually seeks to resolve their conflict. The Socratic method of question and answer as displayed in Plato's dialogues is an example. The term can also mean the play of ideas, cunning or hairsplitting disputation, or argumentative skill.

dialogue or **dialog** \ˈdī-ə-ˌlóg, -ˌläg\ [Latin *dialogus*, from Greek *diálogos* conversation, a derivative of *dialégesthai* to converse]   **1.** A written composition in which two or more characters are represented as conversing or reasoning on some topic.   **2.** The conversational element of literary or dramatic composition.

As a literary form, a dialogue is a carefully organized exposition, by means of invented conversation, of contrasting philosophical or intellectual attitudes. The oldest known dialogues are the Sicilian mimes, written in rhythmic prose by Sophron of Syracuse in the early 5th century BC. Although none of these has survived, Plato knew and admired them. But the form of philosophic dialogue that he perfected by 400 BC was sufficiently original to be an independent literary creation. With due attention to characterization and the dramatic situations from which the discussions arise, Plato's dialogues develop dialectically the main tenets of Platonic philosophy. From Lucian in the 2nd century AD the dialogue acquired a new tone and function. His influential *Dialogues of the Dead*, with their coolly satirical tone, inspired innumerable imitations in England and France during the 17th and 18th centuries, *e.g.*, dialogues by the French writers Bernard de Fontenelle (1683) and François Fénelon (1700–12).

The revival of interest in Plato during the Renaissance encouraged numerous imitations and adaptations of the Platonic dialogue. In Spain, Juan de Valdés used it to discuss problems of patriotism and humanism in 1533, and Vincenzo Carducci, theories of painting in 1633. In Italy, dialogues on the Platonic model were written by Torquato Tasso in 1580, Giordano Bruno in 1584, and Galileo in 1632.

In the 16th and 17th centuries, the dialogue lent itself easily and frequently to the presentation of controversial religious, political, and economic ideas. George Berkeley's *Three Dialogues Between Hylas and Philonous* (1713) is perhaps the best of the English imitations of Plato. The best-known 19th-century examples are Walter Savage Landor's *Imaginary Conversations* (vols. 1 and 2, 1824; vol. 3, 1828; thereafter sporadically to 1853), sensitive re-creations of such historical personages as Dante and Beatrice. André Gide's *Interviews imaginaires* (1943), which explore the psychology of the supposed participants, and George Santayana's *Dialogues in Limbo* (1925) illustrate the survival of this ancient form in tne 20th century.

Dialogue of the Ancients   *see* THE COLLOQUY OF THE OLD MEN.

Dialogues des Carmélites \dyà-,lòg-dä-kàr-mä-'lēt\ Screenplay by Georges BERNANOS, published posthumously in French as a drama in 1949 and translated both as *The Fearless Heart* and *The Carmelites*. In *Dialogues des Carmélites*, Bernanos examined the religious themes of innocence, sacrifice, and death. Based on Gertrud von Le Fort's novel *Die Letzte am Schafott* (1931; *The Song at the Scaffold*) and on a scenario by Robert P. Brückberger and Phillipe Agostini, it tells the story of the martyrdom of 16 Carmelite nuns from Compiègne, France, who were executed by guillotine on July 17, 1794, during the French Revolution.

diamb \'dī-,am, -,amb\ or **diiamb** \,dī-'ī-,am, -,amb\ [Greek *diíambos*]   In prosody, a metrical foot consisting of two iambs, or an iambic dipody reckoned as a single compound foot (∪ ′ ∪ ′).

Diamond as Big as the Ritz, The \'rits\   Allegorical short story about lost illusions, by F. Scott FITZGERALD, published in 1922 in *Tales of the Jazz Age.*

John T. Unger is a student at an exclusive Massachusetts prep school. He befriends Percy Washington, a new classmate who boasts that his father is "the richest man in the world" and who invites John to spend the summer at his family's home in the Montana Rockies. The Washington mansion is built upon a secret diamond mine that contains a single diamond one cubic mile in size; the site is well hidden and visible only from the air.

After a squadron of government aircraft locates the diamond mine, military climbers begin to scale the mountain. Rather than allow his private empire to be invaded and appropriated by the government, Percy's father blows up the diamond mountain, killing himself and his wife, the invaders, and Percy, as John and the Washington sisters watch helplessly, horror-struck.

Diana \dī-'an-ə\   In Roman mythology, goddess of wild animals and the hunt, virtually indistinguishable from the Greek ARTEMIS. Her name is akin to the Latin words *dium* ("sky") and *dius* ("daylight"). Like her Greek counterpart, she was also a goddess of domestic animals. As a fertility deity she was invoked by women to aid conception and delivery.

Perhaps originally an indigenous woodland goddess, Diana was early identified with Artemis. She later absorbed Artemis' identification with both SELENE (Luna) and HECATE; hence the characterization *triformis* sometimes used in Latin literature.

Diana of the Crossways \dī-'an-ə\   Novel by George MEREDITH, 26 chapters of which were published serially in 1884 in the *Fortnightly Review*. A "considerably enlarged" three-volume book was published in 1885.

Diana of the Crossways examines the unhappy marriage of the title character Diana Warwick and is loosely based on events in the life of Caroline Norton (playwright Richard Brinsley Sheridan's granddaughter), who was suspected of revealing an important political secret that she had acquired from her lover. Although Meredith was forced to attach a disclaimer to the novel, his story is less about political scandal than about his protagonist's inner life and motives.

diary \'dī-ə-rē\, *also called* journal \'jər-nəl\ [Latin *diarium*, a derivative of *dies* day]   A record of events, transactions, or observations kept daily or at frequent intervals; especially a daily record of personal activities, reflections, or feelings. Written primarily for the writer's use alone, the diary usually offers a frankness not found in writing done for publication.

The diary form began to flower in the late Renaissance. In addition to revealing the diarist's personality, diaries are important for the recording of social and political history. For example, *Journal d'un bourgeois de Paris*, kept by an anonymous French priest from 1409 to 1431 and continued by another hand to 1449, is invaluable to the historian of the reigns of Charles VI and Charles VII. The English diarist John Evelyn is surpassed only by the greatest diarist of all, Samuel Pepys, whose diary from Jan. 1, 1660 to May 31, 1669, gives both an astonishingly frank picture of his foibles and frailties and a stunning picture of life in London.

An 18th-century diary of extraordinary emotional interest was that of Jonathan Swift, published as *Journal to Stella* (written 1710–13; published posthumously 1766–68). It is a surprising amalgam of ambition, affection, wit, and freakishness. Other notable English diaries of the late 18th century were those of the novelist Fanny Burney, published posthumously in 1842–46, and James Boswell's *Journal of a Tour to the Hebrides* (1785), a genuine diary though somewhat expanded, which was one of the first diaries to be published in its author's lifetime.

Interest in the diary increased greatly in the first part of the 19th century. Those of unusual literary interest, all published posthumously, include the *Journal* of Sir Walter Scott (1890), the *Journals* of Dorothy Wordsworth (1855), and the diary of Henry Crabb Robinson (1869). The posthumous publication of the diaries of the Russian artist Marie Bashkirtseff produced a great sensation in 1887, as did the publication of the diary of the Goncourt brothers, beginning in 1888.

André Gide's journal was published in several volumes in his lifetime. Other notable examples from the 20th century, all published posthumously, include the *Journal* of Katherine Mansfield (1927), *Het Achterhuis* (1947; *The Diary of a Young Girl*) by Anne Frank, and the five-volume *Diary of Virginia Woolf* (1977–84).

Diary of a Country Priest, The   Novel by Georges BERNANOS, published in French as *Journal d'un curé de campagne* in 1936.

The narrative mainly takes the form of a journal kept by a young parish priest during the last year of his troubled life. He records his spiritual struggle over what he perceives as the ineffectuality of his efforts to improve the lives of his impoverished and misguided parishioners. Physically, he battles a stomach ailment that local gossip attributes to drunkenness. His role in the conversion of a wealthy countess, who suddenly dies, aggravates his moral ambivalence and draws reproof from his superiors, as well as from the woman's family. His stomach condition worsens, and he seeks medical attention too late. In the deathbed ritual of absolution, however, he expresses an abiding faith that transcends his own and his fellows' failures.

Diary of a Madman   Short story by Nikolay GOGOL, published in 1835 as "Zapiski sumasshedshego."

Diary of a Madman, a first-person narrative presented in the form of a diary, is the tale of Poprishchin, a government clerk who gradually descends into insanity. At the outset, the narrator records his frustrations and humiliations straightforwardly, rationalizing various affronts to his dignity. Over time, however, reason gives way to delusion. His intermittent encounters with Sophie, the radiant daughter of his official superior, provoke an obsession that leads to his "overhearing" two dogs discussing his hopelessness. As such hallucinations become more frequent, he finds solace—and his ultimate rationale—in a new identity as the rightful king of Spain, whose enemies have engineered his exile. Throughout the story, interludes of sanity provide striking counterpoint to the deepening psychosis.

diastole \dī-'as-tə-lē\ [Greek *diastolē* the act of expanding or dilating]   In prosody, the lengthening of a short quantity or syllable for metric regularity. It is the opposite of SYSTOLE.

Dib \'dēb\, Mohammed (b. July 21, 1920, Tlemcen, Alg.)   Algerian novelist, poet, and playwright who is known for his early trilogy on Algeria—*La Grande Maison* (1952; "The Big House"), *L'Incendie* (1954; "The Fire"), and *Le Métier à tisser* (1957; "The Loom")—in which he described the Algerian people awakening to a consciousness of self and to the impending struggle for independence.

Dib wrote of the poor Algerian worker and peasant in his early realistic novels. From the time of his exile from Algeria in 1959, Dib lived in France. Most of Dib's later novels are marked by the use of symbol, myth, allegory, and fantasy to portray the French colonial repression of the Algerian people, the search for the authentic expression of an Algerian personality, the War of Independence and its effects, the new Algeria after independence and the struggle of the technocrats for control, and the plight of the Algerian emigrant worker in France. These novels—*La Danse du roi* (1960; "The Dance of the King"), *Qui se souvient de la mer* (1962; *Who Remembers the Sea*), *Cours sur la rive sauvage* (1964; "Run on the Wild Shore"), *Dieu en barbarie* (1970; "God in Barbary"), *Le Maître de chasse* (1973; "The Hunt Master"), and *Habel* (1977)—like the early novels, express Dib's optimism.

Though he worked in a variety of genres, Dib viewed himself as essentially a poet. His collections of poetry include *Ombre gardienne* (1961; "Guardian Shadow"), *Formulaires* (1970), and *Omneros* (1975), and he published two collections of novellas, *Au café* (1956; "In the Café") and *Le Talisman* (1966). Dib was also the author of a film scenario and several plays.

dichoree \,dī-'kȯr-ē, ,dī-kȯr-'ē\ [Greek *dichóreios,* from *di-* two + *choreîos* choreus]   *see* DITROCHEE.

dichronous \'dī-krō-nəs\ [Greek *díchronos,* from *di-* two + *chrónos* time]   In classical prosody, capable of being occupied by either a long or a short syllable, or a syllable that can be scanned as either long or short. *See also* ANCEPS.

Dick \'dik\, Philip K., *in full* Kindred (b. Dec. 16, 1928, Chicago, Ill., U.S.—d. March 2, 1982, Santa Ana, Calif.)   American science-fiction writer whose novels and short stories often depict the psychological struggles of characters trapped in illusory environments.

Dick worked briefly in radio before studying at the University of California at Berkeley for one year. The publication of his first story, "Beyond Lies the Wub," in 1952 launched his full-time writing career. He published his first novel, *Solar Lottery*, three years later. The theme of a reality at variance with

what it appears or was intended to be emerged early in Dick's work and remained his central preoccupation. In such novels as *Time Out of Joint* (1959), *The Man in the High Castle* (1962; Hugo Award winner), and *The Three Stigmata of Palmer Eldritch* (1965), the protagonists must determine their own orientation in an "alternate world." Beginning with *The Simulacra* (1964) and culminating in *Do Androids Dream of Electric Sheep?* (1968; adapted for film as *Blade Runner*, 1982), the illusion centers on artificial creatures at large in a real world of the future.

Among Dick's numerous story collections are *A Handful of Darkness* (1955), *The Variable Man and Other Stories* (1957), *The Preserving Machine* (1969), and the posthumously published *I Hope I Shall Arrive Soon* (1985).

Dick, Mr. \'dik\, *byname of* Richard Babley \'rich-ərd-'bab-lē\   Fictional character in Charles Dickens' novel DAVID COPPERFIELD, a simpleminded but kind man who is a distant relative and treasured friend of David's Aunt Betsey Trotwood.

Dickens \'dik-ənz\, Charles (John Huffam) (b. Feb. 7, 1812, Portsmouth, Hampshire, Eng.—d. June 9, 1870, Gad's Hill, near Chatham, Kent)   English novelist, generally considered the greatest of the Victorian period.

Bettmann Archive

Dickens' father, a clerk in the navy pay office, was well paid, but he often brought the family to financial embarrassment or disaster. In 1824 the elder Dickens was thrown into debtors prison, and Charles was withdrawn from school and forced to work in a factory. It is notable that the images of the prison and of the lost, oppressed, or bewildered child recur in many of his novels.

As a young man, Dickens worked as a reporter, successively, in the law courts, in Parliament, and on London newspapers. These years left him with a lasting affection for journalism and contempt both for the law and for Parliament. His career as a writer of fiction began in 1833 with short stories and essays in periodicals, reprinted as SKETCHES BY "BOZ" (1836). In 1836 he married Catherine Hogarth and began a large family, of which nine children survived.

His comic novel THE PICKWICK PAPERS (1837) made him the most popular author of his time in England. His novels OLIVER TWIST (1838) and NICHOLAS NICKLEBY (1839) were followed in 1841 by THE OLD CURIOSITY SHOP and BARNABY RUDGE. Exhausted, Dickens took a five-month vacation in the United States, where he was lionized. His reactions to America—many negative—found expression in AMERICAN NOTES (1842) and MARTIN CHUZZLEWIT (1844). A CHRISTMAS CAROL (1843), written in a few weeks, entered immediately into modern mythology. It was the first and the best of his annual Christmas novels and stories, which also included THE CRICKET ON THE HEARTH (1846).

In many of his novels of the 1840s, including DOMBEY AND SON (1848), his heightened concern with vulgarity and evil coexists with his basic optimism, which appears in perhaps its purest form in the semiautobiographical DAVID COPPERFIELD (1850). Afterward, however, in BLEAK HOUSE (1853), HARD TIMES (1854), LITTLE DORRIT (1857), GREAT EXPECTATIONS (1861), and OUR MUTUAL FRIEND (1865), the inhuman aspect of Victorian industrial society becomes predominant, and the comic spirit, where it can be detected at all, is satirical. His historical novel of the French Revolution, A TALE OF TWO CITIES, appeared in 1859.

Dickens' journalistic ambitions found a permanent form in his self-published weekly miscellany of fiction, poetry, and essays entitled HOUSEHOLD WORDS (which ran from 1850 to 1859) and its successor, *All the Year Round* (1859–88). Dickens contributed several serialized novels and many items on current political and social affairs.

Dickens' marriage began to unravel in the mid-1850s. In 1858 he separated from his wife and began a protracted affair with Ellen Ternan, a young actress. At this time he achieved great popularity for his public readings, in which his emotional involvement was intense. His last novel, THE MYSTERY OF EDWIN DROOD (1870), was left unfinished at his death.

Dickens' works are characterized by attacks on social evils and inadequate institutions, topical references, an encyclopedic knowledge of London, pathos, a vein of the macabre, a delight in Christmas, a pervasive spirit of benevolence and geniality, inexhaustible powers of character creation, an acute ear for characteristic speech, a strong narrative impulse, and a prose style that, if sometimes overdependent on a few comic mannerisms, is highly individual and inventive.

Dickensian \di-'ken-zē-ən\   Characteristic of or having the qualities of the writings of Charles Dickens with respect to humor and pathos in the portrayal of odd, often extravagant, and picturesque character types usually from the lower economic strata of 19th-century English society.

Dickey \'dik-ē\, James, *in full* James Lafayette Dickey (b. Feb. 2, 1923, Atlanta, Ga., U.S.)   American poet, novelist, and critic best known for his poetry combining themes of nature mysticism, religion, and history and for his powerful novel *Deliverance* (1970).

Dickey served as a fighter-bomber pilot in the U.S. Army Air Forces during World War II. After the war he earned B.A. (1949) and M.A. (1950) degrees from Vanderbilt University. By his own account, Dickey began writing poetry at the age of 24 with little awareness of formal poetics. After pursuing graduate studies and working for a time in advertising, he published his first book of poems, *Into the Stone*, in 1960. He was a teacher and writer-in-residence at a number of U.S. colleges and universities. From 1966 to 1968 he served as poetry consultant to the Library of Congress.

Dickey's other collections of poetry include *Drowning with Others* (1962), *Helmets* (1964), *Buckdancer's Choice* (1965), *Poems 1957-1967* (1967), *The Zodiac* (1976), and *The Whole Motion* (1992; collected poems 1949–92). Of his works of nonfiction prose, *Babel to Byzantium: Poets & Poetry Now* (1968), the autobiographical *Self-Interviews* (1970), and *Jericho: The South Beheld* (1974) are notable.

His poetry is noted for its lyrical portrayal of a world in conflict—predator with prey, soldier with soldier, the self with itself.

Dickinson \'dik-ən-sən\, Emily (Elizabeth) (b. Dec. 10, 1830, Amherst, Mass., U.S.—d. May 15, 1886, Amherst)   American lyric poet who is noted for her eloquent, concise, and deceptively simple verses.

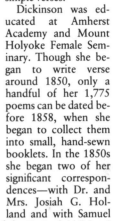

Bettmann Archive

Dickinson was educated at Amherst Academy and Mount Holyoke Female Seminary. Though she began to write verse around 1850, only a handful of her 1,775 poems can be dated before 1858, when she began to collect them into small, hand-sewn booklets. In the 1850s she began two of her significant correspondences—with Dr. and Mrs. Josiah G. Holland and with Samuel Bowles. The two men were editors of the *Springfield* (Mass.) *Republican*, a paper that took an interest in literary matters.

Dickinson's poems of the 1850s are fairly conventional in sentiment and form, but beginning about 1860 she began to experiment with both language and prosody. Her prevailing poetic form was the quatrain of three iambic feet, but she used many other forms as well, lending complexity to even the simpler hymnbook measures by constantly altering the metrical beat to fit her thought. She broke new ground in her wide use of off-rhymes. In striving for an epigrammatic conciseness, she stripped her language of superfluous words. She tampered freely with syntax and liked to place a familiar word in an extraordinary context.

In 1862 Dickinson wrote to a literary man, Thomas Wentworth Higginson, asking his opinion of her work. Higginson, although he advised Emily not to publish, recognized the originality of her poems and remained her "preceptor" for the rest of her life. After 1862 she resisted all efforts by her friends to put her verse before the public. Only seven poems were published during her lifetime, five of them in the *Springfield Republican*.

In 1864 and 1865 persistent eye trouble caused her to live several months in Cambridge, Mass., where she sought treatment. Once back in Amherst she never traveled again and after the late 1860s never left the boundaries of the family's property. After the Civil War, she sought increasingly to regulate her life by the rules of art. Her letters, some of them equal in artistry to her poems, classicize daily experience in an epigrammatic style. By 1870 she was dressing only in white and saw few of the callers who came to the homestead; her seclusion was fiercely guarded by her devoted sister, Lavinia.

Soon after Dickinson's death Lavinia determined to have Emily's poems published. In 1890 *Poems by Emily Dickinson*, edited by T.W. Higginson and Mabel Loomis Todd, appeared. Other volumes of Dickinson poems, edited chiefly by Mabel Loomis Todd, Martha Dickinson Bianchi (Emily's niece), and Millicent Todd Bingham, were published between 1891 and 1957, and in 1955 Thomas H. Johnson edited all the surviving poems and their variant versions.

dicolon \dī-'kō-lən\ *plural* dicola \-'kō-lə\ A verse or rhythmic period having two colons.

diction \'dik-shən\ [Latin *dictio* oratorical style, literally, the act of speaking, a derivative of *dicere* to say] Choice of words, especially with regard to correctness, clearness, or effectiveness. Any of the four generally accepted levels of diction—formal, informal, colloquial, or slang—may be correct in a particular context but incorrect in another or when mixed unintentionally. Most ideas have a number of alternate words that the writer can select to suit a particular purpose. "Children," "kids," "youngsters," "youths," and "brats," for example, all have different evocative values.

The widest scope for literary style is offered at the level of word choice. Writers such as Samuel Johnson, who believed that great thoughts were always general and that it was not the business of poets to "number the streaks of the tulips," use general, abstract, nonemotive words. Other writers, however, prefer particular, concrete, and emotive words and take advantage of the evocative values of technical, dialect, colloquial, or archaic terms when it suits their purpose.

Dictys Cretensis \'dik-tis-krē-'ten-sis\ Alleged author of a spurious chronicle of the Trojan War. Dictys was supposed to have accompanied the Cretan leader Idomeneus from Knossos to the siege of Troy and to have written a pro-Greek account of the Trojan War. His manuscript was said to have been "discovered" during the 1st century AD and to have been transliterated from Phoenician into Greek. Probably in the 4th century one Lucius Septimius put out a translation of Dictys' supposed eyewitness account (which in fact probably dates from the 2nd or 3rd century AD). This fantastic work, the *Ephemeris belli Trojani*, together with a similar but pro-Trojan account by Dares Phrygius, was a major sourcebook for medieval handlings of the Trojan story. *See also* TROY.

didactic \dī-'dak-tik, di-\ or **didactical** \-ti-kəl\ [Greek *didaktikós* apt at teaching] Of literature or other art, intended to convey instruction and information. The word is often used to refer to texts that are overburdened with instructive or factual matter to the exclusion of graceful and pleasing detail so that they are pompously dull and erudite. Some literature, however, is both entertaining and consciously didactic, as for example proverbs and gnomic poetry.

didascaly \dī-'das-kə-lē, di-\ [Greek *didaskalía* teaching, instruction, a derivative of *didáskalos* teacher] The instruction or training of the chorus in ancient Greek drama. The Greek plural noun *didaskaliai* ("instructions") came to refer to records of dramatic performances, containing names of authors and dates, in the form of the original inscriptions or as later published by Alexandrian scholars.

Diderot \dēd-'rō\, Denis (b. Oct. 5, 1713, Langres, Fr.—d. July 31, 1784, Paris) French man of letters and philosopher who, from 1745 to 1772, served as chief editor of the L'ENCYCLOPÉDIE, one of the principal works of the Age of Enlightenment.

Diderot was first educated by the Jesuits and received the master of arts degree from the University of Paris in 1732. In 1745 the publisher André Le Breton approached Diderot with a view to bringing out a French translation of Ephraim Chambers' *Cyclopaedia*. Diderot undertook the task with the distinguished mathematician Jean Le Rond d'Alembert as coeditor and profoundly changed the nature of the publication, broadening its scope and turning it into an important organ of radical and revolutionary opinion. The *encyclopédistes* sought to further knowledge and, by so doing, to strike a resounding blow against reactionary forces in the church and the state.

While editing the *Encyclopédie*, Diderot composed most of his own important works as well. In 1751 he published *Lettre sur les sourds et muets* ("Letter on the Deaf and Dumb"), which studies the function of language and deals with points of aesthetics, and in 1754 he published the *Pensées sur l'interprétation de la nature* ("Thoughts on the Interpretation of Nature"), acclaimed as the method of philosophical inquiry of the 18th century. Among his philosophical works, special mention may be made of *L'Entretien entre d'Alembert et Diderot* ("Conversation Between d'Alembert and Diderot"), *Le Rêve de d'Alembert* ("D'Alembert's Dream"), and the *Eléments de physiologie*.

His essays, among them "Regrets sur ma vieille robe de chambre" ("Regrets over My Old Bathrobe") and "Entretien d'un père avec ses enfants" ("Conversation of a Father with His Children"), based on personal experience, have the qualities of form and style of his short stories and novels: *La Religieuse* (1796; written 1760; "The Nun"), *Jacques le fataliste* (1796; written 1773), and *Le Neveu de Rameau* (RAMEAU'S NEPHEW). He wrote several plays and expounded his theories on drama in *Entretiens sur le fils naturel* (1757; "Discussion on the Natural Son") and *Discours sur la poésie dramatique* (1758; "Discourse on Dramatic Poetry").

Although he wrote some literary criticism, it is as the first great art critic, covering the salons, or annual art exhibitions, that he is best remembered. His analysis of art, artists, and the technique of painting, together with the excellence of his taste and his style, won him posthumous fame; especially admired was his *Essai sur la peinture* (1796; written 1765; "Essay on Painting").

Didion \'did-ē-ən\, Joan (b. Dec. 5, 1934, Sacramento, Calif., U.S.) American novelist and essayist known for her lucid prose style and incisive depictions of social and psychological fragmentation.

Didion graduated from the University of California at Berkeley in 1956 and then worked for *Vogue* magazine from 1956 to 1963, first as a copywriter and later as an editor. During this period she wrote her first novel, *Run River* (1963), which examines the disintegration of a California family. While in New York, she met and married the writer John Gregory Dunne, with whom she returned to California in 1964. A collection of magazine columns published as *Slouching Towards Bethlehem* (1968) established Didion's reputation as an essayist and confirmed her preoccupation with the forces of disorder. In a second collection, *The White Album* (1979), Didion continued her analysis of the turbulent 1960s. The inner decay of the Establishment is a major theme of the essays constituting the volume *After Henry* (1992; also published as *Sentimental Journeys*). Didion's fiction, also centering on personal and social unrest, includes the short novels *Play It as It Lays* (1970), *A Book of Common Prayer* (1977), *Democracy* (1984), and the extended essays *Salvador* (1983) and *Miami* (1987).

Dido \'dī-,dō\, *also called* Elissa \i-'lis-ə\ In Greek legend, the reputed founder of Carthage, daughter of the Tyrian king Mutto (or Belus), and wife of Sychaeus (or Acerbas). After her husband was slain by her brother Pygmalion, Dido fled to the coast of Africa where she purchased from a local chieftain, Iarbas, a piece of land on which she founded Carthage. The city soon prospered, and Iarbas sought Dido's hand in marriage. To escape from him, Dido constructed a funeral pyre on which she stabbed herself before the people. Virgil, however, made Dido a contemporary of Aeneas, whose descendants founded Rome. Dido fell in love with Aeneas after his landing in Africa, and Virgil attributes her suicide to her abandonment by him. Dido was identified with the Virgo Caelestis (*i.e.*, Tanit, the tutelary goddess of Carthage).

Dido, Queen of Carthage \'dī-ˌdō . . . 'kär-thij\ (*in full* The Tragedy of Dido, Queen of Carthage) Play in five acts by Christopher MARLOWE and Thomas Nashe, published in 1594.

The play is based on the story of Dido and Aeneas as told in the fourth book of Virgil's *Aeneid*. In the play, Dido, the queen of Carthage, is in love with Aeneas, who has taken refuge in Carthage after the fall of Troy. He refuses to marry her, however, and as he sails from Carthage, the despairing Dido kills herself. The play adds a significant character from Greek legend to Virgil's story: Iarbas, a barbarian chieftain who himself wants Dido for his bride.

Didymus Chalcenterus \'did-i-məs-kal-'sen-tə-rəs\ (fl. *c.* 80–10 BC, Alexandria) Greek scholar and grammarian, one of the chief links between ancient and modern classical scholarship. His industry, as the reputed author of 3,500 books, earned him the nickname of Chalcenterus ("Brass Guts"). His output included work on the text of Homer, exegetical commentaries on numerous Greek authors, and lexicographical compilations.

diectasis \dī-'ek-tə-sis\ [Greek *dia-* through, completely + *éktasis* stretching, lengthening of a short syllable] In prosody, lengthening by an interpolated syllable.

Diego, \dē-'ā-gō\, Gerardo, *surname in full* Diego Cendoya \thän-'dō-yä\ (b. Oct. 3, 1896, Santander, Spain—d. July 8, 1987, Madrid) Spanish anthologist, musicologist, and prolific, innovative poet.

Diego received a doctorate from the University of Madrid in 1920. During the 1920s he wrote experimental poetry and joined the avant-garde Ultraísmo and Creacionismo movements. He taught for a time in the ancient town of Soria in north-central Spain; the location inspired the poems of *Imagen* (1922), *Soria* (1923), and *Versos humanos* (1925; "Human Verses"). In *Vía crucis* (1931; "Way of the Cross") Diego explored religious themes. *Angeles de Compostela* (1940; rev. ed., 1961), which also contained religious poetry, and *Alondra de verdad* (1941; "Lark of Truth"), a diary in 42 sonnets, have been called his best work; both collections are relatively traditional and classical in tone.

From 1939 to 1966 Diego was a professor at the Beatriz Galindo Institute in Madrid, where he continued to produce new poems at an astonishing rate. *Paisaje con figuras* (1956; "Landscape with Figures") won the second of his national literary awards, and in 1979 he shared the Cervantes Prize with Jorge Luis Borges.

Dietrich von Bern \'dē-trik-fòn-'bern\ Heroic figure of Germanic legend, apparently derived from Theodoric the Great, an Ostrogothic king of Italy who reigned from 493 to 526 AD.

Dietrich's exploits are related in a number of south German songs preserved in DAS HELDENBUCH ("The Book of Heroes")—including *Dietrichs Flucht* ("Dietrich's Flight"), *Die Rabenschlacht* ("The Battle of Ravenna"), *Alpharts Tod* ("Alphart's Death"), and a number of additional stories—and, more fully, in the 13th-century Icelandic prose *Thithriks saga*. This legend also has a connection with the Middle High German epic Nibelungenlied. References to Dietrich in Anglo-Saxon records are few and obscure.

Driven by Ermenrich (Ermanaric) from his kingdom of Bern (Verona), Dietrich lives for many years at the court of Etzel (Attila), until he returns with a Hunnish army to defeat Ermenrich at Ravenna. Etzel's two sons fall in the fight, and Dietrich returns to Etzel to answer for their deaths. Later he has his revenge by slaying Ermenrich. Dietrich's long stay with Etzel represents Theodoric's youth spent at the Byzantine court.

Dietrich typifies the wise and just ruler as opposed to the tyrannical Ermenrich. Many of the incidents told about him have no basis in the story of Theodoric, although some could be related to the experiences of Theodoric's father, Theodemir. Other figures in the Dietrich cycle are his weapons master, Hildebrand, with his nephews Alphart and Wolfhart; Wittich and Heime, Dietrich's traitorous vassals; and Biterolf and Dietleib, the king of Toledo and his son, who join Dietrich in battle at Worms.

Digenis Akritas \thē-yen-'ēs-ä-'krē-täs\, *also called* Digenis Akritas Basileios \vä-'sē-lē-ōs\ Byzantine epic hero celebrated in folk (Akritic) ballads and in an epic relating his parentage, boyhood adventures, manhood, and death. Based on a historical character who died about 788, the epic—a blend of Greek, Byzantine, and Oriental motifs—originated in the 10th century and was popularized by itinerant folksingers. It was recorded in several versions from the 12th to the 17th century, the oldest of which is a linguistic mixture of popular and literary language.

Digenis Akritas, the ideal medieval Greek hero, is a bold warrior of the Euphrates frontier, the son of a Saracen amir converted to Christianity by the daughter of a Byzantine general. He was a proficient warrior by the age of three and spent the rest of his life valiantly defending the Byzantine Empire from frontier invaders. The feeling for nature and strong family affections that permeate the epic anticipate the great mid-17th-century Cretan national romance, *Erotókritos* by Vitzéntzos Kornáros, and much modern Greek popular poetry.

digest \'dī-jest\ [Latin *digesta* systematic arrangement of laws, from neuter plural of *digestus,* past participle of *digerere* to disperse, arrange, organize] **1.** A summation or condensation of a body of information on a specific subject, such as a periodical devoted to condensed versions of previously published works. **2.** A product of digestion, such as a literary condensation or abridgment.

digression \dī-'gresh-ən, di-\ [Latin *digressio,* a derivative of *digredi* to go off, digress] **1.** The act of digressing, or turning aside from the main subject of attention, in a discourse or other usually organized literary work. The writers Laurence Sterne and Jonathan Swift were particularly well known for their use of this technique. **2.** The portion of the discourse in which such a change of topic is made.

diiamb *see* DIAMB.

dilemma tale *also called* judgment tale. Typical African form of short story that has a morally ambiguous ending, thus allowing the audience to comment or speculate upon the correct solution to the problem posed in the tale. Issues raised include conflicts of loyalty, the necessity of choosing a just response to a difficult situation, and the question of where to lay the blame when several parties seem equally guilty. An example is the story of a young boy who in a time of crisis must choose between loyalty to his own father, who is a cruel and unjust man, and loyalty to the kindly foster father who brought him up.

Another tale deals with a man who died while hunting an ox to feed his three wives. The first wife learns through a dream what has happened to him, the second leads her fellow wives to the place where he died, and the third restores him to life. The audience must decide which of the three most deserves his praise.

A final example is the Wolof tale of three brothers, all married to the same girl, who journey together to a strange land. One night the girl is murdered by a robber, and the eldest brother, with whom she is sleeping, is condemned to death on suspicion. He begs leave to visit his father before he dies. When he is late in returning, the second brother offers to die in his place, but as he is about to be executed, the third brother steps forward and "confesses" that he is the murderer. At that moment the eldest brother rides in, just in time to embrace his fate. Which of the brothers, the listeners are asked, is the most noble?

As these examples show, dilemma tales function both as instruction and entertainment, and they help to establish social norms for the audience.

Dillard \'dil-ərd\, Annie, *original surname* Doak \'dōk\ (b. April 30, 1945, Pittsburgh, Pa., U.S.)   American writer best known for her meditative essays on the natural world.

Dillard attended Hollins College in Virginia. She was a scholar-in-residence at Western Washington University in Bellingham from 1975 to 1978 and on the faculty of Wesleyan University in Middletown, Conn., from 1979 to 1981.

Dillard's first published book was a collection of poetry, *Tickets for a Prayer Wheel* (1974). It was as an essayist, however, that she earned critical as well as popular acclaim. In her Pulitzer Prize-winning collection *Pilgrim at Tinker Creek* (1974), she distilled from keen observations of her own habitat the essential enigmas of religious mysticism. Critics hailed the work as an American original in the spirit of Henry David Thoreau's *Walden. Holy the Firm* (1977) and *Teaching a Stone to Talk* (1982) explored similar themes. *Living by Fiction* (1982), *Encounters with Chinese Writers* (1984), and *The Writing Life* (1989) present her views of literary craftsmanship and the writer's role in society. She published an autobiographical narrative, *An American Childhood*, in 1987. When her first novel, *The Living*, appeared in 1992, reviewers found in its depictions of the logging culture of the turn-of-the-century Pacific Northwest the same visionary realism that distinguished the author's nonfiction.

dime novel   A type of inexpensive, usually paperback, melodramatic novel of adventure popular in the United States roughly between 1860 and 1915; it often featured a western theme. One of the best-known authors of such works was E.Z.C. Judson, whose stories, some based on his own adventures, were written under the pseudonym of Ned Buntline. The dime novels were eventually replaced by pulp magazines. *Compare* PENNY DREADFUL.

dimeter \'dim-ə-tər\   In prosody, a line consisting of two metrical feet or of two dipodies.

Dimmesdale, Arthur \'är-thər-'dimz-dāl\   Fictional character, a tormented Boston minister in THE SCARLET LETTER by Nathaniel Hawthorne. Having fathered Hester Prynne's illegitimate child, the bachelor Dimmesdale vacillates between the hunger for cleansing confession and the Puritan zeal fueled by his secret sin.

Dindshenchas or **Dinnsheanchas** \din-'hen-ə-ḵəs\ ("Lore of Places")   Studies in Gaelic prose and verse of the etymology and history of place-names in Ireland—*e.g.*, of streams, raths (strongholds of ancient Irish chiefs), mounds, and rocks. They were preserved in variant forms in monastic manuscripts dating from as early as the 12th century. These place-lore stories contain much pre-Christian mythology, especially stories of gods and fairies. The most famous collection is the *Dindshenchas* ascribed to Amhairgin mac Amhalgaidh, a poet to King Diarmaid in the 6th century. It describes the naming of more than 200 locations and was an important source for Irish poets, who were expected to be familiar with the lore of each area.

Dinesen \'dē-nə-sən, *Angl also* 'din-ə-\, Isak, *pseudonym of* Karen Christence Dinesen, Baroness Blixen-Finecke (b. April 17, 1885, Rungsted, Den.—d. Sept. 7, 1962, Rungsted)   Danish writer whose finely crafted stories, set in the past and per-

vaded with an aura of supernaturalism, incorporate the themes of eros and dreams.

Educated privately and at the Academy of Fine Arts, Copenhagen, Dinesen married her cousin, Baron Bror Blixen-

Archive Photos

Finecke, in 1914 and went with him to Africa. There they owned and directed a coffee plantation in Kenya and became big-game hunters. After her divorce in 1921 she continued to operate the plantation for 10 years until mismanagement, drought, and the falling price of coffee forced her return to Denmark.

Her years in Kenya are recorded in a nonfiction book, OUT OF AFRICA (1937; *Den afrikanske farm*). These highly regarded memoirs of her years in Kenya reveal an almost mystical love of Africa and its people. In 1944 she produced her only novel, *Gengældelsens veje* (*The Angelic Avengers*), under the pseudonym Pierre Andrézel. It is a melodramatic tale of innocents who defeat their apparently benevolent but actually evil captor, but Danish readers saw in it a clever satire of Nazi-occupied Denmark.

She initially wrote first in English and then rewrote her books in Danish, but her later books usually appeared simultaneously in both languages. Dinesen's characteristic writings were in the form of tales—highly polished narratives in the Romantic tradition. Collections include SEVEN GOTHIC TALES (1934; *Syv fantastiske fortællinger*), WINTER'S TALES (1942; *Vintereventyr*), and *Last Tales* (1957; *Sidste fortællinger*). *Carnival: Entertainments and Posthumous Tales* (1977) includes uncollected or hitherto unpublished stories. Her other posthumously published works include *Daguerreotypes, and Other Essays* (1979) and *Letters from Africa, 1914–31* (1981).

dingdong \'diŋ-ˌdȯŋ, -ˌdäŋ\   A verse or poem having a singsong monotonous character, such as a jingle.

Dingelstedt \'diŋ-əl-ˌshtet\, Franz Ferdinand, Count (Freiherr) von (b. June 30, 1814, Halsdorf, Hesse-Kassel [Germany]—d. May 15, 1881, Vienna, Austria-Hungary)   German poet, playwright, and theatrical producer known for his biting political satires.

A member of the liberal Young Germany movement, Dingelstedt wrote political satires against the German princes, notably *Die Neuen Argonauten* (1839; "The New Argonauts"), and a collection of satirical poems, *Lieder eines Kosmopolitischen Nachtwächters* (1841; "Songs of a Cosmopolitan Nightwatchman"). Publication of the former book led to his dismissal from his job as a teacher in 1841. Between 1841 and 1843 he was a correspondent in Paris and London and underwent a political conversion that marked the beginning of his career as a state official. Dingelstedt was appointed manager of the court theaters at Munich and Weimar and, later, director of the opera and Hofburgtheater at Vienna. He was responsible for acclaimed new productions of the German classics and of William Shakespeare. He was also the founder of the German Shakespeare Society, and he translated many of Shakespeare's plays. Dingelstedt wrote novels—including *Die Amazone* (1869)—and an autobiographical sketch, *Münchener Bilderbogen* (1879; "Picture Sheet of Munich").

Ding Ling or **Ting Ling** \'diŋ-'liŋ\, *pseudonym of* Jiang Weizhi \'jäŋ-'wā-'jər\ (b. 1904, Changde, Hunan province, China—d. March 4, 1986, Beijing)   Chinese writer noted for her highly successful short stories centering on young, unconventional Chinese women.

Born into a declining gentry family, Ding Ling received her education in Hunan provincial schools. Thereafter she journeyed in 1921 to Shanghai and Nanjing. After a stint at Shanghai University, she went to Beijing, where in 1925 she fell in love with the leftist would-be poet Hu Yepin.

Cheng Ming/Encyclopedia of China

Influenced by Gustave Flaubert's *Madame Bovary* and other European novels, Ding Ling began writing partly autobiographical short stories in which she developed a new kind of Chinese heroine—daring, independent, and passionate, yet perplexed and emotionally unfulfilled in her search for the meaning of life. These chronicles of modern Chinese women were an immediate success. By 1930 Ding Ling had completed three collections of short stories and a novelette.

Meanwhile, Hu Yepin, making little progress in his literary career, had turned his attention to politics and had joined the League of Leftist Writers. He then joined the Chinese Communist Party, was arrested by Nationalist authorities, and was executed in 1931. Ding Ling herself joined the Communist Party that same year and edited journals of the League of Leftist Writers.

Ding Ling's conversion to Marxism resulted in the proletarian-oriented *Shui* (1931; "Flood"), acclaimed as a model of Socialist Realist fiction in China. She was abducted by agents of the Nationalist Party in 1933 and imprisoned until 1936, when, disguised as a soldier, she escaped and joined the Communists at Yenan. There she became friends with Mao Zedong. She was not completely uncritical of the Communist movement, however, expressing her dissatisfactions openly through her stories and in journal articles, for which she was censured by Mao.

Ding Ling continued her criticism of the party, especially in regard to women's rights. She was officially censured and expelled from the party as a rightist in 1957 and was imprisoned for five years during the Cultural Revolution. In 1975 she was freed, and her membership in the Communist Party was restored in 1979. Her later publications include several critical essays, short stories, and longer fictional prose, some of which was published in *I Myself Am a Woman* (1989).

Dinis \'dē-,nēsh\, Júlio, *pseudonym of* Joaquim Guilherme Gomes Coelho \'gō-mesh-'kwā-lyü\ (b. Nov. 14, 1839, Porto, Port.—d. Sept. 12, 1871, Porto) Portuguese poet, playwright, and novelist, the first great novelist of modern middle-class Portuguese society.

Dinis's first attacks of tuberculosis forced him to resign as deputy professor at the medical school of Porto. He had already published several tales of country life in the *Jornal do Porto*. Retiring to the coastal town of Ovar for his health, he wrote the novel for which he is best known, *As pupilas do Senhor Reitor* (1867; "The Pupils of the Dean"), depicting country life and scenery in a simple and appealing style. It was based on his own family situation (his mother being English) and described the influence of the English on Portuguese culture. Encouraged by its immediate success, he published *Uma família inglesa* (1868; "An English Family"), a novel describing English society in Porto.

Dinis' poems and plays were published posthumously, but he is best remembered for his novels.

Dinnsheanchas   *see* DINDSHENCHAS.

Diomedes \,dī-ə-'mē-dēz\ In Greek legend, commander of 80 Argive ships and one of the most respected leaders in the Trojan War. His famous exploits include the wounding of Aphrodite, the slaughter of Rhesus and his Thracians, and the seizure of the Trojan Palladium, the sacred image of the goddess Pallas Athena that protected Troy. After the war Diomedes returned home to find that his wife had been unfaithful (Aphrodite's punishment) and that his claim to the throne of Argos was disputed. Fleeing for his life, he sailed to Italy and founded Argyripa (later Arpi) in Apulia, eventually making peace with the Trojans. He was worshiped as a hero in Argos and Metapontum. According to Roman sources, his companions were turned into birds by Aphrodite, and, hostile to all but Greeks, they lived on the Isles of Diomedes off the Apulian coast.

Dion \'dī-,ăn\ Chrysostom \'kris-ə-stəm, kri-'săs-təm\, *also called* Dion Chrysostomos, Dio Chrysostomus, Dio Prusaeus, *or* Dio Cocceianus (b. *c.* AD 40, Prusa, Bithynia—d. *c.* 112) Greek rhetorician and philosopher who won fame in Rome and throughout the empire for his writings and speeches. The name Chrysostom means "golden-mouthed."

For political reasons Dion was banished in AD 82 from both Bithynia and Italy. He wandered for 14 years through the lands near the Black Sea, adopting the life of poverty advocated by the Cynics. With the death of the emperor Domitian, his exile ended and he revitalized his career.

A collection of 80 "orations" with fragments of others survives, but some are dialogues or moral essays and 2 are spurious. Four are speeches addressed to Trajan. In *Olympicus*, the sculptor Phidias explains the principles he followed in his famous statue of Zeus, one passage being supposed by some to have suggested the German dramatist Gotthold Lessing's *Laokoon*. In *On Aeschylus, Sophocles and Euripides*, Dion compares the treatment of the story of Philoctetes by each tragedian. Best known is the *Euboicus*, depicting country life on the island of Euboea, an important document for social and economic history.

A patriotic Greek who accepted Roman rule, Dion typified the revival of Greek self-confidence under the Roman Empire that marked the beginning of the new, or second, sophistic movement in the 2nd century AD.

Dione \dī-'ō-nē\ In Greek mythology, a consort and, in one remote region, cult partner of Zeus. Since the partner and wife of Zeus was normally the goddess Hera, it has been conjectured that Dione is an older figure than Hera. Dione was variously described. In the *Iliad* she is mentioned as the mother of the goddess Aphrodite by Zeus; in Hesiod's *Theogony*, however, she is simply identified as a daughter of Oceanus.

Dionysian \,dī-ə-'nizh-ən, -'nish-, -'nī-sē-\ Characteristic of the god Dionysus or the cult of worship of Dionysus; specifically, of a sensuous, frenzied, or orgiastic character. The philosopher Friedrich Nietzsche used the terms Dionysian and Apollonian to analyse and explain the character of Greek tragedy in his book *The Birth of Tragedy*. According to Nietzsche, Greek tragedy was the result of a fusion of Dionysian and Apollonian elements, with the Apollonian representing reason, restraint, and harmony. *See also* APOLLONIAN.

Dionysius or **Dionysios** \,dī-ə-'nish-ē-əs, -sē-əs, -shəs; -'nī-sē-əs; -'niz-ē-əs\ of Halicarnassus \,hal-i-,kär-'nas-əs\ (fl. *c.* 20 BC; b. Halicarnassus, Caria, Asia Minor) Greek historian and teacher of rhetoric whose history of Rome, from its origins to the First Punic War (264–241 BC), is, with Livy's, the most valuable source for early Roman history.

Dionysius migrated to Rome in 30 BC, and his history, which sought to justify the Romans to the Greeks, began to appear in 7 BC. Of its 20 books, only the first 9 and parts of 10 and 11 are extant. His literary and rhetorical theories are propounded in several extant treatises: *On Imitation* (containing assessments of individual authors), *Commentaries on the Ancient Orators*, and *On the Arrangement of Words*, the only surviving ancient study of the principles of word order and euphony.

Dionysus \ˌdī-ə-'nī-səs, -'nē-\, *also called* Bacchus \'bak-əs, 'bäk-\ In Greek and Roman mythology, a nature god of fruitfulness and vegetation, especially known as a god of wine and ecstasy.

According to the most popular tradition, Dionysus was the son of Zeus and Semele, a daughter of Cadmus (king of Thebes), but in origin a Phrygian earth goddess. Hera, Zeus's jealous wife, persuaded Semele to prove her lover's divinity by requesting him to appear in his real person. Zeus complied, but his power was too great for the mortal Semele, who was blasted with thunderbolts. Zeus, however, saved his son by sewing him up in his thigh, keeping him there until he reached maturity, so that he was twice born. Dionysus was then conveyed by the god Hermes to be brought up by the bacchantes (maenads, or Thyiads) of Nysa, a purely imaginary spot.

Because Dionysus apparently represented the sap, juice, or lifeblood element in nature, lavish festal orgies in his honor were widely instituted. These festivals, known as Dionysia (or Bacchanalia), quickly won converts among the women in the post-Mycenaean world, but the men were hostile to the events. *See also* BACCHANTE.

Diop \'jòp\, Birago Ismael (b. Dec. 11, 1906, Dakar, French West Africa [now in Senegal]—d. Nov. 25, 1989, Dakar) Senegalese poet and recorder of traditional folktales and legends of the Wolof people.

Diop received his education in Dakar and Saint-Louis, Senegal, and then studied veterinary medicine at the University of Toulouse (France) until 1933. This was followed by a series of tours as government veterinary surgeon in The Sudan, Côte d'Ivoire, Upper Volta (now Burkina Faso), and Mauritania. From 1961 to 1965 he served as newly independent Senegal's ambassador to Tunisia.

He is known for his small but beautifully composed output of lyric poetry. With his compatriot Léopold Sédar Senghor, Diop was active in the Negritude movement in the 1930s, which sought a return to African cultural values. Diop explored the mystique of African life in *Leurres et lueurs* ("Lures and Glimmerings"), a selection of his verse written between 1925 and 1960.

Diop received literary awards in 1964 for *Les Contes d'Amadou Koumba* (1947; *Tales of Amadou Koumba*) and *Les Nouveaux Contes d'Amadou Koumba* (1958), both reprinted in the 1960s, and for *Contes et lavanes* (1963; *Tales and Commentaries*). These books contained tales that were first told him by his family's griot (a storyteller whose role is to preserve the oral traditions of his tribe). Diop's skill in rendering the nuances of dialogue and gesture furthered the popularity of his books, selections from which were reprinted in a school-text edition in 1967. *Les Contes d'Awa* ("Tales of Awa") appeared in 1978. His autobiography, *La Plume raboutée* (*The Spliced Pen*), was also published in 1978.

Diop \'jòp\, David (b. July 9, 1927, Bordeaux, Fr.—d. 1960, Dakar, Senegal) One of the most talented of the younger French West African poets of the 1950s, whose tragic death in an airplane crash cut short a promising career.

Diop's works in *Coups de pilon* (1956; "Pounding"), his only surviving collection, are angry poems of protest against European cultural values. They enumerate the sufferings of Africans first under the slave trade and then under the domination of colonial rule and call for revolution to lead to a glorious future for Africa. He was among the more radical of the Negritude writers, rejecting the notion of any positive results from the colonial experience and asserting that political freedom precedes cultural and economic revival.

Although he grew up and lived most of his life in France, Diop rejected European culture and spent the last few years of his life in Africa, teaching school first in Senegal and later in Guinea. The Martinique poet Aimé Césaire was a dominant influence on his verse, which first appeared in the journal *Présence Africaine* and in Léopold Sédar Senghor's *Anthologie de la nouvelle poésie nègre et malgache.*

Dioscuri \ˌdī-ə-'skùr-ē, -'skyùr-; dī-'äs-kùr-ē, -kyùr-\, *also called* Castor and Pollux (in Rome) *or* Castor and Polydeuces (in Greece). In Greek and Roman mythology, twin deities who aided shipwrecked sailors and received sacrifices for favorable winds. They were the children of Leda and either Zeus or Tyndareus, Leda's husband. According to some versions, Castor was the son of Tyndareus and thus a mortal, while Pollux was the son of Zeus.

The twins were inseparable and became renowned for their athletic ability. A dispute between them, however, led to bloodshed; although the details are variously recorded, authorities agree that Castor was slain. After Pollux refused immortality because Castor had to remain in the netherworld, Zeus allowed them to remain together alternately in the heavens and the netherworld. Later he transformed them into the constellation Gemini.

Diphilus \'dif-i-ləs\ (b. Sinope [now Sinop, Tur.]; fl. late 4th century BC, Athens—d. Smyrna? [now İzmir, Tur.]) Greek poet of the nonpolitical and realistic Athenian school of New Comedy, the ancestor of the comedy of manners.

Diphilus lived and worked at Athens and was an elder contemporary of the dramatist Menander. His work, of which about 60 titles are known, survives in Greek fragments and in Latin adaptations by the two masters of classical Roman drama, Plautus (in *Casina* and *Rudens*) and Terence (in *Adelphi*). Diphilus excelled in scenes of action and spectacle, and his style is especially marked by its vivid imagery.

diplasic \dī-'plas-ik, -'plaz-\ [Greek *diplásios* twofold, double] *in classical prosody* **1.** Two to one in proportion, that is, having a thesis twice the length of the arsis. **2.** Containing the repetition of a metrical pattern.

diplomatic \'dip-lə-'mat-ik\ Exactly reproducing the original, as in a *diplomatic* edition of a text. The word *diplomatic* originally meant "pertaining to the original copies of official documents," a diploma being originally any official document. *Compare* PARADIPLOMATIC.

dipody \'dip-ə-dē\ [Greek *dipodía*, a derivative of *dípous* twofooted, from *di-* two + *pod-*, *poús* foot] In classical prosody, a pair of metrical feet that is taken as a single unit. Trochaic, iambic, and anapestic verse are all measured by dipodies. In them, a monometer consists of one dipody (or two feet), a dimeter of four feet, a trimeter of six feet, and a tetrameter of eight feet. When trochaic or iambic verse is measured by single feet it is called tripody (three feet), tetrapody (four feet), hexapody (six feet).

Di Prima \di-'prē-mə\, Diane (b. Aug. 6, 1934, New York, N.Y., U.S.) American poet, one of the few women of the Beat movement to attain prominence.

After attending Swarthmore College, Di Prima lived in New York City's Greenwich Village, leading the bohemian lifestyle that typified the Beat movement. Her first book of poetry, *This Kind of Bird Flies Backward*, was published in 1958. In 1961 Di Prima and LeRoi Jones (now Amiri Baraka) began a monthly poetry journal, *Floating Bear*, that featured their own poetry and that of other notable Beat writers such as Jack Kerouac and William Burroughs. Di Prima also founded two publishing houses that specialized in works by avant-garde poets—The Poets Press and Eidolon Editions. From 1974 she was an instructor at the Naropa Institute in Boulder, Colo.

Although Di Prima's career reflected the political and social upheaval of the United States during the decades of the 1960s and '70s, her writing was of a more personal nature; poems about her relationships, her children, and the experiences of everyday life figured prominently. Much of Di Prima's later writing reflected her interests in Eastern religions, alchemy, and female archetypes. Her later collections of poetry include *The New Handbook of Heaven* (1963), *Poems for Freddie* (1966; later published as *Freddie Poems*), *Earthsong: Poems 1957–59* (1968), *The Book of Hours* (1970), *Loba, Parts 1–8* (1978), and *Pieces of a Song* (1990). She also wrote a book of short stories published as *Dinners and Nightmares* (1961; rev. ed., 1974), an autobiographical book entitled *Memoirs of a Beatnik* (1969), and a number of plays, collected in *ZipCode* (1992).

dipsas \'dip-səs\ *plural* dipsades \-sə-ˌdēz\ [Greek *dipsás*, a derivative of *dípsa* thirst] A serpent with a bite said to produce intense thirst. The snake was the subject of a story told by several Greek authors, including Sophocles. According to the legend, Zeus was grateful to those who revealed to him the identity of the god who had stolen fire. He rewarded the informants by giving them the antidote to old age, which they packed onto the back of an ass that was then allowed to depart alone. The ass became very thirsty and stopped at a spring guarded by the snake. After first refusing him water, the snake then offered to trade it for the contents of the ass's load. The snake, after receiving the contents, shed his skin, and the ass was relieved of his thirst.

dirge \'dərj\ [Middle English *dirige, derge*, from Latin *dirige* (singular imperative of *dirigere* to direct), the first word of an antiphon in the Office of the Dead adapted from Psalm 5:9 (Vulgate)] 1. A song or hymn of grief or lamentation; especially, one intended to accompany funeral or memorial rites. 2. A piece of writing resembling a dirge in being expressive of deep and solemn grief or sense of loss; especially, a poem of this kind. *Compare* ELEGY.

Discordia *see* ERIS.

discourse \'dis-ˌkȯrs\ Formal and orderly and usually extended expression of thought on a subject. Also, a linguistic unit (such as a conversation or story) larger than a sentence.

diseme \'dī-ˌsēm\ [Greek *dísēmos* having two beats or morae, from *di-* two + *sêma* sign] In classical prosody, a long syllable that is regarded as two short ones. This may be scanned ‿‿ in resolution, when a normally long syllable becomes two shorts, or ‿‿ in contraction, when two normally short syllables become one long.

dispositio \ˌdis-pə-'zish-ē-ˌō, -'zit-\ [Latin, literally, arrangement] The rhetorical and logical arrangement of the matter or the discrete elements of a discourse, especially in classical and Renaissance rhetorical systems.

disputatio \ˌdis-pü-'tä-tē-ō\ *plural* disputationes \-ˌtä-tē-'ō-ˌnās\ [Latin, discussion, dispute] Disputation, especially in medieval or Renaissance rhetorical principle or practice.

disquisition \ˌdis-kwə-'zish-ən\ [Latin *disquisitio* inquiry] A formal or systematic inquiry into or discussion of a subject; specifically, an elaborate analytical or explanatory essay or discussion.

Disraeli \diz-'rā-lē, dis-\, Benjamin, Earl of Beaconsfield, Viscount Hughenden of Hughenden \'hyü-ən-dən\ (b. Dec. 21, 1804, London, Eng.—d. April 19, 1881, London) British statesman and novelist who was prime minister of England in 1868 and again in 1874–80.

Of Italian-Jewish descent, Disraeli was baptized a Christian, a decision by his father that later enabled him to enter Parliament. At the age of 17 he worked for a firm of solicitors, but speculation in a dubious moneymaking scheme put him deeply in debt. His reputation suffered further when he was unmasked as the author of the anonymously published novel *Vivian Grey* (1826–27), which fictionalized another of his financial imbroglios. This novel, with its indiscretions, set a pattern, intertwining Disraeli's fiction with his personal and political fortunes. For the next four years, Disraeli accomplished little, but he did produce another extravagant novel, *The Young Duke*, in 1831. In 1830 he undertook 16 months of travel in the Mediterranean countries and the Middle East.

Back in England, he cut a striking if not always popular figure, and his novel of that period, *Contarini Fleming* (1832), is of considerable autobiographical interest. In the early 1830s he attempted several times to obtain a seat in Parliament, but his generally dubious reputation kept him out of office until 1837. He soon proved himself a skillful speaker and a master of Parliamentary politics. His extravagant behavior added to his notoriety, as did his open affair with a married woman (the prototype of the heroine in his novel *Henrietta Temple* [1837]).

When Conservative leader Sir Robert Peel shut him out of his Cabinet, Disraeli responded with CONINGSBY (1844), in which the pragmatic, humdrum, middle-class Conservatives are contrasted with Disraeli's supporters, a group of aristocratic, nostalgic, and romantic young Tories, nicknamed Young England. The novel was the first of a trilogy that included *Sybil* (1845) and *Tancred* (1847). Disraeli took over the leadership of the Conservative cause with Peel's downfall and, in 1868, became prime minister. He was opposed by the Liberals' William E. Gladstone, who held office between Disraeli's two terms. In 1870 Disraeli published the three-volume novel *Lothair*, a political comedy that was criticized as being undignified.

In 1874, at the age of 70, Disraeli began his second administration. With his health failing, he accepted a peerage, taking the title Earl of Beaconsfield, and he moved to the less onerous position of leader of the House of Lords. Thereafter his fortunes waned, and the Conservatives were heavily defeated in the general election of 1880. He kept his party leadership and finished the three-volume *Endymion* (1880), a mellow, nostalgic political novel recalling his early career.

dissociation of sensibility Phrase used by T.S. Eliot in the essay "The Metaphysical Poets" (1921) to explain the change that occurred in English poetry after the heyday of the Metaphysical poets. According to Eliot, the dissociation of sensibility was a result of the natural development of poetry after the Metaphysical poets, who had felt "their thought as immediately as the odour of a rose"; this phenomenon—the "direct sensuous apprehension of thought," or the fusion of thought and feeling—which Eliot called a mechanism of sensibility, was lost by later poets. Eliot gave evidence of the dissociation of sensibility in the more elevated language and cruder emotions of later poets.

distancing effect *see* ALIENATION EFFECT.

Distant Relations Experimental novel by Carlos FUENTES, published in 1980 as *Una familia lejana*, exploring the idea of alternate and shifting realities.

The main portion of the novel is told to the narrator one afternoon in Paris by a highly cultured French aristocrat, the Comte de Branly. Branly explains that, while visiting Toltec ruins in Mexico, he had befriended the archaeologist Hugo Heredia and his son Víctor. Months later, when Branly had returned to Paris, he met a Frenchman also named Victor Heredia. The second Victor appeared to be a phantom; the identity of his son André fused with that of the son of Hugo Heredia. At the novel's close, the narrator is revealed to be the double of Carlos Fuentes, living out an alternate life.

distich \'dis-tik\ [Greek *dístichon,* from neuter of *dístichos* having two rows, of two verses, from *di-* two + *stíchos* row, line, verse]   A strophic unit of two lines.

disyllabic \ˌdī-sə-'lab-ik, ˌdis-ə-\   Consisting of or having two syllables.

dit \'dē\ *plural* dits \'dē, 'dēz\ [Old French, word, speech, dit, from past participle of *dire* to say]   A short, usually didactic, sometimes satirical poem in medieval French literature often dealing with simple subjects.

dithyramb \'dith-i-ˌram, -ˌramb\ [Greek *dithýrambos*]   A choric poem, chant, or hymn of ancient Greece sung by revelers at the festival in honor of the god Dionysus.

The form originated about the 7th century BC in the songs of banqueters under the leadership of a man who, according to Archilochus, was "wit-stricken by the thunderbolt of wine." It was contrasted with the more sober paean, sung in honor of Apollo. The dithyramb began to achieve literary distinction about 600 BC, when the poet Arion composed works of this type, gave them names, and formally presented them at the Great Dionysia competitions at Corinth.

By the end of the 6th century BC, the dithyramb was a fully recognized literary genre. Its most famous exponent was Lasus of Hermione (b. *c.* 548), who is said to have been one of Pindar's teachers. The great age of the dithyramb was also the great age of Greek choral lyric poetry in general; Simonides of Ceos, Pindar, and Bacchylides all composed them. Bacchylides' Ode 18 is unusual in that it contains a dialogue between a chorus and a soloist. This attempt to increase the dramatic interest of the narrative may explain why the classical dithyramb gave way to the more vivid methods of tragedy.

From about 450 BC onward, dithyrambic poets employed ever-more-startling devices of language and music, until for ancient literary critics "dithyrambic" acquired the connotations of "turgid" and "bombastic." True dithyrambs are rare in modern poetry, although John Dryden's "Alexander's Feast" (1697) may be said to bear a coincidental resemblance to the form.

Dithyramb may also refer to any poem in an inspired wild irregular strain, or to a statement or piece of writing in an exalted impassioned style usually in praise of a particular subject.

divan or **diwan** \di-'van, -'vän; dī-'van, 'dī-ˌvan\ [Turkish, from Persian *dīwān* council, account book, collection of poems]   A collection of poems especially in Persian or Arabic; specifically, a series of poems by one author, such as the *Dīwān* of Moḥammad Shams od-Dīn Ḥāfez.

Diver, Dick and Nicole \dik-'dī-vər . . . ni-'kōl\   Fictional characters, an ill-fated American couple in Europe in TENDER IS THE NIGHT by F. Scott Fitzgerald.

Dick is a charming young psychiatrist who marries a schizophrenic patient, the wealthy Nicole Warren. Dick was based both on Fitzgerald himself and on his friend Gerald Murphy, while Nicole was modeled on Fitzgerald's wife, Zelda, who also suffered nervous breakdowns.

Divine Comedy, The   Long narrative poem originally titled *Commedia* (about 1555 printed as *La divina commedia*) written about 1310–14 by DANTE. The work is divided into three major sections—*Inferno, Purgatorio,* and *Paradiso*—which trace the journey of a man from darkness and error to the rev-

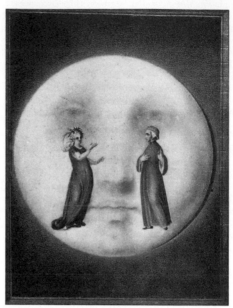

Detail of a Ferrarese illuminated manuscript by Franco de' Russi and the Giraldis, *c.* 1480
Vatican Library

elation of the divine light, culminating in the beatific vision of God. It is usually held to be one of the world's greatest works of literature.

The plot of *The Divine Comedy* is simple: a man is miraculously enabled to visit the souls in Hell, Purgatory, and Paradise. He has two guides: Virgil, who leads him through the *Inferno* and *Purgatorio,* and Beatrice, who introduces him to *Paradiso.* Through these fictional encounters taking place from Good Friday evening in 1300 through Easter Sunday and slightly beyond, Dante the character learns of the exile that is awaiting him (an actual exile that had already occurred at the time of writing). This device allowed Dante not only to create a story out of his exile but also to explain how he came to cope with personal calamity and to offer suggestions for the resolution of Italy's troubles as well. Thus, Dante's story is historically specific as well as paradigmatic; his exile serves as a microcosm of the problems of a country, and it also becomes representative of the Fall of Man.

The basic structural component of *The Divine Comedy* is the canto. The poem consists of 100 cantos, which are grouped into the three major sections, or canticles. Technically there are 33 cantos in each canticle and one additional canto, contained in the *Inferno,* that serves as an introduction to the entire poem. For the most part the cantos range from 136 to 151 lines. The poem's rhyme scheme is the terza rima (*aba, bcb, cdc,* etc.) Thus, the divine number three is present in every part of the work.

Dante adopts the classical convention of a visit to the land of the dead, but he adapts it to a Christian worldview by beginning his journey there. The *Inferno* represents a false start during which Dante, the character, must be disabused of harmful values that somehow prevent him from rising above his fallen world. Despite the regressive nature of the *Inferno,* Dante's meetings with the damned are among the most memorable moments of the poem: the Neutrals, the virtuous pagans,

Francesca da Rimini, Filipo Argenti, Farinata degli Uberti, Piero delle Vigne, Brunetto Latini, the simoniacal popes, Ulysses, and Ugolino impose themselves upon the reader's imagination with tremendous force. Nonetheless, the journey through the *Inferno* primarily signifies a process of separation and thus is only the initial step in a fuller development.

In the *Purgatorio* the protagonist's spiritual rehabilitation commences. There Dante subdues his own personality so that he will be able to ascend. He comes to accept the essential Christian image of life as a pilgrimage, and he joins the other penitents on the road of life. At the summit of Purgatory, where repentant sinners are purged of their sins, Virgil departs, having led Dante as far as human knowledge is able—to the threshold of Paradise. Beatrice, who embodies the knowledge of divine mysteries bestowed by Grace, continues Dante's tour.

In the *Paradiso* true heroic fulfillment is achieved. Dante's poem gives expression to those figures from the past who seem to defy death and who inspire in their followers a feeling of exaltation and a desire for identification. The *Paradiso* is consequently a poem of fulfillment and of completion.

Dixon \'dik-sən\, Thomas (b. Jan. 11, 1864, Shelby, N.C., U.S.—d. April 3, 1946, Raleigh, N.C.)   American novelist, dramatist, and legislator who vigorously propagated ideas of white supremacy. He is chiefly remembered for his novel *The Clansman* (1905), which presented a sympathetic picture of the Ku Klux Klan. Dixon's friend, D.W. Griffith, used the novel as the basis for the epic film *The Birth of a Nation* (1915).

Dixon was admitted to the bar in 1886. He spent a year as a member of the North Carolina legislature but resigned to become a Baptist minister, serving in Raleigh, N.C., Boston, and New York City (1889–99). His first novel was *The Leopard's Spots* (1902); with *The Clansman* and *The Traitor* (1907), it forms a trilogy about the South during Reconstruction. He wrote other novels and some plays, and as late as 1939 he wrote yet another fictional account of black-white relations in the United States, *The Flaming Sword*. He also wrote nonfiction.

dizain \dē-'zaⁿ, *Angl* di-'zān\ or **dizaine** \dē-'zan\ [French *dizain,* from Middle French, a derivative of *dix* ten]   A French poem or stanza of 10 octosyllabic or decasyllabic lines.

Djebar \jə-'bâr\, Assia, *original name* Fatima-Zohra Imalayan \ē-mà-là-'yán\ (b. Aug. 4, 1936, Cherchell, Alg.)   One of the most talented and prolific of contemporary Algerian women writers.

Djebar's career as a novelist began in 1957 with the publication of her first novel, *La Soif* (*The Mischief*). It was followed by *Les Impatients* (1958; "The Impatient Ones"), which similarly dealt with the colonial Algerian bourgeois milieu.

Two later novels, *Les Enfants du nouveau monde* (1962; "The Children of the New World") and the sequel *Les Alouettes naïves* (1967; "The Naive Larks"), chronicle the growth of Algerian women's collective consciousness and describe her countrywomen's contributions to the war for independence from France that took place from 1954 to 1962. Djebar collaborated with her husband, Walid Garn, on the play *Rouge l'aube* ("Red is the Dawn"), published in the review *Promesses* in 1969. A collection of her poems, *Poèmes pour l'Algérie heureuse* ("Poems for a Happy Algeria"), was also published that year.

Djebar spent most of the war years outside Algeria, but afterward she taught history at the University of Algiers, was made department head of the French section at the university, and became a filmmaker for the national television station. In 1978 she continued her analysis of Algerian women in her film *Nouba des femmes du mont Chenoua,* the story of an Algerian woman engineer returned to Algeria after a long Western exile. *Femmes d'Alger dans leur appartement* (1980; *Women of*

Algiers in Their Apartment, including additional stories, essays, and bibliography), a collection of novellas, was another exploration of the feminine world. Later works include *L'Amour, la fantasia* (1985; *Fantasia: An Algerian Cavalcade*), *Ombre Sultane* (1987; *A Sister to Scheherazade*), and *Loin de Médine: Filles d'Ismäel* (1991; "Far from Medina: Daughters of Ishmael").

Dobell \dō-'bel\, Sydney Thompson, *pseudonym* Sydney Yendys \'yen-dis\ (b. April 5, 1824, Cranbrook, Kent, Eng.—d. Aug. 22, 1874, Nailsworth, Gloucestershire)   English writer of erratic poetry characterized by formlessness, chaotic imagery, and exaggerations of passion—one of a group of poets of what Charles Kingsley called the Spasmodic school. Dobell's long dramatic poem *The Roman* (1850) was hailed by critics and secured for its author the acquaintance of many notable figures in liberal politics and in literature. *The Roman* celebrated the revolutionary year of 1848 (a year that saw a series of republican revolts against European monarchies). Another long poem, *Balder* (intended as part of a trilogy), was not appreciated and was burlesqued in *Firmiliam: . . . a Spasmodic Tragedy* by W.E. Aytoun. The vague aesthetic of the Spasmodic school was expressed by Dobell in a number of essays collected in 1876 as *Thoughts on Art, Philosophy and Religion.* Dobell also wrote lyrics and, with Alexander Smith, a sonnet sequence on the Crimean War.

Döblin \'dœ-,blēn, dœ-'blēn\, Alfred (b. Aug. 10, 1878, Stettin, Ger.—d. June 26, 1957, Emmendingen, near Freiburg im Breisgau, W.Ger.)   German novelist and essayist, the most talented narrative writer of the German Expressionist movement.

Döblin studied medicine at the universities of Berlin and Freiburg and became a doctor, practicing psychiatry in the workers' district of the Alexanderplatz in Berlin. His Jewish ancestry and socialist views obliged him to leave Germany for France in 1933 after the Nazi takeover, and in 1940 he escaped to the United States, where he converted to Roman Catholicism in 1941. He resettled in Paris in the early 1950s.

Although Döblin's technique and style vary, the urge to expose the hollowness of a civilization heading toward its own destruction and a quasi-religious urge to provide a means of salvation for suffering humanity were two of his constant preoccupations. His first successful novel, *Die drei Sprünge des Wang-lun* (1915; *The Three Leaps of Wang-lun*), is set in China and describes a rebellion that is crushed by the tyrannical power of the state. *Wallenstein* (1920) is a historical novel, and *Berge, Meere und Giganten* (1924; "Mountains, Seas, and Giants"; republished as *Giganten* in 1932) is a merciless antiutopian satire.

In his best-known and most Expressionistic novel, BERLIN ALEXANDERPLATZ (1929), he powerfully dramatizes the human condition in a disintegrating social order. Döblin's subsequent books include *Babylonische Wandrung* (1934; "Babylonian Wandering"), sometimes described as a late masterwork of German Surrealism; *Pardon wird nicht gegeben* (1935; *Men Without Mercy*); and two unsuccessful trilogies of historical novels. He also wrote essays on political and literary topics, and his *Reise in Polen* (1926; *Journey to Poland*) is a stimulating account of a trip to Poland. Döblin recounted his flight from France in 1940 and his observations of postwar Germany in the book *Schicksalsreise* (1949; *Destiny's Journey*).

Dobrolyubov \,də-,brə-'lyū-bəf\, Nikolay Aleksandrovich (b. Jan. 24 [Feb. 5, New Style], 1836, Nizhny Novgorod, Russia—d. Nov. 17 [Nov. 29], 1861, St. Petersburg)   Radical Russian utilitarian critic who rejected traditional and Romantic literature.

Dobrolyubov, the son of a priest, was educated at a seminary and a pedagogical institute. Early in his life he rejected traditionalism and found his ideal in progress as represented by Western science. In 1856 Dobrolyubov began contributing to *Sovremennik* ("The Contemporary"), an influential liberal periodical, and from 1857 until his death he was chief critic for the journal. He was probably the most influential critic after Vissarion Belinsky among the radical intelligentsia. He is perhaps best known for his essay "What is Oblomovism" (1859–60). The essay deals with the phenomenon represented by the character Oblomov in Ivan Goncharov's novel of that name. It established the term Oblomovism as a name for the superfluous man of Russian life and literature.

Dobson \'däb-sən\, Austin, *in full* Henry Austin Dobson (b. Jan. 18, 1840, Plymouth, Devonshire, Eng.—d. Sept. 2, 1921, London)   English poet, critic, and biographer whose love and knowledge of the 18th century lent a graceful elegance to his poetry and inspired his critical studies.

In 1856 Dobson entered the Board of Trade, where he remained until his retirement in 1901. His first collection of poems, *Vignettes in Rhyme* (1873), was followed by *Proverbs in Porcelain* (1877). In these and in *At the Sign of the Lyre* (1885), he showed the polish, wit, and restrained pathos that made his verses popular. The ease with which he handled the artificial French forms—the ballade, the triolet, and the rondeau—helped to revive their use in English.

After 1885 Dobson was chiefly occupied with biographical and critical works. His books on Henry Fielding, Thomas Bewick, Sir Richard Steele, Oliver Goldsmith, Horace Walpole, William Hogarth, Samuel Richardson, and Fanny Burney reveal careful research into, and sympathy with, 18th-century life. Three series of *Eighteenth Century Vignettes* (1892–96) and *A Paladin of Philanthropy* (1899 and 1901) typify his delicate prose style.

Dobyns \'däb-inz\, Stephen (b. Feb. 19, 1941, Orange, N.J., U.S.)   American poet and novelist whose works are characterized by a cool realism laced with pungent wit.

Dobyns attended Shimer College in Mount Carroll, Ill., and graduated from Wayne State University and the University of Iowa. He taught English for a year before becoming a reporter for the *Detroit News* in 1969. From 1973, while writing fiction and poetry, he served as visiting lecturer and teacher at several American colleges and universities.

Dobyns' first collection of poetry, *Concurring Beasts*, appeared in 1971. The following year he published the novel *A Man of Little Evils*, and from that point on he alternated between poetry and crime fiction, publishing roughly a book a year. Subsequent poetry volumes included *Griffon* (1976), *Heat Death* (1980), *Black Dog, Red Dog* (1984), *Cemetery Nights* (1987), and *Velocities: New and Selected Poems, 1966–1992* (1994). Among his other novels are *Saratoga Longshot* (1976), *Dancer with One Leg* (1983), *Cold Dog Soup* (1985), *The Two Deaths of Señora Puccini* (1988), *After Shocks—Near Escapes* (1991), and *The Wrestler's Cruel Study* (1993).

dochmiac \'däk-mē-,ak\ or **dochmius** \-mē-əs\ *plural* dochmii \-mē-ī\ [Greek *dóchmios*, from *dochmós, dóchmios* slanted, oblique]   In classical prosody, a foot of five syllables typically having the first and fourth short and the rest long (∪ − − ∪ −). Dochmiac verse is based on this pattern and occurs mainly in Greek drama.

Doctor Faustus \'faùs-təs, 'fōs-\ (*in full* The Tragicall History of D. Faustus)   Tragedy in five acts by Christopher MARLOWE, published in 1604 but first performed a decade or so earlier. Marlowe's play followed by only a few years the first translation into English of the medieval legend on which it is based. In *Doctor Faustus* Marlowe retells the story of Faust, the doctor-turned-necromancer, who makes a pact with the

devil in order to obtain knowledge and power. Both Doctor Faustus and Mephistopheles, who is the devil's intermediary in the play, are subtly and powerfully portrayed. Marlowe examines Faustus' grandiose intellectual ambitions, revealing them as futile, self-destructive, and absurd. *See also* FAUST; MEPHISTOPHELES.

Doctor Faustus \'faùs-təs, 'fōs-\   Novel by Thomas MANN, published in German as *Doktor Faustus* in 1947.

The novel tells the life story of a German composer, Adrian Leverkühn (1885–1940), who lives the last 10 years of his life in extreme alienation. A solitary, estranged figure, he "speaks" the experience of his times in his music, and the story of Leverkühn's compositions is that of German culture in the two decades before 1930—the collapse of traditional humanism and the victory of the mixture of sophisticated nihilism and barbaric primitivism that undermine it. These developments are expressed in the new musical forms and themes of Leverkühn's compositions up to the final work, a setting of the lament of Doctor Faustus (in the 16th-century version of the Faust legend), who, in hope, had made a pact with the devil, but in the end is reduced to hopelessness. Mann relates Leverkühn's personal tragedy (and that of Faust) to the tragedy of Germany's arrogance, isolation, and destruction in World War II.

Doctorow \'däk-tə-,rō\, E.L., *in full* Edgar Laurence (b. Jan. 6, 1931, New York, N.Y., U.S.)   American novelist known for his skillful manipulation of traditional genres.

Doctorow graduated from Kenyon College and later attended Columbia University. In 1959 he joined the editorial staff of New American Library, leaving that post five years later to become editor in chief at Dial Press. He subsequently taught at several colleges and universities, including Sarah Lawrence College and New York University.

Doctorow's first novel, *Welcome to Hard Times* (1960), was a philosophical turn on the western genre. In his next book, *Big As Life* (1966), he used science fiction to explore the human response to crisis. *The Book of Daniel* (1971) is a fictionalized treatment of the execution of Julius and Ethel Rosenberg for espionage in 1953. In *Ragtime* (1975; film, 1981), his most commercially successful work, actual figures of early 20th-century America share the spotlight with emblematic Anglo, Jewish, and African-American characters. The later novels *Loon Lake* (1980), *World's Fair* (1985), and *Billy Bathgate* (1989; film, 1991) examine the milieu of the Great Depression and its aftermath, and *The Waterworks* (1994) concerns life in 19th-century New York. Doctorow also wrote a play and published *Lives of the Poets* (1984), a collection of short fiction.

Doctor's Dilemma, The   Drama in four acts and an epilogue by George Bernard SHAW, performed in 1906 and published in 1911. The play satirizes the medical profession and comments wryly on the general public's inability to distinguish between an artist's behavior and achievement.

A question of medical ethics is central to *The Doctor's Dilemma*: Dr. Colenso Ridgeon must choose between saving Louis Dubedat, a talented and charming artist who has borrowed money with no intention of repayment and has deceived his devoted wife Jennifer, and helping a poverty-stricken doctor who treats indigent patients. The dilemma is further complicated when the doctor falls in love with Jennifer.

Doctor Thorne \'thȯrn\   Novel by Anthony TROLLOPE, published in three volumes in 1858. The book was the third in the series of BARSETSHIRE NOVELS, in which Trollope explored the fictional English county of Barset.

Doctor Zhivago \zhi-'vä-gō, *Russian* zhȧ-'vä-gə\   Novel by Boris PASTERNAK, published in Italy in 1957. This epic tale about the effects of the Russian Revolution and its aftermath on a bourgeois family was not published in the Soviet Union until 1987. One of the results of its publication in the West was Pasternak's complete rejection by Soviet authorities; when he was awarded the Nobel Prize for Literature in 1958 he was compelled to decline it. The book quickly became an international best-seller.

Dr. Yury Zhivago, Pasternak's alter ego, is a poet, philosopher, and physician whose life is disrupted by the war and by his love for Lara, the wife of a revolutionary. His artistic nature makes him vulnerable to the brutality and harshness of the Bolsheviks; wandering throughout Russia, he is unable to take control of his fate, and dies in utter poverty. The poems he leaves behind constitute some of the most beautiful writing in the novel.

documentary novel \,däk-yŭ-'men-tə-rē\ Fiction that features a large amount of documentary material such as newspaper stories, trial transcripts, and legal reports. Examples include the works of Theodore Dreiser.

documentary theater *see* THEATER OF FACT.

dodecasyllable \,dō-,dek-ə-'sil-ə-bəl\ [Greek *dōdeka* twelve] In poetry, a line of 12 syllables.

Doderer \'dō-dər-ər\, Heimito von (b. Sept. 6, 1896, Weidlingau, near Vienna, Austria-Hungary—d. Dec. 23, 1966, Vienna) Austrian novelist who achieved international fame with his novel *Die Dämonen* (1956; *The Demons*), in which he explores the society and mood of Vienna in 1926–27.

Doderer served as an officer in the Imperial Austrian Dragoons in World War I and was captured by the Russians. He spent several years in Siberia working as a lumberjack before his repatriation in 1920. He received a doctorate in history from the University of Vienna in 1925. An involved psychological thriller, *Ein Mord, den jeder begeht* (1938; *Every Man a Murderer*), and several other novels that followed attracted little attention. In the 1930s Doderer was briefly a member of the then-outlawed National Socialist Party in Austria, which he described in a book of reminiscences, *Tangenten* (1964; "Tangents"). In World War II he was a Luftwaffe captain. *Die Strudlhofstiege* (1951; "The Strudlhof Stairs"), which covered the Vienna of 1910–11 and 1923–25, sets the stage for *Die Dämonen*, which was a success and established Doderer's reputation. *Die Wasserfälle von Slunj* (1963; *The Waterfalls of Slunj*) was the first novel in an intended tetralogy spanning life in Vienna from 1880 to 1960 and collectively entitled *Roman Nr. 7* ("Novel No. 7"). The second volume, *Der Grenzwald* ("The Frontier Forest"), unfinished, appeared posthumously in 1967.

Dodge \'däj\, Mary Mapes \'māps\, *original name* Mary Elizabeth Mapes (b. Jan. 26, 1831, New York, N.Y., U.S.—d. Aug. 21, 1905, Onteora Park, N.Y.) American author of children's books and first editor of *St. Nicholas* magazine.

At the age of 20 Mary Mapes married William Dodge, a lawyer, and they had two sons. To maintain her independence after she was suddenly widowed seven years later, she started writing children's stories. Her first collection, *Irvington Stories* (1864), centered on the American colonial family. The following year Dodge's beloved classic, HANS BRINKER, appeared.

In 1873, in the midst of an economic depression, Dodge was asked to become editor of a new publishing venture, the children's magazine *St. Nicholas*. Its subsequent success stemmed from Dodge's high literary and moral standards. Dodge's editorial excellence enabled *St. Nicholas* to attract such well-known contemporary writers as Mark Twain, Bret Harte, Lucretia Peabody Hale, Louisa May Alcott, Robert Louis Stevenson, and Rudyard Kipling.

Dodgson, Charles Lutwidge.   Real name of Lewis CARROLL.

Dodona \dō-'dō-nə\ Ancient sanctuary of Zeus in Epirus (Greece). Dodona is first mentioned in the *Iliad*, where its priests are called the Selloi (or Helloi) and are described as "of unwashen feet, sleeping on the ground." The description suggests worshipers or servants of an earth goddess or of some chthonian (underworld) power with whom they kept in continual contact, day and night. Homer was also the first to mention (in the *Odyssey*) the oracle at Dodona. A tree (or trees) was reputed to give oracles, presumably through the rustling of its leaves and other sounds it emitted. Herodotus, but no earlier writer, mentions priestesses, whom he describes as the givers of the oracles, doubtless under some kind of inspiration from the god.

A further peculiarity of Dodona was the "bronze," a large gong set vibrating at every breeze by a scourge held in the hand of a figure standing over it; the persistent ringing passed into a Greek proverbial phrase—*Khalkos Dodones* ("Brass of Dodona")—for a continuous talker who has nothing to say.

dodrans \'dō-,dranz\ [Latin, three quarters] In classical prosody, a unit of six syllables of aeolic meter. The nucleus of a dodrans is a choriamb, which is either preceded or followed by an iamb or a trochee. Thus dodrans is scanned as ⌣ ⌣ – ⌣ ⌣ – or – ⌣ ⌣ – ⌣ ⌣ .

Dodsley \'dädz-lē\, Robert (b. 1703, near Mansfield, Nottinghamshire, Eng.—d. Sept. 23, 1764, Durham, Durham) British author, London bookseller, publisher, playwright, and editor who was influential in mid-18th-century literary England. He is associated with the publication of works by Samuel Johnson, Alexander Pope, Thomas Gray, and Oliver Goldsmith.

While serving as a footman, Dodsley published the poem *Servitude* (1729), which was later reissued as *The Muse in Livery; or, The Footman's Miscellany* (1732). Financed by his friends, who included Alexander Pope, he established himself as a publisher in 1735, publishing Johnson's poem *London* (1738) and suggesting and backing Johnson's *Dictionary of the English Language*.

Dodsley founded several literary periodicals, including *The Annual Register* (1758), edited by the political philosopher Edmund Burke. Dodsley himself edited two major collections: *A Select Collection of Old English Plays* (1744) and *A Collection of Poems, By Several Hands* (1748). In 1758 his tragedy *Cleone* began a long run at London's Covent Garden.

Dodson \'däd-sən\, Owen (Vincent) (b. Nov. 28, 1914, Brooklyn, N.Y., U.S.—d. June 21, 1983, New York, N.Y.) African-American poet, teacher, director, and playwright, and a leading figure in black theater.

The son of a journalist, Dodson began writing poetry and directing plays while attending Bates College and Yale University. As an enlistee in the U.S. Navy during World War II he wrote naval history plays for black seamen; the verse chorale *The Ballad of Dorie Miller* (1943), about an African-American Navy hero; and the poem "Black Mother Praying in the Summer of 1943," a plea for racial integration. Dodson's black history pageant *New World A-Coming* was performed at New York's Madison Square Garden in 1944. His first poetry collection, *Powerful Long Ladder*, appeared in 1946 and was widely praised. The next year he began teaching at Howard University, where he remained for 23 years. Dodson wrote the novels *Boy at the Window* (1951) and *Come Home Early, Child* (1977), and more than 35 plays and opera librettos; his verse dramas *Divine Comedy* (produced 1938) and *Bayou Legend* (produced 1948) are especially notable. Dodson himself considered *The Confession Stone* (1970), a song cycle written in the voice of Mary about the life of Jesus, which is often performed as an Easter play, to be his masterpiece.

Dodsworth \\'dädz-,wərth\\ Novel by Sinclair LEWIS, published in 1929. The book's protagonist, Sam Dodsworth, is an American automobile manufacturer who sells his company and takes an extended European vacation with his wife, Fran. *Dodsworth* recounts their reactions to Europeans and European values, their various relationships with others, their estrangement, and their brief reconciliation.

Dogberry \\'dȯg-,ber-ē, 'däg-, -bə-rē\\ Fictional character, an ill-spoken, comic figure who is the constable in William Shakespeare's MUCH ADO ABOUT NOTHING.

doggerel or **doggrel** \\'dȯg-ə-rəl, 'dȯg-rəl, 'däg-\\ [Middle English (*rym*) *dogerel,* perhaps a derivative of *dogge* dog] Verse that is loosely constructed and often metrically irregular. (The term is sometimes used as an epithet for trivial or bad poetry.)

Doggerel appears in most literatures and societies as a useful form for comedy and satire. It is characteristic of the rhymes of children's games from ancient times to the present and of most nursery rhymes.

One of the earliest uses of the word is found in the 14th century in the works of Geoffrey Chaucer, who applied the term "rym doggerel" to his "Tale of Sir Thopas," a burlesque of the long-winded medieval romance.

John Skelton, caught in the transition between Chaucer's medieval language and the beginning of the English Renaissance, wrote verse long considered to be doggerel. He defended himself in *Colin Clout*:

> For though my rhyme be ragged,
> Tattered and jagged,
> Rudely rain-beaten,
> Rusty and moth-eaten,
> If ye take well therewith,
> It hath in it some pith.

Doggerel has been employed in the comic verse of such poets as Samuel Butler, Jonathan Swift, and Ogden Nash, and it is commonly heard in limericks and nonsense verse, popular songs, and commercial jingles.

In German, doggerel is called *Knüttelvers* (literally "cudgel verse"). It was popular during the Renaissance and was later used for comic effect by such poets as J.W. von Goethe and Friedrich von Schiller.

dolce stil nuovo \\'dōl-chā-stēl-'nwō-vō\\ or **dolce stil novo** \\'nō-vō\\ [Italian, literally, sweet new style] The style of a group of 13th–14th-century Italian poets, mostly Florentines, whose vernacular sonnets, canzones, and ballate celebrate a spiritual and idealized view of love and womanhood in a way that was considered sincere, delicate, and musical. The Bolognese poet Guido Guinizelli is considered a forerunner of the *stilnovisti* ("writers of the new style"), and the most brilliant poets of the group are Guido CAVALCANTI and DANTE himself (in his lyric works).

Several influences prepared the way for the development of the *dolce stil nuovo*: the troubadour poetry of Provence, which celebrated courtly love and used poetic forms that evolved into the Italian sonnet and canzone; the simplicity and mysticism of St. Francis and his followers; the 13th-century Sicilian school of poets, who created the sonnet and canzone from Provençal forms and who were the first poets in Italy to use the vernacular; and the philosophical doctrines of Thomism, Aristotelianism, and Platonism, with which all the *stilnovisti* had contact. Guinizelli's contribution was his own gentle style of poetry as well as an exalted view of woman and love.

Cavalcanti, the poet of the complexities of love, contributed some of the most stunning examples of the *dolce stil nuovo*, as for example the sonnet that begins "Who is she coming, whom all gaze upon." Cavalcanti was also the author of a famous and difficult canzone analyzing the nature of love, called "Donna mi prega" ("A lady entreats me").

The influence of the *stilnovisti* was felt for centuries; their impact can be seen on the poetry of Petrarch and Lorenzo de' Medici (who consciously imitated them), as well as that of Michelangelo, Pietro Bembo, Torquato Tasso, Dante Gabriel Rossetti, and Ezra Pound.

Dolittle, Doctor \\'dü-lit-əl\\ Fictional character, the hero of a series of children's books by Hugh LOFTING.

Dr. Dolittle is an eccentric veterinarian who learns from his parrot, Polynesia, how to speak the language of animals so that he can treat their complaints more effectively.

Created by Lofting during World War I in letters sent to his children from the front, Dr. Dolittle first appeared in *The Story of Doctor Dolittle, Being the History of His Peculiar Life at Home and Astonishing Adventures in Foreign Parts* (1920). From 1922 to 1928 Lofting published one Dolittle book a year. The last of the series, *Doctor Dolittle and the Secret Lake*, was published posthumously in 1948. The original works also were illustrated by Lofting.

Doll's House, A Play in three acts by Henrik IBSEN, published in Norwegian as *Et dukkehjem* in 1879 and performed the same year. The play centers on an ordinary family—Torvald Helmer, a bank lawyer, his wife Nora, and their three little children. Torvald supposes himself the ethical member of the family, while his wife assumes the role of the pretty and irresponsible little woman in order to flatter him. Into this arrangement intrude several hard-minded outsiders, one of whom threatens to expose a fraud that Nora had once committed without her husband's knowledge in order to obtain a loan needed to save his life. When Nora's act is revealed, Torvald reacts with outrage and repudiates her out of concern for his own social reputation. Utterly disillusioned about her husband, whom she now sees as a hollow fraud, Nora declares her independence of him and their children and leaves them, slamming the door of the house behind her.

Dolphin, The Book of confessional poetry by Robert LOWELL, published in 1973. It was awarded a Pulitzer Prize in 1974. The poems concern the author's third marriage, the son it produced, and the response to these matters by his previous wife of 20 years. The poems are unrhymed sonnets, and in subject matter and narrative content they recall late Victorian love sonnets.

Dombey and Son \\'däm-bē\\ (*in full* Dealings with the Firm of Dombey and Son, Wholesale, Retail, and for Exportation) Novel by Charles DICKENS, published in 20 monthly installments during 1846–48 and in book form in 1848. It was a crucial novel in his development, a product of more thorough planning and maturer thought than his earlier serialized books.

The title character, Mr. Dombey, is a wealthy shipping merchant whose wife dies giving birth to their second child, a long-hoped-for son and heir, Paul. The elder child, Florence, being female, is neglected by her father. When Paul's health is broken by the rigors of boarding school and he dies, Dombey's hopes are dashed. In her grief, Florence draws emotional support from her father's employee Walter Gay. Resentful of their relationship, Dombey sends Gay to the West Indies, where he is shipwrecked and presumed lost. Dombey then takes a new wife—the poor but proud widow Edith Granger—who eventually runs off with Dombey's trusted assistant. After his ultimately empty pursuit of the pair, Dombey returns bereft and bankrupt. Walter Gay, meanwhile, has returned with the story of his rescue by a China clipper and asked Florence to marry him. They set sail for the East, returning a few years later with a baby son—named Paul—to find Mr. Dombey on the brink of suicide. The family's reconciliation concludes the book in a typically Dickensian glow.

Dombrowska   *see* DĄBROWSKA.

domestic tragedy   Drama in which the tragic protagonists are ordinary middle-class or lower-class individuals, in contrast to classical and Neoclassical tragedy, in which the protagonists are of kingly or aristocratic rank and their downfall is an affair of state as well as a personal matter. The earliest known examples of domestic tragedy are three anonymous late Elizabethan dramas: *Arden of Feversham* (*c.* 1591), the story of the murder of Mr. Arden by his wife and her lover and their subsequent execution; *A Warning for Faire Women* (1599), which deals with the murder of a merchant by his wife; and *A Yorkshire Tragedy* (*c.* 1606), in which a father destroys his family. Domestic tragedy did not take hold, however, until reintroduced in the 18th century by George Lillo with *The London Merchant; or, The History of George Barnwell* (1731). The popularity of this sordid drama of an apprentice who murders his uncle-guardian influenced domestic tragedy in France and Germany as well.

Domestic tragedy found its mature expression in the plays of Henrik Ibsen toward the end of the 19th century. In earlier domestic dramas by other playwrights the protagonists were sometimes villains and at other times merely pathetic, but the bourgeois heroes of Ibsen's *Brand* (1866), *Rosmersholm* (1886), *The Master Builder* (1892), and *When We Dead Awaken* (1899) are endowed with some of the isolated grandeur of the heroes of classical tragedy.

The tragedy *Woyzeck*, written in 1836 by the German dramatist Georg Büchner, took as its subject the poor and oppressed. *Woyzeck*, however, was well in advance of its time, since domestic tragedy set in the milieu of the lower classes did not come to the fore until the turn of the 20th century with such works as Gerhart Hauptmann's *Die Weber* (1892; *The Weavers*) and *Rose Bernd* (1903). Examples of 20th-century domestic tragedies are Arthur Miller's *Death of a Salesman* (1949) and Eugene O'Neill's *Long Day's Journey into Night* (1956).

Dominique \dō-mē-'nēk\   Novel by Eugène FROMENTIN, published in French in 1862 in *Revue des deux mondes*. The work is known for its psychological analysis of characters who content themselves with the second best in life and love.

This poetic novel tells the story of Dominique, who falls in love with the unattainable Madeleine, a young friend's married cousin, and throws himself into a Paris literary career to try to overcome his despair. He realizes, however, that his work is mediocre. Eventually the two become friends, and, years later, Madeleine confesses her love yet advises him to leave her. He does and contents himself with a quiet country life and marriage to another.

Donalbain \'dän-əl-,bān\   Fictional character, a son of Duncan, the king of Scotland who is murdered near the beginning of William Shakespeare's MACBETH. Donalbain and his brother Malcolm both fear for their own lives; Donalbain goes to Ireland and is not seen again.

Donatus \də-'nā-təs\, Aelius (fl. mid-4th century AD)   Famous grammarian and teacher of rhetoric at Rome, one of whose pupils was Eusebius Hieronymus (later St. Jerome).

Donatus wrote a large and a small school grammar, *Ars maior* and *Ars minor*. The latter was written for young students and gives, by question and answer, elementary instruction in the eight parts of speech. It remained in use throughout the European Middle Ages, and its author's name in the forms *donat* and *donet* came to mean "grammar" or any kind of "lesson." The larger work, in three parts, deals with the elements of grammar,

the eight parts of speech, and errors and beauties of language. Donatus has little claim to originality, but his grammar was often cited by other authors, and many commentaries were written on it. Donatus also wrote commentaries on the authors Terence and Virgil.

Aelius Donatus is to be distinguished from Tiberius Claudius Donatus, probably late 4th century AD, author of the *Interpretationes Vergilianae*, a commentary on the *Aeneid*.

Donelaitis \,dȯ-ne-'lä-ē-tis\ or **Duonelaitis** \,dwä-\, Kristijonas (b. Jan. 1, 1714, near Gumbinnen, East Prussia [now Gusev, Russia]—d. Feb. 18, 1780, Tolmingkehmen [now Chistyye Prudy])   One of the greatest Lithuanian poets and the first to be appreciated outside his country.

Donelaitis studied theology and classical languages at the University of Königsberg (1736–40) and in 1743 became pastor of the village of Tolmingkehmen. His main work, *Metai* (1818; *The Seasons*), 2,997 lines in length, was written in hexameters, never before used in Lithuanian verse. It depicts realistically and in their own dialect the life of the serfs and the countryside of 18th-century Prussian Lithuania. The poem was first published in an incomplete edition with a German translation (*Das Jahr in Vier Gesängen*; "The Year in Four Cantos") by Ludwig Rhesa in Königsberg in 1818. Donelaitis' other literary works include six fables and a tale in verse, *Pričkaus pasaka apie lietuvišką svodbą* (1865; "Pričkus' Tale about a Lithuanian Wedding").

Don Juan \'dän-'hwän, 'wän, *chiefly Brit and in poetry* dän-'jü-ən\   Fictitious character who is a symbol of libertinism. Originating in popular legend, he was first given literary personality in the tragic drama *El burlador de Sevilla* (1630; "The Seducer of Seville"), attributed to the Spanish dramatist Tirso de Molina. Through Tirso's tragedy, Don Juan became a universal character, as familiar as Don Quixote, Hamlet, and Faust. The legend of Don Juan tells how, at the height of his licentious career, he seduced a girl of noble family and killed her father, who had tried to avenge her. Later, seeing a commemorative effigy on the father's tomb, he flippantly invited it to dine with him, and the stone ghost duly arrived for dinner as a harbinger of Don Juan's death. In the original Spanish tragedy, Don Juan's attractive qualities—his vitality, his arrogant courage, and his sense of humor—heighten the dramatic value of the catastrophe. The power of the drama derives from its rapid pace, the impression it gives of cumulative tension as Don Juan's enemies gradually hound him to destruction, and the awareness that the Don is goaded to defy even the ghostly forces of the unknown. In the end he refuses to repent and falls to eternal damnation.

In the 17th century strolling Italian players carried the Don Juan story to France, and by the 19th century many foreign versions of the Don Juan legend existed. The French versions include Molière's *Le Festin de pierre* (1665; "The Stone Feast"), based on earlier French arrangements; Prosper Mérimée's short story "Les Âmes du Purgatoire" ("The Souls of Purgatory"); and the drama *Don Juan de Marana* (1836) by Alexander Dumas *père*. Early English versions—Thomas Shadwell's *The Libertine* (1675), for example—are considered uninspired, but later the character reappears with a new force in Lord Byron's long satiric poem *Don Juan* (1819–24) and in George Bernard Shaw's drama *Man and Superman* (1903). Later Spanish versions retain Don Juan's likable qualities and avoid the calculated cynicism of certain foreign versions.

The highly popular *Don Juan Tenorio* (1844) of José Zorrilla y Moral, still traditionally performed in Spain, borrowed lavishly from French sources. Zorrilla's play is said to sentimentalize the legend by furnishing a pious heroine and a serious love interest and by procuring Don Juan's repentance and salvation.

Don Juan \,dän-'jü-ən\ Epic poem written in ottava rima by Lord BYRON. Left unfinished at his death, the poem, which was published between 1819 and 1824, comprises 16 cantos and a fragment of a 17th. Byron's comic tale of the charming Don Juan's picaresque adventures with women, war, pirates, and politics is a study of the eternal struggle between nature and civilization. Unlike the character found in earlier versions of the Don Juan story, Byron's hero is not calculating and manipulative but is a "natural" man whose instincts toward love and life are constantly being thwarted by brutality, hypocrisy, and deadening conventionality. The poet's masterful use of the rhyme scheme to express different moods and the sheer narrative brilliance of the epic have made *Don Juan* one of the most influential works of the English language.

Don Juan in Hell \'dän-'hwän, 'wän, *chiefly Brit and in poetry* dän-'jü-ən\ The third act of MAN AND SUPERMAN by George Bernard Shaw. Set off from the main action of the play, this act is a nonrealistic dream episode. A dialogue for four actors, it is spoken theater at its most operatic and is often performed as a separate piece.

Don Juan Tenorio \,dōŋ-'kwän-tä-'nō-rē-ō\ Spanish drama in seven acts by José ZORRILLA, produced and published in 1844. The play, a variation of the traditional Don Juan story, was the most popular play of 19th-century Spain.

Zorrilla's Romantic style and sensibility are revealed in the rollicking story of the young nobleman Don Juan who drinks, duels, and wenches his way through Seville. The young novice Ines chastely falls in love with Don Juan, then dies after he abandons her. Don Juan later kills her father, Don Gonzalo. Years later, a statue of Don Gonzalo—the requisite "stone guest" of Don Juan tales—appears to Don Juan and shows him a vision of hell. Ines also appears to him and asks him to repent; as in no other versions of the story, he does so, though not until he is dying.

While Zorrilla's Don Juan is as selfish and lusty as his other literary counterparts, he is more an enchanter than a calculating seducer, and his vivid last-minute conversion adds a moral air to the play.

Donleavy \,dən-'lē-vē\, J.P., *in full* James Patrick (b. April 23, 1926, Brooklyn, N.Y., U.S.) American-born author of the lusty comic novel *The Ginger Man* (Paris, 1955; U.S., 1958), which introduced Dangerfield, the coarse, comic antihero. Donleavy is noted for characters who display heroism in the face of a mad universe and remain deeply attached to life despite its flaws.

Donleavy served with the U.S. Navy during World War II, studied microbiology at Trinity College, Dublin, and became an Irish citizen in 1967. *A Singular Man* (1963), *The Saddest Summer of Samuel S.* (1966), *The Beastly Beatitudes of Balthasar B* (1968), and later works continued to develop the prose style of *The Ginger Man*, which is distinguished by alliteration and an original treatment of voice. Action occurs in the third person while thoughts are conveyed in the first, allowing the character to speak both as observer and observed. Later works include *The Onion Eaters* (1971), *A Fairy Tale of New York* (1973), *The Destinies of Darcy Dancer, Gentleman* (1977), *Schultz* (1979), *Leila: Further in the Destinies of Darcy Dancer* (1983), and *Are You Listening Rabbi Löw* (1987).

Donnay \dȯ-'nā\, Maurice(-Charles) (b. Oct. 12, 1859, Paris, Fr.—d. March 31, 1945, Paris) French playwright whose dramas deal with love and adultery, social problems, and the manners of his time.

Donnay's dramatic career began with monologues written for the literary cabaret Le Chat-Noir. He made his name in the theater with *Amants* (1895; "Lovers"), one of his best plays

and the first work of a series called "Théâtre d'Amour," which also includes *La Douloureuse* (1897; "The Sorrowful Woman") and *L'Affranchie* (1898; "The Freedwoman"), both of which are dramas about women whose loves are spoiled by lies. A second cycle of plays, including *Le Retour de Jérusalem* (1903; "The Return from Jerusalem") and *Les Éclaireuses* (1913; "The Girl Scouts"), deals with current social problems; and another group, including *La Chasse à l'homme* (1919; "The Manhunt") and *La Reprise* (1924), are comedies of manners depicting France after World War I.

Among Donnay's other works are several autobiographical publications, including *Mon Journal, 1919–30* (1953).

Donne \'dən, *commonly* 'dän\, John (b. sometime between Jan. 24 and June 19, 1572, London, Eng.—d. March 31, 1631, London) Leading English poet of the Metaphysical school who is noted for his excellent love poetry, his religious verse and treatises, and his sermons.

Detail of an oil painting by an unknown artist after I. Oliver, c. 1616

National Portrait Gallery, London

Donne was born of Roman Catholic parents. He matriculated at Oxford at the age of 12 and after three years transferred to the University of Cambridge. He then enrolled as a student of the law in London. By the beginning of 1598 Donne had become a secretary to Sir Thomas Egerton, lord keeper of the great seal, in an office that was then a recognized path to high public appointments.

Donne had by this time written much of his poetry, most of it in imitation of ancient Latin poets. The classical models, however, are so transformed by his wit and daring imagination that the verses are thoroughly original. He had also composed numerous love lyrics in various moods by 1601, the year in which he married Anne More. This marriage took place without her father's consent, an offense against both civil and canon law. When in February 1602 Donne told her father of the marriage, he was briefly imprisoned, lost his position, and struggled for many years in poverty.

His writings of this period include several well-known secular poems, notably SONG ("Go and catch a falling star"); A VALEDICTION: FORBIDDING MOURNING ("As virtuous men pass mildly away"); "The Bait" ("Come live with me, and be my love"); THE CANONIZATION ("For God's sake hold your tongue, and let me love"); "To His Mistress Going to Bed" ("Come, madam, come, all rest my powers defy"); and "The Anniversary" ("All kings, and all their favourites").

In a casuistical work, *Biathanatos* (written *c.* 1608; published 1646), Donne argued the grounds on which one could rightly take one's own life. He was in the throes of a deep, personal religious struggle that he expressed in poems written between 1607 and 1613. These HOLY SONNETS include "Thou hast made me," "At the round earth's imagined corners, blow," DEATH, BE NOT PROUD, and BATTER MY HEART.

Convinced finally that he was called to the ministry, Donne was ordained early in 1615. From October 1616 he was reader (preacher and spiritual director) at Lincoln's Inn. His preaching soon developed great power and eloquence. In 1621 he was installed as dean of St. Paul's Cathedral in London.

After his ordination his creative talents were occupied almost wholly in preaching and in composing the prose *Devotions upon Emergent Occasions* (1624). Included in the *Devotions* is the famous passage that begins "No man is an island" and concludes with "and therefore never send to know for whom the bell tolls; it tolls for thee." *See also* METAPHYSICAL POETRY.

donnée \dȯ-'nā\ *plural* données *same or* -'nāz\ [French, from feminine past participle of *donner* to give] The set of assumptions (such as a widely held belief or a body of common knowledge) or a given subject or motif (such as a plot situation or a quirk of character) on which a work of fiction or drama proceeds.

Donnelly \'dän-əl-ē\, Ignatius (b. Nov. 3, 1831, Philadelphia, Pa., U.S.—d. Jan. 1, 1901, Minneapolis, Minn.) American novelist, orator, and social reformer; one of the leading advocates of the theory that Francis Bacon was the author of William Shakespeare's plays.

Donnelly grew up in Philadelphia, where he became a lawyer. In 1856 he moved to Minnesota, where, with another ex-Philadelphian, John Nininger, he founded Nininger City, intended as both a cultural and an industrial center. There he edited the erudite *Emigrant Aid Journal*, published in both English and German, to attract settlers. The scheme was briefly successful, but a panic in 1857 caused abandonment of the town, leaving Donnelly as its only resident.

He entered politics and served as lieutenant governor of Minnesota and as a U.S. congressman from 1863 to 1869. His first and most popular book was *Atlantis* (1882), which traced the origin of civilization to the legendary submerged continent of Atlantis. It was followed in 1883 by another work of speculation, *Ragnarok: The Age of Fire and Gravel*, which attempted to relate certain gravel and till deposits to an ancient near-collision of the Earth and a huge comet. In *The Great Cryptogram* (1888) and *The Cipher in the Plays and on the Tombstone* (1899), he attempted to prove that Bacon was the author of the plays attributed to Shakespeare by deciphering a code he discovered in Shakespeare's works. He also ascribed the plays of Christopher Marlowe and the essays of Michel de Montaigne to Bacon. Donnelly's utopian novel *Caesar's Column* (1891), which predicted such developments as radio, television, and poison gas, portrays the United States in 1988 as ruled by a ruthless financial oligarchy and peopled by an abject working class.

Donoso \dȯ-'nō-sō\, José (b. Oct. 5, 1924, Santiago, Chile) Chilean novelist and short-story writer important in the development of the new Latin-American novel.

Donoso studied in Santiago and in the United States at Princeton University (B.A., 1951). He taught during the 1950s and toward the end of the decade began to work as a journalist. After lecturing at the University of Iowa (1965–67), he took up residence in Spain. He published two short-story collections, *Veraneo y otros cuentos* (1955; "Summer Vacation and Other Stories") and *El charleston* (1960; *Charleston and Other Stories*).

Donoso's first novel, *Coronación* (1957; *Coronation*), established his reputation. It presents the moral collapse of an aristocratic family and suggests that an insidious loss of values affects all sectors of society. Donoso's second and third novels, *Este domingo* (1966; *This Sunday*) and *El lugar sin límites* (1966; *Hell Has No Limits*), depicted characters barely able to subsist in an atmosphere of desolation and anguish.

Donoso's masterpiece, *El obsceno pájaro de la noche* (1970; *The Obscene Bird of Night*), presented a hallucinatory, often grotesque, world and captured the fears, frustrations, dreams, and obsessions of his characters with profound psychological insight. Later works include the novella collection *Tres novelitas burguesas* (1973; "Three Bourgeois Novellas"; *Sacred*

Families: Three Novellas) and the novels *Casa de campo* (1978; *A House in the Country*), *La desesperanza* (1986; "Hopelessness"; *Curfew*), *El jardín de al lado* (1981; *The Garden Next Door*), and *Tartuta: Naturaleza muerta con cachimba* (1990; *Tartuta; and Still Life With Pipe*). Donoso returned to live in Chile in 1982.

Don Quixote \,dän-kē-'hō-tē, *British* ,dän-'kwik-sət, *Spanish* ,dȯn-kē-'ko̱-tä\ Novel by Miguel de CERVANTES, one of the most widely read classics of Western literature. The novel was published in two parts: the first part, in full *El ingenioso hidalgo Don Quixote de la Mancha* ("The Ingenious Hidalgo Don Quixote de la Mancha"), was published in 1605; the second part, *Segunda parte del ingenioso cavallero Don Quixote de la Mancha*, in 1615.

Originally conceived as a comic satire against the chivalric romances then in literary vogue, the novel describes realistically what befalls an elderly knight who, his head bemused by reading romances, sets out on his old horse Rosinante, with his pragmatic squire Sancho Panza, to seek adventure. In the process, he also finds love in the person of the peasant Dulcinea.

Contemporaries evidently did not take the book as seriously as later generations have done, but by the end of the 17th century it was deemed highly significant, especially abroad. It came to be seen as a mock epic in prose, and the "grave and serious air" of the author's irony was much admired.

In the history of the modern novel the role of *Don Quixote* is recognized as seminal. Evidence of its influence may be seen in the works of Daniel Defoe, Henry Fielding, Tobias Smollett, and Laurence Sterne. Connections also have been noticed with major works by a great many of the classic novelists of the 19th century, including Sir Walter Scott, Charles Dickens, Gustave Flaubert, Benito Pérez Galdós, Herman Melville, and Fyodor Dostoyevsky. The same is true, in different ways, in the case of many postrealist writers of the 20th century, from James Joyce to Jorge Luis Borges.

Doolittle \'dü-,lit-əl\, Hilda, *byname* H.D. (b. Sept. 10, 1886, Bethlehem, Pa., U.S.—d. Sept. 27, 1961, Zürich, Switz.) American modernist poet, known initially as an Imagist, whose poetry reflected classicism and classical themes. She was also a translator, novelist, playwright, and self-proclaimed "pagan mystic."

Doolittle went to Europe in 1911, and she remained abroad, except for brief visits, for the remainder of her life. William Carlos Williams was an early acquaintance, and, while at Bryn Mawr in 1905–06, she met and, for a brief time, became engaged to Ezra Pound. She was married to Richard Aldington from 1913 to 1938. Her friends included D.H. Lawrence, Marianne Moore, T.S. Eliot, Amy Lowell, the Sitwells, and the poet and novelist Bryher (Annie Winifred Ellerman), with whom she had a lifelong association.

H.D.'s first book of poetry, *Sea Garden* (1916), was followed by *Hymen* (1921), *Heliodora and Other Poems* (1924), *Red Roses for Bronze* (1929), and *Trilogy* (1944–46). She was one of the first Imagists, and she wrote clear, impersonal, and sensuous verse. Her later work was somewhat looser and more passionate, though it remained erudite and symbolic. The *Collected Poems of H.D.* (1925 and 1940), *Selected Poems of H.D.* (1957), and *Collected Poems 1912–1944* (1983) secured her position as a major 20th-century poet. She won additional acclaim for her translations (*Choruses from the Iphigeneia in Aulis and the Hippolytus of Euripides* [1919] and *Euripides' Ion* [1937]), for her verse drama (*Hippolytus Temporizes* [1927]), and for such prose works as *Palimpsest* (1926), *Hedylus* (1928), and *The Gift* (1982). Several of her books were autobiographical—including *Tribute to Freud* (1956), *Bid Me to Live* (1960), and *End to Torment* (1979).

Doolittle, Eliza \i-ˈlī-zə-ˈdü-lit-əl\ Cockney flower girl who is transformed into a woman of poise and polish in PYGMALION by George Bernard Shaw.

Doon de Mayence \dō-ˈóⁿ-də-mä-ˈyäⁿs\ Hero baron of the medieval epic poems in Old French known as chansons de geste, which together form the core of the Charlemagne legends. Doon's story is told in a chanson belonging to a cycle called *Geste de Doon de Mayence*. It tells of Charlemagne's rebellious barons and contains the stories of heroes such as Girart de Roussillon, Raoul de Cambrai, Renaud de Montauban, and Ogier the Dane, all of whom are represented as opposing Charlemagne (though the emperor's name is probably often used to stand for his weaker successor, Louis). The chanson dealing with Doon himself first gives a romantic account of his childhood; the second half, describing his wars in Saxony, may have a historical basis.

Doone, Lorna \ˈlôr-nə-ˈdün\ Fictional heroine of the historical romance LORNA DOONE by R.D. Blackmore.

doppelgänger \ˈdäp-əl-ˌgaŋ-ər, *German* ˈdóp-əl-ˌgeŋ-ər\ [German, from *doppel-* double + *-gänger* goer; coined by Jean Paul in the novel *Siebenkäs* (1796)] In German folklore, a wraith, or apparition, of a living person, as distinguished from a ghost. The concept of the existence of a spirit double, an exact but usually invisible replica of every person, bird, or beast, is an ancient and widespread belief. To meet one's double is a sign that one's death is imminent. The doppelgänger became a popular symbol in 18th- and 19th-century horror literature, and the theme took on considerable complexity. One of the masters of the double figure was the German writer of fantastic tales E.T.A. Hoffmann. His first novel, *Die Elixiere des Teufels*, 2 vol. (1815–16; *The Devil's Elixir*), was one of the earliest expositions of the theme. Another, perhaps better-known, version of the doppelgänger occurs in Fyodor Dostoyevsky's novel *Dvoynik* (1846; *The Double*).

Other themes related to the doppelgänger theme in folklore and literature include the mirror image, the shadow image, and the multiple personality.

Dorat or **Daurat** \dō-ˈrä\, Jean, *pseudonym* Auratus \au̇-ˈrä-tu̇s\ (b. 1508, Le Dorat, near Limoges, Fr.—d. Nov. 1, 1588, Paris) French humanist, a brilliant Hellenist, one of the poets of La Pléiade and their mentor for many years.

After studying at the Collège de Limoges, Dorat became tutor to the pages of Francis I. He tutored Jean-Antoine de Baïf, whose father he succeeded as director of the Collège de Coqueret. There, besides Baïf, his pupils included Pierre de Ronsard, Rémy Belleau, and Pontus de Tyard. Joachim du Bellay was added to this group by Ronsard, and these five young poets, along with and under the direction of Dorat, formed a society for the reform of French language and literature. They increased their number to seven with the dramatist Étienne Jodelle and named themselves La Pléiade, in emulation of the seven Greek tragic poets of Alexandria. The election of Dorat as their president proved his personal influence, but as a writer of French verse he is the least important of the seven.

Dorat stimulated his students to intensive study of Greek and Latin poetry, while he himself wrote incessantly in both languages. He is said to have composed more than 15,000 Greek and Latin verses. His influence and fame as a scholar extended to England, Italy, and Germany. In 1556 he was appointed professor of Greek at the Collège Royal, a post that he held until he retired in 1567. He published a collection of the best of his Greek and Latin verse in 1586.

Dorothy \ˈdôr-thē, ˈdôr-ə-\ Fictional character, the youthful heroine of *The Wonderful Wizard of Oz* (1900), a book-length tale for children by L. Frank BAUM. Dorothy's down-to-earth Kansas upbringing serves her well in the fantastic Land of Oz, where she travels in the company of the Scarecrow, the Tin Woodman, the Cowardly Lion, and her little dog Toto.

Dorrit, Amy \ˈā-mē-ˈdôr-it\ Fictional character, the protagonist of the novel LITTLE DORRIT by Charles Dickens.

Dorst \ˈdôrst\, Tankred (b. Dec. 19, 1925, Oberlind, Thuringia, Ger.) German author whose experiments with theatrical forms, translations, and political plays and novels marked him as an original.

Dorst studied at the University of Munich, where he became interested in marionettes and "illusionary theater," in which reality is seen as merely another role to be played. His earliest plays were experiments with these forms. His 1960 drama *Gesellschaft im Herbst* ("Party in Autumn"), about a crafty businessman who fools the owner of an ancestral castle into thinking that the castle holds buried treasure, is a satire on contemporary German society's obsession with romantic myths. During the mid-to-late 1960s, Dorst introduced a number of foreign works to the German theater and translated or adapted plays by Thomas Dekker, Denis Diderot, Molière, and Sean O'Casey, among others.

Dorst's transformation into a political writer occurred with his 1968 play *Toller*, a drama based on the life of the writer Ernst Toller that examines the relationship between literature and politics. In the 1970s Dorst began to collaborate with Ursula Ehler on a series of plays and novels. Most important was the Merz cycle, chronicling the life of a middle-class German family during the 20th century and using a variety of forms—including stage plays, radio and television drama, and novels—He returned to his original interest in mythology and fantasy with *Merlin, oder das wüste Land* (1981; "Merlin: Or, The Wasteland"), an epic 10-hour takeoff on the Arthurian myths. Dorst and Ehler's subsequent works, such as *Ich, Feuerbach* (1986; "I, Feuerbach"), are concerned with the artist's struggle to exist amid political chaos. In 1990 he and Ehler published a collection of plays based on fairy tales and myths.

Dos Passos \däs-ˈpas-əs, dəs-\, John (Roderigo) (b. Jan. 14, 1896, Chicago, Ill., U.S.—d. Sept. 28, 1970, Baltimore, Md.) American writer, one of the major novelists of the post-World War I "lost generation," whose reputation as a social historian and as a radical critic of the quality of American life rests primarily on his trilogy U.S.A.

The son of a wealthy lawyer, Dos Passos graduated from Harvard University (1916) and was an ambulance driver in World War I. His early works were basically portraits of the artist recoiling from the shock of his encounter with a brutal world. Extensive travel as a newspaper correspondent in the postwar years enlarged his sense of history, sharpened his social perception, and confirmed his radical sympathies. His writing began to develop a larger and tougher objective realism.

The execution of Nicola Sacco and Bartolomeo Vanzetti in 1927 crystallized for Dos Passos an image of the United States as "two nations"—one of the rich and privileged and one of the poor and powerless. *U.S.A.* is the portrait of these two nations.

U.S.A. was followed by a less ambitious trilogy, *District of Columbia*, which chronicles Dos Passos' disillusion with the labor movement, radical politics, and New Deal liberalism.

Dostoyevsky or **Dostoevsky** \də-stə-ˈyef-skʸē, *Angl* däs-tə-ˈyef-skē, -ˈyev-\, Fyodor Mikhaylovich (b. Oct. 30 [Nov. 11, New Style], 1821, Moscow, Russia—d. Jan. 28 [Feb. 9], 1881, St. Petersburg) Russian novelist, journalist, and short-story writer whose psychological penetration into the darkest recesses of the human heart had a profound and universal influence on the 20th-century novel.

Dostoyevsky was born into a middle-class family. He graduated as a military engineer but resigned his commission to devote himself to writing. The novel *Dvoynik* (1846; THE DOUBLE), which was less well received than his earlier *Bednyye lyudi*

Embassy of the Russian Federation

(1846; *Poor Folk*), introduced the concept of the split personality or divided self that would become a common psychological feature of the characters of Dostoyevsky's later novels. A series of sketches, short stories, and another short novel followed. In 1849 Dostoyevsky was arrested for subversion for his participation in the Petrashevsky Circle, a radical intellectual discussion group. His sentence of death was commuted to imprisonment in Siberia. Accepting his punishment as a necessary atonement for what he believed was a serious crime, Dostoyevsky spent four years at hard labor and four years as a soldier. The only reading material he was allowed in prison was the New Testament, and frequent readings increased Dostoyevsky's Christian faith. *Zapiski iz myortvogo doma* (1861–62; *The House of the Dead*) is a fictionalized account of this experience.

Released in 1854, Dostoyevsky returned to St. Petersburg. He married a widow in 1857 in what proved to be an unfortunate match. He began to write again, producing the short novel *Selo Stepanchikovo i yego obitateli* (1859; *The Friend of the Family*). In 1860 he and his brother founded the magazine *Vremya*, in which were published *The House of the Dead* and *Unizhennyye i oskorblyonnyye* (1861; *The Insulted and Injured*). When *Vremya* was suppressed, the brothers founded another magazine, *Epokha*, in which they published *Zapiski iz podpolya* (1864; NOTES FROM THE UNDERGROUND).

In 1864–65 Dostoyevsky's wife and brother died, the magazine collapsed, and Dostoyevsky was burdened with overwhelming debt. He attempted without success to raise money by gambling, and he had several love affairs that came to nothing. Soon afterwards, however, he produced *Prestupleniye i nakazaniye* (1866; CRIME AND PUNISHMENT), the first of his major novels. In the next year he married his stenographer Anna Snitkina, and the union proved to be a devoted one. From the turmoil of this period emerged two great novels, *Idiot* (1868–69; THE IDIOT) and *Besy* (1872; THE POSSESSED).

In 1873 prominent friends helped to secure for Dostoyevsky the editorship of the conservative weekly *Grazhdanin* ("The

Citizen"). He resigned his editorship after a year, but in 1876 he revived as a separate monthly publication a column entitled "Dnevnik pisatelya" ("The Diary of a Writer"), which he had contributed to *Grazhdanin*. He continued the publication for over a year, with a few additional issues in 1880 and 1881. It is devoted mostly to his views on significant current events, literary reminiscences and criticism, and occasional sketches and short stories, of which two are among his best: "Krotkaya" (1876; "A Gentle Spirit") and "Son smeshnogo cheloveka" (1877; THE DREAM OF A RIDICULOUS MAN). By the time he published his last work, *Bratya Karamazovy* (1879–80; THE BROTHERS KARAMAZOV), often considered his masterpiece, he was recognized in his own country as one of its greatest writers.

Dottore \dōt-'tō-rä\, *also called* Gratiano *or* Graziano \grät-'syä-nō\   Stock character of the Italian COMMEDIA DELL'ARTE, who was a loquacious caricature of pedantic learning. The Dottore was at times a legal scholar, ready with advice for any occasion, whose bungled and inept courtroom arguments were the basis for comic dialogues; at other times he was a physician armed with a huge syringe and a roster of preposterous cures for any ailment; he also could be a rhetorician or grammarian. When he appeared as a physician, he wore a large turned-up hat and was called Dottore Balanzone Lombardi, after two famous 16th-century actors of this part.

Dottore's contribution to the action of the play consisted of a kind of ineffectual wandering about while talking continuously. His long-winded disquisitions, scholarly puns, and malapropisms were spoken in a jargon of Latin jumbled with local dialect.

Double, The   Novel by Fyodor DOSTOYEVSKY, published in 1846 in Russian as *Dvoynik*.

The Double is the first of many works by Dostoyevsky to reveal his fascination with psychological doubles. The morbidly sensitive and pretentious clerk Golyadkin, already clinically deranged by the social pressures of his office and by unrequited love, suffers a growing persecution mania, which leads him to encounter another man looking exactly like him who is the leader of a conspiracy against him. He is finally driven to a madhouse by a series of encounters with this being, who is sometimes clearly his own reflection in a glass, sometimes the embodiment of his own aggressive fantasies, sometimes an unpleasant ordinary mortal who happens to have the same name and appearance, and sometimes, in some supernatural way, himself.

double ballade   A ballade having six stanzas and usually an envoi, or shortened final dedicatory stanza. *See also* BALLADE.

double dactyls *also called* higgledy-piggledy \‚hig-əl-dē-'pig-əl-dē\ *or* jiggery-pokery \‚jig-ə-rē-'pō-kə-rē\   A light-verse form consisting of eight lines of two dactyls each, arranged in two stanzas. The first line of the poem must be a jingle, often "Higgledy-piggledy" or "Jiggery-pokery"; the second line must be a name; the last lines of each stanza are truncated and they should rhyme; and one line in the second stanza must consist of a single word. The following example by R. McHenry illustrates the form:

> Higgledy-piggledy
> Emily Dickinson
> Amherst had nothing more
> Noble than she.
>
> 'Sconced in her house with the
> Curtains pulled back just so:
> Monochromatically
> Serving up tea.

Double Dealer, The American literary magazine founded in New Orleans, La., and published from January 1921 until May 1926. From July 1921 it was subtitled *A National Magazine from the South.*

The Double Dealer, sometimes rendered *The Double-Dealer*, was named after a William Congreve play. Enjoying the support of H.L. Mencken and Sherwood Anderson, it was the first magazine to publish the fiction of Ernest Hemingway (May 1922) and the second magazine to publish William Faulkner's verse (June 1922). It also helped launch the careers of Hart Crane, Thornton Wilder, Jean Toomer, and Kenneth Fearing. Among the other writers it published were Robert Penn Warren, Edmund Wilson, Amy Lowell, John Crowe Ransom, Richard Aldington, Hilda Doolittle (H.D.), Joseph Campbell, Mary Austin, and Ben Hecht.

double rhyme *see* FEMININE RHYME.

Douglas \\'dəg-ləs\\, Gawin *or* Gavin (b. 1475?—d. September 1522, London, Eng.) Scottish poet and first British translator of Virgil's *Aeneid.*

Four surviving works attributed to Douglas reflect his moral earnestness and his command of difficult metrical forms. Besides the *Aeneid* they include a long poem, *Conscience*, and two moral allegories, *The Palice of Honour* (1501) and *King Hart. The Palice of Honour* is a dream allegory on the theme "where does true honour lie?" *King Hart* (ascribed without certainty to Douglas) describes vigorously and graphically the progress of Hart (the human soul) from a youthful enslavement to pleasure through the inevitable assaults of conscience, age, and death. Douglas' last literary work was the first direct translation of the whole *Aeneid* to be made in Britain. Although Douglas casually updated Virgil and lacked "classical" diction and gravity of tone, his translation is technically sound and sensitive to linguistic differences. Each book also contains a notable original prologue.

After the Battle of Flodden (1513), in which James IV of Scotland was killed, Douglas abandoned his literary career for political activities. The marriage of the king's widow, Margaret Tudor, sister of Henry VIII, to Douglas' nephew aligned the Douglas family with the pro-English faction in Scotland. In 1521 he was forced by political enemies to flee to England, where he remained in exile until his death in London from the plague.

Douglas \\'dəg-ləs\\, George, *pseudonym of* George Douglas Brown \\'braún\\ (b. Jan. 26, 1869, Ochiltree, Ayrshire, Scot.—d. Aug. 28, 1902, London, Eng.) Scottish novelist who was instrumental in the realistic movement in literature of the early 20th century. Educated at Glasgow University and Balliol College, Oxford, he was a brilliant student who won many awards. After graduation in 1895 he traveled to London to write for metropolitan newspapers, eventually becoming a publisher's reader.

Douglas' novel *The House with the Green Shutters* (1901), one of the first literary works to forego romance or adventure, received much attention for its realistic study of contemporary Scottish life. Another novel, *Love and a Sword* (1899), was not nearly so influential. He died suddenly, at the height of his career.

Douglas \\'dəg-ləs\\, Keith Castellain (b. Jan. 20, 1920, Royal Tunbridge Wells, Kent, Eng.—d. June 9, 1944, Normandy, Fr.) British poet who is remembered for the irony, eloquence, and simple, direct language he used to express the misery and waste of war, to which he was to fall victim.

Douglas' education at Oxford University was cut short by the outbreak of war. By 1941 he was serving as a tank commander in North Africa, where some of his most powerful poems were written (*Alamein to Zem-Zem*, 1946). He was moved back to Britain in 1944 to take part in the invasion of Normandy, on the third day of which he was killed in combat. His posthumous *Collected Poems* (1951) enhanced his reputation as a war poet, but in 1964 Ted Hughes's edition of Douglas' *Selected Poems* established him as a poet of universal significance.

Douglas \\'dəg-ləs\\, Norman, *in full* George Norman Douglas (b. Dec. 8, 1868, Thüringen, Austria—d. Feb. 9, 1952, Capri, Italy) Essayist and novelist who wrote of southern Italy, where he lived for many years. In his later years he lived on the island of Capri, which is the setting of his most famous book, *South Wind* (1917). All his books, whether fiction, topography, essays, or autobiography, have a charm arising from Douglas' uninhibited expression of a bohemian, aristocratic personality. His prose is considered an excellent example of the conversational style.

Douglas was born of an old Scottish landowning family, which had intermarried with German aristocrats, and he attended the *Gymnasium* at Karlsruhe, Ger., where he showed a precocious gift for both languages and natural science. He entered the British Foreign Office in 1893 but spent only about three years in diplomatic service (in Russia), after which he traveled widely in India, Italy, and North Africa.

His first notable book was *Siren Land* (1911) and his first popular success the satirical novel *South Wind*. Perhaps the richest of his books is *Old Calabria* (1915) and the most self-revealing, his informal autobiography *Looking Back* (1933).

Douglass \\'dəg-ləs\\, Frederick, *original name* Frederick Augustus Washington Bailey \\'bā-lē\\ (b. Feb. 7, 1817, Tuckahoe, Md., U.S.—d. Feb. 20, 1895, Washington, D.C.) African-American who started life as a slave but was thrust by his oratorical and literary brilliance into the forefront of the U.S. abolition movement.

The son of a slave mother (from whom he was early separated) and a white father he never knew, Frederick lived with his grandmother on a Maryland plantation until the age of eight. He worked as a house servant and later as a field hand, and along the way he learned to read and write. In 1838 he managed to flee to New York City and then to New Bedford, Mass., where he worked as a laborer for three years, eluding slave hunters by changing his name to Douglass.

At an antislavery convention in 1841, Douglass was asked to speak extemporaneously about his own experiences; his remarks were so poignant and naturally eloquent that he was catapulted into a new career as agent for the Massachusetts Anti-Slavery Society. To counter skeptics who doubted that he could ever have been a slave, Douglass wrote his autobiography in 1845, revised and completed in 1882 as *Life and Times of Frederick Douglass*. Douglass' account became a classic of American literature as well as a primary source about slavery from the bondsman's viewpoint. After a two-year speaking tour of Great Britain and Ireland, Douglass returned with funds to purchase his freedom and also to start his own antislavery newspaper, the *North Star* (later *Frederick Douglass's Paper*), which he published from 1847 to 1860 in Rochester, N.Y.

During the American Civil War, Douglass was a consultant to President Abraham Lincoln. Throughout Reconstruction (1865–77), he fought for full civil rights for freedmen and vigorously supported the women's rights movement. After Reconstruction, Douglass held several government positions, including U.S. minister and consul general to Haiti from 1889 to 1891.

Dove \\'dəv\\, Rita (Frances) (b. Aug. 28, 1952, Akron, Ohio) African-American writer and teacher who was named poet laureate of the United States in 1993.

Dove graduated from Miami University in Ohio and studied subsequently at Tübingen University in Germany. She studied creative writing at the University of Iowa and published the first of several chapbooks of her poetry in 1977. From 1981 to 1989 Dove taught at Arizona State University, leaving that post to teach at the University of Virginia. She was writer-in-residence at Tuskegee (Ala.) Institute in 1982.

In her poetry collections, including *The Yellow House on the Corner* (1980) and *Museum* (1983), as well as a volume of short stories entitled *Fifth Sunday* (1985), Dove focused her attention on the particulars of family life and personal struggle, addressing the larger social and political dimensions of black experience primarily by indirection. The Pulitzer Prize-winning *Thomas and Beulah* (1986) is a cycle of poems chronicling the lives of the author's maternal grandparents, born in the Deep South at the turn of the century. Subsequent works include the poetry collections *The Other Side of the House* (1988) and *Grace Notes* (1989) and the novel *Through the Ivory Gate* (1992).

Dover Beach \'dō-vər\   Poem by Matthew ARNOLD, published in *New Poems* in 1867. The most celebrated of the author's works, this poem of 39 lines addresses the decline of religious faith in the modern world and offers the fidelity of affection as its successor.

Dowden \'daud-ən\, Edward (b. May 3, 1843, Cork, County Cork, Ire.—d. April 4, 1913, Dublin)   Irish critic, biographer, and poet, noted for his critical work on William Shakespeare.

Educated at Queen's College, Cork, and Trinity College, Dublin, Dowden became professor of English literature at Trinity in 1867 and lectured at Oxford (1890–93) and Cambridge (1893–96). His *Shakspere: A Critical Study of His Mind and Art* (1875) was the first book in English to attempt a unified and rounded picture of Shakespeare's development as an artist, studying him in terms of successive periods. Dowden produced numerous other works on Shakespeare, and he is remembered in addition for his *Life of Shelley* (1886). He also was among the first to appreciate Walt Whitman, with whom he became good friends.

Down and Out in Paris and London \'par-is . . . 'lən-dən\   Autobiographical work by George ORWELL, published in 1933. Orwell's first published book, it contains essays in which actual events are recounted in a fictionalized form.

The book recounts that to atone for the guilt he feels about the conditions under which the disenfranchised and downtrodden peoples of the world exist, Orwell decides to live and work as one of them. Dressed as a beggar, he takes whatever employment might be available to a poverty-stricken outcast of Europe. In Paris he lives in a slum and works as a dishwasher. The essay "How the Poor Die" describes conditions at a charity hospital there. In London's East End, he dresses and lives like his neighbors, who are paupers and the poorest of working-class laborers. Dressed as a tramp, he travels throughout England with hoboes and migrant laborers.

Dowson \'daus-ən\, Ernest (Christopher) (b. Aug. 2, 1867, Lee, Kent, Eng.—d. Feb. 23, 1900, Lewisham, London)   One of the most gifted of the circle of English poets of the 1890s known as the Decadents.

In 1886 Dowson entered Queen's College, Oxford, but left in 1888 when he was obliged to work at his father's dock in the Limehouse district in London. Dowson was an active member of the Rhymers' Club, a group of "decadents" that included William Butler Yeats, Arthur Symons, and Aubrey Beardsley. In 1891 he met Adelaide Foltinowicz, a young waitress with whom he fell in love and who was to be the inspiration for much of his poetry. In that same year he published his best-known poem, "Non Sum Qualis Eram Bonae sub Regno Cy-narae," popularly known from its refrain as "I have been faithful to thee, Cynara, in my fashion." Adelaide, who was 12 years old when they met, declined his offer of marriage, but he remained faithful to her, in his fashion, for the next six years.

In 1894 his father died, his mother committed suicide, and Dowson discovered the symptoms of his tuberculosis. In 1897 Adelaide married another man; after that, Dowson lived mostly in France, supporting himself by ill-paid translations. He was discovered wretched and penniless, addicted to absinthe, and ill, by a friend, R.H. Sherard, who brought him back to London, where he died in Sherard's house.

Although Dowson published two novels in collaboration with Arthur Moore, *A Comedy of Masks* (1893) and *Adrian Rome* (1899), and a book of short stories, *Dilemmas* (1895), his reputation rests on his poetry, *Verses* (1896) and *Decorations* (1899). His lyrics, marked by meticulous attention to melody and cadence, are polished and often charming. Yeats acknowledged that much of his own technical development was due to Dowson, whose influence can also be traced in the early work of Rupert Brooke.

Doyle \'doil\, Sir Arthur Conan \'kō-nən, *commonly* 'kä-\ (b. May 22, 1859, Edinburgh, Scot.—d. July 7, 1930, Crowborough, Sussex, Eng.)   Writer best known for his creation of the detective Sherlock HOLMES.

Conan Doyle practiced medicine until 1891 after graduating from the University of Edinburgh, and the character of Holmes, who first appeared in *A Study in Scarlet* (1887), partly derives from a teacher at Edinburgh noted for his deductive reasoning. Short stories about Holmes began to appear regularly in the *Strand Magazine* in 1891 and later made up several collections, including *The Adventures of Sherlock Holmes* (1892), *The Memoirs of Sherlock Holmes* (1894), *The Return of Sherlock Holmes* (1905), and *The Case-Book of Sherlock Holmes* (1927). Conan Doyle wearied of him and devised his death in 1893—only to be forced by public demand to restore him ingeniously to life. The other Holmes novels include *The Mystery of Cloomber* (1889), *The Sign of Four* (1890), *The Doings of Raffles Haw* (1892), THE HOUND OF THE BASKERVILLES (1902), and *The Valley of Fear* (1915). The continuing popularity of Sherlock Holmes has put the author's other works—chiefly historical romances—somewhat in the shade.

Conan Doyle was knighted in 1902 for his work with a field hospital in Bloemfontein, S.Af., and for other activities concerning the South African (Boer) War. After the death of his son from wounds incurred in World War I, he dedicated himself to the cause of spiritualism.

Drabble \'drab-əl\, Margaret (b. June 5, 1939, Sheffield, Yorkshire, Eng.)   English writer of novels that are skillfully modulated variations on the theme of a girl's development toward maturity through her experiences of love, marriage, and motherhood.

The daughter of a judge and sister of novelist A.S. Byatt, Margaret Drabble began writing after leaving Cambridge University. The central characters of her novels, although widely different in character and circumstance, are shown in situations of tension and stress that are the necessary conditions for their moral growth. Drabble is concerned with the individual's attempt to define the self, but she is also interested in social change. She writes in the tradition of such authors as George Eliot, Henry James, and Arnold Bennett. Her novels include *A Summer Bird-cage* (1962), *The Garrick Year* (1964), *The Millstone* (1965), *The Needle's Eye* (1972), *The Realms of Gold* (1975), *The Ice Age* (1977), *The Middle Ground* (1980), and a trilogy composed of *The Radiant Way* (1987), *A Natural Curiosity* (1989), and *The Gates of Ivory* (1991).

In addition to her novels Drabble has written and edited several books on the general subject of literature, as well as journal articles and screenplays.

Drachmann \'dräk-mən\, Holger Henrik Herholdt (b. Oct. 9, 1846, Copenhagen, Den.—d. Jan. 14, 1908, Hornbæk) Writer best known for his lyrical poetry, which placed him in the front rank of late 19th-century Danish poets.

The son of a physician, Drachmann studied painting and began to write, then developed an interest in social problems and joined the new radical literary movement led by Georg Brandes. *Digte* (1872), a collection of poems, expressed Drachmann's social theories.

Drachmann established his position as the greatest poet of the Danish modern movement of his time with such collections as *Dæmpede melodier* (1875; "Muted Melodies"), *Sange ved havet* (1877; "Songs by the Sea"), *Venezia* (1877; "Venice"), and *Ranker og roser* (1879; "Weeds and Roses"). However, in the prose *Derovre fra grænsen* (1877; "From Over the Border") and the verse fairy tale *Prinsessen og det halve kongerige* (1878; "The Princess and Half the Kingdom") his writing showed a patriotic and romantic trend that brought him into conflict with the Brandes group.

Drachmann's output was of great variety, including verse, short stories, novels, and plays, but his lyric verse is of major importance. He forsook classical prosody for a freer meter and a lively rhythm that reflected the cadences of natural speech. Apart from love, his favorite subjects are the sea and its life. The best later collections are *Gamle guder og nye* (1881; "Old and New Gods"), *Sangenes bog* (1889; "The Book of Songs"), and *Den hellige ild* (1899; "The Holy Flame"). His novels are often partly autobiographical, with characters who are artists or writers, as in the novel considered his most important, *Forskrevet*, 2 vol. (1890; "Pledged"). Among his plays was the fantasy *Der var engang* (1885; "Once upon a Time") was popular, though chiefly because of Peter Lange-Müller's music.

Dracontius \drə-'kän-shē-əs, -shəs\, Blossius Aemilius (fl. 5th century AD) The foremost Christian Latin poet of Africa, who lived at the time of the literary revival that took place under Vandal rule in the latter part of the 5th century.

At Carthage, Dracontius received the traditional rhetorical education and practiced as a lawyer. Though his family was initially favored by the Vandals, he eventually suffered imprisonment and confiscation of his property because of a poem in which he praised the emperor rather than the Vandal king Gunthamund (484–496).

Dracontius' earlier verse is represented by the *Romulea*, a collection of nine pieces principally on mythological themes. The highly rhetorical flavor of these poems reappears in his elegiac *Satisfactio*, a plea for pardon addressed to Gunthamund during his imprisonment, and is evident even in his most religious poem, *De laudibus dei*. This last poem, his most important work, comprises 2,327 hexameters in three books. Book I describes the Creation and Fall and the evidence for immortality; Book II treats the benevolence of God as shown by the preservation and redemption of the world; and Book III is concerned with the dealings of God with humans. The account of the Creation was separately circulated in the Middle Ages under the title *Hexaëmeron*. Dracontius shows wide familiarity with secular Latin literature and with the Bible.

Dracula \'drak-yŭl-ə\ Gothic novel by Bram STOKER, published in 1897. The most popular literary work derived from vampire legends, *Dracula* became the basis for an entire genre of literature and film.

Count Dracula, an "undead" villain from Transylvania, uses his supernatural powers to lure and prey upon innocent victims from whom he gains the blood on which he lives. The novel is written chiefly in the form of journals kept by the principal characters—Jonathan Harker, who contacts the vampire in his Transylvanian castle; Harker's fiancée (later his wife), Mina, adored by the Count; the well-meaning Dr. Seward; and Lucy Westenra, a victim who herself becomes a vampire. The doctor and friends destroy Dracula in the end, but only after they drive a stake through Lucy's heart to save her soul.

Dracula combined central European folktales of the *nosferatu*, or undead, with historical accounts of the 15th-century prince Vlad the Impaler, who allegedly speared 100,000 victims and was given the epithet Dracula (a derivative of Romanian *drac*, or "devil"). Critics have seen the story's vampirism as a lurid Victorian literary sublimation of sexuality.

dragon \'drag-ən\ [Old French *dragun, dragon,* from Latin *dracon-, draco* snake, dragon, from Greek *drákōn,* a derivative from the base of *dérkesthai* to see clearly, look at] In Western folklore, a fabulous animal generally represented as a monstrous winged and scaly serpent or saurian with a crested head, enormous claws, and a barbed tail. In Chinese mythology, the dragon is a beneficent supernatural creature whose presence is associated with rain and floods.

Belief in these creatures apparently arose without the slightest knowledge on the part of the ancients of the gigantic, prehistoric, dragonlike reptiles. In general, in the Middle Eastern world, where snakes are large and often deadly, the serpent or dragon was symbolic of the principle of evil. Thus, the Egyptian god Apepi was the great serpent of the world of darkness. But the Greeks and Romans, though accepting the Middle Eastern idea of the serpent as an evil power, also at times conceived the *drakontes* as beneficent powers—sharp-eyed dwellers in the inner parts of the Earth. On the whole, however, the image of dragons as evil was more potent and it outlasted the more benign image. Christianity condemned the serpent deities outright, and in Christian art the dragon came to be symbolic of sin and paganism and, as such, was depicted prostrate beneath the heels of saints and martyrs.

The Chinese dragon, *lung,* represents yang, the principle of heaven, activity, and maleness in the yin-yang of Chinese cosmology. From ancient times, it was the emblem of the Imperial family, and until the founding of the republic (1911) the dragon adorned the Chinese flag. The dragon came to Japan with much of the rest of Chinese culture, and there (as *ryū* or *tatsu*) it became capable of changing its size at will, even to the point of becoming invisible. Both Chinese and Japanese dragons, though regarded as powers of the air, are usually wingless. They are among the deified forces of nature in Taoism.

Drake \'drāk\, Joseph Rodman (b. Aug. 7, 1795, New York, N.Y., U.S.—d. Sept. 21, 1820, New York City) Romantic poet who contributed to the beginnings of an American national literature by a few memorable lyrics before his early death.

Drake graduated from medical school in New York in 1816, after which he married an heiress, honeymooned in Europe, and returned to New York to open a pharmacy. While a student, he had become friends with another poet, Fitz-Greene Halleck, with whom he began collaborating in 1819 on topical satirical verses; the result was the "Croaker Papers," published under a pseudonym in the New York *Evening Post.* These lampoons of public personages appeared in book form in 1860.

Drake died of tuberculosis in 1820. Although he had asked his wife to destroy his unpublished poems after his death, she kept them, and his daughter saw to the publication of 19 of his verses in 1835 as *The Culprit Fay and Other Poems.* The title poem, considered his best, deals with the theme of the fairy lover in a Hudson River setting. The volume also contains two fine nature poems, "Niagara" and "Bronx." These and other poems appeared in his *Life and Works* (1935), edited by F.L. Pleadwell.

drama \'dräm-ə, 'dram-\ [Greek *drâma* deed, action on the stage, play, a derivative of *drân* to do, act]　A composition in verse or prose intended to portray life or character or to tell a story usually involving conflicts and emotions through action and dialogue and typically designed for theatrical performance. *See also* COMEDY; TRAGEDY.

dramatic irony　A plot device; a type of IRONY that is produced when the audience's or reader's knowledge of events or individuals surpasses that of the characters. The words and actions of the characters therefore take on a different meaning for the audience or reader than they have for the play's characters. This may happen when, for example, a character reacts in an inappropriate or foolish way or when a character lacks self-awareness and thus acts under false assumptions.

The device abounds in works of tragedy. In the Oedipus cycle, for example, the audience knows that Oedipus' acts are tragic mistakes long before he recognizes his own errors. Later writers who mastered dramatic irony include William Shakespeare (as in Othello's trust of Iago), Voltaire, Jonathan Swift, Henry Fielding, Thomas Hardy, and Henry James. Dramatic irony can also be seen in such works as O. Henry's short story "The Gift of the Magi." In Anton Chekhov's story "Lady with the Dog," an accomplished Don Juan engages in a routine flirtation only to find himself seduced into a passionate lifelong commitment to a woman who is no different from all the others.

dramatic literature　The texts of plays that can be read, as distinct from being seen and heard in performance.

The relationship between dramatic text and performance is complex. In the case of the Greek dramatists of the 5th century BC, the texts now available are a small selection made by later copying and preservation. Scholars cannot ascertain how, precisely, these are related to the compositions made available for the original productions. The problem here as in many later periods is the relation between the words written to be spoken or sung by the performers and the many other elements of dramatic composition—in movement, in scene and costume, and occasionally in music—the performance would include. Some of these can be inferred from the particular styles of writing, but most have to be studied from other kinds of surviving accounts.

In the drama of the English Renaissance few plays were published as literary works, but the importance of the dramatic writing of the period eventually established many of the plays as texts. In later periods, and notably from the 19th century onward, it became habitual to include in the written text of a play, and especially in its independently published form, details not only of scene and stage movement but also of the appearance of the characters and of the states of mind intended to accompany or to punctuate the spoken words.

Most drama is a form of writing for oral and actual performance, and it is in periods when imaginative writing has been taken to be coterminous with "literature," and particularly with printed literature, that some of its elements have been most persistently misunderstood. The phrase dramatic literature has elements in common with the phrase oral literature, especially in times such as the present when the silent reading of print has come to seem the normal means for the reception and study of imaginative writing. The name for work within these conditions—"literature"—was applied to these other forms of writing intended primarily for oral communication. The need for understanding the conditions of oral performance is now more widely recognized. At the same time, given this recognition, the texts of the great plays are still read as dramatic literature, with a proper emphasis on the distinguishing features of the dramatic.

Remnants of the art of drama before it occurs as text, or dramatic literature, may be seen in the storytelling traditions of ancient cultures, in which gesture and often dance and song, as well as the individual style of the storyteller, are essential elements of the narrative.

dramatic monologue　A poem written in the form of a speech of an individual character to an imaginary audience; it compresses into a single vivid scene a narrative sense of the speaker's history and psychological insight into his character. Though the form is chiefly associated with Robert BROWNING, who raised it to a highly sophisticated level in such poems as "My Last Duchess," "The Bishop Orders His Tomb at St. Praxed's Church," and "Fra Lippo Lippi," it is actually much older. Many Old English poems are dramatic monologues—for instance, "The Wanderer" and "The Seafarer." The form is also common in folk ballads, a tradition that Robert Burns imitated with broad satiric effect in "Holy Willie's Prayer."

Browning's contribution to the form is one of subtlety of characterization and complexity of the dramatic situation, which the reader gradually pieces together from the casual remarks or digressions of the speaker. The subject discussed is usually far less interesting than what is inadvertently revealed about the speaker himself.

The dramatic monologue form parallels the novelistic experiments with point of view in which the reader is left to assess the intelligence and reliability of the narrator. Later poets who successfully used the form were Ezra Pound ("The River Merchant's Wife: A Letter"), T.S. Eliot ("Love Song of J. Alfred Prufrock"), and Robert Frost ("The Pauper Witch of Grafton"). *Compare* SOLILOQUY.

dramatic unities　The unity of time, unity of place, and unity of action. *See* UNITY.

dramatism \'dram-ə-,tiz-əm, 'dräm-\　A technique of analysis of language and thought as basically modes of action rather than as means of conveying information. It is associated with the critic Kenneth Burke.

dramatis personae \'dram-ə-tis-pər-'sō-nē, 'dräm-, -,nī\ [New Latin]　**1.** The characters or actors in a drama.　**2.** *singular in construction*　A list of the characters or actors in a drama.

dramatist \'dram-ə-tist, 'dräm-\　*see* PLAYWRIGHT.

dramatization \,dram-ə-tə-'zā-shən, ,dräm-\　An adaptation for theatrical presentation.

dramaturge \'dram-ə-,tərj, 'dräm-\ [German *Dramaturg,* from Greek *dramatourgós* contriver (taken to mean literally "dramatist"), from *dramat-, drâma* drama, play + *-ourgos* maker]　A specialist in dramaturgy. The term is sometimes used specifically to mean an individual employed by a theater company as an adviser in choosing and interpreting the plays it presents.

dramaturgy \'dram-ə-,tər-jē, 'dräm-\ [German *Dramaturgie,* from Greek *dramatourgía* dramatic composition, action of a play, from *dramat-, drâma* drama, play + *-ourgia* making, production]　The art or technique of dramatic composition or theatrical representation. In this sense English *dramaturgy* and French *dramaturgie* are both borrowed from German *Dramaturgie,* a word used by the German dramatist and critic Gotthold Lessing in an influential series of essays entitled *Hamburgische Dramaturgie* ("The Hamburg Dramaturgy") published from 1767 to 1769.

drame bourgeois \ˌdrȧm-bür̄zh-'wȧ\ [French, bourgeois drama] Type of play that enjoyed brief popularity in France in the late 18th century. Written for and about the middle class and based upon the theories of the French essayist and encyclopedist Denis Diderot, the *drame bourgeois* was conceived of as occupying a place between tragedy and comedy. It was designed as a serious depiction of middle-class problems, especially social abuses, but usually included a conventional happy ending. Diderot wrote two *drames* illustrating his theories, *Le Fils naturel* (1757; *Dorval; or, The Test of Virtue*) and *Le Père de famille* (1758; *The Father*), adapting them from the earlier *comédie larmoyante* ("tearful comedy") of Pierre-Claude Nivelle de La Chaussée.

Most of the plays in this genre, including those of Diderot's successors, Michel-Jean Sedaine and Louis-Sébastien Mercier, are regarded by critics today as sentimental and humorless, full of inflated dialogue and pompous sermonizing. *Drame bourgeois*, however, was important to the development of French acting; it led to more natural styles of speech and gesture and attempted greater historical accuracy in costumes and scenery. Diderot and his followers are also seen as distant precursors of the earliest writers of a drama known as the problem play.

drawing-room comedy Theatrical genre popular in the early 20th century, so called because the plays were usually set indoors, often actually in a drawing room. Such comedies generally portrayed upper-class society and were a form of COMEDY OF MANNERS. The plays of George Bernard Shaw, Noël Coward, and Philip Barry are examples of the genre.

Drayton \'drāt-ən\, Michael (b. 1563, Hartshill, Warwickshire, Eng.—d. 1631, London) Poet who was the first to write English odes in the manner of Horace.

Drayton spent his early years in the service of Sir Henry Goodere, to whom he owed his education, and whose daughter, Anne, he celebrated as Idea in his poems. His first published work, *The Harmonie of the Church* (1591), contains biblical paraphrases in an antiquated style. His next works conformed more nearly to contemporary fashion: in the pastoral, with *Idea, The Shepheards Garland* (1593); in the sonnet, with *Ideas Mirrour* (1594); in the erotic idyll, with *Endimion and Phoebe* (1595); and in the historical heroic poem, with *Robert, Duke of Normandy* (1596) and *Mortimeriados* (1596). The last, originally written in rhyme royal, was recast in Ludovico Ariosto's ottava rima verse as *The Barrons Warres* (1603).

Drayton's most original poems of this period are *Englands Heroicall Epistles* (1597), a series of pairs of letters exchanged between famous lovers in English history. In his first collected poems, published as *Poems* (1605), and in *Poemes Lyrick and Pastorall* (1606) he introduced a new mode with the "odes," modeled on Horace. Further collected editions culminated in his most important book, *Poems* (1619). In that volume Drayton reprinted most of what he chose to preserve, often much revised, with many new poems and sonnets. His most ambitious work, *Poly-Olbion* (1612–22), is a catalog of the glories of England. In his old age he wrote the delightful works *Nymphidia* (1627) and *The Muses Elizium* (1630).

dreadful \'dred-fəl\ A cheap and sensational story or periodical; especially, a story of crime or desperadoes such as was popular in mid-to-late Victorian England. *See also* PENNY DREADFUL.

Dream of a Ridiculous Man, The Short story by Fyodor DOSTOYEVSKY, published in Russian in 1877 as "Son smeshnogo cheloveka." It addresses questions about original sin, human perfectibility, and the striving toward an ideal society. The inability of the rationalist to provide answers to all of life's questions is also touched on.

The unnamed narrator sees himself as he knows others do: a once merely ridiculous man who has deteriorated into madness. At one time, desperate to the point of suicide, he fell asleep and had a dream that he had killed himself, was buried and exhumed, and traveled to a planet that was a duplicate of Earth, except that it was perfect and untainted. However, his own presence began to corrupt the society, which became exactly like that of the Earth. He implored the people to crucify him, hoping that his sacrifice would return them to their previous state. They threatened him with imprisonment as a madman if he continued ranting about the possibility of an ideal society. The narrator awakened, convinced that humanity was not intrinsically evil but had only fallen from grace.

Dream of John Ball, A \'jän-'bȯl\ A romantic fantasy in prose by William MORRIS, published in serial form in *The Commonweal* in 1886–87 and in book form in 1888.

The historical figure referred to in the title was a 14th-century English priest who preached inflammatory sermons advocating a classless society; in 1381 he was hanged for being a leader of the Peasants' Revolt. In *A Dream of John Ball* a 19th-century man dreams that he is a scholar in Kent, England, during the revolt. He sees Ball inspire a crowd of peasants to defeat the sheriff's men in battle and later has a conversation with Ball in which they discuss the future. As Ball hears of the decline of feudalism, the rise of the Industrial Revolution, and 19th-century commercial society, he realizes that even in the future his hopes for an egalitarian society have yet to be fulfilled. The tale is considered a forerunner of Morris' utopian novel *News from Nowhere*.

Dream of the Red Chamber Novel by CAO ZHAN written in Chinese as *Honglou meng* and generally considered to be the greatest of all Chinese novels.

The work, published in English as *Dream of the Red Chamber* (1929), first appeared in manuscript form in Beijing during Cao Zhan's lifetime. In 1791, almost 30 years after Cao Zhan's death, the novel was published in a complete version of 120 chapters prepared by Gao Ê and Cheng Weiyuan. Uncertainty remains about the final 40 chapters of the book. They may have been forged by Gao, substantially written by Cao Zhan and simply discovered and put into final form by Gao and Cheng, or perhaps composed by an unknown author. *The Story of the Stone* (1973) is a complete five-volume English translation.

The novel is a blend of realism and romance, psychological motivation and fate, daily life and supernatural occurrences. A series of episodes rather than a strongly plotted work, it details the decline of the Jia family, including 30 main characters and more than 400 minor ones. The major focus, however, is on young Baoyu, the gifted but obstinate heir of the clan. Spoiled by his mother and grandmother, he is continually reprimanded by his strict Confucian father, who especially abhors Baoyu's intimacy with his numerous female cousins and maidservants. Most notable among these relations are the melancholy Daiyu, Baoyu's ill-fated love, and the vivacious Baochai, Baoyu's eventual wife. The work and the character Baoyu himself are generally thought to be semiautobiographical creations of Cao Zhan. His portrait of the extended family reflects a faithful image of upper-class life in the early Ching dynasty (1644–1911/12), while the variety of individual character portraits reveals a psychological depth not previously approached in Chinese literature.

Dream of the Rood, The Old English lyric, the earliest dream poem and one of the finest religious poems in the English language. The poem was once (but is no longer) attributed to Caedmon or Cynewulf. In a dream the poet beholds a beautiful tree—the rood, or cross, on which Christ died. The rood tells him its own story. Forced to be the instrument of the Savior's death, it describes how it suffered the nail wounds, spear shafts, and insults along with Christ to fulfill God's will. Once bloodstained and horrible, it is now the resplendent sign of human redemption. The poem was originally known only in fragmentary form from some 8th-century runic inscriptions on the Ruthwell Cross, now standing in the parish church of Ruthwell in Scotland. The complete version, found in the 10th-century codex known as the Vercelli Book, was discovered in 1822 in northern Italy.

Dream Play, A Fantasy play in 14 scenes by August STRINDBERG, published in Swedish as *Ett drömspel* in 1902 and first produced in 1907. Presented as a dream, this fluid tableau of human foibles is a poignant lament that humans are to be pitied.

As the play opens, the daughter of the Vedic god Indra arrives on Earth with the intention of determining if human complaints are justified. She encounters a host of tormented characters and herself is enmeshed in a wrenching marriage. Only the Poet, who has created the dream, seems unaffected by human suffering.

Dream Songs, The Masterwork of John BERRYMAN, published in 1969 as a compilation of his earlier works *77 Dream Songs* (1964) and *His Toy, His Dream, His Rest* (1968).

Dreamtime *also called* The Dreaming *or* World Dawn. In Australian Aboriginal mythology, the time of Creation when the natural environment was shaped and humanized by the actions of mythic beings known as Ancestors. Many of these beings took the form of humans or of animals; some changed their forms. They were credited with having established the local social order and its laws. Some, especially the great fertility mothers, but also male genitors, were responsible for creating human life—*i.e.*, the first people.

The expression "Dreamtime" is perhaps a translation of the word *altyerrenge* (usually anglicized as *Alcheringa* or *Alchuringa*) in the language of the Aranda, a people of the Alice Springs region, Northern Territory, whose culture was described in classic studies by the anthropologists W.B. Spencer and F.J. Gillen early in the 20th century. Semantically related words exist in other Aboriginal languages.

Mythic beings of the Dreamtime are eternal. Though in the myths some Ancestors were killed or disappeared beyond the boundaries of the people who sang about them, and others were metamorphosed as physiographic features (for example, a rocky outcrop or a waterhole) or manifested as or through sacred ritual objects usually of wood or stone (in Aranda *tywerrenge*, anglicized *churinga*), their essential quality remains undiminished. In Aboriginal belief, they are spiritually as much alive today as ever. The places where the mythic beings performed some action or were transformed became sacred sites upon which ritual was focused.

Dream Variation *also called* Dream Variations. Poem by Langston HUGHES, published in 1926 in *The Weary Blues*, his first poetry collection. The poem articulates the dream of African-Americans as the speaker yearns for freedom and for acceptance in American society. It ends with the well-known lines: "Night coming tenderly/ Black like me."

dream vision *also called* dream allegory. A type of poetic narrative or narrative framework that was especially popular in medieval literature. It was so named because the poet pictured himself falling asleep and envisioning in his dream a series of allegorical people and events. The device made more acceptable the fantastic and sometimes bizarre world of personifications and symbolic objects characteristic of medieval allegory.

Well-known dream visions include the first part of *Roman de la rose* (13th century); Geoffrey Chaucer's *Book of the Duchesse* (1369/70); *Pearl* (late 14th century); *Piers Plowman* (c. 1362–c. 1387), attributed to William Langland; William Dunbar's *The Thrissill and the Rois* and *The Goldyn Targe* (early 16th century); and John Bunyan's *The Pilgrim's Progress* (1678).

Dreiser \ˈdrīz-ər, *commonly* ˈdrīs-\, Theodore (b. Aug. 27, 1871, Terre Haute, Ind., U.S.—d. Dec. 28, 1945, Hollywood, Calif.) Novelist who was the outstanding American practitioner of naturalism. He led a national literary movement that replaced a Victorian sense of propriety with the unflinching presentation of real-life subject matter.

Dreiser was born into poverty, and harsh experiences would become dominant themes in his novels. He spent a year at Indiana University before becoming a newspaper reporter. During this period he came to believe that humans are helpless in the grip of instincts and social forces beyond their control.

SISTER CARRIE (1900), Dreiser's first novel, concerned the life of a young kept woman whose behavior goes unpunished; the book sold fewer than 500 copies. Within the next nine years, Dreiser achieved financial success as an editor in chief of several women's magazines. He was forced to resign in 1910, however, because of an office imbroglio involving an assistant's daughter.

In 1911 Dreiser's second novel, JENNIE GERHARDT, was published, followed by the first two volumes of a projected trilogy of novels, based on the life of the American transportation magnate Charles T. Yerkes, THE FINANCIER (1912) and *The Titan* (1914). In his next major novel, *The 'Genius'* (1915), he transformed his own life and numerous love affairs into a sprawling semiautobiographical chronicle that was censured by the New York Society for the Suppression of Vice. Other published works include a short-story collection, *Free and Other Stories* (1918); a book of sketches, *Twelve Men* (1919); philosophical essays, *Hey-Rub-a-Dub-Dub* (1920); a rhapsodic description of New York, *The Color of A Great City* (1923); works of drama, including *Plays of the Natural and Supernatural* (1916) and *The Hand of the Potter* (1918); and the autobiographical works *A Hoosier Holiday* (1916) and *A Book About Myself* (1922).

In 1925 Dreiser published his first novel in a decade, AN AMERICAN TRAGEDY, based on a celebrated murder case. The

Brown Brothers

book brought Dreiser a degree of critical and commercial success he had never before attained and would not thereafter equal. The book's highly critical view of the American legal system made him the adopted champion of social reformers. In the 1930s he published the autobiographical *Dawn* (1931), one of the most candid self-revelations by any major writer. He completed most of *The Stoic*, the long-postponed third volume of his trilogy, in the weeks before his death.

Drew, Nancy \'nan-sē-'drü\ A fictional teenage amateur detective in an extended series of children's mystery books written by Carolyn Keene (a collective pseudonym, used by Edward Stratemeyer and, among many others, by his daughter Harriet S. Adams). Nancy Drew's intelligence, courage, and independence made her a popular role model for many generations of young readers.

The Secret of the Old Clock (1930), written by Mildred Augustine Wirt Benson, was followed by four additional Nancy Drew Mystery Stories that same year and more than 100 novels in the following 60 years. A new series, The "Nancy Drew Files" Mystery Series, began publication in 1986. *See also* Edward STRATEMEYER.

Dreyfus \drā-'füēs\, Alfred (b. Oct. 19, 1859, Mulhouse, Fr.—d. July 12, 1935, Paris) French army officer whose trial for treason began a 12-year controversy, known as the Dreyfus Affair, that deeply marked the political and social history of the French Third Republic. Dreyfus was the son of a wealthy Jewish textile manufacturer and had risen to the rank of captain in the French army by 1889. He was accused of selling military secrets to the Germans and was convicted and sentenced to life imprisonment on insufficient evidence in a highly irregular trial. On the whole, public opinion and the press, led by a virulently anti-Semitic faction, welcomed the verdict and used it as a pretext to question the loyalty of all French Jews.

The case attracted the support of such writers as Anatole France, Marcel Proust, and Émile Zola. Zola's open letter, J'ACCUSE, published on the front page of the paper *L'Aurore*, galvanized public opinion about the case and eventually led to a new trial and exoneration for Dreyfus.

Dr. Heidegger's Experiment \'däk-tər-'hī-dəg-ər\ Story by Nathaniel HAWTHORNE, published in *Twice-Told Tales* (1837).

Elderly Dr. Heidegger and four of his contemporaries participate in his scientific experiment on aging. Dr. Heidegger applies water from the Fountain of Youth to a faded rose; the flower regains its freshness and beauty. After drinking some of the fabled water, the three male participants revert to young manhood and woo the sole female subject, whose youthful beauty has been revived. After the vial of water is spilled accidentally, the rose and the experimenters wither and become old. The experiment has taught Dr. Heidegger not to desire the transient headiness of youth. However, his four friends intend to search for the Fountain of Youth.

Drieu La Rochelle \drē-, œ -lä-rò-'shel\, Pierre (b. Jan. 3, 1893, Paris, Fr.—d. March 15, 1945, Paris) French writer whose life and works illustrate the malaise common among European youth after World War I.

Drieu's plan to enter diplomatic service was interrupted by World War I, in which he fought and was wounded. Like many others of his generation, he emerged from the war disillusioned. Characteristic novels of his Surrealist period include his first novel, *L'Homme couvert de femmes* (1925; "The Man Covered With Women"), and *Le Feu follet* (1931; *The Fire Within*, or *Will o' the Wisp*; film, 1963). *Le Feu follet* is the story of the last hours in the life of a young bourgeois Parisian addict who kills himself.

Later works include a war memoir, *La Comédie de Charleroi* (1934; *The Comedy of Charleroi and Other Stories*); *Rêveuse bourgeoisie* (1937; "Dreamworld Bourgeoisie"); and, perhaps his best-known novel, *Gilles* (1939). Drieu eventually became a fascist and collaborated with the Vichy government during World War II; shortly after the liberation of France, he committed suicide. His *Récit secret* (1961; *Secret Journal and Other Writings*) and *Mémoires de Dirk Raspe* (1966) were published posthumously.

Drinkwater \'driŋk-,wȯt-ər, -,wät-\, John (b. June 1, 1882, Leytonstone, Essex, Eng.—d. March 25, 1937, London) English poet, playwright, and critic, a typical man of letters of the Georgian Age of the 1910s and '20s. Drinkwater promoted repertory theater in England and wrote popular chronicle dramas. In 1907 he became manager and producer for the Pilgrim Players, which developed into the Birmingham Repertory Theatre Company. His published verse includes *The Collected Poems*, 2 vol. (1923). He wrote critical studies (*William Morris*, 1912; *Swinburne*, 1913; and others); several historical plays, one of which, *Abraham Lincoln* (1918), was produced with great success both in London and the United States; and autobiographical works, *Inheritance*, 2 vol. (1931), and *Discovery* (1932).

Driving Miss Daisy \,mis-'dā-zē\ One-act play by Alfred Uhry, produced and published in 1987. The play won the 1988 Pulitzer Prize for drama. It is the story of a friendship that develops over a 25-year period between Daisy Werthan, an elderly Jewish widow living in Atlanta, and Hoke Coleburn, the African-American chauffeur her son hires for her. Set during the years of the civil-rights movement, the drama was hailed for its quiet, unsentimental examination of its elderly characters and for its balanced depiction of gradually changing political sensibilities in the South.

Uhry won an Academy Award for his screenplay adaptation of *Driving Miss Daisy*, produced in 1989.

Dr. Jekyll and Mr. Hyde \'jek-əl, 'jēk-...'hīd\ (*in full* The Strange Case of Dr. Jekyll and Mr. Hyde) Novella by Robert Louis STEVENSON, published in 1886. The work is known for its vivid portrayal of the psychopathology of a "split personality."

The calm, respectable Dr. Jekyll develops a potion that will allow him to separate his good and evil aspects for scientific study. At first Jekyll has no difficulty abandoning the drug-induced persona of the repulsive Mr. Hyde, but as the experiments continue the evil personality wrests control from Jekyll and commits murder. Afraid of being discovered, he takes his life; Hyde's body is found, together with a confession written in Jekyll's hand.

The phrase "Jekyll and Hyde" has become shorthand for the exhibition of wildly contradictory behavior, especially between private and public selves.

droll \'drōl\ A short comical scene performed in an English public house during the mid-17th century when the theaters were closed by the government and the performance of plays was not permitted. Drolls, or droll humors, often consisted of scenes adapted from full-length plays, though they were sometimes improvised by the actors.

drollery \'drōl-ə-rē\ An artistic or intellectual production of a light and humorous character.

Droll Stories Collection of short stories by Honoré de BALZAC, published in three sets of 10 stories each, in 1832, 1833, and 1837, as *Contes drolatiques*.

Rabelaisian in theme, the stories are written with great vitality in a pastiche of 16th-century language. The tales are fully

Illustration by Boris Artzybasheff for an American edition of *Droll Stories*

as lively as the author's masterful *Comédie humaine* series, but they stand apart for their good-humored licentiousness and historical wordplay.

Drood, Edwin \'ed-win-'drüd\   Fictional character, the alleged victim in the unfinished novel THE MYSTERY OF EDWIN DROOD by Charles Dickens.

Drost \'dròst\, Aernout (b. March 15, 1810, Amsterdam, Neth.—d. Nov. 5, 1834, Amsterdam)   Dutch writer whose historical novels were the first important works of the 19th-century Romantic movement in The Netherlands.

Drost's first novel, *Hermingard van de Eikenterpen* (1832; "Hermingard of the Oak Burial Mounds"), portraying the conversion of a Germanic woman to Christianity in 4th-century Holland, gave him scope for the development of his Romantic ideals and religious concepts. Drost died at the age of 24. His posthumously published works include *Schetsen en verhalen* (1835–36; "Sketches and Stories"), of which the most important is "De pestilentie te Katwijk" ("The Plague at Katwijk"). Drost's founding of the journal *De muzen* (1834; "The Muses"), precursor of *De Nieuwe Gids* ("The New Guide"), was a significant step toward the later Dutch literary revival.

Droste-Hülshoff \'drò-stə-'huels-hòf\, Annette, Baroness (Freiin) von, *original name* Anna Elisabeth Franziska Adolphine Wilhelmine Louise Maria, Freiin von Droste zu Hülshoff (b. Jan. 10, 1797, Schloss Hülshoff, near Münster, Westphalia [Ger.]—d. May 25, 1848, Meersburg, Baden)   One of the great women poets of Germany, author of prose tales that are considered the forerunner of the 19th-century realistic short story.

Droste-Hülshoff was educated by tutors and lived most of her life in isolation. Her first collection of poetry, *Gedichte* (1838; "Poems"), included poems of a deeply religious nature. Between 1829 and 1839 she wrote a cycle of religious poems, *Das geistliche Jahr* (1851; "The Spiritual Year"), which contains some of the most earnest religious poetry of the 19th century.

Her fame rests chiefly on the poetry dealing with her native Westphalian landscape. Her only complete prose work, a novella, *Die Judenbuche* (1842; *The Jew's Beech*), is a psychological study of a Westphalian villager who murders a Jew. It is the first example in German literature of the hero's fate portrayed as arising from his social environment; the crime becomes understandable within the context of life in the village.

drott-kvaett \'dròt-,kvet\ [Old Norse *drótt-kvætt*, from neuter of *dróttkvæthr* composed in drott-kvaett meter, from *drótt* retinue + *kvæthi* poem]   A medieval Scandinavian verse form used in skaldic poetry. Drott-kvaett consists of stanzas of eight regular lines, each of which has three stresses and ends with a trochee. The form exhibits a complex pattern of internal and terminal rhyme, alliteration, and especially alternation of consonance with full rhyme at the ends of lines.

Dr. Seuss   Pseudonym of Theodor Seuss GEISEL.

druid \'drü-id\ [Greek *Dryídēs* (singular) or Latin *druides, druidae* (plural), of Celtic origin]   A member of an ancient Celtic priesthood with divinatory, educational, judicial, and shamanic duties and much political influence. In early Irish religious literature *druí* (plural *druíd*) is used to translate Latin *magus* ("wizard"), and the druids play a role in medieval Irish tales such as those of the Ulster cycle. The character of Merlin in Arthurian literature represents at several removes a figure from druidic tradition.

druidess \'drü-i-dəs\   A female druid.

Drum   South African literary magazine, published in English monthly from 1951, that focused on the concerns of black writers. Originating in Sophiatown, a black neighborhood near Johannesburg, it came to symbolize an era of protest literature that vehemently opposed the apartheid legislation of the 1950s. Together with the companion publication *Trust*, the journal circulated in several African nations.

Drum launched the careers of such writers as Can Themba and Nat Nakasa; contributors included Bloke Modisane, Es-'kia Mphahlele, Jordan K. Ngubane, and Alex La Guma.

Drummond \'drəm-ənd\, William, *in full* William Drummond of Hawthornden \'hò-thòrn-dən\ (b. Dec. 13, 1585, Hawthornden, near Edinburgh, Scot.—d. Dec. 4, 1649, Hawthornden)   First notable poet in Scotland to write deliberately in English. He also was the first to use the canzone, an Italian metrical form, in English verse.

Drummond studied at Edinburgh and in France. On the death of his father, first laird of Hawthornden, in 1610, he settled down on his Hawthornden estate, leaving law for literature and devoting himself to the life of a cultured and rather detached man of means.

He wrote *Poems* (1614, 1616), *Flowres of Sion* (1623), and *Forth Feasting* (1617), a poem celebrating James I's visit to Scotland in that year, and he was apparently the author of *Polemo-Medinia inter Vitarvam et Nebernam* (1645?), a macaronic piece intermingling Scots and Latin. His prose writings include a group of Royalist political pamphlets, *The History of Scotland, From The Year 1423 Until the Year 1542* (1655), and *A Cypresse Grove* (1623; earlier version, *A Midnight's Trance*, 1619), a meditation on death and mutability.

Drummond \'drəm-ənd\, William Henry (b. April 13, 1854, Mohill, County Leitrim, Ire.—d. April 6, 1907, Cobalt, Ont., Can.)   Writer of humorous dialect poems conveying a sympathetic but sentimentalized picture of "habitants," or French-Canadian farmers.

Drummond emigrated with his parents to Canada about 1864. He left school at age 15 to help support his family, but at age 30 took a degree in medicine at Bishop's College in Quebec. After four years in country practice he moved to Montreal, where he gave well-received public readings of his poems. His first collection, *The Habitant* (1897), was followed by several others, all of which were published together as *The Poetical Works of William Henry Drummond* (1912).

Drummond, Hugh "Bulldog" \'hyü-'bùl-,dòg-'drəm-ənd\   A fictional character, the English hero of a popular series of

English mystery novels (from 1920) by SAPPER. Drummond, a two-fisted man of action, made his first appearance in a short story published in *Strand Magazine*. He next appeared in the novel *Bull-dog Drummond: The Adventures of a Demobilized Officer Who Found Peace Dull.* (The author later removed the hyphen from the nickname.) Drummond was a former British Army captain who craved adventure and excitement. He was the prototype of what the author called "the Breed": a patriotic, athletic Englishman, educated at a public school, who was physically strong and vigorous, did well at games, and had contempt for and distrust of intellectuals. He was also xenophobic. The Bulldog Drummond books were crudely written, with weak plots and little style, but in the 1920s and '30s Drummond was an enormously popular character.

Drummond de Andrade \\'drü-mȯn-dē-âⁿn-'dräj-ē\\, Carlos (b. Oct. 31, 1902, Itabira, Braz.—d. Aug. 17, 1987, Rio de Janeiro)   Poet, journalist, author of *crônicas* (a short fiction-essay genre widely employed in Brazil), and literary critic, considered one of the most accomplished and influential poets of mid-20th-century Brazil. His experiments with poetic form (including laying the foundation of what later became concrete poetry) and his often ironic treatment of realistic themes reflected his concern with the modern human struggle for freedom and dignity. His *crônicas* reveal a special concern for children and the urban poor.

After receiving a degree in pharmacy in 1925, Drummond de Andrade turned to poetry and joined the new group of Brazilian modernists who were introducing colloquial language and unconventional syntax in their free-verse forms. He helped found the literary magazine *A revista* ("Review") in 1925. The first of many poetry collections, *Alguma poesia* (1930; "Some Poetry"), shows both his own strong poetic personality and his affinity with Modernismo.

When he retired from government service in 1962, Drummond de Andrade was a director of the National Historical and Artistic Heritage Service of Brazil. He published approximately 15 volumes of poetry and a half-dozen collections of *crônicas*.

An English-language collection of his works, including translations by American poets Elizabeth Bishop and Mark Strand, was published as *Traveling in the Family* (1986).

Drums at Dusk   Historical novel by Arna BONTEMPS, published in 1939.

Set in Haiti in the late 18th century, the work is based on the uprising of black slaves that occurred at the time of the French Revolution of 1789, securing independence for their country. A young Frenchman living in Haiti is sympathetic to the plight of the blacks but is nonetheless marked for revenge. Aided by his black friend Toussaint l'Ouverture, he escapes from Haiti with the girl he loves.

Drum-Taps   Collection of poems in free verse, most on the subject of the American Civil War, by Walt WHITMAN, published in May 1865. The mood of the poetry moves from excitement at the falling-in and arming of the young soldiers at the beginning of the war to the troubled realization of the war's true significance. The disillusion of the Battle of Bull Run is reflected in "Beat! Beat! Drums!" while an understanding of the depth of suffering of the wounded informs "Vigil Strange I Kept on the Field One Night."

Sequel to Drum-Taps, published in the fall of 1865 (the title page reads 1865–66), includes "Pioneers! O Pioneers!" and Whitman's poems on the death of Abraham Lincoln, O CAPTAIN! MY CAPTAIN! and the elegy WHEN LILACS LAST IN THE DOORYARD BLOOM'D. Both *Drum-Taps* and *Sequel to Drum-Taps* were incorporated into the fourth (1867) edition of LEAVES OF GRASS.

Drunken Boat, The   Poem by Arthur RIMBAUD, written in 1871 at age 16 as "Le Bateau ivre" and often considered his finest poem. The poem was written under the sponsorship of the poet Paul Verlaine, who first published it in his study of Rimbaud that appeared in the review *Lutèce* in 1883.

"The Drunken Boat" is written in the first person from the point of view of a boat that is adrift after all of its passengers have been massacred. The description of the vessel's erratic course, its assault by storms, and the vast wastes of the ocean reflect the torment of the poet's soul. The poem was written in part to counter Charles Baudelaire's poem "Le Voyage," in which that poet made a distinction between art and reality.

dryad \\'drī-əd, -ˌad\\ [Greek *dryad-, dryás,* a derivative of *drŷs* tree] *see* WOOD NYMPH.

Dryasdust *in full* Dr. Jonas Dryasdust \\'jō-nəs-'drī-əz-ˌdəst\\ Fictional character, an antiquarian created by Sir Walter SCOTT writing pseudonymously as "Editor," or "Antiquary," in the prefaces to several works, such as *The Antiquary* (1816). A dull expert on rare books, Dryasdust is a friend of the "Editor," with whom he discusses the intents and uses of history.

Dryden \\'drīd-ən\\, John (b. Aug. 19, 1631, Aldwinkle, Northamptonshire, Eng.—d. May 1, 1700, London)   English poet, dramatist, and literary critic who so dominated the literary scene of his day that it came to be known as the Age of Dryden.

When in 1660 Charles II was restored to the throne, Dryden celebrated by publishing *Astraea Redux.* His coronation poem *To His Sacred Majesty* (1661) and *Annus Mirabilis* (1667) so pleased the king that Dryden was appointed poet laureate in 1668 and, two years later, royal historiographer.

Detail of oil painting by James Maubert

National Portrait Gallery, London

Charles reopened the theaters, which had been closed since 1642. Dryden's first play, *The Wild Gallant*, a farcical comedy, was produced in 1663, and he collaborated with Sir Robert Howard on *The Indian-Queen* (1665), a heroic tragedy. In 1665 Dryden's *The Indian Emperour*, a sequel to *The Indian-Queen*, was an outstanding success. In 1667 he had another remarkable hit with the tragicomedy *Secret Love, or the Maiden Queen.*

In 1668 Dryden published *Of Dramatick Poesie, an Essay*, the first substantial piece of modern dramatic criticism. He defends English drama against the champions of both ancient classical drama and the Neoclassical French theater; he also attempts to discover general principles of dramatic criticism.

Dryden's play *Tyrannick Love* appeared in June 1669. In December 1670 came the first part of *The Conquest of Granada by the Spaniards*, followed by the second part about a month later. He abandoned crowd-pleasing rant and bombast in 1672 with the staging of his brilliant comedy MARRIAGE A-LA-MODE. In November 1675, Dryden staged his last and most intelligent example of the heroic genre, *Aureng-Zebe.* Equally fine was his tragedy *All for Love* (1677), based on William Shakespeare's *Antony and Cleopatra.*

Dryden soon turned from playwriting and in the space of two years had made his name as England's greatest verse satirist.

With the publication in 1681 of ABSALOM AND ACHITO-PHEL and in 1682 of MAC FLECKNOE, Dryden not only helped change the course of history but also established himself as a brilliant poet.

In 1685, after the newly acceded king James II seemed to be moving to Catholic toleration, Dryden was received into the Roman Catholic church. In his longest poem, the beast fable *The Hind and the Panther* (1687), he argued the case for his adopted religion. The abdication of James II in 1688 destroyed Dryden's political prospects, and he lost his laureateship to his enemy Thomas Shadwell.

Dryden turned to the theater again with the tragedy *Don Sebastian* (1689). Although it failed, *Amphitryon* (1690), helped by the music of Henry Purcell, succeeded. Dryden collaborated again with Purcell in the dramatic opera *King Arthur* (1691). With the failure of the tragicomedy *Love Triumphant* in 1694, Dryden stopped writing for the stage.

In the 1680s and '90s Dryden supervised poetical miscellanies and translated the works of Juvenal and Persius. But his great late work was his translation of Virgil, published in 1697. His last publication was *Fables Ancient and Modern* (1700), mainly verse adaptations from the writings of Ovid, Geoffrey Chaucer, and Giovanni Boccaccio, introduced with a critical preface.

Dry Salvages, The   Poem by T.S. ELIOT, first published in 1941 in the *New English Weekly* and in pamphlet form. The third of the four poems in THE FOUR QUARTETS, it was written in strong-stress "native" meter and divided into five sections. "The Dry Salvages" (pronounced to rhyme with *assuages*) resumes the themes of time and history set forth in "Burnt Norton" and "East Coker."

The title of the poem refers to a formation of rocks near Cape Ann, Mass., which Eliot visited as a child. In addition to its images of the Atlantic Ocean, the work describes the continuous power of the Mississippi River, another memory from Eliot's childhood in St. Louis.

The poem is primarily concerned with experience and the human response to Christian doctrines, particularly the Incarnation. Like the other three poems, "The Dry Salvages" struggles with what it acknowledges are difficult, often contradictory concepts that can only be partially understood:

> But to apprehend
> The point of intersection of the timeless
> With time, is an occupation for the saint.

duan \ˈdü-ən, ˈt͟hü-\ [Irish and Scottish Gaelic]   A poem or song in Irish and Scottish Gaelic literature. The word was used by James Macpherson for major divisions of his Ossianic verse and hence was taken to be the Scottish Gaelic equivalent of "canto."

Duarte \ˈdwär-chē\, Fausto (Castilho) (b. 1903, Praia, Saõ Tiago, Cape Verde Islands—d. 1953, Portugal)   Government official and writer whose early work, written in Portuguese, established him as one of the earliest African novelists.

Duarte was educated under the official program of *assimilaçao* ("assimilation"), which after 1921 aimed for social and political equality for Africans in the Portuguese sphere of influence. He was then sent to Portuguese Guinea (now Guinea-Bissau) as a government administrator.

Duarte wrote about African indigenous culture. His first novel, *Auá: novela negra* (1934; "Auá: Black Novel"), is set among the Fulani peoples of Guinea. He wrote three other novels—*O Negro sem alma* (1935; "The Black Without Soul"), *Rumo ao degrêdo* (1939; "Adrift as an Exile"), and *A revolta* (1945; "The Revolution")—and a book of short stories—*Foram estes os vencidos* (1945; "To Move is to Conquer").

Dube \ˈdü-ˌbe\, John Langalibalele (b. Feb. 22, 1871, near Inanda Mission Station, Natal [now in South Africa]—d. Feb. 11, 1946, Umhlanga, Natal)   South African minister, educator, journalist, and author of *Insila ka Shaka* (1930; *Jeqe, the Bodyservant of King Shaka*), the first novel published by a Zulu in his native language.

After studying at Oberlin College, Oberlin, Ohio, U.S., and being ordained a minister, Dube returned to Natal with the goal of establishing a school for his fellow Africans similar to Alabama's Tuskegee Institute. In the early 1900s he founded Ohlange Institute, near Durban, S.Af., and several years later he founded a girls' school nearby. He became widely known from his work with the institute and on *Ilanga lase Natal* ("The Natal Sun"), the first Zulu newspaper (which he helped to found in 1904). In 1912 he was elected the first president general of the South African Native National Congress (later the African National Congress).

Political involvement occupied much of the rest of his life. He wrote a biography of the prophet Isaiah Shembe (*U-Shembe*) and *Insila ka Shaka*, a historical novel about Shaka, the great 19th-century Zulu chief.

Dubliners \ˈdəb-lin-ərz\   Short-story collection by James JOYCE, written in 1904–07, published in 1914. Joyce used three stories published under the pseudonym Stephen Dedalus as the basis for *Dubliners*.

Dubliners has a well-defined structure along with interweaving, recurring symbols. The first three stories, narrated in the first person, portray children; the next four deal with young adults, and, like the remaining stories, are told by a third person, whose tone and sensibility shifts to reflect that of the changing protagonists; the following four stories concern mature life from middle age onward; and the next three, the public life of politics, art, and religion. The fifteenth and final story, THE DEAD, is considered not only the jewel of the collection but also a world masterpiece.

Du Bois \dü-ˈbȯis, dyü-\, W.E.B., *in full* William Edward Burghardt (b. Feb. 23, 1868, Great Barrington, Mass., U.S.—d. Aug. 27, 1963, Accra, Ghana)   American sociologist, the most important black protest leader in the United States during the first half of the 20th century. He helped create the National Association for the Advancement of Colored People (NAACP) in 1909 and edited *The Crisis*, its magazine, from 1910 to 1934.

Du Bois graduated from Fisk University, Nashville, Tenn., and received a doctorate from Harvard University. For more than a decade he devoted himself to sociological investigations of the condition of blacks in America, producing 16 research monographs published between 1897 and 1914 at Atlanta University, where he was a professor, as well as *The Philadelphia Negro; A Social Study* (1899), the first case study of a black community in the United States.

Du Bois's black nationalism took several forms, including a belief in the importance of cultural nationalism. As the editor of *The Crisis* he encouraged the development of black literature and art and urged his readers to see "Beauty in Black."

He resigned from the editorship and from the NAACP in 1934 because of ideological differences within the organization and returned to Atlanta University to teach and write. In 1940 he founded the magazine *Phylon*, the university's "Review of Race and Culture." During this period he also produced two major books: *Black Reconstruction* (1935), a Marxist interpretation of the post-Civil War era, and *Dusk at Dawn* (1940), in which he viewed his career as an ideological case study illuminating the complexity of black-white conflict.

From 1944 to 1948 Du Bois returned to the NAACP, but following a second bitter quarrel he severed his connection and thereafter moved steadily leftward politically. In 1961 he joined the Communist Party and, moving to Ghana, renounced his American citizenship more than a year later. *The Autobiography of W.E.B. Du Bois* was published in 1968.

du Bois \dü-'bwä, düE-\, William Pène (Sherman) (b. May 9, 1916, Nutley, N.J., U.S.—d. Feb. 5, 1993, Nice, Fr.) American author and illustrator of children's books noted for his comic coterie of peculiar characters. In 1948 he was awarded the Newbery Medal for *The Twenty-One Balloons* (1947).

Born into a family of artists, du Bois studied art in France and published books for children from the mid-1930s. He served in World War II as a correspondent for *Yank* and other magazines and became the first art director of *The Paris Review* in 1953. *The Twenty-One Balloons* is about a retired math teacher who refuses to tell anyone but the Western American Explorer's Club about his fantastic journey by hot-air balloon to the volcano of Krakatoa.

In his uncompleted series about the seven deadly sins, du Bois profiled sloth in *Lazy Tommy Pumpkinhead* (1966), pride in *Pretty Pretty Peggy Moffitt* (1968), gluttony in *Porko von Popbutton* (1969), and avarice in *Call Me Bandicoot* (1970). *The Alligator Case* (1965) and *The Horse in the Camel Suit* (1967) parody the detective novels of Raymond Chandler. Several of du Bois's books feature bears, such as *Bear Party* (1951), *Bear Circus* (1971), and the semiautobiographical *Gentleman Bear* (1983). His other works included *The Flying Locomotive* (1941), *Peter Graves* (1950), *Lion* (1956), and *The Forbidden Forest* (1978). He also illustrated editions of books by such notable authors as Edward Lear, Jules Verne, Arthur Conan Doyle, Isaac Bashevis Singer, Roald Dahl, and Mark Strand.

DuBois, Blanche \'blanch-dü-'bwä\ Character in A STREETCAR NAMED DESIRE, a Pulitzer Prize-winning drama by Tennessee Williams.

An alcoholic nymphomaniac posing as the epitome of genteel Southern womanhood, Blanche has, from her first appearance, a fragile hold on reality. When her brutish brother-in-law Stanley Kowalski rapes her, she loses her last vestiges of sanity. Trying to maintain her affected refinement to the end, she says to a doctor, "I have always depended on the kindness of strangers."

Du Bos \düE-'bōs, -'bō\, Charles (b. Oct. 27, 1882, Paris, Fr.—d. Aug. 5, 1939, La Celle-Saint-Cloud) French critic of French, English, and German literature whose writings on William Shakespeare, Percy Bysshe Shelley, and Lord Byron helped turn French attention toward English authors.

Because his mother was English, Du Bos was exposed to English literature at an early age. He studied at the University of Oxford for a year (1900–01) and also in Germany. Among his works are studies of J.W. von Goethe and of the French authors Gustave Flaubert, Prosper Mérimée, and François Mauriac. His correspondence with his friend André Gide was published as *Le Dialogue avec André Gide* (1929; 2nd edition, retitled, 1950). His chief interest was in what he called the "soul" of a work and its effects in the "soul" of a reader. As he became older, this concern became increasingly religious, and his *Journal intime*, 6 vol. (1946–55), written partly in English, is an account of the spiritual evolution that brought him into the Roman Catholic church in 1927.

Dubus \də-'byüs\, Andre (b. Aug. 11, 1936, Lake Charles, La., U.S.) American short-story writer and novelist who was noted as a chronicler of the struggles of contemporary American men whose lives seem inexplicably to have gone wrong.

After graduating from McNeese State College (now University), Lake Charles, La., Dubus served six years in the Marine Corps and then took an M.F.A. degree from the University of Iowa. He taught literature and creative writing at Bradford (Mass.) College from 1966 to 1984. Dubus wrote of the emotional complexities of ordinary people in ordinary settings, who find that the traditional American virtues they assumed would lead to happiness do not do so. Most of his characters suffer compulsions or addictions focused on cigarettes, alcohol, food, coffee, drugs, or even weight lifting. When these fail to provide enough distraction, the male characters often turn to violence.

Dubus' first collection of stories, *Separate Flights* (1975), was praised for its craft, strong sympathy with its characters, and detailed evocation of setting, as was *Adultery and Other Choices* (1977). "Andromache," from the latter collection, was cited as the best of his many stories about the Marine Corps. "The Fat Girl" and "Graduation" (from *Adultery and Other Choices*) and the 1984 novella *Voices from the Moon* are cited as his best attempts to develop the point of view of his female characters. He also wrote *The Times Are Never So Bad* (1983) and *We Don't Live Here Anymore* (1984).

Du Camp \düE-'kän\, Maxime (b. Feb. 8, 1822, Paris, Fr.—d. Feb. 9, 1894, Baden-Baden, Ger.) French writer and photographer who is chiefly known for his vivid accounts of 19th-century French life.

Du Camp pioneered in photography and published works in virtually every literary genre. He traveled widely with his friend, the novelist Gustave Flaubert (1844–45 and 1849–51), and his *Égypte, Nubie, Palestine et Syrie* (1852), written after one of their journeys, is among the first books illustrated with photographs. During the revolutionary year 1848 he was wounded and then decorated for counterrevolutionary activity in France. His *Expédition des deux-Siciles* (1861; "Expedition to the Two Sicilies") recounts his experiences as a volunteer with the Italian revolutionary Giuseppe Garibaldi.

In 1851 Du Camp founded the *Revue de Paris* and in it published Flaubert's great novel, *Madame Bovary*; disputes arising from the publication of the novel ended their friendship. He also wrote poems (*Les Chants modernes*, 1855; "Modern Songs"), art criticism, novels, a monograph on his friend, the writer Théophile Gautier, and *Souvenirs littéraires*, 2 vol. (1882–83; "Literary Recollections"), which included previously unrevealed information about Flaubert and his struggles with epilepsy.

Duchess, the Fictional character in ALICE'S ADVENTURES IN WONDERLAND by Lewis Carroll.

An ugly old woman who is a member of Wonderland royalty, the Duchess appears twice in the story. In the first instance, she is dealing with a baby who cries and frequently sneezes (because of the Cook's heavy use of pepper, which fills the air). The Duchess shakes the baby violently while attempting to placate it with loud lullabies, notably

> "Speak roughly to your little boy
> And beat him when he sneezes:
> He only does it to annoy
> Because he knows it teases."

When the baby is put into Alice's arms, it turns into a pig, and the pig runs away.

The Duchess reappears at the Red Queen's croquet game, where the mallets are live flamingos and the balls are live hedgehogs.

Duchess of Malfi, The \'mal-fè\ Five-act tragedy by English dramatist John WEBSTER, performed 1613/14 and published in 1623.

Written after William Shakespeare had completed his final play, *The Duchess of Malfi* is regarded as the last great Elizabethan tragedy. There is no evidence that Webster had read or seen the play that Spanish dramatist Lope de Vega wrote about the duchess. Webster's play tells of the spirited duchess and her love for her trustworthy steward Antonio. They marry secretly, despite the opposition of her two brothers, Ferdinand (the Duke of Calabria) and the Cardinal. Although she bears three children, she refuses to name the father. Eventually betrayed by Bosola, a spy, the duchess and her family flee but are intercepted; Antonio and the oldest child, a boy, escape. Ferdinand orders Bosola to strangle the duchess, her two younger children, and her maid, then goes mad with guilt. In typical fashion for revenge tragedy, the final act is one of carnage. All are killed except for the eldest son of the duchess and Antonio, who is named ruler of Malfi.

Webster used dense symbolic imagery in this moving romantic tragedy. The duchess, by far the strongest character in the play, is a passionate, noble woman who rejects her brothers' demands for the sake of love. Unbroken by cruel treatment she proclaims before her death, "I am the duchess of Malfi still."

Ducis \dɪ̄-'sēs, -'sē\, Jean-François (b. Aug. 22, 1733, Versailles, Fr.—d. March 31, 1816, Versailles)   French dramatist who made the first sustained effort to present William Shakespeare's tragedies on the French stage. Although he remodeled the tragedies to the French taste for witty, epigrammatic style and attempted to confine the plays within the "classical unities" (of time, place, and action), such critics as Voltaire still disliked Shakespeare's "barbarous histrionics." Ducis achieved great success with his principal adaptations—including *Hamlet* (1769), *Roméo et Juliette* (1772), *Le Roi Lear* (1783), *Macbeth* (1784), and *Othello* (1792).

Ducis came from a bourgeois family, rising through his position as the secretary of several powerful figures of the court. He knew no English and thus was hampered from the start by having to work with the mediocre translations of Pierre-Antoine de La Place (1707–93) and Pierre Le Tourneur (1736–88). Aware of his uncomfortable position between an audience with specific tastes and a body of brilliant but largely unfamiliar works in an alien style, he attempted to compromise the plays, buying exposure for them by revising the texts and, in some cases, even by changing the catastrophes.

Of Ducis' original tragedies, *Oedipe chez Admète* (1778; "Oedipus at the Home of Admetus") and *Abufar* (1795) are considered his best; the first earned him election to the Académie Française, in succession, ironically, to Voltaire. His complete works, including his beautifully written letters, were edited and published by his friend François-Vincent Campenon (1818 and 1826).

Dudek \'dyū-dek\, Louis (b. Feb. 6, 1918, Montreal, Que., Can.)   Canadian poet noted for his support of Canadian small-press publishing and the development of the nonnarrative long poem.

Educated at McGill University (where he later taught) and Columbia University, Dudek was an editor and critic. His poetic output included *East of the City* (1946), *The Transparent Sea* (1956), love poems, and *Laughing Stalks* (1958), a social satire that includes parodies of certain Canadian poets and critics. His *Collected Poems* appeared in 1971. The influence of Ezra Pound is evident in *Europe* (1954), a travelogue poem in 99 cantos inspired by observations of several countries on the European continent, and in other works. Another collection, *Cross-Section* (1980), contains poems written between 1940 and 1980. Dudek's prose works include *The Theory of the Image in Modern Poetry* (1981), *Ideas for Poetry* (1983), and *In Defence of Art* (1988; a collection of critical essays and reviews). Later collections of poetry include *Zembla's Rocks* (1986) and *Small Perfect Things* (1991).

Dudek also cofounded Contact Press, Delta Canada, and D.C. Books (all small presses), *Delta* literary magazine, and the McGill Poetry Series.

Du Fu or **Tu Fu** \'dū-'fū\ (b. 712, China—d. 770, Hunan) Chinese poet, considered by many to be the greatest of all time.

Du Fu received a traditional Confucian education but failed in the imperial examinations of 736. As a result, he spent much of his youth traveling, during which he won renown as a poet and met the other poets of the period, including the great Li Bo. During the 740s Du Fu was a well-regarded member of a group of high officials, even though he was without money and official position himself and failed a second time in an imperial examination. Between 751 and 755 he tried to attract imperial attention by submitting a succession of literary products in which political advice was offered, couched in a language of ornamental flattery, a device that eventually resulted in a nominal position at court. He married, probably in 752, and acquired some farmland; but by then he showed signs of a lung ailment. In 755, during the An Lushan Rebellion, he experienced extreme personal hardships. He escaped, however, and in 757 joined the exiled court, being given the position of censor. He was eventually relieved of his post and underwent another period of poverty and hunger. Wandering about until the mid-760s, he served a local warlord, a position that enabled him to acquire some landed property and to become a gentleman farmer, but in 768 he again started traveling aimlessly toward the south. Popular legend attributes his death to overindulgence in food and wine after a 10-day fast.

Du Fu's early poetry celebrated the beauties of the natural world and bemoaned the passage of time. He soon began to write bitingly of war, as in "Bingqu xing" ("Ballad of the Army Carts"), a poem about conscription, and with hidden satire, as in "Liren xing" ("The Beautiful Woman"), which speaks of the conspicuous luxury of the court. As he matured, and especially during the years of extreme personal and national turmoil of 755 to 759, his verse began to sound a note of profound compassion for humanity caught in the grip of senseless war.

Du Fu's paramount position in the history of Chinese literature rests, finally, on his superb classicism. He was highly erudite, and his intimate acquaintance with the literary tradition of the past was equaled only by his complete ease in handling the rules of prosody. His dense, compressed language makes use of all the connotative overtones of a phrase and of all the intonational potentials of the individual word, qualities that no translation can ever reveal. He was an expert in all poetic genres current in his day, but his mastery was at its height in the *lüshi*, or "regulated verse," which he refined to a point of glowing intensity.

Dugan \'dū-gən\, Alan (b. Feb. 12, 1923, New York, N.Y., U.S.)   American poet who wrote with bemused sarcasm about mundane topics, infusing them with an ironic depth. A fully developed style was evident in his first verse collection, *Poems* (1961), which in 1962 won a National Book Award and a Pulitzer Prize.

Dugan served in World War II and attended Queens College in New York and Olivet College in Michigan before graduating from Mexico City College. Propelled by the success of *Poems*, he accepted grants to travel and to continue publishing. He taught at Sarah Lawrence College in Bronxville, N.Y., from 1967 until 1971, when he joined the faculty at the Fine Arts Work Center in Provincetown, Mass. Among his later books were *Poems 2* (1963), *Poems 3* (1967), *Poems 4* (1974), *Sequence* (1976), and *Poems Six* (1989).

Dugan examined the triviality of war, the bleakness of ordinary life, the ignorance of humanity, and the nature of beauty and love. As a result of his terse cadences, ironic detachment, and colloquial style, his works have an understated humor. His poetry was compiled in *Collected Poems* (1969), *New and Collected Poems 1961–1983* (1983), and *Ten Years of Poems* (1987).

Duhamel \dᴦ-à-'mel\, Georges (b. June 30, 1884, Paris, Fr.—d. April 13, 1966, Valmondois, near Paris)   French author most noted for two novel cycles: *Vie et aventures de Salavin*, 5 vol. (1920–32), and *Chronique des Pasquier*, 10 vol. (1933–44).

Duhamel began by writing poetry, plays, and literary criticism, and in 1906 he joined with several other writers and artists in founding a short-lived community at Créteil-sur-Marne, known as the Abbaye. He took a science degree in 1908 and qualified as a doctor of medicine in 1909, later serving as a front-line surgeon during World War I. Deeply affected by the sufferings and futility of war, he recorded his wartime experiences in two short-story collections, *Vie des martyrs* (1917; *The New Book of Martyrs*) and *Civilisation 1914–1917* (1918); the latter book was awarded the Goncourt Prize.

From 1920 Duhamel wrote novels and a great variety of essays and miscellaneous works on social and moral issues. His writings include a five-volume autobiography, *Lumières sur ma vie* ("Lights on My Life"). His two novel cycles also contain many reflections of his own experiences. Duhamel became a member of the Académie Française in 1935.

Duino Elegies \'dwē-nō\   Series of 10 poems by Rainer Maria RILKE, published in German as *Duineser Elegien* in 1923.

Acknowledged as Rilke's finest achievement (with the possible exception of his *Sonnets to Orpheus*) and one of the century's poetic masterpieces, the *Duino Elegies* is praised for its supple language, its experimentation with meter and rhyme, and its profound meditation on human existence. Scholars note that the poems are more elegiac in mood than in form.

The cycle was conceived as a whole, although the poems were composed over a period of 10 years. Rilke wrote the first two elegies, and began the third, while visiting the castle of Duino on the Adriatic in 1912; he finished the third in Paris in 1913 and completed the fourth and began the fifth in Munich in 1915. Emotionally paralyzed by World War I and its aftermath, Rilke wrote little more until February 1922, when in a burst of nearly manic productivity he revised the fifth poem, completed the remaining five of the cycle, and wrote the 55 poems that comprise the *Sonnets to Orpheus*, all in a span of three weeks.

Dujardin \dᴦ-zhár-'daⁿ\, Édouard(-Émile-Louis) (b. Nov. 10, 1861, Saint-Gervais-la-Forêt, Fr.—d. Oct. 31, 1949, Paris)   French writer and journalist who is best known for his novel *Les Lauriers sont coupés* (1888; "The Laurels Are Cut Down"; *We'll to the Woods No More*), which was the first work to employ the interior monologue from which James Joyce derived the stream-of-consciousness technique he used in *Ulysses*.

Dujardin was associated with the Symbolist movement from its beginning and published Symbolist verse and drama. He also founded several literary reviews, wrote criticism, and was noted as a lecturer and writer on primitive Judaism and Christianity.

Duke and the Dauphin, The *also called* the King and the Duke.   Fictional characters, a comic pair of swindlers who pretend to be long-lost royalty in HUCKLEBERRY FINN by Mark Twain. The two charlatans present themselves to Huck Finn and the runaway slave Jim as the 30-year-old Duke of Bridgewater and the 70-year-old King of France. They make their living by swindling gullible townspeople by various schemes.

Duke of Omnium \'äm-nē-əm\   Fictional character in the PALLISER NOVELS by Anthony Trollope. The Duke, who was born Plantagenet Palliser, figures most prominently in *Can You Forgive Her?*, the first book of the series. A stuffy yet decent-minded man, he is politically ambitious and neglectful of his beautiful and spirited young wife, Lady Glencora. He matures emotionally as a result of their troubled marriage and eventual reconciliation; in Trollope's subsequent Palliser novels, the Duke and his wife are important figures in the world of Parliament and its political and social intrigues.

Duke's Children, The Novel by Anthony TROLLOPE, published serially in 1879–80 and in book form in 1880; it is the final volume of the PALLISER NOVELS.

Plantagenet Palliser, Duke of Omnium and former prime minister of England, is now a widower. He is concerned that his three children—Lord Silverbridge, Lord Gerald, and Lady Mary—will not uphold the values of their ancient lineage. Though their politics, sense of their place in society, and choice of marital partners all cause him considerable anxiety, the novel ends on an optimistic note.

Dulcibella \,dəl-si-'bel-ə\, *also called* Dowsabel \'daùs-ə-,bel\   In English poetry, generic name for an idealized sweetheart, based on the Latin word *dulcis* ("sweet"). Dulcibella, like Dulcinea, represents beauty, inspiration, and virtuous love. The name was used in medieval literature and it appeared with some frequency in the 16th century, but it was obsolete by the 18th century.

Dulcinea \,dül-thē-'nä-ä\, *in full* Dulcinea del Toboso \thel-tō-'bō-sō\   Fictional character in the picaresque novel DON QUIXOTE by Miguel de Cervantes. Aldonza Lorenzo, a sturdy Spanish peasant girl, is renamed Dulcinea by the crazed knight-errant Don Quixote when he selects her to be his ladylove. In Don Quixote's mind, Dulcinea is a golden-haired, highborn young woman of incomparable loveliness for whom he will perform brave deeds as her paladin.

The name Dulcinea, like Dulcibella, came to be used generically for mistress or sweetheart.

Dumas \dᴦ-'mä, *Angl* dü-'mä, dyü-; 'dü-,mä, 'dyü-\, Alexandre, *known as* Dumas *fils* ("son") (b. July 27, 1824, Paris, Fr.—d. Nov. 27, 1895, Marly-le-Roi)   French playwright and novelist, one of the founders of the "problem play"—that is, of the middle-class realistic drama treating some contemporary ill and offering suggestions for its remedy.

Dumas *fils*, the illegitimate son of Alexandre Dumas *père*, possessed a good measure of his father's literary fecundity, but the work of the two men could scarcely be more different. The first success of the younger Dumas was a novel, *La Dame aux camélias* (1848; *The Lady of the Camillias*), but he found his vocation when he adapted the story into a play, known in English as *Camille*, first performed in 1852. (Giuseppe Verdi based his opera *La traviata*, first performed in 1853, on this play.) Although his father had written colorful historical plays and novels, Dumas *fils* specialized in drama set in the present. The unhappy witness of the ruin brought on his father by illicit love affairs, Dumas *fils* devoted his plays to sermons on the sanctity of the family and of marriage; *Le Demi-Monde* (performed 1855), for example, dealt with the threat to the institution of marriage posed by prostitutes. He was admitted to the Académie Française in 1875.

His other plays include *Le Fils naturel* (1858; "The Natural Son") and *Un Père prodigue* (1859; "A Prodigal Father"), a dramatization of Dumas's interpretation of his father's character.

Dumas \dᴦ-'mä, *Angl* dü-'mä, dyü-; 'dü-,mä, 'dyü-\, Alexandre, *known as* Dumas *père* (b. July 24, 1802, Villers-Cotterêts, Aisne, Fr.—d. Dec. 5, 1870, Puys, near Dieppe)   One of the most prolific and most popular French authors of the 19th century. Without ever attaining indisputable literary merit, Dumas succeeded in gaining a great reputation first as a dramatist and then as a historical novelist. He was the father of the dramatist and novelist Alexandre Dumas, called Dumas *fils*.

Dumas's father assumed the name Dumas in 1786 and later became a general in Napoleon's army. The family fell on hard times, however, especially after General Dumas's death in 1806; and the young Alexandre went to Paris to attempt to make a living as a lawyer. He obtained a post in the household of the Duke d'Orléans (the future King Louis-Philippe) but tried his fortune in the theater.

Dumas's plays, when judged from a modern viewpoint, are crude, brash, and melodramatic, but they were received with rapture in his lifetime. *Henri III et sa cour* (1829) portrayed the French Renaissance in garish colors; *Napoléon Bonaparte* (1831) played its part in making a legend of the recently dead emperor; and *Antony* (1831) enacted a contemporary drama of adultery and honor.

Though he continued to write plays, Dumas later turned his attention to the historical novel, often working with collaborators (especially Auguste Maquet).

The best known of Dumas's works are *Les Trois Mousquetaires* (1844; THE THREE MUSKETEERS), a romance about four swashbuckling heroes in the age of Cardinal Richelieu; *Vingt Ans après* (1845; "Twenty Years After"); *Le Comte de Monte-Cristo* (1844–45; THE COUNT OF MONTE CRISTO); *Dix Ans plus tard ou le Vicomte de Bragelonne* (1848–50; "Ten Years Later; or, The Vicomte de Bragelonne"); and *La Tulipe noire* (1850; "The Black Tulip"). His memoirs, written with a mixture of candor, mendacity, and boastfulness, recount the events of his extraordinary life and also provide a unique insight into French literary life during the Romantic period.

Dumas \dü-'mä\, Henry (b. July 20, 1934, Sweet Home, Ark., U.S.—d. May 23, 1968, New York, N.Y.) African-American author of poetry and fiction who wrote about the clash between black and white cultures.

Dumas grew up in Arkansas and in New York City's Harlem. While in the U.S. Air Force (1953–57) he won creative-writing awards for his contributions to Air Force periodicals. Religion (especially Christianity), African-American folklore and music, and the civil-rights movement, in which he was active, were important influences on his writing.

The vulnerability of black children amid the Southern white lynch-mob mentality, a young sharecropper encountering a civil-rights worker, and whites experiencing the mystical force of black music are among the subjects Dumas examined in his short stories, many of which were collected in *Ark of Bones* (1970) and *Rope of Wind* (1979). Nature, revolutionary politics, and music are especially frequent subjects of his poetry, which is noted for its faithfulness to the language and cadence of black American speech. *Poetry for My People* (1970; republished as *Play Ebony, Play Ivory*, 1974) is a collection of blues-influenced verse. Dumas, who was murdered, left an unfinished novel, *Jonoah and the Green Stone*, which was published in 1976.

du Maurier \dü-'mȯr-ē-,ā, dyü-\, Dame Daphne, *married name* Lady Daphne Browning \'braú-niŋ\ (b. May 13, 1907, London, Eng.—d. April 19, 1989, Par, Cornwall) English novelist and playwright, daughter of actor-manager Sir Gerald du Maurier and granddaughter of caricaturist George du Maurier, best known for her novel REBECCA (1938; film, 1940).

Du Maurier's first novel, *The Loving Spirit* (1931), was followed by many successful, usually romantic tales set on the wild coast of Cornwall, where she came to live. She also wrote

historical fiction, several plays, and *Vanishing Cornwall* (1967), a travel guide. Du Maurier was made a Dame Commander in the Order of the British Empire in 1969. She published an autobiography, *Growing Pains*, in 1977; the collection *The Rendezvous and Other Stories* in 1980; and a literary reminiscence, *The Rebecca Notebook and Other Memories*, in 1981.

du Maurier \dü-'mȯr-ē-,ā, dyü-\, George (Louis Palmella Busson) (b. March 6, 1834, Paris, Fr.—d. Oct. 6, 1896, London, Eng.) British caricaturist whose illustrations for *Punch* were acute commentaries on the Victorian scene. He also wrote three successful novels.

Du Maurier's happy childhood at Passy, Fr., is recalled in *Peter Ibbetson* (1891), and his full-blooded enjoyment of student life in the Latin Quarter of Paris is reflected in TRILBY (1894). In *The Martian* (1897), there is a poignant episode based on his own experience of the loss of sight in one eye. The misfortune obliged him to abandon painting in favor of drawing. In 1860 he moved to London, where his skilled draftsmanship and engaging personality quickly established his success. His gently satiric caricatures were mainly aimed at the growing nouveau riche class and at the Aesthetes, led by Oscar Wilde. His book illustrations and drawings for such periodicals as *Once a Week* and *The Leisure Hour*, however, are sometimes considered his best work. His granddaughter, Daphne du Maurier, edited *The Young George du Maurier: A Selection of His Letters, 1860–1867* in 1951.

Dumb Waiter, The Drama in one act by Harold PINTER, produced in 1959 and published in 1960. It projected the uneasy feeling of comic menace that was prevalent in Pinter's early plays.

The Dumb Waiter is a two-character play set in the basement of an old rooming house, connected to the rooms above by a dumbwaiter and an intercom. Ben and Gus make small talk and wait. It becomes obvious that they are hired killers who are waiting for their victim, whose identity they have not yet been told. The dumbwaiter goes up and down, bearing notes ordering food that the two men cannot possibly provide. Ben and Gus rehearse the murder they are about to commit. Gus leaves the room. Answering a call on the intercom, Ben is ordered to shoot the first person who comes in the room. He calls for Gus: they have their orders. Ben points his gun at the door, ready to shoot, as Gus enters the room. The two men stare at each other in terror.

Dunash ben Labrat \dü-'näsh-ben-lə-'brät\, Labrat *also spelled* Librat, *also called* al-Abrad \ȧl-'ȧb-rȧd\ *or* Adonina ha-Levi \,ȧ-dō-'nē-nə-hä-'lä-vē\ (b. *c.* 920—d. *c.* 990, Córdoba?) Hebrew poet, grammarian, and polemicist who was the first to use Arabic meters in his verse, thus inaugurating a new mode in Hebrew poetry.

Dunash was born in either Fès (now in Morocco) or Baghdad (now in Iraq) and after traveling to Sura, Babylonia, studied there under a renowned master of Jewish learning, Saʿadia ben Joseph. There he first composed his poems in Arabic meters, an innovation that amazed Saʿadia.

After a time Dunash migrated to Córdoba in Moorish Spain, then experiencing a renaissance of Jewish culture under a powerful Jewish statesman and adviser to the caliph, Ḥisdai ibn Shaprut (*c.* 915–975?). While in Córdoba, Dunash became involved in philological matters. His criticism of Menahem ben Saruq, the author of the first Hebrew dictionary, resulted in a fresh examination of Hebrew grammar.

Dunbar \'dən-,bär\, Paul Laurence (b. June 27, 1872, Dayton, Ohio, U.S.—d. Feb. 9, 1906, Dayton) American author whose reputation rests upon his verse and short stories written in black dialect. He was the first black writer in the United

States to attempt to support himself by writing and one of the first to attain national prominence.

Both of Dunbar's parents were former slaves; his father escaped to Canada and then returned to the U.S. to fight in the Civil War. Dunbar published his first volume of poetry, *Oak and Ivy* (1893), at his own expense while working as an elevator operator and sold copies to his passengers to pay for the printing. His second volume, *Majors and Minors* (1895), attracted the favorable notice of the novelist and critic William Dean Howells, who also introduced Dunbar's next book, *Lyrics of Lowly Life* (1896), which contained some of the finest verses of the first two volumes.

Dunbar's poems gained a large popular audience, and he read to audiences in the United States and England. He was given a job in the reading room of the Library of Congress in Washington, D.C. (1897–98). In all, he published four collections of short stories and four novels before his early death.

Writing for a largely white readership, Dunbar depicted the pre-Civil War South in pastoral, idyllic tones. Only in a few of his later stories did a suggestion of racial disquiet appear. His first three novels—including *The Uncalled* (1898), which reflected his own spiritual problems—were about white characters. His last novel, sometimes considered his best, was *The Sport of the Gods* (1902), concerning an uprooted black family in the urban North.

Dunbar \'dən-ˌbär\, William (b. 1460/65, Scotland—d. before 1530) Middle Scots poet attached to the court of James IV who was the dominant makar, or Scottish Chaucerian, in the golden age of Scottish poetry.

Dunbar was probably of the family of the earls of Dunbar and March and may have received an M.A. degree from St. Andrews in 1479. It is believed that he was a Franciscan novice and traveled to England and France in the king's service. In 1501 he was certainly in England, probably in connection with the arrangements for the marriage of James IV and Margaret Tudor, which took place in 1503. In 1500 he was granted a pension of £10 by the king. By 1504 he was in priest's orders, and in 1510 he received, as a mark of royal esteem, a pension of £80. After the king's death at the Battle of Flodden (1513), Dunbar evidently received the benefice for which he had so often asked in verse, as there is no record of his pension after 1513.

With few exceptions the more than 100 poems attributed to Dunbar are short and occasional pieces inspired by personal moods or events at court. They range from gross satire to hymns of religious exaltation. Of his longer works, some, such as the charming dream allegory *The Goldyn Targe*, are courtly Chaucerian pieces. *The Thrissill and the Rois* is a nuptial song celebrating the marriage of James IV and Margaret Tudor.

In a quite different vein, the alliterative *The Flyting of Dunbar and Kennedie* is a virtuoso demonstration of personal abuse directed against his professional rival Walter Kennedy. Dunbar's most celebrated and shocking satire is the alliterative *Tretis of the Tua Mariit Wemen and the Wedo* ("Treatise of the Two Married Women and the Widow").

Dunbar was at ease in hymn and satire, morality and obscene comedy, panegyric and begging complaint, elegy and lampoon. His poetic vocabulary ranged through several levels, and he moved freely from one to another for satiric effect. He wrote with uncommon frankness and wit, manipulating old themes and forms with imagination and originality.

Dunbar Nelson \'dən-ˌbär-'nel-sən\, Alice, *original name in full* Alice Ruth Moore \'môr\ (b. July 19, 1875, New Orleans, La., U.S.—d. Sept. 18, 1935, Philadelphia, Pa.) Novelist, poet, essayist, and critic associated with the early period of the Harlem Renaissance of the 1920s and '30s.

The daughter of a Creole seaman and a black seamstress, Moore completed a two-year teacher-training program at Straight University by age 17. She further studied at Cornell University, the Pennsylvania School of Industrial Art, and the University of Pennsylvania. She taught at the elementary, secondary, and college levels until 1931.

Her first collection of stories, poems, and essays, *Violets, and Other Tales*, was published in 1895. She later moved to New York, where she taught and helped establish the White Rose Mission in Harlem. In 1898 she married the writer Paul Laurence Dunbar.

Her short-story collection *The Goodness of St. Rocque, and Other Stories* was published as a companion piece to her husband's *Poems of Cabin and Field* in 1899. She moved to Delaware after she and Dunbar separated in 1902; he died four years later. She married a fellow teacher in 1910 and divorced him the following year; in 1916 she married the journalist Robert J. Nelson.

While not considered a major figure in the Harlem Renaissance for her own literary contributions, Dunbar Nelson influenced the work of other black writers not only by her own precise, incisive literary style but also through her numerous reviews of such writers as Langston Hughes.

Duncan \'dəŋk-ən\ Fictional character, the Scottish king who is murdered by Macbeth in William Shakespeare's MACBETH.

Duncan \'dəŋ-kən\, Robert Edward, *original name* Edward Howard Duncan, *adopted name* Robert Edward Symmes (b. Jan. 7, 1919, Oakland, Calif., U.S.—d. Feb. 3, 1988, San Francisco, Calif.) American poet, a leader of the Black Mountain group of poets in the 1950s.

Duncan attended the University of California at Berkeley in 1936–38 and 1948–50. He edited the *Experimental Review* from 1938 to 1940 and traveled widely thereafter, lecturing on poetry in the United States and Canada throughout the 1950s. He taught at Black Mountain College in North Carolina in 1956. He was a longtime resident of San Francisco and was active in that city's poetry community.

Duncan's poetry is evocative and highly musical and uses a rich fabric of associations and mythic images whose meanings are sometimes obscure. His thematic concerns include strong social and political statements. His collections include *The Years as Catches: First Poems, 1939–1946* (1966) and *Derivations: Selected Poems, 1950–56* (1968). *The Opening of the Field* (1960), *Roots and Branches* (1964), *Bending the Bow* (1968), and *Ground Work* (1984) contain his finest poems. He also wrote plays, including *Medea at Kolchis* (1965).

Duncan \'dəŋ-kən\, Ronald (Frederick Henry) (b. Aug. 6, 1914, Salisbury, Rhodesia [now Harare, Zimb.]—d. June 3, 1982, Barnstaple, Devon, Eng.) British playwright, poet, and man of letters whose verse plays express the contrast between traditional religious faith and the materialism and skepticism of modern times.

From an early interest in socialism, Duncan moved to the expression of Christian and Buddhist convictions in his literary work. His plays include *This Way to the Tomb* (1945), *Stratton* (1949), *Our Lady's Tumbler* (1951), *Don Juan* (1953), *The Death of Satan* (1954), and *The Catalyst* (1958). His *Collected Plays* appeared in 1971. Duncan also wrote television plays, verse, short stories, novels, and many works of nonfiction, including three volumes of autobiography (*All Men Are Islands*, 1964; *How to Make Enemies*, 1968; and *Obsessed*, 1975), *The Encyclopaedia of Ignorance*, 2 vol. (1977), and *A Memoir of Benjamin Britten* (1981). He wrote the libretto for Benjamin Britten's opera *The Rape of Lucretia* (1946), and he was a founder in 1955 of the English Stage Company. He served as poetry editor of *The Townsman*, a literary magazine he founded, from 1938 to 1946.

Dunciad, The \'dən-sē-,ad\   Poem by Alexander POPE, published anonymously in three books in 1728. Written largely in iambic pentameters, it is a masterpiece of mock-heroic verse.

After Pope had edited the works of William Shakespeare to adapt them to 18th-century tastes, the scholar Lewis Theobald attacked him in *Shakespeare Restored* (1726). Pope responded by writing the first of four books of his *Dunciad*, in which Theobald appears as Tibbald, favorite son of the Goddess of Dullness (Dulness), a suitable hero for what Pope considered the reign of pedantry. The work is much more than the vengeance of an aggrieved crank, however, for Pope writes with much facility, wit, and verve. The poem was reissued in 1729 as *The Dunciad Variorum*; the reissue included elaborate false footnotes, appendices, errata, and prefaces, as if the *Dunciad* itself had fallen into the hands of an artless pedant. Both versions were published anonymously, and Pope did not own up to the work until 1735. By then he had a new victim: the poet laureate Colley Cibber, who was recast as the dubious hero of the first three books and an added fourth, which appeared as *The New Dunciad* in 1742. The final version, *The Dunciad in Four Books*, was released in 1743.

Dunn \'dən\, Douglas (Eaglesham) (b. Oct. 23, 1942, Inchinnan, Renfrewshire, Scot.)   Scottish writer and critic, best known for his poems evoking working-class British life.

Dunn left school at 17 to become a junior library assistant. He worked at libraries in Britain and the United States before completing his higher education at the University of Hull, England. He worked as an assistant librarian at the university before leaving in 1971 to pursue his writing.

Dunn's first book of poetry, *Terry Street* (1969), was widely hailed for its evocation of working-class Hull. Critics praised Dunn's dry humor and his ability to capture the sordid with precision, free of sentimentality. *Backwaters* and *Night* (both 1971), *The Happier Life* (1972), and *Love or Nothing* (1974) were not as well received. *Barbarians* (1979) was a highly political volume, attacking the sovereignty of the propertied class and Oxbridge intellectuals while arguing for the robustness of "barbarian" working-class culture. Although most critics generally admired the work, they had greater praise for *St. Kilda's Parliament* (1981), noting Dunn's mastery of blank verse and his treatment of Scottish themes. *Europa's Lover* (1982) was a long poem celebrating the best of European values.

Dunn's *Elegies* (1985) contains moving, unflinching poems on the death of his first wife in 1981. *Northlight* (1988) marked Dunn's return to social subjects. In addition to several television and radio plays, Dunn also published a collection of short stories, *Secret Villages* (1985), and edited a number of poetry anthologies.

Dunne \'dən\, Finley Peter (b. July 10, 1867, Chicago, Ill., U.S.—d. April 24, 1936, New York, N.Y.)   American journalist and humorist who created the homely philosopher Mr. Dooley.

Dunne was born of Irish immigrant parents. In 1884 he began working for various Chicago newspapers, specializing eventually in political reporting and editorial writing. In 1892 he began contributing Irish-dialect sketches to the *Chicago Evening Post* and five years later to the *Chicago Journal*. In these Dunne introduced Martin Dooley, a saloonkeeper who commented in a rich Irish brogue on politics and society. Dunne's witty penetration of shams and hypocrisies made Mr. Dooley a force for clear thinking and tolerance in public affairs. Many of Mr. Dooley's remarks, such as "Thrust ivrybody, but cut th' cards," became part of American lore. Dunne wrote more than

700 dialect essays, some of which were republished in eight volumes from 1898 to 1919.

Dunne \'dən\, John Gregory (b. May 25, 1932, Hartford, Conn., U.S.)   American writer who was noted for his works of social satire, personal analysis, and Irish-American life.

After graduating from Princeton University, Dunne briefly served in the military and became a staff writer for *Time* magazine in New York City. He married novelist Joan Didion in 1964 and moved to California, where he wrote screenplays and contributed to numerous magazines—including a joint column with his wife in the *Saturday Evening Post* (1967–69).

Dunne's first book, *Delano: The Story of the California Grape Strike* (1967; rev. ed., 1971), examines the labor and social issues surrounding the grape-pickers' strike of the mid-1960s. *The Studio* (1969) is a telling portrait of the motion-picture industry. *Vegas: A Memoir of a Dark Season* (1974) describes the narrator's nervous breakdown in a story about three colorful inhabitants of Las Vegas. Dunne examined Irish-American communities in a gritty trilogy of novels: *True Confessions* (1977), *Dutch Shea, Jr.* (1982), and *The Red White and Blue* (1987). His other works include the autobiographical *Harp* (1988) and two collections of essays, *Quintana & Friends* (1978) and *Crooning* (1990).

Dunsany \,dən-'sän-ē\, Edward John Moreton Drax Plunkett \'pləŋ-kit\, 18th Baron of (b. July 24, 1878, London, Eng.—d. Oct. 25, 1957, Dublin, Ire.)   Irish dramatist and storyteller of great imagination.

Educated at Eton and Sandhurst, Dunsany served in the South African (Boer) War and World War I. His early work included a book of short stories, *The Gods of Pegana* (1905), and two plays, *The Glittering Gate* (produced 1909) and *The Gods of the Mountain* (produced 1911). In these works as well as in his more than 50 subsequent verse plays, novels, short stories, and memoirs, Dunsany explored mysterious kingdoms of fairies and gods in a richly colored prose; he also introduced a characteristic element of the macabre. His autobiography, *Patches of Sunlight*, was published in 1938.

duologue \'dü-ə-,lȯg, -,läg\ [Latin *duo* two + English *-logue* (as in *dialogue*)]   **1.** A dialogue between two persons.   **2.** A dramatic or musical piece for two participants.

Duonelaitis   *see* DONELAITIS.

Dupin, C. Auguste \sä-ō-gœst-dœ-'paⁿ\   Fictional detective appearing in three stories by Edgar Allan Poe. Dupin was the original model for the detective in literature.

Based on the roguish François-Eugène Vidocq, onetime criminal and founder and chief of the French police detective organization Sûreté, C. Auguste Dupin is a Paris gentleman of leisure who uses "analysis" for his own amusement to help the police solve crimes. In the highly popular short stories THE MURDERS IN THE RUE MORGUE and THE PURLOINED LETTER, as well as the less successful "The Mystery of Marie Roget," Dupin is depicted as an eccentric, a reclusive amateur poet who prefers to work at night by candlelight and who smokes a meerschaum pipe—foreshadowing the nocturnal Sherlock Holmes. Like Holmes, Dupin is accompanied by a rather obtuse sidekick, though Dupin's companion, unlike Dr. Watson, remains a nameless narrator.

duple \'dü-pəl, 'dyü-\   In prosody, consisting of a meter based on disyllabic feet.

Durán \dü-'rän\, Agustín (b. Oct. 14, 1793, Madrid, Spain—d. Dec. 1, 1862, Madrid)   Spanish literary critic, bibliographer, librarian, writer, and editor who was one of the major opponents of Neoclassicism and a major theoretician of Spanish Romanticism.

Durán was sent to the seminary at Vergara, studied at the University of Seville, and was admitted to the bar at Valladolid. He held a post in the education department at Madrid (1821–23) but was suspended for his political opinions. In 1834 he became secretary of the board for the censorship of the press and shortly afterwards obtained a post in the national library at Madrid. Dismissed during the revolution of 1840, Durán was reinstated in 1843.

Perhaps Durán's best-known piece of criticism was his academy speech, *Sobre el influjo que ha tenido la crítica moderna en la decadencia del teatro antiguo español* (1828; "On the Influence That Modern Criticism Has Had on the Decadence of the Old Spanish Theater"), which proposed that Spanish medieval and classical drama was more poetic than and so otherwise unlike the classical drama of Greece and France as to demand appreciation by different rules. Between 1828 and 1832 Durán compiled and edited two collections of ballads, *Colección de romances antiguos* ("Collection of Ancient Ballads") and *Colección de romances castellanas anteriores al siglo XVIII* ("Collection of Castilian Ballads Prior to the 18th Century"), better known as *Romancero general*, or *Romancero de Durán*. He also was at least partly responsible for reviving the work of the Spanish dramatists Tirso de Molina and Lope de Vega.

Durão \dū-'raůⁿ\, José de Santa Rita (b. 1722?, Cata Prêta, Braz.—d. Jan. 24, 1784, Lisbon, Port.) Brazilian epic poet, best known for his long poem *Caramúru*, a fictitious treatment of the discovery of Bahia (northeastern Brazil). Durão was a pioneer in his use of South American Indians as subjects of literature.

Durão was educated at the Jesuit college in Rio de Janeiro and at the University of Coimbra in Portugal. In 1758 he entered the Gratian convent of the Order of St. Augustine. Because of his open expression of support for the Jesuits, who had been expelled from Portugal and Brazil in 1759, Durão was forced to leave the country, and after detention in Spain as a spy he went to Rome, where he acted as a papal librarian. In 1778 he returned to Portugal, soon retiring to the Gratian convent and becoming its prior.

In 1781 he published in Lisbon his epic *Caramúru: Poema épico do descubrimento da Bahia* ("Caramúru: Epic Poem of the Discovery of Bahia"), a poetic treatment in 10 cantos. Caramúru ("Dragon of the Sea") is the name bestowed on the explorer Diogo Álvares by the Indians. The poem is notable for its descriptions of South American scenery and Indian life and the love it expresses for Brazil. Embittered by its failure to win immediate recognition, Durão burned most of his other works.

Duras \dᴜᴇ-'ràs\, Marguerite, *pseudonym of* Marguerite Donnadieu \dô-nà-'dyœ\ (b. April 4, 1914, Gia Dinh, Cochinchina [Vietnam]) French novelist, screenwriter, scenarist, playwright, and film director, internationally known for her screenplays of *Hiroshima mon amour* (1959) and *India Song* (play, 1973; screenplay, 1975).

Duras spent most of her childhood in Indochina, but at the age of 17 she moved to France to study at the University of Paris, Sorbonne. She began writing in 1942. *Un Barrage contre le Pacifique* (1950; *The Sea Wall*), her third novel and first success, dealt with a poor French family in Indochina, reflecting the novels by Erskine Caldwell and John Steinbeck then popular in France. Her next successes, *Le Marin de Gibraltar* (1952; *The Sailor from Gibraltar*) and *Moderato cantabile* (1958), were more lyrical and complex and more given to dialogue. She wrote the dialogue for the original screenplay of Alain Resnais's critically acclaimed film *Hiroshima mon amour*, and, in the following decades, she wrote several more screenplays, some of them adaptations of her own work.

Duras' writing grew increasingly minimal and abstract. Her major novels include *L'Après-midi de Monsieur Andesmas* (1962; *The Afternoon of Monsieur Andesmas*), *Le Ravissement de Lol V. Stein* (1964; *The Ravishing of Lol Stein*), *Détruire, dit-elle* (1969; *Destroy, She Said*), *L'Amour* (1971), and *L'Amant* (1984; *The Lover;* film, 1992). A later novel was *La Pluie d'été* (1990; *Summer Rain*). Collections of her plays are included in *Théâtre I* (1965), *Théâtre II* (1968), and *Théâtre III* (1984).

Durbeyfield, Tess \'tes-'dər-bē-,fēld\ Fictional character, the protagonist of Thomas Hardy's novel TESS OF THE D'URBERVILLES. Tess is an innocent young girl whose life is changed dramatically when her family discovers its noble lineage and she becomes involved with a neighbor who bears the family's aristocratic name.

D'Urfey \'dər-fē\, Thomas (b. 1653, Exeter?, Devon, Eng.—d. February 1723, London) English dramatist, satirist, and songwriter with a light satirical touch whose plays were very popular in their time; his comedies, with their complicated plots and lively dialogue, to some extent point the way to sentimental comedy of the later 18th century.

Patronized by King Charles II, whom he entertained as a jester and singer, and more cautiously by James II, D'Urfey changed his religious and political allegiance on the accession of William and Mary and was, in turn, favored by them. He wrote 32 plays between 1676 and 1688. D'Urfey also wrote some 500 songs, a number of texts to be set to music by Henry Purcell, and an epilogue for Purcell's opera *Dido and Aeneas*.

Durgā \'dūr-gə\ (Sanskrit: "the Inaccessible") In Hindu mythology, one of the many forms of the goddess Śakti, and the wife of Śiva. Her best-known feat was the slaying of the buffalo-demon Mahiṣāsura. According to legend she was created for this purpose out of flames that issued from the mouths of Brahmā, Vishnu, Śiva, and the lesser gods. She was born fully grown and beautiful; nevertheless, she presents a fierce, menacing form to her enemies. She is usually depicted in painting and sculpture riding a lion (sometimes a tiger), with 8 or 10 arms, each holding the special weapon of one or another of the gods, who gave them to her for her battle against the buffalo-demon.

Durrell \'də-rəl, US also 'dür-əl, 'dər-\, Lawrence (George) (b. Feb. 27, 1912, Jullundur, India—d. Nov. 7, 1990, Sommières, Fr.) English writer who is best known as the author of THE ALEXANDRIA QUARTET, a series of four interconnected novels.

Durrell spent most of his life outside England and had little sympathy with the English character. He was educated in India until he reached age 11 and moved in 1935 to the island of Corfu. During World War II he served as press attaché to the British embassies in Cairo and Alexandria, and after the war he spent time in Yugoslavia, Rhodes, Cyprus, and the south of France.

Durrell wrote several books of poetry and prose before the publication of *The Alexandria Quartet*, composed of *Justine* (1957), *Balthazar* (1958), *Mountolive* (1958), and *Clea* (1960). The tetralogy explored the erotic lives of a group of exotic characters living in Alexandria. It became a best-seller and won high critical esteem.

Durrell's later fiction was less well received. He first gained recognition as a poet with *A Private Country* (1943), and his reputation was established by *Cities, Plains and People* (1946), *The Tree of Idleness* (1953), and *The Ikons* (1966). His *Collected Poems 1931–74* appeared in 1980. In the nonfiction works *Prospero's Cell* (1945), *Reflections on a Marine Venus* (1953), and *Bitter Lemons* (1957), Durrell describes the Greek islands of Corfu, Rhodes, and Cyprus. Many critics regard his poetry and nonfiction books as his most enduring achievements.

Dürrenmatt \\'dʊer-ən-ˌmät\\, Friedrich (b. Jan. 5, 1921, Konolfingen, near Bern, Switz.—d. Dec. 14, 1990, Neuchâtel)   Swiss playwright, novelist, and essayist whose tragicomic plays were central to the post-World War II revival of German-language theater.

Dürrenmatt, who was educated in Zürich and Bern, became a full-time writer in 1947. Dürrenmatt's vision of the world as essentially absurd gave a comic flavor to his plays. Writing on the theater in *Theaterprobleme* (1955; *Problems of the Theatre*), he described the primary conflict in his tragicomedies as humanity's comic attempts to escape from the tragic fate inherent in the human condition.

His plays often have bizarre settings. His first play, *Es steht geschrieben* (1947; "It Is Written"), is about the Anabaptist suppression in Münster in 1534–36. In it, as in *Der Blinde* (1948; "The Blind Man") and *Romulus der Grosse* (1949; *Romulus the Great*), comic liberties are taken with the historical facts. *Die Ehe des Herrn Mississippi* (1952; *The Marriage of Mr. Mississippi*; U.S. title, *Fools Are Passing Through*), a serious play in the guise of an old-fashioned melodrama, established his international reputation. Other plays include *Der Besuch der alten Dame* (1956; THE VISIT); *Die Physiker* (1962; THE PHYSICISTS), a modern morality play about science, generally considered his best play; *Der Meteor* (1966; *The Meteor*); and *Porträt eines Planeten* (1970; *Portrait of a Planet*). In addition to plays, Dürrenmatt wrote detective novels, radio plays, and critical essays. His works, written in German, were translated into more than 50 languages.

Duse \\'dü-zā\\, Eleonora (b. Oct. 3, 1858, near or in Vigevano, Lombardy, Austrian Empire [now in Italy]—d. April 21, 1924, Pittsburgh, Pa., U.S.)   Italian actress who was acclaimed in many countries and found her greatest interpretive roles in the heroines of the Italian playwright Gabriele D'Annunzio and of the Norwegian playwright Henrik Ibsen.

Having acted from the age of four, Duse was a well-traveled sophisticate by 1894, when she met and fell in love with the rising young poet Gabriele D'Annunzio. He wrote a number of plays for her. Her belief in his talent was boundless, and his cult of beauty added another dimension to her acting. D'Annunzio eventually broke off the relationship and told the story of their love in his novel *Il fuoco* (1900; *The Flame of Life*).

Dust Tracks on a Road   Autobiography of Zora Neale HURSTON, published in 1942.

Controversial for its refusal to examine the effects of racism or segregation, *Dust Tracks on a Road* opens with the author's childhood in Eatonville, Fla., the site of the first organized African-American effort at self-government. It follows her through an expanding world of experience and intellectual growth to Howard University, where the writer Charles S. Johnson discovers her work and publishes two stories. The most notable of her patrons thereafter are Fannie Hurst, a white writer for whom she works as a secretary, and anthropologist Franz Boas, who encourages and arranges a fellowship for her research of black folklore. This research formed the basis of her well-received book *Mules and Men* (1935).

Hurston maintains a sunny, invincible attitude throughout the book. White readers seemed to like her lack of comment on racial problems; black critics, however, found this unconscionable and accused her of playing up to whites. In fact, critical comments on U.S. race relations and U.S. foreign policy had been excised by the book's editors.

Dutchman   One-act drama by Amiri BARAKA, produced and published in 1964 under the playwright's original name LeRoi Jones. *Dutchman* presents a stylized encounter that illustrates hatred between blacks and whites in America as well as the po-

litical and psychological conflicts facing black American men in the 1960s. The play won an Obie Award as best American off-Broadway play of 1964; it was made into a film in 1967. Set in a New York City subway car, the play involves Clay, a young, middle-class black man who is approached seductively by Lula, a white fellow passenger. Lula provokes Clay to anger and finally murders him.

Du Toit \\dœ-'tȯi\\, Jakob Daniel, *pseudonym* Totius \\'tō-tē-ùs\\ (b. Feb. 21, 1877, Paarl, Cape Colony, S.Af.—d. July 1, 1953, Pretoria, Transvaal)   Afrikaner poet, pastor, biblical scholar, and compiler of an Afrikaans Psalter (1936) that is regarded as one of the finest poetic achievements of its kind in Afrikaans.

Du Toit was educated in Pretoria, Rustenburg, and Daljosafat, and at the theological seminary at Burgesdorp. On the outbreak of the South African (Boer) War he joined the Boer forces as chaplain. In 1900 he went to the Free University, Amsterdam, where he received a doctor's degree in theology in 1903 and then entered the ministry. From 1911 he taught at the University of Potchefstroom, Transvaal.

Du Toit was responsible for the greater part of the translation of the Bible into Afrikaans, completed in 1932. His poetry includes the patriotic verses in *Trekkerswee* (1915; "Trekkers' Grief") and the personal lyrics in *Passieblomme* (1934; "Passion Flowers") and *Skemering* (1948; "Twilight").

Dutt   see DATTA.

Duun \\'dün\\, Olav (b. Nov. 21, 1876, Fosnes, Jøa Island, Nor.—d. Sept. 13, 1939, Tønsberg)   Novelist who, along with Knut Hamsun and Sigrid Undset, is one of the outstanding names in 20th-century Norwegian fiction. His works were influential in raising Nynorsk, a language based on spoken dialects, to literary eminence.

Duun was a cattle herder and fisherman before entering a seminary at the age of 26. He worked as a teacher until 1926, when he retired to Holmestrand on the Oslo Fjord to devote himself to writing. His many novels analyze the psychological and spiritual characteristics of peasant life. His masterpiece is a series of novels, collectively entitled *Juvikfolke* (1918–23; *The People of Juvik*), describing the development of a peasant family through six generations, from 1814 to 1914, and symbolically tracing the development of the Norwegian people from a state of unselfconscious primitivism to a state of civilized humanism. The novels in the series have been translated as *Trough of the Waves* (1930), *The Blind Man* (1931), *The Big Wedding* (1932), *Odin in Fairyland* (1932), *Odin Grows Up* (1934), and *Storm* (1935).

Duyckinck \\'dī-ˌkiŋk\\, Evert Augustus (b. Nov. 23, 1816, New York, N.Y., U.S.—d. Aug. 13, 1878, New York City)   American biographer, editor, and critic who focused scholarly attention on American writing and contributed to the advance of American literature in the mid-19th century with such works as the two-volume *Cyclopaedia of American Literature* (1855; supplement 1866), written with his brother George.

Duyckinck graduated from Columbia in 1835, studied law for two years, and was admitted to the bar but never practiced. He studied in Europe and upon his return to New York City became coeditor of *Arcturus: A Journal of Books and Opinion*. In 1848 he and his brother bought the journal *Literary World* and edited it together, making it the most influential literary weekly of the time until, despite its high quality, it failed financially in 1853.

Duyckinck came to know most of the important writers of the day and fostered the careers of many—among them Herman Melville. Duyckinck wrote several popular biographical compilations, including the *Lives and Portraits of the Presidents of the United States* and *Portrait Gallery of Eminent Men and Women of Europe and America*, 2 vol. (1873).

dwarf \'dwȯrf\ *plural* dwarfs *or* dwarves \'dwȯrvz\ In folklore, a legendary humanlike being of small stature, usually misshapen and ugly and skilled as an artificer.

In Teutonic and especially Scandinavian mythology and folklore, the term dwarf denoted a species of fairy inhabiting the interiors of mountains and the lower levels of mines. Dwarfs were of various types, all of small stature, some no more than 18 inches (45 cm) tall and others about the height of a two-year-old child. In appearance they were sometimes beautiful, but more often they resembled grave old men with long beards and, in some cases, humped backs.

The mountain dwarfs lived in subterranean halls, believed to be full of gold and precious stones. They were principally famous for their skill in metalwork and the forging of magical swords and rings, but they were also credited with profound wisdom and secret knowledge, having powers to foresee the future, assume other forms, and make themselves invisible. One such dwarf was Alberich of the German epic *Nibelungenlied*.

Dwarf, The Novel by Pär LAGERKVIST, published in Swedish in 1944 as *Dvärgen*. Set during the Italian Renaissance and cast in the form of a journal, it is a study of the psychology of evil.

The narrator, Piccoline, always referred to as "the Dwarf," is a minor retainer at the court of an Italian Renaissance prince, a position he has obtained by strangling his predecessor. He keeps a journal of his observations and impressions. A bitter outsider, he sees all events as distorted by his misanthropy, and he poisons his enemies and betrays those who confide in him. The Dwarf makes his final entries from the dungeon where he is imprisoned for complicity in the deaths of the prince's wife and daughter and the latter's lover.

Dwight \'dwīt\ Timothy (b. May 14, 1752, Northampton, Mass., U.S.—d. Jan. 11, 1817, New Haven, Conn.) American educator, theologian, and poet who had a strong influence on education in his time.

Educated by his mother, a daughter of the preacher Jonathan Edwards, Dwight entered Yale at age 13 and graduated in 1769. He then pursued a variety of occupations—he was a tutor at Yale, a school principal, a Massachusetts legislator, and a chaplain with the Continental Army. In 1783 he began a successful school in Greenfield Hill, Conn., where he became pastor of the Congregational Church and began to write poetry. His works include *Greenfield Hill* (1794), a popular history of and tribute to the village, and epics such as *The Conquest of Canaan* (1785), a biblical allegory of the taking of Connecticut from the British, which some critics regard as the first American epic poem. Dwight's political satire marks him as a Hartford wit. He served as president of Yale from 1795 to 1817.

Dybbuk, The \'dib-ůk\ Expressionistic drama in four acts by S. ANSKY, performed in 1920 in Yiddish as *Der Dibek* and published the following year. Originally titled *Tsvishn Tsvey Veltn* ("Between Two Worlds"), the play was based on the mystical concept from Ḥasidic Jewish folklore of the dybbuk, a disembodied human spirit that, because of former sins, wanders restlessly until it finds a haven in the body of a living person. The translation of the play into several languages contributed to worldwide interest in the dybbuk.

The plot centers on a young woman, Leah, who on the day of her wedding is possessed by a dybbuk. This proves to be none other than the spirit of Channon, a young Ḥasidic scholar who had loved her and who had died upon learning of her betrothal to another man. The dybbuk, which can be expelled only by exorcism, at first refuses to leave Leah but is eventu-

ally persuaded to do so. In the end Leah dies, and her soul and Channon's rise and are united forever.

Dyce \'dīs\ Alexander (b. June 30, 1798, Edinburgh, Scot.—d. May 15, 1869, London, Eng.) Scottish editor whose works contributed to the growing interest in William Shakespeare and his contemporaries during the 19th century.

As an undergraduate at the University of Oxford, Dyce edited a dictionary of the language of Shakespeare. After serving as a curate in Cornwall and Suffolk, he settled in London, where he completed William Gifford's *Dramatic Works and Poems of James Shirley* (1833) and revised his own *Works of John Ford* (1869). Dyce edited the works of the dramatists George Peele, John Webster, Robert Greene, Thomas Middleton, Francis Beaumont and John Fletcher, and Christopher Marlowe. His six-volume edition of the works of Shakespeare (1857; rev. ed., 1864–67) was a notable contribution to Shakespearean scholarship. Dyce also published many 17th- and 18th-century works and an edition of John Skelton (1843).

Dyer \'dī-ər\ Sir Edward (b. October 1543, Sharpham Park, Somerset, Eng.—d. May 1607, London) English courtier and poet whose reputation rests on a small number of lyrics ascribed to him in which critics have found great dexterity and sweetness. Educated at the University of Oxford, Dyer went to court under the patronage of the Earl of Leicester. Dyer was employed on diplomatic missions to the Netherlands (1584) and Denmark (1589) and was knighted in 1596. His contemporary reputation as a poet was high, but little of his work, published anonymously or under initials in collections, can be ascribed to him with certainty. His best-known poem is "My Mynd to Me a Kingdom Is."

Dyer \'dī-ər\ John (baptized Aug. 13, 1699, Aberglasney, Carmarthenshire, Wales—d. December 1757, Coningsby, Lincolnshire, Eng.) British poet chiefly remembered for "Grongar Hill" (1726), a short descriptive and meditative poem that limns the view from a hill overlooking the vale of Towy and uses this as a starting point for meditation on the human lot:

> A little rule, a little sway,
> A sunbeam in a winter's day,
> Is all the proud and mighty have
> Between the cradle and the grave.

Dygasiński \dig-ä-'shyĕⁿ-sk⁷ē\ Adolf (b. March 7, 1839, Niegosławice, Poland, Russian Empire—d. June 3, 1902, Grodzisk Mazowiecki) One of the outstanding Polish naturalist writers. A teacher and a devotee of science, Dygasiński published about 50 volumes of short stories, the best of which deal with the lives of animals. His masterpiece is *Gody życia* (1902; "Feast of Life"), an allegorical prose poem about the struggle between a small bird and a powerful eagle-owl.

Dynasts, The (*in full* The Dynasts, A Drama of the Napoleonic Wars, in Three Parts, Nineteen Acts, and One Hundred and Thirty Scenes) Verse drama by Thomas HARDY, published in three parts in 1903, 1906, and 1908 and together in one volume in 1910. The monumental work, written mostly in blank verse with some scenes, descriptive connecting sequences, and stage directions written in prose, depicts the career of Napoleon Bonaparte from 1805 until his defeat at Waterloo in 1815. The work illustrates Hardy's stoical pessimism and is a clear statement of his belief in "Immanent Will," a blind and indifferent force that determines the fates (and generally blights the lives) of the privileged and the common people alike.

dystopia \dis-'tō-pē-ə\ [*dys-* bad + u*topia*], *also called* antiutopia. An imaginary place where people lead dehumanized and often fearful lives. *Compare* UTOPIA.

Earle \'ərl\ or **Earles** \'ərlz\, John (b. 1601?, York, Eng.—d. Nov. 17, 1665) Anglican clergyman, best known as the chief author of *Micro-cosmographie; or, A Peece of the World Discovered; in Essayes and Characters* (1628; enlarged 1629 and 1630).

At the University of Oxford as a student from about 1616 and as a fellow from 1619, Earle wrote occasional verse. His *Micro-cosmographie*, written while he was at Oxford, is outstanding; it avoids didacticism and displays genuine personalities, such as a "child," a "Good old Man," a "young raw Preacher," and a "Grave Divine." It is alive with humor, perception, and epigrammatic brilliance. Earle's wit, learning, and tolerance were widely praised, and, though a Royalist Anglican, he tried to conciliate Nonconformists. Meanwhile he translated into Latin the *Eikon Basilike* ("Royal Image"), an extremely popular book of meditations supposedly by Charles I, and Richard Hooker's *Of the Lawes of Ecclesiasticall Politie*. He was exiled in 1644–60, but, after the Restoration, he became bishop successively of Worcester and of Salisbury.

Earnshaw family \'ərn-,shȯ\ Fictional family, the sponsors of the foundling Heathcliff in Emily Brontë's novel WUTHERING HEIGHTS. The family consists of Mr. and Mrs. Earnshaw and their son Hindley and daughter Catherine (Cathy). It is the frustrated love between Cathy and Heathcliff that propels the plot of the novel.

Earth Spirit Drama in four acts by Frank WEDEKIND, published in 1895 as *Der Erdgeist* after his publisher refused the complete manuscript of *Die Büchse der Pandora: Eine Monstretragödie* ("Pandora's Box: A Monster Tragedy"). *Erdgeist* was first performed in 1898.

Together with *Die Büchse der Pandora* (PANDORA'S BOX), the second part of the original work, *Earth Spirit* relates the experiences of Lulu, an amoral femme fatale. In *Earth Spirit*, Lulu's first husband dies when he finds her with another man, her second husband kills himself, and she kills the third. She also ensnares the lesbian Countess Geschwitz.

Earwicker, Humphrey Chimpden \'həm-frē-'chimp-dən-'ir-wik-ər\ Fictional character, a middle-aged tavern owner who is the protagonist of James Joyce's novel FINNEGANS WAKE. Earwicker (often designated by variations on his initials, H.C.E., one form of which is "Here Comes Everybody") is Joyce's Everyman. His wife Anna (also called Anna Livia Plurabelle and A.L.P.) is his female counterpart.

East Coker \,ēst-'kō-kər\ Poem by T.S. ELIOT, originally appearing in 1940, first in the *New English Weekly* and then in pamphlet form. It is the second of the four poems in THE FOUR QUARTETS. Like the other three poems, "East Coker" was written in strong-stress meter and organized into five sections. Continuing the study of cyclical patterns begun in "Burnt Norton," it examines the nature of history and spiritual renewal.

"East Coker" is named after the hamlet in Somersetshire where Eliot's ancestors lived before immigrating to America in the 1660s. The poem is bleak in tone, with images of deserted streets, subterranean shelters, and hospitals. It closes with the determination that "For us, there is only the trying. The rest is not our business."

Easter 1916 Poem by William Butler YEATS, published separately in 1916 and collected in *Michael Robartes and the Dancer* (1921). It commemorates the martyrs of the Easter Rising, an insurrection against the British government in Ireland in 1916, which resulted in the execution of several Irish nationalists whom Yeats knew personally.

The poem examines the nature of heroism and its incongruity with everyday life. Although Yeats questions the fanaticism of the rebels and the necessity of their actions, he admires their steadfast determination. He reluctantly celebrates their martyrdom with the repeated line "A terrible beauty is born."

Eastman \'ēst-mən\, Max (Forrester) (b. Jan. 12, 1883, Canandaigua, N.Y., U.S.—d. March 25, 1969, Bridgetown, Barbados) American poet, editor, and prominent radical before and after World War I.

Eastman was educated at Williams College, Williamstown, Mass. He taught at Columbia University for four years, and he was the founder of the first men's league for woman suffrage in 1910. Eastman edited and published *The Masses*, a radical political and literary periodical. Its editors were brought to trial twice in 1918 because of their editorial opposition to the entry of the United States into World War I, but both trials ended with hung juries. He then edited and published *The Liberator*, a similar magazine, until 1922, when he traveled to Russia to study the Soviet regime. He married Eliena Krylenko, a sister of the Soviet minister of justice, but returned to the United States believing that the original purpose of the October Revolution (1917) had been subverted by corrupt leaders. In the 1920s and '30s he wrote several books attacking developments in the Soviet Union: *Since Lenin Died* (1925), *The End of Socialism in Russia* (1937), and *Stalin's Russia and the Crisis in Socialism* (1939).

From 1941 he was a roving editor for *Reader's Digest*. His many other books include *Enjoyment of Poetry* (23 eds., 1913–48), *Enjoyment of Laughter* (1936), and two autobiographical works, *Enjoyment of Living* (1948) and *Love and Revolution: My Journey Through an Epoch* (1965).

East of Eden \'ēd-ən\ Novel by John STEINBECK, published in 1952. It is a symbolic recreation of the biblical story of Cain and Abel woven into a history of California's Salinas Valley. With *East of Eden* Steinbeck hoped to reclaim his standing as a major novelist, but his broad depictions of good and evil come at the expense of subtlety in characterization and plot and it was not a critical success.

Spanning the period between the American Civil War and the end of World War I, the novel highlights the conflicts of two generations of brothers; the first being the kind, gentle Adam Trask and his wild brother Charles. Adam eventually marries Cathy Ames, an evil, manipulative, and beautiful prostitute; she betrays him, joining Charles on the very night of their wedding. Later, after giving birth to twin boys, she shoots Adam and leaves him to return to her former profession. In the shadow of this heritage Adam raises their sons, the fair-haired, winning, yet intractable Aron, and the dark, clever Caleb. This second generation of brothers vie for their father's approval. In bitterness Caleb reveals the truth about their mother to Aron, who then joins the army and is killed in France.

Eben *also called* Eben Fardd *see* Ebenezer THOMAS.

Eberhart \'eb-ər-,härt\, Richard (b. April 5, 1904, Austin, Minn., U.S.) American poet and teacher, a founder of the Poet's Theatre, Cambridge, Mass. (1951).

Educated at Dartmouth College, Cambridge, and Harvard, Eberhart published his first book of poems, *A Bravery of Earth*, in 1930. In the 1930s he also became tutor to the son of King Prajadhipok of Siam (now Thailand) and afterward taught at several U.S. colleges, particularly at Dartmouth (1956–70). He was consultant in poetry at the Library of Congress (1959–61). In 1962 he was cowinner, with John Hall Wheelock, of the Bollingen Prize in Poetry. His *Collected Poems, 1930–1986* was published in 1988 and *Maine Poems* followed in 1989.

Ebner-Eschenbach \\'äb-nər-'esh-ən-,bäḵ\\, Marie, Baroness (Freifrau) von, *original name* Marie Dubsky \\'dŭp-skē\\ (b. Sept. 13, 1830, Zdislavič, Moravia [now in Czech Republic]— d. March 12, 1916, Vienna, Austria-Hungary) Austrian novelist known for her perceptive portrayals of the lives of a broad spectrum of her compatriots.

Her first literary venture was the drama *Maria Stuart in Schottland* (1860), but she found her true sphere in narrative. In *Die Prinzessin von Banalien* (1872), *Božena* (1876), and *Das Gemeindekind* (1887; *The Child of the Parish*), her masterpiece, she graphically depicted the surroundings of her Moravian home and showed a true sympathy for the poor and an unsentimental understanding of children. *Lotti, die Uhrmacherin* (1879; "Lotti, The Watchmaker"), *Zwei Comtessen* (1885; "Two Countesses"), and *Unsühnbar* (1890; "Inexpiable" or "Not Atonable") described with equal insight the life of the Austrian aristocracy. She wrote many more novels and short stories, as well as some works of autobiography.

Eça de Queirós or **Eça de Queiroz** \\'ĕ-sȧ-də-'kä-,rŭsh\\, José Maria (b. Nov. 25, 1845, Póvoa do Varzim, Port.—d. Aug. 16, 1900, Paris, Fr.) Novelist committed to social reform who introduced naturalism and realism to Portugal. He was the leading 19th-century Portuguese novelist and is often considered to be the greatest Portuguese novelist of all.

The illegitimate son of a prominent magistrate, Eça de Queirós received his degree in law from the University of Coimbra. His father helped him make a start in the legal profession. Eça de Queirós' real interest lay in literature, however, and soon his short stories—ironic, fantastic, macabre, and often gratuitously shocking—and essays on a wide variety of subjects began to appear in the *Gazeta de Portugal*.

By 1871 he had become closely associated with a group of Portuguese intellectuals committed to social and artistic reform and known as the Generation of '70. During the 1870s and '80s Eça de Queirós, while serving on diplomatic missions, wrote the novels for which he is best remembered. His first, *O Crime do Padre Amaro* (1876; *The Sin of Father Amaro*), describes the destructive effects of celibacy on a priest of weak character and the dangers of fanaticism. A biting satire on the romantic ideal of passion and its tragic consequences appears in his next novel, *O Primo Basílio* (1878; *Cousin Bazilio*).

Satire also characterizes the novel that is generally considered Eça de Queirós' masterpiece, *Os Maias* (1888; *The Maias*). Its subject is the degeneration of a traditional family whose last offspring are led into a series of tangled sexual relationships by the actions of their parents, who are symbols of the decadence of Portuguese society.

Unlike his earlier work, his last novels are sentimental. *A cidade e as serras* (1901; *The City and the Mountains*) extols the beauty of the Portuguese countryside and the joys of rural life. Eça de Queirós was appointed consul in Paris in 1888, where he served until his death.

Ecclesiastes \\i-,klē-zē-'as-tēz\\, *Hebrew* Qohelet \\kō-'hel-et\\ ("Preacher") An Old Testament book of wisdom literature that is placed in the third section of the biblical canon, known as the Ketuvim (Writings). In the Hebrew Bible, Ecclesiastes stands between the Song of Solomon and Lamentations and with them belongs to the Megillot, five scrolls that are read at various festivals of the Jewish religious year. The common Christian English translations follow the Septuagint in placing Ecclesiastes between Proverbs and the Song of Solomon, an order reflecting the old tradition that Solomon wrote all three.

Ecclesiastes reflects the ideas of one who questioned the doctrine of retributive justice associated with wisdom theology. His observations on life convinced him that "the race is

not to the swift, nor the battle to the strong, nor bread to the wise, nor riches to the intelligent, nor favor to the men of skill; but time and chance happen to them all" (Ecclesiastes 9:11). Human fate, the author maintains, does not depend on righteous or wicked conduct but is an inscrutable mystery that remains hidden in God. All attempts to penetrate this mystery and thereby gain the wisdom necessary to secure one's fate are "vanity," or futile.

Echegaray y Eizaguirre \\,ā-chä-gä-'rī-ē-,ā-thä-'gēr-rä\\, José (b. April 19, 1832, Madrid, Spain—d. Sept. 4, 1916, Madrid) The leading Spanish dramatist of the last quarter of the 19th century. Along with the Provençal poet Frédéric Mistral, he was awarded the Nobel Prize for Literature in 1904.

A professor of mathematics in his early life, Echegaray y Eizaguirre entered government service in 1868, holding various positions. He was named minister of finance in 1874 and played a major role in developing the Banco de España.

His first play, *El libro talonario* ("The Checkbook"), was not produced until 1874, when he was 42, but he then produced an average of two plays a year for the rest of his life. His early work is almost wholly romantic, but he turned to the problem play (thesis play) in his later work. He often displayed his thesis by use of a satiric reversal; in *O locura o santidad* (1877; *Madman or Saint*), for example, he showed that honesty is condemned as madness by society. In all his plays his manner is melodramatic. Though forgotten now, he achieved tremendous popularity in his day because of his fertile imagination, which generally compensated for his lack of dramatic force. His use of skillfully contrived stage effects did much to revolutionize the scope of the Spanish theater.

Echidna \\i-'kid-nə\\ In Greek mythology, a monster that was half-woman and half-serpent. Among Echidna's progeny by the 100-headed Typhon were Ladon (the dragon said to have protected the Golden Apples of the Hesperides), the dragon who protected the Golden Fleece, the Hydra, the Chimera, and the infernal hounds Orthus and Cerberus. The Sphinx and the Nemean lion, both sired by Orthus, were also among her offspring.

Echo \\'ek-ō\\ In Greek mythology, a mountain nymph, or oread. Ovid relates in his *Metamorphoses* that Echo offended the goddess Hera by keeping her in conversation, thus distracting her from spying on one of Zeus's many extramarital amours; to punish Echo for this act, Hera deprived her of speech, except for the power to repeat the last words of another. Echo's hopeless love for Narcissus, who fell in love with his own image, caused her to fade away until all that was left of her was her voice.

According to the Greek writer Longus, Echo rejected the advances of the god Pan; he thereupon drove the shepherds mad, and they tore her to pieces. Gaea (Earth) buried her limbs but allowed her to retain the power of song.

echo \\'ek-ō\\ In literature, the repetition of a sound, syllable, word, or phrase for rhetorical or poetic purposes. Assonance, consonance, and all rhymes are types of echo.

echo verse Verse in which repetition of the end of a line or stanza imitates an echo. The repetition usually constitutes the entire following line and changes the meaning of the part being repeated. This device was popular in the 16th and 17th centuries in France, England, and Italy. The best-known examples are George Herbert's poem "Heaven" and Jonathan Swift's "A Gentle Echo on Woman."

Eckermann \\'ek-ər-,män\\, Johann Peter (b. Sept. 21, 1792, Winsen, Hanover [now in Germany]—d. Dec. 3, 1854, Weimar, Prussia [now in Germany]) German writer, chiefly remembered as the close associate of J.W. von Goethe; his *Gespräche* *mit Goethe in den letzten Jahren seines Lebens, 1823–32,* 3 vol. (1836–48; "Conversations with Goethe in the Last Years of His Life"), is comparable to James Boswell's *Life of Johnson.*

Reared in great poverty, Eckermann served in the northern German War of Liberation (1813–14) against Napoleon and became a clerk in the war department at Hanover. At an early age Goethe became his idol. He published a book of poems in 1821 and in 1823 attracted Goethe's attention by sending him the manuscript of his *Beiträge zur Poesie mit besonderer Hinweisung auf Goethe* ("Helps Toward Understanding Poetry with Special Instructions on Goethe"), which contained sensitive appreciations of Goethe's work. Goethe invited Eckermann to Weimar, and he there gave up his own ambition of becoming an original poet to become Goethe's unpaid literary assistant. In 1838 Eckermann also acquired an appointment at the Weimar court and the position of librarian.

Eckermann's *Gespräche* has been translated into every major European language. The first English translation, *Conversations with Goethe* (1839), was made by the American critic and teacher Margaret Fuller. Based on notes taken with Goethe's permission, Eckermann's work is a selective arrangement of information on Goethe's life and thought. Eckermann also acted as Goethe's literary executor and, with F.W. Riemer, prepared the first complete edition of Goethe's works.

eclogue \'ek-ˌlôg, -ˌläg\ [Latin *ecloga* short extract from a literary work, short poem, from Greek *eklogē* extract from a literary work, literally, choice, selection] A short, usually pastoral, poem in the form of a dialogue or soliloquy. The eclogue first appeared as a specifically pastoral form in the idylls of the Greek poet Theocritus (*c.* 310–250 BC), generally recognized as the inventor of pastoral poetry. The Roman poet Virgil (70–19 BC) adopted the form for his 10 *Eclogues,* also known as *Bucolics.* The eclogue was revived during the Renaissance by the Italians Dante, Petrarch, Giovanni Boccaccio, and Battista Spagnoli (also called Baptista Mantuanas or Mantuan).

Edmund Spenser's series of 12 eclogues, *The Shepheardes Calender* (1579), is the first outstanding pastoral poem in English. By the 17th century less formal eclogues were being written by such poets as Richard Lovelace, Robert Herrick, and Andrew Marvell. Marvell's "Nymph Complaining for the Death of her Fawn" (1681) climaxed the eclogue tradition of combining rural freshness with learned imitation. In the 18th century English poets began to use the eclogue for ironic verse on nonpastoral subjects, such as in Jonathan Swift's "A Town Eclogue. 1710. Scene, The Royal Exchange." Since then a distinction has been made between the terms *eclogue* and *pastoral,* with *eclogue* referring only to the dialogue or soliloquy form.

The eclogue eventually fell from favor, but it has occasionally been revived for special purposes by modern poets, as in Louis MacNeice's ironic eclogues in his *Collected Poems, 1925–1948* (1949). *See also* IDYLL.

Eco \'ā-kō, *Angl* 'ek-ō\, Umberto (b. Jan. 5, 1932, Alessandria, Italy) Italian literary critic, novelist, and semiotician (student of signs and symbols).

After receiving a doctoral degree from the University of Turin, Eco worked as a cultural editor for Italian Radio-Television and also lectured for several years at the University of Turin. He then taught in Florence and Milan and later, in 1971, assumed a professorial post at the University of Bologna. His initial studies and researches were in aesthetics, his principal work in this area being *Opera aperta* (1962; rev. ed., 1972, 1976; *The Open Work*). It suggests that in much modern music, Symbolist verse, and literature of controlled disorder (Franz Kafka, James Joyce) the messages are fundamentally ambiguous and invite the audience to participate more actively in the interpre-

tive and creative process. From this work he went on to explore other areas of communication and semiotics in such volumes as *A Theory of Semiotics* (1976), *Semiotics and the Philosophy of Language* (1984), and *The Limits of Interpretation* (1991), all written in English.

His erudite murder mystery *Il nome della rosa* (1980; THE NAME OF THE ROSE; film, 1986) became an international bestseller. He also wrote the novel *Il pendolo di Foucault* (1988; *Foucault's Pendulum*).

ecthlipsis \ek-'thlip-sis\ *plural* ecthlipses \-ˌsēz\ [Greek *ekthlípsis* loss of a sound or letter in a word, literally, the act of squeezing out, a derivative of *ekthlíbein* to squeeze out] In Latin prosody, the elision or suppression of a final *m* and a preceding short vowel before a word beginning with *h* or a vowel.

Edda \'ed-ə\ Body of ancient Icelandic literature contained in two 13th-century books commonly distinguished as the *Prose Edda* (*Younger Edda*) and the *Poetic Edda* (*Elder Edda*). It is the fullest and most detailed source for modern knowledge of Germanic mythology.

The Prose Edda. The *Prose Edda* (less commonly known by the name *Snorra-Edda*) was written by the Icelandic chieftain, poet, and historian SNORRI STURLUSON, probably in 1222–23. It is a textbook on poetics intended to instruct young poets in the difficult meters of the early Icelandic skalds (court poets) and to provide for a Christian age an understanding of the mythological subjects treated or alluded to in early poetry. It consists of a prologue and three parts. Two of the sections—*Skáldskaparmál* ("The Language of Poetry"), dealing with the elaborate, riddle-like kennings and circumlocutions of the skalds, and *Háttatal* ("A Catalog of Meters"), giving examples of 102 meters known to Snorri—are of interest chiefly to specialists. The remaining section, *Gylfaginning* ("The Deceiving of Gylfi"), cast in the form of a dialogue, describes the visit of Gylfi, a king of the Swedes, to Asgard, the citadel of the gods. In answer to his questions, the gods tell Gylfi the Norse myths about the beginning of the world, the adventures of the gods, and the fate in store for all in the Ragnarǫk ("Doom of the Gods"). The tales are told with dramatic artistry, humor, and charm.

The Poetic Edda. The *Poetic Edda* (sometimes called *Sæmundar Edda*) is a later manuscript dating from the second half of the 13th century but containing older materials (hence its better known alternative title, the *Elder Edda*). It is a collection of mythological and heroic poems of unknown authorship, composed over a long period (AD 800–1100). They are usually dramatic dialogues in a terse, simple, archaic style that is in decided contrast to the artful poetry of the skalds.

The mythological cycle is introduced by VǪLUSPÁ ("Sibyl's Prophecy"), a sweeping cosmogonic myth. It is followed by HÁVAMÁL ("Sayings of the High One"), a group of gnomic poems—disconnected, fragmentary, didactic poems concerning Odin. One of the finest poems is the humorous THRYMSKVITHA ("Lay of Thrym"), which recounts Thor's retrieval of his stolen hammer while disguised as a bride.

The second half of the *Poetic Edda* contains a number of heroic poems. The first are a group known as the Helgi poems, which concern the Viking Helgi Hjorvardsson and Svava, a Valkyrie whom he loves. The next collection is dominated by stories of the hero Sigurd (Siegfried), recounting his youth, his marriage to Gudrun, his death, and the tragic fate of the Burgundians (Nibelungs). The remainder of the poems are stories of Brynhild (Brunhild) and Gudrun.

These lays are the oldest surviving poetic forms of the Germanic legend of deceit, slaughter, and revenge that forms the core of the great medieval German epic NIBELUNGENLIED.

Unlike the *Nibelungenlied*, which stands on the threshold of romance, the austere Eddic poems dwell on cruel and violent deeds with a grim stoicism that is unrelieved by any civilizing influences.

Eddic \\'ed-ik\\ or **Eddaic** \\e-'dā-ik\\ **1.** Of or relating to the Old Norse *Edda*, a 13th-century collection of mythological, heroic, and gnomic poems, many of which were composed at a much earlier date. **2.** Having the characteristics of the alliterative strophic poetry of the *Edda* that is relatively simple in syntax and imagery. *Compare* SKALDIC POETRY.

Eddison \\'ed-i-sən\\, E.R., *in full* Eric Rucker (b. Nov. 24, 1882, St. Helen's, Adel, Yorkshire, Eng.—d. Aug. 18, 1945) English novelist and scholar of Icelandic literature whose works in the genre of romantic fantasy influenced the English fantasist J.R.R. Tolkien.

Eddison attended Eton College and then Trinity College, Oxford. From 1906 he worked for the Board of Trade.

In Eddison's most famous work, *The Worm Ouroboros* (1922), a tale of magic and wizardry, the hero travels to a planet named Mercury whose culture contains a blend of Eastern and Western feudal, classical, and modern cultures. Eddison's Zimiamvia trilogy—*Mistress of Mistresses* (1935), *A Fish Dinner in Memison* (1941), and *The Mezentian Gate* (1958; posthumously gathered from notes)—takes place in the heaven he first described in *The Worm Ouroboros*.

Eddison's knowledge of Northern sagas and myths is evident in *Styrbiorn the Strong* (1926) and in his translation of the Icelandic *Egils saga* (1930). His ornate, heavily rhythmic and archaic style is reflected in that of Tolkien's *The Lord of the Rings* (1954–56).

Edel \\'ā-,del, -dəl\\, Leon, *in full* Joseph Leon Edel (b. Sept. 9, 1907, Pittsburgh, Pa., U.S.) American literary critic and biographer, notably of Henry James.

Edel grew up in Saskatchewan, Can., and graduated from McGill University. He received a doctorate of letters from the University of Paris. During the 1930s he held a variety of jobs and then served in the U.S. Army from 1943 to 1947. He taught English at New York University and at the University of Hawaii.

Edel edited James's *Complete Tales*, 12 vol. (1963–65), and wrote the definitive biography of James in five volumes (1953–72). He also edited James's *Complete Plays* (1949) and James's letters, 4 vol. (1974–84). His other books include *Willa Cather: A Critical Biography* (1953), written with E.K. Brown; *The Psychological Novel, 1900–1950* (1955; rev. ed., *The Modern Psychological Novel*, 1964); and *Literary Biography* (1957). His psychological portrait of the Bloomsbury group, entitled *Bloomsbury: A House of Lions*, was published in 1979 and *Writing Lives* in 1984.

Eden *see* GARDEN OF EDEN.

Edgeworth \\'ej-wərth\\, Maria (b. Jan. 1, 1767, Blackbourton, Oxfordshire, Eng.—d. May 22, 1849, Edgeworthstown, Ire.) Anglo-Irish writer, known for her children's stories and for her novels of Irish life.

Edgeworth lived in England until 1782, when her family went to Edgeworthstown, northwest of Dublin, where Maria, then 15 and the eldest daughter, assisted her father in managing his estate. In this way she acquired the knowledge of rural economy and of the Irish peasantry that was to be the backbone of her novels. Encouraged by her father, Edgeworth began her writing, and the 21 other children in the family provided material and audience for her stories. She published them in 1796 as *The Parent's Assistant*. Even the intrusive moralizing, attributed to her father's editing, does not wholly suppress their vitality,

and the children who appear in them, especially the impetuous Rosamond, are the first real children in English literature since William Shakespeare.

Her first novel, CASTLE RACKRENT (1800), reveals her gift for social observation, character sketch, and authentic dialogue. Sir Walter Scott acknowledged his debt to Edgeworth in writing *Waverley*. Her next work, *Belinda* (1801), a society novel unfortunately marred by her father's insistence on a happy ending, was particularly admired by Jane Austen.

Between 1809 and 1812 Edgeworth published her *Tales of Fashionable Life* in six volumes. They include one of her best novels, *The Absentee*, which focused attention on a great contemporary abuse: absentee English landowning.

Before her father's death in 1817 she published three more novels, two of them, *Patronage* (1814) and *Ormond* (1817), of considerable power. After 1817 she wrote less, completing her father's *Memoirs* (1820) and devoting herself to the estate. Her last years were saddened by the Irish famine of 1846, during which she worked for the relief of stricken peasants.

A selection of her letters, *Maria Edgeworth in France and Switzerland*, was published in 1979.

Edib Adıvar \\ā-'dip-ā-də-'väsh\\, Halide, *also called* (1901–10) Halide Salih \\hä-li-'dā-sä-'lih\\, *original name* Halide Edib (b. 1883, Constantinople, Ottoman Empire [now Istanbul, Tur.]— d. Jan. 9, 1964, Istanbul) Novelist and pioneer in the emancipation of women in Turkey.

Educated by private tutors and at the American College for Girls in Istanbul, Edib became actively engaged in Turkish literary, political, and social movements. An ardent patriot, she wrote *Yeni Turan* (1912; "The New Turan"), on the nationalistic Pan-Turkish movement. She also worked to raise Turkish educational standards and encourage social and economic progress. Her famous novel *Handan* ("Family") concerns the problems of an educated woman.

After educational work in the Ottoman province of Syria during World War I, she and her husband joined the Turkish nationalists and played a vital role in the war of independence in Anatolia. Her most famous novel, *Ateşten gömlek* (1922; *The Daughter of Smyrna*), is the story of a young woman who works for the liberation of her country and of the two men who love her.

Among her other important novels are *Zeyno'nun Oğlu* (1926; "Zeyno's Son") and *Sinekli Bakkal* (1936; originally written in English as *The Clown and His Daughter*, 1935). Other important works in English are *The Turkish Ordeal* (1928), *Conflict of East and West in Turkey* (1935), and *Turkey Faces West* (1930), in which she examines the ideological conflicts facing the young Turkish Republic.

Edinburgh Review, The \\'ed-in-,bər-ə\\ (*in full* The Edinburgh Review, or The Critical Journal) Scottish magazine that was published from 1802 to 1929 and which contributed to the development of the modern periodical and to modern standards of literary criticism. *The Edinburgh Review* was founded by Francis Jeffrey, Sydney Smith, and Henry Brougham as a quarterly publication, with Jeffrey as its first and longtime editor. It was intended as an outlet for liberal views in Edinburgh. The magazine soon earned wide esteem for its political and literary criticism, and by 1818 it had attained a circulation of 13,500. Its contributors included the novelist Sir Walter Scott, the essayist William Hazlitt, and the historian Thomas Babington Macaulay. *The Edinburgh Review*'s prestige and authority among British periodicals during the 19th century were matched only by that of *The Quarterly Review*.

edition \\ə-'dish-ən\\ [Latin *editio* published version of a literary work, literally, the act of emitting or bringing forth] **1.** A set of copies differing in some way from others of the same published text, as in a paperback edition or an illustrated edition. **2.** The whole number of bound copies of a work printed from a single setting of type or from plates made therefrom. The term *edition* is usually distinguished from *printing*; a printing refers to one continuous operation of the printing process, and thus a single edition may have several printings if the same plates are used more than once.   **3.** A printed work that has the same title as an earlier production but with substantial changes in or additions to the text.

editio princeps \ă-'dit-ē-,ō-'prin-,keps, ə-'dish-ē-,ō-'prin-,seps \ *plural* editiones principes \ă-,dit-ē-'ō-,năs-'prin-ki-,păs, ə-,dish-ē-'ō-nēz-'prin-sə-,pēz \ [New Latin, literally, first edition]   The first printed edition especially of a work that circulated in manuscript before printing became common.

education novel   Genre popular in the late 18th and early 19th centuries in which a plan of education was set forth for a young person. The education novel was similar to the BILDUNGSROMAN but less well developed in terms of characters and plot and narrower in scope. Examples include Henry Brooke's *The Fool of Quality* and Jean-Jacques Rousseau's *Émile.*

Education of Henry Adams, The   Autobiographical work by Henry ADAMS that was privately printed in 1906 and published in 1918. Considered to be one of the most distinguished examples of the genre, the *Education* combines autobiography, bildungsroman, and critical evaluation of an age. Its chapter entitled "The Dynamo and the Virgin" contrasts the Virgin Mary, the unifying force acting on the European Middle Ages, with the dynamo, as representative of the forces of technology and industry acting upon civilization in the early 20th century. Adams marks the destruction of the human values that supported the achievements of his forebears and fears a future age driven by corruption and greed.

Éducation sentimentale, L' \lā-due-kā-'syôⁿ-sāⁿ-tē-mäⁿ-'täl \ *see* A SENTIMENTAL EDUCATION.

Edward II \'ed-wərd\ (*in full* The Troublesome Raigne and Lamentable Death of Edward the Second)   Tragedy in five acts by Christopher MARLOWE. One of the first Elizabethan plays on a British historical theme, it was performed about 1592 and published in 1594.

The drama's principal characters are Edward II, the stubborn, petty, weak-minded king of England; the frivolous Piers Gaveston, who is the king's favorite; the younger Lord Roger de Mortimer, who leads the barons' revolt against Edward; and Edward's neglected wife, Queen Isabella. Edward's infatuation with Gaveston, to the detriment of his duties as king, is the source of the tragedy. He bestows titles and honors on Gaveston, insults the queen and the royal courtiers, and sentences an enemy of Gaveston to death. Hoping to win her husband back, Isabella aids the barons' plots against Gaveston. Mortimer gradually develops a hunger for power and is steadily corrupted. Death follows death: Gaveston is killed; the king is imprisoned, tortured, and murdered; his son Edward III avenges him.

Along with the excitement of the quest for glory, Marlowe is concerned with the issues of social responsibility, power's corrupting qualities, and the suffering that power produces.

Edwards \'ed-wərdz\, Jonathan (b. Oct. 5, 1703, East Windsor, Conn. [U.S.]—d. March 22, 1758, Princeton, N.J.)   Greatest theologian and philosopher of Puritanism and stimulator of the religious revival known as the "Great Awakening."

Edwards' father and grandfather were ministers. He graduated from Yale College in 1720 and received an M.A. degree

in 1723. In 1727 he became his grandfather's colleague in the Congregational church at Northampton, Mass. At his grandfather's death in 1729, Edwards became sole occupant of the Northampton pulpit. In his first published sermon, entitled *God Glorified in the Work of Redemption, by the Greatness of Man's Dependence upon Him, in the Whole of It*, Edwards blamed New England's moral ills on its assumption of religious and moral self-sufficiency.

Against the prevailing heretical tendencies, Edwards delivered a series of sermons on "Justification by Faith Alone" in November 1734. The result was a great revival in the winter and spring of 1734–35. His subsequent report, *A Faithful Narrative of the Surprising Work of God* (1737), made a profound impression in America and Europe, particularly through his description of the types and stages of conversion experience.

In 1740–42 came the Great Awakening throughout the colonies. Dating from this period is the sermon "Sinners in the Hands of an Angry God" (1741), with its arresting image of the unredeemed, like loathsome insects, deserving to be flung into the fires of hell. In defense and criticism of the Awakening, which produced not only conversions but also excesses and disorders, Edwards wrote *The Distinguishing Marks of a Work of the Spirit of God* (1741), *Some Thoughts Concerning the Present Revival of Religion in New England* (1742), and *A Treatise Concerning Religious Affections* (1746).

Meanwhile, Edwards' relations with his own congregation had become strained because of his narrowing of the requirements for participation in the Eucharist, or Lord's Supper, and he was eventually dismissed. In the course of this controversy he wrote two books, *Qualifications for Communion* (1749) and *Misrepresentations Corrected, and Truth Vindicated, in a Reply to the Rev. Mr. Solomon Williams's Book* (1752).

In 1751 Edwards was sent into virtual exile as pastor of the frontier church at Stockbridge, Mass., and missionary to the Indians there. Hampered by many difficulties, he nevertheless discharged his pastoral duties and found time to write his famous work *Freedom of Will* (1754).

Late in 1757 Edwards accepted the presidency of the College of New Jersey (later Princeton University) and arrived there in January. He had hardly assumed his duties when he contracted smallpox from a primitive attempt at vaccination and died.

Edwards \'ed-wərdz\, Jorge (b. July 29, 1931, Santiago, Chile)   Chilean writer, literary critic, and diplomat who gained notoriety with the publication of *Persona non grata* (1973), a memoir of his experiences as the Chilean ambassador to Cuba in the early 1970s.

After receiving a law degree at the University of Chile in 1958, Edwards began his career as a diplomat and continued his education at Princeton University. His collections of short fiction, which include *El patio* (1952; "The Backyard"), *Gente de la ciudad* (1961; "City People"), *Las máscaras* (1967; "The Masks"), and *Temas y variaciones* (1969; "Themes and Variations"), departed from prevailing Chilean literature in that the stories did not deal with rural life but with the anguish of middle-class bureaucrats. Critical of the revolutionary regime of Cuba's Fidel Castro, *Persona non grata* created a controversy among Latin-American writers. Edwards' novels about Chile include *El peso de la noche* (1965; "Night's Burden"), about the decay of the middle-class family; *Los convidados de piedra* (1978; "The Stone Guests"), a story set during the 1973 military coup; *El museo de cera* (1981; "Wax Museum"), a political allegory; *La mujer imaginaria* (1985; "The Imaginary Woman"), about the liberation of a female artist; and *El anfitrión* (1987; "The Host"), a modern retelling of the Faust story. In 1990 he published *Adiós, poeta* ("Good-bye, Poet"), a study of Pablo Neruda.

Edwards \\'ed-wərdz\\, Lewis (b. Oct. 27, 1809, Penllwyn, Cardiganshire, Wales—d. July 19, 1887) Welsh educator and minister of the Calvinistic Methodist Church of Wales whose literary and theological essays greatly influenced the development of Welsh culture.

After ordination in 1837, Edwards married the granddaughter of Thomas Charles of Bala, a Methodist clergyman and Welsh Bible editor. With his brother-in-law David Charles, he opened the Bala Calvinistic Methodist College to prepare men for the ministry; in 1867 this became the theological college for his church in North Wales. Through Edwards' influence his denomination adopted a more presbyterian form of church government on the Scottish model.

Periodicals in Welsh that he established include *Yr Esboniwr* ("The Expositor," from 1844) and *Y Traethodydd* ("The Essayist," from 1845).

A man of considerable critical faculties, Edwards produced works on J.W. von Goethe and the Welsh clergyman-poet Goronwy Owen. He also translated a number of English hymns into Welsh.

Edwards \\'ed-wərdz\\, Sir Owen Morgan (b. Dec. 25, 1858, Llanuwchllyn, Merioneth, Wales—d. May 15, 1920, Llanuwchllyn) Welsh writer and educator who greatly influenced the revival of Welsh literature and the development of Welsh national consciousness.

After attending colleges in Wales and Scotland, Edwards studied history at the University of Oxford until 1887. As a teacher of modern history at Oxford (1889–1907), he founded and edited three Welsh magazines for popular circulation. He was knighted in 1916.

Though a scholar himself, he wrote books in a natural, charming, lucid style that reached a universal Welsh audience. They were often descriptive works dealing informally with Welsh regions, manners, history, and character, or comparisons of Welsh life with life abroad, such as *O'r Bala i Geneva* (1889; "From Bala to Geneva"). His major work in English was *Wales* (1901). As chief inspector of Welsh education (1907–20), he tirelessly worked to secure the study of Welsh culture in the Welsh schools.

Eeden \\vän-'ād-ən\\, Frederik Willem van (b. April 3, 1860, Haarlem, Neth.—d. June 16, 1932, Bussum) Dutch writer and physician whose works reflect his lifelong search for a social and ethical philosophy.

Van Eeden studied medicine at Amsterdam and, with writers Willem Kloos and Albert Verwey, founded *De Nieuwe Gids*, a literary periodical devoted to modern authors and new social ideas, in 1885. Later he practiced medicine at Bussum, near Hilversum, where he started a clinic for physical therapy. In 1898 he founded Walden, an agricultural colony based on the ideas of Henry David Thoreau.

Although in his early days van Eeden was chiefly known outside his own country for his idealistic social theories, his fame is based on his literary work. He first attracted attention with *De kleine Johannes* (1885; *The Quest*), a symbolic fairy tale. *Het lied van schijn en wezen* ("Song of Semblance and Substance"), the first part of which appeared in 1895, is a long philosophical poem. His psychiatric experience provided material for the novel *Van de koele meren des doods* (1900; *The Deeps of Deliverance*). Van Eeden's criticism and social treatises were collected in *Studies*, 6 vol. (1890–1918). He also wrote many plays.

Eekhoud \\'āk-,haût\\, Georges (b. May 27, 1854, Antwerp, Belg.—d. May 29, 1927, Schaerbeek) One of the first important Belgian regionalist novelists.

Originally a poet, Eekhoud worked with Max Waller's review *La Jeune Belgique* ("Young Belgium") in the 1880s to bring new life to Belgian literature. He turned to prose to express his views on the reform of society. As a novelist Eekhoud lacked the ability to construct satisfactory stories, and his characters rarely came alive. His strength lay in his descriptive realism. Even his best novel, *La nouvelle Carthage* (1888; "The New Carthage"), set in Antwerp, is saved only by the brilliance of its various episodes.

Unlike many regionalists, Eekhoud was able to evoke both urban and rural scenes. His cycles of stories, *Kermesses* (1884; "Country Fair") and *Nouvelles kermesses* (1887), graphically describe the seamy side of peasant life; his city novels explore the worlds of the working classes and of social outcasts.

Eeyore \\'ē-,yôr\\ Fictional character, a donkey in several popular children's stories by A.A. MILNE. Eeyore, whose tail is attached by a nail, is one of Christopher Robin's many toy animals whose adventures are detailed in the stories in *Winnie-the-Pooh* and *The House at Pooh Corner*. A melancholy misanthrope, Eeyore frequently makes bitter, self-deprecating comments that make him an excellent foil for Winnie-the-Pooh, the affectionate, bumbling Bear of Very Little Brain.

Effect of Gamma Rays on Man-in-the-Moon Marigolds, The

Naturalistic drama in two acts by Paul ZINDEL, produced in 1965. It won the Pulitzer Prize when it was published in 1971. Largely autobiographical, the play is noted for its sympathetic characterizations.

The story centers on Beatrice Hunsdorfer, an impractical, embittered widow living with her two awkward teenage daughters in a ramshackle house where she makes a living by nursing an elderly invalid. Alternately charming and abrasive, Beatrice is generally selfish like her elder daughter, Ruth, who suffers from convulsions brought on by a childhood trauma. The younger daughter, Tillie, is an eccentric outcast who earns respect by winning her school science project.

Effen \\vän-'ef-ən\\, Justus van (b. Feb. 21, 1684, Utrecht, Neth.—d. Sept. 18, 1735, 's-Hertogenbosch) Dutch essayist and journalist whose straightforward didactic pieces had a wholesome influence on the contemporary Dutch fashion of rococo writing.

Van Effen worked as a private tutor, a secretary at the Netherlands embassy in London in 1715 and 1727, and a clerk in the Dutch government's warehouses in 1732. An admirer of the English press and of *The Spectator* in particular, he launched first *Le Spectateur français* (1725) and then in his native language *De hollandsche Spectator* (1731), a weekly that he edited for the rest of his life. The descriptive realism and homely prose of his essays on common life and customs influenced the emerging novelists of the Dutch domestic scene.

Effi Briest \\'ef-ē-'brēst\\ Novel by Theodor FONTANE, written in 1891–93; published in installments in *Deutsche Rundschau* from October 1894 to March 1895 and in book form in 1895. Known for its deft characterization and accurate portrayal of Brandenburg society, the novel examines the place of women in society by following the corruption and downfall of Effi, married at age 17 to a 38-year-old bureaucrat. Considered Fontane's best novel, *Effi Briest* is free of didacticism, drawing no clear distinctions between good and evil in its characters while developing sympathy for its female protagonist.

efreet *see* AFREET.

Egan \\'ē-gən\\, Pierce, *known as* The Elder (b. 1772, London, Eng.—d. Aug. 3, 1849, London) Sporting writer whose works were considered indispensable reading for English men-about-town in the early 19th century.

Egan made his reputation as a boxing reporter. His best-known work is *Boxiana* (1818–24), a racy but accurate account of the lives of famous pugilists. Egan also developed a flair for sensational literature describing the contemporary "fast" life.

Eggleston \'eg-əl-stən\, Edward (b. Dec. 10, 1837, Vevay, Ind., U.S.—d. Sept. 4, 1902, Lake George, N.Y.) Clergyman, novelist, and historian who realistically portrayed various regions of the United States in such books as THE HOOSIER SCHOOL-MASTER (1871).

By the age of 19, Eggleston had become an itinerant preacher (or "circuit rider"), but the taxing activity broke his health. He held various pastorates, serving from 1874 to 1879 in Brooklyn; he was an editor of the juvenile paper *Little Corporal* (1866–67), the *National Sunday School Teacher* (1867–73), and other periodicals.

In all of his work he sought to write with "photographic exactness" of the real West. The most popular of his books for adults was *The Hoosier School-Master,* a vivid study of backwoods Indiana. His other novels include *The End of the World* (1872), *The Mystery of Metropolisville* (1873), *Roxy* (1878), and *The Graysons* (1888). His later works are considered less significant. After a trip to Europe in 1879 he turned to the writing of history. His *Beginners of a Nation* (1896) and *Transit of Civilization from England to America* (1900) contributed to the growth of the study of social history.

Egill Skallagrímsson \'ā-yil-'skä-hlä-grim-,sòn\, Skallagrímsson *also* Skalla-Grímsson (b. *c.* 910, Borg, Ice.—d. 990) One of the greatest of Icelandic skaldic poets, whose adventurous life and verses are preserved in the *Egils saga,* which is attributed to Snorri Sturluson.

The saga portrays Egill as having a dual nature derived from his mixed descent from fair, extroverted Vikings and dark, taciturn Lapps. He was headstrong, vengeful, and greedy for gold, but also a loyal friend, shy lover, and devoted father. As a young man he killed the son of King Erik Bloodax and placed a curse upon the king, which he inscribed on a pole in magic runes. Later, shipwrecked off the coast of Northumbria, Eng., he fell into Erik's hands (*c.* 948) but saved his own life by composing in a single night the long praise poem *Hǫfuthlausn* ("Head Ransom") praising Erik in a unique end-rhymed meter.

Shortly after the death of two of his sons, Egill locked himself in his enclosed bed and refused food. When his daughter coaxed him into writing a poem, he composed the deeply personal lament *Sonatorrek* (*c.* 961; "Loss of Sons" or "Revenge Denied"). The poem is also a family portrait in which he recalls the deaths of his sons and of his parents as well; in it desire for revenge and hatred of the gods overwhelm him, but gradually his anger dissipates. Egill apparently lived a long life and eventually wrote many more poems, one late verse being a lament on his encroaching senility.

egis *see* AEGIS.

Egmont \'eg-,mänt\ Tragic drama in five acts by J.W. von GOETHE, published in 1788 and produced in 1789. The hero is based upon the historical figure of Lamoraal, Count of Egmond (Egmont), a 16th-century Dutch leader during the Counter-Reformation. The work had great appeal for European audiences excited by the new movements toward democracy and nationalism.

The play is set during the period in which the Netherlands was suffering under the harsh rule of Roman Catholic Spain. The story pits the sympathetic and tolerant Egmont against the fierce and brutal Spanish Duke of Alva, sent to repress further Protestant rebellion. Egmont proves to be no match for the scheming Alva, and he is sentenced to die. At the conclusion of the play, however, he has a vision of the eventual triumph of freedom.

Egoist, The (*in full* The Egoist: A Comedy in Narrative) Comic novel by George MEREDITH, published in three volumes in 1879. One of Meredith's most popular works, the novel concerns the egoism of Sir Willoughby Patterne, an inane and conceited man who wants to marry someone worthy of him. Constantia Durham, his selected fiancée, humiliates him by eloping with an officer of the hussars when she discovers Patterne's shallow nature. Patterne then pursues Clara Middleton, meanwhile encouraging the tender feelings of Laetitia Dale. Clara rejects him after learning of his duplicity; she has also fallen in love with another man. Laetitia truly loves Patterne, but, wounded by his shabby and calculating treatment of her, she too rejects him. Humbled at last, Patterne honestly courts Laetitia and convinces her to marry him.

Egoist, The Avant-garde British literary periodical founded in 1914 by Harriet Shaw Weaver and Dora Marsden as a feminist paper named *The New Freewoman: An Individualist Review.* The periodical changed its name as well as its direction under the editorial influence of Ezra Pound. *The Egoist* published articles on all the modern arts and became known as the journal of Imagist poets. James Joyce's novel *A Portrait of the Artist as a Young Man* was first published there in 1914–15. Initially issued every two weeks, *The Egoist* became a monthly periodical until it ceased publication at the end of 1919.

Eguren \ā-'gü-ren\, José María (b. July 7, 1874, Lima, Peru—d. April 19, 1942, Lima) Author considered one of the leading postmodernist poets of Peru.

His first book of poetry, *Simbólicas* (1911; "Symbolisms"), signaled a break with the Modernismo tradition, while still maintaining affinities with the work of Romantic and early French Symbolist poets who had influenced the movement. Many of the poems describe in musical and highly pictorial language a medieval world of adventure peopled with knights and princesses. His second book, *La canción de las figuras* (1916; "The Ballad of the Figures"), a collection of highly personal and hermetic poems, continues in the same tradition.

With the appearance of Peruvian poet César Vallejo's *Trilce* (1922), poets like Eguren were censured for their escapism. The communist editor José Carlos Mariátegui, who published a collection of Eguren's poems, *Poesías* (1929; "Poetry"), admired his technical mastery but considered him out of touch with reality. After 1929 Eguren wrote mostly prose criticism, collected in *Motivos estéticos* (1959; "Aesthetic Motifs").

Egyptian, The Historical novel by Mika WALTARI, published in Finnish in 1945 as *Sinuhe, egyptiläinen.*

The novel is set in Egypt during the 18th dynasty when Akhnaton, who ruled from 1353 to 1336 BC, established a new monotheistic cult. Narrated by its protagonist, a physician named Sinuhe who is in contact with both rich and poor, the novel describes the daily life, religion, and politics of the era. His travels take him as far away as Syria and Crete. A confidante of pharaohs, he eventually lives in permanent exile.

Ehrenburg \i-rʸin-'bủrk\, Ilya Grigoryevich (b. Jan. 15 [Jan. 27, New Style], 1891, Kiev, Ukraine, Russian Empire—d. Aug. 31, 1967, Moscow, Russian S.F.S.R., U.S.S.R.) Prolific writer and journalist who was an effective spokesman to the West for Soviet issues and attitudes.

Born into a middle-class Jewish family, Ehrenburg became involved as a youth in revolutionary activity and was arrested in his early teens. He immigrated to Paris, where he began publishing poetry in 1910. During World War I he was a war correspondent at the front, returning to Russia in 1917. He lived in Ukraine during the civil war and, between 1917 and 1921, wavered between supporting and opposing the Bolsheviks. His first novel—generally considered his best work—was the philosophical-satirical *Neobychaynyye khozhdeniya Khulio Khurenito i yego uchenikov* (1922; *The Extraordinary Adventures of Julio Jurenito and His Disciples*). Having lived for a time in Europe, he was permitted to return to the Soviet Union. Soon he was sent back to Europe as foreign editor of several Soviet newspapers. In 1941 he returned to the Soviet Union, where his *Padeniye Parizha* (1941; *The Fall of Paris*)—a bitter attack on the West—was published, winning the 1942 Stalin Prize. Ehrenburg also wrote poetry, short stories, essays, travelogues, and memoirs.

After his embrace of the Soviet regime, he adapted his writing to Soviet political demands and was successful in avoiding the purges that destroyed many other writers and artists. In 1946–47 he won a second Stalin Prize, for *Burya* (*The Storm*), and in 1951–52 another major novel was published, *Devyaty val* (*The Ninth Wave*). Shortly after Joseph Stalin's death Ehrenburg produced the novel *Ottepel* (1954; *The Thaw*), which dealt realistically with Soviet life and provoked intense controversy in the Soviet press. In his autobiography, *Lyudi, gody, zhizn* ("People, Years, Life"), Ehrenburg examined many topics (*e.g.*, Western art) and people (*e.g.*, writers lost in the purges of the 1930s) not considered proper material for Soviet authors. Although this boldness brought official censure in 1963 when the "thaw" began to reverse, Ehrenburg survived and remained prominent in Soviet literary circles until his death.

Eichendorff \ˈī-kən-ˌdȯrf\, Joseph, Baron (Freiherr) von (b. March 10, 1788, near Ratibor, Prussia [now Racibórz, Pol.]—d. Nov. 26, 1857, Neisse [now Nysa]) Poet and novelist, considered one of the great German Romantic lyricists.

Eichendorff studied law at Heidelberg, where he published his first verse and became acquainted with the circle of Romantics. Continuing his studies in Berlin, he met the national leaders of the Romantic movement. When the Prussian war of liberation broke out in 1813, Eichendorff enlisted in the Lützowsche Freikorps and fought against Napoleon.

The French Revolution appears in the novella *Das Schloss Dürande* (1837; "Castle Dürande") and in the epic poem *Robert und Guiscard* (1855). The Napoleonic Wars, which brought about the decline of the Eichendorff family and the loss of the Lubowitz castle, are the sources of nostalgia in his poetry. During these war years he wrote two of his most important prose works: a long Romantic novel, *Ahnung und Gegenwart*, (1819; "Premonition and Present"), which is pervaded by hopelessness and despair, and *Novellen des Marmorbilds* (1819; "Novellas of a Marble Statue"), which contains supernatural elements. After the war he held posts in the Prussian civil service. His poetry of this period (*Gedichte*, 1837) gained the popularity of folk songs and inspired such composers as Robert Schumann, Felix Mendelssohn, and Richard Strauss. In 1826 he published his most important prose work, *Aus dem Leben eines Taugenichts* (*Memoirs of a Good-for-Nothing*), which, with its combination of the dreamlike and the realistic, is considered a high point of Romantic fiction. From 1844 he devoted himself entirely to his writing.

Eileithyia \ī-lī-ˈthī-ə\ Pre-Hellenic goddess of childbirth, who hindered or facilitated the procedure according to her disposition. Cretan excavations indicate that she was worshiped continuously from Neolithic to Roman times. In Homer's works she appears, sometimes in the plural, as a personification of birth pangs and is described as the daughter of Hera. In later times Eileithyia tended to be identified with Hera or Artemis, goddesses who were also associated with marriage and childbirth.

Eilhart von Oberg \ˈīl-ˌhärt-ˌfȯn-ˈō-ˌberg\ (fl. late 12th century AD) German poet important in the history of the court epic

and the development of the Tristram and Isolde story in romance literature.

Eilhart was a member of a Brunswick family mentioned in records of Henry the Lion. His epic, *Tristrant und Isalde*, a labored version of an Old French source now lost, dates from the last quarter of the 12th century. It is not known if Eilhart's work preceded that of the Flemish author Heinrich von Veldeke. Precedence, the corruptness of the early fragment, and later complete but modified versions of his epic make it difficult to assess Eilhart's importance. His epic was popular, for it provided the basis of a 15th-century prose novel, *Tristan und Isalde*, and a tragedy by Hans Sachs. Its relationship to the classic epic by Gottfried von Strassburg (fl. 1210) is clear but less significant.

Einhard \ˈīn-ˌhärt\, *also called* Eginhard \ˈā-gin-ˌhärt\ (b. *c.* 770, Maingau, Franconia [Ger.]—d. March 14, 840, Seligenstadt, Franconia) Frankish historian and court scholar whose writings constitute an invaluable source of information on the life of Charlemagne and the Carolingian Empire.

Einhard was educated after 779 in the monastery of Fulda. His brilliance was soon recognized, and in 791 he was sent to Charlemagne's Palace School at Aachen, where he quickly became the trusted friend and adviser of the king. His political prominence increased after Charlemagne's death in 814 and the succession of Louis I the Pious, whom Einhard had been influential in raising to the throne.

The *Vita Karoli Magni* ("Life of Charles the Great"; *Life of Charlemagne*) was probably written about 830–833, after Einhard had left Aachen and was living in Seligenstadt. Based on 23 years of service to Charlemagne and on research in the royal annals, the book was expressly intended to convey Einhard's gratitude and admiration for Charlemagne's aid to his education. Following the model of Suetonius' *De vita Caesarum* (*Lives of the Caesars*), particularly the "Life of Augustus," it was composed in an excellent Latin style and analyzed Charlemagne's family, his foreign and domestic achievements, his personal tastes, and his death. Brief and limited in scope and detail, it provides a generally accurate and direct account of the period. As an example of the classical renaissance at the Carolingian court and as the first medieval biography of a lay figure, the work was highly admired and copied in its own time.

eisteddfod \ī-ˈsteth-ˌvȯd, ā-\, *plural* eisteddfods *or* eisteddfodau \-ˌsteth-ˈvȯ-ˌdī\ [Welsh, literally, session] Formal assembly of Welsh bards and minstrels that originated in the traditions of court bards of medieval times. The modern National Eisteddfod, revived in the 19th century and held each summer alternately in a site in North or South Wales, has been broadened to include awards for music, prose, drama, and art, but the chairing and investiture of the winning poet remains its high point.

Earlier assemblies were competitions of musicians (especially harpists) and poets from which new musical, literary, and oratorical forms emerged. The assembly at Carmarthen in 1451 is famous for establishing the arrangement of the strict meters of Welsh poetry in forms that are still authoritative. In the 17th century the custom fell into disuse, though poetry remained a popular art and a form of eisteddfod survived in informal gatherings of rhymesters who met to compose verses on impromptu subjects. In the 18th century, when local eisteddfods were revived, it was apparent that many farmers and workers were still sufficiently skilled in the complicated craftsmanship of bardic versification to win prizes. Though the bardic forms were preserved, the quality of eisteddfod poetry was normally mediocre and degenerated to its lowest level in the late 19th century. The subjects assigned for the competition were celebrations of

Welsh history or the Welsh countryside, biblical subjects such as the Resurrection, or abstract subjects such as almsgiving. Such poetry was necessarily impersonal and resulted in lengthy, descriptive compositions in which form was the major concern and content and emotional depth were secondary. With World War I and the Depression of the 1930s, many Welsh poets turned to more personal poetry, and the eisteddfod became primarily a forum for a youthful poet to gain a hearing. *See also* AWDL.

Ekelöf \'ek-e-ˌlœf\, Gunnar (b. Sept. 15, 1907, Stockholm, Swed.—d. March 16, 1968, Sigtuna) Outstanding Swedish poet and essayist whose radically modern style was influenced by such poets as Charles Baudelaire, Arthur Rimbaud, Ezra Pound, and T.S. Eliot.

In his early poetry, such as *Sent på jorden* (1932; "Late on Earth"), Ekelöf was drawn to the Surrealist technique of automatic writing, but his work also reflects an interest in musical forms and Oriental mysticism. A student of Oriental languages, Ekelöf felt divided between mystical tendencies and rationalism. This conflict is apparent in *Färjesång* (1941; "Ferry Song") and *Non Serviam* (1945; "I Will Not Serve"). One of Ekelöf's most important works is *En Mölna-elegi* (1960; "A Mölna Elegy"), published in several earlier versions from the mid-1940s. Its starting point is within the mind of the poet, sitting at Mölna dock on a summer day in 1940. Personal memories from his past intermingle with incidents from history in an endless panorama.

In the 1950s Ekelöf turned away from finished compositions to work in fragmentary forms, as in *Strountes* (1955; "Nonsense"). His Akritas trilogy—*Dīwān över Fursten av Emgión* (1965; "Diwan over the Prince of Emgión"), *Sagan om Fatumeh* (1966; "The Tale of Fatumeh"; *Selected Poems*), and *Vägvisare till underjorden* (1967; *Guide to the Underworld*)—contains his finest poetic expression of the simultaneous experience of presence and transitoriness. In 1958 Ekelöf became a member of the Swedish Royal Academy.

Ekkehard I or **Ekkehart I** \'ek-ə-ˌhärt\, *called* The Elder, *also called* Ekkehard I of St. Gall (b. *c.* 910, Toggenburg?, Alemannia [now in Switz.]—d. Jan. 14, 973, Sankt Gallen) Teacher, monk, hymnist, and poet who until about 1941 was regarded as the author of *Waltharius*, a celebrated Latin heroic poem based on the life of King Walter of Aquitaine.

Of noble birth, Ekkehard was educated at the Swiss Benedictine monastery of Sankt Gallen (St. Gall), then one of Europe's greatest centers of learning, at which he later taught. He was elected dean of the monastery in 957 and for a time was in Rome. He retired to Sankt Gallen and was chosen abbot but declined the position. A noted economist, Ekkehard rejuvenated the intellectual and ecclesiastical prestige that had distinguished Sankt Gallen for centuries.

Among Ekkehard's extant hymns are those honoring the Trinity and Saints Columban, John the Baptist, and Stephen. The belief that Ekkehard was also the author of the famous *Waltharius* epic stems from a statement in the *Casus Sancti Galli*, a history of Sankt Gallen written in part by Ekkehard IV, that Ekkehard I—while still in abbey school—composed a *Vitam Waltharii manu fortis* as a school exercise for his master Geraldus. That an individual named Geraldus, or Gerald, dedicated the work to Bishop Erkanbald of Strasbourg is clear; scholars now tend to attribute the entire 1,456-line *Waltharius* epic to Geraldus.

Ekrem \e-'krem\, Recaizade Mahmud (b. March 1, 1847, Constantinople, Ottoman Empire [now Istanbul, Tur.]—d. Jan. 31, 1914, Constantinople) Writer who was one of the outstanding figures in 19th-century Turkish literature.

Ekrem was apprenticed to a number of government offices after his formal education. Later he became an official in the Council of State and a teacher at the renowned Galatasaray Lycée and at the Imperial School of Political Science in Constantinople. After the Young Turk Revolution in 1908, he held several government posts, finally becoming senator.

Writing in the traditional Ottoman classical style early in his literary career, he came under the influence of the famous Turkish modernist Namık Kemal. Although never a great poet himself, Ekrem strove to redefine art and poetical form. Writing for *Servet-i Fünun*, an avant-garde literary periodical, Ekrem developed a great following among younger poets. "Art for art's sake" was a major tenet, as it was for much of the French Parnassian school of poetry. Among Ekrem's most important works are *Talim-i Edebiyat* (1882; "The Teaching of Literature"), literary criticism and theory; and *Tefekkür* (1888; "Meditations"), poems and prose. He also wrote plays and made translations from the French.

Ekwensi \ə-'kwän-sē\, Cyprian (Odiatu Duaka) (b. Sept. 26, 1921, Minna, Nigeria) Igbo (Ibo) novelist, short-story writer, and children's author whose strength lies in his realistic depiction of the forces that have shaped the African city dweller.

Ekwensi was educated at Ibadan University College in Nigeria and at the Chelsea School of Pharmacy in London. His early works include the novellas *When Love Whispers* (1947) and *The Leopard's Claw* (1950), which combine a fascination for urban life with earnest exhortations to avoid its pitfalls. *People of the City* (1954; rev. ed., 1969) is a commentary on the problems of corruption, bribery, and despotism as seen through the eyes of a crime reporter and dance-band leader in Lagos.

Jagua Nana (1961), Ekwensi's most successful novel, has as its protagonist Jagua, a charming, colorful, and impressive prostitute. Around her, Ekwensi sets in motion a whole panoply of vibrant, amoral characters who have rejected their rural pasts and have adopted the opportunistic, pleasure-seeking urban code. Similar characters and themes emerge from *Lokotown and Other Stories* (1966), where the glitter and excitement of Lagos life is sharply contrasted with its seediness and degradation. *Burning Grass* (1962) concerns the Fulani cattlemen in the north of Nigeria. *Jagua Nana's Daughter* (1986) is a sequel to *Jagua Nana*. Ekwensi also wrote a number of children's books and a collection of Igbo folktales.

Elaine or **Elayne** \i-'lān\ Character of Arthurian legend, first portrayed in *Le Morte Darthur* (1485) by Sir Thomas Malory.

In Malory's sprawling work, Elaine (or Elayne) is the name of five women with overlapping identities. The best known and most cited of these is Elaine Le Blank, known as the Fair Maid of Astolat, who falls in love with Lancelot, provokes Guinevere's jealousy, and eventually dies of love for the knight. Elayne the Fair, or Sans Pere ("the Peerless"), daughter of King Pelles, takes on the likeness of Guinevere for a night and, by Lancelot, becomes the mother of Galahad, the pure and noble knight who later finds the Holy Grail. A third Elayne is the sister of Morgawse and Morgan le Fay in the opening pages of the epic. Lancelot's mother, the wife of King Ban, is also named Elaine; yet another Elayne appears as a minor character, the daughter of King Pellinore.

The character also appears in two works by Alfred, Lord Tennyson. In "The Lady of Shalott" (1832), Tennyson develops Malory's Elaine Le Blank. In "Lancelot and Elaine" (1859; part of *Idylls of the King*) she is called "the lily maid of Astolat." By her request her dead body is placed on a barge, a lily in her right hand and a letter avowing her love and Lancelot's innocence in her left.

Eldorado \ˌel-də-ˈräd-ō, -ˈräd-, *Spanish* ˌel-dō-ˈrä-<u>th</u>ō \ (Spanish: "The Gilded One")   Originally, the legendary ruler of an Indian town near Bogotá, who was believed to coat his naked body with gold dust during festivals, then plunge into Lake Guatavita to wash off the dust after the ceremonies; his subjects were said to throw jewels and golden objects into the lake. Spanish conquistadores heard the tale before 1530, and one of them reported that he had visited Eldorado himself in a city called Omagua.

As the search for Eldorado led into the Orinoco and Amazon valleys, the name came to mean an entire fabulous country of gold with legendary cities named Manoa and Omagua. In this quest, Gonzalo Pizarro crossed the Andes from Quito (1539), Francisco de Orellana sailed down the Napo and the Amazon (1541–42), and Gonzalo Jiménez de Quesada explored eastward from Bogotá (1569–72). Sir Walter Raleigh searched for Manoa in the Orinoco lowlands (1595), while Spaniards sought Omagua nearby. In 1603 the Portuguese Pêro Coelho de Sousa explored northward from Pernambuco, and the golden city of Eldorado was shown on maps of Brazil and the Guianas for years thereafter.

Eldorado was only one of the many mythical regions of great riches, the search for which led to the rapid conquest of much of the Americas. Since then, Eldorado has come to mean any place where wealth can be quickly and easily gained.

Electra \i-ˈlek-trə\ ("Bright One")   In Greek mythology, the daughter of Agamemnon and Clytemnestra, who saves the life of her young brother Orestes by sending him away when their father (Agamemnon) is murdered. Orestes later returns, and Electra helps him to slay their mother (Clytemnestra) and their mother's lover (Aegisthus). The plays entitled *Electra* by Sophocles and Euripides and the *Libation Bearers* by Aeschylus vary the theme in detail. Later interpretations of the myth include Benito Pérez Galdós' *Electra* (1901) and Eugene O'Neill's *Mourning Becomes Electra* (1931).

Electra \i-ˈlek-trə\ (*Greek* Ēlektra)   Tragedy by SOPHOCLES. The date of its first performance is unknown.

As in Aeschylus' *Libation Bearers*, the action of *Electra* follows the return of Orestes to kill his mother, Clytemnestra, and her lover Aegisthus in retribution for their murder of Agamemnon. Sophocles, however, chose to examine the character of Orestes' sister Electra and her anguished participation in her brother's plans for vengeance. In order to gain admittance to the palace, Orestes spreads false news of his own death. Believing this report, the despairing Electra unsuccessfully tries to enlist her sister Chrysothemis in an attempt to murder their mother. In a dramatic scene, Orestes then enters in disguise and hands Electra the urn that is supposed to contain his own ashes. Moved by his sister's display of grief, Orestes reveals his true identity to her and then strikes down Clytemnestra and Aegisthus.

Electra \i-ˈlek-trə\ (*Greek* Ēlektra)   Drama by EURIPIDES, performed about 418 BC. In Euripides' version of the Greek legend, Electra and Orestes murder their mother, Clytemnestra, in retribution for her murder of their father, Agamemnon. Electra is portrayed as a frustrated and resentful woman who finally lures her mother to her death by appealing to her maternal instincts. After the horrible murder both Electra and Orestes, who is here portrayed as her reluctant accomplice, are consumed by remorse. Euripides' bitterly realistic and antiheroic play is a convincing portrait of Electra's wretchedness.

elegiac \ˌel-ə-ˈjī-ək, -ˌak; i-ˈlē-jē-ˌak\ or **elegiacal** \ˌel-ə-ˈjī-ə-kəl\ [Greek *elegeiakós*, a derivative of *elegeîon* elegiac couplet, elegy]   **1.** In classical prosody, of, relating to, consisting of, or noted for verse written in elegiac meter.   **2.** Of or relat-ing to the period in Greece around the 7th century BC when poetry written in elegiac meter flourished.   **3.** Of, relating to, befitting, or comprising elegy or an elegy; especially, expressing sorrow or lamentation, often for something past.

elegiac meter \ˌel-ə-ˈjī-ək, -ˌak; i-ˈlē-jē-ˌak\   **1.** In classical prosody, a distich (two lines), the first line of which is a dactylic hexameter and the second of which is often misleadingly called pentameter (it lacks the arsis, or short elements, in the third and sixth feet). In actuality, the second line is made up of two hemiepe, or two and a half dactyls followed by another two and a half dactyls. Elegiac meter is scanned:

$$- \cup \cup \mid - \cup \cup \mid - \cup \cup \mid - \cup \cup \mid - \cup \cup \mid - -$$
$$- \cup \cup \mid - \cup \cup \mid - \mid - \cup \cup \mid - \cup \cup \mid -$$

2. The meter characteristic of a kinah, a Hebrew elegy or dirge. *Compare* KINAH METER.

elegiac stanza   In poetry, a quatrain in iambic pentameter with alternate lines rhyming. The older and more general term for this is heroic stanza, but the form became associated specifically with elegiac poetry when Thomas Gray used it to perfection in *An Elegy Written in a Country Church Yard* (1751). From the mid-18th to the mid-19th century the form was usually used for elegiac verse, of which the best-known example is Gray's poem, which begins

> The curfew tolls the knell of parting day,
> The lowing herd wind slowly o'er the lea,
> The plowman homeward plods his weary way,
> And leaves the world to darkness and to me.

elegiambus \ˌel-ə-jī-ˈam-bəs\ *plural* elegiambi \-ˌbī\ [Late Greek *elegíambos*, from Greek *elegeîon* elegiac couplet + *íambos* iamb]   In classical prosody, a verse composed of the dactylic $- \cup \cup - \cup \cup -$, as in the elegiac pentameter, and iambics. It is sometimes applied to the length $- \cup \cup - \cup \cup \mid - \cup - \cup - -$.

elegy \ˈel-ə-jē\ [Greek *elegeía, elegeîon* elegiac couplet, elegy, a derivative of *élegos* song accompanied by the flute]   **1.** A poem in elegiac couplets.   **2.** A song or poem expressing sorrow or lamentation, especially for one who is dead.   **3.** A pensive or reflective poem that is usually nostalgic or melancholy.

In classical literature an elegy was simply any poem written in the elegiac meter (alternating lines of dactylic hexameter and pentameter) and was not restricted as to subject. Though some classical elegies were laments, many others were love poems. In some modern literatures, such as German, in which the classical elegiac meter has been adapted to the language, the term elegy refers to this meter, rather than to the poem's content. Thus, Rainer Maria Rilke's famous *Duineser Elegien* are not laments; they deal with the poet's search for spiritual values. In English literature since the 16th century, however, an elegy has come to mean specifically a poem of lamentation. It may be written in any meter the poet chooses.

A distinct kind of elegy is the pastoral elegy, which borrows the classical convention of representing its subject as an idealized shepherd in an idealized pastoral background and follows a rather formal pattern. It begins with an expression of grief and an invocation to the Muse to aid the poet in expressing his suffering. It usually contains a funeral procession, a description of sympathetic mourning throughout nature, and musings on the unkindness of death. It ends with acceptance, often a very affirmative justification, of nature's law. The outstanding example of the English pastoral elegy is John Milton's "Lycidas" (1638), written to commemorate the death of Edward King, a college friend.

Other elegies observe no set patterns or conventions. In the 18th century the English GRAVEYARD SCHOOL of poets wrote generalized reflections on death and immortality combining gloomy, sometimes ghoulish imagery of human impermanence with philosophical speculation. Representative works are Edward Young's *Night Thoughts* (1742–45) and Robert Blair's *The Grave* (1743), but the best known of these poems is Thomas Gray's more tastefully subdued creation *An Elegy Written in a Country Church Yard* (1751), which pays tribute to the generations of humble and unknown villagers buried in the church cemetery.

In modern poetry the elegy remains a frequent and important poetic statement. Its range and variation can be seen in such poems as A.E. Housman's "To an Athlete Dying Young," W.H. Auden's "In Memory of W.B. Yeats," John Peale Bishop's "The Hours" (on F. Scott Fitzgerald), and Robert Lowell's "The Quaker Graveyard in Nantucket."

Elegy Written in a Country Church Yard, An   Meditative poem written in iambic pentameter quatrains by Thomas GRAY, published in 1751.

A meditation on unused human potential, the conditions of country life, and mortality, *An Elegy Written in a Country Church Yard* is one of the best-known elegies in the language. It exhibits the gentle melancholy that is characteristic of the English poets of the graveyard school of the 1740s and '50s. The poem contains some of the best-known lines of English literature, notably "Full many a flower is born to blush unseen" and "Far from the madding Crowd's ignoble Strife."

The elegy opens with the narrator musing in a graveyard at close of day; he speculates about the obscure lives of the villagers who lie buried and suggests that they may have been full of rich promise that was ultimately stunted by poverty or ignorance. The churchyard in the poem is believed to be that of Stoke Poges, Buckinghamshire, which Gray visited often, and where he now lies buried.

Eleusinian Mysteries \ˌel-yü-'sin-ē-ən\   Most famous of the secret religious rites of ancient Greece. According to the myth told in the Homeric *Hymn to Demeter*, the earth goddess Demeter went to Eleusis in search of her daughter Persephone (Kore), who had been abducted by Hades (Pluto), god of the underworld. Befriended by the royal family of Eleusis, she agreed to rear the queen's son. She was, however, prevented by the queen's fear from making the boy immortal and eternally young. After this occasion, she revealed her identity to the royal family and commanded that a temple be built for her into which she retired.

According to the *Hymn to Demeter*, the Mysteries at Eleusis originated in the twofold story of Demeter's life—her separation from and reunion with her daughter and her failure to make the queen's son immortal. After Eleusis was incorporated, the city of Athens took responsibility for the festival, but the festival never lost its local associations.

The Mysteries began with the march of the *mystai* (initiates) in solemn procession from Athens to Eleusis. The rites that they then performed in the Telesterion, or Hall of Initiation, were and remain a secret. Something was recited, something was revealed, and acts were performed, but there is no sure evidence of what the rites actually were, though some garbled information was given by later Christian writers who tried to condemn the Mysteries as pagan abominations. It is clear, however, that neophytes were initiated in stages and that the annual process began with purification rites at what were called the Lesser Mysteries held at Agrai (Agrae) on the stream of Ilissos, outside of Athens, in the month of Anthesterion (February–March). The Greater Mysteries at Eleusis was celebrated annually in the month of Boedromion (September–October). It included a ritual bath in the sea, three days of fasting, and completion of the still-mysterious central rite.

elf \'elf\ *plural* **elves** \'elvz\ *or* **elfs** [Middle English, from Old English *ælf;* akin to Middle High German *alp* incubus, Old Norse *alfr* elf]   In Germanic folklore, originally, a spirit of any kind, later specialized into a diminutive creature, usually in tiny human form. In the *Prose Edda*, elves were classified as light elves (who were fair) and dark elves (who were darker than pitch); these classifications are roughly equivalent to the Scottish seelie court and unseelie court. The notable characteristics of elves were mischief and volatility. They were believed at various times and in various regions to cause diseases in humans and cattle, to sit upon the breast of a sleeper and give him bad dreams (the German word for nightmare is *Alpdrücken,* or "elf-pressure"), and to steal human children and substitute changelings (deformed or weak elf or fairy children). Elves occasionally also were benevolent and helpful. In time, elves came to be indistinct from fairies, though such classics as J.W. von Goethe's poem "Der Erlkönig" ("The Elf King" or "The Erl King") and J.R.R. Tolkien's *The Lord of the Rings* still treat elves as a distinct type. *See also* FAIRY; PIXIE.

Elia \'el-ē-ə, *commonly* 'ēl-\   Pseudonym of Charles LAMB. Lamb used the name of a clerk who worked with his brother John and created a persona to reflect his own thoughts on a variety of subjects. The work of Elia initially appeared in *London Magazine;* two volumes of essays by Elia eventually were published, the first in 1823 and the second in 1833.

Elijah \i-'lī-jə\, *also spelled* Elias \i-'lī-əs\ *or* Elia \i-'lī-ə\, *Hebrew* Eliyyahu (fl. 9th century BC)   Hebrew prophet who ranks with Moses as a savior of the Yahweh religion from corruption. Elijah was also a pioneer in teaching God's transcendence and the idea of salvation being bestowed on a purified "remnant" of the people. He linked faith with reason and morality.

According to tradition, Elijah lived during the reign of King Ahab, whose Phoenician wife, Jezebel, promoted Baal worship at Yahweh's expense; Elijah proclaimed a drought in punishment for the foreign cult. He later met 450 prophets of Baal in a contest on Mount Carmel and vanquished them, simultaneously announcing the end of the drought. Though later disheartened in his struggle, Elijah soon was renewed, and he upheld the moral law in denouncing Ahab's judicial murder of Naboth and confiscation of his vineyard. Elijah was finally taken to heaven in a whirlwind. Many authors—including Geoffrey Chaucer, John Milton, and William Blake—have referred to the character in their works.

Eliot \'el-ē-ət\, George, *pseudonym of* Mary Ann (or Marian) Cross \'krôs\, *original surname* Evans \'ev-ənz\ (b. Nov. 22, 1819, Chilvers Coton, Warwickshire, Eng.—d. Dec. 22, 1880,

Chalk drawing by F.W. Burton, 1865
National Portrait Gallery, London

London)   Victorian novelist who developed the method of psychological analysis characteristic of modern fiction.

Evans was sent to several schools, including Mrs. Wallington's School at Nuneaton, which she attended from 1828 to 1832. There she developed a strong evangelical piety. In 1841 she moved with her father to Coventry, where she lived with him until his death in 1849. In Coventry she became acquainted with Charles Bray, a self-taught freethinker who campaigned for radical causes. His brother-in-law, Charles Hennell, was the author of *An Inquiry Concerning the Origin of Christianity* (1838), a book that precipitated Evans' break with orthodoxy.

The Brays and the Hennells introduced her to many new religious and political ideas. When Hennell married in 1843, Evans completed his wife's translation of D.F. Strauss's *Das Leben Jesu kritisch bearbeitet*, published anonymously as *The Life of Jesus Critically Examined*, 3 vol. (1846). John Chapman, who published the translation, got her a chance to review a book in *The Westminster Review* (January 1851), and she decided to settle in London as a freelance writer. In January 1851 she went to board with the Chapmans. Chapman eventually bought *The Westminster Review*, and for three years, until 1854, Evans served as its subeditor. Under her influence the review enjoyed its most brilliant run since the days of John Stuart Mill. During this period she became associated with George Henry LEWES, a married journalist who would be her companion until his death in 1878.

At Weimar and Berlin, Evans wrote some of her best essays for *The Westminster Review* and translated Spinoza's *Ethics* (still unpublished), while Lewes worked on his groundbreaking life of J.W. von Goethe. Evans then turned to early memories and, encouraged by Lewes, wrote a story about a childhood episode in Chilvers Coton parish. Published in *Blackwood's Magazine* (1857) as "The Sad Fortunes of the Reverend Amos Barton," it was an instant success. Two more tales, also based on local events, appeared serially in the same year, and all three were published under the pseudonym George Eliot as SCENES OF CLERICAL LIFE, 2 vol. (1858).

ADAM BEDE (1859), her first long novel, was set in the countryside, while in THE MILL ON THE FLOSS, 3 vol. (1860), she returned again to the scenes of her early life. Her other novels include SILAS MARNER (1861), ROMOLA (1863), FELIX HOLT, THE RADICAL (1866), and DANIEL DERONDA (1876). MIDDLEMARCH (1871–72) is by general consent George Eliot's masterpiece.

In 1863 Lewes and Evans bought the Priory in Regent's Park, where their Sunday afternoons became a brilliant feature of Victorian life. Lewes died on Nov. 30, 1878. For some years Evans' investments had been in the hands of John Walter Cross (1840–1924), whose mother had died a week after Lewes. Drawn by sympathy and the need for advice, Evans soon began to lean on Cross for affection too. On May 6, 1880, some seven months before her death, they were married. After a wedding trip in Italy they settled in London.

Eliot \'el-ē-ət\ T.S., *in full* Thomas Stearns (b. Sept. 26, 1888, St. Louis, Mo., U.S.—d. Jan. 4, 1965, London, Eng.) American-English poet, playwright, and literary critic, a leader of the modernist movement in poetry. In 1948 he was awarded the Nobel Prize for Literature.

One of Eliot's ancestors arrived in Boston in 1670. Although by the time of the poet's birth the Eliots had been in Missouri 54 years, they retained their New England political and theological culture. Eliot graduated from Harvard after three years. He spent a year studying in France, and from 1911 to 1914 he was back at Harvard reading Indian philosophy and studying Sanskrit. In 1914 he met Ezra Pound and moved to England.

Eliot's first important publication, and the first masterpiece of modernism in English, was the poem THE LOVE SONG OF J. ALFRED PRUFROCK. From the appearance of Eliot's first volume, *Prufrock and Other Observations*, in 1917, one may date the maturity of the 20th-century poetic revolution. Together Pound and Eliot set about reforming poetic diction.

Eliot taught for a year before he began his brief career as a bank clerk in Lloyds Bank Ltd. in London. Meanwhile he was also a prolific reviewer and essayist. In 1919 he published *Poems*, which contained the unique "Gerontion," a meditative interior monologue in blank verse.

With the publication in 1922 of THE WASTE LAND, his best-known poem, Eliot won an international reputation. The poem, in five parts, proceeds on a principle of "rhetorical discontinuity" that reflects the fragmented experience of the 20th-century sensibility of the great modern cities of the West.

Archive Photos

Eliot's work as a critic is probably best represented by his first critical volume, THE SACRED WOOD (1920). The essays discuss the poet and tradition and introduce two phrases that were much discussed in later critical theory—OBJECTIVE CORRELATIVE (the use of an external object, event, or situation to evoke emotion in the reader) and DISSOCIATION OF SENSIBILITY, a phrase he invented to explain the change that came over English poetry after John Donne and Andrew Marvell. Shortly before the publication of his *The Use of Poetry and the Use of Criticism* (1933)—his Charles Eliot Norton lectures at Harvard—his interests had broadened into theology and sociology. Three short books, or long essays, were the result: *Thoughts After Lambeth* (1931), *The Idea of a Christian Society* (1939), and NOTES TOWARDS THE DEFINITION OF CULTURE (1948). These book-essays, along with his *Dante* (1929), proposed the view that whether a work is poetry must be decided by literary standards; whether it is great poetry must be decided by standards higher than the literary.

Eliot's masterpiece is THE FOUR QUARTETS, taken as a single work, though each "quartet" is a complete poem. The four parts, published at intervals between 1936 and 1942, were issued as a book in 1943.

His plays, which begin with SWEENEY AGONISTES (1932) and include such poetic dramas as THE COCKTAIL PARTY (1950), are, with the exception of MURDER IN THE CATHEDRAL (1935), inferior to his lyric and meditative poetry. Eliot's career as editor was ancillary to his main interests, but his quarterly review, *The Criterion* (1922–39), was a distinguished international critical journal of the period. He was a "director," or working editor, of the publishing firm of Faber & Faber Ltd. from the early 1920s until his death.

Eliot always kept his private life rigorously in the background. In 1915 he married Vivian Haigh-Wood; after 1933 she was mentally ill, and they lived apart; she died in 1947. In January 1957 he married Valerie Fletcher, with whom he lived happily until his death.

Elisha \i-'lī-shə\, *also called* Elisaios \,el-ē-'sī-əs\, *also spelled* Eliseus \,el-ē-'sē-əs\ In the Hebrew scriptures, Israelite prophet, the student and, about 851 BC, the successor to the prophet Elijah. He instigated and directed Jehu's revolt against the house of Omri, which was marked by a bloodbath at Jezreel in which King Ahab of Israel and his family were slaughtered.

The popular traditions about Elisha found in chapters 2–13 of Kings II sketch a charismatic, quasi-ecstatic figure, very similar to Elijah. Like his mentor, Elisha was a passionate exponent of the ancient religious and cultural traditions of Israel that both men felt to be threatened by the ruling dynasty of Omri, which was in alliance with Phoenicia. (King Ahab's wife, the Tyrian princess Jezebel, was then trying to introduce the worship of Baal into Israel.) As a prophet, Elisha was a political activist and revolutionary. He led a "holy war" that extinguished the house of Omri in Jerusalem as well as in Samaria.

In popular estimation Elisha remains partly in Elijah's shadow: though Elisha recruited Jehu to revolt against and succeed Ahab, it was Elijah who was instructed to anoint Jehu as Israel's king. The story of Elisha's apprenticeship and the account in which he becomes Elijah's heir and successor both feature a mantle, the cultic garment of the prophet that connotes power and authority. In the first, Elijah casts it upon his pupil; in the second, Elisha picks it up.

elision \i-ˈlizh-ən\ [Late Latin *elisio* (translation of Greek *ékthlipsis*), a derivative of Latin *elidere* to eject, force out]   In prosody, the slurring or omission of a final unstressed vowel that precedes either another vowel or a weak consonant sound, as in the word *heav'n*. It may also be the dropping of a consonant between vowels, as in the word *o'er* for *over*. Elision is used to fit words into a metrical scheme, to smooth the rhythm of a poem, or to ease the pronunciation of words. In classical Greek poetry, an apostrophe (') is substituted for an elided letter, as it is frequently in English verse.

Elissa   *see* DIDO.

Elizabeth and Essex \i-ˈliz-ə-bəth . . . ˈes-iks\   Biography of Elizabeth I, Queen of England, by Lytton STRACHEY, published in 1928. Subtitled "A Tragic History," it chronicles the relationship between the aged Elizabeth and young Robert Devereux, 2nd Earl of Essex. Strachey's experimental psychoanalysis of the queen, which met with mixed reviews, was more narrowly focused and provocative than the analyses found in his previous biographies.

Elizabethan literature   The body of works written during the reign of Elizabeth I of England (1558–1603), probably the most splendid age in the history of English literature. Elizabethan literature encompasses the work of Sir Philip Sidney, Edmund Spenser, Roger Ascham, Bishop Richard Hooker, Christopher Marlowe, William Shakespeare, and others. The epithet Elizabethan can only suggest the immense vitality and richness of English literature produced in the late 16th and early 17th centuries and does not describe any special characteristic of the writing. The Elizabethan Age saw the flowering of poetry (the sonnet, the Spenserian stanza, dramatic blank verse), was a golden age of drama (especially for the plays of Shakespeare), and inspired a wide variety of splendid prose (from historical chronicles, versions of the Holy Scriptures, pamphlets, and literary criticism to the first English novels). From about the beginning of the 17th century a sudden darkening of tone became noticeable in most forms of literary expression, especially in drama, and the change more or less coincided with the death of Elizabeth. English literature during the reign of James I (1603–25) is properly called Jacobean. But, insofar as 16th-century themes and patterns were carried over into the 17th century, the writing is sometimes referred to as "Jacobethan."

Elkin \ˈel-kin\, Stanley (Lawrence) (b. May 11, 1930, New York, N.Y., U.S.)   American writer known for his extraordinary flights of language and imaginative tragicomic explorations of contemporary life.

Elkin grew up in a Jewish family in Chicago. He was educated at the University of Illinois at Champaign-Urbana, completing a dissertation on William Faulkner. From 1960 he taught at Washington University in St. Louis.

Elkin's first novel, *Boswell, A Modern Comedy* (1964), tells of an ordinary man who founds a club for famous individuals, hoping like his namesake to bask in reflected glory. *Criers and Kibitzers, Kibitzers and Criers* (1966), a collection of comic short stories on Jewish themes and characters, was well received. Elkin further develops the rift between family ties and the lure of assimilation in *A Bad Man* (1967).

The Franchiser (1976), considered one of Elkin's strongest works, tells of Ben Flesh, an orphaned bachelor adopted as an adult into the absurd Finsberg family of 18 twins and triplets, all with rare and incurable diseases. Like Elkin himself, Ben suffers from multiple sclerosis, and he comes to terms with his disease as his brothers and sisters die from theirs. *The Living End* (1979), a collection of three interwoven novellas about heaven, hell, and Minnesota's twin cities of Minneapolis and St. Paul, is perhaps Elkin's best-known work. Baroque in detail, *The Living End* portrays God as a petulant creator who destroys the world because He was misunderstood. Elkin gained further critical acclaim for *Stanley Elkin's The Magic Kingdom* (1985), in which Eddy Bale arranges a trip to Disney World for seven terminally ill British children, in honor of his young son's death. In *The MacGuffin* (1991) Elkin attempted a more conventional narrative structure while maintaining his usual style as he tracks the life of City Commissioner Robert Druff over a period of 48 hours.

Elliot family \ˈel-ē-ət\   Fictional characters in the novel PERSUASION by Jane Austen. The head of the family is Sir Walter Elliot of Kellynch Hall, who is immensely vain on account of his good looks and distinguished ancestry. His oldest daughter, Elizabeth, is a snob like her father; unable to find a worthy suitor, she remains unmarried. His youngest daughter, Mary, is also self-centered but has stooped to marry the son of the local squire. Anne, the middle daughter, is the novel's heroine. Decent but timid and neglected, she asserts her independence by the novel's end.

ellipsis \i-ˈlip-sis, e-\ [Greek *élleipsis*, literally, a falling short, defect, a derivative of *elleípein* to leave out, fall short]   The omission of one or more words that are understood but that must be supplied to make a construction semantically complete, as in "No! I am not Prince Hamlet, nor was meant to be" from T.S. Eliot's poem "The Love Song of J. Alfred Prufrock."

elliptical \i-ˈlip-tik-əl\ or **elliptic** \i-ˈlip-tik\   **1.** Of, relating to, or marked by extreme economy of speech or writing. The style is exemplified in W.H. Auden's poem "This Lunar Beauty":

> But this was never
> A ghost's endeavor
> Nor finished this,
> Was ghost at ease;
> And till it pass
> Love shall not near
> The sweetness here
> Nor sorrow take
> His endless look.

2. Of or relating to deliberate obscurity (as of literary or conversational style).

Ellison \ˈel-i-sən\, Harlan (Jay) (b. May 27, 1934, Cleveland, Ohio, U.S.)   American writer of short stories, novels, essays, and television and film scripts; he is best known for his science-fiction writing and editing.

Ellison became a prolific contributor of science fiction, crime and sex fiction, and true confessions for genre magazines. After serving in the U.S. Army from 1957 to 1959, he edited *Rogue* magazine from 1959 to 1960 before becoming a successful television scriptwriter.

Ellison's reputation as an important science-fiction writer rests on short stories such as " 'Repent, Harlequin!' Said the Ticktockman" (1965), "A Boy and His Dog" (1969), and those in collections like *I Have No Mouth and I Must Scream* (1967) and *The Beast That Shouted Love at the Heart of the World* (1969). As an editor he published several important anthologies; for each of the stories he commissioned for *Dangerous Visions* (1967) and *Again, Dangerous Visions* (1972) he added a personal introductory essay that revealed as much about himself as it did about the work in question. His other works include *Deathbird Stories: A Pantheon of Modern Gods* (1975), *All the Lies That Are My Life* (1980), and *The Harlan Ellison Hornbook* (1990).

Ellison \'el-i-sən\, Ralph (Waldo) (b. March 1, 1914, Oklahoma City, Okla., U.S.—d. April 16, 1994, New York, N.Y.) American teacher and writer who won eminence with his first and only published novel, INVISIBLE MAN (1952), about race relations in the United States in the 20th century.

Exhibiting an early interest in jazz as well as in writing, Ellison left Tuskegee Institute (Alabama) in 1936 after three years' study of music and joined the Federal Writers' Project in New York City. Encouraged by novelist Richard Wright, in 1939 he began contributing short stories, reviews, and essays to various periodicals. He served in the Merchant Marines during World War II, thereafter producing *Invisible Man*, which won the 1953 National Book Award for fiction. After his novel appeared, Ellison published only two collections of essays, *Shadow and Act* (1964) and *Going to the Territory* (1986). He lectured widely on black culture, folklore, and creative writing and taught at various American colleges and universities. His second novel was left unfinished at his death.

Ellmann \'el-mən\, Richard (David) (b. March 15, 1918, Highland Park, Mich., U.S.—d. May 13, 1987, Oxford, Oxfordshire, Eng.) American literary critic and scholar, an expert on the life and works of James Joyce, William Butler Yeats, Oscar Wilde, and other modern British and Irish writers.

Ellmann graduated from Yale University and taught at Northwestern University, Evanston, Ill., from 1951 to 1968, at Yale University from 1968 to 1970, and at the University of Oxford from 1970 to 1984. His book *Yeats: The Man and the Masks* (1948) is a study of one of Yeats's intense conflicts, the dichotomy between the self of everyday life and the self of fantasy. The book revealed Yeats as a timid and confused man behind a facade of arrogance. Other books on Yeats included *The Identity of Yeats* (1954), which focused on his poems, and *Eminent Domain* (1967), on Yeats' relationships with several contemporary writers. Ellmann's definitive biography *James Joyce* (1959; new and rev. ed., 1982) explores in detail aspects of the writer's life and thought; his work on this biography led to his editing Joyce's letters (1966) and other works on Joyce. He also edited several books, including *The Artist as Critic: Critical Writings of Oscar Wilde* (1969) and *The New Oxford Book of American Verse* (1976). Ellmann's biography *Oscar Wilde* appeared posthumously in 1988.

Elmer Gantry \'el-mər-'gan-trē\ Novel by Sinclair LEWIS, a satiric indictment of fundamentalist religion that caused an uproar upon its publication in 1927.

The title character of *Elmer Gantry* starts out as a greedy, shallow, philandering Baptist minister, turns to evangelism, and eventually becomes the leader of a large Methodist congregation. Throughout the novel Gantry encounters fellow religious hypocrites, including Mrs. Evans Riddle, Judson Roberts, and Sharon Falconer, with whom he becomes romantically involved. Although he is often exposed as a fraud, Gantry is never fully discredited.

elocution \,el-ə-'kyū-shən\ [Latin *elocutio* expression of an idea in words] *archaic* **1.** Literary style or expression. **2.** Impressive writing or style; eloquence.

eloge \ā-'lōzh, -'lòzh\ *plural* eloges [Middle French, eulogy, from Latin *elogium* elegiac couplet, epitaph] A panegyrical, or laudatory, funeral oration. The term is also an archaic synonym for EULOGY.

El Saadawi \,el-sä-ä-'dä-wē\, Nawal, *Arabic* Nawāl al-Saʿadāwī (b. Oct. 27, 1931, Kafr Tahla, Egypt) Egyptian writer, physician, and feminist who is sometimes described as "the Simone de Beauvoir of the Arab world."

Educated at Cairo University (M.D., 1955) and Columbia University in New York City (M.P.H., 1966), El Saadawi also attended ʿAin Shams University in Cairo. She worked as a physician at the University of Cairo and at a rural health center, and she was editor in chief of *Health* magazine from 1968 to 1972. She was employed by the United Nations in several capacities, including a two-year directorship of African training and research for women in Addis Ababa, Ethiopia. From 1980 she was a practicing psychiatrist.

Expelled from her professional position in the Cairo ministry of health in 1972 because of her feminism, El Saadawi was imprisoned for the same reason for two months in 1981. In her novels, short stories, and nonfiction, she deals chiefly with the status of Arab women, as in *Mudhakkirāt tabība* (1960; *Memoirs of a Woman Doctor*), *Mawt al-rajul al-waḥīd ʿalā 'l-arḍ* (1974; *God Dies By the Nile*), *Imraʾah ʿind nuqṭat al-ṣifr* (1975; *Woman at Point Zero*), and *Al-wajh al-ʾārī lil-marʾah al-ʾArabiyyah* (1977; *The Hidden Face of Eve*). The oppression of women through religion is the underlying theme of several of El Saadawi's novels, including *Suqūṭ al-Imām* (1988; *The Fall of the Imam*) and *Jannât wa-Iblîs* (1992; *The Innocence of the Devil*).

Elsinore \'el-si-,nòr\, *Danish* Helsingør. Danish seaport on Zealand island, the setting for William Shakespeare's tragedy HAMLET. Hamlet mentions Elsinore four times in the play. Kronborg Castle, believed to be the home of the historical Hamlet, still stands in Helsingør today.

Elskamp \'els-,kämp\, Max (b. May 5, 1862, Antwerp, Belg.—d. Dec. 10, 1931, Antwerp) One of the outstanding Belgian Symbolist poets, whose material was the everyday life and folklore of his native city. His poems often reflected his Roman Catholic religious sentiments.

Like most Belgian poets of his generation, Elskamp was deeply influenced by literary developments in France; nevertheless, his subject—the simple and colorful religious experiences of his fellow Belgians—was unique and Belgian in inspiration. He employed a poetic idiom suitable to this subject, echoing the rhythms of the litanies and liturgies of the church.

Elsschot \'el-,skȯt\, Willem, *pseudonym of* Alfons de Ridder \də-'rid-ər\ (b. May 7, 1882, Antwerp, Belg.—d. June 1, 1960, Antwerp) Flemish novelist and poet whose mordant irony and sympathetic reflections on middle-class life won him lasting popularity.

Elsschot's first work, *Villa des roses* (1913), is an exercise in the naturalism of the period. The novel deals with the middle-class world, recounting events in a French boardinghouse. Elsschot's two subsequent novels, *De verlossing* (1921; "The Deliverance") and *Lijmen* (1924; *Soft Soap*), went virtually unnoticed; discouraged, he ceased writing until the 1930s. *Kaas* ("Cheese") was published in 1933, followed by *Tsjip* ("Cheep") in 1934. Laarmans, the protagonist in *Kaas*, had been introduced in *Lijmen* and reappeared in subsequent novels, including Elsschot's masterpiece, *Het dwaallicht* (1946; "Will-o'-the-wisp"). He is a sensitive person who repeatedly fails in business because of his honesty and sympathy for his customers. Elsschot's novels are caustic portrayals of social realities, but a beam of sympathy penetrates the ironic tone. His poetry was published as *Verzen van vroeger* (1934; "Early Verse") and *Verzen* (3rd edition, 1947).

Éluard \ā-'lw⁸ăr, -'lyăr\, Paul, *pseudonym of* Eugène Grindel \graⁿ-'del\ (b. Dec. 14, 1895, Saint-Denis, Paris, Fr.—d. Nov. 18, 1952, Charenton-le-Pont)   A founder of SURREALISM and one of the important lyrical poets of the 20th century.

In 1919 Éluard made the acquaintance of the Surrealist poets André Breton, Philippe Soupault, and Louis Aragon, with whom he remained in close association until 1938. Experiments with new verbal techniques, theories on the relation between dream and reality, and the free expression of thought processes produced *Capitale de la douleur* (1926; "Capital of Sorrow "), his first important work. It was followed by *La Rose publique* (1934; "The Public Rose") and *Les Yeux fertiles* (1936; "The Fertile Eyes"). The poems in these volumes are generally considered the best to have come out of the Surrealist movement.

After the Spanish Civil War Éluard abandoned Surrealist experimentations. His late work reflects his political militance and a deepening of his underlying attitudes: the rejection of tyranny, the search for happiness. In 1942 he joined the French Communist Party. His poems dealing with suffering and brotherhood, *Poésie et vérité* (1942; "Poetry and Truth"), *Au rendez-vous allemand* (1944; "To the German Rendezvous"), and *Dignes de vivre* (1944; "Worthy of Living"), were circulated clandestinely during World War II and served to strengthen the morale of the Resistance. After the war his *Tout dire* (1951; "Say Everything") and *Le Phénix* (1951) contributed to the great body of French popular lyrical poetry.

Elysium \i-'lizh-ē-əm, -'liz-\, *also called* Elysian Fields *or* Elysian Plain \-ən\   In Greek and Roman mythology, the dwelling place of happy souls after death. Elysium was conceived of as either a concrete physical region or a state of existence.

In Homer's writings the Elysian Plain was a land of perfect happiness at the end of the earth, on the banks of the Oceanus River. A similar description was given by Hesiod of the Isles of the Blessed. In the earlier authors, only those specially favored by the gods entered Elysium and were made immortal. By the time of Hesiod, however, Elysium was a place for the blessed dead, and, from Pindar on, entrance to Elysium was gained by having led a righteous life.

Elytis \e-'lē-ˌtēs\, Odysseus, *also spelled* Odysseas Elytēs, *original surname* Alepoudhelis \ā-le-pū-'thel-ˌēs\ (b. Nov. 2, 1911, Iráklion, Crete)   Greek poet and winner of the 1979 Nobel Prize for Literature. Born the scion of a prosperous Cretan family, he abandoned the family name as a young man in order to dissociate his writing from the family soap business.

Elytis studied law at Athens University and periodically worked in the family business. Intrigued by French Surrealism, and particularly by the poet Paul Éluard, he began publishing verse in the 1930s, notably in *Nea grammata*, an avant-garde literary magazine. Elytis' earliest poems exhibited a strong individuality of tone and setting within the Surrealist mode. The volume *Prosanatolismoi* (*Orientations*), published in 1940, is a collection of his works to that date.

When Nazi Germany occupied Greece in 1941, Elytis joined the antifascist resistance to the Italians in Albania. He became something of a bard among young Greeks; one of his poems, *Asma hērōiko kai penthimo gia ton chameno anthypolochago tēs Alvanias* (1945; *Heroic and Elegiac Song for the Lost Second Lieutenant of the Albanian Campaign*), was regarded as an an-

them to the cause of freedom. After the war he lapsed into literary silence for almost 15 years, returning to print in 1959 with *To Axion Esti* ("Worthy It Is"; *The Axion Esti*), a long poem reminiscent of Walt Whitman's *Song of Myself.*

Elytis lived in Paris after the Greek military coup of 1967. His later works include *Ho hēlios ho hēliatoras* (1971; *The Sovereign Sun*), *Ta eterothalē* (1974; "The Stepchildren"), and *Ho mikros nautilos* (1986; *The Little Mariner*).

Elzevir \'el-zə-ˌvir\ *or* **Elsevier** \'el-sə-ˌvēr\   Of, relating to, or being books or editions, especially of the Greek New Testament and the classics, printed, published, and sold by the Elzevir family at Amsterdam, The Hague, Utrecht, or Leiden from roughly 1587 to 1681.

Fifteen members of the Elzevir family were in the book business during that period. Louis (1540?–1617), son of a printer of Louvain (now Leuven, Belgium), settled in Leiden as a Protestant émigré about 1581, set himself up as a bookbinder and bookseller, published more than 100 books, and began the family specialization in learned books. The business in Leiden enjoyed its greatest success between 1622 and 1652 under the management of his son Bonaventura (1583–1652) and grandson Abraham (1592–1652), during which time they became printers to the university. Two notable and widely imitated series were their *Petites Républiques*, 35 volumes concerned with different countries and published between 1625 and 1649, and their literary classics. The Leiden bookshop was closed in 1659, but publishing and printing continued, although in declining quantity and quality, until 1681. Members of the family operated branches under the Elzevirs' name at The Hague (*c.* 1590–1665), Utrecht (*c.* 1603–75), and Amsterdam (1638–81).

After having enjoyed an almost legendary reputation among bibliophiles for excellence of typography and design, the Elzevirs' work is now regarded only as typical of the high quality that prevailed in their day in Holland.

Embla   *see* ASKR AND EMBLA.

emblem book   Collection of symbolic pictures, usually accompanied by mottoes and expositions in verse and often also by a prose commentary. Derived from the medieval allegory and bestiary, the emblem book developed as a pictorial-literary genre in 16th-century Italy and became popular throughout western Europe in the 17th century.

The father of emblem literature was the 16th-century Italian lawyer and humanist Andrea Alciato, whose *Emblemata* (Latin; 1531) appeared in translation and in more than 150 editions. The Plantin press specialized in emblem literature, publishing at Antwerp in 1564 the *Emblemata* of the Hungarian physician and historian Johannes Sambucus; in 1565, that of the Dutch physician Hadrianus Junius (Adriaen de Jonghe); and, at Leiden, the early English emblem book of Geoffrey Whitney, *Choice of Emblemes* (1585), an anthology of emblems from Alciato, Junius, and others. English emblem books were either printed in the Netherlands or made by combining English text with foreign engravings, as in the English edition of the *Amorum Emblemata, Figuris Aeneis Incisa* (1608) of Octavius Vaenius (Otto van Veen), an important early Dutch emblem book.

The Netherlands became the center of the vogue. Vaenius' *Amorum Emblemata* presented metaphors from Ovid and other Latin erotic poets with pictorial representation. The Dutch emblem books were widely translated, plagiarized, and reprinted with different text or engravings. From polyglot editions, begun by Daniël Heinsius' verses in Dutch and Latin and later in French, publication of emblem books became an international enterprise. Books of love emblems were exchanged by lovers and formed attractive little encyclopedias of those "questions of love" that had been the erudite pastime of the academies throughout the Renaissance. Meanwhile, the Dutch emblematists had turned to religious emblems, serving Calvinists as well as Jesuits, who used them for propaganda. In Vaenius' *Amoris Divini Emblemata* (1615), quotations from St. Augustine replace those of Ovid and Cupid reappears as the soul's preceptor.

The only English emblem book to achieve widespread popularity was the *Emblemes and Hieroglyphikes* (1635) of Francis Quarles.

Emecheta \ˌā-mā-'shā-tā\, Buchi (b. July 21, 1944, Lagos, Nigeria) Nigerian sociologist, poet, playwright, essayist, and children's author whose novels were published in English and German.

Emecheta was married at the age of 16 and followed her husband to London in 1962. The difficulties of her impoverished life in London during the early 1960s provide the subject for her first two books, *In the Ditch* (1972) and *Second-Class Citizen* (1974). Both semiautobiographical, they examined the search for first-class citizenship, self-confidence, and dignity as a woman.

Emecheta won several literary awards. *The Bride Price* (1976), *The Slave Girl* (1977), and *The Joys of Motherhood* (1979) are set in the past and deal with the lives of women in male-dominated society. *Destination Biafra* (1982) takes the Nigerian civil war as its topic, and *Double Yoke* (1982) the still unequal position of women in contemporary African society. Her later novels include *The Rape of Shavi* (1983), *Gwendolen* (1989), and *Kehinde* (1994). She also wrote several books for children, including *Titch the Cat* (1979).

emend \ē-'mend\   **1.** To correct (a written work) usually by textual alterations.   **2.** To alter (a literary work) to serve a purpose different from the original.

Emerson \'em-ər-sən\, Ralph Waldo (b. May 25, 1803, Boston, Mass., U.S.—d. April 27, 1882, Concord) American poet, essayist, and lecturer who was the leading exponent of New England Transcendentalism.

Emerson graduated from Harvard College in 1821 and was ordained to the Unitarian ministry in 1829. Although his position seemed secure, he had begun to question Christian doctrines, and grief over the death of his wife in 1831 drove him to further doubts. He had become acquainted with the new biblical criticism and the doubts that had been cast on the historicity of miracles. Emerson's own sermons, from the first, had been unusually free of traditional doctrine and were instead a personal exploration of the uses of spirit. Indeed, they had divested Christianity of all external or historical supports and made its basis one's private intuition of the universal moral law and its test a life of virtuous accomplishment. Unitarianism ceased to fulfill his needs, and in 1832 he resigned from the ministry.

Library of Congress

Emerson helped initiate Transcendentalism by publishing anonymously in Boston in 1836 a little book of 96 pages entitled NATURE. Having found the answers to his spiritual doubts, he formulated his essential philosophy, and almost everything he ever wrote afterward was an extension, amplification, or amendment of the ideas he first affirmed in *Nature*.

In a lecture entitled "The American Scholar" (Aug. 31, 1837), Emerson described the resources and duties of the new liberated intellectual that he himself had become. The address was in effect a challenge to the Harvard intelligentsia, warning against pedantry, imitation, traditionalism, and scholarship unrelated to life. Emerson's later Harvard lecture, "Address at Divinity College" (1838), was another challenge, this time directed against a lifeless Christian tradition. This address alienated many and resulted in his being ostracized by Harvard for many years. Young disciples, however, joined the informal Transcendental Club (founded in 1836) and encouraged him in his activities.

In 1840 he helped launch *The Dial*, first edited by Margaret Fuller and later by himself, thus providing an outlet for the ideas Transcendentalists were trying to present to America. He continued to lecture, publishing two volumes entitled *Essays* (1841; 1844); these included the well-known SELF-RELIANCE and made Emerson internationally famous.

His *Representative Men* (dated 1850) contains biographies of Plato, Swedenborg, Michel de Montaigne, William Shakespeare, Napoleon, and J.W. von Goethe. *The Conduct of Life* (1860), Emerson's most mature work, reveals a developed humanism together with a full awareness of human limitations. Emerson's collected *Poems* (dated 1847) were supplemented by others in *May-Day* (1867), and the two volumes established his reputation as a major American poet.

Eminent Victorians Collection of short biographical sketches by Lytton STRACHEY, published in 1918.

Strachey's portraits of Cardinal Manning, Florence Nightingale, Thomas Arnold, and General Charles "Chinese" Gordon revolutionized English biography. Until Strachey, biographers had kept an awestruck distance from their subjects; anything short of adulation was regarded as disrespect. Strachey, however, announced that he would write lives with "a brevity which excludes everything that is redundant and nothing that is significant," whether flattering to the subject or not. His intensely personal sketches scandalized stuffier readers but delighted many literati.

Strachey's impressionistic portraits occasionally led to inaccuracy, since he selected the facts he liked and had little use for politics or religion. By portraying his "Eminent Victorians" as multifaceted, flawed human beings rather than idols, and by informing public knowledge with private information, Strachey ushered in a new era of biography.

Eminescu \ˌem-ē-'nes-ˌkü\, Mihail, *pseudonym of* Mihail Eminovici \em-'ē-nȯ-vēch\ (b. Jan. 15, 1850, Ipotești, near Botoșani, Moldavia, Ottoman Empire [now in Romania]—d. June 15, 1889, Bucharest, Rom.) Poet who transformed both the form and content of Romanian poetry, creating an influential school of poetry.

Eminescu was educated in the German-Romanian cultural center of Cernăuți (now Chernivtsi, Ukraine) and at the universities of Vienna and Berlin. In 1874 he was appointed school inspector and librarian at the University of Iași but soon resigned to become editor in chief of the conservative paper *Timpul*. His literary activity came to an end in 1883, when he suffered the onset of a mental disorder that later led to his death in an asylum.

Eminescu's talent was first revealed in 1870 by two poems published in *Convorbiri literare*, the organ of the Junimea society in Iași. Other verses followed, and he became recognized as the foremost modern Romanian poet. Mystically inclined and of a melancholy disposition, he found inspiration in the glory of the Romanian medieval past and in folklore, on which he based one of his outstanding poems, "Luceafărul" (1883; "The Evening Star").

Eminescu's poetry has a distinctive simplicity of language, a masterly handling of rhyme and verse form, a profundity of thought, and a plasticity of expression that affected nearly every Romanian writer who followed. His poems have been translated into several languages, including an English translation produced in 1930. Among his prose writings, apart from many studies and essays, his best-known works are the stories "Cezara" and "Sărmanul Dionis" (1872).

Emma \'em-ə\ Novel by Jane AUSTEN, published in three volumes in 1815. Of all Austen's novels, *Emma* is the most consistently comic in tone. It centers on Emma Woodhouse, a wealthy, pretty, self-satisfied young woman who indulges herself with meddlesome and unsuccessful attempts at match-making among her friends and neighbors. After a series of humiliating errors, a chastened Emma finds her destiny in marriage to the mature and protective George Knightley, a neighboring squire who had been her mentor and friend.

Empedocles on Etna \em-'ped-ə-,klēz . . . 'et-nə\ Dramatic poem by Matthew ARNOLD, published anonymously in 1852 in the collection *Empedocles on Etna, and Other Poems. By A.* It is based on legends concerning the death of the Greek philosopher and statesman Empedocles (*c.* 490–430 BC).

Empedocles is portrayed in the poem as a man who can no longer feel joy. He considers himself useless, intellectually as well as politically, and plans to commit suicide by leaping into the crater of Mt. Etna. Two friends try to lift his depression and convince him that life is worth living. But all their persuasive skills fail to restore meaning to Empedocles' life.

Emperor Jones, The \'jōnz\ Drama in eight scenes by Eugene O'NEILL, produced in 1920 and published in 1921. *The Emperor Jones* was the playwright's first foray into Expressionist writing.

Based loosely on an event in Haitian history, the play shows the decline of a former Pullman porter, Brutus Jones, who has escaped from prison to an unnamed Caribbean island. With help from a Cockney adventurer, Jones persuades the superstitious natives that he is a magician, and they crown him emperor. He abuses and exploits his subjects and boasts of his power, insisting that only a silver bullet can kill him. Advised that an uprising is in the offing, Jones flees into the jungle. There he is forced to confront his internal demons; scenes show his private past, as images of his victims assail him. More scenes depict bizarre racial memories, including the sale at a slave auction and the earlier capture in the Congo of his ancestors. Terrified, Jones fires all his ammunition at his ghostly tormentors. In the final scene, the rebels find Jones and shoot him.

While not considered one of O'Neill's finest plays, the work was a sensation and remains a staple of small theater groups.

Empress of Blandings \'blan-diŋz\ Fictional creature, a huge Berkshire sow resembling a balloon with ears and a tail, in stories and novels by P.G. WODEHOUSE. She is the property and pride of Lord EMSWORTH, and she has won three consecutive Fat Pigs silver medals at the Shropshire Agricultural Show. In the course of Wodehouse's many tales set at Blandings Castle, she is stolen, kidnapped, hidden, and even forced to diet.

Empson \'emp-sən\, Sir William (b. Sept. 27, 1906, Hawdon, Yorkshire, Eng.—d. April 15, 1984, London) British poet and critic known for his immense influence on 20th-century literary criticism and for his rational, metaphysical poetry.

Empson attended Cambridge, where he studied mathematics and English literature, the latter under I.A. Richards. From 1931 to 1934 Empson taught at the University of Tokyo, and he subsequently taught at Peking National University in China. He was Chinese editor at the British Broadcasting Corporation during World War II and returned to teach at Peking National University from 1947 to 1952. He taught at Sheffield University from 1953, becoming professor emeritus in 1971. He was knighted in 1979.

Several of the verses published in Empson's *Poems* (1935) reflect his interest in the sciences and technology, which he used as metaphors in his largely pessimistic assessment of the human lot. Much influenced by John Donne, these poems are personal, elliptical, and difficult. Later collections of his poetry include *The Gathering Storm* (1940) and *Collected Poems* (1949; rev. ed., 1955).

Empson's critical work entitled SEVEN TYPES OF AMBIGUITY (1930) was essentially a close examination of poetic texts. The book helped lay the foundation for the influential critical school known as the New Criticism. He applied his critical method to somewhat longer texts in *Some Versions of Pastoral* (1935) and further elaborated it in *The Structure of Complex Words* (1951). Empson's verbal analyses were based on the view that poetry's emotive effect derives primarily from the ambiguities and complexities of its cognitive and tonal meanings.

empyrean \,em-,pī-'rē-ən, -pə-; em-'pir-ē-ən, -'pī-rē-\ The highest heaven or heavenly sphere in ancient and medieval cosmology usually consisting of fire or light. The word was used chiefly by Christian writers (such as John Milton) to signify the true and ultimate heavenly paradise. In a more general sense, it refers to an ideal place or state.

Emsworth \'emz-wərth\, **Lord**, *in full* Clarence Threepwood \'klar-əns-'thrēp-,wûd\, 9th Earl of Emsworth. Fictional character, the elderly, absent-minded ninth proprietor of Blandings Castle, Shropshire, England, the site of many short stories and novels by P.G. WODEHOUSE—from *Something Fresh* (1915) to his final, unfinished *Sunset at Blandings* (1977). Lord Emsworth is almost invariably called upon to save the day, and he is frequently harassed by his snobbish sisters. His only desire is to be left in peace amid the perpetually summery castle gardens to devote himself to his prize pig, EMPRESS OF BLANDINGS.

Encantadas, The \,en-kän-'täd-əz\ Ten fictional sketches by Herman MELVILLE, published in 1854 in *Putnam's Monthly Magazine* as "The Encantadas, or Enchanted Isles," under the pseudonym Salvator R. Tarnmoor.

Seven of the sketches describe the Galapagos Islands in the eastern Pacific Ocean, which Melville had seen when he was a working sailor and about which he had read in Charles Darwin's *The Voyage of the Beagle.* Sailors believed that these islands were enchanted. The other three pieces are sketches of people who reside for a time in the Encantadas, mostly renegades and castaways.

Encina \än-'thē-nä\, Juan del (b. July 12, 1468?, Encinas?, near Salamanca, Castile [Spain]—d. August 1529/30, León?) Playwright, poet, priest, and composer of secular vocal music who was the first Spanish dramatist to write specifically for performance.

After training as a chorister at Salamanca Cathedral (*c.* 1484) and at the University of Salamanca (before 1490), Encina entered the service of the duke of Alba as a resident poet-dramatist-composer in 1492. He wrote for the court a number of *églogas* (short pastoral plays) incorporating music. *Cancionero* (1496; "Songbook") contained eight of his plays and most of his poetry. Thereafter Encina lived primarily in Italy. He was a prior at León from 1523 until his death.

The first half dozen of Encina's *églogas* are little more than dialogues in colloquial peasant speech between mock-realistic shepherds more interested in recreation than work. His later *églogas* introduce other character types and, although still rudimentary in plot, are more complex, refined, and sententious. These later plays, a notable example of which is *Égloga de Plácida y Vitoriano*, show the influence of the *égloga*'s Italian antecedents in their celebration of pagan love and their incorporation of themes from classical mythology.

Enckell \'eŋ-kel\, Rabbe (Arnfinn) (b. March 3, 1903, Tammela, Fin.—d. June 17, 1974, Helsinki) Finnish poet, playwright, and critic, and a leading representative of the Swedish-Finnish poetic revival that began in the 1920s.

Enckell studied art in France and Italy. His first collection of impressionistic nature poems, *Dikter*, appeared in 1923. In this collection and a sequel, *Flöjtblåsarlycka* (1925; "The Flutist's Happiness"), Enckell describes with a painter's eye the exquisite nuances in the phenomena of nature. He was associated with the avant-garde journal *Quosego* in 1928–29. After writing a number of semiautobiographical novels, including *Ljusdunkel* (1930; "Chiaroscuro"), Enckell returned to poetry with *Vårens cistern* (1931; "The Cistern of Spring") and *Tonbrädet* (1935; "The Sounding Board").

Enckell used classical parallels to dramatize the problems of his time in a series of verse plays, including *Orfeus och Eurydike* (1938) and *Alkman* (1959). His most remarkable collection of poetry is *Andedräkt av koppar* (1946; "Breath of Copper"). In 1960 he was made poet laureate of Swedish Finland.

enclosed rhyme *also called* enclosing rhyme. In poetry, the rhyming pattern *abba* found in certain quatrains, such as the first verse of Matthew Arnold's "Shakespeare":

> Others abide our question. Thou art free.
> We ask and ask—thou smilest and art still,
> Out-topping knowledge. For the loftiest hill,
> Who to the stars uncrowns his majesty, . . .

encomiologic \en-ˌkō-mē-ə-'läj-ik\ [Greek *enkōmiologikón* meter used in encomia, from *enkōmion* encomium + *lógos* word, utterance] Of or having to do with a compound verse in Greek and Latin prosody that is made up of two and a half dactylic feet followed by two and a half iambic feet: $- \cup \cup - \cup \cup - \cup - \cup - \underline{\cup}$.

encomium \en-'kō-mē-əm\ *plural* encomia \-mē-ə\ [Greek *enkōmion* laudatory ode, panegyric] A prose or poetic work in which a person, thing, or abstract idea is glorified. The term originally meant a Greek choral song honoring the hero of the Olympic games and sung at the victory celebration at the end of the games. The term later took on the broader meaning of any composition of a laudatory nature. Verse forms of the encomium include the EPINICION and the ODE.

Encyclopédie, L' \län-sē-klō-pā-'dē\ (*in full* Encyclopédie, ou Dictionnaire raisonné des Sciences, des Arts et des Métiers; "Encyclopedia, or Classified Dictionary of Sciences, Arts, and Trades") The 18th-century French encyclopedia that was one of the chief works of the philosophes, a group dedicated to the advancement of science and secular thought and to the new tolerance and open-mindedness of the Enlightenment. The 35-volume *Encyclopédie* was a literary and philosophic enterprise that had profound political, social, and intellectual repercussions in France in the decades just prior to the Revolution. Its contributors were called Encyclopédistes.

The work's publisher was André Le Breton, who in 1745 secured the services of the mathematician Jean Le Rond d'Alembert and of the translator and philosopher Denis Diderot. Diderot undertook the general direction of the work on *L'Encyclopédie*, except for its mathematical parts, which were edited by d'Alembert (who resigned in 1758). Seventeen volumes of *L'Encyclopédie*'s text were published between 1751 and 1765; 11 volumes of plates were also published between 1762 and 1772. These were supplemented in 1776–77 by five more volumes—four of text and one of plates—and by two volumes of index in 1780, all compiled under other editors, since Diderot had refused to edit the supplementary materials. These seven volumes, with the 28 prepared by Diderot, constituted the first edition of *L'Encyclopédie* in 35 folio volumes.

L'Encyclopédie was a showcase for representatives of the new schools of thought in all branches of intellectual activity. Notable for its attitude of tolerance and liberalism, the work gave innovative coverage of the trades and mechanical arts. In its skepticism, its emphasis on scientific determinism, and its criticism of the abuses perpetrated by contemporary legal, judicial, and clerical institutions, *L'Encyclopédie* had widespread influence and served in effect as an intellectual prologue to the French Revolution.

In 1782 the publication of a new, enlarged edition was begun under the title *Encyclopédie méthodique ou par ordre de matières* ("Encyclopedia Arranged Systematically or by Order of Subjects"). Work on this encyclopedia continued through the French Revolution and was completed in 1832 with the appearance of the 166th volume.

Endgame Play in one act by Samuel BECKETT, written in French as *Fin de partie* and produced and published in 1957. It was translated into English by the author. *Endgame* has four characters: Hamm, the master, who is blind, wheelchair-bound, and demanding; Clov, his resentful servant, physically incapable of sitting down; and Hamm's crippled, senile parents, Nagg and Nell, confined to garbage cans. They all live in one room with two windows. The complex relationship between Hamm and Clov is the principal subject of the play. As is characteristic of Beckett's plays, the setting of *Endgame* is spare and the stage directions are copious.

Endō Shūsaku \'en-dō-shə̇-'sä-kù\ (b. March 27, 1923, Tokyo, Japan) A major contemporary Japanese novelist notable for his examination of the relationship between East and West through a unique Christian perspective.

Endō became a Roman Catholic at age 11, with the encouragement of his mother and an aunt. He graduated from Keiō University. His first collections of fiction, *Shiroi hito* (1955; "White Man") and *Kiiroi hito* (1955; "Yellow Man"), like most of his later fiction contrast Japanese and Western experience and perspectives. In *Umi to dokuyaku* (1957; *The Sea and Poison*), he examines the Japanese sense of morality. One of Endō's most powerful novels, *Chimmoku* (1966; SILENCE), is a fictionalized account of Portuguese missionaries and the slaughter of their Japanese converts. This novel and *Samurai* (1980; *The Samurai*) are considered to be his best writing, showing the complexities of the interactions between cultures as well as presenting a supple and well-told narrative.

Endō's other extended fiction includes *Kazan* (1959; *Volcano*), *Kuchibue o fuku toki* (1974; *When I Whistle*), *Sukyandaru* (1986; *Scandal*), and a number of comic novels; he also wrote short stories, drama, essays, and a biography.

End of the Affair, The Novel of psychological realism by Graham GREENE, published in 1951.

The novel is set in wartime London. The narrator Maurice Bendrix, a bitter, sardonic novelist, has a five-year affair with a married woman, Sarah Miles. When a V-1 bomb explodes in front of Bendrix's apartment and Sarah finds Bendrix pinned beneath the front door, she believes him dead. She promises a God in whom she does not believe that she will give Bendrix up if he is allowed to live. Just then, Bendrix walks into the room and Sarah begins her religious journey; she breaks off with Bendrix, railing against God even as she begins to take religious instruction. Gradually she comes to a profound religious faith.

Despite its religious theme, the novel was considered to be scandalous because of its realistic and sympathetic portrayal of the adulterous Sarah.

Endor, Witch of   *see* WITCH OF ENDOR.

end rhyme   In poetry, a rhyme that occurs in the last syllables of verses, as in stanza one of Robert Frost's "Stopping by Woods on a Snowy Evening":

> Whose woods these are I think I know,
> His house is in the village, though;
> He will not see me stopping here
> To watch his woods fill up with snow.

End rhyme is the most common type of rhyme in English poetry. *Compare* BEGINNING RHYME; INTERNAL RHYME.

end-stopped \'end-ˌstäpt\   In poetry, marked by a grammatical pause at the end of a line, as in these lines from Alexander Pope's *An Essay on Criticism*:

> A little learning is a dangerous thing;
> Drink deep, or taste not the Pierian spring.
> There shallow draughts intoxicate the brain,
> And drinking largely sobers us again.

Compare ENJAMBMENT; RUN-ON.

Endymion \en-'dim-ē-ən\   In Greek mythology, a beautiful youth who spent much of his life in perpetual sleep. According to one tradition, Zeus offered him anything that he might desire, and Endymion chose an everlasting sleep in which he might remain youthful forever. According to another version of the myth, Endymion's eternal sleep was a punishment inflicted by Zeus because he had ventured to fall in love with Zeus's wife, Hera. In any case, Endymion was loved by Selene, the goddess of the moon, who visited him every night while he lay asleep in a cave on Mount Latmus in Caria; she bore him 50 daughters. A common form of the myth represents Endymion as having been put to sleep by Selene herself so that she might enjoy his beauty undisturbed. Endymion has been represented in literature by such writers as John Lyly, John Keats, Henry Wadsworth Longfellow, and Edna St. Vincent Millay.

Endymion \en-'dim-ē-ən\   Long poem by John KEATS, published in 1818. Written in loose rhymed couplets, *Endymion* is divided into four books totaling 4,000 lines. The poem recasts the Greek legend of Endymion, a mortal son of Zeus beloved by Selene. In Keats's version, the moon goddess, Diana (or Cynthia), loves Endymion, who is a human shepherd. Keats emphasizes the love of Endymion for the goddess rather than her love for him. Considered an allegory of a poet seeking perfection, the poem expresses the Romantic notion that perfect love may indeed be possible, not just an unattainable ideal.

Enemy of the People, An   Five-act drama by Henrik IBSEN, published in 1882 as *En folkefiende* and performed in 1883.

An Enemy of the People concerns the actions of Doctor Thomas Stockmann, a medical officer charged with inspecting the public baths on which the prosperity of his native town depends. He finds the water to be contaminated. When he refuses to be silenced, he is declared an enemy of the people.

Stockmann served as a spokesman for Ibsen, who felt that his plays gave a true, if not always palatable, picture of life and that truth was more important than critical approbation.

English Bards and Scotch Reviewers   Satire in verse by Lord BYRON, first published anonymously in 1809. The poem was written in response to the adverse criticism that *The Edin-*

burgh Review had given *Hours of Idleness* (1807), Byron's first published volume of poetry.

In *English Bards and Scotch Reviewers*, Byron uses heroic couplets in imitation of Alexander Pope's *The Dunciad* to attack the reigning poets of Romanticism and Lord Francis Jeffrey, the editor of *The Edinburgh Review*. He praises instead such Neoclassical poets as Pope and John Dryden.

English sonnet   *see* SHAKESPEAREAN SONNET.

englyn \'eŋ-lin\   *plural* englyns *or* englynion \eŋ-'lən-yòn\ [Welsh]   A group of strict Welsh poetic meters. The most popular form is the *englyn unodl union* ("direct monorhyme englyn"), which is a combination of a CYWYDD, a type of rhyming couplet, and another form and is written in an intricate pattern of alliteration and rhyme called CYNGHANEDD. The *englyn unodl union* consists of 30 syllables in lines of 10, 6, 7, and 7 syllables. In this form the last syllables of the last three lines rhyme with the 6th, 7th, 8th, or 9th syllable of the first line. The various forms of englyns were among the 24 strict bardic meters available to Welsh poets from about the 14th century.

enjambment *or* **enjambement** \en-'jam-mənt, äⁿ-zhäⁿb-'mäⁿ\ [French *enjamber*, literally, the act of striding over, a derivative of *enjamber* to stride over, straddle, encroach on], *also called* run-on.   In prosody, the continuation of the sense of a phrase beyond the end of a line of verse. T.S. Eliot used enjambment in the opening lines of his poem *The Waste Land*:

> April is the cruelest month, breeding
> Lilacs out of the dead land, mixing
> Memory and desire, stirring
> Dull roots with spring rain.
> Winter kept us warm, covering
> Earth in forgetful snow, feeding
> A little life with dried tubers.

Compare END-STOPPED.

Enlightenment \en-'līt-ən-mənt\, *French* Siècle des Lumières \syekl-də-lᵫm-'yer\ ("Age of the Enlightened"), *German* Aufklärung \aûf-'kler-ùŋ\   A European intellectual movement of the 17th and 18th centuries in which ideas concerning God, reason, nature, and humankind were synthesized into a worldview that gained wide assent and that instigated revolutionary developments in art, philosophy, and politics. Central to Enlightenment thought were the use and the celebration of reason, the power by which the individual understands the universe and improves the human condition. The goals of the rational individual were considered to be knowledge, freedom, and happiness.

Enmerkar \'en-ˌmer-ˌkär\   Ancient Sumerian hero and king of Erech, a city-state in southern Mesopotamia, who is thought to have lived at the end of the 4th or beginning of the 3rd millennium BC. Along with Lugalbanda and Gilgamesh, Enmerkar is one of the three most significant figures in the surviving Sumerian epics.

Scholars have determined that there are three epics related to Enmerkar. Two of these tell the tale of Enmerkar's subjugation of a rival city, Aratta. One is called *Enmerkar and the Lord of Aratta*. The longest Sumerian epic yet discovered, it is the source of important information about the history and culture of the Sumero-Iranian border area. The other epic on the defeat of Aratta is known as *Enmerkar and Ensuhkeshdanna*. A third epic, *Lugalbanda and Enmerkar*, tells of the heroic journey to Aratta made by Lugalbanda in the service of Enmerkar.

ennead \'en-ē-ˌad\ [Greek *ennead-, enneás*, a derivative of *ennéa* nine]   A group of nine; especially, any of several groups of nine gods that were considered to be associated in the mythology and religion of ancient Egypt.

Ennius \'en-ē-əs\, Quintus (b. 239 BC, Rudiae, Calabria [Italy]—d. 169 BC) Epic poet, dramatist, and satirist, the most influential of the early Latin poets and considered the founder of Roman literature. His epic ANNALES, a narrative poem telling the story of Rome from the wanderings of Aeneas to the poet's own day, was the national epic until it was eclipsed by Virgil's *Aeneid*.

Ennius was at home in three languages: Oscan, his native tongue; Greek, in which he was educated; and Latin, the language of the army with which he served in the Second Punic War. In Rome from 204, he earned a meager living as a teacher and by adapting Greek plays, but he was on familiar terms with many of the leading men in Rome, among them Scipio Africanus the Elder. His patron was Marcus Fulvius Nobilior, whose son Quintus obtained Roman citizenship for Ennius. Nothing else of significance is known about his life.

Titles survive of 19 plays that Ennius adapted from the Greek, mostly from Euripides (*e.g.*, *Iphigenia at Aulis*, *Medea*, *Telephus*, and *Thyestes*). His plays on Roman themes were *Sabinae*, *Ambrachia* (on the capture of that city by Fulvius), and *Scipio* (although the status of the two latter works as plays is uncertain).

In the *Saturae* Ennius developed the only literary genre that Rome could call its own. Four books in a variety of meters on diverse subjects, they were mostly concerned with practical wisdom, often driving home a lesson with the help of a fable. More philosophical were two works on the theories of Epicharmus, the Sicilian poet and philosopher. Some epigrams, on himself and Scipio Africanus, are the first Latin elegiac couplets.

Ennius was conversant with the intellectual and literary movements of the Hellenistic world. He created a mode of poetic expression that reached its greatest beauty in Virgil and was to remain preeminent in Latin literature.

Enoch Arden \'ē-nək-'ärd-ən\ Poem by Alfred, Lord TENNYSON, published in 1864. In the poem, Enoch Arden is a happily married fisherman who suffers financial problems and becomes a merchant seaman. He is shipwrecked, and after 10 years on a desert island, he returns home to discover that his beloved wife, believing him dead, has remarried and has a new child. Not wishing to spoil his wife's happiness, he never lets her know that he is alive.

enoplion \e-'näp-lē-,än, -ən\ [Greek *rhythmòs kat' enóplion* martial rhythm] A hemiepes preceded by one or two short syllables or a long syllable, or any of a variety of aeolic lines that expand by the addition of dactyls; this latter form is also known as a *prosodiac*.

Enquist \'eŋ-,kvēst\, Per Olov (b. Sept. 23, 1934, Hjoggböle, Swed.) Swedish novelist, playwright, and journalist noted for his later, "documentary-style," fiction.

Enquist's first novels, *Kristallögat* (1961; "The Crystal Eye") and *Färdvägen* (1963; "The Route Traveled"), reflect his aesthetic interest in the form of the novel and the influence of the French *nouveau roman*, or antinovel. He then began to take a documentary, quasi-scholarly approach in both his novels and dramas, as in *Hess* (1966) and *Legionärerna* (1968; *The Legionnaires*). His novel *Musikanternas uttåg* (1978; *The March of the Musicians*) deals with early unionizing efforts in his native province. His most successful drama, *Tribadernas natt* (1975; *The Night of the Tribades*), presents Enquist's analysis of August Strindberg's marital relationship. Among his later works are *Doktor Mabuses nya testamente* (1982; "Doctor Mabuse's New Testament"), a detective novel written with A. Ehnmark; *I lodjurets timma* (1988; *The Hour of the Lynx*), a play; and *Kapten Nemos Bibliotek* (1991; *Captain Nemo's Library*), a novel.

Enrico IV \en-'rē-kō-'kwär-tō\ A tragedy in three acts by Luigi PIRANDELLO, produced and published in 1922; it is sometimes translated as *Henry IV*. The theme of *Enrico IV* is madness, which lies just under the skin of ordinary life and is, perhaps, superior to ordinary life in its construction of a satisfying reality.

The play tells the story of a modern nobleman who, as a result of a fall from a horse 20 years earlier, believes himself to be the 11th-century Holy Roman emperor Henry IV. He lives in a castle, where he is humored by "courtiers" in period costume who help him maintain his illusion.

In reality the nobleman is sane; he simply prefers the trappings of the Middle Ages to the horrifying modern world. He seals his fate by committing a crime that makes it necessary for him to spend the rest of his life feigning madness.

Enright \'en-,rīt\, D.J., *in full* Dennis Joseph (b. March 11, 1920, Leamington, Warwickshire, Eng.) British poet, novelist, and teacher.

After graduating from Cambridge, Enright taught at several universities throughout the world. *Memoirs of a Mendicant Professor* (1969) tells of his years abroad.

Both his poetry (*Selected Poems*, 1968; *Collected Poems*, 1987; and *Selected Poems*, 1990) and his novels (*Academic Year*, 1955; *Figures of Speech*, 1965) are antisentimental and reflect his broad experience. Much of his later poetry is based on literary works or themes, including the works *Paradise Illustrated* (1978) and *A Faust Book* (1979). He also wrote fiction for children and edited *The Oxford Book of Contemporary Verse 1945–1980* (1980), *The Oxford Book of Death* (1983), and *The Oxford Book of Friendship* (1991).

Entertainer, The Play in 13 parts by John OSBORNE, produced in 1957 and published in 1959. The playwright uses a seedy, third-rate English music-hall comedian and the deteriorating Empire Music Hall as metaphors for Great Britain's decline as a world power. In brief bursts of topical, frequently disjointed Brechtian commentary, *The Entertainer* also decries the rise of pop culture and the chic espousal of radical political views.

entrelacement \,än-trə-,läs-'mäⁿ, -'mänt\ [French, act or product of interlacing, a derivative of *enterlacer* to interlace] Literary technique in which several simultaneous stories are interlaced in one larger narrative. This technique allows digression and presents opportunities for moral and ironic commentary while not disturbing the unity of the whole.

Entwicklungsroman \ent-'vik-,luŋz-rō-,män, *German* -,luns-\ [German, from *Entwicklung* development + *Roman* novel] *see* BILDUNGSROMAN.

enumerative bibliography *see* DESCRIPTIVE BIBLIOGRAPHY.

envelope \'en-və-,lōp, 'än-\ In poetry, a device in which a line or a stanza is repeated so as to enclose a section of verse, as in Sir Thomas Wyat's "Is it Possible?":

> Is it possible
> That so high debate,
> So sharp, so sore, and of such rate,
> Should end so soon and was begun so late?
> Is it possible?

The term can also be used for a quatrain with a rhyme scheme of *abba* because the rhymes of the first and last lines can be said to enclose the other lines.

envoi or **envoy** \'en-,vȯi, 'än-\ [French *envoi*, from Middle French *envoy*, literally, the act of sending, dispatch] The usually explanatory or commendatory concluding remarks to a poem, essay, or book; specifically, a short, fixed final stanza of a poem (such as a BALLADE) pointing the moral and usually addressing the person to whom the poem is written. Although they are most often associated with the ballade and chant royal—*i.e.*, French poetic forms—envois have also been used by several English poets, including Geoffrey Chaucer, Robert Southey, and Algernon Charles Swinburne.

Eos \'ē-ˌäs\   In Greek mythology, the personification of the dawn. According to the Greek poet Hesiod, Eos was the daughter of the Titans Hyperion and Theia and was the sister of Helios (Sun) and Selene (Moon). By the Titan Astraeus, Eos was the mother of Zephyrus (the West Wind), Notus (the South Wind), and Boreas (the North Wind) and of Hesperus (the Evening Star) and the other stars; by Tithonus of Troy she was the mother of Memnon, king of the Ethiopians. In Roman mythology she was called Aurora.

Eos was also represented as the lover of the hunter Orion and of the youthful hunter Cephalus, who resisted her.

Eötvös \'œt-ˌvœsh\, Baron (Báró) József (b. Sept. 13, 1813, Buda, Hung.—d. Feb. 2, 1871, Pest)   Novelist, essayist, educator, and statesman whose life and writings were devoted to the creation of a modern Hungarian literature and to the establishment of a modern democratic Hungary.

During his studies in Buda, Eötvös became inspired with liberalism and the desire to reform Hungarian society. Between 1836 and 1841 he studied social conditions in England and France and returned deeply impressed by liberal philanthropy, Romanticism, and utopian socialism. His first novel, *A karthausi* (1839–41; "The Carthusians"), which expresses disappointment at the July Revolution in France (1830), was intended as a criticism of feudalism in Hungary. *A falu jegyzője* (1845; *The Village Notary*) bitterly satirizes old Hungary, and a historical novel about the 16th-century Hungarian peasant rebellion, *Magyarország 1514-ben* (1847; "Hungary in 1514"), mobilized public opinion against serfdom.

Eötvös became minister of education in the revolutionary government of 1848, but he resigned later that year. Until 1851 he lived in Munich, where he began his greatest work, *A tizenkilencedik század uralkodó eszméinek befolyása az álladalomra* (1851–54; "The Influence of the Ruling Ideas of the 19th Century on the State").

Eötvös's later years were devoted to political and philosophical activity. After the revolution of 1848, he wrote no poetry and only one novel, *Nővérek* (1857; "The Sisters"), which explained his ideas on education. His literary work, however, is of great importance. His short stories mark the beginning of a new portrayal of the peasant in Hungarian literature, and he was a pioneer of realism at a time when the romantic novel was in fashion.

epanalepsis \ˌep-ə-nə-'lep-sis\   [Greek *epanálēpsis* resumption, repetition, a derivative of *epalambánein* to take up again, repeat]   Repetition of a word or phrase after intervening language, as in the first line of Algernon Charles Swinburne's "Itylus":

> Swallow, my sister, O sister swallow,
> How can thine heart be full of the spring?

epanodos \e-'pan-ə-ˌdäs\   [Greek *epánodos* recapitulation, literally, ascent, return]   A figure of speech in which a word is repeated within a sentence, as in "Because I do not hope to turn again/Because I do not hope" from T.S. Eliot's poem "Ash Wednesday."

Ephialtes \ˌef-ē-'al-tēz\   In Greek mythology, one of the twin sons of Iphimedia by the god Poseidon. He also appears as one of the giants of the ninth circle of hell in Dante's *Inferno*. *See* ALOADAE.

Ephorus \'ef-ə-rəs\ (b. *c.* 405 BC, Cyme, Aeolis—d. 330 BC)   Greek historian, the author of the first universal history, who, despite his defects, was esteemed in classical times and is considered the best of the historians writing in his period.

According to uncertain tradition, Ephorus was the pupil of Isocrates, whose school rivaled Plato's Academy in fame. Ephorus' *Historiai*, his major work, was completed with a 30th book added by his son Demophilus, who edited the entire work. It began with the return of the Heracleidae to Peloponnesus and ended with the siege of Perinthus (340) by Philip II of Macedonia, with a further extension in the 30th book that centered on the Second Sacred War of 355–46. Ephorus was the first historian to divide his work into books, to each of which he wrote a preface, and he treated his material under subject headings rather than chronologically.

Ephorus' work is no longer extant, but the structure and content of the book are known through the writings of other authors who used it as a source. They include Diodorus Siculus, whose chronological blunders arise in part from trying to reproduce Ephorus in annalistic form, and Polybius, who gave Ephorus credit for knowledge of naval warfare conditions but belittled his descriptions of certain land operations.

Several other works have been attributed to Ephorus, including a treatise on discoveries, another on the history and antiquities of Cyme, and an essay on style.

epic \'ep-ik\ [from *epic*, adjective, pertaining to an epic, from Latin *epicus,* from Greek *epikós*, a derivative of *épē* lines, verses, epic poetry, plural of *épos* word]   Long narrative poem in an elevated style that celebrates heroic achievement and treats themes of historical, national, religious, or legendary significance. It is to be distinguished from the briefer heroic lay, the less elevated, less ambitious folktale and ballad, and the more consistently extravagant and fantastic medieval romance, although in the narrative poetry of Ludovico Ariosto, Matteo Boiardo, and Edmund Spenser the categories tend to merge. One may also distinguish "primary" (also called traditional or classical) epic, shaped from the legends and traditions of a heroic age and part of the oral tradition of literature, from "secondary" (or literary) epic, which was written down from the beginning and was self-consciously produced by sophisticated poets who adapted aspects of traditional epic for specific literary and ideological purposes. Homer's *Iliad* and *Odyssey* are primary epics; Virgil's *Aeneid* and John Milton's *Paradise Lost* are secondary epics.

Although the Mesopotamian verse-narratives of Gilgamesh, dating from the 3rd millennium BC, may constitute the earliest epic, the Homeric poems, which assumed their final form in the period 900–750 BC, are usually regarded as the first important epics and the main source of epic conventions and characteristics in the secondary epics of western Europe. The main aspects of epic convention are the centrality of a hero—sometimes semidivine—of military, national, or religious importance; an extensive, perhaps even cosmic, geographical setting; heroic battle; extended and often exotic journeying; and the involvement of supernatural beings, such as gods, angels, or demons, in the action. Epics tend to treat familiar and traditional subjects. They usually begin with a statement of the subject, invoking the assistance of a muse, and then plunge into the middle of the story, filling in the earlier stages later on with retrospective narrative by figures within the poem. Catalogs and processions of heroes, often associated with specific localities, are common, and when such heroes speak it is often in set speeches delivered in formal circumstances. Epic narrative is often enriched by extended epic similes that go beyond an initial point of correspondence to elaborate a whole scene or episode drawn from a different area of experience.

Primary epics registering heroic experience in the vernacular languages of Europe continued to appear long after Virgil popularized secondary epic. The Spanish *Cantar de mio Cid* celebrates the hero of the wars against the Moors in the 11th century; the French *La Chanson de Roland* (12th century) commemorates an 8th-century battle in the Pyrenees between Charlemagne's army and the Saracens; the 13th-century German *Nibelungenlied* recounts a story deriving ultimately from the war between the Burgundians and the Huns in the 5th century; and the Anglo-Saxon *Beowulf* refers to historical characters and events of the 6th century as it describes Beowulf's struggles against the monsters that threaten the heroic fellowship of the mead hall. But long before these poems assumed the form in which they now exist, the historical elements in them had passed into myth and were influenced by legends from other periods and traditions.

The epic poem was generally regarded as a superseded form in the 20th century, but the scope and majesty of the genre were occasionally suggested by works in other forms, such as the fantasy trilogy *The Lord of the Rings* (1954–55), a prose work by J.R.R. Tolkien that reflects the flavor and forms of Norse saga and Anglo-Saxon poetry in its epic narrative set in the realm of Middle Earth.

epic caesura   A type of feminine caesura. *See* CAESURA.

epicede \'ep-ə-ˌsēd\ or **epicedium** \ˌep-ə-'sē-dē-əm\ *plural* epicedes *or* epicedia \-dē-ə\ [Greek *epikédeion,* from *epí* on, upon + *kêdos* funeral rites, mourning]   In ancient Greece, a funeral song or ode that was performed in the presence of the corpse, as opposed to a dirge, which could be sung anywhere.

Epicharmus \ˌep-i-'kär-məs\ (b. *c.* 530 BC—d. *c.* 440 BC) Greek poet who, according to the *Suda* lexicon of the 10th century AD, was the originator of Sicilian (or Dorian) comedy. He has been credited with more than 50 plays written in the Sicilian dialect; titles of 35 of his works survive, but the remains are scanty.

Many of Epicharmus' plays were mythological burlesques. His works featured set debates, and the stock characters, such as the parasite and the rustic, were later characteristic of Middle and New Comedy. Some of his titles suggest parodies of tragedies. Though they seem to have had some musical accompaniment, the plays had no chorus. Epicharmus' style was lively. His comedies were apparently short and largely farcical but contained a mixture of philosophical moralizing in the form of gnomic maxims. Ancient authorities also attributed to him works on ethics and medicine.

epic simile *also called* Homeric simile.   An extended simile often running to several lines used typically in epic poetry to intensify the heroic stature of the subject and to serve as decoration. An example from the *Iliad* follows:

> But swift Aias the son Oïleus would not at all now
> take his stand apart from Telamonian Aias,
> not even a little; but as two wine-coloured oxen straining
> with even force drag the compacted plough through the fallow
>   land,
> and for both of them at the base of the horns the dense sweat
>   gushes;
> only the width of the polished yoke keeps a space between them
> as they toil down the furrow till the share cuts the edge of the
>   ploughland;
> so these took their stand in battle, close to each other.

epic theater *also called* epic drama; *German* episches Theater \'ä-pē-shəs-tā-'ät-ər\   Form of drama presenting a series of loosely connected scenes that avoid illusion and often interrupt the action to address the audience directly with analysis or argument (as by a narrator) or with documentation (as by a film). Epic theater is now most often associated with the dramatic theory and practice evolved by the playwright-director Bertolt Brecht in Germany from the 1920s onward. Its dramatic antecedents include the episodic structure and didactic nature of plays by Georg Büchner, the pre-Expressionist drama of Frank Wedekind, and the Expressionist theater of Erwin Piscator and Leopold Jessner, both of whom made exuberant use of the technical effects that came to characterize epic theater.

Brecht's perspective was Marxian, and his intention was to appeal to his audience's intellect in presenting moral problems and in reflecting contemporary social realities on stage. He wished to block their emotional responses and to hinder their tendency to empathize with the characters and to get caught up in the action. To this end, he used "alienating," or "distancing," effects to cause the audience to think objectively about the play, to reflect on its argument, and to draw conclusions. A similar concept was the Living Newspaper, which later became part of the tradition of epic theater. *See also* ALIENATION EFFECT; LIVING NEWSPAPER.

epideictic oratory \ˌep-ə-'dīk-tik\ [Greek *epideiktikós* for display, declamatory, a derivative of *epideiknýnai* to show off, display], *also called* ceremonial oratory.   According to Aristotle, a type of suasive speech designed primarily for rhetorical effect. Epideictic oratory was panegyrical, declamatory, and demonstrative. Its aim was to condemn or to eulogize an individual, a cause, occasion, movement, city, or state. An outstanding example of this type of speech is a funeral oration by Pericles in honor of those killed in the first year of the Peloponnesian War.

epigram \'ep-ə-ˌgram\ [Greek *epígramma* inscription, short poem, epigram, a derivative of *epigráphein* to write on, inscribe]   A short poem treating concisely, pointedly, and often satirically a single thought or event and often ending with a witticism or ingenious turn of thought. By extension the term is also applied to a terse, sage, or witty, often paradoxical saying, usually in the form of a generalization.

Originally an inscription suitable for carving on a monument, the term took on its current meaning by about the 1st century BC. Many of the poems of the period that were collected in the GREEK ANTHOLOGY are examples of the verse form. Catullus (*c.* 84–*c.* 54 BC) originated the Latin epigram, and it was given final form by Martial (*c.* AD 40–103) in some 1,500 pungent and often indecent verses that served as models for French and English epigrammatists of the 17th and 18th centuries.

The epigram was revived by Renaissance scholars and poets such as the French poet Clément Marot, who wrote epigrams in both Latin and the vernacular. In England the form took shape somewhat later, notably in the hands of Ben Jonson and his followers; one of these was Robert Herrick, writer of such graceful examples as the following:

> I saw a Flie within a Beade
> Of Amber cleanly buried:
> The Urne was little, but the room
> More rich than *Cleopatra's* Tombe.

As the century progressed, both English and French epigrams became more astringent and closer in spirit to Martial. The *Maximes* (1665) of François VI, Duke de La Rochefoucauld, marked one of the high points of the epigram in French. It influenced such later practitioners as Voltaire. In England, John Dryden, Alexander Pope, and Jonathan Swift produced some of the most memorable epigrams of their time.

Samuel Taylor Coleridge, writing at the beginning of the 19th century, produced an epigram that neatly sums up the form:

> What is an Epigram? A dwarfish whole,
> Its body brevity, and wit its soul.

The epigram engaged German taste in the 18th and early 19th centuries, culminating in J.W. von Goethe's *Zahme Xenien* (1820; "Gentle Epigrams"). Among later masters of the English epigram were Oscar Wilde and George Bernard Shaw. Wilde became famous for such remarks as "A cynic is a man who knows the price of everything and the value of nothing." Shaw, in his *Annajanska* (1919), commented that "All great truths begin as blasphemies."

epigraph \\'ep-ə-ˌgraf\\ [Greek *epigraphē*, a derivative of *epigráphein* to write on, inscribe]   **1.** An inscription on a statue, a building, or a coin.   **2.** A quotation set at the beginning of a literary work (such as a novel) or a division of a work to suggest its theme.

epilogue or **epilog** \\'ep-ə-ˌlòg, -ˌläg\\ [Greek *epílogos* concluding part of a speech or play, a derivative of *epilégein* to say in addition]   **1.** The conclusion or final part of a nondramatic literary work that serves typically to round out or complete the design of the work—also called *afterword. Compare* FOREWORD; PREFACE.   **2.** A speech often in verse addressed to the audience by one or more of the actors at the end of a play, such as that at the end of William Shakespeare's *Henry VIII*:

> 'Tis ten to one this play can never please
> All that are here. Some come to take their ease,
> And sleep an act or two; but those, we fear,
> We have frighted with our trumpets; so 'tis clear,
> They'll say 'tis naught; others, to hear the city
> Abused extremely, and to cry, "That's witty!"
> Which we have not done neither. That, I fear,
> All the expected good we're like to hear
> For this play at this time is only in
> The merciful construction of good women;
> For such a one we show'd 'em. If they smile,
> And say 'twill do, I know, within a while
> All the best men are ours; for 'tis ill hap,
> If they hold when their ladies bid 'em clap.

The epilogue, at its best, was a witty piece intended to send the audience home in good humor. Its form in the English theater was established by Ben Jonson in *Cynthia's Revels* (c. 1600). Jonson's epilogues typically asserted the merits of his play and defended it from anticipated criticism.

The heyday of the prologue and epilogue in the English theater was the Restoration period. From 1660 to the decline of the drama in the reign of Queen Anne, scarcely a play was produced in London without a prologue and epilogue. Epilogues were rarely written after the 18th century. *Compare* PROLOGUE.   **3.** The final scene of a play whose main action is set within a framework, such as Bertolt Brecht's *The Caucasian Chalk Circle.*

Epimenides \\ˌep-i-'men-ə-ˌdēz\\ (fl. 6th century BC?)   Cretan seer, reputed author of religious and poetical writings. He conducted purificatory rites at Athens about 500 BC according to Plato (about 600 BC according to Aristotle). All surviving fragments, including a line quoted by St. Paul (Titus 1:12), are attributable to other sources. Stories of his advanced age (157 or 299 years), his miraculous sleep of 57 years, and his wanderings outside the body have led some scholars to regard him as a legendary figure of a shamanistic type.

Epimenides is reputed to be the first to record the liar paradox (also called Epimenides' paradox), in which a sentence that is grammatically correct (such as "I am lying") can be logically nonsensical.

Épinay \\dā-pē-'ne\\, Louise-Florence-Pétronille, Dame de La Live d' \\də-lä-'lēv\\, *byname* Madame d'Épinay, *original surname* Tardieu d'Esclavelles \\tär-dyœ-des-klä-'vel\\ (b. March 11, 1726, Valenciennes, Fr.—d. April 17, 1783, Paris)   A distinguished figure in literary circles of 18th-century France.

Though she wrote a good deal herself, she is more famous for her friendships with three of the outstanding French writers and thinkers of her day, Denis Diderot, Baron Friedrich Melchior von Grimm, and Jean-Jacques Rousseau.

Mme d'Épinay interested herself in literature and the welfare of men of letters after the breakdown of her marriage to Denis-Joseph de La Live d'Épinay, a financier. She set up a congenial salon in her country house at La Chevrette, near Montmorency, and offered hospitality to the philosophes, the leading intellectual figures of the period immediately prior to the French Revolution. Her friendship with Grimm was long and untroubled, and Mme d'Épinay collaborated with him on his cultural newsletter. Her association with Rousseau, on the other hand, was brief and stormy: in 1756 he accepted her offer of accommodation in the "Hermitage," a small dwelling near her country house, and wrote his novel *Julie: ou, la nouvelle Héloïse* there. But then he quarreled with his hostess, and the two became implacable foes.

Mme d'Épinay was the author of several novels and works on education, but her writings are of interest now chiefly for their autobiographical revelations.

epinicion \\ˌep-ə-'nis-ē-ˌän, -'nish-\\ or **epinikion** \\-'nik-ē-ˌän, -'nēk-\\ *plural* epinicia or epinikia \\-ē-ə\\ [Greek *epiníkion,* from *epí* on, upon + *níkē* victory]   A song of triumph or a choral lyric ode in honor of a victor in war or in the great Hellenic games. An epinicion was performed as part of the celebration on the victor's triumphal return to the city.

The epinicion had a basis in improvised celebration, but the form as it has survived is highly literary. One of the earliest examples extant is an ode for an Olympic victory in 520 BC that was written by Simonides of Ceos. Though the epinicion's structure is not fixed, there is a certain uniformity in content and arrangement. The occasion demands a reference to the victor and the nature and place of his victory; to this may be added reference to victories of members of his family or, in the case of athletic victory, a compliment to his trainer. Generally there is a myth, more or less elaborate and relevant to the occasion. A gnomic element is also included.

The epinicion ode did not use traditional lines or stanzas, but the meter was formed afresh for each poem and was never used again in exactly the same form. The strophes, or stanzas, either single or in systems of three, were repeated throughout the poem, and often their form was related to the accompanying dance. Its performance required a trained choir and musicians skilled in the lute and the lyre. The epinicion reached its zenith in the odes of Pindar (518 or 522 to after 446 BC). Those of a younger contemporary, Bacchylides, signaled the end of the form's popularity. *See also* ODE.

epiphany \\i-'pif-ə-nē\\ [Greek *epipháneia* appearance, manifestation of a deity, a derivative of *epiphaínesthai* to come into view, appear]   **1.** A usually sudden manifestation or perception of the essential nature or meaning of something; an intuitive grasp of reality through something usually simple and striking (such as a commonplace event or person).   **2.** A literary representation of an epiphany, or a symbolically revealing work or part of a work. The use of the word in relation to literature is associated particularly with James Joyce because of his description of the concept in a draft of the work that became *A Portrait of the Artist as a Young Man.*

Epipsychidion \\ˌep-ē-sī-'kid-ē-ən, -sī-, -psī-, -psi-\\   Poem in couplets by Percy Bysshe SHELLEY, written in 1821 in Pisa (Italy). It is dedicated to Teresa ("Emilia") Viviani, the teenaged daughter of the governor of Pisa who had been confined in a nunnery by her father. Shelley renames her Emily and imagines her living in an ideal *menage à trois* with him and his wife;

eventually, he and Emily would live perfect lives on an island paradise. In his attempts to convey the rapture of his feelings, Shelley lapsed into self-parody and later found the poem something of an embarrassment.

epirrhema \,ep-i-'rē-mə\ [Greek *epírrhēma,* from *epí* on, following + *rhêma* something spoken, word]   In ancient Greek Old Comedy, an address usually about public affairs. It was spoken by the leader of one-half of the chorus after that half of the chorus had sung an ode. It was part of the parabasis, or performance by the chorus, during an interlude in the action of the play.

episode \'ep-i-,sōd\ [Greek *epeisódion* parenthetic addition in a poem or play, episode, from *epí* on, following + *eísodos* entrance]   A usually brief unit of action in a dramatic or literary work, such as the part of an ancient Greek tragedy between two choric songs and equivalent to any developed situation in a modern play; a developed situation that is integral to but separable from a continuous narrative (such as a novel or play); or one of a series of loosely connected stories or scenes.

Episodios nacionales \,ä-pē-sō-'thē-ōs-,nä-thē-ō-'nä-läs\ ("National Episodes")   Vast series of short historical novels, comprising 46 volumes, by Benito PÉREZ GALDÓS, published between 1873 and 1912. The scope and subject matter of these novels—the history and society of 19th-century Spain—put Pérez Galdós in the company of such writers as Honoré de Balzac and Charles Dickens. Based on exacting research, the works are vivid and realistic.

The first grouping, composed of 10 books published from 1873 to 1875, covers the period of Spanish history from 1805 to 1812. The second series, also 10 volumes, treats the period 1812–33 during the reign of Fernando (Ferdinand) VII. The third series covers the Carlist wars; the fourth, 1846 to 1868; and the fifth, comprising only six volumes, the period from 1869 to the Bourbon restoration in 1874. The books of the fifth series showed a decline in Pérez Galdós' mental powers.

epistle \i-'pis-əl\ [Latin *epistula,* literally, letter, dispatch, from Greek *epistolē* message, dispatch, letter, a derivative of *epistéllein* to send to, order]   A composition in prose or poetry written in the form of a letter to a particular person or group.

In literature there are two basic traditions of verse epistles, one derived from Horace's *Epistles* and the other from Ovid's *Epistulae heroidum* (better known as *Heroides*). The first addresses moral and philosophical themes and has been the most popular form since the Renaissance. The form that developed from Ovid deals with romantic and sentimental subjects; it was more popular than the Horatian form during the European Middle Ages. Well-known examples of the Horatian form are the letters of Paul the Apostle (the Pauline epistles incorporated into the Bible) and such works as Alexander Pope's "An Epistle to Dr. Arbuthnot."

Epistle to Dr. Arbuthnot, An \är-'bəth-nət\   Poem by Alexander POPE, published in January 1735. Addressed to Pope's friend John Arbuthnot, the epistle is an apology in which Pope defends his works against the attacks of his detractors, particularly the writers Lady Mary Wortley Montagu, Joseph Addison, and John, Lord Hervey.

Pope wrote this poem in imitation of the poet Horace, skillfully modulating the natural tempo of the rhymed couplets with enjambment, caesuras, and other forms of varied rhythm. The poem satirizes cowardly critics, hypocritical pedants, insipid patrons of the arts, and corrupt sycophants and caricatures Pope's contemporaries.

epistolary novel \i-'pis-tə-,ler-ē, ,ep-i-'stōl-ə-rē\   A novel told through the medium of letters written by one or more of the characters. Originating with Samuel Richardson's *Pamela* (1740), the story of a servant girl's victorious struggle against her master's attempts to seduce her, the epistolary novel was one of the earliest forms of novel to be developed. It remained one of the most popular up to the 19th century. The epistolary novel's reliance on subjective points of view makes it the forerunner of the modern psychological novel.

The advantages of the novel in letter form are that it presents an intimate view of the character's thoughts and feelings without interference from the author and that it conveys the shape of events to come with dramatic immediacy. Also, the presentation of events from several points of view lends the story dimension and verisimilitude. Though the method was most often a vehicle for the SENTIMENTAL NOVEL, it was used in other types of novels as well. Of the outstanding examples of the form, Richardson's *Clarissa* (1747–48) has tragic intensity, Tobias Smollett's *Humphry Clinker* (1771) is a picaresque comedy and social commentary, and Fanny Burney's *Evelina* (1778) is a novel of manners.

Some disadvantages of the form were apparent from the outset. The servant girl Pamela's remarkable literary powers and her propensity for writing on all occasions were cruelly burlesqued in Henry Fielding's *Shamela* (1741), which pictures his heroine in bed scribbling, "I hear him coming in at the Door," as her seducer enters the room. From 1800 on, the popularity of the form declined, though novels combining letters with journals and narrative were still common. In the 20th century, letter fiction was often used to exploit the linguistic humor and unintentional character revelations of such semiliterates as the fatuous ballplayer hero of Ring Lardner's *You Know Me Al* (1916).

epistolography \i-,pis-tə-'läg-rə-fē\   The art or practice of writing epistles, or letters.

epistrophe \e-'pis-trə-fē\ [Greek *epistrophḗ* the act of turning about]   Repetition of a word or expression at the end of successive phrases, clauses, sentences, or verses, especially for rhetorical or poetic effect, as in Abraham Lincoln's "of the people, by the people, for the people." Compare ANAPHORA.

epitaph \'ep-ə-,taf\ [Latin *epitaphium* inscription on a tomb, funeral oration, from Greek *epitáphios* funeral oration, from *epí* on, upon + *táphos* funeral rites, grave, tomb]   An inscription in verse or prose upon a tomb; and, by extension, anything written as if to be inscribed on a tomb.

Probably the earliest surviving are those written on the sarcophagi and coffins of the ancient Egyptians. Ancient Greek epitaphs are often of considerable literary interest, deep and tender in feeling, rich and varied in expression, and epigrammatic in form. They are usually in elegiac verse, though many of the later epitaphs are in prose. Among the most familiar epitaphs are those, ascribed to Simonides of Ceos (*c.* 556–*c.* 468 BC), on the heroes of Thermopylae, the most famous of which has been translated thus:

> Go tell the Spartans, thou that passest by
> That here, obedient to their laws, we lie.

Roman epitaphs, in contrast to the Greek, contained as a rule nothing beyond a record of facts with little variation.

The oldest existing British epitaphs are those of the Roman occupiers and are, of course, in Latin, which continued for many centuries to be the preferred language for epitaphs. In the 13th century, French came into use and English about the middle of the 14th century.

Most of the epitaphs that have survived from before the Reformation were inscribed upon brasses. By Elizabethan times, however, epitaphs upon stone monuments, in English, became much more common and began to assume a more literary character. Thomas Nashe tells how, by the end of the 16th century, the writing of verse epitaphs had become a trade. Many of the best-known epitaphs are primarily literary memorials, not necessarily intended to be placed on a tomb.

Semiliteracy often produces epitaphs that are comic through grammatical accident—for example, "Erected to the memory of/John MacFarlane/Drowned in the Water of Leith/By a few affectionate friends." Far more common, though, are deliberately witty epitaphs, a type abounding in Britain and the United States in the form of acrostics, palindromes, riddles, and puns on names and professions. Benjamin Franklin's epitaph for himself plays on his trade as a printer, hoping that he will "appear once more in a new and more beautiful edition, corrected and amended by the Author"; and that of the antiquary Thomas Fuller has the inscription "Fuller's Earth."

The art of the epitaph was largely lost in the 20th century. Some notable examples of humorous epitaphs were suggested, however, by the 20th-century writer and wit Dorothy Parker; they include "I told you I was sick" and "If you can read this, you're standing too close."

epitasis \ə-'pit-ə-sis\ *plural* epitases \-,sēz\ [Late Greek *epitasis,* from Greek, stretching, increase in intensity]   The part of a play that develops the main action and that leads to the catastrophe or denouement. *Compare* CATASTASIS; PROTASIS.

Epithalamion \,ep-ē-thə-'lā-mē-ˌän, -ən\   Marriage ode by Edmund SPENSER originally published with his sonnet sequence *Amoretti* in 1595. The poem celebrates Spenser's marriage in 1594 to his second wife, Elizabeth Boyle, and it may have been intended as a culmination of the sonnets of *Amoretti.* Taken as a whole, the group of poems is unique among Renaissance sonnet sequences in recording a successful love affair culminating in marriage. *Epithalamion* is considered by many to be the best of Spenser's minor poems.

The 24-stanza poem begins with the predawn invocation of the Muses and follows the events of the wedding day. The poet, reflecting on the private moments of the bride and groom, concludes with a prayer for the fruitfulness of the marriage. The mood of the poem is hopeful, thankful, and very sunny.

epithalamium \,ep-ə-thə-'lā-mē-əm\   or **epithalamion** \-mē-ən, -ˌän\ or **epithalamy** \-'thal-ə-mē\ *plural* epithalamiums *or* epithalamia \-thə-'lā-mē-ə\ *or* epithalamies [Greek *epithalámion,* from *epí* on, upon + *thálamos* room, bridal chamber]   A nuptial song or poem in honor or praise of a bride and bridegroom.

In ancient Greece the singing of such songs was a traditional way of invoking good fortune on the marriage and often of indulging in ribaldry. By derivation, the epithalamium should be sung at the marriage chamber, but the word is also used for the song sung during the wedding procession, containing repeated invocations to Hymen (Hymenaeus), the Greek god of marriage. No special meter has been associated with the epithalamium either in antiquity or in modern times.

The earliest evidence for literary epithalamiums are the fragments from Sappho's seventh book (*c.* 600 BC). The earliest surviving Latin epithalamiums are three by Catullus (*c.* 84–*c.* 54 BC). Epithalamiums based on classical models were written during the Renaissance by Torquato Tasso in Italy and Pierre de Ronsard in France. Among English poets of the same period, Richard Crashaw, John Donne, Sir Philip Sidney, and Ben Jonson used the form. In the 19th century, epithalamiums were written by Gerard Manley Hopkins and Edmund Gosse, and in the 20th, by such poets as A.E. Housman.

epithet \'ep-ə-ˌthet, -thət\ [Greek *epítheton* adjective, epithet, from neuter of *epíthetos* adjectival, literally, additional, added]   An adjective or phrase that is used to express the characteris-

tic of a person or thing, such as Ivan the Terrible. In literature, the term is considered an element of poetic diction, or something that distinguishes the language of poetry from ordinary language. Homer used certain epithets so regularly that they became a standard part of the name of the thing or person described, as in "rosy-fingered Dawn" and "gray-eyed Athena." The device was used by many later poets, including John Keats in his sonnet "On First Looking Into Chapman's Homer":

> Oft of one wide expanse had I been told
>   That deep-browed Homer ruled as his demesne; . . .

epitome \i-'pit-ə-mē\ [Greek *epitomḗ,* a derivative of *epitémnein* to cut short, abridge]   **1.** A summary or an abridgment of a written work.   **2.** A brief presentation of a broad topic, or a compendium.   **3.** A brief statement expressing the essence of something.

epitrite \'ep-ə-ˌtrīt\ [Greek *epítritos,* from *epítritos* (adjective) containing a whole and a third, having a ratio of 4:3, having three long syllables and one short, from *epí* on, upon + *trítos* third]   In classical prosody, a foot consisting of one short and three long syllables, usually in the sequence − ∪ − −. The epitrite is not used as the basis of any rhythm in Latin verse, though it did appear as a rhythm for the clausulae of Ciceronian orations. *Compare* PAEON. Four forms of the epitrite were distinguished, depending on the position of the short syllable: first (∪ − − −), second (− ∪ − −), third (− − ∪ −), and fourth (− − − ∪).

epizeuxis \,ep-ə-'zük-sis\ [Greek *epízeuxis* repetition, literally, the act of fastening together]   In literature, a form of repetition in which a word is repeated immediately for emphasis, as in the first and last lines of "Hark, Hark! the Lark," a song in William Shakespeare's *Cymbeline*:

> Hark, hark! the lark at heaven's gate sings,
>   And Phoebus gins arise,
> His steeds to water at those springs
>   On chaliced flowers that lies;
> And winking Mary-buds begin
>   To ope their golden eyes:
> With every thing that pretty is,
>   My lady sweet, arise:
> Arise, arise!

Epoch   American literary journal founded in 1947. *Epoch* published fiction and poetry of high caliber by unknown as well as established writers. Its first issue contained works by E.E. Cummings and John Ciardi. Subsequent issues included the writings of, among others, Hayden Carruth, David Ignatow, Anne Sexton, May Swenson, Diane Ackerman, William Kennedy, Leslie Fiedler, Ray Bradbury, Joyce Carol Oates, Philip Roth, Richard Farina, and Thomas Pynchon.

Beginning with its Spring 1956 issue, when publication was taken over by Cornell University, *Epoch* published two or three times yearly. Later issues were devoted in large measure to special topics.

epode \'ep-ˌōd\ [Greek *epōidós,* from *epōidós* (adjective) sung or said after]   **1.** A verse form composed of two lines differing in construction and often in meter, the second shorter than the first.   **2.** In Greek lyric odes, the third part of the three-part structure of the poem, following the strophe and the antistrophe.

eponym \'ep-ə-ˌnim\ [Greek *epṓnymos* person whose name has been given to something, from *epṓnymos* (adjective) giving one's name to something, surnamed, from *epí* on, upon + *ónoma, ónyma* name]   One for whom or which something is or is believed to be named. The word can refer, for example, to the usually mythical ancestor or totem animal or object that a social group (such as a tribe) holds to be the origin of its name. In its most familiar use, *eponym* denotes a person for whom a place or thing is named, as in describing James Monroe as the eponym of Monrovia, Liberia. The derivative adjective is *eponymous*. An eponymous hero of a work of literature is one whose name is the title of the work, such as Anne Brontë's *Agnes Grey*, Charles Dickens' *David Copperfield*, and John Fowles's *Daniel Martin*.

epopee \'ep-ə-,pē\ [French *épopée,* from Greek *epopoiía,* a derivative of *epopoiós* epic poet, from *épē* epic poetry + *poieîn* to make] An epic, especially an epic poem.

epos \'ep-,äs\ [Greek *épos* word, speech, tale] **1.** An epic. **2.** A body of poetry expressing the tradition of a people; specifically, a number of poems that treat an epic theme but are not formally united.

epyllion \e-'pil-ē-ən, -,än\ *plural* epyllia \-ē-ə\ *or* epyllions [Greek *epýllion* short verse, short epic poem, diminutive of *épos* word, speech, line of verse] A brief narrative poem in dactylic hexameter, usually dealing with mythological and romantic themes. The epyllion is characterized by lively description, scholarly allusion, and an elevated tone similar to that of the epic.

Such poems were especially popular during the Greek Alexandrian period (*c.* 4th–3rd century BC), as seen in the works of Callimachus and Theocritus, although the term *epyllion* was not applied to them until the 19th century. William Shakespeare's *Lucrece* and Matthew Arnold's "Sohrab and Rustum" are examples of epyllions in English.

Equiano \,ek-wē-'än-ō, ,äk-\, Olaudah (b. *c.* 1750, Essaka, Benin [now in Nigeria]—d. April/May 1797, England) Igbo (Ibo) who was sold into slavery and later freed. His autobiography, *The Interesting Narrative of the Life of Olaudah Equiano, or Gustavus Vassa, the African* (1789), with a strong abolitionist stance and an interesting and detailed description of his youth in Africa, was so popular that by 1794 it had run through eight English editions and one American edition.

Captured at age 12, Equiano was taken to the West Indies, where he traveled widely with his master and received some education before he was freed. Once in England he became an active abolitionist, agitating and lecturing against the cruelty of British slave owners in Jamaica. In 1787 he was appointed commissary aboard the *Vernon,* which was carrying 500 to 600 freed slaves to Freetown, Sierra Leone, to establish a settlement there. Publication of his autobiography was aided by British abolitionists who were collecting evidence on the sufferings of slaves. In that book and in the later *Miscellaneous Verses,* he idealizes his African past and shows a great pride in his race while attacking those Africans who trafficked in slavery. He cites not only the injustices and humiliations of his fellow slaves but also the kindness of his own master and of English women who befriended him.

equivalence \i-'kwiv-ə-ləns\ *or* **equivalency** \-lən-sē\ *plural* equivalences *or* equivalencies. In classical prosody, the principle that one long syllable is equal to two short ones. The principle is used as the basis for SUBSTITUTION in quantitative verse.

Equus \'ek-wəs\ Drama in two acts by Peter SHAFFER, produced and published in 1973. It depicts a psychiatrist's fascination with a disturbed teenager's mythopoeic obsession with horses.

The drama unfolds through the eyes of Martin Dysart, a psychiatrist and amateur mythologist, who narrates the events of his rehabilitation of Alan Strang, a 17-year-old stable boy who has been arrested for blinding six horses. Confused by the conflict between his father's agnosticism and voyeurism and his mother's secretive religious devotion, Alan has grown to worship horses as deities of great religious and sexual power. When a stable girl attempts to seduce Alan, he is impotent in the presence of the horses and blinds them in a fit of uncontrolled anger and guilt. Dysart grows to appreciate the depth and power of Alan's feelings and to regret that his successful treatment of the boy will rob him of his creative vitality.

Erasmus \i-'raz-məs\, Desiderius (b. Oct. 27, 1469, Rotterdam, Holland [The Netherlands]—d. July 12, 1536, Basel, Switz.) Humanist who was the greatest scholar of the northern Renaissance, the compiler of the first edition of the Greek New Testament to be printed and distributed. He is also an important figure in patristics and classical literature.

Erasmus attended schools at Gouda, Deventer, and Utrecht. Later he was educated under the influence of the pietist *devotio moderna* (a late medieval lay religious movement emphasizing education), became an Augustinian canon, and was ordained a priest in 1492. Studies in Paris confirmed his dislike of scholastic theology and brought him into contact with humanist groups. He visited England in 1499–1500, 1505–06, 1509–14, and 1517, lectured at the universities of Oxford and Cambridge, and became well acquainted with Thomas More, John Fisher, and John Colet, who inspired him to study the Bible. Erasmus began to study Greek and visited Italy, where he widened his humanist contacts. He also spent four years at Louvain, Belg., six years at Freiberg, Ger., and the rest of his life in Basel, Switz.

The writings of Erasmus, covering a wide variety of topics, rank him as one of the greatest scholars of his time. The *Adagia* (1500; *Proverbes or Adagies*), containing more than 3,000 proverbs collected from the works of the classical authors, established his reputation, and the *Moriae encomium* (*c.* 1511; *The Praise of Follie*) and his 1516 edition of the New Testament ensured it.

Erato \'er-ə-,tō\ In Greek mythology, one of the nine Muses, the patron of lyric and erotic poetry or hymns. She was often depicted playing a lyre.

Ercilla y Zúñiga \er-'thēl-yä-ē-'thün-yē-gä\, Alonso de (b. Aug. 7, 1533, Madrid [Spain]—d. Nov. 29, 1594, Madrid) Spanish soldier and poet, author of *La Araucana* (1569–89; *The Araucaniad*), the most celebrated Spanish Renaissance epic poem and the first epic poem about America.

Ercilla y Zúñiga received an excellent literary education before going to the New World in 1555. He distinguished himself in Chile in the wars against the Araucanian Indians and while there began the poem based on his experiences. He finished the work after his return to Spain in 1563. *La Araucana* appeared in three installments in 1569, 1578, and 1589 and consisted of 37 cantos; two further cantos were added in 1590. The poem is weak in form, unity, and versification, but it excels in graphic descriptions, particularly of fighting. It shows great sympathy for the brave resistance of the Araucanians.

Erckmann-Chatrian \erk-mån-shå-trē-'yäⁿ\, *pseudonym of* Émile Erckmann \'erk-,mån\ *and* Louis-Alexandre Chatrian \shå-trē-'yäⁿ\ (respectively b. May 20, 1822, Phalsbourg, Fr.—d. March 14, 1899, Lunéville; b. Dec. 18, 1826, Soldatenthal, Fr.—d. Sept. 3, 1890, Paris) Two of the first French regionalist novelists in the 19th century.

The two men were close friends and decided to collaborate in writing novels that are essentially patriotic and popular in character. They chose as their heroes the people of their native province, Alsace, and based their plots on events in its history. Their first joint publication was a collection of short stories, *Contes fantastiques* (1847; "Fantastic Tales"), and they established their reputation with the novels *L'Illustre Docteur*

Mathéus (1859), *Le Fou Yégof* (1862; "Crazy Yégof"), *Madame Thérèse* (1863), and *L'Ami Fritz* (1864; "Friend Fritz"). They often portrayed military life, as in *L'Histoire d'un conscrit de 1813* (1864), about a man called to the colors (drafted) toward the end of the Napoleonic Wars, and in *Waterloo* (1865), in which they grasp the opportunity to decry the horrors of war and to advance their own pacifist views. Erckmann and Chatrian quarreled in 1889 and abandoned their partnership as a result.

Ercles vein \'ər-kləz, -,klēz; 'är-kləz\ A rousing, somewhat bombastic manner of public speaking or writing. In William Shakespeare's *A Midsummer Night's Dream* (Act I, scene 2), "Ercles' vein" is Bottom's expression for the style of speech he considers appropriate to the character of "Ercles," *i.e.*, Hercules.

Erdgeist \'ert-,gīst\ *see* EARTH SPIRIT.

Erdrich \'er-drik\, Louise, *in full* Karen Louise Erdrich (b. June 7, 1954, Little Falls, Minn., U.S.) American author whose principal subject was the Chippewa Indians in the northern Midwest.

Erdrich grew up in Wahpeton, N.D., where her parents taught at a Bureau of Indian Affairs boarding school, and attended Dartmouth College and Johns Hopkins University. She married writer Michael Dorris, her collaborator in her novels. Although she published two volumes of poetry, it was her fiction for which she was best known. After her short story "The World's Greatest Fisherman" won the 1982 Nelson Algren fiction prize, it became the basis of her first novel, *Love Medicine* (1984; expanded edition, 1993). *Love Medicine* began a tetralogy that includes *The Beet Queen* (1986), *Tracks* (1988), and *The Bingo Palace* (1994), about the Indian families on and around a North Dakota Chippewa reservation and the whites they encounter.

Erdrich's novels are noted for their depth of characterization; they are inhabited by a variety of characters, some of which reappear in several stories. White culture, which brings such forces as alcohol, Roman Catholicism, and government policies, acts to destroy the Indian community; tradition and loyalty to family and heritage are what work to keep it intact. Erdrich also wrote short stories, and she and Dorris were coauthors of the novel *The Crown of Columbus* (1991).

Erec \'ē-rek, 'ā-\ Middle High German epic poem by HARTMANN von Aue, written about 1180–85 and considered the first Arthurian romance in German. This poem of some 10,-000 lines is a loose translation of a work by Chrétien de Troyes about one of the knights of the Round Table. The story concerns the duties and proper behavior of a knight and reflects the ideals of restraint and moderation that Hartmann valued.

When the knight Erec realizes that devotion to his new wife, Enite, has caused him to become neglectful of his knightly duties, he sets out on a series of adventures, taking Enite with him. He eventually learns to achieve a balance between his two chivalrous duties.

Erechtheus \i-'rek-,thüs, -thē-əs\ Legendary king and probably also a divinity of Athens. According to Homer's *Iliad*, he was born from "the fertile corn-land" and raised by the goddess Athena, who established him in her temple at Athens. In later times only a great snake was thought to share the temple with Athena, and there is evidence that Erechtheus was or became a snake or an earth or ancestor spirit.

The earliest Athenian kings tended to have similar names, suggesting a connection with the earth (*chthōn*; *e.g.*, Erichthonius, Erysichthon), to have been born of the earth and raised by Athena, and to have something serpentine about them. Snakes were often earth or ancestor spirits, so that Athena's sharing her temple with Erechtheus, whom she herself nurtured, may have been the mythical way of expressing her guardianship of the ancient royal house of Athens and of the land itself and its fertility, with which ancient kingship was intimately connected.

In his lost play *Erechtheus*, Euripides gave that king three daughters, one of whom was appropriately named Chthonia. At war with neighboring Eleusis and its ally King Eumolpus, Erechtheus learned from the god Apollo that Athens would win if he sacrificed his daughter. He sacrificed Chthonia and won but apparently gained little by it, for he was destroyed by Poseidon or by a thunderbolt from Zeus.

Erewhon \'er-ə-,hwän, -,hwən, -,wän, -,wən\ (*in full* Erewhon; or, Over the Range) Satirical novel by Samuel BUTLER, first published anonymously in 1872. During Butler's lifetime, his reputation rested on the success of *Erewhon*, which he claimed as his own when it met with immediate approval. It was the only work from which Butler earned a profit.

The name of the realm in which the novel is set, Erewhon, is an anagram for "nowhere." The novel begins as an adventure story, using the convention of travel in an imaginary country. To the story's narrator, Erewhon at first seems utopian in its disregard for money—which lends status but has no purchasing value—and machines—which have been outlawed as dangerous competitors in the struggle for existence. Erewhon has also declared disease a crime for which the sick are imprisoned, and crime is considered a disease for which criminals are sent to the hospital. As the unnamed narrator further examines the institutions of Erewhon, his illusions of utopia and eternal progress are stripped away.

The novel's two main themes, religion and evolution, are examined in "The Musical Banks" (representing the Anglican church) and in chapters called "Some Erewhonian Trials" and "The Book of the Machines" (which grew out of Butler's reading of Charles Darwin).

Butler's sequel, entitled *Erewhon Revisited* (1901), lacks the freshness of the original, which remains a noteworthy satire of life and thought in Victorian England.

Erh-ya *see* ERYA.

Eridu Genesis \e-'rē-dū-'jen-ə-sis\ In Mesopotamian literature, ancient Sumerian epic primarily concerned with the Creation of the world, the establishment and development of the human race, and the Flood. According to the epic, which was named for one of the earliest settlements in the area, after the universe was created out of the primeval sea and the gods were given birth, the deities in turn fashioned humans from clay to cultivate the ground, care for flocks, and perpetuate the worship of the gods.

Cities were soon built and kingship was instituted. For some reason, however, the gods determined to destroy mortals with a flood. The god Enki, who did not agree with the decree, revealed it to Ziusudra, a man well known for his humility and obedience. Ziusudra built a huge boat, in which he successfully rode out the Flood. Afterward, he prostrated himself before the gods An and Enlil and, as a reward for living a godly life, was given immortality.

Erigone \e-'rig-ə-nē\ In Greek mythology, daughter of Icarius, the hero of the Attic deme (township) of Icaria. Her father, who had been taught by the god Dionysus to make wine, gave some to several shepherds, who became intoxicated. Their companions, thinking they had been poisoned, killed Icarius and buried him under a tree. Erigone, guided by her dog Maera, found his grave and hanged herself on the tree. Dionysus sent a plague on the land, and all the maidens of Athens, in a fit of madness, hanged themselves. To propitiate Icarius and Erigone, the festival called Aiora ("the Swing") was instituted.

During this festival various small images were swung from trees, and offerings of fruit were made.

Erinna \i-'rin-ə\ (fl. end of 4th century BC?)   Greek poet whose verse was almost as well known in antiquity as that of Sappho.

Erinna lived on an island (probably Telos) off the coast of Asia Minor. Only six poems and fragments survive, three on papyrus and three in quotation by other ancient writers. Of these, three concern a friend's death after marriage. The longest of her surviving works is a hexameter poem of lament for a friend that is written in the local Dorian dialect. Erinna herself is sometimes said to have died at the age of 19, but evidence does not support this supposition.

Erinys \i-'rin-is, -'rīn-\ *plural* Erinyes \i-'rin-ē-ˌēz\ (Greco-Roman mythology)   *see* FURY.

Eris \'er-is, 'ē-ris\, *also called* Discordia \dis-'kȯr-dē-ə\   In Greco-Roman mythology, the personification of strife. She was the daughter of Nyx and the sister and companion of Ares, or the Roman Mars. Eris is best known for her part in starting the Trojan War. When she alone of the gods was not invited to the marriage of Peleus and Thetis, she threw among the guests a golden apple inscribed "For the most beautiful." Hera, Athena, and Aphrodite each claimed it, and Zeus assigned the decision to Paris. Paris awarded the apple to Aphrodite, who then helped him win Helen of Troy. In the war that resulted, Hera and Athena remained implacable enemies of Troy.

Erlingsson \'er-liŋ-ˌsȯn\, Thorsteinn (b. Sept. 27, 1858, Fljótshlíd, Ice.—d. Sept. 28, 1914, Reykjavík)   Icelandic poet known for both lyrical romantic poetry and satirical verse in which he attacked the political and religious orders of the day.

Although he spent 13 years in Copenhagen, much of the time studying at the University of Copenhagen, Erlingsson never took a degree. He lived in poverty and in 1896 returned to Iceland, where he worked as an editor of several provincial journals. In 1900 he settled in Reykjavík and eked out a writer's pension by private teaching. Living at a time when the Danish regime imposed great hardship on the Icelanders, Erlingsson embraced socialism.

His two major publications were *Thyrnar* (1897; "Thorns"), later enlarged, and *Eithurinn* (1913; "The Oath"). *Thyrnar* is a collection of poems ranging from exquisite love lyrics to scathing political and religious satire. *Eithurinn* is an unfinished group of narrative poems that interprets the 17th-century tragic love story of Ragnheithur, the defiant daughter of Bishop Brynjólfur Sveinsson of Skálholt, who gives birth to the child of a lover whom she has been forced to forswear.

Erl-king, The \'erl-ˌkiŋ, 'ȯrl-\, *also called* The Elf-king.   Dramatic ballad by J.W. von GOETHE, written in 1782 and published as *Erlkönig*. The poem is based on the Germanic legend of a malevolent elf who haunts the Black Forest, luring children to destruction. It was translated into English by Sir Walter Scott and set to music in a famous song by Franz Schubert.

In the ballad, a father and son are journeying homeward on horseback at night. The son is ill with a fever and believes he sees and hears the erl-king. The father tells him that the form he sees is only the fog and the sound he hears is only the rustling leaves. Nonetheless, the erl-king wheedles, trying to tempt the boy to come with him. But when the boy again expresses his fear, the erl-king says that if the boy does not come of his own accord, he will be taken forcibly. The father, feeling his son's fear, spurs his horse on, but when they arrive home, the boy is dead.

Goethe masterfully recreates in the poem's cadence the galloping of the horses' hooves. The poem is one of several of Goethe's early works expressing the poet's conviction that the powers of nature are filled with unconscious elements capable of overwhelming humans.

Ern Malley hoax \'ərn-'mal-ē\   Literary fraud perpetrated in 1943–44 on the Australian literary periodical *Angry Penguins* by two antimodern poets, James McAuley and Harold Stewart. In order to parody what the hoaxers saw as the meaninglessness of experimental verse and to discredit the magazine and its editor Max Harris, the two wrote to *Angry Penguins* under the name Ethel Malley, the sister of a deceased mechanic and poet named Ernest (Ern) Malley. Claiming to have found the poetry in her late brother's effects, "Miss Malley" submitted some 17 poems to the magazine for an opinion as to their worth. Harris received the work enthusiastically, publishing a special edition of the magazine and a volume of the collected poems under the title *The Darkening Ecliptic* (1944). About nine months after first contacting the magazine, McAuley and Stewart revealed their hoax, listing as the sources of Malley's poetry patches of William Shakespeare, medical journals, government reports, and other random text. The generally unsympathetic press made much of the event. Despite the efforts of McAuley and Stewart, however, at least some of the verses can be considered to have merit, and the Malley poetry and its worth continue to be subjects of debate.

Ernst \'ernst, *Angl* 'ərnst\, Paul (Karl Friedrich) (b. March 7, 1866, Elbingerode, Saxony [Germany]—d. May 13, 1933, Sankt Georgen, Austria)   German writer known particularly for his short stories and for hundreds of essays on philosophical, economic, and literary problems.

Ernst studied for the ministry but quickly became disillusioned with theology. He became a militant Marxist and the editor of the *Berliner Volkstribüne*. He severed his Marxist connections at the turn of the century, however, and repudiated the doctrine in *Der Zusammenbruch des Marxismus* (1919; "The Collapse of Marxism"). He had already expressed his antagonism toward naturalism in art and called for a return to classicism in his essay *Der Weg zur Form* (1906; "The Road to Form"). His search for eternal truths led him through German idealist philosophy back to a form of Christianity that he dramatized in what he called redemption drama, best exemplified by *Ariadne auf Naxos* (1912).

Although Ernst believed his greatest literary contribution was in the theater, he became popular through his novels and won critical acclaim only in his short stories. The autobiographical novel *Der schmale Weg zum Glück* (1904; "The Narrow Road to Happiness") passed through more than 10 editions, and *Jugenderinnerungen* (1930; "Recollections of Youth") and *Grün aus Trümmern* (1933; "Green Out of Ruins"), of folkloric inspiration, were almost as popular. His best collection of short stories is *Komödianten- und Spitzbubengeschichten* (1927; "Tales of Comedians and Rogues"). *Erdachte Gespräche* (1921; "Imagined Conversations") is his best-known essay collection.

Eros \'er-ˌäs, 'ir-\   In Greek mythology, god of love, similar to the Roman god CUPID. In the *Theogony* of Hesiod (fl. *c.* 700 BC), Eros was a primeval god, son of Chaos, the original primeval emptiness of the universe. Later tradition made him the son of Aphrodite, variously by Zeus, Ares, Hermes, or others. Eros was god not simply of passion but also of fertility. His brother was Anteros, the god of mutual love, who was sometimes described as his opponent. The chief associates of Eros were Pothos and Himeros (Longing and Desire). Later writers assumed the existence of a number of Eroses (like the several versions of the Roman Amor).

In Alexandrian poetry the image of Eros degenerated into that of a mischievous child. In archaic art he was represented as a beautiful winged youth but tended to be made younger and younger until, by the Hellenistic period, he was an infant.

erotica \i-'rät-i-kə\ [Greek *erōtiká*, plural of *erōtikós* erotic, pertaining to sexual love, a derivative of *erōt-, éros* sexual love] Literary or artistic works having an erotic theme; especially, books treating of sexual love in a sensuous or voluptuous manner. The word erotica typically applies to works in which the sexual element is regarded as part of the larger aesthetic aspect. It is usually distinguished from pornography, which can also have literary merit but which is usually understood to have sexual arousal as its main purpose. *Compare* PORNOGRAPHY.

There are erotic elements in literary works of all times and all countries. Among the best-known examples of erotic literature are the *Kāma-sūtra* and other Sanskrit literature from about the 5th century AD, Persian lyric poems called ghazels, Ovid's *Ars Amatoria*, parts of Geoffrey Chaucer's *The Canterbury Tales*, Giovanni Boccaccio's *Decameron*, the 16th-century Chinese novel *Jin ping*, William Shakespeare's *Venus and Adonis*, the writings of the Marquis de Sade, and D.H. Lawrence's *Lady Chatterley's Lover*.

Erskine \'ər-skin\, John (b. Oct. 5, 1879, New York, N.Y., U.S.—d. June 2, 1951, New York City)   American educator, novelist, and musician noted for energetic, skilled work in several different fields.

Erskine attended Columbia University and taught there from 1909 to 1937, earning a reputation as a learned, witty teacher and lecturer specializing in Elizabethan literature.

In the 1920s Erskine appeared as a piano soloist with the New York Philharmonic, beginning a distinguished career as a concert pianist. He also served as president of the Juilliard School of Music, director of the Juilliard Musical Foundation, and director of the Metropolitan Opera Association.

Erskine wrote more than 45 books. He was particularly successful with his early satirical novels, which are legends retold with updated views on morality and society. These works include *The Private Life of Helen of Troy* (1925) and *Adam and Eve* (1927), the story of how Adam adjusts to life with women (in the novel, first Lilith and then Eve). Erskine also coedited the *Cambridge History of American Literature*, 3 vol. (1917–19). He described various facets of his life in *The Memory of Certain Persons* (1947), *My Life as a Teacher* (1948), and *My Life in Music* (1950).

Ervine \'ər-vin\, Saint John (Greer) (b. Dec. 28, 1883, Belfast, Ire.—d. Jan. 24, 1971, London, Eng.)   British playwright, novelist, and critic who was one of the first to write dramas in the style of local realism fostered by the Irish literary renaissance.

Ervine's best-known plays are *Mixed Marriage* (performed 1911) and the domestic tragedies *Jane Clegg* (1913) and *John Ferguson* (1915). Later plays include such comedies as *The First Mrs. Fraser* (1928), a rousing London success; *Robert's Wife* (1937); and a reactionary play on nationalization, *Private Enterprise* (1947). In 1915 he became associated with the Abbey Theatre. After World War I, Ervine settled in London and was a drama critic for *The Observer*. His books on drama include *The Organized Theatre* (1924) and *The Theatre in My Time* (1933).

Ervine also wrote biographies of Salvation Army general William Booth and of Oscar Wilde and George Bernard Shaw. His novels include *Francis Place, The Tailor of Charing Cross* (1912) and *Alice and a Family* (1915).

Erya or **Erh-ya** \'er-'yä\   An early Chinese lexicon that is considered a classic work of Chinese literature and is sometimes ranked with the *Wu jing* ("Five Classics") in importance and influence. The *Erya*, possibly assembled in the Qin (221–206 BC) or early Han (206 BC–AD 220) dynasty, is a compilation of words found in texts from the Zhou dynasty (traditionally 1122–256/255 BC) and is organized into 19 categories. The entries are accompanied by definitions and information on usage. Both the form and the content of the work influenced the creation of later Chinese lexicons.

Erziehungsroman \ert-'sē-,ûŋz-rō-,män, *German* -,ûŋs-\ [German, literally, novel of upbringing]   *see* BILDUNGSROMAN.

Esau \'ē-,sȯ\, *also called* Edom \'ē-dəm\   In the Old Testament book of Genesis, a son of Isaac and Rebekah and the elder twin brother of Jacob. In Hebrew tradition he is the ancestor of the Edomites.

At birth, Esau was red and hairy, and he grew to become a wandering hunter, while his twin Jacob was a shepherd. Although younger, Jacob dominated him by deception. In one notable incident, when Esau returned hungry from a hunt, Jacob bought Esau's birthright (*i.e.*, the rights due him as the eldest son) for some pottage (soup). When Isaac was dying, Jacob, with Rebekah's help, cheated Esau out of his father's blessing. Esau would have killed Jacob, but Jacob fled; when he returned 20 years later, Esau forgave him.

The story reflects the relationship of Israel and Edom, the land bordering ancient Israel (in what is now southwestern Jordan). It sought to explain why Israel dominated the kingdom of Edom, although the latter was older.

Escola Velha \esh-'kō-lə-'väl-yə\ [Portuguese, literally, old school]   Spanish dramatists in the early 16th century who were influenced by the Portuguese dramatist Gil VICENTE. Their designation as a school was the work of later critics. Although in form Vicente was a medieval dramatist, his skill in comedy and character portrayal and the varied subject matter of his plays made him a forerunner of the modern drama. He wrote 12 of 44 plays entirely in Spanish and 18 more in both Spanish and Portuguese, but the Inquisition proved to be the death of popular theater in Portugal and Vicente's real influence was felt in Spain.

esemplastic \,es-,em-'plas-tik, -əm-\ [Greek *es, eis* into + *hén*, neuter of *heîs* one + *plastikós* capable of molding, plastic] Shaping or having the power to shape disparate things into a unified whole. The word, coined by Samuel Taylor Coleridge to describe a faculty of the imagination, was probably suggested by *Ineinsbildung*, a term used by the German philosopher Friedrich Schelling.

Esenin   *see* YESENIN.

Esmond, Henry \'hen-rē-'ez-mənd\   Fictional character, the protagonist of William Makepeace Thackeray's novel HENRY ESMOND.

Espinel \,ä-spē-'nel\, Vicente (Martínez) (baptized Dec. 28, 1550, Ronda, Málaga, Spain—d. Feb. 4, 1624, Madrid)   Spanish writer and musician remembered chiefly for his picaresque novel *La vida del Escudero Marcos de Obregón* (1618; "Life of Squire Marcos of Obregón"), upon which the French novelist Alain-René Lesage based parts of his popular *Histoire de Gil Blas de Santillane* (1715–35; *The Adventures of Gil Blas of Santillane*).

After his expulsion from the University of Salamanca in 1572, Espinel entered the army and led a roguish life very much like that of his character Marcos, visiting Italy, Flanders, and the Netherlands. He returned to Spain in 1584 and was ordained to the priesthood in 1587. He is thought to have added the fifth string to the Spanish guitar.

Espinosa \,ä-spē-'nō-sä\, Pedro de (b. 1578, Antequera, Spain—d. Oct. 21, 1650, Sanlúcar de Barrameda)   Spanish poet and editor of the anthology *Flores de poetas ilustres de*

España (1605; "Flowers from the Illustrious Poets of Spain"), in which most of the important poets of Spain's Golden Age (*c.* 1500–1650) were published. Espinosa's own poetry clearly showed the Baroque influences of highly ornamental language and subtlety bordering on the esoteric. His long poem *Fábula del Genil* is considered one of the better poems in the Baroque mode.

Espronceda y Delgado \ˌäs-prȯn-ˈthä-ē-ˌthel-ˈgä-thō\, José de (b. March 25, 1808, Almendralejo, Spain—d. May 23, 1842, Madrid) Romantic poet and revolutionary, often called the Spanish Lord Byron.

Espronceda fled Spain in 1826 for revolutionary activities and in London began a tempestuous affair with Teresa Mancha (the subject of *Canto a Teresa*), which dominated the next 10 years of his life. He participated in the July Revolution of France (1830) and was later allowed to return to Spain, where he was a founding member of the Republican Party and was imprisoned several times for revolutionary activities. His historical novel *Sancho Saldaña* (1834), influenced by Sir Walter Scott, was written in prison in Badajoz. *Estudiante de Salamanca* (1839; *The Student of Salamanca*), a milestone of Iberian Romanticism, is a variant of the Don Juan legend. Espronceda was most admired for his lyric poetry, and his *Poesías* (1840; *Poems*) shows the influence of both Byron and Scott. The unfinished poem *El diablo mundo* (1840; "The Devilish World") contains ideological reflections and is considered one of his best works. He also wrote several plays.

Esquire \ˈes-ˌkwīr\ American monthly magazine, founded in 1933 by Arnold Gingrich, that began production as an oversized magazine for men, featuring drawings of scantily clad young women. It later abandoned its titillating role but continued to cultivate the image of refined taste. In 1943 the U.S. postmaster general attempted to withdraw *Esquire*'s second-class mailing privileges (an economy generally essential to a magazine's survival) because he did not believe the magazine made a "special contribution to the public welfare." Gingrich and his associates eventually won their case in the U.S. Supreme Court.

Esquire was a pioneer in the use of unconventional topics and feature stories. As it began to publish the work of Thomas Wolfe, Ernest Hemingway, William Faulkner, John Steinbeck, Truman Capote, and Norman Mailer, the magazine's risqué image gradually receded. It provided an outlet for new writers of fiction and nonfiction, and its topical features, satiric humor, and excellent book, movie, and music reviews filled a void between literary and opinion periodicals in the American market.

essay \ˈes-ˌā\ [Middle French *essai,* literally, trial, test] An analytic, interpretative, or critical literary composition usually much shorter and less systematic and formal than a dissertation or thesis and usually dealing with its subject from a limited and often personal point of view.

Some early treatises—such as those of Cicero on the pleasantness of old age or on the art of "divination," Seneca on anger or clemency, and Plutarch on the passing of oracles—presage to a certain degree the form and tone of the essay, but not until the Renaissance was the flexible and deliberately nonchalant and versatile form of the essay perfected by Montaigne. Choosing the name *essai* to emphasize that his compositions were attempts or endeavors, a groping toward the expression of his personal thoughts and experiences, Montaigne used the essay as a means of self-discovery. Later writers who most nearly recall the charm of Montaigne include, in England, Robert Burton, though his whimsicality is more erudite, Sir Thomas Browne, and Laurence Sterne, and in France, with more self-consciousness and pose, André Gide and Jean Cocteau.

At the beginning of the 17th century, social manners, the cultivation of politeness, and the training of an accomplished gentleman became the theme of many essayists. This theme was first exploited by the Italian Baldassare Castiglione in his *Il libro del cortegiano* (1528; *The Book of the Courtier*). The influence of the essay and of genres allied to it, such as maxims, portraits, and sketches, proved second to none in molding the behavior of the cultured classes.

With the advent of a keener political awareness with the age of Enlightenment, in the 18th century, the essay became all-important as the vehicle for a criticism of society and of religion. Because of its flexibility, its brevity, and its potential both for ambiguity and for allusions to current events and conditions, it was an ideal tool for philosophical reformers. *The Federalist Papers* in America and the tracts of the French Revolutionaries, are among the countless examples of attempts during this period to improve the human condition through the essay.

While in several countries the essay became the chosen vehicle of literary and social criticism, in other countries the genre became semipolitical, earnestly nationalistic, and often polemical, playful, or bitter. Essayists such as Robert Louis Stevenson and Willa Cather wrote with grace on several lighter subjects, and many writers—including Virginia Woolf, Edmund Wilson, and Charles du Bos mastered the essay as a form of literary criticism.

Essay on Criticism, An Didactic poem in heroic couplets by Alexander POPE, first published anonymously in 1711 when the author was 22 years old. Although inspired by Horace's *Ars poetica*, this work of literary criticism borrowed from the writers of the Augustan Age. In it Pope sets out poetic rules, a Neoclassical compendium of maxims, with a combination of ambitious argument and great stylistic assurance. The poem received much attention and brought Pope a wider circle of friends, notably Joseph Addison and Richard Steele, who were then collaborating on *The Spectator*.

The first of the poem's three sections opens with the argument that good taste derives from Nature and that critics should imitate the ancient rules established by classical writers. The second section lists the many ways in which critics have deviated from these rules. The final section, which discusses the characteristics of a good critic, concludes with a short history of literary criticism and a catalog of famous critics.

The work's brilliantly polished epigrams (*e.g.,* "A little learning is a dangerous thing," "To err is human, to forgive, divine," and "For fools rush in where angels fear to tread"), while not original, have become part of the proverbial heritage of the English language.

Essay on Man, An Philosophical essay written in heroic couplets of iambic pentameter by Alexander POPE. Published in 1733–34, it was conceived as part of a larger work that Pope never completed.

The poem consists of four epistles. The first epistle surveys relations between humans and the universe; the second discusses humans as individuals. The third addresses the relationship between the individual and society, and the fourth questions the potential of the individual for happiness. *An Essay on Man* describes the order of the universe in terms of a hierarchy, or chain, of being. By virtue of reason, humans are placed above animals and plants in the hierarchy.

Essays *also spelled* Essayes. Work by Francis BACON originally consisting of 10 essays published in 1597. The collection was reissued in 1612, enlarged to 38 essays, and published as *The Essaies of Sr Francis Bacon Knight*. A third edition, published in 1625, included 58 essays and was retitled *The Essayes or Counsels, Civill and Morall*.

The 1625 edition covers a wide range of topics, including such titles as "Of Seditions and Troubles," "Of Travel," "Of Friendship," "Of Nature in Men," "Of Gardens," and "Of Regimen in Health." Though some of his topics were weighty, Bacon's prose style was distinctively aphoristic, allusive, witty, and rich. The work was much admired by his contemporaries, and many of his aphorisms—such as "Cure the disease and kill the patient"—are current today.

Essays Series of short prose reflections by Michel de MONTAIGNE, published in French as *Essais* in three books; the first two, comprising, respectively, 57 and 37 chapters of greatly varying lengths, were published in 1580, and the third, 13 chapters in length, was published with enlarged versions of Books I and II in 1588. The work is considered to be one of the most captivating and intimate self-portraits ever written.

Montaigne saw his age as one of dissimulation, corruption, violence, and hypocrisy. It was his perception of humans as creatures of weakness and failure, of inconstancy and uncertainty, of incapacity and fragmentation, that led him to seek understanding through self-examination. His skepticism is reflected in the French title of his work, *Essais*, or "Attempts," which implies a project of trial and error, of tentative exploration. Montaigne's book inaugurated the term *essay* for the short prose composition treating a given subject in a rather informal and personal manner.

The essays move freely from one topic to the next and cover such diverse subjects as friendship, solitude, politics, sleep, fear, death, sadness, and moderation. As disparate in theme as the topics seem, however, the essays reveal an inner order leading to a final acceptance of and enthusiasm for the boundlessness of human nature.

Essays in Idleness Collection of 243 short prose pieces by YOSHIDA Kenkō, composed as *Tsurezuregusa* about 1330, though it may have been started as early as 1319. The work, written in a time of turmoil in Japanese history, looks back nostalgically to the past, seeking out the survivals of happier days. Kenkō's appreciation of the perishable and the incomplete and his other aesthetic judgments are often based on a worldly awareness considered surprising in a Buddhist priest. *Tsurezuregusa* gained wide currency, especially after the 17th century.

Estaunié \es-tō-'nyā\, Edouard (b. Feb. 4, 1862, Dijon, Fr.— d. April 1, 1942, Paris) French writer known for his novels of character.

Estaunié was by profession an engineer and ended his career as inspector general of telegraphs. He was elected to the Académie Française in 1923. The recurrent theme in Estaunié's 12 novels is expressed by the title of one of them, *La Vie secrète* (1908; "The Secret Life"); it was his thesis that each individual's outward life masks another ill-understood and usually much more important life, which may break through the mask unexpectedly to take temporary control. Estaunié's novels gain distinction from their profound and detailed psychological analysis. The more important of them include *L'Empreinte* (1895; "The Stamp"), *Les Choses voient* (1912; "Things See"), *L'Ascension de M. Baslèvre* (1920; "The Ascent of Mr. Baslèvre"), and *L'Appel de la route* (1922; *The Call of the Road*).

Estébanez Calderón or **Estévanes Calderón** \ā-'stā-bā-näth-käl-dā-'rôn\, Serafín, *pseudonym* El Solitario \,el-,sō-lē-'tā-rē-ō\ ("The Solitary One") (b. Dec. 27, 1799, Málaga, Spain— d. Feb. 5, 1867, Madrid) One of the best known of the costumbristas, Spanish writers who depicted in short articles the typical customs of the people. He moved to Madrid in 1830, where he published newspaper articles under his pseudonym and pursued a career that combined Arabic studies, poetry, and the collecting of manuscripts. His *Escenas andaluzas* ("Andalu-

sian Sketches") was published in 1847. He was also influential in the government.

Estella \es-'tel-ə\ Fictional character in the novel GREAT EXPECTATIONS by Charles Dickens. Estella is reared by her guardian, the eccentric Miss Havisham, to wreak vengeance on men in retaliation for Miss Havisham's having been jilted by her fiancé.

Esther \'es-tər\ Biblical character, the beautiful Jewish wife of the Persian king Ahasuerus (Xerxes I) in the Old Testament Book of Esther. The story of Esther is read on the Jewish festival of Purim, which commemorates the rescue of the Jews from Haman's plottings.

The Book of Esther recounts how Esther and her cousin Mordecai persuade Ahasuerus to retract an order for the general annihilation of Jews throughout the empire. The massacre had been plotted by the king's chief minister, Haman, and the date decided by casting lots (*purim*). Haman is hanged on the gallows he had built for Mordecai, and on the day planned for their annihilation the Jews instead destroy their enemies. Esther became a legendary figure epitomizing bravery, steadfastness, and loyalty.

Etana Epic \ā-'tän-,ä\ Ancient Mesopotamian tale concerned with the question of dynastic succession. In the beginning, according to the epic, there was no king on the earth. The gods thus set out to find one and apparently chose Etana, who proved to be an able ruler until he discovered that his wife, though pregnant, was unable to give birth and that he thus had no heir to the throne. The one known remedy was the birth plant, which Etana was required to bring down personally from heaven. Etana, therefore, prayed to the god Shamash, who heard his request and directed him to a mountain where a maimed eagle, languishing in a pit, would help him obtain the special plant. Etana rescued the eagle, and as a reward it carried him high up into the sky.

The result of Etana's quest is uncertain because of the incomplete state of the texts. According to one fragment, Etana reached heaven and prostrated himself before the gods. According to another fragment, however, Etana either became dizzy or lost his nerve before reaching heaven and crashed to the ground. If, as many scholars believe, Etana was successful, the myth may have been used to support early dynastic claims.

Etana of the myth is probably the Etana who ruled Kish in southern Mesopotamia sometime in the first half of the 3rd millennium BC.

Eteocles \i-'tē-ə-,klēz\ In Greek legend, the son of Oedipus and Jocasta and the brother of Polyneices, Antigone, and Ismene. After Oedipus' forced exile, Eteocles refuses to share the Theban throne with Polyneices. The city is attacked by Polyneices, who has raised an army, and the two brothers kill each other. The story is the subject of *Seven Against Thebes*, the third (and only extant) play in a trilogy by Aeschylus.

Eternal Curse on the Reader of These Pages Novel by Manuel PUIG, written in English and then translated by the author as *Maldición eterna a quien lea estas páginas* (1980). With the exception of the letters that form the epilogue, the novel consists entirely of dialogue between two men in New York City—an elderly Argentine invalid and the young American who cares for him. Their relationship is revealed through a dense, sometimes confusing narrative that blends reality and fantasy.

Ethan Frome \'ē-thən-'frōm\ Tragic novel by Edith WHARTON, published in 1911. Wharton's original style and her use of hard-edged irony and the flashback technique set *Ethan Frome* apart from the work of her contemporaries.

The main characters are Ethan Frome, his wife Zenobia, called Zeena, and her young cousin Mattie Silver. Frome and Zeena marry after she nurses his mother in his last illness. Although Frome seems ambitious and intelligent, Zeena holds him back. When her young cousin Mattie comes to stay on their New England farm, Frome falls in love with her. But the social conventions of the day doom their love and their hopes. The story forcefully conveys Wharton's abhorrence of society's unbending standards of loyalty. Written while Wharton lived in France but before her divorce (1913), *Ethan Frome* became one of the best known and most popular of her works.

Etherege \'eth-ə-rij\, Sir George (b. *c.* 1635, Maidenhead, Berkshire, Eng.?—d. *c.* May 10, 1692) Originator of the English Restoration COMEDY OF MANNERS.

Etherege's first comedy, *The Comical Revenge; or, Love in a Tub*, was premiered at Lincoln's Inn Fields Theatre in 1664. An immediate success, it was novel in its exploitation of contemporary manners, especially in the intrigue of the stylish Sir Frederick Frollick. Written in heroic couplets and blank verse, it nonetheless followed earlier tradition, with its romantic plot and its farcical subplot in prose. Its success gave Etherege an entrance into the world of fashion, where he became the boon companion of the literary rakes Sir Charles Sedley, the Earl of Rochester, and the Earl of Dorset. *She Wou'd if She Cou'd*, Etherege's second comedy (1668), was the first comedy of manners to attain unity of tone by shedding the incongruous romantic verse element.

Etherege wrote the prologue for the opening in 1671 of the new Dorset Garden Theatre. There his last and wittiest comedy, *The Man of Mode, or, Sir Fopling Flutter*, was produced with acclaim in 1676. He was knighted in 1680.

Etherege's style of comedy was successfully cultivated by his successors and has persisted to modern times. His own plays, however, failed to hold the stage after the mid-18th century. His love lyrics are among the most charming of their day.

ethos \'ē-,thäs, -,thòs\ [Greek *êthos* disposition, character] In rhetoric, the character or emotions of a speaker or writer that are expressed in the attempt to persuade an audience. It is distinguished from pathos, which is the emotion the speaker or writer hopes to induce in the audience. The two words were distinguished in a broader sense by ancient classical authors, who used *pathos* when referring to the violent emotions and *ethos* to mean the calmer ones. Ethos was the natural disposition or moral character, an abiding quality, and pathos a temporary and often violent emotional state. For Renaissance writers the distinction was a different one: ethos described character and pathos an emotional appeal.

Ettrick Shepherd, The \'et-rik\ Byname of Scottish poet James HOGG.

Etzel *see* ATTILA.

eudaemon or **eudemon** \,yü-'dē-mən\ [Greek *eudaímōn* having a good attendant spirit, happy (from *eu-* well, good + *daímōn* divinity, spirit), mistakenly taken to mean literally "good spirit"] A good spirit or angel. The opposing spirit is the CACODAEMON.

Euemeros *see* EUHEMERUS.

Eugene Onegin \yü-'jēn-ōn-'yā-gin\ or **Yevgeny Onegin** \yiv-'gʸe-nʸe-,ə-'nʸe-gʸin\ Verse novel by Aleksandr PUSHKIN, written from 1823 to 1831 and published in Russian in 1833 as *Yevgeny Onegin*.

Eugene Onegin is a disillusioned aristocrat who moves from St. Petersburg to a rural estate. Through Lensky, a neighboring landowner and poet, Onegin meets Tatyana, a romantic, unpolished young woman who falls in love with him at first sight. Onegin rejects her love. He needlessly allows himself to be drawn into a duel with Lensky, whom he kills. Tatyana enters a loveless marriage of convenience that is, to her, a binding commitment.

Years later, Onegin and Tatyana meet again. She is now a member of high Russian society. Onegin falls in love with Tatyana but she rejects him, admitting that although she still loves him, she must remain faithful to her marriage vows.

Peter Ilich Tchaikovsky's opera *Eugene Onegin*, written in 1877–78, is one of the best-known Russian operas.

Eugénie Grandet \œ-zha-nē-grânⁿ-'dā\ Novel by Honoré de BALZAC, first published in 1833 (revised edition, 1839). When Balzac later grouped many of his novels into schema in his multivolume *La Comédie humaine* (1834–37), *Eugénie Grandet* was included among the "scenes of provincial life" under the category "Studies of Manners."

The action of the novel concerns the adult life of the title character, the daughter of a wealthy but miserly man living a simple life in the provincial town of Saumur. Eugénie's inexperience leads her to fall in love with an unworthy man; she eventually pays his debts so that he can marry another woman. At the novel's end, Eugénie is alone, living out a solitary, pinched life in the provincial house she has inherited.

euhemerism \yü-'hēm-ə-,riz-əm, -'hem-\ **1.** A theory held by the 4th-century-BC Greek mythographer Euhemerus that the gods of mythology were but deified mortals. **2.** Interpretation of myths as traditional accounts of historical persons and events. The word *euhemeristic* is applied to such explanations of primitive myths.

There is no doubt an element of truth in the euhemeristic approach, for, among the Romans, the gradual deification of ancestors and emperors was a prominent feature of religious development. Among preliterate people, family and tribal gods sometimes originate as great chiefs and warriors. But euhemerism is not accepted by students of comparative religion as the sole or even chief explanation of the origin of gods.

Euhemerus \yü-'hēm-ər-əs, -'hem-\ or **Euemeros** \yü-'ēm-, -'em-\ or **Evemerus** \e-'vēm-, -'vem-\ (fl. 300 BC) Greek mythographer who established the tradition of seeking an actual historical basis for mythical beings and events.

It is thought Euhemerus was born at Messina, though some claim he was born at Chios, Tegea, or Messene in the Peloponnesus. He lived at the court of Cassander, king of Macedonia, from approximately 301 to 297 BC. He is chiefly known by his *Sacred History*, a philosophic romance based upon archaic inscriptions that he claimed to have found during his travels in various parts of Greece. In this work he systematized for the first time an old Oriental (perhaps Phoenician) method of interpreting the popular myths; he asserted that the gods were originally heroes and conquerors who had earned a claim to the veneration of their subjects. This system spread widely, and the early Christians, especially, used it as a confirmation of their belief that ancient mythology was merely an aggregate of fables of human invention.

Eulenspiegel, Till \,til-'ôœl-ən-,shpē-gəl, *Angl* 'ôil-ən-,spē-gəl\ *Low German* Dyl Ulenspegel \,dil-'ül-ən-,shpē-gəl\ German peasant trickster whose merry pranks were the source of numerous folk and literary tales. The historical figure is said to have been born at Kneitlingen, Brunswick, and to have died in 1350 at Mölln, Schleswig-Holstein, where his gravestone has been pointed out since the 16th century. Anecdotes associated with his name were printed about 1500 in one or more Low German–language versions. The earliest extant text is a High German version, *Ein kurtzweilig Lesen von Dyl Vlenspiegel* (Antwerp, 1515; "An Amusing Book About Till Eulenspiegel"); the sole surviving copy is in the British Library, London. The jests and practical jokes are broadly farcical, often brutal, sometimes obscene; but they have a serious theme. In the figure of Eulenspiegel, the individual gets back at society; the stupid yet cunning peasant demonstrates his superiority to the narrow, dishonest, condescending townsman, as well as to the clergy and nobility.

The Low German text, or parts of it, was translated into Dutch and English (*c.* 1520), French (1532), and Latin (1558). A later English version, *Here Beginneth a Merye Jest of a Man That was Called Howleglas,* appeared about 1560. Eulenspiegel has been the subject of musical and literary works, notably Charles de Coster's *The Glorious Adventures of Tyl Ulenspiegl* (in French; 1867), Richard Strauss's symphonic poem *Till Eulenspiegels lustige Streiche* (1894–95; *Till Eulenspiegel's Merry Pranks*), and Gerhart Hauptmann's epic poem *Till Eulenspiegel* (1928).

eulogy \'yū-lə-jē\ [Greek *eulogía* praise, eulogy, from *eu-* well + *lógos* word, speech]   A composition or an oration in commendation of someone or something (such as of the character and accomplishments of a deceased person); a synonym for ENCOMIUM.

Eumenes   *see* FURY.

Eumenides \yū-'men-i-,dēz\ ("Kind Goddesses")   Play by Aeschylus, third play of the trilogy known as the ORESTEIA.

Eumenius \yū-'men-ē-əs\ (fl. *c.* AD 300; b. Augustodunum, Gaul [now Autun, Fr.])   Roman orator and teacher of rhetoric, who was the author of *Oratio pro instaurandis scholis* ("Oration on the Restoration of the Schools"), an interesting document on the education of his time as well as a vigorous panegyric on Emperor Constantius Chlorus. The oration was delivered in 298 to promote the restoration of the university college at Augustodunum, which, like the city, had been damaged in the disturbances and siege of 269. The oration actually amounts to an expression of appreciation to the emperor Constantius Chlorus for his plans for reconstruction, which included appointment of Eumenius as principal of the college.

From the 16th century onward, other contemporary speeches in the *Panegyrici Latini,* a collection of addresses to emperors from the 3rd and 4th centuries, have been ascribed to Eumenius—but without evidence or probability. In his *Oration* the frigid affectations of panegyric are enlivened by personal enthusiasm.

eumolpique \ǣ-môl-'pēk\ [French, from Greek *eúmolpos* sweetly singing, from *eu-* well + *mélpein* to sing]   Poetic measure devised by the French poet and composer Antoine Fabre d'Olivet (1767–1825). It consists of two unrhymed alexandrines (lines of iambic hexameter), the first verse of 12 syllables ending in masculine (stressed) rhyme, the second of 13 syllables ending in feminine (unstressed) rhyme.

Eumolpus \yū-'mäl-pəs\   Mythical ancestor of the priestly clan of the Eumolpids at Eleusis, a city in ancient Greece, that was the site of the Eleusinian Mysteries, the best known of the Greek mystery cults. His name (meaning "good" or "strong singer"; *i.e.,* a priest who could chant his litanies clearly and well) was a personification of the clan's hereditary functions. His legend fluctuated so greatly that three identities for Eumolpus have been assumed:

1. Being a "sweet singer," he was connected with Thrace, the country of Orpheus. He was the son of the god Poseidon and Chione ("Snow Girl"), daughter of the north wind, Boreas; after various adventures he became king in Thrace but was killed while helping the Eleusinians in their war against Erechtheus of Athens.

2. As one of the originators of the Eleusinian Mysteries, he was an Eleusinian, a son of Gaea (Earth), father of Ceryx, and the mythical ancestor of the Ceryces (Heralds).

3. Because Orpheus and his followers were closely connected with mysteries of all sorts, Eumolpus was believed to be the son, father, or pupil of Musaeus, a mythical singer closely allied with Orpheus.

euphemism \'yū-fə-,miz-əm\ [Greek *euphēmismós,* a derivative of *euphēmízesthai* to use words of good omen, from *eu-* good + *phēmízein* to spread a report, name, call]   The substitution of an agreeable or inoffensive expression for one that may offend or suggest something unpleasant.

euphony \'yū-fə-nē\ [Greek *euphōnía,* a derivative of *eúphōnos* sweet-voiced, musical, from *eu-* well + *phōnḗ* sound of the voice, voice]   Pleasing, harmonious, or sweet sound, the acoustic effect produced by words so formed and combined as to please the ear. Euphony is achieved through the use of vowel sounds in words of generally serene imagery. Vowels are considered more euphonious than consonants and back vowels (ü, u̇, ō, ȯ) more euphonious than front vowels (ē, i, ā, e). Liquid consonants and the semivowel sounds (l, m, n, r, y, w) are also considered euphonious. An example may be seen in Alfred Tennyson's "The Lotos-Eaters": "The mild-eyed melancholy Lotos-eaters came." Euphony is the opposite of CACOPHONY.

Euphorion \yū-'fōr-ē-ən\ (b. *c.* 275 BC?)   Greek poet and grammarian, of Chalcis in Euboea, whose poetry was highly regarded in Hellenistic literary circles and later among Catullus' generation of Roman poets in the 1st century BC.

Euphorion studied philosophy at Athens. Soon after 223 BC, Antiochus the Great, king of Syria, gave him the coveted post of royal librarian at Antioch. His works include small-scale epics (epyllia) on mythological themes, poetic invectives and epigrams, and scholarly treatises. Surviving fragments reveal him as a plagiarist possessed of a willfully obscure and turgid style.

Euphues \'yū-fyū-ēz\ (*in full* Euphues: The Anatomy of Wit)   Prose romance by John LYLY, published in 1578. *Euphues* is a romantic intrigue told in letters interspersed with general discussions on such topics as religion, love, and epistolary style. Euphues is a clever young man who disregards advice to temper his wit with wisdom and to beware the pitfalls that await him if he continues to commit certain indiscretions. Despite this advice, Euphues betrays the trust of his friend Philautus' by stealing the affections of Philautus' fiancée and is himself soon abandoned by her for yet another man. Having learned a valuable lesson, Euphues begins to acquire wisdom.

In Lyly's sequel, *Euphues and His England* (1580), the older, more temperate Euphues goes to England to observe English life and customs. With his old friend Philautus and others, he debates the nature of love, religion, and philosophy.

Lyly's frequent use of similes drawn from classical mythology and his artificial and affected prose—full of such devices as antithesis, alliteration, similes, and a pervading straining after elegance—inspired a short-lived Elizabethan literary style called "euphuism."

euphuism \'yū-fyū-,iz-əm\   An elegant Elizabethan literary style marked by excessive use of balance, antithesis, and alliteration and by frequent use of similes drawn from mythology and nature. The word is also used to convey artificial elegance of language. It was derived from the name of a character in the prose romances *Euphues: The Anatomy of Wit* (1578) and *Euphues and his England* (1580) by the English author John Lyly. Although the style soon fell out of fashion, it played an important role in the development of English prose. It appeared at a time of experimentation with prose styles, and it offered prose that was lighter and more fanciful than previous writing. The influence of euphuism can be seen in the works of such writers as Robert Greene and William Shakespeare, both of whom imitated the style in some works and parodied it in others.

Eupolidean \,yū-,păl-ə-'dē-ən, -pəl-; ,yū-pə-'lid-ē-ən\ [Greek *eupolídeion,* from neuter of *eupolídeios* in the style of Eupolis] In classical prosody, the characteristic meter used by the Greek writer Eupolis (5th century BC). The meter was used, *e.g.,* by Aristophanes, as a stichic length (measured by line rather than by stanza) as well as in strophic verse. It consists either of the aeolic pattern | ⏓ ᵛᵛ ⏟ ⎯ ⏑ ⎮ | ⎯ ∪ ∪ ⎯ — in which four variable syllables precede the choriambic nucleus (⎯ ∪ ∪ ⎯) and create what is called *choriambic dimeter,* or the same pattern lacking the final syllable (catalectic). A full Eupolidean line is scanned: ᵛᵛ ⏟ ⎯ ⏑ ⎮ | ⎯ ∪ ∪ ⎯ | ⏟ ⎯ ⏑ ⎮ | ⎯ ∪ ⎯.

Eupolis \'yū-pə-ləs\ (fl. second half of 5th century BC, Athens) One of the leading Athenian poets of the vigorous and satirical Old Comedy and a rival of Aristophanes.

Eupolis' first play was produced in 429 BC. Of his work 19 titles and more than 460 fragments survive. Objects of his satire included the demagogues Cleon and Hyperbolus and the wealthy Callias and Alcibiades and their fashionable circle. In his last play, *The Demes,* written just after the disastrous Athenian expedition led by Alcibiades to Sicily during the Peloponnesian War (412 BC), he addressed himself with patriotic fervor to the problem of how the fortunes of Athens were to be restored. He died young, about 410 BC, probably on active service at the Hellespont.

Euripides \yū-'rip-ə-,dēz\ (b. *c.* 484 BC, Athens [Greece]—d. 406, Macedonia) One of classical Athens' three great tragic dramatists.

Euripides was the son of Mnesarchus (or Mnesarchides) and Cleito; there is indirect evidence that his family was well-to-do.

Marble herm copied from a Greek original, *c.* 340–330 BC; in the Museo Archeologico Nazionale, Naples

Soprintendenza alle Antichità della Campania, Naples

The general impression of Euripides left by tradition is of a figure austere and not convivial.

Euripides was first chosen to compete in the dramatic festival of Dionysus in 455 BC, and he won his first victory in 441. In all he competed on 22 occasions, submitting four plays at each. In 408 he left Athens to live at the court of Archelaus, king of Macedonia, who was a noted patron of the arts.

The ancients knew of 92 plays composed by Euripides. Nineteen of them survive, if one of disputed authorship is included. Among the most notable are MEDEA (produced 431 BC), HIPPOLYTUS (produced 428), ELECTRA (produced 418), TROJAN WOMEN (produced 415), ION (produced 413), IPHIGENIA AT AULIS (produced 406), and BACCHAE (produced 406). In his plays Euripides took the heroic figures of ancient legend and transformed them into ordinary people with contemporary attitudes.

Euripides' plays exhibit his iconoclastic, rationalizing attitude toward both religious belief and the ancient legends and myths that formed the traditional subject matter for Greek drama. He frequently depicts the gods as irrational, petulant, and singularly uninterested in meting out "divine justice."

Unlike Aeschylus and Sophocles, Euripides made his characters' tragic fates stem almost entirely from their own flawed natures and uncontrolled passions. Chance, disorder, and human irrationality and immorality frequently result in apparently meaningless suffering that is looked upon with indifference by the gods.

The chief structural peculiarities of Euripides' plays are his use of prologues and of the providential appearance of a god (deus ex machina) at the play's end. Almost all of the plays start with a monologue that is in effect a bare chronicle explaining the situation and characters with which the action begins. Similarly, the god's epilogue at the end of the play serves to reveal the future fortunes of the characters. Another striking feature of his plays is that over time Euripides found less and less use for the chorus.

In the works written after 415 BC his lyrics underwent a change, becoming more emotional and luxuriant. At its worst the style is hardly distinguishable from Aristophanes' parody of it in his comedy *Frogs,* but where frenzied emotion is appropriate, as in the tragedy *Bacchae,* Euripides' songs are unsurpassed in their power and beauty.

See also ALCESTIS; ANDROMACHE; CHILDREN OF HERACLES; CYCLOPS; HECUBA; HELEN; IPHIGENIA AMONG THE TAURIANS; THE MADNESS OF HERACLES; ORESTES; PHOENICIAN WOMEN; SUPPLIANTS.

Europa \yū-'rō-pə\ In Greek mythology, the daughter either of Phoenix or of Agenor, king of Phoenicia. The beauty of Europa inspired the love of Zeus, who approached her in the form of a white bull and carried her away from Phoenicia to Crete. There she bore three sons: King Minos of Crete, King Rhadamanthus of the Cyclades Islands, and, according to some legends, Prince Sarpedon of Lycia. She later married the king of Crete, who adopted her sons, and she was worshiped under the name of Hellotis in Crete, where the festival Hellotia was held in her honor.

Eurydice \yū-'rid-ə-sē\ In Greek legend, the wife of Orpheus. Her husband's attempt to retrieve Eurydice from Hades forms the basis of one of the most popular Greek legends. *See* ORPHEUS.

Eusden \'yūs-dən\, Laurence (baptized Sept. 6, 1688, Spofforth, Yorkshire, Eng.—d. Sept. 27, 1730, Coningsby, Lincolnshire) British poet who, by flattering the Duke of Newcastle, was made poet laureate in 1718. He became rector of Coningsby and held the laureateship until his death. Alexander Pope satirized him frequently and derisively.

Eustace Diamonds, The \'yū-stəs\ Novel by Anthony TROLLOPE, published serially from 1871 to 1873 and in book form in New York in 1872. It is a satirical study of the influence of money on marital and sexual relations.

The story follows two contrasting women and their courtships. Lizzie Eustace and Lucy Morris are both hampered in their love affairs by their lack of money. Lizzie's trickery and deceit, however, contrast with Lucy's constancy. Trollope was understood to be commenting on the malaise in Victorian England that allowed a character like Lizzie, who marries for money, steals the family diamonds, and behaves despicably throughout, to rise unscathed in society. The work is the third of Trollope's six PALLISER NOVELS.

Euterpe \yū-'tər-pē\ In Greek mythology, one of the nine Muses, patron of music or flute playing. She is often depicted playing flutes.

Evangeline \i-'van-jə-,lēn\ (*in full* Evangeline, A Tale of Acadie) Narrative poem by Henry Wadsworth LONGFELLOW, published in 1847. The poem tells a sentimental tale of two lovers separated when British soldiers expel the Acadians (French colonists) from what is now Nova Scotia. The lovers, Evangeline and Gabriel, are reunited years later as Gabriel is dying. After both die, they are finally buried together.

Written in classical hexameters, the poem intentionally echoes such epics as Homer's *Odyssey*. Although it is considered overly sentimental by many critics, *Evangeline* is respected for its sense of the vast North American landscape and its evocation of an earlier time.

Evans \'ev-ənz\, Mari (b. July 16, 1923, Toledo, Ohio, U.S.) African-American author of poetry, children's literature, and plays.

Evans attended the University of Toledo and later taught at several schools in the Midwest and East. She began five years of writing, producing, and directing for an Indianapolis television program, "The Black Experience," in 1968, the same year her first poetry collection, *Where Is All the Music?*, was published. With her second collection, *I Am a Black Woman* (1970), she gained acclaim as an important new poet. Her poem "Who Can Be Born Black" was often anthologized.

Her later collections include *Nightstar: 1973–1978* (1981), whose poems praise blues artists and community heroes and heroines, and *A Dark and Splendid Mass* (1992). Evans also wrote works for juvenile readers and several plays, including *River of My Song* (produced 1977) and the musical *Eyes* (produced 1979), an adaptation of Zora Neale Hurston's *Their Eyes Were Watching God*. She edited the anthology *Black Women Writers (1950–1980): A Critical Evaluation* (1984).

Evans, Mary Ann *or* Marian.   Real name of George ELIOT.

Eve   *see* ADAM AND EVE.

Evelina \,ev-ə-'lē-nə\ (*in full* Evelina; or The History of a Young Lady's Entrance Into the World)   Novel of manners by Fanny BURNEY, published anonymously in 1778.

The novel was Burney's first work, and it revealed its author to be a keen social commentator with an ear for dialect. *Evelina* traces the social development of a young girl who is subject to errors of manners and judgment but eventually overcomes her deficiencies to marry. Innovative in its cooly detached treatment of contemporary manners and its use of the erring and uncertain conduct of the heroine for its plot development, *Evelina* pointed the way for the novels of Jane Austen.

Evelyn \'ēv-lən, 'ev-\, John (b. Oct. 31, 1620, Wotton, Surrey, Eng.—d. Feb. 27, 1706, Wotton)   English country gentleman, author of some 30 books on the fine arts, forestry, and various religious topics. His *Diary*, kept all his life, is considered an invaluable source of information on the social, cultural, religious, and political life of 17th-century England.

Evelyn was the son of a wealthy landowner. After studying in the Middle Temple, London, and at Balliol College, Oxford, he decided not to join the Royalist cause in the English Civil Wars for fear of endangering his brother's estate at Wotton, then in parliamentary territory. In 1643, therefore, he went abroad. In 1652, during the Commonwealth, he returned to England and acquired his father-in-law's estate, Sayes Court, at Deptford. In 1659 he published two Royalist pamphlets.

At the Restoration of the monarchy in 1660, Evelyn was well received by Charles II; he served on a variety of commissions. In 1664 he produced for the commissioners of the navy *Sylva, or a Discourse of Forest-trees, and the Propagation of Timber*, a description of the various kinds of trees, their cultivation, and uses. In 1662 Evelyn produced *Sculptura*, a small book on engraving and etching, in which he announced a new process, the mezzotint. His *Life of Mrs. Godolphin* (1847) is one of the most moving of 17th-century biographies. Evelyn's last important

book, *Numismata*, was published in 1697. His *Diary*, begun when he was 11 years old, was first published in 1818. It was written for himself alone but contained relatively little about himself in it. The diary ranges from bald memoranda to elaborate set pieces. It bears witness to more than 50 years of English life and, as such, is of great historical value.

Evemerus   *see* EUHEMERUS.

Eve of St. Agnes, The \'ag-nis\   Narrative poem in 42 Spenserian stanzas by John KEATS, written in 1819 and published in 1820 in *Lamia, Isabella, The Eve of St. Agnes, and Other Poems*. The poem brims with sensuality and vivid description.

According to a medieval legend, on the eve of St. Agnes' feast day (January 20, said to be the coldest night of winter) a young maiden will receive a vision of her true love while she is asleep. Madeline dreams of Porphyro, whose family and hers are enemies. Porphyro is at her bedside when she awakens, having convinced her nurse to hide him in his beloved's room. The lovers elope, disappearing into the wintry night.

Everdene, Bathsheba \bath-'shē-bə-'ev-ər-,dēn\   Fictional character, heroine of the pastoral novel FAR FROM THE MADDING CROWD by Thomas Hardy. Owner of a small farm, Bathsheba has several suitors: the abusive ne'er-do-well Sergeant Francis Troy, whom she marries; William Boldwood, a neighboring farmer who kills Troy; and Gabriel Oak, a shepherd who truly loves her and becomes her second husband.

Evergreen Review   Literary magazine published from 1957 to 1973 in the United States. Its editor, Barney Rosset, developed the progressive periodical into a forum for radical expression of ideas on topics from sex to politics. The magazine was known for publishing erotic—some said pornographic—material. Some of the more noteworthy contributors to the magazine included Che Guevara, Vladimir Nabokov, Jack Kerouac, Allen Ginsberg, Samuel Beckett, Henry Miller, and E.E. Cummings.

Everson \'ē-vər-sən\, William (Oliver), *byname* Brother Antoninus \,an-tō-'nī-nəs\ (b. Sept. 10, 1912, Sacramento, Calif., U.S.—d. June 3, 1994, Santa Cruz, Calif.)   American Roman Catholic poet whose works recorded a personal search for religious vision in a violent, corrupt world.

Raised by Christian Scientist parents, Everson became an agnostic in his teens; while attending Fresno (Calif.) State College, he resolved to become a poet. His first book, *These Are the Ravens*, was published in 1935. He was drafted during World War II but served at a work camp for conscientious objectors in Waldport, Oregon, where he cofounded the Untide Press and printed his own poetry. After marrying his second wife, poet Mary Fabilli, he converted to Roman Catholicism and he became a Dominican lay brother in 1951. For the next seven years he lived in monastic withdrawal. His literary silence was broken in 1957 with the composition of his long poem *River-Root* (1976), which depicts sexual love as a form of religious contemplation. He became identified with the San Francisco poetry renaissance of the Beat movement. After 1957 Everson published most of his poetry as Brother Antoninus, until 1969, when he returned to secular life and married for a third time.

Emphatic assertions, rugged landscapes, and harsh juxtapositions mark Everson's poetry. He considered his lifetime of work to form a trilogy, which he called *The Crooked Lines of God* and which was composed of *The Residual Years: Poems 1934–1948* (1968), his early nature poetry; *The Veritable Years: Poems 1949–1966* (1978), his religious poetry; and a projected third volume to be entitled *The Integral Years* and intended to contain his post-1966 poetry. In the 1980s he began writing an autobiographical epic, beginning with the cantos of *In Medias*

Res (1984). His final collection, *The Blood of the Poet*, was published in 1994.

Everyman \\'ev-rē-,man\\ An English morality play of the 15th century, probably a version of a Dutch play, *Elckerlyc*. It achieves a beautiful, simple solemnity in treating allegorically the theme of death and the fate of the human soul—of Everyman's soul. Though morality plays on the whole failed to achieve the vigorous realism of scriptural drama in the Middle Ages, this short play (about 900 lines) contains vivid characterization that gives it dramatic energy and makes it more than an allegorical sermon. It is generally regarded as the finest of the morality plays.

Every Man in His Humour Comic drama in five acts that established the reputation of Ben JONSON, performed in 1598 and revised before its publication in the folio edition of 1616. With its galleries of grotesques, its scornful detachment, and its rather academic effect, the play introduced to the English stage a vigorous anatomizing of "the time's deformities"—the language, habits, and humors of the London scene.

The characters in *Every Man in His Humour* are based on the four humors of medieval physiology, bodily fluids that were held to influence personality or temperament. They are driven by their unchangeable personalities and tend to avoid interaction. *See also* COMEDY OF HUMORS.

Every Man out of His Humour Comic drama in five acts by Ben JONSON, performed in 1599 and published in 1600. Although the play was modeled after its successful predecessor, *Every Man in His Humor*, it was a critical failure that forced Jonson to abandon the public stage for private theater. Jonson wrote *Every Man out of His Humour* as a contribution to the so-called war of the theaters, in which he satirized the playwrights Thomas Dekker and John Marston. The play is a convoluted but self-confident work that supports Jonson's definition of comedy as a reflection of nature, an image of truth.

In *Every Man out of His Humour* Jonson continued his study of personalities and mannerisms in terms of medieval physiology. Each of the characters plagued by a particular humor eventually overcomes his personal disorder. *See also* COMEDY OF HUMORS; WAR OF THE THEATERS.

Everything That Rises Must Converge Collection of nine short stories by Flannery O'CONNOR, published posthumously in 1965. The flawed characters of each story are fully revealed in apocalyptic moments of conflict and violence that are presented with comic detachment.

The title story is a tragicomedy about social pride, racial bigotry, generational conflict, false liberalism, and filial dependence. The protagonist Julian Chestny is hypocritically disdainful of his mother's prejudices. His smug selfishness is replaced with childish fear when she suffers a fatal stroke after being struck by a black woman she has insulted out of oblivious ignorance rather than malice. Similarly, "The Comforts of Home" is about an intellectual son with an Oedipus complex. Driven by the voice of his dead father, the son accidentally kills his sentimental mother in an attempt to murder a harlot.

The other stories are "A View of the Woods," "Parker's Back," "The Enduring Chill," "Greenleaf," "The Lame Shall Enter First," "Revelation," and "Judgment Day."

Evtushenko *see* YEVTUSHENKO.

Ewald \\'ā-vəlt\\, Johannes (b. Nov. 18, 1743, Copenhagen, Den.—d. March 17, 1781, Copenhagen) One of Denmark's greatest lyric poets and the first to use themes from early Scandinavian myths and sagas.

At 19 Ewald was already becoming known as a writer of prose and occasional poetry. When finishing *Adam og Eva* (1769), a dramatic poem in the style of French tragedy, he met the German epic poet Friedrich Klopstock. He also read William Shakespeare's plays and James Macpherson's so-called translations of works by Ossian (Oisín). Their influence resulted in the historical drama *Rolf Krage* (1770), taken from an old Danish legend recorded by the medieval historian Saxo Grammaticus.

Beset by addiction to alcohol, in the spring of 1773 he was moved from Copenhagen to the relative isolation of Rungsted by his mother and a friend. There he produced his first mature works: *Rungsteds lyksaligheder* (1773; "The Joys of Rungsted"), a lyric in the elevated new style of the ode; *Balders død* (1774; *The Death of Balder*), a lyric drama on a subject from Saxo and Old Norse mythology; and the first chapters of his memoirs, *Levnet og meninger* ("Life and Opinions"). In 1775 he was transferred to a still more solitary place near Elsinore, where he underwent a religious crisis. In 1777 he returned to Copenhagen. On his deathbed he wrote the heroic Pietist hymn "Udrust dig, helt fra Golgotha" ("Gird Thyself, Hero of Golgotha").

Of Ewald's dramatic works, only *Fiskerne* (1779; "The Fishermen"), an operetta, is still performed. His greatest work in prose is his memoirs, published posthumously in 1804. Ewald renewed Danish poetry in all of its genres, however. He is best known as a lyric poet, especially for his great personal odes and for songs such as "Kong Kristian stod ved højen Mast" (translated by Henry Wadsworth Longfellow as "King Christian Stood by the Lofty Mast"), which is used as a national anthem, and "Lille Gunver," the first Danish romance. Ewald's poetry heralded the works of Adam Oehlenschläger and the Romantic movement by its emotionalism and its use of themes drawn from Old Norse literature.

Ewart \\'yū-ərt\\, Gavin (Buchanan) (b. Feb. 4, 1916, London, Eng.) British poet noted for his light verse, which frequently dealt with sexual themes. He wrote children's poems and poetry on serious subjects as well.

Soon after Ewart's 17th birthday his poem "Phallus in Wonderland" was published, beginning a long career of writing poetry that ranged from whimsical to bawdy. He published his first collection, *Poems and Songs*, in 1939. For the next 25 years he almost completely abandoned poetry; he served in the Royal Artillery during World War II and worked as an advertising copywriter (1952–71). His second collection, *Londoners* (1964), was in general more serious in tone and showed affinities with the poetry of John Betjeman.

With *Pleasures of the Flesh* (1966) and *The Deceptive Grin of the Gravel Porters* (1968) Ewart's characteristic approach was set; he intermingled poems of serious autobiography, social satire, and sexual humor. A strain of melancholy pervades his later poetry, in which he examined such topics as cruelty and death. Several of his collections, including *The Learned Hippopotamus* (1986) and *Caterpillar Stew* (1990), were written for children, and his verse was gathered in *The Collected Ewart 1933–1980* (1980) and *Collected Poems 1980–1990* (1991). Ewart also edited several poetry anthologies.

examen \\ig-'zā-mən\\ [Late Latin, examination] A critical study (such as of a writer or a phenomenon).

Examiner, The Influential British magazine that was known for its radical, reformist positions on significant issues of the time, including opposition to the slave trade and support of Roman Catholic emancipation. It was published weekly from 1808 until 1881. Among its notable contributors were John Keats, Percy Bysshe Shelley, and William Hazlitt. Leigh Hunt, who cofounded *The Examiner* with his brother John, was its editor until 1821.

Excalibur \ek-'skal-i-bər\ In Arthurian legend, King Arthur's sword. As a boy Arthur alone was able to draw the sword out of a stone in which it had been magically fixed. This account is contained in Sir Thomas Malory's 15th-century prose rendering of the Arthurian legend, but another story in the same work suggests that it was given to Arthur by the Lady of the Lake and that, when the king lay mortally wounded after his last battle, he ordered the faithful Sir Bedivere to go to the water and throw the sword into it.

There was a famous sword in Irish legend called *Caladbolg*, from which *Excalibur* is evidently derived by way of Geoffrey of Monmouth, whose 12th-century *Historia regum Britanniae* refers to Arthur's sword as *Caliburn*. Malory said that Excalibur means "cut-steel."

excerpt \'ek-,sərpt, 'eg-,zərpt\ [Latin *excerptum*, from neuter of *excerptus*, past participle of *excerpere* to pick out, select] A selection or fragment (such as from a writing or a work of music); a chosen portion or sample.

excursion [Latin *excursio* sortie, sally] Part of a stage direction. *See* ALARUMS AND EXCURSIONS.

exegesis \,ek-sə-'jē-sis, 'ek-sə-jē-\ *plural* exegeses \-,sēz\ [Greek *exégēsis*, a derivative of *exēgeîsthai* to explain, interpret] An explanation or interpretation of a portion of Scripture.

Doctrinal and polemical intentions often influence interpretive results; a given text may yield a number of very different interpretations according to the exegetical presuppositions and techniques applied to it. The study of these methodological principles themselves constitutes the field of HERMENEUTICS.

Although at times the Hebrew and Greek of the Bible have been treated as sacred languages, and the history contained in the text has been regarded as somehow different from "ordinary" history, most forms of biblical exegesis employed in the modern era are applicable to many other bodies of literature. *Textual criticism* is concerned with establishing the original texts of the biblical books. *Philological criticism* is the study of the biblical languages in respect to grammar, vocabulary, and style. *Literary criticism* attempts to use internal and external evidence to establish the literary genre, date, authorship, and intended audience of the various biblical texts. *Tradition criticism* attempts to analyze the various sources of the biblical materials in such a way as to discover the oral traditions that lie behind them and to trace their gradual development. *Form criticism*, the major exegetical method of the 20th century, assumes that literary material, written or oral, takes certain forms according to the function the material serves within the community which preserves it. *Redaction criticism* examines the way the various pieces of the tradition have been assembled into the final literary composition by an author or editor and can reveal something of the author's intentions. *Historical criticism* places the biblical documents within their historical context and examines them in the light of contemporary documents.

The word exegesis has also been used in a more general sense to mean an analysis of any literary text. *See* EXPLICATION DE TEXTE.

exemplum \ig-'zem-pləm, eg-\ *plural* exempla \-plə\ [Late Latin, from Latin, model, example] An anecdote or short narrative used to point to a moral or sustain an argument. Exempla were used in medieval sermons and were eventually incorporated into literature in such works as Geoffrey Chaucer's "The Nun's Priest's Tale" and "The Pardoner's Tale."

Exeter Book \'ek-sə-tər\ The largest extant collection of Old English poetry. Copied about 975, the manuscript was given to Exeter Cathedral by Bishop Leofric (d. 1072). It begins with several long religious poems: *Christ*, in three parts;

two poems on St. Guthlac; the fragmentary "Azarius"; and the allegorical *Phoenix*. Following these are a number of shorter religious verses intermingled with poems of types that have survived only in this codex. All the extant Anglo-Saxon lyrics, or elegies, as they are usually called—"The Wanderer," "The Seafarer," "The Wife's Lament," "The Husband's Message," and "The Ruin"—are found here. These are secular poems evoking a poignant sense of desolation and loneliness, although some of them also function as religious allegories. In addition, the Exeter Book preserves 95 riddles, a genre that would otherwise have been represented in Old English by a solitary example.

The remaining part of the Exeter Book includes "The Rhyming Poem," which is the only example of its kind; gnomic verses; "Widsith," the heroic narrative of a fictitious bard; and two refrain poems, "Deor" and "Wulf and Eadwacer." The book is believed to be copied from an earlier collection. *See also* DEOR; THE HUSBAND'S MESSAGE; WIDSITH.

existentialism \,ek-si-'sten-chə-,liz-əm, ,eg-zi-\ [German *Existentialismus*, a derivative of *existentiell* grounded in existence, existential] A family of philosophies devoted to an interpretation of human existence in the world that stresses its concreteness and its problematic character. As a self-conscious movement it is primarily a 20th-century phenomenon, embracing the theories of Martin Heidegger, Karl Jaspers, Jean-Paul Sartre, Gabriel Marcel, and Maurice Merleau-Ponty, but its characteristic features occurred earlier, especially in the 19th-century thinkers Friedrich Nietzsche and Søren Kierkegaard.

Existentialism is largely a coherent development within traditional philosophy. It rejects traditional attempts to ground human knowledge in the external world, however. According to existentialists, human beings are not solely or even primarily knowers; they also care, desire, manipulate, and, above all, choose and act. Second, the self, or ego, required by some if not all traditional epistemological doctrines, is not a fundamental entity but rather emerges from experience.

It is an important tenet of existentialism that the individual is not a detached observer of the world, but "in the world." A person "exists" in a special sense in which entities like stones and trees do not; a human being is "open" to the world and to objects in it. Further, humans, unlike other entities, make themselves what they are by choices, choices of ways of life (Kierkegaard) or of particular actions (Sartre).

Existentialism inspired a large body of imaginative literature, such as that of Sartre, Albert Camus, and Simone de Beauvoir. Existentialist writers are characterized by their concern with "being," which contrasts not only with knowing but also with abstract concepts, which cannot fully capture what is individual and specific. The existentialist movement also provided a means of articulating and interpreting these same themes as discerned in works of literature from all periods.

exodos \'ek-sə-,däs, 'eg-zə-\ [Greek *éxodos*, literally, close, end, departure, exit] The last part of a Greek drama. The exodus follows the last song of the chorus, and it is during the exodus that the deus ex machina appears.

exordium \eg-'zȯr-dē-əm\ *plural* exordiums *or* exordia \-dē-ə\ [Latin, literally, warp laid on a loom before the web is begun, starting point] The introductory part of a discourse or composition. The term originally referred specifically to one of the traditional divisions of a speech established by classical rhetoricians.

explication de texte \ek-splē-kä-'syōⁿ-də-'tekst\ *plural* explications de texte *same*\ [French, literally, explanation of text] **1.** A method of literary criticism involving a detailed examination of each part of a work, such as structure, style, and imagery, and an exposition of the relationship of these parts to each other and to the whole work. The method was originally used to teach literature in France and has since become a tool for use by literary critics in other countries, particularly by practitioners of New Criticism. **2.** A critical analysis employing explication de texte.

explicit \ 'eks-pli-sit, -kit \   A device added to the end of some manuscripts and incunabula by the author or scribe and providing such information as the title of the work and the name or initials of its author or scribe. Explicits were soon incorporated into or completely replaced by the COLOPHON, information about the printer, printing materials, and typeface, and, often, the printer's emblem.

In medieval Latin works, the word *explicit* meant "here ends . . . ." Originally, it may have been an abbreviation for *explicitus est liber* ("the book is unrolled"), but by analogy with *incipit* ("here begins . . . "), it was taken as a present-tense, third-singular verb form.

Expressionism \ ek-'spresh-ə-,niz-əm \   An artistic theory or practice of the late 19th and early 20th centuries in which the subjective or subconscious thoughts and emotions of the artist, the struggle of abstract forces, or the inner realities of life are presented by a wide variety of nonnaturalistic techniques that include abstraction, distortion, exaggeration, primitivism, fantasy, and symbolism. It arose as a reaction against complaints of materialism, complacent bourgeois prosperity, rapid mechanization and urbanization, and the domination of the family within pre-World War I European society.

In forging a drama of social protest, Expressionist writers were concerned with general truths rather than with particular situations; hence they explored the predicaments of representative symbolic types rather than of fully developed individualized characters. Emphasis in Expressionist drama is laid not on the outer world, which is merely sketched in and barely defined in place or time, but on the internal, on an individual's mental state. The leading character in an Expressionist play often delivers long monologues couched in a concentrated, elliptical language.

August Strindberg and Frank Wedekind were notable forerunners of Expressionist drama, but the first full-fledged Expressionist play was Reinhard Johannes Sorge's *Der Bettler* ("The Beggar"), which was written in 1912 but not performed until 1917. The other principal playwrights of the movement were Georg Kaiser, Ernst Toller, Paul Kornfeld, Fritz von Unruh, and Walter Hasenclever, all of Germany. Outside Germany, playwrights who used Expressionist dramatic techniques included the American authors Eugene O'Neill and Elmer Rice.

Expressionist poetry was similarly nonreferential and sought an ecstatic, hymnlike lyricism that would have considerable associative power. This condensed, stripped-down poetry, utilizing strings of nouns with only a few adjectives and infinitive verbs, eliminated narrative and description to get at the essence of feeling. The principal Expressionist poets were Georg Heym, Ernst Stadler, August Stramm, Gottfried Benn, Georg Trakl, Else Lasker-Schüler, and Franz Werfel. The dominant theme of Expressionist verse was horror over urban life and apocalyptic visions of the collapse of civilization.

The decline of Expressionism was hastened by the vagueness of its longing for a better world, by its use of highly poetic language, and in general by the intensely personal and inaccessible nature of its mode of presentation. In Germany, the movement was effectively killed by the Nazi regime, which labeled Expressionism decadent and forbade its exhibition and publication.

expurgate \ 'ek-spər-,gāt \   To expunge obscene or otherwise objectionable parts of a written or dramatic work before publication or presentation.

extraliterary \ ,ek-strə-'lit-ə-,rer-ē \   Lying outside what is literary, or lying outside the province of literature.

extrametrical \ ,ek-strə-'met-ri-kəl \   In prosody, exceeding the usual or prescribed number of syllables in a given meter. Also, in reference to a syllable or syllables not counted in metrical analysis. In the following final couplet from a sonnet by William Shakespeare, the ending syllables are extrametrical:

> Yet him for this my love no whit disdaineth;
> Suns of the world may stain when heaven's sun staineth.

extravaganza \ ek-,strav-ə-'gan-zə \ [Italian *estravaganza, stravaganza*, literally, extravagance]   **1.** A literary or musical work marked by extreme freedom of style and structure and usually by elements of burlesque or parody, such as Samuel Butler's *Hudibras*.   **2.** An elaborate and spectacular theatrical production. The term once specifically referred to a type of 19th-century English drama made popular by J.R. Planché, a British playwright and antiquary who wrote fanciful portrayals of fairy tales and other poetic subjects based on similar French productions. Planché's productions included dancing and music and influenced such later writers as W.S. Gilbert.

eye dialect   The use of misspellings that are based on standard pronunciations (such as *sez* for *says* or *kow* for *cow*) but are usually intended to suggest a speaker's illiteracy or his use of generally nonstandard pronunciations. It is sometimes used in literature for comic effect.

Eyeless in Gaza \ 'gaz-ə, 'gäz- \   Novel of ideas by Aldous HUXLEY, published in 1936. This semiautobiographical novel criticized the dearth of spiritual values in contemporary society.

In nonchronological fashion, the novel covers more than 30 years in the lives of a group of upper-middle-class English friends, especially Anthony Beavis and his longtime married lover, Helen. His intense prep-school friendships continue at Oxford; most important are his relationships with Brian Foxe, who later commits suicide; with Hugh Ledwidge, who marries Helen; and with Mark Staithes, who becomes a Marxist and with whom Beavis goes to Mexico to fight in a revolution. While in Mexico, Beavis adopts a Buddhist-centered philosophy, practices meditation, and becomes a pacifist.

eye rhyme   In poetry, an imperfect rhyme in which two words are spelled similarly but pronounced differently (such as *move* and *love*, *bough* and *though*, *come* and *home*, and *laughter* and *daughter*). Some of these (such as *flood* and *brood*) are referred to as historical rhymes because at one time they probably had the same pronunciation.

Eyre, Jane \ 'jān-'ār \   A fictional character, heroine of the novel JANE EYRE by Charlotte Brontë.

Ezekiel \ ē-'zē-kē-əl \, *also spelled* Ezechiel, *Hebrew* Yeḥezqel (fl. early 6th century BC)   Prophet-priest of ancient Israel and the subject and in part the author of an Old Testament book that bears his name. Ezekiel's early oracles (from c. 592) in Jerusalem are pronouncements of violence and destruction; his later statements address the hopes of the Israelites exiled in Babylon. More than any of the classical biblical prophets, Ezekiel was given to trances; symbolic actions, such as eating a scroll on which words of prophecy are written in order to symbolize his appropriation of the message, or lying down for an extended time to symbolize Israel's punishment; and strange visions, including one of the throne of God, which he describes as being supported by a kind of chariot featuring a series of wheels within wheels. The many writers who have incorporated this vision and other aspects of the story of Ezekiel into their works include Geoffrey Chaucer, John Milton, William Blake, W.B. Yeats, and Flannery O'Connor.

fable \\'fā-bəl\\ [Old French, from Latin *fabula* talk, narrative, fable]   **1.** A story of supernatural or marvelous happenings (as in legend, myth, or folklore).   **2.** A narration intended to enforce a useful truth; especially, one in which animals or inanimate objects speak and act like human beings. The fable differs from the ordinary folktale in that it has a moral that is woven into the story and often explicitly formulated at the end.

The Western tradition of the fable effectively began in Greece with tales ascribed to AESOP, almost certainly a legendary figure. The Aesopian fables emphasize the social interactions of human beings, and the morals they draw tend to embody advice on the best way to deal with the competitive realities of life.

Fable flourished in the European Middle Ages, as did all forms of allegory. A notable collection of fables was made in the late 12th century by Marie de France. The medieval fable gave rise to an expanded form known as the BEAST EPIC—a lengthy, episodic animal story replete with hero, villain, victim, and an endless stream of heroic endeavor, parodying epic grandeur. In the Renaissance, Edmund Spenser made use of this kind of material in "Prosopopoia, or Mother Hubberd's Tale" (1591).

The fable has traditionally been of modest length, however. The shorter form reached its zenith in 17th-century France in the work of Jean de La Fontaine, whose theme was the folly of human vanity. In the 19th century fable found a new audience with the rise of literature for children. Among the celebrated authors who employed the form were Lewis Carroll, Kenneth Grahame, Rudyard Kipling, Hilaire Belloc, Joel Chandler Harris, Beatrix Potter, and, though not writing primarily for children, Hans Christian Andersen, Oscar Wilde, Antoine de Saint-Exupéry, J.R.R. Tolkien, and James Thurber.

The oral tradition of fable in India may date as far back as the 5th century BC. The *Pañca-tantra*, a Sanskrit compilation of beast fables, has survived only in an 8th-century Arabic translation known as the *Kalīlah wa Dimnah*, after two jackals that figure in one of the tales.

In China the full development of fable was hindered by traditions of thought that prohibited the Chinese from accepting any notion of animals behaving and thinking as humans. Between the 4th and the 6th century, however, Chinese Buddhists adapted fables from Buddhist India as a way to further the understanding of religious doctrines. Their compilation is known as *Boyu jing*.

In Japan the 8th-century histories *Kojiki*, ("Records of Ancient Matters") and *Nihon shoki* ("Chronicles of Japan") are studded with fables, many on the theme of small but intelligent animals getting the better of large and stupid ones. The form reached its height in the Kamakura period (1192–1333). *See also* FOLKTALE; TRICKSTER.

Fable for Critics, A   A satire in verse by James Russell LOWELL, published anonymously in 1848. In the poem Apollo, the god of poetry, asks a critic about the leading American writers. The critic replies with summary reviews of William Cullen Bryant, Ralph Waldo Emerson, Nathaniel Hawthorne, John Greenleaf Whittier, and others, including Lowell himself. Though the tone of the poem is amiable, Lowell's perceptive criticisms punctured some reputations.

Fables   Work by Jean de LA FONTAINE, published as *Fables choisies, mises en vers* ("Selected Fables, Set in Verse") from 1668 to 1694. The first six books, known as the *premier recueil* ("first collection"), were published in 1668 and were followed by five more books (the *second recueil*) in 1678–79 and a 12th book in 1694.

Taking his material chiefly from the Aesopic tradition and, in the second collection, from the East Asian, La Fontaine enriched the tales immeasurably by subordinating their narrowly didactic original intent. He contrived delightful miniature comedies and dramas excelling in rapid characterization. Within the compass of about 240 poems, La Fontaine presents a wide range of forms. Some of the poems are fables only in name and are really elegies, idylls, epistles, or poetic meditations. The subject matter of the poems is equally diverse. Often La Fontaine held up a mirror to the social hierarchy of his day, and some of the poems occasionally reflect contemporary political issues and intellectual preoccupations. But his chief and most comprehensive theme remains that of the traditional fable: the fundamental, everyday moral experience of humanity throughout the ages.

Fables of Bidpai, The \\'bid-ˌpī\\   *see* PAÑCA-TANTRA.

fabliau \\'fab-lē-ˌō\\ or **fableau** \\fa-'blō\\ *plural* fabliaux \\-ˌō, -ˌōz\\ *or* fableaux \\-'blō, -'blōz\\ [French, from Old French (Picard dialect) *fabliau* (in other dialects *fablel, fableau*), diminutive of *fable* fable]   A short metrical tale made popular in medieval France by the jongleurs, or professional storytellers. Fabliaux were characterized by vivid detail and realistic observation and were usually comic, coarse, and often cynical, especially in their treatment of women.

About 150 fabliaux are extant. Many are based on simple jokes or puns or on wry situations, such as one in which a man is rescued from drowning but has his eye put out by the boat hook that saves him. The majority of fabliaux are erotic, and the merriment often depends on situations and adventures that are either indecorous or frankly obscene.

It was once widely held that fabliaux represented the literature of the bourgeois and common people. This, however, is unlikely, since they frequently contain a substantial element of burlesque (or mockery and parody) that depends, for its appreciation, on considerable knowledge of courtly society, love, and manners.

Some of the subject matter in the fabliaux has parallels in other times and other countries: many of the plots stem from folklore, some have classical affinities, and a few can be traced to Oriental sources. The earliest fabliau, *Richeut*, dates from about 1175, but the main period of their composition was the 13th century, extending into the first half of the 14th. Most fabliaux are 200 to 400 lines in length, though there are extremes of fewer than 20 lines and of more than 1,300. Their authors included amateur writers (notably Philippe de Beaumanoir) and professionals (*e.g.*, Jehan Bodel and Rutebeuf). Verse tales analogous to the fabliaux exist in other languages. Geoffrey Chaucer's "The Reeve's Tale," for example, is based on a known fabliau.

Fabre \\'fābr, *Angl* 'fāb-rə\\, Émile (b. March 24, 1869, Metz, Fr.—d. Sept. 25, 1955, Paris)   French playwright and administrator of the Comédie-Française (1915–36) who developed it into a vehicle for classical and contemporary repertoire.

Fabre began writing and producing plays at the age of 13. *Comme ils sont tous* (1894; "As They All Are"), his first success, was followed by a series of popular political and social satires: *L'Argent* (1895; "Silver"), *La Vie publique* (1905; "Public Life"), *Les Ventres dorés* (1905; "The Golden Bowels"), and *Les Sauterelles* (1911; "The Grasshoppers"), which attacked colonial administration. His other plays include a series of family tragedies and adaptations of two novels by Honoré de Balzac.

Fabre d'Églantine \\fä-brä-dā-glän-'tēn\\, Philippe(-François-Nazaire) (b. July 28, 1750, Carcassonne, Fr.—d. April 5, 1794,

Paris) French political satirist who wrote dramas and who helped create the Republican calendar.

Fabre was an actor in the provinces before going to Paris. After publishing the poem *Étude de la nature* (1783; "Study of Nature"), he wrote many comedies. Only one of these, *Le Philinte de Molière* (1790), which Fabre presented as a sequel to Molière's *Misanthrope*, retains some reputation. Fabre's best-known work is the song "Il pleut, il pleut, bergère" ("It's raining, it's raining, shepherdess"), which French children still sing today.

fabula \ˈfab-yə-lə, ˈfäb-yu̇-lä\ *plural* fabulae \-ˌlē, -ˌlī\ [Latin] In addition to meaning "talk," "story," or "fable," Latin *fabula* was a general word for "play"; particular types included the *fabula Atellana* \ˌat-ə-ˈlän-ə\, *fabula crepidata* \ˌkrā-pi-ˈdät-ə\, *fabula palliata* \ˌpal-ē-ˈät-ə\, *fabula praetexta* \prē-ˈteks-tə\, and *fabula togata* \tō-ˈgät-ə\.

The *fabula Atellana* ("Atellan play") was the earliest form of native farce in ancient Italy. These fabulae were presumably rustic improvisational comedies featuring masked stock characters. The farces derived their name from the town Atella in Campania. They became a popular entertainment in ancient republican and early imperial Rome. They became a literary genre in the 1st century BC, but only a few fragments survive of works by Lucian Pomponius of Bononia, Novius, and other writers. They feature stock characters, including Maccus, the clown; Bucco ("Fat-cheeks"), the simpleton; and Pappus, the old fool. Certain of the stock characters of the 16th-century Italian commedia dell'arte reflect the influence of the Atellan plays.

The *fabula crepidata* was a form of Roman tragedy based on Greek models. The name was derived from the *crepida*, a kind of thick-soled Greek shoe presumably worn by the actors.

The *fabula palliata* was an ancient Roman comedy based on Greek New Comedy and treating a Greek subject. The name derives from *pallium*, a cloak, and means roughly "play in Greek dress." The form was developed by the playwright Gnaeus Naevius in the 3rd century BC.

The *fabulae palliatae* retained the Greek stock characters and conventionalized plots of romantic intrigue as a framework for the satire of everyday contemporary life. These comedies became more than mere translation in the works of Plautus, Terence, and Statius Caecilius. It is through the *fabulae palliatae* of Plautus and Terence that Greek New Comedy was preserved and influenced succeeding generations of comedy in Europe from the Renaissance on.

The *fabula praetexta*, or *fabula praetextata*, was an ancient Roman drama with a theme from Roman history or legend. It was introduced in the 3rd century BC and took its name from the *praetexta*, an outer garment bordered with purple worn by Roman officials.

The *fabula togata* (from the Roman *toga*, hence "play in Roman dress") replaced the *fabula palliata* by about the 2nd century BC. The *togata* form was also a comedy based on Greek models, but it featured Roman life and characters. No complete work of this form survives.

fabulist \ˈfab-yu̇-list\ A creator or writer of fables.

facetiae \fə-ˈsē-shē-ˌē, -ˌī\ [Latin, cleverness, wittiness, plural of *facetia* joke] Witty or humorous writings or sayings.

faction \ˈfak-shən\ [blend of *fact* and *fiction*] Literary work based on fact but using the narrative techniques of fiction. *See also* NONFICTION NOVEL.

Fadeyev or **Fadeev** \ˌfə-ˈdʸā-yəf\, Aleksandr (b. Dec. 11 [Dec. 24, New Style], 1901, Kimry, near Tver, Russia—d. May 13, 1956, Moscow, U.S.S.R.) Russian novelist, leading exponent and theoretician of proletarian literature.

Fadeyev joined the Communist Party in 1918 and fought in Siberia against both the anticommunist White armies and the Japanese. Drawing on this experience he wrote his first important novel, *Razgrom* (1927; *The Nineteen*), which deals with a ragged band of guerrilla fighters trapped between the Whites and the Japanese. Siberia is also the setting of an unfinished multivolume novel *Posledny iz Udege* (1929–41; "The Last of the Udege").

After becoming a member of the board of the Union of Soviet Writers, Fadeyev wrote little fiction. From 1946 to 1954 he was general secretary and chairman of the executive board of the union. After World War II he published *Molodaya gvardiya* (1945, rev. ed., 1951; *The Young Guard*), dealing with youthful guerrilla fighters in German-occupied Ukraine. The extent to which Fadeyev was responsible for the purges of writers and artists in the 1930s and '40s has not been ascertained, but he zealously supported the cultural purge of 1946–1948, personally attacking Boris Pasternak and Mikhail Zoshchenko. When Stalin died, Fadeyev eulogized him. After the official denunciation of Stalin in 1956, Fadeyev ended a long drinking bout by killing himself.

faerie or **faery** \ˈfā-ə-rē, ˈfā-rē, ˈfar-ē\ *plural* faeries. The imagined realm of fairies; an imaginary land of enchantment.

Faerie Queene, The Epic poem that was published between 1590 and 1609 by Edmund SPENSER. It is the central poem of the Elizabethan period and is one of the great long poems in the English language. A celebration of Protestant nationalism, it represents infidels and papists as villains, King Arthur as the hero, and married chastity as its central value.

The form of *The Faerie Queene* fuses the medieval allegory with the Italian romantic epic. The plan was for 12 books (of which six were completed), focusing on 12 virtues exemplified in the quests of 12 knights from the court of Gloriana, the Faerie Queene, a symbol for Elizabeth I herself. Arthur, in quest of Gloriana's love, would appear in each book and come to exemplify Magnificence, the complete man. Spenser took the decorative chivalry of the Elizabethan court festivals and reworked it through a constantly shifting veil of allegory, so that the knight's adventures and loves build into a complex, multileveled portrayal of the moral life. The verse, a spacious and slow-moving nine-lined stanza (see SPENSERIAN STANZA), and Spenser's archaic language frequently rise to an unrivaled sensuousness.

The first installment of the poem (Books I–III) was published in 1590; the second, which contained Books I–III and Books IV–VI, in 1596. The first folio edition, with Books I–VI and the MUTABILITIE CANTOS fragment, appeared in 1609.

Faesi \ˈfes-ē\, Robert (b. April 10, 1883, Zürich, Switz.—d. Sept. 18, 1972, Zollikon) Swiss poet, dramatist, short-story writer, and literary critic.

From 1922 to 1953 Faesi combined his literary activity with a professorship of German literature at the University of Zürich. His poems in the collections *Aus der Brandung* (1917; "From the Surge") and *Der brennende Busch* (1928; "The Burning Bush") are socially significant products of World War I and postwar Expressionism. Faesi treats life in Zürich during the 18th century in *Zürcher Idylle* (1908; rev. ed., 1950; "The Zürich Idyll") and in his important three-volume series—*Die Stadt der Väter, Die Stadt der Freiheit, Die Stadt des Friedens* (1941–52; "The City of the Fathers," "The City of Freedom," "The City of Peace"). In 1949 he wrote the libretto for Willy Burkhard's opera *Die schwarze Spinne* ("The Black Spider"). Faesi also wrote important critical studies of Rainer Maria Rilke, Gottfried Keller, Thomas Mann, and others. His correspondence with Mann was published in 1962.

Fafnir \ˈfäf-nir, ˈfäv-\ Fictional character, a dragon who guards the treasure of the Nibelungs and who is killed by Siegfried in the German epic NIBELUNGENLIED.

Fagin \ˈfā-gin\ Fictional character, one of the villains in Charles Dickens' novel OLIVER TWIST and one of the most notorious anti-Semitic portraits in English literature.

Fagin is an old man in London who teaches young homeless boys how to be pickpockets and then fences their stolen goods. Although a miser and exploiter, he shows a certain loyalty and solicitude toward the boys.

Faguet \fä-ˈge\, Émile (b. Dec. 17, 1847, La Roche-sur-Yon, Fr.—d. June 6, 1916, Paris) French literary historian and a provocative critic.

Faguet was appointed to a chair at the Sorbonne in 1890 and elected to the Académie Française in 1900. He contributed to a number of major French journals and was drama critic (1888–1907) for the *Journal des débats*.

Faguet's most remarkable work is *Politiques et moralistes du XIX siècle*, 3 vol. (1891–1900; "Moralists and Political Thinkers of the 19th Century"). Among his nonliterary works are *L'Anticléricalisme* (1906), *Le Pacifisme* (1908), and *Le Féminisme* (1910).

Fagunwa \fä-ˈgün-wä\, D.O., *in full* Daniel Olorunfemi (b. 1903 or *c.* 1910, Okeigbo, near Ondo, Yorubaland [now in Nigeria]—d. Dec. 9, 1963, near Bida) Yoruba chief whose series of fantastic novels made him Nigeria's most popular writer. He was also a teacher.

Fagunwa's first novel, *Ogboju Ode Ninu Igbo Irunmale* (1938; *The Forest of a Thousand Daemons*), was the first full-length novel published in the Yoruba language. His second, *Igbo Olodumare* ("The Forest of God"), was published in 1949. He also wrote the novels *Ireke Onibudo* (1949; "The Sugarcane of the Guardian"), *Irinkerindo Ninu Igbo Elegbeje* (1954; "Wanderings in the Forest of Elegbeje"), and *Adiitu Olodumare* (1961; "The Secret of the Almighty"), as well as short stories and two travel books.

Fagunwa's works characteristically take the form of loosely constructed picaresque fairy tales containing many folkloric elements: spirits, monsters, gods, magic, and witchcraft. Every event points up a moral; this moral tone is reinforced by his use of Christian concepts as well as traditional and invented proverbs. His imagery, humor, wordplay, and rhetoric reveal an extensive knowledge of "deep" (classical) Yoruba.

fair copy A neat and exact copy of a written work, especially of a corrected or revised draft of a document.

Fairfax \ˈfar-ˌfaks\, Edward (b. *c.* 1575, Leeds, Yorkshire, Eng.—d. Jan. 27, 1635) English poet whose *Godfrey of Bulloigne; or, the Recoverie of Jerusalem* (1600), a translation of Torquato Tasso's epic poem *Gerusalemme liberata*, won fame and was praised by John Dryden. The poem contributed to the development of the English couplet and influenced the poets Edmund Waller and John Milton. Among Fairfax's other works were 12 eclogues, of which only two and most of a third are known to have survived. The finest, "Hermes and Lycaon," is a singing match between worldly and spiritual lovers.

Fairfax, Mrs. Alice \ˈal-is-ˈfar-ˌfaks\ Fictional character, the housekeeper at Thornfield Hall in the novel JANE EYRE by Charlotte Brontë.

fairy \ˈfar-ē\ *or* **faerie** *or* **faery** \ˈfā-ə-rē, ˈfā-rē, ˈfar-ē\ *plural* **fairies** *or* **faeries** [Middle English *fairie* fairyland, fairy people, from Old French *faerie*, a derivative of *fee, feie* fairy, from Latin *Fata* goddess of fate] A mythical being of folklore and romance usually having magic powers and dwelling on earth in close relationship with humans. It can appear as a dwarf creature typically having green clothes and hair, living underground or in stone heaps, and usually exercising magic powers to benevolent ends; as a diminutive sprite usually in the shape of a delicate, beautiful, ageless winged woman dressed in diaphanous white clothing, inhabiting fairyland, but making usually benevolent intervention in personal human affairs; or as a tiny, mischievous, and protective creature usually associated with a household hearth. *Compare* BROWNIE; DWARF; ELF; GOBLIN; KOBOLD; LEPRECHAUN; PIXIE; PUCK.

While the term *fairy* goes back only to the Middle Ages in Europe, analogues to these beings in varying forms appear in both written and oral literature, from the Sanskrit Gandharva (semidivine celestial musicians) to the nymphs of Greek mythology and Homer, the jinni of Arabic mythology, and similar folk characters of the Eskimos and other indigenous American peoples and of the Samoans.

The common modern depiction of fairies in children's stories represents a bowdlerization of what was once a serious and even sinister folkloric tradition. The fairies of the past were feared as dangerous and powerful beings who were sometimes friendly to humans but could also be cruel or mischievous.

Fairies were usually conceived of as being characteristically beautiful or handsome and as having lives corresponding to those of human beings, though longer. They were said to have no souls and at death they simply perished. They were believed to carry off human children, leaving CHANGELING substitutes, and they also transported adults to fairyland, which resembled pre-Christian abodes of the dead.

Fairy lore is particularly prevalent in Ireland, Cornwall, Wales, and Scotland. Fairies are common in literature from the Middle Ages on and appear in the works of many well-known writers, including the Italians Matteo Boiardo and Ludovico Ariosto, the English poet Edmund Spenser, the Frenchman Charles Perrault, the Scotsman Andrew Lang, and the Dane Hans Christian Andersen. *See also* MÄRCHEN.

fairy tale *also called* fairy story **1.** A simple narrative dealing with supernatural beings (such as fairies, magicians, ogres, or dragons) that is typically of folk origin and written or told for the amusement of children. **2.** A more sophisticated narrative containing supernatural or obviously improbable events, scenes, and personages and often having a whimsical, satirical, or moralistic character.

The term embraces such popular folktales (also called MÄRCHEN) as "Cinderella" and "Puss in Boots" and art fairy tales (*Kunstmärchen*) of later invention, such as *The Happy Prince* (1888), by Oscar Wilde. It is often difficult to distinguish between tales of literary and oral origin, because folktales have received literary treatment from early times, and, conversely, literary tales can often be traced back into the oral tradition. Early Italian collections such as *Le piacevoli notti* (1550, vol. 1; 1553, vol. 2; "The Pleasant Nights") of Gianfrancesco Straparòla and the *Il pentamerone* (1636; orig. pub. [1634] in Neapolitan dialect as *Lo cunto de li cunti* ["The Story of Stories"]) of Giambattista Basile contain reworkings in a highly literary style of such stories as "Snow White," "Sleeping Beauty," and "The Maiden in the Tower." A later French collection, Charles Perrault's *Contes de ma mère l'oye* (1697; *Tales of Mother Goose*), including "Cinderella," "Little Red Riding Hood," and "Beauty and the Beast," remains faithful to the oral tradition, while the *Kinder- und Hausmärchen* (1812–15; "Children's and Household Tales"; generally known as *Grimm's Fairy Tales*) of the Brothers Grimm are transcribed directly from oral renderings.

Art fairy tales were cultivated in the period of German Romanticism by J.W. von Goethe, Ludwig Tieck, Clemens Brentano, and E.T.A. Hoffmann and in Victorian England by

John Ruskin and Charles Kingsley, but few of these tales have found permanent popularity. The master of the art fairy tale is the Danish writer Hans Christian Andersen.

fakelore \\'fāk-ˌlȯr\\ [blend of *fake* and *folklore*] Imitation folklore (such as tales or songs) created to pass as genuinely traditional.

Falkberget \\'fälk-ˌber-ge\\, Johan Petter, *pseudonym of* Johan Petter Lillebakken \\'lil-ə-ˌbäk-kən\\ (b. Sept. 30, 1879, near Røros, Nor.—d. April 5, 1967, Tyvol, near Røros) Regional novelist of life in the central eastern mountains of Norway.

The self-educated son of a miner, Falkberget worked in the copper mines himself from the age of eight until he was 27. His novels about the mountain peasants, miners, and railway workers deal realistically with their hard lives. *Den fjerde nattevakt* (1923; *The Fourth Night Watch*) deals with life in Røros between 1807 and 1825. *Christianus Sextus* (1927–35), a trilogy set in the 18th century, dramatizes the history of a mine by that name. In 1940 Falkberget escaped the German occupation of Norway by walking to Sweden, carrying with him the manuscript that was to become his second trilogy, *Nattens brød* (1940–59; "Bread of Night").

Falke \\'fäl-kə\\, Gustav (b. Jan. 11, 1853, Lübeck [Germany]—d. Feb. 8, 1916, Grossborstel, near Hamburg) German poet and novelist prominent among the new lyric poets of his time. His verses were influenced by folk songs and the Romantic poets.

Falke worked as a bookseller and then as a music teacher until a pension from the Hamburg government enabled him to devote his time to writing. His best-known poems are contained in *Mynheer der Tod* (1892; "Mynheer Death"), *Hohe Sommertage* (1902; "High Summer Days"), and *Frohe Fracht* (1907; "Happy Load"). His novels include *Der Mann im Nebel* (1899; "The Man in the Fog") and *Die Kinder aus Ohlsens Gang* (1908; "The Children from Ohlsen's Passage"). He also published volumes of short stories, *Geelgösch* (1910) and *Der Spanier* (1910; "The Spaniard"), and the autobiographical *Stadt mit den goldenen Türmen* (1912; "City with the Golden Towers").

Fall, The Novel by Albert CAMUS, published in 1956 in French as *La Chute*. One of the author's most brilliant technical achievements, the novel is set in an Amsterdam bar. It consists of a one-sided conversation over the course of several days between an unidentified stranger and Jean-Baptiste Clamence, a former Parisian lawyer. Clamence begins the conversation as a confession of his own deeds but soon his confession extends to embrace the human dilemma—addressing such topics as alienation and the inadequacy of traditional values.

falling action In a play or other work of literature, the events that follow the climax and lead to the catastrophe or denouement. It is in contrast to *rising action*, the events leading up to the plot's climax.

falling rhythm *also called* descending rhythm. In prosody, rhythm established by a metric foot in which the first syllable is accented, as in trochaic and dactylic feet. It is the opposite of rising, or ascending, rhythm. *See also* CADENCE.

Fall of the House of Usher, The \\'əsh-ər\\ Story of supernatural horror by Edgar Allan POE, published in 1839 in *Burton's Gentleman's Magazine* and issued in *Tales* (1845). One of Poe's most terrifying tales, "The Fall of the House of Usher" is narrated by a man who has been invited to visit his childhood friend Roderick Usher. Usher gradually makes clear that his twin sister Madeline has been placed in the family vault not quite dead. When she reappears in her blood-stained shroud, the visitor rushes to leave as the entire house splits and sinks into a lake.

Falstaff \\'fȯl-ˌstaf\\, *in full* Sir John Falstaff. Fictional character, a father substitute of license and good fellowship for Prince Hal in William Shakespeare's two-part play HENRY IV. Falstaff comments on the political action of the play with inglorious, reckless, egotistical good sense.

Shakespeare had originally called this character Sir John Oldcastle in the first version of *Henry IV*, Part 1, following his source play, the anonymous *Famous Victories of Henry the Fifth*. He changed the name before the play was registered, however, doubtless because descendants of the historical Sir John Oldcastle (an English Lollard leader at the turn of the 14th century), who were then prominent at court, protested. He chose the name Falstaff partly because it contained echoes of the name Sir John Fastolf, which he had earlier given to a cowardly knight in *Henry VI*, Part 1.

The character of Falstaff, whose death is movingly reported in *Henry V*, later appeared in Shakespeare's THE MERRY WIVES OF WINDSOR.

Fama \\'fā-mə, 'fä-\\, *Greek* Pheme \\'fē-ˌmē\\ In Greek and Roman mythology, the personification of popular rumor. The Greek poet Hesiod portrayed her as an evildoer, easily stirred up but impossible to quell. The Athenian orator Aeschines distinguished Popular Rumor (Pheme) from Chicanery (Sykophantia) and Slander (Diabole). In Roman literature she was imaginatively conceived: Virgil described her (*Aeneid*, Book IV) as a swift, birdlike monster with as many eyes, lips, tongues, and ears as feathers, traveling on the ground but with her head in the clouds. According to Ovid in *Metamorphoses*, she inhabited a reverberating mountaintop palace of brass.

Family Moskat, The \\'mōs-kät\\ Novel by Isaac Bashevis SINGER, first published in installments from 1945 to 1948 in the Yiddish-language daily newspaper *Forverts* and in book form (two volumes) as *Di familye Mushkat* in 1950. A one-volume English translation was published in 1950.

Panoramic in sweep, the novel follows many characters and story lines in depicting Jewish life in Warsaw from 1911 to the late 1930s. Singer examines Hasidism, Orthodoxy, the rise of secularism, the breakdown of 19th-century traditions, assimilation, Marxism, and Zionism.

family sagas *see* ICELANDERS' SAGAS.

fancy \\'fan-sē\\ [ME *fantsy*, contraction of *fantasie* imagination, mental image, ultimately from Greek *phantasía*, a derivative of *phantázein* to make visible, present to the mind] **1.** The power of conception and representation used in artistic expression (such as through the use of figures of speech by a poet). Sometimes used as a synonym for imagination, especially in the sense of the power of conceiving and giving artistic form to that which is not existent, known, or experienced. **2.** The invention of the novel and the unreal by recombining the elements found in reality so that life is represented in alien surroundings or essentially changed in natural physical and mental constitution (as in centaurs or giants)—distinguished from *imagination*. **3.** The conceiving power that concerns itself with imagery (as figures of speech and details of a decorative design); synonymous with *conceit*.

The concepts of fancy and imagination have always been closely related, but at least since the Middle Ages distinctions have been made between the two. In England, John Dryden, Sir Joshua Reynolds, David Hume, and others set forth views of the differences, generally giving imagination a broader and more important role than fancy. Samuel Taylor Coleridge stated the theory that has had the most lasting influence. According to Coleridge, imagination is the faculty associated with creativity and the power to shape and unify, while fancy, dependent on and inferior to imagination, is merely "associative."

Fanny Hill \\'fan-ē-'hil\\ Notorious erotic novel by John CLELAND, first published in two volumes in 1748–49 as *Memoirs of a Woman of Pleasure*. The novel, published in an expurgated version as *Memoirs of Fanny Hill* in 1750 and commonly known simply as *Fanny Hill*, chronicles the life of a London prostitute, describing with scatological and clinical precision many varieties of sexual behavior. Although elegantly written, the novel was suppressed from its initial publication. It was kept in print surreptitiously, however, and for almost two centuries *Fanny Hill* enjoyed a salacious reputation. The book was not published legally until 1963 in the United States and 1970 in England.

Fanshawe \\'fan-ˌshȯ\\ First novel by Nathaniel HAWTHORNE, published in 1828 at his own expense. Hawthorne wrote *Fanshawe* while a student at Bowdoin College in Brunswick, Maine. Soon after he deemed the work to be of such derivative and mediocre quality that he attempted, unsuccessfully, to destroy all existing copies. The book's treatment of plot and character development were derived chiefly from the conventions of gothic novels and the works of Sir Walter Scott.

Fanshawe \\'fan-ˌshȯ\\, Sir Richard, 1st Baronet (b. June 1608, Ware Park, Hertfordshire, Eng.—d. June 16, 1666, Madrid, Spain) English poet, translator, and diplomat whose version of Luís de Camões' *Os Lusíadas* (*The Lusiads*) is a major achievement of English verse translation.

Educated at Cambridge, Fanshawe was appointed secretary to the English embassy at Madrid in 1635. He later served in a series of government and diplomatic posts, including ambassador to Portugal.

Fanshawe's *The Faithfull Shepherd*, a translation of Battista Guarini's *Il pastor fido*, was published in 1647. A second edition "with divers other poems" (1648) included his version of the fourth book of Virgil's *Aeneid*, in Spenserian stanza. His *Selected Parts of Horace* appeared in 1652. The great work of his retirement was his translation, published in 1655, of the *Os Lusíadas*, which retained Camões' original meter.

fantasy or **phantasy** \\'fan-tə-sē, -zē\\ Imaginative fiction dependent for effect on strangeness of setting (such as other worlds or times) and of characters (such as supernatural or unnatural beings). Examples include William Shakespeare's *A Midsummer Night's Dream*, Jonathan Swift's *Gulliver's Travels*, J.R.R. Tolkien's *Lord of the Rings* trilogy, and T.H. White's *The Once and Future King*. Science fiction can be seen as a form of fantasy, but the terms are not interchangeable, as science fiction usually is set in the future and is based on some aspect of science or technology while fantasy is set in an imaginary world and features the magic of mythical beings.

Farah \\'fä-rə\\, Nuruddin (b. 1945, Baidoa, Italian Somaliland [now in Somalia]) Somali writer who was the first novelist and the first English-language author of his country.

Farah was educated in Ethiopia and at the colonial-era Institutio Magistrale in Mogadishu, Somalia. He later studied at Panjab University in Chandīgarh, India. There he wrote his first published novel, *From a Crooked Rib* (1970), the story of a woman's determination to maintain her dignity in a sexist society.

In *A Naked Needle* (1976) Farah used a flimsy tale of interracial and cross-cultural love to reveal a lurid picture of Somali life in the postrevolutionary mid-1970s. He next wrote a trilogy—*Sweet and Sour Milk* (1979), *Sardines* (1981), and *Close Sesame* (1983)—about life under a distinctively African dictatorship, in which ideological slogans barely disguise an almost surreal society and human ties have been severed by dread and terror. His novel *Maps* (1986) examines issues of identity

and boundaries. The political nature of his fiction forced him into exile, and he taught in Europe, North America, and elsewhere in Africa.

Farazdaq, al- \\ˌal-fä-'räz-dȧk\\ ("The Lump of Dough"), byname of Tammām ibn Ghālib abū Firās \\täm-'mäm-ˌib-ən-'gä-lēb-ȧ-'bū-fē-'räs\\ (b. *c.* 641, Yamāmah region, Arabia [now in Saudi Arabia]—d. *c.* 728 or 730) Arab poet famous for his satires in a period when poetry was still a political instrument. With his rival Jarīr, he represents the transitional period between Bedouin traditional culture and the new Muslim society.

Living in Basra, al-Farazdaq composed satires on the Banū Nashal and Banū Fuqaim tribes, and when a member of the latter tribe became governor of Iraq in 669, he was forced to flee to Medina, where he remained for several years. He returned to Basra but fell out of favor again in 694. Later, however, al-Farazdaq became official poet to the caliph al-Walīd (reigned 705–715), to whom he dedicated a number of panegyrics. He also enjoyed the favor of the caliph Sulaymān (715–717) and that of Yazīd II (720–724).

His *Dīwān*, the collection of his poetry, contains several thousand verses, including laudatory and satirical poems and laments. Most of them are characterized by a happy sincerity, though some of his satires are notably obscene.

farce \\'färs\\ **1.** A light dramatic composition that uses highly improbable situations, stereotyped characters, extravagant exaggeration, and violent horseplay. Also, the class or form of drama made up of such compositions. **2.** The broad humor characteristic of theatrical farce. Also, a passage containing such comic element.

Farce is generally regarded as intellectually and aesthetically inferior to comedy in its crude characterizations and implausible plots, but it has been sustained by its popularity in performance. Antecedents of farce are found in ancient Greek and Roman theater, both in the comedies of Aristophanes and Plautus and in the popular native Italian *fabula Atellana*.

It was in 15th-century France that the term *farce* was first used to describe the elements of clowning, acrobatics, caricature, and indecency found together within a single form of entertainment. Such pieces were initially bits of impromptu buffoonery inserted by actors into the texts of religious plays—hence the use of the Old French word *farce*, "stuffing." Such works were afterward written independently. French farce spread quickly throughout Europe, notable examples being the interludes of John Heywood in 16th-century England.

Farce remained popular throughout the 18th and 19th centuries; in France, Eugène-Marin Labiche's *Le Chapeau de paille d'Italie* (1851; *The Italian Straw Hat*) and Georges Feydeau's *La Puce à l'oreille* (1907; *A Flea in Her Ear*) were notable successes.

Farce survived in the late 19th and early 20th centuries in such plays as *Charley's Aunt* (1892) by Brandon Thomas and found new expression in film comedies with Charlie Chaplin, the Keystone Kops, and the Marx Brothers. Farce continued to be produced in theaters throughout the 20th century. Two examples from the second half of the century are the Italian Dario Fo's *Morte accidentale di un anarchico* (1974; *Accidental Death of an Anarchist*) and Michael Frayn's *Noises Off* (1982).

farce-comedy Comedy of a marked farcical character or a comic work that employs elements of farce. Examples include Oscar Wilde's *The Importance of Being Earnest* and several of William Shakespeare's plays.

farceur \\fär-'sər\\ [French] A writer or actor of farce.

Farès \\fä-'res\\, Nabile (b. 1940, Collo, Alg.) Kabylian novelist and poet known for his abstruse, poetic, and dreamlike style. Rebellion against both the established religious traditions and the newly formed conventions of Algeria since independence is central to his work.

In his first novel, *Yahia, pas de chance* (1970; "Yahia, No Chance"), Farès introduced a quest that was to haunt his later works—the search for the self, which takes him back to his childhood, and further still, to the pre-Islāmic voices of inspiration tied to the earth. Farès' successive novels—*Un Passager de l'Occident* (1971; "A Passenger from the West") and the trilogy *La Découverte du nouveau monde* ("The Discovery of the New World"), including *Le Champs des oliviers* (1972; "The Olivetree Groves"), *Mémoire de l'absent* (1974; "Memory of the Absent"), and *L'Exil et le désarroi* (1976; "Exile and Disorder")—carry forward his diffuse style and themes of lost innocence and delirium.

In his novels Farès sought to create a style that would match the rebellious quality of his theme. To that end he used a variety of experimental techniques, including stream-of-consciousness narration and unconventional punctuation and capitalization.

Farès' collections of poetry include *Le Chant d'Akli* (1971; "The Song of Akli"), *Chants d'histoire et de vie pour des roses de sable: Texte bilingue pour un peuple sahrawi* (1978), and *L'Exil au féminin* (1986; "Exile to the Feminine").

Farewell to Arms, A   Novel by Ernest HEMINGWAY, published in 1929. Like his early short stories and his novel *The Sun Also Rises*, the work is full of the disillusionment of the "lost generation" expatriates.

While serving with the Italian ambulance service during World War I, the American lieutenant Frederick Henry falls in love with the English nurse Catherine Barkley, who tends him after he is wounded. She becomes pregnant but refuses to marry him, and he returns to his post. Henry deserts during the Italians' retreat after the Battle of Caporetto, and the reunited couple flee into Switzerland. There, however, Catherine and her baby die during childbirth, leaving Henry desolate.

Far from the Madding Crowd   Novel by Thomas HARDY, published serially and anonymously in 1874 in *The Cornhill Magazine* and published in book form under Hardy's name the same year. It was his first popular success.

The plot centers on Bathsheba Everdene, a farm owner, and her three suitors, Gabriel Oak (a generous shepherd), Sergeant Troy (a young, handsome, and inconsiderate soldier), and William Boldwood (the owner of the neighboring farm). The contrasting relationships between Bathsheba and her suitors are a study of the many faces of love, including honest, heartfelt love and unscrupulous and manipulative adoration.

Fargue \\'färg\\, Léon-Paul (b. March 4, 1876, Paris, Fr.—d. Nov. 25, 1947, Paris)   French poet and essayist whose work spanned numerous literary movements.

Before he reached 20 years of age, Fargue had already published his important poem *Tancrède* in the magazine *Pan* (1895; published in book form in 1911) and had become a member of the Symbolist circle connected with the journal *Le Mercure de France*. His first collection of verse, *Poèmes*, was published in 1912 and reissued in 1918. Later works include *Pour la musique* (1919; "For Music"), *Espaces* (1929; "Spaces"), and *Sous la lampe* (1929; "Under the Lamp").

After 1930 Fargue devoted himself almost exclusively to journalism, writing newspaper columns and longer lyrical essays about Parisian life. It is for these and the prose-poem memoirs collected in *Le Piéton de Paris* (1939; "The Parisian Pedestrian") that he is chiefly remembered.

Fargue's works have been linked with the Dadaists (for their juxtaposition of images), the Cubists (for their dislocation and deformation of words), and the Surrealists (for their fascination with dreams). Fargue helped found *La Nouvelle Revue française*

in 1912, contributed to the first issue of the Surrealist magazine *Littérature* in 1919, and codirected the experimental journal *Commerce* in the 1920s.

Fariña \\fä-'rēn-yə\\, Richard (b. April 30, 1936?, Brooklyn, N.Y., U.S.—d. April 30, 1966, Carmel, Calif.)   American folksinger, songwriter, and novelist. He was killed in a motorcycle accident just after the publication of his first novel, *Been Down So Long It Looks Like Up to Me* (1966).

Fariña studied engineering and literature at Cornell University, served with the Irish Republican Army in the mid-1950s, and later served briefly with guerrillas in Cuba.

Among the folk songs he composed were "Pack Up Your Sorrows" and "Hard Lovin' Loser." His first novel was a comic work about the meaning of life, partially set at Cornell during the late 1950s. His novel *Long Time Coming and a Long Time Gone*, with a foreword by the folksinger Joan Baez, was published posthumously in 1969.

Farjeon \\'fär-jən\\, Eleanor (b. Feb. 13, 1881, London, Eng.—d. June 5, 1965, Hampstead, London)   English writer for children whose magical but unsentimental tales, which often mock the behavior of adults, earned her a revered place in many British nurseries.

Farjeon grew up in the bohemian literary and dramatic circles of London. She came to public attention at 16 as the librettist of an opera by her brother Harry, which was produced by the Royal Academy of Music.

Her success with *Nursery Rhymes of London Town* (1916), simple tunes originally for adults but adapted and sung in schools throughout England, spurred her writing. In addition to such favorites as *Martin Pippin in the Apple-Orchard* (1921) and *The Little Bookroom* (1955), Farjeon produced children's educational books, among them *Kings and Queens* (1932; with Herbert Farjeon), and memoirs, notably *A Nursery in the Nineties* (1935; rev. ed., 1960).

Farquhar \\'fär-kər, -kwər, -ˌkwär\\, George (b. 1678, Londonderry, County Derry, Ire.—d. April 29, 1707, London, Eng.)   Irish playwright of great comic power who stood out from his contemporaries by originality of dialogue and a stage sense that stemmed from experience as an actor.

Farquhar entered Trinity College, Dublin, but he preferred to spend his energies as an unsuccessful actor at the Smock Alley Theatre in Dublin. After an incident in which a fellow actor was gravely wounded, he abandoned acting and decided to go to London to write comedy. His early plays were, in the main, spirited variations on a theme: young men have their fling for four acts and reform, unconvincingly, in the fifth.

His first play, *Love and a Bottle*, was well received at London's Drury Lane Theatre in 1699 and was followed in the same year by *The Constant Couple*. A sequel to the latter, *Sir Harry Wildair*, appeared in 1701. Between 1702 and 1704 he wrote *The Inconstant* (adapted from John Fletcher's *Wild-Goose Chase*), *The Twin-Rivals*, and *The Stage-Coach*, a farce translated from French.

Farquhar's real contribution to English drama came in 1706 with *The Recruiting Officer* and, in the following year, with THE BEAUX' STRATAGEM. In these plays he introduced a verbal vigor and love of character that are more usually associated with Elizabethan dramatists.

Farrar \\'far-ər\\, Frederic William (b. Aug. 7, 1831, Bombay, India—d. March 22, 1903, Canterbury, Kent, Eng.)   Popular English religious writer and author of a sentimental novel of school life, *Eric; or, Little by Little* (1858).

In 1856 Farrar became a fellow of Trinity College, Cambridge, and he later accepted an assistant mastership at Harrow School. His first novel was followed by *Julian Home* (1859) and

St. Winifred's (1862). Farrar was an expert philologist; his *Essay on the Origin of Language* (1860) earned him a fellowship of the Royal Society. His *Life of Christ* (1874) ran through 30 editions in as many years. In 1876 Farrar became canon of Westminster Cathedral and in 1883 archdeacon. He was dean of Canterbury from 1895.

Farrell \'far-əl\, James Thomas (b. Feb. 27, 1904, Chicago, Ill., U.S.—d. Aug. 22, 1979, New York, N.Y.) American novelist and short-story writer known for his realistic portraits of the lower-middle-class Irish in Chicago, drawn from his own experiences.

E.B. Inc.

Farrell attended the University of Chicago from 1925 to 1929. In 1932 he moved to New York City. That year the first volume of his well-known STUDS LONIGAN trilogy, *Young Lonigan*, was published. It was followed by *The Young Manhood of Studs Lonigan* in 1934 and *Judgment Day* in 1935. Danny O'Neill, a character introduced in *Studs Lonigan*, is the subject of a later series, published between 1936 and 1953, in which he reflects Farrell's acquired faith in humanitarian values and man's power to cope with circumstances. *The Face of Time* (1953) is considered another of Farrell's best works.

After 1958 Farrell worked on what was to be a 25-volume cycle, *A Universe of Time*, of which he completed 10 volumes. His complete works include 25 novels, 17 collections of short stories, and such works of nonfiction as *A Note on Literary Criticism* (1936) and *Reflections at Fifty* (1954), a collection of personal essays.

farsa \'fär-sä\ [Oromo (Cushitic language of East Africa) *faarsaa* singer, song] *see* BOASTING POEM.

fashionable novel Early 19th-century subgenre of the comedy of manners portraying the English upper class, usually by members of that class. One author particularly known for his fashionable novels was Theodore Hook.

fast \'fast\ Of a dramatic or literary work, holding the reader's interest by reason of sustained conflict, vivid writing, or the rapid advancement of the story.

Fastnachtsspiel \'fäst-,näkt-,shpēl\ *plural* Fastnachtsspiele \-,shpē-lə\ [German, from *Fastnacht* Shrove Tuesday + *Spiel* play] Carnival or Shrovetide play that emerged in the 15th century as the first truly secular drama of pre-Reformation Germany. Usually performed on platform stages in the open air by amateur actors, students, and artisans, the *Fastnachtsspiele* consisted of a mixture of popular and religious elements. The plays often contained satirical attacks on greedy clergymen and other traditional dislikes of the German burghers, an element that relates them to the Feast of Fools (a medieval festival during which ecclesiastical ritual was parodied) and the French *sotie*. In addition to features borrowed from liturgical drama and bits of comedy that were no doubt brought in by the wandering minstrels, the *Fastnachtsspiele*, according to many scholars, contain themes and influences from German folk traditions of the pre-Christian era.

Hans Rosenplüt of Nürnberg and his younger contemporary Hans Folz of Worms, who also settled in Nürnberg, were the most notable purveyors of *Fastnachtsspiele* in the mid-15th century. In the 16th century the plays reached a level of greater respectability when Hans Sachs wrote many *Fastnachtsspiele* among his 208 plays.

Fata Morgana \'fä-tə-mȯr-'gä-nə\ A mirage that appeared periodically in the Strait of Messina between Sicily and Italy, named in Italian after the legendary enchantress MORGAN LE FAY of Arthurian romance.

Fate \'fāt\, *also called* Moira or Parca. In Greek and Roman mythology, one of the goddesses of fate or destiny supposed to determine the course of human life and in particular the span of a person's life and allotment of misery and suffering. The term is usually used in the plural.

Homer speaks of fate (*moira*) in the singular as an impersonal power and sometimes makes its functions interchangeable with those of the Olympian gods. Hesiod was the first to personify the Fates as three very old women who spin the threads of human destiny. Their names were Clotho ("Spinner"), Lachesis ("Allotter"), and Atropos ("Inflexible"). Much later, some fanciful writers assigned distinct tasks to the three goddesses: Clotho spun the "thread" of human fate, Lachesis dispensed it, and Atropos cut it. The Romans identified the Parcae, originally personifications of childbirth, with the three Greek Fates. The individual names of the Roman goddesses were Nona, Decuma, and Morta.

fate tragedy or **fate drama** (German: *Schicksalstragödie*) A type of play especially popular in early 19th-century Germany in which a malignant destiny drives the protagonist to commit a horrible crime, often unsuspectingly. Adolf Müllner's *Der neunundzwanzigste Februar* (1812; "February 29") and *Die Schuld* (1813; "The Debt") and Zacharias Werner's *Der vierundzwanzigste Februar* (1806; "February 24") are among the best-known examples.

Father, The Tragic drama in three acts by August STRINDBERG, published in 1887 as *Fadren* and performed the same year. Strindberg had come to believe that life is a series of struggles between weaker and stronger wills, and the influences of Strindberg's misogyny and naturalistic fiction are evident in this play, one of his most important works.

The Captain, a scientist and freethinker whose marriage has gone sour, is engaged in a power struggle with his wife, Laura, over their daughter. He wants to send the girl away to school; Laura is determined to keep her at home under her influence. Laura resolves to drive her husband to insanity, and she begins by insinuating that he is not the father of the child.

Father and Son Autobiography by Edmund GOSSE, published anonymously in 1907. Considered a minor masterpiece, *Father and Son* is a sensitive study of the clash between religious fundamentalism and intellectual curiosity. The book recounts Gosse's austere childhood, particularly his relationship to his father, the eminent zoologist Philip Henry Gosse. In the conflict between his rigid fundamentalism and mounting scientific knowledge, the elder Gosse rejected science for his faith. The younger Gosse, with his vast thirst for knowledge of the broader world, was finally unable to accept his father's beliefs.

Father Christmas *chiefly British* The Christmas spirit personified. *See* SANTA CLAUS.

Fathers and Sons Novel by Ivan TURGENEV, published in 1862 as *Ottsy i deti*. Quite controversial at the time of its publication, *Fathers and Sons* concerns the inevitable conflict between generations and between the values of traditionalists and intellectuals. The physician Bazarov, the novel's protagonist, is the most powerful of Turgenev's creations. He is a nihilist, denying the validity of all laws save those of the natural sciences. Uncouth and forthright in his opinions, he is nonetheless susceptible to love and by that fact doomed to unhappiness. In sociopolitical terms he represents the victory of the revolutionary nongentry intelligentsia over the gentry intelligentsia to which Turgenev belonged. At the novel's first appearance the radical younger generation attacked it bitterly as a slander, and conservatives condemned it as too lenient in its characterization of nihilism.

Father Time   The personification of time, especially as a bald, bearded old man holding a scythe and water jar or sometimes an hourglass.

Faulkner \'fôk-nər\, William (Cuthbert), *original surname* (until 1924) Falkner \'fôk-nər, 'fôlk-\ (b. Sept. 25, 1897, New

Robert Capa—Magnum

Albany, Miss., U.S.—d. July 6, 1962, near Oxford, Miss.) American novelist and short-story writer best known for his Yoknapatawpha cycle, developed as a fable of the American South and of human destiny. He won the Nobel Prize for Literature in 1949.

Faulkner dropped out of high school in his second year and later endured a very brief stint at the University of Mississippi. A neighbor put up most of the money for the publication of Faulkner's first book, a cycle of pastoral poems, *The Marble Faun* (1924). His first novel, *Soldier's Pay* (1926), is about the return to Georgia of a fatally wounded aviator. His second novel, *Mosquitoes* (1927), is a heavily satirical picture of the New Orleans literary circle. A third novel, *Flags in the Dust*, was refused by the publisher of the other two. Given a new title, SARTORIS, the manuscript was accepted by another publisher, and it appeared in January 1929. THE SOUND AND THE FURY, the first of his masterworks, appeared in October of the same year.

In the years from 1930 to 1942 Faulkner published two collections of stories, a second and last book of poems (*A Green Bough*, 1933), and nine novels—AS I LAY DYING (1930); SANCTUARY (1931); LIGHT IN AUGUST (1932); *Pylon* (1935); ABSALOM, ABSALOM! (1936); *The Unvanquished* (1938); *The Wild Palms* (1939); THE HAMLET (1940); and GO DOWN, MOSES (1942), which includes the story THE BEAR. By 1945, how-

ever, his novels were effectively out of print, and Faulkner accepted a contract to write movie scripts in Hollywood. His second period of success began with the publication in 1946 of *The Portable Faulkner*, which presented his Yoknapatawpha legend as a whole. In 1948 Faulkner published another novel, INTRUDER IN THE DUST. *Collected Stories*, published early in 1950, won the National Book Award.

In 1951 a sequel to *Sanctuary* was published; a three-act play, *Requiem for a Nun*, with a narrative prologue to each act, it had the effect of a novel. In 1954 Faulkner's longest novel, *A Fable*, on which he had been working for nearly 10 years, was published. Faulkner rounded out the Yoknapatawpha story with THE TOWN (1957) and THE MANSION (1959).

faun \'fôn, 'fän\ [Latin *fauni,* plural of *Faunus* Faunus]   An ancient Italic deity of fields and herds represented as having human shape, with pointed ears, small horns, and sometimes a goat's tail, or as half goat and half man.

Fauntleroy, Lord \'fônt-lə-ˌrói\, *in full* Cedric Errol, Lord Fauntleroy \'sed-rik-'er-əl, 'sĕd-\   Fictional character, a young American boy who becomes heir to an English earldom in Frances Hodgson Burnett's sentimental novel LITTLE LORD FAUNTLEROY (1886).

Faunus \'fôn-əs, 'fän-\   Ancient Italic rural deity whose attributes in classical Roman times were identified with those of the Greek god PAN. Faunus was originally worshiped in the countryside as a bestower of fruitfulness on fields and flocks. He eventually became primarily a woodland deity. A grandson of Saturn, Faunus was typically represented as half man and half goat (a borrowing from the Greek satyr) and was depicted in the company of similar creatures, known as fauns.

Fauriel \fôr-'yel\, Claude(-Charles) (b. Oct. 21, 1772, Saint-Étienne, Fr.—d. July 15, 1844, Paris)   French scholar and writer who developed the study of comparative literature and helped revive interest in literary-historical studies.

During the French Revolution, Fauriel served in the army and in 1799 became private secretary to the minister of police. He resigned after three years. At about this time, his first literary efforts—articles in the *Décade Philosophique*—were noticed and approved by Mme de Staël.

Fauriel's *Chants populaires de la Grèce moderne*, 2 vol. (1824–25; "Popular Songs of Modern Greece"), served the dual causes of poetry and Greek independence. His other works include *Histoire de la Gaule méridionale sous la domination des conquérants germains*, 4 vol. (1836; "History of Southern Gaul Under the Rule of the German Conquerors"); a translation of a Provençal poem on the Albigensian Crusade—*Histoire de la croisade contre les hérétiques albigeois* (1837; "History of the Crusade Against the Albigensian Heretics"); and two posthumously published works, *Histoire de la poésie provençale*, 3 vol. (1846; *History of Provençal Poetry*), and *Dante et les origines de la langue et de la littérature italiennes*, 2 vol. (1854; "Dante and the Origins of the Italian Language and Literature"). Fauriel's memoirs were published under the title *Les Derniers Jours du consulat* (1886; "The Last Days of the Consulate").

Fauset \'fôs-ət\, Jesse Redmon, *married name* Harris \'har-is\ (b. April 27, 1882, Snow Hill, N.J., U.S.—d. April 30, 1961, Philadelphia, Pa.)   African-American novelist, critic, poet, and editor known for her discovery and encouragement of several writers of the Harlem Renaissance.

Fauset graduated from Cornell University (B.A., 1905), and she later earned a master's degree from the University of Pennsylvania (1919). She taught French in an all-black secondary school in Washington, D.C., for several years. While there she published articles in *The Crisis* magazine, the journal of the

National Association for the Advancement of Colored People (NAACP). Its editor, W.E.B. Du Bois, persuaded her to move to New York City to become the magazine's literary editor.

Library of Congress

In that capacity, from 1919 to 1926, she published the works of such writers as Langston Hughes, Countee Cullen, Claude McKay, and Jean Toomer. She also edited and wrote for *The Brownies' Book*, a short-lived periodical for black children.

In her own work Fauset portrayed mostly middle-class black characters forced to deal with self-hate as well as racial prejudice. In her best-known novel, *Comedy: American Style* (1933), Olivia Carey, the protagonist, is a black woman who longs to be white, while her son and husband take pride in their cultural heritage. Fauset's other novels include *There Is Confusion* (1924), *Plum Bun* (1928), and *The Chinaberry Tree* (1931).

Faust \'faust\, *also called* Faustus \'faus-təs, 'fôs-\ *or* Doctor Faustus.   Hero of one of the most durable legends in Western folklore and literature, the story of a German necromancer who sells his soul to the devil in exchange for knowledge and power.

There was a historical Faust, indeed perhaps two, one of whom more than once alluded to the devil as his *Schwager*, or crony. One or both died about 1540, leaving a tangled legend of sorcery and alchemy, astrology and soothsaying, studies theological and diabolical, necromancy and sodomy. Contemporary references indicate that he was widely traveled and fairly well known, but all observers testify to his evil reputation.

Faust owes his posthumous fame to the anonymous author of the first *Faustbuch* (1587), a collection of tales about the ancient magi. In the *Faustbuch* the acts were attributed to Faust. The author's intense descriptions of hell and of the fearful state of mind of his merciless hero, as well as his creation of the ruthless, savage, embittered, yet remorseful fiend MEPHISTOPHELES, were so realistic that they inspired a certain terror in the reader.

The *Faustbuch* was speedily translated and read throughout Europe. An English prose translation of 1592 inspired DOCTOR FAUSTUS (1604) by Christopher Marlowe, who, for the first time, invested the Faust legend with tragic dignity. Marlowe, however, retained much of the coarse humor and many clownish episodes of the *Faustbuch*, and German versions of Marlowe's play compounded them. This association of tragedy and buffoonery remained an inherent part of the Faust dramas and puppet plays that were popular for two centuries. In the early versions, Faust's eternal damnation was never in doubt.

The publication of magic manuals bearing Faust's name later became a lucrative trade. The books included careful instructions on how to avoid making a bilateral pact with the Devil or, if need be, how to break such a pact.

The German writer Gotthold Lessing undertook the salvation of Faust in an unfinished play (1780). Lessing, a rationalist, saw Faust's pursuit of knowledge as noble and arranged for the hero's reconciliation with God. This was the approach also adopted by J.W. von Goethe, who was the outstanding chronicler of the Faust legend. His FAUST (Part I, 1808; Part II, 1832) makes of the Faust legend a profoundly serious but highly ironic commentary on the contradictory possibilities of the Western cultural heritage.

Faust was the figure in which the Romantic age recognized its mind and soul, and the character, in his self-consciousness and crisis of identity, continued to appeal to writers through the centuries. In the 19th and 20th centuries, those who retold the Faust legend without Goethe's happy ending included Adelbert von Chamisso, *Faust, Ein Versuch* (1804); Christian Grabbe, *Don Juan und Faust* (1829); Nikolaus Lenau, *Faust: Ein Gedicht* (1836); Heinrich Heine, *Der Doktor Faust: Ein Tanzpoem* (1851); and Paul Valéry, *Mon Faust* (1946). Perhaps the most eloquent 20th-century version of the story is Thomas Mann's *Doktor Faustus* (1947; DOCTOR FAUSTUS).

Faust \'faust\   Two-part dramatic work by J.W. von GOETHE. Part I was published in 1808 and Part II in 1832, after the author's death. The supreme work of Goethe's later years, *Faust* is sometimes considered Germany's greatest contribution to world literature.

Part I sets out the magician Faust's despair, his pact with Mephistopheles, and his love for Gretchen; Part II covers his life at court, the wooing and winning of Helen of Troy, and his purification and salvation.

In earlier eras the play was often decried as formless because of its array of lyric, epic, dramatic, operatic, and balletic elements. It includes almost every known poetic meter, from doggerel through terza rima to six-foot trimeter (a line of verse consisting of three measures), and a number of styles ranging from Greek tragedy through medieval mystery, baroque allegory, Renaissance masque, and commedia dell'arte to something akin to the modern revue. This mixture of forms and styles suggests to modern critics, however, a deliberate attempt to create a vehicle of cultural comment rather than an inability to create a coherent form of his own, and the content with which Goethe invests his forms bears this out. He draws on an immense variety of cultural material—theological, mythological, philosophical, political, economic, scientific, aesthetic, musical, literary—for the more realistic Part I no less than for the more symbolic Part II.

Favart \fä-'vår\, Charles-Simon (b. Nov. 13, 1710, Paris, Fr.—d. May 12, 1792, Belleville)   French dramatist and theater director who was one of the creators of the opéra-comique (French form of opera in which spoken dialogue alternates with self-contained musical numbers).

Favart became stage manager of the Théâtre de l'Opéra-Comique in 1743 and director of the company in 1758.

His best play, *Les Trois Sultanes* (1761), is a comedy based on a love triangle. In it, song and dance are less important than in his other works, the best of which is *La Chercheuse d'esprit* (1741; "The Woman in Search of Spirit"). Favart had a special talent for pastoral plays, one of which, *Bastien et Bastienne* (1753), was later given a musical setting by W.A. Mozart.

Fawley, Jude \'jüd-'fôl-ē\   Fictional character, the unfortunate stonemason who is the protagonist of Thomas Hardy's novel JUDE THE OBSCURE.

Fearing \'fir-iŋ\, Kenneth (Flexner) (b. July 28, 1902, Oak Park, Ill., U.S.—d. June 26, 1961, New York, N.Y.)   American poet and novelist who used an array of topical idioms in his satires of urban life.

In 1924 Fearing moved to New York City and worked as a commercial freelance writer for the rest of his life. In his poetry he depicts a mechanized society devoid of belief, faith, and love. His work, acclaimed for its power, vividness, and wit, appeared in *Poetry* magazine and *The New Yorker*. His books include *Stranger at Coney Island* (1948) and *New and Selected Poems* (1956).

During the 1940s Fearing's readership shifted from his poetry to his psycho-thriller fiction. His most successful book, *The Big Clock* (1946; film, 1948), is a satire about a magazine publisher who commits murder and then sets his top reporter to hunt down a suspect, who is the reporter himself.

Federal Theatre Project *see* WPA FEDERAL THEATRE PROJECT.

Federal Writers' Project *see* WPA FEDERAL WRITERS' PROJECT.

Federer \'fā-dǝr-ǝr\, Heinrich (b. Oct. 6/7, 1866, Brienz, Switz.—d. April 29, 1928, Zürich)   Novelist who imparted new vigor to Christian fiction in Switzerland.

Federer started to write in 1899 when asthma, from which he suffered all his life, put an end to his work as a priest. He then worked as a journalist in Zürich and after 1907 as an independent writer. He had been raised in the Roman Catholic tradition among peasants and in mountains of the Sarner region, and this background influenced the themes that were predominant in his books.

Federer's wide reading kept his delightful, realistic art free from the narrow outlook of *Heimatkunst*, the genre of a group of Swiss local colorists. His novels include *Der heilige Franz von Assisi* (1908; "Saint Francis of Assisi"), *Lachweiler Geschichten* (1911; "Lachweil Stories"), *Berge und Menschen* (1911; "Mountains and Men"), *Sisto e Sesto* (1913; "Sixtus and Sesto"), *Umbrische Reisegeschichtlein* (1921; "Umbrian Travel Stories"), *Papst und Kaiser im Dorfe* (1925; "Pope and Emperor in the Village"), and the autobiographical *Am Fenster* (1927; "On the Window"). His complete works were published in 12 volumes (1931–38).

Federici \fā-dā-'rē-chē\, Camillo, *original name* Giovanni Battista Viassolo \vyäs-'sō-lō\ (b. April 9, 1749, Garessio, Piedmont [Italy]—d. Dec. 23, 1802, Padua, Austrian Empire [now in Italy])   Italian dramatist and actor whose comedies were highly popular in the late 18th century.

Federici was educated at Turin and showed at an early age a great fondness for literature and especially for the theater. The praises bestowed on his early attempts determined his choice of a career, and he obtained engagements with several companies both as writer and actor. He settled at Padua, and the reputation of his comedies rapidly spread in Italy. Most of his pieces were somewhat melodramatic, but he caught something of the new spirit that was manifesting itself in German dramatic literature in the works of Friedrich von Schiller and August von Kotzebue. Federici fell ill in 1791 and was disabled for several years, and his works, in the absence of copyright law, were published without his permission. In 1802 he undertook to prepare a collected edition, but only four volumes were completed by the time of his death.

Fedin \'f²ā-d⁽ʲ⁾in\, Konstantin Aleksandrovich (b. Feb. 12 [Feb. 24, New Style], 1892, Saratov, Russia—d. July 15, 1977, Moscow, U.S.S.R.)   Soviet writer noted primarily for his early novels that portrayed the difficulties of intellectuals in Soviet Russia.

During the 1920s, Fedin belonged to a literary group called the Serapion Brothers, the members of which accepted the Russian Revolution but demanded freedom for art and literature. His first novel, *Goroda i gody* (1924; "Cities and Years"), based partly on his experiences as an internee in Germany during World War I, was a social-psychological study of the reaction of the intelligentsia to the Russian Revolution. Gradually, however, he accepted official Soviet literary policies, and he became first secretary of the steering committee of the Union of Soviet Writers in 1959 and chairman of the executive board in 1971.

His major work is generally considered to be the trilogy composed of *Pervyye radosti* (1945; *First Joys*), *Neobyknovennoye leto* (1947–48; *An Unusual Summer*), and *Kostyor* (1961–65; *The Conflagration*). Though they are works of Socialist Realism, they are fresh and vital and are free from the simplistic psychological portrayals that abound in Soviet novels.

Feijóo y Montenegro \fā-'ḵō-ō-ē-,mȯn-tā-'nā-ḡrō\, Benito Jerónimo (b. Oct. 8, 1676, Casdemiro, Spain—d. Sept. 26, 1764, Oviedo)   Teacher and essayist, a leading 18th-century Spanish stylist.

A Benedictine monk, Feijóo taught philosophy and theology at the University of Oviedo. His essays publicized and encouraged the spread of scientific knowledge. His two principal works, *Teatro crítico universal* (1726–39) and *Cartas eruditas y curiosas* (1742–60), treat an encyclopedic variety of subjects: natural science, education, law, medicine, philology, and popular beliefs or superstitions.

Feinstein \'fīn-,stīn\, Elaine, *original surname* Cooklin \'kůk-lin\ (b. Oct. 24, 1930, Bootle, Eng.)   British writer and translator who examined her own eastern European heritage in a number of novels and collections of poetry.

Feinstein's first published work was a collection of poetry, *In a Green Eye* (1966). After translating some of the poetry of Marina Tsvetayeva, she began to find her own distinct voice. Her second volume of verse, *The Magic Apple Tree* (1971), was preceded by a novel, *The Circle* (1970).

Characters in Feinstein's work are changed and controlled by their dreams and memories. In several of her books a woman searches for identity within and outside her family. One of Feinstein's best-known novels is *The Survivors* (1982), a multigenerational saga of two Jewish families who flee Russia for England. Her other novels include *Children of the Rose* (1975), *The Shadow Master* (1978) and *All You Need* (1989). Her volumes of poetry include *The Feast of Eurydice* (1980), *Badlands* (1986), and *City Music* (1990).

Félibre \fā-'lē-brǝ, *French* -'lĕbr *with* r *as a uvular trill*\ *plural* Felibres *same or* -brǝz\ [French, from Provençal *felibre*]   A member or supporter of the Félibrige.

Félibrige \fā-lē-'brēzh\ [French, from Provençal *Felibrige,* a derivative of *felibre* Félibre]   Association organized in the 19th century for the maintenance of the Provençal customs and language. The Félibrige was founded in 1854 by seven poets—Joseph ROUMANILLE, Frédéric MISTRAL, Théodore Aubanel, Anselme Mathieu, Jean Brunet, Alphonse Tavan, and Paul Giéra—who took their name from a Provençal tale in which Jesus is discovered in the Temple disputing with "Seven Doctors of the Law" ("li sèt felibre de la léi"). The group met near Avignon under the guidance of Roumanille, who, from the mid-1840s, had produced secular verse and delightfully humorous prose works in his native Provençal dialect. In 1852 he had also collected and published *Li Prouvençalo,* an anthology of writing in Provençal. Mistral was inspired by Roumanille to devote his energy to restoring the glory of the Provençal language, and he became the most powerful personality of its renaissance. In 1855 he cofounded with Roumanille the *Armana Prouvençau* ("Provençal Almanac"), an annual periodical that for 80 years published the best contemporary Provençal writing. Later, Mistral compiled a huge Provençal dictionary, *Lou Tresor dóu Félibrige,* 2 vol. (1878).

The Félibrige grew considerably in the period after Mistral, attracting followers not only from Provence but also from other southern provinces, such as Gascony, Languedoc, Limousin, and Aquitaine, as well as from Catalonia in Spain. The vigorous regional movement that resulted exerted a strong influence well into the 20th century.

Felix Holt \\'fē-liks-'hōlt\\ (*in full* Felix Holt, the Radical) Novel by George ELIOT, published in three volumes in 1866.

The novel is set in England in the early 1830s, at the time of agitation for passage of the Reform Bill, a measure designed to reform the electoral system in Britain. Despite his education, Felix Holt has chosen to work as an artisan, hoping to inspire his fellow workers to take charge of their own destiny. His austerity and passionate idealism are contrasted with the political ambitions of Harold Transome, who arrives home in Loamshire to claim his family's estate and stand as a candidate for the Radicals (those who support parliamentary reform and universal suffrage). Esther, the heroine, believes herself to be the daughter of a Nonconformist minister, but she is in fact the true heir of the Transome estate. Esther falls in love with Felix but must choose between him and Transome after Felix is imprisoned for killing a man (albeit accidentally) while trying to pacify a riot. Eventually she chooses Felix and renounces her claim to the Transome legacy.

Felix Krull \\'fā-liks-'krŭl\\ (*in full* The Confessions of Felix Krull, Confidence Man) Novel by Thomas MANN, originally published in German as *Die Bekenntnisse des Hochstaplers Felix Krull* in 1954; the first few chapters were published in 1922 as a short story.

The novel, which was unfinished at Mann's death, is the story of a confidence man who wins the favor of others by performing the roles they desire of him. The story is a good example of Mann's often-used theme of the immorality of the artist. Krull makes an art of his criminality and is motivated less by greed than by the sheer joy of a job well done.

fellow traveler [translation of Russian *poputchik*] Originally, a writer in the Soviet Union who was not against the Bolshevik Revolution of 1917 but did not actively support it as a propagandist. The term was used in this sense by Leon Trotsky in *Literature and the Revolution* (1925) and was not meant to be pejorative. Implicit in the designation was the recognition of the artist's need for intellectual freedom and his dependence on links with the cultural traditions of the past. In the 1920s some of the most gifted and popular Soviet writers, such as Osip Mandelstam, Leonid Leonov, Boris Pilnyak, Isaak Babel, Ilya Ehrenburg, and members of the Serapion Brothers, were fellow travelers. They were opposed bitterly by champions of a new proletarian art, and by the end of the decade the term came to be practically synonymous with a counterrevolutionary.

Outside the Soviet Union the term was widely used in the Cold War era of the 1950s, especially in the U.S., as a political label to refer to any person who, while not thought to be an actual "card-carrying" member of the Communist Party, was in sympathy with its aims and supported its doctrines.

Felltham \\'fel-thəm\\, Owen (b. 1602?—d. Feb. 23, 1668, London, Eng.) English essayist and poet, best known for his *Resolves Divine, Morall, and Politicall*, in which the striking images (some borrowed by the poet Henry Vaughan) are more original than the ideas. Felltham wrote the first edition of *Resolves* (1623), which contained 100 essays, when he was 18. The second edition, *Resolves, a Second Centurie* (1628), contained a further 100 essays. In addition to the *Resolves*, Felltham printed *A Brief Character of the Low Countries under the States* in 1652. It appeared in a reissue of the *Resolves* in 1661 together with 41 poems, some letters, and occasional pieces.

Femina Prize *see* PRIX FÉMINA.

feminine caesura In verse, a caesura that follows an unstressed or short syllable. *See* CAESURA.

feminine ending In prosody, having an unstressed and usually extrametrical syllable at the end of a line of verse. In the opening lines from Robert Frost's poem "Directive," the fourth line has a feminine ending while the rest are masculine:

> Back out of all this now too much for us,
> Back in a time made simple by the loss
> Of detail, burned, dissolved, and broken off
> Like graveyard marble sculpture in the weather,
> There is a house that is no more a house
> Upon a farm that is no more a farm
> And in a town that is no more a town.

feminine rhyme *also called* double rhyme. In poetry, a rhyme involving two syllables (as in *motion* and *ocean* or *willow* and *billow*). The term feminine rhyme is also sometimes applied to triple rhymes, or rhymes involving three syllables (such as *exciting* and *inviting*). *Compare* MASCULINE RHYME. Robert Browning alternates feminine and masculine rhymes in his "Soliloquy of the Spanish Cloister":

> Gr-r-r—there go, my heart's abhorrence!
> Water your damned flower-pots, do!
> If hate killed men, Brother Lawrence,
> God's blood, would not mine kill you!
> What? your myrtle-bush wants trimming?
> Oh, that rose has prior claims—
> Needs its leaden vase filled brimming?
> Hell dry you up with flames!

feminist criticism Any of a variety of approaches to literary criticism that attempt to examine the ways in which literature has been shaped according to issues of gender.

Feminist literary theory originated largely in the women's movement that followed World War II. Two of the earliest documents of feminist theory are Simone de Beauvoir's book *Le Deuxième Sexe* (1949; *The Second Sex*) and Kate Millett's *Sexual Politics* (1970). Feminist criticism established several aims: to critique the established canon of Western literature and to expose the standards on which it is based as patriarchal; to recover forgotten and neglected texts by women in order to reevaluate them; to establish "gynocriticism," the study of woman-centered writing, and to establish a women's canon; and to explore the cultural construction of gender and identity.

Feminist critics are extremely varied in their approaches. Among the writers who have had a great impact on feminist critical discourse are Ellen Moers, Carolyn Heilbrun, Sandra Gilbert, Susan Gubar, Annette Kolodny, Adrienne Rich, Elaine Showalter, Nina Baym, Alice Jardine, Catherine Stimpson, Gayatri Spivak, Hélène Cixous, Luce Irigaray, and Julia Kristeva.

Fences Play in two acts by August WILSON, performed in 1985 and published in 1986. It won the Pulitzer Prize for drama in 1987. Set in 1957, it is the second in Wilson's projected series of plays depicting African-American life in the 20th century.

The protagonist of *Fences* is Troy Maxson, who had been an outstanding baseball player at a time when the major leagues were closed to black players; he bitterly resents his lost opportunities. An ex-convict as well, Troy is now a garbage collector. He is married to Rose and is the father of teenaged Cory. An emotional, hard-drinking man, Troy ranges from tyrannical fury to delicacy as his preconceived ideas are challenged.

Fénelon \\fän-'lōⁿ\\, François de Salignac de La Mothe- (b. Aug. 6, 1651, Château de Fénelon, Périgord, Fr.—d. Jan. 7, 1715, Cambrai) French archbishop, theologian, and man of letters whose liberal views on politics and education exerted a lasting influence on French culture.

Fénelon began his higher studies in Paris in about 1672 at Saint-Sulpice seminary. Ordained a priest in 1676, he was appointed director of Nouvelles Catholiques ("New Catholics"), a college for women who instructed converts from French Protestantism.

From his pedagogical experiences at Nouvelles Catholiques, he wrote his first important work, *Traité de l'éducation des filles* (1687; "Treatise on the Education of Girls"). In 1689 Fénelon became tutor to Louis, Duke of Bourgogne, grandson and heir to Louis XIV. For the prince's education, Fénelon composed his best-known work, *Les Aventures de Télémaque* (1699), in which the adventures of Telemachus in search of his father, Odysseus, symbolically express Fénelon's fundamental political ideas. He was elected to the Académie Française in 1693.

Fénelon lost favor at court when he turned to Mme Guyon, the leading exponent of the Quietist school of prayer, for guidance in his spiritual life. When Mme Guyon's teaching and personal life were attacked, Fénelon responded with *Explication des maximes des saints sur la vie intérieure* (1697; "Explanation of the Sayings of the Saints on the Interior Life"). Fénelon not only lost Bossuet's friendship but also exposed himself to Bossuet's public denunciation. As a result, Fénelon's *Maximes des saints* was condemned by the pope and he was exiled to his diocese.

Fenestella \,fen-ə-'stel-ə\ (b. 52 BC—d. AD 19, or b. 35 BC—d. AD 36) Latin poet and annalist whose lost work, the *Annales*, was used as a source by the 1st-century-AD historian Pliny the Elder, the 2nd-century biographer Suetonius, and the 4th-century grammarian Diomedes.

Fenestella's *Annales* was in at least 22 books and certainly included the year 59 BC, although the exact period it covered is unknown. The few surviving fragments ascribed to Fenestella refer to such varied subjects as the origin of the appeal to the people (*provocatio*), the use of elephants in the games, the wearing of gold rings, the material for making the toga, and details of the lives of Terence and Cicero.

Fenian cycle \'fē-nē-ən\, *also called* Fionn cycle \'fin\ *or* Ossianic cycle \,äsh-ē-'an-ik, ,äs-\ In Irish literature, tales and ballads centering on the deeds of the legendary Finn MacCumhaill (MacCool) and his war band, the Fianna Éireann. An elite volunteer corps of warriors and huntsmen, skilled in poetry, Fianna flourished under the reign of Cormac mac Airt in the 3rd century AD. Fenian lore attained its greatest popularity about 1200, when the cycle's outstanding story, THE COLLOQUY OF THE OLD MEN, was written down. Other earlier tales were recorded in manuscripts such as THE BOOK OF THE DUN COW (*c.* 1100) and THE BOOK OF LEINSTER (*c.* 1160). The Fenian cycle remains a vital part of Irish folklore and contains many of the best-loved folktales of the country.

An early tale, *The Boyish Exploits of Finn* (*Macgnímartha Finn*), tells how, after Cumhaill (Cool), chief of the Fianna, is killed, his posthumous son is reared secretly in a forest and earns the name Finn ("The Fair") by his exploits. He grows up to triumph over his father's slayer, Goll MacMorna, to become head of the Fianna, which later includes his son Oisín (Ossian), the poet, his grandson Oscar, the handsome Diarmaid (Dermot), and his former clan enemy Goll MacMorna.

The other tales of the cycle deal with Fianna's rise and fall. Its disintegration begins when Diarmaid elopes with Gráinne (Grace), a king's daughter whom Finn, as an old man, wishes to marry. Later, when Diarmaid is wounded, Finn lets him die for lack of water. The king and people finally turn against the overbearing Fianna, a conflict that culminates in the Battle of Gabhra, in which the Fianna is destroyed. Related to the Fenian sagas is a series of tales concerning Cormac mac Airt, his grandfather Conn of the Hundred Battles, and his son Cairbré of the Liffey.

Fenoglio \fā-'nōl-yō\, Beppe (b. March 1, 1922, Alba, Italy—d. Feb. 18, 1963, Turin) Italian novelist who wrote of the struggle against fascism and Nazism during World War II.

Fenoglio spent most of his life in Alba. His studies at the University of Turin were cut short by service in the army. After World War II he became a wine merchant.

Fenoglio's first book, *I ventitré giorni della città di Alba* (1952; "The 23 Days of the City of Alba"), includes 12 short stories about the partisans of his native town. His first novel, *La Malora* (1954; *Ruin*), shows the difficult and harsh lives of peasants near Alba. The last of Fenoglio's works to be published in his lifetime was *Primavera di bellezza* (1959; "Spring of Beauty"), which he said he originally wrote in English, then translated into Italian.

Among his posthumously published works are translations of Samuel Taylor Coleridge's "Rime of the Ancient Mariner" and Emily Brontë's *Wuthering Heights* and his best-known book, the novel *Il partigiano Johnny* (1968; "Johnny the Partisan").

Fenrir \'fen-rər\ Monstrous wolf of Norse mythology. He was the son of the trickster god Loki and a giantess, Angerboda.

Fearing Fenrir's strength and knowing that only evil could be expected of him, the Æsir bound him with a magical chain made of the sound of a cat's footsteps, the beard of a woman, the breath of fish, and the spittle of a bird. When the chain was placed on him, Fenrir bit off the hand of the god Tyr. He was then gagged with a sword and was destined to lie bound to a rock until the Ragnarök ("Doom of the Gods"), when he will break his bonds and fall upon the gods. According to one version of the myth, Fenrir will devour the sun, and in the Ragnarök he will fight against Odin and swallow him. Odin's son Vidar will avenge his father, stabbing the wolf to the heart according to one account and tearing his jaws asunder according to another. Fenrir figures prominently in Norwegian and Icelandic poetry of the 10th and 11th centuries.

Fenton \'fent-ən\, Elijah (b. May 20, 1683, Shelton, Staffordshire, Eng.—d. July 16, 1730, Easthampstead, Berkshire) English poet perhaps best known for his collaboration in a translation of the Greek epic poem *Odyssey* with Alexander Pope and William Broome.

After graduating from Cambridge, Fenton became a teacher and later served as a children's tutor to various noble families. His *Poems on Several Occasions* (1717) was admired by Pope, who asked Fenton if he would assist in a translation of the *Odyssey*. Fenton translated books 1, 4, 19, and 20. He also wrote the *Life of John Milton* (1725), edited the poems of Edmund Waller (1729), and wrote *Mariamne* (1723), a tragedy.

Feraoun \fer-â-'ün\, Mouloud (b. 1913, Tizi-Hibel, Alg.—d. 1962, El-Biar) Kabyle novelist and teacher whose works give vivid and warm portraits of Berber life and values.

The son of a peasant farmer, Feraoun passed his youth in the Kabylie mountains. His early successes at school led to a teaching degree from the École Normale at Algiers. His support of Algerian independence resulted in his assassination by terrorists.

Feraoun's works all describe Kabyle peasant life. *Le Fils du pauvre* (1950; "The Poor Man's Son") is a semiautobiographical story of a Berber youth struggling against poverty and hardship to achieve an education and self-advancement. *La Terre et le sang* (1953; "Earth and Blood") deals with an émigré whose life in France is burdened by the segregation of his proud countrymen and with the importance of *nif* ("honor"), the basis of traditional Berber morality and the source of the sense of self-worth, dignity, pride, and community. *Les Chemins qui montent* (1957; "The Upward Roads") carries forward in more bitter tones the themes of the resignation, resistance, and endurance of the fellah (peasant) faced with the realities of colonial society. Feraoun's devotion to his culture is also evident in a collection of portraits and sketches in a translation of 19th-century Kabyle poetry and in his journal.

Ferber \'fər-bər\, Edna (b. Aug. 15, 1887, Kalamazoo, Mich., U.S.—d. April 16, 1968, New York, N.Y.)   American novelist and short-story writer who wrote with compassion and curiosity of the middle-class Midwestern American experience.

Ferber began her career at 17 as a reporter in Wisconsin. Her early stories introduced a traveling petticoat saleswoman named Emma McChesney, whose adventures are collected in several books, including *Emma McChesney & Co.* (1915). Although her books are somewhat superficial in their careful attention to exterior detail at the expense of profound ideas, they do offer an accurate, lively portrait of America in the 1920s and '30s. After SO BIG (1924), for which she won a Pulitzer Prize, and SHOW BOAT (1926), which became a popular play, critics hailed her as the greatest woman novelist of the period. Her autobiography, *A Peculiar Treasure* (1939), evinces her genuine and encompassing love for the United States. Her later works include the novel GIANT (1952).

Ferdowsī \fər-'daù-sē\, *also spelled* Firdawsī, Firdusi \-'dü-\, *or* Firdousi, *pseudonym of* Abū ol-Qasem Manṣūr \män-'sūr\ (b. *c.* 935, near Ṭūs, Persia [Iran]—d. *c.* 1020/26, Ṭūs)   Persian poet, author of the Persian national epic entitled the SHĀH-NĀMEH ("Book of Kings"), which he gave final and enduring form.

Many legends have been woven around Ferdowsī's name, but very little is known about his life. The only reliable source is Neẓāmī-ye ʿArūẓī, a 12th-century poet who in 1116 or 1117 collected the traditional stories that were current in his birthplace less than a century after his death. According to ʿArūẓī, Ferdowsī was a *dehqān* ("landowner"). He had only one child, a daughter, and to provide her with a dowry he set his hand to the task that was to occupy him for 35 years. The *Shāh-nāmeh* of Ferdowsī was finally completed in 1010 and was presented to the celebrated sultan Maḥmūd of Ghazna, who by that time had made himself master of Khūrāsān, Ferdowsī's homeland. According to ʿArūẓī, Ferdowsī went to Ghazna in person and was able to secure the sultan's acceptance of the poem. Unfortunately, Ferdowsī received only a pittance and showed his bitter disappointment. Fearing the sultan's wrath, he fled and found refuge at the court of the Sepahbād Shahreyār. There Ferdowsī composed a satire of 100 verses on Sultan Maḥmūd that he inserted in the preface of the *Shāh-nāmeh* before offering to rededicate the poem to Shahreyār. Shahreyār, however, persuaded him to leave the dedication to Maḥmūd, bought the satire from him for 1,000 dirhams a verse, and had it expunged from the poem. The whole text of the satire, bearing every mark of authenticity, has survived to the present.

According to the narrative of ʿArūẓī, Ferdowsī died inopportunely just as Sultan Maḥmūd had determined to make amends for his shabby treatment of the poet by sending him 60,000 dinars' worth of indigo.

Fergusson \'fər-gə-sən\, Robert (b. Sept 5, 1750, Edinburgh, Scot.—d. Oct. 16, 1774, Edinburgh)   Scottish poet who was one of the leading figures of the 18th-century revival of Scots vernacular writing and the chief forerunner of Robert Burns.

Fergusson was educated at St. Andrews University and became a copying clerk in a lawyer's office in Edinburgh. In 1771 he began to contribute poems to Ruddiman's *Weekly Magazine*. From 1773 his good spirits gave way to fits of depression and religious guilt, and after being severely injured in the head by a fall he became insane. He died in the Edinburgh asylum at the age of 24.

Fergusson wrote in both Scots and English, but the English verse has little value. His Scots poems—racy, realistic, wittily descriptive, and humorous—had a stimulating effect on Burns, whose "The Holy Fair" and "The Cotter's Saturday Night" stem from Fergusson's "Leith Races" and "The Farmer's Ingle." Fergusson's vigorous poems like "The Daft Days," "Address to the Tron Kirk Bell," and the famous "Auld Reekie" stand in their own right.

Ferlinghetti \ˌfer-liŋ-'get-ē\, Lawrence (b. March 24, 1920, Yonkers, N.Y., U.S.)   American poet, one of the founders of the BEAT MOVEMENT in San Francisco in the mid-1950s. His City Lights bookstore was an early gathering place of the Beats, and the publishing arm of City Lights was the first to print the Beats' books of poetry.

Ferlinghetti was reared by a female relative in France and later on a Long Island, N.Y., estate on which she was employed as a governess. He was a U.S. naval officer during World War II, and he attended the University of North Carolina, Columbia University, and the Sorbonne.

Ferlinghetti composed his poetry mainly to be read aloud. It was popular in coffeehouses and on college campuses, where it struck a responsive chord in disaffected youth. *Pictures of the Gone World* (1955) and *A Coney Island of the Mind* (1958), with its notable verse "Autobiography," were highly popular, as was the long poem *Tentative Description of a Dinner Given to Promote the Impeachment of President Eisenhower* (1958). His later poems continued to be politically oriented, as indicated by such titles as *One Thousand Fearful Words for Fidel Castro* (1961), *Where Is Vietnam?* (1965), *Tyrannus Nix?* (1969), and *Who Are We Now?* (1976). Selected poems were printed in *Endless Love* (1981).

Fernández \fer-'nän-däth\, Lucas (b. 1474?, Salamanca, Castile [Spain]—d. 1542)   Spanish dramatist and musician whose plays are notable for their effective dialogue, simple humor, and skillful use of interpolated songs and music.

Fernández was educated at Salamanca and was professor of music there from 1522 until his death. His six plays show clearly the influence of his rival Juan del Encina. His most impressive work is the *Auto de la Pasión*, an Easter play. His *Diálogo para cantar* (1514; "Dialogue for Singing") is the first example of a rudimentary zarzuela.

Fernández de Avellaneda \fer-'nän-däs-ṯhä-ˌäb-äl-yä-'nä-ṯhä\, Alonso.   Probably the pseudonym of the otherwise unknown author of *Segundo tomo del ingenioso hidalgo Don Quijote de la Mancha* (1614; "Second Book of the Ingenious Knight Don Quixote of La Mancha"), a fraudulent sequel to the first volume of Miguel de Cervantes' *Don Quixote* (1605). Suggestions of the author's identity include Fray Luis de Aliaga (confessor of Philip III), Lope de Vega, and even Cervantes himself.

Fernández de Lizardi \fer-'nän-däs-ṯhä-lē-'sär-ṯhē\, José Joaquín (b. Nov. 15, 1776, Mexico City [Mexico]—d. June 21, 1827)   Mexican editor, pamphleteer, and novelist, and a leading literary figure in Mexico's national liberation movement.

Largely self-taught, Fernández de Lizardi wrote as "the Mexican thinker," taking this pseudonym from the title of his radical journal, *El pensador mexicano* (1812). His *El periquillo sarniento* (1816; *The Itching Parrot*), the first picaresque novel of Latin America, is a colorful depiction of Mexican society and reflects the ideas of the French Enlightenment and of Jean-Jacques Rousseau on education. He also wrote *La Quijotita y su prima* (1819; "Miss Quixote and Her Cousin") and *Las noches tristes y días alegres* (1823; "Sad Nights and Happy Days").

Fernández de Moratín \fer-'nän-däs-ṯhä-ˌmō-rä-'tēn\, Leandro (b. March 10, 1760, Madrid, Spain—d. July 21, 1828, Paris, Fr.)   Dramatist and poet, the most influential Neoclassic literary figure of the Spanish Enlightenment.

Fernández de Moratín was an apologist of the French Encyclopédistes, a translator of Molière and William Shakespeare,
and a satirist of contemporary society. The two predominant
themes of his plays are dramatic criticism, as seen in *La comedia nueva* (1792; "The New Comedy"), in which he satirizes the
absurd characters and plots of contemporary plays, and attacks
on excessive parental authority and marriages of convenience,
as seen in *El sí de las niñas* (1806; *The Maiden's Consent*). Because of political and ecclesiastical opposition to his French
sympathies, he spent most of his life after 1814 in France.

Fernández Retamar \fer-'nän-däs-rä-'tä-mär\, Roberto (b.
June 9, 1930, Havana, Cuba)   Cuban poet, essayist, and literary critic and cultural spokesman for the Castro revolution.

After first studying art and architecture, Fernández Retamar
studied literature in Havana, Paris, and London and then taught
at the University of Havana from 1955. He also taught briefly
at Yale University (from 1957 to 1958) and lectured at several American universities. For almost three decades he edited
the magazine *Casa de las Américas*. Fernández Retamar became
one of the most eloquent spokesmen of the Castro revolution.

His commitment to the revolution is reflected in his poetry,
though *Poesía reunida* (1966; "Poetry Reunited"), a collection
of his poetry written from 1948 to 1965, and *A quien pueda in-
teresar (poesía 1958–1970)* (1970; "To Whom It May Concern")
maintain a balance between ideology and artistic expression.
Other volumes of poetry include *Buena suerte viviendo* (1967;
"Good Luck in Living"), *Qué veremos arder* (1970; "What We
Will See Burning"), *Cuaderno paralelo* (1973; "Parallel Frame"),
Revolución nuestra, amor nuestro (1976; "Our Revolution, Our
Love"), *Palabra de mi pueblo* (1980; "Words on My People"),
and *Poeta en La Habana* (1982; "Poet in Havana").

Fernández Retamar's greatest impact was as an essayist. *En-
sayo de otro mundo* (1967; "Examination of Another World")
redefines Modernismo. His best-known work is a study of
culture in Latin America, *Calibán* (1971; *Caliban and Other
Essays*). He also wrote such works of criticism as *La poesía
contemporánea en Cuba (1927–1953)* (1954) and *Para una teoría
de la literatura hispanoamericana y otras aproximaciones* (1975).

Fern Hill   Poem by Dylan THOMAS that evokes the joy and
the inevitable loss of the world of childhood. It was first published in 1946 in his collection *Deaths and Entrances*.

"Fern Hill" is narrated by the mature poet, who reflects systematically on the delights of childhood and its symbiotic relationship with the natural world, on the adolescent's nascent
sexuality, and, ultimately, on the loss of childhood innocence
and the realization of mortality.

Ferrars, Edward \'ed-wərd-'fer-ərz\   Fictional character, the
suitor of Elinor Dashwood in Jane Austen's novel SENSE AND
SENSIBILITY.

Ferreira \fer-'rā-rə\, António (b. 1528, Lisbon, Port.—d.
1569, Lisbon)   Portuguese poet who was influential in fostering the new Renaissance style of poetry and who strongly
advocated the use of Portuguese, rather than Spanish or Latin,
as the literary language.

Ferreira was a disciple of the poet Francisco de Sá de Miranda, who had introduced Renaissance styles of poetry into
Portugal. His verse epistles, inspired by the moral and aesthetic
tenets of humanism, reveal his integrity as a critic of society as
well as his clear and vigorous style. His tragedy *Castro* (written
c. 1558), one of the first in modern European literature, deals
with the Portuguese national heroine Inês de Castro.

Ferreira \fer-'rā-rə\, Manuel (b. 1917, Gândara dos Oli-
vais, Leiria, Port.—d. March 17, 1992, Linda-a-Velha)   Portuguese-born scholar and fiction writer whose work centered

on African themes. He was an authority on Lusophone (Portuguese-language) African literature.

After his graduation from the Technical University of Lisbon, Ferreira went to Cape Verde (1941–47) and later to Angola on military duty. There he developed a deep appreciation
of African cultures. His study of Cape Verdean culture and
literature, *A aventura crioula* (1967; "The Creole Adventure"),
was the most thorough work to date on the subject. His three-
volume anthology of Portuguese-language African poetry, *No
reino de Caliban* (1975–81; "On the Kingdom of Caliban"),
contains a wealth of biographical and historical information.
He also compiled a two-volume history of African literatures
written in Portuguese, *Literaturas africanas de expressão portuguesa* (1977). A professor of African literature at the University of Lisbon, Ferreira in 1978 founded the Lisbon-based
quarterly *África*. Among his short stories and novels on Cape
Verdean themes was *Morabeza: Contos de Cabo Verde* (1957).

Ferreira \fer-'rā-rə\, Vergílio *or* Virgilio (b. Jan. 28, 1916,
Melo, Port.)   Portuguese teacher and novelist who turned
from an early social realism to more experimental and inward-
looking forms of the novel.

Ferreira's literary career began during World War II, and
his early novels were written in the prevailing social-realist (or
Neorealist) style. Works published during this phase of his career are *Onde tudo foi morrendo* (1944; "Where All Was Dying")
and *Vagão J* (1946; "Car J"). Beginning with *Mudança* (1949;
"Change"), however, Ferreira moved toward an increasingly introspective and existential focus.

In his later psychological novels, Ferreira probed the recesses
of the human condition in a search for meaning and the means
of self-discovery. Of the novels of this period *Aparição* (1959;
"Apparition") is the best known. Others include *Manhã subm-
ersa* (1954; "Submerged Morning"), *Cântico final* (1959; "Final
Song"), *Estrela polar* (1962; "Polar Star"), and *Alegria breve*
(1965; "Brief Joy").

Ferreira de Castro \fer-'rā-rə-dē-'käsh-trō\, José Maria (b.
May 24, 1898, Salgueiros, Port.—d. June 29, 1974, Porto)
Journalist and novelist considered to be one of the fathers of
contemporary Portuguese social-realist (or Neorealist) fiction.

Ferreira de Castro drew widely on his nine years' residence
in the Amazon jungles of Brazil (1911–19) to vividly depict the
Portuguese emigrant experience and the relationships among
rubber workers of various regions and social classes. Two novels—*Emigrantes* (1928; "Emigrants") and *A selva* (1930; "The
Jungle")—launched Ferreira de Castro's literary career. In later
novels the author turned his attention to regional Portuguese
themes from rural areas; typical of this period are *Terra fria*
(1934; "Cold Land"), *A lã e a neve* (1947; "The Wool and
the Snow"), and *A curva da estrada* (1950; "The Curve in the
Road").

Ferreira de Castro had a long and active career in journalism,
and he considered his fiction writing to be an extension of documentary reporting.

Ferrier \'fer-ē-ər\, Susan Edmonstone (b. Sept. 7, 1782, Edinburgh, Scot.—d. Nov. 5, 1854, Edinburgh)   Novelist who
described the pretensions of Scottish society in the early 19th
century.

The daughter of James Ferrier, principal clerk of the Court of
Session and a colleague of Sir Walter Scott, she was acquainted
with Edinburgh intellectual circles. Scott greatly admired her
writing and in his *Tales of My Landlord* (1816–19) called her his
sister shadow. Ferrier's three anonymously published novels—
Marriage (1818); *The Inheritance* (1824), often considered her
best work; and *Destiny; or, The Chief's Daughter* (1831)—are
distinguished by their vigor and sardonic wit.

Fescennine verse \'fes-ə-ˌnīn, -nin\, *Latin* Fescennini versus, *also called* carmina Fescennina.   Early native Italic jocular dialogue in Latin verse. At vintage and harvest, and probably at other rustic festivals, they were sung by masked dancers. They were similar to the often ribald wedding songs called epithalamia. (*Compare* EPITHALAMIUM.) It is clear from the literary imitations by Catullus (*c.* 84–*c.* 54 BC) that Fescennine verses were very free, even obscene, in language.

It was believed that the verses averted the evil eye; hence, some early authors connected the name with *fascinum* ("charm, bewitchment"). The true derivation may be from Fescennia, an Etruscan city. Whether they developed into the dramatic *satura* (medley, or hodgepodge) that was the forerunner of Roman drama has been debated by modern scholars.

Festschrift \'fest-ˌshrift\ *plural* Festschriften \-ˌshrif-tən\ *or* Festschrifts [German, from *Fest* festival + *Schrift* writings]   A usually miscellaneous volume of writings by different authors presented as a tribute or memorial; especially, a volume of learned essays contributed by students, colleagues, and admirers to honor a scholar on a special anniversary.

Festus \'fes-təs\, Sextus Pompeius (fl. 2nd or 3rd century AD, Narbo, Gaul [now Narbonne, Fr.])   Latin grammarian who made an abridgment in 20 books of Marcus Verrius Flaccus' *De significatu verborum* ("On the Meaning of Words"), a work that is otherwise lost. It also preserves by quotation the work of other authors that has not survived elsewhere. The first half of Festus' work, too, is lost, but a further abridgment of it by Paul the Deacon in the 8th century survives. In his abridgment Festus made a few insertions of his own and removed obsolete Latin words with the intention of publishing them in a separate work, but it is doubtful whether this was ever written. The remains of his abridgment exist in only one manuscript, the Codex Festi Farnesianus, at Naples. The glosses on it of Josephus Justus Scaliger (1565) were one of the first examples of modern classical scholarship.

Fet *or* **Foeth** \'fʲet\, Afanasy Afanasyevich, *legitimized surname* Shenshin \shən-'shēn\ (b. Nov. 23 [Dec. 5, New Style], 1820, Novosyolki, near Mtsensk, Russia—d. Nov. 21 [Dec. 3], 1892, Moscow)   Russian poet and translator whose sincere and passionate lyric poetry strongly influenced later Russian poets, particularly the Symbolist Aleksandr Blok.

Fet was still a student at the University of Moscow when, in 1842, he published several admirable lyrics in the literary magazine *Moskvityanin.* In 1850 a volume of his poems appeared, followed by another in 1856. He served several years in the army, retiring in 1856.

His intense and brief lyrics, which aimed to convey vivid momentary sensations, were taken up by the later Symbolists, but during his lifetime his reactionary political views and somewhat unattractive personality limited his influence. After 1863 he published very little, but he continued to write nature poetry and love lyrics (published posthumously in a four-volume collected edition, 1894). His works also include translations of Ovid, Virgil, J.W. von Goethe's *Faust,* and Arthur Schopenhauer's *The World as Will and Idea.*

Feuchtwanger \'foikt-ˌväŋ-ər\, Lion (b. July 7, 1884, Munich, Ger.—d. Dec. 21, 1958, Los Angeles, Calif., U.S.)   German novelist and playwright known for his historical romances.

Born of a Jewish family, Feuchtwanger studied philology and literature at Berlin and Munich (1903–07) and took his doctorate in 1918. In 1918 he founded a literary paper, *Der Spiegel.* His first historical novel was *Die hässliche Herzogin* (1923; *The Ugly Duchess*), about Margarete Maultasch, duchess of Tirol. His finest novel, *Jud Süss* (1925; U.K. title, *Jew Süss*; U.S. title, *Power*), set in 18th-century Germany, was the first of his

works to reveal his deep psychological understanding. This gift for psychological analysis remained characteristic of his subsequent work—the *Josephus-Trilogie* (*Der jüdische Krieg* [1932; "The Jewish War"], *Die Söhne* [1935; "The Sons"], *Der Tag wird kommen* [1945; "The Day Will Come"]), *Die Geschwister Oppenheim* (1933; *The Oppermanns*), a novel of modern life, and *Der falsche Nero* (1936; *The Pretender*).

Feuchtwanger was exiled in 1933 and moved to France, from which he escaped to the United States in 1940 after some months in a concentration camp, described in *The Devil in France* (1941). Of his later works the best known are *Proud Destiny* (1947), *Goya oder der arge Weg der Erkenntnis* (1951; *This Is the Hour*), and *Jepta und seine Tochter* (1957; *Jephthah and His Daughter*).

feuilleton \fœy-'tōⁿ, *Angl* ˌfə-yə-'tōn, ˌfər-\ [French, literally, lower part of a newspaper page reserved for feature articles, third of a paper sheet printed in duodecimo format, a diminutive of *feuillet* leaf, folio sheet]   **1.** A part of a European newspaper or magazine devoted to material designed to entertain the general reader. It is presented as a supplement or a feature section.   **2.** A piece of writing (such as an installment of a serialized novel) printed in a feuilleton.   **3.** A novel printed in installments, also called a *serial.*   **4.** A work of fiction that caters to popular taste.   **5.** A short literary composition often having a familiar tone and reminiscent content, also called a *sketch.*

Feverel, Richard \'rich-ərd-'fev-ər-əl\   Fictional character, the protagonist of the novel THE ORDEAL OF RICHARD FEVEREL by George Meredith.

Feydeau \fā-'dō\, Georges(-Léon-Jules-Marie) (b. Dec. 8, 1862, Paris, Fr.—d. June 5, 1921, Paris)   French dramatist whose farces delighted Parisian audiences in the years before World War I and are still regularly performed.

Feydeau was an able actor and director and wrote 39 plays between 1881 and 1916. Working in the tradition of the comic dramatist Eugène-Marin Labiche, he took the farce to new heights on the French stage. Though not a serious social critic, he made satirical capital out of every new fashion.

Feydeau's farces are masterpieces of improbable contrivance, usually dependent on far-fetched cases of mistaken identity. His favorite theme is the anxious and comic efforts of an unfaithful spouse to conceal amorous escapades, and his favorite comic device is the meeting of characters who are assiduously trying to avoid each other. Among his plays are *La Dame de chez Maxim* (1899; *The Girl from Maxim's*), *La Puce à l'oreille* (1907; *A Flea in Her Ear*), and *Occupe-toi d'Amélie!* (1908; *Keep an Eye on Amélie!*). Feydeau's farces have maintained their place in the repertory of the Comédie-Française in Paris.

Fezziwig \'fez-i-wig\   Fictional character, the generous employer of the young Ebenezer Scrooge in A CHRISTMAS CAROL by Charles Dickens. Fezziwig appears during Scrooge's encounter with the Ghost of Christmas Past, when Scrooge and the ghost visit Fezziwig's workplace, where Scrooge was an apprentice, on Christmas Eve.

Fialho de Almeida \'fyäl-yu-de-äl-'ma-də\, José Valentim (b. May 7, 1857, Vila de Frades, Alentejo, Port.—d. March 4, 1911, Vila de Frades)   Portuguese short-story writer and political essayist noted for the dramatic, poetic, and fantastic elements in his storytelling.

While in medical school in Lisbon, Fialho supported himself with his writing. He published *Contos* ("Poems") in 1881 and a book of stories a year later, but he was unable to find a patron. This circumstance may have prompted him to write his serial story collection *Os gatos* (1889–93; "The Cats"). The collection attacks the monarchy and satirizes Lisbon life and the customs of the period. He tired of his attempts to achieve independence and in 1893 married a wealthy woman who soon left him a wealthy widower.

In *O país das uvas* (1893; "Vineyard Country") and other short-story collections, he offers lively, earthy descriptions of rural Portuguese life, which he contrasts favorably with the decadence of the cities. Other collections are *Pasquinadas* (1890; "Lampoons"), *Vida irônica* (1892; "Ironic Life"), and *Lisboa galante* (1890; "Courtly Lisbon").

fiction \'fik-shən\ **1.** Literature created from the imagination, not presented as fact, though it may be based on a true story or situation. **2.** A work of fiction; especially a NOVEL, SHORT STORY, or NOVELLA.

fictionalize \'fik-shə-nə-,līz\ or **fictionize** \'fik-shə-,nīz\ To make into or treat in the manner of fiction.

fictioneer \,fik-shə-'nir\ One who writes fiction, especially in quantity.

Fiedler \'fēd-lər\, Leslie A., *in full* Aaron (b. March 8, 1917, Newark, N.J., U.S.) American literary critic who applied psychological (chiefly Freudian) and social theories to American literature.

Fiedler attended the University of Wisconsin (M.A., 1939; Ph.D., 1941), and, after service in the U.S. Naval Reserve from 1942 to 1946, he did further research at Harvard University. Thereafter he taught at many universities, chiefly at the State University of New York at Buffalo.

Fiedler propounded many ingenious but controversial theories. He gained considerable notoriety with his essay "Come Back to the Raft Ag'in, Huck Honey!" later republished in *An End to Innocence* (1955). His major work, *Love and Death in the American Novel* (1960), argued that much of American literature embodies themes of innocent (presexual), but often homoerotic, male bonding and escape from a domestic, female-dominated society. This idea is further explored in *Waiting for the End* (1964) and *The Return of the Vanishing American* (1968). His later critical works include *The Inadvertent Epic: From Uncle Tom's Cabin to Roots* (1979) and *Fiedler on the Roof: Essays on Literature and Jewish Identity* (1990), as well as the books *The Stranger in Shakespeare* (1972) and *What Was Literature?: Class, Culture, and Mass Society* (1982).

Field \'fēld\, Eugene (b. Sept. 2, 1850, St. Louis, Mo., U.S.—d. Nov. 4, 1895, Chicago, Ill.) American poet and journalist, best known, to his disgust, as the "poet of childhood."

Field worked for a variety of newspapers, including the *Denver Tribune*. Comic paragraphs from his *Tribune* column, "Odds and Ends," formed his first book, *The Tribune Primer* (1882), journalistic joking in the tradition of Artemus Ward and Josh Billings. These squibs served as apprentice work for his "Sharps and Flats" column in the *Chicago Morning News* (renamed the *Record* in 1890). Here Field satirized the cultural pretensions of Chicago's newly rich. *A Little Book of Western Verse* (1889), drawn in part from his column, included poems in rural dialect, verses for children in an affected Old English dialect, translations of Horace, and the well-known "Little Boy Blue" and "Dutch Lullaby" ("Wynken, Blynken, and Nod"). Field's collected works in 10 volumes were published the year after his death, and two more volumes were added in 1900.

Field \'fēld\, Nathan or Nat, *byname of* Nathaniel Field (baptized Oct. 17, 1587, London, Eng.—d. June/August 1619?) One of the principal actors of England's Elizabethan stage.

About 1600 Field became a member of the Children of the Queen's Revels, remaining with this theater company throughout its various changes of name and composition until 1616–17, when he joined the King's Men. His name appears on the list of actors given in the First Folio (1623) of Shakespeare's plays. Field also wrote two comedies, *A Woman Is a Weathercock* (1612) and *Amends for Ladies* (1618), and he collaborated with Francis Beaumont and John Fletcher and with Philip Massinger on other plays.

Fielding \'fēl-diŋ\, Henry (b. April 22, 1707, Sharpham Park, Somerset, Eng.—d. Oct. 8, 1754, Lisbon, Port.) Novelist and playwright, one of the founders of the English novel.

Leaving Eton College at age 17, Fielding lost his family's financial support and turned to the theater. In all, he wrote some 25 plays. His *Historical Register, For the Year 1736* (1737), which ridiculed the prime minister, effectively ended his career as a playwright. To restore his fortunes, Fielding began to read for the bar. Meanwhile he was editing, and very largely writing, a thrice-weekly newspaper, the *Champion; or, British Mercury*, which ran from November 1739 to June 1741.

In 1740 Samuel Richardson had published his highly successful epistolary novel *Pamela*. In April 1741 a parody known as SHAMELA was published pseudonymously; it ruthlessly satirizes Richardson's sentimentality and prudish morality. Though Fielding never claimed it, *Shamela* was generally accepted in his lifetime as his work. Like *Shamela*, JOSEPH ANDREWS (1742) parodies Richardson's novel, but at the same time it is entertaining and original in its own right.

In 1743 Fielding published three volumes of *Miscellanies*, works old and new. Of these, by far the most important is *The Life of Mr. Jonathan Wild the Great*, in which Fielding satirizes the human penchant for mistaking power for greatness.

In 1745 Fielding published an anti-Jacobite pamphlet, and he was rewarded for his loyalty in 1748, when he was appointed justice of the peace (or magistrate) for Westminster and Middlesex, with his own courthouse. Together with his half brother Sir John Fielding, who succeeded him, he established a new tradition of justice and suppression of crime in London.

Fielding published TOM JONES in 1749. With its great comic gusto, vast gallery of characters, and contrasted scenes of high and low life, it has always been the most popular of his works. Two years later *Amelia*, a much more somber work, was published. The study of a relationship between a man and his wife and a celebration of womanly virtues, it anticipates the Victorian domestic novel.

Fields, The Novel by Conrad Richter, published in 1946. It was the second novel in a trilogy published collectively as *The Awakening Land*. The other novels in the trilogy are *The Trees* and THE TOWN.

Fiennes \'fīnz\, Celia (b. June 7, 1662, Newton Toney, Wiltshire, Eng.—d. April 10, 1741, Hackney, London) English travel writer whose journals are an invaluable source for social and economic historians.

Fiennes made an extended trip through northern England in 1697, traveling more than 600 miles (1,000 km) in six weeks. This trip was followed by others that eventually took her to every county in England. Her journeys extended over the period from about 1685 to about 1712.

Fiennes was an indefatigable and meticulous observer who paid special attention to urban life, industry, and the growing material prosperity of her country. Her journals were written in 1702 from notes she had made during her travels. These provide the first comprehensive eyewitness account of England written since Elizabethan times.

The Illustrated Journeys of Celia Fiennes, 1685–c. 1712 was published in 1982.

Fifth Business First of a series of novels known collectively as THE DEPTFORD TRILOGY by Robertson Davies.

Figaro \'fig-ə-ˌrō, 'feg-\ Comic character, a barber turned valet who is the hero of three plays of Pierre-Augustin Beaumarchais. The two most popular of these are THE BARBER OF SEVILLE and THE MARRIAGE OF FIGARO; both were adapted for the opera, the former by Giovanni Paisiello in 1782 and by Gioacchino Rossini in 1816 and the latter by W.A. Mozart in 1786.

Figes \'fī-jez\, Eva, *original surname* Unger \'ən-gər\ (b. April 15, 1932, Berlin, Ger.) English novelist, social critic, and translator who reacted against traditional realist literature by inventing new forms for her own works.

Figes' poetic novels explore the inner lives of her characters, often through a stream-of-consciousness technique. *Equinox* (1966) examines the breakup of a marriage and the protagonist's subsequent struggle to rebuild her world. *Winter Journey* (1967) relates a day in the life of an isolated old man. Each of the seven chapters of *Waking* (1981) begins with a woman awaking at a different stage in her life, from idyllic childhood to approaching death. Her later novels include *Light* (1983), *The Seven Ages* (1986), *Ghosts* (1988), *The Tree of Knowledge* (1990), and *The Tenancy* (1993).

In addition to fiction, Figes wrote several books of criticism, including *Patriarchal Attitudes: Women in Society* (1970) and *Sex and Subterfuge: Women Novelists to 1850* (1982), and an autobiography, *Little Eden* (1978).

Figulus \'fig-yə-ləs\, Publius Nigidius (fl. not later than 98–45 BC) Roman savant and writer, next to Marcus Terentius Varro the most learned Roman of his age.

Figulus sought to revive Pythagorean doctrines of mathematics, astronomy, and astrology, and even the magic arts. Suetonius and Lucius Apuleius tell of Figulus' supernatural powers. Saint Jerome calls him *Pythagoricus et magus* ("Pythagorean and Magician"). Figulus wrote the earliest comprehensive work on Roman religion, *De diis* ("Concerning the Gods"). His other works include *Commentarii grammatici*, in at least 29 books, a loose collection of notes concerned with, among other matters, synonyms, inflection, orthography, word formation, syntax, and etymology; *De extis* ("Concerning Sacrificial Meats"); *Augurium privatum*, a work on augury; *De ventis* ("Concerning Winds"), in at least four books; and a rhetorical treatise, *De gestu* ("Concerning Gesture"). His writings survive only in fragments quoted by other authors, especially Aulus Gellius.

figurative \'fig-yər-ə-tiv, 'fig-ər-\ Of language or writing, characterized by figures of speech (such as metaphor and simile) or elaborate expression, as opposed to literal language.

figure of speech A form of expression used to convey meaning or heighten effect, often by comparing or identifying one thing with another that has a meaning or connotation familiar to the reader or listener. An integral part of language, figures of speech are found in oral literatures, as well as in polished poetry and prose and in everyday speech. Greeting-card rhymes, advertising slogans, newspaper headlines, the captions of cartoons, and the mottos of families and institutions often use figures of speech, generally for humorous, mnemonic, or eye-catching purposes. The argots of sports, jazz, business, politics, or any specialized groups abound in figurative language.

In European languages figures of speech are generally classified in five major categories: (1) figures of resemblance or relationship (*e.g.*, simile, metaphor, kenning, conceit, parallelism, personification, metonymy, synecdoche, and euphemism); (2) figures of emphasis or understatement (*e.g.*, hyperbole, litotes, rhetorical question, antithesis, climax, bathos, paradox, oxymoron, and irony); (3) figures of sound (*e.g.*, alliteration, repetition, anaphora, and onomatopoeia); (4) verbal games and gymnastics (*e.g.*, pun and anagram); and (5) errors (*e.g.*,

malapropism, periphrasis, and spoonerism). Figures involving a change in sense, such as metaphor, simile, and irony, are called tropes.

fili \'fē-lē, *Modern Irish* 'fē-lə\ *plural* filid \'fē-'lē, *Old Irish* 'fē-ləth\ [Old Irish, seer, diviner, poet] A professional poet in ancient Ireland whose official duties were to know and preserve the tales and genealogies and to compose poems recalling the past and present glory of the ruling class. The filid constituted a large aristocratic class, and they were severely censured for their extravagant demands as early as 575. Their power was not checked, however, since they could enforce their demands by the feared lampoon (*áer*), or poet's curse, which not only could take away a person's reputation but, according to a widely held belief, could cause physical damage or even death. After the Christianization of Ireland in the 5th century, filid assumed the poetic function of the outlawed Druids.

Although at first the filid wrote in a verse form similar to the poetry of Germanic languages (two half-lines linked by alliteration), they later developed intricate rules of prosody and rigid and complicated verse forms. By the 12th century filid were composing lyrical nature poetry and personal poems, and they no longer strictly adhered to set rules of prosody. *See also* BARD.

Financier, The Novel by Theodore DREISER, published in 1912, the first book of an epic trilogy that Dreiser intended to call the Trilogy of Desire, based on the life of Charles T. Yerkes, an American transportation magnate. The other two volumes were *The Titan* (1914) and *The Stoic*, which was completed by Dreiser's wife after his death and published posthumously in 1947.

The Financier begins the saga of Frank Algernon Cowperwood. Driven, vital, and unscrupulous, he sees himself bound for greatness. The novel describes his career in the brokerage business, his advantageous but ultimately doomed marriage, his deals with corrupt politicians, and his relationship with his mistress, whose father eventually uses political influence to ruin Cowperwood and send him to prison. Out of prison in little more than a year, Cowperwood recoups his fortune during the panic of 1873 and moves to Chicago.

The remaining two novels follow Cowperwood to Chicago and London through a series of shady deals, love affairs, and intrigues until, after his death, his empire collapses and his life is seen to have been meaningless.

Finch, Anne *see* Anne Finch, Countess of WINCHILSEA.

Finch \'finch\, Robert (Duer Claydon) (b. May 14, 1900, Freeport, N.Y., U.S.) A leading Canadian lyric poet whose poetry is characterized by metaphysical wit, complex imagery, and a strong sense of form.

Finch's first collection, *Poems* (1946), won a Governor General's Award, as did *Acis in Oxford* (1961), a series of meditations inspired by a performance of G.F. Handel's dramatic oratorio *Acis and Galatea*. *Dover Beach Revisited* (1961), treating the World War II evacuation of Dunkirk and issues of faith, contains 11 variations on Matthew Arnold's poem. In another collection, *Variations and Theme* (1980), Finch describes in 14 variations the fate of a rare pink water lily. His later works include *Has and Is* (1981), *The Grand Duke of Moscow's Favorite Solo* (1983), and *Sail-boat and Lake* (1988).

Finching, Flora \'flôr-ə-'fin-chiŋ\ Fictional character in the novel LITTLE DORRIT by Charles Dickens. Flora is a widow who was once a sweetheart of Arthur Clennam and still cherishes a passion for him. Now middle-aged, Flora retains a fluttery girlishness; though silly, she is nevertheless kind-hearted and sympathetic.

fin de siècle \faⁿ-də-'syekl, *Angl* ˌfan-də-sē-'ek-əl, -lə\ [French *fin de siècle* end of the century]   Of, relating to, characteristic of, or resembling the late 19th-century literary and artistic climate of sophistication, escapism, extreme aestheticism, world-weariness, and fashionable despair. When used in reference to literature, the term essentially describes the movement inaugurated by the Decadent poets of France and the movement called Aestheticism in England during this period.

Findley \'find-lē\, Timothy (b. Oct. 30, 1930, Toronto, Can.)   Canadian author of novels about people's troubled, often violent, relationships.

At age 17 Findley began a 15-year acting career. He also began writing short stories during the late 1950s. His first two novels, *The Last of the Crazy People* (1967) and *The Butterfly Plague* (1969), are set in southern California.

Findley's two most acclaimed novels were *The Wars* (1977), which features the struggle of a soldier in the midst of World War I as he attempts to save 130 doomed horses, and *Famous Last Words* (1981), narrated by Hugh Selwyn Mauberley, a character created by Ezra Pound. Findley's later novels include *Not Wanted on the Voyage* (1984), *The Telling of Lies* (1986), and *Headhunter* (1993). He also published several radio and television scripts and a number of plays; the short-story collections *Dinner Along the Amazon* (1984), *Stones* (1988), and *Any Time at All* (1993); and *Inside Memory: Pages from a Writer's Workbook* (1990).

Fink \'fiŋk\, Mike (b. 1770/80, Fort Pitt [Pittsburgh], Pa. [U.S.]—d. 1823, Fort Henry? [North Dakota])   Frontiersman and legendary hero of the American tall tale.

As a youth Fink won fame as a marksman and Indian scout around Fort Pitt. Later, when keelboats became the chief vessels of commerce on the Ohio and Mississippi rivers, he became "the king of the keelboatmen," renowned as a marksman, roisterer, and champion rough-and-tumble fighter.

Mythic stories about Mike Fink spread his fame widely between about 1829 and the American Civil War, though thereafter his fame declined. In tall tales, sketches, short stories, romances, plays, and even poems, he was a symbol of the boastfulness, playfulness, physical strength, and violence of frontiersmen.

Finn \'fin\, *in full* Finn (Fionn) MacCumhaill *or* Finn MacCool \mə-'kūl\   Legendary Irish hero, leader of the group of warriors known as the Fianna Éireann. *See* FENIAN CYCLE.

Finn, Huckleberry \'hək-əl-ˌber-ē-'fin\   One of the enduring characters in American fiction, the protagonist of Mark Twain's HUCKLEBERRY FINN (1884) who was introduced in *Tom Sawyer* (1876). Huck Finn is an uneducated, superstitious boy, the son of the town drunkard. Although he sometimes is deceived by tall tales, Huck is a shrewd judge of character. He has a sunny disposition and a well-developed, if naively natural, sense of morality.

Finnegans Wake \'fin-ə-gənz-'wāk\   Experimental novel by James JOYCE. Extracts of the work appeared as *Work in Progress* from 1928 to 1937, and it was published in its entirety as *Finnegans Wake* in 1939.

The book is, in one sense, the story of a publican in Chapelizod (near Dublin), his wife, and their three children; but Mr. Humphrey Chimpden Earwicker, Mrs. Anna Livia Plurabelle, and Kevin, Jerry, and Isabel are every family of mankind. The motive idea of the novel, inspired by the 18th-century Italian philosopher Giambattista Vico, is that history is cyclic; to demonstrate this the book begins with the end of a sentence left unfinished on the last page. Languages merge: Anna Livia has "vlossyhair"—*włosy* being Polish for "hair"; "a bad of

wind" blows—*băd* being Persian for "wind." Characters from literature and history appear and merge and disappear. On another level, the protagonists are the city of Dublin and the River Liffey standing as representatives of the history of Ireland and, by extension, of all human history.

As he had in his earlier work *Ulysses*, Joyce drew upon an encyclopedic range of literary works. His strange polyglot idiom of puns and portmanteau words is intended to convey not only the relationship between the conscious and the unconscious but also the interweaving of Irish language and mythology with the languages and mythologies of many other cultures.

Fionn cycle   *see* FENIAN CYCLE.

Firbank \'fər-ˌbaŋk\, Ronald, *in full* Arthur Annesley Ronald Firbank (b. Jan. 17, 1886, London, Eng.—d. May 21, 1926, Rome, Italy)   English novelist who was a literary innovator.

Firbank's eccentricities, drinking, and witty remarks made him a well-known, even legendary, figure in London intellectual and bohemian life. His most notable novels are *Vainglory* (1915), *Inclinations* (1916), *Caprice* (1917), *Valmouth* (1919), *The Flower Beneath the Foot* (1923), *Sorrow in Sunlight* (1924), and *Concerning the Eccentricities of Cardinal Pirelli* (1926).

Firbank's writing has a fantastic and perverse humor. His wit largely depends upon the shape and cadence of the sentence and upon an eccentric vocabulary. He influenced the later novelists Evelyn Waugh and Ivy Compton-Burnett.

Firdawsī *also spelled* Firdusi *or* Firdousi   *see* FERDOWSĪ.

Fire!!   Magazine that exerted a marked impact on the Harlem Renaissance of the 1920s and early '30s despite its demise after the first issue (November 1926).

The idea for the experimental, apolitical Negro literary journal was conceived in Washington, D.C., by poet Langston Hughes and writer and graphic artist Richard Nugent. The two, along with an editorial board comprising Zora Neale Hurston, Gwendolyn Bennett, John Davis, and Aaron Douglas, selected the brilliant young critic and novelist Wallace Henry Thurman to edit the publication. Thurman solicited art, poetry, fiction, drama, and essays from his editorial advisers, as well as from such leading figures of the New Negro movement as Countee Cullen and Arna Bontemps. Responses to the magazine ranged from minimal notice in the white press to heated contention among African-American critics. *See also* HARLEM RENAISSANCE.

firedrake \'fīr-ˌdrāk\, *also called* firedragon \'fīr-ˌdrag-ən\ [Old English *fȳrdraca*, from *fȳr* fire + *draca* dragon]   A fire-breathing dragon. The firedrake is known especially in Germanic mythology as the guardian of a treasure and in folktales as the abductor or guardian of maidens.

Fire Next Time, The   Nonfiction book, published in 1963, comprising two previously published essays in letter form by James BALDWIN. In these essays Baldwin warned that, if white America did not change its attitudes and policies toward black Americans and alter the conditions under which blacks were forced to live, violence would result.

In the brief first essay, "My Dungeon Shook: Letter to My Nephew on the One Hundredth Anniversary of the Emancipation," the author attacks the idea that blacks are inferior to whites and emphasizes the intrinsic dignity of black people. In the second essay, "Down at the Cross: Letter from a Region in My Mind," Baldwin recounts his coming-of-age in Harlem, appraises the Black Muslim (Nation of Islam) movement, and gives a statement of his personal beliefs.

Firishtah \ˌfē-'resh-tä\, *also called* Muḥammad Qāsim Hindūshāh \'hin-dū-ˌshä\ (b. *c.* 1570—d. *c.* 1620)   One of Muslim India's most famous writers.

Very little is known about Firishtah's life except that he was captain of the guard to Murtazā Niẓām Shāh, Muslim Indian ruler of Ahmadnagar (1565–88). It was during this period that Firishtah conceived his history of Indo-Muslim rulers and saints. Written in Persian after 1589, this history is called *Golshan-e Ebrāhīmī* ("The Garden of Ibrāhīm"; Eng. trans., *Mahomedan Power in India*). It is also known under the title *Tārīkh-e Fereshteh* ("Firishtah's Chronicle"). The second of the two versions in which it was written often appears under still another title, the *Nowras-nāmeh* ("New Book"). The history covers the famous Muslim rulers of India from the 10th century to the time of the author and also contains information concerning the famous Hindu rulers of the time, Hindu history, and a geography of the lands under Hindu control.

In time the work lost its status as an authority for early Indo-Muslim history, but it remains a valuable source. Firishtah is also known for his treatise on pharmacology and therapy techniques, with information on physiology and the humors. It appears under two titles, *Dastūr ol-Aṭebbāʾ* ("Memorandum for Doctors") and *Ekhtīārāt-e Qāsemī* ("Selections by Qāsim").

First Circle, The, Novel by Aleksandr SOLZHENITSYN, originally titled *V kruge pervom*. The original manuscript, reflecting Solzhenitsyn's own imprisonment, was 96 chapters long; hoping to avoid censorship the author deleted nine chapters, but though it was accepted for publication by the literary journal *Novy mir*, it was not published until 1968, and then only in the West. A decade later the complete novel was published in Russian in the United States, and in 1990 it was openly published in Russia.

Referring to the schema of Dante's *Inferno*, the title *The First Circle* reflects the relatively privileged Soviet prison in which the protagonist, Gleb Nerzhin, is incarcerated. This prison is a research laboratory in which prisoners are required to invent despicable gadgets (such as a device that identifies even disguised voices over the telephone) in the service of their captors, Joseph Stalin's secret police. Heroism is criminal in the secret police's perverse hierarchy of values, and cruelty and betrayal are rewarded.

first edition   1. All of the copies of a literary work printed from the first setting of type for that work and issued at the same time.   2. A single copy from a first edition.

First Folio   The first published edition (1623) of the collected works of William SHAKESPEARE, originally published as *Mr. William Shakespeares Comedies, Histories & Tragedies*. It is the major source for contemporary texts of his plays.

The publication of drama in the early 17th century was usually left to the poorer members of the Stationers' Company (which issued licenses) and to outright pirates. The would-be publisher had only to get hold of a manuscript, by fair means or foul, enter it as his copy (or dispense with the formality), and have it printed. Such a man was Thomas Thorpe, the publisher of Shakespeare's sonnets (1609).

The first Shakespeare play to be published (*Titus Andronicus*, 1594) was printed by a notorious pirate, John Danter, who also brought out, anonymously, a defective *Romeo and Juliet* (1597), largely from shorthand notes made during performance. Eighteen of Shakespeare's plays were printed in quartos (books about half the size of a modern magazine) both "good" and "bad" before the First Folio (a large-format book) was published in 1623. The bad quartos are defective editions, usually with badly garbled or missing text.

For the First Folio, a large undertaking of more than 900 pages, a syndicate of five men was formed, headed by Edward Blount and William Jaggard. The actors John Heminge and Henry Condell undertook the collection of 36 of Shake-

speare's plays, and about 1,000 copies of the First Folio were printed, none too well, by Jaggard's son, Isaac.

In 1632 a second folio was issued and in 1663 a third. The second printing (1664) of the latter included *Pericles* (which otherwise exists only in a bad quarto) and several other plays of dubious attribution, including *The Two Noble Kinsmen* (which appeared in a quarto of 1634) and *Cardenio* (now lost), as well as *The London Prodigal* and *The History of Thomas Lord Cromwell*. In 1685 the fourth and final folio was published.

first person   *see* POINT OF VIEW.

Fischart \'fish-ˌärt\, Johann (b. 1546/47, Strassburg [now Strasbourg, Fr.]—d. 1590, Forbach, Lorraine [France])   German satirist, the principal German literary opponent of the Counter-Reformation.

Fischart received a good education and traveled widely, visiting the Netherlands and probably England, and studying in Paris, Strassburg, and Siena [Italy]. In 1574 he received a law degree in Basel, Switz. Three years in Speyer (now in Germany) as advocate at the *Reichskammergericht* (imperial court of justice) were followed by appointment in 1583 as magistrate at Forbach, Lorraine.

Of his main works, the earliest are attacks on the papacy, Franciscans, and Dominicans. Two of the latest are polemical satires against the Roman Catholic church and especially the Jesuits. Beginning as a Lutheran, he came to defend Calvinist doctrines—the only major German writer to do so.

Fischart's principal literary work is the *Affentheurliche und ungeheurliche Geschichtsschrift* (1575)—renamed *Geschichtklitterung* in later editions (1582, 1590)—a greatly expanded prose version of François Rabelais's *Gargantua*. Also noteworthy is his *Das glückhafft Schiff von Zürich* (1576; "The Ship of Good Fortune from Zürich"), a carefully constructed poem commemorating the boatload of citizens who carried a basin of porridge from Zürich to Strassburg.

Fish \'fish\, Stanley (Eugene) (b. April 19, 1938, Providence, R.I., U.S.)   Literary critic who is particularly associated with reader-response criticism, according to which the meaning of a text is created, rather than discovered, by the reader.

Fish was educated at the University of Pennsylvania and Yale University. He taught at Johns Hopkins University from 1974 to 1985 and at Duke University thereafter.

In *Surprised by Sin: The Reader in "Paradise Lost"* (1967), Fish suggested that the subject of John Milton's masterpiece is in fact the reader, who is forced to undergo spiritual self-examination when led by Milton down the path taken by Adam, Eve, and Satan. In *Is There a Text in This Class? The Authority of Interpretive Communities* (1980), Fish further developed his theory. The essays in *Doing What Comes Naturally: Change, Rhetoric, and the Practice of Theory in Literary and Legal Studies* (1989) discuss a number of beliefs in literary theory.

Fisher \'fish-ər\, Dorothy Canfield, *original name* Dorothea Frances Canfield \'kan-ˌfēld\, *pen name* Dorothy Canfield (b. Feb. 17, 1879, Lawrence, Kan., U.S.—d. Nov. 9, 1958, Arlington, Vt.)   Prolific author of novels, short stories, children's books, educational works, and memoirs.

Canfield received a Ph.D. in Romance languages from Columbia University in 1904, a rare accomplishment for a woman of her generation. In 1907 she married John Redwood Fisher and published her first novel, *Gunhild*. In the same year she inherited her great-grandfather's farm in Arlington, Vt.; the town appears (often with the skimpiest of literary veils) in many of her works, including *Hillsboro People* (1915), written with poet Sarah N. Cleghorn, and *The Bent Twig* (1915).

In 1912 Fisher met Maria Montessori in Italy and was impressed by the educator's theories. *A Montessori Mother* (1912),

The Montessori Manual (1913), and *Mothers and Children* (1914) were the results of their friendship. Her experiences in French clinics and war camps resulted in three volumes of short stories, including *Home Fires in France* (1918).

After returning to the United States, Fisher translated Giovanni Papini's *Life of Christ* (1923) and during the 1920s and '30s produced a string of marriage-and-family stories and novels. *Her Son's Wife* (1926) is one of the best-regarded of her longer works. In the 1940s and '50s, Fisher worked for numerous environmental, children's, and educational causes, while writing several historical children's books, including *Paul Revere and the Minute Men* (1950).

Fisher \'fish-ər\, M.F.K., *original name in full* Mary Frances Kennedy (b. July 3, 1908, Albion, Mich., U.S.—d. June 22, 1992, Glen Ellen, Calif.)   Writer whose compelling style, wit, and interest in the gastronomical made her one of the major American writers on the subject of food. In her 15 celebrated books, Fisher created a new genre: the food essay. Seeing food as a cultural metaphor, she proved to be both an insightful philosopher of food and a writer of fine prose.

Kennedy was reared in Whittier, Calif., and became accomplished in the kitchen. She married in 1929 and moved to Dijon, France, where she reveled in French cooking and culture. Her first book of essays celebrating food, *Serve It Forth*, was published in 1937. Other early works include *Consider the Oyster* (1941) and *How to Cook a Wolf* (1942), in which she encourages readers to make the most of whatever they can afford.

While all of Fisher's books were well received, critics point to *The Gastronomical Me* (1943) as one of her best early efforts. Her 1949 translation of French gastronomist Jean Anthelme Brillat-Savarin's *The Physiology of Taste* is regarded as the definitive English version. *An Alphabet for Gourmets* (1949) is superbly witty, and *A Cordiall Water* (1961), a discourse on folk remedies, became something of a cult classic. Her 1971 memoir, *Among Friends*, details her early years. *Sister Age* (1983) is a meditation on growing older.

fit \'fit\ [Old English *fitt*]   *archaic*   A division of a poem or song; a canto or a similar division. The word is of Old English date and has an exact correspondent in Old Saxon *fittea*, which occurs in the Latin preface of the *Heliand*. It probably represents figurative use of a common Germanic noun referring to the unraveled edge of a fabric.

Fitch \'fich\, Clyde, *in full* William Clyde Fitch (b. May 2, 1865, Elmira, N.Y., U.S.—d. Sept. 4, 1909, Châlons-sur-Marne, Fr.)   American playwright best known for plays of social satire and character study.

Fitch began writing short stories for magazines in New York City. He was a prolific writer, producing 33 original plays and 22 adaptations. His earlier plays were largely melodramas and historical plays of lesser significance. Among the more important later plays were *Beau Brummel* (1890), written for the actor Richard Mansfield, *The Climbers* (1901), *Captain Jinks of the Horse Marines* (1901), *The Girl with the Green Eyes* (1902), *The Truth* (1907), and *The City* (1909).

Fitton \'fit-ən\, Mary (baptized June 24, 1578, Gawsworth, Cheshire, Eng.—d. *c.* 1647)   English lady considered by some to be the still-mysterious "dark lady" of William Shakespeare's sonnets, though her authenticated biography does not suggest acquaintance with Shakespeare. She became maid of honor to Elizabeth I in about 1595 and mistress to William Herbert (later earl of Pembroke) and to Sir Richard Leveson. She was twice married and widowed.

Fitts \'fits\, Dudley (b. April 28, 1903, Boston, Mass., U.S.—d. July 10, 1968, Lawrence, Mass.)   American teacher, critic, poet, and translator, best known for his contemporary English versions of classical Greek works.

Fitts began publishing poetry and criticism in periodicals such as *Poetry, transition,* and *Atlantic Monthly.* With poet Robert Fitzgerald he translated *The Alcestis of Euripides* (1936; first performed over BBC radio, 1937) and *The Antigone of Sophocles* (1939; first performed over NBC radio, U.S., 1939). The New Directions press, founded by James Laughlin, a former student of Fitts, published his *Poems 1929–1936* (1937) and his translations *One Hundred Poems from the Palatine Anthology* (1938) and *More Poems from the Palatine Anthology in English Paraphrase* (1941).

While Fitts also translated Latin, Spanish, and Latin-American writings into English, his translations of ancient Greek works became particularly noted. He later translated plays of Aristophanes, including *Lysistrata* (1954), *The Frogs* (1955), *The Birds* (1957), and *Ladies' Day* (1959); *Sixty Poems of Martial* (1967); and, with Fitzgerald, Sophocles' *Oedipus Rex* (1949). He also edited anthologies of poetry translations and, in 1960–68, the Yale Series of Younger Poets.

FitzGerald \fits-'jer-əld\, Edward (b. March 31, 1809, Bredfield, near Woodbridge, Suffolk, Eng.—d. June 14, 1883, Merton, Norfolk)   English writer, best known for his THE RUBÁIYÁT OF OMAR KHAYYÁM, which, though it is a free adaptation and selection from the 12th-century Persian poet's verses, stands on its own as a classic of English literature. Many of its images, such as "A jug of wine, a loaf of bread, and thou" and "The moving finger writes," have passed into common currency.

After graduating from Trinity College, Cambridge, in 1830, FitzGerald lived chiefly in seclusion, though he kept up a steady correspondence with many intimate friends—including Alfred, Lord Tennyson, William Makepeace Thackeray, and Thomas Carlyle.

FitzGerald published a few works anonymously, then freely translated *Six Dramas of Calderón* (1853) before turning to Oriental studies and mastering Persian. In March 1859 the *Rubáiyát* was published in an unpretentious, anonymous pamphlet. The poem attracted no attention until it was discovered by Dante Gabriel Rossetti in 1860 and by Algernon Swinburne soon thereafter. *See also* OMAR KHAYYAM.

Fitzgerald \fits-'jer-əld\, F. Scott, *in full* Francis Scott Key Fitzgerald (b. Sept. 24, 1896, St. Paul, Minn., U.S.—d. Dec. 21, 1940, Hollywood, Calif.)   American short-story writer and novelist known for his depictions of the Jazz Age (the 1920s).

Fitzgerald attended Princeton University, where he nearly realized his dream of brilliant social and literary success, but because of his poor academic record he left in 1917. In Novem-

ber of that year he joined the U.S. Army. In 1918 he met Zelda Sayre, the daughter of an Alabama Supreme Court judge. To prove himself and win her, Fitzgerald rewrote the novel he had begun at Princeton; in 1920 THIS SIDE OF PARADISE was published and Fitzgerald married Zelda.

Publication of the novel gave Fitzgerald an entrée to literary magazines, such as *Scribner's*, and high-paying general magazines, such as *The Saturday Evening Post.*

In them he published early stories such as THE DIAMOND AS BIG AS THE RITZ, later collected in TALES OF THE JAZZ AGE (1922). Fame and prosperity were both welcome and frightening; in THE BEAUTIFUL AND DAMNED (1922), Fitzgerald describes the life he and Zelda feared, a descent into ennui and dissipation.

The Fitzgeralds moved in 1924 to the Riviera, where they fell in with a group of American expatriates. Fitzgerald describes this society in his last completed novel, TENDER IS THE NIGHT (1934). Shortly after their arrival in France, Fitzgerald completed THE GREAT GATSBY (1925), the most profoundly American novel of its time. It poignantly captures Fitzgerald's own ambivalence about American life, at once vulgar and dazzlingly promising. Some of Fitzgerald's finest short stories, particularly "The Rich Boy" and "Absolution," appeared in *All the Sad Young Men* (1926).

Fitzgerald soon began to drink excessively, and in 1930 Zelda had a mental breakdown. In 1932 she had another, from which she never fully recovered. Fitzgerald told the story of his downward slide in THE CRACK-UP (1945). By 1937, however, he had become a scriptwriter in Hollywood, where he met Sheilah Graham, a well-known Hollywood gossip columnist with whom he lived for the rest of his life. In 1939 he began a novel about Hollywood, THE LAST TYCOON (1941), but he died before it was finished.

Fitzgerald \fits-'jer-əld\, Penelope, *original surname* Knox \'näks\ (b. Dec. 17, 1916, Lincoln, Eng.)   English novelist and biographer noted for her deft characterizations and for her ability to note the telling detail.

Fitzgerald's father, Edmund Knox, was the editor of *Punch*; her uncle Ronald translated the Bible and wrote detective stories. After her graduation from Somerville College, Oxford, in 1939, she worked as a journalist and tutor and for the BBC. She wrote two biographies, *Edward Burne-Jones* (1975) and *The Knox Brothers* (1977), before publishing her first work of fiction. In 1984 her biography, *Charlotte Mew and Her Friends*, was published.

Fitzgerald's first novel, *The Golden Child* (1977), was a detective story of murder in a museum. *The Bookshop* (1978) was praised for its mordant wit. In *Offshore* (1979), Fitzgerald's characters live on houseboats; this taut portrayal of a closed community won her the Booker Prize. *Human Voices* (1980), a humorous account of the BBC in 1940, successfully evoked wartime Britain. Fitzgerald's later works include *At Freddie's* (1982), about a school for child actors; *Innocence* (1986), a love story set in Florence; *The Beginning of Spring* (1988), set in czarist Moscow; and *The Gate of Angels* (1990). She also edited an unfinished novel by William Morris, *The Novel on Blue Paper* (1982).

FitzGerald \fits-'jer-əld\, R.D., *in full* Robert David (b. Feb. 22, 1902, Hunter's Hill, N.S.W., Australia—May 24, 1987, Glenn Innes, N.S.W.)   Australian poet known for his technical skill and seriousness.

FitzGerald's literary work steadily progressed from his second collection of poetry, *To Meet the Sun* (1929), now considered rather dated and derivative, to *Moonlight Acre* (1938), which included the philosophical poem "Essay on Memory." *Between Two Tides* (1952) is a long metaphorical narrative. "Heemskerck Shoals" is included in *A Night's Orbit* (1953). His later verse was published in *Product* (1977). He also wrote a book of criticism, *The Elements of Poetry* (1963), and a volume of essays, *Of Places and Poetry* (1976).

Perceived by some critics to be a graceless writer or simply difficult, FitzGerald was nonetheless a major influence on the tone of Australian poetry.

Five Women Who Loved Love   Story collection written by IHARA Saikaku, published in Japanese in 1686 as *Kōshoku gonin onna*, and considered a masterwork of the Tokugawa period (1603–1867).

Five Women Who Loved Love is composed of five separate tales, each divided into five individually titled chapters. They consist of vignettes that reveal the sensual and—of equal interest—financial activities of members of the leisure class, demimonde, and merchant class.

fixed form   In poetry, any form that has set rules governing most elements of its composition, including length, meter, and rhyme scheme. Such forms include the sonnet, the ballade, the chant royal, and the limerick.

Fixer, The   Novel by Bernard MALAMUD, published in 1966. It received the Pulitzer Prize in 1967.

Considered by some to be the author's finest novel, *The Fixer* is the story of a Jewish handyman, or fixer, who discovers that there is no rational reason for human cruelty; he also learns that freedom requires constant vigilance. As in Malamud's other works, the condition of the Jews serves as a metaphor for the condition of humanity.

The novel, set in czarist Russia in the early 20th century, tells the story of Yakov Bok. Bok says of himself that he fixes what's broken—except in the heart. His tinkering includes altruistic acts of kindness to others, but his generosity is repaid with misfortune and vilification. Most of the novel takes place while Bok is imprisoned awaiting trial for a murder he did not commit.

Fjǫrgyn   *see* JǫRD.

Flags in the Dust   *see* SARTORIS.

Flaiano \flä-'yä-nō\, Ennio (b. March 5, 1910, Pescara, Italy—d. Nov. 20, 1972, Rome)   Italian screenwriter, playwright, novelist, journalist, and drama critic who was especially noted for his social satires.

Flaiano contributed critical essays to such magazines as *Mondo* and *L'Espresso*. His first play, *La guerra spiegata ai poveri* (1946; "War Explained to the Poor"), displays his sharp, subtle humor. His first novel, *Tempo di uccidere* (1947; *A Time to Kill*), won him the Strega Prize in 1947. He began writing film scripts during World War II and, with writer Tullio Pinelli, brought a sense of realism to such Federico Fellini films as *La strada* (1954), *La dolce vita* (1960), and *Otto e mezzo* (1963; 8½).

Flaiano's other books include the short-story collections *Diario notturno* (1956; "Night Journal") and *Una e una notte* (1959; "One and One Night"), as well as the play *La conversazione continuamente interrotta* (performed 1972; "A Continually Interrupted Conversation").

flam \'flam\ [probably short for *flimflam*]   *obsolete*   A fanciful bit of writing.

Flanders, Moll \'mäl-'flan-dərz\   A fictional character, the lusty, ambitious heroine of English writer Daniel Defoe's picaresque novel MOLL FLANDERS.

Flanner \'flan-ər\, Janet, *pseudonym* Genêt \zhə-'nä\ (b. March 13, 1892, Indianapolis, Ind., U.S.—d. Nov. 7, 1978, New York City)   American writer and Paris correspondent for *The New Yorker* magazine from 1925 to 1975 (except for the war years 1939–44). Hers was some of the most sophisticated, insightful, and cosmopolitan reportage from Paris during the period.

A friend of Harold Ross, Flanner was hired by him in 1925 to write a periodic "Letter from Paris" for his new magazine, *The New Yorker*. Signed by "Genêt," the articles contained observations on politics, art, theater, and the general quality of

French life. In the 1930s she also began writing an occasional "Letter from London." Her first novel, *The Cubical City*, appeared in 1926.

Most of her essays were collected in *American in Paris; Profile of an Interlude Between Two Wars* (1940), *Paris Journal, 1944–1965* (1966), *Paris Journal, 1965–1971* (1971), and *Janet Flanner's World: Uncollected Writings 1932–1975* (1979).

flashback \'flash-,bak\ **1.** A literary or theatrical technique that involves interruption of the chronological sequence of events by interjection of events or scenes of earlier occurrence, often in the form of reminiscence. **2.** An instance of flashback—called also *backflash*.

flash-forward \'flash-'fôr-wərd\ [*flash*back + *forward*] A literary or theatrical technique that involves interruption of the chronological sequence of events by interjection of events or scenes of future occurrence.

flat and round characters Characters as described by the course of their development in a work of literature. Flat characters, as it were, are two-dimensional in that they are relatively uncomplicated and do not change throughout the course of a work. By contrast, round characters are complex and undergo development, sometimes sufficiently to surprise the reader.

The two types are described by E.M. Forster in his book *Aspects of the Novel*.

Flaubert \flō-'ber\, Gustave (b. Dec. 12, 1821, Rouen, Fr.—d. May 8, 1880, Croisset) Novelist regarded as the foremost exponent of the realist school of French literature and best known for the work that is generally regarded as his masterpiece, MADAME BOVARY (1857).

Flaubert's first published work appeared in a little review in 1837. In November 1841 he was enrolled as a student at

Detail of a drawing by E.F. von Liphart, 1880
Bibliothèque Municipale, Rouen

the Faculty of Law in Paris. At the age of 22, however, he was recognized to be suffering from a nervous disease and he abandoned the law for literature. After the deaths of his father and sister he retired to Croisset, near Rouen, on the Seine. He was to spend nearly all the rest of his life there.

On a visit to Paris in 1846, Flaubert met the writer Louise Colet. She became his mistress, but their relationship did not go smoothly, and they parted with great bitterness in 1855. In 1847 Flaubert went on a walking tour along the Loire and the coast of Brittany with the writer Maxime du Camp. Flaubert's account of this tour was published after his death as *Par les champs et par les grèves* (1886; "Over the Fields and over the Shores").

From November 1849 to April 1851 Flaubert traveled with du Camp in Egypt, Palestine, Syria, Turkey, Greece, and Italy. On his return he began *Madame Bovary*, which took him five years to complete. It was published in installments in the *Revue* from Oct. 1 to Dec. 15, 1856. Having scandalized the author-

ities with his probing, sympathetic, and realistic account of a bourgeois woman's adultery, Flaubert was brought to trial in 1857 and narrowly escaped conviction. He immediately afterward began work on SALAMMBÔ (1862), a novel about ancient Carthage. A play, *Le Château des coeurs* (*The Castle of Hearts*), written in 1863, was not printed until 1880.

In 1869, a few months before the outbreak of the Franco-Prussian War, Flaubert published *L'Education sentimentale* (A SENTIMENTAL EDUCATION), a panorama of France under the July Monarchy. It was not well received, and two plays, *Le Sexe faible* (1910; "The Feeble Sex") and *Le Candidat* (1874; *The Candidate*), likewise had no success. There followed in 1874 the novel *La Tentation de Saint Antoine* (THE TEMPTATION OF SAINT ANTHONY), actually the fourth version of a work begun in 1839.

Flaubert temporarily abandoned work on the long novel *Bouvard et Pécuchet* (1881) in order to write *Trois contes* (1877; *Three Tales*), containing the three short stories "Un Coeur simple" ("A Simple Heart"), "La Légende de Saint Julien l'Hospitalier," and "Hérodias." This work, through the diversity of the stories' themes, shows Flaubert's talent in all its aspects and has actually been held by some to be his masterpiece. *Bouvard et Pécuchet*, which concerns two men who, suddenly liberated from their workaday jobs, undertake several scientific experiments but are thwarted by bad judgment, was left unfinished at Flaubert's death.

Flecknoe \'flek-nō\, Richard (b. *c.* 1600—d. *c.* 1678) English poet, dramatist, and traveler whose writings are notable for both the praise and the ridicule they evoked.

The most authentic information about Flecknoe is contained in his *Relation of Ten Years' Travels in Europe, Asia, Affrique, and America* (1654?). Flecknoe's picture of himself as a ladies' man contrasts with Andrew Marvell's account in his poem "Flecknoe, an English Priest at Rome," which ridicules Flecknoe's threadbare asceticism and bad verses. John Dryden lampooned him in his hostile *MacFlecknoe* (1682) as being "Through all the realms of Nonsense, absolute." Neither Flecknoe's poems in *Epigrams of All Sorts* (1670) nor his prose sketches in *Enigmatical Characters* (1658) warrant such an attack. His *The Short Treatise of the English Stage*, appended to a revision of his play *Love's Kingdom* (1664), is of historical interest.

Fleming \'flem-iŋ\, Ian (Lancaster) (b. May 28, 1908, London, Eng.—d. Aug. 12, 1964, Canterbury, Kent) Internationally popular suspense novelist whose character James BOND, the stylish, high-living British secret service agent 007, became one of the most successful heroes of 20th-century fiction.

Educated in England, Germany, and Switzerland, Fleming was a journalist in Moscow (1929–33), a banker and stockbroker (1935–39), and a high-ranking officer in British naval intelligence during World War II. After the war he was foreign manager of the London *Sunday Times*.

Casino Royale (1953) was the first of 12 James Bond novels, which were packed with violent action, hairbreadth escapes, international espionage, terror, and sex. The books sold more than 18,000,000 copies and were translated into 11 languages. All the Bond novels, notably *From Russia, with Love* (1957), *Dr. No* (1958), *Goldfinger* (1959), and *Thunderball* (1961), were made into popular motion pictures. Fleming also published two collections of short stories featuring Bond. His successful children's book, the only work he wrote in that genre, was entitled *Chitty Chitty Bang Bang* (1964).

Fleming \'flem-iŋ\, Paul (b. Oct. 5, 1609, Hartenstein, Saxony [Germany]—d. April 2, 1640, Hamburg) Outstanding lyric poet of 17th-century Germany. He brought a new immediacy and sincerity to the meter and stanza introduced by his teacher, Martin Opitz.

Fleming was studying medicine and composing Latin verse at Leipzig when he met Opitz and became his ardent disciple. He wrote some of the century's finest poetry: love lyrics that were unique for their time in their freshness and depth of feeling and religious hymns distinguished for their fervor and stoical dignity. Some of them—*e.g.*, "In allen meinen Taten" ("In All My Deeds")—appear in hymnals today. Fleming excelled in the sonnet form and was the first German to use it effectively. His *Teutsche Poemata* ("German Poems") and *Geist und weltliche Poemata* ("Spiritual and Worldly Poems") appeared posthumously in 1642 and in 1651.

fleshly school of poetry Epithet applied to a group of late 19th-century English poets associated with Dante Gabriel Rossetti. The term was invented by Robert Williams Buchanan and appeared as the title of an article in the *Contemporary Review* (October 1871) in which he castigated the poetry of Rossetti and his colleagues, notably Algernon Swinburne, for its "morbid deviation from the healthy forms of life." In Buchanan's view, these poets exhibited "weary wasting, yet exquisite sensuality; nothing virile, nothing tender, nothing completely sane; a superfluity of extreme sensibility." He reviled their decadence, their "amatory forms" and "carnal images." Rossetti replied with "The Stealthy School of Criticism" in *The Athenaeum*, in December 1871, and Swinburne with a pamphlet, "Under the Microscope," in 1872.

Fletcher \'flech-ər\, Giles, the Elder (b. *c.* 1548, Cranbrook, Kent, Eng.—buried March 11, 1611, London) English poet and author, father of the poets Phineas and Giles Fletcher.

Educated at King's College, Cambridge, Fletcher served as a diplomat. In 1588 he was sent to Russia to the court of the czar, Fyodor I, with instructions to conclude an alliance between England and Russia, to restore English trade, and to obtain better conditions for the English Muscovy Company. He returned to England in 1589 and in 1591 published *Of the Russe Common Wealth*, a comprehensive account of Russian geography, government, law, methods of warfare, religion, and manners that continues to be of interest in modern times.

Fletcher \'flech-ər\, Giles, the Younger (b. *c.* 1585, London, Eng.—d. 1623, Alderton, Suffolk) English poet principally known for his great devotional poem *Christs Victorie*.

Fletcher was the younger son of Giles Fletcher the Elder. He was educated at Westminster School and at Trinity College, Cambridge. After his ordination, he became known for his sermons at the Church of St. Mary the Great. He left Cambridge about 1618 and soon after received the rectory of Alderton, Suffolk.

The theme of Fletcher's masterpiece, *Christs Victorie, and Triumph in Heaven, and Earth, over, and After Death* (1610), bears some resemblance to that of the religious epic *La Semaine* (1578; *Devine Weekes and Workes*) of the French Protestant poet Guillaume du Bartas; but the devotion, passionate lyricism, and exquisite vision of paradise that critics have praised are Fletcher's own. The poem is written in eight-line stanzas somewhat derivative of Edmund Spenser.

Fletcher \'flech-ər\, John (baptized Dec. 20, 1579, Rye, Sussex, Eng.—d. Aug. 29, 1625, London) English dramatist who collaborated with Francis BEAUMONT and others on comedies and tragedies between about 1606 and 1625.

When not quite 12, Fletcher was apparently admitted to Bene't (now Corpus Christi) College, Cambridge. From 1596 until 1607 nothing is known of him. His name is first linked with Beaumont's in Ben Jonson's *Volpone* (1607), to which both men contributed encomiums.

Fletcher and Beaumont first worked for the Children of the Queen's Revels and its successor company and then (from about 1609 until Beaumont's retirement in 1613) mainly for the King's Men at the Globe and Blackfriars theaters. After 1613 Fletcher was often assisted, or his plays were revised, by Philip Massinger; other collaborators included Nathaniel Field and William Rowley. Throughout his career he also wrote plays unaided. He died in the great London plague of 1625.

The canon of the Beaumont and Fletcher plays is approximately represented by the 52 plays in the folio *Fifty Comedies and Tragedies* (1679), except that James Shirley's *Coronation* must be omitted and *Henry VIII, Sir John van Olden Barnavelt*, and *A Very Woman* must be added. Of these 54 plays not more than 12 are by Beaumont or by Beaumont and Fletcher in collaboration. Another three were probably collaborations with both Beaumont and Massinger. The others represent Fletcher either unaided or in collaboration with dramatists other than Beaumont, principally Massinger.

The masterpieces of the Beaumont and Fletcher collaboration—PHILASTER, *The Maides Tragedy*, and *A King and No King*—show, most clearly in the last, the emergence of the features that distinguish the Fletcherian mode from that of William Shakespeare, George Chapman, or John Webster: the remote, often pseudo-historical, fairy-tale setting; the clear, smooth speech rising to great emotional arias of declamatory rhetoric; the basically sensational or bizarre plot; and the sacrifice of consistency and plausibility in characterization so that emotional states shift constantly and piquant situations can be prolonged.

Of Fletcher's unaided plays, *The Faithfull Shepheardesse*, *The Mad Lover*, *The Loyall Subject*, *The Humorous Lieutenant*, *Women Pleas'd*, *The Island Princesse*, and *A Wife for a Moneth* (all between *c.* 1608 and *c.* 1624) are perhaps the best. *The Wild-Goose Chase*, a play that is notable for its irony and easy wit, is the most urbane and consistent in tone of his comedies. Lastly, there are the Fletcherian plays in which others besides Beaumont had a hand. Of the numerous plays in this group, the best are probably *The False One* and *The Beggars Bush*.

Fletcher \'flech-ər\, Phineas (baptized April 8, 1582, Cranbrook, Kent, Eng.—d. 1650, Hilgay, Norfolk) English poet best known for his religious and scientific poem *The Purple Island*.

Fletcher was the elder son of Giles Fletcher the Elder and brother of Giles Fletcher the Younger. He was educated at King's College, Cambridge, and became chaplain to Sir Henry Willoughby. In 1621 he accepted the rectory of Hilgay, Norfolk. His greatest work, *The Purple Island*, was published with *Piscatorie Eclogs and Other Poeticall Miscellanies* in 1633. *The Purple Island, or the Isle of Man* allegorically describes in 12 cantos the human physiology and soul. The chief charm of the poem is considered by critics to be its descriptions of rural scenery. The *Piscatorie Eclogs* are pastorals whose characters are represented as fisherboys on the banks of the Cam.

fleur du mal \flœr-dœ-'mâl\ *plural* fleurs du mal *same*\ [French, literally, flower of evil] A morbid or scandalous creation in literature or art. The phrase alludes to *Les Fleurs du mal* (1857), a volume of Decadent poetry by French poet Charles Baudelaire.

Fleurs du mal, Les \lā-flœr-dœ-'mâl\ ("The Flowers of Evil") Collection of poems published in 1857 by Charles BAUDELAIRE. A second edition, published in 1861, was greatly enlarged and enhanced but omitted six poems that had been banned. (These were first republished in 1866 in Belgium in the collection *Les Épaves*, but they remained banned in France until 1949.) The otherwise definitive edition of *Les Fleurs du mal* was published posthumously in 1868. Contemporary scholars consider the work to be the fullest expression of French Romantic poetry.

Les Fleurs du mal is composed of six sections, each with a theme—a structure that was new to French poetry. The sections are "Spleen et idéal," "Tableaux parisiens," "Le Vin," "Fleurs du mal," "Révolte," and "La Mort." Shifting in style from the rhetorical to the impressionistic, from the abstract to the intensely physical, Baudelaire balances banality and originality, the prosaic and the melodic, to emphasize the eternal interdependence of opposites.

Flint \'flint\, F.S., *in full* Frank Stuart (b. Dec. 19, 1885, London, Eng.—d. Feb. 28, 1960, Berkshire) English poet and translator, prominent in the movement known as IMAGISM.

Flint left school at age 13 and worked at a variety of jobs. At the age of 17 his reading of a volume by John Keats fired his enthusiasm for poetry. He learned French and Latin (eventually he mastered 10 languages) and after World War I rose to become a high official in the Ministry of Labour.

Flint's first volume of poetry, *In the Net of the Stars* (1909), was a collection of love lyrics, clearly showing the influence of Keats and Percy Bysshe Shelley. The same year he and a group of young poets, all dissatisfied with the state of English poetry, began working to overthrow conventional versification and to replace strict meter with unrhymed cadence (a term he appropriated). His friendship with the English poet T.E. Hulme and the expatriate American poet Ezra Pound helped him to develop further his own distinctive poetic style. *Cadences* (1915) and *Otherworld* (1925) established him as a leading member of the Imagists.

Flintwinch, Jeremiah \ˌjer-ə-'mī-ə-'flint-ˌwich\ Fictional character in the novel LITTLE DORRIT by Charles Dickens. Originally the family butler, Flintwinch becomes the business partner of Mrs. Clennam after he comes into possession of confidential information about the family and its financial dealings. His gullible wife, Affery, is the Clennan family maid.

Fløgstad \'flœg-ˌstä\, Kjartan, *pseudonym* K. Villum \'vel-ˌlüm\ (b. June 7, 1944, Sauda, Nor.) Norwegian writer best known for his novel *Dalen Portland* (1977; "Portland Valley"; *Dollar Road*).

Some of Fløgstad's deepest affinities were with Latin-American writers. He translated the Chilean poet Pablo Neruda in *Dikt i utval* (1972; "Selected Poems"), as well as various Cuban poets in *Dikt frå Cuba* (1973; "Poems from Cuba"). Fløgstad's own poetry, published in *Valfart* (1968; "Pilgrimage") and *Seremoniar* (1969; "Ceremonies"), is a skillful mixture of symbolism, wide and eclectic reading, humor, and a responsiveness to both city and village life. In his collection of essays and short fictions, *Den hemmelege jubel* (1970; "The Secret Enthusiasm"), Fløgstad defended literature, art, and the imagination against both the political right and left. *Fangliner* (1972; "Prison Lines") is a collection of short stories that take a hard and unsentimental look at the lives of fishermen and factory workers. His first novel was the semiautobiographical *Rasmus* (1974). *Dalen Portland* recounts the lives of small-town factory workers and sailors with lyrical realism. His later novels, including *Fyr og flamme* (1980; "All Fired Up"), *U3* (1983), and *Kniven på strupen* (1991; "At Knife-point"), strengthened his reputation.

Floire et Blancheflor \'flwär-ā-blä(n)sh-'flôr\ French metrical romance known in two versions from the 12th and 13th centuries and thought to be of Greco-Byzantine or Moorish origin. Its theme of separation and reunion of young lovers resembles that of AUCASSIN ET NICOLETTE, though the roles and religion of the two main characters are reversed. Floire is

the son of a Saracen king; Blancheflor, his beloved, is a Christian. The English account, *Floris and Blancheflur* (or *Flores and Blancheflour*), was composed in the East Midlands dialect about 1250 and is one of the most charming romances in Middle English.

Florio \'flôr-ē-ō\, John, *also called* Giovanni Florio (b. *c.* 1553, London, Eng.—d. *c.* 1625, Fulham, near London) English lexicographer and translator of Michel de Montaigne.

Son of a Protestant refugee of Tuscan origin, Florio studied at Oxford. From 1604 to 1619 he was groom of the privy chamber to Queen Anne.

In 1580 Florio translated, as *Navigations and Discoveries* (1580), Giovanni Battista Ramusio's account of the voyages of Jacques Cartier. *Florio His Firste Fruites* (1578), a grammar and a series of dialogues in Italian and English, was followed in 1591 by *Florio's Second Frutes* and by *Giardino di ricreatione*, a collection of more than 6,000 proverbs in Italian. His Italian-English dictionary, *A World of Wordes* (1598), for which he drew heavily upon the works of Giordano Bruno, contains about 46,000 definitions. The second edition, *Queen Anna's New World of Words* (1611), was greatly enlarged. In 1603 Florio produced his major translation of the *Essais* of Michel de Montaigne, which he revised in 1613.

Florus \'flôr-əs\, Publius Annius (fl. late 1st and early 2nd century AD, b. Africa—d. Rome?) Historian of Rome and poet, important as the first of a number of African writers who influenced Latin literature in the 2nd century. He was also the first of the "new-fashioned" poets of Hadrian's reign, who used lighter and more graceful meters than those of the poets they displaced.

Florus compiled a brief sketch of the history of Rome from its founding to the time of Augustus, based chiefly on Livy. The work, called in some manuscripts *Epitome de T. Livio bellorum omnium annorum DCC libri duo*, is a rhetorical panegyric of the greatness of Rome that has almost no historical value by modern standards. In the manuscripts the writer is variously identified, but stylistic similarity to a dialogue *Vergilius orator an poeta*, known to be the work of Florus, authenticates his authorship of the history. It is generally agreed that he is the Florus said to have addressed the well-known lines to Hadrian that begin, "I do not wish to be a Caesar," which provoked Hadrian's satirical parody, "I do not wish to be a Florus," as quoted by Spartianus. Twenty-six trochaic tetrameters, *De qualitate vitae*, and five graceful hexameters, *De rosis*, are also attributed to him.

flourish \'flər-ish\ A florid bit of writing or speech, such as a complicated figure of speech or an ornate metaphor.

flower \'flaủ-ər\ A florid insertion or interpolation in a text; a figure of speech or other ornament of literary style.

Flowering Judas \'jü-dəs\ Short story by Katherine Anne PORTER, published in *Hound and Horn* magazine in 1930. It is the title story of Porter's first and most popular collection, which was published in the same year. When the collection was reissued in 1935, four stories were added to make a total of 10.

Set in Mexico in 1920 during the Mexican Revolution, "Flowering Judas" concerns the attempts of Laura, a beautiful, young American teacher of Indian children and a clandestine worker for the revolutionary cause, to rationalize her actions as she faces the loss of her ideals.

fluid \'flü-id\ Characterized by or employing a smooth, easy style or producing such an effect, especially in literature or art.

Flying Dutchman In European maritime legend, specter ship doomed to sail forever; its appearance to seamen is believed to signal imminent disaster. In the most common version, the captain gambles his salvation on a rash pledge to round the Cape of Good Hope during a storm and so is condemned to that course for eternity; this rendering forms the basis of the opera *Der fliegende Holländer* (1843) by Richard Wagner.

Another legend depicts a captain sailing forever through the North Sea, playing at dice for his soul with the devil. The dice-game motif recurs in *The Rime of the Ancient Mariner* (1798) by Samuel Taylor Coleridge. Sir Walter Scott adapted the legend in his narrative poem *Rokeby* (1813), in which murder is committed on shipboard and plague breaks out among the crew, closing all ports to the ship.

flyting \'flī-tiŋ\ [Scots, literally, quarreling, contention] A dispute or exchange of personal abuse or ridicule in verse form between two characters in a poem (as an early epic) or between two of the Scottish makaris (plural of MAKAR—i.e., poet) of the 15th and 16th centuries.

In the Scottish poetic competition two highly skilled rivals engaged in a contest of verbal abuse, remarkable for its fierceness and extravagance. The tradition seems to be derived from the Gaelic filid (a class of professional poets), who composed savage tirades against persons who slighted them. Although the flyting became obsolete in Scottish literature after the European Middle Ages, the tradition itself never died out among writers of Celtic background. The style and language of Robert Burns's "To a Louse" ("Ye ugly, creepin, blastit wonner/Detested, shunn'd by saunt an' sinner") parodies earlier Scots flyting, and James Joyce's poem "The Holy Office" is a bard's curse on the society that spurns him.

Fo \'fō\, Dario (b. March 24, 1926, Leggiuno-Sangiamo, Italy) Prolific Italian playwright, manager-director, and actor-mime.

Fo early collaborated on satirical revues for small cabarets and theaters. He and his wife, the actress Franca Rame, founded the Campagnia Dario Fo–Franca Rame in 1959. They gradually developed an agitprop theater of politics, often blasphemous and scatological, but rooted in the tradition of commedia dell'arte. In 1968 they founded another acting group, Nuova Scena, with ties to the Italian Communist Party, and in 1970 they started the Collettivo Teatrale La Comune.

Fo wrote more than 40 plays, some with Rame. Among his most popular are *Morte accidentale di un anarchico* (1974; *Accidental Death of an Anarchist*) and *Non si paga, non si paga!* (1974; *We Can't Pay? We Won't Pay!*). As a performer, Fo is best known for his solo tour de force *Mistero Buffo* (1974; "Comic Mystery"), based on medieval mystery plays but so topical that it changed with each audience. His later works include *Tutta casa, letto e chiesa* (1978; "All House, Bed, and Church"; *Adult Orgasm Escapes from the Zoo*) and *L'uomo nudo e l'uomo in frak* (1985; *One was Nude and One Wore Tails*) and (with Rame) *Female Parts* (1981) and *Coppia aperta* (1983; *The Open Couple—Wide Open Even*).

Fodor \'fō-ˌdòr, -dər\, Eugene (b. Oct. 14, 1905, Léva, Hung. [now Levice, Slovakia.]—d. Feb. 18, 1991, Torrington, Conn., U.S.) Hungarian-born American travel writer who created a series of popular tourist guidebooks that provided historical background and cultural insights into the people and places described, as well as reliable, practical information designed to assist inexperienced travelers.

Fodor studied in Czechoslovakia, France, and Germany. He then worked as an interpreter for a French shipping company, in his spare time writing articles about exotic ports of call and life aboard ship. He was a travel correspondent and editor in Prague (1930–33) and London (1934–38). His first book, *1936—On the Continent*, was a best-seller in Europe and the United States. Fodor became a naturalized U.S. citizen in 1942 and served in the U.S. Army. In 1949 he settled in Paris

and founded Fodor's Modern Guides, Inc. He returned to the United States in 1964 and sold his company in 1968.

Foeth *see* FET.

Fogazzaro \ˌfō-gät-'tsä-rō\, Antonio (b. March 25, 1842, Vicenza, Republic of Venice [Italy]—d. March 7, 1911, Vicenza) Italian novelist whose works reflect the conflict between reason and faith.

Fogazzaro established his reputation as a novelist only late in life with *Malombra* (1881; *The Woman*), *Daniele Cortis* (1885), and *Il mistero del poeta* (1888; *The Poet's Mystery*). His best-known work, *Piccolo mondo antico* (1896; *The Little World of the Past*), was acclaimed even by critics unsympathetic to his religious and philosophical ideas. He was the author of short stories and plays as well as of novels, and his poetry is collected in *Valsolda* (1886).

Fogg, Phileas \'fil-ē-əs-'fòg, 'fäg\ Fictional character, a wealthy, eccentric Englishman who wagers that he can travel around the world in 80 days in Jules Verne's novel AROUND THE WORLD IN EIGHTY DAYS.

foil \'fòil\ In literature, a character who is presented as a contrast to a second character so as to point to or show to advantage some aspect of the second character. An obvious example is the character of Dr. Watson in Sir Arthur Conan Doyle's Sherlock Holmes stories. Watson is a perfect foil for Holmes because his relative obtuseness makes Holmes's deductions seem more brilliant.

Folengo \fō-'läŋ-gō\, Teofilo, *original name* Girolamo Folengo (b. Nov. 8, 1491, Mantua [Italy]—d. Dec. 9, 1544, near Bassano Campese, Republic of Venice) Italian popularizer of MACARONIC verse form, a synthetic combination of Italian and Latin first written by Tisi degli Odassi in the late 15th century.

Folengo entered the Benedictine order as a young man, taking the name Teofilo, by which he is known. He left the order about 1525. After 1530 he lived as a hermit near Sorrento, then was readmitted to the Benedictine order in 1534, where he remained until his death.

Though he wrote much poetry in various forms, Folengo's masterpiece is *Baldus*, a poem in macaronic hexameters, published under the pseudonym Merlin Cocai (Cocaio). The original edition had 17 books, the later editions 25. Four versions of *Baldus* are known, published in 1517, 1521, 1539–40, and 1552 (modern edition, *Le maccheronee*, 1927–28). The poem narrates the adventures of a rustic hero, Baldus, a descendant of Rinaldo, cousin of the medieval epic hero Roland.

folio \'fō-lē-ō\ [Latin, ablative of *folium* leaf] In printing, a sheet of paper folded in half. The term also refers to a book made up of folio sheets, which is the largest regular book size. The collected works of William Shakespeare were first published in a folio edition in 1623, and several other such editions followed. *See also* FIRST FOLIO.

folk drama *also called* folk theater. A form of theater blending performance art and oral literature that is characterized by dances, many of them elaborate, with masks portraying animal or human characters. Folk drama is common in many parts of the preliterate world.

Folk drama has long been used as a method of transmitting traditions and teachings, as in the ancient Greek mysteries and in secret societies down to the present time. Some ancient folk dramas, however, were part of a public cult. Thus, in ancient Greece the feast of Dionysus led eventually to classical Greek drama, and in medieval Europe the dramatic celebrations of the Christian church developed into folk dramas and at length into the literary drama of the Renaissance and later.

folk literature *also called* oral tradition *or* folklore. The traditional knowledge and beliefs of cultures that are transmitted by word of mouth. It consists of both prose and verse narratives, poems and songs, myths, dramas, rituals, fables, proverbs, riddles, and the like. Folk literature exists side by side with the growing written record.

The individuals who led societies in a variety of ways—shamans, priests and priestesses, rulers, and warriors—provided the greatest stimulus for folk literature, for the telling of and listening to myths, tales, and songs. The medieval romances, especially the Breton lays, drew freely and sometimes directly on these folk sources as did many epics, such as the Anglo-Saxon *Beowulf* and the Finnish *Kalevala*. In literary forms such as the *fabliaux* the tales were often reworked by writers, but in the 16th and 17th centuries, writers such as Gianfrancesco Straparola and Giambattista Basile went directly to folk literature for much of their material.

Folk literature is characterized by the presence of devices to aid memory, such as repetition, formulaic expressions ("once upon a time," "married and lived happily ever after"), and a variety of conventional motifs and episodes that constitute a formula of structure in the form of familiar plots. It also typically contains enough realism to support the marvelous in tale or song, violent actions, and simple, strong emotions. Its manifestations may vary greatly from region to region; for example, some ethnic groups may favor folk songs while others excel in storytelling.

folklore \ˈfōk-ˌlȯr\   The sum total of traditionally derived and orally transmitted literature, material culture, and custom of subcultures within predominantly literate and technologically advanced societies; comparable study among wholly or mainly nonliterate societies belongs to the disciplines of ethnology and anthropology. The word folklore is sometimes restricted to the tradition of oral literature.

Folklore studies began in the early 19th century. The first folklorists concentrated exclusively upon rural peasants, preferably uneducated, and the few other groups relatively untouched by modern ways (*e.g.*, Gypsies). Their aim was to trace preserved archaic customs and beliefs to their remote origins in order to trace the history of human thought. In Germany, Jacob Grimm used folklore to illuminate Germanic religion of the Dark Ages. In Britain, Sir Edward Tylor, Andrew Lang, and others combined data from anthropology and folklore to "reconstruct" the beliefs and rituals of prehistoric peoples. The best-known work of this type is Sir James Frazer's *The Golden Bough* (1890).

Large collections of material—fairy tales and other types of folktales, ballads and songs, oral epics, folk plays, riddles, proverbs—were amassed in the course of these efforts. The underlying impulse often was nationalistic; since the folklore of a group reinforced its sense of ethnic identity, it figured prominently in many struggles for political independence and national unity.

As the scholarship of folklore developed, an important advance was the classification of material for comparative analysis. Standards of identification were devised, notably for ballads (by Francis J. Child) and for the plots and component motifs of folktales and myths (by Antti Aarne and Stith Thompson). Using these, Finnish scholars, led by Kaarle Krohn, developed the "historical-geographical" method of research, in which every known variant of a particular tale, ballad, riddle, or other item was classified as to place and date of collection in order to study distribution patterns and reconstruct "original" forms.

After World War II the study of folklore lost its restrictions of class and even of educational level; any group that expressed its inner cohesion by maintaining shared traditions qualified as a "folk," whether the linking factor was occupation, language, place of residence, age, religion, or ethnic origin. Emphasis also shifted from the past to the present, from the search for origins to the investigation of present meaning and function.

folk song   A traditional or composed song typically characterized by stanzaic form, refrain, and simplicity of melody. A form of folk literature, folk songs are essentially expressions of commonly shared ideas or feelings. Narrative folk songs are found chiefly in major Western and Asian civilizations, where they have long been cultivated by the most skillful singers. In the course of time these songs of warfare, of adventure, or of domestic life have formed local cycles, with characteristic metrical forms and formulas of plot and verbal expression.

folktale \ˈfōk-ˌtāl\   A characteristically anonymous, timeless, and placeless tale circulated orally among a people.

The existence of such tales is practically universal both in time and place. Certain peoples tell very simple stories and others tales of great complexity, but the basic elements of storyteller and audience are universal in history. A folktale travels with great ease even through language boundaries because it is characterized by a simple formula and by narrative motifs rather than by its verbal form. In many preliterate cultures folktales are hardly to be distinguished from myths, since, especially in tales of tricksters and heroes, they presuppose a background of belief about tribal origins and the relation of mortals and gods. Conscious fictions, however, enter into such stories. Animals abound, whether in their natural form or anthropomorphized. Adventure stories, exaggerations, marvels of all kinds, such as otherworld journeys, and narratives of marriage or sexual adventure, usually between human beings and animals, are common.

Follen \ˈfȯl-ən\, Adolf Ludwig, *also called* August Adolf Follenius \fȯ-ˈlā-nē-əs\ (b. Jan. 21, 1794, Giessen, Hesse [Germany]—d. Dec. 26, 1855, Bern, Switz.)   German political and Romantic poet, an important founder and leader of radical student groups in the early 19th century.

While studying at Giessen in 1814, he founded the democratic Deutsche Lesegesellschaft ("German Reading Society"). Expelled for his political views in 1815, he went to Heidelberg, where he was a founder of the political student association Teutonia. With his brother, Karl, he was also the leader of the Unbedingten ("Uncompromising Ones"), or Schwarzen ("Blacks"), a radical student group whose ideas resulted in the assassination of the dramatist August Kotzebue in 1819. He expressed his political ideas in the collection of songs *Freye Stimmen frischer Jugend* (1819; "Free Voices of Fresh Youth").

Banished after a political trial, Follen moved to Switzerland, where he published *Harfen-Grüsse aus Deutschland und der Schweiz* (1823; "Harp Greetings from Germany and Switzerland"). Follen also wrote nonpolitical poetry, inspired, like his political ideas, by a Romantic enthusiasm for the Middle Ages. His last important work was the epic poem *Tristans Eltern* (1857; "Tristan's Parents").

Folquet de Marseille \fȯl-ke-də-mȧr-ˈsey\, *also called* Foulques de Toulouse \fülk-də-tü-ˈlüs\ (b. *c.* 1155, Marseille?, Provence [France]—d. Dec. 25, 1231, Toulouse)   Provençal troubadour and cleric.

Born into a Genoese merchant family, Folquet became a poet about 1180. His works, which include love lyrics, crusading songs, and religious poems, demonstrate a classical education and careful metrical forms. In 1195 Folquet, with his wife and children, entered a Cistercian abbey and renounced his love poetry. He became abbot and, about 1205, bishop of Toulouse, in which capacity he engaged in persecuting the heretical Albigensians and helped to found the University of Toulouse.

Fomorian \fō-'wȯr-ē-ən, -'mȯr-\ [Middle Irish *fomóir* Fomorian, pirate, giant]   One of a race of sea robbers in Celtic legend who originally were probably gods representing the powers of evil and darkness.

Fonseca \dȧ-fūn-'sek-ə\, Manuel da (b. Oct. 15, 1911, Santiago-do-Cacém, Port.—d. March 11, 1993, Lisbon)   Portuguese novelist and poet who wrote realistic works about his homeland, the agricultural province of Alentejo.

Da Fonseca's literary career began with the publication of the poem "Rosa dos ventos" ("Rose of the Winds") in 1940. His best-known novel was *Cerromaior* (1943; "Biggest Hill"). Among his other books are *O fogo e as cinzas* (1952; "The Fire and the Ashes"), *Seara de vento* (1958; "Harvest of Wind"), *Um anjo no trapézio* (1968; "An Angel on the Trapeze"), *Tempo de solidão* (1969; "Time of Solitude"), and *Crónicas algarvias* (1986; "Constant Gibberish"), as well as the verse collections *Poemas completos* (1963) and *Obra poética* (1984).

Fontane \fȯn-'tä-nə\, Theodor (b. Dec. 30, 1819, Neuruppin, Brandenburg [Germany]—d. Sept. 20, 1898, Berlin)   Writer who is considered the first master of modern realistic fiction in Germany.

Fontane began his writing career in 1848 as a journalist, and he served for several years in England as correspondent for two Prussian newspapers. From this vantage he wrote many books on English life, including *Ein Sommer in London* (1854; "A Summer in London") and *Jenseits des Tweed* (1860; *Across the Tweed: A Tour of Mid-Victorian Scotland*). Between 1862 and 1882 he published a four-volume account of his travels in the borderlands of Brandenburg. He also wrote *Männer und Helden* (1850; "Men and Heroes") and *Balladen* (1861; "Ballads"), stirring celebrations of heroic and dramatic events.

Fontane produced his best work after he became the drama critic for the liberal newspaper *Vossische Zeitung*. Turning to the novel late in life, he wrote *Vor dem Sturm* (1878; *Before the Storm*), considered to be a masterpiece in the genre of the historical novel. In several of his novels Fontane wrote sympathetically of women in circumscribed domestic lives; *L'Adultera* (1882; *The Woman Taken in Adultery*), *Irrungen, Wirrungen* (1888; "Trials and Tribulations"; *Entanglements*), *Frau Jenny Treibel* (1893), and EFFI BRIEST (1895) are among his best. His other major works include *Der Stechlin* (1899), noted for its charming style, and *Schach von Wuthenow* (1883; *A Man of Honor*), in which he portrayed the weaknesses of the Prussian upper class.

Fontenelle \fȯⁿt-'nel\, Bernard Le Bovier, Sieur (Lord) de (b. Feb. 11, 1657, Rouen, Fr.—d. Jan. 9, 1757, Paris)   French scientist and man of letters.

Fontenelle settled in Paris after he had passed the age of 30 and had become famous as the writer of operatic librettos. His literary activity during the years 1683–88 won him a great reputation. *Lettres galantes* (1683; expanded edition, 1685) contributed to his fame, but *Nouveaux Dialogues des morts* (1683; "New Dialogues of the Dead"; 2nd part, 1684) enjoyed a greater success. The *Dialogues* were a series of conversations modeled on the dialogues of Lucian, between such figures as Socrates and Michel de Montaigne or Lucius Seneca and Paul Scarron.

Fontenelle's most famous work was *Entretiens sur la pluralité des mondes* (1686; *A Plurality of Worlds*). These charming and sophisticated dialogues were more influential than any other work in securing acceptance of the Copernican system. Fontenelle was elected to the Académie Française in 1691.

He was a close friend of Montesquieu and well known to Voltaire, who mocked him in his *Micromégas* (1752). Fontenelle's most original contribution was in his approach to

historiography, shown in his *De l'origine des fables* (1724; "Of the Origin of Fables"), in which he supports the theory that similar fables arise independently in several cultures.

Fonvizin \ˌfǒn-'vʸē-zʸin\, Denis Ivanovich (b. April 3 [April 14, New Style], 1744/45, Moscow, Russia—d. Dec. 1 [Dec. 12], 1792, St. Petersburg)   The foremost 18th-century Russian dramatist, who is noted for satirizing the cultural pretensions and privileged coarseness of the nobility.

Fonvizin worked as a government translator until 1769. Beginning by translating fables, Fonvizin later wrote original satirical fables, such as *Lisitsa-Koznodey* ("The Fox-Preacher"), published in 1787, but written long before. Fonvizin's wit and his knowledge of French and German classics made him a favorite in the court of Catherine the Great. His first important comedy, *Brigadir* (1769; "Brigadier"), ridiculed the contemporary fashion of aping French manners and speech. His masterpiece, *Nedorosl* (1783; "The Minor"), is considered the first truly Russian drama, and it is still performed. It deals with a gentry family so ignorant and brutish that they survive only through the industry of their ill-treated serfs. In 1783 Fonvizin criticized the Russian aristocracy and fell out of favor with Catherine. Thereafter, his works were banned, and his last years were spent in travel.

fool \'fül\, *also called* jester \'jes-tər\   A comic entertainer whose madness or imbecility, real or pretended, made him a source of amusement and gave him license to abuse and poke fun at even the most exalted of his patrons. Professional fools flourished from the days of the Egyptian pharaohs until well into the 18th century, finding a place in societies as diverse as that of the Aztecs of Mexico and the courts of medieval Europe. Often deformed, dwarfed, or crippled, fools may have been kept for luck as well as for amusement, in the belief that deformity can avert the evil eye and that abusive raillery can transfer ill luck from the abused to the abuser. Fool figures played a part in the religious rituals of India and pre-Christian Europe, and, in some societies, they were regarded as being inspired with poetic and prophetic powers.

The clown-player in William Shakespeare's dramatic company, Robert Armin, published a historical account of household fools in 1605. His knowledge may have influenced the playwright, who produced some of the best-known fools in literature, among them Touchstone in *As You Like It* and the Fool in *King Lear*.

Fool for Love   One-act play by Sam SHEPARD, produced and published in 1983. It is a romantic tragedy about the tumultuous love between a rodeo performer and his half sister. The father they have in common, a character called Old Man, acts as narrator and chorus.

fool's literature   Allegorical satires popular throughout Europe from the 15th to the 17th century, featuring the fool, or jester, who represented the weaknesses, vices, and grotesqueries of contemporary society. The first outstanding example of fool's literature was Sebastian Brant's DAS NARRENSCHIFF (1494; *The Ship of Fools*), which inspired such biting moral satires as Thomas Murner's poem *Narrenbeschwörung* (1512; "Exorcism of Fools") and Erasmus' *Encomium moriae* (1509; *The Praise of Folly*).

foot \'füt\ *plural* feet \'fēt\ [translation of Latin *pes* or Greek *poús*]   In poetry, the basic unit of verse meter consisting of any of various fixed combinations or groups of stressed and unstressed or long and short syllables. *Compare* CADENCE; METER.

The prevailing kind and number of feet, revealed by SCANSION, determines the meter of a poem. In classical (or quantitative) verse, a foot, or metron, is a combination of two or more long (written −) and short (◡) syllables. There are 28 different feet in classical verse, ranging from the pyrrhic (two short syllables) to the dispondee (four long syllables). The adaptation of classical metrics to the strongly accented Germanic languages, such as English, is in some ways problematic. The terminology persists, however, a foot usually being defined as a group of one stressed (′) and one or two unstressed (◡) syllables. An exception is the spondee, which consists of two stressed syllables; in English verse, this is usually two monosyllables, such as the phrase "He who." The most common feet in English verse are the iamb, an unstressed followed by a stressed syllable, as in:

re | port;

the trochee, a stressed followed by an unstressed syllable, as in:

dai | ly;

the anapest, two unstressed syllables fol-lowed by a stressed syllable, as in:

ser | e | nade;

and the dactyl, a stressed syllable followed by two unstressed syllables, as in:

mer | ri | ly.

If a single line of a poem contains only one foot, it is called monometer; two feet, dimeter; three feet, trimeter; four feet, tetrameter; five feet, pentameter; six feet, hexameter; seven feet, heptameter; eight feet, octameter. More than six, however, is rare.

Foote \'fut\, Shelby (b. Nov. 17, 1916, Greenville, Miss., U.S.) Historian, novelist, and short-story writer known for his works treating the United States Civil War and the American South.

Foote attended the University of North Carolina for two years, and he served in the U.S. Army during World War II. His first novel, *Tournament*, was published in 1949. Like many of Foote's later novels, it is set in Bristol, Miss., a fictional town modeled on Foote's hometown.

Follow Me Down (1950), considered by many critics to be his best novel, was based on an actual murder trial. *Love in a Dry Season* (1951) was set against the changing fortunes of the South from the 1920s to World War II. *Shiloh* (1952) was Foote's first popular success. It used the monologues of six soldiers to recreate the Civil War battle of the title. Foote next set out to write what proved to be his masterwork, *The Civil War: A Narrative* (1958–74), which consists of three volumes—*Fort Sumter to Perryville* (1958), *Fredericksburg to Meridian* (1963), *Red River to Appomattox* (1974). Considered a masterpiece by many critics, it was also criticized by academics for its lack of footnotes and other scholarly conventions. Foote appeared as narrator and commentator in Ken Burns's 11-hour television documentary *The Civil War* (1990).

Forché \fȯr-'shā\, Carolyn (Louise), *original surname* Sidlosky \sid-'läs-kē\ (b. April 28, 1950, Detroit, Mich., U.S.) American poet whose concern for human rights was reflected in her writing, especially in the collection *The Country Between Us* (1981), which examines events she witnessed in El Salvador.

Forché was educated at Michigan State and Bowling Green State universities. Her first collection of poetry, *Gathering the Tribes* (1976), evoked her childhood, her Slovak ancestry, and reflections on sexuality, family, and race.

From 1978 to 1980 Forché was a journalist in El Salvador, where, in addition to her involvement in Amnesty International as a human-rights advocate, she translated works by Salvadoran poets. The later five-part book-length poem *The Angel of History* (1994) is a compelling distillation of Forché's intensely moral sensibility.

In addition to her own writings, she edited several books, including *Against Forgetting: Twentieth-Century Poetry of Witness* (1993). She also translated the poetry of Claribel Alegría.

Ford \'fȯrd\, Ford Madox, *original name* Ford Hermann Hueffer \'hū-fər, 'hwef-ər\, *also called* Ford Madox Hueffer (b. Dec. 17, 1873, Merton, Surrey, Eng.—d. June 26, 1939, Deauville, Fr.) English novelist, editor, and critic, and an international influence in early 20th-century literature.

Ford's first novel was *The Shifting of Fire* (1892). His acquaintance with Joseph Conrad in 1897 led to their collaboration on *The Inheritors* (1901) and *Romance* (1903). In 1908 he founded the *English Review*, publishing pieces by both famous and then little-known contemporary British authors. At the same time, Ford produced works of his own: a trilogy of historical novels about the ill-fated Catherine Howard (the fifth wife of King Henry VIII) and novels of contemporary life in which he experimented with technique and style. It was not until THE GOOD SOLDIER (1915) that he matched an assured, controlled technique with powerful content. In it and many later works, his subject is the demise of aristocratic England in the course of war.

Ford served in World War I, in which he was gassed and shell-shocked. Afterward he changed his name from Hueffer to Ford and tried farming in Sussex and Left Bank life in Paris. While in Paris he edited the *Transatlantic Review* (January 1924–January 1925). Of more than 70 published works, those on which Ford's reputation rests are *The Good Soldier* and the tetralogy PARADE'S END (1950; comprising *Some Do Not* [1924], *No More Parades* [1925], *A Man Could Stand Up* [1926], and *Last Post* [1928]).

Ford \'fȯrd\, John (baptized April 17, 1586, Ilsington, Devon, Eng.—d. 1639?) Major English dramatist of the Caroline period, whose revenge tragedies are characterized by scenes of austere beauty, insight into human passions, and poetic diction of a high order.

In 1602 Ford was admitted to the Middle Temple (a training college for lawyers), and he remained there, except for a period of suspension (1606–08), until at least 1617. He published an elegy on the Earl of Devonshire and a prose pamphlet in 1606. Ford collaborated with Thomas Dekker on *The Sun's Darling* (1624), perhaps also on *The Welsh Ambassador* (1623), and on three other plays, now lost, of about the same date; he also may have contributed to Thomas Middleton's and William Rowley's *Spanish Gypsy* (1623), John Fletcher's *Fair Maid of the Inn* (1626), and other plays of Francis Beaumont and Fletcher.

Ford's own plays, only two of which can be definitely dated, were written between about 1627 and 1638: *The Broken Heart*; *The Lover's Melancholy* (1628); 'TIS PITY SHE'S A WHORE; *Perkin Warbeck*; *The Queen*; *The Fancies, Chaste and Noble*; *Love's Sacrifice*; and *The Lady's Trial* (1638). There is no certain record of him after 1639.

Ford \'fȯrd\, Richard (b. Feb. 16, 1944, Jackson, Miss., U.S.) American writer of novels and short stories.

Ford attended Michigan State University, Washington University Law School, and the University of California, Irvine, and subsequently taught in several American colleges and universities. In his first novel, *A Piece of My Heart* (1976), critics noted the influence of William Faulkner. *The Ultimate Good Luck* (1981) presents an American in Mexico who is drawn reluctantly into violence and murder as he tries to get his girlfriend's brother out of jail. In the early 1980s Ford worked for a sports magazine; the protagonist of his novel *The Sportswriter* (1986) is an alienated, middle-aged sportswriter reflecting on his life.

Ford also wrote short stories about lonely and damaged people, collected in *Rock Springs* (1987). In his fourth novel,

Wildlife (1990), a teenager in rugged Montana country witnesses the breakup of his parents' marriage.

forensic oratory \fŏr-'en-sik\, *also called* legal oratory. Type of suasive speech most often used in the defense of individual freedom and resistance to prosecution. It was the most characteristic type of oratory in ancient Athens, where laws stipulated that litigants should defend their own causes. In the 1st century BC of ancient Rome, Cicero became the foremost forensic orator and exerted a lasting influence on later Western oratory and prose style.

foreshadowing \ˌfŏr-'shad-ō-iŋ\   The organization and presentation of events and scenes in a work of fiction or drama so that the reader or observer is prepared to some degree for what occurs later in the work. This can be part of the general atmosphere of the work, or it can be a specific scene or object that gives a clue or hint as to a later development of the plot. The disastrous flood that occurs at the end of George Eliot's *The Mill on the Floss*, for example, is foreshadowed by many references to the river and to water in general throughout the book.

foreshortening \fŏr-'shŏrt-ən-iŋ\   Representation in art or literature that is compact, abridged, or shortened.

Forester \'fŏr-ə-stər\, C.S., *in full* Cecil Scott (b. Aug. 27, 1899, Cairo, Egypt—d. April 2, 1966, Fullerton, Calif., U.S.)   British historical novelist and journalist, best known as the creator of the British naval officer Horatio HORNBLOWER, whose rise from midshipman to admiral and peer during the Napoleonic Wars is told in a series of 12 novels.

Forester abandoned medicine for writing and achieved success with his first novel, *Payment Deferred* (1926); others include *Brown on Resolution* (1929), *The Gun* (1933), *The General* (1936), and *The Ship* (1943). Many of his novels were adapted to motion pictures; most notable among these is THE AFRICAN QUEEN (1935). Forester also wrote biographies and history, including *Hunting the Bismarck* (1959; U.S. title, *The Last Nine Days of the Bismarck* or *Sink the Bismarck!*). Forester described the genesis and progress of the Hornblower series in the self-revealing *Hornblower Companion* (1964).

foreword \'fŏr-wərd\   Prefatory comments (as for a book), especially when written by someone other than the author.

formalism \'fŏr-mə-ˌliz-əm\   Marked attention to arrangement, style, or artistic means (as in art or literature), usually with corresponding de-emphasis of content. The word is used to refer to the approach taken by literary critics who emphasize the formal aspects of a literary work, in particular the Russian school of literary criticism that flourished from 1914 to 1928.

Formalism \'fŏr-mə-ˌliz-əm\, *also called* Russian Formalism. Twentieth-century Russian school of literary criticism that flourished from 1914 to 1928. It began in two groups: OPOYAZ (an acronym for Russian words meaning "Society for the Study of Poetic Language"), founded in 1914 at St. Petersburg and led by the literary critic Viktor Shklovsky; and the Moscow Linguistic Circle, founded in 1915. Both groups made use of the linguistic techniques of Ferdinand de SAUSSURE. Although they based their approach largely on Symbolist notions concerning the autonomy of the text and the discontinuity between literary and other uses of language, the Formalists sought to make their analyses more objective and scientific than those of Symbolist criticism. Closely allied to the Russian Futurists and opposed to sociological criticism, the Formalists analyzed the text itself, apart from its psychological, sociological, biographical, and historical elements.

Formalism was a powerful influence in the Soviet Union until 1929, when it was condemned for its lack of political perspective. Later, largely through the work of the structuralist linguist Roman Jakobson, it became highly influential in the West, notably in Anglo-American New Criticism, which is sometimes called formalism, and in structuralism.

form criticism   A method of biblical criticism that seeks to classify units of scripture into literary patterns (such as love poems, parables, sayings, elegies, legends) and that attempts to trace each type to its period of oral transmission in an effort to determine the original form.

fornaldarsǫgur \'fŏr-näl-ˌdär-'sœ- gœr\ [Old Norse, sagas of old times]   Icelandic sagas dealing with the ancient myths and legends of Germania, with the adventures of Vikings, or with other exotic adventures in foreign lands. The stories take place on the European continent before the settlement of Iceland. Though the existing *fornaldarsǫgur* were written between 1250 and 1350, after the Icelanders' sagas (written between 1200 and 1220), they are thought to be of earlier oral composition.

The *fornaldarsǫgur* do not have the same literary value as the Icelanders' sagas, but, because they are based on lost heroic poetry, they are of great antiquarian interest. The most important of these is the VǪLSUNGA SAGA. *Compare* ICELANDERS' SAGAS.

Forner \ˌfŏr-'ner\, Juan Pablo (b. Feb. 23, 1756, Mérida, Spain—d. March 17, 1797, Madrid)   The foremost literary polemicist of the 18th century in Spain. He often used his brilliant wit against fads, affectations, and muddleheadedness.

Forner's brilliant wit and biting sarcasm are evident in his early work *Sátira contra los abusos introducidos en la poesía castellana* (1782; "Satire Against the Abuses Introduced into Castilian Poetry"), an attack against the innovations of verse styles such as *gongorismo*. In *El asno erudito* (1782; "The Erudite Ass") Forner viciously attacked the dramatist Tomás de Iriarte and his work. He was forbidden to write satires after 1785. His two most important works are *Exequias de la lengua castellana* (1795; "Exequies of the Castilian Language"), a defense of Castilian literature, and *Oración apologética por la España y su mérito literario* (1786; "Arguments on Behalf of Spain and Her Literary Merits").

Forrest \'fŏr-əst\, Leon (b. Jan. 8, 1937, Chicago, Ill., U.S.) African-American author of large, inventive novels that fuse myth, history, legend, and contemporary realism.

From 1965 to 1973 Forrest worked as a journalist for various papers, including the Nation of Islam's weekly *Muhammad Speaks*. He also published excerpts from his first novel, *There Is a Tree More Ancient than Eden*, which was issued in book form in 1973.

There Is a Tree portrays the tangled relationships between the illegitimate offspring of a onetime slave-owning family; several of the book's distinctive characters reappear in subsequent Forrest novels. Echoes of Greek and Latin mythology are present in *The Bloodworth Orphans* (1977), about the search by three orphaned siblings for roots and understanding amid turmoil. In *Two Wings to Veil My Face* (1983) an ex-slave tells her life story to her great-grandson. Forrest's most ambitious novel, *Divine Days* (1992), concerns the efforts of an African-American playwright to investigate the disappearance of a fellow black. A book of collected essays, *Relocations of the Spirit*, was published in 1994.

Forsaken Merman, The   Poem by Matthew ARNOLD, published in 1849 in *The Strayed Reveller, and Other Poems. By A.*, the author's first verse collection. The merman of the poem grieves for his human wife, who, after hearing the church bells at Easter, has abandoned him and their children to live on land among humans, never to return. The poem is suffused with feelings of melancholy and loss.

Forster \\'fȯr-stər\\, E.M., *in full* Edward Morgan (b. Jan. 1, 1879, London, Eng.—d. June 7, 1970, Coventry, Warwickshire) British novelist, essayist, and social and literary critic.

Forster attended King's College, Cambridge, where he became a member of the Apostles, an elite, semisecret group of intellectuals.

His first essays and short stories began to appear in 1903 in the liberal *Independent Review*. By 1910 Forster

had written four novels, *Where Angels Fear to Tread* (1905), *The Longest Journey* (1907), A ROOM WITH A VIEW (1908), and HOWARDS END (1910). From the first his novels showed a strong strain of social comment, based on acute observation of middle-class life. Forster's strength as a novelist lay in his ability to personify archetypes, his depictions of the struggle between the base and noble aspects of human nature, his memorable, rounded characters, and his stylistic clar-

BBC Hulton Picture Library

ity. These first four novels were followed by a number of short stories and by MAURICE, a novel with a homosexual theme, which was published posthumously in 1971.

Forster visited India in 1912–13. From 1915 to 1919 he served with the Red Cross in Alexandria, Egypt, and in 1921 he returned to India. His experiences in these two colonial settings, along with his lifelong exploration of the ambiguities of character, inform what most consider to be his masterwork, A PASSAGE TO INDIA (1924).

In his middle years Forster turned to literary criticism. His ASPECTS OF THE NOVEL (1927) is a classic discussion of aesthetics and the creative process. His collections of essays, sketches, and biographies include *Abinger Harvest* (1936), *Two Cheers for Democracy* (1951), and *The Hill of Devi* (1953).

Forster \\'fȯr-stər\\, Georg, *in full* Johann Georg Adam Forster (b. Nov. 26, 1754, Nassenhuben, near Danzig [now Gdańsk, Poland]—d. Jan. 12, 1794, Paris, Fr.) Explorer and scientist who helped to establish the literary travel book as a favored genre in German literature.

With his father, Johann Reinhold Forster, he immigrated to England in 1766. Both accompanied Captain James Cook on his second voyage around the world (1772–75). Forster's account of the journey, *A Voyage Round the World* (1777), was based on his father's journals; it later appeared in a German version, *Reise um die Welt* (1778–80). The book established Forster as an advanced thinker and accomplished stylist and influenced much German scientific and literary writing.

He held professorships at the University of Kassel and at the university in Wilno (now Vilnius, Lithuania) before becoming librarian at the University of Mainz. Sympathetic with the French Revolution, he championed the republican government in Mainz, occupied by the French in 1792, and in 1793 he went to Paris to negotiate on its behalf. Forster spent his final days in Paris disillusioned by the excesses of the Reign of Terror.

Forster \\'fȯr-stər\\, John (b. April 2, 1812, Newcastle upon Tyne, Northumberland, Eng.—d. Feb. 2, 1876, London) Writer and journalist who, through his friendship with the influential editor Leigh Hunt, became adviser, agent, and proof-

reader to many leading writers of the day. A close friend of Charles Dickens, he wrote *The Life of Dickens* (1872–74), an essential sourcebook and a literary masterpiece, despite its flaws.

After early contributions to an encyclopedia and to periodicals, he joined *The Examiner* (1833) and was its editor (1847–55). In 1855 he became secretary to the lunacy commissioners and in 1861 became a commissioner. Apart from his now superseded historical treatises on the 17th century, Forster's *Life and Adventures of Oliver Goldsmith* (1848; expanded into *The Life and Times . . .*, 1854), *Walter Savage Landor* (1869), and the unfinished *Life of Jonathan Swift* (1876) remain authoritative.

Forster \\'fȯr-stər\\, Margaret (b. May 25, 1938, Carlisle, Cumberland, Eng.) British novelist and biographer whose books are known for their detailed characterizations.

Forster's novels generally featured ordinary heroines struggling with issues of love and family. Beginning with *Dames' Delight* (1964) and *Georgy Girl* (1965; film, 1970), she published novels with regularity. *Mother Can You Hear Me?* (1979) and *Have the Men Had Enough?* (1989) are both about a family's efforts to care for an elder member. *The Bride of Lowther Fell* (1980) and *Lady's Maid* (1990) are set in the Victorian era.

Among Forster's other novels are *The Travels of Maudie Tipstaff* (1967), *Mr. Bone's Retreat* (1971), *Marital Rites* (1981), and *The Battle for Christabel* (1991). *Significant Sisters: The Grassroots of Active Feminism 1839–1939* (1984) profiles a number of famous women. Forster also wrote biographies of several writers.

Forsyte family \\'fȯr-ˌsīt\\ A fictional upper-middle-class English family created by John Galsworthy in his trilogy *The Forsyte Saga* and further treated in *A Modern Comedy* (1929), a trilogy set in the post-World War I era and consisting of *The White Monkey* (1924), *The Silver Spoon* (1926), and *Swan Song* (1928).

Forsyte Saga, The \\'fȯr-ˌsīt\\ Sequence of three novels linked by two interludes by John GALSWORTHY. The saga chronicles the lives of three generations of a monied, middle-class English family at the turn of the century. As published in 1922, *The Forsyte Saga* consisted of the novel *The Man of Property* (1906); the interlude (a short story) "Indian Summer of a Forsyte" (1918); the novel *In Chancery* (1920); the interlude "Awakening" (1920); and the novel *To Let* (1921).

Soames Forsyte, a solicitor and "the man of property," is married to the beautiful, penniless Irene, who falls in love with Philip Bosinney, the French architect whom Soames had hired to build a country house. Soames rapes Irene and proceeds to ruin Bosinney, who subsequently dies in a traffic accident in London. Irene returns to Soames.

In Chancery concerns the love between Irene and Young Jolyon Forsyte, Soames's cousin. (The story of the last days of Old Jolyon, his father, is told in "Indian Summer of a Forsyte.") Irene and Soames divorce; she marries Jolyon and bears a son, Jon. Soames and his second wife, Annette Lamotte, have a daughter, Fleur.

In *To Let*, Fleur and Jon grow up and fall in love; Jolyon informs his son of Irene and Soames's past relationship. Although Fleur is determined to marry Jon, he refuses. Fleur becomes the wife of Michael Mont, son of a baronet. Jolyon dies, and Irene leaves England. Soames discovers that Annette is involved in an affair with a Frenchman, as Irene had been.

Forsyth \\'fȯr-ˌsīth\\, Frederick (b. Aug. 25, 1938, Ashford, Kent, Eng.) British author of best-selling thriller novels noted for their journalistic style and their fast-paced plots based on international political affairs and personalities.

Forsyth was a reporter for the *Eastern Daily Press* from 1958 to 1961 and a European correspondent for Reuters News

Agency from 1961 to 1965. He worked as a correspondent for the BBC until 1968. *The Biafra Story* (1969) is his nonfiction history of the Biafran war.

Forsyth's first and most admired novel, *The Day of the Jackal* (1971), was based on rumors he had heard of an actual assassination attempt on the life of French president Charles de Gaulle. Several other carefully researched thrillers followed, including *The Odessa File* (1972), about a search for a Nazi war criminal, and *The Dogs of War* (1974), about an uprising in an African nation. His later works include the novels *The Devil's Alternative* (1979), *The Fourth Protocol* (1984), and *The Negotiator* (1989) and the short-story collection *No Comebacks* (1982).

Fort \'fôr\, Paul (b. Feb. 1, 1872, Reims, Fr.—d. April 20, 1960, Argenlieu) French poet usually associated with the Symbolist movement.

At the age of 18, reacting against the naturalistic theater, Fort founded the Théâtre d'Art (1890–93), in which formalized backcloths and stylized performances were substituted for realistic settings and acting. He also founded and edited the review *Vers et Prose* (1905–14), which published the work of Paul Valéry and other important Symbolist writers. Between 1897 and 1924 Fort produced 30 volumes of ballads. His ballad stanzas were printed in the form of prose paragraphs to emphasize the importance of rhythm and assonance over rhyme.

For the Union Dead Title poem of a collection by Robert LOWELL, published in 1964. Lowell originally titled the poem "Colonel Shaw and the Massachusetts 54th" to commemorate Robert Gould Shaw, a white Bostonian who had commanded a battalion of black Union troops during the American Civil War, and published it in the 1960 edition of *Life Studies*.

The poem alludes to three significant incidents of the previous 100 years: Shaw's death and anonymous burial; the dedication, in Boston in the 1890s, of a memorial to Shaw and others who died for the Union; and the violent resistance to school integration in contemporary America.

Fortuna \fôr-'tü-nə\ In Roman mythology, goddess of chance or lot who became identified with the Greek TYCHE. The original Italian deity was probably regarded as the bearer of prosperity and abundance. Frequently she was an oracular goddess consulted in various ways regarding the future. Fortuna was sometimes referred to as Fors Fortuna, combining Fors, the male symbol of chance, and Fortuna, the female symbol, originally separate but later regarded as one entity with both male and female aspects.

Fortunata y Jacinta \,fôr-tü-'nä-tä-ē-ḵä-'thēn-tä, -'sēn-\ Naturalistic novel by Benito PÉREZ GALDÓS, published in four volumes in 1886–87 and considered a masterwork of Spanish fiction. *Fortunata y Jacinta* offers deft characterizations and incisive details of the social, personal, and psychological aspects of its era. The novel was part of Pérez Galdós' lengthy series of *novelas españolas contemporáneas* ("contemporary Spanish novels") and established many characters who would reappear in subsequent novels.

The main plot concerns two unhappily married Spanish women of different classes. Fortunata is the working-class wife of Maxi Rubín and the mistress of Juanito Santa Cruz, a self-indulgent Madrileño (citizen of Madrid). Middle-class Jacinta is Santa Cruz's wife. Ironically, Fortunata bears Santa Cruz children out of wedlock but is childless with her husband; the marriage of Jacinta and Santa Cruz is similarly barren. After sundry vicissitudes, now on her deathbed, Fortunata sends her newborn child to Jacinta.

Fortunatus \,fôr-chə-'nä-təs\, Venantius (Honorius Clementianus) (b. *c.* 540, Treviso, near Venice [Italy]—d. *c.* 600,

Poitiers, Aquitaine [now in France]) Poet and churchman whose Latin poems and hymns combine echoes of classical Latin poets with a medieval tone.

Probably in fulfillment of a vow, Fortunatus crossed the European continent, visiting Metz, Paris, and Tours. In 567 he reached Poitiers, where Radegunda, former queen consort of Chlotar I, had founded a monastery. Impressed by her holiness and that of Agnes, the abbess, he became a priest and subsequently bishop of Poitiers.

The extant works of Fortunatus are the *Vita S. Martini*, his prose biographies of saints (including the *Vita Radegundis*), and 11 books of poems (with an appendix of 34 poems). His early poems include addresses to bishops and officials, panegyrics, an epithalamium, epigrams, and occasional poems. Their dominant characteristic is a strongly rhetorical flavor. The influence of rhetoric is especially effective in a later poem celebrating the installation of Agnes as abbess. Of his six poems on the subject of the Cross, two splendid hymns, the *Pange lingua* and the *Vexilla regis*, have been translated into English as "Sing, My Tongue, the Glorious Battle" and "The Royal Banners Forward Go."

fortune \'fôr-chən\ [Latin *fortuna,* derivative from the root of *fors* chance, luck] A hypothetical force or power that unpredictably determines events and issues favorably or unfavorably. It is often personified as Fortuna.

Fortune Theatre \'fôr-chən, 'fôr-,tyün\ Elizabethan public playhouse in northern London, built in 1600 by Philip Henslowe to compete with Cuthbert Burbage's new Globe Theatre. It was named after the goddess of fortune, whose statue stood over the front doorway.

The Fortune opened in 1600 with a performance by the theatrical company known as the Admiral's Men. After the Puritans closed the public theaters in 1642, the Fortune was used occasionally for clandestine performances. The theater was torn down in 1661.

Forverts \'fôr-,verts\, *also called* Jewish Daily Forward. Yiddish-language newspaper founded in 1897 and published in New York City.

The newspaper was established by Abraham Cahan and the Jewish Socialist Press Federation as a civic aid and a unifying device for Jewish immigrants from Europe. It carried socialist-oriented columns on government and politics and covered subjects intended to familiarize readers with American culture. It also published short stories and novels in serial form, most notably those of Isaac Bashevis Singer.

At the height of its influence, the *Forverts* had a daily circulation of some 200,000 in several regional editions, but by the late 20th century readership was greatly reduced. In 1984 the paper changed from a daily to a weekly, and in 1990 the editors began publishing an English-language version entitled *Forward*.

For Whom the Bell Tolls Novel by Ernest HEMINGWAY, published in 1940.

Set near Segovia, Spain, in 1937, the novel tells the story of American teacher Robert Jordan, who has joined the antifascist Loyalist army. Jordan has been sent to make contact with a guerrilla band and blow up a bridge to advance a Loyalist offensive. The action takes place during Jordan's 72 hours at the guerrilla camp. During this period he falls in love with Maria, and he befriends the shrewd but cowardly guerrilla leader Pablo and his courageous wife Pilar. Jordan manages to destroy the bridge; Pablo, Pilar, Maria, and two other guerrillas escape, but Jordan is injured. Proclaiming his love to Maria once more, he awaits the fascist troops and certain death.

The title is from a sermon by John Donne containing the famous words "No man is an Iland, intire of it selfe; every man is a peece of the Continent. . . . And therefore never send to know for whom the bell tolls; it tolls for thee."

Fosco, Count \\'fôs-kō, 'fäs-\\, *in full* Count Isidore Ottavio Baldassore Fosco. Fictional character, a refined but implacable villain in THE WOMAN IN WHITE by Wilkie Collins. He is considered the original of the fat, cultured villain who later became a common type in crime novels.

Foscolo \\'fôs-kō-lō\\, Ugo, *original name* Niccolò Foscolo (b. Feb. 6 [Jan. 26, Greek calendar], 1778, Zacynthus, Venetian republic [now Zákinthos, Greece]—d. Sept. 10, 1827, Turnham Green, near London, Eng.) Poet and novelist whose works rank among the masterpieces of Italian literature.

Foscolo was educated at Spalato (now Split, Croatia) and Padua in Italy, and about 1793, with his family, he took up residence in Venice. In 1797 the performance of his tragedy *Tieste* ("Thyestes") made him famous.

Foscolo's early enthusiasm for Napoleon, proclaimed in his ode *A Bonaparte liberatore* (1797; "To Bonaparte the Liberator"), quickly turned to disillusionment when Napoleon ceded Venetia to Austria in 1797. Foscolo's highly popular novel *Ultime lettere di Jacopo Ortis* (1802; *The Last Letters of Jacopo Ortis*) contains a bitter denunciation of the transaction. Some critics consider this story the first modern Italian novel.

When the Austrians and Russians invaded Italy in 1799, Foscolo, with other Italian patriots, joined the French side. In 1804 he was sent to serve in France. While there he translated several classical works and Laurence Sterne's *A Sentimental Journey* into Italian and wrote odes and sonnets. In 1807 Foscolo returned to Milan and published *Dei sepolcri* ("Of the Sepulchres"), a patriotic poem in blank verse, written as a protest against Napoleon's decree forbidding tomb inscriptions. Its publication won for its author the chair of Italian rhetoric at the University of Padua in 1808. When the chair was abolished by Napoleon the next year, Foscolo moved to Milan. The satirical references to Napoleon in his tragedy *Aiace* (first performed 1811; "Ajax") again brought suspicion on him; in 1812 he moved to Florence, where he wrote another tragedy, *Ricciarda*, and most of his highly acclaimed unfinished poem *Le grazie* (published in fragments 1803 and 1818, in full 1822; "The Graces"). In 1813 Foscolo returned to Milan.

Napoleon fell the following year, the Austrians returned to Italy, and Foscolo, refusing to swear allegiance, fled first to Switzerland and in 1816 to England. He supported himself by teaching and writing commentaries on Dante, Boccaccio, and Petrarch for *The Edinburgh Review* and *The Quarterly Review*.

Foucault \\fü-'kō\\, Michel (Paul) (b. Oct. 15, 1926, Poitiers, Fr.—d. June 25, 1984, Paris) French structuralist (and, later, poststructuralist) theorist noted for his examination of the concepts and codes by which societies operate.

Foucault studied under the Marxist philosopher Louis Althusser at the École Normale Supérieure in Paris. He taught at the University of Clermont-Ferrand and at the University of Paris-Vincennes. From 1970 until his death he was a professor at the Collège de France.

In several books, including *Folie et déraison: histoire de la folie à l'âge classique* (1961; *Madness and Civilization*) and *Surveiller et punir: naissance de la prison* (1975; *Discipline and Punish: The Birth of the Prison*), Foucault theorizes that institutions such as asylums, hospitals, and prisons are society's devices for exclusion and that by surveying social attitudes in relation to these institutions one can examine the development and uses of power.

Among Foucault's other works are *Les Mots et les choses: une archéologie des sciences humaines* (1966; *The Order of Things: An Archaeologie of Human Sciences*) and *L'Archéologie du savoir*

(1969; *The Archaeology of Knowledge*). His three-volume *Histoire de la sexualité* (1976–84; *History of Sexuality*) examines the history of Western attitudes toward sexuality since the ancient Greeks. His theories of discourse analysis were highly influential in subsequent literary theory and criticism.

Foulques *see* FOLQUET.

found poem A poem consisting of words found in a nonpoetic context (such as a product label) and usually broken into lines that convey a verse rhythm. Both the term and the concept are modeled on the *objet trouvé* (French: "found object"), an artifact not created as art or a natural object that is held to have aesthetic value when taken out of its context.

Fountainhead, The Novel by Ayn RAND, published in 1943. An exposition of the author's anticommunist philosophy of "objectivism," *The Fountainhead* tells of the struggle of genius architect Howard Roark—said to be based on Frank Lloyd Wright—as he confronts conformist mediocrity.

In Rand's world, suppression of individual creativity is the greatest evil. Roark is expelled from architectural school for his nonconformist ideas, but he pursues his vision undaunted.

Fouqué \\fü-'kā\\, Friedrich Heinrich Karl de La Motte, Baron (b. Feb. 12, 1777, Brandenburg [Germany]—d. Jan. 23, 1843, Berlin) German novelist and playwright remembered chiefly as the author of the popular fairy tale *Undine* (1811).

Fouqué's writings expressed heroic ideals of chivalry designed to arouse a sense of German tradition and national character in his contemporaries during the Napoleonic era. He gathered much of his material from Scandinavian sagas and myths. His dramatic trilogy *Der Held des Nordens* (1808–10; "Hero of the North") is the first modern dramatic treatment of the Nibelung story and a source for the later dramas of Friedrich Hebbel and the operas of Richard Wagner. His most lasting success, however, has been the story of Undine, a water sprite who marries the knight Hildebrand to acquire a soul and thus become human but who later loses this love to treachery.

Four Branches of the Mabinogi, The \\,mab-i-'nō-gē\\ (*Welsh* Pedair Cainc y Mabinogi) Four distinct but linked Welsh narratives compiled some time between the latter half of the 11th century and the early 13th century. Believed to be the work of a single redactor, the Four Branches have roots in Celtic myth and folklore, while at the same time the courtly settings and generally courteous behavior of the characters—quite distinct from the frequently unvarnished ferocity of Irish saga—are a link to the continental romances of Chrétien de Troyes. *Pwyll Pendefig Dyfed* ("Pwyll Prince of Dyfed") describes Pwyll's wooing of a fairy princess, Rhiannon, and Rhiannon's loss and recovery of their child Pryderi, whom she is falsely accused of murdering after he is supernaturally abducted the night of his birth. *Branwen ferch Llŷr* ("Branwen Daughter of Llŷr") relates the marriage of Branwen, sister of Brân the Blessed, king of Britain, to Matholwch, the king of Ireland, and the treacherous acts of Efnisien, Brân's half-brother, which result in a devastating war between Ireland and Britain from which only Branwen, the wounded Brân, and seven other men escape alive back to Wales. *Manawydan fab Llŷr* ("Manawydan Son of Llŷr") comprises the further adventures of two of the escapees, Manawydan (Brân and Branwen's brother) and Pryderi, who with his wife Cigfa and mother Rhiannon combat an enchantment placed over Pryderi's realm. *Math fab Mathonwy* ("Math Son of Mathonwy") is a complex tale focusing on Math, a prince of northern Wales, his nephew Gwydion, and Gwydion's nephew Lleu Llaw Gyffes ("Lleu Skilled Hand"); among many other events, Gwydion's magic and duplicity lead to the death of Pryderi. *See also* MABINOGION.

Four Quartets, The Series of four poems by T.S. ELIOT, published individually from 1936 to 1942, and in book form in 1943; the work is considered to be Eliot's masterpiece.

Each of the quartets has five "movements" and each is titled by a place name—BURNT NORTON (1936), EAST COKER (1940), THE DRY SALVAGES (1941), and LITTLE GIDDING (1942). Eliot's insights into the cyclical nature of life are revealed through themes and images deftly woven throughout the four poems. The work addresses the connections of the personal and historical present and past, spiritual renewal, and the very nature of experience; it is considered the poet's clearest exposition of his Christian beliefs.

Four Saints in Three Acts Opera consisting of a prologue and four acts, with libretto by Gertrude STEIN and music by Virgil Thomson. Stein completed the libretto in 1927, the score was published in 1934, and the opera was first performed in 1934.

Thomson divided Stein's libretto into scenes and acts, and added two figures representing the laity to the cast of characters. The plotless opera, set in 16th-century Spain, treats the Spaniards St. Theresa of Avila, St. Ignatius of Loyola, and two fictional figures, St. Settlement and St. Chavez.

fourteener \ˌfȯr-ˈtē-nər\ A poetic line of 14 syllables; especially, such a line consisting of seven iambic feet. The form is also called a heptameter or septenary. It was used in Greek and Latin prosody and flourished in Elizabethan English narrative verse but since then has been used only rarely. When each fourteener is written as two lines of eight and six syllables, it becomes the standard ballad meter, as in Samuel Taylor Coleridge's "The Rime of the Ancient Mariner."

Fowles \ˈfaùlz\, John (Robert) (b. March 31, 1926, Leigh upon Sea, Essex, Eng.) English novelist whose richly allusive and descriptive works combine psychological probings—chiefly of sex and love—with an interest in the social and philosophical context of human behavior.

Fowles's first novel, *The Collector* (1963; film, 1965), about a shy man who kidnaps a girl and keeps her captive in a hapless search for love, was immediately successful. A Greek island is the setting of his second novel, *The Magus* (1966, rev. ed., 1977; film, 1968). THE FRENCH LIEUTENANT'S WOMAN (1969; film, 1981) is a love story set in Victorian England, which, by use of authorial intrusion and parodies of early novelistic devices, richly documents the social mores of that time. A volume of collected novellas, *The Ebony Tower*, was published in 1974. His later novels include *Daniel Martin* (1977), *Mantissa* (1982), and *A Maggot* (1985).

Foxe \ˈfäks\, John (b. 1516, Boston, Lincolnshire, Eng.—d. April 18, 1587, Cripplegate, London) English Puritan preacher and author of *The Book of Martyrs* (1563), a graphic and polemic account of those who suffered for the cause of Protestantism from the 14th century through the reign of Queen Mary I in Foxe's own time. It helped shape popular opinion about Roman Catholicism for at least a century.

In London, Foxe became tutor to the grandchildren of the Duke of Norfolk. He was ordained a deacon of the Church of England. Foxe worked for the Reformation, writing several tracts. He also began his account of martyrs, but the accession of the Roman Catholic queen Mary I in 1553 forced him to flee overseas. In Strasbourg, Fr., he published his partly completed martyrology in Latin as *Commentarii rerum in ecclesia gestarum* (1554; "Commentaries on Affairs Within the Church"). He later went to Basel, where he wrote a burning appeal to the English nobility to restrain the queen from persecuting Protestants: *Ad inclytos ac praepotentes Angliae proceres* (1557; "To the Renowned and Powerful Nobles of England"). With the aid of manuscripts sent to him from England, he expanded his account of the martyrs and had it printed in 1559.

Foxe's translation into English of his Latin original was printed in March 1563 under the title *Actes and Monuments of these Latter and Perillous Dayes*. It immediately acquired the popular name *The Book of Martyrs*. In 1570 he produced his greatly improved second edition. This was the crown of his achievement; he made few changes in his third (1576) and fourth (1583) editions.

Foxe was ordained an Anglican priest in 1560, but having Puritan scruples he refused all offices. He often preached, however, and a sermon delivered at Paul's Cross (*A Sermon, Of Christ Crucified* [1570]) had a wide sale.

fragmentist \ˈfrag-mən-tist\ A writer of a literary fragment.

Fra Lippo Lippi \ˌfrä-ˈlē-pō-ˈlē-pē\ Poem by Robert BROWNING, published in the two-volume collection *Men and Women* in 1855.

Considered one of Browning's finest dramatic monologues, "Fra Lippo Lippi" is loosely based on the life of Florentine painter Filippo Lippi (c. 1406–69) as described in Giorgio Vasari's 16th-century *Lives of the Painters*. In the poem, Lippi's impoverished aunt had placed him in a monastery because she could not afford to raise him. His patron Cosimo de' Medici later tries to lock the carousing monk in his quarters at night, but when Lippi escapes through a window, Cosimo grants him freedom.

frame \ˈfrām\ **1.** An event or set of events or circumstances that form the background for the action of a novel or dramatic work. **2.** A literary device used in a story or dramatic work to unite the matter of the story or drama or to provide a plausible excuse for relating or presenting it; especially, such a device that is not essential to the story or dramatic action itself. A work that uses such a device is called a *frame story*.

Frame \ˈfrām\, Janet, *in full* Janet Paterson Frame Clutha \ˈklü-thə\ (b. Aug. 28, 1924, Dunedin, N.Z.) Leading New Zealand writer of novels, short fiction, and poetry.

Frame's early memories of poverty, the deaths of two sisters, and several stays in psychiatric hospitals provided much of the impetus for her work.

Her first book, *The Lagoon* (1951), was a collection of short stories expressing the sense of isolation and insecurity of those who feel they do not fit into a normal world. *Owls Do Cry* (1957), an experimental novel, incorporates both poetry and prose and investigates the ambiguous border between sanity and madness. Among her other novels are *Faces in the Water* (1961), *The Edge of the Alphabet* (1962), *Snowman, Snowman: Fables and Fantasies* (1963), *Scented Gardens for the Blind* (1963), *The Adaptable Man* (1965), *A State of Siege* (1966), *The Rainbirds* (1968), *Intensive Care* (1970), *Daughter Buffalo* (1972), and *Living in the Maniototo* (1979).

She wrote three volumes of memoirs, *To the Is-land* (1982), *An Angel at My Table* (1984), and *The Envoy from Mirror City* (1985).

frame story *also called* frame tale [translation of German *Rahmenerzählung*] Overall unifying story within which one or more tales are related. In the single story, the opening and closing constitutes a frame. In the cyclical frame story—that is, a story in which several tales are related—some frames are externally imposed and only loosely bind the diversified stories. *The Thousand and One Nights*, in which Scheherazade (Shahrazad) avoids death by telling her royal husband a story every night and leaving it incomplete, is an example of a frame story. Other frames are an integral part of the tales, as in Giovanni Boccaccio's *Decameron*, in which the stories are woven together by a common theme. Another famous example is Geoffrey Chaucer's *The Canterbury Tales*, in which the pilgrimage frame brings together the varied tellers of the tales.

Framley Parsonage \'fram-lē\ Novel by Anthony TROL-LOPE, published serially from January 1860 to April 1861 and in three volumes in 1861, the fourth of his six BARSETSHIRE NOVELS.

France \'fräⁿs\, Anatole, *pseudonym of* Jacques-Anatole-François Thibault \tē-'bō\ (b. April 16, 1844, Paris, Fr.—d. Oct. 12, 1924, Saint-Cyr-sur-Loire) Writer and ironic, skeptical, and urbane critic who was considered in his day the ideal French man of letters. He was elected to the Académie Française in 1896 and was awarded the Nobel Prize for Literature in 1921.

France's characteristic skepticism appears in such early works as *Le Crime de Sylvestre Bonnard* (1881), a novel about a philologist in love with his books and bewildered by everyday life; *La Rôtisserie de la Reine Pédauque* (1893; *At the Sign of the Reine Pédauque*), which discreetly mocks belief in the occult; and *Les Opinions de M. Jérôme Coignard* (1893), in which an ironic and perspicacious critic examines the great institutions of the state.

France underwent considerable turmoil in his personal life. His marriage ended in divorce in 1893. He had earlier met Mme Arman de Caillavet, and their liaison inspired his novels *Thaïs* (1890), a tale set in Egypt of a courtesan who becomes a saint, and *Le Lys rouge* (1894; *The Red Lily*), a love story.

A marked change in France's work first appears in four volumes collected under the title *L'Histoire contemporaine* (1897–1901). The first three volumes—*L'Orme du mail* (1897; *The Elm-Tree on the Mall*), *Le Mannequin d'osier* (1897; *The Wicker Work Woman*), and *L'Anneau d'améthyste* (1899; *The Amethyst Ring*)—depict the intrigues of a provincial town. The last volume, *Monsieur Bergeret à Paris* (1901; *Monsieur Bergeret in Paris*), concerns the participation of the hero in the Dreyfus Affair—a 12-year controversy involving false charges of treason against French army officer Alfred Dreyfus and virulent anti-Semitism. *Monsieur Bergeret* is the story of France himself, who felt compelled to support Dreyfus. After 1900 he introduced his social preoccupations into most of his stories. *Crainquebille* (1903), a comedy in three acts adapted by France from an earlier short story, proclaims the hostility toward the bourgeois order that led France eventually to embrace socialism. Toward the end of his life his sympathies were drawn to communism. However, *Les Dieux ont soif* (1912; *The Gods Are Athirst*) and *L'Île des Pingouins* (1908; *Penguin Island*) show little belief in the ultimate arrival of a fraternal society. *Le Petit Pierre* (1918; *Little Pierre*) and *La Vie en fleur* (1922; *The Bloom of Life*) complete the cycle started in *Le Livre de mon ami* (1885; *My Friend's Book*).

Francesca da Rimini \frän-'chäs-kä-dä-'rē-mē-,nē\, *original name* Francesca da Polenta \pō-'län-tä\ (d. 1283/84, Rimini, Romagna [Italy]) Daughter of Guido da Polenta, lord of Ravenna, and wife of Gianciotto Malatesta, ruler of Rimini. Married to Gianciotto for reasons of state, she was murdered by him when he discovered her affair with his brother Paolo, whom he also killed.

Dante was the first to make a literary reference to the tragedy; in Canto 5 of the *Inferno* he encounters the lovers Francesca and Paolo on the second circle. Their love and death have also been celebrated in plays by Silvio Pellico and Gabriele D'Annunzio, in operas by Hermann Götz and Sergey Rachmaninoff, and in works by many other writers, painters, and composers.

Francien \fräⁿ-'syaⁿ\ [French] The dialect of French used in the Middle Ages in the region of Île-de-France that furnishes

the basis for the literary and official form of the modern French language. The French word *francien* was coined in the later 19th century by Romance scholars, there having been no contemporary term in Old French to refer to this dialect.

Francis \'fran-sis\, Dick (b. Oct. 31, 1920, Tenby, Wales) British mystery writer known for his realistic plots centered on the sport of horse racing.

Francis was the son of a jockey, and in 1946 he took up steeplechase riding, turning professional in 1948. In 1957 he had an accident that cut short his riding career. That same year he published *The Sport of Queens: The Autobiography of Dick Francis*, and until 1973 he was a racing correspondent for London's *Sunday Express*.

In 1962 Francis turned to fiction with a successful first novel, *Dead Cert*. Thereafter he averaged a book a year, all set in the world of horse racing. His books usually feature an amateur sleuth who uses classic deductive reasoning while becoming emotionally involved with the case. The typical Francis villain is a pretentious snob whose smooth exterior masks his vices. Among the novels are *Nerve* (1964), *Forfeit* (1968), which won an Edgar (mystery writers) award, *Reflex* (1980), and *Hot Money* (1987), considered one of his best works.

Frank \'fräŋk, *Angl* 'fraŋk\, Anne, *in full* Annelies Marie Frank (b. June 12, 1929, Frankfurt am Main, Ger.—d. March 1945, Bergen-Belsen concentration camp, near Hannover) Young Jewish girl whose diary records the two years that her family spent in hiding to escape the persecutions of the German Nazis.

Early in the Nazi regime of Adolf Hitler, Anne Frank's father, Otto Frank (1889–1980), a German businessman, took his wife and two daughters to live in Amsterdam. Faced with deportation, the Franks went into hiding with four other Jews. Gentile friends smuggled in supplies, and they hid until Aug. 4, 1944, when the Gestapo, acting on a tip from informers, discovered them.

The family was transported to the Auschwitz concentration camp in Poland, where Anne's mother died. Anne and her sister were transferred to Bergen-Belsen and died there of typhus. Otto Frank was found hospitalized at Auschwitz when it was liberated by Russian troops. Friends who had searched their hiding place later gave Otto Frank the papers left behind by the Gestapo; among them he found Anne's diary. He had it published in 1947 as *Het Achterhuis* (*The Diary of a Young Girl*). Precocious in style and insight, it traces her emotional growth amid adversity and records her assertion that "In spite of everything I still believe that people are really good at heart." The diary has been translated into more than 30 languages and has been widely read and dramatized.

Frank \'fräŋk\, Leonhard (b. Sept. 4, 1882, Würzburg, Ger.—d. Aug. 18, 1961, Munich, W.Ger.) German Expressionist novelist and playwright who used sensationalism and a compact and austere prose style to dramatize a favorite theme—the destruction of the individual spirit by bourgeois society.

In 1914, having fled to Switzerland to avoid World War I, Frank published his first book, *Die Räuberbande* (1914; *The Robber Band*), the story of rebellious young boys who seek to create the ideal society but end up as "good citizens." While in Switzerland he also published *Die Ursache* (1915; *The Cause of the Crime*), an attack on repressive educational systems, and *Der Mensch ist gut* (1917; "Man Is Good"), a revolutionary denunciation of war.

Frank returned to Germany in 1918. His belief in the necessity of the establishment of socialism was expressed in his novel *Der Bürger* (1924; *A Middle-Class Man*) and in *Das ochsenfurter Männerquartett* (1927; *The Singers*). During the same period he wrote his masterpiece, *Karl und Anna* (1926; *Carl and Anna*), a realistic, if sentimental, account of a soldier who seduces his comrade's wife.

In 1933 Frank's books were banned and burned by the Nazis, and he emigrated again to Switzerland. From there he went to Paris, where in 1940 he was confined in an internment camp. After several escapes and reinternments, he fled to the United States. He returned to Germany in 1950 and two years later published his last important work, the thinly disguised autobiographical novel *Links, wo das Herz ist* (1952; *Heart on the Left*).

Frankenstein \\'fraŋk-ən-ˌstīn\\ (*in full* Frankenstein; or, the Modern Prometheus)   Novel by Mary Wollstonecraft SHELLEY, published in 1818, in which she invented what was to become one of the Western world's best-known monsters.

A combination of gothic romance and science fiction, the book tells the story of Victor Frankenstein, a Swiss student of natural science who creates an artificial man from pieces of corpses and brings his creature to life. Rejected and reviled for his hideous appearance, the creature learns the ways of humans, but he cannot find companionship. Increasingly brutal, the monster haunts Frankenstein and insists that he create a female companion. Frankenstein almost complies but in the end cannot perform the deed. The monster eventually brings about the scientist's destruction. The name Frankenstein has become popularly attached to the creature itself.

Frankfurt School \\'fräŋk-ˌfûrt, *Angl* 'fraŋk-fərt\\   Group of German Neo-Marxists associated from the mid-1920s with the Institute of Social Research at the University of Frankfurt. The Frankfurt School's members helped develop western Marxism, which was critical of both moderate socialism and of dogmatic communism. By the 1930s, their initial focus on economics broadened to include such disciplines as literary theory. They viewed literature under capitalism as part of the industry of culture dominated by the existing social order. They searched for revolutionary elements in literature, describing them as reflections of sociopolitical realities.

Notable members of the Frankfurt School included Max Horkheimer, Theodor Adorno, Walter Benjamin, Erich Fromm, Leo Lowenthal, and Herbert Marcuse. With the rise of Nazism in Germany, the Institute of Social Research briefly relocated to Geneva before settling at Columbia University in New York City. Although its members began publishing in English, the institute retained its distance from American Marxists and, in 1951, returned to Frankfurt.

Franklin \\'fraŋ-klən\\, Benjamin, *pseudonym* Richard Saunders \\'sòn-dərz\\ (b. Jan. 6 [Jan. 17, New Style], 1706, Boston [Mass., U.S.]—d. April 17, 1790, Philadelphia, Pa.)   American printer and publisher, author, inventor and scientist, and diplomat. Franklin invented the Franklin stove, bifocal spectacles, and the lightning rod and contributed to science with his experiments in electricity.

Franklin ended his formal education at the age of 10, and at 12 he was apprenticed to his brother, a printer. His first enthusiasm was for poetry, but he soon turned to prose. He achieved much of what was to become his characteristic style from imitation of the writing in *The Spectator*, Joseph Addison and Richard Steele's famous periodical of essays. About 1729 Franklin became the printer of paper currency for the colony of Pennsylvania and some of the other colonies. At that time he began publication of the *Pennsylvania Gazette*, a colonial newspaper generally acknowledged as among the best of such publications, and *Poor Richard's* (1732–57), a series of almanacs in which he printed numerous proverbs praising prudence, industry, and honesty. In 1748 he gave up the management of his publications to devote himself to science, but in 1753 he

served as deputy postmaster general for the northern colonies. He wrote many additional papers and essays of significance as well as an incomplete autobiography.

Franklin spent the years from 1757 to 1762 in London representing the colony of Pennsylvania in a dispute over the lands held by the Penn family. In 1764 he was sent back to London, and in March 1775, aware that there might be war between the colonies and Great Britain, he left England. Back in Philadelphia he served as a delegate to the Second Continental Congress, in which he helped draft the Declaration of Independence. In 1776 Franklin went to France to seek military and financial aid for the colonies. There he became a hero to the French people, the personification of the unsophisticated nobility of the New World. At the close of the Revolutionary War, Franklin was one of the diplomats chosen to negotiate peace with Great Britain, and he was instrumental in achieving the adoption of the U.S. Constitution.

Franklin \\'fraŋ-klən\\, Miles, *in full* Stella Maria Sarah Miles Franklin, *pseudonyms* Brent of Bin Bin \\'brent . . . 'bin-ˌbin\\ *and* Mrs. Ogniblat l'Artsau \\lärt-'sò\\ (b. Oct. 14, 1879, Talbingo, N.S.W., Australia—d. Sept. 19, 1954, Sydney, N.S.W.)   Australian author of historical fiction who wrote from feminist and nationalist perspectives.

Franklin grew up in isolated bush regions of New South Wales that were much like the glum setting of her first novel, *My Brilliant Career* (1901; film, 1980). Franklin's feminism and her outright rejection of traditional women's roles made her books controversial in Australia. In fact, the book *My Career Goes Bung*, the sequel to her first novel, was judged so audacious that it was not published until 1946. In 1906 she moved to the United States, worked as an editor and as secretary for the National Women's Trade Union League, and wrote the novel *Some Everyday Folk and Dawn* (1909). She moved to England in 1915.

Returning to Australia in 1927, Franklin published six chronicle novels of pioneer years in Australia, using the pseudonym Brent of Bin Bin: *Up the Country* (1928), *Ten Creeks Run* (1930), *Back to Bool Bool* (1931), *Prelude to Waking* (1950), *Cockatoos* (1954), and *Gentlemen at Gyang Gyang* (1956). She also wrote five more novels using her own name, including *All That Swagger* (1936), noted for its portrayal of the barrenness of bush life. She bequeathed her estate to found the prestigious Miles Franklin Award for Australian fiction.

Franklin's Tale, The   One of the 24 stories in THE CANTERBURY TALES by Geoffrey Chaucer.

The tale told by the Franklin centers upon the narrative motif of the "rash promise." While her husband Arveragus is away, Dorigen is assiduously courted by a squire, Aurelius. She promises to return his love if he can accomplish the task of removing every rock from the coast of Brittany so that her husband may have a safe return from sea. With a magician's help, Aurelius creates the illusion that the rocks have disappeared. Dorigen's husband insists that she fulfill her promise. But Aurelius, moved by her love for her husband, releases her from her obligation with a noble farewell.

Although Chaucer suggested that the story was borrowed from a Breton lay, its source more likely is Giovanni Boccaccio's *Il filocolo*.

Franko \\'frän-kò\\, Ivan (Yakovych) (b. Aug. 27, 1856, Nahuyevychi, Galicia, Austrian Empire [now Ivana-Franka, Ukraine]—d. May 28, 1916, Lemberg, Galicia [now Lviv, Ukraine])   Ukrainian author, scholar, journalist, and political activist who gained preeminence among Ukrainian writers at the end of the 19th century. He wrote dramas, lyric poetry, short stories, essays, translations, and children's verse, but his naturalistic novels chronicling contemporary Galician society and his long narrative poems mark the height of his literary achievement.

Franko attended the university in Lemberg (later Ivan Franko University), where he became a socialist and contributed to political and literary journals and to populist newspapers. Active political involvement and occasional imprisonment interrupted his studies, which were completed at the University of Vienna in 1891. In his later years he grew critical of Marxist socialism and supported Ukrainian nationalism.

Franko's literary career was characterized by a gradual shift from Romanticism to realism. He wrote more than 40 long poems, notably *Panski zharty* (1887; *The Master's Jests*), *Ivan Vyshensky* (1900; *Ivan Vyshensky*), and *Moysey* (1905; *Moses*). His collections of verse included *Ziv'yale lystya* (1886; "Withered Leaves"), *Miy izmarahd* (1897; "My Emerald"), and *Iz dniv zhurby* (1900; "From the Days of Sorrow"). He wrote some 100 works of prose, including the novels *Boryslav smiyetsya* (1882; "Boryslav Laughs"), *Zakhar Berkut* (1883), *Osnovy suspilnosti* (1895; "Pillars of Society"), and *Perekhresni stezhky* (1900; "Crossed Paths").

Franny and Zooey \\'fran-ē . . . 'zü-ē\\ Volume containing two interrelated stories by J.D. SALINGER, published in book form in 1961. The stories, originally published in *The New Yorker* magazine, concern Franny and Zooey Glass, two members of the family that was the subject of most of Salinger's short fiction.

Franny is an intellectually precocious late adolescent who tries to attain spiritual purification by obsessively reiterating the "Jesus prayer" as an antidote to the perceived superficiality and corruptness of life. She subsequently suffers a nervous breakdown. In the second story, her next older brother, Zooey, attempts to heal Franny by pointing out that her constant repetition of the "Jesus prayer" is as self-involved and egotistical as the egotism against which she rails.

Franzén \\frȧnt-'sän\\, Frans Mikael (b. Feb. 9, 1772, Uleåborg, Swedish Finland [now Oulu, Fin.]—d. Aug. 14, 1847, Härnösand, Swed.) Finnish-Swedish poet, a forerunner of the Romantic movement in Sweden.

Franzén studied and later taught at Åbo, Fin. In 1811 Franzén went to Sweden. In 1831 he was appointed bishop of Härnösand, where he lived until his death.

Franzén, inspired by William Shakespeare, John Milton, and Thomas Gray, was a master of a new poetic style in Swedish literature. His work consists chiefly of simple, idyllic lyrics, the best of which embody the imaginative spirit of the Romantic era.

Frashëri \\frä-she-'rē\\, Sami, *Turkish* Şemseddin Sami \\,shemsed-'dēn-sä-'mē\\ (b. June 1, 1850, Frashër, near Janina, Ottoman Empire [now Ioánnina, Greece]—d. June 18, 1904, Constantinople [now Istanbul, Tur.]) Author and lexicographer who was a leading figure in the Albanian nationalist movement and in 19th-century Turkish literature.

Born into an established Albanian Muslim family, Frashëri was educated at the Greek school of Janina and was also given lessons in Turkish, Persian, and Arabic by private tutors. After moving to Istanbul, he began a career in journalism and founded the newspaper *Sabah* ("Morning") in 1875. He also became associated with the new Turkish writers. He translated works from French and wrote several novels and plays, notably *Taaşşuk-ı Talat ve Fitnet* (1872), a novel that condemns Turkish marriage customs, and three plays, *Besa Yahut Ahde Vefa* (1875), *Seydi Yahya* (1875), and *Ĝave* (1876). The last play, which was considered too outspoken, led to a two-year exile in North Africa.

On his return, Frashëri began working on what are considered his greatest contributions, his lexicographical works *Kamus-ı Fransevi* (1882, 1905), a French-Turkish, Turkish-French dictionary; the six-volume *Kamusü'l-Âlam* (1889–98; "Universal Dictionary"); and the two-volume *Kamus-ı Türki* (1899–1900; "Turkish Dictionary").

Frauenlob \\'frau̇-ən-,lōp\\, *byname of* Heinrich von Meissen \\'hīn-riḳ-fȯn-'mī-sən\\ (b. *c.* 1260, Meissen, Thuringia [Germany]—d. Nov. 29, 1318, Mainz, Franconia [Germany]) Late Middle High German poet, who was the original representative of the school of middle-class poets succeeding the courtly minnesingers and adapting the minnesinger traditions to theological mysteries, scientific lore, and philosophy. His nickname, meaning "extoller of ladies," supposedly derives from his championing of the title *Vrowe* ("lady") over *Wip* ("woman") in a contest with a rival poet.

Well-educated and precocious, Frauenlob became a wandering court minstrel, lived for some time in Prague, and settled in Mainz (*c.* 1312), where he founded the first meistersinger school. Though it is unlikely that this school had the rigid structure of the later meistersinger *Singschulen*, the strained ingenuity and mannered conceits of Frauenlob's verses make him the true model of the meistersingers. His best-known poem, *Marienleich* ("Mary's Song"), is an impressive display of virtuosity in which the Virgin is praised in complex language that combines traditional religious imagery, double meanings, and esoteric philosophical allusions.

Frayn \\'frān\\, Michael (b. Sept. 8, 1933, London, Eng.) British playwright, novelist, and translator whose work was often compared to that of Anton Chekhov. Frayn was perhaps best known for his long-running stage farce *Noises Off* (1982), a frenetic play-within-a-play about the antics of an English theatrical company performing a typically English sex farce.

Frayn worked as a newspaper reporter, columnist, and critic for the *Manchester Guardian* and London *Observer*. In the early 1960s several collections of essays from his newspaper columns were published. Frayn wrote novels, plays, documentary films, and teleplays. He also translated and adapted several plays by Anton Chekhov.

Frayn's own plays are primarily comedies or tragicomedies. *Alphabetical Order* (1976) concerns the dehumanization that occurs when a chaotic newspaper office is transformed by an overly efficient employee. In *Make and Break* (1980) a salesman loses his humanity though he gains business success. Other plays include *Donkeys' Years* (1977) and *Benefactors* (1984). Among his novels are *The Tin Men* (1965), *The Russian Interpreter* (1966), *A Very Private Life* (1968), *The Trick of It* (1989), and *Now You Know* (1992).

Frazer \\'frā-zər\\, Sir James George (b. Jan. 1, 1854, Glasgow, Scot.—d. May 7, 1941, Cambridge, Cambridgeshire, Eng.) British anthropologist, folklorist, and classical scholar, best remembered as the author of THE GOLDEN BOUGH.

Frazer attended Glasgow University and Trinity College, Cambridge, where he eventually became a fellow. In 1907 he was appointed professor at Liverpool, but he returned to Cambridge after one session, remaining there for the rest of his life.

His outstanding position among anthropologists was established by the publication in 1890 of *The Golden Bough* (enlarged to 12 vol., 1911–15). The underlying theme of the work is Frazer's theory of a general development of modes of thought from the magical to the religious and, finally, to the scientific. Frazer's interpretation had a wide influence among men of letters. His other works include *Totemism and Exogamy* (1910) and *Folk-Lore in the Old Testament* (1918). He was knighted in 1914.

Fréchette \frā-'shet\, Louis-Honoré (b. Nov. 16, 1839, Lévis, Que. [Canada]—d. May 31, 1908, Montreal) Preeminent French-Canadian poet of the 19th century, noted for his patriotic poems.

Fréchette studied law at Laval University, Quebec, and was admitted to the bar in 1864. He worked as a journalist until he was discharged for liberal views. During a sojourn in Chicago (1866–71) he wrote *La Voix d'un exilé* (1866–68; "The Voice of an Exile"), a poem attacking the political and clerical dealings in Quebec during the period of Canadian confederation. Returning to Lévis in 1871, Fréchette entered politics, representing that city in the federal House of Commons (1874–78) and serving from 1889 until his death as clerk of the provincial Legislative Council in Quebec City.

In 1880 his *Les Fleurs boréales* (1879; "The Northern Flowers") and *Les Oiseaux de neige* (1879; "The Snow Birds") became the first works by a Canadian to be awarded a prize by the Académie Française. Fréchette then wrote *La Légende d'un peuple* (1887), his famous cycle of poems that are an epic chronicle of Canadian history. Other works include *Poésies choisies* (1908; "Selected Poems"); the prose stories in *Originaux et détraqués* (1892; "Eccentrics and Lunatics") and *Le Noël au Canada* (1899; *Christmas in French Canada*); the dramas *Félix Poutré* (1871), *Papineau* (1880), and *Véronica* (1908); and the polemical *Lettres à Basile* (1872).

Frederic \'fred-rik\, Harold (b. Aug. 19, 1856, Utica, N.Y., U.S.—d. Oct. 19, 1898, Henley-on-Thames, Oxfordshire, Eng.) American journalist, foreign correspondent, and author of several historical novels.

Frederic became a reporter and by 1882 was editor of the *Albany Evening Journal*. In 1884 he went to London as the correspondent for *The New York Times*. London remained his base for the rest of his life.

His historical novels ranged in setting from the American Revolution (*In the Valley*, 1890) to the American Civil War (*The Copperhead*, 1893, and *Marsena and Other Stories*, 1894). Of his New York State novels, *The Damnation of Theron Ware* (1896; U.K. title, *Illumination*), the story of the decline and fall of a Methodist minister, brought him his greatest fame. Three other novels, *March Hares* (1896), *Gloria Mundi* (1898), and *The Market Place* (1899), are about English life.

Fredro \'fre-drȯ\, Aleksander (b. June 20, 1793, Surochów, Galicia [now in Poland]—d. July 15, 1876, Lwów, Austrian Galicia [now Lviv, Ukraine]) Polish comic dramatist whose work, influenced by Molière and by Carlo Goldoni, is remarkable for its brilliant characterization, ingenious construction, and skillful handling of verse meters.

Born to a wealthy and powerful landed family, Fredro was educated by private tutors. At the age of 16 he joined the Napoleonic troops of the duchy of Warsaw. After leaving the army in 1815 to care for his estate at home, he began to write seriously. Among his more notable plays are *Mąż i żona* (produced 1822; "Husband and Wife"), a comedy of marital infidelity; *Śluby panieńskie* (1833; "Maidens' Vows"), concerned with psychological development; and *Zemsta* (1834; "Vengeance"), a brilliantly constructed comedy, considered to be his masterpiece. He abruptly stopped writing in 1835 after receiving harsh criticism from the extremist Romantic poet Seweryn Goszczyński. Fredro resumed writing much later with several interesting plays; these did not, however, compare to his earlier productions. His memoirs, *Trzy po trzy* ("Topsy Turvy Talk"), are considered to be among the most brilliant works of Polish prose.

Freeman \'frē-mən\, Douglas Southall (b. May 16, 1886, Lynchburg, Va., U.S.—d. June 13, 1953, Westbourne, Hampton Gardens, near Richmond, Va.) American journalist, educator, and author noted for writings on the Confederacy.

After receiving degrees from Johns Hopkins and Washington and Lee universities, Freeman began a long and distinguished teaching career. From 1936 he was a lecturer at the Army War College. From 1915 to 1949 he also edited the Richmond (Va.) *News Leader*.

In 1935 Freeman won the Pulitzer Prize for his four-volume biography, *R.E. Lee*. His other works include *Virginia—A Gentle Dominion* (1924); *The Last Parade* (1932); *The South to Posterity: An Introduction to the Writings of Confederate History* (1939); *Lee's Lieutenants, A Study in Command*, 3 vol. (1942–44); *John Steward Bryan* (1947); and *George Washington*, 7 vol. (1948–57), the final volume of which was prepared by his assistants after his death—the whole work earning him a second, posthumous Pulitzer Prize in 1958.

Freeman \'frē-mən\, Mary Eleanor Wilkins (b. Oct. 31, 1852, Randolph, Mass., U.S.—d. March 13, 1930, Metuchen, N.J.) American writer known for her stories and novels of frustrated lives in New England villages.

In 1867 the Wilkins family moved to Brattleboro, Vt. Mary began writing stories and verse for children to help support her family, and she quickly became successful. Returning to Randolph, she did her best writing there in the 1880s and '90s. Although she produced a dozen volumes of short stories and as many novels, Freeman is remembered chiefly for the first two collections of stories, *A Humble Romance and Other Stories* (1887) and *A New England Nun and Other Stories* (1891), and for the novel *Pembroke* (1894).

Freeman \'frē-mən\, Richard Austin (b. 1862, London, Eng.—d. Sept. 30, 1943, Gravesend, Kent) Popular English author of novels and short stories featuring the fictional character John Thorndyke, a pathologist-detective.

Educated as a physician and surgeon, Freeman practiced in the Gold Coast (now Ghana), where he contracted a disease. Forced by ill health to retire from practice in 1904, he began to write fiction. *The Red Thumb Mark* (1907) was the first of many works featuring Thorndyke.

free verse Poetry organized to the cadences of speech and image patterns rather than according to a regular metrical scheme. Its rhythms are based on patterned elements such as sounds, words, phrases, sentences, and paragraphs, rather than on the traditional prosodic units of metrical feet per line. Free verse, therefore, eliminates much of the artificiality and some of the aesthetic distance of poetic expression and substitutes a flexible formal organization suited to the modern idiom and more casual tonality of the language.

Although the term is loosely applied to the poetry of Walt Whitman and even earlier experiments with irregular meters, it was originally a literal translation of VERS LIBRE, the name of a movement that originated in France in the 1880s. The first English-language poets to be influenced by vers libre, notably T.E. Hulme, F.S. Flint, Richard Aldington, Ezra Pound, and T.S. Eliot, were students of French poetry. IMAGISM, started in England in 1912 by Aldington, Pound, Flint, and Hilda Doolittle (H.D.), was concerned with more than versification, but one of its principles was "to compose in sequence of the musical phrase, not in sequence of the metronome." Carl Sandburg, William Carlos Williams, Marianne Moore, and Wallace Stevens all wrote some variety of free verse; the versification of Williams and Moore most closely resembles that of the vers libre poets of France.

Freidank \'frī-ˌdäŋk\ (fl. early 13th century) German didactic poet whose work came to be regarded as a standard repository of moral precepts.

Freidank was a wandering minstrel of burgher origin, born probably in Alemannic or Swabian territory (near the modern-day region where Germany, France, and Switzerland meet). He took part in the crusade of Frederick II in 1228–29. Several of the impressions left by these experiences are recorded in the one work by which he is known, *Bescheidenheit* ("Moderation"), a collection of gnomic (aphoristic) verse, which seems to have been written about 1230. The sources on which Freidank drew were common property, but in his formulation they acquired the authority of proverbs.

Freie Bühne \'frī-ə-'būe-nə\ ("Free Stage") Independent theater founded by the critic and director Otto Brahm in 1889 in Berlin for the purpose of staging new, naturalistic plays. The Freie Bühne's first production was of Henrik Ibsen's *Gengangere* (1881) in September 1889. A month later, Brahm staged Gerhart Hauptmann's first play, *Vor Sonnenaufgang* (1889), a tragedy of working-class people. During the following seasons, Brahm's presentations included an important naturalist drama dealing with a degenerate family, *Die Familie selicke* (1890) by Arno Holz, as well as plays by Leo Tolstoy, Émile Zola, and August Strindberg. Although the Freie Bühne was a success, it lasted for only three seasons, largely because Berlin's commercial theater had by then embraced the new theatrical movement of naturalism.

Freiligrath \'frī-lēg-,rät, -lik-\, Ferdinand, *in full* Hermann Ferdinand Freiligrath (b. June 17, 1810, Detmold, Westphalia [Germany]—d. March 18, 1876, Cannstatt, near Stuttgart) One of the outstanding German political poets of the 19th century, whose verse gave poetic expression to radical sentiments.

After working as an accountant, Freiligrath abandoned commerce for literature with the success of his first poems, the Romantic *Gedichte* (1838; *Poems*). Influenced by the writings of Victor Hugo, these early poems were characterized by vividly imaginative and evocative exotic scenes and by technical virtuosity; they won him a pension from the Prussian king Frederick William IV. His views became increasingly radical, however, and he renounced the pension upon the publication of his collection of political poems *Glaubensbekenntnis* (1844; "Statement of Conscience"). His poetry was banned, and he was forced to leave Germany. His poems in *Ça ira* (1846) and *Neuere politische und soziale Gedichte* (1849 and 1851; "Newer Political and Social Poetry"), celebrating the Revolution of 1848, which brought him back to Germany, were even more strongly socialistic and antimonarchical. The poem *Die Toten an die Lebenden* (1848; "From the Dead to the Living") resulted in his arrest for subversion, but he was acquitted. He formed a long-standing friendship with Karl Marx, with whom he edited the *Neue rheinische Zeitung* ("New Rhenish Newspaper"). In 1851 he went to England to escape further political persecution. In 1868 a public subscription raised in Germany enabled him to return.

Among Freiligrath's other important works were his translations of the social poetry of William Wordsworth, Henry Wadsworth Longfellow, Walt Whitman, Robert Burns, Victor Hugo, and Molière.

French Academy   *see* ACADÉMIE FRANÇAISE.

French Lieutenant's Woman, The   Novel by John FOWLES, published in 1969. A pastiche of a historical romance, it juxtaposes the ethos of the Victorian characters living in 1867 with the ironic commentary of the author writing in 1967.

The plot centers on Charles Smithson, an amateur Victorian paleontologist. He is engaged to Ernestina Freeman, a conventional, wealthy woman, but he breaks off the engagement after a series of clandestine trysts with the beautiful, mysterious Sarah Woodruff, a social outcast known locally as the forsaken

lover of a French lieutenant. The author, who continually intrudes on the narration, presents three different endings, encouraging his readers to reach their own conclusions.

French Revolution, The   Three-volume narrative history by British essayist and historian Thomas CARLYLE, first published in 1837.

The French Revolution established Carlyle's reputation. Its creation was beset with difficulty; after spending months on the manuscript in 1834, Carlyle lent his only draft to philosopher John Stuart Mill, who accidentally burned it. After Mill confessed what had happened, Carlyle responded in a generous and uncharacteristically lighthearted manner. He immediately began to reconstruct the work.

The three volumes are individually titled "The Bastille," "The Constitution," and "The Guillotine," covering the events from 1774 to 1795. Carlyle believed that the excesses of the French Revolution were a divine judgment upon a selfish monarchy and nobility. His work contains many outstanding set pieces and character studies, including those of General Lafayette and Robespierre. Carlyle's history was admired by Charles Dickens and helped inspire *A Tale of Two Cities*.

Freneau \fre-'nō\, Philip (Morin) (b. Jan. 2, 1752, New York City [U.S.]—d. Dec. 18, 1832, Monmouth County, N.J.) Poet, essayist, and editor, known as the "poet of the American Revolution."

After the outbreak of the Revolution, Freneau began to write vitriolic satire against the British and Tories. He spent two years in the Caribbean islands, where he produced two of his most ambitious poems, "The Beauties of Santa Cruz" and "The House of Night." On his return he became an active participant in the war. Captured and imprisoned by the British in 1780, he bitterly recounted the experience in the poem *The British Prison-Ship* (1781), written after his release.

During the next several years he contributed to the *Freeman's Journal* in Philadelphia. Freneau became a sea captain until 1790, when he again entered partisan journalism, ultimately as editor from 1791 to 1793 of the strongly Republican *National Gazette* in Philadelphia.

Well schooled in the classics and in the Neoclassical English poetry of the period, Freneau strove for a fresh idiom that would be unmistakably American, but, except in a few poems, he failed to achieve it.

Frenssen \'fren-sən\, Gustav (b. Oct. 19, 1863, Barlt, Holstein [Germany]—d. April 11, 1945, Barlt)   Novelist who was the foremost exponent of *Heimatkunst* (local color or regionalist movement) in German fiction.

Frenssen was a Lutheran pastor for 10 years. His critical attitude toward orthodoxy, however, developed into a total rejection of Christianity, and together with the resounding success of his third novel, *Jörn Uhl* (1901), it led him to resign his pastorate and devote all his time to writing. He owed his success, in large part, to the vitality of his characters and the charm and beauty he lent to the locale of his novels—the shores of the North Sea.

About half of Frenssen's novels were translated into English. Among them are *Die drei Getreuen* (1898; *The Three Comrades*), *Jörn Uhl, Hilligenlei* (1905; *Holyland*), *Der Pastor von Poggsee* (1921; *The Pastor of Poggsee*), *Klaus Heinrich Baas* (1909), *Peter Moors Fahrt nach Südwest* (1907; *Peter Moor's Journey to Southwest Africa*), and the autobiographical *Otto Babendiek* (1926; abridged, *The Anvil*).

Frere \'frir, 'frer\, John Hookham, *pseudonym* William and Robert Whistlecraft \'wis-əl-,kraft\ (b. May 21, 1769, London, Eng.—d. Jan. 7, 1846, Valletta, Malta)   British diplomat and man of letters.

Frere was educated at Eton and at Cambridge University. He entered the Foreign Office, in 1799 becoming undersecretary of state for foreign affairs and in 1800 going to Portugal as envoy extraordinary. His diplomatic career ended disastrously in 1808, when he was blamed for endangering the British Army by advising against retreat from the French to La Coruña, Spain.

Frere is remembered for witty parodies in *The Anti-Jacobin* (1797–98), a weekly that opposed revolution in England and abroad, as well as for his brilliance as a translator and for his experiments with meter. He reintroduced into English verse the Italian ottava rima, an eight-line stanza with a skillfully interwoven rhyme scheme, which he used effectively in his mock-heroic Arthurian epic *The Monks and the Giants* (1817–18). He also showed mastery of meter in his translations of four plays by Aristophanes.

Freud \'froit, *Angl* 'fróid \, Sigmund (b. May 6, 1856, Freiberg, Moravia, Austrian Empire [now Příbor, Czech Republic]—d. Sept. 23, 1939, London, Eng.)   Austrian neurologist, founder of psychoanalysis. Freudian theory has had a great impact on psychology, psychiatry, literary criticism, and other fields.

Freud entered the University of Vienna in 1873 as a medical student and received his degree in 1881. In 1885 he went to Paris to study with the neurologist Jean-Martin Charcot, which proved a turning point in his career. Charcot's work with patients classified as hysterics introduced Freud to the possibility that mental disorders might be caused by purely psychological factors rather than by organic brain disease.

Upon his return to Vienna he entered into a partnership with the physician Josef Breuer. They collaborated on *Studien über Hysterie* (1895; *Studies in Hysteria*), which contains a presentation of Freud's pioneering psychoanalytic method of free association. This method allowed Freud to develop theories of the unconscious and of neuroses. In 1899 he published *Die Traumdeutung* (*The Interpretation of Dreams*), in which he analyzed the highly complex symbolic processes underlying dream formation. In 1905 appeared his controversial study *Drei Abhandlungen zur Sexualtheorie* (*Three Essays on the Theory of Sexuality*), in which he presented discoveries concerning infantile sexuality and in which he proposed several complicated stages of psychosexual development, including the formation of the Oedipus complex. His theories, including what some see as a male view of sexuality, have since been criticized on a number of grounds.

Freud also applied his psychoanalytic insights to mythological, anthropological, cultural, and religious phenomena. Among his most noted works in this vein are *Totem und Tabu* (1913; *Totem and Taboo*) and *Das Unbehagen in der Kultur* (1930; *Civilization and Its Discontents*).

Freudian criticism \'frói-dē-ən\   Literary criticism that uses the psychoanalytic theory of Sigmund Freud to interpret a work in terms of the known psychological conflicts of its author or, conversely, to construct the author's psychic life from unconscious revelations in his work.

Freud himself examined several literary characters in psychoanalytic terms, for example, Oedipus and Hamlet (in *The Interpretation of Dreams*). The Freudian critics who followed departed from the traditional scope of criticism in reconstructing an author's psychic life on the basis of his or her writings. Edmund Wilson explored this realm in his *The Wound and the Bow* (1941), and Frederick Crews did the same in several works, including *The Sins of the Fathers: Hawthorne's Psychological Themes* (1966). This approach as applied to biography is known as psychobiography, *e.g.*, Van Wyck Brooks's *The Ordeal of Mark Twain* (1920). Professional analysts have applied these techniques to literature, notably Ernest Jones in *Hamlet*

and Oedipus (1910 and 1949), which traces the famous problem of Hamlet's irresolution back to William Shakespeare's own Oedipal guilt. *See also* PSYCHOANALYTIC CRITICISM.

Frey \'frī\, Adolf (b. Feb. 18, 1855, Külligen, near Aarau, Switz.—d. Feb. 12, 1920, Zürich)   Swiss writer whose most lasting achievements are his biographies of Swiss authors and his Swiss-German dialect poetry.

As a biographer Frey showed a predilection for rich character studies in the manner of the 19th-century realists. Because he knew many of his subjects personally, his verbal portraits of them contain much unique material. Among these biographies are *Erinnerungen an G. Keller* (1892; "Memories of G. Keller"), *C.F. Meyer* (1899), *A. Böcklin* (1903), and *Der Tiermaler R. Koller* (1906; "The Animal Painter R. Koller"). His collections of poetry, notably the Swiss-dialect *Duss und underm Rafe* (1891), are rooted in the style of the folk song. His plays and his historical novels, such as *Die Jungfer von Wattenwil* (1912; "The Maid of Wattenwil"), are considered to be of less importance.

Freyja \'frā-yə\ ("Lady"), *also called* Mardöll, Hörn, Gefn, *or* Syr.   Most renowned of the goddesses of Norse mythology, the sister and female counterpart of Freyr. Freyja had charge of love, fertility, battle, and death. Her father was Njörd, the sea god. Pigs were sacred to her, and she rode on a boar with golden bristles or in a chariot drawn by cats. It was Freyja's privilege to choose half of the heroes slain in battle to take to her great hall in the Fólkvangar (Odin took the other half to Valhalla). She possessed a famous necklace called Brísingamen, which Loki stole and Heimdall, the gods' watchman, recovered. Greedy and lascivious, Freyja was also credited with teaching witchcraft to the Æsir.

Freyr \'frār\ or **Frey** \'frā\, *also called* Yngvi \'iŋ-vē\   In Norse mythology, the god of peace, fertility, rain, and sunshine and the son of the sea god Njörd. Although originally one of the Vanir tribe, he was included with the Æsir. Gerd, daughter of the giant Gymir, was his wife. Worshiped especially in Sweden, he was also well known in Norway and Iceland. His sister and female counterpart, Freyja, was goddess of love, fertility, battle, and death. The boar was sacred to both.

Freyre or **Freire** \'frā-rə\, Gilberto (de Mello) (b. March 15, 1900, Recife, Braz.—d. July 18, 1987, Recife)   Writer and sociologist, leader of the NORTHEASTERN SCHOOL of Brazilian writers.

In 1926 Freyre organized the first northeastern regionalist congress in Recife and published the "Regionalist Manifesto." He was joined in this endeavor by the writers Jorge de Lima, José Américo de Almeida, and José Lins do Rego, among others.

The best known of Freyre's works is *Casa-grande e senzala* (1933; "The Big House and the Slave Quarters"; *The Masters and the Slaves*), an account of the relationship between Brazil's Portuguese colonizers and their African slaves. His other works include *Sobrados e mucambos* (1936; "The Rich and the Servants"; *The Mansions and the Shanties*), *Brazil: An Interpretation* (1945; revised and expanded as *New World in the Tropics*, 1980), *Nordeste* (1937; "The Northeast"), and *Ordem e progresso* (1959; *Order and Progress*).

Freytag \'frī-ˌtäk\, Gustav (b. July 13, 1816, Kreuzburg, Silesia, Prussia [Germany]—d. April 30, 1895, Wiesbaden, Ger.)   German writer of realistic novels celebrating the merits of the middle classes.

Freytag became privatdocent (lecturer) in German literature at the University of Breslau in 1839, but he resigned after eight years to devote himself to writing. He was much excited by the revolutions of 1848 and became, with Julian Schmidt, joint editor of the Leipzig weekly *Die Grenzboten*, which he made into the leading organ of the middle-class liberals.

He made his name with the comedy *Die Journalisten* (1854; *The Journalists*), still regarded as one of the most successful German comedies, and he acquired an international reputation with his widely translated novel *Soll und Haben* (1855; *Debit and Credit*), celebrating solid bourgeois values. He attempted to realize a similar intention with *Die verlorene Handschrift* (1864; *The Lost Manuscript*), which depicted Leipzig university life in the same realistic manner, but it was less successful. His most ambitious literary work was the novel cycle *Die Ahnen*, 6 vol. (1873–81; "The Ancestors"), which traced the story of a German family from the 4th century AD up to Freytag's own time. His *Bilder aus der deutschen Vergangenheit*, 5 vol. (1859–67; partial Eng. trans. *Pictures of German Life*) stressed the idea of folk character as determinative in history. His collected works, *Gesammelte Werke*, 22 vol. (1886–88), were reissued in 12 volumes, edited by E. Elster, in 1926.

Freytag's pyramid \'frī-,täks\   A device created by the German writer and critic Gustav Freytag in his book *Die Technik des Dramas* (1863) to illustrate the structure of a typical five-act play. According to Freytag, the typical plot consists of an introduction, rising action that leads to a climax followed by falling action, and finally a catastrophe (or denouement).

Friar's Tale, The   One of the 24 stories in THE CANTERBURY TALES by Geoffrey Chaucer.

The Friar relates the comeuppance of a corrupt summoner—an ecclesiastical court officer—in a story based on a medieval French fabliau. The summoner befriends a bailiff, who is the devil in disguise, and the two agree to share the proceeds of their extortions. In one of several humorous scenes, the summoner hears a frustrated man mutter, "The devil take all, cart, horse and hay in one!" and urges the devil to take up the offer, but the devil declines, explaining to his overeager friend that it was not meant as a literal request. When the summoner tries to extract a bribe from a poor widow, and she too asks for the devil to carry him away, the devil asks her if she really means it. When she agrees, he whisks the summoner off to hell.

Friday \'frī-,dā\   Fictional character, a native who befriends and then serves the hero in Daniel Defoe's novel ROBINSON CRUSOE. The character is named for the day of the week on which he was rescued.

Friedman \'frēd-mən\, Bruce Jay (b. April 26, 1930, New York, N.Y., U.S.)   American comic author whose dark, mocking humor and social criticism was directed at the concerns and behavior of American Jews.

Friedman worked in publishing for several years before achieving success with his first novel, *Stern* (1962). The title character is a luckless descendent of the biblical Job, unable to assimilate into mainstream American life. Although most of his characters are Jewish by birth, they feel marginal to both Jewish and American culture.

Friedman's works include the novels *A Mother's Kisses* (1964), *The Dick* (1970), *About Harry Towns* (1974), *Tokyo Woes* (1985), *Violencia* (1988), and *The Current Climate* (1989); the short-story collections *Far from the City of Class* (1963), *Black Angels* (1966), and *Let's Hear It for a Beautiful Guy* (1984); essays such as *The Lonely Guy's Book of Life* (1978); the plays *Scuba Duba: A Tense Comedy* (1967) and *Steambath* (1971); and several screenplays.

Friel \'frēl\, Brian (b. Jan. 9, 1929, near Omagh, County Tyrone, N.Ire.)   Playwright noted for his portrayals of Roman Catholic conditions in both Ireland and Northern Ireland.

Friel taught school in Londonderry for 10 years. After *The New Yorker* began regular publication of his stories, he turned to writing full time in 1960. His first dramatic success was *Philadelphia, Here I Come!* (produced 1964). The play tells of a young Irishman's ambivalence about immigration to America.

Friel had plays produced almost yearly for the next decade. After writing *The Loves of Cass McGuire* (1966), *Lovers* (1967), *Crystal and Fox* (1968), and *The Mundy Scheme* (1969), he turned to more political themes, relating the dilemmas of Irish life and the troubles in Northern Ireland in such plays as *The Freedom of the City* (1973), *Volunteers* (1975), *Living Quarters* (1977), and *Making History* (1988). Many of his plays—notably *Aristocrats* (1979), *Translations* (1980), and the Tony award-winning *Dancing at Lughnasa* (1990)—deal with family ties and with mythmaking as a human need.

Frigg \'frig\, *also called* Friia, Frija \'frē-ə\, *or* Frea \'frā-ə\   In Norse mythology, the wife of Odin and mother of Balder. She was a promoter of marriage and of fertility. In Icelandic stories, she tried to save her son's life but failed. Some myths depict her as the weeping and loving mother, while others stress her loose morals.

Frisch \'frish\, Max (Rudolf) (b. May 15, 1911, Zürich, Switz.—d. April 4, 1991, Zürich)   Swiss dramatist and novelist, noted for his Expressionist depictions of the moral dilemmas of 20th-century life.

In 1933 Frisch withdrew from the University of Zürich and became a newspaper correspondent. He worked for some years as an architect but then abandoned architecture in 1955 to devote himself full-time to writing.

One of Frisch's earliest dramas was the morality play *Nun singen sie wieder* (1946, rev. ed., 1955, 1972; *Now They Sing Again*), in which Surrealistic tableaux reveal the effects of the assassination of hostages by German Nazis. *Santa Cruz* (1947) established the central theme of his subsequent works: the predicament of the complicated, skeptical individual in modern society. His other historical melodramas include *Die chinesische Mauer* (1947, 2nd rev. ed., 1972; *The Chinese Wall*) and the bleak *Als der Krieg zu Ende war* (1949; *When the War Was Over*). Reality and dream are used to depict the terrorist fantasies of a responsible government prosecutor in *Graf Öderland* (1951, rev. ed., 1961; *Count Oederland*), while *Don Juan oder die Liebe zur Geometrie* (1953, rev. ed. 1962; *Don Juan, or The Love of Geometry*) is a reinterpretation of the legend of the famous lover. In *Biedermann und die Brandstifter* (1958; U.K. title, *The Fire Raisers*; U.S. title, *The Firebugs*), arsonists insinuate themselves into the house of the weak-willed, complacent Biedermann, who allows them to destroy his home and his world rather than confront them. Frisch's later plays include *Andorra* (1961) and *Biografie* (1967, rev. ed., 1985; *Biography*).

Frisch's early novels *Stiller* (1954; *I'm Not Stiller*), *Homo Faber* (1957), and *Mein Name sei Gantenbein* (1964; *A Wilderness of Mirrors*) portray aspects of modern intellectual life and examine the theme of identity. Frisch's autobiographical works include two noteworthy diaries, *Tagebuch 1946–1949* (1950; *Sketchbook 1946–1949*) and *Tagebuch 1966–1971* (1972; *Sketchbook 1966–1971*). His later novels include *Montauk* (1975), *Der Mensch erscheint im Holozän* (1979; *Man in the Holocene*), and *Blaubart* (1982; *Bluebeard*).

Fröding \'frœ-diŋ\, Gustaf (b. Aug. 22, 1860, Alster, Värmland, Swed.—d. Feb. 8, 1911, Stockholm)   Lyrical poet who, by uniting colloquial language with a rich musical form, liberated Swedish verse from traditional patterns.

Fröding worked for 10 years as a journalist but spent long periods in sanatoriums for treatment of nervous disorders. Stimulated by the revolt against naturalism, in 1891 he published his first collection of poems, *Guitarr och dragharmonika* (*Guitar and Concertina*). It was followed by *Nya dikter* (1894; "New Poems") and *Stänk och flikar* (1896; "Splashes and Spray"). These three volumes contain the essential Fröding. Passages in the last led to his prosecution for pornography, and, although he was acquitted, the experience was disastrous to a man so scrupulous and sensitive. He managed to publish two more small books of poems, *Nytt och gammalt* (1897; "New and Old [Pieces]") and *Gralstänk* (1898; "Splashes of Grail"), before a final breakdown. A collection of verse and prose, *Efterskörd* ("Aftermath"), appeared in 1910, and a posthumous collection, *Reconvalescentia*, in 1913.

Fröding's poetic style showed a virtuosity new to Swedish literature and an unusual technical perfection. He was a master of humorous verse, and his drolleries are as effective as the bitter pathos or evocative magic of his serious poetry.

Frogs (*Greek* Batrachoi) A literary comedy by ARISTOPHANES, produced in 405 BC. The play tells the story of Dionysus, the god of drama, who is mourning the quality of present-day tragedy in Athens after the death of his recent favorite, Euripides. Disguising himself as the hero Heracles, Dionysus goes down to Hades to bring Euripides back to the land of the living. A competition between Euripides and his predecessor, Aeschylus, however, convinces Dionysus that Aeschylus is the writer more likely to help Athens in its troubles, and, leaving Euripides behind, Dionysus returns to earth with Aeschylus.

Froissart \frwȧ-'sȧr, *Angl* 'frȯi-,sȧrt\, Jean (b. 1333?, Valenciennes, Brabant [now in France]—d. 1400/01, Chimay, Hainaut [now in Belgium]) European medieval poet and court historian whose *Chroniques* (*Chronicles*) of the 14th century remain the most important and detailed documents of feudal times and the best contemporary exposition of chivalric and courtly ideals.

As a scholar, Froissart lived among the nobility of several European courts. He also traveled to Scotland, Italy, France, and the Iberian Peninsula.

The main subject of Froissart's *Chroniques* was the "honourable adventures and feats of arms" of the Hundred Years' War. The firsthand narrative covers weddings, funerals, and great battles from 1325 to 1400 and concerns events in Flanders, Spain, Portugal, France, and England. Book I was based on the work of the Flemish writer Jean le Bel and later rewritten.

In addition to the *Chroniques*, Froissart wrote allegorical poetry celebrating courtly love. *L'Horloge amoureux* compares the heart to a clock, and *Méliador* is a chivalrous romance. He also wrote ballades and rondeaux.

Frome, Ethan \'ē-thən-'frōm\ Fictional character, the protagonist of Edith Wharton's novel ETHAN FROME.

Fromentin \frō-mäⁿ-'taⁿ\, Eugène (b. Oct. 24, 1820, La Rochelle, Fr.—d. Aug. 27, 1876, La Rochelle) French painter and author, known for his depictions of the land and people of Algeria.

As a writer Fromentin is best known for his novel DOMINIQUE, first published in the *Revue des deux mondes* in 1862 and dedicated to George Sand. Fromentin's other literary works are *Visites artistiques ou simples pélerinages* (1852–56; "Artistic Visits or Simple Pilgrimages"), *Un Été dans le Sahara* (1857; "A Summer in the Sahara"), *Une Année dans le Sahel* (1858; "A Year in the Sahel"), and *Les Maîtres d'autrefois* (1876; *The Old Masters of Belgium* or *The Masters of Past Time*).

From the Earth to the Moon Novel by Jules VERNE, published as *De la Terre à la Lune* (1865) and also published as *The Baltimore Gun Club* and *The American Gun Club*. Although the novel was subtitled *Trajet direct en 97 heures 20 minutes* ("Direct Passage in Ninety-Seven Hours and Twenty Minutes"), the actual journey to the Moon was depicted in the book's sequel, *Autour de la Lune* (1870; *Round the Moon*).

From the Earth to the Moon concerns a group of obsessive American Civil War veterans, members of the Baltimore Gun Club, who conceive the idea of creating an enormous cannon in order to shoot a "space-bullet" to the Moon from a site in Florida.

frontier humor Vital and exuberant literature that was generated by the westward expansion of the United States in the late 18th and the 19th centuries. The spontaneity, sense of fun, exaggeration, fierce individuality, and irreverence for traditional Eastern values in frontier humor reflected the optimistic spirit of pre-Civil War America. Frontier humor appears mainly in tall tales of exaggerated feats of strength, rough practical jokes (especially on citified Easterners and greenhorns), and tales of encounters with panthers, bears, and snakes.

Classic characters of frontier humor include Mike Fink, the semilegendary king of the Mississippi River keelboatmen, Paul Bunyan, hero of the northwestern loggers, and Davy Crockett, an actual historical figure whose *Narrative* (1834) is a combination of tall tales, comic self-portraiture, and humorous proverbs. Representative writers of Southern frontier humor were A.B. Longstreet, Thomas B. Thorpe, Johnson Jones Hooper, and George Washington Harris. Mark Twain represents a culmination of the tradition. *See also* LOCAL COLOR.

Fronto \'frän-tō\, Marcus Cornelius (b. *c.* AD 100, Cirta, Numidia [now Constantine, Alg.]—d. *c.* 166, Rome?) Prominent Roman orator, rhetorician, and grammarian whose high reputation—equal in ancient times to those of Cato, Cicero, and Quintilian—was based chiefly on his orations, all of which are lost.

In addition to his orations, Fronto's grammatical and rhetorical studies won him a number of followers, called the Frontoniani. Modern evaluations of Fronto's mastery of language are based on the information contained in the *Noctes Atticae* of Aulus Gellius, a member of Fronto's circle; on a collection of Fronto's letters; and on miscellaneous pieces discovered in 1815 in the Ambrosian Library in Milan.

Fronto tried to reinvigorate the decaying Latin of his day by reviving the vocabulary of earlier republican Roman writers. The resulting *elocutio novella* ("new elocution") was often artificial and pedantic, but it had widespread influence and gave new vitality to Latin prose writing.

Frost \'frȯst\, Robert (Lee) (b. March 26, 1874, San Francisco, Calif., U.S.—d. Jan. 29, 1963, Boston, Mass.) American poet best known for his use of colloquial language, familiar rhythms, and symbols taken from common life to express the simple values of New England life. Generations of students have been introduced to poetry by the accessible images of poems such as STOPPING BY WOODS ON A SNOWY EVENING, THE ROAD NOT TAKEN, THE DEATH OF THE HIRED MAN, and MENDING WALL.

Frost briefly attended Dartmouth and Harvard colleges. He settled on a family farm in Derry, N.H., but sold the farm and in 1912 moved to England, where his first collection of poems, *A Boy's Will* (1913), was published. After the outbreak of World War I, Frost returned to the United States and bought a farm in Franconia, N.H.

Frost's poetry reveals his almost mystical attachment to the fields and farms of New England. An ardent naturalist and botanist, he acutely observed the details of rural life and endowed them with universal, even metaphysical, meaning.

Frost's distinguished career as a teacher and poet-in-residence took him to Amherst College, the University of Michigan, Harvard, and Dartmouth. His poetry collections include *Mountain Interval* (1916), *New Hampshire* (1923), *West-Running Brook* (1928), *A Further Range* (1936), *A Witness Tree* (1942), *Steeple Bush* (1947), and *In the Clearing* (1962).

Frost at Midnight Poem by Samuel Taylor COLERIDGE, published in LYRICAL BALLADS (1798), in which Coleridge pioneered a new, informal mode of poetry unified by conversational tone and rhythm.

In the winter of 1798 Coleridge composed the four-stanza poem in the presence of his sleeping infant son, Hartley. The soliloquy begins with the description of a silent frosty night and proceeds through a meditation on the relationship between the quiet work of frost and the quiet breathing of the sleeping baby at the poet's side, to conclude in a resolve that his child shall be brought up as a "child of nature," so that the sympathies the poet has come to detect may be reinforced throughout the child's education.

Fry \\'frī\\, Christopher, *original name* Christopher Harris \\'har-is\\ (b. Dec. 18, 1907, Bristol, Gloucestershire, Eng.) British writer of verse plays.

Fry adopted his mother's surname after he became a schoolteacher at age 18, his father having died many years earlier. He was for many years an actor, director, and writer of revues and plays before he gained fame as a playwright with THE LADY'S NOT FOR BURNING (1948), an ironic medieval comedy whose heroine is charged with being a witch. *A Phoenix Too Frequent* (1946) retells a tale from Petronius Arbiter. *The Boy with a Cart* (1950) is a legend of miracle and faith in the style of the mystery plays. *A Sleep of Prisoners* (1951) and *The Dark Is Light Enough* (1954) explore religious themes. After many years of translating and adapting plays—including *Ring Round the Moon* (produced 1950; adapted from Jean Anouilh's *L'Invitation au château*), *Duel of Angels* (produced 1958; adapted from Jean Giraudoux's *Pour Lucrèce*), and *Peer Gynt* (produced 1970; based on Johan Fillinger's translation of Henrik Ibsen's play)—Fry wrote *A Yard of Sun*, which was produced in 1970. He collaborated on a number of screenplays, including *Ben Hur* (1959) and *Barabbas* (1962), and wrote both radio and television plays. His *Can You Find Me: A Family History* was published in 1978.

Frye \\'frī\\, Northrop, *in full* Herman Northrop Frye (b. July 14, 1912, Sherbrooke, Que., Can.—d. Jan. 23, 1991, Toronto, Ont.) Canadian educator and literary critic, author of influential theories of criticism.

Frye was educated at the University of Toronto, Emmanuel College in Toronto, and Merton College, Oxford. He taught at Victoria College from 1939.

In 1947 he published *Fearful Symmetry: A Study of William Blake*, a sweeping study of Blake's visionary symbolism. In ANATOMY OF CRITICISM (1957), he analyzed various modes of literary criticism and stressed the recurring importance of archetypal symbols in literature. In later works Frye studied T.S. Eliot (1963), John Milton's epics (1965), Shakespearean comedy (1965) and tragedy (1967), and English Romanticism (1968). *The Stubborn Structure: Essays on Criticism and Society* appeared in 1970, and *The Great Code: The Bible and Literature*, a study of the mythology and structure of the Bible, was published in 1982. Frye's other critical works include *The Well-Tempered Critic* (1963), *The Secular Scripture: A Study of the Structure of Romance* (1976), *Northrop Frye on Shakespeare* (1986), and *Words with Power: Being a Second Study of "The Bible and Literature"* (1990).

fu \\'fü\\ [Chinese (Beijing dialect) *fù*] Chinese literary form combining elements of poetry and prose. The form developed during the Han dynasty (206 BC–AD 220) from its origins in the long poem *Li sao* ("On Encountering Sorrow") by Qu Yuan (c. 343–c. 289 BC). It was particularly suitable for description and exposition, in contrast to the more subjective, lyrical *sao*. The elements of the *fu* form include a long line, caesura, and the use of balanced parallel phrases. The use of rhyme places it somewhere between poetry and prose.

While some Han writers used the form quite skillfully, it was often abused for purposes of trivial and hackneyed description. Hundreds of years later, during the Song dynasty (960–1279), the *fu* was enriched by the skill of Ouyang Xiu (1007–72) and Su Dongpo (1036–1101), who used it to express philosophical concerns.

Fuentes \\fü-'en-,tās\\, Carlos (b. Nov. 11, 1928, Mexico City) Mexican novelist, short-story writer, playwright, critic, and diplomat whose experimental novels won him an international literary reputation.

Fuentes studied law at the University of Mexico, Mexico City, and later attended the Institute of Advanced International Studies in Geneva. He held a series of diplomatic posts in the 1950s. He also cofounded and edited several periodicals, including *Revista Mexicana de literatura* (1954–58; "Mexican Review of Literature").

The stories in Fuentes' first collection, *Los días enmascarados* (1954, 2nd ed., 1966; "The Masked Days"), blended elements of the realistic and the fantastic. His first novel, *La región más transparente* (1958; *Where the Air Is Clear*), which treated the theme of national identity and bitterly indicted Mexican society, won him national prestige.

The novel *Las buenas conciencias* (1959; *The Good Conscience*) emphasized the moral compromises that mark the transition from a rural economy to a complex, middle-class urban one. In *Aura* (1962) Fuentes skillfully fused reality and fantasy in a short, powerful narrative. *La muerte de Artemio Cruz* (1962; THE DEATH OF ARTEMIO CRUZ), which presents the agony of the last hours of a wealthy survivor of the Mexican Revolution, established Fuentes' international reputation as a major novelist.

The novel *Cambio de piel* (1967; *A Change of Skin*) defined existentially a collective Mexican consciousness by exploring and reinterpreting the country's myths. *La nueva novela hispanoamericana* (1969; "The New Hispano-American Novel") was Fuentes' chief work of literary criticism. The novel *Terra nostra* (1975; "Our Land"; *Terra Nostra*) explored the cultural substrata of the New and Old Worlds, using Jungian archetypal symbolism. Among his later novels are *La cabeza de la hidra* (1978; THE HYDRA HEAD), filled with the theme of the double; *Una familia lejana* (1980; DISTANT RELATIONS); *Gringo viejo* (1985; *The Old Gringo*); and *Cristóbal nonato* (1987; *Christopher Unborn*). In 1992 Fuentes' book-length essay on Hispanic cultures was published simultaneously in Spanish (*El espejo enterrado*) and English (*The Buried Mirror*).

Fugard \\'fü-,gärd\\, Athol, *in full* Harold Athol Lannigan Fugard (b. June 11, 1932, Middleburg, S.Af.) South African dramatist, actor, and director whose theater group in Port Elizabeth produced plays defiantly indicting apartheid.

Fugard's earliest plays were *No-Good Friday* and *Nongogo* (both published in *Dimetos and Two Early Plays*, 1977), but it was *The Blood Knot* (1963), produced for stage (1961) and television (1967) in both London and New York City, that established his international reputation. *The Blood Knot*, dealing with brothers who fall on opposite sides of the racial color line, was the first in a sequence Fugard called "The Family Trilogy." The series continued with *Hello and Goodbye* (1966) and *Boesman and Lena* (1969) and was later published under the title *Three Port Elizabeth Plays* (1974).

Fugard later experimented with a more imagist approach to drama, not using a rigid script but merely giving actors what he called "a mandate" to work around "a cluster of images." From this technique derived the imaginative if shapeless drama of *Orestes* (published in *Theatre One: New South African Drama*, 1978), and the documentary expressiveness of *Sizwe Bansi Is Dead*, *The Island*, and *Statements After an Arrest Under the Immorality Act* (all published in *Statements: Three Plays*, 1974).

A much more traditionally structured play, *Dimetos* (1977), was performed at the 1975 Edinburgh Festival. Other plays include *A Lesson from Aloes* (published 1981), *"Master Harold" and the Boys* (1982), and *The Road to Mecca* (1985). *My Children! My Africa! and Selected Shorter Plays* was published in 1990. *Tsotsi* (1980) is Fugard's only novel, and his only work of nonfiction is *Notebooks, 1960–1977* (1983).

Fugitive \'fyū-jə-tiv\ Any of a group of young poets and critics formed shortly after World War I at Vanderbilt University in Nashville, Tenn. The group, led by the poet and critic John Crowe RANSOM, published a bimonthly magazine, *The Fugitive* (1922–25), edited by poet Allen Tate. Other important members of the group were Donald Davidson and Robert Penn Warren. Outstanding selections from the magazine were collected in the *Fugitive Anthology* (1928).

Acutely aware of their Southern heritage, the Fugitives advocated a form of literary regionalism. Many of the Fugitives went on to become leaders in the Agrarian movement of the 1930s, which sought to resist the inroads of industrialism by a return to the agricultural economy of the Old South. Their views were published as a symposium in *I'll Take My Stand: The South and the Agrarian Tradition* (1930).

Fujiwara \,fū-jē-'wä-rä\ Sadaie, *also called* Teika \'tā-kə\ *or* Fujiwara Teika (b. 1162, Japan—d. Sept. 26, 1241, Kyōto) One of the greatest poets of his age and Japan's most influential poetic theorist and critic until modern times.

The son and poetic heir of the influential Shunzei (or Fujiwara Toshinari), Teika was a supremely accomplished and original poet. His ideal of *yōen* ("ethereal beauty") was a unique contribution to a poetic tradition that accepted innovation slowly. In his poems, Teika employed traditional language in startling new ways, showing that the prescriptive ideal of "old diction, new treatment" inherited from Shunzei might accommodate innovation and experimentation.

During his 40s, Teika underwent a profound inner conflict that greatly hindered his creativity and modified his poetic ideals. The chief poetic ideal of his later years was *ushin* ("conviction of feeling"), an ideal advocating poetry in more direct, simple styles than the technically complex poetry of *yōen*.

The best known of Teika's treatises and anthologies, regarded as scripture by generations of court poets, are *Eiga taigai* (1216; "Essentials of Poetic Composition"), *Hyakunin isshū* (c. 1235; "Single Poems by One Hundred Poets"), *Kindai shūka* (1209; "Superior Poems of Our Time"), and *Maigetsu shō* (1219; "Monthly Notes"). He also participated in the compilation of two Imperial anthologies, *Shin kokinshū* (c. 1205, "New Collection of Ancient and Modern Times") and *Shin chokusenshū* (1235; "New Imperial Collection").

Fujiwara \,fū-jē-'wä-rä\ Toshinari, *also called* Fujiwara Shunzei \'shūn-,zā\, *original name* Fujiwara Akihiro \,ä-kē-'hē-rō\ (b. 1114, Japan—d. Dec. 22, 1204, Kyoto) Major Japanese poet and critic, an innovator of *waka* (classical court poems) and compiler of the *Senzaishū* ("Collection of a Thousand Years"), the seventh Imperial anthology of classical Japanese poetry.

Shunzei began writing while young; over the decades he employed a variety of styles. Despite his neoclassical orientation,

he was more than an imitator of old styles and meters. Chinese descriptive poetry, especially that of the late Tang dynasty (618–907), and his Buddhist faith were important influences on his art. Shunzei is generally considered one of the first major *waka* poets; his son Fujiwara Sadaie and his granddaughter Fujiwara Toshinari no Musume, whom he helped rear, were also early practitioners of the *waka* style.

After 1150 Shunzei was noted for his appearances at poetry contests. He especially emphasized the ideal of *yūgen*, the subtle communication of romantic beauty with complex overtones of memory and, often, melancholy. In 1187 he was honored with the assignment to compile the *Senzaishū*. *Korai fūteishō* (1197, revised 1201; "Notes on Poetic Style Through the Ages") is considered his major critical work.

Fulgentius \fəl-'jen-shē-əs, -shəs\, Fabius Planciades (fl. late 5th and early 6th centuries AD) Christian Latin writer of African origin, a mythographer and allegorical interpreter of Virgil. Though his style is mediocre and his subject matter largely fantastic, Fulgentius exerted great influence on medieval European scholars.

Fulgentius is the author of the *Mythologiarum libri iii*, containing allegorical interpretations of myths supported by absurd etymologies, and of an *Expositio Virgilianae continentiae*, in which he makes Virgil himself appear in order to reveal the mystic meaning of the *Aeneid*. He also wrote an *Expositio sermonum antiquorum*, explanations of 62 rare Latin words supported by quotations, some of them from authors and works that never existed, and a *Liber absque litteris de aetatibus mundi et hominis*, a bizarre work in which human history is divided into 23 periods.

Fuller \'fül-ər\, Charles, *in full* Charles H. Fuller, Jr. (b. March 5, 1939, Philadelphia, Pa., U.S.) American playwright who is best known for A SOLDIER'S PLAY (1981), which won the 1982 Pulitzer Prize for drama.

In 1967 Fuller cofounded the Afro-American Arts Theatre in Philadelphia, and he was codirector from 1967 to 1971. During the 1970s he wrote plays for the Henry Street Settlement theater in New York, and in 1974 the Negro Ensemble Company produced his *In the Deepest Part of Sleep*. He based *The Brownsville Raid* (1975) on an actual incident involving the dishonorable discharge in 1906 of an entire black U.S. Army regiment.

In *Zooman and the Sign* (produced 1980; published 1982) Fuller presented a father's search for the killer of his daughter. *A Soldier's Play* follows the investigation by a black army captain of the murder of a black soldier at a base in Louisiana.

Fuller \'fül-ər\, Henry Blake (b. Jan. 9, 1857, Chicago, Ill., U.S.—d. July 28, 1929, Chicago) American novelist who wrote about his native city of Chicago.

Fuller came from a prosperous Chicago family. His first two novels—*The Chevalier of Pensieri-Vani* (1890; written under the pseudonym Stanton Page) and *The Chatelaine of La Trinité* (1892)—were gracefully told, brief but unhurried tales about Europe.

Fuller took a decidedly different direction with *The Cliff-Dwellers* (1893), a realistic novel, called the first important American city novel, about people in a Chicago skyscraper. *With the Procession* (1895) was another realistic novel about a wealthy Chicago merchant family. His other fiction set in Chicago includes *Under the Skylights* (1901), short stories about the city's artistic life; *On the Stairs* (1918), a novel about two men, one going up in life, the other down; and *Bertram Cope's Year* (1919), which is about an instructor at the University of Chicago. Fuller continued his European-based fiction with *Waldo Trench and Others* (1908), collected stories about Americans in Italy, and *Gardens of This World* (1929), which extends the tale begun in his first book.

Fuller \\'fu̇l-ər\\, Margaret, *in full* Sarah Margaret Fuller, *married name* Marchesa (Marchioness) Ossoli \\'ȯs-sō-lē\\ (b. May

23, 1810, Cambridgeport, Mass., U.S.—d. July 19, 1850, at sea) American critic, teacher, and woman of letters whose efforts to civilize the taste and enrich the lives of her contemporaries make her significant in the history of American culture.

Fuller taught in Bronson Alcott's Temple School in Boston, 1836–37, and in Providence,

Library of Congress

R.I., 1837–39. In 1839 she published a translation of J.P. Eckermann's *Conversations with Goethe*; her most cherished project, never completed, was a biography of J.W. von Goethe. From 1840 to 1842 she was editor of *The Dial*, a magazine launched by the Transcendentalists, for which she wrote poetry, reviews, and critiques.

Woman in the Nineteenth Century (1845) is a tract on feminism that was both a demand for political equality and an ardent plea for the emotional, intellectual, and spiritual fulfillment of women. It was published by Horace Greeley, who had admired her *Summer on the Lakes, in 1843* (1844), a perceptive study of frontier life in Illinois and Wisconsin.

In 1844 Margaret Fuller became literary critic on Greeley's newspaper, the *New York Tribune*. Before she sailed for Europe in 1846, some of her essays appeared as *Papers on Literature and Art*, which assured the cordial welcome she received in English and French circles. America's first woman foreign correspondent, she reported on her travels for the *Tribune*; the "letters" were later published in *At Home and Abroad* (1856). Settling in Italy in 1847, she was caught up in the cause of the Italian revolutionists, led by Guiseppe Mazzini, and was secretly married to Giovanni Angelo, Marchese Ossoli. Following the suppression of the republic she sailed for America with her husband and infant son, Angelo. They perished in a shipwreck off Fire Island (N.Y.), and with them was lost her manuscript history of the revolution.

Fuller \\'fu̇l-ər\\, Roy (Broadbent) (b. Feb. 11, 1912, Oldham, Lancashire, Eng.—d. Sept. 27, 1991, London) British poet and novelist, best known for his concise verse chronicling the daily routines of home and office.

Educated privately in Lancashire, Fuller became a solicitor in 1934 and served in the Royal Navy (1941–45) during World War II. After the war he pursued a dual career as a lawyer and a man of letters.

Fuller's first volume of poetry appeared in 1939. The poems published in *The Middle of a War* (1942) and *A Lost Season* (1944) chronicle his wartime service and show him intensely concerned with the social and political conditions of his time. *Epitaphs and Occasions* (1949) satirized the postwar world, but in *Brutus's Orchard* (1957) and *Collected Poems 1936–61* (1962) Fuller adopted a more reflective tone and showed greater interest in psychological and philosophical subjects. A lucid and detached tone persists in such later volumes as *Buff* (1965), *New Poems* (1968), and *From the Joke Shop* (1975) as the poet sardonically reflects on old age. *New and Collected Poems 1934–84* (1985) is an authoritative collection of his verse. *Available for*

Dreams (1989) was the last volume of poetry to be published during his lifetime; *Last Poems* was published in 1993.

Fuller wrote several novels, including *Image of a Society* (1956), *The Ruined Boys* (1959), and *My Child, My Sister* (1965), and his memoirs were published in four volumes from 1980 to 1991.

Fuller \\'fu̇l-ər\\, Thomas (b. June 19, 1608, Aldwincle, Northamptonshire, Eng.—d. Aug. 16, 1661, London) British scholar and preacher, and one of the most witty and prolific authors of the 17th century.

Fuller was educated at Queens' College, Cambridge, and was appointed preacher at the Chapel Royal, Savoy, London, in 1641. He left London in 1643, and for a time during the English Civil Wars he served as chaplain to the Royalist army. He returned to London in 1646 and wrote *Andronicus, or the Unfortunate Politician* (1646), a satire against Oliver Cromwell. In 1649 he was given the parish of Waltham Abbey, Essex.

Fuller was again appointed to a pulpit in London in 1652. There he completed *The Church-History of Britain* (1655) and added to it *The History of the University of Cambridge* and *The History of Waltham-Abbey in Essex*.

By enriching his factual accounts with descriptions of psychological oddities and other details of human interest, Fuller widened the scope of English biographical writing. His *History of the Worthies of England*, published posthumously in 1662, was the first attempt at a dictionary of national biography.

For the modern reader, Fuller's most interesting work is probably *The Holy State, the Profane State* (1642), an entertaining collection of character sketches.

Fu Manchu, Dr. \\'fu̇-man-'chu̇\\ Fictional character, a Chinese criminal genius who was the hero-villain of short stories by Sax ROHMER. The sinister Dr. Fu personified the genre of the "yellow peril" mystery, which expressed Western fears of Asian power and influence.

Fu Manchu made his first appearance in the short story "The Zayat Kiss," in the *Story-Teller* (1912). For 45 years, story collections appeared, including *Dr. Fu Manchu* (1913), *The Devil Doctor* (1916), *The Trail of Fu Manchu* (1934), and *Emperor Fu Manchu* (1959).

Furetière \\fuėr-'tyer\\, Antoine (b. Dec. 28, 1619, Paris, Fr.—d. March 14, 1688, Paris) French novelist, satirist, and lexicographer.

Furetière entered the legal profession, but he soon took holy orders to provide himself with an income that would enable him to pursue his literary vocation. After publishing three books of comic and satirical verse, he wrote *Nouvelle allégorique* (1658; "Allegorical Novella"; *The Rebellion*), a facetious survey of the contemporary Parisian world of letters, in which he wrote so favorably of the members of the Académie Française that he was, in 1662, himself elected.

The good will of his colleagues, however, was sorely tested when his groundbreaking *Le Roman bourgeois* (1666; "The Bourgeois Novel"; *Scarron's City Romance*) was published. The work dealt realistically with the Parisian middle classes, a subject matter deemed unworthy of an academician.

Furetière incurred greater displeasure when, late in 1684, he revealed his intention of publishing his own dictionary of the French language, on which he had been working some 40 years. This enterprise infuriated fellow academicians, whose own long-projected dictionary was still incomplete. They expelled him from the academy, and the rest of Furetière's life was spent in controversy with his former colleagues. His great *Dictionnaire universel*, soon to be recognized as more comprehensive and much more useful than the academy's, was first printed in Holland in three volumes in 1690.

Furies　*see* FURY.

Furnished Room, The　Short story by O. HENRY, published serially in 1904 and then collected in *The Four Million* (1906). Set in New York City, it is a melodramatic tale about a young man who, after a futile search for his missing girlfriend, commits suicide in his rented room, not knowing that it is the same room in which his girlfriend had killed herself one week earlier.

Furphy \'fər-fē\, Joseph, *pseudonym* Tom Collins \'käl-ənz\ (b. Sept. 26, 1843, Yering, near Yarra Glen, Vic., Australia—d. Sept. 13, 1912, Claremont, W. Aus., Australia)　Australian author whose novels combine an acute sense of local Australian life and color with the eclectic philosophy and literary ideas of a self-taught workingman.

The son of Irish immigrants, Furphy worked as a thresher, teamster, and gold miner before settling down in 1884 at his brother's foundry at Shepparton. There he completed a picaresque novel, *Such Is Life* (1903), written as excerpts from the diary of Tom Collins. Furphy's other major works, *Rigby's Romance* (serialized 1905; published in book form, 1921) and *The Buln Buln and the Brolga* (published posthumously in 1948), were written from chapters cut from the original of *Such Is Life*. His *Poems* was published in 1916.

Fury \'fyùr-ē\ *plural* Furies.　In Greco-Roman mythology, any of the goddesses of vengeance. Known in Greek as Erinyes (*singular* Erinys), they were probably personified curses, but possibly were originally conceived of as ghosts of the murdered. According to the Greek poet Hesiod they were the daughters of Gaea (Earth) and sprang from the blood of her mutilated spouse Uranus; in Aeschylus they were the daughters of Nyx; in Sophocles, of Darkness and of Gaea. Euripides was the first to speak of them as three in number. Later writers named them Alecto ("Unceasing in Anger"), Tisiphone ("Avenger of Murder"), and Megaera ("Jealous"). Because the Greeks feared to utter the dreaded name Erinyes, the goddesses were often addressed by the euphemistic names Eumenides ("Kind Ones") or Semnai Theai ("Venerable Goddesses"). In Latin the Erinyes were known as the Furiae or Dirae; it is unclear if they possessed a cult independent of imported Greek belief.

Futabatei \fū-'tä-bä-tä\ Shimei, *pseudonym of* Hasegawa Tatsunosuke \tät-sə-'nōs-ke\ (b. April 4, 1864, Edo [now Tokyo], Japan—d. May 10, 1909, at sea in Bay of Bengal)　Japanese novelist and translator of Russian literature; his UKIGUMO (1887–89; "The Drifting Clouds") brought modern realism to the Japanese novel.

Born to an aristocratic samurai family, Futabatei studied Russian at the Tokyo School of Foreign Languages (1881–86). He began his literary career soon after leaving school. Although Futabatei wrote three novels and translated many stories, he is best known for *Ukigumo*, his first novel, and for his earliest translations of stories by Ivan Turgenev, *Aibiki* ("The Rendezvous") and *Meguriai* ("Chance Meetings"), both published in 1888. In these works Futabatei used a style called *gembun itchi* ("unification of spoken and written language"), one of the first attempts to employ modern colloquial idiom.

Futabatei was displeased with *Ukigumo* (although both it and his translations were well received), and so in 1889 he joined the staff of the government gazette *Kampō*, where he remained until 1897. He did not write another novel for nearly 10 years. From 1898 to 1902 he taught Russian and worked for government agencies, later going to Harbin and Beijing in China. After returning to Japan in 1903, he resumed translating fiction professionally. Between 1896 and 1909 his output included translations of stories by Turgenev, Nikolay Gogol, Leo Tolstoy, and Maksim Gorky; articles on literary criticism

and social conditions; and two novels, *Sono omokage* (1906; *An Adopted Husband*) and *Heibon* (1907; *Mediocrity*).

Futurism \'fyü-chə-,riz-əm\, *Italian* Futurismo \,fü-tü-'rēz-mō\, *Russian* Futurizm \fü-tü-'rʸēzm\　An artistic movement begun in Italy about 1909 and marked especially by violent rejection of tradition and an effort to give formal expression to the dynamic energy and movement of mechanical processes.

Futurism was first announced on Feb. 20, 1909, when the Paris newspaper *Le Figaro* published a manifesto by Filippo Tommaso Marinetti, who coined the name. The manifesto's rhetoric was passionately bombastic, and its tone was aggressive and inflammatory.

Marinetti had founded the journal *Poesia* in Paris in 1905, and he later founded a press with the same name to publish Futurist works. Among those who were influenced by him were Wyndham Lewis, the English founder of Vorticism, and the French poet Guillaume Apollinaire.

Russian Futurism went beyond its Italian model in its revolutionary social and political outlook. Marinetti influenced the two Russian writers considered the founders of Russian Futurism, Velimir Khlebnikov and the younger Vladimir Mayakovsky. The Russians published their own manifesto in December 1912, entitled *Poshchochina obshchestvennomu vkusu* ("A Slap in the Face of Public Taste"). The Russian Futurists repudiated Aleksandr Pushkin, Fyodor Dostoyevsky, and Leo Tolstoy and then-current Russian Symbolist verse and called for the creation of new techniques for writing poetry.

Both the Russian and the Italian Futurist poets discarded logical sentence construction and traditional grammar and syntax; they frequently presented an incoherent string of words stripped of their meaning and used for their sound alone. As the first group of artists to identify wholeheartedly with the Bolshevik Revolution of 1917, the Russian Futurists were given several important cultural posts. But their challenging literary techniques and their theoretical premises of revolt and innovation proved too unstable a foundation upon which to build a broader literary movement, and their influence was negligible by the time of Mayakovsky's death in 1930.

Fuzuli \fü-zü-'lē\ or **Fuḍūlī** \fü-dü-'lē\, Mehmed bin Süleyman (b. c. 1480, Karbalā' [Iraq]—d. 1556, Karbalā')　Turkish poet and greatest figure in the classical school of Turkish literature.

Fuzuli apparently came from a family of religious officials and was well versed in the thought of his day, but very little is known about his life. Among his early patrons was the shāh Ismā'īl I, founder of the Ṣafavid dynasty of Iran and conqueror of Baghdad in 1508. Twenty-six years later, when the Ottoman sultan Süleyman I took Baghdad, Fuzuli attempted to curry favor and henceforth wrote in the name of the Ottoman sovereign. It seems that he was never able to move to the Ottoman capital at Constantinople (Istanbul), and in his famous *Şikâyetname* ("Complaint"), he caustically commented on not being given the status of court poet.

Fuzuli composed poetry with equal facility and elegance in Turkish, Persian, and Arabic. The works for which he is famous include his melodic and sensitive rendition of the great Muslim classic *Leylâ ve Mecnun*, a celebrated allegorical romance depicting the attraction of Majnūn (the human spirit) for Laylā (divine beauty). Fuzuli also wrote two divans (collections of poems), one in Azerbaijani Turkish and one in Persian. These anthologies contain his most lyrical verses. His poetic expression, characterized by sincerity, passion, and a pervasive strain of melancholy, transcended the highly formalized classical Islāmic literary aesthetic, and his works influenced many poets up to the 19th century.

Gabler, Hedda \'hed-då-'gåb-lər\   Fictional character, the protagonist of Henrik Ibsen's drama HEDDA GABLER.

Gaboriau \gå-bȯr-'yō\, Émile (b. Nov. 9, 1832?, Saujon, Fr.—d. c. Oct. 1, 1873, Paris)   French novelist who is best known as the father of the *roman policier* ("detective novel").

Gaboriau made his reputation with the publication in 1866 of *L'Affaire Lerouge* (*The Widow Lerouge*) after having published several other books and miscellaneous writings. His later books, many of them classics of their kind, include *Le Crime d'Orcival* (1867; *The Mystery of Orcival*), *Monsieur Lecoq* (1868), *Les Esclaves de Paris* (1868; *The Slaves of Paris*), and *L'Argent des autres* (1874; *Other People's Money*).

Gabriel \'gā-brē-əl\, *Hebrew* Gavri'el, *Arabic* Gibrā'īl, Jabra'il, *or* Jibrīl.   In the Bible and the Qur'ān, one of the archangels. Gabriel was employed to announce the birth of John the Baptist to Zechariah and to announce the imminent birth of Jesus to the Virgin Mary. In John Milton's *Paradise Lost*, Gabriel was the leader of the angels in heaven.

Gadda \'gäd-dä\, Carlo Emilio (b. Nov. 14, 1893, Milan, Italy—d. May 21, 1973, Rome)   Italian essayist, short-story writer, and novelist outstanding particularly for his original and innovative style.

Gadda began writing in the 1930s and from the first demonstrated a fascination with and facility for language as well as a gift for unemotional and acute psychological and sociological analysis. His first works were collected in *I sogni e la folgore* (1955; "The Dreams and the Lightning"). Gadda's best-known and most successful novel, *Quer pasticciaccio brutto de via Merulana* (1957; *That Awful Mess on Via Merulana*), is a story of a murder and burglary in fascist Rome and of the subsequent investigation. The language of the novel, known to Italians as *Il pasticciaccio* ("The Pastiche"), is literary Italian, with an admixture of three Roman dialects and puns, technical jargon, foreign words, parodies, made-up words, and classical allusions.

Gaddis \'gad-əs\, William (Thomas) (b. Dec. 29, 1922, New York, N.Y., U.S.)   American novelist whose long, experimental works portray the contemporary human condition.

Gaddis first gained note as an author with publication of his controversial novel *The Recognitions* (1955). The book, rich in language and imagery, began as a parody of Faust but developed into a multileveled examination of spiritual bankruptcy. Discouraged by the harsh critical reception of his book, Gaddis published nothing for 20 years and instead worked as a freelance writer for various corporations. His second novel, *JR* (1975), uses long stretches of cacophonous dialogue to depict what its author viewed as the greed, hypocrisy, and banality of the world of American business. Gaddis' third novel, *Carpenter's Gothic* (1985), is even more pessimistic in its depiction of moral chaos in modern American society.

Gaddis' fiction contains long dialogues and monologues related by a minimum of plot and structured by scant punctuation. It shows the influence of the writings of James Joyce and, in turn, influenced the work of Thomas Pynchon.

Gaea \'jē-ə\ *or* **Ge** \'jē\   Greek personification of the Earth as a goddess. Mother and wife of URANUS (Heaven), from whom the Titan CRONUS, her last born child by him, separated her, she was also mother of the other Titans, the Giants (Gigantes), the Furies, the Hecatoncheires, and the Cyclopes.

Gaelic revival \'gāl-ik, 'gal-, 'gäl-\   Resurgence of interest in Irish language, literature, history, and folklore inspired by the growing Irish nationalism of the early 19th century.

With the English military conquest and settlement of Ireland early in the 17th century, Irish became the language of an oppressed people. Schools did not teach the literary language, and no native nobility existed to support Irish writing. By the mid-19th century there was little literary activity, and almost all speakers of Irish were illiterate.

About the same time, translations of heroic tales from ancient Irish manuscripts (*e.g.*, *The Annals of the Four Masters*) caught the imagination of the educated classes. Anglo-Irish poets began to write verses with Gaelic patterns and rhythms that echoed the passion and rich imagery of ancient bardic verse. In 1842 the patriotic organization known as Young Ireland founded *The Nation*, a paper that published the works of Thomas Osborne Davis, a master of prose and verse, and of such poets as Thomas D'Arcy McGee, Richard D'Alton Williams, and Speranza (the pseudonym of Lady Wilde, mother of Oscar Wilde). The *Dublin University Magazine* (1833–80), another important literary publication, often included the work of James Clarence Mangan, who translated Gaelic poems into English and also wrote original verse in the Gaelic style.

The Gaelic revival laid the scholarly and nationalistic groundwork for the IRISH LITERARY RENAISSANCE, the great flowering of Irish literary talent at the end of the 19th and beginning of the 20th century.

Gaines \'gānz\, Ernest J., *in full* James (b. Jan. 15, 1933, Oscar, La., U.S.)   American writer whose fiction, as exemplified by THE AUTOBIOGRAPHY OF MISS JANE PITTMAN (1971), his most acclaimed work, reflected African-American experience and the oral tradition of his rural Louisiana childhood.

When Gaines was 15, his family moved to California. He graduated from San Francisco State College (now San Francisco State University) in 1957 and attended graduate school at Stanford University. He taught or was writer-in-residence at several schools, including Denison and Stanford universities.

Gaines's novels are set in rural Louisiana, often in a fictional plantation area named Bayonne that some critics have compared to William Faulkner's Yoknapatawpha County. In addition to *The Autobiography of Miss Jane Pittman*, his novels include *Catherine Carmier* (1964), *Of Love and Dust* (1967), *In My Father's House* (1978), and *A Gathering of Old Men* (1983).

gai saber \'gī-så-'ber\ *or* **gay science**   The art of composing love poetry; especially the art of the Provençal troubadours as set forth in a 14th-century work called the *Leys d'amors*. The Old Provençal phrase *gai saber* ("gay knowledge" or "gay science") is associated with the *Consistòri del Gai Saber*, originally the *Sobregaya compannia dels VII Trobadors de Tolosa* ("Very Gay Company of the Seven Troubadours of Toulouse"), a group of seven citizens of Toulouse who in 1323 organized yearly competitions to encourage troubadour poetry, by then in serious decline.

Galahad \'gal-ə-,had\   The pure knight in Arthurian romance, son of LANCELOT and Elaine (daughter of Pelles), who achieved the vision of God through the Holy GRAIL.

In the first romance treatments of the Grail story (*e.g.*, Chrétien de Troyes's late 12th-century *Le Conte du Graal*), Perceval was the Grail hero. But during the 13th century a new, austerely spiritual significance was given to the Grail theme, and a new Grail winner was required whose genealogy could be traced back to the House of David in the Old Testament. For this purpose Galahad was created. His grandfather Pelles was said to have been a descendant of Joseph of Arimathea, the original keeper of the Grail. This version of the Grail story appeared in the *Queste del Saint Graal* ("Quest for the Holy Grail"), which forms part of the Prose *Lancelot* section of the Vulgate cycle.

Galanthis   *see* GALINTHIAS.

Galatea \\,gal-ə-'tē-ə\ In Greek mythology, a Nereid who was loved by the Cyclops Polyphemus. Galatea, however, loved the youth Acis. When Polyphemus discovered Acis and Galatea together, he crushed Acis to death with a boulder. In some versions of the Pygmalion story, Galatea is also the name of the statue that Pygmalion creates and then falls in love with.

Gale \'gāl\, Zona (b. Aug. 26, 1874, Portage, Wis., U.S.—d. Dec. 27, 1938, Chicago, Ill.) American novelist and playwright whose *Miss Lulu Bett* (1920) established her as a realistic chronicler of Midwestern village life.

Gale graduated from the University of Wisconsin and worked as a reporter, first for various Milwaukee newspapers and later for the *New York World*. After the publication of her first short story, in 1903, she gave her full time to writing.

Gale's books include *Friendship Village* (1908), *A Daughter of the Morning* (1917), *Birth* (1918), and *Preface to a Life* (1926). Her early writings were sentimental evocations of the virtues of small-town life and fall within the local-color tradition. Her later writings, however, reveal her interest in progressive causes and are increasingly critical of small-town provincialism. The dramatization of *Miss Lulu Bett*, a study of an unmarried woman's attempts at self-assertion in the face of a constricting social environment, won Gale the Pulitzer Prize in 1921.

Galib Dede \gä-'lēp-de-'de\, *also called* Şeyh Galib \'she-gä-'lēp\, *pseudonyms of* Mehmed Esad \e-'sät\ (b. 1758, Constantinople, Ottoman Empire [now Istanbul, Tur.]—d. Jan. 4, 1799, Constantinople) Turkish poet, one of the last great classical poets of Ottoman literature.

Galib Dede was born into a family that was well connected with the Ottoman government. He continued the family tradition by becoming an official in the Ottoman imperial council, though he later gave up this government position and became the sheikh (superior) of the Galata monastery in Constantinople. In addition to his *Divan* (collection of poems), Galib Dede is known for his masterpiece, *Hüsn ü Aşk* ("Beauty and Love"). This allegorical romance describes the courtship of a youth (Hüsn, or "Beauty") and a girl (Aşk, or "Love"). After many tribulations, the couple are finally brought together, allegorizing the fundamental unity of love and beauty.

Galinthias \gə-'lin-thē-əs\ or **Galanthis** \gə-'lan-this\ In Greek mythology, a friend, or servant, of Alcmene, who bore Zeus's son Heracles (Hercules). While Alcmene was in labor, Zeus's jealous wife, Hera (goddess of childbirth), was clasping her hands, thus by magic preventing delivery. To foil Hera, Galinthias falsely announced that Alcmene had given birth to a son, so causing Hera to relax. Thus the charm was broken, and Alcmene gave birth to Heracles. As punishment, Hera transformed Galinthias into a weasel or (according to Ovid) a lizard.

Gallagher \'gal-ə-gər\, Tess, *original surname* Bond \'bänd\ (b. July 21, 1943, Port Angeles, Wash., U.S.) American poet known for her introspective verses about self-discovery, womanhood, and family life.

Gallagher studied at the Universities of Washington and Iowa. Her first full-length volume of verse, *Instructions to the Double* (1976), is a confessional work about her efforts to synthesize her past life with her future career as a poet.

In 1978 Gallagher published three collections of poems: *Portable Kisses*, *On Your Own*, and *Under Stars*. Several poems in *Willingly* (1984) eulogize her late father, including "Boat Ride" and "3 A.M. Kitchen: My Father Talking." The collections *Amplitude* (1987) and *Moon Crossing Bridge* (1992) focus on her relationship with her third husband, author Raymond Carver. In addition to her poetry and several plays for film and television, she wrote *The Lover of Horses and Other Stories* (1986), a book of short fiction.

Galland \gä-'läⁿ\, Antoine (b. 1646, Rollot, near Montdidier, Fr.—d. 1715, Paris) French Orientalist and scholar, best known for his adaptation of the Middle Eastern tales *Alf laylah wa laylah* in *Les Mille et une nuits* (1704–17; THE THOUSAND AND ONE NIGHTS).

Galland attended the College of Noyon and the Collège de France in Paris. He accompanied the French ambassador to Constantinople during the years 1670–75, learned Arabic, Persian, and Turkish, and wrote a journal of his travels.

In addition to his work on dictionaries and academic writings, Galland translated the Qur'ān and in 1694 wrote *Les Paroles remarquables, les bons mots et les maximes des Orientaux* (*The Remarkable Sayings, Apothegms, and Maxims of the Eastern Nations*), a compendium of Eastern wisdom. His major work, the *Les Mille et une nuits*, was a popular version freely translated from Syrian manuscripts.

Gallant \ga-'lant\, Mavis, *original name* Mavis de Trafford Young \'yəŋ\ (b. Aug. 11, 1922, Montreal, Can.) Canadian-born writer of essays, novels, plays, and especially short stories. In unsentimental prose and with trenchant wit she delineated the isolation, detachment, and fear that afflict rootless North American and European expatriates.

Following graduation from high school in New York City, Gallant worked in Montreal at the National Film Board and as a newspaper reporter for the *Montreal Standard*.

From 1950 she lived mostly in Europe, eventually settling in France. In the 1950s she became a regular contributor to *The New Yorker* magazine, which through the years published more than 100 of her short stories and much of her nonfiction. Collections of her well-constructed, perceptive, often humorous short stories include *My Heart Is Broken* (1964), *The Pegnitz Junction* (1973), *Home Truths: Selected Canadian Stories* (1981), *Overhead in a Balloon: Stories of Paris* (1985), *In Transit* (1988), and *Across the Bridge* (1993).

Gallegos \gä-'yä-gōs, -'gōh\, Rómulo, *surname in full* Gallegos Freire \'frā-rā\ (b. Aug. 2, 1884, Caracas, Venez.—d. April 4, 1969, Caracas) Novelist and president of Venezuela in 1948, best known for his forceful novels that dramatize the overpowering natural aspects of the Venezuelan llanos (prairies) and the local folklore.

Gallegos won an international reputation as one of the leading novelists of Latin America with *Doña Bárbara* (1929), the story of the ruthless woman boss of a hacienda. Other major novels are *Cantaclaro* (1934; "Chanticleer"), dealing with a ballad singer of the llanos, and *Canaima* (1935), a story of the tropical forest, named after the evil spirit that pervades the jungle.

In 1936 Gallegos began a political career that eventually led to his inauguration as president of Venezuela in February 1948. His government was overthrown by a military coup in November 1948, however, and he was sent into exile; he returned to Venezuela in 1958.

galliambic \,gal-ē-'am-bik\ [Latin *galliambus* galliambic meter, from *gallus* priest of Cybele + *iambus* iamb] In classical prosody, consisting of four Ionic feet, each consisting of two accented and two unaccented syllables. The last of the feet is catalectic (incomplete or truncated). The galliambic meter is scanned as ∪∪−̆ − | ∪̆∪ −− ‖ ∪∪−̆ ∪̄ | ∪̆∪ −, with a diaeresis after the second foot. Some of the feet may be varied by resolution and contraction. The meter was named for the priests known as the *galli* because it reproduced the rhythm of their chants during the worship of Cybele, Great Mother of the Gods. It was used occasionally by Hellenistic Greek poets and, in Latin, by the Roman poet Catullus, who usually altered it to scan as ∪∪−∪ | −∪−− ‖ ∪∪−− | ∪∪−.

Gallimard \gȧ-lē-'mȧr\, Gaston (b. Jan. 18, 1881, Paris, Fr.—d. Dec. 25, 1975, Paris)   French publisher whose firm was one of the most influential publishing houses of the 20th century.

Gallimard studied law and literature at the University of Paris and turned to journalism soon afterward. In 1908, with André Gide and Jean Schlumberger, he founded the literary review *La Nouvelle Revue française*, and in 1911 the three men established a publishing house for the works of contributors to their review. The firm was called La Nouvelle Revue Française–Librairie Gallimard until 1919, when it was renamed simply Librairie Gallimard. In addition to major works by such contemporary writers as Gide, Marcel Proust, André Malraux, Jean-Paul Sartre, Albert Camus, and many lesser French authors, the firm published the well-known *La Pléiade* series of French literary classics.

Gallus \'gal-əs\, Gaius Cornelius (b. *c.* 70 BC, Forum Julii, Gaul—d. 26 BC, Egypt)   Roman soldier and poet, famous for four books of poems to his mistress "Lycoris," which, in ancient opinion, made him one of the greatest Roman elegiac poets. Only a single line of his verse survives.

Gallus was a friend of Augustus and Virgil and, having distinguished himself in the war against Mark Antony, was made governor of Egypt. There, however, his imprudent conduct led to his disgrace and suicide. Quintilian ranked him with Albius Tibullus, Sextus Propertius, and Ovid.

Galsworthy \'gȯlz-,wər-t͟hē, *commonly* 'galz-\, John (b. Aug. 14, 1867, Kingston Hill, Surrey, Eng.—d. Jan. 31, 1933, Grove Lodge, Hampstead)   English novelist and playwright, winner of the Nobel Prize for Literature in 1932.

Educated at Harrow and New College, Oxford, Galsworthy was called to the bar in 1890. He found law uncongenial, however, and took to writing. His first works, a collection of short stories and the novel *Jocelyn* (1898), were published at his own expense under the pseudonym John Sinjohn. *The Island Pharisees* (1904) was the first book to appear under his own name. *The Man of Property* (1906) began the novel sequence to be known as THE FORSYTE SAGA, the long chronicle novel by which Galsworthy is chiefly remembered. The story of the Forsyte family was continued in *The White Monkey* (1924), *The Silver Spoon* (1926), and *Swan Song* (1928), collected in *A Modern Comedy* (1929).

Galsworthy was also a successful dramatist; his plays, written in a naturalistic style, usually examined a controversial ethical or social problem. They include *The Silver Box* (1906), *Strife* (1909), *Justice* (1910), and *Loyalties* (1922). In 1921 he founded PEN (now International PEN), a worldwide organization of writers.

Galt \'gȯlt\, John (b. May 2, 1779, Irvine, Ayrshire, Scot.—d. April 11, 1839, Greenock, Renfrewshire)   Prolific Scottish novelist admired for his depiction of country life.

Galt settled in London in 1804. Commissioned by a merchant firm to establish trade agreements, he traveled to the Mediterranean area, where he met the poet Lord Byron, with whom he traveled to Malta and later to Athens. Other commercial ventures took him to France and The Netherlands (1814) and to Canada (1826). All his life he had been a voluminous writer, and when he finally returned home for good, he devoted himself entirely to literature.

His masterpieces are *The Ayrshire Legatees* (1820), *The Annals of the Parish* (1821), *Sir Andrew Wylie* (1822), *The Provost* (1822), *The Entail* (1823), and *Lawrie Todd* (1830), novels of Scottish rural life that foreshadowed the Kailyard (kitchen garden) school of fiction of the late 19th century.

Galt, John \'jän-'gȯlt\   Fictional character, a hero of ATLAS SHRUGGED by Ayn Rand. Galt, a talented research engineer, expounds Rand's theories of objectivism, or ethical egoism, which value reason and individualism over collectivism and mysticism.

Gálvez \'gäl-ḇās\, Manuel (b. July 18, 1882, Paraná, Arg.—d. Nov. 14, 1962, Buenos Aires)   Novelist and biographer whose documentation of a wide range of social ills in Argentina in the first half of the 20th century earned him an important position in modern Latin-American literature.

Gálvez studied law at the National University of Buenos Aires and was an inspector of secondary education from 1906 to 1931. He founded and began directing the literary magazine *Ideas* in 1903.

Gálvez is best remembered for his realistic novels of Argentine life, which deal with conflict in urban society. In *La maestra normal* (1914; "The Schoolmistress"), his first and generally considered his best novel, he captures the pettiness and monotony of life in a small Argentine city before the quickening pace of modernity shattered old provincial ways.

Gama \'gä-mə\, Basílio da, *in full* José Basílio da Gama (b. 1740, São José do Rio das Mortes, Braz.—d. July 31, 1795, Lisbon, Port.)   Neoclassical poet and author of the Brazilian epic poem *O Uraguai* (1769), an account of the Portuguese-Spanish expedition against the Jesuit-controlled reservation Indians of the Uruguay River basin.

Gama completed his novitiate with the Jesuits in 1759. In that same year the order was expelled from Brazil and all other Portuguese possessions, and he eventually left Brazil for Rome. When he returned to Brazil in 1767, he was sent by the Inquisition to Lisbon, where, as a Jesuit, he faced deportation to Angola. He won a pardon from the Marquês de Pombal by composing a poem for the wedding of Pombal's daughter, and he further ingratiated himself by revising the slant of the originally pro-Jesuit *O Uraguai*.

In spite of its questionable historicity, the poem became the most important Brazilian work of the colonial period. Gama showed himself to be a sensitive and original poet in breaking away from the strict epic model established by Luis de Camões, Portugal's great 16th-century poet, and creating a Brazilian epic in blank verse.

Gamelyn, The Tale of \'gam-ə-lin\   Anonymous English metrical romance written about 1350. The poem, which consists entirely of rhymed couplets, is some 900 lines long and is written in the East Midland dialect of Middle English. Based on English folklore, it tells of Gamelyn, son of Sir John de Boundys, who is deprived of his inheritance by his brother and becomes an outlaw in the forest.

The Tale of Gamelyn is of special interest for its connections with the English ballads of the outlaw Robin Hood. It was a source of such later works as William Shakespeare's *As You Like It* and Geoffrey Chaucer's "Cook's Tale" in *The Canterbury Tales*.

Gamp, Sairey \'sā-rē-'gamp\   Comic fictional character in Charles Dickens' novel MARTIN CHUZZLEWIT. A high-spirited old Cockney, Mrs. Sarah Gamp (called Sairey) is a sketchily trained nurse-midwife who is as enthusiastic at laying out a corpse as she is at delivering a baby.

Gandalf \'gän-,dȧlf, 'gan-\   Fictional character, a wise magician who guides and advises the hobbits Bilbo and Frodo Baggins throughout their many adventures in J.R.R. Tolkien's THE HOBBIT and THE LORD OF THE RINGS trilogy.

Gaṇeśa or **Ganesha** \gə-'nā-shə\, *also called* Gaṇapati \,gə-nə-pə-'tē\   Elephant-headed Hindu god, the son of Śiva and Pārvatī. Gaṇeśa, considered the remover of obstacles, is the first god invoked at the beginning of worship or a new enterprise, and his image is often seen at the entrance of temples or houses. He is a patron of letters and learning, and he is the legendary scribe who wrote down the *Mahābhārata* ("Great Epic of the Bharata Dynasty") from Vyāsa's dictation. Gaṇeśa is usually depicted as colored red; he is potbellied, has one tusk broken, and has four arms that may hold a noose, a goad, a pot of rice or sweetmeats, and his broken tusk, or that may bestow boons or protection. He rides on a rat.

Ganivet \ˌgä-nē-'bet\, Ángel, *surname in full* Ganivet y García \ē-ˌgär-'thē-ä\ (b. Dec. 13, 1865, Granada, Spain—d. Nov. 29, 1898, Riga, Latvia, Russian Empire)   Spanish essayist and novelist, considered a member (or, sometimes, a precursor) of the Generation of '98 because of his concern for the spiritual regeneration of his country. Fluent in five languages, he served with the Spanish consular service in Antwerp (Belg.), Helsinki (Fin.), and Riga (Latvia). An anguished and skeptical man facing an uncertain prognosis of a progressive disease, and disillusioned in love, he drowned himself in the Dvina River.

Ganivet's most important work is the *Idearium español* (1897; *Spain, an Interpretation*), an essay that examines the Spanish temperament and the historical basis of the political situation in his country.

Gant, Eugene \yü-'jĕn-'gant, 'yü-jĕn\   Autobiographical character, an alienated young artist in Thomas Wolfe's novels LOOK HOMEWARD, ANGEL and OF TIME AND THE RIVER.

Ganymede \'gan-i-ˌmēd\, *Greek* Ganymēdēs \ˌgan-i-'mē-dēz\, *Latin* Ganymedes *same*\ *or* Catamitus \ˌkat-ə-'mī-təs\   In Greek legend, the son of Tros, king of Troy. (In other versions he is said to be the son of Laomedon, the son of Ilus, or of others.) Because of his great beauty, he was carried off either by the gods or by Zeus, disguised as an eagle, or, according to a Cretan account, by Minos, to serve as Zeus's cupbearer.

From early times it was believed that Ganymede's kidnapper had a homosexual passion for him, hence the term *catamite*, derived from the popular Latin form of his name. Reference to this aspect of the Ganymede myth is made in Aristophanes' *Peace*, Plato's *Phaedrus* (one of two dialogues on human passions), and other works of literature.

Gao Ming *or* **Kao Ming** \'gaú-'miŋ\ (b. *c.* 1305, Yongjia [Ruian], China—d. *c.* 1370, Ninghai, Zhejiang province)   Chinese poet and playwright whose sole surviving opera, *Pipa ji* ("Lute Story"), became the model for Ming-dynasty drama.

Quitting a frustrating official career under the Mongol regime in 1356, Gao found a new vocation in the theater. As a southerner, he shunned the fashionable *zaju*, or "variety theater," which was flourishing in the north under Mongol patronage, and instead wrote for the *nanxi*, or "southern drama," an operatic folk theater associated with the former Song capital of Hangzhou. His opera *Pipa ji*, completed about 1367, won the favor of the founding Ming emperor and enjoyed sufficient popularity to restore this regional theater to national stature. A moralistic tragicomedy, the opera tells how a devoted young wife, Zhao Wuniang, wanders as an itinerant lute player searching for her husband, Cai Bojie, an ambitious scholar who has abandoned her and his aging parents in quest of fame at court. The work won renown both for its libretto, which elevated the popular operatic verse into a polished poetic medium, and for its melodious, romantic southern music.

Garborg \'gär-bòrg\, Arne (*or* Adne) Evensen (b. Jan. 25, 1851, Time, Nor.—d. Jan. 14, 1924, Asker)   Novelist, poet, playwright, and essayist, one of the first great writers to show the literary possibilities of Nynorsk (New Norwegian language).

Educated at a teachers' seminary, Garborg taught school and edited newspapers before studying at King Frederick's Univer-

sity. An unusually versatile and prolific writer, Garborg established himself as one of the great authors of his time with his second novel, *Bondestudentar* (1883; "Peasant Students"), a depiction of the cultural clash between country and city life as embodied in the struggles of a peasant student living in the capital. Garborg's masterpiece is a poetic cycle in Nynorsk, *Haugtussa* (1895; "The Mound Elf"), which describes a young girl's belief in the supernatural.

Garção \gär-'saúⁿ\, Pedro António Correia (b. April 29, 1724, Lisbon, Port.—d. Nov. 10, 1772, Lisbon)   One of Portugal's principal Neoclassical poets.

Garção studied law at Coimbra but apparently took no degree. In 1756 he became a member of Arcádia Lusitana, a literary society founded to rid Portuguese poetry of the archaisms, conceits, and windy rhetoric still persisting from the 17th century. From 1760 to 1762 he edited the *Gazeta de Lisboa*.

Taking the ancient Latin poet Horace as his model, Garção adopted a classical simplicity. His verse play *Teatro novo* (1766; "New Theater") attacked foreign influences in the theater, and his *Assembléia ou partida* ("Meeting or Parting") satirized the social life of Lisbon. In the "Cantata de Dido," included in the latter work, he combined the spirit of classical art with perfection of form to produce one of the most celebrated 18th-century Portuguese poems.

García Calderón \gär-'sē-ä-ˌkäl-dā-'rōn\, Ventura (b. 1885, Paris, Fr.—d. Oct. 28, 1959, Paris)   Peruvian writer and diplomat who composed in both Spanish and French.

The son of a Peruvian president who was driven into exile in a military coup, García Calderón spent most of his life in France and elsewhere in Europe, writing novels, short stories, and criticism and holding various government posts. In his best literary work he wrote about the regional native highlands of Peru, suggesting how little upper-class Peruvians knew about their rural compatriots. Among his chief works were *La venganza del cóndor* (1924; "The Vengeance of the Condor") and *Couleur de sang* (1931; "Color of Blood").

García de la Huerta \gär-'thē-ä-thä-lä-'wer-tä\, Vicente (Antonio) (b. March 9, 1734, Zafra, Spain—d. March 12, 1787, Madrid)   Playwright, poet, and critic whose Neoclassical tragedy *Raquel* (1778) was once considered the most distinguished tragic drama of 18th-century Spain.

García held a position in the Royal (later National) Library and was a political prisoner in Oran, where *Raquel* was performed. Although he was learned and translated Sophocles and Voltaire, his critical ability was not sound. His 16-volume *Teatro español* (1785–86; "Spanish Theater"), a collection of plays of the Spanish Golden Age (*c.* 1500–*c.* 1680), omitted such important dramatists as Lope de Vega and Juan Ruiz de Alarcón.

García Gutiérrez \gär-'thē-ä-gü-'tyer-rāth\, Antonio (b. July 5, 1813, Chiclana, Spain—d. Aug. 26, 1884, Madrid)   Dramatist whose play *El trovador* (1836; "The Troubadour") was the most popular and successful drama of the Romantic period in Spain.

After studying medicine briefly in Cádiz, García Gutiérrez went to Madrid, hoping to gain success as a playwright. The initial reaction by his colleagues to *El trovador* was so discouraging that García Gutiérrez enlisted in the army; however, when the play was performed it was an instant success, and he decided to devote himself to writing. Few of his subsequent works were as successful as *El trovador*, though his *Simón Bocanegra* (1843) was popular, and two of his later plays, *Venganza catalana* (1864; "Catalan Vengeance") and *Juan Lorenzo* (1865), are considered among his best works.

García Lorca \gär-'thē-ä-'lȯr-kä\, Federico (b. June 5, 1898, Fuente Vaqueros, Spain—d. Aug. 19/20, 1936, Granada) Spanish poet and dramatist noted for his poems of death and for his dramatic trilogy: *Bodas de sangre* (produced 1933; BLOOD WEDDING), YERMA (produced 1934), and *La casa de Bernarda Alba* (produced 1936; THE HOUSE OF BERNARDA ALBA).

Lorca read law at the University of Granada but soon abandoned this pursuit to study literature, painting, and music. In 1919 he entered the *residencia de estudiantes* ("residence of scholars") at the University of Madrid. During his first two years at the *residencia*, Lorca's poetry became known in literary circles throughout Spain. At the same time he was composing the experimental poems that would later be published as *Libro de poemas* (1921; "Book of Poems"), *Primeras canciones* (1936; "First Songs"), and *Canciones* (1927; "Songs"), he was also writing his first play, *El maleficio de la mariposa* (*Butterfly's Evil Spell*), which opened in 1920 but closed after one night.

Lorca found his true genius when he collaborated with the distinguished composer Manuel de Falla on the folk music festival Fiesta de Cante Jondo, held at Granada in 1922. In the traditions of folk and gypsy music, Lorca seemed to find a resolution of his musical, poetical, and spiritual impulses. *Poema del Cante Jondo* (written 1922, published 1931; "Poem of the Cante Jondo") and *Romancero gitano* (1928; THE GYPSY BALLADS) were to be the lyrical expression of this resolution.

Lorca's first successful play was the 1927 production of *Mariana Pineda*, a poetic and romantic verse drama, with scenery by Salvador Dalí. The publication of *Romancero gitano* brought Lorca international fame but little happiness. He sought relief in the United States and Cuba in 1929–30. The trip inspired *Poeta en Nueva York* (*Poet in New York*), published posthumously in 1940.

By 1931 Lorca was back in Spain, where he began the poems to be published as *Diván del Tamarit* (1936; "Divan of Tamarit") and again wrote for the theater. The result was *Bodas de sangre*, the first of a trilogy of folk dramas, with its tragic theme inspired by a news item.

In 1934 the goring and subsequent death of a bullfighter who had been Lorca's friend inspired *Llanto por Ignacio Sánchez Mejías* (1935; "Lament for Ignacio Sánchez Mejías"; LAMENT FOR THE DEATH OF A BULLFIGHTER). Later that year, *Yerma*—the second in Lorca's folk-drama trilogy and, along with *Bodas de sangre*, one of the few successful poetic tragedies of the 20th century—was produced. The final play of the trilogy, *La casa de Bernarda Alba*, is about five frustrated sisters.

In July, alarmed by the outbreak of the Spanish Civil War, Lorca left Madrid for Granada. His fate fulfilled the premonition of violent death that haunts his works, for Lorca was shot to death at night without trial by the Nationalists.

García Márquez \gär-'sē-ä-'mär-käs\, Gabriel (b. March 6, 1928, Aracataca, Colom.) Latin-American author of novels and short stories, a central figure in the so-called MAGIC REALISM movement in Latin-American literature. He was awarded the Nobel Prize for Literature in 1982.

García Márquez studied law and journalism at the National University of Colombia in Bogotá and at the University of Cartagena. He began his career as a journalist in 1948, working for the next 10 years in Cartagena, Barranquilla, Bogotá, Rome, Paris, and Caracas. In the 1960s he worked as a screenwriter, journalist, and publicist in Mexico City. He moved to Barcelona in 1973 and in the later 1970s returned to Mexico.

García Márquez began writing short stories in the late 1940s. His first major publication was the novella *La hojarasca* (1955; translated in the collection *Leaf Storm and Other Stories*). This story introduced the fictional Colombian village of Ma-

condo—the setting of much of his later work—and the combination of realism and fantasy characteristic of his style.

His story *El coronel no tiene quien le escriba* (1961), which first appeared in the Colombian magazine *Mito* in 1958, was translated together with a collection of short stories, *Los funerales de la Mamá Grande* (1962), under the title *No One Writes to the Colonel and Other Stories* (1968).

Lutfi Ozkok

It was during his first stay in Mexico that García Márquez wrote his best-known novel, *Cien años de soledad* (1967; ONE HUNDRED YEARS OF SOLITUDE), which recounts the history of Macondo and its founders, the Buendía family.

García Márquez's subsequent novels include *El otoño del patriarca* (1975; *The Autumn of the Patriarch*), *Crónica de una muerte anunciada* (1981; *Chronicle of a Death Foretold*), *El amor en los tiempos del cólera* (1985; LOVE IN THE TIME OF CHOLERA), and *El general en su laberinto* (1989; *The General in His Labyrinth*). *Doce cuentos peregrinos* (1992) is a collection of 12 short stories that he wrote between 1974 and 1992.

Garcilaso de la Vega \gär-thē-'lä-sō-thä-lä-'b̦ä-gä\ (b. 1503, Toledo, Spain—d. Oct. 14, 1536, Nice, duchy of Savoy [now in France]) The first major poet in the Golden Age of Spanish literature (c. 1500–c. 1680).

Garcilaso was born into an aristocratic family. Entering court life at an early age, he distinguished himself as a soldier. Serving under the viceroy in southern France, he was mortally wounded in an assault on a fortified position and died several days later.

Although his earliest poetry was written in rather conventional Spanish meters, Garcilaso was made aware of Italianate meters by the poet Juan Boscán. Garcilaso, a consummate craftsman, transformed the Italianate meters into Spanish verse of high lyric quality. Many of Garcilaso's poems express the melancholy laments and misfortunes of romantic love. His small body of work was published with that of Boscán, by the latter's widow, in 1543. These works largely determined the course of lyric poetry throughout Spain's Golden Age.

Garden of Eden \'ē-dən\ In the Old Testament Book of Genesis, the earthly paradise inhabited by the first man and woman, Adam and Eve, before their expulsion for their disobedience to God. In English literature, Eden is usually equated with a lost Paradise, whether mythic, metaphoric, or historical. John Milton's epic poem *Paradise Lost* contains perhaps the most significant literary depiction of Eden.

Garden Party, The Short story by Katherine MANSFIELD, published as the title story in *The Garden Party, and Other Stories* (1922).

The story centers on Laura Sheridan's response to the accidental death of a neighborhood workman; Laura suggests that, out of respect for the man's family, Laura's family cancel their lavish garden party. Dismissing Laura's feelings as inappropriate and overwrought, her family proceeds with the festivities. After the party, Laura takes a basket of leftover food to the dead neighbor's bereaved family, views the body, observes the family's grief, and begins to ponder the meaning of life and death.

Gardner \'gärd-nər\, Erle Stanley (b. July 17, 1889, Malden, Mass., U.S.—d. March 11, 1970, Temecula, Calif.) Prolific American author and lawyer whose best-known works center on the lawyer-detective Perry MASON.

Gardner dropped out of Valparaiso University, Ind., after a brief time and settled in California, where he worked as a typist in a law firm. After three years he was admitted to the California bar.

While practicing trial law in Ventura, Calif., Gardner began writing for the pulp magazines popular at the time, creating accurate courtroom scenes and brilliant legal maneuvers resembling his own legal tactics. With the successful publication of the first Perry Mason detective stories, *The Case of the Velvet Claws* (1933) and *The Case of the Sulky Girl* (1933), he gave up the law. Eighty Perry Mason novels followed. Gardner also wrote two other series of detective stories, one under the pseudonym A.A. Fair.

Gardner \'gärd-nər\, John, *in full* John Champlin Gardner, Jr. (b. July 21, 1933, Batavia, N.Y., U.S.—d. Sept. 14, 1982, near Susquehanna, Pa.) American novelist and poet whose philosophical fiction reveals his characters' inner conflicts.

Gardner attended Washington University, St. Louis and the University of Iowa and then taught at various colleges and universities throughout the United States, including Oberlin College, Ohio; Bennington College, Vermont; and the University of Rochester.

Gardner published two novels, *The Resurrection* (1966) and *The Wreckage of Agathon* (1970), before his reputation was established with the appearance of *Grendel* (1971), a retelling of the Beowulf story from the point of view of the monster. His next novel, *The Sunlight Dialogues* (1972), is an ambitious epic with a large cast of characters. Later novels include *October Light* (1976; National Book Critics Circle Award), *Freddy's Book* (1980), and *Mickelsson's Ghosts* (1982). Gardner was also a gifted poet and a critic who published several books on Old and Middle English poetry. He expressed his views about writing in *On Moral Fiction* (1978), in which he deplored the tendency of many modern writers toward pessimism, believing that the goal of true art is a celebration of life.

Gargantua and Pantagruel \gär-'gan-chů-ə . . . ,pan-tə-'grü-əl, pan-'tag-rů-el, ,pan-tə-grü-'wel\ Collective title of five comic novels by François RABELAIS, published between 1532 and 1564. The novels present the comic and satiric story of the giant Gargantua and his son Pantagruel. The first two novels were published under the anagrammatic pseudonym Alcofribas (Alcofrybas) Nasier.

The first book, commonly called *Pantagruel* (1532), deals with some of the fantastic incidents of the early years of Pantagruel. While at the University of Paris he receives a letter from his father that is still considered an essential exposition of French Renaissance ideals. In Paris Pantagruel also meets the cunning rogue Panurge, who becomes his companion throughout the series.

In *Gargantua* (1534), old-fashioned scholastic pedagogy is ridiculed and contrasted with the humanist ideal of King Francis I, whose efforts to reform the French church Rabelais supported.

Le Tiers Livre (1546; "The Third Book") is Rabelais's most profound and erudite work. In it Pantagruel has become a sage; Panurge is self-absorbed and bedeviled, wondering if he should marry. He consults various prognosticators, allowing Rabelais to hold forth on sex, love, and marriage, and to satirize fortune

tellers, judges, and poets. Panurge persuades Pantagruel and friends to join him on a voyage to the Oracle of the Holy Bottle in Cathay for an answer. This they do in *Le Quart Livre* (1552; "The Fourth Book"), which reflects the era's interest in exploration; the Pantagruelians encounter a series of islands that present opportunities for the author to satirize the religious and political forces wreaking havoc on 16th-century Christendom. In a fifth book, *Le Cinquième Livre* (1564; of doubtful authenticity), the band arrives at the temple of the Holy Bottle, where the oracle answers Panurge with a single word: "Drink!"

Gargery, Joe \'jō-'gär-jə-rē\ Fictional character, the simple, kind-hearted, and loyal blacksmith who is married to the hero Pip's mean-spirited sister in the novel GREAT EXPECTATIONS by Charles Dickens.

Garland \'gär-lənd\, Hamlin, *in full* Hannibal Hamlin Garland (b. Sept. 14, 1860, West Salem, Wis., U.S.—d. March 4, 1940, Hollywood, Calif.) American author perhaps best remembered for his short stories and his autobiographical "Middle Border" series of narratives. He is considered one of the foremost representatives of Midwestern Regionalism.

As his farming family moved progressively westward from Wisconsin, Garland rebelled against the vicissitudes of pioneering and went to Boston in 1884. There he gradually won a place for himself in the literary set of Boston and Cambridge and was influenced by the novelist William Dean Howells. Garland recorded the physical oppression and economic frustrations of pioneer life on the Great Plains in the short stories collected in *Main-Travelled Roads* (1891), one of his best works. The short stories he published in *Prairie Folk* (1892) and *Wayside Courtships* (1897) were later combined in *Other Main-Travelled Roads* (1910). His novel *Rose of Dutcher's Coolly* (1895) tells the story of a sensitive young woman who rebels against the drudgery of farm life and goes to Chicago to pursue her talent for literature. After producing a series of mediocre novels that were serialized in the popular "slick magazines," Garland wrote the acclaimed autobiographical tale *A Son of the Middle Border* in 1917. Its sequels and his later novels were lesser efforts.

Garneau \gär-'nō\, Hector de Saint-Denys (b. June 13, 1912, Sainte-Catherine de Fossanbault, Que., Can.—d. Oct. 24, 1943, Sainte-Catherine de Fossanbault) Poet whose intense and introspective verse, filled with images of death and suicide, stood out from the prevailing regionalism of Canadian literature and strongly influenced the poets who followed.

In his early 20s Garneau suffered a heart attack, and he lived thereafter in increasing solitude, writing poetry that reflects the despair he felt over his joyless life. He published only one volume of poetry, *Regards et jeux dans l'espace* (1937; "Glances and Games in Space") in his lifetime. His *Poésies complètes* (1949; "Complete Poetry") and *Journal* (1954), an intimate record of his life between 1935 and 1939, appeared posthumously.

Garner \'gär-nər\, Alan (b. Oct. 17, 1934, Congleton, Cheshire, Eng.) British writer whose works, noted for their somewhat idiosyncratic style, appeal primarily to young readers.

Garner spent two years in the Royal Artillery and attended Magdalen College, Oxford. His first book, *The Weirdstone of Brisingamen: A Tale of Alderley* (1960), is a conventional fantasy for young readers set in Alderley Edge in his native Cheshire. His next two novels—*The Moon of Gomrath* (1963) and *Elidor* (1965)—shift back and forth in time but remain anchored both in local legend and in contemporary England. His later works for young readers include *The Stone Book* (1976), *Alan Garner's Fairy Tales of Gold* (1979), and *Alan Garner's Book of British Fairy Tales* (1984).

Garnett \\'gär-nət\\, Constance (Clara), *original surname* Black \\'blak\\ (b. Dec. 19, 1861, Brighton, East Sussex, Eng.—d. Dec. 17, 1946, Edenbridge, Kent)   English translator who made the great works of Russian literature available in the English language in the first half of the 20th century. The first to render Fyodor Dostoyevsky and Anton Chekhov into English, she also translated the complete works of Ivan Turgenev and Nikolay Gogol and major works of Leo Tolstoy.

In 1879, when advanced education for women was unusual, she won a scholarship to Newnham College, Cambridge. In 1892, she began her career as a translator with Ivan Goncharov's *Obyknovennaya istoriya* (1847), which she rendered as *Common Story* (1894). Altogether she produced about 70 volumes of translations from Russian literature. Although her translations are not considered to be definitive, they were a significant influence on the English-language public.

Garnett \\'gär-nət\\, David (b. March 9, 1892, Brighton, East Sussex, Eng.—d. Feb. 17, 1981, Le Verger Charry, Montcuq, Fr.)   English novelist, son of Edward and Constance Garnett.

A prolific writer, Garnett is best known for his satirical fantasies *Lady into Fox* (1922), the tale of a man whose wife is suddenly transformed into a fox, and *A Man in the Zoo* (1924), concerned with a man who is accepted by the London Zoo to be exhibited as an example of *Homo sapiens*. Later novels, which were not fantastic, were less successful. In *The Golden Echo* (1953), *The Flowers of the Forest* (1955), *The Familiar Faces* (1962), and *Great Friends: Portraits of Seventeen Writers* (1980), Garnett described his memories of the English literary coterie—including the Bloomsbury group—of which he was a member during the period of World War I and the 1920s.

Garnett \\'gär-nət\\, Edward (William) (b. Feb. 19, 1868, London, Eng.—d. Feb. 21, 1937, London)   Influential English critic who discovered, advised, and tutored many of the great British writers of the early 20th century.

The son of the writer and librarian Richard Garnett, he was more influenced by his family's literary interests than by his slight formal education. Through extensive reading Garnett developed a nearly unerring ability to recognize genuine and original literary talent. Among the authors he discovered or befriended were Joseph Conrad, D.H. Lawrence, John Galsworthy, Ford Madox Ford, W.H. Hudson, and Stephen Crane. His own fiction, which he produced in quantity, was unsuccessful.

Garnett \\'gär-nət\\, Richard (b. Feb. 27, 1835, Lichfield, Staffordshire, Eng.—d. April 13, 1906, London)   English writer and librarian. From the age of 15 until his retirement in 1899 he was in the employ of the British Museum.

Largely through Garnett's efforts, a general catalog of the British Museum was published in 1905, after 25 years of preparation. His own writing was chiefly biographical and historical, but he also wrote poetry, translations, and essays. Best known among his works of fiction is *The Twilight of the Gods, and Other Tales* (1888), a collection of fables in the style of the Greek writer Lucian.

Garnier \\gärn-'yā\\, Robert (b. *c.* 1545, La Ferté Bernard, Fr.—d. Sept. 20, 1590, Le Mans)   Outstanding French tragic dramatist of his time.

While a law student at Toulouse, Garnier won prizes for his poetry. He published his first collection of lyrical pieces, now lost, in 1565.

In his early plays Garnier was a follower of the Senecan school. His pieces in this style are *Porcie* (1568), *Hippolyte* (1573), and *Cornélie* (1574). His next group of tragedies—*Marc-Antoine* (1578), *La Troade* (1579), *Antigone* (1580)—are more technically accomplished in that the rhetoric is accompanied by action.

In 1582 and 1583 he produced his two masterpieces, *Bradamante* and *Les Juives* ("The Jews"). In *Bradamante*, the first important French tragicomedy, Ludovico Ariosto's romantic story becomes an effective drama. *Les Juives* is the story of the barbarous vengeance of Nebuchadnezzar on King Zedekiah and his children.

Garrett \\'gä-ret\\, João Baptista da Silva Leitão de Almeida, Viscount (Visconde) de Almeida Garrett (b. Feb. 4, 1799, Porto, Port.—d. Dec. 9, 1854, Lisbon)   Writer, orator, and statesman who was one of Portugal's finest writers and a major Romantic poet.

Garrett graduated with a degree in law from the University of Coimbra in 1820, having already gained a name for himself as a playwright and a fervent liberal. In 1823 his liberalism forced him into exile in England and later France, where he developed an interest in romanticism and Portuguese themes that was reflected in his long poem *Camões* (1825).

Garrett returned to Portugal in 1832 and distinguished himself as a liberal statesman and writer. He was asked by the government to revive a native theater tradition that had been moribund for centuries. To this end he wrote a series of historical prose dramas that have become classics. Among them are *Um auto de Gil Vicente* (1838; "A Short Play of Gil Vicente") and *O Alfageme de Santarém* (1841; "The Armorer of Santarém"). Another work, *Frei Luís de Sousa* (1843; "Friar Luís de Sousa"), is considered one of the greatest Portuguese plays of the 19th century. An excursion Garrett took to Santarém in July 1843 resulted in a prose masterpiece describing his journey, *Viagens na minha terra* (1846; "Voyage to My Land"). His historical romance *O arco de Sant'Ana*, 2 vol. (1845–50), was probably the first Romantic novel produced in Portugal.

His other works include *Folhas Caídas* (1853), a collection of short love poems that are among the best Portuguese lyric poems of the Romantic period.

Garros \\gä-'rōs\\, Pey de (b. *c.* 1530, Lectoure, near Agen, Fr.—d. 1585, Pau)   Provençal poet whose work raised the Gascon dialect to the rank of a literary language in 16th-century France.

Garros studied law at Toulouse and later became *avocat-général* of Pau. In the preface to his *Poesias gasconas* (1567), he chided his fellow countrymen for preferring French to Gascon and pleaded for a restoration of the native dialect. He published a rhymed Gascon translation of the Psalms of David in 1565. His *Églogues* go beyond the imitation of classical models, attempting to capture the true flavor of Gascon peasant life.

Garshin \\'gär-shən\\, Vsevolod Mikhaylovich (Feb. 2 [Feb. 14, New Style], 1855, Bakhmutsky district, Russian Empire—d. March 24 [April 5], 1888, St. Petersburg, Russia)   Russian short-story writer whose works helped to foster the vogue enjoyed by that genre in Russia in the late 19th century.

Garshin served in the army from 1877 to 1878 and later used his wartime experiences as material for his stories. He wrote of the plight of an injured soldier in his first story, "Chetyre dnya" (1877; "Four Days"). It is a first-person narrative of a wounded soldier lying for four days unattended on the battlefield, near the body of his victim. In perhaps his most famous story, "Krasny tsvetok" (1883; "The Red Flower"), a madman dies after destroying a flower he believes to contain all of the world's evil. Haunted by similar delusions in his own life, Garshin committed suicide by throwing himself down a stairwell.

Gary \\gä-'rē\\, Romain, *original surname* Kacew \\kä-'chə\\ (b. May 8, 1914, Vilna, Russian Empire [now Vilnius, Lithuania]—d. Dec. 2, 1980, Paris, Fr.)   French novelist whose first work, *L'Éducation européenne* (1945; *Forest of Anger*), won him immediate acclaim. The novel was later revised and reissued in English as *Nothing Important Ever Dies* (1960).

During World War II, Gary served with the Free French Forces in Europe and North Africa. For 20 years following the war, he served in the French diplomatic service.

Gary's novels mix humor with tragedy and faith with cynicism. *Les Couleurs du jour* (1952; *The Colors of the Day*), set in Nice at carnival time, and *La Danse de Gengis Cohn* (1967; *The Dance of Genghis Cohn*), in which the ghost of a Jewish stand-up comedian takes possession of his Nazi executioner, are comic novels informed by serious moral considerations. *Les Racines du ciel* (1956; *The Roots of Heaven*), winner of the Prix Goncourt, balances a visionary conception of freedom and justice against a pessimistic comprehension of human cruelty and greed. Other works by Gary include *Lady L* (1959), a social satire; *La Promesse de l'aube* (1960; *Promise at Dawn*), an autobiography; and *Les Cerf-volants* (1980; "The Kite").

Gascoigne \'gas-ˌkȯin, *perhaps originally* 'gas-kin \, George (b. c. 1525, Cardington, Bedfordshire, Eng.—d. Oct. 7, 1577, Bernack, near Stamford, Lincolnshire)   English poet and a major literary innovator.

Gascoigne attended the University of Cambridge and then studied law at Gray's Inn in 1555. He thereafter pursued careers as a politician, country gentleman, courtier, soldier of fortune, and man of letters, all with moderate distinction.

Gascoigne's chief importance, however, is as a pioneer of the English Renaissance who had a remarkable aptitude for domesticating foreign literary genres. He foreshadowed the English sonnet sequences with groups of linked sonnets in his first published work, *A Hundreth Sundrie Flowres* (1573), a collection of verse and prose. He wrote "Certayne Notes of Instruction" (1575), the first treatise on prosody in English and also the first original nondramatic English blank verse. "The Adventures of Master F.J.," published in *A Hundreth Sundrie Flowres*, was the first original prose narrative of the English Renaissance.

Gascoyne \'gas-ˌkȯin \, David (Emery) (b. Oct. 10, 1916, Harrow, Middlesex, Eng.)   English poet deeply influenced by the French Surrealist movement of the 1930s. Through his translations and critical writings he did much to make the movement known in Britain.

Gascoyne's first book of poems, *Roman Balcony*, appeared in 1932, and his only novel, *Opening Day*, was published the next year. His important introductory work, *A Short Survey of Surrealism* (1935), and his verses *Man's Life Is This Meat* (1936) were milestones of the Surrealist movement in England. *Poems 1937–42* (1943) marked the beginning of his religious verse and contain his noted good-bye to the 1930s—his "Farewell Chorus." *Night Thoughts*, a long, semidramatic poem, was broadcast in 1955 and published the next year.

Gaskell \'gas-kəl \, Elizabeth Cleghorn, *original surname* Stevenson \'stēv-ən-sən \ (b. Sept. 29, 1810, Chelsea, London, Eng.—d. Nov. 12, 1865, near Alton, Hampshire)   English novelist and short-story writer, and first biographer of Charlotte Brontë.

Mrs. Gaskell (as she is generally known) was the daughter of a Unitarian minister. When her mother died, she was brought up by an aunt in an atmosphere of rural gentility. In 1832 she married William Gaskell, a Unitarian minister, and settled in Manchester. Domestic life and the obligations of a minister's wife kept her from beginning her literary career until middle age. Her first novel, MARY BARTON (1848), reflects the temper of Manchester in the late 1830s. It prompted Charles Dickens to invite her to contribute to his magazine, *Household Words*, where her next major work, CRANFORD (1853), appeared. Mrs. Gaskell's next novel, *Ruth* (1853), received mixed reaction because it offered a sympathetic alternative to the traditional narrative of the seduced girl's progress to prostitution

and an early grave. NORTH AND SOUTH (1855) also examines social issues, in this case, the cotton-mill industry.

Among the many friends attracted by Mrs. Gaskell was Charlotte Brontë, who died in 1855 and whose biography Charlotte's father, Patrick Brontë, urged her to write. *The Life of Charlotte Brontë* was published in 1857. The book was at once a work of art, an indispensable sourcebook, and a well-documented, though partial, interpretation of its subject.

Among her later works, *Sylvia's Lovers* (1863), dealing with the impact of the Napoleonic Wars upon simple people, is notable. Her last and longest novel, WIVES AND DAUGHTERS (1864–66; unfinished at her death), is considered by many to be her finest.

Gaspar \'gas-ˌpär, -pər \ or **Casper** \'kas-pər \   Legendary figure, said to have been one of the MAGI.

Gaspé \gås-'pā \, Philippe Aubert de (b. Oct. 30, 1786, Quebec—d. Jan. 29, 1871, Quebec)   Author of the first important French-Canadian novel.

Gaspé received a classical education in Quebec, studied law there, and later became sheriff. Bankruptcy forced his withdrawal from public life in his 40s into a quiet life of reading and meditation. When he was 76 years old, he was inspired by a rebirth of Canadian nationalism to write *Les Anciens Canadiens* (1863; *The Canadians of Old*), a romantic historical novel set in Canada at the time of the British conquest (1760). Its themes of idealization of the past, the farmer's loyalty to the soil, and distrust of English Canada influenced the Canadian regionalist school of literature.

Gass \'gas \, William Howard (b. July 30, 1924, Fargo, N.D., U.S.)   American writer and critic noted for his experimentation with stylistic devices.

Gass called his fiction works "experimental constructions," and each of his books contains stylistic innovations. His first novel, *Omensetter's Luck* (1966), concerns a man who is maliciously and falsely connected to a mysterious death. Piecing together various viewpoints without the use of quotation marks to distinguish speakers, Gass creates levels of insight into character and setting. His novella *Willie Masters' Lonesome Wife* (1968) makes use of typographical and other visual devices.

Gass's other work includes *In the Heart of the Heart of the Country* (1968), short stories; *On Being Blue* (1976), imaginative interpretations of the color blue; *China Through a Writer's Eye* (1985), a travel book with text and photos by Gass; and several collections of critical essays.

Gates \'gāts \, Henry Louis, Jr. (b. Sept. 16, 1950, Keyser, W.Va., U.S.)   African-American critic and scholar known for his pioneering theories of black literature. He used the term "signifyin' " to represent African and African-American literary history as a continuing reflection and reinterpretation of what has gone before. Gates was at the forefront of the discovery and restoration of many lost works by black writers—such as Harriet E. Wilson's *Our Nig* (1859), the earliest known novel by an African American—and he argued in *Loose Canons* (1992) and elsewhere for the inclusion of African-American literature in the Western canon.

Gates visited Africa while attending Yale University and did advanced studies at Clare College, Cambridge, where his tutor was the Nigerian writer Wole Soyinka. Gates later taught at several American universities, including Yale and Harvard.

Gates's theory of signifyin' traces black Caribbean and American culture back through the "talking book," the central method for recording slave narratives, and the early "signifying monkey" storyteller to Esu, the trickster figure of the West African Yoruba. Black culture, Gates held, maintains an ongoing dialogue, often humorous, insulting, or provocative, with what has preceded it, and all works of black writers must be seen in this context. Gates's fullest exposition of signifyin' was found in *Figures in Black: Words, Signs, and the "Racial" Self* (1987) and *The Signifying Monkey: A Theory of Afro-American Literary Criticism* (1988). He applied his theory to many texts, including those of Soyinka, the slave narratives, Frederick Douglass, and the 18th-century poet Phillis Wheatley.

gathering \'gath-ə-riŋ *also* 'geth- *or* 'gäth-\ **1.** A collection (as of money for charity) or compilation (as of literary fragments). **2.** In printing, the process of collecting together signatures (groups of pages created by folding a single printer's sheet a certain number of times) to be bound into a book. The term is sometimes used in reference to the signature itself.

Gatsby, Jay \'jā-'gats-bē\ Fictional character, the rich, mysterious protagonist of F. Scott Fitzgerald's novel THE GREAT GATSBY.

gaucho literature \'gaù-chō\ Latin-American poetic genre that imitates the *payadas* ("ballads") traditionally sung to guitar accompaniment by the wandering gaucho minstrels of Argentina and Uruguay. By extension, the term includes the body of Latin-American literature that treats the gaucho way of life and philosophy. The gaucho's story found its highest poetic expression in Rafael Obligado's poems (1887) on the legendary gaucho minstrel Santos Vega. The gaucho was humorously portrayed in the mock epic *Fausto* (1866) by Estanislao del Campo. Later the gaucho aroused the national conscience and received epic treatment in the classic poem *El gaucho Martín Fierro* (1872) by José Hernández.

In prose the first serious use of gaucho lore was made by Domingo Faustino Sarmiento in *Civilización y barbarie: vida de Juan Facundo Quiroga, y aspecto físico, costumbres, y hábitos de la República Argentina* (1845), a classic account of the cultural clash between the Pampas and the civilizing forces of the city. This theme of conflict between old and new informs a rich literature that ranges from the somber descriptive short stories of Uruguay's Javier de Viana and the keen psychological portrayal of rural types in Carlos Reyles' *El terruño* (1916; "The Native Soil") to the simple humorous narrative of *El inglés de los güesos* (1924; "The Englishman of the Bones") by Argentina's Benito Lynch.

Gautier \gō-'tyā\, Léon, *in full* Émile-Théodore-Léon Gautier (b. Aug. 8, 1832, Le Havre, Fr.—d. Aug. 25, 1897, Paris) Literary historian who revived an interest in early French literature, particularly with his translation and critical discussion of the *Chanson de Roland* (1872) and with his research on the chansons de geste.

In 1859 Gautier became keeper of the imperial archives in Paris. In 1871 he became professor of paleography at the École des Chartres, the school in which he had been educated (1852–55). He was made chief of the historical section of the national archives in 1893. His works include *Les Épopées françaises*, 3 vol. (1886–88; "The French Epics"; 2nd ed., 5 vol., 1878–97, with a bibliography of chansons de geste).

Gautier \gō-tyā\, Théophile, *byname* Le Bon Théo \lə-bōⁿ-tā-'ō\ (b. Aug. 31, 1811, Tarbes, Fr.—d. Oct. 23, 1872, Neuilly-sur-Seine) French poet, novelist, critic, and journalist whose influence was strongly felt from the early Romantic period until the end of the 19th century.

Gautier lived most of his life in Paris. He studied painting but soon decided that his true vocation was poetry. He was sympathetic to the Romantic movement and took part in the cultural battles over it. He humorously recalled this period in *Histoire du romantisme* (1874; "History of Romanticism") and *Portraits contemporains* (1874; "Contemporary Portraits").

Gautier's first poems appeared in 1830. *Albertus*, a long narrative about a young painter who falls into the hands of a sorcerer, was published in 1832. At this time he turned from Romanticism and became an advocate of art for art's sake. The preface to *Albertus* and the novel *Mademoiselle de Maupin* (1835) state his disregard of conventional morality.

A trip to Spain in 1840 inspired some of his best poetry, in *España* (1845), and prose, in *Voyage en Espagne* (1845). From 1836 to 1855 he was a weekly contributor to *La Presse* and *Le Moniteur Universel*. He also contributed to many other periodicals and papers.

Gautier developed a technique in poetry that he called *transposition d'art* ("transposing art"), recording his exact impressions when experiencing a painting or other work of art. These poems, published in *Émaux et camées* (1852; "Enamels and Cameos"), are among his finest. They inspired other French Aesthetes, including Théodore de Banville, Leconte de Lisle, and Charles Baudelaire.

Gautier's poetic and fantastic imagination is seen to advantage in his fiction—for example, in his evocations of ancient Pompeii or Egypt and in his stories of the supernatural, *La Mort amoureuse, Avatar* (1857; "The Dead Lover, Avatar"). His prodigious output includes extraordinary art and dramatic criticism that is partly reprinted in *Les Beaux-Arts en Europe* (1855) and in the six-volume *Histoire de l'art dramatique en France depuis vingt-cinq ans* (1858–59; "History of Drama in France for Twenty-Five Years").

Gautier d'Arras \gō-tyā-dá-'räs\ (d. 1185) Author of early French romances. His work, emphasizing human action and its psychological foundations, exercised an important influence on the genre known as *roman d'aventure* ("romance of adventure").

His romance *Eracle*, a mythical life of the Byzantine emperor Heraclius, was begun in 1176–78 and finished about 1179–81. *Ille et Galeron*, a Breton romance, was written for Beatrix of Vienne, the wife of Frederick I Barbarossa.

Gautier de Metz \gō-tyā-də-'mets\ or **Gauthier** de Més en Loherains \də-mä-zäⁿ-lō-ə-'raⁿ\ (fl. 13th century) French poet and priest who is usually credited with the authorship of a treatise about the universe, *L'Image du monde* (c. 1246; "The Mirror of the World"; also called *Mappemonde*), based on the medieval Latin text *Imago mundi* by Honorius Inclusus. Gautier's poem is one of several medieval "encyclopedic" works that describe the world's creation, geography, and astronomy with factual as well as imaginary passages.

Gawain \gə-'wän; 'gä-ˌwän, -wən\ Hero of Arthurian legend and romance. A nephew and loyal supporter of King Arthur, Gawain appears in the earliest Arthurian literature as a model of knightly perfection, against whom all other knights are measured. In the 12th-century *Historia regum Britanniae*, by Geoffrey of Monmouth, Gawain (or Walgainus) is Arthur's ambassador to Rome. In the 12th-century verse romances of Chrétien de Troyes, he is a leading character whose prowess was surpassed only by that of Lancelot (who was inspired by courtly love) and Perceval (who was inspired by his quest for the Grail).

When the Grail theme began to emerge as an important element of Arthurian romance, in the 13th century, Gawain's character changed. In the *Queste del Saint Graal* especially, he cannot perceive the spiritual significance of the Grail, relies on his own prowess, and fails utterly in the quest. This deterioration is even more marked in later romances, such as the prose *Tristan*, which depicts him as treacherous and brutal to women. These darker aspects of his character are also reflected in Sir Thomas Malory's late 15th-century prose work *Le Morte Darthur*.

In Middle English poetry, however, Gawain is generally regarded as a brave and loyal knight. Perhaps his most important single adventure is that described in the anonymous 14th-century poem SIR GAWAYNE AND THE GRENE KNIGHT.

In several of the romances and in Malory, Gawain's strength waxes and wanes with the Sun, a characteristic that links him with Gwalchmei, the solar deity of Celtic mythology. *See also* ARTHURIAN LEGEND; GRAIL.

Gay \'gā\, John (b. June 30, 1685, Barnstaple, Devon, Eng.—d. Dec. 4, 1732, London)   English poet and dramatist, chiefly remembered as the author of THE BEGGAR'S OPERA (1728).

Gay went to London as an apprentice to a silk merchant and settled there after being released from his indentures. Among his early literary friends were Aaron Hill and Eustace Budgell, whom he helped in the production of *The British Apollo*, a question-and-answer journal of the day.

From 1712 to 1714 Gay was steward in the household of the Duchess of Monmouth, which gave him leisure and security to write. He had produced a burlesque of the Miltonic style, *Wine*, in 1708, and in 1713 his first important poem, *Rural Sports*, appeared. His finest poem, *Trivia: or, The Art of Walking the Streets of London* (1716), displays an assured and precise craftsmanship in which rhythm and diction underline whatever facet of experience he is describing. *The Shepherd's Week* (1714) is a series of mock-classical poems in pastoral setting; the *Fables* (two series, 1727 and 1738) are brief, octosyllabic illustrations of moral themes, often satirical in tone.

The Beggar's Opera, which was produced in 1728, is a story of thieves and highwaymen and was intended to mirror the moral degradation of society.

Gay \'ge, 'gā\, Sophie, *in full* Marie-Françoise-Sophie Nichault de Lavalette Gay (b. July 1, 1776, Paris, Fr.—d. March 5, 1852, Paris)   French writer and grande dame who wrote romantic novels and plays about aristocratic French society in the early 19th century.

She published the novel *Laure d'Estell* in 1802 but did little other writing for 11 years. Among her numerous later novels are *Léonie de Montbreuse* (1813), *Malheurs d'un amant heureux* (1818, 1823; "Misfortunes of a Happy Lover"), *Le Moqueur amoureux* (1830; "The Amorous Mocker"), *La Physiologie du ridicule* (1833; "The Physiology of Ridicule"), and *Le Mari confident* (1849; "The Confident Husband"). She also wrote for the theater, both drama and comic opera, and her play *La Duchesse de Châteauroux* (1834) was a great success.

gayatri \'gä-yə-‚trē\ [Sanskrit *gāyatrī*, a derivative of *gāyatra* song, hymn]   An ancient Vedic meter of 24 syllables generally arranged in a triplet, or three-line verse.

Gee \'jē\, Maurice (b. Aug. 22, 1931, Whaketane, N.Z.)   Novelist best known for his realistic evocations of New Zealand life. He also wrote popular books for juveniles.

Gee's adult fiction focuses on small-town New Zealand society, especially its men, whom he characterizes as beer swillers obsessed with rugby and racing. Relations between the sexes are distorted by personal limitations and social expectations. Gee's first novel, *The Big Season* (1962), and his short-story collection *A Glorious Morning, Comrade* (1975) were set in this milieu. Gee's best-known work is his Plumb trilogy, which examines the lives of three generations of a New Zealand family. The first book, *Plumb* (1978), covers the period from the 1890s through 1949; it is based on the career of Gee's grandfather, a Presbyterian minister who was tried for heresy by his church and jailed for sedition by the state. Like the succeeding volumes of the trilogy, *Plumb* is narrated by the main character, who interweaves the historical past, the personal past, and the narrative present. The remaining volumes, which carry

the story through the 1980s, are *Meg* (1981) and *Sole Survivor* (1983). Gee's later works include *Prowlers* (1987) and *The Burning Boy* (1990). He also wrote a number of "Tolkienesque" works in the fantasy science-fiction genre for juvenile readers. Notable among the latter is a series known as the "O" trilogy—*The Halfmen of O* (1982), *The Priests of Ferris* (1984), and *Motherstone* (1985).

Geibel \'gī-bəl\, Emanuel von, *in full* Franz Emanuel August von Geibel (b. Oct. 17, 1815, Lübeck [Germany]—d. April 6, 1884, Lübeck)   German poet and dramatist who was the center of a circle of literary figures belonging to the Gesellschaft der Krokodile ("Society of the Crocodiles"), a literary society that cultivated traditional poetic themes and forms.

After completing university studies, Geibel devoted himself to travel. In 1838 he became tutor to the Russian ambassador in Athens. Two years later his extremely successful *Gedichte* ("Poems") appeared. It ran to 100 editions in his lifetime. Returning to Lübeck, he taught secondary school until 1852, when Maximilian called him to Munich as an honorary professor of German literature and aesthetics.

Geibel's lyrics—*Zeitstimmen* (1841; "Voices of the Times"), *Junius-Lieder* (1848; "June Songs"), and *Spätherbstblätter* (1877; "Leaves of Late Autumn")—reflect the taste of the time: classical, idealistic, and nontopical. He also published excellent translations of Romantic and ancient poets in *Spanisches Liederbuch* (1852; "Spanish Songbook") and, with Paul von Heyse, in *Klassisches Liederbuch* (1875; "Classical Songbook").

Geisel \'gī-zəl\, Theodor Seuss, *pseudonym* Dr. Seuss \'süs\ (b. March 2, 1904, Springfield, Mass., U.S.—d. Sept. 24, 1991, La Jolla, Calif.)   American writer and illustrator of immensely popular children's books.

Geisel initially worked as a freelance cartoonist, illustrator, and writer for several American publications. The first book he published under his pseudonym was *And To Think That I Saw It on Mulberry Street* (1937). His lively children's books were a major departure from mainstream writing for children. They were peopled with invented creatures and were brimming with nonsense words and humorous situations. In 1957 he published *The Cat in the Hat*, a book specifically designed for beginning readers.

Among his many popular works are *Horton Hatches the Egg* (1940), *How the Grinch Stole Christmas* (1957), *Yertle the Turtle* (1958), *Green Eggs and Ham* (1960), and *Hop on Pop* (1963).

Geisel also designed and produced animated cartoons for television, many of them based on his books.

Gelber \'gel-bər\, Jack (b. April 12, 1932, Chicago, Ill., U.S.)   American playwright and teacher known for *The Connection* (performed 1959, published 1960), and for his association with THE LIVING THEATRE, an innovative, experimental theater group.

After graduating from the University of Illinois, Champaign-Urbana, Gelber began working with the struggling Living Theatre group in New York City. His first play, *The Connection*, is historically important for its disregard of the traditional relationship between audience and actor; it was a breakthrough for The Living Theatre, and both the production and the playwright received wide notice.

Set in a slum apartment, the play was staged to suggest a naturalistic scene, with actors already on stage as the audience arrived (as if the audience were seeing life, not a play, in progress). This nontraditional staging was supported by other techniques: by presenting an actor as an audience member; by using the theater aisles as a performance area; and by having the actors (who represented drug addicts) panhandle the audience during the play's intermission. The play was imaginatively and brilliantly produced, though for all its appearance of improvisation, it was tightly structured.

The Apple (1961), Gelber's second play, also was written expressly for The Living Theatre. His later works continued to challenge theatrical conventions, but none matched the popular or critical success of his first play.

Gelert or **Gellert** \\'gel-ərt\\ In Welsh tradition, the trusted hound of Prince Llewellyn the Great of Wales. Having been left to guard his master's infant son, Gelert killed a wolf that attempted to attack the child. Llewellyn, returning home to find an upset cradle and Gelert's muzzle stained with blood, assumed that the dog had destroyed his son and stabbed it. When he found the child unharmed beneath the cradle, with the wolf's corpse beside him, the remorseful prince caused Gelert to be honorably buried.

The story is a late Welsh version of an ancient Indian folktale recounted in the Sanskrit *Pañca-tantra*. The legend is found in various forms in many European countries. It also exists in the Persian, Hebrew, and Buddhist traditions.

Gellert \\'gel-ərt\\, Christian Fürchtegott (b. July 4, 1715, Hainchen, Saxony [Germany]—d. Dec. 13, 1769, Leipzig) Poet and novelist who was a prominent representative of the German Enlightenment.

After working as a tutor, Gellert studied at the University of Leipzig, where he later taught. Gellert was best known for his *Fabeln und Erzählungen* (1746–48; "Fables and Tales"), a collection of naïvely realistic fables and moralizing stories charming for their directness and simplicity. Equally popular was *Geistliche Oden und Lieder* (1757; "Spiritual Odes and Songs"), poems and hymns that combined religious feeling with the rationalism of the Enlightenment. Gellert also wrote a sentimental novel, *Das Leben der schwedischen Gräfin von G* (1748; "The Life of the Swedish Countess of G"), which combined the late 17th-century novel of exotic adventure with the character novel of modern literature and introduced the moralistic "family novel" in German literature.

Gellius \\'jel-ē-əs\\, Aulus (fl. 2nd century AD) Latin author remembered for his miscellany *Noctes Atticae* ("Attic Nights"), in which many fragments of lost works are preserved. The work is an interesting source on the state of knowledge and scholarship of the time and contains many anecdotes about the distinguished men who were his teachers and friends in Rome and Athens.

Gelosi \\jā-'lō-sē\\ (*in full* Compagnia dei Gelosi) One of the earliest and most famous of the commedia dell'arte companies of 16th-century Italy. The name was derived from the troupe's motto, *Virtù, fama ed honor ne fèr gelosi* ("Virtue, fame, and honor make us jealous").

Gemara *see* TALMUD.

gender studies A field of criticism that studies the influence, conscious or unconscious, of gender upon works of art. It emerged in the mid-1980s as a development of feminist criticism. The principal influence upon gender studies was the publication in 1976 of the first volume of Michel Foucault's *Histoire de la sexualité* (*The History of Sexuality*), which delineates the differences between sex and gender. Although an individual's sex in itself may have little relevance in a work of art, gender—that person's socialization or experience as male or female—may determine his or her responses and choices. Gender studies is a heterogenous field, including advances in feminist criticism, men's studies that use the innovations of women's studies, and certain gay and lesbian studies.

Generation of 1927 *Spanish* Generación del 1927. Group of Spanish writers, chiefly poets, who rose to prominence in the late 1920s and who derived their collective name from the year in which several of them produced important commemorative editions of the poetry of Luis de Góngora on the tercentenary of his death.

Chief among the members of the Generation of 1927 were Federico García Lorca, Rafael Alberti, Jorge Guillén, Vicente Aleixandre, Luis Cernuda, Pedro Salinas, Gerardo Diego, and Dámaso Alonso. Generally speaking, they were influenced by Symbolism, Futurism, and Surrealism, and they helped introduce the tenets of these movements into Spanish literature. They rejected the use of traditional meter and rhyme and discarded anecdotal treatment and strictly logical descriptions in their poems. Instead, they made frequent and audacious use of metaphor, coined new words, and introduced highly symbolic or suggestive images into their poems in an effort to convey aspects of inner personal experience.

Although they differed in individual style and concerns, the poets of the Generation of 1927 formed what can be considered the dominant trend in Spanish poetry during the 1920s, '30s, and early '40s. After the Spanish Civil War (1936–39), Spanish poetry turned away from their highly cultivated and abstruse aestheticism.

Generation of '98 *also called* Generation of 1898, *Spanish* Generación del '98 *or* Generación del 1898. In Spain, the novelists, poets, essayists, and thinkers active at the time of the Spanish-American War (1898) who reinvigorated Spanish letters and restored Spain to a position of intellectual and literary prominence.

The shock of Spain's defeat in the war provided an impetus for many writers and thinkers to embark on a period of self-searching. The term Generation of '98 was used loosely at the turn of the century but was elaborated on by the literary critic AZORÍN in critical essays that appeared in various periodicals. Never an organized movement or school, the Generation of '98 had no representative form or style, but all associated with it desired to restore a sense of national pride.

Joaquín Costa, Ángel Ganivet, and Miguel de Unamuno are generally considered precursors of the Generation of '98, but many literary historians consider Ganivet and, usually, Unamuno as members of the group proper. Other outstanding figures were Azorín himself, the philosopher and critic José Ortega y Gasset, the novelists Pío Baroja, Vicente Blasco Ibáñez, and Ramón María del Valle-Inclán, and the poets Antonio Machado and Manuel Machado.

género chico \\'kä-nä-rō-'chē-kō\\ [Spanish, literally, little genre] Spanish literary genre of light dramatic or operatic one-act playlets, as contrasted with the *género grande* of serious drama or opera. Developed primarily in the theaters of Madrid during the late 19th century, *género chico* works usually dealt with Madrid's lower classes, whose way of life was regarded with mingled sentimentality and satiric humor. Carlos Arniches, Ricardo de la Vega, and Tomás Luceño were the chief writers in the genre.

Genêt Pseudonym of American writer Janet FLANNER.

Genet \\zhə-'ne, -'nā\\, Jean (b. Dec. 19, 1910, Paris, Fr.—d. April 15, 1986, Paris) French criminal and social outcast turned writer who, as a novelist, transformed erotic and often obscene subject matter into a poetic and anarchic vision of the universe and, as a dramatist, became a leading figure in the avant-garde theater.

Genet, an illegitimate child abandoned by his mother, was raised by a family of peasants. Caught stealing at the age of 10, he spent part of his adolescence at a notorious reform school, Mettray, where he experienced much that was later described in the novel *Miracle de la rose* (1945–46; *Miracle of the Rose*).

His autobiographical *Journal du voleur* (1949; *The Thief's Journal*) gives a complete and uninhibited account of his life as

Jerry Bauer

a tramp, pickpocket, and male prostitute during the 1930s. It also reveals him as an aesthete and an existentialist.

Genet began to write in 1942 while imprisoned for burglary at Fresnes and produced the novel *Notre-Dame des fleurs* (1944; OUR LADY OF THE FLOWERS), which vividly portrays the prewar Montmartre underworld of thugs, pimps, and perverts. When in 1948 Genet was convicted of burglary for the 10th time and condemned to automatic life imprisonment, a delegation of well-known French writers appealed on his behalf to the president and he was reprieved.

After writing two other novels, *Pompes funèbres* (1947; *Funeral Rites*) and *Querelle de Brest* (1947; *Querelle of Brest*; film, 1982), Genet began to experiment with drama. His early attempts, with their compact, Neoclassical, one-act structure, reveal the strong influence of Jean-Paul Sartre. *Haute Surveillance* (1949; *Deathwatch*) continued his interest in the prison world. In *Les Bonnes* (1947; *The Maids*), however, he began to explore the complex problems of identity that were soon to preoccupy other avant-garde dramatists, such as Samuel Beckett and Eugène Ionesco. With this play Genet was established as an outstanding figure in the Theater of the Absurd.

His subsequent plays, *Le Balcon* (1956; THE BALCONY), *Les Nègres* (1958; *The Blacks*), and *Les Paravents* (1961; *The Screens*), are large-scale, stylized dramas in the Expressionist manner, designed to shock and implicate an audience by revealing its hypocrisy and complicity.

Geneva school \jə-'nē-və\, *French* École de Genève \ā-kôl-də-zhə-'nev\ A group of critics whose response to literature and approaches to criticism began to be defined in the 1930s. Emphasizing the individual consciousness of the writer, the various members of the Geneva school examined an author's entire body of work as a means of getting at the person's vision of his own self and the world. Their philosophy was in direct opposition to the strictly textual examination that was popular in such objectivist schools as New Criticism.

The first critics to use this phenomenological approach were Marcel Raymond, Albert Béguin, and Georges Poulet, who were friends and correspondants.

genie or **genii** \'jē-nē\ *plural* **genies** or **genii** \'jē-nē, -nē-ˌī\ [French *génie* attendant spirit, from Latin *genius* (associated by French translators of *The Thousand and One Nights* with Arabic *jinnīy* jinni)] *see* JINNI.

genius loci \-'lō-ˌsī, -ˌkē\ [Latin] A tutelary deity or spirit of a place.

Genius of Christianity, The Five-volume treatise by François-Auguste-René CHATEAUBRIAND, published in French as *Le Génie du christianisme, ou beautés de la religion chrétienne* in 1802. It included the novels *Atala* (1801) and *René* (1805, with a revised edition of *Atala*). Written shortly after the death of his mother, the work reveals Chateaubriand's own struggle to reconcile rationalism and religion and his eventual return to traditional Christianity. In response to the rationalism of

Enlightenment writers, Chateaubriand defends Christianity by stressing its capacity to nurture and stimulate European culture, architecture, art, and literature.

Genji monogatari \'gen-jē-'mō-nō-gä-tä-rē\ *see* THE TALE OF GENJI.

genre \'zhän-rə, 'zhäⁿr, 'jän-rə\ [French, kind, sort] A distinctive type or category of literary composition, such as the epic, tragedy, comedy, novel, and short story.

Despite critics' attempts to systematize the art of literature, such categories must retain a degree of flexibility, for they can break down on closer scrutiny. For example, hybrid forms such as the tragicomedy and prose poem are possible. Newly created forms, such as Vikram Seth's *The Golden Gate* (a novel written in rhyming verse form) and John Fuller's *Flying to Nowhere* (a novel written in highly poetic prose), and numerous prose works of intermediate or very specific length (such as the novella and the short-short) are a clear indication of the difficulty of too close a reliance on genre as a category.

genteel comedy Early 18th-century subgenre of the comedy of manners that reflected the behavior of the British upper class. Contrasted with Restoration comedy, the genteel comedy was somewhat artificial and sentimental. Colley Cibber's play *The Careless Husband* is an example of the type.

Gentleman's Magazine, The Popular English periodical that was published for nearly two centuries (1731–1907). It gave the name *magazine* to its genre. The first general periodical in England, it was founded by Edward Cave as a storehouse, or magazine, of essays and articles culled from other publications, often from books and pamphlets. Samuel Johnson joined *The Gentleman's Magazine* in 1738, and a short time later it began to publish parliamentary reports and original writing.

gentry \'jen-trē\ In parts of Ireland, a collective name for the fairies, comparable to "good folk" or "good people" denoting the fairies elsewhere in the British Isles.

Geoffrey \'jef-rē\ of Monmouth \'män-məth\ (d. 1155) Medieval English chronicler and bishop of St. Asaph (1152), whose major work, the HISTORIA REGUM BRITANNIAE (*History of the Kings of Britain*), brought the figure of Arthur into European literature.

In three passages of the *Historia*, Geoffrey describes himself as "Galfridus Monemutensis," an indication that he probably came from Monmouth. Geoffrey alleges that the *Historia* was translated from a "very old book in the British tongue" brought by Walter, archdeacon of Oxford, from Brittany. This seems a pure fabrication, but it is clear that Geoffrey was for most of his life an Oxford cleric, closely connected with Walter and sharing with him a taste for letters.

The *Historia regum Britanniae*, written sometime between 1135 and 1139, was one of the most popular books of the Middle Ages. Its historical value is almost nil, however. In the book he introduced the enchanter Merlin, whose story he related in the later *Vita Merlini*. Written in ornate Latin hexameters, probably between 1148 and 1151, *Vita Merlini* is based on genuine Celtic material about a madman with a gift for divination.

Denounced from the first by other historians, Geoffrey's fictional history nevertheless had an enormous influence on later chroniclers. Romanticized versions in the vernacular, the so-called *Bruts*, were in circulation from about 1150. Writers of the later Middle Ages gave the material a wide currency, and indeed Geoffrey's influence was at its greatest after the accession of the Tudors. The text, with an English translation, was published in 1929 by Acton Griscom and Robert Ellis Jones. J.J. Parry produced an edition of the *Vita Merlini* in 1925. *See also* BRUT.

Geoffrin \zhȯ-'fraⁿ\, Marie-Thérèse Rodet (b. 1699, Paris, Fr.—d. 1777, Paris)   French hostess whose salon in the Hôtel de Rambouillet became an international meeting place of artists and men of letters from 1749 to 1777.

Mme Geoffrin inherited the salon of the more unconventional Mme de Tencin, gave it an added tone of respectability, and became a generous, motherly patron to her guests and protégés, offering them criticism and advice. She ruled her domain with tact and strictness; neither religion nor politics as a subject of conversation was permitted. On Mondays such artists as François Boucher, Maurice-Quentin de La Tour, and Jean-Baptiste Greuze attended; on Wednesdays writers, including Horace Walpole, Pierre Marivaux, Bernard de Fontenelle, and Claude-Adrien Helvétius, were present. Mme Geoffrin's salon was also a center for the Encyclopédistes, the compilers of L'Encyclopedie whose vast project she subsidized.

Geography III   Collection of poetry by Elizabeth BISHOP, published in 1976. The poems offer meditations on the need for self-exploration, on the significance of art, especially poetry, to human life, and on human responsibility in a chaotic world. The collection includes some of Bishop's best-known poems, among them "In the Waiting Room," "Crusoe in England," and the villanelle "One Art." The book won the 1976 National Book Critics' Circle Award.

Geometres \jē-'äm-ə-ˌtrēz\, John, *also called* John Kyriotes \kēr-'yō-tēs, *Angl* ˌkir-ē-'ō-tēz\ (fl. 10th century)   Byzantine poet, official, and bishop, known for his short poems in classical meter. Geometres held the post of *protospatharios* (commander of the guards) at the Byzantine court and later was ordained priest. His poems, on both contemporary politics and religious subjects, are distinguished by considerable charm and appreciation of natural beauty. His prose works, most of which remained unpublished, include a life of the Virgin Mary consisting of sermons for her feast days and an encomium on Eve's apple.

George \'jȯrj\ the Pisidian \pə-'sid-ē-ən\, *Greek* Georgios Pisides \'yȯrḡ-yȯs-pē-'sē-ᴛhēs\ (fl. early 7th century)   Byzantine epic poet, historian, and cleric whose classically structured verse lyricizing the military, philosophical, and religious themes of his day was acclaimed as a model for medieval Greek poetry but whose imitativeness and pretentious imagery was later decried.

A deacon and archivist of Constantinople's cathedral Hagia Sophia, George chronicled imperial events and the deeds of his ruler, the emperor Heraclius (610–641). He eulogized the Byzantine resurgence in "The Expedition of Heraclius Against the Persians" (622) and "The Heracliad" (627), an ode commemorating the victory over the Parthians.

George's major work, the *Hexaëmeron* ("Six Days"), a rhapsody on the beauty of the Creation and on the Creator's wisdom, was popularized through translations into Armenian and Slavic languages. His other writings include the moralistic elegy "De vanitate vitae" ("On the Vanity of Life") and "Hymn to the Resurrection."

George \'jȯrj\, Saint (fl. probably 3rd century; d. probably Diospolis, Palestine)   Christian martyr who became the patron saint of England. Though nothing of his life or deeds can be established, George's legends, dating from the 6th century, became popular and increasingly extravagant, as in Jacobus de Voragine's *Legenda aurea* (1265–66; *Golden Legend*), which tells of his rescuing a maiden from a dragon—a theme much represented in art.

George \gā-'ȯr-gə\, Stefan (b. July 12, 1868, Büdesheim, near Bingen, Hesse [Germany]—d. Dec. 4, 1933, Minusio, near Locarno, Switz.)   Lyric poet who was chiefly responsible for the revival of German poetry at the close of the 19th century.

George studied in Paris, Munich, and Berlin and traveled widely, becoming associated with Stéphane Mallarmé and the Symbolists in Paris and with the Pre-Raphaelites in London. Returning to Germany, he founded a literary school of his own, the George-Kreis. Many well-known writers belonged to it or contributed to its journal, *Blätter für die Kunst*, published from 1892 to 1919. The chief aim of the journal was to revitalize German literary language.

George imposed a new set of poetic ideals to serve as a protest not only against the debasement of the language but also against materialism and naturalism. He preached a humanism inspired by Greece, which he hoped would be realized in a new society. His ideas, and the affectations into which they led some of his disciples, his claim of superiority, and his obsession with power were ridiculed, attacked, and misused by those who misunderstood them. When the Nazi government offered George money and honors, he refused them and went into exile.

His collected works fill 18 volumes (*Gesamtausgabe*, 1927–34), including five of translations and one of prose sketches. His collections of poetry are the most significant of the volumes, showing his poetic and spiritual development.

Georgian poetry   Any of a number of lyrical poems produced in the early 20th century by an assortment of British poets, including Lascelles Abercrombie, Hilaire Belloc, Edmund Charles Blunden, Rupert Brooke, William Henry Davies, John Drinkwater, James Elroy Flecker, Ralph Hodgson, Wilfred Wilson Gibson, Robert Graves, Walter de la Mare, Harold Monro (editor of *The Poetry Review*), Siegfried Sassoon, Sir J.C. Squire, and Edward Thomas.

Brooke and Sir Edward Marsh felt a need to make new poetry more accessible to the public, and with Monro, Drinkwater, and Gibson they planned a series of anthologies, applying the name "Georgian" to suggest the opening of a new poetic age with the accession (1910) of George V. Five volumes of *Georgian Poetry*, edited by Marsh, were published between 1912 and 1922.

The real gifts of Brooke, Davies, de la Mare, Blunden, and Hodgson should not be overlooked, but, taken as a whole, much of the Georgians' work was lifeless. It took inspiration from the countryside and nature, and in the hands of less gifted poets, the resulting poetry was diluted and middlebrow conventional verse of late Romantic character. "Georgian" came to be a pejorative term, used in a sense not intended by its progenitors: rooted in its period and looking backward rather than forward.

georgic \'jȯr-jik\   A poem dealing with practical aspects of agriculture and rural affairs. The model for such verse in postclassical literature was Virgil's *Georgica*, itself modeled on a now lost *Geōrgika* (Greek: "agricultural things") by the 2nd-century-BC Greek poet Nicander of Colophon.

Gerard \'jer-ˌärd, -ərd; jə-'rärd\ of Cremona \krā-'mō-nä\ (b. *c.* 1114, Cremona, Lombardy [Italy]—d. 1187, Toledo, kingdom of Castile [Spain])   European medieval scholar who translated the works of many major Greek and Arabic writers into Latin.

Gerard went to Toledo to learn Arabic in order to read the *Almagest* of the 2nd-century-AD Greek mathematician and astronomer Ptolemy, which was not then available in Latin; he remained in Toledo for the rest of his life. About 80 translations from the Arabic have been attributed to him, but it has been suggested that he was in charge of a school of translators responsible for some of the translations. Gerard's translation of the *Almagest* (printed in 1515) was finished in 1175. Among other Greek authors translated from Arabic versions by Gerard (according to tradition) are Aristotle, Euclid, and Galen. Translations of original Arabic texts attributed to him include works on medicine, notably the *Canon* of Avicenna.

Gérin-Lajoie \zhā-raⁿ-lá-'zhwä\, Antoine (b. Aug. 4, 1824, Yamachiche, Que., Lower Canada—d. Aug. 4, 1882, Ottawa, Ont., Can.)   Writer, librarian, and leader in the early literary movement of French Canada.

While a college student, Gérin-Lajoie wrote the first French-Canadian play, *Le Jeune Latour* (1844; "The Young Latour"). He later served as translator to the legislative assembly of Canada (1852–56) and as assistant librarian of Parliament (1856–80).

Gérin-Lajoie was one of the founders of the Institut Canadien of Montreal and of the literary magazines *Les Soirées canadiennes* (1861–65; "Canadian Evenings") and *Le Foyer canadien* (1863–66; "The Canadian Home"). He was the author of *Catechisme politique* (1851; "Political Catechism") and *Dix Ans au Canada, de 1840 à 1850* (1888; "Ten Years in Canada, from 1840 to 1850"), the history of the advent of "responsible government" (with the colonial executive responsible to the Canadian assembly) in the colony. He also wrote a novel in two parts, *Jean Rivard, le défricheur* (1862; "Jean Rivard, the Reclaimer") and *Jean Rivard, l'économiste* (1864; "Jean Rivard, the Economist"), which portrays rural life in French Canada in the mid-19th century.

Germinal \zher-mē-'näl\   Novel by Émile Zola, first published in 1885. The work is one of a series of 20 novels known collectively as the ROUGON-MACQUART CYCLE.

Gernsback \'gərnz-,bak\, Hugo (b. Aug. 16, 1884, Luxembourg, Lux.—d. Aug. 19, 1967, New York, N.Y., U.S.) American inventor and publisher who was largely responsible for the establishment of SCIENCE FICTION as an independent literary form.

After receiving a technical education in Luxembourg and Germany, Gernsback traveled to the United States in 1904 to market an improved dry battery that he had invented. He formed a radio supply house, and in 1908 he founded *Modern Electrics* (later absorbed by *Popular Science*), a pioneer magazine for radio enthusiasts.

In 1926 Gernsback began publishing *Amazing Stories*, the first magazine devoted exclusively to what he referred to as "scientifiction." The stories were often crudely written, but the very existence of the magazine and its successors, including *Wonder Stories*, encouraged the development and refinement of the genre. His contribution was later recognized with the establishment of the annual Hugo Award for the best science fiction.

Gerstenberg \'ger-stən-,berk\, Heinrich Wilhelm von (b. Jan. 3, 1737, Tondern, Den.—d. Nov. 1, 1823, Altona, near Hamburg [Germany])   German poet, critic, and theorist of the Sturm und Drang literary movement, whose *Briefe über die Merkwürdigkeiten der Literatur* (1866–67; "Letters About the Peculiarities of Literature") contained the first definite formulation of the critical principles of this movement.

After studying law and completing military service, Gerstenberg spent 12 years in Copenhagen, where he became a friend of Friedrich Gottlieb Klopstock, the leading writer of the German Enlightenment. During that time he wrote *Gedicht eines Skalden* (1766; "Poems of an Old Norse Bard"), in which he introduced bardic poetry into German literature with the use of material and themes from Norse antiquity. His powerful and gruesome tragedy *Ugolino* (1768) ranges in its expression from the heroic to the macabre. During his Copenhagen years he also wrote the text of a cantata, *Ariadne auf Naxos* (1767), that was set to music by Johann Adolph Scheibe and Johann Christian Bach. It was later adapted by Georg Benda for a well-known duodrama (a drama for two performers in which the dialogue is spoken with an instrumental accompaniment).

Gerusalemme liberata \jä-,rü-zä-'lem-mä-,lē-bä-'rä-tä\ ("Jerusalem Liberated")   Heroic epic poem in ottava rima, the masterpiece of Torquato TASSO. He completed it in 1575, then spent several years revising it. While he was incarcerated in the asylum of Santa Anna, part of the poem was published without his knowledge as *Il Goffredo*; he published the complete epic in 1581. It was published in English as *Jerusalem Delivered*.

Gerusalemme liberata tells of the Christian army led by Godfrey of Bouillon during the last months of the First Crusade, which recovered Jerusalem from the Turks in 1099. To the poem's principal historical action, Tasso added imaginary characters and episodes that freely expressed his lyrical and hedonistic imagination.

Tasso tried to balance the moral aspirations of the times with his own sensuous inspiration and the formal rules of the epic with his lyrical fancy. *Gerusalemme conquistata*, a new version of the epic written to submit to the era's moral and literary prejudices, was published in 1593 but poetically it was judged a failure.

Gervase \'jər-vəs\ of Tilbury \'til-bə-rē\ (b. *c.* 1152—d. *c.* 1220)   Scholar and courtier who wrote the *Otia imperialia*, a book of marvels intended as a compendium of geography, history, and natural history.

Gervase studied at Bologna and afterward taught canon law there. He returned to England about 1180 and served in a series of royal households. He later received an appointment from the Holy Roman emperor Otto IV as marshal of the kingdom of Arles, and he appears to have remained in the imperial service until Otto's death in 1218. Soon afterward Gervase returned to England, where he retired to an unnamed house of regular canons.

Gervase's claim to fame rests upon the *Otia imperialia*, dedicated to Otto IV. The work was still in progress in 1215 and cannot have been presented to the emperor until near the end of his life. Extracts have been published from the 17th century onward, and an edition of the whole work was published by the German philosopher G.W. Leibniz in 1707 and 1710.

Geryon \'jē-rē-ən, 'ger-ē-\ or **Geryones** \jē-'rī-ō-,nēz\   In Greek mythology, a monster with three heads or three bodies who lived on the island of Erytheia in the west and kept large herds of cattle. The cattle were guarded by a herdsman named Eurytion (or Eurythion) and the infernal hound Orthus (or Orthrus, the son of Typhon and Echidna). One of the labors of Heracles was to steal the cattle, which he did after killing Eurytion, Orthus, and Geryon.

gesaku \gä-'sä-kü\ [Japanese]   Popular Japanese fiction written between approximately the 1770s to about the late 19th century. It was characterized by a flippant tone and a certain erudition. Initially the writers of *gesaku* (called *gesakusha*) were typically sophisticated, educated men who were familiar with popular Chinese literature. They engaged in wordplay and wrote light, rather gossipy stories of events in entertainment quarters. They usually kept their *gesaku* separate from their serious (*i.e.*, nonfiction) writing. Hiraga Gennai is generally acknowledged as the founder of the movement.

Later *gesakusha* were largely motivated by profit. They aimed at as wide a public as possible and followed a successful book with as many sequels as the public would accept. Among the distinct genres within *gesaku* are the humorous books called *sharebon* ("witty books") and *kokkeibon* ("funny books"); the love stories, or *ninjōbon*; the nonillustrated volumes, or *yomihon* ("reading books"); and the illustrated books, or *kibyōshi* ("yellow covers").

Gessner \'ges-nər\, Salomon (b. April 1, 1730, Zürich [Switz.]—d. March 2, 1788, Zürich) Swiss writer, translator, painter, and etcher known throughout Europe for literary works on pastoral themes in the Rococo style.

Gessner ran an important publishing house, from which he published his books with his own excellent etchings. The pastoral prose *Idyllen* (1756–72) and the epic poem *Der Tod Abels* (1758; "The Death of Abel") were his most renowned works, making him the most successful and typical representative of the Rococo literary movement. Gessner also translated part of Alexander Pope's "Pastorals" and two tales by Denis Diderot. The final collection of his works was published at Zürich in 1841.

gest or **geste** \'jest\ [Old French *geste, jeste* narrative, tale, deed, exploit, from Latin *gesta* (plural) deeds, exploits] A story of achievements or adventures. Among several famous medieval collections of gests are Fulcher of Chartres's *Gesta Francorum*, Saxo Grammaticus' *Gesta Danorum*, and the compilation known as the *Gesta Romanorum*. The term was also used to refer to a romance in verse.

Gesta Danorum \'jes-tə-dä-'nō-rəm\ ("Story of the Danes") History of Denmark by SAXO GRAMMATICUS, written between 1185 and 1222 and considered the greatest work of medieval Danish literature. It traces Danish history from the legendary King Dan to Canute IV in 1185. The first nine books of the *Gesta Danorum* give an account of some 60 legendary Danish kings. For this part Saxo depended on ancient lays, romantic sagas, and the accounts of Icelanders. His legend of *Amleth* is thought to be the source of William Shakespeare's *Hamlet*; his Toke the Archer, the prototype of William Tell. Three heroic poems translated by Saxo into Latin hexameters are especially noteworthy. These oldest-known Danish poems are *Bjarkemaalet*, a battle hymn designed to arouse warlike feelings; *Ingjaldskvadet*, a poem warning of the dangers of luxury and its ability to corrupt the traditional Viking spirit; and *Hagbard and Signe*, a tragedy of love and family feuds. The final seven books contain Saxo's account of the historical period, but he achieves independent authority only when writing of events close to his own time. His work is noteworthy for its sense of patriotic purpose based on a belief in the unifying influence of the monarchy.

Gesta Romanorum \'jes-tə-,rō-mə-'nō-rəm\ ("Deeds of the Romans") Latin collection of anecdotes and tales, probably compiled early in the 14th century in England. It was one of the most popular books of the time and the source, directly or indirectly, of much later literature. Of its authorship nothing certain is known, but its didactic nature and the allegorical explanations attached to the stories in the early versions suggest that it was intended as a manual for preachers.

The title is only partially appropriate because it contains, in addition to stories from classical history and legend, many others from a variety of sources, Oriental and European in particular. The collection is full of the kinds of stories popular in the Middle Ages—tales of magicians and monsters, ladies in distress, escapes from perilous situations—all unified by their moral purpose and made real by details drawn from observation of nature and everyday life. Among its variety of material are found the germ of the romance of Guy of Warwick; the story of Darius and his three sons, versified by Thomas Hoccleve; part of Geoffrey Chaucer's "The Man of Law's Tale"; and a tale of the emperor Theodosius, the same in its main features as that of King Lear. William Shakespeare's *Pericles* probably was based on John Gower's version of a story about

Apollonius of Tyre, derived from the collection, and the three-caskets plot in *The Merchant of Venice* is also thought to be based on a tale from the *Gesta Romanorum*. The narrative structure enabled the easy insertion of additional stories by a transcriber, and therefore the manuscripts show considerable variety. The earliest printed editions were produced at Utrecht [now in The Netherlands] and Cologne [now in Germany] late in the 15th century, but their exact dates are unknown.

Geste, Beau \,bō-'zhest\ Fictional character, the English protagonist of the novel BEAU GESTE by Percival C. Wren.

Gevers \'gā-vərs\, Marie, *original name* Maria Theresia Carolina Fanny Gevers (b. Dec. 30, 1883, Edegem, Belg.—d. March 9, 1975, Edegem) Franco-Belgian novelist and poet whose work, almost without exception, evokes Kempenland, a rural area near Antwerp where she spent most of her life.

Gevers' first works were lyrical poems constructed out of everyday incidents of her tranquil life. Her volumes of verse include *Les Arbres et le vent* (1923; "The Trees and the Wind") and *Antoinette* (1925). Gevers' novels are notable for their descriptions of the Kempenland region and for their reworkings of local myths and legends. Among her most successful novels are *La Comtesse des digues* (1931; "The Countess of the Dikes"), *Madame Orpha* (1933), and *La Ligne de vie* (1937; "Lifeline"). Her best-known work is *Vie et mort d'un étang* (1961; "Life and Death of a Pond").

Gezelle \kə-'zel-ə\, Guido (b. May 1, 1830, Bruges [Belgium]—d. Nov. 27, 1899, Bruges) Flemish priest and poet who was one of the masters of 19th-century European lyric poetry.

Gezelle was ordained in 1854 while already a teacher at Roulers, where he remained until 1860, when he was transferred to Bruges. He worked to inspire his students with his religious, poetic, and Flemish-nationalist idealism.

Gezelle was a lively, sometimes reckless political journalist, writing in his own weekly, *'t Jaer 30*, and in other papers. He founded and edited a cultural weekly, *Rond den Heerd*, in 1865. On the verge of a mental breakdown, he was transferred in 1872 as curate to Courtrai, where he recovered his balance and again began to write poetry. In 1881 he founded and edited *Loquela*, a philological review, and in 1886 he published a masterly translation of Henry Wadsworth Longfellow's poem *The Song of Hiawatha*. From about 1877 until his death his output of poetry continued to be constant.

From 1850 to 1870, Gezelle's poetry was the expression of a sensitive, passionate, and versatile personality who was ill-adjusted to life yet who delighted in the beauty of nature and found spiritual exaltation in the love of God. The poetry of his second period (1877–99) was more mature and controlled in construction. Gezelle showed considerable originality in his use of language and imagery, and his poetry had great lyrical purity and intensity.

Ghālib \'gȯ-leb\, Mīrzā Asadullāh Khān (b. Dec. 27, 1797, Āgra, India—d. Feb. 15, 1869, Delhi) The preeminent Indian poet of his time writing in Persian, equally renowned for poems, letters, and prose pieces in Urdu.

Ghālib's best poems were written in three forms: ghazel (love lyric), *masnawī* (description or narrative in rhyming couplets), and qasida (panegyric). His critics accused him of writing in an obscure and ornamental style of Persian incomprehensible to the common reader. His verses affirm God's omnipotence while questioning the misery of the phenomenal world.

In 1850 Ghālib was appointed poet laureate to the last Mughal emperor, Bahādur Shāh II.

Ghassaniy, al- *see* MUYAKA.

ghazel *also spelled* ghazal, gazel, gasal, *or* ghasel \'gaz-al, -el; 'gäz-əl; 'gȧ-zȧl\ [Arabic *ghazal*] In Islāmic literature, a lyric poem, generally short and graceful in form and typically dealing with themes of love.

As a genre the ghazel developed in Arabia in the late 7th century from the *nasib*, which itself was an often amorous prelude to the qasida (ode). The poems begin with a rhymed couplet whose rhyme is repeated in all subsequent even lines. The odd lines are unrhymed. The two main types of ghazel are native to Hejaz and Iraq.

The ghazels by 'Umar ibn Abī Rabī'ah (died 712/719) of the Quraysh tribe of Mecca are some of the oldest. 'Umar's poems, based largely on his own life and experiences, are realistic, lively, and urbane in character. They continue to be popular with modern readers.

What became a classic theme of the ghazel was introduced by Jamīl (died 701), a member of the 'Udhrah tribe from Hejaz. Jamīl's lyrics tell of hopeless, idealistic lovers pining for each other unto death. These enormously popular works were imitated not only in Arabic but also in Persian, Turkish, and Urdu poetry until the 18th century.

Of additional note is the work of Ḥāfeẓ (also spelled Ḥāfiz; died 1389/90), considered among the finest lyric poets of Persia, whose depth of imagery and multilayered metaphors revitalized and perfected the genre. The form was introduced to Western literature by German Romantics, notably Friedrich von Schlegel and J.W. von Goethe.

Ghelderode \də-'kel-də-,rō-də\, Michel de (b. April 3, 1898, Ixelles, Belg.—d. April 1, 1962, Brussels) Eccentric Belgian dramatist whose folkish morality plays resound with violence, demonism, holy madness, and Rabelaisian humor.

Ghelderode scored an early success with his *Images de la vie de Saint François d'Assise* (1927; "Scenes from the Life of St. Francis of Assisi"), in which the life and death of the saint are told with sincere faith but with little traditional reverence. He then wrote *Barabbas* (1928) for performance during Holy Week. The style of the dialogue is as striking as the daring conception of events, the avant-garde staging, and the strange mixture of piety and ribaldry. Ghelderode wrote many other plays, but because he was something of a recluse who was content to write for the ordinary people of his native Flanders, he was little known even in France until after World War II, when he was belatedly recognized as a master of the avant-garde theater.

Ghose \'gōz\, Zulfikar \'zůl-fē-,kär\ (b. March 13, 1935, Sialkot, India [now Pakistan]) Pakistani-American author of novels, poetry, and criticism about cultural alienation.

Ghose grew up a Muslim in Sialkot and in largely Hindu Bombay, then moved with his family to England. He graduated from the University of Keele in 1959 and married an artist, Helena de la Fontaine, from Brazil (later the setting for six of his novels). In 1969 he moved to the United States to teach at the University of Texas.

His first novel, *The Contradictions* (1966), explores differences between Western and Eastern attitudes and ways of life. In *The Murder of Aziz Khan* (1967) a small farmer tries to save his traditional land from greedy developers. Ghose's trilogy *The Incredible Brazilian*, comprising *The Native* (1972), *The Beautiful Empire* (1975), and *A Different World* (1978), presents the picaresque adventures, often violent or sexually perverse, of a man who goes through several reincarnations. Ghose's other novels include *Crump's Terms* (1975), *Hulme's Investigations into the Bogart Script* (1981), *A New History of Torments* (1982), *Don Bueno* (1983), *Figures of Enchantment* (1986), and *The Triple Mirror of the Self* (1992). His poems, from those in *The Loss of India* (1964) to the *Selected Poems* (1991), are of-

ten about the travels and memories of a self-aware alien. He also wrote an early autobiography, *Confessions of a Native-Alien* (1965).

ghost \'gōst\ Soul or specter of a dead person, usually believed to inhabit the netherworld and to be capable of returning in some form to the world of the living. According to descriptions or depictions provided by believers, a ghost may appear as a living being or as a nebulous likeness of the deceased and, occasionally, in other forms. The traditional visual manifestations of haunting include ghostly apparitions, the displacement of objects, or the appearance of strange lights; auditory signs include disembodied laughter and screams, footsteps, ringing bells, and the spontaneous emanation of sounds from musical instruments.

Tales of ghosts are still common in living folklore worldwide. *Compare* GHOUL; KOBOLD; POLTERGEIST.

Ghosts A drama in three acts by Henrik IBSEN, published in 1881 as *Gengangere* and performed the following year. The play is an attack on conventional morality and on the results of hypocrisy.

Ostensibly a discussion of congenital venereal disease, *Ghosts* also deals with the power of ingrained moral contamination to undermine the most determined idealism. Although the lecherous Captain Alving is in his grave, his ghost will not be laid to rest. The memorial that Helen, his conventionally minded widow, has erected to his memory burns down even as his son Oswald goes insane from inherited syphilis and his illegitimate daughter slips inexorably toward her destiny in a brothel.

Ghost Sonata, The One-act drama in three scenes by August STRINDBERG, written and published as *Spöksonaten* in 1907 and performed the following year. The drama is considered the best of Strindberg's four chamber plays, and it is one of the most macabre, wrathful works in all of world literature. The playwright's antirealist invocation of ghosts, vampires, and evil spirits helped usher in Expressionist drama.

The work concerns the vampirish Hummel, seeking to destroy the Colonel, who years ago seduced the woman Hummel loved. Hummel introduces a Student to his peculiar coterie, which includes both the Colonel's wife (known as the Mummy) and her frail daughter, who draws life from hyacinths. At an elaborate "ghost supper" in the Colonel's apartment, Hummel humiliates the Colonel and tells the guests that the hyacinth girl is his child, but when the Mummy reveals Hummel's sordid past he hangs himself. Later, as the girl slowly dies, the Student declaims how appearances can mask evil; he turns to the audience and warns them that they, too, cannot escape their sins.

ghost story A tale about ghosts. More generally, the phrase may refer to a tale based on imagination rather than fact. Ghost stories exist in all kinds of literature, from folktales to religious works to modern horror stories, and in most cultures. They can be used as isolated episodes or interpolated stories within a larger narrative, as in Lucius Apuleius' *The Golden Ass*, Geoffrey Chaucer's "The Nun's Priest's Tale," William Shakespeare's *Hamlet*, and many Renaissance plays and gothic novels, or they can be the main focus of a work, such as the stories of Sheridan Le Fanu's *In a Glass Darkly*, Henry James's novella *The Turn of the Screw* and Kingsley Amis' novel *The Green Man*.

ghostwriter \'gōst-,rī-tər\ One who writes for and in the name of another.

ghoul \'gül\ [Arabic *ghūl*] In popular legend, demonic being believed to inhabit burial grounds and other deserted places. In ancient Arabic folklore, *ghūl*s belonged to a diabolic class of jinn (spirits) and were said to be the offspring of Iblīs, the Muslim prince of darkness. They were capable of constantly changing form, but their presence was always recognizable by their unalterable feature: ass's hooves.

The *ghūl*, as a vivid figure in the Bedouin imagination, appeared in pre-Islāmic Arabic poetry, notably that of Ta'abbata Sharran. In North Africa, it was easily assimilated into an ancient Berber folklore already rich in demons and fantastic creatures. Modern Arabs use *ghūl* to designate a human or demonic cannibal and frequently employ the word to frighten disobedient children.

Anglicized as "ghoul," the word entered English tradition and was further identified as a grave-robbing creature that feeds on dead bodies and on children. In the West ghouls have no specific image and have been described by Edgar Allan Poe as "neither man nor woman . . . neither brute nor human." They are thought to assume disguises, to ride on dogs and hares, and to set fires at night to lure travelers away from the main roads. *See also* JINNI.

Giacomo da Lentini \\'jä-kō-mō-dä-len-'tē-nē\\, *also called* Jacopo da Lentini \\'yä-kō-pō\\ (fl. 1st half of 13th century) Senior poet of the SICILIAN SCHOOL and notary at the court of the Holy Roman emperor Frederick II. Celebrated during his life, he was acclaimed as a master by the poets of the following generation, including Dante, who memorialized him in the *Purgatorio* (XXIV, 55–57).

Giacomo is traditionally credited with the invention of the sonnet, and his works in that form remain the earliest known. He adapted the themes, style, and language of Provençal poetry to Italian, infusing it with his own aristocratic and exclusive tastes. All his extant poetry—some 40 lyrics, including sonnets, canzone, *tenzoni* (poetic debates), and one *discordo* (poetic disagreement)—concerns the theme of love, which, in the courtly tradition, is seen in feudal terms as the service of the lover to his lady.

Giacosa \\jä-'kō-zä\\, Giuseppe (b. Oct. 21, 1847, Colleretto Parella, near Turin, Piedmont [Italy]—d. Sept. 1, 1906, Colleretto Parella) Italian dramatist who collaborated with Luigi Illica to write the libretti for three of Giacomo Puccini's most famous operas.

Giacosa's first successful comedy, *Una partita a scacchi* (1873; "A Game of Chess"), was set in the European Middle Ages. Giacosa followed this with several more comedies and light historical dramas. He then gradually turned to examining contemporary social problems in the manner of Henrik Ibsen. Giacosa's best plays, among which are *I diritti dell'anima* (1894; *Sacred Ground*) and *Come le foglie* (1900; *Like Falling Leaves*), are psychological investigations of people in crisis.

In 1891 Giacosa was one of several writers asked to work on the libretto for Puccini's opera *Manon Lescaut*. Giacosa suggested that Illica assist him, and this led to a collaboration between the two men on the texts of *La bohème* (1896), *Tosca* (1900), and *Madama Butterfly* (1904). Illica devised the operas' structure and first draft, which Giacosa then polished and converted into verse.

giant \\'jī-ənt\\ [Middle English *geaunt, giaunt,* from Middle French *geant,* ultimately from Latin *gigant-, gigas,* from Greek *gígas*] In folklore, a huge mythical being, usually humanlike in form. The term derives (through Latin) from the Giants (Gigantes) of Greek mythology, who were monstrous, savage creatures often depicted with men's bodies terminating in serpentine legs.

According to Hesiod, the giants were sons of Gaea (Earth) and were born from the blood of Uranus (Heaven) after his son, the Titan Cronus, had wounded him. After Cronus and the other Titans were defeated in a long series of battles against the gods, who were led by Zeus, the giants attempted to avenge the Titans. The Gigantomachy was a desperate struggle between the Giants and the Olympians. The gods finally prevailed, and the Giants were slain. The Gigantomachy was interpreted as a symbol of the triumph of Hellenism over barbarism, of good over evil.

The giants of Norse mythology were primeval beings existing before the gods and overcome by them. Giants in folklore were mortals who inhabited the world in early times. Israelite spies in Canaan saw giants (Numbers 13:32–33), and such beings, according to legend, once roamed throughout Cornwall in Britain.

European medieval towns often had tutelary giants whose effigies were carried in procession. In London the giant figures of Gog and Magog are said to represent two Cornish giants made captive by Brutus, the legendary founder of Britain. The 40-foot (12-meter) effigy of Druon Antigonus at Antwerp and the 22-foot (7-meter) figure of Gayant at Douai, Fr., preserve similar traditions.

In most European tales giants appear as cruel and stupid, given to cannibalism, and often one-eyed. Heroes who best them often do so more by wit than by strength, as in the *Odyssey*, in which Odysseus manages to escape from the Cyclops Polyphemus by outsmarting him. Although kindly giants occur (*e.g.,* Rübezahl, who is said to have lived in the Bohemian forest), most are feared and hated.

In literature giants appear in many folktales, including "Jack and the Beanstalk" and the legend of Paul Bunyan, as well as in such classic satires as Jonathan Swift's *Gulliver's Travels* and François Rabelais's *Gargantua* and *Pantagruel*.

Giant Novel about two generations of wealthy Texans by Edna FERBER, published in 1952.

The story unfolds as Leslie Lynnton, a patrician Virginian, marries Bick Benedict, a Texas cattle baron. The reader experiences Texas from Leslie's point of view, as she attempts to understand and to adapt to the customs and expansive way of life of Texans. Alongside her vivid descriptions of the crudeness of the newly rich oil men and cattle barons, Ferber observes their exploitation of the impoverished Mexicans who work for them.

Giants in the Earth (*in full* Giants in the Earth: A Saga of the Prairie) Novel by O.E. RØLVAAG that chronicles the struggles of Norwegian immigrant settlers in the Dakota territory in the 1870s. First published in Norway in two volumes as *I de Dage* (1924; "In Those Days") and *Riket grundlæges* (1925; "The Kingdom Is Founded"), the novel was published in English as a single volume in 1927 as *Giants in the Earth*. It had two sequels, *Peder Seier* (1928; *Peder Victorious*) and *Den signede dag* (1931; *Their Fathers' God*).

The book's indomitable protagonist, Per Hansa, his wife Beret, their children, and three other Norwegian immigrant families settle at Spring Creek, living in makeshift sod huts. Surviving the winters' fierce blizzards, they see their crops destroyed by locusts in summer. They nonetheless persist; new settlers arrive, and the community grows. Beret, who cannot adapt to life on the prairie, almost dies giving birth to the son Per names Peder Victorious. Cheered when a traveling minister baptizes Peder, Beret eventually becomes obsessively religious. When another settler lies dying, Beret insists that Per find a minister for him, but Per is caught in a fierce snowstorm and dies.

Gibbon \\'gib-ən\\, Edward (b. April 27 [May 8, New Style], 1737, Putney, Surrey, Eng.—d. Jan. 16, 1794, London) English rationalist historian and scholar best known as the author of THE DECLINE AND FALL OF THE ROMAN EMPIRE (1776–88), often considered the greatest historical work written in English.

Entering Magdalen College, Oxford, in 1752, Gibbon horrified his father by converting to Roman Catholicism. He was packed off to Calvinist Lausanne, Switz., and was persuaded to return to orthodox Protestantism the following year. His views of religion were thereafter somewhat jaded.

Gibbon's first publication was in French, *Essai sur l'étude de la littérature* (1761; *An Essay on the Study of Literature*). Subsequent publications in French included *Mémoires littéraires de la Grande Bretagne*, 2 vol. (1768–69), which was cowritten with Georges Deyverdun. In Lausanne and in Paris he met the leading intellectual lights of the era, and in England he was a member of The Club, the brilliant circle that was formed around Samuel Johnson.

On a trip to Rome in 1764, Gibbon was inspired to write of the decline and fall of the city. In its material decay he found both the effect and symbol of moral decadence. The first volume of the history was published to general acclaim that was tempered by the reaction to his ironical treatment of the rise of Christianity. He further answered objections to alleged falsification of evidence in *A Vindication of Some Passages in the Fifteenth and Sixteenth Chapters of the Decline and Fall of the Roman Empire* (1779). The second and third volumes of the history followed in 1781 and the last three volumes in 1788. Although subsequent scholarship has applied materials unknown to Gibbon and his conclusions have been modified, his acumen, command of historical perspective, and superb literary style have preserved his place at the forefront of English historiographers. His *Memoirs* was published posthumously in 1796.

Gibbon \'gib-ən\, Lewis Grassic, *pseudonym of* James Leslie Mitchell \'mich-əl\ (b. Feb. 13, 1901, at or near Auchterless, Aberdeenshire, Scot.—d. Feb. 7, 1935, Welwyn Garden City, Hertfordshire, Eng.)   Scottish novelist whose work signaled a 20th-century revival of Scottish themes. He was also a respected historian.

Mitchell was interested in archaeology from an early age, and this interest is evident in the tales of adventure that he wrote. He achieved real fame with his trilogy *A Scots Quair*—consisting of *Sunset Song* (1932), *Cloud Howe* (1933), and *Grey Granite* (1934)—which traces Scottish life in all "its sourness, its harshness, in its beauty, and its sorrow" from the prewar Scottish countryside through postwar depression and social crises. *Scottish Scene* (1934; written in collaboration with poet Hugh MacDiarmid) provides a multifaceted picture of Scotland through a variety of literary vehicles such as poems, plays, short stories, and essays. His "Scottish" books were written under the pseudonym by which he is best known.

His scientific and historical works, published under his real name, include *Niger: The Life of Mungo Park* (1934) and *The Conquest of the Maya* (1934).

Gibbons \'gib-ənz\, Stella (Dorothea) (b. Jan. 5, 1902, London, Eng.—d. Dec. 19, 1989, London)   English novelist and poet whose first novel, COLD COMFORT FARM (1932), a burlesque of the rural novel, won her immediate fame.

Gibbons studied journalism at University College, London. After graduation she worked for a time for the *British United Press* as a cable decoder and held various other jobs over a period of 10 years (1923–33), including those of drama and literary critic, reporter, and fashion writer.

Cold Comfort Farm was a popular and critical success but was never equaled by her later work. Gibbons wrote several other novels, including *Westwood; or, The Gentle Powers* (1946) and *Here Be Dragons* (1956), two works that deal with a young woman's disillusionment and education, as well as *The Charmers* (1965) and *The Woods in Winter* (1970). She also published poetry and four collections of short stories.

Gibran or **Jibran** \ji-'brän\, Khalil or Kahlil, *Arabic name in full* Jubrān Khalīl Jubrān (b. Jan. 6, 1883, Bsharrī, Lebanon—d. April 10, 1931, New York, N.Y., U.S.)   Lebanese-American philosophical essayist, novelist, mystic poet, and artist.

Gibran immigrated with his parents to Boston in 1895. After studying in Beirut, he returned to Boston, and in 1912 he settled in New York City, where he devoted himself to writing essays and short stories, both in Arabic and in English, and to painting.

Gibran's writings are full of lyrical outpourings and are expressive of his deeply religious and mystical nature. His principal works in Arabic are *Dam'ah wa ibtisāmah* (1914; *A Tear and a Smile*), *Al-Arwāḥ al-mutamarridah* (1920; *Spirits Rebellious*), *Al-Ajniḥah al-mutakassirah* (1922; *The Broken Wings*), and *Al-Mawākib* (1923; *The Procession*), a collection of poems. His principal works in English are *The Madman* (1918), *The Forerunner* (1920), THE PROPHET (1923), *Sand and Foam* (1926), and *Jesus, the Son of Man* (1928).

Gibson \'gib-sən\, Wilfred Wilson (b. Oct. 2, 1878, Hexham, Northumberland, Eng.—d. May 26, 1962, Virginia Water, Surrey)   British poet who drew his inspiration from the workaday life of provincial English families.

Gibson was educated privately, served briefly in World War I, and thereafter devoted his life to poetry. His first poem appeared in *The Spectator* in 1897, but it was with his realistic presentation of the lives of country folk in *Stonefolds* and *On the Threshold* (both 1907) that he first exploited the themes of contemporary life which distinguished his major works. These include *Daily Bread* (1910; a series of 18 short verse plays), the narrative poem *Fires* (1912), *Borderlands* (1914), *Livelihood* (1917), *Krindlesyke* (1922), *Kestrel Edge* (1924), *Coming and Going* (1938), and *The Outpost* (1944).

Gibson \'gib-sən\, William (Ford) (b. March 17, 1948, Conway, S.C., U.S.)   Writer of science fiction who was the leader of the genre's CYBERPUNK movement.

Many of Gibson's early stories were published in *Omni* magazine. With the publication of his first novel, *Neuromancer* (1984), Gibson emerged as a leading exponent of "cyberpunk," a new school of science-fiction writing. Gibson's creation of "cyberspace," a computer-simulated reality that shows the nature of information, is considered the author's major contribution to the genre.

Count Zero (1986) was set on the same world as *Neuromancer*, but seven years later. The characters of *Mona Lisa Overdrive* (1988) can "die" into computers, where they may support or sabotage outer reality. After collaborating with writer Bruce Sterling on *The Difference Engine* (1990), a story set in Victorian England, Gibson returned to the subject of cyberspace in *Virtual Light* (1993).

Gide \'zhēd\, André(-Paul-Guillaume) (b. Nov. 22, 1869, Paris, Fr.—d. Feb. 19, 1951, Paris)   French writer, humanist, and moralist, who received the Nobel Prize for Literature in 1947.

Gide's first work was an autobiographical study of youthful unrest entitled *Les Cahiers d'André Walter* (1891; *The Notebooks of André Walter*). In 1891 Gide was introduced into French Symbolist circles, and for a time he was influenced by Symbolist aesthetic theories. His works *Le Traité du Narcisse* (1891; "Narcissus" in *The Return of the Prodigal*), *Le Voyage d'Urien* (1893; *Urien's Voyage*), and *La Tentative amoureuse* (1893; "The Lovers' Attempt" in *The Return of the Prodigal*) belong to this period. In 1893 and 1894 Gide traveled to North Africa. His contact with the Arab world and its radically different moral standards helped to liberate him from Victorian conventions. One result of this nascent intellectual revolt was his growing awareness of his homosexuality. In 1895 Gide married his cousin Madeleine Rondeaux, to whom he was deeply attached and who had earlier refused him.

Gide's great creative period began with *L'Immoraliste* (1902; THE IMMORALIST) and *La Porte étroite* (1909; STRAIT IS THE GATE). The works mark an important stage in his development because they adapt treatment and style to the subject—his concern with psychological problems. In them Gide mastered classical construction and a pure, simple style. In 1908 he was foremost among those who founded *La Nouvelle Revue française*, the literary review that was to unite progressive French writers for 30 years.

World War I intensified Gide's anguish, and early in 1916 he began to keep a second journal (published in 1926 as *Numquid et tu?*), in which he recorded his search for God. Finally, however, unable to resolve his religious dilemma, he resolved to achieve his own ethic. He began his autobiography, *Si le grain ne meurt* (1924; IF IT DIE . . .), an account of his life from birth to marriage that is among the great works of confessional literature. In 1918 his friendship with the young Marc Allégret caused a serious crisis in his marriage.

Work on his autobiography and the completion in 1918 of *Corydon* (a Socratic dialogue in defense of homosexuality begun earlier) gave Gide some measure of peace. *Corydon*'s publication in 1924 was disastrous, however, and he was violently attacked, even by his closest friends.

Gide titled his next work *Les Faux-Monnayeurs* (1926; THE COUNTERFEITERS). He called it his only novel, meaning that in conception, range, and scope it was on a larger scale than his other tales.

About the mid-1920s, Gide became a champion of society's victims and outcasts, demanding equality for women and more humane conditions for criminals. In 1938 Madeleine died—after a long estrangement they had been brought together by her final illness. With the outbreak of World War II, Gide began to realize the value of tradition and to appreciate the past. In a series of fictitious interviews written in 1941 and 1942 for *Le Figaro*, he expressed a new concept of liberty, declaring that absolute freedom destroys both the individual and society.

Gide began to receive honors in the late 1940s. These culminated in his acceptance of the Nobel Prize for Literature. In 1950 he published the last volume of his *Journal*.

Gids, De \də-ˈkits\ ("The Guide")   Dutch literary journal, published from 1837, that encouraged an emerging national consciousness in The Netherlands. It flourished under the early leadership of Everhardus Johannes POTGIETER, whose sharp criticism was often moralistic. Printed with a blue cover, *De Gids* was known as *de blauwe beul* ("the blue butcher") for its merciless treatment of complacency, but by the late 19th century it was regarded as a traditionalist magazine. Among the contemporary writers published in *De Gids* were Martinus Nijhoff, Herman Teirlinck, and Karel van de Woestijne.

Gifford \ˈgif-ərd\, William (b. April 1756, Ashburton, Devonshire, Eng.—d. Dec. 31, 1826, London)   English satirical poet, classical scholar, and early editor of 17th-century English playwrights, remembered as first editor (1809–25) of *The Quarterly Review*.

Orphaned at age 11, Gifford owed his education at Oxford University to patronage. In *The Baviad* (1791) and *The Maeviad* (1795), verse satires attacking a group of minor English writers of the 1780s, he shows his resentment of those to whom entry to the world of letters, so difficult for him, had been undeservedly easy.

Gifford was both self-important and small-minded; while editor of *The Quarterly*, he offended eminent contributors by

rewriting their literary reviews to introduce political abuse. This practice provoked William Hazlitt to attack him in *A Letter to William Gifford, Esq.* (1819) and to immortalize him in a portrait etched in vitriol in *The Spirit of the Age* (1825).

Gift, The   Novel by Vladimir NABOKOV, originally published serially (in expurgated form in Russian) as *Dar* in 1937–38. It was published in its complete form as a book in 1952. *The Gift* was set in post-World War I Berlin, where Nabokov himself had been an émigré. Steeped in satiric detail about the Russian émigré community, the novel tells parallel stories of the protagonist Fyodor's maturation as a gifted young writer and of his love affair with Zina, a fellow émigré.

giftbook \ˈgift-ˌbu̇k\, *also called* annual *or* keepsake.   An illustrated literary miscellany, or collection of verse, tales, and sketches. The giftbook was popular in England and the United States during the second quarter of the 19th century and was published annually in ornamental format.

Gift of the Magi, The   Short story by O. HENRY, published in the *New York Sunday World* in 1905 and then collected in *The Four Million* (1906).

The story concerns James and Della Dillingham Young, a young couple who, despite their poverty, individually resolve to give each other an elegant gift on Christmas Eve. Della sells her beautiful long hair in order to buy a platinum fob chain for Jim's antique gold watch. Meanwhile, Jim pawns his treasured watch to purchase jeweled tortoiseshell combs for Della's precious tresses. The tale concludes with the exchange of gifts and the couple's recognition of the irony of their sacrifices.

Gigi \zhē-ˈzhē, *Angl* ˈjē-jē\   Comedy of manners by COLETTE, published in 1944.

While Gigi's mother works as a second-rate theater singer, Gigi is left in the care of her grandmother and great-aunt, both retired courtesans. They endeavor to teach Gigi the family business. The two decide to ask Gaston, the bored, fatuous, wealthy son of one of the grandmother's former lovers, to initiate Gigi into her courtesan career. Gigi, furious, refuses, but after Gaston reappears she realizes that she loves him and tells him so. He proposes marriage, and love conquers all.

Gilbert \ˈgil-bərt\, W.S., *in full* Sir William Schwenk Gilbert (b. Nov. 18, 1836, London, Eng.—d. May 29, 1911, Harrow Weald, Middlesex)   English playwright and humorist best known for his collaboration with composer Sir Arthur Sullivan in comic operas.

In 1861 Gilbert began to contribute to the magazine *Fun* a series of comic verses that were later collected as *The Bab Ballads* (1869), followed by *More Bab Ballads* (1873); the two collections were combined in one volume entitled *Songs of a Savoyard* (1898).

Gilbert's dramatic career began when a playwright, Thomas William Robertson, recommended him as someone who could produce a bright Christmas piece in only two weeks. Gilbert promptly wrote *Dulcamara, or the Little Duck and the Great Quack*, a commercial success; other commissions followed. In 1870 Gilbert met Sullivan, and they started working together the following year. *Thespis, or the Gods Grown Old* (first performance 1871) and *Trial by Jury* (1875), a brilliant one-act piece, were followed by four productions staged by Richard D'Oyly Carte: *The Sorcerer* (1877), *H.M.S. Pinafore* (1878), *The Pirates of Penzance* (1879, New York; 1880, London), and *Patience, or Bunthorne's Bride* (1881). Carte built the Savoy Theatre in 1881 for productions of the partners' works, which collectively became known as the "Savoy Operas"; they included *Iolanthe, or the Peer and the Peri* (1882), *Princess Ida, or Castle Adamant* (1884), *The Mikado, or the Town of Titipu* (1885), *Ruddigore, or the Witch's Curse* (1887), *The Yeomen of the Guard* (1888), and *The Gondoliers* (1889). By then, however, relations between the partners had become strained. The two were estranged until 1893, when they again collaborated, producing *Utopia Limited* and, later, *The Grand Duke* (1896). Gilbert was knighted in 1907. He had meanwhile written librettos for other composers; the music for his last opera, *Fallen Fairies, or the Wicked World* (1909), was by Edward German.

Gil Blas \zhēl-'blås\ (*in full* Histoire de Gil Blas de Santillane) Picaresque novel by Alain-René LESAGE, published in four volumes, the first two in 1715, the third in 1724, and the fourth in 1735.

Considered one of literature's first realistic novels, *Gil Blas* takes an ordinary man through a series of adventures in high and low society. The work helped to popularize the picaresque novel, which was already widespread in Spain, though the work's happy ending, in which the hero achieves wealth and respectability, gave a new twist to the picaresque tradition.

Gilded Age Period of gross materialism and blatant political corruption in American history during the 1870s that gave rise to important novels of social and political criticism. The period takes its name from the earliest of these, *The Gilded Age* (1873), written by Mark Twain in collaboration with Charles Dudley Warner. Twain's satire was followed in 1880 by *Democracy*, a political novel published anonymously by the historian Henry Adams. *An American Politician*, by F. Marion Crawford (1884), was another product of the period.

The political novels of the Gilded Age represent the beginnings of a new strain in American literature, the novel as a vehicle of social protest. The trend grew in the late 19th and early 20th centuries with the works of the muckrakers and culminated in the proletarian novelists.

Giles Goat-Boy \'jīlz-'gōt-,bòi\ (*in full* Giles Goat-Boy; or, The Revised New Syllabus) Satiric allegorical novel by John BARTH, published in 1966. The book is set in a vast university that is a symbol for the world.

The novel's protagonist, Billy Bockfuss (also called George Giles, the goat-boy), was raised with herds of goats on a university farm after being found as a baby in the bowels of the giant West Campus Automatic Computer (WESCAC). The WESCAC plans to create a being called GILES (Grand-Tutorial Ideal, Laboratory Eugenical Specimen) that would possess superhuman abilities. Billy's foster father, who tends the herd, suspects Billy of being GILES but tries to groom him to be humanity's savior and to stop WESCAC's domination over humans.

Gilgamesh \'gil-gə-,mesh, gil-'gäm-əsh\ The best known of all ancient Mesopotamian heroes.

The fullest extant text of the Gilgamesh epic is on 12 incomplete Akkadian-language tablets found at Nineveh in the library of the Assyrian king Ashurbanipal (reigned 668–627 BC). The gaps that occur in the tablets have been partly filled by various fragments found elsewhere in Mesopotamia and Anatolia. In addition, five short poems in the Sumerian language are known from tablets that were written during the first half of the 2nd millennium BC; the poems have been entitled "Gilgamesh and Huwawa," "Gilgamesh and the Bull of Heaven," "Gilgamesh and Agga of Kish," "Gilgamesh, Enkidu, and the Nether World," and "The Death of Gilgamesh."

The Gilgamesh of the poems and epic tablets was probably the Gilgamesh who ruled in southern Mesopotamia sometime during the first half of the 3rd millennium BC, though there is no historical evidence for the exploits narrated in the poems and epic.

Gill \'gil\, Brendan (b. Oct. 4, 1914, Hartford, Conn., U.S.) Critic and writer chiefly known for his work as critic of film, drama, and architecture for *The New Yorker*.

Gill began writing for *The New Yorker* immediately after finishing college in 1936. His witty essays often appeared anonymously in the magazine's "Talk of the Town" column, and he served as staff film critic from 1960 to 1967, theater critic from 1968 to 1987, and architecture critic thereafter. *Here at The New Yorker* (1975), a rich collection of anecdotes, photographs, and drawings recalling his years at the magazine, exhibited Gill's pointed wit and sparkling prose. *Ways of Loving: Two Novellas and Eighteen Short Stories* (1974) was praised for its urbanity, although some critics found the work lacking in substance. *A New York Life: Of Friends and Others* (1990) contains elegant, witty sketches of many of Gill's friends and acquaintances—including Dorothy Parker, Eleanor Roosevelt, Alec Waugh, and Man Ray. He also wrote biographies, poems, novels, and plays.

Gilliatt \'gil-ē-ət\, Penelope (Ann Douglass) (b. March 25, 1932, London, Eng.—d. May 9, 1993, London) English writer of essays, short stories, screenplays, and novels. Her fiction was noted for its sensitive, sometimes wry look at modern life.

After winning a fiction-writing award from British *Vogue*, Gilliatt joined the magazine's staff and became its features editor. She later worked as a film critic for *The Observer* and *The New Yorker*. Her essays were collected in *Unholy Fools* (1973), *Three-Quarter Face* (1980), and *To Wit: Skin and Bones of Comedy* (1990).

Gilliatt wrote the screenplay *Sunday, Bloody Sunday* (1971), about a middle-aged man and woman and the young male lover they share. The ménage à trois theme appeared throughout her novels—*One by One* (1965), *A State of Change* (1967), *The Cutting Edge* (1978), *Mortal Matters* (1983), and *A Woman of Singular Occupation* (1988). Her short stories were collected in the volumes *What's It Like Out?* (1968), *Nobody's Business* (1972), *Splendid Lives* (1977), *Quotations from Other Lives* (1982), *They Sleep Without Dreaming* (1985), *22 Stories* (1986), and *Lingo* (1990).

Gilman \'gil-mən\, Charlotte Perkins, *original name* Charlotte Anna Perkins \'pər-kinz\, *married names* Stetson, Gilman (b. July 3, 1860, Hartford, Conn., U.S.—d. Aug. 17, 1935, Pasadena, Calif.) Leading theorist of the women's movement in the United States.

Gilman began her literary career in the 1890s with the publication of poetry, short stories, and essays of social analysis. She also gained worldwide fame as a lecturer, speaking on topics concerning women, ethics, labor, and society. In *Women and Economics* (1898), the work for which she is best known, she proposed that the sexual and maternal roles of women had been overemphasized to the detriment of their social and economic potential and that only economic independence could bring true freedom.

Gilman's autobiography, *The Living of Charlotte Perkins Gilman*, appeared in 1935. Among her other publications were a frequently anthologized short story, THE YELLOW WALLPAPER (1899), *The Home* (1903), *The Man-Made World* (1911), and *His Religion and Hers* (1923).

Gimpel the Fool \'gim-pəl\ Short story by Isaac Bashevis SINGER, published in 1945 in Yiddish as "Gimpl tam." It was later published in Singer's collection *Gimpel the Fool and Other Stories* (1957). Set in a bygone era in an eastern European shtetl (Jewish small town), the tale concerns Gimpel, a gullible man who responds to a lifetime of betrayal, heckling, and deception with childlike acceptance and complete faith.

Gin Game, The Two-act play by American dramatist D.L. Coburn, produced in 1976. Coburn's first play, it won the Pulitzer Prize for Drama in 1978, the year it was published.

The Gin Game centers on two lonely residents of a retirement home. While playing a series of gin rummy games, they undergo a painful review of their lives. Their four card games are marked by violent exchanges that intensify until ultimately their friendship is ruined.

Ginsberg \'ginz-ˌbərg\, Allen (b. June 3, 1926, Newark, N.J., U.S.) American poet whose epic poem HOWL (1956) is considered to be one of the most significant products of the BEAT MOVEMENT.

Ginsberg studied at Columbia University, where he became close friends with Jack Kerouac and William Burroughs, who were later to be numbered among the Beats. *Howl*, his first published book, laments what Ginsberg believed to have been the destruction by insanity of the "best minds of [his] generation." *Empty Mirror*, a collection of earlier poems, appeared in 1961 along with *Kaddish and Other Poems*, followed by REALITY SANDWICHES in 1963. KADDISH, a long confessional poem, is one of Ginsberg's most important works. He became an influential guru of the American youth counterculture in the late 1960s.

His later volumes of poetry include *Planet News* (1968); *The Fall of America: Poems of These States, 1965–1971* (1972); *Mind Breaths: Poems 1972–1977* (1978); and *White Shroud: Poems 1980–1985* (1986). His *Collected Poems 1947–1980* appeared in 1984.

Ginzberg, Asher *see* AḤAD HAʿAM.

Ginzburg \'gĕnts-ˌbürg\, Natalia, *original surname* Levi \'lä-vē\ (b. July 14, 1916, Palermo, Italy—d. Oct. 7, 1991, Rome) Italian writer noted for her unsentimental treatment of family relationships.

Ginzburg's literary career began with the publication of short stories in the Florentine periodical *Solaria*. Her first novella, *La strada che va in città* (1942; *The Road to the City*), is the story of a young peasant girl who, lured by the excitement of the city, is seduced by and marries a man she does not love. A second novella, *È stato così* (1947; *The Dry Heart*), also deals with an unhappy marriage. In *Tutti i nostri ieri* (1952; U.K. title, *Dead Yesterdays*; U.S. titles, *A Light for Fools* and *All Our Yesterdays*), Ginzburg portrayed the crises of the Italian younger generation during the Fascist period. *Lessico famigliare* (1963; *Family Sayings*) is a novelistic memoir.

Ginzberg also wrote several dramas, notable among which are *Ti ho sposato per allegria* (performed 1966; *I Married You for the Fun of It*) and *L'inserzione* (performed 1968; *The Advertisement*); several collections of critical essays, including *Mai devi domandarmi* (1970; *Never Must You Ask Me*); and a biography of the poet and novelist Alessandro Manzoni, *La famiglia Manzoni* (1983). In 1990 she published *Serena Cruz, o la vera giustizia* ("Serena Cruz, or True Justice").

Giono \zhyȯ-'nō\, Jean (b. March 30, 1895, Manosque, Fr.—d. Oct. 8, 1970, Manosque) French novelist, a celebrant of nature, most of whose works are set in Provence.

A love of nature came to Giono from his mountain town and from the shepherd family with whom, as a boy, he spent his summers. An infantryman in World War I, he later described the horrors of war in *Le Grand Troupeau* (1931; *To the Slaughterhouse*).

His popularity grew in the late 1920s with a series of regionalist, anti-intellectual novels about the nobility of simple people. The series culminated in such works as the trilogy *Le Chant du monde* (1934; *Song of the World*), which, like most of his work, was a protest against modern civilization.

After World War II, Giono developed a new style: concise, lean, and concentrated on storytelling. Among his best works of these years are *Le Hussard sur le toit* (1952; *The Horseman on the Roof*) and *Le Bonheur fou* (1957; *The Straw Man*). The later novels *Deux cavaliers de l'orage* (1965; *Two Riders of the Storm*) and *Ennemonde et autres caractères* (1968; *Ennemonde*) are lyrical portrayals of the people and countryside of Provence.

Giovanni \jĕ-ō-'vän-ē\, Nikki, *byname of* Yolande Cornelia Giovanni, Jr. (b. June 7, 1943, Knoxville, Tenn., U.S.) African-American poet whose writings ranged from calls for violent revolution to poems for children and intimate personal statements.

Giovanni entered Nashville's Fisk University in 1960. By 1967, when she received her B.A., she was firmly committed to the civil-rights movement and the concept of black power. In her first three collections of poems, *Black Feeling, Black Talk* (1968), *Black Judgement* (1968), and *Re: Creation* (1970), her content is urgently revolutionary and suffused with deliberate interpretation of experience through a black consciousness.

Giovanni's experiences as a single mother then began to influence her poetry. *Spin a Soft Black Song* (1971), *Ego-Tripping* (1973), and *Vacation Time* (1980) were collections of poems for children. She returned to political concerns in *Those Who Ride the Night Winds* (1983), with dedications to African-American heroes and heroines. In *Gemini* (1971) she presents autobiographical reminiscences, and *Sacred Cows . . . and Other Edibles* (1988) is a collection of her essays.

Giovanni's Room \jō-'vän-ē\ Novel by James BALDWIN, published in 1956, about the conflict in the sexual identity of a young expatriate American in Paris.

After a single homosexual experience in adolescence, David represses his unacceptable impulses. In Paris, he meets Hella Lincoln. He is determined to live the life that he thinks is expected of a male in white, middle-class Western culture. He and Hella have an affair, and David proposes marriage.

While Hella is in Spain considering his proposal, David has an affair lasting several months with Giovanni, an Italian bartender. Still unable to reconcile homosexuality with the life he envisions for himself, David rejects Giovanni. David and Hella go to the south of France. She finds him in a homosexual bar with a sailor and realizes what David's relationship with Giovanni had been. David is left alone, abandoned by Hella, and still in conflict over his sexuality.

Gippius \'gʲepʲ-i-ús\ *or* **Hippius** \'hʲepʲ-\, Zinaida Nikolayevna (b. Nov. 8 [Nov. 20, New Style], 1869, Belyov, Russia—d. Sept. 9, 1945, Paris, Fr.) Russian Symbolist poet who wrote in a metaphysical vein.

The wife of the poet and novelist Dmitry MEREZHKOVSKY, who was a leader among the Symbolists of the early 1900s, Gippius made her own place in Russian literature. In addition to poetry, she wrote plays, novels, short stories, and critical and political essays.

During the Revolution of 1905, Gippius and her husband became zealous revolutionaries and she wrote political verse. With the failure of the revolution, the couple emigrated to Paris; they returned to Russia before the outbreak of World War I but took a vehemently anti-Bolshevik attitude. In late 1919 they left the Soviet Union, settling in Paris. Gippius continued to write and produced several bitter, angry works against the Bolsheviks.

Giraldi \jē-'räl-dē\, Giambattista, *also called* Cynthius \'sin-thē-əs\, *Italian* Cinzio \'chĕnt-sē-yō\ *or* Cinthio \'sin-thē-ō\ (b. 1504, Ferrara [Italy]—d. Dec. 30, 1573, Ferrara) Italian poet and dramatist who wrote the first modern tragedy on classical principles to appear on the Italian stage (*Orbecche*), and who was one of the first writers of tragicomedy.

Giraldi was influenced by the revival of Aristotelian literary principles after the publication in Latin of the original text of Aristotle's *Poetics* in 1536. In his poem *Ercole* (1557; "Hercules") he tried to reconcile the Aristotelian rules with modern taste. In his own tragedies—*Orbecche* (1541), his only strictly Senecan tragedy; *Didone* (1542); *Altile* (1543); *Cleopatra* (1543); *Selene*; *Eufimia*; *Arrenopia*; *Epitia*, from which William Shakespeare's *Measure for Measure* derives; and *Antivalomeni* (1549)—he included new dramatic elements while conforming to the Aristotelian rules.

Writing for a popular audience, he gave them horror and violence, but he altered the Senecan model to provide a happy ending, thus producing tragicomedy. His *Ecatommiti* (1565), 112 moralistic stories collected according to the pattern of Giovanni Boccaccio's *Decameron*, showed a preference for direct narrative. These stories were imitated in France, Spain, and England, and Shakespeare's *Othello* derives from one of them.

Giraudoux \zhē-rō-'dü\, Jean, *in full* Hyppolyte-Jean Giraudoux (b. Oct. 29, 1882, Bellac, Fr.—d. Jan. 31, 1944, Paris) French novelist, essayist, and playwright who created an impressionistic form of drama by emphasizing dialogue and style rather than realism.

Giraudoux became known as an avant-garde writer with a group of early poetic novels, such as *Suzanne et le Pacifique* (1921). Giraudoux's theatrical career began in 1928 with *Siegfried*, a dramatization of his novel *Siegfried et le limousin* (1922). Plays such as *Électre* (1937) were adapted from the classical tradition, such as *Cantique des cantiques* (1938; "Song of Songs") from the biblical tradition, and such as *Ondine* (1939) from the folk tradition.

Among Giraudoux's other important works are *La Guerre de Troie n'aura pas lieu* (1935; *Tiger at the Gates*) and *La Folle de Chaillot* (1946; *The Madwoman of Chaillot*), in which a tribunal of elderly, eccentric Parisian ladies, assisted by a ragpicker, wipe out a world of speculators. He also wrote film scripts.

Girls of Slender Means, The   Novel by Muriel SPARK, published in a shortened version in 1963 in the *Saturday Evening Post* and published in book form later that year.

The novel, set primarily in London during World War II, focuses on the inhabitants of a residential club for unmarried women and on the friendship of several of them with a young man named Nicholas Farringdon. When tragedy strikes and 13 of the women are killed, Nicholas realizes that there is no safety anywhere, especially for those on whom fortune had once seemed to smile. This epiphany stimulates his conversion to Roman Catholicism. Years later, he dies in Haiti, where he has gone as a missionary.

Girodias \zhē-ród-'yàs\, Maurice, *original surname* Kahane \kə-'hản\ (b. April 12, 1919, Paris, Fr.—d. July 3, 1990, Paris) French publisher of banned books, including many classics of modern literature.

As a young man Girodias worked closely with his father, Jack Kahane, whose Obelisk Press published such classics of erotica as Henry Miller's *Tropic of Cancer* (1934) and Frank Harris' *My Life and Loves*, 3 vol. (1923–27). Girodias, who took his mother's non-Jewish maiden name during World War II, was unable to regain control of Obelisk after the war, and in 1953 he founded Olympia Press. He quickly built a reputation for publishing books of merit that were censored or banned in other countries, including Vladimir Nabokov's *Lolita* (1955) and various works by Miller, Samuel Beckett, J.P. Donleavy, Lawrence Durrell, Jean Genet, Nikos Kazantzakis, William Burroughs, Georges Bataille, and the Marquis de Sade.

Gironella \ˌkē-rō-'nãl-yä\, José María (b. Dec. 31, 1917, Darníus, Gerona, Spain)   Spanish author best remembered for his

historical novel *Los cipreses creen en Dios* (1953; *The Cypresses Believe in God*), in which the conflicts within a fictitious family symbolize the dissension that overtook the people of Spain during the years preceding the Civil War of 1936–39.

Gironella served in the Nationalist army during the Civil War and later worked as a newspaper reporter and correspondent. In 1945 he published a volume of poetry and in 1946 his first novel, *Un hombre* (*Where the Soil Was Shallow*).

The chronicle begun in *Los cipreses* was continued with *Un millón de muertos* (1961; *One Million Dead*), *Ha estallado la paz* (1966; *Peace After War*), and *Los hombres lloran solos* (1986; "The Men Cry Alone"). Gironella also wrote short stories, memoirs, travel books, and essays.

Gísla saga \'gēs-lə\   Icelandic saga set in northwestern Iceland and written probably before the middle of the 13th century, which tells of an outlaw poet Gísli Súrsson (d. *c.* 980), who was himself killed for avenging his wife's brother by killing his sister's husband. The saga reveals Christian influence, for Gísli chose loyalty to his wife over loyalty to his blood kin.

Gissing \'gis-iŋ\, George (Robert) (b. Nov. 22, 1857, Wakefield, Yorkshire, Eng.—d. Dec. 28, 1903, Saint-Jean de Luz, Fr.)   English novelist, noted for the realism of his novels about lower-middle-class life and for his acute perception of the social position and psychology of women.

Gissing was educated at a Quaker boarding school and at Owens College, Manchester, where his academic career was brilliant. Yet his personal life was, until the last few years, mostly unhappy; twice involved in miserable marriages, he led the life of near poverty and constant drudgery that he described in the novels NEW GRUB STREET, 3 vol. (1891), and *The Private Papers of Henry Ryecroft* (1903). Before he was 21 he conceived the ambition of writing a long series of novels, somewhat in the manner of Honoré de Balzac, whom he admired. The first of these, *Workers in the Dawn*, appeared in 1880, to be followed by 21 others. Between 1886 and 1895 he published one or more novels every year, among them *Demos* (1886), *The Emancipated* (1890), *Born in Exile* (1892), *The Odd Women* (1893), and *In the Year of Jubilee* (1894). He also wrote *Charles Dickens: A Critical Study* (1898), a perceptive piece of literary criticism.

Gītāñjali \gē-'tän-jə-lē\   A collection of poetry, the most famous work by Rabindranath TAGORE, published in India in 1910. Tagore then translated it into prose poems in English, as *Gitanjali: Song Offerings*, and it was published in 1912 with an introduction by William Butler Yeats. Medieval Indian lyrics of devotion provided Tagore's model for the poems of *Gītāñjali*. Love is the principal subject, although some poems detail the internal conflict between spiritual longings and earthly desires. Much of his imagery is drawn from nature.

Giusti \'jüs-tē\, Giuseppe (b. May 13, 1809, Monsummano, Tuscany [Italy]—d. March 31, 1850, Florence)   Northern Italian poet who is known for his satires on Austrian rule during the early years of Italy's nationalistic movement (the Risorgimento).

Giusti's first collections of satirical poems had to be printed outside Italy without the author's name. His first notable satire, written in 1833, was *La guigliottina a vapore* ("The Steam Guillotine"), which announced that the Chinese had invented a steam guillotine which would make decapitation much more efficient for dictators. Other satires defended Italy or bemoaned its political and social state.

Giusti also wrote satires on the death in 1835 of the Austrian emperor Francis I and on the crowning of the new emperor. *Sant'Ambrogio* (*c.* 1846), in which the poet's hostility toward Austrian troops attending a mass turns into a feeling of sympathy and solidarity with them as they join in singing a chorus by

Giuseppe Verdi, is a very moving poem and is often considered his masterpiece.

Gjellerup \'gyel-ə-rüp\, Karl Adolph (b. June 2, 1857, Roholte, Den.—d. Oct. 11, 1919, Klotzsche, Ger.) Danish poet and novelist who together with his compatriot Henrik Pontoppidan won the Nobel Prize for Literature in 1917.

The son of a parson, Gjellerup studied theology, but after coming under the influence of Darwinism and the new radical ideas of the critic Georg Brandes, he thought of himself as an atheist. This atheism was proclaimed in his first book, *En idealist shildring af Epigonus* (1878; "An Idealist, A Description of Epigonus"), and in his farewell to theology, *Germanernes lærling* (1882; "The Teutons' Apprentice"). The latter book, however, indicated the path that was to take him, via German idealist philosophy and Romanticism, back to a conscious search for religion. He finally found satisfaction in studying Buddhism and other Oriental religions. This last period of his life is represented by two books: *Minna* (1889), a novel of contemporary Germany, where Gjellerup lived in his later years, and *Pilgrimen Kamanita* (1906; *The Pilgrim Kamanita*), an exotic tale of reincarnation set in India.

Gladkov \ˌglət-'kòf\, Fyodor Vasilyevich (b. June 9 [June 21, New Style], 1883, Chernavka, near Saratov, Russia—d. Dec. 20, 1958, Moscow, U.S.S.R.) Russian writer best known for *Tsement* (1925; *Cement*), the first postrevolutionary novel to dramatize Soviet industrial development. Although crudely written, the work anticipated in two important ways the future trends of Soviet literature. Its theme of reconstruction was to become commonplace in Soviet fiction following an official demand in 1928 for "five-year-plan novels"; and its positive hero, whose confidence overcomes apathy and despair, became a model for the heroes of Socialist Realism.

Outstanding among Gladkov's later works is his volume of personal reminiscences, *Povest o detstve* (1949; "Story of Childhood"), which was awarded the Stalin Prize in 1950.

glaistig or **glastig** \'glas-tik, 'glash-, -tig\ [Scottish Gaelic *glaistig*] A female sprite in Celtic mythology.

Glan-y-gors, Jac. Pseudonym of John JONES.

Glasgow \'glas-gō\, Ellen (Anderson Gholson) (b. April 22, 1873, Richmond, Va., U.S.—d. Nov. 21, 1945, Richmond) Pulitzer Prize-winning American novelist whose realistic depiction of life in her native Virginia helped direct Southern literature away from sentimentality and nostalgia.

Glasgow was irregularly schooled because of delicate health but otherwise lived the life of a Southern belle except for her intense seriousness about becoming a novelist of stature. In *The Voice of the People* (1900) she began a planned social history of Virginia from 1850. The series also included *The Battle-Ground* (1902), *The Deliverance* (1904), *The Romance of a Plain Man* (1909), and *Virginia* (1913).

Glasgow was past the age of 50 when she first gained serious attention from the critics with *Barren Ground* (1925), a story of the Piedmont countryside of Virginia. She then published a trilogy of ironic novels of manners set in Richmond (disguised as "Queenborough"): *The Romantic Comedians* (1926), *They Stooped to Folly* (1929), and *The Sheltered Life* (1932), the last often linked with *Barren Ground* as her best work. Glasgow's memoirs, *The Woman Within* (1954), and her *Letters* (1958) were published after her death. *The Collected Stories* appeared in 1963.

Glaspell \'glas-pel\, Susan (b. July 1, 1882, Davenport, Iowa, U.S.—d. July 27, 1948, Provincetown, Mass.) American dramatist and novelist who, with her husband, George Cram COOK, founded the influential Provincetown Players in 1915.

Glaspell's first novel was *The Glory of the Conquered* (1909), and some of her short stories were collected in *Lifted Masks* (1912). Cook, whom she married in 1913, interested her in socialist ideas, which figured in her next novel, *The Visioning* (1911). While summering in Provincetown in 1915, Glaspell and Cook launched the Provincetown Players, ostensibly to produce their one-act play *Suppressed Desires*, a satire on psychoanalysis. Two of Glaspell's full-length plays—*Inheritors* (1921) and *The Verge* (1922)—were also produced by the Provincetown group.

After Cook's death in 1924, Glaspell settled in Provincetown. In *The Road to the Temple* (1926), she gave a romantic account of her husband's life. Her last play was the Pulitzer Prize-winning *Alison's House* (1931), which is about the impact of a great poet (said to be patterned on Emily Dickinson) on her family 18 years after her death. Her later novels include *The Fugitive's Return* (1929) and *The Morning Is Near Us* (1940).

Glass Bead Game, The Final novel by Hermann HESSE, published in two volumes in 1943 in German as *Das Glasperlenspiel*, and sometimes translated as *Magister Ludi*. The book is an intricate bildungsroman about humanity's eternal quest for enlightenment and for synthesis of the intellectual and the participatory life.

Set in the 23rd century, the novel purports to be a biography of Josef Knecht ("servant" in German), who has been reared in Castalia, the remote place his society has provided for the intellectual elite to grow and flourish. Since childhood, Knecht has been consumed with mastering the Glass Bead Game, which requires a synthesis of aesthetics and scientific arts, such as mathematics, music, logic, and philosophy. This he achieves in adulthood, becoming a Magister Ludi (Master of the Game).

Glassco \'glas-kō\, John, *pseudonyms* Sylvia Bayer \'bā-ər, 'ber\, George Colman \'kōl-mən\, Jean de Saint-Luc \saⁿ-'lük\, *and* Miles Underwood \'ən-dər-ˌwùd\ (b. Dec. 15, 1909, Montreal, Que., Can.—d. Jan. 29, 1981, Montreal) Canadian author whose poetry, short stories, novels, memoirs, and translations were notable for their versatility and sophistication.

Glassco abandoned his studies at McGill University to join the expatriote community in Paris, an experience he chronicled in the celebrated *Memoirs of Montparnasse* (1970). He earned acclaim for his first published work, the poem "Conan's Fig," which appeared in the international quarterly *transition* in 1928. After contracting tuberculosis, he returned to Quebec in the early 1930s.

While his poetry dealt with the simplicity of rural life in the Eastern Townships of Quebec, his prose, inspired by the Decadents of the 19th century, was heavy with irony and eroticism. He wrote *Under the Hill* (1959), the completion of an unfinished romance by Aubrey Beardsley; *English Governess* (1960; also published as *Harriet Marwood, Governess*), a parody of Victorian pornography; and *The Fatal Woman* (1974), a collection of three novellas that explore the dehumanization of sexual fantasies. His verse collections, elegant and classical, include *The Deficit Made Flesh* (1958), *A Point of Sky* (1964), and *Selected Poems* (1971).

Glass family \'glas\ A fictional family composed of precocious and unhappy adolescents and troubled adults whose lives and philosophies dominated the short stories of J.D. SALINGER. Originally published in *The New Yorker* magazine from the late 1940s to the early 1960s, the short fiction about the Glass family was collected in *Nine Stories* (1953), *Franny and Zooey* (1961), and *Raise High the Roof Beam, Carpenters* and *Seymour: An Introduction* (published together in 1963). The most prominent members of the family are Bessie Glass and her children Seymour, Buddy, Zooey (born Zachary), and Franny.

Glass Menagerie, The One-act drama by Tennessee WILLIAMS, produced in 1944 and published in 1945. Considered by some critics to be Williams' finest drama, *The Glass Menagerie* launched his career.

Amanda Wingfield lives in a St. Louis tenement, clinging to the myth of her early years as a Southern belle. Her daughter Laura, who wears a leg brace, is painfully shy and often seeks solace in her collection of small glass animals. Amanda's son Tom is desperate to escape his stifling home life and his warehouse job. Amanda encourages him to bring "gentleman callers" home to his sister. When Tom brings Jim O'Connor for dinner, Amanda believes that her prayers have been answered. Laura blossoms during Jim's visit, flattered by his attention. After kissing her, however, he confesses that he is engaged. Laura retreats to her shell, and Amanda blames Tom, who leaves home for good after a final fight with his mother.

Glatigny \glȧ-tēn-'yē\, Albert-Alexandre, *in full* Joseph-Albert-Alexandre Glatigny (b. May 21, 1839, Lillebonne, Fr.—d. April 16, 1873, Sèvres) French poet of the Parnassian school, known for his poems of satirical comment and for his peripatetic life as a strolling actor and improvisator.

Glatigny wrote a historical drama at age 16 and a year later joined a traveling theater company. While on the road he was inspired to write his first book of poems, *Les Vignes folles* (1860; "The Mad Vines"). Later collections include *Les Flèches d'or* (1864; "The Golden Barbs") and *Gilles et Pasquins* (1872).

His one-act comedy in verse, *L'Illustre Brizacier* (1873; "The Illustrious Brizacier"), was based on his own imprisonment in Corsica when he was mistaken for a wanted criminal. His other plays are *Le Singe* (1872; "The Monkey") and *Les Folies-Marigny* (1872; "The Marigny Madnesses").

Glatstein \'glȧt-,shtēn\, Jacob, *also called* Yankev Glatshteyn (b. Aug. 20, 1896, Lublin, Poland, Russian Empire—d. Nov. 19, 1971, New York, N.Y., U.S.) Yiddish poet, novelist, and literary critic who in 1920 helped establish the Inzikhist ("Introspectivist") literary movement. In later years he was one of the outstanding figures in mid-20th century American Yiddish literature.

Glatstein immigrated to the United States in 1914 and studied law at New York University. In the 1920s he edited and wrote for *In zikh* ("In Oneself"), a modernist poetry journal that celebrated personal experience in free and naturalistic verse, rejecting traditional stylized lyricism and metric elegance. His volume *Yankev Glatshteyn* (1921) was the first collection of Yiddish poems written solely in free verse.

From 1938 Glatstein turned increasingly to elegiac verse mourning the destruction of traditional Jewish life in eastern Europe, as in the poem "A gute nakht, velt" ("Good Night, World"). Among his 12 poetry collections are *Fraye ferzn* (1926; "Free Verses"), *Dem tatns shotn* (1953; "The Father's Shadow"), *Di freyd fun yidishn vort* (1961; "The Joy of the Yiddish Word"), and *A yid fun lublin* (1966; "A Jew from Lublin"). He wrote two autobiographical novels, *Ven Yash iz geforn* (1938; *When Yash Set Out*) and *Ven Yash iz gekumen* (1940; *Homecoming at Twilight*). Many of his essays are collected in the two-volume *In tokh genumen* (1947–56; "The Heart of the Matter").

Glaucus \'glȯ-kəs\ ("Gleaming") Name of several figures in Greek mythology, the most important of whom were the following:

Glaucus, surnamed Pontius, was a sea divinity. Originally a fisherman and diver of Boeotia, he once ate a magical herb and leaped into the sea, where he was changed into a god and endowed with the gift of prophecy. Another version made him spring into the sea for love of the sea god Melicertes.

Glaucus of Potniae near Thebes was the son of Sisyphus (king of Corinth) by his wife Merope and father of the hero Bellerophon. He was known for the manner of his death. According to one legend, he fed his mares on human flesh in order to make them fierce in battle. This angered the gods, who caused him to be thrown from his chariot and torn to pieces by the horses. Another version of the story says that the horses attacked Glaucus because they were made mad by the gods, who wanted to punish Glaucus for keeping the horses from breeding.

Glaucus, the son of the Cretan king Minos and his wife Pasiphae, fell into a jar of honey when a child and was smothered. The seer Polyeidus (Polyidus) finally discovered the child but on confessing his inability to restore him to life was shut up in a vault with the corpse. There he killed a serpent and, seeing it revived by a companion who laid a certain herb upon it, brought the dead Glaucus back to life with the same herb.

Glaucus, grandson of Bellerophon, was a Lycian prince who assisted Priam in the Trojan War.

gleeman \'glē-,man\ [Old English *glēoman,* from *glēo* entertainment, music +*man* man] In Anglo-Saxon times, a professional traveling entertainer who recited poetry to the accompaniment of musical instruments such as the harp. The gleemen sometimes wrote their own poetry, but often the poetry they recited had been written by a scop (a poet attached to a particular court).

Glengarry Glen Ross \,glen-'gar-ē-,glen-'rȯs\ Play in two acts by David MAMET, originally produced in London in 1983 and published in 1984, when it won the Pulitzer Prize for drama. The play concerns a group of ruthless real-estate salesmen who compete to sell lots in Florida developments known as Glengarry Highlands and Glen Ross Farms. Built on the strength of its explosive and often profane dialogue, *Glengarry Glen Ross* depicts the real-estate industry as seedy and unscrupulous.

Glissant \glē-'sän\, Édouard (b. Sept. 21, 1928, Le Lamentin, Martinique) West Indian poet and novelist who wrote in French, one of several members of the Negritude movement from the Antilles.

A disciple and compatriot of the poet Aimé Césaire, who founded the Negritude movement to promote an African culture free of colonial influences, Glissant recorded the awakening of colonized peoples. He combined the accents of revolt and liberation with an epic tone in such volumes of poetry as *Un Champ d'îles* (1953; "An Expanse of Islands") and *Les Indes* (1956; "The Indies"). His *La Lézarde* (1958; "The Crack"; *The Ripening*) was a prizewinning novel. In *Le Quatrième Siècle* (1962; "The Fourth Century"), he retraced the history of slavery in Martinique and the rise of a generation of young West Indians, trained in European universities, who would reclaim their land.

Glissant's other works include the novels *Malemort* (1975) and *La Case du commandeur* (1981; "The Commander's Cabin"); the verse collections *Boises* (1977; "Woods"), *Pays rêvé, pays réel* (1985; "Countries Dreamed, Countries Real"), and *Fastes* (1991; "Annals of Great Deeds"); and the play *Monsieur Toussaint* (1961).

Globe Theatre \'glōb\ Famous London theater in which the plays of William Shakespeare were performed after 1599. It was built by two brothers, Richard and Cuthbert Burbage. Half the shares in the new theater were kept by the Burbages. The rest were assigned equally to Shakespeare and other members of the CHAMBERLAIN'S MEN (the company of players who acted there), of which Richard Burbage was principal actor and of which Shakespeare had been a leading member since late 1594. The theater was destroyed by fire in 1613, rebuilt in 1614, and finally pulled down in 1644.

glosa \'glô-sə\ [Spanish, literally, gloss] Spanish verse form in which an introductory stanza called a *cabeza* is followed by one stanza for each line of the *cabeza*, in which the line is explained or glossed. The form was instituted by court poets of the 14th or 15th century.

gloss \'glôs\ [Greek *glôssa* difficult word requiring explanation, language, tongue] **1.** A translation or a brief explanation or definition of a textual word or expression felt to be difficult or obscure. Glosses can appear in the margin or between the lines of a text or in a separate vocabulary book based on the text. For example, ancient Greek manuscripts were often published with Latin translations of difficult words, and medieval manuscripts often included vernacular translations of Latin words. **2.** An expanded interpretation of or commentary on a textual word, expression, or passage.

Gloucester, Earl of \'glôs-tər\ Fictional character, a gullible father in William Shakespeare's KING LEAR. Gloucester's story provides a parallel subplot to the tragedy of Lear. Like the king, the Earl of Gloucester is a father suffering from filial ingratitude and from his false judgment of his children.

Głowacki, Aleksander. Real name of Bolesław PRUS.

Glubdubdrib \ˌgləb-'dəb-ˌdrib\ The Island of Sorcerers in the third section of GULLIVER'S TRAVELS by Jonathan Swift. On the island, hero Lemuel Gulliver can summon the great men of old; he thereby discovers the many deceptions of history.

Glück \'glik\, Louise (Elisabeth) (b. April 22, 1943, New York, N.Y., U.S.) Poet known for her insights into the self and for her severe lyricism. Glück was noted for her willingness to confront in her writing the horrible, the difficult, and the painful.

After attending Sarah Lawrence College and Columbia University, from 1971 Glück taught poetry at numerous colleges and universities. Her first collection of poetry, *Firstborn* (1968), used a variety of first-person personae, all disaffected or angry. The collection's tone disturbed many critics, but Glück's exquisitely controlled language and imaginative use of rhyme and meter delighted others. Although its outlook was equally grim, her collection *The House on Marshland* (1975) showed a greater mastery of voice. Her adoption of different perspectives became increasingly imaginative; for example, in "The Sick Child," from the collection *Descending Figure* (1980), her voice is that of a mother in a museum painting looking out at the bright gallery. The poems in *The Triumph of Achilles* (1985), which won the National Book Critics Circle Award for poetry, address archetypal concerns of classic myth, fairy tales, and the Bible. These concerns are also evident in *Ararat* (1990), which was praised for searing honesty in its examination of the family and the self. *The Wild Iris* was published in 1992.

Glueckel \'glük-əl\ of Hameln \'häm-əln\ (b. 1646, Hamburg [Germany]—d. 1724, Metz, Lorraine [France]) German-Jewish diarist whose seven books of memoirs, *Zikhroynes*, written in Yiddish with passages in Hebrew, reveal much about the history, culture, and everyday life of contemporary Jews in central Europe. Glueckel wrote the first five sections between 1691 and 1699. She resumed writing in 1715, finishing the final two sections in 1719.

After the Jews were expelled from Hamburg in 1649, Glueckel's family moved to Altona, where she received a traditional religious education. At age 14 she was married to Ḥayyim of Hameln, with whom she had 12 children. After her husband's death in 1689, she successfully managed his business, but in 1700 she married Cerf Lévy, a wealthy banker of Metz, who soon lost his own fortune as well as hers.

Memoirs of Glueckel of Hameln contains information about the lives of court Jews and wealthy Jewish merchants and about the status of ordinary women. Interspersed with family history and visits to such cities as Hanover, Berlin, and Amsterdam are pious sayings, devotional prayers, folk tales, and parables. The memoirs are a significant source for linguistic and philological studies of pre-Modern Yiddish.

glyconic \glī-'kän-ik\ [Greek *Glykôneus,* a derivative of *Glykôn,* Greek poet of unknown date] The most common Aeolic verse form used for Greek and Latin lyric poetry and named for the Greek poet Glycon, about whom little is known. The glyconic is usually scanned as ⏓ ⏓ | — ∪ ∪ — | ⏓ —. The catalectic form (⏓ ⏓ | — ∪ ∪ — | —) is known as a pherecratic. The glyconic was sometimes extended by adding a dactyl (— ∪ ∪), a cretic (— ∪ —), or a choriamb (— ∪ ∪ —) at the beginning, middle, or end. The result, used, for example, by Sappho and Alcaeus, was called *Asclepiadean* and was scanned ⏓ ⏓ | — ∪ ∪ — — ∪ ∪ — | ⏓ — or ⏓ ⏓ | — ∪ ∪ — — ∪ ∪ — | ⏓ —.

Glyn \'glin\, Elinor, *original surname* Sutherland \'səth-ər-lənd\ (b. Oct. 17, 1864, Jersey, Channel Islands—d. Sept. 23, 1943, London) English novelist and short-story writer known for her highly romantic tales with luxurious settings and improbable plots.

Glyn's first book, *The Visits of Elizabeth*, was an epistolary novel, consisting of a group of letters from a young girl to her mother, that described the foibles and philanderings of a group of European aristocrats. First serialized in the *World*, it was published in book form in 1900. Encouraged by its wide success, she wrote several more "society novels" before turning to romances. *Three Weeks* (1907), the story of an adulterous relationship between a Balkan queen and an Englishman, caused a sensation. It was widely read and widely condemned. *His Hour* (1910; U.S. title, *When His Hour Came*), one of her best romances, was set in the court of St. Petersburg. *The Career of Katherine Bush* (1916) was her first novel in which the heroine was not of aristocratic birth.

In 1920 she began her career as a scriptwriter in Hollywood, where a number of her own novels were filmed. These included *Three Weeks* and *It* (1927), which was set in the United States. Glyn completed her autobiography, *Romantic Adventure,* in 1936.

gnome \'nōm, 'nō-ˌmē\ *plural* gnomes *or* gnomae \'nō-ˌmē, -ˌmī\ [Greek *gnômē* thought, opinion, maxim] A brief reflection or maxim such as an APHORISM or PROVERB.

The form of such statements may be either imperative, as in the famous command "know thyself," or indicative, as in the English adage "Too many cooks spoil the broth." Gnomes are found in the literature of many cultures; among the best-known examples are those contained in the biblical book of Proverbs. They are found in early Greek literature, both poetry and prose, from the time of Homer and Hesiod onward.

Gnomes appear frequently in Old English epic and lyric poetry. In *Beowulf* they are often interjected into the narrative, drawing a moral from the hero's actions with such phrases as "Thus a man ought to act." The main collections of Old English gnomes are to be found in the Exeter Book and the 11th-century Cotton Psalter.

gnome \'nōm\ [New Latin *gnomus*] In European tradition, a dwarfish, subterranean goblin or earth spirit who guards mines of precious treasures hidden in the earth. Gnomes are represented in medieval mythologies as small, physically deformed (usually hunchbacked) creatures resembling dry, gnarled old humans. Gob, the king of the gnome race, ruled with a magic sword and is said, as an elemental figure associated with earth (and thus the humor black bile), to have influenced the melancholic temperament of humans.

The word first appears in the works of the 16th-century alchemist Paracelsus, in which gnomes were described as able to move through solid earth as fish move through water.

gnomic \\'nō-mik\\ [Greek *gnōmikós,* a derivative of *gnṓmē* maxim]   **1.** Characterized by or expressive of aphorism or sententious wisdom, especially concerning the human condition or human conduct.   **2.** Of a poet, given to the composition of gnomic poetry.

gnomic poetry   Aphoristic verse containing short, memorable statements of traditional wisdom and morality. Gnomic poetry is most commonly associated with the 6th-century-BC poets Solon and Simonides and with the elegiac couplets of Theognis and Phocylides. Their aphorisms were collected into anthologies, called *gnomologia* (or gnomologies), and used in instructing the young. One of the best-known *gnomologia* was compiled by Stobaeus in the 5th century AD, and such collections remained popular in the Middle Ages.

Alexander Pope's *An Essay on Man* (1733–34) offers a more modern example of the use of couplets of distilled wisdom interspersed throughout a long poem.

Go and catch a falling star   Poem by John Donne, also known as SONG.

gobbet \\'gäb-ət\\   A fragment or extract of literature or music.

goblin \\'gäb-lin\\ [Middle English *gobelin* demon, incubus, from Old French *gobelin* or Medieval Latin *gobelinus,* perhaps ultimately from Greek *kóbalos* scamp, rogue, demon invoked by rogues]   In folklore, an ugly or grotesque wandering sprite, sometimes conceived as evil and malicious and sometimes as merely playful and mischievous.

Goblin Market   Poem by Christina ROSSETTI, published in 1862 in the collection *Goblin Market and Other Poems.* Comprising 567 irregularly rhyming lines, the poem recounts the plight of Laura, who succumbs to the enticement of the goblins and eats the fruit they sell. Her sister, Lizzie, resists the "fruit-call" as she watches Laura grow sick from her indulgence. At last, Lizzie revisits the goblins' glen to buy more fruit for Laura and withstands an assault by the malevolent beings without tasting a drop of the "goblin pulp and goblin dew." Her victory redeems Laura and drives the goblins from the glen.

Illustration by Laurence Housman for the 1893 edition of *Goblin Market*

god \\'gäd, 'gȯd\\ [Old English]   A being or object believed to have more than natural attributes and powers and to require human worship; specifically, one controlling a particular aspect or part of reality.

Godden \\'gäd-ən\\, Rumer, *in full* Margaret Rumer Godden Haynes-Dixon \\'hānz-'dik-sən\\ (b. Dec. 10, 1907, Eastbourne, Sussex, Eng.)   Writer whose many works reflect her personal experiences in colonial India and in England.

She was taken in infancy to India and lived there until adolescence, when she was sent to a boarding school in England. She eventually returned to India and wrote several books, beginning with *Chinese Puzzle* (1936). In later life she moved to Scotland, where she continued to write.

Black Narcissus (1939; film, 1946) concerns a group of English nuns who found a mission in the Himalayas. Underlying the plot are problems of cultures in conflict and obsessive love, both recurring themes in Godden's fiction. She introduced the first of many child protagonists in *Breakfast with the Nikolides* (1942), followed by *An Episode of Sparrows* (1955), *The Greengage Summer* (1958), and *China Court* (1961). *The River* (1946; film, 1951) depicts English children growing up in Bengal. *In This House of Brede* (1969) portrays contemporary life in an English Benedictine convent.

Among Godden's almost two dozen books for children are *The Doll's House* (1947), *The Fairy Doll* (1956), *The Story of Holly and Ivy* (1958), and *Miss Happiness and Miss Flower* (1961). With her sister Jon Godden, she wrote the memoirs *Two Under the Indian Sun* (1966) and *Shiva's Pigeons: An Experience of India* (1972), as well as the story collection *Mercy, Pity, Peace, and Love* (1989). She also published two volumes of autobiography, *A Time to Dance, No Time to Weep* (1987) and *A House with Four Rooms* (1989).

goddess \\'gäd-əs, 'gȯd-\\   A female god.

Godey's Lady's Book \\'gō-dē\\   A magazine that was one of the most successful and influential periodicals in the United States for much of the 19th century. Founded by Louis Antoine Godey in Philadelphia in 1830, *Godey's Lady's Book* was an important arbiter of fashion and etiquette. The magazine also published works by such American authors as Ralph Waldo Emerson, Henry Wadsworth Longfellow, Edgar Allan Poe, Nathaniel Hawthorne, and Harriet Beecher Stowe.

Edited by Godey until 1836, the magazine was then edited by Sarah Josepha Hale until 1877. In 1892, *Godey's* was moved to New York City and renamed *Godey's Magazine.* It published fiction by popular writers of the period until it ceased publication in 1898.

Godiva \\gə-'dī-və\\, Lady, *Old English* Godgifu \\'gȯd-yē-ˌvü\\ (fl. *c.* 1040–80)   Anglo-Saxon gentlewoman famous for her legendary ride while nude through Coventry, Warwickshire.

Godiva was the wife of Leofric, Earl of Mercia. The chronicler Florence of Worcester (d. 1118) mentions Leofric and Godiva with respect, but does not refer to the ride. There is no evidence connecting the rider with the historical Godiva.

The earliest extant source for the story is the *Chronica* (for the year 1057) of Roger of Wendover (d. 1236). He recounts that her husband, in exasperation over her ceaseless imploring that he reduce Coventry's heavy taxes, declared he would do so if she rode naked through the crowded marketplace. She did so, her hair covering all of her body except her legs. Ranulf Higden (d. 1364), in his *Polychronicon,* says that as a result Leofric freed the town from all tolls save those on horses. A later chronicle asserted that Godiva required the townsmen to remain indoors at the time fixed for her ride. Peeping Tom, a citizen who looked out his window, apparently became a part of the legend in the 17th century.

godling \'gȯd-liŋ, 'gäd-\ An inferior or purely local deity, particularly a supernatural being midway between a god and a fetish (an object regarded with superstitious reverence).

Godolphin \gə-'däl-fin\, Sidney (baptized Jan. 15, 1610—d. Feb. 9, 1643, Chagford, Devon, Eng.) English poet and royalist during the reign of Charles I.

Godolphin was educated at Exeter College, Oxford. He was elected a member of the House of Commons in 1628 and was again elected to the Short Parliament in March 1640 and to the Long Parliament in October 1640. During the first of the English Civil Wars, he joined the Royalist forces of Sir Ralph Hopton and, at age 33, was killed in action.

A few of Godolphin's poems were published in the 17th century; of these, the chief is *The Passion of Dido for Aeneas*, a translation from Virgil's fourth book of the *Aeneid*, apparently unfinished at Godolphin's death and completed and published by the poet Edmund Waller (1658). Other poems survived in manuscript collections. The first complete edition was by George Saintsbury, in *Minor Poets of the Caroline Period*, 3 vol. (1905–21).

Go Down, Moses \'mō-zəz, -zəs\ A collection of seven stories by William FAULKNER, first published in 1942 as a novel under the inaccurate title *Go Down, Moses, and Other Stories*; the title was corrected for the second printing. Set in Faulkner's fictional Yoknapatawpha County, the book contains some of the author's best writing.

The voices of Faulkner's South—black and white, comic and tragic—ring through this sprawling tale of the McCaslin clan. The tone ranges from the farcical to the profound. As the title suggests, the stories are rife with biblical themes. Although the seven stories were originally published separately, *Go Down, Moses* is best read as a novel of interconnecting generations, races, and dreams.

The first story, "Was," is considered a comic masterpiece. It opens with a raucous fox chase that suggests the theme and action of the story. Buck and Buddy, twin sons of Carothers McCaslin, chase their slave and half-brother, Turl; Turl chases his girlfriend Tennie, slave of Hubert and his sister Sibbey Beauchamp; and Sibbey, the only white woman in the countryside, pursues Buck. A poker game decides the fate of the couples and ownership of the slaves. "The Fire and the Hearth" establishes the dignity of Lucas Beauchamp, son of Turl and Tennie. "Pantaloon in Black," the story of a black man lynched for killing a deceitful white, has little relation to the other stories, but echoes their themes of love, loss, and racial tension. "The Old People" and THE BEAR feature Ike McCaslin's confrontations with nature. In "Delta Autumn," Ike, at age 79, is forced to confront his role in perpetuating the exploitation of his own black relatives. In the final story, "Go Down, Moses," Faulkner focuses not on inner family struggles but on the entire community.

God's Grandeur Sonnet by Gerard Manley HOPKINS, written in 1877 and published posthumously in 1918 in the collection *Poems of Gerard Manley Hopkins*. This celebratory poem suggests that God has imbued nature with an eternal freshness that is able to withstand the heavy burden of humanity.

God's Trombones (*in full* God's Trombones: Seven Negro Sermons in Verse) Volume of poetry by James Weldon JOHNSON, published in 1927. The work represents what the author called an "art-governed expression" of the traditional black preaching style. The constituent poems are an introductory prayer, "Listen, Lord—A Prayer," and seven verse sermons entitled "The Creation," "The Prodigal Son," "Go Down Death—A Funeral Sermon," "Noah Built the Ark," "The Crucifixion," "Let My People Go," and "The Judgment Day."

Although he identified himself as an agnostic, Johnson drew heavily throughout his career from the oral tradition and biblical poetry of his Christian upbringing. In *God's Trombones*, he conveys the raw power of fire-and-brimstone oratory while avoiding the hackneyed devices of dialectal transcription that had marred previous literature in the black idiom.

Godunov, Boris \ˌbȯ-'rʸēs-gə-dù-'nȯf, *Angl* 'bȯr-is-'gùd-ə-ˌnȯf\ The protagonist of Aleksandr Pushkin's historical tragedy BORIS GODUNOV.

Godwin \'gäd-win\, Francis (b. 1562, Hannington, Northamptonshire, Eng.—d. April 1633, Whitbourne, Herefordshire) Bishop and historian who wrote the first story of space travel in English literature, *The Man in the Moone; or, A Discourse of a Voyage Thither by Domingo Gonsales, the Speedy Messenger* (1638).

Godwin was a student at Christ Church, Oxford, at the time when the Italian philosopher Giordano Bruno was introducing his revolutionary ideas to the university. In his story Godwin accepts the new cosmology of Nicolaus Copernicus and Johannes Kepler and the new ideas of Galileo.

His other writings include *A Catalogue of the Bishops of England* (1601; Latin translation, by Godwin, *De Praesulibus Angliae*, 1616, 1743), containing thumbnail character studies, and *Rerum Anglicarum, Henrico VIII, Edwardo VI, et Maria Regnantibus* (1616), chronicling the English Reformation in a detached manner.

Godwin \'gäd-win\, Gail (Kathleen) (b. June 18, 1937, Birmingham, Ala., U.S.) American novelist who wrote about women searching for a personal identity and for meaning in their lives.

After graduating from the University of North Carolina in 1959, Godwin worked as a reporter for the Miami *Herald* and then worked from 1962 to 1965 at the U.S. embassy in London. Returning to the United States, she attended the University of Iowa. She examined the experiences of women smothered by marriage in the violent novel *The Perfectionists* (1970), which was based on her own brief marriage, and in *Glass People* (1972).

The protagonist of Godwin's widely admired *The Odd Woman* (1974) is a college teacher who attempts to come to terms with her family and her married lover. The three principal characters of *A Mother and Two Daughters* (1982) have close relationships with each other, yet grow in separate ways to self-fulfillment. Godwin also wrote the novels *Violet Clay* (1978), *The Finishing School* (1984), *A Southern Family* (1987), *Father Melancholy's Daughter* (1991), and *The Good Husband* (1994).

Goetel \'gœt-əl\, Ferdynand (b. May 15, 1890, Sucha, Galicia, Austria-Hungary [now in Poland]—d. Nov. 24, 1960, London, Eng.) Polish novelist and essayist.

Goetel became a writer after World War I when he returned to his liberated country from Russian Turkistan, where he had spent several years as a prisoner of war. In 1924 he published his memoir *Przez płonący Wschód* ("Through the Blazing East"), in which he describes his experiences in Russia during the Revolution of 1917 and the following civil war. His short stories, including "Pątnik Karapeta" (1923; "Karapeta the Pilgrim") and "Ludzkość" (1925; "Mankind"), were based on his observations of the Turkic peoples. *Z dnia na dzień* (1926; *From Day to Day*) is a novel interesting for its use of the diary form within the main narrative as a means of exploring character. In his political essay "Pod znakiem faszyzmu" (1939; "Under the Banner of Fascism") he did not hide his admiration for the Italian fascist Benito Mussolini.

Goethe \\'gœ̄-tə, *Angl* 'gər-, 'gā-\\, Johann Wolfgang von (b. Aug. 28, 1749, Frankfurt am Main [Germany]—d. March 22, 1832, Weimar, Saxe-Weimar) German poet, novelist, playwright, and natural philosopher, the greatest figure of the German Romantic period and the most influential man of letters of his era.

Library of Congress

Goethe studied law in the cosmopolitan cities of Leipzig and Strassburg, where in addition he received a splendid introduction to literature, society, and the arts. His earliest writings took the form of fashionable Rococo songs and lyric poems; he also tried his hand at verse plays. In 1773 he provided the turbulent Sturm und Drang movement with its first major drama, GÖTZ VON BERLICHINGEN, which he wrote in conscious imitation of William Shakespeare, and in 1774 with its first novel, *Die Leiden des jungen Werthers* (THE SORROWS OF YOUNG WERTHER). In the sensitive, ill-fated Werther, Goethe created the prototype of the Romantic hero.

After 1775 Goethe resided in Weimar, where he fell in love with Charlotte von Stein, who inspired some of his finest lyrics. His creativity found expression in an outpouring of lyrics in praise of natural beauty and ballads such as "Erlkönig" (ERL-KING) echoing folk themes. Direct contact with classical Greek and Roman culture during an Italian sojourn of 1786 helped to shape his plays *Iphigenie auf Tauris* (1787) and *Torquato Tasso* (1790) and the poems known as the "Römische Elegien" (1795; ROMAN ELEGIES). Other plays of this period include EGMONT (1788) and *Faust, Ein Fragment* (1790), his first version of the famous play; he also published the bildungsroman *Wilhelm Meisters Lehrjahre* (1795–96; WILHELM MEISTER'S APPRENTICESHIP).

Goethe's aesthetic theories were sharpened by his friendship and correspondence with the poet Friedrich von Schiller. He contributed to Schiller's journal *Die Horen* (1795–97) and after its demise continued his writings on the ideals of arts and literature in his journal *Propyläen* (1798–1800). Although not wholly sympathetic to the Romantic movement, Goethe approved of the Romantics' receptivity to foreign literatures and sought a rapprochement with Eastern culture in the poems of *West-östlicher Divan* (1819; *Divan of West and East*).

Remaining astonishingly creative, Goethe in his last years wrote the novel *Wilhelm Meisters Wanderjahre* (1821, final version 1829; *Wilhelm Meister's Travels*) and completed his greatest drama, FAUST (Part I, 1808; Part II, 1832).

Gogarty \\'gō-gər-tē\\, Oliver St. John (b. Aug. 17, 1878, Dublin, Ire.—d. Sept. 22, 1957, New York, N.Y., U.S.) Writer whose memoirs vividly recreate the Dublin of his youth.

Gogarty attended Royal University (now University College, Dublin), where he was a fellow student of James Joyce. Gogarty practiced as a surgeon and throat specialist in Dublin, and he became acquainted with W.B. Yeats, George Moore, Æ (George Russell), and other leaders of the Irish Literary Renaissance. He wrote the entertaining memoirs *As I Was Going Down Sackville Street* (1937), *Tumbling in the Hay* (1939), and *It Isn't This Time of Year at All* (1954).

Gogol \\'gȯ-gəlʲ, *Angl* 'gȯ-gəl, 'gō-ˌgȯl\\, Nikolay (Vasilyevich) (b. March 19 [March 31, New Style], 1809, Sorochintsy, near Poltava, Ukraine, Russian Empire—d. Feb. 21 [March 4], 1852, Moscow) Russian humorist, dramatist, and novelist, whose novel *Myortvye dushi* (1842; DEAD SOULS) and short story "Shinel" (1842; THE OVERCOAT) are considered the foundations of 19th-century Russian realism.

While working at minor government jobs in St. Petersburg, Gogol wrote occasionally for periodicals, taking for his subject the people and traditions of the Ukrainian countryside. His story collections *Mirgorod* and *Arabeski* (*Arabesques*) appeared in 1835. The former volume includes TARAS BULBA, a vivid narrative of the Cossack past, and the latter the story "Zapiski sumasshedshego" (DIARY OF A MADMAN), in which the hero is a frustrated office drudge who ends up in a lunatic asylum.

Bettmann Archive

In 1836 Gogol published several stories in Aleksandr Pushkin's journal *Sovremennik*. Not only did he find Pushkin's opinions valuable, but he also received from Pushkin the themes for his two principal works, *Revizor* (1836; THE GOVERNMENT INSPECTOR) and *Dead Souls*.

In 1842 the first edition of Gogol's collected works was published. The acclaim that followed made Gogol one of the most popular Russian writers. He began to feel that God had given him a great literary talent in order to make him not only castigate abuses through laughter but also to reveal to Russia the righteous way of living in an evil world.

His creative powers began to fail, however, and his attempt to guide his countrymen—especially in the ill-starred *Vybrannye mesta iz perepiski s druzyami* (1847; *Selected Passages from Correspondence with My Friends*)—brought the scorn of former admirers. Crushed by this rejection, Gogol began to wander from place to place. He finally settled in Moscow, where he came under the influence of a fanatical priest who seems to have practiced on Gogol a type of spiritual sadism. Under the priest's influence, Gogol burned the presumably completed manuscript of the second volume of *Dead Souls* just 10 days before he died on the verge of madness.

Góis \\'gȯish\\, Damião de (b. Feb. 2, 1502, Alenquer, Port.—d. Jan. 30, 1574, Alenquer?) Leading Portuguese humanist, noted for his encyclopedic and analytical mind.

Born of a noble family, Góis was appointed to a secretarial post at a Portuguese trading establishment in Antwerp in 1523. He carried out a series of diplomatic and commercial missions throughout Europe between 1528 and 1531. In 1533 he resigned from government service to devote himself exclusively to humanistic pursuits. Góis studied in Padua between 1534 and 1538 and was acquainted with the Italian humanists Pietro Bembo and Lazzaro Buonamico. He eventually returned to Portugal and was appointed chief keeper of the national archive. In 1558 he was chosen to write the official chronicle of King Manuel, which was completed in 1567. In 1571 Góis faced the charges of the Inquisition and was subjected to imprisonment and a series of hearings lasting nearly two years. Abandoned by his family, he is thought to have died in his birthplace, Alenquer.

Góis's major works, in both Latin and Portuguese, are histories. They include the *Crônica do felicíssimo Rei Dom Manuel* (4 parts, 1566–67; "Chronicle of the Most Happy King Dom Manuel") and the *Crônica do Príncipe Dom João* (1567; "Chronicle of Prince Dom John").

Gökalp \gœ-'kälp\, Ziya, *pseudonym of* Mehmed Ziya \zē-'yä\ (b. March 23, 1876, Diyarbakır, Ottoman Empire [now in Turkey]—d. Oct. 25, 1924, Constantinople [now Istanbul]) Sociologist and writer, one of the most important intellectuals and spokesmen of the Turkish nationalist movement.

Gökalp was imprisoned for his revolutionary activities while he was a student. After the Young Turk Revolution in 1908, he moved to Salonika, where he taught in a secondary school and became an intellectual leader. During that period he contributed to the avant-garde periodicals *Genç kalemler* ("The Young Pens") and *Yeni mecmua* ("New Magazine"), both vehicles for the dissemination of revolutionary nationalist ideas. After the 1918 armistice ending World War I, Gökalp was exiled to Malta with other leading Turkish activists. Freed in 1921, he settled in Ankara.

Gökalp's best-known works include the verse collection *Kızıl elma* (1915; "The Red Apple"). The title poem deals with an ancient Turkish myth in which universal sovereignty, symbolized in the apple, devolves on the Turks. Other writings are *Yeni hayat* (1918; "The New Life"), an anthology of poems; the prose work *Türkeşmek, İslamlaşmak, muasırlaşmak* (1918; "Turkification, Islāmization, and Modernization"); fables in prose and poetry, *Altın ışık* (1923; "The Golden Light"); the prose work *Türkçülüğün esasları* (1923 and 1970; *Principles of Turkism*); his unfinished *Türk medeniyeti tarihi* ("A History of Turkish Civilization," vol. 1, 1925); and *Malta mektublar* (1931; "Maltese Letters").

Goldbarth \'gōld-,bärth\, Albert (b. Jan. 31, 1948, Chicago, Ill., U.S.) American poet noted for his erudition and wit and whose compulsive wordiness brought comparisons with Walt Whitman.

Educated at the University of Illinois at Chicago, the University of Iowa, and the University of Utah, Goldbarth taught at several schools, notably the University of Texas, Austin, and Wichita State University in Kansas.

Goldbarth often published one or more collections of poems annually. His collections include *Coprolites* (1973), a group of meditations on human leavings; *Opticks* (1974), a long poem about glass, light, and perception; *Comings Back* (1976); *Curve: Overlapping Narratives* (1977); *Different Fleshes* (1979), subtitled "A Novel/Poem"; *Ink, Blood, Semen* (1980); *Faith* (1981); and *Heaven and Earth: A Cosmology* (1991).

Gold Bug, The Mystery story by Edgar Allan POE, published in 1843 in the Philadelphia *Dollar Magazine*; it was later published in the collection *Tales* (1845). The central character, William Legrand, has sequestered himself on Sullivan's Island, South Carolina, after a series of economic setbacks. With his servant Jupiter he finds a golden beetle. The parchment in which he captured it is later revealed to be inscribed with cryptic writing and an emblem similar to the death's-head marking on the insect. Legrand deciphers the message and follows its strange instructions, which lead him to uncover the buried treasure of Captain Kidd.

Golden Age In Latin literature, the period, from approximately 70 BC to AD 18, during which the Latin language was brought to perfection as a literary medium and many classical Latin masterpieces were composed. The Golden Age can be subdivided into the CICERONIAN PERIOD (70–43 BC), dominated by Marcus Tullius Cicero, and the AUGUSTAN AGE (43 BC–AD 18), a period of mature literary achievements by such writers as Virgil, Horace, and Livy. *See also* SILVER AGE.

Golden Age ("Siglo de Oro") The period from the early 16th century to the late 17th century, generally considered the high point in Spain's literary history. The Golden Age began with the political unification of Spain about 1500, and its literature is characterized by patriotic and religious fervor, heightened realism, and a new interest in earlier epics and ballads.

During the Golden Age such forms as the chivalric and pastoral novels were replaced by the PICARESQUE NOVEL, which was exemplified by the anonymous *Lazarillo de Tormes* (1554) and by the works of Mateo Alemán and Francisco Gómez de Quevedo. The monumental novel *Don Quixote* (Part I, 1605; Part II, 1615) by Miguel de CERVANTES remains the single most important literary work produced during the Golden Age. Poetry during the period was initially marked by the adoption of Italian meters and verse forms such as those used by Garcilaso de la Vega. Eventually it was characterized by the elaborate conceits and wordplay of the Baroque movements known as CULTERANISMO and CONCEPTISMO, whose chief practitioners were Luis de Góngora and Quevedo, respectively. The Golden Age also witnessed the almost single-handed creation of the Spanish national theater by the prolific playwright Lope de VEGA. The Spanish dramatic tradition he established was further developed by Tirso de Molina and by Pedro CALDERÓN. The end of the Golden Age is marked by Calderón's death in 1681.

Golden Apples, The Collection of short stories by Eudora WELTY, published in 1949. The stories had all been published previously, and Welty added one novella-length story, "Main Families in Morgana."

Symbolism from Greek mythology unifies the stories, all of which are set in the Mississippi Delta town of Morgana over a 40-year period. The hero of "Moon Lake" and the guitarist in "Music from Spain" are Perseus figures. King MacLain, the protagonist of "Shower of Gold," is a sexually adventurous Zeus figure.

Golden Ass, The Prose narrative of the 2nd century AD by Lucius APULEIUS, who called it *Metamorphoses*.

In all probability Apuleius used material from a lost *Metamorphoses* by Lucius of Patrae, which is cited by some as the source for an extant Greek work on a similar theme, the brief *Lucius, or the Ass* (attributed to the Greek rhetorician Lucian). Though Apuleius' picaresque novel is fiction, its hero has been seen as a partial portrait of its author. It is particularly valuable for its description of the ancient religious mysteries. Considered a rare portrait of ancient manners, the work has been valued also for its entertaining and at times bawdy episodes that alternate between the dignified, the ludicrous, the voluptuous, and the horrible. Its "Cupid and Psyche" tale (books 4–6) has been frequently imitated by later writers, notably William Morris in *The Earthly Paradise* and C.S. Lewis in the novel *Till We Have Faces*. Some of Lucius' adventures reappear in Giovanni Boccaccio's *Decameron*, Miguel de Cervantes' *Don Quixote*, and Alain-René Lesage's *Gil Blas*.

Golden Bough, The A study of comparative religion by Sir James FRAZER. Originally published in two volumes in 1890 with the subtitle *A Study in Comparative Religion*, it was enlarged and republished with the subtitle *A Study in Magic and*

Religion, (12 volumes, 1911–15). *Aftermath, a supplement* appeared in 1936. This massive work surveys the spiritual beliefs, practices, and institutions of cultures worldwide and posits a natural progression from magic to religion to science. The author provides detailed descriptions of esoteric rites and ceremonies, analysis of recurrent motifs in myth, and interpretation of the "primitive" worldview. Although the evolutionary sequence of magical, religious, and scientific thought is no longer accepted, Frazer's work enabled him to synthesize and compare a wider range of information about religious and magical practices than has been achieved subsequently by any other single anthropologist. This material also had a profound impact on the literature and art of the modernist period.

Golden Bowl, The   Novel by Henry JAMES, published in 1904.

Wealthy American widower Adam Verver and his daughter Maggie live in Europe, where they collect art and relish each other's company. Through the efforts of the manipulative Fanny Assingham, Maggie becomes engaged to Amerigo, an Italian prince in reduced circumstances, but remains blind to his rekindled affair with her longtime friend Charlotte Stant. Maggie and Amerigo marry, and later, after Charlotte and Adam have also wed, both spouses learn of the ongoing affair, though neither seeks a confrontation. Not until Maggie buys the gilded crystal bowl of the title as a birthday present for Adam does truth crack the veneer of propriety.

Golden Boy   Drama in three acts by Clifford ODETS, produced and published in 1937. It traces the downfall of Joe Bonaparte, a gifted young musician who becomes corrupted by money and brutality when he chooses to become a prizefighter rather than a classical violinist.

Golden Fleece   In Greek mythology, the prize sought by Jason and the Argonauts; its capture would enable Jason to win the throne to which he was rightful heir.

According to the legend, Jason's uncle Athamas had two children, Phrixus and Helle, by his first wife, Nephele. Ino, his second wife, hated the children of Nephele and persuaded Athamas to sacrifice Phrixus in order to alleviate a famine. Before the sacrifice, the ghost of Nephele appeared to Phrixus, bringing a ram with a golden fleece on which he and Helle tried to escape over the sea. Helle fell off and was drowned in the strait that thenceforth was called the Hellespont. Phrixus safely reached the other side, and, proceeding to Colchis, he sacrificed the ram and hung up its fleece in the grove of Ares, where it was guarded by a sleepless dragon.

When Jason tried to claim the throne from his uncle Pelias, who had usurped it from Jason's father, Pelias imposed on Jason the task of fetching the Golden Fleece. Jason then assembled the Argonauts and together they faced many obstacles. When they finally reached their destination, they were forced to perform several additional tasks, but Aëtes (Aeetes), the king, still refused to give up the fleece. Medea, his daughter, had by that time fallen in love with Jason, and to help him she caused the dragon to sleep. Jason then took the fleece and Medea and returned home.

Golden Lotus   An English translation of the classic Chinese novel JIN PING MEI.

Golden Notebook, The   Novel by Doris LESSING, published in 1962.

The novel presents the crisis of a woman novelist, Anna Wulf, suffering from writer's block. Immensely self-analytical, she seeks to probe her disorderly life by keeping four notebooks: a black one covering her early years in British colonial Africa; a red one about her years as a communist; a yellow

one with the fictional story of her alter ego, Ella; and a blue one with her diary. Excerpts from these notebooks mingle with excerpts from an ostensibly fictional work, "Free Women," which features a character named Anna Wulf. As the separate lines of plot development progress toward resolution, the novelist integrates her fragmented experiences and unifies the separate threads of her writing into a single golden notebook.

Goldfaden \\'gōld-ˌfäd-ən\\, Abraham, *original surname* Goldenfoden \\'gōld-ən-ˌfōd-ən\\, *Yiddish* Avrom Goldfadn (b. July 12 [July 24, New Style], 1840, Starokonstantinov, Ukraine, Russia [now Starokostyantinyv, Ukraine]—d. Jan. 9, 1908, New York, N.Y., U.S.)   Hebrew and Yiddish poet and playwright and originator of Yiddish theater.

Goldfaden published volumes of Hebrew and Yiddish poems before his graduation from a rabbinical seminary at Zhitomir in 1866. He then taught in Russia until he migrated to Poland and then to Romania, where he organized at Iaşi, in 1876, what is generally recognized as the first Yiddish theater. In 1887 he migrated to New York City, where he established the first illustrated Yiddish periodical. He next went to London to reorganize the Yiddish theater there. In 1903 he finally settled in New York, where he opened a drama school. Among his many plays are *Shulamis* (1880), considered his masterwork, and *Bar Kokhva* (1887).

Golding \\'gōl-diŋ\\, Louis (b. Nov. 19, 1895, Manchester, Eng.—d. Aug. 9, 1958, London)   English novelist and essayist, an interpreter of British Jewish life.

The son of poor Jewish parents who had emigrated to Britain from Russia, Golding attended Queen's College, Oxford, where he first began to write. He published his first novel, *Forward from Babylon*, in 1920.

Golding produced at least a book a year. The best known was *Magnolia Street* (1932), a story of working-class life among Jews and Gentiles in a Manchester back street. In 1934 it was produced as a play. His book *The Jewish Problem* (1938) was a study of anti-Semitism. A broadcaster and lecturer, he also wrote film scripts, verse, short stories, and books on boxing.

Golding \\'gōl-diŋ\\, William, *in full* Sir William Gerald Golding (b. Sept. 19, 1911, St. Columb Minor, near Newquay, Cornwall, Eng.—d. June 19, 1993, Perranarworthal)   English novelist who in 1983 won the Nobel Prize for Literature for his parables of the human condition.

Educated at Brasenose College, Oxford, Golding graduated in 1935 and became a master at Bishop Wordsworth's School, Salisbury. He joined the Royal Navy in 1940. After the war he returned to teaching and remained in that profession until 1960.

Golding's first published novel was LORD OF THE FLIES (1954; film, 1963 and 1990), the story of a group of schoolboys isolated on a coral island who revert to savagery. *The Inheritors* (1955), set in the last days of Neanderthal culture, is another story of the essential violence and depravity of human nature. *Pincher Martin* (1956) concerns the guilt-filled reflections of a naval officer, who faces an agonizing death on his torpedoed ship. Two other novels, *Free Fall* (1959) and *The Spire* (1964), also demonstrate Golding's belief that "man produces evil as a bee produces honey." His later works include *Darkness Visible* (1979); *Rites of Passage* (1980), which won the Booker McConnell Prize; *A Moving Target* (1982; essays); *The Paper Men* (1983); and *Close Quarters* (1987), a sequel to *Rites of Passage*. Golding was knighted in 1988.

Goldoni \\gōl-'dō-nē\\, Carlo (b. Feb. 25, 1707, Venice, Venetian republic [Italy]—d. Feb. 6, 1793, Paris, Fr.)   Prolific dramatist who seriously altered the commedia dell'arte dramatic form by creating realistic characters, tightly constructed plots, and a new spirit of gaiety and spontaneity. For these innovations Goldoni is considered the founder of Italian realistic comedy.

Although Goldoni practiced law for a number of years and held diplomatic appointments, his real interest was in writing plays. His early plays veer between the old style and the new, and he dispensed with masked characters altogether in such plays as *La Pamela* (performed 1750; *Pamela*), based on Samuel Richardson's novel. During the 1750–51 season he produced some of his best comedies, notably *I pettegolezzi delle donne* ("Women's Gossip"), a play in Venetian dialect; *Il bugiardo* (*The Liar*), in commedia dell'arte style; and *Il vero amico* ("The True Friend"), a comedy of manners.

From 1753 to 1762 Goldoni wrote for the Teatro San Luca (now Teatro Goldoni). His important plays from this period are *La locandiera* (performed 1753; *Mine Hostess*) and two fine plays in Venetian dialect, *I rusteghi* (performed 1760; "The Tyrants") and *Le baruffe chiozzote* (performed 1762; "Quarrels at Chioggia").

In 1762 Goldoni left Venice for Paris to direct the Comédie-Italienne. Subsequently, he rewrote all of his French plays for Venetian audiences; his French *L'Éventail* (performed 1763) became in Italian one of his finest plays, *Il ventaglio* (performed 1764; *The Fan*). Goldoni retired in 1764 to teach Italian to the princesses at Versailles. In 1783 he began his celebrated *Mémoires* in French (1787).

Goldschmidt \'gŏlt-,shmit\, Meïr Aron (b. Oct. 26, 1819, Vordingborg, Den.—d. Aug. 15, 1887, Copenhagen) Danish writer of Jewish descent whose work foreshadowed later realism.

Goldschmidt went to school in Copenhagen and became a journalist. In 1840 he founded *Corsaren*, an influential satirical weekly expressing his radical ideas. A feud with the philosopher Søren Kierkegaard caused him to give up the paper and go abroad in 1846. His first novel, *En Jøde* (1845; *The Jew of Denmark*), described the gulf between the Jew and Danish society. Returning in 1847, Goldschmidt abandoned radicalism and founded a new periodical, *Nord og Syd*, in which his novel *Hjemløs* (which he later translated as *Homeless*, 3 vol.) was serialized (1853–57).

Goldschmidt's finest descriptions of Jewish life are to be found in his short stories, notably in *Fortællinger* (1846; "Tales"). In *Ravnen* (1867), one of the outstanding Danish novels of the 19th century, he depicts Jews with an unusual blend of sympathy and irony. His philosophy of retributive justice, or nemesis, underlies most of his novels and his memoirs (1877).

Goldsmith \'gōld-,smith\, Oliver (b. Nov. 10, 1730, Kilkenny West, County Westmeath, Ire.—d. April 4, 1774, London, Eng.) British essayist, poet, novelist, dramatist, and eccentric, notable for his graceful and lively writing style.

After an unhappy childhood, Goldsmith attended Trinity College, Dublin, and he left Ireland in 1752 to study medicine in Edinburgh. He took no degree (although he was later known as Dr. Goldsmith), and after leaving school he wandered through Europe until he arrived in London early in 1756.

Goldsmith soon emerged as an essayist in *The Bee* and other periodicals, and in 1762 he published his *Life of Richard Nash, of Bath, Esq.* In 1764 he became one of the nine founding members of the famous Club, a select body, including Sir Joshua Reynolds, Samuel Johnson, and Edmund Burke, that met weekly for supper and conversation. Despite Goldsmith's growing means, he was forced by his extravagance to undertake hack work. He thus produced histories of England and of ancient Rome and Greece, biographies, verse anthologies, translations, and works of popular science. These were mainly

compilations of works by other authors, enlivened by Goldsmith's fine writing.

By 1762 Goldsmith had established himself as an essayist with his collection *The Citizen of the World; or, Letters from a Chinese Philosopher*, in which he used the device of satirizing Western society through the eyes of an Oriental visitor to London. By 1764 he had won a reputation as a poet with *The Traveller*, the verses of which embodied both his memories of tramping through Europe and his political ideas. In 1770 he confirmed that reputation with the more famous THE DESERTED VILLAGE. In 1766 he revealed himself as a novelist with THE VICAR OF WAKEFIELD. Goldsmith turned to the theater with *The Good Natur'd Man* (1768), which was followed in 1773 by the much more effective SHE STOOPS TO CONQUER.

During his last decade Goldsmith's conversational encounters with Johnson and others, his foolishness, and his wit were preserved in Boswell's *Life of Johnson*.

golem \'gō-ləm, 'gȯi-\ [Yiddish *goylem*, from Hebrew *gōlem* something shapeless] In Jewish folklore, an artificial figure constructed to represent a human being and endowed with life; specifically, such a figure created in the 16th century by the cabalist Rabbi Löw of Prague. Golems sometimes helped their creators but often became uncontrollable and had to be destroyed. The basic idea of the golem has been adapted by many authors and has appeared in various forms in literature, notably in Mary Shelley's *Frankenstein*, Karel Čapek's *R.U.R.*, and Isaac Bashevis Singer's *The Golem*.

Golgotha *see* CALVARY.

goliard \'gōl-yərd, -,yärd\ [Medieval Latin *goliardus*, from Old French *golias, gouliart* gourmand, glutton, riotous liver, perhaps ultimately from a Germanic verb akin to Middle High German *goln* to shout, jest, behave unrestrainedly, Gothic *goljan* to greet; influenced in sense by association with Old French *gole* throat, gluttony] Any of the wandering students and clerics in medieval England, France, and Germany, remembered for their satirical verses and poems in praise of debauchery. The goliards described themselves as followers of the legendary Bishop Golias; they were renegade clerics of no fixed abode who were chiefly interested in riotous living.

Goliard satires were almost uniformly directed against the church and the pope. In 1227 the Council of Trier forbade priests to permit goliards to take part in chanting the service. After several further decrees the privileges of clergy were finally withdrawn from the goliards.

The word *goliard* eventually lost its clerical association, passing into French and English literature of the 14th century in the general meaning of jongleur, or minstrel (its meaning in *Piers Plowman* and in Geoffrey Chaucer's works).

A remarkable collection of the goliards' Latin poems and songs in praise of wine and riotous living was published in the late 19th century under the title CARMINA BURANA, taken from the 13th-century manuscript of that title at Munich. Many of the works were translated by John Addington Symonds as *Wine, Women, and Song* (1884). The collection also includes the only two complete surviving texts of medieval Passion dramas—one with and one without music. *Compare* JONGLEUR; TROUVÈRE.

Golias \gōl-'yȧs\ Stock character in medieval French literature derived from the legendary Bishop Golias, patron of the goliard. Golias is an insubordinate, roistering, bibulous lecher who is redeemed by his wit and bonhomie.

Goliath \gə-'lī-əth\ In the Bible (I Samuel 17), a Philistine giant slain by the youthful David, who thereby achieved renown. The Philistines had encamped to make war against Saul and the

Israelites, and Goliath came forth day by day to challenge men to single combat. Only David ventured to respond and, armed with a sling and pebbles, he slew Goliath.

Gollum \'gäl-əm, 'gȯl-\ Fictional character in J.R.R. Tolkien's novels THE HOBBIT and THE LORD OF THE RINGS trilogy. Gollum, who usually speaks in a sibilant whisper, is a vaguely reptilian creature who is obsessed with the ring that is the focus of much of the action of the books.

Gombrowicz \gōm-'brȯ-vēch\, Witold (b. Aug. 4, 1904, Małoszyce, near Opatów, Poland, Russian Empire—d. July 25, 1969, Vence, Fr.) Polish novelist, story writer, and dramatist best known for his novel *Ferdydurke* (1937) and other absurdist satires.

Gombrowicz spent 24 years (1939–63) in voluntary exile in Buenos Aires. His writings were banned in turn by the Nazis, the Stalinists, and the Polish government, and though he returned to Europe in 1963, he settled in France rather than his native Poland. He published his postwar works abroad: the novels *Trans-Atlantyk* (1953; *Trans-Atlantyk*), *Pornografia* (1960; "Pornography"), and *Kosmos* (1965; "Cosmos").

The dominant theme of Gombrowicz' writings is human immaturity (which he considered to be innate). He portrayed humanity as incapable of understanding the world without depending on the spurious knowledge and shallow opinions of others. Other notable works include the play *Ślub* (1953; *The Marriage*); the diaries *Dziennik*, 3 vol. (1957–66; *Diary*); and the short-story collections *Pamiętnik z okresu dojrzewania* (1933; "Memoirs of an Adolescent") and *Bakakaj* (1957).

Gómez de Avellaneda \'gō-mās-thä-,ä-vä-yä-'nä-thä, -väl-\, Gertrudis (b. March 23, 1814, Puerto Príncipe, Cuba—d. Feb. 1, 1873, Madrid, Spain) Cuban-Spanish poet and playwright who is considered one of the foremost Romantic writers of the 19th century and one of the greatest women poets.

Gómez de Avellaneda went to Spain in 1836, where, except for a short period from 1859 to 1863, she lived for the rest of her life. Her first poems, originally published under the pseudonym of La Peregrina ("The Pilgrim"), were collected in 1841 in a volume entitled *Poesías* ("Poems"). Tinged with a pessimism born of much personal suffering, the poems rank among the most poignant in all Spanish literature. Her second volume of poetry, also entitled *Poesías*, was published in 1850.

Gómez de Avellaneda's plays are distinctive for their poetic diction and lyrical passages and are based chiefly on historic models. Her play *Alfonso Munio* (1844; rev. ed., *Munio Alfonso*, 1869), based on the life of Alfonso X, and *Saúl* (1849), a biblical drama, achieved popular success. One of her last plays, *Baltasar* (1858; *Belshazzar*), is considered to be a masterpiece. Her nine novels, with the exception of *Sab* (1841), an antislavery work, are now almost completely forgotten.

Gómez de la Serna \'gō-māth-thä-lä-'ser-nä\, Ramón (b. July 5, 1891, Madrid, Spain—d. Jan. 12, 1963, Buenos Aires, Arg.) Spanish writer whose *greguerías*, brief poetic statements characterized by a free association of words, ideas, and objects, had a significant influence on avant-garde literature in Europe and Latin America.

Gómez de la Serna studied law but never practiced. He devoted his life to literature, publishing his first book in 1904. About 1910 he invented the *greguería*, which he defined as "humor plus metaphor"; *e.g.*, "it is only in botanical gardens that trees carry visiting cards." He also wrote biographies, novels, and plays. He founded the important literary magazine *Prometeo* and wrote more than 100 books and countless articles in leading European and Latin-American newspapers and journals.

Gomorrah *see* SODOM AND GOMORRAH.

Gonçalves \gȯⁿ-'säl-vish\, António Aurélio (b. 1901, São Vicente, Cape Verde Islands—d. 1984) Portuguese-African story writer, novelist, critic, and teacher whose works challenge the traditional social role of women in the Cape Verde Islands.

Gonçalves attended the University of Lisbon and later taught history and philosophy in São Vicente. All of Gonçalves' *noveletas* (his coinage for novella) and other works of fiction have Cape Verdean women as central characters, and in this regard he is unique among Portuguese-language African writers. His short story "História de tempo antigo" (1960; "Story of Former Times") involves the death of the narrator's mother and emphasizes familial bonds between mother and child. *O enterro de nhâ Candinha Sena* (1957; "The Burial of Mrs. Candinha Sena") delves into the narrator's childhood relationship with a childless woman of great kindness and character. After a long hiatus, Gonçalves published *Noite de vento* (1970; "Windy Night") and *Virgens loucas* (1971; "Foolish Virgins"), which also have female protagonists.

Gonçalves Dias \gȯⁿ-'säl-vish-'dē-ásh\, Antônio (b. Aug. 10, 1823, Boa Vista, near Caxias, Maranhão, Braz.—d. Nov. 3, 1864, off the coast of Maranhão) Romantic poet generally regarded as the national poet of Brazil.

Though Gonçalves Dias lived much of the time abroad following his education at the University of Coimbra in Portugal, his songs, published as *Primeiros cantos* (1847; "First Poems"), *Segundos cantos* (1848; "More Poems"), and *Últimos cantos* (1851; "Last Poems"), continually celebrated, with exuberance and longing, the New World as a tropical paradise.

In addition to being a poet, Gonçalves Dias was a respected ethnologist and scholar. He published a dictionary of the Tupí Indian language and an unfinished Indian epic, *Os Tambiras* (1857; "The Tambiras"). He also held governmental posts in which he surveyed the school system of northern Brazil.

Goncharov \gən-,chə-'rȯf\, Ivan Aleksandrovich (b. June 6 [June 18, New Style], 1812, Simbirsk, Russia—d. Sept. 15 [Sept. 27], 1891, St. Petersburg) Russian novelist and travel writer whose highly esteemed novels dramatize social change in Russia and contain some of Russian literature's most vivid and memorable characters.

After graduating from Moscow University in 1834, Goncharov served for nearly 30 years as a government official. The only unusual event in his uneventful life was a voyage to Japan made in 1852–55 as secretary to a Russian admiral; this he described in *Fregat Pallada* (1858; *The Frigate Pallada*).

Goncharov's most notable achievement is his fiction. His first novel, *Obyknovennaya istoriya* (1847; *A Common Story*), won instant recognition from the influential critic Vissarion Belinsky. OBLOMOV (1859), a more mature work, is generally accepted as one of the most important Russian novels. It draws a powerful contrast between the aristocratic and capitalistic classes in Russia and attacks the way of life based on serfdom. Goncharov's third novel, *Obryv* (1869; *The Precipice*), though a remarkable book, is inferior to *Oblomov*.

Goncourt \gōⁿ-'kür\, Edmond and Jules, *in full* Edmond-Louis-Antoine Huot de Goncourt *and* Jules-Alfred Huot de Goncourt (respectively b. May 26, 1822, Nancy, Fr.—d. July 16, 1896, Champrosay; b. Dec. 17, 1830, Paris—d. June 20, 1870, Auteuil) French brothers, writers, and constant collaborators who contributed solidly to the naturalistic novel, social history, and art criticism. Above all, they are remembered for their perceptive, revealing *Journal* and for Edmond's legacy, the Académie Goncourt, which annually awards the PRIX GONCOURT to the author of an outstanding work of French literature.

An inheritance enabled the Goncourts to live in modest comfort without working. The brothers, both amateur artists, first made a sketching tour of France, Algeria, and Switzerland. They then turned to playwriting and in 1851 published a novel, *En 18*, all without success. The brothers achieved more success with a series of social histories, which they began publishing in 1854. These works drew on private correspondence, newspaper accounts, brochures, and even dinner menus and dress patterns to re-create the life of specific periods in French history.

Meticulous documentation and attention to detail also went into the Goncourts' novels. The brothers covered a vast range of social environments: the world of journalism and literature in *Charles Demailly* (1860); that of medicine and hospitals in *Soeur Philomène* (1861); upper-middle-class society in *Renée Mauperin* (1864); and the artistic world in *Manette Salomon* (1867). The Goncourts' frank presentation of upper and lower social classes and their clinical dissection of social relations helped establish naturalism. The most lasting of their novels, *Germinie Lacerteux* (1864), was based on the double life of their seemingly impeccable servant, Rose. It is one of the first realistic French novels of working-class life.

The Goncourts began keeping their monumental *Journal* in 1851, and Edmond continued it until his death in 1896, 26 years after Jules had died. Full of critical judgments, scabrous anecdotes, descriptive sketches, literary gossip, and thumbnail portraits, the complete *Journal* is at once a revealing autobiography and a monumental history of social and literary life in 19th-century Paris. The Académie Goncourt, first conceived by the brothers in 1867, was officially constituted in 1903.

Goncourt Prize   *see* PRIX GONCOURT.

Gondal   *see* ANGRIA AND GONDAL.

Goneril \'gän-ə-ril\   Fictional character, one of Lear's two treacherous daughters in William Shakespeare's tragedy KING LEAR.

Gone With the Wind   Novel by Margaret MITCHELL, published in 1936. *Gone With the Wind* is a sweeping, romantic story about the American Civil War from the point of view of the Confederacy. In particular it is the story of Scarlett O'Hara, a headstrong Southern belle who survives the hardships of the war and afterwards manages to establish a successful business by capitalizing on the struggle to rebuild the South. Throughout the book she is motivated by her unfulfilled love for Ashley Wilkes, an honorable man who is happily married. After a series of marriages and failed relationships with other men, notably the dashing Rhett Butler, she has a change of heart and determines to win Rhett back.

Góngora \'gȯn-gō-rä\, Luis de, *surname in full* Góngora y Argote \e̅-är-'gȯ-tä\ (b. July 11, 1561, Córdoba, Spain—d. May 23, 1627, Córdoba)   One of the most influential Spanish poets of his era. His Baroque, convoluted style, known as *gongorismo*, was so exaggerated by less gifted imitators that his own reputation suffered for it until the 20th century.

Góngora attended the University of Salamanca and quickly achieved fame. His letters, as well as some of his satirical verse, show an unhappy and financially distressed life, vexed by the animosity that some of his writings had evoked. He had strong supporters—Lope de Vega was an admirer—and equally powerful enemies, none more so than his rival Francisco de Quevedo, who outdid even Góngora in mordant and unrelenting satire.

Góngora was always successful with his lighter poetry—the *romances* (Spanish folk ballads), *letrillas* (a type of short lyric poem), and sonnets. His longer works, particularly the *Fábula*

de Polifemo y Galatea ("Story of Polyphemus and Galatea") and the *Soledades* ("Solitudes")—both circulated in manuscript in 1613—were written in an intensely difficult and purposely complex style; they provoked the scorn and enmity of many. In both, Góngora elaborated his style by the introduction of numerous Latinisms of vocabulary and syntax and by exceedingly complex imagery and mythological allusions.

gongorismo \ˌgȯŋ-gō-'rēz-mō\ or **Gongorism** \'gȯŋ-gə-ˌriz-əm\   Spanish literary style named for Luis de Góngora, whose poetry exhibited the characteristic features of *culteranismo*—the re-Latinizing of poetic language and themes and the use of classical allusion, syntax, and vocabulary—to their limits. His highly ornate rhetorical style was imitated by lesser poets, and *gongorismo* came to mean obscurant poetry chiefly notable for its literary affectation.

Gong Zizhen or **Kung Tzu-chen** \'gȯŋ-'dzə̄-'jən\, *also called* Gong Dingan \'din-'gän\ (b. Aug. 22, 1792, Hangzhou, Zhejiang province, China—d. Sept. 26, 1841, Nanjing)   A reform-minded Chinese writer and poet whose works both foreshadowed and influenced the modernization movements of the late Qing dynasty (1644–1911).

Born into an eminent family of scholars and officials, Gong passed the state examinations and succeeded to a series of metropolitan posts in the Qing administration. Concern over the Qing failure to deal adequately with Western pressures and internal problems led Gong in 1830 to join other progressives in founding a literary club to agitate for reform. Although his many essays on reform issues had great impact on later intellectuals such as Kang Youwei and Liang Qichao, they were ill-received in the conservative Qing councils of the time. Thus, Gong retired in disillusionment to a life of private letters in 1839. Famed chiefly as a prose stylist, Gong was also a master of lyrical *ci* poetry and published several verse collections, most notably his *Jihai zashi* (1839; "Miscellaneous Verse"). He was given the courtesy name Seren or Eryu.

Gonzaga \gȯⁿ-'zä-gə\, Tomás Antônio, *pseudonym* Dirceu \dēr-'seú\ (b. Aug. 11, 1744, Porto, Port.—d. 1810, Mozambique)   Poet whose popularity in Portugal up to the 20th century was second only to that of Luís de Camões.

Gonzaga completed his law studies at Coimbra (1768) and in 1782 was appointed a judge in Vila Rica, Braz. There he fell in love with Marília, who was mentioned in his lyrics, but on the eve of their marriage (1789) he was arrested on a charge, undoubtedly false, of conspiracy. After three years in prison he was exiled to Mozambique. His fame rests on a single book of pastoral love lyrics, *Marília de Dirceu*. The work was published in three parts in 1792, 1799, and 1812 and chronicles his relationship with Marília.

González Martínez \gȯn-'säl-äs-mär-'tē-näs\, Enrique (b. April 13, 1871, Guadalajara, Mex.—d. Feb. 19, 1952, Mexico City)   Poet, physician, and diplomat who was a major influence in 20th-century Mexican literature.

González Martínez began writing while practicing medicine in the provinces. With the coming of the Mexican Revolution (1911) he entered public life, serving in the Ministry of Education and occupying diplomatic posts in Europe and various Latin-American countries. He became famous for his sonnet "Tuércele el cuello al cisne de engañoso plumaje" ("Wring the neck of the swan with the false plumage"), an attack on the excesses of poetic modernism, published in his collection *Los senderos ocultos* (1911; "The Hidden Ways"). Other poetic works include *La palabra del viento* (1921; "Word of the Wind"), *Poemas truncos* (1935; "Short Poems"), and *Bajo el signo mortal* (1942; "Under the Mortal Sign").

Good-bye, Mr. Chips \\'chips\\   Sentimental novel by James HILTON, published serially and in book form in 1934. The work depicts the career of a gentle schoolteacher at an English public school. Arthur Chipping ("Mr. Chips") is a middle-aged bachelor who falls in love with and marries a young woman whom he has met on a mountaineering vacation. They live happily at Brookfield School until her death, only a few years later. Mr. Chips devotes the rest of his life to educating many generations of boys.

Good-Bye to All That   Autobiography by Robert GRAVES, published in 1929 and revised in 1957. It is considered a classic of the disillusioned postwar generation.

Divided into anecdotal scenes and satiric episodes, *Good-Bye to All That* is infused with a dark humor. It chronicles the author's experiences as a student at Charterhouse School in London and as a teenaged soldier in France during World War I, where he sustained severe wounds in combat. His memoir continues after the war with descriptions of his life in Wales, at Oxford University, and in Egypt.

Good Earth, The   Novel by Pearl BUCK, published in 1931. The novel, about peasant life in China in the 1920s, was awarded the Pulitzer Prize for fiction in 1932.

The Good Earth follows the life of Wang Lung, from his beginnings as an impoverished peasant to his eventual position as a prosperous landowner. He is aided immeasurably by his equally humble wife, O-Lan, with whom he shares a devotion to the land, to duty, and to survival. Buck combines descriptions of marriage, parenthood, and complex human emotions with depictions of Chinese reverence for the land and for a specific way of life.

Good Man Is Hard to Find, A   Volume of short stories by Flannery O'CONNOR, published in 1955. Like much of the author's work, the collection presents vivid, hidebound characters seemingly hounded by a redemption that they often successfully elude. Several of the stories are generally considered masterpieces of the form. These include "The Artificial Nigger," in which the strange sight of a black lawn statue causes a bigoted grandfather to realize a truth about injustice; "Good Country People," in which a young woman's sense of moral superiority proves her downfall; and the title story, whose demonic character the Misfit becomes an instrument of revelation for his most formidable victim.

good-night \\'gùd-'nīt\\   Sensational type of BROADSIDE BALLAD, popular in England from the 16th through the 19th century, purporting to be the farewell statement of a criminal made shortly before his execution. Good-nights are usually repentant in tone, containing a sketchy account of how the criminal first went astray, a detailed account of his grisly crime, his sentence by the judge, the grief of his aged parents, and a warning to others not to follow his example. Enterprising hack writers and broadside publishers often had the good-night printed in advance of the execution, ready for sale at the moment it was accomplished. Many good-nights have been incorporated into the folk tradition.

Goodrich \\'gùd-,rich\\, Samuel Griswold, *pseudonym* Peter Parley \\'pär-lē\\ (b. Aug. 19, 1793, Ridgefield, Conn., U.S.—d. May 9, 1860, New York, N.Y.)   American publisher and author of children's books.

Goodrich became a bookseller and publisher at Hartford and later in Boston. There, beginning in 1828, he published for 15 years an illustrated annual, the *Token*, to which he was a frequent contributor both of prose and verse. The *Token* contained some of the earliest work of Nathaniel Hawthorne and Henry Wadsworth Longfellow. Goodrich published *Pe-*

ter *Parley's Magazine* (1832–44) and then merged it into his *Merry's Museum*, founded in 1841 and for a time edited by Louisa May Alcott.

In 1827 he began, under the name of Peter Parley, his series of books for the young, which embraced geography, biography, history, science, and miscellaneous tales. He was the sole composer of comparatively few of these, but in his *Recollections of a Lifetime*, 2 vol. (1856), he wrote that he was "the author and editor of about 170 volumes," of which some 7,000,000 copies had been sold, and he listed both the works of which he was the author or editor and the spurious works published under his name. He was widely imitated, especially in England.

Good Soldier, The   Tragic novel by Ford Madox FORD, published in 1915.

The novel relates events in the lives of John Dowell, a Philadelphian from a "good" family, and his wife, Florence, who supposedly suffers from heart disease. Florence's condition mandates that the Dowells live in a succession of European health spas. In this setting they develop and maintain a long friendship with the Ashburnhams—Edward, who also apparently suffers from heart disease, and his wife, Leonora. Dowell narrates the story of deception and betrayal. The novel's structure was innovative, built not upon strict chronological development but rather through the random accretion of Dowell's memories, discoveries, and growing awareness.

Good Soldier Schweik, The \\'shvīk\\   Satiric war novel by Jaroslav HAŠEK, published in Czech as *Osudy dobrého vojáka Švejka za světové války* in four volumes in 1921–23. It is also translated as *The Good Soldier Svejk*. Hašek planned to continue *The Good Soldier Schweik* to six volumes, but died after completing the fourth.

The novel reflected the pacifist, antimilitary sentiments of post-World War I Europe. The title character is classified as "feeble-minded"; nevertheless, with the advent of World War I he is drafted into the service of Austria. Naive, instinctively honest, invariably incompetent, and guileless, Schweik is forever colliding with the clumsy, dehumanized military bureaucracy. Schweik's naïveté serves as a contrast to the self-importance and conniving natures of his superior officers and is the main vehicle for Hašek's mockery of authority.

Good Woman of Setzuan, The \\'sech-'wän\\   Drama, a "parable in 10 scenes," by Bertolt BRECHT, produced in 1943 and published in 1953 as *Der gute Mensch von Sezuan*.

The play is set in China between World War I and World War II. The title character, Shen Te, is a poor but warmhearted prostitute. Because she alone was willing to shelter three gods, they have favored her with a gift of money. She purchases a tobacco shop but finds that her kinsfolk and other customers take advantage of her kindness. To save her business, Shen Te adopts an alter ego; dressing as a man and acting the role of her tough, pragmatic cousin Shui Ta, she is able to exact just payment. She is forced to assume this role so often that, as Shui Ta, she is accused of murdering Shen Te. In the climactic trial scene, Shui Ta reveals that he and Shen Te are the same person.

Gorboduc \\'gòr-bo-,dək\\ (*in full* The Tragedie of Gorboduc)   Blank verse play by Thomas Norton and Thomas SACKVILLE, performed in 1561 and published in 1565 and, in 1570 with printing errors corrected, as *The Tragedie of Ferrex and Porrex*. It was the first English play in blank verse and the first English tragedy on a Senecan model. The drama was based on the legend of Gorboduc, a mythic king of ancient Britain.

In the play, Gorboduc, a good ruler, gives his kingdom away during his lifetime to his two sons, Ferrex and Porrex, who quarrel; the younger son (Porrex) kills the elder. Gorboduc's queen, Videna, avenges the death of her more beloved older son by murdering her younger son. Gorboduc and his queen are, in turn, murdered by his horrified former subjects.

Gordimer \\'gȯr-di-mər\\, Nadine (b. Nov. 20, 1923, Springs, Transvaal, S.Af.) South African novelist and short-story

writer whose major theme was exile and alienation. She received the Nobel Prize for Literature in 1991.

Gordimer was writing by the age of 9, and she published her first story in a magazine when she was 15. Her wide reading informed her about the world on the other side of apartheid—the official South African policy of racial segregation—and that discovery in time developed into strong political opposition to apartheid. In addition to writing, she lectured and taught at various schools in the United States during the 1960s and '70s.

Bettmann Archive

Gordimer's first book was *The Soft Voice of the Serpent* (1952), a collection of short stories. In 1953 a novel, *The Lying Days*, was published. Both exhibit the clear, controlled, and unsentimental technique that became her hallmark.

Her novel *The Conservationist* (1974) won the Booker McConnell Prize in 1974. Later works include *Burger's Daughter* (1979), the short-story collection *A Soldier's Embrace* (1980), *July's People* (1981), *A Sport of Nature* (1987), and *My Son's Story* (1990). Gordimer examines how public events affect individual lives, how the dreams of one's youth are corrupted, and how innocence is lost.

Gordon \\'gȯrd-ən\\, Adam Lindsay (b. Oct. 19, 1833, Faial, Azores, Port.—d. June 24, 1870, Brighton, Vic., Australia) One of the first poets to write in a distinctly Australian idiom.

Gordon was so wild as a youth that his father sent him from England to South Australia, where he became a horse breaker and gained a reputation as a fine steeplechase rider. While in South Australia he published two volumes of poems, *Sea Spray and Smoke Drift* (1867) and *Ashtaroth* (1867); neither book had much impact. Early in 1868 Gordon sustained a serious riding injury and suffered the loss of his only child, Annie. In 1869 he moved to Brighton, near Melbourne, and there he published a third volume of poetry, *Bush Ballads and Galloping Rhymes* (1870). Further misfortune befell him, however, and he suffered severe depression. The day after *Bush Ballads* was published, he shot himself on the beach near Brighton.

Gordon's strong rhythms and homespun philosophy make his poetry memorable. His work eventually was widely accepted, and some of his lines have been adopted into the Australian vernacular.

Gordon, Charles William. Real name of Ralph CONNOR.

Gordon \\gȯr-'dōn, *Angl* 'gȯrd-ən\\, Judah Leib, *also called* Leon Gordon, *byname* Yalag \\yä-'läk\\ (b. Dec. 7, 1830, Vilna, Russian Empire [now Vilnius, Lithuania]—d. Sept. 16, 1892, St. Petersburg, Russia) Jewish poet, essayist, and novelist, the leading poet of the Hebrew Enlightenment (Haskala), whose use of biblical and postbiblical Hebrew resulted in a new and influential style of Hebrew-language poetry.

After he left Lithuania, Gordon was imprisoned as a political conspirator by the Russian government. Following his release he became editor of *Ha-Melits* ("The Advocate"). His early poems dealing with biblical subjects were followed by powerful

satires in verse aimed against the harsher aspects of rabbinic Judaism. His last poems reflect bitter disillusionment with the ideals of Haskala. Although Gordon was of limited poetic talent, his advocacy of social and religious reforms proved widely influential, and his skillful use of postbiblical idiom increased the flexibility of modern Hebrew. His poems were collected in *Kol shire Yehudah Leib Gordon* (1883–84; "Collected Poetry of Yehudah Leib Gordon") and his stories in *Kol kitve Yehudah Leib Gordon* (1889).

Gordon \\'gȯrd-ən\\, Mary (Catherine) (b. Dec. 8, 1949, Long Island, N.Y.) Writer whose novels and short fiction deal with growing up as a Roman Catholic and with the nature of goodness and piety as expressed within that tradition.

Gordon was educated at Barnard College and Syracuse University. Her first novel, *Final Payments* (1978), was a critical and popular success. The protagonist, Isabel, is 30 before she leaves home, having cared for her domineering father for 11 years until his death. Soon she has friends, a career as a social worker, and several married lovers. Feeling the need to atone for her "self-indulgence," she becomes the caregiver to her father's former housekeeper, a woman she hates.

In *The Company of Women* (1981), Felicitas is nurtured by a large circle of Catholic women. After attending only parochial schools, Felicitas goes to Columbia University, where she becomes sexually involved with a married professor, gives up her studies, and becomes pregnant. She returns to the company of women, gives birth to her baby, and later marries only to provide a father for her child.

Gordon's later works include a collection of short stories, *Temporary Shelter* (1987), and the three novellas in *The Rest of Life* (1993); the novels *Men and Angels* (1985) and *The Other Side* (1989); and two works of nonfiction, *Spiritual Quests: The Art and Craft of Religious Writing* (1988) and *Good Boys and Dead Girls and Other Essays* (1991).

Gorey \\'gȯr-ē\\, Edward (St. John) (b. Feb. 22, 1925, Chicago, Ill., U.S.) Writer, illustrator, and designer, noted for his arch humor and gothic sensibility. Gorey drew a pen-and-ink world of beady-eyed, blank-faced individuals whose dignified Edwardian demeanor is undercut by silly and often macabre events. His nonsense rhymes recalled those of Edward Lear, and his mock-Victorian prose delighted readers with its ludicrous fustiness. Gorey's work evoked the cosy sensibilities of childhood reading while subverting that feeling with its often grisly humor.

After graduating in 1950 from Harvard, Gorey immersed himself in the New York cultural scene. In 1953 he began writing and illustrating short books. *The Doubtful Guest* (1957), his first book for children, featured a penguinlike creature that moved into a wealthy home: "It came 17 years ago—and to this day/It has shown no intention of going away."

During the 1960s Gorey published under several playful pseudonyms, mostly anagrams such as Ogdred Weary and Mrs. Regera Dowdy. Gorey was fond of illustrated alphabets; his most celebrated was *The Gashlycrumb Tinies* (1962), which disposes of 26 children: "M is for Maud who was swept out to sea/N is for Neville who died of ennui." He illustrated two books by Edward Lear, including *The Dong with a Luminous Nose* (1969). Gorey continued to write his own stories, including *The Hapless Child* (1961), *The Gilded Bat* (1966), and *The Deranged Cousins: or, Whatever* (1969).

From 1970 Gorey concentrated on adult works, although he still wrote children's stories. His anthologies *Amphigorey* (1972), *Amphigorey Too* (1975), and *Amphigorey Also* (1983) sold well; the first two volumes were the basis for a 1978 musical stage adaptation, *Gorey Stories*.

Gorgon \ˈgȯr-gən\ In Greek mythology, a snake-haired female monster whose appearance could turn the beholder into stone. Homer spoke of a single Gorgon, a monster of the underworld, and the Attic tradition regarded the Gorgon as a monster produced by Gaea (Earth) to aid her sons in battle against the gods. The later Greek poet Hesiod increased the number of Gorgons to three—Stheno (the Mighty), Euryale (the Far Springer), and MEDUSA (the Queen)—and made them the daughters of the sea god Phorcys and of his sister-wife Ceto. Medusa was the only one of the three who was mortal.

Goriot, Père \per-gȯr-ˈyō\ Fictional character, the protagonist of Honoré de Balzac's novel LE PÈRE GORIOT.

Gorky or **Gorki** \ˈgȯrʸ-kʸē, *Angl* ˈgȯr-kē\, Maksim *or* Maxim, *pseudonym of* Aleksey Maksimovich Peshkov \ˈpʸesh-kəf\ (b. March 16 [March 28, New Style], 1868, Nizhny Novgorod, Russia—d. June 14, 1936) Russian short-story writer and novelist who first attracted attention with his naturalistic and sympathetic stories of tramps and social outcasts.

Brown Brothers

Gorky had an unhappy childhood, in which he was forced to earn his living from the age of eight. He was frequently beaten by his employers and was nearly always hungry and ill clothed. These early experiences later led him to choose the pseudonym Gorky, meaning bitter. Oppressed by his miserable life, he attempted suicide. At the age of 21 he became a tramp, supporting himself with odd jobs of all kinds during extensive wanderings throughout southern Russia.

While living in Tbilisi, Georgia, Gorky began to publish stories in the provincial press. With the publication of CHELKASH (1895) in a leading St. Petersburg journal, he began to have remarkable success. The story, which combines elements of Romanticism and realism, initiated Gorky's celebrated "tramp period," during which he described (and often sympathized with) the social dregs of Russia. "Dvadtsat shest i odna" (1899; TWENTY-SIX MEN AND A GIRL), describing the

difficult labor conditions in a bakery, is often regarded as his best short story.

He next tried his hand at a series of plays and novels. His first novel, *Foma Gordeyev* (1899), illustrates his admiration for strength of body and will in the masterful barge owner and rising capitalist Ignat Gordeyev, who is contrasted with his relatively feeble and intellectual son Foma, a "seeker after the meaning of life," as are many of Gorky's other characters. From this point, the rise of Russian capitalism became one of Gorky's main fictional interests. *Mat* (1906; *Mother*) holds considerable interest as Gorky's only long work devoted to the Russian revolutionary movement. Gorky also wrote a series of plays, the most famous of which is *Na dne* (1902; THE LOWER DEPTHS).

Between 1899 and 1906 Gorky lived mainly in St. Petersburg, where he became a Marxist and then a Bolshevik. In 1901 he was arrested for publishing a revolutionary poem, "Pesnya o burevestnike" ("Song of the Stormy Petrel"); he was released shortly afterward and went to the Crimea, having developed tuberculosis. He took a prominent part in the Russian Revolution of 1905, was arrested in the following year, and was again quickly released, partly as the result of protests from abroad.

Gorky left Russia in 1906 and spent seven years as a political exile, living mainly in his villa on the Italian island of Capri. He returned to Russia in 1913, and he opposed Russia's participation in World War I. He also criticized the Bolshevik seizure of power in November 1917 and went on to attack the victorious Lenin's dictatorial methods in his newspaper *Novaya zhizn* ("New Life"). In July 1918 his protests were silenced by Lenin's orders. From 1919 onward Gorky cooperated with Lenin's government. In the decade ending in 1923 Gorky's greatest masterpiece appeared—the autobiographical trilogy *Detstvo* (1913–14; MY CHILDHOOD), *V lyudyakh* (1915–16; *In the World*), and *Moi universitety* (1923; *My Universities*).

Gorky lived in Italy from 1921 to 1928 but was eventually persuaded to return to the U.S.S.R. permanently. He became the undisputed leader of Soviet writers; he was the first president of the Union of Soviet Writers, and in that capacity he worked to establish Socialist Realism. His most generally admired work of this later period is a set of reminiscences of Russian writers—*Lev Tolstoy* (1919; *Reminiscences of Leo Nikolaevich Tolstoy*) and *O pisatelyakh* (1928; "About Writers").

Mystery attaches to Gorky's death, which occurred suddenly in 1936 while he was under medical treatment. Accusations have continued to surface that Gorky was murdered on Joseph Stalin's orders, though documentary proof of the charge has not been found.

Gormenghast series \ˈgȯr-mən-ˌgast, -ˌgäst\ Three fantasy novels—*Titus Groan*, *Gormenghast*, and *Titus Alone*—by British author and illustrator Mervyn PEAKE. With the novella *Boy in Darkness* they compose the Gormenghast epic, a bildungsroman about Titus, 77th Earl of Groan.

Titus Groan (1946) tells of Titus's infancy in the dank castle of Gormenghast, a crumbling medieval monstrosity surrounded by the mud huts of the "outer dwellers." Subplots and secondary characters, including his frivolous sister Fuchsia and the guileful, ambitious Steerpike, are the primary objects of attention.

In *Gormenghast* (1950) Titus grows from adolescence to early manhood and becomes conscious of his need for freedom and love. He eventually leaves Gormenghast in search of his destiny.

Though modern elements, including automobiles, airplanes, electronic devices, and glass-and-steel buildings, feature in *Titus Alone* (1959), the novel is no less fantastic or gothic than its predecessors. Peake was planning a fourth Gormenghast novel at the time of his death in 1968.

Görres \'gœr-əs\, Joseph von, *in full* Johann Joseph von Görres (b. Jan. 25, 1776, Koblenz, Archbishopric of Trier [Germany]—d. Jan. 29, 1848, Munich)   German writer who was one of the leading figures of late German Roman Catholic Romanticism.

Görres taught natural science in Koblenz and then lectured at Heidelberg (1806–07), where he became acquainted with the leaders of German Romanticism. With Achim von Arnim and Clemens Brentano, he edited the *Zeitung für Einsiedler* ("Journal for Hermits," renamed *Tröst Einsamkeit*; "Consolation Solitude"), the organ for the Heidelberg Romantics. His interest in German folk literature awakened by this contact, he rediscovered and popularized old German literature in his *Die teutschen Volksbücher* (1807; "The German Folkbooks"), a collection of late medieval narrative prose. Fascination with the Orient, another characteristic of the Romantic movement, engendered his *Mythengeschichte der asiatischen Welt* (1810; "Mythical Stories of the Asiatic World").

In 1808 Görres returned to Koblenz. There, in 1814, he founded the newspaper *Rheinische Merkur*. Considered to be the most influential journal of the time in Germany, it turned first against Napoleon and, after his fall, against the reactionary politics of the German states, all of which led to its suppression in 1816. With the publication of his pamphlet "Teutschland und die Revolution" (1819; "Germany and the Revolution"), he was forced to flee to Strasbourg and to Switzerland. In 1824 he formally returned to the Roman Catholic church and in 1827 became professor of history at Munich. He also wrote the monumental *Christliche Mystik*, 4 vol. (1836–42; "Christian Mysticism").

Gorter \'kôr-tər\, Herman (b. Nov. 26, 1864, Wormerveer, Neth.—d. Sept. 15, 1927, Brussels)   Foremost Dutch poet of the 1880s literary revival, a movement nourished by Aesthetic ideals.

In 1889 Gorter contributed to the movement's periodical *De Nieuwe Gids* ("The New Guide") with his first and most important work, "Mei" ("May"). The poem describes impressionistically the beauty of the Dutch spring landscape on the arrival of the personified May, whose joy is subsequently subdued by disillusion and thus symbolizes Gorter's own spiritual development: from orgiastic abandonment in nature to a quieter, metaphysical longing for peace within humanity.

In his sensitive *Verzen* of 1890 he moved from the retrospection of "Mei" to a direct communication of immediate spiritual and sensuous experience, producing some of the most remarkable poetry in the language. Later, Gorter became a visionary communist, and his Marxist-inspired *Pan* (1916) looks to a new utopia.

Gosse \'gòs\, Sir Edmund (b. Sept. 21, 1849, London, Eng.—d. May 16, 1928, London)   English translator, literary historian, and critic who introduced the work of continental European writers to English readers.

Gosse worked on the library staff of the British Museum from 1865 to 1875, was a translator for the Board of Trade for some 30 years, lectured on English literature at Trinity College, Cambridge, from 1885 to 1890, and finally was librarian to the House of Lords from 1904 to 1914.

Gosse translated Henrik Ibsen's plays, notably *Hedda Gabler* (1891) and *The Master Builder* (1893; with William Archer). He wrote literary histories, such as *18th Century Literature* (1889) and *Modern English Literature* (1897), as well as biographies of Thomas Gray (1884), John Donne (1899), Ibsen (1907), and other writers. Some of his many critical essays were collected in *French Profiles* (1905). His finest book is probably FATHER AND SON (1907), a minor classic of autobiography in which he recounts with grace, irony, and wit his escape from the dominance of a puritanical father to the exhilarating world of letters. Gosse was knighted in 1925.

Go Tell It on the Mountain   Semiautobiographical novel by James BALDWIN, published in 1953. Based on the author's experiences as a teenaged preacher in a small revivalist church, the novel describes two days and a long night in the life of the Grimes family, particularly the 14-year-old John and his stepfather Gabriel. It is a classic of contemporary African-American literature.

Baldwin's description of John's descent into the depths of his young soul was hailed as brilliant, as was his exploration of Gabriel's complex sorrows. The novel teems with biblical references. Though the novel is in part about the position of blacks in American society, some critics felt that Baldwin inadequately addressed racial issues; the novelist, however, said he made a deliberate attempt to break out of the "cage" of black writing.

Gotham \'gäth-əm\   Name given to New York City, or the borough of Manhattan, by Washington Irving in *Salmagundi* (1807–08), a series of satirical essays he published with his brother, William, and James K. Paulding. This nickname for Manhattan has been used continuously ever since.

The name was originally used in an English legend, in which the village of Gotham in Nottinghamshire was expecting a visit from King John (reigned 1199–1216). In order to avoid the expense entailed by the residence of the court, the villagers decided to feign stupidity. Royal messengers found them engaged in ridiculous tasks, such as trying to drown an eel, joining hands around a thornbush to shut in a cuckoo, and attempting to rake the moon out of a pond. Hearing about their foolishness, the king determined to stay elsewhere. The "foles of Gotham" are mentioned in the 15th-century Wakefield plays. *The Merrie Tales of the Mad Men of Gotham*, a collection of their jests, was first published in the 16th century. In reference to this tale, bookseller Frances Steloff named her New York bookstore Gotham Book Mart and used the motto "Wise Men Fish Here."

gothic \'gäth-ik\   **1.** Of or relating to a late 18th- and early 19th-century style of fiction characterized by the use of medieval settings, a murky atmosphere of horror and gloom, and macabre, mysterious, and violent incidents.   **2.** Of or relating to a literary style or an example of such style characterized by grotesque, macabre, or fantastic incidents or by an atmosphere of irrational violence, desolation, and decay. In the mid-20th century, the term SOUTHERN GOTHIC was used to describe such a style as it was adapted by several writers of the American South to portray their vision of the South at that time. The word is sometimes capitalized.

gothic novel   European Romantic, pseudomedieval fiction having a prevailing atmosphere of mystery and terror. Its heyday was the 1790s, but it was frequently revived thereafter. Called gothic because its imaginative impulse was drawn from the rough and primitive grandeur of medieval buildings and ruins, such novels were expected to be dark and tempestuous and full of ghosts, madness, outrage, superstition, and revenge. The settings were often castles or monasteries equipped with subterranean passages, dark battlements, hidden panels, and trapdoors. The vogue was initiated in England by Horace Walpole's immensely successful *Castle of Otranto* (1765). His most respectable follower was Ann Radcliffe, whose *The Mysteries of Udolpho* (1794) and *The Italian* (1797) are among the best examples of the genre. A more sensational type of gothic romance exploiting horror and violence flourished in Germany and was introduced to England by Matthew Gregory Lewis with *The Monk* (1796). The classic horror stories *Frankenstein* (1818), by Mary Wollstonecraft Shelley, and *Dracula* (1897), by Bram Stoker, are written in the gothic tradition but without the specifically gothic trappings.

Easy targets for satire, the early gothic romances died of their own extravagances of plot, but gothic elements continued to haunt the fiction of such major writers as the Brontë sisters, Edgar Allan Poe, and Nathaniel Hawthorne, as well as many modern horror stories. A good deal of early science fiction, like H.G. Wells's *The Island of Doctor Moreau* (1896), also seems to spring out of the gothic movement. In the second half of the 20th century, the term was applied to paperback romances having themes and trappings similar to the original gothic novels.

Gottfried von Strassburg \'gȯt-‚frēt-fȯn-'shträs-‚bu̇rk\ (fl. 1210) One of the greatest medieval German poets, whose courtly epic *Tristan und Isolde* (probably written about 1210) is the classic version of the famous love story.

The only information about Gottfried consists of references to him in the work of other poets and inferences from his own work. However, the breadth of learning displayed in *Tristan und Isolde* reveals that he must have been well educated and accustomed to polite society.

The Celtic legend of Tristan and Iseult (TRISTAN AND ISOLDE) reached Germany through French sources. Gottfried based his work on the Anglo-Norman version of Thomas of Brittany (1160–70).

Gottfried's moral purpose, as he states it in the prologue, is to present to courtiers an ideal of love. The core of this ideal is that love (*Minne*) cnnobles through the suffering with which it is inseparably linked. This ideal Gottfried enshrines in a story in which actions are motivated and justified not by a standard ethic but by the conventions of courtly love. Thus, the love potion, instead of being the direct cause of the tragedy as in primitive versions of the Tristan story, is treated with sophistication as a mere outward symbol of the nature of the lovers' passion—tragic because adulterous but justified by the "courts of love" because of its spontaneity, its exclusiveness, and its completeness.

Although unfinished, Gottfried's is the finest of the medieval versions of the Tristan legend and one of the most perfect creations of the medieval courtly spirit, distinguished alike by the refinement and elevated tone of its content and by the elaborate skill of its poetic technique.

Gotthelf \'gȯt-‚helf\, Jeremias, *pseudonym of* Albert Bitzius \'bit-sē-u̇s\ (b. Oct. 4, 1797, Morat, Switz.—d. Oct. 22, 1854, Lützelflüh) Swiss novelist and short-story writer whose vivid narrative works extol the virtues of Bernese rural people and traditional church and family life.

The son of a pastor, Bitzius studied theology at Bern and Göttingen and took part in the political activities that brought to an end the rule of the aristocracy in Bern.

When radical tendencies began to appear in Swiss liberalism, Bitzius became more conservative. He felt compelled to write about Christian beliefs in a world threatened by materialism. His *Der Bauernspiegel* (1837; "Mirror of the Peasants"), *Leiden und Freuden eines Schulmeisters*, 2 vol. (1838–39; *The Joys and Sorrows of a School-master*), *Die Armennot* (1840; "Needs of the Poor"), *Wie Uli der Knecht glücklich wird* (1841; *Ulric the Farm Servant*), and *Uli der Pächter* (1849; "Ulric the Tenant Farmer") all had rural life and people as subject matter.

Gotthelf's 13 novels and more than 50 short stories reveal not only his genius as an epic writer and his poetic gifts but also his intense interest in people. Psychological observation, imagination, and creative power of language enabled him to achieve vivid portraits.

Göttinger Hain \'gœt-in̄-ər-'hīn\ ("Göttingen Grove"), *also called* Göttinger Hainbund \'hīn-‚bu̇nt\ ("Göttingen Grove Group") A literary association of the era of German "sentimentality" (about 1740 to 1780) that is credited with the reawakening of homely, folk, and nature themes in German lyric and popular national poetry. Members were the young poets—mostly students at the university at Göttingen—H.C. Boie, J.H. VOSS, Ludwig HÖLTY, J.F. Hahn, K.F. Cramer, Friedrich and Christian Stolberg, and J.A. Leisewitz.

Founded in 1772, the group took its name from Friedrich Gottlieb Klopstock's ode *Der Hügel und der Hain* ("The Hill and the Grove"), in which the grove is metaphorically the abode of the German bards, in contrast to the hill as home of the Greek Parnassians, an opposition the Hain felt aptly symbolized their poetic goals. The *Göttinger Musenalmanach* ("Göttingen Muses Journal"), published from 1770, became the literary organ for the circle and the archetype for many similar German literary journals.

The poets of the Göttinger Hain had in common a desire to free poetry from the confines of the rationalism of the Enlightenment and from social convention; they attempted to make poetry free from foreign, especially French, examples. The group disbanded after 1774.

Gottsched \'gȯt-shät\, Johann Christoph (b. Feb. 2, 1700, Judithenkirch, near Königsberg, Prussia [now Kaliningrad, Russia]—d. Dec. 12, 1766, Leipzig, Saxony [Germany]) Literary theorist, critic, and dramatist who introduced French 18th-century classical standards of taste into the literature and theater of Germany.

After studying at Königsberg, Gottsched taught at the University of Leipzig. He brought out his most important theoretical work, *Versuch einer kritischen Dichtkunst vor die Deutschen* ("Essay on a German Critical Poetic Theory") in 1730. It was the first German treatise on the art of poetry to apply the standards of reason and good taste advocated by Nicolas Boileau, the foremost exponent of classicism in France.

Gottsched's most enduring achievement resulted from his collaboration with the actress Caroline Neuber, which led to the establishment of the Leipzig school of acting and criticism. Following classicist models, they effectively transformed the nature of the German theater from coarse entertainment into a respected vehicle for serious literary effort. Gottsched's *Deutsche Schaubühne*, 6 vol. (1741–45), containing chiefly translations from the French, provided the German stage with a classical repertory. His concern for style, advanced by his *Ausführliche Redekunst* (1728; "Complete Rhetoric") and *Grundlegung einer deutschen Sprachkunst* (1748; "Foundation of a German Literary Language"), helped to regularize German as a literary language. Gottsched also issued the first German literary review, *Beiträge zur kritischen Historie der Deutschen Sprache* (1732–44; "Contributions to the History of the German Language").

Götz von Berlichingen \'gœts-fȯn-'ber-lik̄-in̄-ən\ (*in full* Götz von Berlichingen mit der eisernen Hand) Drama in five acts by J.W. von GOETHE, published in 1773 and performed in 1774. The pseudo-Shakespearean tragedy was the first major work of the Sturm und Drang movement. Intending the play as a drama to be read rather than performed, Goethe published it as a shortened version of his drama *Urgötz oder Die Geschichte Gottfriedens von Berlichingen mit der eisernen Hand dramatisiert* (1771; "The Dramatized Story of Gottfried von Berlichingen with the Iron Hand").

The play was based on the autobiography of a Franconian knight who lived from the mid-15th to the mid-16th century and who constantly did battle with various feudal governments. Through Götz's story, Goethe was able to make oblique criticisms of contemporary political tyranny.

Gourmont \gür-'mōⁿ\, Rémy de (b. April 4, 1858, Bazoches-en-Houlmes, Fr.—d. Sept. 27, 1915, Paris) Novelist, poet, playwright, and philosopher who was one of the most intelligent contemporary critics of the French Symbolist movement.

After studying law at Caen, Gourmont accepted a position in 1881 at the Bibliothèque Nationale, where he developed his wide interests and erudition. He was dismissed in 1891, however, for publishing an allegedly unpatriotic article in the *Mercure de France*, a journal he had helped to found. After that he continued to contribute to the *Mercure de France* until he died, but a painful skin disease caused him to be a semi-recluse.

His 50 published volumes are mainly collections of essays. They include *Epilogues* (1903–13), a running commentary on contemporary events and persons; *Promenades littéraires* (1904–27) and *Promenades philosophiques* (1905–09), literary and philosophical essays; and books devoted to studies of style, language, and aesthetics.

Gourmont's strength as a critic was grounded in the completely aesthetic basis of his literary critiques. His approach to literature later influenced the 20th-century poets Ezra Pound and T.S. Eliot. His novels, however, which include *Sixtine* (1890; *Very Woman*), *Les Chevaux de Diomède* (1897; *The Horses of Diomedes*), *Le Songe d'une femme* (1899; *The Dream of a Woman*), and *Un Coeur virginal* (1907; *A Virgin Heart*), have been criticized because the characters seem at times more intellectual symbols than human beings.

Government Inspector, The Farcical drama in five acts by Nikolay GOGOL, originally performed and published as *Revizor* in 1836. The play, sometimes translated as *The Inspector General*, mercilessly lampoons the corrupt officials of an obscure provincial town that is portrayed as a microcosm of the Russian state.

Aleksandr Pushkin provided Gogol with the theme of the drama, in which a well-dressed windbag named Ivan Khlestakov, who has been mistaken for the dreaded government inspector, is bribed and fêted by village officials in the hope of turning his attention away from their maladministration. As they celebrate their apparent success following the bogus inspector's departure, however, the arrival of the real inspector is announced—to the horror of those concerned.

Gower \'gaū-ər, 'gȯr\, John (b. 1330?—d. 1408, London?) Medieval English poet in the tradition of courtly love and moral allegory who strongly influenced the writing of other poets of his day.

Gower's French-language work *Speculum meditantis*, or *Mirour de l'omme* (c. 1374–78; "The Mirror of Man"), is composed of 12-line stanzas and opens impressively with a description of the devil's marriage to the seven daughters of sin; continuing with the marriage of reason and the seven virtues, it ends with a searing examination of the sins of English society just before the Peasants' Revolt of 1381. The denunciatory tone is relieved at the end by a long hymn to the Virgin.

Gower's major Latin poem, the *Vox clamantis* (c. 1385), owes much to Ovid; it is essentially a homily, being in part a criticism of the three estates of society, in part an elegy for a prince. The poet's political doctrines are traditional, but he uses the Latin language with fluency and elegance. Gower wrote several poems in English, including *In Praise of Peace*, in which he pleads urgently with the king to avoid the horrors of war. His greatest English work is the CONFESSIO AMANTIS (begun c. 1386), a collection of exemplary tales of love.

Goytisolo \ˌgȯi-tē-'sō-lō\, Juan (b. Jan. 5, 1931, Barcelona, Spain) Spanish novelist, short-story writer, and essayist whose early Neorealist work evolved into avant-garde fiction using structuralist and formalist techniques.

A young child when his mother was killed during the Spanish Civil War, Goytisolo grew up hating the fascist dictatorship and the country's conservative religious values. From 1948 to 1952 he attended the universities of Barcelona and Madrid. He lived in self-imposed exile in France from the late 1950s until Francisco Franco's death in 1975.

His highly praised first novel, *Juegos de manos* (1954; *The Young Assassins*), concerns a group of students who are intent on murdering a politician and who kill the student they have chosen as the assassin. *Duelo en el Paraíso* (1955; *Children of Chaos*), set just after the Spanish Civil War, is about the violence that ensues when children gain power over a small town. After the publication of the short-story collection *Fin de fiesta* (1962; *The Party's Over*), his style grew more experimental, as in *Señas de identidad* (1966; *Marks of Identity*). *Reivindicación del Conde don Julián* (1970; *Count Julian*), which is considered his masterwork, experimented with transforming the Spanish language, seen as a tool of political power. Later novels include *Juan sin tierra* (1975; *Juan the Landless*) and *Makbara* (1980). Goytisolo also wrote travel narratives, critical essays, and a personal memoir, *Coto vedado* (1985; *Forbidden Territory*).

Gozzano \gȯt-'tsä-nō\, Guido (b. Dec. 19, 1883, Turin, Italy—d. Aug. 9, 1916, Turin) Italian poet, leader of a poetic school known as Crepuscolarismo, which favored a direct, unadorned style to express nostalgic memories.

Gozzano graduated from the National College of Savigliano and briefly attended law school in Turin before beginning a literary career. *La via del rifugio* (1907; "The Road to Shelter"), his first volume of verse, showed the influence of Gabriele D'Annunzio.

The second and last collection Gozzano published during his lifetime was *I colloqui* (1911; *The Colloquies*), which addresses the themes of youth, death, creative repression, nostalgia, regret, and contentment. Much of Gozzano's work was uncollected when he died from tuberculosis at age 32.

Gozzi \'gȯt-tsē\, Carlo, Count (conte) (b. Dec. 13, 1720, Venice [Italy]—d. April 4, 1806, Venice) Poet, prose writer, and dramatist, a fierce and skillful defender of the traditional Italian commedia dell'arte form against the dramatic innovations of Pietro Chiari and Carlo Goldoni.

After serving in the army, Gozzi returned to Venice in 1744, where he wrote satires and miscellaneous prose and joined the reactionary Academy of the Granelleschi, a group determined to preserve Italian literature from being corrupted by foreign influences. Gozzi began his personal crusade for the revival of commedia dell'arte by attacking Goldoni, author of many fine realistic comedies, first in a satirical poem and then in an exotic commedia dell'arte play, *L'amore delle tre melarance* (performed 1761; *The Love for Three Oranges*).

Following the immense success of the play, Gozzi wrote nine other *fiabe* (fantastic plays; literally, "fairy tales"), based upon puppet plays, Oriental stories, popular fables, fairy stories, and the works of such Spanish dramatists as Tirso de Molina, Pedro Calderón de la Barca, and Miguel de Cervantes. Outstanding among these *fiabe* are *Il re cervo* (performed 1762; *The King Stag*), *Turandot* (performed 1762), *La donna serpente* (performed 1762; "The Snake Woman"), and *L'augellin belverde* (performed 1765; "The Pretty Little Green Bird").

Gozzi also wrote a vivid, if immodest, autobiography, *Memorie inutili* (1797; *The Memoirs of Carlo Gozzi*).

Gozzi \'gȯt-tsē\, Gasparo, Count (conte) (b. Dec. 4, 1713, Venice [Italy]—d. Dec. 27, 1786, Padua, Venetia) Italian poet, prose writer, journalist, and critic, remembered for a satire that revived interest in Dante and for his two periodicals, which brought the journalistic style of the 18th-century English essayists Joseph Addison and Sir Richard Steele to Italy.

Gozzi was an early member, with his dramatist brother Carlo Gozzi, of the purist Academy of the Granelleschi, a literary society founded for the purpose of literary reform. He became known for verse satires and *Difesa di Dante* (1758; "Defense of Dante"), an attack on the critic Saviero Bettinelli for preferring Virgil to Dante as a model for Italian poets. More important was Gozzi's publication and, in large part, his writing of two periodicals (the *Gazzetta veneta* and the *Osservatore veneto*) similar in style to those of Addison and Steele. Gozzi also wrote a romance, some occasional verse, translations of French works, and many letters.

Gqoba \'gō-bə, 'kō-; *in Xhosa the first consonant is a type of click*\, William Wellington (b. 1840, near Gaga, Cape Colony [now in South Africa]—d. April 26, 1888)   Black poet, philologist, and journalist, a dominant literary figure among 19th-century African writers, whose poetry reflects the effects of missionaries and education on the Bantu people.

During his short career Gqoba pursued a number of trades: wagon maker, clerk, teacher, translator of Xhosa and English, and pastor. During 1884–88 he was editor of *Isigidimi samaxosa* ("The Kaffir Express"), to which he contributed articles on the history of the Xhosa people.

Fame came to Gqoba after the composition of two long didactic poems, "The Discussion Between the Christian and the Pagan" and "The Great Discussion on Education," both influenced in style by his fellow South African Tiyo Soga's translation of John Bunyan's *Pilgrim's Progress* into Xhosa. In the first poem the traditional conflict is set up between the pleasures and riches of the life advocated by the pagan and the ascetic life advocated by the Christian. Although the Christian's argument is much less convincing, he wins in the end. The second poem depicts a group of young intellectuals who are critical of the educational practices of their day, but, again, the moderate Christian position, which wins out, seems to many less convincing than the radical one.

Grabbe \'gräb-ə\, Christian Dietrich (b. Dec. 11, 1801, Detmold, Westphalia [Germany]—d. Sept. 12, 1836, Detmold)   German dramatist whose plays anticipated Expressionism and film technique.

Grabbe's most important work, *Napoleon oder die Hundert Tage* (1831; "Napoleon or the Hundred Days"), exemplifies the boldly experimental form of his plays, in which he avoided continuous action by the use of a series of vividly depicted and contrasting scenes. His tragedy *Don Juan und Faust* (1829) is an imaginative and daring attempt to combine the two great works of W.A. Mozart and J.W. von Goethe. Like many of his plays, it exceeded the practical demands of the theater. Among his most enduring work is the mordant satire *Scherz, Satire, Ironie und tiefere Bedeutung* (1827; *Comedy, Satire, Irony and Deeper Meaning*). He is also known for *Abhandlung über die Shakespeare-Manie* (1827; "Essay on Shakespeare Mania"), in which he attacks William Shakespeare and advocates an independent national drama.

Graça Aranha \'grä-sə-ä-'rän-yə\, José Pereira da (b. June 21, 1868, São Luís, Braz.—d. Jan. 26, 1931, Rio de Janeiro)   Brazilian novelist and diplomat who is best remembered for his novel *Canaã* (1902; *Canaan*), in which he explored the conflicts of the Brazilian ethnic melting pot. With its philosophical digressions and lyrical descriptions, *Canaã*, a "novel of ideas," was influential in introducing readers throughout the world to the beauties of the Brazilian landscape and the problems of Brazilian society.

A founding member of the Brazilian Academy of Letters, Graça Aranha was a prominent spokesman for social, political, and artistic reform throughout his literary and public career. His innovative spirit did not decline with age: in the 1920s he was closely associated with young radicals of the Modernismo movement in Brazil, and in 1924 he resigned from the Academy because he felt its standards were formalistic and stifling. Constantly experimenting with avant-garde literary techniques, he adopted the modernist idiom in a novel published the year before his death, *A viagem maravilhosa* (1929; "The Marvelous Journey"). His aesthetic views were further publicized in his essays *A estética da vida* (1925; "The Aesthetics of Life") and *O espírito moderno* (1925; "The Modern Spirit").

Grace Abounding   Spiritual autobiography of John BUNYAN, written during the first years of his 12-year imprisonment for Nonconformist religious activities and published in 1666. Bunyan's effort to obtain an absolutely honest, unadorned rendering of the truth about his own spiritual experience caused him to forge a highly original style. His description of the inner life of the Christian is rich in powerful physical imagery; he feels "a clogging and a heat at my breast-bone as if my bowels would have burst out" and states that a preacher's call to abandon the sin of idle pastimes "did benumb the sinews of my best delights."

Graces \'grā-səz\   In Greek religion, a group of goddesses of fertility. The name, a translation of Greek *Charites* or Latin *Gratiae*, refers to the "pleasing" or "charming" appearance of a fertile field or garden. The number of Graces varied in different legends, but usually there were three: Aglaia ("Brightness"), Euphrosyne ("Joyfulness"), and Thalia ("Bloom"). They are said to be daughters of Zeus and Hera (or Eurynome, daughter of Oceanus) or of Helios and Aegle, a daughter of Zeus. The Graces frequently were taken as goddesses of charm or beauty in general and hence were associated with Aphrodite, the goddess of love.

Gracián \gräth-'yän\, Baltasar, *surname in full* Gracián y Morales \ē-mō-'räl-äs\ (b. Jan. 8, 1601, Belmonte de Calayatud, Spain—d. Dec. 6, 1658, Tarazona)   Philosopher and writer known as the leading Spanish exponent of *conceptismo*, a style of dealing with ideas that involves the use of terse and subtle displays of exaggerated wit.

Gracián entered the Jesuit order and later became rector of the Jesuit college at Tarragona. His early works—*El héroe* (1637; *The Hero*), *El discreto* (1646; *The Compleat Gentleman*), and *El oráculo manual y arte de prudencia* (1647; *The Oracle*)—were largely efforts to educate people in the ethics of worldly life. His literary ideas on *conceptismo* and the art of writing in conceits were clearly set forth in *Agudeza y arte de ingenio* (1642; 2nd edition, 1648; "Subtlety and the Art of Genius"). In defiance of his superiors, he published pseudonymously *El criticón* (1651, 1653, 1657; *The Critick*), a three-part philosophical novel. In it he examined society from the standpoint of a savage and gave the clearest statement of his pessimistic philosophy, with its emphasis on willpower and struggle.

gracioso \ˌgrä-thē-'ō-sō, -sē-\ [Spanish, from *gracioso* (adjective) amusing, comical]   A buffoon in Spanish comedy.

Grade \'grä-də\, Chaim \'kī-im\ (b. April 5, 1910, Vilna, Russian Empire [now Vilnius, Lithuania]—d. June 26, 1982, New York, N.Y., U.S.)   Yiddish poet, short-story writer, and novelist.

In Vilna, Grade gave up his religious studies to become a writer. He escaped to Russia after the German invasion in 1941, but he returned to Vilna after the war and discovered that his wife and mother had been killed and the culture in which he had been nurtured had been destroyed. Grade then moved to Paris, where he wrote searing poetry about the Holocaust. In 1948 he settled in New York City.

Most of Grade's subsequent works dealt with issues related to the culture and tradition of his Jewish faith. The short story "Mayn krig mit Hersh Rasseyner" (1950; "My Fight with Hersh Rasseyner") tells of a post-World War II encounter of a secular Jew deeply troubled by the Holocaust with a devout friend from Poland. Grade's novel *Di agune* (1961; *The Agunah*) concerns an Orthodox woman whose husband is missing in action in wartime and who, according to Orthodox Jewish law, is forbidden to remarry. His other fiction includes a novella, *Der brunem* (1967; *The Well*), the ambitious two-volume *Tsemakh Atlas* (1967, 1968; *The Yeshiva*), and many short stories and poems. Grade also published a memoir, *Der mame's Shabosim* (1955; *My Mother's Sabbath Days*).

Gradgrind \'grad-ˌgrīnd\ Fictional character, the proprietor of an experimental school where only facts are taught in Charles Dickens' novel HARD TIMES. For Dickens he embodies the unsympathetic qualities of the Utilitarian social philosophy prevalent in Victorian England.

gradus \'grād-əs, 'grad-\ A dictionary of Greek or Latin prosody and poetic phrases used as an aid in the writing of verse in Greek or Latin. The term is derived from the *Gradus ad Parnassum* ("A Step to Parnassus"), a 17th-century prosody dictionary long used in British schools.

Graf \'gräf\, Oskar Maria (b. July 22, 1894, Berg am Starnberger See, Ger.—d. June 28, 1967, New York, N.Y., U.S.) German regional novelist and poet known for novels and sketches of Bavarian peasant life, such as *Kalender-Geschichten*, 2 vol. (1929, rev. ed., 1957; "Calendar Histories"). Graf's writing is marked by frank realism and by his own socialist and pacifist beliefs, but these are tempered by humorous affection for his subjects.

Graf worked as a director for the Munich Workers' Theater before turning to writing. In 1933 he fled Germany, and in 1938 he left Europe and eventually settled in New York. Graf's early work centered on themes of social revolution and protest. These ideas were never totally absent from his work, but he found his stride in stories of Bavarian folk life. He feared the effects of modernity on traditional lives, a concern that is particularly notable in his utopian novel, *Die Eroberung der Welt* (1949; "The Conquest of the World"), reissued as *Die Erben des Untergangs* (1959; "The Heirs of the Ruins").

graffito \grə-'fē-tō\ *plural* graffiti \-tē\ [Italian, incised inscription, a derivative of *graffiare* to scratch] Any casual writing, rude drawing, or marking on the walls of buildings, as distinguished from a deliberate writing known as an inscription. Centuries-old graffiti have been found in great abundance, *e.g.*, on the monuments of ancient Egypt. Apparently, private owners of property felt the nuisance of the defacement of their walls, for in Rome near the Porta Portese (formerly Porta Portuensis) was found an inscription begging persons not to scribble (*scariphare*) on the walls.

Graffiti are important to the paleographer because they illustrate the forms and corruptions of the various alphabets used by the people and thus may guide the archaeologist to the date of a building. Their chief value, however, is twofold. First, they are important to the linguist since the language of graffiti is closer to the spoken language of the period and place than usual written language. The linguist also learns about other languages, as in the case of the ancient Greek mercenaries who scribbled their names, in the Cypriote dialect and syllabary, on an Egyptian sphinx, or the Greek "tourist" from Pamphylia who carved his name on the great pyramid at Giza. Second,

graffiti are invaluable to the historian for the light they throw on the everyday life of the period and on intimate details of customs and institutions. The graffiti dealing with the gladiatorial shows at Pompeii are in this respect particularly noteworthy.

The most famous graffito is that generally accepted as representing a caricature of Christ upon the cross found on the walls of the Domus Gelotiana on the Palatine in Rome in 1857 (now in the Luigi Pigorini Museum of Prehistoric Ethnography of the Roman College).

Graham \'grā-əm, 'gram\, Jorie (b. May 9, 1951, New York, N.Y., U.S.) American poet whose abstract, intellectual verse was known for its visual imagery, complex metaphors, and philosophical content.

Graham began publishing poems in 1977. Her first volume of verse, *Hybrids of Plants and of Ghosts* (1980), features compact, intricate poems that explore death, beauty, and change. *Erosion* (1983) examines the connection between the body and the soul in such poems as "Reading Plato," "I Watched a Snake," and "The Sense of an Ending." In *The End of Beauty* (1987), Graham experimented with form, constructing subtle, sometimes inaccessible poems divided into series of short, numbered stanzas with missing words and lively enjambment. *Region of Unlikeness* (1991), which is annotated to explain textual obscurities, furthers her exploration of philosophy and religion in such poems as "The Tree of Knowledge," "The Holy Shroud," and "Chaos." She also published *Materialism* (1993) and contributed to several anthologies.

Graham \'grā-əm, 'gram\, Winston (Mawdsley) (b. June 30, 1910, Victoria Park, Manchester, Eng.) English author whose mysteries and historical novels feature suspenseful, psychological plots that often hinge on the discovery of past events.

The subjects of Graham's crime stories are usually ordinary people and amateur detectives who face moral quandaries. The title character and narrator of *Marnie* (1961; film, 1964), perhaps his best-known mystery, is a professional fraud who subconsciously represses a traumatic childhood experience. His other notable crime novels are *The Forgotten Story* (1945), *Take My Life* (1947), *Fortune Is a Woman* (1953), *The Little Walls* (1955), *After the Act* (1965), and *Stephanie* (1992).

Graham's historical novels, set in Cornwall in the 18th and 19th centuries, chronicle several generations of the Poldark family, including Ross POLDARK. These include *Ross Poldark* (1945), *Jeremy Poldark* (1950), *The Grove of Eagles* (1963), *The Black Moon* (1973), *The Miller's Dance* (1982), and *The Twisted Sword* (1990). Graham's nonfiction works include *The Spanish Armadas* (1972) and *Poldark's Cornwall* (1983).

Grahame \'grā-əm, 'gra-əm\, Kenneth (b. March 8, 1859, Edinburgh, Scot.—d. July 6, 1932, Pangbourne, Berkshire, Eng.) Author of THE WIND IN THE WILLOWS (1908), one of the English classics of children's literature. Its animal characters—principally Mole, Rat, Badger, and Toad—combine captivating human traits with authentic animal habits.

While pursuing a career at the Bank of England, Graham contributed articles to such journals as the *St. James Gazette* and the *Yellow Book* and published collections of sketches, stories, and essays—*Pagan Papers* (1893), *The Golden Age* (1895), and *Dream Days* (1898)—all of which reveal his sensitive understanding of childhood. *The Wind in the Willows* made his reputation as a writer of children's books. Parts of it were originally written in letter form to his young son.

Grail \'grāl\, *also called* Holy Grail [Old French *graal,* from Medieval Latin *gradalis*] Object of legendary quest for the knights of Arthurian romance. The term evidently denoted a widemouthed or shallow vessel, though its precise etymology remains uncertain.

The story of the Grail may have been inspired by classical and Celtic mythologies, which abound in horns of plenty, magic life-restoring caldrons, and the like. The first extant text to give such a vessel Christian significance as a mysterious, holy object was Chrétien de Troyes's late 12th-century unfinished romance *Perceval, ou Le Conte du Graal*. The work combines the religious with the fantastic, and in it Chrétien introduces the guileless rustic knight Perceval, whose dominant trait is innocence. Early in the 13th century, Robert de Boron's poem *Joseph d'Arimathie, ou le roman de l'estoire dou Graal* extended the Christian significance of the legend, linking it with the cup used by Christ at the Last Supper and afterward by Joseph of Arimathea to catch the blood flowing from Christ's wounds as he hung upon the Cross. Wolfram von Eschenbach gave the legend profound and mystical expression in his epic *Parzival*, in which the Grail became a precious stone, fallen from heaven. Prose versions of Robert's works began to link the Grail story even more closely with ARTHURIAN LEGEND. A 13th-century German romance, *Diu Krône*, made Sir Gawain the Grail hero, while the *Queste del Saint Graal* (which forms part of what is called the Prose *Lancelot*, a section of the Vulgate cycle) introduced a new hero, the pure Sir Galahad, son of Lancelot. This latter work was to have the widest significance of all, and its essence was transmitted to English-speaking readers through Sir Thomas Malory's late 15th-century prose narrative *Le Morte Darthur*.

Grandbois \grän-'bwä\, Alain (b. May 25, 1900, Saint-Casimir, Que., Can.—d. March 18, 1975, Quebec) French-Canadian poet whose use of unconventional verse forms, abstract metaphors of voyage and death, and colorful imagery influenced younger experimental poets.

Much of Grandbois's early poetry was originally published in volumes such as *Poèmes* (1934) and *Les Îles de la nuit* (1944; "The Isles of the Night"). Among his later collections are *Poèmes* (1963) and *Selected Poems* (1965), containing both the French originals and English translations. In addition to poetry, he wrote biographies of Louis Jolliet, *Né à Québec* (1948; *Born in Quebec*), and Marco Polo, *Les Voyages de Marco Polo* (1942), as well as a volume of short tales, *Avant le chaos* (1945; "Before the Chaos").

Grandet, Eugénie \ē-zhä-nē-grän-'dā\ Fictional character, the protagonist of the novel EUGÉNIE GRANDET by Honoré de Balzac.

grandeza mexicana, La \lä-grän-'dā-sä-mā-hē-'kä-nä\ ("The Grandeur of Mexico") Epistolary poem by Bernardo de BALBUENA, published in 1604. One of the first examples of a poem in the baroque style to be written in the Spanish New World, it is an elaborate description of Mexico City. In an introductory octave and nine chapters of terza rima verse the poem celebrates the culture of the city and its people. The first edition included the "Compendio apologético en alabanza de la poesía" ("Apologetic Compendium in Praise of Poetry"), a treatise on poetics in which Balbuena states his belief that poetry should be a kind of process of defamiliarization achieved through such techniques as describing the commonplace in uncommon terms.

Grand Guignol \grän-gē-'nyòl\ Short plays emphasizing violence, horror, and sadism, popular in Parisian cabarets in the 19th century, especially at the Théâtre du Grand Guignol.

Grand Inquisitor Character invented by Ivan Karamazov in Fyodor Dostoyevsky's novel THE BROTHERS KARAMAZOV. Ivan, in an attempt to shake his brother Alyosha's faith, posits the Grand Inquisitor as the opponent of Christ who questions why God allows human misery to continue.

grand style A literary style marked by a sustained and lofty dignity, sublimity, and eloquence (as often attributed to such epic poets as Homer, Virgil, or John Milton).

grand tour A tour of Europe (including The Netherlands, France, Germany, Austria, Switzerland, and Italy especially) that was considered an essential part of a gentleman's education from about the 16th through the 19th century. Many writers, including Henry Fielding, Tobias Smollett, Laurence Sterne, James Boswell, and J.W. von Goethe toured the European continent and later wrote about their travels.

Grangerford, Emmeline \'em-ə-,līn-'grän-jər-fərd\ Fictional character, a poet and painter in Mark Twain's HUCKLEBERRY FINN. Upon viewing her works, Huck Finn naively echoes his hosts' reverence for Emmeline's maudlin elegies of deceased neighbors and her soppy crayon drawings of young ladies in mourning. One such drawing, a mawkish portrait of a woman weeping over a dead bird, is titled "I Shall Never Hear Thy Sweet Chirrup More Alas."

Emmeline is a parody of Julia A. Moore, "The Sweet Singer of Michigan," a notoriously bad American poet who was popular in the 1870s.

Granville-Barker \'gran-,vil-'bär-kər\, Harley (b. Nov. 25, 1877, London, Eng.—d. Aug. 31, 1946, Paris, Fr.) English dramatist, producer, and critic whose naturalistic stagings in an era of theatrical artificiality profoundly influenced the 20th-century theater.

Granville-Barker began his stage training at age 13 and first appeared on the London stage two years later. In 1904 he became manager of the Court Theatre with J.E. Vedrenne and introduced the plays of Henrik Ibsen, Maurice Maeterlinck, John Galsworthy, and John Masefield, as well as Gilbert Murray's translations from Greek. Granville-Barker's original productions of the early plays of George Bernard Shaw were also important. Among new plays produced were several of his own: *The Voysey Inheritance* (1905); *Prunella* (1906), written with Laurence Housman; *Waste* (1907); and *The Madras House* (1910). He revolutionized the performance of William Shakespeare's plays with his innovative use of continuous action on an open stage and rapid, lightly stressed speech. After World War I, Granville-Baker retired from the theater and moved to Paris, collaborating with his second wife in translating Spanish plays and writing the five series of *Prefaces to Shakespeare* (1927–48). In 1937 he became director of the British Institute of the University of Paris. He fled to Spain in 1940 and then went to the United States and lectured at Harvard University. He returned to Paris in 1946.

Grapes of Wrath, The Novel by John STEINBECK, published in 1939. Set during the Great Depression, it traces the migration of an Oklahoma Dust Bowl family to California and their subsequent hardships as migrant farm workers. It won a Pulitzer Prize in 1940. The work did much to publicize the injustices of migrant labor.

The narrative, interrupted by prose-poem interludes, chronicles the struggles of the Joad family's life on a failing Oklahoma farm, their difficult journey to California, and their disillusionment once they arrive there and fall prey to a parasitic economic system. The insularity of the Joads—Ma's obsession with family togetherness, son Tom's self-centeredness, and daughter Rose of Sharon's materialism—ultimately gives way to a sense of universal community.

graphic \'graf-ik\ [Greek *graphikós,* literally, of or for writing, a derivative of *gráphein* to write] **1.** Marked by clear, lifelike, or vividly realistic description or striking imaginative power. **2.** Vividly or plainly shown or described.

Grass \'gräs\, Günter (Wilhelm) (b. Oct. 16, 1927, Danzig [now Gdańsk, Pol.]) German poet, novelist, playwright, sculptor, and printmaker who, with his extraordinary first novel *Die Blechtrommel* (1959; THE TIN DRUM), became the literary spokesman for the German generation that grew up in the Nazi era.

In his native Danzig, Grass passed through the Hitler Youth movement, was drafted at 16, wounded in battle, and became a prisoner of war. Encouraged by the writers' association Gruppe 47, he produced poems and plays, at first with little success. In 1956 he wrote the exuberant, picaresque novel *Die Blechtrommel*. It was followed by the novella *Katz und Maus* (1961; *Cat and Mouse*) and the epic novel *Hundejahre* (1963; *Dog Years*). The three books together form a trilogy set in Danzig.

His other novels—always politically topical—include *Der Butt* (1977; *The Flounder*), a ribald fable of the war between the sexes from the Stone Age to the present; *Das Treffen in Telgte* (1979; *The Meeting at Telgte*), a hypothetical "Gruppe 1647" meeting of authors at the close of the Thirty Years' War; *Kopfgeburten: oder die Deutschen sterben aus* (1980; *Headbirths, or, the Germans Are Dying Out*); and *Unkenrufe* (1992; *The Call of the Toad*), concerning the uneasy relationship between Poland and reunited Germany.

grateful dead In folktales of many cultures, the spirit of a deceased person who bestows benefits on the one responsible for his burial. In the prototypical story, the protagonist is a traveler who encounters the corpse of a debtor, to whom the honor of proper burial has been denied. After the traveler satisfies the debt or pays for the burial, he goes on his way. In another version of the story, burial is prescribed for religious reasons but prohibited by civil authorities; this version forms the theme of the apocryphal Book of Tobit in the Old Testament.

The hero is soon joined by another traveler (sometimes in the form of an animal or, in the story of Tobit, an angel), who helps him in a dramatic way. The companion ultimately reveals himself as the grateful spirit of the deceased whom the hero helped to bury.

Gratiano or **Graziano** Stock theatrical character in Italian COMMEDIA DELL'ARTE. *See* DOTTORE.

Grau \'graù\, Shirley Ann (b. July 8, 1929, New Orleans, La., U.S.) American novelist and short-story writer noted for her examinations of evil and isolation among American Southerners.

Grau's first book, *The Black Prince, and Other Stories* (1955), had considerable success. Her first novel, *The Hard Blue Sky* (1958), concerns Cajun fishermen and their families. This was followed by *The House on Coliseum Street* (1961) and *The Keepers of the House* (1964), which won a Pulitzer Prize for fiction. It deals with three generations of the Howland family, a once-mighty Southern dynasty. Among her later novels are *The Condor Passes* (1971), *Evidence of Love* (1977), and *Roadwalkers* (1994). Her other short-story collections include *The Wind Shifting West* (1973) and *Nine Women* (1985).

Graustark \'graù-,stärk\ Romantic quasi-historical novel subtitled *The Story of a Love Behind a Throne*, by George Barr MCCUTCHEON, first published in 1901. Modeled on Anthony Hope's popular novel *The Prisoner of Zenda* (1894), *Graustark* is set in the mythical middle-European kingdom of Graustark and is suffused with derring-do, court intrigues, and passionate romance. McCutcheon's further novels about the imaginary principality include *Beverly of Graustark* (1904) and *The Prince of Graustark* (1914).

In its extended senses, the word Graustark is used to refer to an imaginary land of high romance or to a highly romantic piece of writing.

Graves \'grävz\, Robert (von Ranke) (b. July 24/26, 1895, London, Eng.—d. Dec. 7, 1985, Deyá, Majorca, Spain) English poet, novelist, critic, and classical scholar who carried on many of the formal traditions of English verse in a period of experimentation. His more than 120 books also include a notable historical novel, I, CLAUDIUS (1934); an autobiographical classic of World War I, GOOD-BYE TO ALL THAT (1929; rev. ed., 1957); and erudite, controversial studies in mythology.

Graves wrote three books of verse while serving as a British officer during World War I. He was severely wounded in 1916 and remained deeply troubled by his war experiences for at least a decade. In 1929 he met Laura Riding, an American poet with whom he was associated for 13 years. Together they established the Seizin Press (1927–38) and published the journal *Epilogue* (1935–38). They also cowrote *A Survey of Modernist Poetry* (1927, reprinted 1977), in which they developed ideas about close textual analysis.

The success of Graves's *Good-Bye to All That*, war memoirs notable for their grimness, enabled him to make his permanent home on Majorca. Graves's novel *I, Claudius* is an engaging first-person narrative written in the voice of the Roman emperor Claudius. Graves's researches for *The Golden Fleece* (1944; U.S. title, *Hercules, My Shipmate*) led him into a wide-ranging study of myths and to what was his most controversial scholarly work, THE WHITE GODDESS (1948).

Graves was professor of poetry at the University of Oxford from 1961 to 1966. His *Collected Poems* appeared in 1948, with four later revisions. His views on poetry can be found in *The Crowning Privilege* (1955) and *Oxford Addresses on Poetry* (1962).

Graveyard by the Sea, The Poem by Paul VALÉRY, written in French as "Le Cimetière marin" and published in 1922 in the collection *Charmes; ou poèmes*. The poem, set in the cemetery at Sète (where Valéry is now buried), is a meditation on death.

At first, the narrator observes the calm sea under the blazing noontime sun and accepts the inevitability of death. But as the wind begins to stir and waves start forming on the sea, a sign of the energy beneath the surface, the narrator proclaims the necessity of choosing life by choosing eternal change over contemplation. Valéry approached the composition of the poem as if it were a musical form, with the rhythm of the verse mimicking the movement of the sea.

graveyard school Genre of 18th-century British poetry that focused on death and bereavement. The graveyard school consisted largely of imitations of Robert Blair's popular long poem of morbid appeal, *The Grave* (1743), and of Edward Young's celebrated blank-verse dramatic rhapsody *Night Thoughts* (1742–45). These poems express the sorrow and pain of bereavement, evoke the horror of death's physical manifestations, and suggest the transitory nature of human life. The meditative, philosophical tendencies of graveyard poetry found their fullest expression in Thomas Gray's *An Elegy Written in a Country Church Yard* (1751), a dignified, gently melancholy elegy celebrating the graves of humble villagers and suggesting that the lives of rich and poor alike "lead but to the grave." The works of the graveyard school were significant as early precursors of the Romantic movement.

Gravity's Rainbow Novel by Thomas PYNCHON, published in 1973. The sprawling narrative comprises numerous threads having to do either directly or tangentially with the secret development and deployment of a rocket by the Nazis near the end of World War II. Lieutenant Tyrone Slothrop is an American working for Allied Intelligence in London. Agents of the Firm, a clandestine military organization, are investigating an apparent connection between Slothrop's erections and the targeting of incoming V-2 rockets. As a child, Slothrop was the subject of experiments conducted by a Harvard professor who is now a Nazi rocket scientist. Slothrop's quest for the truth behind these implications leads him on a nightmarish journey of either historic discovery or profound paranoia, depending on his own and the reader's interpretation. The novel won the National Book Award for fiction in 1974.

Gray \'grā\, Simon (James Holliday) (b. Oct. 21, 1936, Hayling Island, Hampshire, Eng.) British dramatist whose plays, often set in academia, are noted for their witty, literary dialogue and complex characterizations.

Gray alternately lived in Canada and England. While working as a university lecturer in both countries, he wrote satirical novels and farcical plays for stage and television. His first stage play was *Wise Child* (1968), which featured a criminal transvestite.

Gray's first international success was *Butley* (1971; film, 1974), a play about a petulant university professor whose venomous wit masks an inner emptiness. Similarly, *Otherwise Engaged* (1975) concerns a sardonic publisher who strives to isolate himself. *Quartermaine's Terms* (1981) is the sadly comic story of a gentle, ineffectual English teacher. Among Gray's other plays are *Spoiled* (1971), *The Rear Column* (1978), *The Common Pursuit* (1984), and *Hidden Laughter* (1990).

Gray \'grā\, Thomas (b. Dec. 26, 1716, London, Eng.—d. July 30, 1771, Cambridge, Cambridgeshire) English poet whose AN ELEGY WRITTEN IN A COUNTRY CHURCH YARD (1751) is one of the best known of English lyric poems.

Gray entered Peterhouse College, Cambridge, in 1734, but he left in 1738 without a degree and set out in 1739 on a grand tour of France, Switzerland, and Italy.

In 1742 Gray settled at Cambridge. That same year his friend the poet Richard West died, an event that affected him profoundly. Gray produced some of his best poems about this time, including "Ode on the Spring," "Sonnet on the Death of Mr. Richard West," "Hymn to Adversity," and "Ode on a Distant Prospect of Eton College."

When Gray's famous elegy was published, its success was instantaneous and overwhelming. Its theme that the lives of the rich and poor alike "lead but to the grave" was already familiar, but Gray's treatment—which had the effect of suggesting that it was not only the "rude forefathers of the village" he was mourning but the death of all and of the poet himself—gave the poem its universal appeal. In 1757 two Pindaric odes by Gray were published. The critical response disappointed him, and he virtually ceased to write, becoming increasingly retiring and hypochondriacal.

Gray, Dorian \'dôr-ē-ən-'grā\ Fictional character, the hedonistic protagonist of Oscar Wilde's novel THE PICTURE OF DORIAN GRAY. He exchanges his soul for youth that never fades.

Grayson, David. Pseudonym of Ray Stannard BAKER.

Graziano or **Gratiano** Stock theatrical character in Italian COMMEDIA DELL'ARTE. *See* DOTTORE.

Grazzini \grät-'tsē-nē\, Anton Francesco, *byname* Il Lasca \ĕl-'läs-kä\ ("The Roach") (b. March 22, 1503, Florence [Italy]—d. Feb. 18, 1584, Florence) Italian poet, playwright, and storyteller who was active in the linguistic and literary controversies of his day.

In 1540 Grazzini took part in the founding of the Accademia degli Umidi ("Academy of the Humid"), the first literary society of the time. Grazzini, who was a contentious individual, received his byname from the common name of a fish well known to anglers for putting up a good fight and belonging

to the genus *Leuciscus*, another name by which he was sometimes identified. He was instrumental in founding the CRUSCA ACADEMY in 1582.

In his burlesque verses he strongly opposed humanism and Petrarchism, but he defended pure Tuscan diction in the reform of Italian literary style. His own language is lively, at times approaching dialect, in his seven comedies (written 1540–50) and in *Le cene* ("The Suppers"), a collection of 22 stories in the manner of Giovanni Boccaccio, purporting to be told by a group of young people at a carnival. (D.H. Lawrence translated one, *The Story of Doctor Manente* [1917].)

Grazzini also collected (1559) the *Canti carnascialeschi* ("Carnival Songs") popular in Florence during the time of Lorenzo the Magnificent.

great books Certain classics of literature, philosophy, history, and science that are believed to contain the basic ideas of Western culture. These include works by Homer, Plato, Aristotle, Thucydides, Herodotus, Thomas Aquinas, William Shakespeare, Blaise Pascal, Immanuel Kant, J.S. Mill, and Charles Darwin, among many others. *See also* CANON.

great chain of being *also called* chain of being. The conception of the nature of the universe that had a pervasive influence on Western thought, particularly through the ancient Greek Neoplatonists and derivative philosophies during the European Renaissance and the 17th and early 18th centuries. The term denotes three general features of the universe: plenitude, continuity, and gradation. The principle of plenitude states that the universe is "full," exhibiting the maximal diversity of kinds of existences. The principle of continuity asserts that the universe is composed of an infinite series of forms, each of which shares with its neighbor at least one attribute. According to the principle of linear gradation, this series ranges in hierarchical order from the barest type of existence to the *ens perfectissimum*, or God.

This model of the universe died out in the 19th century but was given renewed currency in the 20th by Arthur O. Lovejoy in *The Great Chain of Being: A Study of the History of an Idea* (1936). A summary of the concept of the great chain of being can be found in the first epistle of Alexander Pope's *An Essay on Man*.

Great Dionysia \,dī-ə-'nish-ə\, *also called* City Dionysia. Ancient drama festival in which tragedy, comedy, and satyric drama originated. It was held in Athens in March in honor of Dionysus, the god of wine. Tragedy of some form was introduced by the tyrant Peisistratus when he refounded the festival (534/531 BC), but the earliest tragedy that survives, Aeschylus' *Persians*, dates from 472 BC.

In the competition for tragedy, three poets wrote, produced, and probably acted in three tragedies on a single theme. Each poet also presented a satyr play, which treated a heroic subject in burlesque fashion. Judges awarded a prize to the best poet. In comedy, introduced in 486 BC, five poets competed for the prize, each with one play. The satyr play was always the work of a tragic poet, and the same poet never wrote both tragedies and comedies.

Great Expectations Novel by Charles DICKENS, first published serially in *All the Year Round* in 1860–61 and issued in book form in 1861. The novel was one of its author's greatest critical and popular successes.

The first-person narrative relates the coming-of-age of Pip (Philip Pirrip). Reared in the marshes of Kent by his disagreeable sister and her sweet-natured husband, the blacksmith Joe Gargery, the young Pip one day helps a convict to escape. Later he is sent to live with Miss Havisham, a woman driven half-mad years earlier by her lover's departure on their wedding day. Her other ward is the orphaned Estella, whom she is teaching to torment men with her beauty. Pip, at first cautious, later falls in love with Estella, to his misfortune. When an anonymous benefactor makes it possible for Pip to go to London for an education, he credits Miss Havisham. He begins to look down on his humble roots, but nonetheless Estella spurns him again and marries instead the ill-tempered Bentley Drummle. Pip's benefactor turns out to have been Abel Magwitch, the convict he once aided, who dies awaiting trial after Pip is unable to help him a second time. Joe rescues Pip from despair and nurses him back to health.

Great Gatsby, The \'gats-bē\ Novel by F. Scott FITZGERALD, published in 1925. The narrator, Nick Carraway, is a young Princeton man who works as a bond broker in Manhattan. His neighbor at West Egg, Long Island, is Jay Gatsby, a self-made Midwesterner of considerable wealth. Nick watches as Gatsby is betrayed by his own dreams, which have been nurtured by a meretricious society.

Great God Brown, The Drama in four acts and a prologue by Eugene O'NEILL, produced and published in 1926. An example of O'Neill's pioneering experiments with Expressionistic theater, the play makes use of multiple masks to illustrate the private and public personas of the characters, as well as the changing tenor of their interior lives.

The action juxtaposes its two central characters, William "Billy" Brown, a mediocre architect, and Dion Anthony, a talented but dissolute artist. Both characters are in love with Margaret, who chooses Dion because she is in love with the sensual, cynical mask he presents to the world. But when he removes his mask to reveal the spiritual, artistic side of his nature, she is repulsed. Frustrated at being unable to realize his artistic promise, Dion sinks deeper into his self-destructive habits and soon dies. Billy, who has always been jealous of Dion's talent, steals Dion's mask and takes on his persona. He marries Margaret, who believes that he is Dion. Billy eventually is accused of the murder of his "old" self and is shot by the police. Margaret continues to worship Dion's mask.

Great Mother of the Gods *also called* Cybele \'sib-ə-lē, *in Byron's work* si-'bē-lē\, Cybebe \'sib-ə-bē\, Dindymene \,din-di-'mē-nē\, *or* Agdistis \ag-'dis-tis\ Ancient Oriental and Greco-Roman deity, known by a variety of local names; the name Cybele or Cybebe predominates in Greek and Roman literature from about the 5th century BC onward. Her full official Roman name was Mater Deum Magna Idaea ("Great Idaean Mother of the Gods"). Her mythical attendants, the Corybantes, were wild, half-demonic beings.

Legends agree in locating the rise of the worship of the Great Mother in the general area of Phrygia in Asia Minor (now in west-central Turkey), and during classical times her cult center was at Pessinus, located on the slopes of Mount Dindymus, or Agdistis (hence her names Dindymene and Agdistis). The Greeks always saw in the Great Mother a resemblance to their own goddess RHEA and finally identified the two completely. The Romans identified the Great Mother with the goddesses Ops, Tellus, and Ceres. By the end of the Roman Republic her worship had attained prominence, and under the empire it became one of the most important cults in the Roman world.

In all of her aspects, Roman, Greek, and Oriental, the Great Mother was the great parent not only of gods but also of human beings and beasts. She was called the Mountain Mother, and special emphasis was placed on her maternity over wild nature; this was manifested by the orgiastic character of her worship.

Cybele's ecstatic rites, as celebrated by her priests (known as *galli*), were at home and fully comprehensible in Asia, but they were too frenzied for cultures farther west. The Great Mother was especially prominent in the art of the empire. She usually appears with mural crown and veil, seated on a throne or in a chariot, and accompanied by two lions.

Mother goddess figures who were usually goddesses only of fertility and reproduction in general should not be confused with the Great Mother of the Gods, who was regarded as the giver of life to gods, human beings, and beasts alike.

Gréban \grā-'bän\, Arnoul (b. 1420, probably Le Mans, Anjou, Fr.—d. 1471, probably Le Mans) French author of an important 15th-century religious drama known as *Mystère de la Passion* (1453/54), dramatizing the events of Jesus' life. The performance of this Passion play, revised by Jean Michel to 65,000 lines, usually took four days. Gréban also collaborated with his brother Simon on a long mystery play about the Acts of the Apostles.

Grecism \'grē-,siz-əm\ Imitation of Greek art, literature, sculpture, or architecture.

Greek Anthology (*Greek* Anthologia Hellēnikē), *also called* Palatine Anthology. Collection of Greek epigrams, songs, epitaphs, and rhetorical exercises that includes about 3,700 short poems, mostly written in elegiac couplets. Some of the poems were written as early as the 7th century BC, others as late as AD 1000. The nucleus of the Anthology is a collection made early in the 1st century BC by Meleager, who called it *Stephanos* (Greek: "Garland" or "Collection of Flowers"); Meleager introduced it with a poem comparing each writer in the collection to a flower. In the late 9th century AD, Constantinus Cephalas joined Meleager's collection to those of Philippus of Thessalonica (1st century AD), Diogenianus (2nd century), and Agathias (6th century). Late in the 10th century, the Cephalas collection was revised and augmented. This revision forms the first 15 books of the Anthology, preserved in the Palatine manuscript, discovered at Heidelberg, Ger. The 16th book is made up of poems culled from another manuscript version of the Cephalas collection (the Planudean manuscript) and compiled by Maximus Planudes in 1301.

The literary value of the Anthology lies in the distinction and charm of perhaps one-sixth of the whole. For the rest, it preserves a good deal that is of historical interest.

Greek mythology The body of myths and stories developed by the ancient Greeks concerning their gods and heroes, the nature of the cosmos, and their own religious practices.

The Greek myths are known today primarily from Greek literature. The oldest known literary sources, the *Iliad* and the *Odyssey* (9th or 8th century BC), focus on events surrounding the Trojan War and the activities of the gods' society on Mt. Olympus. Two poems by Homer's near-contemporary Hesiod, the *Theogony* and the *Works and Days*, contain accounts of the genesis of the cosmos, the succession of divine rulers, the succession of human ages, the origin of human woes, and the origin of sacrificial practices. Myths are also preserved in the Homeric hymns and in fragments of epic poems on the Trojan War; in lyric poems, especially those composed by Pindar; in the works of the tragedians of the 5th century BC, Aeschylus, Sophocles, and Euripides; in writings of scholars and poets of the Hellenistic Age (330–23 BC), such as Callimachus, Euhemerus, and Apollonius of Rhodes; and in writers of the time of the Roman Empire, for example, Ovid, Plutarch, and Pausanias.

Folktales, consisting of popular recurring themes and told for amusement, inevitably found their way into Greek myth. One such theme is that of lost persons (*e.g.*, Odysseus, Paris, Helen of Troy) found or recovered after long and exciting adventures. Another is the journeys to the land of the dead (such as those undertaken by Orpheus, Heracles, Odysseus, and Theseus).

Greek mythology formed the staple of most Greek poetry and epic, as well as of many dramatic works. It also influenced philosophers and historians to a marked degree. The Romans adopted Greek mythology virtually wholesale into their own literature. Through the medium of Latin and, above all, the works of Ovid, Greek myth was stamped indelibly on the medieval imagination. With subsequent revivals and reinterpretations, its influence has permeated Western culture to an unparalleled extent, from the themes of art and literature to the vocabulary of science and technology.

Greek tragedy The form of drama produced in ancient Greece by the authors Aeschylus, Euripides, and Sophocles. The dramas had a fairly rigid structure consisting of an introductory prologos; a parodos, which marks the entrance of the chorus; several episodes constituting the main action of the play; and the exodus, or conclusion, which follows the last song of the chorus. *See also* TRAGEDY.

Green \'grēn\, Anna Katharine (b. Nov. 11, 1846, Brooklyn, N.Y., U.S.—d. April 11, 1935, Buffalo, N.Y.) American writer of detective fiction who helped to make the genre popular in America by creating well-constructed plots based on a good knowledge of criminal law.

Inspired by her father's work as a lawyer, Green began her writing career with the detective story *The Leavenworth Case* (1878), which introduced her detective hero, Ebenezer Gryce, and rapidly became popular. After writing her third detective novel, Green wrote two volumes of poetry. Thereafter she concentrated on detective fiction.

Green's tendency to intersperse romantic characterizations and dialogue in her work sometimes makes her style old-fashioned, but her skillful plotting and technical accuracy are noteworthy. Some of her works are *Lost Man's Lane* (1898), *The Filigree Ball* (1903), *The House of the Whispering Pines* (1910), and *The Step on the Stair* (1923).

Green \'grēn\, Henry, *pseudonym of* Henry Vincent Yorke \'yòrk\ (b. Oct. 29, 1905, near Tewkesbury, Gloucestershire, Eng.—d. Dec. 13, 1973, London) Novelist and industrialist whose sophisticated satires mirrored the changing class structure in post-World War II English society.

While working in his family's engineering firm, Green produced his laconically titled social comedies, *Blindness* (1926), *Living* (1929), *Party Going* (1939), *Caught* (1943), *Loving* (1945), *Back* (1946), *Concluding* (1948), *Nothing* (1950), and *Doting* (1952). Underlying the pleasant surfaces of the novels are disturbing and enigmatic perceptions. An early autobiography, *Pack My Bag*, was published in 1943. *Surviving: The Uncollected Writings of Henry Green*, edited by his grandson Matthew Yorke, was published in 1992.

Green \'grēn\, Julien (Hartridge) (b. Sept. 6, 1900, Paris, Fr.) French-American writer of somber novels that show the influence of the American regional style known as Southern gothic. Written in French and usually set in French provincial towns, they deal with neurotic and obsessive characters whose lives are centered on magnified trivialities. Green was the first person of American parentage to be elected to the Académie Française (1971).

Green's first novel, *Mont-Cinere* (1926; *Avarice House*), was favorably received in both France and the United States. *Adrienne Mesurat* (1927; *The Closed Garden*) was awarded the Femina Bookman Prize. Other fiction includes *Léviathan* (1929; *The Dark Journey*), *Épaves* (1932; *The Strange River*), *Le Visionnaire* (1934; *The Dreamer*), *Minuit* (1936; *Midnight*), *Si j'étais vous* (1947; *If I Were You*), *La Malfaiteur* (1955; *The Transgressor*), *L'Autre* (1971; *The Other One*), *Le Mauvais Lieu* (1977; "The Bad Place"), *Les Pays lointains* (1987; *The Distant Lands*),

and *Les Étoiles du sud* (1989; "The Southern Stars"). Green also wrote plays, one of which, *Sud* (1953; *South*), became the basis of a 1973 opera, with music by Kenton Coe. *Memories of Happy Days* (1942) was Green's only book written in English. His *Journals*, covering the years from 1926, were published in several separate volumes. Other works include collections of essays, collections of short stories, and *La Nuit des fantômes* (1976; "Halloween"), a children's book. In 1970 the Académie Française awarded Green its grand prize for literature.

Green \'grēn\, Paul (Eliot) (b. March 17, 1894, Lillington, N.C., U.S.—d. May 4, 1981, Chapel Hill, N.C.) American novelist and playwright whose characteristic works deal with North Carolina folklore and regional themes; he was one of the first white playwrights to write perceptively about the problems of Southern blacks.

Green began writing plays for the Carolina Playmakers in 1919. His best-known play, *In Abraham's Bosom*, concerns a man's attempt to establish a school for his fellow blacks; it was awarded the Pulitzer Prize in 1927. During the Great Depression, Green's work took on a stronger note of social protest. Among his plays from this period are *Hymn to the Rising Sun*, about a chain gang, and *Johnny Johnson*, an expressionistic, episodic antiwar play for which Kurt Weill wrote the music; both plays were first performed in 1936. In 1941 Green collaborated with Richard Wright in the dramatization of Wright's novel *Native Son*. Green also wrote more than a dozen symphonic dramas, including *The Stephen Foster Story* (1959), *Trumpet in the Land* (1970), and *The Lone Star* (1977), which won wide popularity.

Greenaway \'grē-nə-,wā\, Kate, *byname of* Catherine Greenaway (b. March 17, 1846, London, Eng.—d. Nov. 6, 1901, London) English artist and book illustrator known for her original and charming children's books.

Kate Greenaway began to exhibit drawings in 1868, and her first published illustrations appeared in such magazines as *Little Folks*. In 1879 she produced her first successful book, *Under the Window*. It was followed by *The Birthday Book* (1880), *Mother Goose* (1881), *Little Ann* (1883), and other books for children, which had an enormous success. "Toy-books" though they were, these little works created a revolution in book illustration; they were praised by art critics throughout the world.

In 1890 Greenaway was elected to the Royal Institute of Painters in Water Colours, and in 1891, 1894, and 1898 she exhibited watercolor drawings, including illustrations for her books, at the gallery of the Fine Art Society (which exhibited a representative selection in 1902). From 1883 to 1897, with a break only in 1896, she issued a series of *Kate Greenaway's Almanacs*. Although she illustrated *The Pied Piper of Hamelin* (1889) and other works, the artist preferred to provide her own text.

Greenberg \'grēn-,bərg\, Uri Zvi, *pseudonym* Tur Malka \'tūr-'māl-kä\ (b. Jan. 10, 1894, Biały Kaimień, Galicia, Austria-Hungary [now Bily Kamin, Ukraine]—d. May 8, 1981, Tel Aviv, Israel) Hebrew and Yiddish poet whose strident, Expressionist verse exhorted the Jewish people to redeem their historical destiny; he warned of the impending Holocaust in poems such as "In malkhus fun tselem" (1922; "In the Kingdom of the Cross"). An adherent of the right-wing Revisionist Zionist party, Greenberg used his poetry to espouse a mystical, religious view of Zionism and to further the party's extreme nationalism.

The son of a Ḥasidic rabbi, Greenberg received a traditional Ḥasidic upbringing in Lemberg (now Lviv, Ukraine). In 1920 he became copublisher of Warsaw's *Khalyastre* ("The Gang"), an Expressionist, avant-garde literary journal. He wrote in both

Yiddish and Hebrew until he immigrated to Palestine in 1924; thereafter, he wrote solely in Hebrew.

Greenberg's early Hebrew poetry, such as "Yerushalim shel matah" (1924; "Earthly Jerusalem"), was influenced by Walt Whitman. From the 1930s his work was politicized, as in the collection *Ezor magen u-ne'um ben ha-dam* (1930; "A Shield of Defense and the Word of the Son of Blood"), the poem "Migdal ha-Geviyyot" (1937; "The Tower of Corpses"), and the acclaimed collection *Reḥovot ha-nahar* (1951; "Streets of the River").

Greene \\'grēn\\, Graham, *in full* Henry Graham Greene (b. Oct. 2, 1904, Berkhamsted, Hertfordshire, Eng.—d. April 3, 1991, Vevey, Switz.) English novelist, short-story writer, playwright, and journalist whose novels treat life's moral ambiguities in the context of contemporary political settings.

Bettmann Archive

After studying at Balliol College, Oxford, Greene converted to Roman Catholicism in 1926. His first published work was a book of verse, *Babbling April* (1925), and, while working as a copy editor, he achieved a modest success with his first novel, *The Man Within* (1929). He worked as a journalist, film critic, and literary editor until 1940. He then traveled widely for much of the next three decades as a freelance journalist.

Greene found his voice with his fourth novel, *Stamboul Train* (1932; also entitled *Orient Express*; film, 1934). It was the first of his "entertainments," works similar to thrillers in their language and their suspenseful plots, but possessing greater moral complexity and depth. *Stamboul Train* was followed by the novels *A Gun for Sale* (1936; also entitled *This Gun For Hire*; film, 1942), *The Confidential Agent* (1939; film, 1945), and *The Ministry of Fear* (1943; film, 1945). A fifth entertainment, *The Third Man* (1949; film, 1949), was originally written as a screenplay.

Greene's finest novels—BRIGHTON ROCK (1938; film, 1948), THE POWER AND THE GLORY (1940; film, 1962), THE HEART OF THE MATTER (1948), and THE END OF THE AFFAIR (1951)—all have distinctly religious themes through which he expresses his preoccupation with sin and moral failure. His next four novels were each set in a different Third World nation on the brink of political upheaval: THE QUIET AMERICAN (1955; film, 1957) in Vietnam, OUR MAN IN HAVANA (1958; film, 1959) in Cuba, A BURNT-OUT CASE (1961) in the Belgian Congo, and THE COMEDIANS (1966; film, 1967) in Haiti. His later works include *The Honorary Consul* (1973; film, 1983), *The Human Factor* (1978; film, 1979), *Monsignor Quixote* (1982), and *The Tenth Man* (1985). Greene also published plays and several collections of short stories. His *Collected Essays* appeared in 1969. He produced a memoir entitled *A Sort of Life* (1971), to which *Ways of Escape* (1980) is a sequel.

Despite the grim nature of many of his stories, Greene was one of the most widely read British novelists of the 20th century. His books' unusual popularity is explained largely by his superb gifts as a storyteller, especially his masterful selection of detail and his use of realistic dialogue in a fast-paced narrative.

Greene \\'grēn\\, Robert (b. July 1558?, Norwich, Eng.—d. Sept. 3, 1592, London) One of the most popular English prose writers of the later 16th century and William Shakespeare's most successful predecessor in blank-verse romantic comedy. He was also among the earliest English autobiographers.

Greene wrote more than 35 works between 1580 and 1592. To be certain of supplying material attractive to the public, he at first slavishly followed literary fashions. His first model was John Lyly. In the later 1580s Greene wrote prose pastorals in the manner of Sir Philip Sidney. The best of these is *Pandosto* (1588), the direct source of Shakespeare's *The Winter's Tale.* About 1590 Greene began to compose serious didactic works. Beginning with *Greenes never too late* (1590), he recounted prodigal son stories based on personal experience.

Greene's *The Honorable Historie of frier Bacon, and frier Bongay* (written *c.* 1591, published 1594) is the first successful romantic comedy in English. In *The Scottish Historie of James the fourth, slaine at Flodden* (written *c.* 1590, published 1598), he used an Italian tale but drew on fairy lore for the characters of Oberon and Bohan.

In his last year Greene wrote exposés of the Elizabethan underworld, including *A Notable Discovery of Coosnage* (1591) and the successful and amusing *A disputation betweene a hee conny-catcher and a shee conny-catcher* (1592). His notable *Greenes groats-worth of witte, bought with a million of repentance*—in which (among other things) he insults the work of Shakespeare—was published shortly after his death.

Green Henry \\'hen-rē\\ Autobiographical novel by Gottfried KELLER, first published in German as *Der grüne Heinrich* in 1854–55 and completely revised in 1879–80. The later version is a classic bildungsroman. Green Henry (so called because his frugal mother made all his clothes from a single bolt of green cloth) sets out to become an artist. After some success and many disappointments, he returns to his native city. In the original version he dies at the end. In the revised version, Henry wins a certain respect and contentment in a modest post as a civil servant.

Green Mansions Novel by W.H. HUDSON, published in 1904. An exotic romance set in the jungles of South America, the story is narrated by a man named Abel who as a young man had lived among the Indians. He tells of Rima, a strange bird-like woman with whom he falls in love. A creature of the forest, Rima is eventually destroyed by the superstitious Indians.

Gregory Narekatzi \\'greg-ə-rē-,när-ə-'kät-sē\\, Saint, *also called* Gregory of Narek \\'när-ek\\ (b. 951—d. 1001) Poet and theologian generally considered the first great Armenian poet and the principal literary figure in Armenia during the 10th century. He was renowned for his mystical poems and hymns, biblical commentaries, and sacred elegies.

Gregory \\'greg-ə-rē\\, Horace (Victor) (b. April 10, 1898, Milwaukee, Wis., U.S.—d. March 11, 1982, Shelburne Falls, Mass.) American poet, critic, and editor noted for both conventional and experimental writing.

Gregory began to write poetry while studying Latin in college, and he first contributed to periodicals in the early 1920s. Finding formal verse inadequate, he tried to combine the idiom of modern life with literary influences in *Chelsea Rooming House* (1930), his first success. His poetry also appeared in many avant-garde magazines during the 1920s and '30s. A later volume was *Another Look* (1976).

Gregory wrote biographies of Amy Lowell (1958) and James McNeill Whistler (1959). His *Pilgrim of the Apocalypse* (1933; 2nd ed., 1957) was one of the first important critiques of D.H. Lawrence. Gregory edited the works of many writers, and with his wife, Marya Zaturenska, he wrote *A History of American Poetry, 1900–1940* (1946). His essays are collected in *Spirit of*

Time and Place (1973), and his translated works include *Love Poems of Ovid* (1964).

Gregory \\'greg-ə-rē\\, Isabella Augusta, Lady, *original surname* Persse \\'pərs\\ (b. March 5, 1852, Roxborough, County Galway, Ire.—d. May 22, 1932, Coole) Irish writer and playwright who—by her translations of Irish legends, her peasant comedies and fantasies based on folklore, and her work for the ABBEY THEATRE—played a considerable part in the late 19th-century IRISH LITERARY RENAISSANCE.

In 1880 she married a member of Parliament, Sir William Henry Gregory; her literary career did not begin until after his death (1892). In 1898 she met William Butler YEATS and became his lifelong friend and patron. She took part in the founding of the Irish Literary Theatre (1899) and became a director (1904) of the Abbey Theatre. Her peasant comedies were based on Irish folkways and picturesque peasant speech, offsetting the more tragic tones of the dramas of Yeats and John Millington Synge.

Lady Gregory wrote or translated nearly 40 plays. *Seven Short Plays* (1909), her first dramatic works, are among her best, vivid in dialogue and characterization. The longer comedies, *The Image* and *Damer's Gold*, were published in 1910 and 1913, and her strange, realistic fantasies, *The Golden Apple* and *The Dragon*, in 1916 and 1920. She also arranged and wrote continuous narratives of various versions of Irish sagas, translating them into an Anglo-Irish peasant dialect known as Kiltartan. They were published as *Cuchulain of Muirthemne* (1902) and *Gods and Fighting Men* (1904).

Greiff \\thā-'gräf\\, León de (b. July 22, 1895, Medellín, Colom.—d. July 11, 1976, Bogotá) Latin-American poet notable for his stylistic innovations.

De Greiff's first book, *Tergiversaciones* (1925; "Tergiversations"), while displaying the musicality common to the Latin-American modernist poets, was innovative in its invention of words, use of strange adjectives, and breaking of the flow of language in an attempt to portray a world laden with symbolic meanings. *Libro de los signos* (1930; "Book of Signs") uses the same stylistic devices; the predominant themes of this poetry collection are solitude, the tedium of existence, and the past. *Variaciones alrededor de la nada* (1936; "Variations About Nothing") contains deeply confessional poems with philosophical speculations on the nature of love, the artistic ideal, and the poet's feeling of life as an adventure. De Greiff's poetry is often ironic, humorous, and satirical to the point of self-mockery.

Grein \\'grīn\\, Jack Thomas, *byname of* Jacob Thomas Grein (b. Oct. 11, 1862, Amsterdam, Neth.—d. June 22, 1935, London, Eng.) Critic, playwright, and theater manager who influenced British drama at the turn of the century.

Drawn to the theater as a boy, Grein became a drama critic at 18. Family misfortunes forced him to go to London, where he became a naturalized citizen in 1895. Inspired by André Antoine's naturalistic Théâtre-Libre in Paris, he founded (1891) the Independent Theatre in London, which was dedicated—despite critical opposition—to new plays chosen for their literary and artistic value. Among the works produced by Grein were Henrik Ibsen's *Ghosts* (1891) and George Bernard Shaw's *Widower's Houses* (1892). Grein wrote drama criticism for *Life* (1889–93), *Illustrated London News*, and other publications. His volumes of published criticism appeared from 1898 to 1903 and in 1921 and 1924.

Grendel \\'gren-dəl\\ Fictional character, a monstrous creature defeated by Beowulf in the Old English poem BEOWULF. Descended from the biblical Cain, Grendel is an outcast, doomed to wander the face of the earth. He revenges himself upon humans by terrorizing and occasionally devouring them.

Many critics have seen Grendel as the embodiment of the physical and moral evil of heathenism; Beowulf's struggles to overcome the monster are thought to symbolize Anglo-Saxon England's emerging Christianity. The 20th-century American writer John Gardner told the story of Beowulf from Grendel's point of view in *Grendel* (1971).

Gresset \\grā-'se\\, Jean-Baptiste-Louis (b. Aug. 29, 1709, Amiens, Fr.—d. June 16, 1777, Amiens) French poet and dramatist who is best known for his irreverent comic narrative poem *Ver-Vert* (1734; *Ver-Vert, or the Nunnery Parrot*), describing with wit tinged with malice the adventures of a parrot who attempts to maintain his decorous convent background while on a visit to another convent.

After entering the Jesuit order in 1726, Gresset continued his education in Paris before returning to teach in Amiens and Tours. In spite of the objections of some of his superiors, Gresset continued to write light occasional verse, within a year publishing *La Carême impromptu* ("The Lenten Impromptu") and *Le Lutrin vivant* ("The Living Lectern"). Returning to Paris in 1735 for a year's study of theology, he wrote *La Chartreuse* ("The Carthusian") and *Les Ombres* ("The Shadows"), both lively and detailed accounts of life in a Jesuit college; they led first to his banishment to the provinces and then to his expulsion from the order, as his keen eye for absurdity and his natural frivolity were seen as anticlerical and impious. His first plays—the tragedy *Édouard III* (performed 1740), which included the first murder ever enacted on the French stage, and a verse comedy, *Sidney* (1745)—were not especially successful, but *Le Méchant* (1747; "The Sorry Man"), a witty exposé of salon life, was highly praised for its pithy, polished dialogue. He was admitted to the Académie Française in 1748. In 1759 Gresset wrote *Lettre sur la comédie*, in which he renounced all his previous poetic and dramatic works as irreligious.

Grettis saga \\'gret-is\\ Latest and one of the finest of the ICELANDERS' SAGAS, written about 1320. Its distinction rests on the complex, problematic character of its outlaw hero, Grettir, and on its skillful incorporation into the narrative of numerous motifs from folklore. Its theme is summed up in the gnomic style of the sagas: "Good gifts and good luck are often worlds apart."

Wellborn, brave, and generous but headstrong and trouble-prone, Grettir, at age 14, kills a man in a quarrel and is outlawed for three years. He spends these years in Norway performing many brave deeds. On his return to Iceland he saves the people from the malicious ghost of Glam the shepherd, who is ravaging the countryside. The dying fiend imposes a curse on Grettir, predicting he will grow afraid of the dark. Later, on an errand of mercy, Grettir accidentally sets fire to a hall in which a chieftain's son burns to death and so is outlawed again. Though his life depends on solitary hiding, his growing fear of the dark compels him to seek centers of human society. At last his enemies overwhelm him with the aid of witchcraft. The best English translation of the saga is by D. Fox and H. Pálsson (1974).

Greville \\'grev-il\\, Fulke, 1st Baron Brooke (b. Oct. 3, 1554, Beauchamp Court, Warwickshire, Eng.—d. Sept. 30, 1628, Warwick) English writer who is best remembered as a powerful philosophical poet.

After matriculating at the University of Cambridge in 1568, Greville was given a post in the Court of the Welsh Marches in 1576. He went on several diplomatic missions abroad and was enriched by grants of land and minor offices. In 1598 he became treasurer of the navy. He later restored Warwick Castle (bestowed on him in 1605 by James I) and wrote verse treatises and plays. He was made a baron in 1621.

Greville's *Life of the Renowned Sir Philip Sidney* (1652) is a valuable commentary on Elizabethan politics. His sonnet collection *Caelica* (1633) is realistic and ironic, differing in tone from most Elizabethan cycles. The melancholy and Calvinistic bent of his mind emphasized the "wearisome condition of humanity," and his verse treatises showed how statesmen can best keep order in a wicked world. Other works by Greville are *Certaine learned and elegant workes* (1633) and *Remains* (1670).

Grévin \grā-'vaⁿ\, Jacques (b. 1538, Clermont-en-Beauvais, Fr.—d. Nov. 5, 1570, Turin, Savoy) French poet and dramatist who is credited with writing the first original French plays to observe the form of classical tragedies and comedies.

Before becoming a doctor of medicine, Grévin wrote several successful comedies, including *La Trésorière* (performed 1559; "The Paymistress"). His comedies, licentious in tone, imitated the regular form of the Roman playwrights Plautus and Terence but used contemporary subjects and a Parisian setting. They were published in Grévin's *Théâtre* (1561), along with his *La Mort de César*, a tragedy on the Senecan model, for which he drew material from classical and contemporary sources. A friend and disciple of the poet Pierre de Ronsard, Grévin also wrote love sonnets and satirical sonnets.

Forced to flee France in 1560 because of his Protestant faith, Grévin took refuge at the Turin court of the Duchess of Savoy (Margaret of France), where he wrote medical treatises on antimony and poisons.

Grey \'grā\, Zane, *original name* Pearl Grey (b. Jan. 31, 1872, Zanesville, Ohio, U.S.—d. Oct. 23, 1939, Altadena, Calif.) Prolific writer whose romantic novels of the American West helped create a new literary genre, the WESTERN.

Trained as a dentist, Grey practiced in New York City from 1898 to 1904, when he published privately a novel of pioneer life, *Betty Zane*, based on an ancestor's journal. He published several works before he achieved success with *The Heritage of the Desert* (1910). Grey subsequently wrote more than 80 books, a number of which were published posthumously. The novel *Riders of the Purple Sage* (1912) was the most popular; others include *The Lone Star Ranger* (1915), *The U.P. Trail* (1918), *Call of the Canyon* (1924), and *Code of the West* (1934). Prominent among his nonfiction works is *Tales of Fishing* (1925).

Griboyedov or **Griboedov** \gr^yi-bə-'yed-əf\, Aleksandr Sergeyevich (b. Jan. 4 [Jan. 15, New Style], 1795, Moscow, Russia—d. Feb. 11 [Jan. 30], 1829, Tehrān, Iran) Russian playwright whose comedy *Gore ot uma* (1822–24; *Woe from Wit*) is one of the finest in Russian literature.

Griboyedov was a graduate of Moscow University. He joined the hussars during the war of 1812 against Napoleon. After resigning his commission in 1816, he lived in St. Petersburg, where he joined the diplomatic service and was appointed secretary in the Russian mission in Tehrān. A sympathizer with the Decembrist revolt of 1825 against Nicholas I, he was arrested in the following year but soon released. In 1828 he was appointed Russian minister in Tehrān. He died there at the hands of a mob that attacked the Russian embassy.

Although Griboyedov left an interesting correspondence and several plays, which include *Molodye suprugi* (1815; "Young Married People") and *Student* (1817; "The Student"), his reputation rests solely on the satirical *Gore ot uma*. Production of the play was prohibited and only fragments of it were published during Griboyedov's lifetime. The style is a masterpiece of conciseness, colloquialism, and wit, so that many of Griboyedov's lines have become proverbial.

Grieg \'grēg\, Nordahl Brun, *in full* Johan Nordahl Brun Grieg (b. Nov. 1, 1902, Bergen, Nor.—d. Dec. 2, 1943, over Berlin, Ger.) Lyric poet, dramatist, and novelist whose resistance work and death in World War II made him a national hero.

Grieg's first books were the sea poems *Rundt Kap det Gode Haab* (1922; *Around the Cape of Good Hope*) and the novel *Skibet gaar videre* (1924; *The Ship Sails On*). In spite of a cosmopolitan outlook, he was strongly nationalistic, and his love for Norway was expressed in the poems *Norge i våre hjerter* (1929; "Norway in Our Hearts").

After publishing *De unge døde* (1932; "The Young Dead Ones"), six essays on individual poets, Grieg spent two years in Moscow (1932–34), where he became a communist. Russian theater and especially the techniques of the cinema inspired his most powerful social play, *Vår ære og vår makt* (1935; "Our Power and Our Glory"), which denounced profit-seeking owners of the Norwegian merchant fleet in World War I. *Nederlaget* (1937; *The Defeat*), a play dealing with the Paris Commune of 1870, was inspired by the Republican defeat in the Spanish Civil War. When Germany occupied Norway, Grieg escaped to Britain with the Norwegian government-in-exile and in his war poems (Eng. trans., 1944) and radio talks became the leading voice of free Norway. He also participated actively in the fighting and was killed in an Allied bombing raid over Berlin.

griffin or **griffon** or **gryphon** \'grif-ən\ [Old French *grifun*, a derivative of *grif* griffin, from Late Latin *gryphus*, alteration of Latin *grypus, gryps*, from Greek *grýps*] Composite mythological creature typically having the head, forepart, and wings of an eagle and the body, hind legs, and tail of a lion. The griffin was a favorite decorative motif in the ancient Middle Eastern and Mediterranean lands. Probably originating in the Levant in the 2nd millennium BC, the griffin had spread throughout western Asia and into Greece by the 14th century BC. According to legend, the griffins were in constant battle with the Arimasps (one-eyed men of Scythia) in the Scythian desert, possibly as protectors of Apollo's treasures. Judging from its frequent appearance in sanctuary and tomb furnishings, the griffin was in some sense sacred, but its precise nature or its place in cult and legend remain unknown. There are references to griffins in the works of Herodotus, Pliny the Elder, and Dante, among others. *Compare* SPHINX.

Griffiths, Clyde \'klīd-'grif-iths\ The doomed protagonist of the novel AN AMERICAN TRAGEDY by Theodore Dreiser. Having escaped a constricted religious life, Griffiths finds himself in the grip of events beyond his control.

Grigoryev or **Grigoriev** \gr^yi-'gór^y-yif\, Apollon Aleksandrovich (b. *c.* July 20 [Aug. 1, New Style], 1822, Moscow, Russia—d. Sept. 25 [Oct. 7], 1864, St. Petersburg) Russian literary critic and poet remembered for his theory of organic criticism, in which he argued that the aim of art and literature, rather than being to describe society, should be to synthesize the ideas and feelings of the artist in an organic and intuitively felt unity.

At the University of Moscow, Grigoryev came in contact with the currents of the Romanticism and idealism of the time. From 1850 to 1856 he was the editor of the Moscow journal *Moskvityanin* ("The Muscovite"), in which position he abandoned his earlier Romantic utopian fantasies and came to appreciate the native Russian virtues and the stability of existing institutions. His nationalist sentiments were not well received by the Westernizers of the capital, and he worked as a tutor until about 1861, when he was able to resume journalism with the publication of the literary journal *Vremya* ("Time"). Grigoryev also translated works of Sophocles, William Shakespeare, Lord Byron, J.W. von Goethe, Heinrich Heine, and others.

Grigoryev's poetry is mostly forgotten, but several of his lyrics and ballads based on Russian gypsy songs remain popular.

Grigson \\'grig-sən\\, Geoffrey (Edward Harvey) (b. March 2, 1905, Pelynt, Cornwall, Eng.—d. Nov. 25, 1985, Broad Town, Wiltshire) English editor, poet, and literary critic who became known in the 1930s primarily as the founding editor of the influential periodical *New Verse* (1933–39) and afterward as the editor of many poetry anthologies.

Grigson's later career as polemical journalist, art critic, anthologist, and editor of many varied works tended to obscure his achievement as a poet—he was a miniaturist with a fine and highly individual gift for precise and delicate observation. His poetic output was brought together in *Collected Poems* (1963) and *Collected Poems 1963–80* (1984). He also wrote an autobiography, *The Crest on the Silver* (1950), as well as many critical studies. He edited more than 12 anthologies of poetry, including *The Oxford Book of Satirical Verse* (1980).

Grillparzer \\'gril-ˌpärt-sər\\, Franz (b. Jan. 15, 1791, Vienna [Austria]—d. Jan. 21, 1872, Vienna) Austrian dramatist who wrote tragedies that were belatedly recognized as the greatest works of the Austrian stage.

Grillparzer studied law at the University of Vienna and spent much of his life in government service, retiring in 1856. In 1817 the first performance of Grillparzer's tragedy *Die Ahnfrau* (*The Ancestress*) evoked public interest. It contains many of the outward features of the then popular "fate tragedy" (*Schicksalstragödie*), but the characters are themselves ultimately responsible for their own destruction. In his tragedy *Sappho* (1818), Grillparzer attributes Sappho's tragic fate to her unhappy love for an ordinary man and to her inability to reconcile life and art. Work on the trilogy *Das Goldene Vlies* (1821; *The Golden Fleece*) was interrupted by the suicide of Grillparzer's mother and by his own illness. This drama, with Medea's assertion that life is not worth living, is the most pessimistic of his works.

More satisfying is the historical tragedy *König Ottokars Glück und Ende* (1825; *King Ottocar, His Rise and Fall*). Grillparzer was disappointed at the reception given to this and a following play and became discouraged by the objections of the censor. His private and professional misery during these years is reflected not only in his diaries but also in the impressive cycle of poems entitled *Tristia ex Ponto* (1835).

Des Meeres und der Liebe Wellen (1831; *The Waves of Sea and Love*), often judged to be Grillparzer's greatest tragedy, marks a return to a classical theme in treating the story of Hero and Leander. The psychological insight in this play anticipates the plays of Henrik Ibsen. *Der Traum ein Leben* (1834; *A Dream Is Life*), an Austrian *Faust*, owes much to Grillparzer's intensive and prolonged studies of Spanish drama. His only comedy, *Weh dem, der lügt!* (1838; "Woe to Him Who Lies!"), was a commercial failure. Grillparzer wrote no more for the stage and very little at all after the 1840s. Three tragedies, apparently complete, were found among his papers: *Die Jüdin von Toledo* (*The Jewess of Toledo*), based on a Spanish theme; *Ein Bruderzwist in Habsburg* (*Family Strife in Hapsburg*), a profound and moving historical tragedy; and *Libussa*.

Grillparzer's prose works include critical studies on Spanish drama and a posthumously published autobiography.

Grimald \\'grim-əld\\, Nicholas, *surname also spelled* Grimalde, Grimvald, *or* Grimoald (b. 1519/20, Huntingdonshire, Eng.—d. c. 1559) English scholar and poet, best known as a contributor to *Songes and Sonettes* (1557), also called *Tottel's Miscellany*, an anthology of contemporary poetry.

Grimald was licensed as a preacher in 1551–52 and named chaplain to Nicholas Ridley, bishop of London. After the accession of the Roman Catholic queen Mary I in 1553, Ridley was imprisoned, removed from his bishopric, and, in 1555, executed. Grimald was also imprisoned in 1555 but was released,

presumably because he recanted. In 1558 he is said to have returned to the Protestant belief.

The first edition of *Tottel's Miscellany*, published in June 1557, contained 40 poems by Grimald, including two early examples of English blank verse. Only 10 of his poems appeared in the second edition and in later editions, perhaps because of his religious inconstancy. Grimald also wrote two plays in Latin: a tragicomedy, *Christus Redivivus* (1543), produced at Oxford, and a tragedy about John the Baptist, *Archipropheta* (1548), produced at Cambridge. His plays and his surviving poems, edited by L.R. Merrill, were published in 1925.

Grimké \\'grim-kē\\, Angelina Weld (b. Feb. 27, 1880, Boston, Mass., U.S.—d. June 10, 1958, New York, N.Y.) African-American poet and playwright, an important forerunner of the Harlem Renaissance.

Grimké was born into a prominent biracial family of abolitionists and civil-rights activists; the noted abolitionists Angelina and Sarah Grimké were her great-aunts, and her father was the son of a wealthy white aristocrat and a slave. In the early 1900s she began to write articles and poems to express her concern about racism and the plight of blacks in America. Her play *Rachel*, produced in 1916 and published in 1920, concerns a young woman who is so horrified by racism that she vows never to bring children into the world. Although the play is considered to be overly sentimental and was criticized for its defeatism, it was one of the first plays written by a black author about black issues.

Grimké is best known for her small body of poetry, which has been anthologized in *Negro Poets and Their Poems* (1923), *The Poetry of the Negro* (1949; edited by Langston Hughes), and *Caroling Dusk* (1927; edited by Countee Cullen), among others. Her poems are mainly personal lyrics that draw images from nature and express a sense of isolation or a yearning for love.

Grimm \\'grim\\, Friedrich Melchior, Baron (Freiherr) von (b. Sept. 26, 1723, Ratisbon [Germany]—d. Dec. 19, 1807, Gotha, Saxe-Gotha) Critic of German descent who played an important part in the spread of 18th-century French culture throughout Europe.

In 1748 Grimm went to Paris as escort to the second son of the powerful Schönberg family and, later, worked at various times for the Prince of Saxe-Gotha, the Count of Friesen, and the Duke d'Orléans. At the same time he was admitted to progressive literary and philosophical circles in Paris.

Grimm became a close friend of the encyclopedist Denis Diderot (for whom he wrote an article on lyric poetry) and the lover of Madame d'Épinay, a writer and patron of a Parisian literary circle. In 1753 his position and connections equipped him to launch a cultural newsletter, which he wrote and edited for the benefit of foreign sovereigns and nobility eager to keep abreast of French cultural affairs.

Published in 1812 as *Correspondance littéraire*, it shows sound critical taste and is an invaluable social document, containing information about every aspect of the age. Grimm's carefully nurtured social standing and prosperity were swept away in the French Revolution.

Grimm \\'grim\\, Hans (Emil Wilhelm) (b. March 22, 1875, Wiesbaden, Ger.—d. Sept. 27, 1959, Lippoldsberg) German writer whose works were popular expressions of Pan-Germanism and helped to prepare the climate of opinion in Germany that embraced the nationalist and expansionist policies of Adolf Hitler.

From 1901 to 1910 Grimm was a merchant in Cape Colony, S.Af. His experiences in South Africa furnished material for his literary works, the first of which, *Südafrikanische Novellen*, appeared in 1913. His novel *Volk ohne Raum* (1926; "Nation

Without Room"), in which he contrasts the wide-open spaces of South Africa with Germany's cramped position in Europe, deals with the German settlers in South West Africa (now Namibia), their involvement in the South African War, and their determination to retain their land despite the provisions of the Treaty of Versailles. Grimm's style was influenced by the Old Icelanders' sagas.

Grimm \'grim \, Jacob and Wilhelm, *in full* Jacob Ludwig Carl Grimm and Wilhelm Carl Grimm, *byname* Brothers Grimm,

Jacob (right) and Wilhelm Grimm, oil portrait by Elisabeth Jerichau-Baumann, 1855; in the Nationalgalerie, Berlin
Staatliche Museen, Berlin

German Brüder Grimm (respectively b. Jan. 4, 1785, Hanau, Hesse-Kassel [Germany]—d. Sept. 20, 1863, Berlin; b. Feb. 24, 1786, Hanau—d. Dec. 16, 1859, Berlin)   German brothers famous for their classic collections of folk songs and folktales, especially for *Kinder- und Hausmärchen* (1812–15; "Children's and Household Tales"; generally known as GRIMM'S FAIRY TALES), which helped to establish the science of folklore.

The Grimms first collected folk songs and tales from several literary traditions for their friends Achim von Arnim and Clemens Brentano, who had collaborated on an influential collection of folk lyrics in 1805. Encouraged by Arnim, they published their collected tales as the *Kinder- und Hausmärchen*. The tales in the collection were mostly taken from oral sources. They aimed at a genuine reproduction of the original storyteller's words and ways, but the tales were carefully refined and reshaped. The collection became and remains a model for the collecting of folktales everywhere, and the Grimms' notes to the tales, along with other investigations, indicated a solid basis for the science of the folk narrative and even of folklore.

The Grimms also gave their attention to the written documents of early literature, bringing out new editions of ancient texts. Wilhelm's outstanding contribution was *Die deutsche Heldensage* ("The German Heroic Tale"). While collaborating on these subjects, Jacob also turned to the study of philology, producing an extensive work on the grammar of all the Germanic languages, the *Deutsche Grammatik* (1819–37). In what was to become known as Grimm's law, he demonstrated the principle of the regularity of correspondence among consonants in genetically related languages, a principle previously observed by the Dane Rasmus Rask. Jacob's work on grammar exercised an enormous influence on the contemporary study of

linguistics, Germanic, Romance, and Slavic, and it remains of value and in use even now.

In 1829 the brothers were appointed librarians and professors at the University of Göttingen. Jacob's *Deutsche Mythologie*, written during this period, was to be of far-reaching influence. From poetry, fairy tales, and folkloristic elements, he traced the pre-Christian faith and superstitions of the Germanic peoples, contrasting the ancient beliefs to those of classical mythology and Christianity.

In 1840 the Brothers Grimm accepted an invitation from the king of Prussia, Frederick William IV, to go to Berlin, where as members of the Royal Academy of Sciences they lectured at the university. There they began their most ambitious enterprise, the *Deutsches Wörterbuch*, a large German dictionary intended as a guide for the user of the written and spoken word as well as a scholarly reference work. Jacob lived to see the work proceed to the letter *F*, while Wilhelm only finished the letter *D*. Generations of successors were required to finish the enormous task of compiling the dictionary.

Grimmelshausen \'grim-əls-,hau̇-zən \, Hans Jacob Christoph von, Jacob Christoph *also spelled* Jakob Christoffel (b. 1621/22, Gelnhausen, near Frankfurt am Main [Germany]—d. Aug. 17, 1676, Renchen, Strasbourg)   German novelist whose SIMPLICISSIMUS series is one of the masterworks of his country's literature. Satirical and partially autobiographical, it is a matchless social picture of the often grotesque events of the Thirty Years' War (1618–48).

Grimmelshausen served as a musketeer in the Thirty Years' War, formally joined the imperial army, and in 1639 became secretary to Reinhard von Schauenburg, commandant at Offenburg.

After the war, he worked as a tax collector and tavern-keeper, among other positions. He had begun writing in his army days and published two minor satires in 1658 and 1660. In 1669 he published the first part of his picaresque novel *Der Abentheurliche Simplicissimus* (*The Adventurous Simplicissimus*). His authorship, however, was not established until 1837 from the initials HJCVG, which he used in a sequel to identify himself merely as editor. His sequels to *Simplicissimus* include *Die Landstörtzerin Courasche* (1670; *Courage, the Adventuress*) and *Das wunderbarliche Vogel-Nest* (1672; "The Magical Bird's Nest").

Grimm's Fairy Tales \'grim \   Classic and influential collection of folklore by Jacob and Wilhelm GRIMM, first published in two volumes as *Kinder- und Hausmärchen* (1812–15; "Children's and Household Tales"), and later revised and enlarged seven times between 1819 and 1857. The work was first translated into English as *German Popular Tales*, 2 vol. (1823–26), and has since been translated under numerous titles.

Grimm's Fairy Tales comprises some 200 stories, most of which were adopted from oral sources. The best-known tales include "Hansel and Gretel," "Snow White," "Little Red Riding Hood," "Sleeping Beauty," "Tom Thumb," "Rapunzel," "The Golden Goose," and RUMPELSTILTSKIN. The stories' universal appeal—whether they are considered as psychological archetypes or as fantasy narratives—inspired a myriad of print, theatrical, operatic, balletic, and cinematic adaptations.

Grimshaw \'grim-,shȯ \, Beatrice (Ethel) (b. 1871, County Antrim, Ire.—d. June 30, 1953, Bathurst, N.S.W., Australia)   Irish-born writer and traveler whose many books deal with her adventures in the South Seas.

Grimshaw was commissioned by the London *Daily Graphic* to travel around the world and report her experiences, but she was so attracted by the Pacific islands that the journey was never completed. She settled in Papua in 1907 and became the first white woman to grow tobacco there. She traveled extensively among the islands of the Pacific and the East Indies and made detailed studies of local legends and customs. She wrote more than 33 novels and travel books based on her experiences, of which the best known is the novel *The Red Gods Call* (1910). Another important novel is *The Victorian Family Robinson* (1934), and her travel books include *From the Fiji to the Cannibal Islands* (1907).

Grin \\'grʸēn\\, Aleksandr Stepanovich, *pseudonym of* Aleksandr Stepanovich Grinevsky \\grʸi-'nʸef-skʸē\\ (b. Aug. 11 [Aug. 23, New Style], 1880, Slobodskoy, Russia—d. July 8, 1932, Stary Krym, U.S.S.R. [now in Ukraine]) Soviet prose writer notable for his romantic short stories of adventure and mystery.

Leaving home at 15, Grin traveled to Odessa, where he fell in love with the sea, an important element in many of his stories. In the early 1900s he joined the Socialist Revolutionary Party and was shortly afterward arrested and exiled to Siberia. After his return he devoted himself to writing.

Grin's stories drew on his travels and adventures and reflect his extensive reading of Western writers. His tales, fantastic and whimsical works full of mystery and adventure, are among the most exotic of all Russian literature. Soviet critics named their imaginary romantic and ideal setting "Grin-Land." His writing was generally ignored by the Soviet censors until 1950, when it was condemned as antisocial, bourgeois, and decadent.

Grin is now recognized as a master of the allegorical and symbolic tale and novel, and as the creator of a fantasy world expressive of a profound humanism and moral responsibility. Among his best-known works are the novels *Blistayushchiy mir* (1923; "The Glittering World") and *Doroga nikuda* (1930; "The Road to Nowhere") and the tales *Korabli v Lisse* (1918; "The Ships in Liss") and *Serdtse pustyni* (1923; "Heart of the Desert").

Gringore or **Gringoire** \\graⁿ-'gòr\\, Pierre (b. *c.* 1475, Normandy, Fr.—d. *c.* 1538) French actor-manager and playwright, best known as a writer of soties (satirical farces) for *Les Enfants sans souci,* a famous medieval guild of comic actors. Gringore was for a time its second dignitary, Mère Sotte ("Mother Fool"). As Mère Sotte he enjoyed the favor of Louis XII and took advantage of his fool's costume to launch scathing attacks against the king's enemy Pope Julius II.

Gripenberg \\'grē-pən-ˌberʸ\\, Bertel Johan Sebastian, Baron (Friherre) (b. Sept. 10, 1878, St. Petersburg, Russia—d. May 6, 1947, Sävsjö, Swed.) One of the foremost Finnish poets who wrote in Swedish.

Gripenberg's first collection, *Dikter* (1903; "Poems"), attracted attention for its richness of color and sensualism. This and other early collections, of which the most important were *Gallergrinden* (1905; "The Iron Gate") and *Svarta sonetter* (1908; "Black Sonnets"), show his proud individualism, love of beauty, and skillful handling of the sonnet form. The collections *Drivsnö* (1909; "Loose Snow"), *Aftnar i Tavastland* (1911; "Evenings in Tavastland"), *Skuggspel* (1912; "A Play of Shadows"), and *Spillror* (1917; "Broken Bits") reveal a more tranquil, contemplative attitude than his sometimes angry early verse. Later collections contain some fine patriotic poems. Gripenberg also published prose works, including his memoirs, *Det var de tiderna* (1943; "Those Were the Times").

Griselda \\gri-'zel-də\\, *also spelled* Grisilda, *also called* Griseldis, Grisel, Grissil, *or* Patient Griselda. Character of romance in medieval and Renaissance Europe, noted for her enduring patience and wifely obedience. She was the heroine of the last tale in the *Decameron* by Giovanni Boccaccio, who derived the story from a French source. Petrarch translated Boccaccio's Italian version into Latin in *De obidentia ac fide uxoria*

mythologia, upon which Geoffrey Chaucer based his English version found in "The Clerk's Tale" of *The Canterbury Tales.* The English playwright Thomas Dekker collaborated on another version, *Patient Grissil* (1603).

Grisette \\grē-'zet\\ Stock character in numerous 19th-century French novels, a pretty, young woman who usually works as a laundress, milliner, or seamstress and who is an easy sexual conquest. Typically, such a character is hardworking and lighthearted, her cheerful disposition sometimes masking hunger or malnutrition.

Examples of this stock character appear in works such as *Mimi Pinson* by Alfred de Musset and Henri Murger's *Scènes de la vie de bohème* ("Scenes of Bohemian Life"), the story on which Giacomo Puccini's opera *La Bohème* is based.

Groan, Titus \\'tī-təs-'grōn\\ Fictional character, the titled heir to the crumbling castle Gormenghast in the GORMENGHAST SERIES by Mervyn Peake.

grotesque \\grō-'tesk\\ A decorative style in which animal, human, and vegetative forms are interwoven and deformed to the point of absurdity. This nonliterary sense of the word first entered the English language as a noun. The word comes ultimately from 16th-century Italian *grottesca,* deriving from *grotta* ("cave"), in allusion to certain caves under Rome in which paintings in such a style were found. It came to be used as an adjective describing something in this style and hence to mean bizarre, incongruous, or unnatural, or anything outside the normal.

The term was first used regularly in reference to literature in the 18th century. In literature the style is often used for comedy or satire to show the contradictions and inconsistencies of life. Examples of the grotesque can be found in the characters and situations in the works of Edgar Allan Poe, Evelyn Waugh, Flannery O'Connor, Eugene Ionesco, Mervyn Peake, and Joseph Heller, among many others.

Groth \\'grōt\\, Klaus (b. April 24, 1819, Heide, Holstein [Germany]—d. June 1, 1899, Kiel, Ger.) German regional poet whose book *Quickborn* (1853) first revealed the poetic possibilities of Plattdeutsch (Low German).

Inspired by the Scots dialect poems of Robert Burns and the Swabian-Swiss writings of Johann Peter Hebel, Groth explored the potentials of his native Dithmarschen dialect as a vehicle of lyrical expression. His poems have the simplicity of folk songs and have been set to music by Johannes Brahms and other composers. His work influenced Fritz Reuter, whose novels elevated Plattdeutsch prose to a literary language.

Grotowski \\grō-'tòf-skʸē\\, Jerzy (b. Aug. 11, 1933, Rzeszów, Pol.) International leader of the experimental theater in his role as the director of productions staged by the Polish Laboratory Theater of Wrocław. A leading exponent of audience involvement, he set up emotional confrontations between spectators and actors; the performers were disciplined masters of bodily and vocal contortions, violent but graceful action, and an almost unintelligible dialogue of howls and groans.

Grotowski studied at the National Theatrical Academy in Kraków (1951–59), then joined the Laboratory Theater in 1959, the year it was founded. Grotowski's permanent company first appeared in western Europe in 1966. His productions included *Faustus* (1963), *Hamlet* (1964), and *The Constant Prince* (1965). Grotowski's methods and pronouncements influenced such American experimental theater movements as The Living Theatre, the Open Theatre, and the Performance Group. In 1969 the Laboratory Theater made a successful American debut in New York City with *Akropolis*, based on a 1904 play by Stanisław Wyspiański.

Grotowski's later productions included *Undertaking Mountain* (1977) and *Undertaking Earth* (1977–78), but he created few new works for public performance after 1969.

Group, The   Novel by Mary MCCARTHY, published in 1963, that chronicles the lives of eight Vassar College friends from their graduation in 1933 to the funeral of Kay Strong, the protagonist, in 1940.

The women believe that their superior education has given them control over their lives and the ability to break down existing taboos and limitations. They all believe in progress, modernity, marrying well, and accumulating wealth and possessions. The novel is the story of their subsequent loss of illusion as they discover that both bohemia and high society have their hypocrisies and that resistance to change is universal.

The Group interweaves the stories of the eight group members—Kay Strong, Helena Davison, Dottie Renfrew, Elinor Eastlake, Mary "Pokey" Prothero, Libby MacAusland, Polly Andrews, and Priss Hartshorn—as they encounter the realities of sex, marriage, motherhood, and careers.

Group Portrait with Lady   Novel by Heinrich BÖLL, published in German in 1971 as *Gruppenbild mit Dame*. A sweeping portrayal of German life from World War I until the early 1970s, the novel was cited by the Nobel Prize committee when it awarded Böll the Nobel Prize for Literature in 1972.

The story's anonymous narrator gradually reveals the life—past and present—of Leni Pfeiffer, a war widow who, with her neighbors, is fighting the demolition of the Cologne apartment building in which they reside. Leni and her illegitimate son Lev become the nexus of Cologne's counterculture; they spurn the prevailing work ethic and assail the dehumanization of life under capitalism. In a larger sense, the work attempts both a reconciliation with the past and a condemnation of the pursuit of affluence in present-day Germany.

Group Theatre   Company of stage craftsmen founded in 1931 in New York City by Harold Clurman, Cheryl Crawford, and Lee Strasberg, for the purpose of presenting American plays of social significance. The characteristic Group production was a social protest play with a leftist viewpoint. After its first trial production of Sergey Tretyakov's *Roar China*, the Group staged Paul Green's *House of Connelly*, a play of the decadent Old South as reflected by the disintegrating gentry class. The Group then followed with two anticapitalist plays, *1931* and *Success Story*. Financial and artistic success came two years later with the production of Sidney Kingsley's *Men in White*, which was awarded a Pulitzer Prize.

In 1935 the Group Theatre staged *Waiting for Lefty* by one of its actors, Clifford Odets. The play, suggested by a taxicab drivers' strike of the previous year, used flashback techniques and "plants" in the audience to create the illusion that the strikers' meeting was occurring spontaneously. The Group also staged Odets' *Awake and Sing!*, *Till the Day I Die*, *Paradise Lost*, and *Golden Boy*; other productions included Paul Green's *Johnny Johnson*, Irwin Shaw's *Bury the Dead*, Robert Ardrey's *Thunder Rock*, and William Saroyan's *My Heart's in the Highlands*. The Group was disbanded in 1941.

Grove \'grōv\, Frederick Philip (b. 1871, Russia—d. Aug. 19, 1948, Simcoe, Ont., Can.)   Canadian novelist whose fame rests on somber naturalistic works that deal frankly and realistically with pioneer life on the Canadian prairies.

Grove grew up in Sweden, traveled widely in Europe as a youth, and attended European universities. On a visit to Canada in 1892, he was left stranded there by his father's sudden death. He worked as an itinerant farm laborer from 1892 to 1912 and as a teacher in Manitoba from 1912 to 1924. He worked as an editor in Ottawa before retiring to a farm near Simcoe.

Grove's series of prairie novels, *Settlers of the Marsh* (1925), *Our Daily Bread* (1928), *The Yoke of Life* (1930), and *Fruits of the Earth* (1933), were his most successful works. He also wrote two books of essays on prairie life and an autobiography, *In Search of Myself* (1946).

Grub Street \'grəb\   The world of literary hacks, or usually mediocre, needy writers who write for hire.

The term originated during the 18th century. According to Samuel Johnson's *Dictionary*, Grub Street was "originally the name of a street in Moorfields in London, much inhabited by writers of small histories, dictionaries, and temporary poems; whence any mean production is called grubstreet." The novelist Tobias Smollett, himself engaged much of his life in Grub Street hackwork, provided a memorable scene of a Grub Street dinner party in *Humphry Clinker* (1771). George Gissing's novel *New Grub Street* (1891) also deals with London literary life.

Gruffydd \'grif-ˌith\, William John (b. Feb. 14, 1881, Bethel, Caernarvonshire, Wales—d. Sept. 29, 1954, Caernarvon)   Welsh-language poet and scholar whose works represented first a rebellion against Victorian standards of morality and literature and later a longing for the society he knew as a youth.

Gruffydd's earliest work, with R. Silyn Roberts, the book of poems *Telynegion* (1900; "Lyrics"), naturalized the romantic lyric in Wales. Other works include *Caneuon a Cherddi* (1906; "Songs and Poems"), *Llenyddiaeth Cymru o 1450 hyd 1600* (1922; "History of Welsh Literature, 1450–1600"), *Ynys yr Hud* (1923; "The Enchanted Island"), *Caniadau* (1932; "Poems"), and *Antigone* (verse tragedy, 1950). Gruffydd edited the Welsh quarterly review *Y Llenor* ("The Literary Man") from its inception in 1922 until 1951, when it was discontinued.

Grün \'grün\, Anastasius, *pseudonym of* Anton Alexander, Count (Graf) von Auersperg \fôn-'aů-ərs-pərk\ (b. April 11, 1806, Laibach, Carniola, Austrian Empire [now Ljubljana, Slovenia]—d. Sept. 12, 1876, Graz)   Austrian poet and statesman known for his spirited collections of political poetry.

As a member of the estates of Carniola in the Diet at Laibach, Grün was a critic of the Austrian government, and after 1848 he represented the district of Laibach briefly at the German national assembly at Frankfurt. In 1860 he was summoned to the remodeled Austrian Parliament by the emperor, who in 1861 named him a life member of the upper house (Herrenhaus).

Grün's early works include a significant cycle of poems, *Der letzte Ritter* (1830; *The Last Knight*), celebrating the life and adventures of the Holy Roman emperor Maximilian I. Grün's political poetry was printed in two collections: *Spaziergänge eines Wiener Poeten* (1831; "Promenades of a Viennese Poet") and *Schutt* (1836; "Rubbish"). His epics, *Die Nibelungen im Frack* (1843) and *Der Pfaff vom Kahlenberg* (1850), are characterized by a fine ironic humor. He also produced masterly translations of the popular Slovene songs current in Carniola in *Volkslieder aus Krain* (1850; "Folksongs from Carniola") and of the English poems on Robin Hood (1864).

Grundtvig \'grůent-vē\, N.F.S., *in full* Nikolai Frederik Severin (b. Sept. 8, 1783, Udby, Den.—d. Sept. 2, 1872, Copenhagen)   Danish bishop and poet, founder of a theological movement (Grundtvigianism) that revitalized the Danish church. He was also outstanding as a hymn writer, historian, pioneer of studies on early Scandinavian literature, and educator.

After taking a degree in theology Grundtvig studied the *Edda*s and Icelandic sagas. His *Nordens mythologi* (1808; "Northern Mythology") marks a turning point in this research. Grundtvig's first attempt to write history from a Christian standpoint, *Verdens krønike* (1812; "World Chronicle"), attracted much attention. Because of his criticism of the Lutheran state church he was unable to find a pastorate from 1813 until 1821. During these years he wrote religious poetry and also opened the way for research into Anglo-Saxon literature with his version of Beowulf (1820).

In 1825 Grundtvig became embroiled in religious controversy. His writings were censored, and in 1826 he resigned his pastorate. He expounded his philosophy in a new and inspired *Nordens mythologi* (1832) and in his *Haandbog i verdenshistorien*, 3 vol. (1833–43; "Handbook of World History"). In 1839 Grundtvig was allowed to receive the living of Vartov, Copenhagen, and in 1861 he was given the rank of bishop.

Grundtvig is still considered the greatest Scandinavian hymn writer. His *Sang-værk til den danske kirke*, 5 vol. (1837–81), contains new versions of the hymns of the whole Christian church, as well as a wealth of original hymns.

Grundy, Mrs. \\,mis-iz-'grən-dē\\ Imaginary English character who typifies the censorship effected in everyday life by conventional opinion. She appears (but never onstage) in Thomas Morton's play *Speed the Plough* (produced 1798), in which one character, Dame Ashfield, continually worries about what her neighbor Mrs. Grundy will say. Since then the term Mrs. Grundy has passed into everyday speech as a criterion of rigid respectability.

Gruppe 47 \\'grup-ə-,zē-bən-ùnt-'firt-sig\\ ("Group 47") Informal association of German-speaking writers that was founded in 1947 (hence its name). Gruppe 47 originated with a group of war prisoners in the United States who were concerned with reestablishing the broken traditions of German literature. Feeling that Nazi propaganda had corrupted their language, they advocated a style of sparse, even cold, descriptive realism devoid of pompous or poetic verbiage.

Returning to Germany, they founded the weekly *Der Ruf* ("The Call"), which was suppressed in 1947 by the U.S. military government for political radicalism. As the group's political aims diminished, its literary prestige rose, and its yearly prize conferred high distinction. The last full conference of the group was in 1967.

Grynswth, Syr Meurig. Pseudonym used by John Ceiriog HUGHES.

Gryphius \\'grif-ē-ùs\\, Andreas (b. Oct. 2, 1616, Glogau, Silesia [now Głogów, Pol.]—d. July 16, 1664, Glogau) Lyric poet and dramatist, one of Germany's leading writers in the 17th century.

Gryphius' literary reputation has increased enormously during the 20th century. His plays are distinguished by a deep sense of melancholy and pessimism and are threaded through with a fervent religious strain that borders on despair. He wrote five tragedies: *Leo Armenius* (1646), *Catharina von Georgien*, *Carolus Stuardus*, and *Cardenio und Celinde* (all printed 1657), and *Papinianus* (1659). The plays deal with the themes of stoicism and religious constancy unto martyrdom, of both the Christian ruler and the Machiavellian tyrant, and of illusion and reality. The latter theme also pervades his three comedies, the best of which are *Die geliebte Dornrose* (1660; *The Beloved Hedgerose*) and *Herr Peter Squentz* (1663).

Gryphius' lyric poetry covers a wide range of verse forms and is characterized by technical mastery and assurance and a sincere and compelling portrayal of human emotions in adversity.

Guan Hanqing or **Kuan Han-ch'ing** \\'gwän-'hän-'chiŋ\\ (b. 1241?, Dadu, now Beijing, China—d. 1320?, China) Dramatist who was considered by many critics to be the greatest playwright of the Chinese classical theater.

Guan Hanqing, probably a scholar, belonged to a writers' guild that specialized in writing plays for performing groups. Fourteen of his plays (from more than 60 with known ti-

tles) have been preserved. Several of them are unquestionably masterpieces, and there is little doubt that Guan played an important role in raising the early Chinese drama to a new level of excellence. His close association with performers may have contributed to his understanding of the common people displayed in his works. Many of his characters are women of low social standing, invariably portrayed with great sympathy and painstaking detail. His heroines always act with intelligence, integrity, and courage. Though Guan's plots, following the fashion of his time, are unrealistic, his understanding of his characters and sympathy toward them always shine through. His style is simple and straightforward, probably closer to the spirit of early popular theater than to the style of plays by his contemporaries. The action, often simple everyday happenings, is depicted with humor and poignancy. Some of his better-known dramas include *Doue yuan* (*Injustice to Tou O*), *Hudie meng* (*Butterfly Dream*), and *Jiu feng zhen* ("Saving a Prostitute").

Guare \\'gwar\\, John (b. Feb. 5, 1938, New York, N.Y., U.S.) American playwright known for his innovative and often absurdist dramas.

Guare was educated at Georgetown and Yale universities. He then began staging short plays, primarily in New York City. His first notable works—*Muzeeka* (1968), about American soldiers of the Vietnam War who have television contracts, and *Cop-Out* (1968)—satirized the American media.

In 1971 Guare earned critical acclaim for *The House of Blue Leaves*, a farce about a zookeeper who murders his insane wife after he fails as a songwriter. *Two Gentlemen of Verona* (1972; with Mel Shapiro), a rock-musical modernization of William Shakespeare's comedy, won the Tony and New York Drama Critics Circle awards for best musical of 1971–72. Guare dealt with such issues as success—in *Marco Polo Sings a Solo* (1977) and *Rich and Famous* (1977)—and parent-child relationships—in *Landscape of the Body* (1978) and *Bosoms and Neglect* (1980). The plays *Lydie Breeze* (1982), *Gardenia* (1982), and *Women and Water* (1990) make up a family saga set in Nantucket, Mass., in the second half of the 19th century. Guare also wrote several screenplays.

Guarini \\gwä-'rē-nē\\, Battista, *in full* Giovanni Battista Guarini (b. Dec. 10, 1538, Ferrara [Italy]—d. Oct. 7, 1612, Venice) Renaissance court poet who, along with Torquato Tasso, is credited with establishing a new literary genre, the pastoral drama.

In 1567 Guarini entered the service of Alfonso II, Duke of Ferrara, as courtier and diplomat. He became a friend of Tasso, who was also in the duke's service, and, in 1579, replaced him as court poet when Tasso's erratic behavior resulted in his imprisonment. Guarini retired in 1582 to his ancestral farm, the Villa Guarini, where he wrote his celebrated pastoral tragicomedy, *Il pastor fido* ("The Faithful Shepherd"). Published in 1590 and first performed in 1595, it became one of the most famous and most widely translated and imitated works of the age. For nearly two centuries *Il pastor fido* was regarded as a code of gallantry and a guide to manners. An English adaptation is John Fletcher's *The Faithful Shepherdess* (1609?). Sir Richard Fanshawe's translation (1647) was critically edited in 1964 and 1976.

Gudmundsson \\'gvᴜeth-,mᴜend-sȯn\\, Kristmann (b. Oct. 23, 1901, Thverfell, Ice.—d. Nov. 20, 1983, Reykjavík) Icelandic novelist who gained an international reputation with his many works of romantic fiction, several written in Norwegian.

In 1924 Gudmundsson went to Norway and two years later published in Norwegian a collection of stories, *Islandsk kjærlighet* ("Icelandic Loves"). It was a literary success and astonished the critics by its mastery of Norwegian idiom and style. He followed that success with the publication of several novels, among them the autobiographical *Hvite netter* (1934; "White Nights"). In 1939 he returned to Iceland and began writing in Icelandic. Gudmundsson's fiction drew a great deal on his Icelandic background and on Icelandic literature and social history, but the constant theme in his work is love (both physical and spiritual) between men and women.

Gudmundsson \\'gvʊeth-ˌmʊend-sòn\\, Tómas (b. Jan. 6, 1901, Efri-Brú, Ice.—d. Nov. 14, 1983, Reykjavík) Poet best known for introducing the city as a subject in Icelandic poetry.

Gudmundsson graduated in law from the University of Iceland in Reykjavík and subsequently became a civil servant in 1928. His first work, *Vith sundin blá* (1924; "Beside the Blue Waters"), revealed his control of poetic form and an appealing voice. His next collection, *Fagra veröld* (1933; "The Fair World"), established him as an outstanding poet; it won immediate attention for its appreciation of urban life. Gudmundsson was adopted as poet laureate of the city.

Travel in the Mediterranean gave him a new stimulus, apparent in *Stjörnur vorsins* (1940; "Stars of Spring"). After 1943 he devoted himself to writing. From 1942 to 1955 he edited a literary magazine, *Helgafell*, and from 1956 to 1959 *Nýtt Helgafell*. During this period *Fljótith helga* (1950; "The Holy River") was published. It addressed many of the social issues that were brought to light by World War II and revealed Gudmundsson as a mature philosopher. An edition of his collected poems was published in 1953. His later works include *Heim til thín, Ísland* (1977; "Home to You, Iceland"), containing personal reflections on life and death, as well as several poems written for specific occasions.

Gudrun \\'gvʊeth-ˌrūn\\, *Old Norse* Gudrún. Heroine of several Old Norse legends whose principal theme is revenge. She is the sister of Gunnar (Gunther) and wife of the hero known in Old Norse as Sigurd (better known as Siegfried) and, after Sigurd's death, of Atli. Her sufferings as a wife, sister, and mother are the unifying elements of several poems. The counterpart of KRIEMHILD in the *Nibelungenlied*, she is sometimes confused with the heroine of the Middle High German romance *Gudrun Lied*, an independent Baltic-coast legend of an abduction that ends happily with a rescue and the lovers' reunion. *See also* EDDA; LAY OF ATLI.

Guérin \\gā-'raⁿ\\, Maurice de, *in full* Georges-Maurice de Guérin (b. Aug. 4/5, 1810, Château du Cayla, near Andillac, Fr.—d. July 19?, 1839, Château du Cayla) French Romantic poet who had a cultish following after his death.

Guérin at first studied for a clerical career. By 1831, however, he had decided against a religious life, and he soon went to Brittany to live in a radical community led by the brilliant Roman Catholic rebel Abbé Félicité Lamennais. In his journal *Le Cahier vert* (1861; "The Green Notebook"), Guérin recorded some of the studies and discussions there, which were major influences in his life. Within a year the community was dissolved, and Guérin moved into the social life of Paris, where he wrote his two major prose poems, *La Bacchante* and *Le Centaure*. Both works are remarkable for the richness and depth of their pantheistic descriptions of nature. Guérin died of tuberculosis in 1839.

Recognition came to Guérin in 1840 when some of his works were published posthumously through the efforts of his sister Eugénie and friends. Later, in 1861, a collection of works, *Reliquiae* (2 vol.), appeared. A Guérin cult arose, prompting the publication of every scrap of writing by Maurice and Eugénie. The *Journal et lettres* (1862) of Eugénie de Guérin (1805–1848) show that she possessed gifts as rare as her brother's, but her mysticism assumed a more strictly religious form.

Guermantes family \\ger-'mäⁿt\\ Fictional characters in Marcel Proust's seven-part novel REMEMBRANCE OF THINGS PAST. Just as the family of Charles SWANN signifies, to the narrator Marcel, the wealthy bourgeoisie, the Guermantes family, with its roots deep in French history, signifies the glamorous aristocracy. The family includes the Prince and Princess de Guermantes; the Duke and Duchess de Guermantes; the duke's brother Baron de Charlus, a dissipated and promiscuous homosexual; and Robert de Saint-Loup, a marquis, who introduces Marcel into the Guermantes' social circles.

Guernes \\'gern\\ de Pont-Sainte-Maxence \\də-póⁿ-saⁿt-mâk-'säⁿs\\ (fl. 12th century) Wandering scholar from the Île-de-France, author of the first vernacular life of St. Thomas Becket, which reveals passionate devotion to the saint and shows considerable literary merit. Guernes wrote his *Vie de saint Thomas Becket* (composed in verse about 1174) from Latin sources.

Guerre, Martin \\mär-taⁿ-'ger, *Angl* 'märt-ən-'ger\\ Fictional character, a 16th-century Frenchman from Gascony who, after a decade of marriage to Bertrande de Rols, vanishes from the town. About eight years later, Arnaud du Thil, a man resembling Guerre, arrives and is accepted by Guerre's wife and many of the townspeople as the missing man. A claim surfaces that the real Guerre is in Flanders and a trial ensues. During the trial the real Guerre returns, and subsequently the supposed imposter is executed.

Guest \\'gest\\, Edgar Albert (b. Aug. 20, 1881, Birmingham, Warwickshire, Eng.—d. Aug. 5, 1959, Detroit, Mich., U.S.) Writer whose sentimental verses were widely read.

Guest's family moved to the United States in 1891. Four years later he went to work for the *Detroit Free Press* as an office boy, eventually becoming a reporter and then a writer of daily rhymes. These became so popular that they were eventually syndicated to newspapers throughout the country and made his name a household word. His first book, *A Heap o' Livin'* (1916), became a best-seller and was followed by similar collections of his optimistic rhymes on such subjects as home, mother, and the virtue of hard work.

Guevara \\gā-'ḇä-rä\\, Antonio de (b. *c.* 1480, Treceño, Spain—d. April 3, 1545, Mondoñedo) Spanish court preacher and man of letters whose didactic work *Reloj de príncipes o libro aureo del emperador Marco Aurelio* (1529; *The Golden Boke of Marcus Aurelius* or *The Diall of Princes*), which was an attempt to invent a model for rulers, became one of the most influential books of the 16th century. Guevara falsely attributed parts of the work to Emperor Marcus Aurelius, whose *Meditations* did not come to light until later (1558).

Guevara grew up at the court of Ferdinand and Isabella, serving as page to the prince Don Juan until his death in 1497. Guevara became a Franciscan in 1504, was court preacher in 1521, and was appointed royal chronicler in 1526. A rhetorician, more concerned with developing a golden prose than with content, Guevara wrote mostly about inconsequential subjects, which enabled him to display his wit and affected diction. His other major works include *Epístolas familiares* (1539–42; "Familiar Letters"), *Menosprecio de corte y alabanza de aldea* (1539; "Scorn of Court Life and Praise of Village Life"), and *La década de Césares* (1539; "The Ten Caesars"). Guevara's masterwork was frequently reprinted through the 20th century, but his work is now considered of little more than historical interest.

Guèvremont \\gev-rə-'mōⁿ, gäv-\\, Germaine, *original name* Marianne-Germaine-Grignon \\grē-'nyôⁿ\\ (b. April 16, 1893, Saint-Jérôme, Que., Can.—d. Aug. 21, 1968, Montreal) French-Canadian regional writer, one of the last novelists to skillfully recreate the confined world of rural Quebec.

Grignon published her first article in 1912. She moved to Sorel, Que., with her husband in 1920. She moved to Montreal in 1935 and began to contribute sketches of the rural life she had observed in the region around Sorel for a monthly magazine entitled *Paysana*. Several of these pieces are included in *En Plein Terre* (1942; "On Open Ground"). The same characters and subject matter were presented in novel form in *Le Survenant* (1945; "The Unexpected One"), which inspired a French-Canadian television series, and its sequel, *Marie-Didace* (1947). The two novels were translated and published together as *The Outlander* (1950) in the United States and Canada and as *Monk's Reach* (1950) in the United Kingdom.

Guiccioli \gwē-'chō-lē\, Countess Teresa, *also called* (from 1851) Marquise de Boissy \mär-kēz-də-bwä-'sē\, *original surname* Gamba-Ghiselli \ˌgäm-bä-gē-'zel-lē\ (b. 1800, Ravenna, Papal States [Italy]—d. 1873, Florence, Italy) The last inamorata of the English poet Lord Byron.

Teresa was married in 1818 to the sexagenarian Count Alessandro Guiccioli. In April 1819 she met Byron at Venice, and he fell completely in love with her. When the countess returned to Ravenna, Byron followed her, and later she returned to live with him in Venice. Because of Byron's friendship with her father and brother, he was initiated into the secret revolutionary society of the Carbonari, to which he supplied arms. Her memories of her life with Byron were published in *Lord Byron jugé par les temoins de sa vie* (1868; "Lord Byron Judged by the Evidence of His Life"; *My Recollections of Lord Byron*).

Guide to Kulchur \'kəl-chər\ Prose work by Ezra POUND, published in 1938. A brilliant but fragmentary work, it consists of a series of apparently unrelated essays reflecting his thoughts on various aspects of culture and history.

Guido delle Colonne \'gwē-dō-del-lä-kō-'lōn-nä\ (b. *c.* 1215, Sicily?—d. *c.* 1290, Sicily?) Jurist, poet, and Latin prose writer whose Latin version of the Troy legend was important in bringing the story to Italians and, through various translations, into English literature.

Guido was a poet of the Sicilian school, a group of early Italian vernacular poets who were associated with the courts of the Holy Roman emperor Frederick II and his son Manfred, and was strongly influenced by the poetry of France and Provence. Guido's poetry, though not particularly inspired, was intricate in thought and excellent in form.

Probably more important than Guido's poetry, however, is his *Historia destructionis Troiae* ("History of the Destruction of Troy"), which he completed about 1287. Thought to be a condensed version of the French *Roman de Troie* by Benoît de Sainte-Maure, Guido's work was widely translated throughout Europe. William Caxton translated it from a French source and published it in Bruges about 1474 as *The Recuyell of the Historyes of Troye*, the first book printed in the English language.

Guillaume de Lorris \gē-yōm-də-lō-'rēs\ (fl. 13th century) French author of the first and more poetic section of ROMAN DE LA ROSE, the medieval verse allegory he started about 1230.

Guillaume's work—which makes up the first 4,058 lines—is that of a courtly poet of great perceptiveness in his expression of character through allegorical symbols. Guillaume drew on the traditions of courtly love descended from the troubadours.

Little is known of Guillaume de Lorris except that the last part of his name derives from a village near Orléans.

Guillaume de Machaut \gē-yōm-də-mà-'shō\, Machaut, *also spelled* Machault (b. *c.* 1300, Machaut, Fr.—d. 1377, Reims) French poet and musician who was greatly admired by contemporaries as a master of French versification and is now regarded as one of the leading French composers of the 14th century. He

was the last great poet in France to think of the lyric and its musical setting as a single entity.

Guillaume took holy orders and in 1323 entered the service of John of Luxembourg, king of Bohemia, who in 1337 appointed him canon of Reims cathedral.

In his longer poems, Guillaume did not go beyond the themes and genres already widely employed in his time. They are mostly didactic and allegorical exercises in the well-worked courtly love tradition. An exception among the longer works is *Voir-Dit*, which tells how a young girl of high rank falls in love with the poet because of his fame and creative accomplishments. Guillaume also wrote lays and virelays, and his many rondeaux and ballades were instrumental in establishing these as set forms. His influence—most significantly his technical innovations—spread beyond the borders of France. In England, Geoffrey Chaucer drew heavily upon Guillaume's poetry for elements of *Book of the Duchesse*.

Guillaume d'Orange \gē-yōm-dò-'räⁿzh\ Central hero of some 24 anonymous French epic poems, or chansons de geste, of the 12th and 13th centuries. The poems form what is sometimes called *La Geste de Guillaume d'Orange* and together tell of a family warring against the Spanish Muslims. Modern research suggests that at least part of the Guillaume legend may have been originally localized in the Spanish marches, where sons and nephews of the historical Wilhelmus, a Frankish nobleman (and cousin of the emperor Charlemagne) upon whom the Guillaume of the epics is based, played a part in political events of the 9th century.

Poems in the cycle include the *Couronnement de Louis*, the *Charroi de Nîmes*, the *Prise d'Orange*, the *Chevalerie Vivien*, *Aliscans*, and the *Moniage Guillaume*. The underlying theme is the devotion of Guillaume and his family—to each other, to their championship of Christendom against the infidels in Spain and the south, and, above all, to their ungrateful and uncooperative king, Louis the Pious.

Guillén \gē-'yen\, Jorge (b. Jan. 18, 1893, Valladolid, Spain—d. Feb. 6, 1984, Málaga) Spanish lyric poet who experimented with different meters and used verbs rarely but whose work proved more accessible than that of other experimental poets.

The son of a newspaper publisher, Guillén studied in Switzerland and at the University of Granada before graduating from the University of Madrid in 1913. He taught Spanish at the University of Paris from 1917 to 1923 and began publishing his poetry. He earned a doctorate at the University of Madrid in 1924 and later taught at several universities. He became a member of the Generation of 1927 and in 1928 published his collection *Cántico* ("Canticle"; *Cantico: A Selection of Spanish Poems*), which he expanded in subsequent editions in 1936, 1945, and 1950. He was influenced by Paul Valéry and Juan Ramón Jiménez, who emphasized the musical properties of language over the narrative and didactic.

Guillén went to the United States during the Spanish Civil War and taught Spanish at Wellesley College (1940–57). From 1957 to 1963 he published *Clamor*, a three-volume collection of mature poems that express a sad awareness of the evanescence and limitations of life. His later works include *Homenaje* (1967; "Homage"), *Y otros poemas* (1973, "And Other Poems"), and *Final* (1981). He was also a critic and translator, notably of Valéry. Guillén was awarded the first Cervantes Prize (the highest honor in Hispanic letters) in 1976.

Guillén \gē-'yen\, Nicolás, *surname in full* Guillén Batista \bä-'tēs-tä\ (b. July 10, 1902, Camagüey, Cuba—d. July 16, 1989, Havana) Cuban poet of social protest and a leader of the Afro-Cuban movement in the late 1920s and the '30s. He was the national poet of revolutionary Cuba.

Guillén abandoned his law studies at the University of Havana in 1921 in order to concentrate on poetry. Of mixed African and European descent, he combined a knowledge of traditional literary form with firsthand experience of the speech, legends, songs, and sones (popular dances) of the Afro-Cubans in his first volume of poetry, *Motivos de son* (1930; "Motifs of Son"), which was soon hailed as a masterpiece.

The poems of *Cantos para soldados y sones para turistas* (1937; "Songs for Soldiers and Sones for Tourists") reflect his growing political commitment, and in that year Guillén went to Spain to fight with the Republicans in the Spanish Civil War. From this experience came the poems collected in *España* (1937; "Spain").

Guillén returned to Cuba after the defeat of the Spanish republic and joined the Communist Party. He continued to treat themes of revolution and social protest in such later volumes of poetry as *Elegías* (1958; "Elegies"), *La paloma de vuelo popular* (1959; "The Dove of Popular Flight"), and *Tengo* (1964; "I Have"; Eng. trans., *Tengo*).

Guimarães \gē-mȧ-'rĩⁿsh\, Bernardo (Joaquim da Silva) (b. Aug. 15, 1825, Ouro Prêto, Braz.—d. March 10, 1884, Ouro Prêto) Poet, dramatist, and regional novelist whose works marked a major transition toward greater realism in Brazilian literature and who was popular in his time as a minor Romantic novelist.

After a youthful bohemian life in São Paulo, Guimarães retired to his native Minas Gerais to write and teach school. Guimarães' subject was the Brazilian frontier, which he treated unsentimentally. His antislavery novel *A escrava Isaura* (1875; "The Slave Girl Isaura"), which helped to promote abolitionist sentiment in Brazil, is an early example of Latin-American social-protest literature and was compared to Harriet Beecher Stowe's *Uncle Tom's Cabin* (1852).

Guimarães Rosa \gē-mȧ-'rĩⁿsh-'rō-sə\, João (b. June 27, 1908, Cordisburgo, Braz.—d. Nov. 19, 1967, Rio de Janeiro) Novelist and short-story writer whose innovative prose style, derived from the oral tradition of the *sertão* (hinterland of Brazil), revitalized Brazilian fiction in the mid-20th century. His work reflects the problems of an isolated rural society in adjusting to a modern urban world.

Guimarães Rosa studied medicine at Belo Horizonte and became a physician. His urge to travel, however, soon led him into the Brazilian foreign service, and he served as a diplomat in several world capitals.

With the publication of *Sagarana* (1946), a collection of stories set in the *sertão*, Guimarães Rosa was hailed as a major force in Brazilian literature. Except for writing the seven stories in *Corpo de baile* (1956; "Corps de Ballet"), he devoted the next several years to diplomacy and the creation of his monumental epic novel, *Grande sertão: veredas* (1956; *The Devil to Pay in the Backlands*), which firmly established his international reputation. Turning exclusively to the short story, Guimarães Rosa published several more collections before his death, notably *Primeiras estórias* (1962; *The Third Bank of the River*).

Guimerà \gē-mȧ-'rä\, Àngel (b. May 6, 1847, Santa Cruz de Tenerife, Canary Islands, Spain—d. July 18, 1924, Barcelona) Catalan playwright, poet, orator, and fervent supporter of the Catalan literary revival known as La Renaixensa.

Guimerà's parents took him to Catalonia when he was seven, and the region left its mark on him. He studied in Barcelona before settling in the village of Vendrell. In 1872 he moved permanently to Barcelona, where he later became editor of *La Renaixensa*, a literary magazine. In 1877 he won the highly competitive Catalan poetic contests (*jocs florals*) and was named master troubadour (*mestre en gai saber*).

His public speeches, collected in *Cants a la pàtria* (1906; "Songs to the Fatherland"), his poetry, and most of his plays were concerned with awakening the Catalans' long-submerged pride in their ancient language and culture. His most celebrated play was the widely translated *Terra baixa* (1896; *Marta of the Lowlands*). His other plays include historical and modern tragedies, rural drama, and comedies.

Guinevere \'gwin-ə-,vir, 'gin-\ Wife of Arthur, legendary king of Britain, best known in Arthurian romance through the love that his knight Sir LANCELOT bore for her. In early Welsh literature, a character named Gwenhwyvar was "the first lady of this island"; in Geoffrey of Monmouth's inventive *Historia regum Britanniae* (early 12th century), she was named Guanhumara and was presented as a Roman lady. In some accounts it was suggested that she was Arthur's second wife.

An early tradition of abduction (and infidelity) surrounded the figure of Guinevere. According to the late 11th- or early 12th-century *Vita Gildae*, she was carried off by Melwas, king of Aestiva Regio (literally, "Summer Region"), to be rescued by Arthur and his army. In Chrétien de Troyes's late 12th-century romance *Le Chevalier de la charrette*, she was rescued by Lancelot (a character whom Chrétien had earlier named as one of Arthur's knights) from the land of Gorre, to which she had been taken by Meleagant. In the early part of the 13th-century prose Vulgate cycle, courtly love was exalted through the passion of Lancelot and Guinevere; but, in the austerely spiritual part of the Vulgate cycle, the *Queste del Saint Graal*, their adulterous love stood condemned, and Lancelot was unable to look directly at the Holy Grail because of it.

In the early chronicles and later in prose Arthurian romances, Guinevere was abducted by Mordred, Arthur's nephew (or, in some versions, his son), and this action was closely bound up with the death of Arthur and the end of the knightly fellowship of the Round Table.

Güiraldes \gwē-'räl-dās, -däh\, Ricardo (b. Feb. 13, 1886, Buenos Aires, Arg.—d. Oct. 8, 1927, Paris, Fr.) Argentine novelist and poet best remembered for his novel *Don Segundo Sombra* (1926), a poetic interpretation of the Argentine gaucho (the free-spirited vagabond cattle herder of the Pampas) that has become a classic work of Latin-American literature.

The son of a wealthy landowner, Güiraldes spent his boyhood on his family's ranch, where he learned the complex traditions of the gaucho. His first volume of poetry and prose, *El cencerro de cristal* (1915; "The Crystal Bell"), was harshly received by critics because of its stylistic idiosyncrasies but has since been recognized as the forerunner of post-World War I literary innovation in Argentina.

Güiraldes soon turned almost exclusively to prose, publishing several novels and short stories that combined his sophisticated formal approaches with his deep and sentimental feeling for his native land and its traditional themes. Examples include *Cuentos de muerte y de sangre* (1915; "Tales of Death and of Blood") and *Xaimaca* (1923; "Jamaica").

Guitry \gē-'trē\, Sacha, *byname of* Alexandre-Georges Guitry (b. Feb. 21, 1885, St. Petersburg, Russia—d. July 24, 1957, Paris, Fr.) Prodigious French playwright who generally acted in his own plays.

Sacha was only 21 when he achieved success with his first play, *Nono*. This was followed by *Chez les Zoaques* (1906), *Petite Hollande* (1908), *Le Scandale de Monte Carlo* (1908), *Le Veilleur de nuit* (1911), and *Un Beau Mariage* (1911). His output was enormous: more than 90 of the 130 plays he wrote were produced, including *Deburau* (1918), *Pasteur* (1919), and *Béranger* (1920). He wrote, directed, and acted in many motion pictures, of which the best known was perhaps *Roman d'un tricheur* (1938; "The Story of a Cheat"). His autobiography, *Mémoires d'un tricheur* (*If I Remember Right*), appeared in 1935.

Guittone d'Arezzo \gwē-'tō-nä-dä-'ret-tsō\ (b. *c.* 1230, Arezzo, Tuscia [Italy]—d. 1294, Florence) Founder of the Tuscan school of courtly poetry.

Knowledge of Guittone's life comes mainly from his writings. Born near Arezzo, he traveled for commercial reasons, being an exile from Arezzo after 1256 for his political views. Guittone experimented with elaborate and difficult forms of love poetry in a language that mingled local dialectisms, Latinisms, and Provençalisms. After he entered orders, he gave up love poetry for religious poetry. Guittone's "Ahi, lasso! O e stagion di doler tanto?" ("Ah, alas! How long does so much misery last?"), written after the military defeat (1260) of the political faction he supported, is a noble poem. His later work included sonnets and moral lyrics. He is also known as the creator of the *lauda*, a sacred ballad, in the vernacular. His 41 letters are among the oldest documents of epistolatory prose in Italian.

Gulag Archipelago, The \'gü-,läg, -,lag\ History and memoir of life in the Soviet Union's prison camp system by Russian novelist Aleksandr SOLZHENITSYN, first published in Paris as *Arkhipelag GULag* in three volumes (1973–75). Gulag is a Russian acronym for the Soviet government agency that supervised labor camps; Solzhenitsyn used the word archipelago as a metaphor for the labor camps, which were scattered through the sea of civil society like a chain of islands extending "from the Bering Strait almost to the Bosporus."

An exhaustive and compelling account based on his own eight years in Soviet prison camps, on other prisoners' stories committed to his photographic memory while in detention, and on letters and historical sources, the work represents the author's attempt to compile a literary and historical record; it was subtitled "An Experiment in Literary Investigation." A testimonial to Stalinist atrocities, *The Gulag Archipelago* devastated readers outside the Soviet Union with its descriptions of the brutality of the Soviet regime. The book gave new impetus to critics of the Soviet system and caused many sympathizers to question their position.

After the first volume was published in Paris in 1973, the official Soviet press virulently denounced Solzhenitsyn, who was arrested and exiled from the country in February 1974.

Gulliver's Travels \'gəl-i-vərz-'trav-əlz\ Four-part satirical novel by Jonathan SWIFT, published anonymously in 1726 as *Travels Into Several Remote Nations of the World*.

The novel is ostensibly the story of Lemuel Gulliver, a surgeon and sea captain who visits remote regions of the world. In the beginning Gulliver is shipwrecked on Lilliput, where people are six inches tall. The Lilliputians' utterly serious wars, civil strife, and vanities are human follies so reduced in scale as to be rendered ridiculous. His second voyage takes him to Brobdingnag, where lives a race of giants of great practicality who do not understand abstractions. Gulliver's third voyage takes him to the flying island of Laputa and the nearby continent and capital of Lagado. There he finds pedants obsessed with their own specialized areas of speculation and utterly ignorant of the rest of life. At Glubdubdrib, the Island of Sorcerers, he speaks with great men of the past and learns from them the lies of history. He also meets the Struldbrugs, who are immortal and, as a result, utterly miserable. In the extremely bitter fourth part, Gulliver visits the land of the Houyhnhnms, a race of intelligent, virtuous horses served by brutal, filthy, and degenerate creatures called Yahoos.

Gumilyov or **Gumilev** \gü-mʸi-'lʸȯf\, Nikolay Stepanovich (b. April 15, 1886, Kronshtadt, Russia—d. Aug. 24, 1921, Petrograd [St. Petersburg]) Russian poet and theorist who founded and led the Russian ACMEIST movement.

Gumilyov was educated at the Tsarskoye Selo Lyceum. His earliest published volumes of poetry, *Put konkvistadorov* (1905; "The Path of the Conquistadors"), *Romanticheskiye tsvety* (1908; "Romantic Flowers"), and *Zhemchuga* (1910; "Pearls"), marked him as a talented young poet under the influence of the Symbolist movement. In 1909 he became a founding member of APOLLON, the leading poetry journal in Russia in the years before the war. From 1910 to 1918 he was married to the poet Anna Akhmatova.

In 1912 Gumilyov helped found the Guild of Poets, which included Anna Akhmatova and Osip Mandelstam and which soon formed the nucleus of the emerging Acmeist movement. Gumilyov's poetry collection *Chuzhoye nebo* (1912; "Foreign Sky") established his reputation as a leading Russian poet. He attained his full artistic stature in the poems published in *Kostyor* (1918; "The Pyre"), *Shatyor* (1921; "The Tent"), and *Ognenny stolp* (1921; "The Pillar of Fire"). He had never bothered to hide his antipathy toward the Bolsheviks, and in August 1921 he was arrested and shot for counterrevolutionary activities. He was rehabilitated in the Soviet Union in 1986.

Gumilyov also wrote verse dramas and an important series of literary essays in which he developed the aesthetic canons of the Acmeist movement.

Gundulić \'gůn-dů-lich\, Ivan (Franov) (b. Jan. 8, 1589, Dubrovnik, republic of Venice [now in Croatia]—d. Dec. 8, 1638, Dubrovnik) Croatian poet and dramatist whose epic poem *Osman* (written 1626; first published 1826) was the outstanding achievement of the Renaissance flowering of art and literature that gave Dubrovnik the name of the "South Slav Athens."

A prolific writer, Gundulić also occupied various governmental positions in the Dubrovnik city-republic. Inspired in general by the Italian Renaissance and in particular by Torquato Tasso's *Gerusalemme liberata*, Gundulić's *Osman* describes the Ottoman sultan Osman II's defeat by the Poles at Khotin in Bessarabia (1621).

Gunn \'gən\, Neil Miller (b. Nov. 8, 1891, Dunbeath, Caithness, Scot.—d. Jan. 15, 1973, Inverness) Scottish author whose novels are set in the Highlands and seaside villages of his native land.

Gunn's first novel, *The Grey Coast*, was published in 1926. His third book, *Morning Tide* (1930), about a proud, sensitive boy growing up in the Highlands, was a popular success. Gunn's next two novels were quite different: *The Lost Glen* (1932) is a bitter story of the Highland people's decline, and *Sun Circle* (1933) relates the legend of a pagan Viking attack on Christian Caithness. The popularity of his novel *Highland River* (1937) enabled him to devote himself full-time to writing.

The Silver Darlings (1941), about the Caithness fishing industry in the 19th century, became another best-seller. Beginning with *The Shadow* (1948), Gunn's novels featured complex, often dark themes. *The Lost Chart* (1949) is a desolate Cold War novel, and *The Well at the World's End* (1951) is about a mystical quest. His final novel, *The Other Landscape* (1954), also relies on mystical elements. In addition, Gunn wrote plays and was especially known for his short stories and travel articles. His autobiography, *The Atom of Delight*, appeared in 1956.

Gunn \'gən\, Thom, *byname of* Thomson William Gunn (b. Aug. 29, 1929, Gravesend, Kent, Eng.) Anglo-American poet whose verse is notable for its adroit, terse language.

Gunn graduated from Trinity College, Cambridge, and later studied and taught at Stanford University in California. He also taught at the University of California at Berkeley.

His first volume of verse was *Fighting Terms* (1954; rev. ed., 1962). *The Sense of Movement* (1957) contains one of his best-known poems, "On the Move," a celebration of black-jacketed motorcyclists. In the late 1950s his poetry became more experimental. A selection of his work from this period was published in *Poems, 1950–1966* (1969). In the 1970s Gunn produced both a euphoric volume, *Moly* (1971), and a collection expressing disenchantment, *Jack Straw's Castle* (1976). *Selected Poems 1950–1975* was published in 1979, and *The Passages of Joy* in 1982. *The Occasion of Poetry* (1982) is a collection of essays. *The Man with Night Sweats* (1992) has AIDS as its subject.

Gunnar \'gū-när\ *see* GUNTHER.

Gunnarsson \'gœn-när-sȯn\, Gunnar (b. May 18, 1889, Valthjófsstadur, Ice.—d. Nov. 21, 1975, Reykjavík) Prolific Icelandic novelist and short-story writer who wrote in Danish to gain a wider audience.

Gunnarsson had published two collections of verse in Icelandic before he was 17. He went to Denmark determined to become a professional writer. In 1912 the first volume of his novel *Af Borgslægtens historie* ("The Borg Family Papers") appeared. It became a Scandinavian best-seller. The other three parts appeared from 1912 to 1914 (partial Eng. trans., *Guest the One-Eyed*). Gunnarsson lived and wrote in Denmark until 1939, when he retired to Iceland.

Gunnarsson followed *Af Borgslægtens historie* with more than 40 novels, as well as short stories, articles, and translations. Although he wrote in Danish, he drew exclusively on Icelandic history and his Icelandic background for his novels.

Güntekin \ˌgœn-te-'kin\, Reşat Nuri (b. Nov. 25, 1889, Constantinople, Ottoman Empire [now Istanbul, Tur.]—d. Dec. 6, 1956, London, Eng.) Prolific Turkish novelist, short-story writer, journalist, and playwright. His best-known work is the novel *Çalıkuşu* (1922; "The Wren"; Eng. trans., *The Autobiography of a Turkish Girl*), a picaresque tale that combines romance with realistic description of Anatolia.

Güntekin was educated at a French school in Smyrna and at Istanbul University. His literary career began in 1917 with the publication of short fiction and drama criticism. *Çalıkuşu*, which was serialized in a newspaper before its publication in book form, made his name and won him great popularity. His other novels include *Dudaktan kalbe* (1923; "From Lips to Heart"), *Yeşil gece* (1928; "The Green Night"), and *Miskinler tekkesi* (1946; "The Poor of the Dervish Convent"). His plays include sentimental family dramas, such as *Taş parçası* (1923; "A Piece of Stone") and *Eski şarkı* (1951; "The Old Song"), and social satires such as *Hülleci* (1935; "The Hired Husband").

Gunther \'gun-tər, 'gən-thər\, *also called* Gundicar, Gundicarius, Gunnar, Gundahar, *or* Guntharius (d. 437) Burgundian king who was a hero of many medieval legends.

The historical Gunther led the Burgundians across the Rhine in the early 5th century, establishing a kingdom at Worms. He fell in battle against the Huns in 437.

Gunther (called Gunnar) figures in the Eddaic poem *Lay of Atli*, in which he is slain by Atli (Attila) the Hun and avenged by his sister Gudrun (known in some other sources as Kriemhild), Atli's wife. In the 9th- or 10th-century Latin poem *Waltharius*, Gunther (Guntharius) and his warriors try unsuccessfully to kill the hero (Walter of Aquitaine) and steal his treasure. In the 12th–13th-century German epic *Nibelungenlied*, Siegfried helps Gunther to win Brunhild and in return marries Gunther's sister Kriemhild. *See also* LAY OF ATLI; NIBELUNGENLIED; WALTHARIUS.

Günther \'gœn-tər\, Johann Christian (b. April 8, 1695, Striegau, Silesia [now Strzegom, Poland]—d. March 15, 1723, Jena [Germany]) One of the most important German lyric poets of the period between the European Middle Ages and the late 18th century.

Günther studied medicine at Wittenberg but after two years of dissolute life went to Leipzig in 1717. An effort to secure for him the post of stipendiary poet at the Saxon-Polish court at Dresden ended in a fiasco. In 1719 his father, who for long had opposed his son's poetical ambitions, disinherited him, despite Günther's attempts at reconciliation.

Günther's mature poetry is largely lyrical and occasional. His true poetic quality, however, emerged when he wrote of his personal sufferings in such poems as the *Leonorenlieder* and in the confessional poem in which he pleads to his father for mercy.

Guo Moruo or **Kuo Mo-jo** \'gwȯ-'mwȯ-'rwȯ\, *original name* Guo Kaizhen \'gwȯ-'kī-'jən\ (b. November 1892, Shawan, Luoshan county, Sichuan, China—d. June 12, 1978, Beijing) Chinese scholar, one of the leading writers of 20th-century China, and an important government official.

In 1914 Guo went to Japan to study medicine. There he fell in love with a Japanese woman who became his common-law wife and began to devote himself to the study of foreign languages and literature. His translation of J.W. von Goethe's *Sorrows of Young Werther* gained enormous popularity among Chinese youth soon after its appearance in 1922. Two years later his translation of *Social Organization and Social Revolution*, by the Japanese Marxist Kawakami Hajime, greatly influenced his own thought, and he became an adherent of Marxism. He rejected individualistic literature and called for a "socialist literature that is sympathetic toward the proletariat."

Guo's participation in a failed Communist uprising in 1927 led him to flee to Japan, where for 10 years he pursued scholarly research on Chinese antiquities. In 1937 he returned to China to take part in the resistance against Japan and was given important government posts.

As a writer, Guo was enormously prolific in every genre. Besides his poetry and fiction, his works include plays, nine autobiographical volumes, and numerous translations of the works of Goethe, Friedrich von Schiller, Ivan Turgenev, Leo Tolstoy, Upton Sinclair, and other Western authors. He also produced historical and philosophical treatises, including his monumental study of inscriptions on oracle bones and bronze vessels, *Liang Zhou jin wen ci da xi tu lu kao shi* (1935, rev. ed., 1957; "Corpus of Inscriptions on Bronzes from the Two Zhou [Chou] Dynasties").

After 1949 Guo held many important positions in the People's Republic of China, including the presidency of the Chinese Academy of Sciences.

Gürpınar \ˌgœr-pȯ-'när\, Hüseyin Rahmi (b. Aug. 17, 1864, Constantinople, Ottoman Empire [now Istanbul, Tur.]—d. March 8, 1944, Istanbul) Turkish novelist, a prolific writer known for his sketches of life in Istanbul.

Educated privately and at the School of Political Science in Constantinople, Gürpınar entered on a career in the Turkish civil service, retiring in 1908 at the time of the Young Turk revolution. Afterward, except for short service as a member of Parliament, he lived a solitary life on the island of Heybeli, in the Sea of Marmara.

Influenced by European writers including Alfred de Musset and Guy de Maupassant, Gürpınar gradually developed his own distinctive style. He wrote some 50 novels, about 70 short stories, a few unsuccessful plays, and several translations of French novels. *Mürebbiye* (1897; "The Governess") was an attack on the custom of entrusting children to the care of often domineering governesses. Other well-known novels include *Metres* (1900; "The Mistress"); *İffet* (1897; "Chastity");

Mutallaka (1897; "The Divorcée"); *Son arzu* (1922; "The Last Wish"); and *Ben deli miyim?* (1925; "Am I Mad?").

guslar \\'gūs-ˌlär\\ *plural* guslari \\-ˌlär-ē\\ [Serbo-Croatian *guslar*, a derivative of *gusle* single-stringed fiddle] Any of a group of popular narrative singers of the Balkans who inherit a tradition that dates from the 17th century. Among the few performers continuing the oral tradition of epic poetry in the West, the *guslari* serve as transmitters and interpreters of a repertory of song and epic. The *guslari* accompany themselves on the gusla, or gusle (a one-stringed instrument), and intone their musical stories.

Gustafson \\ˌgəs-'taf-sən\\, Ralph (Barker) (b. Aug. 16, 1909, Lime Ridge, near Sherbrooke, Que., Can.) Canadian poet whose work shows a development from traditional form and manner to an elliptical style that reflects the influence of Anglo-Saxon verse and the metrical experiments of the 19th-century British poet Gerard Manley Hopkins.

Gustafson attended the University of Oxford and then became a tutor and journalist in London. He settled in New York after World War II but later returned to Canada.

Gustafson's early volumes of verse, such as *The Golden Chalice* (1935), *Lyrics Unromantic* (1942), and *Flight into Darkness* (1944), showed a gradually increasing individuality of style and an evolving vision. The later of his numerous works, which are usually considered his better writings, include *Rivers Among Rocks* (1960), *Sift in an Hourglass* (1966), *Ixion's Wheel* (1969), *Conflicts of Spring* (1981), *Plummets and Other Partialities* and *Winter Prophecies* (both 1987), and *Shadows in the Grass* (1991). Gustafson also produced two volumes of short stories, *The Brazen Tower* (1974) and *The Vivid Air* (1980).

Guthrie \\'gəth-rē\\, A.B., *in full* Alfred Bertram Guthrie, Jr. (b. Jan. 13, 1901, Bedford, Ind., U.S.—d. April 26, 1991, Choteau, Mont.) American novelist best known for his writing about the American West.

Guthrie earned a degree in journalism from the University of Montana and later went to work for the *Lexington Leader* newspaper in Kentucky, where between 1926 and 1947 he rose from cub reporter to executive editor. His first book, *Murders at Moon Dance*, was published in 1943. Next came his three most famous novels (often designated a trilogy)—*The Big Sky* (1947), *The Way West* (1949), which won a Pulitzer Prize, and *These Thousand Hills* (1956)—all of which realistically depict the lives of Americans settling along the upper Missouri and Columbia rivers. Guthrie returned permanently to Montana in 1953, where he later successfully blended the Western and detective genres in such books as *Wild Pitch* (1973), *The Genuine Article* (1977), and *No Second Wind* (1980). He also published *The Big It* (1960), a collection of short stories; *The Blue Hen's Chick* (1965), an autobiography; and *A Field Guide to Writing Fiction* (1991).

Gutiérrez Nájera \\gü-'tyer-räs-'nä-ḵä-rä\\, Manuel (b. Dec. 22, 1859, Mexico City, Mex.—d. Feb. 3, 1895, Mexico City) Mexican poet and prose writer whose musical, elegant, and melancholy poetry and restrained rhythmic prose sketches and tales mark the transition in Mexican literature between Romanticism and modernism. His active support of the fledgling Modernismo movement gave encouragement to a generation of younger writers in Mexico.

Gutiérrez Nájera read widely and was strongly influenced by the French poets Alfred de Musset, Théophile Gautier, and Paul Verlaine. His first article appeared in the newspaper *La Iberia* when he was 13, and until his death he wrote several articles a week. In 1894 he founded the *Revista azul* ("Blue Review"), a literary journal that became Mexico's first forum for modernist poetry. Recognized as more of an influence on literary trends than as a major poet in his own right, he is still admired for his *crónicas*, a genre of short story that he created.

Gutiérrez Solana \\gü-'tyer-räth-sō-'lä-nä\\, José (b. Feb. 28, 1886, Madrid, Spain—d. June 24, 1945, Madrid) Painter and writer, a key figure in the Spanish cultural revival of the early 20th century.

The descendant of an old but impoverished family of Santander, Gutiérrez Solana attended art school in Madrid for a short period, but he was primarily self-taught. He spent his days in the slums and suburbs of Madrid and in the Cantabrian harbors, studying and identifying himself with the most wretched aspects of Spanish life. These journeys were the basis for his gloomy and corrosive literary works, the two volumes of *Madrid: escenas y costumbres* (1912, 1918; "Madrid: Scenes and Customs"), and for his intense and dramatic paintings. He first exhibited in 1907 and won medals in 1922, 1929, and 1942. His subjects included bulls, urban landscapes, and, in two famous paintings, prostitutes in "Claudia's Place" and literary life in "La tertulia de Pombo."

Guto'r Glyn \\'git-òr-'glin\\ (fl. *c.* 1440–93) Welsh bard whose works were among the first to show a consciousness of nationhood among the people of Wales. *Gwaith Guto'r Glyn* ("The Works of Guto'r Glyn," first published in 1939) was collected by J.Ll. Williams and edited by Sir Ifor Williams.

Gutzkow \\'gút-skō\\, Karl (Ferdinand) (b. March 17, 1811, Berlin, Prussia [Germany]—d. Dec. 16, 1878, Sachsenhausen, Frankfurt am Main) Novelist and dramatist who was a pioneer of the modern social novel in Germany.

Gutzkow began his career as a journalist and first attracted attention with the publication of *Maha Guru, Geschichte eines Gottes* (1833; "Maha Guru, Story of a God"), a fantastic satirical romance. In 1835 he published *Wally, die Zweiflerin* ("Wally, the Doubter"), an attack on marriage that marked the beginning of the Young Germany revolt against Romanticism. In 1839 Gutzkow produced the tragedy *Richard Savage*, the first in a series of well-constructed and effective plays. His domestic tragedy *Werner oder Herz und Welt* (1840; "Werner or Heart and World") long remained in the repertory of the German theaters.

In 1847 Gutzkow went to Dresden, where he succeeded Ludwig Tieck as literary adviser to the court theater. In 1850 was published the first volume of his nine-volume *Die Ritter vom Geiste* ("The Knights of the Spirit"), now considered the starting point of the modern German social novel; it also anticipated the naturalist movement. His final well-known work, *Der Zauberer von Rom* (1858–61; "The Magician of Rome"), is a powerful study of Roman Catholic life in southern Germany.

guwen or **ku-wen** \\'gǖ-'wən\\ [Chinese *gǔwén*, from *gǔ* ancient + *wén* writing], *also called* wenyan \\'wən-'yan\\ In Chinese literature, classical or literary prose that aims at the standards and styles set by ancient writers and their distinguished followers of subsequent ages, with the Confucian Classics and the early philosophers as supreme models. While the styles may vary with individual writers, the language is always far removed from their spoken tongues. Sanctioned by official requirement for the competitive examinations and dignified by traditional respect for the cultural accomplishments of past ages, this medium became the linguistic tool of practically all Chinese prose writers. *Compare* BAIHUA.

Guy \\'gē\\, Rosa (Cuthbert) (b. Sept. 1, 1925/28, Trinidad, West Indies) African-American writer whose fiction for young adults usually concerned family conflicts and the realities of life in the urban American ghetto as well as life in the West Indies.

After immigrating to the United States with her family in 1932, Guy grew up in New York City's Harlem. She became a writer and studied at New York University. In the late 1940s, with other young black writers, she formed the Harlem Writers' Guild.

Her first novel, *Bird at My Window* (1966), was set in Harlem and dealt with social forces that foster the demoralization of black men; the work also examined the relationship between the black mother and her children. *Children of Longing* (1970), which Guy edited, contained accounts of firsthand experiences and of the aspirations of young black people aged 13 to 23. After publication of these works, Guy traveled in the Caribbean, living in Haiti and Trinidad. Her subsequent novels, such as *The Friends* (1973) and *Ruby* (1976), reflect West Indian and Haitian cultures. Still later works include *The Disappearance* (1979), *A Measure of Time* (1983), *New Guys Around the Block* (1983), *Paris, Pee Wee, and Big Dog* (1984), *My Love, My Love; or, The Peasant Girl* (1985), *And I Heard a Bird Sing* (1987), and *The Ups and Downs of Carl David III* (1989).

Guy of Warwick \'gē . . . 'wȯr-ik, *U.S. also* 'wȯr-wik\ English hero of romance whose story was popular in France and England from the 13th to the 17th century and was told in English broadside ballads as late as the 19th century. The kernel of the story is a single combat in which Guy defeats Colbrand (a champion of the invading Danish kings Anlaf and Gonelaph), thereby delivering Winchester from Danish dominion. The Anlaf of the story is probably the Norwegian Olaf (later King Olaf I Tryggvason), who, with Sweyn I Forkbeard of Denmark, harried the southern counties of England in 994.

Guzmán \gús-'män\, Martín Luis (b. Oct. 6, 1887, Chihuahua, Mex.—d. Dec. 22, 1976, Mexico City) Novelist who was one of the finest writers of the revolutionary period in Mexico.

After studying law at the National Autonomous University of Mexico in Mexico City, Guzmán joined the Mexican Revolution and served as a colonel in the revolutionary forces of Pancho Villa. From 1914 to 1934, he lived in exile in Madrid and New York City, where he was editor of the periodical *El gráfico* ("The Graphic"). His experiences in the revolution were recorded in his volume of memoirs, *El águila y la serpiente* (1928; *The Eagle and the Serpent*). He is also famous for his novel *La sombra del caudillo* (1929; "The Shadow of the Leader"), in which he depicted the political corruption of the 1920s in Mexico. His other major works include *Memorias de Pancho Villa* (1940; *Memoirs of Pancho Villa*), *Mina el mozo, héroe de Navarra* (1932; "Mina the Youth, Hero of Navarre"), *Muertes históricas* (1958; "Historical Deaths"), and *Crónicas de mi destierro* (1963; "Chronicles of My Exile").

Guzmán de Alfarache \gúth-'män-tha-,äl-fä-'rä-chä\ Picaresque novel by Mateo ALEMÁN, published in Spanish in 1599. A second part of the novel appeared in 1604, and the whole work was translated into English as *The Life and Adventures of Guzman de Alfarache; or, The Spanish Rogue*.

One of the earliest and most popular picaresque novels, it is a lengthy and pessimistic saga influenced by Roman Catholic theology. The novel depicts the descent into sin and degradation of Guzmán, a well-born young man from Seville who runs away to Madrid and soon learns how difficult life without money can be. When he is ultimately caught stealing from his employer, Guzmán is condemned to life as a galley slave. This leads to his conversion and consequent redemption.

Gwalchmai ap Meilyr \'gwälk̲-mī-äp-'mī-lir\ (fl. *c.* 1140–80) One of the earliest Welsh court poets (*gogynfeirdd*) at the court of Owain Gwynedd at Aberffraw, Anglesey. His extant poems include traditional eulogies to the Welsh princes Owain Gwynedd and Madog ap Maredudd and a "boasting poem," *Gorhoffedd*, celebrating his prowess in war and with women.

gyascutus \,jī-ə-'skyū-təs, ,gī-, -'skü-\ An imaginary, large, four-legged beast with legs on one side longer than on the other for walking on hillsides. Humorous references to this creature, whose name has countless local variants, first appeared in American newspapers during the 1840s. The word was apparently coined to mimic the Latin taxonomic names of real animals, but its precise origin is unknown.

Gyllenborg \'yœl-lən-,bȯrʸ\, Gustaf Fredrik, Greve (Count) (b. Dec. 6, 1731, Strömsbro, near Linköping, Swed.—d. March 30, 1808, Stockholm) Swedish poet known for his satirical and reflective poetry.

Gyllenborg formed a literary society with the poets Gustav Philip Creutz and Hedvig Charlotta Nordenflycht. The three published two literary anthologies, the first in three volumes (1753, 1754, 1756) and the second in two (1759, 1762). Gyllenborg was one of the original members of the Swedish Academy (founded 1786).

Gyllenborg attacked the weaknesses of modern society in the spirit of the French Romantic philosopher Jean-Jacques Rousseau in such poems as "Verldsföraktaren" (1762; "The Misanthrope"). A pessimism typical of the late 18th century is expressed in his most famous poem, "Menniskans elände" (1762; "Misery of Man"). Gyllenborg wrote most of his important work before 1763, thereafter devoting himself to a civil-service career. His memoirs, *Mitt lefverne 1731–1775*, were published in 1885.

Gyllensten \'yœl-lən-,stän\, Lars (Johan Wictor) (b. Nov. 12, 1921, Stockholm, Swed.) Swedish intellectual, professor of histology, poet, and prolific philosophical novelist.

Gyllensten was reared and educated in Stockholm and was a professor of medicine at the Karolinska Institute for 18 years. The principal theme in his novels is the subjective and relative nature of the human perception of truth. The theme is developed in *Barnabok* (1952; "Children's Book") and in its sequel, *Senilia* (1956). *Sokrates död* (1960; "The Death of Socrates") is a historical novel set in 5th-century-BC Athens. Later works include *Lotus i Hades* (1966; "Lotus in Hades"), *Diarium spirituale* (1968), and *Grottan i öknen* (1973; "The Cave in the Desert"). He explores an ideologically bankrupt world in such novels as *Moderna myter* (1949; "Modern Myths") and *Kains memoarer* (1963; *The Testament of Cain*). In 1986 his *Sju vise mästare om kärleken*, seven tales of love in its many guises, was published, and in 1991 the novel *Det himmelska gästabudet* ("The Heavenly Banquet").

Other works by Gyllensten include *Det blå skeppet* (1950; "The Blue Ship"), *Carnivora* (1953), *Senatorn* (1958; "The Senator"), *Baklängesminnen* (1978; "Memories Backward"), and a collection of essays and lectures on literature, *Så var det sagt* ("As It Was Said"), published in 1992.

Gynt, Peer \'par-'gœnt, *Angl* 'pir-'gint\ Fictional character, the legendary Norwegian folk hero who is the protagonist of Henrik Ibsen's play PEER GYNT.

Gypsy Ballads, The Verse collection by Federico GARCÍA LORCA, written between 1924 and 1927 and first published in Spanish in 1928 as *Romancero gitano*. The collection comprises 18 lyrical poems, 15 of which combine startlingly modern poetic imagery with traditional literary forms; the three remaining poems were classified by Lorca as historical ballads. All 18 poems were written in the traditional ballad meter of eight-syllable lines. Many of the poems were imbued with mythic allusions, Freudian symbolism (green symbolizes sexuality and blue, innocence) and indirect metaphors.

Haasse \ˈhä-sə\, Hella S., *in full* Hella Serafia van Lelyveld-Haasse \vän-ˈlä-lœ-ˌvelt\ (b. Feb. 2, 1918, Batavia, Dutch East Indies [now Jakarta, Indonesia]) Dutch novelist noted for her innovative historical fiction.

Haasse published a volume of poetry, *Stroomversnelling* ("Fast Current"), in 1945. Her novel *Het woud der verwachting* (1949; *In a Dark Wood Wandering*) is about Charles d'Orléans, a French nobleman taken prisoner by the English in 1415. Giovanni Borgia, a 16th-century Italian aristocrat, is the subject of *De scharlaken stad* (1952; *The Scarlet City*), which is narrated with unusual shifts of perspective among characters.

Haasse revived the Marchioness of Merteuil (from Choderlos de Laclos' novel *Les liaisons dangereuses*) in *Een gevaarlijke verhouding of Daal-en-Bergse brieven* (1976; "A Dangerous Liaison, or Letters from Daal-en-Berg"). In novels about the Dutch aristocrat Charlotte-Sophie Bentinck, *Onverenigbaarheid van karakter* (1978; "Incompatibility of Character") and *De groten der aarde* (1981; "Great Figures of History"), Haasse used a collage form, with authentic documents, to tell her story. Haasse also wrote the play *Een draad in het donker* (1963; "A Thread in the Dark"), based on the myth of Theseus and Ariadne, and autobiographical works, including *Zelfportret als legkaart* (1954; "Self-Portrait as Jigsaw Puzzle").

Haavikko \ˈhä-vĕk-kō\, Paavo (b. Jan. 25, 1931, Helsinki, Fin.) Finnish humanist poet, novelist, and dramatist. His work is modernistic, experimental, and linguistically innovative.

With his first collection of poems, *Tiet etäisyyksiin* (1951; "Ways to Far Away"), Haavikko demonstrated a rare command of rhythm and image in his virtuoso handling of the language. In his next collection, *Tuuliöinä* (1953; "On Windy Nights"), he used the wind as the central metaphor for contemporary anxiety and alienation. In *Synnyinmaa* (1955; "Birthplace"), *Lehdet lehtiä* (1958; "Leaves, Pages"), and *Talvipalatsi* (1959; *The Winter Palace*), Haavikko explored the creative process and the role of the poet. Many of his later collections of poetry, such as *Runoja matkalta salmen ylitse* (1973; "Poems from a Voyage Across the Sound") and *Viiniä, kirjoitusta* (1976; "Wine, Writing), examined the subject of power.

In *Yksityisia asioita* (1960; "Private Affairs") Haavikko castigated the mentality that prevailed during the civil war (1918) in Finland. His short stories were collected in *Lasi Claudius Civiliksen salaliittolaisten pöydällä* (1964; "A Glass on the Table in [Rembrandt's painting] *The Conspirators of Claudius Civilis*"), and his stage works in *Näytelmät* (1978; "Plays"). Haavikko also wrote the libretto for Aulis Sallinen's opera *Ratsumies* (1974; *The Horseman*). His later works include *Ikuisen rauhan aika* (1981; "Time of Eternal Peace"), *Viisi pientä draamalista tekstiä* (1981; "Five Small Dramatic Pieces"), *Rauta-aika* (1982; *The Age of Iron*), and *Viisi sarjaa nopeasti virtaavasta elämästä* (1987; "Five Series about Rapidly Flowing Life").

Habima or **Habimah** \hä-ˈbĕ-mä\ ("Stage") Hebrew theater company originally organized as Habima ha-'Ivrit ("The Hebrew Stage") in Białystok, Pol., in 1912 by Nahum Zemach. In 1913 the troupe traveled to Vienna, where it staged Osip Dymov's *Hear O Israel* before the 11th Zionist Congress. In 1917, after the war caused the ensemble to dissolve, Zemach reestablished the group in Moscow, calling it Habima.

Encouraged by Konstantin Stanislavsky, the director of the Moscow Art Theater, and inspired by a fervent desire to transcend the tawdry and superficial Yiddish operettas and melodramas then in vogue, Habima opened in 1918 with a production staged by Yevgeny Vakhtangov, a student of Stanislavsky,

who remained Habima's chief director until his death in 1922. Vakhtangov's production in 1922 of S. Ansky's *The Dybbuk* was an immediate success and established Habima as a theater of the highest artistic excellence. It became one of four studios of the Moscow Art Theater. In 1926, after touring Europe, Habima went to the United States. After a division in its membership, the major part of the group left for Palestine without Zemach and in 1931 permanently established itself in Tel Aviv. In 1958 Habima was designated the National Theater of Israel and awarded an annual state subsidy.

Haddad \ha-ˈdad\, Malek (b. July 5, 1927, Constantine, Alg.—d. June 2, 1978, Algiers) Algerian poet, novelist, and cultural adviser.

Haddad wrote for French and Algerian weeklies and magazines during the Algerian War of Independence. His first published book was a collection of poetry, *Le Malheur en danger* (1956; "Trouble in Danger"). A second collection, *Écoute et je t'appelle* (1961; "Listen and I Will Call"), was introduced by the essay "Les Zéros tournent en rond" ("The Zeros Turn Round in a Circle").

Haddad wrote four novels: *La Dernière Impression* (1958; "Last Impression"), *Je t'offrirai une gazelle* (1959; "I Will Offer You a Gazelle"), *L'Élève et la leçon* (1960; "The Pupil and the Lesson"), and *Le Quai aux fleurs ne répond plus* (1961; "The Flowers Quay No Longer Answers"). Following Algerian independence Haddad continued to write for periodicals until 1968, when he became director of culture at the Ministry of Culture and Information. Among the dominant themes of his works are the fatherland, exile, and happiness.

Hades \ˈhā-dēz\, *Greek* Aïdes, *also called* Pluto \ˈplü-tō\ *or* Pluton \ˈplü-ˌtän\ In Greek religion, son of the Titans Cronus and Rhea, brother of the deities Zeus and Poseidon. After Cronus was overthrown, the kingdom of the underworld fell by lot to Hades. There he ruled with his queen, Persephone, over the infernal powers and over the dead, in what was often called "the House of Hades," or simply Hades. Though he supervised the trial and punishment of the wicked after death, he was not normally one of the judges in the underworld; nor did he personally torture the guilty, a task assigned to the Furies (Erinyes).

Ḥāfeẓ or **Ḥāfiz** \ˈkȯ-fez\, *in full* Moḥammad Shams od-Dīn Ḥāfeẓ (b. 1325/26, Shīrāz, Iran—d. 1389/90, Shīrāz) One of the finest lyric poets of Persia, best known for his *Dīvān.*

Ḥāfeẓ received a traditional religious education, lectured on Qur'ānic and other theological subjects ("Ḥāfeẓ" designates one who has learned the Qur'ān by heart), and wrote commentaries on religious classics. As a court poet he enjoyed the patronage of several rulers of Shīrāz.

About 1368–69 Ḥāfeẓ fell out of favor at the court and did not regain his position until 20 years later, just before his death. In his poetry there are many echoes of historical events as well as biographical descriptions and details of life in Shīrāz. One of the guiding principles of his life was Ṣūfism, an Islāmic mystical movement.

Ḥāfeẓ' principal verse form, one that he brought to perfection, was the ghazal, a lyric poem of 6 to 15 couplets linked by unity of subject and symbolism rather than by a logical sequence of ideas. Traditionally the ghazal had dealt with love and wine, motifs that, in their association with ecstasy and freedom from restraint, lent themselves naturally to the expression of Ṣūfī ideas. Ḥāfeẓ's achievement was to give these conventional subjects a freshness and subtlety that completely relieves his poetry of tedious formalism. An important innovation credited to Ḥāfeẓ was the use of the ghazal instead of the qasida (ode) in panegyrics. The extraordinary popularity of his poetry in all Persian-speaking lands stems from his simple and often colloquial though musical language, free from artificial virtuosity, and his unaffected use of homely images and proverbial expressions.

Ḥāfiẓ Ibrāhīm \'kä-fĕth-ĕ-,brä-'hēm\, Muḥammad (b. 1872, Dayrut, Egypt—d. July 21, 1932, Cairo)　Egyptian author known as the "poet of the Nile."

Ḥāfiẓ wrote nationalistic poems and well-known odes denouncing imperialism. His superb skill as a reciter of poetry won him a prominent place in society, and he became director of literature (1911–31) in the national library in Cairo. Ḥāfiẓ's true talent may have been in prose, as can be seen from his unfinished work *Al-Buʾasāʾ* (1903; "The Miserable Ones").

Hafstein \'häf-,stān\, Hannes (b. Dec. 4, 1861, Mödruvellir, Ice.—d. Dec. 13, 1922, Reykjavík)　Icelandic statesman and poet, a pioneer of literary realism in Iceland.

In 1886 Hafstein became a member of the Althing (parliament). In 1904 he was appointed Icelandic minister of state to the Danish crown, the first Icelander to hold the post.

Most of his poetry was written when he was a young man; it is filled with the vigor and joy of life, his love of country, and his admiration for the heroic, as exemplified by a portrait of Danish critic Georg Brandes in the periodical *Heimdallur* (1884). He also wrote many delicate love lyrics and drinking songs.

hag \'hag\ [Middle English *hagge* old woman, witch]　In European folklore, an ugly and malicious old woman who practices witchcraft, with or without supernatural powers. Hags are often said to be aligned with the devil or the dead.

Hagalín \'hä-ĝä-,lĕn\, Guthmundur Gíslason (b. Oct. 10, 1898, Arnarfjörthur, Ice.—d. Feb. 26, 1985, Akranes)　Icelandic novelist, short-story writer, and essayist. His works constitute a social history of Iceland from World War I to the post–World War II period.

As a young man, Hagalín worked on fishing boats and read widely. At age 18 he went to the Latin School in Reykjavík but left after a year. He turned to journalism and spent three years in Norway, traveling and lecturing on Iceland. In 1927 he returned to Iceland and worked as a librarian.

Hagalín developed a strong prose style to interpret the rough, forthright people of his community. His short stories are models of economy, and in his novels the characters dictate the action. Hagalín was one of the first Icelanders to write fictional biographies based on real people (though the form had its ancestry in the sagas).

Hagalín's best-known novels include *Kristrún í Hamravík* (1933), *Sturla í Vogum* (1938), and *Móthir Ísland* (1945; "Mother Iceland"). He wrote several volumes of autobiography, including *Ég veit ekki betur* (1951; "I Know No Better") and *Hér er kominn Hoffinn* (1954; "Here Hoffinn Is Come").

Hagar \'hā-,gär, -gər\ or **Agar** \'ā-,gär\　In the Old Testament, Abraham's concubine and the mother of his son Ishmael. Purchased in Egypt, she served as a handmaid to Abraham's childless wife, Sarah, who gave her to Abraham to conceive an heir. When Hagar became pregnant, her meekness changed to arrogance; with Abraham's reluctant permission, Sarah treated her so harshly that she fled into the wilderness. There, by a spring of water, she was found by an angel of the Lord, who told her to return home, promising her that she would have many descendants through a son, Ishmael, and saying that he would grow up to be a "wild ass of a man," in constant struggle with all other men. Hagar returned home to bear her child.

About 14 years after the birth of Ishmael, Abraham's son Isaac, with whom God had promised to make a covenant, was born to Sarah. One day Sarah saw Isaac and Ishmael playing together and, fearing that Ishmael would also become an heir, sent the son and mother into the desert. There God sustained them and was with Ishmael until he grew up.

Allusions to Hagar abound in English literature. The rejected handmaid has also furnished the subject of several novels, notably Margaret Laurence's *The Stone Angel* (1964).

Hagedorn \'häg-ə-,dörn\, Friedrich von (b. April 23, 1708, Hamburg [Germany]—d. Oct. 28, 1754, Hamburg)　Poet who introduced a new lightness and grace into German poetry.

Although he is usually grouped with the German anacreontic poets, Hagedorn's model was Horace, and not the Greek poet Anacreon. His best and most popular works appeared in *Versuch in poetischen Fabeln und Erzählungen* (1738; "Attempt at Poetic Fables and Tales") and *Oden und Lieder*, 3 vol. (1742–52; "Odes and Songs"). These fables and tales in verse, influenced by the French poet Jean de La Fontaine, are characterized by neatness of form, graceful lightness of touch, and a feeling for rhythm that sets Hagedorn apart from other poets of his time.

Hagen \'hä-gən\ or **Hagano** \'hä-gə-,nō\ or **Hogni** \'hȯk-nē\　Mythological Germanic hero who plays a variety of roles in a number of northern European legends. In the *Nibelungenlied*, he appears as a vassal of the Burgundian king Gunther and is a grizzled warrior, loyal and wary. He plays a principal role in the epic as the slayer of Siegfried and becomes the chief object of hatred and revenge for Siegfried's widow, Kriemhild. In the Latin heroic epic *Waltharius*, he is called Hagano. In Old Norse poems he is Hogni, the brother of Gunnar; both brothers meet their death at the hands of Atli (Attila). *See* LAY OF ATLI; NIBELUNGENLIED; WALTHARIUS.

Haggada or **Haggadah** \hä-'gäd-ə, -'gȯd-\ *plural* Haggadoth *or* Haggadot \-,dōth, -,dōt\ [Hebrew *haggādhāh*]　**1.** Explanatory matter occurring in rabbinical literature, often taking the form of story, anecdote, legend, or parable, and treating such varied subjects as astronomy, astrology, magic, medicine, and mysticism.　**2.** Explanatory matter in the Talmud interpreting the Scriptures as distinguished from that regulating religious practice.　**3.** The prayer book containing the seder ritual.

Haggard \'hag-ərd\, Sir H. Rider, *in full* Sir Henry Rider Haggard (b. June 22, 1856, Bradenham, Norfolk, Eng.—d. May 14, 1925, London)　English novelist best known for his romantic adventure KING SOLOMON'S MINES (1885).

In 1875 Haggard went to Natal, where he held a series of official posts. In 1881 he returned to England and wrote a history of recent events in southern Africa, entitled *Cetywayo and His White Neighbours* (1882).

After publishing two unsuccessful novels, Haggard captured the public with his African adventure story *King Solomon's Mines*. He followed this with SHE (1887) and further stories of Africa, notably *Allan Quatermain* (1887), *Nada the Lily* (1892), *Queen Sheba's Ring* (1910), *Marie* (1912), and *The Ivory Child* (1916). He also wrote memorably of ancient Egypt in several novels, beginning with *Cleopatra* (1889).

Haggard was also a practical farmer. *A Farmer's Year* (1899) and *Rural England*, 2 vol. (1902), are works of some importance. His autobiography, *The Days of My Life: An Autobiography by Sir H. Rider Haggard* (1926), was published posthumously.

hagiography \,hä-gē-'äg-rə-fē, ,hā-jē-\ or **hagiology** \-'äl-ə-jē\ [Greek *hágios* sacred]　The writings about or study of the lives of the saints. Elements of hagiography include acts of the martyrs; biographies of saintly monks, bishops, princes, or virgins; and accounts of miracles connected with their tombs, relics, icons, or statues. The genre was developed and became popular during the Middle Ages, and many examples survive from that period. Among the noted early hagiographers are Eusebius of Caesarea in the 4th century, Gregory I the Great in the 6th, the Venerable Bede in the 8th, and Aelfric in the 10th. Modern critical hagiography began with the 17th-century Belgian historian Jean Bolland and his followers, who compiled the *Acta Sanctorum. The Lives of the Fathers, Martyrs, and Other Principal Saints* by Alban Butler is a well-known collection from the 18th century.

Hagiwara Sakutarō \hä-'gē-wä-rä-sä-kù-'tä-rō\ (b. Nov. 1, 1886, Maebashi, Japan—d. May 11, 1942, Tokyo)   Japanese poet whose attempt to express his perceptions directly in concrete, often unpretty images, rather than in amorphous descriptions, represented a revolutionary trend in Japanese literature.

Hagiwara began to write while still in high school. He was deeply influenced by the new style of the poet Yosano Akiko, whose *Midaregami (Tangled Hair)* appeared in 1901. He left high school without graduating and went to Tokyo to work on the poetry magazine of the established poet Kitahara Hakushū. In 1916 he started his own magazine and in 1917 brought out his first book of poetry, *Tsuki ni hoeru* ("Barking at the Moon"). His difficult style was not immediately understood. *Atarashiki yokujo* (1922; "New Desires") expressed Hagiwara's sensual philosophy in poetic aphorisms. A collection of his poetry, translated as *Face at the Bottom of the World and Other Poems,* appeared in 1969.

Hahn-Hahn \'hän-'hän\, Ida (Marie Luise Gustave), Countess (Gräfin) von, *original surname* Hahn (b. June 22, 1805, Tressow, Mecklenburg-Schwerin [Germany]—d. Jan. 12, 1880, Mainz)   German author of poetry, travel books, and novels that, although written in an artificial, aristocratic style, often show acute psychological insight.

Hahn-Hahn incorporated many of her own unsuccessful relationships with men into the sentimental plots of her novels. These novels, collected in *Aus der Gesellschaft,* 8 vol. (1835–46; "From Society"), deal with aristocrats of strong, passionate natures who are involved in tragic conflicts with their circumstances. The best of her novels, *Gräfin Faustine* (1841; "Countess Faustine"), deals with the "freedom of feeling" associated with the Young Germany movement that strongly influenced her. Her style was parodied by a rival, Fanny Lewald, in *Diogena* (1847). In 1850 Hahn-Hahn converted to Roman Catholicism and began publishing pious stories and poems. Her *Von Babylon nach Jerusalem* (1851; "From Babylon to Jerusalem") was a justification of her conversion.

haikai \'hī-ˌkī\ *plural* haikai [Japanese, short for *haikai no renga* humorous linked verse]   A comic *renga,* or Japanese linked-verse form. The haikai was developed as early as the 16th century as a diversion from the composition of the more serious *renga* form. *See* RENGA.

haiku \'hī-ˌkü\ *plural* haiku [Japanese]   An unrhymed Japanese poetic form consisting of 17 syllables arranged in three lines containing five, seven, and five syllables, respectively. Also, a poem written in the haiku form or a modification of it but in a language other than Japanese.

The term *haiku* is derived from the first element of the word *haikai* (a humorous form of *renga* [linked-verse poem]) and the second of *hokku* (the initial stanza of a *renga*). The hokku, which set the tone of the poem, had to contain in its three lines mention of such subjects as the season, the time of day, and the dominant features of the landscape, making it almost an independent poem. The hokku (often interchangeably called haikai) became known as the haiku late in the 19th century, when it was entirely divested of its original function of opening a sequence of verse; today, even the earlier hokku are usually

called haiku. The form gained distinction in the 17th century, when the great master Bashō elevated haiku to a highly refined and conscious art. The subject range of the haiku was eventually broadened, but it remained an art of expressing much and suggesting more in the fewest possible words. Other outstanding haiku masters were Buson in the 18th century, Kobayashi Issa in the 18th and 19th centuries, and Masaoka Shiki in the late 19th century. It has remained Japan's most popular poetic form.

In English, the Imagist poets and others wrote haiku or imitated the form.

Hairy Ape, The   Drama in eight scenes by Eugene O'NEILL, produced in 1922 and published the following year. It is considered one of the prime achievements of expressionism on stage.

Yank Smith, a brutish stoker on a transatlantic liner, bullies and despises everyone around him, considering himself superior. He is devastated when a millionaire's daughter is repulsed by his simian ways, and he vows to get even with her. Ashore in New York, Yank schemes to destroy the factory owned by the woman's father, but his plans fail. Yank wanders into a zoo. There, feeling alienated from humanity, he releases an ape (for whom he feels some kinship), and the ape kills him.

Hakīm, al- \ȧl-kä-'kēm\, Tawfīq Ḥusayn (b. Oct. 9, 1898, Alexandria, Egypt—d. July 26, 1987, Cairo)   Founder of contemporary Egyptian drama and a leading figure in modern Arabic literature.

Al-Ḥakīm won fame as a dramatist with *Ahl al-kahf* (1933; *People of the Cave*), a study of the human struggle against time. This introduced his series of "dramas of ideas," which were contrasted with the dramas of entertainment being produced at the time. Al-Ḥakīm's dramas include *Shahrazād* (1934), based on *The Thousand and One Nights,* as well as the plays *Al-Malik Udib* (1939; *King Oedipus*), *Pijmalīyūn* (1942; *Pygmalion*), and *Sulaymān al-Ḥakim* (1943; *The Wisdom of Solomon*). His output of more than 50 plays also includes many on Egyptian social themes, such as *Sirr al-muntahirah* (1937; "The Secret of the Suicide Girl") and *Ruṣāṣah fi al-qalb* (1944; "A Bullet in the Heart"). His boldest drama was the lengthy *Muḥammad* (1936), which was not intended for performance.

Al-Ḥakīm made drama a respected Arabic literary genre. Prior to him, prose plays had been primarily lightweight comedy or farce. Al-Ḥakīm wrote in a flexible, high-quality prose, often interspersed with colloquial Arabic. In addition to dramatic works, he produced an autobiographical novel, *Yawmīyāt nā'ib fi al-aryāf* (1937; *The Maze of Justice*), a satire on Egyptian officialdom.

Hal, Prince \'hal\, *byname of* Henry \'hen-rē\, Prince of Wales, *later* King Henry V, *also called* Harry Monmouth \'män-məth\   Fictional character who first appears in the first part of William Shakespeare's play HENRY IV, where he is portrayed as an irresponsible, fun-loving youth. In Shakespeare's HENRY V he proves a wise, capable, responsible king and wins a great victory over the French at Agincourt.

halcyon \'hal-sē-ən\ [Greek *halkyōn, alkyōn*]   A bird that was fabled by the ancients to occupy a nest floating at sea about the time of the winter solstice and to calm the waves during incubation.

Hale \'hāl\, Edward Everett (b. April 3, 1822, Boston, Mass., U.S.—d. June 10, 1909, Roxbury, Mass.)   American clergyman and author best remembered for his short story "The Man Without a Country."

Hale trained on his father's newspaper, the *Boston Daily Advertiser,* and early on turned to writing. He wrote for such journals as the *North American Review, The Atlantic Monthly,* and *Christian Examiner*. From 1870 to 1875 he published and edited the Unitarian journal *Old and New*. "My Double and How He Undid Me" (1859) established the vein of realistic fantasy that was Hale's forte. It introduced a group of loosely related characters figuring in *If, Yes, and Perhaps* (1868), *The Ingham Papers* (1869), *Sybaris and Other Homes* (1869), *His Level Best* (1872), and other collections. "The Man Without a Country," which appeared first in *The Atlantic Monthly* in 1863, was written to inspire greater patriotism during the Civil War. *East and West* (1892) and *In His Name* (1873) were his most popular novels.

Hale's ministry began in 1846. Many of his 150 books and pamphlets were tracts for such causes as the education of blacks, workers' housing, and world peace. The reminiscent writings of his later years are rich and colorful—*A New England Boyhood* (1893), *James Russell Lowell and His Friends* (1899), and *Memories of a Hundred Years* (1902). His *Works*, in 10 volumes, appeared in 1898–1900.

Hale \ˈhāl\, Lucretia Peabody (b. Sept. 2, 1820, Boston, Mass., U.S.—d. June 12, 1900, Belmont, Mass.)   American novelist and writer of children's books.

Hale produced her first novel, *Struggle for Life*, in 1861. From 1868 to 1883 she wrote about the bumbling but endearing Peterkin family. These tales were eventually gathered into *The Peterkin Papers* (1880), the first American nonsense classic, and *The Last of the Peterkins, with Others of Their Kin* (1886). The success of these stories arose from Hale's skill in combining a realistic depiction of contemporary Bostonian society with a silliness that charmed youngsters.

Hale \ˈhāl\, Sarah Josepha, *original surname* Buell \ˈbyü-əl\ (b. Oct. 24, 1788, Newport, N.H., U.S.—d. April 30, 1879, Philadelphia, Pa.)   American writer who, as the first female editor of a magazine, shaped many of the attitudes and thoughts of women of her period.

Hale turned to writing in 1822 as a widow trying to support her family. Within several years she was invited to edit the *Ladies' Magazine* (1828–37). When the magazine was bought by Louis A. Godey in 1837, Hale was retained as editor for the new magazine entitled *Lady's Book*, later called *Godey's Lady's Book* (1837–77).

One of Hale's more important books is *The Ladies' Wreath* (1837), a collection of poetry by English and American women that sold widely. Her most significant work is *Woman's Record: or, Sketches of All Distinguished Women from "the Beginning" till A.D. 1850* (1853). The 2,500 entries contain valuable, orderly biographical information. Hale is also remembered as the author of the children's verse "Mary Had a Little Lamb" (1830).

ha-Levi *see* JUDAH HA-LEVI.

Halévy \à-lā-ˈvē\, Ludovic (b. Jan. 1, 1834, Paris, Fr.—d. May 8, 1908, Paris)   French librettist and novelist who, in collaboration with Henri Meilhac, wrote the librettos for most of the operettas of Jacques Offenbach. He also wrote satirical comedies about contemporary Parisian life.

Halévy's first real success was his anonymous collaboration on the libretto for Offenbach's operetta *Orphée aux enfers* (1858; "Orpheus in the Underworld"). In 1861 he began a literary partnership with Meilhac that lasted 20 years and that would produce a series of lively and witty works epitomizing the spirit and mores of the Second Empire (characteristic of France under Napoleon III) even while making fun of them. Together the two men wrote the librettos for Offenbach's operettas *La Belle Hélène* (1864), *Barbe bleue* (1866; "Bluebeard"), *La Vie parisienne* (1866; "Parisian Life"), and *La Grande-Duchesse de Gérolstein* (1867). The scripts of these works are characterized by buffoonery, farce, and the light and

ironic mockery of society. Halévy and Meilhac also wrote the libretto for Georges Bizet's opera *Carmen* (1875). Among the best of their entertaining drawing-room comedies are *Fanny* (1868) and *Froufrou* (1869).

The best of Halévy's fiction includes *La Famille Cardinal* (1883), a study of lower-class Parisian life during the early years of the Third Republic, and the sentimental novel *L'Abbé Constantin* (1882), which was a huge success with the public. He was elected to the Académie Française in 1884.

Haley \ˈhā-lē\, Alex (Palmer) (b. Aug. 11, 1921, Ithaca, N.Y., U.S.—d. Feb. 10, 1992, Seattle, Wash.)   American writer whose works of historical fiction and reportage depicted the struggles of American blacks.

Haley's first major work, THE AUTOBIOGRAPHY OF MALCOLM X (1965; film, 1992), was an authoritative and widely read narrative based on Haley's interviews with the Black Muslim spokesman. The work is recognized as a classic of black American autobiography.

Haley's greatest success was ROOTS (1976). This well-researched genealogy—born of the history recited by one of Haley's grandmothers—covers seven American generations, from the enslavement of Haley's African ancestors to his own genealogical quest. In 1977 Haley won a special Pulitzer Prize. *A Different Kind of Christmas* (1988) is a novella about a plantation owner who rejects slavery.

half rhyme   *also called* near rhyme, slant rhyme, *or* oblique rhyme.   In prosody, two words that have only their final consonant sounds and no preceding vowel or consonant sounds in common (such as *stopped* and *wept*, or *parable* and *shell*). The device was common in Welsh, Irish, and Icelandic verse years before it was first used in English by Henry Vaughan. It was not used regularly in English until Gerard Manley Hopkins and William Butler Yeats began to do so.

Haliburton \ˈhal-i-ˌbərt-ən\, Thomas Chandler (b. Dec. 17, 1796, Windsor, Nova Scotia [Canada]—d. Aug. 27, 1865, Isleworth, Middlesex, Eng.)   Canadian writer best known as the creator of Sam Slick, a resourceful Yankee clock peddler and cracker-barrel philosopher whose encounters with a variety of people illuminated Haliburton's conservative view of human nature.

Haliburton, as a member of the Nova Scotia Legislative Assembly (1826–29), led a popular movement for liberal reform. He later reverted to his early Tory convictions. In 1856 he moved to England, where from 1859 until his death he was a member of Parliament.

The escapades of Sam Slick were first revealed serially in the newspaper *Nova Scotian* (1835) but subsequently published in book form (1836, 1838, 1840) as *The Clockmaker; or, The Sayings and Doings of Samuel Slick of Slickville*. The satirical dialogues between Sam Slick and the squire are enriched by the tremendous vitality of Sam's colloquial speech and by his fund of anecdotes and tall tales. Haliburton's subsequent works were *The Attaché; or, Sam Slick in England*, 4 vol. (1843–44), *Sam Slick's Wise Saws and Modern Instances; or, What He Said, Did, or Invented* (1853), and *Nature and Human Nature* (1855).

Hall \ˈhȯl\, Donald, *in full* Donald Andrew Hall, Jr. (b. Sept. 20, 1928, New Haven, Conn., U.S.)   American poet and critic whose poetic style moved from studied formalism to greater emphasis on personal expression.

Hall received bachelor's degrees in literature from both Harvard and Oxford universities He was a junior fellow at Harvard from 1954 to 1957. From 1957 to 1975 he taught at the University of Michigan. His volume of poetry, *Exiles and Marriages* (1955), exhibits the influence of his academic training. In *The Dark Houses* (1958) Hall showed a richer emotional range, presaging the intuitive, often idiosyncratic later work collected in *A Roof of Tiger Lilies* (1964), *The Alligator Bride* (1968), *The Yellow Room* (1971), and *The Town of Hill* (1975). Subsequent volumes include *Kicking the Leaves* (1978), *The One Day: A Poem in Three Parts* (1988) and *Old and New Poems* (1990).

The author's critical views and theories of literature were presented in *Marianne Moore: The Cage and the Animal* (1970), *Writing Well* (1973), *Goatfoot Milktongue Twinbird* (1978), *To Read Literature, Fiction, Poetry, Drama* (1981), and *The Weather for Poetry* (1982), among other works. He also published *String Too Short to Be Saved* (1961; rev. ed., 1979); several books on baseball, notably *Fathers Playing Catch with Sons* (1985); and a biography of the sculptor Henry Moore. He edited *The Oxford Book of American Literary Anecdotes* (1981), *The Oxford Book of Children's Verse in America* (1985), and other anthologies.

Hall \\'hòl\\, Edward (b. *c.* 1498, London, Eng.—d. April 1547, Eng.) English historian whose *Chronicle* was one of the chief sources of William Shakespeare's history plays.

Educated at Eton and at King's College, Cambridge, Hall became common sergeant of London in 1533 and undersheriff in 1535. He was also a member of Parliament for Wenlock (1529) and Bridgnorth (1542) in Shropshire. The value of Hall's great work, of which the full title is *The Union of the Two Noble and Illustrate Fameilies of Lancastre and Yorke* (1548; 2nd ed., 1550), is very considerable for the contemporary reign of Henry VIII, and its literary quality is higher than that of most chronicles of the time.

Hall \\'hòl\\, James (b. Aug. 19, 1793, Philadelphia, Pa., U.S.—d. July 5, 1868, Cincinnati, Ohio) One of the earliest American authors to write of the American frontier.

In 1828 Hall compiled the first western literary annual, the *Western Souvenir*, and he edited the *Illinois Monthly Magazine* (1830–32), which he continued at Cincinnati until 1836 as the *Western Monthly Magazine*.

Hall wrote a travel book, *Letters from the West* (1828); one novel, *The Harpe's Head* (1833); a survey of western exploration, *The Romance of Western History* (1857); and several volumes of short stories. Such tales as "Pete Featherton" and "A Legend of Carondelet" established Hall early on as a short-story writer of distinction. He was particularly successful in sketching life in the French settlements of the Illinois country and in interpreting such authentic figures as the backwoodsman, voyageur, and Indian hater. His best stories appear in *Legends of the West* (1832) and *Tales of the Border* (1835).

Hall \\'hòl\\, Joseph (b. July 1, 1574, Ashby-de-la-Zouch, Leicestershire, Eng.—d. Sept. 8, 1656, Higham, Norfolk) English bishop, moral philosopher, and satirist, remarkable for his literary versatility and innovations.

Educated under Puritan influences at the Ashby School and the University of Cambridge (from 1589), Hall was elected to the university lectureship in rhetoric. He became rector of Hawstead, Suffolk, in 1601.

Hall's *Virgidemiarum: Six Books* (1597–1602; "A Harvest of Blows") was the first English satire successfully modeled on Latin satire, and its couplets anticipated the satiric heroic couplets of John Dryden. With *Characters of Vertues and Vices* (1608), Hall was also the first writer in English to emulate Theophrastus, an ancient Greek philosopher who wrote a book of characters. As a moral philosopher Hall achieved a European reputation for his Christianization of stoicism. *Mundus Alter et Idem* (*c.* 1605; "The World Different and the Same"), an original and entertaining Latin satire that influenced Jonathan Swift's *Gulliver's Travels* (1726), dates from this period, as does *Heaven upon Earth* (1606), a book of moral philosophy.

Hall initially took part in the literary battle (1642) between Anglicans and Puritans, but amid the ensuing exchange of invective he pleaded for unity and tolerance among Christians.

Hall \\'hòl\\, Radclyffe, *byname of* Marguerite Radclyffe-Hall \\'rad-,klif\\ (b. Aug. 12, 1880, Bournemouth, Hampshire, Eng.—d. Oct. 7, 1943, London) English writer best known for her novel *The Well of Loneliness* (1928), which created a scandal for its treatment of lesbianism.

Hall began her literary career by writing verses, which were eventually collected into five volumes. Several of these verses were later set to music by such composers as Conigsby Clarke and Coleridge Taylor. By 1924 she had written her first two novels, *The Forge* and *The Unlit Lamp*. The latter book was her first to treat lesbian love. Hall's *Adam's Breed* (1926), a sensitive novel about the life of a restaurant keeper, won several prizes, including the coveted Prix Fémina. Her fame turned to notoriety with the publication of *The Well of Loneliness*, in which she explored in detail the attachment between a young girl and an older woman. The intense and earnest love story was roundly condemned. A London magistrate, Sir Chartres Biron, ruled that, although it was dignified and restrained, the book presented an appeal to "decent people" not only to recognize lesbianism but also to understand that the person so afflicted was not at fault. He judged the book an "obscene libel" and ordered all copies of it destroyed. Later, a decree handed down in a U.S. court disagreed with Biron, finding that homosexuality was not in itself obscene. The British ban on *The Well of Loneliness* was eventually overturned on appeal after Hall's death.

Among Hall's other works are *Twixt Earth and Stars: Poems* (1906), *Songs of Three Counties and Other Poems* (1913), and the novels *The Master of the House* (1932) and *The Sixth Beatitude* (1936).

Hallam \\'hal-əm\\, Arthur Henry (b. Feb. 1, 1811, London, Eng.—d. Sept. 15, 1833, Vienna [Austria]) English essayist and poet who died of a stroke before his considerable talent developed; he is remembered principally as the friend of Alfred, Lord Tennyson commemorated in Tennyson's elegy *In Memoriam.*

In 1828 Hallam met Tennyson at Trinity College, Cambridge, where they joined other artistically and politically progressive students in the exclusive undergraduate club called the Apostles. Hallam defended Tennyson's early work, *Poems, Chiefly Lyrical* (1830), in a review for *The Englishman's Magazine* and was engaged to Tennyson's sister Emily. Hallam's prize-winning essays and critically acclaimed poems were collected and printed posthumously in *Remains, in Verse and Prose, of Arthur Henry Hallam* (1834).

Halleck \\'hal-ək\\, Fitz-Greene (b. July 8, 1790, Guilford, Conn., U.S.—d. Nov. 19, 1867, Guilford) American poet who was a member of the Knickerbocker school and was known for both his satirical and romantic verse.

In collaboration with Joseph Rodman Drake, Halleck contributed the satirical "Croaker Papers" to the New York *Evening Post* in 1819, and on the death of Drake he wrote the moving tribute beginning "Green be the turf above thee." Other popular works were the feudal romance "Alnwick Castle" (1822), "Burns" (1827), the often recited "Marco Bozzaris" (1825), "Red Jacket" (1828), and "Young America" (1865).

Hallgrímsson \\'hàtl-,grēm-sòn, *Angl* 'hät-əl-, 'häl-\\, Jónas (b. Nov. 16, 1807, Hraun, Öxnadalur, Ice.—d. May 25, 1845, Copenhagen, Den.) One of Iceland's most popular Romantic poets.

In 1835 Hallgrímsson helped to found the periodical *Fjölnir* (1835–47; "The Many-Sided"), in which he published much of his poetry and later his short stories, the first in Icelandic.

He is chiefly remembered for his lyrical poems describing Icelandic scenery. An admirer of the European Romantic poets, he adapted and translated much foreign poetry into Icelandic. He was critical of the rímur (narrative poems in the traditional, artificial form that had long been popular in Iceland), and he strove to purify the language of poetry.

Halpern \\'hal-pərn\\, Moyshe Leyb (b. Jan. 2, 1886, Złoczów, Galicia, Austria-Hungary [now Zolochiv, Ukraine]—d. Aug. 31, 1932, New York, N.Y., U.S.) Yiddish poet whose unsentimental and psychologically complex free verse extols socialism, individual rights, and social justice.

Halpern lived in poverty in Montreal and New York after immigrating to North America in 1908; his first poems were published that same year. He was a member of Di Yunge ("The Young Ones"), a group of young New York-based poets who were attempting to redefine and modernize Yiddish poetry. Like his colleagues, Halpern rejected the idea prevalent in the late 19th century that Yiddish poetry should serve Jewish nationalist and social causes, and instead attempted to assert his individuality.

Halpern was considered a major Yiddish poet after the publication of his first collection, *In Nyu-York* (1919; "In New York"). Until 1924 he worked closely with the Yiddish communist daily *Di frayhayt* ("Freedom"). His second collection, *Di goldene pave* ("The Golden Peacock"), was published in 1924. *Moyshe Leyb Halpern*, a collection of his poems, was published posthumously in 1934.

Ham \\'ham\\ Biblical character from the Old Testament, one of Noah's three sons. In Genesis 5:32, Ham is named as the middle son, the first and third being Shem and Japeth (Japheth). In Genesis 9:24, however, he is identified as the youngest son, who, observing Noah naked and drunk in his tent, reports the fact to his brothers; Shem and Japeth immediately cover their father's nakedness. For this disrespect Noah curses Ham's son Canaan, prophesying that he will be a slave to his uncles—and, by extension, that his descendants will be slaves. The incident is the subject of later works, including Zora Neale Hurston's one-act play *The First One*.

Ham was considered the ancestor of the nations of Cush (Ethiopia), Mizraim (Egypt), Put (modern-day Libya), and Canaan, as well as being the eponymous forerunner of the Hamites. The appellation Ham was used also as a poetic name for Egypt.

Hamadhānī, al- \\,ál-,há-má-'thä-,nē\\, Aḥmad ibn al-Ḥusayn (b. 968, Hamadan, Persia [Iran]—d. 1008, Herāt, Ghaznavid Afghanistan) Arabic-language author credited with introducing the genre known as MAQĀMAH.

Al-Hamadhānī, often known as Badīʿ az-Zamān ("Wonder of the Age"), achieved an early success through a public debate with Abū Bakr al-Khwarizmī, a leading savant, in Nīshāpūr.

Al-Hamadhānī is credited with the composition of some 52 extant *maqāmat* (the number 400 that is usually cited is an idiomatic reference to an indefinite number). An English translation by W.J. Prendergast, *The Maqāmāt of Badīʿ al-Zamān al-Hamadhānī*, was published in 1915 and reprinted in 1973. The pieces are written in a combination of conventional prose, rhymed and rhythmic prose (*sajʿ*), and verse. They typically consist of the encounters of the fictional narrator ʿIsā ibn Hishām with the hero Abū al-Fatḥ al-Iskandarī, a witty orator and talented poet. Al-Hamadhānī's *maqāmat* include travelogues, sermons, letters, and dialogues.

hamadryad \\,ham-ə-'drī-əd, -,ad\\ [Greek *Hamadryad-, Hamadryás,* from *háma* together with + *Dryás* Dryad] A nymph of trees and woods; especially, a nymph whose life begins and ends with that of a particular tree.

Haman \\'hā-mən\\ Biblical character, a court official and villain whose plan to destroy the Jews of Persia was thwarted by ESTHER.

hamartia \\,hä-,mär-'tē-ə\\ [Greek *hamartía* error, fault, a derivative of *hamartánein* to miss the mark, err], *also called* tragic flaw. An inherent defect of character, or the error, guilt, or sin of the tragic hero in a literary work.

Aristotle introduced the term casually in the *Poetics* in describing the tragic hero as one of noble rank and nature whose misfortune is not brought about by villainy but by some "error of judgment" (hamartia). This imperfection later came to be interpreted as a moral flaw, such as Othello's jealousy or Hamlet's irresolution, although most great tragedies defy such a simple interpretation. The hero's suffering and its reverberations are disproportionate to the flaw. An element of cosmic collusion among the hero's flaw, chance, and other external forces is essential to bring about the catastrophe.

In Greek tragedy the nature of the hero's flaw is even more elusive. Often the tragic deeds are committed unwittingly, as when Oedipus unknowingly kills his father and marries his own mother. If the deeds are committed knowingly, they often are not committed by choice; Orestes is under obligation to Apollo to avenge his father's murder by killing his mother. Also, an apparent weakness is often only an excess of virtue, such as an extreme probity or zeal for perfection which, in turn, may suggest that the hero is guilty of hubris—i.e., presumption of being godlike and attempting to overstep human limitations.

Ḥamāsah \\ká-'mä-sə\\ An Arabic anthology compiled by the poet ABŪ TAMMĀM in about 835. It is so called from the title of its first book, which contains poems on bravery in war.

Abū Tammām's anthology consists of 10 books, containing, in all, 884 poems, mostly fragments selected from longer poems: *Al-Ḥamāsah, Al-Marāthī* ("Dirges"), *Al-Adab* ("Manners"), *An-Nasīb* ("Amatory Verses"), *Al-Hijāʿ* ("Satires"), *Al-Adyāf wa al-madīḥ* ("Hospitality and Panegyric"), *Aṣ-Ṣifāt* ("Miscellaneous Descriptions"), *As-Sayr wa an-Nuʿas* ("Journeying and Drowsiness"), *Al-Mulah* ("Pleasantries"), and *Madhammāt an-nisaʾ* ("Dispraise of Women").

The poems, taken from the works of Arab poets of all periods, from the pre-Islāmic to about 832, are extemporaneous or occasional utterances, as distinguished from qasidas (odes). They are short, direct, and generally free of metaphor. The Ḥamāsah is a storehouse of ancient material, and it became a fundamental work for poets seeking to acquire polish. It inspired other anthologies and many commentaries, enumerated by Ḥajjī Khalīfa, the 17th-century historian and bibliographer.

Hamdānī, al- \\ál-,hám-'dä-,nē\\, *in full* Abū Muḥammad al-Ḥasan ibn Aḥmad al-Hamdānī (b. 893?, Ṣanʿāʾ, Yemen—d. *c.* 945?) Arab geographer, poet, grammarian, historian, and astronomer who represented some of the best aspects of Islāmic culture during the last effective years of the ʿAbbāsid caliphate. (The ʿAbbāsids ruled from AD 750 to 1258.)

Most of al-Hamdānī's life was spent in Arabia itself. When he was imprisoned during a political controversy, his influence was sufficient to invoke a tribal rebellion in his behalf to secure his release.

His encyclopedia *Al-Iklīl* ("The Crown"; partially translated as *The Antiquities of South Arabia*) and his other writings are a major source of information on Arabia. They provide a valuable anthology of South Arabian poetry and much genealogical, topographical, and historical information.

Hamerling \\'häm-ər-liŋ\\, Robert, *original name* Rupert Johann Hammerling (b. March 24, 1830, Kirchberg am Walde [Austria]—d. July 13, 1889, Graz) Austrian poet remembered chiefly for his epics.

Hamerling wrote several popular collections of lyrics, including *Ein Schwanenlied der Romantik* (1862; "A Swan Song of the Romantic"), that have attractive rhythms but not much originality. His most important works are his epics: *Ahasver in Rom* (1866; "Ahasuerus in Rome"), a grandiosely romantic retelling of the myth of the Wandering Jew, and *Der König von Sion* (1869; "The King of Zion"), a narrative of the Anabaptist movement of 1534. Hamerling's other works include dramas, a novel, and a few autobiographical writings such as *Stationen meiner Lebenspilgerschaft* (1889; "Stations on My Life's Journey").

Hamilton \ˈham-əl-tən\, Hamish, *original name* James Hamilton (b. Nov. 15, 1900, Indianapolis, Ind., U.S.—d. May 24, 1988, London, Eng.)   British publisher of some of the most renowned authors in Britain, the United States, and France.

Hamilton studied modern languages and law at Cambridge, and in 1926 he became London office manager of the New York-based publisher Harper & Brothers. He worked there until he established Hamish Hamilton Ltd. in 1931. Hamilton lavished personal attention on his authors, who included such Americans as James Thurber, Raymond Chandler, J.D. Salinger, and William Styron. He also published works by the British authors Nancy Mitford and Angela Thirkell, as well as works by the French authors Albert Camus and Jean-Paul Sartre.

Hamilton \ˈham-əl-tən\, Patrick, *in full* Anthony Walter Patrick Hamilton (b. March 17, 1904, Hassocks, Sussex, Eng.—d. Sept. 23, 1962, Sheringham, Norfolk)   English playwright and novelist, notable for his capture of atmosphere and of the Cockney dialect spoken in the East End of London.

Hamilton began acting in 1921 and then, fascinated by theatrical melodrama, took to writing. He became known with the novel *Craven House* (1926). Three very successful motion pictures were based on works by Hamilton: the play *Rope* (performed 1929; U.S. title, *Rope's End*; film, 1948); the play *Gaslight* (1938; also called *Angel Street*; film, 1944); and the novel *Hangover Square* (1941; film, 1945). Hamilton also wrote novels portraying the unpleasantness of the modern city—*The Midnight Bell* (1929) and *The Plains of Cement* (1934), both included in the volume *Twenty Thousand Streets Under the Sky* (1935).

Hamilton \ˈham-əl-tən\, William, *in full* William Hamilton of Gilbertfield \ˈgil-bərt-ˌfēld\ (b. *c.* 1665, Ladyland, Ayr, Scot.—d. May 24, 1751, Latrick, Lanark)   Scottish writer whose vernacular poetry is among the earliest of the 18th-century Scottish literary revival.

Hamilton became closely acquainted with the poet Allan Ramsay, with whom he exchanged "Familiar Epistles" (1719) in verse, after which Robert Burns's similar poetic letters were modeled. Hamilton's modernized version of *Wallace* (1722) by Blind Harry also influenced Burns. Perhaps his most famous poem is "The Braes of Yarrow."

Hamlet \ˈham-lət\   Legendary prince of Denmark and central character in the play of the same name by William Shakespeare.

The Hamlet character corresponds to the figure of Amleth (Amlódi), whose story is narrated in books 3 and 4 of Saxo Grammaticus' late 12th-century history of Denmark. It is possible that Saxo drew on a (lost) Icelandic saga of Amlódi, mentioned by a 10th-century Icelandic poet, for his information. One scholar suggested that the Hamlet story had its origins in the East, being similar to a tale in the 11th-century *Shāh-nāmeh* (1010; "Book of Kings") by the Persian poet Ferdowsī. Others posited a Celtic origin, pointing to the warrior Amhlaide, who is named as the slayer of King Niall Glúndub in the Irish Annals of the year 917.

The Hamlet story was told in volume 5 (1570) of François de Belleforest's *Histoires tragiques*. Shakespeare's play, which was first performed in 1600 or 1601, was evidently preceded by another play on Hamlet, now lost and usually referred to as the *Ur-Hamlet*, of which Thomas Kyd is a conjectured author. *The Hystorie of Hamblet*, an English version of Belleforest's work, was published in London in 1608. None of these sources provides a clue to explain Hamlet's tragic flaw, his famous hesitation (whether it be from reluctance or unreadiness) to avenge his father's murder. This element is central and peculiar to Shakespeare's conception of Hamlet and has long fascinated both directors and critics.

Many post-Shakespearian writers—including Alfred Döblin, Elmer Rice, and Archibald MacLeish—have written works concerning Hamlet; notable is Tom Stoppard's play *Rosencrantz and Guildenstern Are Dead* (produced 1966).

Hamlet \ˈham-lət\ (*in full* Hamlet, Prince of Denmark) Tragedy in five acts by William SHAKESPEARE, performed in 1600–01 and published in a quarto edition in 1603.

As the play opens, Hamlet is mourning his father, who has been killed, and lamenting the behavior of his mother, Gertrude, who married his uncle Claudius within a month of his father's death. The ghost of his father appears to Hamlet, informs him that he was poisoned by Claudius, and asks Hamlet to avenge his death. Hamlet hesitates, desiring further evidence of foul play. His uncertainty and inability to act make him increasingly melancholy, and to everyone around him Hamlet seems to be going mad. To the pompous old courtier Polonius, it appears that Hamlet is lovesick over Polonius' daughter Ophelia.

Despite the apparent guilt of Claudius, Hamlet still cannot bring himself to avenge his father's wrongful murder. He nevertheless terrorizes his mother and kills the eavesdropping Polonius. Justly fearing for his own life, Claudius sends Hamlet to England with Hamlet's friends Rosencrantz and Guildenstern, who carry orders to have Hamlet killed. Hamlet discovers the orders, however, and alters them to make his two friends the victims instead.

Hamlet returns to Denmark. There he hears that Ophelia has killed herself and that her brother Laertes seeks to avenge Polonius' murder. Claudius is only too eager to arrange the duel. Carnage ensues. Both Hamlet and Laertes are struck by the sword that Claudius has had dipped in poison. Gertrude, also present at the duel, mistakenly drinks from the cup of poison that Claudius has placed near Hamlet to insure his death. Before Hamlet dies, he manages to stab Claudius.

Hamlet, The \ˈham-lət\   Novel by William FAULKNER, published in 1940, the first volume of a trilogy including *The Town* (1957) and *The Mansion* (1959). Set in the late 19th century, the narrative depicts the early years of the crude and contemptible Flem Snopes and his clan who by the trilogy's end supplant the dispirited gentry class (represented by the Sartoris family) of Frenchman's Bend, Miss.

Ḥammād ar-Rāwiyah \ḳàm-ˈmäd-àr-ˈrä-wē-yə\ ("Ḥammād the Transmitter [or Reciter]") (b. *c.* 694, Kūfah, Iraq—d. *c.* 772, Kūfah)   Anthologist of Arab antiquities credited with collecting the seven early odes known as AL-MUʿALLAQĀT (*The Seven Odes*).

Ḥammād became one of the most learned men of his time in Arabic verse. He committed vast numbers of poems to memory and studied the associated lore of battles, genealogies, and folk stories. This knowledge won him the favor of al-Walīd II and other Umayyad caliphs, including Hishām, who summoned Ḥammād to Damascus. Despite his renown and popularity Ḥammād was criticized by some Arab scholars because his interest was in poetry rather than philology and grammatical scholarship; moreover, they suspected that he was creating some of the early Arabic poems he collected.

Hammer, Mike \'mīk-'ham-ər\ Fictional character, a brawling, brutal private detective who is the protagonist of a series of hard-boiled mystery books (beginning with *I, the Jury*, 1947) by Mickey SPILLANE.

Hammett \'ham-et\, Dashiell, *in full* Samuel Dashiell Hammett (b. May 27, 1894, St. Mary's county, Md., U.S.—d. Jan. 10, 1961, New York City) American writer who helped to create the hard-boiled school of detective fiction.

Hammett left school at age 13 and worked at a variety of low-paying jobs before working for eight years as a detective for the Pinkerton agency. He began to publish short stories and novelettes in pulp magazines and published two novels—*Red Harvest* and *The Dain Curse* (both 1929)—before writing THE MALTESE FALCON (1930), often considered his finest work. The novel introduced Sam Spade, Hammett's fictional detective, who epitomized the character of the hard-boiled detective. Hammett also wrote *The Glass Key* (1931) and THE THIN MAN (1934), which initiated a series of motion pictures built around his detective couple Nick and Nora Charles. Nora was based on the playwright Lillian Hellman, with whom Hammett formed a romantic alliance in 1930 that lasted until his death. *See also* DETECTIVE STORY; HARD-BOILED FICTION.

Hammond Innes \'ham-ənd-'inz\, Ralph, *pseudonyms* Ralph Hammond *or* Hammond Innes (b. July 15, 1913, Horsham, Sussex, Eng.) English novelist known for adventure stories in which suspense and the forces of nature are strong features.

Hammond Innes began his career in teaching and publishing. In 1978 he was made a Commander of the British Empire. His books often pit his characters against an extreme environment—such as the sea, polar regions, or the desert—in some trial they must endure in order to be redeemed. Hammond Innes' best-known books are *The White South* (1949), *Campbell's Kingdom* (1952), *The Wreck of the "Mary Deare"* (1956), *The Doomed Oasis* (1960), *Atlantic Fury* (1962), *The Conquistadors* (1969), *The Last Voyage: Captain Cook's Lost Diary* (1979), *The Black Tide* (1982), *Medusa* (1988), and *Isvik* (1991). He also wrote television and motion-picture scripts.

Hamsun \'häm-sùn\, Knut, *pseudonym of* Knut Pederson \'ped-er-sòn\ (b. Aug. 4, 1859, Lom, Nor.—d. Feb. 19, 1952, near Grimstad) Norwegian novelist, dramatist, poet, and winner of the Nobel Prize (1920). A leader of the Neoromantic revolt at the turn of the century, he rescued the novel from a tendency toward excessive naturalism.

Of peasant origin, Hamsun had almost no formal education. His first publication, the novel *Sult* (1890; HUNGER), about a starving young writer in Norway, was a great success. Hamsun followed this with a series of lectures attacking such idols as Henrik Ibsen and Leo Tolstoy.

Like the asocial heroes of his early works—*e.g.*, *Mysterier* (1892; *Mysteries*), *Pan* (1894), and *Victoria* (1898)—Hamsun either was indifferent to or took an irreverent view of progress. In a work of his mature style, *Markens grøde* (1917; *Growth of the Soil*), he expresses a back-to-nature philosophy, but his message of fierce individualism remained constant. Consistent to the end in his antipathy to modern Western culture, Hamsun supported the Germans during their occupation of Norway in World War II.

Handful of Dust, A Satirical novel by Evelyn WAUGH, published in 1934. The novel, which is often considered Waugh's best, examines the themes of contemporary amorality and the death of spiritual values. Precipitated by the failure of Waugh's marriage and by his conversion to Roman Catholicism, the novel points up the similarities between the savagery of so-called civilized London society and the barbarity encountered by the hero in the South American jungle.

The novel's protagonist, Tony Last, is bewildered and devastated when, out of boredom, his beloved wife Brenda has an affair and sues Tony for divorce. Tony flees to South America, where he is captured by a demented, illiterate English squatter who keeps Tony a prisoner, forcing him to read aloud continuously from the works of Charles Dickens.

Handke \'hänt-kə\, Peter (b. Dec. 6, 1942, Griffen, Austria) Avant-garde Austrian playwright, novelist, poet, and essayist, one of the most original German-language writers in the second half of the 20th century.

Handke studied law at the University of Graz from 1961 to 1965 and contributed pieces to the avant-garde literary magazine *manuskripte*. He came to public notice as an anticonventional playwright with his first important drama, *Publikumsbeschimpfung* (1966; *Offending the Audience*), in which four actors analyze the nature of theater for an hour and then alternately insult the audience and praise its "performance." Several more plays lacking conventional plot, dialogue, and characters followed. Handke's other most significant dramatic piece was his first full-length play, *Kaspar* (1968), which depicts the foundling Kaspar Hauser as a near-speechless innocent destroyed by society's attempts to impose on him its language and its rational values. Handke's other plays include *Das Mündel will Vormund sein* (1969; "The Ward Wants to Be Guardian"; *My Foot My Tutor*) and *Der Ritt über den Bodensee* (1971; *The Ride across Lake Constance*).

Handke's novels are for the most part ultraobjective, deadpan accounts of characters who are in extreme states of mind. His best-known novel, *Die Angst des Tormanns beim Elfmeter* (1970; *The Goalie's Anxiety at the Penalty Kick*), is an imaginative thriller about a former soccer player who commits a pointless murder and then waits for the police to take him into custody. *Die linkshändige Frau* (1976; *The Left-Handed Woman*) is a dispassionate description of a young mother coping with the disorientation she feels after she has separated from her husband. Handke's memoir about his deceased mother, *Wunschloses Unglück* (1972; "Wishless Misfortune"; *A Sorrow Beyond Dreams*), is another of his most effective works. Handke's later novels include *Der Chinese des Schmerzes* (1983; *Across*), *Die Wiederholung* (1986; *Repetition*), and *Die Abwesenheit* (1987; *Absence*).

Handke also wrote short stories, essays, radio dramas, and autobiographical works. The dominant theme of his writings is that ordinary language, everyday reality, and their accompanying rational order have a constraining and deadening effect on human beings and are underlain by irrationality, confusion, and even madness.

Hannah \'han-ə\, *also called* Anna \'an-ə\ Biblical figure, the mother of SAMUEL.

Hannah \'han-ə\, Barry (b. April 23, 1942, Meridian, Miss., U.S.) American author of darkly comic, often violent novels and short stories set in the Deep South.

Hannah was educated at Mississippi College and the University of Arkansas . He subsequently taught writing at numerous schools, including the universities of Alabama, Iowa, Montana, and Mississippi. His first novel, *Geronimo Rex* (1972), was a raucous coming-of-age story addressing the theme of racism. In the less successful *Nightwatchmen* (1973), both a secret killer and a hurricane are unleashed upon a small college town.

Hannah's reputation as a daring stylist was secured with *Airships*, a collection of short stories that appeared in 1978. The book's recurrent motif of American Civil War valor was developed more fully in the short novel *Ray* (1980). Hannah's later works include *The Tennis Handsome* (1983), which portrays the misadventures of a dissipated professional tennis player; *Captain Maximus* (1985), containing short stories and the outline of an original screenplay; the novel *Hey Jack!* (1987); *Never Die* (1991), an offbeat treatment of the western genre; and a collection of stories entitled *Bats Out of Hell* (1993).

Hansberry \'hanz-bər-ē, -,ber-ē\, Lorraine (b. May 19, 1930, Chicago, Ill., U.S.—d. Jan. 12, 1965, New York City)   American play-

Bettmann Archive

wright whose A RAISIN IN THE SUN (1959) was the first drama by a black woman to be produced on Broadway.

A Raisin in the Sun, is an insightful study of the stresses that both divide and unite a working-class black family when it is presented with a chance for a better life. It won the New York Drama Critics' Circle Award, and the film version of 1961 received a special award at the Cannes festival. Hansberry's next play, THE SIGN IN SIDNEY BRUSTEIN'S WINDOW, a drama of political questioning and affirmation set in the New York City neighborhood of Greenwich Village, where Hansberry had long made her home, had only a modest run on Broadway in 1964. Her promising career was cut short by her early death from cancer.

TO BE YOUNG, GIFTED AND BLACK, adapted by Robert Nemiroff from her writings, was produced Off-Broadway in 1969 and published in book form in 1970.

Hans Brinker \'häns-'briŋ-kər\ (*in full* Hans Brinker; or, The Silver Skates)   Novel for children by Mary Mapes DODGE, published in 1865.

The story is set in The Netherlands and concerns the fortunes of the impoverished Brinker family. The good deeds of the Brinker children (Hans and Gretel) help to restore their father's health and bring about their own good fortune. The plot of the novel, however, is secondary to informative details about Dutch family life and to considerable history and geography of the country, which Dodge had never visited.

Hansen \'han-sən\, Joseph (b. July 19, 1923, Aberdeen, S.D., U.S.)   American writer, author of a series of crime novels featuring the homosexual insurance investigator and detective Dave BRANDSTETTER.

Hansen, who also wrote under the pseudonyms Rose Brock and James Colton, began his career as editor, novelist, and journalist in the mid-1960s. He taught writing through the University of California extension programs from 1977.

In *Fadeout* (1970), the first novel to feature Brandstetter, the detective falls in love with a man whom he clears of murder charges. *Death Claims* (1973) is about surviving the death of a lover. Brandstetter investigates the murder of the owner of a bar for homosexuals in *Troublemaker* (1975). In *Early Graves* (1987) he comes out of retirement to trace a serial killer who murders men with AIDS. Brandstetter also appears in several other novels and in *Brandstetter and Others* (1984), a collection of short stories.

In addition to the Brandstetter series, Hansen wrote the novels *A Smile in His Lifetime* (1981), *Backtrack* (1982), and *Job's Year* (1983), as well as the short-story collections *The Dog and Other Stories* (1979), *Bohannon's Book* (1988), and *Bohannon's Country* (1993).

Hansen \'han-sən\, Martin A., *in full* Martin Jens Alfred Hansen (b. Aug. 20, 1909, Stroby, Den.—d. June 27, 1955, Copenhagen)   One of the most widely read Danish authors of his day.

From two early novels of social consciousness, *Nu opgiver han* (1935; "Now He Gives Up") and *Kolonien* (1937; "The Colony"), Hansen went on to write a tale of extravagant imagery, *Jonatans rejse* (1941; "Jonatan's Journey"), and a historical novel, *Lykkelige Kristoffer* (1945; *Lucky Kristoffer*). After World War II he turned to the psychological novel with *Løgneren* (1950; *The Liar*). He later wrote *Orm og tyr* (1952; "Serpent and Bull"), a consideration of pre- and post-Christian Danish history as seen in its religious monuments. A somewhat conservative strain, a preoccupation with myth, and an awareness of the roots of culture are found in all his works. *Against the Wind* (1979) includes 12 stories of rural life.

Hansson \'hän-sön\, Ola (b. Nov. 12, 1860, Hönsinge, Swed.—d. Sept. 26, 1925, Büyükdere, Tur.)   Poet, prose writer, and critic, belatedly recognized as one of the most original of modern Swedish writers.

In *Dikter* (1884; "Poems") and *Notturno* (1885), Hansson celebrated the natural beauty and folkways of his native province of Skåne. The influence of contemporary psychology led him to produce *Sensitiva Amorosa* (1887), a collection of morbid, erotic sketches that shocked the Sweden of his day. He was embittered by their reception, and he lived abroad from 1889 in Germany, Switzerland, and Turkey. His later works reflect his admiration for Friedrich Nietzsche and the Pan-Germanist Julius Langbehn.

Han Yu or **Han Yü** \'hän-'yue\, *also called* Han Wengong \'hän-'wen-'gůŋ\ (b. 768, Dengzhou, Henan province, China—d. 824, Changan)   Master of Chinese prose, outstanding poet, and the first proponent of what later came to be known as neo-Confucianism, which had wide influence in China and Japan.

At a time when its popularity had greatly declined, Han began a defense of the Confucian doctrine. He attacked Daoism and Buddhism, then at the height of their influence. In defending Confucianism, Han quoted extensively from the *Mengzi*, the *Da Xue* ("Great Learning"), the "Zhongyong" ("Doctrine of the Mean"), and the *Yi jing* ("Classic of Changes"), works that hitherto had been somewhat neglected by Confucians. In so doing, he laid the foundations for later neo-Confucianists who took their basic ideas from these books.

Han advocated the adoption of the free, simple prose of these early philosophers, a style unencumbered by the mannerisms and elaborate verselike regularity of the parallel prose that was prevalent in Han's time. His own essays (*e.g.*, "On the Way," "On Man," "On Spirits") are among the most beautiful ever written in Chinese, and they became the most famous models of the prose style he espoused. In his poetry Han also tried to break out of the existing forms, but many of his efforts at literary reform failed.

hapax legomenon \,hap-,aks-li-'gäm-ə-,nän, ,häp-,äks-, -nən\ *plural* hapax legomena \-nə, -,nä\ [Greek *hápax legómenon* something said only once]   A word or form occurring only once in a document or corpus.

hard-boiled fiction   Of or relating to a tough, unsentimental style of American crime writing characterized by impersonal, matter-of-fact presentation of naturalistic or violent themes or incidents, by a generally unemotional or stoic tone, and often by a total absence of explicit or implied moral judgments. Hard-boiled fiction uses graphic sex and violence, vivid but often sordid urban backgrounds, and fast-paced, slangy dialogue.

The genre was popularized by Dashiell HAMMETT, whose first truly hard-boiled story, "Fly Paper," appeared in the pulp magazine *Black Mask* in 1929. Combining his own experiences with the realistic influence of writers such as Ernest Hemingway and John Dos Passos, Hammett developed a distinctly American type of detective fiction that differed considerably from the more genteel English mystery.

Hammett's innovations were incorporated in the hard-boiled melodramas of James M. Cain, particularly in such early works as *The Postman Always Rings Twice* (1934) and *Double Indemnity* (1936). Successors included Raymond Chandler, with novels such as *The Big Sleep* (1939), *Farewell, My Lovely* (1940), and *The Little Sister* (1949), and Jim Thompson, in such works as *The Killer Inside Me* (1952), *Savage Night* (1953), and *Pop. 1280* (1964). Other important writers of the hard-boiled school were George Harmon Coxe (1901–84), author of such thrillers as *Murder with Pictures* (1935) and *Eye Witness* (1950), and W.R. Burnett (1899–1982), who wrote *Little Caesar* (1929) and *The Asphalt Jungle* (1949). Hard-boiled fiction ultimately degenerated into the extreme sensationalism and undisguised sadism of what *Ellery Queen's Mystery Magazine* called the "guts-gore-and-gals-school," as found in the works of Mickey Spillane, writer of such phenomenal best-sellers as *I, the Jury* (1947). *See also* DETECTIVE STORY.

Hard Times   Novel by Charles DICKENS, published in serial form (as *Hard Times: For These Times*) in the periodical *Household Words* from April to August 1854 and in book form later the same year. The novel is a bitter indictment of industrialization, with its dehumanizing effects on workers and communities in mid-19th-century England.

Louisa and Tom Gradgrind have been harshly raised by their father, an educator, to know nothing but the most factual, pragmatic information. Their lives are devoid of beauty, culture, or imagination, and the two have little or no empathy for others. Louisa marries Josiah Bounderby, a vulgar banker and mill owner. She eventually leaves her husband and returns to her father's house. Tom, unscrupulous and vacuous, robs his brother-in-law's bank. Only after these crises does their father realize that the principles by which he raised his children have corrupted their lives.

Hardwick \ˈhärd-wik\, Elizabeth (b. July 27, 1916, Lexington, Ky., U.S.)   American novelist, short-story writer, and essayist best known for her eloquent literary and social criticism.

Hardwick attended the University of Kentucky and Columbia University in New York City. Her experience as a young Southern woman in Manhattan provided the backdrop for her somber, introspective first novel, *The Ghostly Lover* (1945). As a frequent contributor to the *Partisan Review* and other liberal intellectual journals, she developed the elegant, incisive analytical voice that became her trademark. Her marriage to the poet Robert Lowell lasted from 1949 to 1972, during which period Hardwick wrote her second novel, *The Simple Truth* (1955), edited *The Selected Letters of William James* (1961), published an essay collection entitled *A View of My Own* (1962), and helped to found *The New York Review of Books* (1963). The latter journal became the principal outlet for her criticism, a second volume of which, *Seduction and Betrayal: Women and Literature*, appeared in 1974. She also edited the multivolume *Rediscovered Fiction by American Women* (1977). The novel *Sleepless Nights* (1979) is a partly autobiographical work.

Hardy \är-ˈdē\, Alexandre (b. 1572?, Paris, Fr.—d. 1632?) Playwright, the first Frenchman known to have made his living as a dramatist, who claimed authorship of some 600 plays.

Hardy was a hired poet for troupes of actors both in the provinces and in Paris. His works were widely admired in court circles, where he wrote for royal companies. The actors who bought his plays rarely allowed him to publish them, and fewer than 50 survived. Shortly after Hardy's death his plays ceased to be produced.

Hardy's work neglected the unities of time and place, cut down or eliminated the role of the chorus, and depicted violence on stage. His plots were faster paced than those of the tragedies and pastorals modeled on ancient Greek and Roman works. Action was linked with the psychology of the characters—the protagonists acted rather than declaimed, developed as human beings, and sometimes experienced inner conflict. Many plays were demanded of him, and his style was unpolished.

Unlike other 17th-century playwrights, Hardy took few stories from the Greek and Latin dramatists or the Bible. He drew instead upon such writers as Ovid, Miguel de Cervantes, and Giovanni Boccaccio.

Hardy \ˈhär-dē\, Thomas (b. June 2, 1840, Upper Bockhampton, Dorset, Eng.—d. Jan. 11, 1928, Dorchester, Dorset)   English poet and his nation's foremost regional novelist, whose most impressive novels are set in "Wessex," an imaginary county in southwestern England that were based on the actual county of Dorset.

E.B. Inc.

After leaving school in 1856, Hardy became a pupil of an architect and church restorer in Dorchester. In 1862 he left Dorchester for London, where he lived until 1867. During his years in London, Hardy began seriously to write poetry; some of the poems of this period—for example, "Neutral Tones"—are among his finest and most characteristic work.

In 1870 Hardy went to St. Juliot in Cornwall in connection with the restoration of its church. There he met his future wife, Emma Lavinia Gifford. This meeting and its setting were re-created more than 40 years later, after his wife's death, in his most poignant poems, a group known as *Veteris Vestigiae Flammae* ("Vestiges of an Old Flame").

After his first attempt at a novel was rejected by two publishers, the novelist George Meredith advised Hardy to write a novel with a purely artistic purpose and a more complicated plot—advice that he followed too faithfully in his first published book, *Desperate Remedies*, which met with a mixed reception when it appeared anonymously in 1871. In 1872 Hardy returned to London and architectural work, having meanwhile written the first of the Wessex novels, *Under the Greenwood Tree*, which was published in May of that year.

In 1873 Hardy began FAR FROM THE MADDING CROWD (1874). It is the first "typical" Hardy novel, for, although it has humor and what may pass for a happy ending, its scheme and general tone belong more to tragedy than to comedy. The novel was his first popular success, and he was encouraged by its reception to devote himself entirely to writing.

From 1878 to 1895 Hardy published THE RETURN OF THE NATIVE (1878), *The Trumpet-Major* (1880), THE MAYOR OF

CASTERBRIDGE (1886), THE WOODLANDERS (1887), TESS OF THE D'URBERVILLES (1891), and JUDE THE OBSCURE (1895). They all make plain Hardy's stoical pessimism and his sense of the inevitable tragedy of human life.

With *Tess*, Hardy began to come into conflict with the conventions of Victorian morality. *Jude the Obscure* aroused even greater indignation, and the public reaction to *Jude* so disgusted Hardy that he wrote no more novels, thenceforth devoting his energies to poetry, which he had always regarded as far more important than his fiction. In 1898 *Wessex Poems* was published; *Poems of the Past and the Present* followed in 1901, and several more volumes appeared during the remainder of his life. He also published THE DYNASTS (1910), a huge drama (not intended for performance) of the Napoleonic Wars, written mostly in blank verse.

Hardy Boys \'här-dē\ Fictional characters, the teenage protagonists of a series of juvenile novels. Frank and Joe Hardy are trained in the art of criminal detection by their father, an ex-police detective. The boys solve crimes together, often aided by their father or their friends. Edward STRATEMEYER originally conceived and plotted the series. More than four dozen novels about the Hardys were written by a series of writers using the pseudonym Franklin W. Dixon and were distributed by the Stratemeyer Literary Syndicate. Publication of the series was continuous from 1927, when *The Tower Treasure* and two other Hardy Boys books were first issued. A "Hardy Boys Case Files" series also started publication in 1986 and from 1988 averaged a dozen titles per year. A number of books by Dixon and the likewise pseudonymous Carolyn Keene feature the Hardy Boys and Nancy DREW together.

Hare \'har\, David (b. June 5, 1947, St. Leonards, Sussex, Eng.) British playwright and director noted for his deftly crafted satires examining British society in the post-World War II era.

Hare founded an experimental touring theater group in 1968. He directed and wrote plays for the group. With the plays *How Brophy Made Good* (1969), *Slag* (1970), *The Great Exhibition* (1972), and *Knuckle* (1974), Hare established himself as a talented playwright and a vigorous critic of the mores of British public life. *Teeth 'n' Smiles* (1975) examined the milieu of rock musicians, while the widely acclaimed *Plenty* (1978) was a searching study of the erosion of a woman's personality over a 20-year period, metaphorically evoking Britain's contemporaneous postwar decline. *A Map of the World* (1982), a complexly structured survey of Western and Third World ideologies, received a mixed critical reception, as did *Pravda: A Fleet Street Comedy* (1985), which was a popular success.

Hare also wrote several plays for television and wrote and directed the film *Wetherby* (1985).

Harington \'har-iŋ-tən\, Sir John (b. 1561—d. Nov. 20, 1612, Kelston, Somerset, Eng.) English Elizabethan courtier, translator, author, and wit who also invented a type of flush toilet.

For translating and circulating among the ladies a wanton tale from the 16th-century Italian poet Ludovico Ariosto, Harington was banished from court by Queen Elizabeth I until he finished the translation of Ariosto's epic poem *Orlando furioso*. The translation, published in 1591, remains one of the finest of the age. Probably while translating, he invented a flush toilet and installed one for the queen in her palace at Richmond, Surrey. In 1596, in *The Metamorphosis of Ajax* (a jakes; *i.e.*, privy), Harington described his invention in terms more Rabelaisian than mechanical and was again banished by Elizabeth. In 1599 he went on a military expedition to Ireland, winning a knighthood.

Harīrī, al- \al-kȧ-'rē-rē\, *in full* Abū Muḥammad al-Qāsim ibn 'Alī al-Ḥarīrī (b. 1054, near Basra, Iraq—d. 1122, Basra)

Scholar of Arabic language and literature and government official who is primarily known for the refined style and wit of his collection of tales, the *Maqāmāt*, published in English as *The Assemblies of al-Ḥarīrī* (1867, 1898).

Al-Ḥarīrī's works include a long poem on grammar (*Mulḥat al-i'rāb fī annaḥw*), for which he also wrote a commentary, and a book on errors of expression in Arabic (*Durrat al-ghawwāṣ fī awhām al-khawaṣṣ*). The *Maqāmāt* recounts in the words of the narrator, al-Ḥārith ibn Hammām, his repeated encounters with Abū Zayd as-Sarūjī, an unabashed confidence artist and wanderer possessing all the eloquence, grammatical knowledge, and poetic ability of al-Ḥarīrī himself. Through these tales, filled not only with humor and adventure but with linguistic and poetic feats as well, al-Ḥarīrī's *Maqāmāt* unites the author's experiences as an information officer with his authoritative knowledge of Arabic grammar, style, and verse. Indeed, the *maqāmah* form, which was largely introduced by his predecessor al-Hamadhānī, is considered to have reached its peak and to have become established in the work of al-Ḥarīrī. *See also* MAQĀMAH.

Harishchandra \hə-'resh-,chən-drə\, *also called* Bharatendu \'bär-ə-,ten-dü\ (b. Sept. 9, 1850, Vārānasi, India—d. Jan. 6, 1885, Vārānasi) Indian poet, dramatist, critic, and journalist, commonly referred to as the "father of modern Hindi." His great contributions in founding a new tradition of Hindi prose were recognized even in his short lifetime, and he was admiringly called Bharatendu ("Moon of India").

Harishchandra began his literary career at the age of 17 when he established the first literary magazine in Hindi, the *Kavivachana-sudha*. In 1872 he founded the *Harishchandra Magazine*, later called *Harishchandra Chandrika*. A circle of distinguished poets and litterateurs whom he generously patronized gathered around him, and their work resulted in a radical transformation of Hindi language and literature in the pages of his magazine.

Harishchandra's influence was deep and far-reaching. His works mark the end of the Rīti period of Hindi literature (c. 1650–1850) and usher in what is called the Bharatendu epoch, which in turn leads into the modern period.

Harishchandra's poetry, in contrast to the rather dry poetry of the Rīti period, was simple, deeply felt, and filled with devotional ardor and emotional lyricism. His numerous plays, written partly in modern Hindi and partly in Braj Bhasa (a dialect of Hindi) verse, are among the first in the language and explore a wide range of themes. They include satirical farces and several dramas in which the poet expresses his intense grief at the stultifying poverty of India and the decline of its civilization under centuries of foreign domination and colonialism.

Harizi \hä-'rē-thē\, Judah ben Solomon (b. *c.* 1170, Spain—d. *c.* 1235) Man of letters, last representative of the golden age of Spanish Hebrew poetry. He wandered through Provence and also the Middle East, translating Arabic poetry and scientific works into Hebrew.

His version of *The Guide of the Perplexed* of the philosopher Moses Maimonides is more artistic, if less accurate, than that of Moses ibn Tibbon. His skillful adaptation of the difficult *Maqāmāt* of al-Ḥarīrī, under the title *Maḥberot Iti'el*, encouraged him to compose original Hebrew *maqāmat* (anecdotes usually told in rhymed and rhythmic prose). These *maqāmat*, collected in *Taḥkemoni*, are the works on which his fame primarily rests. His writing is characterized by its rich vocabulary and remarkable linguistic dexterity.

Harjo \'här-jō\, Joy (b. May 9, 1951, Tulsa, Okla., U.S.) American poet, writer, academic, and Native-American activist.

An enrolled member of the Creek tribe, Harjo was the daughter of a Creek father and a Cherokee-French mother. A graduate of the universities of New Mexico and Iowa, she taught at several American colleges and universities.

Harjo used Native-American symbolism, imagery, history, and ideas set within a universal context. Her poetry also dealt with social and personal issues, notably feminism, and with music, particularly jazz. Her poetry collections included *The Last Song* (1975), *What Moon Drove Me to This?* (1979), *She Had Some Horses* (1983), *In Mad Love and War* (1990), and *Fishing* (1993).

Harker, Jonathan \'jän-ə-thən-'här-kər\ Fictional character, an English solicitor who travels to Transylvania on business and encounters the vampire Count Dracula in DRACULA, the classic horror tale by Bram Stoker.

Harlem \'här-ləm\, *also called* A Dream Deferred.   Poem by Langston HUGHES, published in 1951 as part of his *Montage of a Dream Deferred*, an extended poem cycle about life in Harlem. The 11-line poem speculates about the consequences of white society's withholding of equal opportunity. After listing several relatively benign possibilities, the poet suggests that a dream deferred may explode.

Harlem Renaissance \'här-ləm\, *also called* New Negro Movement.   Period of outstanding literary vigor and creativity that took place in the United States during the 1920s. The Harlem Renaissance altered the character of literature created by many black American writers, moving from quaint dialect works and conventional imitations of white writers to sophisticated explorations of black life and culture that revealed and stimulated a new confidence and racial pride. The movement was centered in the vast black ghetto of Harlem, in New York City.

One of the leading figures and chief interpreters of the period was Alain Locke, a teacher, writer, and philosopher. Another leading figure was James Weldon Johnson, author of the pioneering novel *Autobiography of an Ex-Coloured Man* (1912) and *God's Trombones* (1927), a collection of seven sermons in free verse. Johnson acted as mentor to many of the young black writers who formed the core of the Harlem group. Claude McKay, an immigrant from Jamaica, produced an impressive volume of verse, *Harlem Shadows* (1922), and a best-selling novel, *Home to Harlem* (1928), about a young black man's return from World War I. Countee Cullen helped bring more Harlem poets to public notice by editing *Caroling Dusk: An Anthology of Verse by Negro Poets* in 1927. Langston Hughes published his first collection of verse, *The Weary Blues*, in 1926, and his novel *Not Without Laughter* appeared in 1930. He also collaborated on a play (*Mule Bone*, 1931) with Zora Neale Hurston, another writer associated with the movement. Wallace Thurman and William Jourden Rapp collaborated on a popular play, *Harlem*, in 1929. Thurman, one of the most individualistic talents of the period, also wrote a satirical novel, *The Blacker the Berry* (1929), that ridiculed elements of the movement. Another notable writer was Arna Bontemps, whose novel *God Sends Sunday* (1931) is considered the final work of the Harlem Renaissance. The movement was accelerated by philanthropic grants and scholarships and was supported by white writers such as Carl Van Vechten.

Harlequin \'här-lə-kwin, -kin\ or **Arlecchino** \,är-lek-'kē-nō\ or **Arlequin** \'är-lə-kwin, -kin, *French* är-lə-'kaⁿ\ One of the principal stock characters of the Italian COMMEDIA DELL'ARTE; often a facile and witty gentleman's valet and a capricious swain of the serving maid. In the early years of the commedia (mid-16th century), the Harlequin was a zanni (a wily and covetous comic servant), and he was cowardly, super-

stitious, and plagued by a continual lack of money and food. By the early 17th century, Harlequin had become a faithful valet, patient, credulous, and amorous. He was amoral without being vicious.

Harlequin's costume was originally a peasant's shirt and long trousers, both covered with many colored patches. It later developed into a tight-fitting costume decorated with triangles and diamond shapes, and it included a *batte*, or slapstick.

Harlequin occupied a central role in the Comédie-Italienne, the gallicized adaptation of commedia dell'arte. In mid-18th-century England, John Rich incorporated the role into dance pantomimes based on the combination of a commedia plot and a classical fable. Harlequin was also the principal character of the slapstick pantomime form known as a harlequinade in England and elsewhere.

harlequinade \,här-lə-kwi-'nād, -ki-\ Play or scene, usually in pantomime, in which Harlequin, a male character, has the principal role. Derived from the Italian commedia dell'arte, harlequinades came into vogue in early 18th-century England, with a standard plot consisting of a pursuit of the lovers Harlequin and Columbine by the latter's father or guardian, Pantaloon, and his bumpkin servant Pierrot. In the Victorian era the harlequinade was reduced to a plotless epilogue to the main pantomime, which was often a dramatized fairy tale.

Harlot High and Low, A   Novel in four parts by Honoré de BALZAC, published in 1839–47 as *Splendeurs et misères des courtisanes*. It was also translated into English as *The Splendor and Miseries of Courtesans*. It belongs to the "Scenes of Parisian Life" portion of Balzac's *The Human Comedy*, and it is considered one of his greatest works.

Esther Gobseck, the title character, is redeemed from her abandoned life by her love for Lucien de Rubempré, but Lucien is manipulated by the perverse priest Carlos Herrera. Herrera requires Lucien to pursue a wealthy heiress, and in doing so he uses Esther to finance his suit by seducing and swindling a piggish financier. She commits suicide, and Lucien admits his involvement and kills himself. Herrera, who is the central figure of the novel, turns out to be the criminal mastermind Vautrin, also known as Jacques Collin, who met Lucien in Balzac's *Lost Illusions* and also appears in several other Balzac works.

Harlowe, Clarissa \klə-'ris-ə-'här-,lō\ Fictional character, the virtuous, forbearing heroine of Samuel Richardson's novel CLARISSA.

Harmonia \här-'mō-nē-ə\   In Greek mythology, the daughter of Ares and Aphrodite, according to one account; in another she was the daughter of Zeus and the Pleiad Electra. She was carried off by Cadmus, and all the gods honored the wedding with their presence. Cadmus or one of the gods presented the bride with a robe and necklace, the work of Hephaestus. The necklace brought misfortune to all who possessed it, and it played an important part in several later legends. Both Harmonia and Cadmus were ultimately metamorphosed into snakes.

harmony \'här-mə-nē\   A systematic arrangement of parallel literary passages (such as those of the Gospels) for the purpose of showing agreement.

Harper \'här-pər\, Frances E.W., *in full* Ellen Watkins (b. Sept. 24, 1825, Baltimore, Md., U.S.—d. Feb. 22, 1911, Philadelphia, Pa.)   African-American author, orator, and social reformer, notable for her poetry, speeches, and essays on abolitionism, temperance, and woman suffrage.

Harper taught school before becoming a traveling lecturer for abolition and other reform movements. Her lyrical poetry, which she often recited during her lectures, echoed her reformist ideals. Generally written in conventional rhymed quatrains, it was noted for its simple rhythm and biblical imagery. Its narrative voice reflected the storytelling style of the oral tradition. *Forest Leaves* (c. 1845) was her first volume of verse.

Harper's most popular verse collection, *Poems on Miscellaneous Subjects* (1854; enlarged 1855 and 1871), contains the antislavery poem "Bury Me in a Free Land." *Moses: A Story of the Nile* (1869) is a blank-verse allegory of the aspirations of black Americans during Reconstruction. *Sketches of Southern Life* (1872) is a series of poems told in black vernacular by Aunt Chloe, a mother and former slave. Her novel *Iola Leroy; or, Shadows Uplifted* was published in 1892. She also wrote three novels serialized in *The Christian Recorder*, a religious periodical: *Minnie's Sacrifice*, *Sowing and Reaping*, and *Trial and Triumph*, all of which were published in book form in 1994. Harper's works were anthologized in *Complete Poems of Frances E.W. Harper* (1988) and *A Brighter Coming Day: A Frances Ellen Watkins Harper Reader* (1990).

Harper \'här-pər\, Michael S., *in full* Steven (b. March 18, 1938, New York, N.Y., U.S.)   African-American poet whose sensitive, personal verse is concerned with ancestral kinship, jazz and the blues, and the separation of the races in America.

Harper grew up in New York City and in West Los Angeles. He was educated at Los Angeles City College, Los Angeles State College of Applied Arts and Sciences, and the Writers' Workshop at the University of Iowa (M.F.A., 1963). He taught at several West Coast colleges before joining the faculty of Brown University in 1971.

Harper's first book, *Dear John, Dear Coltrane* (1970), addresses the theme of redemption in compact poems that are based both on historical events and figures and on his travels and personal relationships. The poetry in *History Is Your Own Heartbeat* (1971) and *Song: I Want a Witness* (1972) stresses the significance of history to the individual, particularly to black Americans. *Nightmare Begins Responsibility* (1974), one of his most acclaimed and complex works, contains portraits of individual courage. In *Healing Song for the Inner Ear* (1985), Harper gives the theme of personal history an international focus. His other works include *Debridement* (1973), *Images of Kin* (1977), and *Rhode Island* (1981). He edited *The Collected Poems of Sterling A. Brown* (1980) and *Every Shut Eye Ain't Asleep* (1994; with Anthony Walton), an anthology of poetry by African-Americans since 1945.

Harper's Magazine \'här-pərz\   Monthly magazine published in New York City, one of the oldest and most prestigious literary and opinion journals in the United States. It was founded in 1850 as *Harper's New Monthly*, a literary journal, by the printing and publishing firm of the Harper brothers. *Harper's* was the first American magazine extensively to use woodcut illustrations. It was a leader in publishing the writings of the most illustrious British and American authors, and before 1865 it had become the most successful periodical in the United States. In the late 1920s the periodical changed its editorial format to that of a forum on public affairs, balanced with short stories by contemporary writers. Expenses exceeded revenues in the late 1960s, and the magazine's economic problems worsened. Its certain closing in 1980 was averted by grants by a philanthropic organization, the MacArthur Foundation.

Harpur \'har-pər\, Charles (b. Jan 23, 1813, Windsor, N.S.W., Australia—d. June 10, 1868, Windsor)   Early Australian poet whose verse, though often lacking intensity and originality, reflects a gentle and sincere personality.

Both of Harpur's parents were convicts sent from England to Australia; his home life was stable, however, and he had a good education. He eventually moved to Sydney to work as a postal clerk, and in 1842 he went to live with his brother on a farm. He published his first volume of verse, *Thoughts: A Series of Sonnets*, in 1845. In 1853 his second book, *The Bushrangers: A Play in Five Acts, and Other Poems*, appeared, and though the play is considered a failure, the poems are ranked among his best.

Harpy \'här-pē\ [Greek *Hárpyia*]   In Greco-Roman mythology, a fabulous creature, probably a wind spirit. The presence of Harpies as tomb figures, however, makes it possible that they were also conceived of as ghosts. In Homer's *Odyssey* they were winds that carried people away. Elsewhere, they were sometimes connected with the powers of the underworld.

Harris \'har-əs\, Alexander (b. Feb. 7, 1805, London, Eng.—d. Feb. 1, 1874, Copetown, Ont., Can.)   English author whose *Settlers and Convicts; or, Recollections of Sixteen Years' Labour in the Australian Backwoods* (1847) is an outstanding fictional account of life in Australia.

Settlers and Convicts is a fictionalized autobiography. Harris' detailed, unbiased observations and ability to characterize pioneer life with striking realism made the book a historical classic. His real autobiography, written in 1858, was published in 1961 under the title *The Secrets of Alexander Harris*.

Harris \'har-əs\, Frank, *byname of* James Thomas Harris (b. Feb. 14, 1856, County Galway, Ire.—d. Aug. 26, 1931, Nice, Fr.)   Irish-born American journalist and man of letters best known for his unreliable autobiography, *My Life and Loves*, 3 vol. (1923–27), the sexual frankness of which was new for its day and created trouble with censors. He was also an editor of fearless talent, which he sometimes abused by turning out scandal sheets.

Harris moved to the United States at age 15. Later he moved to England and edited a series of important journals, notably the *Saturday Review* (1894–98), for which he hired George Bernard Shaw. He returned to the United States to publish a biography, *Oscar Wilde: His Life and Confessions* (1916), which no one in England would publish, and in 1922 he moved to Nice. Among his other works is a biography of Shaw (1931).

Harris \'har-əs\, George Washington (b. March 20, 1814, Allegheny City, near Pittsburgh, Pa., U.S.—d. Dec. 11, 1869, on a train en route to Knoxville, Tenn.)   American humorist who combined the skill of an oral storyteller with a dramatic imagination.

From 1843 until his death, Harris wrote humorous tales for the New York *Spirit of the Times* and other publications that were reprinted widely throughout the country. The best of them were published in *Sut Lovingood: Yarns Spun by a "Natural Born Durn'd Fool"* (1867) and, according to a leading critic, surpassed anything before Mark Twain, who himself knew and liked the tales. Harris' tales are introduced by his comic narrator, Sut LOVINGOOD.

Harris \'har-əs\, Joel Chandler (b. Dec. 9, 1848, Eatonton, Ga., U.S.—d. July 3, 1908, Atlanta, Ga.)   American author and creator of the folk character UNCLE REMUS.

As apprentice on a weekly paper, *The Countryman*, Harris became familiar with the lore and dialects of the plantation slave. He established a reputation as a brilliant humorist and writer of dialect while employed on various Southern newspapers, notably on the *Atlanta Constitution* for 24 years. In 1879 "Tar-Baby" appeared in the *Atlanta Constitution* and created a vogue for a distinctive type of dialect literature. *Uncle Remus: His Songs and His Sayings* was published in book form in 1880, followed by others. Included in a series of children's books were *Little Mr. Thimblefinger and His Queer Country* (1894), *The Story of Aaron* (1896), and *Aaron in the Wildwoods* (1897). *Mingo, and Other Sketches in Black and White* (1884),

Free Joe and Other Georgian Sketches (1887), *Sister Jane, Her Friends and Acquaintances* (1896), and *Gabriel Tolliver* (1902) reveal Harris' ability to vitalize other Southern types and to delve into issues faced by the South after Reconstruction. From 1907 until his death he edited *Uncle Remus's Magazine*. See also TAR-BABY.

Harris \'har-is\, Wilson, *in full* Theodore Wilson Harris, *byname* Kona Waruk \'kō-nə-'wä-rŭk\ (b. March 24, 1921, New Amsterdam, British Guiana [now Guyana]) Guyanese author noted for the broad vision and abstract complexity of his novels.

Harris first wrote poetry, which was collected in *Fetish* (1951) and *The Well and the Land* (1952). He then wrote and abandoned several manuscripts before publishing *The Guyana Quartet*, composed of *Palace of the Peacock* (1960), *The Far Journey of Oudin* (1961), *The Whole Armour* (1962), and *The Secret Ladder* (1963).

Harris' novels are full of ambiguous metaphors, puns, symbols with changing meanings, and the confusions of memory, imagination, dream, and reality. His characters reflect humanity's wholeness; an archetypical figure such as Ulysses, for example, belongs not to a single culture but to all. Harris' many novels include a trio set in London (*Da Silva da Silva's Cultivated Wilderness*, 1977; *The Tree of the Sun*, 1978; *The Angel at the Gate*, 1982) and another trilogy comprising *Carnival* (1985), *The Infinite Rehearsal* (1987), and *The Four Banks of the River of Space* (1990). He also wrote short stories and essays.

Harrison \'har-i-sən\, Jim, *byname of* James Thomas Harrison (b. Dec. 11, 1937, Grayling, Mich., U.S.) American novelist and poet known for his lyrical treatment of the human struggle between nature and domesticity.

Harrison attended Michigan State University, and he taught English at the State University of New York at Stony Brook. He began his writing career as a poet. In *Plain Song* (1965), *Locations* (1968), *Walking* (1967), and *Outlyer and Ghazals* (1969), critics noted a distinctive amalgam of earthy style and philosophical inquiry. Harrison also experimented with poetic forms, as exemplified by his use of the ghazel of ancient Persia.

Harrison's first novel, *Wolf* (1971), concerns the efforts of a disaffected man to view a wolf in the wilderness, an experience that he believes will cause his luck to change. *A Good Day to Die* (1973) treats the issue of the environment more cynically. Quandaries of love and work illumine *Farmer* (1976) but take on increasingly dark and obsessive overtones in *Legends of the Fall* (1979; three novellas), *Warlock* (1981), and *Sundog* (1984). The novel *Dalva* (1988) and the title novella in *The Woman Lit by Fireflies* (1990) represent the author's first attempts at creating female protagonists. Harrison's later books of poetry include *Letters to Yesenin* (1973), *Returning to Earth* (1977), *Selected and New Poems, 1961–1981* (1982), and *The Theory & Practice of Rivers* (1985).

Harry \'har-ē\ the Minstrel, *also called* Henry \'hen-rē\ the Minstrel *or* Blind Harry (fl. 1470–92) Author of the Scottish historical romance *The Acts and Deeds of the Illustrious and Valiant Champion Sir William Wallace, Knight of Elderslie*, which is preserved in a manuscript dated 1488. He has been traditionally identified with the Blind Harry named among others in William Dunbar's *The Lament for the Makaris* ("poets") and with a "Blin Hary" who is listed from time to time as having received a few shillings from the royal bounty in the treasurer's accounts (1490–92).

Wallace, which runs to 11 books and nearly 12,000 lines, is a historical novel in verse, fabricated from the events of the Scottish war for independence, popular legend about Wallace, and earlier romances. Though Harry claims historicity for his work,

he portrays Wallace on a superhuman scale. Judged simply as a romance, *Wallace* is inferior to John Barbour's epic *The Bruce* in arrangement and literary finish, but, because of its patriotic fervor, it was immensely more popular among the Scots and remained so into the 19th century.

Harsdörfer or **Harsdörffer** \'härs-,dœr-fər\, Georg Philipp (b. Nov. 1, 1607, Nürnberg [Germany]—d. Sept. 22, 1658, Nürnberg) German poet and theorist of the Baroque movement who wrote more than 47 volumes of poetry and prose and, with Johann Klaj, founded the most famous of the numerous Baroque literary societies, Pegnitzer Hirtengesellschaft ("Pegnitz Shepherds").

Harsdörfer undertook university studies and an extended *Bildungsreise* ("educational journey") through England, France, Italy, and the Netherlands. His poetry, typical of the Baroque movement, is characterized by elaborate and sometimes playful rhetoric and exaggerated poetic forms. He laid particular emphasis, in his poetry and in his theoretical work, on *Klangmalerei* ("painting in sound"). His most famous theoretical work, a handbook for the Baroque poets, is ironically titled *Poetischer Trichter, die Teutsche Dicht und Reimkunst, ohne Behuf der Lateinischen Sprache, in sechs Stunden einzugiessen* (1647–53; "A Poetic Funnel for Infusing the Art of German Poetry and Rhyme in Six Hours, Without Benefit of the Latin Language"). *Frauenzimmer Gesprech-Spiele* (1641–49; "Women's Conversation Plays"), which consists of eight dialogues aimed at teaching women how to become useful members of society, was widely read in its time. His *Pegnesisches Schäfergedicht* (1644; "Pegnitz's Idyll"), written with Klaj, popularized pastoral drama. Harsdörfer also translated works from French, Spanish, and Italian.

Hart \'härt\, Heinrich and Julius (respectively b. Dec. 30, 1855, Wesel, Westphalia [Germany]—d. June 11, 1906, Tecklenburg, Ger.; b. April 9, 1859, Münster, Westphalia—d. July 7, 1930, Berlin) Brothers who as critics and writers were key figures of the Berlin group that introduced naturalism into German literature.

The brothers led the movement to modernize German literature by establishing a critical basis for naturalism and providing a forum for its discussion and dissemination. From 1882 to 1884 they published *Kritische Waffengänge*, the periodical that decisively launched the naturalistic movement in Germany. After 1884 they worked for the popularization of naturalism through other journals they edited (*i.e.*, *Berliner Monatshefte*, *Kritisches Jahrbuch*, and *Die Freie Bühne*), in which they published essays on naturalistic aesthetics. In 1886 they organized Durch, an avant-garde literary coterie, and in 1889 they were founding members of the Freie Bühne, a theater group whose performances of controversial modern plays (including some by Henrik Ibsen) marked the climax of German naturalism. The Harts were also lyrical poets, short-story writers, playwrights, and dramatic critics.

Hart \'härt\, Moss (b. Oct. 24, 1904, New York City, N.Y., U.S.—d. Dec. 20, 1961, Palm Springs, Calif.) One of the most successful American playwrights of the 20th century.

Hart wrote his first play, which was unsuccessful, at 18. In 1929 he wrote the first draft of *Once in a Lifetime*, a satire on Hollywood that became a hit the following year, after its exuberant humor had been tempered by the sardonic skill of George S. Kaufman. Hart then wrote books for musicals for Irving Berlin and Cole Porter, but until 1941 he continued to work with Kaufman, a collaboration that produced such popular comedies as *You Can't Take It with You* (1936) and *The Man Who Came to Dinner* (1939). His success continued with his musical play *Lady in the Dark*, which he himself directed in

1941. Among other plays he directed was the long-running *My Fair Lady* (1956). In 1959 he published *Act One*, the story of his theatrical apprenticeship.

Harte \ˈhärt\, Bret, *original name* Francis Brett Harte (b. Aug. 25, 1836, Albany, N.Y., U.S.—d. May 5, 1902, London, Eng.) American writer who helped create the local-color school in American fiction.

In 1854 Harte left New York for California and went into mining country on a brief trip that legend has expanded into a lengthy participation in, and intimate knowledge of, camp life. In 1857 he was employed by the *Northern Californian*, a weekly paper.

In about 1860 he moved to San Francisco and began to write for the *Golden Era*, which published the first of his *Condensed Novels*, brilliant parodies of James Fenimore Cooper, Charles Dickens, Victor Hugo, and others. He edited the periodical *Californian*, for which he engaged Mark Twain to write weekly articles.

In 1868, after publishing a series of Spanish legends akin to Washington Irving's *The Alhambra*, Harte was named editor of the *Overland Monthly*. For it he wrote THE LUCK OF ROARING CAMP and THE OUTCASTS OF POKER FLAT. Following *The Luck of Roaring Camp, and Other Sketches* (1870), he found himself world famous. He furthered his reputation with the poem "Plain Language from Truthful James" (1870), better known as "The Heathen Chinee." On it he based his best play, *Ah Sin* (1877), a collaboration with Twain.

Flushed with success, Harte in 1871 signed with *The Atlantic Monthly* for $10,000 for 12 stories a year, the highest figure offered an American writer up to that time. Harte moved to the East, where he was greeted as an equal by eminent writers of the day. But his work eventually began to slump, and after several years of indifferent success on the lecture circuit, Harte in 1878 accepted consulships in Crefeld, Ger., and later in Glasgow, Scot. In 1885 he retired to London. He found in England a ready audience for his tales of a past or mythical California long after American readers had tired of the formula. "Ingénue of the Sierras" and "A Protégée of Jack Hamlin's" (both 1893) are perhaps better than his earlier stories.

Hartford wit \ˈhärt-fərd\, *also called* Connecticut wit \kə-ˈnet-i-kət\ Any of a group of federalist poets centered in Hartford, Conn., who collaborated to produce a considerable body of political satire just after the American Revolution. Employing burlesque verse modeled upon Samuel Butler's *Hudibras* and Alexander Pope's *The Dunciad*, the wits advocated a strong, conservative central government and attacked such proponents of democratic liberalism as Thomas Jefferson. Leaders of the group, all graduates of Yale College, were John Trumbull, Timothy Dwight, and Joel Barlow, who later turned apostate and espoused Jeffersonian democracy.

The works that the wits produced are generally more notable for patriotic fervor than for literary excellence. Their most important effort was a satirical mock epic entitled *The Anarchiad: A Poem on the Restoration of Chaos and Substantial Night* (1786–87), which attacks states slow to ratify the American Constitution.

Hartleben \ˈhärt-ˌlā-bən\, Otto Erich (b. June 3, 1864, Clausthal, Hanover [Germany]—d. Feb. 11, 1905, Salò, Italy) German poet, dramatist, and short-story writer known for his naturalistic dramas that portray with ironic wit the weaknesses of middle-class society.

The most popular of Hartleben's dramas was the tragedy *Rosenmontag* (1900; *Love's Carnival*), about a Prussian officer in love with a working-class girl. Social criticism in his works gave way to humorous anecdote, satire, and eroticism reminis-

cent of Guy de Maupassant, as seen in the tales *Vom gastfreien Pastor* (1895; "From the Hospitable Pastor"). He also wrote graceful, though superficial, poetry in an impressionistic style, collected in *Meine Verse* (1905; "My Verses").

Hartley \ˈhärt-lē\, L.P., *in full* Leslie Poles (b. Dec. 30, 1895, Fletton Tower, near Peterborough, Northamptonshire, Eng.—d. Dec. 13, 1972, London) English novelist, short-story writer, and critic whose works fuse a subtle observation of manners traditional to the English novel with an interest in psychological nuance.

Hartley first wrote criticism and published short stories, many of them fantastic or macabre. A collection, *Night Fears*, appeared in 1924. His novella *Simonetta Perkins* (1925), a light exercise in cosmopolitan manners, was followed by *The Killing Bottle* (1932), another collection of stories. *The Shrimp and the Anemone* (1944), his first novel in 19 years, was the first part of a trilogy about a brother and sister, Eustace and Hilda. The first volume treats their childhood; the second and third, *The Sixth Heaven* (1946) and *Eustace and Hilda* (1947), follow them in adulthood. Adept at depicting childhood, Hartley focuses the action of another of his novels, *The Go-Between* (1953; film, 1971), on a 12-year-old boy who inadvertently causes a tragedy.

Relations between brothers and sisters were further explored in *My Sisters' Keeper* (1970). Hartley's most complex and fully realized novel is *The Boat* (1949), in which he examines the struggles of a self-isolating person in England during World War II, when group effort and identification were the norm. A volume of essays, *The Novelist's Responsibility*, appeared in 1967 and *The Collected Stories of L.P. Hartley* in 1968.

Hartman \ˈhärt-mən\, Geoffrey H. (b. Aug. 11, 1929, Frankfurt-am-Main, Ger.) American literary critic and theorist who opposed formalism and championed criticism as a creative act. In his writing, noted for its difficulty, he maintained that the greatest writing is infinitely interpretable.

Hartman came to the United States in 1946 and became a U.S. citizen in that year. After studying at Queens College, New York City, the University of Dijon, France, and Yale University, he embarked on a university teaching career, most of it at Yale University. In his first book, *The Unmediated Vision* (1954), he argued that poetry mediates between its readers and direct experience, much as religion had done in more religious eras. Romantic poetry especially interested him; he wrote several books on William Wordsworth.

With his essay collection *The Fate of Reading* (1975) Hartman argued that history, like literature, is open to many interpretations, and therefore is also a kind of "critical energy." In *Criticism in the Wilderness* (1980) he called for uniting the studies of literature, history, and philosophy and disputed the common notion of criticism as a form separate from, and inferior to, creative writing. Among his later writings were *Easy Pieces* (1985) and *Minor Prophecies* (1991).

Hartmann von Aue \ˈhärt-mən-fòn-ˈaú-ə\ (fl. 1190–1210) Middle High German poet who was one of the masters of the courtly epic.

Hartmann's writings indicate that he was educated at a monastery school, that he was a member of a Swabian court, and that he took part in Henry VI's ill-fated crusade of 1197. Hartmann's extant works consist of four extended narrative poems (EREC, *Gregorius*, *Der arme Heinrich*, IWEIN), two shorter allegorical love poems (*Büchlein I* and *II*), and 16 lyrics (13 love songs and 3 crusading songs). *Gregorius* and *Der arme Heinrich* are religious works with an openly didactic purpose. The latter, Hartmann's most perfect poem, tells the story of a leper who is healed by the readiness of a pure young girl to sacrifice her life for him. The two secular epics, *Erec* and *Iwein*, both based on works by Chrétien de Troyes and belonging to the Arthurian cycle, are complementary in that they depict the return to grace of wayward knights.

Moral purpose mattered more to Hartmann than elegance of style, and his narratives are characterized by clarity and directness and by the avoidance of rhetorical devices and displays of poetic virtuosity.

Hartog \də-'här-tȯk\, Jan de (b. April 22, 1914, Haarlem, Neth.) Dutch-American novelist and playwright who wrote adventure stories in both Dutch and English.

De Hartog's first major novel, *Hollands glorie: roman van de zeesleepvaart* (1947; *Captain Jan: A Story of Ocean Tugboats*), tells the humorous tale of a young boy's career in the merchant navy. De Hartog later settled in the United States and wrote entertaining novels in English. Among these are *A Sailor's Life* (1956), *The Inspector* (1960), *The Peaceable Kingdom: An American Saga* (1972), *The Lamb's War* (1980), *The Trail of the Serpent* (1983), *Star of Peace* (1984), and *The Centurion* (1990). Of his plays, the most popular is the comedy *The Fourposter*, produced in 1951.

Hartzenbusch \'härt-säm-ˌbüch, *German* 'härt-sən-ˌbůsh\, Juan Eugenio (b. Sept. 6, 1806, Madrid, Spain—d. Aug. 2, 1880, Madrid) One of the most successful of the Spanish Romantic dramatists, editor of standard editions of Spanish classics, and author of fanciful poetry in a traditional style.

Los amantes de Teruel (1837; *The Lovers of Teruel*), a vivid dramatization of a legend, was followed by *comedias de magia* ("comedies of magic")—*e.g.*, *Los polvos de la madre Celestina* (1840; "Mother Celestina's Powders")—and adaptations of Golden Age plays. Hartzenbusch entered the Spanish Academy in 1847 and became director of the national library in 1862.

Hārūn ar-Rashīd \ˌhä-'rün-ˌär-rȧ-'shēd, *in Tennyson's poetry* al-'rash-id\, *in full* Hārūn ar-Rashīd ibn Muḥammad al-Mahdī ibn al-Manṣūr al-'Abbāsī (b. February 766/March 763, Rayy [Iran]—d. March 24, 809, Ṭūs) Fifth caliph of the 'Abbāsid dynasty (786–809) who ruled Islām at the zenith of its empire, living in Baghdad with a luxury memorialized in *The Thousand and One Nights* (*The Arabian Nights' Entertainment*).

Harvey \'här-vē\ Comedy in three acts by Mary Chase, performed and published in 1944. The play, which was awarded a Pulitzer Prize in 1945, features Elwood P. Dowd, a kindly, alcoholic middle-aged man whose constant companion is a six-foot tall pooka (an imaginary creature) named Harvey. Though his sister attempts to have him committed to a sanatorium, in the end she changes her mind when she realizes that the treatment he would be given would change his personality.

Harvey \'här-vē\, Gabriel (b. 1550?, Saffron Walden, Essex, Eng.—d. 1630) English writer and friend of the Elizabethan poet Edmund Spenser; the latter celebrated their friendship in *The Shepheardes Calender* (1579) through the characters of Hobbinol (Harvey) and Colin Clout (Spenser). Harvey was also noted for his tenacious participation in literary feuds.

In 1592 Harvey published *Foure Letters and Certaine Sonnets*, which contained a malicious account of the death of the writer Robert Greene and which further embroiled him in a long-running pamphlet war with the author Thomas Nashe. The ensuing literary combat with Nashe continued until 1599, when the archbishop of Canterbury ordered each man's satires to be confiscated and prohibited further publication.

Though represented as an argumentative and malicious pedant by some of his contemporaries, Harvey was nonetheless a talented scholar and literary stylist. His few published writings include two lectures on rhetoric, elegies and other verses in Latin, and several elegantly styled letters between himself and Spenser. His chief, though unfulfilled, aim was the introduction of the classical hexameter into English poetry.

Ḥasdai *see* ḤISDAI.

Hašek \'hä-shek\, Jaroslav (b. April 30, 1883, Prague, Bohemia, Austro-Hungarian Empire [now in Czech Republic]—d. Jan. 3, 1923, Lipnice nad Sázavou, Czech. [now in Czech Republic]) Czech writer known for his four-volume novel THE GOOD SOLDIER SCHWEIK, considered one of the greatest masterpieces of satirical writing.

At age 17 Hašek was already writing satirical newspaper articles. Before World War I he published a volume of poetry, *Májové výkřiky* (1903; "Shouts in May"), and wrote 16 volumes of short stories, of which *Dobrý voják Švejk a jiné podivné historky* (1912; "Good Soldier Schweik and Other Strange Stories") is among the best known. Hašek was captured on the Russian front during World War I and became a prisoner of war. After his release he devoted himself to writing *Osudy dobrého vojáka Švejka za světové války* (1920–23; "The Good Soldier Schweik and His Fortunes in the World War"; *The Good Soldier Schweik*), but he died before it was completed.

Hasenclever \'häz-ən-ˌklā-vər\, Walter (b. July 8, 1890, Aachen, Ger.—d. Aug. 15, 1940, Les Milles, Fr.) German Expressionist poet and dramatist whose work protested bourgeois materialism and the war-making state.

While serving in the German army during World War I, Hasenclever feigned mental illness and was discharged. His first play, *Der Sohn* (1914; "The Son"), concerning a youth who becomes a political revolutionary and brings about his father's death, became the manifesto for the German post-World War I generation. It was followed by two antiwar plays, *Der Retter* (1915; "The Savior"), about a poet who tries to stop the war and is executed by a firing squad, and *Antigone* (1917), a pacifist interpretation of Sophocles' play. In his best-known work, *Die Menschen* (1918; "Humanity"), Expressionist techniques are carried to an extreme form. The characters are symbolic types, speech is reduced to staccato monosyllables, and meaning is conveyed by pantomime and stylized overacting. Later, Hasenclever abandoned the Expressionist style and wrote conventional comedies.

Ḥassān ibn Thābit \ḵȧs-'sän-ˌib-ən-'thä-bit\ (b. *c.* 563, Medina, Arabia—d. *c.* 674) Arabian poet who is best known for his poems in defense of the Prophet Muḥammad.

Ḥassān won acclaim at royal courts in Syria and Mesopotamia. He later settled in Medina, where, after the advent of Muḥammad, he accepted Islām at about the age of 60. Ḥassān was Islām's first religious poet, using many phrases from the Qur'ān in his verse. His poetry thrived under the traditional requirement that literary attacks be countered with satires on the offending poets. His writings in defense of Muḥammad contain material that has been useful in documenting the period. Much of the work ascribed to him in his divan, or collection of poetry, appears to be spurious, however.

Hasselt \vän-'häs-əlt\, André van, *in full* André Henri Constant van Hasselt (b. Jan. 5, 1806, Maastricht, Neth.—d. Dec. 1, 1874, Brussels, Belg.) Romantic poet whose works represent one of the highest achievements of French-Belgian literature in the 19th century.

Van Hasselt obtained Belgian nationality in 1833, settling in Brussels. His first book of poems, *Primevères* (1834), was followed by the patriotic *La Belgique* (1842). In his masterpiece, the epic *Les Quatre Incarnations du Christ* (1863; expanded 1867), he presents great historical events as marking the progress of society under the influence of Christianity toward a final establishment of Christ's kingdom upon earth.

Hathaway \'hath-ə-,wā\, Anne, *also called* Agnes Hathwey \'hath-,wā\ (b. *c.* 1556—d. Aug. 6, 1623, Stratford-upon-Avon, Warwickshire, Eng.)   Wife of William Shakespeare.

Hathaway was probably born at Shottery, near Stratford, the daughter of Richard Hathaway, a local landowner. She married Shakespeare in 1582, when he was 18 and she, according to the sole evidence of an inscription on her gravestone, was 26. Their daughter Susanna was born the following May. After the birth (about 1585) of their twins, Hamnet and Judith, Shakespeare moved to London, probably leaving the family at Stratford. About 1596 Anne and the children were installed in New Place, Stratford, where Anne remained until her death.

hātif \'hä-tif\ [Arabic, from *hātif* shouting, calling loudly] In Arabian folklore, a mysterious nocturnal voice that is sometimes prophetic.

Hauch \'haük\, Carsten, *in full* Johannes Carsten Hauch (b. May 12, 1790, Fredrikshald [now Halden], Nor.—d. March 4, 1872, Rome, Italy)   Danish poet, dramatist, and novelist whose works expressed his high moral seriousness and tragic philosophy.

Hauch studied in Paris and Italy. In 1825 he had to have a foot amputated and shortly afterward attempted suicide. On his return to Denmark, he taught at Sorø, Kiel, and Copenhagen. As a dramatist, Hauch wrote mostly historical tragedies about men of destiny—Bajazet, Tiberius, and Gregor den Syvende (Pope Gregory VII), all in 1828—and about great Danish figures such as Svend Grathe (1841) and Marsk Stig (1850). The gloom of his plays, which are filled with suffering, is relieved somewhat by his belief in universal justice. His historical novels include *Vilhelm Zabern* (1834), *Guldmageren* (1836; "The Alchemist"), *En polsk familie* (1839; "A Polish Family"), and *Robert Fulton* (1853). But his greatest success was as a poet, particularly as a writer of odes. His fullest development as a poet came in his later years. One of his most important poetic works was the ballad cycle *Valdemar Atterdag* (1861). Collections of his poems include *Lyriske digte* (1842; "Lyrical Poems"), *Lyriske digte og romancer* (1861; "Lyrical Poems and Romances"), and *Nye digtninger* (1869; "New Poetry").

Hauff \'haüf\, Wilhelm (b. Nov. 29, 1802, Stuttgart, Württemberg [Germany]—d. Nov. 18, 1827, Stuttgart)   German poet and novelist best known for his fairy stories.

In January 1827 Hauff became editor of J.F. Cotta's *Morgenblatt*. Although he died before he was 25, his collected works comprise 36 volumes. Hauff had a narrative and inventive gift and a sense of form; he wrote with ease, combining narrative themes of others with his own. The influence of E.T.A. Hoffmann is strongly evident in his fantasy *Mitteilungen aus den Memoiren des Satans* (1826–27; "Pronouncements from the Memoirs of Satan"). His short story "Die Bettlerin vom Pont des Arts" (1827; "The Beggar Woman from Pont des Arts") has affinities with Ludwig Tieck's "Puss in Boots" and "Bluebeard." His historical romance *Lichtenstein* (1826) was one of the first imitations of Sir Walter Scott. Some of Hauff's fairy stories published in his *Märchenalmanach auf das Jahr 1826* ("Fairy Tale Almanac for the Year 1826"; followed by similar volumes in 1827 and 1828) had lasting popularity.

Hauge \'heü-ge\, Alfred (b. Oct. 17, 1915, Sjernarøy, Nor.—d. Oct. 31, 1986, Stavanger)   Norwegian novelist and poet, best known for his trilogy describing the life of a Norwegian immigrant to the United States in the 1820s: *Hundevakt* (1961; "Midwatch"), *Landkjenning* (1964; "Land Sighting"), and *Ankerfeste* (1965; "Anchoring"). The collected work was published as *Cleng Peerson* in 1968.

Many of Hauge's other books are concerned with religious and moral questions, and all of his works are rooted in Christian

belief and Norse mythology. *Septemberfrost* (1941; "September Frost"), his first novel, focuses on the miserable conditions in Norway before it achieved independence in 1814. *Ropet* (1946; "The Call") depicts the hostility of small-town pietism to art, a conflict that continued to inspire Hauge in several of his subsequent novels. Among them are *Året har ingen vår* (1948; "The Year Has No Spring"), *Fossen og bålet* (1949; "The Waterfall and the Bonfire"), and *Ingen kjenner dagen* (1955; "No One Knows the Day").

Kvinner på galgebakken (1958; "Women on Gallows Hill") is a psychological detective story in which questions of guilt and responsibility are paramount. In the visionary *Mysterium* (1967; "Mystery"), a man suffering from amnesia finds his way to a cloister where he is eventually healed by a perception of religious truth. *Mysterium* was the first of seven works that comprise the Utstein Monastery series. The remaining works are *Legenden om Svein og Maria* (1968; "The Legend of Svein and Maria"); the book of poems *Det evige sekund* (1970; "The Eternal Second"); *Perlemorstrand* (1974; "Mother of Pearl Beach"); *Leviathan* (1979); *I Rinbrads land* (1983), and *Serafen* (1984; "The Seraph"). Hauge also wrote travel books, stories for children, and several volumes of autobiography.

Hauptmann \'haüpt-,män\, Gerhart (Johann Robert) (b. Nov. 15, 1862, Obersalzbrunn [now Bad Salzbrunn], Silesia, Prussia [Germany]—d. June 6, 1946, Agnetendorf, Ger.)   The most prominent German dramatist of the early 20th century. He won the Nobel Prize for Literature in 1912.

Hauptmann became famous overnight with the October 1889 performance of his social drama *Vor Sonnenaufgang* (*Before Daybreak*). Its shocking realism signaled the end of the rhetorical and highly stylized German drama of the 19th century. Encouraged by the controversy he had elicited, Hauptmann wrote in rapid succession a number of outstanding dramas on naturalistic themes (heredity, the plight of the poor, the clash of personal needs with social restrictions). The most gripping of these is *Die Weber* (1892; THE WEAVERS), a compassionate dramatization of the Silesian weavers' revolt of 1844. *Das Friedensfest* (1890; *The Coming of Peace*) is an analysis of the troubled relations within a neurotic family, while *Einsame Menschen* (1891; *Lonely Lives*) describes the tragic end of an unhappy intellectual torn between his wife and a young woman who is his intellectual equal. Hauptmann resumed his treatment of proletarian tragedy with *Fuhrmann Henschel* (1898; *Drayman Henschel*), a claustrophobic study of a workman's personal deterioration caused by the pressures of his domestic life. *Der Biberpelz* (1893; *The Beaver Coat*) centers on a cunning female thief and her successful confrontation with pompous, uncomprehending Prussian officials.

Although Hauptmann had helped to establish naturalism in Germany, he later abandoned naturalistic principles in his plays. His later works mingle elements of the fairy tale and saga with mystical religiosity and mythical symbolism. The culmination of the final phase in Hauptmann's dramas is *Die Atriden-Tetralogie* (written between 1941 and 1944; "The Atridae Tetralogy"), a cycle of works that express through tragic Greek myths Hauptmann's horror of the cruelty of his own time and his disappointment with postwar European society.

Hauptmann also wrote stories, novels, and epic poems that are as varied as his dramatic works and are often thematically similar. The novel *Der Narr in Christo, Emanuel Quint* (1910; *The Fool in Christ, Emanuel Quint*) depicts, in a modern parallel to the life of Christ, the passion of a Silesian carpenter's son possessed by pietistic ecstasy. A contrasting figure is the apostate priest in his most famous story, *Der Ketzer von Soana* (1918; *The Heretic of Soana*), who surrenders himself to a pagan cult of Eros. The unifying element of Hauptmann's vast and varied literary output is his concern for human suffering. His early naturalistic plays are still frequently performed.

Hávamál \\'hä-və-,mäl, 'haủ-və-,maủl\\ ("Sayings of the High One [Odin]") A heterogeneous collection of 164 stanzas of aphorisms, homely wisdom, counsels, and magic charms that are ascribed to the Norse god Odin. The work contains at least five separate fragments not originally discovered together and constitutes a portion of the *Poetic Edda*. Most of the poems are believed to have been composed in Norway in the 9th and 10th centuries.

The collection begins with poetry concerning rules of social conduct. Of perhaps greater general interest are the myths about Odin's erotic affairs, especially his amorous adventure leading to the theft of the precious mead. In another poem, the *Vafthrúdnismal* ("Lay of Vafthrúdnir"), Odin engages in a contest of wits with Vafthrúdnir, an immensely wise giant. The latter part contains the strange myth of how Odin acquired the magical power of the runes (alphabetical characters) by hanging himself from a tree and suffering hunger and thirst for nine nights. The *Hávamál* ends with a list of magic charms.

Havel \\'häv-el\\, Václav (b. Oct. 5, 1936, Prague, Czech. [now Czech Republic]) Prominent Czech playwright, poet, and political dissident, who, following the fall of communism, was president of Czechoslovakia (1989–92) and subsequently of the new Czech Republic.

Havel found work as a stagehand in a Prague theatrical company in 1959 and progressed to the position of resident playwright of the Theater of the Balustrade company by 1968. He was a prominent participant in the liberal reform movement of 1968 (known as the Prague Spring), and, after its repression by the Soviet Union that year, his plays were banned and his passport was confiscated. During the 1970s and '80s he was repeatedly arrested, and he served four years in prison (1979–83) for his dissident activities. His *Dopisy Olze* (1983; *Letters to Olga*) serves as a record of that period.

Havel's first solo play, *Zahradní slavnost* (1963; *The Garden Party*), typifies his work in its absurdist, satirical examination of bureaucratic routines and their dehumanizing effects. In his best-known play, *Vyrozumění* (1965; *The Memorandum*), an incomprehensible artificial language is imposed on a large bureaucratic enterprise, causing the complete breakdown of human relationships and their replacement by unscrupulous struggles for power. Among his later plays are *Ztížená možnost soustředění* (1968; *The Increased Difficulty of Concentration*); the three one-act plays *Audience* (1975), *Vernisáž* (1975; *Private View*), and *Protest* (1978); and *Largo desolato* (1985).

Havelok \\'hav-ə-,läk\\, *also called* Havelok the Dane. Middle English metrical romance of some 3,000 lines, written about 1300. It is extant in a single manuscript, and it offers the first view of ordinary life in the literature that was produced after the Norman Conquest.

Havelok is composed in a Lincolnshire dialect and contains abundant local traditions. There exist two well-known earlier versions of the Havelok story—Geffrei Gaimar's *L'Estoire des Engles* and the anonymous Anglo-Norman *Le Lai d'Havelok*. The Middle English tale, however, is distinct from (and, except for subject matter, probably unrelated to) the earlier versions in, for example, the names of characters, in style (the use of strong mono- and disyllables, common proverbs, internal monologue), and in its emphasis on ordinary people rather than the aristocracy.

The story opens by recounting the circumstances of the English princess Goldeboru (Goldborough), who has been left to the care of her evil guardian Godrich. The narrative continues with the parallel story of Havelok, the orphaned son of the king of Denmark, who is to be set adrift in the sea by his evil guardian Godard; he is saved by Grim, an exiled Danish fisherman who rescues him and raises him on the east coast of England. He grows strong and takes a menial job in a nobleman's kitchen. Eventually married to Goldeboru, Havelok discovers his royalty, raises an army that defeats the Danish usurper, restores his wife's possessions, and becomes king of Denmark and of a portion of England.

Havisham, Miss \\'hav-i-shəm\\ Fictional character, a half-crazed, embittered jilted bride in Charles Dickens' novel GREAT EXPECTATIONS.

Havlíček Borovský \\'häv-,lē-chek-'bō-rō-,skē\\, Karel, *pseudonym* Havel Borovský (b. Oct. 31, 1821, Borová, Bohemia, Austrian Empire [now in Czech Republic]—d. July 29, 1856, Prague) Czech author and political journalist, a master prose stylist who reacted against Romanticism and through his writings gave the Czech language a more modern character.

Havlíček wrote numerous articles advocating constitutional reform and national rights in the 1840s, and in 1851 he was arrested, tried, and banished until 1855. He also wrote a book of brilliant satirical poems, *Křest Svatého Vladimíra* (posthumously published 1876; *The Conversion of St. Vladimir*).

Hawes \\'hôz\\, Stephen (fl. 1502–21) Poet and courtier who served King Henry VII of England and was a follower of the devotional poet John Lydgate.

Little is known of Hawes's life. His main work is a long allegorical poem, *The Passetyme of Pleasure* (1509), the chief theme of which is the education and pilgrimage through life of the knight Graunde Amoure. Another allegory by Hawes, *The Example of Vertu*, is simpler and shorter. Though he shows at times a finer quality of mind than Lydgate, Hawes is not Lydgate's equal in technical accomplishment.

Hawkes \\'hôks\\, John, *in full* John Clendennin Burne Hawkes, Jr. (b. Aug. 17, 1925, Stamford, Conn.) American author whose novels achieve a dreamlike (often nightmarish) intensity through the suspension of traditional narrative constraints.

Hawkes attended Harvard University; he taught there from 1949 to 1958 and for the next 30 years at Brown University.

Hawkes's first novel, *The Cannibal* (1949), depicts harbingers of a future apocalypse amid the rubble of postwar Germany. *The Beetle Leg* (1951) is a surreal parody of the pulp western. In 1954 he published two novellas, *The Goose on the Grave* and *The Owl*, both set in Italy. With *The Lime Twig* (1961), a dark thriller set in postwar London, Hawkes attracted the critical attention that would place him among the front rank of avant-garde American writers. His next novel, *Second Skin* (1964), is the first-person confessional of a retired naval officer. *The Blood Oranges* (1971), *Death, Sleep, & the Traveler* (1974), and *Travesty* (1976) explore the concepts of marriage and freedom. *The Passion Artist* (1979) and *Virginie: Her Two Lives* (1982) are tales of sexual obsession. Later works include *Adventures in the Alaskan Skin Trade* (1985), *Whistlejacket* (1988), and *Sweet William: A Memoir of Old Horse* (1993). Hawkes also published *The Innocent Party* (1966), a collection of short plays, and *Lunar Landscapes* (1969), a volume of short stories and novellas.

Hawkesworth \\'hôks-wərth\\, John (b. 1715?—d. Nov. 16, 1773, London, Eng.) English writer and Samuel Johnson's successor as compiler of parliamentary debates for *The Gentleman's Magazine*.

Hawkesworth collaborated with Johnson (whose prose style he closely imitated) in founding a periodical, *The Adventurer*. He wrote poems and articles, adapted plays for the actor-manager David Garrick, and wrote miscellaneous original dramatic works. He was commissioned by the British Admiralty to compile *An Account of the Voyages Undertaken in the Southern Hemisphere* (1773), dealing chiefly with the voyages of exploration of Captain James Cook.

Hawkins \\'hȯk-ənz\\, Sir John (b. March 30, 1719, London, Eng.—d. May 21, 1789, London)   English magistrate, writer, and author of the first history of music in English. He was knighted in 1772.

Hawkins produced, among other works, an annotated edition of Izaak Walton's *The Compleat Angler* (1760) and legal articles. His biography of Samuel Johnson, published with his 1787 edition of Johnson's works, was surpassed only by James Boswell's. Hawkins was among Johnson's closest friends and was an executor of his will.

Hawkins' *General History of the Science and Practice of Music* occupied him for 16 years. It was published in five volumes in 1776, a few weeks before Charles Burney's celebrated *General History of Music*. Hawkins' book continues to be invaluable as a mine of detailed information, some of it unavailable elsewhere, but it was eclipsed by Burney's.

Hawkins, Jim \\'jim-'hȯk-inz\\   Fictional character, the youthful narrator of Robert Louis Stevenson's novel TREASURE ISLAND. Jim also appears in sequels to *Treasure Island* by writers other than Stevenson.

Hawks, Asa and Sabbath Lily \\'ā-sə-'hȯks ... 'sab-əth-'lil-ē\\   Fictional characters, a grotesque preacher and his innocent yet perverse daughter in the comic novel WISE BLOOD by Flannery O'Connor.

Hawthornden Prize \\'hȯth-ȯrn-dən\\   The oldest British literary prize, established in 1919 by Alice Warrender. The Hawthornden, which includes a financial award of £2,000, is awarded annually to recognize the best work of imaginative literature published during the previous year and is intended to encourage young authors. British authors under the age of 41 are eligible for the prize.

Hawthorne \\'hȯ-ˌthȯrn\\, Nathaniel (b. July 4, 1804, Salem, Mass., U.S.—d. May 19, 1864, Plymouth, N.H.)   American novelist and short-story writer who was a master of the allegorical and symbolic tale. One of the greatest fiction writers in American literature, he is best known for THE SCARLET LETTER (1850) and THE HOUSE OF THE SEVEN GABLES (1851).

Hawthorne grew up in Salem and in Raymond, Maine, on the shores of Sebago Lake. He returned to Salem in 1825 after four years at Bowdoin College, in Brunswick, Maine.

His first work was the amateurish novel FANSHAWE, which he published in 1828 at his own expense—only to decide that it was unworthy of him and to try to destroy all copies. He soon found his own voice, style, and subjects, however, in such impressive and distinctive stories as "The Hollow of the Three Hills" and "An Old Woman's Tale." By 1832, MY KINSMAN, MAJOR MOLINEUX and ROGER MALVIN'S BURIAL, two of his greatest tales, had appeared. YOUNG GOODMAN BROWN, perhaps the greatest tale of witchcraft ever written, appeared in 1835. Even when his first signed book, TWICE-TOLD TALES, was published in 1837, it brought him little financial reward. By 1842, however, Hawthorne's writing was producing a sufficient income to allow him to marry Sophia Peabody; the couple rented the Old Manse in Concord and began a happy three-year period that Hawthorne would later record in his essay "The Old Manse."

Hawthorne welcomed the companionship of his Transcendentalist neighbors—Ralph Waldo Emerson, Henry David Thoreau, Bronson Alcott—but in general he had little confidence in artists and intellectuals. At the Old Manse, Hawthorne continued to write stories, with the same result as before: literary success, monetary failure. His short-story collection MOSSES FROM AN OLD MANSE, which included such stories as RAPPACCINI'S DAUGHTER, was published in two volumes in 1846.

The Granger Collection, New York City

A growing family and mounting debts compelled the family's return in 1845 to Salem, where Hawthorne was appointed surveyor of the Custom House. Three years later Hawthorne lost his job, but in a few months of concentrated effort, he produced his masterpiece, *The Scarlet Letter*, which made him famous and which was eventually recognized as one of the greatest American novels.

Hawthorne then moved to Lenox in western Massachusetts. There he began work on *The House of the Seven Gables*, the story of the Pyncheon family, who for generations had lived under a curse until it was removed at last by love. In the autumn of 1851 Hawthorne moved his family to West Newton, near Boston. There he quickly wrote THE BLITHEDALE ROMANCE (1852), based on his disenchantment with Brook Farm, an agricultural cooperative in West Roxbury, Mass., where he had lived in 1841.

In 1853 Hawthorne was appointed to the consulship in Liverpool, England, by his old college friend, President Franklin Pierce. When his position was terminated in 1857, he spent a year and a half sight-seeing in Italy. He then produced THE MARBLE FAUN (1860).

Hay \\'hā\\, Sir Gilbert, *also called* Sir Gilbert of the Haye (fl. 1456)   Scottish translator of works from the French, whose prose translations are the earliest extant examples of Scots literary prose.

That Hay received a degree as a master of arts, that he became a knight, and that he was at some time chamberlain to the king of France (Charles VII) are facts known from his own description of himself at the beginning of the manuscript of his prose translations. By 1456 he had entered the service of the Earl of Orkney and Caithness, at whose request he began in that year the translation of three of the most popular works of the Middle Ages: Honoré Bonet's *L'Arbre des batailles* (as *The Buke of the Law of Armys*, or *Buke of Bataillis*); *Le Livre de l'ordre de chevalerie*, a French version of Ramon Llull's *Libre de cavayleria* (as *The Buke of the Order of Knyghthood*); and *Le Gouvernement des princes*, a French version of the pseudo-Aristotelian *Secreta secretorum* (as *The Buke of the Governaunce of Princes*). These remained in manuscript until found in Sir Walter Scott's library at Abbotsford, Scot., and edited by D. Laing in 1847.

Hay's only extant poetical work, *The Buik of Alexander the Conqueror*, is a translation of the French *Roman d'Alexandre*.

Hay \\'hā\\, John (Milton) (b. Oct. 8, 1838, Salem, Ind., U.S.—d. July 1, 1905, Newbury, N.H.)   U.S. secretary of state and author of both fiction and historical works.

Hay studied law in Springfield, Ill., where he met the future president Abraham Lincoln. He served as President Lincoln's private secretary from 1861 to 1865, and under succeeding Republican administrations he held various diplomatic posts in

Europe. Following a five-year stint as editorial writer for the *New York Tribune*, Hay returned to government service and was assistant secretary of state from 1879 to 1881. He became nationally prominent with the election of President William McKinley, under whom he served as ambassador to Great Britain (1897–98) and then secretary of state (1898–1905).

Throughout his life Hay found time to exercise his considerable literary talent, and his *Pike County Ballads and Other Pieces* (1871) and his novel *The Bread-Winners* (1883) were well received. In collaboration with John G. Nicolay, he was also responsible for two historical works that remained standard for many years: *Abraham Lincoln: A History* (1890) and an edition of Lincoln's *Complete Works* (1894).

Hayashi Fumiko \'hä-yä-shē-'fü-mē-kō\, *original name* Miyata Fumiko (b. Dec. 31, 1904, Shimonoseki, Japan—d. June 28, 1951, Tokyo) Japanese novelist whose realistic stories deal with urban working-class life.

Hayashi's youthful experiences of hunger and humiliation appear in her first work, *Hōrōkiizen* (1930; "Journal of a Vagabond"), and in *Seihin no sho* (1931; "A Life of Poverty"). Her stories of women who remained undaunted in the face of degradation and instability commanded a strong following. Often near sentimentality, they are saved by a realistic and direct style. She reached the peak of her popularity after World War II, when such stories as *Daun taun* (1948; *Downtown*) and *Ukigumo* (1949; *The Drifting Clouds*) mirrored the harsh postwar scene.

Hayden \'hād-ən\, Robert (Earl), *original name* Asa Bundy Sheffey \'shef-ē\ (b. Aug. 4, 1913, Detroit, Mich., U.S.—d. Feb. 25, 1980, Ann Arbor, Mich.) African-American poet whose subject matter was most often the black experience.

Hayden joined the Federal Writers' Project, researching black folklore and the history of the Underground Railroad in Michigan. His first collection of poems, *Heart-Shape in the Dust*, was published in 1940. He gained a public after his *A Ballad of Remembrance* (1962) won a grand prize at the First World Festival of Negro Arts in 1966 in Dakar, Senegal. In 1976 he became the first African-American to be appointed poetry consultant to the Library of Congress.

Hayden's best-known poem dealing with black history is "Middle Passage," an alternately lyric, narrative, and dramatic view of the slave trade. Hayden's Baha'i beliefs were often reflected in his poetry, which confronted the brutality of racism. He also published the poetry collections *Words in the Mourning Time* (1970), including his tribute to Malcolm X; *The Night-Blooming Cereus* (1972), concerned with the meaning of life; *Angle of Ascent: New and Selected Poems* (1975); and *American Journal* (1980).

Hay Fever Comedy in three acts by Noël COWARD, produced and published in 1925. Coward's first successful comedy, it was the prototype of many of his later plays in its use of eccentric characters and witty dialogue.

Judith and David Bliss—an aging, recently retired actress and a romance novelist—are the parents of a 19-year-old daughter, Sorel, and a son, Simon. The weekend guests at their summer home include Richard, a diplomat who courts Sorel; Jackie, a flapper; Sandy, a young man intrigued by Judith; and Myra, a middle-aged woman of whom Judith disapproves. Quarreling good-naturedly with each other, the eight players soon pair up. But by the end of the play, the Blisses are restored to their family unit and the guests leave furtively.

Hayley \'hā-lē\, William (b. Oct. 29, 1745, Chichester, Sussex, Eng.—d. Nov. 12, 1820, Felpham, near Chichester) English poet, biographer, and patron of the arts. He is best remembered for his friendships with William Blake and William Cowper.

Of independent means and good intentions, Hayley in 1800 invited Blake and his wife to live in a cottage on his Felpham estate and to engrave and print illustrations for his books. Blake realized that Hayley's wish to turn him into a tame poet, engraver, and miniature-painter would eventually destroy his artistic integrity, and so he returned to London in 1803. He immortalized Hayley in the epigram:

> Thy friendship oft has made my heart to ache:
> Do be my Enemy for Friendship's sake.

Hayley's verse includes the didactic *The Triumphs of Temper* (1781). His *Life . . . of William Cowper*, 3 vol. (1803–04), foreshadows the methods of modern biography.

Hayne \'hān\, Paul Hamilton (b. Jan. 1, 1830, Charleston, S.C., U.S.—d. July 6, 1886, Grovetown, Ga.) American poet and editor, one of the best-known poets of the Confederate cause.

Hayne wrote for the *Charleston Evening News* and the Richmond *Southern Literary Messenger* and was associate editor of the weekly *Southern Literary Gazette*. His first collected poems were published at his own expense in 1855. He was coeditor of the influential *Russell's Magazine* (1857–60). During the American Civil War he contributed verse supporting the Southern cause—notably "The Battle of Charleston Harbor"—to the *Southern Illustrated News* of Richmond. Hayne's published works include *Sonnets and Other Poems* (1857), *Legends and Lyrics* (1872), *The Mountain of the Lovers* (1875), and *The Broken Battalions* (1885).

Haywood \'hā-wùd\, Eliza, *original surname* Fowler \'faù-lər\ (b. 1693?—d. Feb. 25, 1756, London, Eng.) Prolific English writer of sensational romantic novels that mirrored contemporary 18th-century scandals.

Haywood adopted the technique of writing novels based on scandals involving leaders of society, whom she denoted by initials. Among such works are *Memoirs of a Certain Island Adjacent to the Kingdom of Utopia* (1725) and *The Secret History of the Present Intrigues of the Court of Caramania* (1727).

Alexander Pope attacked Haywood with coarse brutality in his satirical poem *The Dunciad*, which she attempted to counter with *The Female Dunciad* (1729). Later, she achieved success with *The Female Spectator* (1744–46), the first periodical to be written by a woman, and with her realistic novel *The History of Jemmy and Jenny Jessamy* (1753).

Hazlitt \'hāz-lit, *commonly* 'haz-\, William (b. April 10, 1778, Maidstone, Kent, Eng.—d. Sept. 18, 1830, Soho, London) English writer who is remembered above all for his essays.

Hazlitt originally studied for the ministry, but he soon abandoned that career and turned to painting. His friends, who by 1803 included Charles Lamb, William Wordsworth, and Samuel Taylor Coleridge, encouraged his ambitions as a painter; yet in 1805 he decided to devote himself to metaphysics and the study of philosophy.

By the end of 1811 Hazlitt was penniless. To remedy his poverty, he gave a course of lectures in philosophy in London and began reporting for the *Morning Chronicle*, quickly establishing himself as critic, journalist, and essayist. He also contributed to a number of journals, among them Leigh Hunt's *The Examiner*; this association led to the publication of *The Round Table* (1817), a two-volume collection of 52 essays of which 40 were by Hazlitt. At the same time, he consolidated his reputation as a lecturer, delivering courses entitled *On the English Poets* (1818) and *On the English Comic Writers* (1819).

Hazlitt was married in 1808, but he lived apart from his wife after the end of 1819, and they were divorced in 1822. He fell in love with the daughter of his London landlord, but the affair ended disastrously; Hazlitt described his suffering in the strange *Liber Amoris; or, The New Pygmalion* (1823). Even so, many of his best essays were written during this difficult period, and they were collected in his two most famous books, *Table Talk* (1821) and *The Plain Speaker* (1826).

Hazlitt spent several years abroad in the early 1820s, an experience he recorded in *Notes of a Journey in France and Italy* (1826). In 1825 he published some of his most effective writing in *The Spirit of the Age*. His last book, *Conversations of James Northcote* (1830), records his long friendship with that eccentric painter.

Hazzard \'haz-ərd\, Shirley (b. Jan. 30, 1931, Sydney, Australia)   Australian-born American writer whose novels and short stories were acclaimed for both their literary refinement and their emotional complexity.

Hazzard published her first collection of short stories, *Cliffs of Fall*, in 1963 and won immediate critical praise. Both *The Evening of the Holiday* (1966) and *The Bay of Noon* (1970), her first two novels, are elegiac love stories set in Italy. A collection of character sketches, *People in Glass Houses* (1967), satirizes the intricate, idealistic world of the United Nations, where she had worked from 1952 to 1962. Although Hazzard had long enjoyed critical favor and a modest loyal following, her reputation swelled to fame with the publication of *The Transit of Venus* (1980), an award-winning novel of international scope and rich psychological texture. The book's omniscient narrative voice constitutes by most evaluations a stylistic tour de force. Hazzard also published *Defeat of an Ideal: A Study of the Self-Destruction of the United Nations* (1973).

H.D.   *see* Hilda DOOLITTLE.

Head \'hed\, Bessie, *original name* Bessie Amelia Emery \'em-ə-rē\ (b. July 6, 1937, Pietermaritzburg, S.Af.—d. April 17, 1986, Serowe, Botswana)   African writer who described the contradictions and shortcomings of pre- and postcolonial African society in morally didactic novels and stories.

Head was born of an illegal union between her white mother (institutionalized during her pregnancy) and black father (who then mysteriously disappeared). At age 27, Head abandoned South Africa and moved to Bechuanaland (near Botswana).

Her novels evolved from an objective, affirmative narrative of an exile finding new meaning in an adopted village in *When Rain Clouds Gather* (1969) to a more introspective account of the acceptance won by a light-colored San (Bushman) woman in a black-dominated African society in *Maru* (1971). *A Question of Power* (1973) is a frankly autobiographical account of disorientation and paranoia in which the heroine survives by sheer force of will. *The Collector of Treasures* (1977), a volume of short fiction, includes brief vignettes of traditional Botswanan village life, macabre tales of witchcraft, and passionate attacks on African male chauvinism. *Serowe, Village of the Rainwind* (1981) explores the themes of communal development. The novel *A Bewitched Crossroad: An African Saga* (1984) is a historical chronicle of tribal migration in southern Africa. Another volume of short fiction, *Tales of Tenderness and Power* (1989), and a novella, *The Cardinals, With Meditations and Stories* (1993), were published posthumously.

headless \'hed-ləs\, *also called* acephalous.   In prosody, a line of verse that is lacking the normal first syllable. An iambic line with only one syllable in the first foot is a headless line, as in the third line of the following stanza of A.E. Housman's poem "To An Athlete Dying Young":

> The time you won your town the race
> We chaired you through the market-place;
> Man and boy stood cheering by,
> And home we brought you shoulder-high.

headless horseman   Fictional character, a legendary spirit that supposedly haunts the community of Sleepy Hollow in Washington Irving's story THE LEGEND OF SLEEPY HOLLOW.

head rhyme   *see* ALLITERATION.

Heaney \'hē-nē\, Seamus Justin (b. April 13, 1939, Castledawson, Londonderry, N.Ire.)   Irish poet whose poems are rooted in Northern Irish rural life.

After graduating from Queen's University, Belfast, Heaney taught secondary school and lectured in colleges and universities in Belfast and Dublin. From 1982 to 1989 he taught at Harvard University, Cambridge, Mass., U.S., and thereafter at the University of Oxford.

His prizewinning poetry collection *Death of a Naturalist* (1966) was followed by several volumes, including *Door into the Dark* (1969), *Wintering Out* (1972), *North* (1975), *Field Work* (1979), *Station Island* (1984), *The Haw Lantern* (1987), and *Seeing Things* (1991). His poems evoke Irish history and draw on myth and unique aspects of the Irish experience. Simplicity and clarity distinguish his style.

In essays such as those published as *Preoccupations: Selected Prose, 1968–1978* (1980), Heaney wrote about poetry and poets he admired, including William Wordsworth, Gerard Manley Hopkins, and Robert Lowell, and provided autobiographical insights into his own work.

Hearn \'hərn\, Lafcadio, *in full* Patricio Lafcadio Tessima Carlos Hearn, *also called* (from 1895) Koizumi Yakumo (b. June 27, 1850, Levkás, Ionian Islands, Greece—d. Sept. 26, 1904, Ōkubo, Japan)   Writer, translator, and teacher who introduced the culture and literature of Japan to the West.

Hearn immigrated to the United States at age 19 and settled in Cincinnati, Ohio, where he worked as a reporter and translated stories by the French authors Théophile Gautier and Gustave Flaubert. In 1877 Hearn went to New Orleans to write a series of articles on Louisiana politics; he also translated French authors and wrote original stories and sketches. Two of his earliest works—*Stray Leaves from Strange Literature* (1884) and *Some Chinese Ghosts* (1887)—were adapted from foreign literature. *Chita* (1889), an adventure novel about the only survivor of a tidal wave, dates from this time.

From 1887 to 1889, Hearn was in the West Indies on assignment for *Harper's Magazine*. This experience resulted in *Two Years in the French West Indies* (1890) and his novel *Youma* (1890), a highly original story of a slave insurrection.

In 1890 Hearn traveled to Japan for Harper's. He soon broke with the magazine and worked as a schoolteacher in Izumo in northern Japan. There he met Koizumi Setsuko, a Japanese woman of high samurai rank, whom he married in 1891. Hearn's articles on Japan began appearing in *The Atlantic Monthly* and were syndicated in several U.S. newspapers. These essays and others, reflecting Hearn's initial captivation with the Japanese, were subsequently collected and published in two volumes as *Glimpses of Unfamiliar Japan* (1894).

In 1891 Hearn transferred to the Government College at Kumamoto, where he remained for three years. In 1895 he became a Japanese subject, taking the name Koizumi Yakumo.

Hearn's most brilliant and prolific period was from 1896 to 1903 as professor of English literature at the Imperial University of Tokyo. In four books written during this time—*Exotics and Retrospective* (1898), *In Ghostly Japan* (1899), *Shadowings* (1900), and *A Japanese Miscellany* (1901)—he is informative about the customs, religion, and literature of Japan. *Kwaidan* (1904) is a collection of stories of the supernatural and translations of haiku poetry.

Heartbreak House   Play in three acts by George Bernard SHAW, published in 1919 and produced in 1920. The play's subtitle, "A Fantasia in the Russian Manner on English Themes," acknowledges its resemblance to Anton Chekhov's *The Cherry Orchard*. The action takes place in the decidedly Bohemian household of the elderly Captain Shotover, a dabbler in mysticism. The time, to judge from the zeppelin attack that provides the climax, is World War I, although no direct reference is made to the conflict. The characters—including Shotover's daughters Hesione and Lady Utterword, Hesione's husband Hector, and sundry others—play out their petty deceptions and grand philosophies oblivious of the momentous changes approaching. This combination of eccentrics gives rise to heated discussions of social theory, sexual conflict, and other typically Shavian subjects.

Heart Is a Lonely Hunter, The Novel by Carson MC-CULLERS, published in 1940. With its profound sense of moral isolation and its sensitive glimpses into the inner lives of lonely people, it is considered McCullers' finest work.

The focus of the work is on John Singer, a deaf-mute in a Georgia mill town during the 1930s, and on his effect on the people who confide in him. When Singer's mute Greek companion of 10 years goes insane, Singer is left alone and isolated. He takes a room with the Kelly family, where he is visited by the town's misfits, who turn to him for understanding but have no knowledge of his inner life. When Singer discovers that his Greek friend has died, he realizes that he can communicate with no one and shoots himself.

The author established her reputation with the novel, which was her first. The book's emphasis on individuals who are considered outcasts because of race, politics, disability, or sensibility placed it squarely within the Southern gothic tradition of American literature.

Heart of a Dog, The Dystopian novelette by Mikhail BUL-GAKOV, written in Russian in 1925 as *Sobachye serdtse*. It was published posthumously in the West in 1968, both in Russian and in translation, and in the Soviet Union in 1987.

The book is a satirical examination of one of the goals of the October Revolution of 1917: to create a new breed of man, uncorrupted by the past and above petit bourgeois concerns. In addressing this subject *The Heart of a Dog* savages the rigid Soviet mind-set, science fiction, and a pseudoscientific theory of the 1920s that held out the promise of sexual rejuvenation through surgical transplantation of monkey glands.

Heart of Darkness Novella by Joseph CONRAD, first published in 1902 with the story "Youth" and thereafter published separately. The story reflects the physical and psychological shock Conrad himself experienced in 1890, when he worked briefly in the Belgian Congo.

The narrator, Marlow, describes a journey he took on an African river. Assigned by an ivory company to take command of a cargo boat stranded in the interior, Marlow makes his way through the treacherous forest, witnessing the brutalization of the natives by white traders and hearing tantalizing stories of a Mr. Kurtz, the company's most successful representative. He reaches Kurtz's compound in a remote outpost only to see a row of human heads mounted on poles. In this alien context, unbound by the strictures of his own culture, Kurtz has exchanged his soul for a bloody sovereignty, but a mortal illness is bringing his reign of terror to a close. As Marlow transports him downriver, Kurtz delivers an arrogant and empty explanation of his deeds as a visionary quest. To the narrator Kurtz's dying words, "The horror! The horror!" represent despair at the encounter with human depravity—the heart of darkness.

Heart of Midlothian, The \mid-ˈlō-the̱-ən\ Novel of Scottish history by Sir Walter SCOTT, published in four volumes in 1818. It is often considered to be his finest novel.

The Old Tolbooth prison in Edinburgh is called "the heart of Midlothian," and there Effie Deans is held on charges of murdering her illegitimate son. Her sister, Jeanie Deans, makes a dangerous journey through outlaw-infested regions to London to seek the queen's pardon for Effie. Justice and Scottish Presbyterianism are discussed at length, and issues of conscience provide the novel's themes. Somewhat unusually for a Scott novel, the heroine, Jeanie, is not beautiful, wealthy, or of the upper class. Scott based the plot of *The Heart of Midlothian* on an actual case, and the 1736 Porteous Riots provide the background for the novel's opening chapters.

Heart of the Matter, The Novel by Graham GREENE, published in 1948. The work is considered by some critics to be part of a "Catholic trilogy" that included Greene's *Brighton Rock* (1938) and *The Power and the Glory* (1940).

Set during World War II in a bleak area of West Africa, the novel concerns the moral dilemmas facing Scobie, an honorable and decent deputy commissioner of police who is torn between compassion for his wife Louise and love and pity for Helen, a young widow with whom he has an affair. Scobie gradually loses control of his life. Racked with guilt and self-loathing over his role in the accidental death of his loyal servant, Scobie plans to commit suicide, but, fearing that knowledge of this mortal sin will cause pain to his wife and others, he disguises his death so that he appears to have died of natural causes. The truth is eventually revealed.

Heathcliff \ˈhēth-ˌklif\ Fictional character, the brooding protagonist of Emily Brontë's romantic novel WUTHERING HEIGHTS.

Heath-Stubbs \ˈhēth-ˈstəbz\, John (Francis Alexander) (b. July 9, 1918, London, Eng.) English poet, translator, dramatist, and critic whose poetry is characterized by wide erudition, a strong moral sense, and perfection of style. He also became known as an anthologist.

Heath-Stubbs won first-class honors in English at Oxford. He afterward taught at Leeds University, at the University of Alexandria, Egypt, and at the University of Michigan. He was lecturer in English literature at the College of St. Mark and St. John in Chelsea. From his earliest volumes—*Wounded Thammuz* (1942), *Beauty and the Beast* (1943), *The Divided Ways* (1946), and *The Swarming of the Bees* (1950)—Heath-Stubbs showed a predilection for past cultures, for myth and legend, and for both humanistic and Christian traditions. His later poetry includes *A Charm Against the Toothache* (1954), *The Triumph of the Mule* (1958), *The Blue-Fly in His Head* (1962), *Satires and Epigrams* (1968), *The Watchman's Flute* (1978), *Naming the Beasts* (1982), and *The Game of Love and Death* (1990). His *Collected Poems 1943–1987* was published in 1988.

Heath-Stubbs' translations include a selection of the prose and poetry of the 19th-century Italian poet Giacomo Leopardi (1966) and, with Peter Avery, *The Ruba'iyat of Omar Khayyam* (1979). He also wrote a number of plays, collected in *Helen in Egypt and Other Plays* (1959).

Heat of the Day, The Novel by Elizabeth BOWEN, published in 1949, about the ramifications of an Englishwoman's discovery that her lover is a spy for the Axis powers.

Set in London during World War II, the novel concerns the lovers Stella and Robert, who both work for the British secret service. Harrison, a colleague who informs Stella that Robert is a double agent, attempts to blackmail her into a sexual liaison. Stella confronts Robert with Harrison's allegations, but he vehemently denies them. Robert finally confesses to Stella that he has betrayed his country; soon after, he falls or jumps to his death.

heavy \'hev-ē\ In prosody, having stress or conspicuous sonority—used especially of syllables in accentual verse; contrasted with *light*.

Hebbel \'heb-əl\, Friedrich, *in full* Christian Friedrich Hebbel (b. March 18, 1813, Wesselburen, Schleswig-Holstein [Germany]—d. Dec. 13, 1863, Vienna [Austria]) Poet and dramatist who added a new psychological dimension to German drama and made original use of G.W.F. Hegel's concepts of history and the process of change to dramatize conflicts in his historical tragedies.

Hebbel was brought up in poverty. After his father's death in 1827, he spent seven years as a clerk and messenger to a tyrannical parish bailiff. He founded a literary circle and had his first poems published in a local newspaper and in a Hamburg fashion magazine. At this time he started his *Tagebücher* (1885–87; "Diaries"), which became an important and revealing literary confession. Provided with a small income from his patrons, he went to Heidelberg to study law but soon left for Munich to devote himself to philosophy, history, and literature. Unable to publish his poems, however, he returned to Hamburg penniless and ill.

Hebbel's powerful prose play *Judith*, based on the biblical story, brought him fame in 1840; it was followed by his poetic drama *Genoveva* (1841). Still in need of money, Hebbel received a grant from the Danish king to spend a year in Paris and another in Italy. While in Paris in 1843 he wrote most of the realistic tragedy *Maria Magdalene*; this skillfully constructed play, technically a model "tragedy of common life," is a striking portrayal of the lower middle class.

He wrote the verse play *Herodes und Mariamne* (published 1850, performed 1849) and the prose tragedy *Agnes Bernauer* (1855). *Gyges und sein Ring* (1856; *Gyges and His Ring*) shows Hebbel's predilection for involved psychological problems. His later work *Die Nibelungen* (1862)—including *Der gehörnte Siegfried* ("The Invulnerable Siegfried"), *Siegfrieds Tod* ("Siegfried's Death"), and *Kriemhilds Rache* ("Kriemhild's Revenge")—grandiosely pictures the clash between heathen and Christian.

Hebe \'hē-,bē\ (from Greek *hēbē*, "young maturity," "bloom of youth") In Greek mythology, daughter of Zeus and Hera. In Homer this princess was a divine domestic, appearing most frequently as cupbearer to the gods. The goddess of youth, she was also associated with the hero-god Heracles, whose bride she became when he was received into heaven. Hebe was sometimes identified with the Roman deity Juventas.

Hébert \ā-'ber, 'ā-,ber\, Anne (b. Aug. 1, 1916, Sainte-Catherine-de-Fossambault, Que., Can.) French-Canadian poet, novelist, and playwright, noted for her examination of the lives of the Quebeçois. She wrote about both the brutal and the brutalized and many aspects of violence in modern life.

Hébert began writing poetry in her teens under the tutelage of her father, Maurice-Lang Hébert, a distinguished literary critic, and her cousin, Hector de Saint-Denys-Garneau, a poet. Her early poetry, *Les Songes en équilibre* (1942; "Dreams in Equilibrium") and *Le Tombeau des rois* (1953; *The Tomb of the Kings*), reveals the poet in anguish, trading a child's joy of living for the stifling responsibilities of maturity. *Oeuvre poétique, 1950–1990* was published in 1993.

In the 1950s Hébert moved to Paris. Her first novel, *Les Chambres de bois* (1958; *The Silent Rooms*), and the short stories in *Le Torrent* (1950; *The Torrent*) take place in a world of symbolism and fantasy. She also wrote *Kamouraska* (1970), a suspenseful novel set in 19th-century Quebec, and *Les Enfants du sabbat* (1975; *Children of the Black Sabbath*), a novel of sorcery and demonic possession, which won for Hébert a 1975

Governor General's Award. *Les Fous de bassan* (1982; *In the Shadow of the Wind*; film, 1986) won the Prix Fémina in 1982. Two later outstanding novels are *Le Premier Jardin* (1988; *The First Garden*) and *L'Enfant chargé de songes* (1992; "The Child Burdened with Dreams"). Her plays were collected as *Le Temps sauvage* (1967).

Hebrew Bible, The *see* TANAKH.

Hecataeus \,hek-ə-'tē-əs\ of Miletus \mi-'lē-təs\ (fl. 6th–5th century BC, Ionia) Greek author of an early history and of a book of travels. During the time of the Persian invasion, he tried to dissuade the Ionians from revolt against Persia.

One of his two known works, the *Genealogia*, or *Historiai*, seems to have been a systematic account of the traditions and mythology of the Greeks, but comparatively few fragments of it survive. There are more than 300 fragments, however, of the *Ges periodos*, or *Periegesis* ("Tour Round the World"), which was written in two parts—one covering Europe, the other "Asia" (which included Egypt and North Africa). He was, in general, the pioneer in those geographic and ethnographic fields that remained always attractive to the Greek historians.

Hecate \'hek-ə-tē, *in the work of Shakespeare and Milton usually* 'hek-it\ Goddess accepted at an early date into Greek religion but probably derived from the Carians in southwestern Asia Minor. In Hesiod she is the daughter of the Titan Perses and the nymph Asteria and has power over heaven, earth, and sea; hence, she bestows wealth and all the blessings of daily life.

Hecate was the chief goddess presiding over magic and spells. Pillars called Hecataea stood at crossroads and doorways, perhaps to keep away evil spirits.

Hecatoncheires \,hek-ə-tän-'kī-,rēz\ The three 100-armed, 50-headed creatures born of Gaea, fathered by Uranus. BRIAREUS is the best known of them. The other two are Cottus and Gyes. The name means literally "those with a hundred hands."

Hecht \'hekt\, Ben (b. Feb. 28, 1894, New York, N.Y., U.S.—d. April 18, 1964, New York City) American journalist, novelist, playwright, and film writer. His play *The Front Page* (1928), written with Charles MacArthur, influenced the public's idea of the newspaper world and the newspaperman's idea of himself.

Hecht was the son of Russian-Jewish immigrants. After attending high school in Racine, Wis., he moved to Chicago and worked as a reporter for the *Chicago Journal* and for the *Chicago Daily News*, which sent him to Berlin during the revolutionary upheaval following World War I. From this experience came some of the material for his first novel, *Erik Dorn* (1921). For the *Daily News* he developed a column that formed the basis of his collection of sketches *A Thousand and One Afternoons in Chicago* (1922).

He was associated in Chicago with the novelist and poet Maxwell Bodenheim. Lively reminiscences of these years are found in his *Gaily, Gaily* (1963), *Letters from Bohemia* (1946), and his autobiography, *A Child of the Century* (1954).

Hecht later divided his time between New York City and Hollywood. *Twentieth Century* (produced 1932) was the first successful stage comedy on which he collaborated with MacArthur. In Hollywood he wrote scripts in the 1930s and 40s, often with MacArthur, for a number of successful motion pictures.

Hecht's last Broadway success was *Ladies and Gentlemen* (produced 1939; also with MacArthur). Columns written for the New York newspaper *PM* appeared as *1001 Afternoons in New York* (1941). Among his other works are *A Guide for the Bedevilled* (1944), an analysis of anti-Semitism; *Collected Stories* (1945); and *Perfidy* (1961).

Hector \\'hek-tər\\ In Greek legend, the eldest son of the Trojan king Priam and his queen Hecuba. Hector was the husband of Andromache and the chief warrior of the Trojan army. In Homer's *Iliad* he is represented as an ideal warrior and the mainstay of Troy. His chief exploits during the Trojan War are his defense of the wounded Sarpedon, his fight with Ajax, and the storming of the Greek ramparts. Achilles slays Hector and drags his body behind his chariot in revenge for Hector's slaying of his friend Patroclus. Aphrodite and Apollo preserve Hector's body from corruption and mutilation, and, when Achilles eventually returns the corpse, it is given a hero's burial.

Hecuba \\'hek-yū-bə\\ (*Greek* Hekabē) In Greek legend, the principal wife of the Trojan king Priam, mother of Hector. When Troy was captured by the Greeks, Hecuba was taken prisoner. According to Euripides (in *Hecuba*), she put out the eyes of Polymestor, king of Thrace, and murdered his two sons in revenge for Polymestor's slaughter of her one remaining son. Later, she was turned into a dog, and her grave became a mark for ships.

Hecuba \\'hek-yū-bə\\ (*Greek* Hekabē) Drama by EURIPIDES, performed about 425 BC. Set in the aftermath of the Trojan War, the play traces the humiliation and degradation that reduces the aging Trojan queen Hecuba, now a widowed slave, to a woman driven by brutal and remorseless desire for revenge. She persuades the Greek commander Agamemnon to allow her vengeance against Polymestor, who had killed her son. After she and her women blind Polymestor and murder his two young sons, Agamemnon judges that justice has been done, and Polymestor is led away, but not before he prophesies Hecuba's hideous death and Agamemnon's own murder by Clytemnestra's hand.

Hedāyat \\'hed-,ō-,yat\\ Ṣādeq or Ṣādeq-e (b. Feb. 17, 1903, Tehrān [Iran]—d. April 4, 1951, Paris, Fr.) Iranian author who was influenced by foreign culture and by the history and lore of ancient Persia.

Born into a prominent aristocratic family, Hedāyat was educated in Tehrān, France, and Belgium. He was immensely drawn to the works of Edgar Allan Poe, Guy de Maupassant, his contemporary Franz Kafka, and the 19th-century masters Anton Chekhov and Fyodor Dostoyevsky. He translated many works of Kafka, including *In der Strafkolonie* (*In the Penal Colony*), for which he wrote a revealing introduction called "Payām-e Kafka" ("Kafka's Message"). Returning to Iran in 1930 after four years, he published his first book of short stories, *Zendeh be gūr* (1930; "Buried Alive"), and *Sē qaṭreh-khūn* (1932; "Three Drops of Blood"). He also began to write plays, and in 1930 his first, *Parvīn dokhtar-e Sāsān* ("Parvin Daughter of Sāsān"), appeared.

Hedāyat was the central figure in Tehrān's intellectual circles. He began to develop his interests in Iranian folklore and published *Osāneh* (1931), a collection of popular songs, and *Neyrangestān* (1932). He also translated the works of leading European authors, and he began to study history, starting with the Sāsānian period (224–651), and the Pahlavi (or Middle Persian) language. In 1936–37 he lived in the Parsee Zoroastrian community in Bombay in order to further his knowledge of that ancient Iranian religion.

One of his most famous novels, *Būf-A Kūr* (1937; *The Blind Owl*), is a deeply pessimistic, kafkaesque novel. In 1951, overwhelmed by despair, he left Tehrān and went to Paris, where he took his own life.

Hedberg \\'hed-berʸ, *Angl* -bərg\\ Olle (b. May 31, 1899, Norrköping, Swed.—d. 1974) Swedish novelist who satirized the conventional world of the middle classes with stylistic precision and elegant craftsmanship.

Beginning with *Rymmare och fasttagare* (1930; *Prisoner's Base*), Hedberg produced a full-length novel almost every year for several decades. In his works of the 1940s, a search for moral and religious values, as in *Bekänna färg* (1947; "Confess Color"), takes the place of his otherwise more satiric attitude. In his *Dockan dansar klockan slår* (1955; "The Doll Dances, the Clock Strikes") and *Djur i bur* (1959; *Animals in Cages*), he is strongly disillusioned and mercilessly castigates the hypocrisy and sterility of middle-class society. *Tänk att ha hela livet främför sig* ("Imagine Having Your Entire Life Ahead of You") was published the year he died.

Hedda Gabler \\'hed-då-'gåb-lər\\ Drama in four acts by Henrik IBSEN, published in 1890 and produced the following year. The work reveals Hedda Gabler as a selfish, cynical woman bored by her marriage to the scholar Jørgen Tesman. Her father's pair of pistols provide intermittent diversion, as do the attentions of the ne'er-do-well Judge Brack. When Thea Elvestad, a longtime acquaintance of Hedda's, reveals that she has left her husband for the writer Ejlert Løvborg, who once pursued Hedda, the latter becomes vengeful. Learning that Ejlert has forsworn liquor, Hedda first steers him to a rowdy gathering at Brack's and subsequently burns the reputedly brilliant manuscript that he loses there while drunk. Witnessing his desperation, she sends him one of the pistols and he shoots himself. Brack deduces Hedda's complicity and demands that she become his mistress in exchange for his silence about the matter. Instead, she ends her ennui with the remaining pistol. The work is remarkable for its nonjudgmental depiction of an immoral, destructive character, one of the most vividly realized women in dramatic literature.

Hédelin *see* AUBIGNAC.

Heep, Uriah \\yū-'rī-ə-'hēp\\ Fictional character, the unctuous villain in Charles Dickens' novel DAVID COPPERFIELD whose name has become a byword for a falsely humble hypocrite.

Heiberg \\'hī-berg\\, Gunnar (Edvard Rode) (b. Nov. 18, 1857, Christiania [now Oslo], Nor.—d. Feb. 22, 1929, Oslo) Dramatist and exponent of Expressionism who is considered the most noteworthy Norwegian playwright after Henrik Ibsen.

Heiberg's plays were always highly provocative, and their opening nights caused the greatest scandals in the history of Norwegian theater. *Paradesengen* (1913; "The Catafalque") deals with the exploitation of a famous man's death by his children in such a way that it was clear to contemporary audiences that the dying hero was meant to be the beloved Norwegian writer Bjørnstjerne Bjørnson. His political plays, the ironically titled *Jeg vil værge mit land* (1912; "I Will Defend My Country") and *Folkeraadet* (1897; "The People's Council"), were violently booed.

His erotic plays mainly became known in other countries: *Balkonen* (1894; *The Balcony*) and *Kjærlighetens tragedie* (1904; *The Tragedy of Love*). In Norway, Heiberg's first play, *Tante Ulrikke* (1884; "Aunt Ulrikke"), has remained the most frequently performed of his works.

Heiberg \\'hī-,ber *with* r *labialized*\\, Johan Ludvig (b. Dec. 14, 1791, Copenhagen, Den.—d. Aug. 25, 1860, Bonderup) Playwright, poet, literary historian, and critic who brought the Danish Romantic movement to an end and established a new era of topical, sophisticated, and satirical literature; he also introduced both Hegelian philosophy and vaudeville, or ballad opera, to Denmark.

Heiberg was the son of the political writer Peter Andreas Heiberg and his wife, the novelist Thomasine, Baroness

Gyllembourg-Ehrensvärd. Although he originally planned an academic career and taught Danish at the University of Kiel, he turned to writing about 1825. Heiberg, who was a central figure in Danish literature and criticism for many years, originated Danish vaudeville, a form of popular folk musical in which critical and satirical verses were set to well-known melodies. Besides his vaudeville pieces, Heiberg's most frequently performed plays are *Elverhøj* (1828; "Elfinhill") and *En sjæl efter døden* (1841; *A Soul After Death*), which was his greatest literary success. From 1827 to 1830 Heiberg edited an influential literary paper in Copenhagen in which he introduced many new talents, most significantly Søren Kierkegaard and Hans Christian Andersen.

Heiberg \\'hī-,ber *with r labialized*\\, Peter Andreas (b. Nov. 16, 1758, Vordingborg, Den.—d. April 30, 1841, Paris, Fr.) Danish poet, playwright, and militant spokesman for the radical political ideas generated by the French Revolution.

Heiberg composed verse and prose satires in which he attacked social snobbery and political conservatism. A representative example is his play *De Vonner og de Vanner* (1792; "The Vons and the Vans"). From 1787 to 1793 he published the periodical *Rigsdalersedlens hændelser* ("The Adventures of a Bank Note") as a vehicle for his opinions. Exiled in 1800 for his writings, he spent his last 40 years in France. He was the father of the dramatist Johan Ludvig Heiberg.

Heidelberg Romantics \\'hī-dəl-,berk, *Angl* -bərg\\ Poets of the second phase of Romanticism in Germany, who were centered in Heidelberg about 1806. Their leaders were Clemens Brentano, Achim von Arnim, and Joseph von Görres; their short-lived organ was the *Zeitung für Einsiedler* ("Journal for Hermits"). The most characteristic production of this school was the collection of folk songs entitled *Des Knaben Wunderhorn* (1805–08; "The Boy's Magic Horn"). The group stimulated their compatriots' interest in German history and founded the study of German philology and medieval literature. They also strengthened the national and patriotic spirit and helped prepare the way for the rising against Napoleon.

Heidenstam \\'hīd-ən-stäm\\, Verner von, *in full* Carl Gustaf Verner von Heidenstam (b. July 6, 1859, Olshammar, Swed.—d. May 20, 1940, Övralid) Poet and prose writer who led the literary reaction to the naturalistic movement in Sweden, calling for a renaissance of the literature of fantasy, beauty, and nationalism. He won the Nobel Prize for Literature in 1916.

Heidenstam's first book of poems, *Vallfart och vandringsår* (1888; "Pilgrimage and Wander Years"), full of the fables of the southern lands and the philosophy of the East, was an immediate success. With his essay "Renässans" (1889) he first voiced his opposition to naturalism and the realistic literary program that had been rather short-lived in Sweden.

His efforts toward the realization of a new Swedish literature include two volumes of poems: *Dikter* (1895; "Poems") and his last volume, *Nya dikter* (1915; "New Poems"), many of which are translated in *Sweden's Laureate: Selected Poems of Verner von Heidenstam* (1919). He also wrote several volumes of historical fiction, the most important of which are *Karolinerna*, 2 vol. (1897–98; *The Charles Men*), and *Folkungaträdet* (1905–07; *The Tree of the Folkungs*).

Heidi \\'hī-dē\\ Classic children's novel by Johanna SPYRI, published in two volumes in 1880–81. The title character is a five-year-old orphan who is sent to the Swiss mountains to live with her grandfather. A usually austere man who lives simply in an Alpine hut, he is cheered by the company of his granddaughter. Heidi, who enjoys her isolated, simple life and her friendship with Peter, a young goatherd, is removed by her Aunt Dete to Frankfurt. There she yearns for the mountains,

Peter, and her beloved grandfather, and she is eventually allowed to return to them.

Heights of Macchu Picchu, The \\,mäch-ü-'pēch-ü\\ Poem by Pablo NERUDA, published in 1947 as "Alturas de Macchu Picchu" and later included as part of his epic CANTO GENERAL. It is considered one of Neruda's greatest poetic works.

The 12 sections of *The Heights of Macchu Picchu* represent separate phases of a journey, literally and figuratively. The poet begins by recounting his failure to find the fulfillment in love that he has spent much of his life seeking. After traveling around the country he has returned home, and, seeking creativity in the midst of meaningless death and his own loneliness, he climbs to and views the lost Inca city of Macchu Picchu. He contemplates the ancients who built the city and concludes that their lives were as meaningless and also as noble as those of his contemporaries.

Heijermans \\'hei-ər-mäns, *Angl* 'hā-\\, Herman (b. Dec. 3, 1864, Rotterdam, Neth.—d. Nov. 22, 1924, Zandvoort) Dutch author and playwright whose work attacked all aspects of bourgeois hypocrisy.

After failing in business, Heijermans became a journalist in Amsterdam. His novel *Kamertjeszonde* (1898; "Petty Sin"), published under the pseudonym Koos Habbema, sharply criticizes prevailing sexual attitudes. In his play *Allerzielen* (1905; "All Souls"), Heijermans treats the theme of the repudiation of a "fallen" woman.

Among his more politically oriented plays, *Op hoop van zegen* (1901; *The Good Hope*) has as its theme the exploitation of fishermen, and *Glück auf* (1911; "Good Luck"), the exploitation of miners. In the novel *Diamantstad* (1904; "Diamond Town") Heijermans realistically depicts the life of the Amsterdam diamond cutters.

In addition to these straightforward social critiques, Heijermans wrote satirical sketches under the name Samuel Falkland. His skillful use of irony is also evident in the play *De wijze kater* (1917; "The Wise Tomcat").

Heike monogatari \\'hä-ke-'mō-nō-gä-tä-rē\\ ("The Tale of the Heike") Medieval Japanese heroic epic, which is to Japanese literature what the *Iliad* is to Western literature—a prolific source of later dramas, ballads, and tales. It stems from unwritten traditional tales and variant texts composed in the late 12th and early 13th centuries. They were first gathered together (*c.* 1220) by an unknown author and eventually came to form a single epic of 12 books. Based on the actual historical struggle between the Taira (Heike) and Minamoto (Genji) families that engulfed Japan in civil war during the second half of the 12th century, the *Heike monogatari* features the exploits of Minamoto Yoshitsune, the most popular hero of Japanese legend, and recounts many episodes of the heroism of aristocratic samurai warriors. Its overall theme is the tragic downfall of the Taira family. Throughout, there is a tone of Buddhist skepticism toward the fleeting fortunes of the world.

Heilbrun \\'hīl-,brən\\, Carolyn (Gold), *pseudonym* Amanda Cross \\'krós\\ (b. Jan. 13, 1926, East Orange, N.J., U.S.) American scholar and feminist literary critic who became known for mystery stories written under her pseudonym.

Heilbrun attended Wellesley College and Columbia University, and in 1960 she joined the faculty of Columbia. Among her scholarly works are *The Garnett Family* (1961), about the British literary family that included noted translator Constance Garnett, and *Christopher Isherwood* (1970). Heilbrun also edited *Lady Ottoline's Album* (1976) and coedited *The Representation of Women in Fiction* (1983). In *Toward a Recognition of Androgyny* (1973) and *Reinventing Womanhood* (1979) she examined the effects of rigid gender roles. *Hamlet's Mother and Other Women* (1990) is a collection of her feminist literary essays.

Not until Heilbrun received tenure from Columbia did she reveal that she was the author of the Amanda Cross mysteries, which feature the literate amateur detective Professor Kate Fansler and are typically set in academic surroundings.

Heimdall \ˈhām-ˌdäl\, *also called* Heimdallr \-ˌdäl-ər\   In Norse mythology, the watchman of the gods. Called the shining god and whitest skinned of the gods, Heimdall dwelt at the entry to Asgard, where he guarded Bifrost, the rainbow bridge. Heimdall kept the "ringing" horn, Gjallarhorn, which could be heard throughout heaven, earth, and the lower world; it was believed that he would sound the horn to summon the gods when their enemies, the giants, drew near at the Ragnarǫk, the end of the world of gods and mortals. When that time came, Heimdall and his enemy Loki would slay each other.

Heimkehrerliteratur \ˈhīm-ˌkär-ər-lit-er-ä-ˌtür\ [German, literally, literature of those who have returned home]   In German literature, body of works written after World War II that portray the efforts of soldiers to come to terms with civilian life. An example is Wolfgang Borchert's *Draussen vor der Tür* (1947; *The Man Outside*).

Heimskringla \ˈhāms-ˌkriŋ-lə\ ("Orb of the World")   Collection of sagas of the early Norwegian kings, written about 1220 by the Icelandic poet and chieftain SNORRI STURLUSON. The collection opens with the *Ynglinga saga*, which traces the descent of the Norwegian kings from the god Odin, who is presented by Snorri as a historical figure, a great conqueror and master wizard from the Black Sea region who settled in the Scandinavian Peninsula, where his knowledge of runes and magic made him ruler over all. It continues with 16 lives of high kings, covering the period of the development of the Norsemen as roving Vikings, through their conversion to Christianity and their eventual settling down to the unification and administration of Norway. One-third of the work is devoted to the 15-year reign of Olaf II Haraldsson, the patron saint of Norway. Many of the other lives are abbreviated. Among the more interesting are those of Harald Fairhair, Haakon the Good, and Olaf Tryggvason.

Heine \ˈhī-nə\, Heinrich, *in full* Christian Johann Heinrich Heine, *original name* (until 1825) Harry Heine (b. Dec. 13, 1797, Düsseldorf [Germany]—d. Feb. 17, 1856, Paris, Fr.)   German poet whose international reputation far exceeded appreciation in his homeland, where he provoked controversy.

Brown Brothers

Heine was born of Jewish parents. Though his family preferred that he become a businessman, Heine eventually took a degree in law, and in 1825, in order to make possible a civil service career (closed to Jews at that time), he resentfully converted to Protestantism. Despite these measures, he never practiced law or held a position in government service.

Heine's reputation grew steadily with the publication of his poems. His first collection, *Buch der Lieder* (1827; THE BOOK OF SONGS), was largely inspired by his youthful and unrequited infatuation with one, or possibly two, of his cousins. After a walking tour through the Harz Mountains, he fictionalized his modest adventure, weaving into it elements both of poetic imagination and sharp-eyed social comment. "Die Harzreise" ("The Harz Journey") became the first piece of what were to be four volumes of *Reisebilder* (1826–31; *Pictures of Travel*), a whimsical amalgam of fact and fiction, autobiography, social criticism, and literary polemic that was widely imitated.

In 1831 Heine went to Paris, where he was to live for the rest of his life. There his concern with political and social matters deepened as he watched the development of limited democracy and a capitalist order in the France of the citizen-king, Louis-Philippe. He wrote a series of penetrating newspaper articles about the development of democracy and capitalism in France, which he collected in book form as *Französische Zustände* (1833; "French Affairs"). He followed this with two studies of German culture, *Die romantische Schule* (1836; *The Romantic School*) and "Zur Geschichte der Religion und Philosophie in Deutschland" (1834–35; "On the History of Religion and Philosophy in Germany"), in which he mounted a criticism of Germany's present and recent past and argued the long-range revolutionary potential of the German heritage of the Reformation, the Enlightenment, and modern critical philosophy. The books were conceived with a French audience in mind and were originally published in French. His critical and satirical writings were unacceptable to the German censors, and at the end of 1835 the Federal German Diet tried to enforce a nationwide ban on all his works. Heine was surrounded by police spies, and his voluntary exile became an imposed one. In 1840–43 he wrote another series of newspaper articles about French subjects, which he reedited and published as *Lutezia* (1854).

Heine's second volume of poems, *Neue Gedichte* (1844; *New Poems*), reflected his newfound sense of social engagement. After a visit to Germany, he published a long verse satire, *Deutschland: Ein Wintermärchen* (1844; *Germany, A Winter's Tale*), a stinging attack on reactionary conditions in Germany. He also wrote another long poem, *Atta Troll. Ein Sommernachtstraum* (1847; *Atta Troll, A Midsummer Night's Dream*), a spoof of radical pomposity and the clumsiness of contemporary political verse.

After 1844 Heine suffered financial reversals and painful physical deterioration. His third volume of poems, *Romanzero* (1851), is full of heartrending laments and bleak glosses on the human condition; many of these poems are now regarded as among his finest.

Heinesen \ˈhī-nə-sən\, William (b. Jan. 15, 1900, Tórshavn, Faroe Islands, Den.—d. March 12, 1991, Tórshavn)   Faroese writer of Danish-language poetry and fiction in which he used his remote North Atlantic homeland as a microcosmic setting for universal social, psychological, and cosmic themes.

In 1921 Heinesen published a volume of lyric poetry, *Arktiske Elegier* ("Arctic Elegies"). He wrote three more collections of poetry before he returned to the Faroe Islands in 1932. In his novels, beginning with *Blæsende Gry* (1934; "Windswept Dawn"), he combined elements of tragedy, comedy, satire, allegory, and social criticism to explore such themes as the harshness of nature and the rights of the individual as opposed to the collective good. His other works include the novels *Noatun* (1938; *Niels Peter*), *De fortabte Spillemænd* (1950; *The Lost Musicians*), *Det gode Håb* (1964; "The Good Hope"), and *Tårnet ved Verdens Ende* (1976; *The Tower at the End of the World*), as well as several volumes of short stories. He was elected to the Danish Academy in 1961.

Heinlein \ˈhīn-līn\, Robert Anson (b. July 7, 1907, Butler, Mo., U.S.—d. May 8, 1988, Carmel, Calif.)   Prolific American writer considered to be one of the most sophisticated of science-fiction writers. He did much to develop the genre, producing such novels as *Starship Troopers* (1959), *Stranger in a Strange Land* (1961), *The Moon Is a Harsh Mistress* (1966), and *I Will Fear No Evil* (1970).

Heinlein was an established professional writer from 1939. His first story, "Life-Line," was published in the action-adventure pulp magazine *Astounding Science Fiction*, for which he wrote until 1942, when he began war work as an engineer. Heinlein returned to writing in 1947, with an eye toward a more sophisticated audience. His first book, *Rocket Ship Galileo* (1947), was followed by a large number of novels and story collections, including works for children and young adults. After the 1940s he largely avoided shorter fiction. His popularity probably reached its peak after the publication of his best-known work, *Stranger in a Strange Land*, which attracted a cult audience. Among his more popular books are *The Green Hills of Earth* (1951), *Double Star* (1956), *The Door into Summer* (1957), *Citizen of the Galaxy* (1957), and *Methuselah's Children* (1958). Later works include *Friday* (1982) and *The Cat Who Walks Through Walls: A Comedy of Manners* (1985). Heinlein won an unprecedented four Hugo Awards.

Heinrich von Meissen   *see* FRAUENLOB.

Heinrich von Melk \ˈhīn-riḵ-fȯn-ˈmelk\ (fl. 1150)   Early Middle High German poet, the first satirist in German literature.

A Benedictine lay brother of the Austrian monastery of Melk, he composed the vivid poem *Von des Tôdes gehügede* (c. 1150–60; "Remembrance of Death" or "Memento Mori"). The monkish theme is traditional, but the poem's satiric edge and unflattering description of the contemporary emerging feudal and courtly culture is new. Another poem, *Vom Priesterleben* ("About Priestly Life"), is an ironic picture of the behavior of worldly priests.

Heinrich von Morungen \ˈhīn-riḵ-fȯn-ˈmȯr-ù̇ŋ-ən\ (d. 1222, near Leipzig [Germany])   German minnesinger, one of the few notable courtly poets from east-central Germany.

A native of Thuringia, he spent much of his later life in the service of Duke Dietrich of Meissen. His poems, of which some 33 are to be found in the Heidelberg manuscript, are all devoted to the fashionable cult of love. His poems show more originality and spontaneity than those of his contemporaries because of his vivid imagination and the intensity of his emotion. As a result his poems hold their appeal for the modern reader.

Heinrich von Veldeke \ˈhīn-riḵ-fȯn-ˈvel-dek-ə, ˈfel-\ (fl. 1185; b. near Maastricht, Lower Lorraine [now in The Netherlands])   Middle High German poet of noble birth whose *Eneit* (c. 1170–89), telling the story of Aeneas, was the first German court epic to attain artistic mastery.

Heinrich modeled his *Eneit* on the French *Roman d'Enéas* rather than directly on Virgil's *Aeneid*. *Eneit* was written not in Heinrich's native Flemish but in the Franconian literary language of such works as Eilhart von Oberg's *Tristrant und Isalde*.

In the Dutch Limburg dialect, Heinrich also wrote *Servatius* (c. 1170), a religious epic on the life and miracles of the patron saint of Maastricht, and a number of lyric poems. Because of his borderland dialect, he is also claimed by the Dutch as the earliest known poet in their literature.

Heinrich Julius \ˈhīn-riḵ-ˈyü-lē-ủs, *Angl* ˈjü-lē-əs\ (b. Oct. 15, 1564, Schloss Hessen, near Wolfenbüttel, Saxony [Germany]—d. July 20, 1613, Prague [now in Czech Republic])   Duke of Brunswick, a representative of early Baroque culture who was important in the development of German drama. His work in-

corporated the theatrical effect of English Elizabethan drama and the English clown, or fool, into German theater.

A gifted scholar, theologian, and patron of the arts, Heinrich Julius brought English actors and dramatists (notably Thomas Sackville) to Wolfenbüttel and thereafter maintained a troupe at his court. His moralizing plays—*Von einem Wirthe* (1593; "Of an Innkeeper"), *Von einem Buler und einer Bulerin* (1593; "Of Two Lovers"), and *Von einer Ehebrecherin* (1594; "Of an Adulteress")—influenced by the English tradition, treat topics of everyday middle-class life in a realistic style. An autocrat and a persecutor of Jews, Heinrich wrote in a didactic tone aimed at instilling the ideology of the landed aristocracy.

His best-known tragedy was *Von einem Ungeratnen Sohn* (1594; "Of a Spoiled Son"), and his best work, the comedy *Von Vincentio Ladislao* (1594), showed his skill at characterization.

Heinse \ˈhīn-zə\, Wilhelm, *in full* Johann Jakob Wilhelm Heinse (b. Feb. 16, 1746, Langewiesen, near Ilmenau, Thuringia [Germany]—d. June 22, 1803, Aschaffenburg, near Frankfurt am Main)   German novelist and art critic whose work combined grace with the stormy fervor that is characteristic of literature of the Sturm und Drang period and exerted a strong influence on the Romantics.

In Heinse's famous novel *Ardinghello und die glückseligen Inseln* (1787; "Ardinghell and the Blessed Islands"), the hero is an artist and a dreamer who founds a utopia on a Greek island. Glorifying eroticism and the aesthetic life, it is a forerunner of the *Künstlerroman* ("artist's novel") of the Romantic movement. His second novel, *Hildegard von Hohenthal* (1795–96; "Hildegard of Hohenthal"), in which music plays the role painting had in *Ardinghello*, is considered a contribution to musical criticism. In a critical work, *Über einige Gemälde der Düsseldorfer Galerie* (1776–77; "On Several Paintings in the Düsseldorf Gallery"), Heinse stresses the dependence of artistic production on historical and national circumstances and expresses particular appreciation of Peter Paul Rubens.

Heinsius \ˈhīn-sē-ủs\, Daniël, *pseudonym of* Daniël Heins \ˈheins, *Angl* ˈhīnz\ (b. Jan. [June?] 9, 1580, Ghent [Belgium]—d. Feb. 25, 1655, Leiden, Neth.)   Dutch poet, famous in his day as a classical scholar.

At Leiden, Heinsius produced classical editions, verses, and orations from an early age. By 1614 he was professor of history, librarian, and secretary to the senate, and his advice determined the policy of the publishing firm of Elzever. Attacked after three decades of success, he failed to parry the criticisms evoked by his New Testament commentary (1639), and he published little after 1640. His literary productions, which include the Dutch tragedy *Herodes infanticida* (1632), reveal him as a skillful craftsman without originality or taste. He deserves, however, to be remembered for his edition of Aristotle's *Poetics* (1611), his *De tragoediae constitutione* (1611), which decisively influenced the French classical theater, and his Dutch poetry (1616), which was indebted to the French group La Pléiade.

He Knew He Was Right   Novel by Anthony TROLLOPE, published serially from 1868 to 1869, and in two volumes in 1869. It is the story of a wealthy, emotionally unstable husband and his unwarranted jealousy of his wife.

Louis Trevelyan marries Emily Rowley, daughter of the governor of the Mandarin Islands. Upon the young couple's return to England, Trevelyan becomes increasingly jealous of attentions paid to Emily by an aging roué. Trevelyan abducts their son and takes him to Italy, where Trevelyan suffers a complete emotional breakdown. Although a partial reconciliation takes place, Trevelyan dies shortly after his return to England.

Hektorović \ˌhek-ˈtȯr-ȯv-ich\, Petar (b. 1487, Starigrad, Hvar Island, Dalmatia, Republic of Venice [now in Croatia]—d.

March 13, 1572, Starigrad)   Folk poet and collector of Dalmatian songs, an important figure in the renaissance in South Slavic literature that took place beginning in the mid-15th century.

An aristocratic landowner educated in Italy, Hektorović was impressed by the Italian humanist adaptation of classical forms for vernacular literature. Although he wrote Italian and Latin verse and translated Ovid, he also incorporated popular Dalmatian lyrics into his chief work, *Ribanje i ribarsko prigovaranje* (1555; "Fishing and Fishermen's Talk"), a pastoral and philosophic poem.

Hel \'hel\   In Norse mythology, originally the world of the dead; the term later came to mean the goddess of death. Hel was one of the children of the trickster god Loki, and her kingdom, called Niflheim, or the World of Darkness, was said to lie downward and northward. Those who fell in battle did not go to Hel but rather with Odin to Valhalla or with Freyja to the great hall in the Fólkvanger.

Heldenbuch, Das \däs-'hel-dən-,bů̇k\   ("The Book of Heroes")   Collection of German metrical romances of the 13th century. The individual poems deal with heroic themes of the struggles and conquests of the Germanic tribes during the great migrations. The poems of the *Heldenbuch* belong to two cycles. One group deals with the Ostrogothic sagas of Ermenrich (Ermanaric), Etzel (Attila), and Dietrich von Bern, who is its central figure and the ideal type of German medieval hero. The chief romances of this cycle are *Biterolf und Dietlieb*, *Der Rosengarten*, and *Laurin und der kleine Rosengarten*. The second cycle, probably of Franconian origin, is of less literary value. It includes several long, popular romances, notably those about the heroes Hugdietrich, Ortnit, and Wolfdietrich.

Heldenlieder \'hel-dən-,lē-dər\   ("Songs of Heroes")   Body of short, poignant poetic songs celebrating dramatic, and usually tragic, episodes in the lives of the Germanic heroes. Other themes concerned pagan religious ritual, battle songs, and laments for the dead. The heroic lay originated about 375–500, during the period of the great migrations (*Völkerwanderungen*). Because they were transmitted orally, very few survive. The sole survivor in Old High German is the HILDEBRANDSLIED (*c.* 800), which, though incomplete, reveals a sophisticated technique of dramatic selection and treatment.

Originally composed and recited by *Skofs* ("court poets"), the hero songs survived in the Christian era as an underground literature, despite church disapproval, and were later disseminated by *Spielleute* ("wandering minstrels"). In the 13th century the *Heldenlieder* supplied the subject matter for the great Middle High German epic *Nibelungenlied*.

Helen \'hel-ən\ or **Helene** \he-'lēn, -'län\, *also called* Helen of Troy \'trȯi\   In Greek mythology, the most beautiful woman of Greece and the indirect cause of the Trojan War. She was the daughter of Zeus, either by Leda or by Nemesis, and sister of the Dioscuri. Before she married Menelaus, her mortal father (Leda's husband Tyndareus) had asked all of her suitors to take an oath to accept Helen's choice and to support that man if any wrong were done to him. During an absence of Menelaus, Helen fled to Troy with Paris, son of the Trojan king Priam; when Menelaus discovered this, he called on the Greek men who had taken the oath to join him in attacking Troy. Troy was subsequently captured, and Menelaus and Helen then returned to Sparta, where they lived happily until their deaths. *See also* MENELAUS; PARIS.

Helen appears often in later literature, usually as the ideal of female beauty. Christopher Marlowe's *The Tragicall History of D. Faustus* describes her beauty as "the face that launched a thousand ships."

Helen \'hel-ən\ (*Greek* Helenē)   Play by EURIPIDES, performed in 412 BC. In this frankly light work, Euripides deflated one of the best-known legends of Greek mythology, that Helen ran off adulterously with Paris to Troy. Only a phantom Helen goes with Paris, and the real woman pines faithfully in Egypt. When Menelaus is shipwrecked in Egypt on his way home from Troy, he is baffled by the duplicate Helen until the phantom evaporates and permits his reunion with his real wife. The pair then escape from the Egyptian king Theoclymenus, who wants to marry Helen, by fooling him into believing that Menelaus is a shipwrecked mariner who escaped death when Menelaus died. Theoclymenus allows Helen to bury her husband at sea, equipping her and her disguised husband with a fast ship and all manner of funeral items. After they escape, the king learns of their subterfuge and eventually accepts the loss philosophically.

Helenus \'hel-ə-nəs\   In Greek legend, son of King Priam of Troy and his wife Hecuba, brother of Hector and Paris, and twin of the prophetess Cassandra. According to Homer, Helenus was a seer and warrior. After the death of Paris in the Trojan War, Helenus paid suit to Helen but was rejected and withdrew in indignation to Mount Ida, where he was captured by the Greeks. Other accounts, however, claim that Odysseus captured Helenus, or that he surrendered voluntarily in disgust at the treacherous murder of Achilles.

Heliand \'hä-lē-,änd\ ("Savior")   Epic on the life of Christ written in Old Saxon alliterative verse dating to approximately AD 830. The work was an attempt to make the newly imposed Christian religion intelligible to the warlike Saxons. Christ was made a Germanic king who rewarded his retainers (the disciples) with arm rings; Herod's feast became a drinking bout; and Nazarethburg, Bethleemaburg, and Rumuburg had the homely familiarity of Saxon towns.

Extant in four manuscripts, the *Heliand* consists of almost 6,000 lines. A Latin commentary, published in 1562 but usually dated to the 9th century, stated that the *Heliand* was undertaken by an unnamed, eminent Saxon poet at the behest of Louis the Pious, who reigned as Holy Roman emperor from 813 to 840. It is one of the few surviving works of Old Saxon poetry.

Helicon \'hel-i-,kän, -kən\   Mountain of the Helicon range in Boeotia, Greece, between Lake Kopaïs and the Gulf of Corinth. It was celebrated in classical literature as the favorite haunt of Apollo and the Muses; its eastern, or Boeotian, side was particularly sacred. Nearby were the fountains Aganippe and Hippocrene, the latter (according to legend) created by the imprint of the hooves of the winged horse Pegasus.

Heliodorus \,hē-lē-ō-'dȯr-əs\ of Emesa \i-'mā-sə\ (fl. 3rd century AD)   Greek writer from Emesa in Syria, author of the *Aethiopica*, the longest and most readable of the extant ancient Greek novels.

The *Aethiopica* tells the story of an Ethiopian princess and a Thessalian prince who undergo a series of perils (battles, voyages, piracy, abductions, robbery, and torture) before their eventual happy marriage in the heroine's homeland. The work, written in an imitation of pure Attic dialect, shows an uncommon mastery of narrative technique. The *Aethiopica* is pervaded throughout with the author's deep religious faith, which centers in the book on the sun god Helios, who is identified with Apollo. Popular with Byzantine and Renaissance critics because of its good entertainment value and high moral tone, the work was used as a model by Torquato Tasso and Miguel de Cervantes.

Helios \'hē-lē-əs\ (Greek: "Sun")   In Greek mythology, the sun god. He drove a chariot daily from east to west across the sky and sailed around the northerly stream of ocean each night in a huge cup. From the 5th century BC, Apollo, originally a deity of radiant purity, was increasingly interpreted as a sun god.

Hellenistic romance \\,hel-ə-'nis-tik\\ Adventure tale, usually with a quasi-historical setting, in which a virtuous heroine and her valiant lover are separated by innumerable obstacles of human wickedness and natural catastrophe but are finally reunited. A precursor of the modern novel, the Hellenistic romance is the source for such classic love stories as those of Hero and Leander, Pyramus and Thisbe, Sappho and Phaon, and Daphnis and Chloe.

Introduced in the 1st century BC, the form reached its height in the 2nd and 3rd centuries AD in the works of writers such as Chariton, Xenophon, Longus, and Heliodorus.

Hellens \\'hel-əns\\, Franz, *pseudonym of* Frédéric Van Ermenghem \\vän-'er-men-əm\\ (b. Sept. 8, 1881, Brussels, Belg.—d. Jan. 20, 1972, Brussels)   Prolific Belgian novelist and poet who in 1922 helped found *Le Disque vert* ("The Green Disk"), a literary review that brought new poets before the public eye.

Hellens' early novels were strongly influenced by his love for the city of Ghent; thus, his first novel, *En ville morte* (1906; "In the Dead City"), may be considered a regionalist work. Later, however, the influence of Edgar Allan Poe became paramount, and he produced works in which fantasy, mystery, and external realism were mingled, as in the novel *Mélusine* (1920), which reinterpreted an ancient legend with great originality and daring. *Moreldieu* (1946) is the story of a man named Marcel Morel whose totally immoral aspiration is to become like God (hence the name *Moreldieu*, or "Morel the God").

Heller \\'hel-ər\\, Joseph (b. May 1, 1923, Brooklyn, N.Y., U.S.)   American writer whose novel CATCH-22 (1961) was one of the most significant works of protest literature to appear after World War II. The satirical novel was both a critical and a popular success.

Heller flew 60 combat missions as a bombardier with the U.S. Army Air Forces in Europe. He received a M.A. at Columbia University, New York City, in 1949 and was a Fulbright scholar at Oxford (1949–50). He taught English at Pennsylvania State University (1950–52) and worked as an advertising copywriter for the magazines *Time* (1952–56) and *Look* (1956–58) and as promotion manager for *McCall's* (1958–61), meanwhile writing *Catch-22* in his spare time.

Less successful were his later novels, including *Something Happened* (1974), *Good as Gold* (1979), *God Knows* (1984), and *Closing Time* (1994), a sequel to *Catch-22*. Heller's dramatic work includes the play *We Bombed in New Haven* (1968).

hellhound \\'hel-,haùnd\\   A dog represented in mythology (such as that of ancient Greece and Scandinavia) as standing guard in the underworld. In Greek mythology this was Cerberus, a three-headed, dragon-tailed dog.

Hellman \\'hel-mən\\, Lillian (b. June 20, 1905, New Orleans, La., U.S.—d. June 30, 1984, Vineyard Haven, Martha's Vineyard, Mass.)   American playwright and motion-picture screenwriter whose dramas bitterly and forcefully attacked injustice, exploitation, and selfishness.

Hellman's marriage (1925–32) to the playwright Arthur Kober ended in divorce. (She had already begun an intimate friendship with the novelist Dashiell Hammett that would continue until his death in 1961.)

Her dramas exposed various forms in which evil appears—a malicious child's lies about two schoolteachers (THE CHILDREN'S HOUR, 1934), a ruthless family's exploitation of fellow townspeople and of one another (THE LITTLE FOXES, 1939, and *Another Part of the Forest*, 1947), and the irresponsible self-

ishness of the post-World War I generation (WATCH ON THE RHINE, 1941, and *The Searching Wind*, 1944). In the 1950s she showed her skill in handling the more subtle structure of Chekhovian drama (*The Autumn Garden*, 1951) and in translation and adaptation (Jean Anouilh's *The Lark*, 1955, and Voltaire's *Candide*, 1957, in a musical version). Her play *Toys in the Attic* (1960) was followed by another adaptation, *My Mother, My Father, and Me* (1963; from Burt Blechman's novel *How Much?*). She also edited Anton Chekhov's *Selected Letters* (1955) and a collection of stories and short novels, *The Big Knockover* (1966), by Hammett. Her reminiscences, *An Unfinished Woman* (1969), were continued in *Pentimento* (1973) and *Maybe* (1980). Hellman was a longtime supporter of leftist causes, and in *Scoundrel Time* (1976) she detailed her troubles and those of her friends during U.S. Senator Joseph McCarthy's anticommunist witch-hunt of the 1950s. Her *Collected Plays* was published in 1972.

Hellström \\'hel-strœm\\, Gustaf, *in full* Erik Gustaf Hellström (b. Aug. 28, 1882, Kristianstad, Swed.—d. Feb. 27, 1953, Stockholm)   Swedish realistic novelist, journalist, and literary critic.

As foreign correspondent for several Scandinavian newspapers, Hellström lived in Paris, London, and New York City (1907–35), and these cities form the background for much of his early fiction. His best work deals with Swedish themes. *Snörmakare Lekholm får en idé* (1927; *Lacemaker Lekholm Has an Idea*), considered his masterpiece, is a family chronicle set in a provincial garrison town. He also wrote a fictionalized autobiography, *Stellan Petreus: en man utan humor* (1921–52; "Stellan Petreus: A Man Without Humor").

Helm, Matt \\'mat-'helm\\   Fictional character, the intrepid hero of a series of spy novels (1960–83) by American writer Donald Hamilton. Employed by a secret military organization during World War II, Helm is called upon to spy, to kill, to convey military secrets, and, in general, to save the world.

Helmer, Nora \\'nôr-ə-'hel-mər\\   Fictional character, once-meek wife who asserts her independence, in Henrik Ibsen's play A DOLL'S HOUSE.

Héloïse \\ā-lō-'ēz\\ (b. *c.* 1098—d. May 15, 1164, Paraclete Abbey, near Nogent-sur-Seine, Fr.)   Wife of the theologian and philosopher Peter ABELARD, with whom she was involved in one of the best known love tragedies of history. About 1118 Fulbert, Héloïse's uncle and a canon of Notre-Dame, entrusted Abelard with the education of his brilliant niece. The two fell in love and were secretly married after Héloïse returned to Paris from Brittany, where she had given birth to Abelard's son. Her outraged relatives caused Abelard to be attacked and castrated. He became a monk at the monastery of St. Denis, and Héloïse entered a convent. She eventually became an abbess. In the 1130s she and Abelard compiled a collection of their letters and religious correspondence that became part of the extensive literature about their relationship.

Hel-shoes \\'hel-,shüz\\   In Norse mythology, shoes placed on the dead before burial to aid them on the rough road to Hel.

Hemans \\'hem-ənz\\, Felicia Dorothea, *original surname* Browne \\'braún\\ (b. Sept. 25, 1793, Liverpool, Eng.—d. May 16, 1835, Dublin, Ire.)   English poet who owed the immense popularity of her poems to a talent for treating Romantic themes—nature, the picturesque, childhood innocence, travels abroad, liberty, the heroic—with a fluency that sweeps the reader along. Turning aside from life's darker aspects, she made Romanticism easy and respectable. *Poems* (1808), written when she was between 8 and 13, was the first of a series of 24 volumes of verse; from 1816 to 1834 one or more appeared almost every year.

At 19 she married Captain Alfred Hemans, and when they separated seven years later, her prolific output helped to support her five children. Often diffuse and sentimental, she is at her best in her shorter pieces, notably "The Landing of the Pilgrim Fathers," "Dirge," and the well-known "Casabianca" ("The boy stood on the burning deck. . . .").

hemiepes \ˌhem-ē-ˈep-ēz\ *plural* hemiepe \-pē\ [Late Greek *hēmiepés,* from Greek *hēmi-* half + *épē* lines, verses]   In classical prosody, a meter of three dactylic feet, the last of which is catalectic, or missing the two final short syllables. It is the first part of a line of dactylic hexameter or pentameter. The meter was used chiefly in Greek epic and lyric verse and is scanned as − ∪ ∪ | − ∪ ∪ | −.

Heminge \ˈhem-iŋ\, John, *surname also spelled* Heming, Hemminge, *or* Hemmings (b. *c.* 1556—d. Oct. 10, 1630, London, Eng.)   British actor who, with Henry Condell, prepared and oversaw the First Folio (1623) of William Shakespeare's work.

Heminge was an important and prosperous member of the theatrical company that became the King's Men in 1603, apparently serving as business manager for more than 25 years. He was one of the original proprietors of the Globe and Blackfriars theaters. Along with Condell and Richard Burbage, Heminge was closely associated with Shakespeare throughout his career; the three are listed among the principal actors in his plays.

Hemingway \ˈhem-iŋ-ˌwā\, Ernest (Miller) (b. July 21, 1899, Oak Park, Ill., U.S.—d. July 2, 1961, Ketchum, Idaho)   American novelist and short-story writer, awarded the Nobel Prize for Literature in 1954. His adventuresome life and four marriages were widely publicized.

Brown Brothers

On graduation from high school in 1917, Hemingway became a reporter for the Kansas City *Star.* During World War I he served as an ambulance driver for the American Red Cross. On July 8, 1918, he was injured on the Austro-Italian front and was decorated for heroism.

After recuperating in the United States, Hemingway sailed for France as a foreign correspondent for the *Toronto Star.* In Paris he became part of the coterie of expatriate Americans that included Gertrude Stein, Ezra Pound, and F. Scott Fitzgerald.

In 1925 his first important book, a collection of stories called *In Our Time,* was published. The following year he published THE SUN ALSO RISES, the novel with which he scored his first solid success.

Based in Paris, he traveled widely for the skiing, bullfighting, fishing, and hunting that by then formed the background for much of his writing. His position as a master of short fiction was advanced by *Men Without Women* (1927), which included the story HILLS LIKE WHITE ELEPHANTS, and was confirmed by *Winner Take Nothing* (1933), which included A CLEAN, WELL-LIGHTED PLACE. At least in the public view, however, the novel A FAREWELL TO ARMS (1929), with its powerful fusion of love story with war story, overshadowed both.

Hemingway's love of Spain and his passion for bullfighting are evident in *Death in the Afternoon* (1932), a study of a spectacle he saw more as tragic ceremony than as sport. Similarly, an African safari provided the subject for *Green Hills of Africa* (1935). His TO HAVE AND HAVE NOT (1937) reflected his growing concern with social problems.

Acting again as a correspondent, Hemingway made four trips to Spain, then in the throes of civil war. He raised money for the Loyalists and wrote a play called *The Fifth Column,* set in besieged Madrid, that was published with some of his best short stories, including THE SHORT HAPPY LIFE OF FRANCIS MACOMBER and THE SNOWS OF KILIMANJARO, in *The Fifth Column and the First Forty-Nine Stories* (1938). The harvest of his considerable experience of Spain was the novel FOR WHOM THE BELL TOLLS (1940), the best selling of all his books.

After seeing action in World War II, Hemingway returned to his home in Cuba. In 1953, he received the Pulitzer Prize in fiction for the short novel THE OLD MAN AND THE SEA (1952). This book was as enthusiastically praised as his previous novel, *Across the River and into the Trees* (1950), had been damned.

By 1960 Fidel Castro's revolution had driven Hemingway from Cuba. He then moved to Ketchum, Idaho. Anxiety-ridden and depressed, he eventually took his own life, leaving behind many manuscripts. Two of his posthumously published books are *A Moveable Feast* (1964), the memoir of his apprentice days in Paris, and *Islands in the Stream* (1970), three closely related novellas.

hemistich \ˈhem-i-ˌstik\ [Greek *hēmistíchion,* from *hēmi-* half + *stíchos* line, verse]   Half a poetic line, usually determined by the placement of a caesura. It often forms a metrically independent colon or group of feet of less than regular length. The hemistich is used in drama to build up tension through an exchange of half lines of dialogue between at least two characters. The device, which creates the effect of an argument, is called hemistichomythia.

This was used to great effect by William Shakespeare in the following passage from *Richard III*:

> K. Rich. Now, by the world—
> Q. Eliz. 'Tis full of thy foul wrongs.
> K. Rich. My father's death—
> Q. Eliz. Thy life hath that dishonour'd.
> K. Rich. Then, by myself—
> Q. Eliz. Thyself thyself misusest.
> K. Rich. Why then, by God—
> Q. Eliz. God's wrong is most of all.

Hémon \ā-ˈmôⁿ\, Louis (b. Oct. 12, 1880, Brest, Fr.—d. July 8, 1913, near Chapleau, Ont., Can.)   French author of *Maria Chapdelaine,* the best-known novel of French-Canadian pioneer life.

After a few years in England as a journalist and sportswriter, Hémon went to Canada in 1911 and, while working as a farmhand, completed *Maria Chapdelaine,* a realistic presentation of the struggle of men and women faced with the inhospitable soil and climate of the Lac Saint-Jean area in Quebec. Initially serialized in 1914 in the Paris magazine *Le Temps*, the novel appeared in book form in 1915, went through many editions, and was translated into many languages. Hémon did not live to see its success: he was killed in a train accident before it was published.

Henchard, Michael \ˈmī-kəl-ˈhen-chərd\ Fictional character, a well-to-do grain merchant with a guilty secret in his past who is the protagonist of the novel THE MAYOR OF CASTERBRIDGE by Thomas Hardy.

hendecacolic \ˌhen-ˌdek-ə-ˈkōl-ik, -ˈkäl-\ [Greek *héndeka* eleven + *kôlon* colon] In classical prosody, made up of eleven colons, or rhythmic phrases.

hendecasemic \ˌhen-ˌdek-ə-ˈsē-mik\ [Greek *héndeka* eleven + *sêma* mark, sign] In classical prosody, containing or equivalent to eleven morae, or short syllables.

hendecasyllable \ˌhen-ˈdek-ə-ˌsil-ə-bəl, -ˌdek-ə-ˈsil-\ [Greek *hendekasýllabos* having eleven syllables, from *héndeka* eleven + *syllabē* syllable] In poetry, a line of eleven syllables usually arranged as ∪∪−∪∪−∪−∪−− or ∪−−∪∪−∪−∪−−. Hendecasyllables were used often by Greek and Latin poets, and Dante and Petrarch used them in such forms as ottava rima and terza rima.

Henderson the Rain King \ˈhen-dər-sən\ Seriocomic novel by Saul BELLOW, published in 1959. The novel examines the midlife crisis of Eugene Henderson, an unhappy millionaire.

The story concerns Henderson's search for meaning. A larger-than-life 55-year-old who has accumulated money, position, and a large family, he nonetheless feels unfulfilled. He makes a spiritual journey to Africa, where he draws emotional sustenance from experiences with African tribes. Deciding that his true destiny is as a healer, Henderson returns home, planning to enter medical school.

hendiadys \hen-ˈdī-ə-dis\ [Medieval Latin *endiadis,* modification of Greek (in Latin sources) *hén dià dyoîn,* literally, one through two] The expression of an idea by the use of usually two independent words connected by *and* (as in *nice and warm*) instead of the usual combination of an independent word and its modifier (as in *nicely warm*).

Henley \ˈhen-lē\, Beth, *in full* Elizabeth Becker Henley (b. May 8, 1952, Jackson, Miss., U.S.) American playwright of regional dramas set in provincial Southern towns, the best known of which, CRIMES OF THE HEART (1982; film, 1986), was awarded the Pulitzer Prize in 1981.

Henley turned from acting to writing as a career because she felt that the theater offered few good contemporary roles for Southern women. Her first play, the one-act *Am I Blue*, was produced while she was still an undergraduate. *Crimes of the Heart,* her first full-length play, was first produced in 1979.

Later plays include the two-act *The Miss Firecracker Contest* (1979; film, 1988), which concerns the attempts of a small-town young woman of dubious reputation to gain respect by winning a beauty contest; *The Wake of Jamey Foster* (1983); *The Lucky Spot* (1986); and *Abundance* (1991).

Henley \ˈhen-lē\, William Ernest (b. Aug. 23, 1849, Gloucester, Gloucestershire, Eng.—d. July 11, 1903, Woking, near London) British poet, critic, and editor who in his journals introduced the early work of many of the great English writers of the late 19th and early 20th centuries.

As a child Henley contracted a tubercular disease that later necessitated the amputation of one foot. Forced to stay in an infirmary in Edinburgh for 20 months (1873–75) after surgery to save the other leg, he began writing free-verse impression-

istic poems about hospital life that established his reputation. These were included in *A Book of Verses* (1888). Dating from the same period is his most popular poem, "Invictus" (1875), which concludes with the lines "I am the master of my fate;/I am the captain of my soul." The rest of his best-known work is contained in *London Voluntaries* (1893) and *In Hospital* (1903).

Restored to active life, Henley earned his living as an editor, the most brilliant of his journals being the *Scots Observer* of Edinburgh, of which he became editor in 1889. The journal was transferred to London in 1891 and became the *National Observer.* Though conservative in its political outlook, it was liberal in its literary taste and published the early work of Thomas Hardy, George Bernard Shaw, H.G. Wells, Sir James Barrie, and Rudyard Kipling. Henley also edited, with T.F. Henderson, the centenary edition of the poems of Robert Burns.

Henry IV   *see* ENRICO IV.

Henry IV \ˈhen-rē\ (*in full* Henry IV, Part 1 and Henry IV, Part 2) Two-part history play by William SHAKESPEARE, performed in 1597–98 in London; Part 1 was published from "foul papers" (the author's first complete draft) in a 1598 quarto edition, and Part 2 was published in 1600, also in a quarto edition and from foul papers. *Henry IV* follows *Richard II* in Shakespeare's second tetralogy, or sequence of four history plays.

In both parts King Henry IV is often overshadowed by his son, Prince Hal (later Henry V); Hotspur, the young rebel military leader; and Hal's comic companion Sir John Falstaff. Secondary characters are numerous, from prostitutes and country bumpkins to a lord chief justice and country gentlemen.

Set in the 15th century in a kingdom plagued with rebellion, treachery, and shifting alliances, the two parts show the development of Prince Hal from wastrel to ruler. In Part 1, he is presented as a roisterer who nonetheless defends his father in battle; in Part 2, after the death of the king, Hal assumes the throne, and abandoning his rowdy ways and companions, assumes the dignity of the monarchy.

Henry V \ˈhen-rē\ History play in five acts by William SHAKESPEARE, performed in 1598–99 and published in 1600 in a quarto edition. It continues the action of the two-part *Henry IV.*

The action of the play culminates in Henry's campaign in France with a ragtag army to seize the French crown, but the depiction of the character of Henry V (formerly known as Prince Hal) dominates the play. In the first two acts he is shown at peace and war, politic, angry, confident, sarcastic. There is an account of Falstaff's death and of a nervous watch before the Battle of Agincourt when Henry walks disguised among his fearful soldiers and prays for victory. Though almost all the fighting occurs offstage, the recruits, professional soldiers, dukes, and princes are shown preparing for defeat or victory. The king's speech to his troops before battle on St. Crispin's Day is famous for its evocation of a brotherhood in arms, but Shakespeare has placed it in a context full of ironies and challenging contrasts.

There is no doubt that Kate, the French princess, marries Henry out of political necessity, but Shakespeare develops the comedy and earnestness of their wooing so that the need for human trust is evident. Shakespeare also hedges the patriotic fantasy of English greatness with hesitations and qualifications about the validity of the myth of glorious nationhood offered by the Agincourt story. In the end the chorus reminds the audience that England was to be plunged into civil war during the reign of Henry V's son.

Henry VI \ˈhen-rē\ (*in full* Henry VI, Part 1; Henry VI, Part 2; and Henry VI, Part 3) Three-part history play by William SHAKESPEARE, performed in 1589–92. Part 1 was published in the First Folio of 1623; Part 2 appeared in quarto in 1594 and was printed from revised fair copies in the First Folio; and Part 3 appeared in quarto in 1595 and was printed from revised fair copies in the First Folio.

The second and third parts of *Henry VI* were originally performed as *The Contention*, a two-part chronicle dramatizing the events of the so-called War of the Roses, the struggle between the York and Lancaster families for the English throne. In Part 2 the power struggle swirls around the ineffective King Henry VI, until gradually the Duke of York emerges as contender for the throne. The high moments of Part 3 include the murder of the Duke of York by the Lancastrians and, in the final scene, the murder of King Henry by Richard, York's son and the future Richard III. Part 1, about the early part of the reign of Henry VI, concerns events preceding the opening of Part 2; whether it was a first effort at a historical play, written before *The Contention*, or a supplement to it that was written subsequently, it is less inspired.

With this first sequence of history plays (ending with *Richard III*), Shakespeare's initial patriotic celebration of English valor against the French was soon superseded by a mature, disillusioned understanding of the world of politics, culminating in the devastating portrayal of Richard III.

Henry VIII \'hen-rē\ History play in five acts by William SHAKESPEARE, produced in 1612–13 and published in the First Folio of 1623.

Henry VIII has had a long and interesting stage history, but from the mid-19th century a number of critics have doubted that Shakespeare was the sole author of the play. Many scenes and splendid speeches are written in a style very close to that of John Fletcher. Although a story of English history, *Henry VIII* differs from the histories Shakespeare wrote during the reign of Queen Elizabeth I. It is more episodic—more of a pageant and a series of loosely connected crises—than a skillfully plotted drama. It also has a different type of unity: three tragic episodes involving the deaths of Buckingham, Wolsey, and Queen Katharine lead to the prophecy of a new age.

Henry \'hen-rē\, O., *pseudonym of* William Sydney Porter \'pòr-tər\ (b. Sept. 11, 1862, Greensboro, N.C., U.S.—d. June 5, 1910, New York, N.Y.) American short-story writer whose tales romanticized the commonplace—in particular the life of ordinary people in New York City. His stories expressed the effect of coincidence on character through humor, grim or ironic, and often had surprise endings, a device that became identified with his name and cost him critical favor when its vogue had passed.

Porter began writing sketches about 1887, and in 1894 he started a humorous weekly, *The Rolling Stone*. When the venture failed, Porter joined the *Houston Post* as reporter, columnist, and occasional cartoonist.

Porter was convicted of embezzling bank funds while working as a teller in Austin, Texas, and in 1898 he entered a penitentiary at Columbus, Ohio. While in prison he wrote to earn money for support of his daughter Margaret. His stories of adventure in the U.S. Southwest and in Central America were immediately popular with magazine readers, and by the time he emerged from prison W.S. Porter had become O. Henry.

In 1902 O. Henry arrived in New York City. From December 1903 to January 1906 he produced a story a week for the New York *World*, writing also for magazines. His first book, *Cabbages and Kings* (1904), depicted fantastic characters against exotic Honduran backgrounds. Both *The Four Million* (1906), which included his well-known stories THE GIFT OF THE MAGI and THE FURNISHED ROOM, and *The Trimmed Lamp* (1907), which included THE LAST LEAF, explored the

lives of the multitudes of New York in their daily routines and searchings for romance and adventure. *Heart of the West* (1907) presented accurate and fascinating tales of the Texas range.

O. Henry then published, in rapid succession, *The Voice of the City* (1908), *The Gentle Grafter* (1908), *Roads of Destiny* (1909), *Options* (1909), *Strictly Business* (1910), and *Whirligigs* (1910). *Whirligigs* contains perhaps his funniest story, THE RANSOM OF RED CHIEF.

Despite his popularity, O. Henry's final years were marred by ill health, a desperate financial struggle, and alcoholism. After his death three more collected volumes appeared: *Sixes and Sevens* (1911), *Rolling Stones* (1912), and *Waifs and Strays* (1917).

Henry Esmond \'hen-rē-'ez-mənd\ (*in full* The History of Henry Esmond, Esquire) Historical novel by William Makepeace THACKERAY, published in three volumes in 1852.

The story, narrated by Esmond, begins in 1691 when he is 12 and ends in 1718. Its complexity of incident is given unity by Esmond and his second cousin Beatrix, who stand out against a background of London society and the political life of the time. Beatrix dominates the book. One of Thackeray's great creations, she is a heroine of a new type, emotionally complex and compelling, but not a pattern of virtue. Esmond, a sensitive, brave, aristocratic soldier, falls in love with her but is finally disillusioned. Befriended as an orphan by Beatrix' parents, Lord and Lady Castlewood, Henry initially adores Lady Castlewood as a mother and eventually, in his maturity, marries her.

Henryson \'hen-rē-sən\ *or* **Henderson** \'hen-dər-sən\, Robert (b. 1420/30?—d. *c.* 1506) Scottish poet, the finest of early fabulists in Britain. He is described on some early title pages as schoolmaster of Dunfermline—probably at the Benedictine abbey school—and he appears among the dead poets in William Dunbar's *The Lament for the Makaris*, which was printed about 1508.

Henryson's longest work is *The Morall Fabillis of Esope the Phrygian, Compylit in Eloquent & Ornate Scottis*, a version of 13 fables based mainly on John Lydgate and William Caxton and running to more than 400 seven-line stanzas.

In *The Testament of Cresseid*, a narrative and "complaint" in 86 stanzas, Henryson completes the story of Geoffrey Chaucer's *Troilus and Criseyde*. The *Testament* blends Henryson's concern for justice with an attraction to the grotesque and a refined sense of the variability of human love.

Shorter poems ascribed to Henryson include *Orpheus and Eurydice*; a pastourelle, *Robene and Makyne*; and moral narratives and meditations.

Henshaw \'hen-,shò\, James Ene (b. Aug. 29, 1924, Calabar, Nigeria) Nigerian playwright whose plays written in a simple style treating various aspects of African culture and tradition have been widely read and acted in Nigeria.

Henshaw was a physician who received his medical degree from the National University of Ireland, Dublin, before taking up playwriting. One of his first plays, *The Jewels of the Shrine*, was published in the collection *This Is Our Chance: Plays from West Africa* (1957). His second collection, *Children of the Goddess, and Other Plays* (1964), handled such themes as the inefficiency of a local village court because of the drunkenness of its members and the struggle between local authorities and missionaries over the propagation of Christianity in a 19th-century Nigerian village. *Medicine for Love: A Comedy in Three Acts* (1964) is a satire with serious overtones. Other plays include the comedy *Dinner for Promotion* (1967), *Enough Is Enough: A Play of the Nigerian Civil War* (produced 1975), and *A Song to Mary Charles (Irish Sister of Charity)* (1984).

Henty \'hen-tē\, George Alfred (b. Dec. 8, 1832, Trumpington, Cambridgeshire, Eng.—d. Nov. 16, 1902, on Weymouth harbor, Dorset)   English writer of a series of adventure stories for boys.

Henty fought in the Crimean War, becoming a correspondent to the *Morning Advertiser*, and in 1865 he became a correspondent for the *Standard*, for which he reported several major wars in Europe.

Meanwhile Henty had begun to write books of adventure for boys, often using his own experiences as a background and basing his stories on historical events. *Out on the Pampas* (1870) began a series of some 80 historical novels for boys, including *Under Drake's Flag* (1883), *With Clive in India* (1884), *The Cat of Bubastes* (1889), *On the Irrawaddy* (1897), and *With Roberts to Pretoria* (1902). Henty was a great exponent of "manliness" in boys' books. His books also are notable for their jingoistic tone and their smug idealization of the British Empire.

Hephaestus or **Hephaistos** \hi-'fes-təs\   In Greek mythology, the god of fire. Born lame, Hephaestus was cast from heaven in disgust by his mother, Hera, and again by his father, Zeus, after a family quarrel. His ill-matched consort was Aphrodite or Charis, the personification of Grace.

As god of fire, Hephaestus became the divine smith and patron of craftsmen; the natural volcanic or gaseous fires already connected with him were often considered to be his workshops. His Roman counterpart was VULCAN.

hephthemimeral caesura \ˌhef-thə-'mim-ər-əl\ [Greek *hephthēmimerēs* containing seven halves, containing three and a half feet, from *heptá* seven + *hēmi-* half + *méros* part]   *see* CAESURA.

heptameter \hep-'tam-ə-tər\   In poetry, a line of seven feet. *See* FOURTEENER.

heptastich \'hep-tə-ˌstik\   In poetry, a group, stanza, or poem of seven lines.

heptasyllable \ˌhep-tə-'sil-ə-bəl\   In poetry, a line of seven syllables.

Hera \'hir-ə, 'hēr-, 'her-\   In Greek mythology, a daughter of the Titans Cronus and Rhea, sister and wife of Zeus, and queen of the Olympian gods. The Romans identified her with their own JUNO. Hera played an important part in Greek literature, appearing most frequently as the jealous wife of Zeus and pursuing with vindictive hatred the heroines who were beloved by him. In general, Hera was worshiped in two main capacities: (1) as consort of Zeus and queen of heaven and (2) as goddess of marriage and of the life of women. The animal especially sacred to Hera was the cow. Her sacred bird was first the cuckoo, later the peacock. She was represented as a majestic and severe, though youthful, matron. *See also* ZEUS.

Heracles \'her-ə-ˌklēz\, *Greek* Herakles, *Roman* Hercules. Most famous hero of Greco-Roman mythology. Traditionally, Heracles was the son of Zeus and Alcmene (granddaughter of Perseus). Zeus swore that the next son born of the Perseid house should become ruler of Greece, but by a trick of Zeus's jealous wife, Hera, another child, the sickly Eurystheus, was born first and became king. When Heracles grew up, he had to serve him and also suffer the vengeful persecution of Hera. His first exploit, in fact, was the strangling of two serpents that she had sent to kill him in his cradle.

Later Heracles was obliged to become the servant of Eurystheus, who imposed upon Heracles the famous Labors. These were later arranged in a cycle of 12, usually as follows: (1) the slaying of the Nemean lion, whose skin he thereafter wore; (2) the slaying of the nine-headed Hydra of Lerna; (3) the capture of the elusive hind (or stag) of Arcadia; (4) the capture of the wild boar of Mount Erymanthus; (5) the cleansing, in a single day, of the cattle stables of King Augeas of Elis; (6) the

shooting of the monstrous man-eating birds of the Stymphalian marshes; (7) the capture of the mad bull that terrorized the island of Crete; (8) the capture of the man-eating mares of King Diomedes of the Bistones; (9) the taking of the girdle of Hippolyte, queen of the Amazons; (10) the seizing of the cattle of the three-bodied giant Geryon, who ruled the island Erytheia in the far west; (11) the bringing back of the golden apples kept at the world's end by the Hesperides; and (12) the fetching up from the lower world of the triple-headed dog Cerberus, guardian of its gates.

Heracles was finally overcome by treachery, poisoned by wearing a cloak smeared with the tainted blood of the centaur Nessus, whom he had killed. His body was placed on a pyre on Mount Oeta (modern Greek Oiti), his mortal part being thus consumed and his divine part ascending to heaven. There he was reconciled to Hera and married Hebe.

Many aspects of Heracles' life—including his birth, his wrestling (as an infant) with serpents, his madness, and his death—are the subjects of later literature.

Herbert \'hər-bərt\, A.P., *in full* Sir Alan Patrick (b. Sept. 24, 1890, Elstead, Surrey, Eng.—d. Nov. 11, 1971, London)   English novelist, playwright, poet, and politician, author of more than 50 books, famous for his witty championing of minority causes. As an independent member of Parliament for Oxford University (1935–50), he also introduced the matrimonial-causes bill (enacted in 1937), which radically amended English divorce laws.

Herbert graduated in law at Oxford and during World War I served in the Royal Navy. His first literary success was *The Secret Battle* (1919), a story of frontline warfare. Another novel, *The Water Gipsies* (1930), affectionately described Thames riverside life. In contrast, *Holy Deadlock* (1934) was frankly propagandist, aimed at the anomalies of the divorce laws. A witty lyricist, he wrote many highly successful comic operas and musicals, among them *Riverside Nights* (1926), *La Vie Parisienne* (1929), *Tantivy Towers* (1931), *Helen* (1932), *Derby Day* (1932), *Big Ben* (1946), and *Bless the Bride* (1947). Herbert was knighted in 1945. His last book, *A.P.H.: His Life and Times*, was published in 1970.

Herbert \'hər-bərt\, Frank (Patrick) (b. Oct. 8, 1920, Tacoma, Wash., U.S.—d. Feb. 11, 1986, Madison, Wis.)   American science-fiction writer noted as the author of the best-selling *Dune* series of futuristic novels, a group of highly complex works that explored such themes as ecology, human evolution, the consequences of genetic manipulation, and mystical and psychic possibilities.

Until 1972, when he began to write full-time, Herbert held a variety of jobs while writing socially engaged science fiction. His reputation was made with the publication of the epic *Dune* (1965), which sold more than 12 million copies, and its sequels, *Dune Messiah* (1969), *Children of Dune* (1976), *God-Emperor of Dune* (1981), and *Chapterhouse: Dune* (1985). Included among his more than two dozen novels are the highly acclaimed *Dragon in the Sea* (1956), *The Green Brain* (1966), *The Santaroga Barrier* (1968), *The Heaven Makers* (1968), *The God Makers* (1972), and *The Dosadi Experiment* (1977).

Herbert \'hər-bərt\, George (b. April 3, 1593, Montgomery Castle, Wales—d. March 1, 1633, Bemerton, Wiltshire, Eng.)   One of the major Metaphysical poets who is noted for his mastery of metrical form, his use of allegory and homely analogy, and his unwavering theme of religious devotion.

Herbert was educated at Trinity College, Cambridge. In 1620 he was elected orator of the university and in that position was much involved with the royal court. By 1625 Herbert's sponsors at court were dead or out of favor, and he turned to the church and was ordained deacon. He resigned as orator in 1627, and in 1630 he was ordained and became rector at Bemerton. He became friends with Nicholas Ferrar, who had founded a religious community at nearby Little Gidding, and devoted himself to his rural parish and the reconstruction of his church. Herbert also wrote poems, which he sent to Ferrar from his deathbed, asking him to decide whether to publish or destroy them. Ferrar published them under the title *The Temple: Sacred Poems and Private Ejaculations* in 1633.

Herbert described his poems as "a picture of the many spiritual conflicts that have passed between God and my soul, before I could subject mine to the will of Jesus, my Master, in whose service I have now found perfect freedom." As well as personal poems, *The Temple* includes such doctrinal poems as "The Church Porch" and "The Church Militant." Other poems in the collection are concerned with church ritual. At Bemerton, Herbert also wrote *A Priest to the Temple: Or The Country Parson, His Character and Rule of Life* (1652). Some of Herbert's poems, such as "The Altar" and "Easter Wings," are notable pattern poems, the lines forming the shape of the subject.

Herbert \ˈhər-bərt\, Xavier, *in full* Alfred Francis Xavier Herbert (b. May 15, 1901, Port Hedland, W.Aus., Australia—d. Nov. 10, 1984, Alice Springs, Northern Territory) Australian novelist and short-story writer best known for his first novel, *Capricornia* (1938), a comic chronicle about life in the Northern Territory of Australia and the inhumane treatment suffered by the Aborigines there at the hands of whites.

Herbert knew many Aborigines as a child and learned their language. As a journalist he traveled over northern Australia, also working as a sailor, miner, aviator, deep-sea diver, and stock rider. In 1935 he became Superintendent of Aborigines at Darwin, a position that led to the writing of *Capricornia*.

The novels *Seven Emus* (1959), *Soldiers' Women* (1961), and *Poor Fellow My Country* (1975) and his collected short stories, *Larger than Life* (1963), were less well received than *Capricornia*. His autobiography, *Disturbing Element*, was published in 1983.

Herbert \ˈker-bert\, Zbigniew (b. Oct. 29, 1924, Lwów, Pol. [now Lviv, Ukraine]) Polish poet, dramatist, and essayist, one of Poland's best known and most influential poets.

Herbert obtained a diploma in law after World War II. Although he started writing poetry at the age of 17, he published little before 1956. His first collection of poems, *Struna światła* (1956; "A String of Light"), was followed by *Hermes, pies i gwiazda* (1957; "Hermes, a Dog and a Star"), *Studium przedmiotu* (1961; "A Study of the Object"), *Pan Cogito* (1974; *Mr. Cogito*), and *Raport z oblężonego miata* (1983; *Report from the Besieged City*). Herbert's poetry expresses an ironic moralism in free verse laden with classical and other historical allusions. His most distinguished collection of poetry, *Elegia na odejście* ("Elegy for an Exit"), was published in 1990.

He also wrote a collection of essays, *Barbarzyńca w ogrodzie* (1962; *Barbarian in the Garden*), inspired by his travels to France and Italy. A translation of *Martwa natura z węzidłem* entitled *Still Life with a Bridle* was published in 1991.

Herculano \ˌer-kü-ˈlä-nō\, Alexandre, *surname in full* Herculano de Carvalho e Araújo \dē-kär-ˈväl-yü-ä-ə-ˈraú-zhü\ (b. March 28, 1810, Lisbon, Port.—d. Sept. 13, 1877, Santarém) Historian, novelist, and poet, one of the writers who is credited with introducing Romanticism to Portugal.

As a young man Herculano took part in the unsuccessful rebellion against the absolute rule of Dom Miguel and was forced into exile in England and France. In 1832 he returned to Portugal with the small army that eventually ousted Miguel

and established a liberal regime. Convinced that an important cultural reform should accompany the political change, Herculano abandoned poetry and became editor of *O Panorama* (1837–39), a review that kept abreast of European literary and social trends. In it he published his historical tales, later gathered in two volumes as *Lendas e narrativas* (1851; "Legends and Chronicles"). From 1839, when he became librarian at the Royal Library of Ajuda, he worked on his ambitious *História de Portugal*, his research based on original manuscripts. He also wrote historical novels in the manner of Sir Walter Scott, a genre he introduced to Portugal.

The first volume of *História de Portugal* appeared in 1846. One of the finest achievements of Romantic historiography, it covers the early history of Portugal to 1279 and stresses the origin and rise of the middle class. The fourth and last volume of *História de Portugal* was issued in 1853.

In 1851 Herculano participated in the overthrow of the authoritarian regime of António da Costa Cabral and helped found two newspapers, in which he attacked political centralism and clerical influence. To this period belongs *Da origem e estabelecimento da inquisiça em Portugal* (1854–59; *History of the Origin and Establishment of the Inquisition in Portugal*).

Hercules \ˈhər-kyə-ˌlēz\ *see* HERACLES.

Herczeg \ˈhert-seg\, Ferenc (b. Sept. 22, 1863, Versecz, Hung.—d. Feb. 24, 1954, Budapest) Novelist and playwright, the leading literary exponent of conservative-nationalist opinion in early 20th-century Hungary.

Herczeg was born into a well-to-do family of German origin. In 1895 he founded *Új idők* ("New Times"), which remained for half a century the literary magazine of the conservative upper and middle classes of Hungary. His light novels of manners contained just enough irony, humor, and social criticism to cause a harmless shock to the conservative public for whom they were intended and for whom such criticism was a new experience. The best example of this type is *A Gyurkovics lányok* (1893; "The Gyurkovics Girls"), in which a clever mother marries off her seven daughters. In his later, more serious novels, Herczeg often used historical settings. The most successful such novel is *Az élet kapuja* (1919; "The Gates of Life"), set in Renaissance Italy. His social comedies, such as *A három testőr* (1894; "The Three Bodyguards") and *Kék róka* (1917; "The Blue Fox Stole"), are amusing and skillfully written. *Bizánc* (1904; "Byzantium") and *A híd* (1925; "The Bridge") were notable historical dramas.

Herder \ˈher-dər\, Johann Gottfried von (b. Aug. 25, 1744, Mohrungen, East Prussia [now Morąg, Pol.]—d. Dec. 18, 1803, Weimar, Saxe-Weimar [Germany]) German critic and philosopher, who was the leading figure of the Sturm und Drang literary movement and an innovator in the philosophy of history and culture.

Herder studied theology, philosophy, and literature at Königsberg and then taught and preached in Riga (now in Latvia). There he published his first works, which included a collection of fragments entitled *Kritische Wälder, oder Betrachtungen die Wissenschaft und Kunst des Schönen betreffend* (1769 and 1846; "Critical Forests, or Reflections on the Science and Art of the Beautiful").

During a visit to Strasbourg in 1770, Herder met the young J.W. von Goethe, with whom he was to be associated for many years. The following year Herder went to Bückeburg as court preacher. The works he produced there were fundamental to the Sturm und Drang literary movement. Among these are *Plastik* (1778), which outlines his metaphysics; *Abhandlung über den Ursprung der Sprache* (1772; "Essay on the Origin of Language"), which finds the origin of language in human nature; an essay on William Shakespeare; and "Auszug aus einem Briefwechsel über Ossian und die Lieder alter Völker" (1773; "Extract from a Correspondence About Ossian and the Songs of Ancient Peoples"), published in a manifesto to which Goethe and Justus Möser, a forerunner of Sturm und Drang, also contributed.

Herder moved to Weimar in 1776. There, anticipating Goethe, he developed the foundations of a general morphology, which enabled him to understand how a Shakespearean play, for instance, or the Gospel According to John, in the historical context of each, was bound to assume the individual form that it did instead of another. Herder's work at Weimar reached its peak in *Zerstreute Blätter* (1785–97; "Sporadic Papers") and in the unfinished *Ideen zur Philosophie der Geschichte der Menschheit* (1784–91; *Outlines of a Philosophy of the History of Man*).

Herder and Goethe eventually became estranged from one another, and on Herder's side this resulted in a bitter enmity toward the whole classical movement in German poetry and philosophy. His *Briefe zu Beförderung der Humanität* (1793–97; "Letters for the Advancement of Humanity") and his *Adrastea* (1801–03), containing treatises on history, philosophy, and aesthetics, emphasized the didactic purpose of all poetry, thus contradicting that very theory of the autonomy of the work of art that he himself had helped to establish.

Heredia \ä-'räth-yä\, José María de (b. Nov. 22, 1842, La Fortuna, Cuba—d. Oct. 2, 1905, near Houdan, Fr.)   Cuban-born French poet who was a brilliant master of the sonnet.

The son of a wealthy Spanish coffee plantation owner and a French mother, Heredia claimed France as "the country of my mind and heart"; and, although he went home after finishing his schooling in France, he quickly returned to Paris and studied at the School of Paleography. He was a leading figure in the movement of French poets known as the Parnassians.

Heredia's 118 sonnets and some longer pieces were published as *Les Trophées* (1893). The poems capture in verse a fugitive moment of history (usually classical or Renaissance) or else an objet d'art (a vase, a coin, an ornate book binding), usually in one startling image. A selection of his poems in English translation was published in *The Flute, with Other Translations and Poems* (1977).

In 1894 Heredia was elected to the Académie Française. In 1901 he became librarian of the Bibliothèque de l'Arsenal, Paris. He also completed an edition of the *Bucoliques* by the 18th-century poet André de Chénier.

Hergesheimer \'hər-gə-ˌshī-mər\, Joseph (b. Feb. 15, 1880, Philadelphia, Pa., U.S.—d. April 25, 1954, Sea Isle City, N.J.)   American author whose novels are typically concerned with the decadent and sophisticated milieu of the very wealthy.

After giving up the study of painting, Hergesheimer turned to writing. Beginning with *The Lay Anthony* (1914), he established himself as a popular and prolific writer of novels, short stories, biography, history, and criticism. Of his novels, *The Three Black Pennys* (1917), the story of three generations of the wealthy, mine-owning Penny family; *Java Head* (1919); and *Balisand* (1924) are considered his best. In 1921 a motion picture based on his short story "Tol'able David" was made.

Herman de Valenciennes \er-mäⁿ-də-vȧ-läⁿ-'syäⁿ\ (fl. 12th century)   French poet known for a scriptural poem that was very popular in his time. Born at Valenciennes (now in France), he became a priest and wrote the *Histoire de la Bible* (after 1189), including the Old and New Testaments in an abridged form, and a separate poem on the Assumption of the Virgin. The work is known as *Le Roman de sapience* ("The Story of Wisdom").

Hermans \'her-mäns\, Willem Frederik (b. Sept. 1, 1921, Amsterdam, Neth.)   Dutch satirical novelist who vehemently attacked the ills and hypocrisies of society.

Hermans' early novels and stories are overcast with dark, disillusioned tones. *De tranen der acacia's* (1949; "The Tears of the Acacias"), which features a feckless fighter, satirizes the Dutch Resistance to Nazi occupation during World War II. He returned to the war as a theme for his noted short novel "Het behouden huis" (1952; "The House of Refuge") and the novel *De donkere kamer van Damocles* (1958; *The Dark Room of Damocles*). Hermans rejected the possibility of human virtue, seeing the individual as either predator or prey, and characterized his own philosophy as "creative nihilism."

Hermans, who was a geologist, taught at the University of Groningen from 1953 to 1973 and found subject matter for fiction in his profession. The geologist protagonist of *Nooit meer slapen* (1966; "Never to Sleep Again") comes to doubt the existence of scientific truth, and Hermans satirized academic communities in the novels *Onder professoren* (1975; "Among Professors") and *Uit talloos veel miljoenen* (1981; "From Countless Millions"). He also wrote poetry, plays, criticism, and scientific works. A later novel was *Au pair* (1989).

Hermaphroditus \hər-ˌmaf-rō-'dī-təs\   In Greek mythology, the son of Hermes and Aphrodite. He spurned the nymph Salmacis, and as punishment she embraced him and asked the gods to prevent them from ever being separated. The gods granted her wish and combined their bodies, creating a new one with both male and female characteristics.

hermeneutics \ˌhər-mə-'nü-tiks, -'nyü-\ [Greek *hermeneutikós* interpretative, a derivative of *hermeneúein* to translate, interpret, explain]   The study of the general principles of biblical interpretation. For both Jews and Christians throughout their histories, the primary purpose of hermeneutics, and of the exegetical methods employed in interpretation, has been to discover the truths and values of the Bible.

The sacred status of the Bible rests upon the conviction that it is a receptacle of divine revelation. In the history of biblical interpretation, four major types of hermeneutics have emerged: the literal, moral, allegorical, and anagogical.

Literal interpretation asserts that a biblical text is to be interpreted according to the "plain meaning" conveyed by its grammatical construction and historical context. The literal meaning is held to correspond to the intention of the authors. This type of hermeneutics is often, but not necessarily, associated with belief in the verbal inspiration of the Bible, according to which the individual words of the divine message were divinely chosen. Jerome, an influential 4th-century biblical scholar, and such diverse later figures as Thomas Aquinas, Nicholas of Lyra, John Colet, Martin Luther, and John Calvin favored literal interpretation.

Moral interpretation seeks to establish exegetical principles by which ethical lessons may be drawn from the various parts of the Bible. Allegorization was often employed in this endeavor.

Allegorical interpretation interprets the biblical narratives as having a level of reference beyond those persons, things, and events explicitly mentioned in the text. A particular form of allegorical interpretation is the typological, according to which the key figures, main events, and principal institutions of the Old Testament are seen as "types" or foreshadowings of persons, events, and objects in the New Testament.

The anagogical or mystical interpretation seeks to explain biblical events as they relate to or prefigure the life to come. Such an approach to the Bible is exemplified by the Jewish Kabbala, which sought to disclose the mystical significance of the numerical values of Hebrew letters and words.

Hermes \'hər-,mēz\   In Greek mythology, son of Zeus and Maia; often identified with the Roman god MERCURY.

Both in literature and cult Hermes was associated with the protection of cattle and sheep, and he was often closely connected with deities of vegetation, especially Pan and the nymphs. In the *Odyssey*, however, he appears mainly as the messenger of the gods and the conductor of the dead to Hades. Hermes was also a dream god, and the Greeks offered to him the last libation before sleep. As a messenger, he may also have become the god of roads and doorways, and he was the protector of travelers. Hermes' association with good luck and his function as a deity of gain, honest or dishonest, are natural derivatives of his character as a god of fertility. Like Apollo, Hermes was a patron of music and was credited with the invention of the kithara (a stringed instrument similar to the lyre) and sometimes of music itself. He was also god of eloquence and presided over some kinds of popular divination.

Hermesianax \,hər-mē-'sī-ə-,naks\ (fl. *c.* 300–250 BC)   Greek elegiac poet from Colophon in Ionia, one of the first of the erudite and sophisticated exponents of Alexandrian poetry. His chief work was an elegiac poem in three books, dedicated to and named for his mistress Leontion. Some 98 lines of the poem were preserved by Athenaeus. The poem enumerates with alternating force and tenderness the power of love for both mythological and historical figures.

Hermeticism \hər-'met-ə-,siz-əm\ or **Hermetism** \'hər-mə-,tiz-əm\, *also called* Ermetismo \,er-me-'tēs-,mō\   Modernist poetic movement originating in Italy in the early 20th century. The works produced within the movement are characterized by unorthodox structure, illogical sequences, and highly subjective language. The name was derived from that of Hermes Trismegistos, the reputed author of occult symbolic works. It was used in reference to this particular movement by the critic Francesco Flora in a series of essays collected as *La poesia ermetica* (1936). Although Hermeticism influenced a wide circle of poets, even outside Italy, it remained inaccessible to the larger public.

Hermeticism was rooted in the poetry and poetic theory of the 18th-century German Romantic poet Novalis and of the 19th-century American writer Edgar Allan Poe, as filtered through the French Symbolist poets, particularly Charles Baudelaire, Stéphane Mallarmé, Paul Valéry, and Arthur Rimbaud. The term was particularly applied to the group of 20th-century Italian poets whose forerunner was Arturo Onofri and whose primary exponent and leader was Giuseppe Ungaretti. The formalistic devices of Hermeticism were partly an outgrowth of Futurism, a short-lived but influential movement that encouraged innovation in literary language and content. The cryptic brevity, obscurity, and involution of the Hermetics were forced upon them, however, by fascist censors.

Although two other poets who were to gain international repute, Salvatore Quasimodo and Eugenio Montale, were associated with the movement, its initial leader was Ungaretti, whose education in Paris had introduced him to French Symbolism. In his first volume of poems, *Il porto sepolto* (1916; "The Buried Port"), Ungaretti introduced an intense, purified short lyric, from which punctuation, syntax, and structure had been eliminated to stress the evocative power of individual words. Montale (with *Ossi di seppia*, 1925; "Cuttlefish Bones") and later Quasimodo (with *Acque e terre*, 1930; "Waters and Land") became his disciples.

After World War II all three of Hermeticism's major poets developed their own individual styles. Ungaretti incorporated more structure and a more straightforward tone, Montale moved in the direction of greater human warmth and sim-

plicity, and Quasimodo wrote powerful, socially committed works. In 1959 Quasimodo won the Nobel Prize for Literature, and Montale received the Nobel in 1975. Some Italian poets, such as Leonardo Sinisgalli, Alfonso Gatto, and Mario Luzi, persisted in the introverted, formalized Hermetic manner, but the movement's greatest poets moved on to develop more accessible and universal styles.

Hernández \er-'nän-däs\, José (b. Nov. 10, 1834, Chacra de Pueyrredón, Buenos Aires, Arg.—d. Oct. 21, 1886, Belgrano, near Buenos Aires)   Argentine poet, best known for his depiction of the gauchos.

At the age of 14, because of illness, he left Buenos Aires to live in the Pampas, where he learned the ways of the gauchos. After an unsuccessful revolt against President Domingo Sarmiento's government in 1870, Hernández fled to Brazil in January 1871. On returning to Buenos Aires, he published *El gaucho Martín Fierro* (1872; *The Gaucho Martin Fierro*), a work depicting the life of a persecuted gaucho; it is recognized as the best example of gaucho poetry. In the poetic narrative's second part, *La vuelta de Martín Fierro* (1879; "The Return of Martín Fierro"), the gaucho hero is reintegrated into the society he had abandoned.

Hernández \er-'nän-däth\, Miguel (b. Oct. 30, 1910, Orihuela, Spain—d. March 28, 1942, Alicante)   Spanish poet and dramatist who combined traditional lyric forms with 20th-century subjectivity.

A goatherd in his youth, Hernández joined the Spanish Communist Party in 1936 and fought in the Civil War (1936–39). He was condemned to death by the Nationalists following the war, but his sentence was commuted to life imprisonment after international protests. He died in prison soon afterward, however. Hernández's predominant themes are love—particularly of a sorrowful nature—war, death, and social injustice. He began with a rich, gongoristic style, but his poetry became more intimate, simple, and tragic later in life.

Hernández' collections include the elaborate *Perito en lunas* (1933; "Connoisseur of Moons"); *El rayo que no cesa* (1936; "The Never-Ending Lightning"), his best work, a collection mostly of sonnets of great classical purity; and *El hombre acecha* (1939; "The Man Who Lurks"), a desolate book full of the horror of war and prison. The posthumous *Cancionero y romancero de ausencias* (1958; *Songbook of Absences*) contains poems and lullabies he wrote in prison for his starving wife and son. Several of Hernández' one-act plays of propaganda appeared during the Civil War; the most notable of these is *Pastor de la muerte* (1938; "Shepherd of Death").

Hernani \er-nȧ-'nē\   Poetic tragedy in five acts by Victor HUGO, performed and published in 1830. Although the play retained the classicists' unity of action, it renounced the unities of time and place, and the premiere was disrupted by protests from proponents of classicism. The performance of *Hernani* was a significant victory for the proponents of the new, more naturalistic Romantic drama.

Set in 16th-century Spain, the story extolled the Romantic hero in the form of a noble outlaw at war with society, dedicated to a passionate love and driven by inexorable fate.

Herne \'hərn\, James A., *original name* James Ahern \ə-'hərn\ (b. Feb. 1, 1839, Troy, N.Y., U.S.—d. June 2, 1901, New York City)   American playwright who helped bridge the gap between 19th-century melodrama and the 20th-century drama of ideas. He was especially strong in character delineation.

After several years as a traveling actor, Herne scored an impressive success with his first play, *Hearts of Oak* (1879), written with the young David Belasco. Subsequent dramas, *Drifting Apart* (1885), *The Minute Men* (1886), and *Margaret Fleming*

(1890), did not achieve the same popularity. *Margaret Fleming*, a drama of marital infidelity, has been judged his major achievement. Herne's most popular play, *Shore Acres*, was first presented in 1892.

Herne \\'hərn\\ the Hunter. Phantom hunter who haunts Windsor Great Park, impersonated by Falstaff in William Shakespeare's *The Merry Wives of Windsor*. Though Herne may have been an actual keeper of the forest, he is probably a local manifestation of the Wild Huntsman myth known throughout the world. The usual story associated with the Wild Hunt involves someone excessively fond of the chase who makes a rash pledge or compact with a stranger (the devil) and is thus doomed to hunt forever. Herne is said to ride at night, especially during storms; he wears horns, rattles chains, blasts trees and cattle, and occasionally appears to mortals.

hero \\'hir-ō, 'hē-rō\\ [Greek *hḗrōs*] A mythological or legendary figure often of divine descent who is endowed with great strength or ability, such as those found in early heroic epics like *Gilgamesh*, the *Iliad*, *Beowulf*, or *La Chanson de Roland*. The word is often broadly applied to the principal male character in a literary or dramatic work.

The legendary heroes belong to a princely class existing in an early stage of the history of a people, and they transcend ordinary men in skill, strength, and courage. They are usually born to their role. Some, like the Greek Achilles and the Irish Cú Chulainn (Cuchulain), are of semidivine origin, unusual beauty, and extraordinary precocity. A few, like the Anglo-Saxon Beowulf and the Russian Ilya of Murom, are dark horses, slow to develop.

War or dangerous adventure is the hero's normal occupation. He is surrounded by noble peers and is magnanimous to his followers and ruthless to his enemies. In addition to his prowess in battle, he is resourceful and skillful in many crafts. If shipwrecked, he is an expert swimmer. He is sometimes, like Odysseus, cunning and wise in counsel, but a hero is not usually given to much subtlety. He is a man of action rather than thought and lives by a personal code of honor that admits of no qualification. His responses are usually instinctive, predictable, and inevitable. He accepts challenges and sometimes even courts disaster. Thus baldly stated, the hero's ethos seems oversimple by the standards of a later age. He is childlike in his boasting and rivalry, in his love of reward, and in his concern for his reputation. He is sometimes foolhardy and wrongheaded, risking his life—and the lives of others—for trifles. Roland, for instance, dies because he is too proud to sound his horn for help when he is overwhelmed in battle. Yet the hero still exerts an attraction for sophisticated readers and remains a seminal influence in literature.

Hero Ain't Nothin' but a Sandwich, A Novel for young adults by Alice CHILDRESS, published in 1973. Presented in 23 short narratives, it is the story of an arrogant black teenager whose fragmented domestic life and addiction to heroin lead him into delinquency.

Hero and Leander \\'hir-ō ... lē-'an-dər, 'hē-rō\\ In Greek mythology, two celebrated lovers. Hero, who was a virgin priestess of Aphrodite at Sestos, was seen at a festival by Leander of Abydos; they fell in love, and he swam the Hellespont at night to visit her, guided by a light from her tower. One stormy night the light was extinguished, and Leander was drowned; Hero, seeing his body, drowned herself.

The story is preserved in Ovid, Musaeus, and elsewhere. It was also adapted by later poets, such as Christopher Marlowe (*Hero and Leander*), and was alluded to by Lord Byron (*The Bride of Abydos*).

Herod \\'her-əd\\, *also called* Herod the Great, *Latin* Herodes Magnus (b. 73 BC—d. March/April, 4 BC, Jericho, Judaea) Roman-appointed king of Judaea from 37 to 4 BC who built many fortresses, aqueducts, theaters, and other public buildings and generally raised the prosperity of the land but who was the center of political and family intrigues in his later years. The New Testament portrays him as a tyrant, into whose kingdom Jesus of Nazareth was born. His instability and cruelty are particularly notable in his murder of Mariamne (one of his wives), their two children, and many members of her immediate family, and in his slaughter of the infants of Bethlehem.

Herod has been the subject of many works of literature, including *El tetrarco* (1635) by Pedro Calderón de la Barca, *La vida y muerte de Herodes* (1636) by Tirso de Molina, and *Mariamne* (1725) by Voltaire.

Herodas \\hə-'rō-dəs\\, *also called* Herondas \\hə-'rän-dəs\\ (fl. 3rd century BC) Greek poet, probably of the Aegean island of Cos, and the author of short dramatic scenes in choliambic verse of a world of low life similar to that portrayed in the New Comedy. His work was discovered in manuscript in 1890 and is the largest collection of the genre. It is written in rough iambic meter and in the vigorous, rather earthy language of the common people. His characters use vehement exclamations, emphatic turns of speech, and proverbs.

In pieces of about 100 lines, Herodas portrays vivid and entertaining scenes with the characters clearly drawn. The themes cover a range of city life: a procuress attempts to arrange a tryst for a respectable matron while her husband is away; a jealous woman accuses her favorite slave of infidelity and has him bound and sent to receive 2,000 lashes; a desperate mother drags a truant urchin to the schoolmaster. It is thought that these sketches were recited with considerable improvisation by an actor who took the various roles.

Herodotus \\hə-'räd-ə-təs\\ (b. 484 BC?, Halicarnassus, Asia Minor [now Bodrum, Tur.]?—d. 430–420) Greek author of the first great narrative history produced in the ancient world, the *History* of the Greco-Persian Wars.

Herodotus is thought to have resided in Athens and to have met Sophocles and then to have left for Thurii, a new colony in southern Italy sponsored by Athens. The latest event alluded to in his *History* belongs to 430, but how soon after or where he died is not known. There is good reason to believe that he was in Athens, or at least in central Greece, during the early years of the Peloponnesian War, from 431, and that his work was published and known there before 425.

In the sense that he created a work that is an organic whole, Herodotus was the first of the Greek, and so of European, historians. Herodotus' work is not only an artistic masterpiece; for all his mistakes (and for all his fantasies and inaccuracies) he remains the leading source of original information not only about Greek history of the period between 550 and 479 BC but also about much of that of western Asia and of Egypt.

Héroët \\ā-rȯ-'e\\, Antoine, *byname* La Maison-Neuve \\lä-me-zōⁿ-'nœv\\ (b. 1492?, Paris, Fr.—d. 1568, Digne) Renaissance court poet whose works are representative of the amalgam of Platonism and Christian humanism that produced the modern concept of Platonic love.

A member of the court surrounding Margaret of Angoulême, sister of Francis I and later queen of Navarre, Héroët is chiefly known for his *La Parfaicte Amye* (1542), a subtle, mystical monologue exalting as man's ultimate happiness a love in which the perfect lover seeks spiritual union with his lady. Héroët imitated Plato's *Symposium* in explaining the mystery of the origin of love in his poem *L'Androgyne* (written 1536; published 1542).

heroic couplet   A couplet of rhyming iambic pentameters often forming a distinct rhetorical as well as metrical unit. The origin of the form in English poetry is unknown, but Geoffrey Chaucer in the 14th century was the first to make extensive use of it. The heroic couplet became the principal meter used in drama in about the mid-17th century, and the form was perfected by John Dryden and Alexander Pope in the late 17th and early 18th centuries. An example, from Pope's "Eloisa to Abelard," is:

> Then share thy pain, allow that sad relief;
> Ah, more than share it, give me all thy grief.

heroic drama   Type of tragic play common in England during the Restoration period of the late 17th century. Heroic drama portrayed epic characters and themes of love and honor and was for the most part written in heroic couplets with overblown dialogue and exotic settings. The plays were staged with spectacular scenery and were influenced by the development of opera at that time in England and by French classical drama. John Dryden wrote some of the best-known examples of heroic drama, such as his *Conquest of Granada*. The genre was satirized by George Villiers, Duke of Buckingham, in *The Rehearsal* (1671), and the popularity of the form soon declined.

heroicomic \hir-ˌō-i-ˈkäm-ik\ or **heroicomical** \-ˈkäm-i-kəl\ Comic by being ludicrously noble, bold, or elevated.

heroic poetry   Narrative verse that is elevated in mood and uses a dignified, dramatic, and formal style to describe the deeds of aristocratic warriors and rulers. It is usually composed without the aid of writing and is chanted or recited to the accompaniment of a stringed instrument. It is transmitted orally from bard to bard over generations.

The extant body of heroic poetry ranges from quite ancient to modern works, produced over a widespread geographic area. It includes what are probably the earliest forms of the verse—panegyrics praising a hero's lineage and deeds, and laments on a hero's death. Another type of heroic poem is the short, dramatic lay devoted to a single event, such as the Old English *Battle of Maldon* or the Old High German *Hildebrandslied*. The mature form of heroic poetry is the full-scale epic, such as the *Iliad* or *Odyssey*.

Much ancient heroic poetry has been wholly lost, but the tradition is still alive among certain preliterate and semiliterate peoples living in remote communities.

heroic prose   Narrative prose tales that are the counterpart of heroic poetry in subject, outlook, and dramatic style. Whether composed orally or written down, the stories were meant to be recited, and they employ many of the formulaic expressions of oral tradition. A remarkable body of this prose is the early Irish Ulster cycle of stories, recorded between the 8th and 11th centuries, featuring the hero Cú Chulainn and his associates. A 12th-century group of Irish stories is the Fenian cycle, focusing on the hero Finn MacCumhaill (MacCool), his son (the poet Oisín), and his elite corps of warriors and hunters, the Fianna Éireann.

Other examples of heroic prose are the 13th-century Icelandic sagas. The "heroic sagas," such as the *Völsunga saga* (c. 1270) and the *Thidriks saga* (c. 1250), are based on ancient Germanic oral tradition of the 4th to 6th century and contain many lines from lost heroic lays. Of higher artistic quality are the "Icelanders' sagas," such as the 13th-century *Grettis saga* and *Njáls saga*, dealing with native Icelandic families.

heroic stanza or **heroic quatrain**   In poetry, a rhymed quatrain in heroic verse with rhyme scheme *abab*. The form was used by William Shakespeare and John Dryden among others and was also called an ELEGIAC STANZA after the publication in the mid-18th century of Thomas Gray's poem *An Elegy Written in a Country Church Yard*.

heroic verse or **heroic meter** or **heroic line**   The verse form in which the heroic poetry of a particular language is, or according to critical opinion should be, composed. In classical poetry this was dactylic hexameter; in French, the alexandrine; in Italian, the hendecasyllabic line; and in English, iambic pentameter.

heroine \ˈher-ə-win, ˈhir-\ [Greek *hērōínē,* feminine derivative of *hērōs* hero]   A mythological or legendary woman having the qualities of a HERO. The word is also more broadly applied to the principal female character in a literary or dramatic work.

Herondas   *see* HERODAS.

Hero of Our Time, A   Novel by Mikhail LERMONTOV, published in Russian in 1840 as *Geroy nashego vremeni*. Its psychologically probing portrait of a disillusioned 19th-century aristocrat and its use of a nonchronological and multifaceted narrative structure influenced such later Russian authors as Fyodor Dostoyevsky and Leo Tolstoy and presaged the antiheroes and antinovels of 20th-century fiction.

The novel is set in the Russian Caucasus in the 1830s. Grigory Pechorin is a bored, self-centered, and cynical young army officer who believes in nothing. With impunity he toys with the love of women and the goodwill of men. He is brave, determined, and willful, but his energies and potential are wasted, and he dies in a duel.

Herrera \er-ˈrer-ä\, Fernando de, *byname* El Divino \el-dē-ˈbē-nō\ (b. 1534?, Seville, Spain—d. 1597, Seville)   Lyric poet and man of letters who was one of the leading figures in the first school of Seville, a group of 16th-century Spanish Neoclassical poets and humanists who were concerned with rhetoric and the form of language.

Although never ordained, Herrera took minor orders and was appointed to a benefice in Seville. His aristocratic literary ideas were clearly set forth in his *Anotaciones a las obras de Garcilaso de la Vega* (1580; "Notes on the Works of Garcilaso de la Vega"). In his own poetry, published as *Algunas obras de Fernando de Herrera* (1582; "Some Works of Fernando de Herrera"), he elaborated on the style of Garcilaso and began to move towards *culteranismo* (an ornate and affected poetic style that flourished in Spain in the 16th and 17th centuries and finally developed, in its most extreme form, into *gongorismo*). His most enduring poems are his patriotic odes, rich in Old Testament rhetoric and melodious eclogues. He also composed a history, *Relación de la guerra de Chipre y batalla naval de Lepanto* (1572; "Account of the War of Cyprus and the Naval Battle of Lepanto"), and a biography, *Elogio de la vida y muerte de Tomás Moro* (1592; "Eulogy on the Life and Death of Thomas More").

Herrera y Reissig \er-ˈrer-ä-ē-ˈrā-sēg\, Julio (b. Aug. 1, 1875, Montevideo, Uruguay—d. March 18, 1910, Montevideo)   Uruguayan writer who was one of the most original poets writing in Spanish in the early 20th century. His verse, extremely controversial in its own time for its innovations in form and language, was widely imitated and strongly influenced the development of contemporary Latin-American poetry.

Born into a well-to-do family, Herrera rejected the bourgeois materialism around him. Leading a consciously bohemian, escapist life in Montevideo, he was soon joined by a group of iconoclastic young poets.

Herrera's talent, however, proved to be more lasting than that of his friends; volumes such as *Los maitines de la noche* (1902; "The Matins of the Night") and *Poemas violetas* (1906; "Violet Poems") were recognized by critics for their vividly imaginative evocation of commonplace scenes of everyday life as well as for their innovative use of language. Despite deliberately ludicrous titles, such as *Pianos crepusculares* (1910; "Twilight Pianos"), Herrera frequently depicted the ordinary.

Herrick \'her-ik\, Robert (baptized Aug. 24, 1591, London, Eng.—d. October 1674, Dean Prior, Devonshire) English cleric and poet, the most original of the "sons of Ben [Jonson]," who revived the spirit of the ancient classic lyric. He is best remembered for the line "Gather ye rosebuds while ye may."

During the time he was apprenticed to his uncle, Sir William Herrick, a prosperous and influential goldsmith, he cultivated the society of the London wits. He received an M.A. in 1620 from Cambridge and was ordained in 1623. Herrick returned to London for a time, keeping in touch with court society and enlarging his acquaintance with Ben Jonson and other writers and musicians. He was presented in 1629 with the living of Dean Prior, and, except for the period from 1646 to 1660 (the Restoration), when he was deprived of his post because of his Royalist sympathies, he remained there for the rest of his life.

Herrick became well known as a poet around 1620–30; many manuscript commonplace books from that time contain his poems. The only book Herrick published was *Hesperides*, which included *His Noble Numbers*, a collection of poems on religious subjects with its title page dated 1647 but not printed until 1648. *Hesperides* contained some 1,400 poems, mostly very short, many of them brief epigrams. His work appeared after that time in miscellanies and songbooks, and the 17th-century English composer Henry Lawes and others set some of his songs to music. Herrick wrote elegies, satires, epigrams, love songs to imaginary mistresses, marriage songs, complimentary verse to friends and patrons, and celebrations of rustic and ecclesiastical festivals.

Herself Surprised First novel of an acclaimed trilogy by Joyce CARY, first published in 1941. Followed by *To Be a Pilgrim* (1942) and *The Horse's Mouth* (1944), *Herself Surprised* is narrated by its protagonist, Sara Monday. A passionate woman, Sara is emotionally involved with three men: her husband, Matthew, who dies; Tom Wilcher, the archtraditionalist protagonist of *To Be a Pilgrim*, who is in love with her; and the artist Gulley Jimson (protagonist of *The Horse's Mouth*).

Hersey \'hər-sē\, John (Richard) (b. June 17, 1914, Tianjin, China—d. March 24, 1993, Key West, Fla., U.S.) American novelist and journalist noted for his documentary fiction about catastrophic events in World War II.

Hersey lived in China until the age of 10, at which time his family returned to the United States. He graduated from Yale University in 1936, and he served as a foreign correspondent in the Far East, Italy, and Russia for *Time* and *Life* magazines from 1937 to 1946. His early novel A BELL FOR ADANO (1944), depicting the Allied occupation of a Sicilian town during World War II, won the 1945 Pulitzer Prize. Hersey's next books demonstrated his gift for combining a reporter's skill for relaying facts with imaginative fictionalization. Both THE WALL (1950), about the Warsaw ghetto uprisings, and HIROSHIMA (1946), an objective account of the atomic bomb explosion in that city as experienced by survivors of the blast, are based on fact, but they are also personal stories of survival in Poland and Japan during World War II.

Hersey's later novels include *A Single Pebble* (1956), *The Child Buyer* (1960), *The Conspiracy* (1972), *The Walnut Door* (1977), and *The Call* (1985).

Hertz \'herts\, Henrik, *original name* Heyman Hertz (b. Aug. 25/27, 1797/8, Copenhagen, Den.—d. Feb. 25, 1870, Copenhagen) Dramatist and poet, among the most popular Danish dramatists.

Hertz first imitated Johan Ludwig Heiberg, whom he joined in attacking contemporary Romantics. They regarded perfection of form as more important than content, as is clearly expressed in Hertz's satirical letters, *Gjenganger-breve* (1830; "Letters of a Ghost"), which were a great success. Hertz wrote some 50 plays, of which the best known are *Sparekassen* (1836; "The Savings Bank"), *Svend Dyrings hieus* (1837; "Sven Dyring's House"), and *Kong Renés datter* (1843; *King René's Daughter*). He was also a prolific writer of many kinds of verse.

Hervey \'här-vē, 'hər-\, John, *title in full* Baron Hervey of Ickworth \'ik-wərth\ (b. Oct. 15, 1696—d. Aug. 5, 1743, Ickworth, Suffolk, Eng.) Politician and wit whose *Memoirs of the Reign of George the Second* are of great importance and, along with the writings of Horace Walpole, are largely responsible for many of posterity's impressions of 18th-century England.

Hervey made the customary grand tour of Europe and, at Hanover, Ger., became a firm friend of Frederick Louis (later prince of Wales). Hervey was Whig member of Parliament for Bury St. Edmunds, Suffolk (1725–33) and was then created Baron Hervey of Ickworth.

Hervey's renown lay in the world of fashion and the court rather than in politics. He suffered from delicate health, which improved after a visit to Italy, where he formed a close friendship with Stephen Fox (later Lord Ilchester). This friendship evoked scandalous allusions from Alexander Pope in his "Epistle to Dr. Arbuthnot," a satiric poem in which Hervey figures as "Sporus." His own outspoken *Memoirs* (published posthumously, 1848; edited by R. Sedgwick, 3 vol., 1931; rev. ed., 1963) were, he said, written for those who prefer to see the great when they are "dressing and undressing rather than when they are playing their part on the public stage."

Hervieu \er-'vyœ\, Paul-Ernest (b. Sept. 9, 1857, Neuilly-sur-Seine, Fr.—d. Sept. 25, 1915, Paris) French novelist and playwright, most of whose dramas were tragedies dealing with family conflicts and relationships that were intended to teach a moral lesson.

After training as a lawyer, Hervieu entered the diplomatic service. Later, he began writing novels and short stories, of which the best are *Flirt* (1890) and *Peints par eux-mêmes* (1893). He then turned to writing plays, and for some 20 years he was associated with the Comédie-Française. One of his most successful plays was a historical drama of the French Revolution, *Théroigne de Méricourt*, which he wrote especially for the Comédie's leading actress, Sarah Bernhardt. His best works had a legal background, notably *Les Tenailles* (1895; "The Pincers") and *La Loi de l'homme* (1897; "Man's Law"). *Le Course du flambeau* (1901; *Passing of the Torch*) is a story of maternal love and filial ingratitude. In 1899 Hervieu was elected to the Académie Française.

Herwegh \'her-vek\, Georg (b. May 31, 1817, Stuttgart, Württemberg [Germany]—d. April 7, 1875, Lichtental, Baden) Poet whose appeal for a revolutionary spirit in Germany was strengthened by a lyric sensitivity unusual among the poets of the period.

Herwegh began his literary career as a journalist. Called up for military duty, he insulted an officer and was forced to flee to Switzerland. There he found a publisher for his best-known collection, the two-volume *Gedichte eines Lebendigen* (1841, 1843; "Poems of One Living"), political poems expressing the aspirations of German youth. Although the book was confiscated, it made Herwegh's reputation overnight and ran through several editions. When he returned to Germany in 1842, he was enthusiastically welcomed by popular demonstrations of sympathy; the Prussian king Frederick William IV received him in an amicable spirit. But when a new journal Herwegh was planning was suppressed, he wrote a tactless letter to the king and was immediately expelled from Prussia. He lived in Zürich and Paris until an amnesty in 1866 permitted him to return to Germany. He also translated the works of Alphonse de Lamartine and wrote poetry collected in the posthumously published *Neue Gedichte* (1877; "New Poems").

Herzog \'hǝrt-ˌsóg, 'hert-, -ˌsäg\ Novel by Saul BELLOW, published in 1964. The work was awarded the National Book Award for fiction in 1965.

Moses Herzog, like many of Bellow's heroes, is a Jewish intellectual who confronts a world peopled by sanguine, incorrigible realists. Much of the action of the novel takes place within the hero's disturbed consciousness, including a series of flashbacks, many of which involve his sexual and marital past.

Like much of Bellow's work, *Herzog* was praised for its combination of erudition and street smarts, for its lively, Yiddish-influenced prose, and for its narrative drive, though some critics felt Herzog's wives and lovers were not fully realized.

Hesiod \'hēs-ē-ǝd, 'hes-\, *Greek* Hesiodos, *Latin* Hesiodus (fl. *c.* 700 BC) One of the earliest Greek poets, often called the father of Greek didactic poetry. Two of his complete epics have survived, the THEOGONY, relating the myths of the gods, and the WORKS AND DAYS, describing peasant life.

Hesiod was a native of Boeotia, a district of central Greece. He may at first have been a rhapsodist (a professional reciter of poetry), learning the technique and vocabulary of the epic by memorizing and reciting heroic songs. He himself attributes his poetic gifts to the Muses, who appeared to him while he was tending his sheep. That his epics won renown during his lifetime is shown by his participation in the contest of songs at the funeral games of Amphidamas at Chalcis on the island of Euboea.

Of Hesiod's two extant epics, the *Theogony* is clearly the earlier. Hesiod's authorship of the *Theogony* has been questioned but is no longer doubted, though the work does include sections inserted by later poets and rhapsodists. The discovery of a Hurrian theogony similar to Hesiod's seems to indicate that Hesiod's theogony owes significant episodes to Middle Eastern models. Nonetheless, the Uranus–Cronus–Zeus succession as told by Hesiod approximates the pattern of a classical Greek tragic trilogy. Hesiod's other epic poem, the *Works and Days*, has a more personal character as it expresses his views on the proper conduct of men.

Such was the power of Hesiod's name that epics by other poets were soon attributed to him; these works, particularly the *Catalogues of Women* and the *Shield of Heracles*, are often included in editions of his works.

Hesperides \hes-'per-i-ˌdēz\ (Greek: "Daughters of Evening"), *singular* Hesperis \'hes-pǝr-is\ In Greek mythology, clear-voiced maidens who guarded the tree bearing golden apples that Gaea gave to Hera at her marriage to Zeus. They were usually three in number, Aegle, Erytheia, and Hespere (or Hesperethusa), but by some accounts were as many as seven. They were said to live among the Hyperboreans. The golden apples were also guarded by the dragon Ladon, the offspring of Phorcys and Ceto. The golden apples that Aphrodite gave to Hippomenes before his race with Atalanta were from the garden of the Hesperides.

Hesperus or **Hesperos** \'hes-pǝ-rǝs\, *Latin* Vesper \'vespǝr\ In Greco-Roman mythology, the evening star, son or brother of Atlas. He was later identified with the morning star, Phosphorus, or Eosphorus (Latin: Lucifer), the bringer of light. Hesperus is variously described by different authors as the father of the Hesperides (the guardians of the golden apples) or of their mother, Hesperis.

Hesse \'hes-ǝ, *Angl* 'hes\, Hermann (b. July 2, 1877, Calw, Ger.—d. Aug. 9, 1962, Montagnola, Switz.) German novelist, poet, and winner of the Nobel Prize for Literature in 1946, who principally deals with the individual's break with society to find spiritual fulfillment. With his appeal for self-realization and his celebration of Eastern mysticism, Hesse posthumously became a cult figure.

Hesse entered a seminary but was unable to adapt to the life there; he then was apprenticed in a Calw factory and later in a Tübingen bookstore. His disgust with conventional schooling was later expressed in the novel *Unterm Rad* (1906; *Beneath the Wheel*), in which an overly diligent student is driven to self-destruction.

Hesse became a freelance writer in 1904, when he brought out his first novel, *Peter Camenzind*, about a failed and dissipated writer. The inward and outward search of the artist is further explored in *Gertrud* (1910) and *Rosshalde* (1914). A visit to India during these years was later reflected in SIDDHARTHA (1922), a lyric novel based on the early life of Buddha.

During World War I, Hesse lived in neutral Switzerland, wrote denunciations of militarism and nationalism, and edited a journal for German war prisoners and internees. He became a permanent resident of Switzerland in 1919 and a citizen in 1923, settling in Montagnola.

A deepening sense of personal crisis had led Hesse to psychoanalysis in 1916. The influence of analysis appears in *Demian* (1919), an examination of the achievement of self-awareness by a troubled adolescent. The novel made its author famous. Hesse's later work shows his interest in Jungian psychology. He was particularly interested in the duality of human nature.

Der Steppenwolf (1927; STEPPENWOLF) describes the conflict between bourgeois acceptance and spiritual self-realization. In *Narziss und Goldmund* (1930; *Narcissus and Goldmund*), an intellectual ascetic who is content with established religious faith is contrasted with an artistic sensualist pursuing his own form of salvation. In his last and longest novel, *Das Glasperlenspiel* (1943; English trans., THE GLASS BEAD GAME, or *Magister Ludi*), Hesse again explores the dualism of the contemplative and the active life, this time through the figure of a supremely gifted intellectual.

Hestia \'hes-tē-ǝ, -chǝ\ Greek goddess of the hearth, daughter of Cronus and Rhea, and one of the 12 Olympian deities. When the gods Apollo and Poseidon became suitors for her hand she swore to remain a maiden forever, whereupon Zeus, the king of the gods, bestowed upon her the honor of presiding over all sacrifices.

She was worshiped chiefly as goddess of the family hearth and was often closely connected with Zeus, god of the family in its external relation of hospitality and its internal unity. She was also sometimes associated with Hermes, the two representing domestic life on the one hand and business and outdoor life on the other. Her Roman counterpart was VESTA. In later philosophy Hestia became the hearth goddess of the universe.

hexameter \hek-'sam-ǝ-tǝr\ In classical prosody, a line of six metrical feet (Greek) or of six metra (Latin), usually dactyls (− ∪ ∪). Dactylic hexameter is the oldest known form of Greek poetry and is the preeminent meter of narrative and didactic poetry in Greek and Latin, in which its position is comparable to that of iambic pentameter in English versification. The epics of Homer and of Virgil are composed in dactylic hexameter, as are the didactic poems of Hesiod and Lucretius. A dactylic hexameter line is scanned as: − ∪∪ | − ∪∪ | − ∪∪ | − ∪∪ | − ∪∪ | − ∪.

Hexapla \'hek-sǝ-plǝ\ [Late Latin, from Greek *Hexaplâ*, from neuter plural of *hexaplóos* sixfold, having six parts] An edition or work in six texts or versions in parallel columns. The term is derived from the title of a version of the Old Testament compiled about the 2nd century AD by Origen, a theologian and biblical scholar of the early Greek church.

Origen's *Hexapla* was a synopsis of six Old Testament versions: the Hebrew text, a transliteration of the Hebrew in Greek letters, the Septuagint (an authoritative Greek version of the Old Testament), and the versions of Aquila, Symmachus, and Theodotion. In the case of some books, Psalms for instance, as many as three more versions were added.

hexapody \hek-'sap-ə-dē\ [Greek *hexapod-, hexápous* (of a line of verse) having six feet] In classical prosody, a prosodic line or group consisting of six feet, often a line of trochaic or iambic verse measured by single feet instead of the more usual dipodies, or a line of dactylic hexameter in which foot and metron coincide.

hexastich \'hek-sə-ˌstik\ or **hexastichon** \hek-'sas-tə-ˌkän\ *plural* hexastichs *or* hexasticha \hek-'sas-tik-ə\ [New Latin *hexastichon,* ultimately from Greek *hexástichos* having six lines], *also called* sextet. A group, stanza, or poem of six lines. *See also* SESTET; SESTINA.

Heyse \'hī-zə\, Paul Johann Ludwig von (b. March 15, 1830, Berlin [Germany]—d. April 2, 1914, Munich) German writer and prominent member of the traditionalist Munich school who received the Nobel Prize for Literature in 1910.

After completing his studies Heyse became an independent scholar and was called to Munich by Maximilian II of Bavaria. There, with the poet Emanuel von Geibel, he became the head of the Munich circle of writers, who sought to preserve traditional artistic values from the encroachments of political radicalism, materialism, and realism. Chief among his carefully wrought short stories is *L'Arrabiata* (1855). He also published novels (including *Kinder der Welt,* 1873; *Children of the World*) and many unsuccessful plays. Among his best works are his translations of Giacomo Leopardi and other Italian poets. In 1871 he formulated a definition of the novella form, the "Falkentheorie" ("falcon theory," from Giovanni Boccaccio's model novella, *Tale of a Falcon*). Heyse, who was given to idealization and who refused to portray the dark side of life, became an embittered opponent of the growing school of naturalism, and his popularity had greatly decreased by the time he received the Nobel Prize.

Heyward \'hā-wərd\, DuBose, *in full* Edwin DuBose Heyward (b. Aug. 31, 1885, Charleston, S.C., U.S.—d. June 16, 1940, Tryon, N.C.) American novelist, dramatist, and poet whose first novel, PORGY (1925), was the basis for a highly successful play, an opera, and a motion picture.

At the age of 17 Heyward worked on the waterfront, where he observed the people who were to become the subjects of his writing. His works of poetry include *Carolina Chansons* (1922), a joint publication with Hervey Allen; *Skylines and Horizons* (1924); and *Jasbo Brown* (1931). In addition to *Porgy,* which is set in a Charleston tenement, Heyward wrote the novels *Angel* (1926), about mountain people in North Carolina; *Peter Ashley* (1932), about pre-Civil War Charleston; and *Star-Spangled Virgin* (1939), concerned with the Virgin Islands during the New Deal.

In 1935 the opera *Porgy and Bess* was produced with libretto and words by Heyward and Ira Gershwin and music by George Gershwin. A motion-picture version appeared in 1959.

Heywood \'hā-ˌwûd\, Jasper (b. 1535, London, Eng.—d. Jan. 9, 1598, Naples [Italy]) Priest and poet whose translations of the Roman playwright Seneca's *Troades* (1559), *Thyestes* (1560), and *Hercules furens* (1561) were included in a collection

issued as *Seneca His Tenne Tragedies Translated into English* (1581). A son of the playwright John Heywood, he was educated at the University of Oxford, joined the Jesuits in Rome (1562), and became professor at the Jesuit college at Dillingen, Ger., in 1564. Head of the Jesuit mission to England from 1581, he was imprisoned during 1583–85 and then exiled.

Heywood \'hā-ˌwûd\, John (b. 1497?, London, Eng.?—d. after 1575, Mechelen, Belg.) Playwright who, by humanizing characterization, helped put English drama on the road to the fully developed comedy of the Elizabethans. One of the first dramatists who was not an ecclesiastic, he replaced biblical allegory with representations of everyday life and manners.

Heywood's works for the stage were interludes—entertainments popular in 15th- and 16th-century England, consisting of dialogues on a set subject. Interludes were performed separately, or preceding or following a play, or between the acts. The four interludes to which Heywood's name is attached are witty, satirical debates in verse, ending on a didactic note like others of their genre and reflecting the influence of French farce and of Geoffrey Chaucer.

The Playe Called the Foure P.P.: A Palmer, a Pardoner, a Potycary, a Pedler (not dated but printed *c.* 1544) is a contest in lying. *The Play of the Wether,* printed in 1533, describes the chaotic results of Jupiter's attempts to suit the weather to different people's desires. *A Play of Love* and *Wytty and Wytless,* both printed in 1533, complete the list of interludes definitely ascribed to Heywood. Two others printed in the same year without an author's name are generally considered to be by Heywood: *A Mery Play Between the Pardoner, the Frere, the Curate and Neybour Pratte* and *A Mery Play Betwene Johan Johan the Husbande, Tyb His Wyfe, and Syr Jhan the Preest.* Heywood's other works include *A Dialogue Conteining the Number in Effect of All the Proverbes in the English Tongue* (1549) and collections of epigrams, published together as *John Heywoodes Woorkes* in 1562; ballads, among them "The Willow Garland," sung by Desdemona in William Shakespeare's *Othello*; and a long verse allegory, *The Spider and the Flie* (1556).

Despite several episodes of oppression, Heywood remained a Roman Catholic. In 1564, leaving his property in the hands of his son-in-law, John Donne (father of the poet), he fled to Belgium, where he died.

Heywood \'hā-ˌwûd\, Thomas (b. 1574?, Lincolnshire, Eng.—d. Aug. 16, 1641, London) English actor and playwright whose career spans the peak periods of Elizabethan and Jacobean drama.

After arriving in London some time before 1598, Heywood joined Philip Henslowe's theatrical company and was active in London as a playwright and actor for the rest of his life. He claimed to have had "either an entire hand, or at least a maine finger" in 220 plays. Of these, 24 survive that are generally accepted as wholly or partly his.

Most of Heywood's plays are sentimental in theme but realistic in setting and reveal an affectionate regard for the daily sights, sounds, and activities of London. He wrote romances such as *The Captives* and *A Pleasant Comedy, Called a Maidenhead Well Lost* (both in 1634); adventure plays such as *The Fair Maid of the West* (1631); and seven lord mayor's pageants, completed between 1631 and 1639. He also wrote masques, mythological cycles, and chronicle histories. His most popular history play, *If You Know Not Me, You Know Nobody* (1605–06), is about Elizabeth I. His masterpiece, *A Woman Killed with Kindness* (1607), is one of the earliest middle-class tragedies. Heywood's most important prose work is *An Apology for Actors* (1612), an account of actors' place and dignity and their function in society since antiquity.

hiatus \hī-'ā-təs\ [Latin, literally, opening, chasm] In prosody, a break in sound between two vowels that occur together without an intervening consonant, both vowels being clearly enunciated. The two vowels may be either within one word, as in the words V*ie*nna and n*ai*ve, or the final and initial vowels of two successive words, as in the phrases "*see it*" and "*go in*." Hiatus is the opposite of elision, the dropping or blurring of the second vowel; it is also distinct from diphthongization, in which the vowels blend to form one sound.

The word also refers to a gap in a sentence or verse that destroys the sense or meaning of the sentence, or, in logic, to a missing step in a proof. *See also* LACUNA.

Hiawatha \,hī-ə-'wōth-ə, ,hē-, -'wäth-\ (*in full* The Song of Hiawatha) Long narrative poem by Henry Wadsworth LONGFELLOW, published in 1855. It is especially notable for its relentless use of trochaic meter, which Longfellow adapted from the meter of the Finnish epic *Kalevala*.

As background for the work, Longfellow consulted two books on the Indian tribes of North America by Henry Rowe Schoolcraft. He perpetuated an error of Schoolcraft's that placed Hiawatha among the forest tribes of the northern Midwest; the historical Hiawatha was chief (*c.* 1450) of the Onondaga tribe, who lived well to the east.

Longfellow's Hiawatha is an Ojibwa Indian, raised by Nokomis, his wrinkled and wise grandmother, "daughter of the Moon." When he grows up, Hiawatha wants to avenge the wrong done by his father, the West Wind, to his mother, Wenonah. Father and son eventually reconcile. Hiawatha becomes his people's leader and marries Minnehaha, of the former enemy Dakota tribe. An era of peace and enlightenment ensues under his reign. Later, disease and famine afflict the tribe and Minnehaha dies. Before Hiawatha takes his leave of the tribe to go to the Isles of the Blessed, he tells his people to heed those who will come with a new religion.

Some of the poem's lines are among the best known of American poetry: "By the shores of Gitche Gumee,/ By the shining Big-Sea-Water,/ Stood the wigwam of Nokomis,/ Daughter of the Moon, Nokomis." The poem, and its sing-song meter, have been frequent objects of parody.

Hicks \'hiks\, Granville (b. Sept. 9, 1901, Exeter, N.H., U.S.—d. June 18, 1982, Franklin Park, N.J.) Critic, novelist, and teacher who was one of the foremost practitioners of Marxist criticism in American literature.

After graduating from Harvard and studying for two years for the ministry, Hicks joined the Communist Party in 1934. As literary editor of the *New Masses*, he became one of the party's chief cultural spokespersons. His book *The Great Tradition* (1933) evaluated American literature since the Civil War from a Marxist point of view.

Hicks was dismissed from his teaching position at Rensselaer Polytechnic Institute in 1935 and consequently became the center of a storm of controversy over academic freedom in the United States. In 1939 he broke with the communists after the Nazi-Soviet pact, explaining his growing dissatisfaction with the party's uncritical endorsement of Soviet policy in a letter to *The New Republic* magazine. He remained an active writer; *Part of the Truth: An Autobiography* was published in 1965, and *Literary Horizons*, a collection of his book reviews over the preceding 25 years, was published in 1970.

hierography \,hī-ə-'räg-rə-fē\ [Greek *hierós* sacred] Descriptive writing on sacred subjects, or a treatise on religion.

hierology \,hī-ə-'räl-ə-jē\ [Greek *hierós* sacred] A body of knowledge of sacred things, specifically the literary or traditional embodiment of the religious beliefs of a people, such as the Bible or the Qur'ān.

Higgins, Henry \'hen-rē-'hig-inz\ Fictional character, a professor of phonetics who instructs Cockney Eliza Doolittle in proper English, in George Bernard Shaw's play PYGMALION.

higgledy-piggledy *see* DOUBLE DACTYLS.

high \'hī\ 1. Of an artistic style or movement, advanced toward its acme or fullest extent; specifically, constituting the late, fully developed, or most creative stage or period. 2. Intensely moving, or characterized by sublime, heroic, or stirring events or subject matter, as in the phrase "high drama."

high comedy Comedy characterized by grace and wit and an appeal to the intellect, as in a comedy of manners. It often takes the form of satirizing human folly and inconsistencies, *e.g.*, the plays of George Bernard Shaw and the novels of George Meredith. The latter helped define the concept of high comedy when he wrote in his lecture later published as *An Essay on Comedy and the Uses of the Comic Spirit* that true comedy should "awaken thoughtful laughter." *Compare* LOW COMEDY.

Highsmith \'hī-,smith\, Patricia, *original name* Mary Patricia Plangman \'plaŋ-mən\ (b. Jan. 19, 1921, Fort Worth, Tex., U.S.—d. Feb. 4, 1995, Locarno, Switz.) American novelist and short-story writer who was best known for her psychological thrillers in which she delved into the nature of guilt, innocence, goodness, and evil.

Highsmith graduated from Barnard College in 1942. In 1950 she published *Strangers on a Train*, an intriguing story of two men, one ostensibly good and the other ostensibly evil, who undergo character reversals. *The Talented Mr. Ripley* (1955) was the first of several books featuring the adventures of a likeable murderer, Tom RIPLEY, who takes on the identities of his victims. Ripley also appears in *Ripley Under Ground* (1970), *Ripley's Game* (1974), *The Boy Who Followed Ripley* (1980), and *Ripley Under Water* (1991). Highsmith's collections of short stories include *The Black House* (1981) and *Tales of Natural and Unnatural Catastrophes* (1987).

In her *Plotting and Writing Suspense Fiction* (1966; revised and enlarged 1981), Highsmith held that "art has nothing to do with morality, convention or moralizing."

Higuchi Ichiyō \'hē-gù-chē-ē-'chē-yō\, *pseudonym of* Higuchi Natsu \'nät-sù\, *also called* Higuchi Natsuko \'nät-sə-kō\ (b. May 2, 1872, Tokyo, Japan—d. Nov. 23, 1896, Tokyo) Poet and novelist, the most important Japanese woman writer of her period, whose characteristic works dealt with the licensed pleasure quarters of Tokyo.

Upon the death of her father in 1889, she suddenly found herself the sole support of her mother and younger sister, and she lived in hardship and poverty until her own death at the age of 24. She had studied classical literature for several years before she tried writing as a means of earning a living.

In 1891 she was introduced to a minor novelist, Nakarai Tōsui, who became an important inspiration for the literary diary she kept from 1891 to 1896, published as *Wakabakage* ("The Shadow of Young Leaves"). In her own distinctive classical prose style, Ichiyō wrote with sensitivity chiefly of the women of the old Tokyo downtown area, at a time when traditional society was giving way to industrialization. Her works include *Ōtsugomori* (1894; *The Last Day of the Year*) and her masterpiece, *Takekurabe* (1895; *Growing Up*), a delicate story of children being reared on the fringes of the pleasure district.

Hijuelos \ē-'kwä-lōs\, Oscar (b. Aug. 24, 1951, New York, N.Y., U.S.) Novelist whose writing chronicles the pre-Castro Cuban immigrant experience in the United States, particularly in New York.

Hijuelos was a full-time writer of fiction from 1984. He won critical acclaim for his first novel, *Our House in the Last*

World (1983), and was awarded the 1990 Pulitzer Prize for fiction for his second novel, *The Mambo Kings Play Songs of Love* (1989; film, 1992).

Our House in the Last World concerns members of the immigrant Santinio family who try to integrate into their Cuban identity and values the rhythms and culture of life in New York's Spanish Harlem. In the novel Hijuelos employs surreal effects suggestive of Latin-American fiction. *The Mambo Kings Play Songs of Love* also chronicles Cuban immigrants, their quest for the American dream, and their eventual disillusionment. It vividly recreates the musical and social environment of North America in the 1950s. A later novel was *The Fourteen Sisters of Emilio Montez O'Brien* (1993).

Hikmet, Nazım   *see* NÂZIM HİKMET.

Hilarius \hə-'lar-ē-əs\ (fl. 1125)   Medieval poet and wandering scholar, a pupil of Peter Abelard who was associated with Angers, Anjou.

Hilarius wrote light verse of great charm in Latin, including poems dedicated to English persons—which has led to the otherwise unsupported theory that he was English himself. His fame rests on three Latin religious plays, two of which, like two of his poems, have French refrains. Those on the raising of Lazarus and on Daniel were written to be performed at matins or vespers, and both follow the biblical narrative fairly closely. The third play, which bears no trace of liturgical performance, is on a nonbiblical subject: the legend of the image of St. Nicholas. All three plays show variety of meter, great liveliness, and dramatic power.

Hildebrandslied \'hil-də-ˌbränts-ˌlēt\ ("Song of Hildebrand")   Old High German alliterative heroic ballad on the fatalistic theme of a duel of honor between a father and a son. The fragmentary ballad, dating to about 800, is the sole surviving record of Old High German heroic poetry. Its hero, Hildebrand, appears in Germanic legend as an elder warrior, as a magician, and as an adviser and weapons master to Dietrich von Bern. In the *Hildebrandslied* the hero is forced into a duel by the aggressions of a young warrior, Hadubrand, who does not know that Hildebrand is his father. Though the fragment stops short of a conclusion, it leaves no doubt that Hildebrand kills his son.

An inferior 15th-century version, *The Younger Lay of Hildebrand*, ends in the reconciliation of the two men. *See also* HELDENLIEDER.

Hildegard von Bingen \'hil-də-ˌgärt-fȯn-'biŋ-ən\, *byname* Sibyl of the Rhine (b. 1098, Böckelheim, West Franconia [Germany]—d. Sept. 17, 1179, Rupertsberg, near Bingen)   German abbess and visionary mystic.

Hildegard was educated at the Benedictine cloister of Disibodenberg and became prioress there in 1136. Having experienced visions since she was a child, Hildegard at the age of 43 consulted her confessor, who in turn reported the matter to the archbishop of Mainz. A committee of theologians subsequently confirmed the authenticity of Hildegard's visions, and a monk was appointed to help her record them in writing. The finished work, *Scivias* (1141–52), consisted of 26 visions, prophetic, symbolic, and apocalyptic in form. About 1147 she left Disibodenberg to found a new convent at Rupertsberg, where she continued to prophesy and to record her visions in writing.

Hildegard's numerous other writings include a morality play, a book of saints' lives, two treatises on medicine and natural history, and extensive correspondence, in which are to be found further prophecies and allegorical treatises. Her lyrical poetry, gathered in *Symphonia armonie celestium revelationum*, consists of 77 poems (all with music), and together they form a liturgical cycle.

Hill \'hil\, Aaron (b. Feb. 10, 1685, London, Eng.—d. Feb. 8, 1750, London)   English poet, dramatist, and essayist whose adaptations of Voltaire's plays *Zaïre* (*The Tragedy of Zara*, 1736) and *Mérope* (1749) enjoyed considerable success.

After leaving school Hill traveled in the Middle East, afterward publishing *A Full Account of the Present State of the Ottoman Empire* (1709). He produced G.F. Handel's opera *Rinaldo* (having himself translated the Italian libretto) at London's Haymarket Theatre. In 1718 he wrote the poem *The Northern Star*, dedicated to Peter the Great of Russia, which the tsar acknowledged by ordering a gold medal for Hill (the medal never arrived). Alexander Pope satirized Hill in *The Dunciad*, to which Hill retorted with *The Progress of Wit* (1730). His letters to Pope and others were published in 1751.

Hill, Fanny \'fan-ē-'hil\   Fictional character, the protagonist of the novel FANNY HILL by John Cleland.

Hills Like White Elephants   Short story by Ernest HEMINGWAY, published in 1927 in the periodical *transition* and later that year in the collection *Men Without Women*. The themes of this sparsely written vignette about an American couple waiting for a train in Spain are almost entirely implicit. Largely devoid of plot, the story is notable for its use of irony, symbolism, and repetition.

Hilton \'hilt-ən\, James (Glen Trevor) (b. Sept. 9, 1900, Leigh, Lancashire, Eng.—d. Dec. 20, 1954, Long Beach, Calif., U.S.)   English novelist whose popular works include LOST HORIZON (1933), GOOD-BYE, MR. CHIPS (1934), and *Random Harvest* (1941), all of which were made into highly successful motion pictures.

Hilton was contributing articles to newspapers and had his first novel (*Catherine Herself*) published before he graduated from the University of Cambridge in 1921. He became a journalist and wrote several more novels. His deftly written, sentimental novella *Good-bye, Mr. Chips* was published in the *British Weekly* in 1934 and became enormously popular after it was reprinted in *The Atlantic Monthly* that same year. Hilton's novels *Knight Without Armour* and *Lost Horizon* were quickly reissued and also attracted wide readerships. Hilton eventually moved to California, where he wrote film adaptations of his own and others' novels.

Himes \'hīmz\, Chester (Bomar) (b. July 29, 1909, Jefferson City, Mo., U.S.—d. Nov. 12, 1984, Moraira, Spain)   African-American writer whose novels reflect his encounters with racism.

Himes attended Ohio State University. From 1929 to 1936 he was incarcerated for armed robbery at the Ohio State Penitentiary, and while there he began to write fiction. A number of his stories appeared in *Esquire* and other American magazines. After his release from prison, he joined the Works Progress Administration, eventually serving as a writer with the Ohio Writers' Project. His first two novels, IF HE HOLLERS LET HIM GO (1945) and *Lonely Crusade* (1947), concern racism in the defense industry and the labor movement, respectively. *Cast the First Stone* (1952) portrays prison life, and *The Third Generation* (1954) examines family life.

In the mid-1950s Himes moved to Paris. There he wrote chiefly murder mysteries set in Harlem. These include *The Crazy Kill* (1959), *Cotton Comes to Harlem* (1965; film, 1970), and *Blind Man with a Pistol* (1969; later retitled *Hot Day, Hot Night*). Among his other works are *Run Man, Run* (1966), a thriller; *Pinktoes* (1961), a satirical work of interracial erotica; and *Black on Black* (1973), a collection of stories. He also published two volumes of autobiography, *The Quality of Hurt* (1972) and *My Life as Absurdity* (1976).

Hippel \'hip-əl\, Theodor Gottlieb von (b. Jan. 31, 1741, Gerdauen, Prussia [now Zheleznodorozhny, Russia]—d. April 23, 1796, Königsberg [now Kaliningrad, Russia]) German writer of the late Enlightenment and a disciple of the philosopher Immanuel Kant.

In 1780 Hippel was appointed mayor of Königsberg, becoming president of the town in 1786. The influence of Laurence Sterne can be seen in his largely autobiographical novel *Lebensläufe nach aufsteigender Linie* (1778–81; "Careers in an Ascending Line"). *Kreuz- und Querzüge des Ritters A bis Z* (1793–94; "The Knight's Crisscrossing Journeys from A to Z") portrays the prejudice and pride of the nobility in the misadventures and ultimate reconciliation with society of a quixotic hero. Hippel's two essays *Über die Ehe* (1774; "On Marriage") and *Über die bürgerliche Verbesserung der Weiber* (1792; "On the Civic Betterment of Women") attracted much attention with their emphasis on the emancipation of women. He also published two comedies; a number of legal, Masonic, and moral works; and hymns.

Hippius *see* GIPPIUS.

hippocampus \,hip-ə-'kam-pəs\ [Greek *hippókampos* sea horse, legendary sea monster, from *híppos* horse + *kámpos* sea monster] A legendary creature with the head and forequarters of a horse and the tail of a dolphin or fish.

hippogriff \'hip-ə-,grif\ [French *hippogriffe,* from Italian *ippogrifo,* from *ippo-* (from Greek *híppos* horse) + *grifo* griffin] A legendary animal that has the foreparts of a winged griffin and the body and hindquarters of a horse. The creature was invented by Ludovico Ariosto in his *Orlando furioso* and was based on a proverbial phrase about crossing a griffin with a horse that was used to signify an impossibility or incongruity.

Hippolyte \hi-'päl-ə-tē\ or **Hippolyta** \-tə\ In Greek mythology, a queen of the Amazons. One of the legendary Labors of Heracles was to steal her girdle, and according to one story, in the process of doing so he killed her. According to another legend, she was the mother of Hippolytus by Theseus.

Hippolytus \hi-'päl-ə-təs\ Minor god in Greek mythology. He was the son of Theseus by Hippolyte (or Antiope) and was a follower of Artemis (the chaste hunter). Jealous of his devotion to Artemis, Aphrodite caused Phaedra, Hippolytus' stepmother, to fall passionately in love with Hippolytus. Ashamed, Phaedra accused Hippolytus of attempted rape and then hanged herself. Theseus banished his son and caused him to be killed before he learned the truth from Artemis.

Later writers who treated the subject include Robert Garnier, Edmund Spenser (in *The Faerie Queene*), Friedrich von Schiller, Hilda Doolittle (H.D.), and Eugene O'Neill (in *Desire Under the Elms*). The theme is that of the biblical story of Joseph and Potiphar's wife and of the story, in the *Iliad*, of Bellerophon and Anteia (Stheneboea).

Hippolytus \hi-'päl-ə-təs\ (*Greek* Hippolytos) Play by EURIPIDES, performed in 428 BC. The action concerns the revenge of Aphrodite, the goddess of love and sexual desire, on Hippolytus, a hunter and sportsman who is repelled by sexual passion and who is instead devoted to the virgin huntress Artemis.

hipponactean \,hip-ə-,nak-'tē-ən\ Of or relating to the 6th-century-BC Greek poet Hipponax, who is said to have invented the metrical form known as the choliamb (or *scazon*), the "limping" iambic or trochaic trimeter in which the last three syllables are long.

hircocervus \,hər-kō-'sər-vəs\ [Late Latin, from Latin *hircus* he-goat + *cervus* stag; translation of Greek *tragélaphos*] A legendary creature that is half goat and half stag.

Hiroshima \,hē-rō-'shē-mä, hē-'rō-shē-mä\ Report by John HERSEY of the explosion of an atomic bomb over Hiroshima, Japan, by the U.S. Army Air Forces on August 6, 1945, and of the aftermath of the explosion. First published in *The New Yorker* magazine as the entire editorial content of its issue of August 31, 1946, the account was objective rather than sensational, focusing on six survivors of the atomic blast and on the horrors they witnessed and endured. Hersey's article was published in book form in November 1946.

Hirsch \'hərsh\, E.D., Jr., *in full* Eric Donald (b. March 22, 1928, Memphis, Tenn., U.S.) American literary critic and educator who is best known for his work on cultural literacy, notably for *Cultural Literacy: What Every American Needs to Know* (1987). He cowrote *The Dictionary of Cultural Literacy* (1988; with Joseph F. Kett and James Trefil) and was the main editor of *A First Dictionary of Cultural Literacy* (1989).

Hirsch graduated from Cornell University and earned a doctorate from Yale in 1957. He taught at Yale for a decade before accepting a professorship at the University of Virginia in 1966. His works of criticism include books on Romantic literature as well as *Validity in Interpretation* (1967), *The Aims of Interpretation* (1976), and *The Philosophy of Composition* (1977).

Based on his own teaching experience, Hirsch concluded that many American students lacked the basic knowledge of cultural terms and concepts that are necessary for academic advancement. His dictionaries provided what he claimed was the necessary information.

Ḥisdai ibn Shaprut \kis-'dī-,ib-ən-shäp-'rüt\, *in full* Ḥisdai abu Yusuf ben Isaac ben Ezra ibn Shaprut, Ḥisdai *also spelled* Ḥasdai \käs-'dī\ (b. c. 915, Jaén, Spain—d. c. 975, Córdoba) Jewish physician, translator, and political figure who helped inaugurate the golden age of Hebrew letters in Moorish Spain.

After becoming court physician to caliph 'Abd ar-Raḥmān III, Ḥisdai gradually gained eminence in the Arab world, acting as vizier without title. He used his linguistic talents (he knew Hebrew, Arabic, and Latin) and persuasive personality in delicate diplomatic missions between Muslim and Christian rulers. After 'Abd ar-Raḥmān died in 961, Ḥisdai continued to perform important services for his son and successor, al-Ḥakam II.

Ḥisdai helped inaugurate the golden age of Spanish Judaism, gathering under his patronage such major literary figures as Dunash ben Labrat (c. 920–c. 990) and Menahem ben Saruq (c. 910–c. 970), who helped establish scientific Hebrew grammar and a new mode in Hebrew poetry. Ḥisdai fostered the study of Jewish law and the Talmud, thereby making Spanish Jewry relatively independent of the Eastern Talmudic academies.

Ḥisdai's written correspondence with a Jewish Khazar king, Joseph, is of historic importance. The Khazars, a Turkic people dwelling in southern Russia, had converted to Judaism in the middle of the 8th century AD. Ḥisdai's letter (which was actually written by Menahem ben Saruq) and the king's response had a shadowy existence until the 16th century.

Hisperic \his-'per-ik\ [Medieval Latin *Hispericus,* alteration of *Hespericus* western, Italian, hence probably (in reference to Latin style) urbane, elegant] Belonging to or constituting a style of Latin writing that probably originated in the British Isles in the 7th century. It is characterized by extreme obscurity intentionally produced by periphrasis (preference for a longer phrase over a shorter, equally adequate phrase), coinage of new words, and very liberal use of loanwords to express quite ordinary meanings. The style takes its name from the *Hisperica famina* ("Hisperic Sayings"), a work probably composed in Ireland in the mid-7th century.

Historia regum Britanniae \his-'tȯr-ē-ə-'rā-gu̇m-bri-'tan-ē-,ī\ ("History of the Kings of Britain") Fictional history of Britain written by GEOFFREY of Monmouth sometime between 1135 and 1139. The *Historia regum Britanniae* was one of the most popular books of the Middle Ages. The story begins with the settlement of Britain by Brutus the Trojan, great-grandson of Aeneas, and by the Trojan Corineus, the eponymous founder of Cornwall, who exterminate giants inhabiting Britain. Then follow the reigns of the early kings down to the Roman conquest. It includes such episodes as the founding of Bath by Bladud and of Leicester by Leir (Lear). The story of the Saxon infiltration during the reign of the wicked usurper Vortigern, of the successful resistance of the Saxons by Vortimer, and of the restoration of the rightful line, followed by the great reigns of Aurelius and his brother Uther Pendragon, leads up to the account of Arthur's conquests, the culminating point of the work. Chapters 106–111 introduce the enchanter Merlin, who predicts, in an obscure and apocalyptic manner, the future political history of Britain. These chapters were first published separately, before 1136. They gave rise to the genre of political prophecies attributed to Merlin.

historical criticism   Criticism in the light of historical evidence, or criticism based on the context in which a work was written, including facts about the author's life and the historical and social circumstances of the time. This is in contrast to other types of criticism, such as textual and formal, in which emphasis is placed on examining the text itself while outside influences on the text are disregarded. New historicism is a particular form of historical criticism. *See also* LITERARY CRITICISM.

historical novel   A novel that has as its setting a period of history and that attempts to convey the spirit, manners, and social conditions of a past age with realistic detail and fidelity to historical fact.

The work may deal with actual historical personages, as does Robert Graves's *I, Claudius* (1934), or it may contain a mixture of fictional and historical characters. It may focus on a single historic event, as does Franz Werfel's *The Forty Days of Musa Dagh* (1933). More often it attempts to portray a broader view of a past society in which great events are reflected by their impact on the private lives of fictional individuals. Since the appearance of the first historical novel, Sir Walter Scott's *Waverley* (1814), this type of fiction has remained popular. Though some historical novels, such as Leo Tolstoy's *War and Peace* (1865–69), are of the highest artistic quality, many are mediocre—the purely escapist costume romance makes no pretense to historicity but uses a setting in the past to lend credibility to improbable characters and adventures.

historical rhyme   A form of eye rhyme, in which two words appear to rhyme but in fact are pronounced differently, where the two words were pronounced the same at one time, as in *flood* and *brood* or *far* and *war*.

historiette \ˌhis-ˌtȯr-ē-'et\ [French, a derivative of *histoire* history, influenced in form by Latin *historia*]   A short history or story.

History   Novel by Elsa MORANTE, published in Italian as *La storia* in 1974.

Set in Rome during and after World War II, the work is centered on the lives of an epileptic Italian woman named Ida, who is half-Jewish; her sons Useppe (Giuseppe)—born as the result of her rape by a German soldier—and Nino, first a fascist then a partisan; and the people whose lives intersect with theirs. Each of the novel's eight sections begins and ends with a brief history of the progress of the war. These sections include graphic descriptions of air raids, deportations, rape, hunger, and homelessness. The author emphasizes that culpability extends far beyond fascist oppressors to munitions manufacturers and other less obvious wielders of power.

History of New York, A \nū-'yȯrk\ (*in full* A History of New York from the Beginning of the World to the End of the Dutch Dynasty, by Diedrich Knickerbocker)   A satirical history by Washington IRVING, published in 1809 and revised in 1812, 1819, and 1848. Originally intended as a burlesque of historical methodology and heroic styles of epic poetry, the work became more serious as the author proceeded.

Diedrich Knickerbocker, the putative narrator, begins with a mock-pedantic cosmogony and proceeds to a history of New Netherlands, often ignoring or altering facts. Descriptions of early New Amsterdam landmarks and old Dutch-American legends are included in the history, as are the discovery of America, the voyage of Henry Hudson, the founding of New Amsterdam, and the hostility of the British, who were based in nearby Connecticut. The book's portrait of the overeducated, belligerent governor William the Testy (Willem Kieft) is actually a Federalist satire of Thomas Jefferson. The history concludes with the rule of Peter the Headstrong (Peter Stuyvesant) and the fall of New Amsterdam to the British in 1664.

History of Sir Charles Grandison, The \'chärlz-'gran-di-sən\   Epistolary novel by Samuel RICHARDSON, published in seven volumes in 1754. His last completed novel, it anticipated the novel of manners of such authors as Jane Austen.

Sir Charles Grandison is a gallant nobleman known for his heroic integrity and magnanimity. He rescues the honorable Harriet Byron when she is kidnapped by Sir Hargrave Pollexfen, her spurned suitor. Eventually, Grandison and Byron fall in love.

history play   *see* CHRONICLE PLAY.

Hlódyn   *see* JÖRD.

Hoagland \'hōg-lənd\, Edward (b. Dec. 21, 1932, New York, N.Y., U.S.)   American novelist, travel writer, and essayist, noted especially for his writings about nature and wildlife.

Hoagland sold his first novel, *Cat Man* (1956), shortly before graduating from Harvard University. The novels *The Circle Home* (1960), set in a seedy boxing milieu, and *The Peacock's Tail* (1965) were noted for their sympathetic portrayals of impoverished, struggling people. His fourth novel, *Seven Rivers West* (1986), tells of the cultural collision between white railroad builders and Indians in western Canada during the 1880s. He also published the short-story collections *City Tales* (1986) and *The Final Fate of the Alligators* (1992).

Hoagland turned a diary into *Notes from the Century Before: A Journal from British Columbia* (1969); *African Calliope: A Journey to the Sudan* (1979) was a later travel book. Perhaps his best work was his nature essays and editorials, which combined a lifelong fondness for wilderness with his characteristic close observation. His essays were collected in *The Courage of Turtles* (1971), *Walking the Dead Diamond River* (1973), *The Moose on the Wall: Field Notes from the Vermont Wilderness* (1974), *Red Wolves and Black Bears* (1976), *The Edward Hoagland Reader* (1979), and *Balancing Acts* (1992).

Hoban \'hō-ˌban\, Russell (Conwell) (b. Feb. 4, 1925, Lannsdale, Pa., U.S.)   Novelist and children's writer who combined myth, fantasy, humor, and philosophy to explore issues of self-identity.

Hoban attended the Philadelphia Museum School of Industrial Art before beginning his career as an advertising artist and copywriter. He moved to London in 1969. His first book, *What Does It Do and How Does It Work?* (1959), developed from his drawings of construction machinery. He then started writing fiction for children. One of his most enduring creations is the anthropomorphic badger Frances, who is featured with her family and friends in a series of books beginning with *Bedtime for Frances* (1960). Fear and mortality intrude on the fantasy story *The Mouse and His Child* (1967), another of Hoban's best-known books. His other notable works for children include *The Sorely Trying Day* (1964), *Charlie the Tramp* (1967), *Emmet Otter's Jug-Band Christmas* (1971), *How Tom Beat Captain Najork and His Hired Sportsmen* (1974), and *Dinner at Alberta's* (1975).

Among Hoban's adult-oriented novels are *The Lion of Boaz-Jachin and Jachin-Boaz* (1973), *Kleinzeit* (1974), and *Turtle Diary* (1975; film, 1985). *Riddley Walker* (1980), probably Hoban's best-known novel, is set in the future in an England devastated by nuclear war. Events are narrated in a futuristic form of English. Hoban's later writings include the novels *Pilgermann* (1983) and *The Medusa Frequency* (1987).

Hobbit, The \'häb-it\   Fantasy novel by J.R.R. TOLKIEN, published in 1937. The novel introduced Tolkien's richly imagined world of Middle Earth and served as a prologue to his trilogy THE LORD OF THE RINGS.

A race of small humanlike creatures, hobbits characteristically value peace, simplicity, and cozy homes, yet they are capable of incredible feats of courage and resourcefulness. The unwilling hero of *The Hobbit*, Bilbo Baggins, is persuaded to join Thorin and his 12 dwarfs to recover their stolen treasure, which is being guarded by the dragon Smaug. During the expedition, Bilbo finds a magical ring that renders the wearer invisible, which figures prominently in *The Lord of the Rings*. *The Hobbit* is the story of Bilbo's maturing from a seeker of warmth and comforts to a fighter, however humble, for the greater good.

Hobbs, Roy \'rȯi-'häbz\   Fictional character, the ambitious, talented, but flawed baseball player who is the protagonist of THE NATURAL, the first novel by Bernard Malamud.

Hobgoblin \'häb-ˌgäb-lən\   In medieval English folklore, a mischievous fairy, also called PUCK.

Hobson \'häb-sən\, Laura Z., *original name* Laura Kean Zametkin \zə-'met-kin\ (b. June 18/19, 1900, New York, N.Y., U.S.—d. Feb. 28, 1986, New York City)   American novelist and short-story writer noted for her novel *Gentleman's Agreement* (1947; film, 1947), a best-selling study of anti-Semitism.

The daughter of Jewish socialist parents, she was educated at Cornell University, Ithaca, N.Y. In the early 1930s she began writing advertising copy and short stories, and in 1934 she joined the promotional staff of the Henry R. Luce publications (*Time*, *Life*, and *Fortune* magazines). After 1940 she devoted herself entirely to writing, producing a total of nine novels and hundreds of short stories and magazine articles. Hobson is best known for *Gentleman's Agreement*, the story of a journalist who poses as a Jew in order to gain a firsthand experience of anti-Semitism. The book is a scathing depiction of the subtle and insidious manifestations of anti-Semitism in American society at that time. Hobson's other novels include *The Trespassers* (1943) and *Consenting Adult* (1975). The first volume of her autobiography, *Laura Z.: A Life*, was published in 1983. A second volume remained unfinished at her death.

Hoby \'hō-bē\, Sir Thomas (b. 1530—d. July 13, 1566, Paris, Fr.)   English diplomat and translator of Baldassare Castiglione's *Il libro del cortegiano*; his translation was entitled *The Courtyer of Count Baldessar Castilio* (1561).

Hoby traveled extensively on the European continent. By 1552 he was at work on his translation of *Il cortegiano*. The influence of Hoby's translation in England was enormous, not only on the social pattern of life at court but on such writers as William Shakespeare and Sir Philip Sidney. Hoby's other works include a translation of a Latin work on the Church of England and an autobiography.

Hoccleve \'häk-ˌlēv\ or **Occleve** \'äk-ˌlēv\, Thomas (b. 1368/69, London, Eng.—d. *c.* 1450?, Southwick)   English poet who was a contemporary and imitator of Geoffrey Chaucer. His work has little literary merit but much value as social history.

At age 18 or 19 Hoccleve obtained a clerkship in the privy-seal office in London, which he retained intermittently for about 35 years. His earliest dated poem, a translation of Christine de Pisan's *L'Épitre au Dieu d'amours*, appeared in 1402 as "The Letter of Cupid." His poem *La Mâle Règle* (1406; "The Male Regimen") presents a vivid picture of the delights of a bachelor's evening amusements in the taverns and cookshops of Westminster.

In 1411 he produced *De regimine principum*, or *The Regement of Princes*, culled from a 13th-century work of the same name, for Henry, Prince of Wales. A tedious homily, it contains a touching accolade to Chaucer, whose portrait Hoccleve had painted on the manuscript. In his later years Hoccleve turned to serious religious verse and to recording the ills of the day in a literal-minded manner that presents a clear picture of the time.

Hocktide play \'häk-ˌtīd\   A folk play formerly given at Coventry, Eng., on Hock Tuesday (the second Tuesday after Easter). The play was suppressed at the Reformation because of the public revels it incited but was revived for the entertainment of Queen Elizabeth I at the Kenilworth Revels in 1575. The action of the play consisted mainly of a mock battle between parties of men representing English and Danish knights, in which the Danes were defeated and led away as captives by English women. This was meant to represent the massacre of the Danes by King Ethelred II in 1002, although some scholars believe that the play had its beginnings in hocking, a still older custom of the folk festivals. On Hock Monday women went out with ropes, hocking, or capturing, any man they met and exacting a forfeit. Men were allowed to retaliate in kind on Hock Tuesday.

Hodgson \'häj-sən\, Ralph (b. Sept. 9, 1871, Yorkshire, Eng.—d. Nov. 3, 1962, Minerva, Ohio, U.S.)   Poet noted for simple and mystical lyrics that express a love of nature and a concern for humanity's alienation from it.

While working as a journalist in London and later as the editor of *Fry's Magazine*, Hodgson belonged to the loosely connected group of poets known as the Georgians. After teaching English literature in Japan (1924–38), he immigrated to the United States. Most of Hodgson's works were written between 1907 and 1917. He achieved fame as a poet with the publication of the frequently anthologized "The Bull" in 1913. His collections include *The Last Blackbird and Other Lines* (1907), *Eve* (1913), *Poems* (1917), *The Skylark and Other Poems* (1958), and *Collected Poems* (1961).

Hoel \'hü-əl\, Sigurd (b. Dec. 14, 1890, Nord-Odal, Nor.—d. Oct. 14, 1960, Oslo)   Novelist who is considered most representative of the interwar generation of fiction writers in Norway.

Hoel's first great success was a satirical novel, *Syndere i sommersol* (1927; *Sinners in Summertime*), in which he ridiculed the popular use of psychoanalytic terms. Hoel was himself influenced by Freudian psychoanalytic theory, as is shown in *En dag i oktober* (1931; *One Day in October*). He even attempted to attribute the tyranny of Nazism to the restrictions of childhood in *Møte ved milepelen* (1947; *Meeting at the Milestone*). *Veien til verdens ende* (1933; "Road to the World's End"), a novel of childhood, proved the best-loved of his works in Norway.

Hœnir \'hœ̄-nir, 'hər-\   In Norse mythology, one of two gods (the other was Mimir) sent by the Æsir as security to the Vanir. Little is known of him, but he is often mentioned as a companion of Loki and Odin.

Hoffman \'hȯf-mən\, Alice (b. March 16, 1952, New York, N.Y., U.S.)   American novelist whose books about women in search of their identities mixed realism and the supernatural.

Hoffman began her professional writing career by contributing short stories to magazines. Her first novel, *Property Of* (1977), which traces the one-year relationship of a suburban girl and a gang leader, is both gritty and romantic. In *The Drowning Season* (1979), she presented a modern fairy tale about a grandmother, Esther the White, and her granddaughter, Esther the Black. *Angel Landing* (1980) is a love story set near a nuclear power plant on Long Island.

Hoffman's *Fortune's Daughter* (1985) relates a sentimental tale about the healing friendship between Rae, a pregnant young woman, and Lila, a middle-aged fortune-teller. *Illumination Night* (1987), the story of a young couple whose marriage is challenged by a teenaged girl, was noted for its subtle characterizations. In *At Risk* (1988) a young girl with AIDS sparks varied reactions from her family and community. *Seventh Heaven* (1990) concerns an unconventional divorcée in a Long Island suburb in 1959–60, while *Turtle Moon* (1992) contemplates the status of single mothers.

Hoffmann \'hȯf-män\, E.T.A., *in full* Ernst Theodor Amadeus, *original name* Ernst Theodor Wilhelm Hoffmann (b. Jan. 24, 1776, Königsberg, Prussia [now Kaliningrad, Russia]—d. June 25, 1822, Berlin [Germany])   German writer, composer, and painter known for his stories in which supernatural and sinister characters move in and out of people's lives, ironically revealing tragic or grotesque sides of human nature.

Hoffmann was educated in law and became a Prussian law officer in the Polish provinces in 1800, serving until 1806. He then turned to his chief interest, music, and held several positions as conductor, critic, and theatrical musical director in Bamberg and Dresden until 1814. He composed the ballet *Arlequin* (1811) and the opera *Undine* (performed in 1816) and wrote the stories in *Phantasiestücke in Callots Manier*, 4 vol. (1814–15; "Fantasy Pieces in the Style of Callot"), which established his reputation as a writer.

Although he wrote two novels, *Die Elixiere des Teufels*, 2 vol. (1815–16; *The Devil's Elixir*), and *Lebens-Ansichten des Katers Murr nebst fragmentarischer Biographie des Kapellmeisters Johannes Kreisler*, 2 vol. (1820–22; "The Life and Opinions of Kater Murr, with a Fragmentary Biography of Conductor Johannes Kreisler"), and more than 50 short stories before his death from progressive paralysis, he continued to support himself as a legal official in Berlin. The struggle within Hoffmann between the ideal world of his art and his daily life as a bureaucrat is evident in many of his stories, in which characters are possessed by their art. His later stories were collected in *Nachtstücke*, 2 parts (1817; *Hoffmann's Strange Stories*), and *Die Serapionsbrüder*, 4 vol. (1819–21; *The Serapion Brethren*).

Hoffmann \'hȯf-män\, Heinrich, *surname in full* Hoffmann-Donner \'dȯn-ər\, *pseudonyms* Reimerich Kinderlieb, Heinrich Kinderlieb, Peter Struwwel, Heulalius von Heulenburg, Polykarpus Gastfenger, *and* Zwiebel (b. June 13, 1809, Frankfurt am Main [Germany]—d. Sept. 20, 1894, Frankfurt am Main)   German physician and writer who is best known for his work DER STRUWWELPETER (1845; *Slovenly Peter*), the story of a boy known for his wild appearance and unruly behavior.

Hoffmann practiced medicine and taught, and he directed the state mental hospital in Frankfurt am Main (1851–88). He wrote *Der Struwwelpeter*, a book of cautionary tales, as a

Christmas gift for his four-year-old son. Hoffmann also wrote poetry, humor, and satire, as well as other children's books and books on medicine and psychiatry.

Hoffmann von Fallersleben \'hȯf-män-fȯn-'fäl-ərs-,lā-bən\, August Heinrich (b. April 2, 1798, Fallersleben, near Braunschweig, Hanover [Germany]—d. Jan. 19, 1874, Corvey Castle, near Höxter)   German patriotic poet, philologist, and literary historian whose poem "Deutschland, Deutschland über Alles" was adopted as the German national anthem after World War I. His uncomplicated verses, expressing his deep love of country and strong fellow feeling, were of great significance to the German student movement.

Having studied at the universities of Göttingen and Bonn, Hoffmann was custodian of the university library at Breslau (1823–38). He became extraordinary professor of German language and literature there in 1830 and ordinary professor in 1835 but was removed by the Prussian authorities in 1842 for his *Unpolitische Lieder* (1840–41; "Nonpolitical Songs"), which was interpreted, despite its title, as political. He was allowed to return to his position after the Revolution of 1848. In 1860 he was appointed librarian to the Duke of Ratibor at Corvey Castle.

Hoffmann was among the earliest and most effective of the poets who prepared the way for the revolutionary movement of 1848. He also composed melodies for many of his songs, which were sung throughout Germany. His patriotic poem "Deutschland, Deutschland über Alles," written in 1841, is typical in its expression of popular feeling—the wish for national unity.

As a student of ancient Germanic literature, Hoffmann ranks among the most persevering and cultivated of German scholars. His *Deutsche Philologie im Grundriss* (1836; "Outline of German Philology") made a valuable contribution to philological research.

Hofmann \'hȯf-män\, Gert (b. Jan. 29, 1931, Limbach, Saxony, Ger.—d. July 1, 1993, near Munich)   German novelist who examined morality and the resonances of Nazism in postwar Germany.

Hofmann studied at the universities of Leipzig and Freiburg, and he taught in Austria, England, and the United States. For years he wrote theater and radio plays in which he introduced his moral and social concerns; the skill he acquired at writing dialogue was essential to his fiction, for which he is best known. His first novel, *Die Denunziation* (1979), presents two brothers' memories of their participation in war crimes. *Die Fistelstimme* (1980; "The Falsetto") consists of a monologue by a professor who is gradually disintegrating in a perverse society. Honoré de Balzac and Casanova are among the historical figures represented in the four stories of Hofmann's *Gespräch über Balzacs Pferd* (1981; *Balzac's Horse and Other Stories*).

Hofmann mingled mordant wit and horror in novels such as his suspenseful *Auf dem Turm* (1982; *The Spectacle at the Tower*), in which impoverished villagers commit unspeakable depravities in hopes of amusing a pair of stranded tourists, and *Unsere Eroberung* (1984; *Our Conquest*). Among his other notable works are *Der Blindensturz* (1985; *The Parable of the Blind*), *Veilchenfeld* (1986; "Field of Violets"), *Fuhlrotts Vergesslichkeit* (1981; "Fuhlrott's Forgetfulness"), *Vor der Regenzeit* (1988; "Before the Rainy Season"), and a collection of essays entitled *Tolstois Kopf* (1991; "Tolstoy's Head").

Hofmannsthal \'hȯf-mäns-,täl\, Hugo von (b. Feb. 1, 1874, Vienna, Austro-Hungarian Empire [now in Austria]—d. July 15, 1929, Rodaun, a suburb of Vienna)   Austrian poet, dramatist, and essayist. He made his reputation with his lyrical poems and plays and became internationally famous for his collaboration with the German operatic composer Richard Strauss.

At age 16 Hofmannsthal published his first poems, under the pseudonym Loris. They created a stir in Vienna and in Germany with their lyrical beauty, magically evocative language, and dreamlike quality.

Between 1891 and 1899 Hofmannsthal wrote a number of short verse plays, including *Gestern* (1891; "Yesterday"), *Der Tod des Tizian* (1892; *The Death of Titian*), *Der Tor und der Tod* (1893; *Death and the Fool*), *Das kleine Welttheater* (1897; *The Little Theater of the World*), *Der weisse Fächer* (1897; partially translated as *The White Fan*), *Die Frau im Fenster* (1897; *Madonna Dianora*), *Der Abenteurer und die Sängerin* (1899; *The Adventurer and the Singer*), and *Die Hochzeit der Sobeide* (1899; *The Marriage of Sobeide*). These playlets are lyric reflections on appearance and reality, transience and timelessness, and continuity and change within the human personality—themes constantly recurring in Hofmannsthal's later works. In 1902, however, he renounced purely lyrical forms in his essay "Ein Brief" (also called "Chandos Brief"). This essay has come to be recognized as symptomatic of the crisis that undermined the aesthetic Symbolist movement of the end of the century.

During a period of reorientation and transition Hofmannsthal experimented with Elizabethan and classical tragic forms, adapting Thomas Otway's *Venice Preserv'd* (1682) as *Das gerettete Venedig* (1905) and writing *Elektra* (1904). At the same time he began a novel, *Andreas* (1932; *The United*), which he never completed. The theater increasingly became his medium. To the end of his life he collaborated with Strauss, writing the librettos for the operas *Der Rosenkavalier* (1910; "The Cavalier of the Rose"), *Ariadne auf Naxos* (1912; *Ariadne on Naxos*), *Die Frau ohne Schatten* (1919; *The Woman Without a Shadow*), *Die ägyptische Helena* (1928; *Helen in Egypt* or *The Egyptian Helen*), and *Arabella* (1933).

After World War I, with the theatrical producer and designer Max Reinhardt, he founded the Salzburg Festival, at which performances have regularly been given of his *Jedermann* (1911; *Everyman*) and *Das Salzburger grosse Welttheater* (1922; *The Great Salzburg Theatre of the World*). His comedies, *Cristinas Heimreise* (1910; *Christina's Journey Home*), *Der Schwierige* (1921; *The Difficult Man*), and *Der Unbestechliche* (performed 1923, published 1956; "The Incorruptible"), are written in Viennese dialect and set in contemporary Austrian society.

Hofmannsthal's reflections on the crisis and disintegration of European civilization after World War I found expression in his political drama *Der Turm* (1925; *The Tower*) and in several essays that were prophetic of the future of Western culture.

Hofmann von Hofmannswaldau \'hȯf-män-fȯn-ˌhȯf-mäns-'väl-ˌdau̇\, Christian (b. Dec. 25, 1617, Breslau, Silesia [now Wrocław, Poland]—d. April 18, 1679, Breslau) Poet who was the leading representative of the "Second Silesian School," the German counterpart to the Baroque extravagance of the Italian poets Giambattista Marino and Battista Guarini and the Spanish poet Luis de Góngora.

While studying at Danzig, Hofmann met and was influenced by the great writer and theorist Martin Opitz. He wrote a quantity of verse, both religious and secular, characterized by eroticism and by exaggerated, high-flown expression. His most characteristic work is *Heldenbriefe* (1663; "Heroes' Letters"), a collection of prose and verse love letters giving full rein to his lascivious, extravagant style. He also published another collection of verse, *Grabschriften* (1643; "Epitaphs"), and *Deutsche Übersetzungen und Gedichte* (1673; "German Translations and Poetry"); his translations include Guarini's famous poem *Il pastor fido*.

Hogg \'hȯg\, James (baptized Dec. 9, 1770, Ettrick, Selkirkshire, Scot.—d. Nov. 21, 1835, Altrive, Yarrow, Selkirkshire)

Scottish poet, known as the "Ettrick Shepherd," who enjoyed a vogue during the ballad revival that accompanied the Romantic movement.

Hogg spent most of his youth and early manhood as a shepherd and was almost entirely self-educated. His talent was discovered early by Sir Walter Scott, to whom he supplied material for Scott's *Minstrelsy of the Scottish Border*. *The Queen's Wake* (1813), a book of poems about Mary Stuart, contains only a few narrative poems and ballads of lasting value. Probably a more important work is Hogg's novel *The Private Memoirs and Confessions of a Justified Sinner* (1824), a macabre tale of a psychopath that anticipates the modern psychological thriller.

Hogg \'hȯg\, Thomas Jefferson (b. May 24, 1792, Norton, Durham, Eng.—d. Aug. 27, 1862, London) English writer best known as the first biographer of his friend Percy Bysshe Shelley.

Hogg first met Shelley at Oxford and was expelled with him in 1811 for his share in writing a pamphlet called *The Necessity of Atheism*. After Shelley's death in 1822, Hogg was commissioned by the poet's family to write a biography of him, the first two volumes of which appeared in 1858 under the title *The Life of Shelley*. This work throws much light on the poet's character through the use of anecdotes and letters. It was to have been in four volumes, but the Shelley family, objecting to the first two volumes' focus on Hogg himself, refused him access to sources necessary for completing the *Life*.

hokku \'hȯk-ˌkü\ [Japanese, from *hok-* opening, first + *ku* stanza] Originally, the opening stanza of a *renga* (linked-verse poem), which developed into an independent poem later called a HAIKU.

Holberg \'hōl-ˌber *with* r *labialized*\, Ludvig, Baron (Friherre) (b. Dec. 3, 1684, Bergen, Nor.—d. Jan. 28, 1754, Copenhagen, Den.) The outstanding Scandinavian literary figure of the Enlightenment period, claimed by both Norway and Denmark as one of the founders of their literatures.

After taking a degree from the University of Copenhagen, Holberg returned to Norway. In 1706 he left for London and Oxford, where he studied for two years. While there, he must have begun his *Introduction til de fornemste europæiske rigers historier* ("Introduction to the History of the Principal Kingdoms of Europe"), which was not published until 1711. After more travels he returned to Denmark again in 1716, and in 1717 he was appointed professor at the University of Copenhagen.

Seized with a "poetic fit," Holberg began to create, under the pseudonym Hans Mikkelsen, an entirely new class of humorous literature. The seriocomic epic *Peder Paars*, a parody of Virgil's *Aeneid* and the earliest classic of the Danish language, appeared in 1719. In 1722 Holberg began to produce for the theater the steady flow of comedies that resulted in his being called the "Molière of the North." Their freshness is such that many are still performed on the Danish stage. Among the best are *Den politiske kandestøber* (1723; *The Political Tinker*), *Den vægelsindede* (1723; *The Weathercock*), *Jean de France* (1723), *Jeppe på Bjerget* (1723; *Jeppe of the Hill*), *Den stundesløse* (1731; *The Fussy Man*), and *Erasmus Montanus* (1731). These plays' characters are often stock types, based on the Miles Gloriosus (braggart soldier) of Plautus or on the cuckold Sganarelle of Molière, but the manners are Danish and the subjects of his satire are both contemporary and universal. A favorite target was the pretensions and pedantry of the learned. In 1731 he published his performed comedies and five additional plays.

Thereafter, he turned to other forms of writing, notably an imaginary voyage in the satirical novel *Nicolai Klimii iter subterraneum* (1741; *The Journey of Niels Klim to the World Underground*). In 1747 he was created Baron Holberg.

Holcroft \\'hōl-ˌkróft\\, Thomas (b. Dec. 10, 1745, London, Eng.—d. March 23, 1809, London)   English dramatist, novelist, journalist, and actor.

Holcroft is remembered for his melodrama *The Road to Ruin* (1792); his translation of Pierre de Beaumarchais's play *Le Mariage de Figaro* under the title *The Follies of a Day* (performed 1784), in which Holcroft played the part of Figaro; and his autobiography, edited in 1816 by his friend William Hazlitt. The autobiography tells the story of a life of struggle against adversity and reveals the gentleness and humor that won him the friendship of a number of leading early Romantic writers.

Hölderlin \\'hœl-dər-ˌlēn\\, Friedrich, *in full* Johann Christian Friedrich Hölderlin (b. March 20, 1770, Lauffen am Neckar, Württemberg [Germany]—d. June 7, 1843, Tübingen)   One of the greatest German lyric poets, especially admired for his success in naturalizing the forms of classical Greek verse in the German language and in melding Christian and classical themes.

Pastel by Franz Karl Hiemer, 1792

Schiller-Nationalmuseum, Marbach, Germany

Hölderlin studied at the theological seminary at the University of Tübingen, where he obtained a master's degree and qualified for ordination, but he was more drawn to Greek mythology than to Christian dogma.

In 1793 Hölderlin was introduced to Friedrich von Schiller, who helped him obtain the first of several posts as a tutor and who published some of the poetry that Hölderlin had begun to write, as well as a fragment of his novel HYPERION.

In December 1795 Hölderlin took a post in the house of a wealthy Frankfurt banker. Before long, he was deeply in love with his employer's wife, Susette, who returned his affection. Susette appears in his poems and in *Hyperion*, but their happiness was short-lived; after a painful scene with Susette's husband, Hölderlin had to leave Frankfurt in 1798.

From 1798 to 1801, though he was physically and mentally shaken, Hölderlin went through a period of intense creativity. He finished the second volume of *Hyperion* and began a tragedy, *Der Tod des Empedokles* (*The Death of Empedocles*), which he never completed. In addition to a number of noble odes, he also produced the great elegies "Menons Klagen um Diotima" ("Menon's Lament for Diotima") and "Brot und Wein" ("Bread and Wine") during this period.

Hölderlin next accepted a post as tutor at Bordeaux in France, but in the summer of 1802 he suddenly left and traveled homeward on foot through France, arriving at Nürtingen in an advanced stage of schizophrenia. The poems of the period 1802–06, including "Friedensfeier" ("Celebration of Peace"), "Der Einzige" ("The Only One"), and "Patmos," are apocalyptic visions of unique grandeur. In 1804 he also completed verse translations of two plays by Sophocles. By 1805 Hölderlin had succumbed irretrievably to his illness. After a spell in a clinic in Tübingen, he was moved to a carpenter's house, where he passed the last 36 years of his life under the shadow of insanity.

Holinshed \\'häl-ən-ˌshed, *perhaps originally* 'häl-ənz-ˌhed\\, Raphael (d. *c.* 1580)   English chronicler, remembered chiefly because his *Chronicles* enjoyed great popularity. They became a quarry for many Elizabethan dramatists, especially William Shakespeare, who found, in the second edition, material for many of his historical plays.

From about 1560 Holinshed lived in London, where he was employed as a translator by Reginald Wolfe, who was preparing a universal history. After Wolfe's death in 1573, the scope of the work was abridged, and it appeared, with many illustrations, as the *Chronicles of England, Scotlande, and Irelande*, 2 vol. (1577). The *Chronicles* was compiled largely uncritically from many sources of varying degrees of trustworthiness. The texts of the first and second (1587) editions were expurgated by order of the Privy Council, and the excisions from the second edition were published separately in 1723. An edition of the complete text of the 1587 edition was published in six volumes (1807–08).

Holm \\'hōlm\\, Sven (b. April 13, 1940, Copenhagen, Den.) Danish modernist novelist and short-story writer.

In the title story of his first collection, *Den store fjende* (1961; "The Great Enemy"), Holm described how a village church on a precipice is gradually crumbling and falling into the sea; the village is a metaphor for society. In *Det private liv* (1974; "The Private Life") the realization dawns on the main character during a marital crisis that material things have usurped the central meaning in his life.

Holm's novels deal with such issues as corruption of language, in *Jomfrutur* (1966; "Maiden Voyage"); ignorance, in *Termush, Atlanterhavskysten* (1967; *Termush*); and poverty, in *Syg og munter* (1972; "Sick and Happy"). In his intense prose poem on the theme of human suffering, *Syv passioner* (1971; "Seven Passions"), Holm offered a utopian alternative to the psychological breakdown and envisioned collapse of the Western way of life. Later works include the play *Hans Egede* (1979) and *Koster det sol?* (1981; "Does the Sun Cost?").

Holmes \\'hōlmz, 'hōmz\\, Oliver Wendell (b. Aug. 29, 1809, Cambridge, Mass., U.S.—d. Oct. 7, 1894, Cambridge)   American physician, poet, and humorist chiefly remembered for a few poems and for his "Breakfast-Table" series of essays.

Holmes received a degree from Harvard in 1836. He practiced medicine for 10 years, taught anatomy at Dartmouth College (Hanover, N.H.), and in 1847 became professor of anatomy and physiology at Harvard. He was later made dean of the Harvard Medical School.

Holmes achieved his greatest fame, however, as a humorist and poet. He won national acclaim with the publication of "Old Ironsides" (1830), which aroused public sentiment against destruction of the USS *Constitution*, an American fighting ship from the War of 1812. Beginning in 1857, he contributed his "Breakfast-Table" papers to *The Atlantic Monthly* and subsequently published *The Autocrat of the Breakfast-Table* (1858), *The Professor of the Breakfast-Table* (1860), *The Poet of the Breakfast-Table* (1872), and *Over the Teacups* (1891).

Among his other works are the poems THE CHAMBERED NAUTILUS (1858) and THE WONDERFUL ONE-HOSS SHAY (1858) and the psychological novel *Elsie Venner* (1861).

Holmes, Sherlock \\'shər-ˌläk-'hōmz, *U.S. commonly* 'hōlmz\\ Fictional character who was created for *A Study in Scarlet* in 1887 by Sir Arthur Conan DOYLE and who became the prototype for the modern mastermind detective. The character generated the most enduring tradition in detective fiction.

Conan Doyle modeled the characteristics of his great detective on the methods and mannerisms of his former teacher in medical school, Dr. Joseph Bell of Edinburgh. A slim, nervously intense, hawk-nosed man, Holmes uses purely scientific reasoning to solve mysteries and can make the most startling deductions from trivial details and bits of physical evidence overlooked by others. He also smokes a pipe, wears a deerstalker cap, plays the violin, and uses cocaine when bored. He lives at 221B Baker Street.

His partner and best friend, Dr. John H. Watson, is the genial but obtuse narrator of the Holmesian stories. Holmes's most formidable opponent is the criminal mastermind Professor Moriarty.

holograph \\'häl-ə-ˌgraf, 'hōl-\\ [Late Greek *hológraphos* written entirely in the same hand, from Greek *hólos* whole + *-graphos* written] A manuscript or document wholly handwritten by the person in whose name it appears.

Holroyd \\'häl-ˌròid, 'hōl-\\, Michael (de Courcy Fraser) (b. Aug. 27, 1935, London, Eng.) Author and editor whose full-scale critical biographies of Lytton Strachey, Augustus John, and George Bernard Shaw are considered superb examples of the genre.

A novelist (*A Dog's Life*, 1969), essayist (*Unreceived Opinions*, 1973), and editor, Holroyd was best-known for his meticulous, scholarly biographies of three of Britain's outstanding literary and artistic figures. His exhaustive two-volume work *Lytton Strachey: A Critical Biography* (1967, 1968; rev. ed., 1973) stands as Strachey's definitive biography. His two-volume *Augustus John* (1974, 1975; rev. ed., 1976) is a study of the painter's personal as well as artistic life. Holroyd's four-volume biography of Shaw, *Bernard Shaw* (1988, 1989, 1991, 1992), took 15 years to research. Holroyd was commended by critics as being judicious, scholarly, and knowledgeable. In 1982 he married the author Margaret Drabble.

Holt, Felix \\'fē-liks-'hōlt\\ Fictional character, the protagonist of George Eliot's novel FELIX HOLT, THE RADICAL.

Holtei \\'hòl-ˌtī\\, Karl von (b. Jan. 24, 1798, Breslau, Silesia [now Wrocław, Poland]—d. Feb. 12, 1880, Breslau) Author who achieved success by his "vaudevilles," or ballad operas, and by his recitations.

Holtei led a varied and unsettled life, traveling between the cities of Hamburg (Ger.), Paris, and Graz (Austria) as a playwright, actor, and theater manager, a life vividly described in his autobiography, *Vierzig Jahre* (1843–50; "Forty Years"). Two of his best plays, *Der alte Freiherr* (1825; "The Old Baron") and *Lenore* (1829), a dramatization of Gottfried August Bürger's poem, achieved great popularity. Also successful were his *Schlesische Gedichte* (1830; "Silesian Poems"), written in his native dialect. He also wrote novels, including *Die Vagabunden* (1851; "The Vagabonds") and *Der letzte Komödiant* (1863; "The Last Comedian"), that are interesting when they draw on his own experience. As a reciter he was unequaled, especially in his interpretation of speeches from William Shakespeare.

Hölty \\'hœl-tē\\, Ludwig Heinrich Christoph (b. Dec. 21, 1748, Mariensee, Hanover [Germany]—d. Sept. 1, 1776, Mariensee) German poet who is considered the most gifted lyric poet of the Göttinger Hain; his work is characterized by love of nature and the expression of national feeling.

In 1769 Hölty went to Göttingen to study theology. There he became close friends with the poets Johann Martin Miller, Johann Heinrich Voss, Heinrich Boie, and Christian and Friedrich Leopold Stolberg. Together they organized the Göttinger Hain. Hölty's poems in the society's mouthpiece, the *Göttinger Musenalmanach* ("Göttingen Muses Journal"), encompassed a wide variety of forms. Influenced by Thomas Gray's *An Elegy Written in a Country Church Yard*, he introduced an element of social criticism into the elegy by his comparison of city and village life in *Elegie auf einen Dorfkirchhof* and *Elegie auf einen Stadtkirchhof* (both 1771; "Elegy on a Village Churchyard" and "Elegy on a City Churchyard"). His sense of closeness to the peasants, delight in nature, and long-

ing for the simple and natural life found skillful expression in his poetry. His lyrics are characterized by strains of melancholy and by sincere religious faith.

Holub \\'hō-lūb\\, Miroslav (b. Sept. 3, 1923, Plzeň, Czech. [now Czech Republic]) Czech poet noted for his detached, lyrical reflections on humanist and scientific subjects.

Holub was a clinical pathologist and immunologist by profession. His first poem was published in 1947; by the mid-1950s he was associated with the young writers of the literary magazine *Květen* who opposed the bombastic Socialist Realism promoted by Czechoslovakia's communist rulers. His first verse collection was *Denní služba* (1958; "Day Duty"), and by 1971 he wrote 10 additional collections, including *Achilles a želva* (1960; "Achilles and the Tortoise"), *Tak zvané srdce* (1963; "The So-Called Heart"), and *Ačkoli* (1969; *Although*).

Among his prose writings are *Anděl na kolečkách: poloreportáž z USA* (1963; "Angel on Wheels: Sketches from the U.S.A.") and *Žít v New Yorku* (1969; "To Live in New York"). By the late 1960s some of his poetry had been translated into English, including his *Selected Poems* (1967). Other collections published in English include *Notes of a Clay Pigeon* (1977), *On the Contrary* (1984), and *Poems Before and After* (1990).

Holy Grail *see* GRAIL.

Holy Sonnets *also called* Divine Meditations *or* Divine Sonnets. Series of 19 devotional poems by John DONNE that were published posthumously in 1633 in the first edition of *Songs and Sonnets*. Characterized by innovative rhythm and imagery, they constitute a forceful, immediate, personal, and passionate examination of Donne's love for God, depicting his doubts, fears, and sense of spiritual unworthiness.

Among the best-known verses of the series are "Thou hast made me," "I am a little world," "At the round earth's imagined corners," "If poisonous minerals," DEATH, BE NOT PROUD, BATTER MY HEART, and "Show me, dear Christ." Most of the poems are highly personal, such as "Holy Sonnet 17," an elegy to Donne's wife, who died in 1617.

Holy War, The Allegory by John BUNYAN, published in 1682. It unfolds the story of the town of Mansoul, which is besieged by the hosts of the devil, is relieved by the army of Emanuel, and is later undermined by further diabolic attacks and plots against his rule. The metaphor works on several levels; it represents the conversion and backslidings of the individual soul, as well as the story of humanity from the Fall to the Redemption and the Last Judgment. There is even a more precise historical level of allegory related to the persecution of Nonconformists under Charles II. While its epic structure is carefully wrought, it is lacking in the spontaneous inward note of *The Pilgrim's Progress*.

Homage to Catalonia \\ˌkat-ə-'lō-nē-ə\\ Autobiographical account by George ORWELL of his experience as a volunteer for the Republicans in the Spanish Civil War, published in 1938.

Unlike other foreign intellectual leftists, Orwell and his wife did not join the International Brigade but instead enlisted in the Workers' Party of Marxist Unification (Partido Obrero de Unificación Marxista; POUM). The book chronicles both his observations of the drudgery of the daily life of a soldier and his disillusionment with political infighting and totalitarianism.

Homage to Clio \\'klī-ō, 'klē-\\ Collection of light verse by W.H. AUDEN, published in 1960. The collection is known for its austere craftsmanship, stylistic variety, and ironic wit.

Like many of Auden's later collections of poetry, *Homage to Clio* is arranged around a theme, in this case, history. The book's only prose piece, "Interlude: An Unwritten Poem," is a witty discourse about the nature of romantic poetry. The poem

"On Installing an American Kitchen in Lower Austria" later became the centerpiece of "Thanksgiving for a Habitat," a sequence of poems that appeared in *About the House* (1965). The last section, entitled "Addendum: Academic Graffiti," contains humorous clerihews, notably about literary figures.

Homage to Mistress Bradstreet \ˈbrad-ˌstrēt\   Long poem by John BERRYMAN, written in 1948–53 and published in 1956. Noted for its intensity, it is a tribute to colonial poet Anne Bradstreet that also reveals much about the author.

The poem examines the tension between Bradstreet's personal life and her artistic life, concluding in a spirit of fatalism. It shows throughout a loving and intimate grasp of the details of American history. The work primarily examines creative repression, religious apostasy, and the temptation to adultery.

Home \ˈhyūm, ˈhōm\, John (b. Sept. 21, 1722, Leith, Scot.—d. Sept. 5, 1808, Merchiston Bank, near Edinburgh)   Scottish dramatist whose play *Douglas*, according to Thomas Gray, "retrieved the true language of the stage."

Home entered the church, then fought against the Jacobites in the 1745 uprising led by Charles Edward Stuart (Bonnie Prince Charlie). His play *Douglas* was produced in Edinburgh in 1756, and in 1757 it had a great success at London's Covent Garden theater, where the actor-manager David Garrick later produced other plays by Home. Home took up soldiering in later life, joining a regiment formed by the Duke of Buccleuch, but retired after a horseback-riding accident, afterward devoting himself to *The History of the Rebellion of 1745* (1802).

Homecoming, The   Two-act drama by Harold PINTER, published and produced in 1965. *The Homecoming* focuses on the return to his London home of Teddy, a university professor, who brings his wife, Ruth, to meet his father, Max, his brothers Lenny and Joey, and his uncle Sam. Ruth's presence exposes a tangle of rage and confused sexuality in this all-male household.

Home Journal   One of the earliest general-circulation magazines in the United States, founded in 1846 by Nathaniel Parker Willis and George P. Morris. Intended for readers in high society, the magazine was an attempt to provide both society news and intellectual stimulation. In its early years it published works by such American authors as Edgar Allan Poe, James Fenimore Cooper, and Washington Irving; among the transatlantic authors it introduced were Honoré de Balzac, Victor Hugo, Thomas Carlyle, and Thomas de Quincey. In 1901 the journal's name was changed to *Town and Country*, and its emphasis became largely the lifestyle of the wealthy.

Homer \ˈhō-mər\ (fl. 9th or 8th century BC?, Ionia?)   Presumed author of the ILIAD and ODYSSEY, the two greatest epic poems of ancient Greece.

Virtually nothing is known about the life of Homer. Scholars generally agree, however, that he was probably an Ionian who lived in the 9th or 8th century BC. There is also a tradition that he was blind. In the judgment of most modern scholars, he composed (but probably did not literally write) the *Iliad*, most likely relying on oral traditions, and he at least inspired the composition of the *Odyssey*. Ancient Greeks esteemed these epics as symbols of Hellenistic unity and heroism and as sources of moral and practical instruction. Since that time the *Iliad* and *Odyssey* have had a profound influence on Western literature and have been translated into modern languages countless times. Their value lies chiefly in the poetry itself, which often moves from sublime passages dealing with gods and heroic exploits to passages expressing deep human emotion.

Homeric Hymns \hō-ˈmer-ik\   Collection of 34 ancient Greek poems in heroic hexameters, all addressed to gods. As-cribed in antiquity to Homer, the poems actually differ widely in date and are of unknown authorship. Most end with an indication that the singer intends to begin another song, therefore suggesting that they were used by rhapsodists as preludes to recitals of heroic poetry.

Homeric simile   *see* EPIC SIMILE.

Homerids \ˈhō-mər-ˌidz\ or **Homeridae** \hō-ˈmer-i-ˌdē, -ˌdī\   A historical clan whose members claimed to be descendants of the ancient Greek poet Homer. They claimed to have brought the *Iliad* and *Odyssey* attributed to him from Ionia to the Greek mainland, as early as the 6th century BC. They may have preserved texts of poems ascribed to Homer. Originally, they were rhapsodists (singer-reciters of Homeric epics), but by the 4th century BC they had apparently ceased to perform and had become judges of rhapsodists competing at the Panathenaea. Authorship of a few Homeric Hymns, preludes, and mythical tales of the gods have been attributed to them.

Home to Harlem \ˈhär-ləm\   First novel by Claude McKAY, published in 1928. In it and its sequel, *Banjo*, McKay attempted to capture the vitality of the black vagabonds of urban America and Europe.

Jake Brown, the protagonist of *Home to Harlem*, deserts the U.S. Army during World War I and lives in London until a race riot inspires him to return to Harlem. On his first night home he meets the prostitute Felice, for whom he spends much of the rest of the novel searching. Amid his adventures in Harlem, a gallery of rough, lusty, heavy-drinking characters appear to vivid effect. While working as a dining-car waiter Jake encounters another point of view in Ray, a pessimistic, college-educated Haitian immigrant who advocates behavior based on racial pride.

homoeomeral \ˌhōm-ē-ˈäm-ə-rəl, ˌhäm-\ [Greek *homoiomerēs* consisting of equal parts]   In prosody, having parts that are metrically similar, as in the repetition of a stanza form.

homoeoteleuton \ˌhōm-ē-ō-tə-ˈlū-ˌtän, ˌhäm-, -tel-ˈyū-\ [Greek *homoiotéleuton,* from neuter of *homoiotéleutos* having the same ending]   An occurrence in writing of the same or similar endings close together (as in the phrase *fairly commonly*). Homoeoteleutons may occur either by chance or by intention (*e.g.,* for rhythmic effect). They may occur in neighboring words, clauses, or lines.

homometrical \ˌhōm-ō-ˈmet-ri-kəl, ˌhäm-\   In prosody, having the same meter throughout.

Hong Shen or **Hung Shen** \ˈhùŋ-ˈshən\ (b. Dec. 31, 1894, Changzhou, Jiangsu province, China—d. Aug. 29, 1955, Beijing)   Pioneering Chinese dramatist and filmmaker.

Educated in Beijing and at Harvard University in the United States, Hong Shen taught dramatic arts and Western literature at various universities after his return to China in 1922. Invited to join the Shanghai Dramatic Society in 1923, he soon began directing plays there by modern Chinese authors, including himself, and by Western writers whom he translated.

In 1930 Hong Shen joined the Star Motion Picture Company and produced one of China's first sound films. An active member of the Left-wing Dramatists League in the 1930s, Hong Shen often included a strong political message in his carefully staged productions. During the Sino-Japanese War (1937–45), he directed tour companies in plays boosting wartime morale for the Nationalist government.

Honwana \ȯⁿn-ˈwän-ä\, Luís Bernardo (b. November 1942, Lourenço Marques, Mozambique)   Journalist and short-story writer who has been praised for his portrayal of village life in his native Mozambique.

Honwana held jobs as a government cartographer and as reporter and then editor of two newspapers in Beira (Mozambique's second largest city) while working toward his secondary degree. After completing high school he devoted himself to literary activities. In the collection *Nós matámos a Cão Tinhosa* (1964; *We Killed Mangy-Dog & Other Stories*), he is never didactic, but beneath the deceptively simple surface of his narrative is a deep understanding of human experiences and needs and an implied criticism of a society that has adopted the wrong values. Honwana's writing was interrupted by imprisonment (1964–67) for his political activities. Upon his release he lived abroad but returned home to work with the transitional government that assumed power with Mozambique's independence (1975). By 1984 he was chief of staff to the president of Mozambique and had completed a novel. He also made several documentary films.

Hood \ˈhůd\, Thomas (b. May 23, 1799, London, Eng.—d. May 3, 1845, London)   English poet whose humanitarian verses, such as "The Song of the Shirt," served as models for a whole school of social-protest poets. He also is notable as a writer of comic verse, having originated several durable forms in that genre.

Hood worked in London as an engraver and became a "sort of sub-editor" of the *London Magazine* during its heyday, when its circle of brilliant contributors included Charles Lamb, Thomas De Quincey, and William Hazlitt. In 1827 he published *The Plea of the Midsummer Fairies*, a volume of poems strongly influenced by John Keats. Several of the poems in it suggest that Hood might possibly have become a poet of the first rank. However, the success of his amusing *Odes and Addresses to Great People* (1825), written in collaboration with his brother-in-law, J.H. Reynolds, virtually obliged him to concentrate on humorous writing for the rest of his life. Hood was famous for his punning, which appears at times to be almost a reflex action, serving as a defense against painful emotion. Of his later poems, the grim ballads "The Dream of Eugene Aram, the Murderer," "The Last Man," "The Song of the Shirt," "The Lay of the Labourer," and "The Bridge of Sighs" are moving protests against social evils of the day—sweated labor, unemployment, and the double sexual standard.

Hooft \ˈhōft\, Pieter Corneliszoon (b. March 16, 1581, Amsterdam [The Netherlands]—d. May 21, 1647, The Hague)   Dutch dramatist and poet, regarded by many as the most brilliant writer of the Dutch Renaissance. Hooft's prose style continued to serve as a model into the 19th century.

During three years spent in France and Italy, Hooft came completely under the spell of the new learning and art. The impact of that experience is shown in the poetry he wrote after his return—love lyrics and the pastoral play *Grandida* (1605). The play is noted for the delicacy of its poetry and the simplicity of its moral—that individuals and nations can be at peace only when rulers and subjects alike shun ambition and seek to serve.

Hooft's pragmatic personal ethic is more explicit in his *Sticht-rijmen* (1618 or 1619; "Edifying Verses") and two Senecan tragedies. *Geeraert van Velsen* (1613) is a quasi-historical dramatization of the murder of Count Floris V, and *Baeto* (1617) portrays an Aeneas-type hero who goes into exile rather than cause civil war. Both plays reveal Hooft's pacifist hatred of tyranny.

In *Nederlandse historiën*, 20 vol. (1642, a continuation in 1654), the glory of the epic hero, the prince of Orange, is reflected in Hooft's affection for the commoners who fought for the new democracy in Holland. Tacitus was his model for this monumental work, on which he spent 19 years chronicling the period from 1555 to 1585.

Hook \ˈhůk\, Theodore Edward (b. Sept. 22, 1788, London, Eng.—d. Aug. 24, 1841, London)   Prolific English playwright and novelist, the best remembered of the fashionable novelists who described society life in the early 19th century.

Hook was the son of a popular songwriter, and, while a schoolboy at Harrow, he wrote the words for his father's comic operas. He later wrote farces and melodramas, ran into debt, and became dissolute, but in 1813 his friend the prince regent procured him the post of accountant general to Mauritius.

In 1817 some £12,000 was found to have been stolen, and Hook, although guilty only of negligence, was recalled to England, tried for mismanagement of public money, and imprisoned from 1823 to 1825. He took to novel writing in an attempt to pay off the legal costs of his trial. The success in 1824 of his *Sayings and Doings*, tales with a fashionable setting, each illustrating a proverb, was such that he extended their three volumes to nine in 1828. From 1824 to 1841 he wrote some 40 fictional works in a similar style.

Hook, Captain \ˈhůk\   Fictional character, a pirate captain and the nemesis of Peter Pan and the lost boys in James M. Barrie's play PETER PAN. Named for the metal hook he wears as a prosthesis on his lower right arm, the captain is relentlessly pursued by the crocodile that wounded him.

Hoosier School-Master, The   Regional novel by Edward EGGLESTON, first serialized in *Hearth and Home* in 1871 and published in book form the same year.

The novel is primarily of interest for its naturalism, its setting in rural Indiana, and its extensive use of Hoosier dialect. Based partially on the experiences of the author's brother, the novel relates episodes in the lives of inhabitants of a backwoods Indiana town as well as the experiences of the young man who is hired to be the only teacher in the town's school.

Hope \ˈhōp\, A.D., *in full* Alec Derwent (b. July 21, 1907, Cooma, N.S.W., Australia)   Australian poet who is best known for his witty, satirical, and allusive verse delivered in a style that is comparable to that of John Dryden.

Hope was educated in Australia and at the University of Oxford and taught at various Australian universities until his retirement in 1969. Though traditional in form, his poetry is thoroughly modern, two outstanding examples being "Conquistador" (1947) and "The Return from the Freudian Isles" (1944). Though he began to publish his verse in literary periodicals as early as 1930, his first book of poems, *The Wandering Islands*, did not appear until 1955. Thereafter he produced several collections of poetry, including *Collected Poetry 1930–1965* (1966), *The Damnation of Byron* (1973), and *The Age of Reason* (1985). He also wrote essays and criticism, including *A Midsummer Eve's Dream* (1970), *The Cave and the Spring* (1965), *Native Companions* (1974), *The New Cratylus: Notes on the Craft of Poetry* (1979), and *Directions in Australian Poetry* (1984). A play, *Ladies from the Sea*, was published in 1987.

Hope \ˈhōp\, Anthony, *in full* Sir Anthony Hope Hawkins (b. Feb. 9, 1863, London, Eng.—d. July 8, 1933, Walton-on-the-Hill, Surrey)   English author of cloak-and-sword romances, of which the best known is THE PRISONER OF ZENDA (1894).

Educated at Marlborough and at Balliol College, Oxford, Hope became a lawyer in 1887. The immediate success of *The Prisoner of Zenda*, his fourth work—and its sequel, *Rupert of Hentzau* (1898)—turned him entirely to writing. His other works include the high-society conversations *The Dolly Dialogues* (1894) and a series of problem novels, such as *The God in the Car* (1894), which was based on the career of Cecil Rhodes, the empire builder of British South Africa. He was knighted in 1918.

Hopkins \ˈhäp-kinz\, Gerard Manley (b. July 28, 1844, Stratford, Essex, Eng.—d. June 8, 1889, Dublin, Ire.)   English poet, one of the most individual of Victorian writers.

Hopkins was awarded a grant to study at Balliol College, Oxford. In 1866 he was received into the Roman Catholic church and he decided to become a priest. He entered the Jesuit novitiate in 1868 and burned his youthful verses, determining "to write no more, as not belonging to my profession."

In 1874 Hopkins went to St. Beuno's College in North Wales to study theology. There he learned Welsh, and, encouraged by his superior, he began to write verse again. Moved by the death of five Franciscan nuns in a shipwreck in 1875, he broke a seven-year silence to write the long poem THE WRECK OF THE DEUTSCHLAND. He also wrote a series of sonnets strikingly original in their richness of language and use of rhythm, including PIED BEAUTY, GOD'S GRANDEUR, and THE WINDHOVER. He continued to write poetry, but it was read only in manuscript by his friends and fellow poets, including Robert Bridges and Coventry Patmore. Ordained to the priesthood in 1877, Hopkins served in various Jesuit churches and institutions in England, Scotland, and Ireland. From 1885 he wrote another series of sonnets, beginning with CARRION COMFORT. These poems, known as the "terrible sonnets," reveal strong tensions between his delight in the sensuous world and his powerful sense of religious vocation.

Hopkins died of typhoid fever, and after his death Robert Bridges began to publish a few of his most mature poems in anthologies. In 1918 Bridges (who was then poet laureate) published the first collected edition. In 1930 a second edition was issued, and thereafter Hopkins' work was recognized as among the most original, powerful, and influential literary accomplishments of his century.

Hopkins' exploitation of the verbal subtleties and music of English and his use of echo, alliteration, and repetition, as well as a highly compressed syntax, were all in the interest of projecting deep personal experiences. He called the energizing prosodic element of his verse SPRUNG RHYTHM, in which each foot may consist of one stressed syllable and any number of unstressed syllables.

Hopkins \ˈhäp-kinz\, Pauline (Elizabeth) (b. 1859, Portland, Maine, U.S.—d. Aug. 13, 1930, Cambridge, Mass.)   African-American novelist, playwright, journalist, and editor. She was a pioneer in her use of traditional romance novels as a medium for exploring racial and social themes. Her work reflects the influence of W.E.B. Du Bois.

In 1880 Hopkins joined her mother and stepfather in performing her first work, a musical entitled *Slaves' Escape; or, The Underground Railroad* (also called *Peculiar Sam*). She then spent several years touring with her family's singing group, Hopkins' Colored Troubadors. Her second play, *One Scene from the Drama of Early Days*, based on the biblical character Daniel, was also written about this time. The difficulties of blacks amid the racist violence of post-Civil War America provided a theme for her first novel, CONTENDING FORCES (1900). She also wrote short stories and biographical articles for the *Colored American Magazine*, of which she was women's editor and literary editor from approximately 1900 to 1904.

Hopkins' novels include *Hagar's Daughter* (published serially in 1901–02 under the pseudonym Sarah A. Allen), *Winona: A Tale of Negro Life in the South and Southwest* (published serially in 1902), and the fantasy *Of One Blood; or, The Hidden Self* (published serially in 1902–03). Her final work was the novella *Topsy Templeton* (published serially in 1916).

Hopkins \ˈhäp-kinz\, Sarah Winnemucca, *also known as* Sarah Hopkins Winnemucca \ˌwin-ə-ˈmək-ə\, Sally Winnemucca, Thocmectony *or* Tocmectone \täk-ˈmek-tə-nē\ ("shell flower") (b. *c.* 1844, Humboldt Sink, Mex. [now in Nevada, U.S.]—d. Oct. 16, 1891, Monida, Mont.)   Native American educator, lecturer, tribal leader, and writer best known for her book *Life Among the Piutes; Their Wrongs and Claims* (1883). Her writings, valuable for their description of Northern Paiute life and for their insights into the impact of white settlement, are among the few contemporary Native American works.

A granddaughter of Truckee and daughter of Winnemucca, both Northern Paiute chiefs, she was encouraged to learn about whites. She lived with a white family, learned fluent English, and attended a convent school in San Jose, Calif., until bigotry forced her removal. As an interpreter and scout for the U.S. Army, Hopkins led a group of Paiutes, including her father, to safety during the Bannock War of 1878; she was awarded tribal honors for bravery.

To protest official government policy toward Native Americans, she toured the East in the early 1880s, giving some 300 lectures. To Hopkins, the U.S. military was a fairer and abler manager of Indian matters than the federal Bureau of Indian Affairs, an agency she considered corrupt and self-serving. Hopkins taught Indian children at an army post in Vancouver, Wash.; she later returned to Nevada and founded an Indian school with private donations, but lack of money and ill health ended this endeavor.

Hopscotch   Novel by Julio CORTÁZAR, published in 1963 as *Rayuela*. Considered to be Cortázar's masterwork, it is an open-ended novel; after reading the first 56 chapters, the reader is asked to reread the chapters in a different order, this time including the many short, later chapters, beginning with chapter 73 and proceeding to chapters 1, 2, 116, and so forth.

The novel's antihero is Horacio Oliveira, an Argentine existentialist who lives among cultured expatriates in Paris while searching for his telepathic mistress. Returning to Buenos Aires, Oliveira meets Traveler and Talita, who are the doubles of his mistress and himself. None of the characters understands or cares more than superficially about the others, and impulse motivates their choices and actions. Narrative progress in the story is insignificant and its end is inconclusive.

Hora \ˈhȯr-ə\ *plural* Horae \ˈhȯr-ˌē, -ˌī\   In Greco-Roman mythology, any one of the personifications of the seasons and goddesses of natural order. According to the Greek poet Hesiod, the Horae were the children of Zeus and the Titaness Themis, and their names (Eunomia, Dike, Eirene—*i.e.*, Good Order, Justice, Peace) indicate the extension of their functions from nature to the events of human life. At Athens they were apparently two in number: Thallo and Carpo, the goddesses of the flowers of spring and of the fruits of summer. In later mythology the Horae became the four seasons, each represented with the conventional attributes.

Horace \ˈhȯr-əs, ˈhär-\, *Latin in full* Quintus Horatius Flaccus (b. December 65 BC, Venusia, Apulia [now Venosa, Italy]—d. Nov. 27, 8 BC, Rome)   Outstanding Latin lyric poet and satirist. The most frequent themes of his *Odes* and verse *Epistles* are love, friendship, philosophy, and the art of poetry.

Horace's father was a former slave who could afford to take his son to Rome to be educated. About 46 BC Horace went to Athens, attending lectures at the Academy. In the civil upheaval after Julius Caesar's murder in March 44, Horace joined Brutus' army and was made *tribunus militum*. When Brutus was defeated in 42, Horace fled back to Rome, which was controlled by Brutus' conqueror, Octavian (later styled Augustus). Through Gaius Maecenas, one of Octavian's principal political advisers, Horace came to Octavian's notice.

During these years Horace was working on Book I of the *Satires*, 10 poems written in hexameter verse and published in 35. The *Satires* drew on Greek roots, stating Horace's rejection of public life firmly and aiming at wisdom through serenity. His 17 *Epodes* were also under way, attacking social abuses. Horace published his *Epodes* in 31 and a second book of eight *Satires* in 30–29. Then he turned to the *Odes*, publishing three books, comprising 88 short poems, in 23. In the *Odes*, Horace represented himself as heir to earlier Greek lyric poets but displayed a sensitive, economical mastery of words all his own.

The last of his epistles to appear in the *Odes* (in Book II, published 20–19) are literary "letters" that were more mature and profound versions of the *Satires*. They announce his abandonment of "frivolous" lyric poetry for this more moralistic kind of verse. In three further epistles, Horace abandoned all satirical elements for a sensible, gently ironical stance. Two epistles make up a second book, and the third, the *Epistle to the Pisos* (*c.*19–18; also called *Epistle to the Pisones*), was also known, at least subsequently, as the ARS POETICA. These last three epistles embody literary criticism in a loose, conversational frame.

By this time Horace was virtually in the position of poet laureate, and in 17 he composed the *Secular Hymn (Carmen saeculare)* for ancient ceremonies called the Secular Games. Horace next completed a fourth book of 15 *Odes*, mainly of a more serious (and political) character than their predecessors. The latest of these poems was completed in 13. In 8 Maecenas died. A month or two later, Horace himself died.

The excellence of Horace's *Odes* was so great that they had few ancient lyrical successors, until some early Christian writers—Ambrose, Prudentius, and Paulinus—occasionally echoed his forms, though with a difference in spirit. Thereafter, the medieval epoch had little use for the *Odes*, which did not appeal to its piety, although his *Satires* and *Epistles* were read because of their predominantly moralistic tones. The *Odes* came into their own again with the Renaissance and, along with the *Ars poetica*, exerted much influence on Western poetry through the 19th century.

Horace \ō-'ràs\ Verse tragedy in five acts by Pierre CORNEILLE, produced in 1640 and published in 1641. It was also translated into English under the title *Horatius*.

Although the character Sabine (Horace's wife) was invented by Corneille, the drama is based on an actual incident mentioned in Livy's history of Rome. To avert all-out war, two cities agree that each will send its three bravest warriors to fight each other in hand-to-hand combat. Curiace and his brothers are chosen to represent Alba, Horace and his brothers to represent Rome. This creates a wrenching dilemma: Curiace is engaged to marry Horace's sister, and Horace's wife is Curiace's sister. Tragedy ensues when the demands of patriotism clash with the bonds of family loyalty.

Horatian ode \hə-'rā-shən\ Short lyric poem written in stanzas of two or four lines in the manner of the 1st-century-BC Latin poet Horace. In contrast to the lofty, heroic epinicion odes of the Greek poet Pindar, most of Horace's odes are intimate and reflective.

Horace introduced early Greek lyrics into Latin by adapting Greek meters, regularizing them, and writing his romanized versions with a discipline that caused some loss of spontaneity and a sense of detachment but that also produced elegance and dignity. His *carmina*, written in stanzas of two or four lines, are now universally called odes, but they have nothing in common with the passionate brilliance of Pindaric odes. Horace's tone is generally serious and serene, often touched with irony and melancholy but sometimes with gentle humor. In later periods, when technical felicity was more highly regarded than imagina-

tion and spontaneity, Horace's odes were prized and imitated. Among the preservers of the Horatian tradition were Pierre de Ronsard, Nicolas Boileau, Jean de La Fontaine, Michael Drayton, and Andrew Marvell. *See also* ODE; PINDARIC ODE.

Horatian satire \hə-'rā-shən\ Urbane and amusing satire of contemporary society that seeks to correct by gentle laughter rather than by bitter condemnation. Horatian satire takes its name from its originator, Horace, the Latin lyricist and satirist of the 1st century BC, whose verse satires on Roman society were suffused with charm and warm humanity. In three of his *Satires*, Horace discusses the tone appropriate to the satirist who out of a moral concern attacks the vice and folly he sees around him. As opposed to the harshness of earlier satirists such as Gaius Lucilius, Horace opts for mild mockery and playful wit as the means most effective for his ends. This type of satire has been used in poetry, by Nicolas Boileau, John Dryden, and Alexander Pope, among others; in drama, in such forms as the comedy of manners; and in prose fiction, in the novels of such authors as Miguel de Cervantes and Jane Austen. *Compare* JUVENALIAN SATIRE.

Horatio \hə-'rā-shō, -shē-ō\ Fictional character, loyal friend and confidant of Prince HAMLET in William Shakespeare's HAMLET.

Horgan \'hȯr-gən\, Paul (b. Aug. 1, 1903, Buffalo, N.Y., U.S.) Versatile American author noted especially for histories and historical fiction about the southwestern United States.

Horgan moved with his family to New Mexico in 1915. His career as a novelist began with the publication of the satirical novel *The Fault of Angels* (1933), about a Russian emigré's attempt to bring high culture to an American city. His trilogy *Mountain Standard Time* (1962), consisting of *Main Line West* (1936), *Far From Cibola* (1938), and *The Common Heart* (1942), depicts life in the Southwest in the early 1900s. *A Distant Trumpet* (1960) concerns late-19th-century soldiers who fought the Apaches. His short stories were collected in *The Return of the Weed* (1936), *Figures in a Landscape* (1940), and *The Peach Stone* (1967).

In addition to novels Horgan wrote historical sketches and books that sympathetically depicted the Native American, Spanish, Mexican, and Anglo-American frontier cultures of the Southwest. Both his two-volume *Great River: The Rio Grande in North American History* (1954) and the biography *Lamy of Santa Fe* (1975) won Pulitzer Prizes for history. He also produced poetry, drama, and children's books.

Horizon Magazine first issued in 1940 in England as a medium for literature during World War II. Founded in 1939 by Cyril Connolly, Stephen Spender, and Peter Watson, it was published until 1950. Among the contributors to *Horizon* were some of the foremost writers of the 20th century, including Evelyn Waugh, W.H. Auden, and George Orwell.

Horla, The \'hȯr-lə\ Short story by Guy de MAUPASSANT that is considered a masterly tale of the fantastic. Originally published as "Lettre d'un fou" ("Letter from a Madman") in 1885, the story was revised, retitled "Le Horla," and published in October 1886; the third and definitive version was published in May 1887. Presented in the form of a diary, it energetically details the hallucinatory obsessions of a madman.

The narrator becomes convinced that a mysterious, invisible parasite is draining away his life force through his lips. Unable to destroy the creature by setting fire to his house, he commits suicide. Some critics have seen a parallel in the author's degeneration from syphilis.

Hornblower, Horatio \hə-'rā-shō-'hȯrn-,blō-ər\ Fictional character, a British naval officer who is the hero of 12 books (mostly novels) by C.S. FORESTER that are set at the time of the Napoleonic Wars. The Hornblower novels begin with *The Happy Return* (1937; U.S. title, *Beat to Quarters*) and conclude with the unfinished novel *Hornblower and the Crisis* (1967; U.S. title, *Hornblower During the Crisis and Two Stories: Hornblower's Temptation and The Last Encounter*).

Other novels in the series include *A Ship of the Line* (1938), *Flying Colours* (1938), and *Lord Hornblower* (1946). *The Hornblower Companion* (1964) is a book of anecdotes and maps that provides background on the series.

hornbook \\'hȯrn-ˌbu̇k\\ Children's primer common in England from the mid-15th to the 18th century and in the colonial United States. It consisted of a paddle-shaped wooden board on which was mounted a printed sheet of vellum or paper. The printed page was protected with thin, transparent sheets of horn.

The printed material usually included such information as the alphabet, numerals, simple words, the blessing "In the name of the Father and of the Son and of the Holy Ghost, Amen," and the Lord's Prayer. Thomas Dekker satirized the hornbook in "The Guls Horne-booke" (1609), a spoof primer for young dandies of the time.

horror story A story in which the focus is on creating a feeling of fear. Such tales are of ancient origin and form a substantial part of the body of folk literature. They can feature supernatural elements such as ghosts, witches, or vampires, or they can address more realistic psychological fears. In Western literature, the literary cultivation of fear and curiosity for its own sake began to emerge in the 18th-century pre-Romantic era with the gothic novel. The genre was invented by Horace Walpole, whose *Castle of Otranto* (1765) may be said to have founded the horror story as a legitimate form. Mary Wollstonecraft Shelley introduced the pseudoscientific note in her famous novel *Frankenstein* (1818), about the creation of a monster that ultimately destroys its creator, Dr. Frankenstein.

In the Romantic era the German storyteller E.T.A. Hoffmann and the American Edgar Allan Poe raised the horror story to a level far above mere entertainment through their skillful intermingling of reason and madness, eerie atmosphere and everyday reality. They invested their specters, doubles, and haunted houses with a psychological symbolism that gave their tales a haunting credibility.

The gothic influence persisted throughout the 19th century in such works as Sheridan Le Fanu's *The House by the Churchyard* and "Green Tea," Wilkie Collins' *The Moonstone*, and Bram Stoker's vampire tale *Dracula*. The influence was revived in the 20th century by science-fiction and fantasy writers such as Mervyn Peake in his Gormenghast series. Other masters of the horror tale were Ambrose Bierce, Arthur Machen, Algernon Blackwood, H.P. Lovecraft, and Stephen King. Isolated masterpieces have been produced by writers not usually associated with the genre, for example, Guy de Maupassant's "Le Horla," A.E. Coppard's "Adam and Eve and Pinch Me," and Saki's "Sredni Vashtar" and "The Open Window." Some of the best-known horror stories owe their power to their development of full-bodied characters in a realistic social environment and the very absence of mysterious atmosphere. In this category are Aleksandr Pushkin's "The Queen of Spades" and W.W. Jacobs' "The Monkey's Paw."

Horse's Mouth, The Comic novel by Joyce CARY, published in 1944. It was the third volume in a trilogy that included *Herself Surprised* (1941) and *To Be a Pilgrim* (1942).

The book's protagonist, Gulley Jimson, is an iconoclastic artist consumed with the creative process who rejects the predictable and conventional in art. He does not hesitate to use people to achieve his ends, involving Sara Monday, his former model and lover, in art theft. After accidentally killing Sara, Jimson works feverishly in a vain attempt to finish a final masterwork before the police come to arrest him. He falls, suffers a stroke, and laughs at his fate.

Horton \\'hȯrt-ən\\, George Moses (b. 1797?, Northampton county, N.C., U.S.—d. 1883?) African-American poet who wrote sentimental love poems and antislavery protests. He was one of the first professional black writers in America.

A slave from birth, Horton was relocated, in 1800, to a plantation near Chapel Hill, seat of the University of North Carolina, where he regularly came into contact with the university students. From the 1820s, they regularly commissioned him to create love poems, including clever acrostic compositions based on the names of their lovers. He received literary training from Caroline Lee Hentz, a student who also published his verse in newspapers and unsuccessfully attempted to engineer his release from slavery.

Horton's first book of poetry, *The Hope of Liberty* (1829; retitled *Poems by a Slave*), includes several love lyrics originally written for students, as well as hopeful poems about freedom. Probably because of fears of punishment, *The Poetical Works of George M. Horton, The Colored Bard of North Carolina* (1845) addressed the issue of slavery in a subtle manner. His last and largest volume of verse was *Naked Genius* (1865).

Horus \\'hȯr-əs\\ In ancient Egyptian religion, the son of Isis by Osiris. He took the form of a falcon whose eyes were the sun and the moon. Falcon cults were widespread in Egypt. At Nekhen, however, the conception arose that the reigning king was a manifestation of Horus and, after Egypt had been united, this conception became a generally accepted dogma.

From the 1st dynasty (c. 2925–2775 BC), Horus and the god Seth were understood to be perpetual antagonists who were reconciled in the harmony of Upper and Lower Egypt. In the myth of Osiris, who became prominent later in the third millenium BC, Horus was the son of Osiris. He was also the opponent of Seth, who murdered Osiris and contested Horus' heritage, the royal throne of Egypt. Horus finally defeated Seth, thus avenging his father and assuming the throne.

Horváth \\'hȯr-ˌvät\\, Ödön Edmund Josef von (b. Dec. 9, 1901, Fiume, Croatia, Austria-Hungary [now Rijeka, Croatia]—d. June 1, 1938, Paris, Fr.) Hungarian-born novelist and playwright who was one of the most promising German-language dramatists of the 1930s and one of the earliest antifascist writers in Germany.

Horváth, the son of a Hungarian career diplomat, attended schools in Budapest, Vienna, and Munich before settling in Germany. His early plays, such as *Revolte auf Côte 3018* (produced 1927; "Revolt on Hill 3018"; rewritten as *Die Bergbahn*, produced 1929, "The Mountain Railway"), show a fascination with the folk culture and political history of his adopted country. His interest soon grew into concern over the rising tide of fascism and the moral decay that contributed to it. His most important plays were *Italienische Nacht* (1930; "Italian Night"), a farce about complacent townspeople and bumbling but effective Nazis, and *Geschichten aus dem Wiener Wald* (1930; *Tales from the Vienna Woods*), a tragic folktale.

In 1933 Horváth fled to Austria, where he continued to write plays and novels, including *Die Unbekannte aus der Seine* (written 1933; "The Stranger from the Seine") and *Figaro lässt sich scheiden* (written 1933; "Figaro Gets a Divorce").

Ho Sho *see* YOSANO Akiko.

Hospital \\'häs-pi-təl\\, Janette Turner, *pseudonym* Alex Juniper \\'jü-ni-pər\\ (b. Nov. 12, 1942, Melbourne, Vic., Australia) Australian novelist and short-story writer who explored the political, cultural, and interpersonal boundaries that separate different peoples.

Hospital graduated from the University of Queensland in Australia and Queen's University in Ontario, Canada. She taught in several colleges and universities in Canada, the United States, and Australia and lived for a while in India. In childhood she became sensitive to the clashes between her strict, fundamentalist upbringing and the dominant secular society, and her subsequent experiences living on several continents enhanced her sensitivity to cultural differences.

Hospital's first novel, *The Ivory Swing* (1982), concerns a troubled Canadian family living in India. In *Tiger in the Tiger Pit* (1983) a reunion provides a setting for family members to examine their wounds. *Borderline* (1985) is a suspenseful novel that begins with a refugee's attempt to cross the U.S.–Canadian border in a meat truck and evolves into a mystery on several levels while also exploring issues of responsibility. The protagonist of *Charades* (1988) seeks answers to both personal and metaphysical dilemmas. Like her previous novels, *The Last Magician* (1992) offers a diversity of ideas along with the mystery at its plot's center. *A Very Proper Death* (1990) was published under the name Alex Juniper. Her short stories were collected in *Dislocations* (1986) and *Isobars* (1990).

Hostage, The   Play in three acts by Brendan BEHAN, produced in 1958 and published in 1962. Considered Behan's masterwork, the play employs ballads, slapstick, and fantasies to satirize social conditions and warfare. In the play, an English soldier is held hostage in a brothel by members of the Irish Republican Army (IRA), who hope thus to prevent the execution of one of their own men.

Hotspur \'hät-‚spər\, *byname of* Henry Percy \'hen-rē-'pər-sē\ Fictional character, the irascible foil to Prince Hal in *Henry IV*, Part 1, and *Richard II* by William Shakespeare. *See* HENRY IV; RICHARD II.

Houghton \'haút-ən, 'hót-, *U.S. also* 'hōt-\ of Great Houghton, Richard Monckton Milnes \'milz, 'milnz\, 1st Baron (b. June 19, 1809, London, Eng.—d. Aug. 11, 1885, Vichy, Fr.)   Eclectic English Victorian poet and man of letters who considerably influenced public taste in literature in his day.

At Trinity College, Cambridge, where he took his M.A. degree in 1831, Houghton joined the socially and artistically progressive club called the Apostles, which included among its members the poets Alfred (later Lord) Tennyson and Arthur Henry Hallam. From 1837 to 1863 he served as a member of Parliament and was made a peer in 1863. In the House of Lords Houghton defended the Oxford Movement in the Church of England, and he favored reform of the franchise (the right to vote).

Houghton was a generous and discriminating patron of writers. He published the pioneer *Life, Letters, and Literary Remains of John Keats* (1848), secured a pension for Tennyson, made the American sage Ralph Waldo Emerson known in England, and was an early champion of the poet Algernon Charles Swinburne. Considered a capable writer, he published two volumes of poetry (1876) and numerous articles on subjects from politics to travel.

Hound and Horn   American quarterly of the arts cofounded and edited by Lincoln Kirstein. It was published from 1927 to 1934. Initially published at Harvard University, *Hound and Horn* became a widely inclusive American arts review by its third issue (1928), and it moved to New York in 1930. The philosophical perspective of the *Hound and Horn* fluctuated drastically, from humanism to Southern agrarianism to Marxism, but it continued to publish works by leading modern poets, writers, and critics, including its staff editors R.P. Blackmur and Yvor Winters.

Hound of the Baskervilles, The \'bas-kər-vilz\   One of the best known of the Sherlock Holmes novels, written by Arthur Conan DOYLE in 1901. The novel was serialized in *Strand* (1901–02) and was published in book form in 1902. Based on a local legend of a spectral hound that haunted Dartmoor in Devonshire, England, the story is set in the moors at Baskerville Hall and the nearby Grimpen Mire, and the action takes place mostly at night, when the terrifying hound howls for blood. Holmes's assistant, Dr. John Watson, narrates the story, which uncharacteristically emphasizes the eerie setting and mysterious atmosphere rather than the hero's deductive ingenuity.

houri \'hū-rē, 'húr-ē\, *also spelled* huri, *Arabic* ḥawrā', *plural* ḥūr.   In Islām, a beautiful maiden who awaits the devout Muslim man in paradise. The Qur'ān describes them as "purified wives" and "spotless virgins." Tradition elaborated on the sensual image of the houri and defined some of her functions; on entering paradise, for example, the believer is presented with a large number of houri, with each of whom he may cohabit once for each day he has fasted in Ramaḍān and once for each good work he has performed.

Hours of Idleness   First collection of poems by Lord BYRON, published in 1807 when he was 19 years old. The poems are generally regarded as commonplace at best. A sneering review published in *The Edinburgh Review* in 1808 dismissed his efforts as the self-indulgent work of a titled youth. In response Byron published, anonymously, his satiric poem *English Bards and Scotch Reviewers* (1809).

House by the Medlar Tree, The   Realist (verismo) novel of Sicilian life by Giovanni VERGA, published in 1881 as *I Malavoglia*. The book concerns the dangers of economic and social upheaval. It was the first volume of a projected five-novel series that Verga never completed. The author's objective narrative and extensive use of dialogue to advance the action and reveal character represented a new style in Italian fiction.

The action centers on the Malavoglia family, who borrow money from the local usurer against unreceived goods they expect to resell. When the shipment is lost at sea, the family must nonetheless repay the debt. A series of setbacks and losses follow, as the family encounters trouble from every quarter. The house is lost and heroic sacrifices are required of both the men and women until the debt is repaid. At the novel's end the family retakes possession of the house by the medlar tree.

house dramatist   A writer of plays for a particular theater.

House for Mr. Biswas, A \'bis-‚wäs\   Novel by V.S. NAIPAUL, published in 1961, in which a poor West Indian Hindu achieves his symbol of success and independence— owning his own house.

The novel begins with the death of Mohun Biswas of heart disease at age 46. A descendant of East Indians brought to Trinidad as indentured laborers, Mr. Biswas has been dogged by misfortune and humiliation. Homeless and loveless, he has wandered from place to place, with every small success matched by a humiliation. His wife is a member of the vast Tulsi clan, to whom she has always given her loyalty and who have treated him with contempt. Mr. Biswas rashly purchases a ramshackle house that he can ill afford; however, it is his own and represents a declaration of independence from the smothering Tulsis. His death leaves his wife and children penniless. His house stands empty.

Household \'haús-‚hōld\, Geoffrey (Edward West) (b. Nov. 30, 1900, Bristol, Eng.—d. Oct. 4, 1988, Banbury, Oxfordshire)

British novelist best known for his psychological thriller *Rogue Male* (1939; also published as *Man Hunt*).

Household was educated at Clifton College, Bristol, and at Magdalen College, Oxford. He traveled in the United States, Europe, the Middle East, and Latin America, places he later used as settings for his novels. During this time the charming stories he wrote for *The Atlantic Monthly* met with considerable success, and in 1935 he began to write full-time. His first novel, *The Terror of Villadonga* (1936; revised and reissued as *The Spanish Cave*), was a work for children. After publishing *The Third Hour* (1937) and a collection of stories entitled *The Salvation of Pisco Gabar* (1938), he served in the Intelligence Corps in Greece, Palestine, Syria, and Iraq. He published 22 novels, usually with a gentlemanly, erudite first-person narrator, as well as several collections of short stories, juvenile books, and an autobiography, *Against the Wind* (1958). *Rogue Justice*, a sequel to *Rogue Male*, was published in 1982.

Household Words   Weekly periodical published in London by Charles DICKENS from March 30, 1850 to May 28, 1859. Priced at twopence and occasionally reaching a circulation of 300,000, the popular magazine addressed a broad readership with weekly miscellanies of fiction, poetry, and essays. Although Dickens was a co-owner with William Bradbury and Frederick Evans, he exerted total editorial control and eventually bought out his partners in order to shut down *Household Words* and replace it with *All the Year Round*.

Dickens himself wrote a great deal for *Household Words*, contributing serialized books, including *Hard Times* (1854) and *Great Expectations* (1860–61), essays, and other miscellaneous pieces. Other distinguished novelists who contributed serials included Mrs. Gaskell, Wilkie Collins, Charles Reade, and Edward Bulwer-Lytton.

House in Paris, The \'par-is\   Novel by Elizabeth BOWEN, published in 1935, in which the plot complexities of infidelity and family tragedy are revealed mainly through the eyes of two children, Leopold and Henrietta, who meet at Naomi Fisher's house in Paris.

House of Bernarda Alba, The \bər-'när-də-'al-bə, *Spanish* ber-'när-thä-'äl-b̤ä\   Three-act tragedy by Federico GARCÍA LORCA, published as *La casa de Bernarda Alba: Drama de mujeres en los pueblos de España* (subtitled "Drama of Women in the Villages of Spain") in 1936. It constitutes the third play of Lorca's dramatic trilogy that also includes *Blood Wedding* and *Yerma*, and it was first produced in Buenos Aires in 1945.

The play tells the story of a repressive and domineering widow who forces her five unmarried daughters to remain in mourning for their father, sequestered with her on the family estate, for eight years. Frustrated and angry, the women respond in their individual ways to their mother's cruelty, and the play ends in violence.

House of Mirth, The   Novel by Edith WHARTON, published in 1905.

The story concerns the tragic fate of the beautiful and well-connected but penniless Lily Bart, who at age 29 lacks a husband to secure her position in society. Maneuvering to correct this situation, she encounters both Simon Rosedale, a rich man outside her class, and Lawrence Selden, who is personally appealing and socially acceptable but not wealthy. She becomes indebted to an unscrupulous man, has her reputation sullied by a promiscuous acquaintance, and slides into genteel poverty. Unable or unwilling to ally herself with either Rosedale or Selden, she finally despairs and takes an overdose of pills.

House of the Seven Gables, The   Romance by Nathaniel HAWTHORNE, published in 1851. Set in mid-19th-century Salem, Mass., the work is a somber study in hereditary sin based on the legend of a curse pronounced on Hawthorne's own family by a woman condemned to death during the infamous Salem witchcraft trials. The greed and arrogant pride of the novel's Pyncheon family through the generations is mirrored in the gloomy decay of their seven-gabled mansion, in which the family's enfeebled and impoverished relations live. At the book's end the descendant of a family long ago defrauded by the Pyncheons lifts his ancestors' curse on the mansion and marries a young niece of the family.

Housman \'haüs-mən\, A.E., *in full* Alfred Edward (b. March 26, 1859, Fockbury, Worcestershire, Eng.—d. April 30, 1936, Cambridge)   English scholar and celebrated poet whose lyrics express a Romantic pessimism in a spare, simple style.

Housman attended Oxford and from 1882 to 1892 worked as a clerk in the Patent Office in London. In the evenings he studied Latin texts in the British Museum reading room and developed a consummate gift for correcting errors in them. Articles he wrote for journals caught the attention of scholars and led to his appointment in 1892 as professor of Latin at University College, London. Having recognized his homosexuality while at Oxford and having experienced a traumatic episode of unrequited love, Housman was apparently convinced that he must live without love, and he became increasingly reclusive.

For solace he turned to his notebooks, in which he had begun to write the poems that eventually made up A SHROPSHIRE LAD (1896). The popularity of the collection grew slowly but surely, and when Housman's second volume of lyrics, *Last Poems*, was published in 1922, it had astonishing success for a book of verse. Housman's major scholarly effort was an annotated edition of Marcus Manilius (1903–30), whose poetry he did not like but who gave him ample scope for emendation. Some of the asperity and directness that appears in Housman's lyrics also is found in his scholarship, in which he defended common sense with a sarcastic wit.

A lecture, *The Name and Nature of Poetry* (1933), gives Housman's considered views of th art. His brother Laurence selected the verses for the posthumous volume *More Poems* (1936). Housman's *Letters* appeared in 1971.

Housman \'haüs-mən\, Laurence (b. July 18, 1865, Bromsgrove, Worcestershire, Eng.—d. Feb. 20, 1959, Glastonbury, Somerset)   English artist and dramatist noted for a series of plays about the Victorian era.

Housman, who was the younger brother of the poet A.E. Housman, studied art in London. Among his earliest works were illustrations for Christina Rossetti's *Goblin Market and Other Poems*. His first writings were fairy tales and poems, which he illustrated himself. *Bethlehem*, his first play, was privately produced in 1902 but, like many of his dramatic works, was for some years withheld by censorship from public performance. He collaborated with Harley Granville-Barker on *Prunella* (1906), a charming fantasy that was the notable exception to that rule. It was not, however, until 1922 that Housman's fame was secured with the publication of the first of three collections entitled *Little Plays of St. Francis*. In the early 1930s, Housman began writing a series of short plays about Queen Victoria. These were collected, along with the previously published *Angels & Ministers* (1921), as *Victoria Regina* in 1934. This series of vignettes was staged with great success in the United States before the censor's ban was lifted in England in 1937. The note of satire that in varying degrees pervaded much of his writing was dominant in several novels, including *Trimblerigg* (1924), of which David Lloyd George was the thinly disguised butt. Housman's autobiography, *The Unexpected Years*, was published in 1936.

Hout \vän-'haȯt\, Jan van (b. Dec. 14, 1542, Leiden, Holland [now in The Netherlands]—d. Dec. 12, 1609, Leiden)   Humanist, translator, historian, and poet who was the first Dutch Renaissance figure to distinguish himself from his contemporaries in the field of literary theory. He foresaw the line of development that European literature was to take and wrote from the first in iambic meter. His "modernity" is also seen in his intense interest in his Germanic past and in his vigorous campaigns against the dry rhetoric and set conventions that characterized the literature of the time.

Most of van Hout's poetry has been lost, but his few surviving prose works show a remarkable individuality of style and an enlightened outlook. His prose introduction to his now lost translation of the Scottish humanist George Buchanan's *Franciscanus* (c. 1575) is a highly ironic invective against the then corrupt Franciscan order and the Roman Catholic church. As a historian, van Hout rose above the medieval tradition of mere chronology with his clarity of thought, his contempt for irrelevancies, and his search for objective truth.

Houyhnhnm \'hwin-əm, hū-'i-nəm\   Any member of a fictional race of intelligent, rational horses described by Jonathan Swift in the satirical GULLIVER'S TRAVELS. The Houyhnhnms are contrasted with the monstrous Yahoos, members of a brutish humanoid race that the Houyhnhnms have tamed into submission.

hovering accent *also called* hovering stress.   A distribution of energy, pitch, or duration in two adjacent syllables when a heavy syllable occurs next to a syllable bearing the metrical ictus so that the stress seems to be divided or diffused nearly equally over both syllables, as *cornfield* in the line

"that o'er/the green/cornfield/did pass."

Hovering accents are common in English verse.

Hovey \'hǝv-ē\, Richard (b. May 4, 1864, Normal, Ill., U.S.—d. Feb. 24, 1900, New York, N.Y.)   American poet, translator, and dramatist whose works consistently reflected his optimism and his faith in a vital United States.

After graduating in 1885 from Dartmouth, Hovey studied art and theology. In 1887 he met the poet Bliss Carman, with whom he later collaborated. Hovey lectured on aesthetics at the Farmington School of Philosophy in Connecticut and at Columbia University, New York City, where he held a post as professor of English at Barnard College.

Hovey's first major work was *Launcelot and Guenevere: A Poem in Dramas* (1891); it was the first part of a planned three-trilogy scheme—each trilogy to consist of a masque, a tragedy, and a drama. Hovey managed to complete the first trilogy and only the masque, *Taliesin* (1896), of the second trilogy. With his friend Carman he collaborated on a series of books of verse, *Songs from Vagabondia* (1894), *More Songs from Vagabondia* (1896), and *Last Songs from Vagabondia* (1901, published posthumously). Hovey's other works include *Seaward* (1893), an elegy on the poet and Dante scholar Thomas William Parsons, and *Along the Trail* (1898), a book of verse on the Spanish-American War.

Howard \'haȯ-ərd\, Bronson (Crocker) (b. Oct. 7, 1842, Detroit, Mich., U.S.—d. Aug. 4, 1908, Avon, N.J.)   American journalist, dramatist, and founder-president of the first society for playwrights in the United States.

Howard had his first success with *Saratoga*, produced in 1870 at a time when dramas of American life written by Americans were practically nonexistent; its success encouraged other native playwrights. *The Henrietta* (1887), a satire on business, and *Shenandoah* (1889), which established Charles Frohman, as

a great producer, were also successes. Howard's other plays include *The Banker's Daughter* (1878), first produced in 1873 as *Lillian's Last Love*; *Wives* (1879); *Young Mrs. Winthrop* (1882); and *One of Our Girls* (1885). He described his craft in *Autobiography of a Play* (1914).

Howard \'haȯ-ərd\, Elizabeth Jane (b. March 26, 1923, London, Eng.)   English writer of novels and shorter fiction who was praised for her deft characterizations of alienated people and her sensitivity to the nuances of family relationships.

Howard's writing was acclaimed for its technique as well as for its evocative, tightly drawn scenes delineating tensions and secrets between parents and children and between spouses. Among her novels are *The Beautiful Visit* (1950), *The Long View* (1956), *The Sea Change* (1959), *After Julius* (1965), and *Something in Disguise* (1969). The last two were later adapted as television plays for which Howard wrote the scripts. Other novels include *Odd Girl Out* (1972), *Getting It Right* (1982), *The Light Years* (1990), and *Marking Time* (1991). Among her works of short fiction are *We Are for the Dark* (1951), a collection of ghost stories, and *Mr. Wrong* (1975), a volume of collected short stories. In addition to writing fiction, Howard edited *The Lover's Companion* (1978) and *Green Shades: An Anthology of Plants, Gardens, and Gardeners* (1991). She also composed scripts for television, including *Upstairs, Downstairs*. She was married for a time to the novelist Kingsley Amis.

Howard, Henry   *see* Henry Howard, Earl of SURREY.

Howard \'haȯ-ərd\, Richard (b. Oct. 13, 1929, Cleveland, Ohio, U.S.)   Poet, critic, and translator who was influential in introducing modern French poetry and experimental novels to American readers and whose own volume of verse, *Untitled Subjects* (1969), won the Pulitzer Prize for poetry in 1970.

Educated at Columbia University and the Sorbonne, Howard worked as a lexicographer before becoming a freelance critic and translator. He also taught comparative literature at the University of Cincinnati and was a fellow at Yale University.

Beginning with his first volume, *Quantities* (1962), much of Howard's poetry was in the form of dramatic monologues in which historic and literary personages address the reader directly. Howard's other volumes of poetry include *Two-Part Inventions* (1974), *Misgivings* (1979), *Lining Up* (1984), *No Traveller* (1989), and *Selected Poems* (1991).

In *Alone with America: Essays on the Art of Poetry in the United States Since 1950* (1969), Howard offers a critical analysis of the work and styles of 41 American poets. He translated a vast body of work from the French, including works by Simone de Beauvoir, Roland Barthes, Alain Robbe-Grillet, Claude Simon, Jean Genet, and Jean Cocteau. Howard's translation of Charles Baudelaire's *Les Fleurs du Mal: The Complete Text of The Flowers of Evil* won an American Book Award in 1984.

Howard \'haȯ-ərd\, Sir Robert (b. 1626, England—d. Sept. 3, 1698)   English dramatist remembered chiefly for his dispute with John Dryden on the use of rhymed verse in drama.

Of Howard's plays, the best were *The Indian-Queen* (1665), a tragedy written in collaboration with Dryden, and *The Committee* (first performed 1662), a comedy of humors that satirized the Commonwealth regime and gained durable popularity from the character of the Irish footman Teague.

Howard's preface to *Four New Plays* began his dispute with Dryden. Howard opposed Dryden's dedicatory epistle to *The Rival Ladies* (1664) that held rhyme to be better suited to heroic tragedy than blank verse. Dryden replied in *Of Dramatick Poesie, an Essay* (1668). In the preface to *The Duke of Lerma*, Howard replied in a rather more personal tone, but Dryden had the final word in the crushing *Defence of an Essay of Dramatick Poesie* prefaced to *The Indian Emperour* (performed 1665).

Howard \\'haú-ərd\\, Sidney (Coe) (b. June 26, 1891, Oakland, Calif., U.S.—d. Aug. 23, 1939, Tyringham, Mass.) American playwright whose works helped to bring psychological as well as theatrical realism to the stage.

Howard graduated from the University of California, Berkeley, in 1915 and studied under George Pierce Baker at his Harvard 47 Workshop. He was on the editorial staff of the magazine *Life* in 1919–22 and in 1923 was a feature writer for William Randolph Hearst's *International Magazine.*

One of Howard's best-known plays is *They Knew What They Wanted* (1924), the story of an aging Italian immigrant in California and his mail-order bride. The play won the Pulitzer Prize in 1925 and was the basis of Frank Loesser's musical *The Most Happy Fella* (1957). Other well-known plays are *The Silver Cord* (1926) and *Yellow Jack* (1934, in collaboration with Paul de Kruif), a dramatized documentary of the conquest of yellow fever. Howard also wrote *Lute Song* (1930; with Will Irwin), *The Late Christopher Bean* (1932; an adaptation from a French play by René Fauchois), and *Dodsworth* (1934; adapted from Sinclair Lewis' novel). He translated and adapted a number of European dramas, including *Salvation* (1928; with Charles MacArthur).

Howards End \\'haú-ərdz-'end\\ Novel by E.M. FORSTER, published in 1910. The narrative concerns the relationships that develop between the imaginative, life-loving Schlegel family—Margaret, Helen, and their brother Tibby—and the apparently cool, pragmatic Wilcoxes—Henry and Ruth and their children Charles, Paul, and Evie. Margaret finds a soul mate in Ruth, who before dying declares in a note that her family country house, Howards End, should go to Margaret. Her survivors choose to ignore her wishes, but after marrying Henry, Margaret ultimately does come to own the house. In a symbolic ending, Margaret brings Henry back to Howards End after several traumatic events have left him a broken man.

Howe \\'haú\\, E.W., *in full* Edgar Watson (b. May 3, 1853, Treaty, Ind., U.S.—d. Oct. 3, 1937, Atchison, Kan.) American editor, novelist, and essayist known for his iconoclasm and pessimism.

An apprentice printer at age 12, Howe worked at the trade in Missouri, Iowa, Nebraska, and Utah (1867–72). At 19 he was publisher of the *Golden* (Colo.) *Globe* and in 1877 founded the *Atchison* (Kan.) *Daily Globe*, which was made famous by the frequent reprinting throughout the United States of articles and comments he published in it. His first and most successful novel, *The Story of a Country Town* (1883), was the first realistic novel of Midwestern small-town life. He published and edited *Howe's Monthly* (1911–33) and wrote essays, travel books, and an autobiography, *Plain People* (1929). His journalistic writing was collected in *The Indignations of E.W. Howe* (1933) and other books.

Howe \\'haú\\, Irving (b. June 11, 1920, New York, N.Y., U.S.—d. May 5, 1993, New York City) American literary and social critic and educator noted for probing into social and political viewpoints in literary criticism.

Howe was educated at the City College of New York. He taught at Brandeis and Stanford universities and the City University of New York at Hunter College. He wrote critical works on Sherwood Anderson (1951), William Faulkner (1952), and Thomas Hardy (1967), and he synthesized his political and literary interests in *Politics and the Novel* (1957) and *A World More Attractive: A View of Modern Literature and Politics* (1963). He edited the works of George Gissing, Edith Wharton, Leon Trotsky, and George Orwell and from 1953 was editor of the periodical *Dissent*. He also edited *Favorite Yiddish Stories* (1974; with Eliezer Greenberg), *The Best of Sholom Aleichem*

(1979; with Ruth R. Wisse), and *The Penguin Book of Modern Yiddish Verse* (1987; with Khone Shmeruk and Wisse).

His *World of Our Fathers* (1976) is a sociocultural study of eastern European Jews who immigrated to the United States between 1880 and 1924. *Celebrations and Attacks* (1978) is a collection of his critical articles, and *A Margin of Hope: An Intellectual Biography* (1982) deals with his involvement with culture and politics. *Selected Writings 1950–1990* was published in 1990.

Howe \\'haú\\, Julia Ward (b. May 27, 1819, New York, N.Y., U.S.—d. Oct. 17, 1910, Newport, R.I.) American author and lecturer best known for her "Battle Hymn of the Republic." The "Battle Hymn," composed to the rhythm of the folk song "John Brown's Body," was first published in *The Atlantic Monthly* in February 1862. Moved by the economic plight of Civil War widows, Howe worked for equal educational, professional, and business opportunities for women. She was the author of travel books, drama, and verse and composed songs for children.

Howell \\'haú-əl\\, James (b. *c.* 1594, probably in Abernant, Carmarthenshire, Wales—d. 1666, London, Eng.) Anglo-Welsh writer known for his *Epistolae Ho-Elianae*, 4 vol. (1645–55), early and lively essays in letter form.

Though vividly recording contemporary phenomena, Howell's essays lack historical reliability because of plagiarizing and the addition of fictitious dates—despite the author's position as historiographer royal, a post created for him at the restoration of the monarchy in 1660. He also did translations and wrote dictionaries, imaginative works, and political pamphlets.

Howells \\'haú-əlz\\, William Dean (b. March 1, 1837, Martins Ferry, Ohio, U.S.—d. May 11, 1920, New York City) American novelist and critic, preeminent in late 19th-century American letters.

Howells grew up in various Ohio towns and began work early as a typesetter and later as a reporter. Meanwhile, he taught himself languages, becoming well read in German, Spanish, and English classics, and began contributing poems to *The Atlantic Monthly*. His campaign biography of Abraham Lincoln (1860) financed a trip to New England, where he met the great men of the literary establishment, including Oliver Wendell Holmes, Nathaniel Hawthorne, and Ralph Waldo Emerson. Following Lincoln's victory, Howells received a consulship at Venice (1861–65), which enabled him to marry. On his return to the U.S. he became assistant editor (1866–71) and then editor (1871–81) of *The Atlantic Monthly*, in which he began publishing reviews and articles interpreting American writers. He immediately recognized the worth of Henry James, and he was the first to take Mark Twain seriously as an artist.

Their Wedding Journey (1872) and *A Chance Acquaintance* (1873) were his first realistic novels of uneventful middle-class life. There followed several international novels, contrasting American and European manners. Howells' best work depicts the American scene as it changed from a simple, egalitarian society where luck and pluck were rewarded to one in which social and economic gulfs were becoming unbridgeable. He also wrote *A Modern Instance* (1882), a powerful novel that tells the story of the disintegration of a marriage. His best-known work, THE RISE OF SILAS LAPHAM (1885), deals with a self-made businessman's efforts to fit into Boston society. In 1887 he made a plea for clemency for the condemned Haymarket anarchists, a group of labor leaders who were convicted of murder after a violent riot in Chicago in 1886. He risked both livelihood and reputation in the cause, believing that they had been convicted for their political beliefs. In 1888 he left Boston for New York.

His deeply shaken social faith was reflected in his later novels, such as the strongly pro-labor *Annie Kilburn* (1888) and *A Hazard of New Fortunes* (1890). The latter, generally considered one of his finest works, dramatizes the competitive life of New York, where a representative group of characters try to establish a magazine.

Howl   Poem in three sections by Allen GINSBERG, published in *Howl and Other Poems* in 1956. It is considered the foremost poetic expression of the Beat movement of the 1950s.

A denunciation of the weaknesses and failings of American society, *Howl* is a combination lamentation, jeremiad, and vision. The poem opens with a run-on sentence that describes the despair and frustration of American youths, beginning "I saw the best minds of my generation destroyed by madness, starving/hysterical naked,/dragging themselves through the negro streets at dawn looking for an/angry fix."

The poem was praised for its incantatory rhythms and raw emotion; critics noted the influences of Ginsberg's mentor William Carlos Williams (who wrote an introduction to the 1959 edition of the book), Walt Whitman, and William S. Burroughs. *Howl* also was an unabashed celebration and critique of the masculine. Its frank references to heterosexual and homosexual coupling landed its publisher, Lawrence Ferlinghetti, in court on charges of distributing obscene material, but he was acquitted in 1957 in a landmark decision.

Hrabal \\'hrȧ-bȧl\\, Bohumil (b. March 28, 1914, Brünn, Moravia, Austria-Hungary [now Brno, Czech Republic]) Czech author of comic, slightly surreal tales about poor workers, eccentrics, failures, and nonconformists.

Though Hrabal received a law degree in 1946 from Charles University, Prague, he never practiced law. His early short stories, collected in *Perlička na dně* (1964; "A Pearl at the Bottom"), *Pábitelé* (1964; "Palaverers"), and *Automat svět* (1966; *The Death of Mr. Baltisberger*), are plotless, darkly humorous free-association anecdotes, typically about social misfits and happily disreputable people. In *Taneční hodiny pro starší a pokročilé* (1964; "Dancing Lessons for Seniors and the Advanced"), an elderly man tells his life story in a single 90-page unfinished sentence. Hrabal's best-known work was his most conventional in form: the novel *Ostře sledované vlaky* (1965; *Closely Watched Trains*; film, 1966).

Hrabal's unconventional writings were banned after the Soviet Union invaded Czechoslovakia in 1969. When Soviet domination ended in 1989, his works from the 1970s were at last published there, including *Příliš hlučná samota* (1989; *Too Loud a Solitude*) and *Obsluhoval jsem anglického krále* (1990; *I Served the King of England*).

Hrosvitha or **Roswitha** \\rȯs-'vē-tä\\ (b. *c.* 935—d. *c.* 1000) Regarded as the first German woman poet.

Of noble birth, Hrosvitha spent most of her life as a nun in the Benedictine convent at Gandersheim. In an effort to counteract the pagan morality expressed in classical works, Hrosvitha wrote (c. 960) six comedies in Latin, based in form on the Roman comic dramatist Terence but embodying Christian themes. Written in a rough, partly rhymed prose, they were meant to provide edification for her sister nuns. Hrosvitha reproached those who prefer the vain pleasure of well-written secular books to the solid worth of sacred subjects. Hrosvitha's comedies were also meant for reading rather than performance. Hrosvitha's other works include narrative poems based on Christian legends and two verse chronicles: one on the feats of Otto the Great and the other on the history of the convent of Gandersheim from its founding in 856 to the year 919.

Hsiao-ching   *see* XIAOJING.

Hsia Yen   *see* XIA YAN.

Hsieh Ling-yün   *see* XIE LINGYUN.

Hsin Ch'i-chi   *see* XIN QIJI.

Hsiung Fo-hsi   *see* XIONG FOXI.

Hsi-yu chi   *see* XIYOU JI.

Hsü Chih-mo   *see* XU ZHIMO.

Huainanzi or **Huai-nan-tzu** \\'hwī-'nän-'tsü\\ ("Master Huai Nan")   Important Chinese classic written in the 2nd century BC under the patronage of the nobleman Huainanzi (Liu An). It is a compilation of 21 loosely connected chapters on metaphysics, cosmology, matters of state, and conduct. Although it contains little that is not included in two earlier Daoist classics, the *Daode jing* and *Zhuangzi*, its cosmogony is more elaborate and more definite than that of the earlier works and has been retained as orthodox doctrine not only by Daoist philosophers but also by later Confucianists.

huaju or **hua-chü** \\'hwä-'jūe\\ [Chinese *huàjù*, from *huà* word, talk + *jù* drama]   Form of Chinese drama featuring realistic spoken dialogue rather than the sung poetic dialogue of the traditional Chinese dramatic forms. *Huaju* was developed in the early 20th century by intellectuals who wanted to replace the traditional Chinese forms with Western-style drama. The first full-length play of this kind was an adaptation of Lin Shu's *Heinu yu tian lu* (1901; "The Black Slave Cries Out to Heaven"), itself a version of *Uncle Tom's Cabin*; it was produced by a group of Chinese students in Japan in 1907. At first the *huaju* plays consisted exclusively of translations or adaptations of Western works intended for the appreciation of Western-educated intellectuals, but the appeal of *huaju* was later broadened through the efforts of the China Traveling Dramatic Troupe. In 1936 the troupe performed *Leiyu* (*Thunderstorm*), an original four-act tragedy by Cao Yu, one of the most successful *huaju* writers.

Huang Zunxian or **Huang Tsun-hsien** \\'hwäŋ-'zwùn-'shyen\\ (b. 1848, Jiaying [now Meixian], Guangdong province, China—d. March 28, 1905, Jiaying)   Chinese poet and government official.

In his career as a diplomat, Huang Zunxian traveled to Japan, the United States, and England, accumulating new material for his poetry and prose works, but the new style that made his poetry popular originated in his hometown of Jiaying. There he observed the speech of the common people and the styles and rhythms of the local folk songs, incorporating these new patterns in his poetry. Huang Zunxian's use of vernacular Chinese and the folk-ballad style was a major innovation in Chinese verse.

Hubbard \\'hǝb-ǝrd\\, Elbert (Green) (b. June 19, 1856, Bloomington, Ill., U.S.—d. May 7, 1915, at sea off Ireland)   American editor, publisher, and author of the moralistic essay "A Message to Garcia" (1899).

A freelance newspaperman and businessman, Hubbard retired in 1892 and founded the Roycroft Press in 1895 at East Aurora, N.Y., based on the model of William Morris' communal Kelmscott Press. Beginning in 1895 he issued the famous monthly "Little Journey" booklets. These were pleasant biographical essays on famous persons, in which fact was interwoven with comment and satire. Hubbard also began publishing *The Philistine*, an avant-garde magazine, which he ultimately wrote single-handedly. "A Message to Garcia," in which the importance of perseverance was drawn as a moral from a Spanish-American War incident, appeared in an 1899 number of *The Philistine*. In 1908 Hubbard began to edit and publish a second monthly, *The Fra*.

Valuable collections of Hubbard's writings are *Little Journeys*, 14 vol. (1915), and *Selected Writings*, 14 vol. (1923). His *Scrap Book* (1923) and *Note Book* (1927) were published posthumously.

hubris \\'hyū-bris\\ or **hybris** \\'hī-\\ [Greek *hýbris*] In classical Greek ethical and religious thought, overweening presumption suggesting impious disregard of the limits governing human action in an orderly universe. It is the sin to which the great and gifted are most susceptible, and in Greek tragedy it is usually the hero's tragic flaw.

Huckleberry Finn \\'hək-əl-,ber-ē-'fin\\ (*in full* The Adventures of Huckleberry Finn) Novel by Mark TWAIN, pub-

Illustration for an 1884 edition by E.W. Kemble
Bettmann Archive

lished in 1884. The book's narrator is Huckleberry FINN, a youngster whose artless vernacular speech is admirably adapted to detailed and poetic descriptions of scenes and narrative renditions that are both broadly comic and subtly ironic.

Huck runs away from his abusive father and, with his companion, the runaway slave Jim, makes a long and frequently interrupted voyage down the Mississippi River on a raft. During the journey Huck encounters a variety of characters and types in whom the book memorably portrays almost every class living on or along the river. As a result of these experiences Huck overcomes conventional racial prejudices and learns to respect and love Jim. The book's pages are dotted with idyllic descriptions of the great river and the surrounding forests, and Huck's good nature and unconscious humor permeate the whole. But a thread that runs through adventure after adventure is that of human cruelty, which shows itself both in the acts of individuals and in their unthinking acceptance of such institutions as slavery. The natural goodness of Huck is continually contrasted with the effects of a corrupt society.

Hudibras \\'hyū-di-,bras\\ Satiric poem by Samuel BUTLER, published in several parts beginning in 1663. The immediate success of the first part resulted in a spurious second part

appearing within the year; the authentic second part was published in 1664. The two parts, plus "The Heroical Epistle of Hudibras to Sidrophel," were reprinted together in 1674. In 1678 a third (and last) part was published. The work is directed against the fanaticism, pretentiousness, pedantry, and hypocrisy Butler saw in militant Puritanism.

The eponymous hero of *Hudibras* is a Presbyterian knight who goes "a-coloneling" with his squire, Ralpho, an Independent. They constantly squabble over religious questions and, in a series of grotesque adventures, are shown to be ignorant, wrongheaded, cowardly, and dishonest. Butler derived his outline from Miguel de Cervantes, and his burlesque method from Paul Scarron. However, his brilliant handling of the octosyllabic meter, his witty, clattering rhymes, his delight in strange words and esoteric learning, and his enormous zest and vigor create effects that are entirely original.

Hudibrastic \\,hyū-də-'bras-tik\\ Written in humorous octosyllabic couplets. The term is derived from Samuel Butler's *Hudibras*, a mock-heroic satirical poem in octosyllabic couplets. *See also* MOCK-EPIC.

Hudson \\'həd-sən\\, W.H., *in full* William Henry (b. Aug. 4, 1841, near Buenos Aires, Arg.—d. Aug. 18, 1922, London, Eng.) British author and naturalist, best known for his exotic romances, especially GREEN MANSIONS (1904).

Hudson's parents were originally New Englanders who took up sheep farming in Argentina. He spent his childhood—lovingly recalled in *Far Away and Long Ago* (1918)—freely roaming the Pampas, studying the plant and animal life, and observing both natural and human dramas on what was then a lawless frontier. After an illness at age 15 permanently affected his health, he became introspective and studious. His reading of Charles Darwin's *Origin of Species*, which confirmed his own observations of nature, had a particularly strong impact. After his parents' death, he led a wandering life. Little is known of this period or of his early years in England, where he settled in 1869 (and was naturalized in 1900).

His early books, romances with a South American setting, are weak in characterization but imbued with a brooding sense of nature's power. Although Hudson's reputation now rests chiefly on these novels, when published they attracted little attention. The first, *The Purple Land that England Lost*, 2 vol. (1885), was followed by several long short stories, collected in 1902 as *El Ombú*. His last romance, *Green Mansions*, is the love story of Rima, a strange, mysterious creature of the forest, half bird and half human.

Hudson's books on ornithological studies (*Argentine Ornithology*, 1888–89; *British Birds*, 1895; etc.) brought recognition from the statesman Sir Edward Grey, who procured him a state pension in 1901. He finally achieved fame with his books on the English countryside—*Afoot in England* (1909), *A Shepherd's Life* (1910), *Dead Man's Plack* (1920), *A Traveller in Little Things* (1921), and *A Hind in Richmond Park* (1922). By their detailed, imaginative descriptions, these works did much to foster the "back-to-nature" movement of the 1920s and '30s but were subsequently little read.

Hudson, Roderick \\'räd-ər-ik-'həd-sən\\ Fictional character, the protagonist of the novel RODERICK HUDSON by Henry James.

Hu Feng \\'hü-'fəŋ\\, *pseudonym of* Zhang Guangren \\'zhäŋ-'gwän-'grən\\ (b. Nov. 1, 1902, Qichuan, Hubei province, China—d. June 8, 1985, Beijing) Chinese critic, poet, and essayist who followed Marxist theory in political and social matters but not in literature.

Zhang studied literature at Beijing University and Qinghua University and went to Japan in 1929 to study English literature at Keiō University. There he joined the Japan Anti-War League, a left-wing writers' organization, and the Japanese Communist Party. In 1933 he returned to China, where he joined the Left-wing Writers' League and worked closely with Lu Xun. During this period he published several collections of essays, including *Wenyi bitan* (1936; "Random Notes on Literature"). After the death of Lu Xun, Hu Feng compiled and published many of Lu Xun's unpublished works. He also edited the literary magazines *Qiwue* ("July") and *Xiwang* ("Hope"). Collections of criticism of those years include *Jian/wenyi/renmin* (1943; "Sword/Literature/People") and *Zai hunluan limian* (1945; "In the Midst of Chaos"). They were followed by *Niliude rizi* (1947; "Days of the Adverse Current") and *Lun xianshizhuyide lu* (1948; "On the Road of Realism"). In the early 1950s, during the drive against intellectuals, Hu Feng was subjected to a campaign of criticism for the emphasis he placed on the subjective nature of creative writing. Ultimately, his views were condemned, and he was convicted and imprisoned for several years. He was rehabilitated in 1980. A three-volume collection, *Hu Feng pinglunji* ("Hu Feng's Essays of Literary Criticism"), was published in 1984–85. His poetry was collected in *Wei zuguo er ge* (1942; "Singing for the Fatherland").

Hughes \\'hyūz, 'yūz\\, John Ceiriog, *pseudonym* Ceiriog \\'kir-yȯg\\ *or* Syr Meurig Grynswth \\sir-'mā-rig-'grən-ˌsūth\\ (b. Sept. 25, 1832, Llanarmon Dyffryn Ceiriog, Denbighshire, Wales—d. April 23, 1887, Caersws, Montgomeryshire) Poet and folk musicologist who wrote outstanding Welsh-language lyrics.

Hughes began winning poetry prizes in the 1850s and thereafter published several volumes of verse, the first being *Oriau'r Hwyr* (1860; "Evening Hours"). Many of his lighthearted lyrics (totaling about 600) were adapted to old Welsh tunes; others were set to original music by various composers. He investigated the history of old Welsh airs and of the harpists with whom the tunes were identified. Of his projected four-volume compendium of Welsh airs, only one volume, *Cant o Ganeuon* (1863; "A Hundred Poems"), appeared. He also wrote many satirical prose letters, collected and edited by Hugh Bevan in *Gohebiaethau Syr Meurig Grynswth* (1948; "Correspondence of Syr Meurig Grynswth").

Hughes \\'hyūz, 'yūz\\, Langston, *in full* James Mercer Langston Hughes (b. Feb. 1, 1902, Joplin, Mo., U.S.—d. May 22, 1967, New York, N.Y.) African-American poet and writer who became one of the foremost interpreters to the world of the black experience in the United States.

Hughes first came to notice when his poem THE NEGRO SPEAKS OF RIVERS, written the summer after his graduation from high school in Cleveland, was published in the African-American journal *Crisis* (1921). After attending Columbia University (1921–22) in New York City, he worked as a steward on a freighter bound for Africa. Upon his return to the United States he took a variety of menial jobs and continued writing.

While working as a busboy in a hotel in Washington, D.C., Hughes put three of his own poems beside the plate of American poet Vachel Lindsay in the dining room. The next day, newspapers around the country reported that Lindsay had discovered a Negro busboy poet. A scholarship to Lincoln University in Pennsylvania followed, and before Hughes received his degree in 1929, his first two books had been published.

Library of Congress

The Weary Blues (1926), which includes DREAM VARIATION, was warmly received. *Fine Clothes to the Jew* (1927) was criticized harshly for its title and for its frankness, but Hughes himself felt it represented a step forward. A few months after graduation *Not Without Laughter* (1930), his first prose work, had a cordial reception. In 1931 he collaborated with Zora Neale Hurston on the play MULE BONE. He then traveled widely in the Soviet Union, Haiti, and Japan and served as a newspaper correspondent (1937) in the Spanish Civil War; his poetry of the 1930s was highly political. He published a collection of short stories, *The Ways of White Folks* (1934), and *The Big Sea* (1940), his autobiography up to the age of 28.

Hughes's *Montage of a Dream Deferred*, containing the famous poem HARLEM, was published in 1951. He wrote *A Pictorial History of the Negro in America* (1956) and edited the anthologies *The Poetry of the Negro* (1949) and *The Book of Negro Folklore* (1958; with Arna Bontemps). He also wrote numerous works for the stage, including the lyrics for *Street Scene*, an opera with music by Kurt Weill. A posthumous book of poems, *The Panther and the Lash* (1967), reflected the black anger and militancy of the 1960s. Hughes translated the poetry of Federico García Lorca and Gabriela Mistral. He was also widely known for his comic character Jesse B. Semple, familiarly called Simple, who appeared in Hughes's columns in the *Chicago Defender* and the New York *Post*. Hughes later published a collection entitled *The Best of Simple* (1961).

Hughes \\'hyūz, 'yūz\\, Richard (Arthur Warren) (b. April 19, 1900, Weybridge, Surrey, Eng.—d. April 28, 1976, near Harlech, Gwynedd, Wales) British writer whose novel *A High Wind in Jamaica* (1929; film, 1965; original title *The Innocent Voyage*) is a minor classic of 20th-century English literature.

Hughes graduate from Oriel College, Oxford, in 1922, the same year in which his one-act play *The Sister's Tragedy* was produced in London. In 1924 his play *Danger*, believed to be the first radio play, was broadcast by the BBC. *Gipsy-Night, and Other Poems* (1922) was followed four years later by a collection of verses, *Confessio Juvenis*, and of short stories, *A Moment of Time*.

Hughes traveled widely in the United States and the Caribbean, contributed to literary journals, and in the early 1930s was vice-chairman of the Welsh National Theatre. His first novel, *A High Wind in Jamaica*, is a fresh and unsentimental adventure story about a group of children who are captured by pirates. After this novel came *In Hazard* (1938), an allegorical novel of the sea. His *Fox in the Attic* (1961) was the first part of a projected trilogy, *The Human Predicament*, dealing with upper-class English and Germans between World Wars I and II; the second volume, *The Wooden Shepherdess*, was published in 1973, but the third volume was left incomplete at his death. His books for children include *The Spider's Palace* (1931) and *Gertrude's Child* (1966).

Hughes \\'hyūz, 'yūz\\, Ted, *byname of* Edward J. Hughes (b. Aug. 16, 1930, Mytholmroyd, Yorkshire, Eng.) English poet whose most characteristic work is without sentimentality, emphasizing the cunning and savagery of animal life in harsh, sometimes disjunctive lines.

The dialect of Hughes's native West Riding area of Yorkshire set the tone of his verse. At Pembroke College, Cambridge, he found folklore and anthropology of particular interest, a concern that was reflected in a number of his poems. In 1956 he married the American poet Sylvia Plath. In 1957, his first volume of verse, *The Hawk in the Rain*, was published. *Selected Poems*, with Thom Gunn (a poet whose work is frequently associated with Hughes's as marking a new turn in English verse), was published in 1962.

Hughes stopped writing poetry almost completely for nearly three years following Plath's suicide in 1963 (the couple had separated earlier), but thereafter he published prolifically, often in collaboration with photographers and illustrators, as in *Remains of Elmet* (1979), in which he recalled the world of his childhood, and *River* (1983). Other collections include *Moortown* (1979) and *Wolfwatching* (1989). He wrote many volumes for children, including *Under the North Star* (1981) and *What Is Truth? A Farmyard Fable for the Young* (1984).

From 1965 Hughes was coeditor of the magazine *Modern Poetry in Translation* in London. In 1984 he was appointed Britain's poet laureate, and in 1992 his *Rain-Charm for the Duchy and Other Laureate Poems* was published.

Hughes \'hyūz, 'yūz\, Thomas (b. Oct. 20, 1822, Uffington, Berkshire, Eng.—d. March 22, 1896, Brighton, Sussex) British jurist, reformer, and novelist best known for TOM BROWN'S SCHOOL DAYS (1857).

Hughes was educated at Rugby School from 1834 to 1842. His love for the great Rugby headmaster Thomas Arnold and for games and boyish high spirits are admirably captured in *Tom Brown's School Days*. The book did much to create an enduring image of the typical public-school boy and to popularize the doctrine of "muscular Christianity."

From 1842 to 1845 Hughes was at Oriel College, Oxford, and *Tom Brown at Oxford* (1861), a less-successful sequel, gives a picture of life there at the time. Hughes's admiration for the religious reformer Frederick Denison Maurice led him to join the Christian Socialists and, in 1854, to become a founding member of the Working Men's College, of which he was principal from 1872 to 1883. His simple, earnest approach to religion and his robust patriotism show plainly in his tracts *A Layman's Faith* (1868) and *The Manliness of Christ* (1879).

Hugh Selwyn Mauberley \'hyū-'sel-win-'mȯb-ər-lē\ Long dramatic poem by Ezra POUND, published in 1920, that provides a finely chiselled "portrait" of one aspect of British literary culture of the time.

Pound referred to *Mauberley* as an attempt "to condense a [Henry] James novel." The subject of the opening section is the gaudiness, corruption, and deterioration of culture in modern commercial society. The fictional Mauberley appears in the poem's second section. He represents the worst failings of contemporary artists and serves as the springboard for Pound's plea that form and style be reinstated as the bearers of authentic meaning.

Hugo \ᴤ-'gō\, Victor(-Marie) (b. Feb. 26, 1802, Besançon, Fr.—d. May 22, 1885, Paris) Poet, dramatist, and novelist, the most important of the French Romantic writers and, in later life, a politician and noted political writer.

Hugo was the son of an officer in Napoleon's army. From 1816, at least, Hugo had conceived ambitions other than the law, in which he was matriculating. He founded a review, the *Conservateur Littéraire* (1819–21), in which his own articles on the poets Alphonse de Lamartine and André de Chénier stand out. In 1822 Hugo married a childhood friend, Adèle Foucher. In that same year he published his first book of poems, *Odes et poésies diverses*, which earned him a pension from Louis XVIII. In 1823 he published his first novel, *Han d'Islande* (*Hans of Iceland*, illustrated by George Cruikshank). During this time Hugo was drawn into a group of friends, all devotees of Romanticism, who met regularly at the Arsenal Library and who were known as the Petit Cénacle. He emerged as a true Romantic with the publication in 1827 of his verse drama *Cromwell*.

The defense of freedom and the cult of an idealized Napoleon in such poems as "Lui" and the ode "À la Colonne" brought Hugo in touch with liberal writers on the newspaper *Le Globe*, and his move toward liberalism was strengthened by Charles X's restrictions on the liberty of the press as well as by the censor's prohibiting the performance of his

play *Marion de Lorme* (1829), the story of a courtesan purified by love. He immediately retorted with HERNANI, the first performance of which, on Feb. 25, 1830, gained victory for the young Romantics over the traditional classicists in a literary battle.

Hugo gained wider fame in 1831 with his historical novel *Notre-Dame de Paris* (1831; THE HUNCHBACK OF NOTRE DAME), an evocation of medieval life under the reign of Louis XI. The book touched the public consciousness more deeply than had his previous novel, *Le Dernier Jour d'un condamné* (1829; *The Last Day of a Condemned Man*), in which Hugo launched a humanitarian protest against the death penalty. He later renewed this theme in *Claude Gueux* (1834).

Archives Photographiques

Hugo produced four books of poems in the period of the July Monarchy: *Les Feuilles d'automne* (1831; "Autumn Leaves"), intimate and personal in inspiration; *Les Chants du crépuscule* (1835; "Twilight Songs"), overtly political; *Les Voix intérieures* (1837; "Inner Voices"), both personal and philosophical; and *Les Rayons et les ombres* (1840; "Lights and Shadows").

Having at last achieved a production of *Marion de Lorme* in 1831, he continued to pour out plays, in part as vehicles for a young and beautiful actress, Juliette Drouet, with whom he had begun a liaison in 1833.

In 1841 Hugo was elected, after three unsuccessful attempts, to the Académie Française. Two years later his daughter was accidentally drowned with her husband. His intense grief is revealed in poems that later appeared in *Les Contemplations* (1856).

When in December 1851 a coup d'état took place, Hugo fled to Brussels and then to Jersey and Guernsey. Enforced at the beginning, exile later became a voluntary gesture and, after the amnesty of 1859, an act of pride. During his exile of nearly 20 years he produced the most extensive part of all his writings and the most original. These included LES CHÂTIMENTS (1853; "The Punishments"), which ranks as one of the most powerful collections of satirical poems in the French language; such epic or metaphysical poems as *La Fin de Satan* ("Satan Redeemed") and *Dieu* ("God")—poems of vast scope that, written between 1854 and 1860, were not published until after his death; and the first two volumes of short epics based on history and legend, the "Petites Épopées" of *La Légende des siècles* (1859; *The Legend of the Centuries*). These, which for Hugo himself formed a single poem with the metaphysical epics, are the summit of his art; they display all his spiritual power without sacrificing his exuberant capacity to tell a story.

He then turned to prose and took up his abandoned novel, LES MISÉRABLES (1862), which he had begun shortly after his daughter's death. Its extraordinary success with readers of every type brought him instant popularity in his own country and its speedy translation into many languages won him fame abroad.

The defeat of France in the Franco-Prussian War and the proclamation of the Third Republic brought Hugo back to Paris. Though he still fought for his old ideals, he no longer possessed the same energy. Increasingly detached from life around him, the poet of *L'Année terrible* (1872), in which he recounted the siege of Paris during the "terrible year" of 1870, had become a national hero. He was in Brussels during the period of the Paris Commune, and he was expelled for giving shelter to the defeated rebels. After a temporary refuge in Luxembourg he returned to Paris, where he was elected senator. During 1872–73 he was in Guernsey for the writing of *Quatre-vingt-treize* (1874; *Ninety-three*) and the preparation of his remaining works for publication. At his death he was given a national funeral and was buried in the Panthéon.

Hugo Award \\'hyū-gō, 'yū-\\, *byname of* Science Fiction Achievement Award. Any of several trophies awarded annually by a professional organization for notable achievement in science fiction or science fantasy. The award is given in five writing categories—novel, novella, novelette, short story, and nonfiction. An award for best new writer and special awards are also occasionally presented. The award was established in 1953 in honor of Hugo Gernsback, who founded the first magazine exclusively for science fiction, which he called "scientifiction."

Huidobro \\wē-'thō-bro\\, Vicente García, *surname in full* Huidobro Fernández \\fer-'nän-däs\\ (b. Jan. 10, 1893, Santiago, Chile—d. Jan. 2, 1948, Santiago) Chilean poet, self-proclaimed father of the short-lived avant-garde movement known as *Creacionismo.*

In 1916, after publishing several collections of poetry in Chile and achieving recognition and notoriety for such literary manifestos as *Non serviam* (1914; "I Will Not Serve"), in which he rejected the entire poetic past, Huidobro went to Paris. There he collaborated with the avant-garde French poets Guillaume Apollinaire and Pierre Reverdy on the influential literary review *Nord-Sud* ("North-South"). It was during this period that *Creacionismo* was invented. In *Poemas árticos* (1918; "Arctic Poems") and *Saisons choisies* (1921; "Chosen Seasons"), the latter in French, he exemplified his theories with incongruous juxtapositions of striking images and random, seemingly irrational, sequences of words and letters of the alphabet.

Huidobro went to Madrid in 1918, where, in 1921, he was one of the founders of *Ultraísmo*, the Spanish offshoot of *Creacionismo.* Traveling frequently between Europe and Chile, he was largely responsible for creating the climate of literary experimentation, based on French models, that prevailed in post-World War I Chile.

Continuing to write in the idiom of *Creacionismo* in such novels as *Sátiro o el poder de las palabras* (1939; "Satyr or the Power of Words"), Huidobro also remained a prolific poet in that style long after the movement had faded.

huitain \\wᵉē-'teⁿ\\ [French, from Middle French, a derivative of *huit* eight] French verse form consisting of an eight-line stanza with 8 or 10 syllables in each line. The form was written on three rhymes, one of which appeared four times. Typical rhyme schemes were *ababbcbc* and *abbaacac.* The huitain was popular in France in the 15th and early 16th centuries with such poets as François Villon and Clément Marot.

Hulme \\'hyūm\\, Keri, Keri *originally spelled* Kerry (b. March 9, 1947, Christchurch, N.Z.) New Zealand novelist, poet, and short-story writer, chiefly known for her first novel, *The Bone People* (1983), which won the Booker Prize in 1985.

Much of Hulme's writing dealt with the language and culture of the native Maori people of New Zealand. Although Hulme was born of mostly mixed Orkney and English descent, she identified closely with the Kai Tahu tribe of the Maori,

of which she claimed one-eighth ancestry. Her first book, *The Silences Between: Moeraki Conversations* (1982), is a verse collection noted for its unique and varied use of language. *The Bone People*, Hulme's most acclaimed work, features three characters she first created as an 18-year-old: Kerewin Holmes, a reclusive painter based on the author herself; Simon, a young mute boy who is washed ashore after a shipwreck; and Joe Gillayley, a Maori factory worker. The book was praised for its Maori mysticism and lyrical originality. Hulme also published *Te Kaihau/The Windeater* (1986), a collection of short stories, and two collections of poetry, *Lost Possessions* (1985) and *Strands* (1992).

Hulme \\'hyūm\\, T.E., *in full* Thomas Ernest (b. Sept. 16, 1883, Endon, Staffordshire, Eng.—killed in action, Sept. 28, 1917, France) English aesthetician, literary critic, and poet, one of the founders of the Imagist movement and a major 20th-century literary influence.

Hulme went to St. John's College, Cambridge, but was expelled for rowdyism in 1904. Thereafter he lived mainly in London, where, in addition to translating the works of the philosopher Henri Bergson and the historian Albert Sorel, he joined with Ezra Pound, F.S. Flint, and Hilda Doolittle (H.D.) in instigating the Imagist movement. Five of his poems were published in *New Age* (January 1912) and reprinted at the end of Pound's *Ripostes.* Before his death while fighting in World War I, Hulme defended militarism against the pacifism of philosopher Bertrand Russell.

Hulme suggested that post-Renaissance humanism was coming to an end and believed that its view of humanity as without inherent limitations and imperfections was based on false premises. His hatred of romantic optimism, his view of humanity as limited and absurd, and his advocacy of a "hard, dry" kind of art and poetry foreshadowed the disillusionment of many writers of the 1920s.

Hulme published little in his lifetime, but his work and ideas gained fame in 1924 when his friend Herbert Read assembled some of his notes and fragmentary essays under the title *Speculations.* Additional compilations were edited by Read (*Notes on Language and Style*, 1929) and by Sam Hynes (*Further Speculations*, 1955).

Human Comedy, The A vast series of some 90 novels and novellas by Honoré de BALZAC, known in the original French as *La Comédie humaine.* The books that made up the series were published between 1829 and 1847.

Balzac's plan to produce a unified series of books that would comprehend the whole of contemporary society was not clearly formulated until about 1834, although he had issued several volumes by that time. He elaborated three general categories of novels: *Études analytiques* ("Analytic Studies"), dealing with the principles governing human life and society; *Études philosophiques* ("Philosophical Studies"), revealing the causes determining human action; and *Études de moeurs* ("Studies of Manners"), showing the effects of those causes, and themselves to be divided into six kinds of *scènes*—private, provincial, Parisian, political, military, and country life. The entire project resulted in a total of 12 volumes published between 1834 and 1837. By 1837 Balzac had written much more, and by 1840 he had hit upon the comprehensive title *La Comédie humaine.* He negotiated with a consortium of publishers for an edition under this name, 17 volumes of which appeared between 1842 and 1848, including a famous foreword written in 1842. A "definitive edition," including many new works, was published, in 24 volumes, between 1869 and 1876.

The whole is an examination of French society from the French Revolution to the eve of the Revolution of 1848, in which Balzac analyzed the underlying principles of this constantly developing world. Balzac ranged back and forth, often within the same novel, from the philosophical to the social, the economic, the legal; from Paris to the provinces; and from the summit of society to the petite bourgeoisie.

No theme is more typically Balzacian than that of the ambitious young provincial fighting for advancement in the competitive world of Paris. Balzac was both fascinated and appalled by the French social system of his time, in which the bourgeois values of material acquisitiveness and gain were steadily replacing what he viewed as the more stable moral values of the old-time aristocracy.

These topics provided material largely unknown, or unexplored, by earlier writers of French fiction. Individuals in Balzac's stories are continually affected by the pressures of material difficulties and social ambitions. They are capable of expending their tremendous vitality in ways Balzac viewed as socially destructive and self-destructive. Linked with this idea of the potentially destructive power of passionate will, emotion, and thought is Balzac's peculiar notion of a vital fluid concentrated inside the person, a store of energy that can be husbanded or squandered at will. Indeed, most of Balzac's characters are spendthrifts of this vital force, as can be seen in his many monomaniacs who are both victim and embodiment of some ruling passion; avarice, as in the main character of *Gobseck* (1835), a usurer gloating over his sense of power, or the miserly father obsessed with riches in EUGÉNIE GRANDET (1833); excessive paternal affection, as in the idolatrous Lear-like father in LE PÈRE GORIOT (1835); feminine vindictiveness, as evidenced in *La Cousine Bette* (1846; COUSIN BETTE) and a half-dozen other novels; the mania of the art collector, as in *Le Cousin Pons* (1847; COUSIN PONS); the artist's desire for perfection, as in *Le Chef-d'oeuvre inconnu* (1831; *The Unknown Masterpiece*); the curiosity of the scientist, as in the fanatical chemist of *Le Recherche de l'absolu* (1834; *The Quest of the Absolute*); or the vaulting and frustrated ambition of the astonishingly resourceful criminal mastermind Vautrin in *Illusions perdues* (1837–43; *Lost Illusions*) and *Splendeurs et misères des courtisanes* (1839–47; A HARLOT HIGH AND LOW). Once such an obsession has gained a hold, Balzac shows it growing irresistibly in power and blinding the person concerned to all other considerations.

Other notable novels in the series include *Les Chouans* (1829), *La Peau de chagrin* (1831; THE WILD ASS'S SKIN), and *Le Médecin de campagne* (1833; THE COUNTRY DOCTOR).

Human Comedy, The Sentimental novel of life in a small California town by William SAROYAN, published in 1943.

The narrator of the story, 14-year-old Homer Macauley, lives with his widowed mother, his sister Bess, and his little brother Ulysses; his older brother has left home to fight in World War II. While family relationships and domestic situations are in the foreground, the events of the outside world, including the cataclysmic war, are never entirely out of the picture.

humanism \'hyü-mə-ˌniz-əm, 'yü-\ The learning or cultural impulse that is characterized by a revival of classical letters, an individualistic and critical spirit, and a shift of emphasis from religious to secular concerns that flowered during the Renaissance.

Renaissance humanism is traceable to the 14th-century Italian poet Petrarch, whose scholarship and enthusiasm for classic Latin writings ("the humanities") gave great impetus to a movement that eventually spread from Italy to all of western Europe. The diffusion of humanism was facilitated by the universal use of Latin and by the invention of movable type. Although hu-

manism gradually became identified with classroom studies of the classics, it more properly embraced any attitude that exalted man's relationship to God, free will, and human superiority over nature.

humanities \hyü-'man-i-tēz, yü-\ The branches of learning (such as philosophy or languages) that investigate human constructs and concerns as opposed to natural processes (such as physics or chemistry).

Humbert, Humbert \'həm-bərt-'həm-bərt\ Fictional character, the pedophile protagonist of Vladimir Nabokov's novel LOLITA.

Humboldt's Gift \'həm-ˌbōlt\ Novel by Saul BELLOW, published in 1975. The novel, which won the Nobel Prize for Literature in 1976, is a self-described "comic book about death," whose title character is modeled on the self-destructive lyric poet Delmore Schwartz.

Charlie Citrine, an intellectual, middle-aged author of award-winning biographies and plays, contemplates two significant figures and philosophies in his life: Von Humboldt Fleisher, a dead poet who had been his mentor, and Rinaldo Cantabile, a very-much-alive minor mafioso who has been the bane of Humboldt's existence. Humboldt had taught Charlie that art is powerful and that one should be true to one's creative spirit. Rinaldo, Charlie's self-appointed financial adviser, has always urged Charlie to use his art to turn a profit. At the novel's end, Charlie has managed to set his own course.

Hume \'hyüm\, Alexander (b. *c.* 1560, Polwarth, Berwick, Scot.—d. Dec. 4, 1609, Logie, near Stirling, Stirling) Scots poet known for a collection of religious poems.

Hume probably attended the University of St. Andrews. After practicing law in Edinburgh and trying his fortune at the Scottish court, he was ordained; in 1590 he became minister of Logie, where he remained until his death. He wrote several ardent and puritanical religious tracts and published in Scots a small collection of poems, *Hymns, or Sacred Songs* (1599). He is remembered chiefly for the evocatively descriptive "Of the Day Estival." "Epistle to Maister Gilbert Mont-Crief" is an interesting early example of autobiography.

humors \'hyü-mərz, 'yü-\ [Latin *umor, humor* moisture, bodily fluid] The four main fluids present in the human body according to the theory of physiology during the Middle Ages and the Renaissance. The humors were blood, phlegm, yellow bile, and black bile. A person's temperament, disposition, and morality were thought to be determined by the relative proportions of the humors in the body as they released vapors that affected the brain. The four main temperaments, depending on which humor was dominant, were sanguine, phlegmatic, choleric, and melancholic. The theory was carried over to literature in the creation of characters based on the relative balance of the humors and in the development of the COMEDY OF HUMORS.

Humphreys \'həm-frēz\, Josephine (b. Feb. 2, 1945, Charleston, S.C., U.S.) American novelist noted for her sensitive evocations of family life in the southern United States.

Humphreys studied creative writing at Duke University and attended Yale University and the University of Texas. From 1970 to 1977, before beginning her writing career, she taught at Baptist College in Charleston. Her first novel, *Dreams of Sleep* (1983), examines a faltering marriage that is saved by a third party. Her later novels include *Rich in Love* (1987) and *The Fireman's Fair* (1991).

Humphry Clinker \'həm-frē-'kliŋ-kər\ (*in full* The Expedition of Humphry Clinker) Humorous epistolary novel by Tobias SMOLLETT, his major work, written in 1770 and published in three volumes in 1771, the year of his death.

Written in the form of letters that view episodes from differing perspectives, *Humphry Clinker* tells of a journey the cantankerous but essentially generous Matthew Bramble makes—accompanied by various family members and servants—from his estate in Wales to Bath, London, Scotland, and back home. On their journey they meet several eccentrics, including poverty-stricken young Humphry Clinker, who is naive and inclined to preach Methodism wherever he can gather a crowd. Bramble eventually recognizes Clinker as his natural son. As a picture of 18th-century British life, *Humphry Clinker* is particularly rewarding, for Smollett evokes the sights, sounds, and smells of the parts of Britain his characters visit.

Humpty Dumpty \ˈhəmp-tē-ˈdəmp-tē\ Fictional character, a large egg with human features in Lewis Carroll's THROUGH THE LOOKING-GLASS. As in the nursery rhyme, Humpty Dumpty is sitting atop a wall when Alice encounters him.

Hunchback of Notre Dame, The \ˌnō-trə-ˈdäm, ˌnō-tər-ˈdäm, *French* nȯ-trȧ-ˈdȧm\ Historical novel by Victor HUGO, published in French as *Notre-Dame de Paris* in 1831.

Set in 15th-century Paris, the novel powerfully evokes life in medieval Paris during the reign of Louis XI. Quasimodo is the hunchbacked, horribly deformed bell ringer at the cathedral of Notre-Dame. Once beaten and pilloried by an angry mob, he has fallen in love with the beautiful gypsy Esmeralda, who took pity on him during this ordeal. When the scheming archdeacon Frollo, who is also obsessed with Esmeralda, discovers that she favors Captain Phoebus, he stabs the captain and Esmeralda is accused of the crime. Quasimodo attempts to shelter Esmeralda in the cathedral, but she eventually hangs; in his grief and despair, Quasimodo throws Frollo from the cathedral tower. Later, two skeletons are found in Esmeralda's tomb—that of a hunchback embracing that of a woman.

Hunger Novel by Knut HAMSUN, published in 1890 as *Sult*. It is the semiautobiographical chronicle of the physical and psychological hunger experienced by an aspiring writer in late 19th-century Norway. The unnamed narrator of this plotless, episodic work is an introspective young man whose hunger to succeed as a writer matches his intense physical hunger. He lacks human contact and at times seems demented. Although he has occasional hunger-induced hallucinations, he neither feels sorry for himself nor tries to rectify his situation.

The book's impulsive, lyrical style marked a clear departure from the then-prevalent social realism and had an electrifying effect on European writers.

Hung Shen *see* HONG SHEN.

Hunt \ˈhənt\, Leigh, *in full* James Henry Leigh Hunt (b. Oct. 19, 1784, Southgate, Middlesex, Eng.—d. Aug. 28, 1859, Putney, London) English essayist, critic, journalist, and poet, who was an editor of influential journals in an age when the periodical was at the height of its power. He was also a friend and supporter of the poets Percy Bysshe Shelley and John Keats. Of Hunt's poems, "Abou Ben Adhem" and "Jenny Kissed Me" are probably the best known.

Though he falls short of greatness, Hunt at his best, in various essays and in his *Autobiography* (1850; a rewriting of *Lord Byron and Some of His Contemporaries*, 1828), has a charm that has gained him a high place in his readers' affection. He excels in perceptive judgments of his contemporaries. As a radical journalist, though not much interested in politics, he attacks oppression with indignation.

The poems in *Juvenilia* (1801), his first volume, show his love for Italian literature. In *The Story of Rimini* (1816), he reintroduced a freedom of movement in English couplet verse lost in the 18th century. From him Keats derived his delight in color

and imaginative sensual experience and a first acquaintance with Italian poetry.

In 1808 Hunt and his brother John launched the reformist weekly *The Examiner*. For their attacks on the unpopular prince regent, the brothers were imprisoned in 1813. Hunt, who continued to write *The Examiner* in prison, was regarded as a martyr in the cause of liberty. After his release (1815) he moved to Hampstead, home of Keats, whom he introduced in 1817 to Shelley, a friend since 1811. *The Examiner* supported the new Romantic poets against attacks by *Blackwood's Magazine* on what it called "the Cockney school of poetry."

In Hunt's writings for the quarterly *The Reflector* (1810–11), politics was combined with criticism of the theater and of the fine arts. *Imagination and Fancy* (1844) draws interesting parallels between painting and poetry. It was in the weekly *The Indicator* (1819–21) and *The Companion* (1828) that Hunt published some of his best essays.

Hunter \ˈhən-tər\, Evan, *original name* Salvatore A. Lombino \lȯm-ˈbē-nō\, *pseudonyms* Ed McBain, Curt Cannon, Ezra Hannon, Hunt Collins, *and* Richard Marsten (b. Oct. 15, 1926, New York, N.Y., U.S.) Prolific American writer of best-selling fiction, of which more than 50 books were crime stories published under the pseudonym McBain.

Hunter graduated from Hunter College (1950). His best-known novel was among his earliest: *The Blackboard Jungle* (1954), a story of violence in a New York high school that was the basis of a popular film. After his *Strangers When We Meet* (1958) and *A Matter of Conviction* (1959; U.S. title, *The Young Savages*) became best-sellers, Hunter wrote the screenplays for both (1960–61), as well as for Alfred Hitchcock's *The Birds* (1962) and several later films. Hunter wrote several novels on the theme of family tensions between generations, including *Mothers and Daughters* (1961), *Last Summer* (1968), *Sons* (1969), and *Streets of Gold* (1974).

Hunter was most prolific as a crime novelist. Nearly all of his books using the pseudonym McBain are novels of police procedure, set in a city much like New York. They include *Cop Hater* (1956), *Fuzz* (1968), *Widows* (1991), and *Mischief* (1993). Hunter also wrote children's stories and stage plays.

Hunter \ˈhən-tər\, Kristin (b. Sept. 12, 1931, Philadelphia, Pa., U.S.) African-American novelist who examined black life and racial relations in the United States in both children's stories and works for adults.

Hunter began writing for *The Pittsburgh Courier*, an important black newspaper, when she was 14 and continued until the year after she graduated from the University of Pennsylvania (1951). While working as an advertising copywriter, she won a 1955 television contest with her script *Minority of One*, about black-white school integration; fearing controversy, the network rewrote the story to show a French-speaking immigrant entering an all-white school. In Hunter's first and best-known novel, *God Bless the Child* (1964), three generations of women confront choices forced upon them by their skin tones.

Despite harshly realistic settings, Hunter's subsequent fiction tended to optimism. *The Landlord* (1966) presents a misanthropic white landlord transformed by his new black tenants. In *The Survivors* (1975) a lonely, prosperous middle-aged dressmaker befriends a neglected 13-year-old boy despite his involvement with dishonest, sometimes brutal acquaintances. Her first book for young readers, *The Soul Brothers and Sister Lou* (1968), was about a musical group inspired by a group of youths who sang together nightly in the alley below her apartment. Its sequel was *Lou in the Limelight* (1981). She has also written *Boss Cat* (1971) and *Guests in the Promised Land* (1973) for young readers.

Hunting of the Snark, The \\'snärk\\ (*in full* The Hunting of the Snark: An Agony in Eight Fits)   Nonsense poem by Lewis CARROLL, first published in 1876.

The fanciful eight-canto poem describes the sea voyage of a bellman, boots (bootblack), bonnet maker, barrister, broker, billiard marker, banker, beaver, baker, and butcher, and their search for the elusive, undefined snark. While scholars have attributed to the work hidden meanings from political subversion to existential agony, Carroll maintained that it was intended simply as nonsense. Painter Henry Holiday illustrated the first edition; however, the poet refused to include any picture of the snark, preferring that readers rely on their own imaginations.

Huon de Bordeaux \\wʸȯⁿ-də-bȯr-'dō, yȯⁿ\\   Old French poem, written in epic meter, dating from the first half of the 13th century. Charlot, son of the emperor Charlemagne, lays an ambush for Huon, son of Séguin of Bordeaux, but Huon kills Charlot without being aware of his identity. Huon is then saved from hanging by performing a series of seemingly impossible tasks.

Thought to be based on *Huon d'Auvergne*—a hypothetical earlier version that told a much grimmer otherworldly story—*Huon de Bordeaux* marks the transition from the epic chanson de geste, based on national history, to the *roman d'aventure*, or romance. *Huon de Bordeaux* had a great vogue in England through a prose translation by John Bourchier, Lord Berners, that was printed about 1534. This translation was used as a sourcebook by Edmund Spenser, William Shakespeare, and John Keats. *See also* OBERON.

Hurst \\'hərst\\, Fannie (b. Oct. 18, 1889, Hamilton, Ohio, U.S.—d. Feb. 23, 1968, New York City)   American novelist, dramatist, and movie scenarist. Hurst's first book of short stories, *Just Around the Corner* (1914), was followed by more than 40 novels and story collections, noted for sympathetic but shallow portrayals of women of various social levels. A number of her books were made into films, some with scripts by her. Her autobiography, *Anatomy of Me*, appeared in 1958.

Hurston \\'hər-stən\\, Zora Neale (b. Jan. 7, 1903, Eatonville, Fla., U.S.—d. Jan. 28, 1960, Fort Pierce, Fla.)   African-American folklorist and writer who celebrated black culture in the voice of the rural South.

At age 16, Hurston joined a traveling theatrical company, ending up in New York City during the Harlem Renaissance. She studied anthropology with Franz Boas at Columbia University, taking a scientific approach to ethnicity. As an ethnologist, Hurston traveled to Haiti to study voodoo. She ultimately rejected the conventional viewpoint of the scholar in favor of personal involvement with her heritage. In 1931 she collaborated with Langston Hughes on the play MULE BONE. Her first novel, *Jonah's Gourd Vine* (1934), was well received though some critics considered it uneven. Her second novel, THEIR EYES WERE WATCHING GOD (1937), was both widely acclaimed and highly controversial. It was criticized by blacks because, although Hurston refused to endorse the myth of black inferiority, neither did she portray blacks as victims of this myth.

Brown Brothers

The tone of Hurston's work is celebratory, rooted in a rural black South reminiscent of her hometown. Her characters act freely within their rich heritage and narrow social position. Hurston influenced such contemporary black authors as Ralph Ellison and Toni Morrison. Her autobiography is titled DUST TRACKS ON A ROAD (1942), and an anthology of her work, *I Love Myself When I Am Laughing and Then Again When I Am Looking Mean and Impressive*, was released in 1979.

Husband's Message, The *also called* The Lover's Message. Old English lyric preserved in the Exeter Book, one of the few surviving love lyrics from the Anglo-Saxon period. It is remarkable for its ingenious form and for its emotive power. The speaker is a wooden staff on which a message from an exiled husband to his wife has been carved in runic letters. The staff tells how it grew as a sapling beside the sea, never dreaming that it would have the power of speech, until a man carved a secret message on it. The husband's message tells of how he was forced to flee because of a feud but now has wealth and power in a new land and longs for his wife. It implores her to set sail and join him. *See also* EXETER BOOK.

Hu Shi or **Hu Shih** \\'hü-'shə̀, 'shē\\ (b. Dec. 17, 1891, Shanghai, China—d. Feb. 24, 1962, Taiwan)   Chinese Nationalist diplomat and scholar who in 1922 helped establish the vernacular (*baihua*) as China's official written language.

By the time Hu Shi began his schooling, traditional Chinese education had solidified into a rigid orthodoxy, remote from contemporary life and learning. The emphasis on literary form over content had begun to seriously hamper the development of new ideas. In 1910 Hu went to the United States to study at Cornell University, and he then became a student of John Dewey at Columbia University. Under the influence of Dewey's pragmatic philosophy, Hu returned to China in 1917 and joined the faculty of Beijing National University. His "Wenxue gailiang chuyi" ("Tentative Proposal for Literary Reform") was published in 1917. In the article Hu made himself the champion of the *baihua* movement. He proposed a new, living literature liberated from the tyranny of the "dead" language and style of classical Chinese, accessible to the people, and flexible enough to express all kinds of new ideas. Hu's collection of verse, *Changshi ji* (1920; *A Book of Experiments*), was just the beginning of a flood of new literature in the vernacular. Despite attacks from traditionalists, vernacular literature spread rapidly. By 1922 the government had proclaimed *baihua* as the national language.

Hu's *Zhongguo zhexue shi dagang* (1919; *Outline of the History of Chinese Philosophy*), which examined the logic of the ancient philosophers, and his later studies of the old vernacular literature, which verified authorship and authenticity, demonstrated how the scientific method could be applied in the study of traditional Chinese literature. So effective was Hu's advocacy of pragmatic methodology that it led to the examination and destruction of many of the accepted—and invalid—versions of ancient Chinese history.

Soon after the May Fourth incident (in 1919), when patriotic, anti-Japanese sentiment exploded into a student demonstration against the decision of the Versailles Peace Conference to support Japan's claims to Shantung province, Hu's split from the leftists became clear. Advocating gradualism and shunning reliance on such abstract formulas as Marxism and anarchism, Hu not only made himself the declared antagonist of the Chinese communists but also found himself frequently in uneasy relationships with the Nationalists. It was not until war with Japan broke out in 1937 that a modus vivendi was reached between Hu and the Nationalist government. He served as its ambassador to the United States from 1938 to 1942 and in

1945 was appointed chancellor of Beijing University. After the establishment of the Chinese Communist government in 1949, Hu lived in New York City, where in 1957 he served as Nationalist China's representative to the United Nations. In 1958 he assumed the presidency of Taiwan's Academia Sinica.

Hutchinson \ˈhəch-ən-sən\, Alfred (b. 1924, Hectorspruit, Transvaal, S.Af.—d. Oct. 14, 1972, Nigeria) Writer and teacher noted for his highly acclaimed autobiography, *Road to Ghana*. It tells of his escape from Johannesburg, South Africa (via East Africa and Ghana), to the United Kingdom after he had been imprisoned in 1952 and charged with high treason in 1956 for opposing apartheid.

Hutchinson was educated at the University College of Fort Hare, S.Af., and the University of Sussex, England. He taught in England until he moved to Nigeria in 1971. Hutchinson wrote a play, *The Rain-Killers* (1964), about the tensions between new and old ways of thought in a Swazi village, a number of radio dramas, including "Fusane's Trial," and several widely anthologized articles and short stories. *Road to Ghana*, however, is considered his most important work.

Huxley \ˈhəks-lē\, Aldous (Leonard) (b. July 26, 1894, Godalming, Surrey, Eng.—d. Nov. 22, 1963, Los Angeles, Calif., U.S.) English novelist and critic whose works are notable for their elegance, wit, and pessimistic satire.

Huxley was a grandson of the prominent biologist T.H. Huxley and was the third child of the biographer and man of letters Leonard Huxley. While attending Eton he became partially blind from keratitis, but he retained enough eyesight to read with difficulty. He graduated from Balliol College, Oxford, in 1916. He published his first book in 1916 and worked on the periodical *Athenaeum* from 1919 to 1921. Thereafter he devoted himself largely to his own writing.

Huxley established himself as a major author in his first two published novels, CROME YELLOW (1921) and ANTIC HAY (1923), both witty and malicious satires on the pretensions of the English literary and intellectual coteries of his day. *Those Barren Leaves* (1925) and POINT COUNTER POINT (1928) are works in a similar vein. Huxley's deep distrust of 20th-century trends in both politics and technology found expression in BRAVE NEW WORLD (1932). The novel EYELESS IN GAZA (1936) continued to shoot barbs at the emptiness and aimlessness of contemporary society, but it also showed Huxley's growing interest in Hindu philosophy and mysticism. Many of his subsequent works reflected this preoccupation, notably *The Perennial Philosophy* (1946). AFTER MANY A SUMMER DIES THE SWAN (1939) examined American culture and the emphasis on youth.

Huxley's most important later works are *The Devils of Loudun* (1952) and *The Doors of Perception* (1954).

Huygens \ˈhœ͞e-kəns *Angl* ˈhī-gənz, ˈhȯi-\, Constantijn (b. Sept. 4, 1596, The Hague [The Netherlands]—d. March 28, 1687, The Hague) The most versatile and the last of the true Dutch Renaissance virtuosos, who made notable contributions in the fields of diplomacy, scholarship, music, poetry, and science.

Huygens' diplomatic service took him several times to England, where he met and was greatly influenced by John Donne and other English writers. He translated 19 of Donne's poems and wrote a volume of character sketches similar to those of the writer Sir Thomas Overbury.

Among Huygens' writings, at one extreme stands *Costelyck mal* (1622; "Exquisitely Foolish"), a satire of the ostentatious finery of the townswomen, and, at the other extreme, *Scheepspraet* (1625; "Ship's Talk"), in the language of the lower deck, and *Trijntje Cornelis* (1653), an earthy farce.

Huygens saw poetry only as "a small pastime," as the titles of his poetry collections indicate: *Otia of ledighe uren* (1625; "Idleness; or, Empty Hours") and *Korenbloemen* (1658 and 1672; "Cornflowers"). *Dagwerck* (1639; "Daily Work"), one of his three autobiographical works, provides insight into the contemporary intellectual climate.

Huysmans *French* wᵉēs-ˈmäⁿs, hwᵉēs-; *Dutch* ˈhœ͞es-mäns\, Joris-Karl, *original name* Charles-Marie-Georges Huysmans (b. Feb. 5, 1848, Paris, Fr.—d. May 12, 1907, Paris) French writer whose major novels epitomized successive phases of the aesthetic, spiritual, and intellectual life of late 19th-century France.

Detail of an oil painting by Jean-Louis Forain
J.E. Bulloz

Huysmans' early work, influenced by contemporary naturalistic novelists, included the novel *Marthe, histoire d'une fille* (1876; *Marthe*), about his liaison with a soubrette, and the novella *Sac au dos* (1880; "Pack on Back"), based on his experience in the Franco-Prussian War. The latter was published in *Les Soirées de Médan* (1880), war stories written by members of Émile Zola's "Médan" group of naturalistic writers. Huysmans soon broke with the group, however, publishing a series of novels too individual in content and violent in style to be classed as naturalistic literature.

The first such novel was *À vau-l'eau* (1882; *Down Stream*), a tragicomic account of the misfortunes, largely sexual, of a humble civil servant, Folantin. *À rebours* (1884; AGAINST THE GRAIN), Huysmans' best-known novel, relates the experiments in aesthetic decadence undertaken by the bored survivor of a noble line. The ambitious and controversial *Là-bas* (1891; *Down There*) tells of the occultist revival that occurred in France in the 1880s. A tale of 19th-century satanists interwoven with a life of the medieval satanist Gilles de Rais, the book introduces Durtal, clearly an autobiographical protagonist. Durtal reappears in Huysmans' last three novels—*En route* (1895), *La Cathédrale* (1898), and *L'Oblat* (1903; "The Lay Monk")—which together constitute a spiritual odyssey that ends in disappointment.

Hviezdoslav \ˈhvyez-dō-ˌsläv\, *pseudonym of* Pál Országh \ˈȯr-ˌsäg\ (b. Feb. 2, 1849, Vyšný Kubín, Austrian Empire [now in Slovakia]—d. Nov. 8, 1921, Vyšný Kubín) One of the most powerful and versatile of Slovak poets.

Hviezdoslav originally wrote in Hungarian and was a Hungarian patriot, but in the 1860s he turned to Slovakia and the Slovak language. His contribution to the development of Slovak poetry was of decisive importance. In his main epics— *Hájnikova žena* (1886; "The Gamekeeper's Wife") and *Ežo Vlkolinský* (1890)—he treated local themes in a style that combined realistic descriptive power with lyric echoes from folk song. In his voluminous lyric output he forged a characteristic style, interwoven with neologisms and dialect elements. Most memorable are his moving *Krvavé sonety* (1919; "Blood-Red Sonnets"), which embody his attitude toward World War I. He also translated much Hungarian, Russian, German, and English literature into Slovak.

Hyacinthus \ˌhī-ə-ˈsinth-əs\ In Greek mythology, a young man of Amyclae in Laconia. According to the usual version, his great beauty attracted the love of Apollo, who killed him accidentally while teaching him to throw the discus; others said that Zephyrus (or Boreas) out of jealousy deflected the discus so that it hit Hyacinthus on the head and killed him. Out of his blood there grew the flower called *hyacinthos* (perhaps a fritillary; not the modern hyacinth). The flower was also said to have sprung from the blood of Ajax, the son of Telamon.

Hyades \ˈhī-ə-ˌdēz\ In Greek mythology, the five (or more) daughters of Atlas and sisters of the Pleiades who nursed the infant wine god, Dionysus, and as a reward were made the five stars in the head of the constellation Taurus, the bull. According to another version, they so bitterly lamented the death of their brother Hyas that Zeus, out of compassion, changed them into stars.

Hyde \ˈhīd\, Douglas, *Gaelic* Dubhghlas de hÍde; *pseudonym* An Craoibhín Aoibhinn \än-ˈkrā-ˌvēn-ē-viŋ\ (b. Jan. 17, 1860, Frenchpark, County Roscommon, Ire.—d. July 12, 1949, Dublin) Distinguished Gaelic scholar and writer and the first president (1938–44) of the Republic of Ireland (Éire). He was the outstanding figure in the struggle for the preservation and extension of the Irish language from 1893, when he founded the nationalist Gaelic League, until 1922, when the founding of the Irish Free State accorded the Irish language equal status with English.

In 1884 Hyde graduated from Trinity College in Dublin, where he first studied early Irish. He became the first professor of modern Irish at University College, Dublin, in 1909 and held the chair until his retirement in 1932. His most important works of scholarship are *The Love Songs of Connacht* (1893; *Abhráin grádh chúige Connacht*) and *A Literary History of Ireland* (1899). Other works include *Pleusgadh na bulgóide* (1903; *The Bursting of the Bubble*) and *Legends of Saints and Sinners* (1915).

Hyde, Mr. Edward \ˈed-wərd-ˈhīd\ The evil alter ego of Dr. Henry Jekyll, a fictional character in Robert Louis Stevenson's DR. JEKYLL AND MR. HYDE.

Hydra \ˈhī-drə\ In Greek legend, the offspring of Typhon and Echidna, a gigantic monster with nine heads (the number varies), the center head being immortal. The destruction of Hydra was one of the 12 Labors of Heracles, which he accomplished with the assistance of Iolaus. As one head was cut off, two grew in its place, but they finally burned out the roots with firebrands and at last severed the immortal head from the body. The arrows dipped by Heracles in Hydra's poisonous blood or gall inflicted fatal wounds.

Hydra Head, The Novel of international intrigue by Carlos FUENTES, published in 1978 as *La cabeza de la hidra.*

Set in Mexico, the book features the Mexican secret service. The story concerns the attempt by the Mexican government to retain control of a recently discovered Mexican oil field. Secret agents from Arab lands, Israel, and the United States attempt to wrest control of the source for their own purposes. In a plot thick with dirty tricks, violence, sex, amazing coincidences, and betrayals, the novel's movie-loving hero, Felix Maldonado, confronts the villains.

Hygieia or **Hygea** or **Hygiea** \hī-ˈjē-ə\ In Greek mythology, the goddess of health. The cult of Hygieia spread with that of Asclepius, the god of medicine. Hygieia came gradually to be identified with Salus, the Roman goddess of safety and health. In later times, Hygieia and Asclepius became protecting deities. Hygieia's animal was a serpent, sometimes shown drinking from a saucer held in her hand.

Hymen \ˈhī-men\, *also called* Hymenaeus \ˌhī-mə-ˈnē-əs\ In Greek mythology, the god of marriage, whose name derives from the refrain of an ancient marriage song. He is usually held to be a son of Apollo by a Muse, perhaps Calliope; other accounts make him the son of Dionysus and Aphrodite, and as such he is a god of fruitfulness. In one of several legends that explain his connection with marriage songs he is a beautiful youth who rescues a group of women, including the girl he loves, from a band of pirates. As a reward he obtains the girl in marriage, and their happy life causes him ever afterward to be invoked in marriage songs.

hymenaic meter \ˌhī-mə-ˈnā-ik\ [Late Latin *hymenaicum metrum,* from Greek *hyménaios* marriage song] In classical prosody, a dactylic dimeter (scanned as − ∪ ∪ / − ∪ ∪).

Hymn to Intellectual Beauty Poem in seven stanzas by Percy Bysshe SHELLEY, written in the summer of 1816. A philosophical musing, the poem contains references to Shelley's childhood, when he first recognized the intangible spirit of beauty alive in the world. "Intellectual beauty" refers to a mysterious, intangible awareness that is not accessible through the senses but that is capable of increasing the potency of the natural world. In the first four stanzas, Shelley describes "The awful shadow of some unseen Power" that passes over the face of the earth, to which humans give the name of "God and ghosts and Heaven." In the last three stanzas, Shelley recounts his boyhood dedication to this spirit and rededicates himself to intellectual beauty in the present.

hyperbaton \hī-ˈpər-bə-ˌtän\ [Greek *hyperbáton,* from neuter of *hyperbatós* transposed, inverted, a derivative of *hyperbaínein* to step over, overstep, transgress] A transposition or inversion of usual word order. The device is often used in poetry, as in line 13 from Canto II of Alexander Pope's *The Rape of the Lock:* "Bright as the sun, her eyes the gazers strike."

hyperbole \hī-ˈpər-bə-lē\ [Greek *hyperbolē* excess, hyperbole, a derivative of *hyperbállein* to exceed] A figure of speech that is an intentional exaggeration for emphasis or comic effect. Hyperbole is common in love poetry— an example is the following passage from William Shakespeare's *The Merchant of Venice*:

> Why, if two gods should play some heavenly match
> And on the wager lay two earthly women,
> And Portia one, there must be something else
> Pawned with the other, for the poor rude world
> Hath not her fellow.

Hyperborean \ˌhī-pər-ˈbȯr-ē-ən, -bō-ˈrē-ən\ In Greek mythology, one of a mythical people intimately connected with the worship of Apollo at Delphi and of Artemis at Delos. The Hyperboreans were named with reference to Boreas, the north wind, and their home was placed in a paradisiacal region beyond the north wind. According to Herodotus, several Hyperborean maidens had been sent with offerings to Delos, but, the offerings having been delivered, the maidens died. Thereafter, the Hyperboreans wrapped their offerings in wheat straw and requested that their neighbors hand them on, from nation to nation, until their offerings finally reached Delos.

hypercatalexis \ˌhī-pər-ˌkat-ə-ˈlek-sis\ In prosody, the occurrence of an additional syllable at the end of a line of verse after the line is metrically complete; especially (in verse measured by dipodies), the occurrence of a syllable after the last complete dipody. A feminine ending is a form of hypercatalexis. *See* FEMININE ENDING.

Hyperion \hᵫ-ˈpä-rē-ˌȯn, *Angl* hī-ˈpir-ē-ən\ Epistolary novel by Friedrich HÖLDERLIN, published in German as *Hyperion, oder Der Eremit aus Griechenland* ("Hyperion; or The Hermit in Greece") in two separate volumes in 1797 and in 1799. Fragments of the work had been published in 1794 in Friedrich von Schiller's periodical *Die neue Thalia.* Hölderlin's only novel, *Hyperion* is the elegiac story of a disillusioned fighter for the liberation of Greece. It is noted for its philosophical classicism and expressive imagery.

Told largely in the form of Hyperion's letters to his love and to a friend, the book recounts the protagonist's attempts to help overthrow Turkish control of Greece. He grows disillusioned with the rebellion, survives a deadly sea battle, and is devastated when Diotima, his love, dies of a broken heart before they can be reunited.

Hyperion \hī-'pir-ē-ən\ Fragmentary poetic epic by John KEATS that exists in two versions. The first was begun in 1818 and published, unfinished, in 1820. The second, *The Fall of Hyperion*, a revised edition with a long prologue, was also left unfinished and was published posthumously in 1856. The poem is the last of Keats's many attempts to come to terms with the conflict between absolute value and mortal decay.

The first poem narrates the story of Hyperion, the sun god of the Titans, the earlier race of gods who were supplanted by the Olympians. When the poem begins, the Titans have already been deposed. Their one hope for regaining their former influence lies with Hyperion, who has retained his powers. But the Titans' era ends with the coming of Apollo, the Olympian god of poetry, music, and knowledge.

The Fall of Hyperion is narrated by the poet who, in a dream, is allowed to enter a shrine. The goddess Moneta reveals to the dreamer that the function of the poet in the world is to separate himself from the mere dreamer and to enter into and embrace the suffering of humanity.

Hypermestra \,hī-pər-'mes-trə\ or **Hypermnestra** \,hī-pərm-'nes-trə\ In Greek mythology, one of the daughters of Danaus known as the Danaïds. Hypermestra was the only one of the 50 Danaïds who did not kill her husband, Lynceus, when Danaus told her to. Her story was told in literature by Aeschylus and Geoffrey Chaucer, among others.

hypermeter \hī-'pər-mi-tər\ or **hypermetron** \-,trän\ **1.** A hypercatalectic verse. **2.** In classical prosody, a period comprising more than two or three colons (rhythmical units of an utterance).

hypermetric Having one or more syllables beyond the required measure at the end of a line or other metrical unit. In classical prosody, having metrical continuity from one line to the next, usually as the result of the elision of a final vowel of one line with the opening line of the next, producing synapheia, the fastening of two lines into one period by avoiding a pause between them.

Hypnos \'hip-nəs, -,nōs\ In Greek mythology, the god of sleep and the counterpart of the Roman Somnus. Hypnos was the son of Nyx (Night) and the brother of Thanatos (Death). He is variously described as living in the underworld, in the land of the Cimmerians, or in a dark, misty cave on the island of Lemnos. The waters of Lethe, the river of forgetfulness and oblivion, flowed through this chamber. Hypnos lay on his soft couch, surrounded by his many sons, who were the bringers of dreams. Chief among his sons were Morpheus, who brought dreams of humans; Phobetor (Icelus), who brought dreams of animals; and Phantasus, who brought dreams of inanimate things.

hyporrhythmic \,hī-pō-'rith-mik, ,hip-ō-\ In Greek and Latin prosody, deficient as to rhythm. The term is used of a hexameter in which the end of a word coincides with the end of each foot and which accordingly has no true caesura.

hypotaxis \,hī-pō-'tak-sis, ,hip-ō-\ [Greek *hypótaxis* postposing, subjection, a derivative of *hypotássein* to place under, subjoin] The arrangement of clauses and phrases in a pattern of syntactic subordination (as by the use of conjunctions or relative pronouns). *Compare* PARATAXIS.

Hypsipyle \hip-'sip-ə-lē\ In Greek mythology, daughter of Dionysus' son Thoas, king of the island of Lemnos. When the women of Lemnos killed all the men on the island, Hypsipyle saved her father by hiding him in a hollow chest that was set afloat on the sea. Hypsipyle later became queen of the island and bore two sons to the Argonaut Jason, who was her lover. Not long afterward, pirates sold her to Lycurgus, king of Nemea, whose son Opheltes she nursed. The infant was killed by a poisonous snake while Hypsipyle was momentarily distracted from watching him. Lycurgus wanted her put to death in retaliation, but her sons, sent by Dionysus, rescued her, and the Nemean Games were instituted in memory of the dead child.

Euripides' tragedy *Hypsipyle*, of which a fragment survives, was based on the legend.

Hywel ab Owain Gwynedd \'hə-wel-,äb-'ō-wīn-'gwin-eth\ (d. 1170) Welsh warrior-prince and lyric poet whose eight extant compositions include the only love poems found in the works of the early Welsh court poets. Also included among the eight are poems expressing love of country, perhaps the first such works in Welsh literature. The son of Owain Gwynedd, Hywel played a major part in the occupation of Ceredigion (Cardiganshire) by the house of Gwynedd (*c.* 1153). He probably died in battle against his half brothers near Pentraeth, Anglesey.

I

Iago \ē-'ä-gō\ Fictional character, the villain of William Shakespeare's tragedy OTHELLO. An intelligent and quick-witted ensign serving under Othello, Iago ostensibly acts out of resentment of Othello's promotion of Cassio ahead of him. Feigning honesty, he plants doubts about the fidelity of Othello's wife, Desdemona, that fester in his commander's mind. One of Shakespeare's most intriguing villains, he frequently takes the audience or reader into his confidence, manipulates his prey, and watches his deceptions wreak havoc.

iamb \'ī-,am, -,amb\ or **iambus** \ī-'am-bəs\ [Greek *íambos*] In prosody, a metrical foot consisting of one short syllable (as in classical or quantitative verse) or one unstressed syllable (as in modern or accentual verse) followed by one long or stressed syllable, as in the word be|cause.

Considered by the ancient Greeks to approximate the natural rhythm of speech, iambic meters were used extensively for dramatic dialogue, invective, satire, and fables. Also suited to the cadence of the English language, iambic rhythms, especially iambic tetrameter and pentameter, are the preeminent meters of English verse. An example of iambic meter is the English ballad, composed of quatrains written in alternating lines of iambic tetrameter and iambic trimeter:

There lived | a wife | at Ush | er's Well,

And a weal | thy wife | was she:

She had | three stout | and stal | wart sons,

And sent | them o'er | the sea.

The iamb is scanned ∪ — in classical verse and ∪ ′ in modern prosody. *Compare* TROCHEE.

iambe \'yäⁿb\ [French, literally, iamb]   French satiric verse form consisting of alternating lines of 8 and 12 syllables. Greek writers, especially Archilochus, had used iambics as a vehicle for satire, but the name came into use as a French form in the late 18th and early 19th centuries when André Chénier's *Ïambes* and Auguste Barbier's *Les Ïambes* were published.

iambelegus \ī-,am-'bel-ə-gəs\ [Greek *iambélegos,* from *íambos* iamb + *élegos* song accompanied by the flute]   In classical prosody, a line of verse that consists of an iambic dimeter and half an elegiac pentameter, which is made up of dactylic elements − ∪ ∪ − ∪ ∪ −. In Greek lyric, an iambelegus is usually ∪̱ − ∪ − ∪̱ | − ∪ ∪ − ∪ ∪ − and is most often found in dactylo-epitrites as used especially by Pindar, where the iambic elements vary in length. In Latin verse, Horace used a longer version in his 13th epode: ∪ − ∪ − ∪ − ∪ ∪̱ | − ∪ ∪ − ∪ ∪ −.

iambic \ī-'am-bik\   A lampoon or piece of usually satiric verse written in iambs (such as that developed by the Ionian Greeks in the period succeeding the epic).

Ianthe \ī-'an-thē\   In Greek mythology, a Cretan woman who married Iphis, a woman who had been raised as a man and was changed into a man so that they could marry.

Iapetus \ī-'ap-ə-təs\   In Greek mythology, one of the Titans, son of Uranus and Gaea. Iapetus was the father of Atlas, Prometheus, Menoetius, and Epimetheus by Clymene. According to other accounts, his wife was Asia or Asopis.

Iasion \ī-'ā-zē-ən\ or **Iasios** \-zē-əs\   In Greek mythology, son of Zeus and Electra who loved Demeter, the goddess of agriculture. In some legends his love is not returned, and he attempts to ravish the goddess but is struck by lightning hurled by Zeus. In most versions, however, Iasion and Demeter consummate their love in a thrice-plowed fallow field. The result of their union is Plutus, the god of wealth and abundance.

Ibara   *see* IHARA.

Ibarbourou \,ē-bär-'bō-rō\, Juana de, *original name* Juanita Fernández Morales \fer-'nän-däs-mō-'rä-läs\ (b. March 8, 1895, Melo, Uruguay—d. July 1979)   Uruguayan poet, one of the most famous South American women poets.

Ibarbourou's poetry, rich in sensual images and expressed in simple language, deals with the themes of love and nature. A note of narcissism and eroticism present in her early works, such as *Las lenguas de diamante* (1919; "Tongues of Diamond") and *Raíz salvaje* (1922; "Wild Root"), gave way later, in *La rosa de los vientos* (1930; "The Rose of the Winds"), to a sense of declining beauty and vitality and, finally, in *Perdida* (1950; "Lost"), to an expression of despair in old age.

Ibn al-Abbār \,ib-nál-âb-'bär\, *in full* Abū 'Abd Allāh Muhammad al-Qudā'ī (b. February 1199, Valencia, Emirate of Balansiya [now part of Spain]—d. Jan. 6, 1260, Tunis [Tunisia])   Historian, theologian, and humorist who became one of the most famous students of Islāmic Spain.

After the fall of Valencia (September 1238), Ibn al-Abbār settled in Tunisia and was employed as the head of the chancellery by Abū Zakarīyā' Yahyā, the founder of the Hafsid dynasty (13th–16th centuries), and his successor, al-Mustansir.

Ibn al-Abbār's *Tuhfat al-qadīm* is a major study of the Islāmic poets of Muslim Spain. He was also a humorist and a satirist of considerable ability. His fall from power and subsequent execution may have resulted from a satirical poem he directed against al-Mustansir.

Ibn al-Fārid \,ib-nál-'fä-rid\, *in full* Sharif ad-dīn Abū Hafs 'Umar ibn al Fārid (b. March 22, 1181, or March 11, 1182, Cairo [Egypt]—d. Jan. 23, 1235, Cairo)   Arab poet whose expression of Sūfī mysticism is regarded as the finest in the Arabic language.

Ibn al-Fārid led a solitary religious life in the hills near Cairo. He spent some years in or near Mecca and was venerated as a saint during his lifetime.

Many of Ibn al-Fārid's poems are qasidas (odes) on the lover's longing for reunion with his beloved. He expresses through this convention his yearning for a return to Mecca and, at a deeper level, a desire to be assimilated into the spirit of Muhammad. Ibn al-Fārid developed the theme at length in *Nazm as-sulūk* (*The Poem of the Way*). Almost equally famous is his "Khamrīyah" ("Wine Ode"), which describes the effects of the wine of divine love. Although Ibn al-Fārid's poetry is mannered in style, with rhetorical embellishments and conventional imagery, his poems contain passages of striking beauty and deep religious feeling.

Ibn al-Kalbī \,ib-nál-'kál-,bē\, *also called* Abū al-Mundhir \á-'bū-ál-'mūn-thir\, *in full* Hishām ibn Muhammad ibn al-Sā'id al-Kalbī (b. before 747, Kūfah [Iraq]—d. 819/821, Kūfah)   Scholar of the customs, lineage, and battles of the early Arabs.

Ibn al-Kalbī wrote extensively on the early Arabs and on religion. His extant writings include *Al-Khayl* ("Horses"), which contains short accounts of famous horses and poems on horses; *Jamharat an-nasab* ("Genealogical Collection"), a work of great importance about the politics, religion, and literature of the pre-Islāmic and early Muslim Arabs; and *Kitāb al-asnām* (*The Book of Idols*), in which he discusses the gods of the pre-Islāmic Arabs. The discussions in the latter are supplemented by relevant excerpts from pre-Islāmic poetry.

Ibn Battūtah \,ib-ən-bat-'tū-tə\, *in full* Abū 'Abd Allāh Muhammad ibn 'Abd Allāh al Lawātī at-Tanjī ibn Battūtah (b. Feb. 24, 1304, Tangier, Mor.—d. 1368/69, Morocco)   The greatest medieval Arab traveler and the author of one of the most famous travel books, the *Rihlah* (TRAVELS), which describes his extensive journeys covering some 75,000 miles (more than 120,000 km).

Ibn Battūtah received the traditional juristic and literary education in Tangier. In 1325, at the age of 21, he went on a pilgrimage to Mecca. Having determined to visit as many parts of the world as possible for the sheer pleasure of new experience, he decided "never to travel any road a second time." He traveled throughout the Middle East, exploring parts of Africa, Asia, and Europe as well. Ibn Battūtah's wandrings lasted some 27 years. Toward the end of 1353 Ibn Battūtah returned to Morocco and, at the sultan's request, dictated his reminiscences. After that he passed from sight, and it is known only that at his death he held the office of *qādī* somewhere in Morocco.

Ibn Ezra \,ib-ən-'ez-rə\, Abraham ben Meir (b. 1092/93, Tudela, Emirate of Saragossa—d. 1167, Calahorra, Spain)   Hispano-Hebrew poet, grammarian, philosopher, and astronomer, best known as a biblical exegete whose commentaries contributed to the golden age of Spanish Judaism.

Initially known as a scholar and poet, about 1140 Ibn Ezra began a lifelong series of wanderings throughout Europe, in the course of which he disseminated biblical lore and produced distinguished works of biblical exegesis.

His biblical commentaries include expositions of the Book of Job, the Book of Daniel, and the Psalms and, most importantly, a commentary on the Pentateuch that is sometimes ranked with the classic 11th-century commentaries by Rashi on the Talmud. Ibn Ezra also translated the Hispano-Hebrew grammarians who had written in Arabic, and he wrote grammatical treatises.

Ibn Ezra \,ib-ən-'ez-rə \, Moses (ben Jacob ha-Sallaḥ), *known in Arabic as* Abū Hārūn Mūsā \'ä-bü-hä-'rün-'mü-,sä \ (b. *c.* 1060, Granada, Spain—d. *c.* 1139) Hispano-Hebrew poet and critic, one of the finest poets of the flowering of Hebrew letters in Moorish Spain (900–1200). He was one of the first Jewish poets to write secular verse.

Ibn Ezra was related to the poet and biblical interpreter Abraham ibn Ezra. His poetry is generally considered to be unsurpassed in mastery of the Hebrew language, poetic structure, and style. Much of his secular verse is found in the cycle *Tarshish*. In it he celebrates love, the pleasures of wine, and the beauty of birdsong and bemoans faithlessness and the onset of old age. His later works were mostly penitential prayers of an introspective, melancholy cast; many of them are included in the liturgy of the Sefardim (Jews of Spanish or Portuguese descent) for the New Year and the Day of Atonement. He also wrote a moving elegy when a woman he had loved died in childbirth.

Ibn Ezra wrote an important treatise in Arabic on the poetic art, *Kitāb al-muḥāḍarah wa al-mudhākarah* ("Conversations and Recollections"; translated into Hebrew as *Shirat Yisra'el*, or "Song of Israel"). An important Spanish literary history, the work deals with Arabic, Castilian, and Jewish poetry.

Ibn Gabirol \,ib-ən-gä-'bē-ròl \, *in full* Solomon ben Yehuda ibn Gabirol, *Arabic* Abū Ayyūb Sulaymān ibn Yaḥyā ibn Gabirūt, *also called* Avicebron \,av-i-'seb-rən \ *or* Avencebrol \,av-ən-'seb-rəl \ (b. *c.* 1022, Málaga, Caliphate of Córdoba [Spain]—d. *c.* 1058/1070, Valencia, Kingdom of Valencia) One of the outstanding figures of the Hebrew school of religious and secular poetry that flourished in Moorish Spain. He was also an important Neoplatonic philosopher.

Ibn Gabirol received his higher education in Saragossa, where he joined the learned circle of other Cordoban refugees established there around famed scholars and the influential courtier Yekutiel ibn Ḥasan. Protected by this patron, whom Ibn Gabirol immortalized in poems of loving praise, the 16-year-old poet became famous for his religious hymns in masterly Hebrew. He made, however, the mistake of lampooning Samuel ha-Nagid, a rising Jewish statesman and vizier in the Berber kingdom of Granada, who was also a talented poet, Talmudist, strategist, and model writer of letters. After making poetical amends, Ibn Gabirol won ha-Nagid's favor and subsequently became his main court encomiast.

He composed *Mukhtār al-jawāhir* ("Choice of Pearls"), a collection of proverbs in Arabic, and a more original, though dated, ethical treatise, also in Arabic, *Kitāb iṣlāḥ al-akhlāq* ("The Improvement of the Moral Qualities").

After 1039 Ibn Gabirol secured a position as a court poet with Samuel ha-Nagid. He composed poems with a messianic tinge for Samuel and for Jehoseph (Yūsuf), his son and successor. All other biographical data about Ibn Gabirol except his place of death must be extrapolated from his poetry, which, like that of the entire contemporary Hebrew school, is modeled after the Arabic. Metrics, rhyme systems, and most of the highly developed imagery follow the Arabic school, but the biblical language adds a particular tinge.

Ibn Gabirol's secular topics include exaggerated, Arab-inspired self-praise; love poems; praise of his noble and learned protectors, together with scathingly satirical reproach of others; dirges; wine songs; spring and rain poems; flower portraits; the agonizingly realistic description of a skin ailment; and a long didactic poem on Hebrew grammar. Of his very rich production, about 200 secular poems and more than 200 religious poems were preserved, though no collection of his poems has survived.

Ibn Ḥazm \,ib-ən-'ḵàz-əm \, *in full* Abū Muḥammad 'Alī ibn Aḥmad ibn Sa'īd ibn Ḥazm (b. Nov. 7, 994, Córdoba, Caliphate of Córdoba [now part of Spain]—d. Aug. 15, 1064, Manta Līsham, near Seville) Muslim litterateur, historian, jurist, and theologian of Islāmic Spain who was famed for his literary productivity, breadth of learning, and mastery of the Arabic language.

After the collapse in AD 1008 of the Andalusian Umayyad dynasty (which had ruled since 756), Ibn Ḥazm was frequently imprisoned for his support of Umayyad claimants to the office of caliph. By 1031 he began to express his convictions by writing, and he became a controversial figure. Fewer than 40 of his works of nonfiction are extant. His appreciation of the Arabic language and his skillful use of poetry and prose are evident in all his works. One delightful example is *Ṭawq al-ḥamāmah* (*The Ring of the Dove*), on the art of love. Ibn Ḥazm is probably best known for his work in the philosophy of law and theology, for which the basic qualification was a thorough knowledge of the Qur'ān and Ḥadīth (Tradition). He became one of the leading exponents of the Ẓāhirī (literalist) school of jurisprudence, creatively extending the Ẓāhirī principle to theology.

Ibn Jubayr \,ib-ən-zhü-'bīr \, *in full* Abū al-Ḥusayn Muḥammad ibn Aḥmad ibn Jubayr (b. 1145, Valencia, Emirate of Balansiya [now part of Spain]—d. Nov. 29, 1217, Alexandria [Egypt]) Spanish Muslim known for a book recounting his pilgrimage to Mecca.

Ibn Jubayr's pilgrimage was begun in 1183 and ended with his return to Granada in 1185. His lively account of this journey, *Riḥlah* (*The Travels of Ibn Jubayr*), is a valuable source for the history of the time; it contains memorable descriptions of his voyages across the Mediterranean in Genoese ships, his unhappy encounters with both Christian and Muslim customs collectors, the Cairo of Saladin, his trip up the Nile to Upper Egypt and across the Red Sea to Jidda, Mecca, and Medina, and his return by way of Iraq, Syria, and Sicily.

Ibn Miskawayh   *see* MISKAWAYH.

Ibn Qutaybah \,ib-ən-kù-'tä-bə, -'tī- \, *in full* Abū Muḥammad 'Abd Allāh ibn Muslim ad-Dīnawarī ibn Qutaybah (b. 828, Kūfah [Iraq]—d. 889, Baghdad) Writer of *adab* literature—that is, of literature exhibiting wide secular erudition—and also of theology, philology, and literary criticism. He introduced an Arabic prose style outstanding for its simplicity and ease.

The 14 surviving volumes definitively ascribed to Ibn Qutaybah include the *Kitāb adab al-kātib* ("Secretary's Guide"), a compendium of Arabic usage and vocabulary; *Kitāb al-'Arab* ("Arab Book"), an argument in favor of Arab rather than Iranian cultural preeminence in the caliphate; *Kitāb al-ma'ārif* ("Book of Knowledge"), a handbook of history; *Kitāb ash-shi'r wa ash-shu'arā'* ("Book of Poetry and Poets"), a chronological anthology of early Arabic poetry; and *Kitāb 'uyūn al-akhbar* ("Book of Choice Narratives"), a collection of *adab* studies dealing with the authority of the overlord, the conduct of war, nobility, character, eloquence, and friendship that is valued for its wealth of examples from history, poetry, and proverbs.

Ibn Shaddād \,ib-ən-shȧd-'dȧd\, *in full* Abū al Maḥāsin Yūsuf ibn Rāfiʻ ibn Shaddād Bahāʼ ad-Dīn (b. 1145, Mosul [Iraq]—d. 1234, Aleppo [Syria])   Arab writer and statesman, author of the *Sirat Salāḥ ad-Dīn* ("Life of Saladin").

In 1187, after making the pilgrimage to Mecca, Ibn Shaddād entered the service of Saladin, the Muslim sultan. He was employed on various embassies and in departments of the civil government, being appointed judge of the army and judge of Jerusalem. After Saladin's death Ibn Shaddād was appointed judge of Aleppo. There he employed some of his wealth in the foundation of colleges.

Ibn Tibbon \,ib-ən-'tib-ən\, Moses ben Samuel (b. Marseille, Fr., fl. 1240–83)   Jewish physician and an important translator of Arabic-language works into Hebrew. His translations served to disseminate Greek and Arab culture throughout Europe. Besides original works, which included commentaries on the Pentateuch (Torah), the Song of Songs, and Aggadic passages (those not dealing with Jewish law) in the Talmud, he also translated Arabic-language works dealing with philosophy, mathematics, astronomy, and medicine.

Ibn Tibbon translated from the Arabic a number of works by the medieval Jewish philosopher Maimonides. These included portions of Maimonides' commentary on the Mishna (one of two parts of the Talmud); his treatises on hygiene, poisons, and logic; and his *Sefer ha-mitsvot*, an analysis of the 613 commandments of the Pentateuch.

Among Arabic writings, Ibn Tibbon translated the commentaries on Aristotle by Averroës, a philosopher who later had a marked influence on Christian theologians; a medical digest by the Persian philosopher and physician Avicenna; and a philosophical work (known in English as the "Book of Principles") by the Muslim philosopher and Aristotelian disciple al-Fārābī . He also translated Euclid's *Elements*.

Ibsen \'ip-sən, *Angl* 'ib-sən\, Henrik (Johan) (b. March 20, 1828, Skien, Nor.—d. May 23, 1906, Kristiania [now Oslo])   Norwegian playwright who introduced to the European stage a new order of moral analysis that was placed against a severely realistic middle-class background and developed with economy of action, penetrating dialogue, and rigorous thought.

Ibsen's first play, *Catilina* (1850; *Catiline*), embodied themes—the rebellious hero, his destructive mistress—that would preoccupy him for all of his career. At the age of only 23 he was hired to work in a new theater at Bergen as director and playwright, in which capacity he had to write a new play every year.

Ibsen was expected to create a national drama out of the heroic literature of Iceland, the then-popular drawing-room drama of France, and the actors, acting traditions, and language of Denmark. First at Bergen and then at the Norwegian Theater in Christiania from 1857 to 1862, Ibsen tried to make palatable dramatic fare out of these incongruous ingredients. Two of the last plays he wrote for the Norwegian stage—*Kjaerlighedens komedie* (1862; *Love's Comedy*) and *Kongsemnerne* (1863; *The Pretenders*)—showed signs of new spiritual energy.

When the theater in Christiania went bankrupt, Ibsen was free to write for himself. In April 1864 he left Norway for Italy. For the next 27 years he lived abroad, mainly in Rome, Dresden, and Munich, returning to Norway only for short visits in 1874 and 1885. Ibsen took with him into exile the fragments of a long semidramatic poem that came to be named BRAND (1866). This tragedy of a rural pastor whose uncompromising dedication carries the seeds of his destruction was highly popular in Norway.

PEER GYNT (1867), another drama in rhymed couplets, presented an utterly antithetical view of human nature; the hero

is buoyant, self-centered, and aimless and a wholly unprincipled opportunist, yet he is also a lovable and beloved rascal. A 10-act philosophical-historical drama, a modern satire, and the prose satire PILLARS OF SOCIETY (1877) were among the works that followed.

Classic Ibsen was born with *Et dukkehjem* (1879; A DOLL'S HOUSE), an unsentimental story of a woman's shattered illusions about marriage and loyalty. Ibsen's next play, *Gengangere* (1881; GHOSTS), created even more of a furor among audiences and critics than had *A Doll's House*. Ibsen's response to his more conventionally minded critics took the form of a direct dramatic counterattack in Doctor Stockmann, the hero of *En folkefiende* (1882; AN ENEMY OF THE PEOPLE). Though portrayed as a victim, Stockmann also carries within him a deep strain of destructiveness. *Vildanden* (1884; THE WILD DUCK) features a gratuitous, destructive truth-teller whose compulsion brings catastrophic misery to a family of helpless innocents. Each of this series of Ibsen's classic modern dramas grows by extension or reversal out of its predecessor. The last of the sequence is ROSMERSHOLM (1886), in which variants of the destructive saint (Brand) and the all-too-human rogue (Peer Gynt) once more strive to define their identities.

Ibsen's writing thereafter became more self-analytic and symbolic. Among his later plays were *Fruen fra havet* (1888; THE LADY FROM THE SEA), HEDDA GABLER (1890), *Bygmester Solness* (1892; THE MASTER BUILDER), *Lille Eyolf* (1894; LITTLE EYOLF), *John Gabriel Borkman* (1896), and *Naar vi døde vaagner* (1899; WHEN WE DEAD AWAKEN). An obsessive personage in the late plays is an aging artist who is bitterly aware of his failing powers. After his return to Norway in 1891, Ibsen continued to write plays until a stroke in 1900 and another a year later made him an invalid.

Ibuse Masuji \'ē-bə̇-sē-'mä-sə̇-jē\ (b. Feb. 15, 1898, Kamo, Hiroshima prefecture, Japan—d. July 10, 1993, Tokyo)   Japanese novelist noted for his sharp but sympathetic short portraits of the foibles of ordinary people.

Ibuse was known in the 1930s for such stories as the satirical "Sanshōuo" (1929; "Salamander" in *Salamander and Other Stories*) and the historical novel *Jon Manjirō hyōryūki* (1937; *John Manjirō, the Cast-Away: His Life and Adventures*), but he achieved his greatest popularity after World War II.

Ibuse's wide interests were apparent in his variety of styles, notably in his intellectual fantasies employing animal allegories, historical fiction, and tales of country life. "Honjitsu kyūshin" (1949; "No Consultations Today"; film, 1952), in which he characterized a town by the patients who come to the doctor's office, and "Yōhai taichō" (1950; "Lieutenant Lookeast"), an antimilitary satire, were later published in a bilingual edition. Ibuse received a National Culture Award for the novel *Kuroi ame* (1965; *Black Rain*; film, 1989), which deals with the long-lasting social effects of the bombing of Hiroshima.

Ibycus or **Ibykos** \'ib-i-kəs, 'ĭb-\ (fl. 6th century BC, Samos, Ionia [Greece])   Lyric poet from the Greek colony of Rhegium in Italy, one of the nine lyric poets recognized by later Greek criticism.

Ibycus left Rhegium for the Aegean island of Samos, where the tyrant Polycrates became his patron. Ancient authorities found it hard to distinguish his early work from that of Stesichorus. The most prominent fragments describe the charms of handsome youths and reveal the aging poet's fear of falling in love. Modern critics find similarities between his poetry and the erotic lyrics of Sappho and Anacreon.

Icarus \'ik-ə-rəs\   In Greek mythology, son of the inventor DAEDALUS who perished by flying too near the Sun with waxen wings. Icarus was the subject of many 20th-century poems, including those by W.H. Auden, Stephen Spender, William Carlos Williams, and Muriel Rukeyser.

Icaza \ē-'kä-sä\, Jorge, *surname in full* Icaza Coronel \ˌkō-rō-'nel\ (b. July 10, 1906, Quito, Ecuador—d. May 26, 1978, Quito) Ecuadorean novelist and playwright whose brutally realistic portrayals of the exploitation of his country's Indians brought him international recognition as a spokesman for the oppressed.

Icaza started writing for the theater, but when he was censured for a 1933 dramatic script, *El dictador*, he turned his attention to the novel. He gained immediate fame with his first novel, *Huasipungo* (1934; rev. ed., 1951; *Huasipungo: The Villagers*, or *The Villagers*). The title is an Indian term for the small plot of land given to the Indian worker by a landowner in return for the worker's labor on the estate. The book was greeted with outrage by the upper classes in Ecuador and quickly became a tool of left-wing propaganda. Many critics have acclaimed it as a masterpiece of realism.

Icaza continued to dramatize the struggles of the poor in novels and plays, notably in the novels *En las calles* (1934; "In the Streets"), *Media vida deslumbrados* (1942; "Half a Life Amazed"), *Huairapamushcas* (1948), and *El chulla Romero y Flores* (1958; "The Social Climber Romero y Flores").

Icelanders' sagas *also called* family sagas. The class of heroic prose narratives written during the 13th century about the great families who lived in Iceland from 930 to 1030. They are a unique contribution to Western literature and are far in advance of any medieval literature in their realism, their controlled, objective style, their powers of character delineation, and their overwhelming tragic dignity. The family sagas represent the highest development of the classical age of Icelandic saga writing. Their artistic unity, length, and complexity have convinced most modern scholars that they are written works by individual authors, although the theory that they were composed orally still has adherents.

The Icelanders' sagas can be subdivided into several categories according to the social and ethical status of the principal heroes. In some, the hero is a poet and a lover who sets out from the rural society of his native land in search of fame and adventure to become the retainer of some foreign ruler. To this group belong some of the early 13th-century sagas, including *Kormáks saga*, *Hallfredar saga*, and *Bjarnar saga Hítdaelakappa*. *Fostbraeda saga* ("The Blood-Brothers' Saga") describes two contrasting heroes: one a poet and lover, the other a ruthless killer. *Egils saga* offers a brilliant study of a complex personality—a ruthless Viking who is also a sensitive poet. In several sagas the hero becomes an outlaw fighting a hopeless battle against the social forces that have rejected him. To this group belong *Hardar saga ok Hólmverja* and *Droplaugarsona saga*, but the greatest of the outlaw sagas are *Gísla saga* and *Grettis saga*.

Most of the Icelanders' sagas, however, are concerned with fully integrated members of society, either as ordinary farmers or as farmers who also act as chieftains. *Hrafnkels saga* describes a chieftain who murders his shepherd, is then tortured and humiliated for his crime, and finally takes cruel revenge on one of his tormentors. The central plot in *Laxdæla saga* is a love triangle, in which the jealous heroine forces her husband to kill his best friend. *Eyrbyggja saga* describes a complex series of feuds between several related families, and *Hávardar saga* is about an old farmer who takes revenge on his son's killer, the local chieftain. *Víga-Glúms saga* tells of a ruthless chieftain who commits several killings and swears an ambiguous oath in order to cover his guilt, while *Vatnsdæla saga* is the story of a noble chieftain whose last act is to help his killer escape.

In the Icelanders' sagas, justice, rather than courage, is often the primary virtue. This theme is an underlying one in NJÁLS SAGA, the greatest of all the sagas.

Iceman Cometh, The Tragedy in four acts by Eugene O'NEILL, written in 1939 and produced and published in 1946. Considered by many to be his finest work, the drama exposes the human need for illusion and hope as antidotes to the natural condition of despair.

O'Neill mined the tragedies of his own life for this depiction of a ragged collection of alcoholics in a rundown New York tavern-hotel run by Harry Hope. The saloon regulars numb themselves with whiskey and make grandiose plans, but they do nothing. They await the arrival of big-spending Theodore Hickman ("Hickey"), who forces his cronies to pursue their much-discussed plans, hoping that real failure will make them face reality. Hickey finally confesses that he killed his long-suffering wife just hours before he arrived at Harry's, and he turns himself in to the police. The others slip back into an alcoholic haze, clinging to their dreams once more.

I Ching *see* YI JING.

ichor \'ī-ˌkȯr, - ˌkər\ [Greek *íchōr* serum, fluid in the veins of the gods] In Greek mythology, an ethereal fluid that takes the place of blood in the veins of the gods.

I, Claudius \'klȯd-ē-əs\ Historical novel set in 1st-century-AD Rome by Robert GRAVES, published in 1934.

The book is written as an autobiographical memoir by Roman emperor Claudius. Physically weak, afflicted with stammering, and inclined to drool, Claudius is an embarrassment to his family and is shunted to the background of imperial affairs. The benefits of his seeming ineffectuality are twofold: he becomes a scholar and historian, and he is spared the worst cruelties inflicted on the imperial family by its own members during the reigns of Augustus, Tiberius, and Caligula.

Palace intrigues and murders surround him. Claudius' informal narration serves to emphasize the banality of the imperial family's endless greed and lust. The story concludes with Claudius ascending to the imperial throne. A sequel, *Claudius, the God and His Wife Messalina* (1935), covers Claudius' years as Roman emperor.

icon \'ī-ˌkän, -kən\ A sign (such as a word or graphic symbol) whose form suggests its meaning. The word was brought into common academic use by those who study semiotics (the study of signs). Some literary critics, especially those associated with New Criticism, referred to poems as verbal icons in the sense that the meaning of a poem is contained in or expressed by the structure and mechanics of its language, including the arrangement of images, the meter, and the use of figures of speech such as metaphor. W.K. Wimsatt expressed this view in the essay collection *The Verbal Icon: Studies in the Meaning of Poetry* (1954).

ictus \'ik-təs\ [Latin, literally, stroke, blow] **1.** The recurring stress or beat in a rhythmic or metrical series of sounds. Metrical accent. **2.** The place of the stress or beat in a metrical foot. *Compare* ARSIS; THESIS.

idealism \ī-'dē-ə-ˌliz-əm\ Literary or artistic theory or practice that values ideal or subjective types or aspects of beauty more than formal or sensible qualities. It may also affirm the preeminent value of imagination as compared with the faithful copying of nature. *Compare* REALISM.

idée reçue \ē-ˌdā-rə-'süē\ [French, received idea] An idea that is unexamined, a phrase particularly associated with Gustave Flaubert, who in his *Le Dictionnaire des idées reçues* (1913; *Flaubert's Dictionary of Accepted Ideas*) mocked the use of clichés and the uncritical reliance on accepted ideas. The so-called dictionary was compiled with the help of the young philosopher Alfred Le Poittevin. Together they invented a grotesque imaginary character called "le Garçon" ("the Boy"), to whom they attributed whatever sort of remark seemed to them most debased.

identical rhyme *see* RIME RICHE.

idiom \'id-ē-əm\ [Greek *idíōma* peculiarity, peculiarity of style, idiom, a derivative of *idioûsthai* to make one's own, a derivative of *ídios* one's own, peculiar] A style or form of artistic expression that is characteristic of an individual, a period or movement, or a medium or instrument.

Idiot, The Novel by Fyodor DOSTOYEVSKY, published in Russian as *Idiot* in 1868–69. The narrative concerns the unsettling effect of the "primitive" Prince Myshkin on the sophisticated, conservative Yepanchin family and their friends. Myshkin visits the Yepanchins, where his odd manner and lack of concern for appearances quickly make him an object of fascination. His hosts, who are given to sensuality, acquisitiveness, and crime, test Myshkin's moral feelings. Myshkin maintains a guileless benevolence toward all, but his message of service, compassion, and brotherly love finally fails, and he lapses into idiocy.

Idomeneus \ī-'däm-i-ˌnūs, ˌī-də-mi-'nē-əs\ In Greek mythology, son of Deucalion, grandson of Minos and Pasiphae, and king of Crete. He courted Helen and played a distinguished part in the Trojan War. According to the *Odyssey*, Idomeneus returned home safely. A later tradition reports that he sacrificed his son to Poseidon, as a consequence of which a plague developed and Idomeneus was driven out of Crete.

Idrīs \'id-rēs\, Yūsuf (b. May 19, 1927, Al-Bayrum, Egypt—d. Aug. 1, 1991, London, Eng.) Egyptian playwright and novelist who broke with traditional Arabic literature by mixing colloquial dialect with conventional classical Arabic narration in the writing of realistic stories about ordinary villagers.

Idrīs' first anthology of stories, *Arkhas layali* (*The Cheapest Nights*), appeared in 1954 and was quickly followed by several more volumes, including *A-laysa kadhalik* (1957; "Isn't That So?"). In the 1960s he sought to create a uniquely Egyptian dramatic form using colloquial language and elements of traditional folk drama and shadow theater. He presented this plan in a series of three essays entitled "Towards a New Arabic Theater," and he tried to put it into practice in his own plays, notably *Al-Farafir* (1964; *The Farfoors* in *Modern Egyptian Drama*). Idrīs' other major works include the novels *Al-Haram* (1959; *The Sinners*) and *Al-'Ayb* (1962; "The Sin"). *In the Eye of the Beholder: Tales of Egyptian Life from the Writings of Yusuf Idris* (1978) and *Rings of Burnished Brass* (1984) were two collections of his works published in translation.

Idun or **Idunn** \'ē-ˌthūn, *Angl* -ˌdün\ or **Iduna** \'ē-ˌthü-nə, *Angl* 'ē-ˌdü-nə, i-'dü-\ In Norse mythology, the goddess of spring or rejuvenation and the wife of Bragi, the god of poetry. Idun was the keeper of the magic apples of immortality, which the gods had to eat to preserve their youth.

idunit \ˌī-'dən-it, 'ī-\ [alteration of *I done it*] An autobiographical or confessional account usually of a sensational character. The word, apparently modeled on the more widely used "whodunit," had little vogue after the 1950s.

idyll or **idyl** \'īd-əl, 'id-\ [Latin *idyllium*, from Greek *eidýllion*, diminutive of *eîdos* shape, form, literary form] **1.** A short descriptive poem usually dealing with pastoral or rural life. *See also* ECLOGUE. **2.** A simple descriptive work either in poetry or prose that deals with rustic life or pastoral scenes or suggests

a mood of peace and contentment. **3.** A narrative poem (such as Alfred, Lord Tennyson's *Idylls of the King*) that treats more or less fully an epic, romantic, or tragic theme.

The term idyll was used in Greco-Roman antiquity to designate a variety of brief poems on simple subjects in which the description of natural objects was introduced. The conventions of the pastoral were developed by the Alexandrian school of poetry, particularly by Theocritus, Bion, and Moschus, in the 3rd–2nd century BC.

The word was revived during the Renaissance, when some poets employed it to distinguish narrative pastorals from those in dialogue. The general use, or misuse, of the word arose in the 19th century, when the word was used indiscriminately to refer to works on a variety of subjects.

Idylls of the King Poetic treatment of the Arthurian legend by Alfred, Lord TENNYSON, comprising 12 poems published in various fragments and combinations between 1842 and 1888. Four books—"Enid," "Vivien," "Elaine," and "Guinevere"—were published as *Idylls of the King* in 1859.

Based largely on Thomas Malory's *Le Morte Darthur*, the work spans the full scope of Arthur's career, from his first encounter with Guinevere, who would become his queen, to his final battle with Mordred. It offers a somber vision of an idealistic community in decay. Tennyson attributes the decline of the Round Table in part to Guinevere's betrayal of Arthur with the knight Lancelot. The poems encompass numerous minor characters and romantic exploits, notably the quest for the Holy Grail.

Iffland \'if-ˌlänt\, August Wilhelm (b. April 19, 1759, Hanover, Hanover [Germany]—d. Sept. 22, 1814, Berlin, Prussia) German actor, dramatist, and manager who exerted a major influence on German theater.

Although he is probably better known as an actor, Iffland achieved some success as an author of domestic dramas and sentimental comedies, notably *Die Jäger* (1787; *The Foresters*) and *Die Hagestolzen* (1799; *The Bachelors*). In 1798 he was appointed manager of the Berlin National Theater, and in 1811 he became director-general of all the royal theaters in Prussia. His collected works were published in 17 volumes between 1798 and 1807, and his autobiography was titled *Meine theatralische Laufbahn* (1798; "My Career in the Theater").

If He Hollers Let Him Go First novel by Chester HIMES, published in 1945, often considered to be his most powerful work.

Bob Jones, a sensitive black man, is driven to the brink by the humiliation he endures from the racism he encounters while working in a defense plant during World War II. Dishonesty and violence mark his relationship with his demanding fiancée; a greater threat is a white female coworker who insults, then entices him.

If It Die . . . Autobiographical work by André GIDE, published as *Si le grain ne meurt*. Initially printed privately in 1920, it was published commercially in 1924. The work is a memoir of Gide's childhood and of his emotional and psychosexual development.

Gide described his father as a solicitous, gentle person who was devoted to him as a child, but who relegated his rearing to his mother, a severe woman who controlled her son's life until her death when he was 25. Although largely incapable of sexual relationships with women, Gide maintained a lifelong emotional and intellectual attachment to his cousin Madeleine, whom he married in 1895. *If It Die . . .* also contains accounts of two trips Gide made to North Africa in the 1890s and of his homosexual experiences there.

If on a Winter's Night a Traveler　Avant-garde novel by Italo CALVINO, published in 1979 as *Se una notte d'inverno un viaggiatore*. Using shifting structures, a succession of tales, and different points of view, the book probes the nature of change and chance and the interdependence of fiction and reality.

The novel, which is nonlinear, begins with a man discovering that the copy of a novel he has recently purchased is defective, a Polish novel having been bound within its pages. He returns to the bookshop the following day and meets a young woman who is on an identical mission. They both profess a preference for the Polish novel. Interposed between the chapters in which the two strangers attempt to authenticate their texts are 10 excerpts that parody genres of contemporary world fiction, such as the Latin-American novel and the political novel of eastern Europe.

Ignatow \ig-'nä-tō\, David (b. Feb. 7, 1914, Brooklyn, N.Y., U.S.)　American poet whose works addressed social as well as personal issues in meditative, vernacular free verse.

Ignatow worked for a time as a journalist with the WPA Federal Writers' Project. His first book of poetry, entitled *Poems* (1948), was followed by *The Gentle Weight Lifter* (1955). Many of the pieces in the latter collection, as well as many in *Say Pardon* (1961) and *Figures of the Human* (1964), are written in the form of parables. From the 1960s, Ignatow taught poetry at several American colleges and universities.

Ignatow's thematic range, as well as his reputation, expanded significantly with *Rescue the Dead* (1968), which explored family, marriage, nature, and society. In *Facing the Tree* (1975), *The Animal in the Bush* (1977), and *Tread the Dark* (1978), he further examined death and the art of poetry. Later collections includes *Whisper to the Earth* (1981), *Leaving the Door Open* (1984), and *Shadowing the Ground* (1991). *The Notebooks of David Ignatow* was published in 1973, and he published *The One in the Many: A Poet's Memoirs* in 1988.

Igor's Campaign, The Song of \'ē-gȯr\, *Russian* Slovo o polku Igoreve, *also translated as* Lay of Igor's Campaign. Masterpiece of Old Russian literature, an account of the unsuccessful campaign in 1185 of Prince Igor of Novgorod-Seversky against the Polovtsy (Kipchaks, or Cumans), a Euro-Asian tribal confederation. As in the great French epic *La Chanson de Roland*, Igor's heroic pride draws him into a combat in which the odds are too great for him. Though defeated, Igor escapes and returns to his people. The tale was written anonymously (1185–87) and preserved in a single manuscript, which was discovered in 1795, published in 1800, and lost during Napoleon's invasion of Russia in 1812.

The tale is not easily classified; its uniqueness has led some scholars to challenge its authenticity. An English translation of it by Vladimir Nabokov was published in 1960.

Igraine \ē-'grān\, *also spelled* Ygaerne, Igerne, *or* Ygerne \ē-'ger-nə, -'gern\　In ARTHURIAN LEGEND, the mother of Arthur. She was impregnated by Uther Pendragon, who appeared to her disguised as her husband.

Ihara Saikaku \ē-'hä-rä-'sī-,kä-kù\, Ihara *also spelled* Ibara \ē-'bä-rä\, *original name probably* Hirayama Tōgo \,hē-'rä-yä-mä-'tō-,gō\ (b. 1642, Ōsaka, Japan—d. Sept. 9, 1693, Ōsaka) Poet and novelist, one of the most brilliant figures of the 17th-century revival in Japanese literature. He enchanted his readers with racy accounts of the amorous and financial affairs of the merchant class and the demimonde.

Saikaku first won fame for his facility in composing haikai, humorous *renga* (linked-verse) poems from which the 17-syllable haiku was derived. Not satisfied with composing at the rate of one verse a minute, he steadily increased his speed, reaching 23,500 in 24 hours in 1684.

Saikaku is best known, however, for his novels, written in a swift, allusive, elliptical style that stemmed from his training as a haikai poet. Their contents reflect the tastes of the prevailing Japanese merchant class. *Kōshoku ichidai otoko* (1682; *The Life of an Amorous Man*) relates the erotic adventures of its hero, Yonosuke, from age 6 to 60. Of other works in a similar vein (including *Kōshoku ichidai onna* [1686; *The Life of an Amorous Woman*] and *Nanshoku ōkagami* [1687; *The Mirror of Love Between Men*]), the best is thought to be *Kōshoku gonin onna* (1686; FIVE WOMEN WHO LOVED LOVE).

Saikaku also wrote novels about the samurai (aristocratic warrior caste), but they were generally considered inferior to his erotic tales or to his accounts of tradesmen's lives.

Ihimaera \,ē-hə-'mir-ə\, Witi \'wit-ē\ (Tame) (b. Feb. 7, 1944, Gisborne, New Zealand)　Maori author whose novels and short stories explore the clash between Maori and Pakeha (white, European-derived) values in New Zealand.

Ihimaera's first short-story collection, *Pounamu, Pounamu* (1972; "Greenstone, Greenstone"), written for secondary school students, presented one of his characteristic themes—traditional, communal Maori society confronted by mechanized, individualistic Pakeha society. His *Tangi* (1973; "Mourning") was the first novel in English by a Maori author. The novel *Whanau* (1974; "Family") presents a day in the life of a Maori village.

Ihimaera surveyed Maori life in the nonfiction *Maori* (1975). He also coedited anthologies of Maori writing. His later writings include the novels *The Matriarch* (1986) and *The Whale Rider* (1987) and the short-story collections *The New Net Goes Fishing (1977)* and *Dear Miss Mansfield: A Tribute to Kathleen Mansfield Beauchamp* (1989).

Iio Sōgi　*see* SŌGI.

Ikbāl　*see* Iqbal.

Ilf \'ēlʸf\, Ilya and **Petrov** \pʸē-'trȯf\, Yevgeny, *pseudonyms, respectively, of* Ilya Arnoldovich Faynzilberg \'fīn-zʸilʸ-bʸirk\ and Yevgeny Petrovich Katayev \,kə-'tä-yif\ (respectively b. Oct. 3 [Oct. 15, New Style], 1897, Odessa, Ukraine, Russian Empire—d. April 13, 1937, Moscow, Russian S.F.S.R., U.S.S.R.; b. Nov. 30 [Dec. 13], 1903, Odessa—d. July 2, 1942, Crimea, Crimean Autonomous S.S.R.)　Soviet humorists, whose intimate literary collaboration at the end of the 1920s and in the 1930s resulted in a number of immensely popular satirical works.

Ilf and Petrov arrived in Moscow seperately in 1923. Initially, Ilf worked on the staff of *Gudok* ("The Whistle"), the central rail-workers' newspaper, while Petrov worked on the satirical journal *Krasny perets* ("Red Pepper"). In 1926, Petrov transferred to *Gudok*, and he and Ilf formed their literary partnership.

In 1928 they published *Dvenadtsat stulyev* (*The Twelve Chairs*), a rollicking picaresque novel of farcical adventures within a framework of telling satire on Soviet life during the 1920s. The work was an instant success, and its rogue-hero—the irrepressible Ostap Bender—became one of the most popular personages in Russian fiction. A sequel, *Zolotoy telyonok* (1931; *The Little Golden Calf*), is an equally humorous but more serious and trenchant satire.

In 1936, following a tour of the United States, Ilf and Petrov wrote *Odnoetazhnaya Amerika* ("One-Storied America"), a witty exposé of American life. The long story *Tonya* (1937), which portrays with appropriate satiric touches the life of Soviet people compelled to live in a capitalist society, was a kind of sequel to this work. From 1932 Ilf and Petrov collaborated on a number of humorous and satiric sketches for the newspaper *Pravda*.

After Ilf died in 1937, Petrov continued his literary work, writing for the newspaper *Literaturnaya gazeta* ("Literary Gazette") and the magazine *Ogonyok* ("Little Light").

I li *see* YI LI.

Iliad \'il-ē-əd, -ˌad\ Highly influential epic poem on the Trojan War, traditionally attributed to the ancient Greek poet HOMER. The poem, divided into 24 books, is set during the Trojan War and is the story of the wrath of Achilles, the greatest of the Greek warriors. The word has also come to mean, in a more general sense, a long narrative, especially an epic in the Homeric tradition.

The *Iliad* is not merely a distillation of the whole protracted war against Troy but also an exploration of the heroic ideal with all its contradictions. The work begins with an explanation of the quarrel between King Agamemnon and Achilles, who, as a result, deserts the Greek forces, taking his friend Patroclus and his Myrmidon followers with him. Without Achilles the Greeks suffer many losses. Unable to stand by any longer when the Trojans set fire to the Greek ships, Patroclus asks for Achilles' permission to rejoin the fight and Achilles agrees, lending Patroclus his armor. When Patroclus is killed by the Trojan hero Hector, in revenge Achilles kills Hector. After Patroclus is buried, Hector's father, King Priam, comes to Achilles and asks for his son's body so that he too can be buried properly. Achilles agrees, as his anger is spent. The work ends with Hector's funeral.

Much of the poetry between the first book, in which the quarrel flares up, and the 16th, in which Achilles makes the crucial concession of allowing his friend Patroclus to fight on his behalf, consists of long scenes of battle, in which individual encounters alternate with mass movements of the opposing armies. The battle poetry is based on typical and frequently recurring elements and motifs, but it is also subtly varied by highly individualized episodes and set pieces, such as the catalog of troop contingents, Agamemnon inspecting his troops, and Hector's famous meeting in Troy with his wife Andromache.

illuminati \i-ˌlü-mi-'nä-tē\ [New Latin, plural of *illuminatus*, from Latin, past participle of *illuminare* to illuminate, reveal] Any of various groups of persons who are or claim to be unusually enlightened. One such group was formed in Bavaria in 1776 by Adam Weishaupt and included J.G. von Herder, Johann Pestalozzi, and J.W. von Goethe.

Illuminations \ē-lū̄e-mē-nä-'syôⁿ\ Collection of 40 prose poems and two free verse poems by Arthur RIMBAUD. Although the poems are undated, they are believed to have been written in 1872–74 when he was between 17 and 19 years of age. Paul Verlaine published the poems without the author's knowledge as the work of "the late Arthur Rimbaud" in 1886, even though Rimbaud was alive at the time.

In *Illuminations*, Rimbaud intended to abolish the distinction between reality and hallucination. In his attempt to revolutionize poetry, he used words for their evocative power rather than for their usual denotative meanings.

Illyés \'el-ˌyäsh\, Gyula (b. Nov. 2, 1902, Racegres, Austria-Hungary [now in Hungary]—d. April 14, 1983, Budapest) Hungarian poet, novelist, dramatist, and dissident, a leading literary figure in Hungary during the 20th century.

Illyés contributed to the literary review *Nyugat* ("The West"), which was edited from 1929 by his friend and mentor Mihály Babits. Eventually becoming editor of the magazine, Illyés renamed it *Magyar csillag* ("Hungarian Star") in 1941. His major novel, *Puszták népe* (1936; *People of the Puszta*), describes the misery suffered by the Hungarian peasantry. In 1950 he wrote "Egy mondat a zsarnokságról" ("One Sentence on

Tyranny"), a poem that is critical of Mátyás Rákosi's Stalinist regime. It was published during the October 1956 uprising.

Other works published in English include Illyés' *Selected Poems* (1971) and his 1936 biography of the 19th-century Hungarian poet Sándor Petőfi, which was translated into English in 1973. His *Hungarian Folk-tales* was published in 1980.

Ilos or **Ilus** \'ī-ləs\ In Greek mythology, the founder of Ilion (*Latin* Ilium, later called Troy). According to legend, the king of Phrygia gave Ilos a spotted cow as a wrestling prize, with the advice that he found a city wherever the cow first lay down. The animal chose the hill of Ate, where Ilos marked out the boundaries of Ilion. His son Laomedon succeeded him as ruler of the city, and his grandson Priam was the last king of Ilion.

Il Penseroso \ˌil-ˌpen-se-'rō-sō\ Poem written in 1631 by John MILTON, published in his *Poems* (1645). It was written in rhymed octosyllabics and has a 10-line prelude. In contrast to his companion poem "L'Allegro," "Il Penseroso" invokes the goddess Melancholy and describes the satisfactions of solitude, music, epic poetry, tragic drama, and the meditative life in general.

Ilya \ə-'lyä\ of Murom \'mùr-əm\ or **Ilya Muromets** \'mü-rə-mʸits\ A hero of the oldest known Old Russian byliny, traditional heroic folk chants. He is presented as the principal bogatyr (knight-errant) at the 10th-century court of Saint Vladimir I of Kiev.

Unlike the aristocratic heroes of most epics, Ilya was of peasant origin. He was a decidedly unpromising child who could not walk until he was more than 30 years old, when he discovered the use of his legs through the miraculous advice of some pilgrims. He was then given a splendid magic horse that became his inseparable companion, and he left his parents' home for Vladimir's court. There he became the head of Vladimir's retainers and performed astonishing feats of strength. Because of his simple heart, rough honesty, and obstinate strength, Ilya has remained a durable symbol to the eastern Slavs.

imagery \'im-ij-rē, -ə-rē\ Representation of objects, feelings, or ideas, either literally or through the use of figurative language; specifically, the often peculiarly individual concrete or figurative diction used by a writer in those portions of text where a particular effect (such as a special emotional appeal or a train of intellectual associations) is desired.

In "The Second Coming," William Butler Yeats invokes a powerful image of encroaching anarchy:

> Turning and turning in the widening gyre
> The falcon cannot hear the falconer;
> Things fall apart . . .

Imaginary Invalid, The Comedy in three acts by MOLIÈRE, produced in 1673 and published in 1674 as *Le Malade imaginaire*. It was also translated as *The Hypochondriac*. Molière wrote the play while ill and collapsed during his own performance of the title role, that of Argan, a hypochondriac who fears death and doctors. (Molière died later that day.)

The Imaginary Invalid is powerful in its delineation of medical cant and self-serving professionalism, of the fatuity of a would-be doctor with no sense, and of the contrasting normality of the young and sensible lovers.

imagination [Latin *imaginatio*, a derivative of *imaginari* to imagine, form a mental image of, a derivative of *imago* representation, image] *see* FANCY.

Imaginism \i-'maj-ə-ˌniz-əm\ [Russian *imazhinizm*, probably from French *imaginer* to imagine] Russian poetic movement of the postrevolutionary period that advocated poetry based on a series of arresting and unusual images. It is sometimes called Imagism but is unrelated to the 20th-century Anglo-American movement of that name. The Imaginist movement was founded in 1919 by its leading poet, Sergey Aleksandrovich Yesenin. Like the Futurists, the Imaginists read poetry in cafés during a time of social upheaval when few books were published, but, unlike the Futurists, they were unable to adapt to the demands of Soviet life. The Imaginists dissolved at the time of Yesenin's suicide in 1925, and their techniques had little lasting effect on Soviet poetry, although Yesenin himself remained a popular poet and cultural hero.

Imagism \ 'im-i-,jiz-əm \   A movement of American and English poets whose verse was characterized by concrete language and figures of speech, modern subject matter, freedom in the use of meter, and avoidance of romantic or mystical themes.

Imagism was a successor to the French Symbolist movement. The Imagist credo was formulated about 1912 by Ezra Pound—in conjunction with fellow poets Hilda Doolittle (H.D.), Richard Aldington, and F.S. Flint—and was inspired by the critical views of T.E. Hulme.

The Imagists wrote succinct verse of dry clarity and hard outline in which an exact visual image made a total poetic statement. In 1914 Pound turned to Vorticism, and Amy Lowell largely took over the spiritual leadership of the group. Among others who wrote Imagist poetry were John Gould Fletcher and Harriet Monroe. The movement influenced the poetry of Conrad Aiken, Marianne Moore, Wallace Stevens, D.H. Lawrence, and T.S. Eliot.

The four anthologies (*Des Imagistes*, 1914; *Some Imagists*, 1915, 1916, 1917), and the magazines *Poetry* (from 1912) and *The Egoist* (from 1914), in the United States and England, respectively, published the work of a dozen Imagist poets. *Compare* SYMBOLISM.

I Malavoglia \ ē-,mä-lä-'vōl-yä \   *see* THE HOUSE BY THE MEDLAR TREE.

Imber \ 'im-bər \, Naphtali Herz (b. 1856, Złoczów, Galicia, Austria-Hungary [now Zolochiv, Ukraine]—d. 1909, U.S.) Itinerant Hebrew poet whose poem "Ha-Tikvah" ("The Hope"), set to music, became the official Zionist-movement anthem in 1933 and Israel's unofficial national anthem in 1948.

A collection of his poems, *Barkai* (1886; *Morning Star*), includes "Ha-Tikvah" and another popular Zionist song, "Mishmar ha-Yarden" ("The Watch on the Jordan").

imitation \ ,im-ə-'tā-shən \   A literary work designed to reproduce the style of another author. *See also* MIMESIS.

Immanuel ben Solomon \ i-'man-yü-əl-ben-'säl-ə-mən \, *also called* Immanuel of Rome (b. *c.* 1260—d. *c.* 1328)   Hebrew poet who lived mainly in Rome, considered the founder of secular poetic writing in Hebrew.

Probably a wandering teacher by profession, Immanuel ben Solomon was a prolific writer of Hebrew verse, sacred and secular (some of the latter being highly erotic), which he collected within a rough narrative framework in *Maḥbarot 'Imanu'el* ("The Compositions of Immanuel"), published frequently after 1491. The last section of the work, inspired by Dante's visions of heaven and of hell, was composed immediately after Dante's death in 1321. In addition, Immanuel ben Solomon wrote Italian poetry and philosophical commentaries on certain books of the Bible. He introduced the sonnet form, thereafter very popular, into Hebrew.

Immermann \ 'im-ər-,män \, Karl Leberecht (b. April 24, 1796, Magdeburg, Saxony [Germany]—d. Aug. 25, 1840, Düsseldorf, Prussia)   Dramatist and novelist whose works included two archetypes in German literary history: *Die Epigonen* ("Those Born After") as a novel of the contemporary social scene and *Der Oberhof* ("The Manor") as a realistic story of village life.

In Düsseldorf, Immermann designed and built a "model" theater where, in accordance with J.W. von Goethe's theories, he mounted experimental productions of masterpieces of drama, including works by William Shakespeare and Pedro Calderón de la Barca. Immermann published his own record of his theatrical experiments as *Düsseldorfer Anfänge* (1840; "Düsseldorf Beginnings").

Immermann's writing is deeply marked by the transitional nature of his time. His dramatic works include *Das Trauerspiel in Tyrol* (1828; later revised and retitled *Andreas Hofer*); *Merlin* (1832); the trilogy *Alexis* (1832); and the comic epic *Tulifäntchen* (1830), a witty parody of the decline of the nobility and of romantic chivalry. Immermann's novels, however, are more important than his plays. *Die Epigonen*, 3 vol. (1836), is a pessimistic picture of society on the brink of a painful adjustment to industrialized mass society. The four-volume novel *Münchhausen* (1838–39) consists of two parts: a highly satiric and ludicrous portrayal of an idle and mendacious aristocrat, and a solidly visualized portrayal of peasants rooted in their work and in their countryside. In the latter section (the "Oberhof" section, published separately in 1863) Immermann glorifies the sturdy respectability of the peasantry, in whom he saw the strength of the German national heritage and the means for its regeneration. His epic *Tristan und Isolde* was left unfinished at his death.

immetrical \ im-'met-ri-kəl \   Lacking meter; unmetrical.

Immoralist, The   Novella by André GIDE, published as *L'Immoraliste* in 1902, one of the tales Gide called *récits*.

Inspired by Nietzschean philosophy, Gide undertook the work as an examination of the point at which concern for the self must be superseded by moral principles based on empathy for others. *The Immoralist* is largely the story of Michel, who marries Marceline, a family friend, to cheer his dying father and provide for his own needs. While recovering from tuberculosis in North Africa, Michel finds himself drawn sexually to young Arab boys. Back in France a friend urges him to ignore convention and indulge his passions. When the pregnant Marceline develops a case of tuberculosis, he neglects her in order to gratify his own desires. Marceline, who has become an impediment to Michel, suffers a miscarriage and later dies as Michel watches.

immortal \ i-'mȯr-təl \   **1.** An immortal being; one exempt from death. **2.** The gods of the Greek and Roman pantheon. **3.** Any of the 40 members of the Académie Française.

Importance of Being Earnest, The \ 'ər-nəst \ (*in full* The Importance of Being Earnest: A Trivial Comedy for Serious People)   Play in three acts by Oscar WILDE, performed in 1895 and published in 1899. A satire of Victorian social hypocrisy, the witty play is considered Wilde's greatest dramatic achievement.

Jack Worthing is a fashionable young man who lives in the country with his ward Cecily Cardew. He has invented a rakish brother named Ernest whose supposed exploits give Jack an excuse to travel to London periodically. Jack is in love with Gwendolen Fairfax, the cousin of his friend Algernon Moncrieff. Gwendolen, who thinks Jack's name is Ernest, returns his love, but her mother, Lady Bracknell, objects to their marriage because Jack is an orphan who was found in a handbag at Victoria Station. Jack discovers that Algernon has been impersonating Ernest in order to woo Cecily, who has always been in love with the imaginary Ernest. Ultimately it is revealed that Jack is really Lady Bracknell's nephew, that his real name is Ernest, and that Algernon is actually his brother. The play ends with both couples happily united.

Imposter, The   Play better known in English as TARTUFFE, a comedy in five acts by Molière.

impressionism \im-'presh-ə-ˌniz-əm\   **1.** The depiction (as in literature) of a scene, emotion, or character by details intended to achieve a vividness or effectiveness more by evoking subjective and sensory impressions than by re-creating or representing an objective reality. The term is sometimes applied to writers—such as Dorothy Richardson, Virginia Woolf, and James Joyce—who employ stream-of-consciousness techniques.   **2.** In literary criticism, the practice of presenting and elaborating one's subjective reactions to a work of art. Also, a critical theory that advocates or defends such a practice as the only valid one in criticism.

imram or **immram** \'im-ˌräv\ *plural* immrama \-ˌräv-ä\ (Old Irish: "act of rowing," or "voyaging")   In early Irish literature, a story about an adventurous voyage. This type of story includes tales of Irish saints traveling to Iceland or Greenland, as well as fabulous tales of pagan heroes journeying to the otherworld (*eachtra* or *echtra*). An outstanding example of an *imram* is *Immram Brain Maic Febail* (*The Voyage of Bran, Son of Febal*), which describes a trip to the enchanted Land of Women.

Imru' al-Qays \im-'rū-âl-'kīs\, *in full* Imru' al-Qays ibn Ḥujr (d. *c.* 550)   Arab author acknowledged as the most distinguished poet of pre-Islāmic times by the Prophet Muḥammad and author of one of the seven odes in the famed collection of pre-Islāmic poetry AL-MUʿALLAQĀT.

The predominant legend cites Imru' al-Qays as the youngest son of Ḥujr, the last king of Kindah. He was twice expelled from his father's court for writing erotic poetry, and he assumed the life of a vagabond. After his father was murdered by a rebel Bedouin tribe, the Banū Asad, Imru' al-Qays was single-minded in his pursuit of revenge. Legend has it that the Byzantine emperor Justinian I sent him a poisoned cloak that caused his death at Ancyra (modern Ankara).

The philologists of the Basra school regarded Imru' al-Qays not only as the greatest of the poets of the Muʿallaqāt but also as the inventor of the form of the classical ode, or qasida. There were at least three collections (*dīwān*s, or divans) of his poetry made by medieval Arab scholars, numbering as many as 68 poems; the authenticity of most of them, however, is doubtful.

incantation \ˌin-ˌkan-'tā-shən\ [Late Latin *incantatio* spell, enchantment, a derivative of Latin *incantare* to put a spell on, enchant]   **1.** A formula of words chanted or recited in a magic ritual and designed to produce a particular effect. An example of this is the recipe recited by the witches in William Shakespeare's *Macbeth*.   **2.** An expression (as of music or poetry) designed to move rather than amuse or convince.

Inchbald \'inch-ˌbôld\, Elizabeth, *original surname* Simpson \'simp-sən\ (b. Oct. 16, 1753, Suffolk, Eng.—d. Aug. 1, 1821, London)   English novelist, playwright, and actress whose highly successful prose romances, *A Simple Story* (1791) and *Nature and Art* (1796), are early examples of the novel of passion.

After launching an acting career, Inchbald began adapting plays and writing original farces and comedies, including *I'll Tell You What* (1785). She was much admired for her beauty and personality.

incident \'in-sə-dənt\   An occurrence or related group of occurrences that are subordinate to a main narrative plot. *See also* EPISODE.

Incidents in the Life of a Slave Girl, Written by Herself   Autobiographical narrative by Harriet Jacobs (1813–1897), a former North Carolina slave, published in 1861.

Jacobs' narrator and alter ego, Linda Brent, is a racially mixed slave owned by sadistic Dr. Flint, a pious churchgoer who repeatedly beats and rapes Linda and also sells her children. Her narrative includes graphic scenes of brutality, slave auctions, and the cruelty of slave owners' wives to their husbands' slave children. Written after Jacobs' own escape to freedom, the book derives its power from the unflinching accuracy of its portrayal of the lives of the slaves.

incipit \'in-sə-pit, 'iŋ-ki-\   The introductory words or part of a medieval Western manuscript or early printed book. In the absence of a title page, the text may be recognized, referred to, and recorded by its incipit. As in the title pages or main divisions of later printed books, incipits (Latin for "here begins") provide an occasion for display letters and much calligraphic ornament.

The end of the text in a medieval manuscript was announced by the word *explicit*, probably a reshaping (after *incipit*) of an earlier Latin phrase such as *explicitum est volumen* ("the book has been completely unrolled"), a reminder of the scroll form of the book used in the West before the codex format was adopted in about AD 300.

incremental repetition   A device used in poetry of the oral tradition, especially English and Scottish ballads, in which a line is repeated in a changed context or with minor changes in the repeated part. The device is illustrated in the following stanzas from the ballad "Lord Randal":

> "O where ha' you been, Lord Randal, my son?
> And where ha' you been, my handsome young man?"
> "I ha' been at the greenwood; mother, mak my bed soon,
> For I'm wearied wi' huntin', and fain wad lie down."

> "And wha met ye there, Lord Randal, my son?
> And wha met you there, my handsome young man?"
> O I met wi' my true-love; mother, mak my bed soon,
> For I'm wearied wi' huntin', and fain wad lie down."

incubus \'iŋ-kyə-bəs\ *plural* incubi \-ˌbī, -ˌbē\ *or* incubuses [Medieval Latin, alteration of Latin *incubo* spirit alleged to alight on and suffocate people in their sleep, a derivative of *incubare* to lie on]   A demon in male form that seeks to have sexual intercourse with sleeping women; the corresponding spirit in female form is called a succubus. In medieval Europe, union with an incubus was supposed by some to result in the birth of witches, demons, and deformed human offspring. The legendary magician Merlin was said to have been fathered by an incubus. *Compare* SUCCUBUS.

incult \in-'kəlt\ [Latin *incultus*, literally, not tilled, untended]   Lacking finish or polish; uncultivated, crude, or disordered. The term is used especially of literary style or its products or producers.

incunabulum \ˌin-kyə-'nab-yə-ləm\ *or* **incunable** \in-'kyü-nə-bəl\ *plural* incunabula \ˌin-kyə-'nab-yə-lə\ [Latin *incunabula* a person's earliest years, literally, bands used to hold a baby in a cradle], *also called* cradle book *or* fifteener.   A book printed before 1501. The date, though convenient, is arbitrary, unconnected as it is to any development in the printing art; the initial period of printing, a restless, highly competitive free-for-all, ran well into the 16th century. Printing began to become regulated from within and controlled from without only after about 1550. Use of the word incunabula for early printing in general seems to have first appeared about 1650.

The total number of editions produced by the 15th-century European presses is generally put at about 35,000 or upward, to which must be added a considerable percentage for ephemeral literature (*e.g.*, single sheets, cheap romances, ballads, and devotional tracts), which has either perished completely or exists only in fragments of waste lining bindings and in other unexpected places.

indeterminacy \,in-də-'tər-min-ə-sē\ The quality or state of being not definitely or precisely determined or fixed. Deconstruction theorists gave the word a specifically literary application, using it to refer to the multiplicity of possible interpretations of given textual elements. Indeterminacy is similar to ambiguity as described by the New Critics, but it is applied not only to literature but also to interpretation of texts.

index \'in-,deks\ A usually alphabetical list that includes all or nearly all items (such as authors, subjects, or keywords) that are considered pertinent and are discussed or mentioned in a printed or written work (such as a book, catalog, or dissertation) or an electronic database. An index gives with each item the location of its mention in the work. The index is usually at or near the end of a printed work.

Index librorum prohibitorum \'in-deks-lī-'brō-rəm-prō-,hib-i-'tō-rəm\ ("Index of Forbidden Books") List of books once forbidden by Roman Catholic church authority as dangerous to the faith or morals of Roman Catholics. Publication of the list ceased in 1966, and it was relegated to the status of a historical document.

The origin of the church's legislation concerning the censorship of books is unclear, but books were a source of concern as early as the scriptural account of the burning of superstitious books at Ephesus by the new converts of St. Paul (Acts of the Apostles 19:19). The decree of Pope Gelasius I about 496, which contained lists of recommended as well as banned books, has been described as the first Roman *Index*. The last and 20th edition of the *Index* appeared in 1948.

Indianista novel \ēn-jä-'nēsh-tə\ [Portuguese *indianista*, literally, advocate of Indians or specialist in Indian cultures] Brazilian literary genre of the 19th century that idealizes the simple life of the South American Indian. The tone of the *Indianista* novel is one of languid nostalgia and *saudade*, a brooding melancholy and reverence for nature characteristic of Portuguese and Brazilian literature. José de Alencar initiated the vogue of the Brazilian *Indianista* novel by contributing two of the most popular works to the genre, *O Guarani* (1857) and *Iracema* (1865), romantic tales of love between Indians and whites and of the conflict between the Indians and their Portuguese conquerors.

indite \in-'dīt\ [Middle English *enditen*, from Old French *enditer* to write down, compose, tell] **1.** To make up or compose (a work such as a poem or story). **2.** To give literary or formal expression to. **3.** To put down in writing. **4.** *obsolete* To dictate.

Indra \'in-drə\ Chief of the Vedic gods of India. A warlike, typically Aryan god, he conquered innumerable human and demon enemies, vanquished the sun, and killed the dragon Vṛtra, who had prevented the monsoon from breaking.

His weapons are lightning and the thunderbolt, and his mount is the four-tusked white elephant Airāvata. Among his allies are the Rudras (or Maruts), who ride the clouds and direct storms; the Aśvins, twin horsemen; and Vishnu, who later evolved into one of the three principal gods of Hinduism. In later Hinduism, Indra plays little part. The *Purāṇas* record some rivalry between Indra and Krishna. Indra is father to Arjuna, hero of the *Mahābhārata*. Indra is sometimes referred to as "the thousand-eyed," because of the thousand marks on his body resembling eyes (actually yonis, or symbols of female genitalia), a result of a curse by a sage whose wife Indra seduced.

induction \in-'dək-shən\ A preface, prologue, or introductory scene, especially of an early English play.

inedita \in-'ed-i-tə\ Unpublished literary material.

Infant Phenomenon Byname of the fictional child performer Ninetta Crummles who appears in the novel NICHOLAS NICKLEBY by Charles Dickens. Ninetta is the beloved eight-year-old daughter of the manager-actors of a troupe of strolling players in which Nicholas Nickleby is a performer.

infernal \in-'fər-nəl\ [Latin *infernus* lower, underground, of the nether world] Relating or belonging to a nether world of the dead and of earth deities. The term is sometimes a synonym for chthonic. *Compare* HADES.

Informer, The Novel of betrayal set during the Irish "troubles" of the 1920s by Liam O'FLAHERTY, published in 1925.

The novel tells the story of Gypo Nolan's betrayal of a friend to the police, his fatal wounding by his former comrades, and his ultimate redemption just before his death.

Inge \'ing\, William (Motter) (b. May 3, 1913, Independence, Kan., U.S.—d. June 10, 1973, Hollywood Hills, Calif.) American playwright best known for his plays *Come Back, Little Sheba* (1950; film, 1952); PICNIC (1953; film, 1956), for which he won a Pulitzer Prize; and BUS STOP (1955; film, 1956).

Inge's first play, *Farther Off from Heaven* (1947), was produced with the help of Tennessee Williams; 10 years later it was revised for Broadway as *The Dark at the Top of the Stairs* (film, 1960).

Inge was one of the first American dramatists to deal with the quality of life in the small towns of the Midwest, and he achieved notable success throughout the 1950s. His later plays—*A Loss of Roses* (1960; film, *The Stripper*, 1963), *Natural Affection* (1963), *Where's Daddy?* (1966), and *The Last Pad* (1970)—were less successful. Inge received an Academy Award for his original screenplay *Splendor in the Grass* (1961). His shorter works include *Glory in the Flower* (1958), *To Bobolink, for Her Spirit* (1962), *The Boy in the Basement* (1962), and *Bus Riley's Back in Town* (1962).

Ingemann \'ēŋ-ə-mȧn\, Bernhard Severin (b. May 28, 1789, Torkilstrup, Den.—d. Feb. 24, 1862, Sorø) Historical novelist and poet whose works glorifying Denmark's medieval past were popular for generations. Most of his works have not won enduring acclaim, but *Morgen og aftensange* (1837–39; "Morning and Evening Songs") and his patriotic verse cycle *Holger Danske* (1837; "Holger the Dane") are much admired in Denmark.

Ingemann produced a series of six historical novels, of which the first, *Valdemar den store og hans mænd* (1824; "Waldemar the Great and his Men"), and the last, *Dronning Margrethe* (1836; "Queen Margrethe"), are in verse, the other four in prose. He is also the author of a hymn, "Through the Night of Doubt and Sorrow," well known in English translation.

initial rhyme *see* ALLITERATION; BEGINNING RHYME.

in medias res \in-'med-ē-,äs-'räs, -'mē-dē-əs-'rāz\ [Latin, into the midst of things] In or into the middle of a narrative or plot without the formality of an introduction or other preliminary. The principle of opening a narrative *in medias res* is based on the practice of Homer, who in the *Iliad*, for example, begins dramatically with the quarrel between Achilles and Agamemnon. The Latin poet and critic Horace has pointed out the immediate interest created by this opening in contrast to beginning the story *ab ovo* ("from the egg"). *Compare* AB OVO.

In Memoriam \,in-mə-'mȯr-ē-əm\ (*in full* In Memoriam A.H.H.) Poem by Alfred, Lord TENNYSON, written between the years 1833 and 1850 and published anonymously in 1850. Consisting of 131 sections, a prologue, and an epilogue, this chiefly elegiac work examines the stages of Tennyson's period of mourning over the death of his close friend Arthur Henry Hallam. *In Memoriam* reflects the Victorian struggle to reconcile traditional religious faith with the emerging theories of evolution and modern geology. The verses show the development of the poet's acceptance and understanding of his friend's death and conclude with an epilogue, a marriage song on the occasion of the wedding of the poet's sister Cecilia.

An enormous critical and popular success, the poem also won Tennyson the friendship of Queen Victoria and helped bring about, in the year of its publication (1850), his appointment as poet laureate.

In Memoriam stanza   A quatrain in iambic tetrameter with a rhyme scheme of *abba*. The form was named for the pattern used by Alfred, Lord Tennyson in his poem *In Memoriam*, which, following an 11-stanza introduction, begins

> I held it truth, with him who sings
> To one clear harp in divers tones,
> That men may rise on stepping-stones
> Of their dead selves to higher things.

Innes, Michael.   Pseudonym of J.I.M. STEWART.

Innocents Abroad, The (*in full* The Innocents Abroad; or, The New Pilgrims' Progress)   A humorous travel narrative by Mark TWAIN, published in 1869 and based on Twain's letters to newspapers about his 1867 steamship voyage to Europe, Egypt, and the Holy Land.

The Innocents Abroad sharply satirized tourists who learn what they should see and feel by reading guidebooks. Assuming the role of a keen-eyed, shrewd Westerner, Twain was refreshingly honest and vivid in describing foreign scenes and his reactions to them. He alternated serious passages—history, statistics, description, explanation, argumentation—with risible ones. The humor itself was varied, sometimes in the vein of the Southwestern yarn spinners, sometimes in that of contemporaneous humorists such as Artemus Ward and Josh Billings, who chiefly used burlesque and parody and other verbal devices.

Inoue   Yasushi \ē-'nō-wä-'yä-sü-shē\   (b. May 6, 1907, Asahikawa, Japan—d. Jan. 29, 1991, Tokyo)   Japanese novelist known for his historical fiction, notably *Tempyō no iraka* (1957; *The Roof Tile of Tempyō*), which depicts the drama of 8th-century Japanese monks traveling to China and returning with Buddhist texts and other artifacts.

Inoue was literary editor of the *Mainichi shimbun* newspaper for 12 years except for a brief period of military service in northern China in 1937, when he became fascinated by China and its history. His first work, *Ryōjū* (1949; *The Hunting Gun*), about loneliness in the modern world, attracted critical acclaim; it was followed by *Tōgyū* (1949; "The Bullfight"), which secured his reputation. Among his many other successes was the novel *Tonkō* (1959; *Tun-huang*), which re-creates 11th-century China and centers on the Buddhist treasures hidden in the Dunhuang caves, and an autobiographical narrative, *Waga haha no ki* (1975; *Chronicle of My Mother*), a moving and humorous account of his mother's decline.

I novel \'ī\, *Japanese* watakushi shōsetsu \wä-'tä-kə-shē-'shō-,se-tsü\ *or* shishōsetsu \shə-'shō-,se-tsü\   Form or genre of 20th-century Japanese literature that is characterized by self-revealing narration, with the author usually as the central character.

The I novel grew out of the naturalistic movement that dominated Japanese literature during the early decades of the 20th century. The term is used to describe two different types of novel, the confessional novel (characterized by prolonged, often self-abasing, revelation) and the "mental attitude" novel

(in which the writer probes innermost thoughts or attitudes toward everyday events in life). Notable I novelists include Shiga Naoya, Kasai Zenzō, Uno Kōji, Takii Kōsaku, and Ozaki Kazuo.

inscape \'in-,skāp\   The essential character or quality belonging to objects or events in nature and human experience, especially as perceived by the blended observation and introspection of the poet and in turn embodied in patterns of such specific poetic elements as imagery, rhythm, rhyme, assonance, sound symbolism, and allusion. The term was coined by the poet Gerard Manley Hopkins; the formative *-scape* suggests both the second element of *landscape* and the word *shape*.

Inspector General, The   *see* THE GOVERNMENT INSPECTOR.

installment or **instalment** \in-'stól-mənt\   One part of a serial.

intentional fallacy   The fallacy that the value or meaning of a work of art (such as a poem) may be judged or defined in terms of the artist's intention. The term originated in a 1946 essay by New Critics W.K. Wimsatt and Monroe Beardsley. The fallacy originates in the attempt "to derive the standard of criticism from the psychological *causes* of the poem and ends in biography and relativism."

intentionality \in-,ten-chə-'nal-ə-tē\   In modern literary theory, the study of authorial intention in a literary work and its corresponding relevance to textual interpretation. With the ascendancy of New Criticism after World War I, much of the debate on intentionality addressed whether or not information external to the text could help determine the writer's purpose, and whether or not it was even possible or desirable to determine that purpose.

With the publication of their influential essay "The Intentional Fallacy" in *The Sewanee Review* (1946), authors W.K. Wimsatt and Monroe Beardsley questioned further the value of searching for authorial intention. Other critics stressed that knowledge of the intention of the author is a necessary criterion by which to judge a work; without that knowledge, it is not possible to determine to what extent the work satisfies the original intention and to what extent, therefore, it is successful.

intercalation \in-,tər-kə-'lā-shən\   The insertion or introduction of something among other existing or original things; also, that which is so inserted.

interchapter \'in-tər-,chap-tər\   An intervening or inserted chapter.

interior monologue   A usually extended representation in monologue of a fictional character's sequence of thought and feeling. These ideas may be either loosely related impressions that approach free association or more rationally ordered sequences of thought and emotion.

Interior monologues encompass several forms, including dramatized inner conflicts, self-analysis, imagined dialogue, and rationalization. An interior monologue may be a direct first-person expression, apparently devoid of the author's selection and control, or a third-person treatment that begins with a phrase such as "he thought" or "his thoughts turned to."

The term interior monologue is often used interchangeably with "stream of consciousness." But while an interior monologue may mirror all the half thoughts, impressions, and associations that impinge upon the character's consciousness, it may also be restricted to an organized presentation of his rational thoughts. Closely related to the soliloquy and dramatic monologue, the interior monologue was first used extensively by Édouard Dujardin in *Les Lauriers sont coupés* (1888; *We'll to the Woods No More*) and later became a characteristic device of 20th-century psychological novels. *See also* STREAM OF CONSCIOUSNESS.

interlude \'in-tər-,lüd\ [Medieval Latin *interludium,* from Latin *inter-* between + *ludus* play]   Early form of English dramatic entertainment, sometimes considered as the transition between medieval morality plays and Tudor dramas. Interludes were performed at court or at "great houses" by professional minstrels or amateurs. They were performed at intervals between some other form of entertainment, such as a banquet, or preceding or following a play, or between acts. John Heywood, one of the most famous writers of interludes, brought the genre to its peak in his *The Play of the Wether* (1533) and *The Playe Called the Foure P.P.* (*c.* 1544).

internal rhyme   Rhyme between a word within a line and another word either at the end of the same line or within another line, as in the following quatrain from the last stanza of Percy Bysshe Shelley's "The Cloud":

> I am the daughter of Earth and Water,
> And the nursling of the Sky;
> I pass through the pores of the ocean and shores;
> I change, but I cannot die.

interpretation \in-,tər-prə-'tā-shən\   **1.** The act or the result of interpreting, such as translation from one language into another (used of oral translation by interpreters). Also, the explanation of actions, events, or statements by the examination of inner relationships or motives or by relating particulars to general principles.   **2.** Representation in performance, delivery, or criticism of the thought and mood in a work of art or its producer, especially as filtered through the personality of the interpreter.

intertextuality \,in-tər-,teks-chù-'wal-ə-tē\ [translation of French *intertextualité*]   In literary theory, a text's quality of interdependence with all previous and future discourse. Literary critic Julia Kristeva in the 1960s introduced the term to express the idea that every new literary text is an intersection of texts—that it has absorbed and transformed previous works and that it will be absorbed and transformed by future texts. The term has been applied differently by other literary theorists.

In the Penal Colony   Novella by Franz KAFKA, written in 1914 and published in German as *In der Strafkolonie* in 1919. An allegorical fantasy about law and punishment, it was also viewed as an existential comment on human torment and on strict devotion to an ambiguous task.

The tale is dispassionately narrated by a traveling anthropologist who visits a penal colony that was formerly led by a sadistic disciplinarian who constructed a torturous apparatus for execution. The purposefulness of the old commander sharply contrasts with the slackness of the new, more humane commander. The death machine is operated by a fanatical officer who in the end demonstrates his devotion to duty by submitting himself to an appalling, clinically described mutilation by the machine during which the machine falls apart.

intimist \'in-tim-ist\ [French *intimiste,* a derivative of *intime* intimate]   Of fiction, dealing chiefly with intimate and private, especially psychological, experiences.

intrigue \'in-,trēg, in-'trēg\ [French, crafty scheme, plot, love affair, from Italian *intrigo*]   The plot of a literary or dramatic work that is especially marked by an intricacy of design or action or by a complex interrelation of events.

introverted \'in-trə-,vər-təd\   Of a quatrain, having an enclosed rhyme. An example of an introverted quatrain is the *In Memoriam* stanza (named for the poem by Alfred, Lord Ten-

nyson), which has an *abba* rhyme scheme. An introverted stanza may also be called an *envelope.*

Intruder in the Dust   Novel by William FAULKNER, published in 1948. Set in Faulkner's fictional Yoknapatawpha County, the novel combines the solution of a murder mystery with an exploration of race relations in the South. Charles ("Chick") Mallison, a 16-year-old white boy, feels that he must repay a debt of honor to Lucas Beauchamp, an elderly black man who has helped him but spurns his offers of payment. When Beauchamp is arrested for the murder of a white man, Chick searches for the real killer to save Beauchamp from being lynched.

intrusive narrator   *see* NARRATOR.

inversion \in-'vər-zhən\, *also called* anastrophe.   In literary style and rhetoric, the syntactical reversal of the normal order of the words and phrases in a sentence. In English, inversion is evident in the placing of an adjective after the noun it modifies ("the form divine"); a verb before its subject ("Came the dawn"); or a noun preceding its preposition ("worlds between"). Inversion is most commonly used in poetry in which it may both satisfy the demands of the meter and achieve emphasis, as in Samuel Coleridge's "Kubla Khan":

> In Xanadu did Kubla Khan
> A stately pleasure dome decree:

The word *inversion* is also used in a metrical sense to describe a change in cadence from rising to falling or from falling to rising rhythm. *See also* COUNTERPOINT RHYTHM.

Invisible Cities   Novel by Italo CALVINO, published in 1972 in Italian as *Le città invisibili.* It consists of a conversation between Marco Polo and Kublai Khan in which Marco Polo describes a series of wondrous, surreal cities in the khan's domain. Each city is characterized by a unique quality or concept. The interplay of reality and imagination and the craft of fiction itself are among the work's underlying issues.

Invisible Man   A novel by Ralph ELLISON, published in 1952.

The narrator of *Invisible Man* is a nameless young black man who moves in a 20th-century America where reality is surreal and who can survive only through pretense. Because the people he encounters "see only my surroundings, themselves, or figments of their imagination," he is effectively invisible. He leaves the racist South for New York City, but his encounters continue to disgust him. Ultimately, he retreats to a hole in the ground, which he furnishes and makes his home.

Invisible Man, The   Science-fiction novel by H.G. WELLS, published in 1897. The story concerns the life and death of a scientist named Griffin who has gone mad. Having learned how to make himself invisible, Griffin begins to use his invisibility for nefarious purposes, including murder. When he is finally killed, his body becomes visible again.

Invitation to a Beheading   Anti-utopian novel by Vladimir NABOKOV, published serially in Russian as *Priglasheniye na kazn* from 1935 to 1936 and in book form in 1938.

Set in a mythical totalitarian country, the novel presents the thoughts of Cincinnatus, a former teacher who has been convicted of "gnostic turpitude" for being different from his mediocre fellow countrymen. Sentenced to be executed at an unknown date, Cincinnatus sits in his prison cell and records in his diary his private thoughts and intuitions about an ideal world that he considers to be his "true" home. He sees the world around him as delusional and himself as the only "real" person in the universe. As the ax falls and he is executed, he, or his spirit, rises toward other beings like himself.

invocation \,in-vō-'kā-shən\ [Latin *invocatio,* a derivative of *invocare* to summon, call upon] A convention of classical literature and of epics in particular, in which an appeal for aid (especially for inspiration) is made to a muse or deity, usually at or near the beginning of the work. Homer's *Odyssey,* for instance, begins:

> Tell me, Muse, of the man of many ways, who was driven
> far journeys, after he had sacked Troy's sacred citadel.

involuted novel *see* REFLEXIVE NOVEL.

Io \'ī-ō\ In Greek mythology, daughter of Inachus, the river god of Argos. Zeus fell in love with Io and, to protect her from the wrath of Hera, changed her into a white heifer. Hera persuaded Zeus to give her the heifer and sent Argus Panoptes ("Argus the All-Seeing") to watch her. Zeus thereupon sent Hermes, who lulled Argus to sleep and then killed him. Hera responded by sending a gadfly to bother Io, who therefore wandered over the earth; Io crossed what is now the Ionian Sea, swam the strait that was thereafter known as the Bosporus ("Ox Ford"), and at last reached Egypt. There she was restored to her original form and became the mother of Epaphus. Io was thus identified with the Egyptian goddess Isis, and Epaphus with Apis, the sacred bull.

Ion \'ī-,än, -ən\ Tragicomedy by EURIPIDES, performed about 413 BC. Its somber action is reversed in a recognition scene.

The drama is set at Delphi, where the title character has grown up as a temple slave. Creusa, the queen of Athens, conceived, bore, and abandoned the child years earlier after being raped by Apollo. Now married to Xuthus, an Achaean king, Creusa has produced no further children. The couple's childlessness brings them to Delphi. When Ion and Creusa meet, they feel a strong affinity. The Delphic oracle states that Ion is the son of Xuthus. All assume that Ion was the fruit of a youthful affair of the king's. The queen in her despair plots to kill the young stranger who threatens her inheritance. Her plot is discovered, and Ion is about to have her punished, but at the last minute a priestess comes forth with a cradle and other artifacts remaining from Ion's first appearance at the temple. Creusa identifies the items, and mother and son embrace.

Ionesco \yȯ-nes-'kō\, Eugène, *Romanian* Eugen Ionescu \yō-'nes-kü\ (b. Nov. 26, 1909, Slatina, Rom.—d. March 28, 1994, Paris, Fr.) Romanian-born French dramatist whose one-act "antiplay" *La Cantatrice chauve* (produced 1950; THE BALD SOPRANO) inspired a revolution in dramatic techniques and helped inaugurate the Theater of the Absurd. He was elected to the Académie Française in 1970.

Ionesco attended the University of Bucharest and was awarded a doctorate in Paris, where, from 1945, he made his home. While learning English, Ionesco was inspired by the stilted commonplaces of his textbook to write the masterly catalog of senseless platitudes that constitutes *The Bald Soprano.* In rapid succession he wrote a number of plays, all developing the "antilogical" ideas present in *The Bald Soprano;* these included brief and violently irrational sketches and also a series of more elaborate one-act plays in which many of his later themes—especially the fear and horror of death—begin to make their appearance. *La Leçon* (produced 1951; THE LESSON), *Les Chaises* (1952; *The Chairs*), and *Le Nouveau Locataire* (1955; *The New Tenant*) are among the notable successes. His early full-length plays *Amédée* (1954), *Tueur sans gages* (1959; *The Killer*), and *Le Rhinocéros* (1959; RHINOCEROS) dispensed with dramatic unity. He had success with *Le Roi se meurt* (1962; *Exit the King*), which was followed by one of his best and most spectacular flights of philosophical fantasy, *Le Piéton*

de l'air (1963; *A Stroll in the Air*). He wrote *Jeux de massacre* (1970; *Killing Game*); *Macbett* (1972), a retelling of William Shakespeare's *Macbeth*; and *Ce Formidable Bordel* (1973; *A Hell of a Mess*). During his long career he also published essays, textbooks for children, and the novel *Le Solitaire* (1973; *The Hermit*). He was elected to the Académie Française in 1970.

ionic \ī-'än-ik\ **1.** *capitalized* A dialect of ancient Greece used especially in Ionia and the Cyclades that was the vehicle of an important body of literature. **2.** A foot of verse that consists of either two long and two short syllables (also called *major ionic* or *a maiore*) or two short and two long syllables (also called *minor ionic* or *a minore*).

Iphigeneia or **Iphigenia** \,if-ə-jə-'nī-ə\ In Greek mythology, eldest daughter of Agamemnon, king of Mycenae, and his wife Clytemnestra. She was sacrificed by her father to the goddess Artemis in order that his ships would be favored by the goddess.

Iphigeneia served as a key figure in certain Greek tragedies: in the *Agamemnon* of Aeschylus, in the *Electra* of Sophocles, and in Euripides' unfinished *Iphigenia at Aulis.* In Euripides' earlier play *Iphigenia Among the Taurians,* she was saved by Artemis, who instead accepted the sacrifice of a deer. In some localities she was identified with Artemis, and some ancient writers claimed that Iphigeneia was originally the goddess Hecate.

Iphigeneia's story was also popular with later dramatists, providing the plot of *Iphigénie* by Jean Racine and of *Ihigenie auf Tauris* by J.W. von Goethe.

Iphigenia Among the Taurians \,if-ə-jə-'nī-ə . . . 'tȯr-ē-ənz\ (*Greek* Iphigeneia en Taurois, *Latin* Iphigenia in Tauris) The title is also translated as *Iphigenia in Tauris.* Tragicomedy by EURIPIDES, performed about 413 BC and consisting chiefly of a recognition scene followed by a clever escape.

In the play Iphigenia has been saved by the goddess Artemis from sacrifice and now serves the goddess' temple at Tauris in Thrace. Her brother Orestes, who is still seeking to appease the Furies for his crime of matricide, is ordered by Apollo to obtain the statue of Artemis from Tauris and to return it to Athens. Knowing that all strangers in Tauris are to be sacrificed to the goddess, Orestes nonetheless journeys to Thrace, where he is delivered to Iphigenia for sacrifice. She recognizes him and with the help of Athena they escape from Tauris with the statue.

Iphigenia at Aulis \,if-ə-jə-'nī-ə . . . 'ȯl-is\ (*Greek* Iphigeneia en Aulidi) Tragedy by EURIPIDES, performed about 406 BC.

The story concerns the legendary sacrifice of Iphigenia by her father Agamemnon. When the Greek fleet is becalmed at Aulis, thus preventing movement of the expeditionary force against Troy, Agamemnon is told that he must sacrifice Iphigenia to appease the goddess Artemis, who has caused the unfavorable weather. Agamemnon lures his daughter to Aulis by pretending that she will marry Achilles. Once she learns the truth, Iphigenia begs for her life, but eventually she goes willingly to her death.

Jean Racine's *Iphigénie* is an adaptation of Euripides' play, but with a love plot and a happy ending. Euripides was also the inspiration for Jean Moreas' verse play *Iphigénie à Aulide.*

I promessi sposi \,ē-prō-'mes-sē-'spō-sē\ Novel by Alessandro MANZONI, published in three volumes in 1825–26; the complete edition was issued in 1827. Initially translated into English as *The Betrothed Lovers,* it was more commonly translated as *The Betrothed.* Set in early 17th-century Lombardy during the period of the Thirty Years' War and the plague, the novel is a sympathetic portrayal of the struggle of two peasant lovers whose wish to marry is thwarted by a vicious local tyrant and the cowardice of their parish priest. A courageous friar takes up the lovers' cause and helps them through many adventures to safety and marriage. The novel brought Manzoni immediate acclaim and had enormous patriotic appeal for Italians of the nationalistic Risorgimento period. It became the model for many later Italian writers.

Iqbāl or Ikbāl \'ik-ˌbȧl\, Sir Muḥammad (b. Nov. 9, 1877, Siālkot, Punjab, India [now in Pakistan]—d. April 21, 1938, Lahore, Punjab)   Indian poet and philosopher, known for his efforts toward the establishment of a separate Muslim state. He was knighted in 1922.

Iqbāl was educated at Lahore (now in Pakistan) and at the universities of Cambridge and Munich. Upon his return from Europe he practiced law, but his fame came from his poetry, which was written in the classical style for public recitation. His poetry soon became widely known, even among the illiterate.

His early poetry affirmed Indian nationalism, as in *Nayā shawālā* ("The New Altar"); but time away from India caused him to shift his perspective, and his hopes took a Pan-Islāmic direction. The recurrent themes of Iqbāl's poetry are the vanished glories of Islām, complaint about its present decadence, and a call to unity and reform.

Notoriety came in 1915 with the publication of his long poem *Asrār-e khūdī* (*The Secrets of the Self*), which he wrote in Persian in order to address his appeal to the entire Muslim world. In the work he presented a theory of the self that is the antithesis of the self-negating quietism of classical Islāmic mysticism; his criticism shocked many and excited controversy.

The dialectical quality of his thinking was expressed by the next long Persian poem, *Rumūz-e bīkhūdī* (1918; *The Mysteries of Selflessness*). Written as a counterpoint to the individualism preached in the *Asrār-e khūdī*, this poem called for self-surrender, finding in the mystery of selflessness the hidden strength of Islām.

Later, he published three more Persian volumes: *Payām-e Mashriq* (1923; "Message of the East"); *Zabūr-e ʿAjam* (1927; "Persian Psalms"), which demonstrated his talent for writing the ghazel, or love poem; and *Jāvīd-nāmeh* (1932; "The Song of Eternity"), Iqbāl's masterpiece. The theme of *Jāvīd-nāmeh* is the ascent of the poet, guided by the great 13th-century Persian mystic Jalāl ad-Dīn ar-Rūmī, through all the realms of thought and experience to the final encounter. Iqbāl's later publications of poetry in Urdu were *Bāl-e Jibrīl* (1935; "Gabriel's Wing"), *Zarb-e kalīm* (1937; "The Blow of Moses"), and the posthumous *Armaghān-e Hijāz* (1938; "Gift of the Hejaz"), which contained verses in both Urdu and Persian. He is considered the greatest poet in Urdu of the 20th century.

Iqbāl's philosophical position was articulated in *The Reconstruction of Religious Thought in Islam* (1934), a volume based on six lectures delivered in 1928–29. During this time Iqbāl began working with the Muslim League. In an address to the league in 1930 he made the famous call for the Muslims of northwestern India to demand status as a separate state. In 1940 the Muslim League voted for the establishment of Pakistan, which became a reality in 1947. Iqbāl since has been acclaimed as the father of Pakistan.

ʿIrāqī \'er-ˌō-ˌkē, *Persian* ˮer-\, *in full* Fakhr ad-Dīn Ibrāhīm ʿIrāqī Hamadānī (b. *c.* 1211, Hamadān, Iran—d. November 1289, Damascus [now in Syria])   One of the outstanding poets of 13th-century Persia.

Very little is known about ʿIrāqī's early life. There is evidence that he abandoned a teaching career to follow a group of wandering Ṣūfīs (Muslim mystics) as far as India in search of higher mystical knowledge. After studying for 25 years with his master, Bahāʾ ad-Dīn Zakariyyā, in Multān, he journeyed to the Hejaz and to the city of Konya in Anatolia (now in

Turkey). At Konya he wrote what is considered to be his greatest work, *Kitāb al-lamaʿāt* ("The Book of Light Beams"), a profound work in both poetry and prose. ʿIrāqī later went to Egypt and finally to Syria. A great poet of mystical love, he also is famous for his *Dīvān* ("Collected Poems") and his *ʿUshshāq-nāmeh* (edited and translated by A.J. Arberry as *The Song of The Lovers: ʿUshshāqnāma*), a mystical work written in *maṣnawī* (rhymed couplets) interspersed with ghazels (lyric poems).

Ireland \'īr-lənd\, John, *also called* Johannes de Irlandia \ir-'lan-dē-ə\ (b. *c.* 1435—d. *c.* 1500)   Scottish writer, theologian, and diplomatist, whose treatise *The Meroure of Wyssdome* is the earliest extant example of original Scots prose.

Ireland lived in France until 1483–84, becoming a doctor of theology and being sent on several diplomatic missions by Louis XI. On Louis's death he returned to Scotland and became private chaplain to James III. He was rector of Yarrow and sat in the Scottish parliament. When James died in 1488, he continued as chaplain to the young James IV and in 1490 wrote for his edification the work that is his chief claim to fame, *The Meroure of Wyssdome*, a hortatory and pious treatise on the value of wisdom to temporal rulers.

Irigaray \ē-rē-gȧ-'rä, *Angl* 'ir-i-ˌgar-ē, i-'rig-ə-ˌrä\, Luce (b. 1932?, Belgium)   French feminist psychoanalyst and philosopher who examined the uses and misuses of language in relation to women.

Irigaray was a member of the Freudian School of Paris, founded by Jacques Lacan, and taught at the University of Paris VIII—Vincennes until she was dismissed in 1974 because of her doctoral thesis. Entitled *Speculum de l'autre femme* (*Speculum of the Other Woman*), it argued that history and culture are written in patriarchal language and centered on men, thereby excluding women's needs and desires, and that the thinking of Sigmund Freud was based in misogyny.

Like Irigaray's first book, *Le Langage des déments* (1973; "The Language of the Demented"), *Parler n'est jamais neutre* (1985; "Speaking is Never Neutral") examines the language of schizophrenics, concluding that meaning derives from individual differences in gender, history, and environment. She discusses the mother-daughter relationship and attacks Freud's concept of the Oedipus complex in *Et l'une ne bouge pas sans l'autre* (1979; "And the One Does Not Stir Without the Other"). Her other writings include *Passions élémentaires* (1982; *Elemental Passions*), *L'Ethique de la différence sexuelle* (1984; *An Ethics of Sexual Differences*), *Le Temps de la différence: pour une révolution pacifique* (1989; *Thinking the Difference: For a Peaceful Revolution*), and *Je, tu, nous: pour une culture de la différence* (1990; *Je, tu, nous: Toward a Culture of Difference*).

Iris \'ī-rəs\   In Greek mythology, the personification of the rainbow and a messenger of the gods. According to the Greek poet Hesiod, she carried water from the River Styx for the oath-taking ceremony of the gods. The water would render unconscious for one year any god or goddess who lied.

Irish Literary Renaissance   The flowering of Irish literary talent at the end of the 19th and the beginning of the 20th century that was closely allied with a strong political nationalism and a revival of interest in Ireland's Gaelic literary heritage. The renaissance was inspired by the nationalistic pride of the GAELIC REVIVAL; by the retelling of ancient heroic legends in books such as the two-volume *History of Ireland* (1878, 1880) by Standish O'Grady and *A Literary History of Ireland* (1899) by Douglas Hyde; and by the Gaelic League, which was formed in 1893 to revive the Irish language and culture. The early leaders of the renaissance, most of whom were members of the privileged class, wrote rich and passionate verse, filled with the grandeur of Ireland's past and the music and mysticism of Gaelic poetry.

The movement developed into a vigorous literary force centered on William Butler YEATS. Though he contributed to the foundation of the Irish Literary Theatre (which later developed into the Abbey Theatre, the first Irish national theater), he wrote only a few plays, which were beautiful but difficult to stage. His chief colleague at the Abbey was Isabella Augusta, Lady GREGORY, who wrote many plays, mostly peasant comedies. The greatest dramatist of the movement was John Millington SYNGE, who wrote plays of great beauty and power in a stylized peasant dialect. Later, the theater turned mostly toward rural realism. In reaction to peasant realism, Sean O'Casey wrote three great dramas of the Dublin slums: *The Shadow of a Gunman* (1923), *Juno and the Paycock* (1924), and *The Plough and the Stars* (1926).

The two major poets associated with the movement were Yeats and Æ (George Russell), a mystic, patriot, and agricultural reformer. Notable among their younger contemporaries were Padraic Colum, Austin Clarke, Seumas O'Sullivan (James Sullivan Starkey), F.R. Higgins, and Oliver St. John Gogarty.

Iron, Ralph.   Pseudonym of South African writer Olive SCHREINER.

Iron Heel, The   Novel by Jack LONDON, published in 1908, describing the fall of the United States to the cruel fascist dictatorship of the Iron Heel, a group of monopoly capitalists. Fearing the popularity of socialism, the plutocrats of the Iron Heel conspire to eliminate democracy and, with their secret police and military, terrorize the citizenry. They instigate a German attack on Hawaii on Dec. 4, 1912; as socialist revolutions topple capitalist governments around the world, the Iron Heel has 52 socialist members of the U.S. Congress imprisoned for treason. Elements of London's vision of fascism, civil war, and governmental oppression proved to be prophetic in the first half of the 20th century.

irony \'ī-rə-nē\ [Latin *ironia,* from Greek *eirōneía* feigned ignorance, irony, a derivative of *eírōn* dissembler], *also called* verbal irony.   The use of words to express something other than and especially the opposite of the literal meaning (as when expressions of praise are used where blame is meant). Also, this mode of expression as a literary style or form. Verbal irony arises from a sophisticated or resigned awareness of contrast between what is and what ought to be and expresses a controlled pathos without sentimentality. It is a form of indirection that avoids overt praise or censure. The term *irony* has its roots in the Greek comic character Eiron, a clever underdog who by his wit repeatedly triumphs over the boastful character Alazon.

In drama, irony is produced when the audience has information unknown to the characters. *See also* DRAMATIC IRONY.

irrational \ir-'rash-ə-nəl\   In classical prosody, of or relating to a syllable having a quantity other than that required by the meter, such as a long syllable that takes the place of a short one.

irregular ode   A rhymed ode that follows neither the three-part form of the Pindaric ode nor the two- or four-line stanza that typifies the Horatian ode. It is also called *pseudo-Pindaric ode* or *Cowleyan ode* (after Abraham Cowley). *See also* HORATIAN ODE; ODE; PINDARIC ODE.

Irving \'ər-viŋ\, John (Winslow) (b. March 2, 1942, Exeter, N.H., U.S.)   American novelist and short-story writer who established his reputation with the novel *The World According to Garp* (1978; film, 1982). Characteristic of his other works, it was noted for its engaging story line, colorful characterizations, macabre humor, and examination of contemporary issues.

After graduating from Phillips Exeter Academy, Irving attended the universities of Pittsburgh, Vienna, New Hampshire, and Iowa. He taught until the late 1970s, when he began to write full-time. His early novels—*Setting Free the Bears* (1969), *The Water-Method Man* (1972), and *The 158-Pound Marriage* (1974)—did not achieve the success of *The World According to Garp.* Infused with comedy and violence, his breakthrough book chronicles the tragic life and death of the novelist T.S. Garp. Irving's later novels include *The Hotel New Hampshire* (1981), *The Cider House Rules* (1985), *A Prayer for Owen Meany* (1989), and *A Son of the Circus* (1994); his short-story collection *Nowhere Man* was published in 1992.

Irving \'ər-viŋ\, Washington (b. April 3, 1783, New York, N.Y., U.S.—d. Nov. 28, 1859, Tarrytown, N.Y.)   Writer called the "first American man of letters." He is best known for the short stories THE LEGEND OF SLEEPY HOLLOW and RIP VAN WINKLE.

The favorite and last of 11 children, Irving avoided a college education but intermittently read law. A series of his whimsically satirical essays appeared over the signature of Jonathan Oldstyle, Gent., in the *Morning Chronicle* during 1802–03.

In 1806 he passed the bar examination and soon set up as a lawyer. In 1807–08, however, his chief occupation was the writing (with his brother William and James K. Paulding) of a series of 20 periodical essays entitled SALMAGUNDI.

Irving next wrote A HISTORY OF NEW YORK, a comic history of the Dutch regime in New York, prefaced by a mock-pedantic account of the world from creation onward. He produced little original work for the next decade, then published THE SKETCH BOOK (1819–20), a collection of stories and essays that mix satire and whimsicality with fact and fiction. Its tremendous success in both England and the United States assured Irving that he could live by his pen. In 1822 he produced *Bracebridge Hall,* a sequel to *The Sketch Book.*

Early in 1826 he accepted an invitation to attach himself to the American legation in Spain, where he wrote *Columbus* (1828), followed by *The Companions of Columbus* (1831). Meanwhile, Irving had become absorbed in the legends of the Moorish past and wrote *A Chronicle of the Conquest of Granada* (1829) and *The Alhambra* (1832), a Spanish counterpart of *The Sketch Book.*

After a 17-year absence, Irving returned to New York in 1832, where he was warmly received. He made a journey west and produced in rapid succession *A Tour of the Prairies* (1835), *Astoria* (1836), and *The Adventures of Captain Bonneville* (1837). Except for four years (1842–46) as minister to Spain, Irving spent the remainder of his life at his home on the Hudson River, "Sunnyside" in Tarrytown, where he devoted his time to literary pursuits.

Irzykowski \ē-zhi-'kôf-skᵉē\, Karol (b. Jan. 25, 1873, Błażkowa, near Tarnów, Austro-Hungarian Empire [now in Poland]—d. Nov. 2, 1944, Żyrardów, Pol.)   Polish novelist and literary critic.

Irzykowski joined the editorial board of *Nowa Reforma,* a liberal newspaper in Kraków. After World War I he moved to Warsaw, where he contributed articles and theatrical reviews to *Robotnik,* a socialist daily. During the German occupation of Poland he was active in the Polish underground and died as a result of serious wounds received during the Warsaw Uprising.

Described as one of the most eccentric figures of the Polish Neoromantic literary world, Irzykowski is remembered as the author of *Pałuba* (1903; "The Hag"), a huge novel that combines a penetrating psychological analysis of its characters with a series of digressions on novel writing. Krzykowski's diaries were published in 1964.

Isaac \ˈī-zik, -zək\ In the Old Testament book of Genesis, the second of the patriarchs of Israel, the only son of Abraham and Sarah, and the father of Esau and Jacob. Although Sarah was past the age of childbearing, God promised Abraham and Sarah that they would have a son and Isaac was born. Later, to test Abraham's obedience, God commanded Abraham to sacrifice the boy. Abraham made all the preparations for the ritual sacrifice, but God spared Isaac at the last moment.

Isaacs \ˈī-zəks, *Spanish* ē-ˈsäks\, Jorge (b. April 1, 1837, Cali, Cauca, Colom.—d. April 17, 1895, Ibagué) Colombian poet and novelist whose best work, *María* (1867; *Maria: A South American Romance*), was one of the most famous Latin-American novels of the 19th century.

During the early 1860s, a period of great civil unrest, Isaacs was reduced to poverty by the destruction of his estates. Settling in Bogotá in 1864, he published a slight volume of poetry, *Poesías*, that attracted considerable attention and, in 1867, the romantic, probably autobiographical novel *María*, which won immediate recognition and remains his best-known work.

Ise monogatari \ˈē-se-ˈmō-nō-gä-tä-rē\ ("Tales of Ise") Classical Japanese work of the Heian period (794–1185), written about 980. It is one of the *uta monogatari* ("poem tales") that emerged as a literary genre in the late 10th century and is related to the literary diary form that preceded it. *Ise monogatari* consists of 143 episodes, each containing one or more poems and an explanation in prose of the circumstances of its composition. The brevity and often the ambiguity of the tanka (a five-line, fixed-form verse) gave rise to a need for such explanations, and when these explanations became extended or (as in the case of *Ise monogatari*) were interpreted as biographical information about one poet (Ariwara Narihira), they approached the realm of fiction. The work was published in English as *Tales of Ise*.

Isengrim \ˈē-sən-ˌgrim, -zən-\ or **Ysengrin** \-ˌgrin\ Greedy and dull-witted wolf who is a prominent character in many medieval European beast epics. Often cast as a worldly and corrupt churchman, he appears first as the main character in both the Latin *Ecbasis captivi* (*c.* 940), in which the beasts are unnamed, and under his own name in Nivard of Ghent's *Ysengrimus* (1152). In the first he is represented as a monk to symbolize slothful and degenerate clergy of the period; in one episode of *Ysengrimus* he is tricked into becoming a monk by Reynard the Fox's report of the good food in monasteries. In beast epics written after *Ysengrimus*, Reynard the Fox supplants the wolf as the chief character. In these tales the clever animals have French traits of manner and speech, while the uncouth Isengrim is German.

Iṣfahānī, al- *see* ABŪ AL-FARAJ AL-IṢBAHĀNĪ.

Isherwood \ˈish-ər-ˌwu̇d\, Christopher, *byname of* Christopher William Bradshaw-Isherwood \ˈbrad-ˌshȯ\ (b. Aug. 26, 1904, High Lane, Cheshire, Eng.—d. Jan. 4, 1986, Santa Monica, Calif., U.S.) Anglo-American novelist and playwright best known for his novels about Berlin in the early 1930s.

Isherwood gained recognition with his first two novels, *All the Conspirators* (1928) and *The Memorial* (1932). During the 1930s he collaborated with W.H. Auden on three verse dramas, including THE ASCENT OF F6 (1936). Living in Berlin from 1929 to 1933, he observed the decay of the Weimar Republic and the rise of Nazism; his novels about this period—*Mr. Norris Changes Trains* (1935; U.S. title, *The Last of Mr. Norris*) and *Goodbye to Berlin* (1939), later published together as THE BERLIN STORIES—established his reputation. In 1938 Isherwood published *Lions and Shadows*, an account of his early life and friendships while at the University of Cambridge.

The coming of World War II prompted Isherwood to immigrate to the United States. In 1939 he settled in southern California, where he taught and wrote for Hollywood films. That same year Isherwood turned to pacifism and the self-abnegation of Indian Vedānta, becoming a follower of Swami Prabhavananda. In the following decades, he produced several works on Vedānta and translations with Prabhavananda, including one of the *Bhagavadgītā*.

Isherwood was naturalized in 1946. *A Single Man* (1964), a brief but highly regarded novel, presents a single day in the life of a lonely, middle-aged homosexual. His avowedly autobiographical works include a self-revealing memoir of his parents, *Kathleen and Frank* (1971); a retrospective biography of himself in the 1930s, *Christopher and His Kind* (1977); and a study of his relationship with Prabhavananda and Vedānta, *My Guru and His Disciple* (1980).

Ishiguro \ē-ˈshē-gə̇-rō\, Kazuo (b. Nov. 8, 1954, Nagasaki, Japan) Novelist known for his lyrical tales of regret fused with subtle optimism.

In 1960 Ishiguro's family immigrated to Britain, where he attended the Universities of Kent and East Anglia. He initially gained literary notice when he contributed three short stories to the anthology *Introduction 7: Stories by New Writers* (1981).

Ishiguro's first novel, *A Pale View of Hills* (1982), details the postwar memories of Etsuko, a Japanese woman trying to deal with the suicide of her daughter Keiko. Set in an increasingly Westernized Japan following World War II, *An Artist of the Floating World* (1986) chronicles the life of elderly Masuji Ono, who reviews his past career as a political artist of imperialist propaganda. Ishiguro's Booker Prize-winning *Remains of the Day* (1989; film, 1993) is a first-person narrative, the reminiscences of an elderly English butler whose prim mask of formality has shut him off from understanding and intimacy.

Ishikawa Takuboku \ē-ˈshi-kä-wä-tä-ˈkü-bō-kü\, *original name* Ishikawa Hajime \ˈhä-jē-mä\ (b. Oct. 28, 1886, Hinoto, Iwate prefecture, Japan—d. April 13, 1912, Tokyo) Japanese poet who was a master of tanka (a traditional Japanese verse form) and whose works enjoyed immediate popularity for their freshness and startling imagery.

Through extensive reading Takuboku acquired familiarity with both Japanese and Western literature. He published his first collection of poetry, *Akogare* ("Yearning"), in 1905. In 1908 he settled in Tokyo, where he gradually shifted toward naturalism and eventually turned to politically oriented writing.

In 1910 his first important collection, *Ichiaku no suna* (*A Handful of Sand*), appeared. The 551 poems were written in the traditional tanka form but were expressed in vivid, nontraditional language. Takuboku gave the tanka an intellectual, often cynical, content, though he is also noted for the deeply personal tone of his poetry. In Tokyo he eked out a living as a proofreader and poetry editor of the *Asahi* newspaper. His life during this period is unforgettably described in his diaries, particularly *Rōmaji nikki* (first published in full in 1954; partial trans., *The Romaji Diary*). In this work, which he wrote in Roman letters so that his wife could not read it, Takuboku recorded his complex emotional and intellectual life.

He also published fiction and a collection of poems in nontraditional forms, *Yobuko no fue* (1912; "The Flute"). His *Kanashiki gangu* (1912; *A Sad Toy*) was published posthumously.

Ishmael \ˈish-ˌmā-əl, -mē-\ Fictional character, the hardworking, courageous sailor who narrates the novel MOBY-DICK by Herman Melville.

Opening the story with the words "Call me Ishmael," the narrator—whose real name is not revealed—is a philosophically inclined teacher who takes to the sea whenever he feels restless. Fascinated with the whaling life, he examines in a leisurely, good-humored manner all aspects of life aboard the *Pequod* and further reflects upon theology, morality, free will and destiny, human diversity, and the meaning of the great whale Moby-Dick.

Ishtar \'ish-,tär\ In Mesopotamian mythology, goddess of war and sexual love. Ishtar is the Akkadian counterpart of the West Semitic goddess Astarte. Ishtar's primary legacy from the Sumerian tradition is the role of fertility figure; she evolved, however, into a more complex character, surrounded in myth by death and disaster, a goddess of contradictory connotations and forces: fire and fire-quenching, rejoicing and tears, fair play and enmity. The Akkadian Ishtar is also an astral deity, associated with the planet Venus. In this manifestation she was the protectress of prostitutes and the patroness of the alehouse.

I Sing the Body Electric Poem by Walt WHITMAN, published without a title in *Leaves of Grass* (1855 edition), later appearing as "Poem of the Body," and acquiring its present title in 1867. The poem is a paean to the human form in all its manifestations of soundness. The respective vigors of male and female, youth and age are equally celebrated and ultimately equated with the soul.

Isis \'ī-səs\ One of the most important goddesses of ancient Egypt.

Little is known of Isis' early cult. In the collection of ancient Egyptian prayers, hymns, and spells known as the Pyramid Texts, she is the mourner for her murdered husband, the god Osiris. In her role as the wife of Osiris, she discovered and reunited the pieces of her dead husband's body and through her magical power brought him back to life.

Isis hid her son, Horus, from Seth, the murderer of Osiris, until Horus was fully grown and could avenge his father. But because Isis was also Seth's sister, she wavered during the eventual battle between Horus and Seth. Despite this ambivalence, Isis and Horus were regarded by the Egyptians as the perfect mother and son. Her chief aspect was that of a great magician, whose power transcended that of all other deities. She was invoked on behalf of the sick and was one of the protectors of the dead.

Iskander \i-,skən-'dʸär\, Fazil (Abdulovich) (b. March 6, 1929, Sukhumi, Georgian S.S.R., U.S.S.R. [now in Georgia]) Abkhazian author writing in Russian who used gentle humor to expose and satirize a variety of social ills.

Though Iskander is known mostly for his prose works, he started his career as a poet, publishing five volumes of verse between 1957 and 1964. His first two collections of stories, *Zapretny plod* (*Forbidden Fruit and Other Stories*) and *Trinadtsaty podvig Gerakla* (*The Thirteenth Labor of Heracles*), were published in 1966. His allegory *Kroliki i udavy* (1982; *Rabbits and Boa Constrictors*) was compared to George Orwell's *Animal Farm*.

Iskander's major work of satire was the novel *Sozvezdiye kozlotura* (1966; *The Goatibex Constellation*), which focused on the experiments in agricultural genetics conducted while Nikita Khrushchev led the Soviet Union. Iskander spent many years writing the epic novel *Sandro iz Chegema* (*Sandro of Chegem*), which consists of a series of anecdotes about the life of an Abkhazian folk character named Uncle Sandro. Excerpts from it were published in 1973; then, unable to issue an unabridged version in the Soviet Union, Iskander published a complete Russian-language edition in the West in 1978. Because he contributed to a banned anthology in 1979, his writings were denied circulation in the Soviet Union, but he published additional sections of *Sandro iz Chegema* in the West in 1981. A

version of the book was published in Russia in three volumes in 1989, even though Iskander continued to work on it. *Put* (1987; "The Path") is a selection of his poetry from the 1950s to the 1980s.

Isla \'ēs-lä\, José Francisco de, *surname in full* de Isla de la Torre y Rojo \thä-'ēs-lä-thä-lä-'tôr-rä-ē-'rō-ḳō\, *byname* El Padre Isla \el-'päth-rä-'ēs-lä\ (b. March 24, 1703, Vidanes, Spain—d. Nov. 2, 1781, Bologna, Papal States [Italy]) Spanish satirist and preacher noted for his novel *Fray Gerundio*.

Isla entered the Jesuit order as a novice in 1719, studying at the University of Salamanca. He was named professor of sacred literature in 1727 and taught the subject until 1754, when he retired to begin work on his masterpiece, *Historia del famoso predicador Fray Gerundio de Campazas, alias Zotes* (1758; *History of the Famous Preacher Friar Gerundio of Campazas, alias Zotes*). The work is a brilliant satire on the vain and tastelessly bombastic preaching that predominated in Spanish churches. It provoked a controversy and was banned by the Inquisition in 1760. Father Isla was exiled from Spain with the general expulsion of the Jesuits in 1767. Among his other works is a masterly Spanish translation of *Gil Blas* by the French novelist Alain-René Lesage.

Islwyn *see* William THOMAS.

Ismene \is-'mē-nē\ In Greek mythology, sister of Antigone, Eteocles, and Polyneices and daughter of Oedipus and Jocasta. She is a minor character in Sophocles' *Antigone*, *Oedipus the King*, and *Oedipus at Colonus*.

isochronism \ī-'säk-rə-,niz-əm\ or **isochrony** \ī-'säk-rə-nē\ [Greek *isóchronos* consisting of units equal in duration] Equal duration of prosodic units (such as metrical feet). The term is generally used to describe quantitative (usually classical) verse rather than accentual or syllabic poetry. Some theorists have maintained that isochronism is a natural feature of the English language and thus that two-syllable and three-syllable feet occupy approximately the same amount of time in English.

isocolon \'ī-sə-,kō-lən\ [Greek *isókolon*, from neuter of *isókolos* having equal members] 1. In Greek prosody, a rhythmical unit (period) consisting of single metrical phrases (colons) of equal length. 2. The use of equal colons in immediate succession.

Isocrates \ī-'säk-rə-,tēz\ (b. 436 BC, Athens [Greece]—d. 338, Athens) Ancient Athenian orator, rhetorician, and teacher whose writings are an important historical source for the intellectual and political life of the Athens of his day. He perfected a periodic prose style that, through its influence on Latin style, was widely accepted as a pattern, and he helped give rhetoric its predominance in the educational system of the ancient world.

Isocrates was born into a prosperous family and grew up during the uncertain times that followed the death of Pericles. Having lost his inherited wealth at the close of the Peloponnesian War, he started a career as an speechwriter, then became a teacher.

Isolde *see* TRISTRAM AND ISOLDE.

isometric \,ī-sə-'met-rik\ Of a stanza or a strophe, having lines of equal metrical measure. *Compare* ANISOMETRIC.

Israel Potter \'iz-rē-əl-'pät-ər\ (*in full* Israel Potter: His Fifty Years of Exile) Fictionalized story of an American who fought in the War of Independence and of his subsequent struggles for survival, by Herman MELVILLE. Published serially in 1854–55 in *Putnam's Monthly Magazine* and in 1855 in book form, this short picaresque novel was based on a historical Israel Potter, whose autobiographical narrative Melville had read.

Israel Potter lived a life of adventure, serving bravely as a regular soldier in the American Revolution. Later, he served under John Paul Jones in the new American navy and was a secret courier for Benjamin Franklin. In exile in Europe, Potter lived a poverty-stricken existence. Upon his return to the United States, his request for a pension was denied. He died forgotten and destitute. Melville turned Potter into a picaresque hero and embellished the facts of his life, satirizing his encounters with Franklin and adding a vignette about Ethan Allen.

Issa *see* KOBAYASHI ISSA.

Italian, The (*in full* The Italian, or The Confessional of the Black Penitents. A Romance) Novel by Ann RADCLIFFE, published in three volumes in 1797. A notable example of gothic literature, the novel's great strength is its depiction of the villain, the sinister monk Schedoni.

The main plot concerns the attempts of various characters to prevent the marriage of Vincentio di Vivaldi, a gallant and persistent nobleman, to Ellena di Rosalba, a fair maiden of unknown ancestry. Although Radcliffe avoided supernatural elements in the work, its romantic story line and dramatic suspense are typical of the genre.

Italian sonnet *see* PETRARCHAN SONNET.

It Can't Happen Here Novel by Sinclair LEWIS, published in 1935. It is a cautionary tale about the rise of fascism in the United States.

During the presidential election of 1936, Doremus Jessup, a newspaper editor, observes with dismay that many of the people he knows support the candidacy of a fascist, Berzelius Windrip. When Windrip wins the election, he forcibly gains control of Congress and the Supreme Court, and, with the aid of his personal paramilitary storm troopers, turns the United States into a totalitarian state. Jessup opposes him, is captured, and escapes to Canada.

ithyphallic \,ith-i-'fal-ik \ [Greek *ithyphallikós*, a derivative of *ithýphallos* ode performed at festivals of Bacchus, literally, the erect phallus carried in these festivals] Having a meter typically used in hymns sung at ancient festivals honoring Bacchus; specifically, having the meter of a trochaic dimeter brachycatalectic ($-$ ∪ $-$ ∪ $-$ $-$).

Ivanhoe \'īv-ən-,hō\ Historical romance by Sir Walter SCOTT, published in 1819. It concerns the life of Sir Wilfred of Ivanhoe, a fictional Saxon knight.

Ivanhoe, a chivalrous knight, returns to England from the Crusades. Disinherited by his father for falling in love with Rowena, who was betrothed to another, Ivanhoe travels in disguise, wins a knightly tournament, and accepts the prize from Rowena. In the end, Ivanhoe and Rowena are united, and they leave England for Spain.

Ivanov \ə-'vȧ-nəf\, Vsevolod Vyacheslavovich (b. Feb. 12 [Feb. 24, New Style], 1895, Lebyazhye, Russia—d. Aug. 15, 1963, Moscow, U.S.S.R.) Soviet prose writer noted for his vivid naturalistic realism, one of the most original writers of the 1920s.

Born into a poor family, Ivanov ran away from home to become a clown in a traveling circus. He held many jobs and served in the Red Army during the civil war that followed the Revolution of 1917. In 1920 Ivanov went to Petrograd (St. Petersburg), where he came under the influence of the literary group known as the Serapion Brothers and of Maksim Gorky. Ivanov's graphic stories of the civil war—*Partizany* (1921; "Partisans"), *Bronepoezd 14–69* (1922; *Armoured Train 14–69*), *Tsvetnyye vetra* (1922; "Colored Winds")—quickly established his reputation as a writer. Set in Asiatic Russia, the stories have a distinctive regional flavor.

In the late 1920s Ivanov was required to revise his works in compliance with offical literary policy. In 1927 he reworked *Armoured Train 14–69*—which had been severely criticized for neglecting the role of the Communist Party in the partisan movement—into a play. The drama became one of the classics of the Soviet repertoire. Ivanov's major later works include a collection of tales, *Taynoye taynykh* (1927; "The Secret of Secrets"), and an autobiographical novel, *Pokhozhdeniya fakira* (1934–35; *The Adventures of a Fakir*).

Ivanov \ə-'vȧ-nəf\, Vyacheslav Ivanovich (b. Feb. 16 [Feb. 28, New Style], 1866, Moscow, Russia—d. July 16, 1949, Rome, Italy) Philosopher, classical scholar, and leading poet of the Russian Symbolist movement.

After studying in Moscow and Berlin, Ivanov lived primarily in Italy, where he continued his research and poetry composition. His first volume of lyric poetry, *Kormchiye zvyozdy* ("Pilot Stars"), appeared in 1903, immediately establishing him as a key figure among the Russian Symbolists. Further volumes—*Prozrachnost* (1904; "Translucency"), *Eros* (1907), and *Cor Ardens* (1911), the latter his most important poetical achievement—strengthened his position as high priest of the movement. He returned to Russia in 1905, and from 1905 to 1910 his "Wednesdays" in his St. Petersburg "tower" became an important gathering place of Russian literati. In 1912 he published another important collection of poems, *Nezhnaya tayna* ("The Sweet Secret").

After further sojourns in Europe, Ivanov returned to Moscow in 1913, remaining in Russia throughout World War I and the Revolution of 1917. In 1921 his *Zimniye sonety* ("Winter Sonnets") was published in Berlin, and in 1924 Ivanov left Russia for Rome, where he became a convert to the Roman Catholic church. His sonnet sequence *Rimskiye sonety* (1926; "Roman Sonnets") is a poetic account of this religious experience. Ivanov's later poetic works include the lyrical-philosophical cycle *Chelovek* (1939; "Man") and *Svet vecherniy* (1944; "Evening Light"). He also wrote two poetic dramas, several collections of essays, and a critical study of Mikhail Lermontov. His translations included works by Sappho and Aeschylus.

ivory tower **1.** An impractical, often escapist, attitude marked by aloof lack of concern with or interest in practical matters or urgent problems. **2.** A secluded place that affords the means of viewing practical issues with an impractical, often escapist attitude. The term is used especially of a place of learning. The phrase *ivory tower* is a translation of the French *tour d'ivoire*, used by the critic Charles Sainte-Beuve to refer to the reclusive lifestyle of the poet Alfred de Vigny.

Iwaszkiewicz \ē-vȧsh-'kʸev-ĕch\, Jarosław (b. Feb. 20, 1894, Kalnik, Ukraine, Russian Empire—d. March 2, 1980, Stawisko, near Warsaw, Pol.) Polish poet, novelist, essayist, playwright, and man of letters.

In 1918 Iwaszkiewicz settled in Warsaw, where he was a cofounder of Skamander, a group of lyrical poets. For two years (1923–25) he was private secretary to Maciej Rataj, the Sejm (parliament) speaker, later joining the Ministry of Foreign Affairs. He served as a member at the Polish legations in Copenhagen and Brussels, returning afterwards to writing.

During and after World War II, Iwaszkiewicz avoided political activities. He agreed in 1953, however, to be chairman of the Polish Committee to Defend Peace and a nonparty member of the Sejm. He twice presided over the Polish Writers' Union (1945–49 and 1959–80). From 1955 he was editor in chief of *Twórczość* ("Creation"), a monthly literary periodical.

Iwaszkiewicz's poems, published in such volumes as *Oktostychy* (1919), *Księga dnia i księga nocy* (1922; "The Book of Day and the Book of Night"), and *Wiersze zebrane* (1968; "Collected Poems"), are frequently lyrical evocations of the Polish landscape. His prose—essays, plays, biographies, short stories, novels, and translations—includes the short-story collection *Opowiadania* (1954; "Stories") and the novel *Sława i chwała*, 3 vol. (1956–62; "Fame and Glory"), an examination of the turbulent Polish society from 1914 to 1945.

Iwein \i-'wān\   Middle High German Arthurian epic poem by HARTMANN von Aue, written about 1200. The poem, which is about 8,000 lines long, was based on a work by Chrétien de Troyes. It treats the medieval knight's conflict between private inclination and public responsibility.

The title character, a knight, marries the widowed Queen Laudine with the help of her maid Lunete. Iwein then leaves to pursue his knightly duties, promising to return in one year. When he does not return at the appointed time, Lunete seeks him out and reminds him of his promise. Filled with remorse, Iwein goes mad and wanders in a forest until eventually he regains his senses. In the end he is reunited with Laudine.

Ixion \ik-'sī-ən, 'ik-sē-ən\   In Greek mythology, son either of the god Ares or of Phlegyas, king of the Lapiths in Thessaly. (Some versions suggest other fathers.) He murdered his father-in-law and could find no one to purify him until Zeus did so and admitted him as a guest to Olympus. Ixion abused his pardon by trying to seduce Hera. To test him, Zeus made a cloud in Hera's likeness. Ixion seduced the pseudo-Hera, who conceived and bore the centaurs. Zeus, to punish Ixion for his ingratitude, bound him on a fiery wheel, which rolled unceasingly through the air or, according to another tradition, in the underworld.

Literary references to Ixion include a poem by that name by Robert Browning and a burlesque by Benjamin Disraeli.

Izanagi and Izanami \ē-'zä-nä-gē . . . ē-'zä-nä-mē\ ("He Who Invites and She Who Invites")   The central deities in the Japanese creation myth. They were the eighth pair of brother and sister gods to appear after heaven and earth separated out of chaos. By standing on the floating bridge of heaven and stirring the primeval ocean with a heavenly jeweled spear, they created the first landmass.

Their first attempt at sexual union resulted in a deformed child, Hiruko ("Leech Child," known in later Shintō mythology as the god Ebisu), and they set him adrift in a boat. Attributing the mistake to a ritual error on the part of Izanami, who as a woman should never have spoken first, they began again and produced numerous islands and deities. In the act of giving birth to the fire god, Kagutsuchi (or Homusubi), Izanami was fatally burned and went to Yomi, the land of darkness. Izanagi followed her there, but she had eaten the food of that place and could not leave. She became angry when he lit a fire and saw her rotting and covered with maggots, and the two were divorced.

Izanagi bathed in the sea to purify himself from contact with the dead. As he bathed, a number of deities came into being. The sun goddess Amaterasu was born from his left eye, the moon god Tsukiyomi was born from his right eye, and the storm god Susanoo was born from his nose. In the Shintō religion, Izanagi's bath is regarded as the founding of *harai*, the important purification practices of Shintō.

Izumi \'ē-zū-mē\ Kyōka, *original name* Izumi Kyōtarō \'kyō-,tä-,rō\ (b. Nov. 4, 1873, Kanazawa, Japan—d. Sept. 7, 1939, Tokyo)   Prolific Japanese short-story writer who created his own romantic, often mystical world and peopled it with characters representing his ideal moral values.

Kyōka went to Tokyo in 1890, hoping to be accepted as a disciple of the then leader of the literary scene, Ozaki Kōyō. A year later he was taken in, and he lived with Kōyō's other pupils until 1894. *Yakō junsa* (1895; "Police Night Patrol") and *Gekashitsu* (1895; "Surgical Room") present Kyōka's ideal values in the classic struggle between duty and human emotions. *Kōya hijiri* (1900; *The Saint of Mt. Koya*) exemplifies his fascination with strange and mysterious situations. In 1899 Kyōka met a geisha, whom he later married; stories such as *Onna keizu* (1907; "The Genealogy of Women"), *Uta andon* (1910; *The Song of the Troubadour*), *Shirasagi* (1909; "Snowy Heron"), and *Sannin mekura hanashi* (1912; *A Tale of Three Who Were Blind*) are idealized images of the geisha world. At one time very popular, Kyōka remained aloof from changes in literary taste.

Jabberwock \'jab-ər-,wäk\   Fictional character, a ferocious monster described in the nonsense poem "Jabberwocky," which appears in the novel THROUGH THE LOOKING-GLASS by Lewis Carroll.

jabberwocky \'jab-ər-,wäk-ē\   Nonsensical or unintelligible speech or writing. The term is derived from the poem "Jabberwocky" in Lewis Carroll's *Through the Looking-Glass*, which begins:

> 'Twas brillig, and the slithy toves
>   Did gyre and gimble in the wabe;
> All mimsy were the borogroves,
>   And the mome raths outgrabe.

J'accuse \zhȧ-'kǖz\   Celebrated open letter by Émile ZOLA to the president of the French Republic in defense of Alfred Dreyfus, a Jewish officer who had been accused of treason by the French army. It was published in the newspaper *L'Aurore* on Jan. 13, 1898. The letter, which began with the denunciatory phrase "*J'accuse*" ("I accuse"), blamed the army for covering up its mistaken conviction of Dreyfus. It was instrumental in generating public response to what became known as the Dreyfus Affair. Zola was brought to trial on Feb. 7, 1898, and was sentenced to one year's imprisonment and a fine of 3,000 francs after being found guilty of libel. As a result of the new attention focused on the affair, Dreyfus underwent a new court martial.

Jacinto \zhä-'sē^n-tü\, António, *byname of* António Jacinto do Amaral Martins \dü-ȧ-'mȧ-rəl-mär-'tē^nsh\, *pseudonym* Orlando Tavora \tä-'vō-rə\ (b. Sept. 28, 1924, São Paulo de Luanda, Portuguese West Africa [now Luanda, Angola]—d. June 23, 1991, Lisbon, Port.)   White Angolan poet, short-story writer, and nationalist leader who campaigned for Angolan solidarity and independence from Portugal through political action and powerful lyric poetry.

The son of Portuguese settlers in Angola, Jacinto became associated with militant movements against Portuguese colonial rule. He contributed militant anticolonial poetry, often under his pseudonym, to Angolan magazines and newspapers. His first verse collection, *Colectânea de poemas*, was published in Lisbon in 1961, the same year he was arrested. He served 14 years in a prison camp at Tarrafal in the Cape Verde Islands, an experience he later described in *Sobrevivir em Tarrafal de Santiago* (1982; "Surviving in Tarrafal de Santiago").

Jackson \'jak-sən\, Helen (Maria) Hunt, *original surname* Fiske \'fisk\ (b. Oct. 15, 1830, Amherst, Mass., U.S.—d. Aug. 12, 1885, San Francisco, Calif.)   American poet and novelist best known for her novel *Ramona* (1884).

She turned to writing after the deaths of her first husband, Captain Edward Hunt, and her two sons. She later married William Jackson and moved to Colorado. A prolific writer, Jackson is remembered primarily for her efforts on behalf of American Indians. *A Century of Dishonor* (1881) arraigned government Indian policy; her subsequent appointment to a federal commission investigating the plight of Indians on missions provided material for *Ramona*. The novel aroused public sentiment but has been admired chiefly for its romantic picture of old California.

Jackson \'jak-sən\, Shirley (Hardie) (b. Dec. 14, 1916, San Francisco, Calif., U.S.—d. Aug. 8, 1965, North Bennington, Vt.)   American novelist and short-story writer best known for her story THE LOTTERY (1948).

Jackson graduated from Syracuse University, N.Y., in 1940 and married the American literary critic Stanley Edgar Hyman. *Life Among the Savages* (1953) and *Raising Demons* (1957) are fictionalized memoirs about their life with their four children. Their light, comic tone contrasts sharply with the dark pessimism of Jackson's other works. "The Lottery," a chilling tale whose meaning has been much debated, provoked widespread public outrage when it was first published in *The New Yorker* in 1948. Jackson's six finished novels, especially *The Haunting of Hill House* (1959) and *We Have Always Lived in the Castle* (1962), further established her reputation as a master of gothic horror and psychological suspense.

Jack the Ripper \'jak\   Pseudonymous murderer of at least seven women, all prostitutes, in or near the Whitechapel district of London's East End, from Aug. 7 to Nov. 10, 1888. One of the most famous unsolved mysteries of English crime, the case has retained its hold on the popular imagination.

Jack the Ripper has provided themes for numerous literary and dramatic works. Perhaps the most notable was *The Lodger* (1913), a horror novel by Mrs. Belloc Lowndes.

Jacob \'jā-kəb\ (*Hebrew* Ya'aqov, *Arabic* Ya'qūb), *also called* Israel \'iz-rē-əl, -rā-\ (*Hebrew* Yisra'el, *Arabic* Isrā'īl)   Hebrew patriarch who was the grandson of Abraham, the son of Isaac and Rebekah, and the traditional ancestor of the people of Israel.

According to the Hebrew scripture, Jacob was the younger twin brother of Esau, who was the ancestor of Edom and the Edomites. After obtaining his brother's birthright from their father by means of an elaborate deception, Jacob fled from his angry brother and settled among kinfolk in Mesopotamia. He fell in love with his cousin Rachel and contracted to work for his uncle Laban for seven years to obtain her hand in marriage. When Rachel's older sister Leah was substituted at the wedding ceremony, Jacob was required to work another seven years for Rachel. Staying on for several more years, Jacob amassed a large amount of property; he then set out with his wives and children to return to Palestine. On the way Jacob wrestled with a mysterious stranger, a divine being who changed Jacob's name to

Israel. Jacob then met and was reconciled with Esau and settled in Canaan. Jacob had 13 children, 10 of whom were founders of tribes of Israel.

Jacob \zhä-'kòb\, Max (b. July 12, 1876, Quimper, Fr.—d. March 5, 1944, Drancy)   Poet who played a decisive role in the new directions of early 20th-century French poetry.

Jacob left his native Brittany in 1894 to go to Paris, where he became an important figure in Montmartre during the formative period of Cubism. Jacob converted to Christianity in 1909 and became a Roman Catholic in 1915. In 1921 he retired into semimonastic seclusion at Saint Benoît-sur-Loire. During World War II he was interned in the concentration camp at Drancy, near Paris, where he died.

Outstanding in his voluminous production are *Le Cornet à dés* (1917; "Dice Box"), a collection of prose poems in the Surrealist manner; *Le Laboratoire central* (1921), "stoppered phials" of lyrical poetry; and his Breton *Poèmes de Morvan le Gaëlique* (1953). *La Défense de Tartufe* (1919), which with the novel *Saint Matorel* (1909) describes his religious experience, *Le Sacrifice impérial* (1929), and his *Correspondance* (1953–55) show his unrelenting self-examination, his fantasy, and his verbal clowning, which concealed the profound torment of a convert, fearful of damnation and longing for heaven.

Jacobean \jak-ə-'bē-ən\ [New Latin *Jacobus* James]   Of or relating to the reign of James I of England (1603–25), or to the writers or literature of his time.

Many of the themes and patterns of Jacobean literature were carried over from the preceding Elizabethan era. Though rich, Jacobean literature is often darkly questioning. William Shakespeare's greatest tragedies were written between about 1600 and 1607. Other Jacobean dramatic writers became preoccupied with the problem of evil; the plays of John Webster, Cyril Tourneur, Thomas Middleton, and William Rowley induce all the terror of tragedy but little of its pity. Comedy was best represented by the acid satire of Ben Jonson and by the varied works of Francis Beaumont and John Fletcher. Another feature of drama at this time, however, was the development of the extravagant courtly entertainment known as the masque. Jonson's comparatively lucid and graceful verse and the writings of his Cavalier successors constituted one of the two main streams of Jacobean poetry. The other poetic stream lay in the intellectual complexity of John Donne and the Metaphysical poets. In prose, Francis Bacon and Robert Burton were among the writers who displayed a new toughness and flexibility of style. The monumental prose achievement of the era was the great King James Version of the Bible, which first appeared in 1611.

Jacobs \'jā-kəbz\, Joseph (b. Aug. 29, 1854, Sydney, N.S.W. [Australia]—d. Jan. 30, 1916, Yonkers, N.Y., U.S.)   Australian-born English folklore scholar and one of the most popular 19th-century adapters of children's fairy tales.

After attending primary school in Sydney, Jacobs immigrated to England in 1872. He graduated from the University of Cambridge in 1876 and between 1882 and 1900 was secretary of the Russo-Jewish Committee (London), formed to improve the social and political conditions of Jews in Russia. He edited the journal *Folk-Lore* from 1889 to 1900. In 1900 he immigrated with his family to the United States, where he worked as revising editor of the *Jewish Encyclopedia*.

A prolific author, Jacobs is generally best known for such scholarly and popular works on folklore as *English Fairy Tales* (1890), *Celtic Fairy Tales* (1892), *Indian Fairy Tales* (1892), *The Fables of Aesop* (1894), *The Book of Wonder Voyages* (1896), and *Europa's Fairy Book* (1916).

Jacobs \'jā-kəbz\, W.W., *in full* William Wymark (b. Sept. 8, 1863, London, Eng.—d. Sept. 1, 1943, London)   English short-story writer best known for his classic horror story THE MONKEY'S PAW (1902).

Jacobs drew on his boyhood memories of seafaring men and dockworkers to create the stories that were to establish him as a writer. His first volume, *Many Cargoes* (1896), had an immediate success and was followed by two others, *The Skipper's Wooing* (1897) and *Sea Urchins* (1898). "The Monkey's Paw," a tale of superstition and terror unfolding within a realistic setting of domestic warmth and coziness, is an example of Jacobs' ability to combine everyday life and gentle humor with exotic adventure and dread. An omnibus, *Snug Harbour*, containing some 17 volumes of Jacobs' work, was published in 1931.

Jacobsen \ˈyä-kŏp-sən\, Jens Peter (b. April 7, 1847, Thisted, Jutland, Den.—d. April 30, 1885, Thisted) Danish novelist and poet who inaugurated the naturalist movement in Denmark and was himself its most famous representative.

While at the University of Copenhagen, Jacobsen heard the lectures of Georg Brandes, an advocate of realism, naturalism, and socially conscious art. Jacobsen's story collection *Mogens* (1872) is considered the first naturalist writing in Danish literature and was greatly admired by Brandes. Jacobsen's first novel, *Fru Marie Grubbe* (1876), is a psychological study of a 17th-century woman whose natural instincts are stronger than her social instincts, resulting in her descent on the social scale from a viceroy's consort to the wife of a ferryman. *Niels Lyhne* (1880), his second novel, is a contemporary story of a man's vain struggle to acquire a philosophy of life. His poems were collected and published posthumously in 1886.

Jacobson \ˈjā-kəb-sən\, Dan (b. March 7, 1929, Johannesburg, S.Af.) South African-born novelist and short-story writer.

Jacobson was the son of eastern European Jewish immigrants. After graduation from the University of Witwatersrand, he worked in public relations and in the family cattle-feed milling business. He then lived and worked in Israel before going to live in England in 1954.

In England he wrote with both humor and pathos of his troubled land of birth. His first novels—*The Trap* (1955), *A Dance in the Sun* (1956), and *The Price of Diamonds* (1957)—form a complex mosaic that provides a peculiarly incisive view of racially divided South African society. Much of his best work is in his short stories, especially in the collections *The Zulu and the Zeide* (1959) and *Beggar My Neighbor* (1964).

With *The Beginners* (1965), a long generational novel paralleling his own family history, Jacobson began to withdraw from writing about South Africa. *The Rape of Tamar* (1970) is a biblical novel, and *The Confessions of Josef Baisz* (1977) is set in a country only "something like" South Africa. His later novels, *Her Story* (1987) and *Hidden In the Heart* (1991), continue to make use of both his political consciousness and his gift for irony.

Jacob's Room \ˈjā-kəb\ Impressionistic novel by Virginia WOOLF, published in 1922. Experimental in form, it centers on the character of Jacob Flanders, a lonely young man unable to synthesize his love of classical culture with the chaotic reality of contemporary society, notably the turbulence of World War I.

The novel is an examination of character development and the meaning of a life by means of a series of brief impressions and conversations, stream of consciousness, internal monologue, and Jacob's letters to his mother. In zealous pursuit of classicism, Jacob studies the ancients at Cambridge and travels to Greece. He either idealizes or ignores the women who admire him. At the end of the novel all that remains of Jacob's life are scattered objects in an abandoned room.

Jacopo da Lentini. *see* GIACOMO da Lentini.

Jacopone da Todi \yä-kō-ˈpō-nä-dä-ˈtō-dē\, *original name* Jacopo dei Benedetti \ˈyä-kō-pō-ˌdä-bä-nä-ˈdet-tē\ (b. *c.* 1230, Todi, Duchy of Spoleto [Italy]—d. Dec. 25, 1306, Collazzone) Italian religious poet, author of more than 100 mystical poems of great power and originality.

Jacopone practiced law until his wife's sudden death in about 1268 precipitated his conversion to an ascetic life. He disposed of his belongings, dedicated himself to God, and in 1278 became a lay brother of the Franciscan order. When he wrote violent satirical verse against Pope Boniface VIII and then signed the manifesto that declared Boniface's election invalid, Boniface retaliated by first excommunicating and then, in 1298, imprisoning him. After Boniface died in 1303, Jacopone was released.

Most of Jacopone's poetic work is in the Italian vernacular. A notable exception is the Latin *lauda* ("canticle") *Stabat mater dolorosa* that has long been attributed to him. His many *laudi spirituali*, some written during his imprisonment, are vivid and original outpourings of many moods, ranging from bitter anger to mystical ecstasy.

Jæger \ˈyeg-er\, Hans Henrik (b. Sept. 2, 1854, Drammen, Nor.—d. Feb. 8, 1910, Kristiania [now Oslo]) Novelist, ultranaturalist, and leader of the Norwegian "Bohème," a group of urban artists and writers in revolt against conventional morality.

An advocate of sexual freedom, Jæger believed that the restrictions and frustrations of monogamy were a source of social evil. In 1885 he created a sensation with his novel *Fra Kristiania-Bohêmen* ("From Bohemian Kristiania"), which was confiscated as pornography. Although his novel was of no literary merit, it became a cause célèbre, dividing the Norwegian literary world between champions of freedom of speech and advocates of good taste and high standards.

Jaggers, Mr. \ˈjag-ərz\ Fictional character in the novel GREAT EXPECTATIONS by Charles Dickens. Mr. Jaggers is the honest and pragmatic lawyer who handles the affairs of most of the characters in the book.

Jāḥiẓ, al- \ˈäl-ˈzhä-ketḥ\, *in full* Abū ʿUthmān ʿAmr ibn Baḥr ibn Maḥbūb al-Jāḥiẓ (b. *c.* 776, Basra, Iraq—d. 868/869, Basra) Islāmic theologian, intellectual, and litterateur known for his individual and masterful Arabic prose.

During the reign of the caliph al-Maʾmūn (813–833), al-Jāḥiẓ moved to the capital, Baghdad, where he supported himself, at least in part, with contributions from patrons, often of high rank, in return for the dedications of his books.

Few of his treatises on theology and politics are extant; some are known only from quotations by other authors. His prose masterpieces, however, have survived intact. They take the form of essays that are at the same time anthologies in which poetry, jokes, and anecdotes—however obscure or daring—were introduced by al-Jāḥiẓ to illustrate his points. His unfinished *Kitāb al-ḥayawān* ("Animals"), in seven volumes, is a bestiary drawing on Aristotle and also an anthology of Arabic literature with animal themes to which theological, sociological, and linguistic discussions have been added. *Kitāb al-bayān wa al-tabyīn* ("Elegance of Expression and Clarity of Exposition"), another long work, treats literary style and the effective use of language. *Kitāb al-bukhalāʾ* ("Book of Misers") is a collection of stories about the avaricious. Al-Jāḥiẓ, in effect, provides in his works an entire education in the humanities of his time.

Jalāl ad-Dīn ar-Rūmī *see* RŪMĪ.

Jamalzadeh \ˈjam-ˌŏl-ˌzŏ-deh\, Mohammad Ali, *Persian* Moḥammad ʿAlī Jamālzādeh, Jamalzadeh *also transliterated* Jamalzada, Jamāl-Zādeh, *or* Jamālzādah (b. 1892, Eṣfahān [Isfahan], Iran) Prose writer who became one of the most important figures in 20th-century Persian literature.

Jamalzadeh was educated in Beirut and in Europe. After studying law in France, he went to Berlin and wrote for the respected periodical *Kāva*; there he published his early stories and historical pieces. His first successful story was "Farsi shakar ast" ("Persian Is Sugar"), which was reprinted in 1921/22 in *Yakī būd yakī nabūd* (*Once Upon a Time*), a collection of short stories that laid the foundation for modern Persian prose. The collection caused a great stir, not only because of its innovative prose style, modern diction, and use of colloquial Persian but also for its satirical, outspoken criticism of society.

For the next 20 years Jamalzadeh pursued a nonliterary career. Most of Jamalzadeh's writing was done during and after World War II. His satirical novel *Dār al-majānīn* (1942; "The Madhouse") was followed by the novel *Qultashan-e dīvān* (1946; "The Custodian of the Divan"), a scathing attack on contemporary Iranian values and culture. Other important works include *Rāh-ye āb-nāmeh* (1947; "The Story of the Water Channel") and memoirs of his early years in Eṣfahān, *Sar ū tah-ye yak karbās yā Eṣfahān-nāmeh* (1956; "The Beginning and End of a Web, or the Book of Eṣfahān," translated as *Isfahan Is Half the World: Memories of a Persian Boyhood*). Jamalzadeh also wrote historical, sociopolitical, and economic works.

James \\'jāmz\\, Henry (b. April 15, 1843, New York, N.Y., U.S.—d. Feb. 28, 1916, London, Eng.) American novelist and, as a naturalized English citizen from 1915, a great figure in transatlantic culture. His fundamental theme was the innocence and exuberance of the New World in conflict with the corruption and wisdom of the Old.

Smith College Archives

James grew up in Manhattan but also spent much of his childhood abroad. After briefly attending Harvard Law School, he devoted himself to literature, publishing his first story at the age of 21. When William Dean Howells became editor of *The Atlantic Monthly*, James found in him a friend and mentor. Between them, James and Howells inaugurated the era of American realism.

James made the first of many trips to Europe as an adult in 1869, and within five years he had decided to live abroad permanently. Thus began his long expatriation, heralded by publication in 1876 of the novel RODERICK HUDSON; *Transatlantic Sketches*—his first collection of travel writings—and a collection of tales. During 1875–76 James lived in Paris, writing literary and topical letters for the *New York Tribune* and working on his novel THE AMERICAN (1877). Late in 1876 he crossed to London, where he later was to write the major fiction of his middle years. In 1878 he achieved international renown with his story of an American flirt in Rome, DAISY MILLER (1879), and he further enhanced his prestige with *The Europeans* that same year.

James's reputation was founded on his versatile studies of "the American girl." In a series of witty tales he pictured the "self-made" young woman, the bold and brash American innocent who insists upon American standards in European society. James ended this first phase of his career by producing his masterpiece, THE PORTRAIT OF A LADY (1881).

In the middle phase of his career, James wrote two novels dealing with social reformers and revolutionaries, THE BOSTONIANS (1886) and THE PRINCESS CASAMASSIMA (1886). These were followed by THE TRAGIC MUSE (1890), in which James projected a study of the London and Paris art studios and the stage. After a failed attempt to win success as a playwright, James spent several years seeking to adapt the techniques of drama to his fiction (as evidenced by WASHINGTON SQUARE [1880]). The result was a complete change in his storytelling methods. In THE SPOILS OF POYNTON (1897), WHAT MAISIE KNEW (1897), THE TURN OF THE SCREW (1898), and THE AWKWARD AGE (1899), James began to use the methods of alternating "picture" and dramatic scene, close adherence to a given angle of vision, and a withholding of information from the reader, presenting only that which the characters see.

The experiments of this "transition" phase led to three great novels that represent James's final phase: THE WINGS OF THE DOVE (1902), THE AMBASSADORS (1903), and THE GOLDEN BOWL (1904). James's other major works include the essay THE ART OF FICTION (1884), the novelette THE ASPERN PAPERS (1888), and the short story THE BEAST IN THE JUNGLE (1903).

James \\'jāmz\\, P.D., *byname of* Phyllis Dorothy James, Baroness James, *married name* White \\'wīt, 'hwīt\\ (b. Aug. 3, 1920, Oxford, Oxfordshire, Eng.) British mystery novelist best known for her fictional detective Adam Dalgliesh of Scotland Yard.

In 1941 James married a medical student, who came home from wartime service mentally deranged and spent much of the rest of his life in psychiatric hospitals. To support her family (which included two children), she took work in hospital administration and, after her husband's death in 1964, became a civil servant in the criminal section of the Department of Home Affairs. Her first mystery novel, *Cover Her Face*, appeared in 1962 and was followed by six more mysteries before she retired from government service in 1979 to devote her time to writing.

James is noted for the strength of her characterizations and for her acute sense of atmosphere. Among the books featuring Dalgliesh are *Unnatural Causes* (1967), *The Black Tower* (1975), and *Devices and Desires* (1989). James also wrote several books featuring a young detective named Cordelia Gray, including *An Unsuitable Job for a Woman* (1972) and *The Skull Beneath the Skin* (1982). Also notable is *Innocent Blood* (1980).

Jāmī \\'jȯ-,mē\\, *in full* Mowlanā Nūr od-Dīn 'Abd or-Raḥmān ebn Aḥmad (b. Nov. 7, 1414, district of Jam [Afghanistan]—d. Nov. 9, 1492, Herāt, Timurid Afghanistan) Persian scholar, mystic, and poet who is often regarded as the last great mystical poet of Iran.

Jāmī spent most of his life in Herāt. During his lifetime his fame as a scholar resulted in offers of patronage by many contemporary Islāmic rulers. He declined most of these offers, preferring the simple life of a mystic and scholar to that of a court poet. His prose deals with a variety of subjects ranging from Qur'ānic commentaries to treatises on Ṣūfism (Islāmic mysticism) and music. Perhaps the most famous is his mystical treatise *Lava'iḥ* (*Flashes of Light*), a clear and precise exposition of the Ṣūfī doctrines of *waḥdat al-wujūd* (the existential unity of being), together with a commentary on the experiences of other famous mystics.

Jāmī's poetical works express his ethical and philosophical doctrines. His poetry is fresh and graceful and is not marred by unduly esoteric language. His most famous collection of poetry is a seven-part compendium entitled *Haft Awrang* ("The Seven Thrones," or "Ursa Major").

Jammes \\zhäm\\, Francis (b. Dec. 2, 1868, Tournay, Fr.—d. Nov. 1, 1938, Hasparren, near Bayonne) French poet and novelist whose simple rustic themes were a contrast to the decadent element in French literature of the turn of the century.

Jammes's poetry reacted against Symbolism and followed a new poetic trend known as naturism. It urged a return to nature, to the small daily happenings of life, to a childlike simplicity. He first attracted attention with *De l'Angélus de l'aube à l'Angélus du soir* (1898; "From the Morning Angelus to the Evening Angelus"). His conversion to Roman Catholicism (1905), under the guidance of the poet Paul Claudel, led him to a growing piety. *Les Géorgiques chrétiennes*, 3 vol. (1911–12; "The Christian Georgics"), is the saga of a religious peasant family told in everyday language. Short stories, novels, and his memoirs (published in 1923) complete his literary production, all written in the same pastoral and intimate tone.

Jane Eyre \\'jän-'är\\ Novel by Charlotte BRONTË, first published in 1847 under the pseudonym Currer Bell.

The title character of the novel is a strong-willed orphan who, after surviving several miserable years at a charity school,

Illustration by Fritz Eichenberg for an American edition of *Jane Eyre*

becomes the governess to a ward of the mysterious Mr. Rochester. She and Mr. Rochester fall in love, but before they can be married it is revealed that he is already married and that his wife, who is insane, is confined in the attic of the estate. Jane leaves but is ultimately reunited with Mr. Rochester after learning of the death of his wife.

Jean Rhys's novel *Wide Sargasso Sea* (1966) offers an account of Mr. Rochester's first marriage.

Janeite or **Janite** \\'jā-,nīt\\ An enthusiastic admirer of the writings of Jane Austen.

Jansson \\'yän-sȯn\\, Tove (Marika) (b. Aug. 9, 1914, Helsinki, Fin., Russian Empire) Finnish artist and writer-illustrator of children's books in Swedish. In her books Jansson created the fantastic self-contained world of Moomintrolls.

Her comic strip "Moomin" ran in the *Evening News*, London, from 1953 to 1960. Her Moomin world was praised for its individualistic characters, complicated plots, and sophisticated humor. Jansson won several national awards for her children's books.

Her first book, *Småtrollen och den stora översvämningen* ("The Small Trolls and the Large Flood"), was published in 1945. This was followed by the first of many Moomin books, *Kometjakten* (1945; *Comet in Moominland*). She also wrote two plays for children, an autobiography (*Bildhuggarens dotter*, 1968; *Sculptor's Daughter*), short stories, and adult fiction.

Janus \\'jā-nəs\\ In Roman religion, the animistic spirit of doorways (*januae*) and archways (*jani*). The worship of Janus was traditionally dated to Romulus and to a period even before the actual founding of the city of Rome.

Some scholars regard Janus as the god of all beginnings and believe that his association with doorways is derivative. He was invoked as the first of any gods in regular liturgies. The beginning of the day, month, and year were sacred to him. The month of January is named for him. Janus was usually represented in art by a double-faced head.

Jaques \\'jāks, 'jaks, *in Shakespeare's work* 'jāks, 'jā-kis, *commonly* 'jāk-wiz, -wēz\\ Fictional character, a cynical and philosophical nobleman in the entourage of the banished Duke in William Shakespeare's pastoral comedy AS YOU LIKE IT.

Jarīr \\zhȧ-'rēr\\, *in full* Jarīr ibn ʿAṭīyah ibn al-Khaṭafā (b. *c.* 650, Uthayfiyah, Yamāmah region, Arabia [now in Saudi Arabia]—d. *c.* 729, Yamāmah) One of the greatest Arab poets of the Umayyad period (661–750), whose career and poetry show the continued vitality of the pre-Islāmic Bedouin tradition.

Jarīr's special skill lay in poems insulting personal rivals or the enemies of his patrons. After sharp verbal clashes in Arabia in defense of Kulayb, his tribe, Jarīr moved to Iraq. There he won the favor of the governor, al-Ḥajjāj, and wrote a number of poems in his praise. He also met the poet al-Farazdaq, with whom he had already begun a battle of poems that is said to have lasted 40 years. The results were collected in the following century as *naqāʾid* ("slanging-matches on parallel themes"). The governor's goodwill earned Jarīr entry at the Umayyad court in Damascus. Jarīr was not able, however, to dislodge the poet al-Akhṭal from the esteem of the caliph ʿAbd al-Malik, and another poetic battle ensued, also producing *naqāʾid*.

Many of Jarīr's satires and panegyrics are in the conventional qasida (ode) form, usually consisting of a travel account sandwiched between a love poem as prologue and a panegyric as conclusion. Jarīr also wrote elegies, wisdom poetry, and epigrams.

Jarndyce family \\'järn-,dīs\\ Among the principal characters of the novel BLEAK HOUSE by Charles Dickens. The dreary, seemingly endless *Jarndyce* v. *Jarndyce* lawsuit contesting a will provides the background for the novel.

Jarnés \\kär-'näs\\, Benjamín, *surname in full* Jarnés y Millán \\ē-mēl-'yän\\ (b. Oct. 7, 1888, Codo, Spain—d. Aug. 11, 1949, Madrid) Spanish novelist and biographer.

Jarnés served in the army from 1910 to 1920, after which he settled in Madrid. His first novel was *Mosén Pedro* (1924), but his reputation was established by his second book, *El profesor inútil* (1926; "The Useless Professor"), a series of episodes with little narrative action that point out a professor's ineptitude and inability to tell reality from unreality. Similar motifs occur in *El convidado de papel* (1928; "The Paper Guest"). In 1929 Jarnés joined the editorial board of *La Gaceta literaria* ("The Literary Gazette") and began to write biographies. He continued to write novels, such as the surrealistic *Teoría del zumbel* (1930; "Theory of the Top-Spinning String"). During the Spanish Civil War he fled to Mexico, where he continued to write fiction but devoted increasing attention to biographies of such people as Stefan Zweig and Miguel de Cervantes, as well as Mexican literary figures. In 1948 he returned to Spain.

Jarrell \ja-'rel\, Randall (b. May 6, 1914, Nashville, Tenn., U.S.—d. Oct. 14, 1965, Chapel Hill, N.C.) American poet, novelist, and critic who is noted for revitalizing the reputations of Robert Frost, Walt Whitman, and William Carlos Williams in the 1950s.

Childhood was one of the major themes of Jarrell's verse, and he wrote about his own extensively in *The Lost World* (1965). In 1942 he joined the U.S. Army Air Forces, and his first book of verse, *Blood for a Stranger*, was published. Many of his best poems appeared in *Little Friend, Little Friend* (1945) and *Losses* (1948), both of which dwell on his wartime experiences.

Jarrell taught at Sarah Lawrence College, Bronxville, N.Y. (1946–47), and his only novel, the sharply satirical *Pictures from an Institution* (1954), is about a similar progressive girls' college. He was a teacher at the University of North Carolina at Greensboro from 1947 until his death.

Jarrell's criticism has been collected in *Poetry and the Age* (1953), *A Sad Heart at the Supermarket* (1962), and *The Third Book of Criticism* (1969). Jarrell's later poetry collections include *The Seven-League Crutches* (1951), *The Woman at the Washington Zoo* (1960), and *The Lost World*. His *Complete Poems* appeared in 1969.

Jarry \zhȧ-'rē\, Alfred (b. Sept. 8, 1873, Laval, Fr.—d. Nov. 1, 1907, Paris) French writer known mainly as the creator of the grotesque and wild satirical farce UBU ROI (1896; "King Ubu"), which was a forerunner of the Theater of the Absurd.

A brilliant youth who had gone to Paris at 18 to live on a small family inheritance, Jarry frequented the literary salons and began to write. His fortune was soon dissipated, and he lapsed into a chaotic and anarchic existence in which he met the demands of day-to-day life with self-conscious buffoonery.

Ubu roi was presented on Dec. 10, 1896, at the Théâtre de l'Oeuvre. The main character is the grotesque and repulsive Père Ubu, who becomes king of Poland. Jarry's sequels to *Ubu roi* included *Ubu enchaîné* (1900; "Ubu Bound") and *Ubu cocu* (published posthumously in 1944; "Ubu Cuckolded").

Jarry also published stories, novels, and poems, but the brilliant imagery and wit of these works usually lapse into incoherence and a meaningless and often scatological symbolism.

Jasmin \zhȧs-'maⁿ\, Jacques, *pseudonym of* Jacques Boé \bō-'ā\ (b. March 6, 1798, Agen, Fr.—d. Oct 4, 1864, Agen) French dialect poet who achieved popular fame for his touching verse portraits of humble people and places.

Jasmin spent most of his life as a barber and wigmaker in his native southern France. His first collection of poems, *Lou chilibari* (1825; "Tin-Kettle Music"), was followed, beginning in 1835, by four volumes of *Las papilhôtos* ("Curl-papers"); in addition to a few poems written cautiously in French, they contained his better works, written in Occitan, his native dialect. Included in this collection was a poem of great pathos—"L'Abuglo de Castel-Culié" ("The Blind Girl of Casterculier")—which captured the public imagination after Jasmin began public readings and singings in Toulouse and Bordeaux. Some of his major poems include "Mous soubenis" (1835; "Souvenirs"), "Françouneto" (1840; "Franconette"), and "Maltro l'Innoucento" (1844; "Maltro the Simple").

Jason \'jās-ən\ In Greek mythology, leader of the Argonauts and son of Aeson, king of Iolcos in Thessaly. According to legend, Aeson's throne had been usurped by his half brother Pelias, and Jason was sent to stay with the centaur Chiron for protection. Returning as a young man to claim his inheritance, Jason was assured that he would receive it if he fetched the Golden Fleece (which was guarded by a sleepless dragon) for Pelias.

Jason embarked for Colchis, where the fleece was kept, with 50 of the noblest heroes of Greece in the ship *Argo*. They met with a number of adventures along the way, and when they finally reached Colchis, they found that the king, Aëtes (Aeetes), would not give up the fleece until Jason yoked the king's fire-snorting bulls to a plow and plowed the field of Ares. That accomplished, the field was to be sown with the dragon's teeth, from which armed men were to spring. Aëtes' daughter, the sorceress MEDEA, who had fallen in love with Jason, helped him accomplish these tasks, but Aëtes still refused to give over the fleece. Medea, however, put the dragon to sleep, and Jason was able to abscond with the fleece and Medea. Eventually the *Argo* reached Iolcos. *See also* ARGONAUT.

On their return Medea murdered Pelias, but she and Jason were driven out by Pelias' son and had to take refuge with King Creon of Corinth. They had two sons. Later Jason deserted Medea for Creon's daughter; this desertion and its consequences formed the subject of Euripides' *Medea*. Jason died at Corinth.

Jastrun \'yȧ-strün\, Mieczysław (b. Oct. 29, 1903, Korolówka, near Tarnopol, Austro-Hungarian Empire [now Ternopol, Ukraine]—d. Feb. 23, 1983, Warsaw, Pol.) Polish poet and essayist.

Jastrun received his doctorate in Polish literature at the Jagiellonian University of Kraków. The dozen volumes of poems that he published between the two world wars show his growth from an imitator of the poets of the Skamander group to an independent and mature poet with a mastery of form. He survived World War II by remaining in hiding in Warsaw. His wartime poems were published in 1944 under the title *Godzina strzeżona* ("A Curfew Hour"), but his best poems—for instance, *Gorący popiół* (1956; "Hot Ashes") and *Genezy* (1959; "Genesis")—were written after the "thaw" of 1956, a period of relative liberalization.

Jātaka \'jä-tə-kə\ ("Birth") Any of the extremely popular stories of former lives of the Buddha that are preserved in all branches of Buddhism. Some *Jātaka* tales are scattered in various sections of the Pāli canon of Buddhist writings. A Sinhalese commentary of the 5th or 6th century that is questionably attributed to a Buddhist scholar named Buddhaghosa and called the *Jātakaṭṭhavaṇṇanā*, or *Jātakaṭṭhakathā*, gathers together about 550 *Jātaka* stories, some of which are quite brief while others are as long as novelettes.

Each tale begins with an introductory story describing the occasion that prompted the telling of that particular *Jātaka* and ends with the Buddha identifying the lives of the people in the introductory story with those of people from the past. There is humor in the stories and considerable variety. The future Buddha may appear in them as a king, an outcast, a god, an elephant—but, in whatever form, he exhibits some virtue that the tale thereby inculcates.

Many *Jātakas* have parallels in the *Mahābhārata* ("Great Epic of the Bhārata Dynasty"), the *Pañca-tantra* (animal fables), the *Purāṇas* (collections of legends), and elsewhere in non-Buddhist Indian literature. Some turn up again in such places as Aesop's fables. The stories have also been illustrated in sculpture and painting throughout the Buddhist world.

Jayadeva \jä-yä-'dä-wə\ (fl. 12th–13th century, eastern India, possibly Bengal) Sanskrit-language poet noted for his *Gītagovinda* ("Cowherd Song").

Both the date and place of birth of Jayadeva have been the source of controversy. It is known that his work was immediately popular and that it was associated with temple ritual in much of India. The *Gītagovinda* is composed of 12 cantos (*sarghas*) divided into 24 loosely connected songs (*prabandhas*) in which the poet recounts the youthful loves of the cowherd hero and god Krishna. Although the subject matter of the work is largely based on the story as told in the *Bhāgavata-Purāṇa*, the *Gītagovinda* differs from older sources in developing, thus largely creating, the character of Rādhā, whose role in Krishna's life is emphasized over the role of the *gopis*. The *Gītagovinda* is sometimes classified as a *mahākāvya*, although it is less grammatically rigid than other *mahākāvya*s.

jazz poetry \'jaz\ Poetry that is read to the accompaniment of jazz music. Authors of such poetry attempt to emulate the rhythms and freedom of the music in the poetry. Forerunners of the style included Vachel Lindsay, who read his poetry in a syncopated and rhythmic style for audiences, and Langston Hughes, who collaborated with musicians. Later poets known for their interest in combining the two forms included Kenneth Patchen, Kenneth Rexroth, Amiri Baraka, and Christopher Logue as well as many of the poets of the Beat movement.

J.B. \'jā-'bē\ Verse drama by Archibald MACLEISH, produced and published in 1958. Acclaimed for its emotional intensity and poetic drama, the play is a modern retelling of the Old Testament's Book of Job. It won MacLeish his third Pulitzer Prize.

Jean de Meun or **Jean** de Meung \zhäⁿ-də-'mœⁿ\ (b. *c.* 1240, Meung-sur-Loire, Fr.—d. before 1305) French poet famous for his continuation of the ROMAN DE LA ROSE, an allegorical poem in the courtly love tradition begun by Guillaume de Lorris about 1230.

De Meun's original name was Clopinel, or Chopinel, but he became known by the name of his birthplace. Little is known of his life. His works are satirical, coarse, at times immoral, but fearless and outspoken in attacking the abuses of the age. His strong antifeminism and censures on the vices of the church were bitterly resented.

Jean-Christophe \‚zhäⁿ-krē-'stôf\ Multivolume novel by Romain ROLLAND, published in French in 10 volumes in the revue *Les Cahiers de la Quinzaine* from 1904 to 1912. It was published in book form in three volumes.

An epic in construction and style, rich in poetic feeling, *Jean-Christophe* presents the successive crises confronting a creative genius. The novel's protagonist, Jean-Christophe Krafft, is a composer of German birth—modeled in part on Ludwig van Beethoven and in part on Rolland himself—who, despite discouragement and the stresses of his own turbulent personality, is inspired by love of life.

Jean Paul \zhäⁿ-'pôl\, *pseudonym of* Johann Paul Friedrich Richter \'rik̯-tər\ (b. March 21, 1763, Wunsiedel, Principality of Bayreuth [Germany]—d. Nov. 14, 1825, Bayreuth, Bavaria) German novelist whose works were immensely popular in the first 20 years of the 19th century. His writing bridged the shift in literature from the formal ideals of Weimar classicism to early Romanticism.

The son of a poor teacher and pastor, Richter studied theology at Leipzig until lack of money forced him to support himself as a private tutor (1787–90) and schoolmaster (1790–94). His reputation began with the novels *Auswahl aus des Teufels Papieren nebst einem nöthigen Aviso vom Juden Mendel* (1789;

"Selections from the Devil's Papers Together with a Required Notice from the Jew Mendel") and *Die unsichtbare Loge*, 2 parts (1793; *The Invisible Lodge*), and was established by *Hesperus, oder 45 Hundsposttage*, 3 issues (1795; *Hesperus; or Forty-five Dog-Post-Days*).

The second period in Jean Paul's work is marked by his attempts to reconcile the comic realist and the sentimental enthusiast in himself. The novels of this period include *Blumen-, Frucht-, und Dornenstücke*, 3 vol. (1796; *Flower, Fruit and Thorn Pieces*), commonly known for its hero as *Siebenkäs*; *Leben des Quintus Fixlein, aus fünfzehn Zettelkästen gezogen* (1796; *Life of Quintus Fixlein, Extracted from Fifteen Letter-Boxes*); *Titan*, 4 vol. (1800–03), which he considered his classical masterpiece; and the unfinished *Flegeljahre*, 4 vol. (1804–05; *Walt and Vult*).

The novels of his third period mirror his disillusionment with both classicism and Romanticism, but his idyllic novels, always marked by humor, treat his predicament in a comic style. *Dr. Katzenbergers Badereise*, 2 vol. (1809; "Dr. Katzenberger's Journey to the Spa"), and *Des Feldpredigers Schmelzle Reise nach Flätz mit fortgehenden Noten* (1809; *Army Chaplain Schmelzle's Journey*) were the last of his extremely popular novels.

Jeeves \'jēvz\, *in full* Reginald Jeeves. Fictional character, an English valet who is the consummate "gentleman's gentleman" to the somewhat dim but kindhearted English socialite Bertie Wooster, in a series of short stories and comic novels set mostly in the late Edwardian era, by P.G. WODEHOUSE.

The first Bertie-and-Jeeves short story to be published was "Extricating Young Gussie" (1915). Most of the early stories appeared in the collections *My Man Jeeves* (1919), *The Inimitable Jeeves* (1923), and *Very Good, Jeeves* (1930). *Thank You, Jeeves*, published in 1934, was Wodehouse's first novel featuring the character. *The Code of the Woosters* (1938) is considered one of the finest of the series. *Much Obliged, Jeeves* (1971) was the last collection.

Jefferies \'jef-rēz\, Richard, *in full* John Richard Jefferies (b. Nov. 6, 1848, near Swindon, Wiltshire, Eng.—d. Aug. 14, 1887, Goring-by-Sea, Sussex) English naturalist, novelist, and essayist whose prophetic vision was unappreciated in his own Victorian Age but has been increasingly recognized and admired since his death.

The son of a yeoman farmer, Jefferies in 1866 became a reporter on the *North Wilts Herald*, seeking escape whenever possible in the open space of the Wiltshire Downs. From his experiences as a reporter came *Hodge and His Masters* (1880), a classic record of Victorian countrymen, from the landowner to the laborer.

The years from 1882 to his death in 1887 were his most creative, though he was both ill and poor. Outstanding are *Bevis: The Story of a Boy* (1882), one of the best boys' books in English, which includes memories of Coate Farm, his birthplace, and its surrounding countryside, and *The Story of My Heart* (1883), his autobiography. In this late period also he wrote moving essays in an introspective style, collected in *The Life of the Fields* (1884), *The Open Air* (1885), and *Field and Hedgerow* (1889). He also dictated a novel, *Amaryllis at the Fair* (1887), which is sometimes compared to Thomas Hardy's regional novels. Earlier novels by Jefferies include the beautiful *Dewy Morn*, 2 vol. (1884), and *Green Ferne Farm* (1880).

Jeffers \'jef-ərz\, Robinson, *in full* John Robinson Jeffers (b. Jan. 10, 1887, Pittsburgh, Pa., U.S.—d. Jan. 20, 1962, Carmel, Calif.) One of the most controversial American poets of the 20th century, who viewed human life as a frantic, often contemptible struggle within a net of passions.

Educated in English literature, medicine, and forestry, Jeffers inherited money, which allowed him to write poetry. His third book, *Tamar and Other Poems* (1924), which brought him immediate fame, revealed the unique style and eccentric ideas developed in such later volumes as *Cawdor* (1928), *Thurso's Landing* (1932), and *Be Angry at the Sun* (1941). The shorter lyrics as well as his sprawling narrative poems celebrate the coastal scenery near Carmel, where Jeffers and his wife moved in 1916. He made a brilliant adaptation of Euripides' *Medea* that was produced in 1946.

Jeffrey \'jef-rē\, Francis Jeffrey, Lord (b. Oct. 23, 1773, Edinburgh, Scot.—d. Jan. 26, 1850, Edinburgh)   Literary critic and Scottish judge, best known as the editor of *The Edinburgh Review.*

Admitted in 1794 to the Scottish bar, Jeffrey discovered that his liberal Whig politics hampered his professional advancement. In 1802, still struggling for success in law, he joined with Sydney Smith and other friends to establish a critical periodical, *The Edinburgh Review.* Jeffrey served as editor from 1803 until 1829, after which he continued to contribute essays on criticism, biography, politics, and ethics.

Jekyll, Dr. Henry \'hen-rē-'jek-əl, 'jĕk-\   Fictional character, the rational, humanistic protagonist of the novel DR. JEKYLL AND MR. HYDE by Robert Louis Stevenson. His alter ego is the evil, barely human Mr. Hyde.

Jellyby, Mrs. \'jel-ē-bē\   Satiric character in the novel BLEAK HOUSE by Charles Dickens. Matronly Mrs. Jellyby is a philanthropist who devotes her time and energy to setting up a mission in Africa while ignoring the needy in her own family and neighborhood.

Jena Romanticism \'yā-nə\, *German* Jenaer Romantik \'yā-nă-ər-rō-'män-tik\   The first phase of Romanticism in German literature, centered in Jena from about 1798 to 1804. The Jena Romantics were led by the versatile writer Ludwig Tieck. Two members of the group, the brothers August Wilhelm and Friedrich von Schlegel, laid down the theoretical basis for Romanticism in the circle's organ, the *Athenaeum.*

The greatest imaginative achievement of the circle is to be found in the lyrics and fragmentary novels of Novalis. The works of Johann Gottlieb Fichte and Friedrich von Schelling expounded the Romantic doctrine in philosophy, while the theologian Friedrich Schleiermacher demonstrated the necessity of individualism in religious thought.

Jennie Gerhardt \'jen-ē-'ger-,härt\   Novel by Theodore DREISER, published in 1911. It exemplifies the naturalism of which Dreiser was a proponent, telling the unhappy story of a working-class woman who accepts all the adversity life visits on her and becomes the mistress of two wealthy and powerful men in order to help her impoverished family.

Jennings \'jen-iŋz\, Elizabeth (Joan) (b. July 18, 1926, Boston, Lincolnshire, Eng.)   English poet whose works treat intensely personal matters in a plainspoken, traditional, and objective style. Her verse frequently reflects her devout Roman Catholicism and her love of Italy.

Jennings' first pamphlet, *Poems,* appeared in 1953, followed by *A Way of Looking* (1955), both of which won awards. *Song for a Birth or a Death* (1961) marked a new development, with a confessional tone and more savage view of love. She suffered a breakdown in the early 1960s, and some of the best of her later poems concern this crisis and its aftermath. *Collected Poems* (1967) was followed by *The Animals' Arrival* (1969), *Lucidities* (1970), and *Relationships* (1972). A translation, *The Sonnets of Michelangelo* (1961), was revised in 1969. Jennings also published poetry for children, criticism, and a biography of Robert Frost. Her book *Collected Poems 1953–1985* was published in 1986 and *Tributes,* another book of verse, in 1989.

Jensen \'yen-sən\, Johannes Vilhelm (b. Jan. 20, 1873, Farsø, Den.—d. Nov. 25, 1950, Copenhagen)   Danish novelist, poet, essayist, and writer of many myths who provoked much debate in his later years through his attempt to depict human development in the light of an idealized Darwinian theory. He received the Nobel Prize for Literature in 1944.

The son of a veterinarian, Jensen went to Copenhagen to study medicine but turned to writing. He first made an impression as a writer of tales. These works fall into three groups: tales from the Himmerland, tales from Jensen's travels in the Far East, and more than 100 tales published under the recurrent title *Myter* ("Myths"). His early writings also include a historical trilogy, *Kongens Fald* (1900–01; *The Fall of the King*), a fictional biography of King Christian II of Denmark. In 1906 he published a volume of poems, and late in life he returned to poetry, producing *Digte, 1901–43* ("Poems 1901–43").

Jensen is best known, however, for the six novels that bear the common title *Den lange rejse,* 6 vol. (1908–22; *The Long Journey*). This story of the rise of humankind from the most primitive times to the voyages of Christopher Columbus exhibits both his imagination and his skill as an amateur anthropologist.

Jeremiah \jer-ə-'mī-ə\, *Hebrew* Yirmeyahu, *Latin Vulgate* Jeremias (b. probably after 650 BC, Anathoth, Judah—d. *c.* 570 BC, Egypt)   Hebrew prophet, reformer, and author of *The Book of Jeremiah* in Hebrew scripture. His spiritual leadership helped his people survive the capture of Jerusalem by the Babylonians in 586 BC and the exile of many Judaeans to Babylonia.

Jeremiah's early messages to the people were condemnations of their false worship and social injustice, with summonses to repentance. The prophet's despondency was expressed in the wish that he had never been born or that he might run away and live alone in the desert.

The unhappy aspects of his prophecy have given rise to the noun *jeremiad,* a prolonged lamentation or complaint, or a cautionary or angry harangue.

Jerome \jə-'rōm\, Jerome Klapka (b. May 2, 1859, Walsall, Staffordshire, Eng.—d. June 14, 1927, Northampton, Northamptonshire)   English novelist and playwright whose humor—warm, unsatirical, and unintellectual—won him a wide following.

Jerome's first book, *On the Stage—and Off,* was published in 1885, but it was with the publication of his next books, *The Idle Thoughts of an Idle Fellow* (1886) and *Three Men in a Boat* (1889), that he achieved great success; both books were widely translated. From 1892 to 1897 he was a coeditor (with Robert Barr and George Brown Burgin) of *The Idler,* a monthly magazine he had helped found that featured contributions by writers such as Eden Phillpotts, Mark Twain, and Bret Harte.

Jerome's many other works include *Three Men on the Bummel* (1900) and *Paul Kelver* (1902), an autobiographical novel. He also wrote a number of plays. A book of Jerome's memoirs, *My Life and Times,* was published in 1926 and a biography by J. Connolly in 1982.

Jerrold \'jer-əld\, Douglas William (b. Jan. 3, 1803, London, Eng.—d. June 8, 1857, London)   English playwright, journalist, and humorist.

Jerrold achieved success in the theater with *Black-Eyed Susan* (1829), a nautical melodrama based on an 18th-century ballad by John Gay. He also mastered a special brand of Victorian humor in a series of articles called "Mrs. Caudle's Curtain Lectures" (1845) for *Punch* magazine, to which he was a regular contributor. More plays with a nautical theme followed *Black-Eyed Susan,* but Jerrold was ambitious to write high comedy, at which he was less successful. A prolific journalist, he wrote much that is bitter and personal, in sharp contrast to the geniality of his "Curtain Lectures," which appeared in book form in 1846 and were regularly reprinted.

Jesuit drama \\'jez-ù-ət, 'jezh-, -yù-\\ Program of theater developed for educational and propagandist purposes in the colleges of the Society of Jesus during the 16th, 17th, and 18th centuries.

The earliest recorded performance of a Jesuit play was in 1551, at the newly founded Collegio Mamertino at Messina, in Sicily. In less than 20 years, plays were being performed at Jesuit colleges across the European continent.

Originally the plays were to be pious in nature, expressing true religious and moral doctrines; they were to be acted in Latin, decorously, and with little elaboration; and no female characters or costumes were to appear. All these rules were relaxed or revised as Jesuit drama evolved. Favorite subjects came from biblical histories, the lives of saints and martyrs, and incidents in the life of Christ, but Jesuit playwrights also reinterpreted material from pagan mythology, ancient history, and contemporary events. The plays became increasingly elaborate, and their stagecraft kept pace with all the newest technical developments of European theater.

The extravagance and luxury of many of the Jesuit productions came under heavy attack. Opponents of the Jesuit order made these objections part of the wave of anti-Jesuit feeling that grew in the mid-18th century. Dramatic performances ceased altogether in 1773, when the Society of Jesus was temporarily suppressed.

Jesus Christ \\'jē-zəs-'krīst\\, *also called* Jesus of Galilee \\'gal-i-lē\\ *or* Jesus of Nazareth \\'naz-ə-reth\\ (b. *c.* 6 BC, Judaea—d. *c.* AD 30, Jerusalem) Founder of Christianity whose deeds and message are recorded in the New Testament.

According to the biblical Gospel accounts, miraculous events surrounded the conception and birth of Jesus. He is believed by his followers to have been miraculously conceived by his mother, Mary. Tradition has it that he was born in Bethlehem. He grew up in Nazareth and as a young man followed his father's trade as a carpenter. During his lifetime Palestine was experiencing great distress under the rule of three sons of Herod and oppressive Roman procurators. Wandering through settlements in Galilee and the neighboring countryside in the company of 12 disciples, Jesus preached a message of religious reform and divine love. He was received with enthusiasm by common people because of his extraordinary healing powers, his effective teaching by parables, and his message of the redeeming love of God for every person. Many miracles were attributed to him. His growing influence alarmed Jewish and Roman authorities alike; regarded by some of his followers as the long-expected Messiah, he was suspected by the Jewish and Roman authorities of having revolutionary aims. After a brief ministry in Galilee, Jesus went with his disciples to Jerusalem to observe Passover. After the Last Supper with his disciples, he was betrayed by one of them, Judas Iscariot, and was arrested by Roman soldiers. Examined by the high priests and the Sanhedrin (a Jewish council with religious, political, and judicial functions), Jesus was condemned as a blasphemer deserving death. Under Roman law he was crucified at Golgotha as a political rebel and was buried in the tomb of Joseph of Arimathea. Belief in his Resurrection from the dead became the focus of the religion that developed around his teachings.

The term Jesus Christ designates not only a historical person who lived in Palestine during the reigns of the Roman emperors Augustus and Tiberius but also one who has been the object of Christian faith and worship for almost 20 centuries. These two designations may be distinguished but they cannot be sepa-

rated, for almost everything known about the historical person comes from the reports of those who were his followers.

Most Western religious literature deals in some way with the person and beliefs of Jesus Christ, notably John Milton's *Paradise Lost* and *Paradise Regained*. Not until about the 19th century did the Christ figure—a character resembling Christ in some essential way, as through innocent suffering—become a protagonist in popular literature. He appears in such works as William Faulkner's *A Fable*, Graham Greene's *The Power and the Glory*, and John Steinbeck's *The Grapes of Wrath*. Another body of modern literature examines the possibility of Christ's appearance in contemporary society.

Jeu de Saint Nicolas, Le \\lə-,zhœ̄-də-saⁿ-nē-kȯ-'lȧ\\ Mystery play by Jehan BODEL, performed in 1201. *Le Jeu de Saint Nicolas* treats a theme earlier presented in Latin, notably by Hilarius (flourished 1125), giving it new form and meaning by relating it to the Crusades. In Bodel's play the saint's image, to which the sole survivor of a Christian army is found praying, becomes the agent of a miracle that causes the Saracen king and his people to convert to Christianity.

The play is notable for its crusading fervor, piety, and satirical wit. It is also of importance for its introduction of comic scenes based on contemporary life and as one of the first Latin school dramas to be translated into the vernacular.

Jeune Belgique, La \\lȧ-zhœ̄n-bel-'zhēk\\ ("Young Belgium") Influential review (1881–97), edited by poet Max Waller; it gave its name to a literary movement (though never a formal "school") that aimed to express a genuinely Belgian consciousness and to free the literature of Belgium from outworn Romanticism. Among writers associated with the movement were Maurice Maeterlinck, Émile Verhaeren, and Max Elskamp—all poets of international stature.

Jeune Parque, La \\lȧ-zhœn-'pȧrk\\ ("The Young Fate") Poem by Paul VALÉRY, published in 1917. An enigmatic work noted for both its difficulty and its formal beauty, it presents in 500 lines the musings of Clotho, the youngest of the three Fates, as she stands at the seashore just before dawn. She stands uncertain whether to remain a serene immortal or to choose the pains and pleasures of human life.

Jewett \\'jü-ət\\, Sarah Orne (b. Sept. 3, 1849, South Berwick, Maine, U.S.—d. June 24, 1909, South Berwick) American writer of regional fiction.

Early in her teens Jewett determined to write about the rapidly disappearing traditions of provincial life about her, and by the age of 28 she was an established writer. Outstanding among her 20 volumes are *Deephaven* (1877) and THE COUNTRY OF THE POINTED FIRS (1896), the latter often regarded as her finest achievement. The books contain realistic sketches of aging Maine natives, whose manners, idioms, and pithiness she recorded with pungency and humor, sympathetically but without sentimentality. A disabling accident virtually ended her writing career in 1902.

Jewish Daily Forward Yiddish-language newspaper better known by its Yiddish name, FORVERTS.

Jew of Malta, The \\'mȯl-tə\\ (*in full* The Famous Tragedy of the Rich Jew of Malta) Five-act tragedy in blank verse by Christopher MARLOWE, produced about 1590 and published in 1633.

In order to raise tribute demanded by the Turks, Ferneze, the Christian governor of Malta, seizes half the property of all Jews living on Malta. When Barabas, a wealthy Jewish merchant, protests, his entire estate is confiscated. Seeking revenge on his enemies, Barabas plots their destruction, but in the end he is betrayed and dies the death he had planned for his enemies.

Jezebel or **Jezabel** \'jez-ə-,bel\ (d. *c.* 843 BC) In the Old Testament (Kings I and II), the non-Israelite wife of King Ahab, who ruled the kingdom of Israel. By interfering with the exclusive worship of the Hebrew god Yahweh, disregarding the rights of the commoners, and defying the great prophets Elijah and Elisha, she provoked the internecine strife that enfeebled Israel for decades. She has come to be an archetype of the wicked woman.

Jhabvala \'jäb-väl-ə\, Ruth Prawer, *original surname* Prawer \'prä-vər\ (b. May 7, 1927, Cologne, Ger.) Novelist and screenwriter, well known for her witty and insightful portrayals of contemporary Indian lives.

A Polish Jew, Jhabvala immigrated to England with her family in 1939. After receiving an M.A. in English (1951) from Queen Mary College, London, she married an Indian architect and moved to India, where she lived for the next 24 years. After 1975 she lived in New York City.

Jhabvala's first two novels, *To Whom She Will* (1955; U.S. title, *Amrita*) and *The Nature of Passion* (1956), won much critical acclaim for their comic depiction of Indian society and manners. Her position as both insider and detached observer allowed her a unique, sometimes satirical perspective when describing Indian family life, India's struggle to adapt to a new social mobility, and the clash between Eastern and Western ideals. Her novel *Heat and Dust* (1975) tells parallel stories of colonial and contemporary India. Her first departure from Indian subject matter occurred in *In Search of Love and Beauty* (1983), which portrays Austrian and German refugees searching for spiritual truths in New York. *Poet and Dancer* (1993) is the story of a destructive friendship between two women living in New York City.

In addition to several original screenplays, Jhabvala wrote film adaptations of many novels, including Henry James's *The Bostonians* (1984) and E.M. Forster's *A Room With A View* (1985) and *Howards End* (1992).

Jibran *see* GIBRAN.

jiggery-pokery *see* DOUBLE DACTYLS.

Jim \'jim\ Fictional character, an unschooled but honorable runaway slave in HUCKLEBERRY FINN by Mark Twain. Some critics accuse Twain of creating a one-dimensional racist caricature while others find Jim a complex, compassionate character. The relationship between Jim and Huck forms the crux of the novel, with Jim acting as a surrogate for Huck's loathsome father.

Jiménez \ḵē-'mä-näs\, Juan Ramón (b. Dec. 24, 1881, Moguer, Spain—d. May 29, 1958, San Juan, P.R.) Spanish poet awarded the Nobel Prize for Literature in 1956.

After studying briefly at the University of Salamanca, Jiménez went to Madrid in 1900. His first two volumes of poetry, *Almas de violeta* ("Souls of Violet") and *Ninfeas* ("Waterlilies"), came out that same year. The excessive sentiment of the two books so embarrassed Jiménez in his later years that he destroyed every copy he could find. His published volumes of that early period, including *Jardines lejanos* (1905; "Distant Gardens"), *Elegías puras* (1908; "Pure Elegies"), and *Pastorales* (1911), clearly reflect the influence of Rubén Darío.

Jiménez worked briefly as an editor before visiting New York City. There he married Zenobia Camprubí Aymar, the Spanish translator of the Hindu poet Rabindranath Tagore. Shortly after his return to Spain, he published *Diario de un poeta recién casado* (1917; "Diary of a Poet Recently Married"), issued in 1948 under the title *Diario de un poeta y mar* ("Diary of a Poet and the Sea"). The volume marked his transition to what he called "*la poesía desnuda*" ("naked poetry"), an at-

tempt to strip his poetry of all extraneous matter and formal meters. During the Spanish Civil War (1936–39) he allied himself with the Republican forces until he voluntarily exiled himself to Puerto Rico, where he spent most of the rest of his life.

Although primarily a poet, Jiménez achieved popularity in America with the translation of his prose work *Platero y yo* (1917; *Platero and I*), the story of a man and his donkey. He also collaborated with his wife in the translation of the Irish playwright John Millington Synge's *Riders to the Sea* (1920). His poetic output during his life was immense. Among his better-known works are *Sonetos espirituales 1914–1915* (1916; "Spiritual Sonnets, 1914–15"), *Piedra y cielo* (1919; "Stone and Sky"), *Poesía, en verso, 1917–1923* (1923), *Poesía en prosa y verso* (1932; "Poetry in Prose and Verse"), *Voces de mi copla* (1945; "Voices of My Song"), and *Animal de fondo* (1947; "Animal at Bottom").

Jimson, Gulley \'gəl-ē-'jim-sən\ Fictional character, the talented but disreputable artist protagonist and narrator of Joyce Cary's novel THE HORSE'S MOUTH, the third volume in a trilogy about art.

Jindyworobak movement \jin-dē-'wor-ə-,bak\ Brief nationalistic Australian literary movement of the 1930s to mid-1940s that sought to promote native ideas and traditions, especially in literature.

The movement was swelled by several circumstances: the Australian depression years focused attention on comparable hardships of an earlier era (the early 1890s); the influx of "alien" culture threatened to overwhelm the young literature then in the making; and travelers described with wonder the little known Australian outback. Among the discoveries of the period was a romantic notion of the spirit of place and the literary importance of what could still be discerned of Aboriginal culture. Xavier Herbert's *Capricornia* (1938) typifies the goals of the Jindyworobak movement.

The poet and novelist James Devaney (1890–1976) took the name Jindyworobak from a 19th-century vocabulary of Wuywurung (an Aboriginal language formerly spoken in the Melbourne region), in which *jindi woraback* is said to mean "to annex."

jingle \'jiŋ-gəl\ A short verse or song marked by catchy repetition of such elements as rhyme, alliterative sounds, and cadences. This is often the form of nursery rhymes, such as "Hickory, Dickory, Dock."

jingxi or **ching-hsi** \jiŋ-'shē\ [Chinese *jīngxì*, from *jīng* capital, Beijing + *xì* play, drama], *also called* Peking opera \'pē-'kiŋ, 'pä-\ Popular Chinese theatrical form that developed during the mid-17th to the mid-19th centuries and is still performed today. It gradually replaced *kunqu*, a traditional drama form that had previously dominated the Chinese theater. Performed in the dialect of Beijing and of the traditional elite, the *jingxi* plays came to be produced throughout China, although most provinces and many major cities developed their own operatic variants using local dialect.

Essentially, *jingxi* came into being as a mixture of southern dramatic traditions and clapper opera (an opera form in which clappers provide an essential musical feature), and it is characterized by elaborate and stylized costumes and makeup, spectacular dance and acrobatic routines, a limited melodic range, lyrics in more colloquial language, and musical accompaniment that emphasizes percussion instruments.

jinni \'jin-ē, ji-'nē\ or **jinn** \'jin\ *plural* jinn or jinns [Arabic *jinnīy*] In Arabic mythology, a supernatural spirit below the level of angels and devils. The word is sometimes anglicized as genie or genii. Ghouls (treacherous spirits of changing shape), afreets (diabolic, evil spirits), and *sīˈlā* (treacherous spirits of invariable form) constitute classes of jinn. Beings of flame or air, jinn are capable of assuming human or animal form and are said to dwell in all conceivable inanimate objects. Jinn delight in punishing humans for any harm done them, intentionally or unintentionally, and are said to be responsible for many diseases and all kinds of accidents; however, those human beings who know the proper magical procedure can exploit the jinn to their advantage.

Belief in the existence of jinn was common in early Arabia, where they were thought to inspire poets and soothsayers. Jinn, especially through their association with magic, have always been favorite figures in North African, Egyptian, Syrian, Persian, and Turkish folklore and have become the center of an immense popular literature, appearing notably in *The Thousand and One Nights*. In India and Indonesia they have entered local Muslim imaginations by way of Qurʾānic descriptions and Arabic literature. They have appeared in Western literature as well, as in Victor Hugo's poem "Les Djinns" and Alain Robbe-Grillet's *Djinn. See also* AFREET; GHOUL.

Jin ping mei or **Chin p'ing mei** \ˈjinˈpiŋˈmä\ ("The Plum in the Golden Vase")   The first realistic social novel to appear in China. It is the work of an unknown author of the Ming dynasty, and its earliest extant version is dated 1617. Two English versions were published in 1939 under the titles *The Golden Lotus* and *Chin P'ing Mei: The Adventurous History of Hsi Men and His Six Wives*.

The first Chinese novel not derived from popular legend and historical event, *Jin ping mei* describes in naturalistic detail the life of the family of a well-to-do businessman, Qing Ximen, who has acquired his wealth largely through dishonest means. He devotes himself to the pursuit of carnal pleasure and heavy drinking. To these ends he acquires six wives and numerous maidservants. The debauchery of Ximen is presented in vivid detail, leading many readers to dismiss the novel as pornography. Others, however, regard the erotic passages as central to the author's moral purpose of exposing the vanity of pleasure. Despite unofficial censorship because of its eroticism, *Jin ping mei* became one of China's most popular novels.

Jirásek \ˈyēˌräˌsek\, Alois (b. Aug. 23, 1851, Hronov, Bohemia, Austrian Empire [now in Czech Republic]—d. March 12, 1930, Prague)   The most important Czech novelist in the period before World War I, as well as a great national figure.

Jirásek was a secondary-school teacher until his retirement in 1909. He wrote a series of historical novels imbued with faith in his nation and in progress toward freedom and justice. He was particularly attracted by the Hussite period of Bohemian history (15th century), to which he devoted his most famous work, the trilogy *Mezi proudy* (1891; "Between the Currents"), *Proti všem* (1894; "Against All the World"), and *Bratrstvo* (1899–1908; "Brotherhood"). Perhaps of greater artistic significance is his portrayal of the 19th-century Czech national revival in *F.L. Věk* (1888–1906). His best work is probably his last major novel, *Temno* (1915; "Darkness"), in which he painted a vivid picture of Bohemia in the grip of the Counter-Reformation. His literary output also included plays and short stories.

Joad family \ˈjōd\   Fictional family of dispossessed tenant farmers, the main characters in THE GRAPES OF WRATH, John Steinbeck's novel of the Great Depression.

Joan \ˈjōn\ of Arc \ˈärk\, Saint, *byname* The Maid of Orléans, *French* Sainte Jeanne d'Arc \zhän-ˈdärk\ *or* La Pucelle d'Orléans \lä-pü-ˈsel-dôr-lä-ˈäⁿ\ (b. *c.* 1412, Domrémy, Bar, Fr.—d. May 30, 1431, Rouen)   National heroine of France, a peasant girl who, acting under what she believed to be divine inspiration, led the French to a momentous victory that was a turning point in the Hundred Years' War. She has been the subject of many works of literature by a wide range of authors, including Voltaire, Robert Southey, George Bernard Shaw, and Jean Anouilh.

Joaquin \hwä-ˈkēn, kwä-\, Nick, *byname of* Nicomedes Joaquin (b. May 4, 1917, Paco, Manila, Philippines)   Filipino novelist, poet, playwright, essayist, and biographer whose works present the diverse heritage of the Filipino people.

Starting as a proofreader for the Philippines *Free Press*, Joaquin rose to contributing editor and essayist under the nom de plume "Quijano de Manila" ("Manila Old-Timer"). He was well known as a historian of the brief Golden Age of Spain in the Philippines, as a writer of short stories suffused with folk Roman Catholicism, as a playwright, and as a novelist.

The novel *The Woman Who Had Two Navels* (1961) examines his country's various heritages. *A Portrait of the Artist as Filipino* (1966), a celebrated play, attempts to reconcile historical events with dynamic change. *The Aquinos of Tarlac: An Essay on History as Three Generations* (1983) presents a biography of Benigno Aquino, the assassinated presidential candidate. The action of the novel *Cave and Shadows* (1983) occurs in the period of martial law under Ferdinand Marcos. Joaquin's other works include the short-story collections *Tropical Gothic* (1972) and *Stories for Groovy Kids* (1979), the play *Tropical Baroque* (1979), and the collections of poetry *The Ballad of the Five Battles* (1981) and *Collected Verse* (1987).

Job \ˈjōb\   Biblical character, an upright and prosperous man who loses all his possessions, his children, and his health and yet refuses to curse God. His story is told in THE BOOK OF JOB.

Jocasta \jō-ˈkas-tə\, *also called* Iocaste \ē-ō-ˈkas-tē\ *or* Epicaste \ˌep-ē-ˈkas-tē\   In Greek mythology, the wife of Laius, king of Thebes, who later unwittingly marries her own son, OEDIPUS.

Jochumsson \ˈyȯk-ʉem-sȯn\, Matthías (b. Nov. 11, 1835, Skógar, Thorskafjördur, Ice.—d. Dec. 18, 1920, Akureyri)   Icelandic poet, translator, journalist, and dramatist.

The son of a poor farmer, Jochumsson at age 30 was ordained at the Lutheran theological college in Reykjavík. He spent his working life as a clergyman until he retired on a poet's pension in 1900.

Through his religious poetry, his hymns and funeral elegies, and in his heroic narrative poems, Jochumsson preached Christian faith and humanity alongside the pagan virtues of the saga age. His innumerable translations of didactic lyrics, patriotic poems, and hymns from the Scandinavian languages, and from English and German as well, illustrate the same virtues. Jochumsson's intellectual integrity and rich humanity ultimately established him as a national figure.

Jodelle \zhȯ-ˈdel\, Étienne (b. 1532, Paris, Fr.—d. July 1573, Paris)   French dramatist and poet, one of the seven members of the literary circle known as La Pléiade.

Jodelle aimed at creating a classical drama that in every respect would be different from the moralities and mysteries then occupying the French stage; he succeeded in producing the first modern French tragedy and comedy. These plays have the reputation of being unactable and unreadable, but they set a new example that prepared the ground for the great Neoclassical tragedians Pierre Corneille and Jean Racine. His first play, *Cléopâtre captive*, a tragedy in verse, was presented before the court at Paris in 1553. Jodelle wrote two other plays, *Eugène* (1552), a comedy, and *Didon se sacrifiant*, another verse tragedy, based on Virgil's account of Dido.

Joe Turner's Come and Gone \ˈjō-ˈtər-nər\   Play in two acts by August WILSON, performed in 1986 and published in

1988. Set in 1911, it is the third in Wilson's projected series of plays depicting African-American life in each decade of the 20th century.

The play is set in a Pittsburgh boardinghouse whose inhabitants are all from the rural South, new to the industrial North, separated from their families and from their heritage. Each is engaged in a search for identity and equilibrium; all maintain links with African traditions as they try to find their places in post-Civil War society.

Johannes von Tepl \yō-'hän-əs-fȯn-'tep-əl\, *also called* Johannes von Saaz \fȯn-'zäts\ (b. *c.* 1350, Tepl or Schüttwa, Bohemia [Czech Republic]—d. *c.* 1415, Prague) Bohemian author of the remarkable dialogue *Der Ackermann aus Böhmen* (c. 1400; *Death and the Ploughman*), the first important prose work in Modern German.

After taking a degree at Prague University, Johannes was appointed, probably before 1378, a notary in Saaz (Žatec), and he became headmaster of the grammar school there in 1383.

Ackermann, which is described in a Latin dedication as an exercise in rhetoric, probably arose from the death of the author's first wife in 1400. In the story a plowman, representing Man, bitterly accuses Death of unjust dealings toward humanity. Death convinces the plowman that his work is necessary, though the plowman still champions human nobility against Death's more negative view. God, the judge, awards Death the victory but Man the honor. The complex structure and elaborately artificial but vigorous rhythmical prose of this work make it—despite the uncertain state of the text—unique in medieval German literature.

Johansson \yō-'hȧn-sȯn\, Lars, *pseudonym* Lucidor \'lū̠-si-‚dȯr\ (b. Oct. 18, 1638, Stockholm, Swed.—d. Aug. 13, 1674, Stockholm) Swedish lyric poet who composed some of the most powerful poems of the Swedish Baroque period.

After studying abroad, Johansson returned to Sweden and became known as a writer of funeral elegies and epithalamiums. His most personal poems are drinking songs and funeral hymns—a typically Baroque combination. His models were the German Baroque poets, but his best works surpass theirs in intensity of feeling and power of expression. His most famous song is "Skulle jag sörja så vore jag tokot" ("Were I to Grieve, Then I Were a Fool"). Johansson's poetry was posthumously published in *Helicons blomster* (1689; "Helicon's Flowers").

John \'jän\, Errol (b. Dec. 20, 1924, Port-of-Spain, Trinidad—d. July 10, 1988, London, Eng.) Trinidad-born actor and playwright.

A founding member of the Whitehall Players in Port-of-Spain, John pursued his acting career from 1950 in London. His play *Moon on a Rainbow Shawl*, about a man's struggle to escape a Port-of-Spain slum, was first produced in London in 1958 and then revised for a production in New York City in 1962. His other plays include *The Tout* (1966) and the three plays published together in *Force Majeure, The Dispossessed, Hasta Luego* (1967). For television he wrote *The Emperor Jones* (1953), *Teleclub* (1954), and *Dawn* (1963).

John \'jän\ of the Cross, Saint, *original name* Juan de Yepes y Álvarez \'ḵwän-t̲h̲ā-'yā-pās-ē-'äl-b̲ä-räth\ (b. June 24, 1542, Fontiveros, Spain—d. Dec. 14, 1591, Ubeda) One of the greatest Christian mystics and Spanish poets.

John became a Carmelite monk at Medina del Campo, Spain, in 1563 and was ordained priest in 1567. In 1568 Teresa of Ávila, the celebrated mystic, enlisted his help in her restoration of Carmelite life to its original observance of austerity. A year later, at Duruelo, he founded the contemplative order of Discalced Carmelites and opened its first monastery. Reform, however, caused friction within the order and led to his impris-

onment, first in 1576 and again in 1577 at Toledo, where he wrote some of his finest poetry. He escaped in August 1578. Eventually he won high office in the order, but further dissension caused his withdrawal to absolute solitude. He was canonized in 1726.

John schematized the steps of mystical ascent—a process that leads from the distractions of the world to the sublime peace of reunion of the soul and God. In such intense poems as "Cántico espiritual" ("The Spiritual Canticle"), "Noche obscura del alma" ("The Dark Night of the Soul"), and "Llama de amor viva" ("The Living Flame of Love"), he expressed the experience of the mystical union between the soul and Christ.

In the eight-stanza "Noche" ("Night"), perhaps his best-known work, he described the process by which the soul sheds its attachment to everything and eventually passes through a personal experience of Christ's Crucifixion to his glory. John's exposition of "the dark night of the soul"—a period of passivity and spiritual suffering that God uses to purge the soul of sin—is considered a masterpiece of mystical literature.

John Brown's Body \jän-'braůn\ Epic poem in eight sections about the American Civil War by Stephen Vincent BENÉT, published in 1928 and subsequently awarded a Pulitzer Prize.

The scrupulously researched narrative begins just before John Brown's raid on Harpers Ferry and ends after the assassination of President Abraham Lincoln. Benét's tone is one of reconciliation. From his viewpoint there are few villains and many heroes; the North and the South are afforded equal respect. Along with historical figures like Lincoln and Robert E. Lee, Benét presents Americans of many backgrounds, occupations, and opinions, from Southern aristocrats and their slaves to farm-boy soldiers from Pennsylvania and Illinois.

John Bull \'jän-'bůl\ In literature and political caricature, a conventional personification of England or of English character. Bull was invented by the Scottish mathematician and physician John Arbuthnot as a character in an extended allegory that appeared in a series of five pamphlets in 1712 and was published collectively in 1727 as *The History of John Bull*; he appeared as an honest clothier, bringing action with his linen-draper friend Nicholas Frog (Holland) against Lewis Baboon (Louis XIV, king of France) for interfering with trade.

The caricature was used throughout the 18th century to represent various political views, but John Bull's widest recognition came in the middle and late 19th century, especially through the influential cartoons portraying him in the periodical *Punch*. The most familiar and frequent representation was that developed by *Punch* cartoonists John Leech and Sir John Tenniel: the jovial and honest farmer figure, solid and foursquare, sometimes in Union Jack waistcoat and with bulldog at heel. John Bull had by then become so universally familiar that the name frequently appeared in book, play, and periodical titles and pictorially as a brand name or trademark for manufactured goods.

Johnson \'jän-sən\, Charles S., *in full* Spurgeon (b. July 24, 1893, Bristol, Va., U.S.—d. Oct. 27, 1956, Louisville, Ky.) American sociologist, authority on race relations, and the first black president (1946–56) of Fisk University, Nashville, Tenn. He was the founder and from 1923 to 1928 the editor of the intellectual magazine OPPORTUNITY, a major voice of the Harlem Renaissance of the 1920s.

Johnson \'jän-sən\, Colin, *Aboriginal name* Mudrooroo \məd-'rü̠-‚rü̠\, *also called* Mudrooroo Narogin *or* Mudrooroo Nyoongah (b. 1939, Beverley, W.Aus., Australia) Australian Aboriginal novelist and poet who depicts the struggles of modern Aborigines to adapt to life in a society dominated by whites.

Johnson, who was part Aborigine, was educated in a Roman Catholic orphanage in Australia. He traveled widely, including a six-year stay in India, where he lived for some time as a Buddhist monk.

Johnson's first novel, *Wild Cat Falling* (1965), is the story of a young half-Aboriginal outcast who is searching for his identity. It was the first Australian novel by someone of Aboriginal descent. The protagonist of *Long Live Sandawara* (1979) attempts to establish his own resistance movement in the slums of Perth. *Doctor Wooreddy's Prescription for Enduring the Ending of the World* (1983) concerns the annihilation of the Tasmanian Aborigines in the 19th century. Later novels include *Doin Wildcat* (1988) and *The Kwinkan* (1994). He also wrote poetry— including the volumes *Song Circle of Jacky* (1986), *Dalwurra, the Black Bittern* (1988), and *Collected Poems* (1991)—and the plays *Big Sunday* (1987) and *Mutjinggaba: The Place of the Old Woman* (1989). He published his later work under his adopted Aboriginal name. Johnson's nonfiction include *Before the Invasion: Aboriginal Life to 1788* (1980) and *Writing from the Fringe: A Study of Modern Aboriginal Literature* (1990).

Johnson \\ˈjän-sən \\, Diane, *in full* Diane Lain Johnson Murray \\ˈmər-ē\\ (b. April 28, 1934, Moline, Ill., U.S.) American writer and academic, best known for worldly and satiric novels set in California that portray contemporary women in crisis.

Johnson was educated at Stephens College, the University of Utah, and the University of California. From 1968 she was a professor of English at the University of California at Davis.

The heroine of her first novel, *Fair Game* (1965), conscious of having been exploited by a series of lovers, eventually finds a man who will foster her desire to grow into a more complete person. In *Loving Hands at Home* (1968) a woman leaves her Mormon husband and his family, with whom she feels no spiritual kinship, but fails to succeed on her own in the wider world. *Burning* (1971) satirizes the southern California way of life. *The Shadow Knows* (1974) concerns a divorced mother whose secure life is shattered when she becomes convinced that she is marked for violence. *Lying Low* (1978) chronicles four days in the lives of three markedly different women. Later novels include *Persian Nights* (1987) and *Health and Happiness* (1990).

Johnson wrote a well-received novelistic biography of writer George Meredith's first wife, *The True History of the First Mrs. Meredith and Other Lesser Lives* (1972), and the biography *Dashiell Hammett: A Life* (1983). She also wrote screenplays (with Stanley Kubrick, *The Shining*, 1980) and a collection of essays, *Terrorists and Novelists* (1982).

Johnson \\ˈyōn-sòn \\, Eyvind (b. July 29, 1900, Svartbjörnsbyn, near Boden, Swed.—d. Aug. 25, 1976, Stockholm) Working-class novelist who not only brought new themes and points of view to Swedish literature but also experimented with new forms and techniques. With Harry Edmund Martinson he was awarded the Nobel Prize for Literature in 1974.

Johnson's early novels, in which the influence of Marcel Proust, André Gide, and James Joyce can be discerned, are mainly concerned with feelings of frustration. In *Bobinack* (1932), an exposé of the machinations of modern capitalism, *Regn i gryningen* (1933; "Rain at Daybreak"), an attack on modern office drudgery and its effects, and *Romanen om Olof*, 4 vol. (1934–37), which tells of his experiences as a logger in the sub-Arctic, he began to seek out the causes for that frustration. *Strändernas svall* (1946; *Return to Ithaca*) and *Hans nådes tid* (1960; *The Days of His Grace*) have been translated into many languages.

Johnson \\ˈjän-sən \\, James Weldon (b. June 17, 1871, Jacksonville, Fla., U.S.—d. June 26, 1938, Wiscasset, Maine) Poet, diplomat, and anthologist of African-American culture.

Johnson graduated from Atlanta (Ga.) University. He later read law, was admitted to the Florida bar in 1897, and began practicing there. During this period, he and his brother, John Rosamond Johnson (1873–1954), a composer, began writing songs, and in 1901 the two went to New York, where they wrote some 200 songs for the Broadway stage.

From 1906 to 1914 he held various diplomatic posts, and he later taught at Fisk University in Nashville, Tenn. His novel AUTOBIOGRAPHY OF AN EX-COLORED MAN (published anonymously, 1912) attracted little attention until it was reissued under his own name in 1927.

Fifty Years and Other Poems (1917) was followed by his pioneering anthology *Book of American Negro Poetry* (1922) and *American Negro Spirituals* (1925, 1926), collaborations with his brother. His best-known work is GOD'S TROMBONES (1927), a group of black dialect sermons in verse. His *Along This Way* (1933) is an autobiography.

Johnson \\ˈjän-sən \\, Lionel Pigot (b. March 15, 1867, Broadstairs, Kent, Eng.—d. Oct. 4, 1902, London) English poet and critic who is mainly remembered as a typical representative of the "tragic generation" of the 1890s, which suffered from fin-de-siècle decadence and melancholy.

Johnson studied at Winchester College and at New College, Oxford, and then went to London to pursue a literary career and to work as a writer and critic for a number of periodicals. Johnson wrote the first solid study of novelist and poet Thomas Hardy, and his *Poetical Works* were edited in 1915 by Ezra Pound. He died at age 35 after falling on a public street and fracturing his skull.

Johnson \\ˈjän-sən \\, Louis Albert (b. Sept. 27, 1924, Wellington, N.Z.—d. Nov. 1, 1988, Winchester, Hampshire, Eng.) New Zealand poet who rejected the rural themes and parochialism of traditional New Zealand verse, instead taking as his subjects suburban life and ordinary human relationships.

After attending Wellington Teachers' Training College, Johnson worked as a schoolteacher, journalist, and editor of several publications, including the *New Zealand Poetry Yearbook* (1951–64), *Numbers* (1954–60), and *Antipodes New Writing* (1987). His early poetry, often characterized as abstract, was included in such collections as *Stanza and Scene* (1945), *The Sun Among the Ruins* (1951), *Roughshod Among the Lilies* (1952), and *New Worlds for Old* (1957). His constant poetic output became increasingly concrete and colloquial. His later works include *Bread and a Pension* (1964), *Onion* (1972), *Coming & Going* (1982), and *Winter Apples* (1984). Johnson received the first New Zealand Book Award for poetry for *Fires and Patterns* (1975). His volume *Last Poems* (1990) was published posthumously.

Johnson \\ˈjän-sən \\, Pamela Hansford (b. May 29, 1912, London, Eng.—d. June 18, 1981, London) English novelist who treated moral concerns with a light but sure touch. In her novels, starting with *The Unspeakable Skipton* (1959), she mined a rich vein of satire.

Johnson's novel *This Bed Thy Centre* (1935) was a popular and critical success. Among her most fully realized novels are *Too Dear for My Possessing* (1940), *An Avenue of Stone* (1947), and *A Summer to Decide* (1948), a trilogy that follows the fortunes of a group of friends from the 1920s to the end of the 1940s.

Johnson examined the implications of modern permissiveness in her novel *Cork Street, Next to the Hatter's* (1965) and in her nonfiction work *On Iniquity* (1967), which contains her reflections on a contemporary murder case involving sexual sadism. *The Good Listener* (1975) and *The Good Husband* (1978) tell the story of a younger man in love with and married to a glamorous older woman. Her other works include a volume of essays, *Important to Me* (1974), and the novel *A Bonfire* (1981).

Johnson \'jän-sən\, Richard (baptized May 24, 1573, London, Eng.—d. 1659?) English author of popular romances, notably *The Most Famous History of the Seaven Champions of Christendome* (vol 1., 1596; vol. 2, 1597), which was so successful that one or two further parts were added later.

Almost nothing is known of Johnson's life, though in his *Nine Worthies of London* (1592) he referred to himself as an apprentice. Among his many other works is a book of ballads, *The Crowne Garland of Golden Roses* (1612).

Johnson \'jän-sən\, Samuel, *byname* Dr. Johnson (b. Sept. 18, 1709, Lichfield, Staffordshire, Eng.—d. Dec. 13, 1784, London) English poet, essayist, critic, journalist, lexicographer, and conversationalist, regarded as one of the outstanding figures of 18th-century life and letters. His *A Dictionary of the English Language*, 2 vol. (1755), was the first major English dictionary to use illustrative historical quotations.

Johnson, the son of a bookseller, was educated at the University of Oxford and set up a school near Lichfield, which was not a success. In 1737 he went to London with a former pupil, David Garrick. There he made friends with poet and satirist Richard Savage, whose biography, *An Account of the Life of Mr Richard Savage*, he was to publish anonymously in 1744. Johnson's early writings were articles for the *The Gentleman's Magazine*. He came to public notice with attacks on Robert Walpole's ministry. In 1745 he turned his attention to William Shakespeare, publishing *Miscellaneous Observations on the Tragedy of Macbeth*. He published his didactic poem *The Vanity of Human Wishes* in 1749. In 1746 Johnson signed a contract to prepare his *Dictionary of the English Language*. The *Dictionary* greatly enhanced his reputation, but it did not free him from reliance upon the journalism and hack writing he produced for a living. He published a paper called *The Rambler* from 1750 to 1752 and wrote a weekly column entitled "The Idler" for the *Universal Chronicle* from 1758 to 1760. His philosophical tale RASSELAS was published in 1759 in order to meet a pressing demand for money. His four-volume *The Lives of the Most Eminent English Poets* (1781) shows Johnson's power to lift hackwork to the level of sustained literary criticism.

In 1763 Johnson met James Boswell, with whom he formed one of the most famous friendships in literary history. In 1773 they journeyed together through the Highlands of Scotland and to the Western Isles, and both left entertaining accounts of the trip. Johnson's version was titled A JOURNEY TO THE WESTERN ISLANDS OF SCOTLAND (1775). In 1765 Johnson's edition of Shakespeare was completed, and in the year of its publication Trinity College, Dublin, conferred the LL.D. degree on him. Brilliant as Johnson was as a writer, he was reportedly even more brilliant as a conversationalist.

Johnson \'yōn-zȯn\, Uwe (b. July 20, 1934, Cammin, Ger.—d. March 12, 1984, Sheerness, Kent, Eng.) German author, many of whose novels explore the contradictions of life in a Germany divided after World War II.

Johnson studied German at the universities of Rostock and Leipzig. He translated the work of several American and British authors before beginning to write himself. After his first novel, *Ingrid Babendererde*, was refused by East German publishers when he declined to make various alterations to it, he moved to West Berlin in 1959. His subsequent work focused on the estrangement between people in the two Germanys.

Once in the West, Johnson published *Mutmassungen über Jakob* (1959; *Speculations About Jakob*), *Das dritte Buch über Achim* (1961; *The Third Book About Achim*), shorter fiction in *Karsch, und andere Prosa* (1964; "Karsch, and Other Prose"),

and *Zwei Ansichten* (1965; *Two Views*). All of Johnson's work was experimental: the narrative abruptly shifts from one consciousness or place to another, and words assume different meanings when used by different characters. In the tetralogy *Jahrestage: Aus dem Leben von Gesine Cresspahl* (1970–83; "Anniversaries: From the Life of Gesine Cresspahl"), Johnson used a montage technique to describe problems in New York in the 1960s and events in German history between the 1920s and 1960s. His later works include an essay on the poet Ingeborg Bachmann, *Eine Reise nach Klagenfurt* (1974; "A Journey to Klagenfurt"); a volume of essays, *Berliner Sachen* (1975; "Berlin Affairs"); and *Begleitumstände: Frankfurter Vorlesungen* (1980; "Circumstances: Frankfurt Lectures").

Johnsonese \ˌjän-sə-'nēz, -'nēs\ A literary style that bears characteristics of the writings of 18th-century English lexicographer and writer Samuel Johnson, having balanced phraseology and Latinate diction.

Johnston \'jän-stən\, Jennifer (Prudence) (b. Jan. 12, 1930, Dublin, Ire.) Irish novelist whose works deal with political and cultural tensions in Ireland, with an emphasis on the problems of the Anglo-Irish.

Johnston's first published book, *The Captains and the Kings* (1972), was actually written after *The Gates* (1973); both novels feature the Anglo-Irish setting of a decaying manor house. Johnston's third novel, *How Many Miles to Babylon?* (1974), concerns the complex friendship of two young men who are sentenced to death during World War I. *Shadows on Our Skin* (1977) and *The Railway Station Man* (1984) focus on violence in Northern Ireland, while *The Old Jest* (1979) and *Fool's Sanctuary* (1987) are set during the emergence of modern Ireland in the 1920s. The protagonist of *The Christmas Tree* (1981) attempts to salvage her troubled life before it is cut short by leukemia. Johnston's novel *The Invisible Worm* was published in 1991. She also wrote short stories and plays.

joint author A person who collaborates with one or more persons in the production of a literary work.

Joinville \zhwăⁿ-'vēl\, Jean, Sire de (b. *c.* 1224, Joinville, Champagne [France]—d. Dec. 24, 1317, Joinville) Author of the famous *Histoire de Saint Louis*, a chronicle in French prose that provides a supreme account of the Seventh Crusade (1248–54).

A member of the lesser nobility of Champagne, Joinville took the crusader's cross at the same time as the king, Louis IX, in 1244, and set out with him in August of 1248 on his expedition to Egypt, from where the crusaders planned to attack Syria. Captured with the entire army, Louis and Joinville were ransomed, and Joinville became friends with Louis during the king's subsequent stay at Acre. They returned to France in 1254. The *Histoire de Saint Louis*, completed about 1309, is a personal account in which Joinville reveals himself as a deeply moving man: simple, honest, straightforward, affectionate. Although the short narratives of Louis's life and reign are valuable because of the author's proximity to them, the heart of the book lies in its lengthy central section, the account of the Seventh Crusade. Besides telling of the financial hardships, the dangers of sea voyages, and the ravages of disease, he vividly describes the confusion and lack of discipline in the crusading army. In addition, the book describes Muslim customs.

The original manuscript of the work disappeared from all records shortly after its composition. Most recent editions are based on a text constructed by Natalis de Wailly (1874). Translations into English include Joan Evans, *The History of St. Louis, by Jean, Sire de Joinville* (1938), and René Hague, *The Life of St. Louis by Jean of Joinville* (1955).

Jókai \\'yō-ˌkȯi\\, Mór (b. Feb. 18, 1825, Komárom, Hungary, Austrian Empire—d. May 5, 1904, Budapest) The most important Hungarian novelist of the 19th century. Jókai's collected works (published 1894–98), which did not include his considerable journalistic writing, filled 100 volumes. Early works such as *Hétköznapok* (1845; "Weekdays") show the influence of French Romanticism, but his mature novels are more realistic and concerned with personal experience. *Egy magyar nábob* (1853–54; "A Hungarian Nabob") and *Az aranyember* (1873; "A Man of Gold") deal with contemporary Hungary.

Jolas \\zhō-'lä\\, Eugene and Maria, Maria Jolas *née* Maria McDonald \\mǝk-'dän-ǝld\\ (respectively b. Oct. 26, 1894, Union City, N.J., U.S.—d. May 26, 1952, Paris, Fr.; b. January 1893, Louisville, Ky., U.S.—d. March 4, 1987, Paris) American founders, with Elliot Paul, of the revolutionary literary quarterly TRANSITION.

Raised in Lorraine, France, Eugene Jolas worked as a journalist both in the United States and France. Maria McDonald moved to Europe to study voice in 1913. She was in the United States during World War I but then returned to Europe. The two met in the United States and were married in 1926. Soon after the marriage the Jolases moved to Paris, where Eugene sought to provide a forum for international writers with the establishment of the periodical *transition*. In addition to his role as the chief editor, Jolas wrote poetry reflecting his beliefs that language should be re-created and should rely upon dreams and the subconscious for inspiration. His best volume was *The Language of Night* (1932).

Maria Jolas's work on *transition* was less visible than her husband's; she was essentially the managing and production editor as well as a translator of the foreign pieces that appeared in the magazine. Her other work included the establishment of the Bilingual School of Neuilly (1932–40) and the translation of 12 novels by Nathalie Sarraute.

Jolley \\'jäl-ē\\, Elizabeth, *original name in full* Monica Elizabeth Knight \\'nīt\\ (b. June 4, 1923, Birmingham, Eng.) Australian novelist and short-story writer whose dryly comic work features eccentric characters and examines relationships between women.

Jolley moved from England to Australia in 1959, and her work often features contrasts between a stagnant Europe and a brash, vital Australia. She began writing her first novel, *Palomino*, in the late 1950s, but because publishers were wary of the story, which concerns a lesbian relationship between a 60-year-old doctor and a much younger woman pregnant with her own brother's child, it was not printed until 1980. *The Newspaper of Claremont Street* (1981) was praised for its humor and somber insight into the characters' psychopathology.

The publication of her third and fourth novels earned Jolley admiration outside Australia for her effortless comic style and deft storytelling. In *Mr. Scobie's Riddle* (1983), set in a nursing home, outcast patients come to terms with their own alienation and imminent death. *Miss Peabody's Inheritance* (1983) explores her two favorite themes: love between women and the contrast between the Old World and the New. Later novels include *Foxybaby* (1985), *The Well* (1986), *The Sugar Mother* (1988), and *My Father's Moon* (1989).

Jolley wrote several radio plays, including a dramatization of her short story "Woman in a Lampshade." The 1983 collection of the same name, while considered uneven, was praised for its innovative writing.

Jonah \\'jō-nǝ\\, *also called* Jonas \\'jō-nǝs\\ Biblical character, the recalcitrant minor prophet whose story, probably written sometime between 500 and 350 BCE, contains a message of protest against the exclusiveness of postexilic Judaism. As the story is told in the Old Testament, Jonah is called by God to go to Nineveh (a great Assyrian city) and prophesy disaster caused by the city's excessive wickedness. Jonah thinks that the city must inevitably fall because of God's judgment against it, and he does not want to prophesy for fear that Nineveh might repent and thereby be saved. He takes passage in a ship that will carry him in the opposite direction, hoping to escape God. A storm of unprecedented severity strikes the ship, and the frightened sailors draw lots to discover who is the cause of their unfortunate and calamitous condition. Jonah draws the unlucky lot and is thrown overboard. Swallowed by a great fish, Jonah stays inside the animal for three days and nights. After he cries to the Lord for mercy, the fish vomits him out onto dry land. Though still reluctant, Jonah performs his appointed mission in Nineveh. Much to his displeasure (because he hates the Assyrians), his call to repentance is heard and the city is saved.

Jonah has figured in works by such authors as Thomas Lodge, Francis Quarles, Herman Melville, James Bridie, Robert Frost, Aldous Huxley, and A.M. Klein.

Jónasson \\'yō-näs-sôn\\, Jóhannes Bjarni, *pseudonym* Jóhannes úr Kötlum \\'yō-hän-nes-ür-'kœt-luem\\ (b. Nov. 4, 1899, Goddastadir, Dalasýsla, Ice.—d. April 27, 1972, Rekyjavík) Poet and reformer whose works reflect his resistance to the political and economic trends that he perceived as threatening Iceland's traditional democracy.

Jónasson's poetic development mirrors the major literary and social trends in 20th-century Iceland. Two early works, *Bí bí og blaka* (1926; "Sleep Baby Sleep") and *Álftirnar kvaka* (1929; "The Swans are Singing"), are Neoromantic and lyrical in form and express a love of nature. Neoromanticism gave way to socialism in the 1930s, and his third volume of poetry, *Ég læt sem ég sofi* (1932; "I Pretend to Sleep"), reflects the change. The poem "Frelsi" ("Freedom") was featured in the first volume of *Rauðir pennar* (1935; "Red Pens"), a socialist literary periodical.

The mood and style of Jónasson's poetry underwent another change with the volume *Sjödægra* (1955; "Book of Seven Days"), written not in traditional verse form but using modernist imagery. Although he attacked the resignation and apathy of the welfare society, in his last volume, *Ný og nid* (1970; "Waxing Moon and Waning Moon"), Jónasson voiced his hope in Iceland's new generation.

Jónasson also published four novels and *Annarlegar tungur* ("Strange Tongues"), which included translations of such modern poets as T.S. Eliot and E.E. Cummings.

Jones \\'jōnz\\, Henry Arthur (b. Sept. 20, 1851, Grandborough, Buckinghamshire, Eng.—d. Jan. 7, 1929, London) English playwright who first achieved prominence in the field of melodrama and who later contributed to Victorian "society" drama.

In 1879 Jones's play *Hearts of Oak* was produced in the provinces, and he won fame in London with *The Silver King*, written with Henry Herman and performed in 1882. More popular melodramatic plays followed, including *Michael and His Lost Angel* (1896). Jones was by then moving in high society, and he began to produce works reflecting a more sophisticated comedy, as in *The Case of Rebellious Susan* (1894) and *The Liars* (1897). His plays, however, continued to display acceptance of a rigid Victorian moral code, a conservative attitude that lost him the sympathy of audiences attending the theater of playwrights like George Bernard Shaw and William Archer. Jones wrote and lectured widely about the function of theater, notably in *The Renaissance of the English Drama, 1883–94* (1895).

Jones \\'jōnz\\, James (b. Nov. 6, 1921, Robinson, Ill., U.S.—d. May 9, 1977, Southampton, Long Island, N.Y.) American novelist best known for *From Here to Eternity* (1951), set in Hawaii just before the Pearl Harbor attack.

The strongest influence on Jones's writing was his service in the U.S. Army from 1939 to 1945. He used his knowledge of day-to-day life in the military in his first novel, *From Here to Eternity*, which describes the experiences of a charismatic serviceman who dies shortly after the outbreak of war in the Pacific. In his second novel, *Some Came Running* (1957), Jones drew on his life in Illinois after the war. His next two novels, *The Pistol* (1958) and *The Thin Red Line* (1962), however, return to his wartime experiences. Jones was an expatriate in Paris from 1958 until 1975, when he returned to the United States. *Whistle*, published posthumously in 1978, is the last in the trilogy that includes *From Here to Eternity* and *The Thin Red Line*.

Jones \\'jōnz\\, John, *pseudonym* Jac Glan-y-gors \\'jak-'glan-ə-'gȯrs\\ (b. Nov. 10, 1766, Glanygors near Cerrigydruidion, Denbighshire, Wales—d. May 21, 1821, London, Eng.) Welsh-language satirical poet and social reformer who produced some of the earliest Welsh political writings. Greatly influenced by the essays on the American and French revolutions by propagandist Thomas Paine, Jones published two pamphlets: *Seren tan Gwmwl* (1795; "A Star Under Cloud") and *Toriad y Dydd* (1797; "The Break of Day").

Jones settled in London in 1789 and became a member of the Gwyneddigion, a literary society of Welshmen living in London. Other works include the poems "Sessiwn yng Nghymru," a satire on the difficulties arising from the use of the English language to administer law in Wales, and "Dic Siôn Dafydd" (1803), a satiric characterization of a Welshman who feigns ignorance of his native tongue.

Jones, LeRoi *see* Amiri BARAKA.

Jones \\'jōnz\\, Thomas Gwynn (b. Oct. 10, 1871, Abergele, Denbighshire, Wales—d. March 7, 1949, Aberystwyth, Cardiganshire) Welsh-language poet and scholar best known for his narrative poems on traditional Celtic themes.

Critics have held Jones's greatest achievement to be the poems *Tir na n-Og*, a lyrical play with music; "Broséliâwnd," set in the forest of Broceliande; "Anatiomaros," set in a district of ancient Gaul; "Argoed," depicting an ideal community; and "Cynddilig," about the 6th-century Welshman Llywarch Hen. His translations of J.W. von Goethe's *Faust* (1922) and his collection of Greek poems and Latin epigrams, *Blodau o Hen Ardd* (1927; with H.J. Rose; "Flowers from an Ancient Garden"), are considered to be among the most successful renderings of ancient literature into Welsh.

Jones, Tom \\'täm-'jōnz\\ Fictional character, the lusty protagonist of Henry Fielding's picaresque novel TOM JONES.

jongleur \\zhōⁿ-'glœ̄r, *Angl* -'glər, 'jäŋ-glər\\ [French, from Old French, alteration (influenced by *jangleor* chatterer, braggart) of *juglere* buffoon, minstrel, from Latin *joculator* buffoon] Professional storyteller or public entertainer in medieval France. The role of the jongleur included that of musician, juggler, and acrobat, as well as reciter of such literary works as fabliaux, chansons de geste, and lays, as well as other metrical romances that were sometimes of his own composition. Jongleurs performed in marketplaces on public holidays, in abbeys, and in castles of nobles, who sometimes retained them in permanent employment. In such a case the jongleur became known as a *ménestrel* and devoted more of his time to literary creation than to entertainment. Fraternities of jongleurs became known as *puys*, groups that held competitions for lyric poets. The jongleur reached the height of his importance in the 13th century but lapsed into decline in the 14th, when various facets of his complex role were disseminated

among other performers—*e.g.*, musicians, actors, and acrobats. *Compare* GOLIARD.

Jonson \\'jän-sən\\, Ben, *byname of* Benjamin Jonson (b. June 11?, 1572, London, Eng.—d. Aug. 6, 1637, London) English Jacobean dramatist, lyric poet, and literary critic. He is generally regarded as the second most important English dramatist, after William Shakespeare, during the reign of James I.

National Portrait Gallery, London

Jonson's formal education ended early. He worked briefly as a bricklayer and as a soldier in the Netherlands. On returning to England he became an actor and playwright, following the life of a strolling player and writing for Philip Henslowe, the leading impresario for the public theater. When EVERY MAN IN HIS HUMOUR (performed 1598) was successfully presented by the Lord Chamberlain's theatrical company, Jonson's reputation was established. In the play he tried to bring the spirit and manner of Latin comedy to the English popular stage. Following this success, the same company acted Jonson's EVERY MAN OUT OF HIS HUMOUR (performed 1599), which proved a disaster.

In 1605 Jonson's *The Masque of Blackness* was presented at court. The "masque," a quasi-dramatic entertainment that was much elaborated during the reign of James I, was given its characteristic shape and style by Jonson in collaboration with Inigo Jones, who specialized in costumes and scenic effects. Jonson's early masques were clearly successful, for during the following years he was repeatedly called upon to function as poet at court. Among his masques were *Hymenaei* (1606), *Hue and Cry After Cupid* (1608), *The Masque of Beauty* (1608), and *The Masque of Queens* (1609). Jonson also invented the "antimasque," which preceded the masque proper and which featured grotesques or comics who were primarily actors rather than dancers and singers. After Jones and Jonson quarreled, however, Jonson lost favor at court.

During this period, nevertheless, he made a mark second only to Shakespeare's in the public theater. VOLPONE (performed 1605/1606) and THE ALCHEMIST (performed 1610) were among the most popular and esteemed plays of the time. Both plays are eloquent and compact, sharp-tongued but controlled. Jonson was noted for engaging in "wit-combats" with Shakespeare, and first at the Mermaid Tavern and then at the Devil Tavern, Jonson reigned supreme. It was a young man's ultimate honor to be regarded as one of the Tribe of Ben.

Jonson's major comedies express a strong distaste for the world in which he lived and a delight in exposing its follies and vices. He was easily the most learned dramatist of his time, and he was also a master of theatrical plot, language, and characterization. His chief plays are still very good theater. He exerted a great influence on the playwrights who immediately followed him, and he alone gave the essential impulse to dramatic characterization in the comedy of the Restoration and also in the plays of the 18th and 19th centuries.

Jónsson \\'yōns-sȯn\\, Arngrímur, *also called* Arngrímur Jónsson Vídalín \\'vē-dä-lēn\\, *byname* Arngrímur the Learned \\'ärn-grē-mu̇er\\ (b. 1568, Vídidalur, Ice.—d. 1648, Hólar) Scholar and historian who brought the treasures of Icelandic literature to the attention of Danish and Swedish scholars.

Jónsson studied at Copenhagen University and returned to Iceland to be head of the Latin school at Hólar, which had become a general center of learning. There, Jónsson collected Icelandic manuscripts on which he based his studies of Icelandic and Scandinavian history.

In 1597 Jónsson produced for the Danish government a digest of his studies, which presented virtually a new history of Norway and Denmark and threw light on the early history of Sweden. *Crymogaea* (1609) and *Specimen Islandiae Historicum et Magna ex Parte Chorographicum* (1643), which described Iceland and its history, were his most widely read publications.

Jónsson \\'yōns-sȯn\\, Hjálmar, *also called* Bólu-Hjálmar \\'bȯ-lʉ-'hyal-mär\\ (b. 1796, Eyjafjördur, Ice.—d. July 25, 1875, Breidumýri)   Icelandic folk poet of brilliant satiric power who depicted his hard life in noteworthy poems.

The illegitimate son of a servant girl and a farmhand, Jónsson had little education, but he soon became an avid reader of the ancient Icelandic sagas and *Edda*s. Miserably poor all his life, he was first a farmhand, then a small tenant farmer. Jónsson was notable as a scathing critic of bureaucracy and the church, and he used a rough invective that made some of his verse unprintable, though it was common currency in the oral tradition of Iceland long after he died. The first collection of his poems was not published until 1879. His collected poems were published in two volumes (1915, 1919) and his collected works in four volumes (1949).

Jǫrd \\'yœrth, *Angl* 'yȯrth, 'yȯrth\\ ("Earth"), *also called* Fjǫrgyn \\'fyœr-gin, *Angl* 'fyȯr-, 'fyȯr-\\ *or* Hlódyn \\'hlȯ-thin\\   In Norse mythology, a giantess, mother of the deity Thor and mistress of the god Odin. In the late pre-Christian era she was believed to have had a husband of the same name, perhaps indicating her transformation into a masculine personality.

Jordan \\'jȯrd-ən\\, A.C., *in full* Archibald Campbell (b. Oct. 30, 1906, Mbokothwana Mission, Cape Colony [now in South Africa]—d. Oct. 20, 1968, Madison, Wis., U.S.)   Xhosa novelist and educator who belonged to the second generation of South African black writers.

Jordan served as lecturer in Bantu languages and African studies at the University of Cape Town until 1961, when he immigrated to the United States. He wrote a series of articles entitled *Towards an African Literature*, which originally appeared in the periodical *Africa South* and were later published in book form. They discuss such topics as traditional praise poems, riddles and proverbs, the history of Xhosa literature, and various important individual Bantu writers. His novel *Ingqumbo yeminyanya* (1940; *The Wrath of the Ancestors*) goes much beyond earlier Xhosa novels in its attempt to reveal the workings of a modern black African mind in its fight against conservative tribal forces. Before his death, Jordan completed two more novels and a collection of short stories; the stories were published in 1974 under the title *Kwezo mpindo zeTsitsa* ("Along the Bends of the Tsitsa").

Jordan \\'jȯrd-ən\\, June, *married surname* Meyer \\'mī-ər\\ (b. July 9, 1936, New York, N.Y., U.S.)   Versatile African-American author who investigated both social and personal concerns through poetry, essays, and drama.

Jordan grew up in Brooklyn, N.Y., and attended Barnard College and the University of Chicago; beginning in 1967 she taught English and literature. She fought for the inclusion of black studies and third world studies in university curricula and advocated acceptance of Black English. Her first poetry collection, *Who Look at Me*, appeared in 1969; among her subsequent collections of poems were *Some Changes* (1971), *Things*

That I Do in the Dark (1977), *Living Room* (1985), and *Naming Our Destiny* (1989).

In the 1970s Jordan wrote books for children and young adults, including the novel *His Own Where* (1971) and the biography *Fannie Lou Hamer* (1972). As a journalist and poet Jordan wrote about feminism and the struggles against racism and for freedom of choice and opportunity for minorities. Her essays are collected in the books *Civil Wars* (1981), *On Call* (1985), and *Technical Difficulties: African-American Notes on the State of the Union* (1992).

Jordan \\'jȯrd-ən\\, Thomas (b. 1612?, London, Eng.—d. 1685?, London)   Poet, playwright, and prolific Royalist pamphleteer.

In 1637 Jordan published his first volume of poems, entitled *Poeticall Varieties*, and in the same year appeared *A Pill to Purge Melancholy*. He wrote many volumes of verse and, after the Restoration in 1660, many plays, in at least one of which, *Money Is an Asse* (produced 1668), he acted.

In 1671 Jordan was appointed laureate to the city of London; from this date on he annually composed a panegyric on the lord mayor and arranged the pagentry of the lord mayor's shows, which he celebrated in verse. Many volumes of these curious productions are preserved in the British Library.

Jørgensen \\'yœr-gən-sən\\, Johannes, *in full* Jens Johannes Jørgensen (b. Nov. 6, 1866, Svendborg, Den.—d. May 29, 1956, Svendborg)   Writer known in Denmark mainly for his poetry (*Digte 1894–98* [1898] and *Udvalte Digte* [1944]), but best known in other countries for his biographies of St. Francis of Assisi (1907) and St. Catherine of Siena (1915).

As a student at the University of Copenhagen, Jørgensen became a follower of the influential critic Georg Brandes but soon became an outspoken critic of Brandes' materialistic realism. He became an advocate of poetic symbolism and, soon after, developed an interest in mystical and religious literature. He converted to Roman Catholicism in 1896. His later life was largely spent writing his autobiography, *Mit livs legende*, 7 vol. (1916–28; *Jørgensen: An Autobiography*, 2 vol.).

Jǫrmungand \\'yœr-mȯn-gänd\\ *or* **Jǫrmungandr** \\-,gänd-ər\\   In Germanic mythology, the evil serpent that surrounds the world. Jǫrmungand was one of the offspring of the trickster god Loki and Angerboda. Because Thor failed in an attempt to kill Jǫrmungand, the two are destined to meet and destroy each other during the Ragnarǫk ("Doom of the Gods").

Jorrocks's Jaunts and Jollities \\'jär-ək\\ (*in full* Jorrocks's Jaunts and Jollities; or, The Hunting, Shooting, Racing, Driving, Sailing, Eating, Eccentric and Extravagant Exploits of that Renowned Sporting Citizen, Mr. John Jorrocks, of St. Botolph Lane and Great Coram Street)   Series of picaresque comic tales by Robert Smith SURTEES, originally published as individual stories in his *New Sporting Magazine* between 1831 and 1834 and collected in book form in 1838.

The ebullient Jorrocks is a vulgar Cockney grocer, a city man who loves the sporting life in the country. Jorrocks is surrounded by a variety of eccentric characters as comical as he is. The adventures of Jorrocks continued in two novels: *Handley Cross* (1843; expanded edition, 1854) and *Hillingdon Hall* (1845). A revised and enlarged version of *Jorrocks's Jaunts and Jollities* was published posthumously in 1869.

jōruri \\'jȯ-,rū-rē\\   In Japanese literature and music, a type of chanted recitative; often the script for a bunraku puppet drama. Its name derives from the *Jōrurihime monogatari*, a 15th-century romantic ballad, the leading character of which is Lady Jōruri. At first it was chanted to the accompaniment of the four-string biwa (Japanese lute); with the introduction of the three-stringed, plucked samisen (or *shamisen*) in the 16th century, both the music and the scripts developed. When puppets were added at the end of the 16th century, the *jōruri* expanded to add a dramatic quality. Themes of loyalty, vengeance, filial piety, love, and religious miracles were included; dialogue and descriptive commentary took an increasingly large role. The chanter was at first more important than the writer of the script, until the appearance of one of Japan's greatest playwrights, Chikamatsu Monzaemon, in the late 17th and early 18th centuries. A 30-year collaboration between Chikamatsu and the chanter Takemoto Gidayū (1651–1714) raised the puppet theater to a high art.

Joseph \\'jō-səf, -zəf\\ of Arimathea \\,ar-i-mə-'thē-ə\\ (b. Arimathea, Samaria; fl. *c.* AD 30) According to all four biblical Gospels, a secret disciple of Jesus, whose body he buried in his own tomb.

Joseph is accorded much attention in later literature. In the apocryphal *Gospel of Peter* (2nd century), he is a friend of Jesus and of Pilate. In Robert de Boron's verse romance *Joseph d'Arimathie* (*c.* 1200), he is entrusted with the Holy Grail (a chalice used during the Last Supper) and is said to have caught the blood that flowed from Jesus' wounds. In Sir Thomas Malory's *Le Morte Darthur* (15th century), when Galahad receives the vision of the Grail, he sees Joseph standing at the altar dressed as a bishop. *See also* GRAIL.

Joseph and His Brothers \\'jō-səf, -zəf\\ Series of four novels by Thomas MANN that formed an epic bildungsroman about the biblical figure Joseph. Known collectively in German as *Joseph und seine Brüder*, the tetralogy consists of *Die Geschichten Jaakobs* (1933; U.K. title, *The Tales of Jacob*; U.S. title, *Joseph and His Brothers*), *Der junge Joseph* (1934; *Young Joseph*), *Joseph in Ägypten* (1936; *Joseph in Egypt*), and *Joseph der Ernährer* (1943; *Joseph the Provider*). The four novels were published together in English in 1948.

Joseph and His Brothers reinterprets the biblical story as told in the Book of Genesis, employing psychological insight and wide-ranging knowledge of myth, history, and geography.

Joseph Andrews \\'jō-səf-'an-,drūz, 'jō-zəf\\ (*in full* The History of the Adventures of Joseph Andrews and of His Friend Mr. Abraham Adams) Novel by Henry FIELDING, published in 1742. It was written as a reaction against Samuel Richardson's novel *Pamela; or, Virtue Rewarded* (1740). *Joseph Andrews* begins as a burlesque of *Pamela*, but the parodic intention of the novel soon becomes secondary, and it develops into a masterpiece of sustained irony and social criticism. At its center is Parson Adams, one of the great comic figures of literature. Joseph and the parson have a series of adventures, in all of which they manage to expose the hypocrisy and affectation of others through their own innocence and guilelessness.

Joseph K. \\'jō-səf-'kä, -zəf\\ Protagonist of the allegorical novel THE TRIAL by Franz Kafka.

Josephson \\'jō-səf-sən, -zəf-\\, Matthew (b. Feb. 15, 1899, Brooklyn, N.Y., U.S.—d. March 13, 1978, Santa Cruz, Calif.) American biographer whose clear writing was based on sound and thorough scholarship.

As an expatriate in Paris in the 1920s, Josephson was an associate editor of *Broom* (1922–24), which featured both American and European writers, and he later served as an editor for the magazine *transition* (1928–29).

His first book was a well-researched and authoritative biography of Émile Zola, *Zola and His Time: The History of His Martial Career in Letters* (1928). Other highly praised biographies followed. His interest in 19th-century French literature appeared in such works as *Victor Hugo* (1942) and *Stendhal*

(1946), which helped to regenerate American interest in Stendhal's work. He addressed another favorite topic, American economics, in what is perhaps his best-known work, *The Robber Barons: The Great American Capitalists, 1861–1901* (1934). The book chronicles the lives of John D. Rockefeller, Andrew Carnegie, and other barons of industry in the late 19th century.

Josipovici \\,jō-zē-pō-'vē-chē\\, Gabriel (David) (b. Oct. 8, 1940, Nice, Fr.) French-born British novelist, literary theorist, dramatist, and short-story writer whose work was characterized by its experimental form and its attention to language.

From 1945 Josipovici was reared in Egypt. He was educated at Victoria College, Cairo, and attended Cheltenham College in England and St. Edmund Hall, Oxford. He joined the faculty of the University of Sussex in 1963.

Josipovici laid the philosophical framework for his fiction in his books of criticism, including *The World and the Book* (1971), *The Lessons of Modernism* (1977), *Writing and the Body* (1982), *The Mirror of Criticism* (1983), *The Book of God* (1988), and *Text and Voice* (1992). His novels grew progressively experimental. The first three—*The Inventory* (1968), *Words* (1971), and *The Present* (1975)—were written mostly in dialogue, while *Migrations* (1977) and *The Air We Breathe* (1981) were composed of a series of images and sound patterns following a loosely narrative form. Among his other novels were *The Echo Chamber* (1980), *Conversations in Another Room* (1984), *Contre-Jour* (1986), *The Big Glass* (1991), and *In a Hotel Garden* (1993). The radio play *Vergil Dying* (1981) was perhaps his most acclaimed drama. He also wrote the short-fiction collections *Mobius the Stripper* (1974), *Four Stories* (1977), and *In the Fertile Land* (1987).

journal \\'jərn-əl\\ 1. An account of day-to-day events or a record of experiences, ideas, or reflections kept regularly for private use that is similar to, but sometimes less personal than, a DIARY. 2. A daily newspaper or a periodical publication especially dealing with matters of current interest. The word is often used of official or semiofficial publications of special groups.

journalism \\'jər-nə-,liz-əm\\ Writing designed for publication in a newspaper or magazine. Such writing is sometimes characterized by a direct presentation of facts or description of events without an attempt at interpretation.

Journal of a Tour to the Hebrides, The \\'heb-ri-,dēz\\ (*in full* The Journal of a Tour to the Hebrides, with Samuel Johnson, LL.D.) Work by James BOSWELL, published in 1785. The book is an account of the trip that Boswell took with Samuel Johnson to Scotland in 1773. The journal is mainly Boswell's record of Johnson's reactions to the people, landscapes, and customs they encountered along the way. Johnson published his own account of the trip in *A Journey to the Western Islands of Scotland* (1775).

Journal of the Plague Year, A An account of the Great Plague of London in 1664–65, written by Daniel DEFOE and published in 1722. Narrated by "H.F.," an inhabitant of London who purportedly was an eyewitness to the devastation that followed the outbreak of bubonic plague, the book was a historical and fictional reconstruction by Defoe.

Journal to Stella \\'stel-ə\\ Series of letters written (1710–13) from Jonathan SWIFT in London to Esther Johnson and her companion, Rebecca Dingley, in Ireland.

Esther (Stella) was the daughter of the widowed companion of Sir William Temple's sister. Swift, who was employed by Sir William, was Stella's tutor when she was a child, and he formed a lifelong attachment to her. Swift wrote to Stella about current political and social events and his reactions to them. Swift's letters contain his comments on eminent people as well as reflective, often humorous descriptions of occurrences and personalities and warm, affectionate personal messages.

Journey to the Center of the Earth, A
Novel by Jules VERNE, published in 1864 in French as *Voyage au centre de la Terre*. It is the second book in his popular science-fiction series *Voyages extraordinaires* (1863–1910).

Otto Lidenbrock, an impetuous German professor of geology, discovers an encoded manuscript in which a 16th-century explorer claims to have found a passageway to the center of the Earth. Otto impulsively prepares a subterranean expedition, enlisting his young nephew Axel and a stoic Icelandic guide, Hans Bjelke. After descending into an extinct volcano in Iceland, the men spend several months in a underground world of luminous rocks, antediluvian forests, and fantastic sea creatures until they ride a volcanic eruption out of Stromboli Island, off the coast of Italy.

Journey to the Western Islands of Scotland, A \'skät-lənd\
Book by Samuel JOHNSON, published in 1775. The *Journey* was the result of a three-month trip to Scotland that Johnson took with James Boswell in 1773. It contains Johnson's descriptions of the customs, religion, education, trade, and agriculture of a society that was new to him. The account in Boswell's diary, published after Johnson's death as *The Journal of a Tour to the Hebrides, with Samuel Johnson, LL.D.* (1785), offers an intimate personal record of Johnson's behavior and conversation during the trip.

Journey Without Maps
Autobiographical travel book by Graham GREENE, published in 1936, that describes his first journey to Africa. Drawn from the journals Greene kept on his travels in West Africa, the book examines the internal as well as external maps people use to chart their experiences.

Jouve \'zhūv\
Pierre-Jean (b. Oct. 11, 1887, Arras, Fr.—d. Jan. 8, 1976, Paris)   French poet, novelist, and critic.

Jouve's earliest verses, *Les Muses romaines et florentines* (1910; "Roman and Florentine Muses"), *Présences* (1912; "Presences"), and *Parler* (1913; "Speaking"), were inspired by Symbolism.

Prevented by ill health from serving in World War I, Jouve spent the war years in Switzerland, serving as a volunteer hospital orderly and writing pacifist verses. Works of this period include *Vous êtes des hommes* (1915; "You Are Men") and *Danse des morts* (1917; "Dance of the Dead"). In 1924 Jouve converted to Roman Catholicism and, concurrently, became fascinated with psychoanalysis—events that caused him to explore the themes of guilt, sexuality, and death. Spirituality and eroticism were merged in *Les Mystérieuses Noces* (1925; "Mysterious Weddings"), *Nouvelles Noces* (1926; "New Weddings"), and *Sueur de sang* (1935; "Sweat of Blood") and in the prose works *Paulina 1880* (1925), *Le Monde désert* (1927; "The Deserted World"), and *La Scène capitale* (1935; "The Crucial Scene").

Jouve spent the World War II years in Geneva, where he wrote *La Vierge de Paris* (1944; "The Virgin of Paris"). The postwar years, spent in Paris, saw the publication of other important collections of verse and explorations of language such as *Ode* (1950), *Langue* (1952; "Language"), *Lyrique* (1956), and *Moires* (1962; "Watered Silk"). He also wrote critical essays on 19th-century French writers and artists and was an adept translator. He was awarded the Académie Française's Grand Prix de Poésie in 1966.

Jowett \'jaủ-ət\
Benjamin (b. April 15, 1817, London, Eng.—d. Oct. 1, 1893, Headley Park, Hampshire)   English classical scholar who was considered one of the greatest teachers of the 19th century. He was renowned for his translations of Plato.

Jowett was educated at St. Paul's School, London, and Balliol College, Oxford. He was made a fellow at Balliol in 1838 and was appointed a tutor in the college in 1842.

Jowett's book *The Epistles of St. Paul* (1855) was controversial, and his contribution to *Essays and Reviews* (1860) caused his opponents to accuse him of heresy. During this period his lectures on the *Republic* stimulated intense interest in Plato. His translations include *The Dialogues of Plato*, in 1871; Thucydides' *History*, in 1881; and Aristotle's *Poetics*, in 1885. His edition of Plato's *Republic*, on which he had worked for 30 years, was published posthumously in 1894.

Joyce \'jȯis\
James (Augustine Aloysius) (b. Feb. 2, 1882, Dublin, Ire.—d. Jan. 13, 1941, Zürich, Switz.)   Irish novel-

Gisèle Freund

ist noted for his experimental use of language and exploration of new literary methods in such works of fiction as ULYSSES (1922) and FINNEGANS WAKE (1939).

Joyce was the eldest of 10 children in his family to survive infancy. His early formal education was spotty, but he entered University College, Dublin, where he read widely and took an active part in the college's Literary and Historical Society. Greatly admiring Henrik Ibsen, he learned Dano-Norwegian to read the original and had an article, "Ibsen's New Drama"—a review of the play *When We Dead Awaken*—published in the London *Fortnightly Review* just after his 18th birthday. This early success confirmed Joyce in his resolution to become a writer. He graduated in 1902 and went to Paris.

Joyce's real efforts during and after his college years went toward mastering the art of writing. He wrote verses and experimented with short prose passages called "epiphanies," by which he meant accounts of moments when the truth about a person or an event was revealed. To support himself while writing, he decided to become a doctor, but he soon abandoned the idea of medical studies, wrote several book reviews, and studied in the Sainte-Geneviève Library.

Recalled home in April 1903 because his mother was dying, he tried various occupations, including teaching, and lived at various addresses, including the Martello Tower at Sandycove, now Ireland's Joyce Museum. Although he had begun writing a lengthy naturalistic novel, *Stephen Hero*, based on the events of his own life, he interrupted the work to publish the stories that would make up THE DUBLINERS (1914). Meanwhile, Joyce had met a young woman named Nora Barnacle and persuaded her to leave Ireland with him, although he refused, on principle, to marry.

Joyce and Barnacle left Dublin in October 1904. They stayed briefly in Pola (Pula), Austria-Hungary, then in Trieste, where their children, George and Lucia, were born. The next years were frustrating and Joyce's financial difficulties increased. He continued to write, however, and reworked *Stephen Hero* into "a work in five chapters" under the title A PORTRAIT OF THE ARTIST AS A YOUNG MAN (1916).

When Italy declared war in 1915, Joyce took his family to Zürich, where he first gave private lessons in English and worked on the early chapters of *Ulysses*. He was helped financially by a grant from the Royal Literary Fund, then by a large grant from Edith Rockefeller McCormick, and finally by a series of grants from Harriet Shaw Weaver, editor of *The Egoist* magazine, which by 1930 had amounted to more than £23,000. He had to contend with eye diseases that never left him. From February 1917 until 1930 he endured a series of 25 operations for iritis, glaucoma, and cataracts, sometimes being totally blind for short intervals.

Unable to find an English printer willing to set up *A Portrait of the Artist* for book publication, Weaver used an American printer and published it herself in 1916. Encouraged by the acclaim given to the book, in March 1918 the American *Little Review* began to publish episodes from *Ulysses*, continuing until the work was banned in December 1920. In July 1920 Joyce went to Paris. *Ulysses* was published there by Sylvia Beach, proprietor of Shakespeare and Co. bookshop, in 1922. The book, already notorious for its censorship troubles, became immediately famous.

In Paris Joyce worked on *Finnegans Wake*, the title of which was kept secret, the novel being known simply as "Work in Progress" until it was published in its entirety in May 1939. In addition to his chronic eye troubles, Joyce suffered great and prolonged anxiety over his daughter's mental health. It became necessary finally to place her in a mental hospital near Paris. In 1931 he and Nora were married. After the fall of France in World War II (1940), Joyce returned to Zürich, where he died, still disappointed with the reception given to his last book. In addition to the novels and short stories for which he is famous, Joyce published three volumes of poetry and a play.

József \'yō-zhef\, Attila (b. April 11, 1905, Budapest, Austria-Hungary—d. Dec. 3, 1937, Balatonszárszó)   One of the greatest Hungarian poets of the 20th century.

József was attracted by Marxist ideology and became a member of the then-illegal Communist Party. In 1932 he launched a short-lived literary periodical, *Valóság*, and in 1936 he became one of the cofounders of the review *Szép Szó*. In his own poetry József presented intimate pictures of proletarian life. He immortalized his mother, a poor washerwoman, and made her a symbol of the working class. He created a style of melancholy realism, infused with irrationality, through which he was able to express the complex feelings of modern men and women and reveal his own faith in life's essential beauty and harmony.

Juan Manuel \'kwän-män-'wel\, Don (b. May 5, 1282, Escalona, New Castile [Spain]—d. 1348, Córdoba)   Nobleman and man of letters who has been called the most important prose writer of 14th-century Spain.

Juan Manuel is best known for his *Libro de los enxiemplos del conde Lucanor et de Patronio* (1328–35; *Count Lucanor; or, The Fifty Pleasant Stories of Patronio*), a treatise on morals in the form of 50 short tales. The work was written in a lucid and straightforward manner, with an informal prose style that

was almost completely free of the ornate language of the day. It greatly influenced the development of Spanish prose. Of Juan Manuel's 12 books, several are lost. Outstanding among his extant works are *Libro de los estados* ("Book of States"), a treatise on politics, and *Libro del caballero y del escudero* ("Book of the Knight and the Squire"), a treatise on society.

Judah ha-Levi \'jü-də-,hä-'lē-,vī, -'lev-ē\, *Hebrew in full* Yehuda ben Shemuel ha-Levi (b. *c.* 1075, Tudela, Kingdom of Pamplona [Spain]—d. July 1141, Egypt)   Jewish poet and religious philosopher. His works were the culmination of the development of Hebrew poetry within the Arabic cultural sphere. Among his major works are the poems collected in *Dīwān*, the "Zionide" poems celebrating Zion, and the *Sefer ha-Kuzari* ("Book of the Khazar"), presenting his philosophy of Judaism in dialogue form.

At the time of his birth, most of Spain, including his native town, was still under Muslim rule. Although there were pockets of flourishing Jewish culture and prosperity, Jews were often caught in the struggle between Muslims and Christians. Judah ha-Levi lived for a time in Andalusia, in Toledo, and in Córdoba, at the center of Jewish cultural life. He had a wide circle of acquaintances and maintained relationships with many famous contemporaries in Spain as well as abroad. As old age approached he felt an increasing need to travel to Jerusalem, writing about the city at length in verse and prose. The epilogue of the *Kuzari* explains his attachment to Zion and reads as a farewell to Spain. Among his many poems celebrating the Holy Land is "Zionide" ("Ode to Zion"), his most famous work and the most widely translated medieval Hebrew poem.

Judah ha-Levi set out for the Holy Land via Egypt but died before he reached his destination. The legend that he was killed in Zion by a hostile Muslim found wide circulation and was repeated in detail by two 19th-century poets, in German by Heinrich Heine in the *Romanzero* of 1851 and in Hebrew by Micah-Joseph Lebensohn in *Rabi Yehudah ha-Levi* in 1869.

Judas Iscariot \'jü-dəs-is-'kar-ē-ət\ (d. *c.* AD 30)   In Christianity, one of the 12 Apostles, notorious for having betrayed Jesus. Other than his apostleship, his act of betrayal, and his death, little is known about him.

Judas disclosed Jesus' whereabouts to the chief priests and elders for 30 pieces of silver. The officials then provided the armed guard that Judas took to the Garden of Gethsemane, near Jerusalem, where Jesus had gone to pray with the other Apostles after the Last Supper. There Judas identified Jesus with a kiss, addressing him as "master."

There are variant traditions about Judas' death. According to Matthew 27:3–10, he repented after seeing Jesus condemned to death, then returned the silver and hanged himself (traditionally from the Judas tree [*Cercis*]). In Acts 1:18, he "bought a field with the reward of his wickedness; and falling headlong he burst open in the middle and all his bowels gushed out," implying that he threw himself down purposely.

In Dante's *Inferno*, Judas appears in the deepest chasm of hell with Julius Caesar's assassins, Brutus and Cassius. In Muslim polemic literature, however, Judas ceases to be a traitor; instead, he supposedly lied to the Jews in order to defend Jesus (who was not crucified). The 14th-century cosmographer Ad-Dimashqī maintained that Judas assumed Jesus' likeness and was crucified in his place. The 2nd-century apocryphal *Gospel of Judas* favorably evaluates him.

His name has subsequently become associated with traitor (a Judas) and treacherous kiss (a Judas kiss).

Jude the Obscure \'jüd\   Novel by Thomas HARDY, published in 1894–95 in *Harper's New Monthly* as *Hearts Insurgent*; published in book form in 1895.

Hardy's last work of fiction, *Jude the Obscure* is also one of his most gloomily fatalistic, depicting the lives of individuals who are trapped by forces beyond their control. Jude Fawley, a poor villager, wants to enter the divinity school at Christminster (Oxford University). Sidetracked by Arabella Donn, an earthy country girl who pretends to be pregnant by him, Jude marries her and is then deserted. He earns a living as a stonemason at Christminster; there he falls in love with his independent-minded cousin, Sue Bridehead. Out of a sense of obligation, Sue marries the schoolmaster Phillotson, who has helped her. Unable to bear living with Phillotson, she returns to live with Jude and eventually bears his children out of wedlock. Their poverty and the weight of society's disapproval begin to take a toll on Sue and Jude; the climax occurs when Jude's son by Arabella hangs Sue and Jude's children and himself. In penance, Sue returns to Phillotson and the church. Jude returns to Arabella and eventually dies miserably.

The novel's sexual frankness shocked the public, as did Hardy's criticisms of marriage, the university system, and the church. Hardy was so distressed by its reception that he wrote no more fiction, concentrating solely on his poetry.

judgment tale *see* DILEMMA TALE.

Judith \ˈjü-dith\   Biblical character, the beautiful widow whose story is told in the apocryphal Book of Judith.

At the siege of the Jewish city of Bethulia, a general named Achior warns Holofernes, leader of the Assyrian expedition, of the danger of attacking the Jews. Judith leaves the besieged city in pretended flight and foretells to Holofernes that he will be victorious. Invited into his tent, she cuts off his head as he lies in drunken sleep. A Jewish victory over the leaderless Assyrian forces follows. Judith has been portrayed in literature by such authors as Geoffrey Chaucer, Friedrich Hebbel, Arnold Bennett, and Jean Giraudoux.

Judson \ˈjəd-sən\, E.Z.C., *in full* Edward Zane Carroll, *pseudonym* Ned Buntline \ˈbənt-ˌlīn\ (b. March 20, 1823, Stamford, N.Y., U.S.—d. July 16, 1886, Stamford)   American adventurer and writer, an originator of the so-called dime novels that were popular during the late 19th century.

Judson's earlier stories were based on the exploits of his own picaresque career, which began as a cabin boy in the U.S. Navy. In 1844 he left the navy, reputedly to fight Indians and travel in the West. He contributed stories to the *Knickerbocker Magazine* and in 1844 established the short-lived *Ned Buntline's Magazine* in Cincinnati, Ohio. He later went to Nashville, Tenn., and founded the sensational newspaper *Ned Buntline's Own.*

Judson joined the Union Army during the Civil War but was dishonorably discharged in 1864 for drunkenness. He later met William F. Cody, whom he styled "Buffalo Bill" and portrayed as the hero of a number of his dime novels. He also wrote a play for Cody, *The Scouts of the Plains* (1872; also published as *The Scouts of the Prairies*), patterned on his life.

Judson's hundreds of dime novels and serials were sensational stories of swashbuckling heroes and violence and had such titles as *The Mysteries and Miseries of New York* (1848), *Ned Buntline's Life Yarn* (1848), *Stella Delorme; or, The Comanche's Dream* (1860), and *Buffalo Bill's First Trial; or, Will Cody, the Pony Express Rider* (1888).

Judy \ˈjü-dē\   Puppet character, wife of the brutal, deceitful Punch. *See* PUNCH.

jueju or **chüeh-chü** \ˈjwe-ˈjǖ\ [Chinese *juéjù,* from *juè* to cut off, sever + *jù* sentence]   A Chinese verse form that was popular during the Tang dynasty (618–907). An outgrowth of the *lüshi,* it was a four-line poem, each line of which consisted of five or seven words; it omitted either the first four lines, the

last four lines, the first two and the last two lines, or the middle four lines of the *lüshi.* Thus it retained the tonal quality of the *lüshi,* but the antithetical structure was made optional.

Julian \ˈjü-lē-ən\ of Norwich \ˈnȯr-ij, -ich, -wich\, *also called* Juliana \ˌjü-lē-ˈän-ə, -ˈan-\ (b. 1342, probably Norwich, Norfolk, Eng.—d. after 1416)   Celebrated mystic whose *Revelations of Divine Love* is generally considered one of the most remarkable documents of medieval religious experience.

According to Julian's report, on May 13, 1373, she was healed of a serious illness after experiencing a series of visions of Christ's suffering and of the Blessed Virgin, about which she wrote two accounts; the second, longer version was composed 20 or 30 years after the first. Unparalleled in English religious literature, the *Revelations* addresses the most profound mysteries of the Christian faith—such as the problems of predestination, the foreknowledge of God, and the existence of evil. The work is noted for its clarity and depth of perception and its sincerity and beauty of expression.

Juliet \ˈjü-lē-ət\, *in full* Juliet Capulet \ˈkap-yü-lət\   One of the two ill-fated lovers who are the protagonists of William Shakespeare's tragedy ROMEO AND JULIET.

Julius Caesar \ˈjü-lē-əs-ˈsē-zər\   Tragedy in five acts by William SHAKESPEARE, produced in 1599–1600 and published in the First Folio of 1623 from a transcript of a promptbook.

The drama takes place in 44 BC, after Caesar has returned to Rome. Fearing Caesar's ambition, Cassius forms a conspiracy among Roman republicans. He convinces the reluctant Brutus to join them. Caesar is slain in the Senate on March 15, "the ides of March." His friend Mark Antony gives a stirring funeral oration that inspires the crowd to turn against the conspirators. Octavius, Caesar's nephew, is restored to power; Brutus and Cassius are eventually defeated at the Battle of Philippi, where they kill themselves to avoid further dishonor.

Jung \ˈyu̇ŋ\, Carl (Gustav) (b. July 26, 1875, Kesswil, Switz.—d. June 6, 1961, Küsnacht)   Swiss psychologist and psychiatrist whose theories were the basis of a form of literary criticism known as ARCHETYPAL CRITICISM. His work has been influential in psychiatry and in the study of religion, literature, and related fields.

Jung was a student at the universities of Basel and Zürich (M.D., 1902). He joined the staff of the Burghölzli Asylum of the University of Zürich (1900), where he began pioneering studies of patients' seemingly peculiar and illogical responses to stimulus words. Jung found that the responses were caused by emotionally charged clusters of associations withheld from consciousness because of their disagreeable, (perceived) immoral, and frequently sexual content. He used the now famous term *complex* (German *Komplex*) to describe such conditions.

From 1907 to 1912, Jung was Sigmund Freud's close collaborator, but he broke with Freud largely over the latter's insistence on the sexual bases of neurosis. A serious disagreement came in 1912, with the publication of Jung's *Wandlungen und Symbole der Libido* (*Psychology of the Unconscious*), which ran counter to many of Freud's ideas.

Jung differentiated two types of people according to attitude: extroverted (outward-looking) and introverted (inward-looking). Later he differentiated four functions of the mind—thinking, feeling, sensation, and intuition—one or more of which predominate in any given person. The results of this study were embodied in *Psychologische Typen* (1921; *Psychological Types*).

In an attempt to explain the source of images in dreams and fantasies, he developed the theory of the collective unconscious. This much-contested conception was combined with his theory of archetypes, which Jung believed were of fundamental importance for the study of the psychology of religion. In Jung's terms, archetypes are instinctive patterns having a universal character, expressed in behavior and images.

Jung gave fresh importance to the so-called Hermetic tradition. He believed that the Christian religion was part of a historic process necessary for the development of consciousness, but he thought that the heretical movements, starting with Gnosticism and ending in alchemy, were manifestations of unconscious archetypal elements not adequately expressed in Christianity. He was particularly impressed with his finding that alchemical-like symbols could be found frequently in modern dreams and fantasies, and he thought that alchemists had constructed a kind of textbook of the collective unconscious. He fully explored these ideas in the four large volumes of his *Collected Works*.

In later years Jung taught psychology at the Federal Polytechnical University in Zürich and at the University of Basel.

Jünger \'yʉŋ-ər\, Ernst (b. March 29, 1895, Heidelberg, Ger.) German novelist and essayist, a formerly ardent militarist and nihilist whose outlook in mid-career changed to an equally ardent belief in peace, European federation, and individual dignity. The change was manifested in *Der Friede* (1946; *The Peace*), dedicated to the memory of his son who died fighting in Italy.

Jünger ran away from home in 1912 to join the French Foreign Legion and later served as a German soldier in both world wars. In 1920 he published *In Stahlgewittern* (*The Storm of Steel*), which argued that Germany's tribulations in World War I were a prelude to rebirth and victory.

Despite his militarism, he resisted Adolf Hitler's offers of friendship in the late 1920s. Indeed, during Hitler's chancellorship, he wrote an allegory on barbarian devastation of a peaceful land (*Auf den Marmorklippen*, 1939; *On the Marble Cliffs*), which, surprisingly, passed the censors.

Jünger's later writings include *Gläserne Bienen* (1957; *The Glass Bees*), a disturbing story of a jobless veteran in an overmechanized world symbolized by artificial bees and marionettes. Later works include *Siebzig verweht*, 2 vol. (1980–81; "Seventy Drifts Away"), *Aladins Problem* (1983; *Aladdin's Problem*), and *Eine gefährliche Begegnung* (1985; "A Dangerous Encounter"). Jünger also wrote essays and other works of nonfiction (including war diaries) and edited several books.

Jungle, The Novel by Upton SINCLAIR, published privately by Sinclair in 1906 after commercial publishers refused the manuscript. The most famous, influential, and enduring of all muckraking novels, *The Jungle* was an exposé of conditions in the Chicago stockyards. Because of public response, the U.S. Pure Food and Drug Act was passed and conditions in the slaughterhouses were improved.

The novel was written when Sinclair was sent by the socialist weekly newspaper *Appeal to Reason* to investigate working conditions in the meatpacking industry. Although Sinclair's chief goal was to expose abusive labor conditions, the American public was most horrified by the novel's descriptions of unsanitary conditions in the meat-processing plants.

Jungle Book, The Collection of stories by Rudyard KIPLING, published in 1894. *The Second Jungle Book*, published in 1895, contains stories linked by poems.

The stories tell mostly of Mowgli, an Indian boy who is raised by wolves from infancy and who learns self-sufficiency and wisdom from the jungle animals. The book describes the social life of the wolf pack and, more fancifully, the justice and natural order of life in the jungle. Among the animals whose tales are related in the work are Akela the wolf; Baloo the brown bear; Shere Khan, the boastful Bengal tiger who is

Mowgli's enemy; Kaa the python; Bagheera the panther; and Rikki-tikki-tavi the mongoose.

Jung-Stilling \'yu̇ŋ-'shtil-iŋ\, Johann Heinrich, *original name* Johann Heinrich Jung, *also called* Heinrich Stilling (b. Sept. 12, 1740, Grund, Westphalia [Germany]—d. April 2, 1817, Karlsruhe) German writer best known for his autobiography, *Heinrich Stillings Leben* (5 vol., 1806; "Heinrich Stilling's Life"), the first two volumes of which give a vividly realistic picture of village life in an 18th-century Pietistic family.

Jung-Stilling studied medicine at Strasbourg, where he met J.W. von Goethe, who was impressed by him and published the first, and best, volume of his autobiography, *Heinrich Stillings Jugend* (1777; "Heinrich Stilling's Youth"). The devoutness and simplicity of the work influenced the Pietistic tide opposed to the rationalism of the Enlightenment. In 1772 Jung-Stilling settled as a physician at Elberfeld. In 1778 he became a lecturer in economics and related subjects in Kaiserslautern and then in 1787 in Marburg. In addition to his autobiography and economic textbooks, he wrote mystical-pietistic works and novels, the best known of which is the allegorical novel *Das Heimweh* (1794–96; "Homesickness").

Junius manuscript *see* CAEDMON MANUSCRIPT.

Juno \'jü-nō\ In Roman mythology, chief goddess and female counterpart of Jupiter, closely resembling the Greek HERA, with whom she was universally identified. Juno was connected with all aspects of the life of women, most particularly married life. As Juno Lucina, goddess of childbirth, she had a temple on the Esquiline from the 4th century BC. Individualized, she became a female guardian angel; as every man had his *genius*, so every woman had her *juno*. Thus, she represented, in a sense, the female life principle. As her cult expanded she assumed wider functions and became, like Hera, the principal female divinity of the state.

Juno and the Paycock \'jü-nō ... 'pā-,kȯk\ Tragicomedy in three acts by Sean O'CASEY, produced in 1924 and published the following year. Set in the grim slums of Dublin during the Irish civil war of 1922–23, the play chronicles the fortunes of the impoverished Boyle family, which represents for O'Casey all of the strengths and shortcomings of Irish character. A violent death and the grim realities of tenement life throw into relief the swagger and inflated rhetoric of the men struggling for Irish independence.

Junot \zhᴇ-'nō\, Laure, Duchess d'Abrantès, *original surname* Permon \per-'mōⁿ\ (b. Nov. 6, 1784, Montpellier, Fr.—d. June 7, 1838, Paris) French author of a volume of famous memoirs.

After her father died in 1795, Laure lived with her mother, Madame Permon, who established a distinguished Parisian salon that was frequented by Napoleon Bonaparte. It was Napoleon who arranged the marriage in 1800 between Laure and his aide-de-camp Andoche Junot. The marriage was unhappy, and Laure had affairs with Prince Metternich, Austrian ambassador to Paris from 1806 to 1809, and, later, with a Royalist aristocrat. Always generous to the Junots, Napoleon became annoyed with Laure's entertaining former émigrés and ordered her to leave Paris following her husband's death in 1813. After many years in Rome, she returned to Paris, where she completed her *Mémoires sur Napoléon, la Révolution, le Consulat, l'Empire et la Restauration*, 8 vol. (1831–35). Noted as a vehicle of caustic wit and extravagance, her memoirs, often incorrect, are also often malicious, especially with regard to Napoleon.

Junqueiro \zhū̇ⁿ-'kā-rū\, Abílio Manuel Guerra (b. Sept. 17, 1850, Freixo-de-Espada à Cinta, Trás-os-Montes, Port.—d.

July 7, 1923, Lisbon) Poet whose themes of social protest and reform, expressed in a blend of grandiloquence and satire, have identified him as the poet *par excellence* of the Portuguese revolution of 1910.

Junqueiro was a leader among the revolutionary group of students at the University of Coimbra known as the Generation of Coimbra, who accomplished, first, the overthrow of Portuguese literary Romanticism and, later, the overthrow of the monarchy. His reputation as a poet dates from his abandonment of an early Romantic style for the realism of *A morte de D. João* (1874; "The Death of Don Juan"), in which he portrays the great lover as a debased seducer, the symbol of false sentimentality perpetuated, like social corruption, by Romanticism. He then produced *A velhice do Padre Eterno* (1885; "The Old Age of the Eternal Father"), which attacked the image of God with the same ruthlessness. In a less polemical phase, he celebrated Portuguese rural and village life in *Os simples* (1892; "The Simple Ones"), in which his lyrical quality is at its purest.

Jupiter \\'jü-pit-ər\\, *also called* Jove \\'jōv\\, Iuppiter, Iovis, *or* Diespiter. The chief ancient Roman and Italian god. Like ZEUS, the Greek god whose name is etymologically related, Jupiter was a sky god. His female counterpart was JUNO.

Jupiter was not only the great protecting deity of the race but also one whose worship embodied a distinct moral conception. He was especially concerned with oaths, treaties, and leagues, and it was in the presence of his priest that the most ancient and sacred form of marriage (*confarreatio*) took place. This connection with the conscience, with the sense of obligation and right dealing, was never completely lost throughout Roman history.

Jurgen \\'yər-gən\\ (*in full* Jurgen: A Comedy of Justice) Novel by James Branch CABELL, published in 1919. The New York Society for the Prevention of Vice declared *Jurgen* obscene and banned all displays and sales of the book. Both *Jurgen* and Cabell achieved considerable notoriety during the two years the book could not be sold legally; when the case came to trial, the judge recommended acquittal.

One of a series of novels Cabell wrote about the mythical medieval kingdom of Poictesme, the book chronicles the adventures of a pawnbroker named Jurgen who, motivated by guilt and gossip, sets off reluctantly in search of Dame Lisa, his loquacious, nagging wife who has been abducted by the Devil. Along the way, Jurgen encounters Dorothy, the love of his youth, who does not recognize him. Through the power granted him by the earth goddess, he relives one day with Dorothy. Jurgen and legendary women such as Guinevere share erotic experiences. Jurgen and his wife are ultimately reunited.

Justice \\'jəs-tis\\, Donald (Rodney) (b. Aug. 12, 1925, Miami, Fla., U.S.) American poet and editor best known for finely crafted verse that frequently illuminates the pain of loss and the desolation of an unlived life.

Educated at the University of Miami, the University of North Carolina, and the University of Iowa, Justice taught English and writing at several American universities.

Justice's poetry collections include *The Summer Anniversaries* (1960), *Night Light* (1967), *Departures* (1973), and *Selected Poems* (1979), which won a Pulitzer Prize. He also published *Platonic Scripts* (1984), a collection of essays, and *The Sunset Maker: Poems, Stories, A Memoir* (1987). Having considered becoming a composer when he was a young man, Justice retained a lifelong interest in music, writing the libretto for *The Death of Lincoln* (1988), a musical work by A. Thomas Taylor. Among books Justice edited or coedited are *The Collected Poems of Weldon Kees* (1960), *Contemporary French Poetry* (1965), and *Syracuse Poems* (1968). He also translated Eugène

Guillevic's *L'Homme qui se ferme* (1973; *The Man Closing Up*) from the French.

Justin \\'jəs-tən\\, *in full* Marcus Junianus Justinus \\jəs-'tī-nəs\\ (fl. 3rd century AD) Roman historian who was the author of *Epitome*, an abridgment of the *Historiae Philippicae* by Pompeius Trogus, whose work is lost. Trogus' book (chiefly a history of Macedonia and the Hellenistic monarchies, with Parthia) preserves material that has proved increasingly valuable to students of the Hellenistic world. It was much used in the Middle Ages.

Justine \\jəs-'tēn, *French* zhūēs-'tēn\\ (*in full* Justine; or, The Misfortunes of Virtue) Erotic novel by the Marquis de SADE, originally published in French as *Justine, ou les malheurs de la vertu*. He wrote an early version of the work, entitled *Les Infortunes de la vertu*, while imprisoned in the Bastille in 1787 and completed the novel in 1791 while free. Featuring graphically described sexual encounters, it is his most famous work.

In de Sade's philosophy, God is evil, wickedness is the source of human activity, and the misfortunes suffered by the heroine result from her failure to recognize these truths. By contrast Justine's sister Juliette delights in evil and therefore thrives in the sequel, *Juliette, ou Les Prospérités du vice* (1798).

Just So Stories A collection of children's animal fables linked by poems by Rudyard KIPLING, published in 1902. Most

Kipling's illustration for "The Elephant's Child," from *Just So Stories* by Rudyard Kipling, 1902

of the stories include far-fetched descriptions of how certain animals developed their peculiar physical characteristics, as in "How the Leopard Got His Spots." In the stories Kipling parodied the subject matter and style of several traditional works, such as the Buddhist *Jātaka* tales and *The Thousand and One Nights*.

Juvenal, \\'jü-vən-əl\\, *Latin in full* Decimus Junius Juvenalis \\jü-və-'nā-lis\\ (b. AD 55–60?, Aquinum [Italy]—d. probably in or after 127) One of the most powerful of Roman satiric poets. Many of his phrases and epigrams have entered common parlance—for example, "bread and circuses" and "who will guard the guards themselves?"

One contemporary source and a number of biographies apparently composed long after his death imply that Juvenal's family was well-to-do. He became an officer in the army as a first step to a career in the administrative service of the emperor Domitian (AD 81–96) but failed to obtain promotion and grew embittered. He wrote a satire declaring that court favorites had undue influence in the promotion of officers, for which he was banished and his property was confiscated. In 96, after Domitian's assassination, Juvenal returned to Rome, but, without money or a career, he was reduced to living as a "client" on the grudging charity of the rich. After some years his situation improved, for autobiographical remarks in one of his satires show him, then elderly, living in modest comfort in Rome and possessing a farm at Tibur (now Tivoli) with servants and livestock. Although still pessimistic, the later satires show a marked change of tone and touches of human kindness, as though he had found consolation at last.

Juvenal's 16 SATIRES deal mainly with life in Rome under the much-dreaded emperor Domitian and his more humane successors Nerva (96–98), Trajan (98–117), and Hadrian (117–138). They were published at intervals in five separate books.

His work was forgotten for a time after his death. Later it began to be read and quoted, first by the Christian propagandist Tertullian—who lived and wrote about AD 200 and was as full of passionate indignation as was Juvenal—then by others. A commentary (which survives) was compiled some time between 350 and 420. Thenceforward Juvenal has never ceased to be studied and admired, and he has been imitated by many satirists, including Giovanni Boccaccio, Nicolas Boileau, and Lord Byron.

Juvenalian satire \ˌjü-və-'nāl-yən\ In literature, any bitter and ironic criticism of contemporary persons and institutions that is filled with personal invective, angry moral indignation, and pessimism. The name alludes to the Latin satirist Juvenal, who, in the 1st century AD, brilliantly denounced Roman society, the rich and powerful, and the discomforts and dangers of city life. Samuel Johnson modeled his poem *London* on Juvenal's third satire and *The Vanity of Human Wishes* on the 10th. *Gulliver's Travels* established Jonathan Swift as the master of Juvenalian satire. In the 20th century, Karl Kraus's indictments of the corruption in post-World War I Austria were in the Juvenalian tradition. *Compare* HORATIAN SATIRE.

juvenilia \ˌjü-və-'nil-ē-ə\ **1.** Artistic or literary compositions produced in the author's youth and typically marked by immaturity of style, treatment, or thought. An example is Lord Byron's *Hours of Idleness*, written when he was 18. **2.** Artistic or literary compositions suited to or designed for the young.

Juventas \jü-'ven-təs, -täs\ The Roman goddess of youth. She was identified with the Greek goddess HEBE.

kabuki \kä-'bü-kē\ [Japanese, from earlier *kabuki* (verb) to act dissolutely] Popular Japanese form of theater that is a rich blending of realism and formalism, of music, dance, mime, and spectacular staging and costuming. In modern Japanese, the word is written with three characters: *ka*, signifying "song"; *bu*, "dance"; and *ki*, "skill."

The kabuki form dates from the early 17th century, and its strongest ties are to the Nō and to the bunraku puppet theater. Nō, the prevailing and established form of theater, had long been the exclusive domain of the nobility and the warrior-aristocrats known as samurai; kabuki therefore became the theater of the townspeople and the farmers. Kabuki derived much of its material from the Nō, and when kabuki was banned in 1652, it reestablished itself by adapting and parodying *kyōgen* (plays that provided comic interludes during Nō performances).

Kabuki, which is performed by all-male casts, finds its material in domestic stories and in popular history and often includes a didactic element. The actors, without masks, move and speak freely, yet without attempting to be realistic. The highly lyrical plays are regarded less as literature than as vehicles for its actors to demonstrate their enormous range of skills in visual and vocal performance. Notable exceptions include the Chūshingura cycle and the works of Chikamatsu Monzaemon, Tsuruya Namboku IV, Kawatake Mokuami, and Okamoto Kidō.

Kadare \ˌkä-'dä-rä\, Ismail (b. Jan. 27, 1936, Gjirokastër, Alb.) Albanian novelist and poet who gained an international readership.

Kadare studied at the University of Tiranë and later at the Gorky Institute of World Literature in Moscow until 1960. Upon returning to Albania, he became a journalist and also embarked on a literary career.

Kadare first won fame in Albania as a poet, but it is his prose works that are known internationally. His best-known novel is *Gjenerali i ushtërisë së vdekur* (1963; *The General of the Dead Army*), a study of postwar Albania as seen through the eyes of an Italian general who descends into madness while repatriating the remains of his country's soldiers who had died in Albania during World War II. Among Kadare's other novels dealing with Albanian history are *Dasma* (1968; *The Wedding*), about a peasant girl who rejects the traditional custom of arranged marriages after she is exposed to socialist doctrines, and *Dimri i madh* (1977; "The Great Winter"), a panoramic view of events leading to the rift in Soviet-Albanian relations that began in 1961. Among his semiautobiographical works is *Kronikë në gur* (1976; *Chronicle in Stone*), about his childhood in the town of Gjirokastër. Later works include *Ura me tri harqe* (1978; "The Three-Arched Bridge"), *Avril brise* (1982; *Broken April*), *Dosja H.* (1990; "Dossier H."), and *Nëpunësi i pallatit të ëndrrave* (1981; *The Palace of Dreams*). Another novel, *Përbindëshi* (1965; "The Monster"), was reissued in 1991.

Kaddish \'kä-dish\ Long poem in five parts by Allen GINSBERG, published in 1961 in *Kaddish and Other Poems: 1958–1960*. Taking the name of a Jewish hymn of praise to God that traditionally is recited by mourners, it is an emotionally driven, personal eulogy for Ginsberg's unstable mother, Naomi, who died insane in 1956. It was composed in the late 1950s under the influence of hallucinogenic drugs.

Kaden-Bandrowski \'kä-den-bän-'drȯf-sk^{y}ē\, Juliusz (b. Feb. 24, 1885, Rzeszów, Galicia, Austria-Hungary [now in Poland]—d. Aug. 6 or 10, 1944, Warsaw, Pol.) Polish novelist and short-story writer whose experimental, realist works savagely satirized Polish society after World War I.

The novels for which Kaden-Bandrowski is best known include *Czarne skrzydła* (1928–29; "Black Wings") and *Mateusz*

Bigda (1933; "Matthew Bigda"), works that describe society in Poland's coal-mining regions and life in Polish government circles. An earlier volume of short stories, *Miasto mojej matki* (1925; "My Mother's Town"), consists of childhood reminiscences.

Kafka \'käf-kä\, Franz (b. July 3, 1883, Prague, Bohemia, Austria-Hungary [now in Czech Republic]—d. June 3, 1924, Kierling, near Vienna, Austria) Czech-born German writer of visionary fiction whose posthumously published novels express the anxieties and alienation of 20th-century man.

Kafka was born into a middle-class Jewish family. He was a timid, guilt-ridden, and obedient child who, though he did well in school, rebelled against the authoritarian institution and the dehumanized curriculum, with its emphasis on rote learning and classical languages. As an adolescent, he declared himself a socialist as well as an atheist. As a Jew,

Archiv für Kunst und Geschichte, Berlin

Kafka was isolated from the German community in Prague, but as a modern intellectual he was also alienated from his own Jewish heritage. In 1902 he met Max Brod, who eventually became the most intimate and solicitous of Kafka's friends as well as his promoter, interpreter, translator, and most influential biographer.

Kafka received a doctorate in 1906, and from 1907 until his retirement in 1922 he worked in the insurance business. In 1923 he went to Berlin to devote himself to writing, but his stay was cut short by the deterioration of his health due to tuberculosis, which ultimately caused his death.

Kafka reluctantly published a few of his writings during his lifetime. These include two sections, published in 1909, from *Beschreibung eines Kampfes* (1936; *Description of a Struggle*); *Betrachtung* (1913; *Meditation*), a collection of short prose pieces; and other works representative of Kafka's maturity as an artist—*Das Urteil* (1916; *The Judgment*), a long story written in 1912; the story "Vor dem Gesetz" (1914; "Before the Law"); two further long stories, *Die Verwandlung* (1915; THE METAMORPHOSIS) and *In der Strafkolonie* (1919; IN THE PENAL COLONY); and a collection of short prose, *Ein Landarzt* (1919; *A Country Doctor*). *Ein Hungerkünstler* (1924; *A Hunger Artist*), four stories exhibiting the concision and lucidity characteristic of Kafka's late style, had been prepared by the author but did not appear until after his death.

Misgivings about his work caused Kafka before his death to request that all of his unpublished manuscripts be destroyed; his literary executor, Brod, disregarded his instructions, however. Brod published the novels *Der Prozess* (THE TRIAL), *Das Schloss* (THE CASTLE), and AMERIKA in 1925, 1926, and 1927, respectively, and a collection of shorter pieces, *Beim Bau der chinesischen Mauer* (*The Great Wall of China*), in 1931.

kafkaesque \,käf-kə-'esk, ,kaf-\ Of, relating to, or suggestive of Franz Kafka or his writings—especially, having a nightmarishly complex, bizarre, or illogical quality.

Kagame \kä-'gä-mā\, Alexis *or* Alegisi (b. May 15, 1912, Kiyanza, Rwanda) Rwandan poet, historian, and Roman Catholic priest who introduced written language, his own (Kinyarwanda) and French, to Rwanda.

Kagame was ordained a priest in 1941 and earned his doctorate at the Pontifical Gregorian University in Rome in 1955. He taught and edited the journal *Kinyamateka* ("The Herald").

Kagame's major books include *Inganji Karinga* (1943; "The Victorious Drums"), a history of the ancient Rwandans; *Isoko y'amājyambere*, 3 vol. (1949–51; "Sources of Progress"), an epic poem; *La Poésie dynastique au Rwanda* (1951; "Dynastic Poetry of Rwanda"); and *Introduction aux grands genres lyriques de l'ancien Rwanda* (1969; "Introduction to the Great Lyrical Poems of Ancient Rwanda"). His masterwork, a long narrative Christian epic, is the only partially published *Umulirimbyi wa Nyili-ibiremwa* ("The Singer of the Lord of Creation"). Lesser-known works include a novella, *Matabaro Ajya Iburayi* (1938–39; "Matabaro Leaves for Europe"); a historical poem, *Umwaduko w'Abazungu muli Afrika yo hagati* (1947; "The Arrival of the Europeans in Central Africa"); and some lighter, humorous works. A collection of poetry on Rwandan social life and customs, *Amazina y'inka*, was published in 1988.

Kagawa Kageki \'kä-gä-wä-'kä-gä-kē\, *also called* Keien \'kä-,en\ (b. May 25, 1768, Tottori, Japan—d. April 26, 1843, Japan) Japanese poet and literary scholar of the late Tokugawa period (1603–1867) who founded the Keien school of poetry.

At the age of 25 Kageki left home and became the student of Kagawa Kagetomo in Kyōto. He was adopted by the Kagawa family but later broke with Kagetomo.

In 1796 he met Ozawa Roan, whose rejection of the traditional and formal poetic style and advocacy of simple and honest expression of feelings greatly influenced him. He began advocating the concept of *shirabe* ("tuning"), stating that the tone of a poem was more important than its intellectual content. In the early 19th century Kageki became the leading poet of Kyōto and established the Keien school. In *Niimanabi iken* (1811), he criticized the poetic style of Kamo Mabuchi. Many of his poems of this period were published in the anthology *Keien isshi* (1828). The Keien school remained a major force in Japanese poetry until the late 19th century.

Kahiga \kä-'hē-gä\, Samuel (b. Aug. 1946, Thika, Kenya) Kenyan novelist and short-story writer.

Kahiga's most widely known early work is *Potent Ash* (1968), a volume of short stories on which he collaborated with his brother Leonard Kibera. Kahiga's seven stories in the collection reflect his experience of growing up in the rural area north of Nairobi, of life there during the struggle for independence in the mid-1950s, and of later middle-class existence in the Westernized urban scene of modern Kenya. He wrote several popular, melodramatic novels about urban life—including *The Girl From Abroad* (1974), *Lover in the Sky* (1975), and *When the Stars Are Scattered* (1979). Some of his later short stories were published as *Flight to Juba* (1979).

Kahn \'kän\, Gustave (b. Dec. 21, 1859, Metz, Fr.—d. Sept. 5, 1936, Paris) French poet and literary theorist who claimed to be the inventor of vers libre ("free verse").

Kahn began writing as a student in Paris. He helped found or edit several literary reviews, including *La Vogue, Le Symboliste,* and *La Revue Indépendante,* which printed his poems and discussed the various theories surrounding the Symbolist movement. Kahn explained his theory of vers libre in the preface to his *Premiers poèmes* (1897), a collection that included the earlier volumes *Les Palais nomades* (1887; "The Wandering Palaces"), *Chansons d'amant* (1891; "A Lover's Songs"), and *Domaine de fée* (1895; "Fairy World"). Kahn was undoubtedly the first and most persuasive advocate of vers libre. He broke with the tradition of the alexandrine line and sought to make rhythm more dependent on the movement of the poem's thoughts than on traditional rules of prosody. He also wrote a highly personal contribution to the history of French poetry, *Symbolistes et décadents* (1902).

Kailyard school \ˈkālˌyärd\   Late 19th-century movement in Scottish fiction characterized by a sentimental idealization of humble village life. Its name derives from Scots *kailyaird*, a kitchen garden usually adjacent to a cottage. The Kailyard novels of prominent writers such as Sir James Barrie, author of *Auld Licht Idylls* (1888) and *A Window to Thrums* (1889), Ian Maclaren (pseudonym of John Watson), and S.R. Crockett were widely read throughout Scotland, England, and the United States and inspired hundreds of imitators. The natural and unsophisticated style and parochial viewpoint quickly degenerated into mawkish sentimentality.

Kaiser \ˈkī-zər\, Georg (b. Nov. 25, 1878, Magdeburg, Ger.—d. June 4, 1945, Ascona, Switz.)   Leading German Expressionist dramatist.

Kaiser's first plays, mainly satirical comedies, attracted little attention. His first success was *Die Bürger von Calais* (1914; *The Burghers of Calais*). Produced in 1917 at the height of World War I, the play was an appeal for peace in which Kaiser revealed his outstanding gift for constructing close-knit drama expressed in trenchant and impassioned language. He followed this with a series of plays in which he showed humans in deadly conflict with the modern world of money and machines: *Von Morgens bis Mitternachts* (1916; *From Morn to Midnight*) and the *Gas* trilogy, consisting of *Die Koralle* (1917; *The Coral*), *Gas* (1918), and *Gas II* (1920). Written in terse and fragmented prose, these plays established him as a leader of the Expressionist movement.

Kaiser's later plays are more intimate and embody a deep experience of love: *Oktobertag* (1928; *The Phantom Lover*), *Der Gärtner von Toulouse* (1938; "The Gardener of Toulouse"), *Alain und Elise* (1940), and others. In 1938, Kaiser went into exile in Switzerland, where he continued his prolific output of more than 60 plays until his death. His last work was a mythological trilogy, *Zweimal Amphitryon* ("Twice Amphitryon"), *Pygmalion*, and *Bellerophon* (1948).

Kakinomoto Hitomaro \ˈkä-kē-nō-ˌmō-tō-ˈhē-tō-ˌmä-rō\, *also called* Kakinomoto no Hitomaro (d. 708, Japan)   Poet who was also Japan's first great literary figure.

Hitomaro is believed to have been born and reared near Nara. He entered the service of the court in a minor capacity; imperial activities are celebrated in some of his most famous poems. Later he became a provincial official, and he is believed to have died in Iwami province (now Shimane prefecture).

Among Hitomaro's surviving works are poems in the two major Japanese poetic forms of his day—tanka and *chōka*. He also probably wrote *sedōka* ("head-repeated poem," consisting of two three-line verses of 5, 7, 7 syllables), a relatively minor song form that seems to have been first adapted to literary purposes by Hitomaro. All of the poems accepted as indisputably his (61 tanka and 16 *chōka*), as well as a large number of others attributed to him, are to be found in the *Man'yōshū*, the first and largest of Japan's anthologies of native poetry.

Standing on the threshold of Japan's emergence from a preliterate to a literate, civilized society, Hitomaro achieved in his poems a splendid balance between the homely qualities of primitive song and the more sophisticated interests and literary techniques of a new age.

All of Hitomaro's poems are suffused with a deep personal lyricism and with a broad humanity and sense of identity with his fellowman. Outstanding among his works are his poem on the ruined capital at Ōmi; his celebration of Prince Karu's journey to the plains of Aki; two poems each on the death of his

first wife and on parting from his second; his lament on the death of Prince Takechi; and his poem composed on finding the body of a man on the island of Samine.

Kalevala \ˈkä-lä-ˌvä-lä\   Finnish national epic compiled from old Finnish ballads, lyrical songs, and incantations that were a part of Finnish oral tradition.

The *Kalevala* was compiled by Elias LÖNNROT, who published the folk material in two editions (32 cantos, 1835; enlarged into 50 cantos, 1849). Kalevala, the dwelling place of the poem's chief characters, is a poetic name for Finland meaning "land of heroes." The leader of the "sons of Kaleva" is the old and wise Väinämöinen, a powerful seer with supernatural origins, who is a master of the harplike kantele. Other characters include the skilled smith Ilmarinen, one of those who forged the "lids of heaven" when the world was created; Lemminkäinen, the carefree adventurer-warrior and charmer of women; Louhi, the female ruler of Pohjola, a powerful land in the north; and the tragic hero Kullervo, who is forced by fate to be a slave from childhood.

Among the main dramas of the poem are the creation of the world and the adventurous journeys of Väinämöinen, Ilmarinen, and Lemminkäinen to Pohjola to woo the beautiful daughter of Louhi, during which the miraculous *sampo*—a mill that produces salt, meal, and gold and is a talisman of happiness and prosperity—is forged and recovered for the people of Kalevala. The last canto seems to predict the decline of paganism: the maid Marjatta gives birth to a son who is baptized king of Karelia, and the pagan Väinämöinen makes way for him, departing from Finland without his kantele and songs.

The *Kalevala* is written in unrhymed octosyllabic trochees and dactyls (the *Kalevala* meter), and its style is characterized by alliteration, parallelism, and repetition. It inspired the paintings of Akseli Gallén-Kallela and the musical compositions of Jean Sibelius. The epic style and meter of the poem *The Song of Hiawatha* by Henry Wadsworth Longfellow also reflect the influence of the *Kalevala*.

Kalevipoeg \ˌkȯ-lä-vē-ˈpō-eg\ ("The Son of Kalevi")   Estonian national epic compiled in 1857–61 by Estonian folklorist and poet F. Reinhold KREUTZWALD. The work became the focus of the nascent 19th-century Estonian nationalism and independence movement. It was translated as *Kalevipoeg: An Ancient Estonian Tale* (1982).

In response to growing nationalistic feelings in his country, F.R. Faehlmann (Fählmann) consciously set about to produce an Estonian nationalist epic. He and many others collected thousands of Estonian folktales and folk songs. Kreutzwald combined these materials with original poetry and published it as *Kalevipoeg*. Kalevipoeg, the hero of the epic, is the symbol of ancient Estonian independence, and the plot revolves around his romantic adventures.

Kālī \ˈkä-lē\ ("Black")   In Hindu mythology, a devouring, destructive goddess. In accordance with the Indian predilection for bringing together seemingly contradictory aspects of life, Kālī is a fierce, terrifying aspect of Devī (the supreme goddess), who in other forms is represented as tranquil and pacific. Kālī is depicted as a hideous, black-faced hag smeared with blood, with bared teeth and protruding tongue. Her four hands hold, variously, a sword, a shield, the severed hand of a giant, or a strangling noose, or they are stretched in a gesture of assurance. Kālī is naked except for her ornaments, which consist of a garland of skulls and a girdle of severed hands. She is often depicted dancing on the inert body of Śiva, her consort.

Kālidāsa \ˌkäl-ē-ˈdäs-ə\ (fl. *c.* 5th century AD, India)   Sanskrit poet and dramatist, probably the greatest Indian writer of any epoch. The six works of his that are identified as genuine are the dramas ABHIJÑĀNAŚAKUNTALA ("The Recognition of Śakuntalā"), VIKRAMORVAŚĪ ("Urvaśī Won by Valor"), and MĀLAVIKĀGNIMITRA ("Mālavikā and Agnimitra"); the epic poems RAGHUVAṂŚA ("Dynasty of Raghu") and KUMĀRĀSAMBHAVĀ ("Birth of the War God"); and the lyric MEGHADŪTA ("Cloud Messenger").

As with most classical Indian authors, little is known about Kālidāsa's person or his historical relationships. His poems suggest but nowhere declare that he was a Brahman (priest). It is certain only that the poet lived sometime between the reign of Agnimitra, the second Śuṅga king (*c.* 170 BC), the hero of one of his dramas, and the Aiholę inscription of AD 634, which lauds Kālidāsa.

Many works are traditionally ascribed to the poet, but scholars have identified only six as genuine and one more as likely ("Ṛtusaṃhāra," the "Garland of the Seasons," perhaps a youthful work). He has become the archetype for Sanskrit literary composition. In drama, his *Abhijñānaśakuntala* is the most famous and is usually judged the best Indian literary effort of any period. The second drama, *Vikramorvaśī,* tells a legend as old as the Veda (earliest Hindu scripture), though very differently. The third of Kālidāsa's dramas, *Mālavikāgnimitra,* is of a different stamp—a harem intrigue, comical, playful, and accomplished.

Kālidāsa's efforts in the literary style known as kavya are of uniform quality. Examples of the epic are *Raghuvaṃśa* and *Kumārāsambhavā,* whose stories are mere pretext for the poet to enchain stanzas, each metrically and grammatically complete, redounding with complex and reposeful imagery. Kālidāsa's mastery of Sanskrit as a poetic medium is nowhere more marked. The lyric poem "Meghadūta" contains, interspersed in a message from a lover to his absent beloved, an extraordinary series of unexcelled and informative vignettes, describing the mountains, rivers, and forests of northern India.

Kalliope *see* CALLIOPE.

Kálvos \\'käl-vōs\\, Andréas Ioannídis (b. April 1792, Zacynthus, Venetian republic [now Zákinthos, Greece]—d. Nov. 3, 1869, London, Eng.) Greek poet who brought an Italian Neoclassical influence to the Ionian school of poets (the school of Romantics from the seven Ionian islands).

Kálvos was brought up in Livorno, Tuscany (1802–12), and lived most of his life in Italy and England. While in Italy he became secretary (1812–17) to the Italian poet and patriot Ugo Foscolo, a fellow native of Zacynthus. Kálvos' first works, including two tragedies, were written in Italian. In 1826 he went to Corfu, where he founded his own private school. He spent his last years in England.

Kálvos published 20 patriotic odes in two fascicles: *Líra* ("The Lyre") at Geneva in 1824 and *Néas Odás* ("New Odes") at Paris in 1826. He wrote of an idealized Greece, a Greece of the old virtues but a Greece viewed from outside. Although he sometimes used Demotic Greek (the vernacular tongue), he was generally a purist given to an austere and moralizing poetry and to various archaisms.

Kāma \\'käm-ə\\ In the mythology of India, the god of love. In Vedic works he personifies cosmic desire or the creative impulse, and he is called the firstborn of the primeval chaos that makes all later creation possible. In later periods he is depicted as a handsome youth, attended by heavenly nymphs, who shoots love-producing flower-arrows.

The term kama (from Sanskrit *kāma*) also refers to one of the proper pursuits of man in his role as a householder, that of pleasure and love. A classic textbook on erotics and other forms of human pleasure, the *Kāma-sūtra,* is attributed to the sage Vātsyāyana.

Kamban \\'käm-bän\\, Gudmundur (Jonsson Hallgrimsson) (b. June 8, 1888, Álfranes, Ice.—d. May 5, 1945, Copenhagen, Den.) One of Iceland's most important 20th-century dramatists and novelists. His work, anchored in a deep historical awareness, often criticized modern Western values and advocated compassion and understanding. He wrote in both Icelandic and Danish.

Kamban's greatest work is the four-volume historical novel *Skálholt* (1930–32; Eng. trans. of vol. 1 and 2, *The Virgin of Skalholt*). Another important work is *Jeg ser et stort skönt land* (1936; *I See a Wondrous Land*), a historical novel that recounts the Viking expeditions to Greenland and America. Among Kamban's most important plays are *Hadda Padda* (1914), on the theme of erotic love, and *Vi mordere* (1920; *We Murderers*), which focuses attention on the penal system and raises questions concerning the legitimacy of punishment.

Kamban was inadvertently shot and killed by the Danish resistance as they attempted to arrest him in order to question him concerning his alleged Nazi sympathies.

Kamo Chōmei \\'kä-mō-'chō-ˌmä\\, *also called* Kamo no Chōmei (b. 1155, Japan—d. July 24, 1216, Kyōto) Poet and critic of Japanese vernacular poetry, one of the major figures in the history of Japanese poetics. He is best known as a classic example of the man of sensibility turned recluse and as the author of *Hōjōki* (1212; AN ACCOUNT OF MY HUT), a description of his life in seclusion.

Chōmei was given a thorough artistic training. His poetic gifts brought him grudging recognition from the court and, eventually, a court-appointed office. Chōmei took Buddhist orders in 1204 and turned his back on the world. He lived for four or five years in the hills of Ōhara and then built his tiny hermit's hut in the Hino foothills southeast of the capital and completed his *Hōjōki.*

Chōmei, in fact, kept in touch with the court and the poetic world after his retirement. In 1205, to his great delight, 10 of his poems were included in the first draft of the *Shin kokinshū,* the eighth imperial anthology of court poetry. About 1208/09 he began work on his *Mumyōshō* ("Nameless Notes"), an extremely valuable collection of critical comments, anecdotes, and poetic lore. In 1214 or 1215 he is believed to have completed his *Hosshinshū* ("Examples of Religious Vocation"). His other works include a selection of his own poems (probably compiled in 1181) and the *Iseki* ("Record of a Journey to Ise"), no longer extant. Chōmei's poetry is representative of the best of an age that produced many poets of the first rank.

Kamo \\'kä-mō\\ Mabuchi (b. 1697, Iba, Japan—d. Oct. 31, 1769, Edo [now Tokyo]) One of the earliest representatives of the Kokugaku ("National Learning") school, a movement to restore the true Japanese spirit by a return to ancient traditions and culture.

Mabuchi was born into a branch of the old Shintō Kamo family, who served as priests of the famous Kamo shrine near Kyōto. Through his studies he became convinced of the importance of the earliest collection of Japanese poems, the Man'yōshū, and of the collection of Shintō rituals called *Norito.* Insisting that these ancient works were representative of the pure Japanese spirit, he helped foster a revival of the early poetic style. His chief original work, the *Kokuikō,* contains a biting rejection of Chinese thought and literature and a hymnal glorification of Japanese antiquity. His writings, collected in 12 volumes, are made up primarily of commentaries on Old Japanese literature.

Kampan \\'käm-ˌpän\\ (b. *c.* 1180, Thanjāvūr district, India—d. 1250) Tamil poet whose principal achievement was the epic *Irāmāvatāram* ("Rāma's Incarnation").

Little is known about Kampan's life. His epic reveals that he was a masterful poet, well versed in Tamil and Sanskrit literary traditions. Based on the Sanskrit *Rāmāyaṇa* by Vālmīki, *Irāmāvatāram* is a blend of earlier *caṅkam* poetry, Tamil epics, the fervor of personal *bhakti* (devotion) toward Rāma, folk motifs, and Sanskrit stories, meters, and poetic devices. Instead of a just king and a perfect man, Rāma is an incarnation of Vishnu and an intense object of devotion, dwarfing the Vedic gods; yet Kampan's emphasis is not on Vishnu but on *dharma* ("the law"), localized and Tamilized.

Kampan revels in elaborate metaphor, hyperbole, and fanciful descriptions of virtue and nature in the *Irāmāvatāram*. The poem is 40,000 lines long; the *Yuttakāṇṭam* ("War Canto") alone, with 14 battles, equals the *Iliad* in length. In northern Kerala, 32 plays based on Kampan are enacted ritually with marionettes in Śiva temples.

Kanagaki Robun \'kä-nä-gä-kē-'rō-bùn\, *original name* Bunzō Nozaki \'bùn-zō-'nō-zä-kē\ (b. Jan. 6, 1829, Edo [now Tokyo], Japan—d. Oct. 8, 1894, Tokyo)   Japanese writer of humorous light fiction who brought a traditional satirical art to bear on the peculiarities of Japanese society in the process of Westernization.

Kanagaki became a disciple of Hanagasa Bunkyō, a writer in the *gesaku* tradition (light, witty writing intended for the entertainment of the merchant and working classes of Edo). Eventually Kanagaki was recognized as a leading *gesaku* writer, noted for such works as *Kokkei Fuji mōde* (1860–61; "A Comic Mount Fuji Pilgrimage"), a parody of popular works on pilgrimages to famous places, and *Aguranabe* (1871; *The Beefeater*).

Kan'ami Kiyotsugu \'kän-ä-'mē-kē-'yō-tsə̇-gə̇\, *original name* Yūsaki Kiyotsugu \'yū-ˌsä-kē\, *also called* Miyomaru \'mē-yō-'mä-rū\ *or* Kanze Kiyotsugu \'kän-ze\ (b. 1333, Iga province, Japan—d. June 8, 1384, Suruga province)   Japanese actor and playwright who was one of the founders of Nō drama.

Kan'ami organized a theater group in Obata to perform *sarugaku*, plays with dialogue, acrobatics, and dances. He moved his troupe to Yamato and formed the Yūzaki Theatrical Company, which eventually became the highly influential Kanze school of Nō. His popularity spread, and he began traveling to Kyōto to perform there as well, where he came under the patronage of shogun Ashikaga Yoshimitsu.

Kan'ami was the first to incorporate *kusemai* (a popular song and dance form with a strong irregular beat) in the drama. He also used music and dances of the *dengaku* (rustic harvest celebrations). Thus he brought together the two principal tributaries to Nō in his plays, which also set new standards of literary quality for drama. Some of the outstanding works attributed to him are *Komachi, Ji'nen koji, Shii no shōshō, Matsukaze,* and *Eguchi*. His son Zeami (Kanze Motokiyo) became the foremost theorist of the Nō theater. He succeeded his father as director of the Kanze school.

Kane \'kàn\, Sheikh Hamidou, Sheikh *also spelled* Cheikh (b. April 3, 1928, Matam, River Region, Senegal)   Senegalese writer best known for his autobiographical novel *L'Aventure ambiguë* (1961; *Ambiguous Adventure*).

Kane studied law at the Sorbonne in Paris. He received degrees in law and philosophy from the École Nationale de la France d'Outre-Mer. After his return to his homeland in 1959, he served in a series of government positions.

The theme of *L'Aventure ambiguë* involves a young man caught between the traditional Islāmic faith of his ancestors and the soulless and materialistic Western culture to which he has become acculturated. What gives the work strength and individuality is the clarity with which Kane poses the conflicting values.

Kanık \kä-'nə̇k\, Orhan Veli (b. April 14, 1914, Bekoz, Constantinople, Ottoman Empire [now Istanbul, Tur.]—d. Nov. 14, 1950, Istanbul)   One of the most innovative poets in 20th-century Turkish literature.

Educated at Istanbul University, he worked briefly as a teaching assistant before joining the Turkish postal administration in Ankara (1936–42). Because he had a good command of French, he worked for the Ministry of Education in the translation office for two years and later translated the works of several major French poets and playwrights. In 1950 he was editor of the literary review *Yaprak* ("Folio" or "Leaf").

Kanık first wrote under the pen name Mehmet Ali Sel and published his early poems in the avant-garde literary review *Varlık* ("Existence"). In 1941 he published a volume of poetry, *Garip* ("Strange"), in collaboration with the poets Oktay Rifat and Melih Cevdet Anday. The work created a break with everything associated with Turkish poetry to that time; conventional meter, rhyme, language, style, and themes were discarded. Introducing everyday spoken Turkish and making use of folk poems and popular song motifs, Kanık encountered violent opposition, but by the time of his death his work and reputation were firmly established. Other works include *Vazgeçemediğim* (1945; "What I Cannot Give Up"), *Destan gibi* (1946; "Like an Epic"), *Yenisi* (1947; "The New One"), and *Karşı* (1949; "Against"). English translations of poems selected from all his works appear in *I Am Listening to Istanbul* (1971).

Kantemir \kən-t'ï-'mʸēr\, Antiokh Dmitriyevich, *also spelled* Antioch Dmitrievich Cantemir (b. Sept. 10 [Sept. 21, New Style], 1708, Constantinople, Ottoman Empire [now Istanbul, Tur.]—d. March 31 [April 11], 1744, Paris, Fr.)   Russian statesman who was his country's first secular poet and one of the leading writers of the classical school.

Kantemir was the son of statesman, scientist, and historian Dmitry Kantemir. Between 1729 and 1731 Kantemir wrote two satires, "To His Own Mind: On Those Who Blame Education" and "On the Envy and Pride of Evil-Minded Courtiers." These poems denounced the opposition to the reforms of the emperor Peter the Great and enjoyed great success when circulated in manuscript (they were not printed until 1762). As ambassador to England (1732–36), he took to London the manuscript of his father's history of the Ottoman Empire, furnishing a biography of his father for the English translation.

From 1736 until his death, Kantemir was minister plenipotentiary in Paris, where he continued to write satires and fables. His Russian translations of several classical and contemporary authors included his 1740 translation of Bernard Le Bovier de Fontenelle's *Entretiens sur la pluralité des mondes* (1686; "Interviews on the Plurality of the World"), which was suppressed as heretical. He also wrote a philosophical work, *O prirode i cheloveke* (1742; "Letters on Nature and Man"), and a tract on the old syllabic system of Russian verse composition (1744).

Kantor \'kan-tər\, MacKinlay, *original name* Benjamin McKinlay Kantor (b. Feb. 4, 1904, Webster City, Iowa, U.S.—d. Oct. 11, 1977, Sarasota, Fla.)   American author whose more than 30 novels and numerous popular short stories included the highly acclaimed *Andersonville* (1955), a Pulitzer Prize-winning novel about the American Civil War.

After finishing high school, Kantor became a reporter on *The Webster City Daily News*, of which his mother was an editor. He moved to Chicago for a number of years before returning to Iowa as a columnist for the *Des Moines Tribune*. He wrote many short stories and achieved recognition for his first historical novel, *Long Remember* (1934), a story about Gettysburg.

After service in World War II he became a screenwriter in Hollywood, where he adapted *Glory for Me* (1945), his verse novel about three American servicemen returning to civilian life, for the film *The Best Years of Our Lives* (1946).

In his long career Kantor also published nonfiction and several collections of short stories on subjects ranging from Chicago gangsters to life in the Ozarks. His historical novels include *Spirit Lake* (1961) and *Valley Forge* (1975).

Kanze school \\'kän-zä\\, *Japanese* Kanze-ryū \\-'ryū\\ School of Nō drama known for its emphasis on beauty and elegance. The school was founded in the 14th century by Kan'ami, who founded the Yūzaki Theatrical Company, the precursor of the Kanze school. Zeami, Kan'ami's son, completed the basic form of the art.

Since the Muromachi period (1338–1573), the Kanze school has been the largest Nō group in Japan—registering several hundred Nō musicians and more than half the dues-paying Nō enthusiasts of Japan.

Kao Ming *see* GAO MING.

Kaplan \\'kap-lən\\, Justin (b. Sept. 5, 1925, New York, N.Y., U.S.) American writer, biographer, and book editor, best known for his acclaimed literary biographies of Mark Twain, Lincoln Steffens, and Walt Whitman.

Kaplan graduated from Harvard in 1944. He left graduate school in 1946 and worked for a publishing house, eventually becoming a senior editor. In that capacity he worked with authors such as Bertrand Russell, Will Durant, Níkos Kazantzákis, and the sociologist C. Wright Mills.

Kaplan's first book, a biography of Mark Twain entitled *Mr. Clemens and Mark Twain* (1966), won both a Pulitzer Prize and a National Book Award. Also well regarded were Kaplan's *Lincoln Steffens, A Biography* (1974), about the prominent journalist and muckraker of the late 19th and early 20th centuries, and *Walt Whitman: A Life* (1980).

Kaplan lectured at Harvard and at Emerson College, Boston, Mass., and was biographer in residence at the Institute for Modern Biography at Griffith University, Brisbane, Australia. He edited several anthologies and was general editor for the 16th edition of *Bartlett's Familiar Quotations* (1992).

Karagöz \\kä-rä-'gœz\\ ("Black Eyes" or "Gypsy") Type of Turkish shadow play, named for its stock hero, Karagöz. The comically risqué plays are improvised from scenarios for local audiences in private homes, coffee shops, public squares, and inn yards. The Karagöz play apparently was highly developed in Turkey by the 16th century and was adapted in Greece and North Africa. Their performance in Turkey has been mostly confined to the Muslim holy month of Ramaḍān.

The character of Karagöz is a good-natured underdog who usually gets his turban knocked off in fights. He exchanges satiric and vulgar repartee with his friend Hacivot, a pompous Turk with an affected accent, and with other stock characters, such as a newly rich peasant, a conniving dervish, and a Jewish merchant.

Karamazov brothers \\kə-ˌrə-'mä-zəf, *Angl* ˌkar-ə-'mä-zôf\\ Fictional characters, the central figures in Fyodor Dostoyevsky's novel THE BROTHERS KARAMAZOV.

Karamzin \\kə-ˌrəm-'zʸēn\\, Nikolay Mikhaylovich (b. Dec. 1 [Dec. 12, New Style], 1766, Mikhaylovka, Simbirsk province, Russia—d. May 22 [June 3], 1826, St. Petersburg) Russian historian, poet, and journalist who was the leading exponent of the sentimental school.

From an early age, Karamzin was interested in Enlightenment philosophy and western European literature. After extensive travel in western Europe, he described his impressions in *Pisma russkogo puteshestvennika* (*Letters of a Russian Traveller, 1789–1790*), published in the monthly review *Moskovsky*

zhurnal (1791–92; "Moscow Journal"), which he founded on his return. Written in a self-revealing style influenced by Jean-Jacques Rousseau and Laurence Sterne, the *Letters* helped introduce to Russia the sentimental style then popular in western Europe. Karamzin's tale *Bednaya Liza* (1792; "Poor Liza"), about a village girl who commits suicide after a tragic love affair, soon became the most celebrated work of the Russian sentimental school.

In 1803 Karamzin's friendship with the emperor Alexander I resulted in his appointment as court historian. The rest of his life was devoted to his 12-volume *Istoriya gosudarstva rossiyskogo* (1816–29; "History of the Russian State"). Conceived as a literary rather than an academic work, the history is, in effect, an apology for Russian autocracy. It is the first such Russian work to have drawn on a great number of documents, including foreign accounts of historical incidents. Karamzin's "History" is considered to have contributed much to the development of Russian literary language, for in it he sought to bring written Russian—then rife with cumbrous locutions—closer to the rhythms and conciseness of educated speech and to equip the language with a full cultural vocabulary.

Karaosmanoğlu \\kä-ˌrä-ō-smä-nō-'ğlū\\, Yakup Kadri (b. March 27, 1889, Cairo, Egypt—d. Dec. 13, 1974, Ankara, Tur.) Writer and translator, one of the most renowned figures in modern Turkish literature, noted for vigorous studies of 20th-century Turkish life.

Educated in Cairo and in İzmir (now in Turkey), Karaosmanoğlu moved to Constantinople (now Istanbul) in 1908. He attracted attention for his outstanding prose poems, and he became connected with the Fecr-i âti ("Dawn of the Future") literary school, which was formed after the Young Turk Revolution of 1908. His first book, a collection of short stories, was published in 1913. A journalist during the Turkish war of independence (1919–22), he became a member of parliament and later had an extensive diplomatic career (1934–54).

His novels are powerful studies of Turkish society since the advent of the republic. In *Hüküm gecesi* (1927; "The Night of Judgment"), he describes the interparty struggles after the adoption of the constitution of 1908. *Sodom ve Gomore* (1928; "Sodom and Gomorrah") is about life in occupied Constantinople after World War I. *Yaban* (1932; "The Stranger"), perhaps his best-known novel, deals with the psychological distance between the Turkish peasant and the urban intellectual. He also wrote poetry and several works of nonfiction.

Karenina, Anna \\'än-ə-kä-'ren-yin-ə, *Russian* 'än-nə-ˌkə-'rʸenʸ-i-nə\\ Fictional character, the tragic heroine of ANNA KARENINA by Leo Tolstoy.

Kariotákis *see* KARYOTÁKIS.

Karkavítsas \\kär-kä-'vēt-säs\\, Andréas (b. 1866, Lekhainá, Greece—d. Oct. 10, 1922, Amaroúsion) Greek novelist and short-story writer whose subject was village life.

Karkavítsas studied medicine at Athens and became an army doctor. In this capacity he traveled to many villages in the provinces, and his short stories tell of the life, traditions, and legends of the villages. He belonged to the National Language Society, which worked for the acceptance of the Demotic, or spoken, language in literature. His greatest achievement is thought to be his realistic novel *O zitiános* (1899; "The Beggar").

Karlfeldt \\'kärl-felt\\, Erik Axel (b. July 20, 1864, Folkärna, Swed.—d. April 8, 1931, Stockholm) Swedish poet whose essentially regional, tradition-bound poetry was extremely popular and won him the Nobel Prize for Literature posthumously in 1931; he had refused the Nobel in 1918.

Karlfeldt's strong ties to the peasant culture of his rural homeland remained a dominant influence all his life. He published his most important works in six volumes of verse: *Vildmarks- och kärleksvisor* (1895; "Songs of Wilderness and of Love"), *Fridolins visor* (1898; "Fridolin's Songs"), *Fridolins lustgård* (1901; "Fridolin's Pleasure Garden"), *Flora och Pomona* (1906), *Flora och Bellona* (1918), and finally, four years before his death, *Hösthorn* (1927; "The Horn of Autumn"). Some of his poems have been published in English translation in *Arcadia Borealis: Selected Poems of Erik Axel Karlfeldt* (1938).

Karm \'kärm\, Dun, *pseudonym of* Carmelo Psaila \'psī-lə\ (b. Oct. 18, 1871, Zebbug, Gozo, Malta—d. Oct. 13, 1961, Valletta) Malta's national poet, whose work has both Romantic and classical affinities. His love of nature and of his native land together with his religious sensibility exemplify the former; his fondness for traditional meter (notably in his sonnets, which are considered particularly fine) exemplifies the latter.

Karm was ordained a priest at the age of 23 and worked as a seminary lecturer and diocesan grammar-school teacher until his dismissal in 1921. He then became assistant director of the National Library, retiring in 1936. He subsequently worked as lexicographer on the official English-Maltese dictionary.

He had already won distinction as a writer in Italian before being invited by the journal *Il-Habib* ("The Friend"), in 1912, to contribute verse in Maltese. Karm influenced several generations of Maltese writers and has been considered instrumental in paving the way for the adoption of Maltese as the official language of the island in 1934. He wrote the lyrics of the national anthem, *Innu Malti* (1923; "Hymn of Malta"). Karm translated into Maltese the poem *I sepolcri* (*The Sepulchres*) by the late 18th- and early 19th-century Italian poet Ugo Foscolo, adding a coda of his own.

Karpiński \kär-'pēⁿ-skʸē\, Franciszek (b. Oct. 4, 1741, Holosków, Kingdom of Poland—d. Sept. 16, 1825, Chorowszczyzna, near Grodno, Russian Empire [now Hrodna, Belarus]) Minor Polish lyric poet who is best known for his religious and patriotic verses.

Karpiński served as a court poet for the princely Czartoryski family until he retired to his family farm. Some of his verse was set to music, including many of his simple morning and evening prayers. His celebrated, much-sung Christmas carol *Bóg się rodzi* ("God is Born") was the first of its type to be written in Polish. He is also known for the secular pastoral ballad *Laura i Filon* ("Laura and Filon") and the patriotic poem *Żale Sarmaty nad grobem Zygmunta Augusta* (1797; "A Sarmatian's Lament at the Tomb of Sigismund Augustus"), in which he mourns the partition of Poland in 1795. He wrote *Pamiętniki*, his memoirs, after his retirement.

Karyotákis or **Kariotákis** \kär-yō-'tä-kēs\, Kóstas (b. 1896, Trípolis, Greece—d. July 20, 1928, Préveza) Greek poet influenced by the French Symbolist poets.

Karyotákis spent most of his lonely childhood in Crete. He read law at Athens and was admitted to the bar in 1919. He served as a member of parliament for three years, and then he worked as a government clerk in Athens, where he developed a friendship with the young poet Maria Polidoúri. Later he was transferred to Pátrai and then to Préveza, where he shot himself in despair over his ill health and unhappy life.

The three volumes of Karyotákis' poetry that were published in his lifetime show the influence of the "new school of Athens," founded in about 1880 by Kostís Palamás. The movement revolted against Katharevusa, the stilted and archaic official language of Greece, and against the emotionalism of the Romantics. His poetry also reveals the Symbolist influence in addition to the loneliness and despair of his childhood.

Kaschnitz \'käsh-nits\, Marie Luise, *in full* Marie Luise von Kaschnitz-Weinberg \'wīn-bərk\, *original surname* von Holzing Berstett \fŏn-'hŏlt-siŋ-'ber-,shtet\ (b. Jan. 31, 1901, Karlsruhe, Ger.—d. Oct. 10, 1974, Rome, Italy) German poet and novelist noted for her hopeful and compassionate viewpoint.

After completing her education and working as a book dealer in Rome, Kaschnitz traveled widely with her archaeologist husband, and the awareness of the classical past she acquired greatly influenced her writing. Before World War II she wrote two novels, both describing the romantic problems of young women: *Liebe beginnt* (1933; "Love Begins") and *Elissa* (1937). After the war, however, she emerged as an important lyric poet who combined modern and traditional verse forms with a highly original diction. In such works as *Totentanz und Gedichte zur Zeit* (1947; "Dance of Death and Poems of the Times") and *Zukunftsmusik* (1950; "Music of the Future"), she expressed an anguished, unflinching vision of the modern world that was nevertheless tempered by guarded feelings of optimism and hope. Such later collections of poems as *Dein Schweigen, meine Stimme* (1962; "Your Silence, My Voice") reflect her sorrow and loneliness after the death of her husband, and her subsequent search for meaning and stability in her life.

Kaschnitz also wrote autobiographical novels, including *Wohin denn ich* (1963; "Whither Then I"), the short-story collection *Lange Schatten* (1960; "Long Shadows"), essays, and radio and stage plays.

Kasperle \'käs-pər-lə\ Most prominent puppet character in Germany and Austria, where *Kasperltheater* became synonymous with puppet theater. The character developed in late 17th-century Austria from Hanswurst, the cunning peasant servant of the Viennese popular theater. Named Kasperle in the early 18th century, he was brought to Germany by traveling puppeteers and became an extraneous but popular character in marionette productions of *Faust*. Kasperle was established as a hand puppet in the mid-19th century when he was given his workingman's identity and traditional yellow-trimmed red jacket.

Kasprowicz \kä-'sprô-vēch\, Jan (b. Dec. 12, 1860, Szymborze, German Poland—d. Aug. 1, 1926, Zakopane, Pol.) The first great Polish poet of peasant origin and a translator who made an enormous range of classical and modern European literature available to Polish readers.

After studying at the universities of Leipzig and Breslau, Kasprowicz moved to Lwów, Pol. (now Lviv, Ukraine), in 1889 to escape Prussian persecution for his radical activities. In 1909 he became a professor of comparative literature at the University of Lwów.

His earliest poetry depicts the suffering, poverty, and ignorance of the peasants and is marked by a concern for social justice. Subsequently, in *Krzak dzikiej róży* (1898; "The Wild Rose Bush"), he lyrically describes the countryside of Poland in the Tatra Mountains area. *Ginącemu światu* (1901; "To a Dying World") is a cycle of poems that expresses his concern with humanity's sufferings and contains metaphysical longings. Later works such as *Księga ubogich* (1916; "Book of the Poor") reveal a mellowing temper and a newfound religious faith. The astonishing range of his translations included the complete works of William Shakespeare, Aeschylus, and Euripides, as well as works by Percy Bysshe Shelley, Algernon Charles Swinburne, William Blake, Robert Browning, and William Butler Yeats. He also translated voluminously from German, French, and Italian.

Kassák \'kôsh-,shäk\, Lajos (b. March 21, 1887, Érsekújvár, Hungary, Austria-Hungary—d. July 22, 1967, Budapest) Poet and novelist, the first important Hungarian working-class writer.

At the age of 20 Kassák began traveling on foot throughout Europe and so gained a cosmopolitan outlook. In 1915 he founded the journal *Tett* ("Action") to express his pacifist views. A socialist, he welcomed the first communist regime of Béla Kun in 1919. After its collapse, Kassák immigrated to Vienna, where he edited a journal of radical opinion, *Ma* ("Today").

Kassák published several novels and volumes of poetry, but his most important work is his eight-volume autobiography, *Egy ember élete* (1928–39; "A Man's Life"). He generally found favor with the government of post-World War II Hungary, although censors deleted from later editions of Kassák's autobiography the chapters dealing with his growing disenchantment with communism. Kassák's contribution was later reevaluated, and in the last decade of his life he enjoyed full official recognition.

Kästner \\'kest-nər\\, Erich (b. Feb. 23, 1899, Dresden, Ger.— d. July 29, 1974, Munich)   German satirist, poet, and novelist who is especially known for his children's books. He was a master of the style of witty, laconic writing associated with the highbrow cabaret of the period and with the Berlin weekly *Die Weltbühne* ("The World Stage").

Kästner studied at Rostock, Leipzig, and Berlin and became a freelance writer (1927). Four volumes of light but fundamentally serious poetry appeared before 1933. He also wrote the remarkable tragic novel *Fabian* (1931). His children's books are notable for their humor and respect for the child's moral seriousness. The most famous of these, *Emil und die Detektive* (1929; *Emil and the Detectives*), was several times dramatized and filmed. Prevented by the Nazis from publishing in Germany from 1933 to 1945, he had his works published in Switzerland. After the war Kästner became magazine editor of *Die Neue Zeitung* ("The New Newspaper") of Munich and subsequently founded a children's paper. His post-World War II works are characterized by a greater emphasis on social philosophy but do not sacrifice their elegance and entertaining qualities. These include *Das doppelte Lottchen* (1950; "The Double Lottie"), *Zu treuen Händen* (1950; "Into Faithful Hands"), the play *Die Schule der Diktatoren* (1956; "The School of Dictators"), and *Als ich ein kleiner Junge war* (1957; "When I Was a Young Man"). Kästner's collected works, *Gesammelte Schriften*, 7 vol., appeared in 1959.

katauta \\,kä-tä-'ü-tä\\ [Japanese]   A Japanese poetic form that consists of 17 or 19 syllables arranged in three lines of either 5, 7, and 5 or 5, 7, and 7 syllables. The form was used for poems addressed to a lover, and a single *katauta* was considered incomplete or a half poem. A pair of *katauta*s of the 5,7,7 type were called a *sedōka*; the 5,7,5 *katauta* may have been the top part of the early tanka. The form was rarely used after about the 8th century AD.

Katayev or **Kataev** \\,kə-'tä-yif\\, Valentin (Petrovich) (b. Jan. 16 [Jan. 28, New Style], 1897, Odessa, Ukraine, Russian Empire—d. April 12, 1986, Moscow)   Soviet novelist and playwright whose lighthearted, satirical treatment of postrevolutionary social conditions rose above the generally uninspired official Soviet style.

Katayev began writing short stories in 1916. In 1922 he moved to Moscow, working on the staff of *Gudok* ("The Whistle"). His novel *Rastratchiki* (1926; *The Embezzlers*) is a picaresque tale of two adventurers in the tradition of Nikolay Gogol. His comic play *Kvadratura kruga* (1928; *Squaring the Circle*) portrays the effect of the housing shortage on two married couples who share a room. *Beleyet parus odinoky* (1936; *Lonely White Sail*, or *A White Sail Gleams*), another novel, treats the 1905 revolution from the viewpoint of two Odessa

schoolboys; it was the basis of a classic Soviet film. Katayev's *Vremya, vperyod!* (1932; *Time, Forward!*) is considered among the most readable of Soviet novels of that era.

During the 1950s and '60s Katayev edited the magazine *Yunost* ("Youth") and opened its pages to the most promising literary talent of the young generation, including Yevgeny Yevtushenko and Bella Akhmadulina. In 1966 the literary magazine *Novy mir* ("New World") printed his *Svyatoy kolodets* (1967; *The Holy Well*), a lyrical-philosophical account of dreams experienced while the narrator is under anaesthesia for surgery, clearly reflecting the influence of Marcel Proust, James Joyce, and Franz Kafka.

Kateb \\'kat-eb\\ Yacine (b. Aug. 6, 1929, Constantine, Alg.— d. Oct. 28, 1989, Grenoble, Fr.)   Algerian poet, novelist, and playwright who was one of North Africa's most respected literary figures.

Kateb's first novel, *Nedjma* (1956), is undoubtedly the one work that has most influenced the course of Francophone North African literature. *Nedjma* recounts a tale of intraclan conflict against the background of violence and disunity characteristic of Algerian society under French colonial rule. It incorporates local legends and popular religious beliefs and treats the quest for a restored Algeria in a mythic manner. The discontinuous chronology and multiple narrative voices found in *Nedjma* greatly influenced a younger generation of North African writers.

Another novel (*Le Polygone étoilé*, 1966; "The Starry Polygon"), a collection of plays (*Le Cercle des représailles*, 1959; "The Circle of Reprisals"), and many of his poems take up the same themes and characters as *Nedjma*. Later plays, however, turned to different concerns. Among these works is *L'Homme aux sandales de caoutchouc* (1970; "The Man in the Rubber Sandals"), the Vietnamese hero of which is Ho Chi Minh. Several of Kateb's plays were produced in France and in Algeria, where he led a popular theater group.

Katherine Group \\'kath-ə-rin\\   A group of five Middle English prose devotional works dating from about 1180 to 1210. It consists of accounts of the lives of Saints Katherine, Margaret, and Juliana (found together in a single manuscript) and two treatises, "Hali Meidenhad" ("Holy Maidenhood") and "Sawles Warde" ("The Guardianship of the Soul"). They were all written near Herefordshire, and a single author may have written more than one of the works.

Katona \\'kŏ-tō-nŏ\\, József (b. Nov. 11, 1791, Kecskemét, Hungary, Holy Roman Empire—d. April 16, 1830, Kecskemét)   Hungarian lawyer and playwright whose historical tragedy *Bánk bán* achieved its great reputation only after his death.

A lawyer, Katona was also interested in the stage and wrote several plays of little literary merit. In 1815 he wrote *Bánk bán*, which though he entered it for a literary prize and in 1820 had it printed, remained unnoticed until the mid-1830s.

Bánk bán is the finest Hungarian drama of the 19th century, and an opera based on it has remained popular in Hungary. Its central figure, Bánk, the highest dignitary (*bán*) at the court of Andrew II (1205–35), tries in the king's absence to prevent a rebellion against the German-born queen Gertrude. Meanwhile the queen's brother Otto tries to seduce Bánk's wife and finally rapes her. Bánk unjustly suspects the queen of connivance in the crime and kills her. Bánk's complex character and the conflict between duty and personal grief make *Bánk bán* a tense and poignant drama.

Kaufman \\'kȯf-mən\\, Bob, *in full* Robert Garnell Kaufman (b. April 18, 1925, New Orleans, La., U.S.—d. Jan. 12, 1986, San Francisco, Calif.)   Innovative African-American poet who became an important figure of the Beat movement.

With a Roman Catholic mother, a German-Jewish father, and a grandmother who believed in voodoo, Kaufman was exposed to a wide variety of religious influences; he eventually adopted the Buddhist religion. After settling in San Francisco in 1958 he became involved in the city's bohemian artistic community and wrote witty, surreal poetry inspired by the rhythms of bebop jazz. Three broadside poems that were published by Kaufman in 1959 were later included in his collection *Solitudes Crowded with Loneliness* (1965). He also was a cofounder of the poetry magazine *Beatitude*.

In the early 1960s Kaufman was one of the most popular American poets among European readers; his second collection, *Golden Sardine*, was published in 1967. After seeing the televised assassination of President John F. Kennedy in 1963, Kaufman took a vow of silence, and he remained silent, neither speaking nor writing, until the end of the Vietnam War. After that he wrote prolifically, producing poems with literary themes that were published with earlier works in *The Ancient Rain: Poems, 1956–1978* (1981). In 1978 he resumed his silence, which he seldom broke for the rest of his life.

Kaufman \ˈkôf-mən\, George S. *in full* Simon (b. Nov. 16, 1889, Pittsburgh, Pa., U.S.—d. June 2, 1961, New York, N.Y.) American playwright and journalist noted for his collaboration with a number of other authors on some of the most successful plays and musical comedies of the 1920s and '30s.

After attending public school in Pittsburgh and Paterson, N.J., Kaufman worked briefly as a salesman. He contributed to the satirical column of Franklin P. Adams ("F.P.A.") in the New York *Evening Mail* and, in 1912, on Adams' recommendation, was given a column of his own in the *Washington Times*. He was a drama critic for *The New York Times* from 1917 to 1930. During this time he also became a member of the Algonquin Round Table.

His first successful play, written in collaboration with Marc CONNELLY, was *Dulcy* (1921), a comedy based on a central character of Adams' column. *The Butter and Egg Man* (1925), a satire on theatrical production, was the only play Kaufman wrote alone. His plays with Connelly included *Beggar on Horseback* (1924) and *Merton of the Movies* (1922), one of the first satires on Hollywood. Among his other collaborations were *Of Thee I Sing* (1931), with Morrie Ryskind and Ira Gershwin (with music by George Gershwin); *Dinner at Eight* (1932) and *The Land Is Bright* (1941), with Edna Ferber; *The Solid Gold Cadillac* (1953), with Howard Teichmann; and a number of memorable successes with Moss Hart that included *Once in a Lifetime* (1930), *You Can't Take It with You* (1936), and *The Man Who Came to Dinner* (1939).

Kaufman was twice winner of the Pulitzer Prize for plays of which he was coauthor. His range was wide, varying in tone with his collaborators, but brilliant satire and caustic wit were his forte.

Kavan \kə-ˈvan\, Anna, *original name* Helen Woods \ˈwŭdz\, *married surnames* Ferguson \ˈfər-gə-sən\, Edmonds \ˈed-məndz\ (b. 1904, Cannes, Alpes-Maritimes, Fr.—d. Dec. 5, 1968, London, Eng.) British novelist and short-story writer known for her semiautobiographical surreal fiction dealing with the themes of mental breakdown and self-destruction.

She was born into a wealthy family and traveled widely as a child. Under the name Helen Ferguson, she wrote six novels, most notably *Let Me Alone* (1930), a portrait of a troubled woman in a violent marriage. Ferguson legally changed her name to Anna Kavan, the name she had given to the heroine of *Let Me Alone* and *A Stranger Still* (1935). After her second divorce, Kavan entered various mental institutions, and by World War II she was a registered heroin addict in England.

Kavan received critical acclaim for a series of sketches called *Asylum Piece* (1940), which she followed with the novel *Change the Name* (1941), the short-story collection *I Am Lazarus* (1945), and the autobiographical *The House of Sleep* (1947). Her reputation declined after the war until the publication of *Who Are You?* (1963), a disturbing novel about a nightmarish marriage, and *Ice* (1967), a surreal novel about a man in pursuit of a woman across a frozen wilderness. Two collections appeared after her heroin-related death: *Julia and the Bazooka* (1970) and *My Soul in China* (1975).

Kavanagh \ˈkav-ə-nə, -ˌnä\, Patrick (b. 1905, near Inniskeen, County Monaghan, Ire.—d. Nov. 30, 1967, Dublin) Poet whose long poem *The Great Hunger* put him in the front rank of modern Irish poets.

Kavanagh was self-educated and worked for a while on a farm in his home county, which provided the setting for a novel, *Tarry Flynn* (1948), later dramatized and presented at the Abbey Theatre, Dublin. After moving to Dublin, where he spent most of his life as a journalist, Kavanagh wrote *The Great Hunger* (1942), an epic about an Irish farm boy that contains impassioned satirical passages recalling D.H. Lawrence. Two volumes of verse followed—*A Soul for Sale* (1947) and *Come Dance with Kitty Stobling* (1960). His *Collected Poems* appeared in 1964 and *Collected Prose* in 1967. An early work of autobiography was *A Green Fool* (1939).

kavya \ˈkäv-yə\ [Sanskrit *kāvyaṃ* poetic composition, a noun derivative of *kāvyaḥ* (adjective) of a sage or poet, poetic, a derivative of *kaviḥ* seer, sage, poet] Highly artificial Sanskrit literary style employed chiefly in the court epic of India from the early centuries AD. It evolved an elaborate poetics of figures of speech, among which the metaphor and simile predominated. Other characteristics were the careful use of language, a tendency to use compound nouns, a sometimes ostentatious display of erudition in the arts and sciences, and an adroitness in the use of varied and complicated meters—all applied to traditional themes and to the rendering of emotions.

The style finds its classical expression in the so-called *mahākāvya* ("great poem"), the strophic lyric (a lyric based on a rhythmic system of two or more lines repeated as a unit), and the Sanskrit theater. The great masters of the kavya form (which was also exported to Java) were Aśvaghoṣa, Kālidāsa, Bāṇa, Daṇḍin, Māgha, Bhavabhūti, and Bhāravi.

The earliest surviving kavya literature was written by Aśvaghoṣa, a Buddhist. Two works by Aśvaghoṣa, both in the style of *mahākāvya*, are extant: the *Buddhacarita* ("Life of the Buddha") and the *Saundarānanda* ("Of Sundarī and Nanda"). In his mastery of the intricacies of prosody and the subtleties of grammar and vocabulary, Aśvaghoṣa anticipated the style of the Hindu *mahākāvya* authors. *See also* MAHĀKĀVYA.

Kawabata Yasunari \ˈkä-wä-ˌbä-tä-yä-ˈsü-nä-rē\ (b. June 11, 1899, Ōsaka, Japan—d. April 16, 1972, Zushi) Japanese novelist who won the Nobel Prize for Literature in 1968. The sense of loneliness and preoccupation with death that permeates much of his mature writing possibly derives from the loneliness of his childhood (he was orphaned early and lost all near relatives while still in his youth).

Kawabata made his entrance into the literary world with the semiautobiographical *Izu no odoriko* (1926; *The Izu Dancer*). The work appeared in the journal *Bungei jidai* ("Literary Age"), which he founded in 1924 with the writer Yokomitsu Riichi and which became the organ of the New Sensationalist school with which Kawabata was early associated. This school is said to have derived much of its aesthetic from such French literary currents as Dadaism, Expressionism, and Cubism. Their influence on Kawabata's work may be seen in abrupt transitions, in imagery that is frequently startling in its mixture of incongruous impressions, and in his juxtaposition of the beautiful and the ugly. The same qualities, however, are present in Japanese prose of the 17th century and in the *renga* (linked verse) of the 15th century. It is to the latter that Kawabata's fiction seemed to draw nearer in later years.

There is a formlessness about much of Kawabata's writing, reminiscent of the fluid composition of *renga*. His best-known novel, *Yukiguni* (1948; SNOW COUNTRY), was begun in 1935 but not published in its final form until 1948. *Sembazuru* (THOUSAND CRANES), intended partly as a sequel to *Yukiguni*, was begun in 1949 and published with the novel *Yama no oto* (THE SOUND OF THE MOUNTAIN) in 1952. These three are considered to be his best novels.

Kawabata committed suicide shortly after the suicide of his friend Mishima Yukio.

Kawahigashi Hekigotō \\,kä-wä-hē-'gä-shē-,hä-kē-gō-'tō\\, *original name* Kawahigashi Heigorō \\'hä-gō-,rō\\ (b. Feb. 26, 1873, Matsuyama, Ehime prefecture, Japan—d. Feb. 1, 1937, Tokyo)   Japanese poet who was a pioneer of modern haiku.

Kawahigashi and his friend Takahama Kyoshi were the leading disciples of Masaoka Shiki, a leader of the modern haiku movement. Kawahigashi became haiku editor of the magazines *Shinsei* (in 1896) and *Nihon* (in 1902), and he published the books *Haiku hyōshaku* and *Shoku haiku hyōshaku* in 1899. After the death of Shiki, Kawahigashi called for a more modern kind of haiku, one that abandoned the traditional metric pattern of 5, 7, and 5 syllables and the conventional use of "season words." He toured Japan in 1907 and 1909–11 to promote the new poetry.

Kawahigashi published accounts of his travels in *Sanzenri* (1906). The haiku collection *Hekigotō kushū* (1916) is also among his principal works. His poetic abilities declined and his disciples abandoned him, and he ceased writing in 1933.

Kawatake Mokuami \\'kä-wä-,tä-ke-mō-'kü-ä-mē\\, *original name* Yoshimura Shinshichi \\yō-'shē-mḁ-rä-'shēn-,shē-chē\\, *also called* Kawatake Shinshichi II *or* Furukawa Mokuami \\'fü-rü-,kä-wä\\ (b. March 1, 1816, Edo [now Tokyo], Japan—d. Jan. 22, 1893, Tokyo)   Versatile and prolific Japanese dramatist, the last great kabuki playwright of the Tokugawa period (1603–1867).

Kawatake became a student of the kabuki playwright Tsuruya Namboku V and wrote many kinds of plays during a long apprenticeship. He became the chief playwright for the Kawarasaki Theater in 1843. During his 40s, Kawatake established his reputation writing domestic plays (*sewamono*) and picaresque plays (*shiranamimono*).

Following the Meiji Restoration (1868), Kawatake began producing *katsurekimono* (modified versions of traditional history plays, or *jidaimono*), emphasizing factual accuracy in his works. He also pioneered in producing a new kind of domestic play (*zangirimono*), which explicitly described the modernization and Westernization of early Meiji society. When he officially retired from active playwrighting in 1881, he relinquished the title of Kawatake Shinshichi.

Kawatake was one of the most prolific of all dramatists, writing more than 360 plays. His plays are still frequently performed and comprise almost half of the current kabuki repertory.

kayak   American literary magazine founded in San Francisco in 1964 by poet George Hitchcock as a forum for surrealist, imagist, and political poems. The magazine, which eventually published short fiction and essays as well, was known for its irreverence and its openness to experimentation, including found poems (verses made from other printed matter such as flyers or discarded letters). Attention was directed especially to the nature of poetry itself, which was addressed in a number of poems and essays throughout the magazine's history. The magazine moved its headquarters to Santa Cruz, Calif., in 1970. The last issue was produced in 1984. Regular contributors included W.S. Merwin, Wendell Berry, Robert Bly, David Ignatow, James Tate, Margaret Atwood, Raymond Carver, Carolyn Kizer, Charles Simic, and Sharon Olds.

Kaye-Smith \\'kā-'smith\\, Sheila, *in full* Emily Sheila Kaye-Smith (b. Feb. 4, 1887, St. Leonard's-on-Sea, Sussex, Eng.—d. Jan. 14, 1956, Northiam, near Rye, Sussex)   British novelist, best known for novels depicting her native rural Sussex.

Kaye-Smith began writing as a youth, publishing her first novel, *The Tramping Methodist* (1908), at age 21. Other novels and a book of verse were followed by *Sussex Gorse: The Story of a Fight* (1916), her first critical success and perhaps her finest novel. It concerns a ruthlessly ambitious farmer and landowner who alienates family and friends. *Tamarisk Town* (1919) and *Joanna Godden* (1921) similarly deal with struggle and survival in rural Sussex.

In 1918 Kaye-Smith joined the Anglican church, and in 1929 she and her husband, an Anglican clergyman, converted to Roman Catholicism. The deep influence of religion is seen in such works as *The End of the House of Alard* (1923) and *The History of Susan Spray, the Female Preacher* (1931). In all, she wrote more than 40 books, including collections of short stories, three volumes of autobiography, two biographical studies (in collaboration with G.B. Stern) of novelist Jane Austen, and several other works of nonfiction.

Kazakov \\kḁ-,zḁ-'kȯf\\, Yury (Pavlovich) (b. Aug. 8, 1927, Moscow, Russian S.F.S.R., U.S.S.R.)   Soviet short-story writer who worked in the classic Russian lyrical style.

Kazakov was initially a jazz musician, but he began to publish short stories in 1952. He graduated from the Gorky Institute of World Literature in 1958. His early short stories marked a notable departure from the tenets of Socialist Realism. The stories in such collections as *Man'ka* (1958), *Na polustanke* (1959; "At the Station"), *Po doroge* (1961; "Along the Road"), and *Goluboe i zelyonoe* (1963; "The Blue and the Green") focus on the subtle and complex emotional reactions of rural characters during moments of inspiration, communion, betrayal, or loss. Kazakov treats questions of conscience and emphasizes the importance of the individual's harmonious coexistence with nature.

Kazantzákis \\kä-zänt-'zä-kēs\\, Níkos (b. Dec. 2, 1885, Megalokastro, Ottoman Empire [now Iráklion, Crete]—d. Oct. 26, 1957, Freiburg im Breisgau [Germany])   Greek writer whose prolific output and wide variety of work represent a major contribution to modern Greek literature.

Kazantzákis studied law at the University of Athens (1902–06) and philosophy under Henri Bergson in Paris (1907–09). He then traveled widely, settling before World War II on the island of Aegina. He served as a minister in the Greek government (1945) and worked for the United Nations Educational, Scientific and Cultural Organization (UNESCO) in Paris (1947–48).

Kazantzákis' works cover a vast range, including essays, travel books, tragedies, and translations of such classics as Dante's *The Divine Comedy* and J.W. von Goethe's *Faust*. He produced lyric poetry and the epic *Odíssa* (1938; *Odyssey*), a 33,333-line sequel to the Homeric epic.

Kazantzákis is perhaps best known for his widely translated novels. They include *Víos kai politía tou Aléxi Zormpá* (1946; ZORBA THE GREEK; film, 1964), *O Kapetán Mikhális* (1950; *Freedom or Death*), *O Khristós Xanastavrónetai* (1954; *The Greek Passion*), and *O televtaíos pirasmós* (1955; *The Last Temptation of Christ*; film, 1988). Published after his death was the autobiographical *Anaforá stóv Gréko* (1961; *Report to Greco*).

Kazin \\'kāz-ən\\, Alfred (b. June 5, 1915, Brooklyn, N.Y., U.S.) American teacher, editor, and literary critic.

Kazin attended the City College of New York and then worked as a freelance book reviewer for various periodicals. At age 27 he wrote a sweeping historical study of modern American literature, *On Native Grounds* (1942), that won him instant recognition as a perceptive critic with a distinct point of view. The book traced the social and political movements that inspired successive stages of literary development in America.

Many of Kazin's later works dealt with the forces that drive an individual to write. Kazin felt that with increasing technological domination of society, literature had diminished in importance as a vehicle of personal growth and political definition. Kazin's sketches of literary personalities revealed much about both the writers and their eras. His critical and political sensibilities were inextricably intertwined. Among the books he edited were *The Portable Blake* (1946), *The Stature of Theodore Dreiser* (1955), and *The Works of Anne Frank* (1959). His other writings include *Starting Out in the Thirties* (1965), *Bright Book of Life* (1973), *New York Jew* (1978), *An American Procession* (1984), and *A Writer's America* (1988).

Kazinczy \\'kȯ-zēn-tsē\\, Ferenc (b. Oct. 27, 1759, Érsemlyén, Hungary, Holy Roman Empire—d. August 1831, Széphalom) Hungarian man of letters who reformed the Hungarian language and attempted to improve literary style.

Born of a well-to-do family of the nobility, Kazinczy learned German and French as a child and acquired an extensive knowledge of foreign literature. He published his first book, a small geography of Hungary, in 1775. Later he studied law and became a civil servant, all the while immersed in literary studies and writing. He helped to found one literary review, then founded another. He also translated a number of plays into Hungarian for a newly founded Hungarian theatrical company.

Kazinczy was arrested for participating in a political conspiracy in December of 1794 and was condemned to death, even though his role had been minor. His sentence was later commuted to imprisonment, and in 1801 he was released. He had by that time determined to devote his life to the improvement of Hungarian literature.

Kazinczy tried, through a voluminous correspondence with other European writers and his own writings, to banish from literature everything he considered vulgar and uncouth. His writings included biting epigrams published in *Tȯvisek és virágok* (1811; "Thorns and Flowers") and many sonnets, a poetical form he introduced into Hungary.

Kazinczy's position as self-styled censor involved him in endless controversies. His most famous battle was fought to improve the language: he initiated reforms of grammar, spelling, and style that made Hungarian a more flexible literary medium. He served on the committee that founded the Hungarian Academy in 1828 and was elected a member in 1830.

Keane \\'kēn\\, Molly, *in full* Mary Nesta Keane, *original surname* Skrine \\'skrīn\\, *pseudonym* M.J. Farrell \\'far-əl\\ (b. July 4, 1904, County Kildare, Ireland) Novelist and playwright whose subject was the leisure class of her native Ireland.

The daughter of an estate owner and the poet Moira O'Neill, Keane began writing novels while in her 20s, using the pseudonym M.J. Farrell. In novels such as *Young Entry* (1928), *Devoted Ladies* (1934), and *The Rising Tide* (1937), she explored the lives of Ireland's rural gentry, amid their horses, foxhunts, loves, and sorrows. The success of her comedy *Spring Meeting* (1938; written with John Perry) led to a career as a playwright. *Treasure Hunt* (1950), also written with Perry, was another success, which Keane turned into a novel (1952). After 1961, however, she abandoned writing for nearly two decades.

Using the name Molly Keane, she returned in 1981 with the acclaimed novel *Good Behaviour*, in which an unattractive, unloved woman murders her domineering mother. *Time After Time*, a novel about four handicapped siblings, was published in 1983. Keane's later novels include *Loving and Giving* (1988; U.S. title, *Queen Lear*) and *Conversation Piece* (1991).

Keats \\'kēts\\, John (b. Oct. 31, 1795, London, Eng.—d. Feb. 23, 1821, Rome [Italy]) English Romantic lyric poet who de-

Detail of an oil painting by Joseph Severn, 1821
National Portrait Gallery, London

voted his short life to the perfection of a poetry marked by vivid imagery, great sensuous appeal, and an attempt to express a philosophy through classical legend.

The son of a livery-stable manager, Keats received relatively little formal education. Throughout his short life he had close emotional ties to his sister, Fanny, and his two brothers, George and Tom. After the breakup of their mother's second marriage, the Keats children lived with their widowed grandmother. John attended a school run by John Clarke, whose son Charles Cowden Clarke did much to encourage Keats's literary aspirations. Keats was apprenticed to a surgeon in 1811, but he broke off the apprenticeship in 1814 and went to live in London, where he worked as a dresser, or junior house surgeon. After 1817 he devoted himself entirely to poetry.

Keats's first mature poem was the sonnet ON FIRST LOOKING INTO CHAPMAN'S HOMER (1816), which was inspired by his excited reading of George Chapman's classic translation of the *Iliad* and *Odyssey*. Clarke also introduced Keats to the journalist and contemporary poet Leigh Hunt and his influential circle. Keats's first book, *Poems*, was published in March 1817. The most interesting poem in the volume was "Sleep and Poetry"; otherwise the work was remarkable only for some delicate natural observation and for obvious Spenserian influences. In 1817 Keats began work on ENDYMION, his first long poem, which appeared in 1818.

In the summer of 1818 Keats went on a walking tour in the Lake District and in Scotland with his friend Charles Brown, and the trip brought on the first symptoms of the tuberculosis of which he was to die. On his return to London a brutal criticism of his early poems appeared in *Blackwood's Magazine*, followed by a similar attack on *Endymion* in the *Quarterly Re-*

view. Contrary to later assertions, Keats met these reviews with a calm assertion of his own talents, and he went on steadily writing poetry. In about October 1819 Keats became engaged to Fanny Brawne, a young woman to whom he had formed a powerful attachment.

It was during the year 1819 that Keats's greatest poetry was written—LAMIA, THE EVE OF ST. AGNES, the great odes (ODE ON INDOLENCE, ODE ON A GRECIAN URN, ODE TO PSYCHE, ODE TO A NIGHTINGALE, ODE ON MELANCHOLY, and TO AUTUMN), and the two versions of HYPERION. The poetry, composed under the strain of illness and his growing love for Brawne, is an astonishing body of work, marked by careful and considered development, technical, emotional, and intellectual. The odes are Keats's most distinctive poetic achievement. They are essentially lyrical meditations on an object or quality that prompts the poet to confront the conflicting impulses of his inner being and to reflect upon his own longings and their relations to the wider world around him. With their rich and exquisitely sensuous detail and their meditative depth, the odes are among the greatest achievements of Romantic poetry. With them should be mentioned the ballad LA BELLE DAME SANS MERCI, which reveals the obverse and destructive side of the idyllic love seen in "The Eve of St. Agnes."

The poems "Isabella," "Lamia," "The Eve of St. Agnes," *Hyperion,* and the odes were all published in the famous 1820 volume *Lamia, Isabella, The Eve of St. Agnes, and Other Poems.* The work appeared in July, by which time Keats's health was doomed. He had been increasingly ill throughout 1819, and by the beginning of 1820 the evidence of tuberculosis was clear. His friends Brown and Hunt and Brawne and her mother nursed him assiduously throughout the year. When he was ordered south for the winter, his friend Joseph Severn undertook to accompany him to Rome, where, faithfully tended by Severn to the last, he died.

keepsake \\'kēp-,sāk\\   A GIFTBOOK, or more specifically, a giftbook made up for a particular group or occasion and serving as a specimen of fine printing.

Kell, Joseph   *see* Anthony BURGESS.

Keller \\'kel-ər\\, Gottfried (b. July 19, 1819, Zürich, Switz.—d. July 16, 1890, Zürich)   The greatest German-Swiss narrative writer of the late 19th-century realistic school.

His father died in Keller's early childhood, but his strong-willed, devoted mother struggled to provide him with an education. After being expelled from secondary school for a prank, he took up landscape painting. When two years of study in Munich (1840–42) brought little success, he returned to Zürich, where he published his first poems in 1846. From 1848 to 1850 the Zürich government sponsored his studies at Heidelberg.

Intending to write for the theater, Keller wrote instead the long autobiographical novel *Der grüne Heinrich* (1854–55; rev. ed., 1879–80; GREEN HENRY), on which his reputation rests. Keller returned to Zürich in 1855 and became clerk to the canton (1861–76).

Keller is also well known for his short stories, some of which are collected in *Die Leute von Seldwyla* (1856–74; *The People of Seldwyla*) and *Sieben Legenden* (1872; *Seven Legends*). His last novel, *Martin Salander* (1886), deals with political life in Switzerland in Keller's time.

Kellermann \\'kel-ər-,män\\, Bernhard (b. March 4, 1879, Fürth, Ger.—d. Oct. 17, 1951, Potsdam, E.Ger.)   German journalist and writer best known for his novel *Der Tunnel* (1913; *The Tunnel*), a sensational technical-utopian work.

Kellermann's early novels, *Yester und Li* (1904), *Ingeborg* (1906), and *Der Tor* (1909; *The Fool*), were written in a Neoromantic, Impressionist manner. The renowned *Tunnel* was

followed by *Der 9. November* (1921; *The Ninth of November*), inspired by the German revolution of 1918; *Das blaue Band* (1938; "The Blue Band"), based on the sinking of the ocean liner *Titanic;* and *Totentanz* (1948; "Dance of Death").

As a foreign correspondent for the *Berliner Tageblatt* during World War I, Kellermann wrote two additional novels, *Der Krieg im Westen* (1915; "The War in the West") and *Der Krieg im Argonnerwald* (1916; "The War in the Argonne Forest"), as well as a number of travel books.

Kellgren \\'kel-grän\\, Johan Henrik (b. Dec. 1, 1751, Floby, Swed.—d. April 20, 1795, Stockholm)   Poet considered the greatest literary figure of the Swedish Enlightenment.

A talented young man, Kellgren soon found his way to the court of Gustav III. For some time he acted as private secretary to the king, who appointed him one of the first members of the Swedish Academy when it was founded in 1786. Kellgren's earliest works, which were erotic poems, appeared in 1773, but he won fame with the satiric poem *Mina löjen* (1778; "My Laughter"). In the 1780s he wrote a number of verse dramas on themes suggested by Gustav. This collaboration culminated in *Gustaf Wasa* (1786), a successful patriotic opera. The following year he wrote what is considered his greatest poem, *Den nya skapelsen, eller inbillningensvärld* (1790; "The New Creation, or the World of the Imagination"), in which he exalts the power of the imagination while describing a rich experience of romantic love. From 1778 until the time of his death, Kellgren was associated with the influential literary journal *Stockholmsposten.*

Kelly \\'kel-ē\\, George (Edward) (b. Jan. 16, 1887, Philadelphia, Pa., U.S.—d. June 18, 1974, Bryn Mawr, Pa.)   American playwright, actor, and director whose dramas of the 1920s depict the foibles of the American middle class with a telling accuracy.

Kelly followed his elder brother Walter into vaudeville as an actor, writing his first sketches for his own performance. His first success on Broadway was *The Torchbearers* (performed 1922), a satire on the social and aesthetic pretensions of the little-theater movement then flourishing in the United States. His next play, *The Show-Off* (1924), became an American comedy classic, and was made as a film three times (1926, 1934, 1946). In *Craig's Wife* (1925), a savage drama, Kelly shifted his vision to the upper middle class.

Kelly also wrote film scripts, among them those for the motion-picture versions of his plays, including *Craig's Wife* (1936), remade as *Harriet Craig* (1950).

Kelly \\'kel-ē\\, Hugh (b. 1739, Dublin?, Ire.—d. Feb. 3, 1777, London, Eng.)   British dramatist, critic, and journalist who was, for a time, a serious rival of the playwright Oliver Goldsmith. Kelly's greatest achievement occurred when his play *False Delicacy* (staged in 1768) scored a triumph in opposition to Goldsmith's *The Good Natur'd Man.*

Kelly immigrated to London in 1760 and began contributing essays to several magazines there. He edited *The Court Magazine* from 1761 to 1765 and published a short epistolary novel called *Memoirs of a Magdalen . . .* (1767). His *Thespis,* 2 vol. (1766–67), confirmed his reputation as a controversial critic.

The resounding success of Kelly's first play, *False Delicacy,* staged with the patronage of David Garrick, cost him Goldsmith's friendship and earned the enduring resentment of Samuel Johnson, who had written the prologue for Goldsmith's work. Another comedy by Kelly, *The School for Wives* (1773), and an afterpiece, *The Romance of an Hour* (1774), proved successful. A final comedy, *The Man of Reason* (1776), was a failure, however.

kelpie or **kelpy** \\'kel-pē\\ *plural* kelpies [perhaps from Scottish Gaelic *cailpeach, colpach* heifer, colt]   A water spirit, usually resembling a horse, that is held especially in Scottish folklore to delight in or bring about the drowning of travelers.

Kemal \ke-'mäl\, Namık, *in full* Mehmed Namık Kemal (b. Dec. 2, 1840, Tekirdağ, Ottoman Empire [now Turkey]—d. Dec. 2, 1888, Sakız [now Chios, Greece]) Turkish prose writer and poet who greatly influenced the Turkish nationalist movements and contributed to the Westernization of Turkish literature.

An aristocrat by birth, Kemal was educated privately, learning Persian, Arabic, and French. His knowledge of languages resulted in his working for the Ottoman government as a translator. Kemal became acquainted with the leading poets of the day and began to write poetry in the classical Ottoman style. He joined the nationalist organization known as the Young Ottomans, and in 1867, when the group was exiled because of revolutionary activities, he fled abroad. Kemal spent his time studying and translating works of such French authors as Victor Hugo, Jean-Jacques Rousseau, and Charles-Louis Montesquieu into Turkish. When the Young Ottomans returned to Constantinople in 1871, Kemal continued his revolutionary writings as editor of the newspaper *İbret*. At this time he also wrote his most famous play, *Vatan yahut Silistre* (1873; "Fatherland; or, Silistria"), a drama that revealed Kemal's ideas of patriotism and liberalism.

Kemal's best-known novels include *İntibah yahut Ali Beyin sergüzeşiti* (1874; "Awakening; or, Ali Bey's Experiences") and *Cezmi* (1880), a novel based on the life of the 16th-century khan of the Crimean Tatars, 'Âdil Giray. *Rüya* (1887; "The Dream"), expressing his desire for a Turkey free from oppression, was a widely read social work.

Kemény \'kem-,änʸ\, Zsigmond, Baron (Báró) (b. June 12?, 1814, Alvinc [Hungary]—d. Dec. 22, 1875, Pusztakamarás) Hungarian novelist especially noted for his minute psychological analysis.

Kemény's private means and title smoothed the way for his career. In Pest, he served on the staff of the liberal daily newspaper *Pesti Hirlap* from 1847 to 1855. In 1855 he became editor of the *Pesti Napló*, making it the most influential newspaper in Hungarian politics.

Kemény's historical novels include *Gyulai Pál* (1847), *Özvegy és leánya* (1855; "The Widow and Her Daughter"), *A rajongók* (1858–59; "The Fanatics"), and *Zord idő* (1862; "Grim Times"). The works make heavy reading, for there is more description than action, the atmosphere is depressing, and the style is difficult. His novels of contemporary life, such as *Férj és nő* (1852; "Husband and Wife"), are pervaded by the same tragic atmosphere. Kemény's mastery lies in his grasp of motivation and his evocation of historical backgrounds.

Kempe \'kemp\, Margery (b. *c.* 1373—d. *c.* 1440) English religious mystic whose autobiography is one of the earliest in English literature.

The daughter of a mayor of Lynn, she married John Kempe in 1393 and bore 14 children before beginning a series of pilgrimages to Jerusalem, Rome, Germany, and Spain in 1414. The descriptions of her travels and her religious ecstasies, which often included "boystrous" crying spells, are narrated in an unaffected prose style. Apparently illiterate, she dictated her *Book of Margery Kempe* to two clerks from about 1432 to about 1436. The work was first published in a modernized version in 1936. The original Middle English version was published in 1940.

Kendall \'kend-əl\, Henry (b. April 18, 1839, Ulladulla, near Milton, N.S.W., Australia—d. Aug. 1, 1882, Sydney) Australian poet whose verse was a triumph over a life of adversity.

His father, a missionary and linguist, died when Kendall and his twin brother were two years old. Their mother moved with

her sons to a farm, where Kendall remained until 1854, when he went to sea with an uncle for two years. At the age of 17 he returned to Sydney. It was then that he began to write. His first verse appeared in local journals and was later collected in *Poems and Songs* (1862). Friends found him a government job in 1863, and in 1868 he decided to marry. Less than a year later, he resigned his post and moved to Melbourne with his wife.

In Melbourne Kendall tried journalism without success and published *Leaves from Australian Forests* (1869), which was well received critically but sold poorly. In 1880 he published his last volume of poetry, *Songs from the Mountains*.

Keneally \kə-'nē-lē\, Thomas (b. Oct. 7, 1935, Sydney, Australia) Australian writer best known for his historical novels. Keneally's characters are gripped by their historical and personal past, and decent individuals are portrayed at odds with systems of authority.

At age 17 Keneally entered a Roman Catholic seminary, but he left before ordination; the experience influenced his early fiction, including *The Place at Whitton* (1964) and *Three Cheers for the Paraclete* (1968). His reputation as a historical novelist was established with *Bring Larks and Heroes* (1967), about Australia's early years as an English penal colony. *The Chant of Jimmie Blacksmith* (1972; film, 1980) won Keneally international acclaim; it is based on the actual story of a half-caste Aborigine who rebels against white racism by going on a murder spree.

Keneally's range was broad. His well-received *Gossip from the Forest* (1975) examined the World War I armistice through the eyes of a thoughtful, humane German negotiator. He was also praised for his treatment of the American Civil War in *Confederates* (1979). His later fiction includes *A Family Madness* (1985), *To Asmara* (1989), *Flying Hero Class* (1991), and *Woman of the Inner Sea* (1992).

The author's best-known work, *Schindler's Ark* (1982; also published as *Schindler's List*; film, 1993), told the true story of Oskar Schindler, a German industrialist who saved more than 1,300 Jews from the Nazis. Controversy surrounded the book's receipt of the Booker Prize for fiction; detractors argued that the work was mere historical reporting.

Kenilworth \'ken-əl-wərth\ Novel by Sir Walter SCOTT, published in 1821 and considered one of his finest historical novels.

Set in Elizabethan England, the novel relates the disaster that follows an attempt by the Earl of Leicester, a favorite of Queen Elizabeth I, to avoid the queen's displeasure at his marriage. Telling no one that he has married Amy Robsart, he hides his new bride at the home of Richard Varney, whose patron he is. Edmund Tressilian, who had also courted Amy, mistakenly believes that Amy is Varney's mistress and attempts to persuade her to return to her parental home. Tressilian then informs the queen that Varney has seduced Amy; to protect Leicester, Varney claims that Amy is his wife. The tangled web of lies and betrayals ultimately results in Amy's death.

Kennedy \'ken-ə-dē\, John Pendleton, *pseudonym* Mark Littleton \'lit-əl-tən\ (b. Oct. 25, 1795, Baltimore, Md., U.S.—d. Aug. 18, 1870, Newport, R.I.) American statesman and writer whose best-remembered work was his historical fiction.

Kennedy was admitted to the Maryland bar in 1816. From 1821 he served two terms in the Maryland House of Delegates and three terms in the U.S. Congress. He was also secretary of the navy in the cabinet of President Millard Fillmore.

Meanwhile, using the pen name of Mark Littleton, Kennedy wrote historical novels, including *Swallow Barn* (1832), sketches of the post revolutionary life of gentlemen on Virginia plantations, and *Rob of the Bowl* (1838), a tale of colonial Maryland.

Kennedy's major work of nonfiction is *Memoirs of the Life of William Wirt* (1849), about an attorney for the prosecution in the trial of Aaron Burr for treason. He also coedited the satirical magazine *Red Book* (1818–19) and wrote political articles for the *National Intelligencer*.

Kennedy \'ken-ə-dē\, Leo, *in full* John Leo Kennedy (b. Aug. 22, 1907, Liverpool, Eng.) Canadian poet of the modernist Montreal group, which reacted against the traditional and experimented with new techniques and subject matter.

Kennedy's family immigrated to Canada in 1912. Ending his formal education in the sixth grade, he went to work for his father, in the meantime publishing poetry and letters in *The Montreal Star*. By 1928 his poetry had come to the attention of a group of students at McGill University. This association led him to help found and to edit the *Canadian Mercury*, a short-lived experimental literary magazine. The criticism he wrote during this period helped to establish modernism in Canadian poetry. His notable creative work included the mortuary collection, *The Shrouding* (1933).

For the most part Kennedy had stopped publishing verse and other literary works by the 1940s, when he began to work in the United States as a copywriter.

Kennedy \'ken-ə-dē\, Walter (b. *c.* 1460—d. *c.* 1508) Scottish poet, remembered chiefly for his flyting (a poetic exchange of personal abuse or ridicule) with his professional rival William Dunbar. The exchange was recorded in *The Flyting of Dunbar and Kennedie*, the outstanding example of this favorite sport of the 15th- and 16th-century Scots poets.

Kennedy was the younger brother of John, 2nd Lord Kennedy of Dunure in Ayr, and a descendant of Robert III. He graduated from the University of Glasgow in 1476 and received his M.A. in 1478. Little else is known about his life. Dunbar's poetic portrait of Kennedy is a remarkable piece of grotesquerie; it may be realistic caricature, but there is probably no truth in his farcical account of Kennedy's life. The remainder of Kennedy's work is predominantly religious. *See also* William DUNBAR.

Kennedy \'ken-ə-dē\, William (b. Jan. 16, 1928, Albany, N.Y., U.S.) American author and journalist whose *Ironweed* (1983) won him the Pulitzer Prize for fiction in 1984.

Kennedy graduated from Siena College, Loudonville, N.Y., in 1949 and worked as a journalist in New York state and in San Juan, Puerto Rico, where he also began writing fiction. In 1963 he returned to Albany, which he considered the source of his literary inspiration. His first novel, *The Ink Truck* (1969), concerns a colorful columnist named Bailey who leads a strike at his newspaper in Albany.

Kennedy combined history, fiction, and black humor in his next novel, *Legs* (1975), about Jack "Legs" Diamond, an Irish-American gangster who was killed in Albany in 1931. *Billy Phelan's Greatest Game* (1978), also set in Albany, chronicles the life of a small-time streetwise hustler who sidesteps the powerful local political machine. *Ironweed*, which brought Kennedy widespread acclaim, tells the story of the hustler's father, Francis Phelan. Also published in 1983, *O Albany!* is a spirited nonfictional account of the politics and history of the city. Kennedy also wrote the novels *Quinn's Book* (1988) and *Very Old Bones* (1992), as well as the screenplays for *The Cotton Club* (1984, with Francis Ford Coppola) and *Ironweed* (1987).

Kennedy \'ken-ə-dē\, X.J., *pseudonym of* Joseph Charles Kennedy (b. Aug. 21, 1929, Dover, N.J., U.S.) American author of witty verse for children as well as for adults.

Kennedy served in the U.S. Navy and studied at Seton Hall University, Columbia University, and the Sorbonne. He studied and taught at the University of Michigan, served as poetry editor of the *Paris Review*, and wrote and edited several books on literature while teaching at Tufts University.

Beginning with his first collection, *Nude Descending a Staircase: Poems, Song, a Ballad* (1961), and with rare subsequent exceptions, Kennedy's poems are in rhyming stanzas and traditional meters and forms. They exhibit vivid language and frequent humor, including parody and satire. His *Cross Ties: Selected Poems* was published in 1985.

Composing poems and stories for his own children led Kennedy to write *One Winter Night in August and Other Nonsense Jingles* (1975). Children misbehave hilariously and are punished outrageously in his nonsense poems published in *Brats* (1986), *Fresh Brats* (1990), and *Drat These Brats!* (1993); by contrast, *The Kite That Braved Old Orchard Beach: Year-Round Poems for Young People* (1991) includes serious, even poignant verses. With his wife, Dorothy M. Kennedy, he wrote and edited *Knock at a Star: A Child's Introduction to Poetry* (1982) and *Talking Like the Rain: A First Book of Poems* (1992).

Kenner \'ken-ər\, Hugh, *in full* William Hugh Kenner (b. Jan. 7, 1923, Peterborough, Ont., Can.) Canadian literary critic who wrote several witty and readable books on modernist writers. His criticism was often based on the writer's own literary criteria.

Kenner studied at the University of Toronto and at Yale University. He was a faculty member of the University of California at Santa Barbara from 1950 until 1973, when he began teaching at Johns Hopkins University. In his influential books *The Poetry of Ezra Pound* (1951) and *The Pound Era* (1971), Kenner described Pound as the central figure in modernist literature and helped to reestablish the poet's battered reputation. Of comparable importance were his studies of James Joyce in *Dublin's Joyce* (1955), *Flaubert, Joyce and Beckett: The Stoic Comedians* (1962), *Joyce's Voices* (1978), and *Ulysses* (1980).

His other works include *Gnomon: Essays on Contemporary Literature* (1958), *The Counterfeiters: An Historical Comedy* (1968), *A Homemade World: The American Modernist Writers* (1975), *A Colder Eye: The Modern Irish Writers* (1983), and *A Sinking Island: The Modern English Writers* (1988). In particular, he focused on T.S. Eliot, Samuel Beckett, G.K. Chesterton, Wyndham Lewis, and Desmond Egan.

Kennicott, Carol \'kar-əl-'ken-i-ˌkät\ Idealistic young bride who attempts to bring culture to the small town of Gopher Prairie, Minn., in the novel MAIN STREET, by Sinclair Lewis.

kenning \'ken-iŋ\ [Old Norse, a derivative of *kenna* to perceive, know, name] A metaphoric compound word or phrase replacing a common noun, used especially in Old English and other Germanic poetry.

A kenning is commonly a simple stock compound such as "whale-path" or "swan road" for "sea"; "God's beacon" for "sun"; or "ring-giver" for "king." Many kennings are allusions that become unintelligible to later generations. *See also* SKALDIC POETRY.

Kent, Earl of \'kent\ Fictional character, faithful counselor to Lear in William Shakespeare's KING LEAR.

Kenyon Review, The \'ken-yən\ American intellectual serial founded in 1939 as a quarterly magazine of literary criticism by faculty members of Kenyon College, Gambier, Ohio. John Crowe RANSOM was its first editor. Until 1958, *The Kenyon Review* was closely identified with the New Criticism, and as such it soon became one of the most influential magazines of its kind in the country. It attracted writers of international literary reputation, including Allen Tate, Robert Penn Warren, and Mark Van Doren. The *Review* published criticism by Ransom, William Empson, Yvor Winters, I.A Richards, and Cleanth

Brooks and poetry by Marianne Moore, Stephen Spender, Wallace Stevens, John Berryman, and Dylan Thomas.

In 1960, when Robie Macauley assumed the editorship, the *Review* began to publish more fiction, though the emphasis remained on criticism. The magazine ceased publication in 1970 but was revived in 1979.

Ker \'kir\ or **Cer** \'sir\ *plural* Keres \'kē-,rēz\ *or* Ceres \'sē-\ In ancient Greek religion, a destructive spirit. Popular belief attributed death and illness to the action of impersonal powers. The word was also used of an individual's doom, with a meaning resembling the notion of destiny.

Kerner \'ker-nər\, Justinus Andreas Christian (b. Sept. 18, 1786, Ludwigsburg, Württemberg [Germany]—d. Feb. 21, 1862, Weinsberg) German poet and spiritualist writer. He and the poet Ludwig Uhland founded the so-called Swabian group of late Romantic poets.

Kerner studied medicine at Tübingen, where he met Uhland and spent most of his time reading and writing poetry. He became a practicing physician, and after settling in Weinsberg in 1818, he frequently entertained the leading poets of the time. His first book, *Reiseschatten: von dem Schattenspieler Luchs* (1811; "Travel Shadows: of the Shadow Player Luchs"), is characterized by the typically Romantic mixture of poetry and prose, seriousness and humor. His first collection, *Gedichte* (1826; "Poems"), reveals an uncharacteristic melancholy and mystical longing for death. The influence of the *Volkslied* ("folk song") is also clear in this poetry. He examined the somnambulist and clairvoyant Friederike Hauffe from 1826 to 1829 and published his results in *Die Seherin von Prevorst. Eröffnungen über das innere Leben der Menschen und über das Hereinragen einer Geisterwelt in die unsere* (1829; *The Seer of Prevorst. Disclosures About the Inner Life of Men and the Projection of a Spiritworld into Ours*). A fifth and enlarged edition of his poetry, *Lyrische Gedichte*, appeared in 1854.

Kerouac \'ker-ə-,wak\, Jack, *original name* Jean-Louis Kerouac (b. March 12, 1922, Lowell, Mass., U.S.—d. Oct. 21, 1969, St. Petersburg, Fla.) American poet and novelist, leader and spokesman of the BEAT MOVEMENT. Kerouac gave the Beat movement its name and celebrated its code of poverty and freedom in a series of novels, of which the first and best known is ON THE ROAD (1957).

Of French-Canadian descent, Kerouac learned English as a second language as a schoolboy. Discharged from the U.S. Navy during World War II as a schizoid personality, he then served as a merchant seaman. Thereafter he roamed the United States and Mexico before publishing his first novel, *The Town and the City* (1950). Dissatisfied with fictional conventions, Kerouac developed a new, spontaneous, nonstop, unedited method of writing that shocked more polished writers. *On the Road*, written in three weeks, was the first product of the new style.

The book revealed a widespread subterranean culture of poets, folksingers, hipsters, mystics, and eccentrics, including the writers Allen Ginsberg, Gregory Corso, William Burroughs, Gary Snyder, and Philip Whalen, all important contributors to the Beat movement. All of Kerouac's works, including THE DHARMA BUMS (1958), *The Subterraneans* (1958), *Doctor Sax* (1959), *Lonesome Traveler* (1960), and *Desolation Angels* (1965), are autobiographical. The posthumously published *Visions of Cody* (1972) was originally a part of *On the Road*.

Kesey \'kē-zē\, Ken (Elton) (b. Sept. 17, 1935, La Junta, Colo., U.S.) Writer who was a hero of the countercultural revolution and the hippie movement of the 1960s.

Kesey was educated at the University of Oregon and Stanford University. At a Veterans Administration hospital in Menlo Park, Calif., he was a paid volunteer experimental subject, taking mind-altering drugs and reporting on their effects. This experience and his work as an aide at the hospital served as background for his best-known novel, *One Flew Over the Cuckoo's Nest* (1962; film, 1975), which is set in a mental hospital. He further examined values in conflict in *Sometimes a Great Notion* (1964).

In the nonfiction *Kesey's Garage Sale* (1973), *Demon Box* (1986), and *The Further Inquiry* (1990), Kesey wrote of his travels and psychedelic experiences with the Merry Pranksters, a group that traveled together in a bus during the 1960s. Tom Wolfe recounted many of their adventures in *The Electric Kool-Aid Acid Test* (1968).

In 1988 Kesey published a children's book, *Little Tricker the Squirrel Meets Big Double the Bear*. With 13 of his graduate students in creative writing at the University of Oregon he wrote a mystery novel, *Caverns* (1990), under the joint pseudonym of O.U. Levon, which read backwards is "novel U.O. (University of Oregon)."

Ketuvim \kə-tü-'vēm, kə-thü-, kə-sü-\ The third division of the Hebrew Bible, or Old Testament. The four sections of the Ketuvim (Writings) include poetical books (Psalms, Proverbs, and Job), the Megillot, or Scrolls (Song of Solomon, Ruth, Lamentations of Jeremiah, Ecclesiastes, and Esther), prophecy (Daniel), and history (Ezra, Nehemiah, and I and II Chronicles).

A miscellaneous collection of liturgical poetry, secular love poetry, wisdom literature, history, apocalyptic literature, a short story, and a romantic tale, the Ketuvim were composed over a long period of time—from before the Babylonian Exile in the early 6th century BCE to the middle of the 2nd century BCE—and were not entirely accepted as canonical until the 2nd century CE.

Kezilahabi \,kā-zē-lä-'hä-bē\, Euphrase (b. April 13, 1944, Ukerewe, Tanganyika [now in Tanzania]) Tanzanian novelist, poet, and scholar writing in Swahili.

Kezilahabi received a B.A. from the University of Dar es-Salaam in 1970 and later returned to the university to teach in the department of Swahili. He also completed graduate studies at the University of Wisconsin.

Kezilahabi's first novel, *Rosa Mistika* (1971), which dealt with the abuse of schoolgirls by their teachers, was a popular success and was later adopted as a standard book for secondary schools in Tanzania and Kenya. His later novels include *Kichwamaji* (1974; "Waterhead"), *Dunia Uwanja wa Fujo* (1975; "The World Is a Chaotic Place"), and *Gamba la Nyoka* (1979; "The Snake's Skin"). The recurrent theme of Kezilahabi's fiction is the difficulty of an individual's integration into Tanzanian society, undergoing the stresses brought on not only by development and urbanization but also by the experiment with African socialism, begun in the late 1960s.

Kezilahabi's poems, such as those in *Kichomi* (1974; "Stabbing Pain"), caused controversy, for he broke with native tradition and became the first Swahili poet to write in blank verse.

Kgositsile \,kȯ-sēt-'sē-lä\, Keorapetse (William) (b. Sept. 19, 1938, Johannesburg, S.Af.) South African poet, essayist, and critic whose writings focus on Pan-African liberation as the fruit of informed heroism and compassionate humanism. Kgositsile's verse uniquely combines indigenous South African and African-American structural and rhetorical traditions.

Kgositsile wrote for the subsequently banned political weekly *New Age*. He began a self-imposed exile in 1961 in Dar es-Salaam, Tanzania, writing for *Spearhead* magazine. From 1962 to 1975 he lived in the United States, first as a graduate student and then as a teacher and poet-in-residence. He returned to Tanzania to lecture in English at the University of Dar es-Salaam.

Kgositsile's poetry includes *Spirits Unchained* (1969), *For Melba* (1970), *My Name Is Afrika* (1971), *The Present Is a Dangerous Place to Live* (1974), *Places and Bloodstains* (1975), *Herzspuren* (1981; "Traces of the Heart"), and *When the Clouds Clear* (1990). He also edited *The Word Is Here: Poetry from Modern Africa* (1973).

khamseh or **khamsa** \'käm-sə, 'käm-\ [Arabic *khamsa* five, group of five] In Persian and Turkish literature, a set of five long epic poems composed in rhyming couplet, or *maṡnawī*, form. *Khamseh* takes its name from the five great epic poems written by NEẒĀMĪ and entitled *Khamseh* ("The Quintuplet"). The first of these five poems is the didactic work *Makhzan al-asrār* (*The Treasury of Mysteries*); the next three are traditional love stories; and the fifth, the *Eskandar-nāmeh*, records the adventures of Alexander the Great. Several other notable poets, including Amīr Khosrow (1253–1325) and ʿAlī Shīr Navaʾī (1441–1501), wrote *khamseh*s in Persian and in Turkish.

Khansāʾ, al- \al-kän-'sä\ ("The Pug-nosed"), *byname of* Tumāḍir bint ʿAmr ibn al-Ḥārith ibn ash-Sharīd \tů-'mä-dēr-,bint-"äm-ər-,ib-nál-'kä-rith-,ib-nåsh-shå-'rēd\ (d. after 630) One of the greatest Arab poets, famous for her elegies.

The deaths of two of her brothers threw al-Khansāʾ into deep mourning; it was her elegies on their deaths and that of her father which made her the most celebrated poet of her time. When her four sons were slain in the Battle of Qādisīyah (637), the caliph ʿUmar is said to have congratulated her on their heroism and assigned her a pension.

The collected poetry of al-Khansāʾ, the *Dīwān*, reflects the pagan fatalism of the tribes of pre-Islāmic Arabia. The poems characteristically are short and imbued with a strong and traditional sense of despair at the irretrievable loss of life. The elegies of al-Khansāʾ were highly influential, especially among later elegists.

Khāqānī \al-,kä-'kä-,nē\, *in full* Afẓal od-Dīn Bādel Ebrāhīm ebn ʿAlī Khāqānī Shīrvānī (b. *c.* 1121, Shīrvān, Seljuq empire [now Azerbaijan]—d. *c.* 1198, Tabrīz, Iran) Persian poet whose importance rests mainly on his brilliant court poems, satires, and epigrams.

Khāqānī's father was a carpenter and a Muslim, and his mother was of Nestorian Christian origin. As a young man he composed lyrics under the name Ḥaqāʾiqī ("Seeker of Truth"). He then gained entry into the court of the ruler of Shīrvān, the *khāqān*, Manūchehr, from whom he took his pen name, Khāqānī.

Embittered by personal disputes and court intrigues, he set out on the pilgrimage to Mecca in 1156/57, after which he composed one of his greatest works, a *maṡnawī* (long poem in rhyming couplets), the *Tuḥfat al-ʿIrāqayn* ("Gift of the Two Iraqs"). It consists of five parts and is essentially a description of the poet's travels.

Returning to the court, Khāqānī was imprisoned for reasons that are not clear. His sufferings moved him to write a *ḥabsīyah* ("jail ballad") that is considered one of the finest of its kind. In 1171 he made another pilgrimage to Mecca, after which he returned to the court of Shīrvān. After the deaths of his son and wife in 1175, he made another pilgrimage and then settled in the city of Tabrīz, writing much of the poetry in his divan. Khāqānī filled his poems with Christian imagery, one of the few Persian poets to have done so.

Khatibi \kä-tē-bē\, Abdelkebir (b. 1938, Mazagan [now El-Jadida], Mor.) Moroccan educator, literary critic, and novelist belonging to the angry young generation of the 1960s.

Khatibi completed his secondary education in Morocco and then pursued a degree at the Sorbonne in Paris. His doctoral dissertation, *Le Roman maghrébin* ("The Maghribian Novel"), was published in 1968. From the outset Khatibi was concerned with the issue of political commitment and literature. He argued for the need to create on the cultural level of the educated masses, while avoiding popular demagoguery. His first novel, *La Mémoire tatouée* (1971; "The Tattooed Memory"), deals semiautobiographically with the typically Maghribian themes of acculturation and decolonization.

Khatibi's early views on the use of French by Maghribian authors reflected the revolutionary tone of the late 1960s: he saw writing as a means of passing beyond the contradictions of Western culture by destroying and re-creating the French language, thus attacking the heart of the culture from within with what Khatibi called a *littérature sauvage*.

Two plays, *La Mort des artistes* (1964; "The Death of the Artists") and *Le Prophète voilé* (1979; "The Veiled Prophet"), and a novel, *Le Livre du sang* (1979; "The Book of Blood"), demonstrate his theoretical approach to literature. The novel is a poetic search for identity inspired by the myth of Orpheus. *De la mille et troisième nuit* ("Of the Thousand and Third Night") was published in 1980. Another novel, *Amour bilingue* (1983; *Love in Two Languages*), is a symbol-filled story of love between a North African man and a French woman.

Khatr-Eddine \'kät-ər-ə-'dēn\, Mohammed (b. 1941, Tafraout, Mor.) Moroccan poet and novelist, a leading voice among postindependence writers.

Khatr-Eddine completed his secondary studies in Casablanca and then worked for the government in Agadir, helping to restore order after an earthquake there. This experience led to his novel *Agadir* (1967), in which the earthquake comes to represent the "seismic" upheavals that had recently taken place in Moroccan society. Other well-known works by Khatr-Eddine include the novels *Corps négatif* (1968; "Negative Body"), *Moi l'aigre* (1970; "I, the Surly One"), and *Le Déterreur* (1973; "The Disentomber") and the collections of poetry *Soleil arachnide* (1969; "Arachnid Sun") and *Ce Maroc* (1975; "This Morocco").

Khatr-Eddine's style, which is often referred to as "linguistic guerrilla warfare," is notable for its use of invented words and of words borrowed from Arabic, its exploding of conventional syntax, its violent and confrontational imagery, and its confusion of literary genres (often combining poetry, reportage, drama, and personal confession). This technique supports the themes of cultural disorientation, loss of personal values, and political conflict and hypocrisy.

Kheraskov \kʸi-'rà-skəf\, Mikhail Matveyevich (b. Oct. 25 [Nov. 5, New Style], 1733, Pereyaslav [now Pereyaslav-Khmelnytskyy], Ukraine, Russian Empire—d. Sept. 27 [Oct. 9], 1807, Moscow, Russia) Epic poet, playwright, and influential representative of Russian classicism who was known in his own day as the Russian Homer.

The son of a Walachian noble who had settled in Russia, Kheraskov became director of Moscow University in 1763. He determined to give Russia a national epic. *Rossiyada* (1771–79; "Russian Epic") is based on the capture of Kazan (1552) by Ivan the Terrible, and *Vladimir vozrozhdyonny* (1785; "Vladimir Reborn") is concerned with St. Vladimir's introduction of Christianity to Russia. Kheraskov composed 20 plays and edited literary magazines. His didactic poem *Plody nauk* (1761; "The Fruits of the Sciences") was a polemic against Jean-Jacques Rousseau's attack on scientific progress.

Khlebnikov \'klʸeb-nʸi-kəf\, Velimir Vladimirovich, *original name* Viktor Vladimirovich Khlebnikov (b. Oct. 28 [Nov. 9, New Style], 1885, Tundutov, Russia—d. June 28, 1922, Santalovo, Novgorod province) Poet who was the founder of Russian Futurism and whose esoteric verses exerted a significant influence on Soviet poetry.

Khlebnikov studied both mathematics and linguistics during his university years. At that time he also began developing ideas for a renovation of poetic language. About 1912 he met the poet Vladimir Mayakovsky and became involved in the Futurist literary movement, which was directed against the mysticism and narrowness of Symbolism and which regarded art as a social utility.

Khlebnikov, unlike other Futurists, retained a form of mysticism—of things and words rather than of ideas and symbols. Through his verbal experimentation he devised a "translogical language," creating a "new world of words" in his verse that makes it fresh and invigorating but difficult for the general reader.

Khlebnikov's popularity began to decline after the Russian Revolution, although his influence did not, as the works of Mayakovsky, Boris Pasternak, Osip Mandelstam, and others clearly show. After World War II he was attacked by Soviet critics as a "formalist" and "decadent," and his name fell into complete oblivion. Following the death of Joseph Stalin, however, he was rehabilitated. A new edition of his collected works was published in English in 1987.

Khomyakov \kə-m‿yi-ˈkòf\, Aleksey Stepanovich (b. May 1 [May 13, New Style], 1804, Moscow, Russia—d. Sept. 23 [Oct. 5], 1860, Ryazan, near Moscow) Russian poet and founder of the 19th-century Slavophile movement that extolled the Russian way of life. He was also an influential lay theologian of the Russian Orthodox church.

Khomyakov's education gave him a mastery of French, German, English, Greek, and Latin. He also learned Sanskrit and compiled a Russian-Sanskrit dictionary. He served with distinction in the Russo-Turkish war of 1828–29.

Khomyakov composed poetry and wrote philosophical and political essays and treatises on economics, sociology, and theology. A successful landlord, he won prizes in England for the construction of agricultural machinery. He was also a self-taught doctor who treated many of the peasants on his estates. He died from cholera, which he caught while doctoring.

Ki Tsurayuki \ˈkē-tsu̇-ˈrä-yə̇-kē\ (b. 868, Japan—d. *c.* 945) Court noble, government official, and noted man of letters in Japan during the Heian period (794–1185).

While serving as chief of the Imperial Documents Division, Tsurayuki took part in the compilation of the first imperial poetry anthology, KOKINSHŪ (905). In a prose introduction, Tsurayuki discussed the general nature of poetry and the styles of the poets represented. The introduction, which was written in the newly developed cursive kana syllabic alphabet, is regarded as one of the early masterpieces of Japanese prose. Tsurayuki was himself a prolific and highly respected writer of Japanese verse (*uta*), and he ranks among the "36 Japanese poets," the most illustrious poets of the 8th to the 10th century. In 935 he wrote *Tosa nikki* (*The Tosa Diary*), a travel book.

Kickham \ˈkik-əm\, Charles Joseph (b. 1826, Mullinahone, County Tipperary, Ire.—d. Aug. 21, 1882, Blackrock, near Dublin) Irish poet and novelist whose nationalistic writings were immensely popular in Ireland in the 19th century.

In 1860 Kickham joined the Fenians, an Irish revolutionary group, and soon rose to the leadership. In 1865 he was sentenced to 14 years in prison for his involvement in the outlawed organization. While interned he wrote the novel *Sally Cavanagh, or the Untenanted Graves* (1869). Released after four years because of ill health, he wrote many popular songs, ballads, and novels, including *Poems, Sketches, and Narratives Illustrative of Irish Life* (1870), *Knocknagow; or, The Homes of Tipperary* (1879), and *For the Old Land: A Tale of Twenty Years Ago* (1886).

Kidnapped Novel by Robert Louis STEVENSON, first published in serial form in the magazine *Young Folks* in 1886. *Kidnapped* and its sequel, *Catriona* (1893; U.S. title, *David Balfour*), are both set in Scotland in the middle 1700s.

After the death of his father, young David Balfour discovers that his uncle Ebenezer has cheated him out of his inheritance. Subsequently, his uncle has David kidnapped and placed on a ship bound for the Carolinas. Aboard ship, Balfour and Alan

"At Queen's Ferry," painting by N.C. Wyeth for a 1913 edition of *Kidnapped*
New York Public Library

Breck, a political rebel, become friends. Balfour eventually reclaims his inheritance and also aids Breck's cause. Balfour's adventures are continued in *Catriona*.

Kielland \ˈk‿yel-ˌlän\, Alexander Lange (b. Feb. 18, 1849, Stavanger, Nor.—d. April 6, 1906, Bergen) Novelist, short-story writer, and dramatist, one of "the four great ones" (with Henrik Ibsen, Bjørnstjerne Bjørnson, and Jonas Lie) of 19th-century Norwegian literature.

Kielland went to Paris in 1878 and the next year published a collection of his short stories. He read widely in the literature of 19th-century liberalism, and he dedicated his creative energies to social criticism and reform.

Kielland was perhaps the foremost Norwegian prose stylist of his day, and the witty and ironic temper of his work often took the edge off his biting social criticism. His most important novels are *Garman & Worse* (1880), in which he depicts the life of his native city of Stavanger; *Arbeidsfolk* (1881; "Working People"), in which he attacks Norway's state bureaucracy; *Skipper Worse* (1882), another portrait of his native Stavanger; and *Sankt Hans Fest* (1887; "St. John's Festival"), in which he satirizes the hypocrisy of Norway's clergy.

Kikuchi Kan \ˈkē-ku̇-chē-ˈkän\, *original name* Kikuchi Hiroshi \ˈhē-rō-shē\ (b. Dec. 26, 1888, Takamatsu, Japan—d.

March 6, 1948, Tokyo) Playwright, novelist, and founder of one of the major publishing companies in Japan.

As a student at the First Higher School in Tokyo, Kikuchi became acquainted with the future novelists Akutagawa Ryūnosuke and Kume Masao. Later, while attending Kyōto Imperial University, he worked with them on the famous literary magazine *Shinshichō* ("New Currents of Thought"). His story "Mumei sakka no nikki" (1918; "Diary of an Unknown Writer") reveals his frank envy of the success of his former classmates. His other well-known works are the story "Tadanao-kyō gyōjō ki" (1918; "On the Conduct of Lord Tadanao"), the plays *Chichi kaeru* (1917; *The Father Returns*) and *Okujō no kyōjin* (1916; *The Madman on the Roof*), and the novel *Shinju fujin* (1920; "Madame Pearl"). In 1923 he established *Bungei shunjū*, a popular literary magazine that gave rise to a large publishing company. Through the magazine Kikuchi set up two of the most prestigious literary awards given to new Japanese writers, the Akutagawa and Naoki prizes.

killcrop \'kil-ˌkräp\ [Low German *kīlkrop*] An infant with a voracious appetite, believed in folklore to be a fairy changeling.

Killigrew \'kil-i-ˌgrü\, Thomas (b. Feb. 7, 1612, London, Eng.—d. March 19, 1683, London) English dramatist and playhouse manager who was better known for his wit than for his plays, although some of the jokes in *The Parson's Wedding* (acted *c.* 1640) were appropriated by the playwright William Congreve.

In 1641 Killigrew published two tragicomedies, *The Prisoners* and *Claracilla*, both probably produced before 1636. In 1647 he followed Prince Charles (the future King Charles II) into exile and was favored with court appointments after the Restoration. In 1660 he received, with Sir William Davenant, a patent for two new playhouses; Killigrew's company became known as the King's Men.

In 1663 Killigrew built the original Theatre Royal in Drury Lane, London. In 1664 his plays were published, and in 1673 he became master of the revels.

Kilmer \'kil-mər\, Joyce, *in full* Alfred Joyce Kilmer (b. Dec. 6, 1886, New Brunswick, N.J., U.S.—d. July 30, 1918, near Seringes, Fr.) American poet known chiefly for his 12-line verse entitled "Trees."

Kilmer's first volume of verse, *Summer of Love* (1911), showed the influence of William Butler Yeats and the Irish poets. After his conversion to Roman Catholicism, Kilmer attempted to model his poetry upon that of Coventry Patmore and the 17th-century Metaphysical poets. "Trees" first appeared in *Poetry* magazine in 1913. His books include *Trees and Other Poems* (1914), *The Circus and Other Essays* (1916), *Main Street and Other Poems* (1917), and *Literature in the Making* (1917). Kilmer joined the staff of *The New York Times* in 1913. In 1917 he edited *Dreams and Images*, an anthology of modern Catholic poetry. Kilmer was killed in action during World War I and was posthumously awarded the Croix de Guerre.

Kilpi \'kēl-pē\, Volter (Adalbert) (b. Dec. 12, 1874, Kustavi, Fin.—d. June 13, 1939, Turku) Finnish novelist and social critic who was an exponent of the modern experimental novel.

Beginning as an "aesthetic" novelist, Kilpi turned to descriptions of 19th-century Finnish island life. In his important novel *Alastalon salissa* (1933; "In the Parlor at Alastalo"), he used interior monologues, long flashback episodes, and exact, detailed description to give an account of the events in a six-hour period. Kilpi uses his experimental technique in a broad, realistic depiction of a timeless, hierarchial social system.

Kim \'kim\ Novel by Rudyard KIPLING, published in 1901. His final and most famous novel, *Kim* chronicles the adventures of an Irish orphan in India who becomes the disciple of a Tibetan monk while learning espionage from the British secret service. The book is noteworthy for its nostalgic, colorful depiction of Indian culture, especially the diverse exotica of street life.

kinah meter \kē-'nä\ [Hebrew *qīnāh* dirge, lamentation] A Hebrew poetic meter typically having the line divided into two parts, with three stresses in the first part and two stresses in the second.

Kinck \'kiŋk\, Hans Ernst (b. Oct. 11, 1865, Øksfjord, Nor.—d. Oct. 13, 1926, Oslo) Prolific Norwegian novelist, short-story writer, dramatist, essayist, and Neoromanticist whose works reflect his preoccupation with the past and his lifelong interest in national psychology.

Kinck was strongly interested in Norwegian folklore. He used philology and history to uncover what he called the hidden forces behind the development of nations. He published the volumes of short stories *Fra hav til hei* (1897; "From Sea to Mountain") and *Flaggermus-vinger* (1895; "Bat's Wings"), but his principal work is the three-volume novel *Sneskavlen brast* (1918–19; "The Avalanche Broke"), dealing with the clash between the peasantry and the professional classes.

King \'kiŋ\, Henry (baptized Jan. 16, 1592, Worminghall, Buckinghamshire, Eng.—d. Sept. 30, 1669, Chichester, Sussex) English poet and Anglican bishop whose elegy for his wife is considered one of the best in the English language.

King was educated at Westminster and at Christ Church, Oxford, and he became bishop of Chichester in 1642. A friend and an executor of the estate of John Donne, his poetry was as much influenced by Ben Jonson as by Donne. He is best known for the poem "An Exequy to his Matchless Never to be Forgotten Friend."

King \'kiŋ\, Stephen (Edwin) (b. Sept. 21, 1947, Portland, Maine, U.S.) American novelist and short-story writer whose enormously popular books were credited with reviving the genre of horror fiction in the late 20th century.

King graduated from the University of Maine in 1970. His first published novel, *Carrie*, about a tormented teenage girl gifted with telekinetic powers, appeared in 1974 and was an immediate popular success. *Carrie* was the first of many novels in which King blended horror, the macabre, fantasy, and science fiction. Among such works were *Salem's Lot* (1975), *The Shining* (1977), *The Stand* (1978), *The Dead Zone* (1979), *Firestarter* (1980), *Cujo* (1981), *Christine* (1983), *It* (1986), *Misery* (1987), *The Tommyknockers* (1987), and *The Dark Half* (1989). King also wrote the short stories collected in *Night Shift* (1978), as well as several novellas and motion-picture screenplays. Many of his works were made into films.

Kingis Quair, The \'kiŋ-iz-'kwīr\ ("The King's Book") Love-dream allegory written about 1423 in Early Scots and attributed to James I of Scotland. It marks the beginning of the golden age of Scottish literature and reflects and acknowledges Geoffrey Chaucer's influence.

The story parallels the life of James I, who was captured and imprisoned for 18 years in England, where he met and married Joan Beaufort.

King James Version \'kiŋ-'jāmz\, *also called* Authorized Version. English translation of the Bible published in 1611 under the auspices of James I of England. Of 54 scholars approved by James, 47 labored in six groups at three locations for seven years, making use of previous English translations and texts in the original languages. The resulting translation had a marked influence on English style and was generally accepted as the standard English Bible for more than three centuries.

King John \'jän\ History play in five acts by William SHAKESPEARE, produced in 1596–97 and published in the First Folio of 1623 from an authorial fair copy.

The title character provides the central focus of the play, which ends with his death. The playwright surrounds him with such characters as the son of Sir Robert Faulconbridge, known as the Bastard, who supports the king and yet mocks all political and moral pretensions. Shakespeare depicts King John on a rapidly changing course, surrounded by many contrasting characters, so that the king's unsteady mind seems no more than one small element in an almost comic jumble of events.

King Lear \'lir\ Tragedy in five acts by William SHAKESPEARE, performed in 1605–06 and published in a quarto edition in 1608. One of Shakespeare's finest tragedies, the work displays a pessimism and nihilism that make it a 20th-century favorite.

The aging King Lear decides to divide his kingdom among his three daughters, allotting each a portion in proportion to the eloquence of her declaration of love. The hypocritical Goneril and Regan make grand pronouncements and are rewarded; Cordelia, the youngest daughter, who truly loves Lear, refuses to make an insincere speech to prove her love and is disinherited. The two older sisters mock Lear and renege on their promise to support him. Cast out, the king slips into madness and wanders about accompanied by his faithful Fool. He is aided by the Earl of Kent, who, though banished from the kingdom for having supported Cordelia, has remained in Britain disguised as a peasant. Kent brings Lear to Cordelia, who cares for him and helps him regain his reason.

The Earl of Gloucester likewise spurns his honest son, Edgar, and believes his conniving illegitimate son, Edmund. Edmund allies himself with Regan and Goneril to defend Britain against the French army mobilized by Cordelia. He turns his father over to Cornwall—who gouges out Gloucester's eyes—then imprisons Cordelia and Lear, but he is defeated in battle by Edgar. Jealous of Edmund's romantic attentions to Regan, Goneril poisons her and commits suicide. Cordelia is hanged. Lear, broken, dies with her body in his arms.

Kingo \'kiŋ-gō\, Thomas (b. Dec. 15, 1634, Slangerup, Den.—d. April 10, 1703, Odense) Clergyman and poet whose works are considered the high point of Danish Baroque poetry.

In his youth, Kingo wrote a series of poems picturing humorous scenes in village life as well as a pastoral poem entitled "Chrysillis." After graduating with a degree in theology, he taught briefly. In 1677 King Frederick III made Kingo bishop of Fyn. Thereafter, he wrote only hymns and religious poems and occasional poetry in honor of the royal family. His religious poems were collected in two volumes collectively entitled *Aandelige sjunge-kor* (1674 and 1681; "Spiritual Chorus"). The best known are the morning and evening songs and "Far, verden, far vel" ("Fare, World, Farewell"). He is remembered today mainly for what is popularly known as Kingo's hymnbook, a collection that appeared in 1699 and contained at least 85 of his own poems.

King, Queen, Knave Novel by Vladimir NABOKOV, first published in Russian in 1928 as *Korol, dama, valet*. With this novel, Nabokov began his career-long obsession with gamesmanship, word play in several languages, and multiple, surreal images and characterizations.

The image of a deck of playing cards is used throughout the novel. Franz, an unsophisticated young man, works in the department store of his rich uncle Dreyer. Out of boredom Martha, the uncle's young wife, seduces Franz. The lovers subsequently plot to drown Dreyer and marry each other. Martha changes her mind abruptly when she learns that an invention

by Dreyer stands to increase his wealth, but she then dies suddenly from pneumonia. Her husband never discovers his wife's duplicity.

Kingsley \'kinz-lē\, Charles (b. June 12, 1819, Holne Vicarage, Devon, Eng.—d. Jan. 23, 1875, Eversley, Hampshire) Anglican clergyman, teacher, and writer whose novels influenced social developments in Victorian Britain.

After graduating from Magdalene College, Cambridge, Kingsley was ordained in 1842 as curate of Eversley and two years later became parish priest there. His first novel, *Yeast* (printed in *Fraser's Magazine*, 1848; in book form, 1851), deals with the relations of the landed gentry to the rural poor. His second, *Alton Locke* (1850), is the story of a tailor-poet who becomes a leader of the Chartist movement (a British working-class movement for parliamentary reform).

Kingsley soon turned to writing his immensely popular historical novels: *Hypatia* (1853), a story of 5th-century Alexandria; *Westward Ho!* (1855), an anti-Catholic adventure set in the Elizabethan period; and *Hereward the Wake* (1866), about the Norman Conquest, also with an anti-Catholic slant. Kingsley's fear of the trend within the church toward Roman Catholicism, growing out of the Oxford movement, led to a notorious controversy with John Henry (later Cardinal) Newman. In answer to an attack by Kingsley, Newman wrote the *Apologia pro Vita Sua* (1864), the history of his religious development. Kingsley's long-popular children's book, *The Water-Babies* (1863), was inspired by his thoughts on evolution.

Kingsley \'kinz-lē\, Henry (b. Jan. 2, 1830, Barnack, Northamptonshire, Eng.—d. May 24, 1876, Cuckfield, Sussex) English novelist who is best known for *Ravenshoe* (1861) and *The Hillyars and the Burtons* (1865).

Kingsley was the brother of the writer and clergyman Charles Kingsley. After leaving the University of Oxford without taking a degree, he set out for the Australian goldfields. He was unsuccessful and returned to England after five years to write *The Recollections of Geoffrey Hamlyn* (1859), a novel of Australian life. He edited the *Edinburgh Review* for a time and was its war correspondent during the Franco-Prussian War of 1870–71.

King's Men An English theater company known by that name after it came under royal patronage in 1603. It had previously been known as the Lord Chamberlain's Men. William Shakespeare was its leading dramatist and Richard Burbage its principal actor. *See* CHAMBERLAIN'S MEN.

King Solomon's Mines \'säl-ə-mən\ Novel by H. Rider HAGGARD, published in 1885. One of the first African adventure stories, it concerns the efforts of a group of Englishmen to find the legendary diamond mines of King Solomon. The explorer Allan Quatermain agrees to take Sir Henry Curtis and a friend on an expedition deep into the interior of Africa to find Curtis' brother, who disappeared while searching for the mines. They find the mines and escape with some of the diamonds; on the way home they find Curtis' brother alive but injured. All four then return safely to Quatermain's home, where they divide the diamonds.

Kingsolver \'kiŋ-,sȯl-vər, -,säl-\, Barbara (b. April 8, 1955, Annapolis, Md., U.S.) American writer and political activist whose novels concern the strength and endurance of the poor and disenfranchised people of the American Southwest.

Kingsolver grew up in eastern Kentucky, the daughter of a physician who treated the rural poor. After graduating from DePauw University, Greencastle, Ind., she traveled and worked in Europe and then returned to the United States.

Kingsolver's novel *The Bean Trees* (1988) concerns a woman who makes a meaningful life for herself and a young Cherokee girl with whom she moves from rural Kentucky to the Southwest. In *Animal Dreams* (1990) a disconnected woman finds purpose and moral challenges when she returns to live in her small Arizona hometown. *Pigs in Heaven* (1993), a sequel to her first novel, deals with the protagonist's attempts to defend her adoption of her Native American daughter. Kingsolver also wrote the nonfictional *Holding the Line: Women in the Great Arizona Mine Strike of 1983* (1989) and a short-story collection, *Homeland and Other Stories* (1989). Her poetry collection, *Another America (Otra America)* (1991), in English with Spanish translation, concerns the struggles, primarily of impoverished women, against sexual and political abuse, war, and death.

Kingston \\'kiŋz-tən, 'kiŋ-stən\\, Maxine Hong, *original surname* Hong \\'hôŋ\\ (b. Oct. 27, 1940, Stockton, Calif., U.S.) Writer whose novels and nonfiction works explore the myths, realities, and cultural identities of Chinese and American families, as well as the role of women in Chinese culture.

The daughter of Chinese immigrants, Kingston was educated at the University of California at Berkeley. She taught at a number of schools, including the University of Hawaii and the University of California at Berkeley.

Kingston's first book, *The Woman Warrior: Memoirs of a Girlhood Among Ghosts* (1976), recalls her own girlhood, blending fact and fantasy in recreating the history of her female relatives in China. In *China Men* (1980), Kingston used biographical, mythological, and fantasy elements to tell the story of her father's life in China and his accommodations to life in America. The protagonist of her novel *Tripmaster Monkey: His Fake Book* (1988) is a young Chinese-American man who lives without regard to consequences.

Kinkel \\'kiŋ-kəl\\, Gottfried (b. Aug. 11, 1815, Oberkassel, near Bonn [Germany]—d. Nov. 13, 1882, Zürich, Switz.) German poet who owes his reputation chiefly to his sympathy with the Revolutions of 1848 (a series of failed revolts against several European monarchies).

Kinkel's *Gedichte* ("Poems") appeared in 1843 and was favorably received. One of his poetic epics, *Otto der Schütz* (1846; "Otto the Marksman"), was published in more than 70 editions and was mainly responsible for his influence on his contemporaries. His poetry is characterized by a sentimentality similar to that found in German literature of the mid-19th century.

In 1845 Kinkel became a professor of art and cultural history in Bonn, and in 1848 he turned to journalism, founding the newspaper *Demokratischer Verein* ("Democratic Union"). Kinkel took an active part in the uprising in Baden in 1849 and was sentenced to imprisonment for life. He eventually escaped to London.

Kinnell \\kə-'nel\\, Galway (b. Feb. 1, 1927, Providence, R.I., U.S.) American poet who examined the primitive bases of existence that are obscured by the overlay of civilization. His poems search for significance in such circumstances as an individual's personal relationship with violence and inevitable death, attempts to hold death at bay, the plight of the urban dispossessed, and the regenerative power of nature.

Educated at Princeton University and the University of Rochester, Kinnell worked for the University of Chicago in the early 1950s. Thereafter he taught and was poet-in-residence or poetry consultant at a number of colleges and universities.

His collections of poetry include *What a Kingdom It Was* (1960), *Flower Herding on Mount Monadnock* (1964), *Body Rags* (1967), *The Avenue Bearing the Initial of Christ into the New World: Poems 1946–64* (1974), *Selected Poems* (1982), for which he won both a National Book Award and a Pulitzer Prize, and *When One Has Lived a Long Time Alone* (1990). Kinnell also wrote a novel, *Black Light* (1966; revised 1980).

Kinoshita Junji \\kē-'nō-shə-tä-'jūn-jē\\ (b. Aug. 2, 1914, Tokyo, Japan) Playwright, a leader in the attempt to revitalize the post-World War II Japanese theater.

Kinoshita graduated from Tokyo University. His first play, *Fūrō* ("Wind and Waves"), which he began to write in 1939, was a historical drama of the Meiji Restoration (the reestablishment of Imperial rule after the downfall of the Tokugawa Shogunate); it was not published until 1947. As wartime censorship grew in rigidity, he turned from contemporary or historical themes to folklore and created his own unique genre of "folk plays." *Yūzuru* (1949; *Twilight Crane*) is an outstanding example and the play with which Kinoshita is most closely identified. After the war he investigated the role of guilt—especially over war—and responsibility in human actions in such plays as *Kaeru shōten* (1951; "Ascension of the Frog"), *Okinawa* (1961), and *Shimpan* (1970; *The Judgment*). *Shigosen no matsuri* (1977; "The Dirge of the Meridian") is a historical play whose protagonist represents Kinoshita's ideas on the dramatic hero. He is also noted for his studies of the Japanese language, translations of Western playwrights, including William Shakespeare, and essays on the theater.

Kinsella \\'kin-sel-ə\\, Thomas (b. May 4, 1928, Dublin, Ire.) Irish poet whose sensitive lyrics deal with primal aspects of the human experience.

After attending University College in Dublin, Kinsella served in the Irish civil service. He taught at Southern Illinois University, Carbondale, and at Temple University in Philadelphia. He also founded his own publishing company, Peppercanister, in Dublin.

His early volumes, *Poems* (1956) and *Another September* (1958; rev. ed., 1962), established him as a poet of note. Such later volumes as *Downstream* (1962) often focus on war and the political and social disruption of modern Ireland. Kinsella's translation of the early Irish saga *The Cattle Raid of Cooley* was published in 1969. *New Poems 1956–73* (1973) and *One and Other Poems* (1979) skillfully extend the themes of love, death, and rejuvenation. Later collections include *Blood and Family* (1988) and *Madonna: and Other Poems* (1991).

Kipling \\'kip-liŋ\\, Rudyard, *in full* Joseph Rudyard Kipling (b. Dec. 30, 1865, Bombay, India—d. Jan. 18, 1936, London, Eng.) English novelist, short-story writer, and poet chiefly remem-

Elliot and Fry

bered for his celebration of British imperialism, his tales and poems of British soldiers in India and Burma (now Myanmar), and his tales for children, particularly the JUST SO STORIES (1902). He received the Nobel Prize for Literature in 1907.

Kipling was taken to England by his parents at the age of six and was left for five years at a foster home at Southsea, the horrors of which he described in the story "Baa Baa, Black Sheep" (1888). He then went to a boarding school in North Devon that was featured as the unruly paradise celebrated in *Stalky & Co.* (1899) and in related stories.

Kipling returned to India in 1882 and worked for seven years as a journalist. He was a keen observer of the thronging spectacle of India, submitting both prose sketches and light verse to his employers. He published *Departmental Ditties* in 1886 and *Plain Tales from the Hills* in 1888 (including the well-known story THE MAN WHO WOULD BE KING), and between 1887 and 1889 he brought out six volumes of short stories. When he returned to England in 1889, his reputation had preceded him, and his fame was redoubled upon the publication of BARRACK-ROOM BALLADS in 1892.

In 1892 Kipling married Caroline Balestier, the sister of Wolcott Balestier, an American publisher and writer with whom he had collaborated in the romance *The Naulahka* (1892). The young couple moved to the United States but were unaccustomed to life in America and eventually returned to England. During his years in the United States, he published THE LIGHT THAT FAILED (1890), THE JUNGLE BOOK (1894), *The Second Jungle Book* (1895), CAPTAINS COURAGEOUS (1897), and KIM (1901).

In 1902 Kipling moved to Sussex, which provided the background for much of his later writing—especially *Puck of Pook's Hill* (1906) and *Rewards and Fairies* (1910). Kipling also spent a considerable amount of time in South Africa, where he was given a house by Cecil Rhodes, the South African statesman. This association fostered Kipling's imperialist persuasions, which were to grow stronger with the years. Kipling's ideas were not in accord with much that was liberal in the thought of the age, and as he grew older he became an increasingly isolated figure.

Although Kipling's poetry was extremely popular in his lifetime, its effect is rhetorical rather than imaginative. His prose, however, developed steadily throughout his life. Though his later work is compressed and elliptical in manner and somber in theme (and thus unlikely to be popular), it is subtle, complex, and, on the whole, highly effective.

Kirby \'kər-bē\, William (b. Oct. 13, 1817, Kingston upon Hull, Yorkshire, Eng.—d. June 23, 1906, Niagara, Ont., Can.) Writer whose historical novel *The Golden Dog* (1877; authorized version, 1896) is a classic of Canadian literature.

In 1832 Kirby's family moved to the United States and in 1839 to Canada. Kirby eventually settled in Niagara, where he worked as editor of the Niagara *Mail* from 1850 to 1871 and as collector of customs from 1871 to 1895.

Kirby was a fervent Loyalist (favoring retention of Canada as part of the British Empire) and in the 1840s wrote several works intensely pro-British in sentiment. Topical history was the subject of his *Annals of Niagara* (1896) and of his verse epic *The U.E.: A Tale of Upper Canada in XII Cantos* (1859).

His masterpiece, *The Golden Dog*, contains historical information and materials from French-Canadian legend that are fused into a skillful plot dealing with British ascendancy in Quebec at the time of Louis XV.

Kireyevsky or **Kireevsky** \kʲi-rʲi-'yef-skĕ\, Ivan Vasilyevich (b. March 10 [March 22, New Style], 1806, Dolbino, Russia—d. May 30 [June 11], 1856, St. Petersburg)   Philosopher,

critic, and writer who was one of the leading ideologists of the Slavophile movement in Russia.

Kireyevsky studied metaphysics in Germany in 1830. Upon his return to Russia he founded, in 1832, a literary journal called *Yevropeyets* ("The European"), which was banned by the government after two issues. He later converted to Orthodox Christianity and lost much of the Western outlook of his youth. In 1845 he served as editor of the journal *Moskvityanin* ("The Muscovite") for three issues.

Together with A.S. Khomyakov, Kireyevsky in the early 1840s articulated the classic arguments of Slavophilism, asserting the superiority of the Russian way of life and arguing that Russia should follow its own path of development based on the values and institutions derived from the country's early history.

Kirkland \'kərk-lənd\, Joseph (b. Jan. 7, 1830, Geneva, N.Y., U.S.—d. April 29, 1894, Chicago, Ill.)   American novelist whose only work, a trilogy of Midwestern pioneer life, contributed to the development of realistic fiction.

Kirkland was influenced by the English realist Thomas Hardy and by his own mother, Caroline Kirkland, whose realistic accounts of the family's life in backwoods Michigan were published in the 1840s. *Zury: The Meanest Man in Spring County* (1887) was the first book of the trilogy. *The McVeys* (1888), depicting village life, and *The Captain of Company K* (1891), about the American Civil War, complete the trilogy.

Kirkwood \'kərk-ˌwûd\, James (b. Aug. 22, 1924, Los Angeles, Calif., U.S.—d. April 21, 1989, New York, N.Y.)   American librettist, actor, author, and playwright who, together with Nicholas Dante, wrote the text for the Broadway musical *A Chorus Line* (1975), which in 1983 became the longest-running musical in the history of Broadway.

Kirkwood appeared on Broadway in *Junior Miss*, *Small Wonder*, and *Welcome Darling* and in such films as *Oh God, Book II* (1980) and *Mommie Dearest* (1981). For *A Chorus Line*, a story about dancers auditioning for a musical, Kirkwood won both a Tony award and a Pulitzer Prize in 1976. Kirkwood also wrote such plays as *U.T.B.U.: Unhealthy To Be Unpleasant* (1966) and the comedy *Legends* (1987). Among his books are *There Must Be a Pony!* (1960), *Good Times/Bad Times* (1968), *P.S. Your Cat Is Dead!* (1972), *Some Kind of Hero* (1975), and *Hit Me with A Rainbow* (1979). His autobiography, *Diary of a Mad Playwright*, was published in 1989.

Kirst \'kirst\, Hans Hellmut (b. Dec. 5, 1914, Osterode, East Prussia [Germany]—d. Feb. 23, 1989, Bremen, W.Ger.)   West German novelist who wrote more than 40 popular novels, mainly political thrillers and military satires.

Kirst served in the German army from 1933 to 1945. Disillusioned by his military experiences, he turned to fiction with the anti-Nazi novel *Wir nannten ihn Galgenstrick* (1950; *The Lieutenant Must Be Mad*). Kirst gained international acclaim for the satiric trilogy *Null-acht fünfzehn* (1954–55; *Zero Eight Fifteen*), about Private Gunner Asch and his personal battle with the absurdities of the German military system. Kirst was perhaps best known for *Die Nacht der Generale* (1962; *The Night of the Generals*; film, 1967). Many of his novels conveyed a collective guilt over German complacency under Nazism.

Kirstein \'kər-ˌstēn\, Lincoln (b. May 4, 1907, Rochester, N.Y., U.S.)   American dance authority and writer who collaborated with George Balanchine to found and direct the various ballet companies that eventually became the world-renowned New York City Ballet. He is known to literature for his establishment of HOUND AND HORN, a literary magazine.

While a student at Harvard University, he founded and edited (1927–34) *Hound and Horn*, whose contributors included T.S. Eliot, Ezra Pound, and E.E. Cummings.

Kirstein became involved in ballet when he helped Romola Nijinsky write the biography of her famous husband. In 1933, he persuaded a young member of Diaghilev's Ballets Russes, George Balanchine, to come to the United States. The two founded the School of American Ballet and several companies that had a profound effect on ballet in the United States. Kirstein's books include *Dance* (1935), *The Classic Ballet* (1952; with Muriel Stuart), *Movement and Metaphor* (1970), *The New York City Ballet* (1974), *Nijinsky Dancing* (1975), and *Thirty Years with the New York City Ballet* (1978). From 1942 to 1948 he edited *Dance Index*, a scholarly magazine that published illustrated and annotated monographs on dance.

Kisfaludy \'kēsh-fȯl-ŭ-dē\, Károly (b. Feb. 6, 1788, Tét, Hung.—d. Nov. 21, 1830, Pest)   Romantic dramatist, the first Hungarian playwright to achieve considerable popular success.

In 1811, while leading a precarious existence as a painter in Vienna, Kisfaludy wrote a historical drama, *A tatárok Magyarországon* ("The Tartars in Hungary"). The play remained unknown until eight years later, when it was performed by a repertory company in a provincial town; they repeated their performance in Pest, making Kisfaludy famous overnight.

Among Kisfaludy's most important works are the tragedy *Iréne* (1820) and the comedy *A kérők* (1817; "The Suitors"). In 1822 Kisfaludy founded a literary almanac, *Aurora*, which became the chief literary vehicle of the coming generation of Hungarian Romantics: József Bajza, Mihály Vörösmarty, and Ferenc Kölcsey.

Kiss of the Spider Woman   Novel by Manuel PUIG, published in 1976 as *El beso de la mujer araña*. Mostly consisting of dialogue between two men in an Argentine jail cell, the novel traces the development of their unlikely friendship. Molina is a middle-aged homosexual who passes the long hours in prison by acting out scenes from his favorite movies. Valentín is a young socialist revolutionary, who initially berates Molina for his effeminacy and his lack of political conviction. Sharing the hardships of a six-month prison term, the two eventually forge a strong relationship that becomes sexual. In an ironic role reversal at the end of the novel, Molina dies as a result of his involvement in politics while Valentín escapes the pain of torture by retreating into a dream world.

Kitahara Hakushū \'kē-tä-,hä-rä-'hä-kü-,shü\, *original name* Kitahara Ryūkichi \'ryū-,kē-chē\ (b. Jan. 25, 1885, Fukuoka, Japan—d. Nov. 2, 1942, Tokyo)   Japanese poet who was a major influence in modern Japanese poetry with his aesthetic and symbolic style.

In 1906 he joined the Shinshisha ("New Poetry Association") and published poems in its magazine, *Myōjō*, which brought him instant fame as a rising young poet. In 1909 he founded the Pan no Kai ("The Pan Society") in opposition to the naturalism that dominated literary circles at that time.

His first collection of poems, *Jashūmon* (1909; "Heretics"), which depicted Christian missionaries in 16th-century Japan, won him much praise for the exotic and sensuous beauty of his writing. In 1911 a collection of his lyric poems, *Omoide* ("Memories"), was published and also received great praise. Kitahara introduced a new symbolic, decadent style into the genre of the traditional 31-syllable tanka with the publication of the collection *Kiri no hana* ("Paulownia Blossoms") in 1913. He founded several magazines, including an innovative tanka magazine entitled *Tama*, and published nearly 200 volumes of poetry in his lifetime.

Kit-Cat Club \'kit-,kat\   Club founded by leading members of the Whig Party in London in the early 18th century. Its members included such literary figures as Joseph Addison, Sir Richard Steele, William Congreve, and Sir John Vanbrugh. The

club met at a pastry shop owned by Christopher Cat (or Kat), who served pastries known as Kit-Cats.

kitchen-sink \,kich-ən-'siŋk\   *chiefly British*   Portraying or emphasizing the squalid aspects of modern life. In literature the term has somewhat negative connotations and has been applied mainly to the dramas of the so-called Angry Young Men, who wrote realistically of working-class life in the mid-1950s.

kitsch \'kich\ [German]   Artistic or literary material held to be of low quality, often produced to appeal to popular taste, and marked especially by sentimentalism, sensationalism, and slickness.

Kivi \'kē-vē\, Aleksis, *pseudonym of* Aleksis Stenvall \'stän-,vȧl\ (b. Oct. 10, 1834, Nurmijärvi, Russian Finland [now in Finland]—d. Dec. 31, 1872, Tuusula)   Father of the Finnish novel, dramatist, and the creator of Finland's modern literary language.

Kivi entered the University of Helsinki in 1857. In 1860 he won the Finnish Literary Society's drama competition with his tragedy *Kullervo*, based on a theme taken from the Finnish national epic *Kalevala*. His most famous plays are the rural comedies *Nummisuutarit* (1864; "Shoemakers of the Heath") and *Kihlaus* (1867; "Fugitives"). Kivi's *Seitsemän veljestä* (1870; *Seven Brothers*) was the first novel written in Finnish. As Finland's first professional writer, Kivi struggled throughout his life against poverty and hostile criticism. Though his works are now regarded as classics, a collection of his poems, *Kanervala* (1866; "Land of the Heathen"), did not begin to be fully appreciated until almost a century after his death.

Kizer \'kī-zər\, Carolyn (Ashley) (b. Dec. 10, 1925, Spokane, Wash., U.S.)   American poet whose work reflected her advocacy of feminism and her concern for human rights. She was awarded the Pulitzer Prize for poetry in 1985 for her collection *Yin: New Poems* (1984).

After attending Sarah Lawrence College, Kizer did graduate work at Columbia University and at the University of Washington. In 1959 she cofounded *Poetry Northwest*, which she also edited from 1959 to 1965. After serving in Pakistan as literary specialist for the U.S. State Department from 1964 to 1965 and from 1966 to 1970, she was the first director of literary programs for the National Endowment for the Arts. Kizer lectured, taught, or was poet-in-residence at several universities.

Her collections include *Poems* (1959), *The Ungrateful Garden* (1961), *Knock upon Silence* (1965), *Midnight Was My Cry* (1971), *Mermaids in the Basement: Poems for Women* (1984), and *The Nearness of You* (1986). "Pro Femina," one of her best-known poems, is a satiric work about women writers.

Klabund \klä-'bŭnt\, *pseudonym of* Alfred Henschke \'hensh-kə\ (b. Nov. 4, 1890, Crossen, Ger.—d. Aug. 14, 1928, Davos, Switz.)   Expressionist poet, playwright, and novelist who influenced German literature with his adaptations of Chinese, Japanese, and Persian literature. Notable among his free, imaginative renderings are *Li-tai-pe* (1916), *Lao-tse* (1921), and *Der Kreidekreis* (1924; *The Circle of Chalk*), a successful drama later adapted by Bertolt Brecht in his play *Der kaukasische Kreidekreis* (*The Caucasian Chalk Circle*).

Henschke identified with the eternally seeking wandering poet and called himself Klabund, a name derived from *Klabautermann* ("hobgoblin") and *Vagabund* ("vagabond"). He composed poetry in a variety of forms, and he created a new prose form, the "Expressionist novella." Notable in this genre are his autobiographical "novels of longing," with themes of sickness and love; biographical "novels of passion," with sensual portraits of historical figures (*e.g.*, *Pjotr*, 1923; *Peter the Czar*); and his greatest achievements in prose, two "novels of fulfillment"—*Bracke* (1918; *Brackie, the Fool*) and *Borgia* (1928; *The Incredible Borgias*).

Klaj \'klī\, Johann, *Latin* Johannes Clajus \'klä-yus\ (b. 1616, Meissen, Saxony [Germany]—d. 1656, Kitzingen, near Würzburg, Franconia) German poet who helped make mid-17th-century Nürnberg a center of German literature.

In 1644, with Georg Philipp Harsdörfer, Klaj founded the Nürnberg literary society known as Pegnitzer Hirtengesellschaft ("Pegnitz Shepherds"). He specialized in pastoral poetry and wrote, jointly with Harsdörfer, the *Pegnesisches Schäfergedicht* (1644; "Pegnitz's Idyll") and, with Harsdörfer and Sigmund von Birken, the *Fortsetzung der Pegnitzschäferey* (1645; "The Pursuit of Pegnitz's Meadows"). He also wrote religious oratorios and mystery plays, including *Die Auferstehung Jesu Christi* (1644; "The Resurrection of Jesus Christ"), *Freudengedicht auf die Geburt Christi* (1645; "Joyful Verses on the Birth of Christ"), *Trauerspiel vom leidenden Christus* (1645; "The Tragedy of the Sorrows of Christ"), and *Herodes* (1645).

Klein \'klīn\, A.M., *in full* Abraham Moses (b. 1909, Ratno, Volhynia, Russian Empire [now in Ukraine]—d. Aug. 21, 1972, Montreal, Que., Can.) Canadian poet whose verse reflects his strong involvement with Jewish culture and history. He was a member of the Montreal group, a coterie of poets who advocated a break with traditional picturesque landscape poetry.

Klein practiced law in Montreal and at various times edited the *Canadian Jewish Chronicle*, lectured at McGill University, and was active in the Co-operative Commonwealth Federation (now the New Democratic Party). Following a nervous breakdown in the mid-1950s, he lived in seclusion until his death.

An ardent supporter of Zionism, Klein made the Jewish experience a vehicle for his artistic expressions. *Hath Not a Jew . . .* (1940), *Poems* (1944), and *The Hitleriad* (1944) deal with persecution of the Jews by the Russians and Nazis. After a visit to Israel he wrote about its creation in *The Second Scroll* (1951), a symbolic novel that carries overtones of the techniques of James Joyce, on whom Klein was an authority. *The Rocking Chair and Other Poems* (1948) describes the change wrought by industrialization on Quebec.

Kleist \'klīst\, Ewald Christian von (b. March 7, 1715, Zeblin, Pomerania [now in Poland]—d. Aug. 24, 1759, Frankfurt an der Oder, Brandenburg [Germany]) German lyric poet best known for his long poem *Der Frühling* (1749; "Spring"), which, with its realistically observed details of nature, contributed to the development of a new poetic style.

In Potsdam, while serving as an army officer, von Kleist met Johann Wilhelm Ludwig Gleim, through whose influence and friendship he became a poet. In about 1757 he became close friends with the writer Gotthold Ephraim Lessing and came in contact with the literary circle in Leipzig. From this period come his patriotic and heroic poems, inspired by his experience in the Seven Years' War: *Ode an die Preussische Armee* (1757) and the short epic *Cessides und Paches* (1759). *Der Frühling* is typical of his heartfelt nature poetry. Wounded in the battle of Kunersdorf, he died the "death for the fatherland" of which he had written in his poetry.

Kleist \'klīst\, Heinrich von, *in full* Bernd Heinrich Wilhelm von Kleist (b. Oct. 18, 1777, Frankfurt an der Oder, Brandenburg [Germany]—d. Nov. 21, 1811, Wannsee, near Berlin) The first of the great German dramatists of the 19th century.

Kleist's reading of the philosophy of Immanuel Kant destroyed his faith in the value of knowledge. Despairing of reason, he decided to place his trust in emotion. The conflict between reason and emotion lies at the heart of his work.

Kleist's first work, the tragedy *Die Familie Schroffenstein* (1803; "The Schroffenstein Family"), depicts pathological states with ruthless clarity. His recurring theme is the fallibility of human perception and the inability of the human intellect by itself to apprehend truth.

In Dresden, where he lived from 1807 to 1809, Kleist became a member of a large circle of writers, painters, and patrons. While he was in prison, accused of being a spy, his adaptation of Molière's *Amphitryon* (published in 1807) attracted attention, and in 1808 he published *Penthesilia*, a tragic drama about the passionate love of the queen of the Amazons for Achilles. Although this play received little acclaim, it is now thought to contain some of Kleist's most powerful poetry, with the grimness of plot and intensity of feeling that have made his place unique among German poets. In 1808 Kleist's one-act comedy in verse, *Der zerbrochene Krug* (*The Broken Pitcher*), was unsuccessfully produced by J.W. von Goethe in Weimar. The play, with its vividly portrayed rustic characters, skillful dialogue, earthy humor, and subtle realism, ranks among the masterpieces of German dramatic comedy. Toward the end of 1808, inspired by a threatened rising against Napoleon, Kleist wrote several savage war poems and a political and patriotic tragedy, *Die Hermannsschlacht* (1821; "The Warrior's Battle"). Between 1810 and 1811 his *Das Käthchen von Heilbronn* (1810; *Katherine of Heilbronn*), a drama set in Swabia during the Middle Ages, was performed in Vienna, Graz, and Bamberg.

Kleist also wrote eight masterly novellas, collected in *Erzählungen* (1810–11; "Stories"), of which *Michael Kohlhaas*, *Das Erdbeben in Chili* (*The Earthquake in Chili*), and *Die Marquise von O* (THE MARQUISE OF O) became well known as tales of violence and mystery. In Kleist's last drama, *Prinz Friedrich von Homburg* (published posthumously in 1821), the problematic hero reflects the author's own conflicts between heroism and cowardice, dreaming and action.

Klephtic ballad \'klef-tik\ Any of the songs and poems extolling the adventures of the Klephts, Greek nationalists living as outlaws in the mountains during the period of Turkish domination over Greece from 1453 to 1828. Containing some of the most beautiful and vivid verse in Modern Greek, the songs, mainly from the 18th century, are an entirely spontaneous poetry, composed in popular language and in 15-syllable verse, rhymed and unrhymed. They are pervaded with the spirit of the forests and the mountains and, like so much of Greek popular poetry, personify trees, rocks, and rivers.

Klíma \'klē-mä\, Ivan (b. Sept. 14, 1931, Prague, Czech.) Czech author whose fiction and plays portray morals and ideals under attack from political ideology.

Klíma spent three years in a Nazi concentration camp during World War II, an experience he recorded in his first published writing in 1945. His first book, *Mezi třemi hranicemi* (1960; "Between Three Borders"), was a nonfiction work on Slovakia. During the 1960s he wrote stories for animated films, served as editor for *Literární noviny* ("Literary News"), edited a book of essays by Karel Čapek, and wrote fiction, including the short stories of *Milenci na jednu noc* (1964; "Lovers for One Night") and the novel *Lod' jménem Naděje* (1969; *A Ship Named Hope*). His play *Zámek* (1964; "The Castle") was considered a parable on communist morality. *Porota* (1969; *The Jury*) portrays a dilemma of responsibility versus despotism. His subsequent plays were banned in Czechoslovakia.

Klíma's one-act plays, such as *Klára a dva páni* (1968; "Klara"), *Cukrárna Myriam* (1971; "Sweetshop Myriam"), and *Hry* (1975; "Games"), are distinguished by tense plots and absurd situations. His later fiction includes the novel *Milostné léto* (1972; "A Summer Affair") and a collection of four linked short stories titled *Moje první lásky* (1985; *My First Loves*).

Klinger \\'kliŋ-ər\\, Friedrich Maximilian von (b. Feb. 17, 1752, Frankfurt am Main [Germany]—d. March 9, 1831, Derpt, Livonia province, Russian Empire [now Tartu, Estonia]) Dramatist and novelist, a representative of the German literary revolt against rationalism in favor of emotionalism known as the Sturm und Drang movement. Indeed, the movement took its name from his play *Der Wirrwarr, oder Sturm und Drang* (1776; "Confusion, or Storm and Stress").

The reckless, rebellious style of Klinger's early life seems the very embodiment of Sturm und Drang in its simpler interpretation. His numerous plays, written in the fury of inspiration, are usually built around a Promethean hero, but they lack probability, psychological depth, and dramatic form. The best of these works, *Die Zwillinge* (1776; "The Twins"), deals with a favorite theme of the period, the enmity of brothers.

In his later years, having outgrown the angry resentment of his early period, Klinger wrote two tragedies on the Medea theme and a cycle of nine romances that express a Rousseauistic longing for simplicity and idyllic nature.

Klonowic \\klô-'nô-vēts\\, Sebastian (Fabian), *pseudonym* Acernus \\ä-'tser-nüs\\ (b. *c.* 1545, Sulmierzyce, Pol.—d. Aug. 29, 1602, Lublin) Polish poet whose work in Latin and Polish is valuable chiefly as cultural history.

Klonowic settled in Lublin, where he became mayor and a municipal juror. The Latin poem "Roxolania" (written 1584) gave the first complete account of the geography, landscape, and people of Ruthenia. The Polish poem *Flis* (1595; "The Boatmen") described the valley of the Vistula River and the life and customs of its raftsmen. *Worek Judaszów* (1600; "Judas' Sack"), satirized the lowlife of Lublin. The Latin poem *Victoria deorum* (1587; "The Victory of the Gods") contends that true nobility depends not upon birth but upon character.

Kloos \\'klōs\\, Willem (Johan Theodoor) (b. May 6, 1859, Amsterdam, Neth.—d. March 31, 1938, The Hague) Dutch poet and critic who was the driving intellectual force of the 1880s Dutch literary revival and the cofounder and mainstay of its periodical, *De Nieuwe Gids* ("The New Guide"). A ruthless critic of the rhetorical, passionless nature of traditional Dutch writing, Kloos continually championed the idea of beauty as the highest value in art and life. Kloos's maxim "poetry alone makes life worth living" is regarded as the manifesto of the 1880s movement.

An admirer of the English Romantic poets, Kloos determined to reestablish the sonnet as a valid art form with a new rhythmic freedom. His own early sonnets were collected in *Verzen* (1894). Kloos evolved the dictum that poetry should be "the most individual expression of the most individual emotion." This aspect of the 1880s movement eventually proved the spiritual downfall of Kloos, for, unlike his fellow poets Herman Gorter and Albert Verwey, he did not develop beyond this stage.

Klopstock \\'klôp-shtôk\\, Friedrich Gottlieb (b. July 2, 1724, Quedlinburg, Saxony [Germany]—d. March 14, 1803, Hamburg) German epic and lyric poet whose subjective vision marked a break with the rationalism that had dominated German literature in the early 18th century.

In 1749 the first three cantos of Klopstock's epic poem *Der Messias* (*The Messiah*), written in unrhymed hexameters, appeared. The emotional handling of the theme created a sensation.

Klopstock left his studies at the University of Leipzig and became a private tutor at Langensalza, Thuringia. An invitation and an annuity from Frederick V of Denmark took him to Copenhagen, where he remained for 20 years. In 1754 he married Margarethe (Meta) Moller of Hamburg, who was the

"Cidli" of his odes, a collection of which, *Oden*, was published in 1771. In 1770 he retired to Hamburg, where the last five cantos of *Der Messias* were produced with waning inspiration three years later.

Despite the success of *Der Messias*—the work was translated into 17 languages—it is chiefly as a lyric poet that Klopstock established his reputation.

knack   *obsolete*   An ingenious literary device or CONCEIT.

Knebel \\'knā-bəl\\, Karl Ludwig von (b. Nov. 30, 1744, Castle Wallerstein, near Nordlingen, Franconia [Germany]—d. Feb. 23, 1834, Jena, Saxony) German poet who was a close friend of J.W. von Goethe and was one of the most talented of the Weimar circle of Neoclassicists.

After serving in the Prussian army, Knebel became tutor to Prince Konstantine of Saxe-Weimar-Eisenach. Knebel's work on Pindar and his translations of the poetry of Propertius and Lucretius inspired Goethe to study them. Knebel also took part in the first performance of Goethe's *Iphigenie auf Tauris*. The author of graceful sonnets, Knebel collected his poetry in *Sammlung Kleiner Gedichte* (published anonymously in 1815; "Collection of Short Poems") and in *Distichen* (1827; "Couplets").

Kniaźnin \\'knʸâzh-nʸen\\, Franciszek Dionizy (b. Oct. 4, 1750, Vitebsk, Pol. [now Vitsebsk, Belarus]—d. Aug. 25, 1807, Końskowola, near Puławy, Galicia, Austrian Empire [now in Poland]) Minor Polish poet, playwright, and translator who was a court poet of the princely Czartoryski family.

Kniaźnin was educated in a Jesuit college and entered the noviate. When the order was disbanded, he was attached in 1783 to the Czartoryskis, for whom he produced lyric poetry, odes, love poems, fables, plays, and verses of a religious or patriotic nature. While in residence at the Puławy palace, he wrote *Na rewolucję 1794 roku* ("For the 1794 [Kościuszko] Revolution") and his best-known poem, *Hejnał na dzień 3 maja* (1791; "Bugle Call to the Third of May"). He is perhaps best remembered for his short lyrical poems.

Knickerbocker, Diedrich \\dē-drik-'nik-ər-,bäk-ər\\   Persona invented by Washington Irving to narrate the burlesque A HISTORY OF NEW YORK. An eccentric 25-year-old scholar, Knickerbocker also narrated Irving's story "Rip Van Winkle."

The word Knickerbocker became synonymous with Dutch-Americans in New York state, and later, with all residents of the state. The word also came to describe the knee breeches that characters wore in the original illustrated text of *A History of New York*.

Knickerbocker school \\'nik-ər-,bäk-ər\\   Group of writers active in and around New York City during the first half of the 19th century. Taking its name from Washington Irving's *A History of New York* "by Diedrich Knickerbocker" (1809), the group sought to promote a genuinely American national culture and establish New York City as its literary center. The most important members of the group were Irving, his friend the novelist J.K. Paulding, James Fenimore Cooper, and William Cullen Bryant. *The Knickerbocker Magazine* (1833–65), a literary monthly edited by Lewis G. and Willis G. Clark, though not an official organ of the group, published members' work.

Knight \\'nīt\\, Etheridge (b. April 19, 1931, Corinth, Miss., U.S.—d. March 10, 1991, Indianapolis, Ind.) African-American poet who emerged as a robust voice of the black aesthetic movement with his first volume of verse, *Poems from Prison* (1968). His poetry combined the energy and bravado of African-American "toasts" (long narrative poems that were recited in a mixture of street slang, specialized argot, and obscenities) with a sensitive concern for freedom from oppression.

Arrested for robbery in 1960, Knight was imprisoned for eight years—an experience that he recounted in verse in *Poems from Prison* and in prose in the anthology *Black Voices from Prison* (1970; originally published two years earlier in Italian as *Voce negre dal carcere*). After his release from prison, Knight taught at various universities and contributed to several magazines. He experimented with rhythmic forms of punctuation in *Belly Song and Other Poems* (1973), which addressed the themes of ancestry, racism, and love. In *Born of a Woman* (1980)—a work that balances personal suffering with affirmation—he introduced the concept of the poet as a "meddler" who forms a trinity with the poem and the reader. Much of his verse was collected in *The Essential Etheridge Knight* (1986).

Knight \'nīt\, Sarah Kemble, *byname* Madame Knight (b. April 19, 1666, Boston, Mass. [U.S.]—d. Sept. 25, 1727, New London, Conn.) American colonial teacher and businesswoman whose vivid and often humorous diary of her unchaperoned journey on horseback from Boston to New York in 1704 is considered one of the most authentic chronicles of 18th-century colonial life in America. *The Journal of Mme Knight* was published posthumously in 1825.

The Journal was one of very few published works of the era not written by a clergyman. It also was a precursor of a type of literature based on regional caricature.

Knightley, George \'jȯrj-'nīt-lē\ Fictional character, the squire who attempts to guide and eventually proposes marriage to Emma Woodhouse in Jane Austen's EMMA.

Knight's Tale, The One of the 24 stories in THE CANTERBURY TALES by Geoffrey Chaucer.

This chivalric romance was based on Giovanni Boccaccio's *Teseida*, and though it was not originally written as part of the Canterbury collection, Chaucer adapted it to fit the character of the Knight. In the tale, the cousins Palamon and Arcite both fall in love with Emelye, sister of Hippolyta, queen of the Amazons, who is married to their captor Theseus. Theseus arranges a tournament for the two rivals to compete for Emelye's hand. Although Arcite wins, he is thrown from his horse and dies. After a period of mourning, Palamon and Emelye marry.

Knopf \kə-'nəpf, *commonly* -'nȯpf\, Alfred A. (b. Sept. 12, 1892, New York, N.Y., U.S.—d. Aug. 11, 1984, Purchase, N.Y.) American publisher, the founder and longtime chairman of the prestigious publishing house Alfred A. Knopf, Inc.

Knopf graduated from Columbia University. After working for a short time at the publishing house of Doubleday, Page, & Company, he started his own firm in 1915. Knopf's appreciation of contemporary literature and his broad range of literary contacts in the United States and abroad helped to make his publishing house renowned for the high literary quality of the cosmopolitan works he published. By the time of Knopf's death in 1984 the authors published by the Knopf house had garnered a total of 16 Nobel and 27 Pulitzer prizes. From 1924 to 1934 Knopf also served as publisher of the *American Mercury*, an influential periodical founded by him, H.L. Mencken, and George Jean Nathan in 1924.

Knowles \'nōlz\, John (b. Sept. 16, 1926, Fairmont, W.Va., U.S.) American author who gained prominence for his first published novel, A SEPARATE PEACE (1959). Most of his novels were psychological examinations of characters caught in conflict between the wild and the pragmatic sides of their personalities.

Knowles contributed articles to various publications during the 1950s before becoming a full-time writer. *A Separate Peace* chronicles the competitive friendship of two students at a New England preparatory school during World War II. Its se-

quel, *Peace Breaks Out* (1981), is viewed from the perspective of a troubled young teacher who has recently returned from World War II.

Other novels include *Indian Summer* (1966), *The Paragon* (1971), *A Vein of Riches* (1978), *Morning in Antibes* (1962), *Spreading Fires* (1974), *A Stolen Past* (1983), and *The Private Life of Axie Reed* (1986). He also wrote the travelogue *Double Vision* (1964) and *Phineas* (1968), a collection of six short stories.

Kobayashi Hideo \kō-'bä-yä-shē-hē-'dä-ō\ (b. April 11, 1902, Tokyo, Japan—d. March 1, 1983, Tokyo) One of the most influential critics in the Japanese cultural world.

Kobayashi graduated in 1927 from Tokyo Imperial University, where he had concentrated on French literature. In the early 1930s he was associated with the novelists Kawabata Yasunari and Yokomitsu Riichi on the journal *Bungaku-kai* ("The Literary Circle"); he became editor in 1935, after the arrest of its previous editor in the growing nationalist tide before World War II. During the war he turned from modern literary criticism and social commentary to studies of Japanese classical art and later to music and philosophy. His major works include studies on Fyodor Dostoyevsky, W.A. Mozart, and Vincent van Gogh and on the Japanese literary genre of the *shishōsetsu*, the autobiographical novel.

Kobayashi Issa \kō-'bä-yä-shē-'ēs-sä\, *also called* Kobayashi Yatarō \yä-'tä-ˌrō\, *original name* Kobayashi Nobuyuki \nō-'bū-yŭ-kē\ (b. June 15, 1763, Kashiwabara, Shinano province, Japan—d. Jan. 5, 1827, Kashiwabara) Japanese poet whose works in simple, unadorned language capture the spiritual loneliness of the common individual.

As a boy Issa was sent by his father to Edo (present-day Tokyo), where he studied haiku under the poet Nirokuan Chikua. He took the pen name Issa (he had many others) in 1793 and traveled extensively through southwestern Japan, afterward publishing a collection of verse, *Tabishūi* (1795; "Travel Gleanings").

In Issa's poetry everyday subjects are treated with ordinary language but take on a lyrical quality through his sharp critical eye and sympathetic tone. His other important works are *Chichi no shūen nikki* (1801; "Diary of My Father's Death") and *Oraga haru* (1819; *The Year of My Life*).

Kobayashi Takiji \kō-'bä-yä-shē-'tä-kē-jē\ (b. Oct. 13, 1903, Shimo Kawazoe, Japan—d. Feb. 20, 1933, Tokyo) Outstanding writer of the proletarian literary movement in pre-World War II Japan.

Kobayashi was deeply impressed by the writings of Shiga Naoya, whose realism, as well as the humanitarianism of the Shirakaba ("White Birch") group with which Shiga was associated, provided a model for his own idealistic concern with social problems. Kobayashi's intimate knowledge of police brutality as a result of an arrest appeared in *Senkyūhyaku nijū hachinen sangatsu jūgo nichi* ("The Fifteenth of March, 1928"), recording the local events of an infamous national police crackdown. The story, along with *Shimen no tameni* ("For the Sake of the Citizen"), *Fuzai-jinushi* ("Absentee Landlord"), and *Kani-kōsen* ("The Cannery Boat"), established him as the best of the new proletarian writers. He went to Tokyo in 1930, where he participated in increasingly radical political activities. Kobayashi went underground in 1932 but continued to publish under pseudonyms. Betrayed by a police spy, he was called in for questioning, and he died in jail the next day as a result of the brutality of the interrogation.

His contribution to literature lies in his attempt to add literary value to political propaganda through the controlled realism with which he expressed his deep anger over social injustice. His work was published in English in 1933 as *The Cannery Boat and Other Japanese Short Stories.*

kobold \'kō-ˌbold, -bōld\ [German] **1.** A gnome held, especially in German folklore, to inhabit underground places. **2.** In German folklore, a mischievous household spirit who usually helps with chores and gives other valuable services but who often hides household and farm tools or kicks over stooping persons. He is temperamental and becomes outraged when he is not properly fed. *See also* POLTERGEIST.

Koch \'käch\, Frederick Henry (b. Sept. 12, 1877, Covington, Ky., U.S.—d. Aug. 16, 1944, Miami Beach, Fla.) Founder of the Carolina Playmakers at the University of North Carolina and considered the father of American folk drama.

Koch attended Ohio Wesleyan University and Harvard University. In 1905 he began teaching at the University of North Dakota, forming the Dakota Playmakers in 1910. Joining the faculty of the University of North Carolina in 1918, he established the Playmakers, whose theater became the first state-subsidized playhouse in the United States. The company toured the Southeast presenting folk plays. Eleven volumes of folk plays appeared under his editorship. Koch also founded and directed a Canadian playwriting school at Banff, Alta., and he is considered a significant force in the American little theater movement.

Koch \'kōk\, Kenneth (b. Feb. 27, 1925, Cincinnati, Ohio, U.S.) American teacher and author noted especially for his witty, often surreal, sometimes epic, poetry. He was also an accomplished playwright.

Koch attended Harvard University and Columbia University, where he subsequently taught for many years. With the publication of *Poems* (1953), his first collection, he became one of the leading poets of the so-called New York school, a loose-knit group that included poets Frank O'Hara and John Ashbery. His work was noted for its rather whimsical humor and unusual juxtapositions.

Koch wrote two Byronic epics in ottava rima: *Ko; or, A Season on Earth* (1959), and *The Duplications* (1977). He also composed the long prose poem *The Burning Mystery of Anna in 1951* (1979), as well as many shorter verses, including those collected in *Selected Poems* (1991). Two dozen of his plays, which are often short, and 10 of his screenplays were collected in *A Change of Hearts: Plays, Films, and Other Dramatic Works 1951–1971* (1973). Koch is also noted for teaching poetry writing and appreciation to children and retirees, as described in his books *Wishes, Lies, and Dreams: Teaching Children to Write Poetry* (1970), *Rose, Where Did You Get That Red? Teaching Great Poetry to Children* (1973), and *I Never Told Anybody: Teaching Poetry Writing in a Nursing Home* (1977). He also wrote the novel *The Red Robins* (1975) and the short stories of *Hotel Lambosa* (1993).

Koch \'kòk, 'kōk\, Martin (b. Dec. 23, 1882, Stockholm, Swed.—d. June 22, 1940, Hedemora) Swedish novelist who was first among the so-called proletarian authors to make a deep impression on his fellow Swedes.

Koch came from a lower-middle-class family, which his father deserted when the children were very young. The young Koch worked as a laborer's helper and studied art. His first publication was the novelette *Ellen* (1911). The most important of his works are the novels *Arbetare, en historia om hat* (1912; "Workers, A Story of Hatred"), *Timmerdalen, en historia om kultur* (1913; "The Timber Valley, A Story of Culture"), and *Guds vackra värld, en historia om rätt och Orätt*, 2 vol. (1916; "God's Beautiful World, A Story of Right and Wrong"). Just before his death a collection of autobiographical tales, *Mauritz* (1939), was published.

Kochanowski \kò-kà-'nòf-skʸē\, Jan (b. 1530, Sycyna, Pol.—d. Aug. 22, 1584, Lublin) Humanist poet who dominated the culture of Renaissance Poland.

Kochanowski studied at the Jagiellonian University in Kraków and later at Padua in Italy. On his return to Poland in 1557, he served as royal secretary in Kraków.

Kochanowski's first poems, mostly elegies, were written in Latin, but he soon turned to the vernacular. Because there was no Polish literary language at the time, he invented his patterns and poetic syntax. His crowning achievement is *Treny* (1580; *Laments*), 19 poems inspired by the death (1579) of his infant daughter. Kochanowski was also the author of the first Polish tragedy, *Odprawa posłów greckich* (1578; *The Dismissal of the Greek Envoys*).

Kochowski \kò-'kòf-skʸē\, Wespazjan (b. 1633, Gaj, Pol.—d. June 6, 1700, Kraków) Polish poet and historian.

During his years in military service (1650–61), Kochowski fought against the Cossacks and the Swedes. He later became court historian for King John III Sobieski. His deep sense of patriotism was best expressed in his epic *Psalmodia polska* (1695; "Polish Psalmody"). The major theme of the 36 psalms is Poland's messianic role in the salvation of the world.

Kock \'kòk\, Charles-Paul de (b. May 21, 1793, Passy, Fr.—d. April 27, 1871, Paris) Prolific French author whose discreetly pornographic novels about Parisian life were, in his day, popular reading throughout Europe.

The son of a refugee Dutch banker who was guillotined during the French Revolution, Kock became a bank clerk in 1808. He published his first book, *L'Enfant de ma femme* (1812; *The Child of My Wife*), at his own expense. Among his most successful subsequent books were *Georgette, ou la nièce de Tabillion* (1820), *Gustave, ou le mauvais sujet* (1821; *Gustavus; or, The Young Rake*), *La Femme, le mari et l'amant* (1829; "The Wife, the Husband, and the Lover"), and *Moeurs parisiennes* (1837; *Scenes of Parisian Life*). His collected works were published between 1835 and 1844.

Kōda Rohan \'kō-ˌdä-rō-'hän\, *pseudonym of* Kōda Shigeyuki \shē-'gä-yù-kē\ (b. Aug. 20, 1867, Edo [now Tokyo], Japan—d. July 30, 1947, Ichikawa, Chiba prefecture) Japanese novelist and essayist whose stories of heroic characters balanced the more romantic tendency of his rival, Ozaki Kōyō, in creating a new literature for early modern Japan.

Rohan's early education was strong in the Japanese and Chinese classics. "Fūryū Butsu" (1889; "The Elegant Buddha"), a poetic tale of mystic ideal love, brought him fame. *Gojū no tō* (1891–92; *The Pagoda*) deals with the single-minded devotion that enables a simple artisan to accomplish an extraordinary feat. Rohan's aesthetic world emphasized strong will and the powers of imagination. The more realistic *Sora utsu nami* (1903–05; "Waves Dashing Against the Sky") was left uncompleted. Rohan's last major work, an annotation of the works of the haiku master Matsuo Bashō, was completed the year of his death.

Koestler \'kest-lər\, Arthur (b. Sept. 5, 1905, Budapest, Austria-Hungary—death reported on March 3, 1983, London, Eng.) Hungarian-born British novelist, journalist, and critic, best known for his novel DARKNESS AT NOON (1940).

Serving as a war correspondent for the British newspaper *News Chronicle* during the Spanish Civil War (1936–39), Koestler was imprisoned by the fascists, an experience he recounted in *Spanish Testament* (1937). This experience and those leading to his break with the Communist Party are reflected in *Darkness at Noon*. Other works of this period, such as *The Gladiators* (1939) and *Arrival and Departure* (1943), deal with similar questions of morality and political responsibility.

Memorable essays are included in *The Yogi and the Commissar and Other Essays* (1945), and in the collection *The God That Failed* (1949), edited by R. Crossman, Koestler wrote of his disillusionment with communism.

Koestler took stock of his early life in the memoirs *Arrow in the Blue* (1952) and *The Invisible Writing* (1954). *The Act of Creation* (1964) is perhaps the best-known book of his scientific and philosophical period. Other works include *The Lotus and the Robot* (1960), *The Ghost in the Machine* (1967), and *The Thirteenth Tribe* (1976). *Bricks to Babel*, a collection of his writings, was published in 1981.

Kojiki \'kō-jē-kē\ ("Records of Ancient Matters")   Together with the NIHON SHOKI, the first written record in Japan, part of which is considered a sacred text of the Shintō religion. The *Kojiki* text was compiled from oral tradition in 712.

The *Kojiki* is an important sourcebook for ceremonies and customs, divination, and magical practices of ancient Japan. It includes myths, legends, and historical accounts of the Imperial court from the earliest days of its creation up to the reign of Empress Suiko (628). Much of Shintō thought is based on interpretations of the mythology contained in the *Kojiki*. It was written using Chinese characters to represent Japanese sounds, inasmuch as no native means of recording Japan's spoken language had yet been devised.

Kokinshū \kō-'kēn-,shū\ ("Collection from Ancient and Modern Times")   The first anthology of Japanese poetry compiled upon Imperial order, by poet KI Tsurayuki and others in 905. It was the first major literary work written in the kana writing system. The *Kokinshū* comprises 1,111 poems, many of them anonymous, divided into 20 books arranged by topics. These include six books of seasonal poems, five books of love poems, and single books devoted to such subjects as travel, mourning, and congratulations.

The best verses in the *Kokinshū* are flawlessly turned miniatures that captivate the reader by their perceptivity and tonal beauty. Subsequent critics enforced the use of the standard poetic diction of some 2,000 words established by the *Kokinshū* and insisted on absolute adherence to the poetic conventions it embodied. As a result, only a skilled critic can distinguish a poem of the 10th century from one of the 18th century.

Kölcsey \'kœl-chä\, Ferenc (b. Aug. 8, 1790, Sződemeter, Hungary, Holy Roman Empire—d. Aug. 24, 1838, Cseke)   Hungarian poet, critic, orator, and able parliamentarian, whose poem "Hymnus" became the national anthem of Hungary.

Kölcsey's critical essays laid the foundation of systematic literary criticism and aesthetics in Hungary. As a member of the Diet (legislature) between 1832 and 1834, he supported liberal causes. His poetry displayed moral strength and devotion to Hungary. The first collected edition of his works appeared in 1886–87.

Kollár \'kôl-lär\, Ján (b. July 29, 1793, Mošovce, Slovakia, Holy Roman Empire—d. Jan. 24, 1852, Vienna [Austria])   Slovak poet who played an important part in the national and literary revival of the Slavs in the early 19th century.

Educated at the University of Jena, Kollár was pastor (1819–49) to the Slovak community in Pest; the last three years of his life were spent in Vienna as professor of Slavonic archaeology. He devoted much of his life to the encouragement of cultural unity among the Slavonic peoples, as in the lyric-epic poem *Slávy dcera* ("The Daughter of Sláva").

Kolodny \kə-'läd-nē\, Annette (b. Aug. 21, 1941, New York, N.Y., U.S.)   American literary critic, one of the first to use feminist criticism to interpret American literary works and cultural history.

Kolodny was educated at Brooklyn College of the City University of New York and the University of California at Berkeley. Her seminal essay "Some Notes on Defining a 'Feminist' Literary Criticism" was published in *Critical Inquiry* in 1975. Kolodny used her politicized feminist perspective to write of her outrage for the ravaged American environment in *The Lay of the Land: Metaphor as Experience and History in American Life and Letters* (1975) and *The Land Before Her: Fantasy and Experience of the American Frontiers, 1630–1860* (1984). "Dancing Through the Minefield: Some Observations on the Theory, Method, and Politics in Feminist Literary Criticism" (1983) combines feminist social history with Kolodny's personal history—she had won a judgment against the University of New Hampshire, which she accused of anti-Semitism and sex discrimination in denying her promotion and tenure.

Koltsov \,kəlʸ-'tsôf\, Aleksey Vasilyevich (b. Oct. 3 [Oct. 15, New Style], 1809, Voronezh, Russian Empire—d. Oct. 29 [Nov. 10], 1842, Voronezh)   Poet whose works describe the sorrows and hardships of the Russian peasant life.

The son of a cattle dealer who treated him harshly, Koltsov began to publish in Moscow periodicals in 1831 and attracted the attention of the noted literary critic Vissarion Belinsky. With Belinsky's help a volume of Koltsov's poems was published in 1835. Koltsov is noted for his success in introducing into Russian verse the authentic language of the Russian peasant.

kommos or **commos** \'käm-əs, 'kôm-\ [Greek *kommós*, literally, beating of the head and breast in grief, a derivative of *kóptein* to beat]   In Greek tragedy, a lament sung in parts alternating between chief actor and chorus.

Komparu Zempō \'kōm-,pä-rù-'zem-,pō\, *also called* Hachiro Motoyasu \hä-'chē-rō-,mō-'tō-yä-sù\ (b. 1454, Japan—d. *c.* 1520, Japan)   Nō dramatist and actor, grandson of Nō actor and dramatist Komparu Zenchiku.

Zempō was one of the last dramatists of Nō's classic period. He wrote one play, *Hatsuyuki* ("First Snow"), in the restrained and poetic manner of his grandfather. Most of his work, however, such as *Arashiyama*, was written to appeal to a wide popular audience through the use of novelty and action-filled plots. Zempō was head teacher of the Komparu school, which under his father had favored a conservative style of performance called *shimogakari* and had waned in popularity. Under Zempō it revived and once again presented performances at the court in Kyōto.

Komparu Zenchiku \'kōm-,pä-rù-'zen-,chē-kú\, *original name* Shichirō Ujinobu \shē-'chē-,rō-ù-'jē-,nō-bù\ (b. 1405, Japan—d. *c.* 1470, Nara, Japan)   Nō actor and playwright who also wrote critical works on drama. Zenchiku, who married a daughter of the actor Zeami (Kanze Motokiyo), was trained in drama by Zeami and Zeami's son Motomasa.

Zenchiku was a talented actor who passed on the teachings of Zeami to the Komparu family school of Nō drama. He wrote more than 20 plays, including the masterpieces *Basho*, *Tamakazura*, *Go'on sankyoku shū*, and *Ugetsu*, all of which were influenced by Zen Buddhist thought. His major critical works—*Shidō yōshō*, *Rokurin ichiro no ki*, and *Shūgyoku tokka*—are important historical sources on the development of Nō drama.

König Rother \'kœ̄-nik-'rō-tər\ ("King Rother")   Medieval German romance from about 1160 that is the earliest record of the type of popular entertainment literature circulated by wandering minstrels. It combines elements from German heroic literature (without the grimness of the older tales) with Orientalisms derived from the Crusades. The story recounts the efforts of King Rother to win the hand of the Byzantine emperor's daughter.

Konopnicka \kò-nòp-'nʸēt-skȧ\, Maria, *original name* Marja Wasiłowska \vȧ-sʸē-'lòf-skȧ\, *pseudonym* Jan Sawa \'sȧ-vȧ\ (b. May 12, 1842, Suwałki, Poland, Russian Empire—d. Oct. 8, 1910, Lwów, Austria-Hungary [now Lviv, Ukraine]) Polish poet and short-story writer.

In exile from Russian-dominated Poland for much of her life, Konopnicka developed strong patriotic convictions. Her sympathy with the oppressed peasantry, however, often led her into sentimentality. *Pan Balcer w Brazylji* (1892–1909; "Mr. Balcer in Brazil"), one of her most ambitious works, is a near-epic description of the disillusionment of a Polish peasant emigrant with the New World. The poem cycle *Italia* (1901; "Italy") contains some of her most beautiful verses. Her short stories are considered among the best in Polish literature. "Niemczaki" ("The German Children") and "Nasza szkapa" ("Our Old Mare") are among the best known.

Konrad von Würzburg \'kòn-rät-fòn-'vuerts-,bürk\ (b. *c.* 1225, Würzburg [Germany]—d. Aug. 31, 1287, Basel, Switz.) Middle High German poet who, during the decline of chivalry, sought to preserve the ideals of courtly life.

Konrad served a succession of patrons as a professional poet and settled in Basel. His works range from love lyrics and short didactic poems (*Sprüche*) to full-scale epics, such as *Partonopier und Meliur*, on the fairy-lover theme, and *Der Trojanerkrieg* (*The Trojan War*), a tedious account of the Trojan War. He is at his best in his shorter narrative poems, the secular romances *Englehart, Dasz Herzmaere* (*The Heart's Tidings*), and *Keiser Otte mit dem Barte* (*Kaiser Otte with the Beard*) and the religious legends *Silvester, Alexius,* and *Pantaleon.*

Konwicki \kòn-'vʸēt-skʸē\, Tadeusz (b. June 22, 1926, Nowa Wilejka, Pol. [now Naujoji Vilnia, Lith.]) Polish writer, screenwriter, and film director known for his bitter novels about the devastations of war and ideology.

A teenager during World War II, Konwicki joined the Polish resistance movement, fighting first the occupying Nazi army and then the Soviets. When his native province was awarded to Lithuania after the war, he and many other ethnic Poles were "repatriated" to Poland.

Konwicki followed the official Communist Party line. His first work, *Przy budowie* (1950; "At the Construction Site"), won the State Prize for Literature. He began a career as a filmmaker and scriptwriter in 1956; his film *Ostatni dzień lata* ("The Last Day of Summer") won the Venice Film Festival Grand Prix in 1958. By the late 1960s he had quit the Communist Party and had become active in the opposition movement.

Konwicki's work is suffused with guilt and anxiety, colored by his wartime experiences and a sense of helplessness in confronting a corrupt and repressive society. Chief among his novels are *Rojsty* (1956; "The Marshes") and *Sennik współczesny* (1963; *A Dreambook for Our Time*), a book that writer and critic Czesław Miłosz called "one of the most terrifying novels of postwar Polish literature." His other works of this period are *Wniebowstąpienie* (1967; "Ascension") and *Zwierzoczłekoupiór* (1969; *The Anthropos-Spectre-Beast*). His later books—including *Kompleks polski* (1977; *The Polish Complex*), the bitterly mocking *Mała apokalipsa* (1979; *A Minor Apocalypse*), and the lyrical *Bohiń* (1987; *Bohin Manor*)—confronted Poland's social cataclysms of the late 1970s and the 1980s. The autobiographical *Wschody i zachody księżyca* (1981; *Moonrise, Moonset*) recounts some of Konwicki's experiences during the period of martial law in Poland.

Kopisch \'kō-pish\, August (b. May 26, 1799, Breslau, Silesia, Prussia [now Wrocław, Pol.]—d. Feb. 3, 1853, Berlin [Germany]) German painter and poet known for his *Gedichte* (1836; "Poems") and *Allerlei Geister* (1848; "All Kinds of Spirits"), poetry based on legends and fairy tales and written with a simplicity and appeal that made it widely popular.

Kopisch studied painting and archaeology in Italy from 1823 to 1828 and in 1826 rediscovered with Ernst Fries the Blue Grotto at Capri, which, though known in Roman times, had been forgotten for centuries. An injury to his hand ended his career as a painter, and in 1847 he was given a court position at Potsdam, where he wrote a history of the royal gardens (published posthumously in 1854).

Kopit \'kō-pit\, Arthur (Lee) (b. May 10, 1937, New York, N.Y., U.S.) American playwright best known for *Oh Dad, Poor Dad, Mama's Hung You in the Closet and I'm Feelin' So Sad* (1960). Subtitled "a pseudoclassical tragifarce in a bastard French tradition," the play parodies the Theater of the Absurd and the conventions of avant-garde drama.

Kopit attended Harvard University, where seven of his plays were produced while he was still a student. He later served as playwright-in-residence at Wesleyan University and adjunct professor of playwrighting at Yale University and at City College, New York.

Praised for his ease with language, impressive theatricality, and his skewering of American popular culture, Kopit wrote plays on a range of subjects. Among the works contained in *The Day the Whores Came Out to Play Tennis and Other Plays* (1965) are the one-act title play, *Chamber Music*, and *Sing to Me Through Open Windows*. Kopit's other plays include *Indians* (1969), *Wings* (1978), the parodic *The End of the World* (1984), and *The Road to Nirvana* (1991), a racy satire of Hollywood.

Köprülü \koe-,prūe-'lūe\, Fuad, *in full* Mehmed Fuad Köprülü, *also called* Köprülüzade \koe-,prūe-,lūe-zä-'de\ (b. Dec. 4, 1890, Constantinople, Ottoman Empire [now Istanbul, Tur.]— d. June 28, 1966, Istanbul) Scholar, historian, and statesman who made important contributions to the history of Turkey and its literature.

A descendant of a famous family of 17th-century Ottoman prime ministers (grand viziers), Köprülü began teaching at the Galatasaray Lycée (secondary school) in Constantinople and in 1913 occupied the chair of Turkish literature at Istanbul University. Later he became dean of the Faculty of Letters there and the founder and first director of the Türkiyat Enstitüsü (Institute of Turkology).

Turning to politics in 1936, he became a member of parliament and finally foreign minister (1950–54). His many books on Turkish literature and history include *Türk edebiyatında ilk mutasavvıflar* (1919; "The First Mystics in Turkish Literature") and *Les Origines de l'empire Ottoman* (1935; "The Origins of the Ottoman Empire").

Kops \'käps\, Bernard (b. Nov. 28, 1926, London, Eng.) English playwright and novelist known for his works of unabashed sentimentality.

Kops established himself with his first play, *The Hamlet of Stepney Green* (1959), a reversal of the family relationships depicted in William Shakespeare's *Hamlet*, ending happily in an affirmation of the human spirit. Among his other plays are *The Dream of Peter Mann* (1960) and *Enter Solly Gold* (1961). His novels include *Awake for Mourning* (1958) and *The Dissent of Dominick Shapiro* (1966). He also wrote an autobiography, *The World Is a Wedding* (1963), radio plays, and other fiction, as well as a surrealistic play *Ezra* (produced 1981).

Koraïs \kò-'rä-ēs\, Adamántios (b. April 27, 1748, Smyrna, Anatolia [now İzmir, Tur.]—d. April 6, 1833, Paris, Fr.) Humanist scholar and father of Modern Greek literature, whose advocacy of a revived classicism laid the intellectual foundations for the Greek struggle for independence. His influence on modern Greek language and culture has been compared to that of Dante on Italian and Martin Luther on German.

The son of a merchant, Koraïs studied medicine at the University of Montpellier, Fr., and in 1788 moved to Paris to pursue a literary career. His main literary works are a 17-volume *Library of Greek Literature*, collected between 1805 and 1826, and the nine-volume *Parerga*, collected between 1809 and 1827. He also translated the historian Herodotus into Modern Greek.

Convinced that modern Greeks could find strength and unity only through a revival of their classical heritage, Koraïs made his writings an instrument for awakening his compatriots to the significance of that heritage for their national aspirations. He created a new Greek literary language: purifying the vernacular (Demotic) of foreign elements, he combined its best elements with Classical Greek. His *Atakta*, composed between 1828 and 1835, was the first Modern Greek dictionary.

Koran　*see* QUR'ĀN.

Kornbluth \'kòrn-,blùth\, C.M., *original name* Cyril Kornbluth (b. 1923, New York, N.Y., U.S.—d. March 21, 1958, Waverly, N.Y.)　American writer whose science-fiction stories reflect a dark, acerbic view of the future.

Kornbluth published science-fiction stories as a teenager. Called the Futurians, he and other young writers, including Isaac Asimov and Frederik Pohl (his frequent coauthor), composed and edited most of the tales in such sci-fi magazines as *Astonishing Stories* and *Super Science Stories*. Kornbluth wrote under almost 20 pseudonyms. After army service during World War II, he attended the University of Chicago.

His well-plotted fiction was acclaimed for its vision and social concerns. Critical of stories in which science was presented as the ultimate savior of humanity, Kornbluth instead examined the dangers of sophisticated technologies allowed to run amok. His essay "The Failure of the Science Fiction Novel as Social Criticism" was published posthumously in 1959. Much of his work was serialized in *Galaxy Science Fiction*. In collaboration with Judith Merril he wrote such works as *Outpost Mars* (1952; revised as *Sin in Space*, 1961) and *Gunner Cade* (1952). Among the books he published with Pohl were *Search the Sky* (1954) and *Gladiator-at-Law* (1955). Kornbluth also wrote *Takeoff* (1952), a science-fiction detective novel about the first space flight, and *The Syndic* (1953), about organized crime in a futuristic United States.

Körner \'kœr-nər\, Theodor, *in full* Karl Theodor Körner (b. Sept. 23, 1791, Dresden, Saxony [Germany]—d. Aug. 26, 1813, Gadebusch, Mecklenburg)　German patriotic poet of the war of liberation against Napoleon in 1813 whose early death in that war made him a popular hero.

By 1812 the Vienna Burgtheater had produced three of Körner's dramatic works, the most ambitious of which, *Zriny* (1812), with its glorification of love for the homeland, made him famous throughout Germany. His dramas, however, are now largely forgotten. After his death at the age of 22, his father collected the best of his militantly passionate patriotic poetry in *Leyer und Schwert* (1814; "Lyre and Sword"), which was received enthusiastically.

Korolenko \kə-,rə-'lʸen-kə\, Vladimir Galaktionovich (b. July 15 [July 27, New Style], 1853, Zhitomir [now Zhytomyr], Ukraine, Russian Empire—d. Dec. 25, 1921, Poltava, Ukraine)　Russian short-story writer and journalist whose works are memorable in showing compassion for the downtrodden.

In 1879 Korolenko was exiled to the Yakut region of Siberia, where he encountered the tramps, thieves, pilgrims, and social outcasts that were to figure prominently in his stories. Released

after five years, he published his best-known story, *Son Makara* (1885; *Makar's Dream*). During his editorship (about 1904 to 1918, with interruptions) of the influential review *Russkoe Bogatstvo* ("Russian Wealth"), Korolenko championed minorities and befriended younger writers, including Maksim Gorky. Unwilling to cooperate with the Bolshevik government, he retired after the October Revolution in 1917 to the Ukraine.

korrigan \'kòr-i-gän\ [Breton, feminine of *korrig* gnome, diminutive of *korr* dwarf]　A long-haired nocturnal, often malevolent Breton fairy sorceress.

Kosinski \kō-'sin-skē\, Jerzy (Nikodem) (b. June 14, 1933, Łódź, Pol.—d. May 3, 1991, New York, N.Y., U.S.)　Polish-born American writer whose novels were sociological studies of individuals in controlling and bureaucratic societies.

At the age of six, upon the outbreak of World War II, Kosinski was separated from his parents and wandered through Poland and Russia, living by his wits and under continual suspicion. He became mute and did not regain his speech until 1947. He studied at the University of Łódź, receiving degrees in history and political science, and from 1955 to 1957 he was professor of sociology at the Polish Academy of Sciences. In 1957 he immigrated to the United States (settling in New York), taught himself English, and published two nonfiction works, *The Future Is Ours, Comrade: Conversations with the Russians* (1960) and *No Third Path* (1962), both under the pen name Joseph Novak.

Kosinski then published the novel THE PAINTED BIRD (1965), followed by *Steps* (1968), which won the National Book Award, and *Being There* (1970; film, 1979). Later novels include *The Devil Tree* (1973; revised 1981), *Cockpit* (1975), *Passion Play* (1979), *Pinball* (1981), and *The Hermit of 69th Street* (1988).

Kostelanetz \,kòs-tə-'lä-nəts\, Richard (Cory) (b. May 14, 1940, New York, N.Y., U.S.)　Avant-garde writer, artist, critic, and editor who was productive in many fields.

Kostelanetz attended Brown University, Columbia University, and King's College, London. He served as visiting professor or guest artist at a variety of institutions and lectured widely.

In 1971, employing a radically formalist approach, Kostelanetz produced the novel *In the Beginning*, which consists of the alphabet, in single- and double-letter combinations, unfolding over 30 pages. Most of his other literary work also challenges the reader in unconventional ways.

Among his other works are *Recyclings: A Literary Autobiography* (1974, 1984), *Politics in the African-American Novel* (1991), *Published Encomia, 1967–91* (1991), and *On Innovative Art(ist)s* (1992). He also made films and issued many audio recordings.

Kosztolányi \'kō-stō-,län-yē\, Dezső (b. March 29, 1885, Szabadka, Hung., Austria-Hungary—d. Nov. 3, 1936, Budapest, Hung.)　Poet, novelist, and critic, considered to be the outstanding impressionist in Hungarian literature.

Kosztolányi published his first volume of poetry in 1907 and joined the circle of the literary magazine *Nyugat* ("The West"; founded 1908). He won immediate recognition in 1910 with the publication of a cycle of poems, *A szegény kisgyermek panaszai* ("The Complaints of a Poor Little Child").

Kosztolányi's work reveals him to be a sympathetic observer of human frailty with a gentle humor and a penchant for the macabre. He wrote lucid and simple poetry as well as accomplished short stories and novels. *Édes Anna* (1926; *Wonder Maid*) is perhaps his best novel. He translated poetry from several European languages and also from Chinese and Japanese.

Kötlum, Jóhannes úr.　Pseudonym of Jóhannes Bjarni JÓNASSON.

Kotlyarevsky or **Kotliarevsky** *Ukrainian* kŏt-l^yȧ-'reŭ-skĕ, *Russian* kət-l^yi-'r^yef-sk^yĕ\\, Ivan (Petrovich) (b. Aug 29 [Sept. 9, New Style], 1769, Poltava, Ukraine, Russian Empire—d. Oct. 29 [Nov. 10], 1838, Poltava)   Author whose burlesque travesty of Virgil's *Aeneid* was the first extended literary composition written in the Ukrainian language; it distinguished him as the father of modern Ukrainian literature. The *Eneida* (1798) transmutes the gods into Ukrainian landowners and Aeneas and the Trojans into dispossessed Cossacks of the period after the suppression of the Zaporozhian Sich (Cossack territory) in 1775. Kotlyarevsky held a position in Poltava's bureaucracy and also wrote several plays that still form a part of the classic Ukrainian repertoire.

Kotsyubinsky or **Kotsiubinsky** *Ukrainian* kȯ-ts^yü-'bȧn-skĕ, *Russian* kə-tsyü-'b^yēn-sk^yĕ\\, Mikhaylo (Mikhaylovich) (b. Sept. 5 [Sept. 17, New Style], 1864, Vinnitsa [now Vinnytsya], Ukraine, Russian Empire—d. April 12 [April 25], 1913, Chernigov [now Chernihiv], Ukraine)   Novelist and short-story writer whose work was one of the highest achievements of Ukrainian modernism.

Kotsyubinsky graduated from Shargorod Seminary in 1880. He did not begin to publish his writing until 10 years later, working in the interim as a teacher and statistician. Kotsyubinsky's philosophical and stylistic evolution from populist realism to impressionism was the result of western European influences and reflected his concern that Ukrainian writing be integrated into the European literary mainstream. His greatest novel, *Fata Morgana* (1904–10), represented a new approach to the traditional theme of social conflict in a small village. Subsequent works used the abortive 1905 revolution as the background for psychological investigations of people at the extremity of emotional experience.

Kotzebue \\'kȯt-sə-,bü\\, August (Friedrich Ferdinand) von (b. May 3, 1761, Weimar, Saxony [Germany]—d. March 23, 1819, Mannheim, Baden)   German playwright widely influential in popularizing poetic drama, which he infused with melodramatic sensationalism and sentimental philosophizing.

Kotzebue's first comedy gave him entrée into court literary circles in Weimar, but in 1781 he was forced to go into exile for a reason that is not clear. In 1783 he entered government service in Russia. Some of his greatest successes—*Adelheid von Wulfingen* (1789), *Menschenhass und Reue* (1789; *The Stranger*), *Die Indianer in England* (1790; *The Indian Exiles*)—were written while he lived in Russia. *Die Spanier in Peru* (1796) also proved a great success.

In 1801 he returned to Weimar, but he was not on good terms with J.W. von Goethe or with the Romantics; he went back to Russia in 1806. In 1817, while abroad, Kotzbebue was denounced by political radicals as a spy and was assassinated.

His more than 200 plays include such comedies as *Der Wildfang* (1798; "The Trapping of Game") and *Die deutschen Kleinstädter* (1803; "The German Small-towner"), which contain admirable pictures of provincial German life.

Kourouma \\kü-rü-'mä\\, Ahmadou (b. 1938, Boundiali, Côte d'Ivoire)   West African novelist and playwright who was a prominent postindependence "disillusionist" writer.

Kourouma's novel *Les Soleils des indépendances* (1968; *The Suns of Independence*) satirizes contemporary African politics. Narrated in a French flavored with pungent folk aphorisms of the Malinke (a West African people), the story follows the last of a line of tribal princes as he is mistreated by French colonial as well as postindependence African authorities. Kourouma's play *Tougnantigui ou le diseur de vérité* ("Tougnantigui, or The Speaker of Truth") was first performed in 1972. A later novel was *Monnè, outrages et défis* (1990; *Monnew*).

Kowalski, Stanley \\'stan-lē-kə-'wäl-skē\\   Fictional character, the primitive but powerful husband of Stella and brother-in-law of Blanche DuBois in the play A STREETCAR NAMED DESIRE by Tennessee Williams.

kraken \\'krä-kən\\ [Norwegian]   A fabulous Scandinavian sea monster perhaps imagined on the basis of chance sightings of giant squids. It appears in literature in a poem of Alfred Tennyson's juvenilia called "The Kraken."

Král' \\'krȧl^y\\, Janko (b. April 24, 1822, Liptovský Mikuláš, Slovakia, Austrian Empire [now in Slovak Republic]—d. May 23, 1876, Zlaté Moravce)   Slovak poet, jurist, and revolutionary whose ballads, epics, and lyrics are among the most original products of Slavic Romanticism. His work also contributed to the popularization of the new Slovak literary language. Král's participation in a Slovak uprising during the 1848 revolution, for which he narrowly escaped execution by the Hungarians, made him a legendary figure in the memory of his countrymen. Among his verse collections are *Pieseň bez mena* (1844; "Song Without a Name"), *Zverbovaný* (1844; "Recruit"), *Orol* (1845; "The Eagle"), and *Zajasal blesk jasnej zory* (1861; "The Gleam of a Clear Dawn Approached").

Kramer \\'krä-mər\\, Dame Leonie Judith, *original surname* Gibson \\'gib-sən\\ (b. Oct. 1, 1924, Melbourne, Vic., Australia)   Australian literary scholar and educator.

Kramer studied at the University of Melbourne and at the University of Oxford and thereafter taught Australian literature at various universities, serving as professor at the University of Sydney from 1968. She wrote several authoritative works on the Australian novelist Henry Handel Richardson and was the editor of *The Oxford History of Australian Literature* (1981).

Krapp's Last Tape \\'krap\\   One-act monodrama by Samuel BECKETT, written in English, produced in 1958, and published in 1959. Krapp sits at a cluttered desk and listens to tape recordings he made decades earlier when he was in the prime of life, leaving only occasionally to imbibe liquor offstage. To Krapp, the voice in the recorded diary is that of a naive and foolish stranger. Although he comments savagely on the young Krapp's hope and idealism, he is drawn to the recorded voice of his younger, more hopeful self.

Krasicki \\krȧ-'shyēts-k^yē\\, Ignacy (b. Feb. 3, 1735, Dubiecko, Polish Galicia [now in Poland]—d. March 14, 1801, Berlin [Germany])   Greatest Polish poet of the 18th century.

Born to an aristocratic but impoverished family, Krasicki was educated at a seminary in Warsaw and became bishop of Warmia (Ermeland) at age 32. He served as chaplain to King Stanisław II Poniatowski and in 1795 was named archbishop of Gniezno.

Krasicki was scholarly, skeptical, and critical but fundamentally optimistic and never cynical. His fables are among his best work. His satires (first collection published in 1779) concentrate on vices such as drunkenness and greediness, as in *Pijaństwo* ("Drunkenness"), in which Krasicki portrays the gradual process of alcohol addiction. His mock-heroic poems include *Monachomachia* (1778; "War of Monks"), a satirical attack on ignorant and dissolute monks.

Krasicki also introduced the modern novel to Poland with *Mikołaja Doświadczyńskiego przypadki* (1776; "The Adventures of Nicholas Try-all"), which reflects the influence of Daniel Defoe, Jonathan Swift, and Jean-Jacques Rousseau.

Krasiński \\krȧ-'shyēⁿ-sk^yē\\, Zygmunt, Count, *in full* Napoleon Stanisław Adam Ludwik Zygmunt Krasiński (b. Feb. 19, 1812, Paris, Fr.—d. Feb. 23, 1859, Paris)   Poet and dramatist, with Adam Mickiewicz and Juliusz Słowacki a member of Poland's triad of Romantic messianic poets.

Krasiński lived most of his life abroad and published his work anonymously. The conflict of loyalty arising from his aristocratic father's support of Russian imperialism and his own desire for Poland's independence is central to the poet's thought.

Krasiński's reputation rests primarily on two tragic dramas, *Nieboska komedia* (1835; *The Undivine Comedy*) and *Irydion* (1836; *Iridion*).

Krasiński's best-known poem, *Przedświt* (1843; "The Moment Before Dawn"), pictures Poland's partition as a sacrifice for the sins of the entire world but optimistically predicts Poland's resurrection and emergence as a world leader.

Kraszewski \krȧ-'shef-skʸē\, Józef Ignacy, *pseudonym* Bogdan Bolesławita (b. July 28, 1812, Warsaw, Duchy of Warsaw [now in Poland]—d. March 19, 1887, Geneva, Switz.)   Polish novelist, poet, literary critic, dramatist, historian, and journalist who was the dominant figure during Poland's Romantic period.

Kraszewski attended the University of Vilna, was imprisoned in 1830 on a charge of conspiracy against the Russian government, and was released in 1832. He lived in Volhynia (now in Ukraine) from 1834 to 1859, dividing his time between writing, farming, and social work. From 1841 he edited, and from 1849 to 1851 edited and published, the *Athenaeum* review. In 1859 he moved to Warsaw, and between 1859 and 1862 he edited the daily *Gazeta Codzienna* (later *Gazeta Polska*). Kraszewski was forced to leave Warsaw in January 1863 because he had offended the head of the government in an editorial. He settled in Dresden, Germany. In 1883 the German government arrested him on a charge of espionage on behalf of France, and in 1884 he was imprisoned. Released in 1885, he went to Geneva, where he died.

Kraszewski's works fill more than 600 volumes. His uneven but enduring works influenced other writers to support Polish nationalism. His writings include nine novels dealing with the issue of serfdom, seven historical novels set against the background of Poland under the Saxon kings, and a cycle of 29 novels covering Polish history.

Kraus \'kraủs\, Karl (b. April 28, 1874, Gitschin, Bohemia, Austria Empire [now Jičín, Czech Republic]—d. June 12, 1936, Vienna, Austria)   Austrian journalist, critic, playwright, and poet who has been compared with Juvenal and Jonathan Swift for his satiric vision and command of language. Because his work is almost untranslatably idiomatic, his talents have not been widely recognized.

In 1899 Kraus founded the literary and political review *Die Fackel*, of which he was sole author from 1911 and which ceased publication in 1936 with the rise of Nazism in Austria. Kraus believed that language was of great moral as well as aesthetic importance. He himself wrote with masterly precision, notably in such collections of aphorisms as *Sprüche und Widersprüche* (1909; "Proverbs and Contradictions") and *Nachts* (1919; "Nights") and in such essay collections as *Sittlichkeit und Kriminalität* (1908; "Morality and Criminality"), *Literatur und Lüge* (1929; "Literature and Lie"), and *Die Sprache* (1937; "Language"). His writing occasionally rose to apocalyptic heights, as in the lengthy satirical drama *Die letzten Tage der Menschheit* (1922; "The Last Days of Humanity"). Kraus also wrote poetry (the nine-volume *Worte in Versen*, 1916–30), epigrams (1927), and dramatic parodies.

Kréa \'krä-ə\, Henri (b. Nov. 6, 1933, Algiers [Algeria])   Algerian-born poet, dramatist, and novelist.

Like the hero of his first and only novel, *Djamal* (1961), Kréa was the product of a marriage between a French father and an Algerian mother. In 1956 he became a journalist and settled permanently in Paris.

Kréa published more than 20 collections of poetry, including *Liberté première* (1957; "First Freedom"), *La Révolution et la poésie sont une seule et même chose* (1957; "Revolution and Poetry Are One and the Same"), and *La Conjuration des égaux* (1964; "The Plot of the Peers"). His plays include *Le Séisme* (1958; "Earthquake") and *Théâtre algérien* (1962). *Tombeau de Jugurtha* (1968; "Fall of Jugurtha") is a historical biography. Kréa's work deals with alienation and identity, nature, heroism, and moral and social change in Algeria.

Kretzer \'kret-sər\, Max (b. June 7, 1854, Posen, Prussia [now Poznań, Poland]—d. July 15, 1941, Berlin, Ger.)   German Expressionist writer who excelled in describing working conditions of the Berlin industrial proletariat in the 1880s and '90s.

Kretzer went to work in a factory at the age of 13, educated himself, and began to write when he was 25. *Der Fassadenraphael* (1911; "The Raphael of the Façades") describes his experience as a sign painter and *Der alte Andreas* (1911; "Old Andrew") records his work in a lamp factory. In other novels he treats pressing social problems of the day: prostitution in *Die Betrogenen* (1882; "The Deceived"); the fate of the urban workers in *Die Verkommenen* (1883; "The Depraved"). *Meister Timpe* (1888; "Master Timpe") is considered his best novel.

Kreutzwald \'kräts-ˌväld\, F. Reinhold, *in full* Friedrich Reinhold Kreutzwald (b. Dec. 26, 1803, Kadrina, Russian Estonia [now in Estonia]—d. Aug. 25, 1882, Derpt [now Tartu]) Physician, folklorist, and poet who compiled the Estonian national epic poem KALEVIPOEG (1857–61, "The Son of Kalevi").

A graduate of the university at Derpt, Kreutzwald was municipal health officer in Voru for more than 40 years. In 1838, F.R. Faehlmann organized the Estonian Learned Society, which collected narrative folk songs for an epic in the tradition of Finland's *Kalevala*. Kreutzwald, a student and translator of German Romantic literature, wrote the epic, combining the collected material with original poetry.

Krėvė-Mickevičius \'kre-vʸe-mits-'kä-ve-chủs\, Vincas, *also called* Vincas Krėvė (b. Oct. 19, 1882, Subartonys, Russian Lithuania—d. July 7, 1954, Broomall, Pa., U.S.)   Lithuanian poet, philologist, novelist, and playwright whose mastery of style gave him a foremost place in Lithuanian literature.

After serving as Lithuanian consul in Azerbaijan, Krėvė became professor of Slavic languages and literature in Kaunas (1922–39) and later in Vilnius. He went into exile in 1944, shortened his name to Vincas Krėvė, and from 1947 was professor at the University of Pennsylvania.

Krėvė became internationally known by his collection of Lithuanian folk songs (*dainos*). *Šarūnas, Dainavos kunigaikštis* (1911; "Sharunas, Prince of Dainava"), *Skirgaila* (1925; "Prince Skirgaila"), *Likimo keliais* (1926–29; "Along the Paths of Destiny"), and *Karaliaus Mindaugo mirtis* (1935; "The Death of King Mindaugas") present a romantic view of the past. His realism is evident in his village drama *Žentas* (1921; "The Son-in-Law") and in his short-story collections *Sutemose* (1921; "Twilight") and *Šiaudinėj pastogėj* (1921; "Under a Thatched Roof"). He adapted Lithuanian legends in *Dainavos šalies senų žmonių padavimai* (1912; "Legends of the Old People of Dainava") and themes from Oriental legends in *Rytų pasakos* (1930; "Tales of the Orient"). *Dangaus ir žemės sūnūs* (1949; "The Sons of Heaven and Earth") shows great power of expression in portraying Hebrew life in Herod's time.

Krieger \'krē-gər\, Murray (b. Nov. 27, 1923, Newark, N.J., U.S.)   American literary critic known for his studies of the special nature of the language of imaginative literature.

Krieger attended Rutgers University, the University of Chicago, and Ohio State University. He taught at the universities of Minnesota and Illinois before his appointment to the first American chaired professorship in literary criticism, at the University of Iowa. He also taught in the University of California system, and in 1967 he founded the influential School of Criticism and Theory while he was at the university's Irvine campus.

Krieger believed that poetic language has a unique capacity to reveal vision and meaning, a capacity beyond the scope of everyday language. He set forth his philosophy of literature in *The New Apologists for Poetry* (1956), *The Tragic Vision* (1960), and *The Classic Vision* (1971), which were later published together as *Visions of Extremity in Modern Literature* (1973). Krieger was among the earliest literary critics to insist on the importance of literary theory; he also stated, in *The Play and Place of Criticism* (1967), that language provides order and meaning to human experience. Among his later works are *Theory of Criticism: A Tradition and Its System* (1976), *Poetic Presence and Illusion* (1979), *Arts on the Level* (1981), *Words About Words About Words* (1988), *A Reopening of Closure* (1989), and *Ekphrasis: The Illusion of the Natural Sign* (1992).

Kriemhild \\'krēm-,hilt, -,hild\\   In Germanic heroic legend, sister of the Burgundian kings Gunther, Gernot, and Giselher. In Norse legend she is called Gudrun. In the German *Nibelungenlied*, she is the central character, introduced as a gentle princess courted by Siegfried.

The origin of Kriemhild's legend may be traced to two historical events. In 437 a Burgundian king, Gundahar (Gunther), and his followers were wiped out by Huns, and in 453 the Hunnish king Attila died in his sleep at the side of his new bride, a German girl. These two events became fused in popular legend.

In Old Norse legend, Atli (Attila) is murdered by his bride, Gudrun, in revenge for his treacherous murder of her brothers. *See* LAY OF ATLI; NIBELUNGENLIED.

Krige \\'krig-ə\\, Uys, *in full* Mattheus Uys Krige (b. Feb. 4, 1910, Bonteboskloof, near Swellendam, Cape Province, S.Af.—d. Aug. 10, 1987, near Hermanus, Cape Province)   South African dramatist, poet, translator, and short-story writer.

Krige began to make his reputation as a creative writer with a book of verse, *Kentering* (1935; "Turnings"); a play, *Magdelena Retief* (1938); and a volume of poetic tales, *Die palmboom* (1940; "The Palm Tree"). He served as a war correspondent with the South African forces in North Africa from 1940 to 1941 and was captured at the Battle of Tobruk [now in Libya]. His escape from a prisoner-of-war camp in Italy two years later became the basis for his first English-language book, *The Way Out* (1946). His earlier short stories were collected as *The Dream and the Desert* (1953), and his later short stories were published as *Orphan of the Desert* (1967). His plays *The Wall of Death* (1960), *The Sniper* (1962), and *The Two Lamps* (1964) solidified his international reputation as a dramatist.

Part of Krige's importance as a writer rests with his pivotal position in South African literature as one who bridged the gulf, both political and linguistic, between Afrikaans and English. In 1968 he coedited *The Penguin Book of South African Verse*, which included translations of African-language poetry as well as Afrikaans poetry. Krige also translated a number of works in English, Spanish, and Italian literature into Afrikaans.

Krishna \\'krish-nə\\, *Sanskrit* Kṛṣṇa.   One of the most widely revered and most popular of all Indian divinities, worshiped as the eighth incarnation (avatar, or *avatāra*) of the Hindu god Vishnu and also as a supreme god in his own right. The basic sources of Krishna's mythology are the epic *Mahābhārata* and its 5th-century-AD appendix, the *Harivaṃśa*, and the *Purāṇas*, particularly Book 10 of the *Bhāgavata-Purāṇa*. The sources tell how Krishna (literally "black," or "dark as a cloud") was born

into the Yādava clan, the son of Vasudeva and Devakī, sister of Kaṃsa, the wicked king of Mathura (in modern Uttar Pradesh). Kaṃsa, hearing a prophecy that he should be destroyed by Devakī's child, tried to slay her children, but Krishna was smuggled across the Yamuna River to Gokula (or Vraja, modern Gokul), where he was raised by the leader of the cowherds, Nanda, and his wife Yaśodā.

After slaying Kamsa, Krishna led the Yādavas to the western coast of Kāthiāwār and established his court at Dvāraka (modern Dwārkā, Gujarāt). He married the princess Rukmiṇī and took other wives as well.

Krishna refused to bear arms in the great war between the Kauravas and the Pāṇḍavas but offered a choice of his personal attendance to one side and the loan of his army to the other. On his return to Dvāraka, a brawl broke out one day among the Yādava chiefs in which Krishna's brother and son were slain. As the god sat in the forest lamenting, a huntsman, mistaking him for a deer, shot him in the heel, his one vulnerable spot, and killed him.

Kristensen \\'kris-ten-sən\\, Tom, *in full* Aage Tom Kristensen (b. Aug. 4, 1893, London, Eng.—d. June 4, 1974, Thurø, near Svendborg, Den.)   Danish poet, novelist, and critic who was one of the central literary figures of the disillusioned generation after World War I.

Kristensen was particularly influential as a literary critic for the left-wing Copenhagen daily *Politiken* (1924–63). He also translated much literature into Danish, including works by Friedrich von Schiller, Theodore Dreiser, D.H. Lawrence, and Erich Maria Remarque. His work was considered radical both politically and artistically. His first two volumes of poetry were *Fribytterdrømme* (1920; "Pirate Dreams") and *Påfuglefjeren* (1922; "The Peacock Feather"). A later volume of poetry, *Den sidste lygte* (1954; "The Last Lantern"), is meditative and philosophical. *Hærværk* (1930; *Havoc*), his best-known novel, is a bitter examination of conscience and an account of the interwar years of his generation. His autobiography *En bogorms barndom* ("A Bookworm's Boyhood") appeared in 1955.

Kristeva \\kris-'tā-və, *French* krē-stä-'vá\\, Julia (b. June 24, 1941, Sliven, Bulgaria)   Bulgarian-born French psychoanalyst, critic, and educator best known for her writings in structuralist linguistics, psychoanalysis, semiotics, and feminism.

Educated in Bulgaria, in 1966 Kristeva immigrated to France where she was research assistant to the structuralist and Marxist critic Lucien Goldmann. The critic Roland Barthes became her mentor. Her doctoral dissertation, *La Révolution du langage poétique* (1974; partial translation, *Revolution in Poetic Language*), was hailed for its application of psychoanalytic theory to language and literature. Kristeva held the professorial chair in linguistics at the University of Paris VII.

Kristeva's theories synthesized elements from such dissimilar thinkers as Jacques Lacan, Michel Foucault, and Mikhail Bakhtin. Two distinct trends characterize her writings: an early structuralist-semiotic phase and a psychoanalytic-feminist phase. Her writings include *Sēmeiōtikē: recherches pour une sémanalyse* (1969) and *Polylogue* (1977), which were in part translated as *Desire in Language: A Semiotic Approach to Literature and Art* (1980). Other works include *Des Chinoises* (1974; *About Chinese Women*), *Au commencement était l'amour: psychanalyse et foi* (1985; *In the Beginning Was Love: Psychoanalysis and Faith*), *Soleil noir: dépression et mélancolie* (1987; *Black Sun: Depression and Melancholia*), and *Étrangers à nous-mêmes* (1988; *Strangers to Ourselves*). Her novels include *Les Samouraïs* (1990; *The Samurai*), about the student riots of the late 1960s, and *Le Vieil Homme et les loups* (1991; *The Old Man and the Wolves*).

Kristin Lavransdatter \\'kris-tin-'låv-råns-ˌdåt-ər\   Historical novel in three volumes by Sigrid UNDSET, published from 1920 to 1922. For this work Undset was awarded the Nobel Prize for Literature in 1928. Set in medieval Norway, the trilogy consists of *Kransen* (1920; *The Bridal Wreath*; U.K. title, *The Garland*), *Husfrue* (1921; *The Mistress of Husaby*), and *Korset* (1922; *The Cross*). A one-volume English edition was published in 1929.

In *The Bridal Wreath*, Kristin Lavransdatter enjoys a happy childhood and youth. *The Mistress of Husaby* concerns Kristin's unhappy marriage. In *The Cross* the family must start over. After her husband dies in an armed confrontation, Kristin gives the keys to her house to her son's wife and enters a convent. In 1349 she dies of the Black Death.

Krleža \\'kər-le-zhå\, Miroslav (b. July 7, 1893, Zagreb, Croatia-Slavonia, Austria-Hungary [now Croatia]—d. Dec. 29, 1981, Zagreb)   Novelist and playwright who was a dominant figure in modern Croatian literature.

Krleža founded a left-wing review in 1919. After World War II he was elected vice president of the Yugoslav Academy of Science and Art and later became director of the Croatian Institute of Lexicography and president of the Yugoslav Writers' Union. Typical works are the dramatic trilogy *Glembajevi* (1932; "The Glembaj Family"), an indictment of the decadence of the Croatian bourgeoisie under the Austrian Empire, and the novel *Povratak Filipa Latinovicza* (1932; *The Return of Philip Latinovicz*). Other works concern the past exploitation and sufferings of the Croatian peasants, *e.g.*, the stories in the collection *Hrvatski bog Mars* (1922; "The Croatian God Mars") and the *Balade Petrice Kerempuha* (1936; "Ballads of Petrice Kerempuha").

Kröger, Tonio \\'tō-nē-ō-'krœg-ər\   A fictional character, the protagonist of Thomas Mann's novella TONIO KRÖGER.

Krokodil \krə-ˌkə-'dʸēl\ ("Crocodile")   Humor magazine published in Moscow, noted for its satire and cartoons.

From 1922 to 1932 the periodical was published as a weekly supplement to the newspaper *Rabochaya gazeta* ("The Worker's Press"; published for its first three months as *Rabochy* ["The Worker"]). From 1932 until 1992 the magazine was published thrice-monthly but thereafter it was forced by economic hardship to cut back to monthly publication.

Krokodil's humor was chiefly directed against what it termed Western imperialism and bourgeois ideology, but it also assailed "undesirable elements" in Soviet society. Vitaly Goryayev, one of its best-known cartoonists, became known for his comic portrayal of the "capitalist warmongers." *Krokodil* was published by *Pravda*, which until 1991 was the official newspaper of the Communist Party.

Kronos   *see* CRONUS.

Kruczkowski \krūch-'kōf-skʸē\, Leon (b. June 28, 1900, Kraków, Poland, Austria-Hungary—d. Aug. 1, 1962, Warsaw) Polish novelist and playwright.

Politically a socialist, Kruczkowski became famous upon the publication of his first novel, *Kordian i cham* (1932; "Kordian and the Churl"), which—as the author himself put it—was "an attempt to show the peasant question in Poland from the broad perspectives of historical development." *Pawie pióra* (1935; "Peacock's Feathers") is another book about the peasant movement, and *Sidła* (1937; "The Trap") concerns the condition of white-collar workers.

Kruczkowski spent World War II in a prison camp. After the war he joined the Polish Workers' Party and was a prominent activist in state and party affairs. His play *Niemcy* (1949; "The Germans") analyzed the process of the rapid spread of Nazi

ideology among the German people. Subsequent plays were *Pierwszy dzień wolności* (1960; "The First Day of Freedom") and *Śmierć gubernatora* (1961; "Death of a Governor").

Krutch \'krŭch\, Joseph Wood (b. Nov. 25, 1893, Knoxville, Tenn., U.S.—d. May 22, 1970, Tucson, Ariz.)   American writer, critic, naturalist, and conservationist.

Krutch attended the University of Tennessee and Columbia University, N.Y. He taught at Brooklyn Polytechnic and began to contribute book reviews and essays to periodicals. From 1924 through 1952, during which time he was drama critic for *The Nation*, he taught and lectured at various schools in the New York area and wrote a number of books, including *The Modern Temper* (1929). In the 1940s he wrote two critical biographies, *Samuel Johnson* (1944) and *Henry David Thoreau* (1948), which reflected his growing interest in commonsense philosophy and natural history. His later work included *The Measure of Man* (1954), *The Great Chain of Life* (1956), and his autobiography, *More Lives Than One* (1962).

Krylov \krə-'lôf\, Ivan Andreyevich (b. Feb. 2 [Feb. 13, New Style], 1768/69, Moscow, Russia—d. Nov. 9 [Nov. 21], 1844, St. Petersburg)   Writer of innocent-sounding fables that satirized contemporary social types in the guise of beasts. His command of colloquial idiom brought a note of realism to Russian classical literature. Many of his aphorisms have become part of everyday Russian speech.

Born to an impoverished family, Krylov had little formal education and began to work as a clerk at the age of nine. In 1805 he began translating the fables of Jean de La Fontaine but found that his true medium was writing fables of his own. The publication of his first book of fables in 1809 gained him the patronage of the imperial family and a post in the St. Petersburg public library, which he maintained for 30 years. He produced eight additional books of fables, all written in verse.

Although some of his themes were borrowed from Aesop and La Fontaine, his foxes and crows, wolves and sheep, were always recognizable Russian types. His salty, down-to-earth parables made him one of the first Russian writers to reach a broad audience.

Kuan Han-ch'ing   *see* GUAN HANQING.

Kubla Khan \'kŭb-lə-'kän, 'kŭb-\ (*in full* Kubla Khan; or, a Vision in a Dream)   Poetic fragment by Samuel Taylor COLERIDGE, published in 1816. According to Coleridge, he composed the 54-line work while under the influence of laudanum. Coleridge believed that several hundred lines of the poem had come to him in a dream, but he was able to remember only this fragment after waking.

The poem begins with these well-known lines: "In Xanadu did Kubla Khan/A stately pleasure dome decree:/Where Alph, the sacred river, ran/Through caverns measureless to man/Down to a sunless sea." Because of the exotic imagery and rhythmic cadence of the poem, early critics decided that poem should be read simply as a reverie and enjoyed for its vivid and sensual qualities. After studying Coleridge's mythological and psychological interests, later critics held that the work had a complex structure of meaning and was basically a poem about the nature of human genius.

Kulchur \'kəl-chər\   A review of contemporary arts, important for the vital nature of its writing and for its role as the representative of the avant-garde arts community in New York City. It was published in New York from spring 1960 to winter 1965–66 and was named for Ezra Pound's *Guide to Kulchur*. Unlike other avant-garde "little" magazines of its time, *Kulchur* concentrated on presenting criticism rather than fiction. Poetry, painting and sculpture, experimental film and theater, dance, jazz and contemporary classical music, sex, and politics were among the subjects that fell within its scope, and the 12th issue was devoted to writings on the subject of civil rights.

Kulhwch and Olwen   *see* CULHWCH AND OLWEN.

Kumārāsambhavā \kŭ-'mä-rə-'səm-bə-və\ ("Birth of the War God")   Epic poem by KĀLIDĀSA written in the 5th century AD. The work describes the courting of the ascetic Śiva, who is meditating in the mountains, by Pārvatī, the daughter of the Himalayas; the conflagration of Kāma (the god of desire)—after his arrow struck Śiva—by the fire from Śiva's third eye; the wedding and lovemaking of Śiva and Pārvatī; and the subsequent birth of Kumāra (Skanda), the war god. The original poem is in eight cantos, but a sequel was added by an imitator.

Kume Masao \'kŭ-me-,mä-'sä-ō\ (b. Nov. 23, 1891, Ueda, Japan—d. March 1, 1952, Kamakura)   Novelist and playwright, one of Japan's most popular writers of the 1920s and '30s.

As a student, Kume was associated with the writers Akutagawa Ryūnosuke and Kikuchi Kan on the famous school literary journal *Shinshichō* ("New Currents of Thought"). He published a book of poetry in 1914, but, before graduating from Tokyo Imperial University in 1916, he had turned to theater. A notable success during this time was the play *Gyūnyūya no kyōdai* (1914; "The Milkman's Younger Brother"). With Akutagawa, he became a disciple of the novelist Natsume Sōseki. *Jūkensei no shūki* (1916; "Notes of a Student Examinee"), *Tora* (1918; "The Tiger"), and *Hasen* (1922; "Shipwreck") are among his best works.

Kumin \'kyŭ-min\, Maxine, *original surname* Winokur \'win-ə-kər\ (b. June 6, 1925, Philadelphia, Pa., U.S.)   Pulitzer Prize-winning poet, novelist, and children's author. Kumin's novels were praised in literary circles, but she was best known for her poetry, written primarily in traditional forms, on loss, fragility, family, and the cycles of life and nature.

After graduating from Radcliffe College, Kumin taught English at several colleges. In the 1950s she met the poet Anne Sexton, who influenced her stylistic development and with whom she collaborated on several children's books. Kumin's first book of poetry, *Halfway*, was published in 1961; *The Privilege* (1965) and *The Nightmare Factory* (1970) address issues of Jewish identity and family and of love between men and women. Kumin's New Hampshire farm was the inspiration for her collection *Up Country: Poems of New England, New and Selected* (1972; Pulitzer Prize, 1973). Critics compared Kumin to Robert Frost and Henry David Thoreau for her precise, unsentimental evocations of rural New England and the rhythms of daily life. The poet's later works include the acclaimed *The Retrieval System* (1978) and *Our Ground Time Here Will Be Brief* (1982).

Kumin's numerous children's books also reflected her love of nature and interest in family, and her short-story collection, *Why Can't We Live Together Like Civilized Human Beings?* (1982), further explored issues of loss and relationships between men and women. Kumin served as poetry consultant to the Library of Congress from 1981 to 1982.

Kuncewicz \kŭnt-'sev-ich\, Maria, *original surname* Szczepańska \che-'pän-skä\, *married name* Kuncewiczowa \kŭnt-sev-i-'chō-vä\ (b. Oct. 30, 1899, Samara, Russia—d. July 15, 1989, Kazimierz Dolny, Pol.)   Polish writer of novels, essays, plays, and short stories.

Kuncewicz studied at the universities of Kraków and Warsaw in Poland and at the University of Nancy, Fr. Her first novel, *Twarz mężczyzny* (1928; "The Face of the Male"), established her gift for penetrating psychological portraits, subtle

irony, and poetical lyricism. *Cudzoziemka* (1936; *The Stranger*) is considered to be her masterpiece. Episodes from her novel *Dni powszednie państwa Kowalskich* (1937; "The Everyday Life of Mr. and Mrs. Jones") were broadcast by radio in Poland.

In 1939 she escaped from Warsaw to Paris, and in 1940 she went to England, where she wrote *Klucze* (1943; *The Keys*), a literary diary subtitled in the English version *A Journey Through Europe at War*. In 1956 she moved to the United States, where she published an anthology of stories and essays entitled *The Modern Polish Mind* (1962) and taught Polish language and literature at the University of Chicago (1961–64). She continued to write novels, including *Gaj oliwny* (1961; *The Olive Grove*) and *Don Kichot i niańki* (1965; "Don Quixote and the Nannies").

k'un-ch'ü   *see* KUNQU.

Kundera \'kŭn-de-rä\, Milan (b. April 1, 1929, Brno, Czech. [now Czech Republic])   Czech novelist, short-story writer, playwright, and poet who wrote various works combining erotic comedy with political criticism.

Kundera's poetry collections *Člověk zahrada širá* (1953; "Man: A Broad Garden"), *Poslední máj* (1955; "The Last May"), and *Monology* (1957; "Monologues"), were condemned by the Czech authorities because of their ironic tone and eroticism. He was at times a member of the Communist Party (1948–50, 1956–70) and studied and taught in the Film Faculty of Prague's Academy of Music and Dramatic Arts.

Several volumes of short stories and a highly successful one-act play, *Majitelé klíčů* (1962; "The Owners of the Keys"), were followed by one of his greatest works, *Žert* (1967; *The Joke*), an ironic novel about life under Joseph Stalin. His second novel, *Život je jinde* (1969; *Life Is Elsewhere*), was forbidden Czech publication. Kundera participated in the brief liberalization of Czechoslovakia in 1967–68, and after the Soviet occupation of the country he was attacked by the authorities, who banned all his works, fired him from his teaching positions, and ousted him from the Communist Party.

In 1975 Kundera was allowed to emigrate (with his wife, Vera Hrabankova) from Czechoslovakia to teach at the University of Rennes in France; in 1979 the Czech government stripped him of his citizenship. His subsequent novels, including *Valčík na rozloučenou* (1976; "Farewell Waltz"; *The Farewell Party*), *Kniha smíchu a zapomnění* (1979; THE BOOK OF LAUGHTER AND FORGETTING), and *Nesnesitelná lehkost byti* (1984; THE UNBEARABLE LIGHTNESS OF BEING), were published in France and elsewhere abroad but until 1989 were banned in his homeland. A translation of Kundera's reflections on the art of the novel was published in 1988. Other works include the play *Jacques et son maître* (1981; *Jacques and His Master*) and the novel *Nesmrtelnost* (1990; *Immortality*).

Kunene \kŭ-'nä-nä\, Mazisi (Raymond) (b. May 12, 1930, Durban, S.Af.)   South African poet who wrote in the Zulu language and used traditional forms, later translating his own work into English.

Kunene began writing in the Zulu language when he was a child and by age 11 had published a number of poems in newspapers and magazines. In his University of Natal master's thesis, "An Analytical Survey of Zulu Poetry, Both Traditional and Modern," Kunene criticized several tendencies in modern Zulu literature.

In 1959 Kunene went to the University of London to complete his doctorate, but he soon became involved in politics and never completed his studies. While abroad he became the official representative of the African National Congress to the United Nations, and he later taught at several American universities.

Kunene's collection *Zulu Poems* (1979) was praised by critics for the freshness of his English renderings of patterns and imagery from Zulu vernacular traditions. His later translations include two epic poems—*Emperor Shaka the Great* (1979) and *Anthem of the Decades* (1981), a work dealing with Zulu religion and cosmology—as well as a collection of short lyrics, *The Ancestors & the Sacred Mountain* (1982).

Kung Tzu-chen *see* GONG ZIZHEN.

Kunikida Doppo \kŭ-'nē-kē-dä-'dŏp-pȯ\, *also called* Kunikida Kamekichi \kä-'mä-kē-chē\ (b. Aug. 30, 1871, Chōshi, Chiba prefecture, Japan—d. June 23, 1908, Chigasaki, Kanagawa prefecture) Writer whose short stories, deeply imbued with a Wordsworthian awareness of nature, brought to Japanese literature a new attitude toward the individual.

Kunikida attended Tokyo Senmon Gakkō (later Waseda University). He had already started to read the works of Ivan Turgenev, Thomas Carlyle, and Ralph Waldo Emerson when he went in 1893 to teach school on the southern Japanese island of Kyushu. That year was crucial in the development of his passionate devotion to nature, which was reinforced by his reading of William Wordsworth's poetry. He returned to Tokyo, where he became a war correspondent for the newspaper of the influential critic and historian Tokutomi Sohō during the Sino-Japanese War (1894–95). His dispatches were collected and entitled *Aitei tsūshin* ("Letters to My Dear Brother"). *Azamukazaru no ki* ("Diary Without Deceit") covered the personally tormented years of 1893–97, during which he married and was deserted by his first wife, who later served as the model for the heroine of the novel *Aru onna* (1919; *A Certain Woman*) by Arishima Takeo.

Other works include *Musashino* (1898; "The Musashi Plain"), *Gyūniku to bareisho* (1901; *Meat and Potatoes*), *Gen oji* (1897; *Old Gen*), and *Haru no tori* (1904; *Spring Birds*).

Kunitz \'kyü-nits\, Stanley (Jasspon) (b. July 29, 1905, Worcester, Mass., U.S.) American poet noted for his subtle craftsmanship and his treatment of complex themes.

Kunitz attended Harvard University. While working as an editor, he contributed poems to magazines, eventually compiling them in his first book, *Intellectual Things* (1930). His collection *Passport to the War* (1944), like his first book, contained meticulously crafted, intellectual verse. Most of the poems from these first two works were reprinted in *Selected Poems 1928–1958* (1958), which won him the Pulitzer Prize in 1959.

With *The Testing-Tree* (1971), Kunitz departed from the formal structure and rational approach of his earlier verse and wrote shorter, looser, and more emotional poetry. Included in the book are "The Illumination" and "King of the River." His later books of poetry include *The Terrible Threshold* (1974), *The Coat Without a Seam* (1974), *The Lincoln Relics* (1978), *The Poems of Stanley Kunitz* (1979), *The Wellfleet Whale and Companion Poems* (1983), and *Next-to-Last Things* (1985), which contains essays as well as verse. Kunitz also edited numerous literary anthologies and translated Russian literature.

kunqu or **k'un-ch'ü** \'kün-'chē\ [Chinese *kūnqŭ*, from *kūn* Kunshan + *qŭ* song, tune] Form of Chinese drama that was developed in the 16th century. *Kunqu* was essentially the *chuanqi* form set to a new type of music, which was created by Wei Liangfu of Kunshan. Important *kunqu* dramatists were Tang Xianzu, who was noted for the delicate sensitivity of his poetry; Shen Jing, who excelled in versification; and Li Yu, known for his effective theatrical pieces.

Kunqu had begun as a genuinely popular opera form, and it became the predominant *chuanqi* form through the end of the 18th century. It had, however, turned into a theater of the literati, its poetic forms too esoteric and its music too refined for the common audience. It was gradually replaced in popularity by the form known as *jingxi*, or Peking opera.

Künstlerroman \'kŭnst-lər-rō-,män\ [German, literally, artist novel] Class of BILDUNGSROMAN, or apprenticeship novel, that deals with the youth and development of an individual who becomes—or is on the threshold of becoming—a painter, musician, or poet. The classic example is James Joyce's *Portrait of the Artist as a Young Man* (1916). The type originated in the period of German Romanticism with Ludwig Tieck's *Franz Sternbalds Wanderungen* (1798; "Franz Sternbald's Travels"). Later examples are Knut Hamsun's *Hunger* (1890) and Thomas Wolfe's *Look Homeward, Angel* (1929).

Kuo Mo-jo *see* GUO MORUO.

Kuprin \kŭ-'prᵞēn\, Aleksandr Ivanovich (b. Aug. 26 [Sept. 7, New Style], 1870, Narovchat, Russia—d. Aug. 25, 1938, Leningrad) Russian novelist and short-story writer, one of the last exponents of the great tradition of Russian critical realism.

Literary fame came to Kuprin with *Poyedinok* (1905; *The Duel*), a realistically sordid picture of the emptiness of life in a remote military garrison. Kuprin wrote prolifically; his subjects might be best described by the title of one of his best-known stories, *Reka zhizni* (1906; "The River of Life"). His best-known novel, *Yama* (1909–15; *Yama: The Pit*), dwells with enthusiasm on the minutiae of the everyday life of prostitutes, their housekeeping, economics, and social stratification.

After the Russian Revolution, Kuprin became one of the many Russian émigrés in Paris, where he continued to write. In 1937 he was allowed to return to the Soviet Union.

Kürenberger \der-'kē̄-rən-,ber-gər\, Der, *also called* Der von Kürenberg \der-fȯn-'kē̄-rən-,berk\ (fl. 1160) The earliest of the minnesingers, German poet-musicians, to be known by name.

All that is known of Kürenberger is that he was an Austrian nobleman from near Linz. In his proud and imperious love songs there is no evidence of the homage to women expressed by the later minnesingers and their French or Provençal models. His poems are written in stanzas of four lines, rhymed in pairs, and divided into half lines by a caesura (pause). Because this is the form (known as the Nibelungenlied strophe) in which the German heroic epic the *Nibelungenlied* was written and because Kürenberger's style has an epic-dramatic quality, it has been conjectured that he may have written a lost German epic on which the unknown author of the *Nibelungenlied* based his poem.

Kürnberger \'kŭrn-,ber-gər\, Ferdinand (b. July 3, 1821, Vienna, Austria—d. Oct. 14, 1879, Munich, Ger.) Austrian writer known for his participation in the Austrian revolution of 1848 and the Dresden rebellion of 1849.

Kürnberger was forced to leave Austria after his participation in the first rebellion and was jailed for his involvement in the second. His best-known play is *Catilina* (1855). Novels and critical essays include *Der Amerika-Müde* (1855; "The One Who Is Tired of America"), *Der Haustyrann* (1876; "The House Tyrant"), *Das Schloss der Frevel* (1904; "Frevel's Castle"), and two books of essays, *Siegelringe* (1874; "Signet Rings") and *Literarische Herzenssachen* (1877; "Literary Matters of the Heart").

Kurtz, Mr. \'kȯrts\ Fictional character, the manager of a trading station in the interior of the Belgian Congo, in Joseph Conrad's HEART OF DARKNESS.

Kurz \'kůrts\, Hermann (b. Nov. 30, 1813, Reutlingen, kingdom of Württemberg [Germany]—d. Oct. 10, 1873, Tübingen) German writer chiefly known for two powerful historical novels, *Schillers Heimatjahre* (1843; "Schiller's Homeland Years") and *Der Sonnenwirt* (1855; "The Proprietor of the Sun Inn"), both critical of the existing social order, and for his satirically humorous tales of Swabian life in *Erzählungen* (1858–63; "Tales").

Because the quality of his work went unrecognized, he was forced to make his living by translating. He produced excellent translations of Ludovico Ariosto's epic *Orlando furioso* (1840–41) and, from the Middle High German, of Gottfried von Strassburg's epic *Tristan und Isolde* (1844).

Kusanagi \kŭ-'sä-nä-gē\ ("Grass-Mower") In Japanese mythology, the miraculous sword that the sun goddess Amaterasu gave to her grandson Ninigi when he descended to earth to become ruler of Japan, thus establishing the divine link between the Imperial house and the sun. The sword was discovered by the storm god Susanoo in the body of the eight-headed dragon (which he killed) and presented by him to his sister Amaterasu. It derives its name from an incident in which the hero Yamato Takeru was attacked by Ainu warriors. They started a grass fire around him, from which he escaped by cutting down the burning brush with the marvelous sword.

A sword, along with a mirror and a jeweled necklace, still forms one of the three Imperial Treasures of Japan.

ku-wen *see* GUWEN.

Kuznetsov \kŭz-n\y/it-'sòf\, Anatoly Vasilyevich, *pseudonym* A. Anatoli \,ə-,nə-'tô-l\y/ē\ (b. Aug. 18, 1929, Kiev, Ukraine, U.S.S.R.—d. June 13, 1979, London, Eng.) Soviet writer noted for the autobiographical novel BABI YAR, one of the most important literary works to come out of World War II.

Kuznetsov was 12 years old in 1941 when the invading German army occupied his home city of Kiev in Ukraine. His first literary success, *Prodolzheniye legendy* (1957; *Sequel to a Legend*), was based on his experiences as a laborer in Siberia; the book helped start the genre of "youth stories" that subsequently became popular in the Soviet Union. In 1966 Kuznetsov's controversial novel *Babi Yar* was published in the Soviet Union in a heavily censored form.

Kuznetsov defected to the West during a trip to London in 1969. In 1970 the full and uncensored version of *Babi Yar* was published in New York. Kuznetsov was promptly denounced as a traitor in the Soviet Union because of the book's condemnation of both German and Soviet policies toward Ukraine in the 1940s.

Kvaran \'kvä-rån\, Einar Hjörleifsson (b. Dec. 6, 1859, Vallanes, Ice.—d. May 21, 1938, Reykjavík) Icelandic journalist, novelist, short-story writer, playwright, and poet.

Kvaran studied at the University of Copenhagen and there joined a group of young Icelandic radicals. He went to Winnipeg, Man., Can., in 1885 and for 10 years was a leading journalist and editor in the Icelandic immigrant community there. He spent the rest of his life as a journalist and writer in Reykjavík.

A popular success, Kvaran expressed the contemporary longing for political independence, a better social structure, and better education. Kvaran's novels were often written to a thesis and were peopled with characters who were little more than spokespersons for various ideas. His masterly short stories show him at his best.

Kvasir \'kvä-sir\ In Norse mythology, a poet-god known for his wisdom. His blood, when mixed with honey by Suttung, a giant, formed the mead that gave wisdom and poetic inspiration to those who drank it. Kvasir was born of the saliva of two rival groups of gods, the Æsir and the Vanir, when they performed the ancient peace ritual of spitting into a common vessel. Two dwarfs, Fjalar and Galar, who were weary of academics and learning, killed Kvasir and distilled his blood in Odhrǫrir, the magic caldron. The story of Kvasir's murder is told in the *Braga Rœdur* ("Conversations of Bragi").

Kyd \'kid\, Thomas (baptized Nov. 6, 1558, London, Eng.—d. *c.* December 1594, London) English dramatist who, with *The Spanish Tragedie* (sometimes called *Hieronimo*, or *Jeronimo*, after its protagonist), initiated the REVENGE TRAGEDY of his day. Kyd anticipated the structure of many later plays, including the development of middle and final climaxes. In addition, Kyd revealed an instinctive sense of tragic situation, while his characterization of Hieronimo in *The Spanish Tragedie* prepared the way for William Shakespeare's psychological study of Hamlet.

Kyd's *The Spanish Tragedie* was entered in the Stationers' Register in October 1592, and the undated first quarto edition almost certainly appeared in that year. It remained one of the most popular plays of the age and was often reprinted.

The only other play certainly by Kyd is *Cornelia* (1594), an essay in Senecan tragedy, translated from the French of Robert Garnier's academic *Cornélie*. Kyd may also have written an earlier version of *Hamlet*, known to scholars as the *Ur-Hamlet*, and his hand has sometimes been detected in the anonymous *Arden of Feversham*, one of the first domestic tragedies, and in a number of other plays.

On May 13, 1593, Kyd was arrested and then tortured, being suspected of treasonable activity. His room had been searched and certain "atheistical" documents found there. He claimed later, in a letter, that the papers had belonged to Christopher Marlowe, with whom he had earlier shared lodgings.

kylin *see* QILIN.

Kynewulf *see* CYNEWULF.

kyōgen \'kyō-,gen\ [Japanese] Brief farce or comic interlude played during a Japanese Nō (lyric drama) cycle, expressed in the vernacular of the second half of the 16th century. Its effect is to relieve the tension of the drama. It is performed in ordinary dress and without masks (unless these are used in parody). There are normally four *kyōgen* interspersed among the usual five Nō pieces.

kyōka \'kyō-,kä\ [Japanese] Form of Japanese poetry, a comic or satirical version of the TANKA.

kyrielle \kĕr-'yel\ *plural* kyrielle [French, literally, repeated series of words or phrases, litany, from Old French *kiriele*, a derivative of *kyrie* kyrie (a Christian liturgical prayer)] A French verse form in short, usually octosyllabic, rhyming couplets. The couplets are often paired in quatrains and are characterized by a refrain that is sometimes a single word and sometimes the full second line of the couplet or the full fourth line of the quatrain.

Kyriotes *see* GEOMETRES.

Labé \là-'bā\, Louise, *original surname* Charly \shàr-'lē\ (b. *c.* 1524, Lyon, Fr.—d. 1566, Parcieux-en-Dombes) French poet who was a member of the 16th-century Lyon school of humanist poets dominated by Maurice Scève. Her wit, charm, and accomplishments and the freedom she enjoyed provoked unverifiable legends, such as those claiming that she rode to war and was a cultured courtesan.

In 1555 Labé published a book of love sonnets that were emotionally intense and stylistically simple. The same volume also contained a prose dialogue, *Débat de Folie et d'Amour* ("Debate Between Madness and Love"), in which was vindicated the "ancient league" between Madness and Love.

Laberius \lǝ-'bir-ē-ǝs\, Decimus (b. *c.* 105 BC—d. 43 BC) Roman knight with a caustic wit who was one of the two leading writers of mimes. The titles of some 42 of his mimes have been preserved, with fragments.

Labiche \là-'bēsh\, Eugène-Marin (b. May 5, 1815, Paris, Fr.—d. Jan. 23, 1888, Paris) Comic playwright who wrote many of the most popular and amusing light comedies of the 19th-century French stage.

Labiche briefly worked as a journalist before writing plays. Of his early plays, *Monsieur de Coislin*, written in collaboration with Marc Michel, was his first great success. A long series of hilarious full-length and one-act plays followed.

Typically, his plays are based on an improbable incident evolving into an imbroglio that brings out the folly and frailty of the characters. The best of his works include *Le Chapeau de paille d'Italie* (1851; *The Italian Straw Hat*), *Le Misanthrope et l'Auvergnat* (1852), *Le Voyage de M. Perrichon* (1860), and *La Poudre aux yeux* (1861; "The Bluff"). Full of dramatic devices, the plays nonetheless show real insight into human nature.

With the publication of his 10-volume *Théâtre complet* (1878–83) while he was in retirement, he was engulfed by new acclaims and success, including election to the Académie Française. Sound and entertaining, his works raised the lowly farce to a much higher level of literary accomplishment.

La Bruyère \là-brœ-'yer\, Jean de (b. August 1645, Paris, Fr.—d. May 10/11, 1696, Versailles) French satiric moralist who is best known for one work, *Les Caractères de Théophraste traduits du grec avec les caractères ou les moeurs de ce siècle* (1688; *The Characters, or Manners of the Age, with the Characters of Theophrastus*), which is considered to be one of the masterpieces of French literature.

La Bruyère became one of the tutors to the Duke de Bourbon, grandson of the Prince de Condé, and remained in the Condé household as librarian at Chantilly. He was bitter about his inferior position, but it allowed him a unique vantage point from which to observe the perils of aristocratic idleness, fads, and fashions.

La Bruyère's masterpiece appeared as an appendage to his translation of the 4th-century-BC character writer Theophrastus in 1688. His method was that of Theophrastus: to define qualities such as dissimulation, flattery, or rusticity and then to give instances of them in actual people, making reflections on the "characteristics" of the time, for the purpose of reforming manners. His satire is constantly sharpened by variety of presentation, and he achieves vivid stylistic effects. Eight editions of the *Caractères* appeared during La Bruyère's life. Although the topical allusions in his book made his election to the Académie Française difficult, he was eventually elected in 1693.

La Calprenède \là-kàl-prǝ-'ned\, Gaultier de Coste, Seigneur de (b. *c.* 1610, château of Toulgon, near Sarlat, Fr.—d. 1663, Grand-Andely) French author of sentimental, adventurous, pseudohistorical romances that were popular to the end of the 18th century. To this rambling and diffuse genre he imparted vitality through swift-moving plots.

Pursuing military and literary careers simultaneously from 1635 to 1641, La Calprenède wrote tragedies and tragicomedies, some based on episodes in English history, including *Jeanne Reyne d'Angleterre* (1636; "Jane, Queen of England") and *Le Comte d'Essex* (1638; "The Earl of Essex"). In 1642 he began a series of novels glorifying love and war: *Cassandre*, 10 vol. (1642–45), a history of the decline of the Persian empire; *Cléopâtre*, 12 vol. (1647–58), a story of Cleopatra's alleged daughter by Antony; and *Faramond*, 12 vol. (1661–70), a Merovingian history completed after his death by Pierre d'Ortigue de Vaumorière.

Lacan \là-'kän\, Jacques (Marie Émile) (b. April 13, 1901, Paris, Fr.—d. Sept. 9, 1981, Paris) French psychoanalyst who gained an international reputation as an original interpreter of Sigmund Freud's work.

Lacan earned a medical degree in 1932 and was a practicing psychiatrist and psychoanalyst in Paris for much of his career. He helped introduce Freudian theory into France in the 1930s, but he reached prominence only after he began conducting regular seminars at the University of Paris in 1953. He acquired celebrity status in France after the publication of his essays and lectures in *Écrits* (1966; *The Language of the Self: The Function of Language in Psychoanalysis*).

Lacan emphasized the primacy of language as the mirror of the unconscious mind, and he introduced the study of language (as practiced particularly in the semiotics of Ferdinand de Saussure) into psychoanalytic theory. His major achievement was his reinterpretation of Freud's work in terms of structural linguistics. His influence extended well beyond the field of psychoanalysis to make him one of the dominant figures in French cultural life during the 1970s.

La Chaussée \là-shō-'sā\, Pierre-Claude Nivelle de (b. 1692, Paris, Fr.—d. March 14, 1754, Paris) French playwright who created the COMÉDIE LARMOYANTE ("tearful comedy"), a verse-drama form merging tearful, sentimental scenes with an invariably happy ending.

La Chaussée embarked on a literary career in middle age; his first play, *La Fausse Antipathie* ("False Antipathy"), was written when he was 41 years old. He wrote nine *comédies larmoyantes*—among them *Mélanide* (1741), *Le Préjugé à la mode* (1735; "Fashionable Prejudice"), and *L'École des mères* (1744; "Mothers' School")—in addition to other comedies and several tragedies. He was elected to the Académie Française in 1736.

Laclos \là-'klō\, Pierre Choderlos de, *in full* Pierre-Ambroise-François Choderlos de Laclos (b. Oct. 18, 1741, Amiens, Fr.—d. Nov. 5, 1803, Taranto, Parthenopean Republic [now in Italy]) French soldier and writer, author of the classic *Les Liaisons dangereuses* (1782; DANGEROUS LIAISONS), one of the earliest examples of the psychological novel.

Laclos chose a career in the army but soon left it to become a writer. *Les Liaisons dangereuses*, which was his first novel, caused an immediate sensation. Written in epistolary form, the story deals with a seducer, Valmont, and his accomplice, Mme de Merteuil, who take unscrupulous delight in their victims' misery. Laclos's second novel was *De l'éducation des femmes* (1785; "On the Education of Women"). His *Lettre à MM. de l'Académie Française sur l'éloge de M. le Maréchal de Vauban* (1786; "Letter to the Gentlemen of the French Academy on the Praise of the Marshal of Vauban") mocked the French army and its outdated methods of defense and, as a result, lost him his army commission. He again joined the army in

1792, however, and ultimately rose to the rank of general under Napoleon.

Lacretelle \lā-krə-'tel\, Jacques de (b. July 14, 1888, Cormatin, Fr.—d. Jan. 2, 1985, Paris) French novelist who was the third member of his family to be elected to the Académie Française (1936).

Lacretelle's first novel, *La Vie inquiète de Jean Hermelin* (1920; "The Troubled Life of Jean Hermelin"), is an autobiographical novel of adolescence. His next novel, *Silbermann* (1922), recounts the story of a Jewish boy's persecution during the time of the Dreyfus Affair. Following the publication of *La Bonifas* (1925; *Marie Bonifas*), a minutely detailed study of provincial life, he wrote *Amour nuptiale* (1929; *A Man's Life*), a psychological study of a marriage. From 1930 to 1935 Lacretelle wrote *Les Hauts-Ponts* ("High Bridges"), a long family saga set during the 19th century. *Sabine* (1932), the first of the four volumes in the series, was hailed as a masterpiece, though the other three were less well received. Lacretelle worked throughout the war years as a journalist for *Le Figaro*, of which he was a director. His postwar works include an autobiographical novel, *Le Pour et le contre* (1946; "For and Against"); a memoir, *Le Tiroir secret* (1959; "The Secret Drawer"); and the antinovel *Les Vivants et leur ombre* (1977; "The Living and Their Shadows").

lacuna \lə-'kū-nə, -'kyū-\ *plural* lacunae \-,nē, -,nī\ *or* lacunas [Latin, gap, deficiency, literally, depression, pit] In a text or manuscript, a blank or missing section.

Ladies' Home Journal American monthly magazine, one of the oldest in the country and long the trendsetter among women's magazines. It was founded in 1883 as a women's supplement to the *Tribune and Farmer* (1879–85) of Cyrus H.K. Curtis. The *Journal* began independent publication in 1884 with a pious and demure editorial posture and a sentimental literary diet. Edward W. Bok became editor in 1889, and under him the *Journal* attracted great writers from Europe and the United States—including W.D. Howells, Hamlin Garland, Mark Twain, Bret Harte, Rudyard Kipling, Sarah Orne Jewett, and Arthur Conan Doyle.

Ladipo \lä-'dē-pō\, Duro (b. Dec. 18, 1931, Oshogbo, Nigeria—d. Mar. 11, 1978, Oshogbo) Nigerian dramatist whose innovative folk operas helped establish a unique Yoruba tradition of traveling opera companies.

In 1962 Ladipo founded a club in Oshogbo that was similar to Ibadan's Mbari Club, and for its inauguration his new theater company performed his first opera, *Oba moro* ("Ghost-Catcher King"). He premiered *Oba kò so* ("The King Did Not Hang") at the club's first anniversary, and a year later introduced *Oba wa ja* ("The King Is Dead"). The three plays, based on the history of the Oyo kingdom, were translated into English and published together in *Three Yoruba Plays* (1964).

Earlier Yoruba operas had been mostly based on biblical stories or folktales, but Ladipo produced reliable cultural and historical records. He also dispensed with the traditional dances and the opening and closing "glees" usually associated with Yoruba operas.

Ladislaw, Will \'wil-'lad-i-,slô\ Fictional character, a young headstrong idealist in MIDDLEMARCH, a novel by George Eliot. Ladislaw is set in stark contrast to Edward Casaubon, his middle-aged and pedantic cousin, both of whom are attracted to Dorothea Brooke.

Lady Chatterley's Lover \'chat-ər-lē\ Novel by D.H. LAWRENCE, published in a limited English-language edition in Florence (1928) and in Paris (1929). It was first published in England in an expurgated version in 1932. The full text was only published in 1959 in New York City and in 1960 in London, when it was the subject of a landmark obscenity trial (*Regina* v. *Penguin Books Limited*) that turned largely on the justification of the use in the novel of until-then taboo sexual terms. This last of Lawrence's novels reflects the author's belief that men and women must overcome the deadening restrictions of industrialized society and follow their natural instincts to passionate love.

Constance (Connie) Chatterley is married to Sir Clifford, a wealthy landowner who is paralyzed from the waist down and is absorbed in his books and his estate, Wragby. After a disappointing affair, Connie turns to the estate's gamekeeper, Oliver Mellors, a symbol of natural man who awakens her passions.

Lady from the Sea, The Play in five acts by Henrik IBSEN, published in Norwegian as *Fruen fra havet* in 1888 and first performed in early 1889. It was the first of several mystical psychological dramas by Ibsen.

The play traces the increasing distraction of Ellida Wangel, the second wife of Dr. Wangel. She is obsessed with images of the sea because she once loved a sailor who promised to someday claim her. When the sailor does arrive, her husband releases her from her wedding vows. This act restores her equilibrium and breaks the sailor's spell over her.

Lady of Shalott, The \shə-'lät\ Narrative poem in four sections by Alfred, Lord TENNYSON, published in 1832 and revised for his 1842 collection *Poems*.

Typically Victorian in its exaltation of an imprisoned maiden who dies for a chaste love, the poem tells of Elaine of Arthurian legend, shut in her father's coldly beautiful castle on the island of Shalott. Tennyson evokes his heroine's dreamlike, monotonous life through incantatory rhyme and meter.

Lady of the Lake, The Poem in six cantos by Sir Walter SCOTT, published in 1810. Composed primarily in octosyllabic tetrameter couplets, it mines Gaelic history to retell a well-known legend about the heroine Ellen Douglas. The poem, which is set in the Scottish Highlands in the 16th century, recounts the banishment and eventual restoration of the noble Douglas family.

Lady's Not for Burning, The Verse comedy in three acts by Christopher FRY, produced in 1948 and published in 1949. Known for its wry characterizations and graceful language, this lighthearted play about 15th-century England brought Fry renown. Evoking spring, it was the first in his series of four plays based on the seasons. (The others are *Venus Observed* [1949; autumn], *The Dark is Light Enough* [1954; winter], and *A Yard of Sun* [1970; summer].)

The plot is set in motion by the disappearance of the town's rag-and-bone man. After many plot twists, the missing man turns up and those who have been arrested as suspects are released.

Lady Windermere's Fan \'win-dər-,mir\ Comedy of manners in four acts by Oscar WILDE, performed in 1892 and published the following year.

Set in Edwardian London, the play's action is put in motion by Lady Windermere's jealousy over her husband's interest in Mrs. Erlynne, a beautiful older woman with a mysterious past. Unknown to Lady Windermere, Mrs. Erlynne is really her divorced mother who, for the past 20 years, has been presumed dead. Lord Windermere is merely hoping to ease the older woman's reentrance into society, which she attempts under a pseudonym. In a fit of pique, Lady Windermere goes to the rooms of her ardent admirer, Lord Darlington. Mrs. Erlynne follows closely, saving her daughter from scandal by an act of generosity that ruins her own chances.

Laertes \la-'er-tēz\ Fictional character, the son of Polonius and brother of Ophelia, who serves as a foil to Prince Hamlet in William Shakespeare's HAMLET.

Laestrygones \les-'trig-ə-,nēz\, *also called* Laestrygonians \,les-tri-'gō-nē-ənz\ Fictional race of cannibalistic giants described in Book 10 of Homer's ODYSSEY. When Odysseus and his men land on the island native to the Laestrygones, the giants pelt Odysseus' ships with boulders, sinking all but Odysseus' own ship.

La Farge \lə-'färzh, -'färj\, Oliver (Hazard Perry) (b. Dec. 19, 1901, New York, N.Y., U.S.—d. Aug. 2, 1963, Albuquerque, N.M.) American anthropologist, short-story writer, and novelist who acted as a spokesman for Native Americans through his political actions and his fiction.

La Farge rejected the popular sentimental image of the Indian in contemporary literature. His first novel, *Laughing Boy* (1929; film, 1934), is a poetic but realistic story of the clash of cultures; it was awarded the Pulitzer Prize in 1929. La Farge's autobiography, *Raw Material*, was published in 1945.

La Fayette \lä-fä-'yet, *Angl* ,läf-ē-'et, ,laf-\, Marie-Madeleine, Countess (comtesse) de, *byname* Madame de La Fayette, *original surname* Pioche de la Vergne \pyòsh-də-lä-'vernʸ\ (baptized March 18, 1634, Paris, Fr.—d. May 25, 1693, Paris) French writer whose LA PRINCESSE DE CLÈVES, published anonymously in 1678, is a landmark of French fiction.

Throughout the 1660s Madame de La Fayette was a favorite of Henrietta Anne of England, Duchess d'Orléans. During this time she also began what was to be a lasting and intimate friendship with the Duke de La Rochefoucauld, author of the famous *Maximes*. With him she formed a distinguished literary circle. After producing two conventional romances, she wrote her masterpiece, *La Princesse de Clèves*, considered to be France's first serious "historical" novel.

La Fontaine \lä-fòⁿ-'tan\, Jean de (b. July 8?, 1621, Château-Thierry, Fr.—d. April 13, 1695, Paris) Poet whose FABLES (1668–94) rank among the masterpieces of French literature.

Detail of an oil painting by François De Troy
Bibliothèque Publique et Universitaire, Geneva

La Fontaine made important contacts in Paris, and it was there he spent his most productive years as a writer and was able to attract patrons. In 1657 he became one of the protégés of Nicolas Fouquet, the wealthy superintendent of finance. From 1664 to 1672 he served as gentleman-in-waiting to the dowager duchess d'Orléans in Luxembourg. For 20 years, from 1673, he was a member of the household of Mme de La Sabliere, whose salon was a celebrated meeting place of scholars, philosophers, and writers. In 1683 he was elected to the Académie Française, after opposition by the king to his unconventional character.

La Fontaine's *Fables* were published over the last 25 years of his life. They comprise some 240 poems and include timeless stories of simple countryfolk, heroes of Greek mythology, and the familiar animals of the fable. Few of his many other writings are more than poetic exercises or experiments. One exception is the leisurely narrative *Les Amours de Psiché et de Cupidon* (1669; *The Loves of Cupid and Psyche*), notable for the lucid elegance of its prose, its skillful blend of delicate feeling and witty banter, and sly studies of feminine psychology. His *Contes et nouvelles en vers* (*Tales and Novels in Verse*) is essentially a collection of licentious tales borrowed from Italian sources. The first of the tales was published in 1664, the last posthumously.

Laforet \,lä-fò-'ret\, Carmen, *surname in full* Laforet Díaz \'thē-äth\ (b. Sept. 6, 1921, Barcelona, Spain) Spanish novelist and short-story writer who received international recognition for her first novel, *Nada* (1945; "Nothing"; *Andrea*).

Educated in Las Palmas, Canary Islands, Laforet returned to Barcelona immediately after the Spanish Civil War (1936–39). Reflecting her own experience, *Nada* presents the impressions of an adolescent who returns to Barcelona from abroad after the war and discovers a sordid, chaotic atmosphere and intellectual emptiness. The book is written in the postwar narrative style known as *tremendismo*, which is characterized by a tendency to emphasize misery and grotesque imagery.

In contrast to her first novel, Laforet's later works, though better constructed, are sentimental and less intense. In 1952 she published *La isla y los demonios* ("The Island and the Demons"), another novel of initiation. She followed with *La llamada* (1954; "The Call"), a collection of short stories. Her conversion to Roman Catholicism in 1951 is strongly reflected in *La mujer nueva* (1955; "The New Woman"). After 1970 she published little.

Laforgue \lä-'fòrg\, Jules (b. Aug. 16, 1860, Montevideo, Uruguay—d. Aug. 20, 1887, Paris, Fr.) French Symbolist poet, a master of lyrical irony and one of the first advocates of vers libre ("free verse"). The impact of his work was felt by several 20th-century American poets, especially T.S. Eliot.

In 1881 Laforgue was appointed reader to the Empress Augusta in Berlin, and he remained in Germany for almost five years, during which time he wrote most of his works.

In the verse of *Les Complaintes* (1885), *L'Imitation de Notre-Dame la Lune* (1886; "The Imitation of Our Lady the Moon"), and *Le Concile féerique* (1886; "The Fairy Council"), Laforgue gave ironic expression to his obsession with death, his loneliness, and his boredom with daily routine. He forged new words, experimented with common speech, and combined popular songs and music-hall tags with philosophic and scientific terms to create an imagery that appears surprisingly modern. His search for new rhythms culminated in the vers libre that he and his friend Gustave Kahn invented almost simultaneously. He reinterpreted William Shakespeare, Richard Wagner, Gustave Flaubert, and Stéphane Mallarmé in a collection of short stories, *Moralités légendaires* (1887; *Six Moral Tales from Jules Laforgue*). His art criticism, published in the Symbolist reviews and subsequently in *Mélanges posthumes* (1923), testifies to his remarkable understanding of the Impressionist vision.

Lagerkvist \'läg-ər-kvēst\, Pär (Fabian) (b. May 23, 1891, Växjö, Swed.—d. July 11, 1974, Stockholm) One of the major Swedish literary figures of the first half of the 20th century. He was awarded the Nobel Prize for Literature in 1951.

Lagerkvist was involved with socialism and soon began to support artistic and literary radicalism, as demonstrated in his manifesto entitled *Ordkonst och bildkonst* (1913; "Literary and Pictorial Art"). In *Teater* (1918; "Theater"), the three one-act plays *Den svåre stunden* ("The Difficult Hour") illustrate a similar modernism.

Lagerkvist's extreme pessimism gradually subsided beginning with *Det eviga leendet* (1920; *The Eternal Smile*) and his autobiographical novel *Gäst hos verkligheten* (1925; *Guest of Reality*). By the time Lagerkvist had written his great prose monologue *Det besegrade livet* (1927; "The Triumph over Life"), he was able to declare his faith in humanity. His prose work *Bödeln* (1933; *The Hangman*), later dramatized, is a protest against human brutality. The play *Mannen utan själ* (1936; *The Man Without a Soul*) is also an expression of Lagerkvist's indignation with fascism. His most unusual play, sometimes called a "stage oratorio," is *Låt människan leva* (1949; *Let Man Live*), which deals with human readiness throughout history to judge and condemn others.

It was not until his novel *Dvärgen* (1944; THE DWARF) appeared that he had unqualified success with Swedish critics; it became his first best-seller. With the novel BARABBAS (1950) he achieved world recognition.

Lagerlöf \\'läg-ər-ˌlœf\\, Selma (Ottiliana Lovisa) (b. Nov. 20, 1858, Mårbacka, Swed.—d. March 16, 1940, Mårbacka)

Novelist whose work is rooted in legend and saga, and who in 1909 became the first woman and also the first Swedish writer to win the Nobel Prize for Literature.

Lagerlöf's first novel, *Gösta Berlings saga*, 2 vol. (1891), recounts the story of 12 cavaliers, a motley group led by Gösta Berling, a renegade priest of weak character but irresistible charm. A lyrical work set in her native Värmland, it played a part in the Swedish Romantic revival of the 1890s. In 1894 she

Nobel Foundation, Stockholm

published a collection of stories, *Osynliga länkar* (*Invisible Links*). After visiting Italy she published *Antikrists mirakler* (1897; *The Miracles of Antichrist*), a socialist novel about Sicily. Another collection, *En herrgårdssägen* (*Tales of a Manor*), is one of her finest works. A winter in Egypt and Palestine (1899–1900) inspired *Jerusalem*, 2 vol. (1901–02), which established her as the foremost Swedish novelist. In *Mårbacka* (1922), *Ett barns memoarer* (1930; *Memories of My Childhood*), and *Dagbok för Selma Lagerlöf* (1932; *The Diary of Selma Lagerlöf*), she recalled her childhood with subtle artistry. She also produced a Värmland trilogy: *Löwensköldska ringen* (1925; *The Ring of the Löwenskölds*), set in the 18th century; *Charlotte Löwensköld* (1925); and *Anna Svärd* (1928).

La Guma \\lä-'gü-mä\\, Alex, *in full* Justin Alexander La Guma (b. Feb. 20, 1925, Cape Town, S.Af.—d. Oct. 11, 1985, Havana, Cuba)   Black South African novelist and short-story writer whose characteristically brief works gain power through his restraint and his superb eye for detail.

La Guma's first story, *A Walk in the Night* (1962; enlarged edition with other stories, 1967), presents the struggle against oppression by characters in Cape Town's toughest district and, in particular, the moral dissolution of a young man who is unjustly fired from his job. Its general theme of protest is reiterated in *And a Threefold Cord* (1964), which depicts the degrading effect of apartheid, and in *The Stone-Country* (1967), which grew out of La Guma's experiences in prison for political activities. His novel *Time of the Butcherbird* appeared in 1979.

La Harpe or **Laharpe** \\lä-'ärp\\, Jean-François de, *surname also spelled* Delharpe \\de-'lärp\\ *or* Delaharpe \\de-lä-'ärp\\ (b. Nov. 20, 1739, Paris, Fr.—d. Feb. 11, 1803, Paris)   Critic and unsuccessful playwright who wrote severe and provocative criticisms and histories of French literature.

Orphaned at 9 and imprisoned at 19 for allegedly writing a satire against his protectors at college, La Harpe became a bitter man. Of many uninspired plays he wrote, the best are perhaps his first tragedy, *Warwick* (1763), and *Mélanie* (1770), a drama of pathos that was never performed. He wrote criticism for and was editor of the *Mercure de France*. In 1786, after being admitted to the Académie Française, he began to lecture at the newly established Lycée. His lectures, published as *Le Lycée, ou Cours de littérature ancienne or moderne*, 16 vol. (1799–1805), show La Harpe's clear understanding of 17th-century literature, as is also shown in his *Commentaire sur Racine* (1807). His *Oeuvres* were published in 1821.

Lahbabi \\läh-bä-'bē\\, Mohammed Aziz (b. Dec. 25, 1922, Fès, Mor.—d. Aug. 23, 1993, Rabat)   Moroccan novelist, poet, and philosopher.

Lahbabi received a doctorate in philosophy from the Sorbonne and then taught philosophy at the University of Rabat and at the University of Algiers. He also founded the Union of Arab Writers of the Maghrib, over which he presided, and he directed the review *Afâaq* ("Horizons").

Lahbabi attempted to forge a philosophy based on Muslim humanism. From this work came *Le Personnalisme musulman* (1964), an overview of Muslim thought, and *Du Clos à l'ouvert* (1961), a study in culture and civilization. Lahbabi published numerous literary essays, as well as many volumes of poetry and a novel, *Espoir vagabond* (1972; "Vagabond Hope").

lai   *see* LAY.

laisse \\'les, 'läs\\ [French, from Old French, part of a poem spoken or sung without interruption, a derivative of *laissier* to let, leave]   The irregular strophe of Old French poetry; especially, a strophe of the chansons de geste.

Laius \\'lä-əs\\   In Greek mythology, the father of OEDIPUS.

Lake poets   Group of English poets—William Wordsworth, Samuel Taylor Coleridge, and Robert Southey—who lived in the English Lake District of Cumberland and Westmorland (now Cumbria) at the beginning of the 19th century. Southey, however, did not subscribe in his views or work to the theories of poetry expressed by Wordsworth and Coleridge.

Lakṣmī or **Lakshmi** \\'lək-ˌshmē\\, *also called* Śrī \\'shrē\\   In Hindu mythology and religion, the goddess of wealth and good fortune. The wife of Vishnu, she is said to have taken different forms in order to be with him in each of his incarnations. In the most widely received account of Lakṣmī's birth, she rose from the churning of the milky ocean, seated on a lotus and holding another blossom in her hand.

L'Allegro \\lä-'leg-rō\\   Early lyric poem by John MILTON, written in 1631 and published in his *Poems* (1645). It was written in rhymed octosyllabics. A contrasting companion piece to his "Il Penseroso," "L'Allegro" invokes the goddess Mirth, with whom the poet wants to live, first in pastoral simplicity and then amid the "busy hum of men" in cities full of vitality.

Lamartine \\lä-mär-'tēn\\, Alphonse de (b. Oct. 21, 1790, Mâcon, Fr.—d. Feb. 28, 1869, Paris)   French poet and statesman whose lyrics in *Méditations poétiques* (1820) established him as one of the key figures in the Romantic movement in French literature.

Lamartine was educated at the college at Belley. He was drawn to the military, but after brief service for Louis XVIII, he turned to literature, writing tragedies in verse and elegies. In 1816 he met and fell in love with the brilliant but desperately ill Julie Charles. With her vast connections in Paris, she was able to help him find a position. After her death in December 1817, Lamartine, who had already dedicated many strophes to her (notably "Le Lac"), devoted new verses to her memory (particularly "Le Crucifix").

In 1820 he published *Méditations poétiques*, his first collection of poetry. Bringing both intimate and religious themes to French verse, it was immensely successful because of its new romantic tone and sincerity of feeling. Although Lamartine's vocabulary remained that of the somewhat faded rhetoric of the preceding century, the resonance of his sentences, the power of his rhythms, and his evident passion for life sharply contrasted with the poetry of the 18th century. Two years later Lamartine published *Nouvelles méditations poétiques* and *Mort de Socrates*. He was elected to the Académie Française in 1829, and the following year he published the two volumes of *Harmonies poétiques et religieuses*, filled with religious enthusiasm. That same year Lamartine entered politics. After two unsuccessful attempts he was elected deputy in 1833. Within the next few years he published two long poems that he considered to be fragments of larger works, *Jocelyn* (1836) and *La Chute d'un ange* (1838; "The Fall of an Angel").

After a collection published in 1839 under the title *Recueillements poétiques* ("Poetic Meditations"), Lamartine became more active in politics. He spoke for the working classes and believed that a revolution was inevitable. After the revolution of Feb. 24, 1848, the Second Republic was proclaimed in Paris, and Lamartine became, in effect, head of the provisional government. In April 1848 he was elected to the National Assembly. As the months passed and Lamartine proved to be, as he had claimed, the spokesman for the working people and not the clever manipulator and placater the wealthier citizens had hoped he would be, he was thrown out of office and the revolt crushed.

A broken man, Lamartine entered the twilight of his life. He was 60 years old in 1850, and his debts were enormous. For 20 years he struggled desperately, though in vain, against bankruptcy, publishing novels, poetry, and historical works, but he died nearly forgotten by his contemporaries.

Lamb \ˈlam\, Charles (b. Feb. 10, 1775, London, Eng.—d. Dec. 27, 1834, Edmonton, Middlesex) English essayist and critic, best known for his series of miscellaneous "Essays of Elia," but also among the greatest of English letter writers and a perceptive literary critic.

Lamb left school just before the age of 15 and in 1792 found employment as a clerk at India House, remaining there until his retirement in 1825. From 1796 Lamb was guardian of his sister, Mary, who in a fit of madness (which was to prove recurrent) had killed their mother.

Lamb's first appearances in print were as a poet. He also wrote *A Tale of Rosamund Gray* (1798), a prose romance, and *John Woodvil* (1802), a poetic tragedy. None of these works brought him much acclaim. "The Old Familiar Faces" (1789) remains his best-known poem, although "On an Infant Dying As Soon As It Was Born" (1828) is considered to be his finest poetic achievement.

Lamb and his sister published *Tales from Shakespear* (1807), a retelling of the plays for children, and *Mrs. Leicester's School* (1809), a collection of stories supposedly told by schoolchildren. In 1808 Lamb published a children's version of the *Odyssey*, called *The Adventures of Ulysses*. Lamb also published an anthology of selections from Elizabethan dramas and contributed critical papers on William Shakespeare and on the artist William Hogarth to the quarterly *The Reflector*.

Lamb's greatest achievements in prose were the essays he wrote under the pseudonym Elia for *London Magazine*. They are almost wholly autobiographical (though often he appropriated to himself the experiences of others). The persona of Elia predominates in nearly all of the essays. Lamb's style, therefore, is highly personal and mannered, its function being to "create" and delineate this persona with humor and sometimes pathos. The first essays were published separately in 1823; a second series appeared, as *The Last Essays of Elia*, in 1833.

Lamb \ˈlam\, Mary (Ann) (b. Dec. 3, 1764, London, Eng.—d. May 20, 1847, London) English writer known for *Tales from Shakespear* (1807), written with her brother Charles.

From an early age Lamb helped support her family by doing needlework. Her mother, an invalid, was entirely dependent on her care. In 1796, in a fit of madness, Lamb stabbed and killed her mother. She was declared temporarily insane and placed under the guardianship of her brother Charles. For the rest of her life she was subject to recurrent bouts of mental illness.

For *Tales from Shakespear*, a collection of prose adaptations of William Shakespeare's plays, intended for children, Mary wrote the preface and the 14 comedies and histories, and Charles contributed the 6 tragedies; only Charles's name, however, appeared on the title page. In 1809 Charles and Mary published *Mrs. Leicester's School*, a book of children's stories, and *Poetry for Children*.

lament \lə-ˈment\ A nonnarrative poem expressing deep grief or sorrow over a personal loss. The form developed as part of the oral tradition along with heroic poetry and exists in most languages. Examples include *Deor's Lament*, an early Anglo-Saxon poem, and the ancient Sumerian "Lament for the Destruction of Ur." *Compare* COMPLAINT; DIRGE; ELEGY.

Lament for the Death of a Bullfighter Four-part poem by Federico GARCÍA LORCA, written in Spanish as "Llanto por Ignacio Sánchez Mejías" ("Lament for Ignacio Sánchez Mejías") and published in 1935. Each part of the poem is written in a different poetic meter, and each addresses a different aspect of the goring and death of a bullfighter who had been Lorca's friend. A haunting and powerful elegy, it contains the famous, insistent refrain "A las cinco de la tarde" ("At five in the afternoon").

Lamia \ˈlā-mē-ə\ In classical mythology, a female demon who devoured children. According to late myths, she was a queen of Libya who was beloved by Zeus. When Hera robbed her of her children from this union, Lamia killed every child she could get into her power. She was also known to seduce young men in order to devour them.

Lamia \ˈlā-mē-ə\ Narrative poem in rhymed couplets by John KEATS, published in 1820 in *Lamia, Isabella, The Eve of St. Agnes, and Other Poems*. Keats took the story from *Anatomy of Melancholy* (1621) by Robert Burton, who had found it in a work by the ancient Greek writer Flavius Philostratus.

In the poem, Lamia and Lycius fall in love. At their bridal feast Lycius' friend Apollonius recognizes Lamia as an evil sorceress and calls her by name. Lamia screams and vanishes. Heartbroken, Lycius falls dead.

Lamming \ˈlam-iŋ\, George (William) (b. June 8, 1927, Carrington Village, near Bridgetown, Barbados) West Indian novelist and essayist who wrote about decolonization and reconstruction in the Caribbean nations.

Lamming worked in Trinidad from 1946 to 1950 before settling in England. His highly acclaimed first novel, *In the Castle of My Skin* (1953), is an autobiographical bildungsroman set against the backdrop of burgeoning nationalism in the British colonies of the Caribbean in the 1930s and '40s.

Lamming continued to study decolonization in his succeeding three novels: *The Emigrants* (1954), *Of Age and Innocence* (1958), and *Season of Adventure* (1960). *The Pleasures of Exile* (1960) is a collection of essays that examines Caribbean politics, race, and culture. Lamming's later novels include *Water with Berries* (1971) and *Natives of My Person* (1971). His poetry and short stories were published in various anthologies, and *Conversations*, a volume of essays and interviews, was published in 1992.

Lamontagne-Beauregard \lä-mōⁿ-tánʸ-bō-rə-'gär\, Blanche (b. 1889, Les Escoumains, Que., Can.—d. 1958, Canada) French-Canadian poet who is recognized as the first important female poet of French Canada.

Lamontagne-Beauregard's mature writing extols her homeland, the Gaspé Peninsula, in a robust, emotional style. Her collections of lyric poetry include *Visions Gaspésiennes* (1913; "Views of the Gaspé"), *Par nos champs et nos rives* (1917; "Through Our Fields and Shores"), *Ma Gaspésie* (1928; "My Gaspé"), and *Moisson nouvelle* (1926; "New Harvest").

L'Amour \lä-'mòr, -'mùr\, Louis, *original name* Louis Dearborn LaMoore, *pseudonyms* Tex Burns \'bərnz\ *and* Jim Mayo \'mā-ō\ (b. March 22, 1908, Jamestown, N.D., U.S.—d. June 10, 1988, Los Angeles, Calif.)   American writer, prolific and best-selling author of more than 100 books, mostly formula westerns with authentic portrayals of frontier life.

L'Amour began his career as a writer in the 1940s. He stopped using pseudonyms after *Hondo* was published in 1953. More than 30 of his books—including *Kilkenny* (1954), *The Burning Hills* (1956), *Guns of the Timberland* (1955), and *How the West Was Won* (1963)—formed the basis of films. His books sold 200 million copies in 20 languages.

Lampman \'lamp-mən\, Archibald (b. Nov. 17, 1861, Morpeth, Ont. [Canada]—d. Feb. 10, 1899, Ottawa)   Important Canadian poet of the Confederation group, whose most characteristic work sensitively records the feelings evoked by scenes and incidents of the outdoors.

Lampman worked for the Canadian civil service from 1883 until his death. He collaborated with two other Ottawa poets in the writing of a weekly column, "At the Mermaid Inn," in the Toronto *Globe* (1892–93). Repelled by the mechanization of urban life, Lampman wrote nature poems, eventually publishing two volumes of verse, *Among the Millet and Other Poems* (1888) and *Lyrics of Earth* (1893).

lampoon \lam-'pün\ \[French *lampon,* probably from *lampons!* let us gulp down! (a frequent refrain in 17th-century French satirical poems)]   A virulent satire in prose or verse that is a gratuitous and sometimes unjust and malicious attack on an individual. Although the term came into use in the 17th century from the French, examples of the lampoon are found as early as the 3rd century BC in the plays of Aristophanes, who lampooned Euripides in *Frogs* and Socrates in *Clouds*. In English literature the form was particularly popular during the Restoration and the 18th century, as exemplified in the lampoons of John Dryden, Thomas Brown, and John Wilkes.

Lancelot or **Launcelot** \'lan-sə-,lät, -lət\, *also called* Lancelot of the Lake, *French* Lancelot du Lac.   One of the greatest knights in ARTHURIAN LEGEND; in many accounts he is linked with Guinevere (Arthur's queen), and he was the father of the pure knight Sir Galahad.

Lancelot first appeared as one of Arthur's knights in Chrétien de Troyes's 12th-century romance of *Erec*, and the same author later made him one of the heroes in *Lancelot, ou Le Chevalier de la charrette*, which retold a legend about Guinevere's abduction, making Lancelot her rescuer and lover. The work also mentions Lancelot's upbringing by a fairy in a lake, a story that received fuller treatment in the German poem *Lanzelet*. These two themes were developed further in the Prose *Lancelot* of the great 13th-century Vulgate cycle. According to that work, after the death of his father, King Ban of Benoic, Lancelot was carried off by the enchantress Vivien, the Lady of the Lake, who in time sent him to Arthur's court. Her careful education of Lancelot, combined with the inspiring force of his love for Guinevere, produced a knight who was the very model of chivalry.

In later branches of the cycle, Lancelot was displaced as the perfect knight by his son, Sir Galahad. Lancelot's adulterous love for the queen not only causes him to fail in the quest for the Holy Grail, but it also sets in motion the fatal chain of events that brings about the destruction of the knightly fellowship of the Round Table.

In medieval English romance, Lancelot played a leading role in the late 14th-century poem *Le Morte Arthur* and in Sir Thomas Malory's 15th-century prose work *Le Morte Darthur*.

Landnámabók \'län-naù-mä-,bōk\ ("Book of Settlements"), *also called* Landnáma.   Unique Icelandic genealogical record, probably originally compiled in the early 12th century by Ari Thorgilsson the Learned, though it exists in several later versions. It lists the names of 400 original settlers of Iceland, their Norwegian origins, their descendants, and their landholdings. Occasionally the lists of names are enlivened by anecdotes of marriages or feuds or by brief but vivid character sketches. The *Landnámabók* served as the source for many Icelandic sagas.

Landon \'lan-dən\, Letitia Elizabeth, *also called* L.E.L. (b. Aug. 14, 1802, London, Eng.—d. Oct. 15, 1838, Gold Coast Colony [now Ghana])   English poet and novelist who, at a time when women were conventionally restricted in their themes, wrote of passionate love. She is remembered for verse that reveals her lively intelligence.

Landon's first volume of verse came out in 1821. It and the eight collections that followed were extremely popular, and she was in great demand as a contributor to magazines and giftbooks. Her four novels (published 1831–42) were also successful. In 1838 she married George Maclean, then the chief administrator of the Cape Coast settlement (now in Ghana). She died of poisoning, presumably by accident, soon after her arrival in Africa.

Landor \'lan-,dòr\, Walter Savage (b. Jan. 30, 1775, Warwick, Warwickshire, Eng.—d. Sept. 17, 1864, Florence, Italy)   English writer best remembered for *Imaginary Conversations*, prose dialogues between historical personages.

Landor was educated at Rugby School and at the University of Oxford, both of which he left after disagreement with the authorities. A proficient classicist from boyhood, he wrote many of his English works originally in Latin. He wrote lyrics, plays, and heroic poems, but *Imaginary Conversations* (vol. 1 and 2, 1824; vol. 3, 1828; and thereafter sporadically to 1853), was his great work.

Landsmål or **Landsmaal**   *see* NYNORSK.

Landstad \'län-,stä\, Magnus Brostrup (b. Oct. 7, 1802, Måsøy, Nor.—d. Oct. 8, 1880, Kristiania [now Oslo])   Pastor and poet who published the first collection of authentic Norwegian traditional ballads (1853).

After ordination, Landstad served in several parishes before going to Christiania (later Kristiania), where he remained the rest of his life. His *Norske folkeviser* ("Norwegian Folk Ballad") revolves around the adventures of trolls, heroes, knights, and gods. Henrik Ibsen drew many of the themes for his early dramas from the Landstad collection. Landstad's national hymnal, which included about 50 of his own hymns, was completed in 1861.

Lang \\'laŋ\\, Andrew (b. March 31, 1844, Selkirk, Selkirkshire, Scot.—d. July 20, 1912, Banchory, Aberdeenshire) Scottish scholar and man of letters noted for his collections of fairy tales and translations of Homer.

Educated at St. Andrews University and at Balliol College, Oxford, Lang held an open fellowship at Merton College until 1875, when he moved to London. He quickly became famous for his critical articles in *The Daily News* and other papers. He displayed talent as a poet and as a novelist, but he received much acclaim for his 12-volume collection of fairy tales, beginning with *The Blue Fairy Book* (1889) and ending with *The Lilac Fairy Book* (1910). His own fairy tales include *The Gold of Fairnilee* (1888), *Prince Prigio* (1889), and *Prince Ricardo of Pantouflia* (1893).

Lang also did important pioneering work in such volumes as *Custom and Myth* (1884) and *Myth, Ritual and Religion* (1887). He later turned to history and historical mysteries, notably *Pickle the Spy* (1897), *A History of Scotland from the Roman Occupation*, 4 vol. (1900–07), *Historical Mysteries* (1904), and *The Maid of France* (1908). His lifelong devotion to Homer produced well-known prose translations of the *Odyssey* (1879), in collaboration with S.H. Butcher, and of the *Iliad* (1883), with Walter Leaf and Ernest Myers. He defended the theory of the unity of Homeric literature and wrote *World of Homer* (1910).

Lange \\'län-ge\\, Antoni (b. *c.* 1861, Warsaw [Poland]—d. March 17, 1929, Warsaw) Polish poet, literary critic, and translator who was a leader of the Young Poland movement, a group of Neoromantic writers.

Lange studied in Paris, and after his return to Warsaw he became one of the leading personalities in literary circles. He was one of the first to popularize Indian philosophy and literature in Poland. In his *Studia z literatury francuskiej* (1897; "Studies on French Literature") he both wrote about the French Parnassians and Symbolists and made excellent translations of their works into Polish. His own poems did not win him recognition.

Langer \\'läŋ-ər\\, František (b. March 3, 1888, Prague [now in Czech Republic]—d. Aug. 2, 1965, Prague) Physician and writer, one of the outstanding Czech dramatists of the interwar period.

Langer studied medicine in Prague and wrote a collection of short stories and two unsuccessful plays before joining the Austrian army as a surgeon. During World War I, he was taken prisoner by the Russians (1916) and subsequently joined the Czechoslovak Legion, which fought the Bolsheviks in the Russian Civil War. After the war, he served in the medical corps of the Czech army and continued his literary career.

Langer achieved his greatest success with *Velbloud uchem jehly* (1923; *The Camel Through the Needle's Eye*), a comedy about working-class life. Of his later writing, only *Jízdní hlídka* (1935; "The Cavalry Watch") compared with his earlier successes; it was based upon his experiences in the legion. The postwar communist government did not allow him to publish new work until the late 1950s.

Langhorne \\'laŋ-ˌhȯrn\\, John (b. March 1735, Winton, Somerset, Eng.—d. April 1, 1779, Blagdon, Somerset) Poet and English translator of the Greek biographer Plutarch. Langhorne's work anticipates that of George Crabbe in its description of the problems facing the poor. His best work is perhaps *The Country Justice* (3 parts, 1774–77). His translation of Plutarch, written with his brother William, appeared in 1770. Langhorne also contributed reviews to *The Monthly Review* (1761–79) and edited the poems of William Collins (1765).

Langland \\'laŋ-lənd\\, William, *also called* Langley \\'laŋ-lē\\ (b. *c.* 1330—d. *c.* 1400) Presumed author of one of the greatest examples of Middle English alliterative poetry, generally known as PIERS PLOWMAN, an allegorical work with a complex variety of religious themes.

Little is known of Langland's life, but he clearly had a deep knowledge of medieval theology and was interested in the asceticism of St. Bernard of Clairvaux.

language \\'laŋ-gwij\\ Form or manner of verbal expression; more specifically, the style or characteristic mode of expression of an individual speaker or writer.

langue \\'läⁿ, *French* 'läⁿg\\ Language viewed abstractly as a system of forms and conventions used for communication in a community. It is contrasted with *parole*, meaning a language used as a specific individual usage, or a linguistic act. The use of the French word *langue* in this sense was introduced by the linguist Ferdinand de Saussure.

Languish, Lydia \\'lid-ē-ə-'laŋ-gwish\\ Fictional character, the sentimental heroine of Richard Brinsley Sheridan's comic play THE RIVALS.

Lanier \\lə-'nir\\, Sidney (b. Feb. 3, 1842, Macon, Ga., U.S.—d. Sept. 7, 1881, Lynn, N.C.) American musician and poet whose verse often suggests the rhythms and thematic development of music.

In 1867 Lanier published his first book, the novel *Tiger-Lilies*, a mixture of German philosophy, Southern traditional romance, and his own experiences as a soldier in the American Civil War. In 1873 he accepted a position as first flutist in the Peabody Orchestra, Baltimore, Md., and he also played private concerts. With numerous poems already published in magazines, he wrote several potboilers.

"Corn" (1875), treating agricultural conditions in the South, and "The Symphony" (1875), treating industrial conditions in the North, brought national recognition. Adverse criticism of his "Centennial Meditation" in 1876 launched him on an investigation of verse technique that he continued until his death. *The Song of the Chattahoochee*, a volume of poems, was published in 1877. Appointed lecturer at Johns Hopkins University in 1879, he delivered a series of lectures on verse technique, the early English poets, and the English novel, later published as *The Science of English Verse* (1880), *Shakspere and His Forerunners* (1902), and *The English Novel* (1883; rev. ed., 1897).

Laocoön \\lā-'äk-ō-än\\ In Greek legend, a seer and a priest of the god Apollo. Laocoön offended Apollo by breaking his oath of celibacy and begetting children. Thus, while preparing to sacrifice a bull, Laocoön and his twin sons, Antiphas and Thymbraeus (also called Melanthus), were crushed to death by two great sea serpents sent by Apollo. An additional reason for his punishment was that he had warned the Trojans against accepting the wooden horse left by the Greeks. The legend found its most famous literary expression in Virgil's *Aeneid*.

Laomedon \\lā-'äm-ə-dän\\ Legendary king of Troy who reneged on promises to Apollo and Poseidon, who punished him, and to Heracles, who came to his aid. Heracles eventually captured Troy and killed Laomedon and all his sons except Priam.

Lao She \\'laù-'shə\\, *pseudonym of* Shu Sheyou \\'shü-'shə-'yō\\, *original name* Shu Qingchun \\'chiŋ-'chùn\\ (b. Feb. 3, 1899, Beijing, China—d. October 24, 1966, China?) Chinese author of humorous, satiric novels and short stories and, after the onset of the Sino-Japanese War, of lesser patriotic and propagandistic plays and novels.

Lao She served as principal of an elementary school at age 17 and soon worked his way up to district supervisor. In 1924 he went to England, teaching Mandarin Chinese to support himself. By reading the novels of Charles Dickens to improve his English, Lao She was inspired to write his first novel, which enjoyed some success. He also completed two additional humorous, action-packed novels, in which he developed the theme that the strong, hard-working individual could reverse the tide of stagnation and corruption plaguing China.

Lao She returned to China in 1931 and continued to write. In *Niu Tianci zhuan* (1934; "The Life of Niu Tianci"), he reversed his individualist theme and stressed the futility of the individual's struggle against society as a whole. His new theme found its clearest expression in his masterpiece, *Luotuo Xiangzi* (1936; "Camel Xiangzi"), the tragic story of the trials of a ricksha puller in Beijing. *Rickshaw Boy* (1945), an unauthorized and bowdlerized English translation with a happy ending, became a U.S. best-seller.

During the war Lao She headed the All-China Anti-Japanese Writers Federation, encouraging writers to produce patriotic and propagandistic literature. His own works were inferior to his earlier productions and infused with propaganda. In 1946–47 Lao She traveled to the United States on a cultural grant, lecturing and overseeing the translation of several of his novels, including *The Yellow Storm* (1951) and his last novel, *The Drum Singers* (1952), which never appeared in Chinese. Upon his return to China he continued to write propagandistic plays.

Lapham, Silas \'sī-ləs-'lap-əm\ Fictional character, the self-made protagonist of William Dean Howells' novel THE RISE OF SILAS LAPHAM.

Laputa \lə-'pyū-tə\ Fictional place in Jonathan Swift's novel GULLIVER'S TRAVELS, a floating island encountered by Gulliver during his third voyage. The island is populated by philosophers who are so absorbed by abstract thoughts that they are followed around by "flappers," or people who recall the philosophers to reality by flapping inflated bladders at their heads.

Larbaud \lar-'bō\, Valery(-Nicolas) (b. Aug. 29, 1881, Vichy, Fr.—d. Feb. 2, 1957, Vichy) French novelist and critic, an erudite cosmopolitan who became a literary intermediary between France and other European countries.

Larbaud's personal fortune permitted him a life of travel and leisure. His novels and stories are largely based on personal experiences. *Fermina Marquez* (1911) deals with the effects of the visit of a beautiful South American girl to a boys' school, and *A.O. Barnabooth* (1913) is the journal and verse of a South American millionaire—Larbaud's alter ego—a cultivated, sensuous adventurer. *Enfantines* (1918) is a collection of nostalgic childhood reminiscences, and *Amants, heureux amants* (1923; "Lovers, Happy Lovers") deals with men and women in love. His translations include works of Sir Thomas Browne, Samuel Butler, Walt Whitman, and James Joyce. He also wrote two volumes of criticism of English and French literature.

Lardner \'lärd-nər\, Ring, *in full* Ringgold Wilmer Lardner (b. March 6, 1885, Niles, Mich., U.S.—d. Sept. 25, 1933, East Hampton, N.Y.) American writer, one of the most gifted American satirists and storytellers.

Lardner began his writing career in 1905 as a reporter for the *South Bend* (Ind.) *Times*. He went on to work at newspapers in Chicago, where he established a reputation as a sportswriter specializing in baseball stories. From 1913 to 1919 he wrote a daily column for the *Chicago Tribune* and from 1919 to 1927 a humorous weekly column for the Bell syndicate. Meanwhile, in 1914, he had begun publishing fiction and had won popular success with his comic stories about baseball player Jack Keefe, some of which were collected in *You Know Me Al* (1916).

Lardner moved to New York in 1919, and he first attracted serious critical interest with his collection *How to Write Short Stories* (1924). Some of Lardner's best stories—"My Roomy," "Champion," "The Golden Honeymoon," and "Some Like Them Cold"—appeared in the 1924 collection. Equally good was his next collection, *The Love Nest and Other Stories* (1926). He collaborated on two plays that had Broadway runs: *Elmer the Great* (1928) with George M. Cohan and *June Moon* (1929) with George S. Kaufman. His spoof autobiography, *The Story of a Wonder Man*, appeared in 1927.

Larivey \la-rē-'ve\, Pierre de (b. *c.* 1540, Champagne, Fr.—d. Feb. 12, 1619, Troyes) Chief French comic dramatist of the 16th century. Larivey's successful *Comédies facétieuses* (1579, 1611; "Merry Comedies") were free adaptations from Italian playwrights, with French settings and idioms added. These comedies of intrigue were popular for their sudden twists in plot, swift reversals of fortune, and realistic, racy language. Molière used situations from Larivey's *Les Esprits* ("The Ghosts") and *Le Fidèle* ("The Faithful") for his *L'Avare* (*The Miser*) and *Les Femmes savantes* (*The Learned Ladies*).

Larkin \'lär-kin\, Philip (Arthur) (b. Aug. 9, 1922, Coventry, Warwickshire, Eng.—d. Dec. 2, 1985, Kingston upon Hull, Humberside) Most representative and highly regarded of the poets who gave expression to a clipped, antiromantic sensibility prevalent in English verse in the 1950s.

Larkin was educated at Oxford University on a scholarship, an experience that provided material for his first novel, *Jill* (1946; rev. ed., 1964). Another novel, *A Girl in Winter*, followed in 1947. His first and second books of poetry, *The North Ship* and *XX Poems*, were published at his own expense in 1945 and 1951, respectively. Larkin's reputation spread with the publication of *The Less Deceived* (1955), his third volume of verse.

Larkin became librarian at the University of Hull, Yorkshire, in 1955. He was jazz critic for *The Daily Telegraph* from 1961 to 1971, and his writings on jazz were collected in *All What Jazz: A Record Diary 1961–68* (1970). *The Whitsun Weddings* (1964), *High Windows* (1974), and *Aubade* (1980) are his later volumes of poetry. He also edited the *Oxford Book of Twentieth-Century English Verse* (1973). *Required Writing* (1982) is a collection of miscellaneous essays. A biography and a collection of Larkin's letters, both published in 1993, were controversial because they revealed aspects of Larkin's views and character that many readers found offensive.

La Roche \lä-'ròsh\, Sophie von, *original surname* Gutermann \'gü-tər-,män\ (b. Dec. 6, 1731, Kaufbeuren, Bavaria [Germany]—d. Feb. 18, 1807, Offenbach, Hesse) German writer whose first and most important work, *Geschichte des Fräuleins von Sternheim* (1771; *History of Lady Sophia Sternheim*), was the first German novel written by a woman and is considered to be among the best European works of the period.

From 1771 La Roche maintained a literary salon in Ehrenbreitstein to which the young J.W. von Goethe belonged. In that year her close friend and cousin, the well-known writer Christoph Martin Wieland, edited and published her first novel. Fräulein von Sternheim's melancholy moods and the "confessional" aspect lent to the novel by its epistolary form won it fame. This, like all La Roche's works, is imbued with the rational spirit of the Enlightenment and shows her interest in economic and social problems, including women's education.

La Rochefoucauld \lä-ròsh-fü-'kō\, François VI, Duke (duc) de, *also called* (until 1650) Prince de Marcillac (b. Sept. 15, 1613, Paris, Fr.—d. March 16/17, 1680, Paris) French classical author who became the leading exponent of the *maxime*, a French literary form of epigram that expresses a harsh or paradoxical truth with brevity.

La Rochefoucauld joined the army at an early age and was wounded in several battles. Though he later became involved in the Fronde, a series of revolts against the government that took place between 1648 and 1653, he eventually won his way back into royal favor. He became a member of a group of intellectuals whose gatherings were enlivened by a new game that consisted of discussing epigrams on manners and behavior, expressed in the briefest, most pungent manner possible. The care with which La Rochefoucauld kept notes and versions of his thoughts on the moral and intellectual subjects of the game is clear from the surviving manuscripts. When the clandestine publication of one of them in Holland forced him to publish under his own name, it was clear that he had satisfied public taste: five editions of the MAXIMES were to appear within his lifetime, the first in 1665.

La Rochefoucauld has been called an Epicurean but his imaginative insights attached him to no doctrine. Like Michel de Montaigne and Blaise Pascal, he was aware of the mystery surrounding human beings that dwarfs their efforts and mocks their knowledge, of the many things concerning themselves of which humans know nothing. All these insights seem common to the French classical school of which he is so brilliant a member. These insights also accounted for his fame and influence on his disciples: in England, Lord Chesterfield and Thomas Hardy; in Germany, Friedrich Nietzsche and Georg Christoph Lichtenberg; in France, Stendhal, Charles-Augustin Sainte-Beuve, and André Gide.

Though he did a considerable amount of writing over the years La Rochefoucauld actually published only two works, his *Mémoires* and the *Maximes*. In addition, some 150 letters have been collected along with 19 short pieces now known as *Réflexions diverses*.

Larra \'lär-rä\, Mariano José de, *surname in full* Larra y Sánchez de Castro \ē-'sän-chäth-thä-'käs-trō\ (b. March 24, 1809, Madrid, Spain—d. Feb. 13, 1837, Madrid) Spanish journalist and satirist who attacked contemporary society for its social habits, literary tastes, and political ineptitude.

In 1828 Larra published a newspaper, *El duende satírico del día*, for which he wrote his first journalistic essays. He later published another paper, *El pobrecito hablador* (1832–33), and then became drama critic for *La revista española*, under the pen name Fígaro. In 1834 his play *Macías* was produced and he published his only novel, *El doncel de Don Enrique el doliente* ("The Mourner Don Enrique's Page").

Larra's personal life was filled with unhappiness, and his work became increasingly bitter and pessimistic. He married early and unhappily in 1829 and committed suicide after being rejected by a woman with whom he had had a long affair. Unlike most other *costumbristas* (writers of prose sketches of the customs of society), who took a nostalgic approach, Larra exposed in his mordant sketches the pretentiousness and absurdity of contemporary Spanish society. In his journalistic essays and articles he directed his trenchant wit against almost every aspect of Spain's political, social, and intellectual life. The analytical depth and penetration of his criticism and his reforming zeal had a morally constructive emphasis; these qualities prompted the Generation of '98 to hail Larra as a forerunner.

Larreta \lär-'rä-tä\, Enrique Rodríguez (b. March 4, 1875, Buenos Aires, Arg.—d. July 7, 1961, Buenos Aires) Argentine writer famous for the historical novel *La gloria de Don Ramiro* (1908; *The Glory of Don Ramiro*).

Larreta spent five years researching his novel, and he prided himself on its historical accuracy. His other works include *Zogoibi* (1926; "The Unfortunate One"); *Gerardo, o la torre de las damas* (1953; "Gerardo, or the Tower of the Ladies"); its sequel, *En la pampa* (1955; "On the Pampa"); and *La naranja* (1948; "The Orange"), a volume of memoirs and essays.

Larsen \'lär-sən\, Nella, *married surname* Imes \'īmz\ (b. April 13, 1891, Chicago, Ill., U.S.—d. March 30, 1964, New York, N.Y.) Novelist and short-story writer of the Harlem Renaissance.

Larsen was born to a Danish mother and a West Indian father who died when she was two years old. Her first story was published in 1926. Her first novel, *Quicksand* (1928), concerns a young, headstrong biracial woman who seeks love, acceptance, and a sense of purpose, only to be mired in an emotional morass of her own creation. Her second novel, *Passing* (1929), centers on two light-skinned women, one of whom, Irene, marries a black man and lives in Harlem, while the other, Clare, marries a white man but cannot reject her black cultural ties. In 1930 Larsen became the first black woman to be awarded a Guggenheim fellowship. She never published again.

Larsen, Wolf \'wùlf-'lär-sən\ Fictional character, a vicious ship captain in the novel THE SEA-WOLF by Jack London.

La Sale or **La Salle** \lä-'säl\, Antoine de (b. *c.* 1386, near Arles, Provence [France]—d. *c.* 1460) French writer chiefly remembered for his *Petit Jehan de Saintré* (1456; *Little John of Saintre*), a romance marked by a great gift for the observation of court manners and a keen sense of comic situation and dialogue. Modern criticism ascribes an important place to *Saintré* in the development of French prose fiction.

From 1400 to 1448 La Sale served the dukes of Anjou. The Angevin claims to the kingdom of Sicily took him repeatedly into Italy, and his didactic works contain several accounts of his unusual and picturesque experiences there. La Sale visited the Sibyl's mountain near Norcia in Italy, seat of the legend later attached to the German poet Tannhäuser; he relates the legend in great detail in his *Paradis de la reine Sibylle*.

La Sale became governor of the sons of Louis of Luxembourg, count of St. Pol, in 1448. At his patron's estate he wrote *La Salle* (1451), a collection of moral anecdotes; *Le Petit Jehan de Saintré*; *Du Réconfort à Madame de Fresne* (1457; "For the Consolation of Madame de Fresne"), on the death of her young son; and a *Lettre sur les tournois* (1459; "A Letter on the Tournaments").

Lasker-Schüler \'läs-kər-'shü-lər\, Else, *original surname* Schüler (b. Feb. 11, 1869, Elberfeld, Ger.—d. Jan. 22, 1945, Jerusalem, Palestine) Eccentric German writer chiefly noted for her lyric poetry.

Lasker-Schüler frequented Berlin's avant-garde literary circles, and her lyric poems and short stories began appearing in periodicals. Her first book, a poetry collection entitled *Styx* (1902), was followed by *Meine Wunder* (1911; "My Miracles") and several other volumes of lyric poetry. Her other important works are the play *Die Wupper* (1909; "Wupper River"), the autobiographical novel *Mein Herz* (1912; "My Heart"), and the short stories collected in *Der Prinz von Theben* (1914; "The Prince of Thebes") and *Der Wunderrabbiner von Barcelona* (1921; "The Wonder Rabbi of Barcelona").

Lasker-Schüler's poems exploit a rich vein of fantasy and symbolism and alternate between pathos and ecstasy. Many of her short stories reinterpret tales from *The Thousand and One Nights*.

Last Chronicle of Barset, The \'bär-sət\ The final Barsetshire novel by Anthony TROLLOPE, published serially in 1866–67 and in book form in 1867. It is a satirical view of a materialistic society. The principal figures of the novel appeared in earlier BARSETSHIRE NOVELS. It is the story—with elaborate complications—of a poor curate accused of stealing £20.

Last Leaf, The Short story by O. HENRY, published in 1907 in his collection *The Trimmed Lamp and Other Stories*.

"The Last Leaf" concerns Johnsy, a young woman who is seriously ill with pneumonia. She believes that when the ivy vine on the wall outside her window loses all its leaves she will also die. Her neighbor Behrman, an artist, tricks her by painting a leaf on the wall. Johnsy recovers, but Behrman, who caught pneumonia while painting the leaf, dies.

Last of the Mohicans, The \mō-'hē-kənz\ (*in full* The Last of the Mohicans: A Narrative of 1757) The second and most popular novel in the series THE LEATHER-STOCKING TALES by James Fenimore COOPER, first published in two volumes in 1826. In terms of narrative order, it also is the second novel in the series, taking place in 1757, during the French and Indian War. Its principal character is Natty Bumppo, also called Hawkeye, now in middle life and at the height of his powers. The story tells of brutal battles with the Iroquois and their French allies, cruel captures, narrow escapes, and revenge. The beauty of the unspoiled wilderness and sorrow at its disappearance, symbolized in Hawkeye's Mohican Indian friends, the last of their tribe, are important themes of the novel.

Last Tycoon, The Unfinished novel by F. Scott FITZGERALD, published posthumously in 1941. As edited by Edmund Wilson, it contained six completed chapters, an abridged conclusion, and some of Fitzgerald's notes. The work is an indictment of the Hollywood film industry, where Fitzgerald had had a disappointing career as a screenwriter.

Monroe Stahr is a studio executive who has worked obsessively to produce high-quality films without regard to their financial prospects. He takes a personal interest in every aspect of the studio. At age 35 he is almost burned out, and the novel is the story of how he loses control of the studio and his life.

La Taille \lä-'täy\, Jean de (b. *c.* 1540, Bondaroy, Fr.—d. *c.* 1607, Bondaroy) Poet and dramatist who helped to effect the transition from native French drama to classical tragedy.

While studying in Paris, La Taille came under the influence of Pierre de Ronsard and Joachim du Bellay. His chief poems are a satire, *Le Courtisan retiré* ("The Retired Courtier"), and *Le Prince nécessaire*, a portrait of an ideal monarch. A collection of his works appeared in 1572, including his tragedy *Saül le furieux* (1562) and *De l'art de la tragédie*, the most important piece of French dramatic criticism of its time; in it La Taille deprecated the native drama and insisted on the Senecan model. A second collection (1573) included a lesser tragedy, *La Famine, ou les Gabéonites*, plagiarizing Seneca's *Troades*, and two comedies, *Le Négromant*, translated freely from Ludovico Ariosto, and *Les Corrivaux* ("The Rivals"), remarkable for its colloquial prose dialogue.

Latini \lä-'tē-nē\, Brunetto (b. *c.* 1220, Florence? [Italy]—d. 1294, Florence) Florentine scholar who helped disseminate ideas that were fundamental to the development of early Italian poetry.

Between 1262 and 1266 Latini wrote a prose encyclopedia in French, *Li Livres dou trésor* (*The Book of the Treasure*), and an abridged version in Italian verse called the *Tesoretto*. The work had a profound influence on an entire generation, including Guido Cavalcanti, Forese Donati, and Dante.

Li Livres dou Trésor is a repository of classical citation. It contains one of the first translations in a modern European vernacular of Aristotle's *Ethics*. On almost every question or topic of philosophy, ethics, and politics Latini freely quotes from Cicero and Seneca. Almost as frequently, when treating questions of government, he quotes from the Book of Proverbs, as Dante was to do. Latini's legacy includes the appreciation of Cicero (who was seen as not only preaching but as fully exemplifying the intellectual as citizen), the love of glory, and the quest for fame through a wholehearted devotion to excelling.

Latinus \lə-'tī-nəs\ In Roman mythology, king of the aborigines in Latium and eponymous hero of the Latin race. Latinus was a shadowy personality who was perhaps invented to explain the origin of Rome and its relations with Latium. According to the *Aeneid*, the hero Aeneas landed at the mouth of the Tiber River and was welcomed by Latinus, the peaceful ruler whose daughter Lavinia he ultimately married.

Latona *see* LETO.

Lattimore \'lat-i-,mȯr\, Richmond (Alexander) (b. May 6, 1906, Baoding prefecture, China—d. Feb. 26, 1984, Rosemont, Pa., U.S.) American poet and translator renowned for his disciplined yet poetic translations of Greek classics.

While in college, Lattimore wrote poetry that touched on Greek, Anglo-Saxon, and Norse tradition. He later focused on composing lyric poetry. His translations include Homer's *Iliad* (1951) and *Odyssey* (1967) and *The Four Gospels and the Revelation* (1979); he coedited, with David Grene, *Complete Greek Tragedies* (1959). His translations of the works of Aeschylus, Euripides, Aristophanes, and Pindar were particularly highly praised. Lattimore's translation of the *Iliad* is also well regarded.

Lattimore was a professor of Greek at Bryn Mawr (Pa.) College from 1935 to 1971. A collection of his poetry, *Poems from Three Decades*, was published in 1972. He also wrote criticism, such as *Story Patterns in Greek Tragedy* (1964).

lauda \'laú-də\ or **laude** \-dä\ *plural* laude *or* laudi \-dē\ [Italian, from Latin *laudes* praises, eulogy, plural of *laus* praise] A nonliturgical devotional song in praise of the Virgin Mary, Christ, or the saints that constituted an early Italian poetic genre.

The poetic *lauda* was of liturgical origin, and it was popular from about the mid-13th to the 16th century in Italy, where it was used particularly in confraternal groups and for religious celebrations. The first *lauda* in Italian was St. Francis' moving canticle sometimes called *Laudes creaturarum o Cantico del Sole* ("Praises of God's Creatures or the Canticle of the Sun"). Another outstanding early master of the *lauda* was the gifted 13th-century Franciscan poet Jacopone da Todi, who wrote many highly emotional and mystical *laudi spirituali* ("spiritual canticles") in the vernacular. Jacopone is also the reputed author of a famous Latin *lauda*, the *Stabat mater dolorosa*. Another famous 13th-century *lauda* in Latin is the *Dies irae* ("Day of Wrath"), a funeral hymn.

Laude were frequently written in *ballata* form for recitation by religious confraternities. These recitations evolved into dialogues and eventually became part of the Italian version of the miracle play, the *sacra rappresentazione*, a form of religiously inspired drama that became secularized during the Renaissance. The *lauda* remained important in Italian devotional life until the 19th century.

Laughlin \'läk-lin\, James (b. Oct. 30, 1914, Pittsburgh, Pa., U.S.) American publisher and poet, founder of the New Directions press.

In the mid-1930s Laughlin lived in Italy with Ezra Pound, a major influence on his life and work; returning to America, he founded New Directions in 1936. Initially he intended to publish writings by ignored yet influential avant-garde writers of the period; Pound's *The Cantos* and William Carlos Williams' *Paterson* were among the works eventually issued by his press. During the 1940s New Directions also republished out-of-print novels by authors such as Henry James and F. Scott Fitzgerald. Laughlin's editions of such authors as Dylan Thomas, Lawrence Ferlinghetti, Tennessee Williams, and Herman Hesse proved very popular. New Directions also produced a large body of English translations of foreign authors. Laughlin himself wrote poetry noted for its warmth and imagination; his volume *Collected Poems* was published in 1992. Among his prose writings are memoirs of Pound, *Random Essays* (1989), and *Random Stories* (1990).

Laura \'laū-rä, *Angl* 'lȯ-rə\ The beloved of the Italian poet PETRARCH and the subject of his love lyrics, written over a period of 20 years, most of which were included in his *Canzoniere* or *Rime* (1360). Laura has traditionally been identified as a Laura de Noves of Avignon, a married woman and a mother, but this tradition remains unverified.

Petrarch wrote more than 300 Italian sonnets to Laura, as well as other short lyrics and one long poem. They treat a variety of moods and subjects, but particularly his intense psychological reactions to his beloved. Many of his similes, such as burning like fire and freezing like ice, beautifully stated in the sonnet beginning "I find no peace, and all my war is done," were to be frequently repeated by the sonneteers of Elizabethan England and later became poetic clichés.

Petrarch's poems spawned a generation of translators and imitators in Europe and particularly in England, where his example inspired the great love-sonnet cycles of Sir Philip Sidney, Edmund Spenser, Michael Drayton, and William Shakespeare.

Laurence \'lȯr-əns\, Margaret, *original name* Jean Margaret Wemyss \'wē-mis\ (b. July 18, 1926, Neepawa, Man., Can.—d. Jan. 5, 1987, Lakefield, Ont.) Canadian writer best known for her stories and novels depicting the lives of women struggling for self-realization in the male-dominated world of western Canada.

In the 1950s, Laurence lived in Africa; she reflected on her experiences there in her first novel, *This Side Jordan* (1960), which deals with the exchange of power between old colonials and native Africans in the emerging nation of Ghana. *The Prophet's Camel Bell* (1963; U.S. title, *New Wind in a Dry Land*) is an account of Laurence's years in Somaliland (now Somalia). *The Tomorrow-Tamer* (1963), also set in Ghana, is a collection of short stories.

Laurence's next three novels—*The Stone Angel* (1964), *A Jest of God* (1966; U.K. title, *Now I Lay Me Down*), and *The Fire-Dwellers* (1959)—were set in the fictional Canadian prairie town of Manawaka. Each is centered on a woman of considerable strength of character. Other stories about Manawaka were collected in *A Bird in the House* (1970) and *The Diviners* (1974). She published her first children's book, *Jason's Quest*, in 1970 and a collection of occasional essays, *Heart of a Stranger*, in 1976. She twice received the Governor General's Award for fiction.

Lautréamont \lō-trä-ä-'mōⁿ\, Count (comte) de, *pseudonym of* Isidore-Lucien Ducasse \dụē-'kȧs\ (b. April 4, 1846, Montevideo, Uruguay—d. Nov. 4, 1870, Paris, Fr.) Poet, a strange and enigmatic figure in French literature who is recognized as a significant influence on the Surrealists.

He took the name of Lautréamont and his title from the arrogant hero of Eugène Sue's historical novel *Latréaumont* (1837).

The first stanza of his prose poem *Les Chants de Maldoror* was published anonymously in 1868. A complete edition was published in 1869, but the Belgian publisher, alarmed by its violence and fearing prosecution, refused to distribute it to booksellers. The *Poésies*, a shorter work, was printed in 1870.

Maldoror was republished in 1890. The work received little notice until the Surrealists, struck by its disquieting juxtaposition of strange and unrelated images, adopted Lautréamont as one of their exemplars. Above all it was the savagery of protest in *Maldoror*, as if revolt against the human condition had achieved definitive blasphemy, that created a ferment among the poets and painters of the early 20th century.

Lavater \'lä-vä-ter\, Johann Kaspar (b. Nov. 11, 1741, Zürich, Switz.—d. Jan. 2, 1801, Zürich) Swiss writer, Protestant pastor, and founder of physiognomics, an antirational, religious, and literary movement.

Lavater's studies in physiognomy and his interest in "magnetic" trance conditions had their source in his religious beliefs, which drove him to search for demonstrable traces of the divine in human life. His *Physiognomische Fragmente zur Beförderung der Menschenkenntnis und Menschenliebe*, 4 vol. (1775–78; *Essays on Physiognomy*), established his reputation throughout Europe. J.W. von Goethe worked with Lavater on the book, and the two enjoyed a warm friendship that was later severed by Lavater's zeal for conversion. His most important books are *Aussichten in die Ewigkeit* (1768–78; "Prospects in Eternity"), *Geheimes Tagebuch von einem Beobachter seiner selbst* (1772–73; *Secret Journal of a Self Observer*), *Pontius Pilatus* (1782–85), and *Nathanael* (1786). His lyrical and epic poems are imitations of Friedrich Klopstock.

Lawler \'lȯ-lər\, Ray, *in full* Raymond Evenor Lawler (b. 1921?, Footscray, Melbourne, Vic., Australia) Actor and playwright whose *Summer of the Seventeenth Doll* is credited with changing the direction of modern Australian drama.

Lawler joined the National Theatre Company in Melbourne as an actor, writer, and producer. In 1956 Lawler played the lead in his *Summer of the Seventh Doll* in Melbourne; the play's success led to productions in London and New York City. Its criticism of Australian cultural stereotypes—combined with a natural style and a language free of cliché—inspired a new phase of dramatic realism in Australia.

Lawler's other plays include *Cradle of Thunder* (1949), *A Breach in the Wall* (1967), *The Man Who Shot the Albatross* (1972), and two additional plays in "The Doll Trilogy": *Kid Stakes* (1975) and *Other Times* (1976).

Lawrence \'lȯr-əns, 'lär-\, D.H., *in full* David Herbert (b. Sept. 11, 1885, Eastwood, Nottinghamshire, Eng.—d. March 2, 1930, Vence, Fr.) English short-story writer, poet, and essayist, and one of the most important and controversial 20th-century English novelists. His works are notable for their passionate intensity and for a sensuality that centers on, but is not limited to, the erotic.

Lawrence worked as a clerk and as a pupil-teacher before attending University College in Nottingham; he earned his teaching certificate in 1908. Ford Madox Ford published much of Lawrence's early work in the *English Review* and also helped place his first novel, *The White Peacock* (1911).

In 1912 Lawrence met and fell in love with Frieda Weekley. The two began an intensely intimate but difficult relationship that was to form the underlying theme of much of his later fiction. SONS AND LOVERS, Lawrence's first mature novel, was published in 1913, as was his first volume of poems, *Love Poems and Others*. These were followed by *The Prussian Officer and Other Stories* (1914).

The years of World War I were a dark period in Lawrence's life. THE RAINBOW (1915) was banned as obscene. Lawrence's pacifism and his wife's German origins surrounded them with suspicion and hostility. His many unpleasant experiences at the hands of the military authorities are vividly described in *Kangaroo* (1923).

After the war Lawrence went to Italy, where he produced a group of novels consisting of *The Lost Girl* (1920), AARON'S ROD (1922), and the uncompleted *Mr. Noon* (published in its entirety only in 1984). He also wrote his brilliant, if idiosyncratic, STUDIES IN CLASSIC AMERICAN LITERATURE (1923). By this time he had found a publisher willing to reissue *The Rainbow* and to bring out its sequel, WOMEN IN LOVE (1921).

Having wandered about Italy, Germany, and Austria and traveled to Ceylon (Sri Lanka), the Lawrences went on to Australia. In the summer of 1922 they accepted an invitation from a wealthy admirer, Mabel Dodge, to join her at Taos, N.M. Ever restless, in 1923 they moved to Mexico; Lawrence's fascination with Aztec culture resulted in *The Plumed Serpent* (1926). During the winter of 1924–25 Lawrence fell seriously ill with tuberculosis, which had plagued him from an early age.

He returned to Italy in 1925. That same year his short novel *St. Mawr* was published, and he then wrote the posthumously published *Etruscan Places* (1932). He also started LADY CHATTERLEY'S LOVER; privately published in 1928, it led an underground life until legal decisions in New York (1959) and London (1960) made it freely available. The dying Lawrence moved to the south of France in 1929. He was buried in Vence, and his ashes were removed to Taos in 1935.

Lawrence wrote with poetic vividness, attempting to describe subjective states of emotion, sensation, and intuition. His great novels remain difficult because their realism is underlain by obsessive personal metaphors, by elements of mythology, and above all by his desire to express the inexpressible.

Lawrence \'lȯr-əns, 'lär-\, T.E., *in full* Thomas Edward, *byname* Lawrence of Arabia \ə-'rā-bē-ə\, *also called* (from 1927) T.E. Shaw \'shȯ\ (b. Aug. 15, 1888, Tremadoc, Caernarvonshire, Wales—d. May 19, 1935, Clouds Hill, Dorset, Eng.) British archaeological scholar, military strategist, and author best known for his legendary war activities in the Middle East during World War I and for his account of those activities in *The Seven Pillars of Wisdom* (1926).

Lawrence attended Oxford University, where he joined an expedition excavating the Hittite settlement of Carchemish on the Euphrates, working there from 1911 to 1914. At the beginning of the war, experts on Arab affairs were rare and Lawrence was assigned to intelligence. When an Arab leader, Ḥusayn ibn ʿAlī, proclaimed a revolt against the Turks, Lawrence urged his superiors to abet the efforts at rebellion with arms and gold as a method of undermining Germany's Turkish ally. He joined one of the Arab armies as political and liaison officer. Lawrence was not the only officer to become involved in the incipient Arab rising, but he quickly became—especially from his own accounts—its brains, its organizing force, its liaison with Egypt, and its military technician.

The Seven Pillars of Wisdom, though rife with adjectives and often straining for effects and "art," is an action-packed narrative of Lawrence's campaigns in the desert with the Arabs. Lawrence also published an English translation of Homer's *Odyssey* in 1932. Little else by the author was published in his lifetime. His first postwar writings, including a famous essay on guerrilla war, have been published as *Evolution of a Revolt* (1968). An anthology of more than 100 of his poems was published as *Minorities* (1971), and his literary reputation was further substantiated by an immense correspondence.

Lawson \'lȯ-sən\, Henry (Archibald) (b. June 17, 1867, near Grenfell, N.S.W., Australia—d. Sept. 22, 1922, Abbotsford, N.S.W.) Australian writer of short stories and balladlike verse, noted for his realistic portrayals of bush life.

About 1884 Lawson moved to Sydney, where the *Bulletin* published his first stories and verses (1887–88). He worked for several newspapers but also spent much time wandering. Out of these experiences came material for his vivid, realistic writing, which, by its often pessimistic blend of pathos and irony, captured some of the spirit of Australian working life.

Lawson's principal works are collections of poems or stories, including *In the Days When the World Was Wide and Other Verses* (1896), *While the Billy Boils* (1896), *Joe Wilson and His*

Mates (1901), *Children of the Bush* (1902), and *Triangles of Life and Other Stories* (1913).

Lawson \'lȯ-sən\, John Howard (b. Sept. 25, 1894, New York, N.Y., U.S.—d. Aug. 11, 1977, San Francisco, Calif.) American playwright, screenwriter, and member of the "Hollywood Ten," who was jailed (1948–49) and blacklisted for his refusal to tell the House Committee on Un-American Activities about his political allegiances.

Lawson's early plays, such as *Roger Bloomer* (1923) and *Processional* (1925), are notable examples of Expressionism. He later portrayed problems of the working class: *The International* (1928) depicts a world revolution of the proletariat; *Marching Song* (1937) concerns a sit-down strike. Lawson's plays emphasize ideology and innovation.

During the 1930s and '40s Lawson devoted his time to writing screenplays. He wrote such scripts as *Action in the North Atlantic* (1943) and *Sahara* (1943) and was the cofounder and first president of the Screen Writers Guild. In 1949 he published *Theory and Technique of Playwriting and Screenwriting*, a revised edition of his earlier *Theory and Technique of Playwriting* (1936). Lawson explored American cultural tradition in *The Hidden Heritage: A Rediscovery of the Ideas and Forces That Link the Thought of Our Time with the Culture of the Past* (1950).

Laxdæla saga \'läks-,dȧl-ə\ ("Saga of [the Men of] Laxárdal") One of the Icelanders', or family, sagas of the 13th century. It is the tragic story of several generations of an Iceland hero-family from the end of the 9th to the 11th century, and in particular the story of Gudrun, who causes the death of the man she loves.

Laxness \'läks-nes\, Halldór, *pseudonym of* Halldór Kiljan Guthdjónsson \'gvu̇eth-,yȯn-sȯn\ (b. April 23, 1902, Reykjavík, Ice.) Icelandic novelist, awarded the Nobel Prize for Literature in 1955.

His first major novel, *Vefarinn mikli frá Kasmír* (1927; "The Great Weaver from Kashmir"), is about a young man who is torn between his religious faith and the pleasures of the world. During a stay in the United States (1927–29), Laxness turned to socialism, an ideology that is reflected in his novels from the 1930s and '40s. After his return to Iceland, Laxness published a series of novels with subjects drawn from the social life of Iceland: *Salka Valka* (1931–32), *Sjálfstætt fólk* (1934–35; *Independent People*), and *Heimsljós* (1937–40; *World Light*). These novels generated a great deal of controversy. The trilogy *Íslandsklukkan* (1943–46; "Iceland's Bell"), set in the late 17th and early 18th centuries, has an explicitly nationalist theme; its style is influenced by that of the medieval Icelandic sagas. The work firmly established him as the foremost writer of Iceland.

Beginning in the late 1950s, Laxness' novels were more lyrical and introspective. They include *Brekkukotsannáll* (1957; *The Fish Can Sing*), *Paradísarheimt* (1960; *Paradise Reclaimed*), and *Kristnihald undir Jökli* (1968; *Christianity at Glacier*).

In addition to novels, Laxness published plays, poetry, short stories, critical essays, and translations, and he edited several Icelandic sagas. His memoirs include *Sagan af brauddinu dýra* (1987; *The Bread of Life*) and *Dagar hjá múnkum* (1987; "Days with Monks").

lay or **lai** \'lā\ [Old French *lai*] **1.** In medieval French literature, a short romance, usually written in octosyllabic verse, that dealt with subjects thought to be of Celtic origin. The earliest lay narratives were written in the 12th century by Marie de France; her works were largely based on earlier Breton versions thought to have been derived from Celtic legend. The BRETON LAY, a 14th-century English poetic form based on these lays, is exemplified by "The Franklin's Tale" in Geoffrey Chaucer's *The Canterbury Tales*. **2.** A medieval lyric poem. The earliest extant examples are those composed by Gautier de Dargies in the 13th century. These lays had nonuniform stanzas of about 6 to 16 or more lines of 4 to 8 syllables. One or two rhymes were maintained throughout each stanza.   **3.** A simple narrative poem or a ballad, such as those written in the early 19th century by Sir Walter Scott.   **4.** A song or melody.

Layamon \ˈlä-ə-mən\ or **Lawamon** \ˈlȯ-mən\ (fl. 12th century)   Early Middle English poet, author of the romance-chronicle the *Brut* (c. 1200), the outstanding literary product of the 12th-century revival of English literature.

Layamon's source was the *Roman de Brut* by Wace, an Anglo-Norman verse adaptation of Geoffrey of Monmouth's *Historia regum Britanniae*. In some 16,000 long alliterative lines (often broken into short couplets by rhyme), the *Brut* recounts the legendary history of Britain from the landing of Brutus, great-grandson of the Trojan Aeneas, to the final Saxon victory over the Britons in 689. It is the first work in English to treat the "matter of Britain"—i.e., the legends surrounding Arthur and the knights of the Round Table. One-third of the poem deals with Arthurian matter, but Layamon's is not a high chivalric treatment: mass war is the staple.

Laye \ˈlī\, Camara (b. Jan. 1, 1928, Kouroussa, French Guinea [now in Guinea]—d. Feb. 4, 1980, Senegal)   Guinean fiction writer who was one of the first sub-Saharan African authors to achieve an international reputation.

While living in Paris, Laye wrote his first novel, *L'Enfant noir* (1953; *The Dark Child*), which re-creates nostalgically his childhood days in Guinea in a flowing, poetic prose. *Le Regard du roi* (*The Radiance of the King*), which some critics consider to be Laye's best work, was published in 1954. It describes a white man's journey through the jungle in quest of an audience with an African king. Its nightmarish intensity is reminiscent of the works of Franz Kafka and of Amos Tutuola.

In the 10 years following his return to Guinea in 1956, Laye wrote numerous short stories for such periodicals as *Black Orpheus* and *Présence africaine*. The sequel to *L'Enfant noir*, entitled *Dramouss* (1966; *A Dream of Africa*), is heavily weighted with social commentary. Its chief character, returning to his home after six years in Paris, finds that political violence has replaced the values and way of life he had longed for when abroad.

Lay of Atli \ˈät-lē\, *Norse* Atlakvida \ˈät-lä-ˌkvē-də\   Heroic poem in the Norse *Poetic Edda*, an older variant of the tale of slaughter and revenge that is the subject of the German epic *Nibelungenlied*, from which it differs in several respects. In the Norse poem, Atli (the Hunnish king Attila) is the villain, who is slain by his wife, Gudrun, to avenge her brothers. In the German epic the characters of Atli, Gudrun, Gunnar, and Hogni are represented, respectively, by Etzel, Kriemhild, Gunther, and Hagen. *See also* EDDA; NIBELUNGENLIED.

Lay of the Last Minstrel, The   Long narrative poem in six cantos by Sir Walter SCOTT, published in 1805. It was the author's first original poetic romance, and it established his reputation. Scott based it on the old Scottish Border legend of the goblin Gilpin Horner. The poem, set in the 16th century, is full of magical and folk elements and of knightly combat between the English army and Scottish clans. Its narrator is the last of the ancient line of minstrels. He tells the story of a feud between Lady Buccleuch and Lord Cranstoun, who loves the lady's daughter.

Layton \ˈlāt-ən\, Irving (Peter) (b. March 12, 1912, Neamṭ, Rom.)   Poet who treated the Jewish-Canadian experience with rebellious vigor.

Layton's family immigrated to Canada in 1913. His poems, lyrical and romantic in tone and classical in form, developed

from the early descriptive poetry collected in *Here and Now* (1945) and *Now Is the Place* (1948) into the tough and denunciatory expressions of his hatred of the bourgeoisie contained in *In the Midst of My Fever* (1954) and *The Cold Green Element* (1955). He later turned from social satire to concern for the universal human condition—*e.g.*, *The Swinging Flesh* (1961) and *Europe and Other Bad News* (1981). *A Wild Peculiar Joy: Selected Poems 1945–1989* was published in 1989. He also published volumes of prose, including *Engagements* (1972), *Taking Sides* (1978), and *Wild Gooseberries: The Selected Letters of Irving Layton* (1989).

Lazarillo de Tormes \ˌlä-zä-ˈrēl-yō-t͟hä-tȯr-ˈmäs\   Fictional character, the shrewd and ironic protagonist of *La vida de Lazarillo de Tormes* (1554; *The Life of Lazarillo of Tormes* and other translations), by an unknown author. The work is considered the original picaresque novel.

Lazarus \ˈlaz-ə-rəs\   Biblical figure known from the Gospel narrative of John (11:18, 30, 32, 38). Lazarus, the brother of Martha and Mary, lived at Bethany, near Jerusalem. When Lazarus died, he was raised by Jesus from the dead after he had been entombed for four days. The miracle inspired many people to believe in Jesus as the Christ.

Lazarus \ˈlaz-ə-rəs\, Emma (b. July 22, 1849, New York, N.Y., U.S.—d. Nov. 19, 1887, New York City)   American writer best known for her sonnet "The New Colossus" (1883), written to the Statue of Liberty.

Lazarus' first book, *Poems and Translations* (1866), caught the attention of Ralph Waldo Emerson. At 21 she published *Admetus and Other Poems* (1871). She also wrote a prose romance (*Alide*) based on J.W. von Goethe's autobiography, a tragedy (*The Spagnoletto*), and the translation *Poems and Ballads of Heinrich Heine* (1881). About 1881 she began working for the relief of new immigrants in the United States. "The New Colossus," written to express her faith in America as a refuge for the oppressed, closes with the lines:

> Give me your tired, your poor,
> Your huddled masses, yearning to breathe free,
> The wretched refuse of your teeming shore.
> Send these, the homeless, tempest-tost to me,
> I lift my lamp beside the golden door!

This sonnet was chosen to be inscribed on a bronze plaque inside the base of the statue, dedicated in 1886.

lazzo \ˈlät-tsō\ *plural* lazzi \-tsē\   Improvised comic dialogue or action in Italian commedia dell'arte. The word, which means in more general contexts "jest" or "quip" and first appears in Italian in 1660, is of obscure and much debated origin. Lazzi were one of the prime resources of the commedia actors, consisting of verbal asides on current political and literary topics, manifestations of terror, and pratfalls and other acrobatics. Arlecchino is a character particularly congenial to lazzi. Lazzi were implicit in many of the comedies of Molière and those of William Shakespeare, in which they came to be called jigs.

Leacock \ˈlē-ˌkäk\, Stephen (Butler) (b. Dec. 30, 1869, Swanmore, Hampshire, Eng.—d. March 28, 1944, Toronto, Ont., Can.)   Canadian humorist, educator, lecturer, and author of many books of lighthearted sketches and essays.

Leacock immigrated to Canada with his parents at the age of six. He was educated at the University of Toronto and the University of Chicago. He taught economics and political science at McGill University in Montreal from 1903 to 1936. Although Leacock wrote extensively on history and political economy, his true calling was humor, both as a lecturer and as an author.

His fame now rests securely on work begun with the beguiling fantasies of *Literary Lapses* (1910) and *Nonsense Novels*

(1911). Leacock's humor is typically based on a comic perception of social foibles and the incongruity between appearance and reality in human conduct.

Leander   *see* HERO AND LEANDER.

Lear \ˈlir\   Legendary British king and central character of William Shakespeare's play KING LEAR. The story of Lear's kingdom—his division of it among his daughters and the consequences of his action—was told in Geoffrey of Monmouth's early 12th-century *Historia regum Britanniae* (*History of the Kings of Britain*), from which Raphael Holinshed borrowed material when compiling the early part of his *Chronicles* (1577). Shakespeare may have used Holinshed's work when writing *King Lear*, though he was perhaps more directly influenced by an anonymous play, *The True Chronicle History of King Leir*, performed and printed in 1605.

The story of Lear was treated by Edmund Spenser in *The Faerie Queene*, and it was one of the "tragedies" told in the mid-16th-century compilation *A Myrrour for Magistrates*.

Lear \ˈlir\, Edward (b. May 12, 1812, Highgate, near London, Eng.—d. Jan. 29, 1888, San Remo, Italy)   English landscape painter who is more widely known as the writer of an original type of nonsense verse and as the popularizer of the LIMERICK.

Detail of a drawing by William Holman Hunt, 1857

Walker Art Gallery, Liverpool

The youngest of 21 children, Lear from the age of 15 earned his living by drawing. He subsequently worked for the British Museum, made drawings of birds for John Gould, a zoologist, and, during 1832–37, made illustrations of the Earl of Derby's private menagerie at Knowsley, Lancashire. It was for the earl's grandchildren that he produced *Book of Nonsense* (1846; enlarged 1861, 1863), the first of many nonsense volumes.

Lear suffered all his life from epilepsy and melancholia. He was homosexual, and after 1837 he lived mainly abroad. Though naturally timid, he was a constant and intrepid traveler. During his nomadic life he lived, among other places, at Rome, Corfu (Greece), and, finally, with his celebrated cat "Foss," at San Remo.

Lear published several volumes of bird and animal drawings, seven illustrated travel books (notably *Journal of a Landscape Painter in Albania*, 1851), and many books of nonsense—*A Book of Nonsense*; *Nonsense Songs, Stories, Botany and Alphabets* (1871), including THE OWL AND THE PUSSY-CAT; *More Nonsense, Pictures, Rhymes, Botany, etc.* (1872); and *Laughable Lyrics* (1877). Posthumous collections of his work include *Queery Leary Nonsense* (1911), *The Complete Nonsense of Edward Lear* (1947), and *Indian Journal: Watercolours and Extracts from the Diary of Edward Lear (1873–1875)* (1953).

Learned Ladies, The   *see* THE BLUE-STOCKINGS.

Lear of the Steppes, A \ˈlir\   Short story by Ivan TURGENEV, published in 1870 as "Stepnoy Korol Lir"; it has also been translated as "King Lear of the Steppes." A loose adaptation of William Shakespeare's tragedy *King Lear*, set in the Russian countryside, the story concerns the disrespectful treatment the protagonist, Kharlov, receives from his ungrateful daughters and the revenge he wreaks upon them.

Leather-Stocking Tales, The   Series of five novels by James Fenimore COOPER, published between 1823 and 1841. The novels constitute a saga of 18th-century life among Indians and white pioneers on the New York State frontier through their portrayal of the adventures of the main character, Natty Bumppo, who takes on various names throughout the series. The books cover his entire adult life, from young manhood to old age, though they were not written or published in chronological order. The individual novels are THE PIONEERS (1823), THE LAST OF THE MOHICANS (1826), THE PRAIRIE (1827), THE PATHFINDER (1840), and THE DEERSLAYER (1841).

The Pioneers is both the first and finest detailed portrait of frontier life in American literature; it is also the first truly original American novel. The main subject of the book is the conflict between two different views of the frontier—that of Natty Bumppo (here called Leather-Stocking), who sees the land as "God's Wilderness," and that of another main character who wants to tame and cultivate the land. *The Last of the Mohicans* takes the reader back to the French and Indian War of Natty's middle age, when he is at the height of his powers. This work was succeeded by *The Prairie*, in which, by now very old and philosophical, Leather-Stocking dies, facing the westering sun he has so long followed. Identified from the start with the vanishing wilderness and its natives, Leather-Stocking becomes an unalterably elegiac figure.

Cooper intended to bury Leather-Stocking with *The Prairie*, but many years later he resuscitated the character and portrayed his early maturity in *The Pathfinder* and his youth in *The Deerslayer*. While all of *The Leather-Stocking Tales* have been criticized as artless, some critics see *The Deerslayer* as the best of the five novels. Mark Twain mocked it (and *The Pathfinder*) in "Fenimore Cooper's Literary Offences."

Leaven of Malice   Novel by Robertson Davies, the second in a series known collectively as the SALTERTON TRILOGY.

Leaves of Grass   Collection of poetry by American author Walt WHITMAN, first presented as a group of 12 poems published anonymously in 1855. It was followed by five revised and three reissued editions during the author's lifetime. Poems not published in his lifetime were added in 1897. The unconventional language and subjects of the poems exerted strong influence on American and foreign literature but also led to the book's suppression on charges of indecency.

The first edition included noted poems such as SONG OF MYSELF and I SING THE BODY ELECTRIC, celebrating the beauty of the human body, physical health, and sexual passion. In a preface that was deleted from later editions, Whitman maintained that a poet's style should be simple and natural, without orthodox meter or rhyme, like an animal or tree in harmony with its environment.

Among the 122 new poems in the third edition (1860–61) were Whitman's "Calamus" poems, which record an intense homosexual love affair. His Civil War poems, DRUM-TAPS (1865) and *Sequel to Drum-Taps* (1865), were included in the fourth edition (1867). The seventh edition (1881–82) grouped the poems in their final order, and the eighth edition (1889) incorporated his *November Boughs* (1888).

Leavis \ˈlē-vəs\, F.R., *in full* Frank Raymond (b. July 14, 1895, Cambridge, Cambridgeshire, Eng.—d. April 14, 1978, Cambridge)   English literary critic who introduced a new seriousness into the field.

Born in Cambridge, Leavis attended and later taught at the university. In 1932 he cofounded *Scrutiny*, a quarterly journal of criticism that was published until 1953 and is regarded by many as his greatest contribution to English letters.

Leavis' criticism falls into two phases. In the first, influenced by T.S. Eliot, he devoted his attention to English verse. In *New Bearings in English Poetry* (1932) he attacked late Victorian poetry and proclaimed the importance of the work of T.S. Eliot, Ezra Pound, and Gerard Manley Hopkins. In *Revaluation: Tradition and Development in English Poetry* (1936), he extended his survey of English poetry back to the 17th century. In the 1940s his interest moved toward the novel. In *The Great Tradition* (1948) he reassessed English fiction, proclaiming Jane Austen, George Eliot, Henry James, and Joseph Conrad as the great novelists of the past and D.H. Lawrence as their only successor. Other novelists, notably Leo Tolstoy and Charles Dickens, engaged his attention in *Anna Karenina and Other Essays* (1967) and *Dickens the Novelist* (1970), written with his wife. His range is perhaps best shown in the collection *The Common Pursuit* (1952).

Leblanc \lə-'bläⁿ\, Maurice(-Marie-Emile) (b. Dec. 11, 1864, Rouen, Fr.—d. Nov. 6, 1941, Paris)   French author and journalist, known as the creator of Arsène LUPIN, French gentleman-thief turned detective, who is featured in more than 60 of Leblanc's crime novels and short stories.

Leblanc abandoned his law studies to become a pulp crime writer. Commissioned in 1905 to write a crime story for the French periodical *Je sais tout*, he created "L'Arrestation d'Arsène Lupin" and achieved immediate and long-lasting popular success.

Le Braz \lə-'bräz\, Anatole (b. April 2, 1859, Duault, Fr.—d. March 20, 1926, Menton)   Breton folklorist, novelist, and poet who collected and edited the legends and popular beliefs of his native province.

Le Braz was professor of philosophy at several schools and, later, professor of French literature at the University of Rennes (1901–24). One of his major works, *La Légende de la mort* (1893; "The Legend of the Dead"; Eng. trans., *Dealings with the Dead*), includes vividly poetic retellings of the legends of death—stories, traditions, and practices—Le Braz collected in Brittany. He also wrote *Vieilles histoires du pays breton* (1897; "Ancient Stories of Brittany") and a study of Celtic drama, *L'Essai sur l'histoire du théâtre celtique* (1903; "Essay on the History of Celtic Theater"). His artistic works, also based on the traditions of Brittany, include a collection of poems, *La Chanson de la Bretagne* (1892; "The Song of Brittany"), and several novels and stories, *Le Gardien du feu* (1890; "Keeper of the Fire"; Eng. trans., *The Night of the Fires*), *Pâques d'Islande* (1897; "Iceland Easter"), and *Contes du soleil et de la brume* (1905; "Tales of Sun and Mist").

Le Carré \lə-kä-'rā\, John, *pseudonym of* David John Moore Cornwell \'kórn-wôl\ (b. Oct. 19, 1931, Poole, Dorset, Eng.)   English writer known for realistic, suspenseful spy novels based on a wide knowledge of international espionage.

Le Carré was an instructor in French and Latin at Eton College before becoming a member of the British foreign service in West Germany in 1959. He began to devote himself full-time to writing as a result of the success of his third novel of espionage, *The Spy Who Came in from the Cold* (1963; film, 1965). This book was followed by two more espionage novels, *The Looking Glass War* (1965) and *A Small Town in Germany* (1968).

Tinker, Tailor, Soldier, Spy (1974) was the first in a trilogy of spy novels centered on the shrewd but self-effacing British intelligence agent George Smiley, who had appeared in Le Carré's earlier novels, *Call for the Dead* (1961) and *A Murder of Quality* (1962). In the trilogy Smiley's nemesis is the Soviet master spy Karla, and their struggle is continued in *The Honourable School-*

boy (1977) and culminates in *Smiley's People* (1980). *The Little Drummer Girl* (1983) describes a struggle between the Israeli secret service and a Palestinian terrorist. Later novels include *A Perfect Spy* (1986), *The Russia House* (1989), and *The Night Manager* (1993).

Lechoń \'lech-ôn^y\, Jan, *pseudonym of* Leszek Serafinowicz \se-rä-fĕ-'nô-vĕch\ (b. March 13, 1899, Warsaw [Poland]—d. June 8, 1956, New York, N.Y., U.S.)   Poet, editor, diplomat, and political propagandist, and one of the foremost Polish poets of the era.

His first volume, *Karmazynowy poemat* (1920; "The Scarlet Poem"), dealt with patriotic themes; it was followed by *Rzeczpospolita Babińska* (1921; "The Republic of Babin"). In 1924 he collected his lyrical poems in *Srebrne i czarne* ("Silver and Black"). In 1926 he became editor of a satirical weekly, *Cyrulik Warszawski* ("The Barber of Warsaw"), and in 1932 he was appointed cultural attaché to the Polish embassy in Paris, where he remained until France capitulated to the Nazis.

In 1941 Lechoń went to New York City, where for four years he edited a Polish weekly. His *Lutnia po Bekwarku* ("Bekwark's Lute") appeared in 1942 in London; it was followed in 1945 by another volume of verse. From 1952 until his suicide, Lechoń worked for Radio Free Europe, a U.S.-funded operation.

Le Clézio \lə-klāz-'yō\, Jean-Marie(-Gustave) (b. April 13, 1940, Nice, Fr.)   French novelist who achieved fame with his first novel, *Le Procès-verbal* (1963; *The Interrogation*).

Le Clézio at first was identified with the *nouveau roman* ("new novel"), an avant-garde movement in France in the 1950s and '60s, but he later asserted an individual style, expressing in parables the reality of a world of "small adventures." Le Clézio makes evident the inner disorder of humanity as well as human discord with the world. His characters totter on the edge of madness: such is the fate of Adam Pollo in *Le Procès-verbal*. *La Fièvre* (1965; *Fever*) and *La Déluge* (1966; *The Flood*) also examine mental aberration. *L'Extase matérielle* (1967; "The Ecstasy of Matter") is a treatise on Le Clézio's literary ideas. It was followed by *Terra amata* (1967; "Beloved Earth"), an experimental narrative. *La Guerre* (1970; *War*) and *Les Géants* (1973; *The Giants*) set forth what Le Clézio saw as the horrors of modern civilization. Le Clézio's later works include *Mondo et autres histoires* (1978; "Mondo and Other Stories"), *Désert* (1980; "The Desert"), *La Ronde et autres faits divers* (1982; "The Round and Other News-In-Brief Items"), and *Le Chercheur d'or* (1985; "The Gold Seeker").

Leconte de Lisle \lə-kôⁿt-də-'lēl\, Charles-Marie-René (b. Oct. 22, 1818, Saint-Paul, Réunion—d. July 17, 1894, Louveciennes, near Paris, Fr.)   French poet, leader of the anti-Romantic Parnassians.

Leconte de Lisle's theories, which were a reaction against Romanticism, stressed the need for impersonality and discipline in poetry. His epic poetry is often overweighted by erudition and ornamentation, but his shorter poems convey a compelling and individual vision; "Qaïn" (1869; "Cain") is one of the most impressive short epics of the 19th century.

Leconte de Lisle studied law at the Université de Rennes in 1837 but then decided to devote himself to literature. In 1846 he went to work on *La Démocratie pacifique*, a daily journal that propagated the utopian social theories of Charles Fourier. In the next few years he wrote political articles and unsuccessfully attempted practical work for the February Revolution of 1848. Later, while remaining a republican, he became convinced that the poet should not engage in direct political action.

His first volume of poetry was published in 1852. He eventually arranged all of his poems, which appeared in different collections during his lifetime, to form *Poèmes antiques*, *Po-*

èmes barbares, and *Poèmes tragiques*. *Derniers poèmes* was published in 1895.

Leconte de Lisle also published a series of translations from Greek and Latin, three anticlerical and republican booklets (1871–72), and, under the pseudonym Pierre Gosset, *Histoire du Moyen Âge* (1876).

lection \'lek-shən\ [Latin *lectio* act of reading, reading matter] A variant reading of a text.

Leda \'lē-də\ In Greek mythology, mortal woman usually believed to be the mother of Clytemnestra, who became the wife of King Agamemnon, and of Castor, one of the Heavenly Twins (or Dioscuri). She was also believed to have been the mother (by Zeus, who had ravished her in the form of a swan) of the other twin, Pollux, and of Helen, both of whom hatched from eggs. Variant legends gave divine parentage to both the twins and possibly also to Clytemnestra, while yet other legends say that Leda bore the twins to her mortal husband, Tyndareus. In any case, the divine swan's encounter was a popular literary subject. William Butler Yeats, Mona Van Duyn, Rainer Maria Rilke, and Hilda Doolittle (H.D.) all wrote poems on the subject.

Leda and the Swan \'lē-də\ Sonnet by William Butler YEATS, composed in 1923, printed in *The Dial* (June 1924) and published in the collection *The Cat and the Moon and Certain Poems* (1924). The poem is based on the Greek mythological story of beautiful Leda, who gave birth to Helen and Clytemnestra after she was raped by Zeus in the form of a swan.

The poem details the rape of Leda with graphic imagery. At the climax of their sexual union, Yeats tersely outlines the fate of their lineage: "The broken wall, the burning roof and tower/ And Agamemnon dead." By alluding to Helen's involvement with the Trojan War and Clytemnestra's murder of her husband Agamemnon, Yeats suggests that this initial act of violence engendered the later cataclysms.

Lee, Don L. *see* Haki MADHUBUTI.

Lee \'lē\, Laurie (b. June 26, 1914, Stroud, Gloucester, Eng.) English poet and author of both fiction and autobiography, best known for his autobiographical trilogy, including *Cider with Rosie* (1959; U.S. title, *The Edge of Day*), on the author's boyhood in the country; *As I Walked Out One Midsummer Morning* (1969), on his trip to London to seek his fortune; and *A Moment of War* (1991), on his experiences in Spain during the Spanish Civil War (1936–39).

In addition to the trilogy, Lee's works include the poetry collections *The Sun My Monument* (1944), *The Bloom of Candles* (1947), and *My Many-Coated Man* (1955), as well as a collection of stories, *I Can't Stay Long* (1976).

Lee \'lē\, Nathaniel (b. 1649?—buried May 6, 1692, London, Eng.) English playwright whose heroic plays were popular but marred by extravagance. Lee was educated at Westminster School and Trinity College, Cambridge. His earliest play, *Nero*, was performed in 1674. A blank-verse tragedy, *The Rival Queens* (1677), made his reputation; it remained popular until the 19th century. Lee collaborated with John Dryden in *Oedipus* (1678) and *The Duke of Guise* (1682).

Lee \'lē\, Vernon, *pseudonym of* Violet Paget \'paj-it\ (b. Oct. 14, 1856, Boulogne-sur-Mer, Fr.—d. Feb. 13, 1935, San Gervasio Bresciano, Italy) English essayist and novelist who is best known for her works on aesthetics.

Paget was born to cosmopolitan and peripatetic intellectuals who in 1873 settled their family in Florence. In 1878 she determined to publish under a masculine pseudonym in order to be taken seriously, and in 1880 her collection of essays originally published in *Fraser's Magazine* was published under the name

by which she came to be known both personally and professionally. This work, *Studies of the Eighteenth Century in Italy*, brought to life for English readers the hitherto unexplored world of poet-librettist Pietro Metastasio and dramatists Carlo Goldoni and Carlo Gozzi. Her collections of essays *Belcaro* (1881) and *Euphorion* (1884) reveal her scholarship, always enlivened by wit and imagination. In her three-volume novel *Miss Brown* (1884) she brutally caricatured English aesthetic coteries (especially the Pre-Raphaelites).

She wrote more than 30 books, including several collections of stories, among them *Pope Jacynth and other Fantastic Tales* (1904). Her powerful allegorical drama *Satan the Waster* (1920) reveals her ardent pacifism.

Le Fanu \lə-fä-'nüe\, Sheridan, *in full* Joseph Sheridan Le Fanu (b. Aug. 28, 1814, Dublin, Ire.—d. Feb. 7, 1873, Dublin) Irish writer of ghost stories and mystery novels.

The three volumes of *The Purcell Papers* (1880) show his mastery of the supernatural. Between 1845 and 1873 he published 14 novels, of which *Uncle Silas* (1864) and *The House by the Churchyard* (1863) are the best known. Le Fanu contributed numerous short stories, mostly of ghosts and the supernatural, to the *Dublin University Magazine*, which he owned and edited from 1861 to 1869. *In a Glass Darkly* (1872), a book of five long stories, is generally regarded as his best work.

Left Hand of Darkness, The Science-fiction novel by Ursula K. LE GUIN, published in 1969. The book, set on a planet called Gethen, or Winter, is a vehicle for Le Guin's Daoist view of the complementary nature of all relationships. Gethen is inhabited by a race of androgynous humans who may change sexual roles during monthly estrus periods, so that at different times any individual may be either a mother or a father. Interspersed with anthropological comments on the Gethenians as well as extracts from their own folklore and philosophy, the plot follows the exploits of Genly Ai, the first ambassador to Gethen from the Ekumen (the league of known worlds), who with the aid of Estraven, a sympathetic Gethenian, attempts to bring the peoples of Gethen into the Ekumen.

legal oratory *see* FORENSIC ORATORY.

legend \'lej-ənd\ [Medieval Latin *legenda* reading, divine lesson, saint's life, from feminine of Latin *legendus*, gerundive of *legere* to read] **1.** The story or account of the life of a saint, or a collection of such stories. **2.** A story coming down from the past; especially, one handed down from early times by tradition and popularly regarded as historical although not entirely verifiable. Also, the total body of such stories and traditions; especially, the collective stories and traditions of a particular group (such as a people or clan). **3.** A popular myth usually of current or recent origin. **4.** The subject of a legend, or a person around whom such stories and traditions have grown up; specifically, one held to possess extraordinary qualities that are usually partly real and partly mythical.

Some legends are the unique property of the place or person to whom they are attached, such as the story of young George Washington chopping down the cherry tree. But many local legends are actually well-known folktales that have become attached to a particular person or place. For example, a widely distributed folktale of an excellent marksman who is forced to shoot an apple, hazelnut, or some other object from his son's head has become associated with the Swiss hero William Tell. *See also* FOLKTALE.

Legend of Good Women Dream-vision by Geoffrey CHAUCER, written in the 1380s. The fourth and final work of the genre that Chaucer composed, it presents a "Prologue" (existing in two versions) and nine stories. In the "Prologue" the god of love is angry at Chaucer for writing about so many women who betray men. As penance, Chaucer is instructed to write about good women. The stories—concerning such women of antiquity as Cleopatra, Dido, and Lucrece—are brief and rather mechanical, with the betrayal of women by wicked men as a regular theme. As a result, the whole becomes more a legend of bad men than of good women.

Legend of Sleepy Hollow, The   Short story by Washington IRVING, first published in THE SKETCH BOOK in 1819–20.

The protagonist of the story, Ichabod Crane, is a Yankee schoolteacher who lives in Sleepy Hollow, a Dutch enclave on the Hudson River. A suggestible man, Crane believes the ghost stories he has heard and read. He is particularly impressed by the tale of a spectral headless horseman said to haunt the area. Crane is also mercenary; he courts Katrina Van Tassel mostly because she is expected to receive a large inheritance. Abraham Van Brunt (also called Brom Bones) is Crane's jealous rival, who often plays tricks on the schoolmaster. Late one night as Ichabod Crane rides home from a party at Katrina's home, he is suddenly frightened by a ghostlike headless horseman. The ghost pursues him and hurls at him a round object that might be a head but is later revealed to have been a pumpkin. Ichabod Crane is never seen in Sleepy Hollow again.

Legree, Simon \'sī-mən-lə-'grē\   Fictional character, the principal villain in Harriet Beecher Stowe's antislavery novel UNCLE TOM'S CABIN.

Le Guin \lə-'gwin\, Ursula K., *original surname* Kroeber \'krō-bər\ (b. Oct. 21, 1929, Berkeley, Calif., U.S.)   Writer best known for tales of science fiction and fantasy imbued with concern for character development and language.

The daughter of anthropologist Alfred L. Kroeber and writer Theodora Kroeber, Le Guin attended Radcliffe College and Columbia University. The methods of anthropology influenced her science-fiction stories, which often featured highly detailed descriptions of alien societies. Her first three novels, *Rocannon's World* (1966), *Planet of Exile* (1966), and *City of Illusions* (1967), introduced beings from the planet Hain, who established human life on habitable planets, including the Earth. Though her Earthsea series—*A Wizard of Earthsea* (1968), *The Tombs of Atuan* (1971), *The Farthest Shore* (1972), and *Tehanu: The Last Book of Earthsea* (1990)—was written for children, it attracted a large adult readership.

Among Le Guin's most important novels are THE LEFT HAND OF DARKNESS (1969), *The Dispossessed* (1974), *The Word for World Is Forest* (1972), and *Always Coming Home* (1985). Le Guin also wrote non-science fiction and essays on fantasy fiction, feminist issues, and other topics, some of them collected in *The Language of the Night* (1979) and *Dancing at the Edge of the World* (1989).

Lehmann \'lā-mən\, John (Frederick) (b. June 2, 1907, Bourne End, Buckinghamshire, Eng.—d. April 7, 1987, London)   English poet, editor, publisher, and man of letters whose book-periodical *New Writing* and its successor, *Penguin New Writing*, were an important influence on English literature from the late 1930s through the aftermath of World War II.

Lehmann worked as a journalist and poet in Vienna from 1932 to 1936 and then returned to England to found *New Writing*, which was issued until 1950. From 1938 to 1946 Lehmann was general manager of the Hogarth Press, founded by Leonard and Virginia Woolf, and from 1940 to 1945 advisory editor of *The Geographical Magazine*. In 1954 he founded *The London Magazine*, a literary review that he edited until 1961.

His first volume of poems, *A Garden Revisited*, appeared in 1931, and several other volumes preceded his *Collected Poems* (1963). His autobiography, which throws much light on the literary life of his time, appeared in three volumes—*The Whispering Gallery* (1955), *I Am My Brother* (1960), and *The Ample Proposition* (1966)—and in a condensed one-volume version in the United States—*In My Own Time* (1969). He also published a biography of the poet Rupert Brooke in 1980.

Lehmann \'lā-mən, 'lē-\, Rosamond (Nina) (b. Feb. 3, 1901, Bourne End, Buckinghamshire, Eng.—d. March 12, 1990, London)   English novelist noted for her sensitive portrayals of girls and young women on the threshold of adult life. She was the sister of the editor and publisher John Lehmann.

Lehmann's first novel, *Dusty Answer* (1927), is a finely told story of a girl moving through childhood and adolescence to the complexity of mature emotions. *Invitation to the Waltz* (1932) is a slight but wholly realized work about a girl's timid confrontation with social demands. The girl appears again in *The Weather in the Streets* (1936).

Lehmann's style grew more complex and her subject matter more encompassing in her later books, which include *The Ballad and the Source* (1944), *The Echoing Grove* (1953), and *A Sea-Grape Tree* (1976). Her autobiography is entitled *The Swan in the Evening* (1967).

Lehrstück \'lār-,stük\ [German, literally, lesson play]   A form of drama that is specifically didactic in purpose and that is meant to be performed outside of the orthodox theater. Such plays were associated particularly with the epic theater of the German dramatist Bertolt Brecht. In Brecht's *Lehrstücke* the didactic element was political.

Lehtonen \'leh-tȯ-,nen\, Joel (b. Nov. 27, 1881, Sääminki, near Savonlinna, Russian Empire [now in Finland]—d. Nov. 20, 1934, Helsinki)   Finnish writer whose novels and short stories were written in the naturalistic tradition of Émile Zola and Maksim Gorky.

Lehtonen started his career as a journalist, later working as a translator, critic, and freelance writer. His earliest fiction was characterized by the Neoromanticism of the turn of the century, and his first novel, *Paholaisen viula* (1904; "The Devil's Fiddle"), is highly indebted to Selma Lagerlöf's *Gösta Berlings saga* (1891). In *Rakastunut rampa* (1922; "A Cripple in Love"), however, Lehtonen bitterly rejects the tributes to individualism that marked his youthful phase. In the short-story collection *Kuolleet omenapuut* (1918; "The Dead Apple Trees") Lehtonen views the Finnish civil war with disgust. *Putkinotko* (1919–20; "Weedpatch"), his next novel, is suffused with nihilism despite its air of good-humored tolerance. Pessimism over contemporary society appears in his last novel, *Henkien taistelu* (1933; "The Struggle of the Spirits"), and in a volume of poems, *Hyvästijättö lintukodolle* (1934; "Farewell to the Bird's Nest"), which were written shortly before his suicide.

Leiber \'lē-bər\, Fritz, *in full* Fritz Reuter Leiber, Jr. (b. Dec. 24, 1910, Chicago, Ill., U.S.—d. Sept. 5, 1992, San Francisco, Calif.)   American writer noted for his stories of sword-and-sorcery, contemporary horror, and satiric science fiction.

Leiber's first published story, "Two Sought Adventure," appeared in 1939. The story introduced the characters Grey Mouser and Fahfrd, who were featured in a series of swashbuckling adventure fantasies collected in *The Three of Swords* (1989) and *Swords' Masters* (1990). Leiber was also a pioneer of horror stories with modern urban settings, beginning with "Smoke Ghost" (1941) and continuing in his early novels such as *Gather, Darkness!* (1950) and *Conjure Wife* (1953).

In the early 1950s, the height of McCarthyism, the politically liberal Leiber was noted for his savagely satiric works about a chaotic, crumbling America, including the short story "Coming Attraction" (1950) and the novel *The Green Millennium* (1953). The satire is less harsh in his later fiction, which includes *The*

Silver Eggheads (1961) and *A Specter is Haunting Texas* (1969). Leiber's later short stories, which includes "Gonna Roll the Bones" (1967), "Ill Met in Lankhmar" (1970), and "Belsen Express" (1975), are among his most admired works.

Leino \'lā-ˌnō\, Eino, *pseudonym of* Armas Eino Leopold Lönnbohm \'lœn-ˌbûm\ (b. July 6, 1878, Paltamo, Russian Finland—d. Jan. 10, 1926, Tuusula, Fin.) Prolific and versatile poet, a master of Finnish poetic forms.

Leino studied at the University of Helsinki and worked as a journalist, principally as literary and dramatic critic on the liberal newspapers *Päivälehti* and *Helsingin Sanomat*.

In his first collection of poems, *Maaliskuun lauluja* (1896, "Songs of March"), Leino's mood was lighthearted and his style free and melodic. He gradually turned to poems of confession and solitude, critical patriotic poems about the period of Russian oppression, desolate ballad themes, and mythical motifs. The last dominate *Helkavirsiä* (1903–16; *Whitsongs*), Leino's main work, in which he returns to the meter and spirit of folklore.

Other poetry includes *Talviyö* (1905, "Winter Night") and *Halla* (1908, "Frost"), along with the historical poem *Simo hurtta* (1904–19; "Simo the Bloodhound"). Leino also wrote plays, collected in *Naamioita* (1905–11, "Masks"), contemporary novels, animal fables, and critical essays.

Leipoldt \'lā-pòlt\, C. Louis, *in full* Christiaan Frederik Louis Leipoldt (b. Dec. 28, 1880, Worcester, Cape Colony [now in South Africa]—d. April 12, 1947, Cape Town) South African doctor, journalist, and leading poet of the Second Afrikaans Language Movement.

Leipoldt began as a journalist writing for *De Kolonist*, *Het Dagblad*, and the *South African News*, and during the South African (Boer) War he was a war correspondent.

Leipoldt's poetry gave searing expression to the Afrikaners' feelings of humiliation and protest after the war and extolled the beauties of the South African landscape. His best poetry is to be found in *Oom Gert Vertel en ander gedigte* (1911; "Uncle Gert's Story and Other Poems"), *Uit drie wêrelddele* (1923; "From Three Continents"), and *Skoonheidstroos* (1932; "The Consolation of Beauty"). Leipoldt's *Die heks* (1923; "The Witch") and *Die laaste aand* (1930; "The Last Evening") were the first notable dramatic works in Afrikaans.

Leiris \lā-'rēs\, Michel Julien (b. April 20, 1901, Paris, Fr.—d. Sept. 30, 1990, Saint-Hilaire) French writer who was a pioneer in modern confessional literature and was also a noted art critic, anthropologist, and poet.

While associated with the Surrealists, Leiris published the collection of poems *Simulacre* (1925; "Simulacrum"), and, in the late 1920s, he wrote the novel *Aurora*, published in 1946. The novel and his numerous collections of poems all show his fascination with puns and wordplay and with the associative power of language.

In 1939 Leiris published the autobiographical and self-deprecating *L'Âge d'homme* (*Manhood*), which catalogs his physical and moral flaws. In 1948 he began another autobiography, *La Règle du jeu* (*Rules of the Game*), published collectively in 1976, but originally published in individual volumes as *Biffures* (1948; *Scratches*), *Fourbis* (1955; "Odds and Ends"), *Fibrilles* (1966; "Fibrils"), and *Frêle bruit* (1976; "Frail Noise"). The work is replete with memories of childhood humiliations, sexual fantasies, and contemplations of death and physical decrepitude. His *Journal 1922–1989* was published in 1992.

Leisewitz \'lī-zə-ˌvits\, Johann Anton (b. May 9, 1752, Hannover, Hanover [Germany]—d. Sept. 10, 1806, Braunschweig, Brunswick) German dramatist whose most important work, the tragedy *Julius von Tarent* (1776), is the forerunner of

Friedrich von Schiller's famous Sturm und Drang masterpiece *Die Räuber* (1781; *The Robbers*).

Leisewitz' *Julius von Tarent* treats the favorite Sturm und Drang theme of fratricide and asserts a fundamental conflict between the political state and the individual heart. Leisewitz' short dramatic sketches *Die Pfändung* (1775; "The Distraint") and *Der Besuch um Mitternacht* (1775; "The Midnight Visit") pursue the Sturm und Drang trend toward the theme of social injustice.

leitmotiv *or* **leitmotif** \'līt-mō-ˌtēf\ In literature, a dominant recurring phrase, sentence, or theme within a work, such as the repetition of the phrase "only connect" in E.M. Forster's novel *Howards End*. The word (German "leading motif") was originally applied to repeated musical phrases associated with a particular character, situation, or idea in Richard Wagner's music dramas.

Leland \'lē-lənd\, Charles Godfrey (b. Aug. 15, 1824, Philadelphia, Pa., U.S.—d. March 20, 1903, Florence, Italy) American poet and writer of miscellany, best known for the "Hans Breitmann Ballads," which reproduce the dialect and humor of the Philadelphia Germans (also called Pennsylvania Dutch).

Leland studied for two years in Germany, where he became fascinated with German culture. In 1853 he turned to journalism and worked for a number of years on P.T. Barnum's *Illustrated News*, the Philadelphia *Evening Bulletin*, and *Vanity Fair*. He also edited *Graham's Magazine*, where he published the first of his German-English poems, "Hans Breitmann's Barty" (1857). Written in a mixture of German and broken English, the poems were later collected in *The Breitmann Ballads* (complete edition, 1895).

Lélia \lāl-'yä\ Novel by George SAND, published in 1833. It shocked contemporary readers with a heroine who, like George Sand herself, was an iconoclastic, intellectual woman who scorned society's rules.

Independent and sensual, Lélia has had many lovers. Now repelled by physical passion, which represents the means by which men dominate women, Lélia tells her sister Pulchérie, a courtesan, that neither celibacy nor love affairs satisfy her. Pulchérie suggests that Lélia become a courtesan; she may find fulfillment by giving pleasure to others. Lélia tries to seduce Sténio, a young poet who is in love with her; she cannot continue, however, and sends Pulchérie in her stead. As a result of this betrayal, Sténio falls into utter debauchery, and despite attempts to rescue him, he comes to a tragic end.

Lem \'lem\, Stanisław (b. Sept. 12, 1921, Lwów, Poland [now Lviv, Ukraine]) Polish author of science fiction that veers between humanism and despair about human limitations.

Lem studied medicine at Lwów University and at Jagiellonian University in Kraków, but instead of pursuing a career in theoretical biology he began writing. After publishing poetry, scientific essays, and a conventional novel, Lem turned to science fiction. His first success, *Astronauci* (1951; "The Astronauts"), included elements of conventional Socialist Realism. He soon became a prolific writer of short stories, among them an extensive comic series about time traveler Ijon Tichy (some translated in *The Star Diaries*) and the collections *Cyberiada* (1965; *The Cyberiad: Fables for the Cybernetic Age*) and *Opowieści o pilocie Pirxie* (1968; *Tales of Pirx the Pilot*).

One of Lem's major novels was *Solaris* (1961), about a sentient ocean. In *Pamiętnik znaleziony w wannie* (1961; *Memoirs Found in a Bathtub*) an unnamed man battles a gigantic, immensely complicated, and neurotic computer. Lem's other writings include television dramas, science-fiction criticism, and nonfiction speculations about cybernetics and the sciences.

Lemaire de Belges \lə-'mer-də-'belzh\, Jean (b. *c.* 1473, Bavai, Hainaut [now in Belgium]—d. *c.* 1525) Walloon poet, historian, and pamphleteer, who, writing in French, was the last and one of the best of the school of poetic *rhétoriqueurs* and the chief forerunner, both in style and in thought, of the Renaissance humanists in France and Flanders.

Lemaire led a wandering life in the service of various princes. Most of his poems are occasional pieces in memory of various royal figures. His two *Épitres de l'amant vert* (1505) are charming and witty letters in light verse describing the grief of Margaret of Austria's parrot during her mistress's absence. Lemaire, who traveled in Italy and was an admirer of Italian culture, attempted in his *Concorde des deux langages* (after 1510; "Harmony Between Two Languages") to reconcile the influence of the Italian Renaissance with French tradition. His most extensive work is a legendary romance in prose, *Illustrations de Gaule et singularitez de Troye* (*c.* 1510).

Lemaître \lə-'metr, *Angl* -'met-rə\, Jules, *in full* François-Élie-Jules Lemaître (b. April 27, 1853, Vennecy, Fr.—d. Aug. 4, 1914, Tavers) French critic, storyteller, and dramatist, now remembered for his uniquely personal and impressionistic style of literary criticism.

Lemaître's first essay (1894), on the French historian and dramatist Joseph Renan, showed his independence of mind and lively style. His critical essays from the *Journal des débats* were collected in *Les Contemporains* (vol. 1–7, 1885–99; vol. 8, 1918; selections translated into English as *Literary Impressions*) and *Impressions du théâtre* (vol. 1–10, 1888–98; vol. 11, 1920). Lemaître was an enemy of critical dogmatism and critical systems; like his contemporary Anatole France, he emphasized his individual, human perceptions of works, controlled only by knowledge and taste.

His other works include penetrating and authoritative collections of lectures: on philosopher and writer Jean-Jacques Rousseau (1907), on the French tragedian Jean Racine (1908), on the writer and political figure Archbishop François Fénelon (1910), and on a variety of nonliterary subjects. Of his plays, *Revoltée* (1889; "Rebellious Woman"), *Les Rois* (1893; "The Kings"), and *La Massière* (1904; "The Treasurer") had moderate success. His best collections of stories include *Serenus* (1886) and *En marge des vieux livres* (1905–07; *On the Margins of Old Books*).

Lemercier \lə-mer-'syā\, Népomucène, *in full* Louise-Jean Népomucène Lemercier (b. April 21, 1771, Paris, Fr.—d. June 7, 1840, Paris) Poet and dramatist, a late proponent of classical tragedy over Romanticism, and the originator of French historical comedy.

Lemercier's first tragedy, *Méléagre*, was produced at the Comédie-Française before he was 16. His *Tartuffe révolutionnaire* (1795) created a succès de scandale and was suppressed because of its bold political allusions.

The orthodox tragedy *Agamemnon* (1794) was probably Lemercier's most celebrated play. *Pinto* (1800), a historical comedy treating the Portuguese revolution of 1640, was original in attempting to divest historical events of poetic ornament and the high seriousness of tragedy. This more experimental attitude was also shown in *Christophe Colomb* (1809), a Shakespearean comedy, and *Richard III et Jeanne Shore* (1824), an imitation of William Shakespeare and Nicholas Rowe.

The most successful of his later plays was *Frédégonde et Brunehaut* (1821), a "regular" tragedy in which he claimed to portray, from early French history, a modern equivalent of the classic House of Atreus theme.

Lemonnier \lə-mȯ-'nyā\, Camille, *in full* Antoine-Louis-Camille Lemonnier (b. March 24, 1844, Ixelles, near Brussels, Belg.—d. June 13, 1913, Ixelles) Novelist, writer of short stories, and art critic who was one of the outstanding personalities of the 19th-century French literary renaissance in Belgium.

Lemonnier's first outstanding novel, *Un Mâle* (1881; "A Male"), shows the influence of the naturalism of Émile Zola. Like his other novels, *Un Mâle* is a work of great violence, describing characters of unbridled instincts and passions. *Happechair* (1886; "Bloodsucker") deals with the life of drudgery led by mill workers. Many consider *Le Petit Homme de Dieu* (1902; "The Little Man of God"), a late naturalist novel, his masterpiece.

Lenau \'lā-ˌnau̇\, Nikolaus, *pseudonym of* Nikolaus Franz Niembsch \'nēmpsh\, Lord (Edler) von Strehlenau (b. Aug. 13, 1802, Csatád, Hungary, Holy Roman Empire—d. Aug. 22, 1850, Oberdöbling, near Vienna, Austria) Austrian poet known for melancholy lyrical verse that mirrored the pessimism of his time as well as his personal despair.

Lenau's fame rests predominantly on his shorter lyrical poems. The early poems, which were published in *Gedichte* (1832; "Poems") and *Neuere Gedichte* (1838; "Newer Poems"), demonstrate close ties to the Weltschmerz ("world grief") mood of the Romantic period and reveal a personal, almost religious relationship to nature. His later poems, *Gesammelte Gedichte*, 2 vol. (1844; "Collected Poems"), and the religious epics *Savonarola* (1837) and *Die Albigenser* (1842; "The Albigensians") deal with his relentless and unsuccessful search for order and constancy in love, nature, and faith. His *Faust. Ein Gedicht* (1836, rev. ed., 1840) is noticeably derivative of J.W. von Goethe's, but Lenau's Faust confronts an absurd life devoid of absolute values.

Lenau's epic *Don Juan* (1851) appeared posthumously. His letters to Baroness Sophie von Löwenthal, with whom he was in love from 1834 until his death, were published in 1968.

Lenclos or **Lanclos** \də-län-'klō\, Ninon de, *byname of* Anne de Lenclos (b. 1620, Paris, Fr.—d. Oct. 17, 1705, Paris) Celebrated French courtesan.

Portrait by an unknown French artist, 17th century; in the Versailles Museum, France
Giraudon—Art Resource

Ninon de Lenclos is noted for her salon in Paris that attracted a number of the most prominent literary and political figures of the age. De Lenclos's lovers were many and influential; her intellectual admirers included the playwright Molière, the poet Paul Scarron, and the skeptic Saint-Évremond.

De Lenclos's irreligious attitudes caused King Louis XIV's mother, Anne of Austria, to have her confined to a convent in 1656, but her sympathizers quickly secured her release. She defended her philosophy and conduct in her book *La Coquette vengée* (1659; "The Coquette Avenged"). During the 1670s she was protected by Scarron's widow, who later became (as Mme de Maintenon) the wife of Louis XIV.

After she retired from her career as a courtesan in 1671, de Lenclos's receptions became not only fashionable but also highly respectable. François Arouet, father of Voltaire, managed her business dealings during the final years of her life; in her will she left money for books for young Voltaire.

L'Engle \ˈleŋ-gəl\, Madeleine, *original surname* Camp \ˈkamp\, *married name* Franklin \ˈfraŋ-klən\ (b. Nov. 29, 1918, New York, N.Y., U.S.)   American author of imaginative juvenile literature that was often concerned with such themes as the conflict of good and evil, the nature of God, individual responsibility, and family life.

L'Engle pursued a career in the theater before publishing her first book, *The Small Rain* (1945), a novel about an aspiring pianist who chooses her art over her personal relationships. After writing her first children's book, *And Both Were Young* (1949), she began a series of juvenile fictional works about the Austin family—*Meet the Austins* (1960), *The Moon by Night* (1963), *The Twenty-four Days Before Christmas* (1964), *The Young Unicorns* (1968), and *A Ring of Endless Light* (1980).

In A WRINKLE IN TIME (1962), L'Engle introduced a group of young children who engage in a cosmic battle against a great evil that abhors individuality. Their story continued in *A Wind in the Door* (1973), *A Swiftly Tilting Planet* (1978), and *Many Waters* (1986). L'Engle also wrote fiction and poetry for adults. She discussed her life and writing career in *A Circle of Quiet* (1972), *The Summer of the Great-Grandmother* (1974), *The Irrational Season* (1977), *Walking on Water* (1980), and *Two Part Invention* (1988), a series of autobiographical books.

Lennep \ˈlen-ep\, Jacob van (b. March 24, 1802, Amsterdam, Neth.—d. Aug. 25, 1868, Oosterbeek)   Dutch novelist, poet, and leading man of letters in the mid-19th century.

Early in his career van Lennep found his natural genre, the historical novel, and his first such work, *De pleegzoon* (1833; *The Adopted Son*), was set in the 17th century. Like many of his later works it contains a strong element of adventure and a complicated plot. *De lotgevallen van Ferdinand Huyck* (1840; *The Count of Talavera*) is a tale of great charm and ingenuity told with humor and realism. Although he was the most popular Dutch writer of his time, van Lennep was weak in characterization and few of his works appeal to the modern reader.

Lenngren \ˈlen-grän\, Anna Maria, *original surname* Malmstedt \ˈmäm-ˌstet\ (b. June 18, 1754, Uppsala, Swed.—d. March 8, 1817, Stockholm)   Swedish poet whose Neoclassical satires and pastoral idylls show a balance and moderation characteristic of the Enlightenment and are still read for their gaiety and elegance.

Lenngren began to publish poetry when she was 18. In 1780 she married Carl Lenngren, founder (with J.H. Kellgren) and later editor of the influential *Stockholmsposten*, to which she thereafter contributed anonymously.

Her best work was written in the 1790s. Her most famous idylls are "Den glada festen" (1796; "The Merry Festival") and "Pojkarne" (1797; "The Boys"). Of her satires, "Portraiterne" (1796) and "Grefvinnans besök" (1800; "The Countess's Visit") stand out.

Lennox \ˈlen-əks\, Charlotte, *original surname* Ramsay \ˈram-zē\ (b. 1720, New York, N.Y., U.S.—d. Jan. 4, 1804, London, Eng.)   American-born English novelist whose work, especially

The Female Quixote (1752), was much admired by leading literary figures of her time.

In 1735 she was sent to England by her father to be adopted by an aunt. Her aunt proved to be insane, however, and her father died soon after, leaving her on her own. After an attempt at a career in the theater, she married Alexander Lennox in 1748. She made the first comparative study of William Shakespeare's source material, called *Shakespear Illustrated . . .* (1753–54), a project in which she was probably assisted by Samuel Johnson.

Lenormand \lə-nȯr-ˈmäⁿ\, Henri-René (b. May 3, 1882, Paris, Fr.—d. Feb. 16, 1951, Paris)   French dramatist, the most important of those playwrights concerned with subconscious motivation who flourished between World Wars I and II.

Lenormand was educated at the University of Paris and spent much of his adult life writing for the Parisian stage. His first play exploring the tragedy of human destiny was *Le Temps est un songe* (1919; "Time Is a Dream"). His best-known play, *Les Ratés* (1920; "The Failures"), traces the physical and moral disintegration of a playwright and his mistress, a mediocre actress, who, under the pressure of adversity, end their lives in murder and suicide. Lenormand often chose abnormal or pathological types for his characters, and to portray their inner struggles, he made use of tableaux, *i.e.*, a succession of very short scenes serving to show the various facets of the characters' inner personalities.

Lenormand's play *Le Simoun* (1920; "The Simoom") depicts the demoralizing influence of the life and climate of the tropics on a European man who becomes obsessed with an incestuous passion for his adult daughter. *Le Lâche* (1925; "The Coward") is a psychological study of fear in a man about to go to war as a soldier. Two of Lenormand's plays, *Le Mangeur de rêves* (1922; "The Dream Eater") and *L'Homme et ses fantômes* (1924; "Man and His Phantoms"), explore the Oedipus complex. His other plays include *Les Possédés* (1909; "The Possessed"), *À l'Ombre du mal* (1924; "The Shadow of Evil"), *Une Vie secrète* (1929; "A Secret Life"), and *Asie* (1931; "Asia").

Lenz \ˈlents\, Jakob Michael Reinhold (b. Jan. 12, 1751, Sesswegen, Livonia, Russia [now Cesvaine, Latvia]—d. May 24, 1792, Moscow)   Russian-born German poet and dramatist of the Sturm und Drang period, who is considered an important forerunner of 19th-century naturalism and of 20th-century Expressionist theater.

Lenz studied theology at Königsberg University. In Strasbourg he became a member of J.W. von Goethe's circle and was strongly influenced by the Sturm und Drang dramatists. Lenz made his reputation with plays from the Strasbourg years, an eccentric didactic comedy, *Der Hofmeister oder Vortheile der Privaterziehung* (1774; "The Tutor, or the Advantages of Private Education"), and his best play, *Die Soldaten* (1776; "The Soldiers"). *Anmerkungen übers Theater* (1774; "Observations on the Theater") contains a translation of William Shakespeare's *Love's Labour's Lost* and outlines Lenz's theories of dramaturgy, including contempt for classical conventions, particularly the unities of time and place, and a search for utterly realistic depiction of character.

Consumed by the ambition to become Goethe's equal, Lenz made himself ridiculous by imitating both Goethe's writing style and his personal life. His eccentricities were thought to be harmless and amusing until a tactless parody brought about his expulsion from the court in disgrace. The remaining years of his life were spent in aimless drifting and poverty and, eventually, in insanity. Georg Büchner portrayed episodes of Lenz's insanity in his short novel *Lenz* (1839).

León \lā-ˈōn\, Luis de (b. 1527, Belmonte, Cuenca province, Spain—d. Aug. 23, 1591, Madrigal de las Altas)   Spanish mystic and poet who contributed greatly to Spanish Renaissance literature.

León was a monk educated chiefly at Salamanca, where he obtained his first chair in 1561. Academic rivalry between the Dominicans and the Augustinians, whom he had joined in 1544, led to his denunciation to the Inquisition for criticizing the text of the Vulgate. After almost five years' imprisonment (1572–76), he was exonerated and restored to his chair, which, however, he resigned in favor of the man who had replaced him. His prose masterpiece, *De los nombres de Cristo* (1583; "On the Names of Christ"), a treatise on the various names given to Christ in the Scriptures, is the supreme exemplar of Spanish classical prose style: clear, lofty, and, though studied, devoid of affectation. His translations from Greek, Latin, Hebrew, and Italian include the Song of Solomon (modern edition by Jorge Guillén, 1936) and the Book of Job, both with commentary. León's poems, containing many of the motifs of *De los nombres de Cristo*, were published posthumously in 1631. His other works include theological treatises and commentaries in Latin on various psalms and books of the Bible and *La perfecta casada* (1583; "The Perfect Married Woman"), a commentary in Spanish on Proverbs 31, incorporating elements of the medieval ascetic tradition of misogyny interspersed with picturesque glimpses of feminine customs of the day.

Leonard \'len-ərd\, Elmore, *in full* Elmore John Leonard, Jr. (b. Oct. 11, 1925, New Orleans, La., U.S.) American author of popular crime novels known for his use of local color and his uncanny ear for realistic dialogue.

Leonard served in the U.S. Naval Reserve (1943–46), then graduated from the University of Detroit. While composing scripts for advertising and educational films, he began writing western novels and short stories. The 1957 films *3:10 to Yuma* and *The Tall T* were based on his novelettes, and Leonard's novel *Hombre* (1961) was also adapted for film in 1967. His first crime novel, *The Big Bounce*, was published in 1969.

Leonard followed the latter with a series of novels set primarily in Detroit and Florida. Among his outstanding crime novels of the 1970s are *Fifty-two Pickup* (1974), *Swag* (1976; also published as *Ryan's Rules*), *Unknown Man No. 89* (1977), and *The Switch* (1978). His novel *Stick* (1983) became a bestseller. Subsequent novels include *LaBrava* (1983), *Glitz* (1985), *Bandits* (1987), *Freaky Deaky* (1988), and *Rum Punch* (1992).

Leonidas \lē-'än-i-dəs\ of Tarentum \tə-'ren-təm\ (fl. first half of the 3rd century BC) Greek poet more important for his influence on the later Greek epigram than for his own poems.

Leonidas was among the earlier Hellenistic epigrammatists, and about 100 of his epigrams survive, all but two collected in the *Greek Anthology*. Leonidas was a facile versifier but seldom more. Not many of his sepulchral or dedicatory epigrams can have been intended for inscriptions; the deaths often seem contrived, the dedications an excuse for a flourish of fancy adjectives. For generations epigrammatists lacking inspiration aped his manner and composed variations on his poems.

leonine verse \'lē-ə-,nīn\ 1. Latin or French verse in which the last word in the line rhymes with the word just before the caesura (as in "gloria factorum temere conceditus horum"). Such rhymes were already referred to as *rime leonine* in the anonymous 12th-century romance *Guillaume d'Angleterre*. A later tradition imputes their invention to a 12th-century Parisian canon and Latin poet named Leonius or Leoninus, but "leonine" may simply refer to their supposed preeminence over other verse forms. 2. English verse in which the end of the line rhymes with a sound occurring near the middle of the line (as in Alfred, Lord Tennyson's "the long light shakes across the lakes"). *See also* INTERNAL RHYME.

Leonov \lʲi-'ó-nəf\, Leonid Maksimovich (b. May 19 [May 31, New Style], 1899, Moscow, Russia—d. Aug. 8, 1994, Moscow) Soviet novelist and playwright whose work was significant for its psychological portrayals.

From 1915 to 1918 Leonov worked as a journalist in Arkhangelsk, where he published his first poems and sketches. In his approach to characterization and plot construction, he was similar to the 19th-century Russian novelist Fyodor Dostoyevsky. His characters are explored and revealed from within, and the plots are many-leveled. Two of Leonov's major novels are exemplary: *Barsuki* (1924; *The Badgers*), which deals both with prerevolutionary Russia and with the new Russia; and *Vor* (1927; *The Thief*), which portrays various types of Moscow underworld characters during the early 1920s.

A writer most adroit in portraying moral and psychological problems, Leonov tried to adjust to the demands of communist critics for Socialist Realism. The effort was reflected in the novels he wrote in the 1930s, including *Sot* (1930; *Soviet River*), *Skutarevsky* (1932), and *Doroga na okean* (1935; *Road to the Ocean*). Also memorable is the novel *Vzyatiye velikoshumska* (1944; *Chariots of Wrath*). He wrote 12 plays between 1936 and 1946; 11 of them were produced by Moscow theaters, but the 12th did not get by the censors. His long novel *Russky les* (1953; *The Russian Forest*) was awarded a Lenin Prize in 1957. Leonov was elected to the Academy of Sciences in 1972.

Leonowens \'lē-ə-,nō-ənz\, Anna Harriette, *original name* Crawford \'krô-fərd\ (b. Nov. 5, 1834, Carnarvon, Carnarvonshire, Wales—d. Jan. 19, 1914, Montreal, Ont., Can.) British writer best known as the governess employed by King Mongkut (Rama IV) of Siam (now Thailand) for the instruction of his children.

At an early age Anna went to Asia, and there she married Major Thomas Lewis Leonowens of the Indian army. After the major died in 1858, she lived in Singapore with her two children until she was invited by King Mongkut in 1862 to serve as governess to the royal children. For five years she was part of the royal household in Bangkok. After leaving Siam she wrote two books, *The English Governess at the Siamese Court* (1870) and *The Romance of the Harem* (1872).

Her adventures in Siam inspired a popular book by Margaret Landon, *Anna and the King of Siam* (1944), on which was based the musical by Richard Rodgers and Oscar Hammerstein II, *The King and I*, as well as two motion pictures and a television series.

Leontyev or **Leontiev** \lʲe-'òn-tyif\, Konstantin Nikolayevich (b. Jan. 13 [Jan. 25, New Style], 1831, Kudinovo, near Kaluga, Russia—d. Nov. 12 [Nov. 24], 1891, near Moscow) Russian essayist who questioned the benefits to Russia of following contemporary industrial and egalitarian developments in Europe.

Leontyev entered the Russian consular service, where he held posts in Crete, Edirne, and Salonika. In 1879 he became assistant editor of the newspaper *Varshavsky dnevnik* ("Warsaw Diary"), and a year later he joined the staff of the Moscow censorship department.

Leontyev wrote with a clarity and a persistent personal conviction rare among Russian political thinkers. He tried to find in the Russian Empire an alternative that could civilize an Eastern world recoiling from the commercially minded, democratic West. He elaborated his thoughts on the subject in a number of remarkable essays, many of which were collected in the volume *Vostok, Rossiya i slavyanstvo* (1885–86; "The East, Russia and Slavdom"). Leontyev also wrote novels, short stories, and a revealing autobiography, *Moya literaturnaya sudba* (1875; "My Literary Destiny").

Leopard, The   Novel by Giuseppe TOMASI DI LAMPEDUSA, published in 1958 as *Il gattopardo*. The novel is a psychological study of Don Fabrizio, prince of Salina (called the Leopard, after his family crest), who witnesses with detachment the transfer of power in Sicily from the old Bourbon aristocracy to the new Kingdom of Italy and the grasping, unscrupulous liberal bourgeoisie during the 1860s.

While adhering to the Don's conservative viewpoint, the rich narrative unfolds in a series of compelling dramatic scenes. The character of Don Fabrizio is one of the most striking in modern Italian literature.

Leopardi \ˌlā-ō-ˈpär-dē\, Giacomo (b. June 29, 1798, Recanati, Papal States [Italy]—d. June 14, 1837, Naples)   Italian poet, scholar, and philosopher whose outstanding scholarly and philosophical works and superb lyric poetry place him among the great writers of the 19th century.

By the age of 16 Leopardi independently had mastered Greek, Latin, and several modern languages; had translated many classical works; and had written two tragedies, many Italian poems, and several scholarly commentaries. He eventually became blind in one eye and developed a cerebrospinal condition that afflicted him all his life. Forced to suspend his studies for long periods, and wounded by his parents' neglect, he poured out his hopes and his bitterness in poems such as *Appressamento della morte* (written 1816, published 1835; "Approach of Death"), a visionary work in terza rima.

Leopardi was devastated by his frustrated love for his married cousin, Gertrude Cassi (subject of his journal *Diario d'amore* and the elegy "Il primo amore"), and by the death from consumption of Terese Fattorini, subject of one of his greatest lyrics, "A Silvia." His verse collection *Canzoni* was published in 1824, and in 1825 he accepted an offer to edit Cicero's works. He published *Versi* (1826), an enlarged collection of poems, and *Operette morali* (1827; "Minor Moral Works"), an influential philosophical exposition, mainly in dialogue form, of his doctrine of despair. In 1831 he published a further collection of poems, *I canti*. Yet another frustrated love inspired some of his saddest lyrics. He finally settled in Naples in 1833, where, among other works, he wrote *Ginestra* (1836). Leopardi's finest poems are probably the lyrics called "Idillii."

Leopold \ˈlā-ō-ˌpōlt\, Carl Gustaf af (b. March 26, 1756, Stockholm, Swed.—d. Nov. 9, 1829, Stockholm)   Swedish court poet in the service of Gustav III and Gustav IV.

Leopold began his career in 1792 with articles and polemical essays propagating the rational ideas of the Enlightenment and parrying the criticism of the younger generation of Romantics. A member of the Swedish Academy from its foundation in 1786, he became, on the death of the poet and critic J.H. Kellgren (1795), the dominant arbiter of classical taste in Sweden. His philosophical, didactic poetry is typified by his ode "Försynen" (1793; "Providence").

Leopold \ˈlā-ə-ˌpōlt\, Jan Hendrik (b. May 11, 1865, 's-Hertogenbosch, Neth.—d. June 21, 1925, Rotterdam)   Poet whose unique expression and masterly technique set him apart from other heirs to the Dutch literary renaissance of the 1880s. His poetry is often wistful and melancholy in mood, conveying a solitude of spirit that was probably accentuated by his deafness.

Leopold made his debut in the periodical *De Nieuwe Gids* ("The New Guide") in 1893 and later collaborated on Albert Verwey's *Tweemaandelijks tijdschrift* ("Bimonthly Periodical"). His most highly rated work is the epic poem "Cheops" (1915), which describes in rich, musical language the journey of a pharaoh's soul after death.

leprechaun or **leprecaun** or **leprehaun** \ˈlep-rə-ˌkän, -ˌkȯn\ [Irish *leipreachán, lucharachán* puny creature, dwarf, elf, from

Middle Irish *luchrapán, lupraccán,* from Old Irish *luchorpán,* from *lu-* small + *corp* body (from Latin *corpus*) + *-án,* diminutive suffix]   In Irish folklore, a mischievous fairy in the form of a tiny old man. Solitary by nature, he is said to live in remote places and to make shoes. He possesses a hidden crock of gold; if captured he may, if his captor keeps his eyes on him, reveal its hiding place. Usually, however, the captor is tricked into glancing away and the fairy vanishes.

Lermontov \ˈlyer-mən-təf\, Mikhail (Yuryevich) (b. Oct. 3 [Oct. 15, New Style], 1814, Moscow, Russia—d. July 15 [July 27], 1841, Pyatigorsk)   The leading Russian Romantic poet and author of the novel *Geroy nashego vremeni* (1840; A HERO OF OUR TIME), which was to have a profound influence on later Russian writers.

Lermontov's first volume of verse, *Vesna* ("Spring"), was published in 1830. The same year he entered Moscow University, where he wrote many lyrical verses, longer narrative poems, and dramas. In 1832 Lermontov left the university and went to St. Petersburg, where he entered the cadet school, from which he graduated in 1834.

Lermontov was greatly shaken in 1837 by the death of the poet Aleksandr Pushkin in a duel. He wrote an elegy denouncing not only his killer but also the court aristocracy, whom he saw as executioners of freedom. As soon as the verses became known to the court of Nicholas I, Lermontov was arrested and exiled to the Caucasus. He was allowed to return to the capital in 1838, and soon his verses began to appear in the press. Lauded for having suffered and been exiled because of his libertarian verses, Lermontov began to be seen as Pushkin's successor.

In 1840 Lermontov was exiled again, this time to an infantry regiment in the Caucasus. During the journey back to his regiment after a short leave in 1841, he experienced a flood of creative energy: his last notebook contains such masterpieces of Russian lyric poetry as "Utyos" ("The Cliff"), "Spor" ("Argument"), "Svidaniye" ("Meeting"), "Listok" ("A Leaf"), and "Prorok" ("Prophet"), his last work. Lermontov lingered on in the health resort of Pyatigorsk, where he was provoked into fighting a duel that ended in his death.

His freedom-loving sentiments and his bitterly skeptical evaluation of the times in which he lived are embodied in his philosophical lyric poetry—"Duma" ("Thought"), "Ne ver sebe . . . " ("Do Not Trust Yourself . . . ") and are interpreted in an original fashion in the romantic and fantastic images of his Caucasian poems—*Mtsyri* (1840) and *Demon* (1841)—on which the poet worked for the remainder of his life. The novel *Geroy nashego vremeni*, written in superb prose, contains the summary of his reflections on contemporary society and the fortunes of his generation.

Lernet-Holenia \ˈler-net-hō-ˈlā-nyä\, Alexander (b. Oct. 21, 1897, Vienna, Austria—d. July 3, 1976, Vienna)   Popular dramatist, poet, and novelist, noted for his nostalgia for pre-World War I Austria. In particular, his novel *Die Standarte* (1934), which depicts military unrest in Serbia in 1918, illustrates the loss of authority in the disintegrating empire.

Lernet-Holenia wrote several successful plays, ranging from society comedies to farces and melodrama: *Österreichische Komödie* (1927; "Austrian Comedy"), *Ollapotrida* (1926; "Mishmash"), *Erotik* (1927), *Parforce* (1928; "By All Means"), *Die nächtliche Hochzeit* (1929, published as a novel 1930; "The Nightly Marriage"), and *Die Frau des Potiphar* (1934; "Potiphar's Wife"). His poetry, published in such volumes as *Pastorale* (1921), *Das Geheimnis Sankt Michaels* (1927; "St. Michael's Secret"), and *Die goldene Horde* (1935; "The Golden Horde"), mingles the classical tradition and modern influences.

During the 1930s Lernet-Holenia also wrote detective and adventure novels, including *Ich war Jack Mortimer* (1933; "I Was Jack Mortimer") and *Die Auferstehung des Maltravers* (1936; "The Resurrection of Maltraver").

His later works include the novel *Prinz Eugen* (1960) and the collection of short stories *Mayerling* (1960), both of which reflect a nostalgia for the old Austria.

Leroux \lə-'rü\, Gaston (b. May 6, 1868, Paris, Fr.—d. April 15/16, 1927, Nice) French novelist, best known for his *Le Fantôme de l'opéra* (1910; *The Phantom of the Opera*), which later became famous in various film and stage renditions.

By 1890 Leroux had become a full-time journalist, and from 1894 to 1906 he sailed the world as a correspondent, reporting back to Paris various adventures in which he took part, notably during the Russian Revolution of 1905. In the early 1900s he began writing novels, his first success being *Le Mystère de la chambre jaune* (1907; *The Mystery of the Yellow Room*). In 1910 *Le Fantôme de l'opéra* appeared and received only moderate success. The melodrama of a hideous recluse abducting a beautiful young woman in a Paris opera house did not achieve international celebrity until the American actor Lon Chaney created the title role in the silent-film version of 1925.

Lesage or **Le Sage** \lə-'säzh\, Alain-René (b. May 6, 1668, Sarzeau, Fr.—d. Nov. 17, 1747, Boulogne) Prolific French satirical dramatist and author of the classic picaresque novel GIL BLAS, which was influential in making the picaresque form a European literary fashion.

Lesage studied law in Paris but later abandoned his legal clerkship to dedicate himself to literature. He received a pension from the abbot of Lyonne, who also taught him Spanish and interested him in the Spanish theater.

Lesage's early plays were adaptations of Spanish models and included the highly successful comedy *Crispin, rival de son maître* (performed 1707; *Crispin, Rival of His Master*). His prose work *Le Diable boiteux* (1707; *The Devil upon Two Sticks*) is of Spanish inspiration, but its satire is aimed at Parisian society. He composed more than 100 *comédies-vaudevilles* for the popular Théâtre de la Foire, and he is considered the successor to Molière.

Lesage's *Histoire de Gil Blas de Santillane* (1715–1735; *The Adventures of Gil Blas of Santillane*) is one of the earliest realistic novels. It concerns the education and adventures of a young valet as he progresses from one master to the next.

Leskov \lʲi-'skòf\, Nikolay Semyonovich, *pseudonym* Stebnitsky \stʲib-'nʲits-kʲč\ (b. Feb. 4 [Feb. 16, New Style], 1831, Gorokhovo, Russia—d. Feb. 21 [March 5], 1895, St. Petersburg) Novelist and short-story writer who has been described as the greatest of Russian storytellers.

As a child Leskov was taken to various monasteries by his grandmother, and he used those early memories of Russian monastic life with good effect in his most famous novel, *Soboryane* (1872; *Cathedral Folk*).

In 1865 Leskov published his best-known story, *Ledi Makbet Mtsenskogo uezda* (*Lady Macbeth of the Mtsensk District*), the passionate heroine of which lives and dies by violence. His most popular tale, however, remains *Skaz o Tulskom kosom Levshe i o stalnoy Blokhe* (1881; "The Tale of Cross-eyed Lefty from Tula and the Steel Flea"), a masterpiece of Gogolesque comedy in which an illiterate smith from Tula outwits the most advanced British craftsman. Another story, the picaresque *Ocharovanny strannik* (1873; *Enchanted Wanderer*), was written after a visit to the monastic islands on Lake Ladoga in 1872. His early novels *Nekuda* (1864; "Nowhere to Go") and *Na nozhakh* (1870–71; "At Daggers Drawn") were violently attacked for their antirevolutionary attitudes. In 1969 W.B.

Edgerton translated 13 of Leskov's stories into English for the first time and included a new translation of "The Steel Flea."

Leśmian \'leshʸ-myán\, Bolesław, *original surname* Lesman \'les-mán\ (b. Jan. 12, 1878, Warsaw, Poland, Russian Empire—d. Nov. 5, 1937, Warsaw) Lyric poet who was among the first to adapt Symbolism and Expressionism to Polish verse.

Of Jewish origin, Leśmian was educated in Kiev, wrote some of his early poems in Russian, and spent most of his life practicing law in a provincial town.

His small literary output includes *Sąd rozstajny* (1912; "Orchard"); *Łąka* (1920; "The Meadow"), the volume that established his reputation; *Napój cienisty* (1936; "The Shadowy Drink"); and *Dziejba leśna* (1938; "Woodland Tale").

Lespinasse \les-pē-'nàs\, Julie de, *in full* Julie-Jeanne-Éléanore de Lespinasse (b. 1732, Lyon, Fr.—d. May 23, 1776, Paris) Hostess of one of the most brilliant and emancipated of Parisian salons and the author of several volumes of passionate letters that reveal her romantic sensibility and genuine literary gifts.

Mme du Deffand, one of the reigning aristocratic Parisian hostesses, met Lespinasse and, recognizing her intelligence and charm, persuaded her to come to Paris in 1754 and assist at her literary salon. Lespinasse was dismissed in 1764 when Mme du Deffand became jealous of her younger companion's popularity. Lespinasse set up her own salon in the rue Saint-Dominique, and the philosopher and mathematician Jean Le Rond d'Alembert joined her there. She nursed him through a serious illness but never returned his deep love for her. Instead, she was torn between her passions for unworthy men of fashion—the Marquess de Mora and the Count de Guibert. Lespinasse's *Lettres* (1809) show her intensely experienced emotions of love, remorse, and despair. Denis Diderot wrote of her in his *Rêve de d'Alembert*, which she requested he suppress.

Lessing \'les-iŋ\, Doris (May), *original surname* Tayler \'tā-lər\ (b. Oct. 22, 1919, Kermānshāh [now Bākhtarān], Iran) British writer whose novels and short stories are largely concerned with people caught in the social and political upheavals of the 20th century.

Lessing lived on a farm in Southern Rhodesia [now Zimbabwe] from 1924 until she settled in England in 1949. There she began her career as a writer. *In Pursuit of the English* (1960) tells of her initial months in England, and *Going Home* (1957) describes her reaction to Rhodesia on a return visit. She reflected further on this subject in *African Laughter: Four Visits to Zimbabwe* (1992). Her early years (through 1949) are chronicled in *Under My Skin* (1994), an autobiography.

Her first published book, *The Grass Is Singing* (1950), is about a white farmer and his wife and their African servant in Rhodesia. Many critics consider her series of novels about Martha QUEST—who grows up in southern Africa and settles in England—her most substantial work. Called the *Children of Violence*, the series comprises *Martha Quest* (1952), *A Proper Marriage* (1954), *A Ripple from the Storm* (1958), *Landlocked* (1965), and *The Four-Gated City* (1969). THE GOLDEN NOTEBOOK (1962), in which a woman writer attempts to come to terms with her life through her art, is one of the most complex and the most widely read of her novels. A master of the short story, Lessing published several collections; these included *Five* (1953), *The Story of a Non-Marrying Man* (1972; also published as *The Temptation of Jack Orkney*), and her African stories, many of which were collected in *This Was the Old Chief's Country* (1951) and *The Sun Between Their Feet* (1973).

Lessing turned to science fiction in a five-novel sequence titled *Canopus in Argos: Archives* (1979–83). The novels *The Diary of a Good Neighbour* (1983) and *If the Old Could . . .* (1984)

were published under the name Jane Somers to dramatize the problems of unknown writers. Her later novels include *The Good Terrorist* (1985) and *The Fifth Child* (1988).

Lessing \\'les-iŋ\\, Gotthold Ephraim (b. Jan. 22, 1729, Kamenz, Upper Lusatia, Saxony [Germany]—d. Feb. 15, 1781, Braunschweig, Brunswick) German dramatist, critic, and writer on philosophy and aesthetics. He helped free German drama from the influence of classical and French models and wrote the first German plays of lasting importance.

Detail of an oil painting by Georg May, 1768
Gleimhaus, Halberstadt, Germany

In 1746 Lessing entered the University of Leipzig as a student of theology. His real interest, however, lay in literature, philosophy, and art, and he became fascinated by the theater in Leipzig. He wrote several comedies, including *Damon, oder Die wahre Freundschaft* (1747; "Damon; or, True Friendship"), *Die alte Jungfer* (1749; "The Old Maid"), *Die Juden* (1754; "The Jews"), *Der Misogyn* (1755; "The Misogynist"), and *Der Freigeist* (1755; "The Free Thinker"). In 1748 he moved to Berlin, where he made a name for himself through his brilliant and witty criticism for the *Berlinische Privilegirte Zeitung*.

After a brief period in Wittenberg, where he took a degree in medicine, he returned to Berlin. There he published a six-volume edition of his works that included *Miss Sara Sampson* (1755), which is the first major *bürgerliches Trauerspiel*, or domestic tragedy, in German literature. With his friends Moses Mendelssohn and C.F. Nicolai, Lessing conducted a truly epoch-making correspondence (*Briefwechsel über das Trauerspiel*, 1756–57; "Correspondence About Tragedy") on the aesthetic of tragic drama.

In 1760 Lessing went to Breslau, where he studied philosophy and aesthetics, the result being the great treatise *Laokoon: oder über die Grenzen der Malerei und Poesie* (1766; *Laocoön: An Essay on the Limits of Painting and Poetry*). The poetic fruit of Lessing's stay in Breslau was the comic masterpiece *Minna von Barnhelm oder Das Soldatenglück* (1767; *Minna von Barnhelm; or, A Soldier's Fortune*), which marks the birth of classical German comedy. Lessing next accepted the offer of a group of Hamburg merchants to act as adviser and critic in their privately funded venture of a national theater. The project collapsed within a year, but his reviews of more than 50 performances were published, in the form of 104 brief essays on basic principles of the drama, under the title *Hamburgische Dramaturgie* (1767–69; *Hamburg Dramaturgy*).

Lessing's last years were spent at Wolfenbüttel. Among the works of this period were his tragedy *Emilia Galotti*, performed in 1772; a "dramatic poem" in iambic verse, *Nathan der Weise* (*Nathan the Wise*), which appeared in 1779; and Lessing's last work, *Die Erziehung des Menschengeschlechts* (1780; *The Education of the Human Race*), a treatise that expresses his belief in the perfectibility of the human race.

Lesson, The   One-act play by Eugène IONESCO, a comedic parable of the dangers inherent in indoctrination, performed in 1951 as *La Leçon* and published in 1953.

The absurd plot of the play concerns a timid professor who uses the meaning he assigns to words to establish tyrannical dominance over an eager female student.

Lestrade, Inspector \\lə-'sträd\\   Fictional character, the perennially confounded Scotland Yard inspector who must request the help of Sherlock Holmes in the Holmes stories by Sir Arthur Conan DOYLE.

L'Estrange \\lə-'stränj\\, Sir Roger (b. Dec. 17, 1616, Hunstanton, Norfolk, Eng.—d. Dec. 11, 1704, London)   One of the earliest of English journalists and pamphleteers and an ardent supporter of the Royalist cause during the English Civil Wars (1642–51) and Commonwealth period (1649–60).

L'Estrange was strongly implicated in an unsuccessful attempt to recapture the town of Lynn, Norfolk, from anti-Royalist forces in 1644, and he was imprisoned for four years. He later withdrew to the Netherlands. Just before the restoration of the monarchy he attacked the poet John Milton, a leading apologist for the Commonwealth, in a pamphlet called *No Blinde Guides* (1660), a reference to Milton's blindness.

The Revolution of 1688, in which King James II lost the throne, cost L'Estrange his official post of surveyor of the imprimery (printing office). He afterward supported his wife and himself chiefly by translations of many standard authors, including the lively *Fables of Aesop, and Other Eminent Mythologists: With Morals and Reflexions* (1692).

Le Sueur \\lə-'sür\\, Meridel (b. Feb. 22, 1900, Murray, Iowa, U.S.)   American author who espoused feminism and social reform in her fiction, journalism, and poetry.

Le Sueur grew up on the Midwestern plains, where she was influenced by her family's heritage of social and political activism and by the stories and poetry she heard from Native American women. She quit high school, acted in silent films, and began writing fiction and working as a journalist in the late 1920s.

The lives of women during the Great Depression was the subject of her first novel, *The Girl*. Although she wrote it in 1939, the novel was not published until 1978. Le Sueur's short stories, including those collected in *Salute to Spring* (1940), were widely admired. *North Star Country* (1945) is a history of the people of the Midwest in the form of an oral history, and *Crusaders* (1955) is a biography of her parents. In the late 1940s and the 1950s, while under FBI surveillance because of her political views, she wrote children's books on American history and folklore. Her other works include the nonfiction *Conquistadores* (1973) and *The Mound Builders* (1974); *Rites of Ancient Ripening* (1975; poetry); *Harvest: Collected Stories* (1977); and *Ripening: Selected Work, 1927–80* (1982).

Lethe \\'lē-thē\\   In Greek mythology, daughter of Eris (Strife) and the personification of oblivion. Lethe is also the name of a water or plain in the infernal regions.

Leto \\'lē-tō\\, *Latin* Latona \\lə-'tō-nə\\   In classical mythology, a Titan, the daughter of Coeus and Phoebe, and mother of the god Apollo and the goddess Artemis. Leto, pregnant by Zeus, sought a place of refuge where she might safely deliver. She finally reached the barren isle of Delos, which, according to some, was a wandering rock borne about by the waves until it was fixed to the bottom of the sea for the birth of Apollo and Artemis. In later versions the wanderings of Leto were ascribed to the jealousy of Zeus's wife, Hera, who was enraged at Leto's bearing Zeus's children. The foundation of Delphi followed immediately upon the birth of Apollo.

letter \\'let-ər\\, *also called* epistolary literature.   A personal written message to another person. The first notable collection of letters was gathered by Atticus and Tiro, who published nearly 1,000 of Cicero's letters. This gave rise to letter writing as a literary genre. Catullus wrote in verse, and Horace established the verse letter with striking examples in his *Epistles*. The popularity of the letter as a genre has continued down to the present day.

Letters from the Earth Miscellany of fiction, essays, and notes by Mark TWAIN, published posthumously in 1962. Written over a period of 40 years, the pieces in the anthology are characterized by a sense of ironic pessimism.

The title piece comprises letters written by Satan to his fellow angels about the shameless pride and foolishness of humans. "Papers of the Adam Family," a first-person family history of Adam and Eve, traces the first failed attempts at civilization. Other pieces include "A Cat-Tale," an amusing, alliterative bedtime story; "Fenimore Cooper's Literary Offenses," a critique of that author's style; and "The Damned Human Race," a collection of bitter satirical bits.

Let Us Now Praise Famous Men Nonfiction book on the daily lives of Depression-era tenant farmers, with text by James AGEE and black-and-white portraits by documentary photographer Walker Evans, published in 1941.

In 1936, at the request of *Fortune* magazine, Agee and Evans went to Alabama to report on the lives of tenant farmers. During the next five years the project evolved into a visually stunning, multilayered work that conveyed in the first person Agee's responses to his subjects as an involved observer, as well as his difficulties in chronicling their lives in this manner.

Leucothea \lū-'käth-ē-ə\ ("White Goddess [of the Foam]") In Greek mythology, a sea goddess first mentioned in Homer's *Odyssey* for rescuing the Greek hero Odysseus from drowning. She was customarily identified with Ino, daughter of the Phoenician Cadmus; because she cared for the infant god Dionysus, the goddess Hera drove Ino (or her husband, Athamas) mad so that she and her son, Melicertes, leaped terrified into the sea. Both were changed into marine deities—Ino as Leucothea, Melicertes as Palaemon.

Lever \'lē-vər\, Charles James (b. Aug. 31, 1806, Dublin, Ire.—d. June 1, 1872, Trieste, Austria-Hungary [now in Italy]) Irish editor and author of lighthearted, rollicking novels, many on post-Napoleonic Irish life and characters.

In 1831, after study at Trinity College, Cambridge, Lever qualified for the practice of medicine. His gambling and extravagance, however, left him short of money despite his income and his inheritance, and he began to utilize his gifts as a raconteur. In 1837 *The Confessions of Harry Lorrequer* appeared serially in the *Dublin University Magazine*, where it was a popular success. His novel *Charles O'Malley*, which ranges from the west of Ireland to the Iberian Peninsula, appeared in 1841, and *Jack Hinton* and *Tom Burke of "Ours,"* a vigorous story of an Irishman in the service of the French empire, followed in 1843.

In 1842 Lever assumed the editorship of the *Dublin University Magazine* and gathered around him Irish wits. He traveled to the European continent in 1845 and served as British consul at La Spezia (1857) and Trieste (1867). He continued to write novels, among them *The Knight of Gwynne* (1847), *Confessions of Con Cregan* (1849), *Roland Cashel* (1850), *The Fortunes of Glencore* (1857), and *Lord Kilgobbin* (1872).

Levertin \'lā-ver-tēn\, Oscar Ivar (b. July 17, 1862, near Stockholm, Swed.—d. Sept. 22, 1906, Stockholm) Swedish poet and scholar, a leader of the Swedish Romantic movement of the 1890s.

Levertin was educated at Uppsala University and in 1899 became professor of literature at the University of Stockholm. After the death of his first wife and an attack of tuberculo-

sis, which led him to go to Davos, Switz., he abandoned his early naturalism for Romanticism. In Davos he completed his first volume of poems, *Legender och visor* (1891; "Legends and Songs"), which placed him at the head of the new Romantic movement. In *Nya dikter* (1894; "New Poems"), the atmosphere and coloring are less melancholy. *Dikter* (1901) has a simpler and more compressed style and has genuine Swedish themes. His last and perhaps finest poetical work was *Kung Salomo och Morolf* (1905; "King Solomon and Morolf"), based on material drawn from Oriental tales and medieval romances. Levertin also wrote short stories, and from 1897 until his death he was a leading literary critic of the *Svenska Dagbladet* ("Swedish Daily Paper").

Levertov \'lev-ər-,tôf\, Denise (b. Oct. 24, 1923, Ilford, Essex, Eng.) English-born American poet who wrote deceptively matter-of-fact verse.

Levertov became a civilian nurse during World War II, serving in London throughout the bombings. She settled in New York in 1947 with her husband and was naturalized in 1955.

Her first volume of verse, *The Double Image* (1946), was not successful. *Here and Now* (1957) was quickly followed by *Overland to the Islands* (1958), and five more volumes appeared in the 1960s. She also translated the Buddhist work *In Praise of Krishna: Songs from the Bengali* (1967; with Edward Dimock, Jr.). *Relearning the Alphabet* (1970) discloses her concern with social issues. Opposed to the war in Vietnam, she was active in the War Resisters League and edited for it the collection *Out of the War Shadow* (1967).

In *Footprints* (1972) she reverted to the mystical tone of her earlier works. Levertov's later efforts include essays and prose, as in *The Poet in the World* (1973), and several collections of poetry, including *Candles in Babylon* (1982), *Breathing the Water* (1987), *A Door in the Hive* (1989), and *Evening Train* (1992).

Levi \'lā-vē\, Carlo (b. Nov. 29, 1902, Turin, Italy—d. Jan. 4, 1975, Rome) Italian writer, painter, and political journalist whose first documentary novel became an international literary sensation and enhanced the trend toward social realism in postwar Italian literature.

Levi was a painter and a practicing physician when he was exiled to southern Italy for antifascist activities. His *Cristo si è fermato a Eboli* (1945; *Christ Stopped at Eboli*) reflects the visual sensitivity of a painter and the compassionate objectivity of a doctor. Quickly acclaimed a literary masterpiece, it was widely translated.

Though Levi's first novel is unquestionably his masterpiece, he wrote other important nonfiction works. His *Paura della libertà* (1947; *Of Fear and Freedom*) proclaims the necessity of intellectual freedom despite an inherent human dread of it. *L'orologio* (1950; *The Watch*) deals with a postwar cabinet crisis in Rome, *Le parole sono pietre* (1955; *Words Are Stones*) is a study of Sicily, and *La doppia notte dei tigli* (1959; *The Linden Trees*, or *The Two-Fold Night*) examines postwar Germany.

Levi \'lā-vē\, Primo (b. July 31, 1919, Turin, Italy—d. April 11, 1987, Turin) Italian-Jewish writer and chemist, noted for his restrained and moving autobiographical account of and reflections on survival in Nazi concentration camps.

Levi graduated from the University of Turin with a degree in chemistry in 1941. Two years later he attempted to make connection with a resistance movement, but he was captured and sent to Auschwitz. Upon the liberation of Auschwitz by the Soviets in 1945, Levi returned to Turin, where in 1961 he became the general manager of a factory producing paints, enamels, and synthetic resins.

Levi's first book, *Se questo è un uomo* (1947; *If This Is a Man*, or *Survival in Auschwitz*), demonstrated extraordinary qualities of humanity and detachment in its analysis of the atrocities he had witnessed. His later autobiographical works, *La tregua* (1963; U.K. title, *The Truce*; U.S. title, *The Reawakening*) and *I sommersi e i salvati* (1986; *The Drowned and the Saved*), are further reflections on his wartime experiences. His best-known work, *Il sistema periodico* (1975; THE PERIODIC TABLE), is a collection of 21 meditations, each named for a chemical element, on the analogies between the physical, chemical, and moral spheres. He also wrote poetry, science fiction, essays, and short stories. His death was apparently a suicide.

Levin \'lev-in\, Meyer (b. Oct. 8, 1905, Chicago, Ill., U.S.—d. July 9, 1981, Jerusalem, Israel)   American author of novels and nonfiction about the Jewish people and Israel.

Levin first became known with the novel *Yehuda* (1931). One of his most significant works, *The Old Bunch* (1937), traces the lives of several young Chicago Jews from 1921 to 1934. His other notable works are *Citizens* (1940) and *Compulsion* (1956), the latter about the notorious Leopold–Loeb murder case.

Beginning in 1933 Levin worked for *Esquire* magazine, and he was a reporter for the Loyalists in the Spanish Civil War (1936–39). He was also a war correspondent during World War II. After the war he produced a documentary film, *The Illegals* (1948), about the journey of Jewish immigrants from Poland to Israel.

Levin settled in Israel in 1958. His only comic novel, *Gore and Igor*, was published in 1968. His later works on the early settlement of Israel—*The Settlers* (1972) and *The Harvest* (1978)—were not well received. *The Architect*, published posthumously in 1981, was a thinly veiled treatment of the early career of architect Frank Lloyd Wright.

Levin, Konstantine \kən-ˌstən-'tʸēn-'lʸe-vʸin, *Angl* 'kän-stən-ˌtēn-'lev-in\   Fictional character whose happy marriage is presented as a contrast to the tragic love affair of Anna Karenina and Vronsky in Leo Tolstoy's novel ANNA KARENINA.

Levine \lə-'vēn\, Philip (b. Jan. 10, 1928, Detroit, Mich., U.S.)   American poet of urban working-class life.

Levine studied at Wayne State University, Detroit, Mich., and the University of Iowa. He worked at a series of industrial jobs before he began teaching English and poetry at a number of colleges and universities. In his poetry Levine attempted to speak for those whose intelligence, emotions, and imagination are constrained by tedious and harsh working conditions.

Despite Levine's concern with modern life's brutalities, he also wrote poems of love and joy. His numerous poetry collections include *On the Edge* (1963), *They Feed They Lion* (1972), *Ashes: Poems New and Old* (1979), and *A Walk with Tom Jefferson* (1988). Inspired by a visit to Barcelona, he wrote the poems of *The Names of the Lost* (1976) in honor of the Loyalists who fought in the Spanish Civil War (1936–39). He won the 1991 National Book Award for his collection *What Work Is*.

Lévi-Strauss \lā-vē-'strōs\, Claude (b. Nov. 28, 1908, Brussels, Belg.)   French social anthropologist and leading exponent of structuralism, a name applied to the analysis of cultural systems (*e.g.*, kinship and mythical systems) in terms of the structural relations among their elements. Structuralism has influenced not only 20th-century social science but also the study of philosophy, comparative religion, literature, and film.

After studying philosophy and law at the University of Paris (1927–32), Lévi-Strauss taught in a secondary school and was associated with Jean-Paul Sartre's intellectual circle. He later taught at universities in Brazil, the United States, and France.

In 1949 Lévi-Strauss published his first major work, *Les Structures élémentaires de la parenté* (rev. ed., 1967; *The Elementary Structures of Kinship*). He attained popular recognition

with *Tristes tropiques* (1955; *A World on the Wane*), a literary, intellectual autobiography. Other publications include *Anthropologie structurale* (1958; *Structural Anthropology*), *La Pensée Sauvage* (1962; *The Savage Mind*), and *Le Totémisme aujourd'hui* (1962; *Totemism*). His massive *Mythologiques* appeared in four volumes: *Le Cru et le cuit* (1964; *The Raw and the Cooked*), *Du miel aux cendres* (1966; *From Honey to Ashes*), *L'Origine des manières de table* (1968; *The Origin of Table Manners*), and *L'Homme nu* (1971; *The Naked Man*). In 1973 a second volume of *Anthropologie structurale* appeared. In *La Voie des masques*, 2 vol. (1975; *The Way of the Masks*), and *La Poterie jalouse* (1985; *The Jealous Potter*) he studied Native American mythology and art. In 1983 he published a collection of essays, *Le Regard éloigné* (*The View from Afar*). Some of his lectures were collected in *Paroles donées* (1984; *Anthropology and Myth*).

Levitsky \le-'vitsʸ-kē\, Ivan, *pseudonym of* Ivan Nechuy-Levitsky \ne-'chüy\, *also spelled* Nechúi-Levýtsky *or* Nečuj-Levyc'kyj (b. Nov. 25, 1838 [Nov. 13, New Style], 1838, Steblev, Kiev province, Ukraine, Russian Empire—d. April 2 [April 15], 1918, Kiev)   Ukrainian realistic novelist of the reform period following the emancipation of the serfs. Levitsky drew upon his background as a seminary student and a provincial teacher to depict the educated and lower classes in some of the earliest social novels in Ukrainian literature. His works include *Prichepa* (1869; "The Intruder"), *Khmari* (1874; "Clouds"), *Kaydasheva semya* (1879; "The Kaydashev Family"), and *Burlachka* (1881; "A Factory Girl").

Lewald \'lā-ˌvält\, Fanny (b. March 24, 1811, Königsberg, Prussia [now Kaliningrad, Russia]—d. Aug. 5, 1889, Dresden, Ger.)   Popular German novelist and feminist who wrote mainly on the family, marriage, and social problems.

Lewald first began writing at the age of 30. Her novels *Clementine* (1842) and *Jenny* (1843) describe circumscribed lives built around family virtues. *Die Familie Darner*, 3 vol. (1888; "The Darner Family"), and *Von Geschlecht zu Geschlecht*, 8 vol. (1863–65; "From Generation to Generation"), are realistic novels about the lives of family members over several generations. *Diogena* (1847) is a parody of *Gräfin Faustine*, a sentimental novel by Lewald's rival, Ida, Gräfin von Hahn-Hahn. In the historical novel *Prinz Louis Ferdinand*, 3 vol. (1849), Rahel Varnhagen von Ense, an early 19th-century Berlin literary hostess, is the central figure.

Lewald also wrote travel books about Italy, Scotland, and England and an autobiography, *Meine Lebensgeschichte*, 3 vol. (1861–62; "My Life Story").

Lewes \'lü-is\, George Henry (b. April 18, 1817, London, Eng.—d. Nov. 28, 1878, London)   English philosopher, literary critic, dramatist, actor, scientist, and editor remembered chiefly for his decades-long liaison with George Eliot.

In the early 1840s, through his correspondence with John Stuart Mill, Lewes became acquainted with the positivist philosophy of Auguste Comte. In 1850 Lewes and his friend Thornton Leigh Hunt founded a radical weekly called *The Leader*, for which he wrote the literary and theatrical features, and in 1853 his *Comte's Philosophy of the Sciences* was published.

Lewes married in 1841 and the couple lived communally with the Hunts and two other couples. Eventually Mrs. Lewes had two children by Hunt. Lewes willingly registered the first child under his family name and remained on amicable terms with his wife and with Hunt. In 1851, however, after the birth of the second child, Lewes ceased to regard her as his wife. In the same year, after their estrangement, he met Mary Ann Evans (George Eliot). Legal divorce was impossible for Lewes because he had condoned his wife's adultery, but from their separation in 1854 until his death Lewes and Evans lived happily together.

All of Lewes' major writings were stimulated by this association. Before turning to scientific studies, he published his two-volume *Life and Works of Goethe* (1855), still considered the best introduction in English to the poet.

Lewis \\'lū-is\\, Alun (b. July 1, 1915, Aberdare, Glamorganshire, Wales—d. March 5, 1944, Goppe Pass, Arakan, Burma [Myanmar]) Welsh poet who described his experiences as an enlisted man and then an officer during World War II.

Lewis worked as a schoolteacher before entering the army shortly after the outbreak of the war. Most of the poems in *Raiders' Dawn* (1942) are about army life in training camps in England, as are the short stories in *The Last Inspection* (1942). *Ha! Ha! Among the Trumpets* (1945) contains the verse he wrote after leaving England for military duty in Asia, where he was killed. *Letters from India* (1946) and *Selected Poetry and Prose* (1966) were also published posthumously.

Lewis \\'lū-is\\, C.S., *in full* Clive Staples (b. Nov. 29, 1898, Belfast, Ire. [now in Northern Ireland]—d. Nov. 22, 1963, Oxford, Oxfordshire, Eng.) British scholar, novelist, and author of some 40 books, most of them on Christian apologetics, the most widely known being THE SCREWTAPE LETTERS (1942). He also achieved considerable fame with his stories for children, THE CHRONICLES OF NARNIA, which have become classics of fantasy.

Lewis graduated from University College, Oxford. From 1925 to 1954 he taught at Magdalen College, Oxford, and from 1954 to 1963 at the University of Cambridge.

His first work to attract attention was *The Pilgrim's Regress: An Allegorical Apology for Christianity, Reason and Romanticism* (1933). The critical and characteristic *Allegory of Love: A Study in Medieval Tradition*, considered by many to be his greatest work, was published in 1936. The first of his science-fiction novels (a genre then scarcely known), OUT OF THE SILENT PLANET (1938), embraced allegory and apologetics. It was followed by PERELANDRA (1943) and THAT HIDEOUS STRENGTH (1945), the three books forming what many critics consider to be one of the best of all science-fiction trilogies. *The Problem of Pain* (1940) and *Mere Christianity* (1943; revised and enlarged 1952) brought him wide recognition as a lay expositor of Christian apologetics, but they were far exceeded by the fictional best-selling *Screwtape Letters*, purportedly written by an elderly devil to edify his junior in the subtle art of temptation. Lewis' first story for children was *The Lion, the Witch and the Wardrobe* (1950), the first of seven tales about the land of Narnia. Notable among his other books are a volume of autobiography, *Surprised by Joy: The Shape of My Early Life* (1955), and a novel based on the story of Psyche and Cupid, *Till We Have Faces: A Myth Retold* (1956).

Lewis \\'lū-is\\, Matthew Gregory, *byname* Monk Lewis (b. July 9, 1775, London, Eng.—d. May 14, 1818, at sea) English gothic novelist and dramatist who became famous overnight after the sensational success of his novel THE MONK (1796); thus, his byname.

Lewis attended Oxford University and served as a member of Parliament from 1796 to 1802. In 1812 he inherited a fortune and large properties in Jamaica. Sincerely interested in the conditions of his 500 slaves, he made two West Indian voyages, contracted yellow fever on his return from the second, and died at sea.

The Monk, written when Lewis was 19, was influenced by the leading gothic novelist, Ann Radcliffe, and also by contemporary German gothic literature. Its success was followed by a popular musical drama in the same vein, *The Castle Spectre*

(1798), which was produced by the dramatist Richard Brinsley Sheridan. Lewis' other lasting work was a triumph of a very different nature, the *Journal of a West India Proprietor* (published posthumously in 1834).

Lewis \\'lū-is\\, Sinclair, *in full* Harry Sinclair Lewis (b. Feb. 7, 1885, Sauk Center, Minn., U.S.—d. Jan. 10, 1951, near Rome, Italy) American novelist and social critic who punctured American complacency with his broadly drawn, widely popular satirical novels. He won the Nobel Prize for Literature in 1930, the first given to an American.

Lewis graduated from Yale University in 1907. His first novel, *Our Mr. Wrenn* (1914), attracted favorable notice but few readers. At the same time, he was writing with ever-increasing success for such popular magazines as *The Saturday Evening Post* and *Cosmopolitan*. The publication of MAIN STREET in 1920 made his literary reputation. *Main Street* was followed by a string of successful novels, including BABBITT (1922), ARROWSMITH (1925), ELMER GANTRY (1927), and DODSWORTH (1929). Lewis' later books were not up to the standards of his work in the 1920s. IT CAN'T HAPPEN HERE (1935) dramatized the possibilities of a fascist takeover of the United States. It was produced as a play by the Federal Theater with 21 companies in 1936. *Kingsblood Royal* (1947) is a novel of race relations.

Lewis \\'lū-is\\, Wyndham, *in full* Percy Wyndham Lewis (b. Nov. 18, 1882, on a yacht off the coast of Amherst, Nova Scotia, Can.—d. March 7, 1957, London, Eng.) English artist and writer who founded VORTICISM, the abstract movement in painting and literature that sought to relate art to the industrial process.

At the age of 16 Lewis won a scholarship to London's Slade School of Art, but he left three years later without completing his course and went to Paris, where he painted and attended lectures at the Sorbonne. On his return to London in 1909 he began to write stories and to exhibit his paintings. In 1914 he founded a Vorticist review entitled *Blast: Review of the Great English Vortex*, but only two issues appeared.

Lewis' first novel, *Tarr*, was published in 1918; he then worked in seclusion for several years, eventually publishing *The Art of Being Ruled* (1926), a volume of political theory; *The Lion and the Fox* (1926), a study of William Shakespeare and Machiavelli; and *The Wild Body* (1927), a collection of short stories and essays on satire. In 1930 he caused a furor in literary London with the publication of a huge satirical novel, *The Apes of God*, in which he scourged many well-known public figures.

Though Lewis produced some of his most noted paintings and wrote some of his finest books in the 1930s, including his memoirs *Blasting and Bombardiering* (1937) and the novel *The Revenge for Love* (1937), he was deeply in debt by the end of the decade. In 1939 Lewis and his wife journeyed to the United States, where he hoped to recoup his finances with a lecture tour and portrait commissions. The outbreak of World War II made his return to England impossible, and he and his wife lived in poverty in Canada for three years. His 1954 novel *Self Condemned* is a fictionalized account of those years.

At the war's end, Lewis and his wife returned home, and he became art critic for *The Listener*, a publication of the BBC. He also wrote *Rude Assignment* (1950), a second volume of memoirs; *Rotting Hill* (1951), a book of satirical short stories; and *The Human Age* (1955–56), a continuation of a multivolume allegorical fantasy begun in 1928.

Lewys \ˈlü-is\ Glyn Cothi, *also called* Llywelyn y Glyn \ˌhlə-ˈwel-ˌən-ə-ˈglin\ (fl. 1447–86)   Welsh bard whose work reflects an awakening of national consciousness among the Welsh.

Reputedly a native of Carmarthenshire, Lewys was, during the Wars of the Roses, a zealous Lancastrian and partisan of Jasper Tudor, the uncle of Henry VII of England. In 1837 a collection containing 154 of his surviving 230 poems (many written in his own hand) was published in London. Publication of his entire works began in 1953.

Lezama Lima \lā-ˈzä-mä-ˈlē-mä\, José (b. Dec. 19, 1910, Havana, Cuba—d. Aug. 9, 1976, Havana)   Influential Cuban poet, novelist, and essayist.

After studying law in Havana, Lezama became one of the founders and supporters of *Verbum* (1937) and other literary reviews, and he was leader of the literary group associated with *Orígenes* (1944–56). The group published the work of a number of excellent young poets who revolutionized Cuban letters.

His solid foundation in the Spanish classics of the Golden Age (*c.* 1600–*c.* 1680) and his knowledge of the French Symbolists greatly influenced his early work. *Muerte de Narciso* (1937; "Death of Narcissus"), Lezama's first book of poems, reveals his learning. *Enemigo rumor* (1941; "Enemy Rumor"), concerned centrally with the essence of poetry, reveals the poet's belief that the act of creation is laden with religious and metaphysical possibilities. In *Aventuras sigilosas* (1945; "Silent Adventures"), he recreates incidents of his youth. His novel *Paradiso* (1966), which is considered to be his masterpiece, reaffirms faith in his art and in himself.

The poems in *La fijeza* (1949; "Stability") are an attempt to recapture his past experiences. *Analecta del reloj* (1953; "Selected Work of the Clock"), a collection of essays, is notable for "Las imágenes posibles" ("Possible Images"), which expresses his poetic credo. *La expresión americana* (1957) includes essays that attempt to discern the essence of Latin-American reality. His *Tratados en la Habana* ("Treatises on Havana") was published in 1958.

Liang Chenyu or **Liang Ch'en-yü** \ˈlyäŋ-ˈchən-ˈyǖ\ (b. 1520, Kunshan, Jiangsu province, China—d. *c.* 1593, China)   Chinese playwright and author of the first play of the Kun school (*kunqu*) of dramatic singing. When his great actor friend Wei Liangfu developed a new, more subtle and quiet style of dramatic singing, he asked Liang Chenyu to create a showcase for his new style, and Liang Chenyu complied by writing the *Huan sha ji* ("Washing the Silken Gauze"), a *kunqu* drama that initiated the type of theater which was to dominate the Chinese stage until the end of the 18th century.

Liang Shiqiu or **Liang Shih-ch'iu** \ˈlyäŋ-ˈshə-ˈchyü\ (b. Dec. 8, 1902, Beijing, China—d. Nov. 3, 1987, Taipei, Taiwan)   Writer, translator, and literary critic known for his devastating critique of modern romantic Chinese literature and for his insistence on the aesthetic, rather than the propagandistic, purpose of literary expression.

Liang Shiqiu was graduated from Colorado College (in Colorado Springs) in 1924 and went on to study at Columbia and Harvard universities. While at Harvard he outlined the romantic excesses of modern Chinese literature, suggesting that it borrow from the forms of Western literature. He later expanded these ideas into a book-length treatise entitled *Langmandi gudiandi* (1927; "The Romantic and the Classic").

By the time of his return to China in 1926, Liang Shiqiu also felt strongly about the aesthetic and independent purposes of literary creation. In 1927, he and other like-minded writers, including Hu Shi and Xu Zhimo, founded the Crescent Moon Society and published their ideas in the journal *Xinyue* ("Crescent Moon"). Liang Shiqiu taught at Beijing University for a number of years and worked on his translation into vernacular Chinese of the complete works of William Shakespeare (completed in 1967). When the communists took control of China in 1949, he moved to Taiwan.

In addition to his many critical works and his rendition of Shakespeare, Liang Shiqiu produced a number of other excellent translations, making available to Chinese readers such varied works as the 12th-century love letters of the monk Abelard to Héloïse, Sir James Barrie's *Peter Pan*, and Emily Brontë's *Wuthering Heights*. He also wrote a history of English literature in Chinese and compiled a Chinese–English dictionary.

Libation Bearers (*Greek* Choēphoroi)   Play by Aeschylus, second in the trilogy known as the ORESTEIA.

Li Bo or **Li Po** \ˈlē-ˈbwô, *Angl* ˈlē-ˈbō\, *also called* Li Taipo \ˈtī-ˈbwô\ (b. 701, Sichuan province, China—d. 762, Dangtu, Anhui province)   Chinese poet who rivaled Du Fu for the title of China's greatest poet.

At age 19 Li Bo left home and lived with a Daoist recluse. After a period of wandering, he married and lived with his wife's family, north of Hanzhou. He had already begun to write poetry, some of which he showed to various officials in the vain hope of becoming employed as a secretary. A visit to a friend in northeastern China in 734 began another period of wandering. In 742 he arrived at Changan, the Han dynasty capital, where he was accepted into a group of distinguished court poets, though he did not receive an official court post. In the autumn of 744 he began his wanderings again.

In 756 Li Bo became unofficial poet laureate to the military expedition of Prince Lin, the emperor's 16th son. The prince was soon accused of intending to set up an independent kingdom and was executed; Li Bo was arrested and imprisoned at Jiujiang. A high official looked into Li Bo's case, had him released, and made him a staff secretary. In the summer of 758 the charges against Li Bo were revived, and he was banished to Yelang. Before he arrived, he benefited from a general amnesty. He then returned to eastern China, where he died in a relative's house, though popular legend says that he drowned when, sitting drunk in a boat, he tried to seize the moon's reflection in the water.

Li Bo was a romantic in his view of life and in his verse. One of the most famous wine drinkers in China's long tradition of imbibers, Li Bo frequently celebrated the joy of drinking. He also wrote of friendship, solitude, the passage of time, and the joys of nature with brilliance and great freshness of imagination.

Library of Alexandria \ˌal-ig-ˈzan-drē-ə\   The most famous library of classical antiquity. It formed part of the research institute at Alexandria in Egypt that is known as the Museum, or Alexandrian Museum. The Alexandrian museum and library was founded by Ptolemy I Soter (died 283 BC) and further expanded by his son Ptolemy II Philadelphus (308–246 BC). A subsidiary "daughter library" was established about 235 BC by Ptolemy III in the Temple of Sarapis. Scholars do not know how far the ideal of internationality—incorporating not only all Greek literature but also translations into Greek from the other languages of the Mediterranean, the Middle East, and

India—was realized; the only translation recorded was the Septuagint, the earliest extant Greek version of the Old Testament.

The library's editorial program included the establishment of the Alexandrian canon of Greek poets, the division of works into "books" as they are now known (probably to suit the standard length of rolls), and the gradual introduction of systems of punctuation and accentuation. The museum and library were destroyed in the civil war that occurred under Aurelian in the late 3rd century AD; the "daughter library" was destroyed by Christians in AD 391.

libretto \li-'bret-ō\ *plural* librettos *or* libretti \-'bret-ē\ [Italian, literally, booklet, diminutive of *libro* book] Text of an opera or other kind of musical theater. The term is also used, less commonly, of a musical work not intended for the stage.

The earliest operas, beginning in 1597 with Ottavio Rinuccini's *Dafne*, set to music by Jacopo Peri, were court entertainments, and as a commemoration the words were printed in a small book, or "libretto." In the 1630s Venetian opera became a public spectacle, and audiences used printed librettos to follow the drama. The early French and Italian librettists regarded their works as poetic dramas, with the composer expected to pay faithful regard to the accents of the words. A tendency to more lyrical treatment of the text developed in Venice, however, and purely musical demands began to outweigh strict subservience to the poetry.

Perhaps the best example of successful partnership between librettist and composer is that of Hugo von Hofmannsthal and Richard Strauss, who collaborated on *Elektra* (1909), *Der Rosenkavalier* (1911), two versions of *Ariadne auf Naxos* (1912 and 1916; *Ariadne on Naxos*), *Die Frau ohne Schatten* (1919; *The Woman Without a Shadow*), *Die ägyptische Helena* (1928; *The Egyptian Helen*), and *Arabella* (produced—after von Hofmannsthal's death—in 1933).

Among the rare successful uses of spoken-drama texts are Claude Debussy's setting of Maurice Maeterlinck's *Pelléas et Mélisande* (1902) and Richard Strauss's setting of Oscar Wilde's *Salomé* (1905). Other well-known librettists were Emanuel Schikaneder, who wrote the text for W.A. Mozart's *Die Zauberflöte* (1791; *The Magic Flute*); Arrigo Boito, who wrote his own operas and collaborated with other composers to write the text for theirs; and W.S. Gilbert, who wrote a series of light operas with the composer Arthur Sullivan. Composer Virgil Thomson collaborated with avant-garde writer Gertrude Stein in *Four Saints in Three Acts* (1928) and *The Mother of Us All* (1947).

Li Ch'ing-chao *see* LI QINGZHAO.

Lichtenberg \'likt-ən-,berk\, Georg Christoph (b. July 1, 1742, Ober-Ramstadt, near Darmstadt, Hesse [Germany]—d. Feb. 24, 1799, Göttingen, Hanover) German physicist and satirical writer, best known for his ridicule of metaphysical and romantic excesses.

In 1763 Lichtenberg entered Göttingen University, where he later taught and conducted research in a wide variety of fields—including geophysics, volcanology, meteorology, chemistry, astronomy, mathematics, and physics.

Lichtenberg was an excellent satirist, and his biting wit involved him in many controversies with well-known contemporaries. He ridiculed Johann Kaspar Lavater's science of physiognomy, and Johann Heinrich Voss's views on Greek pronunciation called forth the powerful satire *Über die Pronunciation der Schöpse des alten Griechenlandes* (1782; "On the Pronunciation of the Muttonheads of Old Greece"). In 1769 and 1774 he resided for some time in England, and his *Briefe aus England* (1776–78; "Letters from England") are the most attractive of his writings. He contributed to the *Göttinger*

Taschenkalender ("Göttingen Pocket Almanac") from 1778 onward and to the *Göttingisches Magazin der Literatur und Wissenschaft* ("Göttingen Magazine of Literature and Science"), which he edited for three years (1780–82) with J.G.A. Forster.

Lidman \'lēd-màn\, Sara (b. Dec. 30, 1923, Missenträsk, Swed.) Novelist, one of the most acclaimed and widely read of the post-World War II generation of Swedish writers.

Lidman grew up in remote northern Sweden. Her studies at the University of Uppsala were interrupted by tuberculosis, at which time she began to write. Her first two novels, *Tjärdalen* (1953; "The Tar Still") and *Hjortronlandet* (1955; "Cloudberry Land"), deal with the rural life of her childhood and youth. Another well-known work is *Regnspiran* (1958; *The Rain Bird*).

In the 1960s she visited Africa and produced two novels protesting the oppression of blacks. *Samtal i Hanoi* (1966; "Conversations in Hanoi") is a record of her trip to Vietnam, and *Fåglarna i Nam Dinh* (1972; "Birds in Nam Dinh") covers the Vietnam War. Lidman's interest in domestic social issues is apparent in the subject of *Gruva* (1968; "The Mine"), a study of Lapland iron miners. She then returned to the setting of her earliest works, in the 1970s beginning a series of novels about the effects of the Industrial Revolution on the far north of Sweden; among these works are *Din tjänare hör* (1977; "Your Servant Is Listening"), *Nabots sten* (1981; *Naboth's Stone*), and *Järnkronan* (1985; "The Iron Crown").

Lidner \'lēd-nər\, Bengt (b. March 16, 1757, Göteborg, Swed.—d. Jan. 4, 1793, Stockholm) Swedish dramatic and epic poet of early Romanticism, noted for his choice of spectacular subjects.

Lidner's best works were written between 1783 and 1787. *Grefvinnan Spastaras Död* (1783), the text for a cantata, deals with a woman who attempts to rescue her son during an earthquake. Both are killed, and the poem follows the mother to heaven, where she meets Lidner's mother. In the operatic libretto *Medea* (1784), a deceived wife kills her sons on the stage. The heroine of the epic *Yttersta Domen* (1788; "The Last Judgment") is Eve; in its famous opening, images of sound and light combine to evoke an intense atmosphere of death.

Lie \'lē\, Jonas (Lauritz Idemil) (b. Nov. 6, 1833, Hokksund in Eiker, Nor.—d. July 5, 1908, Stavern) Novelist whose goal was to reflect in his writings the nature, the folk life, and the social spirit of his native Norway. He is considered one of "the four great ones" of 19th-century Norwegian literature, together with Henrik Ibsen, Bjørnstjerne Bjørnson, and Alexander Kielland.

With much encouragement from his wife and with her collaboration, Lie wrote his first novel, *Den fremsynte eller billeder fra Nordland* (1870; *The Visionary or Pictures from Nordland*). The first Norwegian story of the sea and of business life, *Tremasteren "Fremtiden" eller liv nordpå* (1872; *The Barque "Future"*), followed. Two novels from his naturalistic period are *Livsslaven* (1883; "The Life Convict"; *One of Life's Slaves*), which tells of the social misfortunes of a boy born out of wedlock, and *Familien paa Gilje* (1883; *The Family at Gilje*), a classic novel that deals with the position of women.

Toward the end of his life Lie wrote two volumes of fairy tales called *Trold* (1891–92; some translated as *Weird Tales from Northern Seas*).

Liezi \'lye-'dzə\ *or* **Lieh-tzu** \-'dzü\, *also called* Chongxu Zhide Zhenjing \'chüŋ-'shūē-'jē-'də-'jen-'jiŋ\ ("True Classic of the Perfect Virtue of Simplicity and Emptiness") Chinese Daoist classic bearing the name of the philosopher Liezi. As in earlier Daoist classics (from which it borrowed heavily), emphasis in the *Liezi* centers on the mysterious Dao (Way) of Daoism, a great unknowable cosmic reality of incessant change to which human life should conform. In its present form, the *Liezi* possibly dates from the 3rd or 4th century AD.

Life of Henry Brulard, The \äⁿ-rē-brüē-'lår, *Angl* 'hen-rē-brü-'lär, -'lärd\ Unfinished autobiography by STENDHAL, which he began writing in November 1835 and abandoned in March 1836. The scribbled manuscript, including the author's sketches and diagrams, was deciphered and published as *Vie de Henry Brulard* in 1890, 48 years after its author's death. The work is a masterpiece of ironic self-searching and self-creation, in which the memories of childhood are closely interwoven with the liberating joy of writing.

Life of Samuel Johnson, LL.D., The \'sam-yù-wəl-'jän-sən\ Generally regarded as the greatest of English biographies, written by James BOSWELL and published in two volumes in 1791.

Boswell, a 22-year-old lawyer from Scotland, first met the 53-year-old Samuel JOHNSON in 1763, and they were friends for the 21 remaining years of Johnson's life. From the beginning, using a self-invented system of shorthand, Boswell kept a record of Johnson's conversations. The record was important, for apart from Johnson's achievements as journalist, poet, lexicographer, and author, he was a forceful, witty talker.

Boswell, himself a superlative reporter, often asked Johnson questions that appeared naive or ignorant in order to prompt his subject to make statements worth preserving. Such conversations and statements make up the bulk of the biography.

Life on the Mississippi \ˌmis-i-'sip-ē\ Memoir of the steamboat era on the Mississippi River before the American Civil War by Mark TWAIN, published in 1883.

The book begins with a brief history of the river from its discovery by Hernando de Soto in 1541. Chapters 4–22 describe Twain's career as a Mississippi steamboat pilot, the fulfillment of a childhood dream.

The second half of *Life on the Mississippi* tells of Twain's return, many years after, to travel the river from St. Louis to New Orleans. By then the competition from railroads had made steamboats passé, in spite of improvements in navigation and boat construction. Twain sees new, large cities on the river, and records his observations on greed, gullibility, tragedy, and bad architecture.

Life Studies A collection of poetry and prose by Robert LOWELL, published in 1959. The book marked a major turning point in Lowell's writing and also helped to initiate the 1960s trend to confessional poetry; it was awarded the National Book Award for poetry in 1960. The book is in four sections, including "91 Revere Street," an autobiographical sketch in prose of Lowell's youth amid stormy domestic tensions. The other sections include a series of poems in traditional forms, a group of poems about authors Ford Madox Ford, George Santayana, Delmore Schwartz, and Hart Crane, and "Life Studies," which consists of 15 confessional poems, including the well-known SKUNK HOUR and WAKING IN BLUE.

Ligeia \li-'jē-ə\ Short story by Edgar Allan POE, published in the magazine *American Museum* in 1838 and later included in the two-volume *Tales of the Grotesque and Arabesque* (1840).

In the first half of the story the aristocratic narrator describes the beauty and intelligence of his late wife, dark-haired Ligeia, and how she died convinced that a strong will could stave off death. Distraught after her death, the narrator leaves the Rhine valley for rural England, where he enters into an unhappy marriage with fair-haired Lady Rowena Trevanion, of Tremaine. He uses opium; she falls ill and dies. Sitting with the corpse, he watches in amazement as it rises and sheds the burial shroud, revealing dark-haired Ligeia, reborn.

light comedy Comedy characterized by delicacy and wit. Also, comedy that is lighthearted and amusing and that makes few demands intellectually.

Light in August Novel by William FAULKNER, published in 1932, the seventh in the series set in the fictional Yoknapatawpha County, Mississippi.

The central figure of *Light in August* is the orphan Joe Christmas, whose mixed blood condemns him to life as an outsider, hated or pitied. Joe is frequently whipped by Simon McEachern, the puritanical farmer who raises him, and, after savagely beating his adoptive father, Joe leaves home when he is 18. He then wanders for 15 years, eventually moving in with Joanna Burden, a white woman devoted to helping Negroes. Her evangelism comes to remind Joe of Simon's, and he murders her. Betrayed by his companion Lucas Burch, Joe is hunted down, killed, and castrated.

light stress In prosody, an accent or stress on a word that is not accented in everyday speech. The word *if* in the third line of the following stanza from Samuel Taylor Coleridge's poem "The Rime of the Ancient Mariner" exhibits this kind of stress:

> And every tongue, through utter drought,
> Was withered at the root;
> We could not speak, no more than if
> We had been choked with soot.

Light That Failed, The Novel by Rudyard KIPLING, published in 1890.

The book, which includes autobiographical elements, describes the youth and manhood of Dick Heldar and traces his efforts as a war correspondent and artist whose sketches of British battles in the Sudan become popular. When he returns to London, he begins painting his masterpiece, racing against time because a battle wound has caused his eyesight to progressively fail.

Kipling wrote two separate endings to *The Light That Failed*, a happy ending for the version published in *Lippincott's Monthly Magazine* in January 1890 and an unhappy ending for the version published in book form a few months later.

light verse Verse on trivial or playful themes that is written mainly to amuse and entertain and that often involves nonsense and wordplay. Frequently distinguished by considerable technical competence, wit, sophistication, and elegance, light poetry constitutes a considerable body of verse in all Western languages. The term is a general one that can be applied to such forms as NONSENSE VERSE, LIMERICK, CLERIHEW, EPIGRAM, and MOCK-EPIC.

Ligne \də-'lēnʸ\, Charles-Joseph, prince de (b. May 23, 1735, Brussels [Belgium]—d. Dec. 13, 1814, Vienna [Austria]) Belgian military officer and man of letters whose memoirs and correspondence had an important influence on Belgian literature.

De Ligne was the scion of a family long established in Hainaut and in the Holy Roman Empire. After serving with distinction for Austria in the Seven Years' War (1756–63), he became a trusted adviser of the Holy Roman emperor Joseph II.

De Ligne's memoirs and letters reflect his experiences as a favorite at leading European courts and salons until his exile following the Belgian rebellion of 1789. His works include *Mélanges militaires, littéraires et sentimentaires*, 34 vol. (1795–1811; "Miscellaneous Military, Literary, and Sentimental Memoirs"), *Fragments de l'histoire de ma vie* (1927; "Fragments of the History of My Life"), and *Letters and Memoirs of the Prince de Ligne* (translated by Leigh Ashton).

Li He \'lē-'hə\ or **Li Ho** \'lē-'hō\ (b. 791, China—d. 817, Changgu) Brilliant Chinese poet who showed great promise until his untimely death at age 26.

Literary legend describes Li He as a man of *guicai* ("devilish talent") who composed his haunting verses by jotting down single lines on small slips of paper while on horseback, dropping the slips into an embroidered black bag, and assembling a finished poem each evening. Li He promised to do well on the literary examinations necessary for an official career, but he was excluded from the examinations by a minor technicality; his resulting disappointment was said to have triggered the poor health that led to his death a few years later. Li He's verse is characterized by its vivid imagery, odd diction, striking juxtapositions, and unrelieved pessimism.

Li Houzhu   *see* LI YU (937–978).

Li ji or **Li chi** \\'lē-'jē\\ ("Record of Rites") One of the Five Classics (*Wu jing*) of Chinese Confucian literature, the original text of which is said to have been compiled by the ancient sage Confucius (551–479 BC). The text was later extensively reworked by Elder Dai (Da Dai) and his cousin Younger Dai (Xiao Dai).

In general, *Li ji* underscores moral principles in its treatment of such subjects as royal regulations, development of rites, ritual objects and sacrifices, education, music, the behavior of scholars, and the doctrine of the mean (*zhong yong*). In 1190 Zhu Xi, a Neo-Confucian philosopher, gave two chapters of *Li ji* separate titles and published them together with two other Confucian texts under the name *Si shu* ("Four Books"). This collection is generally used to introduce Chinese students to Confucian literature.

Liliencron \\'lē-lyən-ˌkrōn\\, Detlev, Baron (Freiherr) von, *in full* Friedrich Adolf Axel Detlev, Baron von Liliencron (b. June 3, 1844, Kiel, Holstein [Germany]—d. July 22, 1909, Alt-Rahlstedt, near Hamburg) German writer whose poetry in *Adjutantenritte und andere Gedichte* (1883; "Rides of the Adjutant and Other Poems") was the starting point for a lyric revival. His fresh and unconventional verse was a challenge to the long Romantic tradition and a forerunner of realism.

Liliencron's first volume of poetry, *Adjutantenritte*, struck a new note of optimism and individualism. His poems are characterized by a vividness of impression and accuracy of detail, but he lacked any profound sense of large coherence. He wrote excellent prose in his *Kriegsnovellen* (1895; "War Stories"), in which he painted realistic and arresting pictures of war. His loosely constructed satiric epic *Poggfred, ein kunterbuntes Epos* (1896; "Poggfred, a Topsy-Turvy Epic") achieved some success.

Lilith \\'lil-ith\\ Female demon of Jewish folklore; her name and personality are derived from the Babylonian–Assyrian demon called Lilit, or Lilu. She may also have an association with other early goddesses.

In rabbinic literature Lilith is variously depicted as the mother of Adam's demonic offspring following his separation from Eve or as his first wife, who scoffed at him and left him because he insisted on the male-superior sexual position, the so-called missionary position. Three angels tried in vain to force her to return, and the more docile Eve was created in her place. Refusing to couple with Adam, Lilith was said to have bred with demons, producing 100 offspring a day. She appears in J.W. von Goethe's *Faust* and Dante Gabriel Rossetti's *Eden Bower*.

In the 20th century, Lilith has become something of a feminist symbol for her rebellion against patriarchal ways. *See also* ADAM AND EVE.

Li Liweng   *see* LI YU (1611–*c*. 1680).

Lilliput \\'lil-i-ˌpət, -ˌpùt\\ A fictional kingdom inhabited by tiny people in Jonathan Swift's satire GULLIVER'S TRAVELS.

Lilliput and its rival island, Blefuscu, are thought to be Swift's satiric disguises for England and France, respectively.

Lillo \\'lil-ō\\, George (b. Feb. 4, 1693, London, Eng.—d. Sept. 3, 1739, London) English dramatist known for his innovative domestic tragedy *The London Merchant; or, The History of George Barnwell* (1731), in which members of the middle class replaced the customary aristocratic or royal heroes. The play greatly influenced the rise of bourgeois drama in Germany and France, as well as in England.

Lillo's first piece was *Sylvia; or The Country Burial*, a ballad opera produced in 1730. His other dramas include *The Christian Hero* (1735), *Fatal Curiosity* (1736), and *Marina* (1738).

Lima \\'lē-mə\\, Jorge de (b. April 23, 1895, União dos Palmares, Braz.—d. Nov. 15, 1953, Rio de Janeiro) Brazilian poet and novelist who became one of the foremost regional poets in Brazil in the 1920s.

Lima's earliest verses show the marked influence of the French Parnassian poets, but the volume *O mundo do menino impossível* (1925; "The World of the Impossible Child") signals his endorsement of the Brazilian Modernismo movement. He became active in the northeastern regionalist movement and produced a great deal of so-called Afro-Brazilian poetry throughout the 1930s.

Following his religious conversion in 1935, Lima sought to "restore poetry in Christ" and wrote metaphysical and expressionist poetry and fiction. His best-known collections of poetry include *A túnica inconsútil* (1938; "The Seamless Tunic"), *Poemas negros* (1947; "Black Poems"), and *Invenção de Orfeu* (1952; "The Invention of Orpheus"). His best-known fiction is *Calunga* (1935) and *A mulher obscura* (1939; "The Obscure Woman").

Lima \\'lē-mə\\, Manuel dos Santos (b. Jan. 28, 1935, Silva Porto [now Kuito], Angola) Angolan writer whose work is rooted in his country's struggle for liberation from Portuguese colonialism.

Lima was a military leader of the Popular Army for the Liberation of Angola. Lima's first novel, *As sementes da liberdade* (1965; "The Seeds of Liberty"), was published in Rio de Janeiro, and his second, *As lágrimas e o vento* (1975; "Tears and Wind"), in Lisbon. The latter work is a fictional account of the war that resulted in Angolan independence. Lima's output includes *Kissange* (1961), a volume of poetry; *A pele do diabo* (1977; "The Skin of the Devil"), a play; and *Os añoes e os mendigos* (1984; "Dwarfs and Beggars"), a political fable.

Lima Barreto \\'lē-mə-bȧ-'ret-ü\\, Afonso Henriques de (b. May 13, 1881, Rio de Janeiro, Braz.—d. Nov. 1, 1922, Rio de Janeiro) Brazilian novelist, journalist, short-story writer, and aggressive social critic.

An active journalist and a lifelong Carioca (resident of Rio), Lima Barreto depicts in his novels the main events of the new republic in Brazil (principally the 1890s and the first decade of the 20th century) and the life of that period. His ironic humor is evident in the creation of melancholic, quixotic protagonists who are unable to cope with mechanized urban society, militarism, and governmental organization.

Lima Barreto's best-known novels include *Vida e morte de M.J. Gonzaga de Sá* (1919; "Life and Death of M.J. Gonzaga de Sá"), *Recordações do escrivão Isaías Caminha* (1909; "Memoirs of the Notary Public Isaiah Caminha"), *O triste fim de Policarpo Quaresma* (1915; "The Sad End of Policarp Lent"), *Numa e a ninfa* (1915; "Numa and the Nymph"), and *Clara dos Anjos* (composed in 1904 but published posthumously in 1948).

limerick \\'lim-ə-rik\\ A popular form of short, humorous verse, often nonsensical and frequently ribald. It consists of five lines, rhyming *aabba*, and the dominant meter is anapestic, with two feet in the third and fourth lines and three feet in the others. The origin of the word *limerick* is obscure, but a group of poets in County Limerick, Ireland, wrote limericks in Irish in the 18th century.

The first collections of limericks in English date from about 1820. Edward Lear, who composed and illustrated the limericks in his *Book of Nonsense* (1846), claimed to have gotten the idea from a nursery rhyme beginning "There was an old man of Tobago." An example from Lear's collection is this verse:

> There was an Old Man who supposed
> That the street door was partially closed;
>   But some very large rats
>   Ate his coats and his hats,
> While that futile Old Gentleman dozed.

Toward the end of the 19th century, W.S. Gilbert displayed his skill in a sequence of limericks that Sir Arthur Sullivan set as the familiar song in *The Sorcerer* (1877):

> My name is John Wellington Wells,
> I'm a dealer in magic and spells,
>   In blessings and curses,
>   And ever-fill'd purses,
> In prophecies, witches, and knells.

Gilbert also wrote one of the first offbeat limericks, which were to become nearly as popular as the true kind. Their charm lay in the unexpected jolt caused by failure to find the expected rhyme.

> There was an old man of St. Bees,
> Who was stung in the arm by a wasp,
>   When asked, "Does it hurt?"
>   He replied, "No, it doesn't,
> I'm so glad it wasn't a hornet."

limited edition   An issue of something collectible (such as books, prints, or medals) that is advertised to be limited to a relatively small number of copies.

lin \\'lin, 'lĕn\\ [Chinese (Beijing dialect) *lín*]   In Chinese mythology, a female unicorn.

Lincoln \\'liŋk-ən\\, Abraham, *byname* Honest Abe \\'ăb\\, The Railsplitter, *or* The Great Emancipator (b. Feb. 12, 1809, Hodgenville, Ky., U.S.—d. April 15, 1865, Washington, D.C.)   Sixteenth president of the United States (1861–65), who preserved the Union during the American Civil War and brought about the emancipation of the slaves. Assassinated by John Wilkes Booth in Ford's Theatre in Washington, D.C., he came to be regarded as a hero and martyr. He was the inspiration for much literature, including Walt Whitman's poems "When Lilacs Last in the Dooryard Bloom'd" and "O Captain! My Captain!"

Lindegren \\'lin-də-grän\\, Erik (Johan) (b. Aug. 5, 1910, Luleå, Swed.—d. May 31, 1968, Stockholm)   Swedish modernist poet who made a major contribution to the development of a new Swedish poetry in the 1940s.

The appearance of Lindegren's second volume of poetry, *Mannen utan väg* (1942; *The Man Without a Way*), marked the beginning of a new type of poetry in Sweden. Using unconventional imagery and syntax, the poetry in this volume reflected the stupidities and horrors of the contemporary human scene. His two later volumes of poetry, *Sviter* (1947; "Suites") and *Vinteroffer* (1954; "Winter Sacrifice"), continue to reveal the strength of his commitment to modernism, though they are more lyrical.

In 1947 Lindegren and Karl Vennberg edited the modernist anthology *40-talslyrik* ("Poetry of the 1940s"). Lindegren made notable translations of T.S. Eliot, William Shakespeare, Saint-John Perse, Paul Éluard, Paul Valéry, William Faulkner and Graham Greene. He also translated the librettos of several operas and wrote texts for performance.

Lindgren \\'lind-grän\\, Astrid (b. Nov. 14, 1907, Vimmerby, Swed.)   Influential Swedish writer of children's books.

Lindgren's great popularity began in 1945 with the creation of *Pippi Långstrump* (PIPPI LONGSTOCKING), the first of three books with Pippi as its main character. This unusual redheaded girl stands totally apart from the conformist demands of everyday life and incarnates every child's dream of freedom and power. An equally popular character is found in *Emil in Lönneberga* (1963), which was followed by a sequel in 1970. Other well-known characters include the title character in *Nils Karlsson-Pyssling* (1949), a lonely child in his world of imaginary creatures. In *Mio, min Mio* (1954) and *Bröderna Lejonhjärta* (1973; "The Brothers Lionheart"), Lindgren turned with equal success to the world of folklore.

Lindsay, Sir David   *see* Sir David LYNDSAY.

Lindsay \\'lind-zē\\, Howard and **Crouse** \\'kraús\\, Russel (respectively b. March 29, 1889, Waterford, N.Y., U.S.—d. Feb. 11, 1968, New York, N.Y.; b. Feb. 20, 1893, Findlay, Ohio—d. April 3, 1966, New York, N.Y.)   Team of American playwrights and producers who coauthored successful humorous plays and collaborated on theatrical productions.

Lindsay and Crouse first collaborated on *Anything Goes* (1934). Their longest-playing drama was a 1939 production based on Clarence Day's book *Life with Father*, which ran for 7½ years (3,213 performances) and in which Lindsay played Father opposite his real-life wife, Dorothy Stickney. Lindsay and Crouse produced *Arsenic and Old Lace* in 1940, and the result was another success. In 1946 the pair won the Pulitzer Prize in drama for *State of the Union* (1945), a satire of American politics. They also wrote the libretto for the play *The Sound of Music* (1959).

Lindsay \\'lind-zē\\, Vachel \\'vă-chəl, *commonly* 'vach-əl\\, *in full* Nicholas Vachel Lindsay (b. Nov. 10, 1879, Springfield, Ill., U.S.—d. Dec. 5, 1931, Springfield)   American poet who—in an attempt to revive poetry as an oral art form of the common people—wrote and read to audiences compositions with powerful rhythms that had an immediate appeal.

A part-time lecturer, Lindsay wandered throughout the country reciting his poems in return for food and shelter. He first received widespread recognition in 1913 when *Poetry* magazine published his poem "General William Booth Enters into Heaven," about the founder of the Salvation Army. His poems are studded with vivid imagery and bold rhymes and express both his ardent patriotism and his romantic appreciation of nature.

Lindsay's best volumes of verse include *Rhymes to Be Traded for Bread* (1912), *General William Booth Enters into Heaven and Other Poems* (1913), *The Congo and Other Poems* (1914), and *The Chinese Nightingale and Other Poems* (1917).

line \\'līn\\   A unit in the rhythmic structure of verse that is formed by the grouping together of a number of the smallest units of the rhythm (such as syllables, stress groups, metrical feet) according to some principle or norm supplied by the nature or conventions of that type of verse. For instance, if a poem is written in iambic pentameter the rules of the form dictate that a standard line in the poem will consist of 10 syllables arranged in five iambic feet. Lines in turn are composed or combined into larger structural units (such as strophes or stanzas), either by continuous repetition in series or by arrangement in systematic patterns.

lineation \\‚lin-ē-'ā-shən\\   An arrangement of lines (as of verse).

Linklater \\'liŋk-lə-tər, *commonly* -ˌlā-tər\\, Eric (Robert) (b. March 8, 1899, Dounby, Orkney Islands, Scot.—d. Nov. 7, 1974, Aberdeen) Scottish novelist, poet, and historical writer noted for his satiric wit.

Linklater was assistant editor of the *Times of India* (1925–27) and taught English at his alma mater, Aberdeen University, where he became rector (1945–48). He also served in World Wars I and II.

Linklater's early novels include *White-Maa's Saga* (1929), *Juan in America* (1931), *Men of Ness* (1932), and *Magnus Merriman* (1934). He was a prolific writer, and his 30th book, *The Voyage of the Challenger* (1972), a nonfictional account of the expedition of HMS *Challenger* in 1872–76, has all the verve his early works displayed. Linklater wrote three volumes of autobiography, *The Man on My Back* (1941), *A Year of Space* (1953), and *Fanfare for a Tin Hat* (1970).

Linnankoski \\'lēn-nän-ˌkȯs-kē\\, Johannes, *pseudonym of* Vihtori Peltonen \\'pel-tō-nen\\ (b. Oct. 18, 1869, Askola, Russian Finland—d. Aug. 10, 1913, Helsinki) Novelist, orator, and champion of Finnish independence from Russia; his works were instrumental in forming Finnish national consciousness in the early 20th century.

Linnankoski was of peasant origin and largely self-taught. His finest novel, *Pakolaiset* (1908; "The Fugitives"), is about peasant life. More popular in his day was *Laulu tulipunaisesta kukasta* (1905; *The Song of the Blood-Red Flower*), a lyrical fantasy on the amorous adventures of a lumberjack.

Lins \\'lēⁿnsh\\, Osman (b. July 5, 1924, Vitória de Santo Antão, Braz.—d. July 8, 1978, São Paulo) Novelist and short-story writer, one of the leading innovators of mid-20th century Brazilian fiction.

After publishing two traditional novels and a volume of short stories—*O visitante* (1955; "The Visitor"), *O fiel e a pedra* (1961; "The Plumbline and the Rock"), and *Os gestos* (1957; "Gestures")—Lins broke with linear narration to create the three works that secured his reputation: *Nove, Novena* (1966; "Nine, a Novena"), consisting of nine narratives; *Avalovara* (1973), a novel; and *A rainha dos cárceres da Grécia* (1976; "The Queen of the Grecian Jails"), a novel-essay that integrates short essays on literary theory and criticism within a fictional narrative. Lins also wrote several plays.

Lins do Rego \\'lēⁿnsh-dü-'reg-ü\\, José, *surname in full* Lins do Rego Cavalcanti \\kȧv-əl-'käⁿn-tē\\ (b. June 3, 1901, Pilar, Paraíba, Braz.—d. Sept. 12, 1957, Rio de Janeiro) Novelist of Brazil's Northeastern school of realists, best known for his five-book Sugar Cane cycle describing the clash between the old feudal order of plantation society and the new ways introduced by industrialization.

The first work of the cycle, *Menino de engenho* (1932; *Plantation Boy*), is based on Lins do Rego's own boyhood and family. It was followed by *Doidinho* (1933; "Daffy Boy"), *Banguê* (1934; "Old Plantation"), *O moleque Ricardo* (1935; "Black Boy Richard"), and *Usina* (1936; "The Sugar Refinery"). The first three volumes of the cycle were published in English translation as *Plantation Boy* (1966). The author returned to the plantation setting with *Fogo morto* (1943; "Dead Fire"), now considered to be his masterwork.

Lin Shu \\'lin-'shü\\ (b. Nov. 8, 1852, Fuzhou, Fujian province, China—d. Oct. 9, 1924, Beijing) Translator who first made available to Chinese readers more than 171 works of Western literature, even though he himself had no firsthand knowledge of any foreign language. Working through oral interpreters, Lin Shu translated fiction from England, the United States, France, Russia, Switzerland, Belgium, Spain, Norway, Greece, and Japan into flowing classical Chinese. Because of the second-

hand nature of Lin Shu's translations—indeed, many are translations of translations—they are not completely accurate. Nevertheless, Lin Shu's translations remain important for their role in introducing Western literature to China.

Linton family \\'lin-tən\\ Fictional characters, neighbors of the Earnshaw family, in Emily Brontë's novel WUTHERING HEIGHTS. The family consists of Mr. and Mrs. Linton and their children Edgar and Isabella.

Linus or **Linos** \\'lī-nəs\\ In Greek mythology, the personification of lamentation; the name is also a common noun denoting a song of lamentation. Two principal stories, associated with Argos and Thebes, respectively, arose to explain the origin of the lament.

According to the Argive story, Linus was exposed at birth and was torn to pieces by dogs. In revenge, Apollo (his father) sent a Poine, or avenging spirit, to destroy the Argive children. The hero Coroebus killed the Poine, and a festival, Arnis, otherwise called dog-killing day (*kynophontis*), was instituted, in which stray dogs were killed, sacrifice offered, and mourning made for Linus and his mother Psamathe.

In the Theban version, Linus invented the Linus song but was put to death by Apollo for presuming to be his rival.

Lin Yutang or **Lin Yü-t'ang** \\'lin-'yüē-'tän\\ (b. Oct. 10, 1895, Lunji, Fujian province, China—d. March 26, 1976, Hong Kong) Prolific writer of a wide variety of works in Chinese and English and founder of several Chinese magazines specializing in social satire and Western-style journalism.

The son of a Presbyterian minister, Lin Yutang traveled to the United States and Europe for advanced study. On his return to China, he taught, edited several English-language journals, and contributed essays to Chinese literary magazines.

In 1932, Lin Yutang established the *Lunyu banyuegan* ("Analects Fortnightly"), a type of Western-style satirical magazine totally new to China. It was highly successful, and he soon introduced two more publications. In 1935 Lin Yutang published the first of his many English-language books, *My Country and My People*. It was widely translated and for years regarded as a standard text on China. He moved to New York City in 1936 to meet the popular demand for his historical accounts and novels. *The Wisdom of China and India* appeared in 1942. Lin Yutang also wrote books on Chinese history and philosophy and highly acclaimed English translations of Chinese literary masterpieces.

Lion, the Witch, and the Wardrobe, The Children's novel by C.S. Lewis, the first in the series collectively known as THE CHRONICLES OF NARNIA.

Li Po *see* LI BO.

lipogram \\'lip-ə-ˌgram, 'līp-\\ [Middle Greek *lipográmmatos* lacking a letter, from Greek *leípein* to leave, be lacking + *grámma* letter] A written text deliberately composed of words not having a certain letter (such as the *Odyssey* of Tryphiodorus, which had no alpha in the first book, no beta in the second, and so on).

Li Qingzhao or **Li Ch'ing-chao** \\'lē-'chiŋ-'jau̇\\ (b. 1081, Jinan, Shandong province, China—d. after 1141, Jinhua, Zhejiang province) China's greatest woman poet, whose work, though it survives only in fragments, continues to be as highly regarded as it was in her own day.

Li Qingzhao produced seven volumes of essays and six volumes of poetry, but unfortunately all her work is lost except for some poetry fragments. She was a writer of *ci* poetry, a form of lyric poetry written to music and generally associated with the Song dynasty (960–1279). Li's poetry is noted for its feminine sensibility and striking diction.

Li Shangyin or **Li Shang-yin** \ˈlē-ˈshäŋ-ˈyin, -ˈyēn\ (b. 813, Henei, Henan province, China—d. 858, Zhengzhou, Henan province) Chinese poet remembered for his elegance and obscurity.

Until the second half of the 20th century little of Li Shangyin's poetry had been translated into European languages. To Chinese critics he has been one of the most controversial, difficult, and complex of poets because of his use of exotic imagery, abstruse allusions, political allegory, and personal satire involving both historical and contemporary events and figures.

Lispector \lēsh-pek-ˈtȯr\, Clarice (b. Dec. 10, 1925, Chechlnik, Ukraine, U.S.S.R.—d. Dec. 9, 1977, Rio de Janeiro, Braz.) Novelist and short-story writer, one of Brazil's more important 20th-century literary figures. Her works convey a highly personal, almost existentialist view of the human dilemma and are written in a prose style characterized by a simple vocabulary and an elliptical sentence structure.

Lispector's first novel, *Perto do coração selvagem* (1944; "Near to the Savage Heart"), published when she was 19 years old, won critical acclaim for its sensitive interpretation of adolescence. In her later works, such as *A maçã no escuro* (1961; *The Apple in the Dark*), *A paixão segundo G.H.* (1964; *The Passion According to G.H.*), and *Água viva* (1973; "Living Water"), her characters, searching for meaning in life, gradually gain a sense of awareness of themselves. Lispector's last novel, *A hora da estrela* (1977; *The Hour of the Star*), displays concern for the inhabitants of the northeastern region.

Short-story collections such as *Laços de família* (1960; *Family Ties*) and *A legião estrangeira* (1964; *The Foreign Legion*) focus on personal moments of revelation in everyday life and the lack of meaningful communication among individuals.

Lista \ˈlēs-tä\, Alberto, *surname in full* Lista y Aragón \ē-ˌär-ä-ˈgȯn\ (b. Oct. 15, 1775, Triana, Spain—d. Oct. 5, 1848, Seville) Spanish poet and critic, the foremost member of the second Sevillian Neoclassic school.

At the age of 20, Lista held the chair of mathematics at a college in Seville; later, in 1807, he assumed the chair of rhetoric and poetry at the University of Seville. He founded the periodical *El censor* and the Free University of Madrid.

Lista's *Poesías* (1822, 1837; "Poems") show faint influences of the Romantic movement. Among his best-known works are *El imperio de la estupidez* (1798; "The Empire of Stupidity"), a critical work in the manner of Alexander Pope's *The Dunciad*; *Ensayos literarios y críticos* (1844; "Literary and Critical Essays"); and the lectures *Lecciones de literatura española* (1836; "Lessons in Spanish Literature").

lit crit *see* LITERARY CRITICISM.

literary \ˈlit-ə-ˌrer-ē\ [French *littéraire,* from Latin *litterarius* of reading and writing, a derivative of *litterae* written matter, literary works, plural of *littera* letter of the alphabet] **1.** Of, relating to, or having the characteristics of literature. Of or relating to books. **2.** Having a firsthand knowledge of literature, or being well-read. **3.** Of, relating to, or concerned with men and women of letters or with writing as a profession.

Literary Club, The A dining club founded by Samuel Johnson in 1764 as THE CLUB.

literary criticism *also called* (jocularly, and chiefly in academic contexts) lit crit \ˈlit-ˈkrit\ A discipline concerned with a range of enquiries about literature: criticism asks what literature is, what it does, and what it is worth.

The Western critical tradition began with Plato in the 4th century BC. In the *Republic* he attacked the poets on two fronts: their art is merely imitative, and it appeals to the worst rather than to the best in human nature. A generation later

Aristotle, in his *Poetics,* countered these charges and developed a set of principles of composition that were of lasting importance to European literature. As late as 1674 Nicolas Boileau was still, in *L'Art poétique,* recommending observance of the Aristotelian rules—or unities—of time, action, and place.

European literary criticism from the Renaissance onward has for the most part focused on the same two issues: the moral worth of literature and the nature of its relationship to reality. At the end of the 16th century Sir Philip Sidney argued in *The Defence of Poesie* that it is the special property of literature to express moral and philosophical truths in a way that rescues them from abstraction and makes them immediately graspable. A century later, John Dryden, in *Of Dramatick Poesie, An Essay* (1668), put forward the less idealistic view that the business of literature is primarily to offer an accurate representation of the world "for the delight and instruction of mankind." This remains the assumption of the great critical works of 18th-century England, underlying both Alexander Pope's *An Essay on Criticism* (1711) and the extensive work of Samuel Johnson.

William Wordsworth's assertion in his "Preface" to the second edition of the *Lyrical Ballads* (1800) that the object of poetry is "truth . . . carried alive into the heart by passion" marks a significant change from the ideas of the mid-18th century. Other important statements of critical theory in the Romantic period were Samuel Taylor Coleridge's *Biographia Literaria* (1817) and Percy Bysshe Shelley's *A Defence of Poetry* (written 1821). The later 19th century saw a development in one direction toward an aesthetic theory of art for art's sake and in another direction toward the view, expressed by Matthew Arnold, that the cultural role of literature should be to take over the sort of moral and philosophical functions that had previously been fulfilled by religion.

The volume of literary criticism increased greatly in the 20th century. An early example of this in the English-speaking world was I.A. Richards' *Principles of Literary Criticism* (1924), which became influential as the basis of Practical Criticism. From this developed the New Criticism of the 1940s and '50s, which was associated with such American critics as John Crowe Ransom and Cleanth Brooks. The premise of the New Critics, that a work of literature should be studied as a separate and self-contained entity, set them in opposition both to biographical criticism and to those schools of criticism—Marxist, psychoanalytical, historical, and the like—that set out to examine literature from perspectives external to the text.

The late 20th century witnessed a radical reappraisal of traditional modes of literary criticism. Building on the work of the Russian Formalist critics of the 1920s and the examinations of linguistic structure carried out by the Swiss philologist Ferdinand de Saussure, literary theorists began to call into question the overriding importance of the concept of "the author" as the source of the text's meaning. Structuralist and poststructuralist critics, such as Roland Barthes and Jacques Derrida of France, instead directed attention toward the ways in which meaning is created by the determining structures of language and culture. *See also* CHICAGO CRITICS; DECONSTRUCTION; FEMINIST CRITICISM; FORMALISM; FREUDIAN CRITICISM; GENEVA SCHOOL OF CRITICISM; MARXIST CRITICISM; NEW CRITICISM; NEW HISTORICISM; POSTSTRUCTURALISM; PRACTICAL CRITICISM; READER-RESPONSE CRITICISM; STRUCTURALISM.

literaryism \ˈlit-ə-ˌrer-ē-ˌiz-əm\ An instance of or tendency to use excessive refinement of expression in written compositions.

Literary Research Association *also called* Literary Association, *Chinese* Wenxue yanjiu hui. Chinese literary society founded in Beijing in November 1920 by a group of professors, writers, students, and translators. The Literary Research Association, generally referred to as the realist or "art-for-life's-sake" school, assumed the editorship of the established literary magazine *Xiaoshuo yuebao* ("Fiction Monthly"), in which most major fiction writers published their works throughout the 1920s. The socially reflective writing that characterized this group held sway in China well into the 1940s, when it was gradually eclipsed by more propagandistic literature. *See also* CREATION SOCIETY.

literary sketch   Short prose narrative, often an entertaining account of some aspect of a culture written by someone within that culture for readers outside of it—*e.g.*, anecdotes of a traveler in India published in an English magazine. Relaxed and informal in style, the sketch is less dramatic but more analytic and descriptive than the tale and the short story. One common variation of the sketch is the character sketch, a form of casual biography usually consisting of a series of anecdotes about a real or imaginary person.

literate \\'lit-ə-rət\\ [Latin *litteratus* versed in literature, cultured, a derivative of *litterae* writing, literary works]   **1.** Educated, cultured.   **2.** Able to read and write—opposed to *illiterate*.   **3.** Versed in literature or creative writing.   **4.** Dealing with literature or belles lettres.

literati \\,lit-ə-'rät-ē\\ [Latin, plural of *literatus* a person of culture, from *literatus* (adjective) versed in literature, cultured] The educated class or intelligentsia; specifically, persons interested in literature or the arts. The term was originally used in the 17th century to describe the literate class in China. It later meant members of literary clubs of 18th-century Edinburgh and professional men who were supporters of a particular party within the Church of Scotland, and from there it took on its broader meaning.

literator \\'lit-ə-,rā-tər\\ [in part from Latin *litterator* schoolmaster, in part from French *littérateur*]   *see* LITTERATEUR.

literature \\'lit-ə-rə-,chür, - chər, -,tyur\\ [Latin *litteratura* writing, elements of elementary education, literature, a derivative of *litteratus* versed in literature, cultured]   **1.** *archaic* Knowledge of books; literary culture.   **2.** The production of literary work especially as an occupation.   **3.** Writings in prose or verse; especially, writings having excellence of form or expression and presenting ideas of permanent or universal interest. **4.** The body of written works produced in a particular language, country, or age.   **5.** The body of writings on a particular subject.   **6.** Printed matter (as leaflets, handbills, or circulars).

litotes \\'līt-ə-,tēz, 'lit-; lī-'tō-tēz\\ [Greek *litótēs*, literally, plainness, a derivative of *litós* plain, simple]   A figure of speech by which conscious understatement is used to create emphasis by negation; examples are the expressions "not bad!" and "no mean feat." Litotes is responsible for much of the characteristic stoicism of Old English poetry and the Icelanders' sagas.

litterateur \\,lit-ə-rə-'tər, -'tur\\ or **literator** \\'lit-ə-,rā-tər, ,lit-ə-'rä-,tor\\ [French *littérateur*, a derivative of *littérature* literature] A literary person; especially, a professional writer.

Littérature \\lē-tā-rā-'tuer\\   The most notable of the French periodicals issued by members of the Dada movement. The review, founded by André Breton, Louis Aragon, and Philippe Soupault, was published in Paris from 1919 to 1924.

littérature engagée \\lē-tā-rā-tuer-äⁿ-gå-'zhā\\ ("engaged literature")   The literature of commitment, popularized in the immediate post-World War II era, when the French existentialists, particularly Jean-Paul Sartre, revived the idea of the artist's serious responsibility to society. Engagement was understood as an individual moral challenge that involved the responsibility of adapting freely made choices to socially useful ends, rather than as "taking a position" on particular issues. The existentialist position was a reaction against the creed of "art for art's sake" and against the "bourgeois" writer, whose obligation was to his craft rather than his audience. Sartre defined such terms in his introductory statement to *Les Temps modernes* (1945), a review devoted to *littérature engagée*.

Little Dorrit \\'dor-it\\   Novel by Charles DICKENS, published serially from 1855 to 1857 and in book form in 1857. The novel attacks the injustices of the contemporary English legal system, particularly the institution of debtors' prison.

Amy Dorrit, referred to as Little Dorrit, is born and lives much of her life at the Marshalsea prison where her father is imprisoned for debt. She earns meager wages at jobs outside the prison walls, returning nightly to Marshalsea. One of her jobs is as a seamstress for Mrs. Clennam, whose son Arthur eventually helps free Mr. Dorrit from prison.

Arthur becomes a debtor himself and falls in love with Little Dorrit, but because their financial circumstances are now reversed, he does not ask her to marry him. In the end miserly Mrs. Clenam is forced to reveal that Arthur is not really her son and that she had been keeping money from him and the Dorrits for many years. Little Dorrit and Arthur are then free to marry.

Little Em'ly \\'em-lē\\   Fictional character, the childhood playmate and first love of David Copperfield in Charles Dickens' novel DAVID COPPERFIELD. Later, Em'ly is seduced and abandoned by David's reprobate friend James Steerforth.

Little Eva \\'ē-və\\, *byname of* Evangeline St. Clare \\ē-'van-jə-,līn-sānt-'klar, -sin-\\   Fictional character, the angelic daughter of a Southern slave owner and friend to the black slave Uncle Tom, in UNCLE TOM'S CABIN, by Harriet Beecher Stowe.

Little Eyolf \\'ā-,yolf\\   Play in three acts by Henrik IBSEN, published in Norwegian as *Lille Eyolf* in 1894 and produced the following year. This complex psychological drama is acclaimed for its subtle intricacies and profound ironies.

Alfred Allmers returns from his mountain retreat to discover that his crippled son Eyolf has drowned mysteriously. His relationship with his energetic wife, Rita, begins to deteriorate and he decides to leave. They eventually reunite to piece together the family that was broken by Eyolf's sudden death.

Little Foxes, The   Drama in three acts by Lillian HELLMAN, a chronicle of greed and hate in a ruthless family in the American South, produced and published in 1939.

Set at the turn of the 20th century, the play concerns the manipulative Regina Giddens and her two brothers, Ben and Oscar Hubbard, who want to borrow money from Regina's rich, terminally ill husband Horace so that they can open the first cotton mill in town. When Horace discovers that they have arranged the theft of $80,000 in bonds, instead of prosecuting his brothers-in-law, he informs Regina that he will draw up a new will leaving her only $80,000. The threatened disinheritance causes Regina to reveal all the loathing she feels for Horace. When he suffers an attack, Regina withholds his medication and cold-bloodedly watches him die.

Hellman's play *Another Part of the Forest* (1947) portrays the Hubbard family 20 years prior to the action in *The Little Foxes*.

Little Gidding \\'gid-iŋ\\   Poem by T.S. ELIOT, originally appearing in 1942, both in the *New English Weekly* and in pamphlet form. The next year it was published in a volume with the previous three poems of THE FOUR QUARTETS. Written in five sections in strong-stress meter, "Little Gidding" concludes Eliot's study of human experience, Christian faith, and the nature of time and history.

The title is taken from the name of a village in Huntingdonshire where Nicholas Ferrar established an Anglican community in the 17th century. The poem, set at the Little Gidding chapel in winter and in London during World War II, addresses spiritual renewal.

Little Lord Fauntleroy \\'fănt-lə-,rȯi, 'fȯnt-\\ Sentimental novel for children written by Frances Hodgson BURNETT, published serially in *St. Nicholas* magazine and in book form in 1886.

The novel's protagonist Cedric and his mother, Dearest, live in America until Cedric learns that he is to inherit the title and estate of his paternal grandfather. The mother and son then move to England, where Cedric, as Lord Fauntleroy, charms his embittered grandfather, the Earl of Dorincourt, and everyone else he meets with his open, egalitarian ways.

little magazine Any of various small periodicals devoted to serious literary writings, usually avant-garde and noncommercial. They were published from about 1880 through much of the 20th century and flourished in the United States and England, though French authors (especially the Symbolist poets and critics who wrote about 1880–1900) often had access to a similar type of publication and German literature of the 1920s was also indebted to them. The name signifies most of all a noncommercial manner of editing, managing, and financing.

Foremost in the ranks of such magazines were two American periodicals, *Poetry: a Magazine of Verse* (founded 1912), especially in its early years under the vigorous guidance of Harriet Monroe, and the more erratic and often more sensational *Little Review* (1914–29) of Margaret Anderson; a group of English magazines in the second decade of the 20th century, of which the *Egoist* (1914–19) and *Blast* (1914–15) were most conspicuous; and *transition* (1927–38).

Little Minister, The Popular sentimental novel by James M. BARRIE, published in 1891 and dramatized in 1897.

Set in Thrums, a Scottish weaving village based on Barrie's birthplace, *The Little Minister* concerns Gavin Dishart, a young, impoverished minister with his first congregation. The weavers he serves soon riot in protest against reductions in their wages and harsh working conditions. Warned by Babbie, a beautiful and mysterious Gypsy, that Lord Rintoul, the local laird, has summoned the militia, the weavers prepare for a fight. During the ensuing melee, Dishart rescues Babbie from the soldiers. The minister and the Gypsy fall in love, he never suspecting that she is really a well-born lady who is unwillingly betrothed to the old Lord Rintoul. After many trials the two live happily ever after.

Little Nell \\'nel\\ Fictional character, a frail child who is a major figure in Charles Dickens' novel THE OLD CURIOSITY SHOP.

Little Orphant Annie \\'an-ē\\ One of the best-known poems of James Whitcomb RILEY, first published under the pseudonym "Benj. F. Johnson, of Boone" in the popular collection *The Old Swimmin' Hole and 'Leven More Poems* (1883).

"Little Orphant Annie" was written in the Hoosier dialect of Riley's native Indiana. Sentimental and cheerfully philosophical, the poem concerns an orphaned girl who tells the children in whose house she lives scary stories about "the Gobble-un."

The cartoonist Harold Gray named his comic strip about a similarly plucky girl "Little Orphan Annie."

little people Tiny imaginary beings (such as fairies, elves, and leprechauns) of folklore.

Little Prince, The Fable by Antoine de SAINT-EXUPÉRY, published with his own illustrations in French as *Le Petit Prince* in 1943.

The narrator, a pilot who has crash-landed in a desert, encounters a boy prince from another planet who tells him about his adventures on Earth. The prince has cultivated a precious

Illustration by the author for the original edition of *The Little Prince*
Harcourt, Brace, Jovanovich and Companies

rose back on his planet and is dismayed to discover that roses are so common on Earth. A desert fox convinces the prince, who is generally scornful of logic, that he is responsible for loving the rose and that this act of giving provides his life with meaning. Satisfied, the prince returns to his planet.

Little Review, The Avant-garde American literary magazine founded in Chicago by Margaret ANDERSON, published from 1914 to 1929. Despite minimal financial support and numerous fights with censors, *The Little Review* managed to be the most influential arts magazine of its time. Its contributors included T.S. Eliot, Wyndham Lewis, Gertrude Stein, William Carlos Williams, Ezra Pound, and Wallace Stevens, but the magazine is probably best known for its serialization of James Joyce's novel *Ulysses*.

The first issue, published in March of 1914, featured work by Vachel Lindsay and essays on feminism, Friedrich Nietzsche, and psychoanalysis. In the May 1914 issue Anderson extolled the ideas of anarchist Emma Goldman and called for the abolition of private property; her few financial backers then abandoned her. In 1916 Anderson's companion, artist Jane Heap, joined her as associate editor. Anderson and Heap moved to New York's Greenwich Village in 1917. It was Pound, who was the European editor, who brought *Ulysses* to the magazine. The serialization of *Ulysses* began in the March 1918 issue; over the next three years the U.S. Post Office burned entire press runs of four issues for alleged obscenity.

Financially strapped and demoralized by the tepid response to *Ulysses*, in 1921 Anderson and Heap began to publish *The Little Review* as a quarterly rather than a monthly. In 1922 Anderson turned over the editorship to Heap, who in 1927 relocated the then irregularly published magazine to Paris. With Anderson, she drafted a questionnaire mailed to dozens of artists and writers, including questions such as "What is your attitude toward art today?" More than 50 responded, including Sherwood Anderson, Edith Sitwell, Jean Cocteau, Marianne Moore, and Bernard Russell, and their replies made up the last issue of *The Little Review*.

little theater   Movement in American theater to free dramatic forms and methods of production from the limitations of large commercial theaters by establishing small experimental centers of drama. The movement was influenced by the vital European theater of the late 19th century, especially the revolutionary theories of director Max Reinhardt, the designing concepts of Adolphe Appia and Edward Gordon Craig, and the staging experiments at such theaters as the Théâtre-Libre of Paris, the Freie Bühne in Berlin, and the Moscow Art Theater. Community playhouses such as the Toy Theatre in Boston, the Little Theatre in Chicago, and the Little Theatre, New York City, all founded in 1912, were centers of the experimental activity. The little theaters provided a valuable early opportunity for such playwrights as Eugene O'Neill, George S. Kaufman, Elmer Rice, Maxwell Anderson, and Robert E. Sherwood.

Littleton, Mark.   Pseudonym of John P. KENNEDY.

Little Women (*in full* Little Women, or Meg, Jo, Beth, and Amy)   Novel for children by Louisa May ALCOTT, published in two parts in 1868 and 1869. It initiated a genre of family stories for children.

Meg, Jo, Beth, and Amy March are raised in genteel poverty by their loving mother Marmee in a quiet Massachusetts town while their father serves as an army chaplain during the American Civil War. They befriend Theodore Lawrence (Laurie), the lonely grandson of a rich old man next door. The vital force of the family is Jo, a headstrong tomboy who is the emotional center of the book. In the course of the novel beautiful, vain Meg marries Laurie's tutor John Brooke and starts her own family; quiet, sickly Beth dies from scarlet fever; artistic Amy marries Laurie after he is turned down by Jo; and Jo marries Professor Bhaer, whom she meets while living in a boardinghouse, and together they set up a school for boys.

The novel had two sequels: *Little Men: Life at Plumfield with Jo's Boys* (1871) and *Jo's Boys and How They Turned Out* (1886).

liturgical drama   In the Middle Ages, type of play acted within or near a church and relating stories from the Bible and of the saints. Although they had their roots in the Christian liturgy, such plays were not performed as essential parts of a standard church service. The language of the liturgical drama was Latin, and the dialogue was frequently chanted to simple monophonic melodies. Music was also used incidentally.

The earliest traces of the liturgical drama are found in manuscripts dating from the 10th century. The liturgical drama flourished particularly during the 12th and 13th centuries. Eventually, the connection between the liturgical drama and the church was severed completely as the plays came under secular sponsorship and adopted the vernacular. *See also* MIRACLE PLAY; MORALITY PLAY; MYSTERY PLAY.

Litwos   Pseudonym of Henryk SIENKIEWICZ.

Liu E \'lyü-'ä\ or **Liu O** \'ö\ (b. Oct. 18, 1857, Dantu [now Zhenjiang], China—d. Aug. 23, 1909, Dihua, Xinjiang)   Chinese government functionary and economic promoter famed for the major literary work *Lao Can youji* (1904–07; *The Travels of Lao Ts'an*).

Liu engaged in various government work until he became disillusioned with Imperial attitudes about reform and turned to the promotion of private economic development. Liu was convinced of China's need to modernize using Western technology and business methods. His concerns indirectly shaped much of *Lao Can youji*, a social satire exposing the limitations of the old elite and officialdom. Written in the traditional mode of vernacular novels, this work is preeminent among the satirical fiction that dominated the literature of the late Qing dynasty. Despite its popular success, Liu was convicted on a spurious charge of malfeasance and exiled to Xinjiang, where he died in disgrace.

Liu Zongyuan or **Liu Tsung-yüan** \'lyü-'dzu̇ŋ-'ywen\ (b. 773, Dongguan, Shanxi province, China—d. 819, Liuzhou, Guangxi province)   Chinese poet and prose writer who supported the movement to liberate writers from the highly formalized *pianwen*, the so-called parallel prose style cultivated by the Chinese literati for nearly 1,000 years.

Liu Zongyuan served as a government official for most of his life, acting with integrity and courage despite his politically motivated exile to minor positions in isolated regions of China. He joined the poet and essayist Han Yu in condemning the artificialities and restrictions of the *pianwen* style and in urging a return to the simple and flexible classical prose style. In pursuit of this goal, Liu Zongyuan produced many examples of clear and charming prose.

Lively \'līv-lē\, Penelope (Margaret), *original surname* Low \'lō\ (b. March 17, 1933, Cairo, Egypt)   British writer of well-plotted novels and short stories that stress the significance of memory and historical continuity.

Lively's first book, the children's novel *Astercote* (1970), about modern English villagers who fear a resurgence of medieval plague, was followed by at least 19 other novels for children, many of which were set in rural England, including the award-winning books *The Ghost of Thomas Kempe* (1973) and *A Stitch in Time* (1976).

Her passion for landscape gardening inspired Lively's first work for adults, the nonfiction *The Presence of the Past: An Introduction to Landscape History* (1976). Her first adult novel, *The Road to Lichfield* (1977), in which past truths shift when viewed from a contemporary perspective, reflected her interest in history and in the kinds of evidence on which contemporary views of the past are based. Her other novels for adults include *Treasures of Time* (1979), which won the British National Book Award; *Judgement Day* (1980); *Moon Tiger* (1987; Booker Prize); *Passing On* (1989); *City of the Mind* (1991); and *Cleopatra's Sister* (1993). *Oleander, Jacaranda* (1994) is a memoir of her Egyptian childhood.

Lives   *see* PARALLEL LIVES.

Livesay \'līv-,sā\, Dorothy (Kathleen) (b. Oct. 12, 1909, Winnipeg, Man., Can.)   Canadian lyric poet whose works range from angry protest (*Day and Night*, 1944) to intensely personal evocations (*Selected Poems*, 1957).

Livesay's poetry shows the influence of the French Symbolist poets. A second influence was her experience in Montreal as a social worker during the Depression, intensified by an affinity for the social gospel of such liberal poets of the 1930s as C. Day-Lewis, Stephen Spender, and W.H. Auden. Her other collections of poetry include *Poems for People* (1947), *Call My People Home* (1950), *New Poems* (1955), *The Unquiet Bed* (1967), *Ice Age* (1975), and *Phases of Love* (1983). She twice (1944, 1947) received the Governor General's award for poetry, and in 1947 she received the Lorne Pierce Medal, Canada's greatest literary honor. Her *Collected Poems* appeared in 1972 and *Selected Poems: The Self-Completing Tree* in 1986.

Living Newspaper   Theatrical production consisting of dramatizations of current events, social problems, and controversial issues, with appropriate suggestions for improvement. The technique was used for propaganda in the U.S.S.R. after the Revolution of 1917. It became part of the EPIC THEATER tradition initiated by Erwin Piscator and Bertolt Brecht in Germany in the 1920s.

The Living Newspaper was initiated in the United States in 1935 as part of the WPA FEDERAL THEATRE PROJECT. One of its major supporters was dramatist Elmer Rice. Outstanding productions included *Triple-A Plowed Under*, dealing with the Supreme Court's invalidation of the Agricultural Adjustment Administration (AAA), and *One-Third of a Nation*, dramatizing the plight of the poor. Criticism of the Living Newspaper for alleged communist leanings contributed to the cancellation of the Federal Theatre Project in 1939.

Livings \'liv-iŋz\, Henry (b. Sept. 20, 1929, Prestwich, Lancashire, Eng.) Regional British working-class playwright whose farces, which resemble parables, exhibit both a dazzling comic flair and an unexpected force and profundity that is heightened by his use of colloquial language.

Livings was trained as an actor at Joan Littlewood's Theatre Workshop. His first stage play, *Stop It, Whoever You Are*, about a washroom attendant, was performed in 1961. Among his other plays are *The Quick and the Dead Quick* (produced 1961); *Big Soft Nellie* (produced 1961), whose witless hero creates chaos in a radio repair shop; *Nil Carborundum* (produced 1962), about life in the Royal Air Force; and *Eh?* (1965), in which a teenaged night watchman is put in charge of a huge marine boiler, with disastrous consequences.

Living Theatre, The Theatrical repertory company known for its innovative production of experimental drama, often on radical themes, and for its confrontations with tradition, authority, and audiences. It was formed in New York City in 1951 by Julian Beck and Judith Malina. The group struggled during the 1950s, producing plays by Gertrude Stein, Luigi Pirandello, Alfred Jarry, T.S. Eliot, Jean Cocteau, August Strindberg, and others. Its first big success came with its 1959 production of *The Connection*, Jack Gelber's drama about drug addiction.

Members of the troupe tangled with the federal government over their political (nonviolent and anarchial) views and failure to pay income taxes. Beck and Malina were jailed briefly, and The Living Theatre was closed.

In 1964 the company took up "voluntary exile" in Europe. Influenced by Oriental mysticism, Gestalt psychology, and an Artaudian desire to abolish the distinction between art and life, The Living Theatre moved toward deliberately shocking and confronting its audiences. In 1970 the troupe split into several groups and dispersed.

Livius Andronicus \'liv-ē-əs-,an-drə-'nī-kəs, an-'drän-ik-əs\, Lucius (b. *c.* 284 BC, Tarentum, Magna Graecia [now Taranto, Italy]—d. *c.* 204 BC, Rome?) Founder of Roman epic poetry and drama.

Livius Andronicus was a Greek slave, freed by a member of the Livian family; he earned his living teaching Latin and Greek in Rome. His main work was the *Odusia*, a translation of Homer's *Odyssey*. Written in rude Italian Saturnian meter, it had little poetic merit, to judge from the less than 50 surviving lines and from the comments of Cicero and Horace. It was, however, the first major poem in Latin and the first example of artistic translation.

In 240, as part of the Ludi Romani (the annual games honoring Jupiter), Livius produced a translation of a Greek play, probably a tragedy, and perhaps also a comedy. After this, the first dramatic performance ever given in Rome, he continued to write, stage, and sometimes perform in both tragedies and comedies. Only a few fragments of his three remaining comedies and nine tragedies have survived.

Livy \'liv-ē\, *Latin in full* Titus Livius \'liv-ē-əs\ (b. 59/64 BC, Patavium, Venetia, Italy—d. AD 17, Patavium) With Sallust and Tacitus, one of the three great Roman historians.

Little is known about Livy's life and nothing about his family background. Most of his life must have been spent at Rome,

and at an early stage he attracted the interest of Augustus and was even invited to supervise the literary activities of the young Claudius (the future emperor), presumably about AD 8. He never became closely involved with the literary world of Rome, however, and his lifework was the composition of his history.

Livy's history was divided into 142 books, of which books 11–20 and 46–142 have been lost. Apart from fragments, the books after Book 45 are known only from summaries that were made from the 1st century AD onward.

Previous writers about the history of Rome had been public figures and men of affairs. Livy was unique among Roman historians in that he played no part in politics. The chief effect is that Livy did not seek historical explanations in political terms. The novelty and impact of his history thus lay in the fact that he saw history in terms of human personalities and representative individuals rather than of partisan politics.

Together with Cicero and Tacitus, Livy also set new standards of literary style. The earliest Roman historians had written in Greek, the language of culture. Livy evolved a varied and flexible Latin style in which the language matched the subject matter. He reports bare notices of archival fact in dry and formal language, reserving his poetic and dramatic vocabulary for such events as battles.

Livy's history was deeply rooted in the Augustan revival and owed its success in large measure to its moral seriousness. It was the detached attempt to understand the course of history through character, however, that represents Livy's great achievement.

Li Yu or **Li Yü** \'lē-'yǖ, *Angl* 'yü\, *also called* Li Houzhu \'hō-'jǖ\ (b. 937, Jinling [now Nanjing]—d. Aug. 15 (?), 978, Bian [now Kaifeng, Henan province], China) Chinese poet and the last ruler of the Nan Tang (Southern Tang) dynasty, which lasted from 937 to 975.

Li Yu succeeded his poet father, Li Jing, as ruler in 961. His country was invaded in 974 by Taizu, founder of the Song dynasty (960–1279), and when his capital, Jinling, fell the next year, Li Yu surrendered and was taken to the Song capital, Bian. There he was given a nominal title, but his life was one of misery. When Taizu died in 976, his brother and successor, Taizong, had Li Yu poisoned.

Li Yu was a master of the CI song form. More than 30 of his lyrics have survived. His earlier poems reflect the gay and luxurious life at his court, though some are tinged with romantic melancholy. His middle poems are those written from the time of his wife's death (964) to his captivity (975). Li Yu achieved his greatness, however, in his later poems in which he expressed his grief and despair at the loss of his kingdom.

Li Yu or **Li Yü** \'lē-'yǖ, *Angl* 'yü\, *also called* Li Liweng \'lē-'wəŋ\ (b. 1611, Rugao, Zhejiang province, China—d. *c.* 1680, Hangzhou) Chinese author of fiction and essays known for their narrative directness and psychological insight.

Li Yu spent much of his life traveling throughout China with his own theatrical troupe, which performed his original romances and light comedies in the homes of wealthy patrons. His best-known play was *Fengzheng wu* ("Kite Mishap"). Though his many dramas were soon forgotten in China, his playwriting abilities were admired in Japan long after his death.

During the period of the puritanical Manchu rule, Li Yu was called a writer of lewd works. His irreverent outlook was reflected in his extravagant lifestyle and in his *Xianqing ouji* ("Sketches of Idle Pleasures"), a collection of discourses on health, dramatic theory, feminine beauty, and various other topics. He wrote two novels; one of them, *Rouputuan* (1634?; "The Carnal Prayer Mat"), is an erotic satire on the corruption and immorality of the late Ming dynasty, which fell in 1644.

His other works include a short-story collection and a collection of 12 loosely connected tales known as *Shierlou* ("Twelve Towers"); six tales from the latter work were translated into English as *A Tower for the Summer Heat* (1992).

Llewellyn \\'hlwel-in, hlə-'wel-, *Angl* lü-'wel-in, thlü-\\, Richard, *byname of* Richard Dafydd Vivian Llewellyn Lloyd \\'lóid\\ (b. Dec. 8, 1906, St. David's, Pembrokeshire, Wales—d. Nov. 30, 1983, Dublin, Ire.) Welsh novelist and playwright, known especially for *How Green Was My Valley* (1939; film, 1941), a best-selling novel about a Welsh mining family. It was followed by *Up, Into the Singing Mountain* (1960), *And I Shall Sleep . . . Down Where the Moon Is Small* (1966), and *Green, Green My Valley Now* (1975).

After working in the motion-picture industry and in journalism, Llewellyn wrote two successful mystery plays, *Poison Pen* (1938) and *Noose* (1947). Among his other novels are *None But the Lonely Heart* (1943; film, 1944), *A Few Flowers for Shiner* (1950), and *A Night of Bright Stars* (1979).

Llwyd \\'hlüyd\\, Morgan (b. 1619, Merioneth, Wales—d. June 3, 1659, Wrexham, Denbighshire) Puritan writer whose *Llyfr y Tri Aderyn* (1653; "The Book of the Three Birds") is considered the most important original Welsh work published during the 17th century. The work is in two parts, on the theory of government and on religious liberty. It is in the form of a discourse conducted among the eagle (Oliver Cromwell, or the secular power), the raven (the Anglicans, or organized religion), and the dove (the Nonconformists, or the followers of the inner light). Llwyd also wrote *Llythur ir Cymru Cariadus* (1653; "Letter to the Beloved Welsh").

Llywarch Hen \\'hlə-,wärk-'hän\\ (fl. 6th century) Central figure in a cycle of poems composed by a 9th-century storyteller in Powys (Wales). Set against the background of the struggle of the Welsh of the Kingdom of Powys against the Anglo-Saxons of Mercia, the poems speak of heroic virtues, express laments for fallen heroes, and grieve for the transitoriness of earthly things. In these tales, prose was used for narrative and description and verse for dialogue and soliloquy, but the verse passages are all that remain. They are preserved in *The Red Book of Hergest*, a manuscript of the 15th century.

Llywelyn y Glyn   *see* LEWIS Glyn Cothi.

local color Style of writing marked by the presentation of the features and peculiarities of a particular locality and its inhabitants. The name is given especially to a type of American literature that in its most characteristic form made its appearance just after the Civil War.

The frontier novels of James Fenimore Cooper have been cited as precursors of the local-color story, as have the New York Dutch tales of Washington Irving. Set during the California gold rush, Bret Harte's "The Luck of Roaring Camp" (1868), with its use of miners' dialect and western background, is among the early local-color stories. Many authors first achieved success with vivid descriptions of their own localities: Mark Twain described Mississippi River life; Harriet Beecher Stowe, Rose Terry Cooke, and Sarah Orne Jewett wrote of New England; George Washington Cable, Joel Chandler Harris, and Kate Chopin described the Deep South; T.N. Page did the same for Virginia; Edward Eggleston wrote of Indiana frontier days; Charles E. Craddock told stories of the Tennessee mountaineers; and O. Henry chronicled both the Texas frontier and the streets of New York City.

Lochinvar \\'läk-in-,vär, ,lȯk-in-'vär\\ Fictional romantic hero of the ballad "Marmion" (1808) by Sir Walter SCOTT.

Lochinvar is a brave knight who arrives unannounced at the bridal feast of Ellen, his beloved, who is about to be married to "a laggard in love and a dastard in war." Lochinvar claims one dance with the bride and dances her out the door, swooping her up onto his horse, and they ride off together.

Locke \\'läk\\, Alain (LeRoy) (b. Sept. 13, 1886, Philadelphia, Pa., U.S.—d. June 9, 1954, New York, N.Y.) American educator, writer, and philosopher, best remembered as a leader and one of the chief interpreters of the HARLEM RENAISSANCE.

Graduated in philosophy from Harvard University, Locke was the first black Rhodes scholar, studying at Oxford (1907–10) and the University of Berlin (1910–11). For almost 40 years, as head of the department of philosophy, he taught at Howard University, Washington, D.C.

Locke encouraged black authors to seek subjects in black life and to set high artistic standards for themselves. He familiarized American readers with the Harlem Renaissance by editing a special Harlem issue for *Survey Graphic* (March 1925), which he expanded into *The New Negro* (1925), an anthology of fiction, poetry, drama, and essays.

Locke edited the *Bronze Booklet* studies of cultural achievements by blacks, and he annually reviewed literature by and about blacks in *Opportunity* and *Phylon*. His many works include *Four Negro Poets* (1927), *Frederick Douglass, a Biography of Anti-Slavery* (1935), *Negro Art—Past and Present* (1936), and *The Negro and His Music* (1936). His unfinished materials for a definitive study of blacks in American culture formed the basis for M.J. Butcher's *The Negro in American Culture* (1956).

Lockhart \\'läk-ərt, -,ärt,-,härt\\, John Gibson (b. July 14, 1794, Wishaw, Lanarkshire, Scot.—d. Nov. 25, 1854, Abbotsford, near Melrose, Roxburghshire) Scottish critic, novelist, and biographer, known for his *Life of Sir Walter Scott* (1837–38; enlarged, 1839), one of the great biographies in English.

Lockhart became one of the main contributors to the Tory-oriented *Edinburgh Monthly Magazine* (later *Blackwood's Edinburgh Magazine*) from the time of its founding in 1817. With others, he wrote the "Translation from an Ancient Chaldee Manuscript," which lampooned Scottish celebrities in a parody of Old Testament style, and "On the Cockney School of Poetry," the first of a series of attacks on the English poets John Keats and Percy Bysshe Shelley.

In 1818 Lockhart met Sir Walter Scott. Lockhart married Scott's daughter Sophia in 1820 and became, through Scott's influence, editor (1825–53) of the Tory *Quarterly Review*. Early in his editorship (1828) he produced a biography of Robert Burns. Though his *Life of Sir Walter Scott* was attacked by contemporaries for exposing Scott's faults, it is now regarded as an idealized portrait, depicting Scott's success in brilliant color and indicating his foibles with subtle wit.

Locksley Hall \\'läks-lē\\ Poem in trochaic meter by Alfred, Lord TENNYSON, published in the collection *Poems* (1842). The narrator of this dramatic monologue declaims against marriages made for material gain and worldly prestige.

The narrator revisits Locksley Hall, his childhood home, where he and his cousin Amy had fallen in love. Amy, however, was a shallow young woman who acceded to her parents' desires that she marry a wealthier suitor. The narrator begins the poem by protesting the modern, mechanized world, but ends by reluctantly accepting the inevitability of change.

In Tennyson's sequel, "Locksley Hall Sixty Years After" (1886), the narrator has grown old and has made his peace with the people and the memories of his youth.

locus classicus \\'lō-kəs-'klas-i-kəs\\ *plural* loci classici \\'lō-,sī-'klas-i-,sī\\ [New Latin, literally, classical passage] A passage that has become a standard for the elucidation of a word or subject. The term is also used to refer generally to a classic case or example.

Lodge \'läj\, David (John) (b. Jan. 28, 1935, London, Eng.) English novelist, literary critic, and editor known chiefly for his satiric novels.

Lodge was educated at University College, London, and at the University of Birmingham. His early novels, known mostly in England, include *The Picturegoers* (1960), about a group of Roman Catholics living in London; *Ginger, You're Barmy* (1962), Lodge's novelistic response to his army service in the mid-1950s; and *The British Museum Is Falling Down* (1965), which uses stream-of-consciousness technique. *How Far Can You Go?* (1980; U.S. title, *Souls & Bodies*) is a satiric look at a group of contemporary English Catholics. Several of Lodge's novels satirize academic life and share the same setting and recurring characters; these include *Changing Places: A Tale of Two Campuses* (1975), *Small World: An Academic Romance* (1984), and *Nice Work* (1988). The novel *Paradise News* was published in 1991.

In addition to writing fiction, Lodge coauthored the plays *Between These Four Walls* (produced 1963) and *Slap in the Middle* (produced 1965). His works of literary theory include *Language of Fiction* (1966), *The Novelist at the Crossroads, and Other Essays on Fiction and Criticism* (1971; rev. ed., 1984), *Write On: Occasional Essays* (1986), and *After Bakhtin: Essays in Fiction and Criticism* (1990).

Lodge \'läj\, Thomas (b. *c.* 1557, London?, Eng.—d. 1625, London) British writer remembered for the prose romance *Rosalynde*, the source of William Shakespeare's *As You Like It*.

Lodge published his earliest work, an unlicensed pamphlet (*c.* 1579), in reply to Stephen Gosson's attack on stage plays. *An Alarum Against Usurers* (1584) answered Gosson's attack on his character. Lodge appended to the *Alarum* both a prose tale, *The Delectable Historie of Forbonius and Prisceria*, and a verse lament, *The Lamentable Complaint of Truth over England*. This collection foreshadowed his varied activity for the next 12 years: in verse (*Scillaes Metamorphosis*, 1589; *Phillis*, 1593; *A Fig for Momus*, 1595); in romances (*Rosalynde*, 1590; *Robert, Second Duke of Normandy*, 1591; *Euphues Shadow*, 1592; *William Longbeard*, 1593; *A Margarite of America*, 1596); in pamphlets ("Catharos," 1591; "The Divel Conjured," 1596; *Wits Miserie, and the Worlds Madnesse*, 1596; *Prosopopeia*, 1596); and in plays (*The Wounds of Civill War*, 1594; with Robert Greene, *A Looking Glasse for London and England*, 1594).

Apart from *A Treatise of the Plague* (1603) and *The Poore Mans Talentt*, a manual of domestic medicine (printed 1881), his later works were translations. Many of his well-known lyrics first appeared in his romances. Of these, *Rosalynde* is a dramatically plotted tale combining Senecan motives with the artifice of euphuism and Arcadian romance.

Lofting \'lôf-tiŋ\, Hugh (b. Jan. 14, 1886, Maidenhead, Berkshire, Eng.—d. Sept. 26, 1947, Santa Monica, Calif., U.S.) English-born American author and illustrator of a series of children's classics about Doctor DOLITTLE, a chubby, gentle, eccentric physician to animals.

Lofting lived most of his life in the United States, but the ambience of all his books is English. The character Dr. Dolittle was originally created to entertain Lofting's children in letters he sent from the front during World War I. *The Story of Dr. Dolittle*, the first of his series, appeared in 1920 and won instant success. From 1922 to 1928 he wrote one Dr. Dolittle book a year, and these seven are considered the best of the series—certainly the sunniest. *The Voyages of Dr. Dolittle* (1922) won the Newbery Medal as the best children's book of the year. Wearying of his hero, Lofting tried to get rid of him by sending him to the moon (*Dr. Dolittle in the Moon*, 1928), but popular demand

compelled him to write *Dr. Dolittle's Return* in 1933. The last book of the series was published posthumously.

Lofting also wrote *The Story of Mrs. Tubbs* (1923) and its sequel, *Tommy, Tilly, and Mrs. Tubbs* (1934).

Logan \'lō-gən\, John (b. 1748, Soutra, Midlothian, Scot.—d. Dec. 25, 1788, London, Eng.) Scottish poet and preacher best known for his part in a controversy that arose posthumously over the authorship of a poem entitled "Ode to the Cuckoo," which some claimed was written by Michael BRUCE.

In 1770 Logan edited and published a collection of poetry, including especially five poems written by Bruce and two poems on which the two collaborated. To increase the volume's size, Logan inserted some poems of his own and some from other sources. In his preface he stated that these could easily be distinguished from Bruce's without attribution. When in 1781 Logan published a volume of what he claimed was his own work, he included what some later scholars—beginning in the early 1800s—claimed was Bruce's "Cuckoo."

Several of Logan's sermons and lectures were also published, one of which was proved to be written by another author.

logaoedic \,läg-ə-'ē-dik\ [Late Greek *logaoidikós,* from *lógos* utterance, prose + *aoidē* music, poetry] In prosody, having a metrical rhythm marked by the mixture of several meters; specifically, having a rhythm that uses both dactyls and trochees or anapests and iambs.

Logau \'lō-gaů\, Friedrich, Baron (Freiherr) von, *pseudonym* Salomon von Golaw \'zä-lō-mòn-fòn-'gō-laů\ (b. June 1604, Brockuth, near Nimptsch, Silesia [now in Poland]—d. July 24, 1655, Liegnitz [now Legnica, Poland]) German epigrammatist noted for his direct, unostentatious style.

Logau spent his life in service to the petty courts of Brieg and Liegnitz. Resenting the forced lowliness of his position, he directed much of his satirical wit at courtly life, particularly at foreign (primarily French) cultural customs he saw adopted by the nobility, and at the misguided contempt of the nobility for the German language. His epigrams support the ideals of genuine noblemen and loyal German patriots and decry the futility of bloody rivalries among religious groups. The first collection of epigrams, *Erstes Hundert Teutscher Reimen-Sprüche* (1638; "First Hundred German Proverbs in Rhyme"), appeared in 1654 in a revised and enlarged edition as *Salomons von Golaw Deutscher Sinn-Getichte Drey Tausend*, 3 vol. ("Salomon von Golaw's Three Thousand German Epigrams"; reissued 1872 as *Friedrichs von Logau sämtliche Sinngedichte*; "Friedrich von Logau's Collected Epigrams").

logographer \lō-'gäg-rə-fər\ [Greek *logógraphos* prose writer, from *lógos* utterance, prose + *gráphein* to write] A prose writer in ancient Greece whose purpose was the systematic recording of factual material. As such, logographers are the precursors of historians proper who are said to have started with Herodotus.

Logue \'lōg\, Christopher (b. Nov. 23, 1926, Portsmouth, Hampshire, Eng.) English poet and one of the leaders in the movement to bring poetry closer to popular experience. His own pungent, political verse owes much to the work of Bertolt Brecht and to the English ballad tradition.

Logue's first book of poetry was *The Weakdream Sonnets* (1955). He adapted the verse of Chilean poet Pablo Neruda for *The Man Who Told His Love* (1958) and *Songs* (1959). Subsequent volumes include *Songs from the Lily-White Boys* (1960), *Logue's A.B.C.* (1966), *New Numbers* (1969), and *Fluff* (1984). Among his poems printed on posters are "I Shall Vote Labour" (1966), "Kiss Kiss" (1968), and "Black Dwarf" (1968). He worked on a remarkably fresh adaptation of Homer's *Iliad*, four sections of which have been published: *Patrocleia* (1962), *Pax* (1967), *War Music* (1981), and *Kings* (1991). Logue also wrote plays, screenplays, documentaries, and children's books (such as *The Children's Book of Children's Rhymes*, 1986).

Lohengrin \'lō-ən-₁grēn, *Angl* -₁grin\   The knight of the swan, hero of German versions of a legend widely known in variant forms from the European Middle Ages onward. It seems to bear some relation to the northern European folktale of "The Seven Swans," but its actual origin is uncertain. The basic story tells of a mysterious knight who arrives—in a boat drawn by a swan—to help a noble lady in distress. He marries her but forbids her to ask his origin; she later forgets this promise, and he leaves her, never to return.

The first German version of the legend—which itself probably derives from a fairy tale of seven brothers who are persecuted by a wicked grandmother and then metamorphosed into swans—appeared in Wolfram von Eschenbach's *Parzival* (*c.* 1210). In this account the swan knight Loherangrîn, the son and heir of Parzival, the hero of the Holy Grail, arrives in a swan-drawn boat from the castle of the Grail to aid Elsa of Brabant, marries her, and returns to the Grail castle.

An anonymous Middle High German poem, *Lohengrin* (*c.* 1275–90), set the story in the historical context of the reign of the German king Henry I the Fowler (876?–936). A contemporary poem known as the *Wartburgkrieg* presents the story of Lohengrin as an entry in a storytelling competition. An anonymous 15th-century epic called *Lorengel* was the chief source used by the 19th-century composer Richard Wagner for his opera *Lohengrin* (1850).

In a French version of the legend, the *Chevalier au cygne*, the knight of the swan (here called Helyas) marries Beatrix of Bouillon, the story being arranged and elaborated to glorify the House of Bouillon. English versions of the legend were strongly influenced by this French account.

Lo-Johansson \'lū-'yū-hän-₁sȯn\, Ivar, *in full* Karl Ivar Lo-Johansson (b. Feb. 23, 1901, Ösmo, Swed.—d. April 11, 1990, Stockholm)   Swedish writer and social critic who in his more than 50 "proletarian" novels and short-story collections depicted the lives of working-class people with great compassion.

Lo-Johansson was first recognized in the mid-1930s for his detailed and realistic depiction of the plight of landless Swedish peasants, known as *statare*, in two volumes of short stories, *Statarna I–II* (1936–37; "The Share Croppers"), and in his novel *Jordproletärerna* (1941; "Proletarians of the Earth"). The books helped spur extensive land reforms, including the abolition of indentured farm labor in 1945. Lo-Johansson gave intense expression to individual human suffering, such as his characterization of a farm servant's wife in *Bara en mor* (1939; "Only a Mother"). Significant among his later works is a series of eight autobiographical novels, beginning with a tribute to his father (himself an indentured farm laborer) in *Analfabeten* (1951; "The Illiterate") and concluding with *Proletärförfattaren* (1960; "The Proletarian Writer"). In the 1970s he used short stories in his cycle of tales on the seven deadly sins, and in the 1980s he wrote a series of memoirs.

Loki \'lō-kē\   In Norse mythology, a cunning trickster who had the ability to change his shape and sex. Loki was represented as the companion of the great gods Odin and Thor, helping them with his clever plans but sometimes causing them embarrassment and difficulty. He also appeared as the enemy of the gods; for causing the death of the god Balder, Loki was punished by being bound to a rock. Loki created a female, Angerboda ("Distress Bringer"), and produced three evil progeny: Hel, the goddess of death; Jǫrmungand, the evil serpent surrounding the world; and Fenrir, the wolf.

Lolita \lō-'lē-tə\   Novel by Vladimir NABOKOV, published in 1955 in France. Upon its American publication in 1958 *Lolita* created a cultural and literary sensation.

The novel is presented as the posthumously published memoirs of its antihero Humbert Humbert. A European intellectual and pedophile, Humbert lusts obsessively after 12-year-old nymphet Lolita (real name, Dolores Haze), who becomes his willing inamorata. The work examines love in the light of lechery.

Loman, Willy \'wil-ē-'lō-mən\   Fictional character, an aging traveling salesman who is the protagonist of Arthur Miller's play DEATH OF A SALESMAN.

Lomonosov \lə-₁mə-'nȯ-səf\, Mikhail Vasilyevich (b. Nov. 8 [Nov. 19, New Style], 1711, near Kholmogory [Russia]—d. April 4 [April 15], 1765, St. Petersburg)   Russian poet, scientist, and grammarian who is often considered the first great Russian linguistic reformer.

Lomonosov was educated at the Slavonic–Greek–Latin Academy and the St. Petersburg Academy. He later studied in Germany at the University of Marburg and in Freiberg. His "Ode," dedicated to the empress, and the *Pismo o pravilakh rossiyskogo stikhotvorstva* ("Letter Concerning the Rules of Russian Versification"), in which he established what became the standards for Russian verse, made a considerable impression.

Lomonosov returned to St. Petersburg in 1741 and in 1745 was appointed a professor at the academy, where he subsequently made the many substantial contributions to the natural sciences for which he is known. In addition to his scientific work, Lomonosov continued his literary activity, both as a writer of poems and plays and as a linguist and critic. He wrote *Rossiyskaya grammatika* (1755; "Russian Grammar") and systematized the Russian literary language, which until that time was an amalgam of church Slavic and Russian vernacular. He created the famous "three styles" of poetic diction characteristic of Russian Neoclassicism: the "high" (or grand) style for such verse as heroic poems and odes; the "middle" style for dramatic works demanding colloquial speech; and the "low" style for comedies, epigrams, songs, letters in prose, and precise descriptions. To these achievements were added all the work of reorganizing education, to which Lomonosov accorded much importance. From 1755 he followed closely the development of Moscow University, for which he had drawn up the plans.

His poetic works include occasional verse for various celebrations and official events, several spiritual odes, an unfinished epic on Peter the Great, and the long, didactic poem *Pismo k I.I. Shuvalovu o polze stekla* (1752; "Letter to I.I. Shuvalov Concerning the Usefulness of Glass").

London \'lən-dən\, Jack, *original name* John Griffith Chaney \'chā-nē\ (b. Jan. 12, 1876, San Francisco, Calif., U.S.—d. Nov. 22, 1916, Glen Ellen, Calif.)   American novelist and short-story writer whose works deal romantically with elemental struggles for survival.

Deserted by his father, a roving astrologer, London was raised in Oakland, Calif., by his spiritualist mother and his stepfather, whose surname, London, he took. He worked as a sailor and saw much of the United States as a hobo riding freight trains and as a member of one of the many protest armies of the unemployed born of the panic of 1893. He was jailed for vagrancy and in 1894 became a militant socialist. London educated himself at public libraries, and at age 19 he crammed a four-year high-school course into one year and entered the University of California at Berkeley. After a year he quit school to unsuccessfully seek a fortune in the Klondike gold rush of 1897.

London studied magazines and then set himself an energetic daily schedule of writing. Within two years, stories of his Alaskan adventures, though often crude, began to win acceptance for their fresh subject matter and virile force. His first book, *The Son of the Wolf* (1900), gained a wide audience. His reputation was further enhanced by publication of the short story TO BUILD A FIRE (1908). During the remainder of his life he produced steadily, completing 50 books of fiction and nonfiction in 17 years. He sailed a ketch to the South Pacific, telling of his adventures in THE CRUISE OF THE SNARK (1911). In 1910 he settled in California, where he built his grandiose Wolf House.

Archive Photos

Jack London's hastily written output is of uneven quality. His Alaskan stories—THE CALL OF THE WILD (1903), WHITE FANG (1906), and BURNING DAYLIGHT (1910)—in which he dramatized, in turn, atavism, adaptability, and the appeal of the wilderness are outstanding. His autobiographical novels include *The Road* (1907); *Martin Eden* (1909), perhaps his most enduring work; and *John Barleycorn* (1913). Other important works are THE SEA-WOLF (1904), which features a Nietzschean superman hero, and THE IRON HEEL (1907), a fantasy of the future that is a terrifying anticipation of fascism.

London Magazine, The \'lən-dən\ An English periodical that was dedicated to an adventurous exploration of various subjects, particularly literature and literary criticism. The magazine was published monthly from January 1820 to June 1829.

It initially was edited by John Scott, assisted by William Hazlitt, Thomas Hood, and Mary Russell Mitford. Thomas De Quincey's *Confessions of an English Opium-Eater* and a series of essays by Charles Lamb that were eventually collected as *Essays of Elia,* as well as the work of other young English writers such as Thomas Carlyle, Leigh Hunt, John Keats, and William Wordsworth, were published there. In addition, the magazine published a wide range of foreign literature, including works from Denmark, Serbia, Russia, and Iceland. It competed fiercely with *Blackwood's Edinburgh Magazine,* which insulted Scott's writers; after Scott revealed some of his rival's libels, he was mortally wounded in a duel with one of its representatives.

A later monthly literary review, founded in 1954 by John Lehmann, was also named *The London Magazine.* It was geared toward the common reader who was interested in serious literature, and its scope was later expanded to include coverage of other arts. Its contributors included W.H. Auden, Louis MacNeice, Evelyn Waugh, Derek Walcott, and Jaroslav Seifert.

Lonelyhearts, Miss \'lōn-lē-,härts\ A fictional character, the protagonist and narrator of Nathanael West's novel MISS LONELYHEARTS.

Lonely Passion of Judith Hearne, The \'jü-dith-'hərn\ Novel by Brian MOORE, published in 1955 as *Judith Hearne,* about an aging Irish spinster's disillusionment and her subsequent descent into alcoholism. The U.S. version was published in 1956 as *The Lonely Passion of Judith Hearne.*

Set in Belfast in the early 1950s, the novel is the study of a Roman Catholic woman who tries to gain the affection of James Madden, an unscrupulous retired man she meets at a local pub. Madden sees her as a potential investor in a business scheme, but she mistakenly infers a romantic interest. She begins to drink heavily, and she finds no comfort in her confession to an indifferent priest. Her disintegration is rapid, and she eventually becomes a resident at a nursing home.

Long Day's Journey into Night Drama in four acts by Eugene O'NEILL, written 1939–41 and produced and published, posthumously, in 1956. The play, which is considered an American masterpiece, was awarded a Pulitzer Prize in 1957.

O'Neill's autobiographical play is a shattering depiction of a day in the dreary life of a couple and their two sons. James Tyrone, a semiretired actor, is vain and miserly; his wife Mary feels worthless and retreats into a morphine-induced haze. Jamie, their older son, is a bitter alcoholic. James refuses to acknowledge the illness of his consumptive younger son, Edmund. As Mary sinks into hallucination and madness, father and sons confront each other in searing scenes that reveal their hidden motives and interdependence.

O'Neill wrote *A Moon for the Misbegotten* (1952) as a sequel, charting the subsequent life of Jamie Tyrone.

Longfellow \'lȯŋ-,fel-ō\, Henry Wadsworth (b. Feb. 27, 1807, Portland, Mass. [now in Maine], U.S.—d. March 24, 1882, Cambridge, Mass.) The most popular American poet of the 19th century.

Longfellow graduated from Bowdoin College (Brunswick, Maine) in 1825. In 1829, after traveling in Europe, he returned to the United States to be a professor and librarian at Bowdoin. When he was offered a professorship at Harvard, with another opportunity to go abroad, he accepted, and in 1835 he settled at Heidelberg, where he fell under the influence of German Romanticism.

In 1836 Longfellow returned to Harvard. In 1839 he published *Hyperion,* a romantic novel, and *Voices of the Night,* containing the poems "The Psalm of Life" and "The Light of the Stars," which became immediately popular. "The Wreck of the Hesperus," included in *Ballads and Other Poems* (1841), swept the nation, as did EVANGELINE (1847), an idyll of the former French colony of Acadia.

After presiding over Harvard's modern-language program for 18 years, Longfellow left teaching in 1854. In 1855 he published HIAWATHA, and its appeal was immediate. He translated Dante's *The Divine Comedy,* 3 vol. (1865–67), producing one of the most notable translations to that time, and wrote six sonnets on Dante that are among his finest poems.

The *Tales of a Wayside Inn,* modeled roughly on Geoffrey Chaucer's *The Canterbury Tales* and published in 1863, reveals Longfellow's narrative gift. The first poem, PAUL REVERE'S RIDE, became a national favorite. In 1872 he published what was intended to be his masterpiece, *Christus: A Mystery,* a trilogy dealing with Christianity from its beginnings, and he followed this work with two fragmentary dramatic poems, "Judas Maccabaeus" and "Michael Angelo." Although his genius was not dramatic, these neglected works were later seen to contain some of his most effective writing.

Longford \'lȯŋ-fərd\, Edward Arthur Henry Pakenham, 6th Earl of, Baron Longford, Baron Silchester of Silchester \'silchis-tər\ (b. Dec. 29, 1902, London, Eng.—d. Feb. 4, 1961, Dublin, Ire.) Theater patron and playwright who is best remembered as the director of the Gate Theatre in Dublin.

In 1931 Longford bought up the outstanding shares of the financially unstable Gate Theatre and also became a codirector. Five years later he formed Longford Productions Ltd., an acting company that alternated with that of Hilton Edwards and Micheál Mac Liammóir at the Gate Theatre. Longford subsidized the theater from his own resources, for he wished to keep it a people's theater and to maintain low admission prices.

Longford's own plays performed at the Gate Theatre included *The Melians* (1931), *The Yahoo* (1935), and *Ascendancy* (1935). The company also staged Longford's Gaelic versions of plays by Aeschylus, Sophocles, Euripides, and Molière.

Longinus \län-'jī-nəs\, *also called* Dionysius Longinus *or* Pseudo-Longinus (fl. early 1st century AD)   Name sometimes assigned to the author of ON THE SUBLIME (Greek: *Peri Hypsous*), one of the great, seminal works of literary criticism. The earliest surviving manuscript, from the 10th century, first printed in 1554, ascribes it to Dionysius Longinus. It was later noticed that the index to the manuscript read "Dionysius or Longinus." The problem of authorship embroiled scholars for centuries, and one solution has been to name him Pseudo-Longinus.

long meter or **long measure** *abbreviated* L.M.   In poetry, a quatrain in iambic tetrameter lines with the second and fourth lines rhyming and often the first and third lines rhyming. An example is the following stanza from the poem "When I Survey the Wondrous Cross" by Isaac Watts:

> See, from his head, his hands, his feet,
> Sorrow and love flow mingled down;
> Did e'er such love and sorrow meet,
> Or thorns compose so rich a crown?

Compare BALLAD METER; COMMON METER.

long particular meter *abbreviated* L.P.M.   In verse, a hymn meter of six iambic tetrameter lines to the stanza.

Longus \'läŋ-gəs\ (fl. 2nd–3rd century AD)   Greek writer, author of DAPHNIS AND CHLOE, the first pastoral prose romance and one of the most popular of the Greek erotic romances.

Longus was less concerned with the complications of plot than with describing the way in which love developed between his hero and heroine, from their first naïve and confused feelings of childhood to full sexual maturity. The work displays a penetrating psychological analysis and a notable feeling for nature. *See also* PASTORAL.

Lonigan, Studs \'stədz-'län-i-gən\   A fictional character, the protagonist of James T. Farrell's trilogy STUDS LONIGAN.

Lönnrot \'lœn-rùt\, Elias (b. April 9, 1802, Sammatti, Swedish Finland—d. March 19, 1884, Sammatti, Russian Finland) Folklorist and philologist who created the Finnish national epic, the KALEVALA (1835, enlarged, 1849), from short ballads and lyric poems collected from oral tradition. He also published *Kanteletar* (1840–41; "Old Songs and Ballads of the Finnish People") and other collections.

From 1833 to 1853 Lönnrot lived in Kajaani, in a remote part of eastern Finland, near Russian Karelia. He made field trips among the Lapps, the Estonians, and the Finnic peoples of northwestern Russia and collected evidence of the relationship of the Baltic branches of the Finno-Ugric languages as well as folk poetry. Believing that the short poems he collected were fragments of a continuous epic of which no full version survived, he joined a number of them together with connective material of his own and imposed upon this a unifying plot. The influence of the *Kalevala* on Finnish national consciousness, art, and culture has been immense.

Lönnrot was professor of Finnish language and literature at the University of Helsinki from 1853 to 1862. He promoted Finnish as a national language (Swedish had previously been predominant) and paved the way for the birth of modern Finnish literature.

Lonsdale \'länz-ˌdāl\, Frederick Leonard, *original name* Lionel Frederick Leonard \'len-ərd\ (b. Feb. 5, 1881, St. Helier, Jersey, Channel Islands, U.K.—d. April 4, 1954, London, Eng.) British playwright and librettist whose lightweight comedies of manners have survived because of their epigrammatic wit.

Lonsdale established himself as a librettist of musical comedies, chief among them being *The King of Cadonia* (1908), *The Balkan Princess* (1910), and *The Maid of the Mountains* (1916). During the 1920s, however, he began to produce his most characteristic work, reminiscent of the plays of W. Somerset Maugham. The most successful of these plays were *Aren't We All* (1923), *The Last of Mrs. Cheyney* (1925), *On Approval* (1927), *Canaries Sometimes Sing* (1929), and *Once Is Enough* (1938).

Look Back in Anger   Play in three acts by John OSBORNE, performed in 1956 and published in 1957. A published description of Osborne as an "angry young man" was extended to apply to an entire generation of disaffected young British writers who identified with the lower classes and viewed the upper classes and the established political institutions with disdain.

Although the form of the play was not revolutionary, its content was unexpected. On stage for the first time were the 20- to 30-year-olds of Great Britain who had not participated in World War II and who found its aftermath lacking in promise. The hero, Jimmy Porter, has reached an uncomfortably marginal position on the border of the middle class, from which he can see the traditional possessors of privilege holding the better jobs and threatening his upward climb.

Look Homeward, Angel (*in full* Look Homeward, Angel: A Story of the Buried Life)   Novel by Thomas WOLFE, published in 1929. It is thinly veiled autobiography.

The novel traces the unhappy early years of the introspective protagonist, Eugene Gant, before he sets off for graduate study at Harvard. Wolfe employed a remarkable variety of literary styles in the novel, reflecting Gant's shifting feelings and attitudes: evocative description, acutely realistic dialogue, satire, fantasy, and meandering passages in which the author becomes intoxicated with his own prose. *Of Time and the River: A Legend of Man's Hunger in His Youth* (1935) continued Gant's story.

loose sentence   A sentence in which the principal clause comes first and subordinate modifiers or trailing elements follow. *Compare* PERIODIC SENTENCE.

Looy \vän-'lôi\, Jacobus van (b. Sept. 12, 1855, Haarlem, Neth.—d. Feb. 24, 1930, Haarlem)   Dutch author and painter who personified the close association between art and literature in the late 19th century.

Van Looy wrote first in the direct, personal 1880s style, as in his popular novel *De dood van mijn poes* (1889; "The Death of My Cat"). The influence of the Symbolism of the time is seen in *De nachtcactus* (1888; "The Night Cactus"), with the flower representing ephemeral desire that blooms for one night and then dies. In his later work *Feesten* (1902; "Celebrations"), he appears more objective, describing scenes from lower-middle-class life; and in his autobiographical *Jaapje* (1917), *Jaap* (1923), and *Jacob* (1930), he shows his genius for impressionistic word painting.

Lope de Vega Prize \'lō-pā-ˌthā-'bā-ˌgā\   Literary prize awarded annually to the Spanish or Latin-American playwright of the year's finest play not yet published or performed. The winner of the first prize receives 600,000 pesetas and production of the play at the Teatro Español in Madrid. A second prize is also awarded. The prize was established in 1932 by the Ayuntamiento de Madrid in memory of dramatist Lope de Vega.

Lopes \'lō-pish\, Manuel (b. Dec. 23, 1907, Santo Antão, Cape Verde Islands)   Cape Verdean poet and novelist who portrayed the struggle of his people to live in a land bedeviled by drought, famine, and unemployment.

Lopes was one of the founders of the journal *Claridade*, which in 1936 gave birth to modern Cape Verdean literature. Lopes' story "O galo que cantou na baía" (1936; "The Cock that Crowed in the Bay"; revised and published in 1984 in *Galo cantou na baía e otros contos*) is the first Cape Verdean prose narrative rooted in a social reality that includes traditional folk elements. The novels *Chuva braba* (1956; "Torrential Rains") and *Os flagelados do vento leste* (1960; "Victims of the East Wind") reflect both the anguish and the hope of his people.

Lopes published essays on Cape Verdean culture, as well as two volumes of poetry, *Poemas de quem ficou* (1949; "Poems of One Who Remained Behind") and *Crioulo e outros poemas* (1964; "Creole and Other Poems").

Lopes da Silva \\'lō-pish-də-'sel-və\\, Baltasar *or* Baltazar, *pseudonym* Osvaldo Alcântara \\ȧl-'käⁿ-tȧ-rə\\ (b. April 23, 1907, Vila da Ribeira Brava, São Nicolau, Cape Verde Islands—d. May 28, 1989, Lisbon, Port.) Poet, novelist, and short-story writer who was instrumental in the shaping of modern Cape Verdean literature.

Lopes da Silva's only novel, *Chiquinho* (1947), written in Portuguese, re-creates the experiences of a Cape Verdean who grows up to understand that, in his land, life is a prolonged tragedy given meaning by the assertion of human courage, unselfishness, and dignity. *Chiquinho* marks the advent of realism in the Cape Verdean novel and is now a classic.

Lopes da Silva's poems were published in journals in Cape Verde, Portugal, and Brazil. He was one of the founders of the journal *Claridade* ("Clarity") in 1936. His published nonfiction includes *Cabo Verde visto por Gilberto Freire* (1956), a study of Cape Verdean culture. He also edited an anthology of contemporary Cape Verdean fiction (1960). *Os trabalhos e os dias* ("The Work and the Days") was published in 1987.

Lopez \\'lō-,pez\\, Barry (Holstun) (b. Jan. 6, 1945, Port Chester, N.Y., U.S.) American writer best known for his books on natural history and the environment. In *Of Wolves and Men* (1978) and *Arctic Dreams* (1986), Lopez employed natural history as a metaphor for wider moral issues.

In 1977 Lopez' collection of Native American trickster stories, *Giving Birth to Thunder, Sleeping with His Daughter: Coyote Builds North America*, was published. The critically acclaimed *Of Wolves and Men* combines scientific information, folklore, and essays on the wolf's role in human culture. Lopez' other works include the fictional narratives *Desert Notes: Reflections in the Eye of a Raven* (1976) and *River Notes: The Dance of Herons* (1979); a volume of short fiction, *Winter Count* (1981); and a collection of essays, *Crossing Open Ground* (1988).

López de Ayala \\'lō-pȧth-thȧ-ä-'yä-lä\\, Pedro (b. 1332, Vitoria, Castile [Spain]—d. 1407, Calahorra, Navarre) Spanish poet and court chronicler who observed firsthand the happenings of his time and, unlike earlier chroniclers, recorded them objectively. His *Crónicas* (standard edition, 1779–80) is among the first great Spanish histories.

Ayala had a long and distinguished civil career under four Castilian monarchs, Peter I, Henry II, John I, and Henry III. As a poet he is chiefly remembered for his *Rimado de palacio* (c. 1400; "Poem of Palace Life"), an autobiographical satire on contemporary society and one of the last works written in *cuaderna vía* (Spanish narrative verse form consisting of four-line stanzas, each line having 14 syllables and identical rhyme). Ayala's translations from Livy, Boccaccio, and others gave him a reputation as the first Castilian humanist.

López de Mendoza *see* SANTILLANA.

López Velarde \\'lō-pās-b̧ä-'lär-thä\\, Ramón (b. June 15, 1888, Jerez, Mex.—d. June 19, 1921, Mexico City) Postmodernist Mexican poet who incorporated French Symbolist techniques into the treatment of purely Mexican themes.

López Velarde's first book of poems, *La sangre devota* (1916; "Devout Blood"), treats the simplicity of country life, the tension between sensuality and spirituality, and the poet's love for his cousin Fuensanta (Josefa de los Ríos); the language is often complex and full of daring imagery. *Zozobra* (1919; "Anguish") was colored by the death of Fuensanta in 1917. *El son del corazón* (1932; "The Sound of the Heart") collected the poems not published at the time of López Velarde's death.

López Velarde also wrote the essay collections *El minutero* (1933; "The Minute Hand"), *El don de febrero* (1952; "The Gift of February"), and *Prosa política* (1953; "Political Prose").

López y Fuentes \\'lō-pās-ē-'fwen-tās\\, Gregorio (b. Nov. 17, 1895, La Huasteca, Veracruz, Mex.—d. Dec. 10, 1966, Mexico City) Novelist who was one of the most important chroniclers of the Mexican Revolution (1919–20) and its effects.

After unsuccessful efforts at poetry and novels, López y Fuentes began to draw upon his experiences in the revolution. His first success, the novel *Campamento* (1931; "Military Camp"), was followed by *Tierra* (1932; "Land"), a novel about the Mexican revolutionary Emiliano Zapata; *¡Mi general!* (1934; "My General!"), a work on the lives of generals after the revolution; and *El indio* (1935; "The Indian"; *They That Reap*), his most celebrated work.

Lorde \\'lȯrd\\, Audre (Geraldine), *also called* Gamba Adisa \\'gäm-bə-ə-'dē-sə\\ (b. Feb. 18, 1934, New York, N.Y., U.S.—d. Nov. 17, 1992, St. Croix, Vir.Is.) African-American poet, essayist, and autobiographer known for her passionate writings on lesbian feminism and racial issues.

Lorde's first volume of poetry, *The First Cities* (1968), focused on personal relationships. *Cables to Rage* (1970) explored her anger at social and personal injustice and contained the first poetic expression of her lesbianism. Her next volumes, *From a Land Where Other People Live* (1973) and *New York Head Shop and Museum* (1974), were more rhetorical and political. Most critics consider *The Black Unicorn* (1978) to be her finest poetic work. In it she turned from the urban themes of her early work, looking instead to Africa, and wrote on her role as mother and daughter, using rich imagery and mythology.

The poet's 14-year battle with cancer is examined in *The Cancer Journals* (1980), in which she recorded her early battle with the disease and gave a feminist critique of the medical profession. *A Burst of Light* (1988), which further detailed her struggle, won a National Book Award in 1989. She also wrote the novel *Zami: A New Spelling of My Name* (1982), noted for its clear, evocative imagery. Her last poetry collection, *Undersong: Chosen Poems Old and New*, was published in 1992.

Lord Jim \\'jim\\ Novel by Joseph CONRAD, published in 1900. Originally intended as a short story, the work grew to a full-length novel as Conrad explored in great depth the perplexing, ambiguous problem of lost honor and guilt, expiation and heroism.

The title character is a man haunted by guilt over an act of cowardice. He becomes an agent at an isolated East Indian trading post. There his feelings of inadequacy and responsibility are played out to their logical and inevitable end.

Lord of the Flies Novel by William GOLDING, published in 1954. The book explores the dark side of human nature and stresses the importance of reason and intelligence as tools for dealing with the chaos of existence.

In the novel, children are evacuated from Britain because of a nuclear war. One airplane, with adults and prep-school boys as passengers, crashes on an uninhabited island, and all the adults are killed. As the boys fashion their own society, their attempts at establishing a social order gradually devolve into savagery. Finally abandoning all moral constraints, the boys commit murder before they are rescued and returned to civilization.

Lord of the Rings, The   Trilogy of fantasy novels by J.R.R. TOLKIEN comprising *The Fellowship of the Ring* (1954), *The Two Towers* (1955), and *The Return of the King* (1956). The novels, set in the Third Age of Middle Earth, formed a sequel to Tolkien's THE HOBBIT and were succeeded by his posthumous *The Silmarillion* (1977). The trilogy is the saga of a group of sometimes reluctant heroes who set forth to save their world from consummate evil. Its many worlds and creatures draw their life from Tolkien's extensive knowledge of philology and folklore.

At 33, the age of adulthood among hobbits, Frodo Baggins receives a magic Ring of Invisibility from his uncle Bilbo. A Christlike figure, Frodo learns that the ring has the power to control the entire world and, he discovers, to corrupt its owner. A fellowship of hobbits, elves, dwarfs, and men is formed to destroy the Ring by casting it into the volcanic fires of the Crack of Doom where it was forged. They are opposed on their harrowing mission by the evil Sauron and his Black Riders.

Lord Weary's Castle \'wir-ē\   Collection of poems by Robert LOWELL, published in 1946. It was awarded the Pulitzer Prize in 1947. Some of the poems reflect Lowell's New England roots; others have Roman Catholic themes, and still others recall events that occurred during World War II.

Lorelei \'lȯr-ə-,lī\   Echoing rock in the Rhine River near Sankt Goarshausen, Ger. It is associated with a legend that the Lorelei was a maiden who threw herself into the Rhine in despair over a faithless lover and was transformed into a siren who lured fishermen to destruction. The legend was claimed as his invention by German writer Clemens Brentano in the novel *Godwi* (1801–02). It has been the subject of a number of literary works and songs; the poem *Die Loreley* by Heinrich Heine was set to music by more than 25 composers.

Lorna Doone \'lȯr-nə-'dün\   Historical romance by R.D. BLACKMORE, published in 1869. Set in the wilds of Exmoor (northern Devonshire, Eng.) during the late 17th century, the novel concerns the adventurous life of the yeoman John Ridd and his love for Lorna Doone, a beautiful maiden.

Blackmore considered the novel a romance and studded it with the high adventure, dramatic set pieces, bloody villainy, and obstacles to love that characterize the genre.

Lost Generation   In general, the post-World War I generation, but specifically a group of American writers who came of age during the war and established their literary reputations in the 1920s. The term stems from a remark made by Gertrude Stein to Ernest Hemingway, "You are all a lost generation." Hemingway used the comment as an epigraph to *The Sun Also Rises* (1926). The generation was "lost" in the sense that its inherited values could no longer operate in the postwar world and because of its spiritual alienation from a country that seemed to its members to be hopelessly provincial and emotionally barren. The term embraces Hemingway, F. Scott Fitzgerald, John Dos Passos, E.E. Cummings, Archibald MacLeish, and Hart Crane, among others. The last representative works of the era were Fitzgerald's *Tender Is the Night* (1934) and Dos Passos' *The Big Money* (1936).

Lost Honor of Katharina Blum, The \,kät-ä-'rē-nä-'blùm\   Novel by Heinrich BÖLL, published in 1974 in the German weekly newsmagazine *Der Spiegel* as *Die verlorene Ehre der Katharina Blum*. The novel condemned as irresponsible the coverage of the trial of the Baader-Meinhof group, a German terrorist organization, by the tabloid newspaper *Bild-Zeitung* and rebuked official government attacks on individual civil liberties.

Katharina's ordered life falls into ruins after the *News*, a sensationalist local tabloid, falsely accuses her lover of a single night of terrorism and then names Katharina as his accomplice. Hounded by the press and the police, she shoots and kills the journalist who has tried to exploit her sexually and who has written the lies that have destroyed her life.

Lost Horizon   Novel by James HILTON, published in 1933. Hugh Conway, a veteran member of the British diplomatic service, finds inner peace, love, and a sense of purpose in Shangri-La, a utopian lamasery high in the Himalayas in Tibet.

Lost Lady, A   Novel by Willa CATHER, published in 1923, depicting the decline of the American pioneer spirit and the aridity of small-town life.

The title character, Marian Forrester, is portrayed through the adoring eyes of young Niel Herbert. He initially views Marian, the gracious wife of an industrial magnate and Western pioneer, as the personification of ladylike propriety. In truth she is somewhat less perfect than she seems, and after her husband's death, she drinks too much and looks to other men for emotional and financial support. By the time Niel leaves home to start his adult life in Boston, he feels only a "weary contempt" for her. Niel learns much later, however, that she managed to escape and that she has married a suitable, wealthy man.

Lothario \lō-'thär-ē-ō, -'thar-\   Fictional character, an unfeeling rake and libertine whose chief interest is seducing women. He appeared in *The Fair Penitent* (1703), a tragedy in blank verse by Nicholas Rowe.

Loti \lō-'tē\, Pierre, *pseudonym of* Louis-Marie-Julien Viaud \'vyō\ (b. Jan. 14, 1850, Rochefort, Fr.—d. June 10, 1923, Hendaye)   Novelist whose themes anticipated some of the central preoccupations of French literature between World War I and World War II.

Loti's career as a naval officer took him to the Middle East and East Asia, thus providing him with the exotic settings of his novels and reminiscences. After the publication of his first novel, *Aziyadé* (1879), he won the respect of critics and the devotion of a large public. Other early successes included *Pêcheur d'Islande* (1886; *An Iceland Fisherman*) and *Madame Chrysanthème* (1887; *Japan: Madam Chrysanthemum*).

His books, the novels such as *Ramuntcho* (1897) and *Les Désenchantées* (1906; *Disenchanted*), as well as the volumes in which he himself figured—*Le Roman d'un enfant* (1890; *A Child's Romance*), *Prime Jeunesse* (1919; "Early Childhood"), and *Un Jeune Officier pauvre* (1923; "A Poor Young Officer")—all reflect his passionate nature.

An exceptionally gifted observer, he was able to return from his voyages with a rich store of pictorial images, which he then embodied in simple, musical prose. His literary impressionism, however, served a deeper strain in his nature; death, as much as love, lies at the heart of his work, revealing a profound despair at the passing of sensuous life. This despair was tempered by his tenderness and compassion for the human condition, and such books as *Le Livre de la pitié et de la mort* (1890; *The Book of Pity and of Death*) and *Reflets sur la sombre route* (1889; "Reflections on a Dark Road") are perfect examples of his art.

Lotichius \lō-'tē-kē-ús\, Petrus, *pseudonym of* Petrus Lotz \'lōts\, *also called* Lotichius Secundus \zä-'kùn-dùs\ (b. Nov. 2, 1528, Niederzell, near Schlüchtern, Hesse [Germany]—d. Oct. 22, 1560, Heidelberg, Lower Palatinate)   One of Germany's outstanding neo-Latin Renaissance poets.

Lotichius' elegies, poems, and eulogies were first published in 1551; the complete works, with dedicatory epistle by the scholar-poet Joachim Camerarius, appeared in 1561. The verses, written in Latin, are indebted to Catullus and Ovid and show feeling for the countryside; his love lyrics have an autobiographical directness and exhibit 16th-century sensibilities.

Lotos-Eaters, The Poem by Alfred, Lord TENNYSON, published in the collection *Poems* (1832; dated 1833). The poem is based on an episode in Book 9 of Homer's *Odyssey*.

Odysseus' sailors, returning home after the fall of Troy, are forced to land in a strange country after a strong wind propels them past the island of Cythera. The inhabitants, "the mild-eyed melancholy Lotos-eaters," are sustained solely on the fruit of the lotus plant. The sailors eat the fruit and become lethargic and listless, losing all desire to continue their journey.

Lot's wife \\'lät\\ Biblical character, a disobedient woman who was turned into a pillar of salt for looking back to see the destruction of Sodom and Gomorrah as she and her family were fleeing. Her story is seen as an example of what happens to those who choose a worldly life over salvation. Writers who have used the image of Lot's wife in one sense or another include John Milton, Andrew Marvell, Lord Byron, Charlotte Brontë, William Blake, D.H. Lawrence, and James Joyce.

Lottery, The Short story by Shirley JACKSON, published in *The New Yorker* in June 1948 and included the following year in her collection *The Lottery; or, The Adventures of James Harris*. Much anthologized, the story is a powerful allegory of barbarism and social sacrifice.

Set in a small New England town, the story recounts the events on the day of the town's annual lottery. Mr. Summers and Mr. Graves conduct the lottery drawing, a festive event that, according to nostalgic Old Man Warner, has lost some of its traditional luster. Tessie Hutchinson is announced as the winner; she begins to protest but is silenced when the community surrounds her and stones her to death. The unemotional narrative voice underlines the horror of the final act.

Lotus-Eaters \\'lō-təs-,ē-tərz\\, *Greek* Lotophagoi, *Latin* Lotophagi. In Greek mythology, a tribe encountered by the hero Odysseus on the Libyan coast, after a north wind had driven him and his men from Cape Malea. The local inhabitants, whose distinctive practice is indicated by their name, invited Odysseus' scouts to eat of the mysterious plant. Those who did so were overcome by a blissful forgetfulness; they had to be dragged back to the ship and chained to the rowing benches.

The Greeks called several nonnarcotic plants *lōtos*, but the Homeric reference is probably to a Mediterranean jujube tree (*Ziziphus lotus*). The phrase "to eat lotus" is used metaphorically by numerous ancient writers to mean "to forget," or "to be unmindful."

Louÿs \\'lwēs\\, Pierre, *pseudonym of* Pierre Louis \\'lwē\\ (b. Dec. 10, 1870, Ghent, Belg.—d. June 4, 1925, Paris, Fr.) French novelist and poet whose merit and limitation were to express pagan sensuality with stylistic perfection.

Louÿs founded a number of short-lived literary reviews, notably *La Conque* (1891). His collection *Chansons de Bilitis* (1894), prose poems about lesbian love, purportedly from ancient Greek originals, deceived even experts. *Aphrodite* (1896), a novel depicting courtesan life in ancient Alexandria, made him famous. His best novel is *La Femme et le pantin* (1898; *Woman and Puppet*), set in Spain.

Lovecraft \\'ləv-,kraft\\, H.P., *in full* Howard Phillips (b. Aug. 20, 1890, Providence, R.I., U.S.—d. March 15, 1937, Providence) American author of fantastic and macabre short novels and stories.

Most of Lovecraft's short stories appeared in the magazine *Weird Tales* beginning in 1923. His Cthulhu Mythos series of tales describe ordinary New Englanders' encounters with horrific beings of extraterrestrial origin. His other short stories deal with similar phenomena in which horror and morbid fantasy acquire an unexpected verisimilitude. *The Case of Charles Dexter Ward* (1928), *At the Mountains of Madness* (1931), and *The Shadow Over Innsmouth* (1936) are considered his best short novels. Lovecraft was a master of poetic language, and he attained unusually high literary standards for the genre.

Loved One, The (*in full* The Loved One: An Anglo-American Tragedy) Satiric novel by Evelyn WAUGH, published in 1948. The novel concerns the experiences of a young Englishman living in southern California. It attacks the snobbery of Englishmen and the stupidity, vulgarity, and intellectual sterility of Americans.

Love in the Time of Cholera Novel by Gabriel GARCÍA MARQUEZ, published in 1985 as *El amor en los tiempos del cólera*.

The story, which concerns the themes of love, aging, and death, takes place between the late 1870s and the early 1930s in a South American community troubled by wars and outbreaks of cholera. It is a tale of two lovers, artistic Florentino Ariza and wealthy Fermina Daza, who reunite after a lifetime apart. Their spirit of enduring love contrasts ironically with the surrounding corporeal decay.

Lovelace \\'ləv-,lās\\, Earl (b. July 13, 1935, Toco, Trinidad) West Indian novelist, short-story writer, and playwright celebrated for his descriptive, dramatic fiction about West Indian culture.

Lovelace was raised by his maternal grandparents on Tobago. He attended private schools there and in Port of Spain, Trinidad. After living abroad for a short time, he returned to Trinidad in 1967 and worked as a journalist, novelist, and dramatist.

His acclaimed first novel, *While Gods Are Falling* (1965), features a protagonist who feels that only by returning to his remote village can he truly be himself. *The Schoolmaster* (1968) is a tragic novel about the building of a school in rural Trinidad. *The Dragon Can't Dance* (1979), which Lovelace adapted into a play (produced 1990), concerns the efforts of a group of people to regain their culture and sense of community in poverty-ridden Trinidad. A later novel is *The Wine of Astonishment* (1982). Lovelace also published the short-story collection *A Brief Conversion and Other Stories* (1988) as well as the plays *The New Hardware Store* and *My Name Is Village*, collected in *Jestina's Calypso & Other Plays* (1984).

Lovelace \\'ləv-,lās\\, Richard (b. 1618—d. 1657, London, Eng.) English poet, soldier, and Royalist whose graceful lyrics and dashing career made him the prototype of the perfect Cavalier.

Lovelace was educated at Charterhouse and Oxford, and at age 16 or possibly a little later he wrote *The Scholar*, a comedy acted at Whitefriars, of which only the prologue and epilogue survive. He took part in the expeditions to Scotland (1639–40) at the time of the rebellions against Charles I.

Returning to his estates in Kent, Lovelace was chosen in 1642 to present a Royalist petition to a hostile House of Commons. For this he was imprisoned briefly in the Gatehouse, London, where he wrote "To Althea, from Prison," which contains the well-known lines "Stone walls do not a prison make/Nor iron bars a cage." He passed much of the next four years abroad and was wounded fighting for the French against the Spaniards at Dunkerque (Dunkirk) in 1646. In 1648 he was again imprisoned. During his imprisonment Lovelace prepared

Lucasta (1649)—which included "To Althea" as well as "To Lucasta, Going to the Wars" and "To Aramantha, That She Would Dishevel Her Hair"—for the press. The only other publication of his work was *Lucasta; Posthume Poems of Richard Lovelace, Esq.* (1659).

Lovelace, Robert \\'ləv-lās\\   Fictional character, an aristocratic libertine in the epistolary novel CLARISSA by Samuel Richardson.

Love's Labour's Lost   Early comedy in five acts by William SHAKESPEARE, performed in 1594–95 and published in 1598 in a quarto edition.

The play concerns Ferdinand, the king of Navarre, and three of his noblemen, all dedicated to the study and the renunciation of women. These four meet the princess of France and her three attendants, and, inevitably, the men abandon their absurd principles.

Love Song of J. Alfred Prufrock, The \\jā-'al-frid-'prü-,fräk\\   Dramatic monologue by T.S. ELIOT, published in *Poetry* magazine in 1915 and in book form in *Prufrock and Other Observations* in 1917.

The poem consists of the musings of Prufrock, a weary middle-aged man haunted by the feeling that he has lost both youth and happiness: "I have measured out my life with coffee spoons."

"Prufrock" was both Eliot's first major publication and the first masterpiece of modernism in English. Eliot's experiment with poetic form, meter, rhyme, and voice was a radical departure from the restrictions of established forms and diction.

Love Suicides at Amijima, The \\ä-mē-'jē-mä\\   Classic bunraku (puppet theater) play by CHIKAMATSU Monzaemon, written and performed about 1720 as *Shinjū ten no Amijima*.

Jihei, a paper merchant, falls in love with the prostitute Koharu, but he cannot afford to buy her release from her brothel. Though the lovers' exchanges are amusing in early passages of the play, the complicated tensions of duty and desire lead to a tragic decision: since society makes their love impossible, Jihei and Koharu will seek to be joined in the afterlife.

Lovingood, Sut \\'sət-'ləv-iŋ-,gùd\\   Fictional character, the protagonist of *Sut Lovingood: Yarns Spun by a "Natural Born Durn'd Fool"* (1867), a collection of bawdy backwoods tales by American humorist George Washington HARRIS. Sut, a shiftless, self-deprecating frontiersman, narrates the tales in colorful vernacular. His tales abound with practical jokes, sexual innuendo, and political satire.

low comedy   Dramatic or literary entertainment with no underlying purpose except to provoke laughter by boasting, boisterous jokes, drunkenness, scolding, fighting, buffoonery, and other riotous activity. Used either alone or added as comic relief to more serious forms, low comedy has its origins in the comic improvisations of actors in ancient Greek and Roman comedy. Written forms of low comedy can also be found in medieval religious drama, in the works of William Shakespeare, and in farce and vaudeville.

Lowell \\'lō-əl\\   Amy (b. Feb. 9, 1874, Brookline, Mass., U.S.—d. May 12, 1925, Brookline)   American critic, lecturer, and a leading Imagist poet.

At 28 Lowell began to devote herself seriously to poetry, but she published nothing until 1910. Her first volume, *A Dome of Many-Coloured Glass* (1912), was succeeded by *Sword Blades and Poppy Seed* (1914), which included her first poems in free verse and what she called "polyphonic prose." *A Critical Fable* (1922), an imitation of her kinsman James Russell Lowell's *A Fable for Critics*, was published anonymously and stirred widespread speculation until she revealed her authorship.

Lowell's vivid and powerful personality and her independence and zest made her conspicuous, as did her scorn of convention. A bold experimenter in form and technique, she remained conservative at the core, retaining conventional verse forms and in her last years severing connections with all radical schools of poetry. Her works include *Six French Poets* (1915); *Tendencies in Modern American Poetry* (1917); *Can Grande's Castle* (1918); a two-volume biography, *John Keats* (1925); *What's O'Clock* (1925); and the posthumously published *East Wind* (1926) and *Ballads for Sale* (1927). *Complete Poetical Works* was published in 1955.

Lowell \\'lō-əl\\, James Russell (b. Feb. 22, 1819, Cambridge, Mass., U.S.—d. Aug. 12, 1891, Cambridge)   American poet, critic, essayist, editor, and diplomat whose major significance probably lies in the interest in literature he helped develop in the United States.

Lowell graduated from Harvard in 1838 and in 1840 took his degree in law, which he never practiced. In 1844 he was married to the poet Maria White, who had inspired his poems in *A Year's Life* (1841). Another early work, *Conversations on Some of the Old Poets* (1845), contained a collection of critical essays that included pleas for the abolition of slavery. From 1845 to 1850 he wrote some 50 antislavery articles for periodicals and began serial publication of his BIGLOW PAPERS on the same subject. The year 1848 saw the publication of Lowell's two other most important pieces of writing: THE VISION OF SIR LAUNFAL, an enormously popular long poem extolling the brotherhood of man; and A FABLE FOR CRITICS, a witty verse evaluation of contemporary American authors.

The death of three of Lowell's four children was followed by the death of his wife in 1853. Henceforth his literary production comprised mainly prose essays on topics in literature, history, and politics. In 1855 his lectures on English poets before the Lowell Institute led to his appointment as Smith professor of modern languages at Harvard University, succeeding Henry Wadsworth Longfellow. In 1857 he married Frances Dunlap and began four years as editor of the new *Atlantic Monthly*.

With Charles Eliot Norton, Lowell was editor of *The North American Review* from 1864 to 1872, and during this time he wrote a series of critical essays on major literary figures that were collected with other essays in the two series of *Among My Books* (1870, 1876). He was appointed minister to Spain (1877–80) and ambassador to Great Britain (1880–85). After his second wife died in 1885, Lowell retired from public life.

Lowell \\'lō-əl\\, Robert, *in full* Robert Traill Spence, Jr. (b. March 1, 1917, Boston, Mass., U.S.—d. Sept. 12, 1977, New York, N.Y.)   American poet noted for his complex, confessional poetry.

Lowell graduated from Kenyon College in Gambier, Ohio, in 1940 and that year married the novelist Jean Stafford. Lowell's first major work, LORD WEARY'S CASTLE (1946), won the Pulitzer Prize in 1947. It contains two of his most praised poems: THE QUAKER GRAVEYARD IN NANTUCKET and "Colloquy in Black Rock," celebrating the feast of Corpus Christi.

After being divorced in 1948, Lowell married the writer and critic Elizabeth Hardwick the next year (divorced 1972). He spent a few years abroad and then settled in Boston in 1954. His LIFE STUDIES (1959), which won the National Book Award for poetry, contains an autobiographical essay, "91 Revere Street," as well as a series of 15 confessional poems. Chief among the poems are "Waking in Blue," which tells of his confinement in a mental hospital, and SKUNK HOUR, which dramatically conveys his mental turmoil.

Lowell's activities in the civil-rights and antiwar campaigns of the 1960s lent a more public note to his next three books of poetry: FOR THE UNION DEAD (1964), *Near the Ocean* (1967), and *Notebook 1967–68* (1969). Lowell's trilogy of plays, *The Old Glory*, which views American culture over the span of history, was published in 1965 (rev. ed., 1968). His later poetry volumes include THE DOLPHIN (1973), which won a second Pulitzer Prize, and *Day by Day* (1977). His translations include *Phaedra* (1963) and *Prometheus Bound* (1969); *Imitations* (1961), free renderings of various European poets; and *The Voyage and Other Versions of Poems by Baudelaire* (1968).

Lower Depths, The Drama in four acts by Maksim GORKY, performed in 1902 and published in the same year as *Na dne*. The play's title was also translated into English as *A Night's Lodging* or *At the Bottom*.

Set in the late 19th century in a dilapidated flophouse, the play examines society's outcasts. The denizens of the rooming house are unexpectedly uplifted by a new boarder, Luka, a tramp who listens to their stories, advises them, and spins illusions, thus offering them hope. In the end he wanders off, never to be seen again. Bleak reality sets in: a resident thief kills the landlord and is taken to jail; an alcoholic actor hangs himself.

Lowndes \\'laundz\\, Marie Adelaide, *original name* Belloc \\'bel-,ăk\\, *pseudonym* Mrs. Belloc Lowndes (b. 1868, France—d. Nov. 14, 1947, Eversley Cross, Hampshire, Eng.) English novelist and playwright best known for murder mysteries that were often based on actual cases.

Lowndes published her first story at age 16 and her first novel 20 years later. After a series of historical and fictional character studies—*e.g.*, *The Heart of Penelope* (1904) and *Barbara Rebell* (1905)—she wrote *The Chink in the Armour* (1912), a psychological study of a murder-plot victim. *The Lodger*, published the following year, was a fictional treatment of the Jack the Ripper murders. Her numerous works include an autobiography, *I, Too, Have Lived in Arcadia* (1941).

Lowry \\'lau-rē\\, Malcolm, *in full* Clarence Malcolm Lowry (b. July 28, 1909, Birkenhead, Cheshire, Eng.—d. June 27, 1957, Ripe, Sussex) English novelist, short-story writer, and poet whose masterwork is UNDER THE VOLCANO (1947; reissued 1962).

Lowry rebelled against his conventional bourgeois upbringing and shipped to China as a cabin boy, later continuing his education at the University of Cambridge. While there he wrote *Ultramarine* (1933; reissued 1963), a novel based on his sea voyage.

Lowry went to the United States in 1935, gravitated toward the movie colony in Hollywood, and then moved to Cuernavaca, Mex., the setting of *Under the Volcano*. The technique of the book's narrative, with flashbacks and juxtaposition of contrasting thoughts and images, owes much to the cinema. Lowry later lived in Canada and Italy and, finally, in England.

Lowry's other works include a collection of short stories, *Hear Us O Lord from Heaven Thy Dwelling Place*, which appeared in 1961, and *Selected Poems* the next year. His *Selected Letters* was published in 1965.

Loyal Forty-seven Rōnin, The \\'rō-,nēn\\ (Japanese play cycle) *see* CHŪSHINGURA.

Lucan \\'lü-kən\\, *in full* Marcus Annaeus Lucanus \\lü-'kā-nəs\\ (b. AD 39, Corduba [now Córdoba, Spain]—d. 65, Rome [Italy]) Poet and Roman republican patriot whose historical epic, the *Bellum civile*, better known as the *Pharsalia* because of its vivid account of the Battle of Pharsalus, is remarkable as the single major Latin epic poem that eschewed the intervention of the gods.

Lucan attracted the favorable attention of the emperor Nero because of his early promise of genius as a rhetorician and or-

ator. Shortly, however, Nero became jealous of his ability as a poet and halted further public readings of his poetry. Already disenchanted by Nero's tyranny and embittered by the ban on his recitations, Lucan became one of the leaders in a conspiracy to assassinate Nero. When the conspiracy was discovered, he was compelled to commit suicide.

The *Bellum civile*, his only extant poem, is an account of the war between Julius Caesar and Pompey the Great, carried down to the arrival of Caesar in Egypt after the murder of Pompey, when it stops abruptly in the middle of the 10th book. The work is naturally imitative of Virgil, and although the style and vocabulary are usually commonplace and the meter monotonous, the rhetoric is often lifted into real poetry by its energy and flashes of fire.

Lucan's poetry was popular during the Middle Ages. His work also strongly influenced Pierre Corneille and other French classical dramatists of the 17th century.

Luce \\'lüs\\, Clare Boothe, *original name* Ann Clare Boothe \\'büth, 'bu̲th\\ (b. March 10, 1903, New York, N.Y., U.S.—d. Oct. 9, 1987, Washington, D.C.) American playwright, politician, and celebrity, noted for her satiric wit and for her role in American politics.

Boothe held editorial positions at *Vogue* magazine and at *Vanity Fair* during the early 1930s. Some of her satiric articles for *Vanity Fair* were collected in *Stuffed Shirts* (1931). In 1935 she married magazine publisher Henry R. Luce.

After an earlier play failed, Luce wrote *The Women* (1936), a comedy that ran for 657 performances on Broadway; *Kiss the Boys Goodbye* (1938), a satire on American life; and *Margin for Error* (1939), an anti-Nazi play. All three were adapted into motion pictures.

Luce was elected to the U.S. House of Representatives (1943–47) as a Republican from Connecticut. She was influential in the Republican Party nationally and served as ambassador to Italy from 1953 to 1956.

Lu Chi *see* LU JI.

Lucian \\'lü-shən\\, *Greek* Lucianos, *Latin* Lucianus *or* Lucinus (b. *c.* AD 120, Samosata, Commagene, Syria [now Samsat, Tur.]—d. after 180, Athens) Ancient Greek rhetorician, pamphleteer, and satirist.

Little is known of the life of Lucian; the dating of the events of his life are matters of mere probability. As a young man he acquired a Greek literary education on his travels through western Asia Minor. Although he was raised speaking Aramaic, so successfully did he master the Greek language and culture that he began a career as a public speaker.

Lucian settled in Athens in the late '50s of the 2nd century. During this period he gave up public speaking and began writing critical and satirical essays on the intellectual life of his time, either in the form of Platonic dialogues or, in imitation of Menippus, in a mixture of prose and verse. Thanks to the patronage of his Roman friends, he obtained a lucrative post in Alexandria as *archistator*, a kind of chief court usher. After some years he returned to Athens and took up public speaking again. The date and circumstances of his death are unknown.

Of the 80 prose works traditionally attributed to Lucian, about 10 are spurious. His writings are outstanding for their mordant and malicious wit, embodying a sophisticated and often embittered critique of the shams and follies of the literature, philosophy, and intellectual life of his day. Lucian satirized almost every aspect of human behavior in such works as *Charon, Dialogues of the Dead, Timon, True History*, and *Nigrinus*. He is particularly critical of those whom he considers impostors, especially of philosophers who failed to practice what they preached.

Lucian's best work in the field of literary criticism is his treatise *How to Write History*, which stresses the impartiality, detachment, and rigorous devotion to truth that characterize the ideal historian. Notable too are his *Teacher of Orators* and *Word-Flaunter*.

Lucidor Pseudonym of Lars JOHANSSON.

Lucien Leuwen \lūēs-'yaⁿ-'lœ-ven\ Unfinished novel by STENDHAL, published posthumously in 1894. It is perhaps the most autobiographical of Stendhal's fiction. The book follows the career of Lucien, from his expulsion from the École Polytechnique because of his idealism, through his military career (during which he falls in love with a young widow, Mme de Chasteller, but is forced to renounce her), to his career in government service in Paris. In the last section, which was never written, Stendhal had planned to show Lucien in Italy and to resolve the story with a happy ending based on the return of Mme de Chasteller.

Lucifer \'lū-si-fər\, *also called* Satan \'sāt-ən\ Fictional character in PARADISE LOST and *Paradise Regained* (1671), epic poems by John Milton.

The archangel Lucifer, who has led an unsuccessful revolt in Heaven, becomes known as Satan when he is banished to Hell by God. Out of revenge, Satan uses trickery and temptation to corrupt the first humans, Adam and Eve, who are subsequently cast out of the Garden of Eden. Although Satan is wicked and duplicitous (he disguises himself as a serpent), he possesses the heroic qualities of strong leadership and rebellious individualism.

Lucilius \lū-'sil-ē-əs\, Gaius (b. *c.* 180 BC, Suessa Aurunca, Campania [Italy]—d. *c.* 103 or 102 BC, Neapolis) Effectively, the inventor of poetical satire who gave to the existing, formless Latin medley of drama, prose, and poetry known as *satura* the distinctive character of critical comment that the word satire still implies.

Lucilius was a Roman citizen of good family and education, a friend of learned Greeks, and well acquainted with Greek manners, which afforded him targets for his wit. He began to write only after middle life. His works were collected in a posthumous edition of 30 books. Only about 1,300 lines survive, mostly written in the hexameters that were to influence the development of the later Roman satirists Horace, Persius, and Juvenal.

Luck of Ginger Coffey, The \'jin-jər-'kȯf-ē\ Novel by Brian MOORE, published in 1960. The story concerns an Irishborn Canadian immigrant whose self-deluded, irresponsible behavior nearly breaks up his family.

Luck of Roaring Camp, The Short story by Bret HARTE, published in 1868 in the *Overland Monthly*, which Harte edited.

"The Luck" is a baby boy born to Cherokee Sal, a fallen woman who dies in childbirth at Roaring Camp, a California gold rush settlement. The men of the camp decide to raise the child themselves, and his presence inspires them to stop fighting and gambling and to clean themselves and the camp. When they discover gold, they believe that the child has brought them the fortune. Tragedy strikes, however, when a flood sweeps the camp, killing both the Luck and his protector.

Lucky Jim \'jim\ Best-selling novel by Kingsley AMIS, published in 1954. The novel features the antihero Jim Dixon, a junior faculty member at a provincial university who despises the pretensions of academic life. Dixon epitomizes a newly important social group risen from lower-middle-class and working-class backgrounds only to find the more comfortable perches still occupied by the well born.

Lucretius \lū-'krē-shəs, -shē-əs\, *in full* Titus Lucretius Carus (fl. 1st century BC) Latin poet and philosopher known for his poem *De rerum natura* (ON THE NATURE OF THINGS).

Apart from Lucretius' poem, almost nothing is known about him. The Church Father Jerome stated in his chronicle for the year 94 BC (or possibly 96 or 93) that Lucretius was born in that year and that years later a love potion drove him insane. In lucid intervals he wrote several books, which Cicero afterward emended, and he killed himself in his 44th year (51 or 50).

Lucretius spoke in austere compassion for the ignorant, unhappy human race. He hated the seers who inculcated religious fears by threats of eternal punishment after death and the false philosophers, in which category he included Stoics, Platonists, and Pythagoreans. His moral fervor expressed itself in gratitude to Epicurus, who rejected religion and provided a scientific basis for understanding the world. The influence of Lucretius on Virgil was pervasive, especially in Virgil's *Georgics*.

Ludwig \'lüt-vik̠\, Emil (b. Jan. 25, 1881, Breslau, Ger. [now Wrocław, Pol.]—d. Sept. 17, 1948, near Ascona, Switz.) German writer known for his many popular biographies.

Ludwig was trained in law but at age 25 began writing plays and poems. After serving as foreign correspondent during World War I, he wrote a novel (*Diana*, originally published as two works, 1918–19) and, in 1920, a biography of J.W. von Goethe, which established him as a writer in the "new school" of biography that emphasized the personality of the subject. His biographies appearing in English translation include *Napoleon* (1927); *Bismarck* (1927); *The Son of Man* (1928), a highly controversial biography of Christ; *Lincoln* (1929); *Hindenburg* (1935); *Cleopatra: The Story of a Queen* (1937); *Roosevelt: A Study in Fortune and Power* (1938); *Three Portraits: Hitler, Mussolini, Stalin* (1940); and *Beethoven* (1943).

Ludwig \'ləd-wig\, Jack (Barry) (b. Aug. 30, 1922, Winnipeg, Manitoba, Can.) Canadian author whose fiction, set in Canada and the United States, urged an enthusiastic approach to life and often reflected his Jewish background.

Ludwig was educated at the University of Manitoba and the University of California at Los Angeles; he later taught in several American colleges and universities.

The issues of Ludwig's partly satirical first novel, *Confusions* (1963), are moral, social, sexual, and racial, as a schizophrenic young Jewish man seeks his identity. The hero of *Above Ground* (1968), after spending most of his youth in hospital rooms, finds rejuvenation in sexual encounters with a series of willing women. At the center of *A Woman of Her Age* (1973) is an 85-year-old former radical whose compassion lends strength to those around her. In addition to novels, Ludwig wrote short stories, essays, adaptations of several classic plays, and several volumes on sports.

Ludwig \'lüt-vik̠\, Otto (b. Feb. 11, 1813, Eisfeld, Thuringia [Germany]—d. Feb. 25, 1865, Dresden, Saxony) German novelist, playwright, and critic who is remembered principally for his realistic stories, which contributed to the development of the *Novelle*.

Ludwig early became interested in poetry and music and in 1838 produced an opera, *Die Köhlerin*. After ill health and shyness caused him to forsake a music career, he moved to Dresden and turned to literary studies, writing stories and dramas.

Ludwig's psychological drama *Die Erbförster* (1850) was only partially successful. His more enduring work includes a series of stories on Thuringian life, characterized, as were the dramas, by attention to detail and careful psychological analysis. The most notable are *Die Heiteretei und ihr Widerspiel* (1851; *The Cheerful Ones and Their Opposites*) and *Zwischen Himmel und Erde* (1855; *Between Heaven and Earth*).

Lugalbanda \ˌlü-gäl-ˈbän-dä\ One of the major figures in the surviving Sumerian epics and the hero of the tale called the *Lugalbanda Epic*, or *Lugalbanda and Enmerkar*. *See* ENMERKAR.

Lugones \lü-ˈgō̄-nās, -näh\, Leopoldo (b. June 13, 1874, Villa María del Río Seco, Arg.—d. Feb. 19, 1938, Buenos Aires) Argentine poet, literary and social critic, and cultural ambassador, considered by many the outstanding figure of his age in the cultural life of Argentina.

Lugones began as a socialist journalist, settling in Buenos Aires, where in 1897 he helped found *La montaña* ("The Mountain") and became an active member of the group of modernist experimental poets led by the Nicaraguan poet Rubén Darío. Lugones' first important collection of poems, *Las montañas del oro* (1897; "Mountains of Gold"), reveals his affinity with Modernismo in its use of free verse and exotic imagery, devices he continued in *Los crepúsculos del jardín* (1905; "Twilights in the Garden") and *Lunario sentimental* (1909; "Sentimental Lunar Almanac").

Between 1911 and 1914 Lugones lived in Paris, editing the *Revue sudaméricaine*, but he returned to Argentina at the outbreak of World War I. A change in his political outlook from socialism to an intense conservative nationalism was paralleled in his art by a rejection of modernism in favor of a treatment of national themes in a realistic style. This change, already foreshadowed in the prose sketches of *La guerra gaucha* (1905; "The Gaucho War"), was revealed in the poems of *El libro de los paisajes* (1917; "The Book of Landscapes"), which extolled the beauty of the Argentine countryside. Lugones continued to develop native themes in such prose works as *Cuentos fatales* (1924; "Tales of Fate"), a collection of short stories, and the novel *El ángel de la sombra* (1926; "The Angel of the Shadow").

Lugones was director of the National Council of Education (1914–38). He was also noted for several volumes of Argentine history, for studies of classical Greek literature and culture, and for his Spanish translations of Homer's *Iliad* and *Odyssey*.

Luhan \ˈlü-ˌhän\, Mabel Dodge, *original surname* Ganson \ˈgan-sən\ (b. Feb. 26, 1879, Buffalo, N.Y., U.S.—d. Aug. 13, 1962, Taos, N.M.) American writer whose candid autobiographical volumes, collectively known as *Intimate Memories*, contain much information about well-known Americans of her era.

Luhan's life and writing revolved around the literary, artistic, and political celebrities she gathered about her both in New York City and abroad. She later settled in an artists' colony in Taos, where her home again became a gathering place for celebrated artists and writers. She devoted herself to recording her relationships with such figures as Gertrude Stein, John Reed, and Walter Lippmann, with little regard for propriety or privacy.

The volumes of Luhan's *Intimate Memories* are *Background* (1933), *European Experiences* (1935), *Movers and Shakers* (1936), and *Edge of Taos Desert* (1937).

Lu Hsün *see* LU XUN.

Luiken *see* LUYKEN.

Lu Ji or **Lu Chi** \ˈlü-ˈjē\ (b. 261, southern China—d. 303, China) Renowned Chinese literary critic and the first important writer to emerge from the kingdom of Wu (222–280).

Grandson of the great Lu Xun, one of the founders of the Wu kingdom, Lu Ji remained in obscurity for 10 years after the Wu kingdom was subjugated by the Jin dynasty (265–317). In 290 he traveled to Luoyang, the imperial capital, where he was warmly received by the literary elite and appointed president of the national university. He eventually rose to higher posts and

became a member of the nobility, but he was executed on a false charge of treason.

Although Lu Ji left a considerable body of lyric poetry in imitative style, he is better known as a writer of *fu*, an intricately structured form of poetry mixed with prose. A prime specimen of this form is his *Wen fu* ("On Literature"), a subtle and important work of literary criticism that defines and demonstrates the principles of composition with rare insight and precision.

Lukács \ˈlü-ˌkäch\, György (b. April 13, 1885, Budapest, Austria-Hungary [now Hungary]—d. June 4, 1971, Budapest) Hungarian Marxist philosopher, writer, and literary critic who was a significant influence in European intellectual life during the first half of the 20th century.

Born into a wealthy Jewish family, Lukács joined the Hungarian Communist Party in 1918. In his book *Geschichte und Klassenbewusstsein* (1923; *History and Class Consciousness*), he developed his own Marxist philosophy of history and laid the basis for his critical literary tenets by linking the development of form in art with the history of the class struggle.

Lukács spent most of the years 1929 to 1933 in Berlin, after which he moved to Moscow to attend the Institute of Philosophy. He returned to Hungary in 1945 and became a member of parliament and a professor at the University of Budapest. In 1956 he was a major figure in the Hungarian uprising, serving as minister of culture during the revolt. He was arrested and deported to Romania but was allowed to return to Budapest in 1957, thereafter producing a steady output of critical and philosophical works. His works include *Die Seele und die Formen* (1911; *Soul and Form*), a collection of essays that established his reputation as a critic; *Der historische Roman* (1955; *The Historical Novel*); and books on J.W. von Goethe and aesthetics.

Lulu \ˈlü-ˌlü\ Fictional character, the protagonist of Frank Wedekind's plays *Der Erdgeist* (EARTH SPIRIT) and *Die Büchse der Pandora* (PANDORA'S BOX).

Lulu is a beautiful and desirable but amoral woman bent on sexual conquest, who leaves death and destruction in her wake.

Luna *see* SELENE.

Lundkvist \ˈlůnd-kvist\, Artur (Nils) (b. March 3, 1906, Oderljunga, Swed.—d. Dec. 11, 1991, Stockholm) Poet, novelist, essayist, and influential member of the Swedish Academy.

Lundkvist moved to Stockholm at age 20 and there participated in the group Fem Unga ("Five Young Men") in the late 1920s and early 1930s. His early poetry—in such collections as *Glöd* (1928; "Glowing Embers"), *Svart stad* (1930; "Black City"), and *Floderna flyter mot havet* (1934; "The Rivers Run Toward the Sea")—reflected a type of sexual mysticism such as that espoused by D.H. Lawrence. In the shadow of World War II, however, Lundkvist's writings became marked by pessimism and by a longing for a new kind of human solidarity. Among his more than 70 books are *Det talande trädet* (1960; "The Talking Tree") and *Flykten och överlevandet* (1977; "Escape and Survival"), each of which combines poetry and prose, and the travel books *Vallmor från Tasckent* (1952; "Poppies from Taskent") and *Så lever Kuba* (1965; "This is the Way Cuba Lives").

Lundkvist is notable for having introduced to Swedish readers the works of T.S. Eliot, D.H. Lawrence, and William Faulkner, as well as those of many Spanish and Latin-American writers he himself translated.

Lun yu or **Lun yü** \ˈlůn-ˈyüē\ ("Conversations") One of four Confucian texts that, when published together in 1190 by the Neo-Confucian philosopher Zhu Xi, became the great Chinese classic known as SI SHU. The work has been translated into English as *Analects*.

Lun yu is considered by scholars to be the most reliable source for the doctrine of the sage Confucius (551–479 BC) and is usually the first Confucian text studied in schools. It covers almost all the basic ethical concepts of Confucius—*e.g.*, *ren* ("benevolence"), *junzi* ("the superior man"), *tian* ("Heaven"), *zhong yong* (doctrine of "the mean"), *li* ("proper conduct"), and *zheng ming* ("adjustment to names"). The last inculcates the notion that all phases of a person's conduct should correspond to the true significance of "names"—*e.g.*, marriage should be true marriage, not concubinage.

Lupin, Arsène \är-'sen-lūē-'paⁿ\ Fictional character in stories and novels by Maurice LEBLANC. The debonair Lupin is a former thief, a criminal genius who has turned detective. He is often suspected by the police, who are never convinced that he has reformed, when a daring robbery occurs.

Lurie \'lûr-ē\, Alison (b. Sept. 3, 1926, Chicago, Ill., U.S.) Writer whose urbane and witty novels usually feature upper-middle-class academics in a university setting.

Lurie graduated from Radcliffe College in 1947 and later taught English and then children's literature at Cornell University. One of her best-known books, *The War Between the Tates* (1974; film, 1977), concerns the manner in which the wife of a professor at mythical Corinth University deals with her husband's infidelity. *Foreign Affairs* (1984), winner of the 1985 Pulitzer Prize for fiction, describes the separate, unexpected sexual and romantic affairs of two academics from Corinth University during a sabbatical semester in England. Lurie's other works, almost all set in academia, included *Love and Friendship* (1962), *The Nowhere City* (1965), *Imaginary Friends* (1967), *Real People* (1969), *Only Children* (1979), and *The Truth About Lorin Jones* (1988).

She also wrote books for children, such as *The Heavenly Zoo* (1979), *Clever Gretchen and Other Forgotten Folktales* (1980), and *Fabulous Beasts* (1981), as well as works about children's literature.

lüshi or **lü-shih** \'lūē-'shə\ [Chinese *lùshī*, from *lù* rule, constraint + *shī* poetry, verse] A form of Chinese poetry introduced in the Tang dynasty (618–907). It consists of eight lines of five or seven syllables—each line set down in accordance with strict tonal patterns. Exposition (*qi*) was called for in the first two lines; the development of the theme (*cheng*), in parallel verse structure, in the middle, or second and third, couplets; and the conclusion (*he*) in the final couplet. *Lüshi* provided a new, formal alternative to the long-popular free *gushi* ("ancient style"). The poet Du Fu was particularly associated with *lüshi*, and Bo Juyi also frequently used the form.

The symmetry and lyricism of *lüshi* inspired *jueju*, a condensed form of *lüshi* consisting of quatrains and depending for its artistry on suggestiveness and economy. Another variation, *pailü*, followed most of the rules of *lüshi*, but also allowed the poet to alter the rhyme and elongate the poem.

Lusiads, The \'lū-sē-ədz, -,adz\ Epic poem by Luís de CAMÕES, published in 1572 as *Os Lusíadas*. The work describes the discovery of the sea route to India by Vasco da Gama. The 10 cantos of the poem are in ottava rima and amount to 1,102 stanzas in all.

The action of the poem begins after an introduction, an invocation, and a dedication to King Sebastian. Vasco da Gama's ships are already under way in the Indian Ocean, sailing up the coast of East Africa, and the gods of Greco-Roman mythology gather to discuss the fate of the expedition (which is favored by Venus and attacked by Bacchus). The voyagers spend several days in Melinde on the east coast of Africa, and at the king's request Vasco da Gama recounts the entire history of Portugal from its origins to the inception of their great voyage (Cantos

III, IV, and V). When they reembark, Bacchus tries to arrange the shipwreck of the Portuguese fleet but is prevented by Venus, and Vasco da Gama is able to reach Calicut (Kozhikode, now in Kerala state, southwestern India), the end of his voyage. On their homeward voyage the mariners chance upon the island Venus has created for them, and the nymphs reward them for their labors. One of the nymphs sings of the future deeds of the Portuguese, and the entertainment ends with a description of the universe given by Thetis and Vasco da Gama, after which the sailors embark once more and the nymphs accompany them on their homeward journey.

Luther \'lū-thər\ Drama in three acts by John OSBORNE, performed and published in 1961. The play is a psychological study of the religious reformer Martin Luther, who is portrayed as an angry man struggling with self-doubts and his desire to believe. The drama highlights his work as a scholar, his defiance of church authority at the Diet of Worms, his involvement in the peasants' revolt, and his eventual marriage to an ex-nun.

Luttrell \'lət-rəl\, Henry (b. *c.* 1765—d. Dec. 19, 1851, London, Eng.) A famous London society wit and poet of light verse.

After a brief try at managing his father's estates in the West Indies (about 1802), Luttrell returned to London, where he was introduced into society by the Duchess of Devonshire. He became popular as a fashionable wit and conversationalist. In 1820 he published his *Advice to Julia*, of which a third edition, altered and amplified, appeared in 1822 as *Letters to Julia, in Rhyme*. This poem, suggested by the ode to Lydia in the first book of Horace's *Odes*, was his most important work.

Lu Xun or **Lu Hsün** \'lū-'shūēn\, *pseudonym of* Zhou Shuren \jō-'shū-'rən\ (b. Sept. 25, 1881, Shaoxing, Zhejiang province, China—d. Oct. 19, 1936, Shanghai) Writer commonly considered to be one of the greatest figures in 20th-century Chinese literature.

Although he originally studied to be a doctor, Lu Xun became associated with the nascent Chinese literary movement in 1918, when he published his famous short story "Kuangren riji" ("Diary of a Madman"). With its title taken from Nikolay Gogol, the tale is a condemnation of traditional Confucian culture, which the madman narrator sees as a "man-eating" society. The first Western-style story written wholly in Chinese, it was a tour de force that attracted immediate attention and helped gain acceptance for the short-story form as an effective literary vehicle. "A Q zhengzhuan" (1921; "The True Story of A Q"), which was collected with "Kuangren riji" and other stories in *Nahan* (1923; *Call to Arms*), contains a mixture of humor and pathos in its repudiation of the old order. The term *A Qism* was coined to signify the Chinese penchant for naming defeat a "spiritual victory." Three years after the publication of *Nahan*, Lu Xun published *Panghuang* (1926; *Wandering*) and, in 1936, *Gushi xinbian* ("Old Tales Retold"). He also wrote prose-poems and reminiscences.

Although best known for his works of fiction, Lu Xun was also a master of the prose essay, a vehicle he made use of more and more toward the end of his life. His *Zhongguo xiaoshuo shilüe* ("Outline History of Chinese Fiction") and companion compilations of classical fiction remain standard works. Translations, largely from the Russian, also occupy a large place in his complete works.

Forced by political circumstances to flee Beijing in 1926, he eventually found sanctuary in the Shanghai International Settlement. Although he himself refused to join the Communist Party, he recruited many of his fellow writers and countrymen to the communist cause. Considered a revolutionary hero by present-day Chinese communists, Lu Xun was adopted posthumously as the exemplar of Socialist Realism by the Chinese communist movement.

Luyken or **Luiken** \\'lœœ-kən\\, Jan or Johannes (b. April 16, 1649, Amsterdam [Neth.]—d. April 5, 1712, Amsterdam) Dutch lithographer and poet whose work ranged from hedonistic love songs to introspective religious poetry.

As a young man, Luyken published *De Duytse lier* (1671; "The Dutch Lyre"), a volume of erotic poetry. He was married in 1672 and baptized in the Baptist church the following year. Influenced by the writings of the German mystic Jakob Böhme, Luyken embraced Pietistic Christianity. He worked as a book illustrator but became increasingly ascetic and began to withdraw from society. His later poetry, including *Jezus en de ziel* (1678; "Jesus and the Soul"), was inspired by his mystical vision of life.

Lu You \\'lü-'yō\\ or **Lu Yu** \\'lü-'yü\\, *pseudonym* Fangweng \\'fäŋ-'wəŋ\\ (b. 1125, Shanyin, China—d. 1210, China) One of the most important and prolific Chinese writers of the Southern Song dynasty, who left behind a collection of nearly 10,000 poems as well as numerous prose pieces. Primarily a poet, Lu You gained renown for his simple, direct expression and his attention to detail, features that set him apart from the elevated and allusive style of the prevailing Jiangxi school of poetry. As a conservative in matters of form, however, he wrote many poems in the *gushi*, or "old poetry," mode and excelled at the *lüshi*, or "regulated poetry," form, whose sharply defined tonal and grammatical patterns had been perfected by the great masters of the Tang dynasty.

Traditionally, Lu You has been most admired for the ardor of his patriotic poems, in which he protested the Ruzhen invasion of China that had begun in 1125 and chided the Song court for its failure to drive out the invaders. Because of his hawkish views, expressed at a time when the displaced court was controlled by a peace faction, Lu You did not advance in his career. Four times demoted for his outspoken opinions, Lu You finally resigned his civil service commission and retired to his country estate. During retirement he devoted his poetry entirely to the celebration of rural life.

Luzi \\'lüt-sē\\, Mario (b. Oct. 20, 1914, Castello, near Florence, Italy) Italian poet and literary critic who emerged from the Hermetic movement to become one of the most notable poets of the 20th century.

Luzi published his first book of verse, *La barca* (1935; "The Ship"), before graduating from the University of Florence. Like *La barca*, the collections *Avvento notturno* (1940; "Nocturnal Advent") and *Un brindisi* (1946; "A Toast") have elements of Hermeticism. He abandoned symbolism for direct language and existential themes in *Quaderno gotico* (1947; "Gothic Notebook"), *Primizie del deserto* (1952; "First Fruits of the Desert"), and *Onore del vero* (1957; "Honor of Truth").

Luzi's later verse, with its dramatic dialogues and ruminations on change, was typified by the collection *Nel Magma* (1963; enlarged 1966; "In the Magma"). His other volumes of poetry include *Dal fondo delle campagne* (1965; "From the Bottom of the Field"), *Al fuoco della controversia* (1978; "At the Fire of Controversy"), *Per il battesimo dei nostri frammenti* (1985; *For the Baptism of Our Fragments*), and *Frasi e incisi di un canto salutare* (1990; "Phrases and Digressions of a Salutary Song"). Luzi also wrote *L'inferno e il limbo* (1949; enlarged 1964; "Hell and Limbo"), a book of essays, and the verse drama *Ipazia* (1972).

Luzzatto \\lüt-'tsät-tō\\, Moshe Ḥayyim (b. 1707, Padua, Venetian republic [Italy]—d. May 6, 1747, Acre, Palestine [now 'Akko, Israel]) Jewish cabalist (esoteric Jewish mystic) and writer, one of the founders of modern Hebrew poetry.

Luzzatto wrote lyrics and in about 1727 the drama *Migdal 'oz* ("Tower of Victory"), but he early turned to cabalist studies, eventually becoming convinced that he was the Messiah. After being expelled by the Italian rabbis, he moved to Amsterdam (1736), where he wrote his morality play *La-yesharim tehilah* (*Praise for Uprightness*) and an ethical work, *Mesilat yesharim* (1740; *The Path of the Upright*).

Luzzatto \\lüt-'tsät-tō\\, Samuel David, *also known by the acronym* Shedal \\shä-'däl\\ (b. Aug. 22, 1800, Trieste [Italy]—d. Sept. 30, 1865, Padua) Jewish writer and scholar.

In his writings, which are in Hebrew and Italian, Luzzatto presents an emotional and antiphilosophical concept of Judaism, and his Hebrew poetry is pervaded by national spirit. His chief merit as a scholar lies in biblical exegesis, Hebrew philology, and the history of Hebrew literature.

Lycidas \\'lis-i-dəs\\ Poem by John MILTON, written in 1637 for inclusion in a volume of elegies published in 1638 to commemorate the death of Edward King, who had drowned in a shipwreck in August 1637. "Lycidas" mourns the loss of a virtuous and promising young man about to embark upon a career as a clergyman. Adopting the conventions of the classical pastoral elegy (Lycidas was a shepherd in Virgil's *Eclogues*), Milton muses on fame, the meaning of existence, and heavenly judgment.

Lydgate \\'lid-ˌgāt, -git\\, John (b. *c.* 1370, Lydgate, Suffolk, Eng.—d. *c.* 1450, Bury St. Edmunds?) English poet, known principally for long moralistic and devotional works.

Lydgate had few peers in his sheer productiveness; 145,000 lines of his verse survive. His poems vary from vast narratives such as *Troy Book* and *The Falle of Princis* to occasional poems of a few lines. Of the longer poems, one translated from the French, the allegory *Reason and Sensuality* (*c.* 1408), on the theme of chastity, contains fresh and charming descriptions of nature in well-handled couplets.

Lydgate admired the work of Geoffrey Chaucer and imitated his versification; between 1431 and 1438 he was occupied with *The Falle of Princis*, translated into Chaucerian rhyme royal from a French version of Giovanni Boccaccio's work. He also wrote love allegories, lives of the saints, versions of Aesop's fables, and both religious and secular lyrics.

Lydgate, Tertius \\'tər-shē-əs-'lid-ˌgāt\\ Fictional character, an ambitious, progressive physician in the novel MIDDLEMARCH by George Eliot.

Lyly \\'lil-ē\\, John (b. 1554?, Kent, Eng.—d. November 1606, London) Author considered to be the first English prose stylist to leave an enduring impression upon the language. As a playwright he also contributed to the development of prose dialogue in English comedy.

Lyly was educated at Magdalen College, Oxford, and went to London about 1576. There he gained fame with the publication of two prose romances, EUPHUES (1578) and *Euphues and His England* (1580), which made him the most fashionable English writer in the 1580s.

After 1580 Lyly devoted himself almost entirely to writing comedies. In 1583 he gained control of the first Blackfriars Theatre, in which his earliest plays, *Campaspe* and *Sapho and Phao* (performed 1583–84), were produced. Lyly's finest play is considered to be *Endimion* (performed 1588).

Lyly's comedies mark an enormous advance upon those of his predecessors in English drama. Although their plots are drawn from classical mythology and legend and their characters engage in speeches redolent of Renaissance pedantry, the charm and wit of the dialogues and the light and skillful construction of the plots set new standards.

Lynch \ 'linch, 'lĕnch \, Benito (b. June 25, 1885, Buenos Aires, Arg.—d. Dec. 23, 1951, La Plata) Argentine novelist and short-story writer who brought a new realism to the tradition of the gaucho novel, a genre that portrays the people of the South American grasslands.

Of Irish ancestry, Lynch as a boy lived on a cattle ranch in the province of Buenos Aires, gaining an intimate knowledge of rural life. His first important novel, *Los caranchos de la Florida* (1916; "The Vultures of La Florida"), deals with the conflict between a father, master of a cattle ranch, and his son, who has returned after study in Europe. Lynch's simple, ironic approach is displayed in *Raquela* (1918) and in the novel generally considered his best, *El inglés de los güesos* (1924; "The Englishman of the Bones"), a tragic story of love between an English anthropologist and a gaucho girl.

Lyndon, Barry \ 'bar-ē-'lin-dən \ Fictional character, the roguish Irish protagonist and narrator of William Makepeace Thackeray's BARRY LYNDON.

Lyndsay or **Lindsay** \ 'lind-zē \, Sir David (b. *c.* 1490—d. before April 18, 1555) Scottish poet of the pre-Reformation period whose didactic writings in colloquial Scots were characterized by a combination of moralizing and humor.

Lyndsay was born into an aristocratic family, and most of his verse, along with a work on heraldry, was written during his prosperous years as a member of the royal court. Lyndsay's *Ane Satyre of the Thrie Estaits* is the only surviving complete Scottish morality play. Originally entitled "The mysdemeanours of Busshops Religious persones and preists within the Realme" (1540), it was enlarged and performed in 1552.

The Dreme (1528), Lyndsay's earliest surviving work in verse, is an allegory of the contemporary condition of Scotland, with a delightfully personal epistle to the king. *The Testament and Complaynt of Our Soverane Lordis Papyngo* (completed 1530) is a mixture of satire, comedy, and moral instruction in which the king's dying parrot gives advice to the king and court, and *An Answer quhilk Schir David Lyndsay maid to the Kingis Flyting* (1536) is a ribald example of the game of poetic abuse ("flyting") practiced by Scottish poets. *The Complaynt and Publict Confessioun of the Kingis Auld Hound callit Bagsche* (*c.* 1536) is a short didactic piece satirizing court life through the mouth of a dog, a device later revived by Robert Burns.

Lyonnesse \ ˌlī-ə-'nes \ or **Lennoys** \ li-'nȯis \ or **Leonais** \ ˌlē-ō-'nes \ Mythical "lost" land supposed once to have connected Cornwall in the west of England with the Scilly Isles lying in the English Channel. The name Lyonnesse first appeared in Sir Thomas Malory's late 15th-century prose account of the rise and fall of King Arthur, *Le Morte Darthur*, in which it was the native land of the hero Tristan.

Lyre of Orpheus, The \ 'ȯr-ˌfyüs, -fē-əs \ Novel by Robertson DAVIES, published in 1988. The book is the third in the so-called Cornish trilogy that also includes *The Rebel Angels* (1981) and *What's Bred in the Bone* (1985). This fable about the nature of artistic creation has two major plot lines. One thread concerns the production of an unfinished opera said to have been written by E.T.A. Hoffmann. The other concerns the discovery that the famous art collector Francis Cornish actually passed off one of his own paintings as a 16th-century masterpiece.

lyric \ 'lir-ik \ [Latin *lyrica* lyric poetry, from neuter plural of *lyricus* of lyric poetry, literally, of the lyre, from Greek *lyrikós*, a derivative of *lýra* lyre] A verse or poem that can, or supposedly can, be sung to the accompaniment of a musical instrument (in ancient times, usually a lyre) or that expresses intense personal emotion in a manner suggestive of a song. Lyric poetry expresses the thoughts and feelings of the poet and is some-

times contrasted with narrative poetry and verse drama, which relate events in the form of a story. Elegies, odes, and sonnets are important types of lyric poetry.

Sappho and her contemporary Alcaeus and the later Anacreon were the chief Doric lyric poets. At the close of the 5th century Bacchylides and Pindar developed the tradition of the dithyrambic odes to its highest point. Latin lyrics were written by Catullus and Horace in the 1st century BC.

In medieval Europe the lyric form can be found in the songs of the troubadours, in Christian hymns, and in various ballads. In the Renaissance the most finished form of lyric, the sonnet, was brilliantly developed by Petrarch, William Shakespeare, Edmund Spenser, and John Milton. Especially identified with the lyrical forms of poetry in the late 18th and 19th centuries were the Romantic poets, including such diverse figures as Robert Burns, William Blake, William Wordsworth, John Keats, Percy Bysshe Shelley, Alphonse de Lamartine, Victor Hugo, J.W. von Goethe, and Heinrich Heine. With the exception of some dramatic verse, most Western poetry in the late 19th and the 20th centuries may be classified as lyrical. *See also* ELEGY; ODE; SONNET.

Lyrical Ballads Collection of poems by Samuel Taylor COLERIDGE and William WORDSWORTH; its appearance in 1798 is often designated by scholars as a signal of the beginning of the English Romantic movement. The volume began with Coleridge's "Rime of the Ancient Mariner," continued with poems displaying delight in the powers of nature and the humane instincts of ordinary people, and concluded with Wordsworth's meditative "Tintern Abbey." It contained many controversial poems by Wordsworth, such as "The Idiot Boy," written in common, everyday language.

lyric caesura A type of feminine caesura. *See* CAESURA.

Lysias \ 'lis-ē-əs \ (b. *c.* 445 BC—d. after 380 BC) Greek professional speech writer whose unpretentious simplicity became the model for a plain style of Attic Greek.

Lysias' surviving forensic speeches often deal with crimes against the state—murder, malicious wounding, sacrilege, and taking bribes. He was capable of passionate oratory, as exemplified in his own most famous speech, "Against Eratosthenes," denouncing one of the Thirty Tyrants for his part in the reign of terror that followed the collapse of Athens in 404.

Lysistrata \ li-'sis-trə-tə, lī-; ˌlis-i-'strä-tə \ (*Greek* Lysistratē) \ -tē \ Comedy by ARISTOPHANES, produced in 411 BC.

Lysistrata depicts the seizure of the Athenian Acropolis and of the treasury of Athens by the city's women who, at the instigation of the witty and determined Lysistrata, have banded together with the women of Sparta to declare a ban on sexual contact until their partners end the Peloponnesian War, which has lasted more than 20 years. The women hold out until their desperate partners arrange for peace, and the men and women are then reunited.

Lyttelton \ 'lit-əl-tən \, George, 1st Baron Lyttelton of Frankley \ 'fraŋk-lē \ (b. Jan. 17, 1709, Hagley, Worcestershire, Eng.—d. Aug. 22, 1773, Hagley) British Whig statesman and writer, patron of novelist Henry Fielding and poet James Thomson.

Son of a prominent Whig family, Lyttelton served in a series of official positions and was acquainted with the leading literary figures of his day. He wrote a poetic epistle to Alexander Pope and a description of Thomson included in the poet's *The Castle of Indolence* (1748). Fielding dedicated his novel *Tom Jones* (1749) to Lyttelton, and Tobias Smollett satirized him as Gosling Scragg in *The Adventures of Peregrine Pickle* (1751).

Lytton *see* BULWER-LYTTON.

Ma'arrī, -al \âl-mà-'àr-,rē, *Arabic* -'àr-\, *in full* Abū al-'Alā' Aḥmad ibn 'Abd Allāh al-Ma'arrī (b. December 973, Ma'arrat an-Nu'mān, near Aleppo [Syria]—d. May 1057, Ma'arrat an-Nu'mān) Great Arab poet known for his virtuosity and for the originality and pessimism of his vision.

A childhood disease left al-Ma'arrī virtually blind. His early poems were collected in *Saqṭ az-zand* ("The Tinder Spark"), which gained great popularity. Although he lived in seclusion, he enjoyed respect and authority locally, and many students came to study with him. He also maintained an active correspondence. His extant letters were translated into English by D.S. Margoliouth as *The Letters of Abu 'l-'Alā of Ma'arrat al-Nu'mān* (1898).

Al-Ma'arrī wrote a second, more original collection of poetry, *Luzūm mā lam yalzam* ("Unnecessary Necessity"), or *Luzūmīyāt* ("Necessities"); the title refers to the unnecessary complexity of the rhyme scheme. The skeptical humanism of these poems was also apparent in *Risālat al-ghufrān* (*Risalat ul Ghufran, a Divine Comedy*), in which the poet visits paradise and meets his predecessors, heathen poets who have found forgiveness. *Al-Fuṣūl wa al-ghāyāt* ("Paragraphs and Periods") is a collection of homilies in rhymed prose.

Mab \'mab\, *also called* Queen Mab. In English folklore, the queen of the fairies. Mab is a mischievous but basically benevolent figure. In William Shakespeare's *Romeo and Juliet* she is referred to as the fairies' midwife, who delivers sleeping men of their innermost wishes in the form of dreams. In Michael Drayton's mock-epic *Nymphidia* (1627) she is the wife of the fairy king Oberon and is the queen of the diminutive fairies. Mab is similarly mentioned as a pixielike fairy in works by Ben Jonson, John Milton, and Robert Herrick. Titania later replaced her as queen of the fairies in English folklore.

Mabinogion \mà-bē-'nòg-yən\ Collection of 11 medieval Welsh tales based on mythology, folklore, and heroic legends. The name Mabinogion was given to the collection by Lady Charlotte Guest when she translated the tales in 1838–49. They had been preserved in two ancient manuscripts, *The White Book of Rhydderch* and *The Red Book of Hergest* (c. 1375–1425).

The finest of the tales are the four related stories known as THE FOUR BRANCHES OF THE MABINOGI, or "The Four Branches" (dating from the late 11th century). "The Four Independent Native Tales" show minimal continental influence and include "Culhwch and Olwen," "Lludd and Llefelys," "The Dream of Macsen Wledig," and "The Dream of Rhonabwy." The tales "Owain and Luned" (or "The Lady of the Fountain"), "Geraint and Enid," and "Peredur, the Son of Efrawg" parallel the French romances *Yvain*, *Erec*, and *Perceval* of Chrétien de Troyes.

Macaire \mà-'ker\ Anonymous French medieval epic, or chanson de geste, known from a 14th-century manuscript. It is named after one of its chief characters.

The story concerns Blanchefleur, wife of the aged and infirm emperor Charlemagne, who having repulsed the advances of Macaire, is accused of infidelity and sentenced to perpetual exile. Ultimately her innocence is proved, she pardons her husband, and is reunited with him. The same story was developed in another chanson, known as *La Reine Sebile*, the text of which has been reconstructed from 13th-century fragments discovered in England, Belgium, and Switzerland.

macaronic \,mak-ə-'rän-ik\ [New Latin *macaronicus* or Old Italian *maccaronico* in the style of a macaronic, a derivative of Italian dialect *maccaroni* dumpling, macaroni] Originally, a comic Latin verse form that is characterized by the introduction of vernacular words with appropriate but absurd Latin endings; later variants apply Latinate formations to modern languages. The form was first written by Tisi degli Odassi in the late 15th century and was popularized in the early 16th century by Teofilo Folengo, a dissolute Benedictine monk. His work soon found imitators in Italy and France, and some macaronics were even written in mock Greek.

The outstanding English-language poem in this form is the *Polemo-Medinia inter Vitarvam et Nebernam* (1645?), in which William Drummond subjected Scots dialect to Latin grammatical rules. A modern English derivative of the macaronic pokes fun at the grammatical complexities of ancient languages, as in A.D. Godley's illustration of declension in "Motor Bus":

> Domine defende nos
> Contra hos Motores Bos

("Lord protect us from these motor buses").

In a broader sense, *macaronic* may simply describe a mixture of two languages, with or without comic intent.

MacArthur \mək-'är-thər\, Charles (b. Nov. 5, 1895, Scranton, Pa., U.S.—d. April 21, 1956, New York, N.Y.) American journalist, dramatist, and screenwriter, who is remembered for his comedies written with Ben Hecht.

At the age of 17, MacArthur moved to Chicago to begin a career in journalism, working at the *Chicago Tribune* and the *Chicago Herald-Examiner*, before moving to New York City to work for the *New York American* and to begin writing plays.

MacArthur and Hecht began their long partnership and earned critical acclaim with *The Front Page* (1928), a farce about a star reporter who is drawn into his own story. They also achieved success with *Twentieth Century* (produced 1932), a lively satire of the entertainment industry. Later collaborations included *Jumbo* (1934), *Ladies and Gentlemen* (produced 1939), and *Swan Song* (produced 1946). The pair also wrote many successful screenplays in the 1930s, among them *Crime Without Passion*, *The Scoundrel*, which won an Academy Award for best original story, *Soak the Rich*, *Gunga Din*, and *Wuthering Heights*. MacArthur's solo screenplays included *The Sin of Madelon Claudet* (1931), which featured an Academy Award-winning performance by his second wife, Helen Hayes, *Rasputin and the Empress* (1932), and *The Senator Was Indiscreet* (1947).

Macaulay \mə-'kȯ-lē\, Rose, *in full* Dame Emilie Rose Macaulay (b. Aug. 1, 1881, Rugby, Warwickshire, Eng.—d. Oct. 30, 1958, London) Author of novels and travel books characterized by intelligence, wit, and lively scholarship.

Macaulay first attracted attention as a social satirist with a series of novels, *Potterism* (1920), *Dangerous Ages* (1921), *Told by an Idiot* (1923), *Orphan Island* (1924), *Crewe Train* (1926), and *Keeping Up Appearances* (1928). After 1930 she wrote fewer novels, though the fiction she did produce, such as *Going Abroad* (1934), *The World My Wilderness* (1950), and *The Towers of Trebizond* (1956), conformed to a high standard.

Some Religious Elements in English Literature (1931) and *They Were Defeated* (1932), a study of the poet Robert Herrick, were among her best works of literary criticism. In addition to two travel books, *They Went to Portugal* (1946) and *Fabled Shore* (1949), she also produced three volumes of verse.

Macaulay \mə-'kȯl-ē\, Thomas Babington, *in full* Thomas Babington Macaulay, Baron Macaulay of Rothley \'rȯth-lē\ (b. Oct. 25, 1800, Rothley Temple, Leicestershire, Eng.—d. Dec. 28, 1859, Campden Hill, London) English historian who is best known for his five-volume *History of England* (1849–61), covering the crucial period 1688–1702, when the supremacy of Parliament was established and the monarchy restricted to a constitutional status.

Macaulay attended Trinity College, Cambridge, where he held a fellowship until 1831. In 1825 the first of his essays, that on Milton, was published in *The Edinburgh Review* and brought him immediate fame.

He studied law and was called to the bar in 1826 but never practiced seriously. Aspiring to a political career, in 1830 he entered Parliament as member for Calne in Wiltshire. He was regarded as a leading figure in an age of great orators. He became a member and later the secretary of the Board of Control, which supervised the administration of India by the East India Company. Meanwhile, he found time to write a ballad, "The Armada," as well as eight literary and historical essays for *The Edinburgh Review*.

In 1834 Macaulay accepted an invitation to serve on the recently created Supreme Council of India. He reached India at a vital moment when effective government by the East India Company was being superseded by that of the British crown. In this he was able to play an important part, supporting the liberty of the press and the equality of Europeans and Indians before the law. He inaugurated a national system of education, Western in outlook, and he drafted a penal code that later became the basis of Indian criminal law.

Macaulay returned to England in 1838 and entered Parliament as a member for Edinburgh. He became secretary for war in 1839, but the ministry fell in 1841 and he found the leisure to publish his *Lays of Ancient Rome* (1842) and *Critical and Historical Essays* (1843). He soon retired into private life, settling down to work on his *History of England*, intending to cover the period 1688–1820. The first two volumes appeared in 1849 and achieved an unprecedented success. The third and fourth volumes of his *History* were published in 1855 and at once attained a vast circulation. In 1857 Macaulay was raised to the peerage, with the title of Baron Macaulay of Rothley. The fifth volume of his *History*, edited by his sister Hannah, was published after his death in 1861. Macauley's view of the historical process and his firm, straightforward style remained influential for a century after his death.

Macbeth \mək-'beth, mak-\   Tragedy in five acts by William SHAKESPEARE, performed at the Globe Theatre, London, in 1605–06 and published in the 1623 First Folio. The published edition was based on an actor's promptbook, and some portions of the original text are corrupted or missing. The play chronicles Macbeth's seizing of power and subsequent destruction, his rise and fall both the result of blind ambition.

Macbeth and Banquo, who are generals serving King Duncan of Scotland, meet three witches who prophesy that Macbeth will become thane of Cawdor, then king, and that Banquo will beget kings. Soon thereafter Macbeth is indeed made thane of Cawdor, which leads him to believe the rest of the prophecy. He tells Lady Macbeth, who plots to kill Duncan when he spends a night at Macbeth's castle, Dunsinane. Spurred by his wife, Macbeth kills Duncan, and the murder is discovered by Macduff. Duncan's sons Malcolm and Donalbain flee the country, fearing for their lives. As a result they are suspected of murdering their father, and Macbeth becomes king.

Worried by the witches' prophecy, Macbeth arranges the death of Banquo, though Banquo's son escapes. Banquo's ghost haunts Macbeth, and Lady Macbeth is driven to madness by her guilt. Learning that Macduff is joining Malcolm's army, Macbeth orders the slaughter of Macduff's wife and children. Lady Macbeth dies; Macbeth is killed in battle by Macduff. Malcolm then becomes the rightful king.

MacBeth \mək-'beth, mak-\, George Mann (b. Jan. 19, 1932, Shotts, Lanarkshire, Scot.—d. Feb. 16, 1992, Tuam, County Galway, Ire.)   British poet whose verses encompassed moving

personal elegies, highly contrived poetic jokes, dream fantasies, and macabre satires.

MacBeth published his first collection of poetry as *A Form of Words* (1954). By the end of the 1950s he had become one of the top talk-radio producers with the BBC. He persuaded a wide variety of poets to read their own work on such programs as "The Poet's Voice" (1958–65; renamed "Poetry Now," 1965–76) and "New Comment" (1959–64). He quit the BBC in 1976 shortly after the publication of his first two novels, *The Transformation* and *The Samurai* (both in 1975). His second verse collection, *The Broken Places*, was published in 1963, and from 1965 he published at least one volume of poetry almost every year; these included *The Colour of Blood* (1967), *Shrapnel* (1973), *Poems of Love and Death* (1980), *Anatomy of a Divorce* (1988), and *Trespassing* (1991). He also edited poetry anthologies and wrote children's verse and several more novels, notably *Anna's Book* (1983), *Another Love Story* (1991), and *The Testament of Spencer* (1992).

MacCaig \mə-'käg\, Norman (Alexander) (b. Nov. 14, 1910, Edinburgh, Scot.)   Scottish poet whose mature work sharply recalls the 17th-century Metaphysical poet John Donne.

One element in MacCaig's work is a passionate love for his native Scotland, especially for the Highlands landscape. His early published works were *Far Cry* (1943) and *The Inward Eye* (1946). His characteristic "Donne-ish" voice was first heard in *Riding Lights* (1955) and continued through *Selected Poems* (1971). *Old Maps and New: Selected Poems* was published in 1978 and *The Equal Skies* in 1980. With Alexander Scott he edited *Contemporary Scottish Verse, 1959–1969* (1970).

MacCarthy \mə-'kär-thē\, Desmond, *in full* Sir Desmond Charles Otto MacCarthy (b. May 20, 1877, Plymouth, Devon, Eng.—d. June 8, 1952, Cambridge, Cambridgeshire)   English journalist who, in his nine years of writing weekly columns for the *New Statesman* as the "Affable Hawk," gained a reputation for erudition, sensitive judgment, and literary excellence.

MacCarthy began his career as a freelance journalist, quickly moving to editorial work at the *New Quarterly* (1907–10) and *Eye Witness* (1911–13; later *New Witness*). He worked for the *New Statesman* as drama critic (1913–44), literary editor (1920–27), and weekly columnist (1920–29) and became senior literary critic of the *Sunday Times* in 1928. He was also editor of *Life and Letters* for five years.

MacCarthy the critic was most revealing when his approach was biographical rather than purely literary. He was open to novel visions of reality in literature, helped promote unknown or new authors, and assisted young critics. His seven volumes of collected writings include *Portraits* (1931), *Drama* (1940), and *Shaw* (1951). MacCarthy was knighted in 1951.

MacDiarmid \mək-'dər-mid\, Hugh, *pseudonym of* Christopher Murray Grieve \'grēv\ (b. Aug. 11, 1892, Langholm, Dumfriesshire, Scot.—d. Sept. 9, 1978, Edinburgh)   Preeminent Scottish poet of the first half of the 20th century and leader of the Scottish literary renaissance.

MacDiarmid was a journalist in Montrose, Angus, where he edited three issues of the first postwar Scottish verse anthology, *Northern Numbers* (1921–23). In 1922 he founded the monthly *Scottish Chapbook*, in which he advocated a Scottish literary revival and published the lyrics of "Hugh MacDiarmid," later collected as *Sangschaw* (1925) and *Penny Wheep* (1926). MacDiarmid rejected English as a medium for Scottish poetry; he scrutinized the pretensions and hypocrisies of modern society in verse written in "synthetic Scots," an amalgam of elements from various middle Scots dialects and folk ballads and other sources. He achieved notable success both in his lyrics and in *A Drunk Man Looks at the Thistle* (1926), an extended rhapsody. He returned to standard English in *Stony Limits* (1934) and *Second Hymn to Lenin* (1935). His later style was best represented in *A Kist of Whistles* (1947) and *In Memoriam James Joyce* (1955). Autobiographical volumes include *Lucky Poet* (1943) and *The Company I've Kept* (1966). His *Complete Poems* appeared in 1974.

MacDonagh \mǝk-'dǝn-ǝ, -'dȯn-, -'dän-\, Donagh (b. 1912—d. Jan. 1, 1968, Dublin, Ire.)   Poet, playwright, and balladeer, prominent representative of lively Irish entertainment in the mid-20th century.

MacDonagh's varied literary works include comedies such as *Happy as Larry* (1946) and *God's Gentry* (1951) and poetry such as *Veterans and Other Poems* (1941). Also an authority on the traditional Irish ballad, MacDonagh was a popular radio and stage performer in the 1940s and '50s. With Lennox Robinson, he edited *The Oxford Book of Irish Verse* (1958).

Macdonald \mǝk-'dän-ǝld\, Cynthia (b. Feb. 2, 1928, New York, N.Y., U.S.)   American poet who employed a sardonic tone and used grotesque imagery to comment on the mundane.

Macdonald taught English at Sarah Lawrence College (1970–75) and Johns Hopkins University (1975–78). In 1979 she founded the creative writing program at the University of Houston, serving as codirector.

Amputations (1972), her first published volume of poetry, attracted attention by its startling imagery. Almost all the poems concern freakish people who have undergone amputation—either physical or symbolic—of a body part or who feel amputated from society. Continuing the theme of separateness and alienation, Macdonald places the subjects of her poems in *Transplants* (1976) in threatening environments. *(W)holes* (1980) also focuses on grotesques and incongruous surroundings. Her later works include *Alternate Means of Transport* (1985) and *Living Wills* (1991). She also wrote the libretto for *The Rehearsal* (1978), an opera by Thomas Benjamin.

Macdonald \mǝk-'dän-ǝld\, George (b. Dec. 10, 1824, Huntly, Aberdeen, Scot.—d. Sept. 18, 1905, Ashtead, Surrey, Eng.)   Novelist of Scottish life, poet, and writer of Christian allegories who is remembered chiefly for his fairy stories.

In 1855 Macdonald published a poetic tragedy, *Within and Without*. Of his literature for adults, *Phantastes: A Faerie Romance for Men and Women* (1858) and *Lilith* (1895) are good examples. Although his best-known book for children is *At the Back of the North Wind* (1871), his best and most enduring works are *The Princess and the Goblin* (1872) and its sequel, *The Princess and Curdie* (1873).

MacDonald \mǝk-'dän-ǝld\, John D., *in full* Dann (b. July 24, 1916, Sharon, Pa., U.S.—d. Dec. 28, 1986, Milwaukee, Wis.)   American author of mystery and science-fiction novels and short stories. He is best remembered for his series of 24 crime novels featuring Travis MCGEE.

MacDonald began contributing science-fiction and suspense stories to pulp magazines in the mid-1940s. His first full-length novel was *The Brass Cupcake* (1950).

In *The Deep Blue Good-By* (1964), MacDonald introduced Travis McGee—a tough, eccentric "salvage consultant." Going beyond the usual formula of sex and violence, the author investigates contemporary social and moral concerns through McGee and his erudite sidekick Meyer. Books in the series include *One Fearful Yellow Eye* (1966), *A Tan and Sandy Silence* (1971), and *Cinnamon Skin* (1982). Among his science-fiction novels are *Wine of the Dreamers* (1951), *Ballroom of the Skies* (1952), and *The Girl, the Gold Watch, and Everything* (1962). MacDonald's other notable works include *The Neon Jungle* (1953), *Condominium* (1977), and *One More Sunday* (1984).

Macdonald \mǝk-'dän-ǝld\, Ross, *pseudonym of* Kenneth Millar \'mil-ǝr\, *also called* John Macdonald *or* John Ross Macdonald (b. Dec. 13, 1915, Los Gatos, Calif., U.S.—d. July 11, 1983, Santa Barbara, Calif.)   American mystery writer who is credited with elevating the detective novel to the level of literature with his compactly written tales of murder and despair.

Millar, who adopted a wide array of pseudonyms, wrote his first novels under his real name; these include *The Dark Tunnel* (1944), *Trouble Follows Me* (1946), and *The Three Roads* (1948). Under the name John Macdonald he wrote *The Moving Target* (1949; reissued in 1966 as *Harper*), in which he introduced the shrewd private investigator Lew Archer. Macdonald then assumed the pen name John Ross Macdonald for such Lew Archer mysteries as *The Way Some People Die* (1951), *The Ivory Grin* (1952), *Find a Victim* (1954), and *The Name Is Archer* (1955). Under the name Ross Macdonald he wrote *The Barbarous Coast* (1956), *The Doomsters* (1958), and *The Galton Case* (1959). Such later novels as *The Underground Man* (1971) and *Sleeping Beauty* (1973) reflected Macdonald's abiding interest in conservation.

MacDowell Colony \mǝk-'daů-ǝl\   Permanent summer school for composers, painters, and writers founded in 1907 by pianist Marian Nevins MacDowell (1857–1956), wife of the composer Edward MacDowell (1860–1908), at their summer home in Peterborough, N.H. During her lifetime more than 750 artists used the colony as a working retreat.

Macduff \mǝk-'dǝf\   Fictional character, a nobleman of Scotland who becomes the nemesis of Macbeth in William Shakespeare's MACBETH.

Macedo \mǝ-'sä-dü\, José Agostinho de (b. Sept. 11, 1761, Beja, Port.—d. Oct. 2, 1831, Pedrouços)   Portuguese didactic poet, critic, and pamphleteer notable for his acerbity.

Despite conflicts with religious and secular authorities, Macedo was recognized as the leading pulpit orator of the day and in 1802 was appointed one of the royal preachers.

The best of his didactic poems are *A meditação* ("The Meditation") and *Newton* (1813). He also founded and wrote for a large number of journals, and the tone and temper of these and of his political pamphlets caused one of his biographers to call him the "chief libeler" of Portugal. His malignity reached its height in the satirical poem *Os burros* (1812–14; "The Asses"), in which he pilloried, by name, living and dead men and women of all grades of society.

Mac Flecknoe \mak-'flek-nō\   (*in full* Mac Flecknoe: or, A Satyr upon the True-Blew-Protestant Poet T.S.)   An extended verse satire by John DRYDEN written in the mid-1670s and published anonymously and apparently without Dryden's authority in 1682. It consists of a devastating attack on the Whig playwright Thomas Shadwell that has never been satisfactorily explained; Shadwell's reputation has suffered ever since.

The basis of the satire, which represents Shadwell as a literary dunce, is the disagreement between him and Dryden over the quality of Ben Jonson's wit. This hilarious comic lampoon was both the first English mock-heroic poem and the immediate ancestor of Alexander Pope's *The Dunciad.*

Mácha \'mä-ḵä\, Karel Hynek (b. Nov. 16, 1810, Prague, Bohemia, Austrian Empire [now in Czech Republic]—d. Nov. 5, 1836, Litoměřice)   Poet who is considered the greatest poet of Czech Romanticism.

Mácha was influenced as a student by the Czech national revival and by English and Polish Romantic literature. After schoolboy attempts to write in German, Mácha had begun (1830) to write poems, sketches, and novels in Czech. His best work is the lyrical epic *Máj* (1836; *May*). Coldly received at the time, *Máj* grew in prestige among Czech poets and critics of the 20th century.

Machado \mä-'chä-<u>th</u>ō\, Antonio, *surname in full* Machado y Ruiz \ē-rü-'ēth\ (b. July 26, 1875, Seville, Spain—d. Feb. 22, 1939, Collioure, Fr.) Outstanding Spanish poet and playwright of Spain's Generation of '98.

Machado rejected the modernism of his contemporaries and adopted what he called "eternal poetry," which was informed more by intuition than by intellect. Three stages can be distinguished in his artistic evolution. The first, typified by the poems in *Soledades* (1903; "Solitudes") and *Soledades, galerías, y otros poemas* (1907; "Solitudes, Galleries, and Other Poems"), established his links with Romanticism. These poems are concerned largely with evoking memories and dreams and with the subjective identification of the poet with natural phenomena, especially the sunset. In his second stage Machado turned away from pure introspection, and in *Campos de Castilla* (1912; "Plains of Castile") he sought to capture the stark landscape and spirit of Castile in a severely denuded and somber style. His later works, *Nuevas canciones* (1924; "New Songs") and *Poesías completas* (1928; "Complete Poems"), express profound existential views and reflect on the solitude of the poet. He also wrote plays in collaboration with his brother Manuel and a collection of philosophical reflections, *Juan de Mairena* (1936).

Machado \mä-'chä-<u>th</u>ō\, Manuel, *surname in full* Machado y Ruiz \ē-rü-'ēth\ (b. Aug. 29, 1874, Seville, Spain—d. Jan. 19, 1947, Madrid) Spanish poet and playwright, brother of Antonio Machado. He is best known for his popular poetry inspired by traditional folklore, as in *Cante hondo* (1912; "Singing from the Depths"). He collaborated with his brother on such verse plays as *Desdichas de fortuna o Julianillo Valcárcel* (1926; "Miseries of Fortune; or, Julianillo Valcárcel") and *La Lola se va a los puertos* (1930; "La Lola Is Seen in Doorways").

During his youth he lived in Paris and became a leading figure in the Spanish Modernist movement. His poems of this period, *Alma* (1902; "Soul"), reveal the influence of the Symbolists and Parnassians, especially Paul Verlaine and Rubén Darío. *El mal poema* (1909; "The Evil Poem") is one of the first attempts in Spanish poetry to convey the sordidness of city life through the use of slang and sarcasm. He later became a librarian and achieved success as a journalist.

Machado de Assis \mä-'shä-dō-dē-á-'sēs\, Joaquim Maria (b. June 21, 1839, Rio de Janeiro, Braz.—d. Sept. 29, 1908, Rio de Janeiro) Brazilian poet, novelist, and short-story writer, the classic master of Brazilian literature whose art is rooted in the traditions of European culture.

Machado early worked as a printer's apprentice and began to write in his spare time. Soon he was publishing stories, poems, and novels in the Romantic tradition. By 1869 Machado was a successful Brazilian man of letters. His novel *Memórias póstumas de Brás Cubas* (1881; "The Posthumous Memoirs of Brás Cubas"; *Epitaph of a Small Winner*) is an eccentric first-person narrative in a strikingly original style that marked a clear break with the literary conventions of the day. Machado's reputation also rests on his short stories and two later novels, *Quincas Borba* (1891; *Philosopher or Dog?*) and his masterpiece, *Dom Casmurro* (1899), a haunting and terrible journey into a mind warped by jealousy. Translations of his shorter fiction include *The Devil's Church and Other Stories* (1977) and *The Psychiatrist and Other Stories* (1963).

Machado was the first president of the Brazilian Academy of Letters.

Machaut or **Machault**, Guillaume de   *see* GUILLAUME de Machaut.

Macheath \mǝk-'hēth\ Fictional character, a handsome highwayman in John Gay's THE BEGGAR'S OPERA and a gangster in Bertolt Brecht's THE THREEPENNY OPERA.

Machen \'mak̲-ǝn, 'mak-, *Angl* 'mā-chǝn\, Arthur, *pseudonym of* Arthur Llewellyn Jones \'jōnz\ (b. March 3, 1863, Caerleon, Monmouthshire, Wales—d. Dec. 15, 1947, Beaconsfield, Buckinghamshire, Eng.) Welsh novelist and essayist, a forerunner of 20th-century gothic science fiction.

Machen lived most of his life in poverty as a clerk, teacher, actor, and translator. In 1912, approaching his 50th birthday, he joined the staff of the London *Evening News*. The quality of Machen's writing was demonstrated early in World War I when the newspaper published the short story "The Angel of Mons" from *The Bowmen and Other Legends of War* (1915), which circulated widely as a true story and gave hope to thousands of soldiers in battle. Machen's fantasies are often set in medieval England or Wales, as in the autobiographical *The Hill of Dreams* (1907). His stories set in London are deeply romantic and nostalgic for a preindustrial era. Other works include *The Great God Pan and the Inmost Light* (1894), *The Terror* (1917), *Far Off Things* (1922), and *Things Near and Far* (1923). Machen also translated Giovanni Casanova's *Memoirs*, 12 vol. (1930).

Machiavelli \ˌmäk-ē-ä-'vel-ē, *Angl* ˌmak-\, Niccolò (b. May 3, 1469, Florence [Italy]—d. June 21, 1527, Florence) Italian writer and statesman, Florentine patriot, and original political theorist whose principal work, *Il principe* (1513; THE PRINCE), brought him a reputation of amoral cynicism.

Machiavelli came from a wealthy and prominent family and was made head of the second chancery (*cancelleria*) at the early age of 29. He was sent on several diplomatic missions, including two to Cesare Borgia, the strong sinister prince who was then attempting to create his own principality in central Italy. Borgia caught the imagination of Machiavelli, who adapted his qualities and methods to an ideal new prince who would provide a desperate remedy for the desperate ills of Italy.

Machiavelli later held other influential positions in various Florentine governments, but he lost his position when the Medici family returned to power in Florence. When a conspiracy against the Medici was discovered early in 1513, Machiavelli was accused of complicity. Thrown into prison, he maintained his innocence even under torture. He was finally released from prison, but his freedom was restricted.

Reduced to poverty, Machiavelli sought refuge in the small property near Florence that he had inherited. There he wrote his two most famous works, *Il principe* and a large part of the *Discorsi sopra la prima deca di Tito Livio* ("Discourses on the First 10 Books of Livy"). From this time also dates the comedy first entitled *Commedia di Callimaco e di Lucrezia*, later *La mandragola* (1518; "The Mandrake"), in which human wickedness and corruption are satirized.

Machiavelli's hopes were raised when, on the death of Duke Lorenzo, the Cardinal Giulio de' Medici came to govern Florence. He was presented to the cardinal by Lorenzo Strozzi, to whom in gratitude he dedicated the dialogue *Dell'arte della guerra* (1521; *The Arte of Warre*), which is complementary to his two political treatises. The cardinal agreed to have Machiavelli elected official historiographer of the republic. When Giulio de' Medici later became Pope Clement VII, Machiavelli served him until the sack of Rome by the forces of the Holy Roman emperor.

machine \mǝ-'shēn\ A literary device or contrivance (such as a supernatural agency) introduced for dramatic effect; also, an agency so introduced. *See also* DEUS EX MACHINA.

MacInnes \mǝ-'kin-is\, Tom, *byname of* Thomas Robert Edward McInnes (b. Oct. 29, 1867, Dresden, Ont., Can.—d. Feb.

11, 1951, Vancouver, B.C.) Canadian writer whose works range from vigorous, slangy recollections of the Yukon gold rush, as in *Lonesome Bar* (1909), to a translation of and commentary on the philosophy of Laozi (Lao-tzu), irreverently titled *The Teaching of the Old Boy* (1927). His collected poems include *Complete Poems* (1923) and *In the Old of My Age* (1947). *Chinook Days* (1927), a fictionalized autobiography, also contains history and folklore of British Columbia.

MacKaye \mə-'kī\, Percy (b. March 16, 1875, New York, N.Y., U.S.—d. Aug. 31, 1956, Cornish, N.H.) American poet and playwright whose use of historical and contemporary folk literature furthered the development of the pageant in the United States.

MacKaye was introduced to the theater at an early age by his father, actor Steele MacKaye, with whom he first collaborated. In 1912 he published *The Civic Theatre*, in which he advocated amateur community theatricals. He attempted to bring poetry and drama to large participant groups and to unite the stage arts, music, and poetry by the use of masques and communal chanting. He wrote, among others, the pageants *The Canterbury Pilgrims* (published in 1903) and, as coauthor, *St. Louis: A Civic Masque* (performed 1914 with 7,500 participants).

In 1929 MacKaye became advisory editor to *Folk-Say*, a journal of American folklore. He also conducted research in collaboration with his wife, Marion Morse MacKaye. His most noteworthy contributions to U.S. drama and pageantry are *The Scarecrow* (1908), a historical play; *Caliban* (1916), a pageant-masque; *This Fine Pretty World* (1923), a regional play; and *The Mystery of Hamlet: King of Denmark* (1945), a study of past and present tragedy.

MacKaye \mə-'kī\, Steele, *in full* James Morrison Steele MacKaye (b. June 6, 1842, Buffalo, N.Y., U.S.—d. Feb. 25, 1894, Timpas, Colo.) American playwright, actor, theater manager, and inventor.

MacKaye was the first American to act Hamlet in London (1873). At Harvard, Cornell, and elsewhere he lectured on the philosophy of aesthetics. In New York City he founded the St. James, Madison Square, and Lyceum theaters. MacKaye wrote 30 plays, including the popular *Hazel Kirke*, *Paul Kauvar*, and *Money Mad*, acting in them in 17 different roles. He organized the first school of acting in the U.S., which later became the American Academy of Dramatic Art, and patented more than 100 theatrical inventions, including folding theater seats.

Macken \'mak-ən\, Walter (b. 1915, Galway, Ire.—d. April 22, 1967, Galway) Irish novelist and dramatist whose tales combine an honest and often harsh reflection of the realities of Irish life with a compassionate respect for its people.

Macken was an actor and stage manager in Galway, where he became actor-manager-director of the Gaelic Theatre. He was also connected with the famous Abbey Theatre in Dublin. His novel *Rain on the Wind* (1950) told a story of Galway life. He wrote a trilogy of historical novels, comprising *Seek the Fair Land* (1959), set in Cromwellian Ireland; *The Silent People* (1962), depicting the great Irish potato famine; and *The Scorching Wind* (1964), which brought the story up to the present day. As a dramatist Macken is chiefly known for *Mungo's Mansion*, performed in 1946 at the Abbey Theatre and in 1947 in London as *Galway Handicap*. He also wrote *Home Is the Hero*, which was produced and published in 1953.

Mackenzie \mə-'ken-zē\, Compton, *in full* Sir Edward Montague Compton Mackenzie (b. Jan. 17, 1883, West Hartlepool, Durham, Eng.—d. Nov. 30, 1972, Edinburgh, Scot.) British novelist who suffered critical acclaim and neglect with equal indifference, leaving a prodigious output of more than 100 novels, plays, and biographies.

Mackenzie showed a mastery of cockney humor in *Carnival* (1912) and *Sinister Street* (1913–14). There was a distinctly satiric sting to *Water on the Brain* (1933), in which he attacked the British secret service, which had prosecuted him under the Official Secrets Act for his autobiographical *Greek Memories* (1932). Mackenzie's love of pure fun can be seen in *The Monarch of the Glen* (1941) and *Whisky Galore* (1947). Other novels include *Poor Relations* (1919), *Rich Relatives* (1921), *Vestal Fire* (1927), and *Extraordinary Women* (1928). Among his plays are *The Gentleman in Grey* (1906), *Columbine* (1920), and *The Lost Cause* (1931). The first volume of his memoirs, *My Life and Times: Octave One*, appeared in 1963, and *Octave Ten* in 1971.

An ardent Scottish nationalist, Mackenzie lived in Scotland after 1928. He served as rector of Glasgow University (1931–34), as literary critic for the London *Daily Mail* (1931–35), and as the founder and editor of *Gramophone* magazine (1923–62).

Mackenzie \mə-'ken-zē\, Henry (b. Aug. 26, 1745, Edinburgh, Scot.—d. Jan. 14, 1831, Edinburgh) Scottish novelist, playwright, poet, and editor whose most important novel, *The Man of Feeling*, established him as a major literary figure in Scotland.

Mackenzie's early works include imitations of traditional Scottish ballads, but, on moving to London after 1765, he began to imitate the sentimental style of English novels. His mawkish novel *The Man of Feeling* (1771) was a best-seller. Mackenzie wrote two more novels: *The Man of the World* (1773), and *Julia de Roubigné* (1777), imitating Samuel Richardson's *Clarissa*. He also wrote a play, edited two periodicals, and helped found learned societies.

Macklin \'mak-lin\, Charles, *original name* Charles McLaughlin \mə-'kläk-lin, -'kläk-\ (b. 1690/99, Ireland—d. July 11, 1797) Irish actor and playwright whose career was distinguished though turbulent.

Macklin first appeared as an actor at Bristol and in 1725 went to Lincoln's Inn Fields Theatre, London. He was a pioneer against the stilted declamation of his day, and he set the seal on his stage career at Drury Lane on Feb. 14, 1741, when he played Shylock in *The Merchant of Venice*, giving considerably more dignity to the role than it had had before. Macklin wrote several plays, of which two were outstanding, *Love à la mode* (1759) and *The Man of the World* (1781).

MacLeish \mə-'klēsh\, Archibald (b. May 7, 1892, Glencoe, Ill., U.S.—d. April 20, 1982, Boston, Mass.) American poet, playwright, professor, and public official whose concern for liberal democracy figured in much of his work.

MacLeish was educated at Yale and went to France in 1923 to perfect his poetic craft. The verse he published during his expatriate years—*The Happy Marriage* (1924), *The Pot of Earth* (1925), *Streets in the Moon* (1926), and *The Hamlet of A. MacLeish* (1928)—shows the fashionable influence of Ezra Pound and T.S. Eliot. During this period he wrote his frequently anthologized poem "Ars Poetica" (1926). After returning to the United States in 1928, he published *New Found Land* (1930), which reveals his simple lyric eloquence and includes one of his best-known poems, "You, Andrew Marvell."

In the 1930s MacLeish grew concerned about the menace of fascism. *Conquistador* (1932), about the conquest and exploitation of Mexico, was the first of his "public" poems. Others were collected in *Frescoes for Mr. Rockefeller's City* (1933), *Public Speech* (1936), and *America Was Promises* (1939). His radio verse plays include *The Fall of the City* (1937), *Air Raid* (1938), and *The Great American Fourth of July Parade* (1975).

MacLeish served as librarian of Congress (1939–44) and assistant secretary of state (1944–45). He published his *Collected*

Poems: 1917–1952 in 1952, and his *New and Collected Poems 1917–1976* appeared in 1976. His verse drama J.B., based on the biblical story of Job, was performed on Broadway in 1958. *Riders on the Earth* (1978) is a collection of his essays.

MacLennan \mə-'klen-ən\, Hugh (b. March 20, 1907, Glace Bay, Cape Breton, Nova Scotia, Can.—d. Nov. 7, 1990, Montreal, Que.)   Canadian novelist and essayist whose books offer an incisive critique of Canadian life.

A Rhodes scholar at Oxford, MacLennan studied at Princeton and taught at Lower Canada College, Montreal, and at McGill University. His first novel, *Barometer Rising* (1941), is a moral fable that uses as a background the actual explosion of a munitions ship that partly destroyed the city of Halifax in 1917. His later novels include *Two Solitudes* (1945), *The Precipice* (1948), *The Watch That Ends the Night* (1959), *Return of the Sphinx* (1967), and *Voices in Time* (1980).

Macleod \mə-'klaůd\, Mary, *Gaelic* Màiri Nighean Alasdair Ruaidh (b. 1569, Rowdil, Harris, Inverness, Scot.—d. 1674, Dunvegan, Skye)   Scottish Gaelic poet who was a major representative of the emergent 17th-century poetical school that gradually supplanted the classical Gaelic bards.

Macleod's poetry is written in simple, natural rhythms and incorporates much of the imagery of the bardic poets. It mainly deals with the heroic exploits of the Macleod family. Only a few of her poems survive; among these, her tender and nostalgic elegies are notable.

MacNeice \mək-'nēs\, Louis (b. Sept. 12, 1907, Belfast, Ire.—d. Sept. 3, 1963, London, Eng.)   British poet and playwright, a member, with W.H. Auden, C. Day-Lewis, and Stephen Spender, of a group whose low-keyed, unpoetic, socially committed, and topical verse was the "new poetry" of the 1930s.

After studying at the University of Oxford, MacNeice became a lecturer at the University of Birmingham and at the Bedford College for Women, London. In 1941 he began to write and produce radio plays for the BBC. Foremost among his fine radio verse plays is the dramatic fantasy *The Dark Tower* (1947).

MacNeice's first book of poetry, *Blind Fireworks* (1929), was followed by more than a dozen other volumes, including *Poems* (1935), *Autumn Journal* (1939), *Collected Poems, 1925–1948* (1949), and, posthumously, *The Burning Perch* (1963). An intellectual honesty, Celtic exuberance, and sardonic humor characterized his poetry, which was written with a charming natural lyricism in colloquial speech. Among MacNeice's prose works are *Letters from Iceland* (with W.H. Auden, 1937) and *The Poetry of W.B. Yeats* (1941). He was also a skilled translator, particularly of Horace and Aeschylus (*Agamemnon*, 1936).

Macondo \mä-'kōn-dō\   Fictional Latin-American city in *Cien años de soledad* (ONE HUNDRED YEARS OF SOLITUDE) by Gabriel García Márquez. Founded in the 1820s by the Buendía family, this swampy utopia flourishes until the 1920s, when it is virtually destroyed by an apocalyptic storm.

Macpherson \mək-'fir-sən\, James (b. Oct. 27, 1736, Ruthven, Inverness, Scot.—d. Feb. 17, 1796, Belville, Inverness)   Scottish poet whose initiation of the Ossianic controversy has obscured his genuine contributions to Gaelic studies.

Macpherson's first book of poems, *The Highlander* (1758), was undistinguished. After its publication, however, he gathered an important collection of Scottish Gaelic manuscripts and caused a number of orally transmitted Gaelic poems to be transcribed.

In 1760 he published *Fragments of Ancient Poetry Collected in the Highlands of Scotland and Translated from the Gallic or Erse Language*, claiming that much of their content was based on the works of a 3rd-century Gaelic poet named Ossian. Two

further "translations," *Fingal* (1762) and *Temora* (1763), followed, and the controversy that had begun in 1760 erupted. Macpherson's claim was eventually shown to be preposterous. The earliest fragments of Irish writing dated in their original form to the 6th century AD. Genuine Ossianic ballads can be dated to the 11th and succeeding centuries, although the basic legends are much older. What Macpherson did was to use a number of the ballads he had collected and to add much material of his own. Sometimes his translations were close to the originals, but often he misunderstood these and frequently he changed their entire mood in his attempt to create a doom-laden, romantic atmosphere.

Macpherson avoided publishing his originals during his lifetime. When the Gaelic version appeared in 1807, many people were deceived by it, but it is clear that this version is simply a translation of Macpherson's English. *See also* OSSIAN.

Macpherson \mək-'fərs-ən\, Jay, *in full* Jean Jay Macpherson (b. June 13, 1931, London, Eng.)   Canadian lyric poet who expressed serious religious and philosophical themes in symbolic verse that was often lyrical or comic.

Macpherson's early works, *Nineteen Poems* (1952) and *O Earth Return* (1954), were followed by *The Boatman and Other Poems* (1957, reissued with additional poems, 1968), a collection that established her reputation as a poet.

Her lyrics, often ironic and epigrammatic and linked by recurrent mythical and legendary symbols, reflect the influences of the modern critical theories of Northrop Frye and Robert Graves, Elizabethan songs, the poetry of William Blake, Anglo-Saxon riddles, and traditional ballads. *Four Ages of Man* (1962) is an illustrated account of classical myths, designed for older children. *Welcoming Disaster* (1974) is a collection of her poems from 1970 to 1974. Her study of the pastoral romance, *The Spirit of Solitude: Conventions and Continuities in Late Romance*, was published in 1982.

Macrobius \mə-'krō-bē-əs\, Ambrosius Theodosius (fl. *c.* AD 400)   Latin grammarian and philosopher whose most important work is the *Saturnalia*, the last known example of the long series of symposia headed by the *Symposium* of Plato.

Little is known about Macrobius' life. The *Saturnalia* purports to give an account of discussions in private houses on the day before the *Saturnalia* and on three days of that festival. He also wrote a Neoplatonic commentary in two books on Cicero's "Somnium Scipionis" ("Scipio's Dream") from the *De republica*. Only fragments remain of *De differentiis et societatibus Graeci Latinique verbi* ("On the Differences and Similarities of the Greek and Latin Verb").

Madách \'mò-,däch\, Imre (b. Jan. 21, 1823, Alsósztregova, Hung.—d. Oct. 5, 1864, Alsósztregova)   Hungarian poet whose reputation rests on his ambitious poetic drama *Az ember tragediája* (1861; *The Tragedy of Man*). He is often considered to be Hungary's greatest philosophical poet.

Madách's masterpiece, *Az ember tragediája*, is a Faust-like drama in 15 acts covering the past and future of humankind. The central characters, Adam and Eve, appear throughout the play in the guise of famous historical personalities. They act out humanity's tragic destiny in their constant struggle with Lucifer. Though the drama was intended for reading, its production at the Budapest National Theater in 1883 was the first of many successful performances.

Madame Bovary \bō-vȧ-'rē, *Angl* 'bō-və-rē\   Novel by Gustave FLAUBERT, published in two volumes in 1857. The novel, with the subtitle *Moeurs de province* ("Provincial Customs"), first appeared in installments in the *Revue* from October 1 to December 15, 1856. It ushered in a new age of realism in literature.

In *Madame Bovary*, Flaubert took a commonplace story of adultery and made of it a book that has continued to be read because of its profound humanity. Emma Bovary is a bored and unhappy middle-class wife whose general dissatisfaction with life leads her to act out her romantic fantasies and embark on an ultimately disastrous love affair. She destroys her life by embracing abstractions—passion, happiness—as concrete realities. She ignores material reality itself, as symbolized by money, and is inexorably drawn to financial ruin and suicide.

Mad Hatter Fictional character encountered by Alice at a tea party in Lewis Carroll's ALICE'S ADVENTURES IN WONDERLAND.

Madhubuti \\,mäd-hü-'bü-tē\\, Haki R., *byname of* Don Luther Lee \\'lē\\ (b. Feb. 23, 1942, Little Rock, Ark., U.S.) African-American author, publisher, and teacher.

Lee attended graduate school at the University of Iowa. He taught at several colleges and universities, in 1984 becoming a faculty member at Chicago State University. His poetry, which began to appear in the 1960s, was written in black dialect and slang. His work is characterized both by anger at social and economic injustice and by rejoicing in African-American culture. The verse collection *Don't Cry, Scream* (1969) includes an introduction by poet Gwendolyn Brooks.

Lee founded the Third World Press in 1967, and he established the Institute of Positive Education in Chicago, a school for black children, in 1969. Among his poetry collections published under the Swahili name Haki R. Madhubuti are *Book of Life* (1973) and *Killing Memory, Seeking Ancestors* (1987). He also wrote *From Plan to Planet—Life Studies: The Need for Afrikan Minds and Institutions* (1973) and an essay collection, *Enemies: The Clash of Races* (1978).

Madness of Heracles, The \\'her-ə-,klēz\\ (*Greek Hēraklēs mainomenos, Latin Hercules furens*) Drama by EURIPIDES, performed about 416 BC. Temporarily driven mad by the goddess Hera, Heracles kills his wife and children. When he recovers his reason, he fights suicidal despair and then is taken to spend an honorable retirement at Athens.

Madog or **Madoc** ab Owain Gwynedd \\'mä-,dȯg-,ăb-'ō-wīn-'gwin-eth\\ (fl. 1170) Legendary voyager to America, supposedly a son of Owain Gwynedd (d. 1170), prince of Gwynedd (in North Wales).

A feud over inheritance caused Madog to sail to Ireland and then westward. He returned to Wales after about a year and assembled a group to colonize America. The party set sail in 10 ships and was not seen again. The oldest extant accounts of Madog are in Richard Hakluyt's *Voyages* (1582) and David Powel's *The Historie of Cambria* (1584). In *Letters and Notes on the Manners, Customs, and Condition of the North American Indians* (1841), George Catlin surmised that the members of Madog's expedition were the ancestors of the Mandan Indians. There is a tradition of a "white Indian" settlement at Louisville, Ky., and several 17th- and 18th-century reports were published concerning encounters of frontiersmen with Welsh-speaking Indians. Most anthropologists, however, reject the idea of pre-Columbian European contacts with American Indians.

Elements of Madog's story were used as the basis of two long poems, *Madoc* (1805) by the English poet Robert Southey and *Madog* (1918) by the Welsh writer Thomas Gwynn Jones.

madrigal \\'mad-ri-gəl\\ [Italian *madriale, madrigale,* perhaps from Medieval Latin *matricale,* from neuter of *matricalis simple, natural, native, presumed sense development of Late Latin *matricalis* of the womb, original, a derivative of Latin *matric-, matrix* womb] A medieval short lyrical poem especially of love.

The 14th-century madrigal is based on a relatively constant poetic form of two or three stanzas of three lines each, with 7 or 11 syllables per line. Musically, it is most often set polyphonically (*i.e.,* having more than one voice part) in two parts, with the musical form reflecting the structure of the poem.

The 16th-century madrigal is based on a different poetic form from its precursor and was characteristically of higher literary quality. Not only madrigals but also other poems of fixed form (*e.g.,* canzones, sonnets, sestinas, and ballatas) were set to music. The favorite poets of the madrigal composers were Petrarch, Giovanni Boccaccio, Jacopo Sannazzaro, Pietro Bembo, Ludovico Ariosto, Torquato Tasso, and Battista Guarini.

maenad \\'mē-,nad\\ [Greek *mainad-, mainás,* a derivative of *maínesthai* to rage, be mad] A female participant in orgiastic Dionysian rites. *See also* BACCHANTE.

Maerlant \\'mär-länt\\, Jacob van (b. *c.* 1235, near Brugge [now in Belgium]—d. 1291, Damme) Pioneer of the didactic poetry that flourished in the Netherlands in the 14th century.

Maerlant's early works were versions of medieval romances—*Alexanders Geesten* ("The Heroic Deeds of Alexander"), based on Gautier de Châtillon's Latin *Alexandreis;* the dual work *Historie van den grale* and *Merlijns boeck* (*c.* 1260), freely translated from Robert de Boron's early contributions to the Arthurian cycle; *Roman van Torec* (*c.* 1262); and, most important, the *Die istory van Troyen* (*c.* 1264), from the *Roman de Troie* ascribed to Benoît de Sainte-Maure.

Maerlant's instructive verse turned entirely to Latin sources. His scientific compilation, *Der naturen bloeme* (1266–69?; "The Best of Nature"), was based on Thomas of Cantimpré's *De natura rerum.* A life of St. Francis (before 1273) was based on Bonaventura, and the *Rijmbijbel* (1271; "Verse Bible") was based on Petrus Comestor's *Historia scolastica.* His most important work, *Spieghel historiael* ("Mirror of History"), was an adaptation (with additions of his own) of Vincent de Beauvais's *Speculum historiale,* begun about 1282 and completed after his death by Philippe Utenbroeke and Lodewijk van Velthem.

Maerlant's skills as a religious poet are also fully shown in *Wapene Martijn* (*c.* 1266; "Alas Martin") and in his fervent *Van den lande van ouer zee* ("Of the Country Overseas").

Maeterlinck *Flem* 'mä-tər-liŋk, *Fr* me-ter-'laⁿk, *Angl* 'mät-ər-,liŋk, *also* 'met-, 'mat-\\, Maurice, *in full* Maurice Polydore-Marie-Bernard Maeterlinck, *also called* (from 1932) Count (comte) Maeterlinck (b. Aug. 29, 1862, Ghent, Belg.—d. May 6, 1949, Nice, Fr.) Belgian Symbolist poet and playwright whose rhythmic prose dramas in French are the outstanding works of the Symbolist theater.

Internationally known by the 1890s, Maeterlinck was awarded a Nobel Prize for Literature in 1911. His first important work was *Serres chaudes* (1899; "Hot House Blooms"), a collection of poems in the Symbolist tradition.

Maeterlinck made his greatest impact, however, in the theater. His *Pelléas et Mélisande* (1892; PELLÉAS AND MÉLISANDE) is the unquestioned masterpiece of Symbolist drama, and, in the French composer Claude Debussy's extremely sensitive musical setting (1902), it has remained before the public eye.

Maeterlinck wrote many other plays, including historical dramas such as *Monna Vanna* (1902). Only *L'Oiseau bleu* (1908; THE BLUE BIRD) rivaled *Pelléas et Mélisande* in popularity among contemporary audiences. An allegorical fantasy conceived as a play for children, it portrays a search for happiness in the world. His *Le Bourgmestre de Stilmonde* (1918; *The Burgomaster of Stilmonde*), a patriotic play in which he explores the problems of Flanders under the wartime rule of an unprincipled German officer, briefly enjoyed a great reputation.

Maeterlinck was also a distinguished prose writer, and his works, remarkably blended of philosophical pessimism and interest in the world of nature, were much appreciated during his lifetime. Maeterlinck presented his mystical speculations in *Le Trésor des humbles* (1896; *The Treasure of the Humble*) and *La Sagesse et la destinée* (1898; "Wisdom and Destiny"). His most widely read philosophical works were, however, *La Vie des abeilles* (1901; *The Life of the Bee*) and *L'Intelligence des fleurs* (1907; *The Intelligence of Flowers*).

Maeve, Queen *see* MEDB.

Maeztu \'mīth-tü\, Ramiro de, *surname in full* Maeztu y Whitney \ē-'wēt-nā, *English* 'wit-nē\ (b. May 4, 1875, Vitoria, Spain—d. Oct. 29, 1936, Madrid) Spanish journalist and sociopolitical theorist.

After living in Cuba, Maeztu returned to Spain and became a leading member of the Generation of '98. In 1899 he published his first book, *Hacia otra España* ("Toward Another Spain"), in which he called for Spain to break with its past and enter the European mainstream. Fluent in English, he was the London correspondent for several Spanish newspapers (1905–19) and traveled in France and Germany to cover World War I. Disillusioned by the war, he became convinced that human reason could not solve social problems. He wrote, in English, *Authority, Liberty, and Function in Light of the War*, in which he called for a reliance on authority, tradition, and the institutions of the Roman Catholic church. The work was published in Spanish as *La crisis del humanismo* (1919).

Maeztu published a collection of penetrating literary essays, *Don Quijote, Don Juan y La Celestina* (1926). He was a vehement opponent of the Spanish republic, and in his last work, *La defensa de la hispanidad* (1934; "In Defense of Spanishness"), he called for Spain to recover its 16th-century sense of Roman Catholic mission. Maeztu was shot by the Republicans in the early days of the Spanish Civil War.

Maffei \mäf-'fā\, Francesco Scipione, Marchese di (b. June 1, 1675, Verona, Republic of Venice [Italy]—d. Feb. 11, 1755, Verona) Italian dramatist, archaeologist, and scholar who, in his verse tragedy *Merope* (1713), attempted to introduce Greek and French classical simplicity into Italian drama.

In 1710 Maffei was one of the founders of an influential literary journal, *Giornale dei letterati*, a vehicle for his ideas about reforming Italian drama, as was his later periodical, *Osservazioni letterarie* (1737–40). *Merope* met with astonishing success and, because it was based on Greek mythology and the drama of Euripides and the French Neoclassical period, pointed the way for the later reform of Italian tragedy.

Maffei also wrote a number of scholarly works, librettos, occasional verse, translations of the *Iliad* and the *Aeneid*, and many plays (collected in *Teatro italiano*, 1723). His only other major work, however, aside from *Merope*, is a valuable account of the history and antiquities of his native city: *Verona illustrata*, 4 vol. (1731–32; *A Compleat History of the Ancient Amphitheatres and in Particular That of Verona*).

magazine \,mag-ə-'zēn\, *also called* periodical \,pir-ē-'äd-ə-kəl\ A printed collection of texts (essays, articles, stories, poems), often illustrated, that is produced at regular intervals. The original sense of the English word was "storehouse"; from its use in periodical titles in the figurative sense to mean "storehouse of information" (as in the *Gentleman's Magazine*, first published in 1731), it became the general word for such publications.

The modern magazine has its roots in early printed pamphlets, broadsides, chapbooks, and almanacs, a few of which gradually began appearing at regular intervals. One of the earliest magazines was a German publication, *Erbauliche Monaths-Unterredungen* ("Edifying Monthly Discussions"), issued periodically from 1663 to 1668. Other learned journals soon appeared in France, England, and Italy, and in the early 1670s lighter and more entertaining magazines began to appear, beginning with *Le Mercure galant* (1672; later renamed *Le Mercure de France*) in France. In the early 18th century, Joseph Addison and Richard Steele brought out *The Tatler* and *The Spectator*. These influential periodicals contained essays that continue to be regarded as examples of some of the finest English prose written. At the end of the century specialized periodicals began to appear.

By the early 19th century a different, less learned audience had been identified, and magazines for entertainment and family enjoyment began to appear, among them the popular weekly, the women's weekly, the religious and missionary review, the illustrated magazine, and the children's weekly. Woodcuts and engravings were first extensively used by the weekly *Illustrated London News* (1842).

Magazine publishing benefited in the late 19th and in the 20th centuries from a number of technical improvements, including the production of inexpensive paper, the invention of the rotary press and the halftone block, and the use of advertisements as a means of financial support. *See also* LITTLE MAGAZINE.

Māgha \'mä-gə\ (fl. 8th century AD) Sanskrit poet whose only surviving work is *Śiśupālavadha* ("The Slaying of King Śiśupāla"), an influential *mahākāvya* ("great poem"), a type of classical epic. Māgha was a master of technique in the strict Sanskrit sense of luscious descriptions, intricate syntax, compounds that, depending on how they are split, deliver quite different meanings, and the full register of stylistic embellishments. His *Śiśupālavadha* is considered one of the six model *mahākāvyas*. It is based on an episode of the *Mahābhārata*, in which King Śiśupāla insults the hero-god Krishna, who beheads him in the ensuing duel. Comprising 20 cantos, the *Śiśupālavadha* has a rich vocabulary that allegedly includes every word in the Sanskrit language.

Magi \'mā-jī, 'maj-,ī\, *also called* Wise Men. In Christian tradition, the noble pilgrims "from the East" who followed a miraculous guiding star to Bethlehem, where they paid homage to the infant Jesus as king of the Jews. This event is celebrated in the Eastern church at Christmas and in the West at Epiphany (January 6). Eastern tradition sets the number of Magi at 12, but Western tradition sets their number at 3, probably based on the three gifts of "gold and frankincense and myrrh" (Matthew 2:11) presented to the infant.

The legend of the Magi-Kings was embellished in apocryphal books and Christian folklore. About the 8th century the names of three Magi—Bithisarea, Melichior, and Gathaspa—appeared in a chronicle known as the *Excerpta latina barbari*. They have become known most commonly as Balthasar, Melchior, and Gaspar (or Casper). According to Western church tradition, Balthasar is often represented as a king of Arabia, Melchior as a king of Persia, and Gaspar as a king of India.

Magic Barrel, The Collection of 13 short stories by Bernard MALAMUD, published in 1958. Malamud's first published collection, *The Magic Barrel* won the 1959 National Book Award. The title story, first published in 1954, is considered one of Malamud's finest.

Most of the stories concern impoverished New York Jews. Reflecting the rhythm and style of Yiddish folktales, their settings are often bleak; the plots are ironic and humorous and show the influence of Hasidic tales.

magic carpet A legendary rug or carpet capable of transporting one who stood on it to any place desired. It is spoken of in

Arabic folk literature, perhaps most familiarly in "The History of Prince Ahmed," a story in *The Thousand and One Nights*.

Magician of Lublin, The   Novel by Isaac Bashevis SINGER, published serially as *Der Kuntsnmakher fun Lublin* in the Yiddish-language daily newspaper *Forverts* in 1959 and published in book form in English in 1960. The entire novel did not appear in Yiddish in book form until 1971.

The novel is set in late 19th-century Poland. It concerns Yasha Mazur, an itinerant professional conjurer, tightrope walker, and hypnotist. He loves five women, including his barren and pious wife. To support himself, his assorted women, and his future plans to escape to Italy, he attempts a robbery and fails. Yasha has a crisis of conscience and returns to his wife, becoming a recluse. People begin to refer to him as Jacob the Penitent, and they flock to him as if to a holy man.

Magic Mountain, The   Novel of ideas by Thomas MANN, originally published in German as *Der Zauberberg* in 1924. It is considered a towering example of the bildungsroman, a novel recounting the main character's formative years.

The Magic Mountain tells the story of Hans Castorp, a young German engineer, who goes to visit a cousin in a tuberculosis sanatorium in the mountains of Davos, Switz. Castorp discovers that he has symptoms of the disease and remains at the sanatorium for seven years, until the outbreak of World War I. During this time, he abandons his normal life to submit to the rich seductions of disease, introspection, and death. Through talking with other patients, he gradually becomes aware of and absorbs the predominant political, cultural, and scientific ideas of 20th-century Europe. The sanatorium comes to be the spiritual reflection of the possibilities and dangers of the actual world away from the magic mountain.

magic realism   Latin-American literary phenomenon characterized by the incorporation of fantastic or mythical elements matter-of-factly into otherwise realistic fiction. The term was applied to literature in the late 1940s by Cuban novelist Alejo Carpentier, who recognized the tendency of his region's traditional storytellers as well as contemporary authors to illumine the mundane by means of the fabulous. Prominent among the magic realists, in addition to Carpentier, were the Brazilian Jorge Amado, the Argentines Jorge Luis Borges and Julio Cortázar, the Colombian Gabriel García Márquez, and the Chilean Isabel Allende.

Magister Ludi \mə-'jis-tər-'lü-‚dē\   see THE GLASS BEAD GAME.

Magnificent Ambersons, The \'am-bər-sən\   Novel by Booth TARKINGTON, published in 1918. The book, about life in a Midwestern American town, was awarded a Pulitzer Prize in 1919. It was the second volume in the author's trilogy *Growth*, which included *The Turmoil* (1915) and *The Midlander* (1923, later retitled *National Avenue*).

The novel traces the growth of the United States through the decline of the once-powerful, socially prominent Amberson family. Their fall is contrasted with the rise of new industrial tycoons and land developers, whose power comes not through family connections but through financial dealings and modern manufacturing.

magnum opus \'mag-nəm-'ō-pəs\ [Latin, great work]   A literary or artistic work of importance; more specifically, the greatest achievement of an artist.

Magnússon \'mäg-nūs-‚sŏn, 'mäk-\, Árni \'aůd-nē, *Angl* 'är-nē\ (b. Nov. 13, 1663, Kvennabrekka, Ice.—d. Jan. 7, 1730, Copenhagen, Den.)   Icelandic antiquarian and philologist who built up the most important collection of early Icelandic literary manuscripts.

Magnússon graduated from the University of Copenhagen with a degree in theology in 1685, but he was interested chiefly in the early history and literature of Scandinavia. He traveled extensively in Norway, Sweden, and Iceland, collecting books and manuscripts. His collection was sent to Denmark in 1720. A large part of it perished in the fire of Copenhagen (1728), but the remainder passed to the University of Copenhagen, where it is still housed.

Magnússon \'mäg-nūs-‚sŏn, 'mäk-\, Jón (b. *c.* 1610—d. 1696)   Icelandic parson and author of the *Píslarsaga* ("Passion Story"), one of the strangest documents of cultural and psychic delusion in all literature.

A parson at Eyri in 1655, Magnússon was stricken by an illness he ascribed to the witchcraft of two of his parishioners, a father and son. When he did not recover, even after the "sorcerers" were burned at the stake in 1656, he extended his accusation to a daughter of the family, who was cleared of charges and sued the parson. The *Píslarsaga*, written in protest of this suit, is an eloquent document, both in its fantastic description of Magnússon's sufferings and in its documentation of the belief in witchcraft as the cause of disease. It was not published until 1914.

Magwitch, Abel \'ā-bəl-'mag-wich\   Fictional character, an escaped convict who plays a major role in the growth and development of Pip, the protagonist in Charles Dickens' novel GREAT EXPECTATIONS.

Mahābhārata \mə-‚hä-'bä-rə-tə\ ("Great Epic of the Bharata Dynasty")   One of the two major Sanskrit epics of India, valued for both its high literary merit and its religious inspiration. It consists of a mass of legendary and didactic material surrounding a central heroic narrative that tells of the struggle for supremacy between two groups of cousins, the Kauravas and the Pāṇḍavas. Together with the second major epic, the *Rāmāyaṇa* ("Romance of Rāma"), the *Mahābhārata* is an important source of information about the evolution of Hinduism during the period of about 400 BC–AD 200. Contained within the *Mahābhārata* is the BHAGAVADGĪTĀ ("Song of the Lord"), the single most important religious text of Hinduism.

The poem is made up of almost 100,000 couplets divided into 18 *parvan*s, or sections, to which has been added a supplement entitled *Harivaṃśa* ("Genealogy of the God Hari," *i.e.*, Krishna-Vishnu). Authorship of the poem is traditionally ascribed to the sage VYĀSA, although it is more likely that he compiled existing material. The traditional date for the war that is the central event of the *Mahābhārata* is 3102 BC, but most historians prefer a later date. The poem reached its present form about AD 400.

Above all, the *Mahābhārata* is an exposition on dharma (codes of conduct), including the proper conduct of a king, of a warrior, of a man living in times of calamity, and of a person seeking to attain emancipation from rebirth. The several centuries during which the epic took shape were a period of transition from the religion of Vedic sacrifice to the sectarian, internalized worship of later Hinduism, and different sections of the poem express varying and sometimes contradictory beliefs.

Mahagonny \mä-'häg-ō-nē\ (*in full* Rise and Fall of the City of Mahagonny)   Opera in 20 scenes with music by Kurt Weill and text by Bertolt BRECHT, published in 1929 and performed in German as *Aufstieg und Fall der Stadt Mahagonny* in 1930.

Set in a fictional American frontier town and drawing on the mythology of the Wild West and on the biblical Sodom and Gomorrah story, *Mahagonny* was intended as an allegory of exploitation and hedonism as well as an indictment of a capitalist world that was doomed to end in flaming destruction.

mahākāvya \mə-'hä-ˌkäv-yə\ [Sanskrit *mahākāvyaṃ,* literally, great kāvya] Form of the Sanskrit literary style known as KAVYA. It is a short epic similar to the epyllion and is characterized by elaborate figures of speech.

In its classical form, a *mahākāvya* consists of a variable number of comparatively short cantos, each composed in a meter appropriate to its particular subject matter. The subject matter of the *mahākāvya* is taken from the epic. Most *mahākāvya*s display such set pieces as descriptions of cities, oceans, mountains, the seasons, the rising of the Sun and Moon, games, festivals, weddings, embassies, councils, wars, and triumphs. It is typical of the genre that, while each strophe is intended to be part of a narrative sequence, it more often stands by itself. Traditionally there are several model *mahākāvya*s, including two by Kālidāsa and one each by Bhāravi, Māgha, and Śrīharṣa. The *Bhaṭṭikāvya,* a poem by Bhaṭṭi (probably 6th or 7th century), is sometimes added to the list of model *mahākāvya*s. It illustrates in stanza after stanza the principal rules of Sanskrit grammar and poetics. The *mahākāvya* has been used by modern poets to commemorate such noteworthy individuals as Mahatma Gandhi and Jawaharlal Nehru.

Mahfouz \mä-'füz\, Naguib, *also spelled* Najīb Maḥfūẓ (b. Dec. 11, 1911, Cairo, Egypt) Egyptian writer who was awarded the Nobel Prize for Literature in 1988 and was the first Arabic writer to be so honored.

Mahfouz' early novels, such as *Rādūbīs* (1943; "Radobis"), were historical fiction, but he had turned to describing modern Egyptian society by the time he began his major work, *Al-Thulāthiyya* (1956–57), known as "The Cairo Trilogy." Its three novels—individually titled with the street names *Bayn al-Qaṣrayn* (*Palace Walk*), *Qaṣr al-Shawq* (*Palace of Desire*), and *Al-Sukkari-yah* (*Sukkariyah*)—depict the lives of three generations in Cairo from World War I until after the overthrow of King Farouk I. The trilogy provides a penetrating overview of 20th-century Egyptian thought, attitudes, and social change.

In subsequent works Mahfouz offered critical views of the old Egyptian monarchy, British colonialism, and contemporary Egypt. Several of his more notable novels deal with social issues involving women and political prisoners. His novel *Awlād Ḥāratinā* (1959; *Children of Gebelawi*) was banned in Egypt for a time. His other better-known novels include *Zuqāq al-Midaqq* (1947; *Midaq Alley*), *Bidāya wa Nihāya* (1951; *The Beginning and the End*), *Al-Liṣṣ wa-al-Kilāb* (1961; *The Thief and the Dogs*), *Al-Shaḥḥādh* (1965; *The Beggar*), and *Mīrāmār* (1967; *Miramar*). Mahfouz wrote some 40 novels and short-story collections, as well as more than 30 screenplays and several stage plays.

Maigret, Inspector Jules \zhᴜᴇl-mä-'gre\ Fictional character, an unassuming, compassionate, and streetwise Parisian police commissioner who is the protagonist of more than 80 novels by Georges SIMENON. Simenon's books featuring Maigret include *Pietr-le-Letton* (1931; *The Case of Peter the Lett*), *Le Chien jaune* (1931; *A Face For a Clue*), *Le Fou de Bergerac* (1932; *The Madman of Bergerac*), *Un Noël de Maigret* (1951; *Maigret's Christmas*), *Maigret aux assises* (1960; *Maigret in Court*), and *Maigret et Monsieur Charles* (1972).

Mailáth \'mòi-ˌlät\, János, Count (Gróf) (b. Oct. 5, 1786, Pest, Hungary, Holy Roman Empire [now Budapest, Hung.]—d. Jan. 3, 1855, Lake Starnberg, near Munich [Germany]) Hungarian writer and historian, who interpreted Magyar (Hungarian) culture to the Germans and who wrote a sympathetic account of the Habsburg monarchy (one of the principal sovereign dynasties of Europe from the 15th to the 20th century).

Mailáth edited two important collections of medieval German poetry (1818 and 1819) and wrote some German verse

of his own (1824) before producing his German translations of Hungarian poems (1825 and 1829). Writing in German, he brought out a number of major works, including his *Magyarische Sagen und Märchen* (1825; "Magyar Legends, and Fables") and his five-volume history of the Magyars (also in German, 1828–31). There followed other works on special aspects of Hungarian history and also the perceptive five-volume *Geschichte des oesterreichischen Kaiserstaats* (1834–50; "History of the Austrian Empire").

Mailer \'mā-lər\, Norman (b. Jan. 31, 1923, Long Branch, N.J., U.S.) American novelist who successfully developed a form of journalism that conveys actual events with the subjective richness and imaginative complexity of the novel.

Mailer graduated from Harvard University and was drafted into the army. After his service, he enrolled at the Sorbonne, where he wrote the extraordinarily successful novel THE NAKED AND THE DEAD (1948).

Mailer's second and third novels, *Barbary Shore* (1951) and *The Deer Park* (1955), were greeted with critical hostility and mixed reviews, respectively. His next important work was a long essay, *The White Negro* (1957), a sympathetic study of a marginal social type—the "hipster."

In 1959, Mailer made a bid for attention with *Advertisements for Myself;* the miscellany's naked self-revelation won the admiration of a younger generation. Mailer's subsequent novels, though not critical successes, were widely read as guides to life. *An American Dream* (1965) is about a man who murders his wife, and *Why Are We in Vietnam?* (1967) is about a young man on an Alaskan hunting trip.

A controversial figure whose egotism and belligerence often antagonized both critics and readers, Mailer did not command the same respect for his fiction that he received for his journalism. *The Armies of the Night* (1968), for example, was based on the Washington peace demonstrations of October 1967, during which Mailer was jailed and fined. A similar treatment was given to the Republican and Democratic presidential conventions in *Miami and the Siege of Chicago* (1968) and to the Moon exploration in *Of a Fire on the Moon* (1970).

Among his other works are his essay collections *The Presidential Papers* (1963) and *Cannibals and Christians* (1966); *The Executioner's Song* (1979), a "nonfiction novel" based on the life of convicted murderer Gary Gilmore; *Ancient Evenings* (1983), the first volume of a projected trilogy about Egypt; *Tough Guys Don't Dance* (1984), a contemporary mystery thriller; and the extremely lengthy *Harlot's Ghost* (1991).

Mainard *see* MAYNARD.

Maine Woods, The \'mān\ Collection of three autobiographical narratives by Henry David THOREAU. Each of the essays recounts the details of an excursion in Maine. The collection, edited by Thoreau's friend and frequent touring companion, William Ellery Channing, was issued posthumously in 1864.

The three essays are "Ktaadn and the Maine Woods," "Chesuncook," and "The Allegash and East Branch." The essays describe Thoreau's guides and include detailed studies of the flora, fauna, and history of each geographic area.

Main Street Novel by Sinclair LEWIS, published in 1920. The story of *Main Street* is seen through the eyes of Carol Kennicott, a young woman married to a Midwestern doctor who settles in the Minnesota town of Gopher Prairie (modeled on Lewis' hometown of Sauk Center). The power of the book derives from Lewis' careful rendering of local speech, customs, and social amenities. The satire is double-edged—directed against both the townspeople and the superficial intellectualism of those who despise them.

Mairet \me-'re\, Jean (b. May 10, 1604, Besançon, Fr.—d. Jan. 31, 1686, Besançon)   Classical French dramatist, the forerunner and rival of Pierre Corneille.

Mairet worked chiefly in Paris, where he secured important patrons. Their support enabled him to launch a series of plays catering to the growing enthusiasm for classical, or "regular," drama, which observed rules of place and time and a new standard of verisimilitude and decency. Mairet imitated the *Astrée* of Honoré d'Urfé in his early pastoral plays: *Chryséide et Arimand* (1625), *Sylvie* (1626), and *La Sylvanire; ou, la morte vivre* (1630; "The Wood Nymph; or, The Living Corpse"). These works, with the comedy *Les Galanteries du duc d'Osonne* (1632; "The Gallantries of the Duke of Osonne"), renewed conventional themes by dramatic skill and witty writing. Mairet had even greater success in applying the techniques of classical drama to tragedy: *Virginie* (1633), *Sophonisbe* (1634), *Le Marc-Antoine; ou, la Cleopatre* (1635; "Mark Antony; or, Cleopatra"), *Le Grand et dernier Solyman* (1637; "The Last Great Solomon").

Maironis \mī-'rō-nis\, *pseudonym of* Jonas Mačiulis \mä-'chū-lis\ (b. Nov. 2, 1862, Pasandravys, Lithuania, Russian Empire—d. June 28, 1932, Kaunas)   Poet considered to be the bard of the Lithuanian national renaissance.

In his poetry Maironis expressed the hopes and aspirations of the Lithuanian people at the time of their struggle for independence. He succeeded in replacing the traditional Lithuanian syllabic verse with accentual-syllabic verse, and his sonorous, melodic poetry achieved wide popularity in his lifetime.

All of Maironis' lyric poetry was published in the collection *Pavasario balsai* (1st ed., with 45 poems, 1895; 6th ed., with 131 poems, 1926; "Voices of Spring"). *Jaunoji Lietuva* (1907; "Young Lithuania"), has passages of great lyric beauty. Maironis also wrote three historical dramas on the life of Vytautas the Great (1350–1430), grand duke of Lithuania.

Maitland \'māt-lənd\, Sir Richard, Lord Lethington (b. 1496—d. March 20, 1586)   Scottish poet, lawyer, statesman, and compiler of one of the earliest and most important collections of Scottish poetry.

Maitland's poems reflect the troubled condition of Scotland in the 16th century. Usually dealing with social and political themes, they are either satirical or written with the meditative seriousness of a man who loves his country and who distrusts his more fanatical and intolerant contemporaries. They frequently have a laconic strength and a rhythmic expressiveness. Maitland included his own poems in his valuable collection of Scottish poetry known as the Maitland Folio (begun about 1570), and his daughter added others while she compiled the smaller anthology called the Maitland Quarto (1586). The 183 leaves of the folio and the 138 leaves of the quarto also contain a selection of works by Robert Henryson, William Dunbar, Gawin Douglas, and other important poets of the period.

Máj circle \'mī\   Group of young Czech writers of the mid-19th century whose aim was to create a new Czech literature that would reflect their liberalism and practical nationalism. They published in an almanac called *Máj* (1858; "May") after the lyrical epic poem of the same name by Karel Hynek Mácha, whom the group regarded as the forerunner of their literary revolution. Prominent members of the group were Vítězslav Hálek, Jan Neruda, and Karolina Světlá (Johanna Mužáková).

Major, Major Major \'mā-jər-'mā-jər\   Commander of the 256th Squadron of the U.S. Air Force in Joseph Heller's novel CATCH-22. Major's name was a practical joke by his father; he was promoted by a computer.

Major Barbara \'bär-brə, -bə-rə\   Social satire in three acts by George Bernard SHAW, performed in 1905 and published in 1907, in which Shaw mocked religious hypocrisy and the complicity of society in its own ills.

A major in the Salvation Army, Barbara Undershaft is estranged from her wealthy father, Andrew Undershaft, a munitions manufacturer. Although the Salvation Army condemns war, it gladly accepts a donation of £5,000 from her warmonger father, and she resigns in protest. The Army offers the poor only salvation, while Undershaft takes steps toward eradicating poverty. Barbara later comes to accept her father's views on capitalism and to believe that the greatest evil is the degradation caused by grinding poverty.

makar or **maker** \'māk-ər, 'māk-\ [Middle English (Scots), author, poet, literally, maker] *plural* makaris *or* makeris \-ə-riz\, *also called* Scottish Chaucerian \chō-'sir-ē-ən\ *or* courtly makar.   Any of the Scottish courtly poets who flourished from about 1425 to 1550. The best known are Robert Henryson, William Dunbar, Gawin Douglas, and Sir David Lyndsay; the group is sometimes expanded to include James I of Scotland and Harry the Minstrel (Blind Harry). Because Geoffrey Chaucer was their acknowledged master and they often employed his verse forms and themes, they are usually called "Scottish Chaucerians," but they actually are a product of more than one tradition. Chaucerian influence is apparent in their courtly romances and dream allegories, yet even these display a distinctive "aureate" style, a language richly ornamented by polysyllabic Latinate words.

In addition, the makaris used different styles for different types of poems. The language they used in their poems ranges from courtly aureate English, to mixtures of English and Scots, to the broadest Scots vernacular. The poetry itself might take the form of moral allegory, everyday realism, flyting (a dispute in verse between two characters), or grotesquely comic Celtic fantasy.

Spelled *maker*, the word has also been used more generally as a synonym of *poet*, but it is now archaic in this sense.

Making of Americans, The   Novel by Gertrude STEIN, completed in 1911. Considered to be one of Stein's major works, the novel was not published in book form until 1925 because of its lengthiness and experimental style. *The Making of Americans* lacks plot, dialogue, and action. Subtitled *Being a History of a Family's Progress*, the work is ostensibly a history of three generations of Stein's forebears. By generalizing from her own family, Stein claimed that the book was the history of all Americans. Fitting her prose to the sameness or very slight variations she found in human nature, Stein produced what many readers found to be a repetitious, prolix compilation of vignettes.

Makioka Sisters, The \,mä-kē-'ō-kä\   Novel by TANIZAKI Jun'ichirō, originally published as *Sasameyuki* ("A Light Snowfall"). The work is often considered to be Tanizaki's masterpiece. Serialization of the novel began in 1943 but was suspended by the military government; publication of the complete work was delayed until 1948.

The chief concern of the four Makioka sisters is finding a suitable husband for the third sister, Yukiko, a woman of traditional beliefs who has rejected several suitors. Until Yukiko marries, Taeko, the youngest, most independent, and most Westernized of the sisters, must remain unmarried. More important than the plot of *The Makioka Sisters* is its evocation of middle-class daily life in prewar Ōsaka—Tanizaki's detailed account recalls even the shops and bus routes of the 1930s. Despite the nostalgia, the inescapable influence of the West is felt along with the change from traditional attitudes and lifestyles.

Malade imaginaire, Le   *see* THE IMAGINARY INVALID.

Malamud \\'mal-ə-,məd\\, Bernard (b. April 26, 1914, Brooklyn, N.Y., U.S.—d. March 18, 1986, New York, N.Y.) American novelist and short-story writer who made parables out of Jewish immigrant life.

A son of Russian Jews, Malamud was educated at the City College of New York and Columbia University. His first novel, THE NATURAL (1952), is a fable about a baseball hero who is gifted with miraculous powers. THE ASSISTANT (1957) is about a young Gentile hoodlum and an old Jewish grocer. THE FIXER (1966) won a Pulitzer Prize. His other novels are *A New Life* (1961), *The Tenants* (1971), *Dubin's Lives* (1979), and *God's Grace* (1982).

Malamud's genius is most apparent in his short stories. Though the stories are told in spare, compressed prose, they include bursts of emotional, metaphorical language. Grim city neighborhoods are visited by magical events, and their hardworking residents have glimpses of love and self-sacrifice. Malamud's short-story collections are THE MAGIC BARREL (1958), *Idiots First* (1963), *Pictures of Fidelman* (1969), and *Rembrandt's Hat* (1973).

Malaparte \\mä-lä-'pär-tä\\, Curzio, *pseudonym of* Kurt Erich Suckert \\'sü-kert\\ (b. June 9, 1898, Prato, Italy—d. July 19, 1957, Rome) Journalist, dramatist, short-story writer, and novelist, one of the most powerful Italian writers of the mid-20th century.

In 1924 Malaparte founded the Roman periodical *La Conquista dello stato*, and in 1926 he joined Massimo Bontempelli in founding *900*, an influential, cosmopolitan literary quarterly. He later became coeditor of *Fiera Letteraria*, then editor of *La Stampa* in Turin.

An early convert to fascism, he voiced his political views in his own literary magazine, *Prospettive* (1937), and in many articles written for fascist periodicals. His early fiction—*Avventure di un capitano di Sventura* (1927); *Sodoma e Gomorra* (1931); and *Sangue* (1937)—also showed a fascist slant.

During the 1940s Malaparte repudiated fascism and was expelled from the party. During World War II he worked with the Allied armies. His reports from the Russian front were published as *Il Volga nasce in Europa* (1943; *The Volga Rises in Europe*). He then acquired an international reputation with two passionately written, brilliantly realistic war novels: *Kaputt* (1944) and *La pelle* (1949; *The Skin*).

While continuing to write articles and fiction, Malaparte wrote three realistic dramas, based on the lives of Marcel Proust (*Du côté de chez Proust*, performed 1948) and Karl Marx (*Das Kapital*, performed 1949) and on life in Vienna during the Soviet occupation (*Anche le donne hanno perso la guerra*, performed 1954; "The Women Lost the War Too"). He also wrote a screenplay and published a volume entitled *Racconti italiani* (1957; "Italian Tales").

malapropism \\'mal-ə-,präp-,iz-əm\\ Verbal blunder in which one word is replaced by another similar in sound but different in meaning. The term derives from Richard Brinsley Sheridan's character Mrs. Malaprop, in his play *The Rivals* (1775). Her name is taken from the term *malapropos* (French: "inappropriate") and is typical of Sheridan's practice of concocting names to indicate the essence of a character. Thinking of the geography of contiguous countries, she spoke of the "geometry" of "contagious countries," and she hoped that her daughter might "reprehend" the true meaning of what she was saying.

Mālavikāgnimitra \\'mä-lə-vē-'kãg-nē-'mit-rə\\ ("Mālavikā and Agnimitra") Five-act drama, probably the first of the plays written by KĀLIDĀSA in the 5th century AD. The story is a light tale set in a harem and, unlike Kālidāsa's other works,

sustains a playful and comical mood throughout. It concerns the machinations of King Agnimitra to obtain the hand of Mālavikā, a female dance student with whom he is in love.

Malcolm \\'mal-kəm\\ Fictional character, a son of Duncan, the king of Scotland who is murdered by Macbeth in William Shakespeare's MACBETH.

Malczewski \\mäl-'chef-skʸē\\, Antoni (b. June 3, 1793, Warsaw [Poland], or Knyaginino, near Dubna, Ukraine, Russian Empire—d. May 2, 1826, Warsaw) Polish Romantic poet.

Malczewski served in the Napoleonic Polish army of the duchy of Warsaw. He was demobilized in 1815 and traveled in western Europe before settling in Ukraine. There he became involved with a woman from a neighboring town. Compelled by social pressure, they left and settled in Warsaw, where in 1825 he published *Maria*, a long poem that constitutes his only contribution to Polish poetry. In the poem, Wacław, a young husband, goes to fight the Tatars. After routing the raiders, he hurries home to his wife, Maria, but finds her dead. Its Byronic hero, as well as its picture of Ukraine as a land of somber charm, assured Malczewski both popularity and a high position in Polish literature.

Malherbe \\mä-'lerb\\, Daniel François (b. May 28, 1881, Paarl, Cape Colony [now in South Africa]—d. April 12, 1969, Bloemfontein, Orange Free State) South African novelist, poet, and dramatist whose work helped establish Afrikaans as the cultural language of South Africa. He published many volumes of poetry and drama but is known primarily as a novelist for such works as *Vergeet nil* (1913; "Don't Forget"), an extremely popular novel about the South African (Boer) War; *Die Meulenaar* (1936; "The Miller"); and *Saul* (1933–37), a biblical trilogy. He also wrote *En die wawiele rol* (1945; "And the Wagon Wheels Roll On"), which describes the Great Trek, the mass emigration of Afrikaners from Cape Colony (1835–40) that was a central event in the history of South African nationhood.

Malherbe \\mä-'lerb\\, François de (b. 1555, in or near Caen, Fr.—d. Oct. 16, 1628, Paris) French poet and theoretician whose insistence upon strict form, restraint, and purity of diction prepared the way for French classicism.

Malherbe received a Protestant education but converted to Roman Catholicism. In 1577 he went to Provence as secretary to the governor, Henri d'Angoulême. His first published poem was *Les Larmes de Saint Pierre* (1587; "The Tears of St. Peter"), a florid imitation of Luigi Tansillo's *Lagrime di San Pietro*. In 1600 his ode to the new queen, Marie de Médicis, made his name more widely known.

In 1605 Malherbe went to Paris, where he attained the position of court poet and a modest living from court patronage. He gathered a group of disciples, and much of his critical influence was exercised in the form of sharp verbal thrusts, some of them preserved in the pages devoted to him in Gédéon Tallemant des Réaux's *Historiettes* (*c.* 1659; published 1834–35).

Malherbe's prose writings consist of translations of Livy and Seneca; some 200 letters, of interest for their picture of court life; and his commentary on the works of the poet Philippe Desportes. These notes reveal Malherbe's convictions regarding the necessity for verbal harmony, propriety, and intelligibility and, above all, his conception of the poet as craftsman rather than prophet.

Mallarmé \\mä-lär-'mä\\, Stéphane (b. March 18, 1842, Paris, Fr.—d. Sept. 9, 1898, Valvins, near Fontainebleau) French poet, an originator (with Paul Verlaine) and a leader of the Symbolist movement in poetry.

Mallarmé's early poems, which he began contributing to magazines in 1862, were influenced by those of Charles Baudelaire, who was largely concerned with the subject of escape from reality, a theme that also came to haunt Mallarmé. Although Baudelaire's escapism had been essen-

Archives Photographiques

tially emotional and sensual, Mallarmé's was of a much more intellectual bent. His determination to analyze the nature of the ideal world and its relationship to reality is reflected in the two dramatic poems he began to write in 1864 and 1865, respectively, *Hérodiade* (1869; "Herodias") and *L'Après-midi d'un faune* (1876; "The Afternoon of a Faun").

By 1868 Mallarmé had concluded that, although nothing lies beyond reality, within this nothingness lie the essences of perfect forms; it was the poet's task to perceive and crystallize these essences. Mallarmé devoted himself during the rest of his life to putting his theories into practice in what he called his "Grand oeuvre" ("Great Work"), or "Le Livre" ("The Book"). He never came near to completing this work, but he did complete a number of poems related to the projected "Grand oeuvre," both in their themes and in their extremely evocative use of language. Among these are several elegies, the principal ones being to Baudelaire, Edgar Allan Poe, Richard Wagner, Théophile Gautier, and Verlaine, that Mallarmé was commissioned to write at various times in his career. Mallarmé also wrote about poetry itself, reflecting evocatively on his aims and achievements. A third category of subject matter runs counter to his obsession with the ideal world; this consists of the dozen or so sonnets he addressed to his mistress.

A number of Mallarmé's poems appeared in two volumes (1866; 1871 [dated 1869]) of the anthology *Le Parnasse contemporain*. His work also was published in *Poésies* (1887), a collection of 35 poems selected by Mallarmé; in *Album de vers et de prose* (1887), a selection of nine poems from *Poésies*; in the book *Vers et prose* (1893), an expansion of the above to include 21 poems; and in a second edition of *Poésies* (1899), to which Mallarmé had added about 12 poems and which was published six months after his death.

Mallea \mä-'yä-ä, -'zhä-\, Eduardo (b. Aug. 14, 1903, Bahía Blanca, Arg.—d. Nov. 12, 1982, Buenos Aires) Argentine novelist, essayist, and short-story writer whose psychological novels won critical acclaim.

Mallea began as a short-story writer, first achieving recognition with *Cuentos para una inglesa desesperada* (1926; "Stories for a Desperate Englishwoman"). In 1931 he became editor of the weekly literary magazine of the Buenos Aires newspaper *La nación*. Soon, however, he found the novel a more suitable vehicle for psychological analysis of character and philosophical digression. Often set in Argentina, Mallea's novels were also concerned with national and regional problems, as in *La bahía de silencio* (1940; *The Bay of Silence*) and *Las águilas* (1943; "The Eagles"). In *Todo verdor perecerá* (1941; *All Green Shall Perish*), which many consider his greatest work, he explored the anguish of a woman living in the provinces.

Mallea also wrote several volumes of travel books and essays. His final works were published in the early 1970s.

Mallet-Joris \mȧ-le-yō-'rē\, Françoise, *original name* Françoise-Eugénie-Julienne Lilar \lē-'lȧr\ (b. July 6, 1930, Antwerp, Belg.) Belgian author, a leading contemporary exponent of the traditional French novel of psychological love analysis.

At age 20 Mallet-Joris won unanimous critical approval with her novel *Le Rempart des béguines* (1951; U.S. title, *The Illusionist*; U.K. title, *Into the Labyrinth*), the story of an affair between a girl and her father's mistress, described with clinical detachment in sober, classical prose. This was followed by another novel, *La Chambre rouge* (1953; *The Red Room*), and a book of short stories, *Cordélia* (1956; *Cordelia and Other Stories*). With *Les Mensonges* (1956; *House of Lies*), however, Mallet-Joris's style began to change.

She turned to the historical novel with *Les Personnages* (1960; *The Favourite*), about the intrigues wrought by Cardinal de Richelieu around the love life of King Louis XIII, and with *Marie Mancini le premier amour de Louis XIV* (1964; *The Uncompromising Heart: A Life of Marie Mancini, Louis XIV's First Love*). Bluntly candid about herself, Mallet-Joris told of her personal life, her inner conflicts, and her religious quests in her autobiographical writings, *Lettre à moi-même* (1963; *A Letter to Myself*) and *La Maison de papier* (1970; *The Paper House*). Among her later novels are *Le Jeu de souterrain* (1973; *The Underground Game*), *Allegra* (1976), *Dickie-Roi* (1979; "King Dickie"), *Le Clin d'oeil de l'ange* (1983; "The Angel's Wink"), *Le Rire de Laura* (1985; "Laura's Laughter"), *La Tristesse du cerf-volant* (1988; "The Sadness of the Kite"), and *Divine* (1991). She also wrote a biography of Jeanne Guyon (1978), the 17th-century French mystic.

Malleus maleficarum \'mal-ē-əs-,mal-ə-fi-'kä-rəm, 'mä-lā-u̇s-,mä-lā-fē-'kä-rùm\ ("The Hammer of Witches") Detailed legal and theological document (*c.* 1486) regarded as the standard handbook on witchcraft, including its detection and its extirpation, until well into the 18th century. Its appearance did much to spur on and sustain some two centuries of witch-hunting hysteria in Europe. The *Malleus*, authorized by the pope, was the work of two Dominicans: Johann Sprenger, a German, and Heinrich (Institoris) Kraemer, inquisitor in the Tirol region of Austria.

The *Malleus* codified the folklore and beliefs of the Alpine peasants and was dedicated to the implementation of Exodus 22:18: "You shall not permit a sorceress to live." The work is divided into three parts. In Part I the reality and the depravity of witches is emphasized, and any disbelief in demonology is condemned as heresy. Part II is a compendium of fabulous stories about the activities of witches—*e.g.*, diabolic compacts, sexual relations with devils (incubi and succubi), transvection (night riding), and metamorphosis. Part III is a discussion of the legal procedures to be followed in witch trials. Torture is sanctioned as a means of securing confessions.

The *Malleus* went through 28 editions between 1486 and 1600 and was accepted by Roman Catholics and Protestants alike as an authoritative source of information concerning satanism and as a guide to Christian defense.

Malley, Ern \'ȯrn-'mal-ē\ Fictional author, the central figure of a memorable 20th-century Australian literary hoax. *See* ERN MALLEY HOAX.

Malone \mə-'lōn\, Dumas (b. Jan. 10, 1892, Coldwater, Miss., U.S.—d. Dec. 27, 1986, Charlottesville, Va.) American historian, editor, and the author of an authoritative multivolume biography of Thomas Jefferson.

Malone taught at Yale, Columbia, and the University of Virginia, where he was the Thomas Jefferson Foundation Professor of History. He edited the *Dictionary of American Biography* from 1929 to 1936 and the *Political Science Quarterly* from

1953 to 1958, and he served as director of the Harvard University Press from 1936 to 1943. Malone's masterwork is *Jefferson and His Time*, consisting of *Jefferson the Virginian* (1948), *Jefferson and the Rights of Man* (1951), *Jefferson and the Ordeal of Liberty* (1962), *Jefferson the President: First Term, 1801–1805* (1970), *Jefferson the President: Second Term, 1805–1809* (1974), and *The Sage of Monticello* (1981).

Malone's other writings include *The Public Life of Thomas Cooper* (1926), *Saints in Action* (1939), and *Empire for Liberty*, 2 vol. (1960, with Basil Rauch).

Malone \mə-'lōn\, Edmond (b. Oct. 4, 1741, Dublin, Ire.—d. 1812, London, Eng.)   Irish-born English scholar, editor, and pioneer in efforts to establish an authentic text and chronology of William Shakespeare's works.

After practicing in Ireland as a lawyer and journalist, Malone settled in London in 1777. There he had a wide circle of prominent friends, including Sir Joshua Reynolds, who painted his portrait and whose literary works Malone collected and published (1797).

Malone's "An Attempt to Ascertain the Order in Which the Plays of Shakespeare Were Written" (1778), the first such chronology, and his three supplemental volumes (1780–83) to the Johnson-Steevens edition of Shakespeare, containing apocryphal plays, textual emendations, and the first critical edition of the sonnets, are landmarks in Shakespearean studies. His essay on the Elizabethan stage was the first treatise on English drama based on original sources. His own edition of Shakespeare in 11 volumes appeared in 1790. A new octavo edition, unfinished at his death, was completed by James Boswell, son of Samuel Johnson's biographer, and published in 1821 in 21 volumes.

Malone Dies \mə-'lōn\   Novel by Samuel BECKETT, originally written in French as *Malone meurt* (1951) and translated by the author into English. It is the second narrative in the trilogy that began with MOLLOY and concluded with THE UNNAMABLE. The novel's narrator, Malone, is dying. He spends his time writing an inventory of his meager possessions, a description of his condition, and stories about a character who is clearly an aspect of himself. Malone's struggles to tell his character's story can be viewed as a satire on the creative process as well as an attempt to understand the essence of the self.

Malory \'mal-ə-rē\, Sir Thomas (fl. *c.* 1470)   English writer famous as the author of LE MORTE DARTHUR, the first prose account in English of the rise and fall of King Arthur and the fellowship of the Round Table.

Even in the 16th century Malory's identity was unknown, although he was thought to be a Welshman. In the colophon to *Le Morte Darthur*, the author says that he finished the work in the ninth year of the reign of Edward IV (*i.e.*, March 4, 1469–March 3, 1470) and adds a prayer for "good delyueraunce" from prison. A "Thomas Malorie (or Malarie), knight" was excluded from four general pardons granted by Edward IV in 1468 and 1470. This person is tentatively accepted as the author.

Malouf \mə-'lüf\, David (George Joseph) (b. March 20, 1934, Brisbane, Queen., Australia)   Australian poet and novelist of Lebanese and English descent whose work reflected his ethnic background as well as his Queensland childhood and youth.

Malouf's volumes of poetry include *Bicycle and Other Poems* (1970; U.S. title, *The Year of the Foxes and Other Poems*), *Neighbours in a Thicket* (1974), *Wild Lemons* (1980), and *First Things Last* (1980). Malouf also wrote the libretto for Richard Meale's opera *Voss*, based on the novel by Patrick White.

Malouf's first novel was the autobiographical *Johnno* (1975), set in Brisbane during World War II. *An Imaginary Life* (1978)

recreates the final years of the Roman poet Ovid. *Child's Play* (1981) concerns the metaphysical relationship between a professional assassin and his intended victim. *Fly Away Peter* (1982) is a novella set in Queensland just before World War I. Malouf's later novels include *Harland's Half Acre* (1984), *12 Edmondstone Street* (1985), and *Remembering Babylon* (1993).

Malraux \mål-'rō\, André(-Georges) (b. Nov. 3, 1901, Paris, Fr.—d. Nov. 23, 1976, Paris)   French novelist, art historian, and statesman.

At the age of 21 Malraux went to Cambodia, where he was imprisoned for taking bas-reliefs from a Khmer temple. Mistreatment by the French colonial authorities turned him into a fervent anticolonialist and an advocate of social change. His novel *L'Espoir* (1937; U.K. title, *Days of Hope*; U.S. title, *Man's Hope*), is based on his experience fighting for the Republicans in the Spanish Civil War (1936–39). During World War II, Malraux served in a French tank unit. He was captured but escaped and joined the Resistance, and later, on the Alsatian front, he met General Charles de Gaulle. When de Gaulle came to power in France in 1958, he appointed Malraux minister of cultural affairs, a post he held for 10 years.

Malraux wrote several brilliant and powerful novels, including *Les Conquérants* (1928; *The Conquerors*), a tense and vivid description of a revolutionary strike in Canton. *La Voie royale* (1930; *The Royal Way*) is a thriller set among the Khmer temples of Cambodia. Malraux's masterpiece is *La Condition humaine* (1933; U.K. title, *Man's Estate*; U.S. title, *Man's Fate*), set in Shanghai during the short-lived victory of Chiang Kai-shek and the Nationalists over their former communist allies.

After 1945 Malraux virtually abandoned novel writing for art history and criticism. His major work of this period was *Les Voix du silence* (1951; *The Voices of Silence*), a brilliant and well-documented synthesis of the history of art in all countries and through all ages. He published his autobiography, *Antimémoires* (*Anti-memoirs*), in 1967.

Maltese Falcon, The   Mystery novel by Dashiell HAMMETT, generally considered his finest work. It originally appeared as a serial in *Black Mask* magazine in 1929 and was published in book form the next year.

The novel's sustained tension is created by vivid scenes and by the pace and spareness of the author's style. The other major attraction of *The Maltese Falcon* is its colorful cast of characters; they include the antiheroic detective Sam SPADE; Brigid O'Shaughnessy, a deceptive beauty; Joel Cairo, an effete Levantine whose gun gives him courage; the very fat and jovial but sinister Casper Gutman; and Gutman's "gunsel" Wilmer, eager to be feared. All of them are looking for the Maltese falcon, a fabulously valuable 16th-century artifact.

Malvolio \mal-'vō-lē-ō\   Fictional character, an ambitious steward in William Shakespeare's comedy TWELFTH NIGHT.

Mamet \'mam-it\, David (Alan) (b. Nov. 30, 1947, Chicago, Ill., U.S.)   Playwright, director, and screenwriter noted for his often desperate working-class characters and for his distinctive and colloquial dialogue that is frequently profane.

Mamet began writing plays at Goddard College, Plainfield, Vt. Returning to Chicago, he worked at various factory jobs, at a real estate agency, and as a taxi driver; all these experiences provided background for his plays. In 1973 he cofounded a theater company in Chicago.

Mamet's plays include *Duck Variations* (produced 1972), *Sexual Perversity in Chicago* (produced 1974; filmed as *About Last Night . . .* [1986]), AMERICAN BUFFALO (1976), *A Life in the Theatre* (1977), *The Water Engine* (1978), and *Speed-the-Plow* (1987). GLENGARRY GLEN ROSS (1983; film, 1992) won the 1984 Pulitzer Prize for drama.

Mamet wrote fiction, plays for children, and a number of screenplays. He both wrote and directed the motion pictures *House of Games* (1987) and *Homicide* (1991).

Mammeri \mȧm-ʾrē\, Mouloud (b. Dec. 28, 1917, Taourirt-Mimoun, Alg.—d. Feb. 26, 1989, near Algiers) Kabyle novelist, playwright, and translator who depicted the changing realities of modern-day Algeria.

In his first novel, *La Colline oubliée* (1952; "The Forgotten Hill"), Mammeri records a story of village youths who are stifled under the burden of traditional native customs. With *Le Sommeil du juste* (1955; "The Sleep of the Just"), the scene shifts to the larger world and to the confrontation between Berber and French culture. In *L'Opium et le bâton* (1965; "Opium and the Stick"), Mammeri constructed a story of the Algerian War of Independence, attempting to give the struggle meaning in terms of the essential problem of freedom. His later works include a play, *Le Banquet* (1973), which deals with the destruction of the Aztecs, and *La Traversée* (1982; "The Crossing"), a novel that centers on an alienated journalist's attempt to return to his Berber roots.

mana \ʾmä-nä\ [Maori & Hawaiian] Impersonal supernatural force or power that may be concentrated in objects or persons and that may be inherited, acquired, or conferred. Mana is a central concept of Polynesian mythology.

The term used by Polynesians and Melanesians was appropriated by 19th-century Western anthropologists and applied to that which affected the common processes of nature. Mana was conceptually linked to North American Indian terms that conveyed the same or similar notions—*e.g.*, orenda of the Iroquois, wakan of the Dakota (Sioux), and manitou of the Algonquian. Mana usually issues from persons or is used by them, and the concept of a supernatural sphere as distinct or separate from a natural sphere is seldom recognized by preliterate peoples.

Man and Superman Play in four acts by George Bernard SHAW, published in 1903 and performed (without scene 2 of Act III) in 1905; the first complete performance was in 1915. Basic to *Man and Superman*, which Shaw subtitled *A Comedy and A Philosophy*, is his belief in the conflict between man as spiritual creator and woman as guardian of the biological continuity of the human race. The play incorporates Shaw's concept of the "life force" and satirizes the relationship between the sexes.

The third act is a dream episode entitled "Don Juan in Hell." Based on the Don Juan legend, the act takes the form of a theatrical reading and is often presented independently.

Mānasī \ʾmä-nə-ˌsē\ ("Mind's Creation") Collection of poems by Rabindranath TAGORE, first published in 1890.

Although this collection marked the maturation of Tagore's poetic genius, it nevertheless contains themes of youthful romanticism. Whether addressing nature or love, the work emphasizes duality: the primitive is contrasted with the domesticated, the body with the soul.

Manchild in the Promised Land Autobiographical novel by Claude Brown, published in 1965. The work was noted for its realistic depiction of desperate poverty in Harlem.

Brown's tale of heroin addicts, pimps, and small-time criminals in New York slums shocked readers who were unfamiliar with ghetto life. The autobiographical hero, Sonny, narrates the story of his escape from the addiction and violence that defined his childhood. Sent to the Wiltwyck School for Boys at age nine, Sonny is encouraged to pursue an education. Back home, however, he steals and sells drugs. After more time in reform school, Sonny escapes the neighborhood and immerses himself

in African and African-American culture. Brown's most vivid passages detail Sonny's return visit to Harlem, where he discovers his younger brother mired in a life of crime and both an old friend and a former sweetheart destroyed by heroin addiction.

Manciple's Tale, The One of the 24 stories in THE CANTERBURY TALES by Geoffrey Chaucer.

The Manciple, or steward, tells a story about the origin of the crow, based on the myth of Apollo and Coronis as told in Ovid's *Metamorphoses*. Phebus (Phoebus) kept a snow-white crow that could mimic any human voice. The bird witnesses Phebus' wife with her lover and informs his keeper. After killing his wife in a jealous rage, a remorseful Phebus blames the crow for his madness, plucks out its feathers, and turns the bird black, commending it to the devil. According to the legend, crows have been black ever since.

mandarin \ʾman-də-rin\ A person of position and influence, especially in intellectual or literary circles. The term is often used to refer to an elder and often traditionalist or reactionary member of such a circle.

Mandarins, The Novel by Simone de BEAUVOIR, published in French as *Les Mandarins* in 1954; it won the Prix Goncourt in 1954.

De Beauvoir's semiautobiographical novel addressed the attempts of post-World War II leftist intellectuals to abandon their elite, "mandarin" status and to engage in political activism. The characters of psychologist Anne Dubreuilh and her husband Robert were roughly based on de Beauvoir and her lifelong associate Jean-Paul Sartre; de Beauvoir's account of Anne's affair with the American Lewis Brogan was a thinly veiled account of her own relationship with novelist Nelson Algren.

Mandelshtam or **Mandelstam** \mən-dʸilʸ-ʾshtȧm\, Osip (Emilyevich) (b. Jan. 3 [Jan. 15, New Style], 1891, Warsaw, Poland, Russian Empire—d. Dec. 27, 1938, Vtoraya Rechka, near Vladivostok, Russia, U.S.S.R.) Major Russian poet and literary critic. Most of his works went unpublished in the Soviet Union during the Stalin era (1929–53) and were almost unknown outside that country until the mid-1960s.

Mandelshtam grew up in St. Petersburg in a cultured, middle-class Jewish household. His first poems appeared in the avant-garde journal *Apollon* ("Apollo") in 1910. He was one of the foremost members of the ACMEIST school of poetry, which rejected the mysticism and abstraction of Russian Symbolism. Mandelshtam summed up his poetic credo in his manifesto *Utro Akmeizma* ("The Morning of Acmeism"). In 1913 his first slim volume of verse, *Kamen* ("Stone"), was published. In 1922 his second volume of poetry, *Tristia*, appeared.

Mandelshtam's poetry, which is apolitical and intellectually demanding, distanced him from the official Soviet literary establishment. He turned to children's tales and a collection of autobiographical stories, *Shum vremeni* (1925; "The Noise of Time"). In 1928 a volume of his collected poetry, *Stikhotvoreniya* ("Poems"), and a collection of literary criticism, *O poezii* ("On Poetry"), appeared.

In May 1934 he was arrested for an epigram he had written on Joseph Stalin. Shattered by a fierce interrogation, Mandelshtam was placed under internal exile. He was hospitalized and attempted to kill himself. During this period he composed a long cycle of poems, the *Voronezhskiye tetradi* ("Voronezh Notebooks"), which contain some of his finest lyrics.

In May 1937, having served his sentence, Mandelshtam returned to Moscow. The next year, however, he was arrested again. In a letter that autumn, Mandelshtam reported that he was ill in a transit camp near Vladivostok. Nothing further was ever heard from him. It was largely through the efforts of his widow, who died in 1980, that little of the poetry of Mandelshtam was lost. The two volumes of her memoirs, *Hope Against Hope* (1970) and *Hope Abandoned* (1974), were published in the West.

Mander \\'man-dər\\, Jane, *in full* Mary Jane Mander, *pseudonym* Manda Lloyd \\'lòid\\ (b. 1877, Ramarama, near Drury, Auckland, N.Z.—d. 1949, New Zealand) Writer noted for her realistic novels about her native land and her frank treatment of sexual issues.

Mander grew up on the northern New Zealand frontier and had little formal schooling. In 1912 she moved to New York City in order to study journalism at Columbia University. While in the United States she became involved in the woman suffrage movement and wrote her first three novels, all set in frontier New Zealand. The independent female protagonists of these novels are, in part, self-portraits.

The Story of a New Zealand River (1920) contrasts the life of a cultivated, educated, lonely woman who maintains strict social and moral values in a frontier settlement with that of her uninhibited daughter, who finds employment in Australia and lives with her lover. Mander's other novels include *The Passionate Puritan* (1921), *The Strange Attraction* (1922), *Allen Adair* (1925), *The Besieging City* (1926), and *Pins and Pinnacles* (1928). After 1932 her writing was limited to journalism.

Mandeville \\'män-də-,vil, *Angl* 'man-\\, Bernard de (b. November 1670, Rotterdam, Neth.—d. Jan. 21, 1733, Hackney, London, Eng.) Dutch writer and philosopher who won fame with *The Fable of the Bees*.

Mandeville graduated in medicine from the University of Leiden in 1691. He went to England to learn the language and settled in London. Mandeville's first works in English were burlesque paraphrases from the 17th-century French writers Jean de La Fontaine and Paul Scarron. The 1714 edition of Mandeville's most important work, *The Fable of the Bees*, was subtitled *Private Vices, Publick Benefits*. The 1723 edition included an examination of "The Nature of Society" and provoked a long controversy. The 1729 edition remodeled the entire argument but nevertheless retained something of the original purpose of diverting readers.

Mandeville's argument in *The Fable*, a paradoxical defense of the usefulness of "vices," is based on his definition of all actions as equally vicious in that all are motivated by self-interest; yet, the results of action are often beneficial, since they produce the wealth and comforts of civilization.

Mandeville \\'man-də-,vil\\, Sir John. Purported author of a Middle English collection of traveler's tales from around the world, *The Voyage and Travels of Sir John Mandeville, Knight*, generally known as *The Travels of Sir John Mandeville*, which are selections from the narratives of genuine travelers, embellished with Mandeville's additions and described as his own adventures. The actual author of the tales is unknown.

The book originated in French about 1356–57 and was soon translated into many languages, an English version appearing about 1375. The narrator Mandeville identifies himself as a knight of St. Albans. Incapacitated by arthritic gout, he has undertaken to stave off boredom by writing of his travels, which began on Michaelmas Day (September 29) 1322 and from which he returned in 1356.

It is not certain whether the author himself ever traveled at all, since he selected his materials almost entirely from the encyclopedias and travel books available to him. He enriched these itineraries with accounts of the history, customs, religions, and legends of the regions visited, culled from his remarkably wide reading, transforming and enlivening the originals by his literary skill and genuine creative imagination. The lands he describes include the realm of Prester John, the land of darkness, and the abode of the Ten Lost Tribes of Israel, all legendary. A considerable amount of accurate observation of far-off lands also occurs in the *Travels*, however. The book has always been popular and remains extremely readable.

Manette, Dr. Alexander and Lucie \\,al-ig-'zan-dər-mə-'net . . . 'lü-sē\\ Fictional characters, father and daughter in the novel A TALE OF TWO CITIES by Charles Dickens.

Manfalūṭī \\,mȧn-fȧ-'lü-,tē\\, Muṣṭafā Luṭfī, al- (b. Dec. 30, 1876, Manfalūṭ, Egypt—d. July 25, 1924, Cairo) Egyptian essayist, short-story writer, and pioneer of modern Arabic short prose.

Al-Manfalūṭī was born of a half-Turkish, half-Arab family. He was deeply influenced by pan-Islāmism, Egyptian nationalism, and the Syrian school of writers, who introduced him to Western, particularly French, learning.

Al-Manfalūṭī is best known for his sentimental but elegantly written short prose pieces collected in the three-volume *Al-Naẓarāt* (1910–21; "Views") and in *Al-'Abarāt* (1915; "Tears"). His easy, flowing Arabic style, free from the then-fashionable ornamentation of rhymed prose (*saj'*), formed the basis of the more accomplished modern Arabic narrative of succeeding generations of writers.

Manfred \\'man-fred, -frid\\ Dramatic poem by Lord BYRON, first published in 1817. The poem, Byron's first dramatic work, was clearly influenced by J.W. von Goethe's *Faust*.

Manfred features an archetypal Byronic hero, an outcast in a castle in the Alps. Tortured by remorse for a mysterious sin, Manfred calls on the spirits of the universe, but all deny him the oblivion he seeks. After a failed suicide attempt, he summons the Witch of the Alps and confesses to an incestuous relationship with his sister Astarte. Manfred encounters the spirits of evil, who summon his dead sister and demand his soul in exchange. Unlike Faust, however, Manfred defies the spirits, which vanish, and he then dies.

Mangan \\'maŋ-gən\\, James Clarence (b. May 1, 1803, Dublin, Ire.—d. June 20, 1849, Dublin) A prolific and uneven writer of almost every type of verse whose best work, inspired by a love of Ireland, ranks high in Anglo-Irish poetry.

At the age of 15 Mangan became a copying clerk in a scrivener's office, and he remained a clerk for 10 years. Thereafter living as best he could, he contributed to the prestigious *Dublin University Magazine* and other literary periodicals. His natural melancholy was aggravated by years of ill-paid drudgery and an acute disappointment in love. He became an opium addict and an alcoholic, and the last years of his life were spent in extreme neglect and wretchedness.

Many of Mangan's poems are "translations" from Irish, German, and various Eastern languages (which he probably did not know), often so free that he is in effect using the original as a vehicle for his own emotions. Much of his work has Irish history and legend for its theme, but in a few poems, such as "The Nameless One" and "Twenty Golden Years Ago," he achieves an extraordinary modern note of personal realism and a tragic sincerity of tone. Perhaps his best-known poem is "Dark Rosaleen."

Manganelli \\,män-gä-'nel-lē\\, Giorgio (b. Nov. 11, 1922, Milan, Italy—d. May 28, 1990, Rome) Italian critical theorist and novelist, one of the leaders of the avant-garde in the 1960s.

Manganelli first emerged as a literary innovator in 1964, both as the author of the experimental novel *Hilarotragoedia* and as a member of *Gruppo 63* (Group 63), a school of literature that stressed form over content. In 1967 he published *La letteratura come menzogna* ("Literature as a Lie"), a collection of essays that characterized popular literature as nonsocial, artificial, and nonphilosophical.

Manganelli's other essay collections include *Lunario dell'orfano sannita* (1973; "Almanac of the Sannite Orphan"), *Angosce di stile* (1981; "Anguish of Style"), and *Laboriose inezie* (1986; "Arduous Trifles"). He also wrote the travel guide *Cina e altri orienti* (1974, "China and Other Eastern Places"), as well as *Tutti gli errori* (1986; *All the Errors*), about Milan's La Scala opera house. Among his other works are *Agli dèi ulteriori* (1972; "To Farther Gods"), *A e B* (1975; "A and B"), *Centuria: cento piccoli romanzi fiume* (1979; "Centuria: One Hundred Little Stream-of-Consciousness Novels"), and *Rumori o voci* (1987; "Noises or Voices").

Mangoaela \mäŋ-'gwel-ə\, Z.D., *in full* Zakea Dolphin (b. Feb. 1883, Hohobeng, Cape Colony [now Cape Province, S.Af.]--d. Oct. 25, 1963)   Southern Sotho writer and folklorist whose early work set the stage for much South African indigenous literature.

Mangoaela grew up in Basutoland (now Lesotho). From 1910 he taught and worked at Morija, a mission station, as a bookkeeper and translator and later as editor of the journal *Leselinyana* ("The Little Light").

His first published work, *Tsoe-lopele ea Lesotho* (1911; "The Progress of Lesotho"), is a study of Lesotho under European rule. A collection of 54 hunting stories, *Har'a libatana le linyamat'sane* (1912; "Among Beasts and Animals"), followed. He then contributed to a *Grammar of the Sesuto Language* (1917) and put together 82 praise songs under the title *Lithoko tsa marena a Basotho* (1921; "Praises of the Sotho Chiefs"), giving an early emphasis to an important genre in African oral literature.

manifesto \,man-i-'fes-tō\ [Italian, poster, announcement, manifesto]   A written statement declaring publically the intentions, motives, or views of its issuer. Among many notable literary manifestos are André Breton's *Manifeste du surréalisme* (1924; "Manifesto of Surrealism") and Antonin Artaud's *Manifeste du théâtre de la cruauté* (1932; "Manifesto of the Theater of Cruelty").

Manilius \mə-'nil-ē-əs\, Marcus (fl. early 1st century AD)   Last of the Roman didactic poets. He was the author of *Astronomica*, an unfinished poem on astronomy and astrology probably written between the years AD 14 and 27. Manilius stresses the providential government of the world and the operation of divine reason. The poem's chief interest lies in the attractive prefaces to each book and in the mythological and moralizing digressions.

manitou or **manitu** \'man-ə-,tü\ or **manito** \-,tō\ [Ojibwa *manito,* reinforced by cognate words in other Algonquian languages]   **1.** One of the Algonquian deities or spirits who dominate the forces of nature, or an image or spirit of such a deity. **2.** A supernatural force or spiritual energy that gives power to spirits, deities, and natural forces.

Manley \'man-lē\, Mary de la Riviere (b. April 7, 1663, Jersey, Channel Islands—d. July 11, 1724, London, Eng.)   British writer who achieved notoriety by presenting political scandal in the form of romance. Her *Secret Memoirs and Manners of Several Persons of Quality* (1709) was a chronicle seeking to expose the private vices of Whig ministers. After its publication she was arrested for libel but escaped punishment. In 1711 she succeeded Jonathan Swift as editor of *The Examiner* and in 1714 wrote *The Adventures of Rivella,* her "fictitious autobiography."

Mann \'män, *Angl* 'man\, Heinrich (b. March 27, 1871, Lübeck, Ger.—d. March 12, 1950, Santa Monica, Calif., U.S.)   German novelist and essayist, a socially committed writer whose best-known works are attacks on the authoritarian social structure of German society under William II.

Mann was the elder brother of Thomas Mann. His early novels portray the decadence of high society (*Im Schlaraffenland* [1900; *In the Land of Cockaigne*]), and his later books deal with the greed for wealth, position, and power in William II's Germany. Mann's merciless portrait of a tyrannical provincial schoolmaster, *Professor Unrat* (1905; *Small Town Tyrant*), became widely known through its film version, *Der blaue Engel* (1928; *The Blue Angel*). His *Kaiserreich* trilogy—consisting of *Die Armen* (1917; *The Poor*), *Der Untertan* (1918; *The Patrioteer*), and *Der Kopf* (1925; *The Chief*)—carries even further his indictment of the social types produced by the authoritarian state. A lighter work of this period is *Die kleine Stadt* (1909; *The Little Town*).

After 1918 Mann became a prominent spokesman for radical democracy and published volumes of political essays, *Macht und Mensch* (1919; "Might and Man") and *Geist und Tat* (1931; "Spirit and Act"). He was forced into exile in 1933 when the Nazis came to power, and he spent the rest of his life in France and the United States. His two-part novel *Henri Quatre* (1935 and 1938) represents his ideal of the humane use of power.

Mann \'män\, Thomas (b. June 6, 1875, Lübeck, Ger.—d. Aug. 12, 1955, near Zürich, Switz.)   German novelist and essayist whose early novels earned him the Nobel Prize for Literature in 1929. He is noted for his finely wrought style enriched by humor, irony, and parody and for his subtle and many-layered narratives.

Brown Brothers

Mann's first novel, BUDDENBROOKS (1901), was a tender elegy for the old bourgeois virtues. After publication of the novellas TONIO KRÖGER and TRISTAN (both 1903), he took up the tragic dilemma of the artist with *Der Tod in Venedig* (1912; DEATH IN VENICE), a somber masterpiece. In 1918 Mann published a political treatise, *Betrachtungen eines Unpolitischen* (1918; *Reflections of an Unpolitical Man*), in which he attempted to promote the authoritarian state over democracy, creative irrationalism over "flat" rationalism, and inward culture over moralistic civilization. With the establishment of the Weimar Republic in 1919, Mann slowly revised his outlook. His new position was clarified in the long novel *Der Zauberberg* (1924; THE MAGIC MOUNTAIN).

From this time onward Mann's imaginative effort was directed primarily to the novel, scarcely interrupted by the novellas *Unordnung und frühes Leid* (1926; *Early Sorrow*) and *Mario und der Zauberer* (1930; *Mario and the Magician*). He also undertook a series of essays on such people as Sigmund Freud (1929), J.W. von Goethe (1932), and Friedrich Nietzsche. On Hitler's accession, Mann moved to Switzerland, but he traveled widely, finally, in 1938, establishing residence in the United States. In 1952 he settled again near Zürich. His last major essays—on Goethe (1949), Anton Chekhov (1954), and Friedrich von Schiller (1955)—are impressive evocations of the moral and social responsibilities of writers.

In 1933 he published *Die Geschichten Jaakobs* (U.K. title, *The Tales of Jacob*; U.S. title, *Joseph and His Brothers*), the first part of his tetralogy called *Joseph und seine Brüder* (JOSEPH AND HIS BROTHERS), on the biblical Joseph, continued the following year with *Der junge Joseph* (*Young Joseph*) and two years later with *Joseph in Ägypten* (*Joseph in Egypt*), and completed with *Joseph der Ernährer* (*Joseph the Provider*) in 1943. In *Lotte in Weimar* (1939; U.S. title, *The Beloved Returns*), Mann takes up the story of the heroine of Goethe's *The Sorrows of Young Werther*. Mann's *Doktor Faustus* (1947; DOCTOR FAUSTUS), begun in 1943, was the most directly political of his novels. Relating the fortunes of a German composer, Adrian Leverkühn, to the progressive destruction of German culture in the war, Mann created a work of great power.

Mann documented the composition of the novel in *Die Entstehung des Doktor Faustus* (1949; *The Genesis of a Novel*). He followed this with the novellas *Der Erwählte* (1951; *The Holy Sinner*) and *Die Betrogene* (1953; *The Black Swan*) and the novel *Die Bekenntnisse des Hochstaplers Felix Krull* (1954; FELIX KRULL), the often hilarious story of a confidence man.

Manna-heim *see* MIDGARD.

Manner \'män-ner\, Eeva-Liisa (b. Dec. 5, 1921, Helsinki, Fin.) Lyrical poet and dramatist, a central figure in the Finnish modernist movement of the 1950s.

Manner's first, rather conventional poems appeared in *Mustaa ja punaista* (1944; "Black and Red") and *Kuin tuuli tai pilvi* (1949; "Like the Wind or the Cloud"). Her breakthrough came in 1956 with the influential modernist poems in *Tämä matka* ("This Journey"; rev. ed. 1964). Her poetry is characterized by technical accomplishment, powerful images, and allusiveness. It also displays a rare musicality and sense of harmony.

Manner looked to nature, solitude, and innocence as a source of renewal. In a collection of essays, *Kävelymusiikkia pienille virahevoille* (1957; "Promenade Music for Small Hippopotamuses"), she pointed to Chinese Daoism as an example of balance between rigid organization and chaos. Her appreciation of Oriental philosophy also tempered *Orfiset laulut* (1960; "Orphic Hymns"). In her next collection, *Niin vaihtuivat vuoden ajat* (1964; "Thus Changed the Seasons"), she depicts with grace and simplicity the minute phenomena of nature as proof of an underlying cosmic harmony. Later books of poetry include *Kamala kissa* (1976; "Terrible Cat") and *Runoja 1956–1977* (1980). She also wrote a childhood memoir, *Tyttö taivaan laiturilla* (1951; "The Girl on the Bridge to Heaven").

Manner wrote both verse dramas, such as *Eros ja Psykhe* (1959; "Eros and Psyche"), and traditional plays, such as *Poltettu oranssi* (1968; "Burnt Orange"). A novel, *Varokaa, voittajat* (1972; "Beware, Victors"), is an examination of violence.

Manning \'man-iŋ\, Olivia, *married name* Smith \'smith\ (b. March 2, 1911, Portsmouth, Hampshire, Eng.—d. July 23, 1980, Ryde, Isle of Wight) British journalist and novelist, noted for her ambitious attempt to portray the panorama of modern history in a fictional framework.

Manning's first novel, *The Wind Changes*, was published in 1937. Two years later she married Reginald Donald Smith, drama writer and producer for the BBC. In 1951 she published *School for Love*, the story of a 16-year-old boy in war-ravaged Jerusalem. Her main body of work, however, is THE BALKAN TRILOGY (*The Great Fortune*, 1960; *The Spoilt City*, 1962; *Friends and Heroes*, 1965). The three books are set in Bucharest against a background of the shifting balance of power in Europe. She followed *Balkan Trilogy* with *The Levant Trilogy* (*The Danger Tree*, 1978; *The Battle Lost and Won*, 1979; *The Sum of Things*, 1980).

Mannyng \'man-iŋ\, Robert, *in full* Robert Mannyng of Brunne \'brün-nə\ (fl. *c.* 1330) Early English poet and author of *Handlyng Synne*, a poem of popular morality, and of the chronicle *Story of England*. The author is probably to be identified with a Sir Robert de Brunne, chaplain, who was at the University of Cambridge about 1300.

Handlyng Synne is an adaptation in about 13,000 lines, in short couplets poorly versified, of the *Manuel des péchés* ("Handbook of Sins"), which is usually ascribed to William of Waddington (or Widdington). Like Waddington, Mannyng aimed to provide a handbook that would stimulate careful self-examination as preparation for confession. He deals in turn with the Ten Commandments, the seven deadly sins and the sin of sacrilege, the seven sacraments, the 12 requisites of confession, and the 12 graces of confession. There is much direct instruction, exhortation, and didactic comment; each of the topics is illustrated by one or more tales.

Mannyng's later work, the two-part *Story of England*, is virtually worthless as history. The first part tells the story from the biblical Noah to the death of the British king Caedwalla in 689. The second part traces events up to the death of Edward I in 1307.

Man of Law's Tale, The One of the 24 stories in THE CANTERBURY TALES by Geoffrey Chaucer.

The story describes the sufferings of Constance, daughter of a Christian emperor. When she marries a Syrian sultan who has converted to Christianity, his evil mother conspires to kill all the Christians in the court, including her son. Constance alone survives and is cast adrift. Landing in Northumberland, she converts her host's wife, is falsely accused of killing her, is saved by divine intervention, marries the king, is set adrift by yet another nasty mother-in-law, and, after further misfortunes, is reunited with her husband and father.

man of letters 1. A learned man or scholar. 2. A literary man. Also, an author or a litterateur.

Manon Lescaut \mȧ-,nȯⁿ-les-'kō\ (*in full* Histoire du chevalier des Grieux et de Manon Lescaut) Sentimental novel by Abbé Antoine-François PRÉVOST D'EXILES, published in 1731 as the last installment of Prévost's seven-volume opus *Mémoires et aventures d'un homme de qualité qui s'est retiré du monde* (1728–31; "Memories and Adventures of a Man of Quality Who Has Retired from the World"). The work concerns the downward progress of the chevalier des Grieux, a young seminary student of noble birth. The work tells how des Grieux, a young scapegrace but also a man of the most exquisite sentiment, sacrifices himself to the amoral, delicate, and forever enigmatic courtesan Manon. In this tragic tale love conquers all, but it constantly needs vulgar money to sustain it.

Manrique \män-'rē-kä\, Gómez (b. *c.* 1412, Amusco, Castile [now in Spain]—d. *c.* 1490, Toledo) Soldier, politician, diplomat and poet, chiefly famous as one of the earliest Spanish dramatists whose name is known.

As a poet, Manrique is remembered for songs, elegies, satires such as the *Razonamiento de un rocín a un paje* ("Advice of a Horse to a Page"), and *Regimiento de príncipes* (1495; "Regiment of Princes") and other political poems. He is the only author of liturgical dramas in 15th-century Castile whose work survives. Among these is the *Representación del nacimiento de Nuestro Señor* ("Scenes of the Birth of Our Lord"), a series of dramatic tableaux recounting the birth of Christ.

Manrique \män-'rē-kä\, Jorge (b. 1440, probably at Paredes de Nava, Castile [now in Spain]—d. March 27, 1479, in front of Castle Garci-Muñoz, near Calatrava, Spain) Spanish soldier and writer, best known for his lyric poetry.

Manrique was born into an illustrious Castilian family that numbered among its members the statesman-poet Pedro López de Ayala and the poets Gómez Manrique and the Marquess de

Santillana. His best-known literary work, *Coplas por la muerte de su padre* (1492; "Stanzas for the Death of His Father"), is a lyric poem in honor of his father. It was translated into English by Henry Wadsworth Longfellow as *Coplas de Don Jorge Manrique* (1833). Selections of Manrique's poetry appeared in Hernando de Castillo's anthology *Cancionero general* (1511).

Mansfield \'mans-ˌfēld\, Katherine, *pseudonym of* Kathleen Murry \'mər-ē\, *original name* Kathleen Mansfield Beauchamp

Brown Brothers

\'bē-chəm\ (b. Oct. 14, 1888, Wellington, N.Z.—d. Jan. 9, 1923, Gurdjieff Institute, near Fontainebleau, Fr.) Short-story writer noted for her distinctive prose style with many overtones of poetry. Her delicate stories, focused upon psychological conflicts, have an obliqueness of narration and a subtlety of observation that reveal the influence of Anton Chekhov. She, in turn, had much influence on the development of the short story as a form of literature.

Mansfield left New Zealand at the age of 19 to establish herself in England as a writer. Her initial disillusion is evident in the stories collected in *In a German Pension* (1911). Until 1914 she published stories in *Rhythm* and *The Blue Review*, edited by the critic and essayist John Middleton Murry, whom she married in 1918. *Prelude* (1918) is a series of short stories beautifully evocative of her family memories of New Zealand. These, with others, were collected in *Bliss* (1920), which secured her reputation and is typical of her art.

In the next two years Mansfield did her best work, achieving the height of her powers in *The Garden Party, and Other Stories* (1922), which includes the stories THE GARDEN PARTY, "At the Bay," "The Voyage," "The Stranger" (with New Zealand settings), and the classic "Daughters of the Late Colonel," a subtle account of genteel frustration. Her final work (apart from unfinished material) was published posthumously in *The Dove's Nest* (1923) and *Something Childish* (1924).

Mansfield Park \'manz-ˌfēld\ Novel by Jane AUSTEN, published in three volumes in 1814. In its tone and discussion of religion and religious duty, it is the most serious of Austen's novels. The heroine, Fanny Price, is a self-effacing and unregarded cousin cared for by the Bertram family in their country house. Fanny's moral strength eventually wins her complete acceptance by the family.

Mansion, The Novel by William FAULKNER, first published in 1959 as the third volume of his Snopes trilogy.

The rapacious Snopes family meets its final dissolution in *The Mansion*. In *The Hamlet* (1940) and *The Town* (1957), Faulkner had described the ascent of ruthless Flem Snopes, who clawed his way to power in Jefferson, Miss. *The Mansion* focuses on Linda, Flem's stepdaughter, who is widowed and deafened while fighting for the Loyalists with her husband in the Spanish Civil War, and on her actions when she returns to Jefferson.

Man That Corrupted Hadleyburg, The \'had-lē-ˌbərg\ Short story by Mark TWAIN satirizing the vanity of the virtuous. It was first published in *Harper's Magazine* in 1899 and collected in *The Man That Corrupted Hadleyburg and Other Stories and Sketches* in 1900. The story reflects Twain's disillusionment and pessimism after a period of financial reversals and sadness over the death of his daughter.

A grim tale of revenge, the story relates the downfall of the citizens of a town that boasts of its honesty with the motto "Lead us not into temptation." A mysterious stranger, however, exposes the townspeople's underlying greed and hypocrisy.

manticore \'man-tə-ˌkȯr\, *also spelled* mantichora *or* manticora \ˌman-ti-'kȯr-ə\ *or* mantiger \'man-tij-ər\ [Greek *mantichōras, martichóras,* of Iranian origin; akin to Old Persian *martiya-* man, person, and to Avestan *xvar-* eat, devour] A legendary animal having the head of a man often with horns, the body of a lion, and the tail of a dragon or scorpion. The earliest Greek report of the creature is probably a greatly distorted description of the Caspian tiger, a hypothesis that accords well with the presumed source of the Greek word, an Old Iranian compound meaning "man-eater." Medieval writers used the manticore as a symbol of the devil.

Manticore, The Second of a series of novels by Robertson Davies, known collectively as THE DEPTFORD TRILOGY.

Man Who Loved Children, The Novel by Christina STEAD, published in 1940 and revised in 1965.

Although it went unrecognized for 25 years, *The Man Who Loved Children* is considered Stead's finest novel. Unfolding a harrowing portrait of a disintegrating family, Stead examines the hostility between a husband and wife: Sam Pollit, revealed to be a tyrannical crank far removed from the civilized man he thinks he is, whose claim to love his children lends the ironic title; and Henny, who has become a bitter virago.

Man Who Was Thursday, The (*in full* The Man Who Was Thursday: A Nightmare) Allegorical novel by G.K. CHESTERTON, published in 1908. It relates the experiences of Gabriel Syme, a poet turned detective, who is hired by a shrouded, nameless person to infiltrate a group of anarchists, each named for a day of the week and all determined to destroy the world.

Man Who Would Be King, The Short story by Rudyard KIPLING, collected in *Plain Tales from the Hills* in 1888. Narrated by a British journalist in India, it is about a pair of comic adventurers who briefly establish themselves as godlike leaders of a native tribe in Afghanistan. Exploring the nature of friendship and British imperialism, the story examines the differences between experiences felt and experiences described, ambition and achievement, and reality and fiction.

Man Without Qualities, The Unfinished novel by Robert MUSIL, published as *Der Mann ohne Eigenschaften* in three installments in 1930, 1933, and 1943.

Musil's sprawling masterpiece was his life's work. On the surface a witty, urbane portrait of life in the last days of the Austro-Hungarian Empire, the novel is also a tragic farce that gives account of the slow collapse of a society into anarchy and chaos and an indictment of a society that embraced fascism.

One of the masterpieces of the age, the book ironically dissects modern uncertainty, sham values, and political folly.

Man with the Golden Arm, The Novel by Nelson ALGREN, published in 1949. It won the National Book Award for 1950.

Set in Chicago's West Side, the novel evokes the gritty street life of petty criminals and hustlers. Hero Frankie Machine is a shrewd poker dealer whose "golden arm" shakes as he relies on morphine to overcome the pain of a war injury and to numb the guilt he feels for a drunken spree that put his wife Sophie in a wheelchair. Much of the psychological action centers on Sophie's attempts to manipulate her husband. After Frankie kills his drug dealer and flees, he hangs himself in a seedy hotel.

Man'yōshū \'män-,yō-,shü\ ("Collection of Ten Thousand Leaves") Oldest and greatest of the Imperial anthologies of Japanese poetry. The collection was compiled about 759 AD and contains about 4,500 poems, some dating to the 7th century and perhaps earlier. It was celebrated through the centuries for its *man'yō* spirit, a simple freshness and sincere emotive power not seen later in more polished and stylized Japanese verse. Among the outstanding poets represented are Ōtomo Yakamochi, Kakinomoto Hitomaro, and Yamanoue Okura, all of whom flourished in the 8th century.

Manzoni \män-'zō-nē\, Alessandro (b. March 7, 1785, Milan [Italy]—d. May 22, 1873, Milan) Italian poet and novelist whose novel I PROMESSI SPOSI, 3 vol. (1827; *The Betrothed*), had immense patriotic appeal for Italians of the nationalistic Risorgimento period and is generally ranked among the masterpieces of world literature.

Manzoni spent much of his childhood in religious schools. In 1805 he joined his mother in Paris, where he became a convert to Voltairian skepticism. Soon he married and after a time returned to Roman Catholicism. He wrote a series of religious poems, *Inni sacri* (1815; *The Sacred Hymns*), on the church feasts and a hymn to Mary. The last, and perhaps finest, of the series, "La pentecoste," was published in 1822.

During these years Manzoni also produced an ode on the Piedmontese revolution of 1821, "Marzo 1821," and two historical tragedies influenced by William Shakespeare: *Il conte di Carmagnola* (1820), a romantic work depicting a 15th-century conflict between Venice and Milan; and *Adelchi* (performed 1822), a richly poetic drama about Charlemagne's late 8th- and early 9th-century conquest of Italy.

Prompted by the patriotic urge to forge a language that would be accessible to a wide readership, Manzoni wrote *I promessi sposi* in an idiom as close as possible to contemporary educated Florentine speech. Its prose became the model for many subsequent Italian writers.

Mao Dun or **Mao Tun** \'maü-'dün\, *pseudonym of* Shen Yanbing \'shən-'yän-'biŋ\, *original name* Shen Dehong \'də-'hüŋ\ (b. 1896, Qingzhen, Zhejiang province, China—d. March 27, 1981, Beijing) Editor and author, generally considered China's greatest realistic novelist.

Forced to interrupt his schooling in 1916 because he ran out of money, Shen became a proofreader at the Commercial Press in Shanghai and was soon promoted to editor and translator. In 1920 he and several other young Chinese writers took over editorial control of the 11-year-old journal *Xiaoshuo yuebao* ("Fiction Monthly"). The group revamped the magazine and elected Shen as editor, a post he occupied until 1923.

In 1927 Shen composed three novelettes, first published serially in 1927–28 in *Xiaoshuo yuebao* and in book form as a trilogy under the title *Shi* (1930; "The Canker"). He published *Shi* under the pseudonym Mao Dun, a pun on the Chinese word for "contradiction," and the work was an instant success. Many of his short stories were anthologized, notably "Chuncan" ("Spring Silkworms"), "Chiushou" ("Autumn Harvest"), and "Candong" ("The Last Days of Winter"). Some of these have been translated in *Spring Silkworms and Other Stories* (1956).

In 1930 Mao Dun helped found the League of Left-wing Writers. During the Sino-Japanese War (1937–45), he continued his leftist literary activities, founding and editing two

patriotic literary journals. After the establishment of the communist government in 1949, Mao Dun was active on several literary and cultural committees, but he stopped writing works of fiction. In the 1970s he became vice president of the Chinese Writers' Association and edited a magazine of children's literature. His novel *Hong* (1929) was translated into English as *Rainbow* in 1992.

Mapu \'mä-,pü\, Abraham (b. Jan. 10, 1808, near Kovno, Lithuania, Russian Empire [now Kaunas, Lith.]—d. Oct. 9, 1867, Königsberg, East Prussia [now Kaliningrad, Russia]) Author of the first Hebrew novel, *Ahavat Ziyyon* (1853; *Annou: Prince and Peasant*), an idyllic historical romance set in the days of the prophet Isaiah. Couched in florid biblical language, the novel artfully depicts pastoral life in ancient Israel.

Mapu was an influential advocate of the Jewish social and cultural movement known as the Haskala, or Enlightenment. His novels romanticized a sovereign Israel and indirectly paved the way for the revival of Jewish nationalism. Other novels include ʿAyiṭ tzavuaʿ (1858–69; "The Hypocrite"), an attack on social and religious injustice in a Jewish ghetto; *Ashmat Shomron* (1865; "Guilt of Samaria"), a biblical epic set in the time of King Ahaz (c. 735–720 BCE); and *Hoze ḥezyonot,* (1869; "The Visionary"), an exposé of Ḥasidism (an austere Jewish religious movement with overtones of mysticism) that was confiscated by religious authorities.

maqāmah \má-'kä-mə\ *plural* maqāmat \-mət\ [Arabic, literally, assembly, session] Arabic literary genre in which en-

"The Procession" from the *Maqāmāt* of al-Harīrī; Baghdad school, 13th century

tertaining anecdotes, often about rogues, mountebanks, and beggars, written in an elegant, rhymed prose (*saj*ʿ), are presented in a dramatic or narrative context . The *maqāmah* is the most typical prose expression of the Arabic—and Islāmic—spirit. It tells a basically simple story in an extremely and marvelously complicated style abounding in wordplay, logographs, double entendres, and the like. It is the Arabic genre closest in style to the Western short story.

The first collection of such writings was the *Maqāmāt* of al-HAMADHĀNĪ. It consists mainly of picaresque stories in both rhymed prose and verse. The genre was revived and finally established in the 11th century by al-ḤARĪRĪ of Basra (Iraq), whose *Maqāmāt*, closely imitating al-Hamadhānī's, is regarded as a masterpiece of literary style and learning.

Ma Rainey's Black Bottom \'mä-'rā-nē\ Drama in two acts by August WILSON, performed in 1984 and published in 1985. It was the first of a series of plays in which Wilson portrayed African-American life in the 20th century.

The play features Ma Rainey, a popular blues singer, and the members of her band. Set in a recording studio in Chicago in 1927, *Ma Rainey* comments on the violence perpetrated by blacks against other blacks in their frustration over being excluded from white society.

Marat/Sade \mả-'rả-'såd\ Play in two acts by Peter WEISS, published and performed in 1964 under the title *Die Verfolgung und Ermordung Jean Paul Marats, dargestellt durch die Schauspielgruppe des Hospizes zu Charenton unter Anleitung des Herrn de Sade* (*The Persecution and Assassination of Jean-Paul Marat as Performed by the Inmates of the Asylum of Charenton Under the Direction of the Marquis de Sade*). The title is usually shortened to *Marat/Sade*.

Weiss was an exponent of the Theater of Cruelty: his stated theatrical purpose was to shock his audiences into suffering and atoning for the violent insanity of modern society. Set in 1808, the play concerns a performance by members of the asylum in which the Marquis de Sade was incarcerated from 1801 to 1814. At the warden's suggestion, de Sade directs his fellow inmates in a dramatic recreation of the assassination of Jean-Paul Marat in 1793. What follows is an intense dialectical contest between de Sade and Marat. De Sade personifies anarchy, self-indulgence, and individualism, while Marat, a pre-Marxist revolutionary, believes that the end justifies the means, no matter how violent the means may be.

Marble Faun, The (*in full* The Marble Faun; or, the Romance of Monte Beni) \'mŏn-tä-'bä-nē\ Novel by Nathaniel HAWTHORNE, published in 1860. The novel's central metaphor is a statue of a faun by Praxiteles that Hawthorne had seen in Florence. In the faun's fusing of animal and human characteristics he finds an allegory of the fall of man from amoral innocence to the knowledge of good and evil, a theme that had usually been assumed in his earlier works but that now received direct and philosophic treatment.

The faun of the novel is Donatello, a passionate young Italian who makes the acquaintance of three American artists, Miriam, Kenyon, and Hilda, who are spending time in Rome. When Donatello kills a man who has been shadowing Miriam, he is wracked by guilt until he is arrested by the police and imprisoned. Both of the women are tainted by guilt.

Marcabru \mår-kả-'brū\, *also spelled* Marcabrun \-'brūᵉⁿ\ (b. Gascony [France]; fl. *c.* 1130–48) Gascon poet-musician and the earliest exponent of the *trobar clus*, an allusive and deliberately obscure poetic style in Provençal.

Unlike most successful troubadours, Marcabru was not of the aristocracy, and he served in several courts throughout southern France and Spain without finding a permanent patron. Marcabru's innovative technique and humor are evident in all his verse, and he was widely imitated and admired, despite his consciously obscure imagery and difficult symbolism. More than 40 of his poems are extant, including Crusade songs, satires, romances, and a witty *pastourelle*. Marcabru's favorite subject, however, was the contrast of *fin' amors* (pure, perfect love) and *amars* (the sensual courtly love praised by his contemporaries). A vehement moralist, Marcabru criticized the nobility and other troubadours for distorting the true courtly virtues.

Marcel \mår-'sel\ Fictional character, both the narrator and main character of Marcel Proust's seven-part monumental novel REMEMBRANCE OF THINGS PAST.

March \'márk\, Ausiàs (b. 1397, Valencia, Spain—d. 1459, Valencia) First major poet to write in Catalan.

March's verse describes the conflict between his sensuality and his passionate idealism, expressing an anguished contempt for the flesh and for his own weakness and that of his mistress, Teresa Bou, in yielding to it. Except for Petrarch, all the formative influences on March's poetry and on his attitude toward life—the Provençal troubadours, Scholastic philosophy, and the Italian literary movement known as *dolce stil nuovo*—place him as a writer of the Middle Ages rather than of the Renaissance. March's poems, most fully published in 1543, are by convention divided into *Cants d'amor* and *Cants de mort* ("Songs of Love" and "Songs of Death," respectively, before and after his mistress's death), *Cants morals* ("Moral Songs"), and the great *Cant espiritual* ("Spiritual Song"), in which he at last attains a measure of serenity in the face of death.

March, Augie \'ȯg-ē-'märch\ Fictional character, the protagonist of Saul Bellow's THE ADVENTURES OF AUGIE MARCH.

Märchen \'mer-ḳən\ *plural* Märchen [German, news, report, story, fantastic tale, a diminutive of *Märe* news] Folktale characterized by elements of magic or the supernatural. The German term *Märchen*, used universally by folklorists, also embraces tall tales and humorous anecdotes; although it is often translated as "fairy tale," the fairy is not a requisite motif.

Märchen usually begin with a formula such as "once upon a time," setting the story in an indefinite time and place. Their usual theme is the triumph over difficulty, with or without supernatural aid, of the one least likely to succeed. The characters are stylized—wicked stepmothers, stupid ogres, or handsome princes. The situations are familiar and often reflect the economic and domestic arrangements of peasants and simple workers, such as millers, tailors, or smiths. The hero, however poor or friendless, has easy access to the king and may, through luck, cleverness, or magical intervention, win the king's daughter in marriage and inherit the kingdom.

Versions of these stories, sometimes almost identical, have been found all over the world. The first systematic attempt to transcribe and record *Märchen* verbatim from oral tradition was the collection *Kinder- und Hausmärchen* (1812–15) of the Brothers Grimm, popularly known as *Grimm's Fairy Tales*. *See also* FAIRY TALE.

March family \'märch\ Characters in a series of novels by Louisa May Alcott beginning with LITTLE WOMEN.

The four March sisters are Meg, the oldest, beautiful and rather vain but sweet; Jo, the main focus of the books, a spirited tomboy; Beth, a sickly, gentle musician who dies in the first novel; and Amy, pampered and artistic. Their mother, called Marmee, runs a frugal but happy home while their father is away serving as a chaplain in the American Civil War.

March Hare Fictional character in ALICE'S ADVENTURES IN WONDERLAND by Lewis Carroll. He behaves in a most unpredictable manner as the host of an outdoor tea party that Alice stumbles upon.

Marchmain family \'märch-,mān\ Fictional upper-class Roman Catholic English family featured in the novel BRIDESHEAD REVISITED by Evelyn Waugh. The family consists of Lord Marchmain, who lives in Italy with his mistress, Cara; Lady Marchmain, a devout Roman Catholic who lives at the country estate of Brideshead; and their children, Brideshead (Bridey), Sebastian, Julia, and Cordelia.

Mardi \'mär-dē\ Third novel by Herman MELVILLE, originally published in two volumes as *Mardi: And a Voyage Thither* in 1849. *Mardi* is an uneven and disjointed transitional book that uses allegory to comment on contemporary ideas—about nations, politics, institutions, literature, and religion. It was a dismal failure. The action involves two whaling-ship deserters—the American Taji and Norwegian Jarl—who meet up with a variety of characters, including Yillah, a blonde Pacific Islander who symbolizes Absolute Truth.

mare \'mar\ [Old English] *obsolete* An evil preternatural being conceived of as causing nightmares.

Marechal \ˌmä-rä-'chäl, -'shäl\, Leopoldo (b. June 11, 1900, Buenos Aires, Arg.—d. September, 1970, Buenos Aires) Argentine writer and critic who was best known for his philosophical novels.

In the early 1920s Marechal was part of the *Ultraismo* literary movement, which emphasized free verses, complicated metrical innovations, and nontraditional imagery and symbolism. His first book of poems, *Aguiluchos* (1922; "Eaglets"), employed modernist techniques in the treatment of pastoral themes. In *Días como flechas* (1926; "Days Like Arrows") and *Odas para el hombre y la mujer* (1929; "Odes for Man and Woman"), his metaphors and images became more daring. With *Cinco poemas australes* (1937; "Five Southern Poems"), *Sonetos a Sophia* (1940; "Sonnets to Sophia"), and *El centauro* (1940; "The Centaur"), his poetry showed the influence of Neoplatonic philosophy in its search for balance and order in a chaotic world. The theme continued in the "Canciones Elbitences," love poems addressed to a quintessential woman, Elbiamor. These poems were included in *Antología poética* (1969). Marechal's masterpiece is the novel *Adán Buenosayres* (1948), a precursor of the Latin-American new novel. The mythical voyage of Adán, the hero, his descent into hell, and his constant search for the ideal is at once a roman à clef and a historicized account of Argentina from geologic times.

During the government of Juan Perón, Marechal occupied important government cultural posts. With Perón's fall he went into virtual seclusion but returned to public attention with the novels *El banquete de Severo Arcángelo* (1965; "The Banquet of Severo Arcángelo") and *Megafón o la guerra* (1970; "Megafón, or The War").

Marechera \ˌmä-rä-'chä-rä\, Dambudzo (b. 1952, Rusape, Southern Rhodesia [now Zimbabwe]—d. Aug. 18, 1987, Harare, Zimbabwe) Zimbabwean novelist who won critical acclaim with his collection of stories entitled *The House of Hunger* (1978), a powerful account of life in his country under white rule.

Marechera grew up in poverty. He reacted against his upbringing and adopted an increasingly self-destructive lifestyle. He was expelled from both the University of Rhodesia and New College, Oxford. While living in England, he wrote *The House of Hunger*. In 1980 his novel *Black Sunlight* was published; it is an explosive and chaotic stream-of-consciousness account of a photojournalist's involvement with a revolutionary organization. Marechera returned to Zimbabwe in 1981, but his mental and physical condition deteriorated and he was often homeless. *Mindblast, or The Definitive Buddy* (1984), the last collection published during his lifetime, includes four plays, a prose narrative, poetry, and a section of his Harare journal. A powerful collection of his poetry, entitled *Cemetary of Mind*, was compiled and published posthumously in 1992.

Margaret \'mär-gret, -gə-ret\ of Angoulême \äⁿ-gü-'lem\, *also called* Margaret of Navarre \nȧ-'vȧr\, French Marguerite d'Angoulême *or* de Navarre (b. April 11, 1492, Angoulême, Fr.—d. Dec. 21, 1549, Odos-Bigorre) Queen consort of Henry II of Navarre, who, as both a patron of humanists and religious reformers and an author, was one of the outstanding figures of the French Renaissance.

Margaret extended her protection both to men of artistic and scholarly genius and to advocates of reform within the Roman Catholic church. François Rabelais, Clément Marot, and Bonaventure Des Périers were all in her circle.

The most important of Margaret's own literary works is the *Heptaméron* (published posthumously, 1558–59). It is constructed on the lines of Giovanni Boccaccio's *Decameron*, consisting of 72 tales (out of a planned 100) told by a group of travelers delayed by a flood on their return from a Pyrenean spa. The stories, illustrating the triumphs of virtue, honor, and quick-wittedness, and the frustration of vice and hypocrisy, contain a strong element of satire directed against licentious and grasping monks and clerics.

Although some of Margaret's poetry was published during her lifetime, her best verse was not compiled until 1896, under the title *Les Dernières Poésies* ("Last Poems").

Margaret \'mär-grət, -gə-rət\ of Valois \val-'wä\, *also called* Margaret of France \'frans, 'fräns\ *or* Queen Margot \'märgō\, French Marguerite de Valois, *or* de France, *or* Reine Margot (b. May 14, 1553, Saint-Germain-en-Laye, Fr.—d. March 27, 1615, Paris) Queen consort of the Protestant Henry de Bourbon, king of Navarre (the future Henry IV). She was known for her licentiousness and for her *Mémoires*, a vivid exposition of France during her lifetime.

The daughter of Henry II of France and Catherine de Médicis, Margaret played a secondary part in the prevailing wars between Roman Catholics and Protestants from the moment she took her place at court in 1569. When her husband's growing power and dynastic needs raised the possibility of an annulment of their childless marriage, Margaret withheld her consent until Henry's mistress, Gabrielle d'Estrées, died; she then released Henry to marry Marie de Médicis (1600) but retained her title. In addition to her *Mémoires*, she wrote poems and letters.

marginalia \ˌmär-jə-'nāl-yə\ Notes in the form of commentary or annotation written in the margin of a work by a reader.

Mariana \ˌmar-ē-'an-ə\ Poem by Alfred, Lord TENNYSON, first published in *Poems, Chiefly Lyrical* in 1830.

Suggested by the phrase "Mariana in the moated grange" in William Shakespeare's *Measure for Measure*, the poem skillfully evokes an interior mood by describing exterior scenery—in this case, a bleak grange. Shakespeare's Mariana was spurned by her fiancé Angelo after she lost her dowry, yet she loved him still. Tennyson's poem addresses only this tragic, romantic aspect of the character and not the resolution offered in Shakespeare's comedy. The poem is written in a form of Tennyson's invention: seven stanzas of 12 lines each, ending with variations on a refrain. Tennyson returned to the theme of a lonely woman hopelessly waiting for her lover in the poem "Mariana in the South" (1832).

Mariátegui \ˌmä-rē-'ä-tä-gē\, José Carlos (b. June 14, 1895, Lima, Peru—d. April 16, 1930, Lima) Political leader and essayist who was the first Peruvian intellectual to apply the Marxist model of historical materialism to Peruvian problems.

Mariátegui was sent by the Peruvian government to study in Italy in 1919. While there, he established strong ideological ties with some of the leading socialist thinkers of the time, among them Henri Barbusse, Antonio Gramsci, and Maksim Gorky. He returned to Lima in 1923, and five years later he established the Peruvian Communist Party. He also founded *Amauta* (1926–30), a Marxist cultural and literary journal that published avant-garde writing. In essays in *La escena contemporánea* (1925; "The Contemporary Scene"), Mariátegui attacked fascism and defined the responsibilities of the intellectuals in countries where social oppression and injustices reign.

Mariátegui's masterpiece is the collection of Marxist essays *Siete ensayos de interpretación de la realidad peruana* (1928; *Seven Interpretive Essays on Peruvian Reality*). His *Obras completas* ("Complete Works") was published posthumously in 1959.

Marie de France \mȧ-rē-də-'fräⁿs\ (fl. late 12th century)   Earliest known French woman poet, creator of verse narratives on romantic and magical themes that perhaps inspired the musical lays of the later trouvères, and author of Aesopic and other fables, called *Ysopets*.

Marie's works, of considerable charm and talent, were probably written in England. What little is known about her is taken or inferred from her writings and from a possible allusion or two in contemporary authors. From a line in the epilogue to her fables, Claude Fauchet (1581) drew the name by which she has since been known. Her lays were dedicated to a "noble" king, presumably Henry II of England, but possibly Henry's son, the Young King. Her version of *L'Espurgatoire Seint Patriz* ("St. Patrick's Purgatory") was based on the Latin text (*c.* 1185) of Henry of Saltrey.

Her lays varied in length from the 118 lines of *Chevrefoil* ("The Honeysuckle"), an episode in the Tristram story, to the 1,184 lines of *Eliduc*, a story of the devotion of a first wife whose husband brings a second wife from overseas.

Marin \'mä-rēn\, Biagio (b. June 29, 1891, Grado, Venice, Italy—d. Dec. 24, 1985, Grado)   Italian poet noted for writing with clarity and simplicity in a unique Venetian dialect.

Marin spent his earliest years on Grado, an island in the Lagoon of Venice. He later attended the University of Vienna and was drafted into the Austrian army during World War I; he deserted and then fought on the Italian side. After graduating from the University of Rome he held a variety of jobs, returning in 1968 to Grado, where he spent the rest of his life.

Marin wrote simple poems in traditional forms. He consistently used the Grado dialect, which he adapted somewhat by the use of archaisms and neologisms. His first poetry collection, *Fiuri de tapo* (1912; "Flowers of Cork"), introduced his characteristic subjects, including the sea, the wind, and the rhythms of life in an Italian island village. His poetry collections include *I canti de l'isola* (1951; revised and enlarged, 1970, 1981; "Songs of the Island"), *L'estadela de San Martin* (1958; "The Summer of St. Martin"), *Quanto più moro* (1969; "The More I Die"), and *Poesie* (1972; enlarged ed., 1981; "Poems").

Marinetti \ˌmär-ē-'nät-tē\, Filippo Tommaso (Emilio) (b. Dec. 22, 1876, Alexandria, Egypt—d. Dec. 2, 1944, Bellagio, Italy)   Italian-French prose writer, novelist, poet, and dramatist who was the ideological founder of FUTURISM, an early 20th-century literary, artistic, and political movement.

Marinetti began his literary career working for an Italian-French magazine in Milan. During most of his life his base was in France, though he made frequent trips to Italy and wrote in the languages of both countries. Such early poetry as the French *Destruction* (1904) showed the vigor and anarchic experimentation with form characteristic of his later work. Futurism had its official beginning with the publication of his "Manifeste de Futurisme" in the Paris newspaper *Le Figaro* (Feb. 20, 1909). His ideas were quickly adopted in Italy.

In 1910 Marinetti published a chaotic novel (entitled *Mafarka le Futuriste* in France and *Mafarka il futurista* in Italy) that illustrated and elaborated on his theory. He also applied Futurism to drama in such plays as the French *Le Roi bombance* (performed 1909; "The Feasting King") and the Italian *Antineutralità* (1912; "Anti-Neutrality") and summed up his dramatic theory in the prose work *Teatro sintetico futurista* (1916; "Synthetic Futurist Theater").

In a volume of poems, *Guerra sola igiene del mundo* (1915; "War the Only Hygiene of the World"), Marinetti exulted over the outbreak of World War I and urged that Italy be involved. He became an active fascist and argued in *Futurismo e Fascismo* (1924) that fascism was the natural extension of Futurism. Although his views helped temporarily to ignite Italian patriotism, Marinetti lost most of his following by the end of the decade.

Marinism \'mar-i-ˌniz-əm\ or **marinismo** \ˌmä-rē-'nēz-mō\, *also called* secentismo \ˌsā-chen-'tēz-mō\   A florid, bombastic literary style fashionable in 17th-century Italy marked by extravagant metaphors, far-fetched conceits, hyperbole, fantastic wordplay, original myths, and forced antitheses. A reaction against classicism, it was named for the 17th-century poet Giambattista MARINO and inspired by his collection of lyrical verse, *La lira* (1608–14; "The Lyre").

The style was used in sonnets, madrigals, and narrative poems. Parallel movements were *gongorismo* in Spain, preciosity in France, and Metaphysical poetry in England. *Compare* EUPHUISM; GONGORISMO; METAPHYSICAL POETRY; PRECIOSITY. *See also* Academy of ARCADIA.

Marino \mä-'rē-nō\ or **Marini** \-nē\, Giambattista (b. Oct. 18, 1569, Naples [Italy]—d. March 25, 1625, Naples)   Italian poet, founder of the school of Marinism (later *secentismo*), which dominated 17th-century Italian poetry. Marino's own work, praised throughout Europe, far surpassed that of his imitators, who carried his complicated wordplay and elaborate conceits and metaphors to such extremes that Marinism became a pejorative term.

Marino trained for the law but did not practice his profession. His life after 1590 consisted of wild living, wandering between Italian and French courts, frequent money problems, and immense success with the poetry that he managed to get published despite censorship. Much of his early work was circulated, to great acclaim, in manuscript and published later in his life. In 1596 he wrote *La sampogna* ("The Syrinx"), a series of sensual idylls using mythological and pastoral subjects, but he was unable to publish it until 1620. After 1600 Marino tried to publish some of his voluptuous poems in Parma but was halted by the Inquisition. Finally he was able to publish his early poetry as *Le rime* (1602; "The Rhymes") and *La lira*, 2 vol. (1608 and 1614; "The Lyre").

At Torino (Turin) from 1608 to 1615 he enjoyed the patronage of the duke of Savoy but was resented for his satirical poems against a rival poet, Gaspare Murtola (*La Murtoleide*, 1619; "The Murtoliad"). Murtola had him imprisoned for this offense and others, and, though his friends secured his release, Marino left Torino for Paris in 1615, where he stayed until 1623. Before leaving Paris, Marino published his most important work, a labor of 20 years, *Adone* (1623; definitive edition by R. Balsamo-Crivelli, 1922; *Adonis* [selections]). *Adone*, an enormous poem (45,000 lines), relates, with many digressions, the love story of Venus and Adonis and shows the best and worst of Marino's style.

Other works for which Marino is remembered are *La galeria* (1620; "The Gallery"), an attempt to recreate works of art poetically, and *La strage degli innocenti* (1632; *The Slaughter of the Innocents*).

Marivaux \mȧ-rē-'vō\, Pierre (Carlet de Chamblain de) (b. Feb. 4, 1688, Paris, Fr.—d. Feb. 12, 1763, Paris)   French dramatist, novelist, and journalist whose comedies are, after those of Molière, the most frequently performed in today's French theater.

Most interested in the drama of the courts, Marivaux wrote his first play, *Le Père prudent et équitable, ou Crispin l'heureux fourbe* ("The Prudent and Equitable Father") at age 20, and by 1710 he had joined Parisian salon society. He contributed articles on the various social classes to the *Nouveau Mercure* (1717–19) and modeled his own periodical, *Le Spectateur français* (1720–24), after Joseph Addison and Sir Richard Steele's *The Spectator.*

Marivaux's first plays were written for the Comédie-Française, among them the five-act verse tragedy *Annibal* (1727). But the Italian commedia dell'arte Theatre of Lelio, sponsored in Paris by the regent Philippe d'Orleans, attracted him far more. *Arlequin poli par l'amour* (1723; "Harlequin Brightened by Love") and *Le Jeu de l'amour et du hasard* (1730; *The Game of Love and Chance*) display typical characteristics of his love comedies: romantic settings, an acute sense of nuance and the finer shades of feeling, and deft and witty wordplay. This type of verbal preciousness is still known as *marivaudage.* Marivaux also made notable advances in realism; his servants are given believable feelings, and the social milieu is depicted precisely. Among his 30-odd plays are the satires *L'Île des esclaves* (1725; "Isle of Slaves") and *L'Île de la raison* (1727; "Isle of Reason"), which mock European society after the manner of *Gulliver's Travels. La Nouvelle colonie* (1729; "The New Colony") treats equality between the sexes, while *L'École des mères* (1724; "School for Mothers") studies mother-daughter rapport.

Marivaux's human psychology is best revealed in his romance novels, both unfinished. *La Vie de Marianne* (1731–41), which preceded Samuel Richardson's *Pamela* (1740), anticipates the novel of sensibility in its glorification of a woman's feelings and intuition. *Le Paysan parvenu* (1734–35; "The Fortunate Peasant") is the story of a handsome, opportunistic young peasant who uses his attractiveness to older women to advance in the world. Though Marivaux was elected to the Académie Française in 1743 and became its director in 1759, he was not fully appreciated during his lifetime.

Marjorie Morningstar \ˈmär-jə-rē-ˈmȯr-niŋ-ˌstär\   Novel by Herman WOUK, published in 1955, about a woman who rebels against the confining middle-class values of her industrious American-Jewish family. Her dream of being an actress ends in failure. She ultimately forfeits her illusions and marries a conventional man with whom she finds sufficient contentment as a suburban wife and mother, thus finally coming to accept her parents' values.

Markandaya \ˈmär-kən-ˌdī-ə\, Kamala, *original surname* Purnaiya, *married name* Taylor \ˈtā-lər\ (b. 1924, Chimakurti, India)   Novelist whose works concern the struggles of contemporary Indians with conflicting Eastern and Western values.

A Brahman, Markandaya studied at Madras University, then settled in England in 1948 and married an Englishman. Her first novel, *Nectar in a Sieve* (1954), an Indian peasant's narrative of her difficult life, remains her most popular work. Her next book, *Some Inner Fury* (1955), is set in 1942 during the Indian struggle for independence. Marriage provides the setting for a conflict of values in *A Silence of Desire* (1960).

In Markandaya's fiction Western values typically are viewed as modern and materialistic, and Indian values as spiritual and traditional. Markandaya examines this dichotomy in *Possession* (1963), in which an Indian shepherd-turned-artist is sent to England and nearly destroyed by a titled British lady. Her later works include *A Handful of Rice* (1966), *The Coffer Dams* (1969), *Two Virgins* (1973), and *Pleasure City* (1982; U.S. title, *Shalimar*).

Markham \ˈmär-kəm\, Beryl, *original surname* Clutterbuck \ˈklət-ər-ˌbək\ (b. Oct. 26, 1902, Leicester, Leicestershire, Eng.—d. Aug. 3, 1986, Nairobi, Kenya)   Professional pilot, horse trainer and breeder, writer, and adventurer, best known for her memoir *West with the Night* (1942; reissued 1983).

At age four Markham went with her father to British East Africa, where she received a spotty education while hunting with African tribesmen and learning to speak Swahili and other African languages. At age 18 she became the first woman in Africa to receive a racehorse-trainer's license. While in her late 20s, Markham learned to fly and became a commercial pilot. She made a historic solo flight (1936) across the North Atlantic from England to Cape Breton Island, Canada.

In 1942 she wrote *West with the Night* (possibly with the help of others), and, her reputation having preceded her, she went to Hollywood. After living in California for some years, she returned to Kenya in the early 1950s. In addition to occasionally writing short stories, Markham trained six Kenya Derby winners. Though *West with the Night* had not been a great success when it was originally published, it became a best-seller and brought Markham renewed celebrity after its reissue.

Markham \ˈmär-kəm\, Edwin, *original name* Charles Edward Anson Markham (b. April 23, 1852, Oregon City, Ore., U.S.—d. March 7, 1940, New York, N.Y.)   American poet and lecturer, best known for a poem of social protest, "The Man with the Hoe."

Markham grew up on an isolated ranch in central California. In 1899 he gained national fame with the publication in the *San Francisco Examiner* of "The Man with the Hoe." Inspired by Jean-François Millet's painting, Markham made the French peasant the symbol of the exploited classes throughout the world. Its success enabled Markham to devote himself to writing and lecturing.

His first book of verse, *The Man with the Hoe and Other Poems* (1899), was followed in 1901 by *Lincoln and Other Poems.* Succeeding volumes—*Shoes of Happiness* (1915), *Gates of Paradise* (1920), *New Poems: Eighty Songs at Eighty* (1932), and *The Star of Araby* (1937)—have the commanding rhetoric but lack the passion of the early works.

Markish \mär-ˈkēsh\, Peretz, Peretz *also spelled* Perets *or* Pereẓ (b. Nov. 25 [Dec. 12, New Style], 1895, Polonnoye, Volhynia, Russian Empire [now Polonnye, Ukraine]—d. Aug. 12, 1952, U.S.S.R.)   Soviet Yiddish poet and novelist whose work extols Soviet Russia and mourns the destruction of European Jews in World War II.

Markish served with the Russian army during World War I. After a series of pogroms occurred in Ukraine, he lived in Warsaw and in western Europe. While in Warsaw he coedited the Expressionist literary anthology *Khalyastre* (1922; "The Gang"). A second volume was published two years later in Paris. He returned to the Soviet Union in 1926.

Markish's first poetry collection, *Shveln* (1919; "Thresholds"), established his reputation. His poetry cycle *Di kupe* (1921; "The Heap") was written in response to increasing anti-Semitism in the Soviet Union. Optimistic poems glorifying the communist regime included "Mayn dor" (1927; "My Generation") and the epic *Brider* (1929; "Brothers"). His novel *Dor oys, dor ayn* (1929; "Generation after Generation"), about the genesis of revolution in a small Jewish town, was condemned for "Jewish chauvinism." Awarded the Order of Lenin in 1939, he wrote several paeans to Joseph Stalin, including the 20,000-line epic poem "Milkhome" (1948; "War"). Despite these efforts, Markish was executed in Stalin's anti-Jewish purges of 1952. As a gesture of rehabilitation, the Soviet Union published his poetry in Russian translation in 1957. Several other works were published posthumously, including the novel *Trit fun doyres* (1966; "Footsteps of the Generations"), chronicling the heroism of Polish Jews during World War II.

Marley, Jacob \ˈjā-kəb-ˈmär-lē\   Fictional character, the deceased business partner of Ebenezer Scrooge in A CHRISTMAS

CAROL by Charles Dickens. Marley's ghost visits Scrooge on Christmas Eve at the beginning of the story.

Marlow \'mär-lō\ Fictional character who appears in the novel LORD JIM and in the stories "Youth" and HEART OF DARKNESS by Joseph Conrad.

Marlow, who narrates part of *Lord Jim*, first befriends Jim at the military inquiry following the young man's abandonment of his damaged ship. As the reader follows Marlow's narrative, it becomes clear that his version of events is highly subjective.

This impression of narrative unreliability is heightened in *Heart of Darkness*, where the main story is Marlow's own. He relates the details of his harrowing journey to the interior of the Belgian Congo, where he confronted wretched jungle life and discovered the degeneration of the ivory trader Kurtz.

Marlowe \'mär-ˌlō\, Christopher (baptized Feb. 26, 1564, Canterbury, Kent, Eng.—d. May 30, 1593, Deptford, near

Detail of a portrait thought to be of Christopher Marlowe, dated 1585, artist unknown

The Master, Fellow and Scholars of Corpus Christi College, Cambridge

London) Elizabethan poet and William Shakespeare's most important predecessor in English drama, noted especially for his establishment of dramatic blank verse.

Marlowe graduated from Corpus Christi College, Cambridge, in 1584. After 1587 he was in London, writing for the theaters, occasionally getting into trouble with the authorities because of his violent and disreputable behavior, and probably also engaging himself from time to time in government service. Marlowe was killed at a tavern in Deptford, where, it was alleged, a fight broke out between Marlowe and his killer over the tavern bill.

In a playwriting career that spanned little more than six years, Marlowe's achievements were diverse and splendid. Perhaps before leaving Cambridge he had already written the two-part TAMBURLAINE THE GREAT (1590). Almost certainly during his later Cambridge years, Marlowe had translated Ovid's *Elegies* and the first book of Lucan's *Pharsalia* from the Latin. About this time he also wrote the play DIDO, QUEEN OF CARTHAGE (1594; with Thomas Nashe). With the production of *Tamburlaine*, the only play of his to be published in his lifetime, he received recognition and acclaim, and playwriting became his major concern in the few years that lay ahead. His poem *Hero and Leander*—which is almost certainly the finest nondramatic Elizabethan poem apart from those produced by

Edmund Spenser—was incomplete at his death and was extended by George Chapman; the joint work of the two poets was published in 1598.

Scholars disagree about the order in which the plays subsequent to *Tamburlaine* were written. It is not uncommonly held that his most famous play, DOCTOR FAUSTUS (1604), quickly followed *Tamburlaine* and that Marlowe then turned to a more neutral, more "social" kind of writing in the dramas EDWARD II (1594) and *The Massacre at Paris* (1594?). His last play may have been THE JEW OF MALTA (1633), in which he broke new ground.

Marlowe, Philip \'fil-ip-'mär-ˌlō\ Fictional character, the protagonist of seven novels by Raymond CHANDLER.

Marlowe is a hard-boiled private detective working in the seamy underworld of Los Angeles from the 1930s through the 1950s. The novels, most of which have been made into films, include *The Big Sleep* (1939), *Farewell, My Lovely* (1940), *The Lady in the Lake* (1943), and *The Long Good-Bye* (1953).

Mármol \'mär-mōl\, José (Pedro Crisólogo) (b. Dec. 2, 1817, Buenos Aires, Arg.—d. Aug. 9, 1871, Buenos Aires) Argentine poet and novelist whose outspoken denunciation in verse and prose of the Argentine dictator Juan Manuel de Rosas earned him the title "*verdugo poético de Rosas*" ("poetic hangman of Rosas"), and whose best-known work, *Amalia* (1851–55; *Amalia: A Romance of the Argentine*), is considered by many critics to be the first Argentine novel. He was highly influential in the development of the realistic novel in Latin America.

Mármol, outspoken from his youth in opposition to Rosas, was imprisoned in 1839 for his political views and eventually was forced to flee the country. He wrote most of his works during his years of exile in Montevideo, Uruguay, and in Rio de Janeiro, Brazil. In poetry such as *Rosas: El 25 de mayo de 1850* (1850) Mármol spoke out against the dictator with a forcefulness that made him the hero of liberals throughout Latin America.

Marmontel \ˌmàr-mōⁿ-'tel\, Jean-François (b. July 11, 1723, Bort-les-Orgues, Fr.—d. Dec. 31, 1799, Normandy) French poet, dramatist, novelist, and critic who is remembered for his autobiographical work, *Mémoires d'un père* (1804; "Memoirs of a Father").

In 1745, encouraged by Voltaire, Marmontel settled in Paris, where good management made his career more brilliant than his talent warranted. He was a mediocre dramatist, composing short-lived tragedies and libretti for operas. His *Contes moraux* (1761; "Moral Stories") are more original. He first published them separately in the *Mercure de France*, which he edited between 1758 and 1760. The publication of two philosophical romances, *Bélisaire* (1767) and *Les Incas* (1777), considerably enhanced his reputation.

Marmontel derived from Voltaire the brand of liberal classicism he expounded in his *Éléments de littérature* (1787; "Elements of Literature") and in articles for the *Encyclopédie*. He was elected to the Académie Française in 1763 and became its permanent secretary in 1783.

Marner, Silas \'sī-ləs-'mär-nər\ A fictional character, the protagonist of the novel SILAS MARNER by George Eliot.

Marnix \vän-'mär-niks\, Philips van, Lord (Heer) van Sint Aldegonde \vän-ˌsint-ˌäl-də-'g̣ȯn-də\ (b. 1540, Brussels [Belgium]—d. Dec. 15, 1598, Leiden, Neth.) Dutch theologian and poet whose translation of the Psalms is considered the high point of religious literature in 16th-century Holland. In exile from 1568 to 1572 and a prisoner of the Roman Catholics in 1573 and 1574, Marnix was in the thick of the political and religious struggles of the time.

His first main work was *Den byencorf der H. Roomsche Kercke* (1569; "The Beehive of the Roman Catholic Church"), a polemical tract in prose in which the author, affecting to defend Catholicism, in fact ridicules it. Marnix's translations of the Psalms were first published in 1580, but he spent many years improving them. The language of his version is often moving and powerful, and his identification with the Israelites through his own persecution and exile is strongly evident.

Marot \má-'rō\, Clément (b. 1496?, Cahors, Fr.—d. September 1544, Turin, Savoy) One of the greatest poets of the French Renaissance, whose use of the forms and imagery of Latin poetry had marked influence on the style of his successors.

Marot's father, Jean, was a poet and held a post at the court of Anne de Bretagne and later served Francis I. In 1514 Clément became page to Nicolas de Neufville, seigneur de Villeroi, secretary to the king. He entered the service of Margaret of Angoulême, sister of Francis I and later queen of Navarre. On his father's death, he became valet de chambre to Francis I, a post he held, except for his years of exile, until 1542.

Marot was arrested in 1526 for defying Lenten abstinence regulations, behavior that put him under suspicion of being a Lutheran. A short imprisonment inspired some of his best-known works, especially "L'Enfer" ("The Inferno"), an allegorical satire on justice, and an epistle to his friend Lyon Jamet. In 1527 he was again imprisoned; an epistle, addressed to the king and begging for his deliverance, won his release.

During a period of persecution against Protestants, Marot fled to Navarre and then to Italy, where he stayed until the cessation of harassment in 1537.

When he was not engaged in writing the official poems that his duties at the French court required, Marot spent most of his time translating the Psalms; a first edition of some of these appeared in 1539, another collection in 1542. Although notable for their sober and solemn musicality, they brought about another period of exile for Marot.

Although his early poems were composed entirely in the style of the late medieval poets known as *rhétoriqueurs*, he soon learned to imitate the styles and themes of antiquity, introducing the elegy, the eclogue, the epigram, the epithalamium, and the one-stanza Italian satiric *strambotto* (French *estrabot*) into French poetry, and he was one of the first French poets to attempt the Petrarchan sonnet form.

Marot composed chansons and *cantiques* and originated the *blason*, a satiric verse describing, as a rule, some aspect of the female body in minute detail. In addition to his poems, Marot translated Catullus, Virgil, and Ovid and edited the works of François Villon and the *Roman de la rose.*

Marple, Miss \'mär-pəl\, *in full* Miss Jane Marple. Fictional character, an English detective who is featured in a series of more than 15 detective novels by Agatha CHRISTIE.

Miss Marple is an elderly amateur sleuth who has always lived in St. Mary Mead, a snug English village. A natural busybody, she is skilled at problem solving and has an unsentimental understanding of human nature.

Marquand \'mär-ˌkwänd, -kwənd; mär-'kwänd\, J.P., *in full* John Phillips (b. Nov. 10, 1893, Wilmington, Del., U.S.—d. July 16, 1960, Newburyport, Mass.) American novelist who recorded the shifting patterns of middle- and upper-class American society in the mid-20th century.

Marquand grew up in comfortable circumstances until his father's business failure, when he was sent to live with relatives. This experience of reduced status and security made him acutely conscious of social gradations and their psychological corollaries.

Marquand devoted some 15 years to writing popular fiction, including the widely read adventures of the Japanese intelligence agent Mr. MOTO. He then produced his three most characteristic novels, satirical but sympathetic studies of a crumbling New England gentility: *The Late George Apley* (1937), *Wickford Point* (1939), and *H.M. Pulham, Esquire* (1941). He wrote three novels dealing with the dislocations of wartime America—*So Little Time* (1943), *Repent in Haste* (1945), and *B.F.'s Daughter* (1946)—but in these his social perceptions were somewhat less keen. He came back to his most able level of writing in his next novel, *Point of No Return* (1949), a painstakingly accurate social study of a New England town. Two social types particularly important in the 1950s were depicted in *Melville Goodwin, U.S.A.* (1951), about a professional soldier, and *Sincerely, Willis Wayde* (1955), a sharply satiric portrait of a big-business promoter. His last important novel, *Women and Thomas Harrow* (1958), is partly autobiographical.

Marqués \mär-'käs\, René (b. Oct. 4, 1919, Arecibo, Puerto Rico—d. March 22, 1979, San Juan) Playwright, short-story writer, critic and Puerto Rican nationalist whose work shows deep social and artistic commitment.

Marqués graduated from the College of Agricultural Arts of Mayagüez. He studied at the University of Madrid and at Columbia University in New York City.

His best-known play, *La carreta* (1956; *The Oxcart*), concerns a rural Puerto Rican family that immigrates to New York City in search of its fortune but fails. In 1959 Marqués published three plays together in the collection *Teatro* ("Theater"): *La muerte no entrará en palacio* ("Death Will Not Enter the Palace"), a political allegorical play in which a governor betrays his youthful ideals; *Un niño azul para esa sombra* ("A Blue Child for That Shadow"); and *Los soles truncos* ("Maimed Suns"), one of his most successful plays.

Marqués also published the short-story collections *Otro día nuestro* (1955; "Another of Our Days"), *En una ciudad llamada San Juan* (1960; "In a City Called San Juan"), and *Inmersos en el silencio* (1976; "Immersed in Silence") and the novels *La víspera del hombre* (1959; "The Eve of Man") and *La mirada* (1975; "The Glance"). A collection of his essays, *Ensayos* (1966; some included in *El puertorriqueño dócil* [1967; *The Docile Puerto Rican*]), echoes his imaginative writing in examining the problem of national identity in Puerto Rico.

Marquis \'mar-kwis\, Don, *in full* Donald Robert Perry Marquis (b. July 29, 1878, Walnut, Ill., U.S.—d. Dec. 29, 1937, New York, N.Y.) American newspaperman, poet, and playwright, creator of the literary characters Archy the cockroach and Mehitabel the cat—wry, down-and-out philosophers of the 1920s.

Marquis worked as a reporter on *The Atlanta Journal*. When in 1907 Joel Chandler Harris established *Uncle Remus's Magazine*, Marquis became associate editor.

In 1912 Marquis left Atlanta for New York City, where he became one of the best known of literary journalists. He wrote his columns "The Sun Dial" for the *Evening Sun* and "The Lantern" for the *Herald Tribune*. Stories about Archy and Mehitabel, first published in "The Sun Dial," were later collected in ARCHY AND MEHITABEL (1927).

Among Marquis' published collections of humorous poetry, satirical prose, and plays are *Danny's Own Story* (1912), *Dreams and Dust* (1915), *Hermione* (1916), *The Old Soak* (1916; made into a play, 1926), *Sonnets to a Red Haired Lady* (1922), *The Dark Hours* (1924), and *Out of the Sea* (1927). After Marquis' death *Archy and Mehitabel* was combined with several sequels into an omnibus, *the lives and times of archy and mehitabel* (1940).

Marquise of O, The   Novella by Heinrich von KLEIST, published in 1808 in the literary journal *Phöbus* as *Die Marquise von O*. It was collected in *Erzählungen* (1810–11; "Stories").

Like much of Kleist's fiction, this work is suffused with ambiguity, irony, paradox, and impulsive, erotic passion. The title character, Julietta, is a celibate young widow who finds herself inexplicably pregnant. In desperation, she makes an appeal in a newspaper advertisement for the father of her unborn child to come forward. She is horrified when the man who responds to her advertisement is Count F., an officer in the Russian army who had saved her from being raped by Russian soldiers. After her rescue from this ordeal, Julietta had fainted; Count F. now confesses that he had raped her while she was unconscious. Julietta marries him but refuses to have anything to do with him. After her baby is born Julietta relinquishes her previous ideal of perfection and forgives the count, accepting his genuine contrition and love for her.

Marriage à-la-Mode   Comedy by John DRYDEN, performed in 1672 and published in 1673.

The play has two unrelated plots. One, written in heroic couplets, concerns the princess Palmyra of Sicily, whose usurper father has never seen her, and her childhood sweetheart Leonidas, the rightful heir to the throne. The young pair were raised together in the isolated countryside and have fallen in love; their marriage will right the wrong of Palmyra's father. The other plot is comic. After two years of marriage Rodophil and Doralice have lost interest in each other. Rodophil is attracted to Melanthe, whose affectations annoy her fiancé, Palamede. To complete the square, Palamede is attracted to Doralice. Complications ensue, and in the end the characters reject adultery, preferring their original partners after all.

Marriage of Figaro, The \'fig-ə-,rō\   Comedy in five acts by Pierre-Augustin BEAUMARCHAIS, performed in 1784 as *La Folle Journée; ou, le mariage de Figaro* ("The Madness of a Day, or the Marriage of Figaro"). It is the sequel to THE BARBER OF SEVILLE and is the work upon which Mozart based the opera *Le nozze di Figaro* (1786). Written between 1775 and 1778, *The Marriage of Figaro* reverses the character of Count Almaviva from the romantic hero of *The Barber of Seville* to an unscrupulous villain. The play is generally critical of aristocratic corruption, which it contrasts with lower-class virtue.

In the previous play, Figaro, who is the Count's loyal factotum, helped his master win the hand of Rosine (known as Rosina in the opera), now the Countess Almaviva. Figaro is betrothed to Suzanne, the Countess' maid. Because Count Almaviva wants Suzanne as his mistress, he attempts to prevent the couple's marriage. Suspicious of his master, Figaro sends the Count an anonymous letter informing him that the Countess has a lover. Various intrigues ensue, during which Suzanne and the Countess change places to deceive both the Count and Figaro. Eventually the Count admits his dishonorable intentions and gives his permission for Figaro and Suzanne to marry.

Marryat \'mar-ē-ət\, Frederick (b. July 10, 1792, London, Eng.—d. Aug. 9, 1848, Langham, Norfolk)   Naval officer and the first important English novelist after Tobias Smollett to make full and amusing use of his varied experience at sea.

Marryat entered the Royal Navy at the age of 14 and served with distinction in many parts of the world before retiring in 1830 with a captain's rank. He then began a series of adventure novels marked by a lucid, direct narrative style and an unfailing fund of incident and humor. These include *The King's Own* (1830), *Peter Simple* (1834), *Mr. Midshipman Easy* (1836), and *Poor Jack* (1840). He also wrote a number of children's books, among which *The Children of the New Forest* (1847), a story of the English Civil Wars, is a classic of children's literature.

Mars \'märz\   Ancient Roman deity, in importance second only to Jupiter. By historical times he had developed into a god of war; in Roman literature he was protector of Rome, a nation proud in war. He was also associated with agriculture. Mars was particularly important to the Romans because of his connection with ROMULUS AND REMUS, the legendary founders of Rome. He was the father of these two, and they were aided by a woodpecker and a wolf, both of which were sacred to Mars. In literature and art he is hardly distinguished from the Greek ARES.

Marsh \'märsh\, Ngaio \'ŋā-ē-ō, *Angl* 'nī-yō\, *in full* Dame Edith Ngaio Marsh (b. April 23, 1899, Christchurch, N.Z.— d. Feb, 18, 1982, Christchurch)   One of New Zealand's most popular 20th-century authors who was a major force in raising the detective story to the level of a respectable literary genre. She is known especially for her many mystery stories featuring Inspector Roderick Alleyn of Scotland Yard.

Originally an artist and then an actress in a touring Shakespearean company, Marsh went to England in 1928 and wrote her first novel, *A Man Lay Dead* (1934). She returned to New Zealand, where she produced Shakespearean repertory theater from 1938 to 1964. Her best-known detective novels include *Artists in Crime* (1938), *Overture to Death* (1939), *Final Curtain* (1947), *Opening Night* (1951), *Death of a Fool* (1956), and *Dead Water* (1963). Her autobiography, *Black Beech and Honeydew*, was published in 1966. In 1948 she was made Dame of the Order of the British Empire.

Marshall \'mär-shəl\, Paule, *original surname* Burke \'bərk\ (b. April 9, 1929, Brooklyn, N.Y., U.S.)   Novelist whose works emphasized the need for black Americans to reclaim their African heritage.

The Barbadian background of Marshall's parents was to inform all her work. After graduating from Brooklyn College, she worked briefly as a librarian before joining *Our World* magazine, where she worked from 1953 to 1956. Her autobiographical first novel, BROWN GIRL, BROWNSTONES (1959), tells of the American daughter of Barbadian parents who travels to their homeland as an adult; the book was critically acclaimed for its acute rendition of dialogue.

Soul Clap Hands and Sing, a 1961 collection of four novellas, presents four aging men who come to terms with their earlier refusal to affirm lasting values. Marshall's 1962 short story "Reena" was one of the first pieces of fiction to feature a college-educated, politically active black woman as its protagonist; frequently anthologized, it also was included in the author's 1983 collection *Reena and Other Stories*. *The Chosen Place, the Timeless People* (1969) is set on a fictional Caribbean island and concerns a philanthropic attempt to modernize an impoverished and oppressed society.

Marshall's most eloquent statement of her belief in African-Americans' need to rediscover their heritage was PRAISESONG FOR THE WIDOW, a highly regarded 1983 novel that established her reputation as a major writer. *Daughters* (1991) concerned a West Indian woman in New York who returns home to assist her father's reelection campaign. The protagonist, like those of Marshall's other works, has an epiphany after confronting her personal and cultural past.

Marsman \'märs-mən\, Hendrik (b. Sept. 30, 1899, Zeist, near Utrecht, Neth.—d. June 21, 1940, at sea in the English Channel)   One of the outstanding Dutch poets and critics active between World Wars I and II.

Under the influence of the German Expressionists, Marsman made his literary debut about 1920 with rhythmic free verse, which attracted notice for its aggressive independence. The collection *Verzen* (1923; "Verses") expresses an antihumanist, anti-intellectual rebelliousness, which the poet called "vitalism." As editor of the periodical *De Vrije bladen* ("The Free Press"), in 1925 he became the foremost critic of the younger generation. His next collection of verse appeared in 1927 with the English title *Paradise Regained* and was greeted as a major artistic achievement. Another cycle, *Porta Nigra*, dominated by the idea of death, appeared in 1934. His last book of verse, *Tempel en kruis* (1940; "Temple and Cross"), an autobiographical account of the poet's development, reaffirms humanistic ideals.

Marston \'mär-stən\, John (baptized Oct. 7, 1576, Oxfordshire, Eng.—d. June 25, 1634, London) English dramatist, one of the most vigorous satirists of the Shakespearean era, whose best-known work is *The Malcontent* (1604), in which he rails at the iniquities of a lascivious court.

Marston began his literary career in 1598 with *The Metamorphosis of Pigmalions Image and Certaine Satyres*, a callow, erotic poem that was severely criticized. In the same year, the rough-hewn, obscure verses of *The Scourge of Villanie* were widely acclaimed.

In 1599 Marston turned to writing for the theater, producing *Histrio-mastix* (published in 1610). In his character Chrisoganus, a "Master Pedant" and "translating scholler," the audience was able to recognize the learned Ben Jonson. A brief, bitter literary feud developed between Marston and Jonson—part of "the war of the theaters." Jonson paid him back in *Poetaster* (produced 1601) by depicting Marston as Crispinus, a character who was given a pill that forced him to disgorge a pretentious vocabulary.

For the Children of Paul's, a children's theater company, Marston wrote *The History of Antonio and Mellida* (1602), its sequel, *Antonio's Revenge* (1602), and *What You Will* (1607). Although *What You Will* satirized Jonson, that same year Marston and Jonson collaborated on *Love's Martyr*.

In 1604 Marston became a shareholder in the Children of the Chapel, another children's theater company, for which he wrote his remaining plays. *The Dutch Courtezan* (produced 1603–04) as well as *The Malcontent* earned him his place as a dramatist. The former, with its coarse, farcical counterplot, was considered one of the cleverest comedies of its time.

In 1605 Marston again collaborated with Jonson and with George Chapman on *Eastward Hoe*, a comedy of the contrasts within the life of the city. The play's satiric references to opportunistic Scottish countrymen of the newly crowned James I gave offense, and all three authors were imprisoned.

After another imprisonment in 1608, Marston left unfinished *The Insatiate Countesse*, his most erotic play, and entered the Church of England. He took orders in 1609. In 1633 he apparently insisted upon the removal of his name from the collected edition of six of his plays, *The Workes of John Marston*, which was reissued anonymously the same year as *Tragedies and Comedies*.

Marsyas \'mär-sē-əs\ Legendary Greek satyr of Anatolian origin. According to the usual Greek version, Marsyas found the oboe that the goddess Athena had invented and, after becoming skilled in playing it, challenged Apollo to a contest with his lyre. When King Midas of Phrygia, who had been appointed judge, declared in favor of Marsyas, Apollo punished Midas by changing his ears into ass's ears. In another version the Muses were the judges, and they awarded the victory to Apollo, who tied Marsyas to a tree and flayed him.

Martí \mär-'tē\, José Julián, *in full* José Julián Martí y Pérez \ĕ-'pā-rās\ (b. Jan. 28, 1853, Havana [Cuba]—d. May 19, 1895, Dos Ríos) Poet, essayist, and patriot who became the symbol of Cuba's struggle for independence from Spain.

Martí had published several poems by the age of 15; at 16 he founded a newspaper, *La patria libre* ("The Free Fatherland"). During a revolutionary uprising in 1868, he was sentenced to six months of hard labor, and in 1871 he was deported to Spain. There he continued his education and his writing, receiving a degree in law from the University of Zaragoza. He returned to Cuba in 1878.

Organization of American States

Because of his continued political activities, however, Martí was again exiled to Spain in 1879. From there he eventually went to Venezuela, where he founded the *Revista Venezolana* ("Venezuelan Review"). His political views were also unwelcome in Venezuela, however, and in 1881 Martí went to New York City, where he remained, except for occasional travels, until the year of his death.

He continued to write newspaper articles, poetry, and essays. His regular column in *La nación* of Buenos Aires made him famous throughout Latin America. His poetry, such as the collection *Versos libres* (1913; "Free Verses"), written between 1878 and 1882 on the theme of freedom, reveals a deep sensitivity and an original poetic vision. His essays, considered by most critics his greatest contribution to Latin-American letters, helped to bring about innovations in Spanish prose and to promote better understanding among the American nations. In essays such as *Emerson* (1882), *Whitman* (1887), *Nuestra América* (1881; "Our America"), and *Bolívar* (1893), Martí, who considered himself a citizen of the Americas, expressed his original thoughts in an intensely personal style that is still considered a model of Spanish prose.

Martial \'mär-shəl\, *Latin in full* Marcus Valerius Martialis \,mär-shē-'ā-lis\ (b. March 1, *c.* AD 38–41, Bilbilis, [Spain]—d. *c.* 103) Roman poet whose pointed and sometimes obscene epigrams portrayed human foibles in Roman society during the early empire. He virtually created the modern epigram, and his myriad admirers throughout the centuries have paid him the homage of quotation, translation, and imitation.

Martial was born in a Roman colony in Spain. In his early 20s he made his way to the capital of the empire and attached himself to the powerful and talented family of the Senecas, who were Spaniards like himself. To their circle belonged Lucan, the epic poet, and Calpurnius Piso, chief conspirator in the unsuccessful plot against the emperor Nero in 65. After the latter incident and its consequences, Martial had to look for other patrons. Precisely how Martial lived between 65 and 80, the year in which he published a small volume of poems to celebrate the consecration of the Flavian Amphitheatre, or Colosseum, is not known.

The poverty so often pleaded by the poet is undoubtedly exaggerated. As a mark of special imperial favor, he was awarded a military tribuneship, which he was permitted to resign after six months' service but which entitled him to the privileges of an *eques* (knight) throughout his life. As early as 84 the poet also owned a small country estate northeast of Rome, which may have been given to him by Polla, the widow of Lucan.

Martial's first book, *Liber spectaculorum* (AD 80; *On the Spectacles*), contained more than 30 undistinguished poems, scarcely improved by their gross adulation of the emperor Titus. In the year 84 or 85 appeared two other undistinguished books with Greek titles, *Xenia* and *Apophoreta*. In the next 15 or 16 years, however, he wrote the 12 books of epigrams on which his renown deservedly rests. After 34 years in Rome he returned to Spain, where his last book was published, probably in 102. He died not much over a year later in his early 60s.

Martial was thoroughly acquainted with the great poets of Rome's Golden Age: Catullus, Tibullus, Sextus Propertius, Lucretius, Virgil, and Ovid, but his stress on the simple joys of life—eating, drinking, and conversing with friends—and his famous recipes for contentment and the happy life are chiefly reminiscent of Horace.

Martin Chuzzlewit \'märt-ən-'chəz-əl-,wit\ (*in full* The Life and Adventures of Martin Chuzzlewit) Novel by Charles DICKENS, published serially by "Boz" from 1843 to 1844 and in book form in 1844.

The story's protagonist, Martin Chuzzlewit, is an apprentice architect who is fired by Seth Pecksniff and is also disinherited by his own eccentric, wealthy grandfather. Martin and a servant, Mark Tapley, travel to the United States, where they are swindled by land speculators and have other unpleasant but sometimes comic experiences. Thoroughly disillusioned with the New World, the pair returns to England, where a chastened Martin is reconciled with his grandfather, who gives his approval to Martin's forthcoming marriage to his true love, Mary Graham.

Martin du Gard \mär-tanⁿ-dǖ-'gàr\, Roger (b. March 23, 1881, Neuilly-sur-Seine, Fr.—d. Aug. 22, 1958, Bellême) French novelist, dramatist, and winner of the 1937 Nobel Prize for Literature. Originally trained as a paleographer and archivist, Martin du Gard brought to his works a spirit of objectivity and a scrupulous regard for details. For his concern with documentation and his examination of the relationship of social reality to individual development, he has been linked with the realist and naturalist traditions of the 19th century.

Martin du Gard first attracted attention with *Jean Barois* (1913), which traced the development of an intellectual torn between the Roman Catholic faith of his childhood and the scientific materialism of his maturity. The years between the two world wars were devoted to writing the eight-part novel cycle LES THIBAULT (1922–40; parts 1–6 as *The Thibaults*; parts 7–8 as *Summer 1914*), for which he is best known.

Other works by Martin du Gard include *Vielle France* (1933; *The Postman*), biting sketches of French country life, and *Notes sur André Gide* (1951; *Recollections of André Gide*). Martin du Gard also wrote a somber drama about repressed homosexuality, *Un Taciturne* (1931; "A Silent Man"), and two farces of French peasant life, *Le Testament du père Leleu* (1914; "Old Leleu's Will") and *La Gonfle* (1928; "The Swelling"). In 1941 he began work on *Le Journal du colonel de Maumort*, which was left unfinished at his death.

Martineau \'mär-ti-,nō\, Harriet (b. June 12, 1802, Norwich, Norfolk, Eng.—d. June 27, 1876, near Ambleside, Westmorland) Essayist, novelist, and economic and historical writer who was prominent among English intellectuals of her time.

Martineau first gained a large reading public with an extensive series of anecdotes and dialogues popularizing classical economics, published in several collections, including *Illustrations of Political Economy*, 25 vol. (1832–34), and *Poor Laws and Paupers Illustrated*, 10 vol. (1833–34). After a visit to the United States she wrote *Society in America* (1837) and *Retrospect of Western Travel* (1838). Her best-known novels, includ-

ing DEERBROOK (1839) and *The Hour and the Man* (1841), were also written during this period.

A trip to the Middle East in 1846 led her to study the evolution of religions and to become increasingly skeptical of religious beliefs, including her own liberal Unitarianism. Her chief historical work, *The History of the Thirty Years' Peace, A.D. 1816–1846* (1849), was a widely read popular treatment. She also contributed to several periodicals, and her *Biographical Sketches* (1869, enlarged 1877) was a collection of articles written for the *Daily News* on a number of well-known contemporaries, including Charlotte Brontë. Her three-volume *Autobiography* was published posthumously in 1877.

Martin Eden \'märt-ən-'ēd-ən\ Semiautobiographical novel by Jack LONDON, published in 1909.

The title character becomes a writer, hoping to acquire the respectability sought by his society-girl sweetheart. She spurns him, however, when his writing is rejected by several magazines and when he is falsely accused of being a socialist. She tries to win him back after he achieves fame, but Eden realizes her love is false. Financially successful and robbed of connection to his own class, aware that his quest for bourgeois respectability was hollow, Eden travels to the South Seas, where he jumps from the ship and drowns.

Martínez Estrada \mär-'tē-näs-es-'trä-thä\, Ezequiel (b. Sept. 14, 1895, San José de la Esquina, Arg.—d. Nov. 4, 1964, Bahía Blanca) Leading Argentine writer of the postmodernist generation who influenced many younger writers.

Martínez Estrada began his literary career with essays in the journal *Nosotros* (1917). His first book of poems, *Oro y piedra* (1918; "Gold and Stone"), was followed by *Nefelibal* (1922), *Motivos del cielo* (1924; "Heaven's Reasons"), *Argentina* (1927), and *Humoresca* (1929). The verses are complex, and the language and imagery are often tinted with satire.

Radiografía de la pampa (1933; *X-Ray of the Pampa*), is Martínez Estrada's comprehensive psychological study of the Argentine character laden with fatalistic overtones. *La cabeza de Goliat: microscopia de Buenos Aires* (1940; "The Head of Goliath: A Microscopic Study of Buenos Aires") treats the people of Buenos Aires and continues the themes of *Radiografía*.

Martínez Estrada's many studies of literary figures and texts made him a respected critic. His critical works include *Muerte y transfiguración del Martín Fierro*, 2 vol. (1948; "The Death and Transfiguration of Martin Fierro"), *El mundo maravilloso de Guillermo Enrique Hudson* (1951; "The Wonderful World of William Henry Hudson"), and *El hermano Quiroga* (1957; "Brother Quiroga").

Martínez Sierra \mär-'tē-näth-'syer-rä\, Gregorio (b. May 6, 1881, Madrid, Spain—d. Oct. 1, 1947, Madrid) Poet and playwright whose dramatic works contributed significantly to the revival of the Spanish theater.

Martínez Sierra's first volume of poetry, *El poema del trabajo* (1898; "The Poem of Work"), appeared when he was 17. Short stories reflecting the *modernista* concern with individuality and subjectivity and freedom from archaic forms followed. He turned to drama in 1905 with his *Teatro de ensueño* ("Theater of Dreams"). His masterpiece, *Canción de cuna* (1911; "Song of the Cradle"), was popular in both Spain and Latin America. The most marked feature of his drama, his insight into female characters, has been attributed to his wife and collaborator, María de la O Lejárraga.

Martínez Sierra also edited several important *modernista* periodicals in Madrid and operated Renacimiento, a publishing house that introduced a host of foreign playwrights into Spain. His most important contribution to the Spanish theater was his introduction of the art theater while he was director of the Eslava Theater in Madrid (1917–28). His work there is described in his book *Un teatro de arte en España* (1926; "An Art Theater in Spain").

Martín-Santos \mär-'tēn-'sän-tōs\, Luis (b. Nov. 11, 1924, Larache, Mor.—d. Jan. 21, 1964, San Sebastian, Spain)   Spanish psychiatrist and novelist.

From 1951 until his death, Martín-Santos was director of the Psychiatric Sanitorium in San Sebastián. He tried to develop a psychology of the whole person, and he published his ideas in *Dilthey, Jaspers y la comprensión del enfermo mental* (1955; "Dilthey, Jaspers, and the Understanding of Mental Illness"). In 1962 he published his novel *Tiempo de silencio* ("Time of Silence"), the first of a projected trilogy. The novel is about a medical student, Pedro, thrust among inhabitants of the Madrid slums and confronted with their often violent adaptation to severe conditions. Events force him to confess to a crime of which he is innocent and to face in silence the consequences—even after his innocence has been proved. The novel has been compared in structure and style to James Joyce's *Ulysses*. The sequel, *Tiempo de destrucción* (1975; "Time of Destruction"), was unfinished when Martín-Santos died.

Martinson \'mär-tin-sȯn\, Harry (Edmund) (b. May 6, 1904, Jämshög, Swed.—d. Feb. 11, 1978, Stockholm)   Swedish novelist and poet who was the first self-taught, working-class writer to be elected to the Swedish Academy (1949). With Eyvind Johnson he was awarded the Nobel Prize for Literature in 1974.

Martinson spent his childhood in a series of foster homes and his youth and early adulthood as a merchant seaman, laborer, and vagrant. His first book of poetry, *Spökskepp* ("Ghost Ship"), much influenced by Rudyard Kipling's *The Seven Seas*, appeared in 1929. His early experiences are described in two autobiographical novels, *Nässlorna blomma* (1935; *Flowering Nettle*) and *Vägen ut* (1936; "The Way Out"), and in original and sensitive travel sketches, *Resor utan mål* (1932; "Aimless Journeys") and *Kap Farväl* (1933; *Cape Farewell*). Among his best-known works are *Passad* (1945; "Trade Wind"), a collection of poetry; the novel *Vägen till Klockrike* (1948; *The Road*); and *Aniara* (1956; *Aniara, A Review of Man in Time and Space*), an epic poem about space travel.

Martinson \'mär-tin-sȯn\, Moa \'mü-ə\, *original name* Helga Swartz \'svärts\ (b. Nov. 2, 1890, Vardnass, Swed.—d. Aug. 5, 1964, Södertälje)   Novelist who was among the first to write about the landless agricultural workers of the Swedish countryside. The first half of her life was filled with poverty and misery, but she wrote about the workers with warmth and humor.

The mother of five children, she was widowed at 25 and struggled to support her family. After her second marriage, to the proletarian writer Harry Martinson (divorced 1940), she began a literary career and took the name Moa Martinson. Her most successful work is the autobiographical trilogy *Mor gifter sig* (1936; "Mother Gets Married"), *Kyrkbröllop* (1938; "Church Wedding"), and *Kungens rosor* (1939; "The King's Roses"). Her later novels were about proletarian characters of the 18th and 19th centuries.

Martyn \'märt-ən\, Edward (b. Jan. 30, 1859, Tulira, County Galway, Ire.—d. Dec. 5, 1923, Tulira)   Irish dramatist who with William Butler Yeats and Lady Gregory formed the Irish Literary Theatre (1899), part of the nationalist revival of interest in Ireland's Gaelic literary history known as the Irish Literary Renaissance.

During its three-year existence, the Irish Literary Theatre presented plays by Yeats, George Moore, and Martyn (*The Heather Field* and *Maeve*; both 1899), among others. After the theater closed, Martyn broke with the mainstream of Irish revivalism because of personal conflicts and his dislike of "peasant plays" and "Celtic twilight romanticism." In 1914 he helped found the Irish Theatre in Dublin to produce "nonpeasant" plays, Irish-language plays, and continental drama.

Marulić \'mä-rů-lich\, Marko (b. Aug. 18, 1450, Split, Dalmatia [Croatia]—d. Jan. 6, 1524, Split)   Croatian moral philosopher and poet whose vernacular verse marked the beginnings of Croatian literature.

The scion of a noble family, Marulić studied classical languages and literature and philosophy at Padua (Italy) before returning to his native Split and a life of scholarship. At the age of 60 he withdrew to a Franciscan monastery but returned to Split, disillusioned by the experience, two years later.

Marulić's didactic moral works were written in Latin; they stressed practical Christianity and reflected an appreciation of stoic thought. His most important vernacular poem was *Istorija svete udovice Judit u versih hrvacki složena* (1521; "The History of the Holy Widow Judith"). The first printed Croatian literary work, *Judit* is an epic in six cantos in which Marulić sought by the example of an Old Testament heroine to strengthen his people in their struggles against the Turks.

Marvel, Ik.   Pseudonym of Donald Grant MITCHELL.

Marvell \'mär-vəl\, Andrew (b. March 31, 1621, Winestead, Yorkshire, Eng.—d. Aug. 18, 1678, London)   English poet whose political reputation overshadowed that of his poetry until the 20th century. He is considered to be one of the best secular Metaphysical poets.

Marvell was educated at Cambridge. His father's death in 1641 may have ended Marvell's promising academic career. He was abroad for at least five years (1642–46), presumably as a tutor. In 1651–52 he was tutor to Mary, daughter of Lord Fairfax, the Parliamentary general, at Nun Appleton, Yorkshire, during which time he wrote his notable poems "Upon Appleton House" and "The Garden."

Although earlier opposed to Oliver Cromwell's Commonwealth government, he wrote "An Horatian Ode upon Cromwell's Return from Ireland" (1650), and from 1653 to 1657 he was a tutor to Cromwell's ward William Dutton. In 1657 he became assistant to John Milton as Latin secretary in the foreign office. "The First Anniversary" (1655) and "On the Death of O.C." (1659) showed his continued and growing admiration for Cromwell. In 1659 he was elected member of Parliament for Hull, an office he held until his death.

After the restoration of Charles II in 1660, Marvell turned to political verse satires—the most notable was *Last Instructions to a Painter*, against Lord Clarendon, Charles's lord chancellor—and prose political satire, as exemplified by *The Rehearsal Transpos'd* (1672–73).

At Marvell's death, his housekeeper-servant Mary Palmer claimed to be his widow, although this was undoubtedly a legal fiction. The first publication of his poems in 1681 resulted from a manuscript volume she found among his effects.

Marvell was eclectic: his TO HIS COY MISTRESS is considered a classic of Metaphysical poetry; the Cromwell odes are the work of a classicist; his attitudes are sometimes those of the elegant Cavalier poets; and his nature poems resemble those of the Puritan Platonists.

marwysgafn \mär-'wəs-ˌgävn\ [Welsh, deathbed, deathbed poem, from *marw* dead + *ysgafn* couch, bed]   Welsh religious ode in which the poet, sensing the approach of death, confesses his sins and prays for forgiveness. The *marwysgafn* was popular during the period of the Welsh court poets, called *gogynfeirdd* in the 12th to 14th century.

Marxist criticism \'märk-sist\   A method of literary analysis based on the writings of Karl Marx and Friedrich Engels. Rather than viewing a text as the product of an individual consciousness, Marxist critics examine a work as the product of an ideology particular to a specific historical period. Such critics judge a text on the basis of its portrayal of social actions and institutions and on its representation of class struggle.

The more rigid Marxists have insisted on works that reflected Marxist ideology (*see* SOCIALIST REALISM). Other, more flexible, critics were able to appreciate the great 19th-century realists, despite the distinctly literary nature of their work. Still other Marxist theorists, such as Bertolt Brecht, embraced modernism and shunned realism as lulling the audience into passive acceptance of capitalist ascendency.

Those who are counted among Marxist critics include György Lukács, Walter Benjamin, and Fredric Jameson.

Mary \'mar-ē, 'mā-rē\, *also called* Saint Mary *or* Virgin Mary (fl. beginning of the Christian Era)   The mother of Jesus, an object of veneration in Roman Catholic and Eastern Christianity since the apostolic age, and a favorite subject in Western art, music, and literature. Mary is known from biblical references, which are, however, too sparse to construct a coherent biography. The development of the doctrine of Mary can be traced through titles that have been ascribed to her in the history of Christian communions—guarantee of the incarnation, virgin mother, second Eve, Theotokos (birth-giver of God), mother of God, ever virgin, immaculate, and assumed into heaven. Her humility and obedience to the message of God have made her an exemplar for all ages of Christians. The first mention of Mary is the story of the Annunciation. Other important incidents of her life include the birth of Jesus and the presentation of him in the Temple, the coming of the Magi, and the flight to Egypt. Despite the few incidents of her life that are recorded in the New Testament, Mary's role in Christian tradition grew steadily throughout the centuries, and religious narratives examining various aspects of her character abound.

Mary Barton \'mar-ē-'bärt-ən, 'mā-rē\ (*in full* Mary Barton: A Tale of Manchester Life)   First novel by Elizabeth Cleghorn GASKELL, published in 1848. It is the story of a working-class family that descends into desperation during the depression of 1839. With its vivid description of squalid slums, *Mary Barton* helped awaken the national conscience.

John Barton is a respected laborer who is thrown out of work during hard times. He becomes a union organizer, and he journeys to London with other reformers to present the Chartist petition to Parliament. The unionists get short shrift from government and management, and John's frustration turns to bitter class hatred. He is chosen to carry out a retaliatory murder at the behest of his trade union. His victim is Henry Carson, a mill owner's son who has been paying court to Mary, John's daughter. Mary's working-class lover, Jem Wilson, is indicted for the crime, but Mary helps prove his innocence. John Barton dies, his constitution broken by poverty, remorse, and opium. Mary, Jem, and their friends immigrate to Canada to begin a new life.

Masamune Hakuchō \mä-'sä-mù-ne-'hä-kù-,chō\, *pseudonym of* Masamune Tadao \tä-'dä-ō\ (b. March 3, 1879, Bizen, Okayama prefecture, Japan—d. Oct. 28, 1962, Tokyo)   Writer and critic who was one of the great masters of Japanese naturalist literature.

In 1903 Masamune began writing literary, art, and cultural criticism for the newspaper *Yomiuri*. The novels *Doko-e* (1908; "Whither?") and *Doro ningyo* (1911; The Mud Doll) brought him attention as a writer of fiction. These novels are stories of people living in a gray world devoid of all ambition and hope. *Ushibeya no nioi* (1916; "The Stench of the Stable") and *Shisha*

seisha (1916; "The Dead and the Living") are similar works. Masamune also devoted some time to writing plays, the best known of which is perhaps *Jinsei no kōfuku* (1924; "The Happiness of Human Life").

It is in criticism that Masamune is often considered to have done his best work. In 1932 he published the influential *Bundan jimbutsu hyōron* ("Critical Essays on Literary Figures"). Other outstanding critical works are *Shisō mushisō* (1938; "Thought and Non-Thought") and *Bundanteki jijoden* (1938; "A Literary Autobiography").

Masaoka Shiki \mä-'sä-ō-kä-'shē-kē\, *pseudonym of* Masaoka Tsunenori \tsù-'nä-nō-rē\ (b. Oct. 14, 1867, Matsuyama, Japan—d. Sept. 19, 1902, Tokyo)   Poet and critic who revived haiku and tanka, traditional Japanese poetic forms.

Masaoka began to write poetry in 1885. Four years later he contracted tuberculosis, and he remained an invalid for much of the rest of his life.

As early as 1892 Masaoka began to feel that a new literary spirit was needed to free poetry from centuries-old rules prescribing topics and vocabulary. In an essay entitled "Jojibun" ("Narration"), which appeared in the newspaper *Nihon* in 1900, he introduced the word *shasei* ("delineation from nature") to describe his theory. Through his articles Masaoka also stimulated renewed interest in the 8th-century poetry anthology *Man'yōshū* ("Collection of Ten Thousand Leaves") and in the haiku poet Buson. He frequently wrote of his illness, both in his poems and in such essays as "Byōshō rokushaku" (1902; "The Six-foot Sickbed"), but his work is remarkably detached and almost entirely lacking in self-pity.

masculine caesura   In verse, a caesura that follows a stressed or long syllable. *See* CAESURA.

masculine ending   In poetry, a stressed final syllable at the end of a line of verse. *Compare* FEMININE ENDING.

masculine rhyme   In verse, a monosyllabic rhyme, or a rhyme that occurs only in stressed final syllables (such as *claims, flames* or *rare, despair*). *Compare* FEMININE RHYME. Emily Dickinson used the masculine rhyme to great effect in the last stanza of "After great pain, a formal feeling comes—":

> This is the Hour of Lead—
> Remembered, if outlived,
> As Freezing persons, recollect the Snow—
> First—Chill—then Stupor—then the letting go—

Masefield \'mās-,fēld\, John (b. June 1, 1878, Ledbury, Herefordshire, Eng.—d. May 12, 1967, near Abingdon, Berkshire)   Poet best known for his poems of the sea and for his long narrative poems, such as *The Everlasting Mercy* (1911), which shocked literary orthodoxy with its phrases of a colloquial coarseness hitherto unknown in 20th-century English verse.

Masefield was apprenticed aboard a windjammer that sailed around Cape Horn. He left the sea after that voyage and spent several years living precariously in the United States. His work there in a carpet factory is described in his autobiography, *In the Mill* (1941). He returned to England, worked for a time as a journalist for the *Manchester Guardian*, and settled in London. After he succeeded Robert Bridges as poet laureate in 1930, his poetry became more austere.

Others of Masefield's long narrative poems are *Dauber* (1913) and *Reynard the Fox* (1919). He also wrote novels of adventure—*Sard Harker* (1924), *Odtaa* (1926), and *Basilissa* (1940)—sketches, and works for children. His other works include the poetic dramas *The Tragedy of Nan* (1909) and *The Tragedy of Pompey the Great* (1910) and a further autobiographical volume, *So Long to Learn* (1952).

mask   *see* MASQUE.

mašnawī \'măs-nă-ˌwē\ or **mašnavī** \-ˌvē\ or **mathnavī** \'măth-nă-ˌvē\ [Persian *masnavi* (spelled *mathnawī*), probably a derivative of Arabic *mathnā* two by two]   A series of distichs (couplets) in rhymed pairs (*aa, bb, cc,* and so on) that makes up a characteristic type of Persian verse, used chiefly for heroic, historical, and romantic epic and didactic poetry.

The form originated in the Middle Persian period (roughly from the 3rd century BC to the 9th century AD). It became a favorite poetic form of the Persians and those cultures they influenced. Only a restricted number of meters was employed, and no meter allowed more than 11 syllables in a hemistich (half-line). Meter and diction were prescribed in accordance with the topic. Epic poetry was unknown to the Arabs, who were averse to fiction, whether it was expressed in poetry or in prose. Eventually, however, the *mašnawī* also took root in Arabic literature, where it bore the Arabic name *muzdawij*.

Mason \'mā-sən\, Bobbie Ann (b. May 1, 1940, Mayfield, Ky., U.S.)   Short-story writer and novelist known for her evocation of rural Kentucky life.

Mason was reared on a dairy farm. She graduated from the University of Kentucky and moved to New York City. She attended the State University of New York at Binghamton and the University of Connecticut; her dissertation on Vladimir Nabokov was published as *Nabokov's Garden: A Guide to Ada* (1974). After 1979, she began publishing stories in *The New Yorker*, the *Atlantic Monthly*, and elsewhere.

Mason received critical acclaim for *Shiloh and Other Stories* (1982), her first collection of stories, which described the lives of working-class people in a shifting rural society now dominated by chain stores, television, and superhighways. *In Country* (1985), her first novel, was also steeped in mass culture, leading one critic to speak of Mason's "Shopping Mall Realism." Many critics praised her realistic regional dialogue, although some compared the novel unfavorably to her shorter works. In 1988 Mason published *Spence + Lila*, the story of a long-married couple. *Love Life: Stories* appeared in 1989 and the novel *Feather Crowns* in 1993.

Mason, Bertha \'bər-thə-'mā-sən\   Fictional character, the Creole wife of Edward Rochester in JANE EYRE by Charlotte Brontë and WIDE SARGASSO SEA by Jean Rhys.

Mason, Perry \'per-ē-'mās-ən\   Fictional American trial lawyer and detective, the protagonist of more than 80 mystery novels (beginning with *The Case of the Velvet Claws*, 1933) by American attorney Erle Stanley Gardner. Mason, who almost never lost a case, also had a successful legal career in film, radio (1943–55), and especially on television, as portrayed by Raymond Burr (1957–66 and 1985–93) and by Monte Markham (1973–74).

Perry Mason is assisted by his faithful secretary, Della Street, and has his own private investigator, Paul Drake. Sergeant Holcomb and Lieutenant Tragg of the Los Angeles Police Department appear in each mystery, as does District Attorney Hamilton Burger, whose carefully prepared case for the prosecution is no match for Mason's defense of the accused.

masque or **mask** \'mask\ [Middle French, mask, masquerade]   A short, allegorical dramatic entertainment of the 16th and 17th centuries performed by masked actors. Most likely originating in pre-Christian religious rites and folk ceremonies known as disguising, or mummery, masques evolved into elaborate court spectacles that, under various names, entertained royalty throughout Europe.

During the 16th century the continental European masque traveled to Tudor England, where it became a court entertainment played before the king. Gorgeous costumes, spectacular scenery with elaborate machinery to move it on- and off-

stage, and rich allegorical verse marked the English masque. The masque reached its zenith when Ben Jonson became court poet. He endowed the form with great literary as well as social force. In 1605 Jonson and the scene designer and architect Inigo Jones produced the first of many excellent masques, which they continued to collaborate on until 1634.

Jonson invented the antimasque—also known as the antemasque, the false masque, and the antic masque—and produced the first one in 1609. It took place before the main masque and concentrated on grotesque elements, in direct contrast to the elegance of the masque that followed. In later years the masque developed into opera, and the antimasque became primarily a farce or pantomime. After Jonson's retirement, masques became mainly vehicles for spectacle.

Masque of the Red Death, The   Allegorical short story by Edgar Allen POE, first published in *Graham's Magazine* in April 1842.

In a medieval land ravaged by the Red Death, a plague that causes swift, agonizing death, Prince Prospero retreats to his castle with 1,000 knights and ladies. There he welds the doors and windows shut, confident that he and his guests will escape death. Prospero gives a masquerade ball. At midnight, the grotesquely costumed courtiers find a fearful figure among them, costumed in shrouds and dried blood as the Red Death. Prospero orders the figure's execution, then raises his sword to stab it himself but falls dead. When others try to hold the specter, they find it has no body. They realize that it is the Red Death itself, and one by one they expire.

Massinger \'mas-in-jər\, Philip (b. 1583, near Salisbury, Wiltshire, Eng.—d. March 1639/40, London)   English playwright noted for his social realism and satirical power.

After an indefinite period of apprenticeship—during which he wrote for the theatrical manager Philip Henslowe and collaborated, from about 1613, with fellow playwrights, including John Fletcher—Massinger began about 1620 to work as an independent author. In 1625 he succeeded Fletcher as the chief playwright of the King's Men, a well-known theatrical company. Though apparently not as successful as Fletcher, he remained with the King's Men until his death.

Among the plays Massinger collaborated on with Fletcher is *The False One* (c. 1620), a treatment of the story of Julius Caesar and Cleopatra. Two other important plays written in collaboration are *The Fatal Dowry* (1616–19, with Nathan Field), a domestic tragedy in a French setting, and *The Virgin Martyr* (1620?, with Thomas Dekker), a historical play about the persecution of Christians under the Roman emperor Diocletian. Fifteen plays written solely by Massinger have survived, but many of their dates can only be conjectured. Of these, *The Roman Actor* is considered his best serious play.

The Bondman (1623), about a slave revolt in the Greek city of Syracuse, is one of Massinger's seven tragicomedies and shows his concern for state affairs. The tendency of his serious plays to conform to the standards of the day, however, is contradicted by the mordant realism and satirical force of his two great comedies—*A New Way to Pay Old Debts* and *The City Madam* (1632?).

master \'mas-tər\   In nature-based mythology, a supernatural being who is regarded as the intermediary between humans and a particular species of animal. The master replenishes the species and also sends animals to be killed by deserving hunters.

Master and Margarita, The \ˌmär-gə-'rē-tə\   Novel written by Mikhail BULGAKOV in the 1930s and published as *Master i Margarita* in a censored form in the Soviet Union in 1966–67. The unexpurgated version was published by the Soviets in 1973. It is considered a 20th-century masterpiece.

The novel is witty and ribald, and at the same time a penetrating philosophical work that wrestles with profound and eternal problems of good and evil. It juxtaposes two planes of action—one set in Moscow in the 1930s and the other in Jerusalem at the time of Christ. The three central characters of the contemporary plot are the Devil, disguised as one Professor Woland; the "Master," a repressed novelist; and Margarita, who, though married to a bureaucrat, loves the Master. The Master has burned his manuscript and gone willingly into a psychiatric ward when critics attacked his work—a portrayal of the story of Jesus. Margarita sells her soul to the Devil in order to obtain the Master's release from the psychiatric ward. A parallel plot presents the action of the Master's destroyed novel, the condemnation of Yeshua (Jesus) in Jerusalem.

Master Builder, The   Drama in three acts by Henrik IBSEN, originally published as *Bygmester Solness* in 1892 and first performed in 1893. The play explores the needs of the artist in relation to those of society and the limits of artistic creativity. There is an autobiographical element in the depiction of the aging architect, Halvard Solness, who feels pressure from a younger, more idealistic and ambitious generation of architects and fears the decay of his own creativity.

Master of Ballantrae, The \'bal-ən-,trā\ (*in full* The Master of Ballantrae: A Winter's Tale)   Novel by Scottish writer Robert Louis STEVENSON, first serialized in *Scribner's Magazine* in 1888–89 and in book form in 1889.

The novel is an example of the moral ambiguity Stevenson had explored earlier in *Dr. Jekyll and Mr. Hyde*. Ballantrae is bold and unscrupulous; his younger brother Henry is plodding, good-natured, and honest. While Ballantrae joins the fight to restore the Stuarts to the English throne during the 1745 rebellion, his brother stays behind as a supporter of King George. Ballantrae is believed dead but returns to find Henry in charge of the estate, married to Ballantrae's love. The elder brother begins to persecute the younger, in Scotland and then America; both eventually die in the Adirondacks.

masterpiece \'mas-tər-,pēs\   A work of art of notable excellence or brilliance. A supreme intellectual or artistic achievement; specifically, an artist's most accomplished or climactic work marking the high point of his or her creativity.

Masters \'mas-tərz\, Edgar Lee (b. Aug. 23, 1869, Garnett, Kan., U.S.—d. March 5, 1950, Philadelphia, Pa.)   American poet and novelist, best known as author of SPOON RIVER ANTHOLOGY (1915).

Masters grew up on his grandfather's farm near New Salem, Ill. A volume of his verses appeared in 1898, followed by *Maximilian*, a drama in blank verse (1902); *The New Star Chamber and Other Essays* (1904); *Blood of the Prophets* (1905); and a series of plays issued between 1907 (*Althea*) and 1911 (*The Bread of Idleness*).

In 1909 Masters was introduced to *Epigrams from the Greek Anthology*. He was seized by the idea of composing a similar series of free-verse epitaphs in the form of monologues. The result was *Spoon River Anthology*, in which the former inhabitants of the fictitious community of Spoon River speak from the grave of their bitter, unfulfilled lives in the dreary confines of a small town.

Though Masters continued to publish volumes of verse almost yearly, the quality of his work never again rose to the level of the *Spoon River Anthology*. Among his novels are *Mitch Miller* (1920) and *The Nuptial Flight* (1923). Masters wrote biographies of Abraham Lincoln, Walt Whitman (1937), and Mark Twain (1938). His best effort in this form is *Vachel Lindsay: A Poet in America* (1935), a study of his friend and fellow poet. Also notable are his autobiography, *Across Spoon River*

(1936), and *The Sangamon* (1942), a volume in the "Rivers of America" series.

Mastro-don Gesualdo \'mäs-trō-,dȯn-jez-'wäl-dō\   Realistic novel of Sicilian life by Giovanni VERGA, published in Italian in 1889.

Mastro-don can be translated "Sir-Workman," a title that embodies the story's central dilemma. The protagonist, Gesualdo Motta, is a peasant who becomes a wealthy landowner through hard work and judicious business practices, but he cannot rise socially despite his marriage to the noble Bianca Trao. The decadence of the unbending Trao family is repeatedly contrasted with the honesty, strength, vitality, ingenuity, and ambition of Gesualdo. He is unable to understand why he becomes alienated from both the gentry and the peasantry; this lack of insight is the source of his tragedy.

Masukagami \'mä-sū-'kä-gä-mē\   Historical epic about the Kamakura period (1192–1333) and one of the four best-known *kagami* (records) of Japanese history. The document, which is attributed to NIJŌ Yoshimoto, was written between 1333 and 1376 and narrates the events occurring from the birth of the emperor Go-Toba in 1180 to the return of the emperor Go-Daigo from exile on the Oki Islands in 1334. It includes descriptions of the Mongol invasions of Japan in 1274 and 1281.

Matchmaker, The   Comedy in four acts by Thornton WILDER, produced in 1954 and published in 1955.

The Matchmaker is more traditional than Wilder's earlier plays, although it does employ one of the playwright's favorite nontraditional devices of having the characters address the audience directly.

In the drama, wealthy merchant Horace Vandergelder, a widower, hopes to marry the milliner Irene Molloy. He turns to his late wife's friend Dolly Levi for help, but Dolly wants Horace herself. A series of comic misadventures follow.

In 1964 the play was adapted into the immensely successful musical *Hello Dolly!* (film, 1969).

Matos Guerra \'mȧ-tüsh-'ger-ə\, Gregório de (b. 1623/33, Salvador, Braz.—d. Oct. 19, 1696, Recife)   Poet who was called the Brazilian Villon because of his literary similarity to François Villon, a French lyric poet of the 15th century. Though he produced no single great work, his was the first native Brazilian poetic voice.

Born into the slave-owning gentry, Matos Guerra studied law at Coimbra, Port., and advanced to a high position in Lisbon until he fell into disfavor for using his caustic wit at the expense of court society. Returning to Bahia, Braz., while in his 40s, he practiced law after his own fashion, sometimes defending the poor without charge. His sarcastic epigrams (directed chiefly against the ruling classes, though he did not spare anyone) became increasingly bitter. His satirical verses earned him the nickname *bôca do inferno* ("devil's mouthpiece").

Exiled to the African colony of Angola, Matos Guerra composed a farewell to his native land in which he compared Brazilians to beasts of burden toiling to support Portuguese rascals. He was later permitted to return to Pernambuco.

His poetical works were not printed until 1882. His rebellious spirit made him one of the cultural heroes of Brazil.

matra \'mä-trə\ [Sanskrit *mātrā*, literally, measure, quantity]   A unit of metrical quantity equal to a short vowel in Sanskrit and other Indian languages.

Matsunaga Teitoku \mä-'tsū-nä-gä-'tā-tō-,kü\, *original name* Matsunaga Katsuguma \kä-'tsū-gū-mä\, *also called* Shōyuken \'shō-,yū-,ken\ *or* Chozumaru \chō-'zū-mä-rů\ (b. 1571, Kyōto, Japan—d. Jan. 3, 1654, Kyōto)   Renowned Japanese scholar and haikai poet of the early Tokugawa period (1603–

1867) who founded the Teitoku (or Teimon) school of haikai poetry. Teitoku raised haikai—comic *renga* (linked verses) from which the more serious 17-syllable hokku (later called haiku) of Bashō were derived—to an acceptable literary standard and made them into a popular poetic style.

Teitoku was the son of a professional *renga* poet, and he received an excellent education from some of the best poets of the day. After making the acquaintance of the Neo-Confucian scholar Hayashi Razan, Teitoku began giving public lectures on Japanese classics. In about 1620 he opened the Teitoku school in his home; at first he concentrated on educating children, but gradually he became more interested in tutoring aspiring poets.

Throughout this time he had been composing poems, primarily serious *waka* and *renga* but also lighter haikai. Although reluctant at first, he allowed one of his students to publish a number of his haikai in the anthology *Enoko-shū* (1633; "Puppy Collection"). This volume established him as the leading poet of the early to mid-17th century, and numerous poets were inspired to compose haikai. Several other collections of his poems were published, including *Taka tsukuba* (1638) and *Shinzo inu tsukuba-shu* (1643). Teitoku also set down the rules he had formulated for writing haikai in *Gosan* (1651).

Matter of Britain *see* ARTHURIAN LEGEND.

Matthews \'math-yūz\, Brander, *in full* James Brander Matthews (b. Feb. 21, 1852, New Orleans, La., U.S.—d. March 31, 1929, New York, N.Y.) Essayist, drama critic, novelist, and first American professor of dramatic literature.

Educated at Columbia University, Matthews was professor of literature at Columbia from 1892 to 1900 and of dramatic literature from 1900 to 1924. A prominent figure in New York literary groups, he was the founder of both the Authors' and Players' clubs. Matthews was the author of many short stories and critical essays, was a regular critic for *The New York Times* for a long period, and was the author or editor of more than 40 books. *A Confident Tomorrow* (1899) is considered his best novel. His sound scholarship was revealed in such works as *Molière: His Life and His Works* (1910), *Shakspere as a Playwright* (1913), and *French Dramatists of the 19th Century* (1881).

Matthiessen \'math-ə-sən\, Peter (b. May 22, 1927, New York, N.Y., U.S.) American novelist, naturalist, and wilderness writer whose work dealt with the destructive effects of encroaching technology on preindustrial cultures and the natural environment.

After serving in the U.S. Navy, Matthiessen attended the Sorbonne and Yale University. He moved to Paris, where he helped to found and edit the literary journal *The Paris Review*.

A dedicated naturalist, Matthiessen wrote more than 15 books of nonfiction, including *Wildlife in America* (1959), a history of the destruction of wildlife in North America; *The Cloud Forest: A Chronicle of the South American Wilderness* (1961); *Under the Mountain Wall: A Chronicle of Two Seasons of the Stone Age* (1962), about his experiences as a member of a scientific expedition to New Guinea; *Blue Meridian: The Search for the Great White Shark* (1971); *The Snow Leopard* (1978), set in remote regions of Nepal; and *African Silences* (1991). His book *In the Spirit of Crazy Horse* (1983), about the conflict between federal agents and the American Indian Movement at Wounded Knee, S.D., in 1973, was the subject of a prolonged libel suit that blocked all but an initial printing and was not settled until 1990; in 1991 the book was republished.

Matthiessen's novels include *Race Rock* (1954); the acclaimed *At Play in the Fields of the Lord* (1965; film, 1991), a surrealistic work involving missionaries, Indians, and an expatriate American pilot in the South American rain forest; *Far Tortuga* (1975), a complex work about events leading up to the

death of the crew of a turtle-fishing boat in the Caribbean; and *Killing Mister Watson* (1990).

Matthisson \'mät-i-sön\, Friedrich von (b. Jan. 23, 1761, Hohendodeleben, near Magdeburg, Saxony [Germany]—d. March 12, 1831, Wörlitz, Anhalt-Dessau) German poet whose verses were praised for their melancholy sweetness and pastoral descriptive passages.

Matthisson's poems, which brought him great popularity in his time, were published as *Gedichte* in 1787; their melodious verse exhibits a vigor and warmth combined with delicacy and style. His poem "Adelaide" was set to music as a song by Ludwig van Beethoven.

Maturin \'mat-yŭ-rin\, Charles Robert (b. 1782, Dublin, Ire.—d. Oct. 30, 1824, Dublin) Irish Roman Catholic clergyman, dramatist, and author of gothic romances. He has been called "the last of the Goths," as his best-known work, MELMOTH THE WANDERER (1820), is considered the last of the classic English gothic romances.

Educated at Trinity College, Maturin became curate of St. Peter's in Dublin in 1804. His first popular success was the verse tragedy *Bertram* (1816), produced at London's Drury Lane with Edmund Kean in the title role, but his next two plays were failures. He returned to novels, producing his masterpiece, *Melmoth*, the adventures of an Irish Faust.

Matute \mä-'tū-tā\, Ana María (b. July 26, 1926, Barcelona, Sp.) Spanish novelist whose fiction often featured children or adolescents dealing with such issues as betrayal, isolation, and rites of passage.

Matute's frequent use of biblical allusion, in particular her interest in the story of Cain and Abel, was evident in many of her works, beginning with her first novel, *Los Abel* (1948; "The Abel Family"). Her later novels include *Fiesta al noroeste* (1952; "Celebration in the Northwest"), *Pequeño teatro* (1954; "Little Theater"), and *Los hijos muertos* (1958; *The Lost Children*). Matute also wrote a trilogy consisting of *Primera memoria* (1959; U.K. title, *The Awakening*; U.S. title, *School of the Sun*), about children thrust into an adult world by the Spanish Civil War; a war novel, *Los soldados lloran de noche* (1964; "The Soldiers Cry by Night"); and *La trampa* (1969; "The Trap"), in which the children of *Primera memoria* are grown up.

Matute's short-story collections include *Los niños tontos* (1956; "The Foolish Children") and *Algunos muchachos* (1968; *The Heliotrope Wall*). She also wrote several works for children.

Maud \'mȯd\ Poem by Alfred, Lord TENNYSON, composed in 1854 and published in *Maud and Other Poems* in 1855.

The poem's morbid narrator tells of his father's suicide following financial ruin. Lonely and miserable, he falls in love with Maud, the daughter of the wealthy neighbor who led his father into bankruptcy. After he kills Maud's brother in a duel, the narrator flees the country; he goes mad when he learns of Maud's death but recovers his sanity through service in war.

Many of the poet's admirers were shocked by the morbidity of the poem and by the bellicosity of the hero. It nonetheless contains some of Tennyson's most lyrical passages.

Maugham \'mȯm\, Robin, *byname of* Robert Cecil Romer Maugham, 2nd Viscount Maugham of Hartfield (b. May 17, 1916, London, Eng.—d. March 13, 1981, Brighton) English novelist, playwright, and travel writer, who achieved a certain fame and no little notoriety with his novel *The Servant* (1948).

Maugham was educated at Eton and Trinity College, Cambridge. He served as an intelligence officer in World War II and was severely wounded in 1944. Two nonfiction books based on his war experiences are *Come to Dust* (1945) and *Nomad* (1947).

The Servant, though denounced as obscene, convinced W. Somerset Maugham (Robin's uncle) of his nephew's literary ability. The novel was filmed in 1965. Much of Maugham's work is about homosexuals: a play, *Enemy* (1970), brings a British and a German soldier into confrontation and charts their doomed friendship; and *The Last Encounter* (1972) portrays Charles George Gordon of Khartoum as a man as unsure of his destiny as of his sexual orientation.

Maugham wrote several memoirs, including *Somerset and All the Maughams* (1966) and *Conversations with Willie: Recollections of W. Somerset Maugham* (1978). His autobiographies include *Escape from the Shadows* (1972) and *Search for Nirvana* (1975).

Maugham \'môm\, W. Somerset, *in full* William Somerset Maugham (b. Jan. 25, 1874, Paris, Fr.—d. Dec. 16, 1965, Nice) English novelist, playwright, and short-story writer whose work is characterized by a clear, unadorned style, cosmopolitan settings, and a shrewd understanding of human nature.

After a year at Heidelberg, Maugham entered St. Thomas's medical school, London, and he qualified as a doctor in 1897. He drew upon his experiences as an obstetrician in his first novel, *Liza of Lambeth* (1897), and its success, though small, encouraged him to abandon medicine. In 1908 he achieved a theatrical triumph—four plays running in London at once—that brought him financial security. During World War I he worked as a secret agent. In 1928 he settled in Cape Ferrat in the south of France.

Brown Brothers

His reputation as a novelist rests primarily on four books: OF HUMAN BONDAGE (1915), a semiautobiographical account of a young medical student's painful progress toward maturity; THE MOON AND SIXPENCE (1919), an account of an unconventional artist, suggested by the life of Paul Gauguin; CAKES AND ALE (1930), the story of a famous novelist, which is thought to contain caricatures of Thomas Hardy and Sir Hugh Walpole; and THE RAZOR'S EDGE (1944), the story of a young American war veteran's quest for a satisfying way of life. Maugham's plays, mainly Edwardian social comedies, soon became dated, while his short stories gained popularity. Many of his short stories portray the conflict of Europeans in alien surroundings, and Maugham's skill in handling plot, in the manner of Guy de Maupassant, is distinguished by economy and suspense. In *The Summing Up* (1938) and *A Writer's Notebook* (1949) Maugham explains his philosophy of life as a resigned atheism and a certain skepticism about the extent of the innate goodness and intelligence of humans; it is this that gives his work its astringent cynicism.

Maunick \mō-'nik\, Édouard J., *in full* Édouard Joseph Marc Maunick (b. Sept. 23, 1931, Mauritius) African poet, critic, and translator.

Maunick grew up in the French-speaking minority culture of Mauritius Island, where, as a métis (mulatto), he experienced social discrimination from both blacks and whites. In 1960 he settled in Paris and published frequently in *Présence Africaine* and other European journals.

His first poetry collection was *Les Oiseaux du sang* (1954; "The Birds of Blood"). In *Les Manèges de la mer* (1964; "Tam-

ing the Sea"), he lamented his lonely exile and the persecution of his people. *Mascaret ou le livre de la mer et de la mort* (1966; "Tidal Wave, or The Book of the Sea and of Death") reiterated his sense of isolation. Outraged by the events of the Nigerian war, he published *Fusillez-moi* (1970; "Shoot Me"), a cry of anguish over the slaughter of the Biafran Igbo (Ibo) people.

Maunick's later collections include *Africaines du temps jadis* (1976; "African Women of Times Gone By") and *En mémoire du mémorable suivi de Jusqu'en terre Yoruba* (1979; "A Memory of the Memorable, Followed by As Far as the Land of the Yoruba"). His *Anthologie personnelle* ("Personal Anthology") was published in 1989.

Maupassant \mō-pȧ-'säⁿ\, Guy de, *in full* Henry-René-Albert-Guy de Maupassant (b. Aug. 5, 1850, Château de Miromesnil?,

near Dieppe, Fr.—d. July 6, 1893, Paris) French writer of short stories and novels of the naturalist school who is by general agreement the greatest French short-story writer.

In 1869 Maupassant began law studies in Paris, which were interrupted by the outbreak of the Franco-Prussian War. He volunteered to serve in the army, and his firsthand experience of war was to provide him with the material for some of his finest stories.

The novelist Gustave Flaubert was a friend of

Archives Photographiques

Maupassant's mother, and when Maupassant returned to Paris in 1871 Flaubert was asked to keep an eye on him. This was the beginning of his apprenticeship, during which Flaubert introduced him to some of the leading writers of the time, including Émile Zola, Ivan Turgenev, Édmond de Goncourt, and Henry James. Maupassant published one or two stories under a pseudonym in obscure provincial magazines, but the turning point came in April 1880, when he was one of six writers who each contributed a war story to a volume called *Les Soirées de Médan*. BOULE DE SUIF ("Ball of Fat") was not only by far the best of the six, it is probably the finest story that Maupassant ever wrote. The next 10 years saw the publication of some 300 short stories, six novels, three travel books, Maupassant's only volume of verse, and a fair sprinkling of miscellaneous works. The stories can be categorized by subject; they concern the Franco-Prussian War, the Norman peasantry, the bureaucracy, life on the banks of the Seine, the emotional problems of the different classes, and—somewhat ominously in a late story such as "Le Horla" (1887; THE HORLA)—hallucination. Together, they present a comprehensive picture of French life from 1870 to 1890.

Maupassant's early years in Paris were also the start of his phenomenal promiscuity. When he was in his early 20s, he discovered that he was suffering from syphilis. Although Maupassant appeared to be sturdy and healthy, his letters are full of lamentations about his health. With the passing of the years he became more and more somber. He had begun to travel for pleasure, but these journeys gradually changed into compulsive, symptomatic wanderings until he felt a constant need to be on the move. On Jan. 2, 1892, he tried to commit suicide by cutting his throat. He was committed to an asylum, where he died one month before his 43rd birthday.

Maupin \'mȯ-pin\, Armistead (b. May 13, 1944, Washington, D.C., U.S.)   Novelist known for his *Tales of the City* series.

Maupin's career as a fiction writer was launched when his *Tales of the City* was published as a serial in the *San Francisco Chronicle* in 1976–77, then as a book in 1978. The story, set in San Francisco, focuses on three characters—Mary Ann Singleton, a naive young woman from Cleveland; Michael "Mouse" Tolliver, her homosexual friend; and their motherly landlady, Anna Madrigal, a transsexual. The author's compassion for his characters and his lively, humorous style made *Tales of the City* a cult favorite. Five popular sequels followed: *More Tales of the City* (1980), *Further Tales of the City* (1982), *Baby cakes* (1984), *Significant Others* (1987), and *Sure of You* (1989), all but the last initially serialized in San Francisco newspapers. Although the tone of the books is generally lighthearted, throughout the series characters confront serious personal and political issues including loneliness, parenthood, and the loss of a partner to AIDS. Maupin broke from the series to write *Maybe the Moon* (1992), the story of a dwarf actress.

Mauriac \mȯr-'yȧk\, Claude (b. April 25, 1914, Paris, Fr.) French novelist and critic, a practitioner and interpreter of the avant-garde school of *nouveau roman* ("new novel") writers. It was Mauriac who coined the label *alittérature* ("nonliterature") in his book *L'Alittérature contemporaine* (1958; *The New Literature*) to describe the trend in French fiction.

While a private secretary to Charles de Gaulle (1944–49) and a film and literary critic for the newspaper *Le Figaro*, Mauriac wrote solid and creative critical essays. The eldest son of novelist François Mauriac, he established his own reputation as a novelist with four works published under the general title *Le Dialogue intérieur*, comprising *Toutes les femmes sont fatales* (1957; *All Women Are Fatal*), *Le Dîner en ville* (1959; *The Dinner Party*), *La Marquise sortit à cinq heures* (1961; *The Marquise Went Out at Five*), and *L'Agrandissement* (1963; "The Enlargement"). Mauriac's novels are formless. They may deal simply with the imperceptible gliding of time in the lives of eight people gathered around a dinner table, or they may deal with the absurdity of trying to establish the traditional novel's verisimilitude.

Mauriac published a multivolume "novel of [his] life," consisting of excerpts from letters, documents, and parts of other writers' works interspersed with entries from his own journals. *Le Temps immobile* ("Time Immobilized") was published in 10 volumes between 1974 and 1988. Mauriac also wrote several plays, including *La Conversation* (1964), *Une Certaine Rage* (1977), and *L'Éternité parfois* (1978; "Occasional Eternity").

Mauriac \mȯr-'yȧk\, François (b. Oct. 11, 1885, Bordeaux, Fr.—d. Sept. 1, 1970, Paris)   Novelist, essayist, poet, playwright, and journalist, winner in 1952 of the Nobel Prize for Literature; he belonged to the lineage of French Roman Catholic writers who examined the ugly realities of modern life in the light of eternity. At the heart of every one of his works Mauriac placed a soul grappling with the problems of sin, grace, and salvation.

Mauriac's first published work was a volume of delicately fervent poems, *Les Mains jointes* (1909; "Joined Hands"). His vocation, however, lay with the novel. His first works of fiction, *L'Enfant chargé de chaînes* (1913; *Young Man in Chains*) and *La Robe prétexte* (1914; *The Stuff of Youth*), established his recurring themes. The drab and suffocating strictures of bourgeois life provide the framework for his explorations of the relations of characters deprived of love. *Le Baiser au lépreux* (1922; *The Kiss to the Leper*) established Mauriac as a major novelist. He showed increasing mastery in *Le Désert de l'amour* (1949; *The Desert of Love*) and in *Thérèse Desqueyroux* (1927;

Thérèse). *Le Noeud de vipères* (1932; *Vipers' Tangle*) is often considered Mauriac's masterpiece. It is a marital drama, depicting an old lawyer's rancor toward his family, his passion for money, and his final conversion.

In 1933 Mauriac was elected to the Académie Française. Later novels include the partly autobiographical *Le Mystère Frontenac* (1933; *The Frontenac Mystery*), *Les Chemins de la mer* (1939; *The Unknown Sea*), and *La Pharisienne* (1941; *A Woman of the Pharisees*). In 1938 Mauriac turned to writing plays, beginning with *Asmodée*, in which the hero is a heinous, domineering character who controls weaker souls. Such is also the theme of the less successful *Les Mal-Aimés* (1945; "The Poorly Loved").

A highly sensitive man, Mauriac felt compelled to justify himself before his critics. *Le Romancier et ses personnages* (1933; "The Novelist and His Characters") and the four volumes of his *Journal* (1934–51), followed by three volumes of *Mémoires* (1959–67), describe his intentions, his methods, and his reactions to contemporary moral values. Mauriac tackled the difficult dilemma of the Christian writer—how to portray evil in human nature without placing temptation before his readers—in *Dieu et Mammon* (1929; *God and Mammon*).

Mauriac was also a prominent polemical writer. He intervened vigorously in the 1930s, condemning totalitarianism in all its forms and denouncing fascism in Italy and Spain. In World War II he worked with the writers of the Resistance. After the war he increasingly engaged in political discussion. He wrote *De Gaulle* (1964), having officially supported him from 1962.

Maurice \'mȯr-is, 'mär-; mȯ-'rēs\   Novel by E.M. FORSTER, published posthumously in 1971. Because of the work's homosexual theme, the novel was published only after Forster's death.

Maurice Hall, a student at Cambridge University, reaches maturity and self-awareness when he accepts his homosexuality and also renounces the bourgeois values in which he has always believed. He resolves his conflicts about class consciousness when he takes as a lover Alec Scudder, a gamekeeper on the estate of Maurice's friend Clive.

Maurice \'mȯr-əs, 'mär-; mȯ-'rēs\, Furnley, *pseudonym of* Frank Leslie Thompson Wilmot \'wil-mət, -,mät\ (b. April 6, 1881, Collingwood, Vic., Australia—d. Feb. 22, 1942, Melbourne)   Australian poet, best known for his book *To God: From the Warring Nations* (1917), a powerful indictment of the waste, cruelty, and stupidity of war. He was also the author of lyrics, satiric verses, and essays.

Wilmot began to write poetry before he was 20, contributing his earliest work to the *Tocsin*, a Melbourne labor paper. His first book, *Some Verses*, was published in 1903 under his real name, and a year later *More Verses* appeared but was withdrawn shortly after publication. Neither of these books attracted much attention, and their embarrassed author took the pen name Furnley Maurice. *Unconditioned Songs* (1913) caused a small stir, but it was not until *To God: From the Warring Nations* appeared in 1917 that critics began to take an interest in Wilmot's work. In the same year, he brought out *The Bay and Padie Book: Kiddie Songs*, highly successful children's verse that went through three editions in the next nine years. *Eyes of Vigilance* (1920) contained what is considered some of his best poetry.

Maurois \mȯr-'wȧ\, André, *pseudonym of* Émile Herzog \er-'zȯg, *Angl* 'hərt-,sȯg\ (b. July 26, 1885, Elbeuf, Fr.—d. Oct. 9, 1967, Paris)   Biographer, novelist, essayist, children's writer, and prominent personality in French letters for 50 years.

Maurois came under the formative influence of the stimulating French philosopher and teacher Alain (Émile Chartier).

Maurois's first literary success was a humorous interpretation of the English in *Les Silences du Colonel Bramble* (1918; *The Silence of Colonel Bramble*). His novels depict the crises of a limited bourgeois milieu: in *Bernard Quesnay* (1926), an industrialist facing a strike; and in *Climats* (1928; *Whatever Gods May Be*), the problems of a second marriage. He demonstrated a broad culture in his popular histories: *Histoire de l'Angleterre* (1937; "History of England"), and *Histoire des États-Unis* (1943; "History of the United States"). Maurois is best known for biographies with the narrative interest of novels, including those on Percy Bysshe Shelley (*Ariel*, 1923), Lord Byron (*Don Juan*, 1930; *Byron*), Victor Hugo (*Olympio*, 1954), George Sand (*Lélia*, 1952), and Honoré de Balzac (*Prométhée*, 1965; *Prometheus: The Life of Balzac*). *À la recherche de Marcel Proust* (1949; *The Quest for Proust*) is considered by many his finest biography.

Maurras \mȯ-'räs\, Charles(-Marie-Photius) (b. April 20, 1868, Martigues, Fr.—d. Nov. 16, 1952, Tours) French writer and political theorist whose "integral nationalism" anticipated some of the ideas of fascism.

In 1891, soon after his arrival in Paris, Maurras founded, with Jean Moréas, a group of young poets opposed to the Symbolists and later known as the *école romane* ("Gallo-Roman school"). The group favored classical restraint and clarity over what they considered to be the vague, emotional character of Symbolist work. In 1899 Maurras helped found *L'Action française*, a review devoted to integral nationalism. He also acquired a reputation as the author of *Le Chemin de paradis* (1895; "The Way to Paradise"), philosophical short stories; *Anthinea* (1900), travel essays; and *Les Amants de Venise* (1900; "The Lovers of Venice"), dealing with the love affair of George Sand and Alfred de Musset. After World War I, he was admired in literary quarters as the poet of *La Musique intérieure* (1925; *Music Within Me*), the critic of *Barbarie et poésie* (1925; "Barbarism and Poetry"), and the memorialist of *Au signe de Flore* (1931; "At the Sign of Flora").

Maurras was elected to the Académie Française in 1938. During World War II, he became a strong supporter of the collaborationist government under Philippe Pétain. He was arrested in September 1944 and the following January was sentenced to life imprisonment and excluded from the Académie. In 1952 he was released on grounds of health.

Mavor \'mā-vər\, Elizabeth (Osborne) (b. Dec. 17, 1927, Glasgow, Scot.) British author whose novels and nonfiction works concern relationships between women.

Mavor's first novel, *Summer in the Greenhouse* (1959), considered by some to be her finest, presents a woman's lyrical evocation of a youthful affair. At the end of *The Temple of Flora* (1961), the heroine renounces her married lover. Mavor's third novel, *The Redoubt* (1967), is concerned with betrayal and regrowth; it contrasts the unhappy marriages of two young couples with the contented union of an older couple. In the ironic *A Green Equinox* (1973), the heroine embarks on sequential love affairs with a man, his wife, and his mother. *The White Solitaire* (1988) was published after a hiatus of 15 years.

Mavor's nonfiction includes two historical biographies, *The Virgin Mistress: A Study in Survival* (1964) and *The Ladies of Llangollen* (1971), about two 18th-century Irish gentlewomen who ran away to Wales and lived together for 50 years. She also edited *The Captain's Wife: The South American Journals of Maria Graham 1821–23* (1993), as well as diaries or works by William Beckford, Katherine Wilmot, and Fanny Kemble.

maxim \'mak-sim\ [Medieval Latin *maxima*, short for *maxima propositio* axiom, literally, greatest proposition] A saying of proverbial nature.

Maximes \mȧk-'sēm\ Collection of 500 epigrammatic reflections on human behavior by François de LA ROCHEFOUCAULD, published in five editions between 1665 and 1678. The first edition of the *Maximes* was called *Réflexions ou sentences et maximes morales* and did not contain epigrams exclusively; the most eloquent single item, which appeared only in the first edition and was thereafter removed by the author, is a three-page poetic description of self-interest, a quality he found in all forms of life and in all actions. The manuscripts also contain epigrams embedded in longer reflections; in some cases the various versions show the steps by which a series of connected sentences was filed down to the point of ultimate brevity. Beneath the general single statement, however, can be found a personal reaction, often violent in its expression, to some contemporary political or social issue.

La Rochefoucauld's chief glory is not as thinker but as artist. In the variety and subtlety of his arrangement of words he made the maxime into a jewel.

Maxwell \'maks-,wel, -wəl\, Gavin (b. July 15, 1914, Elrig, near Mochrum, Wigtown, Scot.—d. Sept. 6, 1969, Inverness, Inverness) Scottish author and naturalist.

Maxwell became a freelance journalist, though ornithology remained his special interest. In 1945 he bought the island of Soay and described in *Harpoon at a Venture* (1952; U.S. title, *Harpoon Venture*) his attempt to establish a shark fishery there. Maxwell's prolonged stay in Sicily resulted in two books, *God Protect Me from My Friends* (1956; U.S. title, *Bandit*), about the bandit Salvatore Giuliano, and *The Pains of Death* (1959), on the poverty-stricken lives of the islanders. *A Reed Shaken by the Wind* (1957; U.S. title, *People of the Reeds*) is an account of his travels in Iraq. The best-selling *Ring of Bright Water* (1960) is a gentle story of his life with two pet otters in his seaboard cottage in the western Highlands of Scotland; *The Rocks Remain* (1963) is a continuation of the same story.

Maxwell \'maks-wəl\, William, *original name* William Maxwell Keepers, Jr. \'kē-pərz\ (b. Aug. 16, 1908, Lincoln, Ill., U.S.) American author of spare, evocative short stories and novels about small-town life in the American Midwest.

Maxwell taught English at the University of Illinois before joining the staff of *The New Yorker* magazine, where he worked from 1936 to 1976. His first novel, *Bright Center of Heaven*, was published in 1934. *They Came Like Swallows* (1937) tells how an epidemic of influenza affects a close family. *The Folded Leaf* (1945), perhaps Maxwell's best-known work, describes the friendship of two small-town boys through their adolescence and college years. In *Time Will Darken It* (1948) a long visit from relatives disrupts a family; in *The Château* (1961) American travelers encounter postwar French culture.

Maxwell's collections of short stories include *The Old Man at the Railroad Crossing and Other Tales* (1966), *Over by the River, and Other Stories* (1977), and *Billie Dyer and Other Stories* (1992). His 1980 novel *So Long, See You Tomorrow* returns to the subject of a friendship between two boys, this one disrupted by a parent's murder of his spouse, then suicide.

May \'mī\, Karl (Friedrich) (b. Feb. 25, 1842, Hohenstein-Ernstthal, Saxony [Germany]—d. March 30, 1912, Radebeul, Ger.) German author of remarkably realistic juvenile travel and adventure stories, dealing with desert Arabs or with American Indians in the Wild West.

May worked as a schoolteacher until arrested for petty theft. He later was twice arrested for fraud and spent several years in prison, where he is said to have read voraciously. After his release in 1874 May began to write short stories for various periodicals. His popularity soared upon the appearance of his short-story collections and novels in the early 1890s.

Some of the best known of his more than 60 works are *Der Schatz im Silbersee* (1894; "The Treasure in the Silver Lake"), *Durch die Wüste* (1892; *In the Desert*), *Winnetou*, 3 vol. (1893), *Ardistan und Dschinnistan* (1909; *Ardistan and Djinnistan*), and the autobiography *Mein Leben und Streben* (1910; "My Life and Struggle"). Though virtually unknown in the United States, he is widely read in Europe and is one of the world's all-time best-selling fiction writers.

May \'mā\, Thomas (b. 1595—d. Nov. 13, 1650, London, Eng.) English man of letters known for his defense of the English Parliament in its struggle against King Charles I.

After graduating from Cambridge, May began the study of law at Gray's Inn in 1615. He later abandoned law for literature. *The Heir* (1620), a comedy and his first dramatic work, was followed by another comedy and three tragedies and by translations of Virgil and Martial and (in 1627) of Lucan's *Pharsalia*. This last work impressed Charles I, who requested May to compose verse histories of the reigns of Henry II and Edward III. Disappointment at the rewards from Charles may have contributed to May's sympathy with the Parliamentarians. His *History of the Parliament of England, Which Began Nov. the Third, 1640* (1647) and his *Breviary of the History of the Parliament of England* (1650), although impartial in tone, were, in fact, skillful defenses of the Parliamentarian position.

Mayakovsky \mə-,yə-'kóf-skʸē\, Vladimir Vladimirovich (b. July 7 [July 19, New Style], 1893, Bagdadi, Georgia, Russian Empire—d. April 14, 1930, Moscow, U.S.S.R.) The leading poet of the Russian Revolution of 1917 and of the early Soviet period.

Mayakovsky was repeatedly jailed for subversive activity. He started to write poetry during solitary confinement in 1909. On his release he attended the Moscow Art School and joined the Russian Futurist group and soon became its spokesman. In 1912 the group published a manifesto, *Poshchochina obshchestvennomu vkusu* (*A Slap in the Face of Public Taste*), and Mayakovsky's poetry became conspicuously self-assertive and defiant in form and content.

Between 1914 and 1916 Mayakovsky completed two major poems, "Oblako v shtanakh" (1915; "A Cloud in Trousers") and "Fleytapozvonochnik" (1916; "The Backbone Flute"). He sought to "depoetize" poetry, adopting the language of the streets and using daring technical innovations.

When the Russian Revolution broke out, Mayakovsky was wholeheartedly on the side of the Bolsheviks. Such poems as "Oda revolyutsi" (1918; "Ode to Revolution") and "Levy marsh" (1919; "Left March") became highly popular. So too did his *Misteriya buff* (performed 1921; *Mystery Bouffe*), a drama representing the triumph of the "Unclean" (the proletarians) over the "Clean" (the bourgeoisie).

In 1924 Mayakovsky composed a 3,000-line elegy on the death of Vladimir Lenin. After 1925 he traveled in Europe, the United States, Mexico, and Cuba, recording his impressions in poems and in a booklet of caustic sketches, *Moye otkrytiye Ameriki* (1926; "My Discovery of America"). In his last three years he completed two plays: *Klop* (performed 1929; *The Bedbug*), lampooning the type of philistine that emerged with the new economic policy in the Soviet Union, and *Banya* (performed 1930; *The Bathhouse*), a satire of bureaucratic stupidity and opportunism under Joseph Stalin.

Mayakovsky's poetry was saturated with politics, but no amount of social propaganda could stifle his personal need for love, which burst out again and again because of repeated romantic frustrations. Disappointed in love, increasingly alienated from Soviet reality, and denied a visa to travel abroad, he committed suicide in Moscow. *See also* FUTURISM.

Maynard or **Mainard** \me-'när\, François (b. 1582/83, Toulouse, Fr.—d. Dec. 28, 1646) French poet, leading disciple of François de Malherbe and, like him, concerned with the clarification of the French language.

In 1605 Maynard obtained a post with Margaret of Valois (queen consort of Henry de Bourbon, king of Navarre) and began writing pastoral poetry. *Philandre* belongs to this period, although it was not printed until 1619. He attached himself to Malherbe and helped to spread the latter's ideas on the necessity of a standard grammar, the elimination of personal sentiments in writing, and an objective treatment of the subject matter.

Maynard was made a member of the Académie Française in 1634.

Mayor of Casterbridge, The \'kas-tər-,brij\ Novel by Thomas HARDY, published in 1886, first serially (in the periodical *The Graphic*) and later that year in book form. The fictional city of Casterbridge provides a picture of Dorchester in the 19th century. The novel tells of the rise and fall of Michael Henchard, who, starting from nothing after abandoning his wife and daughter, gains prosperity and respect and is reunited with his family, only to lose everything through his own wrongheadedness, his vengeful nature, and a spate of bad luck.

Mbari Mbayo Club \m-'bä-rē-m-'bä-yō\ Meeting place for African writers, artists, and musicians, founded in Ibadan, Nigeria, in 1961. The first club, known as Mbari Club (*mbari* being the Igbo [Ibo] word for "creation"), was established by a group of young writers with the help of Ulli Beier, a teacher at the University of Ibadan. The club operated an art gallery and theater and published *Black Orpheus*, a journal of African and African-American literature.

Duro Ladipo, a Yoruba playwright, established a similar club in Oshogbo, about 50 miles (80 km) northeast of Ibadan. With Beier's help, Ladipo converted his father's house into an art gallery and a theater, where he produced his plays. The Oshogbo club became a vital part of the community. Ladipo drew upon Yoruba mythology, drumming, dance, and poetry and soon developed a type of Yoruba opera. The name of the club (Mbari Club, like its model) was inadvertently altered when the Igbo word *mbari* was mistaken for a Yoruba phrase, *mbari mbayo*, meaning "when we see it we shall be happy." *See also* BLACK ORPHEUS.

McAlmon \mə-'kòl-mən\, Robert (Menzies) (b. March 9, 1896, Clifton, Kansas, U.S.—d. Feb. 2, 1956, Desert Hot Springs, Calif.) American author and publisher and an exemplar of the literary expatriate in Paris during the 1920s.

In 1920 McAlmon moved to Chicago and then to New York, where he and William Carlos Williams began the little magazine *Contact*. In 1921 McAlmon married the English writer Bryher (Annie Winifred Ellerman) and moved to Paris. After publishing a book of his short stories, *A Hasty Bunch* (1922), at his own expense, he founded his own publishing company; under the name Contact Editions, he published his short-story collection *A Companion Volume* (1923) and his autobiographical novel *Post-Adolescence* (1923), as well as works by Williams, Gertrude Stein, Ernest Hemingway, and Bryher.

McAlmon's best-received work was the novel *Village: As It Happened Through a Fifteen Year Period* (1924), a bleak portrait of the inhabitants of an American town. His later books include *Distinguished Air (Grim Fairy Tales)* (1925), the poetry collection *The Portrait of a Generation* (1926), the epic poem *North America, Continent of Conjecture* (1929), and *Being Geniuses Together: An Autobiography* (1938), a Paris memoir. *McAlmon and the Lost Generation: A Self-Portrait* (1962) is a collection of autobiographical writings.

M'Carthy \mə-'kär-thē\, Justin (b. Nov. 22, 1830, Cork, County Cork, Ire.—d. April 24, 1912, Folkestone, Kent, Eng.) Irish politician and historian who first made his name as a novelist with such successes as *Dear Lady Disdain* (1875) and *Miss Misanthrope* (1878) but then published his *History of Our Own Times* (1879–1905), which won general recognition.

M'Carthy began his career as a journalist, but in 1879 he entered Irish politics and became vice-chairman of the new Home Rule Party under Charles Stuart Parnell. In a crisis over the leadership, M'Carthy became chairman of the anti-Parnellites. In the 1892 general election his party won an overwhelming success, but he had no great political ambitions and in 1896 resigned the leadership. In his final years he became nearly blind, but he continued to write by dictation.

McAuley \mə-'kȯ-lē\, James Phillip (b. Oct. 12, 1917, Lakemba, N.S.W., Australia—d. Oct. 15, 1976, Hobart, Tasmania) Australian poet noted for his classical approach, great technical skill, and academic point of view.

Educated at the University of Sydney, McAuley became a senior lecturer at the Australian School of Pacific Administration, editor of *Quadrant*, a literary journal, and professor of English at the University of Tasmania. McAuley's first volume of poetry, *Under Aldebaran* (1946), was followed by *A Vision of Ceremony* (1956); *Captain Quiros* (1964), a verse narrative of the settlement of Australia; *Surprises of the Sun* (1969); *Collected Poems, 1936–70* (1971); *Music Late at Night: Poems, 1970–1973* (1976); and *A World of Its Own* (1977). His prose works include a volume of literary criticism, *The End of Modernity* (1959); a critical interpretation of an earlier Australian poet, *Christopher Brennan* (1973); and *A Map of Australian Verse* (1975).

McBain, Ed   *see* Evan HUNTER.

McCarthy \mə-'kär-thē\, Cormac, *byname of* Charles McCarthy, Jr. (b. July 20, 1933, Providence, R.I., U.S.) American writer in the Southern gothic tradition whose novels about wayward characters in the rural American South and Southwest are noted for their dark violence and dense prose.

Readers were introduced to McCarthy's difficult narrative style in the novel *The Orchard Keeper* (1965). Later works include *Outer Dark* (1968), about two incestuous siblings; *Child of God* (1974), which tells of a lonely man's descent into depravity; and *Suttree* (1979), about a man who overcomes his fixation on death. After *Blood Meridian* (1985), a violent frontier tale, McCarthy achieved popular fame with *All the Pretty Horses* (1992), winner of the National Book Award. The first volume of "The Border Trilogy," it is the coming-of-age story of two Texans who travel to Mexico. The second installment, *The Crossing* (1994), follows a pair of teenage brothers in southwestern New Mexico.

McCarthy \mə-'kär-thē\, Mary (Therese) (b. June 21, 1912, Seattle, Wash., U.S.—d. Oct. 25, 1989, New York, N.Y.) American novelist and critic noted for bitingly satiric commentaries on marriage, the impotence of intellectuals, and the role of women in contemporary urban America.

McCarthy began her career writing book reviews. She served on the editorial staff of the *Partisan Review* from 1937 to 1948. She married four times, the second time, in 1938, to the noted American critic Edmund Wilson, who encouraged her to begin writing fiction.

Her first novel, THE COMPANY SHE KEEPS (1942), concerns a fashionable woman who experiences divorce and psychoanalysis. *The Oasis* (1949) is about the failure of a utopian community of intellectuals. *The Groves of Academe* (1952) is a satiric examination of American higher education during the era of the anticommunist "witch hunts." THE GROUP (1963), her most popular novel, follows the lives of eight Vassar graduates.

Birds of America (1971) is a post-World War II version of the 19th-century novel in which American innocence is confronted with European sophistication. CANNIBALS AND MISSIONARIES (1979) is about the hijacking of a committee flying to Iran to investigate the shah's atrocities. She also wrote two autobiographies, MEMORIES OF A CATHOLIC GIRLHOOD (1957) and *How I Grew* (1987).

McCrae \mə-'krā\, Hugh (Raymond) (b. Oct. 4, 1876, Melbourne, Vic., Australia—d. Feb. 17, 1958, Sydney, N.S.W.) Australian poet, known for his artificial, romantic, highly polished lyrics on the subjects of love, time, and nature.

McCrae was apprenticed to an architect but left the profession for freelance journalism. After trying unsuccessfully to make his way as a journalist and actor in the United States, he returned to Australia, where he became a successful author and occasional actor. His first book of verse, *Satyrs and Sunlight: Sylvarum Libri* (1909), appeared in a revised edition in 1928. His other works include *Colombine* (1920), *Idyllia* (1922), *The Mimshi Maiden* (1938), *Poems* (1939), *Forests of Pan* (1944), and *Voice of the Forest* (1945).

McCullers \mə-'kəl-ərz\, Carson, *original name* Lula Carson Smith \'smith\ (b. Feb. 19, 1917, Columbus, Ga., U.S.—d. Sept. 29, 1967, Nyack, N.Y.) American writer of novels and stories that depict the inner lives of lonely people.

McCullers' first novel, and in the opinion of many her finest work, THE HEART IS A LONELY HUNTER, appeared in 1940. The book concerns five inhabitants of a small town in Georgia—an adolescent girl with a passion to study music, an unsuccessful socialist agitator, a black physician struggling to maintain his personal dignity, a widower who owns a café, and John Singer, the work's protagonist. In the novel THE MEMBER OF THE WEDDING (1946), a 12-year-old motherless girl yearns to go on her brother's honeymoon. McCullers adapted the latter work into a successful stage play in 1950, and it was made into a film in 1952. Another novel, REFLECTIONS IN A GOLDEN EYE (1941), a highly colored psychological horror story set in a peacetime Southern army camp, was also made into a film, and THE BALLAD OF THE SAD CAFÉ, a novelette published with short stories in 1951, was dramatized by Edward Albee in 1963.

McCutcheon \mə-'kəch-ən\, George Barr (b. July 26, 1866, near Lafayette, Ind., U.S.—d. Oct. 23, 1928, New York, N.Y.) American novelist whose best-known works were GRAUSTARK (1901), a romantic novel set in a mythical middle European kingdom, and *Brewster's Millions* (1902), a comic fantasy.

McCutcheon attended Purdue University briefly, leaving to become a newspaper reporter. City editor of the *Lafayette Daily Courier* from 1893 to 1901, he resigned after *Graustark* achieved popular success. Altogether, McCutcheon published some 40 works of fiction, including more swashbuckling tales of Graustark.

McElroy \'mak-əl-ˌrȯi\, Joseph (Prince) (b. Aug. 21, 1930, New York, N.Y., U.S.) American novelist and short-story writer who was known for intricate, lengthy, and technically complex fiction.

McElroy's first novel, *A Smuggler's Bible* (1966), is made up of eight disconnected chapters that are separated by authorial commentary. *Lookout Cartridge* (1974), perhaps McElroy's best work, is a political thriller about a filmmaker who searches London and New York City in an effort to recover movie footage that may have recorded a crime. *Plus* (1976) is about a rebellious, disembodied brain that operates a computer in outer space. In 1986 McElroy published *Women and Men*, a 1,191-page novel about a journalist and a feminist who live in the same apartment building in New York City but never meet.

More accessible is *The Letter Left to Me* (1988), which centers on a letter of advice written by the late father of a 15-year-old boy.

McEwan \mə-'kyū-ən\, Ian (Russell) (b. June 21, 1948, Aldershot, Eng.) British novelist, short-story writer, and screenwriter whose restrained, refined prose style accentuated the horror of his dark humor and perverse subject matter.

McEwan studied at the University of Sussex and the University of East Anglia. His first two short-story collections, *First Love, Last Rites* (1975) and *In Between the Sheets* (1978), feature disturbing tales of sexual aberrance, black comedy, and macabre obsession. His first novel, *The Cement Garden* (1978), traces the incestuous decline of a family of orphaned children. *The Comfort of Strangers* (1981) is a nightmarish novel about an English couple in Venice.

McEwan's later novels were less sensational: *The Child in Time* (1987) examines a kidnapping; *The Innocent* (1990) concerns international espionage; *Black Dogs* (1992) tells the story of a husband and wife who have lived apart since a honeymoon incident made clear their essential moral antipathy; *The Daydreamer* (1994) explores the imaginary world of a creative 10-year-old boy.

McGahern \mə-'gak-ərn, -'gak-\, John (b. Nov. 12, 1934, Leitrim, Ire.) Irish novelist and short-story writer known for his depictions of Irish men and women constricted and damaged by the conventions of their native land.

After graduation from University College, Dublin, McGahern worked as a laborer and then as a teacher. His first novel, *The Barracks* (1963), told of a terminally ill, unhappily married woman. The novel was praised for its brilliant depiction of Irish life and for its sensitive portrayal of despair. *The Dark* (1965) is a portrait of an adolescent trapped by predatory male relatives in a closed, repressed society. McGahern's frank sexual portrayals earned the wrath of Irish censors, and he was asked not to return to his teaching job. Later novels include *The Leavetaking* (1974), *The Pornographer* (1979), and *Amongst Women* (1990).

His short stories were collected in *Nightlines* (1970), *Getting Through* (1978), and *High Ground* (1985).

McGee \mə-'gē\, Thomas D'Arcy (b. April 13, 1825, Carlingford, County Louth, Ire.—d. April 7, 1868, Ottawa, Ont., Can.) Irish-Canadian writer known for his nationalism.

An Irish patriot, McGee was associated with *The Nation* (1846–48), the literary organ of the Young Ireland political movement (which called for the study of Irish history and the revival of the Irish language). He was implicated in the abortive Irish rebellion of 1848 and fled to the United States, where he established two newspapers, the New York *Nation* and the *American Celt*. He came to advocate peaceful reforms for Ireland rather than revolution, and in 1857 he moved to Canada. He was elected to the Legislative Assembly of Canada in 1858 and served there until his death. According to his belief that literary and cultural nationalism must go along with political involvement, he encouraged the development of a Canadian culture and wrote nationalist poetry. He was assassinated in Ottawa, presumably by Irish nationalists in Canada. Selections from McGee's writings appear in two edited collections: *The Poems of Thomas D'Arcy McGee* (1869) and *D'Arcy McGee: A Collection of Speeches and Addresses* (1937).

McGee, Travis \'trav-is-mə-'gē\ Fictional character, private investigator in a series of 24 crime novels by John D. MACDONALD. McGee, who is tough and intelligent, lives in Florida on the houseboat *The Busted Flush*, calls himself a "salvage consultant," and takes on dangerous assignments.

McGinley \mə-'gin-lē\, Phyllis (b. March 21, 1905, Ontario, Ore., U.S.—d. Feb. 22, 1978, New York, N.Y.) American poet and author of books for juveniles, best known for her light verse celebrating suburban home life.

Starting in the 1920s, McGinley wrote poetry for such magazines as *The New Yorker* and *The Atlantic*. Although her verse is often dismissed as being merely light, it is serious as well as witty. In 1961 she won the Pulitzer Prize in poetry for *Times Three: Selected Verse from Three Decades* (1960). McGinley also wrote a popular series of autobiographical essays about being a wife in the suburbs, titled *Sixpence in Her Shoe* (1964). Her works for juveniles include *The Horse Who Lived Upstairs* (1944) and *The Make-Believe Twins* (1953).

McGuane \mə-'gwän\, Thomas, *in full* Thomas Francis McGuane III (b. Dec. 11, 1939, Wyandotte, Mich., U.S.) American author noted for his novels of violent action.

McGuane's first novels, *The Sporting Club* (1969), *The Bushwhacked Piano* (1971), and *Ninety-two in the Shade* (1973), presented the central plot and theme of his fiction: a man, usually from a secure family, exiles himself from American society and removes himself to an isolated locale; he then finds a reason—alienation, attraction to a woman, rights to territory—to oppose another man in a succession of acts of escalating violence and revenge.

The locales of his novels—Key West, Fla., northern Michigan, Montana—and his scenes of fishing and personal combat suggest the influence of Ernest Hemingway. While McGuane's early novels were noted for their stylistic extravagance, a growing plainness of style developed in his later novels. They include *Panama* (1978), *Nobody's Angel* (1981), *Something To Be Desired* (1984), *Keep the Change* (1989), and *Nothing But Blue Skies* (1992). *An Outside Chance* (1980; rev. ed., 1990) is a collection of his essays on sports.

McKay \mə-'kā\, Claude (b. Sept. 15, 1890, Jamaica, British West Indies—d. May 22, 1948, Chicago, Ill., U.S.) Jamaican-born poet and novelist whose HOME TO HARLEM (1928) was the most popular novel written by an American black to that time.

Library of Congress

Before moving to the United States in 1912, McKay wrote two volumes of Jamaican dialect verse, *Songs of Jamaica* and *Constab Ballads* (1912). After attending Tuskegee (Ala.) Institute and Kansas State Teachers College, he went to New York in 1914, where he contributed to the *Liberator*, then a leading journal of avant-garde politics and art. With the publication of two volumes of poetry, *Spring in New Hampshire* (1920) and *Harlem Shadows* (1922), McKay emerged as the first and most militant voice of the Harlem Renaissance. After 1922 McKay lived abroad, successively in the Soviet Union, France, Spain, and Morocco. In both *Home to Harlem* and *Banjo* (1929) he attempted to capture the vitality of the black vagabonds of urban America and Europe. There followed a collection of short stories, *Gingertown* (1932), and another novel, *Banana Bottom* (1933). In all these works McKay searched among the common folk for a distinctive black identity.

After returning to America in 1934, McKay wrote for various magazines and newspapers, including the *New Leader* and the New York *Amsterdam News*. He also wrote an autobiography, *A Long Way from Home* (1937), and the study *Harlem: Negro Metropolis* (1940). His *Selected Poems* (1953) was issued posthumously.

McMillan \mək-'mil-ən\, Terry (b. Oct. 18, 1951, Port Huron, Mich., U.S.)   African-American novelist whose work often portrays feisty, independent black women and their attempts to find fulfilling relationships with black men.

In McMillan's first novel, *Mama* (1987), a black woman manages to raise five children alone after she forces her drunken husband to leave. *Disappearing Acts* (1989) concerns two dissimilar people who begin an intimate relationship. *Waiting to Exhale* (1992) follows four black middle-class women, each of whom is looking for the love of a worthy man. McMillan edited *Breaking Ice: An Anthology of Contemporary African-American Fiction* (1990).

McMurtry \mək-'mər-trē\, Larry (Jeff) (b. June 3, 1936, Wichita Falls, Tex., U.S.)   American writer noted for his novels set on the frontier, in contemporary small towns, and in increasingly urbanized and industrial areas of Texas.

McMurtry's first novel, *Horseman, Pass By* (1961; filmed as *Hud*, 1963), is set in the Texas ranching country. The isolation and claustrophobia of small-town life are examined in *The Last Picture Show* (1966; film, 1971). McMurtry's frontier epic, *Lonesome Dove* (1985), won a Pulitzer Prize in 1986. A sequel, *Streets of Laredo*, appeared in 1993. Urban Houstonites appear in *Moving On* (1970), *All My Friends Are Going to Be Strangers* (1972), and *Terms of Endearment* (1975; film, 1983). Other novels include *Leaving Cheyenne* (1963; filmed as *Lovin' Molly*, 1974), *Cadillac Jack* (1982), *The Desert Rose* (1983), *Buffalo Girls* (1990), and *The Evening Star* (1992).

McNeile, Herman Cyril   *see* SAPPER.

McPhee \mək-'fē\, John (Angus) (b. March 8, 1931, Princeton, N.J.)   American journalist who wrote accessible, informative books on a wide variety of topics—particularly profiles of figures in sports, science, and the environment.

McPhee was educated at Princeton University. He became an associate editor at *Time* (1957–64) and a staff writer at *The New Yorker* (from 1965). His first book, *A Sense of Where You Are* (1965), was based on an article he wrote for *The New Yorker* on basketball player and Rhodes scholar Bill Bradley. Subjects of his subsequent profiles include tennis players in *Levels of the Game* (1969) and *Arthur Ashe Remembered* (1993); a conservationist in *Encounters with the Archdruid* (1971); and a boat craftsman in *The Survival of the Bark Canoe* (1975).

McPhee focused on central New Jersey in *The Pine Barrens* (1968), the Scottish Highlands in *The Crofter and the Laird* (1970), and Switzerland in *La Place de la Concorde Suisse* (1984). He wrote a series of books on the geology of the western United States, which included *Basin and Range* (1981), *Rising From the Plains* (1986), and *Assembling California* (1993), and he examined the citrus industry in *Oranges* (1967), aeronautical engineering in *The Deltoid Pumpkin Seed* (1973), and nuclear terrorism in *The Curve of Binding Energy* (1974). Among his collections of essays are *A Roomful of Hovings and Other Profiles* (1968), *The John McPhee Reader* (1976), *Giving Good Weight* (1979), and *Table of Contents* (1985).

McPherson \mək-'fir-sən\, James Alan (b. Sept. 16, 1943, Savannah, Ga., U.S.)   African-American short-story writer whose realistic, character-driven fiction examines racial tension, the mysteries of love, and the pain of isolation.

McPherson's short story "Gold Coast" won a contest in the *Atlantic Monthly* in 1968, and he became a contributing editor of the magazine in 1969.

In 1968 McPherson published his first volume of short fiction, *Hue and Cry*. His next collection, *Elbow Room* (1977), won a Pulitzer Prize in 1978. The stories in this book—among them "Elbow Room," "A Loaf of Bread," and "Widows and Orphans"—balance bitterness with hope.

McTeague \mək-'tēg\   Novel by Frank NORRIS, published in 1899. The work was considered to be the first great portrait in American literature of an acquisitive society.

In *McTeague*, Norris sought to describe the influence of heredity and environment on human life. The dentist McTeague marries Trina, whose acquisitiveness is revealed when she wins a lottery. McTeague, initially free of the destructive avarice that defines Trina and his friend and rival Schouler, is a bovine "natural man," brutalized by the more rapacious urban characters. The marriage disintegrates as Trina becomes more and more miserly with her fortune and McTeague drinks heavily. McTeague kills Trina and flees. He later strangles his rival in Death Valley, but not before Schouler handcuffs them together, condemning McTeague to die chained to the body of his enemy.

Measure for Measure   Tragicomedy in five acts by William SHAKESPEARE, produced in 1604–05 and published in the First Folio of 1623. The play examines the nature of mercy and justice, proposing that a good government is one that is flexible and based on common sense.

The play opens with Vincentio, the Duke of Vienna, telling his deputy Angelo to govern his duchy while he travels to Poland. In actuality, the duke remains in Vienna disguised as a friar. Following the letter of the law, Angelo passes the death sentence on Claudio, a nobleman convicted for impregnating his betrothed, Juliet. Claudio's sister Isabella, a novice in a nunnery, pleads his case to Angelo, who offers to spare Claudio in exchange for her favors. On the advice of Vincentio, Isabella schedules the rendezvous but secretly arranges for Angelo's spurned fiancée, Mariana, to take her place. Afterward, Angelo reaffirms the execution. Vincentio comes to the rescue, and in the end Claudio is saved and wed to Juliet, Angelo is discredited and ordered to marry Mariana, and Vincentio asks Isabella to be his wife.

Medb or **Medhbh** \'māv\, *also called* Maeve \'māv\   Legendary queen of Connaught (Connacht) in Ireland. In the Irish epic tale known in English as *The Cattle Raid of Cooley*, Medb led her forces against those of Ulster. Medb is noted for her insatiable sexual appetite, and the list of her mates is impressive; at the time of the battle against Ulster, the king Ailill was her mate, but she also had an affair with the mighty hero Fergus.

Medea \mi-'dē-ə\   In Greek mythology, an enchantress who helped JASON, leader of the Argonauts, to obtain the Golden Fleece from her father, King Aëtes (Aeetes) of Colchis. She was a sorceress and priestess of Hecate and had the gift of prophecy. She married Jason on the return voyage to Iolcus (Iolcos). They were later driven from the region because of the vengeance taken by Medea on King Pelias of Iolcus (who had sent Jason to fetch the fleece) and were granted asylum by Creon of Corinth. There Medea bore Jason two sons, and there Jason fell in love with Creon's daughter and proceeded to divorce Medea. In revenge, Medea murdered Creon, his daughter, and her own two sons by Jason and took refuge with King Aegeus of Athens. The story of Medea's humiliation and revenge is told by Euripides.

Ovid carried the story further in his *Metamorphoses*. After fleeing Corinth, Medea became the wife of Aegeus, who later drove her away after her unsuccessful attempt to poison his son Theseus. The Greek historian Herodotus reported that Medea went from Athens to the region of Asia subsequently called Media, whose inhabitants thereupon changed their name to Medes.

Medea is the subject of later works such as Seneca's *Medea*, a tragedy based on Euripides' drama; Pierre Corneille's *Médée*; and a number of contemporary settings, including plays by Franz Grillparzer and Jean Anouilh.

Medea \mi-'dē-ə\ (*Greek* Mēdeia) Tragedy by EURIPIDES, performed in 431 BC. One of Euripides' most powerful and best-known plays, *Medea* is a remarkable study of injustice and ruthless revenge.

In Euripides' retelling of the legend, the Colchian princess Medea has married the hero Jason. As the play's action begins, Jason has decided to cast off Medea and to marry the daughter of Creon, king of Corinth. After a dreadful struggle between her passionate sense of injury and her love for her children, Medea determines that she will punish Jason by murdering the Corinthian princess and her own sons, leaving Jason to grow old with neither wife nor child. She carries out the murders and escapes in the chariot of her grandfather, the sun-god Helios. Despite the monstrosity of Medea's deeds, Euripides succeeds in evoking sympathy for her.

medieval drama Any of several types of performance popular during the European Middle Ages. *See* INTERLUDE; MIRACLE PLAY; MORALITY PLAY.

medievalism \mē-'dē-və-,liz-əm, mi-, me-, -dē-'ē-və-\ In literature, a spirit of devotion to the institutions, arts, and practices of the Middle Ages; sometimes the devotion is rather to a later age's images of the Middle Ages. This quality can be seen in the works of such authors as Edmund Spenser, John Keats and other Romantic poets, and the Pre-Raphaelite poets.

medieval romance Tale originally composed during the Middle Ages that is based on legend, chivalric love and adventure, or the supernatural. *See* ROMANCE.

meditation \,med-ə-'tā-shən\ A spoken or written discourse treated in a contemplative manner and intended to express its author's reflections or (especially when religious) to guide others in contemplation.

Medusa \mə-'dü-sə, -'dyü-, -zə\ In Greek mythology, the most famous of the monsters known as Gorgons. She was usually represented as a winged female creature having as hair a mass of live snakes. Medusa was the only GORGON who was mortal; hence her slayer, Perseus, was able to kill her by cutting off her head. According to one account, the severed head, which had the power of turning into stone all who looked upon it, was given to Athena, who placed it on her shield.

Medwall \'med-,wȯl\, Henry (fl. 1490) Author remembered for his *Fulgens and Lucrece*, the first known secular play in English.

Medwall was chaplain to Cardinal John Morton, archbishop of Canterbury, and was the rector of Balynghem in the English marches of Calais, in France. His dramatic works were written for the entertainment of the cardinal and his guests. A morality play, *Nature*, a good example of the allegorical type of early drama, displays Medwall's talent for realistic dialogue and his skill as a versifier.

Meghadūta \'mā-gə-'dü-tə\ ("Cloud Messenger") Lyric love poem in some 115 verses composed by KĀLIDĀSA about the 5th century AD. The verse is unique to Sanskrit literature in that the poet attempts to go beyond the strophic unity of the short lyric, normally the form preferred for love poems, by stringing the stanzas into a narrative.

The *Meghadūta* is the lament of an exiled yakṣa (a benevolent nature spirit) who is pining for his beloved on a lonely mountain peak. When a cloud perches on the peak, he asks it to deliver a message to his love in the Himalayan city of Alakā. Most of the poem, composed in an extremely graceful meter, consists of a description of the cloud's journey to Alakā. *Meghadūta* inspired Friedrich von Schiller's *Maria Stuart*.

Meier Helmbrecht \'mī-ər-'helm-,breḳt\ Realistic medieval epic poem dating roughly to 1250, remarkable for its portrayal of the seamy decline of chivalry, when knights became robbers and peasants rebelled against their masters. The poem was written in the region of the Austrian–Bavarian border. Nothing is known of its author, Wernher der Gärtner.

In the poem the young peasant Helmbrecht enters the service of a knight (*i.e.*, a robber). He returns home insufferably proud of his stolen riches and arranges a marriage between his sister and one of his gang. A splendid celebration is held, but the gang is caught at the wedding breakfast. Nine of them are hanged; Helmbrecht is blinded and loses a hand and foot. He returns home, but his father turns him away to wander the forests, where he is caught by peasants and hanged.

Mein Kampf \,mīn-'kämpf\ ("My Struggle") Political manifesto written by the German dictator Adolf Hitler and published in 1925 and 1927. It became the bible of National Socialism (Nazism) in Germany's Third Reich. By 1939 it had sold 5,200,000 copies

The first volume, entitled *Die Abrechnung* ("The Settlement [of Accounts]," or "Revenge"), was written in 1924 in the fortress of Landsberg am Lech, where Hitler was imprisoned after the abortive Beer Hall Putsch of 1923. It treats the world of Hitler's youth, World War I, and the "betrayal" that supposedly led to Germany's collapse in 1918; it also expresses Hitler's racist ideology and declares the need for Germans to seek living space (*Lebensraum*) in the east. The book calls for revenge against France.

The second volume, *Die Nationalsozialistische Bewegung* ("The National Socialist Movement"), written after Hitler's release from prison in December 1924, outlines the political program, including terrorist methods, that National Socialism would pursue in gaining and exercising power in the new Germany.

meiosis \mī-'ō-sis\ [Greek *meiōsis* lessening, diminution] Deliberate understatement, used in literature for emphasis or comic effect.

Meireles \mā-'rel-ish\, Cecília (b. Nov. 7, 1901, Rio de Janeiro, Braz.—d. Nov. 9, 1964, Rio de Janeiro) Poet, teacher, and journalist, whose lyrical and highly personal poetry earned her an important position in 20th-century Brazilian literature. Her poetry is considered by most critics to have found its best expression in such traditional forms as the sonnet.

Meireles established her literary reputation at age 18 with the publication of *Espectros* (1919; "Visions"), a collection of sonnets in the Symbolist tradition. Between 1925 and 1939 Meireles concentrated on her career as a teacher, writing several books for children and in 1934 founding the first children's library in Brazil. That same year she lectured on Brazilian literature in Portugal; in 1936 she was appointed lecturer at the new Federal University in Rio de Janeiro.

Meireles reestablished her reputation as a poet after 14 years of silence with *Viagem* (1939; "Journey"), considered by many critics to mark her attainment of poetic maturity and individuality. Much of her work is collected in *Obra poética* (1958; "Poetic Work").

Meister, Wilhelm \'vil-helm-'mīs-tər\ Fictional hero of two classic epic novels by J.W. von Goethe. *See* WILHELM MEISTER'S APPRENTICESHIP.

meistersinger \\'mīs-tər-,siŋ-ər\\, *German* Meistersinger \\'mīs-tər-,ziŋ-ər\\ *plural* meistersingers, *German plural* Meistersinger [German, from Middle High German, literally, master singer] A member of any of various German guilds, especially of the 15th and 16th centuries, composed chiefly of workingmen and craftsmen and formed for the cultivation of poetry and music.

The meistersingers claimed to be heirs of 12 old masters, poets skilled in the medieval *artes* and in musical theory; the 13th-century poet Frauenlob was said to be their founder. Their true predecessors, however, probably were fraternities of laymen trained to sing in church and elsewhere. Later, these fraternities became *Singschulen* ("song schools"), organized like craft guilds. Their main activity became the holding of singing competitions. Composition was restricted to fitting new words to tunes ascribed to the old masters; subject matter, meter, language, and performance were governed by an increasingly strict code of rules (*Tablatur*). These restrictions led Hans Folz, a barber-surgeon from Worms (d. *c.* 1515), to persuade the Nürnberg Singschule to permit a wider range of subjects and the composition of new tunes. Thenceforth, a member, having passed through the grades of *Schüler*, *Schulfreund*, *Singer*, and *Dichter*, became a "master" by having a tune of his own approved by the *Merkern*, or adjudicators.

Mei Yaochen or **Mei Yao-ch'en** \\'mā-'yaù-'chən\\ (b. 1002, Xuancheng, China—d. 1060, Gaifeng) A leading Chinese poet of the Northern Song dynasty whose verses helped to launch a new poetic style linked with the *guwen*, or "ancient literature," revival.

Although Mei entered government service through the examination system like other statesmen-poets of the Song, his political career was undistinguished. While in office, however, he befriended Ouyang Xiu, then a minor official and a leading advocate of the *guwen* movement. Deeply influenced by Neo-Confucian ideals, proponents of this movement felt that literature should mirror and comment on contemporary life. Mei, whose courtesy name was Shengyu, thus made social and political issues the focus of his poetry and sought subjects in commonplace events and people. Rejecting the then-fashionable *ci* poetry, which derived from romantic ballads and employed elaborate conceits and hyperbole, Mei returned to the old *lüshi*, or "regulated poetry," perfecting a plainer, more prosaic style to gain what he called an "easygoing" voice better suited to his themes and subjects.

Melchior \\'mel-kē-ôr\\ Legendary figure, said to be one of the MAGI.

Meleager \\,mel-ē-'ā-jər\\ (fl. 1st century BC) Greek poet from Gadara in Syria, who compiled the first large collection of epigrams. It formed the basis of the GREEK ANTHOLOGY.

Meleager's collection, entitled *Stephanos* ("Garland"), began with an introductory poem in which he compared each writer to a flower. In addition to some 130 of his own graceful and lucid epigrams, Meleager's collection included the work of some 48 poets. Meleager's own verses, which treat chiefly erotic themes (love of both boys and women), are clever and neatly constructed, though not particularly original.

Meleager \\,mel-ē-'ā-jər\\ In Greek mythology, the leader of the Calydonian boar hunt. The *Iliad* relates how Meleager's father, King Oeneus of Calydon, had omitted to sacrifice to Artemis, who sent a wild boar to ravage the country. Meleager collected a band of heroes to drive it away and eventually killed it himself. Meleager is the subject of the *Meleager* of Euripides, of which only fragments survive.

Meléndez Valdés \\mā-'län-dãth-bãl-'dãs\\, Juan (b. March 11, 1754, Ribera de Fresno, Spain—d. May 24, 1817, Mont-

pellier, Fr.) Poet and politician, the representative poet of the Spanish Neoclassic period. He is best known for sensual, often erotic, poems.

Meléndez Valdés wrote highly eclectic poetry, much influenced by French, Italian, and classical models. He had a genuine feeling for nature and, at his best, displayed a considerable gift. A precursor of Romanticism in bringing the cult of the sentimental to Spain, he also kept alive the tradition of the romance—the dramatic, narrative ballad. In his later years he wrote philosophical odes that reflect the sentiments of the Enlightenment.

melic \\'mel-ik\\ [Greek *melikós* of lyric poetry, a derivative of *mélē* lyric poetry, choral songs, plural of *mélos* song, musical phrase, literally, limb] Of or relating to lyric Greek poetry of the 7th and 6th centuries BC.

Mellors, Oliver \\'äl-i-vər-'mel-ərz\\ Title character of the novel LADY CHATTERLEY'S LOVER by D.H. Lawrence. To Lawrence, Mellors symbolized raw animal passion, natural manhood, and untamed sexuality.

Melmoth the Wanderer \\'mel-məth\\ Novel by Charles Robert MATURIN, published in 1820. Considered the last of the classic English gothic romances, it chronicles the adventures of an Irish Faust, who sells his soul in exchange for prolonged life.

A complex weaving of tales-within-tales, the story is set in the early 19th century, when John Melmoth learns the fate of his ancestor, the title character, by reading a secret document and through his contact with a Spanish sailor. The sailor tells of the Wanderer's many failed attempts to win souls for the devil so as to free himself from his own pact. After the stories are told, the Wanderer himself appears; because he has been unable to win any souls in his 150 years of wandering, he asks to be left to his fate. By the next morning, he has disappeared into the sea.

The book was especially admired in France, notably by Charles Baudelaire. Honoré de Balzac wrote an ironic sequel, *Melmoth réconcilié* (1835; "Melmoth Reconciled").

Melo \\'mel-ù\\, Francisco Manuel de (b. Nov. 23, 1608, Lisbon [Portugal]—d. Oct. 13, 1666, Alcântara, near Lisbon) Portuguese soldier, diplomat, and courtier who won fame as a poet, moralist, historian, and literary critic in both the Spanish and Portuguese languages.

At the outbreak of the Catalan rebellion Melo was chief of staff to the commander of the royal forces, out of which experience came his classic *Historia de la guerra de Cataluña* (1645; "History of the Catalan War"). When Portugal declared its independence from Spain, Melo offered his services to the new Portuguese monarch, John IV. For reasons still obscure he was arrested on Nov. 19, 1644, and was in prison or under police supervision for 11 years. During his imprisonment, Melo wrote constantly; he published some verse in 1649 and a discourse on marriage, *Carta de guia de casados* (1650; *The Government of a Wife*), although he himself never married. He edited 500 of his letters, most of which are a record of his experiences and thoughts in prison, and they were published as *Cartas familiares* (1664; "Personal Letters"). In 1665 he published his *Obras métricas*, which includes Spanish verse, displaying the Baroque conceits and Latinisms conventional in the period, as well as Portuguese sonnets and verse epistles that are notable for their power, sincerity, and perfection of form.

melodrama \\'mel-ə-,dräm-ə. -,dram-\\ [French *mélodrame* drama accompanied by instrumental music, from Greek *mélos* song, musical phrase + French *drame* drama] A play characterized by extravagant theatricality, subordination of characterization to plot, and predominance of physical action. Also, the genre of dramatic literature constituted by such plays.

In Western literature melodramas usually have an improbable plot that generally concerns the vicissitudes suffered by the virtuous at the hands of the villainous but ends happily with virtue triumphant. Featuring stock characters such as the noble hero, the long-suffering heroine, and the cold-blooded, hard-hearted villain, the melodrama emphasizes sensational incident and spectacular staging at the expense of character development.

The pioneer and prime exponent of the 18th-century French melodrama was Guilbert de Pixérécourt. His *Coelina, ou l'enfant de mystère* (1800; "Coelina, or The Child of Mystery") was translated as *A Tale of Mystery* (1802) by Thomas Holcroft, who thereby helped establish the genre in England.

In the early 19th century, melodrama spread throughout the European theater; in Russia the authorities welcomed it, because it diverted popular attention from more serious issues. Among the best known and most representative of the melodramas popular in England and the United States are *The Octoroon* (1859) and *The Colleen Bawn* (1860), both by Dion Boucicault. More sensational were Boucicault's *The Poor of New York* (1857) and Augustin Daly's *Under the Gaslight* (1867). The realistic staging and the social evils touched upon, however perfunctorily and sentimentally, anticipated the later theater of the naturalists.

By the early 20th century motion pictures had become the most popular vehicle for melodramas; later, television also became a popular medium for the form.

melofarce \'mel-ō-ˌfärs\   Melodrama of farcically exaggerated character.

Melpomene \mel-'päm-ə-nē\   In Greek mythology, one of the nine Muses, patron of tragedy and lyre playing. In Greek art her attributes were the tragic mask and the club of Heracles.

Melville \'mel-ˌvil\, Herman, *surname originally spelled* Melvill (b. Aug. 1, 1819, New York, N.Y., U.S.—d. Sept. 28, 1891, New York City)   American author best known for his novels of the sea, including his masterpiece, MOBY-DICK (1851).

A bout of scarlet fever in 1826 left Melville with permanently weakened eyesight. He attended Albany (N.Y.) Classical School in 1835. In 1839 he shipped out as cabin boy on the *St. Lawrence*, a merchant ship bound for Liverpool. In 1841, after a grinding search for work and a brief teaching job, he sailed on the whaler *Acushnet* to the South Seas. In June 1842 the *Acushnet* anchored in the Marquesas Islands, in present-day French Polynesia. Melville's adventures here, somewhat romanticized, became the subject of his first novel, TYPEE (1846). The

voyage was unproductive, and Melville joined an uprising that landed the mutineers in a Tahitian jail, from which he escaped without difficulty. His carefree roving through the islands after his escape confirmed his bitterness against colonial and, especially, missionary debasement of the native Polynesian peoples. Melville based his second book, OMOO (1847), on these events.

In 1847 Melville began MARDI (1849) and became a regular contributor of reviews and other pieces to a literary journal. *Typee* and *Omoo* had provoked immediate enthusiasm and outrage, but when *Mardi* appeared, the public and critics alike found its wild, allegorical fantasy and medley of styles incomprehensible. Concealing his disappointment, Melville quickly wrote REDBURN (1849) and WHITE-JACKET (1850) in the manner expected of him. In 1850 he bought a farm, "Arrowhead," near Nathaniel Hawthorne's home at Pittsfield, Mass. Their relationship at first was close and reanimated Melville's creative energies. On his side, it was dependent, almost mystically intense, but to the cooler, withdrawn Hawthorne, such depth of feeling so persistently and openly declared was uncongenial. The two men gradually drew apart.

Moby-Dick was published in London in October 1851 and a month later in America. It brought its author neither acclaim nor reward. Increasingly a recluse, Melville embarked almost at once on PIERRE (1852). When published, however, it was another critical and financial disaster. ISRAEL POTTER was published in 1855 and enjoyed a modest success. Meanwhile, Melville had published important stories in *Putnam's Monthly Magazine*—BARTLEBY THE SCRIVENER (1853), THE ENCANTADAS (1854), and BENITO CERENO (1855)—reflecting the despair and the contempt for human hypocrisy and materialism that increasingly possessed him. Similar in theme was THE CONFIDENCE-MAN (1857), the last of his novels to be published in his lifetime.

The Civil War furnished the subject of his first volume of verse, *Battle-Pieces and Aspects of the War* (1866), published privately. Four months after it appeared, an appointment as a customs inspector on the New York docks finally brought him a secure income. His second collection of verse, *John Marr, and Other Sailors; With Some Sea-Pieces*, appeared in 1888, again privately published. By then he had been in retirement for three years, assisted by legacies from friends and relatives. *Timoleon* (1891) was his final verse collection. More significant was the return to prose that culminated in his last work, the novel BILLY BUDD, FORETOPMAN, which remained unpublished until 1924. Although by the end of the 1840s he had been among the most celebrated of American writers, his death evoked but a single obituary notice. Only after years of neglect did modern criticism finally secure his reputation with that of the great American writers.

Member of the Wedding, The   Novel by Carson MCCULLERS, published in 1946. It depicts the inner life of 12-year-old Frankie Addams, a Georgia tomboy who imagines that she will be taken by the bride and groom (her brother) on their honeymoon. Frankie finds refuge in the company of two equally isolated characters, her ailing six-year-old cousin John Henry and her father's black housekeeper, Berenice, who serves as both mother figure and oracle. Much of the novel consists of a series of kitchen-table conversations among these three. The threesome is broken by the cousin's death and Berenice's own wedding.

Memento Mori \me-'men-tō-'mȯr-ˌī, 'mō-rē\   Comic and macabre novel by Muriel SPARK, published in 1959. Spark's psychological fantasy was her most widely praised novel. In characteristically spare, exacting prose the author looked unflinchingly at old age.

Several elderly London friends receive anonymous telephone calls with a single message: "Remember you must die." Each hears and interprets the words differently. Old rivalries and romances still color the friends' relations, and Spark makes clear that their personalities in old age are but a continuation of their earlier lives.

Memmi \mem-'mē\, Albert (b. Dec. 15, 1920, Tunis, Tunisia) French-language Tunisian novelist and author of sociological studies of human oppression.

Memmi was born in a poor Jewish section of Tunis, but he studied at an exclusive French secondary school there. He was a Jew among Muslims, an Arab among Europeans, a ghetto dweller among the bourgeoisie, and an *évolué* (one "evolved" in French culture) among tradition-bound family and friends. It was this tension of living in several worlds at once that became the subject of Memmi's autobiographical first novel, *La Statue de sel* (1953; *Pillar of Salt*). Subsequent novels include *Agar* (1955; *Strangers*), which deals with mixed marriage; *Le Scorpion ou la confession imaginaire* (1969; *The Scorpion or the Imaginary Confession*), a tale of psychological introspection; and *Le Désert* (1977; "The Desert"), in which violence and injustice are seen as age-old responses to the pain and uncertainty of the human condition. His novel *Le Pharaoh* ("The Pharaoh") was published in 1988 and a collection of poetry, *Le Mirliton du ciel* ("The Flute of Heaven"), in 1989. Memmi's most influential sociological work was *Portrait du colonisé* (1957; "Portrait of the Colonized"; Eng. trans. *The Colonizer and the Colonized*). Memmi also contributed to North African literature as a critic.

Memnon \'mem-,nän\ In Greek mythology, son of Tithonus (son of Laomedon, king of Troy) and Eos (Dawn) and king of the Ethiopians. After the death of the Trojan warrior Hector, Memnon went to assist his uncle Priam, the last king of Troy, against the Greeks. He performed prodigies of valor but was slain by the Greek hero Achilles. Zeus was moved by the tears of Eos and bestowed immortality upon Memnon. His companions were changed into birds, called Memnonides, that came every year to fight and lament over his grave.

memoir \'mem-,wär, -,wôr\ [French *mémoire*, from Old French *memoire* written account, narrative, masculine derivative of *memoire* (feminine) memory] **1.** *usually plural* A history or narrative composed from or stressing personal experience and acquaintance with the events, scenes, or persons described. The French have excelled at the genre; the Duke de Saint-Simon's *Mémoires* (covering the early 1690s through 1723), are celebrated, as are the Viscount de Chateaubriand's *Mémoires d'outre-tombe* (published posthumously, 1849–50; *The Memoirs of Chateaubriand*). In the 20th century, many distinguished statesmen and military men have described their experiences in memoirs. Notable reminiscences of World War II include the memoirs of Dwight Eisenhower, Viscount Montgomery, and Charles de Gaulle. **2.** *usually plural* An autobiographical account, often anecdotal or intimate in tone, whose focus of attention is usually on the persons, events, or times known to the writer. Contemporary examples of this type of writing include Eudora Welty's *One Writer's Beginnings* (1984) and Malcolm Cowley's *Exile's Return* (1934; rev. ed., 1951). **3.** A biography or biographical sketch, usually based on personal acquaintance with the subject and sometimes having the character of a memorial.

Closely related to, and often confused with, autobiography, a memoir usually differs chiefly in the degree of emphasis placed on external events; whereas writers of autobiography are concerned primarily with themselves as subject matter, writers of memoir are usually persons who have played roles in, or have been close observers of, historical events and whose main purpose is to describe or interpret those events.

Memoirs of a Dutiful Daughter First and best-known book of a four-volume autobiography by Simone de BEAUVOIR, published in French as *Mémoires d'une jeune fille rangée* in 1958.

In *Memoirs of a Dutiful Daughter*, de Beauvoir included travel stories, set pieces, intimate portraits, philosophical musings, and desultory political comments as she described her early years, when she tried to "get other people interested in her soul." The book enjoyed critical and popular success, in part because of its clear prose and its warmth and flashes of humor.

Memoirs of an Egotist Autobiographical work by STENDHAL, published posthumously in France in 1892 as *Souvenirs d'égotisme*. It was also published in the United States as *Memoirs of Egotism*.

Stendhal began writing his memoir in 1832, when he was increasingly aware of his age, isolation, and failing health, and it was left unfinished at his death. *Memoirs of an Egotist* looks back on his life as a Paris bon vivant and with great wit tells of the salons, theaters, concert halls, and museums he frequented. Together with his similarly autobiographical *Vie de Henri Brulard* (1890; also published posthumously), *Memoirs* stands among Stendhal's most original achievements.

Memoirs of Chateaubriand, The \shä-tō-brē-'äⁿ\ Autobiographical work by François-Auguste-René CHATEAUBRIAND, published as *Mémoires d'outre-tombe* ("Memoirs from Beyond the Grave") in 1849–50. The work may have been started as early as 1810, but it was written for posthumous publication.

As much a history of Chateaubriand's thoughts and sensations as it is a conventional narrative of his life, it draws a vivid picture of contemporary French history, of the spirit of the Romantic epoch, and of Chateaubriand's travels. These are complemented by many self-revealing passages in which the author recounts his appreciation of women, his sensitivity to nature, and his lifelong tendency toward melancholy.

Memoirs of Hadrian \'hā-drē-ən\ Historical novel by Marguerite YOURCENAR, published in 1951 as *Mémoires d'Hadrien*.

In the book, Yourcenar creates a vivid and historically accurate portrait of the 2nd-century Roman Empire under Hadrian's rule. The work is a fictional first-person narrative in the form of Hadrian's letters—mostly to his nephew Marcus Aurelius—written shortly before his death. Contemplative and analytical recollections of his accomplishments, his hopes for Rome, and his personal relationships, the letters reveal Hadrian to be a highly intelligent, often wise man, conscious of the great power he wields.

Memoirs of Hecate County \'hek-it\ Collection of six loosely connected short stories by Edmund WILSON, first published in 1946. Because of the frankly sexual nature of the story "The Princess with the Golden Hair," the book was suppressed on obscenity charges until 1959, at which time Wilson published a revised edition.

Some of the stories are narrated by an upper-middle-class intellectual recollecting his past sexual relationships and friendships in Manhattan and in insular, suburban Hecate county. Each story portrays a different aspect of socially dysfunctional America, such as the vapid ritual of the cocktail hour, bogus artists, and the erosion of intellectual rigor by popular culture.

memorialist \mə-'môr-ē-ə-list\ A writer of memorials or memoirs.

Memories of a Catholic Girlhood Autobiography of Mary MCCARTHY, published in 1957.

McCarthy wrote about her troubled childhood with detachment. Wanting to prove herself a "superior girl," McCarthy strove in her formative years for intellectual distinction. Critics noted that *Memories* was more searching, and considerably less acerbic, than her fiction; some considered it her best work.

Mena \'mã-nä\, Juan de (b. 1411, Córdoba, Castile [Spain]—d. 1456, Torrelaguna, Castile)   Poet who was a forerunner of the Renaissance in Spain.

Mena belonged to the literary court of King John II of Castile. He is best known for his poem *Laberinto de Fortuna* (1444; "The Labyrinth of Fortune"), also called *Las trescientas* ("The Three Hundreds") for its length, which owes much to Lucan, Virgil, and Dante. Writing in *arte mayor*, lines of 12 syllables that lend themselves to stately recitation, Mena sought to make the Spanish language a literary vehicle adequate to his epic vision of Spain. His themes are medieval, but his use of Latinisms and rhetorical devices and his references to classical personages suggest an affinity to the new manner of expression that came to be associated with the Renaissance.

Ménage \mã-'näzh\, Gilles (b. Aug. 15, 1613, Angers, Fr.—d. July 23, 1692, Paris)   French scholar and man of letters known for philological works as well as for the *mercuriales*, Wednesday literary meetings, he sponsored for more than 30 years.

Ménage practiced law and frequented Mme de Rambouillet's circle of *précieuses*, who cultivated wit and the art of polite and elegant conversation. He subsequently abandoned law for the church, becoming prior of Montdidier. The *mercuriales* began in 1656 and were attended by poets and critics. Ménage made many enemies, such as the playwright Jean Racine, who prevented his entry to the Académie Française in 1684. Menage's *Requête des dictionnaires* subsequently criticized the academy. He wrote a history of female philosophers (1690) and numerous critical works, including two studies of the French language. *Menagiana* (1693–1715) was a publication of his jokes and judgments, assembled by his friends after his death.

Menahem ben Saruq \mə-'nä-kəm-,ben-sä-'rük\, *in full* Menahem ben Jacob ibn Saruq, Saruq *also spelled* Saruk (b. *c.* 910, Tortosa [Spain]—d. *c.* 970, Córdoba?)   Jewish lexicographer and poet who composed the first Hebrew-language dictionary, the *Maḥberet*, a lexicon of the Bible.

Having as a patron the powerful Jewish statesman Ḥisdai ibn Shaprut, Menahem compiled his famous dictionary. It was severely criticized by the rival philologist and poet Dunash ben Labrat, who, by his bitter attacks, succeeded in turning Ḥisdai against Menahem. Menahem probably died not long after his fall from favor.

Despite its faults, Menahem's dictionary had many virtues and remained in use for many years. Through it the author established that Hebrew is a language with definite, discoverable rules, and he illustrated his principles with many elegantly phrased examples. His dictionary was an invaluable aid to Bible study for European Jews who could not read Arabic.

Menander \mə-'nan-dər\ (b. *c.* 342 BC—d. *c.* 292 BC)   Athenian dramatist whom ancient critics considered the supreme poet of Greek New Comedy—*i.e.*, the last flowering of Athenian stage comedy. He wrote more than 100 plays, winning eight victories at Athenian dramatic festivals.

The known facts of Menander's life are few. In 321 he produced his first play, *Orgē* ("Anger"). In 316 he won a prize at a festival with *Dyscolus* ("Misanthrope"), and he gained his first victory at the Dionysia festival the next year. By 301 Menander had written more than 70 plays.

By the time Menander began to write comedy, the typical subject of comedy had changed from public affairs to fictitious characters from ordinary life. The role of the chorus was generally confined to the performance of interludes between acts. Actors' masks were retained but were elaborated to provide for the wider range of characters required by a comedy of manners. Menander wrote in a refined Attic, which was at the time the literary language of the Greek-speaking world. He was

masterly at presenting such characters as stern fathers, young lovers, greedy demimondaines, intriguing slaves, and others.

Menander's nicety of touch and skill at comedy in a light vein is clearly evident in *Dyscolus* in the character of the gruff misanthrope Knemon. Perhaps his greatest achievement, however, lies in the subtle clash and contrast of character and ethical principle in such plays as *Perikeiromenē* ("The Girl Who Has Her Hair Cut Off") and *Second Adelphoi*.

Menander's works were much adapted by the Roman writers Plautus and Terence, and through them Menander influenced the development of European comedy from the Renaissance on. Their work also supplements much of the lost corpus of his plays, of which no complete text exists except for *Dyscolus*, first printed in 1959 from leaves of a papyrus codex, the so-called Bodmer codex, acquired in Egypt. Since that time large portions of other of Menander's plays have been recovered and published, including much of *Samia* ("The Woman of Samos"), *Aspis* ("The Shield"), and *Misoumenos* ("The Man She Hated").

Ménard \mã-'när\, Louis-Nicolas (b. Oct. 19, 1822, Paris, Fr.—d. Feb. 9, 1901, Paris)   French writer whose vision of ancient Greek religion and philosophy influenced the Parnassian poets.

Ménard was a gifted chemist as well as a painter and historian. He was a socialist republican and was condemned to prison in 1849 for his *Prologue d'une révolution*, which contained radical political opinions and his reminiscences of the June 1848 insurrections in Paris. He escaped abroad, returning to Paris in 1852. Thereafter he devoted himself to classical studies. In 1876 he published *Rêveries d'un païen mystique* ("Reveries of a Mystical Pagan"), which expounds his philosophy.

Ménard's poetic works pale beside those of Charles-Marie-René Leconte de Lisle and José María de Heredia, both of whom he influenced considerably; he also influenced Anatole France and Gustave Flaubert.

Men at Arms   Novel by Evelyn Waugh, originally published in 1952. It is the first volume of the trilogy SWORD OF HONOUR.

Mencius \'men-chē-əs, -chəs\ *or* **Meng-tzu** \'məŋ-'dzü\ *or* **Mengzi** \'məŋ-'dzə\, *original name* Meng ke \'məŋ-'kə\, *posthumous name* Zou gong \'dzō-'gūŋ\ *or* Duke of Zou (b. *c.* 372 BC, ancient state of Zou, China—d. *c.* 289, China)   Early Chinese philosopher whose development of orthodox Confucianism earned him the title "second sage." Chief among his basic tenets was an emphasis on the obligation of rulers to provide for the common people.

Mencius \'men-chē-əs, -chəs\ *or* **Mengzi** \'məŋ-'dzə\ *or* **Meng-tzu** \-'dzü\   Confucian text, named for its author, that earned for the 4th-century-BC philosopher the title *ya sheng* ("second sage"). Though the book was not generally recognized as a classic until the 12th century, a doctoral chair was established as early as the 2nd century BC to teach the *Mencius*. When Zhu Xi, a great Neo-Confucian philosopher, published the *Mencius* together with three other Confucian texts in 1190, he created the classic known as SI SHU ("Four Books").

The book records the doings and sayings of the author and contains statements on the innate goodness of human nature. It also addresses the proper concerns of government and maintains that the welfare of the common people should come before every other consideration.

Mencken \'meŋk-ən\, H.L., *in full* Henry Louis (b. Sept. 12, 1880, Baltimore, Md., U.S.—d. Jan. 29, 1956, Baltimore)   Controversialist, humorous journalist, and pungent critic of American life.

Mencken became a reporter for the *Baltimore Morning Herald* and later joined the staff of the Baltimore *Sun*, for which he worked throughout most of his life. From 1914 to 1923 he coedited (with George Jean Nathan) *The Smart Set*, then the magazine most influential in the growth of American literature. In 1924 he helped found (with Nathan) the AMERICAN MERCURY, and he edited it until 1933.

Mencken was probably the most influential American literary critic in the 1920s, and he often used literary criticism as a point of departure to jab at American weaknesses. His reviews and miscellaneous essays filled six volumes, aptly titled *Prejudices* (1919–27). He fought against writers whom he regarded as fraudulently successful and worked for the recognition of such outstanding newcomers as Theodore Dreiser and Sinclair Lewis. He jeered at American sham, pretension, provincialism, and prudery, and he ridiculed organized religion, business, and the middle class (which he called the "booboisie").

In 1919 Mencken published *The American Language*, an attempt to bring together examples of American expressions and idioms. The book grew with each reissue through the years, and in 1945 and 1948 Mencken published substantial supplements. By the time of his death, he was perhaps the leading authority on the language of his country.

Mencken's autobiographical trilogy, *Happy Days* (1940), *Newspaper Days* (1941), and *Heathen Days* (1943), is devoted to his experiences in journalism. A further volume, *My Life as Author and Editor*, was published in 1993.

Menckenese \ˌmeŋ-kə-ˈnēz, ˌmen-, -ˈnēs\ The peculiarly vigorous, racy, flamboyant, and often caustic style that is characteristic of American journalist H.L. Mencken.

Mendele Moykher Sforim \ˈmen-də-lə-mō-ˈk̲er-sfä-ˈrēm\, *also spelled* Mendele Mokher Sefarim, *pseudonym of* Shalom Jacob Abramovitsh \ə-ˈbräm-ə-ˌvich\ (b. Nov. 20, 1835, Kopyl, near Minsk, Russia [now in Belarus]—d. Dec. 8, 1917, Odessa [now in Ukraine]) Jewish author, founder of both modern Yiddish and modern Hebrew narrative literature and the creator of modern literary Yiddish.

At Berdichev (now Berdychiv) in Ukraine, where he lived from 1858 to 1869, Mendele began to publish fiction in both Hebrew and Yiddish. His first short story in Hebrew was published in 1863, the major novel *Ha-Avot ve-ha-banim* ("Fathers and Sons") in 1868. His first story in Yiddish, *Dos Kleyne mentshele* (1864; "The Little Man"; *The Parasite*), was a significant step in the establishment of standard literary Yiddish.

In 1865 there followed the first version of *Dos Vintshfingerl* ("The Magic Ring"), which was eventually to become his major novel. A play, *Di Takse* (1869; "The Tax"), treated economic and class antagonisms within Jewish society for the first time. A satirical allegory, *Di Klyatshe* (1873; *The Nag*), represents the fate of the Jewish nation in the form of a prince transformed into a broken, maltreated horse. For a time Mendele continued to write stories and plays of social satire in Yiddish. His greatest work, *Kitser masoes Binyomen hashlishi* (1875; *The Travels and Adventures of Benjamin the Third*), is a panorama of Jewish life in Russia. After living from 1869 to 1881 in Zhitomir (now Zhytomyr, Ukraine), where he was trained as a rabbi, he became head of a traditional school (Talmud Torah) at Odessa and was the leading personality of the emerging literary movement. In 1886 he again published a story in Hebrew, but in a new style that was a mixture of all previous periods of Hebrew. While continuing to write in Yiddish, he gradually rewrote most of his former Yiddish works in Hebrew.

Mendès \maⁿ-ˈdes\, Catulle (b. May 22, 1841, Bordeaux, Fr.—d. Feb. 9, 1909, Paris) French poet, playwright, and novelist noted for his association with the Parnassians.

In Paris, Mendès founded *La Revue fantaisiste* (1861), which became a vehicle for the late works of Théophile Gautier and such poets as Charles Baudelaire and Villiers de L'Isle-Adam. He edited *Le Parnasse contemporain*, 3 vol. (1866, 1871, 1876; "The Contemporary Parnassians"), which named the movement, and he became its historian in *La Légende du Parnasse contemporain*.

Mendès' *Poésies* (1892) and *Poésies nouvelles* (1893) imitate many other poets. His plays *Les Mères ennemies* (1882; "The Enemy Mothers") and *La Femme de Tabarin* (1887; "The Woman of Tabarin") were more successful. He also wrote several novels and licentious tales, such as *Pour lire au bain* ("Readings for the Bath"). His critical work *Rapport sur le mouvement poétique français de 1867–1900* (1902; "Thoughts on the French Poetic Movement of 1867–1900") is still read.

Mendes \ˈmeⁿn-dish\, Murilo (b. May 13, 1901, Juiz de Fora, Braz.—d. Aug. 14, 1975, Lisbon, Port.) Brazilian poet and diplomat who played an important role in Brazilian Modernismo after 1930.

Mendes' early poems illuminated the creative, chaotic forces within everyday Brazilian life. His later works show an increasing Surrealist influence. Following his conversion to Roman Catholicism in 1934, he collaborated with Jorge de Lima in the creation of metaphysical poetry (*e.g.*, *Tempo e Eternidade*, 1935; "Time and Eternity").

Much of Mendes' subsequent poetry shows an almost dialectical tension between the objective world and religious transcendence. In poetry published during the last two decades of his life, he sought to incorporate the austere clarity and "dryness" of traditional Iberian Spanish verse.

Mending Wall Poem by Robert FROST, published in the collection *North of Boston* (1914). Written in blank verse, it depicts a pair of neighboring farmers working together on the annual chore of rebuilding their common wall. The wall serves as the symbolic fulcrum of their friendly antagonism; it balances their contrasting philosophies about brotherhood, represented by the sentiments "Good fences make good neighbors" and "Something there is that doesn't love a wall."

Menelaus \ˌmen-ə-ˈlā-əs\ In Greek mythology, king of Sparta and the younger son of Atreus, king of Mycenae; the abduction of his wife, HELEN, led to the Trojan War. After the fall of Troy, Menelaus recovered Helen and brought her home. Menelaus was a prominent figure in the *Iliad* and the *Odyssey*.

Menen \ˈmen-ən\, Aubrey, *in full* Salvator Aubrey Clarence Menen (b. April 22, 1912, London, Eng.—d. Feb. 13, 1989, Trivandrum, Kerala, India) British writer who explored the nature of nationalism and the cultural contrast between his Irish-Indian ancestry and his British upbringing.

After attending University College in London from 1930 to 1932, Menen held a variety of jobs. When World War II began, he was in India, where he organized pro-Allied radio broadcasts and edited film scripts for the Indian government. After the war, he returned to London to work in an advertising agency, but the success of his first novel, *The Prevalence of Witches* (1947), encouraged him to write full-time. His other novels include *The Backward Bride: A Sicilian Scherzo* (1950), *The Fig Tree* (1959), *SheLA* (1962), *A Conspiracy of Women* (1965), and *Fonthill: A Comedy* (1974). Menen's nonfiction includes travel books, essays, and two autobiographies, *Dead Man in the Silver Market* (1953) and *The Space Within the Heart* (1970).

Menéndez y Pelayo \mā-ˈnän-dāth-ē-pā-ˈlā-yō\, Marcelino (b. Nov. 3, 1856, Santander, Spain—d. May 19, 1912, Santander) Spanish literary critic and historian, remarkable for his vast erudition and his elegant and flexible prose.

Menéndez y Pelayo was professor of Spanish literature at Madrid (1878–98) and director of the National Library (1898–1912); his private library of 45,000 volumes forms part of the Library of Menéndez y Pelayo. His works are available in the *Edición nacional de las obras completas de Menéndez y Pelayo*, 43 vol. (1940–46).

Menghistu Lemma \meŋ-'gēs-tū-'lem-mə\, Menghistu *also spelled* Mengistu (b. August 1925, Addis Ababa, Eth.—d. July 1988, Addis Ababa) Ethiopian poet and playwright whose works examine the difficulty of reconciling traditional values and customs with modern Western ideas.

After receiving a Muslim education in Harar, Menghistu Lemma studied in Addis Ababa and in London at the Regent Street Polytechnic and the London School of Economics. He worked in government service, notably as first secretary at the Ethiopian embassy in India (1957–63). His best-known plays, which he also translated into English, were published as *Snatch and Run; or Marriage by Abduction* (produced 1962; published 1963) and *Marriage of Unequals* (produced 1963; published 1970). He also wrote critical essays in both Amharic and English and published a historically important transcription of his father's oral memoirs.

Mengzi or **Meng-tzu** *see* MENCIUS.

Menippean satire \mə-'nip-ē-ən\, *also called* Varronian satire \və-'rō-nē-ən\ Form of satire named for the 3rd-century-BC Greek philosopher Menippus of Gadara, who produced the prototype in his criticism by mixing elements of prose and verse to mock institutions, ideas, and conventions. This type of satire was introduced to Rome by Marcus Terentius Varro in his *Saturae Menippeae* and was further developed by Lucian, who raised Menippean satire to the level of art by his broad, fluent, and seemingly effortless command of the Attic Greek language and literary style. Another instance of Menippean influence can be seen in Jonathan Swift's *Tale of a Tub*, which contains a relatively simple allegory of Reformation history (the *Tale* proper) that is interrupted by a series of editorial digressions.

Menippus \mə-'nip-əs\ (fl. 3rd century BC) Greek philosopher who followed the cynic philosophy of Diogenes and who founded a literary genre known as Menippean satire.

Menippus' writings are lost, but some idea of their character can be gained from his Latin imitators, notably Varro, Seneca, and Lucian. His criticism was an innovation in the presentation of philosophic ideas. Aimed at reaching as wide an audience as possible, it abandoned the dialogue form and conveyed its message in a satiric style. Unusual settings—including a descent into Hades, an auction, and a symposium—were employed with striking effect.

Men of Good Will Epic novel cycle by Jules ROMAINS, published in French in 27 volumes as *Les Hommes de bonne volonté* between 1932 and 1946. The work was an attempt to re-create the spirit of French society from Oct. 6, 1908, to Oct. 7, 1933. There is no central figure or family to provide a focus for the narrative, and the work is populated by a huge cast of characters. Each volume presents a different view of society and distinct incidents, including crimes treated in the manner of a detective story (as in *Le Crime de Quinette*, 1932), domestic scenes (*Éros de Paris*, 1932), and historical events (*Verdun*, 1938). The finest sections, such as the victory parade after World War I, exemplify the interest in collective life and emotion that is the basis of Unanimisme, the literary movement founded by Romains.

Mephistopheles \,mef-i-'stäf-ə-,lēz\ or **Mephisto** \me-'fis-tō\ Familiar spirit of the Devil in late settings of the legend of FAUST. It is probable that the name Mephistopheles was in-

vented for the historical Faust by the anonymous author of the first *Faustbuch* (1587). A latecomer in the infernal hierarchy, Mephistopheles never became an integral part of the tradition of magic and demonology. In *Doctor Faustus* (1604), by the English dramatist Christopher Marlowe, Mephistopheles achieves tragic grandeur as a fallen angel. In the drama *Faust* (Part I, 1808; Part II, 1832) by J.W. von Goethe, he is cold-hearted, cynical, and witty.

Mercer \'mər-sər\, David (b. June 27, 1928, Wakefield, Yorkshire, Eng.—d. Aug. 8, 1980, Haifa, Israel) Playwright who established his reputation on the London stage in the mid-1960s with plays that examine the decay he saw in English society.

Mercer's first play, written for television, was *Where the Difference Begins* (1961); it was the first part of a trilogy, *The Generations* (1964). His *A Suitable Case for Treatment*, televised in 1962, won a Writers' Guild award and was filmed in 1965 as *Morgan!* From that play emerged Mercer's view of the world as anarchic, despairing, and insane, a view also apparent in *The Governor's Lady*, his first stage play (performed 1965), about a man who in utter frustration turned into a baboon and attacked his frigid wife. His other full-length plays include *Ride a Cock Horse* (1965), *Belcher's Luck* (1966), *Flint* (1970), *After Haggerty* (1970), *Duck Song* (1974), and *Cousin Vladimir* (1978).

Merchant of Venice, The \'ven-is\ Comedy in five acts by William SHAKESPEARE, performed about 1596–97, printed in a quarto edition from foul papers in 1600. Much less light-hearted than Shakespeare's other comedies, the work is a serious study of love and marriage and of the abuse of wealth.

Bassanio, a noble but penniless Venetian, asks his wealthy friend Antonio for a loan so as to impress and woo the heiress Portia. Antonio, whose money is invested in foreign ventures, borrows the sum from Shylock, a Jewish moneylender, on the condition that if the loan cannot be repaid in time Antonio will forfeit a pound of flesh. News arrives that Antonio's ships have been destroyed. Unable to collect on his loan, Shylock attempts to claim his pound of flesh. Portia disguises herself as a man to defend Antonio in court. She delivers the famous "quality of mercy" speech, but Shylock is unswayed. Portia admits the validity of his claim but insists that he has a right to the flesh only. If any blood is spilled, she declares, Shylock must die. The contract is cancelled and Shylock is ordered to give half of his estate to Antonio, who agrees not to take the money if Shylock converts to Christianity and restores his disinherited daughter Jessica, who has married a Christian, to his will. Shylock agrees. The play ends with the news that some of Antonio's ships have arrived safely.

Shylock has been the subject of modern scholarly debate over whether the playwright displayed anti-Semitism or religious tolerance in his characterization, for, despite his association with greed and usury, Shylock delivers an eloquent speech ("Hath not a Jew eyes? . . . ") in which he defends himself against his Christian enemies.

Merchant's Tale, The One of the 24 stories in THE CANTERBURY TALES by Geoffrey Chaucer.

The story draws on a folktale of familiar theme, that of an old man whose young wife is unfaithful. Old Januarie is deceived by his young wife May and her lover Damyan after Januarie suddenly goes blind. The lovers sneak up to the branches of a pear tree above Januarie's head and begin to make love. An enraged Pluto instantly restores the old man's sight, but Proserpina allows May to outwit him by explaining that she was fighting with Damyan in the tree because she had been told that by doing so Januarie's sight would be restored.

Mercier \mer-'syā\, Louis-Sébastien (b. June 6, 1740, Paris, Fr.—d. April 25, 1814, Paris) One of the first French writers of *drames bourgeois* (middle-class tragedies). In *Du théâtre* (1773; "About the Theater"), he emphasized the didactic function of the theater, and in his plays he presented a thesis, subordinating dramatic considerations to the didactic end.

Mercier wrote about 60 plays, including a social comedy, *La Brouette du vinaigrier* (1775; "The Barrel-load of the Vinegar Merchant"); such dramas as *Le Faux Ami* (1772; "The False Friend") and the antimilitarist *Le Déserteur* (1770; "The Deserter"); and two historical dramas, *Jean Hennuyer évêque de Lisieux* (1772; "Jean Hennuyer, Bishop of Lisieux") and *La Destruction de la ligue* (1782; "The Destruction of the League"), so anticlerical and antimonarchical that they were not performed until after the French Revolution.

Merck \'merk\, Johann Heinrich (b. April 11, 1741, Darmstadt, Hesse-Darmstadt [Germany]—d. June 27, 1791, Darmstadt) German writer and critic who provided valuable guidance to the young writers of the Sturm und Drang literary movement of the late 18th century.

Merck was influential in German literary circles and sympathetic with the aims of such writers as Friedrich Nicolai, Christoph Martin Wieland, Johann Gottfried von Herder, and J.W. von Goethe, despite his bitingly sarcastic criticism. Merck helped found the periodical *Frankfurter Gelehrte Anzeigen* (1772), in which some of Goethe's earliest pieces were published, and he contributed to Nicolai's journal, *Allgemeine deutsche Bibliothek*, and to Wieland's *Der teutsche Merkur*. His letters provide an invaluable source for the literary life of the times.

Mercure de France, Le \lə-mer-kūēr-də-'fräⁿs\ French literary journal published (with some interruptions) for almost 300 years. Founded by Jean Donneau de Visé as *Le Mercure galant* in 1672, the magazine was renamed *Le Mercure de France* in 1724. It printed poetry, literary criticism, and political commentary in a light, humorous fashion. Napoleon suppressed the publication in 1811; it flourished briefly after his fall in 1815, but it ceased publication in the early 1820s.

Le Mercure de France was revived in 1890 by Alfred Vallette and his friends, who turned it into a strictly literary journal. Vallette became the patron of Symbolism, publishing the most eminent names in French literature, from Stéphane Mallarmé to the absurdist Alfred Jarry. After 1935, despite a brief flourish under the editorship of Georges Duhamel, the *Mercure* fell into decline, and it finally ceased publication in 1965.

Mercury \'mər-kyù-rē\ or **Mercurius** \mər-'kyür-ē-əs\ In Roman mythology, god of merchandise and merchants, commonly identified with the Greek HERMES. The worship of Mercury was introduced early, and his temple on the Aventine Hill in Rome was dedicated in 495 BC. There he was associated with the goddess Maia, who became identified as his mother through her association with the Greek Maia, mother of Hermes.

Mercutio \mər-'kyū-shē-ō\ Fictional character, a kinsman of the prince of Verona and a friend to the Montague Romeo in William Shakespeare's ROMEO AND JULIET.

Merdle, Mr. \'mər-dəl\ Fictional character, a financier, in LITTLE DORRIT by Charles Dickens.

Meredith \'mer-ə-dith\, George (b. Feb. 12, 1828, Portsmouth, Hampshire, Eng.—d. May 18, 1909, Box Hill, Surrey) English Victorian poet and novelist whose novels are noted for their wit, brilliant dialogue, and aphoristic quality of language. Meredith's novels are also distinguished by psychological studies of character and by his extensive use of interior mono-

logue. His best-known works are THE ORDEAL OF RICHARD FEVEREL (1859) and THE EGOIST (1879).

Detail of an oil painting by G.F. Watts, 1893
National Portrait Gallery, London

Meredith's formal education ended at the age of 16, and after several false starts, he was apprenticed at 18 to a London solicitor and was ostensibly launched upon a career in law. He concentrated instead, however, on writing poems and articles and on making translations. He also managed to pay the publication costs of a small collection of verse, entitled *Poems*, in 1851. Because poetry did not pay, Meredith turned his hand to prose, writing a fantasy entitled *The Shaving of Shagpat: An Arabian Entertainment* (1855). Original in conception but imitative of *The Thousand and One Nights* in manner, it baffled many of his readers who did not know whether to regard it as allegory or fairy tale.

Meredith followed *Richard Feverel* with *Evan Harrington* (1860), a comedy in which he used the family tailoring establishment and his own relatives for subject matter. Taking up poetry again, Meredith next published a volume of poems, *Modern Love, and Poems of the English Roadside, with Poems and Ballads* (1862).

Fame and fortune came at last to Meredith with the publication of his next two novels of consequence, *The Egoist* and DIANA OF THE CROSSWAYS (1885). After 1885 he wrote three novels and five volumes of poems that were increasingly more philosophic than poetic.

Meres \'mirz\, Francis (b. 1565, Kirton, Holland, Lincolnshire, Eng.—d. Jan. 29, 1647, Wing, Rutland) English author of the commonplace book *Palladis Tamia: Wits Treasury* (1598), which lists William Shakespeare's dramatic output to 1598. It also includes mention of the deaths of Christopher Marlowe, George Peele, and Robert Greene and briefly records the critical estimation of the poets of the day.

Merezhkovsky \m^yi-r^yish-'kôf-sk^yē, *Angl* ‚mer-əsh-'käf-skē\, Dmitry Sergeyevich (b. Aug. 2 [Aug. 14, New Style], 1865, St. Petersburg, Russia—d. Dec. 9, 1941, Paris, Fr.) Russian poet, novelist, critic, and thinker who played an important role in the revival of religious-philosophical interests among the Russian intelligentsia.

Merezhkovsky published his first volume of poetry in 1888. His essay *O prichinakh upadka i o novykh techeniyakh sovremennoy russkoy literatury* (1893; "On the Causes of the Decline and on the New Trends in Contemporary Russian Literature") was a significant landmark of Russian modernism. At the beginning of the 20th century he and his wife, Zinaida Gippius, edited the magazine *Novy put* (1903–04; "The New Path").

With his trilogy *Khristos i Antikhrist* (1896–1905; "Christ and Antichrist"), Merezhkovsky revived the historical novel in Russia. Its three parts, set in widely separated epochs and geographical areas, serve as vehicles for the author's historical and theological ideas. Another group of fictional works from Russian history—the play *Pavel I* (1908) and the novels *Aleksandr I* (1911–12) and *14 Dekabrya* (1918; *December the Fourteenth*)—also form a trilogy. Merezhkovsky's favorite method was antithesis, which he applied not only in his novels but also in his critical study *Tolstoy i Dostoyevsky* (1901–02), a work of seminal importance and enduring value. His *Gogol i chort* (1906; "Gogol and the Devil") is another noteworthy critical work.

Although Merezhkovsky welcomed the February Revolution of 1917, he opposed the Bolshevik seizure of power. Emigrating in 1920, he eventually settled in Paris, where he published two more historical novels under the general title *Rozhdenie bogov* (1924–25; *Birth of the Gods*) and biographical studies of Napoleon, Jesus Christ, St. Augustine, St. Paul, St. Francis of Assisi, Joan of Arc, Dante, and many others.

Meri \'mä-rē\, Veijo (b. Dec. 31, 1928, Viipuri, Fin.)   Finnish novelist, poet, and dramatist of the generation of the 1960s.

Meri devoted many of his novels and dramas to the depiction of war, but unlike his many Finnish predecessors he did not treat war in the heroic mode. His soldiers existed in an incoherent and farcical world. In *Manillaköysi* (1957; *The Manila Rope*), the main character deserts, taking with him a rope for which he is willing to risk his life, though he has no use for the rope. *Vuoden 1918 taphatumat* (1960; "Incidents 1918") describes the Finnish civil war of 1918 as a chain of confused and disconnected actions. In *Everstin autonkuljettaja* (1966; "The Colonel's Driver") a driver risks his life to retrieve a briefcase. The novels *Peiliin piiretty nainen* (1963; "Woman in the Mirror") and *Suku* (1968; "The Family") deal with contemporary relationships. Meri wrote several collections of short stories, including *Tilanteita* (1962; "Situations"), *Leiri* (1972; "The Camp"), and *Morsiamen sisar* (1972; "The Sister of the Bride"). He also published a volume of poetry, *Mielen lähtölaskenta* (1976; "The Mind's Countdown"), and an autobiography, *Kersantin poika* (1971). His most popular play, *Sotamies Jokisen vihkiloma* (1965; *Private Jokinen's Marriage Leave*), is set in the war years of the 1940s.

Mérimée \mä-rē-'mā\, Prosper (b. Sept. 28, 1803, Paris, Fr.— d. Sept. 23, 1870, Cannes)   French dramatist and master of the short story whose works—romantic in theme but classical in style—were a renewal of classicism in a romantic age.

Mérimée first studied law but preferred to study the Greek, Spanish, English, and Russian languages and their literatures. At 19 he wrote his first play, *Cromwell* (1822).

A collection of his plays, *Le Théâtre de Clara Gazul*, appeared in 1825. Indulging his taste for mystification, he presented them as translations by a certain Joseph L'Estrange of the work of a Spanish actress. His next hoax was *La Guzla* (1827), by "Hyacinthe Maglanowich," ballads about murder, revenge, and vampires, supposedly translated from the Illyrian. Both works deceived even scholars of the day. Inspired by the vogue for historical fiction established by Sir Walter Scott, he wrote *La Jacquerie* (1828; "Peasant Revolt"), 36 dramatic scenes about a peasant insurrection in feudal times, and the novel *La Chronique du règne de Charles IX* (1829), about French court life during war and peace.

Mérimée's short stories, many of which are mysteries, best illustrate his imagination and somber temperament. Spain and Russia were his principal literary sources, and he was the first interpreter of Russian literature in France. Aleksandr Pushkin was his master, especially for his themes of violence and cruelty and the human psychology behind them. In one of Mérimée's best-known stories, *Mateo Falcone* (1829), a father kills a son for betraying the family honor. The collection *Mosaïque* (1833) was followed by his most famous novellas: *Colomba* (1840), the story of a young Corsican girl who forces her brother to commit murder for the sake of a vendetta, and CARMEN (1845), in which an unfaithful Gypsy girl is killed by a soldier who loves her. *Lokis* (1869) and *La Chambre bleue* (1872) show Mérimée's fascination with the supernatural.

In 1831 he met a young girl, Jenny Dacquin, with whom he engaged in a long correspondence, published after his death as *Lettres à une inconnue* (1873; "Letters to an Unknown Girl"). He was also a longtime friend of the Countess of Montijo. In 1853, when her daughter became the empress Eugénie of France, Mérimée was admitted to the royal circle and made a senator. His letters to Sir Anthony Panizzi, principal librarian of the British Museum and Mérimée's closest friend in old age, have been described as a "history of the Second Empire." They were published posthumously as *Lettres à M. Panizzi: 1850–70* (1881). He also wrote several works of literary criticism.

Merlin \'mər-lin\   Enchanter and wise man in Arthurian legend and romance of the Middle Ages, linked with personages in ancient Celtic mythology (especially with Myrddin in Welsh tradition). He appeared in Arthurian legend as an enigmatic figure, fluctuations and inconsistencies in his character being often dictated by the requirements of a particular narrative or by varying attitudes toward magic and witchcraft. Thus, treatments of Merlin reflect different stages in the development of Arthurian romance itself.

Original drawing by Aubrey Beardsley for an 1893 edition of Sir Thomas Malory's *The Birth, Life, and Acts of King Arthur*
Rosenwald Collection, Library of Congress

Geoffrey of Monmouth, in the *Historia regum Britanniae* (written between 1135 and 1139), adapted a story told by the Welsh antiquary Nennius (flourished *c.* 800) of a boy, Ambrosius, who had given advice to the legendary British king Vortigern. In Geoffrey's account Merlin-Ambrosius figured as adviser to Uther Pendragon (King Arthur's father) and afterward to Arthur himself. In a later work, *Vita Merlini*, Geoffrey further developed the story of Merlin by adapting a northern legend about a wild man of the woods gifted with powers of divination. Early in the 13th century, Robert de Boron's verse romance *Merlin* added a Christian dimension to the character, making him the prophet of the Holy Grail. The author of the first part of a version of the Arthurian legend known as the Vulgate cycle made the demonic side of Merlin's character predominant, but in later branches of the Vulgate cycle, Merlin again became the prophet of the Holy Grail, while his role as Arthur's counselor was filled out. It was Merlin, for example, who advised Uther to establish the knightly fellowship of the Round Table and who suggested that Uther's true heir would be revealed by a test that involved drawing a sword from a stone in which it was set. The Vulgate cycle also included a story of the wizard's infatuation with the Lady of the Lake, which eventually brought about his death. *See also* ARTHURIAN LEGEND; GEOFFREY of Monmouth.

Several major Renaissance works—including Ludovico Ariosto's *Orlando furioso*, François Rabelais's *Gargantua*, and Miguel de Cervantes' *Don Quixote*—feature Merlin as a character. Karl Immermann, Alfred, Lord Tennyson, and several later writers also took up the story of Merlin. The most notable of the 20th-century works on Merlin are probably Guillaume Apollinaire's *L'Enchanteur pourrissant*, Jean Cocteau's *Les Chevaliers de la table ronde*, and Tankred Dorst's *Merlin*.

mermaid \'mər-,mād\ [*mere* sea] A fabled marine creature usually represented as having the head, trunk, and arms of a woman and a lower part like the tail of a fish.

Like fairies, mermaids were believed to have magical powers. According to legend, though very long-lived, they were mortal and had no souls. Similar divine or semidivine beings appear in ancient mythologies (*e.g.*, the Mesopotamian sea god Enki or Ea). Mermaids appeared frequently in European folklore, where they were sometimes called sirens because of their love of music and their singing ability. A well-known legend recounts the story of the Lorelei of the Rhine who lured men to death by drowning. Many folktales record marriages between mermaids (who might assume human form) and human men. In most of these tales, the man steals the mermaid's cap, belt, comb, or mirror. While the objects remain hidden from her, she will live with him; if she finds the stolen object, she can return at once to the sea. *Compare* NIX; SIREN.

Mermaid Tavern Famous London meeting place of the Friday Street Club, of which William Shakespeare, Sir Walter Raleigh, John Donne, and Ben Jonson were notable members. It stood to the east of St. Paul's Cathedral.

merman \'mər-,man, - mən\ *plural* mermen \-mən\ [*mere* sea], *also called* manfish. A fabled marine male creature usually represented as having the head, trunk, and arms of a man and a lower part like the tail of a fish. Both Matthew Arnold ("The Forsaken Merman") and Alfred, Lord Tennyson ("The Merman"), among others, wrote poems on mermen.

Merrill \'mer-il\, James (Ingram) (b. March 3, 1926, New York, N.Y., U.S.—d. Feb. 6, 1995, Tucson, Ariz.) American poet known for the fine craftsmanship and wit of his lyric and epic poems.

Merrill attended Amherst College. His first book, *Jim's Book: A Collection of Poems and Short Stories* (1942), and the early books that followed revealed his mastery of poetic form and technique. With the publication of *Water Street* (1962), critics noted a growing ease and the development of a personal vision in his writing. The interactions between art and life and between memory and experience became the major motifs of the transitional stage in his writing.

It was not until the publication of the epic poetry in *Divine Comedies* (1976), *Mirabell: Books of Number* (1978), and *Scripts for the Pageant* (1980)—a trilogy later published in *The Changing Light at Sandover* (1982)—that Merrill achieved a measure of wider public appreciation. He used a Ouija board in composing some of the poetry in the trilogy, which is a serious yet witty summation of his lifelong concerns. A selection of his poetry, *From the First Nine: Poems 1946–1976*, was published in 1982 and *Selected Poems, 1946–1985* in 1992. Merrill also wrote a memoir entitled *A Different Person* (1994). His last volume of poetry, *A Scattering of Salts* (1995), was posthumously published.

Merry Wives of Windsor, The \'wind-zər\ Comedy in five acts by William SHAKESPEARE, produced about 1600–01 and published in a quarto edition in 1602.

Shakespeare used the character of Falstaff, who appears in his historical drama *Henry IV*, in this play. After Falstaff meets Mistresses Page and Ford, two married women said to control their own financial affairs, he writes identical love letters to each of them, never imagining that they will compare notes. When they do, they vow to trick Falstaff. In a climactic scene, Falstaff appears in a silly costume, complete with stag's horns, expecting an assignation—but the women and their husbands have arranged for a group of friends, including the Pages' daughter, all in witch and fairy costumes, to frighten and tease him. All identities are revealed at the end, and in an atmosphere of good humor Falstaff is forgiven.

Merton \'mərt-ən\, Thomas, *original name of* Father M. Louis \'lū-is\ (b. Jan. 31, 1915, Prades, Fr.—d. Dec. 10, 1968, Bangkok, Thai.) Roman Catholic monk known for his prolific writings on spiritual and social themes.

Merton was educated at Cambridge University and Columbia University. After teaching English at Columbia and at St. Bonaventure University near Olean, N.Y., he entered the Cistercian Abbey of Gethsemani (near Louisville, Ky.), housing a contemplative Trappist order. He was ordained a priest in 1949.

Merton's first published works were collections of poems—*Thirty Poems* (1944), *A Man in the Divided Sea* (1946), and *Figures for an Apocalypse* (1948). With the publication of the autobiographical *Seven Storey Mountain* (1948), he gained an international reputation. His early works were strictly spiritual, but in the early 1960s his writings tended toward social criticism, while many of his later works reveal an insight into Oriental philosophy and mysticism unusual in a Westerner. His only novel, *My Argument with the Gestapo*, written in 1941, was published posthumously in 1969. Merton's other writings include *The Waters of Siloe* (1949), a history of the Trappists; *Seeds of Contemplation* (1949); *The Living Bread* (1956), a meditation on the Eucharist; *Contemplation in a World of Action* (1971), an insightful book of essays; and *The Asian Journal of Thomas Merton* (1973).

Merwin \'mər-win\, W.S., *in full* William Stanley (b. Sept. 30, 1927, New York, N.Y., U.S.) American poet and translator known for the spare style of his poetry in which he expressed his concerns about the alienation of humans from their environment.

After graduating from Princeton University, Merwin worked as a tutor and freelance translator. Later he was playwright-in-residence at the Poet's Theatre, Cambridge, Mass., from 1956 to 1957 and poetry editor of *The Nation* (1962).

Critical acclaim for Merwin began with his first collection of poetry, *A Mask for Janus* (1952). His early poems include both lyrical works and philosophical narratives based on myth and folk tales. Subsequent collections include *Green with Beasts* (1956), *The Drunk in the Furnace* (1960), and *The Moving Target* (1963). The poems of *The Lice* (1967) reflect the poet's despair over human mistreatment of the rest of creation. Merwin won a Pulitzer Prize for *The Carrier of Ladders* (1970). Among his later works are *The Compass Flower* (1977), *Finding the Islands* (1982), *The Rain in the Trees* (1988), and *Travels* (1993). Merwin's translations, often done in collaboration with others, range from plays of Euripides and Federico García Lorca to the epics *The Poem of the Cid* and *The Song of Roland* to ancient and modern works from Chinese, Sanskrit, and Japanese.

mesode \'mes-,ōd\ [Greek *mesōidós*, from *mésos* middle + *ōidḗ* song] In poetry, a stanza different in form from the rest of the poem that is inserted between the strophe and the antistrophe of an ode. *Compare* MESYMNION.

Mesrob or **Mesrop** \'mes-,rōb\, Saint, *also called* Mashtots \'mäsh-,tōts\ (b. *c.* 350, Hatzikk, Armenia [now Muş, Tur.]— d. 439/440) Monk, theologian, and linguist who according to tradition devised an alphabet for the Armenian language and employed it in translations of the Bible, laying the foundation for Armenia's golden age of Christian literature.

Mesrob began a monastic existence about 395. He was ordained a priest, maintained a lifelong esteem for the ascetic life, and founded several monasteries. Mesrob devised the first popular Armenian Bible, the "Mesrobian" Bible (*c.* 410). He was personally responsible for the New Testament and the Old Testament Book of Proverbs. Subsequently, he revised the entire text.

A collection of biblical commentaries, translations of patristic works, and liturgical prayers and hymns is credited to Mesrob, corroborating his reputation for having laid the foundation of a national Armenian liturgy. He is also credited with contributing to the origin of the Georgian alphabet.

mesymnion \me-'sim-nē-än\ [Greek *mesýmnion,* from *mésos* middle + *hýmnos* hymn, ode] In classical prosody, a short colon or rhythmic sequence interpolated in a stanza. A mesode is an entire stanza thus composed and occurring within an ode (between the strophe and antistrophe).

Metamorphoses \,met-ə-mòr-'fō-,sēz\ Poem in 15 books, written in Latin about AD 8 by OVID. Written in hexameter verse, it is a collection of mythological and legendary stories, many taken from Greek sources, in which transformation (metamorphosis) plays a role, however minor. The stories, which are unrelated, are told in chronological order from the creation of the world (the first metamorphosis, of chaos into order) to the death and deification of Julius Caesar (the culminating metamorphosis).

The importance of the theme of metamorphosis is more apparent than real; passion is the essential theme of the poem, and passion imparts more unity to the work than do the transformation devices employed by Ovid. The work is noted for its wit, rhetorical brilliance, and narrative and descriptive qualities.

Metamorphoses A prose work by Lucius Apuleius. *See* THE GOLDEN ASS.

Metamorphosis, The Symbolic story by Franz KAFKA, published in German as *Die Verwandlung* in 1915.

The opening sentence of *The Metamorphosis* has become one of the most famous in Western literature: "As Gregor Samsa awoke one morning from uneasy dreams he found himself transformed in his bed into a gigantic insect." Forced by his tyrannical father to hide in his bedroom, Gregor slowly dies from both his family's neglect and his own guilty despair.

metaphor \'met-ə-,fòr\ [Greek *metaphorá* change of a word to a new sense, metaphor, a derivative of *metaphérein* to transfer, change, from *metá* after, beyond + *phérein* to carry] A figure of speech in which a word or phrase denoting one kind of object or action is used in place of another to suggest a likeness or analogy between them (as in *the ship plows the seas* or in *a volley of oaths*). A metaphor is an implied comparison (as in *a marble brow*) in contrast to the explicit comparison of the simile (as in *a brow white as marble*). *Compare* SIMILE.

The metaphor makes a qualitative leap from a reasonable, perhaps prosaic, comparison to an identification or fusion of two objects to make a new entity partaking of the characteristics of both. Metaphor is the fundamental language of poetry, although it is common on all levels and in all kinds of language. Everyday language abounds in phrases and expressions that once were metaphors. For example, "time flies" is an ancient metaphorical expression. When the poet says, "The Bird of Time has but a little way/To flutter—and the Bird is on the Wing" (*The Rubáiyát of Omar Khayyám*), he is constructing a new metaphor on the foundations of an older, stock metaphor. Likewise, when Tennessee Williams entitles his play *Sweet Bird of Youth,* he, too, is referring to the bird of time that flies.

In poetry a metaphor may perform varied functions, from the mere noting of a likeness to the evocation of a swarm of associations; it may exist as a minor beauty, or it may be the central concept and controlling image of the poem. The familiar metaphor "Iron Horse" for train, for example, is the elaborate central concept of one of Emily Dickinson's poems:

> I like to see it lap the Miles—
> And lick the Valleys up—
> And stop to feed itself at Tanks—
> And then—prodigious step
>
> Around a Pile of Mountains—
> And supercilious peer
> In Shanties—by the sides of Roads—
> And then a Quarry pare
>
> To fit its sides
> And crawl between
> Complaining all the while
> In horrid—hooting stanza—
> Then chase itself down Hill—
>
> And neigh like Boanerges—
> Then—prompter than a Star
> Stop—docile and omnipotent
> At its own stable door—

A *mixed metaphor* is the linking of two or more disparate elements, which often results in an unintentionally comic effect produced by the writer's insensitivity to the literal meaning of the words or by the falseness of the comparison. A mixed metaphor may also be used with great effectiveness, however, as in Hamlet's speech:

> Whether 'tis nobler in the mind to suffer
> The slings and arrows of outrageous fortune
> Or to take arms against a sea of troubles . . .

For strictly correct completion of the metaphor, "sea" should be replaced by "host."

metaphrast \'met-ə-,frast\ [Middle Greek *metaphrastḗs,* a derivative of Greek *metaphrázein* to translate, from *metá* after, beyond + *phrázein* to point out, show, tell] A translator; specifically, one who turns verse into a different meter or prose into verse.

Metaphysical poetry \,met-ə-'fiz-i-kəl\ Highly intellectualized poetry written chiefly in 17th-century England. It is marked by bold and ingenious conceits, complexity and subtlety of thought, frequent use of paradox, and often deliberate harshness or rigidity of expression. Metaphysical poetry is chiefly concerned with analyzing feeling. The most notable of the Metaphysical poets is John Donne. Others include George Herbert, Henry Vaughan, Richard Crashaw, Andrew Marvell, John Cleveland, and Abraham Cowley.

Metaphysical poetry is a blend of emotion and intellectual ingenuity, characterized by CONCEIT—that is, by the sometimes forced juxtaposition of apparently unconnected ideas and things so that the reader is startled out of complacency and forced to think through the argument of the poem. The boldness of the literary devices used—especially obliquity, irony, and paradox—is always reinforced by a dramatic directness of language, the rhythm of which is derived from that of living speech.

Metaphysical poetry was especially esteemed in the 1930s and '40s, largely because of T.S. Eliot's influential essay "The Metaphysical Poets" (1921). In their own time, however, the epithet "metaphysical" was used pejoratively: in 1630 the Scottish poet William Drummond of Hawthornden objected to those of his contemporaries who attempted to "abstract poetry to metaphysical ideas and scholastic quiddities." At the end of the century, John Dryden censured Donne for affecting "the metaphysics" and for perplexing "the minds of the fair sex with nice speculations of philosophy when he should engage their hearts . . . with the softnesses of love." Samuel Johnson, in referring to the learning their poetry displays, dubbed them "the metaphysical poets," and the term has continued in use ever since.

Metastasio \,mä-tä-'stäz-yō\, Pietro, *original name* Pietro Armando Dominico Trapassi \trä-'päs-sē\ (b. Jan. 3, 1698, Rome [Italy]—d. April 12, 1782, Vienna [Austria]) Italian poet and librettist. In 1708 his skill in verse improvisation attracted the attention of Gian Vincenzo Gravina, who made him his heir adoptive and Hellenized his name into "Metastasio."

At the age of 14 Metastasio wrote *Giustino*, a tragedy in the Senecan style, and in 1717 he published a book of verses. In 1718 he entered the Academy of Arcadia, and in 1719 he went to Naples, where he gained acceptance in aristocratic circles through his voluptuous wedding poems.

Metastasio composed *Gli orti esperidi* (1721; "The Hesperidean Orchards"), a serenata in which the principal role was taken by Marianna Benti-Bulgarelli, called La Romanina, who became enamored of the poet. In her salon Metastasio came to know such composers as Nicola Porpora and Domenico Sarro, who were later to set his works to music.

At the request of La Romanina, Metastasio composed his first *melodramma*, a lyric tragedy in three acts on the conflict of love and duty, called *Didone abbandonata* (1723; *Dido Forsaken*). *Didone* was followed, between 1726 and 1730, by *Siroe, Catone in Utica, Ezio, Semiramide riconosciuta* ("Semiramide Recognized"), *Alessandro nell'Indie*, and *Artaserse*. In March 1730 he went to Vienna, where he lived the rest of his life as poet laureate to the imperial court.

During the reign of Charles VI, Metastasio wrote the librettos for cantatas, oratorios, and 11 *melodrammi*, some of the best of which were performed as plays in their own right as well as being set to music by virtually every composer from Giovanni Pergolesi to W.A. Mozart. After 1740, with the accession of Maria Theresa, Metastasio's productions were curtailed and his talents gradually went into decline.

Metastasio's other writings include five *canzonette* (16th-century light Italian vocal music), of which *La libertà* (1733; "Liberty") and *La partenza* (1746; "The Departure") are outstanding examples of Italian verse in the Arcadian tradition. He also wrote works of criticism.

Métel *see* BOISROBERT.

meter \'mē-tər\ [Greek *métron* meter, measure] 1. Systematically arranged and measured rhythm in verse, such as rhythm that continuously repeats a single basic pattern (as in iambic meter) or rhythm characterized by regular recurrence of a systematic arrangement of basic patterns in a larger figure (as in ballad meter). 2. A fixed metrical pattern, or a verse form.

Various principles, based on the natural rhythms of language, have been devised to organize poetic lines into rhythmic units. These have produced distinct kinds of versification, among which the most common are quantitative, syllabic, accentual, and accentual-syllabic.

Quantitative verse, the meter of classical Greek and Latin poetry, measures the length of time required to pronounce syllables, regardless of their stress. Various combinations of long and short syllables (the long syllables being roughly equivalent to twice the duration of the short syllables) constitute the basic rhythmic units.

Syllabic verse is most common in languages that are not strongly accented, such as French and Japanese. It is based on a fixed number of syllables within a line, although the number of accents or stresses may be varied. Thus, the classic meter of French poetry is the alexandrine, a line of 12 syllables with a medial caesura (a pause occurring after the 6th syllable). The Japanese haiku is a poem of 17 syllables, composed in three lines of 5, 7, and 5 syllables.

Accentual verse occurs in strongly stressed languages such as the Germanic. It counts only the number of stresses or accented syllables within a line and allows a variable number of unaccented syllables. Old Norse and Old English poetry are based on lines having a fixed number of strongly stressed syllables reinforced by alliteration. Accentual meters are evident in much popular English verse and in nursery rhymes, as in

$$\text{"One, two, Buck} | \text{le my shoe"}$$

In the late 19th century, the English poet Gerard Manley Hopkins used such meters as the basis for his poetic innovation "sprung rhythm."

Accentual-syllabic verse is the usual form of English poetry. It combines Romance syllable counting and Germanic stress counting to produce lines of fixed numbers of alternating stressed and unstressed syllables. Thus, the most common English meter, iambic pentameter, is a line of 10 syllables, or five iambic feet. Each iambic foot is composed of an unstressed syllable followed by a stressed syllable.

Variations within any of these regular meters are not only permissible but also inevitable and desirable. For instance, the words

$$\text{a} | \text{gain and for} | \text{lorn}$$

each constitute an iambic foot, but they are vastly different in quality. Even in the most formal metrical designs, the quality, pitch, and force of certain sounds, along with the interplay of other poetic devices such as assonance, consonance, alliteration, or rhyme, may act to reinforce or obscure the basic metrical pattern.

The function of regular meter in poetry is complex. In its most primitive aspects, as in nursery rhymes or folk ballads, it creates the physical pleasure that all simple rhythmic acts such as rocking, swaying, trotting, or foot tapping provide. Used mimetically, it may be lulling, galloping, staccato, heavy and slow, or quick and light to match the content and emotional tone of the poem. In more sophisticated poetry, regular meter is a subtle and flexible device, organically integrated into the total poem through its sensitive interaction with the natural rhythms of speech and the meaning of words. Although the late 19th century and early 20th century witnessed a widespread rebellion against the restrictions of metrically regular poetry, the challenge of condensing an imaginative impulse into a formal framework still appeals to poets. *See also* SCANSION.

Metge \'met-kä\, Bernat *or* Bernardo (b. 1350, Barcelona [Spain]—d. 1413, Barcelona) Poet and prose writer whose masterpiece, *Lo somni* (1398; "The Dream"), initiated a classical trend in Catalan literature.

In 1376 Metge entered the royal household of Peter IV of Aragon and Catalonia to serve as secretary-mentor to Prince John (later King John I). He was arrested in 1381, and while in prison he translated *Valter e Griselda*, Giovanni Boccaccio's story of Griselda, from Petrarch's Latin version and wrote *Libre de fortuna e prudència* (1381; "The Book of Fortune and Prudence").

When John I became king in 1387, Metge returned to royal service. The victim of court intrigues, the poet was again imprisoned in 1388 and 1396. On the latter occasion he composed *Lo somni*, a series of four prose dialogues in which he reflects on human frailties and ill-fated love. In this work Metge achieved a stylistic masterpiece of Catalan prose that was emulated by Catalan writers for centuries.

Metis \'mē-tis\ In Greek mythology, an Oceanid who was the first wife of Zeus. When she became pregnant, Zeus swallowed her whole because he had been warned that if she bore him a child it would be greater than he. As a result of this act, Hesiod wrote, Athena was born through Zeus's head.

metonymy \me-'tän-i-mē\ [Greek *metōnymía* use of one word for another, metonymy, from *metá* after, beyond + *ónyma* name] Figure of speech that consists of using the name of one thing for something else with which it is associated (as in "I spent the evening reading Shakespeare" or "lands belonging to the crown" or "demanding action by city hall"). Richard Brinsley Sheridan in his speech on the impeachment of Warren Hastings (the first governor-general of India) alludes to Mr. Middleton, who "extended his iron sceptre without resistance." In this sentence the sceptre is an attribute of government; an iron sceptre implies harsh government.

Metonymy is closely related to SYNECDOCHE, the naming of a part for the whole or a whole for the part. The use of synecdoche enables the writer to replace generalities and abstractions with concrete and vivid images.

metreme \'met-ˌrēm\ [probably from French *métrème*, from *mètre* meter + *-ème* (as in *phonème* phoneme)] The minimal unit of metrical structure. *See also* FOOT.

metric \'met-rik\ The part of prosody that deals with metrical structure. The term, now seldom used, is often found in the plural but may be either singular or plural in construction.

metrical romance A medieval verse tale based on legend, chivalric love and adventure, or the supernatural. It was eventually superseded by the prose romance. *See* ROMANCE.

metrification \ˌmet-rə-fi-'kā-shən\ Composition in metrical form.

metrist \'met-rist, 'mēt-\ **1.** A maker of verses. **2.** One skillful in handling meter. **3.** A student of meter or metrics.

metron \'met-ˌrän\ *plural* metra \-rə\ [Greek *métron* measure, meter] In classical prosody, the minimal unit of measure. In some meters there is no difference between a foot and a metron, but in more complex meters a metron can consist of two feet, in which one of the feet is always varied in the same way (such as iambic trimeter, in which the basic unit is two iambs: ◡ — ◡ —). *See also* FOOT.

Mew \'myü\, Charlotte (Mary) (b. Nov. 15, 1869, London, Eng.—d. March 24, 1928, London) English writer who is notable for her short, well-crafted, and highly original poetry.

Mew's life was largely unhappy. Two of her brothers died in infancy and another in boyhood, and a brother and sister were committed to mental hospitals at a young age. Mew and her sister Anne vowed to remain childless so as not to transmit what they believed to be a family disorder.

In the 1890s Mew set about publishing her stories. She adopted many beliefs of the new woman, traveling unescorted to France, smoking cigarettes, and dressing unfashionably, but she remained sexually repressed. When her father died in 1898, Mew and her sister and mother began a slide into genteel poverty. In 1923 several influential admirers, including Thomas Hardy, secured a government pension for her. She eventually poisoned herself.

Mew published short stories and essays in several periodicals before publishing the lyric poetry that secured her reputation. Her first book of poems, *The Farmer's Bride* (1916, expanded 1921; U.S. title, *Saturday Market*), was praised for its natural, direct language, including Wessex country dialect. The title poem and "Madeleine in Church"—in which a prostitute addresses the Virgin Mary—were noted for their then avantgarde conversational rhythms. *The Rambling Sailor* (1929), a posthumous collection of 32 previously uncollected poems, brought the number of Mew's published poems to 60.

Meyer \'mī-ər\, Conrad Ferdinand (b. Oct. 11, 1825, Zürich, Switz.—d. Nov. 28, 1898, Kilchberg) Swiss writer noted for his historical tales and his poetry.

After completing his schooling, Meyer began to study law but suffered from depression. A long stay in French Switzerland gave him a thorough knowledge of French literature and culture; he also took up history, studying abroad in Paris and Italy, then passed the rest of his life in Zürich or nearby. After 1892 he did no more creative work.

Meyer began to write rather late, and his total output was relatively slender. After publishing two minor collections of poetry, he achieved his first success with the powerful poem *Huttens letzte Tage* (1871; "Hutten's Last Days"). The narrative poem *Engelberg* (1872) was followed by his 11 *Novellen* (novellas), among which are *Das Amulett* (1873), *Der Heilige* (1880; *The Saint*), and *Angela Borgia* (1891). His verse was collected in *Gedichte* ("Poems") in 1882.

The material of Meyer's historical narratives was taken almost entirely from the periods of the Renaissance and the Reformation. From these eras he took passionate men of action as his main characters, and through their struggles and tribulations Meyer examined such larger problems as the prevalence of injustice, the power of conscience, and the meaning of destiny. *Der Heilige*, about the conflict between Thomas Becket and Henry II of England, is generally regarded as his best novella.

Meynell \'men-əl, 'mān-; mā-'nel\, Alice (Christiana Gertrude), *original surname* Thompson \'tämp-sən\ (b. Sept. 22, 1847, Barnes, near London, Eng.—d. Nov. 27, 1922, London) English poet and essayist.

Detail of a drawing by John Singer Sargent, 1894
National Portrait Gallery, London

Much of Thompson's childhood was spent in Italy; about 1872 she was converted to Roman Catholicism, which was reflected in her writing. Encouraged by Alfred, Lord Tennyson and Coventry Patmore, she published her first volume of poems, *Preludes*, in 1875.

One sonnet, "My Heart Shall Be Thy Garden," brought her the friendship of Wilfrid Meynell, whom she married in 1877. She continued to pursue her literary activities, also helping her husband, who edited the *Weekly Register*, and in 1883 they launched *Merry England* (1883–95), a monthly for which she wrote many essays.

Meynell's verse is marked by its simple vocabulary and religious sincerity, and it communicates a gentle mournfulness and a sense of the passing of time.

Micawber, Wilkins \'wil-kinz-mi-'kȯb-ər\ Fictional character, a kindhearted, incurable optimist in Charles Dickens' semiautobiographical novel DAVID COPPERFIELD.

Michaels \'mī-kəlz\, Leonard (b. Jan. 2, 1933, New York, N.Y., U.S.)   American short-story writer, novelist, and essayist known for his compelling urban tales of whimsy and tragedy.

Michaels was educated at New York University and at the University of Michigan. He later taught in New York City and at the University of California at Davis. Many of the stories in his first two volumes of short fiction—*Going Places* (1969) and *I Would Have Saved Them If I Could* (1975)—center on Phillip Liebowitz, a picaresque Jewish-American.

In 1981 Michaels published his first novel, *The Men's Club. Shuffle* (1990) is a poignant book of memoirs of the author's mother, father, and first wife, Sylvia, who was also the focus of *Sylvia: A Fictional Memoir* (1992). Michaels also wrote a play, *City Boy* (produced 1985), and a collection of essays, *To Feel These Things* (1993).

Michaux \me-'shō\, Henri (b. May 24, 1899, Namur, Belg.—d. Oct. 18, 1984, Paris, Fr.)   Belgian-born French lyric poet and painter whose domain was the inner world revealed by dreams, fantasies, or hallucinogenic drugs.

Michaux lived intermittently in Paris, where he eventually settled in 1922. He attracted attention with his poems *Qui je fus* (1927; "Who I Was") and held his first painting show in 1937. Michaux's view of the human condition was bleak; his poems emphasize the impossibility of making sense of life as it impinges on the individual person. Against the futility of real life Michaux set the richness of his imagination, and the contradictions of his Surrealistic images serve as a foil to the absurdity of existence. Michaux himself prepared three volumes of selections from his works, *L'Espace du dedans* (1944; "The Space Within"), *Ailleurs* (1948; "Elsewhere"), and *La Vie dans les plis* (1950; "Life Within the Folds"). English translations include *Selected Writings* (1968) and *Poems* (1967).

Michelangelo \,mē-ke-'län-je-,lō, *Angl* ,mīk-əl-'an-jə-,lō, ,mik-\, *in full* Michelangelo di Lodovico Buonarroti Simoni \,bwò-när-'rō-tē-sē-'mō-nē\ (b. March 6, 1475, Caprese, Republic of Florence [Italy]—d. Feb. 18, 1564, Rome)   Italian Renaissance sculptor, painter, architect, and poet who exerted an unparalleled influence on the development of Western art. Although he is best known as the sculptor of such works as the "Pietà," a gigantic marble "David," a "Moses," and the statues of the Medici tomb and as the painter of the ceiling of the Sistine Chapel, he also wrote more than 300 sonnets and madrigals that constitute a compelling spiritual autobiography.

Michener \'mich-nər\, James Albert (b. Feb. 3, 1907?)   American novelist and short-story writer best known for his novels, epic and detailed works classified as fictional documentaries.

Michener served as a naval historian in the South Pacific from 1944 to 1946, and his early fiction is based on this area. He won a Pulitzer Prize in 1948 for the collection *Tales of the South Pacific* (1947), and his *Hawaii* (1959) was a popular success.

Michener's novels were typically detailed and massive in scope, and he researched them extensively, as he did in Spain for *Iberia: Spanish Travels and Reflections* (1968). In his later years, Michener turned his interest to American landscapes in such books as *Centennial* (1974), *Chesapeake* (1978), and *Alaska* (1988). *Space* (1982), a fictional chronicle of the U.S. space program, was another massive opus. His later works include the novels *Poland* (1983) and *Mexico* (1992) and a memoir entitled *The World Is My Home* (1992).

Miciński \myē-'chyēⁿ-skyē\, Tadeusz (b. Nov. 9, 1873, Lódź, Poland, Russian Empire—d. February 1918, near Chirikova, Russia)   Writer, poet, and playwright of the Neoromantic period of Polish literature, a forerunner of Expressionism and Surrealism.

Miciński studied at the University of Kraków and was influenced by Polish messianism and by Friedrich Nietzsche and Fyodor Dostoyevsky. His passionate metaphysical concerns led him to an obsessive concentration on the problem of good and evil. His novel *Nietota: Księga tajemna Tatr* (1910; "Nietota: The Secret Book of the Tatra Mountains") is an imaginary re-creation of Polish life at the beginning of the 20th century. In his novel *Xiądz Faust* (1913; "Father Faust"), Miciński predicted that Polish-Russian solidarity would come about through revolution. At the end of World War I Miciński was assassinated while helping to organize the Polish armed forces.

Mickiewicz \myēts-'kye-vyēch\, Adam (Bernard) (b. Dec. 24, 1798, Zaosye, near Novogrudok, Russian Empire [now Navahrudak, Belarus]—d. Nov. 26, 1855, Constantinople, Ottoman Empire [now Istanbul, Tur.])   One of the greatest poets of Poland and a lifelong apostle of Polish national freedom.

Born into an impoverished noble family, Mickiewicz studied at the University of Vilno (now in Vilnius, Lithuania), where he joined a secret patriotic student organization, the Filomaci, later incorporated into the Filareci. His first volume of poems, *Poezja I* (1822; "Poetry I"), included ballads, romances, and an important preface explaining his admiration for these western European forms and his desire to transplant them to Polish soil. *Poezja II* (1823) contained parts two and four of his *Dziady* (*Forefathers' Eve*), in which he combined folklore and mystic patriotism to create a new kind of Romantic drama. With the other Filareci, Mickiewicz was arrested in 1823 and deported to Russia, where he was befriended by many leading Russian writers, including Aleksandr Pushkin. In 1825 he visited the Crimea and soon after published his erotic *Sonety krymskie* (1826; *Sonnets from the Crimea*).

Mickiewicz was finally able to leave Russia in 1829. In the third part of *Dziady* (1833; part of which was translated as *Improvisation*), which he completed in 1832, Mickiewicz views Poland as fulfilling a messianic role among the nations of western Europe. In 1832 he settled in Paris and there wrote the *Księgi narodu polskiego i pielgrzymstwa polskiego* (*The Books of our Pilgrimage*), a moral interpretation of the history of the Polish people. His masterpiece, the great poetic epic *Pan Tadeusz* (1834; *Master Thaddeus*), describes the life of the Polish gentry in the early 19th century through a fictional account of the feud between two families of Polish nobles.

Mickiewicz taught at the University of Lausanne (Switzerland) and at the Collège de France. For a time he edited the radical newspaper *La Tribune des peuples* ("People's Tribune").

Midas \'mī-dəs\   In classical legend, king known for his foolishness and greed, whose stories were popularized in such works as Ovid's *Metamorphoses.*

According to the myth, Midas captured Silenus, the satyr and companion of the god Dionysus. For his kind treatment of Silenus he was rewarded by Dionysus with a wish. The king wished that all he touched might turn to gold, but when his food became gold and he nearly starved to death as a result, he realized his error and Dionysus then granted him release.

In another story the king was asked to judge a musical contest between Apollo and the satyr Marsyas. When Midas decided against Apollo, the god changed his ears into those of an ass. Midas concealed them under a turban and made his barber swear to tell no one. The barber whispered the secret into a hole in the ground, but reeds grew from the spot and broadcast the sibilant secret—"Midas has ass's ears"—when the wind blew through them.

Middle \'mid-əl\   Constituting a period of a language or literature that is between one called *Old* and one called *New* or *Modern.*

middle article *British* A popular or light literary essay or article of less immediate current significance than an editorial printed in or suitable for printing in a newspaper or weekly.

Middle Comedy Style of drama that prevailed in Athens from about 400 BC to about 320 BC. Preoccupied with social themes, Middle Comedy represented a transition from Old Comedy, which presented literary, political, and philosophical commentary interspersed with scurrilous personal invective, to New Comedy, with its gently satiric observation of contemporary Athenian society, especially domestic life. Aristophanes' last play, *Wealth*, is an extant work that reflects this transition. Antiphanes and Alexis were preeminent Middle Comedy dramatists, but none of their plays has survived complete.

Middle Earth One of the more detailed of all fantasy worlds, the scene of J.R.R. Tolkien's novels THE HOBBIT, the trilogy THE LORD OF THE RINGS, and *The Silmarillion*.

Established in an age before humans acquired dominion over the Earth, Middle Earth is inhabited by a variety of good and evil creatures that include hobbits, elves, dwarfs, humans, monsters, and wizards. The characters as well as the landscape of Middle Earth were derived from mythological models in Greek and northern European traditions.

Middlemarch \'mid-əl-,märch\ (*in full* Middlemarch: A Study of Provincial Life) Novel by George ELIOT, published in eight parts in 1871–72 and also published in four volumes in 1872. Considered to be Eliot's masterpiece, the novel is a complete study of every class of Middlemarch society—from the landed gentry and clergy to the manufacturers and professional men, farmers, and laborers. The focus of the novel is on the thwarted idealism of its two principal characters, Dorothea Brooke and Tertius Lydgate, both of whom marry disastrously.

Dorothea is an earnest, intelligent woman who makes a serious error in judgment when she chooses to marry Edward Casaubon, a scholarly man many years her senior. Lydgate is a young doctor in Middlemarch who becomes involved with and marries the unsuitable Rosamond Vincy. Dorothea discovers her husband to be a pompous fraud and an incompatible and repressive partner. Lydgate finds himself on the brink of financial ruin and personal disgrace because of his ill-considered choice of a wife. The plot of the novel is a long and involved working out of these two misguided decisions. In addition to creating a rich portrait of the life of a small early 19th-century town, Eliot produced an essentially modern novel, with penetrating psychological insights and moral ambiguity.

Middleton \'mid-əl-tən\, Stanley (b. Aug. 1, 1919, Bulwell, Nottingham, Eng.) British writer whose novels examine lower-middle-class marital and familial relationships.

Educated at University College, Nottingham, Middleton served in the British army and in the Army Education Corps. He later taught at High Pavement College, Nottingham.

Middleton won critical respect for his perceptive, restrained treatment of ordinary people and for his honest appraisal of provincial life. His prolific output included *Harris's Requiem* (1960), about a composer who takes great joy in his creativity; *A Serious Woman* (1961) and *Two's Company* (1963), both of which explore compelling sexual attraction; and *Holiday* (1974), a cowinner of the Booker Prize. Middleton's other novels include *The Other Side* (1980), *Valley of Decision* (1985), *Changes and Chances* (1990), and *A Place to Stand* (1992). He also wrote radio plays.

Middleton \'mid-əl-tən\, Thomas (b. April 1570?, London, Eng.—d. July 4, 1627, Newington Butts, Surrey) Late Elizabethan dramatist who drew people as he saw them, with comic gusto or searching irony.

By 1600 Middleton had published three books of verse. He learned to write plays by collaborating with Thomas Dekker, John Webster, and others. A popular playwright, he was often commissioned to write and produce civic entertainments, and in 1620 he was appointed city chronologer. His chief stage success was *A Game at Chaess* (1625), in which the Black King and his men, representing Spain and the Jesuits, are checkmated by the White Knight, Prince Charles. His masterpieces are two tragedies, *Women Beware Women* (1621?; published 1657) and *The Changeling* (1622; with William Rowley; published 1653).

Middleton's comedies picture a society dazzled by money, in which most people grasp for all they can get, by any means. Among the comedies are *Michaelmas Terme* (1605?; published 1607), *A Tricke to Catch the Old-one* (1608), *A Mad World, My Masters* (1608), *A Chast Mayd In Cheape-side* (1613?; published 1630), and *The Roaring Girle* (1611; with Dekker). Middleton also collaborated with Dekker in *The Honest Whore* (1604) and with Rowley and Philip Massinger in *The Old Law* (1618?; published 1656). His tragicomedies are far-fetched in plot but strong in dramatic situations. In *A Faire Quarrell* (1617; with Rowley), Captain Ager, with his conflicts of conscience, is one of Middleton's few heroes.

Midgard \'mēth-,gärth, *Angl* 'mid-,gärd\ or **Midgardr** \-,gär-thər, -,gär-dər\ ("Middle Abode"), *also called* Manna-heim \'män-nä-,häm\ ("Home of Man") In Norse mythology, the Middle Earth, the abode of humans, made from the body of the first created being, the giant Aurgelmir. According to legend, the gods killed Aurgelmir, rolled his body into the central void of the universe, and began fashioning the Midgard. Aurgelmir's flesh became the land, his blood the oceans, his bones the mountains, his teeth the cliffs, his hair the trees, his brains the clouds, and his eyelashes (or eyebrows) the fence that surrounds Midgard. His skull was held up by four dwarfs, Nordri, Sudri, Austri, and Vestri (the four points of the compass), and became the dome of the heavens. The sun, moon, and stars were made of scattered sparks that were caught in the skull.

Midgard is situated halfway between Niflheim on the north, the land of ice, and Muspelheim to the south, the region of fire. Midgard is joined with Asgard, the abode of the deities, by Bifrost, the rainbow bridge.

Midnight's Children Allegorical novel by Salman RUSHDIE, published in 1981. It is a historical chronicle of modern India centering on the inextricably linked fates of two children born within the first hour of independence from Great Britain.

Exactly at midnight on Aug. 15, 1947, two boys are born in a Bombay hospital, where they are switched by a nurse. Saleem Sinai, who will be raised by a well-to-do Muslim couple, is actually the illegitimate son of a low-caste Hindu woman and a departing British colonist. Shiva, the son of the Muslim couple, is given to a poor Hindu street performer whose unfaithful wife has died.

Saleem represents modern India. When he is 30, he writes his memoir, *Midnight's Children*. Shiva is destined to be Saleem's enemy as well as India's most honored war hero. This multilayered novel places Saleem in every significant event that occurred on the Indian subcontinent in the 30 years after independence. *Midnight's Children* was awarded the Booker Prize for fiction in 1981.

midrash \'mid-räsh, -,rash\ [Hebrew *midhrāsh* exposition, explanation] **1.** A haggadic (nonlegal) or halakic (legal) exposition of the underlying significance of a biblical text. **2.** The large collections of materials (midrashim \mi-'drä-shēm, -shim\) deduced from the Hebrew Bible by this exegetical method. **3.** *capitalized* The midrashic literature written during the first millennium CE (Common Era).

Midrash became necessary because the Written Law in the Pentateuch (the first five books of the Old Testament) required reinterpretation in the light of later historical conditions and because of the disagreement between the Pharisees and Sadducees over the status of the Oral Law. Midrash developed into a complex interpretive system used to reconcile biblical contradictions, establish the scriptural bases for new laws, and bring new meaning to the scriptural text. Midrashic activity reached its height in the 2nd century CE with the schools of Rabbi Ishmael ben Elisha and Rabbi Akiba ben Joseph.

Midsummer Night's Dream, A   Comedy in five acts by William SHAKESPEARE, produced in 1595–96 and published in 1600 in a quarto edition from the author's fair copy. It has long been the most popular of Shakespeare's comedies.

Theseus, Duke of Athens, is about to wed Hippolyta, the Amazon queen. Meanwhile, two lovers, Hermia and Lysander, hide in the woods when Hermia's father demands that she marry Demetrius. Hoping to win his favor, Helena tells Demetrius of their whereabouts, and the two go to the woods in search of the fugitives. The forest is also full of fairies who have come for the Duke's wedding. After their king, Oberon, argues with his queen, Titania, he tells his mischievous servant Puck to drop magic juice into her eyes as she sleeps. The magic juice will make her love the first person she sees when she awakes. He also tells Puck to drop the juice into Demetrius' eyes, but Puck confuses Lysander with Demetrius and as a result Lysander falls in love with Helena. So does Demetrius, when Oberon tries to correct Puck's mistake.

In the same woods a group of artisans are rehearsing a play for the Duke's wedding. Ever playful, Puck gives one of the "mechanicals," Bottom, an ass's head; when Titania awakens, she falls in love with Bottom. Oberon's magic then restores Titania and the four lovers to their original states. The Duke invites the two couples to join him and Hippolyta in a triple wedding. The wedding celebration features Bottom's troupe in a comically inept performance of their play, *The Most Lamentable Comedy and Most Cruel Death of Pyramus and Thisbe.*

Midwestern Regionalism   American literary movement of the late 19th century that is characterized by the realistic depiction of Midwestern small-town and rural life. The movement was an early stage in the development of American realistic writing. E.W. Howe's *The Story of a Country Town* (1883) and Joseph Kirkland's *Zury* (1887) and *The McVeys* (1888) foreshadowed the stories and novels of Hamlin Garland, the foremost representative of Midwestern Regionalism. Garland's *Main-Travelled Roads* (1891) and *A Son of the Middle Border* (1917) are works that deal with the poverty and hardship of Midwestern rural life and that explode the myth of the pioneer idyll. Chicago was the focal point of Midwestern realist activity; Garland lived in the city for a time, as did such others as Theodore Dreiser, Edgar Lee Masters, and Sherwood Anderson.

Mikszáth \'mēk-ˌsät\, Kálmán (b. Jan. 16, 1847, Szklabonya, Hung.—d. May 28, 1910, Budapest) Novelist, regarded by contemporaries and succeeding generations alike as the outstanding Hungarian writer of the late 19th and early 20th centuries. In 1887 he was elected to the National Assembly.

Mikszáth had his first success with two volumes of short stories entitled *A tót atyafiak* (1881; "The Slovak Kinsfolk") and *A jó palócok* (1882; "The Good Palócok"). In 1894 he published his first novel, *Beszterce ostroma* ("The Siege of Beszterce"). Mikszáth's early art is romantic in outlook, but he later became more realistic as the writer of everyday life, which he described with understanding and occasional satire.

Mikszáth's two principal works were *Különös házasság* (1900; "A Strange Marriage") and *A Noszty fiú esete Tóth Marival* (1908; "The Noszty Boy and Mary Tóth"). His last work, *A fekete város* (1910; "The Black City"), is the finest of his historical novels.

miles gloriosus \'mē-ˌläz-ˌglȯr-ē-'ō-ˌsüs\ *plural* milites gloriosi \'mē-lē-ˌtäz-ˌglȯr-ē-'ō-ˌsē\ [Latin], *also called* braggart soldier. A boastful soldier; especially, a stock comic character of this type in Roman and Renaissance comedy.

The name derives from a comedy written about 205 BC by the Roman playwright Plautus. It is a complicated farce in which a vain, lustful, and stupid soldier, Pyrgopolynices, is duped by his clever slave and a courtesan. The work was highly popular, and Pyrgopolynices became the prototype for many swaggering cowards of later comedy, such as Capitano in the commedia dell'arte of mid-16th-century Italy and William Shakespeare's Falstaff and Pistol.

Milesian tale \mī-'lē-zhən, -shən\ [translation of Latin *Milesia fabula,* literally, tale of Miletus (alluding to Aristides of Miletus)] One of a class of short salacious tales of Greek and Roman antiquity. Characteristically, a Milesian tale is an erotic or picaresque story of romantic adventure. This type of tale was first written or collected by Aristides of Miletus (*c.* 2nd century BC). In the 1st century BC, Aristides' collection was translated into Latin by Lucius Cornelius Sisenna as *Milesiae fabulae*; this volume served as a model for episodes in Petronius' *Satyricon* (1st century AD) and for *The Golden Ass* (2nd century AD) by Lucius Apuleius. The Greek and Latin Milesian tales later provided prototypes for many tales included in Giovanni Boccaccio's *Decameron* (1353).

Millay \mi-'lā\, Edna St. Vincent (b. Feb. 22, 1892, Rockland, Maine, U.S.—d. Oct. 19, 1950, Austerlitz, N.Y.) American poet and dramatist who came to personify romantic rebellion and bravado in the 1920s.

Brown Brothers

Millay's earliest poems were published in the children's magazine *St. Nicholas.* She grew up in Camden, Maine, and her work is filled with the imagery of coast and countryside. Her first acclaim came when RENASCENCE was included in *The Lyric Year* in 1912; the poem brought Millay to the attention of a benefactor who made it possible for her to attend Vassar. For a time she supported herself in New York City by writing short stories under a pseudonym and as an actress and playwright. In 1923 she married, and she lived thereafter on a farm in the Berkshires.

Her first book, *Renascence and Other Poems* (1917), was full of the romantic and independent temper of youth. The line "My candle burns at both ends," from a poem in *A Few Figs from Thistles* (1920), was taken up as the watchword of the "flaming youth" of the era and brought her a renown she came to despise. In 1921 she published *Second April* as well as three verse plays: *Two Slatterns and a King, The Lamp and the Bell,* and *Aria da Capo.* The title poem of *The Harp Weaver and Other Poems* (1923) is thought to have been inspired by her mother. She also wrote the libretto for Deems Taylor's opera *The King's Henchman,* first presented at the Metropolitan in 1927. Her major later works include *The Buck in the Snow* (1928), *Fatal*

Interview (1931), and *Wine from These Grapes* (1934). Her letters, edited by A.R. Macdougall, were published in 1952.

Miller \'mil-ər\, Arthur (b. Oct. 17, 1915, New York, N.Y., U.S.) American playwright who combined social awareness with a searching concern for his characters' inner lives. He is best known for DEATH OF A SALESMAN (1949).

Miller's first public success was with *Focus* (1945), a novel about anti-Semitism. ALL MY SONS (1947), a drama about a manufacturer of faulty war materials, was his first important play. *Death of a Salesman*, his next major play, is the tragedy of a small man destroyed by false values that are in large part the values of his society.

THE CRUCIBLE (1953) was based on the witchcraft trials in Salem, Mass., in 1692, a period Miller considered relevant to the 1950s, when investigation of subversive activities was widespread. *A Memory of Two Mondays* and another short play, *A View from the Bridge*, were staged on the same bill in 1955. AFTER THE FALL (1964) is concerned with failure in human relationships and its consequences. *The Price* (1968) continued Miller's exploration of the theme of guilt and responsibility by examining the strained relationship between two brothers. *The Archbishop's Ceiling*, produced in 1977, dealt with the Soviet treatment of dissident writers. *The American Clock*, a series of dramatic vignettes about the Great Depression, was produced in 1980. Miller produced several one-act plays in the 1980s, including two—*I Can't Remember Anything* and *Clara*—that were published together as *Danger, Memory! Two Plays* (1986). Later full-length plays include *The Ride Down Mount Morgan* and *The Last Yankee* (both 1991).

Miller also wrote a screenplay, *The Misfits* (1961), for his second wife, the actress Marilyn Monroe. *I Don't Need You Any More*, a collection of his short stories, appeared in 1967, and a collection of theater essays in 1977. His autobiography, *Timebends*, was published in 1987.

Miller \'mil-ər\, Henry (Valentine) (b. Dec. 26, 1891, New York, N.Y., U.S.—d. June 7, 1980, Pacific Palisades, Calif.) American writer and perennial bohemian whose au-

Camera Press

tobiographical novels had a liberating influence on mid-20th-century literature. Because of their sexual frankness, his major works were banned as obscene in Britain and the United States until the 1960s, but they were widely known earlier from copies smuggled in from France.

Miller was brought up in Brooklyn, and he wrote about his childhood experiences there in *Black Spring* (1936). In 1930 he went to France. TROPIC OF CANCER (French edition, 1934; U.S. edition, 1961) is based on his hand-to-mouth existence in depression-ridden Paris. TROPIC OF CAPRICORN (France, 1939; U.S., 1961) draws on his earlier New York phase. In 1964 the U.S. Supreme Court rejected earlier state court findings that the "Tropics" books were obscene.

Miller's visit to Greece in 1939 inspired *The Colossus of Maroussi* (1941). THE AIR-CONDITIONED NIGHTMARE (1945) is a sharply critical account of a tour of the United States. After settling in Big Sur on the California coast, Miller produced his Rosy Crucifixion trilogy, made up of *Sexus*, *Plexus*, and *Nexus* (U.S. edition published as a whole in 1965). It traces the stages by which the hero-narrator becomes a writer.

Other important books by Miller are the collections of essays *The Cosmological Eye* (1939) and *The Wisdom of the Heart* (1941). Various volumes of his correspondence have been published: with Lawrence Durrell (1963), to Anaïs Nin (1965), and with Wallace Fowlie (1975).

Miller \'mil-ər\, J. Hillis, *in full* Joseph (b. March 5, 1928, Newport News, Va., U.S.) American literary critic who was associated with the Geneva group of critics and, later, with deconstruction.

Miller graduated from Oberlin College in 1948. He received an M.A. and Ph.D. from Harvard University in 1949 and 1952, respectively. After teaching English at Williams College for one year, he held positions at Johns Hopkins University from 1953 to 1972, at Yale University from 1972 to 1986, and from 1986 at the University of California at Irvine.

Like the Geneva group of critics, Miller argued that literature is a tool for understanding the mind of the writer. His criticism emphasized theological concerns, as in *Poets of Reality: Six Twentieth-Century Writers* (1965), *The Form of Victorian Fiction: Thackeray, Dickens, Trollope, George Eliot, Meredith, and Hardy* (1968), and *The Disappearance of God: Five Nineteenth-Century Writers* (1963). By 1970, however, he had joined the deconstructionist critics at Yale, and his subsequent scholarship was steeped in arcane language and expressed the belief that language itself is a work's sole reality. Miller's criticism in this vein includes *Fiction and Repetition* (1982) and *The Linguistic Moment* (1985).

Miller \'mil-ər\, Joaquin, *pseudonym of* Cincinnatus Hiner Miller, Hiner *also spelled* Heine (b. Sept. 8, 1837, near Liberty, Ind., U.S.—d. Feb. 17, 1913, Oakland, Calif.) American poet and journalist whose best work conveys a sense of the majesty and excitement of the Old West. His best-known poem is "Columbus," with its refrain, "On, sail on!" once familiar to millions of American schoolchildren.

Miller led a picaresque early life in California among miners and gamblers. In Oregon he owned a newspaper (the *Eugene Democratic Register*) and was a county judge. His first books of poems, *Specimens* (1868) and *Joaquin et al.* (1869), attracted little attention.

In 1870 he traveled to England, where *Pacific Poems* (1871) was privately printed. *Songs of the Sierras* (1871), upon which his reputation mainly rests, was loudly acclaimed in England, while generally derided in the United States for its excessive romanticism. His other books of poetry include *Songs of the Sunlands* (1873), *The Ship in the Desert* (1875), *The Baroness of New York* (1877), *Memorie and Rime* (1884), and the *Complete Poetical Works* (1897).

Miller \'mil-ər\, Johann Martin (b. Dec. 3, 1750, Ulm [Germany]—d. June 21, 1814, Ulm) German poet, novelist, and preacher known for moralizing, sentimental novels and for poems resembling folk songs.

Miller studied theology at Göttingen where, in 1772, he and other students established the Göttinger Hain, a group espousing many of the tenets of the Sturm und Drang movement centered on J.W. von Goethe. Miller published three novels in 1776: *Beytrag zur Geschichte der Zärtlichkeit* ("Contribution to the History of Tenderness"), *Siegwart, eine Klostergeschichte* (*Siegwart, A Tale*), and *Briefwechsel dreyer akademischer Freunde* ("Correspondence of Three Academic Friends").

Miller taught and served as a minister in Ulm. Continuing to write, he published a weekly from 1779 to 1781 and produced two more novels, a book of poems, and two collections of sermons. *See also* GÖTTINGER HAIN.

Miller \\'mil-ər\\, Jonathan (Wolfe) (b. July 21, 1934, London, Eng.) Actor, director, producer, medical doctor, and man of letters noted for his wide-ranging abilities.

Miller made his professional stage debut in 1961 as coauthor of and actor in the satiric review *Beyond the Fringe*. He left the show in 1963 to write television scripts and to direct live theater. His sometimes controversial interpretations of classic works gained him notoriety. He went on to direct operas, most notably, P.I. Tchaikovsky's *Eugene Onegin* and several productions for the English National Theatre. In 1978 he wrote *The Body in Question*, a 13-part series on the history of medicine and of attitudes toward the human body, for the BBC; it also became a best-selling book. From 1988 to 1990 he was artistic director of the Old Vic in London.

Miller \\'mil-ər\\, May, *married surname* Sullivan \\'səl-i-vən\\ (b. Jan. 26, 1899, Washington, D.C., U.S.) African-American playwright and poet associated with the Harlem Renaissance in New York City during the 1920s.

Miller graduated from Howard University in 1920, earning an award for her one-act play *Within the Shadows*. Afterwards she taught secondary school and continued to write. A prizewinning play, *The Bog Guide* (1925), helped establish Miller in the black cultural scene, and she became the most widely published woman playwright of the Harlem Renaissance. She openly addressed racial issues in plays such as *Scratches* (1929), *Stragglers in the Dust* (1930), and *Nails and Thorns* (1933). She also wrote many historical plays, four of which (including *Harriet Tubman* and *Sojourner Truth*) were anthologized in *Negro History in Thirteen Plays* (1935). Miller retired from teaching in 1943 and became a prolific poet, publishing seven volumes that included *Into the Clearing* (1959) and *Dust of Uncertain Journey* (1975).

Miller, Daisy \\'dā-zē-'mil-ər\\ Fictional character, the naive young American who is the protagonist of Henry James's novel DAISY MILLER.

Miller's Tale, The One of the 24 stories in THE CANTERBURY TALES by Geoffrey Chaucer.

This bawdy story of lust and revenge is told by a drunken, churlish Miller. Alison, young wife of a carpenter, takes their boarder Nicholas as her lover. When Nicholas persuades the carpenter that Noah's flood is about to recur, the unwitting husband suspends three tubs from the rafters to serve as lifeboats and uses one for his bed. Alison and Nicholas steal off to her bedroom, only to be interrupted the next morning by her admirer Absolon, who stands under the window and begs her for a kiss. Alison offers her backside. Enraged upon discovering the deception, Absolon returns and pleads once more; this time Nicholas assumes the same pose and is rewarded with a scorching branding iron. His cries for water awaken the carpenter, who assumes that the flood is near; he cuts the rope holding his tub and comes crashing through the attic.

Mill on the Floss, The \\'flös\\ Novel by George ELIOT, published in three volumes in 1860. It sympathetically portrays the vain efforts of Maggie Tulliver to adapt to her provincial world. The tragedy of her plight is underlined by the actions of her brother Tom, whose sense of family honor leads him to forbid her to associate with the one friend who appreciates her intelligence and imagination. When she is caught in a compromising situation, Tom renounces her altogether, but brother and sister are finally reconciled in the end as they try in vain to survive a climactic flood.

Mill on the Po, The \\'pō\\ Trilogy of novels by Riccardo BACCHELLI, first published in Italian as *Il mulino del Po* in 1938–40. The work, considered Bacchelli's masterpiece, dramatizes the conflicts and struggles of several generations of a family of millers. The first two volumes, *Dio ti salve* (1938; "God Bless You") and *La miseria viene in barca* (1939; "Misery Comes to a Boat"), were published in English as *The Mill on the Po*; the third volume, *Mondo vecchio sempre nuovo* (1940), as *Nothing New Under the Sun*.

The first volume covers the period from 1812 to 1848. The second stresses the terrible economic and social effect on the lower classes of the 19th-century Italian struggle for political unity. The third ends with World War I.

Mills, Martin. Pseudonym of Martin á Beckett BOYD.

Milne \\'miln, 'mil\\, A.A., *in full* Alan Alexander (b. Jan. 18, 1882, London, Eng.—d. Jan. 31, 1956, Hartfield, Sussex) English writer, the originator of the immensely popular stories of Christopher Robin and his toy bear, Winnie-the-Pooh.

In 1906 Milne joined the staff of *Punch*, writing humorous verse and whimsical essays. He achieved considerable success with a series of light comedies and wrote one memorable detective novel, *The Red House Mystery* (1922), and a children's play, *Make-Believe* (1918). Some verses written for his son Christopher Robin grew into the collections *When We Were Very Young* (1924) and *Now We Are Six* (1927).

Milne's most popular works were stories about the adventures of Christopher Robin's toy animals, Pooh, Piglet, Kanga, Roo, and Eeyore, as told in WINNIE-THE-POOH (1926) and *The House at Pooh Corner* (1928). A decade later Milne wrote his autobiography, *It's Too Late Now*.

Milnes *see* HOUGHTON.

Miłosz \\'mⁱē-wōsh\\, Czesław (b. June 30, 1911, Šateiniai, Lithuania, Russian Empire) Polish-American author, translator, and critic who received the Nobel Prize for Literature in 1980.

Miłosz completed his university studies in Wilno (Vilnius), which then belonged to Poland. By the time he published his first book of verse, *Poemat o czasie zastygłym* ("Poem of Frozen Time"), at the age of 21, he was both a socialist and a leader of the Catastrophist group of poets, who were so named for their predictions of impending worldwide disaster. During the Nazi occupation Miłosz was active in the Resistance and edited, wrote, or translated numerous clandestine works, such as *Pieśń niepodległa* (1942; "Invincible Song").

His collection of poetry *Ocalenie* (1945; "Rescue") became one of the first books published in communist Poland. After serving as a foreign diplomat, Miłosz sought political asylum in France, before immigrating to the United States, where he taught at the University of California at Berkeley and became a naturalized citizen.

Though Miłosz was primarily a poet, his best-known work became his collection of essays *Zniewolony umysł* (1953; *The Captive Mind*), which condemned the accommodation of many Polish intellectuals to communism. This theme dominated his novel *Zdobycie władzy* (1955; first published in French as *La Prise du pouvoir*, 1953; Eng. trans., *The Seizure of Power*). *Traktat poetycki* (1957; "The Poetic Treatise") combines a defense of poetry with a history of Poland from 1918 to the 1950s.

His other works include his autobiography, *Rodzinna Europa* (1959; *Native Realm*); *Prywatne obowiązki* (1972; "Private Obligations"); the novel *Dolina Issy* (1955; *The Issa Valley*); a history of Polish literature (1969); several volumes of selected poems, including *Bells in Winter* (1978); a series of lectures published as *The Witness of Poetry* (1983); and Polish translations from the Bible.

Milton \\'milt-ən\\, John (b. Dec. 9, 1608, London, Eng.—d. Nov. 8, 1674, Chalfont St. Giles, Buckinghamshire) One of the greatest poets of the English language, best known for his epic poem PARADISE LOST (1667), in which his "grand style" is used with superb power; its characterization of Satan is one of the supreme achievements of world literature. Milton was also a noted historian, scholar, pamphleteer, and civil servant for the Parliamentarians and the Puritan Commonwealth.

Brown Brothers

Milton exhibited scholarly achievement and a devotion to Latin verse at an early age. He was educated at Christ's College, Cambridge (1625–32), where he wrote poetry in Latin, Italian, and English. These include the companion pieces L'ALLEGRO and IL PENSEROSO, which were later published in *Poems* (1645). From 1632 to 1638 Milton retired to his father's home and engaged in private study—producing the masque COMUS (1637), his first dramatization of the conflict of good and evil, and the poem LYCIDAS (1638)—and then toured Italy for a year.

Concerned with the Puritan cause in England, Milton spent much of the period 1641–60 pamphleteering for civil and religious liberty and serving as the secretary for foreign languages in Oliver Cromwell's government. During this time he also produced *Of Education* and AREOPAGITICA (1644). He lost his sight about 1651 but continued in his work, completing *The Second Defence of the People of England* in 1654. After the Restoration of Charles II in 1660, Milton was arrested as a noted defender of the Commonwealth but was soon released. The epics *Paradise Regained* and SAMSON AGONISTES were published together in 1671. His late, long poems were dictated to his daughter, two nephews, friends, disciples, and paid amanuenses, who also corrected copy and read aloud when requested.

Milton's influence on later literature—particularly on 18th-century verse—was immense, though his reputation had waned considerably by the Victorian Age. By the second half of the 20th century, however, his works had regained their place in the canon of Western literature.

mimesis \mi-'mē-sis, mī-\ [Greek *mímēsis* imitation, representation, a derivative of *mimeîsthai* to imitate, a derivative of *mîmos* mime] Imitation, or mimicry. It has long been held to be a basic theoretical principle in the creation of art.

Plato and Aristotle spoke of mimesis as the representation of nature. According to Plato, all artistic creation is a form of imitation: that which truly exists (in the "world of Ideas") is a type created by God; the concrete things humans perceive in daily life are shadowy representations of this ideal type. To Plato artists were imitators of imitations and were therefore twice removed from the truth. Aristotle wrote that tragedy is an "imitation of an action"—that of falling from a higher to a lower estate. Perhaps the best-known modern work on the subject is Erich Auerbach's *Mimesis: Dargestellte Wirklichkeit in der abendländischen Literatur* (1946; *Mimesis: The Representation of Reality in Western Literature*).

Mimir \'mē-mir\, *Old Norse* Mímir. In Norse mythology, the wisest of the gods of the tribe Æsir; he was also believed to be a water spirit. Mimir was sent by the Æsir as a hostage to the rival gods (the Vanir), but he was decapitated and his head

was returned to the Æsir. The god Odin preserved the head in herbs and gained knowledge from it.

According to another story, Mimir resided by a well that stood beneath one of the roots of Yggdrasil, the world tree. The well, sometimes called Mímisbrunnr, contained one of Odin's eyes, which he had pledged in order to drink from the waters and receive wisdom.

Mimnermus \mim-'nər-məs\ (fl. c. 630 BC) Early Greek elegiac poet of Colophon in Asia Minor. One of his extant fragments refers to the struggle of the Ionians against Lydia. His most important poems were a set of elegies addressed to a flute girl named Nanno. Evidently Mimnermus was admired by the ancients; most of the surviving fragments of his works have come from quotations by later authors.

Minamoto Shitagō \mē-'nä-mō-tō-shē-'tä-ˌgō\ (b. 911, Japan—d. 983, Japan) One of the outstanding poets of ancient Japan.

Although Minamoto was a descendant of the emperor Saga, he was barred from high political position because he did not belong to the Fujiwara family, which controlled the government. Instead he devoted himself to scholarly and literary pursuits. He helped compile the collection known as the *Gosenshū* and, as one of the Nashitsubo no Gonin ("Five Men of the Pear Garden"), also engaged in the interpretation of the MAN'YŌSHŪ. *Minamoto no Shitagō shū*, a collection of his works, reveals his discontent and frustration over his lack of success in official life. He also compiled the *Wamyō ruijū shō*, a dictionary of Japanese and Chinese words by categories that was the first dictionary in Japan. UTSUBO MONOGATARI ("The Tale of the Hollow Tree"), written between 956 and 983, was formerly often attributed to Minamoto.

Minderbinder, Milo \'mī-lō-'mīn-dər-ˌbīn-dər\ Fictional character, a black marketer in the satiric World War II novel CATCH-22 by Joseph Heller. Minderbinder, who equates profit with patriotism, exploits his connections as a U.S. Army lieutenant and mess officer to amass personal power and wealth. Corrupt and single-mindedly devoted to his profit margin, he eventually becomes the mayor of several Italian cities, the vice-shah of Oran, and the caliph of Baghdad. He even rents to the German air force fleets of planes that bomb his own base.

Minerva \mi-'nər-və\ In Roman mythology, the goddess of handicrafts, the professions, the arts, and, later, war; she was commonly identified with the Greek ATHENA. Minerva's shrine on the Aventine in Rome was a meeting place for guilds of craftsmen, including at one time dramatic poets and actors.

Miniver Cheevy \'min-i-vər-'chē-vē\ A poem in iambic tetrameter quatrains by Edwin Arlington ROBINSON, published in the collection *The Town Down the River* (1910).

The poem portrays the melancholy Miniver Cheevy who lives in Tilbury Town, an imaginary small town in New England that was a frequent setting for Robinson's poetry. Cheevy has little insight into his personal deficiencies. With exaggerated romantic sadness, he wishes that he had lived in a more gracious era.

minnesinger \'min-ə-ˌziŋ-ər\, *German* Minnesänger \-ˌzeŋ-ər\ Any of certain German poet-musicians of the 12th and 13th centuries. In the usage of these poets themselves, the term *Minnesang* denoted only songs dealing with courtly love (*Minne*). The term has since come to be applied to the entire poetic-musical body, *Sprüche* (political, moral, and religious song) as well as *Minnesang*.

The songs of courtly love, like the concept, came to Germany either directly from Provence or through northern France. The minnesingers, like their Romance counterparts, the troubadours and trouvères, usually composed both words and music and performed their songs in open court. Some were of humble birth; most, however, were *ministeriales*, or members of the lower nobility, who depended on court patronage for their livelihood.

In general the music follows the tripartite form taken over from the Provençal *canso*: two identical sections, called individually *Stollen* and collectively *Aufgesang*, and a third section, or *Abgesang* (the terms were applied by the later Meistersingers); the formal ratio between *Aufgesang* and *Abgesang* is variable.

On a larger scale was the *Leich*, analogous to the French lay. It was an aggregation of short stanzas (versicles), typically couplets, each line of which was sung to the same music and each versicle having its own music. The *Leiche* were often several hundred lines long, and many incorporated religious motifs.

Some of the early songs were probably sung to troubadour melodies, because their texts closely resemble Provençal models. Yet the German songs usually differ in general musical character from the Romance songs. For example, the melodies are more often basically pentatonic (based on a five-tone scale). Popular song and Gregorian chant are other musical roots of the style. *Compare* MEISTERSINGER; TROUBADOUR; TROUVÈRE.

Minos \\'mī-näs, -nəs\\   Legendary ruler of Crete who was the son of Zeus and of Europa. Minos obtained the Cretan throne by the aid of the Greek god Poseidon, and from his capital Knossos (or Gortyn) he gained control over the Aegean islands. He married Pasiphae, the daughter of Helios, who bore him, among others, Androgeos, Ariadne, and Phaedra and who was also the mother of the MINOTAUR. The birth of the Minotaur was a result of the gods' revenge on Minos for his refusal to sacrifice a beautiful bull they had sent him as a sign of their favor.

Minotaur \\'min-ə-ˌtȯr, 'mīn-\\ or **Minotauros** \\-ˌtȯr-əs\\ ("Minos' Bull"), *also called* Asterion \\as-'tir-ē-ən\\ *or* Asterius \\-ē-əs\\   In Greek mythology, a fabulous monster of Crete, half man and half bull. It was the offspring of Pasiphae, the wife of Minos, and a snow-white bull sent to Minos by the god Poseidon for sacrifice. Minos, instead of sacrificing it, kept it alive; as a punishment Poseidon made Pasiphae fall in love with it. Her offspring by the bull was shut up in the Labyrinth created for Minos by Daedalus.

A son of Minos, Androgeos, was later killed by the Athenians. Athenian tradition holds that, to avenge the death of Androgeos, Minos demanded that seven Athenian youths and seven maidens be sent every ninth year (or, according to another version, every year) to be devoured by the Minotaur. When the third time of sacrifice came, the Athenian hero Theseus volunteered to go, and, with the help of Ariadne, daughter of Minos and Pasiphae, he killed the monster.

Many modern writers have taken up the myth of the Minotaur and examined its several elements. In an earlier age the myth became a part of the symbology of cuckoldry and the monstrosity of adultery. Later writers—among them André Gide, Marcel Aymé, Marguerite Yourcenar, Jorge Luis Borges, and Julio Cortázar—examined the Minotaur as a representation of Theseus' self-image, that is, as a frightful aspect of oneself to be faced.

minstrel \\'min-strəl\\ [Old French *menestrel* servant, worker, craftsman, minstrel, from Medieval Latin *ministerialis* servant, official, a derivative of Latin *ministerium* condition or duties of a servant, a derivative of *minister* servant]   One of a class of medieval musical entertainers; especially, a singer of verses to the accompaniment of a harp. The word originally referred to a professional entertainer of any kind, but it began to be used in the more specific sense of a musician about the beginning of

the 17th century. The word *ménestrel* replaced the earlier *jongleur* (from Provençal *joglar*) about the 14th century.

The minstrel profession antedates its name. In earlier centuries the gleeman (from Old English *gléoman*) is heard of among the Angles and the Germanic scop referred to. The Old English poem "Widsith" describes the role of a fictitious scop in Germanic society. Many minstrels were attached to courts. Others, the great majority, traveled widely, staying for short times at places of potential patronage. They performed traditional ballads and epics. Most were unable to write their music down, and consequently little of their music survives.

With the introduction of printing and more simplified musical notation in the late 15th century, the profession began to decline after the 16th century. *Compare* MEISTERSINGER, MINNESINGER, SCOP; TROUBADOUR, TROUVÈRE.

miracle play *also called* saint's play.   One of three principal kinds of vernacular drama of the European Middle Ages (along with the MYSTERY PLAY and the MORALITY PLAY). A miracle play presents a real or fictitious account of the life, miracles, or martyrdom of a saint. The genre evolved from liturgical offices developed during the 10th and 11th centuries to enhance calendar festivals. By the 13th century they had become vernacularized and were performed at public festivals. Almost all surviving miracle plays concern either the Virgin Mary or St. Nicholas, the 4th-century bishop of Myra in Asia Minor, both of whom had active cults during the Middle Ages.

The Mary plays consistently involve her in the role of deus ex machina, coming to the aid of all who invoke her, be they worthy or wanton. The Nicholas plays are similar, an example being Jehan Bodel's *Le Jeu de Saint Nicolas* (c. 1200), which details the deliverance of a crusader and the conversion of a Saracen king. Few English miracle plays are extant, for they were banned by Henry VIII in the mid-16th century and most were subsequently destroyed or lost.

Miranda \\mə-'ran-də\\   Fictional character, the beautiful and naive daughter of Prospero, the rightful duke of Milan, in William Shakespeare's THE TEMPEST. Growing up on a largely uninhabited island with her father and Caliban for company, Miranda is so delighted to meet other humans that in the final act she speaks the famous words "How beauteous mankind is! O brave new world, that has such people in't!"

Mirbeau \\mer-'bō\\, Octave(-Henri-Marie) (b. Feb. 16, 1850, Trévières, Fr.—d. Feb. 16, 1917, Paris)   French writer of novels and plays who unsparingly satirized the clergy and social conditions of his time and was one of the 10 original members of the Académie Goncourt, founded in 1903.

Mirbeau worked as a journalist for Bonapartist and Royalist newspapers. He made his reputation as a storyteller with tales of the Norman peasantry, *Lettres de ma chaumière* (1886; "Letters from My Cottage") and *Le Calvaire* (1887; "The Calvary"). In 1888 he wrote *L'Abbé Jules* ("The Priest Jules") and, in 1890, *Sébastien Roch*, a merciless picture of the Jesuit school he had attended. All of his novels, from *Le Jardin des supplices* (1899; *The Torture Garden*) and *Le Journal d'une femme de chambre* (1900; *Diary of a Chambermaid*) to *La 628-E8* (1907) and *Dingo* (1913), were bitter social satires. His drama *Les Mauvais Bergers* (1897; "The Bad Shepherds") was compared to the work of Henry-Françoise Becque, but his greatest success as a playwright was achieved with *Les Affaires sont les affaires* (1903; "Business Is Business").

Mīrkhwānd or **Mirkhond** \\'mer-ˌkȯnd\\, *byname of* Muhammad ibn Khāvandshāh ibn Mahmūd \\ˌeb-ən-'mak-ˌmūd\\ (b. 1433, Balkh [Afghanistan]—d. June 22, 1498, Herāt)   One of the most important Persian chroniclers of Iran under the Timurid dynasty (15th century).

Spending most of his life in Herāt in the court of the last Timurid sultan, Ḥusayn Bayqarah (1469–1506), Mīrkhwānd enjoyed the protection of Ḥusayn's minister ʿAlī Shīr Navāʾī, a celebrated patron of literature. About 1474, at the request of his patron, he began his general history, *Rowzat oṣ-ṣafāʾ* (Eng. trans. begun as *History of the Early Kings of Persia*, continued as *The Rauzat-us-Safa; or, Garden of Purity*).

The work is composed of seven large volumes and a geographical appendix, sometimes considered an eighth volume. The history begins with the age of the pre-Islāmic Persian kings and surveys the major Muslim rulers of Iran up to the events of 1523. The seventh volume may have been finished by Mīrkhwānd's grandson, the historian Khwāndamīr (Khondamir), and in the 19th century Reẓā Qolī Khān Hedāyat wrote a supplement to the work.

Mīrkhwānd is often criticized for his highly embellished style and for his uncritical approach to sources, but his history preserves sections from earlier works that have since been lost.

Miró \ˈmē-rō\, Gabriel (Francisco Víctor), *surname in full* Miró Ferrer \fer-ˈrer\ (b. July 28, 1879, Alicante, Spain—d. May 27, 1930, Madrid) Spanish writer distinguished for the finely wrought but difficult style and the rich, imaginative vocabulary of his essays, stories, and novels.

In 1922 Miró became secretary of the Concursos Nacionales de Letras y Artes in Madrid. His many novels include *Nuestro padre San Daniel* (1921; *Our Father, Saint Daniel*) and *El obispo leproso* (1926; "The Leprous Bishop"), both of which are critical of religious customs. Among his nonfictional works are *Figuras de la Pasión del Señor* (1916; *Figures of the Passion of Our Lord*) and a series of books describing the culture of his native region.

Misanthrope, Le \lə-mē-zänⁿ-ˈtrȯp\ Satiric comedy in five acts by MOLIÈRE, performed in 1666 and published the following year.

The play is a portrait of Alceste, a painfully forthright 17th-century gentleman utterly intolerant of polite society's flatteries and hypocrisies. He is hopelessly in love with the coquettish Célimène, who proves cruel to her many suitors; all of them leave her except Alceste, who asks her to marry him. She would consent, except that he wishes to live a simple, quiet life, while she cannot abandon the frivolous, false society she loves.

miscellany \ˈmis-ə-ˌlā-nē, mi-ˈsel-ə-nē\ A collection of writings on various subjects. One of the first and best-known miscellanies in English was the collection of poems by various authors published by Richard Tottel in 1557. Thereafter the miscellany became a popular form of publication, and many more appeared in the next 50 years, including *The Paradise of Dainty Devices* (1576), *The Phoenix Nest* (1593), *England's Parnassus* (1600), and *England's Helicon* (1600).

Miser, The Five-act comedy by MOLIÈRE, performed as *L'Avare* in 1668 and published in 1669.

The plot concerns the classic conflict of love and money. The miser Harpagon wishes his daughter Elise to marry a wealthy old man, Anselme, who will accept her without a dowry, but she loves the penniless Valère. Harpagon himself has set his eye on young, impoverished Mariane, whom his son Cléante also loves. Much of the play's action focuses on Harpagon's stinginess. Valère and Mariane are revealed to be Anselme's long-lost children, and they are happily paired with the miser's son and daughter by the play's end, after Harpagon insists that Anselme pay for both weddings.

Although *The Miser* is usually considered to be a comedy, its tone is one of absurdity and incongruity rather than of gaiety. The play, based on the *Aulularia* of Roman comic playwright Plautus, recasts the ancient comic figure of the miser who is in-

human in his worship of money, all too human in his need of respect and affection.

Misérables, Les \lä-mē-zā-ˈrȧbl, *Angl* -ˈräb-lə\ Novel by Victor HUGO, published in French in 1862. It was an instant popular success and was quickly translated into several languages.

Set in the Parisian underworld and plotted like a detective story, the work follows Jean Valjean, a victim of society who has been imprisoned for 19 years for stealing a loaf of bread. A hardened criminal upon his release, he eventually reforms, becoming a successful industrialist and mayor of a northern town. Despite this he is haunted by an impulsive, regretted former crime and is pursued relentlessly by the police inspector Javert. Valjean eventually gives himself up for the sake of his adopted daughter, Cosette, and her husband, Marius.

Les Misérables is a vast panorama of Parisian society and its underworld, and it contains many famous episodes and passages, among them a chapter on the Battle of Waterloo and the description of Valjean's rescue of Marius by means of a flight through the sewers of Paris.

Mishima Yukio \mē-ˈshē-mä-ˈyü-kē-ō\, *pseudonym of* Hiraoka Kimitake \ˌkē-mē-ˈtä-kē\ (b. Jan. 14, 1925, Tokyo, Japan—d. Nov. 25, 1970, Tokyo) Prolific writer who is regarded by many critics as the most important Japanese novelist of the 20th century.

Mrs. Mishima Yukio

Having failed to qualify physically for military service in World War II, Mishima worked in a Tokyo factory and after the war studied law at the University of Tokyo. His highly acclaimed first novel, *Kamen no kokuhaku* (1949; *Confessions of a Mask*), is a partly autobiographical work that describes with stylistic brilliance a homosexual who must mask his sexual orientation.

He followed up his initial success with several novels whose main characters, for physical or psychological reasons, are unable to find happiness. Among these works are *Ai no Kanaki* (1950; *Thirst for Love*), *Kinjiki* (1954; *Forbidden Colors*), *Shiosai* (1954; *The Sound of Waves*), and *Kinkakuji* (1956; THE TEMPLE OF THE GOLDEN PAVILION). In addition to novels, short stories, and essays, Mishima also wrote plays in the form of the Japanese Nō, producing reworked and modernized versions of the traditional stories. His plays include *Sado kōshaku fujin* (1965; *Madame de Sade*) and *Kindai nōgaku shu* (1956; *Five Modern Nō Plays*). Mishima's last work, the four-volume epic *Hōjō no umi* (1965–70; THE SEA OF FERTILITY), is regarded by many as his most lasting achievement.

Deeply attracted to the austere patriotism and martial spirit of Japan's past, Mishima was contemptuous of the materialistic, Westernized society of Japan in the postwar era. Although he maintained an essentially Western lifestyle and had a vast knowledge of Western culture, he raged against Japan's imitation of the West. He formed a controversial private army of about 80 students, the Tate no Kai (Shield Society), with the idea of preserving the Japanese martial spirit and helping to protect the emperor against attack.

On Nov. 25, 1970, Mishima and four Shield Society followers seized control of the commanding general's office at a military headquarters near downtown Tokyo. There Mishima committed seppuku (ritual disembowelment).

Mishna \'mish-nə\, *also spelled* Mishnah ("Repeated Study"), *plural* Mishnayot \,mish-nä-'yōt, -'yōth\ The oldest authoritative postbiblical collection and codification of Jewish oral laws, systematically compiled by numerous scholars over a period of about two centuries. The codification was given final form early in the 3rd century AD by Judah ha-Nasi. The Mishna supplements the written, or scriptural, laws found in the Pentateuch.

Intensive study of the Mishna by subsequent scholars in Palestine and Babylonia resulted in the Talmud, two collections of interpretations and annotations.

Miskawayh \,eb-ən-'mes-,kü-yeh\, Abū 'Alī Aḥmad ibn Muḥammad ibn Ya'qūb (b. *c.* 930—d. Feb. 16?, 1030, Rayy [Iran]) Persian scientist, philosopher, and historian whose scholarly works became models for later generations of Islāmic thinkers.

Some 20 works are attributed to Miskawayh. His moral treatise *Tahdhīb al-akhlāq* ("Treatise on Ethics"), influenced by the Aristotelian concept of the mean, is considered one of the best statements of Islāmic philosophy. As a historian Miskawayh is noted for his Persian nationalist bias and his conviction that the histories of peoples offer moral instruction. He also rejected legends as a source for historical information. His seven-volume universal history, *Kitāb tajarīb al-umam wa ta'aqub al-himam* (*The Eclipse of the Abbasid Caliphate*), greatly stimulated the development of Islāmic historiography.

misline \mis-'līn\ To incorrectly arrange or divide lines (as of poetry) in the process of copying or printing.

Miss Julie \'jü-lē-ə, *Swedish* 'yüē-lē-ə\ Full-length drama in one act by August STRINDBERG, published in Swedish as *Fröken Julie* in 1888 and performed in 1889. Also translated into English as *Countess Julie* and *Lady Julie*, the play substitutes such interludes as a peasant dance and a pantomime for the conventional divisions of acts, scenes, and intermissions.

Julie, an aristocratic young woman, has a brief affair with Jean, her father's valet. After the sexual thrill has dissipated, they realize that they have little or nothing in common. Strindberg portrays Julie as a decaying aristocrat whose era has passed and Jean as an opportunistic social climber to whom the future beckons.

Miss Lonelyhearts \'lōn-lē-,härts\ Novel by Nathanael WEST, published in 1933. It concerns a male newspaper columnist whose attempts to give advice to the lovelorn end in tragedy. The protagonist, known only by his newspaper nom de plume, Miss Lonelyhearts, feels powerless to help his generally hopeless correspondents. His boss, Willie Shrike, relentlessly mocks him for taking his job seriously. When Lonelyhearts tries to become personally involved with one of his correspondents, he is killed.

Mistral \mē-'strál\, Frédéric (b. Sept. 8, 1830, Maillane, Fr.—d. March 25, 1914, Maillane) French poet who led the 19th-century revival of Provençal language and literature and shared the Nobel Prize in 1904 for his contributions in literature and philology.

Mistral attended the Collège Royal of Avignon (later renamed the Lycée Frédéric Mistral); one of his teachers was Joseph Roumanille, who had begun writing poems in the vernacular of Provence. Mistral early decided to devote himself to the rehabilitation of Provençal life and language. In 1854, with several friends, he founded the FÉLIBRIGE, an association for the maintenance of the language and customs of Provence, extended later to include the whole of southern France.

Mistral devoted 20 years' work to a scholarly dictionary of Provençal entitled *Lou Tresor dóu Félibrige*, 2 vol. (1878). His literary output consists of four long narrative poems: *Mirèio* (1859; *Mireio: A Provencal Poem*), *Calendau* (1867), *Nerto* (1884), and *Lou Pouèmo dóu Rose* (1897; *The Song of the Rhône*); a historical tragedy, *La Reino Jano* (1890; "Queen Jane"); two volumes of lyrics, *Lis Isclo d'or* (1876; definitive edition, 1889) and *Lis Oulivado* (1912); and many short stories, collected in *Prose d'Armana*, 3 vol. (1926–29). His first narrative poem, *Li Meissoun*, written in 1848, was published posthumously in the *Revue de France* (July–August 1927).

His volume of memoirs, *Moun espelido* (*Mes origines*, 1906; *Memoirs of Mistral*), is his best-known work, but his claim to greatness rests on his first and last long poems, *Mirèio* and *Lou Pouèmo dóu Rose*, both full-scale epics in 12 cantos.

Mistral \mēs-'trál\, Gabriela, *pseudonym of* Lucila Godoy Alcayaga \gō-'thȯi-,äl-kä-'yä-g̈ä\ (b. April 7, 1889, Vicuña, Chile—d. Jan. 10, 1957, Hempstead, N.Y., U.S.) Chilean poet, the first Latin-American woman to win the Nobel Prize for Literature (1945).

Bettmann Archive

She became a schoolteacher at age 15, advancing later to the rank of college professor. Throughout her life she combined writing with a career as an educator, cultural minister, and diplomat.

Her reputation as a poet was established in 1914 when she won a Chilean prize for three "Sonetos de la muerte" ("Sonnets of Death"). They were signed with the name by which she has since been known, which she coined from those of two of her favorite poets, Gabriele D'Annunzio and Frédéric Mistral. A collection of her early works, *Desolación* (1922; "Desolation"), includes the poem "Dolor," detailing the aftermath of a love affair that was ended by the suicide of her lover. Because of this tragedy she never married, and a haunting, wistful strain of thwarted maternal tenderness informs her work. *Ternura* (1924; enlarged 1945; "Tenderness") and *Tala* (1938; "Destruction") evidence a broader interest in humanity. She also published a book of poems, *Lagar* (1954; "The Wine Press"), and a volume entitled *Lagar II* was published posthumously in 1991.

Mitchell \'mich-əl\, Donald Grant, *pseudonym* Ik Marvel \'mär-vəl\ (b. April 12, 1822, Norwich, Conn., U.S.—d. Dec. 15, 1908) American farmer and writer known for nostalgic, sentimental books on American life, especially *Reveries of a Bachelor* (1850).

Mitchell graduated from Yale and then returned home to farm his ancestral land. In 1844 he was appointed clerk to the U.S. consul at Liverpool, but poor health forced him to resign. Once back in America in 1846, he wrote newspaper articles for the *Morning Courier* and *New York Enquirer* under the pseudonym Ik Marvel, also editing *Lorgnette* (1850), a satirical magazine. His earliest books, *Fresh Gleanings* (1847) and *The Battle Summer* (1850), record incidents of his travels in Europe and the French revolution of 1848. With the publication of *Reveries of a Bachelor* he gained immediate fame, and in 1851 another volume, *Dream Life*, was published. His style is quiet, simple, and archaic, and he has been compared to Jerome K. Jerome, the English author of sentimental works.

In 1853 Mitchell married, and in 1855, with his wife, he bought Edgewood, an estate near New Haven, Conn., intending to farm full-time. He always considered his agricultural projects more important than his writing, and he tried to build a model farm. He wrote several more volumes of essays, mostly on farming life.

Mitchell \'mich-əl\, Margaret (b. 1900, Atlanta, Ga., U.S.—d. Aug. 16, 1949, Atlanta)   American author of the enormously popular novel GONE WITH THE WIND (1936).

Mitchell wrote for *The Atlanta Journal*. After leaving the newspaper she spent 10 years writing her one book, *Gone with the Wind*, a novel about the American Civil War and Reconstruction as seen from the Southern point of view.

Gone with the Wind was almost certainly the largest selling novel in the history of U.S. publishing to that time. In the first six months after publication 1,000,000 copies were sold, 50,-000 of them in one day. Before the author's death sales had totaled 8,000,000 in 40 countries.

Mitchell \'mich-əl\, S. Weir, *in full* Silas (b. Feb. 15, 1829, Philadelphia, Pa., U.S.—d. Jan. 4, 1914, Philadelphia)   American physician and author who excelled in novels of psychology and historical romance.

Mitchell served as an army surgeon during the American Civil War, and his experiences were the basis for "The Case of George Dedlow" (1866), a story about an amputee notable for its psychological insights and realistic war scenes. *Wear and Tear* (1871) and *Fat and Blood* (1877), both medical popularizations, were best-sellers. Mitchell also published short stories, poems, and children's stories anonymously. Of later novels perhaps his most notable are *Roland Blake* (1886), *Hugh Wynne* (1898), *Circumstance* (1901), *Constance Trescott* (1905), and *The Red City* (1908). Mitchell's poetry, which lacks the psychological insight and contemporaneity of his novels, appears in several collections, including the volumes *The Hill of Stones* (1882) and *The Wager* (1900).

Mitchell \'mich-əl\, W.O., *in full* William Ormond (b. March 13, 1914, Weyburn, Sask., Can.)   Writer of stories that deal humorously with the hardships of western Canadian prairie life.

Mitchell received favorable notice for his first novel, *Who Has Seen the Wind* (1947), a sensitive picture of a grim prairie town as seen from the point of view of a small boy. From 1950 to 1958, he wrote weekly scripts for the radio series "Jake and the Kid," which had originated as short stories. Thirteen of these scripts were published as *Jake and the Kid* (1961). His novel *The Kite* (1962) is about a newsman's interview with the oldest and wisest man in western Canada. Another novel, *The Vanishing Point* (1973), deals with a teacher's involvement with Indians in southwestern Alberta. His later novels include *How I Spent My Summer Holidays* (1981), *Ladybug, Ladybug* (1988), and *Roses Are Difficult Here* (1990).

Mitford \'mit-fərd\, Jessica (Lucy) (b. Sept. 11, 1917, Gloucestershire, Eng.)   English-born writer and journalist who is noted for her investigative works on various aspects of American society.

Mitford, sister of the novelist Nancy Mitford, moved to the United States in 1939 and became a naturalized U.S. citizen in 1944. She began to write in the late 1950s, and her second book, *The American Way of Death* (1963), a caustic examination of unscrupulous practices in the American funeral industry, became a best-seller. *The Trial of Dr. Spock* (1969) is an account of the famous pediatrician's trial on conspiracy charges for antiwar activities during the Vietnam War. *Kind and Usual Punishment: The Prison Business* (1973) examines the

American penal system. *Daughters and Rebels* (1960) tells of her childhood and early adult life, while *A Fine Old Conflict* (1977) recalls her experiences as a member of the U.S. Communist Party. In 1992 she published *The American Way of Birth*, about the state of American obstetrical care.

Mitford \'mit-fərd\, Mary Russell (b. Dec. 16, 1787, Alresford, Hampshire, Eng.—d. Jan. 10, 1855, Swallowfield, near Reading)   Dramatist, poet, and essayist, chiefly remembered for her sketches of English village life.

In 1810 Mitford published *Miscellaneous Poems*, and other volumes of mildly romantic verse followed. Her narrative poem *Christina* (1811) was revised by Samuel Taylor Coleridge, who inserted a number of lines. She then turned to the theater, with some success, most notably in the blank-verse tragedy *Rienzi*, which had 34 performances at London's Drury Lane in 1828.

Mitford's reputation, however, rests on the delightful sketches of village life, started in *The Ladies Magazine* (1819), that fill the five volumes of *Our Village*.

Mitford \'mit-fərd\, Nancy, *married name* Honourable Mrs. Peter Rodd \'räd\ (b. Nov. 28, 1904, London, Eng.—d. June 30, 1973, Versailles, Fr.)   English writer noted for her witty novels of upper-class life.

Archive Photos

Nancy Mitford was one of six daughters (and one son) of the 2nd Baron Redesdale. Her sister Jessica became a well-known writer on American society.

Mitford's chief satiric novels are the quasi-autobiographical *The Pursuit of Love* (1945), *Love in a Cold Climate* (1949), *The Blessing* (1951), and *Don't Tell Alfred* (1960). Mitford wrote several biographies, including *Madame de Pompadour* (1954),
Voltaire in Love (1957), and *The Sun King* (1966). One of her most widely read books was *Noblesse Oblige: An Enquiry into the Identifiable Characteristics of the English Aristocracy* (1956), a volume of essays of which she was coeditor and which brought to the attention of the world the distinction between linguistic usages that are U (upper class) and those that are non-U (not upper class).

Mitty, Walter \'wôl-tər-'mit-ē\   Fictional character, the day-dreaming hero of the short story "The Secret Life of Walter Mitty" by James THURBER. In the story, first published in *The New Yorker* magazine in 1939 and collected in *My World—and Welcome to It* (1942), Mitty is a reticent, henpecked proof-reader who is befuddled by everyday life. He weaves elaborate fantasies in which, at different times, he is a daring and heroic pilot, a desperado, and a ship's captain.

mixed metaphor   A figure of speech that combines two or more inconsistent or incongruous metaphors. *See* METAPHOR.

Mixture of Frailties, A   Novel by Robertson Davies, the third in a series known collectively as the SALTERTON TRILOGY.

Mjollnir \'myœl-nir\, *Old Norse* Mjǫllnir.   In Norse mythology, the hammer of the thunder god, Thor, and the symbol of his power.

Mnemosyne \nē-'mäs-i-nē, -'mäz-\   In Greek mythology, a Titan, daughter of Uranus (Heaven) and Gaea (Earth), and, according to the Greek poet Hesiod, the mother (by Zeus) of the nine Muses. Zeus slept with Mnemosyne nine consecutive nights, after which she gave birth to the Muses. Mnemosyne is sometimes held to be a pure abstraction, memory personified.

Mnyampala \m-nyäm-'pä-lä\, Mathias E. (b. 1917, Dodoma, Tanganyika [now Tanzania]—d. June 8, 1969, Dodoma) African poet, scholar, jurist, and author of short fiction who wrote in Swahili.

Mnyampala's first works were intended for the colonial educational system; they include *Mila na Desturi za Wagogo wa Tanganyika* (1954; "History, Traditions, and Customs of the Gogo People of Tanganyika") and *Kisa cha Mrina Asali na Wenzake Wawili* (1961; "The Tale of the Honey Gatherer and His Two Friends"). More notable are his contributions to modern Swahili poetry. He followed the traditional formal patterns of Swahili verse but adapted them to modern—particularly political—themes. His most important poetic works are *Waadhi wa Ushairi* (1960; "Poetic Exhortations"), *Diwani ya Mnyampala* (1960; "Mnyampala's Poetry Book"), *Mashairi ya Hekima* (1965; "Poems of Wisdom"), and *Ngonjera za UKUTA*, 2 vol. (1970–71; "Educational Verses from UKUTA"). (UKUTA is the acronym of the Swahili poets' association that Mnyampala founded.) He also published short fiction and educational essays.

Mo \'mō\, Timothy (b. 1950, Hong Kong)   Anglo-Chinese writer whose critically acclaimed novels explore the intersection of English and Cantonese cultures.

Born to an English mother and a Chinese father, Mo lived in Hong Kong until age 10, when he moved to Britain. He was educated at Oxford University, after which he became a journalist.

Mo's first novel, *The Monkey King* (1978), tells the story of a naive young Portuguese-Chinese in Hong Kong. *Sour Sweet* (1982), which won the Hawthornden Prize in 1982, deals with the immigrant experience in England. The action of *An Insular Possession* (1986) occurs during the 19th-century Opium Wars. Another novel, *The Redundancy of Courage* (1991), is set in a troubled area (recognizable as East Timor) invaded by Indonesian forces and betrayed by Western powers.

Moberg \'mü-berʸ\, Vilhelm, *in full* Carl Artur Vilhelm Moberg (b. Aug. 20, 1898, Algutsboda, Swed.—d. Aug. 8, 1973, Väddö)   Swedish novelist and dramatist, best known for his novels of the Swedish immigration to America.

In the autobiographical novel *Soldat med brutet gevär* (1944; *When I Was a Child*) Moberg wrote about the illiterate class from which he came. His most widely read and translated works include the Knut Toring trilogy (1935–39; *The Earth Is Ours*) and his four-volume epic of the folk migration from Sweden to America in the 1850s, *Utvandrarna* (1949–59; *The Emigrants*), *Invandrarna* (1952; *Unto a Good Land*), *Nybyggarna* (1956), and *Sista brevet till Sverige* (1959). The last two volumes were combined in the translation *The Last Letter Home*. During World War II, Moberg also wrote a novel eloquently attacking tyranny and oppression, *Rid i natt!* (1941; *Ride This Night!*).

Moby-Dick \'mō-bē-'dik\ (*in full* Moby-Dick; or, The Whale)   Novel by Herman MELVILLE, published in London in October 1851 and published a month later in the United States. *Moby-Dick* is generally regarded as its author's masterpiece and one of the greatest American novels.

The basic plot of *Moby-Dick* is simple. The narrator (who asks to be called "Ishmael") tells of the last voyage of the ship *Pequod* out of New Bedford, Mass. Captain Ahab is obsessed with the pursuit of the white whale Moby-Dick, which finally kills him. On that level, the work is an intense, superbly authentic narrative. Its theme and central figure, however, are reminiscent of Job in his search for justice and of Oedipus in his search

Illustration by Rockwell Kent
Rockwell Kent Legacies

for truth. The novel's richly symbolic language and tragic hero are indicative of Melville's deeper concerns: the equivocal defeats and triumphs of the human spirit and its fusion of creative and murderous urges.

Mocatta \mō-'kat-ə\, Frederic David (b. Jan. 15, 1828, London, Eng.—d. Jan. 16, 1905, London)   British philanthropist, historian, bibliophile, and patron of learning.

Mocatta directed the firm of Mocatta and Goldsmid, bullion brokers to the Bank of England. Upon retirement he devoted his time to charitable works and promoting education. Mocatta's chief historical work is *The Jews of Spain and Portugal and the Inquisition* (1877). He bequeathed his fine library of Jewish history and English Judaica to University College, London.

Mochnacki \mōk̯-'nȧt-skʸē\, Maurycy (b. Sept. 13, 1804, Bojanice, Galicia [now in Poland]—d. Dec. 20, 1834, Auxerre, Fr.)   Early Romantic literary critic who was the first Polish critic to define the part literature might play in the spiritual and political life of society.

A journalist in Poland, Mochnacki took part in the insurrection of Nov. 29, 1830, against Russian rule, was wounded, and became an exile in France, where he contributed political articles to *Pamiętnik emigracji polskiej* ("Memoirs of the Polish Émigrés"). His *Powstanie narodu polskiego w latach 1830–1831* ("Insurrection of the Polish Nation in the Years 1830 and 1831") is considered the best eyewitness account of these events. Of his literary articles, *O literaturze polskiej wieku XIX* (1830; "On Polish Literature of the 19th Century") is considered the most important.

mock-epic or **mock-heroic** Form of satire that applies the elevated heroic style of the classical epic to a trivial subject. The tradition, which originated in classical times with an anonymous burlesque of Homer, the *Batrachomyomachia* (*Battle of the Frogs and the Mice*), was honed to a fine art in the late 17th- and early 18th-century Neoclassical period. A double-edged satirical weapon, the mock-epic was sometimes used by the "moderns" of this period to ridicule contemporary "ancients" (classicists). More often it was used by the ancients to point up the unheroic character of the age. The classic example of this use is Nicolas Boileau's *Le Lutrin* (1674, 1683; "The Lectern"), which begins with a quarrel between two ecclesiastical dignitaries about where to place a lectern in a chapel and ends with a battle in a bookstore. Jonathan Swift's "Battle of the Books" (1704) is a variation on the theme in prose. The outstanding English mock-epic is Alexander Pope's tour de force *The Rape of the Lock* (final version, 1714), which concerns a society beau's theft of a lock of hair from a society belle. An American mock-epic, Joel Barlow's *The Hasty Pudding* (1796), celebrates his favorite New England dish, cornmeal mush, in three 400-line cantos.

Mock Turtle Fictional character who describes himself as "the thing mock turtle soup is made from," in Lewis Carroll's ALICE'S ADVENTURES IN WONDERLAND.

model \'mäd-əl\ *archaic* An abstract or summary of a written work. *See also* EPITOME.

Modern \'mäd-ərn\, *also called* New \'nü\ Of, relating to, or having the characteristics of the present or most recent period of development of a language or literature. *Modern* is often applied in distinction to *Old* and *Middle*, as in "Early Modern English," a term used to describe the language and literature of the period immediately following that of Middle English.

moderne gennembrud, det \dā-mō-'der-nə-'gen-nem-,brü\ [Danish, literally, the modern breakthrough] Literary movement that introduced naturalism and realism to Scandinavia.

The movement was dominated by the Danish critic Georg Brandes, who sought to bring Denmark out of its cultural isolation. Brandes' *Hovedstrømninger i det 19de aarhundredes litteratur* (1872–90; *Main Currents in 19th Century Literature*) caused a great sensation throughout Scandinavia. His demands that literature should concern itself with life and reality, and that it should work in the service of progress rather than reaction, provoked much discussion. He influenced both Henrik Ibsen and August Strindberg. Other notable writers influenced by Brandes include Jens Peter Jacobsen, Henrik Pontoppidan, and Herman Bang.

modernism \'mä-dər-,niz-əm\ In literature, a chiefly European movement of the early-to-mid-20th century that represented a self-conscious break with traditional forms and subject matter and a search for a distinctly contemporary mode of expression.

Initially modernism had a radical and utopian spirit stimulated by new ideas in anthropology, psychology, philosophy, political theory, and psychoanalysis. This exuberance can be seen in the works of such writers as Ezra Pound and the other poets of the Imagist movement. The outbreak of World War I had a sobering effect, however, and postwar modernism, as seen in such works as T.S. Eliot's *The Wasteland*, reflected the prevailing sense of fragmentation and disillusion. Other characteristics of later modernism are increasing self-awareness, introspection, and openness to the unconscious and to humanity's darker fears and instincts.

Modernismo \,mō-ther-'nēz-mō\ or **Modernism** \'mäd-ər-,niz-əm\ Late 19th- and early 20th-century Spanish-language literary movement begun in the late 1880s by the Nicaraguan poet Rubén DARÍO.

Modernismo began as a reaction against the sentimental romantic writers then holding sway in Latin America. Young writers across the Americas immersed themselves in the world literary community. Somewhat disparagingly labeled *modernistas* by the older generation, they wrote on exotic themes, often shutting themselves off from their immediate environment in artificial worlds of their own making—the ancient past, the distant Orient, and the lands of childhood fancy and sheer creation. Beauty was their goddess and "art for art's sake" their creed. Influenced by French movements, they followed no regular path; Symbolism, Parnassianism, Decadentism, and other influences coexisted or held sway successively in any given writer.

Foremost among the early *modernistas* were the Mexican Manuel Gutiérrez Nájera, noted for his elegiac verse and restrained rhythmic prose sketches and tales; the Colombian José Asunción Silva, who wrote savagely ironic and elegiac poems; the Cuban Julián del Casal, cultivator of the Parnassian sonnet; and his compatriot José Martí, martyr and symbol of Cuba's struggle for freedom from Spain.

The full flowering of Modernismo came under the leadership of Darío, one of the greatest poets in Spanish. His *Prosas profanas* (1896; "Profane Hymns") represented the high point of the escapist, cosmopolitan phase of the movement. Darío blended the best of modernist formal experimentation with an expression of inner despair or an almost metaphysical joy in *Cantos de vida y esperanza* (1905; "Songs of Life and Hope"). When Spain's empire crumbled in 1898 and mutual sympathy allayed the old distrust between Spain and its former colonies, Darío turned to Hispanic traditions as he had always turned to Hispanic forms, and in the face of U.S. imperialism, he spoke for Hispanic solidarity. Darío and his fellow modernists—including Mexico's Amado Nervo, Peru's José Santos Chocano, Bolivia's Ricardo Jaimes Freyre, Colombia's Guillermo Valencia, and Uruguay's José Enrique Rodó—brought about the greatest revitalization of language and poetic technique in Spanish since the 17th century. Although the movement had run its course by 1920, its influence on both prose and poetry continued well into the 20th century.

Modernismo \mō-,der-'nēz-mü\ In Brazil, a post-World War I aesthetic movement that attempted to create authentically Brazilian methods of expression in the arts. Rebelling against the academicism and European influence they felt dominated the arts in Brazil, the *modernistas* attempted in their works to reflect colloquial Brazilian speech and often treated distinctively Brazilian themes based on native folklore and legend. They experimented with literary form and language, using free verse and unconventional syntax. Their concern with literary reform was often matched by a desire for social reform.

The Modernismo movement first gained wide recognition with its Semana de Arte Moderna ("Week of Modern Art"), held in São Paulo in 1922; the event provoked controversy, with lectures on the aims of Modernismo and readings from works by such poets as Mário de Andrade. The movement soon splintered into several groups with differing goals—some *modernistas*, among them Oswald de Andrade, focused on the nationalistic aims of the movement and agitated for radical social reform; others, such as Manuel BANDEIRA, who is generally considered the greatest of the *modernista* poets, sympathized with its aesthetic principles but lost interest in its political activism. By 1930 Modernismo had lost its coherence as a movement, although its organizers continued to write in the *modernista* idiom. Its influence on the development of contemporary Brazilian literature, however, has been profound.

modernize \'mäd-ər-,nīz\   **1.** To change a text to make it conform to modern usage in spelling and language. Among the authors who have been modernized are Geoffrey Chaucer, whose use of Middle English often makes his meaning unclear to the nonscholar. Sometimes modernization can help the reader surmount the difficulties produced by early printing practices. Early printed books, for example, often used *u* and *v* interchangeably, spelled the same words inconsistently, and (in the very earliest stages) used slashes, colons, and periods more or less interchangeably to indicate pauses.   **2.** To act, write, or speak in a modern manner. The plays of William Shakespeare, for example, are sometimes acted in modern dress, and the actors sometimes substitute elements of modern speech for ease of comprehension.

Modest Proposal, A (*in full* A Modest Proposal For Preventing the Children of Poor People From Being a Burthen to their Parents, Or the Country, and For Making Them Beneficial to the Publick)   A satiric essay by Jonathan SWIFT, published in pamphlet form in 1729.

Presented in the guise of an economic treatise, the essay proposes that the country ameliorate poverty in Ireland by butchering the children of the Irish poor and selling them as food to wealthy English landlords. Swift's proposal is a savage comment on England's legal and economic exploitation of Ireland. The essay is a masterpiece of satire, with a blend of rational deliberation and unthinkable conclusion, and its title has come to symbolize any proposition to solve a problem with an effective but outrageous cure.

Modisane \,mō-dē-'sän\, Bloke, *original name* William Modisane (b. Aug. 28, 1923, Johannesburg, S.Af.)   South African-born British writer, actor, and broadcaster whose moving autobiography, *Blame Me on History* (1963), is a passionate documentation of the degradation of blacks living under apartheid in South Africa.

Educated in Johannesburg, Modisane served on the editorial staff of the *Drum* magazine until he could no longer tolerate life in South Africa. He fled to England in 1959. In London he published short stories, poetry, and articles in a number of periodicals. He also played the lead role in the London production of Jean Genet's *The Blacks*. Modisane's autobiography was well received, and his story "The Dignity of Begging" (1951) was praised for its satire.

Modrzewski \mō-'jef-skʸē\, Andrzej, *in full* Andrzej Frycz-Modrzewski \'frits-\ (b. *c.* 1503, Wołborz, Pol.—d. 1572, Wołborz)   Considered the most eminent Polish writer in Latin of the 16th century.

Modrzewski studied at the Jagiellonian University in Kraków and later at Wittenberg and Nürnberg in Germany. Returning to Poland, he wrote *De poena homicidii* (1543; "The Punishment for Homicide"), a pamphlet urging repeal of the laws that provided heavy prison sentences, large fines, or even death. In a pamphlet of 1545 he sided with the burghers against the gentry, who were monopolizing agriculture. In his most important work, *Commentariorum de republica emendanda libri quinque* (1551–54; "Reform of the Republic"), he elaborated his bold utopian ideals. He also urged a religious reformation uniting the Roman Catholic and Protestant churches. His ideas antagonized both the church and the gentry, who attacked him bitterly and persecuted him.

Moe, Jørgen Engebretsen   *see* Peter Christen ASBJØRNSEN and Jørgen Engebretsen Moe.

Mofolo \mō-'fō-lō\, Thomas Mokopu (b. Dec. 22, 1876, Khojane, Basutoland [now Lesotho]—d. Sept. 8, 1948, Teyateyaneng)   The first important writer from what is now

Lesotho, who created Western-style novels in the Southern Sotho language.

Mofolo's first novel, *Moeti oa Bochabela* (1907; *The Traveller of the East*), is an allegory in which a young black African in search of truth and virtue journeys to a land where he is converted to Christianity. His second novel, *Pitseng* (1910), is also a Christian fable, but in this case his young hero understands that white people have betrayed the promise of their religion. Mofolo's third and last book, *Chaka* (1925), became the classic on which his reputation rests. A historical novel about the Zulu king Shaka, it presents its hero as a fully realized tragic character.

Molière \mōl-'yer\, *original name* Jean-Baptiste Poquelin \pōk-'laⁿ\ (baptized Jan. 15, 1622, Paris, Fr.—d. Feb. 17, 1673, Paris)   French actor and playwright, the greatest of all writers of French comedy.

Brown Brothers

The son of one of the appointed furnishers of the royal household, Molière received a good education but left home in 1643 to become an actor. He toured the French provinces with a theater troupe from 1645 to 1658, writing plays and also acting in them. After returning to Paris he finally achieved success there with his *Les Précieuses Ridicules* (1659; *The Affected Young Ladies*). He soon had his own permanent theater and wrote plays both for bourgeois audiences in Paris and for the court.

Molière wrote little that was intended to be published. His plays were made for the stage, and his early prefaces complain that he had to publish to avoid exploitation. (Two of them were in fact pirated.) He left seven of his plays unpublished, never issued any collected edition, and never (so far as is known) read proofs or took care with his text. Comedies, in his view, were made to be acted. Competition, the fight for existence, was the keynote of Molière's whole career, and his struggle to keep his actors and his audiences was unremitting.

Molière's major plays are *L'École des femmes* (1663; THE SCHOOL FOR WIVES); *Le Tartuffe; ou, l'imposteur* (1669; TARTUFFE), which outraged the religious authorities and was banned until it had been revised; LE MISANTHROPE (1667); *L'Avare* (1669; THE MISER); and *Le Bourgeois Gentilhomme* (1671; THE BOURGEOIS GENTLEMAN). Other plays include *Dom Juan* (1665; *Don John*) and *Les Femmes savantes* (1672; THE BLUE-STOCKINGS).

Molière's theory of comedy was expounded in *La Critique de l'École des femmes* (1663), a play written in response to critics of *L'École des femmes*. In 1673 Molière collapsed onstage during an early performance of his last play, *Le Malade imaginaire* (1674; THE IMAGINARY INVALID), and he died that same night.

Molinet \mò-lē-'ne\, Jean (b. 1435, Desvres, Burgundian Artois [France]—d. Aug. 23, 1507, Valenciennes, Burgundian Hainaut)   Poet and chronicler, leading figure among the Burgundian *rhétoriqueurs*, who is best remembered for his version of *Roman de la Rose*.

About 1464 Molinet entered the service of Charles the Bold, duke of Burgundy, becoming secretary to Georges Chastellain, chronicler and court poet. On the latter's death Molinet took over his post. His duties as chronicler took him to many lands in the wars and on the journeys of the court. His writings also include an *Art de rhétorique* (1492; "Art of Rhetoric," actually concerned with the art of poetry), mysteries, religious poems, occasional verse, and parodies.

Møller \\'mœl-ər\\, Poul Martin (b. March 21, 1794, near Nakskov, Den.—d. March 13, 1838, Copenhagen) Author whose novel of student life, the first in his country's literature to deal with contemporary events, marked an important stage in the history of Danish literature.

Møller began his literary career by translating Homer. A trip to China inspired journals, nostalgic poems about Denmark and Copenhagen, and a witty parody of statistical-topographical descriptions, *Statistisk skildring af Lægdsgaarden i Ølsebymagle*. After his return Møller earned his living by teaching classics and later philosophy at the university in Christiania (now Oslo), Nor., and at Copenhagen.

Møller first read his most famous work, *En dansk students eventyr* ("The Adventures of a Danish Student"), to the students union at Copenhagen in 1824. Other works include "Blade af dødens dagbog" ("Leaves from Death's Diary"), a poetic fragment inspired by Lord Byron, and sketches, such as his witty essay "Quindelighed."

Moll Flanders \\'mäl-'flan-dərz\\ (*in full* The Fortunes and Misfortunes of the Famous Moll Flanders, &c. Who Was Born in Newgate, and During a Life of Continu'd Variety for Threescore Years, Besides her Childhood, was Twelve Year a Whore, Five Times a Wife [Whereof Once to her Own Brother] Twelve Year a Thief, Eight Year a Transported Felon in Virginia, at Last Grew Rich, Liv'd Honest, and Died a Penitent. Written from Her Own Memorandums) Picaresque novel by Daniel DEFOE, published in 1722. The novel recounts the adventures of a lusty and strong-willed woman who is compelled, from earliest childhood, to make her own way in 17th-century England.

Molloy \\mōl-'wä, mə-'lói\\ French prose work by Samuel BECKETT, published in 1951. It was the first book in a trilogy written in French that included *Malone meurt* (1951; MALONE DIES) and *L'Innommable* (1953; THE UNNAMABLE).

Molloy is less a novel than a set of two monologues narrated by Molloy and his pursuer Moran. In the first half of the work, the dying Molloy describes how he lost everything, including the use of his legs, on his journey in search of his mother. The petty bureaucrat Moran assumes the narrative voice in the second half, describing his hunt for Molloy, which leaves him crippled and just as destroyed as his quarry.

Both halves of the book display Beckett's black humor and despairing outlook, as well as literary techniques that became characteristic of his work. *Molloy* was his first major writing in French. Critics noted its sardonic relation to Homer's *Odyssey*.

Molnár \\'mōl-när\\, Ferenc (b. Jan. 12, 1878, Budapest [Hungary]—d. April 1, 1952, New York, N.Y., U.S.) Hungarian playwright and fiction writer who is known for his plays about the contemporary salon life of Budapest and for his moving short stories.

Molnár published his first stories at the age of 19 and achieved his first great success with the play *Az ördög* (1907; *The Devil*). A number of his plays, including *Liliom* (1909), *A hattyú* (1920; *The Swan*), and *A vörös malom* (1923; *The Red Mill*), were successfully performed abroad, particularly in Austria, Germany, and the United States; some were also made into films, though often at the expense of their finely detailed characterizations, bitter cynicism, and biting irony. Some of Molnár's short stories, especially those collected in *Muzsika* (1908; "Music"), are masterpieces; concise and moving, they look be-

neath the glittering facade of society life to the problems of the poor and the underdog. Among his many novels only *A Pál utcai fiúk* (1907; *The Paul Street Boys*) achieved much success. Molnár depicted the victory of evil, egoism, and immorality, but these elements were offset by his light, amusing touch.

molossus \\mō-'läs-əs\\ [Greek *molossós,* from *Molossós* of the Molossians (tribal group of northwestern Greece)] In classical prosody, a foot of three long syllables that occurs as a variant of an iambic metron, as a substitution for a cretic, or as a contracted ionic metron.

moly \\'mō-lē\\ [Greek *móly*] A mythical herb is described by Homer as having a black root and milk-white blossoms; it had magical powers and was given by Hermes to Odysseus to counteract the spells of Circe.

Momaday \\'mäm-ə-‚dā\\, N. Scott, *in full* Navarre (b. Feb. 27, 1934, Lawton, Okla., U.S.) Native-American author of many works centered on his Kiowa Indian heritage.

Momaday grew up on an Oklahoma farm and on Southwestern reservations. He attended the University of New Mexico and Stanford University. His first novel, *House Made of Dawn* (1968), is his best-known work. It narrates, from several different points of view, the dilemma of a young man returning home to his Kiowa pueblo after a stint in the U.S. Army. The book won the 1969 Pulitzer Prize for fiction.

Momaday's limited-edition collection of Kiowa Indian folktales entitled *The Journey of Tai-me* (1967) was enlarged as *The Way to Rainy Mountain* (1969), illustrated by his father, Alfred Momaday. His poetry is collected in *Angle of Geese and Other Poems* (1974) and *The Gourd Dancer* (1976). *The Names: A Memoir* (1976) tells of his early life and of his respect for his Kiowa ancestors. In 1989 he published his second novel, *The Ancient Child. In the Presence of the Sun: Stories and Poems, 1961–1991* appeared in 1992.

Monday, Sara \\'sar-ə-'mən-‚dā, 'sär-\\ Fictional character, the protagonist and narrator in Joyce Cary's novel HERSELF SURPRISED, the first volume of his trilogy on art. Monday is presented as a warmhearted, generous woman who is victimized by the men in her life—the conservative upper-class lawyer Tom Wilcher and the artist and rebel Gulley Jimson.

Monk, The Gothic novel by Matthew Gregory LEWIS, published in 1796. The story's violence and sexual content made it one of the era's best-selling and most influential novels.

The novel is the story of a monk, Ambrosio, who is initiated into a life of depravity by Matilda, a woman who has disguised herself as a man to gain entrance to the monastery. Ambrosio eventually sells his soul to the devil to avoid being tortured by the Spanish Inquisition, but the devil throws him from a precipice to his death on the rocks below.

The book differed from other gothic novels of the time because it concentrated on the sensational and the horrible rather than on romance and because it did not attempt to explain the supernatural events of the plot.

Monkey *see* XIYOU JI.

Monkey's Paw, The Classic tale of horror and superstition, a much-anthologized short story by W.W. JACOBS, published in 1902 in the collection *The Lady of the Barge.*

The story centers on a dried, shrunken monkey's paw that has the power to grant its possessor three wishes; these, however, are always granted in an ironic, sinister fashion.

Monk's Tale, The One of the 24 stories in THE CANTERBURY TALES by Geoffrey Chaucer.

The brawny Monk relates a series of 17 tragedies based on the fall from glory of various biblical, classical, and contemporary figures, including Lucifer and Adam; Nero and Julius Caesar; Zenobia, a 3rd-century queen of Palmyra; and several 14th-century kings. After 775 lines of lugubrious recital, the Knight and the Host interrupt, bored by the list of disasters.

Monk's Tale stanza   A stanza of eight five-stress lines with the rhyme scheme *ababbcbc*. The type was established in "The Monk's Tale" from Geoffrey Chaucer's *The Canterbury Tales*. It bears some similarity to the French ballade form and is thought to have influenced the Spenserian stanza.

monodrama \'män-ə-,dräm-ə, -,dram-\   **1.** A drama acted or designed to be acted by a single person. A number of plays by Samuel Beckett, including *Krapp's Last Tape* and *Happy Days*, are monodramas.   **2.** A dramatic representation of what passes in an individual mind.   **3.** A musical drama for a solo performer.

monody \'män-ə-dē\ [Greek *monōidía,* from *mónos* single, alone + *ōidē* song]   An ode sung by one voice (as by one of the actors in a Greek tragedy).

monogatari \'mō-nō-gä-tä-rē\ [Japanese *mono-gatari* tale, narrative, from *mono* thing + *katari* talk, narration]   Japanese works of fiction, especially those written from the Heian to the Muromachi periods (794–1573).

Monogatari developed from the storytelling of women at court. During the Heian period (794–1185), men wrote in Chinese, and it was women who developed this form of Japanese prose. Some early *monogatari,* however, are believed to have been written by men under women's names. Records describe 11th-century literary competitions where women prepared short *monogatari* for an audience.

The form has many subgenres. *Uta monogatari* (poem tales) are exemplified by the *Ise monogatari* (*c.* 980), consisting of 143 episodes, each containing one or more poems and a prose description of the circumstances of composition. *Tsukuri monogatari* (courtly romance) is exemplified by Murasaki Shikibu's incomparable masterpiece, *Genji monogatari* (*c.* 1010). Like other works of the genre, it incorporates poems and verse fragments.

As the militaristic samurai came to power at the end of the 12th century, women lost favor, and *gunki monogatari* (military tales) developed as a subgenre. The most famous of the military tales is *Heike monogatari,* which describes the warfare between two families; its lengthy, varied text reflects its origins as an improvised story told by priest-entertainers. Later works told of medieval warlords and clan vendettas.

Other types of *monogatari* include *rekishi monogatari* (historical tales), exemplified by the *Ōkagami,* and *setsuwa monogatari* (didactic tales) originating in Buddhist legends but in their secular form often humorous and earthy.

monograph \'män-ə-,graf\ [Greek *mónos* single + *gráphein* to write]   A learned treatise on a small area of learning. Also, a written account of a single subject.

monologue or **monolog** \'män-ə-,lóg, -,läg\ [French *monologue,* from Greek *mónos* single, alone + French *-logue* (as in *dialogue* dialogue)]   An extended speech by one person. The term has several synonyms and distinctive literary uses. A DRAMATIC MONOLOGUE is any speech of some duration addressed by a character to a second person. A SOLILOQUY is a type of monologue in which a character directly addresses an audience or speaks thoughts aloud while alone or while the other actors remain silent. In fiction, an INTERIOR MONOLOGUE is a type of monologue that exhibits the thoughts and feelings passing through a character's mind. *See also* APOSTROPHE.

monometer \mə-'näm-ə-tər\   A rare form of verse in which each line consists of a single metrical unit (a foot or dipody).

The best-known example of an entire poem in monometer is Robert Herrick's "Upon His Departure Hence":

> Thus I
> Passe by,
> And die:
> As One,
> Unknown,
> And gon:
> I'm made
> A shade,
> And laid
> I'th grave,
> There have
> My Cave.
> Where tell
> I dwell,
> *Farewell.*

monopode \'män-ə-,pōd\ [Greek *monopod-, monópous* one-footed, from *mónos* single + *poús* foot]   A one-footed creature; specifically, a fabulous one-footed Ethiopian creature that uses his foot as a sunshade.

monopody \mə-'näp-ə-dē\ [Late Greek *monopodía* measurement by single feet, from Greek *mónos* single + *pod-, poús* foot]   In prosody, a measure consisting of a single metrical foot.

monorhyme or **monorime** \'män-ō-,rīm\   A strophe or poem in which all the lines have the same end rhyme. Monorhymes are rare in English but are a common feature in Latin, Welsh, and Arabic poetry.

monostich \'män-ə-,stik\ [Greek *monóstichon,* from neuter of *monóstichos* consisting of one verse, from *mónos* single + *stíchos* row, line, verse]   A single verse; also, a poem of one verse.

monostrophe \mə-'näs-trə-fē, 'män-ō-,stróf\   **1.** A poem of one stanza.   **2.** A poem in which all the stanzas are of the same metric form.

Monroe \mən-'rō\, Harriet (b. Dec. 23, 1860, Chicago, Ill., U.S.—d. Sept. 26, 1936, Arequipa, Peru)   American founder and longtime editor of POETRY magazine, which, in the first decade of its existence, became the principal organ for modern poetry of the English-speaking world.

Monroe worked on various Chicago newspapers as an art and drama critic while privately writing verse and verse plays. Her poem "Cantata" celebrates Chicago history, and her heroic "Columbian Ode" (1892) was recited at the dedication of Chicago's World's Columbian Exposition. In founding *Poetry* she secured the backing of wealthy Chicago patrons and invited contributions from a wide range of contemporary poets. Monroe served as the magazine's editor, and her open-minded, inclusive editorial policy and her awareness of the importance of the poetic revolution of the early years of the century made her a major influence in the development of modern poetry. Her autobiography, *A Poet's Life: Seventy Years in a Changing World,* was published posthumously in 1938.

Monsarrat \,män-sə-'rat\, Nicholas (John Turney) (b. March 22, 1910, Liverpool, Eng.—d. Aug. 8, 1979, London)   Popular English novelist whose best-known work, *The Cruel Sea* (1951), vividly captured life aboard a small ship in wartime.

Monsarrat's first book, *Think of Tomorrow,* appeared in 1934. From 1940 to 1946 he served with the Royal Navy, chiefly on dangerous Atlantic convoy runs. He afterward put this experience to brilliant account, first in *H.M. Corvette* (1942) and then in his best-seller *The Cruel Sea.* His later work includes *The Story of Esther Costello* (1953), *The Tribe That Lost Its Head* (1956), and *Smith and Jones* (1963). His two-volume *Life Is a Four-Letter Word* (1966, 1970; abridged as *Breaking In,*

Breaking Out) is an autobiography to 1956. His last novel, *The Master Mariner; Running Proud* (1979), was the first book of a projected two-part novel about the British navy.

montage \män-'täzh, mōⁿ-'täzh\   A literary technique, taking its name from cinematic montage, in which images, themes, or fragments of ideas are juxtaposed to produce a single effect. Also, a literary composite made by means of such technique.

Montagu \'män-tə-ˌgyū, 'mən-\, Elizabeth, *original surname* Robinson \'räb-ən-sən\ (b. Oct. 2, 1720, York, Eng.—d. Aug. 25, 1800, London)   One of the first members of the Bluestocking society, a group of English women who organized evenings of conversation. She made her house in London's Mayfair the social center of intellectual society, regularly entertaining such luminaries as Lord Lyttelton, Horace Walpole, Samuel Johnson, and Sir Joshua Reynolds. In 1760 she contributed to Lyttleton's *Dialogues of the Dead*, and in 1769 she published *Essay on the Writings and Genius of Shakespear*.

Montagu \'män-tə-ˌgyū, 'mən-\, Lady Mary Wortley, *original surname* Pierrepont \'pir-pȯnt, -pənt\ (baptized May 26, 1689, London, Eng.—d. Aug. 21, 1762, London)   The most colorful Englishwoman of her time, mainly noted as a prolific letter writer, though she was also a minor poet and essayist.

She eloped with Edward Wortley Montagu, and they eventually settled in London, where she embarked upon a period of intense literary activity. She had earlier written a set of six "town eclogues," witty adaptations of the Roman poet Virgil. Among the works she composed was an anonymous and lively attack on the satirist Jonathan Swift (1734); a play, *Simplicity* (written *c.* 1735); and a series of essays dealing with feminism and the moral cynicism of her time.

Montagu's literary reputation chiefly rests on 52 superb Turkish embassy letters, which she wrote after her return from Constantinople, where her husband was ambassador for two years. The letters, which used her actual letters and journals as source material, were published in 1763 from an unauthorized copy and were acclaimed throughout Europe. *The Complete Letters of Lady Mary Wortley Montagu*, 3 vol. (1965–67), was the first full edition of Montagu's letters.

Montague \'män-tə-ˌgyū, 'mən-\, Charles Edward (b. Jan. 1, 1867, Twickenham, Middlesex, Eng.—d. May 28, 1928, Manchester)   English novelist, journalist, and man of letters particularly noted for writings published in the *Manchester Guardian* and for a number of outstanding works of fiction.

After graduating from the University of Oxford, Montague joined the *Manchester Guardian* and, apart from service with the Royal Fusiliers during World War I, remained there for 35 years. He became well known for his vigorous leading articles and penetrating dramatic criticism, partly collected in *Dramatic Values* (1911). Among his other works are the pre-war novel *A Hind Let Loose* (1910) and two works based on his experiences in World War I—*Disenchantment* (1922) and *Fiery Particles* (1923). His later works include *Rough Justice* (1926), *Right Off the Map* (1927), and *Action* (1927).

Montague family   *see* CAPULET AND MONTAGUE FAMILIES.

Montaigne \mȯⁿ-tenʸ, *Angl* män-'tān\, Michel (Eyquem) de (b. Feb. 28, 1533, Château de Montaigne, near Bordeaux, Fr.—d. Sept. 13, 1592, Château de Montaigne)   French courtier during the reign of Charles IX and author of *Essais* (1580, 1588; ESSAYS), which established a new literary form.

Much care was devoted to Montaigne's education. At the age of six he was sent to the Collège de Guyenne at Bordeaux, where two of the greatest humanists of the time, George Buchanan and M.A. de Muret, were masters. He then studied

law, probably at Toulouse, and in 1557 he became *conseiller* at the *parlement* of Bordeaux. There he met another lawyer, Étienne de La Boëtie, with whom he formed a friendship

that was the outstanding emotional event of his life. La Boëtie's death in 1563 greatly affected Montaigne, who published his friend's works in 1571. Montaigne's translation from Latin to French of the *Theologia naturalis* of Raimond Sebond, made at his father's behest, was published in 1569. In 1571 he retired to his chateau, where he began work on *Essais*.

Montaigne's retirement was far from complete, and despite a chronic and painful illness he made several incursions into the

world of affairs. In particular, he acted as an intermediary between Henry of Navarre (who made him a gentleman of his chamber in 1577) and the court party, a task for which his moderate Roman Catholicism and advocacy of toleration fitted him well. From September 1580 to November 1581 he made the journey through Germany and Italy described in the *Journal du voyage*. He was mayor of Bordeaux during the troubled period 1581–85. In 1588, visiting Paris to supervise publication of a new edition of *Essais*, he was arrested by members of the Protestant League as a suspected agent of Henry of Navarre but was released after a few hours in the Bastille. He spent his last years at his château, continuing to read and to work on his *Essais*.

Montale \mōn-'tä-lā\, Eugenio (b. Oct. 12, 1896, Genoa, Italy—d. Sept. 12, 1981, Milan)   Italian poet, prose writer, editor, and translator who won the Nobel Prize for Literature in 1975.

A veteran of World War I, Montale opposed fascism in the postwar period, when his literary activity began. He was co-founder (1922) of *Primo tempo*, a literary journal, served for several years as director of a library in Florence, and wrote for other journals.

Montale's first book of poems, *Ossi di seppia* (1925; *Cuttlefish Bones*), expressed the bitter pessimism of the postwar period. The works that followed include *La casa dei doganieri e altre poesie* (1932; "The House of the Customs Officer and Other Poems"), *Le occasioni* (1939; "The Occasions"), and *Finisterre* (1943; "Land's End"). Later works, beginning with *La bufera e altro* (1956; *The Storm and Other Poems*), were written with increasing skill and a personal warmth that his earlier works had lacked. Other collections of poems include *Satura* (1962), *Accordi e pastelli* (1962; "Harmony and Pastels"), *Il colpevole* (1966; "The Offender"), and *Xenia* (1966). *Diario de '71 del e '72* appeared in 1973. Montale published three volumes of collected poems (*Poesie*) in 1948, 1949, and 1957.

Montale was considered in the 1930s and '40s to be a Hermetic poet; he was influenced by the French Symbolists and like them sought to convey experiences through the emotional suggestiveness of words and symbolism. In his later poetry, however, his language is more direct and simple.

Montale also rendered into Italian the poetry of William Shakespeare, T.S. Eliot, and Gerard Manley Hopkins, as well as works by Herman Melville, Eugene O'Neill, and others. His newspaper stories and sketches were collected in *La farfalla di Dinard* (1956; *The Butterfly of Dinard*).

Montalvo \mòn-'täl-bō\, Juan (b. April 13, 1832, Ambato, Ecuador—d. Jan. 17, 1889, Paris, Fr.) Ecuadorean essayist, often called one of the finest writers of Spanish-American prose of the 19th century. Montalvo became famous for his *Siete tratados* (1882; "Seven Treatises"), which offered moral standards for the educated person.

Montalvo spent most of his life in exile, writing powerful essays attacking a succession of Ecuador's dictators. His *Capítulos que se le olvidaron a Cervantes* (1895; "Chapters Omitted by Cervantes") was published posthumously and is considered one of the finest imitations of Miguel de Cervantes' *Don Quixote*.

Mont Blanc \ˌmän-'blän, *French* mōⁿ-'bläⁿ\ Poem by Percy Bysshe SHELLEY, published in 1817. Shelley wrote his five-part meditation on power in a godless universe while contemplating the highest mountain in the Alps.

For Shelley, Mont Blanc and the Arve River symbolize the inaccessible mysteries of nature—awe-inspiring, vivifying, destructive—and he uses the landscape to express his romantic atheism. Like William Wordsworth in *Tintern Abbey*, Shelley tried to make the language of the poem suggest the attributes of the landscape observed, violent or serene.

Monteiro Lobato \mōⁿ-'tä-rü-lō-'bä-tü\, José Bento (b. April 18, 1882, Taubaté, Braz.—d. July 4, 1948, São Paulo) Writer and publisher, forerunner of the Modernismo movement in Brazilian literature.

Originally a lawyer and coffee planter in the interior of São Paulo state, Monteiro Lobato wrote to a São Paulo newspaper, describing the droughts and brushfires in the interior. The editor asked for more articles and Lobato replied with sketches and short stories that were later collected in his book *Urupês* (1918; "Mushrooms"). In these he introduced the character Jeca Tatu ("Joe Armadillo"), who became the symbol of the Brazilian backland.

Monteiro Lobato moved to São Paulo, founded the literary review *Revista do Brasil* and a publishing house, and gathered around him a circle of literary talents. Critical and rebellious, he was in and out of prison and exile many times. In addition to his controversial works, he wrote popular children's books.

Montemayor \mōn-tä-mä-'yòr\ or **Montemor** \ˌmòn-tä-'mòr\, Jorge de (b. *c.* 1520, Montemoro-Velho, Coimbra, Port.—d. Feb. 26, 1561, Turin, Duchy of Savoy [Italy]) Portuguese-born author of romances and poetry who wrote the first Spanish pastoral novel.

Montemayor probably went to Spain in 1543 with Philip II's first wife, Mary, as a musician. His most famous literary work, the pastoral novel *Diana* (1559), started a literary fashion in the Renaissance that spread also to France, the Low Countries, Germany, and England, where William Shakespeare used Bartholomew Young's translation as a source for *The Two Gentlemen of Verona*.

Montgomerie \mənt-'gəm-rē, mänt-, -'gäm-\, Alexander (b. 1556?—d. *c.* 1611) Scottish poet, one of the last of the makaris (poets writing in Lowland Scots in the 16th century).

Montgomerie's contemporary reputation was high, and during the 17th and 18th centuries his best-known poem, "The Cherrie and the Slaye," was reprinted many times. This poem, first printed in 1597 and later enlarged, is an allegory in the medieval manner. The poet's dilemma—whether to struggle toward the noble cherry tree on the crag or to be content with the sloe bush at his feet—leads to an intricate debate with such figures as Danger, Dreid, Reason, Curage, and Dispaire. Montgomerie's other poems include the scurrilously invective *The Flytting betwixt Montgomerie and Polwart* (1621), versions of the Psalms, and a large number of sonnets, lyrics, and songs.

Montgomery \mənt-'gəm-rē, mänt-, -'gäm-\, James (b. Nov. 4, 1771, Irvine, Ayrshire, Scot.—d. April 30, 1854, Sheffield, Yorkshire, Eng.) Scottish poet and journalist best remembered for his hymns and versified renderings of the Psalms, which are among the finest in English, uniting fervor and insight in simple verse. The son of a Moravian minister, Montgomery wrote some 22 books of verse.

Montgomery \mənt-'gəm-rē, mänt-, -'gäm-\, L.M., *in full* Lucy Maud (b. Nov. 30, 1874, Clifton [now New London], P.E.I., Can.—d. April 24, 1942, Toronto, Ont.) Canadian regional novelist, known for *Anne of Green Gables* (1908), a sentimentalized story of a spirited, unconventional orphan girl who finds a home with an elderly brother and sister.

Montgomery was reared by her maternal grandparents. She taught school for several years and was briefly a journalist. While caring for her grandmother, she wrote *Anne of Green Gables*, which drew on her girlhood experiences and on the rural life of Prince Edward Island. The book brought her an international following. Six sequels, taking Anne from girlhood to motherhood, were less successful. Montgomery also produced another series of juvenile books, several collections of stories, and two books for adults.

Montherlant \mōⁿ-ter-'läⁿ\, Henry de, *in full* Henry-Marie-Joseph-Millon de Montherlant (b. April 21, 1896, Paris, Fr.—d. Sept. 21, 1972, Paris) French novelist and dramatist whose stylistically concise works reflect his own egocentric and autocratic personality.

Montherlant was born into a noble family of Catalan origin. His early works included *La Relève du matin* (1920; "Morning Exaltation"), which evokes the intense inner life of his schooldays, *Le Songe* (1922; *The Dream*), a semiautobiographical war novel, and *Les Bestiaires* (1926; *The Bullfighters*), a novel about bullfighting.

Montherlant's major work of fiction is a cycle of four novels: *Les Jeunes Filles* and *Pitié pour les femmes* (both 1936; "The Girls" and "Pity for Women"), *Le Démon du bien* (1937; "The Demon of Good"), and *Les Lépreuses* (1939; "The Lepers"). A two-volume English translation was entitled *The Girls: A Tetralogy of Novels*. This sardonic and misogynistic work describes the relationship between a libertine novelist and his adoring female victims. A similar outlook marks Montherlant's *L'Histoire d'amour de la Rose de Sable* (1954; *Desert Love*).

In 1942 Montherlant turned to the theater with the historical drama *La Reine morte* (1942; *Queen After Death*). His best plays are *Malatesta* (1946), *Le Maître de Santiago* (1947; *The Master of Santiago*), *Port-Royal* (1954), *La Ville dont le prince est un enfant* (1951; "The City Whose Prince Is a Child"), and *La Guerre civile* (1965; "The Civil War"). Montherlant was elected to the Académie Française in 1960.

Month in the Country, A Comedy in three acts by Ivan TURGENEV, published in 1855 and first produced professionally in 1872 as *Mesyats v derevne*. The play concerns complications that ensue when Natalya, a married woman, and Vera, her young ward, both fall in love with Belyayev, the naive young tutor of Natalya's son. Considered Turgenev's dramatic masterpiece, the work presaged the psychological realism of Anton Chekhov's plays.

Monti \'mōn-tē\, Vincenzo (b. Feb. 19, 1754, Alfonsine, near Ravenna [Italy]—d. Oct. 13, 1828, Milan) Italian Neoclassical poet, remembered chiefly for his translation of the *Iliad*.

Monti attended the University of Ferrara, then joined the Arcadian Academy (a Neoclassical group) in 1775. Three years later he went to Rome, where as secretary to the pope's nephew he was equivalent to court poet to Pius VI. After his invasion of Italy, Napoleon appointed Monti professor of poetry at the University of Pavia.

Monti's writings include love poetry, three tragedies, works about language, and a translation from Voltaire. Of his topical works the finest is "Al signor di Montgolfier," a beautifully written description of a historic balloon ascension in 1783. His masterpiece, written in fine blank verse, is the *Iliade* (1810), which remains one of the greatest achievements of the Neoclassical age.

Montreal group \‚män-trē-'ól, ‚mən-\ Coterie of poets who during the 1920s and '30s advocated a break with the traditional picturesque landscape poetry that had dominated Canadian poetry since the late 19th century. They encouraged an emulation of the realistic themes, metaphysical complexity, and techniques of the American and British poets Ezra Pound, T.S. Eliot, and W.H. Auden. Based in Montreal, then Canada's most cosmopolitan city, the group included A.M. Klein, A.J.M. Smith, Leo Kennedy, and Francis Reginald Scott, as well as two kindred spirits from Toronto, E.J. Pratt and Robert Finch. First brought together at McGill University in Montreal, the poets founded the *Canadian Mercury* (1928–29), a literary organ for young writers, and subsequently founded, edited, and wrote for a number of other influential journals, including the *McGill Fortnightly Review* and *Canadian Forum*.

Mont-Saint-Michel and Chartres \môⁿ-saⁿ-mē-'shel . . . 'shärt-rə\ Extended essay by Henry ADAMS, printed privately in 1904 and commercially in 1913. It is subtitled *A Study of Thirteenth-Century Unity*.

Mont-Saint-Michel and Chartres is best considered a companion to the author's autobiography, *The Education of Henry Adams* (1918). In *Chartres*, he described the medieval world view as reflected in its cathedrals, which he believed expressed "an emotion, the deepest man ever felt—the struggle of his own littleness to grasp the infinite." Adams was drawn to the ideological unity expressed in Roman Catholicism and symbolized by the Virgin Mary; he contrasted this coherence with the uncertainties of the 20th century.

monument \'män-yə-mənt\ A written tribute or a testimonial.

Moon and Sixpence, The Novel by W. Somerset MAUGHAM, published in 1919. It was loosely based on the life of French artist Paul Gauguin.

The novel's hero, Charles Strickland, is a London stockbroker who renounces his wife, children, and business in order to paint. In Paris, Strickland woos and wins a friend's wife away just so that he can paint her; when she kills herself, he is seemingly unaffected but leaves Paris, later settling in Tahiti with a young native woman. Eventually he dies of leprosy.

Moon for the Misbegotten, A Drama in four acts by Eugene O'NEILL, written in 1943 and published in 1952. It was first performed in New York City posthumously in 1957.

This sequel to O'Neill's masterpiece, *Long Day's Journey into Night*, is set on the Tyrones' Connecticut farm, which has been leased to bullying widower Phil Hogan. Hogan's daughter Josie loves Jim Tyrone, Jr., an alcoholic actor who has come back to the farm after his mother's death. To secure his hold on the farm, Hogan convinces Josie that Jim intends to sell it; he encourages Josie to seduce Jim and force a marriage proposal. Jim spurns her advances, reassures her that he is not going to sell the farm, and confesses that he had been too drunk to attend his mother's funeral. They part, for Josie realizes that Jim lives in misery and that he longs for deliverance in death.

Moonstone, The One of the first English detective novels, written by Wilkie COLLINS and published in 1868.

A debased Englishman steals the moonstone, a sacred gem, from India. It brings bad luck to each of its English possessors. When the gem disappears from a young Englishwoman's room and three sinister Hindus menace her family, the careful, methodical SERGEANT CUFF is assigned to the case.

Several features of *The Moonstone* were to become conventions of the detective story. The reader has all clues before the crime is solved, yet the solution comes as a complete surprise. Several different persons are plausibly suspected of theft. The plot features red herrings, false alibis, suspicious behavior, and thrilling scenes. Collins enhanced the novel's complexity by telling it through several different narrators.

Moore \'mùr, 'mòr\, Brian (b. Aug. 25, 1921, Belfast, N.Ire.) Irish novelist who immigrated to Canada and is best known for his first novel, THE LONELY PASSION OF JUDITH HEARNE (1955).

Moore arrived in Canada in 1948 and wrote for the *Montreal Gazette*. The novel *Judith Hearne* deals with an aging spinster whose crumbling pretensions to gentility are gradually dissolved in alcoholism. *The Feast of Lupercal* (1957) concerns a bachelor schoolteacher, THE LUCK OF GINGER COFFEY (1960) portrays a middle-aged Irish failure who immigrates to Canada to charm his way to fortune, and *The Emperor of Ice Cream* (1965) deals with a boy who is shocked into manhood by the bombing of Belfast in World War II. Among the more impressive of his later novels are *The Doctor's Wife* (1976), *The Color of Blood* (1987), and *Lies of Silence* (1990).

Moore \'mùr, 'mòr\, Clement Clarke (b. July 15, 1779, New York, N.Y., U.S.—d. July 10, 1863, Newport, R.I.) American scholar, now chiefly remembered for the ballad that begins " 'Twas the night before Christmas."

Moore, who was professor of Oriental and Greek literature at the General Theological Seminary, is said to have composed A VISIT FROM ST. NICHOLAS to amuse his children on Christmas 1822, but, unknown to him, a houseguest copied it and gave it to the press. It was first published anonymously in the *Troy* (N.Y.) *Sentinel*, Dec. 23, 1823.

Moore \'mùr, 'mòr\, George (Augustus) (b. Feb. 24, 1852, Ballyglass, County Mayo, Ire.—d. Jan. 21, 1933, London, Eng.) Irish novelist and man of letters who was considered an innovator in fiction in his day.

When he was 18, Moore left Ireland for Paris to become a painter. His *Reminiscences of the Impressionist Painters* (1906) and *Confessions of a Young Man* (1888) are accounts of his years in Paris.

Deciding that he had no talent for painting, he returned to London in 1882 to write. His first novels, *A Modern Lover* (1883) and *A Mummer's Wife* (1885), introduced a new note of French naturalism into the English scene, and he later adopted realism. *Esther Waters* (1894), his best novel, is a story of hardship and humiliation illumined by the novelist's compassion. It was an immediate success, and he followed it with *Evelyn Innes* (1898) and *Sister Teresa* (1901).

In 1901 Moore moved to Dublin, where he contributed notably to the planning of the Abbey Theatre. He also produced a volume of short stories, *The Untilled Field* (1903), and a short poetic novel, *The Lake* (1905), but the real fruits of his stay in Ireland are the volumes of his trilogy *Hail and Farewell— Ave*, 1911; *Salve*, 1912; *Vale*, 1914.

Moore returned to England in 1911. Aiming at epic effect, he produced *The Brook Kerith* (1916), an elaborate and stylish retelling of the Gospel story. His other works include *A Story-Teller's Holiday* (1918), *Conversations in Ebury Street* (1924),

The Pastoral Loves of Daphnis and Chloe (1924), and *Ulick and Soracha* (1926).

Moore \'mȯr, 'mu̇r\, Marianne, *in full* Marianne Craig Moore (b. Nov. 15, 1887, St. Louis, Mo., U.S.—d. Feb. 5, 1972, New

Imogen Cunningham

York, N.Y.) American poet whose work distilled moral and intellectual insights from the close and accurate observation of objective detail. Extremely disciplined in her craft, Moore won the admiration of fellow poets throughout her long career.

Moore graduated in 1909 from Bryn Mawr College (in Pennsylvania). After 1919, living in Brooklyn, N.Y., she devoted herself to writing, contributing poetry and criticism to many journals in the United States and England.

In 1921 her first book, *Poems*, was published in London. Her first American volume was titled *Observations* (1924). These initial collections exhibited Moore's conciseness and her creation of a mosaic of juxtaposed images leading unerringly to a conclusion that, at its best, is both surprising and inevitable. They contain some of her best-known poems, including "To a Steam Roller," "The Fish," "When I Buy Pictures," "Peter," "The Labors of Hercules," and POETRY. The last named is the source of her often-quoted admonition that poets should present imaginary gardens with real toads in them.

In 1925—already well known as one of the leading new poets—she became acting editor of *The Dial*, an influential American journal of literature and arts, and she served in the position until the journal was discontinued in 1929. Her *Collected Poems* appeared in 1951. She also published a translation of *The Fables of La Fontaine* (1954); a volume of critical papers, *Predilections* (1955); and *Idiosyncrasy and Technique: Two Lectures* (1958).

Moore \'mu̇r, 'mȯr\, Nicholas (b. Nov. 16, 1918, Cambridge, Cambridgeshire, Eng.) English poet of the New Apocalypse, a Neoromantic movement of the 1940s.

The son of classicist and Cambridge philosopher G.E. Moore, the young Moore published an important literary review, *Seven* (1938–40), while a Cambridge undergraduate. Most of his work was published in the war years: *The Island and the Cattle* (1941), *A Wish in Season* (1941), *The Cabaret, the Dancer, the Gentleman* (1942), and *The Glass Tower* (1944). *Recollections of the Gala: Selected Poems, 1943–1948* appeared in 1950. After editing poetry magazines in London, he became a horticulturist and wrote very little else until 1963. His *Resolution and Identity* (1970) was published in a limited edition. In *Spleen* (1975), Moore presents 30 variations on one of Charles Baudelaire's famous poems of the same name from *Les Fleurs du mal.*

Moore \'mu̇r, 'mȯr\, Thomas (b. May 28, 1779, Dublin, Ire.—d. Feb. 25, 1852, Wiltshire, Eng.) Irish poet, satirist, composer, and musician.

Moore's major poetic work, *Irish Melodies* (1807–34), contained such titles as "The Last Rose of Summer" and "Believe Me If All Those Endearing Young Charms." The *Melodies,* a group of 130 poems set to the music of Moore and of Sir John Stevenson aroused sympathy and support for the Irish nationalists.

Lalla Rookh (1817), a narrative poem set in an atmosphere of Oriental splendor, gave Moore a reputation among his contemporaries rivaling that of Lord Byron and Sir Walter Scott; it was perhaps the most translated poem of its time. Moore also wrote satirical works, including *The Fudge Family in Paris* (1818).

In 1824 Moore became a participant in one of the most notorious episodes of the Romantic period. He was the recipient of his friend Byron's memoirs, but he and the publisher John Murray burned them, presumably to protect Byron. Moore later brought out the *Letters and Journals of Lord Byron* (1830), in which he included a life of the poet.

mora \'mȯr-ə\ *plural* morae \'mȯr-ē, -ī\ *or* moras [Latin, lapse of time, delay] **1.** The minimal unit of quantitative measure in temporal prosodic systems. The mora is equivalent in time value to an average short syllable. **2.** A unit used in linguistic analysis, especially with reference to vowel length or syllable weight. A syllable ending in a short vowel has the value of one mora, whereas a syllable ending in a long vowel, a diphthong, or a consonant has the value of two morae.

morality play *also called* morality. An allegorical play popular in Europe especially during the 15th and 16th centuries, in which the characters personify moral qualities (such as charity or vice) or abstractions (as death or youth) and in which moral lessons are taught.

With the MYSTERY PLAY and the MIRACLE PLAY, the morality play is one of three main kinds of vernacular drama of the European Middle Ages. The action of the morality play centers on a hero, such as Mankind, whose inherent weaknesses are assaulted by such personified diabolic forces as the Seven Deadly Sins but who may choose redemption and enlist the aid of such figures as the Four Daughters of God (Mercy, Justice, Temperance, and Truth).

Morality plays were a step in the transition from liturgical to professional secular drama and combine elements of each. They were performed by quasi-professional groups of actors who relied on public support; thus the plays were usually short, their serious themes tempered by elements of farce.

The most famous of the French morality plays is Nicolas de la Chesnaye's *Condemnation des banquets* (1507), which argues for moderation by showing the bad end that awaits a company of unrepentant revelers, including Gluttony and Watering Mouth. Among the oldest of morality plays surviving in English is *The Castle of Perseverance* (c. 1425), about the battle for the soul of Humanum Genus. Of all morality plays, EVERYMAN is considered the greatest and is still performed.

Morand \mȯ-'räⁿ\, Paul (b. March 13, 1888, Paris, Fr.—d. July 24, 1976, Paris) French diplomat and novelist.

Morand joined the diplomatic service in 1912, serving as attaché in London, Rome, Madrid, and Siam (Thailand). In his early fiction, *Ouvert la nuit* (1922; *Open All Night*), *Fermé la nuit* (1923; *Closed All Night*), and *Lewis et Irène* (1924; *Lewis and Irene*), he borrowed the cinematic techniques of rapid scene changing, capturing the feverish atmosphere of the 1920s. Later he wrote several collections of short stories and such novels as *L'Homme pressé* (1941; "The Harried Man"), *Le Flagellant de Seville* (1951; "The Flagellant of Seville"), and *Tais-toi* (1965; "Be Quiet"). He also wrote biographies, most notably *Ci-git Sophie Dorothée de Celle* (1968; *The Captive Princess: Sophia Dorothea of Celle*), as well as impressionistic accounts of cities he had visited. He was admitted to the Académie Française in 1968.

Morante \mȯ-'rän-tā\, Elsa (b. Aug. 18, 1918, Rome, Italy—d. Nov. 25, 1985, Rome) Italian novelist, short-story writer, and poet who was known for the epic and mythical quality of her works.

Morante's formal education was incomplete, but her marriage to the novelist Alberto Moravia brought her into association with the leading Italian writers of the day. Her highly acclaimed first novel, *Menzogna e sortilegio* (1948; *House of Liars*), recounts the complex history of a southern Italian family. Morante's next novel, *L'isola di Arturo* (1957; *Arturo's Island*), examines a boy's growth from childhood dreams to the disillusionment of adulthood. Her popular novel *La storia* (1974; HISTORY) depicts the life of a simple, half-Jewish teacher and her son, born of a rape by a German soldier.

Morante also published a volume of short stories, *Lo scialle andaluso* (1963; "The Andalusian Shawl"); a volume of essays, *Il gioco secreto* (1941; "The Secret Game"); and two collections of poetry, *Alibi* (1958) and *Il mondo salvato dai ragazzini* (1968; "The World Saved by Little Children").

Moravia \mō-ˈräv-yä\, Alberto, *pseudonym of* Alberto Pincherle \ˈpēn-ker-lä\ (b. Nov. 28, 1907, Rome, Italy—d. Sept. 26, 1990, Rome)   Italian journalist, short-story writer, and novelist known for his fictional portrayals of social alienation and loveless sexuality. He was a major figure in 20th-century Italian literature.

Moravia was a journalist for a time in Turin and a foreign correspondent in London. His first novel, *Gli indifferenti* (1929; *Time of Indifference*), is a scathingly realistic study of the moral corruption of a middle-class family. The book became a sensation. Moravia was officially censored by Benito Mussolini's fascists (1941), and his works were placed by the Vatican on the *Index librorum prohibitorum* ("Index of Forbidden Books").

Some of his more important novels are *Agostino* (1944; *Two Adolescents*); *La Romana* (1947; *The Woman of Rome*); *La disubbidienza* (1948; *Disobedience*); *Il conformista* (1951; *The Conformist*); *La ciociara* (1957; TWO WOMEN); and *La noia* (1960; *The Empty Canvas*). His books of short stories include *Racconti romani* (1954; *Roman Tales*), *Nuovi racconti romani* (1959; *More Roman Tales*), *Racconti di Alberto Moravia* (1968), *Il paradiso* (1970; "Paradise"), and *Boh* (1976; *The Voice of the Sea and Other Stories*). Moravia's views on literature and realism are expressed in a stimulating book of essays, *L'uomo come fine* (1963; *Man as an End*), and his autobiography, *Alberto Moravia's Life*, was published in 1990.

morceau \mȯr-ˈsō\ *plural* morceaux *same*\ *or* morceaus \-ˈsōz\ [French, piece, morsel]   A short literary or musical piece.

More \ˈmȯr\, Hannah (b. Feb. 2, 1745, Stapleton, Gloucestershire, Eng.—d. Sept. 7, 1833, Bristol, Gloucestershire)   English religious writer, best known as a writer of popular tracts and as an educator of the poor.

As a young woman with literary aspirations, More made the first of her visits to London and was befriended by David Garrick, who produced her plays (*The Inflexible Captive*, 1775; *Percy*, 1777). Later, from her cottage in Somerset, she began to admonish society in a series of treatises beginning with *Thoughts on the Importance of the Manners of the Great to General Society* (1788). In the climate of alarm over the French Revolution, her fresh and forceful defense of traditional values met with strong approval.

Village Politics (1792; under the pseudonym of Will Chip), written to counteract Thomas Paine's *Rights of Man*, was so successful that it led to the production of a series of "Cheap Repository Tracts." Her final popular success as a writer was the didactic novel *Coelebs in Search of a Wife* (1808). The feminist movement in the second half of the 20th century revived interest in her *Strictures on the Modern System of Female Education*, 2 vol. (1799; reissued, edited by Gina Luria, 1974). *See also* BLUESTOCKING.

More \ˈmȯr\, Paul Elmer (b. Dec. 12, 1864, St. Louis, Mo., U.S.—d. March 9, 1937, Princeton, N.J.)   American scholar and conservative critic, one of the leading exponents of the New Humanism in literary criticism.

More was educated at Washington University, St. Louis, Mo., and at Harvard, where he met Irving Babbitt. He taught at Bryn Mawr College, Bryn Mawr, Pa., and was also a literary editor. Like Babbitt, his associate and fellow leader of the New Humanists, More was an uncompromising advocate of traditional critical standards and classical restraint.

More's best-known work is his *Shelburne Essays*, 11 vol. (1904–21), a collection of articles and reviews. Also notable are *Platonism* (1917), *The Religion of Plato* (1921), *Hellenistic Philosophies* (1923), *New Shelburne Essays* (1928–36), and his autobiography, *Pages from an Oxford Diary* (1937). His monumental *Greek Tradition*, 5 vol. (1924–31), is generally thought to be his finest work.

Moréas \mō-rä-ˈäs\, Jean, *pseudonym of* Yánnis Papadiamantópoulos \pä-pä-ᵗhē-ä-män-ˈtō-pü-lōs\ (b. April 15, 1856, Athens, Greece—d. March 31, 1910, Paris, Fr.)   Greek-born poet who played a leading part in the French Symbolist movement.

Moréas moved to Paris in 1879, becoming a familiar figure in literary circles. He published two manifestos that helped establish the name Symbolism for the movement that was replacing Decadence, and in 1886 he founded the periodical *Le Symbolist*.

Having published a volume of verse in both Greek and French in 1878, Moréas produced his first wholly French volumes, *Les Syrtes* (1884) and *Les Cantilènes* (1886). In 1891 Moréas called for a return to the spirit of classicism; he founded the *école romane* ("Roman school") and reverted to classical forms and subject matter. *Énone au clair visage* (1893) and *Eriphyle* (1894) are representative of his work during this period. His verse play *Iphigénie à Aulide* (1903), based on a play by Euripides, met with considerable success. Moréas' last work, *Les Stances* (1899–1920), chronicles his intellectual development.

Morel   *see* Eustache DESCHAMPS.

Moreto \mō-ˈrä-tō\, Agustín, *surname in full* Moreto y Cabaña \ē-kä-ˈbän-yä\ (baptized April 9, 1618, Madrid, Spain—d. Oct. 26/27, 1669, Toledo)   Spanish dramatist who, in his time, was considered the equal of his great near-contemporary Lope de Vega. His reputation, however, has steadily diminished over the years.

Moreto wrote plays with remarkable ease, turning out more than 100 dramas that brought him great popular success. His masterpiece, *El desdén con el desdén* ("Contempt with Contempt"), based on parts of four plays of Lope de Vega, is marked, as are all his best plays, by its elegance and faithfulness to real life. Moreto took minor orders in 1642 and entered a monastery in 1659.

Moretti \mō-ˈret-tē\, Marino (b. July 18, 1885, Cesenatico, Italy—d. July 6, 1979, Cesenatico)   Italian poet and prose writer who was a leader of the Crepuscolarismo movement in the early 20th century.

In 1910 Moretti published his first major collection, *Poesie scritte col lapis* ("Poems Written With a Pencil"), and he was the subject of a landmark essay by Giuseppe Borgese on Crepuscolarismo. His poetry—focused on rural life, remembered youth, and simple pleasures—appeared in such collections as *I poemetti di Marino* (1913; "Marino's Little Poems") and *Il giardino dei frutti* (1916; "The Garden of Fruits"). For more than five decades he concentrated on prose writing and on the revision of his early verse, returning to poetry only with the publication of *L'ultima estate* (1969; "The Last Summer"). Other late collections include *Tre anni e un giorno* (1971; "Three Years and a Day"), *Le poverazze* (1973; "The Mollusks"), and *Diario senza le date* (1974; "Diary Without Dates"). Notable novels include *Il sole del sabato* (1907; "Saturday Sun"), *La voce di Dio* (1921; "The Voice of God"), and *La vedova Fiorvanti* (1941; "The Widow Fiorvanti").

Morgan \'mȯr-gən\, Charles Langbridge (b. Jan. 22, 1894, Bromley, Kent, Eng.—d. Feb. 6, 1958, London) English novelist, playwright, and critic, a distinguished writer of a refined prose who stood apart from the main literary trends of his time.

Morgan entered the Royal Navy in 1907; his first novel, *The Gunroom* (1919), concerns the mistreatment of midshipmen. He worked on the editorial staff of *The Times* of London until the outbreak of World War II, during which he served with the Admiralty.

In *My Name Is Legion* (1925), he reveals a preoccupation with the conflict between the spirit and the flesh and a predilection for a form of secular mysticism. Subsequent novels include *Portrait in a Mirror* (1929), *The Fountain* (1932), *Sparkenbrooke* (1936), *The Voyage* (1940), *The Empty Room* (1941), and *The Judge's Story* (1947). Morgan also wrote three successful plays—*The Flashing Stream* (1938), *The River Line* (1949), and *The Burning Glass* (1953).

Morgan \'mȯr-gən\, Lady Sydney, *original surname* Owenson \'ō-wən-sən\ (b. Dec. 25, 1776, Dublin, Ire.—d. April 16, 1859, London, Eng.) Anglo-Irish novelist who is remembered more for her personality than for her many successful books.

Morgan became established and was lionized as a popular novelist with *The Wild Irish Girl* (1806), a paean of praise to Ireland. After her marriage to Thomas (afterward Sir Thomas) Morgan, she continued to write novels, verse, and essays. *O'Donnel* (1814), considered her best novel for its realistic treatment of Irish peasant life, was followed by *France* (1817), a survey of French society and politics. The success of *France* brought her a request to write a similar account of Italy, which was published in 1821. In 1839 Morgan moved to London, where she eventually gave up writing.

Morgan le Fay \'mȯr-gən-lə-'fā\ Fairy enchantress of ARTHURIAN LEGEND and romance.

Geoffrey of Monmouth's *Vita Merlini* (c. 1150) names her as the ruler of Avalon, a marvelous island where King Arthur was to be healed of his wounds, and it describes her as skilled in the arts of healing and of changing shape. In Chrétien de Troyes's romance *Erec* (c. 1165), she first appears as King Arthur's sister. In 12th- and 13th-century elaborations of Arthurian legend, two themes, of healing and of hostility (owing to unrequited love), were developed: in the early 13th-century Vulgate cycle, for example, Morgan le Fay is responsible for stirring up trouble between Arthur and his queen, Guinevere, yet finally appears as a beneficent figure conveying Arthur to Avalon. Her magic powers are said to have been learned from books and from the enchanter Merlin. Although later versions of the legend place Arthur's death in a Christian context, traditions of a living Arthur being tended by Morgan le Fay (until the time should come for him to return to his kingdom) survive in some 13th- and 14th-century texts.

Morgan, Hank \'haŋk-'mȯr-gən\ Fictional character, the pragmatic protagonist of A CONNECTICUT YANKEE IN KING ARTHUR'S COURT by Mark Twain.

Morgenstern \'mȯr-gən-ˌshtern\, Christian (b. May 6, 1871, Munich, Ger.—d. March 31, 1914, Meran, South Tirol, Austro-Hungarian Empire [now Merano, Italy]) German poet and humorist whose work ranged from the mystical and personally lyrical to nonsense verse.

Morgenstern lived for a time in Norway, where he translated works by such playwrights as Henrik Ibsen, Bjørnstjerne Bjørnson, Knut Hamsun, and August Strindberg. His serious poetry includes *In Phantas Schloss* (1895; "In Phanta's Palace"), *Ich und die Welt* (1898; "I and the World"), *Ein Sommer* (1900; "One Summer"), *Einkehr* (1910; "Introspection"), and *Wir fanden einen Pfad* (1914; "We Found a Path"). His international reputation came from his nonsense verse, including *Galgenlieder* (1905; "Gallows Songs"), *Palmström* (1910), and three volumes published posthumously: *Palma Kunkel* (1916), *Der Gingganz* (1919), and *Die Schallmühle* (1928; "The Noise Mill"), all collected in *Alle Galgenlieder* (1932).

Mori Ōgai \'mō-rē-'ō-ˌgī\, *pseudonym of* Mori Rintarō \'rēn-tä-ˌrō\ (b. Feb. 17, 1862, Tsuwano, Japan—d. July 9, 1922, Tokyo) One of the creators of modern Japanese literature.

The son of a physician of the aristocratic warrior (samurai) class, Ōgai studied medicine in Tokyo and Germany. In 1890 he published the story "Maihime" ("The Dancing Girl"), an account closely based on his own attachment to a German girl. It represented a marked departure from the impersonal fiction of preceding generations and initiated a vogue for autobiographical revelations. Ōgai's most popular novel, *Gan* (1911–13; part of which was translated as *The Wild Goose*), is a story of undeclared love. After 1912 Ōgai abandoned fiction in favor of historical works depicting the samurai code.

Moriarty, Professor \ˌmȯr-ē-'är-tē\ Archcriminal nemesis of Sherlock Holmes in several detective stories and novels by Sir Arthur Conan DOYLE.

Móricz \'mō-rēts\, Zsigmond (b. June 29, 1879, Csécse, Hung., Austro-Hungarian Empire—d. Sept. 4, 1942, Budapest) Hungarian realist novelist who wrote of country towns.

While working as a journalist, Móricz published his first story (1908) in the review *Nyugat* ("The West"), which he later came to edit. Of his many novels and short stories, his greatest works include his first novel, *Sárarany* (1910; "Gold in the Mire"), and *A boldog ember* (1935; "The Happy Man"). *Kivilágos kivirradtig* (1924; "Until the Small Hours of Morning") and *Rokonok* (1930; "Relatives") deal with the decadent nobility. Móricz evokes pure, even idyllic, love in *Légy jó mindhalálig* (1920; "Be Good Until Death"), often considered the finest book about children written in Hungarian, and in *Pillangó* (1925; "Butterfly"). He also wrote the vast historical novels *Erdély* (1922–35; "Transylvania") and *Rózsa Sándor* (1940–42).

Morier \'mȯr-ē-ər, -ē-ˌā\, James Justinian (b. *c.* 1780, Smyrna [now İzmir, Tur.]—d. March 19, 1849, Brighton, Sussex, Eng.) English diplomat and writer whose fame depends on *The Adventures of Hajji Baba of Ispahan* (1824), a picaresque romance of Persian life that long influenced English ideas of Persia. Its Persian translation (1905) led to the development of the modern Persian novel of social criticism.

Mörike \'mœ-rē-kə\, Eduard Friedrich (b. Sept. 8, 1804, Ludwigsburg, Württemberg [Germany]—d. June 4, 1875, Stuttgart) One of Germany's greatest lyric poets, sometimes ranked next to his master, J.W. von Goethe.

After studying theology at Tübingen (1822–26), Mörike held several curacies. In 1834 he became pastor of Cleversulzbach, the remote Württemberg village immortalized in *Der alte Turmhahn*. When only 39, Mörike retired on a pension, which he supplemented by lecturing on German literature.

The variety of Mörike's small output is astonishing. His novel, *Maler Nolten* (1832; "Painter Nolten"), explores the realm of the subconscious and the mysterious forces linking the main character and his early love even beyond the grave. Mörike's poems in folk-song style and his fairy tales show the influence of German Romanticism; his best folktale is *Das Stuttgarter Hutzelmännlein* (1853).

It is, however, as a lyric poet that Mörike was at the height of his powers. The "Peregrina" poems, immortalizing a youthful love of his Tübingen days, and the sonnets to Luise Rau, his onetime betrothed, are among the most exquisite German love lyrics.

Morison \\'mȯr-ə-sən, 'mär-\\, Samuel Eliot (b. July 9, 1887, Boston, Mass., U.S.—d. May 15, 1976, Boston)   American biographer and historian who re-created in vivid prose notable maritime stories of modern history.

Morison was educated at Harvard University and, after further study abroad, returned to teach at Harvard for 40 years. To give authenticity to his writing, Morison undertook numerous voyages himself, sailed the ocean routes followed by Christopher Columbus, and during wartime served on 12 ships as a commissioned officer in the U.S. Naval Reserve.

Morison's writings include *Maritime History of Massachusetts* (1921); *Admiral of the Ocean Sea* (1942), a biography of Columbus for which he was awarded a Pulitzer Prize; *John Paul Jones* (1959), which also received a Pulitzer; the 15-volume *History of U.S. Naval Operations in World War II* (1947–62); *The European Discovery of America: The Northern Voyages A.D. 500–1600* (1971); and *The European Discovery of America: The Southern Voyages A.D. 1492–1616* (1974).

Moritz \\'mō-rits\\, Karl Philipp (b. Sept. 15, 1757, Hameln, Hanover [Germany]—d. July 26, 1793, Berlin)   German novelist whose most important works are his two autobiographical novels, *Andreas Hartknopf* (1786) and *Anton Reiser*, 4 vol. (1785–90). The latter is, with J.W. von Goethe's *Wilhelm Meister*, the most mature 18th-century German novel of contemporary life. He was also an influential writer on aesthetics.

Moritz' family was very poor, but patrons helped him to study theology. After completing his studies he taught in Dessau and Potsdam and in a grammar school in Berlin, where he was briefly editor of the *Vossische Zeitung* (with which the dramatist and critic Gotthold Ephraim Lessing had been associated). In 1786 he traveled to Italy, where he met Goethe, whom he later advised on artistic theory. After his return to Berlin in 1789 he became professor of aesthetics and archaeology at the Academy of Arts.

Morland, Catherine \\'kath-ə-rin-'mȯr-lənd\\   Fictional character, the impressionable heroine of Jane Austen's novel NORTHANGER ABBEY. Catherine's view of the world is colored by her love of gothic stories until she learns the value of controlling her imagination.

Morley \\'mȯr-lē\\, Christopher (Darlington) (b. May 5, 1890, Haverford, Pa., U.S.—d. March 28, 1957, Roslyn Heights, Long Island, N.Y.)   American writer whose versatile works are lighthearted, vigorous displays of the English language.

Morley gained popularity with his literary columns in the *New York Evening Post* and the *Saturday Review of Literature* and from collections of essays and columns such as *Shandygaff* (1918). His novels include the innovative *The Trojan Horse* (1937), a combination of prose, verse, and dramatic dialogue that satirizes human devotion to luxury, and the sentimental best-seller *Kitty Foyle* (1939). *The Old Mandarin* (1947) is a collection of witty free verse. Morley also edited Bartlett's *Familiar Quotations* (1937; 1948).

Morpheus \\'mȯr-ˌfyüs, -fē-əs\\   In Greco-Roman mythology, one of the sons of Hypnos (Somnus), the god of sleep. Morpheus sends human shapes (Greek: *morphai*) of all kinds to the dreamer, while his brothers Phobetor (or Icelus) and Phantasus send the forms of animals and inanimate things, respectively.

Morrell \\'mər-əl, *commonly* mə-'rel\\, Lady Ottoline (Violet Anne), *original surname* Cavendish-Bentinck \\'kav-ən-ˌdish-'ben-tiŋk\\ (b. June 16, 1873, London, Eng.—d. April 21, 1938, Tunbridge Wells, Kent)   Hostess and patron of the arts who brought together some of the most important writers and artists of her day.

The daughter of a general, Morrell broke with her conventionally upper-class background as she formed her circle of artists and intellectuals, which included, among others, D.H. Lawrence, Virginia Woolf, Aldous Huxley, Bertrand Russell, and Augustus John. She and her husband lived in London from 1902 until 1913, when they settled at Garsington Manor, Oxfordshire. Posthumous collections of her writings include *Ottoline* (1963) and *Ottoline at Garsington: Memoirs 1915–18* (1974).

Morris \\'mȯr-əs, 'mär-\\, William (b. March 24, 1834, Walthamstow, near London, Eng.—d. Oct. 3, 1896, Hammersmith, near London)   English designer, poet, and early socialist, whose designs for furniture, wallpaper, and other decorative products generated the Arts and Crafts Movement. Through his friendship with the poet Dante Gabriel Rossetti, Morris was associated with the Pre-Raphaelite Brotherhood, whose interest in medieval subjects was reflected in Morris' poetry as well as his designs.

Morris attended Marlborough College and in 1853 went to Exeter College, Oxford. He took his degree in 1856, and that same year he financed the first 12 monthly issues of *The Oxford and Cambridge Magazine*, where he published many of the poems that were later reprinted in his remarkable THE DEFENCE OF GUENEVERE (1858).

After his marriage to Jane Burden in 1859, Morris commissioned his friend the architect Philip Webb to build what became known as the Red House at Bexleyheath. It was during the furnishing and decorating of this house by Morris and his friends that the idea came to them of founding an association of "fine art workmen." Morris then began creating the designs for which he became famous.

As a poet, he first achieved fame and success with the romantic narrative *The Life and Death of Jason* (1867). Other works of this period were *The Earthly Paradise* (1868–70), a series of narrative poems based on classical and medieval sources; the exquisitely illuminated *Book of Verse* (1870); and his principal poetic achievement, the epic *Story of Sigurd the Volsung and the Fall of the Niblungs* (1876), written after a prolonged study of the Old Norse sagas.

The Morris family moved into Kelmscott House at Hammersmith in 1878. Several years later William became an active socialist; he formed the Socialist League, with its own publication, *The Commonweal*. There his two finest romances—A DREAM OF JOHN BALL (1888) and NEWS FROM NOWHERE (1890), an idyllic vision of a rural socialist utopia—appeared. Subsequently, he founded the Hammersmith Socialist Society.

Morris founded the Kelmscott Press in 1891, and between that year and 1898 it produced 53 titles in 66 volumes. He designed three typestyles for his press, including Geoffrey Chaucer type, in which *The Works of Geoffrey Chaucer* was printed during the last years of Morris' life. One of the greatest examples of the art of the printed book, *Chaucer* is the most highly decorated of the Kelmscott publications.

Morris \\'mȯr-əs, 'mär-\\, Wright (Marion) (b. Jan. 6, 1910, Central City, Neb., U.S.)   American novelist who portrayed the frustration of contemporary life and sought to recapture the American past.

Morris' journeys to see America during the 1920s and '30s led to his first novel, *My Uncle Dudley* (1942), in which a group of people travel across country by car. Morris' other novels include *The Field of Vision* (1956) and *Ceremony in Lone Tree* (1960), books that describe the failed lives of a number of people from a small Midwestern town; the paired novels, *Fire Sermon* (1971) and *A Life* (1973); *The Fork River Space Project* (1977); and *Plains Song, for Female Voices* (1980). Morris also wrote books of nonfiction, including the essay collections *About Fiction* (1975) and *Earthly Delights, Unearthly Adornments* (1978), and several memoirs.

Morris-Jones \'môr-əs-'jōnz, 'mär-\, Sir John, *original name* (until 1918) John Jones (b. Oct. 17, 1864, Llandrygarn, Anglesey, Wales—d. April 16, 1929, Bangor, Caernarvonshire) Teacher, scholar, poet, and linguist who revolutionized Welsh literature and helped restore to Welsh poetry its classical standards.

Jones determined early that he would devote all his time to Welsh language and literature. After graduation from the University of Oxford, he became the first professor of Welsh at the University College of North Wales, Bangor. When he was knighted in 1918, he began styling himself Morris-Jones.

His works include *A Welsh Grammar, Historical and Comparative* (1913), *Cerdd Dafod* (1925; "The Art of Poetry"), *Orgraff yr Iaith Gymraeg* (1928; "The Orthography of the Welsh Language"), and an unfinished study of syntax (1931), published posthumously under the title *Welsh Syntax*. His grammar, though out-of-date in many respects, is still useful and is unlikely to be superseded.

Morrison \'môr-ə-sən, 'mär-\, Arthur (b. Nov. 1, 1863, Kent, Eng.—d. Dec. 4, 1945, Chalfont St. Peter, Buckinghamshire) English writer noted for novels and short stories describing slum life so vividly that they helped bring about changes in British housing legislation.

Morrison began his career as a journalist. He wrote for many of the notable London journals of his time, including the *National Observer*, in which most of the stories in his first major work, *Tales of Mean Streets* (1894), originally appeared. His next important publication was *A Child of the Jago* (1896), a novel credited with precipitating the clearance of the worst London slum of that time. He also wrote detective fiction that featured the lawyer-detective Martin Hewitt. An authority on and collector of Chinese and Japanese art, Morrison also published the authoritative *Painters of Japan* (1911).

Morrison \'môr-ə-sən, 'mär-\, Toni, *original name* Chloe Anthony Wofford \'wäf-ərd\ (b. Feb. 18, 1931, Lorain, Ohio, U.S.) African-American writer noted for her examination of the black experience, particularly the experience of women within the black community. She received the Nobel Prize for Literature in 1993.

Morrison grew up in the Midwest. She attended Howard University in Washington, D.C., and Cornell University in Ithaca, New York. After teaching at Texas Southern University, she taught at Howard for several years. In 1965 she became an editor for a publishing house, also continuing to teach at two branches of the State University of New York.

Her first book, THE BLUEST EYE (1970), is a novel of initiation. In 1973 a second novel, SULA, was

James Keyser

published; it examines (among other issues) the dynamics of friendship and the expectations for conformity within the black community. Morrison used a male narrator for the first time in *Song of Solomon* (1977); its publication brought Morrison to national attention. In 1981 *Tar Baby* was published, and the Pulitzer Prize-winning BELOVED appeared in 1987. Another novel, *Jazz*, and a work of criticism, *Playing in the Dark: Whiteness and the Literary Imagination*, were published in 1992. Morrison's use of fantasy and myth, mastery of ambiguity, and sinuous poetic style gave her works great strength and texture.

Morsztyn \'môr-shtin\, Jan Andrzej (b. *c.* 1613, near Sandomierz [Poland]—d. Jan. 8, 1693, Châteauvillain, Fr.) Polish Baroque poet and diplomat.

Morsztyn was a courtier of Władysław IV and John-Casimir, kings of Poland. He later became leader of the opposition during the reign of John III Sobieski (1674–96) and an agent of King Louis XIV in Poland. As the Count de Châteauvillain, Morsztyn was an émigré in France. He had a lively interest in literature and translated Italian and French poetry and drama into Polish, including Pierre Corneille's *Le Cid*. Throughout his life he wrote short poems, rhymed letters to his friends, and witty epigrams—all gathered in two collections: *Kanikuła albo psia gwiazda* (1647; "The Dog Star") and *Lutnia* (1661; "Lute"). Published for the first time in the 19th century, they secured Morsztyn's place in Polish literature.

Morte Darthur, Le \lə-'môrt-där-'tür, ˌmôrt-'där-thər\ The first account of the Arthurian legend in modern English prose, completed by Sir Thomas MALORY in about 1470 and printed by William Caxton in 1485. The only extant manuscript that predates Caxton's edition is in the British Library, London. The work retells the adventures of the knights of the Round Table in chronological sequence from the birth of Arthur. Based on French romances, Malory's account differs from his models in its emphasis on the brotherhood of the knights rather than on courtly love and on the conflicts of loyalty (brought about by the adultery of Lancelot and Guinevere) that finally destroy the fellowship. *See also* ARTHURIAN LEGEND.

Mortimer \'môr-ti-mər\, John (Clifford) (b. April 21, 1923, Hampstead, London, Eng.) English barrister and writer who wrote plays for the stage, television, radio, and motion pictures, as well as novels.

Educated at Harrow and at Brasenose College, Oxford, Mortimer was called to the bar in 1948. His first novel was *Charade* (1947). Several subsequent novels drew on his legal experience, but it was not until 1957, with a production of his radio play *The Dock Brief*, that his reputation was established. Mortimer wrote many other radio plays and several plays for the stage, including *The Wrong Side of the Park* (performed 1960), *Two Stars for Comfort* (performed 1962), and *The Judge* (performed 1967). He later adapted for television several novels, including his own *Paradise Postponed* (1985; produced 1986) and *Summer's Lease* (1988; produced 1989). One of his finest works is an autobiographical play, *A Voyage Round My Father* (1970).

Throughout his writing career Mortimer maintained a thriving law practice. As a writer, he had his greatest popular success in the late 1970s and 1980s with *Rumpole of the Bailey* and other short stories and television programs that feature the crusty British barrister Horace RUMPOLE and his comical adventures as a defense lawyer.

Mortimer \'môr-ti-mər\, Penelope (Ruth), *original surname* Fletcher \'flech-ər\ (b. Sept. 19, 1918, Rhyl, Flintshire, Wales) British journalist and novelist noted for her compact style and for her depictions of a nightmarish world of neuroses and broken marriages.

After her graduation from the University of London, she began to write poetry, book reviews, and short stories. In 1949 she married the playwright John Mortimer (divorced 1972), with whom she collaborated on the book *Daddy's Gone A-Hunting* (1958). She is perhaps best known for her novel *The Pumpkin Eater* (1962), a story of a woman whose compulsive anxiety to bear children gradually isolates her from her successive husbands. Her other works of fiction include *Saturday Lunch with the Brownings* (1960; stories), *My Friend Says It's Bullet-Proof* (1967), *Long Distance* (1974), and *The Handyman* (1983).

Morus \'môr-is\, Huw, *also called* Eos Ceiriog \'ā-ôs-'kăr-yôg\ (b. 1622, Llangollen?, Denbighshire, Wales—d. August 1709, Llansilin, Denbighshire) One of the finest Welsh poets of the 17th century. Morus wrote during the period when the strict bardic meters were in decline and the free meters of popular poetry were on the rise. He elevated this poetry to new dignity by skillful craftsmanship. Structurally complicated, his works are distinguished by internal rhyme and consonance. Many of his love poems were influenced by the Cavalier poets of England and were easily adapted to popular tunes.

mosaic rhyme A type of multiple rhyme in which one word is made to rhyme with two or more words, as in the rhymes at the ends of the following two lines from W.S. Gilbert's song "The Modern Major-General":

About binomial theorem I'm teeming with a lot o' news,
With interesting facts about the square of the hypotenuse.

Moscherosch \'môsh-ə-ˌrôsh\, Johann Michael, *pseudonym* Philander von Sittewald \fôn-'zit-ə-ˌvält\ (b. March 5, 1601, Willstädt, near Strassburg [now Strasbourg, France]—d. April 4, 1669, Worms [Germany]) German Lutheran satirist whose writings graphically describe life in a Germany ravaged by the Thirty Years' War (1618–48).

Moscherosch was educated at Strassburg, served as a tutor, and held various government offices. His most famous work, *Wunderliche und wahrhafftige Gesichte Philanders von Sittewald* (1641–43; "Peculiar and True Visions of Philander von Sittewald"), lampoons the customs and culture of his day. Almost of equal excellence is the *Insomnis Cura Parentum* (1643), a religious work addressed to his family. Moscherosch was also a member of the Fruchtbringende Gesellschaft ("Productive Society"), founded for the purification of the German language and the fostering of German literature.

Moschus \'mäs-kəs\ or **Moschos** \'môs-ḳôs\ of Syracuse (fl. *c.* 150 BC) Greek pastoral poet of Syracuse, in Sicily. He is said to have been a student of Aristarchus. Moschus' only surviving works are three short extracts from his *Bucolica*; the elegiac poem *Eros the Runaway Slave*, which treats Eros as a plowman; and a short epic poem (166 hexameters) entitled *Europa*. Other works, especially the *Lament for Bion* and *Megara*, are also ascribed to him, almost certainly incorrectly.

Moscow Art Academic Theater \'mäs-ˌkaủ, -ˌkō\, *also called* (until 1920) Moscow Art Theater, *Russian* Moskovsky Khudozhestvenny Akademichesky Teatr *or* Moskovsky Khudozhestvenny Teatr. Outstanding Russian theater specializing in naturalism, founded in 1898 by two teachers of dramatic art, Konstantin Stanislavsky and Vladimir Nemirovich-Danchenko. Its purpose was to establish a theater of new art forms. In 1932 Maksim Gorky's name was added to that of the theater.

The Moscow Art Theater opened with Aleksey Tolstoy's *Tsar Fyodor Ioannovich* in October 1898. For its fifth production it staged Anton Chekhov's *Chayka* (*The Seagull*), its first major success, and thus began a long artistic association with one of Russia's most celebrated playwrights.

Möser \'mœ-zər\, Justus (b. Dec. 14, 1720, Osnabrück, Münster [Germany]—d. Jan. 8, 1794, Osnabrück) German political essayist and poet who was a forerunner of the Sturm und Drang movement of rebellious young German writers.

Educated at the universities of Jena and Göttingen, Möser was named state's attorney at Osnabrück and from 1764 he was virtually head of the government there. In his collection of weekly papers, *Patriotischen Phantasien* (1774–76; "Patriotic Ideas"), he called for the national organic development of a state rather than a system of arbitrary laws imposed by a sovereign. Möser's *Osnabrücke Geschichte*, 2 vol. (1768; "History of Osnabrück"), was a pioneer work, showing the influence of folk traditions on a community. His complete writings are available in *Sämtliche Werke*, 10 vol. (1842–44; "Collected Works").

Moses \'mō-zəs\ of Khoren \'ḳō-ren\, *Armenian* Movses Khorenatzi \'môv-ses-ˌḳō-re-'nät-sē\ Author known as the father of Armenian literature. Traditionally believed to have lived in the 5th century, Moses has also been dated as late as the 9th century. Nothing is known of his life apart from alleged autobiographical details contained in the *History of Armenia*, which bears his name as author. His claims to have been the disciple of St. Sahak (Isaac) and St. Mesrob, to have studied in Edessa and Alexandria after the Council of Edessa (431), and to have been commissioned to write his *History* by the governor Sahak Bagratuni have been rejected by most serious scholars, in large part because of anachronisms in the text. His work, however, is a valuable record of earlier religious tradition in pre-Christian Armenia.

Mosley \'môz-lē, 'mäz-\, Nicholas, *in full* Sir Nicholas Mosley, 7th Baronet, *also called* (from 1966) Lord Ravensdale \'rā-vənz-ˌdāl\ (b. June 25, 1923, London, Eng.) British novelist whose work, often philosophical and Christian in theology, won critical but not popular praise.

Mosley graduated from Eton College, was an officer in the British Army during World War II, and studied at Balliol College, Oxford. His early novels, *Spaces of the Dark* (1951) and *The Rainbearers* (1955), are set in the period following World War II. Other novels include *Corruption* (1957), *Accident* (1965), and *Natalie Natalia* (1971). *Assassins* (1966) is an unorthodox political thriller. The six main characters of *Catastrophe Practice: Plays for Not Acting* (1979) appear in the interlinked but individual novels *Imago Bird* (1980), *Serpent* (1981), *Judith* (1986), and *Hopeful Monsters* (1990). Mosley also wrote nonfiction, including *The Assassination of Trotsky* (1972), first written as a screenplay; *Julian Grenfell: His Life and the Times of His Death 1888–1915* (1976); and family memoirs, *Rules of the Game* (1982) and *Beyond the Pale* (1983).

Mosley \'môz-lē\, Walter (b. 1952, Los Angeles, Calif., U.S.) African-American author of mystery stories noted for their realistic portrayals of segregated inner-city life.

Mosley attended Goddard College and Johnson State College, and he became a computer programmer before publishing his first novel, *Devil in a Blue Dress* (1990). Set in 1948, the novel introduces Ezekiel "Easy" Rawlins, an unwilling amateur detective from the Watts section of Los Angeles. Other novels featuring Rawlins include *A Red Death* (1991), *White Butterfly* (1992), and *Black Betty* (1994). In all of his novels Mosley used period detail and slang to create authentic settings and characters, especially the earnest, complex Rawlins, who continually is faced with personal, social, and moral dilemmas.

Moss \'môs\, Howard (b. Jan. 22, 1922, New York, N.Y., U.S.—d. Sept. 16, 1987, New York City) American poet and editor who was the poetry editor of *The New Yorker* magazine for almost 40 years.

Moss graduated from the University of Wisconsin in 1943 and published the first of 12 volumes of his poetry, *The Wound and the Weather*, in 1946. He joined the staff of *The New Yorker* in 1948, and throughout his tenure there he showcased the works and helped establish the careers of such poets as Sylvia Plath, Richard Wilbur, and Elizabeth Bishop. He won the National Book Award for his *Selected Poems* (1971). Moss also published volumes of criticism and was an accomplished playwright. His plays include *The Folding Green* (1958), *The Oedipus Mah-Jongg Scandal* (1968), and *The Palace at 4 A.M.* (1972).

Mosses from an Old Manse   Collection of short stories by Nathaniel HAWTHORNE, published in two volumes in 1846. Written while Hawthorne lived at the Old Manse in Concord, Mass., the home of Ralph Waldo Emerson's ancestors, the 25 tales and sketches include some of the author's finest short works. Many of the Romantic themes found in Hawthorne's longer fiction are addressed in the stories: for example, the conflict between reason and emotion in the gothic tales RAPPACCINI'S DAUGHTER and "The Birthmark," and between Puritan religion and the supernatural in YOUNG GOODMAN BROWN. Also noteworthy are the title essay describing the parsonage and ROGER MALVIN'S BURIAL, a historical tale.

Motes, Hazel \\'hā-zəl-'mōts\\   Fictional character, a fierce, Jesus-haunted man in Flannery O'Connor's darkly comic novel WISE BLOOD. The work's protagonist, Motes preaches nihilism and the pursuit of sin in his "Church Without Christ." Although at first he rejects conventional religion, he is obsessed with salvation and he eventually blinds himself in an act of atonement.

Mother Courage and Her Children   Play by Bertolt BRECHT, written in German as *Mutter Courage und ihre Kinder: Eine Chronik aus dem Dreissigjährigen Krieg*, produced in 1941 and published in 1949. Composed of 12 scenes, the work is a chronicle play of the Thirty Years' War and is based on the picaresque novel *Simplicissimus* (1669) by Hans Jakob Grimmelshausen. In 1949 Brecht staged *Mother Courage*, with music by Paul Dessau, in the Soviet sector of Berlin.

The plot revolves around a woman who depends on war for her personal survival and who is nicknamed Mother Courage for her coolness in safeguarding her merchandise under enemy fire. One by one her three children die, yet she continues her profiteering.

Mother Goose \\'məth-ər-'güs\\   Fictitious old woman, reputedly the source of the body of traditional children's songs and verses known as nursery rhymes. She is often pictured as a beak-nosed, sharp-chinned elderly woman riding on the back of a flying gander. Mother Goose was first associated with nursery rhymes in an early collection of "the most celebrated Songs and Lullabies of old British nurses," *Mother Goose's Melody; or, Sonnets for the Cradle* (1781), published by the successors of one of the first publishers of children's books, John Newbery. The oldest extant copy dates from 1791, but it is thought that an edition appeared, or was planned, as early as 1765, and it is likely that it was edited by Oliver Goldsmith, who may also have composed some of the verses. The Newbery firm seems to have derived the name "Mother Goose" from the title of Charles Perrault's fairy tales, *Contes de ma mère l'oye* (1697; *Tales of Mother Goose*), a French folk expression roughly equivalent to "old wives' tales."

The persistent legend that Mother Goose was an actual Boston woman is false. The first U.S. edition of Mother Goose rhymes was a 1785 reprint of the Newbery edition.

Mother of Us All, The   Opera in two acts with libretto by American writer Gertrude STEIN and music by American composer Virgil Thomson, first performed and published in 1947. The opera concerns the woman suffrage movement of 19th-century America, as exemplified in the life and work of American suffragist and feminist Susan B. Anthony.

motif \\mō-'tēf\\ [French, from Italian *motivo* musical motif, subject of a painting, reason, cause, from Medieval Latin *motivum* motive, impulse, reason]   A usually recurring salient thematic element, especially a dominant idea or central theme.

Moto, Mr. \\'mō-tō\\   Fictional Japanese detective and secret agent created by American novelist J.P. MARQUAND in *No Hero* (1935). Mr. Moto also was the leading character in five later Marquand mysteries.

An aristocratic, well-educated secret agent, Mr. Moto is short, thin, well-dressed, and well-groomed, with a gold tooth. He is also an astute judge of character and recognizes and respects in an enemy agent the qualities that he values and possesses himself (such as courage, patriotism, and dedication to duty). The books in the series are *Thank You, Mr. Moto* (1936), *Think Fast, Mr. Moto* (1937), *Mr. Moto Is So Sorry* (1938), *Last Laugh, Mr. Moto* (1942), and *Stopover: Tokyo* (1957).

motto \\'mät-ō\\ *plural* mottoes *or* mottos [Italian, saying, word]   A short, usually quoted, passage placed at the beginning of a literary work (such as a novel, essay, or poem) or one of its divisions (such as a chapter or canto) and intended to suggest the subject matter that follows. *Compare* EPIGRAPH.

Mourning Becomes Electra \\i-'lek-trə\\   Trilogy of plays by Eugene O'NEILL, produced and published in 1931. The trilogy, consisting of *Homecoming*, *The Hunted*, and *The Haunted*, was modeled on the *Oresteia* trilogy of Aeschylus and represents O'Neill's most complete use of Greek forms, themes, and characters. O'Neill set his trilogy in the New England of the American Civil War period.

Mourning Bride, The   Tragedy in five acts by William CONGREVE, produced and published in 1697. It is the source of the lines "Music has charms to soothe a savage breast" and "Heav'n has no rage, like love to hatred turn'd,/Nor Hell a fury, like a woman scorn'd."

Congreve's only tragedy, *The Mourning Bride* concerns Almeria, daughter of King Manuel of Granada, who secretly marries Alphonso, the son of her father's enemy, King Anselmo of Valencia. Almeria is separated from her husband in a shipwreck, but they are reunited when Alphonso, in disguise, is captured by Manuel along with the manipulative Moorish queen Zara. Through a series of tragic machinations, Manuel is mistakenly executed by his own orders, Zara commits suicide, and Alphonso helps overthrow the government and publicly regain his bride.

Moviegoer, The   Novel by Walker PERCY, published in 1961. It won a National Book Award. A philosophical exploration of the problem of personal identity, the story is narrated by Binx Bolling, a successful but alienated businessman. Bolling undertakes a search for meaning in his life, first through an obsession with the movies and later through an affair.

Mowgli \\'mau̇-glē, 'mō-\\   Fictional character, an Indian boy raised by wolves who is the central figure in Rudyard Kipling's collection of children's stories included in THE JUNGLE BOOK and its sequel.

A character by the name of Mowgli first appeared in Kipling's story "In the Rukh" (1892; collected in *Many Inventions*, 1893). In this story he is an adult who, from time to time, refers to his unusual childhood.

Mphahlele \\m-pä-'hlä-lä\\, Es'kia, *original name* Ezekiel Mphahlele (b. Dec. 17, 1919, Marabastad, S.Af.)   Novelist, essayist, short-story writer, and teacher whose autobiography, *Down Second Avenue* (1959), has become a South African classic.

Mphahlele attended Adams Teachers Training College in Natal, the University of South Africa, and the University of Denver. His early career as a teacher was terminated for political reasons. He later went into voluntary exile in Nigeria. For a time Mphahlele was coeditor with Ulli Beier and Wole Soyinka of the influential literary periodical *Black Orpheus*. In 1978 he returned to South Africa and the following year became head of the department of African Literature at the University of Witwatersrand in Johannesburg.

Mphahlele's critical writings include two books of essays, *The African Image* (1962) and *Voices in the Whirlwind, and Other Essays* (1972). He helped found the first independent black publishing house in South Africa, coedited the anthology *Modern African Stories* (1964), and edited and contributed to *African Writing Today* (1967). These works were followed by *Let's Talk Writing: Prose* (1985) and *Let's Talk Writing: Poetry* (1986). He also wrote books of short stories and several autobiographical works, including the autobiographical novel *The Wanderers* (1971), and the novel *Chirundu* (1979).

Mqhayi \m-'kä-yē\, Samuel E.K., *in full* Edward Krune (b. Dec. 1, 1875, near Gqumahashe, Cape Colony [South Africa]—d. July 29, 1945, Ntab'ozuko, S.Af.)   South African poet, historian, journalist, biographer, and translator who earned the name "Imbongi Yesizwe Jikelele" ("Xhosa Poet Laureate"). His many publications helped to standardize and purify the Xhosa language.

Mqhayi began his career as a teacher, but he was soon writing and editing newspapers. By 1910 he had worked on the Xhosa Bible Revision Board, published *U-Samson*, his version of the biblical story, and devoted his energy to the task of standardizing Xhosa orthography.

Ityala lamawele (1914; "The Lawsuit of the Twins"), based on his experiences at the Great Place (court) of Chief Nzanzana, brought him immediate fame and is considered a Xhosa classic. He wrote several biographies and in 1927 a book of verse called *Imihobe nemibongo* ("Songs of Joy and Lullabies"), the first published collection of Xhosa poems. His *U-Don Jadu* (1929) describes a fictional utopian state (Mnadi) of the Bantus, and *U-Mqhayi wase ntabozuko* (1939; "Mqhayi of the Mountains of Beauty") is his autobiography. His collected poems, *Inzuzo* ("Cain"), appeared in 1942.

Mr. Flood's Party \'fləd\   Rhymed narrative poem by Edward Arlington ROBINSON, published in his *Collected Poems* (1921). Considered one of Robinson's finest works, the poem is set in Tilbury Town. The narrative concerns lonely, isolated Eben Flood, who climbs a hill above the town one moonlit night and walks down an empty road. Frequently drinking from a jug of liquor, "secure, with only two moons listening," he salutes the harvest moon, the bird on the wing, and old times.

Mrożek \'mrō-zhek\, Sławomir (b. June 26, 1930, Borzęcin, near Kraków, Pol.)   Polish playwright noted for his subtle parody and stylized language.

Mrożek entered journalism as a cartoonist and author of humorous short articles. This same humor is evident in *Słoń* (1958; *The Elephant*), a book of short stories. During the 1950s and '60s Mrożek became a prominent figure in Polish literature by virtue of his plays in the style of the Theater of the Absurd. He left Poland in 1964 and thereafter lived in Paris. Six of his plays—*Policja* (1958; "The Police"), *Męczeństwo Piotra Oheya* (1959; "The Martyrdom of Peter Ohey"), *Na pełnym morzu* (1961; "Out at Sea"), *Karol* (1962; "Charlie"), *Zabawa* (1963; "The Party"), and *Czarowna noc* (1963; "Enchanted Night")—

were translated into English by Nicholas Bethell in *Six Plays* (1967). The most successful of Mrożek's plays, produced in many Western countries, was *Tango* (1964). His later plays included *Wacław* (1970; *Vatzlav: A Play in 77 Scenes*), *Emigranci* (1974; *Emigrés*), *Amor* (1979; "Cupid"), and *Alfa* (1984).

Mr. Sammler's Planet \'sam-lər\   Novel by Saul BELLOW, published in 1970. It won the National Book Award for fiction in 1971.

The setting is New York City during the politically tumultuous late 1960s. Sammler, an elderly Polish Jewish survivor of the Holocaust, is an intellectual who has been injured both physically and psychologically; he has lost the vision in one eye and suffers from a sense of emotional and intellectual alienation. With his intact eye, he views the world, its people, and their insanities. With his blind eye, he internalizes current events, using his historical and philosophical training to analyze and synthesize.

Mrs. Dalloway \'dal-ə-wā\   Novel by Virginia WOOLF, published in 1925.

The novel, which examines one day in the life of Clarissa Dalloway, an upper-class Londoner married to a member of Parliament, is essentially plotless; what action there is takes place mainly in the characters' consciousness. The novel addresses the nature of time in personal experience through two interwoven stories, that of Mrs. Dalloway, preparing for a party, and that of the mentally ill war veteran Septimus Warren Smith.

While never abandoning her omniscient third-person voice, Woolf enters the consciousness of seemingly unconnected characters and brings their feelings to the surface. The characters are connected, and the narrative moves from one to another, through public occurrences that the characters can see or hear, such as an exhibition of skywriting.

Mrs. Warren's Profession \'wȯr-ən\   Play in four acts by George Bernard SHAW, written in 1893 and published in 1898 but not performed until 1902 because of government censorship; the play's subject matter is organized prostitution.

Vivie Warren, a well-educated young woman, discovers that her mother has attained her present status and affluence by rising from poverty through prostitution and that she now has financial interests in several brothels throughout Europe. For years, an aristocratic friend of the family has been her partner. Vivie also discovers that the clergyman father of Frank, her suitor, had once been a client of her mother's.

Mrs. Warren states her position that poverty and a society which condones it are the true immorality. She asserts that life in a brothel is preferable to a life of grinding poverty as a factory worker. Vivie acknowledges her mother's courage in overcoming her past but rejects her continued involvement in prostitution. She severs her relationship with her mother, also rejecting Frank and the possibility of other suitors.

MS. Found in a Bottle *MS. is read as* 'man-yu̇-ˌskript\   Short story by Edgar Allan POE, published in the Baltimore weekly *Saturday Visiter* (October 1833) as the winner of a contest held by the magazine. The story, one of Poe's first notable works, was later published in the two-volume *Tales of the Grotesque and Arabesque* (1840).

The story's narrator, whose journal entries initially reveal him to be a staunch rationalist, begins to accept supernaturalism when a hurricane throws him from his sinking boat onto a large, mystical ship. The crew, made up of extremely aged foreigners who busy themselves with ancient nautical instruments, are oblivious to the narrator, who walks unnoticed among them. The story concludes when the strange ship vanishes into a whirlpool in icy, uncharted waters.

Mtshali \m-'chä-lē\, Oswald Mbuyiseni (b. Jan. 17, 1940, near Vryheid, Natal, S.Af.)   South African poet who wrote in English and Zulu and whose work drew upon life in the Johannesburg township of Soweto.

Mtshali worked as a messenger before publishing *Sounds of a Cowhide Drum* (1971), his first collection of poems. After studying in the United States at the University of Iowa and Columbia University, Mtshali returned to South Africa in 1979 to teach. His second volume of poems, *Fireflames* (1980), was banned by the South African government because it was dedicated to the schoolchildren of Soweto, a reference to the 1976 Soweto uprising.

Mtshali's poetry inevitably reflects his harsh experiences under the apartheid regime. His bitterness finds expression in brilliantly controlled lines etched with an acid irony.

Mu'allaqāt, Al- \äl-mü-,äl-lä-'kät, *Arabic* -,'äl-\   Collection of seven pre-Islāmic Arabic qasida (odes), each considered to be its author's best piece. Since the authors themselves are among the dozen or so most famous poets of the 6th century, the selection enjoys a unique position in Arabic literature, representing the finest of early Arabic poetry. It was translated as *The Seven Golden Odes of Pagan Arabia* (1903) by Lady Anne and Sir Wilfrid Scawen Blunt and as *The Seven Odes* (1957) by A.J. Arberry.

Taken together, the poems of the *Mu'allaqāt* provide an excellent picture of Bedouin life, manners, and modes of thought. The idea of grouping together these particular poems is most commonly attributed to Ḥammād ar-Rāwiyah, who was an 8th-century collector of early poetry. The name *Mu'allaqāt* appeared in about 900 to distinguish the seven poems as a subset in a larger compilation of poems.

The list of poems usually accepted as standard was recorded by Ibn 'Abd Rabbihi and names works by Imru' al-Qays, Ṭarafah, Zuhayr, Labīd, 'Antarah, 'Amr ibn Kulthūm, and al-Ḥārith. Such authorities as Ibn Qutaybah, however, count 'Abid ibn al-Abras as one of the seven, while Abū 'Ubaydah replaces the last two poets of Ibn 'Abd Rabbihi's list with an-Nābighah and al-A'shā.

The *Mu'allaqāt* odes are all in the classical qasida pattern, which some Arab scholars believe to have been created by Imru' al-Qays. After a conventional prelude, the *nasīb*, in which the poet calls to mind the memory of a former ladylove, most of the rest of the ode consists of an arbitrary succession of descriptions of the poet's horse or camel, scenes of desert events, and other aspects of Bedouin life and warfare. The qasida's main theme, or *madīḥ* (panegyric, *i.e.*, the poet's tribute to himself, his tribe, or his patron), is often disguised in these vivid descriptive passages, which are the chief glory of the *Mu'allaqāt*. Their vivid imagery, exact observation, and deep feeling of intimacy with nature in the Arabian Desert contribute to the *Mu'allaqāt*'s standing as a masterpiece of world literature.

Much Ado About Nothing   Comedy in five acts by William SHAKESPEARE, performed in 1598–99 and printed in a quarto edition from the author's fair papers in 1600.

The play takes an ancient theme—that of a woman falsely accused of unfaithfulness—to brilliant comedic heights. Claudio is deceived by his jealous cousin into believing that his lover, Hero, is unfaithful—a plot unveiled by the bumbling constables Dogberry and Verges. Meanwhile, Beatrice and Benedick have "a kind of merry war" between them, matching wits in clever repartee that anticipates other playfully teasing literary couples. Each is tricked into believing that the other is in love, which allows the true affection between them to grow. Both couples are united at the end, after Hero's simulated resurrection from the dead.

In this play Shakespeare eschewed devices of obvious magic or disguise of sex, which he employed in other comedies; the wit and ambiguity of the dialogue and the exquisite pacing of the action sustain the play, which remains popular in repertory.

muckraker \'mǝk-,rā-kǝr\   Any of a group of American writers identified with pre-World War I reform and exposé literature. The name was pejorative when used by President Theodore Roosevelt in his speech of April 14, 1906; he borrowed a passage from John Bunyan's *Pilgrim's Progress*, which referred to the man with the muckrake who "could look no way but downwards." But "muckraker" also came to take on favorable connotations of social concern and courageous exposure of injustice.

The muckrakers' work grew out of the yellow journalism of the 1890s and out of popular magazines. The emergence of muckraking was heralded in the January 1903 issue of *McClure's Magazine* by articles on municipal government, labor, and trusts, written by Lincoln Steffens, Ray Stannard Baker, and Ida M. Tarbell. The movement as such largely disappeared between 1910 and 1912. Among the novels produced by muckrakers were Upton Sinclair's *The Jungle* (1906), about the meatpacking industry in Chicago, and Brand Whitlock's *The Turn of the Balance* (1907), which opposed capital punishment.

Mudrooroo \mǝd-'rü-,rü\, *also called* Mudrooroo Narogin *or* Mudrooroo Nyoongah.   Aboriginal name of Australian writer who originally published under the name Colin JOHNSON.

Mufaddalīyāt, Al- \äl-mü-,fäd-dä-,lē-'yät\   ("The Examination of al-Mufaddal")   Anthology of ancient Arabic poems, compiled between 762 and 784 by al-Mufaddal ibn Muhammad ibn Ya'lah al-Dabbī for his student, the prince (and future caliph) al-Mahdī. *Al-Mufaddalīyāt* is of the highest importance as a record of the thought and poetic art of Arabia in the last two pre-Islāmic centuries.

The anthology is thought to have originally collected 70 to 80 poems and to have been added to in later transmission. The 126 pieces now generally included in the work were written by 68 poets, one of them an anonymous female. The work represents a selection from the composition of those called *al-muqillūn*, "authors of whom little has survived," rather than from the famous poets whose works had been collected in divans. Not all poems of *Al-Mufaddalīyāt* are complete; many are mere fragments, and even in the longest there are often gaps. Al-Mufaddal, however—unlike anthologizers of a later period—always tried to present complete poems as they had been preserved. The collection contains 61 qasidas (polythematic odes), 7 elegies, and 58 miscellaneous monothematic poems.

Mugridge \'mǝg-,rij\   Fictional character, a brutish ship's cook in the novel THE SEA-WOLF by Jack London.

Muhando \mü-'hän-dō\, Penina, *married name* Mlama \m-'lä-mä\ (b. 1948, Kilosa, Tanganyika [now Tanzania])   Tanzanian playwright and scholar, one of the first female dramatists in the Swahili language.

Muhando studied education and theater in Tanzania at the University of Dar es-Salaam, later joining the faculty of the department of theater arts. Her plays include *Hatia* (1972; "Guilt"), *Tambueni haki zetu* (1973; "Reveal Our Rights"), *Heshima yangu* (1974; "My Honor"), *Pambo* (1975), *Nguzo mama* (1982), and *Lina ubani* (1984). The plays explore a variety of themes and situations but generally are concerned with contemporary problems involved in Tanzanian society's rapid adjustment to development and Westernization. In addition to her plays, Muhando wrote several scholarly works dealing with Swahili literature.

Muir \'myū-ər, 'myȯr\, Edwin (b. May 15, 1887, Deerness, Orkney, Scot.—d. Jan. 3, 1959, Cambridge, Cambridgeshire, Eng.)   Literary critic, translator, and one of the chief Scottish poets of his day writing in English.

Muir received an education in Kirkwall. After his marriage in 1919, he went to London, where he wrote literary reviews; he later taught English in Europe.

Muir's stature as a poet did not become widely recognized until the publication of *The Voyage* (1946) and *The Labyrinth* (1949). His *Collected Poems* appeared in 1960. The critical works *Latitudes* (1924) and *Transition* (1927) were notable for their appreciation of D.H. Lawrence. His translations of the works of Franz Kafka, done in collaboration with his wife, established Kafka's reputation in Britain. He also translated works of Sholem Asch, Hermann Broch, and Lion Feuchtwanger. Muir's *Autobiography* was published in 1954.

Mujica Láinez \mū-'ķē-kä-'lä-ē-nās\, Manuel (b. Sept. 11, 1910, Buenos Aires, Arg.—d. April 21, 1984, Córdoba province)   Popular Argentine writer whose novels and short stories blend myth and fantasy with historical figures and events.

Mujica Láinez was educated in Buenos Aires, France, and England. At age 22 he returned to Buenos Aires and became a correspondent of *La Nación*, a newspaper with which he was associated for the remainder of his life.

His first novel, *Don Galaz de Buenos Aires* (1938), is a recreation of city life in the 17th century. *Canto a Buenos Aires* (1943), his first literary success, chronicles the foundation and development of the Argentine capital. Mujica Láinez solidified his reputation in Argentina with a series of novels known as his Buenos Aires cycle. It consists of *Los ídolos* (1953; "The Idols"), *La casa* (1954; "The House"), *Los viajeros* (1955; "The Travelers"), and *Invitados en el paraíso* (1957; "Guests at Paradise"). *Aquí vivieron* (1949; "They Lived Here") and *Misteriosa Buenos Aires* (1950) are collections of short stories.

His masterpiece is the novel *Bomarzo* (1962), about Pier Francesco Orsini, one of the most powerful men of the Italian Renaissance. Mujica Láinez also wrote the libretto for the opera *Bomarzo* by Alberto Ginastera.

Rooted in Latin-American literary tradition, Mujica Láinez's novels are characterized by social satire and an ironic perspective on history. In addition to fiction, Mujica Láinez also wrote biographies and critical studies of many Latin-American artists and poets. His later works include *Cecil* (1972), *El laberinto* (1974; "The Labyrinth"), *Sergio* (1976), and *El gran teatro* (1979; "The Great Theater").

Mukai Kyorai \mū-'kī-'kyō-rī\, *original name* Mukai Kanetoki \kä-'ne-tō-kē\, *also called* Rakushisha \,rä-kü-'shē-shä\ (b. 1651, Nagasaki, Japan—d. Oct. 8, 1704, Kyōto)   Japanese haiku poet of the early Tokugawa period (1603–1867).

Kyorai first trained as a samurai, but at age 23 he gave up martial service and turned to the writing of poetry. In 1684 he met Takarai Kikaku, a disciple of Bashō, and shortly thereafter Kyorai also became a disciple.

Kyorai helped edit two major collections of haiku by Bashō and his followers, *Arano* (1689; "Wilderness") and *Sarumino* (1691; "The Monkey's Raincoat"). After his master's death in 1694 Kyorai devoted himself to teaching haiku and to interpreting Bashō's works. He also published several anthologies of his own poetry and essays, including *Kyorai shō* (1775; "Conversations with Kyorai") and *Tabine ron* (1778; "Discourses of a Weary Traveler").

Mukherjee \'mū-kər-jē\, Bharati (b. July 27, 1940, Calcutta, India)   Indian-born American novelist and short-story writer whose work reflects Indian culture and immigrant experience.

Mukherjee attended the University of Calcutta, the University of Baroda, and the University of Iowa Writers' Workshop. From 1966 to 1980 she lived in Montreal, then moved to the United States and began teaching at the university level.

Mukherjee's work featured not only cultural clashes but undercurrents of violence. Her first novel, *The Tiger's Daughter* (1972), tells of a sheltered Indian woman jolted by immersion in American culture, then again shocked by her return to a violent Calcutta. *Wife* (1975) details the descent into madness of an Indian woman trapped in New York City by the fears and passivity resulting from her upbringing. Mukherjee's first book of short stories, *Darkness* (1985), includes the acclaimed "The World According to Hsü." *The Middleman and Other Stories* (1988) feature third-world immigrants to America, also the subject of two later novels, *Jasmine* (1989) and *The Holder of the World* (1993).

Mule Bone (*in full* Mule Bone: A Comedy of Negro Life in Three Acts)   Play about African-American rural life written collaboratively in 1931 by Zora Neale HURSTON and Langston HUGHES. Drawing on Southern black oral tradition and folklore, the play features such customs as "mule-talking," a type of verbal one-upmanship. (Hurston, an anthropologist as well as a writer, had collected examples of mule-talking in black communities.)

The play remained unfinished and unproduced during the authors' lifetimes; it was published in 1990.

Mulisch \'mūē-lĕsh\, Harry (Kurt Victor) (b. July 29, 1927, Haarlem, Neth.)   Prolific Dutch author known chiefly for his clear, economical prose.

Mulisch's maternal grandmother and great-grandmother died in German concentration camps, while his father was an official of a bank under German control; after the war Mulisch's father was sent to prison as a collaborator. These experiences equipped Mulisch to write about divided loyalties.

Mulisch began writing when World War II interrupted his studies. His first novel, *Archibald Strohalm* (1952), won a literary prize. His novel *Het stenen bruidsbed* (1959; *The Stone Bridal Bed*), in which an American pilot involved in the bombing of Dresden returns to the city years later, won him an international audience. *Twee vrouwen* (1975; *Two Women*) explored love between two women. Perhaps his most popular work is his novel *De aanslag* (1982; *The Assault*), in which one family betrays another during the war. In addition to his many novels, he wrote dramas, essays, and short stories and several books of poetry. His later novels include *Hoogste tijd* (1985; *Last Call*), *De pupil* (1987; *The Pupil*), and *De ontdekking van de hemel* (1992; "The Discovery of Heaven").

Müller \'mūē-lər\, Friedrich, *byname* Maler \'mäl-ər\ ("Painter") Müller (b. Jan. 13, 1749, Kreuznach, Palatinate [Germany]—d. April 23, 1825, Rome [Italy])   German poet, dramatist, and painter who is best known for his prose idylls on country life.

Müller was appointed court painter at Mannheim (1777) but left the next year for Italy. He soon abandoned painting and devoted himself to the history of art. His principal works include *Niobe* (1778), a lyric drama; *Fausts Leben dramatisiert* (1778; "Faust's Life Dramatized"); *Golo und Genoveva* (1811); and the idylls *Die Schafschur* (1775; "The Sheepshearing") and *Das Nusskernen* (1811; "The Nutcracking").

Müller \'mūē-lər\, Wilhelm (b. Oct. 7, 1794, Dessau, duchy of Anhalt [Germany]—d. Sept. 30, 1827, Dessau)   German poet who was known both for his lyrics that helped to arouse sympathy for the Greeks in their struggle for independence from the Turks and for his verse cycles "Die schöne Müllerin" and "Die Winterreise."

After studying at the University of Berlin, Müller volunteered in the Prussian uprising against Napoleon (1813–14). He later taught classics and served as librarian at the ducal library in Dessau.

Müller's reputation was established by the *Gedichte aus den hinterlassenen Papieren eines reisenden Waldhornisten,* 2 vol. (1821–24; "Poems from the Posthumous Papers of a Traveling Bugler"), and *Lieder der Griechen* (1821–24; "Songs of the Greeks"). His other works include *Neugriechische Volkslieder,* 2 vol. (1825; "Modern Greek Folk Songs"), and *Lyrische Reisen und epigrammatische Spaziergänge* (1827; "Lyrical Travels and Epigrammatical Walks"). He also wrote the book *Homerische Vorschule* (1824; "Homeric Preparatory School") and translated Christopher Marlowe's *Doctor Faustus.*

Müllner \'mʊel-nər\, Amadeus Gottfried Adolf (b. Oct. 18, 1774, Langendorf, near Weissenfels, Saxony [Germany]—d. June 11, 1829, Weissenfels, Prussia) German playwright, one of the so-called fate dramatists, who wrote plays in which people perish as a consequence of past behavior.

Müllner's first novel was *Der Incest, oder der Schutzgeist von Avignon* (1799; "The Incest; or, The Guardian Spirit of Avignon"). He next wrote a number of comedies for an amateur theater group in Weissenfels. With his Romantic tragedies, however, *Der neunundzwanzigste Februar* (1812; "February 29") and especially *Die Schuld* (1813; "The Debt"), Müllner became a representative of the fate dramatists, and for several years fate tragedies modeled on *Die Schuld* dominated the German stage. Müllner also edited various journals, and in the year of his death he published the first German detective story, *Der Kaliber* (1829; "The Caliber"). *See also* FATE TRAGEDY.

Multatuli \ˌmʊel-tə-'tǖ-lē\, *pseudonym of* Eduard Douwes Dekker \'daʊ̇-əs-'dek-ər\ (b. March 2, 1820, Amsterdam, Neth.—d. Feb. 19, 1887, Nieder-Ingelheim, Ger.) One of The Netherlands' greatest writers, whose radical ideas and freshness of style eclipsed the Dutch literature of the mid-19th century.

In 1838 Dekker went to the Dutch East Indies, where he held a number of government posts. He resigned in 1856 because the colonial government did not support him in his attempts to protect the Javanese from their own chiefs, and he returned to Europe.

Multatuli (Latin "I have suffered much") became internationally known with his most important work, the novel *Max Havelaar* (1860), which concerns the vain efforts of an enlightened official to expose the Dutch exploitation of the Javanese.

Apart from *Minnebrieven* (1861; "Love Letters"), a fictitious romantic correspondence, his main work was *Ideën,* 7 vol. (1862–77; "Ideas"), in which he gives his radical views on a variety of topics. Included in the *Ideën* is his autobiographical novel *Woutertje Pieterse,* an early work of realism.

mumming play \'məm-iŋ\, *also called* mummers' play \'məm-ərz\ [Middle English *mommen* to speak incoherently, be silent, perform (a mumming play), probably in part a derivative of *mom* an inarticulate sound (of imitative origin), in part from Old French *mommer* to perform wearing masks] Traditional dramatic entertainment, still performed in a few villages of England and Northern Ireland, in which a champion is killed in a fight and is then brought to life by a doctor. It is thought likely that the play has links with primitive ceremonies held to mark important stages in the agricultural year.

Mummers were originally bands of masked persons who during winter festivals in Europe paraded through the streets and entered houses to dance or play dice in silence. "Momerie" was a popular amusement between the 13th and 16th centuries. In the 16th century it was absorbed by Italian carnival masquerading (and hence was a forerunner of the courtly entertainment known as the masque).

It is not known how old the mumming play is. Although contemporary references to it do not begin to appear until the late 18th century, the basic narrative framework is the story of St. George and the Seven Champions of Christendom, which was first popularized in England toward the end of the 16th century. The plot remained essentially the same: St. George, introduced as a gallant Christian hero, fights an infidel knight, and one of them is slain. A doctor restores the dead warrior to life. Other characters include a presenter, a fool in cap and bells, and a man dressed in woman's clothes. Father Christmas also appears.

Münchhausen \'muenk-ˌhaʊ̇z-ən, *Angl* 'mən-ˌchaʊ̇z-ən, 'mün-\, Baron, *in full* Karl Friedrich Hieronymus, Baron (Freiherr) von Münchhausen (b. May 11, 1720, Bodenwerder, Hanover [Germany]—d. Feb. 22, 1797, Bodenwerder) German storyteller, some of whose tales were the basis for *The Adventures of Baron Munchausen.*

Münchhausen served with the Russian army against the Turks and retired to his estates as a country gentleman in 1760. He became famous around Hanover as a raconteur of extraordinary tales about his life as a soldier, hunter, and sportsman. A collection of such tales appeared in *Vademecum für lustige Leute* (1781–83; "Manual for Merry People"), all of them attributed to the baron, though several can be traced to much earlier sources.

Münchhausen, however, was launched as a "type" of tall-story teller by Rudolf Erich RASPE, who used the earlier stories as basic material for a small volume published (anonymously) in London in 1785 under the title *Baron Munchausen's Narrative of His Marvellous Travels and Campaigns in Russia.* Later and much enlarged editions, none of them having much to do with the historical Baron Münchhausen, became widely known and popular in many languages. They are generally known as *The Adventures of Baron Munchausen,* and the English edition of 1793 is now the usual text.

Munday \'mən-dā\, Anthony (b. 1560?, London, Eng.— buried Aug. 9, 1633, London) English poet, dramatist, pamphleteer, and translator.

At age 16 Munday was apprenticed to a printer. After 1579 his writings streamed from the press, including popular ballads, original lyrics, verse, translations of French and Spanish romances, plays, and a number of edifying or moral works.

In 1581–82 he was prominent in the capture and trials of a number of Jesuit emissaries and also wrote several pamphlets justifying the persecution of the Jesuits. His *English Romayne Lyfe* (1582) is a detailed and entertaining, though hostile, description of life and study at the English College at Rome, where Munday had spent some time.

Little is known about Munday's career as actor and playwright. His *Fedele and Fortunio* (1584 at the latest) played at court and was printed in 1585. *John a Kent and John a Cumber,* his earliest surviving original play, was probably written before the middle of 1589.

Munk \'muŋk\, Kaj (Harald Leininger) (b. Jan. 13, 1898, Maribo, Den.—d. Jan. 4, 1944, near Silkeborg) Danish playwright, priest, and patriot who was a rare exponent of religious drama with a strong sense of the theater.

Munk studied at the University of Copenhagen, where he began his first produced play, *En idealist* (1928; *Herod the King*). In 1931 his *Cant* (on the rise and fall of Anne Boleyn) was a success, and *Ordet* (1932; *The Word*), a miracle play set among Jutland peasants, established him as Denmark's leading dramatist. *En idealist, Ordet,* and *Han sidder ved smeltediglen* (1938;

He Sits at the Melting-Pot), a drama of Adolf Hitler's Germany, are his three best plays. *Five Plays*, with preface and translations, was published in 1953.

Munk was a parish priest whose outspoken sermons during World War II led to his being killed by the Nazis.

Munonye \mü-'nōn-yā\, John (b. April 28, 1929, Akokwa, East Central State, Nigeria) African educator and novelist known for his ability to convey the vitality of the contemporary Nigerian scene.

Munonye was educated at Christ the King College in Onitsha and did his university work at Ibadan and at the University of London. He worked for the Nigerian Ministry of Education until 1977 when he left to teach and devote more time to writing.

Munonye's first novel, *The Only Son* (1966), describes the separation of a mother from her son because of religious differences; *Obi* (1969) is a sequel to *The Only Son*. Other novels include *Oil Man of Obange* (1971) and *A Wreath for the Maidens* (1973). *A Dancer of Fortune* (1974) is a satire of modern Nigerian business, and Munonye returned to the family of his first two novels in *Bridge to a Wedding* (1978).

Munro \mən-'rō\ Alice, *original name* Alice Anne Laidlaw \'lād-,lò\ (b. July 10, 1931, Wingham, Ont., Can.) Canadian short-story writer who gained international recognition with her exquisitely drawn stories, usually set in rural Ontario and peopled by characters of Scotch-Irish stock.

Munro attended the University of Western Ontario. Her first collection of stories was published as *Dance of the Happy Shades* (1968). It is one of three collections—the other two being *Who Do You Think You Are?* (1978) and *The Progress of Love* (1986)—awarded the annual Governor General's Literary Award for fiction. Her second collection—*The Lives of Girls and Women* (1971), a group of coming-of-age stories—was followed by *Something I've Been Meaning to Tell You* (1974), *The Beggar Maid: Stories of Flo and Rose* (1978), *The Moons of Jupiter* (1982), *Friend of My Youth* (1986), *Open Secrets* (1994), and *A Wilderness Station* (1994).

Munro, H.H. *in full* Hector Hugh. *see* SAKI.

Munthe \'mùn-te\, Axel Martin Fredrik (b. Oct. 31, 1857, Oskarshamn, Swed.—d. Feb. 11, 1949, Stockholm) Swedish physician, psychiatrist, and writer whose book *The Story of San Michele* (1929), an account of his experiences as a doctor in Paris and Rome and in semiretirement at the villa of San Michele on the island of Capri (Italy), achieved immense popularity in its original English version and in many translations. Its lasting success may be attributed to its intimate revelation of an unusually vital personality and its sympathetic description of suffering.

Munthe studied in Sweden at Uppsala and in France at Montpellier and Paris. After practicing in Paris and Italy he became physician to the Swedish royal family. His other books of reminiscences, *Memories and Vagaries* (1898) and *Letters From a Mourning City* (1887), never achieved the success of *San Michele*.

Murakami Haruki \mü-,rä-'kä-mē-hä-'rü-kē\ (b. Jan. 12, 1949, Kyōto, Japan) Japanese postmodernist novelist and spokesman for a new generation.

As a boy, Murakami rebelled against the study of Japanese literature, instead reading American paperbacks. This early and sustained interest is evident in the structure and nontraditional style of his own novels. His works include *Kaze no uta o kike* (1979; *Hear the Wind*); *Hitsuji o meguru bōken* (1982; *A Wild Sheep Chase*); the allegorical *Sekai no owari to hādoboirudo wandārando* (1985; *The End of the World & Hard-Boiled Won-*

derland), which won the Tanizaki Prize; the realistic *Noruwei no mori* (1987; *Norwegian Wood*); and *Dansu, Dansu, Dansu* (1988; *Dance, Dance, Dance*). He also wrote short stories and several collections of essays.

Murasaki Shikibu \mù-'rä-sä-kē-'shē-kē-bù\ (b. *c.* 978, Kyōto, Japan—d. *c.* 1014, Kyōto) Court lady who was the author of the *Genji monogatari* (THE TALE OF GENJI), generally considered one of the world's oldest and greatest novels.

Her real name is unknown, and it is conjectured that she acquired the sobriquet Murasaki from the name of the heroine of her novel. The main source of knowledge about her life is the diary she kept between 1007 and 1010. The work possesses considerable interest for the delightful glimpses it affords of life at the court of the empress Jōtō mon'in, whom Murasaki served.

Some critics believe that Murasaki wrote the entire *Tale of Genji* between 1001 and 1005, when she began serving at court. More probably, however, the composition of this extremely long and complex novel extended over a much greater period and was not finished until about 1010.

Most of the story is concerned with the loves of Prince Genji and with the different women in his life. The work is supremely sensitive to human emotions and the beauties of nature, but the tone darkens as it proceeds, perhaps reflecting a Buddhist conviction of the vanity of this world. *The Tale of Genji* was translated by Arthur Waley (1925–33) and Edward G. Seidensticker (1976).

Murder in the Cathedral Poetic drama in two parts, with a prose sermon interlude, the most successful play of T.S. ELIOT. The play was performed at Canterbury Cathedral in 1935 and published the same year. Set in December 1170, it is a modern miracle play on the martyrdom of St. Thomas Becket, archbishop of Canterbury.

The play's most striking feature is the use of a chorus in the classical Greek manner. The poor women of Canterbury who make up the chorus nervously await Thomas' return from his seven-year exile, fretting over his volatile relationship with King Henry II. Thomas arrives and must resist four temptations: worldly pleasures, lasting power as chancellor, recognition as a leader of the barons against the king, and eternal glory as a martyr. After Thomas delivers his Christmas morning sermon, four knights in the service of the king accost him and order him to leave the kingdom. When he refuses, they return to slay him in the cathedral.

Murders in the Rue Morgue, The \,rü-'mòrg\ Short story by Edgar Allan POE, first published in *Graham's* magazine in 1841. It is considered the world's first detective story.

The story opens with the discovery of the violent murder of an old woman and her daughter; no grisly detail is spared in the description of the crime scene as it is discovered by neighbors responding to the women's screams. The police are baffled by the fact that the murderer has managed to escape even though the women's apartment appears to have been completely sealed from the inside. The genteel but impoverished C. Auguste DUPIN and his nameless friend—who narrates the story—offer their services to the police and, through a brilliant interpretation of the clues at the scene, identify the murderer—an escaped orangutan.

In its presentation of an amateur detective who uses "ratiocination" to solve a mystery, the story shaped a new genre of fiction. It influenced Sir Arthur Conan Doyle, Dame Agatha Christie, and dozens of writers who borrowed, knowingly or not, Poe's original conception of the detective story.

Murdoch \'mər-,däk\, Iris, *in full* Dame Jean Iris Murdoch, *married name* Mrs. J.O. Bayley \'bā-lē\ (b. July 15, 1919,

Dublin, Ire.) British writer and university lecturer, who attained recognition as a prolific and talented novelist.

Murdoch attended Somerville College, Oxford, and in 1948 she was elected a fellow of St. Anne's College, Oxford. Her

first published work was a critical study, *Sartre, Romantic Rationalist* (1953), which was followed by two novels, *Under the Net* (1954) and *The Flight from the Enchanter* (1956). Other novels include *A Severed Head* (1961), *The Nice and the Good* (1968), *The Black Prince* (1973), *Henry and Cato* (1976), *The Sea, The Sea* (1978), *The Philosopher's Pupil* (1983), *The Good Apprentice* (1985), and *The Book and The Brotherhood* (1987).

Cecil Beaton—Camera Press

Murdoch's second-largest body of works were in the field of philosophy. These include *The Sovereignty of Good* (1970), *The Fire and the Sun: Why Plato Banished the Artists* (1977), and *Metaphysics as a Guide to Morals* (1992).

Murdstone, Edward \'ed-wərd-'mərd-,stōn, -stən\ Fictional character, the cruel stepfather of the title character in Charles Dickens' novel DAVID COPPERFIELD.

Murger \mǖr-'zher\, Henri, *in full* Louis-Henri Murger (b. March 27, 1822, Paris, Fr.—d. Jan. 28, 1861, Paris) French novelist who was among the first to depict bohemian life.

Murger left school at age 13. Later he became secretary to Count Aleksey Tolstoy and was able to improve his education. He began writing poems and became part of the bohemian life in Paris, but he was often destitute and his health deteriorated. Both the gaiety and tragedy of his circumstances are reflected in his best-known work, *Scènes de la vie de bohème* ("Scenes of Bohemian Life"), in which he himself figured as Rodolfe. Published in separate episodes (1847–49), its success enabled Murger to live and write in greater comfort. The work was the basis of Giacomo Puccini's opera *La Bohème*.

Murphy \'mər-fē\ Novel by Samuel BECKETT, published in 1938. The story concerns an Irishman in London who yearns to do nothing more than sit in his rocking chair and daydream. Murphy attempts to avoid all action; he escapes from a girl he is about to marry, takes up with a kind prostitute, and finds a job as a nurse in a mental institution, where he plays nonconfrontational chess. His disengagement from the world is shattered when his fiancée, with a detective and two new lovers in tow, discovers him. He is killed when someone accidentally turns on the gas in his apartment.

Murphy \'mər-fē\, Gerald and Sara, *in full* Gerald Clery Murphy and Sara Sherman Murphy, *original surname* Wiborg \'vē-,bȯrg\ (respectively b. March 25, 1888, Boston, Mass., U.S.—d. Oct. 17, 1964, East Hampton, N.Y.; b. Nov. 7, 1883, Cincinnati, Ohio—d. Oct. 10, 1975, Arlington, Va.) Wealthy American expatriates in Paris and Antibes, Fr., during the 1920s and early 1930s who befriended and hosted such artists and writers as F. Scott Fitzgerald, Ernest Hemingway, John Dos Passos, Archibald MacLeish, Dorothy Parker, Pablo Picasso, Fernand Léger, Igor Stravinsky, and Cole Porter. Fitzgerald's novel *Tender Is the Night* (1934) was dedicated to the couple, and its main characters, Dick and Nicole Diver, were, in part, patterned on the Murphys.

Murray \'mər-ē\, Albert L. (b. May 12, 1916, Nokomis, Ala., U.S.) African-American essayist and critic whose writings assert the vitality and the powerful influence of black people in forming American traditions.

Murray attended Tuskegee Institute and New York University; he also taught at Tuskegee. In 1943 he entered the U.S. air force, from which he retired as a major in 1962. His collection of essays, *The Omni-Americans* (1970), used historical fact, literature, and music to attack false perceptions of black American life. *South to a Very Old Place* (1971) recorded his visit to scenes of his segregated boyhood during the 1920s. In *Stomping the Blues* (1976), he maintained that blues and jazz musical styles developed as affirmative responses to misery. He also cowrote Count Basie's autobiography *Good Morning Blues* (1985) and wrote the novels *Train Whistle Guitar* (1974) and *The Spyglass Tree* (1991).

Murray \'mər-ē\, Gilbert, *in full* George Gilbert Aimé Murray (b. Jan. 2, 1866, Sydney, N.S.W., Australia—d. May 20, 1957, Oxford, Oxfordshire, Eng.) British classical scholar whose translations of the masters of ancient Greek drama—Aeschylus, Sophocles, Euripides, and Aristophanes—brought their works to renewed popularity on the contemporary stage.

In 1908 Murray became professor of Greek at the University of Oxford, where he remained until his retirement in 1936. Between 1904 and 1912 he personally directed many of the productions that made Greek theater once more a living art. By translating into rhymed rather than blank verse, he attempted to give an impression of the rhythmic quality of Greek poetry. Murray also applied insights from the emergent science of anthropology to his other scholarly studies, thus broadening the understanding of Homer and of the older forms of Greek religion. His many works in this vein include *The Rise of the Greek Epic* (1907).

Murray \'mər-ē\, Les, *in full* Leslie Allan Murray (b. Oct. 17, 1938, Nabiac, N.S.W., Australia) Australian poet and essayist whose meditative, lyrical poems capture Australia's psychic and rural landscape as well as its mythic elements.

Murray graduated from Sydney University and worked as a writer-in-residence at several universities. He edited *Poetry Australia* from 1973 to 1979 and also compiled and edited the *New Oxford Book of Australian Verse* (1986).

Murray's poetry celebrates a hoped-for fusion of the Aboriginal (which he called the "senior culture"), the rural, and the urban. The poem "The Buladelah-Taree Holiday Song Cycle," in the collection *Ethnic Radio* (1977), reflects his identification with Australia's Aborigines. *The Boys Who Stole the Funeral* (1979) is a sequence of 140 sonnets about a pair of boys who surreptitiously remove a man's body from a Sydney funeral home for burial in his native outback. Murray's other poetry collections include *Dog Fox Field* (1990), *The Rabbiter's Bounty* (1991), and *The Paperbark Tree* (1992).

Murry \'mər-ē\, John Middleton (b. Aug. 6, 1889, London, Eng.—d. March 13, 1957, Bury St. Edmunds, Suffolk) English journalist and critic whose romantic and biographical approach to literature ran counter to the leading critical tendencies of the day. He wrote at least 40 books and a large body of journalistic works.

Murry was the husband of short-story writer Katherine Mansfield and a close associate of D.H. Lawrence, both of whom influenced his development as a writer. During World War I the Murrys and Lawrences were neighbors in Cornwall, and something of the relationship between the two couples appears in Lawrence's *Women in Love*. Murry also appears, harshly lampooned, as the character Burlap in Aldous Huxley's *Point Counter Point*.

Murry began his career as editor of *Rhythm* while at Brasenose College, Oxford. He was editor of *The Athenaeum* and founding editor in 1923 of *Adelphi*, both literary magazines. Among his numerous critical works are studies of Mansfield (*Katherine Mansfield and Other Literary Portraits*, 1949) and Lawrence (*Son of Woman, the Story of D.H. Lawrence*, 1931), as well as several works on John Keats. Murry's autobiography, *Between Two Worlds* (1935), is strikingly revealing about his own life.

Musäus \mü-'ze-us\, Johann Karl August (b. March 29, 1735, Jena, Saxony [Germany]—d. Oct. 28, 1787, Weimar) German satirist and writer of fairy tales, remembered for his graceful and delicately ironic versions of popular folktales.

Musäus studied theology at Jena but turned instead to literature. His first book, *Grandison der Zweite*, 3 vol. (1760–62; "Grandison the Second"), revised as *Der deutsche Grandison* (1781–82; "The German Grandison"), was a satire of Samuel Richardson's hero Sir Charles Grandison, who had many admirers in Germany. In 1763 Musäus was made master of the court pages at Weimar, and he later became professor at the Weimar Gymnasium.

A second book, *Physiognomische Reisen*, 4 vol. (1778–79; "Physiognomical Travels"), was a satire on Johann Kaspar Lavater's work linking physiognomy to character. His *Volksmärchen der Deutschen*, 5 vol. (1782–86; "Fairy Tales of the Germans"), because it is written in a satirical vein, is not considered genuine folklore.

muse \'myüz\, *plural* muses **1.** *capitalized* Any of the nine sister goddesses in Greek mythology presiding over song and poetry and the arts and sciences. **2.** A source of inspiration; especially, a guiding genius. **3.** A poet.

The Muses are of obscure but ancient origin. They probably were originally the patron goddesses of poets (who in early times were also musicians, providing their own accompaniments), although later their range was extended to include all liberal arts and sciences—hence, their connection with such institutions as the Museum (*Mouseion*, "seat of the Muses") at Alexandria, Egypt. There were nine Muses as early as Homer's *Odyssey*, and Homer invokes either a particular Muse or the Muses collectively from time to time. To begin with, the Muses probably were one of those vague collections of deities, undifferentiated within the group, that are characteristic of presumably early strata of Greek religion.

Differentiation began with the 8th-century-BC poet Hesiod, who mentioned the names of Clio, Euterpe, Thalia, Melpomene, Terpsichore, Erato, Polymnia (Polyhymnia), Urania, and Calliope, who was their chief. Their father was Zeus, and their mother was Mnemosyne ("Memory"). Although Hesiod's list became the standard in later times, it was not the only one; at both Delphi and Sicyon there were only three Muses. All the Hesiodic names are significant; thus, Clio is approximately the "Proclaimer," Euterpe the "Well Pleasing," Thalia the "Blooming," or "Luxuriant," Melpomene the "Songstress," Erato the "Lovely," Polymnia "She of the Many Hymns," Urania the "Heavenly," and Calliope "She of the Beautiful Voice." Because dancing was a regular accompaniment of song, it is not remarkable that Hesiod called one of his nine the "Whirler of the Dance," Terpsichore.

The Muses are often spoken of as unmarried, and they are repeatedly referred to as the mothers of more or less famous sons, such as Orpheus and Eumolpus. In other words, all their myths are secondary, attached for one reason or another to the original vague and nameless group. Hence, there is no consistency in their minor tales—Terpsichore, for example, being named as the mother of several different men by various au-

thors and Orpheus generally being called the son of Calliope but occasionally of Polymnia.

Individual Muses eventually were assigned to the different arts and sciences, especially in Roman times. The lists that have come down are all late and disagree with one another. A common but by no means a definitive list is the following:

Calliope: Muse of heroic or epic poetry.
Clio: Muse of history.
Erato: Muse of lyric and love poetry.
Euterpe: Muse of music or flutes.
Melpomene: Muse of tragedy.
Polymnia: Muse of sacred poetry or of the mimic art.
Terpsichore: Muse of dancing and choral song.
Thalia: Muse of comedy.
Urania: Muse of astronomy.

Musée des Beaux Arts \mü-zā-dā-bō-'zär\ Poem by W.H. AUDEN, published in the collection *Another Time* (1940). In this two-stanza poem Auden comments on the general indifference to suffering in the world. Written in a tone of critical irony, the poem asserts that anguish is most accurately represented in art as a commonplace feeling and not as a dramatic emotion of tragic proportions.

Mushanokōji Saneatsu \mü-'shä-nō-,kō-jē-'sä-nä-,ä-tsü\ (b. May 12, 1885, Tokyo, Japan—d. April 9, 1976, Tokyo) Writer and painter noted for a lifelong philosophy of humanistic optimism.

Mushanokōji attended Tokyo Imperial University, but he left without graduating to join Shiga Naoya, Arishima Takeo, and Satomi Ton in founding the influential literary journal *Shirakaba* ("White Birch"). His reading of Leo Tolstoy and the Bible influenced the development of his humanitarian ideology. Among his early writings was *Omedetaki hito* (1911; "The Good-Natured Soul"). He was also the author of *Ai to shi* (1939; *Love and Death*) and *Aiyoku* (1926; *The Passion*); plays such as *Aru katei* (1910; *A Family Affair*) and *Washi mo shirani* (1914; *I Don't Know Either*); and poetry. In 1918 he founded Atarashii Mura, the New Village, an experiment in communal living that ultimately failed. In later years he turned to painting.

Musil \'mü-zil\, Robert, *also called* Robert, Edler ("Nobleman") von Musil (b. Nov. 6, 1880, Klagenfurt, Austria-Hungary—d. April 15, 1942, Geneva, Switz.) Austrian-German novelist, best known for his monumental unfinished novel *Der Mann ohne Eigenschaften*, 3 vol. (1930, 1933, 1943; THE MAN WITHOUT QUALITIES).

Musil was educated at the University of Berlin and served in the Austrian army in World War I. After the war he eventually supported himself by his writings and freelance journalism. He lived in Berlin, then in Vienna until the Nazi Anschluss, when he fled to Switzerland.

Musil acquired notice in the 1920s writing various fiction and two plays, *Die Schwärmer* (1920; *The Enthusiasts*) and *Vinzenz und die Freundin bedeutender Männer* (1924; "Vincent and the Lady Friend of Important Men"). In 1924 he began his masterwork, *Der Mann ohne Eigenschaften*, a witty and urbane saga of life in the glittering world of the Austro-Hungarian Empire. The First Book was published in 1930, and part of the Second Book in 1933; a remaining portion was published posthumously in 1943.

Muspelheim \'müs-pel-,häm\, *Old Norse* Múspell \'müs-pel\ *or* Múspellheimr \-,häm-ər\ In Norse mythology, a hot, bright, glowing land in the south, guarded by Surt, the fire giant. In the beginning, according to one tradition, the warm air from this region melted the ice of the opposite region, Niflheim, thus giving form to Aurgelmir (Ymir), the father of the evil giants. Sparks from Muspelheim became the Sun, Moon, and stars.

Mussato \mùs-'sä-tō\, Albertino (b. 1261, Padua, March of Verona [Italy]—d. May 31, 1329, Chioggia, Republic of Venice) Italian statesman and writer who was outstanding both as a poet and as a historian of the 14th century.

Mussato was knighted in 1296 and was sent in 1302 as ambassador to Pope Boniface VIII. In 1311 he was a member of an embassy from Padua to Emperor Henry VII in Milan, and, during a long war between Padua and Vicenza, he often served as a negotiator. Mussato was crowned as a poet before the senate and the university of Padua in 1315, the first poet so honored.

Mussato's *Historia Augusta* ("Augustan History"), a chronicle of Henry VII's actions in Italy, and his *De gestis Italicorum post Henricum VII Caesarem* ("Concerning the Deeds of the Italians After Emperor Henry VII") are important sources for the history of 14th-century Italy. His Latin poems and the tragedy *Ecerinis*, based on the life of the Veronese tyrant Ezzelino da Romano, foreshadow Italian humanism.

Musset \mue-'se\, Alfred de, *in full* Louis-Charles-Alfred de Musset (b. Dec. 11, 1810, Paris, Fr.—d. May 2, 1857, Paris) Distinguished French Romantic poet and playwright.

Musset's autobiographical *La Confession d'un enfant du siècle* (1836; *The Confession of a Child of the Century*) presents a striking picture of his youth as a member of a noble family. While still an adolescent, he came under the influence of the leaders of the Romantic movement, and he produced his first work, *Contes d'Espagne et d'Italie* ("Stories of Spain and of Italy"), in 1830.

Oil painting by Charles Landelle; in the Louvre, Paris

Cliché Musées Nationaux, Paris

After the failure of his play *La Nuit vénitienne* (1830; "The Venetian Night"), Musset refused to allow his other plays to be performed, but he continued to publish historical tragedies such as *Lorenzaccio* (1834) and delightful comedies such as *Il ne faut jurer de rien* (1836; "It Isn't Necessary to Promise Anything"). Musset's plays are now performed regularly. He was elected to the Académie Française in 1852.

Above all, Musset is remembered for his poetry. He wrote light satirical pieces and poems of dazzling technical virtuosity as well as lyrics, such as "La Nuit d'octobre" (1837; "The October Night"), that express emotions with passion and eloquence. Though always associated with the Romantic movement, Musset often poked fun at its excesses. His *Lettres de Dupuis et Cotonet* (1836–37), for example, contain a brilliant and illuminating satire of the literary fashions of the day. A love affair with the novelist George Sand inspired some of his finest lyrics, as recounted in his *Confession*.

Mutabilitie Cantos \,myü-tə-'bil-ə-tē\ (*in full* Two Cantos of Mutabilitie: Which, both for Forme and Matter, appear to be parcell of some following Booke of the Faerie Queene, under the legend of Constancie) Two poems and two stanzas of a third by Edmund SPENSER; they are generally considered to constitute a fragmentary Book VII of *The Faerie Queene*. They were first published with the folio edition of *The Faerie Queene* in 1609.

The *Mutabilitie Cantos* employ the new nine-line stanza Spenser had created for *The Faerie Queene*: eight iambic pentameter lines followed by a ninth line of six iambic feet (an alexandrine), the rhyme scheme of which is *ababbcbcc*.

After wreaking havoc on earth, overthrowing the laws of nature, justice, and policy, the poem's central figure, the ambitious Titaness Mutabilitie, hopes to extend her reign to the heavens themselves. She denies the authority of Jove, whose reign is marked by order and beneficence. On Arlo's Hill (Spenser's Irish home) Dame Nature presides over the conflict between titaness and god; she holds that while things in life may fluctuate their fundamental essence does not change.

Mutanabbī, al- \,ál-,mù-tá-'náb-,bē\, *in full* Abū aṭ-Ṭayyib Aḥmad ibn Ḥusayn al-Mutanabbī (b. 915, Kūfah [Iraq]—d. Sept. 23, 965, near Dayr al-ʿĀqūl) Poet regarded by many as the greatest in the Arabic language. Primarily a panegyrist, al-Mutanabbī wrote in a flowery, bombastic style marked by improbable metaphors. His widely quoted verse influenced Arabic poetry until the 19th century and has been translated into English.

Unusual for his time and rank, al-Mutanabbī, received an education. When the Muslim Qarmaṭians (a subsect of the Shīʿite Ismāʿīlites) sacked Kūfah in 924, he joined them and lived among the Bedouin. Claiming to be a prophet—hence the name al-Mutanabbī ("The Would-be Prophet")—he led a Qarmaṭian revolt in Syria in 932. After its suppression and two years' imprisonment, he recanted in 935 and became a wandering poet.

Al-Mutanabbī next began to write panegyrics in the tradition established by the poets Abū Tammām and al-Buḥturī. In 948 he attached himself to Sayf ad-Dawlah, the poet-prince of northern Syria. There he joined a brilliant circle that included al-Fārābi, a philosopher and musician; al-Iṣbahāni, a historian of literature and music; and Ibn Nubātah, a court preacher who delivered fiery sermons in rhymed prose. During his association with Sayf ad-Dawlah, al-Mutanabbī wrote panegyrics that rank as masterpieces of Arabic poetry. The latter part of this period, however, was clouded with intrigues and jealousies that culminated in his departure for Egypt. There he attached himself to the regent, the eunuch Abū al-Misk Kāfūr, who had been born a slave. The poet offended Kāfūr with scurrilous satirical verses, however, and he fled Egypt in 960. He lived in Shīrāz, Iran, until 965, when he returned to Iraq and was killed by bandits.

Al-Mutanabbī's pride and arrogance set the tone for much of his verse, which is ornately rhetorical, yet crafted with consummate skill and artistry. He gave to the traditional qasida, or ode, a freer and more personal development, writing in what can be called a neoclassical style.

Mutiny on the Bounty Romantic novel by Charles Nordhoff and James Norman Hall, published in 1932.

The vivid narrative is based on the actual mutiny against Captain William Bligh of HMS *Bounty* in 1789. Narrated by Roger Byam, a former midshipman and linguist aboard the vessel, the novel describes how Fletcher Christian and 15 others revolted against the petty, tyrannical Bligh, setting him and a number of loyal men adrift in a small craft in the South Seas.

Nordhoff wrote the Polynesian chapters of the novel, Hall the English, although each assisted the other. They collaborated on two sequels, *Men Against the Sea* (1934) and *Pitcairn's Island* (1934), which addressed the fate of the *Bounty* crew.

Mutis \'mü-tēs\, Álvaro, *pseudonym* Álvar de Mattos \thä-'mä-tōs\ (b. Aug. 25, 1923, Bogotá, Colom.) Versatile Colombian poet whose free verse confronts a world of cruelty and suffering.

Influenced in part by French Surrealism, Mutis was among the young poets of the diverse Cántico (Canticle) group that emerged in the 1940s. His poetry is characterized by freedom of meter, often resulting in long lines that are sometimes compared to Walt Whitman's. In his early work Mutis introduced a recurring character, Maqroll el Gaviero, with whom he identified so strongly that Mutis' collected poems (1990) were titled *Summa de Maqroll el Gaviero (1948–1988)*. In *Diario do Lecumberri* (1960; "Lecumberri Diary") Mutis wrote in prose about his experience in a Mexican jail. In later years he wrote fiction, including short stories and the novella *La mansión de Araucaíma* (1973; "Araucaíma Mansion"), which he subtitled "a gothic tale from the hot lands." He expanded on the character of Maqroll de Gaviero in novels, including *La nieve del almirante* (1986; "The Admiral's Snow").

Mutswairo \mū-'tswī-rō\, Solomon M. (b. April 26, 1924, Zawu, Southern Rhodesia [now in Zimbabwe]) Earliest Shona-language novelist and most important Shona poet.

Mutswairo grew up in Northern Rhodesia (now Zambia) and was educated at the University College of Fort Hare, S.Af. He taught and worked as a headmaster before traveling to the United States. He received a doctoral degree from Howard University in 1979, and in 1981 he returned to Zimbabwe.

Mutswairo's first novel, *Feso* (1956), was later banned by government censors; he published his English version of the novel in 1974. Both *Mapondera: Soldier of Zimbabwe* (1978), which celebrates Mapondera's efforts against colonial forces, and the novel *Chaminuka: Prophet of Zimbabwe* (1982) were written in English. Mutswairo's other works include *Murambiwa Goredema* (1959), a novel; *Ambuyamuderere* (1967), Shona nursery rhymes; and an anthology of several Shona poets.

muwashshaḥ \mū-'wȧsh-shȧk̲\ [Arabic, probably a derivative of *wishã* embroidered or painted fabric] An Arabic poetic genre in strophic form developed in Andalusia (part of Muslim Spain) from roughly the 9th to the 12th century. From the 12th century onward, its use spread to North Africa and the Muslim Middle East.

Especially adapted to singing, the *muwashshaḥ* is written in classical Arabic, and its subjects are those of classical Arabic poetry—love, wine, court figures. It sharply differs in form, however, from classical poetry, in which each verse is divided into two metric halves and a single rhyme recurs at the end of each verse. The *muwashshaḥ* is usually divided into five strophes, or stanzas, each numbering four, five, or six lines. A master rhyme appears at the beginning of the poem and at the end of the strophes, somewhat like a refrain; it is interrupted by subordinate rhymes. A possible scheme is *ABcdcdABefef-ABghghABijijABklklAB*. The last *AB*, called *kharjah*, or *markaz*, is usually written in vernacular Arabic or in the Spanish Mozarabic dialect; it is normally rendered in the voice of a girl and expresses her longing for her absent lover. Jewish poets of Spain also wrote *muwashshaḥ*s in Hebrew, with *kharjah*s in Arabic and Spanish. Beginning about the 13th century, Ṣūfī (Muslim mystic) poets began to adapt the form to mystical themes.

Muyaka \mū-'yä-kǝ\ or **al-Ghassaniy** \ȧl-g̲ȧ-'sȧn-ē\, *in full* Muyaka bin Haji al-Ghassaniy (b. 1776—d. 1840) Kenyan author who was the first Swahili-language secular poet known by name.

Muyaka is known particularly as an outstanding composer of quatrains (the most popular Swahili verse form for both philosophical and topical themes). Although he experimented little with prosody, his work ranged widely in type from didactic verse to love poems and from poems on domestic life to political satire. The preface to his collected poems, Diwani ya Muyaka (1940; "Collected Poems of Muyaka"), gives insight into his dual role as a commentator on his times and a voice of contemporary opinion.

Mwangi \'mwäŋ-gē\, Meja (b. December 1948, Nyeri, Kenya) Prolific and popular African novelist.

Mwangi was stimulated to try his hand at writing after reading *Weep Not, Child* by Ngugi wa Thiong'o, Kenya's first novelist. Like his mentor, Mwangi concentrated initially on the Mau Mau rebellion, telling stories of forest guerrillas who struggled, often unsuccessfully, against formidable adversaries. Both *Taste of Death* (his earliest narrative, not published until 1975) and *Carcase for Hounds* (1974) capture the spirit of the resistance movement in the Kikuyu highlands of colonial Kenya.

Mwangi also manifested a lively interest in Kenya's contemporary social problems. In *Kill Me Quick* (1973) he focuses on the plight of young men who, though educated, are unable to find honest employment. In *Going Down River Road* (1976) he deals with the rough-and-tumble life of construction workers in Nairobi, and in *The Cockroach Dance* (1979) he recounts the picaresque adventures of a meter reader coping with the squalor and violence of a slum. Among Mwangi's later works are the thriller *Bread of Sorrow* (1987), *Weapon of Hunger* (1989), *The Return of Shaka* (1989), and *Striving for the Wind* (1990).

My Ántonia \'än-tō-,nē-ǝ\ Novel by Willa CATHER, published in 1918. Her best-known work, it honors the immigrant settlers of the American plains. Narrated by the protagonist's lifelong friend, Jim Burden, the novel recounts the history of Ántonia Shimerda, the daughter of Bohemian immigrants who settled on the Nebraska frontier. The book contains a number of poetic passages about the disappearing frontier and the spirit and courage of frontier people. Many critics consider *My Ántonia* to be Cather's finest achievement.

My Childhood The first book of an autobiographical trilogy by Maksim GORKY, published in Russian in 1913–14 as *Detstvo*. It was also translated into English as *Childhood*.

Like the volumes of autobiography that were to follow, *My Childhood* examines the author's experiences by means of individual portraits and descriptions of events. He reveals that his mother was mostly absent after the death of his father and that his upbringing was in the hands of his brutal grandfather. He also creates a compelling portrait of his unlearned but loving grandmother. Leaving home at age 12, the young Gorky learns self-reliance and begins to educate himself by reading.

The subsequent autobiographical volumes are *V lyudyakh* (1915–16; *In the World*; also published as *My Apprenticeship*) and *Moi universitety* (1923; *My Universities*; also published as *My University Days*). Considered to constitute one of the finest Russian autobiographies, the books reveal Gorky to be an acute observer with great descriptive powers.

Myers \'mī-ǝrz\, L.H., *in full* Leopold Hamilton (b. 1881, Cambridge, Cambridgeshire, Eng.—d. April 8, 1944, Marlow, Buckinghamshire) English philosophical novelist whose most compelling works explore spiritual turmoil and despair.

Myers studied at Eton College, in Germany, and at the University of Cambridge. In 1901, when his father died, he turned his attention exclusively to writing, although he also traveled widely, living for some time in Colorado.

Myers' first novel, *The Orissers* (1922), marked him as an author of distinction. His major work, an Indian tetralogy set in the late 16th century at the time of Akbar the Great, consists of *The Near and the Far* (1929), *Prince Jali* (1931), *The Root and the Flower* (1935), and *The Pool of Vishnu* (1940). The tetralogy was published in 1940 as a single volume entitled *The Near and the Far*.

My Kinsman, Major Molineux \mō-li-'nū, *French* -'nœ̄\ Short story by Nathaniel HAWTHORNE, first published in 1832 in *The Token*, an annual Christmas gift book. The story was collected in *The Snow-Image, and Other Twice-Told Tales* (1851).

The story is set in New England before the American Revolution. Young Robin Molineux seeks out his kinsman, a major in the British army, with the hope of gaining access to power. He finds, however, that his kinsman is scorned, and he is advised to make his own way in the world.

On one level its theme is the loss of innocence. On a second level the story may be interpreted as a political allegory of nascent democratic self-government.

My Last Duchess Poem of 56 lines in rhyming couplets by Robert BROWNING, published in 1842 in *Dramatic Lyrics*, a volume in his *Bells and Pomegranates* series. It is one of Browning's most successful dramatic monologues.

The poem's narrator is the Duke of Ferrara, who comments dispassionately on the portrait of his late wife hanging on the wall, remarking on the duchess's innocence and character. He reveals that the duchess had incurred his displeasure by her expansive friendliness and her refusal to acknowledge his superiority in all things. It becomes apparent at last that he has brought about her death.

My Name Is Aram \ă-'räm\ Book of 14 interconnected short stories by William SAROYAN, published in 1940. The book consists of exuberant, often whimsical episodes in the imaginative life of young Aram Garoghlanian, an Armenian-American boy who is the author's alter ego.

Myrmidon \'mər-mə-,dän, -dən\ Any of a tribe of legendary Thessalian people who accompanied Achilles to the Trojan War. They were fierce and devoted followers of the hero Achilles; their name came to be applied in modern times to subordinates who carry out orders implacably.

According to some authorities, the Myrmidons later went to Aegina. Two derivations are given for the name Myrmidon. One suggests that it derives from a supposed ancestor, the son of Zeus and Eurymedusa (the daughter of King Myrmidon of Thessaly), who was seduced by Zeus in the form of an ant (Greek *myrmēx*). The second derivation refers to the repeopling of Aegina (after all its inhabitants had died of a plague) with ants. The ants were changed into humans by Zeus at the request of Aeacus, king of the island.

Mysteries of Udolpho, The \ŭ-'dŏl-fō, yŭ-\ Novel by Ann RADCLIFFE, published in 1794. One of the most famous of the English gothic novels, the work tells the story of the orphaned Emily St. Aubert, who is subjected to cruelties by her guardians, threatened with the loss of her fortune, and imprisoned but finally freed and united with her lover. Many strange and fearful events (now classic devices of gothic romances) take place in the haunted atmosphere of the solitary castle of Udolpho.

Mysterious Island, The Adventure novel by Jules VERNE, published in French in three volumes as *L'Île mystérieuse* in 1874 and included in his popular science-fiction series *Voyages extraordinaires* (1863–1910). *The Mysterious Island* follows the adventures of a group of castaways who use their survivalist savvy to build a functional community on an uncharted island.

A hot-air balloon carrying five passengers and a dog escapes from Richmond, Va., during the American Civil War. It is blown off course and deposited near an obscure island. One of the castaways nearly dies after a skirmish with pirates; he is saved by the unexplained appearance of medicine after the pirates are unexpectedly routed. The group later discovers that their secret helper is the reclusive Captain Nemo (first introduced in Verne's *Twenty Thousand Leagues Under the Sea*), who dies and is buried at sea in his submarine. The castaways are eventually saved by a passing ship.

Mystery of Edwin Drood, The \'ed-win-'drŭd\ Unfinished novel by Charles DICKENS, published posthumously in 1870. Only 6 of the 12 projected parts had been completed by the time of Dickens' death.

Although Dickens had included touches of the gothic and horrific in his earlier works, *Edwin Drood* was his only true mystery story. He left few clues as to how he intended to end the work, and the solution itself remains a mystery.

Edwin Drood is the ward of Jack Jasper, the choirmaster of Cloisterham and an outwardly respectable opium addict. Jasper secretly loves Drood's fiancée, Rosa Bud. Drood and Rosa no longer love each other and break their engagement; Drood disappears soon thereafter. Neville Landless, also in love with Rosa, is arrested for Drood's murder but is released when no body is found. Jasper confesses his love to Rosa and threatens to incriminate Neville unless she returns his love. Datchery, a stranger, arrives, shadowing and vexing Jasper—then the manuscript ends.

mystery play or **mistery** \'mis-tə-rē\ One of three principal kinds of vernacular drama of the European Middle Ages (with the MORALITY PLAY and the MIRACLE PLAY).

The mystery plays, usually representing biblical subjects, developed from plays presented in Latin by churchmen on church premises. The plays depicted such subjects as the Creation, Adam and Eve, the murder of Abel, and the Last Judgment. During the 13th century, various guilds began producing the plays in the vernacular at sites removed from the churches. Under these conditions, the strictly religious nature of the plays declined, and they became filled with irrelevancies and apocryphal elements. Furthermore, satirical elements were introduced to mock physicians, soldiers, judges, and even monks and priests. In England, over the course of decades, groups of 25 to 50 plays were organized into lengthy cycles. In France a single play, *The Acts of the Apostles* by Arnoul and Simon Gréban, contained 494 speaking parts and 61,908 lines of rhymed verse; it was performed over the course of 40 days.

At their height, the mystery plays were quite elaborate in their production. They did not attempt to achieve unity of time, place, and action, and therefore they could represent any number of different geographic locations and climates in juxtaposition. Mechanical devices, trapdoors, and other artifices were employed to portray flying angels, fire-spouting monsters, miraculous transformations, and graphic martyrdoms.

mystery story Work of fiction in which the evidence related to a crime or to a mysterious event is so presented that the reader has an opportunity to solve the problem, the author's solution being the final phase of the piece.

The mystery story is an age-old popular genre and is related to several other forms. Elements of mystery may be present in narratives of horror or terror, pseudoscientific fantasies, crime stories, accounts of diplomatic intrigue, affairs of codes and ciphers and secret societies, or any situation involving an enigma. By and large, however, the true mystery story is one specifically concerned with a riddle of some kind.

Riddle stories have an ancient heritage. The riddle of Samson, propounded in the Bible (Judges 14:12–18), is a famous early example, but puzzles were also popular among the ancient Egyptians and the Greeks. The distinguishing feature of the riddle story is that the reader be confronted with a number of mysterious facts and situations, explanation of which is reserved until the end of the story.

Edgar Allan Poe's short story "The Gold Bug" is a classic example of one perennially popular type of mystery, the story of a search for lost treasure. Murder mysteries, which are generally among the more sinister mystery stories, also contain elements of riddle-solving. Two notable riddle stories of modern times—"The Lady or the Tiger?" by Frank R. Stockton and "The Mysterious Card" by Cleveland Moffett—offered no solution to the riddle posed and gained wide attention by their novelty.

See also DETECTIVE STORY; HARD-BOILED FICTION; GOTHIC NOVEL; SPY STORY.

myth \'mith\ [Greek *mŷthos* thing said, speech, tale] **1.** A usually traditional story of ostensibly historical events that serves to unfold part of a worldview of a people or a practice, belief, or natural phenomenon. *Compare* EUHEMERISM; FABLE; FOLKTALE. Also, the theme or plot of a mythical tale occurring in forms differing only in detail. **2.** The whole body of myths.

Myths relate the paradigmatic events, conditions, and deeds of gods or superhuman beings that are outside ordinary human life and yet basic to it. These extraordinary events are set in a time altogether different from historical time, often at the beginning of creation or at an early stage of prehistory.

Features of myth are shared by other kinds of literature. Etiological tales explain the origins or causes of various aspects of nature or human society and life. Fairy tales deal with extraordinary beings and events but lack the authority of myth. Sagas and epics claim authority and truth but reflect specific historical settings.

The modern study of myth arose with the Romantic movement of the early 19th century, but interpretations of myth were offered much earlier. The influence of philosophy in ancient Greece led to allegorical views of myth or to the historical reductionism of Euhemerus (fl. 300 BC), who believed that the gods of myth were originally simply great people. The development of comparative philology in the 19th century, together with ethnological discoveries in the 20th, established the main contours of mythology, the science of myth. Since the Romantics, all study of myth has been comparative. Wilhelm Mannhardt, Sir James Frazer, and Stith Thompson employed the comparative approach to collect and classify the themes of folklore and mythology. Bronisław Malinowski emphasized the ways in which myth fulfills common social functions. Claude Lévi-Strauss and other structuralists have compared the formal relations and patterns in myths throughout the world.

Sigmund Freud put forward the idea that symbolic communication does not depend on cultural history alone but also on the workings of the psyche. Thus Freud introduced a transhistorical and biological approach and a view of myth as an expression of repressed ideas. Carl Jung extended Freud's approach with his theory of the "collective unconscious" and the archetypes, often encoded in myth, that arise out of it.

Some scholars, such as Mircea Eliade (a historian of religion) and the German theologian Rudolf Otto, hold that myth is to be understood solely as a religious phenomenon, irreducible to nonreligious categories. Scholars of the so-called Myth and Ritual School contend that any myth functions, or at one time functioned, as the "explanation" of a corresponding ritual.

mythicist \'mith-i-sist\ **1.** A student or interpreter of myths. **2.** An adherent of the view that apparently supernatural persons or events have their origin in human imagination, especially as it is revealed in myth.

mythoclast \'mith-ə-,klast\ [*myth* + *-clast* (as in *iconoclast*)] A decrier of myths.

Myth of Sisyphus, The \'sis-i-fəs\ Philosophical essay by Albert CAMUS, published in French in 1942 as *Le Mythe de Sisyphe*. Published in the same year as Camus's novel *L'Étranger* (*The Stranger*), *The Myth of Sisyphus* contains a sympathetic analysis of contemporary nihilism and touches on the nature of the absurd. Together the two works established his reputation, and they are often seen as thematically complementary.

Influenced by the philosophers Søren Kierkegaard, Arthur Schopenhauer, and Friedrich Nietzsche, Camus argues that life is essentially meaningless, although humans continue to try to impose order on existence and to look for answers to unanswerable questions. Camus uses the Greek legend of Sisyphus, who is condemned by the gods to roll a boulder up a hill for eternity, as a metaphor for the individual's persistent struggle against the essential absurdity of life. According to Camus, the first step an individual must take is to accept the fact of this absurdity. If, as for Sisyphus, suicide is not a possible response, the only alternative is to rebel by rejoicing in the act of rolling the boulder up the hill; with the joyful acceptance of the struggle against defeat the individual gains definition and identity.

mythography \mi-'thäg-rə-fē\ **1.** The representation of mythical subjects in art. **2.** A critical compilation of myths.

mythologem \mi-'thäl-ə-jem\ [Greek *mythológēma* mythical narrative] A basic or recurrent theme of myth.

mythopoeia \,mith-ə-'pē-ə\ [Greek *mythopoiía* the making of tales, a derivative of *mythopoieîn* to relate or invent tales] A creating of myth or a giving rise to myths.

mythopoem \,mith-ə-'pō-əm, -'pōm\ A mythological poem.

mythos \'mī-,thäs\ *plural* mythoi \-,thòi\ **1.** A myth. **2.** Mythology. **3.** The underlying theme or symbolic meaning of a creative work. *See also* MYTH; MYTHOLOGY.

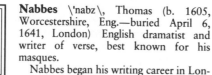

Nabbes \'nabz\, Thomas (b. 1605, Worcestershire, Eng.—buried April 6, 1641, London) English dramatist and writer of verse, best known for his masques.

Nabbes began his writing career in London in about 1630. His first comedy, *Covent Garden*, was performed in 1632 or 1633. The comedies *Totenham Court* (performed 1633) and *The Bride* (performed 1638) met with some success, but his tragedies—especially

The Unfortunate Mother (1640)—were not appreciated. He also wrote a number of masques and occasional verses. All of Nabbes's works, with the exception of his continuation of Richard Knolles's *Generall Historie of the Turkes* (1638), were reprinted in A.H. Bullen's *Old English Plays* (1887).

Nābighah, an- \än-'nä-bē-,gä\, *in full* an-Nābighah adh-Dhubyānī \äth-thú-'byä-,nē\, *original name* Ziyād ibn Muʿāwiyah \zē-'yäd-,ib-ən-mú-"ä-wē-yə\ (fl. *c.* 600) One of the pre-Islāmic Arab poets whose works are believed by some authorities to have been selected for inclusion in the Muʻallaqāt, a collection of 6th-century odes.

One of the most highly respected of the pre-Islāmic poets, an-Nābighah possessed a grave and sensitive style, full of imagination and fine imagery. His verse, mainly eulogies and satires on tribal strife, displays an impressive command of language and its artifices.

Nabokov \nə-ˈbô-kəf, ˈnab-ə-kôf\, Vladimir (Vladimirovich) (b. April 22, 1899, St. Petersburg, Russia—d. July 2, 1977, Montreux, Switz.) Russian-born American novelist and critic. He wrote in both Russian and English, and his best works, including LOLITA (1955), feature intricate, stylish literary effects.

Bettmann Archive

Nabokov began his career as a poet, publishing two collections of verse before leaving Russia in 1919. He graduated from Trinity College, Cambridge, in 1922, and from then until 1940 he lived in Germany and France. By 1925 he had settled upon prose as his main genre. His first novel, *Mashenka* (*Mary*), appeared in 1926; avowedly autobiographical, it contains descriptions of the young Nabokov's first serious romance as well as of the Nabokov family estate, both of which are also described in his autobiography, SPEAK, MEMORY (1951). Nabokov did not again draw so heavily upon personal experience until he wrote PNIN (1957), an episodic novel about an émigré professor in the United States that is partly based on his experiences while teaching at Cornell University, Ithaca, N.Y.

His second novel, *Korol, dama, valet* (1928; KING, QUEEN, KNAVE), marked a turn to the highly stylized form that characterized his art thereafter. The subject matter of Nabokov's novels is principally the problem of art itself presented in various figurative disguises. Thus, *Zashchita Luzhina* (1930; *The Defense*) seemingly is about chess, *Otchayaniye* (1936; *Despair*) about murder, and *Priglasheniye na kazn* (1938; INVITATION TO A BEHEADING) a political story, but all three works make statements about art that are central to understanding the book as a whole. Beginning with *Dar* (published serially 1937–38; THE GIFT), parody became another common feature of his novels.

His first novels in English, THE REAL LIFE OF SEBASTIAN KNIGHT (1941) and BEND SINISTER (1947), do not rank with his best Russian work, but PALE FIRE (1962) extends and completes Nabokov's mastery of unorthodox structure, first shown in *The Gift*. *Lolita* (1955) is another of Nabokov's subtle allegories, and ADA (1969) parodies the family chronicle.

Nabokov's major critical works are an irreverent book about Nikolay Gogol (1944) and a monumental four-volume translation of, and commentary on, Aleksandr Pushkin's *Eugene Onegin* (1964). He also produced a number of short stories and novellas, mostly written in Russian and translated into English.

Naevius \ˈnē-vē-əs\, Gnaeus (b. *c.* 270 BC, Capua, Campania [Italy]—d. *c.* 200 BC, Utica [now Utique, Tunisia]) Early Latin epic poet and dramatist. He was the originator of historical plays (*fabulae praetextae*) based on Roman historical or legendary figures and events. The titles of two *praetextae* are known, *Romulus* and *Clastidium*, the latter celebrating the victory of Marcus Claudius Marcellus in 222.

Naevius produced half a dozen tragedies and more than 30 comedies, many of which are known by their titles alone, as only fragments of his work have survived. Some were translated from Greek plays, and, in adapting them, he created the Latin *fabula palliata* (from *pallium*, a type of Greek cloak), perhaps being the first to introduce song and recitative, transferring elements from one play into another, and adding variety to the meter. He incorporated his own critical remarks on Roman daily life and politics, the latter leading to his imprisonment and perhaps exile. Many of his comedies used the stereotypes of character and plot and the apt and colorful language that would later be characteristic of Plautus.

Nagai Kafū \nä-ˈgī-ˈkä-ˌfū\, *pseudonym of* Nagai Sōkichi \ˈsō-kē-chē\ (b. Dec. 3, 1879, Tokyo, Japan—d. April 30, 1959, Tokyo) Japanese novelist strongly identified with Tokyo and its immediate premodern past.

Kafū failed to finish his university studies and was sent abroad from 1903 to 1908. Before he left, he had produced three novels influenced by French naturalism. After he returned to Japan, he continued to be a student and translator of French literature, principally the Romantic and Symbolist poets. He also did his most important writing at this time, work that seems, in its lyricism and delicate eroticism, nearer 19th-century Japanese literature than French. The lyricism is particularly apparent in *Sumidagawa* (1909; *The River Sumida*), a novelette about the disappearance of the gracious past in Tokyo. For some years after his return, Kafū was a professor at Keiō University in Tokyo and a leader of the literary world. After his resignation in 1916, a stronger note of rancor at what the modern world had done to the old city came into his work. After *Ude Kurabe* (1917; *Geisha in Rivalry*), a caustic study of the geisha's world, he fell into almost complete silence. Only in 1937, with *Bokutō kidan* (*A Strange Tale from East of the River*), did he return to the lyrical vein of his early days.

Nāgarakertāgama \ˈnä-gə-rə-ker-ˈtä-gə-mə\ Javanese epic poem written in 1365 by the Indonesian court poet PRAPAÑCĀ. Considered the most important work of the vernacular literature that developed in the Majapahit era (13th–16th century), it is a long descriptive poem detailing life in the kingdom of Java during the early reign of Rājasanagara (1350–89). It is an invaluable source for the legendary, historical, cultural, political, religious, and social aspects of the old Hindu-Javanese Majapahit empire.

na gCopaleen, Myles.   Pseudonym of Flann O'BRIEN.

nagual \nä-ˈgwäl\ *or* **nahual** \nä-ˈhwäl\ [Spanish, nagual, sorcerer, from Nahuatl *nāhualli* sorcerer]   Personal guardian spirit believed by some Meso-American Indians to reside in an animal, such as a deer, jaguar, or bird. In some areas the nagual is the animal into which certain men can transform themselves to do evil; the word derives from the Nahuatl *nāhualli* ("sorcerer"), applied to the animal forms assumed by sorcerers.

Naḥman ben Simḥah \näk̲-ˈmän-ben-sim-ˈk̲ä\ of Bratslav \ˈbrät-ˌsläv\ (b. *c.* 1772, Medzhibozh, Ukraine, Russian Empire [now Medzhybizh, Ukraine]—d. *c.* 1811, Uman) Ḥasidic rabbi and storyteller, noted for the parables, folklore, and mythic tales that he told to prepare his followers to worship God.

The great-grandson of the Baʻal Shem Tov, the founder of the Ḥasidic movement, Naḥman became a religious leader and teacher at an early age. After studying in Tiberius, Palestine, he declared himself the "true ẓaddik" (righteous man) of his generation, the one who would renew the Ḥasidic movement. He moved to Bratslav in 1802.

Naḥman's disciple, Rabbi Nathan Sternharz, compiled and wrote down his teachings, which emphasized the need to redeem the world from evil through simple faith, prayer, repentance through fasting and self-punishment, and piety expressed through singing and dancing.

Naiad \\'nā-əd, 'nī-, -ˌad\\ *plural* Naiads *or* Naiades \\'nā-ə-ˌdēz, 'nī-\\ [Greek *Naïad-, Naïas,* a derivative of *nân* to flow] In Greek and Roman mythology, one of the beautiful, beneficent nymphs believed to live in and give life and perpetuity to flowing water—springs, rivers, fountains, lakes.

Naʿīmah \\nȧ-'ē-mə, *Arabic* -ˈʿē-\\ *or* **Nouayme** \\nü-'ī-me\\ *or* **Naimy** \\nə-'ī-ˌmē\\, Mikhā'īl (b. Nov. 22, 1889, Biskintā, Lebanon—d. Feb. 28, 1988, Beirut)   Lebanese literary critic, playwright, essayist, and short-story writer who helped introduce modern realism into Arabic prose fiction.

Naʿīmah was educated at schools in Lebanon, Palestine, Russia, and the United States. He settled in New York City and worked as a journalist and critic for Arabic-language publications there. In 1932 he returned to Lebanon a celebrated author. Naʿīmah depicted the problems of Lebanese society realistically and with great technical sophistication. His collections of short stories include *Al-Marāhil* (1933; "The Stages"), *Kana ma kāna* (1937; "Once Upon a Time"), and *Al-Bayādir* (1945; "The Threshing Floors"). His other outstanding books are a highly subjective biography of Khalil Gibran (1934) and his autobiography, *Sabʿūn,* 3 vol. (1959–60; "Seventy").

Naipaul \\'nī-ˌpȯl\\, V.S., *in full* Sir Vidiadhar Surajprasad Naipaul (b. Aug. 17, 1932, Trinidad)   Trinidadian novelist of Indian descent known for works that examine exile and alienation.

Descended from Hindu Indians who had immigrated to Trinidad as indentured servants, Naipaul left Trinidad to attend the University of Oxford in 1950. He subsequently settled in England. His earliest books are ironic and satirical accounts of life in the Caribbean. A HOUSE FOR MR. BISWAS (1961) was a much more important work and won him critical recognition. Naipaul's subsequent novels continued to examine the disintegration and the personal and collective alienation typical of postcolonial nations. The three stories of *In a Free State* (1971) are set in various countries; *Guerrillas* (1975), on a Caribbean island; and A BEND IN THE RIVER (1979), in Central Africa. Naipaul's other novels include *The Mimic Men* (1967) and *The Enigma of Arrival* (1987). *A Way in the World* (1994), considered a novel, is actually more of a spiritual autobiography.

Among Naipaul's nonfiction works are three studies of India, *An Area of Darkness* (1965), *India: A Wounded Civilization* (1977), and *India: A Million Mutinies Now* (1990); *The Middle Passages* (1962); and *The Return of Eva Peron* (1980). Naipaul was knighted in 1989.

Nairne \\'nern\\, Carolina, Baroness Nairne of Nairne, *original surname* Oliphant \\'äl-ə-fənt, 'ȯl-\\ (b. Aug. 16, 1766, Gask, Perth, Scot.—d. Oct. 26, 1845, Gask)   Scottish songwriter and poet who wrote "Charlie Is My Darling," "The Hundred Pipers," "The Land o' the Leal," and "Will Ye No' Come Back Again?"

Nairne followed Robert Burns's example of writing in the folk tradition. Her songs, which helped create the myth that the Stuart cause was the cause of the common people, first appeared in *The Scottish Minstrel* (1821–24) under the pseudonym Mrs. Bogan of Bogan. Their gentle pathos and occasional wit appealed to all tastes, and the songs soon found their way back into the folk repertoire. A collected edition, *Lays from Strathearn* (1846), appeared after her death.

naive narrator   *see* NARRATOR.

Naked and the Dead, The   Novel by Norman MAILER. Published in 1948, the book was hailed as one of the finest American novels to come out of World War II. The story concerns a platoon of 13 American soldiers who are stationed on the Japanese-held island of Anopopei in the Pacific. With almost journalistic detail, Mailer records the lives of men at war, characterizing the soldiers individually in flashbacks that illuminate their past.

Name of the Rose, The   Novel by Umberto ECO, published in Italian as *Il nome della rosa* in 1980. Although the work stands on its own as a murder mystery, it is more accurately seen as a questioning of "truth" from theological, philosophical, scholarly, and historical perspectives.

The story centers on William of Baskerville, a 50-year-old monk who is sent to investigate a death at a Benedictine monastery. During his search, several other monks are killed in a bizarre pattern that reflects the Book of Revelation. Highly rational, Baskerville meets his nemesis in Jorge of Burgos, a doctrinaire blind monk determined to destroy heresy at any cost.

Namora \\nȧ-'mȯr-ə\\, Fernando Gonçalves (b. April 15, 1919, Condeixa, Port.—d. Jan. 31, 1989, Lisbon)   Portuguese writer who wrote Neorealist poetry and fiction, much of it inspired by his experience as a rural doctor.

Namora studied medicine at the University of Coimbra and established a practice in the mountainous Beira Baixa region. He wrote about his attempt to overcome the mistrust of superstitious peasants in *Retalhos da vida de um médico* (1949; *Mountain Doctor;* expanded 1963). In reaction to the oppression and poverty he observed, he turned to writing antifascist Neorealist fiction. He wrote more than 30 novels, including *Minas de São Francisco* (1946; "Mines of São Francisco"), *O trigo e o joio* (1954; *Fields of Fate*), and *Os clandestinos* (1972; "The Secret Ones").

Nana \\nä-'nä\\   Novel by Émile Zola, published in French in 1880. *Nana* is one of a sequence of 20 novels that constitute Zola's ROUGON-MACQUART CYCLE.

The title character grows up in the slums of Paris. She has a brief career as an untalented actress before finding success as a courtesan. Although vulgar and ignorant, she has a destructive sexuality that attracts many rich and powerful men. Cruelly contemptuous of her lovers' emotions, Nana wastes their fortunes, driving many of them to ruin and even suicide.

Nanhu   Pseudonym of XU ZHIMO.

Nansen \\'nȧn-sən\\, Fridtjof (b. Oct. 10, 1861, Store-Frøen, near Christiania [now Oslo], Nor.—d. May 13, 1930, Lysaker, near Oslo)   Norwegian explorer, oceanographer, statesman, and Nobel Prize winner, whose accounts of his many expeditions to the Arctic and in the North Atlantic are classics of Norwegian literature.

A great outdoorsman, Nansen set off in August 1888 with an expedition of six to traverse Greenland from east to west. Forced to winter at Godthåb (Nuuk), Nansen there studied Eskimo culture, later writing *Eskimoliv* (1891; *Eskimo Life*).

In 1893 Nansen initiated a plan to trace the polar current by allowing a specially built ship to freeze into the ice pack off eastern Siberia and to be carried across the Arctic Ocean to Spitsbergen by the currents. Once assured that the ship would continue to drift safely, Nansen started northward with dogsleds and kayaks. On April 8 he turned back from 86°14' N, the highest latitude then reached by humans. The drifting ship reached Norway in 1896. Nansen's two-volume account of the expedition was entitled *Fram over Polhavet* (1897; *Farthest North*).

Nansen made many further contributions to oceanography and exploration. His two-volume *Nord i Tåkeheimen* (1911; *In Northern Mists*) is a critical review of the exploration of the northern regions from early times up to the beginning of the 16th century.

During and after World War I Nansen concentrated his efforts on humanitarian and diplomatic activities. He received the Nobel Prize for Peace in 1922.

nanxi or **nan-hsi** \ˈnän-ˈshē\ [Chinese *nánxì*]   One of the first fully developed forms of Chinese drama. *Nanxi* ("southern drama") emerged in the area around Wenzhou in southern China during the Song dynasty (960–1279). Originally the creation of folk authors, the earliest *nanxi* were a combination of Song plays with local folk songs and ballads. They were characterized by their colloquial language and large numbers of scenes; flexible verses (*qu*) set to popular local music, which made both poetry and music accessible to the ordinary spectator, alternated with vernacular spoken passages. Professional playwrights wrote large numbers of *nanxi* for local troupes. Of these, however, only 283 titles and 20 play texts remain. *Zhang Xie zhuangyuan* ("Top Graduate Zhang Xie") is one of the best-known of the extant texts. The form was the precursor of the *chuanqi* style.

Naoki Prize \nä-ˈō-kē\   Japanese literary prize awarded twice yearly to an outstanding Japanese novelist of popular literature. The Naoki Prize is one of the most prestigious Japanese literary awards. It confers on the winner 1,000,000 yen and a watch.

Kikuchi Kan established the Naoki Prize in 1935 in memory of his friend Naoki Sanjūgo in the hope of elevating the prestige of popular literature.

Napoleon \nə-ˈpō-lē-ən\   Fictional character, a pig who usurps power and becomes dictator over the other animals in ANIMAL FARM, by George Orwell.

Narayan \nə-ˈrī-ən\, R.K., *in full* Rasipuram Krishnaswami, *original surname* Narayanswami \-ˌswä-mē\ (b. Oct. 10, 1906, Madras, India)   One of the finest Indian authors of his generation writing in English.

Reared by his grandmother, Narayan completed his education in 1930 and briefly worked as a teacher before deciding to devote himself full-time to writing. His first novel, *Swami and Friends* (1935), is an episodic narrative recounting the adventures of a group of schoolboys. That book and all of Narayan's later works are set in the fictitious South Indian town of Malgudi. Narayan typically portrays the peculiarities of human relationships and the ironies of Indian daily life, in which modern urban existence clashes with ancient tradition. His style is graceful, marked by genial humor, elegance, and simplicity.

Among his novels are *The English Teacher* (1945), *Waiting for the Mahatma* (1955), *The Guide* (1958), *The Man-Eater of Malgudi* (1961), *The Vendor of Sweets* (1967), *A Tiger for Malgudi* (1983), and *The World of Nagaraj* (1990). Narayan has also written a number of short stories; collections include *Lawley Road* (1956), *A Horse and Two Goats and Other Stories* (1970), *Under the Banyan Tree and Other Stories* (1985), and *Grandmother's Tale* (1992). In addition to works of nonfiction (chiefly memoirs), he also published shortened modern prose versions of two Indian epics, *The Ramayana* (1972) and *The Mahabharata* (1978).

Narcissus \när-ˈsis-əs\   In Greek mythology, the son of the river god Cephissus and the nymph Leiriope; he was distinguished for his beauty. His mother was told that he would have a long life, provided he never looked upon his own features. His rejection, however, of the love of the nymph Echo or of his

lover Ameinias drew upon him the vengeance of the gods. He fell in love with his own reflection in the waters of a spring and pined away (or killed himself); the flower that bears his name grew where he died.

Narnia \ˈnär-nē-ə\   Imaginary setting of THE CHRONICLES OF NARNIA, a series of seven children's books by C.S. Lewis. The magical land is inhabited by spirits, talking animals, unicorns, giants, fauns, werewolves, and other mythical creatures.

narodnost \nə-ˈrȯd-nəsʸt \ [Russian *narodnost'*, a derivative of *narodnyĭ* national, folk, a derivative of *narod* people] (literally "folkness" or "national quality")   Doctrine or national principle, the meaning of which has changed over the course of Russian literary criticism. Originally denoting simply literary fidelity to Russia's distinct cultural heritage, *narodnost*, in the hands of radical critics such as Nikolay Dobrolyubov, came to be the measure of an author's social responsibility, both in portraying the aspirations of the common people and in making literature accessible to the masses. These complementary values of *narodnost* became prescribed elements of Socialist Realism, the officially approved style of writing in the Soviet Union from the early 1930s to the mid-1980s.

narrative verse   A verse or poem that tells a story. It is often contrasted with lyric verse and verse drama. The main forms of narrative verse are the epic and the ballad, both of which are products of the oral tradition.

narratology \ˌnar-ə-ˈtäl-ə-jē\   In literary theory, the study of narrative structure. Like structuralism, from which it derived, narratology is based on the idea of a common literary language, or a universal pattern of codes that operates within the text of a work.

The foundations of narratology were laid in such books as Vladimir Propp's *Morfologiya skazki* (1928; *Morphology of the Folk Tale*), which created a model for folktales based on seven "spheres of action" and 31 "functions" of narrative; Claude Lévi-Strauss's *Anthropologie structurale* (1958; *Structural Anthropology*), which outlined a grammar of mythology; A.J. Greimas' *Sémantique structurale* (1966; *Structural Semantics*), which proposed a system of six structural units called "actants"; and Tzvetan Todorov's *Grammaire du Décaméron* (1969; "The Grammar of the Decameron"), which introduced the term *narratologie*. In *Figures III* (1972; partial translation, *Narrative Discourse*) and *Nouveau Discours de récit* (1983; *Narrative Discourse Revisited*), Gérard Genette codified a system of analysis that examined both the actual narration and the act of narrating as they existed apart from the story or the content. Other influential theorists in narratology were Roland Barthes, Claude Bremond, and Northrop Frye. *See also* ARCHETYPAL CRITICISM; STRUCTURALISM.

narrator \ˈnar-ˌā-tər, -ə-tər; na-ˈrā-tər\ [Latin, a derivative of *narrare* to tell, relate]   One who tells a story. In a work of fiction the narrator determines the story's point of view. If the narrator is a full participant in the story's action, the narrative is said to be in the first person. A story told by a narrator who is not a character in the story is a third-person narrative. *See also* POINT OF VIEW.

Narrators are sometimes categorized by the way in which they present their story. An *intrusive narrator*, a common device in many 18th- and 19th-century works, is one who interrupts the story to provide a commentary to the reader. An *unreliable narrator* is one who does not understand the full import of a situation or one who makes incorrect conclusions and assumptions about events witnessed; this type is exemplified by the narrator of Ford Madox Ford's *The Good Soldier*. A related device is the *naive narrator*, who does not have the sophistication to understand the full import of the story's events, though the reader understands. Such narrators are often children, as in Robert Louis Stevenson's *Treasure Island*. The protagonist of Laurence Sterne's *Tristram Shandy* is the paradigm of the *self-conscious narrator*, who calls attention to the text as fiction.

Narrenschiff, Das \däs-'när-ən-,shift\   Long poem by Sebastian BRANT, published in 1494. It was published in English as *The Ship of Fools*. The work concerns the incidents on a ship carrying more than 100 people to Narragonia, the fools' paradise. An unsparing, bitter, and sweeping satire, especially of

Illustration for the first edition by Albrecht Dürer
Bayerische Staatsbibliothek, Munich

the corruption in the Roman Catholic church, *Das Narrenschiff* was translated into Latin, Low German, Dutch, and French and adapted in English by Alexander Barclay (*The Shyp of Folys of the Worlde*, 1509). In 1962 Katherine Anne Porter used Brant's title for her allegorical novel in which the German ship *Vera* is a microcosm of life. *See also* FOOL'S LITERATURE.

Narrow Road to the Deep North, The   Travel account written by Japanese haiku master BASHŌ as *Oku no hosomichi*, published in 1694.

Considered one of the greatest works of classical Japanese literature, this poetic travelogue was begun in 1689 when Bashō sold his home traveled on foot to the remote northern provinces of Japan. Five months of the journey are described in exquisite prose that combines intimate details of his journey with historical background, fictional anecdotes, literary allusions, and his own emotional responses, often expressed in haiku. Although the work is secular, Bashō clearly seeks spiritual enlightenment and a reaffirmation of values that have been lost in the era of the shoguns.

The first English translation, *Bashō: The Narrow Road to the Deep North and Other Travel Sketches*, by Nobuyuki Yuasa, was published in 1966. The 1968 version by Cid Corman and Kamaike Susumu, called *Back Roads to Far Towns*, was an attempt to provide a more contemporary rendering of the tale. Another translation, *Narrow Road to the Interior* by Sam Hamill, was published in 1991.

Naruszewicz \ˌnä-rü-'she-vʸĕch\, Adam (Stanisław) (b. Oct. 20, 1733, Pinsk, Russia [now in Belarus]—d. July 6, 1796, Janów [Poland])   First Polish historian to use modern methods of scholarship and a poet whose work reflects the transition from the Baroque to the classical style.

Naruszewicz's most important work is *Historia narodu polskiego od przyjęcia chrześcijaństwa*, 7 vol. (1780–86; "The History of the Polish Nation from its Conversion to Christianity"), which records events to the end of the 14th century. Aided in this task by the Polish king Stanisław August, he used as many primary sources as possible and included not only accounts of kings and battles but also descriptions of the economic, social, and cultural life of each period.

Nasby \'naz-bē\, Petroleum V., *in full* Vesuvius, *pseudonym of* David Ross Locke \'läk\ (b. Sept. 20, 1833, Binghamton, N.Y., U.S.—d. Feb. 15, 1888, Toledo, Ohio)   American humorist who had considerable influence on public issues during and after the American Civil War.

From an early age Locke worked for newspapers in New York and Ohio. In 1861, as editor of the *Findlay* (Ohio) *Jeffersonian*, he published the first of many satirical letters purporting to be written by one Petroleum V. Nasby. For more than 20 years Locke contributed "Nasby Letters" to the *Toledo Blade*, which under his editorship gained national circulation. Many of the letters appeared also in book form, including *The Nasby Papers* (1864) and *The Diary of an Office Seeker* (1881).

An ardent Unionist and foe of slavery, Locke vigorously supported the Northern cause. His chief weapon was a heavy irony, with his character Nasby, a coarse and vicious Copperhead, arguing illiterately the Southern position.

Nascimento \ˌnä-shē-'meⁿ-tü\, Francisco Manuel do, *pseudonym* Filinto Elísio \ä-'lēz-yü\ (b. Dec. 23, 1734, Lisbon, Port.—d. Feb. 25, 1819, Paris, Fr.)   The last of the Portuguese Neoclassical poets, whose conversion late in life to Romanticism helped prepare the way for that movement's triumph in his country.

Of humble birth and probably illegitimate, Nascimento in 1768 became tutor to the daughters of the Marquis of Alorna and fell in love with one of them, the "Maria" of his poems. Disapproving of the lowborn poet's affection for his daughter, the marquis may have been ultimately responsible for Nascimento's being denounced to the Inquisition in June 1778. He succeeded in escaping to France, where, except for some four years spent in The Hague, he remained.

The themes of Nascimento's poetry—which is usually in blank verse, polished, robust, but often overladen with archaisms—range from denunciations of the tyranny of the aristocracy, the Inquisition, and the church hierarchy to homely evocations of the joys of life in his native land and laments on the poverty and loneliness of exile. His demonstration of the flexibility and richness of the Portuguese language and his choice of themes influenced the Romantic writers.

Nash \'nash\, Ogden, *in full* Frederic Ogden Nash (b. Aug. 19, 1902, Rye, N.Y., U.S.—d. May 19, 1971, Baltimore, Md.)   American writer of humorous poetry who won a large following for his audacious verse.

Nash sold his first verse (1930) to *The New Yorker*, on whose editorial staff he was employed for a time. With the publication of his first collection, *Hard Lines* (1931), Nash began a 40-year career during which he produced 20 volumes of verse with such titles as *The Bad Parents' Garden of Verse* (1936), *I'm a Stranger Here Myself* (1938), and *Everyone but Thee and Me* (1962). He wrote the lyrics for the musicals *One Touch of Venus* (1943) and *Two's Company* (1952), as well as several children's books.

His rhymes are jarringly off or disconcertingly exact, and his ragged stanzas vary from lines of one word to lines that meander the length of a paragraph, often interrupted by inapposite digressions. Nash said he learned his prosody from the unintentional blunders of poet Julia Moore, the "Sweet Singer of Michigan."

Nashe or **Nash** \'nash\, Thomas (b. 1567, Lowestoft, Suffolk, Eng.—d. *c.* 1601, Yarmouth, Norfolk) Pamphleteer, poet, dramatist, and author of *The Unfortunate Traveller; or, the Life of Jacke Wilton* (1594), the first picaresque novel in English.

Woodcut from *The Trimming of Thomas Nashe Gentleman* by Gabriel Harvey, 1597

About 1588 Nashe went to London, where he became associated with Robert Greene and other authors. In 1589 he wrote *The Anatomie of Absurditie* and the preface to Greene's *Menaphon*.

In *Pierce Penilesse His Supplication to the Divell* (1592) Nashe's prose became a combination of colloquial diction and idiosyncratic coined compounds, ideal for controversy and for his eccentric discussion of the seven deadly sins. In *Christs Teares over Jerusalem* (1593) Nashe ominously warned his countrymen during one of the worst plagues that unless they reformed London would suffer the fate of Jerusalem. *The Terrors of the Night* (1594) was a discursive, sometimes bewildering, attack on demonology.

Pierce Penilesse excepted, Nashe's most successful works were his masque *Summers Last Will and Testament* (1592, published 1600), the picaresque novel *The Unfortunate Traveller; or, The Life of Jacke Wilton*, DIDO, QUEEN OF CARTHAGE (1594;

with Christopher Marlowe), and *Nashes Lenten Stuffe* (1599). *The Unfortunate Traveller* is a brutal and realistic tale of adventure narrated with speed and economy. *Lenten Stuffe*, in praise of herrings, contained a charming description of Yarmouth, Norfolk, which was a herring fishery.

Nāṣir-i Khusraw \'nȯ-se-re-ˈk̇ȯs-ˌrō\, *in full* Abū Muʿīn Nāṣir-i Khusraw al-Marvāzī al-Qubādiyānī (b. 1004, Qubādiyān, Merv, Khorāsān [Iran]—d. *c.* 1072/77, Yumgān, Badakhshān, Central Asia [now in Afghanistan]) Poet, theologian, and religious propagandist, one of the greatest writers in Persian literature.

In 1045 Nāṣir-i Khusraw went on a pilgrimage to Mecca and continued his journey to Palestine and then to Egypt, which was ruled at that time by the Fāṭimid dynasty. The Fāṭimids headed the Ismāʿīlite sect, an offshoot of Shīʿite Islām, and at some point Nāṣir became an Ismāʿīlī missionary. He returned to his homeland, but rival Sunnite Muslims forced him to flee to Badakhshān, where he spent the rest of his days, lamenting in his poetry that he was unable to be an active missionary.

Nāṣir's poetry is of a didactic and devotional character and consists mainly of long odes that are considered to be of high literary quality. His philosophical poetry includes the *Rawshana'iname* (*Book of Lights*). Nāṣir's most celebrated prose work is the *Safarnāme* (*Diary of a Journey Through Syria and Palestine*), a diary describing his seven-year journey. He also wrote more than a dozen treatises expounding the doctrines of the Ismāʿīlīs.

Nathan \'nā-thən\, George Jean (b. Feb. 14, 1882, Fort Wayne, Ind., U.S.—d. April 8, 1958, New York, N.Y.) American author, editor, and drama critic who is credited with raising the standards of producers and playgoers alike.

Beginning in 1906, Nathan was at various times drama critic for numerous magazines and newspapers, but his name is particularly associated with *The Smart Set*, of which he was coeditor (1914–23) with H.L. Mencken, and with the *American Mercury*, which, also with Mencken, he helped to found in 1924. As a critic Nathan championed the plays of Henrik Ibsen, August Strindberg, George Bernard Shaw, Eugene O'Neill, Sean O'Casey, and William Saroyan. He published the *Theatre Book of the Year* annually from 1943 through 1951, as well as more than 30 volumes of lively essays.

National Book Awards Annual awards given to books of the highest quality written by Americans and published by American publishers. The awards were founded in 1950 by the American Book Publishers Council, American Booksellers Association, and Book Manufacturers Institute. From 1976 to 1979 they were administered by the National Book Committee, and in 1980 they were replaced by American Book Awards given by the Association of American Booksellers. They were renamed the National Book Awards, administered by the National Book Foundation, in 1987. Publishers submit selected books to be judged, and fiction, nonfiction, and poetry prizes are awarded.

Native Son Novel by Richard WRIGHT, published in 1940. The novel addresses the issue of white American society's responsibility for the repression of blacks. The plot charts the decline of Bigger Thomas, a young African-American imprisoned for two murders—the accidental smothering of his white employer's daughter and the deliberate killing of his girlfriend to silence her. In his cell Thomas confronts his growing sense of injustice and concludes that violence is the only alternative to submission to white society.

Natsume Sōseki \ˌnä-tsū-ˈmä-ˈsō-ˌse-kē\, *pseudonym of* Natsume Kinnosuke \ˌkēn-ˈnȯ-sȯ-kē\ (b. Feb. 9, 1867, Edo [now Tokyo], Japan—d. Dec. 9, 1916, Tokyo) Outstanding Japanese novelist of the Meiji period (1868–1912) and the first to depict articulately and persuasively the plight of the alienated modern Japanese intellectual. It was through Natsume that the modern realistic novel, which had essentially been a foreign literary genre, found its most natural expression and took root in Japan.

International Society for Educational Information, Inc.

Natsume graduated from the University of Tokyo and taught in the provinces and at the University of Tokyo. His reputation was made with two very successful comic novels, *Wagahaiwa neko de aru* (1905–06; *I Am a Cat*) and *Botchan* (1906; *Botchan: Master Darling*). Both satirize contemporary philistines and intellectual mountebanks. His third book, *Kusamakura* (1906; *The Three-Cornered World*), is a lyrical tour de force about a painter's sojourn in a remote village.

After 1907, when he gave up teaching to devote himself to writing, Natsume produced his more characteristically somber works, which deal with attempts to escape from loneliness. In *Kōjin* (1912–13; *The Wayfarer*) the hero is driven to near madness by his sense of isolation; in *Kokoro* (1914) the hero kills himself; and in *Mon* (1910; "The Gate") the hero is unable to find religious solace. Natsume's last novel, *Michikusa* (1915; *Grass on the Wayside*), was autobiographical.

Natural, The First novel by Bernard MALAMUD, published in 1952. The story of gifted athlete Roy Hobbs and his bat "Wonderboy" is counted among the finest baseball novels.

Hobbs's promising baseball career is cut short when he is shot by a mysterious woman. He turns up some 15 years later to play left field for the New York Knights, whose fortunes suddenly and miraculously improve. Off the playing field, Roy is torn between the dangerous affection of Memo Paris, the niece of team manager Pop Fisher, and Iris Lemon, whose love is genuine. After rejecting Iris for Memo, Hobbs agrees to throw a play-off game. During the game he regrets his decision and decides to play honestly, but Wonderboy is split asunder and Hobbs strikes out, losing the game.

Natural History Encyclopedic scientific work of dubious accuracy by PLINY the Elder, completed in AD 77 as *Naturae historiae* and conventionally known as *Naturalis historia*.

Although Pliny did not distinguish between fact, opinion, and speculation in his 37-volume treatise, he can be credited with creating the first scientific encyclopedia. For centuries, the *Natural History* served as the Western world's primary source of scientific information and theory.

Niccolò Leoniceno's 1492 tract on the errors of Pliny was the first of several works questioning the accuracy and usefulness of the *Natural History*. By the end of the 17th century, as the scientific method of empirical observation replaced speculation, the work had been superseded.

naturalism \ˈnach-ər-ə-ˌliz-əm\ A theory that art or literature should conform exactly to nature or depict every appearance of the subject that comes to the artist's attention; specifically, a theory in literature emphasizing the role of heredity and environment upon human life and character development.

This theory was the basis of a late 19th- and early 20th-century aesthetic movement that, in literature, extended the tradition of realism, aiming at an even more faithful, unselective representation of reality, presented without moral judgment. Naturalism differed from realism in its assumption of scientific determinism, which led naturalistic authors to emphasize the accidental, physiological nature of their characters rather than their moral or rational qualities. Individual characters were seen as helpless products of heredity and environment, motivated by strong instinctual drives from within, and harassed by social and economic pressures from without.

Naturalism originated in France, where the leading exponent of the movement was Émile Zola, whose essay "Le Roman expérimental" (1880; "The Experimental Novel") became the literary manifesto of the school. With Zola's example the naturalistic style became widespread and affected to varying degrees most of the major writers of the period.

Despite their claim to complete objectivity, the naturalists were handicapped by certain biases inherent in their deterministic theories. They depicted nature as "red in tooth and claw," portrayed simple characters dominated by strong, elemental passions, and documented oppressive environments, often in dreary and sordid detail. Finally, they were unable to suppress an element of romantic protest against the social conditions they described.

In American literature, naturalism had a delayed blooming in the work of Hamlin Garland, Stephen Crane, Frank Norris, and Jack London, and it reached its peak in novels of Theodore Dreiser.

Nature Book-length essay by Ralph Waldo EMERSON, published anonymously in 1836. It contains a formulation of his essential philosophy and helped initiate Transcendentalism.

In the essay, Emerson reevalutes traditional views of God and Nature. He asserts the human ability to transcend the materialistic world of sense experience and facts and become conscious of the all-pervading spirit of the universe and the potentialities of human freedom. Although these concepts were not original, Emerson's polished style and breadth of vision lent them a particular vividness.

naṭya \ˈnä-tyə\ [Sanskrit *nāṭyaṃ* dance, acting, drama] The dramatic (narrative) element of Indian classical dance.

Nāṭya-śāstra *in full* Bhārata Nāṭya-śāstra \ˈbä-rə-tə-ˈnä-tyə-ˈshä-strə\ Detailed treatise and handbook on dramatic art that deals with all aspects of the classical Sanskrit theater, including dance, music, poetics, and general aesthetics. It is believed to have been written before the 3rd century by the mythic Brahman sage and priest Bharata. Its primary importance lies in its justification of Indian drama as a vehicle of religious enlightenment.

Naughton \ˈnȯt-ən\, Bill, *in full* William John Francis Naughton (b. June 12, 1910, Ballyhaunis, County Mayo, Ire.—d. Jan. 9, 1992, Ballasalla, Isle of Man) Playwright who is best remembered for a series of working-class comedies he wrote in the 1960s, most notably *Alfie* (1963; film, 1966), an episodic, unsentimental tale of an egocentric Cockney womanizer.

When Naughton was a child, his family moved from Ireland to Bolton, Lancashire. *A Roof over Your Head* (1945), an autobiographical study of life in northern England in the 1920s, was followed by a number of moderately successful novels and short-story collections. In the 1950s he moved to London to write for the humor magazine *Lilliput* and for radio and television.

Naughton drew acclaim for his plays *Alfie* (which was based on his 1962 radio play *Alfie Elkins and His Little Life*), *All in Good Time* (1964; film, *The Family Way*, 1966), and *Spring and Port Wine* (1967; a revision of his earlier play *My Flesh, My Blood*; U.S. title, *Keep It in the Family*; film, 1970).

Nausea First novel by Jean-Paul SARTRE, published in French in 1938 as *La Nausée*. It is considered Sartre's fiction masterwork and is an important statement of existentialist philosophy.

Nausea is written in the form of a diary that narrates the recurring feelings of revulsion that overcome Roquentin, a young historian, as he comes to realize the banality and emptiness of existence. As the attacks of nausea occur more frequently, Roquentin abandons his research and loses his few friends. In an indifferent world, without work, love, or friendship to sustain him, he must discover value and meaning within himself.

Navā'ī or **Nawā'ī** or **Nevā'ī** \nă-,vă-'ē, 'na-,vō-,ē\, 'Alī Shīr, *also called* Mīr 'Alī Shīr \'mēr-'ăl-ē-'shēr\ (b. Feb. 9, 1441, Herāt, Timurid Afghanistan—d. Jan. 3, 1501, Herāt) Turkish poet and scholar who was the greatest representative of Chagatai Turkish literature (written in an eastern Turkic language).

Born into an aristocratic military family, he studied in Mashhad and in Herāt, where he held a number of offices at court and became a patron of the arts. He was also a member of a dervish order, and under his master, the renowned Persian poet Jāmī, he read and studied the works of the great mystics.

Navā'ī devoted the latter part of his life to poetry and scholarship, writing first in Persian and then in Chagatai. He left four great divans, or collections of poems, and five romances. Among his main prose works are the *Muhakamat al-lugatayn* (*The Trial of the Two Languages*), a comparison of Turkish and Persian; the *Majālis an-nafāis* ("Séances of the Exquisite"), about the lives of Turkish poets; and *Mizan al-awzan* ("The Measure of Meters"), a treatise on Turkish prosody. Navā'ī's mastery of the eastern Turkic Chagatai language was such that it came to be known as "the language of Navā'ī." He remains a well-known figure in Uzbekistan, and some of his poetry can be found in popular Uzbek folk songs.

Nāyaṉār \'nă-yə-,năr\ Any of the Tamil poet-musicians of the 7th and 8th centuries AD who composed devotional hymns of great beauty in honor of the Hindu god Shiva (Śiva).

The first of the Nāyaṉārs was the poetess Kāraikkāl Ammaiyār, who called herself a *pēy*, or ghostly minion of Shiva. There were 12 early Nāyaṉār saints. The most important Nāyaṉārs were Appar and Ñanacampantar, in the 7th century, and Cuntaramūrtti, in the 8th. These poets were often known as "the three"; their images are worshiped in South Indian temples as saints. They were approximately contemporary with the Āḷvārs, who worshiped Vishnu.

The hymns of the Nāyaṉārs were collected in the 10th century by Nambi Āṇḍar Nambi under the title *Tēvāram* and set to Dravidian music for incorporation into the services of South Indian temples. Often associated with the Nāyaṉārs, though probably slightly later in date, is the superb devotional poet Māṇikkavācakar.

Naylor \'nā-lər\, Gloria (b. Jan. 25, 1950, New York, N.Y., U.S.) African-American novelist, known for her strong depictions of black women.

Naylor attended Brooklyn College of the City University of New York and Yale University. Her first novel, THE WOMEN OF BREWSTER PLACE (1982), won her instant recognition for its powerful dramatization of the struggles of seven women living in a blighted urban neighborhood. *Linden Hills* (1985) deals with the destructive materialism of upwardly mobile suburban blacks. *Mama Day* (1988) blends stories from William Shakespeare's *The Tempest* with black folklore, and *Bailey's Cafe* (1992) centers on a mythic Brooklyn diner that offers an oasis for the suffering.

Nâzım Hikmet \nä-'zəm-hēk-'met\, *in full* Nâzım Hikmet Ran \'rän\ (b. Jan. 15, 1902, Salonika, Ottoman Empire [now Thessaloníki, Greece]—d. June 3, 1963, Moscow, Russia, U.S.S.R.) Poet who was one of the most important and influential figures in 20th-century Turkish literature.

Nâzım Hikmet studied at the University of Moscow. Returning home as a Marxist, he began to work for a number of journals and started communist propaganda activities. In 1951 he left Turkey forever, and from then on he lived in the Soviet Union and eastern Europe.

Nâzım Hikmet's mastery of language and introduction of free verse and a wide range of poetic themes strongly influenced Turkish literature in the late 1930s. *Simnavna Kadısı Oğlu Şeyh Bedreddin destanı* (1936; *The Epic of Sheik Bedreddin*) concerns a 15th-century revolutionary religious leader in Anatolia and the three-volume *Memleketimden insan manzaraları* (1966–67; *Human Landscapes*) is a 20,000-line epic. Many of his works have been translated into English, including the two volumes entitled *Selected Poems* (1967, 1986), *The Moscow Symphony* (1970), *The Day Before Tomorrow* (1972), *Things I Didn't Know I Loved* (1975), and *Poems of Nazim Hikmet* (1994). Nâzım Hikmet is also known for his Marxist-inspired plays.

Nea grammata \'nā-ä-'grä-mä-tä\ ("New Letters") Greek avant-garde magazine, founded in 1935, that served as the prime vehicle for the poetry of the Generation of the '30s, an influential group that included George Seferis and Odysseus Elytis, who in 1979 won the Nobel Prize for Literature.

near rhyme *see* HALF RHYME.

Necati or **Nejati** \ne-jä-'tē\, Īsa (d. 1509, Constantinople, Ottoman Empire [now Istanbul, Tur.]) The first great lyric poet of Ottoman Turkish literature.

Necati was probably born a slave; while still very young, he went to the city of Kastamonu and began to develop his skill in calligraphy and his reputation as a poet. About 1480, he journeyed to the Ottoman capital, Constantinople, and wrote verses for the Ottoman sultan Mehmed II. After the accession of Sultan Bayezid II in 1481, Necati entered the service of his sovereign's sons, first Prince Abdullah, then Prince Mahmud, in whose service the poet enjoyed great favor.

Apart from a few scattered lines from the many pieces attributed to Necati, the only extant work is his divan, or collection of poems, in which there are numerous examples of his graceful, eloquent, and original verse.

nectar \'nek-tər\ [Greek *néktar*] The drink of the Greek and Roman gods. *Compare* AMBROSIA.

Nedim \nä-'dēm\, Ahmed (b. 1681, Constantinople, Ottoman Empire [now Istanbul, Tur.]—d. 1730, Constantinople) One of the greatest lyric poets of Ottoman Turkish literature.

Nedim was brought up as a religious scholar and teacher, and, winning the patronage of the grand vizier, Nevşehirli İbrahim Paşa, he received an appointment as a librarian. Later, he became the close friend of Sultan Ahmed III (1703–30)—thus his name Nedim, meaning "Boon Companion."

Nedim's qasida (odes) and ghazels (lyrics) are bright and colorful, and he excelled especially in the writing of charming and lively *şarkıs* ("songs"), which are still sung today. His divan, or collection of poems, exhibits his masterly handling of the language and accounts for his popularity.

Nef'î \nä-'fē\, *pseudonym of* Ömer \œ-'mer\, *also called* Nef'î of Erzurum \er-zū-'rūm\ (b. *c.* 1572, Hasankale, Ottoman Empire—d. 1635, Constantinople [now Istanbul, Tur.]) One of the greatest classical Ottoman poets and one of the most famous satirists and panegyrists in Ottoman Turkish literature.

Nef'î became famous as a court panegyrist and also as a powerful satirist during the time of Sultan Murad IV (1623–40). Nef'î attacked the highest public figures in his writings, and his biting invective and witty, satirical sketches were often obscene and vulgar. They earned him many enemies at the court. Bayram Paṣa, deputy prime minister and brother-in-law of the sultan, finally secured his execution in 1635.

Nef'î is considered one of the finest qasida (ode) writers of Ottoman literature. His famous divan, or collection of poems, contains many examples of his eloquent poetic style and his magnificent language. Nef'î also left a Persian divan.

negative capability   As defined by John Keats, a writer's ability to accept "uncertainties, mysteries, doubts, without any irritable reaching after fact and reason." Keats first employed the phrase in an 1817 letter. An author possessing negative capability is objective and not driven by intellectual or philosophical didacticism.

negrismo \nä-'grēz-mō\ [Spanish, a derivative of *negro* black, black person]   Literary movement of the 1920s that sought to emphasize contributions by black artists to Latin-American culture. Nicolás Guillén is one of the better-known authors associated with the movement.

Negritude \nä-grē-'tūēd\ [French *négritude,* a derivative of *nègre* black person]   Literary movement of the 1930s, '40s, and '50s that began among French-speaking African and Caribbean writers living in Paris as a protest against French colonial rule and the policy of assimilation. Its leading figure was Léopold Sédar SENGHOR (elected first president of the Republic of Senegal in 1960), who, along with Aimé CÉSAIRE from Martinique and Léon DAMAS from French Guiana, began to examine Western values critically and to reassess African culture.

The group's quarrel with assimilation was that it assumed the superiority of European culture and civilization over that of Africa (or assumed that Africa had no history or culture). They were also disturbed by the world wars, in which they saw their countrymen not only dying for a cause that was not theirs but being treated as inferiors on the battlefield. These views inspired many of the basic ideas behind Negritude: that Africans must look to their own cultural heritage to determine the values and traditions that are most useful in the modern world; that committed writers should use African subject matter and poetic traditions and should excite a desire for political freedom; that Negritude itself encompasses the whole of African cultural, economic, social, and political values; and that, above all, the value and dignity of African traditions and peoples must be asserted. The movement largely faded in the early 1960s when its political and cultural objectives had been achieved in most African countries.

Negro Speaks of Rivers, The   Poem in free verse by Langston HUGHES, published in the June 1921 issue of *The Crisis.* Hughes's first acclaimed poem, it is a panegyric to people of black African origin throughout history and is written in a style derived from Walt Whitman and Carl Sandburg as well as from African-American spirituals.

Neidhart von Reuenthal \'nīt-,härt-fòn-'ròi-ən-,täl\ (b. *c.* 1180, Bavaria [Germany]—d. *c.* 1250)   Medieval German knightly poet who, in the period of the decline of the courtly love lyric, introduced a new genre called *höfische Dorfpoesie* ("courtly village poetry"). It celebrated, in summer and winter dancing songs, the poet's love of village maidens. The songs often ridicule the boorish peasant youths who are the knight's rivals for the village beauty. The novelty of Neidhart's settings and his coarse humor inspired many imitators, and mockery of the peasants became a popular theme.

Neihardt \'nī-,härt\, John G., *in full* Gneisenau (b. Jan. 8, 1881, near Sharpsburg, Ill., U.S.—d. Nov. 3, 1973, Columbia, Mo.)   American poet, novelist, and short-story writer whose

works focus on the history of Native Americans, especially the Sioux.

Neihardt was a literary critic for various newspapers, worked for the Bureau of Indian Affairs, and taught at the University of Missouri, Columbia. Neihardt's early contact with both whites and Indians in Kansas and Nebraska led him to write such works as *The Lonesome Trail* (1907), a collection of short stories about pioneering heroes and the Omahas. The lyric sequence *A Bundle of Myrrh* (1908) established his reputation as a lyric poet. He also was instrumental in writing down the oral autobiography of Black Elk in BLACK ELK SPEAKS (1932).

Neihardt spent almost 30 years on his major work, *A Cycle of the West* (1949), which contains five book-length narrative poems. The work is a vital picture of the frontier and the people who battled for its control. The novel *When the Tree Flowered* (1951) was one of Neihardt's last works.

Nejati   *see* NECATI.

Nekrasov \nʸi-'krà-səf\, Nikolay Alekseyevich (b. Nov. 28 [Dec. 10, New Style], 1821, Nemirov, Ukraine, Russian Empire—d. Dec. 27, 1877 [Jan. 8, 1878], St. Petersburg, Russia)   Russian poet and journalist whose work centered on the theme of compassion for the sufferings of the peasantry.

Nekrasov studied at St. Petersburg University. His first book of poetry was published in 1840. In 1846 he bought the magazine *Sovremennik* ("The Contemporary"), which had declined after the death of its founder, Aleksandr Pushkin. Nekrasov transformed it into a major literary journal in which both Ivan Turgenev and Leo Tolstoy published their early works. In 1868 Nekrasov, with Mikhail Saltykov (Shchedrin), took over *Otechestvennyye zapiski* ("Notes of the Fatherland"), remaining its editor and publisher until his death.

Nekrasov's major poems have lasting power and originality of expression. *Moroz krasny-nos* (1863; "Red-nosed Frost") gives a vivid picture of a brave and sympathetic peasant woman, and large-scale narrative poem *Komu na Rusi zhit khorosho?* (1879; *Who Can Be Happy and Free in Russia?*) shows his gift for vigorous realistic satire.

Nelligan \nä-lē-'gäⁿ\, Émile (b. Dec. 24, 1879, Montreal, Can.—d. Nov. 18, 1941, Montreal)   French-Canadian poet who was a major figure in the Montreal Literary School.

Nelligan attended the Collège Sainte-Marie in Montreal. His first poem, "Rêve fantasque" ("Whimsical Dream"), was published in the magazine *Le Samedi* ("Saturday") in 1896, and later that year he also published several poems in *Le Monde illustré* ("The Illustrated World"). Nelligan became a member of the Montreal Literary School (known as L'École Littéraire de Montréal), which attempted to modernize French-Canadian literature in both form and theme. The group was influenced by the French Parnassian and Symbolist poets. In 1899 Nelligan entered a mental institution and was eventually transferred to another hospital, where he remained until his death. The first collected edition of Nelligan's poems appeared in 1903, a complete English edition in 1983.

Nemerov \'nem-ər-,ôf\, Howard (b. March 1, 1920, New York, N.Y., U.S.—d. July 5, 1991, University City, near St. Louis, Mo.)   American poet, novelist, and critic whose poetry, marked by irony and self-deprecatory wit, is often about nature. In 1978 Nemerov received the Pulitzer Prize and the National Book Award for *The Collected Poems of Howard Nemerov,* which appeared in 1977.

After graduating from Harvard University, Nemerov served as a pilot in World War II. After the war he taught at various colleges, including Bennington College, Bennington, Vt., and Washington University, St. Louis, Mo. From 1963 to 1964 he was consultant in poetry to the Library of Congress. He was poet laureate of the United States in 1988–89 and again in 1989–90.

Nemerov's first book of verse, *The Image and the Law* (1947), was followed by a number of others, including *The Salt Garden* (1955), *Mirrors and Windows* (1958), *New and Selected Poems* (1960), *Blue Swallows* (1967), *Gnomes and Occasions* (1973), *Sentences* (1980), and *War Stories* (1987). Nemerov's fiction includes *The Melodramatists* (1949); *The Homecoming Game* (1957), a tale of a college professor who flunks a small college's football hero; and *A Commodity of Dreams and Other Stories* (1960). Among his considerable body of critical writing are *Journal of the Fictive Life* (1965), *Reflections on Poetry and Poetics* (1972), and *Figures of Thought: Speculations on the Meaning of Poetry and Other Essays* (1978).

Nemesianus \,nē-mə-sē-'ā-nəs\, Marcus Aurelius Olympius (fl. *c.* AD 280)   Roman poet born in Carthage who wrote pastoral and didactic verse.

Of his works there survive four eclogues and an incomplete poem on hunting (*Cynegetica*). Two small fragments on bird catching (*De aucupio*) are also generally attributed to him. The four eclogues are in the Virgilian tradition and were also influenced by Titus Calpurnius Siculus. They are purely imitative and of conventional form and imagery, yet they are attractive because of their smooth diction and melodious movement.

Nemesis \'nem-ə-sis\   In Greek mythology, two divine conceptions, the first an Attic goddess and the second an abstraction of indignant disapproval, later personified. Nemesis the goddess (perhaps of fertility) was similar to Artemis (a goddess of wild animals, vegetation, childbirth, and the hunt). In post-Homeric mythology, she was pursued by Zeus, who eventually turned himself into a swan and caught her in the form of a goose. According to this version, Nemesis (not Leda) then laid the egg from which Helen of Troy was hatched.

That Nemesis the abstraction was worshiped, at least in later times, is beyond doubt. She signified particularly the disapproval of the gods at human presumption.

Nemirovich-Danchenko \nʸi-mʸi-'rō-vʸech-'dàn-chin-kə\, Vladimir Ivanovich (b. Dec. 11 [Dec. 23, New Style], 1858, Ozurgety, Georgia, Russian Empire [now Makharadze, Georgia]—d. April 25, 1943, Moscow)   Russian playwright, novelist, producer, and cofounder of the famous Moscow Art Theater.

Nemirovich-Danchenko received his formal education at Moscow State University. His plays, which were presented at the Maly Theater (Moscow), were highly praised and respected, and he received at least two awards for playwriting. In 1891 he became an instructor of dramatic art at the Moscow Philharmonic Society. There he expounded his then-remarkable ideas on theatrical art, such as the need for longer, organized rehearsals and a less rigid acting style. In 1897, realizing that the Russian stage was in need of drastic reform, Nemirovich-Danchenko met with Konstantin Stanislavsky to outline aims and policies for an actor's theater, first named the Moscow Art and Popular Theater.

Nemirovich-Danchenko encouraged both Anton Chekhov and Maksim Gorky to write for the theater. His autobiography was translated as *My Life in the Russian Theater* (1936).

Nemo, Captain \'nē-,mō\   Fictional character, the megalomaniacal captain of the submarine *Nautilus* in Jules Verne's novel *Vingt Mille Lieues sous les mers* (1869–70; TWENTY THOUSAND LEAGUES UNDER THE SEA), and also a character in the subsequent *L'Île mystérieuse* (1874; THE MYSTERIOUS ISLAND).

Nemunėlis   *see* BRAZDŽIONIS.

Neoclassicism \,nē-ō-'klas-ə-,siz-əm\   Adherence to or practice of the virtues thought to be characteristic of classical art, literature, and, in modern times, music. These virtues, which include formal elegance and correctness, simplicity, dignity, restraint, order, and proportion, are taken to be universally and enduringly valid. Neoclassicism always refers to the art produced later but inspired by antiquity. Thus the terms classicism and Neoclassicism are often used interchangeably. *Compare* AUGUSTAN AGE.

neologism \nē-'äl-ə-,jiz-əm\ [Greek *néos* new + *lógos* word]   A word, usage, or expression newly introduced into the language.

Neoptolemus \,nē-äp-'täl-ə-məs\   In Greek legend, the son of Achilles, the hero of the Greek army at Troy. In the last year of the Trojan War the Greek hero Odysseus brought him to Troy after the Trojan seer Helenus had declared that the city could not be captured without the aid of a descendant of Aeacus, who had helped to build its walls. Neoptolemus, Aeacus' great-grandson, fought bravely and took part in the capture of Troy but committed the sacrilege of slaying the aged king Priam at an altar.

Neorealism \,nē-ō-'rē-ə-,liz-əm\ or **neorealismo** \,nä-ō-rä-ä-'lēz-mō\   Italian literary movement that flourished especially after World War II and that sought to deal realistically with the events leading up to the war and with their resulting social problems.

The movement was rooted in the 1920s and, though suppressed for nearly two decades by fascist control, emerged in great strength after the fascist regime fell at the end of World War II. Neorealism is similar in general aims to the earlier Italian movement *verismo* ("realism"), from which it originated, but it differs in that its upsurge was brought about by the intense feelings that fascist repression, the Resistance, and the war instilled in its many gifted writers.

Alberto Moravia wrote perhaps the first representative work in *Gli indifferenti* (1929; *Time of Indifference*). During the fascist years many Neorealist writers were driven into hiding (Moravia), put in prison (Cesare Pavese, Elio Vittorini), or sent into exile (Ignazio Silone, Carlo Levi); some joined the Resistance (Vittorini, Italo Calvino, Carlo Cassola); others took refuge in introspective movements such as Hermeticism (Salvatore Quasimodo) or in translating the works of others (Pavese, Vittorini).

After the war the movement exploded in full strength. Vasco Pratolini published one of the finest novels of the Neorealist movement, *Cronache di poveri amanti* (1947; *A Tale of Poor Lovers*). Other notable Neorealist works include *Kaputt* (1944) and *La pelle* (1949; *The Skin*) by Curzio Malaparte; *Uomini e no* (1945; *Men and Not Men*) by Vittorini; *Cristo si è fermato a Eboli* (1945; *Christ Stopped at Eboli*) by Levi; *Giorno dopo giorno* (1947; "Day After Day") by Quasimado; *Il sentiero dei nidi di ragno* (1947; *The Path to the Nest of Spiders*) by Calvino; and *Il taglio del bosco* (1955; "Timber Cutting") and *La ragazza di Bube* (1960; *Bébo's Girl*) by Cassola.

neōteros \nä-'ō-ter-,ôs\ *plural* neōteroi \-ter-,ôi\   Any of a group of poets who sought to break away from the didactic-patriotic tradition of Latin poetry by consciously emulating the forms and content of Alexandrian Greek models. They were referred to as *hoi neōteroi* (Greek: "the younger men") by the Roman author and orator Cicero. The *neōteroi* deplored the excesses of alliteration and onomatopoeia and the ponderous meters that characterized the epics and didactic works of the Latin tradition of Ennius. They wrote meticulously refined epyllia (brief epics), lyrics, epigrams, and elegies. They cultivated a literature of self-expression and entertainment and introduced into Latin literature the aesthetic attitude later known as "art for art's sake."

First arising in the 2nd century BC, the school was essentially non-Roman; it centered on the Milanese poet-teacher Publius Valerius Cato, and most of its adherents came from remote regions of northern Italy. Among them was Gaius Valerius Catullus, who wrote during the Ciceronian period (70 to 43 BC) of the Golden Age. In the Augustan Age (43 BC to AD 18), the influence of the *neōteroi* can be discerned particularly in the pastoral idylls of Virgil and in the elegies of Sextus Propertius and Albius Tibullus.

nepenthe \nə-'pen-thē\ [Greek (*phármakon*) *nēpenthés* (drug) for dispelling grief, neuter of *nēpenthés* dispelling grief, from *nē-* not + *pénthos* grief]   A potion used by the ancients to induce forgetfulness of pain or sorrow.

Neptune \'nep-ˌtün, -ˌtyün\ or **Neptunus** \nep-'tün-ùs, -'tyün-\   In Roman mythology, originally the god of fresh water; by 399 BC he was identified with the Greek POSEIDON and thus became a deity of the sea.

Nereid \'nir-ē-əd\   Any of the 50 (or 100) benign water nymphs held in Greek mythology to be the daughters of Nereus (eldest son of Pontus, a personification of the sea) and Doris, daughter of Oceanus (the god of the water encircling the flat earth). The Nereids were attendants on Poseidon. The best known of them were Amphitrite, consort of Poseidon; Thetis, wife of Peleus (king of the Myrmidons) and mother of the hero Achilles; and Galatea, a Sicilian figure who was loved by the Cyclops Polyphemus.

Nereus \'nir-ē-əs\   In Greek mythology, sea god called "Old Man of the Sea" by Homer; noted for his wisdom, gift of prophecy, and ability to change his shape. He was the eldest son of Pontus, a personification of the sea, and Gaea (Earth). The Nereids (water nymphs) were his daughters by the Oceanid Doris, and he lived with them in the depths of the sea, particularly the Aegean.

Neruda \nā-'rü-thä\, Pablo, *original name* Neftalí Ricardo Reyes Basoalto \'rā-yes-ˌbä-sō-'äl-tō\ (b. July 12, 1904, Parral,

Chile—d. Sept. 23, 1973, Santiago) Chilean poet, diplomat, and Marxist, winner of the Lenin Prize for Peace in 1953 and the Nobel Prize for Literature in 1971.

He began writing poetry when he was 10; in 1920 he began using the name Pablo Neruda, which he was to adopt legally in 1946. In 1921 Neruda moved to Santiago and began publishing his literary works in a magazine issued by the Federation of Chilean Students. In 1923 his first book, *Crepusculario*, was published at his own expense. The following year he published what was to become his most widely read work, *Veinte poemas de amor y una canción desesperada* (1924; TWENTY LOVE POEMS AND A SONG OF DESPAIR). Other works of this early period included *Tentativa del hombre infinito* (1926; "Attempt of the Infinite Man"); *Anillos* (1926; "Rings"), in collaboration with Tomás Lago; and *El hondero entusiasta* (1933; "The Enthusiastic Slingshooter").

In 1927 he was named an honorary consul, and for the next five years he represented Chile in a series of Asian countries. It was during these years in South Asia that he wrote *Residencia en la tierra* (RESIDENCE ON EARTH). Thereafter he was consul to Argentina, Spain, and Mexico.

In 1943 Neruda returned to Chile; two years later he was elected senator and for the next three years devoted as much time to politics as he did to his literary career. His political activity was halted, however, when he lost favor with the Chilean government, which turned to the right. A communist, he was forced along with other leftists into hiding. These years proved to be fruitful ones for his writing, however, and he produced CANTO GENERAL (1950; "General Song"), one of the greatest epic poems written about the American continent. In February 1948 he left Chile and subsequently traveled throughout Europe, the Soviet Union, and Mexico. In 1952, after the order to arrest leftists was rescinded, he returned to Chile.

Nerval \ner-'vål\, Gérard de, *pseudonym of* Gérard Labrunie \lä-brūē-'nē\ (b. May 22, 1808, Paris, Fr.—d. Jan. 26, 1855, Paris)   French poet who was one of the first of the Symbolists and Surrealists in French literature. His writings are a reflection and analysis of his own experiences and dreams, the visions that threatened his grip on sanity.

Nerval attended the Collège de Charlemagne, where he met the poet Théophile Gautier, with whom he formed a lasting friendship. Among his first works were a translation of J.W. von Goethe's *Faust* into French and a collection of stories, *La Main de gloire* (1832; "The Hand of Glory").

In 1842 Nerval traveled to the Levant. The journey resulted one of his best works, *Voyage en Orient* (1843–51; "Voyage to the East"), a travelogue that also examines ancient and folk mythology, symbols, and religion.

During the period of his greatest creativity, Nerval was afflicted with severe mental disorders and was institutionalized at least eight times. *Des Filles du feu* (1854; "Girls of Fire"), which includes the story "Sylvie," evokes his dream of a lost paradise of beauty, innocence, and youth. The 12 sonnets of *Les Chimères* (1854; "The Chimeras") perhaps best convey the musical quality of his writing.

Nervo \'ner-b̲ō\, Amado, *original name* Juan Crisóstomo Ruiz de Nervo \rū-'ēs-t̲hä-'ner-b̲ō\ (b. Aug. 27, 1870, Tepic, Mex.—d. May 24, 1919, Montevideo, Uruguay)   Writer and diplomat, generally considered the most distinguished Mexican poet of the late 19th- and early 20th-century literary movement known as Modernismo. Nervo's introspective verse is characterized by deep religious feeling and simple forms.

In 1888 Nervo began a career as a newspaperman in Mazatlán. In 1894 he moved to Mexico City, where he wrote his first novel, *El bachiller* (1895; "The Baccalaureate"), and his first volume of poetry in the modernist idiom, *Perlas negras* (1898; "Black Pearls"). In 1898 he helped found *La revista moderna* ("The Modern Review"), one of the most influential journals of Modernismo.

Nervo lived in Madrid from 1905 to 1918, but spent a considerable amount of time in Parisian literary circles. During that period he wrote most of the poems, essays, and short stories that have been collected in 29 volumes.

Nesbit \'nez-bit\, E., *in full* Edith (b. Aug. 15, 1858, London, Eng.—d. May 4, 1924, New Romney, Kent)   British children's author, novelist, and poet.

Nesbit led an ordinary country life in Kent, which provided scenes for her books. She was one of the founders of the association known as the Fellowship of New Life, out of which grew the Fabian Society.

Nesbit began writing fiction for children in the early 1890s and eventually produced more than 60 books for juveniles, as well as less successful novels and collections of poetry for adults. Her children's books are marked by vivid characterizations, ingenious plots, and an easy, humorous narrative style. Among her best-known books are *The Story of the Treasure*

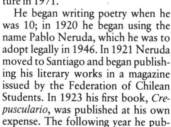

Seekers (1899), *The Wouldbegoods* (1901), *The Revolt of the Toys, and What Comes of Quarreling* (1902), *Five Children and It* (1902), and *The Story of the Amulet* (1906).

Nesimi \nä-sĕ-'mĕ\, Seyid İmadeddin (d. *c.* 1418, Aleppo, Syria) One of the greatest Turkish mystical poets of the late 14th and early 15th centuries, noted for his lyrical and elegant style.

Nesimi became a zealous adherent of the Ḥurūfīs, an extremist religious sect founded by the Iranian mystic Faḳl Allāh of Astarābād. Ḥurūfism (from Arabic *ḥurūf*, "letters") was based on a kabbalistic philosophy associated with the numerological significance attributed to the letters of the alphabet and their combinations. Nesimi was executed for heresy in Aleppo by the ulama—*i.e.*, those learned in the Muslim sciences.

Nesimi wrote two divans (collections of poetry), one in Persian and one in Turkish, and a number of poems in Arabic. The Turkish *Dīvān*, which is considered his most important work, contains 250–300 ghazels (lyrics) and more than 150 rubaiyat (quatrains).

Nestor \'nʸes-tər, *Angl* 'nes-tȯr\ (b. *c.* 1056, Kiev, Kievan Rus [now in Ukraine]—d. Oct. 27, 1113, Kiev) A monk of Kiev's Monastery of the Caves, author of several works of hagiography and an important historical chronicle.

Nestor wrote the lives of Saints Boris and Gleb, the sons of St. Vladimir of Rus, who were murdered in 1015, and the life of St. Theodosius, abbot of the Monastery of the Caves (d. 1074). In about 1112 Nestor completed his much-revised *Povest vremennykh let* ("Tale of Bygone Years"; *The Russian Primary Chronicle: Laurentian Text*), the most important historical work of early medieval Rus. The *Chronicle*, extant in several medieval manuscripts, the earliest dated 1377, relates in detail the earliest history of the eastern Slavs down to the second decade of the 12th century. In Old Russian, the *Chronicle* includes material from translated Byzantine chronicles, west and south Slavonic literary sources, official documents, and oral sagas. This borrowed material is woven with considerable skill into the historical narrative, which is enlivened by vivid description, humor, and a sense of the dramatic.

Nestroy \'nes-trȯi\, Johann (Nepomuk Eduard Ambrosius) (b. Dec. 7, 1801, Vienna, Austria—d. May 25, 1862, Graz) One of Austria's greatest comic dramatists and a brilliant actor who dominated the mid-19th-century Viennese popular stage.

After a career as an opera singer (1822–31) in several European cities, Nestroy returned to Vienna and began writing and acting. His 50 plays, virtually all adaptations of stories from earlier plays or novels, usually center on a brilliant, detached central character. He used satire, irony, and parody to dissect the newly rich bourgeoisie and other figures of Viennese life.

Among his best-known works are *Der böse Geist Lumpazivagabundus oder Das Liederliche Kleeblatt* (1833; "The Evil Spirit Lumpazivagabundus, or the Roguish Trio"); *Der Zerrissene* (1844; *A Man Full of Nothing*); *Das Mädl aus der Vorstadt, oder Ehrlich währt am längsten* (1841; "The Lass from the Suburb or Honesty is the Best Policy"); *Einen Jux will er sich machen* (1842; "He Intends to Have a Fling"), adapted by Thornton Wilder as *The Matchmaker*, and later adapted as the musical play and film *Hello, Dolly!*; and *Kampl oder: Das Mädchen mit den Millionen und die Näherin* (1852; "Kampl; or, The Millionairess and the Seamstress").

Neto \'net-ū\, Agostinho, *in full* Antônio Agostinho Neto (b. Sept. 17, 1922, Icolo e Bengo, Angola—d. Sept. 10, 1979, Moscow, Russia, U.S.S.R.) Poet, physician, and first president of the People's Republic of Angola.

Neto first received recognition in 1948, when he published a volume of poems in Luanda and joined a national cultural movement that was aimed at "rediscovering" indigenous Angolan culture. He was arrested in 1960 because of his militant opposition to the colonial authorities, and he spent the next two years in detention in Cape Verde and in Portugal, where he produced a new volume of verse. In 1962 he escaped to Morocco, where he joined the Angolan liberation movement in exile and was elected president of the Movimento Popular de Libertação de Angola (MPLA). When in 1975 Angola became independent, he was proclaimed president.

Neto was widely recognized as a gifted poet. His work was published in a number of Portuguese and Angolan reviews and was included in Mário de Andrade's *Antologia da poesia negra de expressão portuguesa* (1958).

Neuber \'nȯi-bər\, Caroline, *original name* Friederike Caroline Weissenborn \'vīs-ən-,bȯrn\ (b. March 9, 1697, Reichenbach, Saxony [Germany]—d. Nov. 30, 1760, Laubegast, near Dresden) Actress-manager who exerted a major influence on the development of modern German theater.

In 1727 Neuber and her husband, Johann, formed their own theatrical company. Neuber substituted a careful learning of parts and rehearsal for the heavily improvised farces and harlequinades that then dominated the German stage. Her collaboration with drama reformer Christoph Gottsched, which lasted until 1739, is usually regarded as a turning point in the history of German theater and the beginning of modern German acting. She was immortalized as Madame Nelly in J.W. von Goethe's *Wilhelm Meister*.

Neustadt Prize \'nü-,stat\ (*after 1976* Neustadt International Prize for Literature) Award established in 1969 as the *Books Abroad* International Prize for Literature. It was founded to recognize important achievement in fiction, drama, or poetry. The award is sponsored by the University of Oklahoma and *World Literature Today* (formerly *Books Abroad*), the literary quarterly published by the university, and is conferred every two years. Winners of the prize are chosen by an international jury. Any living writer in any language is eligible for the award as long as a representative sampling of his or her work is available in English or French translation. Winners have included Gabriel García Márquez, Elizabeth Bishop, Czesław Miłosz, and Raja Rao.

Nevā'ī *see* NAVĀ'Ī.

Nevi'im \nə-vē-'ēm\ The second division of the Hebrew Bible, the other two being the Torah (Law) and the Ketuvim (Writings). In the Hebrew canon the Nevi'im (Prophets) are divided into (1) the Former Prophets (Joshua, Judges, Samuel, and Kings) and (2) the Latter Prophets (Isaiah, Jeremiah, Ezekiel, and the Twelve, or Minor, Prophets: Hosea, Joel, Amos, Obadiah, Jonah, Micah, Nahum, Habakkuk, Zephaniah, Haggai, Zechariah, and Malachi). *Compare* OLD TESTAMENT.

Nevins \'nev-inz\, Allan (b. May 20, 1890, Camp Point, Ill., U.S.—d. March 5, 1971, Menlo Park, Calif.) American historian, known especially for his eight-volume history of the American Civil War and his biographies of American political and industrial figures. He also inaugurated the country's first oral history program.

Nevins was educated at the University of Illinois. His first book, *The Life of Robert Rogers* (1914), concerns a Colonial American soldier who fought on the Loyalist side. Nevins joined the New York *Evening Post* as an editorial writer and for nearly 20 years worked as a journalist. During this period he also compiled and edited a collection of documents entitled *American Social History as Recorded by British Travellers* (1923), wrote two works on U.S. history, and produced a biography of explorer John Charles Frémont.

In 1928 he accepted a post at Columbia University in New York City, where he remained for the next 30 years. While at Columbia, Nevins produced an impressive body of work, including two Pulitzer Prize-winning historical biographies: *Grover Cleveland, A Study in Courage* (1932) and *Hamilton Fish, The Inner History of the Grant Administration* (1936). In 1948 he established a project at Columbia for preserving on tape interviews with notable figures whose views of current affairs would interest future historians.

Nevins established himself as a leading authority on the American Civil War with his eight-volume work: *Ordeal of the Union*, 2 vol. (1947), *The Emergence of Lincoln*, 2 vol. (1950), and *The War for Union*, 4 vol. (1959–71). He also wrote notable works on John D. Rockeller and Henry Ford.

New *see* MODERN.

New Apocalypse Literary movement in England during the 1940s that was founded by J.F. Hendry and Henry Treece as a reaction against the politically committed poetry of the 1930s. The movement produced three anthologies inspired by Neoromantic anarchism. The first, *The New Apocalypse* (1940), was edited by Hendry, while the other two—*The White Horseman* (1941) and *The Crown and the Sickle* (1944)—were edited by Hendry and Treece. Treece also wrote a collection of essays entitled *How I See Apocalypse* (1946). Other poets of the New Apocalypse were Nicholas Moore and Vernon Watkins.

Newbery Medal \'nü-bə-rē, -ˌber-ē\ Award given annually to the author of the most distinguished American children's book of the previous year. It was established in 1922 and named for John Newbery, the 18th-century English publisher who was among the first to publish books specifically for children. The award is presented at the annual conference of the American Library Association along with the Caldecott Medal, an award to an artist for the best illustrations for a children's book. Winners of the award include Hugh Lofting, Madeleine L'Engle, and William Pène Du Bois.

New Comedy Greek drama from about 320 BC to the mid-3rd century BC that offers a mildly satiric view of contemporary Athenian society. Unlike Old Comedy, which parodies public figures and events, New Comedy features fictional average citizens in domestic life. Thus, the chorus, the representative of forces larger than life, recedes in importance and becomes a small band of musicians and dancers who periodically provide light entertainment.

The plays commonly deal with the conventionalized situation of thwarted lovers and contain such stock characters as the cunning slave, the wily merchant, the boastful soldier, and the cruel father. Menander introduced the New Comedy in his works about 320 BC and became its most famous exponent. The Roman dramatists Plautus and Terence translated and adapted Greek New Comedy for the Roman stage. Elements of New Comedy influenced European drama down to the 18th century. *See also* MENANDER.

Newcomes, The \'nü-kəmz, 'nyü-\ Novel by William Makepeace THACKERAY, first published in 24 installments from 1853 to 1855 under the title *The Newcomes: Memoirs of a Most Respectable Family*, edited by "Arthur Pendennis, Esq.," the narrator of the story. The novel was published in book form in two volumes in 1854–55.

A tale spanning decades in the lives of a well-to-do, middle-class English family, *The Newcomes* is mainly concerned with Colonel Thomas Newcome and his son Clive. The unheroic but attractive Clive falls in love with his cousin Ethel, but instead marries Rose Mackenzie, who eventually dies in childbirth. The Colonel is ruined financially by the greedy, cold-hearted Barnes Newcome, Ethel's father and head of the family. The Colonel's deathbed scene, described with deep feeling that avoids sentimentality, is one of the most famous in Victorian fiction.

New Criticism *also called* formalism. A type of literary criticism that developed in England and the United States after World War I. New Criticism focused intensively upon the language, imagery, and emotional or intellectual tensions in particular literary works in an attempt to explain their total formal aesthetic organization. New Critics insisted on the intrinsic value of a work of art and focused attention on the work alone as an independent unit of meaning; they were opposed to the critical practice of bringing historical or biographical data to bear on interpretation. To the New Critics, poetry was a special type of discourse, a means of communicating feeling and thought that could not be expressed in any other kind of language. These critics set out to define and formalize the qualities of poetic thought and language, with special emphasis on the connotative and associative values of words and on the multiple functions of figurative language—symbol, metaphor, and image—in the work.

The primary technique employed in New Criticism was analytic (or "close") reading of the text. Seminal works in the tradition were those of the English critics I.A. Richards (*Principles of Literary Criticism*, 1924) and William Empson (*Seven Types of Ambiguity*, 1930), as well as John Crowe Ransom's *The New Criticism* (1941), which loosely organized the principles of this basically linguistic approach to literature. Other figures associated with the movement included Robert Penn Warren, Cleanth Brooks, and Allen Tate.

Newdigate Prize \'nü-di-git, 'nyü-, -ˌgāt\ Poetry prize founded in 1805 by Sir Roger Newdigate and awarded at Oxford University. The award is given annually for the best student poem of up to 300 lines on a given subject. The winner recites the poem at commencement exercises. Winners include Matthew Arnold and John Ruskin.

New Grub Street Realistic novel by George GISSING, published in three volumes in 1891. It portrays the intrigues and the crippling effects of poverty in the literary world.

New Grub Street contrasts the career of Edwin Reardon, a gifted but impoverished author of proven literary merit, with that of Jasper Milvain, a materially successful reviewer and literary hack. The book suggests that self-advertising affords a writer a more certain route to success than does talent.

new historicism \hi-'stȯr-i-ˌsiz-əm\ Modern school of literary criticism that treats the work of literature not so much as a transcendent document worthy of analysis, but as a representation of historical forces. The new historicist takes the social, cultural, and historical implications of the text and extends the analysis to the economic and the political. New historicism makes history itself an object of interpretation; the critic reads literary work to uncover the ideologies that determine culture and law. Foremost among the practitioners of this method are Stephen Greenblatt, Jerome McGann, Marjorie Levinson, and Marilyn Butler.

New Humanism Critical movement in the United States between 1910 and 1930, based on the literary and social theories of the English Victorian poet and critic Matthew Arnold, who sought to recapture the moral quality of past civilizations. Reacting against the scientifically oriented philosophies of literary realism and naturalism, New Humanists argued that: (1) human beings are unique among nature's creatures; (2) the essence of experience is fundamentally moral and ethical; and (3) the human will, although subject to genetic laws and shaped by the environment, is essentially free. Among the New Humanists were Paul Elmer More, Irving Babbitt, Norman Foerster, and Robert Shafer. By the 1930s the New Humanists had come to be regarded as cultural elitists and advocates of social and aesthetic conservatism, and their influence became negligible.

New Life, The *see* LA VITA NUOVA.

Newman \'nū-mən, 'nyū-\, John Henry (b. Feb. 21, 1801, London—d. Aug. 11, 1890, Birmingham, Warwick, Eng.) Influential churchman and man of letters of the 19th century who led the Oxford Movement in the Church of England and later became a cardinal-deacon in the Roman Catholic church. He wrote a number of eloquent books, notably *Apologia pro Vita Sua* (1864; "A Defense of His Life").

Newman attended Oxford University, where he became the effective organizer and intellectual leader of the movement started in 1833 with the object of stressing the Roman Catholic elements in the English religious tradition and of reforming the Church of England. Eventually, in September 1843, Newman resigned his position as vicar of St. Mary's, Oxford, and he preached his last Anglican sermon a week later. On Oct. 9, 1845, he was received into the Roman Catholic church. Newman's quasi-liberal spirit, however, made him suspect among the more rigorous Roman Catholic clergy, and his early career as a Roman Catholic priest was marked by a series of frustrations.

He was delivered from his sense of frustration in 1864 by a challenge from Charles Kingsley to justify the honesty of his life as an Anglican. The resulting history of his religious opinions, *Apologia pro Vita Sua* (1864), was read and approved far beyond the limits of the Roman Catholic church, and by its fairness, candor, and interest and by the beauty of some passages it helped him recapture the almost national status he had once held. The work thus assured Newman's stature in the Roman Catholic church. In 1879 Pope Leo XIII made him cardinal-deacon of St. George in Velabro.

In addition to the *Apologia*, Newman wrote several hymns, including "Lead, Kindly Light," and theological works.

News from Nowhere (*in full* News from Nowhere; or, An Epoch of Rest, Being Some Chapters from a Utopian Romance) Prose work by William MORRIS, published serially in *The Commonweal* in 1890 and as a book later the same year.

Most of the work consists of a vision of England in the year 2090 presented as a dream of William Guest, a thin disguise for Morris himself. Poverty, misery, and the ugliness of factories have vanished, along with money, the legal system, and government itself; labor, art, and nature are ennobled. The improvements are the result of a violent socialist revolution.

newspeak \'nū-,spēk, 'nyū-\ Propagandistic language that is characterized by euphemism, circumlocution, and the inversion of customary meanings. The term was coined by George Orwell in his novel *Nineteen Eighty-four* (1949). Newspeak, "designed to diminish the range of thought," was the language preferred by Big Brother's pervasive enforcers.

New Statesman Political and literary weekly magazine published in London, probably the best known of its kind in England, and one of the world's leading journals of opinion. It was founded in 1913 by Sidney and Beatrice Webb. The journal reflected the viewpoint of the Fabian Socialists and became famous for its aggressive and often satirical analysis of British and world political scenes. Its contributors are drawn from among the most distinguished writers in Britain.

New Testament The second, later, and smaller of the two major divisions of the Christian Bible, and the portion that is canonical only to Christianity.

Christians see in the New Testament the fulfillment of the promise of the Old Testament. The work recounts and interprets the new covenant, represented in the life and death of Jesus, between God and the followers of the Christ. Like the Old Testament, it contains a variety of kinds of writing. Among its 27 books are selected recollections of the life and sayings of Jesus in the four Gospels; a historical narrative of the first years of the Christian church in Acts of the Apostles; Epistles (letters) of advice, instruction, admonition, and exhortation to local groups of Christians; and an apocalyptic description of the intervention of God in history, the Revelation to John.

The books in the New Testament are not arranged chronologically. The Epistles of Paul, for example, which address the immediate problems of local churches shortly after Christ's death, are considered to be the earliest texts. The books are instead arranged in a more logical narrative order—the Gospels telling the life of Jesus and his teachings; the Acts detailing the work of Christ's followers in propagating the Christian faith; the Epistles teaching the meaning and implications of the faith; and Revelation prophesying future events and the culmination of the divine purpose. *Compare* OLD TESTAMENT.

New Worlds British magazine that was a leading innovative force in 1960s science fiction. Founded in 1946 and edited by E.J. Carnell for 18 years, the monthly featured stories by most noted English science-fiction writers, including "The Sentinel" by Arthur C. Clarke, and avant-garde works by young writers such as Brian Aldiss and J.G. Ballard. Under the editorship of Michael Moorcock, *New Worlds* concentrated on experimental science fiction, offered severe social criticism, and published nonfiction essays, concrete poetry, and visual collages. Works published by *New Worlds* included *Bug Jack Barron* by Norman Spinrad, sections of *Stand on Zanzibar* by John Brunner, and "Behold, the Man," by Moorcock himself. The magazine suspended publication in 1970, although several numbers appeared in the late 1970s. A series of anthologies of original stories, most of which were edited by Moorcock, was published in the 1970s and the 1990s.

New Writing International book-periodical that was founded in Vienna and moved to London, where it was edited by John Lehmann. From the spring of 1936, it appeared under a variety of titles: *New Writing* (quarterly; 1936–39), *Folios of New Writing* (1940–41), *Daylight* (1941), *New Writing and Daylight* (annually or semiannually; 1942–46), and *Penguin New Writing* (monthly 1940–42; quarterly 1942–50). The general goal of the magazine was to publish working-class writers.

New Yorker, The \nū-'yȯr-kər\ American weekly magazine, famous for its varied literary fare and humor. It was founded in 1925 by Harold Ross, who was its editor until his death in 1951. *The New Yorker*'s initial focus was on New York City's amusements and social and cultural life, but the magazine gradually acquired a broader scope that encompassed literature, current affairs, and other topics. *The New Yorker* became renowned for its short fiction, essays, foreign reportage, and probing biographical studies, as well as its comic drawings and its detailed reviews of cinema, books, theater, and other arts.

Contributors to the magazine included S.J. Perelman, Robert Benchley, Ogden Nash, E.B. White, John O'Hara, John Hersey, Edmund Wilson, J.D. Salinger, John Updike, Rebecca West, and Dorothy Parker. Among its great cartoonists were Charles Addams, James Thurber (a writer as well), and Rea Irvin, the creator of Eustace Tilley, the early American dandy who is the magazine's trademark.

In 1985 *The New Yorker* was sold to the publisher Samuel I. Newhouse, Jr., this being the first time in its history that the magazine's ownership had changed hands.

New York Intellectuals \nŭ-'yȯrk\   A group of literary critics who were active from the late 1930s through the 1970s in New York City. Characterized by their rejection of bourgeois culture, their adherence to democratic socialism, and their espousal of modernism in literature, the critics were famous for book reviews and essays published in such journals as *The Nation*, *Commentary*, and *Dissent*. The moniker "New York Intellectuals" was coined by Irving Howe in his 1968 essay of the same name. Some of the leading figures in the movement were Lionel Trilling, Philip Rahv, and Alfred Kazin.

Nexø \'nek-sœ̄\, Martin Andersen (b. June 26, 1869, Copenhagen, Den.—d. June 1, 1954, Dresden, E.Ger.)   Writer who, as the first Danish proletarian novelist, helped to raise social consciousness in Denmark and throughout Europe.

Nexø came from an extremely poor family, but with the help of a patron he was able to go to school; after finishing he worked as a teacher in a Grundtvigian folk school until 1901, when he was able to support himself by his writing.

Nexø's two major novels reached an international audience. The first, *Pelle erobreren*, 4 vol. (1906–10; *Pelle the Conqueror*), tells the story of Pelle, the son of a farm laborer, as he moves to Copenhagen and becomes a militant labor leader. The second novel, *Ditte mennskebarn*, 5 vol. (1917–21; *Ditte, Daughter of Man*), depicts the oppressed life of a poor, courageous, and loving woman. A third novel, *Midt i en Jærntid* (1929; *In God's Land*), is critical of wealthy farmers.

Nexø was a great admirer of the Soviet revolutionary experiment; he became a communist after World War I and traveled to the Soviet Union a number of times. His memoirs appeared as *Erindringer*, 2 vol. (1932–39; first part: *Under the Open Sky*). In 1945 he published *Morten hin Røde*, 2 vol. ("Morten the Red"), a sequel to *Pelle erobreren*. Nexø left Denmark in 1949 to live in East Germany.

Nez̧āmī or **Niẓāmī** \'nez-ˌȯ-ˌmē\, *in full* Elyās Yūsof Nez̧āmī Ganjavī \'gan-jav-ˌē\ (b. *c.* 1141, Ganja, Seljuq Empire [now Gyandzha, Azerbaijan]—d. 1209, Ganja)   Greatest romantic epic poet in Persian literature, who brought a colloquial and realistic style to the Persian epic. He is renowned for his originality and clarity of style.

Little is known of Nez̧āmī's life, and only a handful of his qasidas (odes) and ghazels (lyrics) have survived; his reputation rests on his great *Khamseh* ("The Quintuplet"), a group of five poems written in *masnawī* verse form (rhymed couplets) totaling 30,000 couplets. He drew inspiration from the Persian epic poets Ferdowsī and Sanā'ī. The first poem in the group is the didactic *Makhzan al-asrār* (*The Treasury of Mysteries*), the second the romantic epic *Khosrow o-Shīrīn* ("Khosrow and Shīrīn"). The third is his rendition of a well-known story in Islāmic folklore, *Leyli o-Mejnūn* (*The Story of Leyla and Majnun*). The fourth poem, *Haft paykar* (*The Seven Beauties*), is considered his masterwork. The final poem is the *Sikandar* or *Eskandarnāmeh* ("Book of Alexander the Great"; Eng. trans. of part I, *The Sikander Nama*), a philosophical portrait of Alexander.

Ngubane \n̩-gŭ-'bä-nä\, Jordan Kush, Kush *also spelled* Khush (b. Nov. 15, 1917, Ladysmith, Natal, S.Af.—d. 1985?)   Zulu novelist, scholar, and editor for the South African publications *Ilanga lase Natal* ("The Natal Sun," Durban), *Bantu World* (Johannesburg), and *Inkundla ya Bantu* ("Bantu Forum," Verulam).

Ngubane's Zulu-language novel *Uvalo lwezinhlonzi* (1957; "The Fear of Authority") was popular when it appeared and was a required school text before being banned from 1962 to 1967. His nonfictional works include *An African Explains Apartheid* and the essay *Conflict of Minds*. In 1979 he published a long study analyzing similarities and differences between the racial problems in the United States and in South Africa. He also published poetry and short fiction. In 1974 Ngubane published the English-language novel *Ushaba: The Hurtle to Blood River*.

Ngugi wa Thiong'o \n̩-'gŭ-gē-wä-'thyȯn̩-gō\, *original name* James Thiong'o Ngugi (b. Jan. 5, 1938, Limuru, Kenya)   East Africa's leading novelist, whose popular *Weep Not, Child* (1964) was the first major novel in English by an East African. As he became sensitive to the effects of colonialism in Africa, he adopted his traditional name and wrote in the language of Kenya's Kikuyu people.

Ngugi's prizewinning *Weep Not, Child* is the story of a Kikuyu family drawn into the struggle for Kenyan independence. *A Grain of Wheat* (1967), generally held to be artistically more mature, focuses on the many social, moral, and racial issues of the struggle for independence and its aftermath. A third novel, *The River Between* (1965), examines the conflict between Christianity and traditional ways and beliefs. *Petals of Blood* (1977) deals with social and economic problems in East Africa after independence. In a novel written in Kikuyu and English versions, *Caitaani Mutharaba-ini* (1980; *Devil on the Cross*), Ngugi presented these ideas in allegorical form. Written in a manner meant to recall traditional ballad singers, the novel is a partly realistic, partly fantastical account of a meeting between the Devil and various villains who exploit the poor.

The Black Hermit (1968; produced 1962) was the first of several plays, of which *The Trial of Dedan Kimathi* (produced 1974), cowritten with Micere Githae Mugo, is considered by some critics to be his best. Ngugi was also coauthor, with Ngugi wa Mirii, of a play first written in Kikuyu, *Ngaahika Ndeenda* (1977; *I Will Marry When I Want*), the performance of which led to his detention for a year without trial. (His book *Detained: A Writer's Prison Diary*, which was published in 1981, describes his ordeal.) The play attacks capitalism, religious hypocrisy, and corruption among the economic elite. *Matigari ma Njiruungi* (1986; *Matigari*) is a novel in the same vein.

Ngugi presented his ideas on literature, culture, and politics in numerous essays and lectures, the most important of which were collected in *Homecoming* (1972), *Writers in Politics* (1981), and *Barrel of a Pen: Resistance to Repression in Neo-colonial Kenya* (1983). In *Decolonising the Mind: The Politics of Language in African Literature* (1986), Ngugi argued for African-language literature as the only authentic voice for Africans.

Nguyen Du \ŋī-'en-'dü\, *in full* Nguyen-du Thanh-hien, *pen name* To Nhu \'tō-'nü\ (b. 1765, Tien Dien, Vietnam—d. Aug. 10, 1820, Hue)   Vietnamese poet, creator of the epic poem *Kim Van Kieu*.

Considered by some to be the father of Vietnamese literature, Nguyen Du passed the mandarin examinations at the age of 19 and and later held many official posts. While serving in Quang Binh in northern Vietnam in 1813, he attained the rank of Column of the Empire and was subsequently appointed head of a delegation to Peking. During this mission he translated a Chinese novel, dating from the Ming period (1368–1644), into Vietnamese poetry as *Kim Van Kieu* (*The Tale of Kieu: The Classic Vietnamese Verse Novel*). As an exploration of the Buddhist doctrine of karmic retribution for individual sins, the poem expresses his personal suffering and deep humanism. He also wrote "Words of a Young Hat Seller," a shorter poem in a lighter vein; *Chieu hon* ("Address to the Dead"); and many other poems in Chinese.

Niane \'nyȧn\, Djibril Tamsir (b. Jan. 9, 1932, Conakry, French Guinea [now Guinea])   African historian, playwright, and short-story writer.

Niane's first scholarly work, *Recherches sur l'empire du Mali* (1959), was followed by *Histoire de l'Afrique occidentale* (1961;

"History of Western Africa"), coauthored with Jean Suret-Canale. His novel *Soundjata; ou, l'épopée mandingue* (1960; *Sundiata: An Epic of Old Mali*) is a highly successful re-creation of the life and times of the illustrious 13th-century founder of the Mali empire, recounted in the voice of a tribal storyteller. His other works include a collection of short stories, *Mery* (1975), and two historical plays, *Sikasso* and *Chaka.*

Nibelungenlied \'nē-bə-ˌlůŋ-ən-ˌlēt\ ("Song of the Nibelungs") Middle High German epic poem written about 1200 by an unknown poet from the Danube region in what is now Austria. It is preserved in three main 13th-century manuscripts, A (now in Munich), B (St. Gall), and C (Donaueschingen); modern scholars regard B as the most trustworthy. The word Nibelung appears in the first part of the poem as the name of Siegfried's lands and peoples and his treasure, but, throughout the second, it is an alternate name for the Burgundians.

The poem begins with two cantos that introduce Kriemhild, a Burgundian princess of Worms, and Siegfried, a prince from the lower Rhine who is determined to woo her. When he arrives in Worms, he is identified by Hagen, a henchman of Kriemhild's brother King Gunther. Hagen then recounts Siegfried's earlier heroic deeds, including his acquisition of a treasure. When war is declared by the Danes and Saxons, Siegfried leads the Burgundians and distinguishes himself in battle. Upon his return, he meets Kriemhild, and their affections develop during his residence at court.

Hearing of the contest for Brunhild, a queen of outstanding strength and beauty who may be won only by a man capable of matching her athletic prowess, Gunther decides to woo her. He enlists the aid of Siegfried, to whom he promises the hand of Kriemhild if successful. By trickery the two men defeat Brunhild, and she accepts Gunther as her husband. Siegfried and Kriemhild are then married as promised, but Brunhild is suspicious. The two queens soon quarrel, and Kriemhild reveals how Brunhild was deceived. Hagen sides with Brunhild and kills Siegfried.

During these events, Brunhild drops almost unnoticed out of the story. Siegfried's funeral is conducted with great ceremony, and the grief-stricken Kriemhild remains at Worms, though for a long time estranged from Gunther and Hagen. Siegfried's treasure is brought to Worms, but Hagen sinks the treasure in the Rhine.

The second part of the poem deals basically with the conflict between Hagen and Kriemhild and her vengeance against the Burgundians. Etzel (Attila), king of the Huns, asks the hand of Kriemhild, who accepts. After many years, she persuades Etzel to invite her brothers and Hagen to his court. Though Hagen is wary, they all go, and carnage ensues. Kriemhild has Gunther killed and then, with Siegfried's sword, she slays the bound and defenseless Hagen. Kriemhild herself is slain by a knight named Hildebrand.

Elements of great antiquity are discernible in the *Nibelungenlied*. The story of Brunhild appears in Old Norse literature. The brief references to the heroic deeds of Siegfried allude to several ancient stories, many of which are preserved in the Scandinavian *Poetic Edda*, *Vǫlsunga saga*, and *Thithriks saga*, in which Siegfried is called Sigurd. The entire second part of the story appears in an older Eddic poem, the *Atlakvitha* (*Lay of Atli*). Compare EDDA; LAY OF ATLI.

Nicander \ni-'kan-dər, nī-\ (fl. *c.* 2nd century BC, Claros, near Colophon) Greek poet, physician, and grammarian.

Nicander wrote a number of works both in prose and verse, of which two are preserved. The longest, *Theriaca*, is a hexameter poem of 958 lines on the nature of venomous animals

and the wounds they inflict. The details of this work were taken from the prose writings of Apollodorus, an early 3rd-century writer. The other, *Alexipharmaca*, may also have been derived from Apollodorus. It consists of 630 hexameters concerning poisons and their antidotes. Both works are obscurantist, written in unimaginative, archaic language. Among his lost works are *Aetolica*, a prose history of Aetolia; *Heteroeumena*, a mythological epic used by Ovid in the *Metamorphoses*; and *Georgica* and *Melissourgica*, of which considerable fragments are preserved.

Nicholas Nickleby \'nik-ə-ləs-'nik-əl-bē\ (*in full* The Life and Adventures of Nicholas Nickleby) Novel by Charles DICKENS, originally published in 20 monthly installments by "Boz" from 1838 to 1839 and published in book form in 1839.

An early novel, this melodramatic tale of young Nickleby's adventures as he struggles to seek his fortune in Victorian England resembles *The Pickwick Papers* in structure, although not always in tone. Throughout, comic events are interspersed with Dickens' moving indictment of society's ill treatment of children and the cruelty of the educational system.

Nichols \'nik-əlz\, John (b. Feb. 2, 1745, London, Eng.—d. Nov. 26, 1826, London) Writer, printer, and antiquary who, through numerous volumes of literary anecdotes, made an invaluable contribution to posterity's knowledge of the lives and works of 18th-century men of letters in England.

Apprenticed in 1757 to William Bowyer the Younger, known as "the learned printer" (who took him into partnership in 1766), Nichols undertook his first literary work as editor of the works of Jonathan Swift (1775-79). In 1778 Nichols became part manager of the *Gentleman's Magazine* and in 1792 sole managing editor. Of his original work, *Bibliotheca Topographica Britannica* (1780-90) and *The History and Antiquities of the County of Leicester* (1795-1815) are especially valuable. A friend of most of the leading literary figures of his age, he published Samuel Johnson's *Lives of the English Poets*, exercising much editorial influence and supplying a good deal of basic information. His own work as a biographer began with his memoir of Bowyer, expanded into *Biographical and Literary Anecdotes of William Bowyer* (1782). This formed the basis of *Literary Anecdotes of the Eighteenth Century*, 9 vol. (1812-15; completed by his son, John Bowyer Nichols).

Nicholson \'nik-əl-sən\, Reynold Alleyne (b. Aug. 18, 1868, Keighley, Yorkshire, Eng.—d. Aug. 27, 1945, Chester, Cheshire) English orientalist who exercised a lasting influence on Islāmic studies.

Educated at Aberdeen University and the University of Cambridge, Nicholson taught at Cambridge. He was a leading scholar in Islāmic literature and mysticism. His *Literary History of the Arabs* (1907) remains a standard work on the subject in English, while his many text editions and translations of Ṣūfī writings, culminating in his eight-volume *Mathnawi of Jalalu'd-din Rumi* (1925-40), eminently advanced the study of Muslim mystics. He combined exact scholarship with notable literary gifts; some of his versions of Arabic and Persian poetry entitle him to be considered a poet in his own right.

nicker \'nik-ər\ [Old English *nicor*] In Germanic folklore, a demon or monster that lives in the water. It is sometimes represented as half-child, half-horse and sometimes as an old man.

Nickleby, Nicholas \'nik-ə-ləs-'nik-əl-bē\ Fictional character, the protagonist of Charles Dickens' novel NICHOLAS NICKLEBY.

Nicol \'nik-əl\, Abioseh, *pseudonym of* Davidson (Sylvester Hector Willoughby) Nicol (b. Sept. 14, 1924, Freetown, Sierra Leone—d. Sept. 20, 1994, Cambridge, Eng.) Sierra Leonean diplomat, physician, medical researcher, and writer of short stories, poetry, and nonfiction.

Nicol was principal of Fourah Bay College, Freetown (1960–67), vice-chancellor of the University of Sierra Leone, and ambassador to the United Nations (UN). He was president of the World Federation of UN Associations from 1983 to 1987.

Nicol's short stories, simple and realistic presentations of everyday events, are written with astute insight into what he sees as life's mixture of the tragic and the absurd. *Two African Tales* (1965) and *The Truly Married Woman, and Other Stories* (1965) center upon life in government service and upon the interaction of Africans with colonial administrators. His other books include *Africa, A Subjective View* (1964), *Regionalism and the New International Economic Order* (1981), and *Creative Women in Changing Societies* (1982).

Nicolai \ˌnē-kō-'lī, 'nik-ō-ˌlī\, Friedrich, *in full* Christoph Friedrich Nicolai (b. March 18, 1733, Berlin, Prussia [Germany]—d. Jan. 8, 1811, Berlin) Writer and bookseller who, with Gotthold Ephraim Lessing and Moses Mendelssohn, was a leader of the German Enlightenment (*Aufklärung*).

Nicolai learned his father's bookselling business and became acquainted with English literature. In 1752 he took part in a literary controversy over John Milton by defending the English poet against the grammarian Johann Christoph Gottsched. His enthusiasm for English literature gained him the friendship of Lessing and Mendelssohn. He cofounded, with Mendelssohn, the periodical *Bibliothek der schönen Wissenschaften* (1757–60; "Library of Fine Arts") and, with both Lessing and Mendelssohn, *Briefe die neueste Litteratur betreffend* (1761–66; "Letters on the Modern Literary Question"). He also edited the *Allgemeine deutsche Bibliothek* (1765–92), the organ of the "popular philosophers" who fought against authority in religion and what they conceived to be extravagance in literature. He showed a complete incomprehension of the new movement of ideas represented by J.W. von Goethe, Friedrich von Schiller, Immanuel Kant, Johann Gottfried von Herder, and Johann Gottlieb Fichte.

Nicolai's romances are forgotten, although *Das Leben und die Meinungen des Magisters Sebaldus Nothanker* (1773–76; "The Life and Opinions of Master Sebaldus Nothanker") and *Die Freuden des Jungen Werthers* (1775; "The Joys of Young Werther"), his satire on Goethe's *Werther*, were well known in their time. His reflective 12-volume *Die Beschreibung einer Reise durch Deutschland und die Schweiz* (1788–96; "The Description of a Journey Through Germany and Switzerland"), which was widely read, reflects his rather narrow, conservative views.

Nicolson \'nik-əl-sən\, Harold (b. Nov. 21, 1886, Tehrān, Iran—d. May 1, 1968, Sissinghurst Castle, Kent, Eng.) British diplomat and author who wrote more than 125 books, including political essays, travel accounts, and mystery novels.

Nicolson entered the Foreign Office in 1909, where he remained for 20 years. In 1913 he married the poet and novelist Victoria Sackville-West.

In 1929 Nicolson decided to abandon his diplomatic career. He had already published several biographies—*Paul Verlaine* (1921), *Tennyson* (1923), *Byron* (1924), *Swinburne* (1926), and *Some People* (1927)—as well as a novel and other pieces. On Jan. 1, 1930, he became a columnist for Lord Beaverbrook's *London Evening Standard* and also, on that day, began a diary, in which he made daily entries until Oct. 4, 1964. The diaries are a valuable record of British social and political life during their period; they were edited and published by his son Nigel Nicolson in *Diaries and Letters* (3 vol; 1966–68). Along with his newspaper work, he also wrote book reviews and gave

radio talks. From 1935 to 1945 he was a member of Parliament. Some of his later books are *Curzon* (1934), *Politics in the Train* (1936), *Helen's Tower* (1938), *Diplomacy* (1939), *The Congress of Vienna* (1946), *King George V* (1952), and *Journey to Java* (1957).

Nielsen \'nil-sən\, Morten (b. Jan. 3, 1922, Ålborg, Den.—d. Aug. 29, 1944, Copenhagen) Danish poet who became the symbol of his generation's desire for freedom and who was killed as a result of his participation in the organized Danish resistance to the German occupation during World War II.

Although Nielsen was only 22 when he was killed, he had been able to express, in well-formed verse, matters that were engaging the minds of his fellow Danes. The only volume he published before his death was *Krigere uden Vaaben* (1943; "Warriors Without Weapons"). In contrast to most of the poetry of the occupation, Nielsen's verse is still read in Denmark.

Niemcewicz \nʸem-'tse-vʸēch\, Julian Ursyn (b. Feb. 6, 1757/58, Skoki, Pol.—d. May 21, 1841, Paris, Fr.) Polish playwright, poet, novelist, and translator whose writings, inspired by patriotism and concern for social and governmental reform, reflect the turbulent political events of his day.

In 1788 Niemcewicz was elected deputy to the Sejm (parliament) of Poland. In 1790 he wrote *Powrót posła* ("The Deputy's Return"), a political comedy. After participating in the unsuccessful insurrection of 1794, he was captured at Maciejowice and imprisoned in St. Petersburg for two years. While jailed, he translated works of such authors as John Dryden, John Milton, Alexander Pope, and Samuel Johnson. Upon his release he traveled to England and then to the United States, where he remained until 1807, when he returned to Poland. Until 1831 he devoted himself to literary work, publishing *Śpiewy historyczne* (1816; "Historical Songs"), a series of simple song poems that became very popular, and *Lejbe i Sióra* (1821; "Leybe and Syora"), the first Polish novel to discuss the "Jewish question." He also wrote the first Polish historical novel, *Jan z Tęczyna*, 3 vol. (1825; "Jan of Tęczyn"), influenced by Sir Walter Scott. Niemcewicz spent the last years of his life campaigning for Polish freedom. His memoirs appeared posthumously in 1848.

Nietzsche \'nē-chə, *Angl* -chē\, Friedrich (b. Oct. 15, 1844, Röcken, Saxony, Prussia [Germany]—d. Aug. 25, 1900, Weimar) German classical scholar, philosopher, and critic of culture, an impassioned critic of the ethos of his time, especially of Christianity, conformism, and nationalism.

Nietzsche studied classical philology at Bonn and Leipzig (1864–68) and became a Swiss subject and a professor of classics at Basel, Switz., in 1869. There he wrote *Die Geburt der Tragödie aus dem Geiste der Musik* (1872; THE BIRTH OF TRAGEDY), which contains his well-known theory of the Apollonian-Dionysian dichotomy. He resigned from the university permanently in 1879.

During the 10 years following his retirement, Nietzsche published such important works as *Also sprach Zarathustra* (1883–85; THUS SPAKE ZARATHUSTRA), *Jenseits von Gut und Böse* (1886; *Beyond Good and Evil*), and *Zur Genealogie der Moral* (1887; *On the Genealogy of Morals*). While living in Switzerland, Nietzsche had become a friend and admirer of the composer Richard Wagner. Slowly, however, their philosophies diverged, and a formal break was made in 1878. Nietzsche published *Der Fall Wagner* (*The Case of Wagner*) in 1888, the same year that Georg Brandes began lecturing on Nietzsche at the University of Copenhagen. Brandes' lectures were the first significant public notice of Nietzsche's works and thought. In 1889 Nietzsche suffered a mental breakdown and spent a year in an asylum; he spent his last decade in mental darkness attended by his mother and later his sister.

After his death, his sister Elisabeth secured the rights to his literary remains and edited them for publication without scruple or understanding. While she gained a wide audience for her misinterpretations, she withheld his own reflection on his work, *Ecce Homo*, until 1908, 20 years after its composition.

Nieuwe Gids, De \də-'nyü-və-'ḳits\ ("The New Guide") Dutch journal that heralded a literary revival in the northern Netherlands during the 1880s. It was founded on Oct. 1, 1885, by the poets Willem Kloos and Albert Verwey and the prose writer Frederik Willem van Eeden. Unlike the periodical *De Gids*—published from 1837—it pursued an exclusively aesthetic ideal in regard to literature. It also accepted contributions on politics, science, philosophy, and art. Among the leaders of the literary revival were the poets Herman Gorter, Pieter Cornelis Boutens, and Jan Hendrik Leopold; critic Lodewijk van Deyssel; dramatist Herman Heijermans; and the prose writer Louis Marie Anne Couperus.

Gorter's poem "Mei" ("May"), which was first published in *De Nieuwe Gids* in 1889, was regarded as the seminal work of the movement. By 1890 the editorial staff was fragmented over socialist issues. After much infighting, Kloos disbanded the editorial board and published the magazine under his own name from 1893. It declined gradually in popularity and finally ceased publication in 1943 after Kloos's death.

Niflheim \'niv-əl-ˌhām\, *Old Norse* Niflheimr \-ˌhām-ər\ In Norse mythology, the cold, dark, misty world of the dead, ruled by the goddess Hel. In some accounts it was the last of nine worlds, a place into which evil men passed after reaching the region of death (Hel). It was situated below one of the roots of the world tree, Yggdrasil. In the Norse creation story, Niflheim was the misty region north of the void (Ginnungagap) in which the world was created.

Nigger of the "Narcissus," The Novel by Joseph CONRAD, published in 1897. The work was based on Conrad's experiences while serving in the British merchant navy.

All life on board the *Narcissus* revolves around James Wait, a dying black sailor. Other members of the crew include the strong Captain Allistoun; Craik, an Irish religious fanatic; and Donkin, an arrogant, lazy Cockney. The superstitious sailors cater to Wait, even steal food for him, and rescue him when the ship capsizes during a fierce storm. However, he is also the cause of dissension aboard ship, leading to a near mutiny. The novel is notable not only for its vivid picture of life at sea but also as a study of evolving relationships among men amid the most extreme circumstances.

Night Before Christmas, The *see* A VISIT FROM ST. NICHOLAS.

Night of the Iguana, The Three-act drama by Tennessee WILLIAMS, produced and published in 1961. Williams turned from his usual Southern settings and themes in this tale of tourists at a seedy Mexican hotel. The play's first act was noted for its detailed evocation of a dank jungle; some critics found it, and the characters—among them a defrocked priest, a lusty widow, and a dying poet—overblown.

night piece A work of art (such as a picture, composition, or writing) dealing with night.

nihilism \'nī-ə-ˌliz-əm, 'nē-, -hə-ˌliz\ [Latin *nihil* nothing] Any of various philosophical positions that deny that there are objective foundations for human value systems. In 19th-century Russia, nihilism (Russian *nigilizm*) came to be applied to a philosophy of skepticism that originated during the early years of the reign of Alexander II. Fundamentally, nihilism represented a philosophy of negation of all forms of aestheticism; it advocated utilitarianism and scientific rationalism. The so-cial sciences and classical philosophical systems were rejected entirely. Nihilism represented a crude form of positivism and materialism and a revolt against the established social order; it negated all authority exercised by the state, the church, or the family. It based its belief on nothing but scientific truth. All evils, nihilists believed, derived from a single source—ignorance—which science alone would overcome.

In Russian literature *nigilizm* was probably first used by N.I. Nadezhdin, who applied it to Aleksandr Pushkin in an article in the *Messenger of Europe*. Nadezhdin equated nihilism with skepticism, as did V. Bervi later. Mikhail N. Katkov, a well-known conservative journalist, presented nihilism as constituting a social menace by its negation of all moral principles.

If to the conservative elements the nihilists were the curse of the time, to liberals such as N.G. Chernyshevsky they represented a mere transitory factor in the development of national thought, a stage in the struggle for individual freedom. In his celebrated novel *Fathers and Sons* (1862), Ivan Turgenev popularized the term through the figure of Bazarov the nihilist. The nihilists of the 1860s and '70s eventually came to be regarded as disheveled, ragged men who rebelled against tradition and social order. The philosophy of nihilism then began to be associated erroneously with the regicide of Alexander II and the political terror that was employed by those active in clandestine organizations against absolutism. In time, however, nihilism did degenerate into a philosophy of violence. A comparison between Turgenev's hero Bazarov and the hero of Leonid Andreyev's drama *Savva*, written during the early 20th century, reveals the deterioration of nihilist philosophy, which changed from a faith in science into a justification of terror and destruction as a means to attain set goals.

Nihon shoki \nē-'hōŋ-'shō-kē\ or **Nihon-gi** \-'gē\ ("Chronicles of Japan") Text that, together with the KOJIKI, comprises the oldest official history of Japan, covering the period from its mythical origins to AD 697.

The *Nihon shoki*, written in Chinese, reflects the influence of Chinese civilization on Japan. It was compiled in 720 by order of the Imperial court to give the newly Sinicized court a history that could be compared with the annals of the Chinese. It was the first of six officially compiled chronicles that were continued to 887 by Imperial command.

The work consists of 30 chapters. The first part deals with many myths and legends of ancient Japan and is an important source for Shintō thought. The later chapters, for the period from about the 5th century on, are historically more accurate and contain records of several of the powerful clans as well as of the Imperial family.

Nijhoff \'nei-ˌhȯf, *Angl* 'nī-\, Martinus (b. April 20, 1894, The Hague, Neth.—d. Jan. 26, 1953, The Hague) Modernist Dutch poet noted for his intensely original imagery and extraordinary command of poetic technique.

Nijhoff studied at Amsterdam and Utrecht and was for many years editor of the literary periodical *De Gids*. His first volume, *De wandelaar* (1916; "The Walker"), is a collection of symbolic, almost expressionistic poems that reveal in traditional verse an essentially modern anguish and despair. His ambivalence toward the world is also apparent in his second and best-known volume, *Vormen* (1924; "Forms").

His most optimistic verse is published in *Nieuwe gedichten* (1934; "New Poems"); this volume reveals the poet's spiritual renewal and his affirmation of the richness of human existence, particularly in the experimental "Awater." A later volume, *Het uur U* (1942; "Zero Hour"), is a long narrative poem examining a stranger's shattering effect on a self-satisfied community. Nijhoff also wrote dramas and did several translations.

Nijlen \văn-'nei-lən, *Angl* 'nī-\, Jan van (b. Nov. 10, 1884, Antwerp, Belg.—d. Aug. 14, 1965, Forest)   One of the most distinguished Flemish poets of his generation.

Van Nijlen usually published his verse in limited editions. Among his early volumes were *Het angezicht der aarde* (1923; "The Face of the Earth"), *De vogel phoenix* (1928; "The Phoenix Bird"), and *Geheimschrift* (1934; "Secret Writing"). He gained a wider audience when, in 1938, he published a one-volume selection of his poems, *Gedichten, 1904–1938*. Subsequent publications included *De Dauuwtrapper* (1947; "The Dew Trapper") and *Te laat voor deze wereld* (1957; "Too Late for This World").

Van Nijlen's characteristic tone is melancholic and elegiac, reflecting his disillusionment with the modern world. His verses recall the Romantics' longing to escape to a simpler and truer life; they are marked, however, by a classical clarity and finish.

Nijō Yoshimoto \'nē-jō-yō-'shē-mō-tō\ (b. 1320, Japan—d. 1388, Japan)   Government official and *renga* (linked-verse) poet of the early Muromachi period (1338–1573) in Japan who is best known for refining the rules of *renga* composition.

With the assistance of the poet Gusai (Kyūsei), Yoshimoto compiled *Tsukuba-shū* (1356), one of the first collections of *renga*. In 1372 he completed *Ōanshinshiki* (also called *Renga Shinshiki*), which contained new rules for the composition of *renga*. He also wrote *Tsukuba mondō* (1372), a scholarly treatise on linked verse, and contributed numerous poems to such collections as *Kyūshū mondō* (1376) and *Gumon kenchū* (1363). MASUKAGAMI, a historical record of the Kamakura period (1192–1333), is also attributed to him.

Nike \'nī-kē, 'nē-kā\   In Greek mythology, the goddess of victory, daughter of the giant Pallas and of the infernal River Styx. As an attribute of both Athena, the goddess of wisdom or practical reason, and Zeus, Nike was represented in art as a small figure carried in the hand by those divinities. Athena Nike was always wingless; Nike alone was winged.

At Rome, where Nike was called Victoria, she was worshiped from the earliest times. She came to be regarded as the protecting goddess of the Roman Senate.

Nin \'nēn, 'nin\, Anaïs (b. Feb. 21, 1903, Neuilly, Fr.—d. Jan. 14, 1977, Los Angeles, Calif., U.S.)   French-born author of novels and short stories whose literary reputation rests on the eight published volumes of her personal diaries. Her writing shows the influence of the Surrealist movement and her study of psychoanalysis.

Nin launched her literary career with the publication of *D.H. Lawrence: An Unprofessional Study* (1932). In the early 1940s, Nin went to New York City, where she printed and published her novels and short stories at her own expense. Not until 1966, with the appearance of the first volume of her diaries, did she win recognition as a writer. The success of the diary provoked interest in an earlier work entitled *Cities of the Interior* (1959), a five-volume *roman-fleuve*, or continuous novel, which consisted of *Ladders to Fire* (1946); *Children of the Albatross* (1947); *The Four-Chambered Heart* (1950); *A Spy in the House of Love* (1954); and *Solar Barque* (1958).

Nin's literary contribution was a subject of controversy in her lifetime and remained so after her death. Some critics admire her unique expression of femininity, her lyrical style, and her psychological insight, while others dismiss her concern with her own fulfillment as self-indulgent and narcissistic. Her other works of fiction include a collection of short stories, *Under a Glass Bell* (1944); the novels *House of Incest* (1936), *Seduction of the Minotaur* (1961), and *Collages* (1964); and three novelettes collected in *Winter of Artifice* (1939).

Nineteen Eighty-four   Novel by George ORWELL, published in 1949 as a warning about the menaces of totalitarianism.

The novel is set in an imaginary future world that is dominated by three perpetually warring totalitarian police states. The book's hero, Winston Smith, is a minor party functionary in one of these states. His longing for truth and decency leads him to secretly rebel against the government. Smith has a love affair with a like-minded woman, but they are both arrested by the Thought Police. The ensuing imprisonment, torture, and reeducation of Smith are intended not merely to break him physically or make him submit but to root out his independent mental existence and his spiritual dignity.

Orwell's warning of the dangers of totalitarianism made a deep impression on his contemporaries and upon subsequent readers, and the book's title and many of its coinages, such as NEWSPEAK, became bywords for modern political abuses.

Niobe \'nī-ō-bē\   In Greek mythology, the daughter of Tantalus (king of Sipylus in Lydia) and wife of King Amphion of Thebes. According to Homer's *Iliad*, she had six sons and six daughters and boasted of her progenitive superiority to the Titan Leto, who had only two children, the twin deities Apollo and Artemis. As punishment for her pride, Apollo killed all Niobe's sons, and Artemis killed all her daughters. Niobe went back to her Phrygian home, where she was turned into a rock on Mount Sipylus (Yamanlar Dağı, northeast of Izmir, Tur.), which continues to weep when the snow melts above it.

Niobe is the subject of lost tragedies by Aeschylus and Sophocles, and Ovid tells her story in his *Metamorphoses*.

Nishiyama Sōin \,nē-'shē-,yä-mä-'sō-,ēn\, *original name* Nishiyama Toyoichi \,tō-yō-'ē-chē\ (b. 1605, Higo province, Japan—d. May 5, 1682, Kyōto?)   *Renga* (linked-verse) poet of the early Tokugawa period (1603–1867) who founded a school of haikai poetry. Sōin's haikai (comic *renga*) became the transition between the light and clever haikai of Matsunaga Teitoku and the more serious and aesthetic haiku of Matsuo Bashō.

By 1633 Sōin was a professional *renga* poet. His interest in haikai was slow to develop, and it was not until 1673 that his first anthology of haikai, *Sōin senku* ("One Thousand Verses by Sōin"), was published. The poems in this volume, although written in the Teitoku style, demonstrated a higher degree of sophistication than the earlier haikai. Young students—including Ihara Saikaku and Okanishi Ichū—who were dissatisfied with the old school flocked to Sōin's school. His numerous volumes of poetry include *Sōin gohyakku* (1676; "Five Hundred Verses by Sōin") and *Baiō Sōin hokku shū* (1681; "The Collected Hokku of the Plum Old Gentleman Sōin").

nisse \'nis-ə\ *plural* nisser \'nis-ər\ *or* nisses [Swedish, Danish, or Norwegian, alteration of *Nils* (Saint) Nicholas]   In Scandinavian folklore, a friendly goblin or brownie that frequents farm buildings.

Nisus \'nī-səs\   In Greek mythology, a son of King Pandion of Megara. Nisus had a purple lock of hair with magic power, which, if preserved, would guarantee him life and continued possession of his kingdom. When King Minos of Crete besieged Megara, Nisus' daughter Scylla fell in love with Minos (or, in some accounts, was bribed) and betrayed the city by cutting off her father's purple lock. Nisus was killed (or killed himself) and was transformed into a sea eagle. Scylla later drowned, possibly at the hand of Minos, and was changed into a sea bird, possibly a heron, constantly pursued by the sea eagle.

Niven \'niv-ən\, Frederick John (b. March 31, 1878, Valparaíso, Chile—d. Jan. 30, 1944, Vancouver, B.C., Can.)   Regional novelist who wrote more than 30 novels, many of them historical romances, set in Scotland and Canada. Three of his best-known novels—*The Flying Years* (1935), *Mine Inheritance* (1940), and *The Transplanted* (1944)—form a trilogy dealing with the settlement of the Canadian west.

Niven went to Canada about 1900 and worked there in construction camps in the Canadian west. Returning to the British Isles, where he had been educated, he was a writer and journalist in England until after World War I, when he settled permanently in British Columbia. Niven also published two volumes of verse and an autobiography, *Coloured Spectacles* (1938), a collection of essays based on his personal experiences.

nix \'niks\ or **nixie** or **nixy** \'nik-sē\ [German *Nix; nixie* from German *Nixe,* feminine of *Nix*]   In Germanic folklore, a supernatural creature dwelling in freshwater, usually in a beautiful palace, and usually unfriendly to humans.

The nix mingles with humans by assuming a variety of physical forms (such as that of a fair maiden or an old woman) or by making itself invisible. One of three attributes may betray the disguises of nixes: they are music lovers and excellent dancers and they have the gift of prophecy. Though usually malevolent, nixes can easily be propitiated with gifts. In some regions, they are said to abduct human children and to lure people into deep water to drown. According to some sources, nixes can marry human beings and bear human children.

Niẓāmī   *see* NEẒĀMĪ.

Njáls saga \'nyaùls\, *also called* Njála \'nyaù-lä\ or Burnt Njáll \'bərnt-'nyaùl\   One of the longest and generally considered the finest of the 13th-century ICELANDERS' SAGAS. It presents the most comprehensive picture of Icelandic life in the heroic age and has a wide range of complex characters. The work has two heroes—Gunnar (Gunther) and Njáll. Gunnar is a brave, guileless, generous youth like Sigurd (Siegfried) of the heroic legends; Njáll is a wise and prudent man endowed with prophetic gifts. Both are men of peace, but in a society in which the ties of blood impose inescapable obligations and the memories of past injuries may always be rekindled, neither Gunnar's goodwill nor Njáll's wisdom can save them from their fate.

Gunnar meets death at the hands of his enemies when his wife, the beautiful but capricious Hallgerd, in retaliation for a blow he once gave her in anger, refuses him a strand of her hair to string his bow.

Njáll is drawn into a feud through the headstrong actions of his sons. He accepts the consequences stoically in a powerful scene in which he and his family are burned to death in their home by a reluctant "enemy," whose honor demands this vengeance. A third part of the saga deals with the vengeance of Njáll by his son-in-law Kári, the sole survivor of the family.

Njǫrd \'nyœrd, 'nyœrth\, *Old Norse* Njǫrthr \'nyœrth-ər\   In Norse mythology, the god of the wind and of the sea and its riches. His aid was invoked in seafaring and in hunting, and he was considered the god of "wealth-bestowal," or prosperity. He was the father of Freyr and Freyja by his own sister. Traditionally, Njǫrd's native tribe, the Vanir, gave him as a hostage to the rival tribe of Æsir and the giantess Skadi chose him to be her husband. The marriage failed because Njǫrd preferred to live in Nóatún, his home by the sea, while Skadi was happier in her father's mountain home.

Nkosi \ŋ-'kō-sē\, Lewis (b. Dec. 5, 1936, Durban, Natal, S.Af.)   South African author, critic, journalist, and broadcaster.

Nkosi worked as a journalist, first in 1955 for the Zulu-English weekly paper *Ilanga lase Natal* ("Natal Sun") and then for *Drum* magazine, and as chief reporter for its Sunday newspaper, the *Golden City Post*, from 1956 to 1960. In 1961 Nkosi went to Harvard University, and, consequently, he was exiled

from South Africa. From that time he wrote for American, British, and African periodicals. Many of his critical essays were published in *Home and Exile* (1965), which became a standard source for students of African literature.

Nkosi's play *The Rhythm of Violence* (1964), set in Johannesburg in the early 1960s, handles the theme of race relations both ideologically and practically. In addition to this drama, Nkosi produced the BBC radio series "Africa Abroad" from 1962 to 1965 and worked from 1965 to 1968 as literary editor of *The New African*. Nkosi also wrote librettos and was the author of a 1971 radio play entitled "We Can't All Be Martin Luther King." Other late works include essays on South Africa in *The Transplanted Heart* (1975) and the collections *Tasks and Masks: Themes and Styles of African Literature* (1981) and *Home and Exile and Other Selections* (1983). His first novel, *Mating Birds* (1983), brought wide critical attention for its focus on miscegenation in South Africa.

Noah \'nō-ə\, *also spelled* Noe \'nō-ē\   The hero of the biblical Flood story in the Old Testament book of Genesis, the originator of vineyard cultivation, and, as the father of Shem, Ham, and Japeth (Japheth), the representative head of a Semitic genealogical line. A synthesis of at least three biblical source traditions, Noah is the image of the righteous man made party to a covenant with Yahweh, the God of Israel, in which future protection against natural catastrophe is assured. Later literature uses Noah as a symbol of obedience, as a new Adam, as a type of Christ, as a worldly scientist, and in many other related guises. *See also* HAM.

Noailles \nȯ-'äy\, Anna, de, *in full* Anna-Élisabeth de Noailles, Princess Brancovan, Countess (comtesse) Mathieu (b. Nov. 15, 1876, Paris, Fr.—d. April 30, 1933, Paris)   A poet and leading literary figure in France in the pre-World War I period.

The daughter of a Romanian prince and granddaughter of a Turkish pasha, she adopted France and its language for her life and writings. Her friends included the novelists Marcel Proust and Colette and the poets Paul Valéry and Jean Cocteau. Her volumes of poems, *Le Coeur innombrable* (1901; "The Numberless Heart"), *Les Éblouissements* (1907; "Resplendence"), and *L'Honneur de souffrir* (1927; "The Honor of Suffering"), are vibrant with a sensual love of nature. Her later works reflect her fear of the inevitable collapse of her physical powers.

Nobel Prize for Literature \nō-'bel, 'nō-bel\   One of six prizes that are awarded annually by four institutions (three Swedish and one Norwegian) from a fund established under the will of Alfred Bernhard Nobel. The first award was given on Dec. 10, 1901. The institution that awards the prize for literature is the Swedish Academy in Stockholm.

The selection of the prizewinners begins in the early autumn of the year preceding the award, with the prize-awarding institution sending out invitations to nominate candidates to those qualified under the Nobel statutes to do so. The basis of selection is professional competence and international range; self-nomination automatically disqualifies a person. A final decision is made by November 15. An individual may not be nominated posthumously, but a prize duly proposed may be so awarded, as was the case with Erik A. Karlfeldt, winner in 1931.

A prize is either given entire to one person or shared jointly by two or more (in practice never more than three) persons. Prizes have been declined, and in some instances governments have forbidden their nationals to accept Nobel prizes. Those who win a prize but decline are nevertheless entered into the list of Nobel laureates with the remark "declined the prize," as was Boris Pasternak in 1958.

The general principles governing awards were laid down by Nobel in his will. In 1900 supplementary rules of interpretation and administration were agreed upon; these rules have on the whole remained unchanged but have been somewhat modified in application.

noble savage   In literature, an idealized concept of an uncivilized individual who symbolizes the innate goodness of one not exposed to the corrupting influences of civilization.

The glorification of the noble savage is a dominant theme in the Romantic writings of the 18th and 19th centuries, especially in the works of Jean-Jacques Rousseau. For example, *Émile*, 4 vol. (1762), is a long treatise on the corrupting influence of traditional education, and *Rêveries* (1782) contains descriptions of nature and the natural human response to it. The concept of the noble savage, however, can be traced to ancient Greece, where Homer, Pliny, and Xenophon idealized the Arcadians and other primitive groups, both real and imagined. From the 15th to the 19th centuries, the noble savage figured prominently in popular travel accounts and appeared occasionally in English plays such as John Dryden's *The Conquest of Granada* (1672), in which the term *noble savage* was first used, and in Oroonoko (1695) by Thomas Southerne, based on Aphra Behn's novel of the same title.

François Chateaubriand sentimentalized the North American Indian in *Atala* (1801), *René* (1805), and *Les Natchez* (1826), as did James Fenimore Cooper in the Leather-Stocking Tales (1823–41). The three harpooners of the ship *Pequod* in Herman Melville's *Moby-Dick* (1851), Queequeg, Daggoo, and Tashtego, are other examples of the noble savage, as is the character of John the Savage in Aldous Huxley's *Brave New World* (1932).

Nobre \\'nō-brä\\, António (b. Aug. 16, 1867, Porto, Port.—d. March 18, 1900, Foz do Douro)   Portuguese poet whose verse marked a departure from objective realism and social commitment to subjective lyricism and an aesthetic point of view.

From 1890 to 1895 Nobre studied in Paris, where he was influenced by the French Symbolist poets. There he wrote the greater part of *Só* (1892; "Alone"), inspired by nostalgic memories of a childhood spent in the company of peasants and sailors in northern Portugal. *Só* combines the simple lyricism of Portuguese traditional poetry with the more refined perceptiveness of Symbolism. At first it met with a mixed reception, but it became one of the most popular and most imitated works of poetry in Portugal. A final version appeared in 1898. A generation of poets who followed and imitated Nobre was called the Sósino Generation. *Só* was the only volume Nobre published in his lifetime. Two further collections, *Despedidas* (1902; "Farewells") and *Primeiros versos* (1921; "First Poems"), were published posthumously.

node \\'nōd\\ [Latin *nodus,* literally, knot]   An entangling complication (such as in drama); a predicament.

Nodier \\nó-'dyä\\, Charles (b. April 29, 1780, Besançon, Fr.—d. Jan. 27, 1844, Paris)   Writer more important for the influence he had on the French Romantic movement than for his own writings.

In 1824 Nodier settled in Paris after his appointment as director of the Arsenal Library, and he soon became one of the leaders of the literary life of the capital. In his drawing room at the Arsenal, Nodier drew together a cénacle (literary coterie) composed of young men who were to be the leading lights of the Romantic movement: Victor Hugo, Alfred de Musset, and Charles-Augustin Sainte-Beuve. An ardent admirer of J.W. von Goethe and William Shakespeare, he did much to encourage the French Romantics to look abroad for inspiration.

Nodier wrote a great deal, but the only works of his that are still read are his fantastic, masterfully written short stories, rather in the style of the German Romantic E.T.A. Hoffmann.

His election to the Académie Française in 1833 virtually constituted official recognition of Romanticism.

Nō drama or **Noh drama** \\'nō\\   Classic Japanese dance-drama having a heroic theme, a chorus, and highly stylized action, costuming, and scenery. It is one of the oldest extant theatrical forms in the world. Nō, meaning "talent" or "skill," is unlike Western narrative drama in that its performers are simply storytellers who use their visual appearances and their movements to suggest the essence of their tale rather than to enact it. The total effect of a Nō drama is less that of a present action than of a simile or metaphor made visual.

Nō developed from ancient forms of dance-drama and from various types of festival drama at shrines and temples that had emerged by the 12th or 13th century. It became a distinctive form in the 14th century and was continually refined up to the years of the Tokugawa period (1603–1867). Nō gradually became a ceremonial drama performed on auspicious occasions by professional actors for the warrior class. The collapse of the feudal order in 1868 threatened the existence of Nō, but after World War II the form was revived.

The five types of Nō plays are the *kami* ("god") play, which involves a sacred story of a Shintō shrine; the *shura mono* ("fighting play"), which centers on warriors; the *katsura mono* ("wig play"), which has a female protagonist; a fourth type, varied in content, that includes the *gendai mono* ("present-day play")—in which the story is contemporary and "realistic" rather than legendary and supernatural—and the *kyōjo mono* ("madwoman play")—in which the protagonist becomes insane through the loss of a lover or child; and the fifth type, the *kiri*, or *kichiku* ("final," or "demon"), play, in which devils, strange beasts, and supernatural beings are featured.

About 2,000 Nō texts survive in full, of which about 230 remain in the modern repertoire. Zeami and his father, Kan'ami, wrote many of the most beautiful and exemplary of Nō texts. Though gradual changes have been made throughout the years, the form has remained essentially the same.

No Exit   One-act philosophical drama by Jean-Paul SARTRE, performed in 1944 and published in 1945. It is titled in French *Huis clos*, sometimes also translated as *In Camera* or *Dead End*. The play proposes that "hell is other people" rather than a state created by God.

The play begins with a bellman ushering three recently deceased people into a room. They are Garcin, a revolutionary who betrayed his own cause; Estelle, a nymphomaniac who has killed her illegitimate child; and Inez, a predatory lesbian. Each of the three requires another person for self-definition, yet is most attracted to the person who is most likely to cause great distress. Their inability to escape from each other guarantees their eternal torture.

Noma Hiroshi \\'nō-mä-'hē-rō-shē\\ (b. Feb. 23, 1915, Kōbe, Hyōgo prefecture, Japan—d. Jan. 2, 1991, Tokyo)   Japanese novelist who wrote *Shinkū chitai* (1952; *Zone of Emptiness*), which is considered to be one of the finest war novels produced after World War II.

Noma was brought up to succeed his father as head priest of a Buddhist sect, but as a youth he was drawn to Marxist ideology. He became interested in French Symbolist poetry, and, before beginning university work in 1935, he studied under the Symbolist poet Takeuchi Katsutarō. He graduated from Kyōto Imperial University in 1938, where he was heavily involved in the underground student movement and the Kansai labor movement.

Noma attracted attention after the war with the novels *Kurai e* (1946; "Dark Painting") and *Kao no naka no akai tsuki* (1947; *A Red Moon in Her Face*). *Kurai e* combined the techniques of Symbolism and the proletarian literature movement, using stream-of-consciousness prose. *Shinkū chitai* conveys a broad view of the Japanese wartime army by tracing the parallel fate of two soldiers of different classes.

After 1950 Noma employed more straightforward prose in his works. In 1949 he published the first volume of a multivolume work completed in 1971, *Seinen no wa* ("Ring of Youth"), which won the Tanizaki Prize in 1971. Other later works include the autobiographical *Waga tō wa soko ni tatsu* (1961; "My Tower Stands There"), *Shinran* (1973), and *Sayama saiban* (1977; "The Sayama Trial").

nom de plume \,näm-də-'plüm, *French* nôⁿd-'plǖm\ *plural* noms de plume *same or* ,nämz\ *or* nom de plumes *same or* 'plümz\ [French, pen name; probably coined in English] A pseudonym or pen name assumed by a writer, such as George Orwell for Eric Blair and Mark Twain for Samuel Langhorne Clemens.

nominy \'näm-i-nē\ [perhaps from Latin *in nomine* in the name (in formulas such as *in nomine Patris* in the name of the Father, etc.)] In northern England, a formulaic or conventional piece of folk verse, such as counting-out rhymes; the word can also mean rigmarole, or rambling, unconnected speech.

nonce word \'näns\ A word coined and used apparently to suit one particular occasion. Nonce words are sometimes used independently by different writers and speakers, but they are not adopted into general use. James Joyce employed many such words in *Finnegans Wake*, as did Anthony Burgess in *A Clockwork Orange*. *Compare* NEOLOGISM.

nonfiction \,nän-'fik-shən\ Literary works that are based mainly on fact rather than on the imagination, although they may contain fictional elements. Examples are essays and biographies.

nonfiction novel A book-length narrative of actual people and actual events written in the style of a novel. The American writer Truman Capote claimed to have invented the genre with his book *In Cold Blood* (1966). A true story of the brutal murder of a Kansas farm family, the book was based on six years of exacting research. The story is told from the points of view of different "characters," and the author attempts not to insert his own comments or to distort facts. Critics pointed out earlier precedents for this type of journalistic novel, such as John Hersey's *Hiroshima* (1946), an account of the World War II bombing of the Japanese city told through the histories of six survivors.

nonhero *see* ANTIHERO.

Nonnus \'nän-əs\ (fl. 5th century AD; b. Panopolis, Egypt) The most notable Greek epic poet of the Roman period. His chief work is the *Dionysiaca*, a hexameter poem in 48 books; its main subject, submerged in a chaos of subplots, is the expedition of the god Dionysus to India. Nonnus' fertile inventiveness and felicitous descriptive fantasy, which are well served by a unique command of the language and his vast literary knowledge, made him the often-imitated leader of the last Greek epic school. His style, with its ever-recurring, often daring metaphors and unremittingly bombastic tone, appealed to the taste of the time.

nonsense verse Humorous or whimsical verse that features absurd characters and actions and often contains evocative but meaningless nonce words. Nonsense verse differs from other comic verse in its resistance to any rational or allegorical interpretation. Though it often makes use of coined, meaningless words, it is unlike the ritualistic gibberish of

children's counting-out rhymes in that it makes such words sound purposeful. There are various specific forms of nonsense verse, including AMPHIGORY, double dactyl, holorhyme, and LIMERICK.

Skilled literary nonsense verse is rare; most of it has been written for children and is modern, dating from the beginning of the 19th century. The cardinal date could be considered 1846, when *The Book of Nonsense* was published. The work is a collection of limericks composed and illustrated by the artist Edward Lear, who first created them in the 1830s for the children of the Earl of Derby.

Lear's book was followed by the inspired fantasy of Lewis Carroll, whose "Jabberwocky," from *Through the Looking-Glass*, may be the best-known example of nonsense verse.

Hilaire Belloc's volume *The Bad Child's Book of Beasts* (1896) holds an honored place among the classics of English nonsense verse, while, in the United States, Laura E. Richards, a prolific writer of children's books, published verses in *Tirra Lirra* (1932) that have been compared to those of Lear.

Noonuccal, Oodgeroo *see* Kath WALKER.

Noot \,vän-der-'nōt\, Jan Baptista van der, *byname* Jonker Jan \'yôŋ-kər-'yän\ (b. *c.* 1540, Brecht, near Antwerp [now in Belgium]—d. *c.* 1595, Antwerp) The first Dutch poet to realize fully the new French Renaissance poetic style in Holland. He also influenced the English and German poets of his time.

Van der Noot went into political exile in 1567, and his first work—*Het bosken* ("The Little Wood"), a collection of his earliest poetry in the style and form of the Italian poet Petrarch and the French poet Pierre de Ronsard—was published in England in 1570 or 1571. In 1568 one of his main works had appeared, *Het theatre oft toon-neel* ("Theater for Voluptuous Worldlings"), a prose defense of the virtues of Calvinism and a condemnation of the worldliness of Dutch society. It is prefaced by sonnets and epigrams that were translated by Edmund Spenser for an English version. In van der Noot's unique Renaissance production and main poetical work, the *Olympiados* epic, he described in clear, unadorned language his dream of an allegorical journey toward his divine love, Olympia.

Nooteboom \'nō-tə-,bōm\, Cees, *in full* Cornelis Johannes Jacobus Maria Nooteboom (b. July 31, 1933, The Hague, Neth.) Dutch poet, novelist, playwright, travel writer, and essayist who was probably best known for his fiction.

A travel columnist for the Dutch periodicals *Avenue* and *Elsevier*, Nooteboom published a number of collections such as *Een nacht in Tunesie* (1965; "A Night in Tunisia"), *Een avond in Isfahan: Reisverhalen uit Perzie, Gambia, Duitsland, Japan, Engeland, Madeira, en Maleisie* (1978; "An Evening in Isfahan: Travel Writings from Persia, Gambia, Germany, Japan, England, Madeira, and Malaysia"), and *Berlijnse notities* (1990; "Berlin Notes").

Nooteboom's first novel was *Philip en de anderen* (1955; *Philip and the Others*). His later novel *Rituelen* (1980; *Rituals*) is a study of chaos, order, and obsession. Myth and reality are contrasted in *Een lied van schijn en wezen* (1981; *A Song of Truth and Semblance*) and in the fable-novel *In Nederland* (1984; *In the Dutch Mountains*); in both works, the lives of the narrators—who are authors—become interwoven with the lives of their characters. His poetry was largely concerned with the passage of time and with mortality; collections of verse include *Het zwarte gedicht* (1960; "The Black Poem"), *Aas: Gedichten* (1982; "Carrion: Poetry"), and *Rollende stenen* (1991; "Rolling Stones").

Nordal \'nôr-dȧl\, Sigurdur Jóhannesson (b. Sept. 14, 1886, Eyjólfsstadir, Vatnsdalur, Húnavatnssýsla, Ice.—d. Sept. 21, 1974, Reykjavík) Icelandic philologist, critic, and writer in many genres, who played a central role in the cultural life of 20th-century Iceland.

Nordal received his doctorate in Old Norse philology from the University of Copenhagen in 1914 and also studied in Berlin and at the University of Oxford. Upon his return to Iceland in 1918, he taught at the University of Iceland. From 1951 to 1957 he served as Iceland's ambassador to Denmark, and subsequently he taught at several universities in Europe and the United States.

He published fundamental studies of the Eddic poem *Vǫluspá* (1922–23) and many of the Icelanders' sagas. Nordal was instrumental in altering the critical approach to the sagas, showing by careful internal analysis that they are to be regarded more as literary works written by individual writers than as historically accurate products of an oral folk tradition.

He wrote many notable historical works—among them, a life of the medieval writer Snorri Sturluson (1920). He also published essays, novels, short stories, and poems. His collection of short stories *Fornar ástir* (1919; "Old Loves") played a significant role in the development of the modern Icelandic short story, and his Icelandic anthology, *Íslenzk lestrarbók 1400–1900* (1924), was also influential.

Nordenflycht \'nùrd-ən-‚flɛkt\, Hedvig Charlotta (b. Nov. 28, 1718, Stockholm, Swed.—d. June 29, 1763, Lugnet, near Stockholm)   Swedish poet considered to be Sweden's first feminist. Though influenced by Enlightenment ideas, she had a distinct pietistic and sentimental side; both the intellectual and the highly emotional strain are evident in her work.

The deaths of a fiancé in 1737 and of her husband in 1741 (seven months after their marriage) inspired her earliest poems, some of which were published in *Den sörjande turturduvan* (1743; "The Mourning Turtledove"). Nordenflycht became a leading literary figure, publishing four volumes of poetry in the next six years. During the 1750s she formed a literary society, Tankarbyggarorden ("Order of the Thought Builders"), with Gustaf Fredrik Gyllenborg and Finnish-born Gustav Philip Creutz. Their collaboration resulted in two anthologies; the first (in three volumes) was entitled *Våra försök* (1753, 1754, 1756; "Our Attempts"), the second (in two volumes) *Vitterhetsarbeten* (1759, 1762; "Literary Works").

In 1761 she fell in love with a much younger man, but her love was unrequited; Nordenflycht's poems of this period are tender and controlled and are considered to be her highest achievement. Her collected works were published in three volumes (1924–38).

Nordström \'nùrd-‚strœm\, Ludvig Anselm (b. Feb. 25, 1882, Härnösand, Swed.—d. April 15, 1942, Stockholm)   Swedish writer whose realistic, socially conscious works are set in the Norrland region in which he matured.

Nordström was much influenced by English writers, especially Charles Dickens, Thomas Carlyle, Laurence Sterne, H.G. Wells, and G.K. Chesterton. He most delighted his readers with such freshly observed, idiomatic, and lively short stories as those found in *Fiskare* (1907; "Fishermen"), *Borgare* (1909; "Burghers"), *Herrar* (1910; "Gentlemen"), and *Lumpsamlaren* (1910; "The Junk Collector"). His three-volume *Petter Svensks historia* (1923–27; "The Story of Peter Svensk") is the chief work in which he expounds his vision (which he called "totalism") of an anti-individualistic, industrial society in which group and communal values are stressed. In this and other long works of fiction, his sociopolitical views were often put forward at the expense of his art, and most of his long fiction is not memorable. Only two of Nordström's novels, *Landsortsbohème* (1911; "Small-town Bohemia") and *Planeten Markattan* (1937; "The Monkey Planet"), are considered to be of

value. He was able to achieve a certain measure of political influence, however, with two journalistic essays: *Bonde-nöden* (1933; "The Distress of the Peasantry") and *Lort-Sverige* (1938; "Dirt-Sweden"), dealing with the limits of common rural existence and with the filth of the supposedly "clean" Swedish countryside.

Norn \'nôrn\   In Germanic mythology, any of a group of supernatural beings who corresponded to the Greek Fates; they were usually spoken of in the plural and represented as three maidens who spun or wove the fate of mortals. Some sources call them Urd, Verdandi, and Skuld, names that most likely allude to the past (*urthr*, literally, "fate" or "destiny"), present (*verthandi*, literally, "becoming"), and future (*skuld*, literally, "debt"). They were depicted as living by Yggdrasil, the world tree, under Urd's well and were linked with both good and evil. Being frequently attendant at births, they were sometimes associated with midwifery. The name Norn appears only in Scandinavian sources, but the cult of Nornlike beings occurs in several European folklores. In Norse literature the Norns are sometimes called *dísir*.

Norris \'nôr-is, 'när-\, Frank, *in full* Benjamin Franklin Norris (b. March 5, 1870, Chicago, Ill., U.S.—d. Oct. 25, 1902, San Francisco, Calif.)   Novelist and short-story writer who was the first important American author to embrace naturalism.

Norris' first important novel, MCTEAGUE (1899), tells the story of a dentist who murders his miserly wife and then meets his own end while fleeing through Death Valley. Norris' masterpiece, THE OCTOPUS (1901), was the first novel of a projected trilogy, *The Epic of the Wheat*. *The Octopus* pictures the struggle of California wheat growers against a monopolistic railway corporation. The second novel in the trilogy, *The Pit* (1903), deals with wheat speculation on the Chicago Board of Trade. A third novel was unwritten at Norris' death. *Vandover and the Brute*, published posthumously in 1914, is a study of degeneration.

Despite their romanticizing tendencies, Norris' novels present a vividly authentic and highly readable picture of life in California at the turn of the century. His writings were collected in 10 volumes and published in 1928.

Norske folkeeventyr \'nôr-skə-‚fôl-kə-‚ä-ven-‚tœr\ ("Norwegian Folk Tales")   Group of folktales and legends collected by Peter Christen ASBJØRNSEN and Jørgen Engebretsen Moe, published in 1841. The collection was enlarged a number of times, and the final illustrated edition appeared in 1852. The authors, stimulated by a revival of interest in Norway's past, gathered the tales of ghosts, fairies, gods, and mountain trolls that had survived and developed from Old Norse pagan mythology in the mountain and fjord dialects of Norway. They compiled the tales into a brilliant narration that preserved their oral feeling and distinctively Norwegian characteristics even though rendered in standard Norwegian.

Asbjørnsen's vivid prose sketches of folk life and Moe's poems recaptured the folk heritage of Norway for the modern age. The *Norske folkeeventyr* stimulated further research into folktales and ballads and reawakened a sense of national identity.

North \'nôrth\, Roger (b. Sept. 3, 1653, Tostock, Suffolk, Eng.—d. March 1, 1734, Rougham, Suffolk)   English lawyer, historian, and biographer, known primarily for his biographies of three of his brothers and for his own autobiography.

North had a successful legal practice, but in 1696 he retired from official practice to pursue the life of a country gentleman. To vindicate an unfair portrayal of his brother Francis, he wrote *The Life of Francis North*; the preface to this work is the first extensive critical work on biography. He followed the work with biographies of Sir Dudley North and John North. Neither these biographies nor his autobiography was published until after his death.

North \'nȯrth \, Sir Thomas (b. May 28, 1535, London, Eng.—d. 1601?) English translator whose version of Plutarch's *Parallel Lives* was the source for many of William Shakespeare's plays.

In 1557 North was entered at Lincoln's Inn, London, where he joined a group of young lawyers interested in translating. The same year he translated, under the title *The Diall of Princes*, a French version of Antonio de Guevara's purported Spanish translation of the *Meditations* of Marcus Aurelius. Although North retained Guevara's mannered style, he was also capable of quite a different kind of work. His translation of Oriental beast fables from the Italian, *The Morall Philosophie of Doni* (1570), for example, was a rapid and colloquial narrative. His *The Lives of the Noble Grecians and Romanes*, translated in 1579 from Jacques Amyot's French version of Plutarch's *Parallel Lives*, has been described as one of the earliest great masterpieces of English prose. Shakespeare borrowed from North's *Lives* for several plays, and, in fact, he put some of North's prose directly into blank verse, with only minor changes.

North American Review, The American magazine first published in 1815 that became one of the country's leading literary journals of the 19th and 20th centuries. Founded in Boston as *The North American Review and Miscellaneous Journal* (a title it kept until mid-1821), the magazine followed the model of established English and Scottish literary journals. The work of J.W. von Goethe and Friedrich von Schiller first became known to American readers in its pages. It later moved to New York City and became a national periodical, providing an impartial forum in which current public affairs could be discussed. Noted for its outstanding writing on social and political issues, the magazine featured the work of numerous distinguished authors, including Henry George, David Dudley Field, Wendell Phillips, Walt Whitman, William Gladstone, Oliver Wendell Holmes, and H.G. Wells. In 1935 the magazine was sold to Joseph Hilton Smyth, under whose ignominious editorship it ceased publication in 1940. It was resurrected in 1964.

North and South Novel by Elizabeth Cleghorn GASKELL, published anonymously in serial form in *Household Words* from 1854 to 1855 and in book form in 1855. Written at the request of Charles Dickens, this story of the contrast between the values of rural southern England and the industrial north has a psychological complexity that anticipates George Eliot's novels of provincial life.

North & South (*in full* Poems: North & South: A Cold Spring) Collection of poetry by Elizabeth BISHOP, published in 1955. The book, which was awarded a Pulitzer Prize in 1956, was a revision of an earlier collection, *North & South* (1946), to which 17 poems were added. The spare, closely observed verses are marked by a firm grounding in reality, each being set in a recognizable geographic location, such as Nova Scotia, a farm in Maryland, Florida, Paris, and Brazil.

Northanger Abbey \nȯr-'thaŋ-gər, 'nȯr-thaŋ-gər\ Novel by Jane AUSTEN, published posthumously in 1817. *Northanger Abbey*, which was published with *Persuasion* in four volumes, was written about 1798 or 1799, probably under the title "Susan." In 1803 the manuscript of "Susan" was sold to the publisher Richard Crosby, who advertised for it, but unaccountably it was not published at that time.

The novel combines a satire on conventional novels of polite society with one on gothic tales of terror. Catherine Morland, the daughter of a country parson, is the innocent abroad who gains worldly wisdom: first in the fashionable society of Bath and then at Northanger Abbey itself, where she learns not to interpret the world through her reading of gothic thrillers.

Northeastern school Portuguese Colégio Nordestino. Group of 20th-century Brazilian regional writers whose fiction dealt primarily with the culture and social problems of Brazil's hinterland northeast. Stimulated by the revival of modernist-inspired nationalism of the 1920s, the regionalists examined the diverse ethnic and racial cultures of Brazil.

The writers of the Northeastern school included Gilberto Freyre, leader of the movement and author of the monumental *Casa-grande e senzala* (1933; *The Masters and the Slaves*); José Lins do Rego, who depicted the clash of the old and new ways of life in his Sugar Cane cycle of novels (1932–36); and Jorge Amado, who gave Brazil some of its best proletarian literature in such novels as *Cacau* (1933; "Cocoa Bean"), *Jubiabá* (1935), and *Terras do sem fim* (1942; *The Violent Land*). Also associated with the school were Graciliano Ramos and Rachel de Queiroz.

Norton \'nȯrt-ən\, Andre, *original name* Alice Mary Norton (b. Feb. 17, 1912, Cleveland, Ohio, U.S.) Prolific best-selling author of science-fiction and fantasy adventure novels for both juveniles and adults.

Norton spent 18 years as a children's librarian in the Cleveland Public Library, a job that enabled her to become familiar with children's literature. She legally changed her name to Andre Norton in 1934, when her historical fantasy *The Prince Commands* was published; it was the first of nine novels that she published during her librarian years. While working for the science-fiction publisher Gnome Press in the 1950s she wrote her first novel in the genre, *Star Man's Son, 2250 A.D.* (1952).

Norton's fast-moving science fiction and fantasy tales usually feature adolescents undergoing rites of passage—tests of physical, emotional, and moral strength. Her future Earth, distant planets, and fantasy lands are detailed, colorful, and extrapolated from her wide readings in history, biology, travel, archaeology, anthropology, mythology, folklore, and magic. Among her more than 100 books, the most noted include a series of 24 works, beginning with *Witch World* (1963), that are set on a matriarchal planet.

Norton \'nȯrt-ən\, Caroline (Elizabeth Sarah), *original surname* Sheridan \'sher-id-ən\ (b. March 22, 1808, London, Eng.—d. June 15, 1877, London) English poet and novelist whose efforts to secure legal protection for married women made her a notorious figure in mid-Victorian society.

One of three granddaughters of the playwright Richard Brinsley Sheridan, she began to write while in her teens. In 1827 she made an unfortunate marriage to the Honorable George Norton, whom she left after three years. In retaliation, Norton brought action against Lord Melbourne for seducing his wife. When he lost the case, Norton then refused his wife access to their children, and her outcries against this injustice were instrumental in introducing the Infant Custody Bill, which was finally enacted in 1839. In 1855 she was again involved in a lawsuit because her husband not only refused to pay her allowance but also demanded the proceeds of her books. Her eloquent letter of protest to Queen Victoria had great influence on the Marriage and Divorce Act of 1857, abolishing some of the inequities to which married women were subject.

Among her contemporaries, Norton held a high literary reputation. *The Dream, and Other Poems* appeared in 1840 to critical enthusiasm, and *Aunt Carry's Ballads* (1847) was written with tenderness and grace. Her novels—*Stuart of Dunleath* (1851), *Lost and Saved* (1863), and *Old Sir Douglas* (1867)—were based on her own unhappy experiences.

Norton \\'nȯrt-ən\\, Charles Eliot (b. Nov. 16, 1827, Cambridge, Mass., U.S.—d. Oct. 21, 1908, Cambridge) American scholar and man of letters, an idealist and reformer.

Norton opened a night school in Cambridge, was director of a housing experiment in Boston, worked zealously as an editor for the Union cause, and was coeditor (1864–68) of *The North American Review* and one of the founders of *The Nation* (1865). A friend of many literary figures, including Thomas Carlyle, Ralph Waldo Emerson, John Ruskin, Henry Wadsworth Longfellow, and James Russell Lowell, he contributed valuable editions of their letters and other biographical material. Norton also wrote on art and edited collections of poetry, notably the poetry of John Donne (1895–1905). Norton's best literary work probably was his prose translation of Dante's *The Divine Comedy* (1891–92). His letters were published in 1913.

Norton \\'nȯrt-ən\\, Mary, *original surname* Pearson \\'pir-sən\\ (b. Dec 10, 1903, London, Eng.—d. Aug 29, 1992, Hartland, Devonshire) Children's writer most famous for her series on the Borrowers.

Two of Norton's earliest books, *The Magic Bed-knob; or How to Become a Witch in Ten Easy Lessons* (1943) and its sequel, *Bonfires and Broomsticks* (1947), were revised and combined in *Bedknob and Broomstick* (1957). Her most renowned book, THE BORROWERS (1952), featuring the tiny Clock family, quickly became a children's classic. The complete miniature universe that Norton created earned her comparison to such imaginative writers as J.R.R. Tolkien, C.S. Lewis, and Lewis Carroll. Four sequels, *The Borrowers Afield* (1955), *The Borrowers Afloat* (1959), *The Borrowers Aloft* (1961), and *The Borrowers Avenged* (1982), tell of the Clock family's continuing struggles to survive. Constantly in peril, they live by sheer courage and ingenuity.

Norwid \\'nȯr-vēt\\, Cyprian Kamil (b. Sept. 24, 1821, Laskowo-Głuchy, near Warsaw, Poland, Russian Empire—d. May 23, 1883, Paris, Fr.) Polish poet, the most original and innovative of the 19th century.

Norwid lived in exile after the suppression of the Polish insurrection against Russia of 1830–31. From 1842 he lived for a time in Italy, where he studied painting and sculpture. In 1849 he went to Paris and in 1852 to the United States, but in 1854 he returned via England to Paris, where he led a life of penury and obscurity until his death.

His literary failure in his own day resulted from an experimental and difficult style. He wrote poems (*Poezje*, 1863; *Poems*), plays (*Krakus*, 1863; *Wanda*, 1901; *Kleopatra*, 1904), and a treatise on aesthetics, in prose and verse, included in *Poezje*. His poetry is essentially philosophical. Norwid's work was restored to posterity by Zenon Przesmycki, who began publishing his works in 1901. An authentic text of his most important lyrical collection, *Vade-mecum*, was published in 1947.

Nostromo \\näs-'trō-mō\\ (*in full* Nostromo: A Tale of the Seaboard) Novel by Joseph CONRAD, published in 1904. Considered one of Conrad's strongest works, *Nostromo* is a study of revolution, politics, and financial manipulation in a fictional South American republic. The work anticipates many of the political crises of Third World countries in the 20th century.

Notebook of Malte Laurids Brigge, The \\'mäl-tə-'laủ-rits-'brig-ə\\ Nonlinear novel in journal form by Rainer Maria RILKE, published in 1910 in German as *Die Aufzeichnungen des Malte Laurids Brigge*.

The book, which is composed of 71 diary-like entries, contains descriptive, reminiscent, and meditative parts. Brigge, its supposed author, is a 28-year-old poet from a noble Danish family who lives in poverty in Paris. In the first part Brigge records his experiences in Paris and his impressions of the city's horrors: its outcasts and beggars, its disfigured and emotionally wounded, and, above all, the many guises of death he finds there. The second part, beginning with entry 40, relates episodes from Brigge's childhood and youth in Denmark.

Notes from the Underground Short story by Fyodor DOSTOYEVSKY, first published in Russian as *Zapiski iz podpolya* in 1864. The work, which includes extremely misanthropic passages, contains the seeds of nearly all of the moral, religious, political, and social concerns that appear in Dostoyevsky's great novels.

Written as a reaction against Nikolay Chernyshevsky's ideological novel *What Is to Be Done?* (1863), which offered a planned utopia based on "natural" laws of self-interest, *Notes from the Underground* attacks the scientism and rationalism at the heart of Chernyshevsky's novel. The views and actions of Dostoyevsky's underground man demonstrate that in asserting free will humans often act against self-interest. The underground man is profoundly alienated from life, entombed in his room. The hero's views are outlined in Part I, and Part II describes the underground man's conflicts. When he turns to reason for salvation, it fails him, and he concludes that not reason but caprice ultimately prevails in human nature.

Notes Towards the Definition of Culture Critical treatise by T.S. ELIOT, originally appearing as a series of articles in *New England Weekly* in 1943, and published in book form in 1948. In the *Notes*, Eliot presents culture as an organic, shared system of beliefs that cannot be planned or artificially induced. Its chief means of transmission, he holds, is the family. The book has been viewed as a critique of postwar Europe and a defense of conservatism and Christianity.

Nouayme *see* NA'IMAH.

nouveau roman \\nṻ-vō-rō-'mäⁿ\\ ("new novel") In French literature, a form of antinovel developed in the mid-1950s in the work of Alain Robbe-Grillet, Claude Simon, Nathalie Sarraute, Michel Butor, and Marguerite Duras. What was new about these novelists was their systematic rejection of the traditional framework of fiction—chronology, plot, character—and of the omniscient author. In place of these reassuring conventions, they offer texts that demand more of the reader, who is presented with compressed, repetitive, or only partially explained events from which to derive a meaning that will not, in any case, be definitive. In Robbe-Grillet's *La Jalousie* (1957; *Jealousy*), for example, the narrator's suspicions of his wife's infidelity are never confirmed or denied, but their obsessive quality is conveyed by the replacement of a chronological narrative with the insistent repetition of details or events. In *Le Libéra* (1968) by Robert Pinget there is no single narrator, while in the later novels of Jean Cayrol the narrative emanates from the sea, a field, or the desert.

The *nouveau roman* was open to influence from works being written abroad (notably the work of William Faulkner) and from the cinema (Robbe-Grillet and Duras contributed to the *nouvelle vague*, or New Wave, style of filmmaking). By the time Robbe-Grillet's *Pour un nouveau roman* (*Toward a New Novel*) appeared in 1963, it was clear that the term covered a variety of approaches. *See also* ANTINOVEL.

Nouvelle Revue française, La \\lä-nṻ-,vel-rä-,vṻē-fräⁿ-'sez\\ ("The New French Review"), *abbreviated* NRF. Leading French review of literature and the other arts. It was founded in February 1909 (after a false start in November 1908) by a group that included André Gide, Jacques Copeau, and Jean Schlumberger. The *NRF*'s founders wished to publish criticism that emphasized aesthetic issues and to remain independent of any political party or intellectual school. During the period between the two world wars, under the editors Jacques Rivière (1919–25) and Jean Paulhan (1925–40), the *NRF* became France's leading literary journal, publishing works by many notable writers. After the German occupation of France in 1940, Pierre Drieu la Rochelle became editor, and the *NRF* became profascist; it ceased publication in 1943. The review was revived in 1953 as *La Nouvelle Nouvelle Revue française*, under the direction of Paulhan and Michel Arland; it resumed its present name in 1959. The publishing house Editions Gallimard was established in 1911 as an offshoot of the *NRF*.

Novalis \nō-'väl-is\, *pseudonym of* Friedrich Leopold, Baron (Freiherr) von Hardenberg \fȯn-'här-dən-,berk\ (b. May 2, 1772, Oberwiederstedt, Prussian Saxony [Germany]—d. March 25, 1801, Weissenfels, Saxony) Early German Romantic poet and theorist who greatly influenced later Romantic thought.

Novalis, who was born into a family of Protestant Lower Saxon nobility, took his pseudonym from "de Novali," a name his family had formerly used. He studied law at the University of Jena, where he met Friedrich von Schiller, and then at Leipzig, where he formed a friendship with Friedrich von Schlegel. He completed his studies at Wittenberg in 1793.

Detail of an engraving by Edouard Eichens, 1845
Staatliche Museen, Berlin

In 1794–95 Novalis fell in love with and became engaged to the 14-year-old Sophie von Kühn. She died in 1797, however, and Novalis expressed his grief in the beautiful *Hymnen an die Nacht* (1800; *Hymns to the Night*). In these six prose poems interspersed with verse, Novalis celebrates night, or death, as an entry into a higher life in the presence of God and anticipates a mystical and loving union with Sophie and with the universe as a whole after his own death. In 1797 he went to the Academy of Freiberg to study mining. In 1798 Novalis again became engaged, and in 1799 he became a mine inspector, but he died of tuberculosis before he could marry.

Novalis' last years were astonishingly creative, filled with encyclopedic studies, the draft of a philosophical system based on idealism, and his most significant poetic work. Two collections of fragments that appeared during his lifetime, *Blütenstaub* (1798; "Pollen") and *Glauben und Liebe* (1798; "Faith and Love"), indicate his attempt to unite poetry, philosophy, and science in an allegorical interpretation of the world. His celebrated mythical romance *Heinrich von Ofterdingen* (1802; *Henry of Ofterdingen*), set in an idealized vision of the European Middle Ages, describes the mystical and romantic searchings of a young poet. The central image of his visions, a blue flower, became a widely recognized symbol of longing among Novalis' fellow Romantics.

novel \'näv-əl\ [Italian *novella* novella] A fictional prose narrative of considerable length and a certain complexity that deals imaginatively with human experience through a connected sequence of events involving a group of persons in a specific setting. The term also refers to the literary type constituted by such narratives. Within its broad framework, the genre of the novel has encompassed an extensive range of types and styles, including picaresque, epistolary, gothic, romantic, realist, and historical.

Although forerunners of the modern genre are to be found in a number of places, including classical Rome, 10th- and 11th-century Japan, and Elizabethan England, the European novel is usually said to have begun with the *Don Quixote* of Miguel de Cervantes (part I, 1605). In its juxtaposition of impossible idealism and earthy practicality in the figures of the knight and his squire, this work suggests what was to become one of the central concerns of the Western novel.

Although some interesting works were produced in 17th-century France, it was in England that the genre first took permanent root. Daniel Defoe, Samuel Richardson, and Henry Fielding were all writing works in the first half of the 18th century that did much to establish the novel in England. Their popularity soon became a general phenomenon, leading in the 19th century to an extraordinary surge of fiction writing.

In essence the Western novel has remained popular because it can provide a more faithful image of everyday reality than can be achieved by any other literary form. Even the extravagant fantasies of the gothic novel or the modern science-fiction novel depend for their impact on the detailed rendering of surface reality. The history of the novel is in part a history of the changes in conventions established to achieve this verisimilitude. Perhaps because of the novel's realistic bias, its greatest period is usually held to be the mid- to late 19th century, a time when improved literacy rates had increased the size of the potential audience and the modern mass media had not yet arrived to diminish it. During this period and just before, Charles Dickens, William Makepeace Thackeray, and George Eliot were writing in England; Honoré de Balzac, Gustave Flaubert, and Émile Zola in France; Ivan Turgenev, Leo Tolstoy, and Fyodor Dostoyevsky in Russia; and Nathaniel Hawthorne and Herman Melville in the United States.

With the coming of the 20th century the novel began to change somewhat in character. The old certainty that experience could be adequately represented by the language and structures of the conventional novel was increasingly called into question. Writers such as James Joyce, Virginia Woolf, and Dorothy Richardson began to examine the ways in which reality eluded the grasp of literature. In trying to capture the complex and fragmentary quality of experience, some of these writers stretched the limits of the conventional novel to a point at which it became more and more remote from the expectations—and sometimes the comprehension or interest—of the average reader, a process that perhaps culminated in the mid-20th century in the so-called antinovel, or *nouveau roman*. These modernist experiments sometimes produced works of outstanding interest, but they also tended to widen the gap between the popular and the "literary" novel.

See also ANTINOVEL; BILDUNGSROMAN; EPISTOLARY NOVEL; GOTHIC NOVEL; HISTORICAL NOVEL; NOVEL OF MANNERS; NOUVEAU ROMAN; PICARESQUE NOVEL; PROLETARIAN NOVEL; PSYCHOLOGICAL NOVEL; ROMAN À CLEF; SENTIMENTAL NOVEL.

novelese \,näv-ə-'lēz, -'lēs\ A writing style characteristic of bad novels; especially, a style marked by the use of trite expressions.

novelette \,näv-ə-'let\ 1. A work of fiction intermediate in length or complexity between a short story and a novel. 2. *British* A light, usually sentimental, romantic novel.

novelization \,näv-ə-lə-'zā-shən, -,lī-\ The act or process of turning a story into the form of a novel, especially when the story was originally in another form such as a play.

novella \nō-'vel-ə\ *plural* novellas *or* novelle \-'vel-ā, -ē\ [Italian, from feminine of *novello* new] **1.** *plural* novelle. A story with a compact and pointed plot, often realistic and satiric in tone. Originating in Italy during the European Middle Ages, the novella was based on local events, humorous, political, or amorous in nature; the individual tales often were gathered into collections along with anecdotes, legends, and romantic tales. Writers such as Giovanni Boccaccio, Franco Sacchetti, and Matteo Bandello later developed the novella into a psychologically subtle and highly structured short tale, often using a frame story to unify the tales around a common theme.

The novella is an enlarged anecdote like those found in Boccaccio's *Decameron*, the 14th-century Italian classic. During the Elizabethan period, William Shakespeare and other playwrights extracted dramatic plots from the Italian novella. The realistic content and form of these tales influenced the development of the English novel in the 18th century and the short story in the 19th century.

2. *plural usually* novellas. A work of fiction intermediate in length and complexity between a short story and a novel. Leo Tolstoy's *Smert Ivana Ilicha* (*The Death of Ivan Ilich*), Fyodor Dostoyevsky's *Zapiski iz podpolya* (*Notes from the Underground*), Joseph Conrad's *Heart of Darkness*, and Henry James's "The Aspern Papers" are examples of novellas.

Novelle \nō-'vel-ə\ *plural* Novellen \-ən\ [German, from Italian *novella* novella] Genre of German short narrative that flourished in the 18th, 19th, and early 20th centuries in the works of writers such as Heinrich von Kleist, Gerhart Hauptmann, J.W. von Goethe, Thomas Mann, and Franz Kafka. *Novellen* are often encompassed within a frame story based on a striking news item (plague, war, or flood), either real or imaginary. The individual tales are related by various reporter-narrators as a diversion from the present misfortune. Characterized by brevity, self-contained plots that end on a note of irony, a literate and facile style, restraint of emotion, and objective rather than subjective presentation, these tales were a major stimulant to the development of the modern short story in Germany. The *Novelle* also survived as a unique form, although unity of mood and style often replaced the traditional unity of action.

novel of manners Work of fiction that re-creates a social world, conveying with finely detailed observation the customs, values, and mores of a highly developed and complex society. The conventions of the society—codified behavior, acceptable forms of speech, and so on—dominate the story, and characters are differentiated by the degree to which they measure up to or fall below the uniform standard, or ideal, of behavior. The range of a novel of manners may be limited, as in the works of Jane Austen, which deal with the domestic affairs of English country gentry families of the early 19th century and ignore elemental human passions and larger social and political determinations, or sweeping, as in the novels of Honoré de Balzac, which mirror the 19th century in all its complexity in stories dealing with Parisian life, provincial life, private life, public life, and military life. Notable writers of the novel of manners from the end of the 19th century into the 20th include Henry James, Evelyn Waugh, Edith Wharton, H.H. Munro ("Saki"), and John Marquand.

Novikov \nə-vᵛi-'kôf\, Nikolay Ivanovich (b. April 27 [May 8, New Style], 1744, Bronnitsy, near Moscow, Russia—d. July 31 [Aug. 12], 1818, Bronnitsky) Russian writer, philanthropist, and Freemason (member of a secret fraternal order) whose activities were intended to raise the educational and cultural level of the Russian people and included the production of social satires as well as the founding of schools and libraries. Influenced by Freemasonry, Novikov converted his journals

and his ambitious publishing enterprise into vehicles of free-thinking and even criticized Empress Catherine II the Great. As a result, she suspended publication of his journals and had him arrested in 1792. He was released by Emperor Paul in 1796 but was forbidden to resume his journalistic activities.

Novy Mir \'nô-vē-'mʸēr\ ("New World") Literary journal, a highly influential monthly published in Moscow. Founded in 1925, it was an official organ of the writers' union of the U.S.S.R. until the breakup of the Soviet Union. Its pages carried the work of many of the Soviet Union's leading writers, and censorship of the magazine in the 1970s and '80s contributed to the development of a large underground press in the Soviet Union. It continues to publish new fiction and essays. *See also* SAMIZDAT.

Noyes \'nôiz\, Alfred (b. Sept. 16, 1880, Wolverhampton, Staffordshire, Eng.—d. June 28, 1958, Isle of Wight) English poet, a traditionalist remembered chiefly for his lyrical verse.

Noyes's first volume of poems, *The Loom of Years* (1902), published while he was still at Oxford University, was followed by others that showed patriotic fervor and a love for the sea. He taught modern English literature at Princeton (1914–23). Of Noyes's later works, the most notable is the epic trilogy *The Torch-Bearers* (1922–30), which took as its theme the progress of science through the ages. His autobiography, *Two Worlds for Memory*, appeared in 1953.

N-Town plays \'en-,taùn\ An English cycle of 42 scriptural plays, or mystery plays, dating from the second half of the 15th century and so called because an opening proclamation refers to performance "in N. town." Since evidence suggests that the cycle was not peculiar to one city or community but traveled from town to town, the abbreviation "N." would indicate that the appropriate name of the town at which the cycle was being presented would have been inserted by the speaker.

The cycle is preserved in the Hegge Manuscript, named for its 17th-century owner, Sir Robert Hegge, and it is therefore sometimes referred to as the Hegge cycle. On the flyleaf of the Hegge Manuscript is written "Ludus Conventriae" ("Play of Coventry") and for nearly two centuries it was believed that the plays represented the Coventry cycle, but that supposition has since proved false.

The cycle begins with the creation of the angels and the Fall of Lucifer and ends with the Assumption of the Virgin and the Last Judgment. Among the plays with no equivalent in other cycles are one on the death of Cain and five whose central figure is that of the Virgin, with whom the cycle is generally much preoccupied. Typically, the N-Town plays are grave and dignified; the comic relief distinguishing other surviving cycles (from Chester, York, Wakefield) is markedly absent. A basic difference between the N-Town plays and those of the other cycles is that this cycle, because it was a traveling one, was apparently presented by professional actors. It did not use pageant wagons but was given in a single open space, with "mansions" (indicating general scenes) set up about a single acting area. *See also* MYSTERY PLAY.

Nugent \'nū-jənt\, Richard (Bruce), *pseudonyms* Bruce Nugent, Richard Bruce \'brüs\ (b. July 2, 1906, Washington, D.C., U.S.) African-American writer, artist, and actor associated with the Harlem Renaissance in New York City.

Nugent's introduction to Langston Hughes in 1925 signaled the beginning of his lifelong fascination with the arts and his contribution to the literary and political movements of the Harlem Renaissance. He explored issues of sexuality and black identity in his poems, short stories, and erotic drawings. "Shadows," Nugent's first published poem, was anthologized in Countee Cullen's 1927 work *Caroling Dusk: An Anthology of*

Verse by Negro Poets. A one-act musical, "Sadhji: An African Ballet" (based on his earlier short story of the same name), was published in *Plays of Negro Life: A Source-book of Native American Drama* (1927) and produced in 1932. This African morality tale tells of the beautiful Sadhji, a chieftain's wife, beloved by Mrabo, her stepson, who, in turn, is loved by his male friend Numbo. In 1926 Nugent contributed two brush-and-ink drawings and the short story "Smoke, Lilies, and Jade" (published under the name Richard Bruce) to the only issue of *Fire!!* Controversial in its time, the story depicts a 19-year-old artist's sexual encounter with another man.

number \\'nəm-bər\\   **1.** In poetry, metrical structure, or meter.   **2.** A particular musical, theatrical, or literary selection or production.   **3.** A particular issue of a periodical.   **4.** Verses or poetry in general, as in Alexander Pope's statement that he "lisp'd in numbers" to indicate that he began writing poetry at an early age. The term has become almost obsolete, but it was used fairly often in older poetry, for example, in the following lines from Edmund Spenser's "The Ruines of Time":

> For deeds do die, however nobly done,
> And thoughts of men do as themselves decay,
> But wise words taught in numbers for to run,
> Recorded by the Muses, live for ay.

Núñez de Arce \\'nün-yäth-<u>th</u>ā-'är-thā\\, Gaspar (b. Aug. 4, 1832, Valladolid, Spain—d. June 9, 1903, Madrid)   Spanish poet and statesman, once regarded as the great poet of doubt and disillusionment, though his rhetoric is no longer found moving.

Núñez de Arce became a journalist and Liberal deputy, took part in the 1868 revolution, and was colonial minister for a time after the restoration of the monarchy. As a dramatist he had some success, his best play being the historical *El haz de leña* (1872; "The Bundle of Kindling"), on the imprisonment in 1568 of Don Carlos (prince of Asturias [Spain]), but he attained celebrity with *Gritos del combate* (1875; "Cries of Combat")— a volume of verse that tried to give poetic utterance to religious doubts and political issues.

Nun's Priest's Tale, The   One of the 24 stories in THE CANTERBURY TALES by Geoffrey Chaucer.

The protagonist of this mock-heroic story is Chanticleer, a rooster with seven wives, foremost among them the hen Pertelote. Pertelote dismisses Chanticleer's dream of being attacked and tells him to go about his business. A fox soon approaches and flatters him, recalling the exquisite song of Chanticleer's father. The vain rooster is thus tricked into closing his eyes and crowing, only to be seized by the fox and carried off. As Chanticleer's owners and the animals of the barnyard run after them, Chanticleer suggests that his captor yell to tell them to turn back. When the fox opens his mouth, the rooster escapes. The tale ends with a warning against flattery.

The story is based on the medieval tale of Reynard the Fox, common to French, Flemish, and German literature.

nursery rhyme   Verse customarily told or sung to small children. The oral tradition of nursery rhymes is ancient, but new verses have steadily entered the stream. A French poem numbering the days of the month, similar to "Thirty days hath September," was recorded in the 13th century, but such latecomers as "Twinkle, Twinkle, Little Star" (1806) by Ann and Jane Taylor and "Mary Had a Little Lamb" (1830) by Sarah Josepha Hale seem to be just as firmly established in the repertoire. The largest number of nursery rhymes date from the 16th, 17th, and, most frequently, the 18th centuries.

Some of the oldest rhymes are probably those accompanying babies' games, such as "Handy, dandy, prickly, pandy, which hand will you have?" (recorded 1598) and its German equiva-

lent, "Windle, wandle, in welchem Handle, oben oder unt?" Apparently, most were originally composed for adult entertainment. Many were popular ballads and songs. Some were inspired by personalities of the time, and occasionally these can be identified.

The earliest known published collection of nursery rhymes was *Tommy Thumb's (Pretty) Song Book*, 2 vols. (London, 1744). It included "Little Tom Tucker," "Sing a Song of Sixpence," and "Who Killed Cock Robin?" The most influential collection was *Mother Goose's Melody; or, Sonnets for the Cradle*, published by the firm of John Newbery in 1781. Among its 51 rhymes were "Jack and Jill," "Ding Dong Bell," and "Hush-a-bye baby on the tree top." An edition was reprinted in the United States in 1785 by Isaiah Thomas. Its popularity is attested by the fact that these verses are still commonly called "Mother Goose rhymes" in the United States. *See also* ALPHABET RHYME; MOTHER GOOSE.

Nwapa \\'nwä-pä\\, Flora (b. Jan. 13, 1931, Oguta, Nigeria)   Nigerian novelist best known for re-creating Igbo (Ibo) life and customs from a woman's viewpoint.

Nwapa attended University College in Ibadan, Nigeria, and the University of Edinburgh. She worked as a teacher and administrator in Nigeria from 1959 until the Biafran civil war erupted in 1967. After the war she was commissioner for health and social welfare in East Central State before she formed Tana Press/Flora Nwapa Company to publish African books.

Efuru (1966), her first novel, is based on an old folktale of a woman chosen by the gods. *Idu* (1970) centers on a woman whose life is bound up with that of her husband to such an extent that when he dies she seeks him out in the land of the dead. In *This Is Lagos, and Other Stories* (1971) and the later novels *One Is Enough* (1981) and *Women Are Different* (1986), Nwapa continues her compassionate portrayal of women in modern Nigerian society. The novel *Never Again* (1975) and *Wives at War, and Other Stories* (1980) deal with the Biafran conflict. Her sole volume of poetry is *Cassava Song and Rice Song* (1986).

Nye \\'nī\\, Bill, *pseudonym of* Edgar Wilson Nye (b. Aug. 25, 1850, Shirley, Maine, U.S.—d. Feb. 22, 1896, Arden, N.C.)   Journalist and one of the major American humorists in the last half of the 19th century.

Settling in Laramie, Wyo., in 1876, Nye contributed to the *Denver Tribune* and *Cheyenne Sun*. His humorous squibs and tales in the *Laramie Boomerang*, which he helped found in 1881, were widely read and reprinted. Collected, they form the substance of numerous published volumes, from *Bill Nye and Boomerang* (1881) to *Bill Nye's History of the U.S.* (1894). Nye later returned to Wisconsin, where he had grown up, and for several years wrote for the *New York World*. In 1886 he lectured with the poet James Whitcomb Riley, the combination of Nye's wit and Riley's sentiment proving extremely popular.

nymph \\'nimf\\ *plural* nymphs [Greek *nýmphē* bride, girl of marriageable age, nymph]   In Greek mythology, any one of the minor divinities of nature that are represented as beautiful maidens dwelling in the mountains, forests, meadows, and waters. The nymphs were not immortal but were extremely long-lived and were on the whole kindly disposed toward humans. They were distinguished according to the sphere of nature with which they were connected. The Oceanids, for example, were ocean nymphs; the Nereids inhabited both saltwater and freshwater; the Naiads presided over springs, rivers, fountains, and lakes. The Oreads were nymphs of mountains, hills, and grottoes; the Napaeae (from *napē*, "dell") and the Alseids (from *alsos*, "grove") were nymphs of glens and groves; the dryads and hamadryads presided over woods, forests, and trees.

Italy had native divinities of springs and streams and water goddesses (called Lymphae) with whom the Greek nymphs tended to become identified.

Nynorsk \\'nœ-,nȯshk, *Angl* nū-'nȯrsk, nyü- \\, *also called* New Norse *or* Landsmål \\'läns-,mȯl \\ A literary form of Norwegian based on the spoken dialects of Norway. It dates from a grammar and dictionary produced by Ivar Aasen about 1850 and was designed as a national language distinct from that of Denmark. *Nynorsk* literally means "new Norwegian" and *Landsmål* means "country language." *Compare* BOKMÅL.

Nyugat \\'nyü-gȯt \\ ("The West") Hungarian literary periodical founded in 1908 to provide a forum for serious young writers. The magazine, which published its last issue in 1941, also helped to modernize Hungarian literature by exposing its readers to European literature and culture. Endre Ady was the spiritual leader of the group of writers associated with *Nyugat.* Other members of the *Nyugat* school included the poets Mihály Babits, Dezső Kosztolányi, Árpád Tóth, and Gyula Juhász; the novelist Zsigmond Móricz; Frigyes Karinthy, who wrote effective short stories with a strong satirical and grotesque element; and Margit Kaffka, the first major woman writer in Hungary.

Nyx \\'niks \\ In Greek mythology, female personification of night but also a great cosmogonical figure, feared even by Zeus.

According to one tradition, Nyx was the daughter of Chaos and the mother of numerous primordial powers, including Sleep (Hypnos) and Death (Thanatos). Throughout antiquity she caught the imagination of poets and artists but was seldom worshiped.

Nzekwu \\n-'zä-kwü \\, Onuora (b. Feb. 19, 1928, Kafanchan, Nigeria) Nigerian teacher, writer, and editor who explored the internal conflicts inherent in the relationship of the educated Igbo (Ibo) to traditional Igbo culture.

Nzekwu became editor of *Nigeria Magazine* in 1962. Foundation grants he received from the Rockefeller Foundation and UNESCO enabled him to travel in Europe and America.

Nzekwu's first novel, *Wand of Noble Wood* (1961), portrays in moving terms the futility of a Western pragmatic approach to the problems created by an African's traditional religious beliefs. In the hero of *Blade Among the Boys* (1962), traditional practices and beliefs ultimately take precedence over half-absorbed European and Christian values. Nzekwu also wrote a third novel, *Highlife for Lizards* (1965), and coauthored a children's book, *Eze Goes to School* (1963; with Michael Crowder).

Oak, Gabriel \\'gā-brē-əl-'ōk \\ Fictional character, a hardworking, honest young farmer in Thomas Hardy's novel FAR FROM THE MADDING CROWD. Oak is the first of several suitors for the beautiful but seemingly capricious Bathsheba Everdene. Though she rejects his love, he remains loyal to her, and, through the strength of his character, weathers several crises and is rewarded in the end by Bathsheba's hand in marriage.

Oates \\'ōts \\, Joyce Carol (b. June 16, 1938, Lockport, N.Y., U.S.) Prolific American prose writer noted for her depictions of violence and evil in modern society.

Oates studied at Syracuse University and the University of Wisconsin. Her first collection of short stories, *By the North Gate*, was published in 1963, and her first novel, *With Shuddering Fall*, in 1964. She wrote prolifically thereafter, averaging about two books (chiefly short stories and novels) per year. Her more important novels include *A Garden of Earthly Delights* (1967), THEM (1969; winner of a National Book Award), and *Do with Me What You Will* (1973). Also significant is a parodic gothic series that includes *Bellefleur* (1980), *A Bloodsmoor Romance* (1982), and *Mysteries of Winterthurn* (1984). Some of her books are written under the pseudonym Rosamond Smith. She also wrote plays, essays, and literary criticism. She taught at the University of Detroit from 1961 to 1967, at the University of Windsor, Ontario, Can., from 1967 to 1978, and thereafter at Princeton University.

Oates typically portrays people whose intensely experienced lives often end in bloodshed and self-destruction owing to larger forces beyond their control.

obeah \\'ō-bē-ə \\ or **obi** \\'ō-bē \\ [probably from Twi *ɔ-bayifó* magic man, sorcerer, reinforced by words of related sense in other African languages] A system of belief among blacks chiefly of the British West Indies, the Guianas, and the southeastern United States that is characterized by the use of sorcery and magic ritual. In certain cultures of the Caribbean the term denotes witchcraft, usually extremely evil. Potent or bewitched objects buried for the purpose of bringing misfortune upon a particular party are sometimes known as obeah, and use of the word itself has in some areas been prohibited by law.

Oberon \\'ō-bə-,rän, -rən \\, *French* Alberon \\ȧl-be-'rȯⁿ \\ *or* Auberon \\ō-be-'rȯⁿ \\ King of the elves, or of the "faerie," in the medieval French poem *Huon de Bordeaux*. In the poem Auberon is a dwarf-king, living in the woodland, who by magic powers helps the hero to accomplish a seemingly impossible task. In the legendary history of the Merovingian dynasty Oberon is a magician, the brother of the eponymous Merowech (Mérovée).

Lord Berners' prose translation of *Huon de Bordeaux* furnished the name Oberon and the fairy element for William Shakespeare's play *A Midsummer Night's Dream* (performed 1595–96), Ben Jonson's court masque *Oberon, the Faery Prince* (1611), and Christoph Martin Wieland's verse romance *Oberon* (1780).

objective correlative Literary theory first set forth by T.S. ELIOT in the essay "Hamlet and His Problems" and published in THE SACRED WOOD (1920). According to the theory,

> The only way of expressing emotion in the form of art is by finding an "objective correlative"; in other words, a set of objects, a situation, a chain of events which shall be the formula of that *particular* emotion; such that when the external facts, which must terminate in sensory experience, are given, the emotion is immediately evoked.

objectivism \\əb-'jek-tə-,viz-əm \\ The theory or practice of objective art or literature. The term was used by the poet

William Carlos Williams in the 1930s to describe a movement in which emphasis was placed on viewing poems as objects that could be considered and analyzed in terms of mechanical features. According to Williams this meant examining the structural aspects of the poem and considering how it was constructed. Other poets involved in the short-lived movement were Louis Zukofsky, George Oppen, and Charles Reznikoff.

oblique rhyme   *see* HALF RHYME.

Oblomov \ˌə-ˈblō-məf\   Novel by Russian writer Ivan GON-CHAROV, published in 1859. The work is a powerful critique of 19th-century Russia, contrasting aristocrats with the merchant class and condemning the feudal system. Its hero, Oblomov, is a generous but indecisive young nobleman who loses the woman he loves to a vigorous, pragmatic friend. A perpetual daydreamer, he lives his life in his mind and spends his time in bed. From this character derives the Russian term *oblomovshchina*, epitomizing the backwardness, inertia, and futility of 19th-century Russian society. *See also* SUPERFLUOUS MAN.

O'Brien \ō-ˈbrī-ən\, Edna (b. Dec. 15, 1932?, Twamgraney, County Clare, Ire.)   Irish writer whose work was noted for its sensuous, lyrical style, its evocative description, and its sexual candor. Some of her books were banned in Ireland.

O'Brien's popular first novel, *The Country Girls* (1960), was the first volume of THE COUNTRY GIRLS TRILOGY. The subsequent novels—*The Lonely Girl* (1962) and *Girls in Their Married Bliss* (1964)—traced the lives of two Irish women from adolescence to middle age. Her subsequent novels, which also examined restlessness and disillusionment with love, include *Casualties of Peace* (1966), *A Pagan Place* (1971), *Night* (1972), *Johnny I Hardly Knew You* (1977; U.S. title, *I Hardly Knew You*), *The High Road* (1988), and *Time and Tide* (1992).

Among O'Brien's several collections of short stories are *The Love Object* (1968), *A Scandalous Woman and Other Stories* (1974), *A Fanatic Heart* (1984), and *Lantern Slides* (1990). She also wrote plays, screenplays, and nonfiction about Ireland.

O'Brien \ō-ˈbrī-ən\, Fitz-James (b. *c.* 1828, County Limerick, Ire.—d. April 6, 1862, Cumberland, Md., U.S.)   Irish-American journalist, playwright, and author whose psychologically penetrating tales of pseudoscience and the uncanny made him one of the forerunners of modern science fiction.

O'Brien began to work in journalism in London. In 1852 he moved to New York City and soon became an important figure in that city's bohemia. But his work, though published in the leading periodicals of the day, won him neither the reputation he thought he merited nor the financial security he desired. He died from wounds received as a Union soldier during the first year of the American Civil War.

O'Brien's best-known stories include "The Diamond Lens," about a man who falls in love with a being he sees through a microscope in a drop of water; "What Was It?" in which a man is attacked by a thing he apprehends with every sense but sight; and "The Wondersmith," in which robots are fashioned only to turn upon their creators. These three stories appeared in periodicals in 1858 and 1859.

O'Brien \ō-ˈbrī-ən\, Flann, *also called* Brian Ó Nuallain \ō-ˈnō-lən\, *also known as* Myles na gCopaleen \nä-ˈgō-pə-ˌlēn\ (b. Oct. 5, 1911, Strabane, County Tyrone, Ire.—d. April 1, 1966, Dublin)   Irish novelist, dramatist, and, as Myles na gCopaleen, columnist for the *Irish Times* newspaper for 26 years. He is most celebrated for his unusual novel *At Swim-Two-Birds*, which, though it was first published in 1939, achieved fame only after its republication in 1960. *At Swim-Two-Birds* is a rich literary experiment that combines Irish folklore, heroic legend, humor, and poetry in a style replete with linguistic games.

O'Brien's novels *The Hard Life* (1961) and *The Dalkey Archive* (1964; adapted as a play, *When the Saints Go Cycling In*) are likewise amusing. Another novel, *The Third Policeman* (1967), is more somber in tone.

O'Brien \ō-ˈbrī-ən\, Tim, *in full* William Timothy O'Brien (b. Oct. 1, 1946, Austin, Minn., U.S.)   American novelist noted for his writings about American soldiers in the Vietnam War.

O'Brien fought in Vietnam, rising to the rank of sergeant. When he returned to the United States, he worked for the *Washington Post* (1971–74) as a reporter. He collected his newspaper and magazine articles about his war experiences in his first book, *If I Die in a Combat Zone, Box Me Up and Ship Me Home* (1973). By turns meditative and brutally realistic, it was praised for its honest portrayal of a soldier's emotions.

The Vietnam War is present in many of O'Brien's novels. One of the two protagonists in *Northern Lights* (1975) is a wounded war hero. A soldier abandons his platoon in Vietnam to try to walk to Paris in *Going after Cacciato* (1978). A man's lifelong fear of dying from a nuclear bombing is the subject of *The Nuclear Age* (1981), while *The Things They Carried* (1990) returns to the theme of Vietnam War experiences.

obscurantism \əb-ˈskyūr-ən-ˌtiz-əm, ˌäb-skyu̇-ˈran-\ *or* **obscuranticism** \ˌäb-skyu̇-ˈran-tə-ˌsiz-əm\ [French *obscurantisme*, a derivative of *obscurant* one practicing obscurantism, from Latin *obscurant-, obscurans*, present participle of *obscurare* to obscure]   A style (as in literature or art) characterized by deliberate vagueness or abstruseness. In literature this involves the use of difficult allusions, archaic and foreign words, and unfamiliar imagery.

Obstfelder \ˈōpst-ˌfel-dər\, Sigbjørn (b. Nov. 21, 1866, Stavanger, Nor.—d. July 29, 1900, Copenhagen, Den.)   Norwegian Symbolist poet whose unrhymed verse and atmospheric, unfocused imagery marked the first decisive break with naturalistic verse in Norway.

Obstfelder's works include *Digte* (1893; *Poems*), the play *De røde draaber* (1897; "The Red Drops"), several novellas, and the posthumously published fragment *En praests dagbog* (1900; "A Pastor's Diary"). His view is that of a solitary outsider who looks beyond the material world in a search for existential certainty and union with an external spiritual reality. Obstfelder was the model for the diarist hero in the German poet Rainer Maria Rilke's famous *Die Aufzeichnungen des Malte Laurids Brigge* (*The Notebook of Malte Laurids Brigge*).

O Captain! My Captain!   Three-stanza poem by Walt WHITMAN, published in *Sequel to Drum-Taps* in 1865. From 1867 the poem was included in the 1867 and subsequent editions of *Leaves of Grass*.

An elegy on the death of President Abraham Lincoln, "O Captain! My Captain" is noted for its regular form, meter, and rhyme, though it is also known for its sentimentality verging on the maudlin. The poem, which was highly popular, portrays Lincoln as the captain of a sea-worn ship—the Union triumphant after the American Civil War. While "The ship is anchor'd safe and sound, its voyage closed and done," the Captain lies on the deck, "Fallen cold and dead."

O'Casey \ō-ˈkā-sē\, Sean, *original name* John Casey (b. March 30, 1880, Dublin, Ire.—d. Sept. 18, 1964, Torquay, Devon, Eng.)   Irish playwright renowned for realistic dramas of the Dublin slums in war and revolution, in which tragedy and comedy are juxtaposed in a way new to the theater of his time.

O'Casey was born into a lower-middle-class Irish Protestant family. With only three years of formal schooling, he educated himself by reading. He became caught up in the cause of Irish nationalism, and he changed his name to its Irish form and learned Irish Gaelic. He later became active in the labor movement and wrote for the *Irish Worker*. He also joined the Irish Citizen Army, a paramilitary arm of the Irish labor unions, and drew up its constitution in 1914. At this time he became disillusioned with the Irish nationalist movement because its leaders put nationalist ideals before socialist ones.

Disgusted with the existing political parties, O'Casey turned his energies to drama. His tragicomedies reflect in part his mixed feelings about his fellow slum dwellers, seeing them as incapable of giving a socialist direction to the Irish cause, but at the same time admirable for their unconquerable spirit.

After several of his plays had been rejected, the Abbey Theatre in Dublin produced THE SHADOW OF A GUNMAN (1923), set during the guerrilla strife between the Irish Republican Army and British forces. In 1924 the Abbey staged JUNO AND THE PAYCOCK, his most popular play, set during the period of civil war over the terms of Irish independence. THE PLOUGH AND THE STARS (1926), with the anti-British Easter Rising of 1916 as its background, caused riots at the Abbey by patriots who thought the play denigrated Irish heroes. When first produced in the 1920s, these plays had an explosive effect on the audiences at the Abbey and helped to enlarge that theater's reputation.

O'Casey's decision to move to England in 1926 was motivated in part by the Abbey's rejection of *The Silver Tassie*, a partly Expressionist antiwar drama produced in England in 1929. Another Expressionist play, *Within the Gates* (1934), followed, in which the modern world is symbolized by the happenings in a public park. *The Star Turns Red* (1940) is an antifascist play, and the semiautobiographical *Red Roses for Me* (1946) is set in Dublin at the time of the Irish railways strike of 1911.

O'Casey's later plays, given to fantasy and ritual and directed against the life-denying puritanism he thought had beset Ireland, include *Cock-a-Doodle Dandy* (1949), *The Bishop's Bonfire* (1955), and *The Drums of Father Ned* (1958). His last full-length play was a satire on Dublin intellectuals, *Behind the Green Curtains* (1961). Six volumes of O'Casey's autobiography appeared from 1939 to 1956; they were later collected as *Mirror in My House* (1956) in the United States and as *Autobiographies* (1963) in Great Britain.

occasional verse   Poetry written to commemorate a specific occasion or event. This can include poetry written by a poet laureate or other writer on an official occasion, as well as more personal works, such as Edmund Spenser's *Epithalamion*, which he wrote to celebrate his marriage.

Occleve   *see* HOCCLEVE.

occupatio [New Latin, from Latin, preoccupation, prior engagement of a person's interest]   *see* PARALIPSIS.

Occurrence at Owl Creek Bridge, An   Short story by Ambrose BIERCE, published in 1891 in *Tales of Soldiers and Civilians*, a collection that in 1898 was revised, enlarged, and retitled *In the Midst of Life*. The narrative concerns the final thoughts of a Southern planter as he is being hanged by Union soldiers. In the brief period between the tightening of the noose and the actual breaking of his neck, the man imagines his escape.

Oceanid \ō-'sē-ə-nid\ *plural* Oceanids *or* Oceanides \,ō-sē-'an-ə-,dēz\   An ocean nymph, child of the god Oceanus.

Oceanus \ō-'sē-ə-nəs\   In Greek mythology, the river that flowed around the earth (conceived as flat). Beyond it, to the west, were the land of the Cimmerii, where the sun never shone, the country of dreams, and the entrance to the underworld. In Hesiod's *Theogony*, Oceanus was the son of Uranus (Heaven) and Gaea (Earth), the husband of the Titan Tethys,

and the father of 3,000 rivers or stream spirits and 3,000 ocean nymphs. In Homer's works he was the source of the gods.

Ochikubo monogatari \ō-'chē-kü-bō-'mō-nō-,gä-tä-rē\   Japanese novel of the late 10th century, one of the world's earliest extant novels. Its unknown author was probably a man, one of the Heian court's literate elite, writing for an audience of female readers. It was translated into English as *Ochikubo monogatari; or, The Tale of the Lady Ochikubo.*

Ochikubo monogatari is similar to the Cinderella story of Western literature. Lady Ochikubo, the heroine, is treated harshly by her wicked stepmother, who favors her own daughters. Ochikubo's lover helps her escape from the stepmother's house and then subjects her family to vengeance until the merciful Ochikubo insists that he stop. The pair marry and live in happy monogamy, a condition that is rare in Heian court literature. The work's suspenseful narrative is also unusual for its time in that it is a realistic depiction of 10th-century aristocratic life and is devoid of supernatural elements.

O'Clery \ō-'klir-ē\, Michael (b. 1575, Kilbarron, County Donegal, Ire.—d. 1643, Louvain, Brabant [now in Belgium]) Irish chronicler who directed the compilation (completed 1636) of the *Annála Ríoghachta Éireann* (*Annals of the Four Masters*), a chronicle of Irish history from antiquity to 1616.

Assisted by other Irish scholars, in 1620 O'Clery began to collect and to transcribe manuscripts in Ireland. The results were the *Réim Rioghroidhe* (1630; *The Royal List*), a list of kings, their successions, and their pedigrees, with lives and genealogies of saints; the *Leabhar Gabhála* (1631; *Book of Invasions*), an account of the successive settlements of Ireland; and the famous *Annals*. At first a mere record of names, dates, and battles, with occasional quotations from ancient sources, the *Annals* begin to take on the character of modern literary history as they approach the author's own time.

O'Connor \ō-'kän-ər\, Flannery, *in full* Mary Flannery O'Connor (b. March 25, 1925, Savannah, Ga., U.S.—d. Aug. 3, 1964, Milledgeville, Ga.)   American novelist and short-story writer whose works, usually set in the rural South and often depicting human alienation, are concerned with the relationship between the individual and God.

O'Connor's first published work, a short story, appeared in *Accent* in 1946. Her first novel, WISE BLOOD (1952), combines the keen ear for common speech, caustic religious imagination, and flair for the absurd that were to characterize her subsequent work. With the publication of further short stories, first collected in A GOOD MAN IS HARD TO FIND (1955), she came to be regarded as a master of the form. Her other works of fiction are a novel, THE VIOLENT BEAR IT AWAY (1960), and the short-story collection EVERYTHING THAT RISES MUST CONVERGE (1965). A collection of occasional prose pieces, *Mystery and Manners*, appeared in 1969. *The Complete Stories*, published posthumously in 1971, contained several stories that had not previously appeared in book form.

Crippled by lupus erythematosus, which eventually proved fatal, O'Connor lived modestly, writing and raising peafowl on her mother's ancestral farm. Her letters, which provided valuable insight into the role of Roman Catholicism in her life and art, were published as *The Habit of Being* (1979).

O'Connor \ō-'kän-ər\, Frank, *pseudonym of* Michael O'Donovan \ō-'dən-ə-vən, -'dän-\ (b. 1903, Cork, County Cork, Ire.—d. March 10, 1966, Dublin)   Irish writer who, as a critic and as a translator of Gaelic works from the 9th to the 20th century, served as an interpreter of Irish life and literature to the English-speaking world.

O'Connor grew up in poverty, a childhood he recounted in *An Only Child* (1961). He received little formal education before going to work as a librarian and later as a director of the Abbey Theatre, Dublin, in the 1930s, collaborating on many of its productions. He won popularity in the United States for his short stories, which appeared in *The New Yorker* magazine from 1945 to 1961, and he was a visiting professor at several American universities in the 1950s.

Notable among his numerous volumes of short stories, in which he effectively made use of apparently trivial incidents to illuminate Irish life, are *Guests of the Nation* (1931) and *Crab Apple Jelly* (1944). Other collections of tales were published in 1953, 1954, and 1956. *Collected Stories*, including 67 stories, was published in 1981. He also wrote critical studies. O'Connor's English translations from the Gaelic include *The Midnight Court* (1945), a 17th-century satire by Brian Merriman, which is considered by many to be the finest single poem written in Irish. It was included in O'Connor's later collection of translations, *Kings, Lords, and Commons* (1959).

octameter \äk-'tam-ə-tər\   A line of verse consisting of eight metrical feet.

octastich \'äk-tə-,stik\ or **octastichon** \äk-'tas-tə-,kän\ *plural* octastichs *also* octasticha \'äk-'tas-tə-kə\   A verse unit of eight lines. *See also* HUITAIN; OCTAVE.

octastrophic \,äk-tə-'sträf-ik\   Having eight strophes, or stanzas.

octave \'äk-tiv, -,tāv\   **1.** A stanza of eight lines, called OT-TAVA RIMA. **2.** The first two quatrains or first eight lines of an Italian sonnet—also called *octet*. *Compare* SESTET.

octet \äk-'tet\   A stanza or group of eight verse lines; specifically, the first two quatrains or eight lines of an Italian sonnet.

octonarius \,äk-tə-'nar-ē-əs\ *plural* octonarii \-ē-,ī\ [Latin, from *octonarius* (adjective) containing eight]   In early Roman drama (especially comedy), an eight-foot verse (such as a line of four iambic or trochaic metra), in which in certain situations both short elements of the metron can be lengthened and long syllables and anceps (long or short, scanned ⏓) syllables are commonly resolved (*see* RESOLUTION). The scheme of an iambic metron thus is ⏑⏑ ⏑⏑ ⏑⏑ ⏑⏑, the scheme of a trochaic metron ⏑⏑ ⏑⏑ ⏑⏑ ⏑⏑. Both identification and scansion are further complicated by the variety of metra possible, the frequency of elision, and unusual quantities produced by the law of *brevis brevians* (in which a short syllable shortens a following long syllable that is preceded or followed by an accented syllable).

octonary \'äk-tə-,ner-ē\   In poetry, a stanza or group of eight verses; especially, one of the stanzas of the 119th Psalm.

Octopus, The   Novel by Frank NORRIS, published in 1901 and subtitled *A Story of California*. It was the first volume of *The Epic of the Wheat*, his unfinished trilogy about the production, distribution, and consumption of American wheat. *The Octopus* examines the struggle of California wheat farmers in the San Joaquin valley against the powerful Pacific and Southwestern Railroad monopoly. Norris employed the technique of literary naturalism in the novel to dramatize the issues of environmental determinism and social justice.

octosyllable \'äk-tə-,sil-ə-bəl\   A word or line of eight syllables.

Oculi \ō-'kü-lē\, Okello (b. 1942, Dokolo county, Lango district, Uganda)   Ugandan novelist, poet, and chronicler of African rural village life. His writing is filled with authentic snatches of conversation, proverbs, and folk wisdom that confirm African values and denounce European imitations.

Among Oculi's early works were *Prostitute* (1968), a novel dealing with the plight of the uprooted who have left home

for the lure of the city, and *Orphan* (1968), a dramatic, symbolic tale in lively free verse about modern urbanized Africa. His later books include *Kanti Riti* (1974), *Malak* (1977), and *Kookolem* (1978).

O'Curry \ō-'kər-ē\, Eugene (b. 1796, Dunaha, County Clare, Ire.—d. July 30, 1862, Dublin)   Irish Gaelic scholar and industrious copyist and translator of Old Irish manuscripts whose works had an important influence on the revival of the Gaelic language and literature and contributed to the late 19th-century Irish literary renaissance.

O'Curry examined and arranged many of the Irish manuscripts in the Royal Irish Academy, Trinity College library, and British Museum. In 1854 he was appointed professor at the new Catholic University of Ireland. His lectures, which give a full account of the medieval chronicles, historical romances, tales, and poems, were published in 1861. A subsequent three-volume work entitled *On the Manners and Customs of the Ancient Irish* appeared posthumously in 1873.

ode \'ōd\ [Greek (Attic) *ōidḗ*, a contraction of Greek *aoidḗ*, a derivative of *aeídein* to sing]   A ceremonious lyric poem on an occasion of public or private dignity in which personal emotion and general meditation are united. The form is usually marked by particular exaltation of feeling and style and by varying length of line and complexity of stanza forms.

The Greek word *ōidḗ* alluded to a choric song, usually accompanied by a dance. Alcman (7th century BC) originated the strophic arrangement of the ode, which is a rhythmic system composed of two or more lines repeated as a unit. Stesichorus (7th–6th century BC) invented the triadic, or three-part, structure (strophic lines followed by antistrophic lines in the same meter, concluding with a summary line, called an epode, in a different meter) that characterizes the odes of Pindar and Bacchylides. Choral odes were also an integral part of the Greek drama. In Latin the word was not used until about the time of Horace, in the 1st century BC. His *carmina* ("songs"), written in stanzas of two or four lines of polished Greek meters, are now universally called odes. Both Pindaric and Horatian ode forms were revived during the European Renaissance and continued to influence Western lyric poetry into the 20th century.

In pre-Islamic Arabic poetry, the ode flourished in the form of the qasida. Two great collections of these date from the 8th and 9th centuries. *See also* HORATIAN ODE; IRREGULAR ODE; PINDARIC ODE; QASIDA.

Ode: Intimations of Immortality (*in full* Ode: Intimations of Immortality from Recollections of Early Childhood)   Poem by William WORDSWORTH, published in the collection *Poems in Two Volumes* in 1807. One of Wordsworth's masterpieces, the ode sings of the mature narrator's heartbreaking realization that childhood's special relationship to nature and experience has been lost forever, although the unconscious memory of this state of being remains a source of wisdom in the world. The 11-stanza poem is written in the style of the irregular Pindaric ode.

Ode on a Grecian Urn   Poem in five stanzas by John KEATS, published in 1820 in the collection *Lamia, Isabella, The Eve of St. Agnes, and Other Poems*.

Called one of the greatest achievements of Romantic poetry, the ode is also one of the most widely read poems in the English language. The poet describes a scene on an urn that depicts two lovers chasing one another in a pastoral setting, then reflects on the contrast between the transient nature of human love and the enduring nature of art, which has frozen their passion for all time and made it eternal. But the poet also reminds us that the lovers on the urn are unable to consummate their passion—the price they pay for their permanence. The meaning of the enigmatic last two lines—" 'Beauty is truth, truth beauty,'—

that is all/Ye know on earth, and all ye need to know"—has been much debated.

Ode on Indolence   Poem in six stanzas by John KEATS, written in May 1819 and published posthumously in 1848.

The chief event of the ode is a morning vision of three figures in classical dress, passing before the poet as if they were ancient drawings on a spinning urn. The poet recognizes them as Love, Ambition, and Poesy, and their fleeting presence sadly reminds the poet of his recent idleness.

Ode on Melancholy   Poem in three stanzas by John KEATS, published in *Lamia, Isabella, The Eve of St. Agnes, and Other Poems* in 1820. It speaks of the transience of joy and desire and acknowledges that sadness is the inevitable accompaniment of human passion and happiness.

In the work's first two stanzas the poet urges the reader not to give in to death "when the melancholy fit shall fall" but to "glut thy sorrow" and revel in the emotion. The final stanza personifies melancholy as a mysterious goddess who lives in "the very temple of Delight," among the transitory deities of Beauty, Joy, and Pleasure.

Ode to a Nightingale   Poem in eight stanzas by John KEATS, published in *Lamia, Isabella, The Eve of St. Agnes, and Other Poems* (1820). It is a meditation upon art and life inspired by the song of the nightingale, who has made a nest in the poet's garden. The poet's happiness in communing with the bird is contrasted with the dead weight of human grief and sickness and the transience of youth and beauty. The song of the nightingale is seen as a symbol of art that outlasts mortal life.

Ode to Psyche \'sī-kē\   One of the earliest and best-known odes by John KEATS, published in *Lamia, Isabella, The Eve of St. Agnes, and Other Poems* (1820). Based on the myth of Psyche, a mortal who weds the god Cupid, this four-stanza poem is often characterized as an allegorical meditation upon the nature of love. Psyche has also been said to represent the poet's introspection. The poet, upon finding Psyche and Cupid asleep together in the forest, muses that Psyche has no shrine or worshipers and vows that he will be her priest and build a sanctuary for love "in some untrodden region of my mind."

Ode to the West Wind   Poem by Percy Bysshe SHELLEY, written at a single sitting on Oct. 25, 1819. It was published in 1820. Considered a prime example of the poet's passionate language and symbolic imagery, the ode invokes the spirit of the West Wind, "Destroyer and Preserver," the spark of creative vitality. This ode introduced a new stanzaic form composed of five sonnets, each of which has four tercets (units of three lines each). The scheme is based on Italian terza rima, rhyming *aba*, *bcb*, *cdc*, and *ded* followed by a rhyming *ee* couplet.

Odets \ō-'dets\, Clifford (b. July 18, 1906, Philadelphia, Pa., U.S.—d. Aug. 14, 1963, Hollywood, Calif.)   Leading dramatist of the theater of social protest in the United States during the 1930s. As one of its original members, he contributed to the prestige of the Group Theatre from 1931.

Odets' WAITING FOR LEFTY (1935), his first great success, used both the auditorium and the stage for action and was an effective plea for labor unionism. *Awake and Sing!* (1935) was a naturalistic family drama, and GOLDEN BOY (1937) was about an Italian-American prizefighter. *Paradise Lost* (1935) deals with the tragic life of a middle-class family.

Odets moved to Hollywood in the late 1930s to write for motion pictures, and he became a successful director. His later plays include *The Big Knife* (1949), *The Country Girl* (1950; U.K. title, *Winter Journey*), and *The Flowering Peach* (1954).

Odette *in full* Odette Swann \ō-'det-'swän\, *original surname* de Crécy \krā-'sē\   Fictional character, the vulgar wife of Charles Swann in REMEMBRANCE OF THINGS PAST by Marcel Proust. She appears most prominently in the first volume, *Du Côté de chez Swann* (1913; *Swann's Way*).

Odette is a striking beauty, but she is also insensitive, unintelligent, and vain. Formerly a courtesan, she was the wealthy Swann's mistress before she married him; after marriage, she continues to have affairs with other men. After Swann's death Odette remarries and becomes a famed hostess.

Odin \'ōd-ən\   One of the principal gods in Norse mythology. Odin (*Old Norse* Óthinn) is the Scandinavian representative of a common Germanic deity (*Old English* Woden, *Old High German* Wuotan) whose exact nature and role are difficult to determine because of the complex picture of him given by the wealth of iconographical and literary sources. Though Woden was worshiped preeminently, there is not sufficient evidence of his cult to show whether it was practiced by all of the Germanic tribes or to allow conclusions to be drawn about the nature of the god. Later literary sources, however, present a fairly coherent, if complex, picture of Odin as he was worshiped in Scandinavia and Iceland at the end of the pre-Christian period.

From earliest times Odin was a war god, and he appeared in heroic literature as the protector of heroes; fallen warriors joined him in Valhalla. Odin was the great magician among the gods; he rode a magical horse, Sleipnir, and was associated with runes. He was also the god of poets.

O'Dowd \ō-'daùd\, Bernard Patrick (b. April 11, 1866, Beaufort, Vic., Australia—d. Sept. 2, 1953, Melbourne, Vic.)   Poet who gave Australian poetry a more philosophical tone, supplanting traditional bush ballads of old.

In *Dawnward?* (1903), O'Dowd's first book of verse, he expressed strong political convictions. *The Silent Land* followed in 1906, and the philosophical *Dominions of the Boundary* in 1907. In an important prose pamphlet, *Poetry Militant* (1909), he argued that the poet should educate, propagandize, and indoctrinate. His later works include *The Bush* (1912), a long poem about Australia; *Alma Venus! and Other Verses* (1921), a social satire in verse; and *The Poems: Collected Edition* (1941).

Odysseus \ō-'dis-ē-əs, -'dis-,yūs\, *also called* Ulysses \yū-'lis-ēz\, *Latin* Ulixes \yū-'lik-sēz\   Hero of Homer's epic poem the *Odyssey* and one of the most frequently portrayed figures in Western literature. According to Homer, Odysseus was king of Ithaca and father, by his wife, Penelope, of Telemachus. (In later tradition, Odysseus was the son of Sisyphus and fathered sons by Circe, Calypso, and others.)

Homer portrayed Odysseus as a skilled warrior and leader of outstanding wisdom, eloquence, resourcefulness, courage, and endurance. In the *Iliad*, Odysseus appears as the man best fitted to cope with crises in personal relations among the Greeks.

Odyssey \'äd-ə-sē\   One of two great Greek epic poems, a sequel to the *Iliad*. It is attributed to HOMER. Like the *Iliad*, it is essentially an oral poem, developed over a vast period of time. The established version is divided into 24 books. The poem is the story of Odysseus, the king of Ithaca, as he travels home from the Trojan War to recover his house and kingdom.

When the poem opens, Odysseus is on the island of Ogygia, where the nymph Calypso has detained him for seven years. It is 10 years after the end of the Trojan War, and all the other Greeks have returned to their homes. After setting the scene, the rest of Books I–IV shift to Ithaca, where Odysseus' wife Penelope and son Telemachus are struggling to maintain their authority during his prolonged absence. In Book V Zeus orders Calypso to release Odysseus, who promptly sets off on a raft, which is destroyed by the god Poseidon, who hates him. Odysseus is washed ashore on the land of the Phaeacians, which is described in books VI–VIII.

In Books IX–XII Odysseus recounts for the Phaeacians his adventures since leaving Troy: he first comes to the land of the Lotus-Eaters and struggles with lotus-induced lethargy; he blinds Polyphemus the Cyclops, a son of Poseidon; he loses 11 of his 12 ships to the cannibalistic Laestrygones and reaches the island of the enchantress Circe, who has turned some of his companions into swine. Next he visits the Land of Departed Spirits, where he learns from the Theban seer Tiresias how he can expiate Poseidon's wrath. He then encounters the Sirens, Scylla and Charybdis, and the Cattle of the Sun, which his companions, despite warnings, plunder for food. He alone survives the ensuing storm and reaches Calypso's idyllic island.

In Books XIII–XVI the Phaeacians return Odysseus to Ithaca, where the goddess Athena disguises him as a beggar. He reveals his true identity to his son, and together they plot to rid their home of the suitors who have been hounding Penelope. The rest of the poem (Books XVII–XXIV) explains how Odysseus, still in disguise, passes the clever test that Penelope has devised to choose one of the suitors. After passing the test, Odysseus kills the suitors with the help of Telemachus and two faithful servants and is accepted by Penelope as her long-lost husband and as the king of Ithaca.

Ōe Kenzaburō \'ō-e-,ken-'zä-bù-rō\ (b. Jan. 31, 1935, Ehime prefecture, Shikoku, Japan)   Japanese novelist whose rough prose style, at times nearly violating the natural rhythms of the Japanese language, epitomizes the rebellion of the post-World War II generation of which he writes. He was awarded the Nobel Prize for Literature in 1994.

Ōe first attracted literary attention with *Shisha no ogori* (1957; *Lavish Are the Dead*), published in the magazine *Bungakukai*. His first novel, *Memushiri kouchi* (1958; "Pluck the Bud and Destroy the Offspring"), was highly praised, and he won the Akutagawa Prize (a prestigious award given to young writers of fiction) for the story "Shiiku" ("The Catch") in the 1958 collection of the same name. His second novel, *Warera no jidai* (1959; "Our Generation"), was poorly received, however.

Ōe became deeply involved in the politics of the New Left. *Kojinteki-na taiken* (1964; *A Personal Matter*) uses the birth of an abnormal baby to investigate the problem of culturally disinherited postwar youth. After visiting Hiroshima he wrote *Hiroshima nōto* (1965; *Hiroshima Notes*).

Among Oe's other works are *Man'en gannen no futtōbōru* (1967; THE SILENT CRY), a collection of short fiction entitled *Warera no kyōki o ikinobiru michi o oshieyo* (1969; *Teach Us to Outgrow Our Madness*), and the novels *Pinchi rannā chōsho* (1976; "Pinch Runner's Record"), *Dōjidai gēmu* (1979; "Coeval Games"), and *Atarashii hito yo meza meyo* (1983; "Awake, New Man"). Ōe also published *M/T* (1986), a study of regional myths, and *Boku ga hontō ni wakakatta koro* (1992; "When I was Really Young"), a collection of reminiscences.

Oedipus \'ed-i-pǝs, 'ēd-\   In Greek mythology, the king of Thebes who unwittingly killed his father and married his mother. In the post-Homeric tradition, the most familiar literary treatments are Sophocles' plays *Oedipus the King* and *Oedipus at Colonus*.

According to tradition, Laius, the king of Thebes, is warned by an oracle that his son will slay him. Accordingly, when his wife, Jocasta (Iocaste; in Homer, Epicaste), bears a son, he exposes the baby on Mt. Cithaeron, first pinning the baby's ankles together (hence the name Oedipus, meaning Swell-Foot). A shepherd takes pity on the infant, who is adopted by King Polybus of Corinth and his wife and is brought up as their son. In early manhood Oedipus visits Delphi and, learning that he is fated to kill his father and marry his mother, resolves never to return to Corinth.

Traveling toward Thebes, he encounters Laius, who provokes a quarrel in which he is killed by Oedipus. When Oedipus reaches the city, he finds the citizenry terrorized by the Sphinx, who is destroying all passersby who fail to answer her riddle. Oedipus solves the riddle, and he is rewarded with the throne of Thebes and the hand of the widowed queen, his mother, Jocasta. Together they produce four children: Eteocles, Polyneices, Antigone, and Ismene. Later, when the truth is revealed, Jocasta commits suicide. In Homer, Oedipus apparently continues to rule at Thebes until his death. In Sophocles' version of the legend, he blinds himself and leaves Thebes.

The Oedipus legend appears in the folk traditions of Albania, Finland, Cyprus, and Greece. Through Seneca the theme was transmitted to a long succession of playwrights, including Pierre Corneille, John Dryden, and Voltaire. It continued to capture the imagination of writers in the 20th century—particularly after Sigmund Freud chose the term *Oedipus complex* to designate a son's subconscious feeling of love toward his mother and jealousy and hate toward his father—as in André Gide's *Oedipe* and Jean Cocteau's *La Machine infernale*.

Oedipus the King \'ed-i-pǝs, 'ēd-\ (*Greek* Oidipous Tyrannos, *Latin* Oedipus Rex)   Play by SOPHOCLES, performed sometime between 430 and 426 BC, that marks the summit of classical Greek drama's formal achievement, known for its tight construction, mounting tension, and perfect use of the dramatic devices of recognition and discovery. It examines the story of Oedipus, who in attempting to flee from his fate, rushes headlong to meet it.

At the outset of the play, Oedipus is the beloved ruler of the city of Thebes, whose citizens have been stricken by a plague. Consulting the Delphic oracle, Oedipus is told that the plague will cease only when the murderer of Queen Jocasta's first husband, King Laius, has been found and punished for his deed. Oedipus resolves to find Laius' killer. His investigation turns into an obsessive reconstruction of his own hidden past when he discovers that the old man he killed when he first approached Thebes as a youth, was none other than Laius. Finally, Oedipus learns the truth about himself and his past. At the end, Jocasta hangs herself in shame and guilt-stricken Oedipus sticks needles into his eyes, blinding himself.

In Sophocles' later play *Oedipus at Colonus* (produced posthumously 401 BC; *Oidipous epi Kolōnō*), the old, blind Oedipus has spent many years wandering in exile. He ultimately departs to a mysterious death at Colonus, a village close by Athens, where he will become a benevolent source of defense to the land that has given him final refuge. The play is remarkable for the melancholy and beauty of its lyric odes and for its majestic characterization of Oedipus.

Oehlenschläger \'œ-lens-,leg-ǝr\, Adam Gottlob (b. Nov. 14, 1779, Vesterbro, Den.—d. Jan. 20, 1850, Copenhagen)   Poet and dramatist who was a leader of the Romantic movement in Denmark and is considered the great Danish national poet.

Oehlenschläger wrote his famous poem *Guldhornene* (1802; *The Golden Horns*) after meeting the Norwegian scientist and philosopher Henrik Steffens, who was eager to spread the doctrine of Romanticism in Denmark. *Guldhornene* marks a turning point in Danish literature. His first volume of poetry, *Digte* ("Poems"), appeared in 1802 and contained not only *Guldhornene* but also the lyrical drama *Sanct Hansaften-spil* ("A Midsummer Night's Play"). His *Poetiske skrifter* (1805; "Poetic Writings") contains two long cycles of lyric poems and *Aladdin*, a poetic drama on the writer's own life, with the lamp of the story symbolizing intuitive poetic genius.

In the historical plays published in *Nordiske Digte* (1807; "Nordic Poems"), Oehlenschläger turned to Nordic history and mythology for his materials. The work includes *Hakon Jarl hin Rige* ("Earl Haakon the Great") and *Baldur hin Gode* ("Baldur the Good").

After study and travel throughout Europe, Oehlenschläger returned to Copenhagen in 1809 and became a professor of aesthetics at the university there in 1810. His subsequent plays are thought to be inferior to his earlier ones, and his lyric poetry has in general outlived his dramatic verse. Oehlenschläger's most significant later work is the poetic epic *Nordens guder* (1819; *The Gods of the North*), which is a sort of modern Edda.

Oeneus \'ē-,nyūs, -,nūs\ In Greek legend, king of Calydon, husband of Althaea. He is notable for having neglected to sacrifice to Artemis, who sent a wild boar to ravage the country. It is this boar that his son Meleager—the leader of the Calydonian boar hunt—pursued. He was also independently connected with the Greek hero Heracles as the father of Heracles' bride Deianeira, whom he won from the river god Achelous. Oeneus may have been originally a wine god; his name is derived from the Greek word for wine. According to one story, Dionysus, the great god of wine, was the real father of Deianeira.

Oenone \ē-'nō-nē\ In Greek mythology, a fountain nymph of Mount Ida, the daughter of the river god Oeneus or Cebren, and the beloved of Paris, a son of King Priam of Troy. Oenone and Paris had a son, Corythus, but Paris soon deserted her for Helen. Bitterly jealous, Oenone refused to aid the wounded Paris during the Trojan War, even though she was the only one who could cure him. She at last relented but arrived at Troy too late to save him. Overcome with grief, she committed suicide.

oeuvre \'œv-rə, 'ərv- *French* 'œvr *with* r *as a uvular trill*\ *plural* oeuvres *same or* -rəz\ [French, literally, work] A substantial body of work constituting the lifework of a writer, an artist, or a composer.

O'Faolain \ō-'fāl-ən, -'fal-\, Julia (b. June 6, 1932, London, Eng.) Irish author of meticulously researched, often darkly comic novels, short stories, and nonfiction.

O'Faolain, the daughter of authors Sean O'Faolain and Eileen Gould, worked as a language teacher and a translator. In *We Might See Sights!* (1968), Ireland is the setting for several stories satirizing sexual repression; another group of tales in the collection, set in Italy, is concerned with emotional states. Her other short-story collections include *Man in the Cellar* (1974), *Melancholy Baby* (1978), and *Daughters of Passion* (1982). O'Faolain's novel *Godded and Codded* (1970; U.S. title, *Three Lovers*) concerns a young Irish woman's sexual adventures in Paris. *Women in the Wall* (1975) is a fictional account of Queen Radegund, who founded a monastery in Gaul in the 6th century. *No Country for Young Men* (1980), set in Dublin, follows three generations of an Irish family. *The Obedient Wife* (1982), in which an Italian woman ends her affair with a priest and returns to her husband, is set in Los Angeles. The novel *The Judas Cloth* (1992) concerns the 19th-century Roman Catholic clergy. With her husband, Lauro Martines, O'Faolain edited *Not in God's Image: Women in History from the Greeks to the Victorians* (1973). She also translated several works from the Italian under the name Julia Martines.

O'Faolain \ō-'fāl-ən, -'fal-\, Sean, *original name* John Francis Whelan \'wē-lən, 'hwē-\ (b. Feb. 22, 1900, Cork, County Cork, Ire.—d. April 20, 1991, Dublin) Irish writer best known for his carefully crafted, lyrical short stories. He often examined the decline of the nationalist struggle or the oppressive provincialism of Irish Roman Catholicism.

Disturbed by the brutality of the British repression of the Easter Rising of 1916, O'Faolain changed his name, studied Gaelic, and became involved in anti-British activities during the Irish insurrection (1918–21). He graduated from the National University of Ireland and Harvard University.

From 1926 to 1933 O'Faolain taught in Great Britain and the United States. Returning to Ireland, he taught briefly until the success of *Midsummer Night Madness and Other Stories* (1932), his first collection of stories, and the novel *A Nest of Simple Folk* (1933) allowed him to write full-time. O'Faolain produced only four novels, including *Bird Alone* (1936) and *Come Back to Erin* (1940), each portraying a central character who attempts to rebel against and rise above the lower middle class. His well-known works include *A Life of Daniel O'Connell* (1938) and *Vive moi!* (1964), his autobiography. Historical views of the Irish people are contained in *The Irish, a Character Study* (1949; rev. ed., 1969) and *An Irish Journey* (1940).

As the founding editor of *The Bell*, a liberal Dublin literary periodical, O'Faolain also provided a forum for new, untried writers and for established authors, many of whom were in self-exile from Ireland. *Selected Stories* was published in 1978 and the novel *And Again?* in 1979. *The Collected Stories of Sean O'Faolain I* appeared in 1980.

Offa \'of-ə, 'äf-\ of Angel \'aŋ-gəl\ (fl. 4th century AD) Continental Anglian ruler from whom the royal house of Anglo-Saxon Mercia claimed descent.

According to the Old English poem "Widsith," Offa saved his aged father, King Wermund, from Saxon domination by defeating a Saxon king's son in single combat. Offa later became ruler of the large kingdom of Angel. He is probably the same Offa mentioned in the Old English poem *Beowulf*.

Off-Broadway \'of-'bród-,wā, 'äf-\ In the theater of the United States, small professional productions that have served as New York City's alternative to the commercially oriented theaters of Broadway. Off-Broadway plays, usually produced on low budgets in small theaters, have tended to be freer in style and more imaginative than those on Broadway. The designations Broadway and Off-Broadway refer not so much to the location of the theater as to its size and the scale of production.

Off-Broadway theaters enjoyed a surge of growth in quality and importance after 1952, with the success of the director José Quintero's productions at the Circle in the Square Theatre in Greenwich Village. The works of such prizewinning American playwrights as Edward Albee, Charles Gordone, Paul Zindel, Sam Shepard, Lanford Wilson, and John Guare were first produced Off-Broadway, along with the unconventional works of such avant-garde dramatists as Eugène Ionesco, Ugo Betti, Jean Genet, Samuel Beckett, and Harold Pinter.

Like those on Broadway, Off-Broadway theaters began to suffer from soaring costs, which this stimulated the emergence of still less expensive and more daring productions, labeled Off-Off-Broadway. Among the most successful of these groups were The Negro Ensemble Company, La Mama Experimental Theatre Company, the Open Theatre, Manhattan Theatre Club, Ensemble Studio Theatre, and Roundabout.

Officers and Gentlemen Novel by Evelyn Waugh, published in 1955. It is the second volume of the trilogy SWORD OF HONOUR.

Of Human Bondage Semiautobiographical novel by W. Somerset MAUGHAM, published in 1915 and considered his masterwork. It is a perceptive depiction of the emotional isolation of a young man and his eventual insight into life.

Born with a club foot, Philip Carey is acutely sensitive of his handicap. As a medical student in London, he meets selfish and unfaithful Mildred Rogers, a waitress for whom he develops an all-consuming passion and whom he cannot leave, no matter how often she humiliates, betrays, and abandons him. When Philip finishes medical school, he enters a loving relationship with Sally Athelney. Her possible pregnancy forces him to examine his life. Although Sally learns that she is not pregnant, Philip freely chooses to marry her anyway.

O'Flaherty \ō-'flä-hər-tē, -'fla-, -ər-tē; -'fler-tē\, Liam (b. Aug. 28, 1896, Inishmore, Aran Islands, County Galway, Ire.—d. Sept. 7, 1984, Dublin)   Irish novelist and short-story writer whose works combine brutal naturalism, psychological analysis, poetry, and biting satire with an abiding respect for the courage and persistence of the Irish people. He was considered to be a leading figure of the Irish Literary Renaissance.

O'Flaherty embarked on a varied career as a soldier in World War I and a migrant laborer in South America, Canada, the United States, and the Middle East. After taking part in revolutionary activities in Ireland, O'Flaherty settled in England in 1922; he returned to Dublin in the mid-1920s. His books include *Thy Neighbour's Wife* (1923), his successful first novel; *The Black Soul* (1924), the story of a tormented former soldier who seeks tranquillity on a remote western isle; THE INFORMER (1925; film, 1935), about a confused revolutionary who betrays his friend during the Irish "troubles"; *Skerrett* (1932), a critically acclaimed story of conflict between a parish priest and a teacher; *Famine* (1937), a re-creation of the effect of the Irish famine of the 1840s on the individuals of a small community; *Short Stories* (1937; rev. ed., 1956); *Insurrection* (1950), a novel dealing with the Easter Rising of 1916; and *The Pedlar's Revenge and Other Stories* (1976). His autobiography, *Shame the Devil*, was published in 1934.

Of Mice and Men   Novella by John STEINBECK, published in 1937. The tragic story, given poignancy by its objective narrative, is about the complex bond between two migrant laborers. The book, which was adapted by Steinbeck into a three-act play (produced 1937), earned him national renown.

The plot centers on George Milton and Lennie Small, itinerant ranch hands who dream of one day owning a small farm. George acts as a father figure to Lennie, who is large and simpleminded, calming him and helping to rein in his immense physical strength. When Lennie accidentally kills the ranch owner's flirtatious daughter-in-law, George shoots his friend rather than allow him to be captured by a vengeful lynch mob.

Of Time and the River (*in full* Of Time and the River: A Legend of Man's Hunger in His Youth)   Novel by Thomas WOLFE, begun in 1931 and, after extensive editing by Wolfe and editor Maxwell Perkins, published in March 1935 as a sequel to *Look Homeward, Angel* (1929). The book chronicles the maturing of Eugene Gant as he leaves his Southern home for the wider world of Harvard University, New York City, and Europe.

In more than 900 pages, Wolfe examines the passing of time and the creative process. Among the vivid characters Gant encounters are reckless Robert Weaver, eccentric Bascom Pentland, affluent Joel Pierce, and dissolute Francis Starwick.

Ogier the Dane \'ō-jē-ər, ō-'zhyā\, *French* Ogier de Danemarche \ō-zhyā-də-dän-'märk\, *Danish* Holger Danske \'hōl-ğər-'däns-kə\   An important character in the French medieval epic poems known as chansons de geste. His story is told in a cycle of poems known as *Geste de Doon de Mayence*, which deals with the wars of the feudal barons against the emperor Charlemagne. The character of Ogier has a historical prototype in Autcharius, a follower of Carloman, Charlemagne's younger brother, whose kingdom Charlemagne invaded in 771 after Carloman's death. Although Ogier is referred to in the chansons as the son of the Danish king Gaufrey and later became a national hero celebrated in Danish folk song, the surname "of Danemarche" probably originally signified the marches of the Ardennes and not Denmark.

Ogier is the hero of another chanson of the early 12th century, called *La Chevalerie Ogier de Danemarche*, which tells of his reconciliation with Charlemagne. Later in the century, *Les Enfances Ogier* places him at Charlemagne's court, where he is highly esteemed for his military prowess. Stories about Ogier also appeared in Icelandic, Castilian, Catalan, and Italian literature. *See also* CHANSON DE GESTE.

Ogot \ō-'gōt\, Grace (Emily), *original surname* Okinyi \ō-'kin-yē\ (b. May 15, 1930, Butere, near Kisumu, central Nyanza region, Kenya)   Kenyan author of widely anthologized short stories and novels.

A nurse by profession, Okinyi also worked as a scriptwriter and an announcer for the BBC's East African Service, as a columnist in the *East African Standard*, and as a community development officer in Kisumu, among other positions.

One of the few well-known women writers in East Africa, by the early 1970s Ogot was the only woman to have fiction published by the East African Publishing House. Her stories—which have appeared in European and African journals such as *Black Orpheus* and *Transition* and in a collection, *Land Without Thunder* (1968)—give an inside view of traditional life and society among the Luo people and of the conflict of traditional with colonial and modern cultures. Her full-length novel *The Promised Land* (1966) tells of rural Luo immigrants to Tanganyika (now Tanzania) and western Kenya. Her selected short stories were published in 1976 as *The Other Woman*, and her novel *Miaha* (*The Strange Bride*) was published in 1983.

O'Grady \ō-'grā-dē\, Standish James (b. Sept. 18, 1846, Castletown, County Cork, Ire.—d. May 18, 1928, Shanklin, Isle of Wight, Hampshire, Eng.)   Historical novelist and literary historian whose popular English versions of the Irish heroic sagas earned him the title of "father of the Irish literary revival."

O'Grady graduated from Trinity College, Dublin, in 1868. Introduced to the ancient heroic and romantic literature of Ireland through the translations of the Gaelic scholar Eugene O'Curry, O'Grady devoted his career to the study of Irish antiquities. In 1878 he published *History of Ireland: The Heroic Period*; this work was followed in 1880 by *History of Ireland: Cuculain and His Contemporaries*.

The enthusiasm of William Butler Yeats and other young Irish writers eventually brought O'Grady a wider audience and a London publisher. In 1892 he published *Finn and His Companions*, following it two years later with *The Coming of Cuculain*. He also wrote several works of historical fiction, of which *The Bog of Stars* (1893) and *The Flight of the Eagle* (1897) are probably the best. O'Grady's versions of Irish epics have great narrative vigor and imaginative power.

ogre \'ō-gər\ [French, from Old French, epithet for a ferocious pagan, probably alteration (influenced by *bougre* heretic, sodomite) of *orc, from Latin *Orcus*, god of the underworld]   A hideous giant represented in fairy tales and folklore as feeding on human beings. The word gained popularity from its use in the late 17th century by Charles Perrault, the author of *Contes de ma mère l'oye* (*Tales of Mother Goose*). Since then ogres have appeared in many works, including "Tom Thumb"; "Hansel and Gretel," where the witch is a type of ogre because she intends to eat the children; and "Little Red Riding Hood," where the wolf resembles an ogre. The Cyclops of myth and heroic literature who devours humans is a form of ogre.

ogress \'ō-grəs\   A female ogre.

O'Hara \ō-'har-ə\, Frank (b. June 27, 1926, Baltimore, Md., U.S.—d. July 25, 1966, Fire Island, N.Y.)   American poet who gathered images from an urban environment to represent personal experience.

O'Hara was drawn to both poetry and the visual arts for much of his life. During the 1960s, as an assistant curator at the Museum of Modern Art in New York City, O'Hara sent his criticism of current painting and sculpture to such periodicals as *Art News*, and he wrote catalogs for the exhibits he arranged. Meanwhile, local theaters were producing many of his experimental one-act plays, including *Try! Try!* (1960), about a soldier's return to his wife and her new lover.

O'Hara, however, considered himself primarily a poet. His pieces, which mark him as a member of the New York school of poets, are a mixture of quotations, gossip, phone numbers, commercials—any mote of experience that he found appealing. He related what was happening to him rather than trying to clarify experiences for the reader. His first volume of poetry was *A City Winter, and Other Poems* (1952). *The Collected Poems of Frank O'Hara* (1971) was published posthumously.

O'Hara \ō-'har-ə\, **John** (Henry) (b. Jan. 31, 1905, Pottsville, Pa., U.S.—d. April 11, 1970, Princeton, N.J.)   American novelist and short-story writer whose sparingly styled fiction stands as a social history of upwardly mobile Americans from the 1920s through the 1940s.

O'Hara was raised in Pottsville, Pa., which appears in his fiction as Gibbsville, a typical small town in the United States. He worked as a critic and reporter in New York City. The influence of this journalistic experience is seen in the objective and nonexperimental style of his fiction.

O'Hara was fascinated by the effects of class, money, and sexuality on Americans, and his fictional representations of Hollywood and Broadway are thick with the snobbery of social structure. His highly acclaimed first novel, *Appointment in Samarra* (1934), explored the disintegration and death of an upper-class inhabitant of a small city. In 1956 he received a National Book Award for *Ten North Frederick* (1955; film, 1958). Many of his best-selling novels were adapted for stage and screen, including the popular *Butterfield 8* (1935; film, 1960) and *From the Terrace* (1958; film, 1960). O'Hara's short-story collections include *Waiting for Winter* (1966) and *And Other Stories* (1968).

O'Hara, Scarlett \'skär-lit-ō-'har-ə\   Fictional character, the heroine of GONE WITH THE WIND, Margaret Mitchell's romantic novel about the American Civil War. Flirtatious and strong-willed, Scarlett is the quintessential Southern belle.

Okamoto Kidō \ō-'kä-mō-tō-'kē-,dō\, *original name* Okamoto Keiji \'kā-jē\ (b. Oct. 15, 1872, Tokyo, Japan—d. March 1, 1939, Japan)   Japanese dramatist and drama critic who wrote nearly 200 historical kabuki dramas.

While working for the Tokyo newspaper *Nichinichi* ("Daily Daily") in 1908, Okamoto wrote his first play, *Ishin Zengo* ("Before and After the Reformation"), for kabuki theater. He continued writing historical dramas (*jidaimono*), which were noted for their historical accuracy and poetic expression. Some of the best remembered are *Shuzenji monogatari* ("The Tale of Shuzenji"), *Muromachi gosho* ("Muromachi Castle"), *Sasaki Takatsuna, Toribeyama shinjū* ("Double Suicide at Toribeyama"), and *Banchō Sarayashiki* ("The Mansion of the Plates"). In his later years he wrote plays with situations taken from daily life (*sewamono*), such as the popular *Sōma no Kinsan* ("Kin-san of Soma").

In 1937 Okamoto became the first dramatist to be made a member of the Art Academy, and he has since been considered the representative writer of what has been called the New Kabuki (Shin Kabuki). He also wrote more than 100 short stories and several novels, the most popular being *Hanshichi torimono-chō* ("The Casebook of Detective Hanshichi"), a re-counting of cases handled by a detective operating during the late Tokugawa period (1603–1867).

Okara \ō-'kä-rä\, **Gabriel** (Imomotimi Gbaingbain) (b. April 24, 1921, Bumodi, Nigeria)   Nigerian poet and novelist with an acute perception of Africa's problems whose verse was translated into several languages by the early 1960s.

A largely self-educated man, Okara became a bookbinder after leaving school and soon began writing plays and features for radio. In 1953 his poem "The Call of the River Nun" won an award at the Nigerian Festival of Arts. Some of his poems were published in the influential periodical *Black Orpheus*, and by 1960 he was recognized as an accomplished literary craftsman.

Okara incorporated African thought, religion, folklore, and imagery into both his verse and prose. His first novel, *The Voice* (1964), is a remarkable linguistic experiment in which Okara translated directly from the Ijaw language, imposing Ijaw syntax onto the English, in order to give literal expression to African ideas and imagery. The novel creates a symbolic landscape in which the forces of traditional African culture and Western materialism contend. A collection of his poems, *The Fisherman's Invocation*, was published in 1978, and another small collection of poems in 1983.

Okigbo \ō-'kig-bō\, **Christopher** (b. Aug. 16, 1932, Ojoto, Nigeria—d. August 1967, Nigeria)   One of the best and most widely anthologized Nigerian poets.

After graduating from the University of Ibadan, Okigbo held positions as a teacher, librarian at the University of Nigeria, and West African editor of *Transition*, an African literary magazine. He was awarded but declined first prize for poetry at the 1966 Festival of the Negro Arts in Dakar, Senegal. Okigbo's efforts to launch a publishing company in Enugu with the novelist Chinua Achebe came to an abrupt end when he was killed while fighting in the war for Biafran independence from Nigeria.

Okigbo published three volumes of poetry during his short life: *Heavensgate* (1962), *Limits* (1964), and *Silences* (1965). His collected poems appeared posthumously in 1971 under the title *Labyrinths, with Path of Thunder*. His poems are highly personal, richly symbolic renderings of his experiences. He weaves images of his native Igbo (Ibo) landscape into works that are often obscure or allusive but intensely evocative. Okigbo became the most widely translated of all Nigerian poets. His *Collected Poems* was published in 1986.

Okri \ō-krē\, **Ben** (b. March 15, 1959, Minna, Nigeria)   Nigerian author who used the technique of magic realism as a means of conveying the social and political chaos in his country.

Okri's first novels, *Flowers and Shadows* (1980) and *The Landscapes Within* (1981), employ surrealistic images to depict the corruption and lunacy of a politically scarred country. Two volumes of short stories, *Incidents at the Shrine* (1986) and *Stars of the New Curfew* (1988), portray the essential link in Nigerian culture between the world of the spirits and that of physical reality. Okri won the Booker Prize for his novel *The Famished Road* (1991), the story of Azaro, an *abiku* ("spirit child"), and his quest for identity. Okri's first book of poetry, *An African Elegy* (1992), urges Africans to overcome the forces of chaos within their countries, and the novel *Songs of Enchantment* (1993) continues the themes of *The Famished Road*, relating stories of dangerous quests and the struggle to achieve national stability.

Okyeame \,ōk-yä-'ä-mä\   Ghanaian literary magazine published irregularly by the University of Ghana from 1961 to 1972. *Okyeame* was published in English and edited by Efua Sutherland, a Ghanaian writer. Each issue centered on poetry, fiction, or drama and included a writers' forum with essays on African art.

Ólafsson \'ō-läf-sȯn\, Eggert (b. 1726, Snaefellsnes, Ice.—d. May 1768, at sea in the Breidafjördur off the northwestern coast of Iceland) Icelandic poet and antiquarian, an outstanding figure in the history of Iceland's fight to preserve and revivify its language and culture.

Ólafsson studied at the University of Copenhagen; his major interests lay in natural history. His great work *Reise igiennem Island*, 2 vol. (1772; *Travels in Iceland*) recorded a scientific and cultural survey he carried out in 1752–57. His poetry, of historical rather than of literary interest, voices his burning zeal for a cultural and political renaissance in Iceland. His writing had a strong emotional appeal to fellow Icelanders, heightened when he and his bride were drowned on their honeymoon journey home.

Old \'ōld\ Belonging to an early period in the development of a language or literature.

Old Comedy Initial phase of ancient Greek comedy (*c.* 5th century BC), known through the works of Aristophanes. Old Comedy plays are characterized by an exuberant and high-spirited satire of public persons and affairs. Composed of song, dance, personal invective, and buffoonery, the plays consist of loosely related episodes containing outspoken political criticism and comment on literary and philosophical topics. They were first performed in Athens for the religious festival of Dionysus. The plays gradually took on a six-part structure: a prologos, in which the basic fantasy is explained and developed; the parodos, entry of the chorus; the contest, or agon, a ritualized debate between two parties—either an actor and the chorus or two actors, each supported by half of the chorus; the parabasis, or "coming forward," in which the chorus addresses the audience on the topics of the day and hurls scurrilous criticism at prominent citizens; a series of farcical scenes; and a final banquet or wedding.

Old Comedy sometimes is called Aristophanic comedy, for its most famous exponent; 11 of his plays survive intact. The dramatists Cratinus, Phrynichus, and Eupolis also wrote plays of this type.

Old Curiosity Shop, The Novel by Charles DICKENS, first issued serially in 1840–41 in Dickens' own weekly, *Master Humphrey's Clock*; it was published in book form in 1841. The novel was enormously popular in its day but in a later age was scorned for its unabashed sentimentality.

The Old Curiosity Shop is the story of Little Nell Trent and the evil dwarf Quilp. When Little Nell's grandfather gambles away his curiosity shop to his creditor Quilp, the girl and the old man flee London. Nell's friend Kit Nubbles and a mysterious Single Gentleman (who turns out to be the wealthy brother of Nell's grandfather) attempt to find them but are thwarted by Quilp, who drowns while fleeing the law. Little Nell dies before Kit and the Single Gentleman arrive, and her brokenhearted grandfather dies days later.

Old Forest, The Title story of *The Old Forest and Other Stories* (1985) by Peter TAYLOR, a collection of 14 pieces representative of 50 years of the author's fiction. The stories are set in the American South from the 1930s to the middle 1950s; seven were originally published in *The New Yorker*.

"The Old Forest," like much of Taylor's fiction, concerns upper-middle-class Southerners whose privileged, semiagrarian way of life is vanishing because of the industrialization and urbanization of the South. The story is a memory piece in which the action is recalled by the narrator-protagonist after 50 years. On a snowbound day in 1937, one week prior to his marriage to the debutante Caroline Braxley, Nat Ramsey takes Lee Ann Deehart, a girl of "unknown origins," for an innocent ride in his car. The car is involved in an accident, and Lee Ann runs away, disappearing into the old forest. The Braxleys refuse to allow the wedding to take place until Lee Ann is located and any hint of scandal is dissipated.

Oldham \'ōl-dəm\, John (b. Aug. 9, 1653, Shipton Moyne, Gloucestershire, Eng.—d. Dec. 9, 1683, Holm Pierrepont, near Nottingham) Pioneer of the imitation of classical satire in English.

Oldham's poems attracted the attention of John Wilmot, 2nd earl of Rochester, at whose death he wrote the imitation of the *Lament for Bion* (probably wrongly attributed to Moschus). In 1677 he attempted, apparently unsuccessfully, to win recognition at court by writing a poem on the marriage of the Princess Mary to William of Orange. John Dryden mourned Oldham in a noble elegy.

Oldham has a notable place in the development of Augustan poetry of late 17th- and early 18th-century England. The four *Satyrs Upon the Jesuits* (1681), including "Garnet's Ghost," previously published as a broadsheet in 1679, constitute his most widely known work. They are forceful but melodramatic, crowded with coarse images and uneven versification, an attempt to imitate the invective of Juvenal.

Old Man and the Sea, The Short novel by Ernest HEMINGWAY, published in 1952 and awarded the 1953 Pulitzer Prize for fiction. Completed after a 10-year literary drought, it was his last major work of fiction.

The novel is written in Hemingway's characteristically spare prose. It concerns an old Cuban fisherman named Santiago who finally catches a magnificent fish after weeks of not catching anything. After three days of playing the fish, he finally manages to reel it in and lash it to his boat, only to have sharks eat it as he returns to the harbor. The other fishermen marvel at the size of the skeleton; Santiago is spent but triumphant.

Old Mortality Novel by Sir Walter SCOTT, published in 1816. A masterpiece in the genre of historical romance, the story takes place in Scotland in 1679 during a time of political turmoil, when the dissenting Covenanters were up in arms against the English King Charles II. The main character, Henry Morton, is a moderate who is compelled to support the Covenanters when he learns that some of his relatives are dissenters. Representing Scott's own ambiguous feelings toward his native Scotland, Morton is essentially a peacemaker, and his marriage to the granddaughter of a Royalist at the end of the novel symbolizes the hope for a union between the two countries.

Olds \'ōldz\, Sharon (b. Nov. 19, 1942, San Francisco, Calif., U.S.) Poet best known for her powerful, often erotic, imagery of the body and the family.

Olds graduated from Stanford University and from Columbia University and then taught poetry at numerous schools and in workshops.

Olds's first collection, *Satan Says* (1980), described her early sexual life in frank language, making clear that the writer had no use for poetic politesse. *The Dead and the Living* (1984), which received several major poetry awards, refined her poetic voice. Her poems honoring the dead encompassed family members and victims of political violence; those addressed to the living continued her exploration of the life of the body, a theme she further developed in *The Gold Cell* (1987). *The Matter of This World: New and Selected Poems* (1987) and *The Father* (1992) continued her intimate exposition—free of bitterness and self-pity—of her own life.

Old Testament The set of sacred writings shared by Judaism and Christianity. The term implies the Christian addition of a subsequent New Testament. *See also* TANAKH.

Both Christians and Jews are known as "people of the Book," and the Old Testament's profoundly theological interpretation of human life and the universe as creations of the one God is the structure of ideas in which both faiths exist. The term Old Testament was devised by a Christian, Melito of Sardis, c. AD 170 to distinguish this part of the Bible from the Christian New Testament. Except for a few passages in Aramaic, the Old Testament was originally written in Hebrew during the period from 1,200 to 100 BC.

The Hebrew canon recognizes the following main divisions and subdivisions: (1) the Torah, or Pentateuch, contains narratives combined with rules and instructions in the books of Genesis, Exodus, Leviticus, Numbers, and Deuteronomy; (2) the Nevi'im, or Prophets, is subdivided into the Former Prophets, with anecdotes about major Hebrew persons in the books of Joshua, Judges, Samuel, and Kings, and stories of the Latter Prophets exhorting Israel to return to God in Isaiah, Jeremiah, Ezekiel, and the Twelve Minor Prophets; and (3) the Ketuvim, or Writings, consists of devotional and erotic poetry, theology, and drama to be found in Psalms, Proverbs, Job, Song of Songs, Ruth, Lamentations, Ecclesiastes, Esther, Daniel, Ezra-Nehemiah, and Chronicles.

The total number of books in the Hebrew canon is 24, the number of scrolls on which these works were written in ancient times. The Old Testament as adopted by Christianity numbers more works for several reasons. The Roman Catholic canon, derived initially from the Greek-language Septuagint translation of the Hebrew Bible, absorbed a number of books that Jews and Protestants later determined were not canonical (*see* APOCRYPHA). Further, Christians divided some of the original Hebrew works into two or more parts, specifically, Samuel, Kings, and Chronicles (two parts each), Ezra-Nehemiah (two separate books), and the Minor Prophets (12 separate books). The Protestant canon includes 39 books, the Roman Catholic, 46. *Compare* NEW TESTAMENT.

Old Vic \'vik\   London theater company, specializing in productions of William Shakespeare, that eventually became the nucleus of the National Theatre. The company's theater building opened in 1818 as the Royal Coburg and produced mostly popular melodramas. In 1833 it was redecorated and renamed the Royal Victoria and became popularly known as the Old Vic. In 1914 the Old Vic initiated a regular Shakespeare season. By 1918 it was established as the only permanent Shakespearean theater in London. Beginning in the 1940s the Old Vic company presented memorable productions of Shakespeare's plays and other classics, including *Cyrano de Bergerac*, *Oedipus Rex*, *Love for Love*, and *Peer Gynt*. In 1946 the Old Vic School and the Young Vic, a company formed to perform for children, were established. In 1963 the company was dissolved, and until 1976 the Old Vic Theatre was the home of the new National Theatre. The Young Vic was reconstituted in 1970, and by 1976 it had become an independent company. The Old Vic was refurbished and reopened in the late 1980s.

Old Wives' Tale, The   Novel by Arnold BENNETT, published in 1908. This study of the changes wrought by time on the lives of two English sisters during the 19th century is a masterpiece of literary realism.

Constance and Sophia Baines, the daughters of a shopkeeper, grow up in the rural town of Bursley. Sophia eventually runs off and settles in Paris with her husband, who is a cad, and Constance remains behind in England and marries the mild-mannered shop assistant. The sisters are reunited years later when they are old, and Bennett skillfully contrasts what has remained stable in their characters with the differences time and environment have produced in their personalities.

This long and ambitious work established Bennett's reputation as a novelist.

Olesha \ˌɔ-'lʸesh-ə\, Yury Karlovich (b. Feb. 19 [March 3, New Style], 1899, Elizavetgrad, Ukraine, Russian Empire—d. May 10, 1960, Moscow, U.S.S.R.)   Russian writer who examined the conflict between the old mentality and the new in the early years of the Soviet Union.

Olesha served in the pro-Communist Red Army and afterward became a journalist. He published humorous verse and several sharp, critical articles in the early 1920s. In 1927 he produced the novel for which he is remembered, *Zavist* (*Envy*). The work is concerned with a set of six characters, three of whom accept the mechanized, conformist nature of Soviet society and three of whom reject it. Olesha's later works include the short stories "Lyubov" ("Love") and "Liompa" (both 1929), the fairy-tale novel *Tri tolstyaka* (1928; *Three Fat Men*), and the play *Spisok blagodeyany* (1931; "A List of Benefits"). Each is a variation on the theme first presented in *Zavist*.

When in the early 1930s Socialist Realism was made an official aesthetic, Olesha spoke openly of his misgivings at a meeting of the Union of Soviet Writers in 1934. Following this event, Olesha's name vanished from Soviet literature. Little is known of his activities thereafter, and only after Joseph Stalin's death did his name reenter Soviet literature. The publication in 1956 of a selection of his stories signaled his full rehabilitation; since then several volumes of his works, including many never previously published, have appeared.

Oliphant \'äl-i-fənt\, Laurence (b. 1829, Cape Town [now in South Africa]—d. Dec. 23, 1888, Twickenham, Middlesex, Eng.)   British author, traveler, and mystic.

Before the age of 24 Oliphant's travels had provided material for two books, a *Journey to Khatmandu* (1852) and *The Russian Shores of the Black Sea in the Autumn of 1852, with a Voyage Down the Volga, and a Tour Through the Country of the Don Cossacks* (1853). Later experiences in various parts of the world, as a diplomat and as war correspondent for *The Times*, are recorded with verve in *Episodes in a Life of Adventure* (1887) and other books. The *Narrative of the Earl of Elgin's Mission to China and Japan* (1859) gives a fascinating account of 19th-century gunboat diplomacy. Oliphant's satirical novel of London society, *Piccadilly: A Fragment of Contemporary Biography*, appeared in 1865, and in the same year he became a Conservative member of Parliament.

In 1878 he proposed a plan for the Jewish colonization of Palestine (although he was not Jewish himself). The plan was well received by eastern European Jews but was refused by the Ottoman sultan, ruler of Palestine. In 1882 Oliphant and his wife settled in Haifa, where they formed a small community and together wrote the esoteric *Sympneumata; or, Evolutionary Forces Now Active in Man* (1885)—apparently a plea for a purified sex life.

Oliphant \'äl-i-fənt\, Margaret Oliphant (b. April 4, 1828, Wallyford, Midlothian, Scot.—d. June 25, 1897, Windsor, near London, Eng.)   Prolific Scottish novelist, historical writer, and biographer best known for her sympathetic portraits of small-town life.

Between 1849 and her death Oliphant published more than 100 separate books, of which the best known are the *Chronicles of Carlingford*, published anonymously from 1863 to 1866. These four novels include *Miss Marjoribanks* (1866), depicting a young lady's attempts at social climbing, and *Salem Chapel* (1863), concerning a young, intelligent Nonconformist minister's trials with his narrow-minded congregation. The best of her Scottish novels are *Passages in the Life of Mrs. Margaret Maitland* (1849), *Merkland* (1851), and *Kirsteen* (1890). Other works include *A Beleaguered City* (1880) and *A Little Pilgrim in the Unseen* (1882), excursions into the realm of the supernatural. She also published *Annals of a Publishing House: William Blackwood and his Sons* (1897), a work of importance to literary historians.

Oliver \'äl-i-vər\, Mary (b. Sept. 10, 1935, Cleveland, Ohio, U.S.) American poet whose work reflected a deep communion with the natural world.

Oliver worked for a time as a secretary for Edna St. Vincent Millay's sister. Millay's influence is apparent in Oliver's first book of poetry, *No Voyage and Other Poems* (1963). Some of these lyrical nature poems are set in the Ohio of Oliver's youth. Her childhood plays a more central role in *The River Styx, Ohio, and Other Poems* (1972), in which she attempted to recreate the past through memory and myth. *The Night Traveler* (1978) explores the themes of birth, decay, and death through the conceit of a classical journey into the underworld.

Her volume *American Primitive* (1983), which won a Pulitzer Prize, glorifies the natural world, reflecting the American fascination with the ideal of the pastoral life. In *House of Light* (1990) Oliver explores the rewards of solitude in nature. *New and Selected Poems* (1992) is a later collection.

Oliver Twist \'äl-i-vər-'twist\ (*in full* Oliver Twist; or, The Parish Boy's Progress, by "Boz") Novel by Charles DICKENS, published serially from 1837 to 1839 in *Bentley's Miscellany* and in a three-volume book in 1838. The novel was the first of the author's works to depict realistically the impoverished London underworld and to illustrate his belief that poverty leads to crime.

Illustration by George Cruikshank

Written shortly after adoption of the Poor Law of 1834, which halted government payments to the poor unless they entered workhouses, *Oliver Twist* used the tale of a friendless child, the foundling Oliver Twist, as a vehicle for social criticism. While the novel is Victorian in its emotional appeal, it is decidedly unsentimental in its depiction of poverty and the criminal underworld, especially in its portrayal of the cruel Bill Sikes, who kills his kindly girlfriend Nancy for helping Oliver and who is himself accidentally hung by his own rope.

Olmedo \òl-'mā-<u>th</u>ō\, José Joaquín (b. March 20, 1780, Guayaquil, Ecuador—d. Feb. 19, 1847, Guayaquil) Poet and statesman, whose odes captured the revolutionary spirit of his time and inspired a generation of Romantic poets and patriots. His works have remained monuments to the heroic Latin-American figures who helped their countries achieve independence from Spain.

Olmedo was active in political life while writing poetry. The ode for which he is best remembered, *La victoria de Junín: canto a Bolívar* (1825; "The Victory at Junín: Song to Bolívar"), commemorates the decisive battle won there by the forces of the liberator Simón Bolívar against the Spanish armies. Neoclassical in form, yet Romantic in inspiration and imagery, the *Canto a Bolívar* is considered by many critics the finest example of heroic poetry written in Latin America.

When Ecuador became a republic in 1830, Olmedo was elected its first vice president, but he declined the honor, preferring to remain active in local politics. In his later poetry he foresaw and deplored the trend toward the militarism and civil wars that were beginning to undermine the hard-won unity of Latin America.

Olsen \'òl-sən\, Tillie, *original surname* Lerner \'lər-nər\ (b. Jan. 14, 1913, Omaha, Neb., U.S.) American author known for her powerful fiction about the inner lives of the working poor, women, and minorities.

Olsen's early adult life was devoted to political activism and to rearing a family. Her first novel, begun at the age of 19, was set aside for 35 years. Though she found it too painful to finish, Olsen eventually published the reconstructed manuscript as *Yonnondio: From the Thirties* in 1974. The novel tells the story of the Holbrook family, who struggle during the Depression era to survive as coal miners, tenant farmers, and meat packers. *Tell Me A Riddle: A Collection* (1961) contains three short stories and a novella, each a masterpiece in its own right. Olsen used rhythmic, metaphoric language to give a voice to otherwise inarticulate characters.

In her later works Olsen addressed feminist themes and concerns, especially as related to women writers. *Silences* (1978) contains, among other things, a long essay about the author Rebecca Harding Davis, whose career as a writer failed after she married. In 1984 Olsen edited *Mother to Daughter, Daughter to Mother: Mothers on Mothering*.

Olson \'òl-sən\, Charles (John) (b. Dec. 27, 1910, Worcester, Mass., U.S.—d. Jan. 10, 1970, New York, N.Y.) Avant-garde poet and literary theorist, notable for his influence on American poetry during the late 1950s.

Olson was educated at Wesleyan University (Conn.) and Harvard. He taught in Massachusetts at Clark University, Harvard, and Radcliffe College, but his real influence began in the late 1940s as an instructor and then as rector (1951–56) at Black Mountain College in North Carolina.

Olson first gained recognition for *Call Me Ishmael* (1947), a study of the literary influences on Herman Melville's *Moby-Dick*. His concepts of poetry, contained in his 1950 essay *Projective Verse* (published in book form, 1959), influenced such poets as Robert Creeley, Robert Duncan, and Denise Levertov. Olson's *The Maximus Poems* (1953, 1956, combined 1960) is a long sequence of poems continued in subsequent volumes, while *In Cold Hell, in Thicket* (1953) and *The Distances* (1960) contain some of his best-known shorter poems. *See also* BLACK MOUNTAIN POETS.

Olson \'ōl-sən\, Elder (James) (b. March 9, 1909, Chicago, Ill., U.S.—d. July 25, 1992, Albuquerque, N.M.)   American poet, playwright, and literary critic. He was a leading member of the Neo-Aristotelian school of critical theory that came to prominence in the 1940s at the University of Chicago.

After graduating from the University of Chicago, Olson taught for several years at the Armour Institute of Technology (now Illinois Institute of Technology) in Chicago. He returned to the University of Chicago in 1942 and taught there until his retirement in 1977. Along with his teachers and colleagues at Chicago, Richard McKeon, R.S. Crane, and Wayne Booth, Olson became known for his responses to the New Criticism. In *Critics and Criticism* (1952; the Neo-Aristotelian manifesto edited by Crane) and later works that included *Tragedy and the Theory of Drama* (1961) and *The Theory of Comedy* (1968), Olson argued for a systematic, comprehensive, and pluralistic approach to criticism based on the principles of Aristotle's *Poetics*. He attacked the New Critics for focusing on the diction of poetry and argued that criticism should concentrate on poetic wholes instead. *See also* CHICAGO CRITICS.

Although less widely known than his criticism, Olson's poetry is characterized by rich imagery, a serious and elegiac tone, sharp wit, technical dexterity, and metaphysical themes. His works include *Thing of Sorrow* (1934), *The Scarecrow Christ and Other Poems* (1954), *Plays and Poems* (1958), *Olson's Penny Arcade* (1975), and *Last Poems* (1984).

Olympian \ō-'lim-pē-ən\   In classical mythology, one of the gods regarded as inhabiting Mount Olympus.

Olympus \ō-'lim-pəs\, *also called* Mount Olympus.   In Greek mythology, the abode of the gods and the site of the throne of Zeus. The name Olympus was used for several other mountains as well as hills, villages, and mythical personages in Greece and Asia Minor.

The historical Mount Olympus, the highest mountain peak in Greece, is part of the Olympus massif near the Gulf of Thérmai of the Aegean Sea and lies astride the border between the Greek regions of Macedonia and Thessaly.

'Omar Khayyām \ō-,mär-,kī-'yäm, ,ō-mər, ķī-, -'yòm, -'yam\, *Persian in full* Abū ol-Fatḥ 'Omar ebn Ebrahīm ol-Khayyāmī \ōl-'ķī-,yò-,mē\ (b. May 18, 1048, Neyshābūr [Iran]—d. Dec. 4, 1131, Neyshābūr)   Persian poet, mathematician, and astronomer, renowned in his own country and time for his scientific achievements but known to English-speaking readers for his *robāīyāt* ("quatrains") in the version THE RUBÁIYÁT OF OMAR KHAYYÁM, published in 1859 by Edward FitzGerald.

Philosophy, jurisprudence, history, mathematics, medicine, and astronomy are among the subjects he mastered, but few of his prose writings survive. 'Omar Khayyām's fame in the West rests upon the collection of quatrains attributed to him. (The *robā'ī* [or ruba'i, as it is perhaps better known], a Persian verse form, is a quatrain with the rhyme scheme *aaba*.) His poems had attracted comparatively little attention until they inspired FitzGerald to publish his celebrated *The Rubáiyát of Omar Khayyám*. Many of the verses, however, are of doubtful attribution—including the famous quatrain beginning "A Book of Verses Underneath the Bough." Several scholars have attempted to further authenticate 'Omar Khayyām's work and to date most agree on a core group of about 50 quatrains with controversy over some 200 additional quatrains. Each of 'Omar Khayyām's quatrains was originally composed on a particular occasion and forms a complete poem in itself.

Omoo \'ō-,mü\ (*in full* Omoo: A Narrative of Adventures in the South Seas)   Novel by Herman MELVILLE, published in 1847 as a sequel to his novel *Typee*. Based on Melville's own experiences in the South Pacific, this episodic novel, in a more comical vein than that of *Typee*, tells of the narrator's participation in a mutiny on a whale ship and his subsequent wanderings in Tahiti with the former doctor of the ship.

Omotoso \,ō-mō-'tō-sō\, Kole (b. April 21, 1943, Akure, Western State, Nigeria)   Nigerian novelist, playwright, and critic who wrote from a Yoruba background and coupled the folklore he learned as a child with his adult studies in Arabic and English. His major themes include interracial marriage, comic aspects of the Biafran-Nigerian conflict, intertribal friendships, and familial relationships.

After attending local schools, Omotoso attended King's College, Lagos, Nigeria, and the University of Ibadan. His works include the novels *The Edifice* (1971), *The Combat* (1972), *Sacrifice* (1973), *Fella's Choice* (1974), *The Scales* (1974), and *To Borrow A Wandering Leaf* (1978); a collection of shorter tales, *Miracles and Other Stories* (1973); the plays *The Curse* (1976) and *Shadows in the Horizon* (1977); and many critical articles and reviews. His "historical fiction," *Just Before Dawn* (1988), concerns Nigerian history from 1975.

Oña \'ōn-yä\, Pedro de (b. 1570?, Los Confines [Chile]—d. 1643?, Lima [Peru])   First poet known to be born in Chile.

Oña's most famous work, *Primera parte de Arauco domado* (1596; "First Part of the Araucan Conquest"), a verse epic in rhymed couplets, brought him immediate fame. His other works include *El Ignacio de Cantabria* (1639; "Ignatius of Cantabria") and *Temblor de Lima en 1609* ("The Earthquake of Lima in 1609").

Once and Future King, The   Quartet of novels by T.H. WHITE, published in a single volume in 1958. The quartet comprises *The Sword in the Stone* (1938), *The Queen of Air and Darkness*—first published as *The Witch in the Wood* (1939)—*The Ill-Made Knight* (1940), and *The Candle in the Wind* (published in the composite volume, 1958). The series is a retelling of the Arthurian legend, from Arthur's birth to the end of his reign, and is based largely on Sir Thomas Malory's *Le Morte Darthur*.

After White's death, a conclusion to *The Once and Future King* was found among his papers; it was published in 1977 as *The Book of Merlyn*.

Ondaatje \än-'däch-ä\, Michael, *in full* Philip Michael Ondaatje (b. Sept. 12, 1943, Colombo, Ceylon [now Sri Lanka])   Canadian novelist and poet who employed a blend of myth, history, jazz, memoirs, and other forms to create his musical prose and poetry.

Ondaatje immigrated to Montreal when he was 19 and subsequently attended the University of Toronto and Queen's University. His first collection of poetry, *The Dainty Monsters* (1967), is a series of lyrics that juxtapose everyday life with mythology. Ondaatje's fascination with the lore of the American West led to one of his most celebrated works, the 1970 pastiche *The Collected Works of Billy the Kid: Left-Handed Poems*. His collection entitled *Secular Love* (1984) contains poetry about the breakup of his marriage. *The Cinnamon Peeler*, another collection of poetry, was published in 1989.

Ondaatje's prose works, better known than his poetry, include *Coming Through Slaughter* (1976), *In the Skin of a Lion* (1987), and *The English Patient* (1992). The last book, noted for the richly described interior lives of its characters, won Ondaatje international recognition.

Ondine \òn-'dēn\   Fictional character derived from European folklore. *See* UNDINE.

one-act play   A form of drama that is to a full-length play as a short story is to a novel. Originally used as a curtain-raiser, or short play presented before the main show, at the end of the 19th century the form became accepted in its own right.

One Day in the Life of Ivan Denisovich \i-'vän-d^yi-'n^yē-sə-v^yich, *Angl* 'ī-vən-də-'nē-sō-vich\ Short novel by Aleksandr SOLZHENITSYN, published in Russian in 1962 as *Odin den Ivana Denisovicha* in the Soviet literary magazine *Novy Mir*, and published in book form the following year. Solzhenitsyn's first literary work—a treatment of his experiences in the Stalinist labor camps—established his reputation and foreshadowed his masterpiece, *The Gulag Archipelago* (1973–75).

Set in the forced-labor camp in which the author was interned from 1950 to 1953, *Ivan Denisovich* describes a typical day in the life of an inmate. Published during Nikita Khrushchev's de-Stalinization program, the work was released without interference from Soviet government censors and Solzhenitsyn became an instant celebrity.

Onegin, Eugene \yū-'jĕn-ō-'nyeg-in, *Russian* ˌə-'n^yā-g^yin\ Fictional character who is the protagonist of Aleksandr Pushkin's masterpiece EUGENE ONEGIN. Onegin is the original superfluous man, a character type common in 19th-century Russian literature. He is a disillusioned aristocrat who is drawn into tragic situations through his inability or unwillingness to take positive action to prevent them.

120 Days of Sodom, The \'säd-əm\ (*in full* The 120 Days of Sodom: or, The Romance of the School for Libertinage) A sexually explicit account of several months of debauchery, written in 1785 in French as *Les 120 Journées de Sodome, ou l'école du libertinage* by the Marquis de SADE while he was imprisoned in the Bastille. It was not published until 1904.

The book tells the infamous tale of four libertines who kidnap selected victims for a nonstop orgy and subject them to rape, torture, and various mutilations. It was responsible for introducing the term sadism into Western culture and became an underground classic in the 19th century before it was granted legitimacy as a work of literature in the 20th.

One Hundred Years of Solitude Novel by Gabriel GARCÍA MÁRQUEZ, published in Spanish as *Cien años de soledad* in 1967. It was considered the author's masterpiece and the foremost example of his style of magic realism.

The author's epic tale of seven generations of the Buendía family spans a hundred years of turbulent Latin-American history, from the postcolonial 1820s to the 1920s. Patriarch José Arcadio Buendía builds the utopian city of Macondo in the middle of a swamp. At first prosperous, the town attracts gypsy hucksters—and the old gypsy writer Melquíades, a stand-in for the author. A tropical storm lasting nearly five years almost destroys the town, and by the fifth Buendía generation its physical decrepitude is matched by the family's depravity. A hurricane finally erases all traces of the city.

By the end of the novel Melquíades is revealed as the narrator; his mysterious manuscripts are in fact the text of the novel. Critics have noted the influence of Argentine writer Jorge Luis Borges in the book's labyrinthine fantasy.

O'Neill \ō-'nēl\, Eugene (Gladstone) (b. Oct. 16, 1888, New York, N.Y., U.S.—d. Nov. 27, 1953, Boston, Mass.) One of the greatest American playwrights and winner of the Nobel Prize for Literature in 1936.

O'Neill attended Princeton University for one year (1906–07), after which he shipped to sea, lived a derelict's existence on the waterfronts of Buenos Aires, Liverpool, and New York City, submerged himself in alcohol, and attempted suicide. While recovering from tuberculosis at a sanitarium in Wallingford, Conn., he began to write plays.

His first full-length play, *Beyond the Horizon*, was produced on Broadway in 1920. O'Neill's capacity for and commitment to work were staggering. Between 1920 and 1943 he completed 20 long plays and a number of shorter ones. His most distin-

guished short plays include four early sea dramas, *Bound East for Cardiff*, *In the Zone*, *The Long Voyage Home*, and *The Moon of the Caribbees*, which were written between 1913 and 1917 and produced in 1924 under the overall title *S.S. Glencairn*; THE EMPEROR JONES (1921); and THE HAIRY APE (1923).

Mary Evans Picture Library

O'Neill's plays were written from an intensely personal point of view, deriving directly from the scarring effects of his tragic relationships with his family—his mother and father, who loved and tormented each other; his older brother, who both loved and corrupted him and died of alcoholism in middle age; and O'Neill himself, caught and torn between love for and rage at all three.

Among his most celebrated long plays are ANNA CHRISTIE (1922); DESIRE UNDER THE ELMS (1925) and MOURNING BECOMES ELECTRA (1931), both of which evoked the starkness and inevitability of Greek tragedy that he felt in his own life; and THE GREAT GOD BROWN (1926) and STRANGE INTERLUDE (1928), in which O'Neill used experimental techniques such as expressionistic dialogue and spoken asides that have since become accepted on the stage but at the time were revolutionary. Following a long succession of tragic visions, O'Neill's only comedy, the lighthearted and nostalgic AH, WILDERNESS! (1933), appeared on Broadway. THE ICEMAN COMETH (1946), the most complex and perhaps the finest of the O'Neill tragedies, followed.

Even in his last writings, O'Neill's youth continued to absorb his attention. The posthumous production of LONG DAY'S JOURNEY INTO NIGHT in 1956 brought to light an agonizingly autobiographical play, one of O'Neill's greatest. Its sequel, A MOON FOR THE MISBEGOTTEN (1952), was produced the following year.

One of Ours Novel by Willa CATHER, published in 1922. This story of a Nebraska farm boy who dies fighting in France in World War I took four years to write and was a best-seller in its time. It won a Pulitzer Prize in 1923. Cather based the plot on letters written by a cousin who had died in World War I.

Onetti \ō-'net-ē\, Juan Carlos (b. July 1, 1909, Montevideo, Uruguay—d. May 30, 1994, Madrid, Spain) Uruguayan-born novelist and short-story writer who was awarded Uruguay's national literature prize in 1963 and Spain's prestigious Cervantes Prize in 1980.

Onetti moved to Buenos Aires in 1943 and remained there until 1955, working as a reporter for the Reuters News Agency and as a journalist for several publications. His first novella, *El pozo* (1939; "The Well"), depicts the aimless life of a man lost within a city where he is unable to communicate with others and reflects the tenor of the corrupt and bureaucratized Uruguayan national scene of the 1930s. He expanded on the subject of city life devoid of spiritual meaning in the novel *Tierra de nadie* (1942; "No-Man's-Land"). In *La vida breve* (1950; *A Brief Life*), perhaps his best-known work, Onetti created the mythical city of Santa María, which also is the setting of later works. *Un sueño realizado y otros cuentos* ("A Dream Fulfilled and Other Stories"), a collection of stories written in the 1940s, was published in 1951.

After his return to Montevideo in 1955, Onetti wrote the novel *El astillero* (1961; *The Shipyard*), which indicts chaotic Uruguayan political and economic conditions and again attacks the bureaucracy. Onetti's *Obras completas* ("Complete Works") were published in 1970. Later works include the novel *La muerte y la niña* (1973; "Death and the Little Girl"), *Cuentos completos* (1974; "Complete Stories"), the novel *Tiempo de abrazar* (1974; "Time to Embrace"), *Cuando entonces* (1987), and *Cuando ya no importa* (1993; "What's the Use?"). His articles on literary and political figures written between 1939 and 1968 were collected under the title *Réquiem por Faulkner* (1975; "Requiem for Faulkner").

On First Looking into Chapman's Homer \'chap-mən . . . 'hō-mər\ Sonnet by John KEATS, first published in *The Examiner* in 1816 and later published in *Poems* (1817), Keats's first collection. Considered the poet's first mature poem, the sonnet was inspired by Keats's having pored over a 1616 folio edition of George Chapman's English translations of the *Iliad* and the *Odyssey*. It is Keats's response to heroism.

On Heroes, Hero-Worship, and the Heroic in History Six essays by Thomas CARLYLE, published in 1841 and based on a series of lectures he delivered in 1840. The lectures, which glorified great men throughout history, were enormously popular. In the essays he discusses different types of heros and offers examples of each type, including divinities (pagan myths), prophets (Muḥammad), poets (Dante and William Shakespeare), priests (Martin Luther and John Knox), men of letters (Samuel Johnson and Jean-Jacques Rousseau), and rulers (Oliver Cromwell and Napoleon).

Onitsha market literature \ō-'nē-chä\ Subliterary genre of sentimental, moralistic novellas and pamphlets produced in the 20th century by a semiliterate school of writers (students, fledgling journalists, and taxi drivers) and sold at the bustling Onitsha market in eastern Nigeria. Characteristic features of the Onitsha writings include a fascination with Westernized urban life and the desire to warn the newly arrived against the corruption and dangers that accompany it. Typical titles are "Rose Only Loved My Money," "Drunkards Believe Bar as Heaven," "Why Some Rich Men Have No Trust in Some Girls," "How to Get a Lady in Love," and "How John Kennedy Suffered in Life and Death Suddenly." Usually less than 50 pages in length, Onitsha market literature encompasses sentimental novelettes, political tracts, and how-to guides on writing love letters, handling money, and attaining prosperity. As a literary phenomenon the Onitsha market literature, similar in many ways to the chapbooks of 17th- and 18th-century England, are important for the close relationship of writer and audience without reference to a world outside Africa.

On Love Philosophical discourse by STENDHAL, published in 1822 as *De l'amour*. The work was prompted by Stendhal's hopeless love for Métilde Dembowski.

The first part of *On Love* is an analysis of love, in which Stendhal lists four kinds of love: physical love, purely sexual in scope; love as a social game, removed from passion; vanity love, a type necessary for high social standing; and passion, the finest form of love, which the author idealized and to which he devotes most of his attention. Stendhal also outlines seven progressive stages of love, from admiration to "crystallization," or the process by which the lover attributes all types of perfection to the beloved, just as a tree branch, tossed into a salt mine, is covered with salt crystals that shine like diamonds. In the second part of the work Stendhal presents his views, considered radical at the time, against marriage and favoring the full education and moral liberty of women.

onocentaur \ˌän-ə-'sen-ˌtȯr, -ˌtär\ [Greek *onokéntauros* demon inhabiting waste places, from *ónos* ass + *kéntauros* centaur] A mythological creature having the head and arms and upper torso of a human being and the body and legs of an ass.

onomatopoeia \ˌän-ə-ˌmät-ə-'pē-ə, -ˌmat-\ [Greek *onomatopoiía*, from *onomat-*, *ónoma* name + *poieîn* to make] **1.** The naming of a thing or action by a vocal imitation of the sound associated with it (such as *buzz* or *hiss*). **2.** The use of words whose sound suggests the sense. This occurs frequently in poetry, where a line of verse can express a characteristic of the thing being portrayed. The following lines from "The Brook" by Alfred, Lord Tennyson are an example:

> I chatter over stony ways,
> In little sharps and trebles,
> I bubble into eddying bays,
> I babble on the pebbles.

On the Eve Novel by Ivan TURGENEV, published in Russian as *Nakanune* in 1860. It is a major work concerning love amid a time of war and revolutionary social change.

Set in 1853, *On the Eve* deals with the problems facing the younger intelligentsia on the eve of the Crimean War and speculates on the outcome of the emancipation of the serfs in 1861. Elena, its principal character, is a charming yet serious-minded, morally courageous young woman. Her concern for justice finds no outlet in her small circle of family and friends until she is introduced to the young Bulgarian patriot Insarov, whose idealism matches her own and who becomes Elena's companion and the catalyst for the changes in her life.

On the Nature of Things Long poem written in Latin as *De rerum natura* by LUCRETIUS which sets forth the physical theory of the Greek philosopher Epicurus. The title of Lucretius' work translates that of the chief work of Epicurus, *Peri physeōs* (*On Nature*).

Lucretius divided his argument into six books. Books I and II establish the main principles of the atomic universe, refute the rival theories of the pre-Socratic cosmic philosophers Heracleitus, Empedocles, and Anaxagoras, and covertly attack the Stoics, a school of moralists rivaling that of Epicurus. Book III demonstrates the atomic structure and mortality of the soul and ends with a triumphant sermon on the theme "Death is nothing to us." Book IV describes the mechanics of sense perception, thought, and certain bodily functions and condemns sexual passion. Book V describes the creation and working of the world and the celestial bodies and the evolution of life and human society. Book VI explains remarkable phenomena of the earth and sky, in particular, thunder and lightning. The poem ends with a description of the plague at Athens, a somber picture of death that contrasts with the depiction of spring and birth in the invocation to Venus with which the poem opens.

The linguistic style of the poem is notable. Lucretius' aim was to render the bald and abstract Greek prose of Epicurus into Latin hexameters at a time when Latin had no philosophic vocabulary. He succeeded by turning common words to a technical use. When necessary, he invented words. He freely used alliteration and assonance, solemn and often metrically convenient archaic forms, and old constructions. He imitated or echoed Homer, the dramatists Aeschylus and Euripides, the poet Callimachus, the historian Thucydides, and the physician Hippocrates.

On the Road   Novel by Jack KEROUAC, published in 1957. A formless book, it describes a series of frenetic trips back and forth across the United States by a number of penniless young people who are in love with life, beauty, jazz, sex, drugs, speed, and mysticism. The book was one of the first novels associated with the Beat movement of the 1950s.

On the Sublime (*Greek* Peri hypsous)   Treatise on literary criticism by LONGINUS, dating to about the 1st century AD. The earliest surviving manuscript, from the 10th century, was first printed in 1554.

On the Sublime is given a 1st-century-AD date because it was a response to a work of that period by Caecilius of Calacte, a Sicilian rhetorician. It contains 17 chapters on figures of speech, which have occupied critics and poets ever since they were written. About a third of the manuscript is lost.

The author defines sublimity (*hypsos*) in literature as the moral and imaginative power of the writer that pervades his work. This is the first known instance in which greatness in literature is ascribed to qualities innate in the writer rather than his art. The author further suggests that greatness of thought, if not inborn, may be acquired by emulating great authors such as Homer, Demosthenes, and Plato. Illustrative quotations recorded in *On the Sublime* occasionally preserved work that would otherwise now be lost; for example, one of Sappho's odes. *See also* SUBLIME.

Ó Nuallain, Brian.   Pseudonym of Flann O'BRIEN.

Oodgeroo *in full* Oodgeroo Noonuccal \'ü-jə-,rü-'nü-nə-kəl\   Aboriginal name of Australian writer who originally published under the name Kath WALKER.

Ōoka Makoto \'ō-ō-,kä-'mä-kō-,tō\ (b. Feb. 16, 1931, Mishima City, Shizuoka prefecture, Japan)   Prolific Japanese poet and literary critic who was largely responsible for bringing contemporary Japanese poetry to the attention of the Western world.

The son of a tanka poet, Ōoka graduated from Tokyo University in 1953 and subsequently worked as a newspaper reporter and college professor. A book of verse, *Kioku to genzai* (1956; "Memory and the Present"), established his reputation as a poet. He was especially noted for his criticism, however, including that collected in the volume *Nihon shiika kikō* (1978; "Travels Through Japanese Poetry").

In the 1970s Ōoka began experimenting with linked verse (*renga*), in which several poets contribute verses to a single poem. He extended his *renga* experiments to poets in the West as well, and during the 1980s the results were published in a number of anthologies. Translations of Ōoka's poetry were collected and published in English in the volumes *A String Around Autumn* (1982) and *Elegy and Benediction* (1991). His *The Colors of Poetry: Essays in Classic Japanese Verse* (1991) contains eight essays on Japanese poetry. The English translation *A Poet's Anthology* was published in 1993.

Ōoka Shōhei \'ō-ō-,kä-'shō-,hä\ (b. March 6, 1909, Tokyo, Japan—d. Dec. 25, 1988, Tokyo)   Japanese novelist famous for his depiction of the fate of Japanese soldiers during World War II.

Ōoka studied French literature at Kyoto University and was profoundly influenced as a writer by Stendhal, whose works he translated. He was drafted in 1944, fought in the Philippines, and was captured by U.S. soldiers in 1945. His first novel, *Furyoki* (1948; "Prisoner of War"), reflected these experiences. His best-known novel is *Nobi* (1951; *Fires on the Plain*; film, 1952), which tells the story of Tamura, a sick Japanese soldier wandering in the Philippine jungles in the aftermath of the war who eventually goes mad and is saved by his Christian faith. The novel was widely translated and was ranked with the finest works of war literature. *Kaei* (1958–59; "Under the Shadow of the Cherry Blossoms") is a story of a prostitute's suicide. Ōoka also published several collections of essays.

Opaliński \ō-på-'lēⁿ-skʸē\, Krzysztof (b. 1609, Sieraków, Pol.—d. Dec. 7, 1655, Włoszakowice, near Poznań)   Noted Polish satirist.

A highly educated and well-traveled man, and governor (*wojewoda*) of the province of Poznania, Opaliński figured in the history of Polish literature as the author of *Satyry albo przestrogi do naprawy rządu i obyczajów w Polszcze należące* (1650; "Satires or Warnings on the Reform of the Government and Customs in Poland"). In this work, which was widely read in Poland during the 17th century, Opaliński attacked the injustice and abuses afflicting contemporary Polish life and castigated its society in vivid and realistic satires.

Open Boat, The   Short story by Stephen CRANE, published in the collection *The Open Boat and Other Tales of Adventure* in 1898. It recounts the efforts of four survivors of a shipwreck—a newspaper correspondent and the ship's cook, captain, and oiler—as they attempt to remain afloat in a dinghy on the rough seas. Told from a shifting point of view, the narrative reveals nature's indifference.

open couplet or **run-on couplet**   In poetry, a couplet the sense of which requires completion by what follows; a dependent couplet, one that by itself does not contain a complete or relatively complete thought. *See also* COUPLET.

Open Theatre   Experimental United States theater company founded in 1963 in New York City by Peter Feldman and Joseph Chaikan. The group—made up of actors, playwrights, musicians, and choreographers—sought to explore the possibilities of uniting improvisation, pantomime, music, and dance in new dramatic productions. Playwrights worked closely with the entire troupe, and they generated communal works that usually addressed subjects of current political or social relevance.

The best-known Open Theatre productions were *The Serpent* (1969), written by Jean-Claude Van Itallie, and *Terminal* (1969–70), from a text by Susan Yankowitz. The Open Theatre disbanded in 1973.

Open Window, The   Frequently anthologized short story by SAKI, first published in the collection *Beasts and Super-Beasts* in 1914. Vera, a charming 15-year-old, plays a practical joke on a nervous visitor, causing him to flee the house. The story's surprise ending, its witty, concise narrative, and its slightly sinister tone are all trademarks of Saki's fiction.

opera \'äp-rə, 'äp-ə-rə\ [Italian, short for *opera musicale,* literally, musical work]   A drama set to music and made up of vocal pieces with orchestral accompaniment and interludes.

Opera had its origins in the liturgical drama of the Middle Ages, which was combined in 16th-century Florence with contemporary notions of classical Greek tragedy. The subjects chosen by such early operatic composers as Jacopo Peri, Jacopo Corsi, Francesco Cavalli, and Claudio Monteverdi were the ancient myths about figures like Daphne, Ulysses, and Orpheus.

In Paris at the court of Louis XIV the new art was encouraged in the lavish works of Jean-Baptiste Lully, while at the court in Vienna the Italian operas of Pietro Antonio Cesti were performed. In England the development was more sketchy. When opera did become popular in London, in the middle of the 18th century, it was in a form imported from Italy and refined by the German-born composer George Frideric Handel. Meanwhile, the achievements of W.A. Mozart in reconciling music and drama, particularly in comic works like *The Marriage of Figaro* and *The Magic Flute*, set standards that remain unsurpassed. In the 19th century opera developed along national lines. In Italy, Giovanni Bellini's affecting works and Gaetano Donizetti's tragedies and comedies preceded the great achievements of Giuseppi Verdi, whose popular operas include *Rigoletto*, *La traviata*, and *Falstaff*. The great Italian tradition was continued at the turn of the century by Giacomo Puccini's *Tosca*, *La Bohème*, and *Madama Butterfly*. In Germany the most important figure was Richard Wagner, whose music dramas revolutionized opera. His major works—*Die Meistersinger*, *Tristan und Isolde*, *Parsifal*, and *Der Ring des Nibelungen*—remain among the peaks of operatic achievement. In France, Russia, and elsewhere nationalism was also prevalent. Opera has remained a vital art in the 20th century, with composers like Richard Strauss and Alban Berg making major contributions to the form.

opera omnia \ˈōp-ə-rə-ˈäm-nē-ə, ˈäp-\ [Latin, literally, all works] The complete works of a writer.

Ophelia \ō-ˈfēl-yə\ Fictional character in William Shakespeare's tragedy HAMLET. Ophelia is the symbol of innocence gone mad.

Opie \ˈō-pē\, Amelia, *original surname* Alderson \ˈȯl-dər-sən\ (b. Nov. 12, 1769, Norwich, Norfolk, Eng.—d. Dec. 2, 1853, Norwich) British novelist and poet whose best work, *Father and Daughter* (1801), influenced the development of the 19th-century popular novel.

Opie had no formal schooling but moved in intellectual circles that included William Godwin, Mary Wollstonecraft, Sydney Smith, Madame de Staël, and John Horne Tooke. In 1798 she married John Opie, a self-educated painter.

Between 1790 and 1834 Opie wrote 13 works of prose—including *Adeline Mowbray*, 3 vol. (1804), based on the life of Mary Wollstonecraft, and *Valentine's Eve*, 3 vol. (1816)—and five books of verse. She became a Quaker in 1825, working with philanthropist Elizabeth Fry and supporting the antislavery movement. This decision came at some cost to Opie, for she was known as a lover of society.

O Pioneers! Regional novel by American writer Willa CATHER, published in 1913. The work is known for its vivid re-creation of the hardships of prairie life and of the struggle of immigrant pioneer women. The novel was partially based on Cather's Nebraska childhood, and it reflected the author's belief in the primacy of spiritual and moral values over the purely material. Its heroine, Alexandra Bergson, exemplified the courage and purpose Cather felt were necessary to subdue the wild land. The title is taken from Walt Whitman's poem "Pioneers! O Pioneers!" which, like the novel, celebrated frontier virtues of strength and inner spirit.

Opitz \ˈō-pits\, Martin, *surname in full* Opitz von Boberfeld \fȯn-ˈbō-bər-ˌfelt\ (b. Dec. 23, 1597, Bunzlau, Silesia [now Bolesławiec, Poland]—d. Aug. 20, 1639, Danzig [now Gdańsk, Pol.]) German poet and literary theorist who is chiefly known for reforming German poetry.

Opitz studied at the universities of Frankfurt an der Oder, Heidelberg, and Leiden. He then led a wandering life in the service of various territorial nobles. In 1625, as a reward for a requiem poem on the death of Charles Joseph of Austria, he was crowned laureate by the Holy Roman emperor Ferdinand II. In 1629 Opitz was elected to the Fruchtbringende Gesellschaft,

the most important of the literary societies that aimed to reform the German language. From 1635 until his death he lived at Danzig, where Władysław IV of Poland made him his historiographer and secretary.

Opitz was the head of the so-called First Silesian school of poets and during his life was regarded as the greatest German poet. His influential *Buch von der deutschen Poeterey*, written in 1624, established long-standing rules for the "purity" of language, style, verse, and rhyme in poetry. The scholarly, stilted, and courtly style introduced by Opitz and exemplified in his own work dominated German poetry until the middle of the 18th century. Most of Opitz' verse is didactic and descriptive—formal elaborations of carefully considered themes—and the generation of poets who built upon his work far outshone him. He also did a number of significant translations.

Oppen \ˈäp-ən, ˈȯp-\, George (b. April 24, 1908, New Rochelle, N.Y., U.S.—d. July 7, 1984, Sunnyvale, Calif.) American poet and political activist, one of the chief proponents of objectivism.

Oppen grew up in San Francisco and briefly attended Oregon State University, where he met his wife. From 1930 to 1933 Oppen and his wife ran the To Publishers press, which published *An "Objectivist" Anthology* (1932), a seminal work in the history of American poetry. The book was edited by Louis Zukofsky and contained work by Ezra Pound, T.S. Eliot, and William Carlos Williams, among others.

Oppen's own first book of poems, *Discrete Series*, was published in 1934. These spare, precisely written verses earned Oppen a reputation as one of the foremost objectivist poets, who celebrated simplicity over formal structure and rhyme and emphasized the poem as an object in itself, not as a vehicle of meaning or association. Oppen became active in the U.S. Communist Party in the mid-1930s. In 1950 he fled to Mexico City to avoid persecution because of his politics, but he returned in 1958 and began writing again. *The Materials* (1962) was his first book of poetry in 28 years. Most critics agree that Oppen's best work is *Of Being Numerous* (1968), which won a Pulitzer Prize. *The Collected Poems of George Oppen* was published in 1975, and *Primitive*, his last volume of poetry, in 1978.

Oppenheim \ˈäp-ən-ˌhīm\, E. Phillips, *in full* Edward (b. Oct. 22, 1866, London, Eng.—d. Feb. 3, 1946, St. Peter Port, Guernsey, Channel Islands) British author of novels and short stories dealing with international espionage and intrigue, internationally popular for more than 50 years.

Oppenheim's first novel, *Expiation* (1886), and subsequent thrillers won him the attention of a wealthy New York businessman who gave Oppenheim a high-paying job and freed him to devote most of his time to writing. The novels, volumes of short stories, and plays that followed, totaling more than 150 in all, were peopled with sophisticated heroes, adventurous spies, and dashing noblemen. Among his well-known works are *The Long Arm of Mannister* (1910), *The Moving Finger* (1911), and *The Great Impersonation* (1920).

Opportunity (*in full* Opportunity: A Journal of Negro Life) African-American magazine associated with the Harlem Renaissance and published from 1923 to 1949. The editor, Charles S. Johnson, aimed to give voice to black culture, hitherto neglected by mainstream American publishing. Johnson sponsored three literary contests to encourage young writers to submit their work. The 1925 winners included Zora Neale Hurston, Langston Hughes, and Countee Cullen. *Ebony and Topaz, A Collectanea* (1927) was an anthology of the best works published in the magazine. *See also* HARLEM RENAISSANCE.

Optic, Oliver *see* William Taylor ADAMS.

Optimist's Daughter, The Pulitzer Prize-winning short novel by Eudora WELTY, published in 1972. This partially autobiographical story explores the subtle bonds between parent and child and the complexities of love and grief.

opusculum \ō-'pəs-kyə-ləm\ *plural* opuscula \-lə\ [Latin, diminutive of *opus* work] A minor work (as of literature)—normally used in the plural.

oracle \'òr-ə-kəl\ [Latin *oraculum,* a derivative of *orare* to pray to, supplicate] Divine communication delivered in response to a petitioner's request; also, the seat of prophecy itself. In the ancient world, oracles were a branch of divination but differed from the casual pronouncements of augurs by being associated with a definite person or place.

The most famous ancient oracle was that of Apollo at DELPHI, located on the slopes of Mount Parnassus above the Gulf of Corinth. Traditionally, the oracle first belonged to Gaea (Earth) but later was either given to or stolen by Apollo. At Delphi the medium was a woman over 50, known as the Pythia, who lived apart from her husband and dressed in a maiden's clothes. Though the oracle, at first called Pytho, was known to Homer and was the site of a Mycenaean settlement, its fame did not become known throughout the Greek world until the 7th and 6th centuries BC, when Apollo's advice or sanction was sought by lawmakers, colonists, and founders of cults. *See also* DODONA.

oral tradition *see* FOLK LITERATURE.

oratory \'òr-ə-ˌtòr-ē\ [Latin *oratoria,* a derivative of *orator* public speaker, orator] The rationale and practice of persuasive public speaking. Oratory is instrumental and practical, as distinguished from poetic or literary composition, which traditionally aims at beauty and pleasure, and it relies on the use of rhetoric for its effectiveness. *See also* RHETORIC.

orc \'òrk\ A mythical creature (such as a sea monster, giant, or ogre) of horrid form or aspect.

The word *orc* in English has two distinct sources. *Orc* in reference to a vaguely cetacean sea monster is borrowed from one or more Romance words, as French *orque* or Italian *orca,* all ultimately descended from Latin *orca,* which probably denoted a small cetacean such as the grampus. In Ludovico Ariosto's epic *Orlando furioso,* the heroine Angelica is set out as a victim for a man-eating *orca,* in a literary recasting of the Andromeda myth.

A different word *orc,* alluding to a demon or ogre, appears in Old English glosses of about 800 and in the compound word *orcnēas* ("monsters") in the poem *Beowulf.* As with Italian *orco* ("ogre") and the word *ogre* itself, it ultimately derives from Latin *Orcus,* a god of the underworld. The Old English creatures were most likely the inspiration for the orcs that appear in J.R.R. Tolkien's *The Lord of the Rings* trilogy.

Orczy \'òrt-sē\, Baroness Emmuska (b. Sept. 23, 1865, Tarnaörs, Hung.—d. Nov. 12, 1947, London, Eng.) Hungarianborn British novelist, chiefly remembered as the author of THE SCARLET PIMPERNEL, one of the greatest popular successes of the 20th century.

The only child of Baron Felix Orczy, a noted composer and conductor, she was educated in Brussels and Paris. She became famous in 1905 with the publication of *The Scarlet Pimpernel,* set in the times of the French Revolution. Baroness Orczy's sequels to the work were less successful than the original. She also wrote several detective stories, including *Lady Molly of Scotland Yard* (1910) and *Unravelled Knots* (1925).

Ordeal of Richard Feverel, The \'rich-ərd-'fev-ər-əl\ Third novel by George MEREDITH, published in 1859. It is typical of his best work, full of allusion and metaphor, lyrical prose and witty dialogue, with a deep exploration of the psychology

of motive and rationalization. The novel's subject is the relationship between a cruelly manipulative father and a son who loves a girl of a lower social class. Both men are self-deluded and proud, and the story's ending is tragic. When it was first published, some readers considered the novel prurient and, as a result, it was banned by the leading lending libraries.

oread \'òr-ē-əd, -ˌad\ [Greek *oreiad-, oreiás,* a derivative of *óros* mountain] In classical mythology, any of the nymphs of mountains, hills, and grottoes.

Oresteia \ˌòr-es-'tē-ə, -'tī-, -'tā-\ A trilogy of tragic dramas by AESCHYLUS, first performed in 458 BC. It was his last work and is the only complete trilogy of Greek dramas that has survived. The *Oresteia* tells the story of the House of Atreus. The first play, *Agamemnon,* named for its hero, portrays the victorious return of the king from the Trojan War and his murder by his wife, Clytemnestra, and her lover, Aegisthus. At the play's end Clytemnestra and her lover rule Argos. The work has extraordinary, sustained dramatic and poetic power. Particularly notable are the fascinating richness of Clytemnestra's deceitful words and the striking choral songs, which raise in metaphorical and often enigmatic terms the major themes—of theology, politics, and blood relationships—that are elaborated throughout the trilogy.

The second play, *Choēphoroi* (*Libation Bearers*), takes its title from the chorus of women servants who come to pour propitiatory offerings at the tomb of the murdered Agamemnon. It details the revenge of Agamemnon's daughter Electra and his son Orestes. The siblings together invoke the aid of the dead Agamemnon in their plans. Orestes then slays Aegisthus, but Orestes' subsequent murder of Clytemnestra is committed reluctantly, at the god Apollo's bidding. Orestes' attempts at self-justification then falter, and he flees, guilt-wracked, maddened, and pursued by the female incarnations of his mother's curse, the Furies (Erinyes).

The third play, *Eumenides,* opens at the shrine of Apollo at Delphi, where Orestes has taken sanctuary from the Furies. At the command of the Delphic oracle, Orestes journeys to Athens to stand trial for his matricide. There the goddess Athena organizes a trial with a jury of citizens. The Furies are his accusers, Apollo his advocate. The jury is evenly divided in its vote, and Athena casts the tie-breaking vote for Orestes' acquittal. The Furies then turn their vengeful resentment against the city itself, but Athena persuades them, in return for a home and cult, to bless Athens instead and reside there as the Eumenides ("Kind Goddesses") of the play's title. The trilogy thus ends with the cycle of retributive bloodshed closed and supplanted by the rule of law and the justice of the state.

Orestes \ò-'res-tēz\ In Greek mythology, son of Agamemnon (king of Mycenae or Argos) and his wife Clytemnestra. According to Homer, Orestes was away when his father returned from Troy to meet his death at the hands of Aegisthus, his wife's lover. On reaching manhood, Orestes avenged his father by killing Aegisthus and Clytemnestra.

According to the poet Stesichorus, Orestes was a small child at the time of Agamemnon's murder and was smuggled to safety by his nurse. Clytemnestra later was warned of her son's retribution in a dream, and Orestes, for the crime of matricide, was haunted by the Furies (Erinyes) after her death.

The story of Orestes was a favorite in ancient art and literature. Aeschylus' *Oresteia* showed its dramatic potentialities, and these were further exploited by Sophocles and Euripides. Aspects of the story were also featured in the work of such later writers as Hans Sachs, Thomas Dekker and Henry Chettle, Joost van den Vondel, Voltaire, Benito Pérez Galdós, and Gerhart Hauptmann.

Orestes \ô-'res-tēz\   Play by EURIPIDES, performed in 408 BC, that retells the story of the aftermath of Orestes' matricide. Euripides set the play in a world where courts of law already exist. In his version, Orestes, his sister Electra, and his cousin and friend Pylades are condemned to death by the men of Argos for the murder. Their uncle Menelaus is too spineless to defend them, and they plot to kill Menelaus' wife, Helen, and to abduct her innocent daughter. This chaos of violence and attempted murder is only resolved by the deus ex machina Apollo, who finally appears and restores harmony.

organic form   The structure of a work that has grown naturally from the author's subject and materials as opposed to that of a work shaped by and conforming to artificial rules. The concept was developed by Samuel Taylor Coleridge to counter those who claimed that the works of William Shakespeare were formless.

organic unity   In literature, a structural principle first discussed by Plato (in *Phaedrus, Gorgias,* and the *Republic*) and later described and defined by Aristotle. The principle calls for internally consistent thematic and dramatic development, analogous to biological growth, which is the recurrent, guiding metaphor throughout Aristotle's writings. Art was expected to grow naturally from a kernel of thought and to seek its own form. The artist was discouraged from interfering with a work's natural growth by adding ornament, wit, love interest, or some other convention.

Organic form was a preoccupation of the German Romantic poets and was also claimed for the novel by Henry James in *The Art of Fiction* (1884).

Orhon inscriptions \'ôr-ˌhòn\, Orhon *also spelled* Orkhon \'ôr-ḳòn\   Oldest extant Turkic writings, discovered in 1889 in the Orhon River valley of northern Mongolia and deciphered in 1893 by the Danish philologist Vilhelm Thomsen. The writings are on two large monuments, erected in AD 732 and 735 in honor of the Turkish prince Kül (died 731) and his brother the emperor Bilge (died 734) and carved in a script also used for inscriptions found in Mongolia, Siberia, and Turkistan and called by Thomsen "Turkish runes." The inscriptions use epic language to tell of the legendary origins of the Turks, the golden age of their history, their subjugation by the Chinese, and their liberation by Bilge. The polished style of the writings suggests considerable earlier development of the Turkic language.

Orientalia \ˌòr-ē-ən-'tāl-yə\   Materials (such as literary, artistic, and archaeological products and remains) related to the Orient.

Origin (*in full* Origin: A Quarterly for the Creative)   American literary magazine largely devoted to poetry, published and edited by poet Cid Corman as a 64-page quarterly in several intermittent series. The first series, published from 1951 to 1957, included works by such classic modern poets as Wallace Stevens and William Carlos Williams, its primary focus was on such younger postwar poets as Denise Levertov, Robert Duncan, and, especially, Robert Creeley, Charles Olson, and Corman himself. *Origin*'s second series (1961–64) included works by Louis Zukofsky, Gary Snyder, and Michael McClure, and Douglas Woolf's short novel *John-Juan* appeared in the third series (1966–71). In addition, the magazine published translations of troubadour poetry, Chinese and Japanese poetry, and works by 20th-century European and Latin-American poets, including César Vallejo. Corman's anthology *The Gist of Origin* (1975) includes selected works from the magazine.

Orion \ô-'rī-ən\   In Greek mythology, a giant and very handsome hunter who was identified as early as Homer with the constellation known by his name. The story of Orion has many

different versions. According to a late legend, he was born of the earth (from a buried bull hide on which three gods had urinated). Some legends have him as the son of Poseidon. He is associated with the island of Chios, from which he is said to have driven the wild beasts, and with the PLEIADES.

Ørjasaeter \'œr-jä-ˌset-ər\, Tore (b. March 3, 1886, Skjåk, Nor.—d. Feb. 29, 1968, Skjåk)   Norwegian poet who worked in the tradition of the ballad and of folk and nature lyrics.

Ørjasaeter's concern with the conflict between the individual and his heritage is the underlying theme of his main works, *Gudbrand Langleite* (1913), *Brumillom* (1920), and *Skuggen* (1927; "The Shadow"), published as an epic trilogy in a revised edition of his collected works in 1941. Ørjasaeter's finest poetry is found in his collection *Elvesong* (1932; "Song of the River"), a cycle of poems that uses a drop of water on its way to the sea as a symbol for the individual longing for freedom and human solidarity. Ørjasaeter also wrote several dramas, including *Christophoros* (1948) and *Den lange bryllaupsreisa* (1949; "The Long Honeymoon").

Orkan \'òr-kån\, Władysław, *pseudonym of* Franciszek Smreczyński \smre-'chēⁿ-skyē\ (b. Nov. 27, 1875, Poręba Wielka, Austro-Hungarian Empire [now in Poland]—d. May 14, 1930, Kraków, Pol.)   Polish poet and writer.

Born into a family of poor highlanders, Orkan received an incomplete education. Most of his works depict the poverty-stricken lives of the highlanders against a natural landscape of great beauty. In his first volume, *Nowele* (1898; "Short Stories"), as well as in *Komornicy* (1900; "Tenant Farmers"), Orkan gave a naturalistic account of highlander-peasant life in his native Tatra region. Later, influenced by the literary and political Young Poland movement, he wrote *W roztokach* (1903; "In Mountain Valleys") and *Drzewiej* (1912; "In the Old Days"). In the first book he rebelled against the exploitation of the poor highlanders by wealthy farmers, and in the second he presented a poetic story about the first settlers in Podhale. He also wrote a volume of verse, *Z tej smutnej ziemi*, and plays.

Orlando \òr-'lan-dō\   Novel by Virginia WOOLF, published in 1928. The fanciful biographical novel pays homage to the family of Woolf's friend Vita Sackville-West from the time of her ancestor Thomas Sackville (1536–1608) and to the family's country estate at Knole, which Woolf frequented.

The novel is also an affectionate portrait of Sackville-West, who, because she was a woman, could not inherit Knole. Written in a pompous biographical voice, the book pokes fun at a genre the author knew well: her father edited the *Dictionary of National Biography*, and her friend Lytton Strachey had written the revolutionary *Eminent Victorians*. Woolf also parodies the changing styles of English literature and explores issues of androgyny and the creative life of women. *Orlando* marked a turning point in Woolf's career. Not only was it a departure from her more introspective works but its spectacular sales also ended her financial worries. Readers praised the book's fluid style, wit, and complex plot.

Orlando \òr-'lan-dō\, *also called* Roland \'rō-lənd\   Hero of the Charlemagne epics. Later literature that features the character includes Matteo Maria Boiardo's *Orlando innamorato* and Ludovico Ariosto's *Orlando furioso*.

Orlando furioso \òr-'län-dō-fū-rē-'ō-sō\ ("Mad Roland")   Epic poem by Italian poet Ludovico ARIOSTO, published in 1516. Considered the finest expression of the artistic tendencies and spiritual attributes of the Italian Renaissance, the poem was a continuation of Matteo Maria Boiardo's *Orlando innamorato*. Both featured Orlando (the Italian form of Roland), a hero in the so-called Charlemagne epics.

The poem contains three principal nuclei around which are grouped a variety of episodes and themes taken mostly from medieval European literature: Orlando's unrequited love for Angelica (which makes him go mad), the war between Christians and Saracens near Paris, and the secondary love story of Ruggiero and Bradamante.

Ariosto spent much of his adult life writing or revising his masterwork, which he began in 1505. The first two editions consisted of 40 cantos; the definitive third edition of 1532 had 46, written in tightly controlled, subtly nuanced ottava rima verse. A *giunta*, or appendix, known as the *Cinque canti*, or "Five Cantos," was published posthumously in 1545.

Orléans \ȯr-lā-'äⁿ\, Charles, Duke d' (b. Nov. 24, 1394, Paris, Fr.—d. Jan. 4, 1465, Amboise)   The last and one of the greatest of the courtly poets of France, who during exile in England also earned a reputation for his English-language verse. He was the son of Louis, Duke d'Orléans (brother of Charles VI of France).

Charles succeeded to the dukedom in 1407, when his father was assassinated. Henry V of England invaded France in 1415, and in the advance of the French army to Agincourt Charles held high command. Defeated and captured in the ensuing battle, he spent 25 years in England as a prisoner.

His enforced idleness in England gave him leisure to pursue his literary interests; he had written some verse before his capture, and he now composed a complete love-history, mainly in ballades, besides other poems. He also wrote more than 6,000 lines in English, arranged in two love-histories linked by a miscellany.

Charles's release was agreed to on July 2, 1440, and on November 3 he returned to France, where he married Mary of Cleves (his first wife, Isabella, having died in 1409). His son, who became King Louis XII, was born in 1462.

Orley Farm \'ȯr-lē\   Novel by Anthony TROLLOPE, published serially in 1861–62 and in book form in 1862. The story, which revolves around the disputed inheritance of a farm attached to an estate, shows Trollope at his best. In spite of the dramatic and sometimes complicated plot, the novel creates a tranquil portrait of domestic life in mid-Victorian England. Lady Mason, accused of fraud by her husband's child from his first marriage, is a completely realized creation, vacillating between avarice and remorse. Her confession scene is one of the highlights of 19th-century English literature.

Orm \'ȯrm\, *also called* Ormin \'ȯr-min\ (fl. *c.* 1200)   Augustinian canon, author of an early Middle English book of metrical homilies on the Gospels, to which he gave the title *Ormulum*, "because Orm made it." The work (dated on linguistic evidence to about 1200) is of little literary interest but of great value to linguists, for Orm invented an individual and remarkably consistent orthography based on phonetic principles. Intended to help preachers read the work aloud, *Ormulum* shows, for example, the quantity (length) of the vowels by doubling a consonant after a short vowel in a closed syllable, and it distinguishes by three separate symbols sounds that in the Anglo-Celtic or insular script of Old English were all represented by a single symbol.

Oroonoko \ȯr-ù-'nō-kō\ (*in full* Oroonoko; or, The Royal Slave)   Novel by Aphra BEHN, published in 1688. Behn's experiences in the Dutch colony of Surinam in South America provided the plot and the locale for this acclaimed novel about a proud, virtuous African prince who is enslaved and cruelly treated by "civilized" white Christians. Behn's suggestion that "primitive" peoples are morally superior to Europeans was taken by many of her contemporaries as an abolitionist stance. Still her best-known work, the book is one of the earliest examples of the philosophical novel in English, and it influenced the development of the novel in general. *Oroonoko* was adapted for the theater by Thomas Southerne and performed in 1695.

Orpheus \'ȯr-,fyüs, -fē-əs\   Ancient Greek legendary hero endowed with superhuman musical skills. He became the patron of a religious movement based on sacred writings said to be his own.

According to some legends Apollo gave Orpheus his first lyre. Orpheus' singing and playing were so beautiful that animals and even trees and rocks moved about him in dance. Orpheus joined the expedition of the Argonauts, saving them from the music of the Sirens by playing his own, more powerful music. On his return, he married Eurydice, who was soon killed by a snakebite. Overcome with grief, Orpheus ventured to the land of the dead to attempt to bring Eurydice back to life. With his singing and playing he charmed the ferryman Charon and the dog Cerberus, guardians of the River Styx. His music and grief so moved Hades, king of the underworld, that Orpheus was allowed to take Eurydice back with him. Hades' one condition was that neither Orpheus nor Eurydice look back upon leaving the land of the dead. The couple climbed up toward the opening into the land of the living, and Orpheus, seeing the sun again, turned back to share his delight with Eurydice. In that moment, Eurydice disappeared.

Orpheus himself was later killed by the women of Thrace. Accounts of the motive and manner of his death vary, but the earliest known, that of Aeschylus, says that the women were Maenads urged by Dionysus to tear him to pieces in a bacchic orgy because he preferred the worship of the rival god Apollo.

The story of Orpheus was given a happy ending in the anonymous medieval English romance of *Sir Orfeo*. Many later writers, including Pedro Calderón de la Barca (*El divino Orfeo*, 1663), Walter Savage Landor ("Orpheus and Eurydice," 1846–47), and Rainer Maria Rilke (*Die Sonette an Orpheus*, 1923; *Sonnets to Orpheus*), used the story of Orpheus.

Orphic \'ȯr-fik\   Of or relating to Orpheus or to the literature, rites, or doctrines ascribed to him.

Ors y Rovira \'dȯrs-ē-rō-'b̪e-rä\, Eugenio d' (b. Sept. 28, 1882, Barcelona, Spain—d. Sept. 25, 1954, Villanueva y Geltrú)   Catalan essayist, philosopher, and art critic who was a leading ideologue of the Catalan cultural renaissance of the early 20th century.

Ors was by profession a journalist who wrote an influential column (later anthologized) in Catalan called *Glossari*. When he moved to Madrid in 1920, he continued to write *El nuevo glosario* ("The New Glossary") in Castilian. He excelled in a short-essay genre, the *glosa*. In a column in 1906 he coined the term *noucentisme* ("1900-ism") to characterize Catalan culture of the 20th century. He believed that art should be "arbitrary," or subjectivist, breaking with traditional norms. By extending this concept to the political movement of Catalan nationalism, he was able to characterize a whole program of political and cultural renewal for Catalonia. He also wrote a philosophical novel, *La ben plantada* (1911; "Firmly Rooted"), that was one of the most notable works in modern Catalan literature.

Ortega y Gasset \ȯr-'tā-gä-ē-gä-'set\, José (b. May 9, 1883, Madrid, Spain—d. Oct. 18, 1955, Madrid)   Philosopher and humanist who greatly influenced the cultural and literary renaissance of Spain in the 20th century.

Ortega y Gasset studied at Madrid University and in Germany and was influenced by the neo-Kantian philosophical school at Marburg. He diverged from neo-Kantianism in such works as *Adán en el Paraíso* (1910; "Adam in Paradise"), *Meditaciones del Quijote* (1914; *Meditations on Quixote*), and *El tema de nuestro tiempo* (1923; *The Modern Theme*).

Between 1936 and 1945 Ortega y Gasset was a voluntary exile in Europe and Argentina, returning to Spain at the end of World War II. In 1948 he founded the Institute of Humanities in Madrid. Of his other works, the best known are *España invertebrada* (1922; *Invertebrate Spain*) and *La rebelión de las masas* (1929; *The Revolt of the Masses*), in which he characterized 20th-century society as dominated by masses of mediocre and indistinguishable individuals.

orthometry \ȯr-'thäm-ə-trē\ [*ortho-* (as in *orthography*) + Greek *-metria* measurement, meter] The art of correct versification.

Ortigão \ȯr-tē-'gaú\ⁿ\, José Duarte Ramalho (b. Nov. 24, 1836, Porto, Port.—d. Sept. 27, 1915, Lisbon) Portuguese essayist and journalist known for his mastery of Portuguese prose and his critical reflections on his native land.

Ortigão began his literary career at the age of 19 as a contributor to the *Jornal do Porto* ("Porto Journal"). In 1868 he moved to Lisbon to take up an appointment in the office of the Academy of Sciences. In Lisbon he continued writing for Portuguese journals and established contact with progressive intellectuals and writers. Ortigão and his lifelong friend José Eça de Queirós started the satirical review *As farpas* ("The Darts") in 1871, and, after the departure of Eça de Queirós late in 1872, Ortigão produced the review alone until 1888. In his hands, *As farpas* gradually became more didactic and descriptive, a vehicle for disseminating such current intellectual doctrines as humanitarianism, positivism, and aesthetic realism.

Ortigão's outstanding book is probably *A Holanda* (1885; "Holland"), in which he praises the mode of life and achievements of the Dutch people. He opposed the revolution of 1910, which overthrew the monarchy and established a republic, and, in protest, he resigned his public appointments. His complete works were published in 39 volumes (1943–49).

Orton \'ȯrt-ən\, Joe, *byname of* John Kingsley Orton (b. Jan. 1, 1933, Leicester, Leicestershire, Eng.—d. Aug. 9, 1967, London) British playwright noted for his outrageous and macabre farces.

Orton turned to writing in the late 1950s under the encouragement of his lifelong companion, Kenneth Halliwell. A handful of novels the pair wrote at this time were not published, however, and it was not until 1964 that Orton had his first success, when his radio play *The Ruffian on the Stair* was broadcast by the BBC. His three full-length plays, *Entertaining Mr. Sloane* (1964), *Loot* (1965), and *What the Butler Saw* (produced posthumously, 1969), were outrageous black comedies that scandalized audiences with their examination of moral corruption, violence, and sexual rapacity. He also wrote four one-act plays during these years, including *Funeral Games* (1968).

Orton's career was cut short when he was beaten to death by Halliwell, a less successful writer, who immediately afterward committed suicide. John Lahr's *Prick Up Your Ears: The Biography of Joe Orton* was published in 1978.

Orwell \'ȯr-,wel\, George, *pseudonym of* Eric Arthur Blair \'blar\ (b. 1903, Motīhāri, Bengal, India—d. Jan. 21, 1950, London, Eng.) English novelist, essayist, and critic famous for his novels ANIMAL FARM (1945) and NINETEEN EIGHTY-FOUR (1949).

Orwell attended Eton, where he published his first writing in college periodicals. Instead of accepting a scholarship to a university, he decided to follow family tradition and, in 1922, went to Burma (now Myanmar) to serve in the Indian Imperial Police. Later he was to recount his experiences and his reactions to imperial rule in two brilliant autobiographical sketches, "Shooting an Elephant" and "A Hanging," classics of expository prose.

In 1927 Orwell, on leave to England, decided not to return to Burma. Having felt guilty that the barriers of race and caste had prevented his mingling with the Burmese, he thought he could make amends by immersing himself in the life of the poor and outcast of Europe. His subsequent experiences gave Orwell the material for DOWN AND OUT IN PARIS AND LONDON (1933), in which actual incidents are rearranged into something like fiction. Orwell's first novel, *Burmese Days* (1934), established the pattern of his subsequent fiction in its portrayal of a sensitive, conscientious, and emotionally isolated individual who is at odds with an oppressive or dishonest social environment. Other novels of this period were *A Clergyman's Daughter* (1935) and *Keep the Aspidistra Flying* (1936).

During the 1930s he began to consider himself a socialist. By the time his original and unorthodox political treatise *The Road to Wigan Pier* appeared in 1937, Orwell was in Spain, where he had gone to report on the Civil War and stayed to join the Republican militia. In May 1937, after having fought in Barcelona against communists who were trying to suppress their political opponents, he was forced to flee Spain for fear of his life. The experience gave him a lifelong dread of communism, first expressed in the vivid account of his Spanish experiences, HOMAGE TO CATALONIA (1938).

When World War II began, Orwell was rejected for military service, and instead he headed the Indian service of the BBC and then worked as a journalist. The appearance in 1945 of *Animal Farm* made him famous and, for the first time, prosperous. Though it was one of his finest works, it has been overshadowed by his last book, *Nineteen Eighty-four* (1949).

Orzeszkowa \,ȯ-zhe-'shkȯ-vä\, Eliza, *original surname* Pawłowska \pä-'vwȯf-skä\ (b. May 25, 1841, Milkowszczyzna, near Grodno, Russian Empire [now in Belarus]—d. May 18, 1910, Grodno) Polish novelist whose writings are animated by the ideals of social justice, equality, individual freedom.

Born to a family of gentry, she was married at the age of 17 to a landowner, Piotr Orzeszko. When the marriage was annulled 11 years later, she settled in Grodno, where in 1879 she opened a bookshop and publishing house. Her novel *Meir Ezofowicz* (1878; *The Forsaken*) presented a lurid picture of Jewish life in a small town in Belorussia and preached not so much tolerance as assimilation. The Russian authorities closed down her publishing and bookselling operation in 1882, placing her under police surveillance for five years.

Orzeszkowa's well-known peasant novels include *Dziurdziowie* (1885; "The Dziurdzia Family"), a shocking picture of the ignorance and superstition of poor farmers, and *Cham* (1888; "The Boor"), the tragic story of a fisherman's love for a neurotic and sophisticated city girl. *Nad Niemnem* (1888; "On the Banks of the Niemen"), considered her masterpiece, depicts Polish society in Lithuania. *Bene nati* (1892; "Well Born") describes the impoverished gentry of small villages.

Osborne \'äz-bərn, -,bȯrn\, Dorothy, *also called* (from 1655) Lady Temple \'tem-pəl\ (b. 1627, Chicksands Priory, Bedfordshire, Eng.—d. February 1695, Moor Park, near Farnham, Surrey) English gentlewoman best known for the letters she wrote to her future husband, William Temple, before their marriage. The letters are simply written in an easy, conversational style and present an interesting picture of the life of a young English gentlewoman in the Commonwealth period (1649–60). Lively and tender, they are full of good sense, humor, and keen observation.

Temple preserved the group of letters written to him during their prolonged courtship between December 1652 and October 1654, and they remained in manuscript until the 19th century. The best edition of them is by G.C. Moore Smith (1928).

Osborne \\'äz-,bȯrn, -bərn\\, John (James) (b. Dec. 12, 1929, London, Eng.—d. Dec. 24, 1994, Shropshire) British playwright whose LOOK BACK IN ANGER (1957) ushered in a new movement in British drama and made him known as the first ANGRY YOUNG MAN. He reoriented British drama from well-made plays depicting upper-class life to vigorously realistic drama of contemporary blue-collar life.

Osborne briefly attended college but left to take up a career; a job tutoring a touring company of juvenile actors introduced him to the theater. His first play, *The Devil Inside Him*, was written in 1950 with friend and mentor Stella Linden. Osborne made his first appearance as a London actor in 1956, the same year that *Look Back in Anger* was produced. Osborne's next play was THE ENTERTAINER (performed 1957). In 1958 Osborne and director Tony Richardson founded Woodfall Film Productions, which produced motion pictures of *Look Back in Anger* (1959), *The Entertainer* (1959), and, from a film script by Osborne that won an Academy Award, *Tom Jones* (1963), based on the novel by Henry Fielding.

LUTHER (1961), an epic play about the religious reformer, was followed by *Plays for England* (1963): *The Blood of the Bambergs*, a satire on royalty, and *Under Plain Cover*, a study of an incestuous couple playing games of dominance and submission. Later plays include *Inadmissible Evidence* (1965), *A Patriot for Me* (1965), *West of Suez* (1971), and *Déjàvu* (1991), a sequel to *Look Back in Anger*. Osborne also wrote several plays for television as well as two installments of an autobiography, *A Better Class of Person* (1981) and *Almost a Gentleman* (1991).

O'Shaughnessy \\ō-'shȯ-nə-sē\\, Arthur (William Edgar) (b. March 14, 1844, London, Eng.—d. Jan. 30, 1881, London) British poet best known for his much-anthologized "Ode" ("We are the music-makers").

O'Shaughnessy published four volumes of verse: *An Epic of Women* (1870), *Lays of France* (1872), *Music and Moonlight* (1874), and *Songs of a Worker* (1881). He was strongly influenced by the work of Algernon Charles Swinburne and the Pre-Raphaelite artists and writers. He is representative of many Victorian poets for whom a concentration on musicality and emotions was more important than intellectual content.

Osiris \\ō-'sī-rəs\\, *also called* Usiri \\ü-'sē-rē\\ One of the most important gods of ancient Egypt. The origin of Osiris is obscure; he was a local god of Busiris, in Lower Egypt, and may have been a personification of chthonic (underworld) fertility or possibly a deified hero. By about 2400 BC, however, Osiris clearly played a double role: he was both a god of fertility and the embodiment of the dead and resurrected king. This dual role was in turn combined with the Egyptian concept of divine kingship: the king at death became Osiris, god of the underworld; and the dead king's son, the living king, was identified with Horus, a god of the sky. Osiris and Horus were thus father and son. The goddess Isis was the mother of the king and was thus the mother of Horus and consort of Osiris. The god Seth was considered the murderer of Osiris and adversary of Horus.

According to the Greek author Plutarch, Osiris was slain by Seth, who tore the corpse into 14 pieces and flung them over Egypt. Eventually, Isis and her sister Nephthys found and buried all the pieces, except the phallus, thereby giving new life to Osiris, who thenceforth remained in the underworld as ruler and judge. Isis revived Osiris by magical means and conceived her son Horus by him. Horus later successfully fought against Seth and became the new king of Egypt.

Osiris was not only ruler of the dead but also wielded the power that granted all life from the underworld, from sprouting vegetation to the annual flood of the Nile. From about 2000 BC onward it was believed that every man, not just the

deceased kings, became associated with Osiris at death. In this universalized form Osiris' cult spread throughout Egypt, often joining with the cults of local fertility and underworld deities.

Osmond, Gilbert \\'gil-bərt-'äz-mənd\\ Fictional character, an expatriate American who marries Isabel Archer in THE PORTRAIT OF A LADY by Henry James.

Ossian \\'äs-ē-ən; 'ash-ən, 'ȯsh-\\ or **Oisín** \\'ȯsh-yin\\ The Irish warrior-poet of the Fenian cycle of hero tales about Finn and his war band, the Fianna Éireann. The name Ossian became known throughout Europe in 1762, when the Scottish poet James MACPHERSON published what he claimed were translations from 3rd-century Gaelic poems of Oisín. In fact, Macpherson himself had written much of the material. The poems had a considerable effect on early Romantic writers, but they infuriated Irish scholars. Furthermore, Macpherson claimed that the Irish heroes were Caledonians and therefore a tribute to Scotland's past, rather than to Ireland's.

The name Ossian, popularized by Macpherson, superseded Oisín, though they are often used interchangeably. The term Ossianic ballads refers to genuine late Gaelic poems that form part of the common Scots-Irish Gaelic tradition.

Ossianic ballads \\,äs-ē-'an-ik, ,ash-\\ Irish Gaelic and Scottish lyric and narrative poems dealing with the legends of Finn MacCumhaill and his war band. They are named for Oisín (Ossian), the chief bard of the Fenian cycle, a collection of tales and verses on the same subject. The Ossianic ballads belong to a common Scots-Irish Gaelic tradition: some are found in the Scottish Highlands, others in Ireland, but their subjects are of Irish origin. Consisting of more than 80,000 lines, they were formed from the 11th to the 18th century, although their themes of pursuits and rescues, monster slayings, mutually destructive strife, elopements, and magic visitors go back to about the 3rd century AD. Unlike earlier Fenian literature, which reflected a mutual respect between pagan and Christian tradition, the Ossianic ballads are stubbornly pagan and anticlerical, full of lament for past glories and contempt for the Christian present. The earliest collection of these late ballads, made by Sir James MacGregor between 1512 and 1526, is known as *The Book of the Dean of Lismore*.

Ossianic cycle *see* FENIAN CYCLE.

Ostaijen \\vän-'ȯs-tä-yən\\, Paul van (b. Feb. 22, 1896, Antwerp, Belg.—d. March 18, 1928, near Namur) Belgian poet and man of letters whose avant-garde writings in Flemish were influential in Belgium and Holland.

Van Ostaijen's first volume of verse, *Music-hall* (1916), introduced modern city life as a subject for poetry. His second, *Het sienjaal* (1918; "The Signal"), showed the influence of World War I and of German Expressionism and inspired the humanitarian Expressionist movement in Flanders. Compromised as a political activist, van Ostaijen went into exile in Berlin (1918–21). The political and artistic climate there and the hardships he endured made him a nihilist; during this period he wrote *Feesten van angst en pijn* (published posthumously, 1928; *Feasts of Fear and Agony*) and Dadaist-influenced poetry (*Bezette stad*, 1921; "Occupied City"). "Het eerste boek van Schmoll," *The First Book of Schmoll*, part of *Gedichten* (1928; "Poems"), contains his best and most original poems.

Van Ostaijen also wrote a number of influential essays on art and literature, collected and published in two volumes (1929–31). He was the first to publish translations of the work of the German writer Franz Kafka, publishing five of his short prose pieces in Flemish in 1925. Kafka's influence is seen in such works as *Vogelvrij* (1927; "Outlawed") and *Diergaarde voor kinderen van nu* (1932; "Zoo for Today's Children").

Ostrovsky \ˌȯ-'strȯf-skʸē \, Aleksandr Nikolayevich (b. March 31 [April 12, New Style], 1823, Moscow, Russia—d. June 2 [June 14], 1886, Shchelykovo) Russian dramatist who is generally considered the greatest representative of the Russian realistic period.

Ostrovsky wrote his first play, *Kartina semeynogo schastya* ("A Picture of Family Happiness"), in 1847. His next play, *Bankrut* (1850; "The Bankrupt"), written in 1849 and later renamed *Svoi lyudi—sochtyomsya!* (*It's a Family Affair—We'll Settle It Among Ourselves*), provoked an outcry because it exposed bogus bankruptcy cases among Moscow merchants. It brought about Ostrovsky's dismissal from the civil service, and the play was banned for 13 years.

Ostrovsky wrote several historical plays in the 1860s. His main dramatic work, however, was concerned with the Russian merchant class and included two tragedies and numerous comedies, including his masterpieces *Bednost ne porok* (1853; "Poverty Is No Disgrace") and *Groza* (1859; *The Thunderstorm*). His *Snegurochka* (1873; "The Snow Maiden") was adapted as an opera by Nikolay Rimsky-Korsakov in 1882.

Ostrovsky was closely associated with the Maly ("Little") Theater, Moscow's only state theater, where all his plays were first performed under his supervision. In 1885 he became artistic director of the Moscow imperial theaters. The author of 47 original plays, Ostrovsky almost single-handedly created a Russian national repertoire. His dramas are among the most widely read and frequently performed stage pieces in Russia.

Otfrid or **Otfried** \'ȯt-ˌfrēt\ (fl. 9th century) Monk of Weissenburg in Alsace and the earliest German poet whose name is known.

Otfrid's fame rests on his *Evangelienbuch* (c. 870; "Book of the Gospels"), a poem of 7,416 lines. A selective paraphrase of the Gospels, the work interposes short passages of commentary. The poem is an exceptionally valuable document both linguistically and theologically. It is also a milestone in German literary history, because it is the first poem to depart from traditional German alliterative verse and to use end rhymes.

Othello \ə-'thel-ō, ō-\ (*in full* Othello, the Moor of Venice) Tragedy in five acts by William Shakespeare, performed in 1604–05 and published in 1622 in a quarto edition.

The plot of the play is set in motion when Othello, a heroic Moorish general in the service of Venice, appoints Cassio and not Iago as his chief lieutenant. Jealous of Othello's success and envious of Cassio, Iago plots Othello's downfall by falsely implicating Othello's wife, Desdemona, and Cassio in a love affair. Desdemona cannot produce a handkerchief once given her by Othello; thanks to Iago's machinations, it is later found among Cassio's possessions. Overcome with jealousy, Othello kills Desdemona. When he learns, too late, that his wife is blameless, he asks to be remembered as one who "loved not wisely but too well," and kills himself.

Trusting to false appearances and allowing reason to be guided by passion is a theme of many of Shakespeare's comedies. In *Othello* he showed the theme's tragic consequences. Shakespeare adapted the story from an Italian model. His main innovation lay in developing the villainous character of Iago, whose motives are represented as complex and ambiguous.

Others (*in full* Others: A Magazine of New Verse) American literary magazine founded by Alfred Kreymborg and published from July 1915 to July 1919. Created in response to the conservatism of *Poetry*, the most notable of the little magazines, *Others* featured experimental poetry and, from December 1918, prose and artwork. Though the mainstream press received the magazine with hostility, its success as an outlet for modernism resulted in three anthologies and a short-lived theater troupe.

Individual issues of *Others* were devoted to such themes as women writers and writers in Chicago and in Latin America. Its contributors included T.S. Eliot, Mina Loy, Max Bodenheim, Amy Lowell, Wallace Stevens, Marianne Moore, Ezra Pound, Hilda Doolittle (H.D.), Carl Sandburg, Richard Aldington, Conrad Aiken, and Sherwood Anderson.

ottava rima \ō-ˌtäv-ə-'rē-mə, *Italian* ōt-ˌtä-vä-'rē-mä \ *plural* ottava rimas [Italian, stanza of eight lines, literally, eighth stanza] Italian stanza form composed of eight 11-syllable lines, rhyming *abababcc*. It originated in the late 13th and early 14th centuries and was developed by Tuscan poets for religious verse and drama and in troubadour songs. In his romantic epics *Il filostrato* (written c. 1338) and *Teseida* (written 1340–41), Giovanni Boccaccio established ottava rima as the standard form for epic and narrative verse in Italian. The form acquired new flexibility and variety in Ludovico Ariosto's *Orlando furioso* (c. 1507–32) and Torquato Tasso's *Gerusalemme liberata* (1581).

Ottava rima appeared in Spain and Portugal in the 16th century. It was used in 1600 in England (where the lines were shortened to 10 syllables) by Edward Fairfax in his translation of the work of Tasso. In original English verse ottava rima was written in iambic pentameter and used for heroic poetry in the 17th and 18th centuries, but it achieved its greatest effectiveness in Lord Byron's *Beppo* (1818) and *Don Juan* (1819–24). Others who have written poems in the form include Edmund Spenser, John Milton, John Keats, Percy Bysshe Shelley, Robert Browning, and William Butler Yeats.

Otus \'ō-təs\ In Greek mythology, one of the twin sons of Iphimedia by the god Poseidon. *See* ALOADAE.

Otway \'ät-ˌwā\, Thomas (b. March 3, 1652, Trotton, near Midhurst, Sussex, Eng.—d. April 14, 1685, London) English dramatist and poet, one of the forerunners of sentimental drama through his convincing presentation of human emotions in an age of heroic but artificial tragedies. His masterpiece, *Venice Preserv'd*, was one of the greatest theatrical successes of the period.

Otway's first play, a rhyming tragedy called *Alcibiades*, was produced in London in 1675. His second play, *Don Carlos* (produced 1676), had an immense success on the stage and is the best of his rhymed heroic plays. His *Titus and Berenice*, adapted from Molière, and *The Cheats of Scapin*, adapted from Jean Racine, were published together in 1677.

In 1678 Otway obtained a commission in an English regiment serving in the Netherlands, and he was abroad when his first comedy, *Friendship in Fashion*, was staged. His next play, *Caius Marius*, a curious mixture of a story from Plutarch with an adaptation of *Romeo and Juliet*, was staged in 1679. He published his powerful, gloomy autobiographical poem, *The Poet's Complaint of His Muse*, in 1680.

In the spring of 1680 his fine blank-verse domestic tragedy *The Orphan* had great success on the stage. In the same year his best comedy, *The Souldier's Fortune*, was produced. *Venice Preserv'd*, also written in blank verse, was first performed in 1682; until the middle of the 19th century it was probably revived more often than any poetic play except those of William Shakespeare.

Ouida \'wē-də\, *pseudonym of* Maria Louise Ramé *or* de la Ramée \del-ə-rä-'mä\ (b. Jan. 1, 1839, Bury St. Edmunds, Suffolk, Eng.—d. Jan. 25, 1908, Viareggio, Italy) English novelist known for her extravagant melodramatic romances of fashionable life.

The pseudonym Ouida derived from a childhood version of Louisa. Her first novel, *Granville de Vigne* (renamed *Held in Bondage* in 1863), was published serially in 1860. Her stirring narrative style and refreshingly nonjudgmental approach made her books extraordinarily popular. *Strathmore* (1865) and *Chandos* (1866) were followed by *Under Two Flags* (1867). Ouida settled at Florence in 1874. Among her many subsequent novels, *Moths* (1880) was one of her best. She was the author of a number of animal stories, of which *A Dog of Flanders* (1872) was long a children's favorite. Reckless extravagance reduced her to acute poverty in later life.

OuLiPo \ū-lē-'pō\ (*in full* Ouvroir de Littérature Potentielle; "Workshop of Potential Literature") A group of French writers active in the 1970s whose aim was to generate new literary forms and to rejuvenate poetic language through experimentation with linguistic games. They were inspired by Alfred Jarry and Raymond Queneau, whose *Exercices de style* (1947; *Exercises in Style*) consisted of a single anecdote presented in 99 different forms demonstrating different figures of speech, style, and other literary elements. The group's fondness for wordplay and sometimes unbelievably demanding forms can be seen in the work of Georges Perec, whose novel *La Disparition* (1969) was composed entirely without using the letter *e*.

Ouologuem \wō-lō-'gem\, Yambo, *pseudonym* Utto Rodolph \rō-'dolf\ (b. Aug. 22, 1940, Bandiagara, Mopti region, French Sudan [now Mali]) Malian writer who was highly acclaimed for his first novel, *Le Devoir de violence* (1968; *Bound to Violence*), which received the Prix Renaudot. With this work, Ouologuem became the first African writer to receive a major French literary award.

Ouologuem was born to a ruling-class family and studied in Paris. His best-known work, *Le Devoir de violence*, is an epic about a fictitious African empire. The work covers hundreds of years of African history and concludes that three forces—the ancient African emperors, the Arabs, and the European colonial administrators—are responsible for the black African's "slave mentality." These forces combined to produce "négraille" (a word coined by Ouologuem, meaning "nigger rabble" in its translation). Ouologuem viewed the African's lot as a legacy of violence and, in modern times, as a duty of violence toward oppressive white attitudes.

Ouologuem's bitterness about colonialism and its effect on black African psychology also surfaces in some of his poems, and his *Lettre à la France nègre* (1969) attacks the "noble" sentiments of paternalistic French liberals.

His other works include *Les Mille et un bibles du sexe* (1969; "The Thousand and One Bibles of Sex"), published under his pseudonym, Utto Rodolph. Ouologuem also coauthored French-language textbooks for foreigners under the title *Terres de soleil* (1971; "Lands of the Sun").

Our Lady of the Flowers Novel by Jean GENET, written while he was in prison for burglary and published in 1944 in French as *Notre-Dame des fleurs*. The novel and the author were championed by many contemporary writers, including Jean-Paul Sartre and Jean Cocteau, who helped engineer a pardon for Genet.

A wildly imaginative fantasy of the Parisian underworld, the novel tells the story of Divine, a male prostitute who consorts with thieves, pimps, murderers, and other criminals and who has many sexual adventures. Written in lyrical, dreamlike prose, the novel affirms a new moral order, one in which criminals are saints, evil is glorified, and conventional taboos are freely violated.

Our Man in Havana \hə-'van-ə, -'vän-\ Novel by Graham GREENE, published in 1958 and classified by the author as an "entertainment." Set in Cuba before the communist revolution, the book is a comical spy story about a British vacuum-cleaner salesman's misadventures in the British Secret Intelligence Service. Although many critics found fault with the

book's overly farcical style, it was also admired for its skillful rendering of the Cuban locale.

Our Mutual Friend Last completed novel by Charles DICKENS, published serially in 1864–65 and in book form in 1865. Sometimes compared to *Bleak House* because of its subject matter, *Our Mutual Friend* is essentially a critique of Victorian monetary and class values. London is portrayed as grimmer than ever before, and the corruption, complacency, and superficiality of "respectable" society are fiercely attacked. The novel is also notable owing to Dickens' sympathetic portrayal of a Jewish character named Riah, which some critics have seen as Dickens' attempt to atone for the character of Fagin in *Oliver Twist*.

Our Town Pulitzer Prize-winning drama in three acts by Thornton WILDER, produced and published in 1938, considered a classic portrayal of small-town American life.

Set in Grover's Corners, N.H., the play features a narrator, the Stage Manager, who sits at the side of the unadorned stage and explains the action. Through flashbacks, dialogue, and direct monologues the other characters reveal themselves to the audience. The main characters are George Gibbs, a doctor's son, and Emily Webb, daughter of a newspaper editor. The play concerns their courtship and marriage and Emily's death in childbirth, after which she and other inhabitants of the graveyard describe their peace.

Considered enormously innovative for its lack of props and scenery and revered for its sentimental but at bottom realistic depictions of middle-class America, *Our Town* soon became a staple of American theater.

Outcasts of Poker Flat, The Short story by Bret HARTE, first published in the magazine *Overland Monthly* in 1869, later published in the collection *The Luck of Roaring Camp and Other Sketches* (1870); it has become a minor classic of American literature. One of the best examples of Harte's local-color fiction, this story about exiles from an 1850 California mining camp who are caught in a blizzard shows how even the "immoral" members of society are capable of acting unselfishly to help others who are in danger.

Out of Africa \'af-ri-kə, 'äf-\ Memoir by Isak DINESEN, published in English in 1937 and translated the same year by the author into Danish as *Den afrikanske Farm*. It is an autobiographical account of the author's life from 1914 to 1931 after her marriage to Baron Bror Blixen-Finecke, when she managed a coffee plantation in Kenya. In lyrical prose she recounts her profound love of the land, her affection for the fading culture of colonial Africa, her romance with an English hunter, and the eventual failure of the farm. Further insight into the work is provided by the posthumous collection *Letters from Africa, 1914–1931* (1981).

Out of the Cradle Endlessly Rocking Poem by Walt WHITMAN, first published as "A Word Out of the Sea" in the 1860 edition of his collection *Leaves of Grass* and later published in the 1871 version using the final title. This long poem, one of the most powerful in the collection, is written in lyrical free verse. A boy stands by the seashore at night listening to the song of a mockingbird mourning for his mate; at the same time he listens to the death song of the sea and realizes that "my own songs awaked from that hour." The mockingbird, singing to relieve his solitude, is a metaphor for the poetic spirit, while the sea is a symbol of the spiritual world to which poetry is witness.

Out of the Silent Planet Science-fiction novel by C.S. LEWIS, published in 1938. The novel, the first of a trilogy, is in part a retelling of the Christ story. It is an account of the voyage of Ransom, a linguist, to the planet Malacandra (Mars), where he learns that Thulcandra (Earth) is called the silent planet because there has been no communication from it in years. The spiritual being in charge of the latter, having been corrupted, has essentially cut Thulcandra off from the other planets. Ransom is ultimately sent back to Thulcandra with the two earthlings who had kidnapped him and brought him to Malacandra. The novel gives voice to Lewis' concerns about the secularization of society and argues that a return to traditional religious belief is the only means of salvation.

Outremeuse \ū-trə-'mœz\, Jean d' (b. 1338?—d. 1399?) French author of two romanticized but fascinating historical works. The first, *La Geste de Liège*, is a leisurely account, partly in prose, partly in verse, of the mythical history of his native city, Liège. *Ly Myreur des histors* ("The Mirror of History") is even more ambitious, purporting to be a history of the world from the time of the biblical Flood up to the 14th century.

D'Outremeuse's fictionalized accounts of the past offer insights into the workings of a medieval mind and contain unique evidence about the author's time and especially about literature in his age.

outride \'aút-,rīd\   In Gerard Manley Hopkins' system of prosody, an unstressed syllable or group of syllables added to a foot but not counted in the scansion because of its lack of effect upon the rhythmic movement. *See* SPRUNG RHYTHM.

Ouyang Xiu or **Ou-yang Hsiu** \'ō-'yän-'shyū\, *literary name* Zuiweng \'zwē-'wəŋ\ (b. 1007, Mianyang, Sichuan, China—d. 1072, Henan)   Chinese poet, historian, and statesman of the Song (Sung) dynasty (960–1279), who reintroduced *guwen*, the simple ancient style in Chinese literature.

In 1030 Ouyang was appointed a judge at Luoyang, the western capital. There he befriended the renowned essayist Yan Shu and the poet Mei Yaochen, who reinforced for Ouyang the influence of the works of the earlier Han Yu, a writer noted for his pure and easy ancient style.

In 1034 Ouyang Xiu was appointed a collator of texts in the Imperial library at Kaifeng. Two years later his outspokenness resulted in banishment and demotion. During this period he wrote the *Xin Wudai shi* ("New History of the Five Dynasties"), a history of a period of political chaos. He was recalled to the capital in 1043 to become Imperial counselor.

Again demoted and banished in 1045 after a personal scandal, he served as magistrate of one county after another and took to drink. Calling himself the "Old Drunkard," he built a pavilion in Anhui that he named Cuiweng ting ("Old Drunkard Pavilion") and made the subject of an essay which has become one of the most celebrated works in Chinese literature. Ouyang was recalled to the capital in 1054 to become an academician of the Hanlin Academy.

He was first ordered to write the *Xin Tang shu* ("New History of the Tang Dynasty"). A year later, with his work only begun, he was sent as ambassador to the Manchurian Khitans, who ruled most of northern China. In 1057, when he was placed in charge of civil-service examinations, he favored those who wrote in the ancient style and failed those who employed literary embellishments. In this way he set a new course for Chinese literature.

When the "New History" was finished in 1060, he was rapidly promoted to the highest councils of state, leaving a remarkable record in social, financial, and military affairs. His position at court eventually became untenable, however, and at age 60 he was sent as a magistrate successively to Anhui, Shandong, and Henan. In 1071 he was retired with the title of grand preceptor of the crown prince.

Ouyang's advocacy of unembellished prose over the mannered and excessively rhythmic style then popular, and his own writings in the *guwen* style, established a model that was long emulated.

Overbury \'ō-vər-bə-rē, -,ber-ē\, Sir Thomas (baptized June 18, 1581, Compton Scorpion, Warwickshire, Eng.—d. Sept. 15, 1613, London)   English poet and essayist, victim of an infamous intrigue at the court of James I. His poem *A Wife*, which pictured the virtues that a young man should demand of a woman, played a large role in the events that precipitated his murder.

Engraving by Reginald Elstacke, *c.* 1615
Mary Evans Picture Library

In 1606 Overbury became secretary and close adviser to Robert Carr, the king's favorite, who was to become Earl of Somerset. Overbury was knighted in 1608, and Carr became Viscount Rochester in 1611. When Rochester made plans to marry Frances Howard, former wife of the Earl of Essex, Overbury feared that the marriage would reduce his influence over Rochester. Overbury circulated manuscript copies of *A Wife* at court, where the poem was interpreted as an indirect attack on Lady Essex. This act enabled her powerful relatives to have Overbury imprisoned in the Tower. Lady Essex secretly arranged to have Overbury slowly poisoned. Three months after Overbury's death, Rochester married Lady Essex. The couple were convicted of murder (along with four accomplices), but they were pardoned by the king; the four accomplices were executed.

Overbury's *A Wife* was published in 1614 and went through several editions within a year. Its real literary value lies in the *Characters*, ultimately 82, that were added to the second and subsequent editions. These prose portraits of Jacobean types, drawn with wit and satire, give a vivid picture of contemporary society and are an important step in the development of the essay. A few were by Overbury, but most were contributed by John Webster, Thomas Dekker, and John Donne.

Overcoat, The   Short story by Nikolay GOGOL, published in Russian as "Shinel" in 1842. *The Overcoat* is perhaps the best-known and most influential short fiction in all of Russian literature; with the same writer's *Dead Souls*, it is considered the foundation of 19th-century Russian realism.

Gogol's story of government clerk Akaky Akakiyevich Bash-machkin combines a careful eye for detail with biting social satire on the banal evil of bureaucracy. Unattractive, unnoticed, and underpaid, Akaky Akakiyevich decides that he must replace his ancient, worn overcoat. After scrimping for months, he finds a tailor who fashions a fine new coat just in time for winter. On his way home from a party, wearing his new coat for the first time, Akaky Akakiyevich is assaulted by two thugs who steal the garment. The police are indifferent. His coworkers refer him to a Certain Important Personage who becomes outraged by Akaky Akakiyevich's temerity and refuses to help. Coatless, Akaky Akakiyevich catches cold and dies several days later. Soon rumors spread that a ghost is stripping coats from pedestrians; one night, while on the way to visit his mistress, the Certain Important Personage is seized by the collar and relieved of his overcoat. The ghost, satisfied, never returns.

Øverland \' œ̄-vər-ˌlän\, Arnulf (b. April 27, 1889, Kristiansand [now Oslo], Nor.—d. March 25, 1968, Oslo)   Norwegian poet and socialist whose poems helped inspire the Norwegian resistance movement during the German occupation in World War II.

Øverland's first book of poems, *Den ensomme fest* (1911; "The Lonely Feast"), was immediately acclaimed for its style, its clarity, and its economy. After World War I, in his *Brød og vin* (1919; "Bread and Wine"), he developed a radical opposition to bourgeois society and to Christianity and recognized a need to make his poetry into a social weapon. His poems of the 1930s were intended to alert Norwegians to the danger of fascism and Nazism. The best known of these is "Du må ikke sove!" (1937; "You Must Not Sleep!"). His activism led to a four-year imprisonment in a German concentration camp. When he was freed in May 1945, the Norwegian government presented him with the old home of the great national poet Henrik Wergeland as an expression of gratitude.

Overland Monthly   Literary magazine published in San Francisco from 1868 to 1875 and from 1883 to 1935. This ambitious venture, edited for the first two and a half years by Bret Harte, was begun in an attempt to establish Western literature as a legitimate genre. Harte's local-color parables such as "The Luck of Roaring Camp" and "The Outcasts of Poker Flat" first appeared in its pages and solidified his reputation.

Ovid \'äv-id\, *Latin in full* Publius Ovidius Naso (b. March 20, 43 BC, Sulmo, Roman Empire [now Sulmona, Italy]—d. AD 17, Tomis, Moesia [now Constanța, Rom.])   Roman poet noted especially for his ARS AMATORIA (*The Art of Love*) and METAMORPHOSES. His verse had immense influence because of its imaginative interpretations of classical myth and its supreme technical accomplishment.

Mary Evans Picture Library

The main events of Ovid's life are described in an autobiographical poem in *Tristia* (*Sorrows*). As a member of the Roman knightly class, Ovid was destined for an official career. He dutifully held some minor judicial posts, the first steps on the official ladder, but he soon decided that public life did not suit him. From then on he abandoned his official career to cultivate poetry and the society of poets.

Ovid's first work, *Amores* (*The Loves*), a series of short poems depicting the various phases of a love affair with a woman called Corinna, had an immediate success and was followed, in rapid succession, by *Epistolae heroidum*, or *Heroides* (*Epistles of the Heroines*), dramatic monologues about legendary women such as Penelope and Dido; *Medicamina faciei* ("Cosmetics"; *The Art of Beauty*), a witty, frivolous exercise of which only some 100 lines survive; *Ars Amatoria*; and *Remedia amoris* (*Remedies for Love*), a mock recantation of the *Ars Amatoria*.

Having won an assured position among the poets of the day, Ovid turned to more ambitious projects, *Metamorphoses* and *Fasti* ("Calendar"), an account of the Roman year and its religious festivals. The former was nearly complete, the latter half finished, when his life was shattered by a sudden and crushing blow. In AD 8 the emperor Augustus banished him to Tomis on the Black Sea, for reasons that are not fully known.

Exile at Tomis, a half-Greek, half-barbarian port on the extreme confines of the Roman Empire, was a cruel punishment for a man of Ovid's temperament and habits. He never ceased to hope, if not for pardon, at least for mitigation of sentence, keeping up in *Tristia* and *Epistulae ex Ponto* ("Letters from the Black Sea") a ceaseless stream of pathetic pleas, chiefly through his wife and friends, to the emperor. But neither Augustus nor his successor, Tiberius, relented, and hints in the later poems suggest that Ovid was becoming reconciled to his fate.

Owain Cyfeiliog \'ō-wīn-ˌkə-'vīl-yȯg\ (b. *c.* 1130—d. *c.* 1197)   Welsh warrior-prince of Powys and poet of distinct originality among the *gogynfeirdd* (court poets).

Owain ruled over the people of Powys from 1149 to 1195. *Hirlas Owain* ("The Drinking Horn of Owain"), his only extant poem is noteworthy for its dramatic presentation. It is set at court, where his warriors, weary from battle, are gathered at the banquet table. Each stanza begins with instructions to the cupbearer to pour a drink for a hero; he then bestows praise on the man as the drink is poured.

Owen \'ō-ˌwen, *Angl* 'ō-ən\, Alun (Davies) (b. Nov. 24, 1925, Liverpool, Eng.)   Welsh dramatist who wrote for radio, television, screen, and stage and whose work often reflects the cultural and religious conflicts of the city where he was born.

Of Welsh parentage, Owen attended school in Wales and Liverpool and began his theatrical training as an assistant stage manager in repertory theater (1942). He started writing for radio and television in 1957, quickly proving his sharp ear for dialogue and his gift for characterization. His television plays, numbering more than 50, sometimes concentrated on the seamier aspects of city life, as in *No Trams to Lime Street* (1959). A quartet of plays, televised under the title *Male of the Species* (1969), was immensely successful and was produced for the stage in 1974.

Owen won critical acclaim for his stage plays, which included *Progress to the Park* and *The Rough and Ready Lot*, both of which were broadcast in 1958 and produced for the stage in 1959 and which depicted religious and cultural bigotry. From the 1970s on, Owen produced plays mainly for television, although he also continued to write plays for the stage, including *Lucia* (1982) and *Norma* (1983).

Owen \'ō-ˌwen, *Angl* 'ō-ən\, Daniel (b. Oct. 20, 1836, Mold, Flintshire [now in Clwyd], Wales—d. Oct. 22, 1895, Mold)

Writer who is considered the national novelist of Wales. Owen was a natural storyteller whose works, set in his own time, introduced a wealth of vivid and memorable characters that have given him a place in his national literature comparable to that of Charles Dickens in English.

His works include the novels *Hunangofiant Rhys Lewis* (1885; "Autobiography of Rhys Lewis"), *Profedigaethau Enoc Huws* (1891; "The Trials of Enoc Huws"), and *Y Dreflan, ei Phobl a'i Phethau* (1881; "Dreflan, Its People and Its Affairs"), which describes life around the Welsh chapel. *Offrymau Neilltuaeth* (1879; "Offering of Seclusion") is a volume of sermons and portraits of Methodists; *Y Siswrn* (1888; "The Scissors") gathers together poems, essays, and stories. Besides vigorous diction, Owen's works are characterized by pungent humor and freedom from didacticism, qualities not generally found in 19th-century Welsh literature.

Owen \'ō-,wen, *Angl* 'ō-ən\, Goronwy, *also called* Goronwy Ddu o Fôn (b. Jan. 1, 1723, Llanfair Mathafarn Eithaf, Anglesey [now in Gwynedd], Wales—d. July 1769, Brunswick, Va. [U.S.]) Clergyman and poet who revived classicism in modern Welsh literature. He reintroduced the cywydd and the *awdl*, poetic forms used by the medieval Welsh bards.

Among his best-known poems are "Cywydd y Farn Fawr" ("Cywydd of the Great Judgment"), "Cywydd y Gem neu'r Maen Gwerthfawr" ("Cywydd of the Gem or the Precious Stone"), and "Cywydd yn ateb Huw'r Bardd Coch o Fôn" ("Cywydd in Answer to Huw the Red Poet of Anglesey").

Owen \'ō-,wen, *Angl* 'ō-ən\, John, *also called* John Ovenus \ō-'vē-nəs\ *or* Auddenus \ȯ-'dē-nəs\ (b. *c.* 1560, Plas Dhu, Llanarmon, Caernarvonshire [now in Gwynedd], Wales—d. 1622, London, Eng.) Welsh epigrammatist whose perfect mastery of the Latin language brought him the name of "the British Martial," after the ancient Roman poet.

Owen was educated at New College, Oxford, where he was a fellow from 1584 to 1591. He then became a schoolmaster, first at Trelleck, near Monmouth in Wales, and then about 1594 at Warwick.

Owen's *Epigrammata* are divided into 12 books, of which the first four were published in 1606 and the rest at four different times. He became distinguished not only for his mastery of Latin but also for the humor and point of his epigrams. A staunch Protestant, he turned his wit against Roman Catholicism. This practice caused his writings to be placed on the Roman Catholic *Index libroram prohibitorum* ("Index of Forbidden Books") in 1654.

Owen \'ō-ən\, Wilfred (b. March 18, 1893, Oswestry, Shropshire, Eng.—killed in action Nov. 4, 1918, France) English poet noted for his anger at the cruelty and waste of war and his pity for its victims. He also is significant for his technical experiments in assonance, which were particularly influential in the 1930s.

Owen's early poetry, intended for the unpublished collection "Minor Poems—in Minor Keys—by a Minor," are consciously modeled on John Keats; often ambitious, they show enjoyment of poetry as a craft.

In 1915 Owen enlisted in the army. The experience of trench warfare brought him to rapid maturity; the poems written after January 1917 are full of anger at war's brutality, an elegiac pity for "those who die as cattle," and a rare descriptive power. In June 1917 he was wounded and sent home. While in a hospital near Edinburgh he met Siegfried Sassoon; this meeting revolutionized Owen's style and his conception of poetry. He returned to France in August 1918 as a company commander, was awarded the Military Cross in October, and was killed a week before the cessation of active hostilities.

Published posthumously by Sassoon, Owen's single volume of poems contains the most poignant English poetry of the war. His collected poems were published in 1964; his collected letters in 1967.

Owl and the Pussy-cat, The Nonsense poem by Edward LEAR, published in *Nonsense Songs, Stories, Botany and Alpha-*

"The Owl and the Pussy-cat" from *The Complete Nonsense of Edward Lear*; illustration by Lear

bets (1871). One of the best known and most frequently anthologized of Lear's poems, it was written and illustrated for a daughter of the English author John Addington Symonds. The poem was also published as an individual book.

Like much of Lear's nonsense verse, the characters are nonhumans on a journey of discovery: "The Owl and the Pussy-cat went to sea/ In a beautiful pea-green boat,/ They took some honey, and plenty of money/ Wrapped up in a five-pound note."

Ox-Bow Incident, The Novel by Walter van Tilburg CLARK, published in 1940. This psychological study of corrupt leadership and mob rule was read as a parable of fascism when it first appeared. Set in Nevada in 1885, the story concerns the brutal lynching of three characters falsely accused of murder and theft. The strong-willed leader of the lynch mob, Major Tetley, easily takes advantage of the suppressed resentment and boredom of the townspeople.

Oxbridge \'äks-,brij\ General term for Oxford and Cambridge universities. The term refers to characteristics that are common to both schools, particularly the world of the educated elite that is associated with both.

Oxford \'äks-fərd\, Edward de Vere, 17th Earl of (b. April 12, 1550, Castle Hedingham, Essex, Eng.—d. June 24, 1604, Newington, Middlesex) English lyric poet and patron of an acting company, Oxford's Men, who in the 20th century became the strongest candidate proposed (next to William Shakespeare himself) for the authorship of Shakespeare's plays.

Succeeding to the earldom as a minor in 1562, Oxford studied at Queens' College and St. John's College, Cambridge. By the early 1580s his financial position had become very straitened, but in 1586 Queen Elizabeth granted him a handsome annuity.

The theory that Oxford might be the author of Shakespeare's plays was first advanced seriously in J. Thomas Looney's *"Shakespeare" Identified in Edward de Vere, the Seventeenth Earl of Oxford* (1920). He argued that Oxford's poems resembled Shakespeare's early work. Oxford's interest in the drama extended beyond noble patronage, for he himself wrote plays, though there are no known examples extant. His 23 acknowledged poems were written in youth, and, because he was born in 1550, Looney proposed that they were the prelude to his mature work, which began in 1593 with *Venus and Adonis*. The theory is supported by the coincidence that Oxford's poems apparently ceased just before Shakespeare's work began to appear. A major difficulty in the Oxfordian theory, however, is his death date (1604), because, according to standard chronology, 14 of Shakespeare's plays, including many of the most important ones, were first staged after that time.

Oxfordian \äks-'fòr-dē-ən\ Of or relating to Edward de Vere, the 17th Earl of Oxford, or to the doctrine that he was the author of the dramatic works usually attributed to William Shakespeare. *Compare* STRATFORDIAN.

oxymoron \äk-sē-'mòr- än\ [Late Greek *oxýmōron* (in Latin authors), from neuter of *oxýmōros* pointedly foolish, from Greek *oxýs* sharp, keen + *mōrós* dull] *plural* oxymora \-'mòr-ə\ A word or group of words that is self-contradicting, as in *bittersweet* or *plastic glass.* Oxymorons are similar to such other devices as paradox and antithesis. *Compare* ANTITHESIS; PARADOX.

One of the most famous examples of the use of oxymorons is the following speech by Romeo from William Shakespeare's *Romeo and Juliet:*

> Why, then, O brawling love! O loving hate!
> O any thing, of nothing first create!
> O heavy lightness! serious vanity!
> Mis-shapen chaos of well-seeming forms!
> Feather of lead, bright smoke, cold fire, sick health!
> Still-waking sleep, that is not what it is!
> This love feel I, that feel no love in this.

oxytone \'äk-sē-ˌtōn\ [Greek *oxýtonos,* from *oxýs* sharp + *tónos* pitch, accent] Having or characterized by an acute accent or heavy stress on the last syllable.

Oyono \ō-yō-'nō\, Ferdinand Léopold (b. Sept. 14, 1929, Ngoulemakong, Cameroon) African statesman, actor, and comic writer whose two best-known works—*Une Vie de boy* (1956; *Houseboy*) and *Le Vieux nègre et la médaille* (1956; *The Old Man and the Medal*)—reflect the growing sentiment of anticolonialism of the 1950s.

During the 1950s Oyono worked in Paris as an actor on the stage and on television. In 1960 he returned to Cameroon and entered the diplomatic corps. He later took posts in the cabinet. His first novel, *Une Vie de boy,* is the diary of a houseboy in the service of a French commandant. *Le Vieux nègre et la médaille* satirizes colonialism through the eyes of a loyal old villager whose "service" to France—for which he is to receive a medal—consists of the sacrifice of his sons and land. In mocking the foibles of the self-deluded colonial masters as well as the simple villagers, Oyono often paints hilarious portraits. A third, less successful, novel was *Chemin d'Europe* (1960; *Road to Europe*).

Oyono-Mbia \ō-yō-ˌnōm-'byä\, Guillaume (b. 1939, Mvoutessi, Cameroon) Cameroonian dramatist and short-story writer, one of only a few bilingual Cameroonian writers to achieve success both in French and in English.

Oyono-Mbia attended the Collège Évangélique at Limbamba and then went to England, graduating from the University of Keele. From 1969 he taught at the University of Yaoundé in Cameroon and worked for the government. Among Oyono-Mbia's comedies are *Trois prétendants . . . un mari* (1962; *Three Suitors . . . One Husband*), *Until Further Notice* (1967), *Notre fille ne se mariera pas!* (1969; "Our Daughter Will Not Marry!"), and *His Excellency's Special Train* (1969), all written on his favorite theme of youth versus adult, modernity versus tradition. In the 1970s his penchant for satire was also evident in three volumes of amusing tales of life in his native village, *Chroniques de Mvoutessi* (1971–72; "Chronicles of Mvoutessi").

Oz \'äz, 'ōz\, Amos, *original surname* Klausner \'klaůs-nər\ (b. May 4, 1939, Jerusalem) Israeli novelist, short-story writer,

and essayist who edited the *Siaḥ lohamim* ("The Seventh Day"), a collection of soldiers' reflections on the 1967 Six-Day War.

Oz's symbolic, poetic novels reflect the splits and strains in Israeli life. They express a variety of conflicts: between the traditions of intellect and the demands of the flesh; between reality and fantasy; between rural Zionism and the longing for European urbanity; and between the values of the founding settlers and the perceptions of their skeptical offspring. Unable to share the optimism and ideological certainties of Israel's founding generation, Oz presented in his writings an ironic view of reality in which Israeli society is unsentimentally scrutinized. His works of fiction include *Artsot ha-tan* (1965; *Where the Jackals Howl, and Other Stories*), *Mikha'el sheli* (1968; *My Michael*), *La-ga'at ba-mayim, la-ga'at ba-ruaḥ* (1973; *Touch the Water, Touch the Wind*), *Kufsah sheḥora* (1987; *Black Box*), and *Matsav ha-shelishi* (1991; *Fima*). Oz was also known for his controversial political essays.

Ozaki Kōyō \'ō-zä-kē-'kō-ˌyō\, *pseudonym of* Ozaki Tokutarō \'tō-kū-'tä-rō\ (b. Jan. 28, 1869, Tokyo, Japan—d. Oct. 30, 1903, Tokyo) Novelist, essayist, and haiku poet, one of the pioneers of modern Japanese literature.

In 1885, with a group of friends, Kōyō formed the *Kenyūsha,* a magazine and literary association that exercised a major influence in the development of the Japanese novel for nearly 20 years. Through his study of the literature of the Tokugawa period (1603–1867), he led a revival of interest in the 17th-century writer Ihara Saikaku, whose sharp perceptions he adapted to create a style of romantic realism. Kōyō also was active in the movement to create a new colloquial literary language. His elaborate style in early fictional works such as *Ninin bikuni iro zange* (1889; "Amorous Confessions of Two Nuns") and *Kyara makura* (1890; "The Perfumed Pillow") gave way to a more realistic tendency in *Tajō takon* (1896; "Tears and Regrets") and *Kokoro* (1903; "The Heart"). His masterpiece was the novel *Konjiki yasha* (1897–1902; *The Golden Demon*), which portrayed the social cost of modernization.

Ozick \'ō-zik\, Cynthia (b. April 17, 1928, New York, N.Y., U.S.) Novelist and short-story writer whose works seek to define the challenge of remaining Jewish in contemporary American life.

Ozick's first novel, *Trust* (1966), is the story of a woman's rejection of her wealthy American Jewish family and her search for her renegade father in Europe. In subsequent books, such as *Bloodshed and Three Novellas* (1976), Ozick struggled with the idea that the creation of art (a pagan activity) is in direct opposition to principles of Judaism, which forbids the creation of idols. The psychological aftermath of the Holocaust is another theme of Ozick's work, especially in *Levitation: Five Fictions* (1982) and the novel *The Cannibal Galaxy* (1983). Ozick often draws upon traditional Jewish mysticism to expand upon her themes, yet her later works turn away from the theme of the sacred and the profane. Her novel *The Messiah of Stockholm* (1987) is, in part, a meditation on the nature of writing. A collection of essays, *Metaphor and Memory,* was published in 1989.

Ozymandias \ˌäz-ē-'man-dē-əs\ Sonnet by Percy Bysshe SHELLEY, published in 1818. One of Shelley's most famous short works, the poem offers an ironic commentary on the fleeting nature of power. It tells of a ruined statue of Ozymandias (the Greek name for Ramses II of Egypt, who reigned in the 13th century BC), on which is inscribed, "Look on my Works, ye Mighty, and despair!" Around the statue "The lone and level sands stretch far away."

Pacheco \pä-'chä-kō\, José Emilio (b. June 30, 1939, Mexico City)   Mexican critic, novelist, short-story writer, translator, and poet. His poetry transmits his metaphysical concerns in brilliant images.

Pacheco was educated at the National Autonomous University of Mexico. His first published work is a collection of short stories, *La sangre de Medusa* (1958; "The Blood of Medusa"). *Los elementos de la noche* (1963; "The Elements of the Night") and *El reposo del fuego* (1966; "The Sleep of the Fire") are collections of poems. His novel *Morirás lejos* (1967; "You Will Die Far Away") documents the purges of Jews throughout history. The short stories in *El principio del placer* (1972; "The Pleasure Principle") are united by the recurrent theme of anguish.

Pacheco's later books include *Desde entonces: poemas 1975–1978* (1980; "Since Then: Poems 1975–1978") and *Miro la tierra* (1986; "I Look at the Earth"). His works in English include *Tree Between Two Walls* (1969), *The Lost Homeland* (1976), *Signals from the Flames* (1980), and *Selected Poems* (1987). He also edited *La poesía mexicana de siglo XIX* (1965; "Mexican Poetry from the 19th Century") and *Antología del Modernismo, 1884–1921* (1970).

Pa Chin   *see* BA JIN.

Pacuvius \pə-'kü-vē-əs, -'kyü-\, Marcus (b. 220 BC, Brundisium [Italy]—d. *c.* 130, Tarentum [now Taranto])   The greatest Roman tragic dramatist before Lucius Accius.

The bearer of an Oscan name, Pacuvius was probably educated at Tarentum. As a young man he followed his uncle, the poet Quintus Ennius, to Rome, where he joined the circle of Scipio the Younger.

Thirteen titles and fragments amounting to about 440 lines are all that survive of Pacuvius' dramatic output. Apart from one Roman national drama, *Paullus*, the 12 plays that he translated and adapted from original plays by Sophocles and other Greeks may represent his entire output.

As a playwright, Pacuvius was admired by the Romans for his elevated style, his command of pathos, and his scholarly treatment of obscure Greek mythological themes. His plays continued to be produced until the end of the Roman Empire in the 5th century AD.

paean \'pē-ən\ [Greek *paián, paiṓn,* from *Paián, Paiṓn,* epithet of Apollo in such songs]   Solemn choral lyric of invocation, joy, or triumph, originating in ancient Greece where it was addressed to Apollo in his guise as Paean, physician to the gods. Paeans were sung at banquets following the boisterous dithyrambs, at the festivals of Apollo, and at public funerals. It was the custom for them to be sung by an army on the march and before going into battle, when a fleet left the harbor, and after a victory. Paeans were later addressed to other gods as well as to mortals, such as the 5th-century-BC Spartan commander Lysander, who were more or less deified for their achievements.

paeon \'pē-ən, -ăn\ [Greek *paián, paiṓn,* literally, paean]   In classical prosody, a metrical foot consisting of one long and three short syllables. The position of the long syllable determines the designation of the foot as a first ($-\cup\cup\cup$) or fourth ($\cup\cup\cup-$) paeon. (Second and third paeons exist in theory only.) They occur in bacchic or cretic verse, and the fourth paeon occurs as a syncopated iambic or trochaic metron.

Page \'pāj\, Thomas Nelson (b. April 23, 1853, Oakland plantation, near Beaver Dam, Va., U.S.—d. Nov. 1, 1922, Oakland, Calif.)   American author whose work fostered romantic legends of Southern plantation life.

Page attended Washington College (now Washington and Lee University), Va., and the University of Virginia. He practiced law until 1893, when he devoted himself to writing and lecturing. He first won notice with the story "Marse Chan" in the *Century Illustrated Magazine*. This and similar stories were collected in *In Ole Virginia, Marse Chan, and Other Stories* (1887). Among his essays and social studies are *Social Life in Old Virginia* (1897) and *The Old Dominion—Her Making and Her Manners* (1908). His other works include *Two Little Confederates* (1888), a children's tale; *The Burial of the Guns; and Other Stories* (1894); *The Old Gentlemen of the Black Stock* (1897); and *Red Rock* (1898).

pageant \'paj-ənt\ [Middle English *pagent* play in a mystery cycle, movable stage (corresponding to Medieval Latin *pagina, pagenda*), of unknown origin]   An elaborate, colorful exhibition or spectacle, often with music, that consists of a series of tableaux, of a loosely unified theatrical production, or of a procession, usually with floats. In its earlier use the word denoted the vehicle designed for the presentation of religious plays or cycles as well as the presentations themselves. Because these plays were generally accompanied by great ceremony and showmanship, pageant has come to mean also any lavish production, whether indoors or outdoors, without regard to any specifically religious content.

An essential feature of pageantry through the ages has been the element of drama, in which the theme of a procession is illustrated with spoken words or simple dramatic action. Pageant dramas were an integral part of the major festivals of the Roman Catholic church, and these religious pageants gradually developed into the MYSTERY PLAY, the MASQUE, and other theatrical precursors of Western secular drama.

The early 20th century saw a revival of a "pure" form of pageant (one that is first and foremost historical drama), most notably in the works of Louis N. Parker. Parker's insistence on accurate retellings of history, use of natural settings with little or no artificial scenery, and reliance on amateur actors served to repopularize the pageant as historical drama.

pai-hua   *see* BAIHUA.

Painted Bird, The   Semiautobiographical novel by Jerzy KOSINSKI, published in 1965 and revised in 1976. The ordeals of the central character parallel Kosinski's own experiences during World War II. A dark-haired Polish child who is taken for either a Gypsy or a Jew loses his parents in the mayhem of war and wanders through the countryside at the mercy of the brutal, thickheaded peasants he meets in the villages. He learns how to stay alive at any cost, turning survival into a moral imperative. Full of graphic scenes depicting rape, torture, and bestiality, the novel portrays evil in all its manifestations and speaks of human isolation as inevitable.

Painter \'pān-tər\, William (b. *c.* 1540—d. February 1594, London, Eng.)   English author whose collection of tales *The Palace of Pleasure*, based on classical and Italian originals, served as a sourcebook for many Elizabethan dramatists.

Educated at St. John's College, Cambridge, Painter was ordained in 1560. In 1561 he became a clerk of the ordnance in the Tower of London, a position in which he appears to have amassed a fortune out of public funds. In 1591 his son Anthony confessed that he and his father had abused their trust, but Painter retained his office until his death.

The first volume of *The Palace of Pleasure*, which appeared in 1566, contained 60 tales. It was followed in the next year by a volume including 34 new stories. An improved edition (1575) contained seven more new stories. It and similar popular collections are responsible for the high proportion of Elizabethan plays with Italian settings.

The early tragedies *Appius and Virginia* by John Webster and *The Tragedy of Tancred and Gismund* by Robert Wilmot were taken from Painter's book, and it was also the source for William Shakespeare's *Timon of Athens* and *All's Well That Ends Well* (and probably for details in *Romeo and Juliet* and *The Rape of Lucrece*), for Francis Beaumont and John Fletcher's *Triumph of Death*, and for James Shirley's *Loves Crueltie*.

Pa Jen   *see* BAREN.

Palacio Valdés \pä-'läth-ē-ō-väl-'däs\, Armando (b. Oct. 4, 1853, Entralgo, Spain—d. Feb. 3, 1938, Madrid)   One of the most popular 19th-century Spanish novelists, known for his optimism, his charming heroines, and his realism.

After studying law at the University of Madrid, Palacio Valdés began his literary career as a critic but soon turned to the novel. His novels are largely autobiographical, particularly *Riverita* (1886), its sequel *Maximina* (1887), and *La novela de un novelista* (1921; "The Novel of a Novelist"). He had an early interest in science, and his work reveals his experiments in naturalism, notably *La espuma* (1890; *The Froth*) and *La fe* (1892; *Faith*). *Marta y María* (1883), with its biblical Martha and Mary theme, is his most profound work. *José* (1885) is a realistic picture of seafaring life, and *La aldea perdida* (1903; "The Lost Village") shows the destruction of rural life by civilization.

Palais-Royal Theater \pä-le-rwä-'yȧl\   Paris playhouse most noted for 17th-century productions by Molière.

The Palais-Royal traces its history to a small private theater located in the residence of Cardinal Richelieu and known by the name of the residence, the Palais-Cardinal. Following Richelieu's death, the palace became royal property, and, as the Théâtre du Palais-Royal, it was used for courtly entertainments. In 1660 the theater was given to Molière and his troupe, who occupied it until the dramatist-actor's death in 1673. Thereafter, it was used by the Royal Academy of Music. It burned down in 1763, was rebuilt, and burned again in 1781. The entire area was then redeveloped into an amusement area by its owner, the Duke de Chartres. It contained a number of theaters, many called Palais-Royal at various times.

Palamás \ˌpä-lä-'mäs\, Kostís, Kostís *also spelled* Kostes (b. Jan. 13 [Jan. 25, New Style], 1859, Patras, Greece—d. Feb. 27, 1943, Athens)   Greek poet who played an important part in the evolution of modern Greek literature.

Palamás was the central figure in the Demotic movement of the 1880s, which sought to shake off traditionalism and draw inspiration for a new literary and artistic style from the life and language of the people. He became the founder of the "new school of Athens," which condemned romantic exuberance and reverted to a purer and more restrained type of poetry. In 1886 Palamás published his first collection of poems, *Tragoúdia tés patrídos mou* ("Tragedy of My Country"), followed by *Íamboi kai anápaistoi* (1897; "Iambs and Anapaests"), *O táfos* (1898; *The Grave*), *Asálefte zoé* (1904; *Life Immovable*), *Dodecálogos toú gýftou* (1907; *The Twelve Lays of the Gypsy*), and *I flogéra toú vasiliá* (1910; *The King's Flute*). His play, the *Trisévgene* (1903; *Royal Blossom, or, Trisevyene*), has lyric rather than dramatic merits. He also wrote short stories and helped to raise the standard of modern Greek literary criticism.

Palamedes \ˌpal-ə-'mē-dēz\   In Greek mythology, the son of Nauplius, king of Euboea, and a hero of the Trojan War. During the siege of Troy, Palamedes alternated with two other Greek heroes, Odysseus and Diomedes, in leading the army in the field, but his ability aroused their envy. In the epic version they drowned him while fishing or persuaded him to seek treasure in a well, which they thereupon filled with stones.

In the tragic version Agamemnon (king of Mycenae or Argos), Diomedes, and Odysseus had an agent steal into his tent to conceal a letter that contained money and purported to come from King Priam of Troy. They then accused Palamedes of treasonable correspondence with the enemy, and he was stoned to death.

The ancients attributed a number of inventions to Palamedes, including the alphabet, numbers, weights and measures, coinage, and the practice of eating at regular intervals. He is now generally considered to be a personification of Phoenician culture, the source of many of these developments.

Palazzeschi \ˌpä-lät-'tses-kē\, Aldo, *pseudonym of* Aldo Giurlani \jūr-'lä-nē\ (b. Feb. 2, 1885, Florence, Italy—d. Aug. 17, 1974, Rome)   Italian author of witty, avant-garde poetry and fiction who emerged from the literary movements of Crepuscolarismo and Futurism in the early 20th century.

Palazzeschi's early collections of poetry—*I cavalli bianchi* (1905; "The White Knights"), *Lanterna* (1907; "Lantern"), and *Poemi* (1909; enlarged several times as *Poesie*)—emphasized the absurd elements of Crepuscolarismo. He began his association with Futurism with the publication of *L'incendiario* (1910; rev. ed., 1913). His Futurist novel *Il codice di Perelà* (1911; revised in 1954 as *Perelà, uomo di fumo*) was translated as *Perelà, the Man of Smoke*. Other notable novels include *Sorelle Materassi* (1934; U.S. title, *The Sisters Materassi*; U.K. title, *Materassi Sisters*), *I fratelli Cuccoli* (1948; "The Cuccoli Brothers"), and *Stefanino* (1969). Among his works of nonfiction are the memoirs *Due imperi . . . mancati* (1920; "Two Emperors . . . Lost") and *Stampe dell'800* (1932; enlarged 1957; "Nineteenth-Century Engravings").

Pale Fire   Novel in English by Vladimir NABOKOV, published in 1962. It consists of a long poem and a commentary on it by an insane pedant. This brilliant parody of literary scholarship is also an experimental synthesis of Nabokov's talents for both poetry and prose. It extends and completes his mastery of unorthodox structure.

Pale Horse, Pale Rider   A collection of three novellas by Katherine Anne PORTER, published in 1939. The collection consists of "Noon Wine," "Old Mortality," and the title story. For their stylistic grace and sense of life's ambiguity, these stories are considered some of the best Porter wrote.

Palés Matos \pä-'läz-'mä-tōs\, Luis (b. March 20, 1898, Guayama, P.R.—d. Feb. 23, 1959, San Juan)   Writer considered by many to be Puerto Rico's most distinguished lyric poet, who enriched the vocabulary of Spanish verse with words, themes, symbols, images, and rhythms of African folklore and dance.

Palés Matos wrote his first poetry, which was collected in *Azaleas* (1915), in imitation of modernist trends, but he soon found his own direction in his personal interpretation (as a white man) of black culture. His poems on black themes gave impetus to the developing concern of Latin Americans with their African heritage. Although he was best known and most influential for his "Negro" poetry, his reflective and introspective personality found expression in poetry of many other moods and themes. *Poesía, 1915–56* (1957), a collection of much of his poetry, reveals his more personal side as a lyric poet.

Paley \'pā-lē\, Grace, *original surname* Goodside \'gúd-ˌsīd\ (b. Dec. 11, 1922, New York, N.Y., U.S.)   Poet and short-story writer known for her realistic seriocomic portrayals of working-class New Yorkers and for her political activism.

Paley attended Hunter College and the New School for Social Research, both in New York City. She joined the faculty of Sarah Lawrence College in Bronxville, N.Y., in 1966. During the 1960s she was actively involved in the opposition to the Vietnam War and continued her political activism after the war ended.

Her first volume of short stories, *The Little Disturbances of Man: Stories of Men and Women at Love* (1959), was noted for its realistic dialogue. It was followed by *Enormous Changes at the Last Minute* (1974) and *Later the Same Day* (1985), both of which continued her compassionate, often comic, exploration of ordinary individuals struggling against loneliness. All featured the character of Faith, Paley's reputed alter ego. She also published two volumes of poems, *Leaning Forward* (1985) and *Begin Again: New and Collected Poems* (1992).

Palgrave \'pal-ˌgrāv, 'pȯl-\, Francis Turner (b. Sept. 28, 1824, Great Yarmouth, Norfolk, Eng.—d. Oct. 24, 1897, London) English critic and poet, editor of the influential anthology *The Golden Treasury of English Songs and Lyrics* (1861).

Educated at Charterhouse and at Balliol College, Oxford, Palgrave spent many years in the education department of the civil service and taught poetry at the University of Oxford. Of his original verse, *Visions of England* (1880–81) is the best known. His greatest service to poetry, however, was his compilation of *The Golden Treasury*, a comprehensive, well-chosen anthology, carefully arranged in its sequence. Palgrave's choice of poems was made in consultation with his friend Alfred, Lord Tennyson. The anthology had great influence on the poetic taste of several generations and was of particular value in popularizing William Wordsworth.

palimpsest \'pal-imp-ˌsest, pə-'limp-səst\ [Greek *palímpsēston,* from neuter of *palímpsēstos* scraped again, from *pálin* again + *-psēstos,* verbal adjective of *psên* to rub, scrape] Writing material such as parchment that has been used one or more times after earlier writing has been erased or partly erased. The underlying text is said to be "in palimpsest," and, even though the parchment or other surface is much abraded, the older text is recoverable in the laboratory by such means as the use of ultraviolet light. The motive for making palimpsests usually seems to have been economic—reusing parchment was cheaper than preparing a new skin. Another motive may have been directed by Christian piety, as in the conversion of a pagan Greek manuscript to receive the text of a Church Father.

palindrome \'pal-in-ˌdrōm\ [Greek *palíndromos* running back, going backwards, from *pálin* back, again + *-dromos,* a derivative of *drameîn* to run] A word, number, sentence, or verse that reads the same backward or forward. Examples of word palindromes include "civic," "madam," "radar," and "deified." Numerical palindromes include sequences that read the same in reverse order (*e.g.,* 1991), as well as those that can be read upside down and backward (*e.g.,* 1961). Examples of such sentences include "Able was I ere I saw Elba" and "Lewd did I live & evil I did dwel." Examples of palindromic verse include (in Latin) "Roma tibi subito motibus ibit amor" and "Signa te, signa temere me tangis et angis." Some writers have refined the palindrome, composing verses in which each word reads the same backward and forward—for instance, that of William Camden:

> Odo tenet mulum, madidam mappam tenet
> Anna,
> Anna tenet mappam madidam, mulum tenet
> Odo.

Palliser family \'pal-i-sər\ Fictional characters in the Palliser novels, a series of novels published in the late 19th century by Anthony TROLLOPE. The novels trace the slow progress of the marriage between Plantagenet Palliser and Lady Glencora Palliser, formerly Glencora M'Cluskie.

Plantagenet, who chooses a vigorous political career over an idle aristocratic life, is staid and humorless, in contrast to Lady Glencora, who is witty and passionate. Dissatisfied with the arranged marriage, Lady Glencora tells Plantagenet that she still loves her former suitor, charming Burgo Fitzgerald. The Palliser marriage slowly recovers by the end of the first novel, when they start a family. Plantagenet, who succeeds his uncle as Duke of Omnium in the fourth novel, becomes prime minister in the fifth novel.

Palliser novels \'pal-i-sər\ Series of novels by Anthony TROLLOPE. They are united by the fact that each deals with political issues and that the character Plantagenet Palliser appears in each, with other characters recurring periodically. The series consists of CAN YOU FORGIVE HER? (1864–65), PHINEAS FINN (1869), THE EUSTACE DIAMONDS (1872), PHINEAS REDUX (1874), THE PRIME MINISTER (1876), and THE DUKE'S CHILDREN (1880).

Palma \'päl-mä\, Ricardo (b. Feb. 7, 1833, Lima, Peru—d. Oct. 6, 1919, Lima) Peruvian writer best known for his collected legends of colonial Peru, one of the most popular collections in Latin-American literature.

At the age of 20 he joined the Peruvian navy, and in 1860 he was forced by political exigencies to flee to Chile. He returned to Lima to join the revolutionary movement against Spain. Later, during the Chilean occupation of Lima, Palma courageously protested against the wanton destruction, in 1881, of the famous National Library. After the war Palma was commissioned to rebuild the library, and he remained its curator until his death. In 1887 he founded the Peruvian Academy.

Palma's fame derives chiefly from his *Tradiciones peruanas* (1872; "Peruvian Traditions")—short sketches about colonial Peru. The first six volumes of the series appeared between 1872 and 1883; they were followed by *Ropa vieja* (1889; "Old Clothes"), *Ropa apolillada* (1891; "Moth-Eaten Clothes"), *Mis últimas tradiciones* (1906; "My Last Traditions"), and *Apéndice a mis últimas tradiciones* (1910; "Appendix to My Last Traditions").

Palmer \'päm-ər, 'päl-mər\, Vance, *in full* Edward Vance Palmer (b. Aug. 28, 1885, Bundaberg, Queen., Australia—d. July 15, 1959, Melbourne, Vic.) Australian author of novels, short stories, and plays. He is considered one of the founders of Australian drama.

Palmer spent several years working at a variety of jobs in the Australian outback. He also wrote, traveled, and served with Australian forces during World War I. From 1922 to 1926 he helped organize the Pioneer Players, a theatrical company in Melbourne specializing in Australian drama.

Of his novels, *The Passage* (1930), which describes the life of a family, is considered the best. *Golconda* (1948) is the first volume of a political trilogy that includes *Seedtime* (1957) and *The Big Fellow* (1959). Palmer also wrote several plays on political themes. His short stories have been collected in four volumes: *Separate Lives* (1931), *Sea and Spinifex* (1934), *Let the Birds Fly* (1955), and *The Rainbow Bird* (1956). He composed two volumes of balladlike poetry and several volumes of essays and literary criticism.

Palm-Wine Drinkard, The \'driŋ-kərd\ (*in full* The Palm-Wine Drinkard and His Dead Palm-Wine Tapster in the Dead's Town) Novel by Amos TUTUOLA, published in 1952 and since translated into 11 languages. Written in the unorthodox English of the Yoruban oral tradition, the novel was the first Nigerian book to achieve international fame. The story is a classic quest tale in which the hero, a lazy boy who likes to spend his days drinking palm wine, gains wisdom, confronts death, and overcomes many perils in the course of his journey.

It has thematic links to *The Pilgrim's Progress* by John Bunyan, a work that profoundly influenced many Nigerian writers.

Paludan \'pal-ů-dan\, Jacob, *in full* Stig Henning Jacob Puggaard Paludan (b. Feb. 7, 1896, Copenhagen, Den.—d. Sept. 26, 1975, Birkerød, near Copenhagen) Danish novelist and conservative critic whose work expressed a fear of the Americanization of European culture.

Paludan was the leading critic for the conservative Copenhagen newspaper *Dagens Nyheder* and was the editor of *Hasselbalchs Kulturbibliotek*, a book series that popularized arts and letters. He translated several books into Danish, most notably Sinclair Lewis' *Dodsworth*. He is probably best known for his fiction, especially the novels *Fugle omkring fyret* (1925; *Birds Around the Light*), *Markerne modnes* (1927; "The Ripening Fields"), and the monumental epic *Jørgen Stein*, 2 vol. (1932–33).

Paludan-Müller \'pal-ů-dan-'mœl-ər\, Frederik (b. Feb. 7, 1809, Kerteminde, on the island of Funen, Den.—d. Dec. 28, 1876, Copenhagen) Danish poet who achieved early acclaim in the Danish Romantic movement for his Byronic epic *Danserinden* (1833; "The Danseuse").

Paludan-Müller was educated at the University of Copenhagen. His *Adam Homo* (1842–49), a lengthy satirical epic in three parts, is counted among the most important works of Danish literature. Its autobiographical hero, Adam Homo, is said to have been Henrik Ibsen's model for the character of Peer Gynt.

Pamela \'pam-ə-lə\ (*in full* Pamela; or, Virtue Rewarded) Novel in epistolary style by Samuel RICHARDSON, published in 1740 and based on a story about a servant who avoided seduction and was rewarded by marriage.

On the death of Pamela Andrews' mistress, her mistress's son, Mr. B, begins a series of mild stratagems designed to end in Pamela's seduction. These failing, he abducts her and renews his siege in earnest. Pamela spurns his advances, and halfway through the novel Mr. B offers marriage. In the second half of the novel, Pamela wins over those who had disapproved of the misalliance.

Pamela is often credited with being the first English novel. Although the validity of this claim depends on the definition of the term "novel," Richardson was clearly innovative in his concentration on a single action, in this case a courtship.

Pampa \'pām-pä\ (fl. 940) South Indian poet and literary figure, called *ādikavi* ("first poet") in the Kannada language. He created a style that served as the model for all future works in the Kannada language.

Although Pampa's family had been orthodox Hindus for generations, his father, Abhirāmadevarāya, together with his whole family, was converted to the faith of Jainism. True to his rearing, Pampa cared little for material possessions and gave freely of what he had. He highly esteemed his guru, Devendramuni, and his royal patron, Arikēsarī, and lauded both in his writings.

Pampa's great work was the *Ādipurāṇa* ("First [or Original] Scriptures"), in which Jain teaching and tenets are expounded. Another epic of his creation is the *Pampa-Bhārata* (c. 950; Bhārata is both the ancient name for India and the name of a famous king), in which Pampa likened his royal master to the mythical hero Arjuna in the *Mahābhārata* ("Great Epic of the Bhārata Dynasty").

pamphlet \'pam-flət\ [Middle English *pamf(i)let* short written text, small book, from Old French *Pamphilet*, vernacular title (originally, the supposed author) of *Pamphilus seu de amore*, a 12th-century Latin love poem] An unbound printed publication with no cover or with a paper cover. Pamphlets were among the first printed materials, and they were widely used in England, France, and Germany, often for purposes of religious or political propaganda.

The first great age of pamphleteering was inspired by the religious controversies of the early 16th century. In Germany the pamphlet was first used by the leaders of the Protestant Reformation to inflame popular opinion against the pope and the Roman Catholic church.

In France didactic and abusive religious pamphleteering gave way to a more flippant and lively writing that satirized the morals of the court and the chief ministers. The pamphlets of Blaise Pascal, known as *Les Provinciales*, raised the form to the level of literature. In England pamphlets gained increasing propagandist influence during the political and religious controversies of the 17th century.

The pamphlet continued to have a powerful influence throughout the 18th century. In North America, pre-Revolutionary War political agitation stimulated the beginning of extensive pamphleteering; foremost among the writers of political pamphlets was Thomas Paine, whose *Common Sense* appeared in January 1776.

Noted writers of 18th-century France—Voltaire, Jean-Jacques Rousseau, Montesquieu, and Denis Diderot, among others—used pamphlets to express the philosophy of the Enlightenment. Their pamphlets were reasoned discourses, though with the arrival of the French Revolution, pamphlets once again became powerful polemical weapons. The revolution also occasioned one of the outstanding English pamphlets, Edmund Burke's *Reflections on the Revolution in France* (1790). It provoked many replies, the most famous of which is Thomas Paine's *Rights of Man* (1791–92).

In the 19th century pamphlets continued to be used for political propaganda in France and England, but in the 20th century the pamphlet has more often been used for information than for controversy, chiefly by government departments and learned societies.

Pan \'pan\ In Greek mythology, a fertility deity, more or less bestial in form. He was associated by the Romans with FAUNUS. He was originally an Arcadian deity, and his name is a contraction of *pāon-*, a stem that some scholars have seen as akin to *Pūṣan*, the name of a Vedic deity protecting herds. By folk etymology the Greeks associated Pan's name with the word *pan* ("all"). His father was usually said to be Hermes, but, because his mother was often named Penelope (probably not the wife of Odysseus but commonly identified with her), one or another of the characters in the *Odyssey* was sometimes called his father. Pan was generally represented as a vigorous and lustful figure having the horns, legs, and ears of a goat; in later art the human parts of his form were much more emphasized. He haunted the high hills, and his chief concern was with flocks and herds, not with agriculture. Like the shepherds with whom he is associated, he was a piper, and he rested at noon. Pan does not appear often in literature, aside from Hellenistic bucolics, but he was a common subject in ancient art.

Pañca-tantra or **Panchatantra** \,pən-chə-'tən-trə\ ("Five Chapters") Collection of Indian beast fables originally written in Sanskrit that has had extensive circulation throughout the world. In Europe the work was known under the title *The Fables of Bidpai* (after the narrator, an Indian sage named Bidpai, called Vidyāpati in Sanskrit), and one version reached there as early as the 11th century.

In theory, the *Pañca-tantra* is intended as a textbook of *artha* ("worldly wisdom"); the aphorisms tend to glorify shrewdness and cleverness more than the helping of others. The original text is a mixture of Sanskrit prose and stanzas of verse, with the stories contained within one of five frame stories. The introduction, which acts as an enclosing frame for the entire work, attributes the stories to a learned Brahman named Vishṇuśarman, who used the form of animal fables to instruct the three dull-witted sons of a king.

The original Sanskrit work, now lost, may have originated at any time between 100 BC and AD 500. It was translated into Pahlavi (Middle Persian) by the Persian royal physician Burzoe in the 6th century. Although this work also is lost, a Syriac translation of it has survived, together with the famous Arabic translation by Ibn al-Muqaffaʿ (died AD 760), known as *Kalīlah wa Dimnah* after the two jackals that figure in the first story. The *Kalīlah wa Dimnah* led to various other versions, including a second Syriac version and an 11th-century version in Greek, the *Stephanites kai Ichnelates*, from which translations were made into Latin and various Slavic languages. It was the 12th-century Hebrew version of Rabbi Joel, however, that became the source of most European versions.

The 17th-century Turkish translation, the *Hūmayun-name*, was based on a 15th-century Persian version, the *Anwār-e Suhaylī*. The *Pañca-tantra* stories also traveled to Indonesia through Old Javanese written literature and possibly through oral versions. In India the *Hitopadeśa* ("Good Advice"), composed by Nārāyaṇa in the 12th century and circulated mostly in Bengal, appears to be an independent treatment of the *Pañcatantra* material.

Pancks \\'paŋks\\ Fictional character in the novel LITTLE DORRIT by Charles Dickens. Pancks is a clerk who reluctantly collects exorbitant rents for the hypocritical landlord Casby; he is able to appear generous because he makes Pancks act the villain. Finally, tired of his role, Pancks rebels and publicly humiliates Casby.

Pandarus \\'pan-də-rəs\\ In Greek legend, son of Lycaon, a Lycian. In Homer's epic poem the *Iliad*, Pandarus broke the truce between the Trojans and the Greeks by treacherously wounding Menelaus, the king of Sparta; he was finally slain by the warrior Diomedes. In the medieval tale of Troilus and Cressida, as well as in William Shakespeare's play by the same name, Pandarus acted as the lovers' go-between; hence the word "pander."

Pandora \\pan-'dȯr-ə\\ ("All-Giving") In Greek mythology, the first woman. After Prometheus, a fire god and divine trickster, had stolen fire from heaven and bestowed it upon mortals, Zeus determined to counteract this blessing and bring misery on earth. He accordingly commissioned Hephaestus (a god of fire and patron of craftsmen) to fashion a woman out of earth, upon whom the gods bestowed their choicest gifts—beauty, cunning, and so on. She found or was given a vessel—the so-called Pandora's box—containing all manner of misery and evil. Zeus sent her to Prometheus, who refused her. His brother Epimetheus, who forgot Prometheus' warning not to accept any gifts from Zeus, made her his wife. Either with Epimetheus or of her own volition, Pandora opened the jar, and the evils stored in it flew out over the earth. According to another version, Hope alone remained inside, the lid having been shut down before she could escape.

In literature the story of Pandora has been used to illustrate seduction or fatal beauty. Thus, John Milton describing Eve in *Paradise Lost* alludes to Pandora, and many other writers, such as J.W. von Goethe and Frank Wedekind, have used the theme to great effect.

Pandora's Box \\pan-'dȯr-ə, *German* pän-'dō-rə\\ Expressionistic drama in three acts by Frank WEDEKIND, published and performed in German in 1904 as *Die Büchse der Pandora*.

Originally written as the second part of a work similarly titled, the play was censored when it was first published for its explicit scenes of destructive sexuality. The first part of the longer original work had been published in 1895 as *Der Erdgeist* (EARTH SPIRIT). It tells the story of Lulu, an amoral woman who disregards bourgeois values; her amorality and her insistence on sexual freedom are dangerous to all who come in contact with her. *Pandora's Box* tells the sordid story of Lulu after her escape from jail for the murder of her third husband. She becomes a prostitute and is eventually murdered by Jack the Ripper in London.

Panduro \\pan-'dū-rō\\, Leif (b. April 18, 1923, Frederiksberg, Den.—d. Jan. 16, 1977, Asserbo) Danish novelist and dramatist, a social critic who wrote in a satirical, humorous vein.

His first novel, *Av, min guldtand* (1957; "Ow, My Gold Tooth"), was an ironic, at times hilarious description of small-town life. It was followed by *Rend mig i traditionerne* (1958; *Kick Me in the Traditions*) and *De uanstaendige* (1960; "The Indecent Ones"). Panduro's most ambitious novel is *Øgledage* (1961; "Saurian Days"), which makes use of a sophisticated, modernistic narrative technique. The conflict between instinctive energies and the demands of conformity becomes the central theme in several of Panduro's novels from the 1960s—*Fern fra Danmark* (1963; "Far from Denmark"), *Fejltagelsen* (1964; "The Mistake"), and *Den gale mand* (1965; "The Crazy Man").

Panduro produced a number of scripts for radio, television, and film, becoming one of the most successful Scandinavian dramatists of the 1970s with such works as *Farvel, Thomas* (1968; "Good-bye, Thomas") and *I Adams verden* (1973; "In Adam's World").

panegyric \\ˌpan-ə-'jir-ik, -'jīr-\\ [Greek *panēgyrikós*, from *panēgyrikós* (adjective) of or for a festival or assembly, a derivative of *panēgyrís* general or national assembly, from *pan-* all + *ágyris* gathering] Eulogistic oration or laudatory discourse that originally was a speech delivered at an ancient Greek general assembly (panegyris), such as the Olympic and Panathenaic festivals. Speakers frequently took advantage of these occasions, when Greeks of various cities were gathered together, to advocate Hellenic unity. With this end in view and also in order to gratify their audience, they tended to expound on the former glories of Greek cities; hence the elaborate and flowery connotations of the term. The most famous ancient Greek panegyrics to survive intact are the *Panegyricus* (*c.* 380 BC) and the *Panathenaicus* (*c.* 340 BC), both by Isocrates.

In the 2nd century AD, Aelius Aristides, a Greek rhetorician, combined praise of famous cities with eulogy of the reigning Roman emperor. By his time panegyric had probably become specialized in the latter connection and was, therefore, related to the old Roman custom of celebrating at festivals the glories of famous men of the past and of pronouncing *laudationes funebres* at the funerals of eminent persons.

Another kind of Roman eulogistic speech was the *gratiarum actio* ("thanksgiving"), delivered by a successful candidate for public office. Roman writers of the 3rd to the 5th century indiscriminately praised and flattered the emperors in panegyrics that were sometimes written in verse.

Although primarily associated with classical antiquity, panegyrics continued to be written on occasion in the European Middle Ages, often by Christian mystics in praise of God, and in the Renaissance and Baroque periods, especially in Elizabethan England, in Spain during the Golden Age, and in France under the reign of Louis XIV.

Pangloss \\'pan-ˌgläs, -ˌglȯs\\ Fictional character, the pedantic and unfailingly optimistic tutor of Candide, the protagonist of Voltaire's novel CANDIDE, a satire on philosophical optimism.

The name Pangloss—from the Greek elements *pan-*, "all," and *glōssa*, "tongue"—suggests glibness and garrulousness.

panisc or **panisk** \'pan-isk\ [Greek *Panískos,* diminutive of *Pán* Pan] In Greek mythology, a godling of the forest that is half man and half goat and is commonly attendant on the god Pan.

Panneton \pȧn-'tōⁿ\, Philippe, *pseudonym* Ringuet \raⁿ-'gā\ (b. April 30, 1895, Trois-Rivières, Que., Can.—d. Dec. 29, 1960, Lisbon, Port.) French-Canadian novelist whose best-known works present the individual caught in the transition from primitive rural to modern urban life.

Panneton practiced medicine in Montreal and taught medicine at the University of Montreal. He was a cofounder of the French-Canadian Academy. From 1956 until his death, he served as Canadian ambassador to Portugal. *Trente Arpents* (1938; *Thirty Acres*), Panneton's major work, deals with the plight of the small French-Canadian farmer forced by the economic and social upheavals of the late 19th and early 20th centuries to migrate to the city. In other novels, such as *Fausse Monnaie* (1947; "False Money") and *Le Poids du jour* (1948; "The Heaviness of the Day"), he continued his examination of the lives of displaced peasants. He also published a volume of short stories and two historical sketches.

Pantagruel *see* GARGANTUA AND PANTAGRUEL.

Pantaloon \,pan-tə-'lün\ or **Pantalone** \,pän-tä-'lō-nä\ Stock character of the 16th-century Italian COMMEDIA DELL'ARTE—a cunning and rapacious yet often deceived Venetian merchant.

The humor of the role stemmed from Pantaloon's avarice and his amorous entanglements. An abject slave to money, he would starve his servant until he barely cast a shadow. If married, he was a foil for his wife, who was young, pretty, disrespectful, and completely untrustworthy, and he was also a foil for the intrigues and deceits of his daughters and servant girls. Although anxious about his reputation, he engaged in flirtations with young girls who openly mocked him.

In the Italian commedia dell'arte, the character was frequently paired with Dottore as a parent or guardian of one of the lovers. The French variant Pantaloon evolved from the Italian Pantalone when the commedia dell'arte companies played in France. In Elizabethan England, Pantaloon came to mean simply an old man. In 18th-century London, Pantaloon, minus his long coat, was one of the characters of the harlequinade, the English pantomime version of the commedia dell'arte.

pantoum \pan-'tüm\ [French, from Malay *pantun*] A Malaysian poetic form in French and English. The pantoum consists of a series of quatrains rhyming *abab* in which the second and fourth lines of a quatrain recur as the first and third lines in the succeeding quatrain; each quatrain introduces a new second rhyme (as *bcbc, cdcd*). The first line of the series recurs as the last line of the closing quatrain, and in some English examples the third line of the poem recurs as the second line of the closing quatrain, rhyming *xaxa*.

Although the pantoum was introduced into Western literature in the 19th century, it bears some resemblance to older French fixed forms, such as the rondeau and the villanelle. French poets who wrote pantoums include Victor Hugo, Théodore de Banville, and Leconte de Lisle, among others. Austin Dobson was one of the more proficient English practitioners of the form.

pantun or **pantoun** \pan-'tün\ [Malay *pantun*] Indonesian verse consisting of four lines rhyming *abab*; the first two present a figurative suggestion of what is more directly and clearly stated in the final lines.

Panurge \'pan-,ərj, pȧ-'nurzh, *French* pȧ-'nᵫrzh\ Fictional character, the humorous, often roguish companion of Pantagruel in the satirical Pantagruel books by François Rabelais. *See also* GARGANTUA AND PANTAGRUEL.

Panyassis \,pan-ē-'as-əs\ or **Panyasis** \pə-'nī-ə-sis, ,pan-ē-'ā-sis\ (fl. 5th century BC, Ionia) Epic poet from Halicarnassus, on the coast of Asia Minor. The Roman rhetorician Quintilian stated that some later critics regarded Panyassis' work as being second only to that of Homer. His chief poems, extant only in fragments, were the *Heracleia*, describing the mythical adventures of the hero Heracles (Hercules), and the *Ionica*, relating the founding of Ionic Greek colonies in Asia Minor.

Panza, Sancho \'sän-chō-'pän-thä, *Angl* 'pän-zə\ Fictional character, Don Quixote's squire in the novel DON QUIXOTE by Miguel de Cervantes. Panza is a short, pot-bellied peasant whose gross appetite, common sense, and vulgar wit serve as a foil to the mad idealism of his master. He is famous for his many pertinent proverbs. Cervantes used the psychological differences between the two characters to explore the conflict between the ideal and the real and based much of his novel's narrative development on their personal relationship.

pap \'pap\ Something (such as reading matter) that serves only to entertain or is not otherwise intellectually stimulating.

paper \'pā-pər\ A literary composition, especially of brief, occasional, or fragmentary nature—normally used in the plural.

Papini \pä-'pē-nē\, Giovanni (b. Jan. 9, 1881, Florence, Italy—d. July 8, 1956, Florence) Journalist, critic, poet, and novelist, one of the most outspoken and controversial Italian literary figures of the early and mid-20th century.

Papini was a founder of the influential Florentine literary magazine *Leonardo* (1903). During this period he wrote several violently antitraditionalist works, including *Il crepuscolo dei filosofi* (1906; "The Twilight of the Philosophers"). One of his best-known books is the autobiographical novel *Un uomo finito* (1912; *A Man—Finished*; U.S. title, *The Failure*).

Papini became an enthusiastic adherent of Futurism and founded the periodical *Lacerba* (1913) to further its aims. In 1921 he was reconverted to the Roman Catholicism in which he had been reared. A number of religious works followed, notably *Storia di Cristo* (1921; *Life of Christ*); *Pane e vino* (1926; "Bread and Wine"), a volume of religious poetry; and *Sant'-Agostino* (1929; *St. Augustine*).

Papp \'pap\, Joseph, *original surname* Papirofsky \,pap-i-'rȯf-skē\ (b. June 22, 1921, Brooklyn, New York, N.Y., U.S.—d. Oct. 31, 1991, New York, N.Y.) American theatrical producer and director, founder of the New York Shakespeare Festival and the Public Theatre. He was a major innovative force in the American theater in the second half of the 20th century, and he championed many innovative playwrights and talented actors who later achieved prominence.

parabasis \pə-'rab-ə-sis\ *plural* **parabases** \-,sēz\ [Greek *parábasis,* a derivative of *parabaínein* to step forward] An important choral ode in Greek Old Comedy delivered by the chorus at an intermission in the action while facing and moving toward the audience. It was used to express the author's views on political or religious topics of the day.

parable \'par-ə-bəl\ [Greek *parabolē* juxtaposition, comparison, parable, a derivative of *parabállein* to throw or set alongside, compare] A usually short fictitious story that illustrates a moral attitude, a doctrine, a standard of conduct, or a religious principle.

The parable differs from the fable in the inherent plausibility of its story and in the exclusion of anthropomorphism, but resembles it in the essential qualities of brevity and simplicity. The storytelling aspect of a parable is usually subordinated to the analogy it draws between a particular instance of human behavior and human conduct at large. The simple narratives of parables give them a mysterious, suggestive tone and make them especially useful for the teaching of moral and spiritual truths.

Some of the most famous Western parables are in the New Testament; in them, Jesus illustrates his message to his followers by telling a fictitious story that is nevertheless true to life. Parables have a considerable role also in Ṣūfism (Islāmic mysticism), rabbinic (Jewish exegetical) literature, Ḥasidism (Jewish pietism), and Zen Buddhism.

Parade's End Tetralogy by Ford Madox FORD, published in a single volume in 1950 and comprising the novels *Some Do Not* (1924), *No More Parades* (1925), *A Man Could Stand Up* (1926), and *The Last Post* (1928). Set during and after World War I, *Parade's End* shows some of Ford's strongest writing. Its theme is the breakdown of Edwardian culture and the painful emergence of a new world with a new set of values. Christopher Tietjens, the protagonist (thought to be modeled on Ford himself), is a conservative, rather naive, unhappily married landowner who is forced by the irrevocable alterations brought about by World War I to change his way of life. The work's impressionistic narrative style received favorable critical comment, and Tietjens is acknowledged to be one of the great creations of English literature.

paradiplomatic \ˌpar-ə-ˌdip-lə-'mat-ik\ Concerned with or based on evidence apart from strict textual authority. *Compare* DIPLOMATIC.

Paradise Lost Epic poem in blank verse, one of the late works by John MILTON, originally issued in 10 books in 1667 and, with Books 7 and 10 each split into two parts, published in 12 books in the second edition of 1674.

Considered by many scholars to be one of the greatest poems of the English language, *Paradise Lost* tells the biblical story of the fall from grace of Adam and Eve (and, by extension, all humanity) in language that is a supreme achievement of rhythm and sound.

The main characters in the poem are God, Lucifer (Satan), Adam, and Eve. Much has been written about Milton's powerful and sympathetic characterization of Satan. The Romantic poets William Blake and Percy Bysshe Shelley saw Satan as the real hero of the poem and applauded his rebellion against the tyranny of Heaven.

Many other works of art have been inspired by *Paradise Lost*, notably Joseph Haydn's oratorio "The Creation" (1798) and John Keats's long poem "Endymion." Milton wrote a companion piece, *Paradise Regained*, in 1671, which dramatizes the temptation of Christ.

paradox \'par-ə-ˌdäks\ [Greek *parádoxon,* from neuter of *parádoxos* contrary to expectation, from the phrase *parà dóxan* in violation of expectation] **1.** A tenet or proposition contrary to received opinion. **2.** An apparently self-contradictory statement, the underlying meaning of which is revealed only by careful scrutiny. The purpose of a paradox is to arrest attention and provoke fresh thought. The statement "Less is more" is an example. Francis Bacon's comment that "The most corrected copies are commonly the least correct" is an earlier literary example. In George Orwell's anti-utopian satire *Animal Farm* (1945), the first commandment of the animals' commune is revised into a witty paradox: "All animals are equal, but some animals are more equal than others." Paradox has a function in poetry, however, that goes beyond mere wit or attention-getting. Modern critics view it as a device, integral to poetic language, encompassing the tensions of error and truth simultaneously, not necessarily by startling juxtapositions but by subtle and continuous qualifications of the ordinary meaning of words. When a paradox is compressed into two words, as in "loud silence," "lonely crowd," or "living death," it is called an OXYMORON. **3.** Something (such as a person, phenomenon, state of affairs, or action) with seemingly contradictory qualities or phases.

paralipsis \ˌpar-ə-'lip-sis\, *also called* occupatio \ˌäk-yù-'pā-shē-ō, -'pä-tē-ō\ *or* preterition \ˌpret-ə-'rish-ən\ [Greek *paráleipsis,* a derivative of *paraleípein* to neglect, pass over] Rhetorical device by which a speaker or writer draws attention to a subject while professing to ignore or pass over it, as in the use of the phrases "Needless to say" or "It goes without saying" before a statement.

parallelism \'par-ə-lel-ˌiz-əm\ In rhetoric, a component of literary style in both prose and poetry, in which coordinate ideas are arranged in phrases, sentences, and paragraphs that balance one element with another of equal importance and similar wording. The repetition of sounds, meanings, and structures serves to order, emphasize, and point out relations. In its simplest form parallelism may consist of a pair of single words that are synonymous or have a slight variation in meaning: "ordain and establish" or "overtake and surpass." Another variety contains three or more parallel units as in "Reading maketh a full man, conference a ready man, and writing an exact man" (Francis Bacon, "Of Studies"). Chiasmus is a form of parallelism in which the separate clauses are inverted for stronger emphasis; *e.g.,* "I have changed in many things: in this I have not" (John Henry Newman, *Apologia pro Vita Sua*). Parallelism lends wit and authority to the antithetical aphorism; *e.g.,* "We always love those who admire us, but we do not always love those whom we admire" (La Rochefoucauld, *Maximes*).

Parallelism is a prominent figure in Hebrew poetry as well as in most literatures of the ancient Middle East. The Old Testament and New Testament, reflecting the influence of Hebrew poetry, contain many striking examples of parallelism, as in the following lines from Psalms 78:36: "but they flattered him with their mouths; they lied to him with their tongues."

Parallel Lives *also called* Lives. Influential collection of biographies of famous Greek and Roman soldiers, legislators, orators, and statesmen written as *Bioi parállēloi* by the Greek writer PLUTARCH near the end of his life. By comparing a famous Roman with a famous Greek, Plutarch intended to provide model patterns of behavior and to encourage mutual respect between Greeks and Romans. Twenty-two pairs and four single biographies have survived.

The form of *Parallel Lives* was new, not closely linked with either previous biography or Hellenistic history. Plutarch's method was to give details of the birth, youth, achievements, and death of his characters, followed by a formal comparison. His biographies are enriched with frequent ethical reflections and anecdotes. He is essentially a moralist whose aim is to edify the reader.

A well-known English translation by Sir Thomas North in 1579, *Lives of the Noble Grecians and Romans*, was the source of William his Roman history plays and influenced Shakespeare's conception of the tragic hero. Izaak Walton and John Dryden also published translations of the work.

Paramanuchit \ˌpä-rä-'mä-nü-ˌchĕt\, *also called* Paramanujita Jinorasa \ˌpä-rä-ˌmä-nü-'jĕ-tä-jin-ō-'rä-sä\ (b. 1791—d. Dec. 9, 1852) Prince-patriarch of the Siamese Buddhist church who was a prolific writer on patriotic and moralistic themes in verse and prose. He became abbot of Wat Phra Jetubon and was later created *krom somdec-phra Paramanujit,* prince-patriarch of the church.

Paramanuchit's masterpiece is the *Taleng Phai* ("The Defeat of the Mons"), the heroic epic of the struggle of King Naresvara of Ayutthaya to liberate his country from Myanmar (Burmese) rule. His concluding section of the *Samuddhaghosa*, a folktale adapted from a collection called the *Paññāsajātaka*, which had been left unfinished since the 18th century, is distinguished for the beauty of its descriptive passages. His prose is equally valued for its eloquence and descriptive power. His classic models of Siamese poetry were among those collected under the patronage of King Rama III and inscribed on stone at Wat Phra Jetubon (popularly known as Wat Po).

Parandowski \pä-rän-'dōf-sk^yē\, Jan (b. May 11, 1895, Lwów, Galicia, Austria-Hungary [now Lviv, Ukraine]—d. Sept. 26, 1978, Warsaw, Pol.)   Polish writer, essayist, and translator.

Together with the entire Polish elite, Parandowski was transported to Russia when the tsarist army occupied eastern Galicia at the beginning of World War I. Returning home after the Russian Revolution of 1917, he completed his education at the University of Lwów. Shortly afterwards he visited France, Italy, and Greece. He published a dozen books, ranging from historical novels to travelogues, that had Greek or Italian themes or subject matter. One notable exception was a novel, *Niebo w płomieniach* (1936; "Heaven in Flames"), detailing the experiences of a young man who undergoes a religious crisis. He also did a notable prose translation of the *Odyssey*. From 1933 Parandowski was chairman of the Polish branch of PEN, the writers' organization.

paraphrase \'par-ə-ˌfrāz\ [Greek *paráphrasis,* a derivative of *paraphrázein* to retell in other words, from *para-* aside, beyond + *phrázein* to point out, show, tell]   A restatement of a text, passage, or work giving the meaning in another form, usually for clearer and fuller exposition. A paraphrase is a free rendering as opposed to a direct translation from one language to another.

Paráskhos \pä-'räs-ḳōs\, Akhilléfs (b. March 6, 1838, Návplion, Greece—d. Jan. 26, 1895, Athens)   Greek poet who was the central figure of the Greek Romantic school of poetry in its second and last period (*c.* 1850–80).

Paráskhos' unrestrained manner and grandiloquent language owed much to the traditions of the Phanariote poets (Greek poets of Constantinople [Turkey] who gained power through Turkish patronage). Love and patriotism were his favorite themes, and in his numerous lyrics he made use of both "refined" Greek, inherited from the Byzantine scholars, and the spoken language. Perhaps no other modern Greek poet was more admired by his contemporaries. His poems were published in Greek in two volumes (1881, 1904).

parataxis \ˌpar-ə-'tak-sis\ [Greek *parátaxis* act of placing side by side, a derivative of *paratássein* to set side by side]   The placing of clauses or phrases one after another without coordinating or subordinating connectives.

parchment \'pärch-mənt\ [Middle English *parchemin,* from Old French *parchemin, parcamin,* alteration (influenced by *parche, parge,* kind of red leather, from Late Latin *Parthica (pellis),* literally, Parthian skin) of Gallo-Romance **pergamīnus,* ultimately from Greek *pergamēnḗ,* from feminine of *Pergamēnós* of Pergamum]   The processed skins of certain animals—chiefly sheep, goats, and calves—that have been prepared for the purpose of writing on them. Parchment made from the more delicate skins of calf or kid or from stillborn or newly born calf or lamb came to be called vellum, a term that was broadened in its usage to include any especially fine parchment.

The production of parchment facilitated the success of the codex. A sheet of parchment could be cut in a size larger than a sheet of papyrus, it was flexible and durable, and it could better receive writing on both sides. In making a parchment or vellum codex, a large sheet was folded to form a folio of two leaves, a quaternion (quarto) of four, or even an octavo of eight. Gatherings were made from a number of these folded sheets, which were then stitched together to form a book. Because papyrus, on the other hand, was more brittle and could not be made in large enough sheets, the folio collected in quires (*i.e.,* loose sheets) was the limit of its usefulness. At the same time, because of the vertical alignment of the fibers on one side, papyrus was not well adapted for writing on both sides in a horizontal script.

For 400 years the book roll and the codex existed side by side. Contemporary references to the codex date from the 1st century BC, but the earliest actual survivals date from the 2nd century AD. In the 4th century AD parchment as a material and the codex as a form became dominant.

In modern usage, the terms *parchment* and *vellum* may be applied to a type of paper of high quality made chiefly from wood pulp and rags and frequently having a special finish.

Pardo Bazán \'pär-t͟hō-ḅä-'t͟hän\, Emilia, Countess (condesa) de (b. Sept. 16, 1852, La Coruña, Spain—d. May 12, 1921, Madrid)   Spanish author best known for her novels, short stories, and literary criticism. She is generally considered the first naturalist writer in Spain.

Pardo Bazán attained early eminence with her polemical essay *La cuestión palpitante* (1883; "The Burning Question") in which she championed a brand of naturalism that affirmed the free will of the individual. Her finest and most representative novels are *Los pazos de Ulloa* (1886; *The Son of the Bondwoman*) and its sequel, *La madre naturaleza* (1887; "Mother Nature")—studies of physical and moral ruin among the Galician squirearchy. *Insolación* (*Midsummer Madness*) and *Morriña* (*Homesickness*; both 1889) are psychological studies. Her short stories, which were published in eight volumes, were varied in style and subject matter; they are highly regarded. She also wrote several volumes of critical work, including essays on French literature.

Pardo Bazán became a professor at the University of Madrid, and in 1916 she was accorded the distinction—unusual for a woman of her time—of a chair of literature.

Pardoner's Tale, The   One of the 24 stories in THE CANTERBURY TALES by Geoffrey Chaucer.

The cynical Pardoner explains in a witty prologue that he sells indulgences—ecclesiastical pardons of sins—and admits that he preaches against avarice although he practices it himself. His tale relates how three drunken revelers set out to destroy Death after one of their friends had died. An old man tells them that Death can be found under a particular oak tree in a grove, but when they arrive at the tree they discover only a pile of gold florins. Two of the men plot to kill the third so as to have more of the treasure for themselves. However, after they kill their friend, they drink some wine that he had poisoned earlier, and they too die. The Pardoner concludes his tale by speaking in florid rhetoric against the vices of gluttony, gambling, and blasphemy—adding at the end that he will be more than happy to secure divine forgiveness for his listeners, for a price.

Paretsky \pə-'ret-skē\, Sara (b. June 8, 1947, Ames, Iowa, U.S.)   American mystery writer credited with breaking the gender barrier in detective fiction with her popular series of novels featuring V.I. Warshawski, a female private investigator.

Paretsky attended the University of Chicago and then worked for a large insurance company until she began to write full-time in 1985. It was with *Indemnity Only* (1982) that her wisecracking, independent, passionate and compassionate female private detective was created.

Her other V.I. Warshawski novels are *Deadlock* (1984), *Killing Orders* (1985), *Bitter Medicine* (1987), *Blood Shot* (1988), *Burn Marks* (1990), *Guardian Angel* (1992), and *Tunnel Vision* (1994).

In the mid-1980s Paretsky helped found Sisters in Crime to promote the work of other women mystery writers and to challenge the publication of crime stories marred by gratuitous violence against women.

Parini \pä-'rē-nē\, Giuseppe (b. May 22/23, 1729, Bosisio, near Milan [Italy]—d. Aug. 15, 1799, Milan) Italian prose writer and poet remembered for a series of Horatian odes and particularly for *Il giorno* (1763–1801; *The Day*), a satiric poem on the selfishness and superficiality of the Milanese aristocracy.

Of humble origins, Parini was educated in Milan. A volume of Arcadian verse, *Alcune poesie di Ripano Eupilino* (1752), took him into literary circles. In 1754 he was ordained a priest and entered the household of Duke Gabrio Serbelloni as tutor to the duke's oldest son. He remained there until 1762, unhappy and badly treated, but he won ample revenge, first in *Dialogo sopra la nobiltà* (1757), a discussion between the corpse of a nobleman and the corpse of a poet about the true nature of nobility, and next through his masterpiece, *Il giorno*.

The first two parts of *Il giorno* brought Parini literary renown; he became editor of the *Gazzeta di Milano* and then a humanities professor in the Palatine and Brera schools. The most important of Parini's other works are his odes (*Odi*, 1795), composed over a period of about 20 years. He also wrote several literary tracts and an aesthetic treatise.

Paris \'par-is\, *also called* Alexandros \,al-ig-'zan-dròs\ In Greek mythology, son of King Priam of Troy and his wife, Hecuba. A dream regarding his birth was interpreted as an evil portent, and he was consequently expelled from his family when he was an infant. Exposed and left to die, he was raised as a shepherd, unknown to his parents. As a young man he entered a boxing contest at a Trojan festival and defeated Priam's other sons. After his identity was revealed, he was received home again by Priam.

According to legend, Paris was chosen by Zeus to determine which of three goddesses was the most beautiful. Rejecting bribes of kingly power from Hera and military might from Athena, he chose Aphrodite and accepted her bribe to help him win the most beautiful woman alive. His seduction of Helen (the wife of Menelaus, king of Sparta) and refusal to return her was the cause of the Trojan War. During the war Paris seems to have had a secondary role; although a good warrior, he was inferior to his brother Hector and to the Greek leaders whom he faced. Menelaus would have defeated Paris in single combat, but Aphrodite rescued him, and the war continued.

Near the end of the war, Paris shot the arrow that, with Apollo's help, caused the death of the hero Achilles. Soon after, Paris himself received a fatal wound from an arrow shot by the archer Philoctetes. *See also* ERIS; TROY.

Paris Review, The \'par-is\ English-language literary quarterly founded in 1953 and edited by George Plimpton. The co-founders, Peter Matthiessen and Harold Humes, modeled the review on the small literary magazines published in Paris in the 1920s. *The Paris Review* presented quality fiction and poetry by new or relatively unknown writers; it introduced Philip Roth, Jack Kerouac, and Raymond Carver among others. It was also the first American journal to publish Samuel Beckett.

The Paris Review was also known for its interviews with such writers as E.M. Forster, Ernest Hemingway, Aldous Huxley, Nadine Gordimer, T.S. Eliot, and many others. Beginning in 1958, these interviews were published in a series known as *Writers at Work*.

Parker \'pär-kər\, Dorothy, *original surname* Rothschild \'rǒths-,chīld\ (b. Aug. 22, 1893, West End, N.J., U.S.—d. June 7, 1967, New York, N.Y.) American short-story writer and poet who is chiefly remembered for her witty remarks.

Parker became drama critic for *Vanity Fair* and with two other writers for the magazine—Robert Benchley and Robert Sherwood—formed the nucleus of the Algonquin Round Table, an informal luncheon club held at New York City's Algonquin Hotel. From 1927 until 1933 Parker contributed a personal kind of book review to *The New Yorker* magazine as "Constant Reader," and some of these reviews were collected in *A Month of Saturdays* (1971). Three books of her verse, *Enough Rope* (1926), *Sunset Gun* (1928), and *Death and Taxes* (1931), were collected in *Collected Poems: Not So Deep as a Well* (1936). *Laments for the Living* (1930) and *After Such Pleasures* (1933) were collections of her short stories, combined and augmented in 1939 as *Here Lies*. She also worked as a film writer, reported on the Spanish Civil War, and collaborated on several plays.

Parker \'pär-kər\, Stewart, *in full* James Stewart Parker (b. Oct. 20, 1941, East Belfast, N.Ire.—d. Nov. 2, 1988, London, Eng.) Irish playwright whose innovative plays captured the human dimension of the civil conflict in Northern Ireland.

Parker won a scholarship to Queen's University, Belfast. He taught at Hamilton College in Clinton, N.Y., and at Cornell University in Ithaca, N.Y. In 1969 he returned to Belfast and worked as a rock-music columnist for *The Irish Times* while writing plays for theater, radio, and television. His first popularly received work for the stage, *Spokesong* (1980), was produced in 1975. Three of Parker's later plays, *Northern Star* (produced 1984), *Heavenly Bodies* (produced 1986), and *Pentecost* (produced 1987), were published together in *Three Plays for Ireland* (1989).

Parkes \'pärks\, Frank Kobina, *in full* Francis Ernest Kobina Parkes (b. 1932, Korle Bu, Gold Coast [now in Ghana]) Ghanian journalist, broadcaster, and widely anthologized poet.

Parkes was educated in Accra [Ghana] and in Freetown, Sierra Leone. He worked briefly as a newspaper reporter and editor and in 1955 joined the staff of Radio Ghana as a broadcaster. He was president of the Ghana Society of Writers and published a volume of poems, *Songs from the Wilderness* (1965).

His poetry, a rhythmic free verse with much repetition of words and phrases, celebrates all that is African, from the blackness of African skin to indigenous music, dancing, and ritual. It recalls Africa's past sufferings, exhorts the reader to do something about the oppression of blacks, and criticizes world powers for their concern with war and technology rather than with human needs. Also evident is a great faith in the ability of Africans to bring about a glorious future through their own efforts. Although a number of his poems have been collected in anthologies of African and Ghanian poetry—most notably *Messages* (1971) and *Katchikali* (1971)—*Songs from the Wilderness* is Parkes's only published volume of poetry.

Parks \'pärks\, Gordon (b. Nov. 30, 1912, Fort Scott, Kan., U.S.) African-American author, photographer, and film director who documented black American life.

A high-school dropout, Parks worked odd jobs before becoming a photojournalist in the late 1930s. His first books were *Flash Photography* (1947) and *Camera Portraits* (1948). As a staff photographer for *Life* magazine (1948–72), he became known for his portrayals of ghetto life, black nationalists, and the civil-rights movement. A photo essay about a child from a Brazilian slum was expanded into a television documentary (1962) and a book with poetry (1978), both titled *Flavio*. His first work of fiction was *The Learning Tree* (1963).

Parks was noted for his forthright autobiographies, *A Choice of Weapons* (1966), *To Smile in Autumn* (1979), and *Voices in the Mirror* (1990). He combined poetry and photography in *A Poet and His Camera* (1968), *Whispers of Intimate Things* (1971), *In Love* (1971), and *Moments Without Proper Names* (1975). He also wrote *Born Black* (1971), a collection of essays, the novel *Shannon* (1981), and *Arias in Silence* (1994), and he directed several motion pictures.

Parlement of Foules, The \\'pär-lə-mənt . . . 'faŭlz, 'fü-ləz \\ A 699-line poem in rhyme royal by Geoffrey CHAUCER, written in 1380–90. Composed in the tradition of French romances (while at the same time questioning the merits of that tradition), this poem has been called one of the best occasional verses in the English language. Often thought to commemorate the marriage of Richard II to Anne of Bohemia in 1382, it describes a conference of birds who meet to choose their mates on St. Valentine's Day. The narrator falls asleep and dreams about a beautiful garden in which Nature presides over a debate between three high-ranking eagles, all vying for a beautiful female eagle. The other birds, each of whom represents a different aspect of English society, are given a chance to express their opinions; Chaucer uses this device to gently satirize the tradition of courtly love. He handles the debate with humor and deftly characterizes the various birds. Although the debate on love and marriage is never resolved, the poem is complete in itself and ends on a note of joy and satisfaction.

Parley, Peter. Pseudonym of Samuel Griswold GOODRICH.

Parnassian \\pär-'nas-ē-ən \\ or **Parnassien** \\pär-nås-'yeⁿ \\ [French *parnassien* pertaining to the Parnassian school or to poetry in general, literally, of Parnassus, a mountain in central Greece sacred in antiquity to Apollo and the Muses] Of, having the characteristics of, or constituting a school of French poets of the second half of the 19th century that was headed by Leconte de Lisle. The school stressed restraint, objectivity, technical perfection, and precise description as a reaction against the emotionalism and verbal excess of the Romantics. The poetic movement led by the Parnassians resulted in experimentation with meters and verse forms and the revival of the sonnet. Initially taking their themes from contemporary society, the Parnassians later turned to the mythology, epics, and sagas of exotic lands and past civilizations, notably India and ancient Greece, for inspiration. The Parnassians derived their name from the anthology to which they contributed, *Le Parnasse contemporain,* 3 vol. (1866, 1871, 1876), although their principles had been formulated earlier.

The influence of the Parnassians was particularly evident in the Modernismo movement of Spain and Portugal and in the La Jeune Belgique ("Young Belgium") movement.

Parnassus \\pär-'nas-əs \\ Barren limestone spur of the Pindus Mountains, central Greece, in ancient times sacred to the Dorians and in mythology to Apollo and the Corycian nymphs. On a plateau between the summit and Delphi was the Corycian stalactite cave sacred to the nymphs and Pan. For the Roman poets, Parnassus' Castalian spring was a source of inspiration; they favored Parnassus over Mount Helicon as the home of the Muses.

Parnell \\pär-'nel, 'pär-nəl \\, Thomas (b. 1679, Dublin, Ire.—d. 1718, Chester, Eng.) Irish poet, essayist, and friend of Alexander Pope, who relied on Parnell's scholarship in his translation of the *Iliad.* Parnell's poetry, written in heroic couplets, was esteemed by Pope for its lyric quality and stylistic ease. Among his best poems are "An Elegy to an Old Beauty" and "Night Piece on Death," said to have influenced Thomas Gray's *An Elegy Written in a Country Church Yard.*

Parnell contributed to *The Spectator* and the *Guardian* and was a member, with Jonathan Swift and John Gay, of the literary Scriblerus Club. After Parnell's death, Pope collected his poetry and published it in a volume called *Poems on Several Occasions* (1722).

Parnicki \\pär-'nʸēt-skʸē \\, Teodor (b. March 5, 1908, Berlin, Ger.—d. Dec. 5, 1988, Warsaw, Pol.) Polish historical novelist who modernized the genre through his interest in psychoanalysis and his use of innovative narrative techniques.

Parnicki won recognition as a writer with *Aecjusz, ostatni Rzymianin* (1937; "Aetius, the Last Roman"), a picture of the attack by the Huns on a declining Rome in the 5th century AD. *Srebrne orły* (1945; "Silver Eagles") recounts the story of Poland's emergence as an independent state in the 10th and 11th centuries. In *Tylko Beatrycze* (1962; "Only Beatrice"), the author describes the burning of a Cistercian monastery in Poland in 1309. Parnicki also wrote historical novels dealing with Byzantium and ancient Alexandria. With the publication of *Muza dalekich podróży* (1970; "The Muse of Distant Journeys"), Parnicki's work became more imaginative and reflective. A number of his critical works—*Staliśmy jak dwa sny* (1973; "Like Two Dreams"), *Szkice literackie* (1978; "Literary Essays"), and *Historia w literaturę* (1980; "Making History into Literature")—address, among other things, objectivity, creativity, and the nature of the writing of history.

parodos or **parodus** \\'par-ə-dəs \\ *plural* parodoi \\-,dȯi \\ *or* parodi \\-dē \\ [Greek *párodos,* literally, entrance, first entrance of the chorus] The first choral passage in an ancient Greek drama, recited or sung as the chorus entered the orchestra.

parody \\'par-ə-dē \\ [Greek *parōidía,* from *para-* alongside, derivative + *ōidé* song] A literary work in which the style of an author is closely imitated for comic effect or in ridicule.

Differing from burlesque by the depth of its technical penetration and from travesty, which treats dignified subjects in a trivial manner, true parody mercilessly exposes the tricks of manner and thought of its victim yet cannot be written without a thorough appreciation of the work it ridicules.

An anonymous poet of ancient Greece imitated the epic style of Homer in *Batrachomyomachia* (*The Battle of the Frogs and Mice*), one of the earliest examples of parody; Aristophanes parodied the dramatic styles of Aeschylus and Euripides in *Frogs*; Geoffrey Chaucer parodied the chivalric romance in "The Tale of Sir Thopas" (*c.* 1375), as did Miguel de Cervantes in *Don Quixote* (Part I, 1605); François Rabelais parodied the Scholastics in his series of comic novels *Gargantua and Pantagruel* (1532–64); William Shakespeare mimicked Christopher Marlowe's high dramatic style in the players' scene in *Hamlet* and was himself parodied by John Marston, who wrote a parody of *Venus and Adonis* entitled *The Metamorphosis of Pigmalions Image* (1598). Later examples of parody also abound.

The art of parody has been encouraged in the 20th century by such periodicals as *Punch* and *The New Yorker.* The scope of parody has been widened to take in the far more difficult task of parodying prose. One of the most successful examples is Max Beerbohm's *The Christmas Garland* (1912), a series of Christmas stories in the style and spirit of various contemporary writers, most notably Henry James. Other outstanding parodists are Sir Arthur Quiller-Couch, Stephen Leacock, E.B. White, and Frederick Crews, whose *The Pooh Perplex* is a parody of various styles of literary criticism. *Compare* BURLESQUE; TRAVESTY.

paroemia \\pə-'rē-mē-ə \\ [Greek *paroimía,* from *para-* alongside, past + *oimē* song, verse narrative] A rhetorical proverb or adage.

paroemiac \pə-'rē-mē-ˌak\ In classical prosody, an anapestic dimeter catalectic. The verse, which may have been used for proverbs (the word *paroimia* means "proverb"), is scanned as ⏑⏑ – ⏑ ⏑ – ⏑ ⏑ – –.

parole \pə-'rōl\ Language viewed as a specific individual usage. The use of the French word *parole* ("speech") in this sense was introduced by the linguist Ferdinand de Saussure. *Compare* LANGUE.

paronomasia [Greek *paronomasía* derivative, byname, play on words, a derivative of *paronomázein* to call by a slight change of name, from *para-* alongside + *onomázein* to name] *see* PUN.

paroxytone \ˌpär-'äk-sē-ˌtōn\ [Greek *paroxýtonos,* from *para-* to the side of, beyond + *oxýtonos* oxytone] Having or characterized by an acute accent or a heavy stress on the penultimate syllable.

Parra \'pär-rä\, Nicanor (b. Sept. 5, 1914, San Fabian, Chile) One of the most important Latin-American poets of his time and the originator of so-called antipoetry (poetry that opposes traditional poetic techniques or styles).

Parra studied at the University of Chile in Santiago, at Brown University in Providence, R.I. (1943–45), and at the University of Oxford. From 1952 he taught theoretical physics at the University of Chile.

Although Parra later renounced his first book of poetry, *Cancionero sin nombre* (1937; "Songbook Without a Name"), his use of colloquial, often irreverent language, his light treatment of classical forms, and his humorous tone in that volume presaged his later antipoetry. With *Poemas y antipoemas* (1954; *Poems and Antipoems*), Parra's attempts at liberating poetry to make it more accessible to the masses gained him national and international fame. These verses treat common, everyday problems of a grotesque and often absurd world in clear, direct language and with black humor and ironic vision.

After experimenting with the local speech and humor of the Chilean lower classes in *La cueca larga* (1958; "The Long Cueca [Dance]"), Parra published *Versos de salón* (1962; "Verses of the Salon"), which continued the antipoetic techniques of his earlier works. *Obra gruesa* (1969; "Big Work") is a collection of Parra's poems after *Cancionero.* Its tone of dissatisfaction is intensified by the use of cliché and ironic wordplay. In 1967 Parra began to write experimental short poems that he later published as a collection of postcards entitled *Artefactos* (1972; "Artifacts"). In these he attempted to reduce language to its simplest form without destroying its social and philosophical impact. Later collections include *Sermones y prédicas del Cristo de Elqui* (1977; *Sermons and Homilies of the Christ of Elqui*) and *Hojas de Parra* (1985; "Leaves [Pages] of Parra").

Parrington \'par-iŋ-tən\, Vernon Louis (b. Aug. 3, 1871, Aurora, Ill., U.S.—d. June 16, 1929, Winchcombe, Gloucestershire, Eng.) American writer and teacher noted for his far-reaching appraisal of American literary history.

Parrington was educated at the College of Emporia, Kansas, and at Harvard University. He taught at the College of Emporia, the University of Oklahoma, Norman, and the University of Washington, Seattle. Parrington's major work on American literary history was published in *Main Currents in American Thought,* 2 vol. (1927), which won a Pulitzer Prize in 1928. A third volume with the subtitle *The Beginnings of Critical Realism in America,* incomplete at his death, was published in 1930. He also wrote *The Connecticut Wits* (1926) and *Sinclair Lewis, Our Own Diogenes* (1927).

Parsifal *see* PARZIVAL.

Parson's Tale, The The final of the 24 stories in THE CANTERBURY TALES by Geoffrey Chaucer.

The tale is a lengthy prose sermon on the seven deadly sins. Chaucer may have intended the story, with its plethora of pious quotations, as a fitting close to the stories of the religious pilgrims. After reviewing the sins of Pride, Envy, Anger, Sloth, Avarice, Gluttony, and Lechery and their remedies, the Parson urges confession and satisfaction (that is, atonement through such acts as almsgiving, penance, and fasting).

Parthenius \pär-'thē-nē-əs\ of Nicaea (fl. 1st century BC, Rome) Greek poet and grammarian who was described as the "last of the Alexandrians."

Parthenius was captured in the third Mithradatic war and taken to Italy. There he became the Roman poet Virgil's teacher in Greek and exerted an influence on Roman poetry by introducing such Greek authors as Callimachus. His collection of 36 love stories made for the poet Gaius Cornelius Gallus has survived, as have papyrus fragments from two funeral poems. Parthenius also wrote an encomium on his wife Arete in three books, as well as several works on mythological subjects. His verses were favorite reading of the emperors Tiberius and Hadrian.

partimen \'pär-ti-men\ [Old Provençal, literally, division, a derivative of *partir* to divide] A lyric poem of dispute composed by Provençal troubadours in which one poet stated a proposition and a second disputed it. The debate continued, usually for three rounds, after which the question was presented to an arbiter for resolution. The partimen was characterized by a more limited and less personal range of debate than a tenson, a similar form from which the partimen developed. *Compare* TENSON.

Partisan Review American literary quarterly founded by William Phillips and Philip Rahv in 1933 as a vehicle for the communist John Reed Club. It was published irregularly from 1934 to 1962 and quarterly thereafter. During its first years the magazine sought to represent the fight for intellectual and political freedom and asked for contributions by revolutionary writers. Over the years, however, the magazine became more oriented toward literature and art criticism. Works by W.H. Auden, Saul Bellow, Robert Lowell, Mary McCarthy, Denise Levertov, and Susan Sontag among others have been published in its pages.

Parton \'pärt-ən\, Sara Payson Willis, *original name* Grata Payson Willis \'wil-is\, *pseudonym* Fanny Fern \'fərn\ (b. July 9, 1811, Portland, Maine, U.S.—d. Oct. 10, 1872, New York, N.Y.) One of the most popular American women writers in the 19th century.

Parton's sketches, often dealing with domestic life, were originally published in periodicals in Boston and New York City. They were first collected in *Fern Leaves from Fanny's Port-Folio* (1853), which sold a remarkable 100,000 copies its first year. The success of this and other books led to an offer by the *New York Ledger* that made Parton one of the first women newspaper columnists in America.

Parton's writings are considered valuable mostly as a source for social history and as a mirror of popular taste in the mid-19th century. In addition to her articles, Parton wrote a number of best-selling books, including *Ruth Hall* (1855) and *A New Story Book for Children* (1864).

Parzival \'pärt-sē-ˌfäl\ Epic poem, one of the masterpieces of the Middle Ages, written between 1200 and 1210 in Middle High German by WOLFRAM von Eschenbach. The source for this 16-book, 25,000-line poem was probably *Perceval, ou Le Conte du Graal,* an unfinished work by Chrétien de Troyes. Wolfram's version, which introduced the theme of the Holy Grail into German literature, is in part a religious allegory describing Parzival's painful journey from utter ignorance and naïveté to spiritual awareness. The poem is also considered to be the climax of medieval Arthurian tradition. It questions the ultimate value of an education based solely on the code of courtly honor, and it takes its hero beyond the feudal world of knights and lords to the threshold of a higher order.

Parzival, who is eager to become a knight, visits Arthur's court but is judged too raw to become a knight of the Round Table. Later, after numerous adventures, he is granted knighthood. When he visits the ailing Grail King, however, he fails to ask the one question that will release the old man from his suffering: the reason behind his illness. For his ignorance, Parzival is punished by being cursed, and in turn he curses God. When he meets an old hermit who helps him realize the true nature of God, Parzival reaches a turning point in his spiritual education. He returns to the Grail King and this time, having gained wisdom, performs his duties correctly. He is rewarded with the title and duties of the keeper of the Grail.

Wolfram's eccentric style, with its complex rhetorical flourishes, its ambiguous syntax, and its free use of dialect make *Parzival* a difficult but richly rewarding poem. More than 70 manuscript versions of the poem are extant, testifying to its popularity in its own day. Richard Wagner used it as the basis for his last opera, *Parsifal* (1882).

Pascal \pȧs-'kȧl\, Blaise (b. June 19, 1623, Clermont-Ferrand, Fr.—d. Aug. 19, 1662, Paris)   French mathematician, physicist, religious philosopher, and writer who was a master of French prose.

At the age of 17 Pascal published a highly regarded essay on mathematics. He invented the first digital calculator (1642–44) to assist his mathematician father in local administration. Further studies in geometry, hydrodynamics, and hydrostatic and atmospheric pressure led him to invent the syringe and to discover Pascal's law of pressure (1647–54) and the principle of the hydraulic press (1650).

By 1653 Pascal, a strict Roman Catholic, had begun to feel religious scruples. He was drawn to Jansenism, a reform movement within the church, and two years later he entered the convent of Port-Royal, which was the center of the Jansenist movement. Though he never became one of the solitaries at the convent, all of his subsequent works, notably *Les Provinciales* ("Provincial Letters"), a defense of Jansenism against the Jesuits, and the *Pensées* ("Thoughts"), were written for them.

Les Provinciales was an immediate success, and its popularity has remained undiminished. Replacing the bombast and tedious rhetoric of traditional French prose with variety, brevity, tautness, and precision of style, it marks the beginning of modern French prose. The *Pensées* consists of Pascal's notes and manuscript fragments of his Christian apologetics.

Pascoli \'päs-kō-lē\, Giovanni (b. Dec. 31, 1855, San Mauro di Romagna, Kingdom of Sardinia [now in Italy]—d. April 6, 1912, Bologna, Italy)   Sardinian classical scholar and poet whose graceful and melancholy Italian lyric poems, perfect in form, and innovative in diction, were an important influence on the *crepuscolari* ("twilight poets").

Pascoli studied under the poet Giosuè Carducci at the University of Bologna. He was arrested and imprisoned for several months in 1879 for preaching political anarchy. In 1882 he began a career of teaching, first in secondary schools and then in various Italian universities.

Pascoli's first literary work, *Myricae* (1891; "Tamarisks"), a volume of short, delicate, musical lyrics inspired by nature and domestic themes, was a great success. His next volume, *Canti di Castelvecchio* (1903, definitive ed., 1907; "Songs of Castelvecchio"), considered his best work, is a collection of

moving evocations of his sad childhood and celebrations of nature and family life. Subsequent volumes include *Poemi conviviali* (1904), *Primi poemetti* (1904, originally published as *Poemetti*, 1897), and *Nuovi poemetti* (1909). Pascoli's Latin poems, which won prizes, exhibited a fluent skill. During his later years Pascoli wrote several nationalistic and historic poetic works, notably *Poemi del Risorgimento* (1913; "Poems of the Risorgimento [unification movement]"). He also translated English poets.

Pasek \'pȧ-sek\, Jan Chryzostom (b. *c.* 1636, Węgrzynowice, near Rawa Mazowiecka, Kingdom of Poland—d. Aug. 1, 1701, Niedzieliska, near Kraków?)   Polish soldier best remembered for his memoirs, which provide an excellent example of Polish Baroque prose.

Discovered in the 19th century, Pasek's *Pamiętniki* (1836; "Memoirs") is a lively, humorous work that gives a vivid description of the life of an independent, resourceful man of action. In it he relates tales of the 17th-century bloody Polish wars against Sweden and Muscovy, the catastrophic last years of the reign of King John II Casimir Vasa (1648–68), and the incompetent rule of King Michael Wiśniowiecki (1669–73), and he concludes his narrative with the splendid reign of King John III Sobieski (1674–96). Pasek was an excellent raconteur and a keen observer of people.

Pasiphae \pə-'sif-ə-ē\   In Greek mythology, the wife of Minos and the sister of the sorceress Circe. Pasiphae was also the mother of the MINOTAUR, a monster that was half man and half bull.

Poseidon had given Minos a bull that Minos promised to sacrifice to Poseidon. When he did not keep his promise, Poseidon punished him by causing Pasiphae to become infatuated with the bull, and the Minotaur was the result of their union.

Paso \'pä-sō\, Fernando del (b. April 1, 1935, Mexico City, Mex.)   Mexican novelist and artist known for his long, experimental, often humorous novels covering the breadth and history of Mexican culture.

About the time he began painting, del Paso published *Sonetos de lo diario* (1958; "Everyday Sonnets"). His first novel, *José Trigo* (1966), traces the long history of the area north of what is now Puebla, Mexico. *Palinuro de México* (1977; *Palinuro of Mexico*) is a freewheeling, humorous novel in which del Paso creates an entire semimagical universe. *Noticias del imperio* (1987; "News from the Empire") is a re-creation of Mexican history that blends realism with fantasy and horror; the novel has been called one of the most important works of Mexican literature. In 1988 del Paso published a book of children's poetry, *De la A a la Z por un poeta* ("From A to Z by a Poet").

pasquinade \,pas-kwə-'nād\ [Middle French, from Italian *pasquinata,* a derivative of *Pasquino*]   A lampoon or satire in prose or verse usually having a political significance. Pasquino was the popular name for the remains of an ancient Roman statue unearthed in Rome in 1501. It was the focus for bitingly critical political squibs attached to its torso by anonymous satirists that later were collected and published. After the 16th century the vogue of posting pasquinades died out, and the term acquired its more general meaning.

Passage to India, A \'in-dē-ə\   Novel by E.M. FORSTER published in 1924. Considered one of the author's finest works, the novel examines racism and colonialism as well as the need to maintain both ties to the earth and a cerebral life of the imagination.

The book portrays the relationship between the British and the Indians in India and the tensions that arise when a visiting Englishwoman, Adela Quested, accuses a well-respected

Indian man, Dr. Aziz, of attacking her during an outing. Aziz has many defenders, including the compassionate Cecil Fielding, the principal of the local college. During the trial Adela hesitates on the witness stand and then withdraws the charges. Aziz and Fielding go their separate ways, but two years later they have a tentative reunion. As they ride through the jungles, an outcrop of rocks forces them to separate paths, symbolizing the racial politics that caused a breach in their friendship.

Passerat \pås-'rå\, Jean (b. Oct. 18, 1534, Troyes, Fr.—d. Sept. 14, 1602, Paris)   French poet who composed elegant and tender verse and contributed to the *Satire Ménippée*, the manifesto of the moderate Royalist party in support of Henry of Navarre's claim to the throne.

Passerat studied at the University of Paris and taught at the Collège de France, where he wrote scholarly Latin works and commentaries on Catullus, Tibullus, and Propertius. He also composed poetry, his best pieces being his short ode "Du premier jour de mai" ("On the First Day of May") and the charming villanelle "J'ai perdu ma tourterelle" ("I Have Lost My Turtle Dove"). His exact share in the *Satire Ménippée* (1594) is variously stated, but it is generally agreed that he wrote much of the verse. His lines "Sur la journée de Senlis" ("On the Journey From Senlis"), in which he commends the Duke d'Aumale's ability in running away, became a celebrated political song.

Passion play   Religious drama of medieval origin dealing with the suffering, death, and Resurrection of Christ. Early Passion plays (in Latin) consisted of readings from the Gospel with interpolated poetical sections on the events of Christ's Passion and related subjects. Use of the vernacular in these interpolations led to the development of independent vernacular plays, the earliest surviving examples being in German. Such plays were at first only preludes to dramatic presentations of the Resurrection. The introduction of scenes from the Old Testament and the Last Judgment led to development of cyclic plays similar to the Corpus Christi cycles.

The earliest Passion plays of France and Flanders are thought to have their source in a nondramatic narrative poem of the 13th century, the *Passion des jongleurs*. These plays became highly elaborated in the course of their development, culminating in performances lasting more than a week. Confraternities were founded for performance of Passion plays, the most famous being the Confrérie de la Passion (1402). Passion plays were also performed in Spain, Italy, and elsewhere.

By the 16th century, many of the Passion plays, debased by secular influences, had degenerated into mere popular entertainments; many were forbidden by ecclesiastical authorities.

Pasternak \pə-st^yir-'nàk, *Angl* 'pas-tər-,nak, 'pàs-tər-,näk\, Boris (Leonidovich) (b. Jan. 29 [Feb. 10, New Style], 1890, Moscow, Russia—d. May 30, 1960, Peredelkino, near Moscow)   Russian poet whose novel DOCTOR ZHIVAGO helped win him the Nobel Prize for Literature in 1958 but aroused so much opposition in the Soviet Union that he declined the honor. An epic of wandering, spiritual isolation, and love amid the harshness of the Russian Revolution and its aftermath, the novel became an international best-seller but circulated only in secrecy and translation in his own land.

Pasternak studied at Moscow University and the University of Marburg. After the Revolution of 1917 he worked in the library of the Soviet commissariat of education.

His first volume of poetry was published in 1913. In 1917 he brought out a striking second volume, *Poverkh baryerov* ("Over the Barriers"), and with the publication of *Sestra moya—zhizn* (1922; *My Sister—Life*) he was recognized as a major new lyrical voice. His poems of that period reflected Symbolist influences. Though avant-garde and esoteric by Russian standards,

they were successful. From 1933 to 1943, however, the gap between his work and the official modes (such as Socialist Realism) was too wide to permit him to publish. His translations, which were his main livelihood, included renderings of William Shakespeare, J.W. von Goethe, English Romantic poets, Paul Verlaine, and Rainer Maria Rilke.

Pasternak's submission of *Doctor Zhivago* in 1956 to a leading Moscow monthly was rejected. The book reached the West in 1957 through an Italian publishing house. By 1958, the year of its English edition, the book had been translated into 18 languages.

In the Soviet Union, the Nobel Prize brought a campaign of abuse, and Pasternak was ejected from the Union of Soviet Writers. In 1987 the Union of Soviet Writers posthumously reinstated Pasternak, a move that gave his works legitimacy in the Soviet Union and that finally made possible the publication of *Doctor Zhivago* in his native land.

Pasternak's works in English translation include short stories, the autobiographical *Okhrannaya gramota* (1931; *Safe Conduct*), and the full range of his poetic output.

pasticcio   *see* PASTICHE.

pastiche \pas-'tēsh, pàs-\ or **pasticcio** \pas-'tē-chō, pàs-, -chē-ō\ [French *pastiche*, from Italian *pasticcio* muddle, pastiche, literally, pie]   **1.** A literary, artistic, musical, or architectural work that imitates the style of previous work.   **2.** A musical, literary, or artistic composition made up of selections from different works, or a usually incongruous medley of different styles and materials.

pastoral *noun is* ,pas-tə-'räl, -'ral; *adjective is* 'pas-tə-rəl \ [translation of Latin *Bucolica* (plural) the pastoral poems of Virgil or Theocritus]   A literary work (such as a poem or play) dealing with the lives of shepherds or rural life in general and typically drawing a contrast between the innocence and serenity of the simple life and the misery and corruption of city and especially court life. The characters in such works are often used as vehicles for the expression of the author's moral, social, or literary views.

The pastoral convention sometimes uses the device of "singing matches" between two or more shepherds, and it often presents the poet and his friends in the (usually thin) disguises of shepherds and shepherdesses. Its themes often include love and death. Both devices and motifs of pastoral poetry were largely established by Theocritus, whose bucolics are the first examples of pastoral poetry. The tradition was passed on from Greece to Rome, where Virgil alluded to contemporary problems—agrarian, political, and personal—in the rustic society he portrayed. His *Eclogues* exerted a powerful effect on poets of the Renaissance, including Dante, Petrarch, and Giovanni Boccaccio in Italy; Pierre de Ronsard in France; and Garcilaso de la Vega in Spain. The Greek writer Longus' *Daphnis and Chloe*, written in the 2nd–3rd century AD, is considered the first pastoral prose romance. During the 16th and 17th centuries pastoral romance novels (by Jacopo Sannazaro, Jorge de Montemayor, Miguel de Cervantes, and Honoré d'Urfé) appeared, as did the pastoral drama (by Torquato Tasso and Battista Guarini) in the 15th and 16th centuries.

In English poetry the appearance in 1579 of Edmund Spenser's *Shepheardes Calender* brought about a vogue for the pastoral. Sir Philip Sidney, Robert Greene, Thomas Nash, Christopher Marlowe, Michael Drayton, Thomas Dekker, John Donne, Sir Walter Raleigh, Robert Herrick, Andrew Marvell, Thomas Heywood, Thomas Campion, William Browne, William Drummond, and Phineas Fletcher all wrote pastoral poetry. Robert Greene and Thomas Lodge wrote prose romances in the pastoral mode, and playwrights who attempted pastoral drama included William Shakespeare, John Lyly, George Peele, John Fletcher, Ben Jonson, John Day, and James Shirley.

In later centuries, a reaction against the artificialities of the genre, combined with new attitudes to the natural man and the natural scene, resulted in a sometimes bitter injection of reality into the rustic scenes of many poets and novelists. Only the pastoral elegy survived, through Percy Bysshe Shelley and Matthew Arnold. *Compare* ECLOGUE; ELEGY; IDYLL.

pastourelle or **pastorelle** \ˌpas-tə-ˈrel, ˌpäs-\ [French *pastourelle,* from Old French *pasturele,* feminine diminutive of *pastour* shepherd] A conventional form of poetic pastoral composed in Europe during the late Middle Ages and consisting of a love debate between a knight and a shepherdess.

Patchen \ˈpach-ən\, Kenneth (b. Dec. 13, 1911, Niles, Ohio, U.S.—d. Jan. 8, 1972, Palo Alto, Calif.) American experimental poet, novelist, painter, and graphic designer.

Patchen published many collections of verse from 1936 on, notably *Collected Poems* (1968), and several novels, including *The Journal of Albion Moonlight* (1941), *Memoirs of a Shy Pornographer* (1945), and *See You in the Morning* (1948). He also wrote plays and other works, all of which exhibit a combination of high idealism, abhorrence of violence, isolation from the mainstream of American thought, and shock at materialistic secularism. Patchen was one of the more successful practitioners of the poetry-and-jazz movement.

patent theaters \ *British commonly* ˈpāt-ənt, *U.S.* ˈpat-\ Any of several London theaters that, through government licensing, held a monopoly on legitimate dramatic production in London between 1660 and 1843. When he reopened the theaters that had been closed by the Puritans, Charles II issued letters patent to Thomas Killigrew and William Davenant giving them exclusive right to form two acting companies. Killigrew established The King's Servants at Drury Lane. Davenant established The Duke of York's Servants at Lincoln's Inn Fields, from which they moved to Dorset Garden, finally settling at Covent Garden in 1732.

The legality of the patents was confirmed by Parliament with the Licensing Act of 1737, affirming Drury Lane and Covent Garden as the only legitimate theaters in England. Parliament began authorizing theaters outside London in 1768, and in London unlicensed theaters offered undefined "public entertainments" and pantomime. In 1766 a third London patent was issued to Samuel Foote for operation of the Haymarket Theatre during the summer months, and in 1807 the Earl of Dartmouth, as lord chamberlain, loosely interpreted the Licensing Act and began authorizing other theaters in London. The Theatre Regulation Act of 1843 finally abolished the exclusive rights of the patent theaters to present legitimate drama.

Pater \ˈpā-tər\, Walter (Horatio) (b. Aug. 4, 1839, Shadwell, London, Eng.—d. July 30, 1894, Oxford, Oxfordshire) English critic, essayist, and humanist whose advocacy of "art for art's sake" became a cardinal doctrine of the movement known as Aestheticism.

Pater was educated at Queen's College, Oxford, where he studied Greek philosophy and later read with private pupils. In 1864 he was elected to a fellowship at Brasenose College. He began to write for the reviews, and his essays on Leonardo da Vinci, Sandro Botticelli, Pico della Mirandola, Michelangelo, and others were collected in 1873 as *Studies in the History of the Renaissance* (later called simply *The Renaissance*). His delicate, fastidious style and sensitive appreciation of Renaissance art in these essays made his reputation as a scholar and an aesthete, and he became associated with Algernon Swinburne and the Pre-Raphaelites and was the center of a small group of ad-

mirers in Oxford. In the concluding essay in *The Renaissance,* Pater asserted that art exists for the sake of its beauty alone and that it acknowledges neither moral standards nor utilitarian functions as its reason for being.

Marius the Epicurean (1885) is Pater's most substantial work. The book is a philosophical romance in which Pater's ideal of an aesthetic and religious life is scrupulously and elaborately set forth. Several other works, including *Imaginary Portraits* (1887), *Appreciations* (1889), and *Plato and Platonism* (1893), followed during his lifetime, and more were published posthumously. The influence of Pater's style and ideas continued long after his death.

Paterson \ˈpat-ər-sən\ Long poem by William Carlos WILLIAMS, published in five consecutive parts, each a separate book, between 1946 and 1958. Fragments of a sixth volume were published posthumously in 1963.

According to Williams, "a man in himself is a city," and Paterson is both an industrial city in New Jersey and a character of that name. *Paterson* has a mosaic structure, with occasional passages of prose, including letters and a diary, integrated into the poem; it is written in Williams' "variable-foot" free verse.

Paterson \ˈpat-ər-sən\, A.B. *in full* Andrew Barton, *byname* Banjo \ˈban-jō\ (b. Feb. 17, 1864, Narrambla, N.S.W. [Australia]—d. Feb. 5, 1941, Sydney) Australian poet and journalist noted for his composition of the internationally famous song "Waltzing Matilda," which appeared in *Saltbush Bill, J.P., and Other Verses* (1917).

After 1900 Paterson became a journalist, covering the South African (Boer) War and traveling on assignment to China and the Philippines. He became editor of the *Sydney Evening News* in 1904 but left this post two years later to edit the Sydney *Town and Country Journal.* When World War I broke out, he traveled to Europe for the *Sydney Morning Herald.*

Paterson achieved great popular success in Australia with *The Man from Snowy River and Other Verses* (1895), which sold more than 100,000 copies before his death, and *Rio Grande's Last Race and Other Verses* (1902), which also went through many editions. In 1905 he published *The Old Bush Songs: Composed and Sung in the Bushranging.*

pathetic fallacy Poetic practice of attributing human emotion or responses to nature, inanimate objects, or animals. The practice is a form of personification that is as old as poetry, where it has always been common to find smiling flowers, cruel winds, or happy larks. The term was coined by John Ruskin in *Modern Painters* (1843–60). In some classical poetic forms such as the pastoral elegy, the pathetic fallacy is actually a required convention.

Ruskin considered the excessive use of the fallacy the mark of an inferior poet. Later poets, however—especially the Imagists of the early 20th century, as well as T.S. Eliot and Ezra Pound—used the pathetic fallacy freely and effectively.

Pathfinder, The (*in full* The Pathfinder; or, The Inland Sea) Novel by James Fenimore COOPER, published in two volumes in 1840, the fourth of five novels published as THE LEATHER-STOCKING TALES. In terms of the chronological narrative, *The Pathfinder* is third in the series.

Living near Lake Ontario during the French and Indian War, Natty Bumppo is a 40-year-old wilderness scout who comes to the aid of a British colonial garrison under attack. He dearly loves Mabel Dunham, daughter of a sergeant. Mabel refuses his offer of marriage; she loves his friend, Jasper Western, who is under suspicion of being a traitor, in large part because of his fluency in French. The actual traitor, Lieutenant Davy Muir, is eventually killed. At the novel's end Mabel and Jasper are married.

pathos \'pā-,thäs, -,thós, -,thōs\ [Greek *páthos* incident, experience, emotion, passion] An element in artistic representation evoking pity or compassion. *See also* BATHOS. In rhetoric the term describes a certain kind of emotion and is contrasted with ETHOS.

Patmore \'pat-,mór\, Coventry (Kersey Dighton) (b. July 23, 1823, Woodford, Essex, Eng.—d. Nov. 26, 1896, Lymington, Hampshire) English poet and essayist whose best poetry is in *The Unknown Eros and Other Odes* (1877), containing mystical odes of divine love and of married love, which he saw as a reflection of Christ's love for the soul.

Patmore worked in the library of the British Museum, London, for 19 years. One of his most ambitious works was *The Angel in the House*, a vast novel in verse telling the story of two marriages. It was published in two parts, the first consisting of *The Betrothal* (1854) and *The Espousals* (1856), and the second consisting of *Faithful for Ever* (1860) and *The Victories of Love* (1862).

In 1864 Patmore converted to Roman Catholicism. *Amelia* (1878) virtually ended his poetic output, and in later years he primarily wrote original and provocative essays on literature, art, philosophy, and politics, chiefly for the *St. James's Gazette*. These were later partly collected in *Principle in Art* (1889) and *Religio Poetae* (1893). Patmore's last work was a collection of aphorisms, *The Rod, the Root, and the Flower* (1895).

Paton \'pāt-ən\, Alan (Stewart) (b. Jan. 11, 1903, Pietermaritzburg, Natal [South Africa]—d. April 12, 1988, near Durban, Natal) South African writer best known for his first novel, CRY, THE BELOVED COUNTRY (1948), which brought international attention to the issue of apartheid.

Paton attended the University of Natal and then taught for several years. As the principal (1935–48) of Diepkloof Reformatory, which housed several hundred black youths, he introduced controversial progressive reforms.

Both *Cry, the Beloved Country* and his next novel, *Too Late the Phalarope* (1953), exhibit a balanced, economical, rhythmic prose that has, especially in dialogue, a singing tone. In 1953 the Liberal Party of South Africa was formed to offer a nonracial alternative to apartheid; Paton was its national president until its enforced dissolution (a ban on "mixed" racial parties) in 1968. His work for the liberal cause included a fortnightly column, "The Long View," for the liberal journal *Contact*. These pieces, along with public speeches, were collected in *The Long View* (1968) and *Knocking on the Door* (1975). Paton wrote two notable biographies, *Hofmeyr* (1964), a study of cabinet minister Jan Hofmeyr, and *Apartheid and the Archbishop: The Life and Times of Geoffrey Clayton, Archbishop of Cape Town* (1973). In *Ah, But Your Land Is Beautiful* (1981), Paton returned to a fictional account of events in South Africa. His autobiographies were *Towards the Mountain* (1980) and *Journey Continued* (1988).

Patriotic Gore Collection of essays by Edmund WILSON, published in 1962. Subtitled *Studies in the Literature of the American Civil War*, the book contains 16 essays on contemporaries' attitudes toward the Civil War, the effect it had on their lives, and the effects of the postwar Reconstruction period.

Among the subjects of the essays are Oliver Wendell Holmes, Jr.; diaries of Southern women; fiction such as *Poganuc People* by Harriet Beecher Stowe and *Old Creole Days* by George Washington Cable; and memoirs by Union commanders Ulysses S. Grant and William T. Sherman and their Confederate counterparts, Robert E. Lee and John S. Mosby.

pattern poetry *also called* altar poem, figure poem, carmen figuratum \'kär-mən-,fig-yə-'rä-təm\, *or* shaped verse. Verse in which the lines or typography are arranged in an unusual configuration, usually to convey or extend the emotional content of the words. Of ancient (probably Eastern) origin, pattern poems are found in the *Greek Anthology*, which includes work composed between the 7th century BC and the late 10th century. Notable later examples are the wing-shaped "Easter Wings" of the early 17th-century English Metaphysical poet George Herbert:

> Lord, who createdst man in wealth and store,
> Though foolishly he lost the same,
> Decaying more and more
> Till he became
> Most poor:
> With thee
> O let me rise
> As larks, harmoniously,
> And sing this day thy victories;
> Then shall the fall further the flight in me.

In the 19th century, the French Symbolist poet Stéphane Mallarmé employed different type sizes in *Un Coup de dés* (1897; "A Throw of Dice"). Representative poets in the 20th century included Guillaume Apollinaire in France and E.E. Cummings in the United States. In the 20th century, pattern poetry sometimes crossed paths with CONCRETE POETRY; a basic distinction between the two types is the ability of pattern poetry to hold its meaning apart from its typography—*i.e.*, it can be read aloud and still retain its meaning.

Paul \'pól\ the Apostle, *also called* Saint Paul, *original name* Saul \'sól\ of Tarsus \'tär-səs\ (b. AD 10?, Tarsus in Cilicia [now in Turkey]—d. 67?, Rome) First-century Jew who, after being a bitter enemy of the Christian church, became its leading missionary and perhaps its greatest theologian. His extensive travels and his vision of a universal church were responsible for the speed with which Christianity became a world religion. More than half of the biblical book Acts of the Apostles deals with his career, and this, together with the letters written by him or in his name, comprises one-third of the New Testament.

Paul, a Roman citizen, was trained as a rabbi. Although he never met Jesus, he regarded him as a threat to Pharisaic Judaism and persecuted his followers. Converted through a vision he experienced on the road to Damascus (Syria), he accepted the call to be the apostle to the Gentiles. With the Apostles and other Christian leaders, he reached agreement on future missionary policy.

Paul then began a series of three missionary journeys that took him to cities throughout Asia Minor and Greece. He maintained contact with the churches he established by means of letters that taught, corrected, encouraged, and sometimes chided the young Christian communities. Paul was arrested and imprisoned for two years, and, while he was kept in custody awaiting trial, he wrote several more letters.

Paul \'pól\ the Deacon, *also called* Paulus Diaconus \'pól-əs-dī-'ak-ə-nəs\ (b. *c.* 720, Cividale del Friuli, Lombardy [Italy]—d. *c.* 799, Montecassino, Benevento) Lombard historian and poet noted for his *Historia Langobardorum* ("History of the Lombards").

Paul spent many years at the Lombard court in Pavia, serving as councillor under King Desiderius, and in Benevento in southern Italy at the court of Duke Arichis II. Charlemagne insisted that Paul become a member of his court at Aachen, where together with the scholars Alcuin and Einhard he took part in the Frankish king's palace school.

In 786 Paul returned to Italy with Charlemagne, settling at the abbey of Montecassino, where he wrote his Lombard history. Based on written sources and on oral tradition, which would otherwise have been lost, it traces the Lombards to 744. His other works include a history of the bishops of Metz, a collection of homilies for the ecclesiastical year, a commentary on the Rule of St. Benedict, and another history, *Historia Romana.*

Paulding \'pȯl-diŋ\, James Kirke (b. Aug. 22, 1778, Dutchess County, N.Y., U.S.—d. April 6, 1860, Hyde Park, N.Y.) Dramatist and novelist, and public official chiefly remembered for his early advocacy and use of native American material in literature.

Together with the brothers William and Washington Irving, Paulding founded *Salmagundi* (1807–08), a periodical consisting mainly of light satires on local subjects in New York City. He satirized England's conduct toward America during the War of 1812 in *The Diverting History of John Bull and Brother Jonathan* (1812) and in *The Lay of the Scottish Fiddle: A Tale of Havre de Grace* (1813), the latter a burlesque of Sir Walter Scott. He returned to this theme in two later satires: *A Sketch of Old England: By a New England Man* (1822) and *John Bull in America* (1825).

The advantages and hardships of western migration are the theme of "The Backwoodsman" (1818), a poem written to encourage American writers to find literary themes in their own country rather than in Europe. Novels such as *Koningsmarke, the Long Finne, a Story of the New World* (1823), *Westward Ho!* (1832), and *The Old Continental; or, the Price of Liberty* (1846) represent Paulding's attempts to employ the American scene in fiction. In the play *The Lion of the West* (performed 1831; published 1954), he introduced frontier humor to the stage and contributed to the growing legend of Davy Crockett.

Paulinus \pȯ-'lī-nəs\ of Nola \'nō-lə\, Saint, *byname of* Meropius Pontius Anicius Paulinus (b. AD 353, Burdigala, Gaul [now Bordeaux, Fr.]—d. June 22, 431, Nola [Italy]) Bishop of Nola and one of the most important Christian Latin poets of his time.

Paulinus became successively a Roman senator, consul, and governor of Campania, a region of southern Italy. In 395 he was ordained a priest and settled at Nola to live an ascetic life devoted to charity.

Paulinus' act of renunciation caused his old master, the Latin poet and rhetorician Decimus Ausonius, to write reproaches in verse, to which Paulinus replied in poetical epistles. Paulinus' style generally echoes that of such classical authors as Virgil, Horace, and Ovid. His poems (395–407) on the feast day of St. Felix of Nola are particularly charming. About 409 Paulinus was consecrated bishop of Nola.

Some 50 of his extant letters were written to famous contemporaries, including Saints Augustine and Jerome and the celebrated ascetic Sulpicius Severus. Paulinus' prose style is often rhetorical and exuberant.

Paul Revere's Ride \'pȯl-rə-'vir\ Poem by Henry Wadsworth LONGFELLOW, published in 1861 and later collected in *Tales of a Wayside Inn* (1863). Written in anapestic tetrameter meant to suggest the galloping of a horse, this popular folk ballad about a hero of the American Revolution is narrated by the landlord of an inn who remembers the famous "midnight ride" to warn the Americans about the impending British invasion. Although the account of the ride is historically inaccurate, the poem created an American legend.

Paul's Case \'pȯl\ Short story by Willa CATHER, published in *The Troll Garden* in 1905. It recounts the tragic results of a boy's desire to escape what he sees as a stifling environment.

The protagonist is a sensitive high-school student who despises his middle-class family and sees the art world as a glamorous alternative to that life. He frequents art galleries, concert halls, and theaters until his father pulls him out of school and sends him to work in an office. Paul steals money from the firm and runs away to New York, where he buys elegant clothes and

rents a luxurious room in the Waldorf Hotel. When he learns that his father is coming to find him, Paul believes that his idyllic life is over, and he commits suicide.

Pausanias \pȯ-'sā-nē-əs\ (fl. AD 143–176; b. Lydia) Greek traveler and geographer whose *Periegesis Hellados (Description of Greece)* is an invaluable guide to ancient ruins.

Pausanias' *Description* takes the form of a tour of Greece starting from Attica and is divided into 10 books. The first book seems to have been completed after 143, but before 161. No event after 176 is mentioned in the work. Pausanias' account of each important city begins with a sketch of its history; his descriptive narration follows a topographical order. He gives glimpses into the daily life, ceremonial rites, and superstitious customs of the inhabitants and frequently introduces legend and folklore. Works of art, however, are his major concern.

pause \'pȯz\ A break in writing, such as a caesura in verse.

Paustovsky \,pə-ù-'stȯf-sk^yē\, Konstantin Georgiyevich (b. May 19 [May 31, New Style], 1892, Moscow, Russia—d. July 14, 1968, Moscow) Soviet fiction writer best known for his short stories, which carried the prerevolutionary romantic tradition into the Soviet period.

Paustovsky wrote novels, novellas, short stories, and historical and biographical fiction. The short novels *Kara-Bugaz* (1932) and *Kolkhida* (1934) brought him wide popularity. His works reveal a lyrical interest in nature and an intense curiosity about people and are noted for their craftsmanship. His main work, *Rasskaz zhizni* (1946–62; *The Story of a Life*), published in six volumes, is an autobiographical cycle of reminiscences.

Pavese \pä-'vā-sā\, Cesare (b. Sept. 9, 1908, Santo Stefano Belbo, Italy—d. Aug. 27, 1950, Turin) Italian poet, critic, novelist, and translator who introduced many modern American and English writers to Italy.

Pavese translated a number of American writers in the 1930s and '40s—Herman Melville, Sherwood Anderson, Gertrude Stein, John Steinbeck, John Dos Passos, Ernest Hemingway, and William Faulkner—as well as the Irish novelist James Joyce. He also published criticism, posthumously collected in *La letteratura americana e altri saggi* (1951; *American Literature, Essays and Opinions*).

A founder and, until his death, an editor of the publishing house of Einaudi, Pavese also edited the antifascist review *La Cultura.* He was imprisoned by the government in 1935, an experience later recalled in the novellas *Il compagno* (1947; *The Comrade*) and *Il carcere* (*The Political Prisoner,* first published with another novella as *Prima che il gallo canti,* 1949; "Before the Cock Crows"). His first volume of lyric poetry, *Lavorare stanca* (1936; *Hard Labor*), followed his release from prison. An initial novella, *Paesi tuoi* (1941; *The Harvesters*), recalled, as do many of his works, the sacred places of childhood.

The bulk of Pavese's work, mostly short stories and novellas, appeared between the end of World War II and his death by suicide. Partly through the influence of Melville, Pavese became preoccupied with myth, symbol, and archetype. *Dialoghi con Leucò* (1947; *Dialogues with Leucò*) contains poetically written conversations about the human condition. The novel considered his best, *La luna e i falò* (1950; *The Moon and the Bonfire*), is a bleak, yet compassionate story of a hero who tries to find himself at his childhood home. Several other works are notable, especially *La bella estate* (1949; "The Beautiful Summer"), for which he received the Strega Prize.

The Pavese Prize for literature was established in 1957. Among the best work published after his death was the volume of love lyrics *Verrà la morte e avrà i tuoi occhi* (1951; "Death Will Stare at Me out of Your Eyes"), the story collection *Notte di festa* (1953; *Festival Night and Other Stories*), and the diary, *Il mestiere de vivere, diario 1935–1950* (1952; U.K. title, *This Business of Living*; U.S. title, *The Burning Brand: Diaries 1935–1950*). Many collections of Pavese's work have appeared, including *Racconti* (1960; *Told in Confidence and Other Stories*), *Poesie edite e inedite* (1962), and *Lettere* (1966). A poetry collection in English, *A Mania for Solitude, Selected Poems 1930–1950*, was published in 1969.

Pawlikowska-Jasnorzewska \påv-lē-'kôf-skå-yås-nō-'zhef-skå\, Maria (b. Nov. 20, 1893, Krakau, Austria-Hungary [now Kraków, Pol.]—d. July 9, 1945, Manchester, Eng.) One of the finest modern Polish poets.

Pawlikowska-Jasnorzewska's first collection of poems, *Niebieskie migdały* (1922; "Idle Dreams"), was warmly acclaimed by the young poets of the Skamander group. Up to 1939 she published a dozen more small volumes of her lyric poetry—including *Pocałunki* (1926; "Kisses") and *Surowy jedwab* (1932; "Raw Silk")—in which she dealt with such subject matter as the carefree life of a sophisticated modern woman.

During World War II she immigrated to France and later to England, where, lamenting her exile, she expressed her feelings in *Róża i lasy płonące* (1940; "A Rose and Burning Forests") and in *Gołąb ofiarny* (1941; "The Sacrificial Dove").

Payne \'pān\, John Howard (b. June 9, 1791, New York, N.Y., U.S.—d. April 9, 1852, Tunis, Tun.) American-born playwright and actor who followed the techniques and themes of the European Romantic blank-verse dramatists.

A precocious actor and writer, Payne wrote his first play, *Julia; or, The Wanderer*, when he was 15. In 1813 he left for England, where he triumphed onstage at Drury Lane in John Home's *Douglas*; he repeated his success in other European capitals. In Paris, Payne met the actor François-Joseph Talma, who introduced him to French drama (from which many of his more than 60 plays were adapted), and Washington Irving, with whom he was to collaborate on two of his best plays.

The finest play Payne wrote was *Brutus; or, The Fall of Tarquin* (produced 1818). The play remained popular for 70 years. Other important plays were *Clari; or, The Maid of Milan*, which included Payne's famous song "Home, Sweet Home"; *Charles the Second* (1824), written with Irving; and *Thérèse* (1821), a French adaptation.

Paz \'päs, 'päz\, Octavio (b. March 31, 1914, Mexico City, Mex.) Mexican poet, writer, and diplomat who was one of the major literary figures in Latin America after World War II. He received the Nobel Prize for Literature in 1990.

After attending the University of Mexico, Paz published his first book of poetry, *Luna silvestre* ("Savage Moon"), in 1933. In 1937 Paz visited Spain, where he identified strongly with the Republican cause in the Spanish Civil War. He wrote his reflections on that experience in *Bajo tu clara sombra y otros poemas* (1937; "Beneath Your Clear Shadow and Other Poems").

Paz founded and edited several important literary reviews, including *Taller* (1939; "Workshop") and *El hijo pródigo* (1943; "The Prodigal Son"). He edited another review of literature and politics, *Plural*, in the 1970s. His major early poetic publications included *¡No pasaran!* (1937; "They Shall Not Pass!"), *Libertad bajo palabra* (1949; "Freedom Under Parole"), *¿Águila o sol?* (1951; *Eagle or Sun?*), and *Piedra de sol* (1957; *Sun Stone*). In the same period, he produced volumes of essays and literary criticism, including *El laberinto de la soledad* (1950; *The Labyrinth of Solitude*), in which he analyzes the character, history, and culture of Mexico, and *El arco y la lira* (1956; *The Bow and the Lyre*) and *Las peras del olmo* (1957; "The Pears of the Elm"), which are studies of contemporary Spanish-American poetry.

His poetry after 1962 included *Blanco* (1967; "White"), *Ladera este* (1971; "East Slope"), *Air Born/Hijos del aire* (1979; with Charles Tomlinson), and *The Collected Poems of Octavio Paz, 1957–1987* (1987). His later prose works, some written in English, include *Conjunciones y disjunciones* (1970; *Conjunctions and Disjunctions*), *El mono gramático* (1974; *The Monkey Grammarian*), and *One Earth, Four or Five Worlds* (1985).

Paz was influenced in turn by Marxism, surrealism, existentialism, Buddhism, and Hinduism. His most prominent theme was human ability to overcome existential solitude through erotic love and artistic creativity.

p'Bitek \pə-'bē-tek\, Okot (b. 1931, Gulu, Uganda—d. July 19/20, 1982, Kampala) Ugandan poet, novelist, and social anthropologist whose three verse collections—*Song of Lawino* (1966), *Song of Ocol* (1970), and *Two Songs* (1971)—are considered to be among the best African poetry in print.

As a youth p'Bitek published a novel in the Acholi language (later published in English as *White Teeth* [1989]), wrote an opera, and played on Uganda's association football (soccer) team. He took degrees at the University of Bristol in England, the University College of Wales at Aberystwyth, and the Institute of Social Anthropology at Oxford. He taught at various universities in Uganda, Kenya, and Nigeria.

In his first collection of poetry, *Song of Lawino*, p'Bitek addressed the issue of the conflict of cultures. It is the lament of a nonliterate woman over the strange ways of her university-educated husband, whose new ways are incompatible with traditional African concepts of manhood. This book was followed by *Song of Ocol*, which is the husband's response. A third volume, *Two Songs*, includes *Song of a Prisoner* and *Song of Malaya*.

In addition to writing poetry, p'Bitek produced several books on Acholi culture. Some of his essays are collected in *Africa's Cultural Revolution* (1975) and *Artist, The Ruler: Essays on Art, Culture and Values* (1986). *The Horn of My Love* (1974) contains Acholi poetry in both Acholi and English, and *Hare and Hornbill* (1978) is a collection of Acholi folktales that p'Bitek compiled and translated.

Peabody \'pē-,bäd-ē, -bə-dē\, Elizabeth Palmer (b. May 16, 1804, Billerica, Mass., U.S.—d. Jan. 3, 1894, Jamaica Plain, Mass.) American educator and participant in the Transcendental movement.

After being educated at a small private school by her mother, Elizabeth Peabody started her own school in Boston in 1820. From 1825 to 1834 she was secretary to William Ellery Channing, the early leader of Unitarianism in the United States; she then began an association with Bronson Alcott in his Temple School, which she wrote about in *Record of a School* (1835). After two years at the school she became involved in adult education in Boston. In 1839 Peabody opened her West Street bookstore, which became a kind of club for the intellectual community of Boston. On her own printing press she published translations from German by Margaret Fuller and three of Nathaniel Hawthorne's earliest books. For two years she published and wrote articles for *The Dial*, the critical literary monthly and organ of the Transcendental movement; she also wrote for other periodicals.

Peabody's kindergarten, opened in 1860, marked the American adoption of what until then had been primarily a German institution. She devoted herself thereafter to organizing public and private kindergartens and to lecturing and writing in the field. A volume entitled *The Letters of Elizabeth Palmer Peabody* was published in 1984.

Peace (*Greek* Eirēnē) Comedy by ARISTOPHANES, performed at the Great Dionysia in 421 BC. The plot concerns the flight to heaven on a monstrous dung beetle by a war-weary farmer, Trygaeus ("Vintager"), who searches for the lost goddess Peace, only to discover that the God of War has buried her in a pit. With the help of a chorus of farmers, Trygaeus rescues Peace, and the play ends with a joyful celebration of marriage and fertility.

The play was written during the Peloponnesian War fought between Athens and Sparta. *Peace* anticipated, by a few weeks, the ratification of the Peace of Nicias (421 BC), which suspended hostilities between Athens and Sparta for six uneasy years.

Peachum family \\'pē-chəm\\ Fictional characters in John Gay's play THE BEGGAR'S OPERA and in a version of that play adapted 200 years later by Bertolt Brecht, THE THREEPENNY OPERA. The family, consisting of Mr. and Mrs. Peachum and their daughter Polly, lives by dealing in stolen goods.

Peacock \\'pē-ˌkäk\\, Thomas Love (b. Oct. 18, 1785, Weymouth, Dorset, Eng.—d. Jan. 23, 1866, Lower Halliford, Middlesex) English author who satirized the intellectual tendencies of his day in novels in which conversation predominates over character or plot. His best verse is interspersed in his novels.

In 1812 Peacock met Percy Bysshe Shelley, who greatly inspired his writing. Peacock's essay *The Four Ages of Poetry* (1820) provoked Shelley's famous "A Defence of Poetry" (written 1821, published 1840).

Headlong Hall (1816), the first of his seven novels, sets the pattern of all of them: characters seated at table, eating and drinking and embarking on learned and philosophical discussions in which many common opinions of the day are criticized. In his best-known work, *Nightmare Abbey* (1818), romantic melancholy is satirized, with the characters Scythrop drawn from Shelley, Mr. Flosky from Samuel Taylor Coleridge, and Mr. Cypress from Lord Byron.

Peake \\'pēk\\, Mervyn (b. July 9, 1911, Guling, Jiangxi province, China—d. Nov. 17, 1968, Burcot, Oxfordshire, Eng.) English novelist, poet, painter, playwright, and illustrator, best known for the bizarre Titus Groan novels and for his illustrations of his novels and of children's stories.

His Titus Groan novels—consisting of *Titus Groan* (1946), *Gormenghast* (1950), and *Titus Alone* (1959)—display a gallery of eccentric and freakish characters in an idiosyncratic gothic setting. Peake also wrote the poem *The Glassblowers* (1950) and the play *The Wit to Woo* (performed 1957). *See also* GORMENGHAST SERIES.

Pearl An elegiac dream vision known from a single manuscript dated about 1400. The poem is preserved with the chivalric romance *Sir Gawayne and the Grene Knight* and two homiletic poems called *Patience* and *Purity*.

Pearl was composed in stanzaic form, with alliteration used for ornamental effect. Technically it is one of the most complex poems in the language, an attempt to create in words an analogy to the jeweler's art. The jeweler-poet is vouchsafed a heavenly vision in which he sees his pearl, the symbol of a lost infant daughter, who has died to become a bride of Christ. She offers consolation for his grief, expounding the way of salvation and the place of human life in the divine order of things.

Pearl \\'pərl\\ Fictional character, the daughter of the protagonist, Hester Prynne, in the novel THE SCARLET LETTER by Nathaniel Hawthorne. A wild, fey child who is associated throughout the work with nature and the natural, Pearl is Hester's illegitimate child by the minister Arthur Dimmesdale.

Pearl, The Short story by John STEINBECK, published in 1947. It is a parable about a Mexican Indian pearl diver named Kino who finds a valuable pearl and is transformed by the evil it attracts.

Kino sees the pearl as his opportunity for a better life. When the townsfolk of La Paz learn of Kino's find, he is immediately set upon by the greedy priest, doctor, and businessmen. After a series of disasters, Kino throws the pearl back into the ocean. Thereafter his tragedy is legendary in the town.

Pearson \\'pir-sən\\, Hesketh (b. Feb. 20, 1887, Hawford, Worcestershire, Eng.—d. April 9, 1964, London) English actor, director, and biographer.

Pearson, an actor and director, began his career as a writer with *Modern Men and Mummies* (1921), which contained amusing portraits of his prominent contemporaries in the theater. His literary output largely consisted of lively and popular biographies of famous literary and artistic figures. Among such works are *Doctor Darwin* (1930), *Gilbert and Sullivan* (1935), *A Life of Shakespeare* (1942), *G.B.S: A Full-Length Portrait* (1942), *Conan Doyle: His Life and Art* (1943), *The Life of Oscar Wilde* (1946), *The Man Whistler* (1952), and *Henry of Navarre* (1963). A posthumous autobiography, *Hesketh Pearson, by Himself*, appeared in 1965.

Pecksniff, Seth \\'seth-'pek-ˌsnif\\ Fictional character, an unctuous English architect whose insincere behavior made the name Pecksniff synonymous with hypocrisy. He appears in the novel MARTIN CHUZZLEWIT by Charles Dickens.

Pecos Bill \\'pā-kōs-'bil\\ In American folklore, cowboy hero of the Pecos River region of Texas who was an exaggerated personification of Western stamina and values.

Created by journalists, primarily Edward O'Reilly in *Century* magazine, the Pecos Bill character was said to have been born in Texas about 1832 and raised by coyotes after his parents lost him near the Pecos River. As a man he rode a mountain lion and used a rattlesnake as a lasso, besting the toughest of cowboys. Although Pecos Bill stories were read primarily by nonfrontier Americans, they were adopted by cowboys of Australia and Argentina.

Pedrolino Stock theatrical character in Italian COMMEDIA DELL'ARTE. *See* PIERROT.

Peele \\'pēl\\, George (b. 1556, London, Eng.—d. 1596) British dramatist who experimented in many forms of theatrical art: history, melodrama, tragedy, the pastoral, the folk play, and the pageant.

Peele began his varied literary career while at Oxford by translating into English a play of Euripides. In 1581 he moved to London, but he returned to Oxford in 1583 as a technical director for Christ Church's presentation of two spectacles.

About this time Peele joined a group of Oxonians living just outside the London city wall and began to experiment with poetry in various meters. From this association with the so-called University wits came two mythological pastoral plays: *The Arraignment of Paris* (1584) and *The Hunting of Cupid* (1591). He then produced a series of pageants for the city. Of the many playhouse dramas he must have had a hand in, only four can be ascribed to him with certainty: *The Battle of Alcazar* (1594), *The Old Wives' Tale* (1595), *Edward I* (1593), and *The Love of King David and Fair Bethsabe* (1599).

Peer Gynt \\'par-'gænt, *Angl* 'pir-'gint\\ Five-act verse play by Henrik IBSEN, published in Norwegian in 1867 and produced in 1876. The title character, based on a legendary Norwegian folk hero, is a rogue who is saved by the love of a woman.

Peer Gynt is a charming but arrogant peasant youth who leaves his widowed mother in order to seek his fortune. Confident of success, he has one disastrous adventure after another. In one, he attends the wedding of the wealthy young woman he himself might have married. There he meets Solveig, who falls in love with him. He impulsively abducts the bride from her wedding celebration and subsequently abandons her. Peer Gynt embarks on a series of fantastic voyages around the world, finding wealth and fame but never happiness. Finally, as an old, disillusioned man, he returns to Norway, where Solveig, ever faithful, welcomes him lovingly, and he is redeemed.

Pegasus \\'peg-ə-səs\\ In Greek mythology, a winged horse that sprang from the blood of the Gorgon Medusa as she was beheaded by the hero Perseus. Pegasus' father was Poseidon, and with his (or Athena's) help, another Greek hero, Bellerophon, captured Pegasus and first rode him. Bellerophon was later thrown from the winged horse when he attempted to fly with him to heaven. Pegasus then returned to the gods and eventually became a constellation. Pegasus' story was a favorite theme in Greek art and literature, and in late antiquity Pegasus' soaring flight was interpreted as an allegory of the soul's immortality; in modern times it has been regarded as a symbol of poetic inspiration.

Peggotty, Clara \\'klar-ə-'peg-ə-tē\\ Fictional character, devoted servant in the novel DAVID COPPERFIELD by Charles Dickens.

Péguy \\pā-'gē\\, Charles (b. Jan. 7, 1873, Orléans, Fr.—d. Sept. 5, 1914, near Valleroy) French poet and philosopher whose works combined Christianity, socialism, and patriotism.

In 1895 Péguy turned to socialism and abandoned Roman Catholicism, though he retained a fervent religious faith to the end of his life. At this time he wrote his first version of *Jeanne d'Arc* (1897), a dramatic trilogy that formed a declaration and affirmation of his religious and socialist principles. In addition to running a bookstore, in 1900 Péguy began publishing the influential journal *Cahiers de la quinzaine* ("Fortnightly Notebooks"), which exercised a profound influence on French intellectual life for the next 15 years.

Péguy published several collections of his essays, but the most important works of his maturity are his poems. Chief among them are *Le Mystère de la charité de Jeanne d'Arc* (1910), *Mystère des Saints Innocents* (1912), and *Eve* (1913).

Peirithous *see* PIRITHOUS.

Pei-tao *see* BEI DAO.

Peking opera *see* JINGXI.

Peletier \\pel-'tyā\\, Jacques, *also called* Peletier du Mans \\dūe-'mä^n\\ (b. 1517, Le Mans, Fr.—d. 1582, Paris) French poet and critic whose knowledge and love of Greek and Latin poetry influenced La Pléiade, a group of French poetry reformers. In the preface to his translation of Horace's *Ars poetica* (1545) and in his *Art poétique française* (1555), Peletier insisted that poets must imitate the classics if French literature was to rise to great heights. In addition to lyric poetry, Peletier wrote major works on mathematics and on spelling reform.

Peleus \\'pēl-yūs, 'pē-lē-əs\\ In Greek mythology, king of the Myrmidons of Thessaly; he was most famous as the husband of Thetis (a sea nymph) and the father of the hero Achilles, whom he survived.

Peleus, a widower who had previously been married to Antigone, captured Thetis, who was unwilling to marry a mortal. After Thetis bore Achilles, she returned to the depths of the sea, later fetching Peleus to dwell with her.

Pelias \\'pē-lē-əs\\ In Greek mythology, a king of Iolcus (Iolcos) in Thessaly who imposed on his half-nephew Jason the task of capturing the Golden Fleece. Legend relates that on Jason's return with the fleece, his wife Medea, the enchantress, took revenge on Pelias by convincing his daughters (except for

Alcestis) that if they cut up and boiled their father he would recover his youth. To their dismay, he perished.

Pelléas and Mélisande \\pā-lā-'äs . . . mā-lē-'zä^nd\\ Play in five acts by Maurice MAETERLINCK, published in French in 1892 as *Pelléas et Mélisande* and produced in 1893. The play is considered one of the masterpieces of French Symbolist drama. Set in an imaginary land in medieval times, it centers around the tragic love of Pelléas for Mélisande, who is married to his brother. Maeterlinck emphasized atmosphere over plot; impressionistic dialogue is marked by silences and many repetitions of phrases, creating the effect of a litany.

Pellico \\'pel-lē-kō\\, Silvio (b. June 25, 1789, Saluzzo, Kingdom of Sardinia [now part of Italy]—d. Jan. 31, 1854, Turin) Italian patriot, dramatist, and author of *Le mie prigioni* (1832; *My Prisons*), memoirs of his sufferings as a political prisoner, which inspired widespread sympathy for the Italian nationalist movement, the Risorgimento.

Pellico's romantic tragedy *Francesca da Rimini* (published 1818) was a success on its first performance (1815) and was followed by several others. He had already become one of the circle of Romantic revolutionary writers that included Vincenzo Monti, Ugo Foscolo, Giovanni Berchet, and Alessandro Manzoni, and in 1818 he collaborated in founding a liberal and patriotic newspaper, *Il Conciliatore*, of which he became editor. After its suppression by the Austrian police in 1819, he joined a patriotic secret society, the Carbonari, and in 1820 he was arrested for treason and later served eight years in prison. *Le mie prigioni* is admired for its simple, direct style, spiritual revelation, and Christian piety.

Pelops \\'pēl-ˌäps, 'pel-\\ Legendary founder of the Pelopid dynasty at Mycenae in the Greek Peloponnese, which was probably named for him. Pelops was a grandson of Zeus. According to many accounts, his father, Tantalus, cooked and served Pelops to the gods at a banquet. Only Demeter, bereaved over the loss of her daughter, failed to recognize him and partook of his body. When the body was ordered by the gods to be restored, the shoulder, Demeter's portion, was missing; the goddess provided a replacement of ivory.

According to Pindar, however, the sea god Poseidon loved Pelops and took him to heaven; the ghastly feast was merely malicious gossip to account for his disappearance. Pelops, however, had to return to mortal life because his father had abused the favor of the gods by feeding mere mortals with nectar and ambrosia, which were reserved to the gods. Later, according to Pindar, in a chariot chase Pelops won the hand of Hippodamia from her father, King Oenomaus of Pisa in Elis, whom he then killed.

Pembroke \\'pem-brŭk\\, Mary Herbert, Countess of, *original surname* Sidney \\'sid-nē\\ (b. Oct. 27, 1561, near Bewdley, Worcestershire, Eng.—d. Sept. 25, 1621, London) Patroness of the arts and a notable translator. She was the sister of Sir Philip Sidney, who dedicated to her his *Arcadia*. After his death she published it and completed his verse translation of the Psalms.

Lady Pembroke ranked after Queen Elizabeth I as the most admired of Elizabethan *femmes savantes*. Lady Pembroke translated Robert Garnier's tragedy *Marc-Antoine* and Philippe Duplessis-Mornay's *Discours de la vie et de la mort* (both 1592) and elegantly rendered Petrarch's *Trionfo della morte* into terza rima.

PEN, International \\'pen\\ Worldwide organization of writers. The original PEN was founded in London in 1921 by the English novelist John Galsworthy, and, though still headquartered there, it has since grown to include writers worldwide. The name PEN is an acronym standing for "poets, playwrights, editors, essayists, and novelists." International PEN promotes intellectual exchanges and goodwill among writers and promotes freedom of expression. The organization also bestows literary awards, sponsors translations, holds conferences, and publishes pamphlets and newsletters. To become a member of PEN an author normally must have published at least two books, one of considerable literary distinction.

Pendennis \pen-'den-is\ (*in full* The History of Pendennis: His Fortunes and Misfortunes, His Friends and His Greatest Enemy) Semiautobiographical novel by William Makepeace THACKERAY, published serially, monthly from 1848 to 1850, and published in book form in two volumes in 1849–50.

The novel traces the youthful career of Arthur Pendennis (called Pen)—his first love affair, his experiences at "Oxbridge University," his employment as a London journalist, and so on. Pen also appeared in Thackeray's novels *The Newcomes* (1853–55) and *The Adventures of Philip* (1861–62).

Penelope \pə-'nel-ə-pē\ In Greek mythology, a daughter of Icarius of Sparta and the nymph Periboea, faithful wife of the hero Odysseus, and mother of Telemachus. The *Odyssey* tells the story of how, during her husband's long absence from Ithaca after the Trojan War, Penelope warded off the many chieftains of Ithaca and the nearby islands who became her suitors. To spare herself their importunities she insisted that they wait until she had woven a shroud for Laertes, father of Odysseus. Although she worked on the garment every day for several years, she secretly undid her daily work at night in order to delay the date at which she would have to forsake her lost husband by remarrying. She was finally relieved by the return of Odysseus. She is generally a symbol of faithfulness and chastity.

Penna \'pen-nä\, Sandro (b. Jan. 12, 1906, Perugia, Italy—d. Jan. 21, 1977, Rome) Italian poet who celebrated homosexual love, particularly pederasty, with lyrical elegance. Usually written in the form of epigrams, his moody poems often featured the tranquil, homoerotic imagery of young boys at play.

Penna's first collection of verse, *Poesie* ("Poetry"), was published in 1938 and later enlarged, first in 1957 and then in 1970 under the title *Tutte le poesie* ("All the Poetry"). His early verse, influenced by the Italian poets Umberto Saba and Eugenio Montale, borrowed from the school of Hermeticism.

Much of Penna's verse published after the first enlargement of *Poesie* was collected in *Stranezze* (1976; "Oddities"), a book that won him the Bagutta Prize for poetry only a week before his death. His other works of poetry include *Appunti* (1950; "Notes"), *Croce e delizia* (1958; "Suffering and Delight"), *Il viaggiatore insonne* (1977; "The Sleepless Traveler"), and *Peccato di gola* (1989; "The Sin of a Glutton"). English translations of his work include *This Strange Joy* (1982) and *Confused Dream* (1988), which is a partial translation of *Confuso sogno* (1980).

pen name An author's PSEUDONYM or nom de plume.

penny dreadful *plural* penny dreadfuls, *also called* bloods. A novel of violent adventure or crime especially popular in mid-to-late Victorian England and originally costing one penny. They were often issued in eight-page installments. The appellation, like *dime novel* and *shilling shocker*, conveyed second-rate writing as well as gory themes. Among the notably prolific writers of the penny dreadful were James Malcolm Rymer (pseudonym Malcolm J. Errym) and Thomas Peckett Prest. A collection of penny dreadfuls might include such titles as *Vice and Its Victim*, *The Death Grasp, or A Father's Curse*, and *Varney, the Vampire or, The Feast of Blood*. Later penny dreadfuls were more associated with adventure than gore and were often written for boys.

Penny dreadful is also now used to denote more generally any story or periodical characterized by sensationalism and violence.

Penrod \'pen-,räd\ Comic novel by Booth TARKINGTON, published in 1914. Its protagonist, Penrod Schofield, a 12-year-old boy who lives in a small Midwestern city, rebels against his parents and teachers and experiences the baffling ups and downs of preadolescence. Tarkington expertly conveys the speech and behavior of his boyish characters and writes with charm and humor about Penrod's escapades. He wrote two sequels, *Penrod and Sam* (1916) and *Penrod Jashber* (1929).

pensée \pän-'sā\ [French, literally, thought] A thought expressed in literary form. A pensée can be short and in a specific form, such as an aphorism or epigram, or it can be as long as a paragraph or a page. The term was derived from the French mathematician and philosopher Blaise Pascal's *Pensées* (1670), a collection of some 800 to 1,000 notes and manuscript fragments expressing his religious beliefs. The form was particularly popular in French literature, as in Denis Diderot's *Pensées philosophiques* (1746).

pen sketch A literary sketch.

pentalogy \pen-'tal-ə-jē\ A series of five closely related published works.

pentameter \pen-'tam-ə-tər\ In poetry, a line of five metrical feet. In English verse, in which pentameter has been the predominant meter since the 16th century, the preferred foot is the iamb—*i.e.*, an unstressed syllable followed by a stressed one, represented in scansion as ∪ ´.

Geoffrey Chaucer employed iambic pentameter in *The Canterbury Tales* as early as the 14th century. Most English sonnets have been written in iambic pentameter, as in this example from William Shakespeare's 18th sonnet:

> ∪ ´ | ∪ ´ | ∪ ´ | ∪ ´ | ∪ ´
> So long | as men | can breathe | or eyes | can see,
> ∪ ´ | ∪ ´ | ∪ ´ | ∪ ´ | ∪ ´
> So long | lives this | and this | gives life | to thee.

Iambic pentameter is also the meter of heroic verse written in English.

pentapody \pen-'tap-ə-dē\ [*penta-* five + *-pody* (as in *dipody*)] In classical prosody, a metrical unit consisting of five feet.

pentastich \'pen-tə-,stik\ In poetry, a unit, stanza, or poem consisting of five lines.

Pentateuch \'pen-tə-,tük, -,tyük\ The first five books of the Old Testament. *See* TORAH.

penthemimer \,pen-thə-'mim-ər\ [Greek *penthēmimerés,* from *penthēmi-* two and a half (from *pénte* five + *hēmi-* half) + *méros* part] In Greek and Latin prosody, a group of two and a half feet comprising a short colon of five syllables scanned ∪ – ∪ – ∪.

penthemimeral caesura \,pen-thə-'mim-ər-əl\ *see* CAESURA.

Penthesilea \,pen-thə-si-'lē-ə\ In Greek mythology, a queen of the Amazons. Well-respected for her bravery, her skill in weapons, and her wisdom, she led an army of Amazons to Troy to fight against the Greeks. She was said to have killed Achilles, but Zeus brought him back to life and Achilles killed her.

Pepys \'pēps\, Samuel (b. Feb. 23, 1633, London, Eng.—d. May 26, 1703, London) English diarist and naval administrator, celebrated for his *Diary* (1825), which gives a fascinating picture of the upper-class life of Restoration London.

Pepys was sent to St. Paul's School, London, after which he attended Cambridge University. About 1659 he was appointed to a clerkship in the office of the Exchequer, where on Jan. 1, 1660, he began his diary. Shortly after that Pepys received an appointment to work for the navy, and in 1673 he was appointed secretary to the new commission of Admiralty and, as such, the navy's administrative head. He became a member of Parliament in order to represent the Admiralty.

Detail of an oil painting by John Hayls, 1666
National Portrait Gallery, London

Pepys's last years were spent amassing and arranging the library that he ultimately left to Magdalene College, Cambridge, and collecting material for a history of the navy that he never lived to complete, though he published a prelude to it in 1690 entitled *Memoires Relating to the State of the Royal Navy of England for Ten Years Determined December 1688.*

The diary by which Pepys is chiefly known fills six quarto volumes in the Pepys Library. He described with great honesty the Restoration, including the coronation of Charles II, the horrors of the plague, and the Great Fire of London, writing down his account even as his home and its treasures were being threatened with destruction. A number of volumes of Pepys's correspondence have also been published.

Pequod \'pē-,kwäd\   The whaling ship on which most of the action in Herman Melville's novel MOBY-DICK takes place.

Perceval \'pər-sə-vəl\   Hero of Arthurian romance, distinguished by his quality of childlike (often uncouth) innocence, which protects him from worldly temptation and sets him apart from other knights in Arthur's fellowship. This quality also links his story with the primitive folktale theme of a great fool or simple hero. In Chrétien de Troyes's poem *Perceval, ou Le Conte du Graal* (12th century), Perceval's great adventure is a visit to the castle of the wounded king, where he sees a mysterious dish (or grail) but, having previously been scolded for asking too many questions, fails to ask the question that would heal the king. Afterward, he sets off in search of the Grail and gradually learns the true meaning of chivalry and its close connection with the teachings of the church.

The story of Perceval's spiritual development from simpleton to Grail keeper received its finest treatment in Wolfram von Eschenbach's great 13th-century epic PARZIVAL. The poem was the basis of Richard Wagner's last opera, *Parsifal* (1882).

Percy \'pər-sē\, Thomas (b. April 13, 1729, Bridgnorth, Shropshire, Eng.—d. Sept. 30, 1811, Dromore, County Down, Ire.)

English antiquarian and bishop whose collection of ballads, *Reliques of Ancient English Poetry* (1765), awakened widespread interest in English and Scottish traditional songs.

The basis of Percy's collection was a tattered 15th-century manuscript of ballads, to which he added many other ballads, songs, and romances. Publication of the *Reliques* inaugurated the "ballad revival," a flood of collections of ancient songs that proved a source of inspiration to the Romantic poets.

Percy was educated at Christ Church, Oxford, and held livings (benefices) in Northamptonshire. The *Reliques*, dedicated to the Countess of Northumberland, gained him her patronage, and after editing *The Household Book of the Earl of Northumberland in 1512* (1768), he became the earl's chaplain and secretary. In 1778 he acquired the deanery of Carlisle and in 1782 the Irish bishopric of Dromore. Percy's translations from Chinese, Hebrew, Spanish, and Icelandic and his first English version of the Icelandic *Edda* (from Latin, in *Northern Antiquities*, 1770) show his linguistic ability. His correspondence was published in 1946–77.

Percy \'pər-sē\, Walker (b. May 28, 1916, Birmingham, Ala., U.S.—d. May 10, 1990, Covington, La.)   American novelist who wrote of the search for faith and love in the New South, a place transformed by industry and technology.

Percy studied at the University of North Carolina and Columbia University. While working at Bellevue Hospital, New York City, he contracted tuberculosis. During his recuperation he read widely (especially the works of European existentialists), decided on a career in writing, and converted to Roman Catholicism. His conversion and his interest in existentialism were both powerful influences on his works.

During the 1950s Percy wrote articles for philosophical, literary, and psychiatric journals. His first and best-known novel, THE MOVIEGOER (1961), won a National Book Award and introduced Percy's concept of "malaise," a disease of despair born of the rootless modern world. Other fiction includes *Love in the Ruins: The Adventures of a Bad Catholic at a Time Near the End of the World* (1971), *The Second Coming* (1980), and *The Thanatos Syndrome* (1987). He also wrote such nonfiction as *The Message in the Bottle* (1975), a sophisticated philosophical treatment of semantics.

Perec \pe-'rek\, Georges (b. March 7, 1936, Paris, Fr.—d. March 3, 1982, Ivry)   French writer, often called the greatest innovator of form of his generation.

Perec's best-selling first novel was *Les Choses: Une Histoire des années soixante* (1965; *Things: A Story of the Sixties*). In 1967 he joined the Ouvroir de Littérature Potentielle (Workshop of Potential Literature). Known in short as Oulipo, the group dedicated itself to the pursuit of new forms for literature and the revival of old ones. Perec's novel *La Disparition* (1969; "The Disappearance"), written entirely without using the letter "e", was a by-product of his association with OuLiPo. *W, ou le souvenir d'enfance* (1975; *W, or the Memory of Childhood*) is considered a masterpiece of innovative autobiography, using alternating chapters to tell two stories that ultimately converge. By far his most ambitious and most critically acclaimed novel is *La Vie, mode d'emploi* (1978; *Life: A User's Manual*), which describes each unit in a large Parisian apartment building and relates the stories of its inhabitants.

Perec's work in other areas include a highly acclaimed 1979 television film about Ellis Island. *Je me souviens* (1978; "I Remember"), a book of about 480 sentences all beginning with the phrase "I Remember" and recording memories of life in the 1950s, was adapted for the stage. A collection of essays, *Penser/Classer* (1985; "To Think, To Classify"), was published posthumously.

Pereda \pä-'rā-<u>th</u>ä\, José María de (b. Feb. 6, 1833, near Santander, Spain—d. March 1, 1906, Santander) Spanish writer, the acknowledged leader of the modern Spanish regional novelists.

Pereda was given an income by an older brother so that he could become a writer. His first literary effort was the *Escenas montañesas* (1864; "Montaña Scenes"), starkly realistic sketches of the fisherfolk of Santander and the peasants of the Montaña. There followed other sketches and early novels of pronounced controversial spirit, such as *El buey suelto* (1878; "The Unfettered Ox"), *Don Gonzalo González de la Gonzalera* (1879), and *De tal palo tal astilla* (1880; "As the Wood, So the Chip"). With the exception of *Pedro Sánchez* (1883) and *La Montálvez* (1888), all of his novels have a Montaña background. Pereda's best work, one of the finest Spanish novels of the 19th century, was *Sotileza* (1884). A genuine novel of customs, it is an epic of the Santander fisherfolk, exemplified by the haughty, enigmatic fisherwoman Sotileza.

In his virile realism, tinged with human sympathy, Pereda is thoroughly Castilian, and, with his mastery of rich and flexible language, he excels above all as a painter of nature in all its aspects.

Père Goriot, Le \lə-per-gȯr-'yō\ ("Father Goriot") Novel by Honoré de BALZAC, originally published in French in the *Revue de Paris* in 1834 and published in book form in 1835. The novel is considered one of the best works of Balzac's panoramic series *La Comédie humaine* ("The Human Comedy"), and it was the first to feature characters that would reappear in later novels. This pessimistic case study of bourgeois society's ills after the French Revolution tells the intertwined stories of Eugène de Rastignac, an ambitious but penniless young man, and old Goriot, a father who sacrifices everything for his children.

Peregrinatio Etheriae \,per-ā-grē-'nät-ē-ō-ā-'ther-ē-,ī, -'nät-sē-ō; ,per-ə-gri-'nä-shē-ō-ē-'thir-ē-,ē\ ("Pilgrimage of Etheria") An anonymous and incomplete account of a western European nun's travels in the Middle East near the end of the 4th century. It gives important information about religious life and the observances of the church year in the localities visited. It also offers a detailed description of the daily and annual liturgical activities in Jerusalem. *Peregrinatio Etheriae* is an important souce for knowledge of the spoken Latin of the period.

Discovered in 1884 in an 11th-century Latin manuscript at Arezzo, Italy, the account was published in 1887. It was at first attributed to Silvia, a sister of Rufinus (died *c.* 410), a Christian priest, writer, and translator from northern Italy. Later it was determined that the author was probably a Spanish nun called Etheria (also known as Aetheria, Egeria, or Eucheria). According to internal evidence, the account was written between 363 and 540, but most scholars agree that the most likely date was the last years of the 4th century.

Peregrine Pickle \'per-ə-grin-'pik-əl\ (*in full* The Adventures of Peregrine Pickle, In Which Are Included Memoirs of a Lady of Quality) Picaresque novel by Tobias SMOLLETT, published in four volumes in 1751 and modified for a second edition in 1758.

This very long work concerning the adventures of the egotistical scoundrel Peregrine Pickle is a comic and savage portrayal of 18th-century society. Peregrine's journey through Europe, his many debaucheries, and his final repentance all provide scope for Smollett's satire on human cruelty, stupidity, and greed. Smollett also caricatured many of his enemies in the book, most notably Henry Fielding and the actor David Garrick.

Criticized for its excessive viciousness and its libelous tone, the book was not popular in its day. In the second edition Smol-

lett excised many of the more satirical passages; most modern scholars agree, however, that the first version is superior.

Perelandra \,per-ə-'lan-drə\ Second novel in a science-fiction trilogy by C.S. LEWIS, published in 1943. This sequel to *Out of the Silent Planet* (1938) was also published as *Voyage to Venus: Perelandra*. It takes up the adventures of the hero Ransom, who struggles with an evil scientist over the fate of the planet Venus. In an obvious reference to the biblical story of the temptation of Eve, the novel presents the scientist as the tempter of the female ruler of Venus. Sometimes criticized for its sexist view of women, *Perelandra* nevertheless is successful as both science fiction and religious allegory.

Perelman \'per-əl-mən, *commonly* 'pərl-mən\, S.J., *in full* Sidney Joseph (b. Feb. 1, 1904, Brooklyn, N.Y., U.S.—d. Oct. 17, 1979, New York, N.Y.) American humorist who was a master of wordplay in books, movies, plays, and essays.

Perelman graduated from Brown University. He began writing for the early, frenetic Marx Brothers films and helped turn out the screenplays for such classics as *Monkey Business* (1931) and *Horse Feathers* (1932). He also regularly contributed essays to *The New Yorker* magazine under such absurd titles as *Beat Me, Post-Impressionist Daddy* and *No Starch in the Dhoti*. Perelman collaborated on the theatrical comedies *All Good Americans* (1934) and *One Touch of Venus* (1943), and for his collaboration on the film *Around the World in 80 Days* he shared an Academy Award for best screenwriter for 1956. His magazine pieces were collected in a long series of books, including *Strictly from Hunger* (1937), *Westward Ha!; or, Around the World in Eighty Clichés* (1948), and *The Road to Miltown; or, Under the Spreading Atrophy* (1957).

Perelman's humor is characterized by an exquisite sense of cliché and mimicry that is combined with a varied vocabulary to create effects of comic nihilism and literary parody.

Peretz \'per-ets\, Isaac Leib, *also spelled* Yitskhok Leybush Perets, Leib *also spelled* Loeb *or* Löb (b. May 18, 1852, or May 20, 1851, Zamość, Poland, Russian Empire—d. April 3, 1915, Warsaw) Prolific writer of poems, short stories, drama, humorous sketches, and satire who was instrumental in raising the standard of Yiddish literature.

Peretz began writing in Hebrew but soon turned to Yiddish. For his tales of Ḥasidic lore, which he introduced into literature (*e.g.*, the *Silent Souls* series), he drew material from the lives of impoverished Jews of eastern Europe. Critical of their humility and resignation, he urged them to consider their temporal needs while retaining the spiritual grandeur for which he esteemed them. Influenced by Polish Neoromantic and Symbolist writings, Peretz lent new expressive force to the Yiddish language in numerous stories collected in such volumes as *Folkstimlekhe geshikhtn* (1908; "Folktales"). In his drama *Di Goldene keyt* (1909; "The Golden Chain"), he stressed the timeless chain of Jewish culture. To encourage Jews toward a wider knowledge of secular subjects, for several years Peretz wrote articles on physics, chemistry, economics, and other subjects for *Yidishe biblyotek*, which he also edited.

Peretz effectively ushered Yiddish literature into the modern era by exposing it to contemporary trends in western European art and literature. In his stories he viewed Ḥasidic material obliquely from the standpoint of a secular literary intellect, and with this unique perspective the stories became the vehicle for an elegiac contemplation of traditional Jewish values.

Peretz played an important moderating role as deputy chairman at the Yiddish Conference that assembled at Czernowitz in 1908 to promote the status of the language and its culture.

Pérez de Ayala \'pä-rāth-<u>th</u>ä-ä-'yä-lä\, Ramón (b. Aug. 9, 1880, Oviedo, Spain—d. Aug. 5, 1962, Madrid) Spanish novelist, poet, and critic who excelled in philosophical satire and the novel of ideas.

Pérez de Ayala studied at Oviedo University and the University of Madrid. During World War I he worked as a correspondent for the Buenos Aires periodical *La prensa*. He was elected to the Spanish Academy in 1928, and he served as Spanish ambassador to England from 1931 to 1936, when he went into voluntary exile in South America during the Spanish Civil War.

After writing a volume of poetry, *La paz del sendero* (1903; "The Peace of the Path"), he produced a series of four largely autobiographical novels: *Tinieblas en las cumbres* (1907; "Darkness at the Top"), *AMDG* (1910; *i.e.,* the Jesuit motto "Ad Majorem Dei Gloriam," or "To the Greater Glory of God"), *La pata de la raposa* (1912; *The Fox's Paw*), and *Troteras y danzaderas* (1913; "Trotters and Dancers").

Pérez de Ayala's later novels, which are considered his finest works, show a greater mastery of characterization and novelistic technique. *Belarmino y Apolonio* (1921; *Belarmino and Apolonio*) is a symbolic portrayal of the conflict between faith and doubt. *Luna de miel, luna de hiel* (1923; *Honeymoon, Bittermoon*) and its sequel, *Los trabajos de Urbano y Simona* (1923; "The Labors of Urbano and Simona"), treat the contrast between idealistic innocence and the realities of mature romantic love. In *Tigre Juan* (1926; *Tiger Juan*) and its sequel, *El curandero de su honra* (1926; "The Healer of His Honor"), Pérez de Ayala created characters of a universal nature and gave free expression to his delightful and wry humor. He also wrote short stories and essays.

Pérez de Guzmán \\'pā-reth-ˌthā-gūth-'män\\, Fernán (b. *c.* 1378—d. *c.* 1460)　Spanish poet, moralist, and historian, author of the first important work of history and historiography in Spain. His historical portraits of his contemporaries earned him the title of the "Spanish Plutarch."

Pérez de Guzmán devoted himself to letters after being imprisoned by Alvaro de Luna, a counselor to King John II of Castile. Although his poetry went through many editions, it is not as a poet that he is chiefly remembered. His fame rests on his *Mar de historias* (1512; "Sea of Histories"), a collection of biographies of emperors, philosophers, and saints, and primarily on the third part of this collection, which contains historical portraits of 33 prominent men and one woman from the reigns of Henry III to John II (the period 1390 to 1454).

Pérez de Hita \\'pā-rāth-ˌthā-'ē-tä\\, Ginés (b. 1544, Mula, Murcia, Spain—d. 1619)　Spanish writer, author of *Historia de los vandos de los Zegríes y Abencerrages* (1595–1619; "History of the Zegríes and Abencerrages Factions"), usually referred to as *Guerras civiles de Granada* ("The Civil Wars of Granada"). The book is considered the first Spanish historical novel and the last important collection of Moorish border ballads, which are interspersed throughout the book's narrative.

Pérez de Hita fought in the suppression of the revolt of the Moors in the Alpujarras mountains (1568–71), an event that is reflected in the second part of his *Guerras*. The first part deals with Moorish life in Granada before the Christian conquest of that city in 1492. Its portrait of the chivalrous Moorish family of the Abencerrages established the stereotype of the romantic Moor in European literature.

Pérez Galdós \\'pā-rāth-gāl-'dōs\\, Benito (b. May 10, 1843, Las Palmas, Canary Islands, Spain—d. Jan. 4, 1920, Madrid)　Writer who was regarded as the greatest Spanish novelist since Miguel de Cervantes. His enormous output of short novels of 19th-century Spain earned him comparison with Honoré de Balzac and Charles Dickens.

Born into a middle-class family, Pérez Galdós went to Madrid in 1862. After the success of his first novel, *La fontana*

de oro (1870; "The Fountain of Gold"), he began a series of novels based on meticulous research that recount Spain's history from the Battle of Trafalgar (1805) to the restoration of the Bourbons in Spain (1874). The entire cycle of 46 novels would come to be known as the EPISODIOS NACIONALES (1873–1912).

Detail of an oil painting by Joaquín Sorolla y Bastida
Hispanic Society of America

In the 1880s and '90s Pérez Galdós wrote a long series of novels, beginning with *Doña Perfecta* (1876). Known as the *novelas españolas contemporáneas* ("contemporary Spanish novels"), these books include some of his finest works, notably *La desheredada* (1881; *The Disinherited Lady*) and his masterpiece, the four-volume novel FORTUNATA Y JACINTA (1886–87), a study of two unhappily married women from different social classes. Pérez Galdós' earlier novels in the series show a reforming liberal zeal and an intransigent anticlericalism, but after the 1880s he displayed a greater sympathy for his country and its idiosyncracies. He demonstrated a phenomenal knowledge of Madrid, of which he showed himself the supreme chronicler. He also displayed a deep understanding of madness and abnormal psychological states. Pérez Galdós gradually came to admit more elements of spirituality into his work, eventually accepting them as an integral part of reality, as is evident in the important late novels *Nazarín* (1895) and *Misericordia* (1897; *Compassion*) and in a series of novels featuring the character TORQUEMADA. Pérez Galdós also wrote plays, some of which were immensely popular, but their success was largely owing to the political views presented in them rather than to their artistic value.

Pericles \\'per-i-ˌklēz\\ (*in full* Pericles, Prince of Tyre)　Play in five acts by William SHAKESPEARE, first performed in 1608–09 and published in a quarto edition in 1609. The play was based on the classical tale of Appollonius of Tyre as told in book eight of *Confessio amantis* by John Gower. The first scenes of *Pericles* are often feeble in expression, frequently ungrammatical, and sometimes scarcely intelligible, while the second half is well written, in Shakespeare's mature style. It is now generally supposed that the inadequate parts of the play are the result of its being a reconstruction of the text from the actors' imperfect memories. For the second half of the play, either the printer had a manuscript of good quality or the actors' memories were more accurate.

Pericles flees Antioch because he knows about King Antiochus' incestuous love for his own daughter. After aiding the starving people of Tarsus, he is shipwrecked near Pentapolis, where he marries beautiful Thaisa, daughter of King Simonides. He eventually gains the crown of Tyre but loses his wife and later his daughter Marina. Pericles bravely endures many hardships before he and his family are reunited. The play is highly symbolic and filled with imagery of the stormy seas.

pericope \\pə-'rik-ə-pē\\ *plural* pericopes *or* pericopae \\-ˌpē, -ˌpī\\ [Greek *perikopē* section]　A selection or extract from a book; especially, a selection from the Bible appointed to be read in church or used as a text for a sermon.

period \'pir-ē-əd\ [Greek *períodos* circuit, cycle, period in rhetoric] A complete sentence, or an utterance from one full stop to another; usually, a well-proportioned sentence of several clauses.

periodic \,pir-ē-'äd-ik\ Of or relating to a form of construction found in some Greek odes in which the second and third in a group of four strophes are alike in structure and the first and fourth differ from these and from each other.

periodical \,pir-ē-'äd-i-kəl\ A journal or other publication whose issues appear at fixed or regular intervals. *See* MAGAZINE.

periodic sentence A usually complex sentence that has no subordinate or trailing elements following its principal clause, or one in which the main clause comes last, as in "Yesterday, while I was walking down the street, I saw him." *Compare* LOOSE SENTENCE.

Periodic Table, The Collection of memoirs by Primo LEVI, published in Italian as *Il sistema periodico* in 1975. Regarded as his masterwork, it is a cycle of 21 autobiographical stories, each named after and inspired by a chemical element.

To Levi, a chemist as well as a writer, each element had an associative value—its properties symbolizing certain thoughts and triggering specific memories. In "Argon" he draws an analogy between the nonreactivity of this inert gas and the refusal of his Jewish ancestors to assimilate into the Gentile majority of their native Italian Piedmont. "Hydrogen" is an anecdote about his boyhood experiments with this explosive gas. "Vanadium" recounts his unexpected encounter with a former official of Auschwitz, where Levi was imprisoned during World War II. Attacking the fascist myth of racial purity in "Zinc," the author reveals his preference for the "boring metal" when it is in an active state of impurity.

period piece A piece (as of fiction, art, furniture, or music) whose special or chief value lies in its characterization or evocation of a historical period. *See also* HISTORICAL NOVEL.

peripeteia \,per-i-pə-'tē-ə, -'tī-\ or **peripetia** \-'tī-ə\ [Greek *peripéteia* reversal, sudden change, a derivative of *peripetēs* changing suddenly, literally, falling round, falling into] A sudden or unexpected reversal of circumstances or situation in a literary work. Peripeteia is the turning point in a drama after which the plot moves steadily to its denouement. It is discussed by Aristotle in the *Poetics* as the shift of the tragic protagonist's fortune from good to bad, which is essential to the plot of a tragedy. It is often an ironic twist, as in Sophocles' *Oedipus Rex* when a messenger brings Oedipus news about his parents that he thinks will cheer him; the news, instead, slowly brings about the awful recognition that leads to Oedipus' catastrophe. The term is also used to refer to the protagonist's shift from bad fortune to good in a comedy.

periphrasis \pə-'rif-rə-sis\ *plural* periphrases \-,sēz\, *also called* circumlocution \,sər-kəm-lō-'kyü-shən\ [Greek *períphrasis,* a derivative of *periphrázein* to express in a roundabout way, from *perí* around + *phrázein* to point out, show, declare] Use of a longer phrasing in place of a possible shorter form of expression, or a roundabout or indirect way of speaking. In literature it is sometimes used for comic effect, as by Charles Dickens in the speech of the character Wilkins Micawber, who appears in *David Copperfield.*

Perkins \'pər-kinz\, Maxwell (Evarts) (b. Sept. 20, 1884, New York, N.Y., U.S.—d. June 17, 1947, Stamford, Conn.) Influential American editor who discovered many of the most

prominent American writers of the first half of the 20th century.

Perkins graduated from Harvard University in 1907. After working as a reporter for the *New York Times*, he worked in the advertising department of Charles Scribner's Sons. In 1914 he joined the company's editorial staff, later becoming editorial director and vice president.

In 1918 Perkins read the manuscript of F. Scott Fitzgerald's first novel. Scribner's board rejected the book twice, but Perkins made suggestions for its revision and persuaded the company to publish it; the book, *This Side of Paradise* (1920), was a critical and financial success. Perkins worked with Fitzgerald on subsequent novels. He also persuaded Scribner's to publish Ernest Hemingway's first novel and the short stories of Ring Lardner. Perkins is perhaps best known for his work with Thomas Wolfe. In 1928 Wolfe submitted the manuscript of his first novel to Scribner's; the chaotic 1,114-page work had already been rejected by several publishers. Perkins spent months working with Wolfe to cut and restructure it, and in 1929 it was published as *Look Homeward, Angel*. Perkins is also credited with providing the theme and overall structure for Wolfe's second novel, *Of Time and the River* (1935).

Other writers whom Perkins discovered or assisted in their early careers included Erskine Caldwell, Edmund Wilson, John P. Marquand, Alan Paton, and James Jones.

Perrault \pe-'rō\, Charles (b. Jan. 12, 1628, Paris, Fr.—d. May 15/16, 1703, Paris) French poet, prose writer, and storyteller, a leading member of the Académie Française, who played a prominent part in a literary controversy known as the "quarrel of the ancients and moderns." He is best remembered for his collection of fairy stories for children, *Contes de ma mère l'oye* (1697; *Tales of Mother Goose*).

Perrault began to win a literary reputation about 1660 with light verse and love poetry. He spent the rest of his life promoting the study of literature and the arts. In 1671 he was elected to the Académie Française, which soon was sharply divided by the so-called quarrel between the ancients and the moderns. Perrault supported the modern view that as civilization progresses, literature evolves with it and that therefore ancient literature is inevitably more coarse and barbarous than modern literature. His chief opponent in the controversy was Nicolas Boileau-Despréaux, who on the whole had the better of the argument. Nevertheless, Perrault's stand was a landmark in the eventually successful revolt against the confines of the prevailing tradition.

Perrault's charming fairy stories in *Mother Goose* were written to amuse his children. They include "Le Petit Chaperin rouge" ("Little Red Riding Hood"), "La Belle au bois dormant" ("Sleeping Beauty"), "Le Maistre Chat; ou Le Chat botté" ("Puss in Boots"), and "La Barbe bleue" ("Bluebeard"), half-forgotten folktales which Perrault retold in a modern style that is simple and free from affectation.

Perron \dü-pə-'rōn\, Edgar du, *in full* Charles Edgar du Perron (b. Nov. 2, 1899, Meester Cornelis, Java—d. May 14, 1940, Bergen, Neth.) Dutch writer and critic, cofounder with Menno ter Braak of the influential Dutch literary journal *Forum* (1932–35), which aimed to replace superficial elegance of literary style with greater sincerity of literary content. The *Forum* writers resisted National Socialism and Nazi Germany's occupation of The Netherlands.

Du Perron went to Europe in 1921 and lived on the Left Bank in Paris, an experience that provided the background of his novel *Een voorbereiding* (1927; "A Preparation"). Cosmopolitan in outlook, he did much to counteract Dutch provincialism by publicizing the works of the French writers

André Gide and André Malraux. He translated Malraux's *La Condition humaine*, which had been dedicated to him, into Dutch. His collected essays, *De smalle mens* (1934), deal with the precarious position of the individual in the face of the collective attitudes of left and right. His poems, collected in *Parlando* (1941), are characterized by everyday words and a conversational tone. Shortly before World War II, du Perron spent additional years in the Dutch East Indies collecting materials for *De man van Lebak* (1937), a critical biography of the great Dutch novelist Multatuli.

Perry \'per-ē\, Bliss (b. Nov. 25, 1860, Williamstown, Mass., U.S.—d. Feb. 13, 1954, Exeter, N.H.) American scholar and editor, especially noted for his work in American literature.

Perry was educated at Williams College, Williamstown, and the German universities of Berlin and Strassburg (now Strasbourg, Fr.). He taught at Williams, Princeton University, and Harvard University and was Harvard lecturer at the University of Paris. From 1899 to 1909 he edited *The Atlantic Monthly*.

Perry edited many volumes, including the works of Edmund Burke, Sir Walter Scott, and Ralph Waldo Emerson, and he was general editor (1905–09) of the Cambridge edition of the major American poets. He wrote a number of books, including works on Walt Whitman, John Greenleaf Whittier, Thomas Carlyle, Emerson, and others, as well as novels, short fiction, essays, an autobiography, studies of poetry, and collections of fiction and essays.

Persephone \pər-'sef-ə-nē\, *also called* Kore \'kȯr-ē, 'kȯr-ə\ In Greek mythology, daughter of Zeus and DEMETER, the goddess of agriculture and the counterpart of the Roman Proserpina or Proserpine; she was the wife of Hades, king of the underworld. In the Homeric "Hymn to Demeter," the story is told of how Persephone was gathering flowers in the Vale of Nysa when she was seized by Hades and removed to the underworld. Upon learning of the abduction her mother, Demeter, in her misery, became unconcerned with the harvest or the fruitfulness of the earth, so that widespread famine ensued. Zeus intervened, commanding Hades to release Persephone to her mother. Because Persephone had eaten a single pomegranate seed in the underworld, she could not be completely freed but had to remain for one-third of the year with Hades, spending the other two-thirds with her mother. The story that Persephone spent four months of each year in the underworld was no doubt meant to account for the barren appearance of Greek fields for part of the year.

Perseus \'pər-,syüs, -,süs, -sē-əs\ In Greek mythology, the slayer of the Gorgon Medusa and the rescuer of Andromeda from a sea monster. Perseus was the son of Zeus and Danaë, the daughter of Acrisius of Argos. Fearing the fulfillment of a prophecy that he would be killed by his grandson, Acrisius cast both Danaë and the infant Perseus (imprisoned within a chest) into the sea. The vessel was washed up on the island of Seriphus, where Perseus spent his youth. King Polydectes of Seriphus, who desired Danaë, tricked Perseus into promising to obtain the head of Medusa, the only mortal among the Gorgons.

Aided by Hermes and Athena, Perseus forced the Graiae, sisters of the Gorgons, to provide him with winged sandals (which enabled him to fly), the helmet of Hades (which conferred invisibility), a curved sword, or sickle, to decapitate Medusa, and a bag in which to conceal the head. Because the gaze of Medusa turned all who looked at her to stone, Perseus guided himself by her reflection in a shield given him by Athena and beheaded Medusa as she slept. He then returned to Seriphus and rescued his mother by using Medusa's head to turn Polydectes and his supporters to stone.

A further deed attributed to Perseus was his rescue of the princess Andromeda when he was on his way home with Medusa's head. Andromeda's mother, Cassiopeia (Cassiope), had claimed to be more beautiful than the sea nymphs, or Nereids, and Poseidon had punished the kingdom by flooding it and plaguing it with a sea monster. An oracle informed Andromeda's father, King Cepheus, that the ills would cease if he exposed Andromeda to the monster, which he did. Perseus, passing by, saw the princess and fell in love with her. He turned the sea monster to stone by showing it Medusa's head and afterward married Andromeda.

Later Perseus gave the Gorgon's head to Athena, who placed it on her shield, and gave his other accoutrements to Hermes. He accompanied his mother back to her native Argos in order to be reconciled with Acrisius, but Acrisius was not there when they arrived. Soon after this Perseus went to Larissa to compete in an athletic contest. Acrisius, who happened to be there as a spectator, was accidentally struck dead by a discus thrown by Perseus, who thus fulfilled the prophecy that he would kill his grandfather. He subsequently founded Mycenae as his capital, becoming the ancestor of the Perseids, including Heracles.

Persians \'pər-zhənz\ (*Greek* Persai) One of a trilogy of unconnected tragedies presented in 472 BC by AESCHYLUS. *Persians* is unique among surviving tragedies in that it dramatizes recent history rather than events from the distant age of mythical heroes. The play treats the decisive repulse of the Persians from Greece in 480, in particular their defeat at the Battle of Salamis. It is set in the Persian capital, where a messenger brings news to the Persian queen of the disaster at Salamis. After attributing the defeat of Persia to both Greek independence and bravery and to the gods' punishment of Persian folly for going outside the bounds of Asia, the play ends with the return of the broken and humiliated Persian king, Xerxes.

Persius \'pər-shē-əs, -shəs, -sē-əs\, *in full* Aulus Persius Flaccus \'flak-əs\ (b. AD 34, Volaterrae [now Volterra, Italy]—d. 62, Campania) Stoic poet whose Latin satires reached a higher moral tone than those of other classical Latin poets (excepting Juvenal).

A pupil and friend of the stoic philosopher Lucius Annaeus Cornutus and a fellow student of the poet Lucan, who admired all he wrote, Persius discovered his vocation as a satirist through reading the 10th book of Gaius Lucilius. He wrote painstakingly, and his book of satires was still incomplete at his premature death. The book was an immediate success. The six satires, amounting to 650 lines, are in hexameters, but what appears as a prologue, in which Persius (an extremely wealthy man) ironically asserts that he writes to earn his bread, not because he is inspired, is in choliambics. The first satire censures literary tastes of the day, which are seen as reflecting the decadence of national morals. The remaining books are philosophical discussions on themes often treated by Seneca, such as what may rightly be asked of the gods, the necessity of self-knowledge for citizens, and the stoic doctrine of freedom.

persona \pər-'sō-nə\ *plural* personae \-,nē, -,nī\ [Latin, actor's mask, character in a play, person, probably from Etruscan *phersu* mask, from Greek *prósōpa*, plural of *prósōpon* face, mask] In literature, the person who is understood to be speaking (or thinking or writing) a particular work. The persona is almost invariably distinct from the author; it is the voice chosen by the author for a particular artistic purpose. The persona may be a character in the work in question or merely an unnamed narrator, but, insofar as the manner and style of expression in the work exhibit taste, prejudice, emotion, or other characteristics of a human personality, the work may be said to be in the voice of a persona. *See also* NARRATOR.

Personae \pər-'sō-nē, per-'sō-,nī\ (*in full* Personae: The Collected Poems of Ezra Pound) Anthology of short verse by Ezra POUND, published in 1926. The work contains many of his shorter poems, including selections from the earlier collections *A lume spento* (1908), *A Quinzaine for this Yule* (1908), *Personae* (1909), *Exultations* (1909), *Canzoni* (1911), *Ripostes* (1912), and *Lustra* (1916), but the emphasis of the anthology was on his later verse.

personage \'pər-sə-nij\ A dramatic, fictional, or historical character; also, a character as assumed or represented, as in an impersonation.

personification \pər-,sän-ə-fi-'kā-shən\ Figure of speech in which human characteristics are attributed to an abstract quality, animal, or inanimate object. Personification has been used in European poetry since Homer and is particularly common in allegory; for example, the medieval morality play *Everyman* (c. 1500) and the Christian prose allegory *The Pilgrim's Progress* (1678) by John Bunyan contain characters such as Death, Knowledge, Giant Despair, Sloth, and Piety. Personification became almost an automatic mannerism in 18th-century Neoclassical poetry, as exemplified by these lines from Thomas Gray's *An Elegy Written in a Country Church Yard*:

> Here rests his head upon the lap of Earth
> A youth to Fortune and to Fame unknown.
> Fair Science frowned not on his humble birth,
> And Melancholy marked him for her own.

perspectivism \pər-'spek-tə-,viz-əm\ Consciousness of or the process of using different points of view (as in literary criticism or artistic representation).

Persuasion Novel by Jane AUSTEN, published posthumously in 1817. Unlike her novel *Northanger Abbey*, with which it was published, *Persuasion* (written 1815–16) was a work of Austen's maturity. Like *Mansfield Park* and *Emma*, *Persuasion* contains subdued satire and develops the comedy of character and manners.

Persuasion tells the story of a second chance, the reawakening of love between Anne Elliot and Captain Frederick Wentworth, whom eight years earlier she had been persuaded not to marry. Wentworth returns from the Napoleonic Wars with prize money and the social acceptability of naval rank. He is now an eligible suitor acceptable to Anne's snobbish father and his circle, and Anne discovers the continuing strength of her love for him.

Pessanha \pi-'sä^n-yə\, Camilo (b. Sept. 7, 1867, Coimbra, Port.—d. 1926, Macao) Portuguese poet whose work is the representative in Portuguese poetry of Symbolism in its purest and most genuine form and the chief precursor of modernist poetry.

After studying law at the university at Coimbra in 1891, Pessanha taught in the Portuguese colony of Macao in China. He began to practice various Oriental customs, including the use of opium, and learned Cantonese, from which he translated the works in *Oito Elegias Chinesas* ("Eight Chinese Elegies"). His writings on China, in particular the *Introdução a um Estudo sobre a Civilização Chinesa* and the *Elegias*, were collected in *China* (1943).

Although he had begun to write verse in Coimbra, Pessanha was virtually unknown until 1916, when his innovative Symbolist poetry was published in the progressive review *Centauro*. Later collected in *Clépsidra* (1920), it became a breviary for the modernist poets. Pessanha is one of the most lyrical of Portuguese poets.

Pessoa \pes-'sō-ə\, Fernando António Nogueira (b. June 13, 1888, Lisbon, Port.—d. Nov. 30, 1935, Lisbon) Portuguese poet whose part in modernism gave Portuguese literature cachet elsewhere in Europe.

Pessoa lived in Durban, S.Af., where his stepfather was Portuguese consul. He became fluent in English, in which language he wrote his early verse. In 1905 he returned to Lisbon, where he remained, working as a commercial translator while contributing to avant-garde reviews, especially *Orpheu* (1915), the organ of Modernismo, of which Pessoa was a leading aesthetician. He began publishing books of English poetry in 1918, but it was not until 1934 that his first book in Portuguese, *Mensagem*, appeared. It attracted little attention.

Fame came to Pessoa after his death in 1935, when his extraordinarily rich dream world, peopled with several fictional alter egos whose poetry he produced along with his own, became generally known. The most important of his works are *Poesias de Fernando Pessoa* (1942), *Poesias de Álvaro de Campos* (1944), *Poemas de Alberto Caeiro* (1946), and *Odes de Ricardo Reis* (1946).

Included among English translations of his work are *Selected Poems*, 2nd ed. (1982), *Always Astonished: Selected Prose* (1988), and *The Book of Disquiet*.

petasos or **petasus** \'pet-ə-səs\ [Greek *pétasos*] A broad-brimmed low-crowned hat worn by ancient Greeks and Romans. It is especially used in reference to the winged hat of Hermes or Mercury.

Peter Pan \'pē-tər-'pan\ (*in full* Peter Pan; or, The Boy Who Wouldn't Grow Up) Play by James M. BARRIE, first produced in 1904. Although the title character first appeared in Barrie's novel *The Little White Bird* (1902), he is most famous as the protagonist of *Peter Pan*. First composed of three acts, the play was often revised; the definitive version in five acts was published in 1928.

The plot line reveals that, as a baby, Peter Pan fell out of his carriage and was taken by fairies to Never-Never Land. There he can fly and is the champion of the Lost Boys and a friend to the fairy Tinker Bell. Revisiting England, Peter becomes involved with Wendy Darling and her younger brothers, all of whom accompany Peter to Never-Never Land. Peter, the Lost Boys, and the children have many adventures and vanquish the pirate Captain Hook. The Darling children eventually return home, taking the Lost Boys with them and leaving Peter Pan to his perpetual boyhood.

The work was frequently produced as a stage play and a film, and the role of Peter was always played by a woman.

Peter Rabbit \'pē-tər\ Fictional character, a mischievous rabbit featured in Beatrix Potter's THE TALE OF PETER RABBIT, the best-selling children's book on record.

Peters \'pē-tərz\, Ellis, *pseudonym of* Edith Mary Pargeter \'pär-ji-tər\ (b. Sept. 28, 1913, Horsehay, Shropshire, Eng.) Prolific English novelist especially noted for a series of mysteries featuring medieval monastics in Britain and for another featuring a modern family.

Peters began writing novels in the 1930s, and after World War II she became a full-time writer and translator. Though her first crime novel, *Murder in the Dispensary*, was published in 1938 (under the name Jolyon Carr), for most of the next 20 years she concentrated on other genres. Under her own name she published the mystery *Fallen into the Pit* (1951), featuring 13-year-old Dominic Felse. In *Death and the Joyful Woman* (1961) he returns as a 16-year-old whose girlfriend is connected with a murder; the novel, like the many Felse family mysteries that followed it, was published under the name Ellis Peters.

Peters' interest in Shropshire history led her to write the mystery *A Morbid Taste for Bones* (1977), set in the 12th century. It features the monk Brother Cadfael, who before taking his vows had been a lover, sailor, soldier, and fighter in the First Crusade. He returns in *One Corpse Too Many* (1979), and in the 1980s and '90s Peters published more than 15 Cadfael novels. They include *The Virgin in the Ice* (1982) and *The Heretic's Apprentice* (1989). Under her original name Peters wrote crime and historical fiction, including the four-volume "Brothers of Gwynedd" series (1974–77), and translated more than a dozen volumes of prose and poetry from Czech and Slovak into English.

Peters \'pē-tərs\, Lenrie (Wilfred Leopold) (b. Sept. 1, 1932, Bathurst, Gambia [now Banjul, The Gambia]) Physician, novelist, and one of West Africa's most important poets.

Peters was educated at Bathurst, Freetown (Sierra Leone), and at Trinity College, Cambridge, where he earned a medical degree in 1959. His novel *The Second Round* (1965) presents the semiautobiographical story of the disillusionment and alienation of a young doctor returning from England to Freetown after completing his medical studies; he finds his home unsettled and unsettling. Peters' poetry (*Poems*, 1964; *Satellites*, 1967; *Katchikali*, 1971; *Selected Poetry*, 1981; and that found in several anthologies) is generally pessimistic, characterized by irony and sometimes satire. It is marked by grief over the present condition of Africa and a longing for the values of the past.

Petit Testament, Le \lə-pə-,tē-tes-tà-'mäⁿ\ Poem by François VILLON, written as *Le Lais* (*The Legacy*) and retitled when it was published in 1489. It consists of 320 eight-syllable lines grouped in eight-line stanzas. The work probably was written about 1456, about the time Villon was obliged to leave Paris after being implicated in a theft from the Collège de Navarre, and is concerned with his thoughts about his departure.

The poem does not refer to the robbery; rather, in the introduction Villon maintains that he is leaving Paris because of the unhappy end of a love affair. After the introduction Villon makes bequests, upon parting, to friends and acquaintances. To his barber he leaves the clippings from his hair; to "three poor orphans" who prove to be well-known local usurers, some small change; to the clerk of criminal justice, his *branc* (which means both "sword" and "excrement"); and to his beloved, his broken heart. The concluding section of *Le Petit Testament* mocks scholastic language and scholasticism in general.

Petőfi \'pet-ō-fē\, Sándor (b. Jan. 1, 1823, Kiskőrös, Hung.— d. probably 1856, Siberia) One of the greatest Hungarian poets and a revolutionary who symbolized the Hungarian desire for freedom.

Petőfi's first poem was published in 1842. After years of vicissitudes, in 1844 he became an assistant editor of the literary periodical *Pesti Divatlap*. His first volume of poetry, *Versek*, appeared in the same year and made him famous at once, though the tone of his poems scandalized many.

Petőfi played a leading role in the literary life of the period preceding the outbreak of the Hungarian revolution of 1848. A fervent partisan of the French Revolution, he castigated the social conditions of his country, attacking the privileges of the nobles and the monarchy. His poems glowed with political passion, and one of them, "Talpra magyar" ("Rise, Hungarian"), written on the eve of the revolution, became its anthem. During the revolution he became the aide-de-camp of General Jozef Bem, then head of the Transylvanian army. Petőfi disappeared during the Battle of Segesvár, on July 31, 1849. Though for many years his death at Segesvár had been assumed, in the late 1980s Soviet investigators found archives which revealed that he was one of some 1,800 Hungarian prisoners of war who were marched to Siberia. It is believed that he died of tuberculosis in 1856.

Petőfi's poetry is characterized by realism, humor, and descriptive power and is imbued with a peculiar vigor. He intro-

duced a direct, unpretentious style and a clear, unornamented construction adapted from national folk songs. This simplicity was the more arresting as it was used to reveal subtle emotions and political or philosophical ideas. Of his epic poems the *János vitéz* (1845), an entrancing fairy tale, is the most popular. Petőfi's popularity has never diminished in Hungary.

Petrakis \pə-'trä-kis\, Harry Mark (b. June 5, 1923, St. Louis, Mo., U.S.) American novelist and short-story writer whose exuberant and sensitive works deal with the lives of Greek immigrants in urban America.

The son of an Eastern Orthodox priest, Petrakis attended the University of Illinois and held a variety of jobs to support himself while writing. His novels and stories, usually set in Chicago, include *Lion at My Heart* (1959), *The Odyssey of Kostas Volakis* (1963), *A Dream of Kings* (1966), *The Hour of the Bell* (1976), *Nick the Greek* (1979), *Days of Vengeance* (1983), and *Ghost of the Sun* (1990), a sequel to *A Dream of Kings*. He also published collections of short stories, a biography, and an autobiography, *Stelmark: A Family Recollection* (1970).

Petrarch \'pē-,trärk, 'pe-\, *Italian in full* Francesco Petrarca \pe-'trär-kä\ (b. July 20, 1304, Arezzo, Tuscany [Italy]—d. July 18/19, 1374, Arquà, near Padua, Carrara) Italian scholar, poet, and humanist whose poems addressed to LAURA, an idealized beloved, contributed to the Renaissance flowering of lyric poetry. He was regarded as the greatest scholar of his age.

Detail of a portrait by Andrea del Castagno; in the Cenacolo di Sant' Apollonia, Florence

At his father's insistence Petrarch at first studied law, but after his father's death, in 1326, he pursued his interests in literature and in a religious life. Moving to Avignon, he took minor ecclesiastical orders and entered the household of an influential cardinal. This period marked the beginning of his famous chaste love for a woman known now only as Laura. Attempts have been made to identify her, but to no avail. From this love arose the work for which he is most celebrated, the Italian poems (*Rime*) collected and revised throughout his life.

His years in Avignon were years of ambition and unremitting study (notably in the field of classical Latin). Petrarch was a stubborn advocate of the continuity between classical culture and the Christian message. It was in combining the two seemingly conflicting ideals that he can be considered the founder and a great representative of the humanist movement. In 1337 he left Avignon for Vaucluse, a much-loved place of retreat to which he often returned after prolonged periods of traveling. There he produced many of the works that established his reputation. In September 1340 he received invitations from Paris and Rome to be crowned as poet. He chose Rome and was crowned on the Capitoline Hill on April 8, 1341. He returned home in the autumn of 1343, but continued to travel frequently both for his own studies and on diplomatic missions. He visited Verona, Parma, and Padua, made a pilgrimage to Rome, and lived in Milan and Venice before finally settling near Padua about 1367.

Petrarch's influence on literature was enormous and lasting, extending to poets and scholars throughout western Europe. His combined interest in classical culture and Christianity is apparent in his philosophical and religious works. Humanist ideals inspired his Latin poem *Africa* (begun *c.* 1338) and his historical works, but the autobiographical *Secretum meum* (written 1342–58; *Petrarch's Secret*) is most important for a full understanding of his conflicting ideals.

His other major works include *De viris illustribus* (begun *c.* 1337; *On Illustrious Men*), *Rerum memorandum libri* (begun 1342–43; "Books on Matters To Be Remembered"); *De otio religioso* (1345–47; "On Religious Idleness"), *Bucolicum carmen* (begun 1345–47; "Bucolic Song"), *De vita solitaria* (1345–47; "The Life of Solitude"), *Epistolae metricae* (begun *c.* 1345; "Metrical Letters"), and two collections of letters written throughout his life, the *Rerum familiarium libri*, commonly called *Familiares* (*Letters on Familiar Matters*), and *Epistolae seniles*, commonly called *Seniles* (*Letters of Old Age*).

Petrarchan sonnet \pi-'trär-kən, pe-, pē-\, *also called* Italian sonnet.   A poem of 14 lines divided into an octave rhyming *abbaabba* and a sestet with a variable rhyme scheme—it can be *cdecde, cdcdcd,* or *cdcdce,* or some other variation—that never ends in a final couplet. The octave usually presents the theme or problem of the poem, and the sestet presents a change in thought or a resolution of the problem. The sonnet form, developed in 13th-century Italy, reached its highest expression in the works of Petrarch, for whom the Petrarchan sonnet was named. Later brought to England, the Petrarchan sonnet was adapted to create the form now called a SHAKESPEAREAN SONNET. Many English writers continued to write Petrarchan sonnets, however, including William Wordsworth, John Keats, and Elizabeth Barrett Browning. One of the best-known examples of this kind in English is Wordsworth's "The World Is Too Much with Us."

The Petrarchan sonnet exerted a major influence on European poetry. It soon became naturalized in Spain, Portugal, and France and was introduced to Poland, whence it spread to other Slavic literatures. In most cases the form was adapted to the staple meter of the language—*e.g.,* the alexandrine (12-syllable iambic line) in France and iambic pentameter in English.

Petrified Forest, The   Drama in two acts by Robert SHERWOOD, published and produced in 1935. This melodramatic Depression-era tale of frustrated lives and spiritual emptiness is set in a gas station and lunchroom along an Arizona highway. Gabby, the daughter of the station's owner, is unhappy with her life in the desert and longs to go to Paris to paint. She falls in love with Alan Squier, a failed author who stops at the restaurant on his way to California and proposes elopement.

Everything changes when the escaped criminal Duke Mantee arrives and holds them hostage. Though flawed by didacticism and romantic clichés, the play offers insight into the search for values in a decadent civilization.

Petronius Arbiter \pə-'trō-nē-əs-'är-bi-tər\, Gaius, *original name* Titus Petronius Niger \'nī-jər\ (d. AD 66)   Reputed author of the SATYRICON, a literary portrait of Roman society of the 1st century AD.

The most complete and the most authentic account of Petronius' life appears in Tacitus' *Annals.* From his high position in Roman society, it may be assumed that he was wealthy; he belonged to a noble family and was therefore, by Roman standards, a man from whom solid achievements might have been expected. Tacitus' account, however, shows that he belonged to a class of idle pleasure seekers. On the rare occasions when he was appointed to official positions, Petronius showed himself energetic and fully equal to public responsibilities. He served as governor of the Asian province of Bithynia and later held the high office of consul, or first magistrate of Rome.

After his term as consul, Petronius was received by Nero into his most intimate circle as his "director of elegance" (*arbiter elegantiae*), whose word on all matters of taste was law. It is from this title that the epithet "Arbiter" was attached to his name. What Petronius thought of his imperial patron may be indicated by his treatment of the rich vulgarian Trimalchio in the *Satyricon.* Trimalchio is a composite figure, but there are detailed correspondences between him and Nero that strongly suggest that Petronius was sneering at the emperor.

Tacitus records that Nero's friendship ultimately brought on Petronius the enmity of the commander of the emperor's guard, Tigellinus, who in AD 66 denounced him as having been implicated in a conspiracy of the previous year to assassinate Nero and place a rival on the imperial throne. Petronius, though innocent, was arrested at Cumae in southern Italy; he did not wait for the inevitable sentence but took his own life.

Petronius' *Satyricon,* one of the earliest examples of extended prose fiction, is a comic novel written in an episodic style. Interspersed among the adventures of the narrator and two friends are several unrelated stories and digressions in which the author states his own views on a variety of subjects.

Petrov \p^y-'tròf\, Yevgeny.   Writer known for his collaboration with Ilya ILF.

Petruchio \pə-'trü-chē-ō\   Fictional character, a gentleman of Verona who comes to Padua in search of a wife and becomes the aggressive suitor of obstinate Katharina in THE TAMING OF THE SHREW by William Shakespeare.

Petrushka or **Petrouchka** \p^y-'trüsh-kə, *Angl* pə-'trüsh-kə, -'trüch-\   Main character of Russian folk puppet shows, first noted in 17th-century accounts and popular well into the 20th century. Petrushka was typically depicted as a smiling young boy with a large, hooked nose and often was humpbacked.

Petry \'pē-trē\, Ann, *original surname* Lane \'lān\ (b. Oct. 12, 1908, Old Saybrook, Conn., U.S.)   African-American novelist, journalist, and biographer whose works offered a unique perspective on black life in small-town New England.

Petry began her career as a journalist, writing for the *Amsterdam News* and the *Peoples' Voice* of Harlem, and then studied creative writing at Columbia University.

Her first novel, THE STREET (1946), became a best-seller and was critically acclaimed for its portrayal of a working-class black woman, Lutie Johnson, who dreams of getting out of Harlem but is inevitably thwarted by the pressures of poverty and racism. *Country Place* (1947) depicts the disillusionment and corruption among a group of white people in a small town in Connecticut. Her third novel, *The Narrows* (1953), is the story of Link Williams, a Dartmouth-educated black man who tends bar in the black section of Monmouth, Conn., and of his tragic love affair with a rich white woman. Petry's short stories were collected in *Miss Muriel and Other Stories* (1971). Petry also published several historical biographies for children, including *Harriet Tubman, Conductor on the Underground Railroad* (1955) and *Tituba of Salem Village* (1964).

Pétursson \\'pyāt-u␣rs-sôn\\, Hallgrímur (b. 1614, Hólar, Ice.—d. Oct. 27, 1674, Ferstikla)   One of the greatest religious poets of Iceland.

As a boy Hallgrímur ran away to Copenhagen and became a blacksmith's apprentice. Through the influence of Bishop Brynjólfur Sveinsson, he later received a humanistic education. In 1636 he was entrusted with the re-Christianizing of a party of Icelanders who had been held captive by Algerian pirates for nine years. Returning to Iceland, Hallgrímur worked as a laborer and a fisherman but eventually became a parson at Saurbær (1651–69). He contracted leprosy and out of this misery produced his *Passiusálmar* (1666; *The Passion Hymns of Iceland*), which ranks among the greatest religious poetry of the world. In each hymn the poet merges his personal suffering with that of Jesus. The effect of the *Passion Hymns* in bolstering the morale of a desperate people was attested to by their immediate widespread popularity. First printed in 1666 and for the 64th time in 1957, they remain the most cherished devotional songs of the Icelanders.

Phaedra \\'fē-drə\\   In Greek mythology, the half sister of the Minotaur and wife of Theseus, who married her after abandoning her sister Ariadne. Phaedra later became enamored of her stepson Hippolytus, but he refused her advances. Humiliated, she falsely accused him of raping her and then hanged herself.

Works that treat the legend include *Hippolytus* (428 BC) by Euripides, *Phaedra* by Seneca, *Phèdre* (1677) by Jean Racine, *Fedra* (1909) by Gabriele D'Annunzio, *Thésée* (1946) by André Gide, and *The Cretan Woman* (1954) by Robinson Jeffers.

Phaedrus \\'fē-drəs\\ (b. *c.* 15 BC, Thrace—d. *c.* AD 50, Italy)   Roman fabulist who was the first writer to Latinize whole books of fables, producing free versions in iambic meter of Greek prose fables then circulating under the name of Aesop.

The fables of Phaedrus—noted for their charm, brevity, and didacticism—include such favorites as "The Fox and the Sour Grapes," "The Wolf and the Lamb," "The Lion's Share," "The Two Wallets," and "The Pearl in the Dung-Heap." His work became extremely popular in medieval Europe.

In the early 18th century a manuscript was discovered at Parma that contained 64 fables of Phaedrus, of which 30 were new. Another manuscript was later found in the Vatican and published in 1831. Further research identified 30 more fables as written in the iambics of Phaedrus.

Phaethon \\'fā-ə-thən, -,thän\\ ("Shining," or "Radiant")   In Greek mythology, the son of Helios, the sun god, and a woman or nymph variously identified as Clymene, Prote, or Rhode. Phaethon asked his father to be allowed to drive the chariot of the sun through the heavens for a single day. Because he was unable to control the horses of the sun chariot, which came too near to the earth and began to scorch it, Zeus hurled a thunderbolt at Phaethon, who fell to the earth at the mouth of the Eridanus, a river later identified as the Po.

Phèdre \\'fedr, *Angl* 'fed-rə, 'fed\\   Classical tragedy in five acts by Jean RACINE, performed and published in 1677. Based upon the play *Hippolytus* by the Greek playwright Euripides, Racine's work changed the focus from Hippolytus to Phèdre, his stepmother.

Receiving false information that her husband, King Thésée (Theseus), is dead, Phèdre accedes to her nurse Oenone's urging and tells her stepson, Hippolyte (Hippolytus), that she loves him. He rejects her. Thinking that Hippolyte is the aggressor toward Phèdre, Thésée invokes the aid of Neptune to destroy his son. In sorrow and guilt, Phèdre kills herself.

Phelps \\'felps\\, William Lyon (b. Jan. 2, 1865, New Haven, Conn., U.S.—d. Aug. 21, 1943, New Haven)   American scholar and critic who did much to popularize the teaching of contemporary literature.

Phelps attended and taught at Yale and Harvard universities. In 1895, at Yale, he taught the first American college course in the modern novel. Both in this course and in his *Essays on Russian Novelists* (1911), he was influential in introducing Russian novelists to American readers.

Phelps was a popular lecturer and critic, and his literary essays that appeared in *Scribner's Magazine* and other periodicals, together with his syndicated newspaper column, "A Daily Thought," brought him a wide audience. His *Autobiography with Letters* was published in 1939.

Pheme   *see* FAMA.

phenomenological criticism \\fə-,näm-ə-nə-'läj-i-kəl\\   School of criticism based on phenomenology, the philosophy that arose at the turn of the 20th century with the work of Edmund Husserl.

The primary objective of phenomenology was to take a fresh approach to concretely experienced phenomena through the direct investigation of the data of consciousness—without theories about their causal explanation and as free as possible from unexamined presuppositions—and to attempt to describe them as faithfully as possible. Adherents argued that, by carefully exploring examples, it was possible to fathom the essential structures and relationships of phenomena.

As applied to literary criticism, phenomenology is most evident in the theory and practice of the GENEVA SCHOOL. *See also* READER-RESPONSE CRITICISM.

pherecratean \\,fer-ə-'krat-ē-ən\\, *also called* pherecratic \\-'krat-ik\\   **1.** *also called* first pherecratean *or* aristophanic \\ə-,ris-tə-'fan-ik\\   A classical verse or rhythmic system that scans as $- \cup \cup - \cup - \cup$. The pherecratean colon takes its name from the Greek comic poet Pherecrates (5th century BC).   **2.** *also called* second pherecratean.   A classical verse or rhythmic system that scans as $\cup \cup - \cup \cup - \cup$.

Philander \\fi-'lan-dər\\   In Renaissance literature, a common name for a flirtatious male character who has many love affairs.

Philaster *or* **Phylaster** \\fi-'las-tər\\   (*in full* Philaster, or Love Lies A-Bleeding)   Romantic tragicomedy by Francis BEAUMONT and John FLETCHER, produced about 1608–10. The play solidified their joint literary reputation.

The drama's title character is the legitimate heir to the throne of Sicily. He and Arethusa, daughter of the usurper to the throne, are in love, but she is to be married to Pharamond, a lecherous Spanish prince. When Arethusa exposes Pharamond's excesses, the engagement is broken and she is falsely accused of having an affair with her page, Bellario, formerly Philaster's page. Convinced of this, Philaster angrily wounds Arethusa. Bellario, however, is actually Euphrasia, a young woman who is in love with Philaster. At the end, Bellario reveals her true identity and Arethusa and Philaster reconcile. The usurper, fearing a popular uprising, restores Philaster to his throne and returns his lands.

Philemon \\fi-'lē-mən, fī-\\ (b. *c.* 368 BC, Syracuse, Sicily [Italy]—d. *c.* 264 BC)   Poet of the Athenian New Comedy, an elder contemporary and successful rival of Menander.

As a playwright Philemon was noted for his neatly contrived plots, vivid description, dramatic surprises, and platitudinous moralizing. By 328 BC he was producing plays in Athens; he also worked in Alexandria for a time. Of 97 comedies by him, some 60 titles survive in Greek fragments and Latin adaptations.

Philemon and Baucis \fī-'lē-mən, fi-...'bȯs-is\ In Greek mythology, a pious Phrygian couple who hospitably receive two wayfarers—actually Zeus and Hermes in disguise—when their wealthier neighbors turn away the pair. As a reward for their hospitality, Philemon and Baucis are saved from a flood that drowns the rest of the country, their cottage is turned into a temple, and they are granted their wish to die at the same moment, being turned into trees—an oak and a linden.

Philes \'fī-ˌlēz, *Greek* 'fē-ˌlēs\, Manuel (fl. *c.* 1275–1345) Byzantine court poet whose works are of chiefly historical and social interest.

At an early age Philes (who was born in Ephesus) moved to Constantinople (now Istanbul), where he was the pupil of Georgius Pachymeres. Philes' character, as shown in his poems, is that of a begging poet, always pleading poverty and ready to descend to the grossest flattery. He was acquainted with the chief persons of his day and traveled widely. His poems, mostly in iambic trimeters, include verses on church festivals, works of art, and animals, as well as dialogues and occasional pieces.

Philetas or **Philitas** \fi-'lē-təs, fī-\ of Cos \'kȯs, 'käs\ (b. *c.* 330 BC—d. *c.* 270 BC) Greek poet and grammarian who is regarded as the founder of the Hellenistic school of poetry in Alexandria. He is reputed to have been the tutor of Ptolemy II and the poet Theocritus. The Roman poets Sextus Propertius and Ovid mention him as their model, but only fragments of his work have survived. His most important poem appears to have been the *Demeter*, an elegy narrating the wanderings of the Greek goddess of agriculture. He also compiled a dictionary of rare words from Homer, the Greek dialects, and other sources.

Philippe \fē-'lēp\, Charles-Louis (b. Aug. 4, 1874, Cérilly, Fr.—d. Dec. 21, 1909, Paris) French novelist who described from personal experience the sufferings of the poor.

Philippe's novels are set either in Paris or in his native province of Bourbonnais. Of the first group, the most notable is *Bubu de Montparnasse* (1901), which tells the story of a young prostitute's relationship with her procurer and with a young intellectual who tries to save her. The novels of rural poverty include *La Mère et l'enfant* (1900; "The Mother and the Child"), in which the author tenderly recalls his own childhood; *Le Père perdrix* (1902; title page, 1903; "The Father Partridge"), the story of an old, sickly blacksmith and of a young, forthright engineer; and the unfinished *Charles Blanchard* (1913), an evocation of the unhappy childhood of the author's father.

Philips \'fil-ips\, Ambrose (baptized Oct. 9, 1674, Shrewsbury, Shropshire, Eng.—d. June 18, 1749, London) English poet and playwright.

Philips was educated at the University of Cambridge. His first and best-known poems were collected in *Pastorals* and were probably written while he was a fellow at Cambridge, although they were not published until 1710. For *Pastorals*, Philips won immediate praise from several leading men of letters, including Richard Steele and Joseph Addison, but he was strongly attacked by Alexander Pope, whose own *Pastorals* had been published in the same volume as Philips'. His adulatory verses ("Dimpley damsel, sweetly smiling") won Philips the nickname "Namby-Pamby." He also wrote *The Distressed Mother* (1712), an adaptation of Jean Racine's play *Andromaque*.

Phillips \'fil-ips\, Stephen (b. July 28, 1864, Summertown, Oxfordshire, Eng.—d. Dec. 9, 1915, Deal, Kent) English ac-

tor, poet, and dramatist, who was remembered for his play *Paolo and Francesca* (1900).

Phillips joined an acting company in 1885. His first collection of poetry, *Poems* (1897), was followed by several verse dramas, including *Herod* (1901), *Ulysses* (1902), and *Nero* (1906).

Phillpotts \'fil-ˌpäts\, Eden (b. Nov. 4, 1862, Mount Abu, Rājasthān, India—d. Dec. 29, 1960, Broad Clyst, near Exeter, Devon, Eng.) British novelist, poet, and dramatist especially noted for novels evoking their Devonshire setting in a manner reminiscent of the style of Thomas Hardy.

Phillpotts produced more than 100 novels, including *Children of the Mist* (1898), *Sons of the Morning* (1900), and *Widecombe Fair* (1913). He also wrote the autobiographical studies of youth, *The Human Boy* (1899) and *The Waters of the Walla* (1950); the plays *The Farmer's Wife* (1917) and *Yellow Sands* (with his daughter Adelaide, 1926); and the poetry collections *The Iscariot* (1912), *Brother Beast* (1928), and *The Enchanted Wood* (1948). *One Thing and Another* (1954) is a collection of his poems and essays.

Philoctetes \ˌfil-äk-'tē-tēz\ Legendary Greek hero, a notable archer who played a decisive part in the final stages of the Trojan War. Philoctetes (or his father, Poeas) had been bequeathed the bow and arrows of the Greek hero Heracles. Philoctetes used these weapons to slay Paris (son of Priam, king of Troy), and this act eventually brought about the city's fall. The story was used by many writers, including Sophocles, Johan Gottfried Herder, André Gide, and Yannis Ritsos.

Philoctetes \ˌfil-äk-'tē-tēz\ (*Greek* Philoktētēs) Play by SOPHOCLES, performed in 409 BC.

The play opens after the Troy-bound Greeks have cast the title character on the desert island of Lemnos because of an incurable ulcer on his foot. In the course of battle, the Greeks discover that they cannot defeat the Trojans without Philoctetes, who possesses the bow and arrow bequeathed to him by Heracles. A supernatural appearance by Heracles ultimately convinces Philoctetes to go to Troy to both win victory and be healed of his wound.

philology \fi-'läl-ə-jē\ [Greek *philología* love of learning and literature, a derivative of *philólogos* fond of learning, literary, from *phílos* dear + *lógos* word, speech] Study of literature that includes or may include grammar, criticism, literary history, language history, systems of writing, and anything else that is relevant to literature or to language as used in literature. This sense of the term is now rarely used because a distinction is made between literary and linguistic scholarship. When it is used, it is generally a synonym for *linguistics*.

Philombe \fē-'lȯm-bā\, René, *pseudonym of* Philippe-Louis Ombede \ȯm-'bā-dā\ (b. 1930, Ngaoundéré, Cameroon) African novelist, poet, playwright, essayist, and journalist who was noted for his cultural and political activism.

In the mid-1950s, after Philombe was permanently crippled by a spinal disease, he began writing seriously. His *Lettres de ma cambuse* (1964; *Tales from My Hut*), which he had written in 1957, won an award from the Académie Française. He subsequently wrote the novels *Sola, ma chérie* (1966; "Sola, My Darling"), about seemingly unjust marriage customs, and *Un Sorcier blanc à Zangali* (1970; "A White Sorcerer in Zangali"), about the effect of a missionary's clash with the colonial administration in a small village. *Choc anti-choc* (1978) and *Africopolis* (1978) are both thinly veiled allegories of life under a malevolent dictatorship.

In 1960 Philombe helped to found the National Association of Cameroonian Poets and Writers, and he remained its permanent general secretary. Many of his patriotic literary activities earned him long periods in prison, in spite of his infirmities. In 1984 Philombe published a work on Cameroonian books and authors and translated and published his *Tales from Cameroon*.

Philomela \ˌfil-ō-'mē-lə\ In Greek mythology, daughter of Pandion, king of Athens, and sister of Procne. *See* TEREUS.

philosophe \ˌfē-lə-'zȯf\ [French, literally, philosopher] Any of the literary men, scientists, and thinkers of 18th-century France who were united, in spite of divergent personal views, in their conviction of the supremacy and efficacy of human reason.

The philosophes were inspired by the philosophic thought of René Descartes, the skepticism of the libertines, or free-thinkers, and the popularization of science by Bernard de Fontenelle. They expressed support for social, economic, and political reforms that were brought about by sectarian dissensions within the church, the weakening of the absolute monarchy, and the ruinous wars that had occurred toward the end of Louis XIV's reign. In the early part of the 18th century, the movement was dominated by Voltaire and Montesquieu, but this restrained phase gave way to a more volatile one in the second half of the century.

Denis Diderot, Jean-Jacques Rousseau, Georges-Louis Leclerc de Buffon, Étienne Bonnot de Condillac, Anne-Robert-Jacques Turgot, and the Marquis de Condorcet were among the philosophes who compiled *L'Encyclopédie*, one of the great intellectual achievements of the century.

Philostratus \fi-'läs-trə-təs\, Flavius, *called* the Athenian \ə-'thē-nē-ən\ (b. *c.* AD 170—d. *c.* 245) Ancient Greek writer who studied at Athens and sometime after 202 entered the circle of the philosophical Syrian empress of Rome, Julia Domna. On her death he settled in Tyre. He wrote the *Gymnasticus* (a treatise dealing with athletic contests), a life of the Pythagorean philosopher Apollonius of Tyana, *Bioi sophistōn* (*Lives of the Sophists*), a discourse on nature and law, and epistles ("Love Letters").

Philostratus \fi-'läs-trə-təs\ the Lemnian \'lem-nē-ən\ (b. *c.* AD 190) Ancient Greek writer, son-in-law of Flavius Philostratus. He was the author of a letter to Aspasius of Ravenna and of the first series of *Imagines* in two books, discussing 65 real or imaginary paintings on mythological themes in a portico at Naples. They are an important source of information about Hellenistic art.

Philostratus the Younger, grandson of Philostratus the Lemnian, wrote a second series of *Imagines* in the 3rd century AD.

Phineas Finn \'fin-ē-əs-'fin\ (*in full* Phineas Finn: The Irish Member) Novel by Anthony TROLLOPE, first published serially from October 1867 to May 1869 and in two volumes in 1869. It is the second of the PALLISER NOVELS. Trollope based some of the Parliamentary characters that appear in the novel on real-life counterparts, such as Benjamin Disraeli, William Gladstone, and John Bright.

The novel concerns the rapid rise and eventual resignation of Phineas Finn, an impoverished, intelligent, and charming member of Parliament from Ireland. Finn becomes romantically involved with several women: his patron, Lady Laura Standish, who marries another; Violet Effingham, who weds a volatile nobleman; Madame Marie Max Goesler, a wealthy, sophisticated widow; and his patient sweetheart, Mary Flood-Jones.

Phineas Redux \'fin-ē-əs\ Novel by Anthony TROLLOPE, first published serially from July 1873 to January 1874 and in two volumes in 1874. It is a sequel to *Phineas Finn* and the fourth of the PALLISER NOVELS.

The narrative begins after Finn's wife, Mary, has died in childbirth. He resumes his political career and again becomes romantically involved with Lady Laura Standish (now Kennedy) and Madame Marie Max Goesler, whom he eventually marries. An ethical and kind man, Finn is falsely accused of the murder of a rival politician. Eventually acquitted, he leaves political life in disgust.

Phocylides \fō-'sil-ə-ˌdēz\ (fl. *c.* 540 BC) Greek gnomic poet (*i.e.*, writer of pithy moral aphorisms) from Miletus, on the coast of Asia Minor. He is mentioned by the orator Isocrates as the author of "admonitions" (*hypothēkai*), of which a few fragments have survived by quotation. Almost all of the aphorisms are in hexameters and begin with the phrase "This too is Phocylides'."

Phoebe \'fē-bē\ In Greek mythology, a Titan, daughter of Uranus and Gaea. She was the mother of Leto, Asteria, and Hecate. Her epithet was Gold-Crowned, her name signified purity or brightness, and in later mythology she was identified with the moon. *See also* SELENE.

Phoenician Women (*Greek* Phoinissai) Minor drama by EURIPIDES, performed about 409 BC. Set at Thebes, the play concerns the battle between the two sons of Oedipus over control of the city. When Eteocles refuses to give up power to Polyneices, Polyneices brings an army to attack the city. The two brothers eventually kill each other, and when their mother Jocasta discovers their bodies she kills herself. Their uncle Creon takes control and sentences Oedipus, who has been held in the city, to exile.

phoenix \'fē-niks\ [Greek *phoînix*] In ancient Egypt and in classical antiquity, a fabulous bird associated with the worship of the sun. Only one phoenix existed at any time, and it was very long-lived. As its end approached, the phoenix set its nest on fire and was consumed in the flames. From the pyre miraculously sprang a new phoenix, which flew with the ashes to Heliopolis ("City of the Sun") in Egypt, where it deposited them on the altar in the temple of the god of the sun, Re. A variant of the story made the dying phoenix fly to Heliopolis and immolate itself in the altar fire, from which the young phoenix then rose.

The phoenix story probably originated in the Orient and was assimilated to Egyptian sun worship by the priests of Heliopolis. The Egyptians associated the phoenix with immortality, symbolism had a widespread appeal in late antiquity. The story was also widely interpreted as an allegory of resurrection and life after death—ideas that appealed to emergent Christianity. In Islāmic mythology the phoenix was identified as a huge, mysterious bird that was originally created by God with all perfections but that had thereafter become a plague and was killed.

Phoenix \'fē-niks\ In Greek mythology, the son of Agenor and brother of Europa. When Agenor sent Phoenix and his brothers to look for Europa, who had been abducted by Zeus, Phoenix eventually tired of the search and settled in an area that later became the city of Sidon. This was in Phoenicia, which was named for Phoenix.

Phoenix \'fē-niks\ In Greek mythology, a close companion of Achilles. After fleeing from his father Amyntor, who blinded him, Phoenix was taken in by Peleus, who convinced the centaur Chiron to restore his sight. Phoenix later accompanied Achilles to the Trojan War.

Phrynichus \'frin-i-kəs\ (fl. *c.* 420 BC) Athenian poet of Old Comedy.

A contemporary of Aristophanes, Phrynichus began producing plays in 430 and won two victories in the Great Dionysia. Phrynichus' *Monotropos* ("Solitary") placed third in 414, when Aristophanes' *Birds* was second, and his *Muses* placed second to Aristophanes' *Frogs* in 405.

Phrynichus \\'frin-i-kəs\\ (fl. *c.* 500 BC, Athens) Athenian tragic poet, an older contemporary of Aeschylus. Only scant fragments of his work survive.

Phrynichus' first victory probably occurred in about 510, and he is thought to have been the first to introduce the female mask—*i.e.*, women characters—into his plays. After the fall of Miletus in 494 he produced the *Capture of Miletus*, which so harrowed Athenian feelings that he was fined. In 476 his *Phoenissae*, in which news of the battle of Salamis comes to the Persian court, proved a more acceptable subject and won the first prize.

Phrynichus \\'frin-i-kəs\\ Arabius (fl. 2nd century AD, Bithynia) Grammarian and rhetorician who produced *Sophistikē Paraskeuē* ("A Grounding in Sophistic"), of which a few fragments and a summary by Photius survive, and an *Attikistēs* ("Atticist"), extant in an abridged form, called the *Eklogē*. He was critical not only of contemporary deviations from the best Old Attic (ancient Greek dialect) usage but also of what he considered the lapses of his Attic models themselves.

physical poetry Poetry (such as Imagist poetry) that is primarily concerned with the projection of a descriptive image of material things, as in the opening stanza of the poem "Sea Poppies" by Hilda Doolittle (H.D.):

> Amber husk
> fluted with gold
> fruit on the sand
> marked with a rich grain

Physician's Tale, The One of the 24 stories in THE CANTERBURY TALES by Geoffrey Chaucer.

The tale is a version of a story related both by the Roman historian Livy and in the 13th-century *Roman de la Rose*. It concerns the lust of the evil judge Appius for the beautiful, chaste Virginia. Plotting a strategy by which he can possess her, the judge instructs his servant to swear in court that Virginia is a slave whom her father abducted. Her father, seeing through the plot, kills her to save her honor and delivers her head to Appius. Although Appius gives an order for the father's execution, the townspeople rise against the judge and throw him in prison, where he kills himself.

Physicists, The Comedy in two acts by Friedrich DÜRRENMATT, performed and published in German as *Die Physiker* in 1962. Often considered Dürrenmatt's best play, it addresses the ethical dilemma that arises when unscrupulous politicians gain access to scientific knowledge that has the potential to destroy the world.

Three physicists, pretending to be insane, voluntarily commit themselves to an asylum administered by a megalomaniacal psychiatrist, Dr. Mathilde von Zahnd. The ethical physicist Möbius has incarcerated himself to prevent the world from obtaining and misusing his invention. The other two physicists are rival spies, each hoping to obtain Möbius' secret. Möbius convinces the spies that humanity's salvation depends on the three of them remaining secluded together. They discover that Dr. von Zahnd has stolen Möbius' secrets and is now capable of controlling the world. Resigned, the three assume their madmen's roles.

Piano Lesson, The Drama in two acts by August WILSON, produced in 1987 and published in 1990. The play, which was awarded a Pulitzer Prize in 1990, is part of Wilson's cycle about African-American life in the 20th century.

The action takes place in Pittsburgh in 1936 at the house of a family of African-Americans who have migrated from Mississippi. The conflict centers around a piano that was once traded by the family's white master for two of the family's ancestors.

Boy Willie and Berniece, the siblings who inherit the piano (carved to show family history), argue about whether or not to sell it. Berniece's climactic refusal to allow Boy Willie to move the piano exorcises both the literal and figurative ghost of the white slave owner who has been haunting the family.

pianwen or **p'ien-wen** \\'pyen-'wən\\ [Chinese *piánwén,* from *pián* parallel, antithetical + *wén* language, literary composition] Genre of Chinese literature characterized by antithetic construction and balanced tonal patterns without the use of rhyme; the term is suggestive of "a team of paired horses," as is implied in the Chinese word *pian.* Despite the polyphonic effect thus produced, which approximates that of poetry, it has often been made the vehicle of proselike exposition and argumentation.

By the early ninth century, *pianwen* had been cultivated for almost 1,000 years and had become so burdened with restrictive rules as to make forthright expression virtually impossible. Han Yu and his ally Liu Zongyuan advocated the use of Zhou philosophers and early Han writers as models for prose writing. This seemingly conservative reform had, in fact, a liberalizing effect, for the sentence unit in prose writing was freed to seek its own length and structural pattern as logic and content might dictate.

Piazza, The First sketch in the collection *The Piazza Tales* published by Herman MELVILLE in 1856. The sketch describes Melville's farmhouse, "Arrowhead," in Pittsfield, Mass. Supposedly the other tales in the collection, including "Bartleby the Scrivener" and "Benito Cereno," were narrated on the piazza of the farmhouse.

picaresque novel \\,pik-ə-'resk, ,pēk-\\ An early form of the novel, usually a first-person narrative, relating the adventures of a rogue or lowborn adventurer (Spanish: *pícaro*) who drifts from place to place and from one social milieu to another in an effort to survive.

In its episodic structure the picaresque novel resembles the long, rambling romances of medieval chivalry, to which it provided the first realistic counterpart. Unlike the idealistic knight-errant hero, however, the picaro is a cynical and amoral rascal who would rather live by his wits than by honorable work.

The picaresque novel originated in Spain with *Lazarillo de Tormes* (1554; of unknown authorship), in which the poor boy Lázaro describes his services under seven successive lay and clerical masters, each of whom hides his dubious character under a mask of hypocrisy. The next picaresque novel to be published, Mateo Alemán's *Guzmán de Alfarache* (1599), the supposed autobiography of the son of a ruined Genoese moneylender, became the true prototype of the genre and helped establish realism as the dominant trend in the Spanish novel. After about 1625 the picaresque novel in Spain evolved gradually into the novel of adventure.

In the meantime, however, late 16th-century translations of *Lazarillo de Tormes* introduced the picaro into other European literatures. The first picaresque novel in England was Thomas Nashe's *The Unfortunate Traveller; or, The Life of Jacke Wilton* (1594). In Germany the type was represented by H.J. von Grimmelshausen's *Simplicissimus* (1669). The outstanding French example is Alain-René Lesage's *Gil Blas* (1715–35).

In the mid-18th century the growth of the realistic novel with its tighter, more elaborate plot and its greater development of character led to the final decline of the picaresque novel, which came to be considered somewhat inferior in artistry.

Pickle, Peregrine \\'per-ə-,grin-'pik-əl\\ Fictional character, the egotistical hero of the novel PEREGRINE PICKLE by Tobias Smollett.

Pickwick, Samuel \\'sam-yū-əl-'pik-,wik\\ Fictional character, the protagonist of Charles Dickens' novel *The Pickwick Papers*.

Pickwick Papers, The \\'pik-,wik\\ (*in full* The Posthumous Papers of the Pickwick Club) Novel by Charles DICKENS,

"Mr. Pickwick Addresses the Club," a drawing for the original edition of *The Posthumous Papers of the Pickwick Club*

first published serially from 1836 to 1837 under the pseudonym Boz and in book form in 1837. This first fictional work by Dickens was originally commissioned as a series of glorified captions for the work of caricaturist Robert Seymour. His witty, episodic accounts of the kindly, naive Samuel Pickwick and his friends in the Pickwick Club were instantly successful in their own right, however, and made Dickens a literary sensation.

Picnic Drama in three acts by William INGE, produced and published in 1953 and awarded a Pulitzer Prize in the same year. This play about a group of lonely women in a small Kansas town whose lives are disrupted by a virile, charming drifter captures the frustrations of Midwestern life. Inge slightly rewrote the ending in a 1962 version called *Summer Brave*.

Picture of Dorian Gray, The \\'dȯr-ē-ən-'grā\\ Moral fantasy novel by Oscar WILDE, published in an early form in *Lippincott's Magazine* in 1890. The novel had six additional chapters when it appeared in book form in 1891. An archetypal tale of a young man who purchases eternal youth at the expense of his soul, the novel was a romantic exposition of Wilde's Aestheticism.

Dorian Gray is a wealthy Englishman who gradually sinks into a life of dissipation and crime. Despite his unhealthy behavior, his physical appearance remains youthful and unmarked by dissolution. Instead, a portrait of himself catalogues every evil deed by turning his once handsome features into a hideous mask. When Gray destroys the painting, his face turns into a human replica of the portrait, and he dies.

Gray's final negation, "ugliness is the only reality," neatly summarizes Wilde's Aestheticism, both his love of the beautiful

and his fascination with the profane. Publication of the novel scandalized Victorian England, and *The Picture of Dorian Gray* was used as evidence against Wilde in his 1895 trial for homosexuality. The novel became a classic of English literature.

Pictures from Brueghel \\'brü-gəl, 'brȯi-, *Dutch* 'brœ̄-kəl\\ (*in full* Pictures from Brueghel, and Other Poems) Collection of poetry by William Carlos WILLIAMS, published in 1962 and awarded a Pulitzer Prize in 1963. In this volume Williams transcends the objectivist style of his earlier work, treating poetry as a medium for ideas as well as a means of depicting the physical world. Williams also explored new verse forms in the collection. Wanting to find a rhythm suited to American speech, he experimented with a version of free verse he termed *versos sueltos* ("loose verses"), which makes use of the triadic stanza and a "variable foot" measure.

pièce bien faite *see* WELL-MADE PLAY.

Pied Beauty Sonnet by Gerard Manley HOPKINS, composed in the summer of 1877 and published in 1918 in the posthumous collection *Poems of Gerard Manley Hopkins*. One of his best-known poems, it celebrates the singularity and variety of nature, challenging the Platonic ideal of perfect beauty. It is a curtal sonnet, with an opening section of six lines and a closing section of slightly more than four lines.

Pied Piper of Hamelin, The \\'ham-lin, -ə-lin\\ (*in full* The Pied Piper of Hamelin, A Child's Story) Narrative poem of 303 lines by Robert BROWNING, published in 1842 in *Dramatic Lyrics*, part of the *Bells and Pomegranates* series. One of Browning's best-known works, the poem relates the classic legend of the town of Hamelin and its burghers, who engage the mysterious pied piper to lure the town's vermin to their death in the river. When the townspeople refuse to pay the piper for his services, he lures their children away by the same means.

Pien Chih-lin *see* BIAN ZHILIN.

p'ien-wen *see* PIANWEN.

Pierian \\pī-'ir-ē-ən, -'er-\\ **1.** Of or relating to the region of Pieria in ancient Macedonia or to the Muses who were once worshiped there. **2.** Of or relating to learning or poetry, as in the following lines from Alexander Pope's poem *An Essay on Criticism*:

> A little learning is a dangerous thing;
> Drink deep, or taste not the Pierian spring.

Pierre \\pē-'er\\ (*in full* Pierre; or, The Ambiguities) Novel by Herman MELVILLE, published in 1852. An intensely personal work, it reveals the somber mythology of Melville's private life framed in terms of a story of an artist alienated from his society. The artist, Pierre Glendinning, is a well-to-do young man. When he discovers that he has an illegitimate half sister, he tries to provide for her by taking her to live in New York City, where they live in poverty as he attempts to make a living as a writer. He ultimately destroys both of their lives as well as that of his fiancée. The novel, a slightly veiled allegory of Melville's own dark imaginings, was rooted in his relationships with his own family.

Pierrot \\pye-'rō, 'pir-ō\\ *or* **Pedrolino** \\pā-drō-'lē-nō\\ Stock character of the Italian COMMEDIA DELL'ARTE, a simpleminded and honest servant, usually a young and personable valet. One of the comic servants, or *zanni*, Pedrolino functioned as an unsuccessful lover and a victim of the pranks of his fellow comedians. The original Italian character Pedrolino became popular in later French pantomimes as the naive Pierrot.

Piers Plowman \\'pirs-'plau̇-mən\\ (*in full* The Vision of Piers Plowman) Middle English alliterative poem presumed to have been written by William LANGLAND. Three versions of *Piers Plowman* are extant: A, the poem's short, early form, dating from the 1360s; B, a major revision and extension of A made in the late 1370s; and C, a less "literary" version of B dating from the 1380s and apparently intended to focus the work's doctrinal issues. Version C may not be entirely attributable to Langland.

The poem takes the form of a series of dream visions dealing with the social and spiritual predicament of late 14th-century England. In general, the language is simple and colloquial, but some of the imagery is powerful and direct. Realistic and allegorical elements are mingled in a phantasmagoric way, and the writer frequently displays spiritual and didactic impulses. His bitter attacks on political and ecclesiastical corruption (especially among the friars) quickly struck chords with his contemporaries. In the 16th century *Piers Plowman* was issued as a printed book and was used for apologetic purposes by the early Protestants.

Pigeon Feathers (*in full* Pigeon Feathers and Other Stories) Collection of short fiction by John UPDIKE, published in 1962 and comprising the stories "Pigeon Feathers," "Flight," and "Friends from Philadelphia." In these early stories Updike attempted to capture overlooked or unexpected beauty in life. The title story, one of his best known, concerns 14-year-old David Kern's religious doubts, his fear of death, and his triumphant return to faith, the "unexpected gift" that he is granted while shooting pigeons in a barn.

Piglet \'pig-lət\ Fictional character, a small and timorous pig who is a friend of Winnie-the-Pooh, in A.A. Milne's WINNIE-THE-POOH and *The House at Pooh Corner*.

Piglia \'pē-glē-ä\, Ricardo (b. Nov. 24, 1941, Buenos Aires, Arg.) Argentine writer and critic best known for his introduction of the hard-boiled detective novel to the Argentine public.

After attending the University of La Plata, Piglia wrote his first collection of short stories, *La invasión* (1967), which established his reputation as a writer. Another collection of stories, *Nombre falso* (1975; "False Name"), includes "Homenaje a Roberto Arlt," which pays homage to an earlier Argentine writer of crime fiction. His novel *Respiración artificial* (1980; *Artificial Respiration*) is concerned, in part, with cultural dissidents. The 1992 novel *La ciudad ausente* ("The Absent City") is set in the near future in Buenos Aires, where technological advances are accompanied by an increase in political repression.

As a critic, Piglia was a historian of popular culture, and he wrote about such authors as Jorge Luis Borges, Arlt, Julio Cortázar, and Manuel Puig. He also helped promote a series of books, "Serie Negra," that reprinted classic hard-boiled American crime fiction.

Pilgrim, Billy \'bil-ē-'pil-grəm\ Fictional character, protagonist of SLAUGHTERHOUSE-FIVE, a novel by Kurt Vonnegut, Jr.

Pilgrimage Sequence novel by Dorothy M. RICHARDSON, comprising 13 chapter-novels, 11 of which were published separately: *Pointed Roofs* (1915), *Backwater* (1916), *Honeycomb* (1917), *The Tunnel* (1919), *Interim* (1919), *Deadlock* (1921), *Revolving Lights* (1923), *The Trap* (1925), *Oberland* (1927), *Dawn's Left Hand* (1931), and *Clear Horizon* (1935). *Dimple Hill*, the 12th "chapter," appeared in 1938 in a four-volume omnibus under the collective title *Pilgrimage*. A decade after Richardson's death in 1957, *Pilgrimage* was again released in four volumes, this time including an as-yet unpublished 13th chapter, *March Moonlight*. Although some readers thought it inaccessible, the autobiographical work is noted for its pioneering use of stream of consciousness.

Although it does not proceed chronologically, *Pilgrimage* traces the development of Miriam Henderson, a sensitive young woman, across a period of 18 years. She works as a teacher and as a governess, becomes a dental assistant, joins a socialist organization, and studies the lives of Quakers. Her romances with Michael Shatov and, later, with "Hypo" Wilson are ultimately unsatisfactory.

Pilgrimage of Etheria *see* PEREGRINATIO ETHERIAE.

Pilgrim's Progress, The (*in full* The Pilgrim's Progress From This World, to That Which is to Come: Delivered Under the Similitude of a Dream Wherein is Discovered, the Manner of His Setting Out, His Dangerous Journey; and Safe Arrival at the Desired Countrey) Two-part religious allegory by John BUNYAN, at one time second only to the Bible in popularity. It is a symbolic vision of the pilgrimage through life. The first and best-known book, published in 1678, in which the character Christian travels on the road to salvation from the City of Destruction to the Celestial City, is presented as a dream. Written in homely yet dignified biblical prose, the work has some of the qualities of a folktale, and in its humor and realistic portrayals of Mr. Worldly Wiseman, Faithful, Hopeful, Pliant, and Obstinate, it anticipates the 18th-century novel. In *The Pilgrim's Progress, Second Part* (1684), which deals with the effort of Christian's wife and sons to join him, the psychological intensity is relaxed and Bunyan's capacity for humor and realistic observation becomes more evident.

Pillars of Society, The Drama in four acts by Henrik IBSEN, published in Norwegian as *Samfundets støtter* in 1877 and performed the following year.

The play's title initially refers to Karsten Bernick, whose good reputation is threatened by the return to town of his brother-in-law, Johan Tönnesen (onto whom Bernick had earlier displaced the blame for his own misdeeds) and of Johan's half sister, Lona Hessel, whose love Bernick had rejected in order to marry her rich half sister. Bernick concocts a scheme to rid himself of Johan, but when his scheme almost leads to the death of his own son, Bernick has a change of heart and publicly renounces his past sins, prompting Lona to remark that truth and freedom are the real pillars of society.

Pillow Book Title of a book of reminiscences and impressions written as *Makura no sōshi* about 1000 by SEI SHŌNAGON. The entries in the *Pillow Book* are not in chronological order but rather are organized under such headings as "Amusing Things" and "Vexatious Things." Ivan Morris' complete English translation, *The Pillow Book of Sei Shōnagon*, was published in 1967.

The *Pillow Book* belongs to the genre of *zuihitsu* ("random jottings"). *Tsurezure-gusa* (c. 1330; *Essays in Idleness*), by Yoshida Kenkō, is an outstanding 14th-century example of the genre.

Pilnyak or **Pilniak** \pʸilʸ-'nʸȧk\, Boris, *pseudonym of* Boris Andreyevich Vogau \'vō-ˌgaù\ (b. 1894, Mozhaisk, Russia—d. 1937) Soviet writer of Symbolist novels and stories who was prominent in the 1920s.

Pilnyak achieved popularity with the novel *Goly god* (1922; *The Naked Year*), a panorama of the events of the Russian Revolution and the Russian Civil War seen through a series of flashbacks and close-ups of individuals at all levels of society.

In 1926 Pilnyak caused a scandal with his *Povest nepogashennoy luny* (*The Tale of the Unextinguished Moon*), a thinly veiled implication of the highest authorities in the death of Mikhail Frunze, the famous military commander, during an operation. Published by an émigré publishing house in Berlin, Pilnyak's novel *Krasnoye derevo* (1929; "Mahogany") included an idealized portrait of a Trotskyite Communist; it was immediately banned in the Soviet Union.

Pilnyak's dislike of communist goals and methods made him the object of harsh official censure. In an attempt to redeem himself he wrote *Volga vpadayet v Kaspiyskoye more* (1930; *The Volga Falls to the Caspian Sea*), a novel glorifying the five-year plan on the theme of the construction of a Soviet dam. Pilnyak's ambivalence did not escape the authorities, and during 1937—at the height of Joseph Stalin's reign of terror—his name and his works completely disappeared from Soviet literature. Official Soviet sources later acknowledged that he had been arrested in 1937, placing the date of his death in the same year. Although Pilnyak was "posthumously rehabilitated," it was not until 1976 that a volume of his works, offering only a very limited selection, appeared.

Pilot, The (*in full* The Pilot; A Tale of the Sea)   Novel by James Fenimore COOPER, published in two volumes in 1823. Admired for its authentic portrayal of a seafaring life, the work, which takes place during the American Revolutionary War, launched a whole genre of maritime fiction. It features a mysterious and almost superhuman American sea pilot (based on the American hero John Paul Jones) who fights battles off the coast of England against the British and American loyalists. One of the book's themes is the ambiguous nature of loyalty. Although often complicated by nautical terminology and by intrusive philosophical dialogue, the novel is nevertheless noted for its spiritual and moral dimensions.

Pindar \'pin-dər, -ˌdär\, *Greek* Pindaros, *Latin* Pindarus (b. 518/522 BC, Cynoscephalae, Boeotia [Greece]—d. after 446, probably *c.* 438, Argos)   The greatest lyric poet of ancient Greece, the master of epinicia, choral odes celebrating victories achieved in the various official games held throughout Greece.

Pindar was a Boeotian of noble birth and was sent to neighboring Athens to complete his training and education. His early poems have almost all been lost; it is probable, however, that what gave him a growing reputation beyond the borders of Boeotia were hymns in honor of the gods. Pindar was born at the time of the Pythian festival, and from his youth he had a close connection with the Pythian priesthood, which served the oracular shrine of Apollo at Delphi. The first commissions for epinicia came mostly from aristocratic connections, and his progress in winning recognition seems to have been steady, if slow. A significant breakthrough came when Pindar established a link with the court of Theron of Acragas. Theron and Hieron I of Syracuse were to elicit much of Pindar's greatest poetry, and it was through these connections that Pindar's reputation spread throughout the Greek world.

Seventeen volumes of Pindar's poetry, comprising almost every genre of choral lyric, were known in antiquity. Only four books of epinicia have survived complete, but they are supplemented by numerous fragments. Numbering 44 in all, these odes are divided into the Olympian, Pythian, Isthmian, and Nemean—named after the games in which the victories he celebrated were held. The epinicion form, which originally was a relatively simple poem of rejoicing enhanced by touches of realism and humor, is assimilated by Pindar to the religious hymn. The praise and worship of the god whose festival is being celebrated set the tone, and thanksgiving is an integral part of the structure. Pindar's metrical range is exceptionally wide, with no two poems being identical in meter, and he controls difficult and involuted techniques with consummate mastery. His dialect is literary and eclectic, with few Boeotian elements; the vocabulary is enriched, poetic, and highly personal. Pindar's odes make great demands on the modern reader, and it is only in recent times that his art has begun to be appreciated. Yet, ef-

forts to understand the odes are rewarded by at least a glimpse of the poet behind them. The aristocratic society and standards that meant everything to Pindar were dead or dying by his own lifetime, but in his art he re-created them, giving them new and permanent existence and value.

Pindar \'pin-dər, -ˌdär\, Peter, *pseudonym of* John Wolcot \'wùl-kät\ (baptized May 9, 1738, Dodbrooke, Devonshire, Eng.—d. Jan. 14, 1819, London)   English writer of satirical verse on society, politics, and personalities.

Wolcot began his satirical writings about 1778. Despite blindness, he continued to write to the end of his life, producing more than 70 satirical works as well as other poems.

Although Pindar lacked the depth of the great satirists, he was a master of verse caricature, as shown especially in his scurrilous lampoons of George III in *The Lousiad, an Heroi-Comic Poem* (1785–95), *Ode Upon Ode or a Peep at St. James's or New Year's Day* (1787), and *The Royal Visit to Exeter* (1795), a tour de force of Devon dialect humor, and in the virtuosity of his doggerel rhymes. His other targets included writer James Boswell and the painter Benjamin West. He became famous with his *Lyric Odes to the Royal Academicians* (1782–85).

Pindaric ode \pin-'dar-ik\   Ceremonious poem by or in the manner of Pindar, a Greek professional lyric poet of the 5th century BC. Pindar employed the triadic structure of Stesichorus (7th and 6th centuries BC), consisting of a strophe (two or more lines repeated as a unit) followed by a metrically harmonious antistrophe, concluding with a summary line (called an epode) in a different meter. These three parts corresponded to the movement of the chorus to one side of the stage and then to the other and their return to deliver the epode.

Although fragments of Pindar's poems in all of the classical choral forms are extant, it is the collection of four books of epinicion odes that has influenced poets of the Western world since their publication by Aldus Manutius the Elder in 1513. Each of the books is devoted to one of the great series of Greek classical games: the Olympian, Pythian, Isthmian, and Nemean. Celebrating the victory of a winner with a performance of choral chant and dance, these epinicion odes are elaborately complex, rich in metaphor and intensely emotive language.

With the publication of Pierre de Ronsard's four books of French *Odes* (1550), the Pindaric ode began to be adapted to the vernacular languages. Some English poets, notably Ben Jonson, wrote imitation Pindaric odes, while Abraham Cowley's *Pindarique Odes* (1656) introduced a looser version known as Pindarics. These irregular rhymed odes suggest, but do not reproduce, the style and manner of Pindar. The odes are among the greatest in the English language; they include John Dryden's "Alexander's Feast," William Wordsworth's "Ode: Intimations of Immortality," Percy Bysshe Shelley's "Ode to the West Wind," Alfred, Lord Tennyson's "Ode on the Death of the Duke of Wellington," and John Keats's "Ode on a Grecian Urn." *See also* EPINICION; ODE.

Pindemonte \pēn-dā-'mōn-tā\, Ippolito (b. Nov. 13, 1753, Verona, Republic of Venice [Italy]—d. Nov. 18, 1828, Verona) Italian prose writer, translator, and poet remembered for his pre-Romantic lyrics and particularly for his highly prized translation of the *Odyssey*.

Pindemonte's volume of Arcadian verse, *Le stanze* (1779), and one of lyrics, *Poesie campestri* (1788; "Rural Poetry"), both showed a sensitivity to nature and revealed the influence of the contemporary English poets Thomas Gray and Edward Young. A stay in Paris inspired the poem "La Francia" (1789) and a prose satire on political conditions in Europe, *Abaritte* (1790). *Prose campestri*, a companion volume to the earlier poetry, was published in 1794.

In 1805 Pindemonte began his translation of the *Odyssey*, published in 1822 as *Odissea*. Pindemonte also wrote two tragedies and several moralistic letters and sermons.

Pinero \pi-'nir-ō, *commonly* -'ner-\, Sir Arthur Wing (b. May 24, 1855, London, Eng.—d. Nov. 23, 1934, London) A leading playwright of the late Victorian and Edwardian eras in England who helped to create a self-respecting theater by writing "social" dramas that drew a fashionable audience. His farces were literate and superbly constructed, containing a precise, clockwork inevitability of plot and a brilliant use of coincidence.

Pinero began acting at age 19. His first play, *£200 a Year*, was produced in 1877. His best farces, such as *The Magistrate* (1885), *The Schoolmistress* (1886), and *Dandy Dick* (1887), combine wildly improbable events with likable characters. Pinero was at the same time studying serious drama by adapting plays from the French (including *The Iron Master*, 1884, and *Mayfair*, 1885) and also mining a profitable vein of sentiment of his own, as in *The Squire* (1881) and *Sweet Lavender* (1888). Seriousness and sentiment fused in *The Profligate* (1889) and in *The Second Mrs. Tanqueray* (1893), which established Pinero as an important playwright. This was the first of several plays depicting women battling their station in Victorian society. In a less serious vein, *Trelawny of the "Wells"* (produced in 1898) portrayed theatrical company life in the old style of the 1860s, and *The Gay Lord Quex* (1899) was about a theatrical rake. Pinero was knighted in 1909.

Ping Hsin *see* BING XIN.

Pinocchio \pi-'nō-kē-ō, *Italian* pē-'nȯk-kyō\ Fictional character, the puppet hero of the children's story *Le avventure di Pinocchio: Storia di un burattino* ("The Adventures of Pinocchio: The Story of a Puppet") by Carlo COLLODI. The story first appeared in serial form in 1881 in the *Giornale dei bambini* ("Children's Magazine") and was published in book form in 1883. It appeared in English under a variety of titles.

Pinocchio was carved out of a piece of wood by the old wood-carver Gepetto (Geppetto). The puppet acts like a human child: he frequently gets into trouble and is often impulsive and mischievous. When he tells a lie, his nose grows longer, and when he tells the truth, his nose resumes its normal size. The Good Fairy finally grants him his wish to be a real little boy after he learns to care for his "father" Gepetto.

Pinski *or* **Pinsky** \'pin-skē\, David (b. April 5, 1872, Mogilyov, Russia [now Mahilyoŭ, Belarus]—d. Aug. 11, 1959, Haifa, Israel) Yiddish playwright, novelist, and editor, an active member of Jewish and Zionist movements.

Pinski's first short story, "Der Groyser mentshnfraynd" ("The Great Philanthropist"), was published in 1894. He edited a Yiddish anthology, *Literatur un lebn* ("Literature and Life"), and in 1899 he immigrated to the United States, where he wrote for and edited several Jewish labor periodicals. He was president of the Jewish Culture Society (1930–53). In 1949 he moved to Haifa, Israel, and his home became a gathering place for young Yiddish writers.

Pinski's most successful work was the comic play *Der Oytser* (1911; "The Treasure"). His play *Der Eybiker Yid* (1926, "The Eternal Jew") was performed in Moscow by the Hebrew troupe Habima in 1919. His novels include *Dos Hoyz fun Noyekh Edon* (1913; *The Generations of Noah Edon*), which portrays the deterioration of Jewishness in America and argues against assimilation.

Pinsky \'pins-kē\, Robert (b. Oct. 20, 1940, Long Branch, N.J.) American poet and critic whose poems searched for the significance underlying everyday acts.

The title poem of Pinsky's first collection, *Sadness and Happiness* (1975), comments on the poet's own life. His long poem *An Explanation of America* (1979) probes personal and national myths. Vivid imagery characterizes his other collections, which include *History of My Heart* (1984) and *The Want Bone* (1990). *Landor's Poetry* (1968) and *The Situation of Poetry: Contemporary Poetry and Its Tradition* (1976) are among his critical writings. He was poetry editor of *The New Republic* during the late 1970s. Pinsky cotranslated poems by Czesław Miłosz in *The Separate Notebooks* (1984). He devised and published an interactive quest romance called *Mindwheel* to be played on computers. His translation of Dante's *Inferno* (1994) was notable for its gracefulness and its faithfulness to the original terza rima structure.

Pinter \'pin-tər\, Harold (b. Oct. 10, 1930, London, Eng.) English playwright who achieved international renown as one of the most complex and challenging post-World War II dramatists. His plays are noted for their use of understatement, small talk, and reticence—even silence—to convey the substance of a character's thought.

Having begun a career as an actor, after 1956 Pinter began to write for the stage: *The Room* (produced 1957; published 1960) and THE DUMB WAITER (written 1957; published 1960), both one-act dramas, established the mood of comic menace that was to figure in his early plays. His first full-length play was THE BIRTHDAY PARTY (produced 1958).

After Pinter's radio play *A Slight Ache* (produced 1959) was adapted for the stage, his reputation was secured by his second full-length play, THE CARETAKER (1960). His next major play, THE HOMECOMING (1965), further established him as the originator of a unique dramatic idiom. In such later plays as *Landscape* (1968), *Silence* (1969), and *Old Times* (1971), he virtually did away with physical activity on the stage. Pinter's other successes include *No Man's Land* (1975) and *Betrayal* (1978). From the 1970s on, Pinter took up directing of both his own and others' works. His *Poems and Prose 1941–1977* was published in 1978.

Pinter's plays are ambivalent in their plots, presentation of character, and endings, but they are works of undeniable power and originality. They typically begin with a pair of characters whose stereotyped relations and role-playing are disrupted by the entrance of a stranger. The audience sees the psychic stability of the couple break down as their fears, jealousies, hatreds, sexual preoccupations, and loneliness emerge from beneath a screen of commonplace yet bizarre conversation. Dialogue is of central importance in Pinter's plays and is perhaps the key to Pinter's originality.

Pinter also wrote radio and television dramas and a number of successful motion-picture screenplays, including *The Servant* (1963), *Accident* (1967), *The Go-Between* (1971), *The Last Tycoon* (1974), *The French Lieutenant's Woman* (1981), and *Betrayal* (1982). His later plays include *Mountain Language* (1988), *Party Time* (1991), and *Moonlight* (produced 1993).

Pinto \'pēⁿn-tü\, Fernão Mendes (b. *c.* 1510, Monte-mor-o-Velho, Port.—d. July 8, 1583, Almada, near Lisbon) Portuguese adventurer and author of the *Peregrinação* (1614, "Peregrination"; *The Voyages and Adventures of Fernand Mendez Pinto*), a literary masterpiece depicting the impression made on a European by Asian civilization, notably that of China, in the 16th century.

Pinto went to India in 1537 and later claimed to have traveled to almost every part of Asia during the next 21 years and also to have experienced drastic reversals of fortune. The *Peregrinação*, written after Pinto's return to Portugal in 1558, is of great interest for its impressions of Asian culture.

Pioneers, The (*in full* The Pioneers; or, The Sources of the Susquehanna)   The first of five novels in the series THE LEATHER-STOCKING TALES by James Fenimore COOPER, first published in two volumes in 1823. It began the saga of frontiersman Natty Bumppo, also called Leather-Stocking. In this narrative, however, Bumppo is an old man, as is his Indian friend Chingachgook; together they have seen the frontier change from wilderness to settlement, and they know that their way of life is about to vanish.

Piozzi \'pyȯt-tsē\, Hester Lynch, *original surname* Salisbury \'sȯlz-bər-ē, 'sälz-\, *married name* (1763–84) Thrale \'thrāl\, *byname* Mrs. Thrale (b. Jan. 27, 1740, Bodvel, Carnarvonshire, Wales—d. May 2, 1821, Clifton, Bristol, Eng.)   English writer and friend of Samuel Johnson.

She and her first husband, Henry Thrale, became friends with Samuel Johnson, who spent most of the summer of 1766 with them after a severe illness. He gradually became part of the family circle, living about half the time in their homes.

Left a wealthy widow, she soon married Gabriel Piozzi, a man of whom Johnson disapproved, and she was on her honeymoon when she received news of Johnson's death. She hastily compiled and sent back to England copy for *Anecdotes of the Late Samuel Johnson, LL.D., During the Last Twenty Years of His Life* (1786), which thrust her into open rivalry with James Boswell. She brought out a two-volume edition of *Letters to and from the Late Samuel Johnson, LL.D.* in 1788. Although less accurate in some details than Boswell's, her accounts show other aspects of Johnson's character, especially the more human and affectionate side of his nature.

Pip \'pip\   Fictional character, the young orphan whose growth and development are the subject of Charles Dickens' novel GREAT EXPECTATIONS.

Pippa Passes \'pip-ə\   Verse drama in four parts by Robert BROWNING, published in 1841. The poem's sections—Morning, Noon, Evening, and Night—are linked by episodes that either comment on the preceding scene or presage the scene to follow.

On New Year's morning, her only holiday for the entire year, Pippa, an impoverished young winder of silk, sings as she wanders aimlessly. In each section of the poem, people who are at critical points in their lives make significant decisions when they hear Pippa sing as she passes by.

Pippi Longstocking \'pip-ē-'lȯŋ-,stäk-iŋ\   Novel for children by Astrid LINDGREN, published in 1945 in Swedish as *Pippi Långstrump*. A rich young orphan, Pippi is a spirited, freckled redhead who lives independently of adults and possesses great physical strength. Her ingenious solutions to problems always allow her and her friends Annika and Tommy to return home safely from their fantastic adventures. The two sequels were *Pippi Långstrump går ombord* (1946; *Pippi Goes On Board*) and *Pippi Långstrump i Söderhavet* (1948; *Pippi in the South Seas*).

Pirandello \,pē-rän-'del-lō\, Luigi (b. June 28, 1867, Agrigento, Sicily, Italy—d. Dec. 10, 1936, Rome)   Italian playwright, novelist, and short-story writer, winner of the 1934 Nobel Prize for Literature.

Pirandello's earliest works include a collection of verse, *Mal giocondo* (1889; "Painful Joy"); translations of J.W. von Goethe's "Römische Elegien"; and several short stories. The titles of his early collections of short stories—*Amori senza amore* (1894; "Loves Without Love") and *Beffe della morte e della vita* (1902–03; "The Jests of Life and Death")—suggest the wry nature of the realism that is seen also in his first novels: *L'esclusa* (1901; *The Outcast*) and *Il turno* (1902; "The Turn").

Success came with his third novel, often acclaimed as his best, *Il fu Mattia Pascal* (1904; *The Late Mattia Pascal*). This last work already shows the acute psychological observation that was later to be directed toward the exploration of his

Italian Institute, London

characters' subconscious. Pirandello's other novels include *I vecchi e i giovani* (1913; *The Old and the Young*) and *Uno, nessuno e centomila* (1925–26; *One, None and a Hundred-Thousand*). His interest in psychology can be seen in the long essay *L'umorismo* (1908; *On Humor*), in which he examines the principles of his art.

Pirandello first turned to the theater in 1898 with *L'epilogo* ("The Epilogue"), but various accidents prevented its production until 1910 (when it was retitled *La morsa* ["The Vise"]). He then made only sporadic attempts at drama until the success of *Così è (se vi pare)* (RIGHT YOU ARE—IF YOU THINK YOU ARE) in 1917. A demonstration of the relativity of truth, it anticipates Pirandello's two great plays, *Sei personaggi in cerca d'autore* (1921; SIX CHARACTERS IN SEARCH OF AN AUTHOR) and ENRICO IV (1922). The production of the first of these two plays in Paris in 1923 made Pirandello widely known, and his work became one of the central influences on the French theater. Other notable plays include *Tutto per bene* (1920; *All for the Best*), *Vestire gli ignudi* (1923; *To Clothe the Naked*), *Ciascuno a suo modo* (1924; *Each in His Own Way*), and *Questa sera si recita a soggetto* (1930; *Tonight We Improvise*).

pirated edition   An edition of a work reproduced without authorization, especially in infringement of copyright.

Pirithous or **Peirithous** \pī-'rith-ō-əs\   In Greek mythology, the companion and helper of the hero Theseus in his many adventures, including the descent into the underworld (Hades) to carry off Persephone, the daughter of the goddess Demeter.

Pirmez \pėr-'mā\, Octave (b. April 19, 1832, Châtelet, Belg.—d. May 1, 1883, Acoz)   One of the outstanding Belgian men of letters of the period immediately before the literary revival of the 1880s. His works consist primarily of collections of essays, letters, and literary discussions, such as *Pensées et maximes* (1862; "Thoughts and Maxims") and *Heures de philosophie* (1873; "Hours of Thought").

Pirmez was deeply influenced by such French writers as Jean-Jacques Rousseau, Viscount de Chateaubriand, Michel de Montaigne, and Blaise Pascal. His outlook was pessimistic, for he considered that human reason was incapable of controlling sentiments and passions. The hallmark of Pirmez's work is its stylistic elegance and purity.

Piron \pē-'rōⁿ\, Alexis (b. July 19, 1689, Dijon, Fr.—d. Jan. 21, 1773, Paris)   French dramatist and wit, famous for his epigrams and remembered for his comedy *La Métromanie* (1738; "The Poetry Craze").

Piron moved to Paris in 1719, where he worked as a copyist, struggling meanwhile to enter the world of letters. After *Arlequin Deucalion* (1722) and other successful pieces written for the popular Théâtres de la Foire, Piron produced *Les Fils ingrats* ("The Ungrateful Sons") at the Comédie-Française in 1728. *La Métromanie*, a witty, urbane comedy in which he portrays himself as a young poet intoxicated with literary aspirations, was revived at the Comédie-Française until well into the 19th century. It remains his most distinguished play. His tragedies included the moderately successful *Gustave Wasa* (1733). Having achieved a modest fame, Piron acquired noble patrons and the entrée to several literary salons.

King Louis XV vetoed Piron's election to the Académie Française in 1753 because of the licentious *Ode à Priape* ("Ode to Priapus"), which he had written as a young man. He took his revenge on the Académie in his epitaph for himself: "Here lies Piron, who was nothing, Not even a member of the Academy."

Piscator \pis-'kä-tòr\, Erwin (b. Dec. 17, 1893, Ulm, Ger.—d. March 30, 1966, Starnberg, W.Ger.)   German theatrical producer and director famed for his ingenious expressionistic staging techniques; the originator of the epic theater style later developed by the German playwright Bertolt Brecht.

Working in Berlin during the Weimar Republic (1919–33), Piscator used the theater to convey radical political instruction. A bold innovator, he used films and newsreels to enlarge landscapes and convey mass events, and he employed many optical, acoustical, and mechanical devices to create an experience of total theater. In exile during World War II, he headed the Dramatic Workshop of the New School for Social Research in New York City from 1939 until 1951, when he returned to West Germany as director of West Berlin's Volksbühne. He continued to produce sensational works, such as Rolf Hochhuth's *The Deputy* and *The Investigation* by Peter Weiss.

Pisemsky \'pʸē-sʸim-skʸē\, Aleksey Feofilaktovich (b. March 11 [March 23, New Style], 1821, Ramenye, Kostroma province, Russia—d. Jan. 21 [Feb. 2], 1881, Moscow)   Novelist and playwright whom many critics rank with the great masters of Russian realism.

Pisemsky's lack of refinement, reactionary opinions, and general failure to conform to the image of a cultured liberal gentleman estranged him from literary society. One of his most notable works is the novel *Tysyacha dush* (1858; "A Thousand Souls"), a memorable portrait of a "new man," who marries for money instead of love and climbs to the rank of provincial governor. Pisemsky's tragedy *Gorkaya sudbina* (1859; "A Bitter Lot") is considered one of the masterpieces of the Russian theater. His novel *Vzbalamuchennoye more* (1863; "The Stormy Sea") satirized the radical younger generation and further estranged him from his colleagues and public. The politically motivated critical attacks directed against him obscured his achievements.

Pistol   Fictional character, one of the sidekicks of Falstaff who appears in HENRY IV, HENRY V, and THE MERRY WIVES OF WINDSOR.

Pit and the Pendulum, The   Gothic horror story by Edgar Allan POE, first published in *The Gift* (an annual giftbook of occasional verse and stories) in 1843. The work helped secure its author's reputation as a master of lurid gothic suspense.

Like many of Poe's stories, "The Pit and the Pendulum" is a dramatic monologue. Sentenced to death by the Spanish Inquisition, the imprisoned narrator finds himself in absolute darkness, in danger of falling to his death into a pit in the center of the cell. After narrowly escaping the razor-edged blade of a swinging pendulum, he is forced toward the pit by the hot, metal dungeon walls that are closing in. Just as he begins to slip, the walls recede and he is rescued.

Pitoëff \pē-tò-'ef\, Georges (b. Sept. 4, 1884, Tiflis [now Tbilisi], Georgia, Russian Empire—d. Sept. 17, 1939, Geneva, Switz.)   Russian-born director and producer, noted for his popularization in France of the works of contemporary foreign playwrights, especially Luigi Pirandello, George Bernard Shaw, Anton Chekhov, Arthur Schnitzler, and Eugene O'Neill. He was a member of the Cartel des Quatre ("Group of Four"), a group including Louis Jouvet, Charles Dullin, and Gaston Baty, dedicated to rejuvenating the French theater.

Pitoëff formed his first professional theatrical company in 1915 in Geneva and took it on tour to Paris. There, his company performed in various theaters from 1922 to 1934, when they were finally established at the Théâtre des Mathurins. Pitoëff was responsible for nearly 200 productions.

Pixérécourt \pēk-sā-rā-'kür\, Guilbert de, *in full* René-Charles-Guilbert de Pixérécourt (b. Jan. 22, 1773, Nancy, Fr.—d. July 27, 1844, Nancy)   Prolific dramatist who delighted popular audiences in Paris with a succession of more than a hundred plays during the first third of the 19th century. They were performed in the *théâtres des boulevards*, which were patronized by a far less exclusive audience than those of the official theaters and were less bound by convention. His greatest successes were melodramas—*e.g.*, *Victor* (1798) and *Coelina, ou l'enfant de mystère* (1800; "Coelina, or The Child of Mystery")—initiating a theatrical tradition that survived throughout the 19th century.

pixie or **pixy** \'pik-sē\ *plural* pixies.   In the folklore of southwestern England, a fairy; typically conceived of as playing tricks on householders or as dancing in the moonlight.

Plaatje \'pläch-ə\, Sol T., *in full* Solomon Tshekiso Plaatje (b. Oct. 9, 1876, Boshof, Orange Free State [South Africa]—d. June 19, 1932, Kimberley?)   Linguist, journalist, politician, statesman, and writer who was active in African affairs. His native tongue was Tswana, the chief language of Botswana, but he also learned English, Afrikaans, Dutch, German, French, Sotho, Zulu, and Xhosa.

Plaatje used his knowledge of languages in his various roles as war correspondent during the South African (Boer) War (1899–1902), as editor of *Koranta ea Becoana* ("The Tswana Gazette") from 1901 to 1908, as editor of *Tsala ea Batho* ("The Friend of the People") beginning in 1912, as secretary-general of the South African Native National Congress (later African National Congress), and as contributor to various South African English-language newspapers and British journals.

To preserve the traditional Bantu languages, stories, and poetry, Plaatje published his famous *Sechuana Proverbs and Their European Equivalents* (1916), the *Sechuana Phonetic Reader* (with the linguist Daniel Jones) in the same year, and the later collection *Bantu Folk-Tales and Poems*. He also translated a number of William Shakespeare's plays into Tswana. His novel *Mhudi: An Epic of Native Life a Hundred Years Ago* (1930), a story of love and war, is the first English-language novel by a black South African. Set in the 19th century, the narrative is told in the manner of the African oral tradition but also contains elements of Western literature. His diary, *The Boer War Diary of Sol T. Plaatje* (1973), was revised and republished as *Mafeking Diary* in 1990.

plagiarism \'plā-jə-,riz-əm\   An act or instance of plagiarizing (*i.e.*, taking the writings of another person and passing them off as one's own). The fraudulence is closely related to forgery and piracy—practices generally in violation of copyright laws. There is no breach of copyright laws if it can be proved that duplicated wordage was arrived at independently.

Plagiary, Sir Fretful \\'fret-fəl-'plā-jē-,ar-ē\\ Fictional character, the epitome of the vain, talentless playwright, in Richard Brinsley Sheridan's play THE CRITIC. He is based on the English dramatist Richard Cumberland, who had expressed his contempt for Sheridan's *The School for Scandal*.

Plague, The Novel by Albert CAMUS, published in 1947 as *La Peste*. The work is an allegorical account of the determined fight against an epidemic in the town of Oran, Algeria, by characters who embody dignity and fraternity.

plaint A verse lament. *See* COMPLAINT.

Planudes \\plā-'nü-děz, -'nyü-\\, Maximus, *original name* Manuel Planudes (b. 1260, Nicomedia, Anatolia [now İzmit, Tur.]—d. *c.* 1310, Constantinople [now Istanbul]) Greek Orthodox scholar, anthologist, and polemicist. His Greek translations of Latin philosophy and literature and of Arabic mathematics publicized these areas of learning throughout the Greek Byzantine cultural world.

In Constantinople, Planudes established a monastery for laymen and opened a school. Drawing students from the royal family and nobility, the school gained an academic reputation for its thorough humanities curriculum.

Although chiefly known for his theological writings, Planudes made a distinctive contribution to the history of Greek literature with his revision of the Greek Anthology (*Anthologia Hellēnikē*), a renowned collection of Greek literature written between *c.* 700 BC and AD 1000. Although parts of the reconstituted texts show Planudes' personal interpretations, the Anthology helped the development of modern Italian and French by its influence on 15th-century writers. Also influential were his revision of the *Life and Fables of Aesop* and his commentary on Theocritus, the 3rd-century-BC creator of Greek pastoral verse.

Platen \\'plät-ən\\, August, *in full* August Platen, Count (Graf) von Platen-Hallermünde \\'häl-ər-,mœn-də\\, Hallermünde *also spelled* Hallermund \\-,münt\\ (b. Oct. 24, 1796, Ansbach, principality of Ansbach [Germany]—d. Dec. 5, 1835, Syracuse, Sicily [Italy]) German poet and dramatist who, unlike most of his contemporaries, worked for classical purity of style.

In 1819 Platen moved to Erlangen, where he studied under the philosopher of Romanticism, Friedrich Schelling, and made the acquaintance of many of the leading writers of the time, including J.W. von Goethe. He became a first-rate scholar and published a book of poems, *Ghaselen* (1821; "Ghazels"), in which he imitated the style of his friend Friedrich Rückert.

Though Platen was at first influenced as a dramatist by Romanticism, he attacked its extravagances, particularly the *Schicksalstragödie*, or fate tragedy, in his witty comedies written in the manner of Aristophanes: *Die verhängnisvolle Gabel* (1826; "The Fateful Prong") and *Der romantische Oedipus* (1829; "The Romantic Oedipus"). After 1826 Platen lived in Italy, where he wrote his last play, *Die Liga von Cambrai* (1833; "The League of Cambrai"), and the epic fairy tale *Die Abbassiden* (1834; "The Abbasids"). Platen's odes and sonnets and his *Polenlieder* (1831; "Songs of the Poles"), which expressed sympathy for the Poles in their rising against the Russian czar's rule, are counted among the best classical poems of their time.

Plath \\'plath\\, Sylvia (b. Oct. 27, 1932, Boston, Mass., U.S.—d. Feb. 11, 1963, London, Eng.) American poet whose best-known poems are carefully crafted pieces noted for their personal imagery and intense focus. Many concern such themes as

alienation, death, and self-destruction. She was little known at the time of her death by suicide, but by the mid-1970s she was considered a major contemporary poet.

Plath's first major publication was *The Colossus* (1960), a collection of poems written from 1956 to 1960. This was followed by her only novel, THE BELL JAR (1963), which first appeared under a pseudonym. Drawn from Plath's own experiences, the book describes the mental breakdown, attempted suicide, and eventual recovery of a young college girl. Works published posthumously include ARIEL (1965) and *Crossing the Water* (1971), both poetry collections, and *Johnny Panic and the Bible of Dreams* (1977), a book of short stories and other prose. *The Collected Poems*, which includes many previously unpublished poems, appeared in 1981 and was awarded a Pulitzer Prize.

Plato \\'plā-tō\\ (b. 428/427 BC, Athens, or Aegina [Greece]—d. 348/347, Athens) Ancient Greek philosopher who developed a wide-ranging system of philosophy that, while concerned with ethical questions, rested on a metaphysical foundation of eternal Ideas, or Forms, *i.e.*, universals or absolutes. Platonism continued to influence philosophy through the 20th century.

Born of a distinguished Athenian family, Plato had political ambitions until he became convinced that there was no place for men of conscience in active politics. After the execution of Socrates (399 BC), he and other Socratic followers took temporary refuge at Megara. Plato spent the next few years traveling in Greece, Egypt, Italy, and Sicily, where he found a kindred spirit in Dion, brother-in-law of Dionysius I, the ruler of Syracuse. About 387 he founded the Academy in Athens as an institute for the systematic pursuit of philosophical and scientific research. He presided over the Academy for the rest of his life, making it the recognized authority also in mathematics and jurisprudence. On the death of Dionysius I in 367 Plato went to Syracuse at the request of Dion to be the tutor for Dionysius II, but the plan to educate a constitutional king failed, and Plato returned to the Academy.

Although Plato considered the foundation and organization of the Academy his chief work, his importance to later generations derived from his philosophical writings, in the form of dialogues. His dialogues, are divided into two groups on the basis of differences in thought, perhaps indicating the distinction between an earlier, more Socratic thought and a later, more distinctively Platonic thought.

Plato's works listed in their traditional order are *Euthyphrōn* (*Euthyphro*), *Apologia Sōkratous* (*Apology*), *Critōn* (*Crito*), *Phaedōn* (*Phaedo*), *Cratylos* (*Cratylus*), *Theaetētos* (*Theaetetus*), *Sophistēs* (*Sophist*), *Politikos* (*Statesman*), *Parmenidēs*, *Philēbos* (*Philebus*), *Symposion* (*Symposium*), *Phaedros* (*Phaedrus*), *Alkibiadēs* (*Alcibiades*), *Hipparchos* (*Hipparchus*), *Erastai* (*Lovers*), *Charmidēs*, *Lachēs*, *Lysis*, *Euthydēmos* (*Euthydemus*), *Prōtagoras*, *Gorgias*, *Menōn* (*Meno*), *Hippias Meizōn* (*Hippias Major*), *Hippias Elattōn* (*Hippias Minor*), *Iōn*, *Menexenos* (*Menexenus*), *Politeia* (*Republic*), *Timaeos* (*Timaeus*), *Critias*, *Nomoi* (*Laws*), and *Epinomis*.

Platonic models of literary criticism tend to emphasize the moral aspects of a text, in contrast to Aristotelian criticism, which more often stresses logical and formal approaches.

Platter \\'plät-ər\\, Thomas (b. Feb. 10, 1499, Grächen, Switz.—d. Jan. 26, 1582, Basel) Swiss writer and humanist known for his autobiography.

A scholar's assistant in Germany, Platter went to Zürich, where he was introduced to the teachings of the Swiss Reformer Huldrych Zwingli and to the newly discovered world of Greek, Latin, and Hebrew culture. Moving to Basel, Platter taught Hebrew and worked as partner to the printer Andrew

Cratander. His autobiography, completed in 1576, is an important document of the period and tells the story of his lifelong struggle to educate himself.

Plautus \'plȯt-əs\ (b. *c.* 254 BC, Sarsina, Umbria? [Italy]—d. 184)   Roman playwright who ranks with Terence as one of the two great Roman comic dramatists.

Little is known for certain about the life and personality of Plautus. His customarily assigned birth and death dates are largely based on statements made by later Latin writers, notably Cicero in the 1st century BC. Tradition has it that Plautus was associated with the theater from a young age. An early story says that he lost the profits made from his early success as a playwright in an unsuccessful business venture and that for a while afterward he was obliged to earn a living by working in a grain mill.

The Roman predecessors of Plautus in both tragedy and comedy borrowed most of their plots and all of their dramatic techniques from Greece. Though Plautus, like them, took the bulk of his plots from plays written by Greek authors of the late 4th and early 3rd centuries BC, he did not borrow slavishly. The life represented in his plays is superficially Greek but the flavor is Roman, and Plautus incorporated into his adaptations Roman concepts, terms, usages, place-names, laws, and institutions. The action in Plautus' plays is lively and full of slapstick, and in his hands Latin becomes racy and colloquial.

Almost the earliest literary works in Latin to have survived, Plautus' plays were written in verse, as were the Greek originals. Although he used some of the same meters as the Greeks, he varied them, with longer lines and more elaborate rhythms. The original texts of his plays did not survive. Even by the time Roman scholars such as Varro, a contemporary of Cicero, became interested in the playwright, only acting editions of his plays remained. These editions had, of course, been modified for production purposes.

Plautus began to influence European domestic comedy after the Renaissance poet Ariosto had written the first imitations of Plautine comedy in the Italian vernacular. His influence can perhaps be seen at its most sophisticated in the comedies of Molière (whose play *L'Avare*, for instance, was based on *Aulularia*), and it can be traced up to the present day in such adaptations as Jean Giraudoux's *Amphitryon 38* (1929), Cole Porter's musical *Out of This World* (1950), and the musical *A Funny Thing Happened on the Way to the Forum* (1963).

play \'plā\   The stage representation of an action or story, or a dramatic composition. *See also* COMEDY; TRAGEDY.

Playboy of the Western World, The Comedy in three acts by J.M. SYNGE, published and produced in 1907. It is a masterpiece of the Irish Literary Renaissance.

This most famous of Synge's works fused the patois of ordinary Irish villagers with Synge's sophisticated rhetoric and enraged Irish playgoers with its satire of Irish braggadocio. The play follows the mercurial rise and fall of the character Christy Mahon, whose self-reported murder of his father earns him much admiration until his father shows up alive and in pursuit of his cowardly son.

Player Piano First novel by Kurt VONNEGUT, published in 1952 and reissued in 1954 as *Utopia 14*. This anti-utopian novel employs the standard science-fiction formula of a futuristic world run by machines and of one man's futile rebellion against that world.

playwright \'plā-ˌrīt\, *also called* dramatist \'dram-ə-tist, 'dräm-\   A person who writes plays.

Pléiade, La \lä-plā-'yȧd\   Group of seven French writers of the 16th century, led by Pierre de RONSARD, whose aim was to

elevate the French language to the level of the classical tongues as a medium for literary expression. La Pléiade also included Joachim du BELLAY, Jean Dorat, Jean-Antoine de Baïf, Rémy Belleau, Pontus de Tyard, and Étienne Jodelle.

The principles of La Pléiade were authoritatively set forth by du Bellay in *La Défense et illustration de la langue française* (1549; *The Defence and Illustration of the French Language*), a document that advocated the enrichment of the French language by discreet imitation of the classics and the works of the Italian Renaissance—including such forms as the Pindaric and Horatian ode, the Virgilian epic, and the Petrarchan sonnet. Du Bellay also encouraged the revival of archaic and provincial French words, the use of technical terms in literary contexts, the coining of new words, and the development of verse forms new to French literature. The writers of La Pléiade are considered the first representatives of French Renaissance poetry, in part because they revived the alexandrine verse form (12-syllable lines rhyming in alternate masculine and feminine couplets).

Pleiades \'plē-ə-ˌdēz, 'plā-, 'plī-\, *also called* Atlantides \at-'lan-ti-ˌdēz\   In Greek mythology, the seven daughters of the Titan Atlas and the Oceanid Pleione: Maia, Electra, Taygete, Celaeno, Alcyone, Sterope, and Merope. They all fell in love with gods—except Merope, who loved a mortal—and were the mothers of gods. The Pleiades eventually formed a constellation.

pleonasm \'plē-ə-ˌnaz-əm\ [Greek *pleonasmós,* literally, excess, a derivative of *pleonázein* to be in excess, be redundant] **1.** The use of more words than those necessary to denote mere sense (such as *the man he said, saw with his own eyes, true fact*). Pleonasm especially refers to the coincident use of a word and its substitute for the same grammatical function and is similar in meaning to *redundancy* and *tautology.* **2.** An instance or example of such iteration.

Plievier \plē-'vyā\, Theodor, *pseudonym* (until 1933) Theodor Plivier \plē-'vyā\ (b. Feb. 12, 1892, Berlin, Ger.—d. March 12, 1955, Avegno, near Locarno, Switz.)   German war novelist who was one of the first native writers to begin examining Germany's role in World War II.

Plievier served in the German navy in World War I, during which time he participated in the 1918 naval mutiny. An ardent communist, Plievier worked as a left-wing publicist during the 1920s. He described his war experiences in *Des Kaisers Kulis* (1930; *The Kaiser's Coolies*), *Zwölf Mann und ein Kapitän* (1930; "Twelve Men and a Captain"), *Der Kaiser ging, die Generäle blieben* (1932; *The Kaiser Goes, the Generals Remain*), *Der 10. November 1918* (1935; "The 10th of November 1918"), and *Das grosse Abenteuer* (1936; "The Great Adventure"). The only notice his war novels attracted came from the Nazi Party, which banned his books in 1933 and revoked his citizenship in 1934. His most important work is a World War II trilogy that deals with the war on the Eastern Front; it comprises *Stalingrad* (1945), *Moskau* (1952; *Moscow*), and *Berlin* (1954). The novels are shocking in their graphic, naturalistic detail.

Pliny the Elder \'plin-ē\, *Latin in full* Gaius Plinius Secundus (b. AD 23, Novum Comum, Transpadane Gaul—d. Aug. 24, 79, Stabiae, near Mt. Vesuvius)   Roman savant and author of the celebrated *Naturalis historia* (AD 77; NATURAL HISTORY), an encyclopedic work of uneven accuracy that was the European authority on scientific matters up to the Middle Ages.

Pliny, who was descended from a prosperous family, completed his studies in Rome. At the age of 23, he began a military career in which he eventually rose to the rank of cavalry commander. Until near the end of Nero's reign, when he became procurator in Spain, Pliny lived in semiretirement, studying and writing. In AD 69 he returned to Rome and assumed various official positions.

Seven works are ascribed to him, of which only the *Natural History* is extant. There survive, however, a few fragments of earlier writings on grammar, a biography of Pomponius Secundus, a history of Rome, a study of the Roman campaigns in Germany, and a book on hurling the lance. These writings probably were lost in antiquity, and Pliny's fame rests solely on the *Natural History*.

In retrospect, Pliny's influence was based on his ability to assemble in a methodical fashion a number of previously unrelated facts, his perceptiveness in recognizing details ignored by others, and his readable stories, with which he linked together both factual and fictional data. Along with unsupported claims, fables, and exaggerations, Pliny's belief in magic and superstition helped shape scientific and medical theory in subsequent centuries. With the decline of the ancient world and the loss of the Greek texts on which Pliny had so heavily depended, the *Natural History* became a substitute for a general education. In the European Middle Ages many of the larger monastic libraries possessed copies of the work, and these and many abridged versions ensured Pliny's place in European literature.

Pliny \'plin-ē\ the Younger, *Latin in full* Gaius Plinius Caecilius Secundus (b. AD 61 or 62, Comum [Italy]—d. *c.* 113, Bithynia, Asia Minor [now in Turkey])   Roman author and administrator who left a collection of private letters of great literary charm that intimately illustrated public and private life in the heyday of the Roman Empire.

Born into a wealthy family and adopted by his uncle, Pliny the Elder, Pliny began to practice law at 18. His reputation in the civil-law courts placed him in demand in the political court that tried provincial officials for extortion. He later held several high administrative posts.

Between 100 and 109 Pliny published nine books of selected private letters, beginning with those covering events from the death of Emperor Domitian (October 97) to the early part of 100. The 10th book contains addresses to Emperor Trajan on sundry official problems—including a famous letter concerning what to do about the Christians—and the emperor's replies. The private letters are carefully written occasional pieces on diverse topics. Each holds an item of recent social, literary, political, or domestic news, gives an account of an earlier but contemporary historical event, or initiates moral discussion of a problem. Each has a single subject and is written in a style that mixes, in Pliny's terminology, the historical, the poetical, and the oratorical manner to fit the theme. The composition of these *litterae curiosius scriptae* ("letters written with special care") was a fashion among the wealthy, and Pliny developed it into a miniature art form.

Pliny was adept at brief character sketches, his works being less satirical, more kindly, and possibly more complete than those of Tacitus. He was also a devotee of literature, and he left a detailed picture of the amateur literary world of his time and of the salons in which it was the custom to recite one's work and to seek critical revision from one's friends.

ploce \'plōs-ē, 'plŏs-\ [Greek *plokḗ* complication, literally, something twisted]   **1.** Emphatic repetition of a word with particular reference to its special significance (as in "a wife who was a wife indeed").   **2.** In rhetoric, the repetition of a word in an altered grammatical function, as in the line "Why wilt thou sleep the sleep of death?" from William Blake's poem *Jerusalem*, in which the word *sleep* is used as both a verb and a noun. The term also refers to such repetition in general, as in the phrases "pin the pin on" or "dance the dance." *Compare* ANADIPLOSIS.

Plomer \'plü-mər, *commonly and originally in the author's family* 'plō-mər\, William (Charles Franklyn) (b. Dec. 10, 1903, Pietersburg, Transvaal [S.Af.]—d. Sept. 21, 1973, Lewes, East Sussex, Eng.)   South African-born British man of letters.

Plomer's first novel, *Turbott Wolfe* (1925), caused a scandal in South Africa—it touched upon miscegenation and sometimes portrayed white characters in the role of villains. *I Speak of Africa* (1927), a collection of short stories, did not improve his reputation. In collaboration with Laurens Van Der Post and Roy Campbell, he founded the magazine *Voorslag* ("Whiplash") with the intention of excoriating racism in South Africa. When public outrage silenced the journal, Plomer left the country for England.

Plomer wrote two dramatic novels about London, *The Case Is Altered* (1932) and *The Invaders* (1934). Additional publications include a semifictional memoir, *Museum Pieces* (1952), and three volumes of family and personal memoirs, *Double Lives* (1943), *At Home* (1958), and *Autobiography of William Plomer* (1975). He also wrote the librettos for four works by the British composer Benjamin Britten. One of his major works is *Collected Poems* (1960).

plot \'plät\   The plan or the main story of a literary work (such as a novel, play, short story, or poem); also known as narrative structure. Plot involves a considerably higher level of narrative organization than normally occurs in a story or fable. According to E.M. Forster in *Aspects of the Novel* (1927), a story is a "narrative of events arranged in their time-sequence," whereas a plot organizes the events according to a "sense of causality."

In the history of literary criticism, plot has undergone a variety of interpretations. In the *Poetics*, Aristotle assigned primary importance to plot (*mythos*) and considered it the very "soul" of a tragedy. Later critics tended to reduce plot to a more mechanical function, until, in the Romantic era, it was theoretically degraded to an outline on which the content of fiction was hung.

In the 20th century there have been many attempts to redefine plot, and some critics have even reverted to the position of Aristotle in giving it primary importance in fiction. These neo-Aristotelians, following the leadership of Ronald S. Crane, have described plot as the author's control of the reader's emotional responses—the arousal of the reader's interest and anxiety and the control of that anxiety over a duration of time.

Plough and the Stars, The   Tragicomedy in four acts by Sean O'CASEY, performed and published in 1926. The play is set in Dublin during the Easter Rising of 1916, and its premiere at the Abbey Theatre sparked rioting by nationalists who felt that it defamed Irish patriots.

Among the characters who fight to keep their lives intact despite the war's destruction are Nora and Jack Clitheroe. Although Nora is pregnant with their first child, Jack ignores her pleas, goes into the streets to fight for the cause, and is killed. When their baby is stillborn, Nora loses her mind. Her condition prompts Bessie Burgess, an embittered Irish Protestant who has lost a son to the rebels, to become Nora's caretaker. At the play's end Bessie herself is killed by a sniper's bullet.

Plunkett, Edward John Moreton Drax   *see* DUNSANY.

Plunkett \'plən-kit\, James, *pen name of* James Plunkett Kelly \'kel-ē\ (b. May 21, 1920, Dublin, Ire.)   Irish novelist, dramatist, and short-story writer whose works dealt with Ireland's political and labor problems and contained vivid portraits of working-class and middle-class Dubliners.

In the 1940s Plunkett began publishing articles in a number of Irish periodicals, including *The Bell*; his writing was greatly influenced by its editors, Sean O'Faolain and Peader O'Donnell. *Strumpet City* (1969), an acclaimed historical novel, deals with the trade union movement in Dublin prior to World War I. *Farewell Companions* (1977) is a semiautobiographical novel set between the world wars. Plunkett's short-story collections include *The Trusting and the Maimed, and Other Irish Stories* (1955) and *Collected Short Stories* (1977). His three-act play, *The Risen People* (1978), was performed at the Abbey Theatre in 1958. He also wrote several plays for television, including *Memory Harbour* (1963), *The Great O'Neill* (1966), and *The Eagles and the Trumpets* (1984).

Plurabelle, Anna Livia \'an-ə-'liv-ē-ə-'plúr-ə-,bel\ Fictional character in James Joyce's novel FINNEGANS WAKE who symbolizes the eternal and universal female.

Plutarch \'plü-,tärk\, *Greek* Plutarchos, *Latin* Plutarchus (b. *c.* AD 46, Chaeronea, Boeotia [Greece]—d. after 119) Biographer and author writing in Greek whose works strongly influenced the evolution of the essay, biography, and historical writing in Europe from the 16th to the 19th century.

Plutarch was the son of Aristobulus, himself a biographer and philosopher. In 66–67, Plutarch studied mathematics and philosophy at Athens. Public duties later took him several times to Rome.

Plutarch's literary output was immense. The 227 titles in the so-called catalog of Lamprias, a list of Plutarch's works supposedly made by his son, are not all authentic, but neither do they include all he wrote. The order of composition cannot be determined.

His popularity rests primarily on his *Bioi parallēloi* (PARALLEL LIVES), a series of pairs of biographies of famous Greeks and Romans. His surviving writings on ethical, religious, physical, political, and literary topics are collectively known as the *Moralia*, or *Ethica* (Greek *Ēthika*), and amount to more than 60 essays cast mainly in the form of dialogues or diatribes. The literary value of both is enhanced by the frequent quotation of Greek poems, especially verses of Euripides and other dramatists.

Plutarch's interest in religious history and antiquarian problems can be seen in a group of striking essays (usually referred to by their Latin titles), *De superstitione* ("On Superstition"); *De defectu oraculorum* ("On the Failure of the Oracles"); *De E apud Delphos* ("On the E at Delphi"), interpreting the word El at the temple entrance; and *De sera numinis vindicta* ("On the Delays of Divine Justice").

Plutarch's influence has been profound. The *Lives* were translated into French in 1559 by Jacques Amyot, a French bishop and classical scholar, who also translated the *Moralia* (1572). His translations were still being reprinted in the 19th century. Sir Thomas North published an English translation of the *Lives* from Amyot's version in 1579. His vigorous, idiomatic style made his *The Lives of the Noble Grecians and Romanes* an English classic, and it remained the standard English translation for more than a century. North's Plutarch was William Shakespeare's source for his Roman plays and influenced the development of his conception of the tragic hero.

Pluto or **Pluton** *see* HADES.

Plutus \'plü-təs\ In Greek mythology, the god of abundance or wealth, a personification of *ploutos* (Greek: "wealth"). According to the Greek poet Hesiod, Plutus was born in Crete, the son of the goddess of fruitfulness, Demeter, and Iasion.

Pnin \'pnēn\ Novel written in English by Vladimir NABOKOV, published in 1957. It is an episodic story about Timofey Pnin, an older, exiled Russian professor of entomology at the fictional Waindell College in upstate New York. While not considered one of Nabokov's major works, the novel is a comic and tender portrait of a defenseless intellectual trying to deal with the complexities of American life. The character Pnin turns up again as a minor character in *Pale Fire*, another of Nabokov's novels about academic life.

Po Chü-i *see* BO JUYI.

Poe \'pō\, Edgar Allan (b. Jan. 19, 1809, Boston, Mass., U.S.—d. Oct. 7, 1849, Baltimore, Md.) American poet, critic, and short-story writer famous for his cultivation of mystery and the macabre in fiction.

Bettmann Archive

After Poe's mother died in 1811, he was taken into the home of John Allan, a Richmond merchant. He briefly attended the University of Virginia, then went to Boston, where in 1827 he published a pamphlet containing TAMERLANE and other youthful Byronic poems. He then began to write stories, and in 1833 his MS. FOUND IN A BOTTLE won $50 from a Baltimore weekly. By 1835 he was in Richmond as editor of the *Southern Literary Messenger*, the first of several periodicals he was to edit or write for. There he married his cousin Virginia Clemm, who was only 13 years old.

In 1839 he became coeditor of *Burton's Gentleman's Magazine* in Philadelphia, for which he wrote some of his best-known stories of supernatural horror. His *Tales of the Grotesque and Arabesque* appeared later in 1839 (dated 1840). In addition to his stories Poe continued to write poetry, and his most famous poem, THE RAVEN, brought him national fame when it appeared in 1845. Several of his works, including the poem THE BELLS, were published posthumously.

Poe's writing is characterized by a strange duality. On the one hand, he was an idealist and a visionary. His sensitivity to women inspired his most touching lyrics, including ANNABEL LEE. More generally, in such verses as ULALUME and in his prose tales, his familiar mode of escape from the world was through eerie thoughts, impulses, or fears. From these materials he drew the startling effects of his tales of death (THE FALL OF THE HOUSE OF USHER, THE MASQUE OF THE RED DEATH, THE PREMATURE BURIAL), his tales of wickedness and crime (THE BLACK CAT, THE CASK OF AMONTILLADO, THE TELL-TALE HEART), and his tales of survival after dissolution (LIGEIA). Even when his characters are not actually in the clutch of mysterious forces, he uses the anguish of imminent death as the means of causing the nerves to quiver (THE PIT AND THE PENDULUM).

On the other hand, Poe is conspicuous for his close observation of minute details, as in the long narratives (*The Narrative of Arthur Gordon Pym*) and in many of the descriptions that introduce the tales or constitute their settings. Closely connected with this is his power of ratiocination, as manifested in his analytical tales (THE GOLD BUG), detective stories (THE MURDERS IN THE RUE MORGUE), and science-fiction tales.

Poe's genius was early recognized abroad. No one did more to persuade the world and, in the long run, the United States of Poe's greatness than the French poets Charles Baudelaire and Stéphane Mallarmé. Indeed, his role in French literature was that of a poetic master model and guide to criticism. French Symbolism relied on his "The Philosophy of Composition," borrowed from his imagery, and used his examples to generate the modern theory of "pure poetry."

poem \\'pō-əm, -im; 'pōm\\ [Latin *poema,* from Greek *poíēma* work, product, poem, a derivative of *poieîn* to make] A composition in verse. *See also* POETRY.

Poems, Chiefly Lyrical Collection of poems by Alfred, Lord TENNYSON, published in 1830. Many of the poems contain experimental elements such as irregular meters and words employed for their musical or evocative powers rather than for their strict meanings. The collection includes the introspective "The Owl" and "The Kraken" and some of Tennyson's best-known shorter poems, including "Claribel: A Melody," MARIANA, and "A Spirit Haunts the Year's Last Hours."

poesy or **poesie** \\'pō-ə-zē, -sē\\ *plural* poesies [Middle English *poesie,* from Middle French, from Latin *poesis,* from Greek *poíēsis* literally, fabrication, making, a derivative of *poieîn* to make] **1.** A poem or body of poems. **2.** A synonym for POETRY. **3.** Artificial or sentimentalized poetic writing. **4.** Poetic inspiration.

poet \\'pō-ət, -it\\ [Greek *poiētés* maker, composer, poet, a derivative of *poieîn* to make] **1.** One who writes poetry; a maker of verses. **2.** One (such as a writer) having great imaginative and expressive capabilities and possessing a special sensitivity to the medium.

poetaster \\'pō-ə-ˌtas-tər\\ An inferior poet.

poète maudit \\pō-et-mō-'dē\\ [French, literally, accursed poet] In literary criticism, the poet as an outcast of modern society, despised by its rulers who fear the artist's penetrating insights into their spiritual emptiness. The phrase was first applied by Paul Verlaine in *Les Poètes maudits* (1883). This work, published in 1884, included critical and biographical studies that focused on the lives of the then little-known Symbolist poets Tristan Corbière, Stéphane Mallarmé, and Arthur Rimbaud. A revised edition, published in 1888, added material on Marceline Desbordes-Valmore, Auguste Villiers de l'Isle-Adam, and Verlaine himself. Verlaine may have taken *les poètes maudits* from Charles Baudelaire's "Bénédiction," in which a poet is described as untouched by the suffering and contempt he experiences.

poeticism \\pō-'et-ə-ˌsiz-əm\\ An archaic, trite, or strained expression in poetry.

poetic justice An outcome in which vice is punished and virtue rewarded, usually in a manner peculiarly or ironically appropriate. The term was coined by the English literary critic Thomas Rymer in the 17th century, when it was believed that a work of literature should uphold moral principles and instruct the reader in correct moral behavior.

poetics \\pō-'et-iks\\ **1.** A treatise on poetry or aesthetics. **2.** *also* poetic \\pō-'et-ik\\ Poetic theory or practice. **3.** Poetic feelings or utterances.

Poetics \\pō-'et-iks\\ Work on literature and aesthetics written by ARISTOTLE as *Peri poiētikēs.* Only a fragment of the original text survives, its discussion limited to an analysis of tragedy and epic poetry.

Aristotle wrote *Poetics* to counter Plato's indictment of literary art as an appeal to the irrational. He asserts that tragedy is both normal and useful. The tragic poet, he says, is not so much divinely inspired as he is motivated by a universal human need to imitate, and what he imitates is not real objects but rather noble actions. Aristotle holds that such imitation (*mimēsis*) has a civilizing value for those who empathize with it. Thus, while he agrees that tragedy arouses emotions of pity and terror in its audience, he argues that these emotions are purged in the process (*katharsis*) and that literature satisfies and regulates human passions instead of inflaming them.

Using the concept of *mimēsis* as the basis for the discussion of poetry, Aristotle considers poetic art in terms of the characteristics and relationships of the six parts, or components, of tragedy: plot, character, and thought (the objects of imitation); diction and melody (the means of imitation); and spectacle (the manner of imitation). The last four chapters of the *Poetics* return to more general questions of value by means of detailed comparisons of tragedy with comparable poetic works and specifically with the epic.

Aristotle introduced the concept that has most shaped the composition of plays in later ages, namely, the so-called unities—that is, of time, place, and action. Although he was evidently simply describing what he observed—that a typical Greek tragedy had a single plot and action lasting one day (he made no mention at all of unity of place)—Neoclassical critics of the 17th century codified these discussions into rules. *See also* MIMESIS; UNITY.

poet laureate \\'lȯr-ē-ət, 'lär-\\ *plural* poets laureate *or* poet laureates. **1.** A person honored for achievement in the art of poetry. **2.** One regarded by a country or region as its most eminent or representative poet. **3.** A poet appointed for life by an English sovereign as a member of the royal household and formerly expected to compose poems for court and national occasions. The title stems from traditions concerning the laurel and dating to the earliest Greek and Roman times.

In England the office of poet laureate is remarkable for its continuity. It began in 1616 with a pension granted to Ben Jonson by James I. Sixteen months after Jonson's death in 1637, a similar pension for similar services was granted to Sir William Davenant. In 1668 the laureateship was recognized as an established royal office to be filled automatically when vacant.

Thomas Shadwell, inaugurated the custom of producing New Year and birthday odes; this hardened into a tradition between 1690 and about 1820, becoming the principal task of the office. The custom was allowed tacitly to lapse and was finally abolished by Queen Victoria. Her appointment of William Wordsworth in 1843 signified that the laureateship had become the reward for eminence in poetry, and the office since then has carried no specific duties. The laureates from Alfred, Lord Tennyson onward have written poems for royal and national occasions as the spirit has moved them.

The list of poets laureate (with dates of tenure) follows: John Dryden (1668–89), Thomas Shadwell (1689–92), Nahum Tate (1692–1715), Nicholas Rowe (1715–18), Laurence Eusden (1718–30), Colley Cibber (1730–57), William Whitehead (1757–85), Thomas Warton (1785–90), Henry James Pye (1790–1813), Robert Southey (1813–43), William Wordsworth (1843–50), Alfred, Lord Tennyson (1850–92), Alfred Austin (1896–1913), Robert Bridges (1913–30), John Masefield (1930–67), C. Day-Lewis (1968–72), Sir John Betjeman (1972–84), and Ted Hughes (from 1984).

In 1985 the United States government created the title of poet laureate, to be held by the same person who holds the post of consultant in poetry to the Library of Congress.

poetomachia \pō-,et-ə-'māk-ē-ə, -'mak-\ [Greek *poiētēs* poet + *máchē* battle, fight]   A contest of poets; specifically, the literary quarrel known as the WAR OF THE THEATERS involving a number of Elizabethan dramatists.

poetry \'pō-ə-trē\ [Middle English *poetrie,* from Old French, from Medieval Latin *poetria*]   **1.** Metrical writing.   **2.** The productions of a poet; poems.   **3.** Writing that formulates a concentrated imaginative awareness of experience in language chosen and arranged to create a specific emotional response through its meaning, sound, and rhythm.

Poetry may be distinguished from prose literature in terms of form by its compression, by its frequent (though not prescribed) employment of the conventions of meter and rhyme, by its reliance upon the line as a formal unit, by its heightened vocabulary, and by its freedom of syntax. The characteristic emotional content of poetry finds expression through a variety of techniques, from direct description to highly personalized symbolism. One of the most ancient and universal of these techniques is the use of metaphor and simile to alter and expand the reader's imaginative apprehension through implicit or explicit comparison.

Poetry encompasses many modes: narrative, dramatic, aphoristic, celebratory, satiric, descriptive, didactic, erotic, and personal. Within a single work the poet may move from one mode to another, preserving overall unity through the consistency of the formal pattern. The formal patterns available to the poet vary considerably: in English poetry the formal unit may be the single unrhymed line (as in blank verse), the rhymed couplet, the rhymed stanza of four lines or more, or more complex rhyming patterns such as the 14-line sonnet.

Poetry is an ancient mode of expression; it was often used by nonliterate societies who formulated poetic expressions of religious, historical, and cultural significance and transmitted these to the next generation in hymns, incantations, and narrative poems. Something of this early association with the cultural traditions of the tribe has persisted in later theories of poetic inspiration and poetic privilege, though from the time of the Romantics the autonomous creative imagination has been regarded as the source of poetic energy and the guarantee of poetic authenticity. Some modern poets, such as the Surrealists, would claim that the poetic faculty is a mode of access to individual and collective unconscious experience.

In the 19th and 20th centuries Western poetry has responded more to the expressive possibilities of poetic idiom and convention in different traditions. Some poets have experimented with reviving or adapting the subject matter and the verse forms of other times and places. For other poets it has been important to break with tradition and convention and attempt a studied informality of manner, an approximation of the relaxed rhythms and colloquial vocabulary of ordinary speech, and a self-consciously "prosaic" imagery. *Compare* PROSE. *See also* LINE; METER; RHYME.

Poetry   Poem by Marianne MOORE, originally published in a 30-line version in 1921. Moore cut the poem to 13 lines in 1924, replaced most of the excised lines in 1935, and cut it drastically again in 1967. Most critics prefer the 1935 poem published in the collection *Selected Poems* (1935).

Beginning with the famous line "I, too, dislike it," Moore examines her ambivalent feelings toward poetry which, she feels, is not important in itself but can be "useful" if written properly. A "useful" poem, according to Moore, is one that has successfully merged the world of the imagination with the world of the senses; a poet's subject, she holds, should be based on firsthand experience.

Poetry (*in full* Poetry: A Magazine of Verse)   American poetry magazine founded in Chicago in 1912 by Harriet MONROE, who also served for many years as the magazine's editor.

The first issue of *Poetry: A Magazine of Verse* appeared in October 1912. Because its inception coincided with the Midwestern cultural ferment later known as the CHICAGO LITERARY RENAISSANCE, it is often thought of particularly as the vehicle for the raw, original, local-color poetry of Carl Sandburg, Edgar Lee Masters, Vachel Lindsay, and Sherwood Anderson, but it also championed new formalistic movements in verse. The poet and critic Ezra Pound was European correspondent. Imagism, impressionism, and vers libre were expounded in its pages. "The Love Song of J. Alfred Prufrock" by the then-unknown T.S. Eliot appeared in *Poetry* (1915), as did the experimental poems of Wallace Stevens, Marianne Moore, D.H. Lawrence, and William Carlos Williams. *Poetry* survived the withering of the Chicago literary renaissance and World Wars I and II. It remained a highly respected journal even after Monroe's sudden death in 1936.

Poet's Corner   A section of London's Westminster Abbey that contains the tombs of many notable authors and monuments to many others. Among those buried or memorialized there are Geoffrey Chaucer, Edmund Spenser, John Dryden, Samuel Johnson, Alfred, Lord Tennyson, the Brontë sisters, Robert Browning, Henry James, T.S. Eliot, W.H. Auden, and Sir Noël Coward.

Pohl \'pōl\, Frederik (b. Nov. 26, 1919, New York, N.Y., U.S.)   American science-fiction writer whose best work uses the genre as a mode of social criticism and as an exploration of the long-range consequences of technology in an ailing society.

By the late 1930s Pohl was working as an editor of science-fiction magazines. During World War II he served in the U.S. Army Air Forces and then worked briefly in an advertising agency before returning to writing and editing.

Pohl's most famous work, *The Space Merchants* (1953), was written in collaboration with C.M. Kornbluth. It tells the story of Mitchell Courtenay, a "copysmith star class" for a powerful advertising agency, who is made head of a project to colonize Venus in order to create consumers in space. This chilling portrait of a world dominated by the economic perspective of advertising executives made Pohl's reputation. Pohl wrote several other books with Kornbluth; some of their work can be found in *Our Best: The Best of Frederik Pohl and C.M. Kornbluth* (1987). Pohl's other novels include *The Age of the Pussyfoot* (1969), *Man Plus* (1976), and *Chernobyl* (1987). His numerous short-story collections include *The Best of Frederik Pohl* (1975), *Pohlstars* (1984), and *The Gateway Trip: Tales and Vignettes of the Heechee* (1990). Pohl published a memoir, *The Way the Future Was*, in 1978.

Poictesme \pwà-'tem, -'tez-əm\   Mythical medieval French realm that is the setting for JURGEN and several other novels by American author James Branch Cabell—including *The Cream of the Jest* (1917), *Figures of Earth* (1921), and *The High Place* (1923).

Point Counter Point   Novel by Aldous HUXLEY, published in 1928. In his most ambitious and complex work, Huxley offers a vision of life from a number of different points of view, using a large cast of characters who are compared to instruments in an orchestra, each playing his separate portion of the larger piece. One character, Philip Quarles, acts as a guide to Huxley's scheme, explaining the author's motives to the reader and speculating upon the actions of the other characters.

point of view The perspective from which a story is presented to the reader. The three main points of view are first person, third person singular, and third person omniscient. In a first person narrative, the story is told by "I," one of the characters involved in the story, as in Charlotte Brontë's *Jane Eyre*. Third person is the voice in which a story is presented when the narrator is not a character in the story. The term actually refers to either of two narrative voices. A story told in the third person singular is one in which the narrator writes from the point of view of a single character, describing or noticing only what that character has the opportunity to see and hear and know, but not in the voice of that character, as in Henry James's *What Maisie Knew*. A third person omniscient narrator is not limited in viewpoint to any one character and thus can comment on every aspect of the story. George Eliot's *Middlemarch* uses such a narrator. *See also* NARRATOR.

Poirot, Hercule \ˌer-'kyūl-'pwä-rō, pwä-'rō\ Fictional Belgian detective featured in a series of novels by Agatha CHRISTIE.

Short, somewhat vain, with brilliantined hair and a waxed moustache, the aging bachelor Poirot enjoys his creature comforts. Relying on his "little grey cells" to solve crimes, Poirot is notably meticulous in his personal habits and his professional methodology. He appeared in Christie's first novel, *The Mysterious Affair at Styles* (1920), and in dozens of subsequent books, including some of Christie's best-loved works, such as *Murder on the Orient Express* (1933) and *Death on the Nile* (1937). Poirot's final appearance and death occurred in the novel *Curtain* (1975). Christie was said to have based Poirot's mannerisms on her observation of World War I Belgian refugees.

Poldark, Ross \'ròs-'pōl-ˌdärk\ Fictional character who is patriarch of the Poldark dynasty in a series of historical novels by Winston GRAHAM. Ross is an army captain and member of the landed gentry of Cornwall in the late 18th and early 19th centuries. Heroic and temperamental, he struggles to make his tin and copper mines profitable. He appears in *Ross Poldark* (1945), *Demelza* (1946), *Warleggan* (1953), *The Four Swans* (1976), *The Angry Tide* (1977), *The Stranger from the Sea* (1981), and *The Loving Cup* (1984).

polemic \pə-'lem-ik\ [French *polémique,* from *polémique* (adjective) disputatious, from Greek *polemikós* pertaining to war, a derivative of *pólemos* war] An aggressive attack on or refutation of the opinions or principles of another. One of the best-known examples in literature is John Milton's *Areopagitica*.

police procedural *plural* police procedurals. A mystery story written from the point of view of the officer or detective investigating the crime.

Polidoúri or **Polydoúre** \ˌpō-lē-'thü-rē\, Maria (b. 1905, Kalámai, Greece—d. 1930, Athens) Greek poet known for her impassioned, eloquent farewell to life.

Polidoúri was orphaned as a small child, and in 1921 she went to Athens to study law. There she began a friendship with another poet, Kóstas Kariotákis. In 1926 she relocated to Paris, returning two years later, fatally ill. In 1930 she entered a sanatorium near Athens, where she died.

Her two books of poems reflect her awareness of impending death. The tone alternates between bitter questioning and a cold resignation in which she seems to contemplate her own pain from outside herself.

Politian \pō-'lish-ən\, *in full* Angelo Poliziano \pō-ˌlēt-sē-'ä-nō\, *also called* Angelo Ambrogini \ˌäm-brō-'jē-nē\ (b. July 14, 1454, Montepulciano, Tuscany [Italy]—d. Sept. 28/29, 1494, Florence) Italian poet and humanist, the friend and protégé of Lorenzo de' Medici, and one of the foremost classical schol-

ars of the Renaissance. With Lorenzo, he was one of those mainly responsible for the revaluation of vernacular literature.

Sometime before 1469 Politian was sent to Florence, where he wrote Latin and Greek epigrams and attracted the attention of Lorenzo de' Medici. About 1473 he entered the Medici household, and in 1475 he was entrusted with the education of Lorenzo's eldest son, Piero. Politian's translation of the *Iliad*, Books II–V, into Latin hexameters (1470–75) brought him his first renown. Between 1473 and 1478 he produced Latin and Greek verses that are among the best examples of humanist poetry; they include elegies, odes, and epigrams (of particular merit are the elegies *In violas* ["In Violets"] and the ode *In puellam suam* ["In Regard to One's Daughters"]).

Politian's poetic masterpiece of this period is, however, a vernacular poem in ottava rima, *Stanze cominciate per la giostra del Magnifico Giuliano de' Medici* ("Stanzas Begun for the Tournament of the Magnificent Giuliano de' Medici"), composed between 1475 and 1478, which is one of the great works of Italian literature. In it he synthesized the grandeur of classical literature with the spontaneity of Florentine vernacular poetry. The poem describes the love of "Julio" (*i.e.,* Giuliano de' Medici), for "Simonetta" (*i.e.,* Simonetta Cattaneo).

In May 1479, as a result of a quarrel with Lorenzo's wife, Politian was expelled from the Medici household. In Mantua he found a new patron in the person of Cardinal Francesco Gonzaga. There he wrote *Orfeo* (1480; "Orpheus"), a short dramatic composition in the vernacular and based on the myth of Orpheus and Eurydice. In 1480 Politian, after repeatedly entreating Lorenzo, was at last invited to return to Florence and was appointed to the Florentine chair of Latin and Greek (autumn 1480). His best-known works from this period are four inaugural lectures in verse, known collectively as the *Sylvae* ("The Trees"): *Manto* (1482; "The Cloak"), on Virgil's poetry; *Rusticus* (1483; "The Countryside"), on the bucolic poems of Hesiod and Virgil; *Ambra* (1485; "Amber"), on Homer; and *Nutricia* (1486; "The Foster Mother"), on the different genres of Greek and Latin literature.

political verse Byzantine or Modern Greek accentual verse; especially, verse of 15-syllable iambic lines.

Pollio \'päl-ē-ˌō\, Gaius Asinius (b. 76 BC, Italy—d. AD 4, Tusculum, near Rome) Roman orator, poet, and historian whose book of contemporary history (now lost) provided much material for Appian and Plutarch.

Pollio moved in the literary circle of Catullus and entered public life in 56 BC. He joined Caesar at the Rubicon and campaigned in Africa with Curio and from 49 to 45 in Greece, Africa, and Spain with Caesar. On Caesar's death he followed Antony, for whom he governed Cisalpine Gaul. There he was friendly with Virgil and in distributing land to veterans saved the poet's property from confiscation. In 40 he was consul, and Virgil addressed his Fourth Eclogue to him. In 39 Pollio built the first public library in Rome, in the Atrium Libertatis, which he restored. He then retired from public life with full honors and devoted himself to the support of literature.

Pollio, whose speeches are lost, had the reputation of a distinguished orator, combining, according to Tacitus and Seneca, careful composition and dry Atticist elegance in strict presentation of his argument. The style of his speeches displeased Ciceronian critics, however. As a poet he was accepted by Catullus, Helvius Cinna, and Virgil. He also wrote tragedies, which Virgil and Horace praised, but he ceased to write serious verse when he turned to history shortly after 35. His *Historiae* (*History of the Civil Wars*) covered the period from 60 probably to 42, that is, from the First Triumvirate to Philippi, the period in which the Roman Republic fell.

Pollux \\'päl-əks\\   In Greek mythology, one of a set of twin deities. His twin was named Castor. *See* DIOSCURI.

Pollux \\'päl-əks\\, Julius (fl. last half of the 2nd century AD) Greek scholar and rhetorician from Naukratis, Egypt. The emperor Commodus appointed him to a chair of rhetoric in Athens. He is author of an *Onomasticon*, a Greek thesaurus of terms. The 10-volume work, which has survived incomplete, contains rhetorical material and technical terms related to a wide variety of subjects, as well as citations from literature.

Pollyanna *in full* Pollyanna Whittier \\,päl-ē-'an-ə-'hwit-ē-ər, 'wit-\\   Fictional character, the orphaned but ever-optimistic heroine of Eleanor Hodgman Porter's novel *Pollyanna* (1913).

Orphaned at the age of 11, Pollyanna is sent to live with a stern, joyless aunt. Eventually she wins her aunt's love and the goodwill of everyone else she encounters. The character's name has become synonymous with an irrepressible optimism, an unwillingness to face reality, and the desire to find good in every person and situation.

Polo \\'pō-lō\\, Marco (b. *c.* 1254, Venice [Italy], or Curzola, Venetian Dalmatia [now Korčula, Croatia]—d. Jan. 8, 1324, Venice)   Venetian merchant, adventurer, and outstanding traveler, who journeyed from Europe to Asia in 1271–95, remaining in China for 17 of those years, and whose *Il milione* ("The Million"), known in English as the *Travels of Marco Polo*, became a geographical classic.

Marco Polo, title page of the first printed German edition of *Il milione*

Columbia University Libraries, New York

From roughly 1271 to 1295, Polo traveled widely with his father and uncle. Soon after his return to Venice from Asia in 1295, he was taken prisoner by the Genoese—great rivals of the Venetians at sea—during a skirmish or battle in the Mediterranean and was sent to a local prison in Genoa. There he met a prisoner from Pisa—one Rustichello (or Rusticiano)—who was a fairly well-known writer of romances. Polo dictated his story to Rustichello, who compiled *Il milione*, sometimes asserting his own personality and familiar phraseology.

The book was an instant success. It seems to have been conceived as a vast cosmography based on firsthand experience—the book to end all books on Asia. It is now generally conceded that he reported faithfully what he saw and heard, even though much of what he heard was fabulous or distorted. In any case, his account opened new vistas to the medieval mind.

Polonius \\pə-'lō-nē-əs\\   Fictional character, an inquisitive, intrusive old courtier who is the father of Ophelia and Laertes in William Shakespeare's tragedy HAMLET.

Polyaenus \\,päl-ē-'ē-nəs\\ (fl. 2nd century AD)   Macedonian rhetorician and pleader who lived in Rome and was the author of a work entitled *Strategica* (or *Strategemata*), which he dedicated to the emperors Marcus Aurelius and Lucius Verus on the outbreak of the Parthian war (162–165).

The *Strategica* is a historical collection of stratagems and maxims of military strategy written in Greek and strung together in the form of anecdotes; it also includes examples of wisdom, courage, and cunning from civil and political life. Comprising eight books (parts of the sixth and seventh are lost), it originally contained 900 anecdotes, of which 833 are extant.

Polydoúre   *see* POLIDOÚRI.

Polyeucte \\pȯl-'yœ̄kt\\   Neoclassical verse tragedy in five acts by Pierre CORNEILLE, produced about 1641–42 and published in 1643. It is known in English as *Polyeuctes*. With *Le Cid, Horace,* and *Cinna, Polyeucte* forms Corneille's classical tetralogy.

The title character is a recent Christian convert who would rather die a martyr than renounce his new faith. His wife, Pauline, pleads with him, and the Roman soldier Severus attempts to save him, both to no avail. After Polyeucte's execution, Pauline and her father (who executed Polyeucte) are moved by his example to become Christians.

The play is often called Corneille's finest tragedy. Using flexible alexandrine verse, Corneille sets up an elegant, symmetrical argument between two opposing forces: the world of the flesh, represented by the Roman Empire, and the spiritual world that so attracts Polyeucte.

polygraph \\'päl-ē-,graf\\ [French *polygraphe,* from Greek *polýgraphos* writing much or on many topics]   A voluminous or versatile writer.

Polymnia \\pä-'lim-nē-ə\\ or **Polymnis** \\pä-'lim-nis\\ or **Polyhymnia** \\,päl-ē-'him-nē-ə\\   In Greek mythology, one of the nine Muses, patron of sacred poetry or the mimic art. She was said in some legends to have been the mother of Triptolemus (the first priest of Demeter and the inventor of agriculture) by Cheimarrhus or by Celeus, king of Eleusis. In other versions, she was the mother of Orpheus, the legendary lyre-playing hero, or of Eros, the god of love.

Polyneices \\,päl-ē-'nī-sēz\\   In Greek legend, the son of Jocasta and Oedipus and the brother of Antigone, Ismene, and Eteocles. When Oedipus is banished from Thebes, Eteocles and Polyneices agree to share their father's throne, with each ruling for a year at a time. At the end of the first year, however, Eteocles refuses to step down. Polyneices then raises an army, and during his attack on Thebes the brothers kill each other. When the king, their uncle Creon, refuses to bury Polyneices, his sister Antigone buries him anyway and is punished with death. Polyneices' story is told in Sophocles' *Antigone* and Aeschylus' *Seven Against Thebes.*

Polypemon   *see* PROCRUSTES.

Polyphemus \\,päl-ē-'fē-məs\\   In Greek mythology, the most famous of the Cyclops (one-eyed giants), son of Poseidon (god of the sea) and the nymph Thoösa. According to one legend, when the Greek hero Odysseus was cast ashore on the coast of Sicily, he fell into the hands of Polyphemus, who shut him up with 12 of his companions in his cave and blocked the entrance with an enormous rock. Odysseus at length succeeded in making Polyphemus drunk, blinded him by plunging a burning stake into his eye while he lay asleep, and, with six of his friends (the others having been devoured by Polyphemus), made his escape by clinging to the bellies of the sheep let out to pasture.

polyphonic prose   A freely rhythmical form of prose employing characteristic devices of verse other than strict meter (such as alliteration, assonance, rhyme). The form was developed in the early 20th century by Amy Lowell, who demonstrated its techniques in her book *Can Grande's Castle.*

polyptoton \pä-'lip-tə-,tän\ [Late Latin, from Greek *polýptō-ton,* neuter of *polýptōtos* using many inflected forms (of the same word), from *poly-* many + *-ptōtos,* a derivative of *ptôsis* accidence, inflection, literally, the act of falling] The rhetorical repetition within the same sentence of a word in a different case, inflection, or voice or of etymologically related words in different parts of speech. The device is exemplified in the following lines from T.S. Eliot's poem "The Dry Salvages":

> There is no end of it, the voiceless wailing,
> No end to the withering of withered flowers,
> To the movement of pain that is painless and motionless,
> To the drift of the sea and the drifting wreckage,
> The bone's prayer to Death its God. Only the hardly, barely
>   prayable
> Prayer of the one Annunciation.

polyschematist \,päl-ē-'skē-mə-tist\ [Greek *polyschēmátistos* multiform, composed of various meters, from *poly-* many + *schēma* form, shape] In classical prosody, a unit of five to usually eight syllables whose last four syllables form a choriamb (– ∪ ∪ –), with the other syllables being indeterminate (either long or short) and diverse as to quantity. It is considered by many to be the basic figure of all the Greek lyric meters known as aeolic meters, which were used for poetry that was sung rather than recited. A common form was ∪∪ ∪ ∪ ∪ | – ∪ ∪ –. *See also* AEOLIC.

polysyndeton \,päl-ē-'sin-də-,tän\ [Late Greek *polysýndeton,* neuter of *polysýndetos* using many conjunctions, from Greek *poly-* many + *sýndetos* bound together, conjunctive] Repetition of conjunctions in close succession, as in the sentence "We have ships and men and money and stores."

Polyxena \pə-'lik-sē-nə\ In Greek mythology, a daughter of Priam, king of Troy, and his wife Hecuba. According to one legend, she was put to death at the tomb of Achilles, whose ghost had claimed her as his share of the spoils after the fall of Troy. In postclassical times the story was elaborated to include a love affair between Polyxena and Achilles before his death.

Ponder Heart, The \'pän-dər\ Comic novella by Eudora WELTY, published in 1954. Cast as a monologue, it is rich with colloquial speech and descriptive imagery.

The narrator of the story is Miss Edna Earle Ponder, one of the last living members of a once-prominent family, who manages the Beulah Hotel in Clay, Miss. She tells a traveling salesman the history of her family and fellow townsfolk.

Ponge \'pȯⁿzh\, Francis (Jean Gaston Alfred) (b. March 27, 1899, Montpellier, Fr.—d. Aug. 6, 1988, Le Barsur-Loup) French poet who crafted intricate prose poems about everyday objects. He sought to create a "visual equivalence" between language and subject matter by emphasizing word associations and by manipulating the sound, rhythm, and typography of the words to mimic the essential characteristics of the object described.

Ponge was briefly involved with the Surrealist movement in the 1920s. He joined the communist party in 1937 and served as literary and art editor of the communist weekly *Action* from 1944 to 1946, but he left the party in 1947 to concentrate on writing and teaching. He was probably best known for his collection of verse *Le Parti pris des choses* (1942; rev. ed., 1949; *The Voice of Things*) and for the book-length poem *Le Savon* (1967; *Soap*).

Pontano \pȯn-'tä-nō\, Giovanni, *also called* Jovianus Pontanus \,yō-vē-'än-ûs-pȯn-'tän-ûs\ (b. May 7, 1426, Cerreto di Spoleto, near Perugia, Papal States [Italy]—d. September 1503, Naples) Italian prose writer, poet, and royal official whose works reflect the diversity of interests and knowledge of the

Renaissance. His supple and easy Latin style is considered, with that of Politian, to be the best of Renaissance Italy.

Pontano studied language and literature in Perugia. He held various royal appointments, but he was dismissed in 1495 for negotiating peace with the French and, though pardoned, did not return to power.

Pontano became a major literary figure in Naples after 1471 when he assumed leadership of the city's humanist academy. Called the Accademia Pontaniana, it became one of the major Italian literary institutions of the 15th century. Pontano's writings, all in Latin, include a historical work (*De bello neapolitano*); philosophical treatises (*De prudentia, De fortuna*); an astrological poem (*Urania*); dialogues on morality and religion and on philology and literature; and many lyrical poems, of which the most important are *Lepidina,* a charming account of the wedding between a river god and a nymph, and a collection called *De amore coniugali,* a warm and personal series of poems on the joys and sorrows of family life.

Pontifex family \'pän-ti-feks\ Fictional characters, several generations of a self-satisfied, middle-class English family in THE WAY OF ALL FLESH, the autobiographical novel by Samuel Butler that was published in 1903, the year after his death.

The Pontifex family's progenitor is John, a carpenter, whose son George is an authoritarian publisher. George's son Theobald is a skeptic blackmailed by his father into becoming a clergyman. Theobald is similarly repressive in his treatment of his son Ernest, who represents the author and who also becomes a minister.

Pontoppidan \pȯn-'tȯp-ē-dan\, Henrik (b. July 24, 1857, Fredericia, Den.—d. Aug. 21, 1943, Ordrup, near Copenhagen) Realist writer who shared with Karl Gjellerup the Nobel Prize for Literature in 1917. Pontoppidan's novels and short stories—informed with a desire for social progress but despairing, later in his life, of its realization—present an unusually comprehensive picture of his country and his epoch.

Pontoppidan's first collection of stories, *Stækkede vinger* ("Clipped Wings"), was published in 1881, and thereafter he supported himself by writing. His output consists mainly of novels and short stories written in a cold, aloof, epic style. His first books were about country-town life. *Landsbybilleder* (1883; "Village Pictures") and *Skyer* (1890; "Clouds") are characterized by social indignation as well as by ironic appreciation of the complacency and passivity of country people. In the 1890s Pontoppidan wrote short novels on psychological, aesthetic, and moral problems—*e.g.,* *Nattevagt* (1894; "Night Guard"), *Den gamle Adam* (1895; "The Old Adam"), and *Højsang* (1896; "High Song"). These were followed by a major work, the semiautobiographical novel *Lykke-Per* (1898–1904; "Lucky Per").

Pontoppidan wrote several novel cycles, including *De dødes rige,* 5 vol. (1912–16; "The Realm of the Dead"). His last important work was the four volumes of memoirs that he published between 1933 and 1940 and that appeared in a collected and abridged version entitled *Undervejs til mig selv* (1943; "En Route to Myself").

Pooh *see* WINNIE-THE-POOH.

pooka or **phooka** \'pü-kə\ [Irish *púca*] A mischievous or malignant goblin or specter held in Irish folklore to appear in the form of a horse and to haunt bogs and marshes.

Poor Richard \'rich-ərd\ An unschooled but experienced homespun philosopher, a character created by Benjamin FRANKLIN. Franklin used Richard Saunders as his pen name for the annual *Poor Richard's,* an almanac he edited from 1732 to 1757. Although the Poor Richard of the early almanacs is a dim-witted and foolish astronomer, he was soon replaced by Franklin's famous Poor Richard, a country dweller, dutifully pious, quiet, and rather dull, who is a rich source of prudent and witty aphorisms on the value of thrift, hard work, and the simple life. Among his practical proverbs are "God helps those who help themselves" and "Early to bed and early to rise, makes a man healthy, wealthy, and wise."

Popa \'pō-på\, Vasko (b. June 29, 1922, Grebenac, Serbia, Kingdom of Serbs, Croats, and Slovenes [now Yugoslavia]—d. Jan. 5, 1991, Belgrade)   Serbian poet whose modernist style showed the influence of French Surrealism and Serbian folk traditions.

Popa fought with a partisan group during World War II and then studied in Vienna and Bucharest before completing his education at the University of Belgrade. He took a job as an editor in Belgrade, and in 1953 he published his first major verse collection, *Kora* ("Bark"). His other important works include *Nepočin-polje* (1956; "Field of No Rest"), *Sporedno nebo* (1968; "Secondary Heaven"), *Uspravna zemlja* (1972; *Earth Erect*), *Vučja so* (1975; "Wolf's Salt"), and *Od zlata jabuka* (1958; *The Golden Apple*), an anthology of Serbian folk literature. His *Collected Poems, 1943–76*, a compilation in English translation, appeared in 1978.

Pope \'pōp\, Alexander (b. May 21, 1688, London, Eng.—d. May 30, 1744, Twickenham, near London)   Poet and satirist of the English Augustan period.

Pope was mainly self-educated, and he soon began turning out verses in imitation of the poets he read. His first major work was AN ESSAY ON CRITICISM (1711), a poem on the art of writing. He subsequently became associated with Joseph Addison and Sir Richard Steele, the publishers of *The Spectator*. He was clearly influenced by their policy of correcting public morals by witty admonishment, and in this vein he wrote the first version of his mock-epic THE RAPE OF THE LOCK (two cantos, 1712; five cantos, 1714).

National Portrait Gallery, London

As a Roman Catholic, Pope supported Tory rather than Whig positions. His ties with the Whigs Steele and Addison gradually grew looser, and he found new and lasting friends in Tory circles. He was associated with several such men in the Scriblerus Club (1713–14), formed to write joint satires on pedantry. These were also the men who encouraged the greatest labor of his life, his verse translation of the works of Homer. The *Iliad* was completed in six volumes in 1720. The work of translating the *Odyssey* (completed in six volumes in 1726) was shared with William Broome and Elijah Fenton.

Throughout his career Pope found that the life of a wit was perpetual warfare. The fiercest of his many literary battles was fought over an edition of William Shakespeare that he published in 1725. When the scholar Lewis Theobald attacked the edition in *Shakespeare Restored* (1726), Pope replied with the mock-epic THE DUNCIAD (1728).

Pope's next important work was AN ESSAY ON MAN (1733–34), which was intended as the introductory book to a larger work on the relation of man, nature, and society. He was deflected from this project, however, by the need to defend himself again. He chose to adapt for his own defense the first satire of Horace's second book, where the ethics of satire are propounded. The success of his "First Satire of the Second Book of Horace, Imitated" (1733) led to the publication (1734–38) of 10 more paraphrases of Horatian themes adapted to contemporary society and politics. A related work is AN EPISTLE TO DR. ARBUTHNOT (1735), one of the finest of his later poems. His last completed work, *The New Dunciad* (1742), ends in a magnificent but baleful prophecy of anarchy.

Poppins, Mary \'mar-ē-'păp-inz, 'mā-rē\   Fictional character, the heroine of several children's books by P.L. TRAVERS.

Poppins is an efficient, sensible English nanny with magical powers. With humor and good-hearted firmness, she instills in her young charges a sense of wonder, as well as a respect for limits. Her magical abilities include sliding up a bannister and using her umbrella as a parachute.

The character was introduced in the book *Mary Poppins* (1934) and returned in many sequels.

Porgy \'pȯr-gē\   Novel by DuBose HEYWARD, published in 1925. Based partially on Heyward's experiences working on the wharves in Charleston, S.C., this lyrical book records the adventures of Porgy, a crippled black beggar, and his mistress Bess. Narrated in a simple, straightforward style, the authentic rendering of black life on Catfish Row led many readers to assume, mistakenly, that Heyward himself was black. In 1927, collaborating with his wife Dorothy, Heyward dramatized the book. It became the basis for the 1935 opera *Porgy and Bess*, with music by George Gershwin and libretto by Ira Gershwin and Heyward.

pornography \pȯr-'năg-rə-fē\ [Greek *pornográphos* (adjective) writing about prostitutes, from *pórnē* prostitute + *gráphein* to write]   The depiction of erotic behavior intended to cause sexual excitement. *Compare* EROTICA.

Little is known of the origins and earliest forms of pornography. One of the first clear examples of pornography in Western culture can be found in the salacious songs performed in ancient Greece at festivals honoring the god Dionysius. A classic of written pornography is the Roman poet Ovid's *Ars Amatoria* (*The Art of Love*), a treatise on the art of seduction, intrigue, and sensual arousal.

During the Middle Ages pornography was widespread but held in low repute, finding expression mostly in riddles, common jokes, doggerel, and satirical verses. A notable exception is Giovanni Boccaccio's *Decameron*, which contains several licentious stories. A principal theme of medieval pornography was the sexual license of monks and other clerics, along with their attendant displays of hypocrisy.

The invention of printing led to the rebirth of ambitious pornographic written works. They frequently contained elements of humor and romance and were written to entertain as well as to arouse. Many such works harked back to classical writings in their treatment of the joys and sorrows of marital deception and infidelity. The *Heptaméron* of Margaret of Angoulême is similar to the *Decameron* in that it uses the device of a group of people telling stories, some of which are salacious.

In 18th-century Europe there appeared the first modern works that were both devoid of literary value and designed solely to arouse sexual excitement. A small underground traffic in such works became the basis of a separate publishing and bookselling business in England. A classic of this period was John Cleland's widely read *Fanny Hill*.

Pornography flourished in the Victorian era despite, or perhaps because of, the prevailing taboos on sexual topics. A notable work of Victorian pornography is the massive and anonymous autobiography *My Secret Life* (1890), which is both a social chronicle of the underside of a puritanical society and a minutely detailed recounting of an English gentleman's lifelong pursuit of sexual gratification.

Since World War II, written pornography has been largely superseded by explicit visual representations of erotic behavior.

Porter \'pȯr-tər\, Hal (b. Feb. 16, 1911, Albert Park, Vic., Australia—d. Sept. 29, 1984, Melbourne)   Australian writer who is noted for his unusually dense and richly textured style.

Porter taught at various schools until 1951. He then worked as a librarian until he became a full-time writer.

His short stories first appeared in the *Adelaide Advertiser* in 1953 and were later published in several collections, among them *Fredo Fuss Love Life* (1974) and *The Clairvoyant Goat* (1980). Much of his work is characterized by violence, drama, and the grotesque, and Porter's emphasis is on character rather than plot. His most acclaimed novel, *The Tilted Cross* (1961), is about the 19th-century convict-artist Thomas Griffiths Wainewright. Other novels include *A Handful of Pennies* (1958) and *The Right Thing* (1971). Collections of his poems include *The Hexagon* (1956), *Elijah's Ravens* (1968), and *In an Australian Country Graveyard* (1974). Porter is best known for his successful multivolume autobiography, which includes *The Watcher on the Cast-Iron Balcony* (1963), *The Paper Chase* (1966), and *The Extra* (1975).

Porter \'pȯr-tər\, Katherine Anne (b. May 15, 1890, Indian Creek, Texas, U.S.—d. Sept. 18, 1980, Silver Spring, Md.) American novelist and short-story writer, a master stylist whose long short stories have a richness of texture and complexity of character delineation usually achieved only in the novel.

Porter worked as a journalist in Chicago and Denver, Colo., before leaving in 1920 for Mexico, the scene of several of her

Archive Photos

stories. "Maria Concepcion," her first published story (1922), was included in her first collection, FLOWERING JUDAS (1930), enlarged in 1935 by other stories.

The title story of her next collection, PALE HORSE, PALE RIDER (1939), is a poignant tale of youthful romance cruelly thwarted by the young man's death in the influenza epidemic of 1918. In it and the two other stories in the volume, "Noon Wine" and "Old Mortality," there appears for the first time her semiautobiographical heroine, Miranda, a spirited and independent woman. *The Leaning Tower* (1944) depicts in its title story a young Texas artist in Berlin during the rise of Nazism. The ascendancy of Nazism also haunts A SHIP OF FOOLS (1962), Porter's only novel.

Porter's *Collected Short Stories* (1965) won the National Book Award and the Pulitzer Prize for fiction. Her essays, articles, and book reviews were collected in *The Days Before* (1952; augmented 1970). Her last work, published in 1977, was *The Never-Ending Wrong*, dealing with the controversial murder trial (1920–27) of the anarchists Sacco and Vanzetti.

Porter \'pȯr-tər\, Peter (Nevill Frederick) (b. Feb. 16, 1929, Brisbane, Queen., Australia)   Australian-born British poet whose works are characterized by a formal style and by rueful, epigrammatic wit.

Porter's first volumes of poetry, published in the 1960s, reflect a satirical approach to modern society and to his own experiences. Among his many works are *Once Bitten, Twice Bitten* (1961), *A Porter Folio* (1969), *The Last of England* (1970), *A Share of the Market* (1973), *The Cost of Seriousness* (1978), and *English Subtitles* (1981). His *Collected Poems*, published in 1983, were praised for their "bizarre and gaudy mental landscapes." He remained prolific in his later years, writing his own poetry as well as introductions to an illustrated series of monographs on English poets. He also translated some of the poetry of Michaelangelo and, with others, edited *The Fate of Vultures: New Poetry of Africa* (1989).

Porter, William Sydney.   Real name of O. HENRY.

Porthos \'pȯr-thäs, -thȯs, *French* pȯr-'tȯs\   Fictional character, one of the heroes of THE THREE MUSKETEERS by Alexandre Dumas *père*. Porthos, like the other two musketeers, Athos and Aramis, is a swashbuckling French soldier who becomes involved in court intrigue during the reigns of Louis XIII and Louis XIV.

Portia \'pȯr-shə\   Character in William Shakespeare's comedy THE MERCHANT OF VENICE. A wealthy, spirited young woman, Portia marries the noble but impoverished Bassanio. When their friend Antonio's debt to Shylock on Bassanio's behalf cannot be paid, Shylock attempts to claim a pound of flesh. In a famous scene, Portia, disguised as a man, serves as Antonio's lawyer and manages to get Shylock to give up his claim against Antonio.

portmanteau word \pȯrt-'man-tō, ,pȯrt-man-'tō\   A word composed of parts of two or more words (such as *chortle* from *chuckle* and *snort* and *motel* from *motor* and *hotel*). The term was first used by Lewis Carroll to describe many of the unusual words in his *Through the Looking-Glass*, particularly in the poem "Jabberwocky." Other authors who have experimented with such words are James Joyce and Gerard Manley Hopkins. *Compare* NONCE WORD.

Portnoy's Complaint \'pȯrt-,nȯi\   Novel by Philip ROTH, published in 1969. The book became a minor classic of Jewish-American literature. This comic novel is structured as a confession to a psychiatrist by Alexander Portnoy, who relates the details of his adolescent obsession with masturbation and his domination by his over-possessive mother, Sophie. Portnoy's "complaint" refers to the damage done to him by the culture that has shaped him; although he is successful, his achievements are marred by a nagging sense of guilt.

Porto-Riche \pôr-tō-'rēsh\, Georges de (b. May 20, 1849, Bordeaux, Fr.—d. Sept. 5, 1930, Paris) French playwright who began as a writer of historical dramas but made his most original contribution with a number of psychological plays produced in the 1890s.

Porto-Riche came to public notice when *La Chance de Françoise* (*Françoise' Luck*) was produced in 1888. His subsequent works were acute psychological studies of what he considered to be the inevitable conflict between the sexes. His theme was sensual love, which he studied mainly in the maladjusted married couple. This is the subject of his best plays, *Amoureuse* (1891; *A Loving Wife*), *Le Passé* (1897; "The Past"), and *Le Vieil Homme* (1911; "The Old Man"), all of which examine the eternal triangle of the wife, the husband, and the lover. The so-called *théâtre d'amour* that Porto-Riche introduced was highly influential and was much imitated for some years.

Portrait of a Lady, The Novel by Henry JAMES, published in three volumes in 1881. The masterpiece of the first phase of James's career, the novel is a study of Isabel Archer, a young American woman of great promise who travels to Europe and becomes a victim of her own provincialism. It offers a shrewd appraisal of the American character and embodies the national myth of freedom and equality hedged with historical blindness and pride.

Portrait of the Artist as a Young Man, A Autobiographical novel by James JOYCE, published serially in *The Egoist* in 1914–15 and in book form in 1916; considered by many the greatest bildungsroman in the English language. The novel portrays the early years of Stephen Dedalus, who later reappeared as one of the main characters in Joyce's *Ulysses* (1922).

Each of the novel's five sections is written in a third-person voice that reflects the age and emotional state of its protagonist, from the first childhood memories written in simple, childlike language to Stephen's final decision to leave Dublin for Paris to devote his life to art, written in abstruse, Latin-sprinkled, stream-of-consciousness prose.

The novel's rich, symbolic language and brilliant use of stream-of-consciousness foreshadowed Joyce's later work. The work is a drastic revision of an earlier version entitled *Stephen Hero* and is the second part of Joyce's cycle of works chronicling the spiritual history of humans from Adam's Fall through the Redemption. The cycle began with the short-story collection *Dubliners* (1914) and continued with *Ulysses* and *Finnegans Wake* (1939).

Port-Royal \pôr-rwȧ-'yȧl\ Critical work by Charles-Augustin SAINTE-BEUVE, published in three volumes in 1840–48. It was based on a series of lectures given by Sainte-Beuve at the University of Lausanne in 1837–38. This monumental assemblage of scholarship, insights, and historical acumen—a unique work of its kind—chronicles the history of the Cistercian abbey of Port-Royal. The abbey, with its associated community of brilliant scholars and teachers, was famous in the 17th century as a center of Jansenism, a controversial movement within French Roman Catholicism. Saint-Beuve's work covers the religious and literary history of France over half of the 17th century, as glimpsed from the Jansenist perspective.

Poseidon \pō-'sīd-ən\ In Greek mythology, god of the sea and of water generally; he is to be distinguished from Pontus, the personification of the sea and the oldest Greek divinity of the waters. The name Poseidon has been taken etymologically to mean either "husband of earth" or "lord of the earth." Tra-

ditionally, he was a son of Cronus and Rhea and a brother of Zeus and Hades. When the three brothers deposed their father, the kingdom of the sea fell by lot to Poseidon. His weapon was the trident, but it may originally have been a long-handled fish spear. The Romans, ignoring his other aspects, identified him as a sea god with NEPTUNE.

Poseidon was also the god of earthquakes, and many of his oldest places of worship in Greece were inland. He was, in addition, closely associated with horses. He was the father of the winged horse Pegasus by the winged monster Medusa. Most scholars agree that Poseidon was brought to Greece as the god of the earliest Hellenes, who also introduced the first horses to the country.

position \pə-'zish-ən\ In Greek or Latin prosody, the condition of having a short vowel followed by two consonants or a double consonant (such as -*pp*- in Greek *hippos*), which makes its syllable long. Such a syllable is said to be long by position, in contrast to a syllable having a long vowel or a diphthong, which is said to be long by nature.

Possessed, The Novel by Fyodor DOSTOYEVSKY, published in Russian in 1872 as *Besy*. The book, also known in English as *The Devils* and *The Demons*, is a reflection of Dostoyevsky's belief that revolutionists possessed the soul of Russia and that, unless exorcised by a renewed faith in Orthodox Christianity and a pure nationalism, they would drive the country over the precipice. It has become a classic of Russian literature for its searing examination of human evil.

Loosely based on sensational press reports of a Moscow student's murder by fellow revolutionists, *The Possessed* depicts the destructive chaos caused by outside agitators who move into a moribund provincial town. The enigmatic Stavrogin dominates the novel. His magnetic personality influences his tutor, the liberal intellectual poseur Stepan Verkhovensky, and the teacher's revolutionary son Pyotr, as well as other radicals. Stavrogin is portrayed as a man of strength without direction, capable of goodness and nobility. When Stavrogin loses his faith in God, however, he is seized by brutal desires he does not fully understand. In the end, Stavrogin hangs himself in what he believes is an act of generosity, and Stepan Verkhovensky is received into the church on his deathbed.

postmodern \ˌpōst-'mäd-ərn\ Of or relating to any of several artistic movements that have challenged the philosophy and practices of modern arts or literature since about the 1940s. In literature this has amounted to a reaction against an ordered view of the world and therefore against fixed ideas about the form and meaning of texts. This reaction is reflected in eclectic styles of writing through the use of such devices as pastiche and parody as well as in the development of such concepts as the absurd, the antihero and the antinovel, and magic realism. The perception of the relativity of meaning has also led to a proliferation of critical theories, most notably deconstruction and its offshoots.

poststructuralism \ˌpōst-'strek-chə-rə-ˌliz-əm\ Movement in literary criticism conceived in France in the late 1960s. Based on the linguistic theories of Ferdinand de Saussure and the deconstructionist theories of Jacques Derrida, poststructuralism is centered around the idea that language is inherently unreliable and thus cannot possess absolute meaning in itself. Poststructuralists believe that all meaning resides in intertextuality, or the relationship of the text to past and future texts.

Like the practitioners of reader-response, feminist, Marxist, and psychoanalytic criticism, poststructuralists do not support the traditional Western insistence on a single correct reading of a text. Writers associated with the movement include Roland Barthes, Jacques Lacan, Julia Kristeva, and Michel Foucault. *Compare* DECONSTRUCTION; STRUCTURALISM. *See also* INTERTEXTUALITY.

Potgieter \'pȯt-ˌk̄et-ər\, Everhardus Johannes (b. June 27, 1808, Zwolle, Neth.—d. Feb. 3, 1875, Amsterdam) Dutch prose writer and poet who tried to set new literary standards and who anticipated the literary revival of the 1880s.

Potgieter was a thoroughgoing Romantic who eulogized the Holland of the 17th century. He encouraged national consciousness in the journal *De Gids* ("The Guide"), which he founded in 1837.

Potgieter's optimism is evident in *Jan, Jannetje en hun jongste kind* (1842; "Jan, Jannetje and their Youngest Child"), an allegory satirizing Dutch inertia, and in *Het Rijksmuseum* (1844), a homage to 17th-century Holland and to the prose style of Pieter Corneliszoon Hooft, which it imitates. Potgieter's subsequent work includes *Onder weg in den regen* (1864; "On the Way in the Rain"), the best of many subtle and often humorous sketches; *Florence* (1868), a long poem in tercets (three-line stanzas); and *De nalatenschap van den landjonker* (1875; "The Inheritance of the Country Squire"), a poem cycle by a fictitious aristocrat.

Potocki \pō-'tȯt-skʸē\, Wacław (b. 1621, Wola Łużeńska, Pol.—d. July 9, 1696, Łużna) Polish author of a vigorous epic poem, *Wojna chocimska* ("The Chocim War"), and of epigrams.

Potocki, a country squire with little formal education, wrote most of his verse (about 300,000 lines) to please himself. A Unitarian, he was given a choice between exile and conversion to Roman Catholicism when a decree banished all Unitarians from Poland. He chose reluctantly to convert, but his wife refused and he spent many years fearing for her life.

Wojna chocimska, finished in 1670 but not published until 1850, describes the defense of the city of Chocim in 1621 by 65,000 Poles and Cossacks against a Turkish army estimated at 400,000. Historically accurate, though idealizing the Polish heroes, the epic reveals Potocki's gift for poetic condensation. His epigrams were collected in *Ogród fraszek* (written 1670–95; published 1907; "Garden of Rhymes"). The collection gives a lively picture of ideas and manners among the gentry at a time of political and religious conflict.

Potok \'pō-tăk\, Chaim, *original name* Herman Harold Potok (b. Feb. 17, 1929, New York, N.Y., U.S.) Rabbi and author whose novels introduced to American fiction the spiritual and cultural life of Orthodox Jews.

The son of Polish immigrants, Potok was reared in an Orthodox home and attended religious schools. As a young man, he was drawn to the less restrictive Conservative doctrine; after attending Yeshiva University and the Jewish Theological Seminary, he was ordained a Conservative rabbi. He taught until he was named managing editor of *Conservative Judaism* in 1964. He further attended the University of Pennsylvania and in 1965 became editor in chief of the Jewish Publication Society. Throughout his publishing career Potok wrote scholarly and popular articles and reviews.

Potok's first novel was *The Chosen* (1967). The author established his reputation with this story of the son of a Hasidic rabbi and his friend, whose humane Orthodox father encourages him to study secular subjects. *The Promise* (1969) followed the same characters to young adulthood. Potok again turned to the Hasidim in *My Name Is Asher Lev* (1972), which tells of a young artist in conflict with the traditions of his family and community.

Potok's next four novels, the autobiographical *In the Beginning* (1975), *The Book of Lights* (1981), *Davita's Harp* (1985), and *The Gift of Asher Lev* (1990), continued to explore the conflict between religious and secular interests. *I Am the Clay* appeared in 1992, and the illustrated *The Tree of Here* in 1993. Notable among Potok's nonfiction writings is *Wanderings: Chaim Potok's History of the Jews* (1978), in which the author combines impressive scholarship with dramatic narrative.

Potter \'pät-ər\, Beatrix, *in full* Helen Beatrix Potter (b. July 28, 1866, South Kensington, Middlesex, Eng.—d. Dec. 22, 1943, Sawrey, Lancashire) English author and illustrator of children's books who created the characters Peter Rabbit, Jeremy Fisher, Jemima Puddle-Duck, Mrs. Tiggy-Winkle, and others.

Potter spent a lonely and repressed childhood enlivened only by annual holidays in Scotland or the English Lake District, which inspired her love of animals and stimulated her imaginative watercolor drawings. When she was 27, she began sending illustrated animal stories to a sick child of a former governess, and these letters about the Flopsy Bunnies, Tom Kitten, Miss Moppet, and their friends seemed to give such pleasure that she found a commercial publisher. During the next 30 years Frederick Warne & Company brought out the books that made her famous, beginning with THE TALE OF PETER RABBIT (1902), *The Tailor of Gloucester* (1902), *The Tale of Squirrel Nutkin* (1903), and *The Tale of Benjamin Bunny* (1904). The tiny books, which she designed so that even the smallest children could hold them, combined a deceptively simple prose, concealing dry north-country humor, with illustrations in the best English watercolor tradition.

Pottle \'pät-əl\, Frederick Albert (b. Aug. 3, 1897, Lovell, Maine, U.S.—d. May 16, 1987, New Haven, Conn.) American scholar who became the foremost authority on the 18th-century British biographer James Boswell.

Pottle graduated from Colby College, Waterville, Maine. He earned a Ph.D. from Yale University and taught there until his retirement in 1966. Almost all of Pottle's scholarly career was devoted to the editing and publication of Boswell's journals and letters, 13,000 pages of which were purchased by Yale in 1949. The publication of these materials under Pottle's guidance began in 1950 with *Boswell's London Journal, 1762–1763* and continued thereafter, with plans for a total of 30 to 35 volumes. Thirteen such volumes were published under Pottle's editorship. Among his other works are *James Boswell: The Earlier Years, 1740–1769* (1966; reissued 1985).

Poulet \pü-'lā\, Georges (b. Nov. 29, 1902, Chênée, Belg.) Major exponent of the *nouvelle critique* ("new criticism") in French literature that developed after World War II.

Poulet attended the University of Liège. He taught at the University of Edinburgh, Johns Hopkins University, Baltimore, Md., and the University of Zürich.

Poulet was influenced by the ideas of Gaston Bachelard, who explored the relationship of existentialism and psychology to literature. Poulet examined the perception of time in literature in his *Études sur le temps humain* (1949, reprinted 1972; *Studies in Human Time*) and the imagery of the circle in *Les Métamorphoses du cercle* (1961; *The Metamorphoses of the Circle*). Poulet's other works include *La Distance intérieure* (1952; *The Interior Distance*), *L'Espace proustien* (1963; *Proustian Space*), *Trois essais de mythologie romantique* (1966; reprinted 1971; "Three Essays on Romantic Mythology"), *Les Chemins actuels de la critique* (1968; reprinted 1973; "Contemporary Schools of Criticism"), and *La Conscience critique* (1971; "Critical Conscience").

poulter's measure \'pōl-tərz\ A meter in which lines of 12 and 14 syllables alternate. *Poulter* is a now-obsolete variant of *poulterer* (poultry dealer); poulterers would traditionally give one or two extra eggs when counting by the dozen.

Pound \'pau̇nd\, Ezra (Loomis) (b. Oct. 30, 1885, Hailey, Idaho, U.S.—d. Nov. 1, 1972, Venice, Italy) American-born poet and critic, often called the "poet's poet" because of his profound influence on 20th-century writing in English.

Pound graduated from Hamilton College, Clinton, N.Y., in 1905 and the following year received an M.A. degree from the University of Pennsylvania. After teaching briefly at a college in Indiana, he sailed for Europe. In Venice he published, at his own expense, his first book of poems, *A lume spento* (1908). He then went to England, where he published several books of poems, including *Personae*

AP/Wide World

(1909). In 1912 Pound became European correspondent for *Poetry* magazine; he was soon a dominant figure in Anglo-American verse. He also became involved with IMAGISM, editing the first Imagist anthology, *Des Imagistes*, in 1914.

After World War I Pound published two of his most important poetical works, "Homage to Sextus Propertius," in the book *Quia Pauper Amavi* (1919), and HUGH SELWYN MAUBERLEY (1920), and he then moved to Europe. He lived for four years in Paris before moving to Rapallo, Italy, which was to be his home for the next 20 years. At about this time he began publishing volumes of THE CANTOS, a series of poems he was to continue to work on throughout his life, and his compendium volume PERSONAE (1926). He also developed interests outside of literature; his investigations in the areas of culture and history led to his brilliant but fragmentary prose work GUIDE TO KULCHUR (1938). Following the worldwide depression of the 1930s, he turned more and more to history, especially economic history. He became obsessed with monetary reform, involved himself in politics, and declared his admiration for the Italian dictator Benito Mussolini.

Between 1941 and 1943, after Italy and the United States were at war, he made several hundred broadcasts over Rome Radio, often openly condemning the U.S. war effort. He was arrested by U.S. forces in 1945 and spent six months in a prison camp near Pisa. Despite harsh conditions there, he wrote *The Pisan Cantos* (1948), the most moving section of his long poem-in-progress.

Returned to the United States to face trial for treason, he was pronounced "insane and mentally unfit for trial" by a panel of doctors and spent 12 years (1946–58) in Saint Elizabeth's Hospital for the criminally insane in Washington, D.C. After he was released, he returned to Italy, where he spent the rest of his life.

Powell \'pau̇-əl\, Anthony (Dymoke) (b. Dec. 21, 1905, London, Eng.) British novelist best known for the autobiographical and satiric 12-volume series of novels A DANCE TO THE MUSIC OF TIME.

Powell attended Eton College and Balliol College, Oxford, and thereafter joined the London publishing house of Duckworth, which published his first novel, *Afternoon Men* (1931).

Powell left publishing for journalism in 1936, writing for the *Daily Telegraph* and other newspapers. He then published *What's Become of Waring?* (1939), a polished comic treatment of scandal and financial crisis within a minor publishing firm.

After serving in World War II, Powell published *John Aubrey and His Friends* (1948), a biographical study of the 17th-century author of *Brief Lives*. In 1951 he published *A Question of Upbringing*, the first part of his 12-volume series of novels. The series' first-person narrative reflects Powell's own outlook and his experiences of English society in the decades before and after World War II. Powell's later novels include *The Fisher King* (1986). He also wrote several original dramas, a book of criticism, and four volumes of memoirs.

Power and the Glory, The Novel by Graham GREENE, published in 1940. Set in Mexico during the era of anticlerical violence by revolutionaries, the story depicts the martyrdom of the last Roman Catholic priest, who is being hunted by a police lieutenant. The "whisky priest" is a degraded alcoholic who has broken most of his vows but who nevertheless insists upon performing his duties until the very end, when he is finally captured and executed. The book is a Christian parable, pitting God and religion against 20th-century materialism.

Powys \'pō-is\, John Cowper (b. Oct. 8, 1872, Shirley, Derbyshire, Eng.—d. June 17, 1963, Blaenau Ffestiniogg, Merioneth, Wales) Welsh novelist, essayist, and poet, known chiefly for his long panoramic novels, including *Wolf Solent* (1929), *A Glastonbury Romance* (1932), and *Owen Glendower* (1940). He was the brother of the authors T.F. Powys and Llewelyn Powys.

Following his education at the University of Cambridge, Powys was a lecturer for about 40 years, 30 of them in the United States. His works include the striking *Autobiography* (1934) and books of essays, among them *The Meaning of Culture* (1930), *The Pleasures of Literature* (1938), and *The Art of Growing Old* (1943).

Powys \'pō-is\, Llewelyn (b. Aug. 13, 1884, Dorchester, Dorset, Eng.—d. Dec. 2, 1939, Davos, Switz.) British author of essays, travel books, and memoirs.

Powys was the eighth of 11 children of a country clergyman. Unlike his author-brothers T.F. and John Cowper Powys, Llewelyn tended to pursue nonfiction and wrote only one novel, *Apples Be Ripe* (1930), which was a failure. His finest works were *Black Laughter* (1924), a collection of essays reflecting his experiences in Kenya from 1914 to 1919; *Skin for Skin* (1925), a philosophical narrative of his confrontation with tuberculosis (from which he suffered until his death); and *Love and Death* (1939), a partly fictionalized account of and reflection on a love affair.

Powys \'pō-is\, T.F., *in full* Theodore Francis (b. Dec. 20, 1875, Shirley, Derbyshire, Eng.—d. Nov. 27, 1953, Mappowder or Sturminster Newton, Dorset) Novelist and short-story writer whose works dealt mainly with the hardships and brutalities of rural life.

The brother of the authors John Cowper and Llewelyn Powys, he did not go to a university but rather turned to farming for several years. Thereafter he lived frugally on an allowance from his father and on his income from writing. After his marriage in 1905, he settled in Dorset and lived the life of a near-recluse until his death.

Of his eight novels, *Mr. Weston's Good Wine* (1927) is the best known. It is an allegory of the "wines" of Love and Death. His collections of short stories include *The House with the Echo* (1928) and *The White Paternoster* (1930).

practical criticism *also called* applied criticism.   Form of literary criticism with a largely implicit theoretical approach that addresses a particular work or writer. It differs from theoretical criticism in both its methodology and its goal. Early practitioners of this type of criticism included Longinus, Aristotle, and Plato. Other notable practical critics were Samuel Johnson, William Hazlitt, William Coleridge, Matthew Arnold, and Virginia Woolf.

pragmatic criticism   Critical method that judges a work by its success in achieving its intended goal. It concerns the judgment of intention as well as the analysis of an author's strategies.

Prague school \\'präg, 'präg\\, *also called* Prague Linguistic Circle.   School of structuralist linguistic thought and analysis established in Prague during the early 20th century. Among its most prominent members were the linguists Nikolay Trubetskoy and Roman Jakobson.

The Prague school is renowned for its interest in the application of functionalism—the study of how elements of a language accomplish cognition and expression—to syntax and the structure of literary texts. The members designed the first systematic formulation of linguistic structuralism based on the work of Ferdinand de Saussure and constructed a theory of poetic language that was expressed in several significant essays on literature and aesthetics, including one that Jakobson cowrote with Claude Lévi-Strauss on a poem by Charles Baudelaire.

Prairie, The   Novel by James Fenimore COOPER, published in two volumes in 1827, the third of five novels published as THE LEATHER-STOCKING TALES. Chronologically, *The Prairie* is the fifth in the series, ending with the death of the frontiersman Natty Bumppo, or Hawkeye, now an octogenarian.

The Prairie extols the vanishing American wilderness, disappearing because of the westward expansion of the American frontier. It concerns Natty Bumpppo's travels with a party of settlers across the unsettled prairie of the Great Plains. Bumppo ultimately rejects life with the settlers and goes to live out his days in a Pawnee village, away from the encroaching civilization he distrusts.

Prairie Schooner, The *also called* (after 1956) Prairie Schooner.   Quarterly literary magazine founded in 1927 by Lowry Charles Wimberly and associated with the University of Nebraska. At first the journal published only literature and criticism relevant to the Midwest, but it later adopted a broader, more national perspective, publishing authors such as Randall Jarrell, Robert Penn Warren, and Tillie Olsen. The magazine was responsible for establishing Willa Cather's reputation as a serious writer.

praise song   One of the most widely used African poetic forms; a series of laudatory epithets applied to gods, people, animals, plants, and towns that capture the essence of the object being praised. Professional bards, who may be both praise singers to a chief and court historians of their tribe, chant such praise songs. Although expected to know all of the traditional phrases handed down by word of mouth in his tribe, the bard is also free to make additions to existing poems. Thus the praise songs of Shango, the Yoruba god of thunder and lightning, may contain a modern comparison of the god to the power and noise of a railway.

Among some Bantu-speaking peoples, the praise song is an important form of oral literature. The Sotho of Lesotho traditionally required all boys undergoing initiation to compose praises for themselves that set forth the ideals of action or manhood. To the subjects used by the Sotho, the Tswana of Botswana add women, tribal groups, domestic (especially cattle) and wild animals, trees, crops, various features of the landscape, and divining bones. Their praise songs consist of a succession of loose stanzas with an irregular number of lines and a balanced metrical form.

In West Africa praise songs also have been adapted to the times, and a modern praise singer often serves as an entertainer hired to flatter the rich and socially prominent or to act as a master of ceremonies for paramount chiefs at state functions. Thus praise-song poems, though still embodying and preserving a tribe's history, have also been adapted to an increasingly urbanized and Westernized African society.

Praisesong for the Widow   Novel by Paule MARSHALL, published in 1983. Recently widowed Avey (Avatara) Johnson, a wealthy, middle-aged African-American woman, undergoes a spiritual rebirth and finds a vital connection to her past while visiting an island in the Caribbean. Marshall portrays the special anguish of certain blacks who, in their drive to achieve material success, have lost touch with their heritage. Well-received by critics, the work was often compared to the novels of Toni Morrison.

Pramudya Ananta Tur or **Pramoedya Ananta Toer** \\prä-'müd-yä-ä-'nän-tä-'tür\\ (b. Feb. 20, 1925, Blora, Java, Dutch East Indies [now in Indonesia])   Javanese novelist and short-story writer, the preeminent prose writer of postindependence Indonesia.

The son of a schoolteacher, Pramudya went to Jakarta while a teenager and worked as a typist there under the Japanese occupation during World War II. When the Indonesian revolt against renewed Dutch colonial rule broke out in 1945, he joined the nationalists, working in radio and producing an Indonesian-language magazine before he was arrested by the Dutch authorities in 1947. He wrote his first published novel, *Perburuan* (1950; *The Fugitive*), during a two-year term in a Dutch prison camp (1947–49).

After Indonesia gained independence in 1949, Pramudya produced a stream of novels and short stories that established his reputation. The novel *Keluarga gerilja* (1950; "Guerrilla Family") chronicles the tragic consequences of divided political sympathies in a Javanese family during the Indonesian revolution against Dutch rule, while *Mereka jang dilumpuhkan* (1951; "The Paralyzed") depicts the odd assortment of inmates Pramudya became acquainted with in the Dutch prison camp. His short stories were collected in *Subuh* (1950; "Dawn"), *Percikan revolusi* (1950; "Sparks of Revolution"), *Cerita dari Blora* (1952; "Tales of Blora"), and *Cerita dari Jakarta* (1957; "Tales of Jakarta"). In these early works Pramudya evolved a rich prose style that incorporates Javanese everyday speech and images from classical Javanese culture.

By the late 1950s Pramudya had become sympathetic toward the Indonesian Communist Party, and after 1958 he abandoned fiction for essays and cultural criticism that reflect a left-wing viewpoint. He was jailed by the army in the course of its bloody suppression of a communist coup in 1965. Although he was not released until 1979, during his imprisonment he wrote a series of four historical novels that further enhanced his reputation. Two of these, *Bumi manusia* (1980; *This Earth of Mankind*) and *Anak semua bangsa* (1980; *Child of All Nations*), met with great critical and popular acclaim in Indonesia after their publication, although the government subsequently banned them from circulation, and the last two volumes of the tetralogy, *Jejak langkah* (1985; *Footsteps*) and *Rumah kaca* (1988; *House of Glass*), had to be published abroad. These late works depict Javanese society under Dutch colonial rule in the early 20th century.

Prapañcā or **Prapañcha** \\prä-'pän-,chä\\ (fl. 14th century)   Indonesian court poet and historian who was born to a family of Buddhist scholars. Little is known about his life except what is revealed in the NĀGARAKERTĀGAMA (written in 1365), the work for which he is most famous. In his long narrative poem

Prapañca, the son of the Buddhist chaplain to the king of Java, recorded his observations as he traveled throughout the kingdom with his father. The work also venerates King Hayam Wuruk (reigned 1350–89), gives a detailed account of life in the kingdom of Java, and includes information about King Kertanagara (reigned 1268–92), great-grandfather of Hayam Wuruk.

Pratolini \prä-tō-'lē-nē\, Vasco (b. Oct. 19, 1913, Florence, Italy—d. Jan. 12, 1991, Rome) Italian short-story writer and novelist who is known particularly for compassionate portraits of the Florentine poor during the fascist era. He is considered a major figure in Italian Neorealism.

An illness confined Batolini to a sanatorium from 1935 to 1937, and during his confinement he began to write. After moving to Rome, he met the novelist Elio Vittorini, who introduced him into literary circles and became a close friend.

Pratolini's first important novel, *Il quartiere* (1945; *The Naked Streets*), offers a vivid, exciting portrait of a gang of Florentine adolescents. *Cronaca familiare* (1947; *Two Brothers*) is a tender story of Pratolini's dead brother. *Cronache di poveri amanti* (1947; *A Tale of Poor Lovers*), which has been called one of the finest works of Italian Neorealism, became an immediate best-seller and won two international literary prizes. *Un eroe del nostro tempo* (1949; U.S. title, *A Hero of Our Time*; U.K. title, *A Hero of Today*) attacks fascism.

Between 1955 and 1966 Pratolini published three novels covering the period 1875–1945 under the general title *Una storia italiana* ("An Italian Story"): *Metello* (1955), *Lo scialo* (1960; "The Waste"), and *Allegoria e derisione* (1966; "Allegory and Derision").

Pratt \'prat\, E.J., *in full* Edwin John (b. Feb. 4, 1883, Western Bay, Nfd., Can.—d. April 26, 1964, Toronto, Ont.) The leading Canadian poet of his time.

Pratt was trained for the ministry as a youth and taught and preached before enrolling at Victoria College of the University of Toronto, where he went on to teach until his retirement in 1953. His earliest books of poetry were *Rachel* (privately printed 1917), *Newfoundland Verse* (1923), *The Witches' Brew* (1925), and *The Titans* (1926). The latter collection contains "The Cachalot," an account of a whale hunt and one of Pratt's most brilliant and widely read poems.

Pratt reached the pinnacle of his poetic career in *Brébeuf and His Brethren* (1940), a chronicle of the martyrdom of Jesuit missionaries. Later works include *Dunkirk* (1941), *Still Life and Other Verse* (1943), *Collected Poems* (1944), *They Are Returning* (1945), *Behind the Log* (1947), and *Towards the Last Spike* (1952). *E.J. Pratt: Complete Poems* was published in 1989.

Praz \'präts\, Mario (b. Sept. 6, 1896, Rome, Italy—d. March 23, 1982, Rome) Italian literary critic and essayist, a preeminent scholar of English literature.

Praz was educated at the University of Bologna, the universities of Rome and Florence, and the British Museum in London. He taught in England before joining the faculty of the University of Rome in 1934.

Praz established his reputation with the publication of *La carne, la morte e il diavolo nella letteratura romantica* (1930; "Flesh, Death, and the Devil in Romantic Literature"), which was translated into English as *The Romantic Agony*. Among his other notable works are *Penisola pentagonale* (1928; *Unromantic Spain*), *Gusto neoclassico* (1940; *On Neoclassicism*), *Cronache letterarie anglosassoni* (1950–66; "Anglo-Saxon Literary Chronicles"), and *La crisi dell'eroe nel romanzo vittoriano* (1952; *The Hero in Eclipse in Victorian Fiction*). He also edited numerous anthologies and translated many English authors into Italian. His autobiography, *La casa della vita* (*The House of Life*), was published in 1958.

preciosity \,presh-ē-'äs-ə-tē, ,pres-\ [French *préciosité*, literally, preciousness] Fastidious or excessive refinement (as in language); specifically, the affected purism characteristic of the style of thought and expression that was prevalent in the 17th-century French salons. Initially a reaction against the coarse behavior and speech of the aristocracy, this spirit of refinement and bon ton was first instituted by the Marquise de Rambouillet in her salon and gradually extended into literature. The wit and elegance of the *honnête homme* ("cultivated man") became a social ideal, which was expressed in the vivid, polished style of Vincent Voiture's poems and letters and in the eloquent prose works of Jean-Louis Guez de Balzac. The ideal revived the medieval tradition of courtly love, as expressed in the novels of Honoré d'Urfé. The success of his *L'Astrée* (1607–27; *Astrea*), a vast pastoral set in the 5th century, was attributable as much to its charming analysis of the phases of love and the corresponding adventures and complications as to its portraits of members of contemporary society.

While the conceits and circumlocutions of the précieux, or "precious," writers were greatly admired by many, others—such as Molière in his comedy *Les Précieuses ridicules* (1659; *The Affected Young Ladies*)—mocked them for their pedantry and affectation. Preciosity in France was eventually carried to excess and led to exaggeration and affectation (particularly as reflected in burlesque writers), as it did in other countries—seen, for example, in such movements as *gongorismo* in Spain, Marinism in Italy, and euphuism in England.

Precious Bane Novel by Mary WEBB, published in 1924. The story is set in the wild countryside near the Welsh border and is narrated by Prudence Sarn, a young woman whose life has been plagued by her harelip. Prudence's defect forces her to develop an inner strength that supports her when she is betrayed both by her own brother and by the townspeople, who believe she is a witch. Critics noted Webb's use of dialect, her powerful descriptions of nature, and her depictions of rural life, with its abundant legends and superstitions.

précis \prā-'sē, 'prā-,sē\ [French, from *précis* cut short, precise] A concise epitome or abstract of a book, or a brief summary of essential points, statements, or facts.

preface \'pref-əs\ [Middle English, from Old French *prefaice*, from Latin *praefatio*, a derivative of *praefari* to say beforehand] The author's introduction to a work, usually explaining the object and scope of what follows. For works of literature, prefaces can sometimes be extended essays, such as those of Henry James and George Bernard Shaw.

Preil \'prīl\, Gabriel (b. Aug. 21, 1911, Dorpat [now Tartu], Estonia, Russian Empire—d. June 5, 1993, Jerusalem) Poet who was internationally known for his introspective and lyrical poems written in Hebrew. He was a powerful influence on younger Israeli poets both through his own works and through his translations into Hebrew of such American poets as Robert Frost, Carl Sandburg, and Robinson Jeffers.

Preil immigrated to the United States in 1922 and became a citizen in 1928. He settled in New York City, where he attended the Rabbi Isaac Elchanan Theological Seminary and the Teachers Institute (both now part of Yeshiva University). Selections from his verse were gathered in *Nof shemesh u-kefor* (1944; "Landscape of Sun and Frost"), *Ner mul kokhavim* (1954; "Candle Under the Stars"), *Mappat erev* (1960; "Map of Evening"), and *Mi-tokh zeman vanof* (1972; "Of Time and Place"). *Autumn Music* (1979) is a collection of his poems in English translation.

Prelude, The (*in full* The Prelude, or Growth of a Poet's Mind) Autobiographical epic poem in blank verse by William

WORDSWORTH, published posthumously in 1850. Originally planned as an introduction to another work, the poem is organized into 14 sections, or books. Wordsworth first began work on the poem in about 1798. It would absorb him intermittently for the next 40 years, as can be seen in the fact that the poem went through four distinct manuscript versions (1798–99, 1805–06, 1818–20, and 1832–39). *The Prelude* treats as its central subject the narrator's development as a poet, the forces that shaped his imaginative powers, and his spiritual crisis and recovery.

Premature Burial, The Short story by Edgar Allan POE, first published in *Dollar Newspaper* in July 1844.

As a frequent victim of catalepsy, the narrator has obsessive fears and horrible nightmares that he will be buried alive while comatose. As a precaution, he supplies his tomb with escape routes and provisions. Once, upon awakening, he feels trapped in a coffin not of his making. After realizing that he has fallen asleep in a ship's narrow berth, he conquers his morbid fears and suffers no further from catalepsy.

Prem Chand \'prăm-,chənd\, *pseudonym of* Dhanpat Rai Srivastava \srē-'vəs-tə-və\ (b. July 31, 1880, Lamati, near Vārānasi, India—d. Oct. 8, 1936, Vārānasi) Indian author of numerous novels and short stories in Hindi and Urdu who pioneered in adapting Indian themes to Western literary styles.

Prem Chand worked as a teacher until 1921, when he joined Mahatma Gandhi's anticolonial Noncooperation Movement. As a writer, he first gained renown for his Urdu-language novels and his contributions to Urdu journals. His first major Hindi novel, *Sēvāsadana* (1918; "House of Service"), dealt with the problems of prostitution and moral corruption among the Indian middle class. Much of Prem Chand's best work is to be found among his 250 or so short stories, collected in Hindi under the title *Mānasarovar* ("The Holy Lake"). His novels include *Premashram* (1922; "Love Retreat"), *Rangabhūmi* (1924; "The Arena"), *Ghaban* (1928; "Embezzlement"), *Karmabhūmi* (1931; "Arena of Actions"), and *Godan* (1936; *The Gift of a Cow*).

prequel \'prē-kwəl\ [*pre-* + *-quel* (as in *sequel*)] A literary or dramatic work whose story precedes that of an earlier work. For example, Lillian Hellman's play *Another Part of the Forest* (1946) portrays the earlier lives of the characters she first wrote about in *The Little Foxes* (1939) since the action of the later play takes place 20 years before that of *The Little Foxes.*

Pre-Raphaelites \,prē-'răf-ē-ə-,līts, -'răf-\ Group of young British painters, led by Dante Gabriel Rossetti, William Holman Hunt, and John Everett Millais, who banded together in 1848 in reaction against what they conceived to be the unimaginative and artificial historical painting of the Royal Academy and who sought to express a new moral seriousness and sincerity in their works. Their adoption of the name Pre-Raphaelite Brotherhood expressed their admiration for what they saw as the direct and uncomplicated depiction of nature in Italian painting before the High Renaissance. Although the group's active life lasted less than 10 years, its influence on painting in Britain, and ultimately on the decorative arts and literature, was profound.

The Pre-Raphaelite Brotherhood also functioned as a school of writers who linked the incipient Aestheticism of John Keats and Thomas De Quincey to the Decadent movement of the fin de siècle. Rossetti in particular expanded the Brotherhood's aims by linking poetry, painting, and social idealism. Rossetti combined subtle treatments of contemporary life with a new kind of medievalism, seen also in *The Defence of Guenevere* (1858) by William Morris. These writers also used medieval settings as a context that made possible an uninhibited treatment

of sex and violence. The shocking subject matter and vivid imagery of Morris' first volume were further developed by Algernon Charles Swinburne in *Atalanta in Calydon* (1865) and *Poems and Ballads* (1866).

The exquisitely wrought religious poetry of Christina Rossetti is perhaps truer to the original, pious purposes of the Pre-Raphaelite Brotherhood.

pre-Romanticism \,prē-rō-'man-ti-,siz-əm\ Cultural movement in Europe from roughly the 1740s to the 1780s that preceded and presaged the artistic movement known as Romanticism. Chief among the trends of this movement was a shift in public taste away from the grandeur, austerity, nobility, idealization, and elevated sentiments of Neoclassicism toward simpler, more sincere, and more natural forms of expression. A major intellectual precursor of Romanticism was the French philosopher and writer Jean-Jacques Rousseau.

The new emphasis on genuine emotion can be seen in the graveyard school of English poetry; Samuel Richardson's *Pamela* (1740) and other sentimental novels that exploited the reader's capacity for tenderness and compassion; the "novel of sensibility" of the 1760s, with its emphasis on emotional sensitivity and deeply felt personal responses to art and nature; the Sturm und Drang movement in Germany; the English gothic novel of terror, fantasy, and mystery; and, finally, the ambitious efforts to collect and preserve folktales and ballads of all types. By the 1790s pre-Romanticism had been supplanted by Romanticism proper.

Prešeren \,pre-'shä-ren\, France (b. Dec. 3, 1800, Vrba, Slovenia—d. Feb. 8, 1849, Kranj) The outstanding Slovene poet of the Romantic movement. His lyric poems are among the most sensitive, original, and eloquent works in Slovene.

Prešeren studied law in Vienna and later held posts in Ljubljana and Kranj as a civil servant and lawyer. Although he was not a prolific writer, his work gave new life to Slovene literature, the development of which had been checked by political and social conditions. In his *Sonetni venec* (1834; "Garland of Sonnets"), as well as in his later lyrics, he expresses the national consciousness that he sought to stimulate in his compatriots. He also wrote satirical verses and the epic poem *Krst pri Savici* (1836; "The Baptism by the Savica"), which treats the conflict between paganism and the early Slovene converts to Christianity.

preterition [Late Latin *praeteritio,* literally, act of passing by, omission, a derivative of Latin *praeterire* to pass by, omit] *see* PARALIPSIS.

Prévert \prā-'ver\, Jacques(-Henri-Marie) (b. Feb. 4, 1900, Neuilly-sur-Seine, Fr.—d. April 11, 1977, Omonville-la-Petite) French poet who composed ballads of social hope and sentimental love; he also ranked among the foremost of screenwriters, especially during the 1930s and '40s.

Under the influence of Surrealism, Prévert renewed the ancient tradition of oral poetry that led him to a highly popular form of "song poems." These were collected in *Paroles* (1945; "Words"). Many were put to music by Josef Kosma and reached a vast audience of young people who liked Prévert's anticlerical, anarchistic, iconoclastic tone that crackles with humor. Most popular is his *Tentative de description d'un dîner de têtes à Paris-France* (1931; "Attempt at a Description of a Masked Dinner at Paris, France").

He also wrote many excellent film scripts, most notably *Les Enfants du paradis* (1945; *Children of Paradise*). Collections of his poems include *Histoires* (1946; "Stories"), *Spectacle* (1951), *Grand bal du printemps* (1951; "Grand Ball of Spring"), *Charmes de Londres* (1952; "Charms of London"), and *Choses et autres* (1972; "Things and Other Things").

Prévost \prä-'vō\, Marcel, *in full* Eugène-Marcel Prévost (b. May 1, 1862, Paris, Fr.—d. April 8, 1941, Vianne) Novelist who made a sensation in France in the 1890s with stories purporting to show the corrupting effect of Parisian education and Parisian society on young women.

Prévost resigned his post as a civil engineer after the success of his first two novels, *Le Scorpion* (1887) and *Chonchette* (1888). He subsequently wrote 50 more novels, some of which were dramatized and had a moderate success on the stage. The best-known among them was entitled *Les Demi-Vierges* (1894; "The Half-Virgins"); a dramatized version of the book was a great success.

His *Lettres à Françoise* (1902; "Letters to Françoise"), *Lettres à Françoise mariée* (1908; "Letters to Françoise, Married") and *Françoise maman* (1912; "Françoise, Mama")—books of wise counsel to young girls—were even more widely read than his novels. He was elected to the Académie Française in 1909.

Prévost d'Exiles \prä-,vō-däg-'zēl\, Antoine-François, *also called* Abbé Prévost (b. April 1, 1697, Hesdin, Fr.—d. Nov. 25, 1763, Chantilly) Prolific French novelist whose fame rests entirely on one work—MANON LESCAUT (1731).

From an early age, Prévost displayed many of the weaknesses characteristic of the hero of his most famous work. Two enlistments in the army alternated with two entries into the novitiate of the Society of Jesus, from which he was dismissed in 1721. In that year he took vows as a Benedictine monk and in 1726 was ordained a priest. In 1728 he fled to England. One of his numerous love affairs caused him to lose his job there as a tutor and to go to Holland in 1730. In 1735 Prévost returned to England to escape his Dutch creditors, and he was briefly imprisoned in London for forgery. After secretly returning to France, he was reconciled with the Roman Catholic church.

Manon Lescaut, the final installment of a seven-volume novel, *Mémoires et aventures d'un homme de qualité qui s'est retiré du monde* (1728–31; "Memories and Adventures of a Man of Quality Who Has Retired from the World"), is a classic example of the 18th-century sentimental novel.

Priam \'prī-əm, -,am\ In Greek mythology, the last king of Troy. He succeeded his father, Laomedon, as king and extended his control over the Hellespont. He married first Arisbe (a daughter of Merops the seer) and then Hecuba, by whom he had many children, including his favorites, Hector and Paris. Homer described Priam as an old man, powerless but kindly, not even blaming Helen, then the wife of Paris, for his personal losses resulting from the Trojan War. In the final year of the 10-year conflict, Priam saw 13 sons die, including Hector, whose death signified the end of Troy's hopes. Priam's paternal love impelled him to brave the savage anger of Achilles and to ransom the corpse of Hector. When Troy fell, Neoptolemus, the son of Achilles, butchered the old king on an altar.

Priapea or **Priapeia** \,prī-ə-'pē-ə\ Poems in honor of the god of fertility, Priapus. Although there are ancient Greek poems addressed to him, the name *Priapea* is mainly applied to a collection of 85 or 86 short Latin poems composed in various meters. They deal with the fertility god, who, with his sickle, protected gardens and vineyards against thieves and from whose ax-hewn image of fig wood or willow there protruded an erect, red-painted phallus. The majority of the poems, marked by occasional flashes of wit and humor, are remarkable only for their extreme obscenity. Most appear to belong to the Augustan Age (*c.* 43 BC–AD 18) or to a date not much later and show evidence of indebtedness to the poet Ovid. They in turn influenced the poet Martial. Some may originally have been the leisure products of aristocratic voluptuaries; others, genuine inscriptions on shrines of Priapus.

priapean \,prī-ə-'pē-ən\ In Roman poetry, an Aeolic verse composed of a glyconic followed by a pherecrean (also known as a catalectic glyconic). A priapean is scanned ‿‾ | – ‿ ‿ – | ‿ – | ‿‾ | – ‿ ‿ – | –. The meter is so called from its use in Latin poems honoring the fertility god Priapus.

Priapus \prī-'ā-pəs\ In Greek religion, a god of animal and vegetable fertility whose cult was originally located in the Hellespontine regions, centering especially on Lampsacus. He was represented in a caricature of the human form, grotesquely misshapen, with an enormous phallus. The ass was sacrificed in his honor, probably because the ass symbolized lechery and was associated with sexual potency. In Greek mythology his father was Dionysus, the wine god; his mother was either a local nymph or Aphrodite, the goddess of love.

In Hellenistic times Priapus' worship spread throughout the ancient world. Sophisticated urban society tended to regard him with ribald amusement, but in the country he was adopted as a god of gardens, his statue serving as a combined scarecrow and guardian deity.

Price \'prīs\, Reynolds, *in full* Edward Reynolds Price (b. Feb. 1, 1933, Macon, N.C., U.S.) American writer whose stories are set in his home state of North Carolina.

Price attended Duke University in Durham, N.C., and Merton College, Oxford, before he began his long teaching career at Duke. His first novel, *A Long and Happy Life* (1961), introduced his memorable young heroine, the naive, spirited Rosacoke Mustian. Rosacoke also appears in Price's short-story collection *The Names and Faces of Heroes* (1963), and in the novel *A Generous Man* (1966) her brother Milo experiences his sexual awakening. *Good Hearts* (1988) resumes the story of Rosacoke in her middle age. Price's later novels include *Love and Work* (1968), *The Surface of the Earth* (1975), *The Source of Light* (1981), *Kate Vaiden* (1986), *The Tongues of Angels* (1990), and *Blue Calhoun* (1992). He also wrote poetry, plays, two books of memoirs, translations from the Bible, and essays. His *Collected Stories* appeared in 1993 and the autobiographical *A Whole New Life* in 1994.

Price, Fanny \'fan-ē-'prīs\ Fictional character, a poor relation of timid disposition but strong principles who goes to live with the family of Sir Thomas and Lady Bertram, her wealthy uncle and aunt, in Jane Austen's novel MANSFIELD PARK. Fanny is befriended by her cousin Edmund, who becomes a clergyman. Their friendship grows into love, first on her side, and eventually on his.

Prichard \'prich-ərd\, Katharine Susannah (b. Dec. 4, 1883, Levuka, Fiji—d. Oct. 2, 1969, Greenmount, near Perth, W.Aus., Australia) Australian novelist and writer of short stories, plays, and verse, best known for *The Pioneers* (1915; film, 1926).

Prichard's first short story was published when she was only 11 years old. She started her career as a newspaper journalist in Melbourne and Sydney and then freelanced in London, where she also worked on her plays and fiction. Deeply affected by the hunger marches during this period, she returned to Australia in 1916 and joined the Communist Party of Australia. The Marxist influence and her social consciousness remained constant throughout her career. Her skillful use of natural imagery and colloquial language are credited with helping to alter prevailing attitudes toward the Australian Aborigines.

Prichard's novels include *The Black Opal* (1921), *Working Bullocks* (1926), and *Coonardoo* (1929) and a trilogy set in the Western Australian goldfields: *The Roaring Nineties* (1946), *Golden Miles* (1948), and *Winged Seeds* (1950).

Pride and Prejudice Novel by Jane AUSTEN, published anonymously in three volumes in 1813. The narrative, which Austen initially titled "First Impressions," describes the clash between Elizabeth Bennet, the daughter of a country gentleman, and Fitzwilliam Darcy, a rich and aristocratic landowner. Austen reverses the convention of first impressions: "pride" of rank and fortune, and "prejudice" against Elizabeth's inferiority of family, hold Darcy aloof; while Elizabeth is equally fired both by the pride of self-respect and by prejudice against Darcy's snobbery. Ultimately, they come together in love and self-understanding.

Priestley \'prēst-lē\, J.B., *in full* John Boynton (b. Sept. 13, 1894, Bradford, Yorkshire, Eng.—d. Aug. 14, 1984, Alveston, near Stratford-upon-Avon, Warwickshire) British novelist, playwright, and essayist who is noted for his shrewd characterizations.

Priestley fought in World War I and studied at Trinity College, Cambridge. He thereafter worked as a journalist. His early essays were collected in *The English Comic Characters* (1925) and *The English Novel* (1927). *The Good Companions* (1929), a picaresque novel about a group of traveling performers, was a great popular success. Among his other novels are *Angel Pavement* (1930), *Bright Day* (1946), and *Lost Empires* (1965).

Priestley achieved early success on the stage with such comedies as *Laburnum Grove* (1933) and *When We Are Married* (1938). Later dramas include *Time and the Conways* and *I Have Been Here Before* (both 1937), *Johnson over Jordan* (1939), and *An Inspector Calls* (1946). He ultimately produced more than 120 books.

An adept radio speaker, he had a wide audience for his patriotic broadcasts during World War II and for his subsequent Sunday evening programs. A revival of interest in Priestley's work occurred in the 1970s, during which he produced, among other works, *Found, Lost, Found; or The English Way of Life* (1976).

Prime Minister, The Novel by Anthony TROLLOPE, published serially during 1875 and 1876 and in book form in 1876. Considered by modern critics to represent the apex of the PAL-LISER NOVELS, it is the fifth in the series and sustains two plot lines. One records the clash between the Duke of Omnium, now prime minister of a coalition government, and his high-spirited wife, Lady Glencora, whose drive to become the most brilliant hostess in society causes embarrassment for her husband and eventually contributes to his downfall. The second plot relates the machinations of Ferdinand Lopez, an ambitious social climber who wins the support of Lady Glencora—but not her husband—for an election campaign. The novel brilliantly dissects the politics of both marriage and government.

Prime of Miss Jean Brodie, The \'jēn-'brō-dē\ Novel by Muriel SPARK, published in 1961 and adapted for the stage in 1966. The story of an eccentric Edinburgh teacher who inspires cultlike reverence in her young students, the novel was Spark's best-known work. The novel explores themes of innocence, betrayal, and cold rationality opposed to unchecked emotionalism. The story of Miss Brodie's ultimate downfall is told from the unsympathetic perspective of one of her students.

Prince \'prins\, F.T., *in full* Frank Templeton (b. Sept. 13, 1912, Kimberley, Cape Province, S.Af.) British poet whose sensitive, compassionate poetry is written with precision and craftsmanship.

Prince was educated at Balliol College, Oxford, and Princeton University. He later taught in England, Jamaica, and the United States.

Soldiers Bathing and Other Poems (1954) is perhaps his best-known work. Other early poems are collected in *The Doors of Stone: Poems, 1938–1962* (1963). Prince's literary criticism includes *In Defence of English* (1959), *William Shakespeare: The Poems* (1963), and *The Italian Element in Milton's Verse* (1954). He published *Memoirs of Oxford* in verse in 1970, *Drypoints of the Hasidim* (1975), *Afterword on Rupert Brooke* (1976), and *Collected Poems* (1979).

Prince, The Political treatise by Niccolò MACHIAVELLI, published in 1513 as *Il principe*. A short treatise on how to acquire power, create a state, and keep it, the work was an effort to provide a guide for political action based on the lessons of history and his own experience as a foreign secretary in Florence. His belief that politics had its own rules so shocked his readers that the adjectival form of his surname, Machiavellian, came to be used as a synonym for political maneuvers marked by cunning, duplicity, or bad faith.

Prince and the Pauper, The Novel by Mark TWAIN, published in 1881. In it Twain satirizes social conventions, concluding that appearances often hide a person's true value. Despite its saccharine plot, the novel succeeds as a critique of legal and moral injustices.

On a lark two identical-looking boys, Prince Edward Tudor of Wales and street urchin Tom Canty, exchange clothes. In the ensuing mix-up, each is mistaken for the other and both are believed to be mad. Edward learns about the problems of commoners, while Tom learns to play the role of a prince and then a king.

Prince Caspian \'kas-pē-ən\ Children's novel by C.S. Lewis, the second in the series known as THE CHRONICLES OF NARNIA.

Prince Hal *see* HAL.

Princess, The (*in full* The Princess, A Medley) Long poem by Alfred, Lord TENNYSON, published in 1847; a third edition in 1850 added some new lyrics. Well received in its time, this odd fantasy sometimes anticipates 20th-century poetry in its fragmented, nontraditional structure. Seven young men and women gather together on a summer evening to tell the story of a princess who withdraws from the world of men to form a college for women and who does battle with a persistent suitor who invades the college. Each teller adds something new to the plot and characterization. The poem contains interludes of songs that are among the best of Tennyson's lyrics, including "Sweet and Low," "The Splendor Falls," "Tears, Idle Tears," and "Now Sleeps the Crimson Petal." Many of the lyrics have been set to music, and the poem itself was the basis for W.S. Gilbert and Sir Arthur Sullivan's satiric opera *Princess Ida* (1884).

Princess Casamassima, The \,kas-ə-'mas-i-mə, ,kaz-\ Novel by Henry JAMES, published in three volumes in 1886. In the novel James examines the anarchist violence of the late 19th century by depicting the struggle of Hyacinth Robinson, a man who toys with revolution and is destroyed by it. James offers an interesting portrait of an upper-class reformer in the character of the Princess Casamassima, who has rejected the empty social life of her husband and has become involved with reformers and proletarian groups in London.

Princesse de Clèves, La \lä-praⁿ-,ses-də-'klev\ Novel written by Marie-Madeleine, Countess de LA FAYETTE, and published anonymously in 1678. Often called France's first historical novel, the work influenced the course of French fiction. Set during the 16th-century reign of Henry II, it is the story of a virtuous young wife, the title character, who suppresses her passion for a young nobleman. With this simple story, La Fayette launched the novel of character; much more than a story of thwarted love, it is an intimate psychological portrait of a woman's personality. Many 18th- and 19th-century writers used the novel as a model; in its depiction of the princess' move from the sheltered world of her family to the world of intrigue and politics in the court, it is the prototype of the bildungsroman (novel of education).

Pringle \\'priŋ-gəl\\, Thomas (b. Jan. 5, 1789, Blaiklaw, Roxburghshire, Scot.—d. Dec. 5, 1834, London, Eng.) Scottish–South African who was often called the father of South African poetry.

Pringle was educated at the University of Edinburgh. He immigrated to South Africa in 1820 and published a newspaper and a magazine in Cape Town. His reform views eventually caused their suppression. In 1826 he returned to London, spending the rest of his life in the antislavery movement. Pringle's two verse collections, *Ephemerides* (1828) and *African Sketches* (1834), contain many notable poems dealing with the people, wildlife, and landscape of Africa. His autobiography, *Narrative of a Residence in South Africa*, appeared in 1835.

Prioress's Tale, The One of the 24 stories in THE CANTERBURY TALES by Geoffrey Chaucer.

The tale is based on an anti-Semitic legend of unknown origin that was popular among medieval Christians. The Prioress describes how a widow's devout young son is abducted by Jews, who are supposedly prompted by Satan to murder the child to stop him from singing the hymn "O Alma redemptoris" to the Virgin Mary. One of the Jews slits the boy's throat and casts his body into an open sewer. Miraculously, the boy is still able to sing and does so until his mother and a group of Christians find him. A provost condemns the guilty Jews to be executed, and before he dies the boy explains how the Virgin enabled him to continue singing after his throat was slit.

Prism, Miss \\'priz-əm\\ Fictional character, a governess and former nursemaid in Oscar Wilde's comic masterpiece THE IMPORTANCE OF BEING EARNEST.

Prisoner of Chillon, The \\shē-'yōⁿ\\ Historical narrative poem in 14 stanzas by Lord BYRON, published in 1816 in the volume *The Prisoner of Chillon, and Other Poems*. The poem concerns the political imprisonment of the 16th-century Swiss patriot François Bonivard in the dungeon of the château of Chillon on Lake Geneva. Bonivard is chained to a post next to his brothers, whom he watches die one by one. Byron's verse tale, written as a dramatic monologue in a simple, direct style, is a moving indictment of tyranny and a hymn to liberty.

Prisoner of Zenda, The \\'zen-də\\ Novel by Anthony HOPE, published in 1894. This popular late-Victorian romance relates the adventures of Rudolf Rassendyll, an English gentleman living in Ruritania who impersonates the king in order to save him from a treasonous plot. Although the story is improbable, it is saved by Hope's high-spirited and often ironic tone. The book was so successful that Hope gave up his law practice and went on to write a sequel, *Rupert of Hentzau* (1898).

Pritchett \\'prich-it\\, V.S., *in full* Sir Victor Sawdon Pritchett (b. Dec. 16, 1900, Ipswich, Suffolk, Eng.) British novelist, short-story writer, and critic known for his ironic style and his lively portraits of middle-class life.

Pritchett became a full-time journalist in 1922. He was also a literary critic for the *New Statesman* (1928–65) and occasionally wrote travel articles for the *Christian Science Monitor*. He eventually became as well known for his perceptive essays and reviews as for his penetrating and finely crafted short stories. His short stories were published in several volumes, including *You Make Your Own Life* (1938), *Collected Stories* (1956), *Blind Love and Other Stories* (1969), *More Collected Stories* (1983), and *A Careless Widow and Other Stories* (1989). He also wrote

novels, travel books, and a memoir, *Midnight Oil* (1971). Collections of his critical essays include *The Myth Makers* (1979), *A Man of Letters* (1985), *At Home and Abroad* (1989), and *Lasting Impressions* (1990). Pritchett was knighted in 1975.

Private Lives (*in full* Private Lives: An Intimate Comedy) Comedy in three acts by Noël COWARD, published and produced in 1930. This cynical comment on love and marriage is one of Coward's most brilliantly realized plays and is characterized by his trademark witty dialogue. Elyot Chase and his second wife, Sibyl, are honeymooning on the French Riviera when he discovers that his first wife, Amanda, and her second husband, Victor, have the room next to theirs. Elyot and Amanda's attraction to each other is too strong to ignore; they run off to Paris together, only to discover that their love is based on a mutual craving for violent arguments and physical brawls.

Prix Fémina \\‚prē-fä-mē-'nä\\ French literary prize for the best novel published in France each year by a man or woman. The monetary award is 5,000 French francs, and the jury consists of women of letters.

The prize was established in 1904 by the reviews *Fémina* and *Vie Heureuse* as an alternate to the Prix Goncourt, which was then unlikely to be given to works written by women. The Prix Fémina-Vacaresco for nonfiction was established in 1937, and foreign works are awarded the Prix Fémina Étranger.

Prix Goncourt \\‚prē-gōⁿ-'kür\\ One of the most important literary prizes awarded in France. It was first conceived in 1867 by the brothers Edmond and Jules de Goncourt, authors of *Journals*, and created in 1903 by a bequest of Edmond that established the Académie Goncourt, a literary society of 10 members whose chief duty it is to select the winner of the award. Along with a now-inconsiderable 50 francs, the prize confers recognition on the author of an outstanding work of imaginative prose each year; novels are preferred. The prize is awarded each November. Among the writers who have won the Prix Goncourt are Marcel Proust, André Malraux, Elsa Triolet, Simone de Beauvoir, Romain Gary, André Schwarz-Bart, Michel Tournier, and Marguerite Duras.

Prix Renaudot \\‚prē-rä-nȯ-'dō\\ French literary prize awarded to the author of an outstanding original novel published during the previous year. Named for Théophraste Renaudot (1586?–1653), who founded *La Gazette* (later *La Gazette de France*), an influential weekly newspaper, the prize was established in 1925 and first awarded in 1926. Like the Prix Goncourt, with which it competes, the Prix Renaudot is awarded annually at a ceremony in a Parisian restaurant. Its winners have included Michel del Castillo, Jean-Marie Le Clézio, Édouard Glissant, Michel Butor, Jean Cayrol, Louis Aragon, Louis-Ferdinand Céline, and Marcel Aymé.

problem play *also called* thesis play. Type of drama that developed in the 19th century to deal with controversial social issues in a realistic manner, to expose social ills, and to stimulate thought and discussion on the part of the audience.

The genre had its beginnings in the work of the French dramatists Alexandre Dumas *fils* and Émile Augier, who adapted the then-popular formula of Eugène Scribe's "well-made" play to serious subjects, creating somewhat simplistic and didactic thesis plays on subjects such as prostitution, business ethics, illegitimacy, and female emancipation. The problem play reached its maturity in the works of the Norwegian playwright Henrik Ibsen, whose works had artistic merit as well as topical relevance. He exposed the hypocrisy, greed, and hidden corruption of society in a number of masterly plays, including *A Doll's House*, *Ghosts*, *The Wild Duck*, and *An Enemy of the People*.

Ibsen's influence helped encourage the writing of problem plays throughout Europe. Other Scandinavian playwrights, among them August Strindberg, discussed sexual roles and the emancipation of women from both liberal and conservative viewpoints. Eugène Brieux attacked the French judicial system in *The Red Robe*. In England, George Bernard Shaw brought the problem play to its intellectual peak. More recent examples of problem plays are those of the Irish playwright Sean O'Casey, the South African Athol Fugard, the Americans Arthur Miller and August Wilson, and the English dramatists David Hare and Caryl Churchill.

When problem plays advocate a specific response to the problem being discussed, as in Clifford Odets' *Waiting for Lefty*, which is a plea for unionism, they are sometimes called propaganda plays.

The term problem play has also been used in a different sense to describe the plays of William Shakespeare that do not fit neatly into a category such as drama or comedy. These include *All's Well That Ends Well* and *Measure for Measure*.

proceleusmatic \ˌprŏs-ə-lūs-'mat-ik, ˌprō-sə-\ [Greek *prokeleusmatikós*, a derivative of *prokeleúein* to give orders beforehand, from *pro-* before + *keleúein* to urge, drive on, command; probably from the use of proceleusmatics in ancient Greek rowing songs] In classical prosody, a metrical foot consisting of four short syllables.

procephalic \ˌprō-sə-'fal-ik\ [Greek *proképhalos* procephalous] In classical prosody, of a dactylic hexameter (usually scanned as:

‒ ◡ ◡ | ‒ ◡ ◡ | ‒ ◡ ◡ | ‒ ◡ ◡ | ‒ ◡ ◡ | ‒ ◡),

having an extra short syllable at the beginning and scanned:

◡ | ‒ ◡ ◡ | ‒ ◡ ◡ | ‒ ◡ ◡ | ‒ ◡ ◡ | ‒ ◡ ◡ | ‒ ◡.

Procne \'präk-nē\ In Greek mythology, daughter of Pandion and sister of Philomela. *See* TEREUS.

Procopius \prō-'kō-pē-əs\ (b. probably between 490 and 507, Caesarea, Palestine [now in Israel]) Byzantine historian whose works are an indispensable source for his period.

Procopius' writings fall into three divisions: the *Polemon* (*De bellis*; *Wars*), in eight books; *Peri Ktismaton* (*De aedificiis*; *Buildings*), in six books; and the *Anecdota* (*Historia arcana*; *Secret History*), published posthumously.

The *Wars* gives of an account of the wars and conquests of the emperors Justin I and Justinian I in Persia, Africa, Sicily, and Italy. The last book contains a further summary of events down to 553. The *Buildings* tells of the chief public works undertaken during the reign of Justinian down to 560. The *Secret History* purports to be a supplement to the *Wars*, containing explanations and additions that the author could not insert into the latter work for fear of Justinian and Theodora. It is a vehement invective against these sovereigns, with attacks on Belisarius and other noted officials.

Procrustes \prō-'krəs-tēz\, *also called* Polypemon \ˌpäl-i-'pē-män\, Damastes \də-'mas-tēz\, *or* Procoptas \prō-'käp-təs\ In Greek legend, a robber dwelling somewhere in Attica—in some versions, in the neighborhood of Eleusis. Procrustes had an iron bed (or, according to some accounts, two beds) on which he compelled his victims to lie. If a victim was shorter than the bed, Procrustes hammered or racked the body in order to stretch it to fit the bed. Alternatively, if the victim was longer than the bed, he cut off the legs to make the body fit the bed's length. In either event the victim died. Ultimately Procrustes was slain by his own method at the hands of the Attic hero Theseus.

The "bed of Procrustes," or "Procrustean bed," has become proverbial for arbitrarily—and perhaps ruthlessly—forcing someone or something to fit into an unnatural scheme or pattern.

prodelision \ˌprō-di-'lizh-ən\ [Latin *prod-*, variant, before vowels, of *pro-* before, in front of + English *elision*] In classical prosody, the suppression of a short vowel at the beginning of a word when the preceding word ends with a long vowel.

Prodigal Son Biblical character who squandered his patrimony and returned to his father's home in poverty, in a parable attributed to Jesus in the Gospel According to Luke.

The younger of two sons, the destitute Prodigal Son returns home hoping to be accepted as a servant after having wasted his portion of his inheritance. When the father joyfully welcomes his wayward son, commanding that the fatted calf be slain in celebration, the elder son, who has dutifully stayed home and worked for the father, protests. The father responds that a celebration is in order when one who has been thought dead returns to life.

Prodromus \prō-'drō-məs\, Theodore, *also called* Ptochoprodromus \ˌtō-kō-prō-'drō-məs\ ("Poor Prodromus") (d. *c.* 1166) Byzantine writer well known for his prose and poetry, some of which is in the vernacular Greek.

Prodromus wrote many occasional pieces for a widespread circle of patrons at the imperial court during the reigns of John II (1118–43) and Manuel I (1143–80). Prodromus was given a prebend (stipend) by Manuel I, and he ended his life as a monk. His writings, which were often produced on the occasion of a public event, provide the historian with vital information on many aspects of contemporary history. There is a strongly satirical vein in his works, which range from epigrams and dialogues to letters and occasional pieces in both prose and verse. He had a biting sense of humor, and his comments are shrewd and pithy.

proem \'prō-ˌem, -əm\ [Latin *prooemium*, from Greek *prooímion*, from *pro-* before, in front of + *oimē* song] A preliminary discourse to a longer piece of writing or a speech; a preface or a preamble.

Proetus \prō-'ē-təs\ In Greek mythology, a king of Argos, grandson of Danaus. He quarreled with his brother Acrisius and divided the kingdom with him, Proetus taking Tiryns, which he fortified. Proetus' daughters were driven mad either because they insulted the goddess Hera or because they would not accept the new rites of Dionysus. They imagined themselves cows until the seer Melampus cured them, on condition that he be given a third of the kingdom and his brother, Bias, another third. *See also* BELLEROPHON.

Professor, The First novel written by Charlotte BRONTË. She submitted the manuscript for publication in 1847, at the same time that her sisters found publishers for their novels *Agnes Grey* and *Wuthering Heights*. Rejected for publication during the author's lifetime, it was published posthumously in 1857, with a preface by her husband, Arthur Bell Nicholls.

The Professor was based on Brontë's experiences in Brussels as a pupil and teacher at Constantin Héger's school for girls. In the novel William Crimsworth, an Englishman, becomes a teacher in Brussels and falls in love with a fellow teacher. Crimsworth is based on Héger, to whom Brontë was devoted. In her novel *Villette* (1853), she used plot material from *The Professor* and expanded the character of Crimsworth into that of Paul Emanuel.

Professor's House, The Novel by Willa CATHER, published in 1925, in which the protagonist, a university professor, confronts middle age and personal and professional loneliness.

Professor Godfrey St. Peter has completed his significant academic work on Spanish explorers in North America. His daughters have married, his favorite student has died in World War I, and his wife has moved into a new house. The professor prefers to work in his study in the garret of their old house, and there he is almost asphyxiated by a gas leak from a defective stove. He is ready to let go of life when he is saved by Augusta, an old sewing woman who shares his garret. Through Augusta's patience and friendship, he learns to accept life on its own terms.

programma \prō-'gram-ə\ *plural* programmata \-mə-tə\ A preface, especially to a learned literary work.

Prokosch \'prō-,kȯsh\, Frederic (b. May 17, 1908, Madison, Wis., U.S.—d. June 6, 1989, Plan-de-Grasse, Fr.) American writer who became famous for his early novels and whose literary stature subsequently rose as his fame declined.

By the age of 18 Prokosch had received a master's degree from Haverford College (Pa.); he received a Ph.D. from Yale and a second M.A. from the University of Cambridge. Prokosch's first novel, *The Asiatics* (1935), was the picaresque story of a young American who travels from Beirut, Lebanon, across vivid Asian landscapes to China, encountering a variety of distinctive individuals along the way. His other novels of the 1930s, especially the travel adventure entitled *The Seven Who Fled* (1937) and *Night of the Poor* (1939), were also well received. Meanwhile, with his own press he published many of his own poems. His fourth novel, *The Skies of Europe* (1941), includes a portrait of Adolf Hitler as a failed artist.

During World War II Prokosch was cultural attaché of the American legation in Sweden, and he remained in Europe after the war. There he wrote several more novels, including two additional travel adventures, *Storm and Echo* (1948) and *Nine Days to Mukalla* (1953), and *The Missolonghi Manuscript* (1968), a fictional biography of Lord Byron. In addition to publishing four volumes of original poems, he also translated poetry of Euripides, Louise Labé, and Friedrich Hölderlin. His final work, *Voices* (1983), is a memoir of his encounters with leading 20th-century literary figures.

prolegomenon \,prō-li-'gäm-ə-,nän, -nən\ *plural* prolegomena \-nə\ [Greek *prolegómenon*, neuter present passive participle of *prolégein* to say beforehand, from *pro-* before, in advance + *légein* to say] Prefatory remarks; specifically, a formal essay or critical discussion serving to introduce and interpret an extended work.

prolepsis \prō-'lep-sis\ [Greek *prólēpsis* anticipation (in rhetoric), a derivative of *prolambánein* to take in advance, anticipate] A figure of speech in which a future act or development is represented as if already accomplished or presently existing. The following lines from John Keats's "Isabella," for example, proleptically anticipate the assassination of a living character:

> So the two brothers and their murdered man
> Rode past fair Florence

The word may also refer to the anticipation of objections to an argument, a tactic aimed at weakening the force of such objections.

proletarian novel Novel that presents the lives of the working class and that springs out of direct experience of proletarian life. Early examples such as William Godwin's *Caleb Williams* (1794) or Robert Bage's *Hermsprong* (1796)—though, like Charles Dickens' *Hard Times* (1854), sympathetic to the lot of the oppressed worker—are more concerned with the imposition of reform from above than with revolution from within.

The Russian Maksim Gorky, in works such as *Foma Gordeyev* (1899) and *Mat* (1906; *Mother*), as well as many short stories portraying poverty and unemployment, may be taken as an exemplary proletarian writer. The United States has pro-

duced a rich crop of working-class fiction, including that of such socialist writers as Jack London, Upton Sinclair, John Dos Passos, and Edward Dahlberg. England, too, has produced its share of working-class novelists, such as Alan Sillitoe and John Braine.

Proletkult \prə-l^yit-'kül^yt\, *abbreviation of* Proletarskaya Kultura ("Proletarian Culture") Organization established in the Soviet Union in 1917 to provide the foundations for a truly proletarian art—*i.e.*, one that would be created by proletarians for proletarians and would be free of all vestiges of bourgeois culture. Its leading theoretician was Aleksandr Bogdanov. Subsidized by the state, but independent of Communist Party control, the Proletkult established workshops throughout the country where workers were taught to read and encouraged to write plays, novels, and poems. Although the workshops produced a few poets, their styles and techniques were invariably imitative of writers of the past. Vladimir Lenin soon realized the inadvisability of trying to force a new culture and withdrew his support. By 1923 Proletkult was abolished.

prologos \prō-'lō-,gäs\ or **prologus** \-gəs\ *plural* prologoi \-,gȯi\ *or* prologi \-,jī\ [Greek *prólogos,* a derivative of *prolégein* to say beforehand, from *pro-* before + *légein* to speak] In ancient Greek drama, the first part of the play, in which exposition or character development is presented through a monologue or dialogue. The prologos precedes the parodos, the first choral passage in the drama.

prologue or **prolog** \'prō-,lȯg, -,läg\ [Greek *prólogos* prologos] 1. The preface or introduction to a literary work. 2. A speech, often in verse, addressed to the audience by one or more of the actors at the opening of a play. *Compare* EPILOGUE. Also, the actor speaking such a prologue.

The ancient Greek prologos was of wider significance than the modern prologue, effectually taking the place of an explanatory first act. A character, often a deity, appeared on the empty stage to explain events prior to the action of the drama, which consisted mainly of a catastrophe. On the Latin stage, the prologue was generally more elaborately written, as in the case of Plautus' *Rudens*, which contains some of his finest poetry.

In England the mystery and miracle plays began with a homily. In the 16th century Thomas Sackville used a dumb show (pantomime) as a prologue to the first English tragedy, *Gorboduc*; William Shakespeare began *Henry IV, Part 2* with the character of Rumour to set the scene, and *Henry V* began with a chorus. The Plautine prologue was revived by Molière in France during the 17th century.

Though epilogues were rarely written after the 18th century, prologues have been used effectively in such 20th-century plays as Hugo von Hofmannsthal's *Jedermann* (*Everyman*), Thornton Wilder's *Our Town*, Tennessee Williams' *Glass Menagerie*, and Jean Anouilh's *Antigone*.

Prometheus \prō-'mē-thē-əs, -,thyüs\ In Greek religion, one of the Titans, the supreme trickster, and a god of fire. His intellectual side was emphasized by the apparent meaning of his name, Forethinker. In common belief he developed into a master craftsman, and in this connection he was associated with fire and the creation of mortals.

The Greek poet Hesiod related two principal legends concerning Prometheus. The first is that Zeus, who had been tricked by Prometheus into accepting the bones and fat of sacrifice instead of the meat, hid fire from mortals. Prometheus, however, stole it and returned it to Earth once again. As the price of fire, and as a general punishment for mortals, Zeus commissioned the creation of the woman Pandora and sent her down to Epimetheus ("Hindsight"), who, though warned by his brother Prometheus, married her. Pandora took the great lid off the jar she carried, and evils, hard work, and disease flew out to plague mortals. Hope alone remained within. Hesiod relates in his other tale that, as vengeance on Prometheus, Zeus had him chained and sent an eagle to eat his immortal liver, which constantly replenished itself.

Literary treatment of the Prometheus legend continued with *Prometheus Bound* by Aeschylus, who made him not only the bringer of fire and civilization but also their preserver, giving humans all the arts and sciences as well as the means of survival. Prometheus proved to be for later ages an archetypal figure of defiance against tyrannical power. Prometheus in his many aspects has been the inspiration for a large number of other writers, including Lucian, Giovanni Boccaccio, Pedro Calderón de la Barca, J.W. von Goethe, Johann Gottfried von Herder, Percy Bysshe Shelley, and Ramón Pérez de Ayala.

Prometheus Bound \prō-'mē-thē-əs, -,thyūs\ (*Greek* Promēētheus desmōtēs)   Tragedy by AESCHYLUS, the dating of which is uncertain. The play concerns the god Prometheus, who in defiance of Zeus has saved humanity with his gift of fire. For this act Zeus has ordered that he be chained to a remote crag. Despite his seeming isolation, Prometheus is visited by the ancient god Oceanus, by a chorus of Oceanus' daughters, by the "cow-headed" Io (another victim of Zeus), and finally by the god Hermes, who vainly demands from Prometheus his knowledge of a secret that could threaten Zeus's power. After refusing to reveal his secret, Prometheus is cast into the underworld for further torture.

The drama of the play lies in the clash between the irresistible power of Zeus and the immovable will of Prometheus. The most striking and controversial aspect of the play is its depiction of Zeus as a tyrant. In Homeric literature it had been taken for granted that the consequence of defying the gods was severe and inevitable punishment. In questioning the justice of Prometheus' fate and in demonstrating the wrenching choices Prometheus had to face, Aeschylus produced one of the first great tragedies of Western literature.

Prometheus Unbound \prō-'mē-thē-əs, -,thyūs\   Lyrical drama in four acts by Percy Bysshe SHELLEY, published in 1820. The work, considered Shelley's masterpiece, was a reply to Aeschylus' *Prometheus Bound*, in which the Titan Prometheus stole fire from heaven to give to mortals and was punished by Zeus (Jupiter). Shelley's heroic Prometheus strikes against oppression as represented by a power-mad Jupiter. This brilliant but uneven work represented the culmination of the poet's lyrical gifts and political thought.

Prometheus, tortured, is tempted to yield to Jupiter's tyranny but instead forgives him. In this act, Shelley suggests, lies his salvation. Panthea and her sister Asia, symbol of ideal love, decide to free Prometheus by confronting Demogorgon, the volcanic power of the underworld, who vanquishes Jupiter in a violent eruption. Prometheus is reunited with his beloved Asia, and the liberation of human society is foretold. The last act describes this joyful transformation but warns that evil must be checked lest tyranny reign once more.

proode \'prō-,ōd\ [Greek proōidós, from *pro-* before, in front of + ōidē ode]   **1.** A distich with the first line shorter than the second—opposed to *epode*.   **2.** A strophic unit in an ancient ode preceding the strophe and antistrophe and differing from them in structure.

propaganda novel *also called* thesis novel.   A sometimes didactic work that addresses a specific social problem.

propaganda play   A type of PROBLEM PLAY that advocates a specific solution to the conflict dramatized.

proparoxytone \,prō-,pär-'ăk-si-,tōn\ [Greek *proparoxýtonos*, from *pro-* before + *paroxýtonos* paroxytone]   Having or characterized by an acute accent or a heavy stress on the antepenultimate syllable.

Propertius \prō-'pər-shəs, -shē-əs\, Sextus (b. 55–43 BC, Assisium, Umbria [now Assisi, Italy]—d. after 16 BC, Rome)   The greatest elegiac poet of ancient Rome.

The first of Propertius' four books of elegies (the second of which is divided by some editors into two) was published in 29 BC, the year in which he first met his mistress "Cynthia," its heroine. It was known as the *Cynthia* and also as the *Monobiblos*, because it was for a long time afterward sold separately from his other three books.

As Propertius' poetic powers matured with experience, so did his character and interests. In his earliest elegies, love is not only his main theme but is also his religion and philosophy. It is still the principal theme of Book II, but in the latter book he makes clear his concern that he might be considered simply as a gifted scoundrel who is constantly in love and can write of nothing else. In Book II he contemplates writing an epic, is preoccupied with the thought of death, and attacks (in the manner of later satirists, such as Juvenal) the coarse materialism of his time. Although some of his contemporaries accused him of idleness and chided him for contributing little to society, Propertius in elegy 3 of Book III speaks of the significance of the creative process and asserts the artist's great value in human society. In Books III and IV Propertius demonstrates his command of various literary forms, including the diatribe and the hymn. Many of Propertius' verses show the influence of such Alexandrian poets as Callimachus and Philetas. Propertius acknowledges this debt, and his claim to be the "Roman Callimachus," treating Italian themes in the baroque Alexandrian manner, is perhaps best shown in a series of elegies in Book IV that deal with aspects of Roman mythology and history.

Ancient writers valued Propertius' *blanditia*, a vague but expressive word by which they meant softness of outline, warmth of coloring, a fine and almost voluptuous feeling for beauty of every kind, and a pleading and melancholy tenderness. A second and even more remarkable quality is his poetic *facundia*, or command of striking and appropriate language. Not only is his vocabulary extensive but his employment of it is also extraordinarily bold and unconventional.

Prophet, The   Book of 26 poetic essays by Khalil GIBRAN, published in 1923. A best-selling book of popular mysticism, *The Prophet* was translated into more than a dozen languages. Gibran's narrative frame relates that the Prophet, about to board a ship that will take him home after 12 years in a foreign city, is stopped by a group of the city's inhabitants, who ask him to speak to them about the mysteries of life. He does so, discussing love, marriage, beauty, reason and passion, and death, among other topics. Although many critics thought Gibran's poetry mediocre, *The Prophet* achieved cult status among American youth for several generations.

prosaic \prō-'zā-ik\   **1.** Characteristic of prose as distinguished from poetry, *i.e.*, factual or literal.   **2.** Having a dull, flat, unimaginative quality of style or expression.

prose \'prōz\ [Latin *prosa*, short for *prosa oratio*, literally, straightforward speech]   A literary medium distinguished from poetry especially by its greater irregularity and variety of rhythm and its closer correspondence to the patterns of everyday speech. Although prose is readily distinguishable from poetry in that it does not treat a line as a formal unit, the significant differences between prose and poetry are of tone, pace, and object of attention. *Compare* POETRY.

prose poem A work in prose that has some of the technical or literary qualities of a poem (such as regular rhythm, definitely patterned structure, or emotional or imaginative heightening) but that is set on a page as prose.

The form was introduced into French literature by Louis Bertrand, with his *Gaspard de la nuit* (1842; "Gaspard of the Night"). His poetry attracted little interest at the time, but his influence on the Symbolists at the end of the century was acknowledged by Charles Baudelaire in his *Petits Poèmes en prose* (1869; later titled, as Baudelaire intended, *Le Spleen de Paris*). It was this work that gave the form its name, and the *Divagations* (1897) of Stéphane Mallarmé and *Illuminations* (1886) of Arthur Rimbaud firmly established prose poetry in France. Other turn-of-the-century poets who wrote prose poetry were Paul Valéry, Paul Fort, and Paul Claudel.

Prose poems were written in the early 19th century by the German poets Friedrich Hölderlin and Novalis and at the end of the century by Rainer Maria Rilke. The 20th century saw a renewed interest in the form in such works as Pierre Reverdy's *Poèmes en prose* (1915) and in the works of the French poet Saint-John Perse. Amy Lowell's polyphonic prose is a type of prose poetry.

Proserpina \prō-'sər-pi-nə\ or **Proserpine** \'präs-ər-,pin, *in Milton's work* prō-'sər-pin\ *see* PERSEPHONE.

prosodiac \prō-'sō-dē-,ak\ [Greek *prosodiakós* of a prosodion] *see* ENOPLION.

prosodion \prə-'sō-dē-ən\ [Greek *prosódion,* from neuter of *prosódios* processional, a derivative of *prósodos* approach, procession] A procession song that was a form of ancient Greek choral lyric.

prosodist \'präs-ə-dist, 'präz-\ A specialist in prosody.

prosody \'präs-ə-dē, 'präz-\ [Medieval Latin *prosodia* observance of the correct accent and quantity of words in reading and writing, from Latin, accent of a syllable, from Greek *prosōidía* variation in pitch, pronunciation of a syllable on a given pitch, from *pros-* toward, in addition to + *ōidḗ* song] The metrical structure of poetry and the study of such structure.

This study has led to the classification of verse according to metrical structure. The four most common forms of versification are QUANTITATIVE VERSE, which is the system of classical Greek and Latin poetry; SYLLABIC VERSE, used in Romance languages and Japanese; ACCENTUAL VERSE, which is used mainly in Germanic poetry, including Old English and Old Norse; and ACCENTUAL-SYLLABIC VERSE, which is considered the traditional prosody of English literature as it dominated that poetry from the 16th to the 19th century and is still commonly used.

The terminology of "traditional" English prosody was established by Renaissance theorists who sought to impose the rules of classical prosody on vernacular English forms. They merely succeeded in redefining, in classical terms, the elements of an already existing syllable-stress meter.

Nonmetrical prosody is a feature of modern poetry, although many critics deny that it is possible to write poetry without employing some kind of meter. Visual prosodies have been fostered by movements such as Imagism and by such experimenters as E.E. Cummings, who revived the practice of some Metaphysical poets in "shaping" the verse by typographical arrangement.

Prosody entails several important elements other than meter. Rhyme scheme, for example, is one of a variety of effects, including alliteration and assonance, that influence the total "sound meaning" of a poem. Very often, prosodic study involves examining the subtleties of a poem's rhythm, its "flow," a quality rooted in such elements as accent, meter, and tempo but not synonymous with them.

Prosody also takes into account a consideration of the historical period to which a poem belongs, the poetic genre, and the poet's individual style. Finally, the term prosody encompasses the theories that have been developed through the ages about the value of structure: from the emphasis on decorum in the classical age, which identified certain meters as suitable only for particular subjects; to Renaissance formulations of laws restricting modern verse to classical meters; to the 18th-century insistence on the notion that the movement of sound and meter should represent the actions they carry; to Gerard Manley Hopkins' controversial theories of sprung rhythm based on the natural stress of words. Since the publication in 1906–10 of George Saintsbury's *A History of English Prosody*, the subject has been a respected part of literary study. *See also* METER; SCANSION.

prosopopoeia \,prä-sə-'pō-pē-ə, ,prō-\ [Greek *prosōpopoiía,* from *prósōpon* face, person, character + *poieîn* to make] A figure of speech in which an imaginary or absent person is represented as speaking or acting. The word is also sometimes used as a synonym for PERSONIFICATION.

prospect poem Subcategory of TOPOGRAPHICAL POETRY that considers a particular landscape as viewed from an elevated vantage point.

Prospero \'präs-pə-rō\ Fictional character, the rightful Duke of Milan, in the play THE TEMPEST by William Shakespeare.

protagonist \prō-'tag-ə-nist\ [Greek *prōtagōnistḗs,* from *prôtos* first + *agōnistḗs* actor, contestant] In ancient Greek drama, the first or leading actor. The poet Thespis is credited with having invented tragedy when he introduced this first actor into Greek drama, which formerly consisted only of choric dancing and recitation. The protagonist stood opposite the chorus and engaged in an interchange of questions and answers. The term protagonist has since come to be used for the principal character in a novel, story, drama, or poem.

protasis \'prät-ə-sis\ *plural* protases \-,sēz\ [Late Greek *prótasis,* from Greek, something put forward, proposition, problem] **1.** The introductory part of a play or narrative poem; specifically, in a drama, the introduction or part that precedes the EPITASIS. *Compare* CATASTASIS. **2.** The subordinate clause of a conditional statement.

Proteus \'prō-,tyüs, -tē-əs, -,tüs\ In Greek mythology, the prophetic old man of the sea and shepherd of the sea's flocks (*e.g.*, seals). He was subject to the sea god Poseidon. Proteus knew all things—past, present, and future—but those who wished to consult him had first to surprise and bind him during his noonday slumber. Because he had the power to assume whatever shape he pleased, Proteus came to be regarded by some as a symbol of the original matter from which the world was created.

Proulx \'prü\, E. Annie, *in full* Edna (b. Aug. 22, 1935, Norwich, Conn., U.S.) American writer whose darkly comic yet sad fiction was peopled with quirky, memorable individuals and unconventional families.

After publication of her first short-story collection, *Heart Songs and Other Stories* (1988), Proulx turned to writing novels, which better accommodated her dense plots and complex characterizations. *Postcards* (1992), her first novel, used the device of picture postcards mailed from the road over 40 years' time to illustrate changes in American life. In *The Shipping News* (1993), the protagonist Quoyle and his dysfunctional family of two young daughters and a sensible old aunt leave the United States and settle in Newfoundland after the accidental death of his unfaithful wife. *The Shipping News* was awarded both the Pulitzer Prize and the National Book Award.

Proust \'prüst\, Marcel (b. July 10, 1871, Auteuil, Fr.—d. Nov. 18, 1922, Paris) French novelist, author of *À la recherche du temps perdu* (REMEMBRANCE OF THINGS PAST), a novel based on Proust's life, told psychologically and allegorically and often in a stream-of-consciousness style.

Bettmann Archive

Proust, who suffered from asthma throughout his life, attended the Lycée Condorcet and studied at the École des Sciences Politiques. His social connections permitted him to become an observant habitué of the most exclusive drawing rooms of the nobility. In 1896 he published *Les Plaisirs et les jours* (*Pleasures and Days*), a collection of short stories at once precious and profound, most of which had appeared during 1892–93 in the magazines *Le Banquet* and *La Revue Blanche*. From 1895 to 1899 he worked on an autobiographical novel that remained unfinished. A gradual disengagement from social life coincided with growing ill health and with his active support of the movement in 1897–99 to liberate the Jewish army officer Alfred Dreyfus.

At least one early version of Proust's novel was written in 1905–06. Another, begun in 1907, was laid aside in October 1908. This had itself been interrupted by a series of brilliant parodies of Proust's favorite French writers, called "L'Affaire Lemoine" (published in *Le Figaro*). He then wrote *Contre Sainte-Beuve* ("Against Sainte-Beuve"), attacking the French critic's view of literature as a pastime of the cultivated intelligence. In January 1909 there occurred the real-life incident of an involuntary revival of a childhood memory through the taste of tea and a rusk biscuit (which in his novel became madeleine cake), and in July he again began work on *À la recherche du temps perdu*. He retired from the world to write the novel, finishing the first draft in September 1912. Work on the seven-part novel, which brought Proust worldwide fame, occupied the last decade of his life.

proverb \'präv-ərb\ [Latin *proverbium,* from *pro-* before, in front of + *verbum* word] Succinct and pithy saying that is in general use and that expresses commonly held ideas and beliefs. Proverbs are part of every spoken language and folk literature, originating in oral tradition. Often, the same proverb may be found in many variants in different parts of the world, and certain stylistic similarities have been found in proverbs from the same part of the world.

Most literate societies have valued their proverbs and collected them for posterity. There are ancient Egyptian collections dating from as early as 2500 BC. Sumerian inscriptions give grammatical rules in proverbial form. Proverbs were used in ancient China for ethical instruction, and the Vedic writings of India used them to expound philosophical ideas. The biblical Book of Proverbs, traditionally associated with Solomon, actually includes sayings from earlier compilations.

One of the earliest English proverb collections, *The Proverbs of Alfred* (c. 1150–80), contains religious and moral precepts. Proverbs in literature and oratory were at their height in England in the 16th and 17th centuries, used by such practitioners

as John Heywood and Michael Drayton. In North America the best-known collection of proverbs is probably that of *Poor Richard's*, an almanac published annually between 1732 and 1757 by Benjamin Franklin.

Provincetown Players \'präv-ins-ˌtaůn\ Theatrical organization that began performing in 1915 in Provincetown, Mass., U.S. It was founded by a nontheatrical group of writers and artists whose common aim was the production of new and experimental plays. Among the original Provincetowners who staged the first plays in members' homes were Mary Heaton Vorse, George Cram Cook, Susan Glaspell, Hutchins Hapgood, Wilbur Steele, and Robert Edmond Jones.

The group, which took up residence in New York City's Greenwich Village in 1916, discovered and developed the work of such noted writers as Eugene O'Neill, Floyd Dell, Edna St. Vincent Millay, and Paul Green. The Provincetown Players flourished as a noncommercial theater until its demise in 1929.

Prudentius \prü-'den-shē-əs, -shəs\, *in full* Aurelius Clemens Prudentius (b. AD 348, Caesaraugusta [Spain]—d. after 405) Christian Latin poet whose *Psychomachia* ("The Contest of the Soul"), the first completely allegorical poem in European literature, was immensely influential during the Middle Ages.

Prudentius practiced law, held two provincial governorships, and was awarded a high position by the Roman emperor Theodosius. From about 392 he wrote poems on Christian themes. He published a collection of his poems with an autobiographical preface in 405.

Among his many works are the *Cathemerinon* ("Book in Accordance with the Hours"), which comprises 12 lyric poems on various times of the day and on church festivals; the *Apotheosis*, directed against disclaimers of the Trinity and the divinity of Christ; the *Hamartigenia* ("The Origin of Sin"), which attacks Gnostic dualism; and the *Psychomachia*, which describes the struggle of faith, supported by the cardinal virtues, against idolatry and the corresponding vices. He is best known today for writing the lyric for the Christmas plainsong hymn *Divinum Mysterium* ("Of the Father's Love Begotten") and a hymn for Epiphany, "Earth Has Many a Noble City," both from the *Cathemerinon*.

Prudhomme *see* SULLY PRUDHOMME.

Prufrock, J. Alfred \'jā-'al-frid-'prü-ˌfräk\ Fictional character, the indecisive middle-aged man in whose voice T.S. Eliot wrote the dramatic monologue THE LOVE SONG OF J. ALFRED PRUFROCK.

Prus \'prüs\, Bolesław, *pseudonym of* Aleksander Glowacki \gwō-'våt-skʸē\ (b. Aug. 20, 1847, Hrubieszów, Pol., Russian Empire—d. May 19, 1912, Warsaw) Polish journalist, short-story writer, and novelist, one of the leading figures of the positivist period in Polish literature following the failed uprising of 1863.

Throughout much of his life Prus contributed articles called "chronicles" to daily papers and periodicals; these reveal his talent for detailed observation and lively presentation. Among the best known of his tales are *Z legend dawnego Egiptu* ("A Legend of Old Egypt"), *Kamizelka* ("The Waistcoat"), and *Katarynka* ("The Barrel-Organ"). His novels include *Lalka* (1890; *The Doll*), which gives a complex picture of contemporary bourgeois life in Warsaw, and *Faraon* (1897; *The Pharaoh and the Priest*), an ambitious evocation of ancient Egypt.

Prynne, Hester \'hes-tər-'prin\ A fictional character, long-suffering, ennobled protagonist of THE SCARLET LETTER by Nathaniel Hawthorne.

Przyboś \'pshib-ōshʸ\, Julian (b. March 5, 1901, Gwóznica, Rzeszów, Austrian Empire [now in Poland]—d. Oct. 6, 1970,

Warsaw, Pol.)   Polish poet, a leading figure of the Awangarda Krakowska, an avant-garde literary movement that began in Kraków in 1922.

By 1924 Przyboś had begun to publish poetry and prose for the little magazine *Zwrotnica* ("The Switch"), one of the primary vehicles of the Awangarda Krakowska. In his early works, *Śruby* (1925; "Screws") and *Oburącz* (1926; "Twin Grasp"), he introduced his theory of poetry as a new language system characterized by concise but intricate metaphors. In the 1930s he turned to themes of social protest in such collections as *W głąb las* (1932; "Into the Deep Forest") and *Równanie serca* (1938; "Equation of the Heart"). He also wrote for the journal *Linia* ("Line") from 1931 to 1933 and was a member of a group called a.r. ("revolutionary artists") in Łódź from 1930 to 1935.

During World War II, Przyboś wrote poems for the Resistance movement. After the war he served the Polish government as a diplomat and as an emissary to Switzerland (1947–51) and as chairman of the Writers' Union. His postwar verse was published in *Rzut pionowy* (1952; "Vertical Movement"), *Najmniej słów* (1955; "The Minimum of Words"), *Narzędzie ze światła* (1958, "Tools of Light"), and *Próba całości* (1961, "A Try for Completeness"). He was also noted for his critical essays on literature and art.

Przybyszewski \pshi-bi-'shef-sk^yē\, Stanisław (b. May 7, 1868, Łojów, German Poland—d. Nov. 23, 1927, Jaronty, Pol.)   Polish essayist, playwright, and poet.

After attending a German school at Toruń, Przybyszewski in 1889 moved to Berlin, where he became closely associated with a German-Scandinavian artistic circle. In 1898 he settled in Kraków, took over the editorship of *Życie* ("Life"), and became a leader of the Polish modernists.

Przybyszewski's poetry displays a passionate, sensual mysticism, while his prose works describe unusual psychological types and the ambivalence of eroticism. His unconventional philosophical writings and plays enjoyed a meteoric but ephemeral success. His autobiography, *Moi współcześni*, 2 vol. (1926–30; "My Contemporaries"), is an interesting, if not very reliable, account of Central European culture at the turn of the century.

Psalms \'sämz, 'sälmz, 'sòmz, 'sòlmz\   Book of Hebrew literature composed of sacred songs, or of sacred poems meant to be sung. In the Hebrew Bible, the Tehillim ("Songs of Praise") begin the Ketuvim (Writings), the third and last section of the biblical canon. In its present form, the Book of Psalms consists of 150 poems divided into five books (1–41, 42–72, 73–89, 90–106, 107–150), the first four of which are marked off by concluding doxologies (expressions of praise to God). Psalm 150 serves as a doxology for the entire collection. The psalms themselves range in mood and expression of faith from joyous celebration to solemn hymn and bitter protest. They are sometimes classified according to form or type; the major forms include the hymn, the lament, the song of confidence, and the song of thanksgiving. They may also be classified according to subject matter and their use. The dating of individual psalms poses an extremely difficult problem, as does the question of their authorship. They were evidently written over a number of centuries, from the early monarchy to after the Babylonian exile (586–538 BCE).

pseudepigraphy \ˌsü-də-'pig-rə-fē\ [Greek *pseudepígraphos* spuriously titled, not genuine, from *pseudēs* false + *epigráphein* to entitle, ascribe]   The ascription of false names of authors to works, a practice intended to lend to the writings an authority that they would otherwise lack.

Pseudo-Longinus   *see* LONGINUS.

pseudonym \'sü-də-ˌnim\ [Greek *pseudónymos* under a false name, from *pseudēs* false + *ónyma, ónoma* name]   A fictitious name, especially a pen name or such a name used by an author.

Psichari \psē-kä-'rē\, Ernest (b. Sept. 27, 1883, Paris, Fr.—d. Aug. 22, 1914, Rossignol, Belg.)   French writer and soldier whose works combine militaristic sentiments with a semimystical religious devotion.

Psichari's journey toward an acceptance of religious faith was encouraged by the French Roman Catholic intellectuals Maurice Barrès, Charles Péguy, and Jacques Maritain. *L'Appel des armes* (1913; "The Call to Arms"), a military novel that became a guide for nationalist youth before World War I, recorded his experiences as a soldier in Africa (1906–12). He became a Catholic in 1913 and prepared himself for the priesthood, but he was killed at the front in an early engagement of World War I. His autobiographical novel, *Le Voyage du centurion* (1916; "The Voyage of the Centurion"), deals with his conversion while in Africa.

Psyche \'sī-kē\ (Greek: "Soul")   In classical mythology, princess of outstanding beauty who aroused Venus' jealousy and Cupid's love. The fullest version of the tale is that told by the Latin author Lucius Apuleius in his *Metamorphoses* (*The Golden Ass*).

According to Apuleius, the jealous Venus commanded her son Cupid (the god of love) to inspire Psyche with love for the most despicable of men. Instead, Cupid placed Psyche in a remote palace where he could visit her secretly and in total darkness, until one night Psyche discovered Cupid's identity and he fled. Wandering the earth in search of him, Psyche fell into the hands of Venus, who imposed upon her difficult tasks. Finally, touched by Psyche's repentance, Cupid rescued her, and, at his instigation, Jupiter made her immortal and gave her in marriage to Cupid.

psychoanalytic criticism   Literary criticism that uses psychoanalytic theory to analyze readers' responses to literature, to interpret literary works in terms of their authors' psychological conflicts, or to recreate authors' psychic lives from unconscious revelations in their work.

Psychoanalytic criticism originated with the theories of Sigmund Freud. Freud himself was the first to employ this approach in the analysis of literature; other Freudian critics included Ernest Jones, Otto Rank, and Marie Bonaparte. Developments in psychoanalytic theory were reflected in the different approaches to criticism that evolved. Carl Jung's concept of the collective unconscious, which assumes universally similar responses to archetypal human situations, influenced such works as *Archetypal Patterns in Poetry* (1934) by Maud Bodkin and *A Jungian Approach to Literature* (1984) by Bettina L. Knapp. "Ego-psychology," as developed by Norman N. Holland in *The Dynamics of Literary Response* (1968) and *5 Readers Reading* (1975), is an aspect of psychoanalytic criticism that studies how readers respond to texts. Freud was reinterpreted by Norman O. Brown in *Life Against Death* (1959) and *Love's Body* (1966) and by linguist Jacques Lacan, who, in turn, influenced many later critics, including feminist critics Julia Kristeva, Hélène Cixous, and Luce Irigaray.

psychobiography \ˌsī-kō-bī-'äg-rə-fē, -bē-\   A biography written from a psychodynamic or psychoanalytic point of view. Examples include the psychoanalyst Erik Erikson's biographies of Martin Luther and Mohandas Gandhi, Marie Bonaparte's work on Edgar Allan Poe, and Phyllis Greenacre's *Swift and Carroll* (1955), on Jonathan Swift and Lewis Carroll.

psychological novel   Work of fiction in which the thoughts, feelings, and motivations of the characters are of equal or greater interest than is the external action of the narrative. In a psychological novel the internal states of the characters are influenced by and in turn trigger external events. Events may not be presented in chronological order, but rather as they occur in the character's thought associations, memories, fantasies, reveries, contemplations, and dreams.

An overtly psychological approach is found among many novels written from the 18th century on, including Samuel Richardson's *Pamela* (1740), Laurence Sterne's *Tristram Shandy* (1759–67), and the works of Fyodor Dostoyevsky, Leo Tolstoy, George Eliot, and George Meredith. It was not until the 20th century that the psychological novel reached its full potential. Its development coincided with, though it was not necessarily caused by, the growth of interest in psychology and the theories of Sigmund Freud. The detailed recording of the impingement of external events on individual consciousness as practiced by Henry James, the associative memories called up by Marcel Proust, the stream-of-consciousness technique of James Joyce and William Faulkner, and the continuous flow of experience as presented by Virginia Woolf were arrived at relatively independently.

Ptochoprodromus *see* PRODROMUS.

puck \'pək\ [Old English *pūca*] In medieval English folklore, a malicious fairy or demon. In Elizabethan lore he was a mischievous, brownielike fairy, also called Robin Goodfellow or Hobgoblin; he was one of the leading characters in William Shakespeare's *Midsummer Night's Dream*. The Irish pooka, or *púca*, and the Welsh *pwcca* are similar household spirits. *See also* BROWNIE; POLTERGEIST.

Pudd'nhead Wilson \'pùd-ən-,hed-'wil-sən\ (*in full* The Tragedy of Pudd'nhead Wilson, and the Comedy of Those Extraordinary Twins) Novel by Mark TWAIN, originally published as *Pudd'nhead Wilson, A Tale* (1894). A story about miscegenation in the antebellum South, the book is noted for its grim humor and its reflections on racism and responsibility.

Roxana, a light-skinned mixed-race slave, switches her baby with her white owner's baby. Her natural son, Tom Driscoll, grows up in a privileged household to become a criminal who finances his gambling debts by selling her to a slave trader and who later murders his putative uncle. Meanwhile, Roxy raises Valet de Chambre as a slave. David ("Pudd'nhead") Wilson, an eccentric lawyer, determines the true identities of Tom and Valet. As a result Roxy is exposed, Wilson is elected mayor, Tom is sold into slavery, and Valet, unfitted for his newly won freedom, becomes an illiterate, uncouth landholder.

Puig \pói-'ēg, 'pwēg\, Manuel (b. Dec. 28, 1932, General Villegas, Arg.—d. July 22, 1990, Cuernavaca, Mex.) Argentine novelist and motion-picture scriptwriter who achieved international critical and popular acclaim with the publication of *El beso de la mujer araña* (1976; KISS OF THE SPIDER WOMAN).

Puig learned English as a child by seeing every American film he could. He drew upon his childhood for his first novel, *La traición de Rita Hayworth* (1968; BETRAYED BY RITA HAYWORTH), a semiautobiographical account of a boy who escapes the boredom of living on the Pampas by fantasizing about the lives of the stars he has seen in motion pictures. The style of his second novel, *Boquitas pintadas* (1969; "Painted Little Mouths"; *Heartbreak Tango*), parodies the serialized novels popular in Argentina. *The Buenos Aires Affair* (1973) is a detective novel describing the psychopathic behavior of characters who are sexually repressed. *El beso de la mujer araña* is a novel told in dialogues between a middle-aged homosexual and a younger revolutionary who are detained in the same jail cell.

For his novels exploring sexuality and for his overt homosexuality, Puig was branded immoral in Argentina. His later books

include *Pubis angelical* (1979; "Angelic Pubis") and *Maldición eterna a quien lea estas páginas* (1980; ETERNAL CURSE ON THE READER OF THESE PAGES).

Pulci \'pül-chē\, Luigi (b. Aug. 15, 1432, Florence [Italy]—d. November? 1484, Padua, Republic of Venice) Italian poet whose name is chiefly associated with one of the outstanding epics of the Renaissance, *Morgante*, in which French chivalric material is infused with a comic spirit. The use of the ottava rima stanza for the poem helped establish this form as a vehicle for works of a mock-heroic, burlesque character.

For many years Pulci lived under the protection of the Medici family until, at age 38 or 40, he entered the service of a condottiere (mercenary), Roberto Sanseverino. Pulci's masterpiece is the *Morgante*, or *Morgante Maggiore*, an epic in 23 cantos, later expanded to 28, begun about 1460, of which the earliest surviving complete edition is dated 1483.

Pulcinella *see* PUNCH.

Pulitzer Prize \'pül-it-sər, 'pyül-\ Any of a series of annual prizes awarded by Columbia University, New York City, for outstanding public service and achievement in American journalism, letters, and music. Fellowships are also awarded. The prizes, originally endowed with a gift of $500,000 from the newspaper magnate Joseph Pulitzer, are highly esteemed and have been awarded each May since 1917. The awards in letters are for fiction, drama, U.S. history, biography or autobiography, verse, and nonfiction not covered by another category.

pun \'pən\ [perhaps from Italian *puntiglio* quibble, fine point], *also called* paronomasia \,par-ə-nō-'mā-zhə, ,par-,ăn-ə-, -zhē-ə\ A humorous use of a word in such a way as to suggest different meanings or applications, or a play on words, as in the use of the word *rings* in the following nursery rhyme:

> Ride a cock-horse to Banbury Cross,
> To see a fine lady upon a white horse;
> Rings on her fingers and bells on her toes,
> She shall have music wherever she goes.

Common as jokes and in riddles, puns may be used seriously, as in John Donne's "A Hymne to God the Father":

> Sweare by thy selfe, that at my death thy sonne
> Shall shine as he shines now, and heretofore;
> And, having done that, Thou haste done;
> I fear no more.

This quatrain contains two puns, *son/sun* and *done/Donne*.

Punch \'pənch\, *in full* Punchinello \,pən-chi-'nel-ō\, *also called* Pulcinella \,pül-chē-'nel-lä\ Hook-nosed, humpbacked character, the most popular of marionettes and glove puppets and the chief figure in the Punch-and-Judy puppet show. Brutal, vindictive, and deceitful, he is usually at odds with authority. His character had roots in the Roman clown and the comic country bumpkin. More modern origins can be traced to Pulcinella, a character who appeared in the Italian COMMEDIA DELL'ARTE in the 17th century. Polichinelle, the French adaptation of the character, had become firmly established in France by the middle of the 17th century. Diarist Samuel Pepys made the first reference to Punch in England, in 1662. By 1700 practically every puppet show in England featured Punch, and his wife, Judy, originally called Joan, was also a well-known figure. Puppets such as Petrushka (Petrouchka) in Russia developed from the same origins as Punch.

Punch \'pənch\ (*in full* Punch, or the London Charivari \,shär-ē-'vär-ē, shə-'riv-ə-rē\) English illustrated periodical published from 1841 to 1992, famous for its satiric humor, caricatures, and cartoons. The first editors of what was then a weekly radical paper were Henry Mayhew and Mark Lemon. Among the most famous early members of the staff were the authors

William Makepeace Thackeray and Thomas Hood and the illustrator-cartoonists John Leech and Sir John Tenniel.

puppetry \\'pəp-i-trē\\   The making and manipulation of puppets for use in a theatrical show. A puppet is a figure—human, animal, or abstract in form—that is moved by human, and not mechanical, aid. From its beginnings in tribal society, puppetry has been part of every subsequent civilization. *See also* BUNRAKU.

Purāṇa \\pū-'rä-nə\\   In Hindu sacred literature, any of a number of popular encyclopedic collections of myth, legend, and genealogy, varying greatly as to date and origin. *Purāṇa* is the nominalized form of a Sanskrit adjective meaning "old, ancient."

A *Purāṇa* traditionally treats five subjects: primary creation of the universe, secondary creation after periodic annihilation, genealogy of gods and saints, grand epochs, and history of the royal dynasties. Dating from the period AD 400 to 1000, *Purāṇas* are written almost entirely in narrative couplets in much the same easy, flowing style as epic poems.

The 18 principal surviving *Purāṇas* are often grouped loosely according to whether they exalt Vishnu, Śiva (Shiva), or Brahmā. The main *Purāṇas* are usually regarded as (1) the *Viṣṇu-, Nāradīya-, Bhāgavata-, Garuḍa-, Pādma-,* and *Varāha-Purāṇas*; (2) the *Mātsya-, Kūrma-, Liṅga-, Śiva-, Skanda-,* and *Agni-Purāṇas*; and (3) the *Brāhmāṇḍa-, Brahmavaivarta-, Mārkandeya-, Bhaviṣya-, Vāmana-,* and *Brāhma-Purāṇas*. By far the most popular is the BHĀGAVATA-PURĀṆA, which in its treatment of the early life of Krishna had profound influence on the religious beliefs of India. There are also 18 "lesser" *Purāṇas*, or *Upapurāṇas*, that treat similar material and a large number of *sthala-Purāṇas* (or *māhātmyas*) glorifying temples or sacred places.

Purdy \\'pər-dē\\, Al, *in full* Alfred Wellington Purdy (b. Dec. 30, 1918, Wooler, Ont., Can.)   Canadian poet whose erudite, colloquial verse often dealt with the transitory nature of human life.

Purdy's early poetry, collected in *The Enchanted Echo* (1944), *Pressed on Sand* (1955), and *Emu, Remember!* (1956), was conventional and sentimental, but his maturation as a poet was evident in *The Crafte So Longe to Lerne* (1959), *Poems for All the Annettes* (1962), *The Blur in Between* (1962), and *The Cariboo Horses* (1965), a collection of allusive and energetic verse.

The influence of his extensive travels is reflected in many of the poems in the collections *North of Summer* (1967), *Wild Grape Wine* (1968), *Sex and Death* (1973), and *Birdwatching at the Equator* (1982). Poems about his native Ontario are featured in the collections *In Search of Owen Roblin* (1974), *Being Alive* (1978), and *Morning and It's Summer* (1983). His other books of poetry include *Hiroshima Poems* (1972), *Piling Blood* (1984), and *The Woman on the Shore* (1990). In 1990 he published his first novel, *A Splinter in the Heart.*

Purdy \\'pər-dē\\, James (b. July 17, 1923, Ohio, U.S.)   American novelist and short-story writer whose works present a vision of human alienation, indifference, and cruelty.

Purdy's first two works—*Don't Call Me by My Right Name and Other Stories* (1956) and the novella *63: Dream Palace* (1956)—were initially rejected for publication and were privately printed, but later met with critical acclaim.

Purdy's fiction examines the relationships between individuals and the effects of family life. *Malcolm* (1959) is about a 15-year-old boy in a fruitless search for his identity. In *The Nephew* (1960) and *Cabot Wright Begins* (1964), Purdy further develops the bleak worldview that he first propounded in *Malcolm*. In the trilogy *Sleepers in Moon-Crowned Valleys*—consisting of *Jeremy's Vision* (1970), *The House of the Solitary Maggot*

(1974), and *Mourners Below* (1981)—he explores small-town American life and destructive family relationships. Purdy also wrote the novels *I Am Elijah Thrush* (1972), *In a Shallow Grave* (1975), and *Candles of Your Eyes* (1986) and several collections of stories, plays, and poems.

pure poetry   Message-free verse that is concerned with exploring the essential musical nature of the language rather than with conveying a narrative or didactic purpose. The term has been associated particularly with the poems of Edgar Allan Poe. Others who have experimented with the form include Stéphane Mallarmé, Paul Verlaine, Paul Valéry, Juan Ramón Jiménez, and Jorge Guillén.

purism \\'pyŭr-,iz-əm\\ [French *purisme,* a derivative of *pur* pure]   Rigid adherence to or insistence on purity or nicety (as in literary style or use of words). This can refer to an insistence on following fine points of grammar, diction, or style, or it can apply to an effort to purify a language in terms of excluding foreign terms.

Purloined Letter, The   Short story by Edgar Allan POE, first published in an unauthorized version in 1844. An enlarged and authorized version was published in *The Gift* (an annually published gift book containing occasional verse and stories) in 1845 and was collected the same year in Poe's *Tales.*

The Paris police prefect approaches amateur detective C. Auguste Dupin with a puzzle: a cabinet minister has stolen a letter from a woman of royalty whom he is now blackmailing. Despite a painstaking search of the minister's rooms, the police find nothing. When the prefect returns a month later and mentions a large reward for the letter, Dupin casually produces the document. Dupin later explains to his assistant, the story's narrator, that by analyzing the personality and behavior of the minister, he correctly concluded that the letter would be hidden in plain sight.

While the story has been traditionally regarded as an early prototype of detective fiction, it has also been the subject of intense scholarly debate, notably between French philosopher Jacques Derrida, who upheld the story as a model of ambiguous narrative, and French psychoanalyst Jacques Lacan, who maintained that it was a sexual allegory.

purple passage or **purple patch**   1. A passage conspicuous for brilliance or effectiveness in a work that is dull, commonplace, or uninspired.   2. *chiefly British*   A piece of obtrusively ornate writing.

The phrase "purple patch" is a translation from a metaphor in Horace's *Ars poetica*: "Inceptis gravibus plerumque et magna professis / purpureus, late qui splendeat, unus et alter / adsuitur pannus" ("One or two purple patches, which gleam far and wide, are often sewn onto works that were begun seriously and promise many things."). Horace had in mind ornate descriptive passages that violated the stylistic unity of a long narrative poem. The splendor of purple cloth, associated with wealth and power, was proverbial.

Pushkin \\'pūsh-kᵧin, *Angl* 'pŭsh-kən\\, Aleksandr (Sergeyevich) (b. May 26 [June 26, New Style], 1799, Moscow, Russia—d. Jan. 29 [Feb. 10], 1837, St. Petersburg)   Russian author who has often been considered his country's greatest poet and the founder of modern Russian literature.

Pushkin was born into an aristocratic family and attended the Imperial Lyceum at Tsarskoye Selo (later renamed Pushkin), where he began his literary career with the publication in 1814 of his verse epistle "To My Friend, the Poet." While at the Lyceum he also began his first completed major work, the romantic poem *Ruslan i Lyudmila* (1820; RUSLAN AND LUDMILA).

In 1817 Pushkin accepted a post in the foreign office at St. Petersburg, where he was elected to Arzamas, an exclusive literary circle founded by his uncle's friends. Pushkin also became

Mary Evans Picture Library

associated with those who were to take part in the Decembrist uprising of 1825, the unsuccessful culmination of a Russian revolutionary movement in its earliest stage.

For his political poems, in May 1820 Pushkin was banished from St. Petersburg to a remote southern province. There he gathered material for his "southern cycle" of romantic narrative poems: *Kavkazsky plennik* (1820–21; "The Prisoner of the Caucasus"), *Bratya razboyniki* (1821–22; "The Robber Brothers"), and *Bakhchisaraysky fontan* (1823; "The Fountain of Bakhchisaray"). These poems confirmed him as the leading Russian poet of the day and as the leader of the Romantic generation of the 1820s. In May 1823 he started work on his central masterpiece, the novel in verse *Yevgeny Onegin* (1833; EUGENE ONEGIN), on which he continued to work intermittently until 1831.

Pushkin had meanwhile been transferred first to Kishinyov and then to Odessa, and he eventually was again exiled to his mother's estate near Pskov. There he embarked on a close study of Russian history, folktales, and songs. His ballad "Zhenikh" (1825; "The Bridegroom"), based on motifs from Russian folklore, dates from this period, as do *Tsygany* (1824; "The Gypsies"), begun earlier as part of the southern cycle; the provincial chapters of *Yevgeny Onegin*; the poem "Graf Nulin" (1827; "Count Nulin"); and his great historical tragedy BORIS GODUNOV (1831).

The new czar, Nicholas I, allowed Pushkin to return to Moscow in the autumn of 1826. The poet abandoned his revolutionary sentiments and turned to the age of reform at the beginning of the 18th century and to the figure of Peter the Great, whose example he held up to the new czar in the poem "Stansy" (1826; "Stanzas"), in *Arap Petra Velikogo* (1827; *The Negro of Peter the Great*), in the historical poem *Poltava* (1829), and in the poem *Medny vsadnik* (1837; THE BRONZE HORSEMAN).

Because of problems with censorship, Pushkin felt obliged to justify his political position in the poem "Druzyam" (1828; "To My Friends"). The anguish of his spiritual isolation at this time is reflected in a cycle of poems about the poet and the mob (1827–30) and in the unfinished *Yegipetskiye nochi* (1835; "Egyptian Nights"). During this period he wrote the short story "Pikovaya dama" (1834; THE QUEEN OF SPADES); the

four so-called little tragedies: *Skupoy rytsar* (1836; "The Covetous Knight"), *Motsart i Salyeri* (1831; *Mozart and Salieri*), *Kamenny gost* (1839; THE STONE GUEST), *Pir vo vremya chumy* (1832; "Feast in Time of the Plague"); the five short prose tales collected as *Povesti pokoynogo Ivana Petrovicha Belkina* (1831; *Tales of the Late Ivan Petrovich Belkin*); the comic poem of everyday lower-class life *Domik v Kolomne* (1833; "A Small House in Kolomna"); and many lyrics in widely differing styles.

In 1831 Pushkin settled in St. Petersburg. Alongside the theme of Peter the Great, the motif of a popular peasant rising acquired growing importance in his work, as is shown by the unfinished satirical *Istoriya sela Goryukhina* (1837; *The History of the Village of Goryukhino*); the unfinished novel *Dubrovsky* (1841); and finally, the most important of his prose works, the historical novel of the Pugachov Rebellion, *Kapitanskaya dochka* (1836; *The Captain's Daughter*), which had been preceded by a historical study of the rebellion, *Istoriya Pugachova* (1834; "A History of Pugachov").

Pushkin Prize \\'pŭsh-kʸin, *Angl* 'pŭsh-kən\\ Russian literary prize established in 1881 in honor of Aleksandr Pushkin, one of Russia's greatest writers. The prize was awarded to Russian (later Soviet) authors who achieved the highest standard of literary excellence, as exemplified by the prize's namesake. Winners have included Anton Chekhov and Ivan A. Bunin.

Pu Songling or **P'u Sung-ling** \\'pü-'sŭŋ-'liŋ\\ (b. June 5, 1640, Zichuan, Shandong province, China—d. Feb. 25, 1715, Zichuan) Chinese fiction writer whose *Liaozhai zhiyi* (1766; *Strange Stories from a Chinese Studio*) resuscitated the classical genre of short stories.

Pu lived and died as an obscure provincial schoolteacher. When his work was first printed some 50 years after his death, it was immensely popular, inspiring many imitations and creating a new vogue for classical stories. Pu is credited with having adapted several of his tales into "drum songs," a popular dramatic form of the time. His courtesy name is Liuxian or Jianchen.

Pu's impressive collection of 431 tales of the unusual and supernatural was largely completed by 1679, though he added stories to the manuscript as late as 1707. The work departed from the prevailing literary fashion that was dominated by more realistic *huaben* stories written in the colloquial language. Pu instead wrote his stories in the classical idiom, freely adopting forms and themes from the old *chuan qi*, or "marvel tales," of the Tang and Song dynasties.

Puss in Boots Fictional character, the cat in the fairy tale of the same name (in French, "Le Maître Chat ou le chat botté"), as retold by Charles PERRAULT in *Contes de ma mère l'oye* (*Tales of Mother Goose*). The brash Puss in Boots tricks an ogre into transforming himself into a mouse, which Puss promptly gobbles up, so that Puss's master can appropriate the ogre's wealth and win the hand and heart of a beautiful princess. *See also* MOTHER GOOSE.

putative author The author of a work as defined in the work rather than the actual author, or the person or character said to be the author of the work when this is different from the actual author. For example, in William Makepeace Thackeray's *The Newcomes* the character Arthur Pendennis is the narrator and supposed author of the work.

Putnam \\'pət-nəm\\, Samuel (Whitehall) (b. Oct. 10, 1892, Rossville, Ill., U.S.—d. Jan. 15, 1950, Lambertville, N.J.) American editor, publisher, and author best known for his translations of works by authors in Romance languages.

After incomplete studies at the University of Chicago, Putnam worked for various Chicago newspapers and became a literary and art critic for the Chicago *Evening Post* (1920–26). Moving to Europe in 1927, he founded and edited the critical magazine *The New Review* (1931–32) and translated numerous works by French and Italian writers.

Returning to the United States in 1933, Putnam contributed regularly to such left-wing magazines as *Partisan Review*, the *New Masses*, and *The Daily Worker* until the mid-1940s, when his interests shifted to Latin-American and Spanish literature. His authoritative translation of Euclides da Cunha's Brazilian prose epic *Os sertões* appeared in 1944 under the title *Rebellion in the Backlands*, and in 1949 his translation of Miguel Cervantes' *Don Quixote*, on which he had spent 17 years, appeared to high praise. Putnam's survey of the history of Brazilian literature, entitled *Marvelous Journey*, was published in 1948. *Paris Was Our Mistress* (1947) depicts the American expatriate community in Paris in the 1920s and '30s.

Putrament \pū-'trȧ-ment\, Jerzy (b. Nov. 14, 1910, Minsk, Russia—d. June 23, 1986, Warsaw, Pol.)   Polish poet, novelist, journalist, and editor who was also active in politics.

Putrament worked as a journalist during the 1930s, when he was arrested and tried as a communist. His first novel, *Rzeczywistość* (1947; "Reality"), draws on the experiences of his trial. His acclaimed early poetry collections *Wczoraj powrót* (1935; "Yesterday the Return") and *Droga leśna* (1938; "Forest Road") combine sensitivity to his native countryside with his dedication to revolutionary politics. During World War II Putrament escaped to the Soviet Union, where he cofounded the Union of Polish Patriots. He later served in several government posts.

Altogether Putrament wrote some 50 fictional works. Among his best-known writings were the political novels *Rozstaje* (1954; "At the Crossroads") and *Małowierni* (1967; "Those of Little Faith") and the wartime novel *Bołdyn* (1969). As editor of two literary journals he exercised considerable influence on cultural policy from the 1960s onward.

Puttenham \'pət-ən-əm\, George (b. *c.* 1520—d. autumn 1590, London, Eng.)   English courtier, generally acknowledged as the author of the anonymously published *The Arte of English Poesie* (1589), one of the most important critical works of the Elizabethan age.

Little is definitely known of his early life. His knowledge of law and public affairs is shown by *A Justificacion of Queen Elizabeth in Relacion to the Affair of Mary Queen of Scottes*, undertaken at the queen's request and anonymously circulated, but attributed to Puttenham in two of eight extant copies of the manuscript. Puttenham's authorship of *The Arte of English Poesie*—early attributed to him but later disputed in favor of his brother, Richard, and of Lord Lumley—is supported by stylistic and biographical comparisons.

The *Arte* is divided into three books: I, "Of Poets and Poesy," defending and defining poetry; II, "Of Proportion," dealing mainly with prosody as an indispensable formal element of the art of poesy; and III, "Of Ornament," defined as all that renders poetic utterance attractive to eye and ear. The work's importance lies in its treatment of English poetry as an art at a time when this issue was still disputed; in its appeal to "right reason" as the best judge of poetry and the poetic technique; and in its emphasis on the creative, imitative, and "image-forming" faculties of the poet and on poetry's primary purpose as giving pleasure rather than instruction. In its treatment of English prosody and of poetic forms and in its critical estimate of a broad range of English poetry, it is a pioneer work.

Pye \'pī\, Henry James (b. Feb. 20, 1745, London, Eng.—d. Aug. 11, 1813, Pinner, Middlesex)   British poet laureate from 1790 to 1813.

Pye served in Parliament from 1784 to 1790 and became a police magistrate. Fancying himself a poet, he published many volumes of verse; he was made poet laureate in 1790, perhaps as a reward for his faithful support of William Pitt the Younger in the House of Commons. The appointment was looked on as ridiculous, and his birthday odes were a continual source of derision. His most elaborate poem was the epic *Alfred* (1801). Perhaps his most worthy piece was the prose work *Summary of the Duties of a Justice of the Peace Out of Sessions* (1808).

Pygmalion \pig-'māl-yən, -'mā-lē-ən\   In Greek mythology, a king of Cyprus who fell in love with a statue of the goddess Aphrodite. The Roman poet Ovid, in his *Metamorphoses*, invented a more sophisticated version: Pygmalion, a sculptor, made an ivory statue representing his ideal of womanhood and then fell in love with his own creation; the goddess Venus brought the statue to life in answer to his prayer.

Later works give the statue's original substance as marble and name the statue/woman Galatea. The legend has been appropriated by many later authors, notably George Bernard Shaw.

Pygmalion \pig-'māl-yən, -'mā-lē-ən\   Romance in five acts by George Bernard SHAW, produced in German in 1913 in Vienna and in England in 1914, with Mrs. Patrick Campbell as Eliza Doolittle. The play is a humane comedy about love and the English class system.

Henry Higgins, a phonetician, accepts a bet that simply by changing the speech of a Cockney flower seller he will be able, in six months, to pass her off as a duchess. An apt, hardworking pupil, Eliza undergoes grueling training. When she successfully "passes" in high society—having in the process become a lovely young woman of sensitivity and taste—Higgins dismisses her abruptly as a successfully completed experiment. Eliza, who now belongs neither to the upper class nor to the lower class, rejects his dehumanizing attitude.

pygmy or **pigmy** \'pig-mē\ [Greek *Pygmaîoi* (plural), from *pygmaîos* dwarfish, literally, as tall as one *pygmē* (a measure of length, the distance from the elbow to the knuckles)]   One of a fabled race of dwarfs described by ancient Greek authors.

Pyle \'pīl\, Howard (b. March 5, 1853, Wilmington, Del., U.S.—d. Nov. 9, 1911, Florence, Italy)   American illustrator, painter, and author who is best known for his children's books.

Pyle's magazine and book illustrations are among the finest of the turn-of-the-century period in the Art Nouveau style. Many of his children's stories, illustrated by the author with vividness and historical accuracy, have become classics—most notably *The Merry Adventures of Robin Hood* (1883); *Otto of the Silver Hand* (1888); *Jack Ballister's Fortunes* (1895); and his own folktales, *Pepper & Salt* (1886), *The Wonder Clock* (1888), and *The Garden Behind the Moon* (1895).

Pym \'pim\, Barbara (Mary Crampton) (b. June 2, 1913, Oswestry, Shropshire, Eng.—d. Jan. 11, 1980, Oxford)   English novelist, a recorder of post-World War II upper-middle-class life, whose elegant and satiric comedies of manners are marked by poignant observation and psychological insight.

Pym edited the anthropological journal *Africa* for more than 20 years. In her novels she depicted the quiet, uneventful surface of her characters' lives in order to describe human loneliness and the corresponding impulse to love. Her works include *Some Tame Gazelle* (1950), *Excellent Women* (1952), *A Glass of Blessings* (1958), *Quartet in Autumn* (1977), *The Sweet Dove Died* (1978), *A Few Green Leaves* (1980), and *An Unsuitable Attachment* (1982). *A Very Private Eye* (1984) comprises her diaries and letters edited as an autobiography.

Pynchon \'pin-chən\, Thomas (b. May 8, 1937, Glen Cove, Long Island, N.Y., U.S.)   American novelist and short-story writer whose works combine black humor and fantasy to depict human alienation in the chaos of modern society.

Pynchon's first novel, V (1963), is a cynically absurd tale of a middle-aged Englishman's search for "V," an elusive, supernatural adventuress. In his next book, *The Crying of Lot 49* (1966), Pynchon described a woman's strange quest to discover the mysterious, conspiratorial Tristero System in a futuristic world of closed societies. Pynchon's masterpiece, GRAVITY'S RAINBOW (1973), another novel based on the idea of conspiracy, is filled with descriptions of paranoid fantasies, grotesque imagery, and esoteric mathematical language. Pynchon's next novel, *Vineland*, was not published until 1990.

Of his few short stories, most notable are "Entropy" (1960), a neatly structured tale in which Pynchon first used extensive technical language and scientific metaphors, and "The Secret Integration" (1964; collected in *Slow Learner*, 1984), which explores small-town bigotry and racism.

pyŏlgok \\'pyŏl-'gŭk\\, *also called* changga \\'chän-gä\\ [Korean] Korean poetic form that flourished during the Koryŏ period (935–1392). Of folk origin, the *pyŏlgok* was sung chiefly by women, and it was intended for performance on festive occasions. The theme of most of these anonymous poems is love. The *pyŏlgok* is characterized by the presence of a refrain either in the middle or at the end of each stanza. The refrain not only establishes a mood or tone that carries the melody and spirit of the poem but also serves to link the discrete parts and contents of the poem. The *pyŏlgok* entitled "Tongdong" ("Ode on the Seasons") and "Isanggok" ("Winter Night") are among the most moving love lyrics in the Korean language.

Pyramid Texts Collection of Egyptian mortuary prayers, hymns, and spells intended to protect a dead king or queen and to ensure life and sustenance in the hereafter. The texts, inscribed on the walls of the inner chambers of the pyramids, are found at Ṣaqqārah (15 miles south of Cairo) in several 5th- and 6th-dynasty pyramids. The texts, which are thought to have been written between about 2350 and about 2100 BC, constitute the oldest surviving body of Egyptian religious and funerary writings.

Pyramus and Thisbe \\'pir-ə-məs . . . 'thiz-bē\\ Hero and heroine of a Babylonian love story told by Ovid in his *Metamorphoses*. Though their parents refuse to consent to their union, the lovers resolve to flee together and agree to meet under a mulberry tree. Thisbe, first to arrive, is terrified by a lioness, and in her haste to leave she drops her veil, which the lioness tears to pieces with jaws stained with the blood of an ox. Pyra-

mus, upon finding the veil, believes that she has been devoured by the lioness and stabs himself. When Thisbe returns and finds her lover mortally wounded under the mulberry tree, she kills herself. From that time forward, legend relates, the fruit of the mulberry, previously white, was purplish black.

The story of Pyramus and Thisbe was reexamined and retold by such authors as Marie de France in her "Lai de Piramos e Tisbe," William Shakespeare in *A Midsummer Night's Dream*, Luis de Góngora in his parody romance *La fábula de Píramo y Tisbe*, and Théophile de Viau in his tragedy *Pyrame et Thisbé*.

pyrrhic \\'pir-ik\\ [Greek (*poùs*) *pyrrhíchios*, a derivative of *pyrríchē*, a type of dance performed by armed men] In prosody, a foot consisting of two short or unaccented syllables.

pythiambic \\,pith-ē-'am-bik, pith-ī-\\ In classical Latin prosody, a distich, or pair of lines, composed of a pythian, or dactylic hexameter, line followed by an iambic dimeter or trimeter. This distich was used in the *Epodes* of Horace following such Greeks as Archilochus. As Archilochus used it, the iambic line was usually catalectic, or missing the final syllable. In its acatalectic form it scans as:

$$- \cup \cup | - \cup \cup | - \cup \cup | - \cup \cup | - \underset{\smile}{} $$
$$\underset{\smile}{} - \cup - | \underset{\smile}{} - \cup - \text{ (dimeter)}$$
or
$$- \cup \cup | - \cup \cup | - \cup \cup | - \cup \cup | - \underset{\smile}{} $$
$$\cup - \cup - | \cup - \cup - | \cup - \cup - \text{ (trimeter).}$$

Pythian \\'pith-ē-ən\\ Of or relating to Delphi or its oracle of Apollo. Pytho (or Python) was an ancient name for the vicinity of Delphi and was associated with the mythical serpent Python.

Pythian verse \\'pith-ē-ən\\ In classical prosody, name formerly given to dactylic hexameter verse because that was the meter used in the Pythian, or Delphic, oracles. It scans as:

$$- \underset{\smile}{\smile} \underset{\smile}{\smile} | - \underset{\smile}{\smile} \underset{\smile}{\smile} | - \underset{\smile}{\smile} \underset{\smile}{\smile} | - \underset{\smile}{\smile} \underset{\smile}{\smile} | - -,$$

where one long can always substitute for two short syllables and the last foot is invariably a spondee. *See* PYTHIAMBIC.

Pythias *see* DAMON AND PYTHIAS.

Python \\'pī-,thän, -thən\\ In Greek mythology, a huge serpent that was killed by the god Apollo at Delphi either because it refused to let Apollo found an oracle there, being accustomed itself to giving oracles, or because it had persecuted Apollo's mother, Leto, during her pregnancy.

pythoness \\'pīth-ə-nəs, 'pith-\\ [Late Latin *pythonissa*, a derivative of Latin *Pytho, Python* Delphi, the Delphic oracle, from Greek *Pythō, Pythōn*] **1.** A woman who practices divination. **2.** A prophetic priestess of Apollo.

Q Pseudonym of Sir Arthur Thomas QUILLER-COUCH.

Qabbānī, Nizār \\nē-'zär-käb-'bä-,nē\\ (b. March 21, 1923, Damascus, Syria) Syrian diplomat and poet whose subject matter, at first strictly erotic and romantic, grew to embrace political issues as well.

Qabbānī studied law at the University of Damascus, then began his varied career as a diplomat. He served in the Syr-

ian embassies in Egypt, Turkey, Lebanon, Britain, China, and Spain before retiring in 1966 and moving to Beirut, Lebanon, where he founded a publishing company. Meanwhile, he also wrote much poetry, at first in classic forms, then in free verse, which he helped establish in modern Arabic poetry. His poetic language is noted for capturing the rhythms of everyday Syrian speech.

Verses on the beauty and desirability of women filled Qabbānī's first four collections. *Qasā'id min Nizār Qabbānī* (1956; "Poems by Nizār Qabbānī") was a turning point in his art; in it he expressed resentment of male chauvinism. It also included his famed "Bread, Hashish and Moon," a harsh attack on the influence of drug-induced fantasies on weak, impoverished Arab societies. Thereafter, he often wrote from a woman's viewpoint and advocated social freedoms for women. His *'Ala hamish daftar al-naksa* (1967; "Marginal Notes on the Book of Defeat") was a stinging critique of unrealistic Arab leadership during the Six-Day War with Israel. Among his more than 20 poetry collections, the most noted volumes are *Habibati* (1961; "My Beloved") and *Al-rasm bi-al-kalimat* (1966; "Drawing with Words").

qasida or **kasida** \kä-'sē-də\ *plural* qasida *or* kasida [Arabic *qaṣīda*] A poetic form developed in pre-Islāmic Arabia and perpetuated throughout Islāmic literary history. It is a laudatory, elegiac, or satiric poem that is found in Arabic, Persian, and many related Oriental literatures.

The classic qasida is an elaborately structured ode of between 60 and 100 lines (though lengths vary considerably), maintaining a single end rhyme that runs through the entire piece; the same rhyme also occurs at the end of the first hemistich (half line) of the first verse.

The qasida opens with a short prelude (the *nasīb*), which depicts the poet stopping at an old tribal encampment to reminisce; Imru' al-Qays is said to have been the first to use this device, and nearly all subsequent authors imitate him. After this follows the *raḥīl*, which consists of similes and descriptions of desert animals, Bedouin life, and warfare; it may conclude with a piece on *fakhr*, or self-praise. The main theme, the *madīḥ*, or panegyric, often coupled with a *hija'* (satire of enemies), is last and is the poet's tribute to himself, his tribe, or his patron.

The qasida has always been respected as the highest form of the poetic art and as the special forte of the pre-Islāmic poets. By the end of the 8th century the qasida began to decline. It was successfully restored for a brief period in the 10th century by al-Mutanabbī and has continued to be cultivated by the Bedouin. Qasida were also written in Persian, Turkish, and Urdu until the 19th century.

Q.E.D. \,kyū-,ē-'dē\ Short story by Gertrude STEIN, one of her earliest works. Written in 1903, it was published posthumously in 1950 in *Things As They Are*, a novel in three parts.

Q.E.D. is autobiographical, based on an ill-fated relationship between Adele (Stein), an exuberant young woman, and Helen, who seduces her. Helen eventually rejects Adele for Mabel, a manipulative, wealthy woman who uses her money and passionate nature to dominate Helen.

Qian Zhongshu or **Ch'ien Chung-shu** \'chyen-'jŭŋ-'shū\ (b. Nov. 21, 1910, Wuxi, Jiangsu province, China) Chinese scholar and writer.

Qian's prose includes a small volume of essays; *Ren, shou, gui* (1946; "Men, Beasts, and Ghosts"), a collection of short stories; and *Weicheng* (1947; *Fortress Besieged*), a novel. Widely translated, Qian's novel did not receive much recognition in China until the late 1970s. It then became a best-seller in China throughout the 1980s and was made into a TV drama series in 1991. Unlike his creative writings, Qian's scholarly works were greeted with critical acclaim as soon as they came off the press. Such was the case with the new edition of *Tan yi lu* (1948; "Reflections in Appreciation"; revised and enlarged in 1983), *Songshi xuanzhu* (1958; "Selected and Annotated Poems of Song Dynasty"), and the four-volume *Guan zhui bian* (1979). The latter work contains comparative studies in literature and in culture in general, many of which involve several languages and a good number of authors and their creative or scholarly works, both ancient and modern. In 1986 a volume of revisions and addenda was included in volume 4 of the work.

Qian's other writings include *Jiuwen sipian* (1979; "Four Early Articles") and *Qizhui ji* (1984), a collection of scholarly articles.

qilin or **ch'i-lin** \'chē-'lin, -'lēn\ [Chinese (Beijing dialect) *qílín*], *also called* kylin. In Chinese mythology, a unicorn having a yellow belly, a multicolored back, the hooves of a horse, the body of a deer, and the tail of an ox. Gentle of disposition, it never walks on verdant grass or eats living vegetation. Its rare appearance often coincides with the imminent birth or death of a sage or an illustrious ruler. The first *qilin* is said to have appeared in the garden of the legendary Huangdi in 2697 BC. Some three centuries later a pair of *qilin* were reported in the capital of Emperor Yao. Both events bore testimony to the benevolent nature of the rulers. A *qilin* is also said to have appeared to the pregnant mother of Confucius (6th century BC).

Qi Rushan *see* Ch'i Ju-shan.

Quaker Graveyard in Nantucket, The \nan-'tək-it\ Poem by Robert LOWELL, published in 1946 in the collection *Lord Weary's Castle*. This frequently anthologized elegy for a cousin who died at sea during World War II echoes both Herman Melville and Henry David Thoreau in its exploration of innocence, corruption, and redemption. The poem is divided into seven parts and written in rhymed iambic pentameter with occasional trimeter lines.

quantitative verse In prosody, a metrical system based on the duration of the syllables that make up the feet, without regard for accents or stresses. Quantitative verse is made up of long and short syllables, whose duration is determined by the amount of time needed for their pronunciation. It was used mainly by classical Greek and Roman poets. *See also* METER.

quantity \'kwän-tə-tē\ In classical prosody, the relative length or duration of a syllable in a verse based on the length of time it took to pronounce the syllable. Syllables were classified as long, short, or anceps (either long or short at the poet's discretion), and in scansion they were designated by a macron for long (−), a breve for short (⌣), and a combination of the two or an ✕ for anceps (⌒ or ✕). Whereas the meter of modern accentual prosody is based on the pattern of stressed and unstressed syllables in a verse, the meter of classical, or quantitative, verse was determined by the pattern of long and short syllables.

Quare Fellow, The Play in three acts by Brendan BEHAN, performed in 1954 and published in 1956. A tragicomedy concerning the reactions of jailers and prisoners to the imminent hanging of a condemned man (the "Quare Fellow"), the play is an explosive statement on capital punishment and prison life.

Quarles \'kwȯrlz\, Francis (baptized May 8, 1592, Romford, Essex, Eng.—d. Sept. 8, 1644, London) Religious poet remembered for his *Emblemes* (1635), the most notable English-language emblem book (a collection of symbolic pictures, usually with verse and prose).

In *Emblemes*, each emblem consisted of a grotesque engraving and a paraphrase of scripture in ornate and metaphysical language and concluded with an epigrammatic verse. *Emblemes* was so successful that Quarles produced another emblem book, *Hieroglyphikes of the Life of Man* (1638). The two were printed together in 1639, and the work became possibly the most popular book of verse of the 17th century.

Quarles obtained the post of chronologist to London in 1640 and virtually abandoned poetry to employ his pen more lucratively. His first prose work, *Enchiridion* (1640), was a highly popular book of aphorisms. In the English Civil Wars he is said to have suffered for his allegiance and for writing *The Loyall Convert* (1644), a pamphlet defending Charles I's position.

Quarterly Review, The British literary journal, published from 1809 to 1967, that became a major cultural force, especially in its influence on the development of Romanticism in England. Founded by the London publisher John Murray, the magazine was established as a Tory organ to rival the Whig-dominated *Edinburgh Review*. Sir Walter Scott and Robert Southey were both major contributors. The journal developed a reputation for savagery because of its sometimes vicious literary reviews, many of which attacked writers who were currently being championed by *The Edinburgh Review*. *The Quarterly Review* supported William Wordsworth, Washington Irving, and Jane Austen but damned John Keats, William Hazlitt, Percy Bysshe Shelley, Alfred, Lord Tennyson, and Charles Dickens.

quartet \kwȯr-'tet\ In poetry, any group of four lines taken as a unit. The lines may or may not be printed as a separate stanza or QUATRAIN.

quarto \'kwȯr-tō\ [Latin, ablative of *quartus* fourth (of a leaf)] In printing, a sheet of paper folded into quarters. The term also refers to a book made up of quarto signatures. Many of William Shakespeare's plays were originally published as quartos and are sometimes referred to in terms of a specific quarto edition. *Compare* FOLIO.

Quasimodo \,kwäz-ē-'mō-dō, ,kwäs-\ Title character, the deaf, pitably ugly protagonist of Victor Hugo's novel THE HUNCHBACK OF NOTRE DAME. He became a classic symbol of a courageous heart beneath a grotesque exterior.

Quasimodo \kwä-'zē-mō-dō, -'sē-\, Salvatore (b. Aug. 20, 1901, Modica, Italy—d. June 14, 1968, Naples) Italian poet, critic, and translator who was one of the leaders of the Hermetics—poets whose works were characterized by unorthodox structure, illogical sequences, and highly subjective language. He received the Nobel Prize for Literature in 1959.

Quasimodo's first poems appeared in the Florentine periodical *Solaria*. A disciple of the Hermetic poets Giuseppe Ungaretti and Eugenio Montale, Quasimodo gradually became a leader of the movement after the publication of his first poetry collection, *Acque e terre* (1930; "Waters and Land"). After 1935 he abandoned his career as an engineer to teach Italian literature. His later poetry collections—*Oboe sommerso* (1932; "Sunken Oboe"), *Odore di eucalyptus* (1933; "Scent of Eucalyptus"), and *Erato e Apollion* (1936)—have the dry, sophisticated style and abstruse symbolism of Hermeticism but deal with contemporary issues. *Poesie* (1938) and *Ed è subito sera* (1942; "And Suddenly It's Evening") were the last volumes of his Hermetic period.

After World War II Quasimodo's social convictions shaped his work, beginning with *Giorno dopo giorno* (1947; "Day After Day"). Many of his poems recall the injustices of the Fascist regime, the horrors of the war, and Italian guilt, with concrete imagery and simple language. Later volumes include *La terra impareggiabile* (1958; *The Incomparable Earth*), *Tutte le poesie* (1960), and *Dare e avere* (1966; *To Give and To Have and Other Poems*).

Quasimodo published an astonishing range of translations, including classical poetry and drama, six plays of William Shakespeare, Molière's *Tartuffe*, and the poetry of E.E. Cummings and Pablo Neruda. He edited two anthologies of Italian poetry and wrote many significant critical essays, collected in *Il poeta e il politico e altri saggi* (1960; *The Poet and the Politician and Other Essays*) and *Scritti sul teatro* (1961), a collection of drama reviews.

Quatermain, Allan \'al-ən-'kwȯt-ər-,mān\ Fictional character, an explorer and great white hunter who is the protagonist

of KING SOLOMON'S MINES, a romantic adventure novel by H. Rider Haggard, and a subsequent novel, *Allan Quatermain*.

quatorzain \kə-'tȯr-,zān, 'kat-ər-,zān\ [Middle French *quatorzaine* group of fourteen] A poem of 14 lines; specifically, a poem resembling a sonnet but lacking strict sonnet structure.

quatrain \'kwä-,trān, kwä-'trān\ [French, a derivative of *quatre* four] A verse unit of four lines.

quattrocento \,kwät-trō-'chen-tō\ [Italian, literally, four hundred, short for *mille quattrocento* the year 1400] The 15th century; specifically, the 15th-century period in Italian literature and art.

Queeg, Captain \'kwēg\ Fictional character, the unstable skipper of the minesweeper *Caine* in THE CAINE MUTINY by Herman Wouk.

Queen \'kwēn\, Ellery, *pseudonym of* Frederic Dannay \da-'nā\ and Manfred B. Lee \'lē\, *original names, respectively,* Daniel Nathan \'nā-thən\ and Manford Lepofsky \lə-'pȯf-skē\ (respectively b. Oct. 20, 1905, Brooklyn, N.Y., U.S.—d. Sept. 3, 1982, White Plains, N.Y.; b. Jan. 11, 1905, Brooklyn, N.Y.—d. April 3, 1971, near Waterbury, Conn.) American cousins who were coauthors of a series of more than 35 detective novels featuring a character named Ellery Queen.

Dannay and Lee first collaborated on an impulsive entry for a detective-story contest; the success of the result, *The Roman Hat Mystery* (1929), started Ellery Queen on his career. They took turns creating plots and writing stories about the sleuth Queen, whose adventures have been adapted for radio, television, and film. The pair also used the pseudonym Barnaby Ross when writing about their second detective creation, Drury Lane.

Dannay and Lee also cofounded *Ellery Queen's Mystery Magazine* in 1941; edited numerous anthologies, including *101 Years' Entertainment: Great Detective Stories, 1841–1941* (1945); and cofounded Mystery Writers of America.

Queen Mab \'mab\ In English folklore, queen of the fairies. *See* MAB.

Queen Mab \'mab\ (*in full* Queen Mab, A Philosophical Poem: With Notes) Poem in nine cantos by Percy Bysshe SHELLEY, published in 1813. Written in blank verse, Shelley's first major poem is a utopian political epic that exposes as social evils such institutions as monarchy, commerce, and religion and that describes a visionary future in which humanity is liberated from all such vices. Queen Mab, ruler of the fairies, takes the spirit of Ianthe (Shelley's first child) on a journey through time and space to reveal various human follies and errors. The poem is appended with 17 prose notes, essays on such topics as free love, atheism, republicanism, and vegetarianism. It was very popular with members of the working-class radical movement of the 1830s and '40s.

Queen of Hearts Fictional character, the tyrannical monarch in ALICE'S ADVENTURES IN WONDERLAND by Lewis Carroll.

Queen of Spades, The Classic short story by Aleksandr PUSHKIN, published in 1834 as "Pikovaya dama."

In the story, a Russian officer of German ancestry named Hermann learns that an old countess possesses the secret of winning at faro, a high-stakes card game. He begins a liaison with Lizaveta (Elizaveta), the countess's impoverished young ward, to gain access to the old woman, but when the countess refuses to reveal the secret, he threatens her with a pistol and she dies of fright. The night of her funeral, he dreams that the countess has told him the winning cards—three, seven, and ace. Hermann then places bets on the three and seven and wins. Betting everything on the ace, which wins, he is horror-struck to see that he is not holding the ace but the queen of spades, who seems to smile up at him as did the countess from her casket.

Queequeg \\'kwē-kweg\\ Fictional character, a tattooed South Sea Islander and onetime cannibal who is a harpooner aboard the ship *Pequod*, in the novel MOBY-DICK by Herman Melville.

Queiroz \\'kā-rūsh\\, Rachel de (b. Nov. 17, 1910, Fortaleza, Braz.) Brazilian novelist and member of a group of writers known for their novels of social criticism, sometimes called the Northeastern school (for the region of Brazil that is often the setting of their works).

Queiroz was reared on a ranch in the semiarid backlands of northeastern Brazil. Her works vividly describe the life in her native state. Her first book, *O Quinze* (1931; "The Year '15"), deals with families forced to abandon their homes in the drought of 1915. *João Miguel* (1932) is about a poor mestizo who wakes up in jail to learn that he has killed someone in a drunken brawl. Her third novel, *Caminho de pedras* (1937; "Rocky Road"), is the story of a woman who embraces a new sense of independence. *As três Marias* (1939; *The Three Marias*), which follows the lives of three girlhood friends from their meeting in convent school to adulthood, depicts the inadequate educational system and the limited role open to Brazilian women. *Dôra, Doralina* (1975) is a later novel.

Queiroz also published two plays, *Lampião* (1953) and *A beata Maria do Egito* (1958; "Blessed Mary of Egypt"), and several collections of journalistic essays, including *O Brasileiro perplexo* (1963). She also was instrumental in establishing the *crônica* (short-prose) form, and several books of her *crônicas* have been published. Her *O caçador de tatu* (1967; "The Armadillo Hunter") is a selection of chronicles of her life from the mid-1950s. In 1977 Queiroz became the first woman to be elected to the Brazilian Academy of Letters.

Queneau \\kə-'nō\\, Raymond (b. Feb. 21, 1903, Le Havre, Fr.—d. Oct. 25, 1976, Paris) French author who, under the mask of a humorist, produced some of the most important prose and poetry of the mid-20th century.

After working as a reporter for *L'Intransigeant* (1936–38), Queneau became a reader for Gallimard's prestigious *Encyclopédie de la Pléiade*, a scholarly edition of past and present classical authors, and by 1955 he was its director. He was elected to the Académie Goncourt in 1951.

More than 30 works by Queneau have been published, including the fiction *Les Enfants du limon* (1938; "The Children of the Earth"), *Pierrot mon ami* (1943; Eng. trans., *Pierrot*), *Zazie dans le métro* (1959; Eng. trans., *Zazie*), *Les Fleurs bleues* (1965; U.K. title, *Between Blue and Blue*; U.S. title, *The Blue Flowers*), and *Le Vol d'Icare* (1968; *The Flight of Icarus*). His early interest in Surrealism was quelled by a break with its chief proponent, the poet André Breton. The story of their disagreement is told in Queneau's roman à clef *Odile* (1937).

Queneau retained a lifelong interest in verbal play and an appreciation of black humor. He participated in several groups of writers (including, for example, OuLiPo) who enjoyed literary games. One of his most remarkable works of this type is *Exercices de style* (1947; revised and enlarged, 1963; *Exercises in Style*). In it he uses a series of inconsequential events in a young man's day to illustrate 99 different elements of literary style (such as litotes, metaphor, and so on).

Quennell \\'kwin-əl\\, Peter, *in full* Sir Peter Courtney Quennell (b. March 9, 1905, Bickley, Kent [now in Greater London], Eng.—d. Oct. 27, 1993, London) British translator, editor, biographer, and critic who was an authority on Lord Byron and John Ruskin.

Quennell was educated at Balliol College, Oxford. He practiced journalism in London and briefly taught in Tokyo. He was editor of the literary and artistic periodical *The Cornhill Magazine* (1944–51) and was cofounder in 1951 and coeditor for many years of the monthly journal *History Today*.

Among Quennell's most notable works are translations of letters addressed to the 19th-century Austrian statesman Klemens Metternich (1948); critical works such as *Aspects of Seventeenth Century Verse* (1933) and *The Pursuit of Happiness* (1988); and critical and biographical works on William Shakespeare, Lord Byron, John Ruskin, Charles Baudelaire, Alexander Pope, Queen Caroline (the consort of George II), Sir Thomas More, and Vladimir Nabokov. *Customs and Characters* (1982) is a collection of contemporary portraits. His autobiography consists of *The Marble Foot* (1976) and *The Wanton Chase* (1980). He was knighted in 1992.

Quental \\keⁿn-'täl, -'taú\\, Antero Tarquínio de (b. April 18, 1842, Ponta Delgada, Azores—d. Sept. 11, 1891, Ponta Delgada) Portuguese poet who was a leader of the Generation of Coimbra, a group of young poets associated with the University of Coimbra in the 1860s who revolted against Romanticism and struggled to create a new outlook in literature and society.

Between 1858 and 1864, Quental wrote his Romantic early poems, *Raios de extincta luz* ("Rays of Vanishing Light") and the delicate lyrics published in 1872 as *Primaveras românticas* ("Romantic Springtimes"). These were soon followed by *Odes modernas* (1865), a volume of socially critical poetry. His pamphlet *Bom-senso e Bom-gosto* (1865; "Good Sense and Good Taste"), attacking the hidebound formalism of Portuguese literature, marked the opening of a war against the older literary generation that was waged until 1871, when a series of "democratic lectures," organized by Quental and held in the Lisbon Casino, dealt the deathblow to Romanticism.

As a poet Quental made few formal innovations. He was a master of the sonnet, however, and the 109 sonnets of *Os sonetos completos* (1886) are a history of his spiritual progress, giving expression both to his personal anxieties and to the larger ideological issues in Portugal. Quental's *Sonnets and Poems* (1922) was reprinted in 1977.

Quentin Durward \\'kwen-tin-'dər-wərd\\ Novel of adventure and romance by Sir Walter SCOTT, published in 1823. The novel was a popular success and solidified Scott's reputation as a stirring writer. The novel is set in 15th-century France, where the title character saves the life of Louis XI, protects and falls in love with Countess Isabelle de Croye (a Burgundian heiress), helps defeat the king's brutal enemy, and wins Isabelle's hand in marriage.

Querido \\'kvā-rē-,dō\\, Israël (b. Oct. 1, 1872, Amsterdam, Neth.—d. Aug. 5, 1932, Amsterdam) Dutch novelist whose works provide valuable documentary social material.

Querido's observation of the working-class people among whom he lived enabled him to reproduce their way of life in such works as *De Jordaan* (1914), a long epic in four parts.

Socialist elements are evident in his treatment of the human condition in such novels as *Menschenwee* (1903; *Toil of Men*), which provides a detailed description of the miseries he witnessed among the people of Beverwijk. He also wrote rather heavy-handed historical novels such as *De oude wereld* (1919; "The Old World").

quest \\'kwest\\ A chivalrous enterprise in medieval European romance that usually involves an adventurous journey.

Quest, Martha \\'mär-thə-'kwest\\ Fictional protagonist of five semiautobiographical novels by Doris LESSING. Called the *Children of Violence* series, the novels that trace Martha's life from girlhood to middle age are *Martha Quest* (1952), *A Proper Marriage* (1954), *A Ripple from the Storm* (1958), *Landlocked* (1965), and *The Four-Gated City* (1969).

Quested, Adela \\'ad-i-lə-'kwes-tid, ə-'dā-lə\\ Fictional character, a sexually repressed Englishwoman who falsely accuses an Indian physician of attempted rape, in the novel A PASSAGE TO INDIA by E.M. Forster.

Quetzalcóatl \\ˌkets-əl-kō-'ät-əl, ket-ˌsäl-, -'at-\\ (from Nahuatl *quetzalli*, "tail feather of the quetzal" bird [*Pharmoacrus mocinno*] *coatl*, "snake") The Feathered Serpent, one of the major deities of the ancient Mexican pantheon. During the Teotihuacán civilization (3rd to 8th century AD), Quetzalcóatl seems to have been conceived as a vegetation god. Quetzalcóatl's cult later underwent drastic changes. He became the god of the morning and evening star, and in Aztec times (14th through 16th century) Quetzalcóatl was revered as the patron of priests, the inventor of the calendar and of books, and the protector of goldsmiths and other craftsmen.

As the god of learning, of writing, and of books, Quetzalcóatl was particularly venerated in the *calmecac*, religious colleges annexed to the temples, in which the future priests and the sons of the nobility were educated. He figures in much later literature, including D.H. Lawrence's *The Plumed Serpent*.

Quevedo \\kā-'bā-thō\\, Francisco Gómez de, *surname in full* Quevedo y Villegas \\ē-bēl-'yā-gäs\\ (b. Sept. 17, 1580, Madrid, Spain—d. Sept. 8, 1645, Villanueva de los Infantes) Poet and master satirist of Spain's Golden Age (early 16th to late 17th century), who was a virtuoso of language.

Quevedo was versed in several languages, and by the age of 23 he had distinguished himself as a poet and wit. His elder contemporaries, Miguel de Cervantes and Lope de Vega, both expressed their esteem for his poetry, but Quevedo was more interested in a political career. He later fell from political favor and devoted himself to writing, producing a steady stream of satirical verse and prose aimed at the follies of his contemporaries.

Quevedo reveals his complex personality in the extreme variety of tone in his works, ranging from the obscene to the devout, such as treatises on stoic philosophy and translations of Epictetus and Seneca.

He is remembered for his picaresque novel *La vida del buscón* (1626; "The Life of a Scoundrel"), which describes the adventures of "Paul the Sharper" in a grotesque world of thieves, connivers, and impostors. Quevedo's *Sueños* (1627; *Dreams*), fantasies of hell and death, which was written at intervals from 1606 to 1622, shows his development as a master of the then-new Baroque style *conceptismo*, a complicated form of expression depending on puns and elaborate conceits. An anthology of his poems in English translation was published in 1969.

Quickly, Mistress \\'kwik-lē\\ Fictional character, the colorful hostess of a tavern in Eastcheap in William Shakespeare's two-part HENRY IV. She also appears in THE MERRY WIVES OF WINDSOR.

Quiet American, The Novel by Graham GREENE, combining a murder mystery with a cautionary tale of Western involvement in Vietnam. It was first published in 1955, at the beginning of the U.S. involvement in Vietnamese politics, and proved to be prophetic. The novel concerns the relationship between the American Alden Pyle, a quiet, naive CIA operative, and the story's narrator, the world-weary British journalist Thomas Fowler.

Quiller-Couch \\ˌkwil-ər-'kūch\\, Sir Arthur Thomas, *pseudonym* Q \\'kyū\\ (b. Nov. 21, 1863, Bodmin, Cornwall, Eng.—d. May 12, 1944, Fowey, Cornwall) English poet, nov-

elist, and anthologist noted for his compilation of *The Oxford Book of English Verse 1250–1900* (1900; revised 1939) and *The Oxford Book of Ballads* (1910).

Quiller-Couch was educated at Newton Abbot College, Clifton College, and Trinity College, Oxford, where he became lecturer in classics. In 1887 he wrote *Dead Man's Rock*, the first of several novels of Cornwall and the sea. He worked in London for a publishing firm and as assistant editor of *The Speaker*, to which he contributed short stories that were reprinted in book form as *Noughts and Crosses* (1891), the first of a dozen similar volumes. He was knighted in 1910 and in 1912 became a professor at Cambridge and a fellow of Jesus College.

Poems (1930) is a collection of his serious verse; *Green Bays* (1930) contains light verse. His published works, noted for their clear and apparently effortless style, include *On the Art of Writing* (1916), *Shakespeare's Workmanship* (1918), *Studies in Literature* (3 series; 1918, 1922, 1929), *On the Art of Reading* (1920), *Charles Dickens and Other Victorians* (1925), and *The Poet as Citizen, and Other Papers* (1934).

Quilp, Daniel \\'dan-yəl-'kwilp\\ Fictional character, the dwarfish villain of Charles Dickens' novel THE OLD CURIOSITY SHOP.

quindecasyllabic \\ˌkwin-ˌdek-ə-sə-'lab-ik\\ [Latin *quindecim* fifteen] Having 15 syllables.

quintain \\'kwin-ˌtān, kwin-'tān\\ [Latin *quintus* fifth + English *-ain* (as in *quatrain*)] *obsolete* A five-line stanza.

Quintana \\kēn-'tä-nä\\, Manuel José (b. April 11, 1772, Madrid, Spain—d. March 11, 1857, Madrid) Spanish patriot and Neoclassical poet who was esteemed by his countrymen for poems, pamphlets, and proclamations written during the War of Independence from Napoleon. His reputation later declined.

Quintana was active in the Napoleonic Wars and was imprisoned (1814–20) after the return to Spain of Ferdinand VII. Released by the revolutionary forces, he later served as a senator and as tutor to the future Queen Isabella II, who crowned him national poet in 1855.

Quintana's poetry is extremely rhetorical and marked by patriotism and liberalism. The classical ode is his favorite form, and his work is untouched by Romanticism. He is also remembered for his Plutarchian portraits, *Vidas de españoles célebres*, 2 vol. (1807, 1830; "Lives of Famous Spaniards"), for his literary criticism collected in the anthologies *Colección de poesías castellanas* ("Collected Castilian Poems") and *Musa épica* ("Epic Muse"), and also for his few tragedies.

Quintilian \\kwin-'til-ē-ən\\, *Latin in full* Marcus Fabius Quintilianus (b. *c.* AD 35, Calagurris Nassica, Hispania Tarraconensis [Spain]—d. after 96, Rome [Italy]) Latin teacher and writer whose work on rhetoric, *Institutio oratoria*, is a major contribution to educational theory and literary criticism.

Quintilian was probably educated in Rome, where he afterward received practical training in oratory. He then practiced for a time as an advocate in the law courts. Although he settled in his native Spain for about 10 years, he returned to Rome in 68 and began to teach rhetoric, combining this with advocacy in the law courts. Under the emperor Vespasian (ruled 69–79) he became the first person to receive a state salary for teaching Latin rhetoric, and he also held his position as Rome's leading teacher under the emperors Titus and Domitian, retiring probably in 88.

Quintilian's great work *Institutio oratoria*, in 12 books, was published shortly before the end of his life. He believed that the entire educational process was related to the training of an orator. In Book I, therefore, he deals with the stages of education before a boy enters the school of rhetoric itself, which he discusses in Book II. The first two books contain his general observations on educational principles. Books III to XI are concerned with the five traditional "departments" of rhetoric: invention, arrangement, style, memory, and delivery. He also deals with the nature, value, origin, and function of rhetoric and with the different types of oratory. During his general discussion of invention he also considers the successive, formal parts of a speech, including a lively chapter on the art of arousing laughter. Book X contains a well-known and much-praised survey of Greek and Latin authors, recommended to the young orator for study. Book XII concerns the ideal orator in action, after his training is completed: his character, the rules that he must follow in pleading a case, the style of his eloquence, and when he should retire.

Quintus Smyrnaeus \'kwin-təs-smər-'nē-əs\, *also called* Quintus of Smyrna \'smər-nə\ (fl. *c.* AD 375)   Greek epic poet, the author of a hexameter poem in 14 books narrating events at Troy from the funeral of Hector to the departure of the Achaeans after sacking the city (and hence known in English as *Sequel to Homer* [Greek *Ta meth Homeron*, Latin *Posthomerica*]).

Quintus' style is monotonous, and his vocabulary and metrics are traditional, but his very unoriginality makes his work a valuable guide to the content of the lost epics (such as *Aethiopis, Little Iliad,* and *Iliupersis*).

Quiroga \kē-'rō-ğä\, Horacio (b. Dec. 31, 1878, Salto, Uruguay—d. Feb. 19, 1937, Buenos Aires, Arg.)   Uruguayan-born short-story writer whose works imaginatively portray the struggle of humans and animals to survive in the tropical jungle.

Quiroga spent most of his life in Buenos Aires, Arg., taking frequent trips to San Ignacio in the jungle province of Misiones, which provided the material for most of his stories. Such early, imitative works as the collection of prose and verse *Los arrecifes de coral* (1901; "The Coral Reefs") later gave way to success in the form of the short story, influenced at first by Edgar Allan Poe and Rudyard Kipling.

Exploring his view of life as an endless struggle for survival, Quiroga used exotic imagery to depict the primitive and the savage in such collections as *Cuentos de la selva* (1918; *Stories of the Jungle*) and *La gallina degollada y otras cuentos* (1925; *The Decapitated Chicken and Other Stories*). The work generally recognized as his masterpiece, *Anaconda* (1921), portrays realistic, philosophical, and symbolic battles between the nonpoisonous anaconda and the poisonous viper.

Quixote, Don \'dōn-kē-'k̟ō-tä, *Angl* 'dän-kē-'hō-tē; 'kwik-sət, -sōt\   Fictional character, the deluded protagonist of the novel DON QUIXOTE by Miguel de Cervantes.

Quo Vadis? \,kwō-'vä-dis\   Historical novel by Henryk SIENKIEWICZ, published in Polish under its Latin title in 1896. The title means "where are you going?" and alludes to a New Testament verse (John 13:36). The popular novel was widely translated.

Set in ancient Rome during the reign of the emperor Nero, *Quo Vadis?* tells the story of the love that develops between a young Christian woman and a Roman officer who, after meeting her fellow Christians, converts to her religion. Underlying their relationship is the contrast between the worldly opulence of the Roman aristocracy and the poverty, simplicity, and spiritual power of the Christians. The novel has as a subtext the persecution and political subjugation of Poland by Russia.

Qur'ān \kûr-'än, -'an\ *or* **Koran** \kə-'rän, -'ran; 'kôr-,an\   The sacred scripture of Islām, regarded by Muslims as the infallible Word of God, a perfect transcription of an eternal tablet preserved in Heaven and revealed over a period of 20 years to the Prophet Muḥammad (*c.* 570–632).

The intermittent revelations to Muḥammad were first memorized by followers and used in ritual prayers. Although verses were later written down during the Prophet's lifetime, they were first compiled in their present authoritative form during the reign of the third caliph (deputy or successor to the Prophet). As the paramount authority for the Muslim community, the Qur'ān is the ultimate source and continual inspiration of Islām. Its injunctions and their various interpretations have characterized the unique development of Islāmic civilization, and its various interpretations have influenced the direction of the multiple trends within this development.

The Qur'ān consists of 114 *sūrah*s (chapters) of unequal length. The earliest *sūrah*s of the Meccan period are generally shorter and written in dynamic rhymed prose. The *sūrah*s of the later Medinan period are longer and more prosaic. With the exception of the first *sūrah*, the *Fātiḥah* ("Opening"), the *sūrah*s are arranged roughly according to length, with the longer *sūrah*s preceding the shorter ones. Consequently, the present arrangement is, for the most part, an inversion of the text's chronological order. The Meccan *sūrah*s convey an emphatic call to moral and religious obedience in light of the coming Day of Judgment, while the Medinan *sūrah*s provide directives for the creation of a social fabric supportive of the moral life called for by God.

Absolute monotheism governs all Qur'ānic ideas about God. The God who revealed his Word to Muḥammad is identified with the God worshiped by both Jews and Christians, though these communities are said to have failed to hear and incorporate God's revelation to their prophets. The Qur'ān emphasizes God as the absolute creator and sustainer of an ordered universe, an order that reflects His infinite power, wisdom, and authority. The scripture demands absolute submission (*islām*) to God and his word. The Qur'ān provides detailed accounts of the consequences of God's ultimate judgment of each individual: the joys of the gardens of Paradise and the punishment and terror of Hell.

Correct interpretation of the Qur'ān has been a central concern of all schools of Islāmic thought. A special branch of learning, called *tafsīr*, deals exclusively with Qur'ānic exegesis. Commentators use *tafsīr* to study Qur'ānic texts in terms of auxiliary branches of learning such as Arabic grammar, lexicography, and the Prophetic tradition. The Qur'ān, verbally received in Arabic, is regarded as immutable in both form and content, and its translation has traditionally been forbidden. Such translations as have been made are viewed as "paraphrases" to facilitate understanding of the actual scripture.

Qu Yuan *or* **Ch'ü Yüan** \'chю̄-'ywen\ (b. *c.* 343 BC, state of Chu, central China—d. *c.* 289 BC, Chu)   One of the greatest poets of ancient China. His highly original and imaginative verse had an enormous influence on early Chinese poetry.

Qu Yuan was born a member of the ruling house of Chu, a large state in the central valley of the Yangtze River. In his youth he was a favored counselor of Huai-wang, the ruler of Chu, but he was later banished to the south of the Yangtze River by Huai's successor, Jing Xiang. In despair over his banishment Qu Yuan wandered about southern Chu, writing poetry and observing the shamanistic folk rites and legends that greatly influenced his works.

The works of Qu Yuan have survived in an early anthology, the *Chuci* ("Songs of Chu"), much of which has been attributed to later poets writing about the legendary life of Qu Yuan. The anthology begins with the long melancholic poem *Li sao* ("Encountering Sorrow"), Qu Yuan's most famous work.

R

Ra *see* RE.

Raabe \'räb-ə\, Wilhelm, *pseudonym* Jakob Corvinus \kȯr-'vē-nús\ (b. Sept. 8, 1831, Eschershausen, near Hildesheim, Braunschweig [Germany]—d. Nov. 15, 1910, Braunschweig) German writer best known for realistic novels of middle-class life.

Raabe attended lectures at Berlin University, where he wrote his popular first novel, *Die Chronik der Sperlingsgasse* (1857; "The Chronicle of Sperling Street"), which depicts episodes in the lives of the people living on one small street. In 1862 he settled in Stuttgart, where he wrote his most successful novels, *Der Hungerpastor*, 3 vol. (1864; *The Hunger Pastor*), *Abu Telfan, oder Die Heimkehr vom Mondgebirge*, 3 vol. (1868; *Abu Telfan, Return from the Mountains of the Moon*), and *Der Schüdderump*, 3 vol. (1870; "The Rickety Cart"). Raabe later returned to Braunschweig, where he spent the last 40 years of his life. He specialized in short stories and shorter novels, which are now considered his most original works. Notable among them is *Stopfkuchen* (1891, "Stuffing Cake").

Rabassa \rə-'bäs-ə\, Gregory (b. March 9, 1922, Yonkers, N.Y., U.S.) Translator into English of Latin-American fiction who was perhaps best known for his translation of Gabriel García Márquez' *One Hundred Years of Solitude* (1970).

Rabassa was a graduate of Columbia University, and he taught there and at other universities and colleges in New York, including Queens College. His first major translation was of Julio Cortázar's novel *Hopscotch* (1966); subsequently, he translated works of most of the major Latin-American writers. Other translations include *Mulata* (1967; U.K. title, *The Mulatta and Mr. Fly*), by Miguel Asturias; *The Green House* (1968), by Mario Vargas Llosa; a number of books by Gabriel García Márquez; and *Sea of Death* (1984), *Captains of the Sands* (1988), and *Show Down* (1988), by Jorge Amado.

Rabbi Ben Ezra \ben-'ez-rə\ Dramatic monologue by Robert BROWNING, published in the collection *Dramatis Personae* (1864).

Through the personage of Rabbi Ben Ezra, a scholarly and learned Jew, the poem sets forth Browning's religious philosophy. The poem contains a metaphor describing life as a pot that is fashioned by the Master's hand and argues that the value of a person should be measured not by the work done but by the character that has been molded.

rabbinical literature \ra-'bin-i-kəl\ The literature of Hebrew theology and philosophy, including the Talmud and its exegesis.

Rabbit, Run Novel by John UPDIKE, published in 1960. The novel's hero is Harry ("Rabbit") Angstrom, a 26-year-old former high-school athletic star who is disillusioned with his present life and flees from his wife and child in a futile search for grace and order. Three sequels—*Rabbit Redux* (1971), *Rabbit Is Rich* (1981), and *Rabbit at Rest* (1990)—continue the story of Rabbit in the succeeding decades of his life.

Rabe \'räb\, David (William) (b. March 10, 1940, Dubuque, Iowa, U.S.) American playwright whose experiences in a hospital-support unit in Vietnam were the basis for several acclaimed dramas. His work is known for its use of grotesque humor, satire, and surreal fantasy.

Rabe was educated at Loras College, Dubuque, and Villanova University, Pa. His plays about war include *The Basic Training of Pavlo Hummel* (1969), which depicts the ruthlessness of the Viet Cong and the brutalization of American troops; *Sticks and Bones* (1972), in which a blinded, distraught veteran

returns to his middle-American family; and *Streamers* (1975), which concerns violent racial and sexual tensions and prejudices in an army camp in Virginia. Other plays include *The Orphan* (1975), a reworking of the *Orestia*; *In the Boom Boom Room* (1975); *Hurlyburly* (1985) and *Those the River Keeps* (1991), a drama and its prequel about disillusionment in Hollywood; and *Recital of the Dog* (1993).

Rabéarivelo \rä-bā-á-rē-'vä-lō\, Jean-Joseph (b. March 4, 1901, Tananarive [now Antananarivo], Madagascar—d. 1937, Tananarive) Malagasy writer, one of the most important of African poets writing in French, who is considered to be the father of modern literature in his native land. The mythical world created in his poetry is an intensely personal one dominated by visions of death, catastrophe, and alienation mitigated only occasionally by hope of salvation or resurrection. The overall impression is one of a surrealistic otherworld in which natural objects such as birds, trees, stars, cows, and fish have human emotions and human figures seem cosmic or semidivine. He seldom touches upon colonialism, revolution, or the quest for identity, themes that obsessed many later African writers.

Rabéarivelo, a largely self-educated man who earned his living as a proofreader for the Imerina Printing Press, wrote seven volumes of poetry before committing suicide in 1937. *Presque-songes* (1934; "Near-Dreams") and *Traduit de la nuit* (1935; "Translation of the Night") are considered to be the most important. His early work, including his first volume, *La Coupe de cendres* (1924; "Cutting the Ashes"), was imitative of late 19th-century French poetry. His later work, however, exhibited a mature, individual style. A final collection of poems, *Vieilles chansons des pays d'Imerina* ("Old Songs of the Imerina [Merina] Country"), published two years after his death, is based on poetic love dialogues (*hain-teny*) adapted from Malagasy vernacular tradition.

Rabelais \rä-'ble, *Angl* 'rab-ə-,lā, ,rab-ə-'lā\, François, *pseudonym* Alcofribas Nasier (b. *c.* 1494, Poitou, Fr.—d. probably April 9, 1553, Paris) French writer, the author of the comic and satirical masterpieces *Pantagruel* (1532) and *Gargantua* (1534). *See* GARGANTUA AND PANTAGRUEL. His reputation for profound humanist learning was secure in his lifetime.

After apparently studying law, Rabelais became a Franciscan novice, and by 1521 he had taken holy orders. Having run afoul of Franciscan censors, Rabelais left the order and joined the Benedictines. He then took up the study of medicine, probably with the Benedictines in their Hôtel Saint-Denis in Paris and also in Montpellier. He lectured on the works of distinguished ancient Greek physicians, publishing his own editions of Hippocrates' *Aphorisms* and Galen's *Ars parva* ("The Art of Raising Children") in 1532. Rabelais was appointed physician to the hospital of Lyon, the Hôtel-Dieu, in 1532. He followed this profession for the rest of his life.

Detail of an oil painting by an unknown artist, 17th century; in the Musée National du Château de Versailles et des Trianons
Cliché Musées Nationaux, Paris

Fired by the success of an anonymous popular chapbook, *Les Grandes et inestimables cronicques du grant et énorme géant Gargantua*, Rabelais published, pseudonymously, his first novel, *Pantagruel*. Nothing of this quality had been seen before in French in any similar genre. Rabelais displayed his delight in words, his profound sense of the comedy of language itself, his mastery of comic situation, monologue, dialogue, and action, and his genius as a storyteller. Nonetheless, the satirical content of this and subsequent works caused Rabelais to be repeatedly condemned by civil and ecclesiastical authorities. His books were banned in France and placed on the Index of Forbidden Books that were officially proscribed for Roman Catholics. Throughout his career, Rabelais owed his freedom and advancement to the protection of powerful patrons.

Pantagruel was followed by the *Pantagruéline prognostication pour l'an 1533* (1532; *Pantagruel's Prognostication*), a parody of the almanacs and astrological predictions that were becoming increasingly popular, and *Gargantua*, another mockheroic romance. Later volumes in the series are *Le Tiers Livre* (1546) and *Le Quart Livre* (1552), his longest book.

Rabémananjara \rä-bä-má-nän-'jä-rä\, Jacques (b. June 23, 1913, Tananarive [now Antananarivo], Madagascar) Malagasy politician, playwright, and poet who was one of the most prolific writers of the Negritude movement.

Rabémananjara published his first volume of verse, *Sur les marches du soir* ("On the Edges of Evening"), in 1940. The poems of *Antidote* (1961) were written while he was detained in a French colonial prison for alleged antigovernment activity.

In 1956 Rabémananjara was banished, but he returned to Madagascar in 1960, when the country became independent. By the mid-1960s, when he was Madagascar's minister of economic affairs, Rabémananjara had published five volumes of verse and several plays, many of them glorifying the history and culture of his country. He defended and proclaimed the values of African culture, particularly its closeness to nature, contact with ancestral tradition, and ancient rhythm of life. His plays include *Les Dieux malgaches* (1947; "The Malagasy Gods"), *Les Boutriers de l'aurore* (1957; "The Navigators of the Dawn"), and *Les Agapes des dieux* (1962; "Love Feasts of the Gods"). His complete poems were published in French in 1978.

Racan \rä-'kän\, Honorat de Bueil, Seigneur de (b. Feb. 5, 1589, Champmarin, Fr.—d. Jan. 21, 1670, Paris) French poet, one of the earliest members (1635) of the Académie Française.

Racan became a page at the court of Henry IV, served in the army, and in 1639 retired to his country seat in Touraine. His works include the celebrated *Stances sur la retraite* (c. 1618; "Stanzas on Retreat"), which reflects his love of nature and his reluctance to adhere to the poetic discipline of his master, François de Malherbe, whose biography he wrote. Racan's bestknown work is a pastoral drama, *Les Bergeries* ("The Sheepfolds"), sometimes called the finest example of the genre in French; it was performed at the Hôtel de Bourgogne in about 1620 and published in 1625. His other poems are mainly bucolic and religious. Racan also wrote verse paraphrases of the Psalms during his retirement.

race, milieu, and moment According to the French critic Hippolyte Taine, the three principal motives or conditioning factors behind any work of art. Taine sought to establish a scientific approach to literature through the investigation of what created the individual who created the work of art.

By "race" he meant the inherited disposition or temperament that persists stubbornly over thousands of years. By "milieu" he meant the circumstances or environment that modify the inherited racial disposition. By "moment" Taine meant the momentum of past and present cultural traditions.

The literature of a culture, according to Taine, shows the most sensitive and unguarded displays of motive and the psychology of a people.

Racine \rä-'sēn, *Angl* ra-'sēn, rə-\, Jean(-Baptiste) (baptized Dec. 22, 1639, La Ferté-Milon, Fr.—d. April 21,

Detail of an oil painting by an unknown artist, 17th century; in the Musée National du Château de Versailles et des Trianons
Giraudon/Art Resource, New York

1699, Paris) French dramatic poet and master of French classical tragedy. His fame rests on his noble tragedies, BRITANNICUS (1670), BÉRÉNICE (1671), BAJAZET (1672), and PHÈDRE (1677).

Racine, who was reared from age 9 in a Jansenist convent, chose drama as a career in defiance of his upbringing. In 1666, after his first dramatic success, he wrote a bitter defense of his craft in a brilliant anonymous open letter (*Lettre à l'auteur des 'Hérésies imaginaires'*; "Letter to the Author of 'Imaginary Heresies'") in response to his old master Pierre Nicole, who had recently written that a novelist or playwright was a public poisoner.

Racine met Molière, the great comic poet and actor-manager, who accepted his first tragedy, *La Thébaïde ou les frères ennemis* ("The Thebaide or the Enemy Brothers"), which was produced with mediocre success in 1664. *Alexandre le Grand*, produced the year after, was as superficial and fashionable in its use of the themes of love and glory as *La Thébaïde* had been archaic in its gloom and violence. Apparently dissatisfied with Molière's relatively natural acting style, Racine surreptitiously took the script to the oldest of the three permanent theaters then in Paris, the Hôtel de Bourgogne. For this action Molière dropped Racine, who gave all the rest of his commercial plays to the Hôtel de Bourgogne. Molière's star actress, Du Parc, followed Racine and became his mistress. She had the title role in *Andromaque* (first performed 1667), in which Racine found what was to be his most appreciated theme: the tragic folly and blindness of passionate love. The play was far superior to any competitor, and it was a sensational triumph.

There followed Racine's only comedy, the three-act *Les Plaideurs* (1668; *The Litigants*), a slight but witty adaptation of Aristophanes' *Wasps*. Then came the somber *Britannicus* and the touching *Bérénice*, both set in imperial Rome. The first was the occasion of an open breach with Pierre Corneille, the declining idol of an older generation of playgoers, who attended the first night and was openly hostile. Further, *Bérénice* was based on the same historical episode as a play of Corneille produced almost simultaneously with it, such competitions being quite common.

Still trying new directions, Racine used as the subject of his next play, *Bajazet*, recent Turkish history, full of intrigue and danger. *Mithridate* (1673) involves the confrontation between an aging Asiatic despot and a Greek heroine. *Iphigénie* (produced 1674) is an adaptation of *Iphigenia at Aulis* by Euripides, but with a love plot and a happy ending. *Phèdre*, the last, most profound, and most poetic of his tragedies, used Euripides even more successfully.

Racine became a member of the Académie Française in 1672. In 1674 he obtained a sinecure conferring nobility—a treasurership of France. Within eight months of the premiere of *Phèdre*, Racine cut all links with the commercial stage, married a pious, unintellectual young woman, and accepted—with his friend the critic and satirist Nicolas Boileau—the high honor of writing the official history of the reign of the king, Louis XIV. His last two plays, commissioned by the king's wife, Mme de Maintenon, were *Esther* (1689) and *Athalie* (1691), notable for the presence of choral interludes on the Greek model.

Rackham \'rak-əm\, Arthur (b. Sept. 19, 1867, London, Eng.—d. Sept. 6, 1939, Limpsfield, Surrey)   British artist best known for illustrating classic fiction and children's literature.

Rackham studied for seven years at the Lambeth School of Art while also working full-time in an insurance office. While working as a staff artist for a newspaper, he also began illustrating books. He mastered the new halftone process, and his drawings began to reveal a unique range of imagination. Rackham became renowned with the publication of a 1900 edition of the Grimm brothers' *Fairy Tales* featuring his illustrations. In 1908 Rackham was made a full member of the Royal Society of Painters in Water-Colours.

In addition to many collections of fairy tales, Rackham illustrated works of William Shakespeare, Charles Dickens, Jonathan Swift, Izaak Walton, John Milton, Washington Irving, and Edgar Allan Poe.

Radcliffe \'rad-,klif\, Ann, *original surname* Ward \'word\ (b. July 9, 1764, London, Eng.—d. Feb. 7, 1823, London)   English gothic novelist who stands apart in her ability to infuse scenes of terror and suspense with an aura of romantic sensibility.

Radcliffe's first novels, *The Castles of Athlin and Dunbayne* (1789) and *A Sicilian Romance* (1790), were published anonymously. She achieved fame with her third novel, *The Romance of the Forest* (1791). Her next work, THE MYSTERIES OF UDOLPHO (1794), made her the most popular novelist in England. With THE ITALIAN (1797), Radcliffe realized her full powers as a writer. Her characterization of the villain Schedoni, a monk of massive physique and sinister disposition, displays a rare psychological insight. Her later works include a volume of poems (1816) and the posthumous novel *Gaston de Blondeville* (1826).

Raddall \'rad-,ôl\, Thomas Head (b. Nov. 13, 1903, Hythe, Kent, Eng.)   English-Canadian novelist who accurately depicted the history, manners, and idiom of Nova Scotians.

Raddall immigrated with his parents to Nova Scotia in 1913. His first volume of short stories, *The Pied Piper of Dipper Creek* (1939), was followed by the novel *His Majesty's Yankees* (1942), set in Nova Scotia during the American Revolution. He also wrote several other carefully researched historical romances, including *Pride's Fancy* (1946), *The Governor's Lady* (1960), and *Hangman's Beach* (1966). In addition to historical novels he wrote *The Nymph and the Lamp* (1950), a story of contemporary life at a Canadian wireless station; *Halifax, Warden of the North* (1948), a history of Halifax; and several collections of short stories, including *At the Tide's Turn* (1959) and *The Dreamers* (1986). His autobiography, *In My Time*, appeared in 1976.

Rādhā \'rä-,dä\   In Hindu mythology, the mistress of the god Krishna during that period of his life when he lived among the cowherds of Vṛndāvana. Rādhā was the wife of another *gopa* (cowherd) but was the most beloved of Krishna's consorts and his constant companion. In the bhakti (devotional) movement of Vaishnavism, the female, Rādhā, symbolizes the human soul and the male, Krishna, the divine.

The allegorical love of Rādhā has been given expression in the lyrical poetry of many Indian languages. Many Bengali poets composed such poetry, including the supremely lyrical Govinda Dās. The Bengali saint Caitanya was said to be an incarnation of the two lovers; he was Krishna on the inside and Rādhā on the outside. Caitanya's many lyrics celebrating the divine love have not survived. The *Gītagovinda* by Jayadeva was a favorite source of inspiration for the later Rajasthani and Pahari miniature painters.

Radiguet \rå-dē-'ge\, Raymond (b. June 18, 1903, Saint-Maur, Fr.—d. Dec. 12, 1923, Paris)   French novelist and poet who at the age of 17 wrote the masterpiece *Le Diable au corps* (1923; *The Devil in the Flesh*), which remains a unique expression of the poetry and perversity of an adolescent boy's love.

At 16 Radiguet took Paris by storm and joined the frenzied life of the leading figures in the Dadaist and Cubist circles, especially Jean Cocteau, whose protégé he became.

His first literary attempts were poems, *Les Joues en feu* (1920; "The Burning Cheeks"); a short two-act play with music by Georges Auric, *Les Pélicans* (1921); and articles in avant-garde reviews. With *Le Diable au corps* the critics recognized the youth as a master of the Neoclassical tradition. It is the wartime story of a schoolboy of 16 who seduces the wife of a soldier fighting on the front. This book was followed by a second and last novel, *Le Bal du comte d'Orgel* (1924; *Count Orgel Opens the Ball*). Radiguet died at 20 of typhoid.

Radishchev \,rə-'dyēsh-chif\, Aleksandr Nikolayevich (b. Aug. 20 [Aug. 31, New Style], 1749, Moscow [Russia]—d. Sept. 12 [Sept. 24], 1802, St. Petersburg)   Writer who founded the revolutionary tradition in Russian literature and thought.

Radishchev, a nobleman, was educated in Moscow at the St. Petersburg Corps of Pages and in Leipzig, Ger., where he studied law. His most important work, *Puteshestvie iz Peterburga v Moskvu* (1790; *A Journey from St. Petersburg to Moscow*), was an indictment of serfdom, autocracy, and censorship. The unfortunate timing of the book's publication (the year after the French Revolution) led to Radishchev's immediate arrest. He remained in exile in Siberia until 1797. In 1801 he was pardoned by Alexander I and employed by the government to draft legal reforms, but he committed suicide a year later. Though his work has slight claim to literary quality, his fame was great and his thought inspired later generations.

Raffi \'räf-ē\, *pseudonym of* Hakob Meliq-Hakobian \'mel-ēk-hä-'kō-bē-ən\ (b. 1835, Payajïk, Iran—d. 1888, Tiflis, Georgia, Russian Empire)   Celebrated Armenian novelist.

Raffi worked as a schoolmaster and as a journalist associated with the Russian-Armenian paper *Mshak* from 1872 to 1884. An ardent nationalist, he was preoccupied with the lot of his fellow Armenians in Iran and Turkey. His principal novels are *Jalaleddin* (1878), *The Fool* (1880), *David Bek* (1880), *The Golden Cockerel* (1882), *Sparks* (1883–90), and *Samuel* (1885), all originally published in Armenian. He also wrote a number of short stories and historical articles.

Raffles, A.J. \'raf-əlz\   Fictional character, a charming thief who was originally featured in a series of short stories by E.W. Hornung that appeared in the *Strand* and other popular British magazines beginning in the late 1880s.

The Raffles stories are narrated by his accomplice and former schoolmate Bunny Manders. Originally published in two volumes in 1899 and 1901, the collected stories later appeared as *Raffles: the Amateur Cracksman* (1906). In 1932 Barry Perowne began a new series of Raffles stories that were published in various mystery magazines and were later collected in several volumes, including *Raffles in Pursuit* (1934), *Raffles vs. Sexton Blake* (1937), and *Raffles Revisited* (1974).

Ragged Dick \\'dik\\ Children's book by Horatio ALGER, Jr., published serially in 1867 and in book form in 1868. Alternately titled *Street Life in New York with the Bootblacks*, the popular though formulaic story chronicles the successful rise of the title character from rags to respectability. Like most of Alger's novels, *Ragged Dick* served a second purpose as a guide to proper behavior for city youth.

Raghuvaṁśa \\'rä-gü-'väm-shə\\ ("Dynasty of Raghu") One of two great court epics (*mahākāvya*s) written in Sanskrit by KĀLIDĀSA about the 5th century AD. It consists of 19 cantos composed of some 1,570 verses.

The work, which deals with subjects taken from the *Rāmāyaṇa*, describes the vicissitudes of the Solar dynasty of the ancient Indian barons, culminating in the Rāmāyaṇa story of Rāma and Sītā. The *Raghuvaṁśa* is famous for its beautiful descriptions and incidental narratives, which give the poem a somewhat episodic character.

Ragnar Lothbrok \\'räg-när-'lȯth-,brȯk\\, Ragnar *also spelled* Regner *or* Regnar \\'reg-nər\\, Lothbrok *also spelled* Lodbrog *or* Lodbrok (fl. 9th century) Viking hero in medieval European literature, who is largely legendary according to reliable historical sources.

In the Anglo-Saxon Chronicle, Ragnar was said to be the father of three sons, Halfdan, Inwaer (Ivar the Boneless), and Hubba (Ubbe), who led a Viking invasion of East Anglia in 865 seeking to avenge Ragnar's murder. In the European literature of the several centuries following Ragnar's death, his name is surrounded with considerable legend. In the *Gesta Danorum* (c. 1185) of Saxo Grammaticus, he was a 9th-century Danish king whose campaigns included a battle with the Holy Roman emperor Charlemagne. According to Saxo's legendary history, Ragnar was eventually captured by the Anglo-Saxon king Aella of Northumbria and thrown into a snake pit to die. This story is also recounted in the later Icelandic works *Ragnars saga lothbrókar* and *Tháttr af Ragnarssonum*. The 12th-century Icelandic poem *Krákumál* provides a romanticized description of Ragnar's death and links him in marriage with Áslaug, a daughter of Sigurd (Siegfried) and Brynhild (Brunhild), figures from the heroic literature of the ancient Teutons. The actions of Ragnar and his sons are also recounted in the Orkney Islands' poem *Háttalykill*.

Ragnarǫk \\'räg-nə-,rœk, -,räk\\ ("Doom of the Gods") In Scandinavian mythology, the end of the world of gods and mortals. The Ragnarǫk is fully described only in the Icelandic poem *Vǫluspá* ("Sibyl's Prophecy"), probably of the late 10th century, and in the 13th-century *Prose Edda* of Snorri Sturluson, which largely follows the *Vǫluspá*. According to those two sources, the Ragnarǫk was to be preceded by cruel winters and moral chaos. Giants and demons approaching from all points of the compass were to attack the gods, who would meet them and face death like heroes. The sun would be darkened, the stars vanish, and the earth sink into the sea. Afterward, the earth would rise again, the innocent Balder (the slain son of Odin and Frigg) return from the dead, and the hosts of the just live in a hall roofed with gold.

Disjointed allusions to the Ragnarǫk, found in many other sources, show that conceptions of it varied. According to one poem, two human beings, Lif and Lifthrasir ("Life" and "Vitality"), were to emerge from Yggdrasil, the world tree (which would not be destroyed), and repeople the earth.

Rahv \\'räv\\, Philip (b. March 10, 1908, Kupin, Ukraine, Russian Empire—d. Dec. 22, 1973, Cambridge, Mass., U.S.) Ukrainian-born American critic who was cofounder with William Phillips of *Partisan Review*, a journal of literature and social thought.

Rahv immigrated to the United States in 1922 and contributed to *The New Masses, The Nation, The New Republic,* and *The New Leader*. He wrote *Fourteen Essays on Literary Themes* (1949; enlarged, 1957). He also edited many books, including *The Partisan Reader* (1946, with Phillips), *The Discovery of Europe: The Story of the American Experience in the Old World* (1947), *Literature in America* (1958), *Modern Occasions* (1966), and collections of short novels by Henry James, Leo Tolstoy, and other writers.

Raimar *see* RÜCKERT.

Rainbow, The Novel by D.H. LAWRENCE, published in 1915. The novel was officially banned after it was labeled obscene, and unsold copies were confiscated.

The story line traces three generations of the Brangwen family in the Midlands of England from 1840 to 1905. The marriage of farmer Tom Brangwen and foreigner Lydia Lensky eventually breaks down. Likewise, the marriage of Lydia's daughter Anna to Tom's nephew Will gradually fails. The novel is largely devoted to Will and Anna's oldest child, the schoolteacher Ursula, who stops short of marriage when she is unsatisfied by her love affair with the conventional soldier Anton Skrebensky. The appearance of a rainbow at the end of the novel is a sign of hope for Ursula, whose story is continued in Lawrence's *Women in Love*.

rainbow serpent A widely recognized serpent deity of contemporary preliterate societies; it is symbolized by the rainbow, mythically interpreted as a great snake.

Raine \\'rān\\, Kathleen (Jessie) (b. June 14, 1908, London, Eng.) Poet and critic noted for her mystical and visionary poetry.

Raine studied at Girton College, Cambridge, and in the 1930s was one of a group of Cambridge poets. Her gift for exactness of observation and precision of diction is evident in her first book of poems, *Stone and Flower* (1943), as well as in her later poetry. Her work, which has been characterized as meditative and lyrical, is concerned with universal themes such as nature, life, death, and eternity. Raine's many volumes of poems include *The Pythoness* (1949), *The Hollow Hill* (1965), *The Lost Country* (1971), *On a Deserted Shore* (1973), *The Oval Portrait* (1977), *The Oracle in the Heart, and Other Poems, 1975–1978* (1980), *Collected Poems, 1935–1980* (1981), *The Presence: Poems 1984–87* (1987), *Autobiographies* (1991), and *Living with Mystery* (1992). Among her critical works are *Blake and Tradition*, 2 vol. (1968), *From Blake to a Vision* (1978), *The Human Face of God: William Blake and the Book of Job* (1982), and *Yeats the Initiate* (1986). She also published four volumes of autobiography.

Rainis \\'rä-ĕ-nis\\, *pseudonym of* Jānis Pliekšāns \\'plyek-,shänz\\ (b. Sept. 11, 1865, Varslavāni, Latvia, Russian Empire—d. Sept. 12, 1929, Majori, Latvia) Latvian poet and dramatist whose works were outstanding both as literature and for their assertion of national freedom and social consciousness.

From 1891 to 1895 Rainis edited the newspaper *Dienas Lapa*, aimed at promoting social and class consciousness in the peasantry. During the next few years he was banished, returned to Latvia and took part in the unsuccessful revolution of 1905, immigrated to Switzerland, and returned again in 1920, after Latvia had achieved independence.

Rainis' first volume of poetry was *Tālas noskanas zilā vakarā* (1903; "Far-Off Reflections on a Blue Evening"). *Gals un sākums* (1912; "End and Beginning") is imbued with the spirit of Georg Hegel's dialectical philosophy. In his plays Rainis used motifs from folklore as symbols for his political ideals.

Rainis also translated works by William Shakespeare, Friedrich von Schiller, Heinrich Heine, and Aleksandr Pushkin, as well as J.W. von Goethe's *Faust*.

Raisin in the Sun, A Drama in three acts by Lorraine HANSBERRY, published and produced in 1959. The play's title is taken from "Harlem," a poem by Langston Hughes, which examines the question "What happens to a dream deferred? Does it dry up/like a raisin in the sun? . . ." This penetrating psychological study of a working-class black family on the south side of Chicago in the late 1940s reflected Hansberry's own experiences of racial harassment after her prosperous family moved into a white neighborhood.

Walter Lee Younger, a chauffeur, hopes to use his father's life-insurance money to open a liquor store with two partners. His mother, with the support of Walter's pragmatic wife Ruth and independent sister Beneatha, instead uses part of the money as a down payment on a house in an all-white neighborhood. Mama gives the remaining money, including Beneatha's share (which is to be deposited in the bank), to Walter. After one of his partners absconds with the money, Walter despondently contacts Karl Lindner, a representative of the white neighborhood who had earlier tried to buy out the Youngers so as to avoid racial integration, intending to accept his offer. However, Walter finally rejects the proposal.

Raj Quartet, The \\'räj, 'räzh\\ Series of four novels by Paul SCOTT. The tetralogy, composed of *The Jewel in the Crown* (1966), *The Day of the Scorpion* (1968), *The Towers of Silence* (1971), and *A Division of the Spoils* (1975), is set in India during the years leading up to that country's independence from the British raj (sovereignty). The story examines the role of the British in India and the effect of their presence in the country during its struggle for independence. The four novels taken as a whole present a complex portrait of both ruling British and Indian society and the relationship between the two. One of the central incidents of the story is the rape of an Englishwoman, and one of the main characters is the Indian Hari Kumar, who is accused of having participated in the rape. Reared in England where he received an upper-class education, Kumar finds that he is too British to be an Indian but at the same time is excluded from British society because of his race.

rakshasa \\'räk-shə-sə\\ [Sanskrit *rākṣasaḥ,* a derivative of *rakṣaḥ* damage, injury, nocturnal demon] A demon or evil spirit of Hindu mythology.

Ralph Roister Doister \\'ralf-'rȯis-tər-'dȯis-tər, 'räf\\ Earliest known English comedy, a play in five acts written by Nicholas UDALL, produced about 1553 and published in approximately 1566. This farcical tale of a cowardly braggart (or "miles gloriosus") who is egged on by his mischievous friend to pay suit to an engaged widow was the first example of the Roman five-act structure on an English stage. Udall was influenced by the comedies of the Romans Plautus and Terence; one of the subplots, in fact, was adapted from Terence's *Eunuchus*. Written in short, rhymed doggerel, peppered with songs and double entendres, this original blend of classical structure with contemporary English vernacular caused a stir when it was first performed. Subsequent English dramatists were invariably influenced by the play; William Shakespeare used many of Udall's techniques (and borrowed some of his characters) in his own comedies. *Ralph Roister Doister* marks the transition from medieval morality plays into secular drama.

Rāma \\'rä-mə\\ One of the most widely worshiped Hindu deities, the embodiment of chivalry and virtue. Although there are three Rāmas mentioned in Indian tradition (Paraśurāma, Balarāma, and Rāmacandra), the name is specifically associated with Rāmacandra, the seventh incarnation (avatar) of Lord Vishnu. It is possible that Rāma was an actual historical figure, a tribal hero of ancient India who was later deified. His story is told briefly in the MAHĀBHĀRATA ("Great Epic of the Bharata Dynasty") and at great length in the *Rāmāyaṇa* ("Romance of Rāma").

References to Rāma as an incarnation of Vishnu appear in the early centuries AD; it was not until the 14th and 15th centuries that distinct sects appeared venerating him as the supreme god. Rāma's popularity was increased greatly by the retelling of the Sanskrit epics in such works as Tulsīdās' celebrated *Rāmcaritmānas* ("Sacred Lake of the Acts of Rāma").

Rāmāyaṇa \\rä-'mä-yə-nə\\ ("Romance of Rāma") Shorter of the two great epic poems of India, the other being the *Mahābhārata*. The *Rāmāyaṇa* was composed in Sanskrit, probably not before 300 BC, by the poet Vālmīki, and in its present form consists of some 24,000 couplets divided into seven books.

The poem describes the royal birth of Rāma, his tutelage under the sage Viśvāmitra, and his success in bending Śiva's (Shiva's) mighty bow, thus winning Sītā, the daughter of King Janaka, for his wife. After Rāma is banished from his position as heir by an intrigue, he retreats to the forest with his wife and his half brother, Lakṣmaṇa. There Rāvaṇa, the demon-king of Laṅkā, carries off Sītā, who resolutely rejects his attentions. After numerous adventures Rāma slays Rāvaṇa and rescues Sītā. When they return to his kingdom, however, Rāma learns that the people question the queen's chastity, and he banishes her to the forest where she gives birth to Rāma's two sons. The family is reunited when the sons come of age, but Sītā, after again protesting her innocence, asks to be received by the earth, which swallows her up.

The poem enjoys immense popularity in India, where its recitation is considered an act of great merit. Many of its translations into the vernacular languages are themselves works of literary merit, including the Tamil version of Kampaṇ, the Bengali version of Kṛttibās, and the Awadhi version, the *Rāmcaritmānas*, of Tulsīdās.

Rambler, The A twopenny sheet issued twice weekly in London by the publisher John Payne between 1750 and 1752, each issue containing a single anonymous essay. All but five of the 208 periodical essays were written by Samuel Johnson. A majority of the essays deal with the disappointments inherent in life and with setbacks to ambition, and they were intended to instruct, not to entertain.

The Rambler did not sell well as a periodical, though it was an immense success when it was reissued, with the essays revised, in book form in 1753. It also inspired other periodicals, notably John Hawkesworth's *The Adventurer* (1752–54), Edward Moore's lively *The World* (1753–56), George Colman's and Bonnell Thornton's *The Connoisseur* (1754–56), and Henry Mackenzie's Scottish periodical *The Mirror* (1779–80).

Rambouillet \\rän-bü-'ye\\, Catherine de Vivonne, Marquise de (b. 1588, Rome [Italy]—d. Dec. 2, 1665, Paris, Fr.) Aristocratic hostess who exerted a powerful influence on the development of French literature in the first half of the 17th century.

Revolted by the coarseness of the French court under Henry IV and distressed by the amount of political intrigue, Catherine de Vivonne set out to establish at her town house, the Hôtel de Rambouillet, a salon devoted to literature and cultured conversation where the aristocracy and the literati could mingle on an equal footing. With its emphasis on refinement and delicacy in thought and expression, the salon eventually bred the extravagances that Molière pilloried unmercifully in *Les Précieuses ridicules*. Nevertheless, her salon did set a standard for correct and elegant French, and its *habitués* learned the art of exploring human psychology that was to be the basis of French classical literature.

Rāmcaritmānas \'räm-ˌkə-rēt-'mä-nəs\ ("Sacred Lake of the Acts of Rāma") Version written in Awadhi (a language of Uttar Pradesh) of the Sanskrit epic poem the *Rāmāyaṇa*, one of the masterpieces of medieval Hindu literature and a work with significant influence on modern Hinduism. Written in the 16th century by the poet TULSĪDĀS, the poem is distinguished both by its great expression of love for a personal god and by its exemplification through its characters of the ideal conduct of a husband and ruler (Rāma), wife (Sītā), and brother (Lakṣmaṇa).

Rameau's Nephew \rä-'mō\ Novel by Denis DIDEROT, written between 1761 and 1774 but not published during the author's lifetime. J.W. von Goethe translated the text into German in 1805, and it was published in French as *Le Neveu de Rameau* in 1821. The first printing from the original manuscript was not made until 1891.

Set in a café in Paris, the work takes the form of a conversation between "Moi," a representative of the author, and "Lui," a young, cynical bohemian nephew of the French composer Jean-Philippe Rameau. As they display their wit and show off their knowledge, the conversation begins to resemble a chess game with its gambits and sly stratagems. The two men satirize society, in which mediocrity is allowed to flourish, and discuss the nature of genius, music, and art.

Ramos \'rä-müsh\, Graciliano (b. Oct. 27, 1892, Quebrângulo, Braz.—d. March 20, 1953, Rio de Janeiro) Brazilian regional novelist whose works explore the lives of characters shaped by the rural misery of northeastern Brazil.

Ramos spent most of his life in the backlands town of Palmeira dos Índios. His memoirs, *Infância* (1945; "Childhood"), describe the hazards of his family's fortunes in the drought-stricken area, his meager schooling, and his self-education.

In 1934 he published his best-known work, *São Bernardo*, the reflections of Paulo Honório, who has risen by methods ranging from petty deceit to murder to become master of the plantation St. Bernard, where he was once a hired hand.

In 1936 Ramos was arrested and imprisoned on a penal island. No explanation for his arrest was ever given him. On his release from prison he settled in Rio de Janeiro. In 1938 he wrote *Vidas sêcas* (*Barren Lives*), the story of a family's flight from drought to a mysterious land of promise—the city.

Ramsay \'ram-zē\, Allan (b. Oct. 15, 1686, Leadhills, Lanarkshire, Scot.—d. Jan. 7, 1758, Edinburgh) Scottish poet and literary antiquary who maintained national poetic traditions by writing Scots poetry and by preserving the work of earlier Scottish poets.

Ramsay became a wig maker and later a bookseller, and he helped found the Easy Club, a Jacobite literary society. His pen names, first Isaac Bickerstaff and later Gawin Douglas, suggest both Augustan English and medieval Scottish influences. He soon established a reputation as a prolific composer of verse in both English and Scots; and, by collecting and publishing poems by Robert Henryson, William Dunbar, and other late medieval Scottish writers, he made certain of their survival.

In 1721 Ramsay published a subscriber's edition of his own poems; a second volume appeared in 1728. *The Tea-Table Miscellany*, 3 vol. (1724–37), *The Ever Green*, 2 vol. (1724), and *Scots Proverbs* (1737) make up the bulk of his collection of old Scottish songs, poems, and wise sayings.

Ramsay family \'ram-zē\ Fictional characters, the protagonists of Virginia Woolf's experimental novel TO THE LIGHTHOUSE.

Based partly on Woolf's father, Sir Leslie Stephen, Mr. Ramsay is a philosophy professor who is esteemed by his students as an inspiring intellect but disliked by his eight children because of his sarcastic wit and faultfinding. Mrs. Ramsay, the prototypical nurturing mother and wife, is the emotional center of the book. Even after her death, she lives on as an influence on her children and friends and on the household. Among the children are James, the youngest and his mother's favorite; Camilla, called Cam; Prue, who later dies in childbirth; and Andrew, who dies in France during World War I.

Ramuz \rä-'mǖ\, Charles-Ferdinand (b. Sept. 24, 1878, Cully, Switz.—d. May 23, 1947, Pully, near Lausanne) Novelist whose realistic, poetic, and somewhat allegorical stories of people in conflict with nature made him one of the most prominent French-Swiss writers of the 20th century.

A city boy, heir to a refined, middle-class culture, Ramuz nonetheless chose to write about rustic people in a language deliberately simple and earthy. Before World War I he spent a number of years in Paris and struck up a friendship with the composer Igor Stravinsky, for whom he wrote the text of *Histoire du soldat* (1918; *The Soldier's Tale*).

Ramuz's representative theme is of mountaineers, farmers, or villagers fighting heroically but often tragically against catastrophe or the force of myth. In *La Grande Peur dans la montagne* (1925; *Terror on the Mountain*), young villagers challenge fate by grazing their cattle on a mountain pasture despite a curse that hangs over it. Among his other works are *La Beauté sur la terre* (1927; *Beauty on Earth*) and *Derborence* (1934; *When the Mountain Fell*).

Ran \'rän\, *Old Norse* Rán. Norse goddess of the sea and wife of Aegir who was associated with shipwrecks and drowning. She is said to have had nine daughters with Aegir.

Ranaivo \rä-'nī-ˌvō\, Flavien (b. May 13, 1914, Arivonimamo, Madagascar) Lyric poet deeply influenced by Malagasy ballad and song forms, in particular the *hain-teny*, a poetic dialogue usually on the subject of love. Ranaivo also held a number of important civic and government posts.

Ranaivo published three volumes of verse: *L'Ombre et le vent* (1947; "Shadow and Wind"), *Mes chansons de toujours* (1955; "My Lifelong Songs"), and *Le Retour au bercail* (1962; "Return to the Fold").

Ranaivo followed Jean-Joseph Rabearivelo in adapting traditional Malagasy poetry into French, and his crisp and sometimes impudent and slangy use of language reflected the vernacular traditions that inspired him. His poems were personal rather than ideological and were praised for their technical perfection and lyricism.

Rand \'rand\, Ayn \'īn\, *original name* Alice *or* Alissa Rosenbaum \'rō-zən-ˌbȯm\ (b. Feb. 2, 1905, St. Petersburg, Russia—d. March 6, 1982, New York, N.Y., U.S.) Russian-born American writer who, in novels noted for their commercial success, presented her philosophy of objectivism, which held that all real achievement is the product of individual ability and effort, that laissez-faire capitalism is most congenial to the exercise of talent, and that selfishness is a virtue, altruism a vice. Her reversal of the traditional Judeo-Christian ethic won her a cult of followers.

After graduating from the University of Petrograd in 1924, Rand immigrated to the United States in 1926 and worked as a screenwriter in Hollywood. THE FOUNTAINHEAD (1943), her first best-selling novel, depicts a highly romanticized architect-hero, a superior individual whose egoism and genius prevail over timid traditionalism and social conformism. The allegorical ATLAS SHRUGGED (1957) combines science fiction and a political message. Rand also wrote a number of nonfiction works expounding her beliefs, including *For the New Intellectual: The Philosophy of Ayn Rand* (1961), and she edited two journals propounding her ideas, *The Objectivist* (1962–71) and *The Ayn Rand Letter* (1971–76).

Randolph \'ran-,dälf, -,dôlf, -dəlf\, Thomas (b. June 15, 1605, Newnham-cum-Badby, Northamptonshire, Eng.—d. March 1635, Blatherwycke, Northamptonshire) English poet and dramatist who used his knowledge of Aristotelian logic to create a unique kind of comedy.

Randolph's university plays—*Aristippus; or, The Joviall Philosopher* and *The Conceited Pedler*, both comedies—were performed at Cambridge and were published in 1630. *Aristippus* was a debate about the relative virtues of ale and sack (sherry) and was full of the terms of Aristotelian logic and innumerable puns drawn from Randolph's classical learning. *The Jealous Lovers* (1634), a comedy, was well received. *The Muse's Looking-Glass*, performed about 1630, opens and closes with a masque and consists of 15 scenes presented before a comic Puritan couple, with each scene devoted to an Aristotelian vice. *Hey for Honesty*, a comedy adapted from *The Plutus* of Aristophanes, was published in 1651.

Some of Randolph's poetry appeared in collections during his lifetime, notably three poems addressed to Ben Jonson. A posthumous collection (1638) contained *The Muse's Looking-Glass* and *Amyntas*.

Random, Roderick \'räd-ə-rik-'ran-dəm\ A fictional character, the roguish Scottish protagonist of Tobias Smollett's picaresque novel RODERICK RANDOM.

Ransom \'ran-səm\, John Crowe (b. April 30, 1888, Pulaski, Tenn., U.S.—d. July 4, 1974, Gambier, Ohio) American poet and critic, leading theorist of the Southern literary renaissance that began after World War I. Ransom's *The New Criticism* (1941) provided the name for the influential mid-20th-century school of criticism (*see* NEW CRITICISM).

Ransom was educated at Vanderbilt University, Nashville, Tenn., and from 1914 to 1937 he taught English there. At Vanderbilt he also was the leader of the Fugitives, a group of poets who published the influential literary magazine *The Fugitive* (1922–25) and shared a belief in the South and its regional traditions. He was among those Fugitives who became known as the Agrarians. Their *I'll Take My Stand* (1930) criticized the idea that industrialization was the answer to the needs of the South.

Ransom taught from 1937 until his retirement in 1958 at Kenyon College, Gambier, Ohio, where he founded and edited (1939–59) the literary magazine *The Kenyon Review*. Ransom's literary studies include *God Without Thunder* (1930); *The World's Body* (1938), in which he takes the position that poetry and science furnish different but equally valid knowledge about the world; *Poems and Essays* (1955); and *Beating the Bushes: Selected Essays, 1941–1970* (1972). Ransom's poetry is collected in *Chills and Fever* (1924) and *Two Gentlemen in Bonds* (1927).

Ransom, Basil \'baz-əl-'ran-səm, 'bas-, 'bāz-, 'bäs-\ Fictional character, an educated, autocratic, and elegant Confederate army veteran in Henry James's novel THE BOSTONIANS.

Ransome \'ran-səm\, Arthur (Michell) (b. Jan. 18, 1884, Leeds, Yorkshire, Eng.—d. June 3, 1967, Manchester) Writer of children's adventure novels noted for their detailed and colorful accounts of the perception and imagination of children.

Ransome worked in a publishing house and then became a war correspondent during World War I, and in the course of his work he made several trips to Russia. He also traveled in China, Egypt, and the Sudan, and his experiences provided the inspiration for *Old Peter's Russian Tales* (1916) and *Racundra's*

First Cruise (1923), about sailing on the Baltic Sea. Ransome's many other works include *Swallows and Amazons* (1931), *Pigeon Post* (1936), *We Didn't Mean to Go to Sea* (1937), *Missee Lee* (1941), and *Mainly About Fishing* (1959). *The Autobiography of Arthur Ransome* was published in 1976.

Ransom of Red Chief, The Short story by O. HENRY, published in the collection *Whirligigs* in 1910. In the story two kidnappers make off with the young son of a prominent man only to find that the child is more trouble than he is worth; in the end, they agree to pay the boy's father to take him back. This highly popular story reflects the influences of Mark Twain and Ambrose Bierce. Told in the first person in a humorous, energetic style, the story embodies the mischievous spirit of American boyhood.

Rao \'raů\, Raja (b. Nov. 21, 1909, Hassan, Mysore [now Karnātaka], India) Indian writer of English-language novels and short stories.

Descended from a distinguished Brahman family, Rao studied at Nizam College, Hyderābād, and then at age 19 left India for France to study literature and history. His first novel, *Kanthapura* (1938), dealt with the Indian independence movement. Returning to India in 1939, Rao spent the war years editing a journal and engaging in underground activities against the British. Following World War II he alternated between India and France before finally becoming a professor of philosophy at the University of Texas, Austin, in 1965.

Rao's second novel, *The Serpent and the Rope* (1960), considered his masterpiece, is a philosophical and somewhat abstract account of an intellectual Brahman and his wife who are seeking spiritual truth in India, France, and England. Other novels include the allegorical *The Cat and Shakespeare: A Tale of India* (1965), *Comrade Kirillov* (1976), an examination of communism, and *The Chessmaster and His Moves* (1988), peopled by characters from various cultures seeking their identities. Rao's short stories were collected in *The Cow of the Barricades and Other Stories* (1947) and *The Policeman and the Rose* (1978).

Raoul de Houdenc \rȧ-ül-də-ü-'deⁿ\ or **Raoul** de Houdan \ü-däⁿ\ (fl. *c.* 1200–30) Trouvère poet-musician of courtly romances, credited with writing one of the first French romances, told in an ornate, allegorical style.

Little is known of Raoul's life. He was familiar with Paris and seems to have lived as a minstrel, singing sometimes in the street and sometimes at the courts of the minor nobility. His greatest work, the Arthurian romance *Méraugis de Portlesguez*, was constructed on a single theme, developed through myriad, enveloping allegorical details. His *Songe d'enfer* ("Dream of Hell") may have influenced Dante in writing *The Divine Comedy*. Raoul also wrote the *Roman des ailes* ("The Romance of the Wings"), in which he enumerates the qualities necessary for courtly love. Raoul may also have been the author of an allegorical poem, *La Voie de Paradis* ("The Way of Paradise"), and a romance, *Vengeance de Raguidel*.

Rape of the Lock, The Mock-epic poem in heroic couplets by Alexander POPE. The first version, published in 1712, consisted of two cantos; the final version, published in 1714, was expanded to five cantos.

Based on an actual incident and written to reconcile the families that had been estranged by it, *The Rape of the Lock* recounts the story of a young woman who has a lock of hair stolen by an ardent young man. Pope couches the trivial event in terms usually reserved for incidents of great moment—such as the quarrel between the Greeks and the Trojans. The poem marries a rich range of literary allusions and an ironic commentary on the contemporary social world with a sense of suppressed energy threatening to break through the civilized veneer.

RAPP \\'ràp\\, *abbreviation of* Rossiyskaya Assotsiatsiya Proletarskikh Pisateley ("Russian Association of Proletarian Writers")   Soviet association formed (1928) out of various groups of proletarian writers (among them former members of Proletkult). RAPP was dedicated to defining a truly proletarian literature and to eliminating writers whose works were not thoroughly imbued with communist ideology. Under the leadership of Leopold Leonardovich Averbakh, the association managed to seize control of literary activity in 1929, when it received official sanction for its program of establishing the Soviet First Five-Year Plan as the sole theme of Soviet literature. The mechanical literature that was written on assignment and that resulted from RAPP's dictatorship led to an official about-face in 1932, when RAPP was liquidated and the all-inclusive Union of Soviet Writers was founded to promote the doctrine of Socialist Realism.

Rappaccini's Daughter \\,rap-ə-'chē-nē\\   Allegorical short story by Nathaniel HAWTHORNE, first published in *United States Magazine and Democratic Review* (December 1844) and collected in *Mosses from an Old Manse* (1846).

Rappaccini, a scholar-scientist in Padua, grows only poisonous plants in his lush garden. His lovely daughter, Beatrice, has been nurtured on poison and is sustained by her father's toxic plants. Giovanni, a student who lives next door to Rappaccini, falls in love with Beatrice and himself becomes contaminated by the garden's poisonous aura. The antidote he is given cures him; when he gives it to Beatrice, however, she drinks it and dies.

rasa \\'rəs-ə\\ [Sanskrit *rasaḥ* essence, taste, flavor, literally, sap, juice]   In Sanskrit literature, the concept of aesthetic flavor, or an essential element of any work of art that can only be suggested, not described. It is a kind of contemplative abstraction in which the inwardness of human feelings suffuses the surrounding world of embodied forms.

The theory of *rasa* is attributed to Bharata, a sage-priest who may have lived about AD 500. It was developed by the rhetorician and philosopher Abhinavagupta (c. AD 1000), who applied it to all varieties of theater and poetry. The principal human feelings, according to Bharata, are delight, laughter, sorrow, anger, energy, fear, disgust, heroism, and astonishment, all of which may be recast in contemplative form as the various *rasas*: erotic, comic, pathetic, furious, heroic, terrible, odious, marvelous, and quietistic.

Rashōmon \\rä-'shō-mōn\\ ("The Rashō Gate")   Short story by AKUTAGAWA Ryūnosuke, published in Japanese in 1915 in a university literary magazine.

Set in 12th-century Kyōto, the story reveals in spare and elegant language the thoughts of a man on the edge of a life of crime and the incident that pushes him over the brink. Combined with Akutagawa's later story "Yabu no naka" (1921; "In a Grove"), "Rashōmon" was the starting point for Japanese director Kurosawa Akira's classic film *Rashomon* (1951).

Raskolnikov, Rodion \\rə-dʲi-'ȯn-,rə-'skȯlʲ-nʲi-kəf\\   Fictional character who is the protagonist of the novel CRIME AND PUNISHMENT by Fyodor Dostoyevsky. An impoverished student who murders a pawnbroker and her stepsister, Raskolnikov embodies the author's belief that salvation is possible only through atonement.

Rasmussen \\'ràs-,mùs-en, *Angl* 'ras-mə-sən\\, Halfdan (b. Jan. 29, 1915, Copenhagen, Den.)   Danish poet of social protest and writer of nonsense verse.

In Rasmussen's early poetry collections, *Soldat eller menneske* (1941; "Soldier or Human Being") and *Digte under Besaettelsen* (1945; "Poems During the Occupation"), a collection of protest poems published during the German occupation of Denmark, he documents his various experiences from the war years with simplicity and sincerity. His work of the late 1940s is pessimistic and despairing. In *På knae for livet* (1948; "Kneeling to Life") and *Den som har set september* (1949; "The One who Experienced September") the poet rejects all political systems and ideologies. In a didactic poem on his time, "Generation," from the collection *Forventning* (1951; "Expectation"), Rasmussen characterized the despair and anxiety that followed the bombing of Hiroshima. He also wrote poetry about his travels, children's verse, and nonsense verse.

Raspe \\'räs-pə\\, Rudolf Erich (b. 1737, Hannover, Hanover [Germany]—d. 1794, Muckross, County Kerry, Ire.)   German scholar and adventurer best remembered as the author of the popular tall tales about the adventures of Baron MÜNCHHAUSEN.

Raspe worked in several university libraries before 1767, when he was appointed librarian and custodian of the collection of gems and coins owned by the landgraf of Hesse-Kassel. Raspe was one of the first scholars to examine the work of Ossian, the supposed author of epic poetry "discovered" in Scotland, and that of Thomas Percy's *Reliques of Ancient English Poetry*, a collection of old ballads and poems first published in England in 1765. Raspe acquired a reputation for scholarship, and he was elected to the Royal Society in 1769. In 1775, however, he began stealing from the landgraf's gem collection and had to flee to England to escape arrest. While living there as a fugitive, Raspe succeeded in publishing anonymously a collection of humorous and highly colored stories under the title *Baron Munchausen's Narrative of His Marvellous Travels and Campaigns in Russia*. Although Raspe had known the baron in Göttingen, few of the tales were actually derived from him.

In 1786 and again in 1788, the poet G.A. Bürger translated into German and considerably enlarged Raspe's tales. Bürger's translations served to introduce Münchhausen to world literature, and Raspe's authorship of the original was not known until 1847, when Heinrich Döring revealed the fact in his biography of Bürger.

Rasselas \\'ras-i-ləs\\ (*in full* The History of Rasselas, Prince of Abissinia)   Philosophical romance by Samuel JOHNSON published in 1759 as *The Prince of Abissinia*. Supposedly written in the space of a week, *Rasselas* explores and exposes the vanity of the human search for happiness.

The work is addressed to those who "listen with credulity to the whispers of fancy and pursue with eagerness the phantoms of hope." Hoping to learn how he should live, Rasselas meets with men of varied occupations and interests—scholars, astronomers, shepherds, hermits, poets—and explores their manner of life. He finds that complete happiness is elusive and that "while you are making the choice of life, you neglect to live"—which is, perhaps, the most important moral to be drawn from the tale.

rat rhyme *chiefly Scottish*   A scrap of nonsense or doggerel verse.

Rattigan \\'rat-i-gən\\, Sir Terence (Mervyn) (b. June 10, 1911, London, Eng.—d. Nov. 30, 1977, Hamilton, Bermuda)   English playwright who was a master of the well-made play.

Rattigan had early success with two farces, *French Without Tears* (1937) and *While the Sun Shines* (1944). His drama *The Winslow Boy* (1946) was based on a real-life case in which a young boy at the Royal Naval College was unjustly accused of theft. *Separate Tables* (1955), perhaps his best-known work, takes as its theme the isolation and frustration that result from rigidly imposed social conventions. *Ross* (1960) explores the life of T.E. Lawrence (Lawrence of Arabia) and is less traditional in its structure. *A Bequest to the Nation* (1970) reviews the intimate, personal aspects of Lord Nelson's life. His last play, published posthumously, was *Cause Célèbre* (1978).

Ratushinskaya \ˌrä-tü-'shȯn-skə-yə\, Irina Georgiyevna (b. March 4, 1954, Odessa, Ukrainian S.S.R. [now in Ukraine]) Russian lyric poet, essayist, and political dissident who was imprisoned for four years in a Soviet labor camp.

Ratushinskaya was educated at Odessa University and taught physics in Odessa from 1976 to 1978. For her advocacy of human rights, she was sentenced to serve seven years in a labor camp; she was released in 1986 after serving almost four years. After she left the country, her citizenship was revoked.

Ratushinskaya's poetry from before her imprisonment employed much Christian religious imagery and concerned matters of love, creativity, and her response to the beauty of nature. Her later poetry expanded on these themes but took a more political turn. While in prison Ratushinskaya wrote some 250 poems, first scratching them into bars of soap and then, after memorizing them, washing them away. *Stikhi* (1984; *Poems*) was published while she was imprisoned. Other collections of poetry in translation include *No, I'm Not Afraid* (1986), *Beyond the Limit* (1987), *Pencil Letter* (1988), and *Dance With a Shadow* (1992). A memoir of her life in the labor camp was published as *Grey Is the Color of Hope* (1988); *In the Beginning* (1990) records her life up to her imprisonment.

Raven \'rä-vən\, Simon (Arthur Noël) (b. Dec. 28, 1927, Leicester, Leicestershire, Eng.) English novelist, playwright, and journalist, known particularly for his portrayal of the mid-20th-century upper classes of English society in *Alms for Oblivion*.

Raven's most important work is the novel sequence *Alms for Oblivion*, which consists of *The Rich Pay Late* (1964), *Friends in Low Places* (1965), *The Sabre Squadron* (1966), *Fielding Gray* (1967), *The Judas Boy* (1968), *Places Where They Sing* (1970), *Sound the Retreat* (1971), *Come Like Shadows* (1972), *Bring Forth the Body* (1974), and *The Survivors* (1976). His other novels include *The Roses of Picardie* (1980) and *An Inch of Fortune* (1980). In the 1980s Raven began a second series, *The First-Born of Egypt*, with *Morning Star* (1984) and *The Face of the Waters* (1985). His dramatizations for television of Aldous Huxley's *Point Counter Point* (broadcast, 1968) and of Anthony Trollope's *The Way We Live Now* (broadcast, 1969) and *The Pallisers* (broadcast, 1974), as well as *Edward and Mrs. Simpson*, based on Frances Donaldson's *Edward VIII* (broadcast, 1978), reached wide audiences.

Among his other writings are a long essay, *The English Gentleman* (1961), and an autobiography, *Shadows on the Grass* (1982).

Raven, The Best-known poem by Edgar Allan POE, published in 1845 and collected in *The Raven and Other Poems* the same year. Poe achieved instant national fame with the publication of this melancholy evocation of lost love.

On a stormy December midnight, a grieving student is visited by a raven who speaks but one word, "Nevermore." As the student laments his lost love Lenore, the raven's insistent repetition of the word becomes an increasingly harrowing response to the student's own fears and longing.

The poem consists of 18 six-line stanzas; the first five lines of each are written in trochaic octameter, the sixth in trochaic tetrameter. The rhyme pattern, *abcbbb*, enhances the gloom of the lyric; the *b* rhymes are, or rhyme with, "Lenore" and "Nevermore." Poe's 1846 essay "The Philosophy of Composition" describes his careful crafting of the poem.

Raven cycle A collection of oral trickster-transformer tales popular mainly among the Indians of the Northwest Pacific

Coast from Alaska to northwestern Washington. The tales feature Raven as a culture hero, an alternately clever and stupid bird-human whose voracious appetite and eroticism give rise to violent and amorous adventures.

The cycle begins with a boy's birth and relates early adventures that include the seduction of his aunt (some versions substitute the daughter of the Sky Chief) and his flight to the sky to escape the ensuing flood. Raven, his child, falls to earth, where he is adopted by a chief; as an adult he transforms the earth from a dark and arid land inhabited by a variety of ferocious monsters into a land of rivers, lakes, and mountains inhabited by animals and human beings. He later travels about, changing aspects of the physical environment into their present form, often through deception.

rāwī \'rä-ˌwē\ [Arabic, reciter] In Arabic literature, a professional reciter of poetry. The *rāwī*s preserved pre-Islāmic poetry in oral tradition until it was written down in the 8th century.

One or more *rāwī*s attached themselves to a particular poet and learned his works by heart. They then recited and explained the poet's verse before a wider audience. Such an attachment often became an apprenticeship, and, after mastering the poetic technique, some *rāwī*s became poets in their own right. When the great philological schools of Basra and Kūfah in Iraq were formed in the 8th century, the *rāwī*s were sought out by scholars as preservers of an ancient language and poetic style that was falling into disuse.

The method of preserving poetry through *rāwī*s, relying as it did on memory, however, was imperfect, and the poetry of the pre-Islāmic period was subject to mutations, omissions, unauthorized additions, and the transposition of lines and verses.

Rawlings \'rȯ-liŋz\, Marjorie Kinnan (b. Aug. 8, 1896, Washington, D.C., U.S.—d. Dec. 14, 1953, St. Augustine, Fla.) American short-story writer and novelist who founded a regional literature of backwoods Florida.

After graduating from the University of Wisconsin in 1918, Rawlings worked as a journalist for 10 years, meanwhile trying, unsuccessfully, to write stories that would sell. While visiting Florida in 1926, she was enchanted by the landscape, and in 1928 she moved to Cross Creek, Hawthorn, Fla., where she devoted herself to writing fiction. She finally succeeded with her short story "Gal Young Un." Her first novel was *South Moon Under* (1933), followed by *Golden Apples* (1935) and the book for which she is best known, THE YEARLING (1938), which won the Pulitzer Prize for fiction in 1939.

Rawlings took her material from the people and land around her, and her books are less fiction than vivid factual reporting. Rawlings' books have been widely acclaimed for their magical description of the landscape, a quality that is evident in the minor classic *The Yearling*.

Other works include *Cross Creek* (1942), a mystical, autobiographical book describing her discovery of her Florida home, and *The Sojourner* (1953).

Raynouard \rä-'nwär\, François-Juste-Marie (b. Sept. 18, 1761, Brignoles, Fr.—d. Oct. 27, 1836, Passy) French dramatist and philologist who also played a part in the politics of the French Revolution and the Napoleonic period.

Trained as a lawyer, Raynouard was elected to the Legislative Assembly in 1791. In 1793 he was imprisoned, but he was released in 1794 after the end of the Reign of Terror.

Raynouard's first play, *Caton d'Utique* ("Cato of Utica"), was published in 1794. In 1805 his second play, *Les Templiers* ("The Templars"), was a great success, but his *Les États de Blois; ou, la mort du duc de Guise* (1810; "The Estates of Blois; or, The Death of the Duke of Guise") offended Napoleon and was banned. Following the defeat of Napoleon at Waterloo in

1815, Raynouard left politics to devote himself to the study of the medieval troubadour poets of France. His writing in this field proved to be his most important and lasting accomplishment. He wrote *Choix des poésies originales des troubadours*, 6 vol. (1816–21; "Selected Poetry of the Troubadours"). He also wrote a six-volume dictionary, *Lexique roman*, which was published posthumously (1839–44).

Razor's Edge, The   Philosophical novel by W. Somerset MAUGHAM, published in 1944.

The novel is concerned in large part with the search for the meaning of life and with the dichotomy between materialism and spirituality. The main focus of the story is on Larry Darrell, who has returned from service as an aviator in World War I utterly rejecting his prewar values. He is concerned chiefly with discovering the meaning of human existence and eliminating evil in the world. To that end, he spends five years in India seeking—but not finding—answers. *The Razor's Edge* was one of the first contemporary novels to feature a middle-class character who withdrew from Western society in search of non-Western solutions to society's ills.

Re \'rā\, *also called* Ra \'rä\ *or* Phra \'prä\   In ancient Egyptian mythology, god of the sun and creator god. He was believed to travel across the sky in his solar bark and, during the night, to make his passage in another bark through the underworld, where, in order to be born again for the new day, he had to vanquish the evil serpent Apopis (Apepi). As the creator, he rose from the ocean of chaos on the primeval hill, creating himself and then in turn engendering eight other gods.

Read \'rēd\, Herbert, *in full* Sir Herbert Read (b. Dec. 4, 1893, Muscoates Grange, Kirbymoorside, Yorkshire, Eng.—d. June 12, 1968, Malton, Yorkshire [now in North Yorkshire])   Poet and critic who was the chief advocate and interpreter of modern art movements in Great Britain from the 1930s.

Read grew up on a farm; he described his childhood in *The Innocent Eye* (1933), which was incorporated with other autobiographical writings in *The Contrary Experiences* (1963). After working in a bank, he attended the University of Leeds and served for three years as an infantry officer during World War I. War and his lost childhood are frequently examined in his several volumes of poetry, beginning with *Naked Warriors* (1919); his first *Collected Poems* was published in 1926, his last in 1966. He was an important influence among a group of poets of the 1940s known as the New Apocalypse.

Read became an assistant keeper at the Victoria and Albert Museum, London, after World War I, taught briefly at the University of Edinburgh, and edited the *Burlington Magazine*.

Read's many works of art criticism include *Art Now* (1933; rev. ed., 1936, 1948), *Art and Society* (1936), *Education Through Art* (1943), and *The Philosophy of Modern Art* (1952). His *The True Voice of Feeling: Studies in English Romantic Poetry* (1953) helped to revive interest in the Romantic poets. *The Contrary Experience: The Autobiography of Herbert Read* was published posthumously in 1974.

Read \'rēd\, Opie (Percival) (b. Dec. 22, 1852, Nashville, Tenn., U.S.—d. Nov. 2, 1939, Chicago, Ill.)   American journalist, humorist, novelist, and lecturer. Read specialized in the homespun humor of life in Kentucky, Tennessee, and Arkansas.

Inspired by Benjamin Franklin's autobiography, Read became a printer, reporter, and editor. He later edited the Little Rock, Ark., *Gazette* and the *Arkansas Traveler*, a weekly humor and literary journal. His books include *Len Gansett* (1888), a tale of the South; *Jucklins* (1895); *My Young Masters* (1896), about the American Civil War; and many others. His autobiography, *I Remember*, was published in 1930.

Reade \'rēd\, Charles (b. June 8, 1814, near Ipsden, Oxfordshire, Eng.—d. April 11, 1884, London)   English author whose novels expose, with passionate indignation, the social injustices of his times. His greatest work, however, THE CLOISTER AND THE HEARTH (1861), is a brilliant historical romance that recounts the adventures of the father of Desiderius Erasmus.

In 1843 Reade was called to the bar, but he never practiced law. In 1851 he became vice president of Magdalen College, Oxford, but he treated the position as a sinecure.

Although Reade spent a great deal of time and money in writing and staging plays (he wrote 40), they are crippled by crude characterizations and melodrama.

Reade's 14 novels reveal his humanitarianism and concern with social issues. *It Is Never Too Late to Mend* (1856) attacked conditions in prisons, and *Hard Cash* (1863) exposed the ill-treatment of mental patients, especially in private asylums. *Put Yourself in His Place* (1870) dealt with the terrorist activities of trade unionists, and the melodramatic *Foul Play* (1868), written with Dion Boucicault, brought to light the absence of safety measures in shipping.

readerly \'rē-dər-lē\ [translation of French *lisible*]   Of or relating to a text that is straightforward and demands no special effort to understand. Such texts were contrasted with so-called writerly texts by the French critic Roland Barthes in his book *S/Z* (1970). According to Barthes, a readerly text is one that presents a world of easily identifiable characters and events and in which the characters and their actions are understandable. Realistic novels such as those of George Eliot are readerly texts. *Compare* WRITERLY.

reader-response criticism   Critical method that examines the reader and the act of reading rather than the text being read. The reader-response approach evolved out of phenomenological (experiential) and interpretive analyses and is closely related to reception theory; it analyzes the reader's role in the production of meaning when engaged with a written text. Reader-response critics examine, for example, the inferences the reader must supply, the set of assumptions the reader must make, the gaps the reader must fill, the set of schemata the reader must actualize in order to make sense of the text, and the ideologies that determine all of the above.

The major figures of this analytical school initially included I.A. Richards, Louise Rosenblatt, and Walker Gibson and, later, Gerald Prince, Michael Riffaterre, and Georges Poulet. Among other contributors to reader-response theory were Wolfgang Iser, Jonathan Culler, and Norman Holland.

realism \'rē-ə-‚liz-əm\   The theory or practice in art and literature of fidelity to nature or to real life and to accurate representation without idealization of the most typical views, details, and surroundings of the subject. Realism rejects imaginative idealization in favor of a close observation of outward appearances. The word has also been used critically to denote excessive minuteness of detail or preoccupation with trivial, sordid, or squalid subjects in art and literature.

The works of the 18th-century English novelists Daniel Defoe, Henry Fielding, and Tobias Smollett are among the earliest examples in English literature of writings considered to be realistic.

Realism was stimulated by several intellectual developments in the first half of the 19th century, including the anti-Romantic movement in Germany, with its emphasis on the commoner as an artistic subject; Auguste Comte's positivist philosophy, in which the importance of the scientific study of society was emphasized; and the rise of professional journalism, with its ideal of accurate and dispassionate recording of current events.

Realism was a major trend in French novels and paintings between 1850 and 1880. The French proponents of realism uniformly rejected the artificiality of both classicism and Romanticism and insisted that, to be effective, a work must be contemporaneous. They attempted to portray the lives, appearances, problems, customs, and mores of people of the middle and lower classes, and they conscientiously set themselves to reproducing all the hitherto-ignored aspects of contemporary life and society—its attitudes, physical settings, and material conditions.

The novelist Honoré de Balzac was the chief precursor of French realism, notably in his attempt to create a detailed, encyclopedic portrait of the whole range of society in his *La Comédie humaine.* Inspired by the painter Courbet, the French journalist Champfleury wrote a manifesto for writers, *Le Réalisme* (1857), in which he asserted that the hero of a novel should be an ordinary rather than exceptional figure. In 1857 Gustave Flaubert published *Madame Bovary,* with an unrelentingly objective portrait of the bourgeois mentality that became both the principal masterpiece of realism and the work that established the movement in European literature.

Realist tenets—an emphasis on detachment, objectivity, and accurate observation; on lucid but restrained criticism of social environment and mores; and on humane understanding—entered the mainstream of European literature during the 1860s and '70s and became an integral part of the fabric of the modern novel during the height of the genre's development. A significant offshoot of literary realism was naturalism, a late 19th- and early 20th-century movement that aimed at an unselective representation of reality. The French novelist Émile Zola was the leading exponent of naturalism.

Realism in the theater was a general movement in the later 19th century that steered theatrical texts and performances toward greater fidelity to real life. The leaders of this movement included Henrik Ibsen and August Strindberg in Scandinavia and Anton Chekhov and Maksim Gorky in Russia. These and other playwrights rejected the complex and artificial plotting of the so-called well-made play, instead treating the themes and conflicts of contemporary society. They dispensed with poetic language and extravagant diction, using instead action and dialogue that looked and sounded like everyday behavior and speech.

Reality Sandwiches Fourth volume of collected poems by Allen GINSBERG, published in 1963. The poems in the collection are of interest mainly as a record of the Beat lifestyle and of Ginsberg's own experiences.

Real Life of Sebastian Knight, The \sə-'bas-chən-'nīt\ Novel by Vladimir NABOKOV, published in 1941. It was his first prose narrative in English.

The work, which is a satire of literary biography and scholarship, purports to be the true biography of a great writer, the late and neglected Sebastian Knight; it is written by his half brother, V., in response to another biographer's belittling analysis of Sebastian. Before long, however, V.'s "biography" turns into a mystery story, as he searches for the true facts about Sebastian among Sebastian's acquaintances. Himself a mediocre writer, V. eventually has a crisis of identity and his search for the real Sebastian becomes a search for himself.

Reaney \'rā-nē\, James Crerar (b. Sept. 1, 1926, near Stratford, Ont., Can.) Canadian poet and playwright whose works, dealing with Ontario small-town life, transcend their manifest content to move into areas of symbol and dream.

Reaney graduated from the University of Toronto, in 1960 founding *Alphabet,* a literary magazine, and becoming professor of English at the University of Western Ontario. His works include *The Red Heart* (1949), lyric poems; *A Suit of Nettles* (1958), 12 pastoral eclogues; *The Killdeer, and Other Plays* (1962), verse plays; *The Dance of Death at London, Ontario* (1963), a poetic satire of that town; and *Poems* (1972). *Apple Butter and Other Plays* (1973) is a collection of plays for children. He later wrote *Fourteen Barrels from Sea to Sea* (1977), a commentary on Canadian theatrical life in the form of a travel diary.

Rebecca \rə-'bek-ə\ Gothic suspense novel by Daphne DU MAURIER, published in 1938. This highly successful romantic novel is narrated by the unnamed protagonist known only as the second Mrs. de Winter. A shy, awkward young woman, she adores her wealthy, brooding husband, Maxim, with whom she lives at Manderley, his estate in Cornwall. The narrator feels inferior to Rebecca, Maxim's late first wife, who personifies glamor and gaiety, and she thinks that she cannot compete with this dead paragon to win Maxim's love. Mrs. Danvers, the sinister housekeeper, especially wounds the narrator by constantly mentioning how much Maxim had loved, and would always love, Rebecca. The narrator lives under this shadow until she learns the true nature of her husband's first marriage.

Rebel, The Essay by French writer Albert CAMUS, originally published in French as *L'Homme révolté* in 1951. The essay, a treatise against political revolution, was met with disapproval by both Marxists and existentialists and provoked a critical response from French writer Jean-Paul Sartre in the review *Les Temps modernes* (1952).

Rebel Angels, The Novel of ideas by Robertson DAVIES, published in 1981. The novel was the first in a trilogy that included *What's Bred in the Bone* (1985) and *The Lyre of Orpheus* (1988).

Set in a prominent Canadian university, the novel examines the dual themes of the distinction between knowledge and wisdom and the role of the university in contemporary society.

Rebelo \rā-'bel-ū\, Jorge (b. 1940, Lourenço Marques, Portuguese East Africa [now Maputo, Mozambique]) Mozambican poet, lawyer, and journalist who is considered to be the poet of the Mozambican revolution.

Rebelo studied at the University of Coimbra in Portugal, was secretary for information for the Mozambican anti-Portuguese guerrilla group Frelimo, and edited the magazine *Mozambique Revolution.* His poetry is didactic and single-minded, acting as a chronicle of the fight for Mozambican independence, a call to arms, and a rationale for the bloodshed and hardships of war.

Récamier \də-rā-kȧm-'yä\, Madame de, *byname of* Jeanne-Françoise-Julie-Adélaïde, Dame de Récamier, *original surname* Bernard \ber-'nȧr\ (b. Dec. 4, 1777, Lyon, Fr.—d. May 11, 1849, Paris) French hostess of great charm and wit whose salon attracted most of the important political and literary figures of early 19th-century Paris.

Mme de Récamier was the daughter of a prosperous banker and was convent-educated. In 1792 she joined her father in Paris and within the year married a wealthy banker. She began to entertain widely, and her salon soon became a fashionable gathering place for the great and near-great in politics and the arts. Its habitués included many former Royalists and others who were opposed to the government of Napoleon. In 1805 Napoleon ordered her exiled from Paris. She stayed with her good friend Mme de Staël in Geneva and in 1813 went to Rome and Naples. A literary portrait of Mme de Récamier can be found in the novel *Corinne,* written by Mme de Staël during this period.

She returned to Paris following Napoleon's defeat at Waterloo in 1815 but suffered financial losses. Despite her reduced circumstances after 1819, she maintained her salon and continued to receive visitors at the Abbaye-aux-Bois, an old Paris convent in which she took a separate suite. In her later years the French author and political figure François Chateaubriand became her constant companion, as well as the central figure in her salon, where he read from his works.

recension \rē-'sen-shən\ [French *récension* or German *Rezension*, both ultimately from Latin *recensere* to make a review of, enumerate]   **1.** A revision of a text (as of an ancient author) by an editor; especially, a critical revision with intent to establish a definitive text.   **2.** A version of a text established by critical revision.

Rechy \'rich-ē *is the original pronunciation and is the author's own*, 'rech-ē *is preferred by others in the family*\, John (Francisco) (b. March 10, 1934, El Paso, Tex., U.S.)   American novelist whose semiautobiographical works explore the worlds of sexual and social outsiders and occasionally draw on his Mexican-American heritage.

A graduate of Texas Western College, Rechy studied also at the New School for Social Research in New York. He taught creative writing at Occidental College, the University of Southern California, and the University of California at Los Angeles.

In *City of Night* (1963), his first and best-received novel, a young man working as a homosexual hustler makes his way to New Orleans for Mardi Gras. Rechy followed with *Numbers* (1967) and *This Day's Death* (1969), both of which deal with obsession and identity. *The Vampires* (1971) concerns the nature of evil, and *The Fourth Angel* (1972) records the adventures of four thrill-seeking adolescents. The nonfictional *The Sexual Outlaw* (1977) is Rechy's "prose documentary" of three days and nights in the sexual underground. His other novels include *Rushes* (1979), *Bodies and Souls* (1983), and *Marilyn's Daughter* (1988). In *The Miraculous Day of Amalia Gómez* (1991), set in the barrio of Los Angeles, Rechy makes use of the techniques of magic realism.

récit \rā-'sē\ [French, narrative, account]   A brief novel usually with a simple narrative line.

One of the writers who consciously used the form was André Gide. Both *L'Immoraliste* (*The Immoralist*) and *La Porte étroite* (*Strait is the Gate*) are examples of the *récit*. Both are studiedly simple but deeply ironic tales in which the first-person narrator reveals the inherent moral ambiguities of life by means of seemingly innocuous reminiscences.

recognition \,rek-əg-'nish-ən\   An incident or solution of plot in tragedy in which the main character recognizes his own or another character's true identity or discovers the true nature of his own situation. *See* ANAGNORISIS.

recto \'rek-tō\ [New Latin *recto* (*folio*) on the right-hand leaf]   **1.** The side of a leaf (as of a manuscript) that is to be read first.   **2.** A right-hand page. *Compare* VERSO.

redaction \ri-'dak-shən\ [French *rédaction* act of editing, edited work, ultimately from Latin *redigere* (past participle *redactus*) to drive back, convert, reduce to]   An edition or version. A work that has been edited or revised for publication. The word also denotes the act or an instance of editing a work for publication.

Red and the Black, The   Novel by STENDHAL, published in French in 1830 as *Le Rouge et le noir*. Set in France during the Second Restoration (1815–30), the novel is a powerful character study of Julien Sorel, an ambitious young man who uses seduction as a tool for advancement. *The Red and the Black* is generally considered the author's major work and one of the greatest 19th-century novels.

Sorel is a sensitive and intelligent youth who, seeing no road to advancement in the military after Napoleon's fall, endeavors

to make his mark in the church. Viewing himself as an unsentimental opportunist, he sets out to win the affections of Mme de Rênal, whose children he is employed to tutor. After spending time in a seminary, he goes to Paris, where he seduces the aristocratic Mathilde, the daughter of his second employer. The book ends with Sorel's execution for the attempted murder of Mme de Rênal after she had jeopardized his projected marriage to Mathilde.

The title apparently refers to both the tensions in Sorel's character and to the conflicting choice he is faced with in his quest for success: the army (symbolized by the color red) or the church (symbolized by the color black). Incisively and with subtlety, the novel examines careerism, political opportunism, the climate of fear and denunciation in Restoration France, and bourgeois materialistic values.

Red Badge of Courage, The   Novel of the American Civil War by Stephen CRANE, published in 1895 and considered to be his masterwork for its perceptive depiction of warfare and of the psychological turmoil of the soldier. Crane had had no experience of war when he wrote the novel, which he based partly on a popular anthology, *Battles and Leaders of the Civil War*.

The Red Badge of Courage has been called the first modern war novel because, uniquely for its time, it tells of the experience of war from the point of view of an ordinary soldier. Henry Fleming is eager to demonstrate his patriotism in a glorious battle, but when the slaughter starts, he is overwhelmed with fear and flees the battlefield. Ironically, he receives his "red badge of courage" when he is slightly wounded by being struck on the head by a deserter. He witnesses a friend's gruesome death and becomes enraged at the injustice of war. The courage of common soldiers and the agonies of death cure him of his romantic notions. He returns to his regiment and continues to fight on with true courage and without illusions.

Redburn \'red-,bərn\ (*in full* Redburn: His First Voyage)   Novel by Herman MELVILLE, published in 1849. Based on a trip Melville took to Liverpool, Eng., in June 1839, *Redburn* is a hastily written adventure about Wellingborough Redburn, a genteel but impoverished boy from New York City who endures a rough initiation into life as a sailor.

Red Cross Knight   Fictional character, protagonist of Book I of THE FAERIE QUEENE, an epic poem by Edmund Spenser. The Red Cross Knight represents the virtue of holiness, as well as St. George and the Anglican church. He is the chivalric champion and eventual husband of Una, who symbolizes truth and true religion.

rederijkerskamer \'rā-də-,reik-ərs-,käm-ər\ [Dutch, literally, rhetorician's chamber]   Medieval Dutch dramatic society. Modeled after contemporary French dramatic societies (*puys*), such chambers spread rapidly across the French border into Flanders and Holland in the 15th century. At first they were organized democratically; they later acquired sponsorship by the nobility and had a designated leader, assistants, a paid manager, and a jester. Like guilds, they had their own names, slogans, and emblems and were commissioned by the towns that supported them to provide the ceremonial at local festivals.

The *rederijkerskamers* organized national festivals (*landjuwelen*) during which poetry and drama competitions were held. One of the finest plays of this period, *Elckerlyc*, a morality play written about 1485 and attributed to Pieter Doorlant, became well known in England as *Everyman*. In addition to morality plays, the *rederijkerskamers* sponsored miracle plays, farces, and romantic plays.

The poetic style sanctioned by the *rederijkers* (members of the dramatic society), with its emphasis on complex forms and meters, laid the foundation for later Dutch dramatic and heroic verse by perfecting the rhymed alexandrine couplet. The *reder-ijkers* also developed a new poetic form, the *referein*, seen at its best in the poetry of Anna Bijns.

By the end of the 16th century many of the societies had degenerated into mutual admiration societies for poetasters; this, coupled with the new laws against public assemblies and the religious upheavals of the era, led to their decline. The Egelantier ("Wild Briar") and the Wit Lavendel ("White Lavender") *rederijkerskamers*, however, remained popular into the 17th century because of their association with leading Renaissance poets.

redondilla \rä-dōn-'dĕl-yä, -'dē-yä\ [Spanish, a derivative of *redondo* round] A Spanish stanza form consisting of four trochaic lines, usually of eight syllables each, with a rhyme scheme of *abba*. Quatrains in this form with a rhyme scheme of *abab*, sometimes also called redondillas, are more commonly known as *serventesios*. Redondillas have been common in Castilian poetry since the 16th century.

Red Pony, The   Book of four related stories by John STEIN-BECK, published in 1937 and expanded in 1945. The stories chronicle a young boy's maturation.

In "The Gift," the best-known story, young Jody Tiflin is given a red pony by his rancher father. Under ranch hand Billy Buck's guidance, Jody learns to care for and train his pony, which he names Gabilan. Caught in an unexpected rain, Gabilan catches a cold and, despite Billy Buck's ministrations, dies. Jody watches the buzzards alight on the body of his beloved pony, and, distraught at his inability to control events, he kills one of them.

The other stories in *The Red Pony* are "The Great Mountains," "The Promise," and "The Leader of the People," in which Jody develops empathy and also learns from his grandfather about "westering," the migration of people to new places and the urge for new experiences.

Red Queen   Fictional character in THROUGH THE LOOKING-GLASS by Lewis Carroll. The Red Queen has a personality that is the opposite of that of the White Queen, her despotic and chaotic counterpart. The author based the character of the Red Queen on Miss Prickett, the governess of Alice Liddell (the real-life Alice).

Reed \'rēd\, Ishmael (Scott) (b. Feb. 22, 1938, Chattanooga, Tenn., U.S.)   African-American author of poetry, essays, and satiric novels.

Reed grew up in Buffalo, N.Y., and studied at the University of Buffalo. He moved to New York City, where he cofounded the *East Village Other* (1965), an underground newspaper that achieved a national reputation. His first novel, *The Free-Lance Pallbearers*, was published in 1967.

Reed's novels are marked by surrealism, satire, and political and racial commentary. They depict human history as a cycle of battles between oppressed people and their oppressors; the characters and actions are an antic mixture of inverted stereotypes, revisionist history, and prophecy. *Pallbearers* was followed by *Yellow Back Radio Broke-Down* (1969), *Mumbo Jumbo* (1972), *The Last Days of Louisiana Red* (1974), *Flight to Canada* (1976), *The Terrible Twos* (1982), its sequel *The Terrible Threes* (1989), and *Japanese By Spring* (1993). He also wrote several volumes of poetry and collections of essays.

Reed \'rēd\, John (b. Oct. 22, 1887, Portland, Ore., U.S.—d. Oct. 19, 1920, Moscow, Russian S.F.S.R., U.S.S.R.)   American poet-adventurer whose life as a revolutionary writer and activist made him the hero of a generation of radical intellectuals.

Reed, a member of a wealthy Portland family, graduated from Harvard, and in 1913 he began writing for a socialist

newspaper, *The Masses*. In 1914 he covered the revolutionary fighting in Mexico and recorded his impressions in *Insurgent Mexico* (1914). Frequently arrested for organizing and defending strikes, he rapidly became established as a radical leader and helped form the Communist Party in the United States.

Reed covered World War I for *Metropolitan* magazine; out of this experience came *The War in Eastern Europe* (1916). He became a close friend of Vladimir Lenin and was an eyewitness to the 1917 Bolshevik revolution in Russia, recording this event in his best-known book, *Ten Days That Shook the World* (1919).

When the U.S. Communist Party and the Communist Labor Party split in 1919, Reed became the leader of the latter. Indicted for treason, he escaped to the Soviet Union and died of typhus; he was subsequently buried with other Bolshevik heroes beside the Kremlin wall.

Reese \'rēs\, Lizette Woodworth (b. Jan. 9, 1856, Baltimore county, Md., U.S.—d. Dec. 17, 1935, Baltimore, Md.) American poet whose work draws on the images of her rural childhood.

Reese's lyric talent was strikingly evident in her first book, *A Branch of May* (1887); it was followed by *A Handful of Lavendar* (1891). Her fresh images, condensed form, and sincerity of emotion broke with conventional sentimentality and foreshadowed 20th-century lyricism. Her best-known poem is the sonnet "Tears," published in 1899 in *Scribner's* magazine and widely anthologized. *The Selected Poems* (1926) was followed by several other volumes of verse and by two books of reminiscences, *A Victorian Village* (1929) and *The York Road* (1931), as well as a posthumous novel, *Worleys* (1936).

Reeve's Tale, The   One of the 24 stories in THE CANTERBURY TALES by Geoffrey Chaucer. The tale is one of the first English works to use dialect for comic effect. In outline it is similar to one of the stories in Giovanni Boccaccio's *Decameron*.

The old Reeve (bailiff), a woodworker, tells this bawdy tale in response to THE MILLER'S TALE of a cuckolded carpenter. The story tells how two student clerks, speaking broad Northern dialect, avenge themselves on a dishonest miller.

Reflections in a Golden Eye   Novel by Carson MC-CULLERS, published in 1941. Set in the 1930s on a Southern army base, the novel concerns the relationships between self-destructive misfits whose lives end in tragedy and murder.

The cast of characters includes Captain Penderton, a sadomasochistic, latent homosexual officer; his wife, who is having an affair with Major Langdon; the major's wife, who responds to the trauma of her son's death with self-mutilation; Anacleto, a homosexual servant who is befriended by the major's wife; and an army private who engages in voyeurism.

reflexive novel   *also called* involuted novel *or* self-reflexive novel.   A novel that calls attention to the fact that it is a novel and is not meant to be a straightforward reflection of reality. Examples include the works of Samuel Beckett and James Joyce.

refrain \ri-'frān\ [Middle French, alteration of *refrait* melody, liturgical response, repeated subject, a derivative of *refraindre* to break, moderate, echo] A phrase, line, or verse that recurs regularly at intervals throughout a poem or song, especially at the end of each stanza or division. Refrains are found in the ancient Egyptian Book of the Dead and are common in preliterate tribal chants. They appear in literature as varied as ancient Hebrew, Greek, and Latin verse, popular ballads, and Renaissance and Romantic lyrics. Three common refrains are the chorus, recited by more than one person; the burden, in which a whole stanza is repeated; and the repetend, in which the words are re-peated erratically throughout the poem. A refrain may be an exact repetition, or it may exhibit slight variations in meaning.

Regan \'rē-gən\ Fictional character, the king's deceitful middle daughter, in William Shakespeare's tragedy KING LEAR. A sadistic woman who fawns on and then humiliates her father, Regan is eventually poisoned by her equally hypocritical older sister, Goneril.

Régio \'rä-zhyü\, José, *pseudonym of* José Maria dos Reis Pereira \'räs-pi-'rä-rə\ (b. Sept. 17, 1901, Vila do Conde, Port.—d. Dec. 22, 1969, Portalegre) Poet, novelist, drama-tist, and literary critic, generally considered one of the most accomplished literary figures in Portugal in the first half of the 20th century.

Régio began his literary career while still a student with the publication of his lyric-dramatic *Poemas de Deus e do Diabo* (1925; "Poems of God and the Devil"). In 1927 he helped found the literary magazine *Presença*. Régio's novels, plays, and stories are distinguished by their emphasis on character de-lineation and their exploration of good and evil. His deeply introspective works reflect his preoccupation with human es-trangement from the natural world and the human quest for the absolute or the divine. Representative are his novel *O príncipe com orelhas de burro* (1942; "The Prince with Donkey Ears") and the play *Benilde; ou, A virgem-mãe* (1947; "Benilde, or the Virgin Mother"). Between 1945 and 1966 Régio produced his five-novel family saga *A velha casa* ("The Old House"). He wrote several additional volumes of poetry, collections of short stories, and essays on criticism and literature.

regionalism \'rē-jə-nə-,liz-əm\ Emphasis on regional locale and characteristics in art or literature. Regionalism was a signifi-cant movement in Canadian literature early in the 20th century. Other national literatures also had periods in which regional-ism was emphasized. *See also* MIDWESTERN REGIONALISM.

Regnard \rə-'nyàr\, Jean-François (b. Feb. 8, 1655, Paris, Fr.—d. Sept. 4, 1709, Château de Grillon) One of the most successful French playwrights to follow Molière, whose wit and style he openly imitated.

Born into a wealthy family, Regnard traveled extensively as a young man. On one of his trips he was captured by Algerian pirates and imprisoned for seven months until ransomed by his family in 1679. His experiences and impressions provided ma-terial for a series of books.

In 1683 Regnard was named treasurer of France, a profitable post that he held for 20 years. From 1688 on, however, he devoted most of his time to writing, first for the Italian come-dians in Paris and then for the Comédie-Française. He depicted a brilliant but decadent society in a light and facile style free of moralizing. His prime concern was to make an audience laugh as often as possible. His best-known plays are *Le Joueur* (1696; "The Gamester"), *Le Légataire universel* (1708; "The Universal Heir"), and *La Sérénade* (1694).

Régnier \rä-'nyä\, Henri de, *in full* Henri-François-Joseph de Régnier (b. Dec. 28, 1864, Honfleur, Fr.—d. May 23, 1936, Paris) Foremost French poet of the first decade of the 20th century.

Born of an old Norman family, Régnier began to prepare for a career as a diplomat, but while studying law in Paris he came under the influence of the Symbolist poets. He pub-lished his first volume of poems, *Lendemains* ("Tomorrows"), in 1885. Other volumes followed: *Les Jeux rustiques et divins* (1897; "Games—Tough and Divine"), *Les Médailles d'argile* (1900; "Clay Medals"), and *La Sandale ailée* (1906; "The Winged Sandal").

In 1896 Régnier married Marie de Heredia, daughter of an eminent poet, José María de Heredia. Influenced by his father-in-law, Régnier abandoned his earlier free and relatively uncon-trolled writing style in favor of more classical forms. For his themes, however, he continued to draw on the concerns of the Symbolists. He also wrote a number of novels, generally evok-ing a time and place in the past, particularly 14th- and 18th-century Italy and France: *La Double Maîtresse* (1900; "The Double Mistress"), *La Peur de l'amour* (1907; "Fear of Love"), and *Le Voyage d'amour* (1930; "The Journey of Love").

A man of aristocratic bearing and tastes, Régnier became an important figure in French intellectual society in the years fol-lowing the turn of the century. In 1911 he was elected to the Académie Française.

Régnier \rä-'nyä\, Mathurin (b. Dec. 21, 1573, Chartres, Fr.—d. Oct. 22, 1613, Rouen) French satiric poet whose works, written in vigorous, colloquial French, recall those of Horace, Juvenal, Ludovico Ariosto, and Pierre de Ronsard in free and original imitation.

Régnier wrote in alexandrine couplets about typical charac-ters of his time with verve and realism. His talents were fully displayed in *Macette* (1609). An acute critic, Régnier castigated François de Malherbe in an attack on the theory that poetry must conform to precise classical and intellectual standards (Satire IX, *À Monsieur Rapin*).

Reid \'rēd\, Forrest (b. June 24, 1875, Belfast, Ire.—d. Jan. 4, 1947, Warrenpoint, County Down) Irish novelist and critic who early came under the influence of Henry James; he is best known for his romantic and mystical novels about boyhood and adolescence and for a notable autobiography, *Apostate* (1926).

After taking his degree at the University of Cambridge, Reid settled in Belfast. His novels include *The Bracknels* (1911; com-pletely rewritten as *Denis Bracknel*, 1947); *Following Darkness* (1912; revised as *Peter Waring*, 1937); *The Spring Song* (1916); *Pirates of the Spring* (1919); the trilogy *Uncle Stephen* (1931), *The Retreat* (1936), and *Young Tom* (1944); and *Brian Westby* (1934). Reid also wrote studies of William Butler Yeats (1915) and Walter de la Mare (1929).

reification \,rā-ə-fi-'kā-shən, ,rē-\ [Latin *res* thing + *-ification* (as in *personification*)] The treatment of something abstract as a material or concrete thing, as in the following lines from Matthew Arnold's poem "Dover Beach":

> The Sea of Faith
> Was once, too, at the full, and round earth's shore
> Lay like the folds of a bright girdle furled.

Reign of Terror *also called* The Terror, *French* La Terreur \là-te-'rœr\ The period of the French Revolution from Sept. 5, 1793, to July 27, 1794 (9 Thermidor, year II), which has fre-quently been portrayed in literature in such works as Baroness Emmuska Orczy's *The Scarlet Pimpernel* and Charles Dickens' *A Tale of Two Cities.*

Reine Sebile, La \là-,ren-sā-'bēl\ Medieval French chan-son de geste of some 500 lines reconstructed from 13th-century fragments discovered in England, at Mons, Belg., and at Sion, Switz. Its story bears considerable resemblance to the epic ro-mance known as MACAIRE.

Reinmar von Hagenau \'rīn-,mär-fôn-'hä-gə-,naù\, *byname* Reinmar the Elder, *German* Reinmar der Alte \der-'äl-tə\ (d. *c.* 1205) German poet whose delicate and subtle verses constitute the ultimate refinement of the classical, or "pure," *Minnesang* (Middle High German love lyric).

A native of Alsace, Reinmar became court poet of the Baben-berg dukes in Vienna. Among his pupils was Walther von der

Vogelweide, who later became his rival. The purity of Reinmar's rhymes, the evenness of his rhythms, and the fastidious taste that rejected any phrase or emotion which might offend courtly sensibilities made him idolized by his contemporaries as the "nightingale" of his day. His constant theme was unrequited love. Of the numerous lyrics attributed to him, only 30 are now considered authentic.

reizianum \ˌrīt-sē-'an-əm, -'än-, -'än-\   In Greek prosody, usually the aeolic pattern ⏔ | — ⏑ ⏑ — | —, but occasionally the anapestic ⏔. In Latin prosody, *reizianum* refers to any variant of the scheme ⏔ ⏑⏑ ⏔ ⏑⏑ —, usually found in comic verse in an iambic context.

The word *reizianum* is derived from the surname of Friedrich Wilhelm Reiz, an 18th-century German philologist.

Remarque \rə-'märk\, Erich Maria, *pseudonym of* Erich Paul Remark (b. June 22, 1898, Osnabrück, Ger.—d. Sept. 25, 1970, Locarno, Switz.)   Novelist who is chiefly remembered as the author of *Im Westen nichts Neues* (1929; ALL QUIET ON THE WESTERN FRONT), which became perhaps the best-known and most representative novel dealing with World War I.

Remarque was drafted into the German army at the age of 18 and was wounded several times. He drew on these experiences in writing.

All Quiet on the Western Front is a brutally realistic account of the daily routine of ordinary soldiers during a war. It was followed by a sequel, *Der Weg zurück* (1931; *The Road Back*), dealing with the collapse of Germany in 1918.

Remarque left Germany for Switzerland in 1932. His books were banned by the Nazis in 1933. In 1939 he went to the United States, where he was naturalized in 1947. He eventually settled in Porto Ronco, Switz., on Lake Maggiore. He wrote several other novels, most of them dealing with victims of the political upheavals of Europe during World Wars I and II. Some had popular success, but none achieved the critical prestige of his first book.

Remembrance of Things Past   Novel in seven parts by Marcel PROUST, published in French as *À la recherche du temps perdu* from 1913 to 1927. The novel is the story of Proust's own life, told as an allegorical search for truth. It is the major work of French fiction in the early 20th century.

In January 1909 Proust experienced the involuntary recall of a childhood memory when he tasted a rusk (a twice-baked bread, which in his novel became a madeleine) dipped in tea. In July he retired from the world to write his novel, finishing the first draft in September 1912. The first volume, *Du Côté de chez Swann* (*Swann's Way*), was refused by two publishers and was finally issued at the author's expense in November 1913. Proust at this time planned only two further volumes.

During the war years he revised the remainder of his novel, enriching and deepening its feeling, texture, and construction, enhancing the realistic and satirical elements, and tripling its length. In so doing he transformed it into one of the most profound achievements of the human imagination. In June 1919 *À l'ombre des jeunes filles en fleurs* (*Within a Budding Grove*) appeared simultaneously with a reprint of *Swann*. In December 1919 *À l'ombre* received the Prix Goncourt, and Proust suddenly became world famous. Two more installments appeared in his lifetime and had the benefit of his final revision: *Le Côté de Guermantes* (1920; *The Guermantes Way*) and *Sodome et Gomorrhe* (1921; *Cities of the Plain*). The last three parts of *À la recherche* were published posthumously in an advanced but not final stage of revision: *La Prisonnière* (1923; *The Captive*), *Albertine disparue* (1925; *The Sweet Cheat Gone*, originally called *La Fugitive*), and *Le Temps retrouvé* (1927; *Time Regained*). An authoritative edition of the entire work was published in 1954.

The novel begins with the middle-aged narrator's memories of his happy childhood. Marcel tells the story of his life, introducing along the way a series of memorable characters, among them Charles Swann, who forms a stormy alliance with a prostitute, Odette; their daughter, Gilberte Swann, with whom young Marcel falls in love; the aristocratic Guermantes family, including the dissolute Baron de Charlus and his nephew Robert de Saint-Loup; and Albertine, to whom Marcel forms a passionate attachment. Marcel's world expands to encompass both the cultivated and the corrupt, and he sees the full range of human folly and misery. At his lowest ebb, he feels that time is lost; beauty and meaning have faded from all he ever pursued and won; and he renounces the book he has always hoped to write. At a reception after the war, the narrator realizes, through a series of incidents of unconscious memory, that all the beauty he has experienced in the past is eternally alive. Time is regained, and he sets to work, racing against death, to write the very novel the reader has just experienced. In his quest for time lost, he invented nothing but altered everything, selecting, fusing, and transmuting the facts so that their underlying unity and universal significance would be revealed.

Remembrance Rock   Novel by Carl SANDBURG, published in 1948. Sandburg's only novel, the work is a massive chronicle that uses historical facts and both historical and fictional characters to depict American history from 1607 to 1945 in a mythic, passionate tribute to the American people.

Remizov \'rʸä-mʸi-zəf\, Aleksey Mikhaylovich (b. June 24 [July 6, New Style], 1877, Moscow, Russia—d. Nov. 26, 1957, Paris, Fr.)   Symbolist writer whose works had a strong influence on Russian writers before and after the Revolution of 1917.

In 1905 Remizov settled in St. Petersburg, where he immediately began to frequent literary circles, particularly the Symbolist group. His works had begun to appear in various modernist periodicals, but his fame and popularity did not come until the publication in 1909 of *Istoriya Ivana Semyonovicha Stratilatova* ("The Story of Ivan Semyonovich Stratilatov"). This story of provincial life is among his best works, and it embodies many of the characteristics often found in his writing: elements of the weird, the grotesque, and the whimsical. He produced many stories of city and provincial life, others based on folklore and legend, and some using dreams, memoirs, and diaries. Remizov's prose was primarily colloquial; he strove to write in a homespun Russian, eliminating all foreign influences.

Remizov remained aloof from politics, though his works during the Revolution of 1917 and the Russian Civil War showed deep emotional involvement, as in *Slovo o pogibeli zemli Russkoy* (1921; "The Lay of the Destruction of the Land of Russia"). In 1921 he was permitted to leave the country because of ill health. He went first to Berlin and then, in 1923, to Paris, where he continued to write for many years until his death.

Renaissance \ˌren-ə-'säns, -'zäns; ri-'nā-səns\ [French, literally, rebirth]   The transitional period in Europe between medieval and modern times beginning in the 14th century in Italy, lasting into the 17th century, and marked by a humanistic revival of classical influence expressed in a flowering of the arts and literature and by the beginnings of modern science.

In literature, medieval forms continued to dominate the artistic imagination throughout the 15th century. Besides the vast devotional literature of the period—the *ars moriendi*, or books on the art of dying well, the lives of the saints, and manuals of methodical prayer and spiritual consolation—the most popular reading of noble and burgher alike was a 13th-century love allegory, the *Roman de la Rose*. In spite of a promising fecundity in the late Middle Ages—when, for example, England produced William Langland, the *Gawain* poet, John Gower, and, most notably, Geoffrey Chaucer—literary creativity suffered from the domination of Latin as the language of "serious" expression. The result of this circumstance was that, if the vernacular attracted writers, they tended to overload it with Latinisms and artificially applied rhetorical forms. This was the case with the so-called *rhétoriqueurs* of Burgundy and France. A highlight of 15th-century English literature, however, was Sir Thomas Malory's *Le Morte Darthur*. In France there was a vigorous tradition of chronicle writing, which was distinguished by such eminently readable works as the *Chronicles* of Jean Froissart and the *Mémoires* of Philippe de Commynes. Mid-15th-century France also produced the vagabond and great poet François Villon.

The 16th century saw a true renaissance of national literatures. In Protestant countries, the Reformation had an enormous impact upon the quantity and quality of literary output. For Roman Catholics, especially in Spain, the Counter-Reformation was a time of deep religious emotion expressed in art and literature. On all sides of the religious controversy, chroniclers and historians writing in the vernacular were recording their versions for posterity.

While the Reformation was providing a subject matter, the Italian Renaissance was providing literary methods and models. The Petrarchan sonnet inspired French, English, and Spanish poets, while the Renaissance Neoclassical drama finally began to end the reign of the medieval mystery play. Ultimately, of course, the works of true genius were the result of a crossing of native traditions and new forms. The Frenchman François Rabelais assimilated all the themes of his day—and mocked them all—in his story of the giants Gargantua and Pantagruel. The Spaniard Miguel de Cervantes, in *Don Quixote*, drew a composite portrait of the Spanish that caught their exact mixture of idealism and realism. In England, Christopher Marlowe and William Shakespeare used Renaissance drama to probe the deeper levels of English character and experiences.

Renaissance man *also called* Universal man, *Italian* Uomo universale. An ideal that developed in Renaissance Italy from the notion expressed by one of its most accomplished representatives, Leon Battista Alberti, that "a man can do all things if he will." The ideal embodied the basic tenets of Renaissance humanism, which considered humans the center of the universe, limitless in their capacities for development, and led to the notion that all knowledge should be embraced and natural capacities developed as fully as possible.

Thus the gifted individuals of the Renaissance sought to develop skills exemplified in Alberti—who was an accomplished architect, painter, classicist, poet, scientist, and mathematician and who also boasted of his skill as a horseman and in physical feats—and in Leonardo da Vinci, whose gifts were manifest in the fields of art, science, music, invention, and writing.

In the 20th century, the term is still used to refer to an accomplished, well-rounded individual, although contemporary society admits of the occasional Renaissance woman, as well.

Renaixensa, La \lə-,ren-ī-'shen-zə\ Literary and linguistic renascence in Catalan letters that had its origins in 1814, when *Gramática y apologia de la llengua cathalana* ("Grammar and Defense of the Catalan Language") of Josep Pau Ballot i Torres was published. The pioneers of the movement, while promoting the revitalization of the language, did recognize its inability to express more modern spiritual and intellectual ideas. The Institute of Catalan Studies, founded in Barcelona in 1907, played a large part in the enrichment and purifying of the Catalan language.

Among the movement's poetic contributions, Buenaventura Carles Aribau's patriotic *Oda a la patria* (1832; "Ode to the Fatherland") and the verse of Joaquim Rubió i Ors and Victor Balaguer prepared the way for the mysticism of Jacinté Verdaguer Santaló, a great epic poet who wrote *L'Atlántida* (1877) and *Canigó* (1886). Miguel Costa i Llobera cultivated a classical perfection of form. In Joan Maragall i Gorina, Catalonia found its first great modern poet who, in spiritual quality, exerted a powerful influence on later poets.

The foundations of modern Catalan prose were laid by the critical writings of Rubió i Ors, Francisco Pi i Margall, one of the four presidents of the Spanish Republic of 1873, and Josep Torras i Bages, author of *La tradició catalana* (1892; "The Catalan Tradition"). One of the best and most influential writers in prose was the essayist Eugeni d'Ors (pseudonym "Xenius"), whose philosophical novel *La ben plantada* (1911; "Firmly Rooted") was one of the most notable works in modern Catalan literature.

Catalan dramatists produced plays of considerable originality. Àngel Guimerà achieved a European reputation with *Terra baixa* (1896; *Marta of the Lowlands*), which inspired a German and a French opera and was widely translated. The many social dramas of Ignasi Iglésias, inspired by the early works of Gerhart Hauptmann, included one near-masterpiece, *Els Vells* (1903). Adrià Gual, author of several works of fantasy, directed a Catalan-language theater that helped acquaint the public with the great drama of all countries and ages.

Renard \rə-'när\, Jules (b. Feb. 22, 1864, Châlons-sur-Mayenne, Fr.—d. May 22, 1910, Paris) French writer best known for *Poil de carotte* (1894; *Carrots*; U.S. title, *Carrot Top*), a bitterly ironical account of his own childhood, in which a grim humor conceals acute sensibility. His prose, stripped of superfluous words, influenced later French writers, who found in it a corrective to the indiscriminate accretion of detail that was a tendency of the naturalists who preceded him.

After marrying in 1888, Renard devoted himself to writing. Above all an artist (he described himself as a "hunter of images"), he used acutely observed detail in his descriptive writing. His sketches of animal life in *Histoires naturelles* (1896; *Natural Histories*) are models of their kind. Although he spent most of his life in Paris, he never lost touch with his native countryside, and in *Les Philippe* (1907), *Nos frères farouches* (1908; "Our Rustic Brothers"), and *Ragotte* (1908), he depicted rural life with amused penetration and cruel realism. He also wrote plays, including a dramatized version of *Poil de carotte* (1900). He was a founding member of the magazine *Mercure de France* (1890) and was elected to the Académie Goncourt in 1907. His *Journal*, in 17 volumes (1925–27), was translated into English in 1964.

Renart \rə-'när\, Jean (fl. 1200–22) French poet and author of romances of adventure whose work rejected the fey atmosphere and serious morality that had distinguished the poetry of his predecessor Chrétien de Troyes in favor of a half-nostalgic, half-flippant portrayal of high society, with its idyllic picnics, bathing in the spring, tourneying, and lute playing far into the night.

Almost nothing is known of Renart, although he is associated with the village of Dammartin en Goële, near Meaux, a few miles east of Paris. His known works are *L'Escoufle*, a picaresque novel in verse about the adventures of Guillaume and Aelis, betrothed children who flee to France; *Guillaume de Dôle*, the story of a falsely accused bride who cunningly defends her reputation; and *Le Lai de l'ombre* ("The Lay of the Shadow"), about a knight who presses a ring on his lady and, when she refuses it, throws it to her reflection in a well—a gesture that persuades her to accept him. Renart's authorship of the first two works, which had each survived only in a single copy, was first proposed late in the 19th century and was confirmed in 1910, when anagrams of the name Renart were discovered in the final lines of both romances.

Renascence   Poem by Edna St. Vincent MILLAY, first published in 1912 in the anthology *The Lyric Year* and later included as the title poem of her first published collection, *Renascence and Other Poems* (1917).

"Renascence" consists of 214 lines written in octosyllabic couplets. Written when Millay was 20, the poem reflects in simple, direct language the poet's feelings of wonder at the magnitude of the universe and the concepts of God and death.

Renaud de Montauban \rə-nō-də-mōⁿ-tō-ˈbäⁿ\   Hero of an Old French chanson de geste of the same name (also known as *Les Quatre Fils Aymon* ["The Four Sons of Aymon"]), whose story may contain elements of prehistoric myth and whose theme long survived in folktale and ballad throughout western Europe. Renaud slays Charlemagne's nephew after a quarrel over chess, and, mounting his marvelous steed Bayard (which understands human speech), he barricades himself with his brothers in the rock fortress of Montessor. Their father, Aymon, helps to besiege them. They finally escape to Dortmund. Renaud turns to a life of religion and helps in the building of Cologne Cathedral, for which he will accept no wages. His envious fellow workers murder him and throw his body into the Rhine River, where it is conducted upstream by choirs of angels and buried in state.

The French poem, dating from the late 12th or early 13th century, was more than 18,000 lines long; a Middle Dutch version was the ancestor of an early 17th-century *Volksbuch* ("chapbook") version. Spanish "Reinalte," or "Reinaldos," versions (including a play by Lope de Vega) derive partly from French sources and partly from Italian "Rinaldo" poems, which proliferated from the 14th century up to the composition of Torquato Tasso's first epic poem, *Rinaldo*, in the second half of the 16th century.

Renault \ˈren-ō\, Mary, *pseudonym of* Mary Challans \ˈchalənz\ (b. Sept. 4, 1905, London, Eng.—d. Dec. 13, 1983, Cape Town, S.Af.)   British-born South African novelist, best known for her scholarship and her skill in re-creating classical history and legend.

Renault graduated from St. Hugh's College and Radcliffe Infirmary, Oxford. She had begun to write novels but worked as a nurse during World War II.

Renault's best-known sequence of Greek historical novels soon appeared: *The Last of the Wine* (1956), *The King Must Die* (1958), and *The Bull from the Sea* (1962)—all praised for their attention to historical detail. The novels also caused controversy because of their sympathetic handling of male homosexuality. In *Fire from Heaven* (1970), *The Persian Boy* (1972), and *Funeral Games* (1981), Renault retold the history and legend surrounding Alexander the Great; she also examined his psychological background in the biography *The Nature of Alexander* (1975).

Rendell \ˈrend-əl\, Ruth (Barbara), *original surname* Grasemann \ˈgräz-mən\, *pseudonym* Barbara Vine \ˈvīn\ (b. Feb. 17, 1930, London, Eng.)   British writer of mystery novels, psychological novels of crime, and short stories.

Rendell worked as a reporter and subeditor for West Essex newspapers. Her first novel, *From Doon with Death* (1964), introduced Reginald Wexford, the clever detective chief inspector, and his more stodgy associate Mike Burden. The pair appeared in more than a dozen further novels of police procedure, among them *No More Dying Then* (1971), *Murder Being*

Done Once (1972), *An Unkindness of Ravens* (1985), and *The Veiled One* (1988).

In time Rendell's psychological thrillers became at least as popular as her Wexford novels. The thrillers present the inner lives of complex characters as they move incrementally toward violent actions. Sexual obsession, immaturity, exaggerated fantasy lives, and the gap between parent and child are recurring elements in novels such as *A Judgement in Stone* (1977), *The Lake of Darkness* (1980), *Talking to Strange Men* (1987), and *The Bridesmaid* (1989). Rendell also wrote several novels under her pseudonym, including *King Solomon's Carpet* (1991) and *Anna's Book* (1993).

René \rə-ˈnā\   Novel by François-Auguste-René CHATEAUBRIAND, published in French as *René, ou les effets de la passion* in 1805 with a revised edition of *Atala* (1801). It tells the story of a sister who enters a convent rather than surrender to her passion for her brother. In this thinly veiled autobiographical work, Chateaubriand began the Romantic vogue for world-weary, melancholy heroes suffering from vague, unsatisfied yearnings in what has since been called the *mal du siècle* ("the malady of the age").

renga \ˈreŋ-ˌgä\ [Japanese]   Genre of Japanese linked-verse poetry in which two or more poets supplied alternating sections of a poem. The *renga* form began as the composition of a single tanka (a traditional five-line poem) by two people and was a popular pastime from ancient times, even in remote rural areas.

The *Kin'yō-shū* (c. 1125) was the first Imperial anthology to include *renga*, which was at the time simply tanka composed by two poets, one supplying the first three lines of five, seven, and five syllables, and the other the last two of seven syllables each. The first poet often gave obscure or even contradictory details to make it harder for the second to complete the poem intelligibly and, if possible, inventively. These early examples were *tan renga* (short *renga*) and were generally light in tone.

The form developed fully in the 15th century, when a distinction came to be drawn between *ushin renga* (serious *renga*), which followed the conventions of court poetry, and *mushin renga*, or haikai (comic *renga*), which deliberately broke the conventions in vocabulary and diction. Gradually, the composition of *renga* spread to the court poets, who saw the artistic possibilities of this diversion and drew up "codes" intended to establish *renga* as an art. The codes made possible the masterpieces of the 15th century, but their insistence on formalities (*e.g.*, how often a "link" on the moon might appear, and which links must end with a noun and which with a verb) inevitably diluted the vigor and freshness of the early *renga*, itself a reaction against the excessively formal tanka.

The standard length of a *renga* was 100 verses, although there were variations. Verses were linked by verbal and thematic associations, while the mood of the poem drifted subtly as successive poets took up one another's thoughts. An outstanding example of the form is the melancholy *Minase sangin hyakuin* (1488; *Minase Sangin Hyakuin: A Poem of One Hundred Links Composed by Three Poets at Minase*), composed by Sōgi, Shōhaku, and Sōchō. Later the initial verse (hokku) of a *renga* developed into the independent haiku form.

Renn \ˈren\, Ludwig, *pseudonym of* Arnold Friedrich Vieth von Golssenau \ˈfēth-fôn-ˈgôl-sə-ˌnaù\ (b. April 22, 1889, Dresden, Ger.—d. July 21, 1979, East Berlin, E.Ger.)   German novelist best known for *Krieg* (1928; *War*), a semiautobiographical novel based on his World War I battle experiences. (The narrator and principal character of the work is named Ludwig Renn.) The stark simplicity of the novel emphasizes the uncompromising brutality of combat.

Born a Saxon nobleman, Renn himself served as an officer in the Saxon Guards from 1911 through World War I. Inflation in the 1920s wiped out his fortune, and his experience with nascent fascism in Italy led to his becoming a communist in 1928. He was editor of *Linkskurve*, the journal of the Union of Proletarian-Revolutionary Writers. His *Nachkrieg* (1930; *After War*) is a novel about the postwar Weimar Republic. He was arrested by the Nazis on the night of the Reichstag fire, which was blamed on the communists, and served two and a half years in prison.

After his release he escaped in 1936 to Switzerland, where he published the novel *Vor grossen Wandlungen* (1936; *Death Without Battle*). He was leader of the Thälmann Battalion and chief of staff (1936–37) on the Loyalist side in the Spanish Civil War. The novel *Der spanische Krieg* (1956; "The Spanish War") is his account of this experience.

Renn returned to East Germany after World War II and taught at various universities from 1947 to 1951. His later works include children's books, an autobiography, and other novels about war and the military, including *Adel im Untergang* (1944; "Aristocracy in Decline"), *Krieg ohne Schlacht* (1957; "War Without Battle"), and *Auf den Trümmern des Kaiserreichs* (1961; "On the Ruins of the Empire").

repetend \'rep-i-ˌtend, ˌrep-i-'tend\ [Latin *repetendum* something to be repeated] A repeated sound, word, or phrase. In poetry a repetend is a type of refrain, but it differs from the more common variety in that it usually refers to only part of a line and can appear at unexpected points in the poem, unlike the regular placement of the refrain at the end of a stanza.

reportage \ˌrep-òr-'täzh, ri-'pòr-tij\ [French, reporting] Writing intended to give a factual account of directly observed or carefully documented events.

Resende \re-'seⁿn-jē\, Garcia de (b. *c.* 1470, Évora, Port.—d. Feb. 3, 1536, Évora) Portuguese poet, chronicler, and editor whose life was spent in the service of the Portuguese court.

Resende began to serve John II as a page at the age of 10, becoming his private secretary in 1491. He continued to enjoy royal favor under King Manuel and later under John III.

Resende's *Crónica de D. Joao II* (1545; "Chronicle of Don John II"), though largely taken from a work by Rui de Pina (*c.* 1440–*c.* 1523), contains personal anecdotes that give it special interest. Much of his work provides insight into the social life and manners of the period. In the 300 stanzas of his *Miscelânea* ("Miscellany"), he surveys with wonder and pride—and not without social criticism—some of the notable events (including Portuguese overseas exploration) of the age in which he lived. The *Cancioneiro Geral* (1516; "General Songbook")—a vast anthology edited by Resende that also contained compositions of his own—is the chief source of knowledge of late medieval Portuguese verse.

Residence on Earth A unified series of verse collections by Pablo NERUDA. The first collection, published as *Residencia en la tierra* (1933), contained poetry written in 1925–31; the second, published in two volumes in 1935, had the same title but included verses from the period 1925–35; the third, issued in 1947, was entitled *Tercera residencia, 1935–1945*. Written over a period of two decades, the poems helped to establish Neruda as a poet of international significance. The series is remarkable for its philosophical examination of the theme of universal decay. The poet's fierce, anguished tone mixes Surrealistic pessimism with an all-embracing Whitmanesque sensitivity of spirit. Notable individual poems from the series are "España en el corazón" ("Spain in the Heart"), about the Spanish Civil War; the hermetic "Arte Poética" ("Poetic Art"); the vibrant "Galope muerto" ("Dead Gallop"); a despairing poem with the English title "Walking Around"; and the humble "Tres cantos materiales" ("Three Material Songs"), which, like his later odes, celebrates commonplace items.

resolution \ˌrez-ə-'lü-shən\ 1. The division of a prosodic element into its component parts (such as the division of the components of a long syllable in ancient Greek and Latin verse into two short syllables). Also, the substitution in Greek or Latin prosody of two short syllables for a long syllable. *Compare* CONTRACTION. 2. A product of prosodic resolution. 3. The point in a play or other work of literature at which the chief dramatic complication is worked out.

Restif \rā-'tēf\, Nicolas-Edme, *byname* Restif de la Bretonne \rā-tēv-də-là-brə-'tòⁿ\ (b. Oct. 23, 1734, Sacy, near Auxerre, Fr.—d. Feb. 3, 1806, Paris) French novelist whose works are remarkable for their lively, detailed accounts of the sordid aspects of French life and society in the 18th century. Restif set the type for some of his own works—books long prized by collectors for their rarity, quaint typography, and beautiful and curious illustrations.

His novels are rambling and carelessly written. While he parades his moralistic intentions and frequently airs his views on the reform of society, his preoccupation with eroticism, tinged with mysticism, has led to his being called "the Rousseau of the gutter." The author's life formed the basis of much of his writing, as shown in *La Vie de mon père* (1779; *My Father's Life*), a vivid picture of peasant life. In this work, however, as in his autobiography, *Monsieur Nicolas* (1794–97), much of which is set in the Parisian underworld, Restif's vivid imagination has rendered it difficult to separate fact from fiction. Restif recorded his observation of contemporary Parisian life in *Les Contemporaines* (1780–85; "The Modern Women"), while *Le Paysan perverti* (1776; "The Corrupted [Male] Peasant") and *La Paysanne pervertie* (1784; "The Corrupted [Female] Peasant") develop the theme of the demoralization of virtuous country folk in the metropolis.

Restoration literature English literature written after the Restoration of the monarchy in 1660 following the period of the Commonwealth. Some literary historians speak of the era as bounded by the reign of Charles II (1660–85), while others prefer to include within its scope the writings produced during the reign of James II (1685–88). The period led into England's "classical" Augustan Age under Queen Anne (1702–14). Many typical literary forms of the modern world—including the novel, biography, history, travel writing, and journalism—began to develop with sureness during the Restoration period, when new scientific discoveries and philosophic concepts as well as new social and economic conditions came into play. There also was a great outpouring of pamphlet literature, much of it political and religious, while John Bunyan's great allegory, *The Pilgrim's Progress*, also belongs to the period. Much of the best poetry, notably that of John Dryden (the great literary figure of his time, in both poetry and prose), the Earl of Rochester, Samuel Butler, and John Oldham, was satirical and led directly to the later achievements of Alexander Pope, Jonathan Swift, and John Gay in the Augustan Age. The Restoration period excelled, above all, in drama. Heroic plays influenced by principles of French Neoclassicism enjoyed a vogue, but the age is chiefly remembered for its glittering, critical comedies of manners by such playwrights as George Etherege, William Wycherley, Sir John Vanbrugh, and William Congreve.

Return of the Native, The Novel by Thomas HARDY, published in 1878.

The novel is set on Egdon Heath, a barren moor in the fictional Wessex in southwestern England. The native of the title is Clym Yeobright, who has returned to the area to become a schoolmaster after a successful but, in his opinion, shallow career as a jeweler in Paris. He and his cousin Thomasin exemplify the traditional way of life, while Thomasin's husband, Damon Wildeve, and Clym's wife, Eustacia Vye, long for the excitement of city life. Disappointed that Clym is content to remain on the heath, Eustacia, willful and passionate, rekindles her affair with the reckless Damon. After a series of coincidences Eustacia comes to believe that she is responsible for the death of Clym's mother. Convinced that fate has doomed her to cause others pain, Eustacia flees and is drowned (by accident or intent). Damon drowns trying to save her.

In a later edition, to please his readers, Hardy made additions to his novel. Thomasin marries Diggory Venn, a humble, long-time suitor, and Clym becomes an itinerant preacher.

Reuter \'rȯit-ər\, Fritz (b. Nov. 7, 1810, Stavenhagen, Mecklenburg-Schwerin [Germany]—d. July 12, 1874, Eisenach, Ger.) German novelist who helped to initiate the development of regional dialect literature in Germany. His best works, which mirror the contemporary provincial life of Mecklenburg-Schwerin, are written in Plattdeutsch, a north German dialect.

As a youthful member of a student political club, Reuter was arrested when government authorities instituted repressive measures following a student attack on a military guardhouse. He was sentenced to death in 1833, but the sentence was later commuted to 30 years' imprisonment. Released under the amnesty of Frederick William IV after seven years' imprisonment, he never fully regained his health.

The success of Reuter's early Plattdeutsch poems and stories led him to attempt more ambitious works in his native dialect. *Ut de Franzosentid* (1859; "During the Time of the French Conquest") presents, with a mixture of seriousness and humor, life in a Mecklenburg-Schwerin country town during the War of Liberation against Napoleon. *Ut mine Festungstid* (1862; "During the Time of My Incarceration") is an account of his last few years in prison, told without bitterness. *Ut mine Stromtid* (1862–64; "During My Apprenticeship") is considered his masterpiece. In this work, originally issued in three volumes, Reuter's resemblance to Charles Dickens as a great storyteller and as a creator of characters is most apparent.

Reve \'rāv\, Gerard (Kornelis van het) (b. Dec. 14, 1923, Amsterdam, Neth.) Dutch writer noted for his virtuoso style and sardonic humor. His subject matter was occasionally controversial, treating such topics as homosexuality and sadism.

Although Reve invented a fanciful background for himself as the Dutch-born child of Baltic-Russian refugees, he was in fact the son of a Dutch journalist. Reve worked as a reporter for *Het Parool*, a national daily newspaper. His first novel, published under the pseudonym Simon van het Reve, was *De avonden* (1947; "The Evenings"); it was considered the most representative work of fiction of the Dutch postwar generation. Employing a technique he called epistolary autobiography—an amalgam of letter and story, fact and fiction—Reve produced *Op weg naar het einde* (1963; "On the Way to the End") and *Nader tot U* (1966; "Nearer to Thee"), in both of which he explored his homosexuality and his conversion to Roman Catholicism. His other works include *De taal der liefde* (1972; "The Language of Love"), *Ik had hem lief* (1975; "I Loved Him"), and *Bezorgde ouders* (1988; *Parents Worry*). Beginning in the 1980s he published a series of books of correspondence, the first of which was *Brieven aan Wim B., 1968–1975* (1983; "Letters to Wim B.") and continuing through *Brieven van een aardappeleter* (1993; "Letters of a Potato Eater").

Revelation to John \'jän\, *also called* Book of Revelation *or* Apocalypse of John \ə-'päk-ə-,lips\ The last book of the New Testament. It is the only book of the New Testament classified as apocalyptic rather than didactic or historical literature. The designation follows from its extensive use of visions, symbols, and allegory, especially in connection with future events. Revelation to John appears to be a collection of separate units composed by unknown authors who lived during the last quarter of the 1st century, though it purports to have been written by John, "the beloved disciple" of Jesus, at Patmos, in the Aegean Sea.

The book has two main divisions. The first part (chapters 2–3) contains moral admonitions in individual letters addressed to the seven Christian churches of Asia Minor. In the second part (chapters 4–22:5), visions, allegories, and symbols so pervade the text that scholars differ in their interpretations. In all likelihood, the book deals with a contemporary crisis of faith, probably brought on by Roman persecutions. Christians are consequently exhorted to remain steadfast in their faith.

revenge tragedy Drama in which the dominant motive is revenge for a real or imagined injury; it was a favorite form of English tragedy in the Elizabethan and Jacobean eras and found its highest expression in William Shakespeare's *Hamlet*.

The revenge drama derived originally from the Roman tragedies of Seneca but was established on the English stage by Thomas Kyd with *The Spanish Tragedie*. This work, which opens with the Ghost of Don Andrea and the Spirit of Revenge, deals with the predicament of Hieronimo, a Spanish gentleman who is driven to melancholy by the murder of his son. Between spells of madness, he discovers who the murderers are and plans his ingenious revenge. He stages a play in which the murderers take part, and, while enacting his role, Hieronimo actually kills them and then kills himself. The influence of the play, apparent in *Hamlet*, is also evident in other plays of the period, such as John Marston's *Antonios Revenge* and George Chapman's *The Revenge of Bussy d'Ambois*. Most revenge tragedies end with a scene of carnage that disposes of the avenger as well as the victims.

Reverdy \rə-ver-'dē\, Pierre (b. Sept. 13, 1889, Narbonne, Fr.—d. June 17, 1960, Solesmes) French poet and moralist whose complex verse reflects Cubist and Surrealist influence.

In 1910 Reverdy moved to Paris, where he became acquainted with a group of painters and writers that included Pablo Picasso, Georges Braque, and Guillaume Apollinaire. Through their influence he became interested in Cubism, and in 1916 he founded a short-lived review, *Nord-Sud* ("North-South"), to promote the movement. Although he experimented with Surrealism in the 1920s, he later returned to Cubist-inspired poetic techniques. After publishing *Étoiles peintes* (1921; "Painted Stars") and *Les Épaves du ciel* (1924; "Shipwrecks from Heaven"), he retired in 1926 to the Abbaye de Solesmes, remaining there until his death. In solitude he dedicated himself to a search for the spiritual meaning of the physical world, expressing this vocation in the disciplined maxims of the prose works *Le Gant de crin* (1927; "The Horsehair Glove") and *Le Livre de mon bord* (1948; "The Book Beside Me"). A later collection of poetry, *Flaques de verre* ("Glass Puddles"), was published in 1929.

reversed foot A foot in which the prevailing cadence of a metrical series or of an adjacent foot is reversed or inverted by exchanging the positions of stressed and unstressed or long and short elements. *Compare* INVERSION.

review \ri-'vyü\ 1. A critical evaluation (as of a book or play). 2. A magazine devoted chiefly to reviews and essays.

revised edition An edition (as of a book) that incorporates major revisions by the author or an editor and often includes supplementary matter designed to bring it up to date.

Revius \\'rā-vē-ūͤs\\, Jacobus, *pseudonym of* Jacob van Reefsen \\vän-'räf-sən\\ (b. November 1586, Deventer, Neth.—d. Nov. 15, 1658, Leiden)   Dutch Calvinist poet long esteemed only as a theologian but later acknowledged as the greatest Christian lyricist of his period.

Revius was a Dutch Reformed minister who was a vigorous supporter of Protestantism, and his poetry is invariably scriptural or moralistic. His collection *Over-IJsselsche sangen en dichten* (1630; "Overijssel Songs and Poems") shows the stylistic influence of the French Renaissance poet Pierre de Ronsard as well as Revius' affinities with the English Metaphysical poets in his prolific use of stark metaphor and profusion of four-line epigrams. The best-known sonnet from the collection is "Hy droech onse smerten" ("He Bore Our Sorrows"), a moving profession of responsibility for Christ's death.

Revue des Deux Mondes \\rə-vūͤ-dä-dœ-'môⁿd\\   Fortnightly journal of criticism of and commentary on literature and other arts, published in Paris in 1829 and from 1831 to 1944. It was one of a number of journals set up in France following the suspension of censorship in 1828, and it attained a critical influence in that country comparable to the great Scottish and English journals of the day. *Revue des Deux Mondes*, however, limited its concerns to the arts. François Buloz was its editor from 1831 to 1877 and established a tradition of excellence that attracted contributions from such literary eminences as Charles-Augustin Sainte-Beuve, Honoré de Balzac, Victor Hugo, Hippolyte Taine, and Ernest Renan.

Revueltas \\rā-'ḇwäl-täs\\, José (b. Nov. 20, 1914, Durango, Mex.—d. April 14, 1976, Mexico City)   Mexican novelist, short-story writer, and political activist who was one of the originators of the new Mexican novel.

Revueltas was a member of a family of prominent artists. Politically active from the age of 14, Revueltas joined the Mexican Communist Party in 1932 and was twice imprisoned at the infamous Islas Marías penitentiary. *Los muros de agua* (1941; "Walls of Water"), his first novel, is based on his experiences there.

Revueltas' *El luto humano* (1943; *Human Mourning* or *The Stone Knife*) is a powerful novel that uses flashbacks and interior monologues to present the plight of rural Mexicans from the pre-Columbian period up to the 1930s. His novel *Los motivos de Caín* (1957; "Cain's Motives") concerns the brutality of U.S. soldiers during World War II, and *Los errores* (1964; "Mistakes") is a denunciation of the purges of communism. In addition to many more novels, Revueltas also published two short-story collections—*Dios en la tierra* (1944; "God in the Land") and *Dormir en tierra* (1960; "To Sleep in the Land")—essays, and dramas.

Rexroth \\'reks-ₐrȯth\\, Kenneth (b. Dec. 22, 1905, South Bend, Ind., U.S.—d. June 6, 1982, Santa Barbara, Calif.)   American painter, essayist, poet, and translator, an early champion of the Beat movement.

Rexroth's early poetry was experimental, influenced by Surrealism; his later work was praised for its tight form and its wit and humanistic passion. His *Complete Collected Shorter Poems* appeared in 1967 and *Complete Collected Longer Poems* in 1968. *New Poems* was published in 1974. His essays include *Bird in the Bush* (1959), *Assays* (1962), *The Alternative Society* (1970), and *With Eye and Ear* (1970). He wrote the literary history entitled *American Poetry in the Twentieth Century* (1971) and was also a prolific translator of Japanese, Chinese, Greek, Latin, and Spanish poetry. *An Autobiographical Novel* was published in 1966.

Reyes \\'rā-yes\\, Alfonso (b. May 17, 1889, Monterrey, Mex.—d. Dec. 27, 1959, Mexico City)   Poet, short-story writer, essayist, literary scholar and critic, educator, and diplomat, generally considered one of the most distinguished Mexican men of letters of the 20th century.

While still a student, Reyes established himself as an original scholar and an elegant stylist with the publication of *Cuestiones estéticas* (1911; "Aesthetic Questions"). He began his diplomatic career in Paris, then studied and taught in Madrid. He held various diplomatic posts and was also frequently a cultural representative of Mexico. During these years he published both scholarly and creative works, distinguishing himself equally in poetry and prose. The poetry of *Visión de Anáhuac* (1917; "Vision of Anáhuac"), the dialogues and sketches of *El plano oblicuo* (1920; "The Oblique Plane"), and the essays of *Reloj de sol* (1926; "Sundial") reveal Reyes' versatility. In scholarship and criticism he specialized in classical Greek literature and Spanish literature of the Golden Age. He also translated English and French works into Spanish and wrote such general works as *La experiencia literaria* (1942; "The Literary Experience").

Reymont \\'rā-mȯnt\\, Władysław Stanisław, *original surname* Rejment (b. May 7, 1867, Kobiele Wielkie, near Radom, Poland, Russian Empire—d. Dec. 5, 1925, Warsaw)   Polish writer and novelist.

His early writing includes *Ziemia obiecana* (1899; "The Promised Land"), a story set in the rapidly expanding industrial town of Łódź and depicting the lives and psychology of the owners of the textile mills there. His short stories and novels, including *Spotkanie* (1897; "The Meeting") and *Komediantka* (1896; "The Comedienne"), are written in a naturalistic, factual style with short sentences. The novel *Chłopi*, 4 vol. (1904–09; *The Peasants*), is a chronicle of peasant life during the four seasons of a year; written almost entirely in peasant dialect, it has been translated into many languages and won for Reymont the Nobel Prize for Literature (1924). His later work, though less successful, reflects the variety of his interests, including his view of the spiritualist movement in *Wampir* (1911) and his interpretation of Polish political and social life at the close of the 18th century in *Rok 1794*, 3 vol. (1913–18; "The Year 1794").

Reynard the Fox \\'ren-ərd, 'rān-, -ₐärd\\, Reynard *also spelled* Renard *or* Renart \\-ərt, -ₐärt\\   Hero of several medieval European cycles of versified animal tales that satirize contemporary human society. Though Reynard is sly, amoral, cowardly, and self-seeking, he is still a sympathetic hero whose cunning is a necessity for survival. He symbolizes the triumph of craft over brute strength, usually personified by Isengrim, the greedy and dull-witted wolf. Some of the cyclic stories collected around him, such as those telling of the wolf or bear fishing with his tail through a hole in the ice, are found throughout the world; others, like that of the sick lion cured by the wolf's skin, are derived from Greco-Roman sources.

The cycle arose in the area between Flanders and Germany in the 10th and 11th centuries when clerks began to forge Latin beast epics out of popular tales. The Middle High German poem "Fuchs Reinhard" (*c.* 1180) by Heinrich (der Glîchesaere?), a masterpiece of 2,000 lines that was freely adapted from a lost French original, is an early version.

The main literary tradition of Reynard the Fox descends from the extant French "branches" of the *Roman de Renart* (about 30 in number, nearly 40,000 lines of verse). The facetious portrayal of rustic life, the camel as a papal legate speaking broken French, the animals riding on horses and recounting elaborate dreams all suggest the atmosphere of 13th-century France. Because of the popularity of these tales, the nickname *renard* replaced the old word *goupil* ("fox") throughout France.

Rhadamanthus or **Rhadamanthys** \\ₐrad-ə-'man-thəs\\   In Greek mythology, one of the sons of Europa and Zeus.

Rhadamanthus, known for his wisdom and justice, was made one of the judges of the dead along with his brother Minos and Aeacus, another son of Zeus.

rhapsoder \'rap-sō-dər\ *obsolete* A collector of literary pieces.

rhapsodist \'rap-sə-dist\ [Greek *rhapsōidós,* from *rháptein* to sew, stitch together + *ōidē* song] Any of the dramatic reciters of ancient Greece active from the 6th century BC. In the oral epic tradition, rhapsodists were preceded by Homeric singers (*aoidoi*) of their own epic songs and, like them, were musically accompanied on the lyre and aulos.

Rhapsodists recited Homeric poems, but Plato implies in the *Ion* that their repertory may have included works by Hesiod and Archilochus. By the 3rd century BC they were incorporated with actors in the union of the Dionysiac artists. The HOMERIDS, who perpetuated Homer's works, were originally rhapsodists.

rhapsody \'rap-sə-dē\ [Greek *rhapsōidía* activity of a rhapsodist, portion of an epic poem, a derivative of *rhapsōidós* rhapsodist] **1.** A portion of an epic poem adapted for recitation. **2.** *archaic* A miscellaneous collection. **3.** A highly emotional literary work.

Rhea \'rē-ə\ In Greek mythology, an ancient goddess, probably pre-Hellenic in origin, worshiped sporadically throughout the Greek world. A daughter of Uranus (Heaven) and Gaea (Earth), she married her brother Cronus and gave birth to Hestia, Demeter, Hera, Hades, Poseidon, and Zeus.

rhetoric \'ret-ə-rik\ [Greek *rhētorikē,* from feminine of *rhētorikós* rhetorical, oratorical, a derivative of *rhḗtōr* public speaker] The art of speaking or writing effectively. This may entail the study of principles and rules of composition formulated by critics of ancient time. It can also involve the study of writing or speaking as a means of communication or persuasion.

Classical rhetoric was a dual matter of practical application and philosophy. Most historians of rhetoric attribute its invention to the development of democracy in Syracuse in the 5th century BC, when dispossessed landowners were given a chance to argue their claims before a group of fellow citizens. Shrewd speakers sought help from teachers of oratory, called rhetors, who in turn developed theories for successful speechmaking, or rhetoric.

This use of language was also of interest to philosophers because the oratorical arguments called into question the relationships among language, truth, and morality. According to Aristotle, the uses of rhetoric were divided into deliberative speeches, made to advise political assemblies; forensic speeches, made in law courts; and epideictic speeches, made during ceremonies in praise and sometimes in blame. Rome adopted most of this theory in its public life, and Roman rhetoric developed a process of speech composition broken into five categories: invention, or analyzing and researching the speech topic; disposition, or arranging the material into an oration; elocution, fitting words to the situation; pronunciation, or action, delivering the speech orally; and memory, lodging ideas within the mind.

This compartmentalizing of process gave rhetoric a mechanical quality that became more pronounced as the times changed. By the 16th century rhetoric was being applied to letter writing. Through the influence of the French rhetorician Petrus Ramus, rhetoric was reduced to matters of style mainly and became a collection of tropes, or figures of speech, like metaphor, simile, and personification. At this point it gained a reputation for being flowery ornamentation without substance.

Post-Renaissance changes in the theories of knowledge wrought changes in the principles of rhetoric. The classical idea that language reflects an absolute truth or reality has given way to the idea that language largely determines what reality means.

rhetorical criticism \ri-'tȯr-i-kəl\ Critical method that studies a text (or other form of discourse) in the light of the effects it achieves; rhetorical critics examine the structure, forms, devices, and organization of a text and attempt to correlate these elements with the effects produced. Criticism based on rhetoric is a form of reader-response study, and it is one of the oldest methods of examining meaning. *Compare* HERMENEUTICS; READER-RESPONSE CRITICISM.

rhetorician \ˌret-ə-'rish-ən\ **1.** A master or teacher of rhetoric. **2.** An eloquent or grandiloquent writer or speaker.

rhétoriqueur or **grand rhétoriqueur** \grä\u207f-rä-tō-rē-'kœr\ [Middle French, literally, rhetorician] Any of the principal poets of the school that flourished in 15th- and early 16th-century France (particularly in Burgundy), whose poetry, based on historical and moral themes, employed allegory, dreams, symbols, and mythology for didactic effect.

Guillaume de Machaut, who popularized the new lyric genres such as the rondeau, ballade, lay, and virelay in the 14th century, is considered to have been the leader of the new *rhétorique,* or poetic art. The tradition was continued by Eustache Deschamps, Christine de Pisan, and Charles, Duke d'Orléans, as well as by Jean Froissart, the historian, and the political orator Alain Chartier. In his role as chronicler, Froissart was followed by Georges Chastellain, Olivier de La Marche, and Jean Molinet, historiographers of the Burgundian court who became known as the *grands rhétoriqueurs.* They favored a didactic, elegant, and Latinate style in prose and verse. Their short poems exhibited astonishing verbal ingenuity, often relying on the pun, riddle, or acrostic for effects, and they attempted to enrich the French language by multiplying compound words, derivatives, and scholarly diminutives.

Other *rhétoriqueurs* were Jean Bouchet, Jean Marot, Guillaume Crétin, Pierre Gringore, and Jean Lemaire de Belges.

Rhianus \rē-'ā-nəs, rī-\ (b. *c.* 275 BC) Greek poet and scholar from Crete. He is said to have been a slave before receiving an education. His only surviving works are 10 or 11 epigrams preserved in the *Greek Anthology.* He was best known as an epic poet, producing five epics, one mythological (*Heracleia*) and four historical (*Achaeaca, Eliaca, Messeniaca,* and *Thessaliaca*). Only the contents of the *Messeniaca,* dealing with a war in the 7th century BC between Messene and Sparta, are known. He also was an early editor of the *Iliad* and the *Odyssey.*

Rhinoceros Quasi-allegorical play in three acts by Eugène IONESCO, produced in Germany in 1959 and published in French the same year as *Le Rhinocéros.*

At the play's outset, Jean and Bérenger sit at a provincial café, when a solitary rhinoceros runs by them. The next day, townspeople are talking about the strange and sudden proliferation of rhinoceroses and about the metamorphosis of fellow citizens into these creatures. When his friend Jean is transformed, Bérenger attempts to warn everyone, but he appears to be the sole remaining human.

rhopalic or **ropalic** \rō-'pal-ik\ [Greek *rhopalikós,* literally, like a club (i.e., thicker toward the end), a derivative of *rhópalon* club, cudgel], *also called* wedge verse. Having each succeeding unit in a prosodic series larger or longer than the preceding one. For example, a rhopalic may have each successive word in a line or verse longer by one syllable than its predecessor. Each successive line of a stanza may be made longer by the addition of one element (such as a syllable or metrical foot).

rhupunt or **rhupynt** \\'hrē-,pint\\ [Welsh] One of the 24 meters of the Welsh bardic tradition. A rhupunt is a verse composed of three, four, or five four-syllable sections linked by cynghanedd (an intricate system of accentuation, alliteration, and internal rhyme) and rhyme. The first three of the four-syllable sections are made to rhyme with one another and the fourth section to rhyme with the fourth of the next verse. The whole is written as a single line or is divided into as many lines as it has rhyming sections.

rhyme or **rime** \\'rīm\\ [Middle English *rime,* from Old French, of unknown origin] A type of echoing produced by the close placement of two or more words with similarly sounding final syllables. Rhyme is used by poets (and occasionally by prose writers) to produce sounds that appeal to the ear and to unify and establish a poem's stanzaic form. End rhyme (*i.e.,* rhyme used at the end of a line to echo the end of another line) is most common, but internal, interior, or leonine rhyme is frequently used as an occasional embellishment in a poem; a familiar example is William Shakespeare's "Hark; hark! the lark at heaven's gate sings."

Three rhymes are recognized by purists as "true rhymes": *masculine rhyme,* in which the two words end with the same vowel-consonant combination (stand/land); *feminine rhyme* (sometimes called *double rhyme*), in which two syllables rhyme (profession/discretion); and *trisyllabic rhyme,* in which three syllables rhyme (patinate/latinate). The too-regular effect of masculine rhyme is sometimes softened by using *trailing rhyme,* or *semirhyme,* in which one of the two words trails an additional unstressed syllable behind it (trail/failure).

Other types of rhyme include *eye rhyme,* in which syllables are identical in spelling but are pronounced differently (cough/slough), and *pararhyme,* first used systematically by the 20th-century poet Wilfred Owen, in which the two syllables have different vowel sounds but identical penultimate and final consonantal groupings (grand/grind). *Feminine pararhyme* has two forms, one in which both vowel sounds differ (ran in/run on) and one in which only one does (blindness/blandness). *Weakened,* or *unaccented, rhyme* occurs when the relevant syllable of the rhyming word is unstressed (bend/frightened). Because of the way in which lack of stress affects the sound, a rhyme of this kind may often be regarded as consonance, which occurs when the two words are similar only in having identical final consonants (best/least). Another form of near rhyme is assonance, in which only the vowel sounds are identical (grow/home).

Many traditional poetic forms use set rhyme patterns; for example, the sonnet, villanelle, rondeau, ballade, chant royal, triolet, canzone, and sestina. Rhyme seems to have developed in Western poetry as a combination of earlier techniques of end consonance, end assonance, and alliteration. It is found only occasionally in classical Greek and Latin poetry but more frequently in medieval religious Latin verse and in songs from the 4th century (especially those of the Roman Catholic liturgy). Although it has been periodically opposed by devotees of classical verse and of free verse, other poets have continued to introduce new and complicated rhyme schemes. *See also* AL-LITERATION; ASSONANCE; CONSONANCE; POETRY.

rhymer or **rimer** \\'rī-mər\\ One who makes rhymes, a versifier; specifically, a mediocre poet.

rhyme royal or **rime royal** \\'rīm-'rȯi-əl\\ *plural* rhyme royals. A stanza of seven lines in iambic pentameter, rhyming *ababbcc.*

The rhyme royal was first used in English verse in the 14th century by Geoffrey Chaucer in *Troilus and Criseyde* and *The Parlement of Foules.* Rhyme royal became the favorite form for long narrative poems during the 15th and 16th centuries, concluding with William Shakespeare's *The Rape of Lucrece* (1594). John Milton experimented with the form in the 17th century, as did William Morris in the 19th and John Masefield in the 20th. *Compare* BALLADE ROYAL; CHANT ROYAL.

rhyme scheme The formal arrangement of rhymes in a stanza or a poem. It may be identified by the name of a set rhyme pattern (for example, Spenserian stanza). The rhyme scheme is usually notated with lowercase letters of the alphabet (as *ababbcbcc,* in the case of the Spenserian stanza), each different letter representing a different rhyme.

rhymester or **rimester** \\'rīm-stər\\ An inferior poet.

rhyme-tag \\'rīm-,tag\\ A word or phrase used primarily to produce a rhyme. Rhyme-tags are used to comic effect in much light verse, as in W.S. Gilbert's "The Modern Major-Gineral," which reads in part

> I am the very pattern of a modern Major-Gineral,
> I've information vegetable, animal, and mineral;
> I know the kings of England, and I quote the fights historical,
> From Marathon to Waterloo, in order categorical;
> I'm very well acquainted, too, with matters mathematical,
> I understand equations, both the simple and quadratical;
> About binomial theorem I'm teeming with a lot o' news,
> With interesting facts about the square of the hypotenuse.
> I'm very good at integral and differential calculus,
> I know the scientific names of beings animalculous.
> In short, in matters vegetable, animal, and mineral,
> I am the very model of a modern Major-Gineral.

Rhys \\'rēs\\, Ernest Percival (b. July 17, 1859, London, Eng.—d. May 25, 1946, London) English man of letters who, as editor of Everyman's Library, a series of inexpensive editions of world classics, influenced the literary taste of his own and succeeding generations.

In 1886 Rhys became a poet and freelance critic and editor in London. He contributed to reviews and to the two volumes published by the Rhymers' Club, of which he, with William Butler Yeats, was a founding member. He edited a series of lyric poetry (1894–99) for the publisher J.M. Dent, who in 1904 invited him to edit Everyman's Library (a title suggested by Rhys). The first volume came out in 1906, and, by the time of Rhys's death, of the 1,000 volumes planned, 983 had been published. Rhys's own writings include volumes of essays and poems and two volumes of reminiscences, *Everyman Remembers* (1931) and *Wales England Wed* (1940).

Rhys \\'rēs\\, Jean, *original name* Ella Gwendolen Rees William \\'rēs-'wil-yəm\\ (b. Aug. 24, 1890, Roseau, Dominica, Federation of the Leeward Islands —d. May 14, 1979, Exeter, Devon, Eng.) West Indian novelist who earned acclaim for her early works set in the bohemian world of Europe in the 1920s and '30s and for her memorable novel WIDE SARGASSO SEA (1966).

In Paris, Rhys was encouraged to write by the English novelist Ford Madox Ford. Her first book, *The Left Bank* (1927), was a collection of short stories. It was followed by such novels as *Postures* (1928), *After Leaving Mr. Mackenzie* (1931), *Voyage in the Dark* (1934), and *Good Morning, Midnight* (1939).

She moved to Cornwall and disappeared from the public eye, writing little and publishing nothing until *Wide Sargasso Sea,* a novel linked to Charlotte Brontë's *Jane Eyre,* returned her to the limelight. It was followed by the short-story collections *Tigers Are Better-Looking* (1968) and *Sleep It Off Lady* (1976). Rhys's unfinished autobiography, *Smile Please,* was published in 1979.

Rhys \\'rēs\\, Siôn Dafydd, *also called* John David Rhys *or* John Davies (b. 1534, Llanfaethlu, Anglesey, Wales—d. *c.* 1609, Clun Hir?, Brecknockshire) Welsh physician and grammarian whose grammar, *Cambrobrytannicae Cymraecaeve linguae in-*

stitutiones et rudimenta (1592), was the foundation of all later Welsh grammatical studies.

Rhys practiced as a physician at Cardiff, Wales, before devoting all his time to his grammar. He attempted to set down the rules of bardic poetry and the grammar of the Welsh language but did so according to the Latin grammatical structure. His book also includes a greeting in Welsh, a discussion of the poetic art, and a collection of Welsh poetry.

rhythm \'rith-əm\ [Greek *rhythmós* recurrent motion, rhythm] **1.** An ordered, recurrent alternation of strong and weak elements in the flow of sound and silence in speech.

Although rhythm in poetry is difficult to define, it is readily discriminated by the ear and the mind, having as it does a physiological basis. It is universally agreed to involve qualities of movement, repetition, and pattern and to arise from the poem's nature as a temporal structure. Rhythm, by any definition, is essential to poetry; prose may be said to exhibit rhythm but in a much less highly organized sense.

Although it is often equated with rhythm, METER is perhaps more accurately described as one method of organizing a poem's rhythm. Unlike rhythm, meter is not a requisite of poetry; it is, rather, an abstract organization of elements of stress, duration, or number of syllables per line into a specific formal pattern. The interaction of a given metrical pattern with any other aspect of sound in a poem produces a tension, or counterpoint, that creates the rhythm of metrically based poetry.

Compared with the wide variety of metrical schemes, the types of metrically related rhythms are few. *Duple rhythm* occurs in lines composed in two-syllable feet, as in William Shakespeare's line:

Tired with | all these, | for rest | ful death | I cry

In metrical schemes based on three-syllable feet, the rhythm is known as *triple rhythm*, as in Rudyard Kipling's lines:

For the strength | of the Pack | is the Wolf, |

and the strength | of the Wolf | is the Pack

Rising rhythm results when the stress falls on the last syllable of each foot in a line, as in John Milton's line:

When I | consid | er how | my light | is spent

The reverse is *falling rhythm*, as in John Dryden's line:

Bacchus' | blessings | are a | treasure

Running, or *common*, *rhythm* occurs in meters in which stressed and unstressed syllables alternate (duple rhythm, rising or falling). Gerard Manley Hopkins, in reaction against traditional meters, coined the term SPRUNG RHYTHM to apply to verse in which the line is measured by the number of speech-stressed syllables, the number of unstressed syllables being indeterminate.

In free verse, rhythm most commonly arises from the arrangement of linguistic elements into patterns that more nearly approximate the natural cadence of speech and that give symmetry to the verse. The rhythmical resources available to free verse include syntactical patterning; systematic repetition of sound, words, phrases, and lines; and the relative value of temporal junctures occasioned by caesura (a marked pause in the middle of a line), line length, and other determinants of pace. Some authorities recognize in the highly organized patterning of imagery a further source of poetic rhythm.

2. The repetition in a literary work at varying intervals and in an altered form or under changed circumstances of phrase, incident, character type, or symbol. **3.** The effect created by the elements in a play, motion picture, or novel that are related to the temporal development of the action (such as the length and diversity of scenes and language).

Ribas \'rē-bȧs\, Óscar (Bento) (b. Aug. 17, 1909, Luanda, Angola)   Angolan folklorist and novelist who recorded in Portuguese the oral tradition of the Mbundu people of Angola.

Ribas' early work comprised romantic tales. He gradually went blind during his early 20s, but he remained an indefatigable researcher and writer. The publication of his novel *Uangafeitiço* (1951; "The Evil Spell") and the stories in *Ecos da minha terra* (1952; "Echoes of My Land") marked a new African direction in his writing. Both books present a wealth of Mbundu fables, songs, and folk sayings.

Ribas' study of Mbundu culture and religion, *Ilundo: Divindades e ritos angolanos* (1958; "Ilundo: Angolan Divinations and Rites"), appeared after 18 years of research. It was followed by the three-volume *Missosso: Literatura tradicional angolana* (1961–64; "Missosso: Traditional Angolan Literature"), a linguistic work containing a vernacular dictionary and Portuguese versions of Angolan tales (*missosso*), laments, and proverbs. Ribas' autobiography was published as *Tudo isto aconteceu* (1975; "All of This Happened").

Ribeiro \rē-'bā-rü\, Aquilino (Gomes) (b. Sept. 13, 1885, Beira Alta, Port.—d. May 27, 1963, Lisbon)   Novelist who was the mainstay of Portuguese fiction until the surge of Neorealist regionalism that began in 1930.

Ribeiro's revolutionary activism forced him to flee Portugal several times between 1908 and 1932. Much of his time in exile was spent in Paris. He launched his writing career in 1913 with *Jardim das tormentas* ("The Garden of Torments") and *Terras do demo* (1919; "Lands of the Demon"), followed by pieces of shorter fiction subsequently included in *Estrada de Santiago* (1922; "The Road to Santiago"). His later works include *A casa grande de Romarigães* (1957; "The Great House of Romarigães") and *Quando os lobos uivam* (1958; "When the Wolves Howl"). During his 40-year career, Ribeiro published some two dozen novels, most of them notable for the stylistic craft used to depict a geographic region—particularly rural northeastern Portugal—with its rustic slang, archaic forms of speech, human types, fauna, and flora.

Ribeiro \rē-'bā-rü\, Bernardim (b. *c.* 1482, Torrão, Port.—d. October 1552, Lisbon)   Portuguese poet and prose writer who introduced the pastoral style to Portugal in five eclogues, or idylls, and a prose romance. His lyrical treatment of the yearnings of unrequited love provided models for the tradition of the *saudade* (poem of longing) that profoundly influenced the development of Portuguese literature.

Ribeiro, who frequented the royal courts of Manuel I and John III, wrote the chivalric and pastoral romance *Livro das saudades* (1554–57; "Book of Yearnings"). This prose work, better known by its opening words as *Menina e moça* ("Child and Damsel"), is generally considered a masterpiece of Portuguese literature of the Renaissance. Innovative in its use of prose, Ribeiro's tale established a stylistic tradition that has endured as a major force in Portuguese literature.

Ribeiro Couto \rē-'bā-rü-'kü-tü\, Rui (b. March 12, 1898, Santos, Braz.—d. May 30, 1963, Paris, Fr.)   Brazilian poet and short-story writer, who became one of the leading figures of Modernismo in its early years. Originally a Symbolist poet, Ribeiro Couto gravitated toward Modernismo in the early 1920s, publishing poems and short stories concerning themes of humble everyday life. Besides his works in Portuguese, he also wrote fluently in French.

Among Ribeiro Couto's best-known volumes of short stories are *O crime do estudante Batista* (1922: "The Crime of Batista the Student"), *O clube das esposas enganadas* (1933; "The Deceived Wives' Club"), and *O largo da matriz* (1940; "Cathedral Square"). His volumes of poetry include *Um homem na multidão* (1926; "A Man in the Crowd"), *O dia é longo* (1944; "A Long Day"), and *Mar e rio* (1952; "Sea and River").

Ricardo \rē-'kär-dü\, Cassiano, *surname in full* Ricardo Leite \'lā-tē\ (b. July 26, 1895, São José dos Campos, Braz.—d. Jan. 14, 1974, Rio de Janeiro)   Brazilian poet, essayist, literary critic, and journalist, who participated in many literary movements, including Parnassianism, Modernismo, and concretism (the theory and practice of concrete poetry).

Ricardo was a prime mover during the early 1920s in the "Anta" subgroup of Modernismo, which urged a nationalistic rediscovery of the land and its indigenous folkloric traditions. *Martim Cererê* (1928), perhaps his best-known collection of poems, dates from this period. From nationalism, Ricardo evolved toward the compassionate, universal, "post-atomic" worldview evident in *Jeremias sem-chorar* (1964; "Tearless Jeremiah"). He wrote extensively in the area of literary theory and exercised a marked influence on every generation of young poets through the early 1970s.

Rice \'rīs\, Alice Hegan, *in full* Alice Caldwell Hegan Rice (b. Jan. 11, 1870, Shelbyville, Ky., U.S.—d. Feb. 10, 1942, Louisville)   American novelist and short-story writer known for her 1901 best-seller *Mrs. Wiggs of the Cabbage Patch.*

At the age of 16 Rice worked at a mission Sunday school in a Louisville slum known as the Cabbage Patch. With Louise Marshall, she later founded (1910) the Cabbage Patch Settlement House in Louisville. In addition to *Mrs. Wiggs of the Cabbage Patch*, Rice wrote many other novels noted for pathos and humor. Her autobiography, *The Inky Way*, appeared in 1940.

Rice \'rīs\, Elmer, *original surname* Reizenstein \'rīt-sən-,shtīn, *Angl* 'rī-zən-,stīn\ (b. Sept. 28, 1892, New York, N.Y., U.S.—d. May 8, 1967, Southampton, Hampshire, Eng.)   American playwright, director, and novelist noted for his innovative and polemical plays.

Rice's first work, the melodramatic *On Trial* (1914), was the first play to employ on stage the motion-picture technique of flashbacks, in this case to present the recollections of witnesses at a trial. In *The Adding Machine* (1923), Rice adapted techniques from German Expressionist theater. His most important play, STREET SCENE (1929), won a Pulitzer Prize and was adapted into a highly popular musical. *Counsellor-at-Law* (1931) was a rather critical look at the legal profession. In *We, the People* (1933), *Judgment Day* (1934), and several other polemical plays of the 1930s, Rice treated the evils of Nazism, the poverty of the Great Depression, and racism. Rice also wrote several novels and an autobiography, entitled *Minority Report* (1963).

Rice \'rīs\, James (b. Sept. 26, 1843, Northampton, Eng.—d. April 26, 1882, Redhill)   English novelist best known for his literary partnership with Sir Walter BESANT.

In 1868 Rice bought *Once a Week*, which proved a losing venture for him, but which brought him into touch with Besant, who was a contributor. There ensued a close friendship and literary partnership that lasted until Rice's death 10 years later and resulted in a large number of successful novels. To the first, the anonymously published *Ready-money Mortiboy* (1872), Rice contributed the central figure and the leading situation. This work was followed by *My Little Girl* (1873); *This Son of Vulcan* (1876); *The Golden Butterfly* (1876), the most popular of their joint productions; *With Harp and Crown* (1877); *The Monks of Thelema* (1878); *By Celia's Arbour* (1878); *The Seamy Side* (1880); *The Chaplain of the Fleet* (1881); *Sir Richard Whittington* (1881); and a large number of short stories, some of

which were reprinted in *The Case of Mr. Lucraft* (1876), *'Twas in Trafalgar Bay* (1879), and *The Ten Years' Tenant* (1881).

Rich \'rich\, Adrienne (Cecile) (b. May 16, 1929, Baltimore, Md., U.S.)   American poet, scholar, teacher, and critic whose many volumes of poetry trace a stylistic transformation from formal, well-crafted but imitative poetry to a more personal and powerful style.

Rich attended Radcliffe College, and before her graduation her poetry was chosen by W.H. Auden for publication in the Yale Younger Poets series. The resulting volume, *A Change of World* (1951), reflected her mastery of the formal elements of poetry. *The Diamond Cutters and Other Poems* (1955) was followed by *Snapshots of a Daughter-in-Law* (1963), which exhibited a movement away from the restrained and formal to a looser, more personal form. Her fourth collection, *Necessities of Life* (1966), was written almost entirely in free verse. Throughout the 1960s and '70s her increasing commitment to the women's movement and to a lesbian/feminist aesthetic politicized much of her poetry. Among her later volumes of verse are *Leaflets* (1969), *Diving into the Wreck* (1973), *The Dream of a Common Language* (1978), *A Wild Patience Has Taken Me This Far* (1981), and *An Atlas of the Difficult World* (1991). Rich also wrote a number of books of criticism, including *Of Woman Born: Motherhood as Experience and Institution* (1976), *On Lies, Secrets, and Silence* (1979), and *What Is Found There: Notebooks on Poetry and Politics* (1993).

Rich \'rich\, Lady Penelope, *original surname* Devereux \'dev-ə-,rūks, -,reks, -,rū, -,rō, -,rə\ (b. 1562?—d. 1607)   English noblewoman who was the charming "Stella" of Sir Philip Sidney's love poems *Astrophel and Stella* (1591). Party to an arranged marriage that was unhappy from the start, Lady Penelope encouraged Sidney's continued emotional attachment to her.

Richard II \'rich-ərd\ (*in full* The Tragedy of King Richard II)   Play in five acts by William SHAKESPEARE, performed in 1595–96 and published in a quarto edition in 1597 and in the First Folio edition of 1623. It is the first in a sequence of four history plays (the other three being *Henry IV* Parts I and II and *Henry V*), known collectively as the "second tetralogy," treating the early phases of the power struggle between the houses of Lancaster and York.

In contrast with the plays of his earlier "first tetralogy" (*Henry VI* Parts I, II, and III and *Richard III*), which deal with the latter phases of the dynastic struggle, Shakespeare invests *Richard II* with more deeply realized characters and more distinctive dramatic contrasts. Richard, according to Shakespeare, is at first an extravagant, self-indulgent king. He exiles two feuding noblemen, Thomas Mowbray and Henry Bolingbroke. When John of Gaunt dies, Richard seizes his properties to finance a war against the Irish. The seizure gives the resentful, conniving Bolingbroke an excuse to invade England with his own armies. After Richard surrenders and abdicates the throne, he is held prisoner and hammers out the meaning of his life in sustained soliloquy. From this moment of truth, he rediscovers pride, trust, and courage, so that when he is murdered, he dies with an access of strength and an ascending spirit.

Richard III \'rich-ərd\ (*in full* The Tragedy of King Richard III)   Historical tragedy in five acts by William SHAKESPEARE. It was performed in London in 1592–93 and was published in 1597 in a quarto edition reconstructed from an actor's promptbook. *Richard III* was the first of Shakespeare's history plays to have a self-contained narrative unity. In it, Shakespeare emphasized the moment of death as a crisis of conscience in which the individual is capable of great clarity.

The deformed Richard, duke of Gloucester, is among the earliest and most vivid of Shakespeare's sympathetic villains. He plots to become king of England, thereby committing himself to murder, treason, and dissimulation with an inventive imagination that an audience can both relish and condemn. Richard murders King Henry VI; Richard's brother then becomes king of England as Edward IV. Through Richard's machinations his brother George, the duke of Clarence, and Henry's son, the prince of Wales, are murdered. When Edward dies, Richard becomes king and arranges the murder of his principal rivals for the crown, Edward's two young sons. An army led by Henry Tudor, earl of Richmond, challenges Richard's claim to the throne, however. On the night before the Battle of Bosworth Field, Richard is haunted by the ghosts of all whom he has murdered. After a desperate fight, Richard is killed and Richmond becomes King Henry VII.

Richard Cory \'rich-ərd-'kȯr-ē\ Poem by Edwin Arlington ROBINSON, published in the collection *The Children of the Night* (1897). Perhaps Robinson's best-known poem, it is one of several set in Tilbury Town, a fictional New England village.

The Tilbury Town community, represented by the collective "we," narrates the four-stanza poem about Richard Cory, a mysterious fellow villager. The villagers admire him for his wealth, education, and manners. An object of their fascination and envy, he reminds them of royalty. Their ignorance of his troubled soul is underscored by the surprise ending, which reports his suicide with understatement.

Richards \'rich-ərdz\, I.A., *in full* Ivor Armstrong (b. Feb. 26, 1893, Sandbach, Cheshire, Eng.—d. Sept. 7, 1979, Cambridge, Cambridgeshire) English critic, poet, and teacher who was highly influential in developing a new way of reading poetry, which led to the New Criticism. A student of psychology, he concluded that poetry performs a therapeutic function by coordinating a variety of human impulses into an aesthetic whole.

Richards was educated at Magdalene College, Cambridge, and was a lecturer there from 1922 to 1929. During that period he wrote three of his most influential books: *The Meaning of Meaning* (1923; with C.K. Ogden), a pioneer work on semantics, and *Principles of Literary Criticism* (1924) and *Practical Criticism* (1929), companion volumes developing his critical method.

During the 1930s, Richards spent much of his time developing Basic English, a system originated by Ogden that employed only 850 words. Richards believed a universally intelligible language would help to bring about international understanding, and he took Basic English to various institutions in China. In 1942 he published a version of Plato's *Republic* in Basic English. He became professor of English at Harvard University in 1944. His verse was collected in *Internal Colloquies* (1971) and *New and Selected Poems* (1978). His essay collections include *Science and Poetry* (1926; revised as *Poetries and Sciences* [1970]), *Speculative Instruments* (1955), *Beyond* (1974), and *Poetries* (1974). *Complementarities* (1976) includes uncollected essays from 1919 to 1975. *See also* CAMBRIDGE CRITICS.

Richardson \'rich-ərd-sən\, Dorothy M., *in full* Miller, *married name* Odle \'ōd-əl\ (b. May 17, 1873, Abingdon, Berkshire, Eng.—d. June 17, 1957, Beckenham, Kent) English novelist who was a pioneer in stream-of-consciousness fiction.

Richardson passed a relatively secure childhood and youth in late Victorian England. She attended school until age 17, when her father began a slide into bankruptcy. She immediately took a job as a pupil-teacher in Germany and then six months later returned to London and continued to teach until 1895. In November of that year, while under Richardson's care, her mother committed suicide. Determined to make her own way, Richardson moved to Bloomsbury and took a job at a dental office, in the meantime gaining valuable experience writing essays and reviews for publication. In 1908, having broken off a relationship with H.G. Wells, she moved to Sussex and stayed with a Quaker family there.

During this period her fiction writing technique evolved, and she formulated a plan for the multivolume work that would become PILGRIMAGE (complete edition published posthumously in 1967). The first volume (which she termed a chapter), entitled *Pointed Roofs*, was published in 1915. In August 1917 she married Alan Odle, an artist 15 years her junior. Richardson devoted the rest of her life to work on *Pilgrimage*, which traces the developing consciousness of Miriam Henderson. Generally well received and much discussed among her peers during her lifetime, the work is extremely accomplished though it remains little read.

Richardson \'rich-ərd-sən\, Henry Handel, *pseudonym of* Ethel Florence Lindesay Robertson \'räb-ərt-sən\, *original surname* Richardson (b. Jan. 3, 1870, Melbourne, Australia—d. March 20, 1946, Fairlight, Sussex, Eng.) Australian novelist whose trilogy *The Fortunes of Richard Mahony*, combining description of an Australian immigrant's life and work in the goldfields with a powerful character study, is considered the crowning achievement of modern Australian fiction to that time.

Richardson attended the Presbyterian Ladies' College in Melbourne. In 1888 she left Australia to study music in Leipzig, Ger., and she spent the rest of her life abroad, settling in England in 1904.

In Germany Richardson began her first novel, *Maurice Guest* (1908), the story of a young English music student in Leipzig whose career and life are ruined by a tragic love affair. Her second novel, *The Getting of Wisdom* (1910), is an account of her life at the boarding school she attended in Melbourne. *The Fortunes of Richard Mahony* (1930; consisting of *Australia Felix*, 1917; *The Way Home*, 1925; and *Ultima Thule*, 1929) is a detailed and sympathetic account of an immigrant who is unable to adjust to his adopted country. Her last novel, *The Young Cosima* (1939), is a reconstruction of the love triangle of Richard Wagner, Cosima Liszt, and Hans von Bülow. She also wrote a number of short stories, published as *The End of a Childhood and Other Stories* (1934), and an unfinished autobiography, *Myself When Young* (1948).

Richardson \'rich-ərd-sən\, John (b. Oct. 4, 1796, probably Fort George, Upper Canada [now Niagara-on-the-Lake, Ont., Can.]—d. May 12, 1852, New York, N.Y., U.S.) Canadian writer of historical and autobiographical romantic novels.

Richardson was a British volunteer in the War of 1812 and a British officer in England, Barbados, and Spain. He returned to Canada in 1838 and remained there in a variety of positions until 1849, when he moved to New York.

Richardson's first publication was the "metrical romance" *Tecumseh; or, The Warrior of the West* (1828). He wrote his first novel, *Écarté; or, The Salons of Paris*, 3 vol. (1829), in a realistic but somewhat sensational style. Its sequel was *Frascati's; or, Scenes in Paris* (1830). His third novel, *Wacousta; or, The Prophecy*, 2 vol. (1832), a gothic story about Pontiac's War (the Indian uprising of 1763–64), brought him popular acclaim. Its sequel, *The Canadian Brothers; or, The Prophecy Fulfilled*, 2 vol. (1840; U.S. edition, *Matilda Montgomerie*), was less successful. Among his significant works of nonfiction are *Personal Memoirs of Major Richardson* (1838), *War of 1812* (1842), and *Eight Years in Canada* (1847). He also wrote many short stories. His later novels include *The Monk Knight of St. John; A Tale of the Crusades* (1850), *Hardscrabble; or, The Fall of Chicago* (1851), *Wau-nan-gee; or, The Massacre at Chicago* (1852), and *Westbrook, the Outlaw* (1853).

Richardson \'rich-ərd-sən\, Samuel (baptized Aug. 19, 1689, Mackworth, near Derby, Derbyshire, Eng.—d. July 4, 1761, Parson's Green, near London)   English novelist who explored the dramatic possibil-

Detail of an oil painting by Joseph Highmore

National Portrait Gallery, London

ities of the novel by his use of the letter form ("epistolary technique"). His major novels were PAMELA (1740) and CLARISSA (1747–48).

Richardson moved with his family from Derbyshire to London when he was 10. He was bound apprentice to a London printer and later became associated with a printing family whose presses he eventually took over when he set up in business for himself in 1721. During the 1730s his press became known as one of the three best in London, and with prosperity he leased the first of three country houses, in which he entertained a circle of friends that included Samuel Johnson, the painter William Hogarth, the actors Colley Cibber and David Garrick, and Edward Young (many of whose poems he printed, including the celebrated *Night Thoughts*).

In this same decade he began writing in a modest way, undertaking some editing and producing a few pamphlets. More importantly, he was commissioned to write a collection of letters that might serve as models for "country readers," a volume that has become known as *Familiar Letters on Important Occasions*. Occasionally he hit upon the idea of continuing the same subject from one letter to another, a technique he expanded in his novel *Pamela*. He began writing the work in November 1739 and published it as *Pamela: or, Virtue Rewarded* a year later. Richardson published a sequel, *Pamela in her Exalted Condition*, in 1742.

By 1744 Richardson seems to have completed a first draft of his second novel, *Clarissa; or, The History of a Young Lady*, but he spent three years revising it. His third novel, THE HISTORY OF SIR CHARLES GRANDISON (1754), was his bow to requests from correspondents for the hero as a good man, a counterpart to the errant hero of Henry Fielding's *Tom Jones* (1749).

By the end of the 18th century, Richardson's reputation was on the wane, but 20th-century critics appreciated the psychological subtleties of *Pamela* and *Clarissa* and his books were required reading in most courses on the English novel. *See also* EPISTOLARY NOVEL.

Richepin \resh-'paⁿ\, Jean (b. Feb. 4, 1849, Médéa, Alg.—d. Dec. 11, 1926, Paris, Fr.)   French poet, dramatist, and novelist who examined the lower levels of society in sharp, bold language and helped to revolutionize French poetry.

Local authorities responded to the coarse language in Richepin's first book of poetry, *La Chanson des gueux* (1876; "Song of the Poor"), by sentencing him to a month in prison. Despite criticism, Richepin continued to write in his tough style. His works of poetry include *Les Caresses* (1877), *Les Blasphèmes* (1884), and *La Mer* (1886; "The Sea"). He wrote three novels and a number of successful plays. He was elected to the Académie Française in 1908.

Richler \'rich-lər\, Mordecai (b. Jan. 27, 1931, Montreal, Can.)   Prominent Canadian novelist whose incisive and penetrating works explore fundamental human dilemmas and values.

In 1951–52 Richler lived in Paris, where he was influenced and stimulated by existentialist authors. Returning to Canada, he published the novel *The Acrobats* (1954), about a young Canadian painter in Spain with a group of disillusioned expatriates and revolutionaries. Both *Son of a Smaller Hero* (1955) and *A Choice of Enemies* (1957) deal with angry, confused modern heroes. *The Apprenticeship of Duddy Kravitz* (1959) is a bawdy account of a Jewish boy in Montreal and his transformation into a ruthless businessman. Amusing descriptions of the leaders of the communications industries are the subject of *The Incomparable Atuk* (1963). *Cocksure* (1968) and *St. Urbain's Horseman* (1971) both examine North Americans in England. Other works include a collection of humorous essays, *Notes on an Endangered Species and Others* (1974); a children's book, *Jacob Two-Two Meets the Hooded Fang* (1975); and two novels, *Joshua Then and Now* (1980) and *Solomon Gursky Was Here* (1989).

Richter \'rik-tər\, Conrad (Michael) (b. Oct. 13, 1890, Pine Grove, Pa., U.S.—d. Oct. 30, 1968, Pottsville, Pa.)   American short-story writer and novelist known for his lyrical fiction about early America.

Richter became the editor of the Patton (Pa.) *Courier* at age 19. He then worked as a reporter and founded a juvenile magazine that he liquidated before moving to New Mexico in 1928. In an era when many American writers steeped themselves in European culture, Richter was fascinated with American history, and he spent years researching frontier life. He is best known for THE SEA OF GRASS (1936) and his trilogy of pioneer life, *The Trees* (1940), *The Fields* (1946), and THE TOWN (1950), the final volume of which won the Pulitzer Prize for fiction in 1951. Richter's stories are usually told through a contemporary narrator, allowing the reader to see the present and past as a continuum. An autobiographical novel, *The Waters of Kronos* (1960), won the National Book Award in 1961.

riddle \'rid-əl\ [Old English *rǣdelse* opinion, conjecture, riddle]   A deliberately enigmatic or ambiguous question requiring a thoughtful and often witty answer. The riddle is a form of guessing game that has been a part of the folklore of most cultures from ancient times. Western scholars generally recognize two main kinds of riddle: the descriptive riddle and the shrewd or witty question.

The descriptive riddle usually describes an animal, person, plant, or object in an intentionally enigmatic manner, to suggest something different from the correct answer. "What runs about all day and lies under the bed at night?" suggests "A dog," but the answer is "A shoe." Descriptive riddles deal with appearance, not function. Thus, an egg is "A little white house without door or window," not something to eat or something from which a chicken hatches. Paradoxical riddles provide descriptions in terms of action, for example, "What grows bigger the more you take from it?"—"A hole."

Lacking a generic name in English, shrewd or witty questions are classed with riddles. They, too, are of ancient origin. A classical Greek example that has been widely translated is "What is the strongest of all things?"—"Love: iron is strong, but the blacksmith is stronger, and love can subdue the blacksmith." Shrewd questions may be classified by subject and form. Those dealing with letters of the alphabet, words, and symbols are generally statements calling for interpretation: "ICUR YY 4 me" ("I see you are too wise for me"); "What is in the middle of Paris?"—"R"; "Spell 'dry grass' with three letters?"—

"Hay." The influence of the classroom in such riddles (sometimes called "catch riddles") is clear.

Riders to the Sea One-act play by John Millington SYNGE, published in 1903 and produced in 1904. Set in the Aran Islands off the west coast of Ireland and based on a tale Synge had heard there, *Riders to the Sea* won critical acclaim as one of dramatic literature's greatest one-act plays.

The play centers on Maurya, an old woman who has lost to the sea all the male members of her family except Bartley, the last of her six sons. In the course of the play he drowns.

Riding \'rī-diŋ\, Laura, *original surname* Reichenthal \'rī-kən-‚thäl\, *married name* Jackson \'jak-sən\, *pseudonyms* Barbara Rich \'rich\, Madeleine Vara \'vär-ə\, *and* Laura Riding Gottschalk \'gät-‚shók\ (b. Jan. 16, 1901, New York, N.Y., U.S.—d. Sept. 2, 1991, Sebastian, Fla.) American poet, critic, and prose writer who was influential among the literary avant-garde during the 1920s and '30s.

Riding attended Cornell University, Ithaca, N.Y. Early on she came to be associated with the Fugitives, a prominent group of Southern writers. Riding lived abroad from 1926 to 1939, much of the time with the poet and critic Robert Graves; together they established the Seizin Press (1927–38) and published the journal *Epilogue* (1935–38). Their book *A Survey of Modernist Poetry* (1927, reprinted 1977) developed ideas of close textual analysis that influenced New Criticism.

In 1941 Riding married the critic Schuyler B. Jackson, and until his death in 1968 they worked together on lexicographical studies. She completed their "Rational Meaning: A New Foundation for the Definition of Words" in 1974, but it was not published. During this time Riding ceased to write poetry, which she renounced as being "inadequate," but her other writings continued to interest a select audience and her late philosophical work *The Telling* (1972) was highly esteemed among a small readership. Her *Collected Poems*, which was originally published in 1938, was issued in a revised edition in 1980, and *First Awakenings: The Early Poems* was published in 1992.

riding rhyme A rhymed couplet in iambic pentameter. It is an early form of HEROIC COUPLET.

Ridler \'rid-lər\, Anne (Barbara) (b. July 30, 1912, Rugby, Warwickshire, Eng.) English poet and dramatist whose devotional poetry and verse drama is similar to that of T.S. Eliot.

Ridler graduated from King's College, London. From 1935 to 1940 she worked for the publishing house of Faber & Faber, where she was Eliot's secretary for part of the time. Ridler's poetry is filled with complex metaphors, and she has often been called a modern Metaphysical poet. In addition to exploring religious themes, her work celebrates human experience, notably marriage and motherhood. Her books include *Poems* (1939), *Some Time After* (1972), and *New and Selected Poems* (1988). Among her verse plays are *Cain* (1943), *The Trial of Thomas Cranmer* (1956), *The Jesse Tree: A Masque in Verse* (1970), and *The Lambton Worm* (1978).

rifacimento \rē-‚fäch-ē-'men-tō\ or **refacimento** \rā-\ *plural* rifacimenti \-tē\, rifacimentos, refacimenti, *or* refacimentos [Italian *rifacimento* remaking, revision, a derivative of *rifare* to remake] A recasting or adaptation especially of a literary work or musical composition.

Rifbjerg \'rif-‚byer\, Klaus (Thorvald) (b. Dec. 15, 1931, Copenhagen, Den.) Danish author and editor.

Rifbjerg first attracted public notice with an ironic collection of autobiographical prose poems, *Under vejr med mig selv* (1956; "Findings about Myself"). *Efterkrig* (1957; "After the War") contains much of his earliest poetry. His first novel, *Den kroniske uskyld* (1958; "The Chronic Innocence"), is a fur-

ther examination of his past. His later novels include *Anna (jeg) Anna* (1969; *Anna, I, Anna*), *Tak for turen* (1975; "Thanks for the Trip"), and *De hellige aber* (1981; *Witness to the Future*).

Of great importance for Danish poetry of the 1960s were the experimental poems in *Konfrontation* (1960), *Camouflage* (1961), and *Portræt* (1963)—in which Rifbjerg attempted to create new forms of language. His *Amagerdigte* (1965; "Amager Poems") is a collection of realistic poems about the island on which he grew up. *Digte af Klaus Rifbjerg* ("Poems of Klaus Rifbjerg") appeared in 1986.

Rifbjerg was editor in chief for the literary periodical *Vindrosen* (1959–63), and with Jesper Jensen he cowrote a number of satirical revues for the Student Association in Copenhagen. He also wrote for film, radio, and television.

Riffaterre \rĕf-ă-'ter\, Michael (b. Nov. 20, 1924, France) American literary critic whose textual analyses emphasize the responses of the reader rather than such elements as the biography and politics of the author.

Riffaterre was educated in France at the University of Lyon and at the Sorbonne of the University of Paris before moving to the United States to attend Columbia University in New York City. He taught at Columbia from 1955, becoming a full professor in 1964. His first book, *Le Style des Pléiade de Gobineau, Essai d'application d'une méthode stylistique* (1957; *Criteria for Style Analysis*), proposed a new stylistic method of criticism, which he used to examine the effects of irony in the writings of Joseph-Arthur de Gobineau. *Essais de stylistique structurale* (1971; "Essays on Structural Stylistics") stressed the importance of readers' responses to a literary work. Riffaterre defended his structuralist principles in *Semiotics of Poetry* (1978), one of his most notable works. His other books include *La Production du texte* (1979; *Text Production*) and *Fictional Truth* (1989).

Right You Are—If You Think You Are Play in three acts by Luigi PIRANDELLO, produced in Italian in 1917 as *Così è (se vi pare)* and published the following year. The title is sometimes translated as *Right You Are (If You Think So)*, among other variations. This work, like most of Pirandello's plays, contrasts art and life, demonstrating that truth is subjective and relative.

No one has ever seen Signor Ponza's wife and her mother, Signora Frola, together. Councillor Agazzi, Ponza's curious employer, pries into Ponza's private life. Ponza claims that his wife is really his second wife, the first having died in an earthquake that destroyed all verifying documents. Too, his wife only pretends to be Signora Frola's daughter to humor Signora Frola, who, he claims, is insane. Thoroughly bewildered, Agazzi demands to meet Ponza's wife, who arrives, heavily veiled, proclaiming herself as both the daughter of Signora Frola and the second wife of Ponza. The "truth" of the matter remains a mystery.

Riḥlah *see* TRAVELS.

Riksmål or **Riksmaal** *see* BOKMÅL.

Riley \'rī-lē\, James Whitcomb (b. Oct. 7, 1849, Greenfield, Ind., U.S.—d. July 22, 1916, Indianapolis, Ind.) Poet remembered for nostalgic dialect verse and often called "the poet of the common people."

Riley's reputation was first gained by a series of poems in Hoosier dialect ostensibly written by a farmer (Benj. F. Johnson, of Boone) and contributed to the *Indianapolis Daily Journal*. They were later published as *The Old Swimmin' Hole and 'Leven More Poems* (1883). Riley was briefly local editor of the *Anderson* (Ind.) *Democrat*.

Among Riley's numerous volumes of verse are *Pipes o' Pan at Zekesbury* (1888), *Old-Fashioned Roses* (1888), *The Flying Is-*

lands of the Night (1891), *A Child-World* (1896), and *Home Folks* (1900). His best-known poems include "When the Frost Is on the Punkin," LITTLE ORPHANT ANNIE, "The Raggedy Man," and "An Old Sweetheart of Mine." His poems were collected in *Complete Works*, 10 vol. (1916).

Rilke \ˈril-kə\, Rainer Maria, *original name* René Maria Rilke (b. Dec. 4, 1875, Prague, Bohemia, Austria-Hungary [now in Czech Rep.])—d.

Bettmann Archive

Dec. 29, 1926, Valmont, Switz.) Poet who became internationally famous with such works as *Duineser Elegien* (1923; DUINO ELEGIES) and *Die Sonette an Orpheus* (1923; SONNETS TO ORPHEUS).

By the time he left preparatory school, Rilke had already published a volume of poetry (1894). In 1896 he went to Munich in search of an artistic and cosmopolitan milieu, setting the pattern for a life of wandering that took him across Europe. A turning point in his

life was his affair that began in 1897 with Lou Andreas-Salomé; she was the leading influence in his *éducation sentimentale*, and, above all, she introduced Russia to him, which evoked a poetic response that he later said marked the true beginning of his serious work: a long three-part cycle of poems written between 1899 and 1903, *Das Stunden-Buch* (1905; *The Book of Hours*). In these devotional exercises Rilke found his true voice.

Rilke was commissioned by a German publisher to write a book about sculptor Auguste Rodin and went to Paris in 1902. For the next 12 years Paris was the geographic center of his life. But for him it was a city of abysmal, dehumanizing misery, of the faceless and the dispossessed. During his Paris years Rilke developed a new style of lyrical poetry, the so-called *Ding-Gedicht* ("object poem"), which attempts to capture the plastic essence of a physical object. Some of the most successful of these poems are imaginative verbal translations of works of the visual arts, and in them Rilke forced his language to extremes of subtlety and refinement. The experiments, published as *Neue Gedichte* (1907–08; *New Poems*), represented a departure from traditional German lyric poetry. *Die Aufzeichnungen des Malte Laurids Brigge* (1910; THE NOTEBOOK OF MALTE LAURIDS BRIGGE), on which he began work in Rome in 1904, is a prose counterpart.

The price Rilke paid for these masterpieces was a writing block and depression so severe that, aside from a short poetry cycle, *Das Marien-Leben* (1913; *The Life of the Virgin Mary*), he did not publish anything for 13 years. The first works in which he transcended the poems of *Neue Gedichte* were written early in 1912—long poems in the style of elegies, which he wrote while staying at Duino Castle, near Trieste. In the fall of 1915, in addition to a series of new poems, he wrote the fourth Duino elegy.

He did not complete the cycle until 1922, when, within the space of a few days of obsessive productivity, it was finished. Unexpectedly and almost effortlessly, he wrote *Die Sonette an Orpheus*, another superb cycle of 55 poems, closely related in mood and theme to the *Elegies*. In addition to these late works he also wrote a number of simple, almost songlike poems, some short cycles, and four collections in French.

Rimbaud \raⁿ-ˈbō\, Arthur, *in full* Jean-Nicolas-Arthur Rimbaud (b. Oct. 20, 1854, Charleville, Fr.—d. Nov. 10, 1891, Marseille) French poet and adventurer identified with the Symbolists and with a highly original form of prose poem.

Detail from "Un Coin de table,"
oil painting by Henri Fantin-Latour,
1872; in the Louvre, Paris
Giraudon/Art Resource, New York

Rimbaud's first published poem appeared in January 1870 in *La Revue pour tous*. Shortly after the outbreak of the Franco-Prussian War in July 1870, Rimbaud ran away to Paris. He briefly joined the national guard, then wandered through northern France and Belgium. Returned to his home by the police, he again ran away to Paris. When he returned home in March 1871 after a month in Paris, Rimbaud was completely changed. He repudiated his early joyful

verses as false and wrote some of his most violent and blasphemous poems, expressing a disgust with life, a desire to escape into a world of innocence, and a sense of struggle between good and evil. At the same time, he formulated his new aesthetic doctrine, expressed in two letters (May 13 and 15, 1871), later called "Lettres du voyant." The title was based on his belief that the poet must become a seer, a "voyant," who can penetrate infinity and who, by breaking down the restraints and controls that make up the conventional conception of individual personality, must become the instrument for the voice of the eternal.

Rimbaud sent the poet Paul Verlaine specimens of his new poetry, among them the sonnet VOYELLES. Impressed, Verlaine sent money for Rimbaud to join him in Paris. In a burst of self-confidence, Rimbaud composed "Le Bateau ivre" (THE DRUNKEN BOAT), a poem of astonishing verbal virtuosity and of daring choice of images and metaphors.

Arriving in Paris in September 1871, he stayed for three months with Verlaine and his wife and met most of the well-known poets of the day, but he antagonized them all—except Verlaine himself—by his arrogance, boorishness, and obscenity. He became involved in a homosexual relationship with Verlaine.

During 1871–72 Rimbaud composed the last of his poems in verse. Some critics also assign to this creative period the transcendental prose poems contained in ILLUMINATIONS (1886), none of which were dated by Rimbaud.

In July 1872 Verlaine abandoned his wife and fled with Rimbaud to London. In April 1873, back in France, Rimbaud began to write *Une Saison en enfer* (1873; A SEASON IN HELL). After a falling out, Verlaine shot and wounded Rimbaud, an act that resulted in Verlaine's arrest and imprisonment. Rimbaud last saw Verlaine early in 1875, and their meeting ended in a violent quarrel.

In 1875–76 Rimbaud learned several languages and traveled widely. During this period he became known as a poet in France. Verlaine wrote about him in *Les Poètes maudits* (1884; rev. ed., 1888) and published a selection of his poems, which were enthusiastically received. He also published *Illuminations*, which Rimbaud had given him, and further verse poems in the Symbolist periodical *La Vogue*, as the work of "the late Arthur Rimbaud."

In February 1891 Rimbaud fell ill and made his way back to France. Shortly after he arrived at Marseille, his right leg had to be amputated, and in November he died.

Rime of the Ancient Mariner, The   Poem in seven parts by Samuel Taylor COLERIDGE that first appeared in *Lyrical Ballads*, published collaboratively by Coleridge and William Wordsworth in 1798. The title character detains one of three young men on their way to a wedding feast and mesmerizes him with the story of his youthful experience at sea—his slaughter of an albatross, the deaths of his fellow sailors, his suffering, and his eventual redemption.

On an icebound ship near the South Pole, the mariner and his crew are visited by an albatross, considered a favorable omen. The ship breaks free of the ice and sails north, followed by the giant bird. Then, inexplicably, the mariner shoots and kills it, bringing a curse upon the vessel. After some confusion, his shipmates vilify him and hang the bird carcass around his neck. The passing of a ghost ship (a bad omen) causes all but the mariner to die. Lost and alone, he marvels at a life-affirming vision in the moonlight, and his prayer of reverence causes the albatross to fall into the sea. Following his rescue, the mariner understands that his penance for his destructive act will be to wander the world recounting his awful story.

Among the many memorable lines from the poem is the utterance in stanza nine "Water, water, everywhere,/Nor any drop to drink."

rime riche \ˌrēm-'rēsh\ *plural* rimes riches \'rēsh\ [French, literally, rich rhyme]   In French and English prosody, a rhyme produced by agreement in sound not only of the last accented vowel and any succeeding sounds but also of the consonant preceding this rhyming vowel—*also called* identical rhyme. A rime riche may consist of homographs (fair/fair) or homophones (write/right). It is distinguished from *rime suffisante*.

rime suffisante \ˌrēm-ˌsü-fē-'zäⁿt\ *plural* rimes suffisantes \-'zäⁿt\ [French, literally, sufficient rhyme]   In French and English prosody, end rhyme produced by agreement in sound of an accented final vowel and following final consonant or consonants, if any. Examples of rimes suffisantes in English include the rhymes ship/dip and flee/see. It is distinguished from *rime riche*.

rimur or **rímur** \'rē-mər\ [Old Norse *rímur*, plural of *ríma* rhyme, ballad, a derivative of *rím* rhyme, from Middle Low German, from Old French *rime*] *singular* ríma.   Versified sagas, or episodes from the sagas, a form of adaptation that was popular in Iceland from the 15th century.

One of three genres of popular early Icelandic poetry (the other two being dances and ballads), rimur were produced from the 14th to the 19th century. Originally used for dancing, they combine an end-rhymed metrical form derived from Latin hymns with the techniques of syllable counting, alliteration, and internal rhyme used by the earlier Norse court poets, the skalds. Rimur also preserve the skald's elaborate diction but in a stereotyped fashion as though the original meaning of complex epithets had been lost. Most rimur are long narratives based on native tradition or foreign romances. Often a long prose saga was converted into a rimur cycle.

Rinehart \'rīn-ˌhärt\, Mary Roberts, *original surname* Roberts (b. Aug. 12, 1876, Pittsburgh, Pa., U.S.—d. Sept. 22, 1958, New York, N.Y.)   American novelist and playwright best known for her mystery stories.

Rinehart's *The Man in Lower Ten*, serialized in 1907, was followed by her first book, *The Circular Staircase* (1908). In addition to mysteries, she wrote a long series of comic tales about a dauntless spinster named Tish and her adventures with two friends; these appeared in *The Saturday Evening Post* through many years. Of her plays, mostly written in collaboration with Avery Hopwood, the most successful was *The Bat* (1920). She also wrote romances and several books of travel, some of which reflected her experiences as a war correspondent during World War I.

Ring and the Book, The   More than 20,000-line poem by Robert BROWNING, written in blank verse and published in 12 books from 1868 to 1869. Considered his greatest work, it was based on the proceedings of a Roman murder trial in 1698.

Each of the 12 books consists of a dramatic monologue in the voice of a different character involved in the story. Pompilia, a beautiful young woman, is so unhappy in her marriage to Count Franceschini, an older and cruel nobleman, that she prevails upon a young priest to help her return to her parents' home. The count finds them, has Pompilia sent to a convent, and banishes the priest. When Pompilia returns to her parents, the count arranges for the assassination of Pompilia and her parents. The count is arrested, tried, and executed.

Ringuet   Pseudonym of Philippe PANNETON.

Ripley \'rip-lē\, George (b. Oct. 3, 1802, Greenfield, Mass., U.S.—d. July 4, 1880, New York, N.Y.)   Journalist and reformer who was the leading promoter and director of Brook Farm, the celebrated utopian community at West Roxbury, Mass., and a spokesman for the utopian socialist ideas of the French social reformer Charles Fourier. Later, as literary critic for the *New York Tribune*, he was an arbiter of taste and culture for much of the reading public.

Ripley entered the Unitarian ministry after graduating from Harvard Divinity School in 1826. While pastor of Boston's Purchase Street Church, he was a member of the Transcendental Club and an editor of *The Dial*, the prototypical little magazine. In 1841 Ripley left the pulpit to found the Brook Farm community. Brook Farm closed in 1847, and to pay off the community's debts, Ripley took a job with Horace Greeley's *New York Tribune* as book reviewer, city news writer, and translator of foreign news dispatches. His financial position remained precarious until the publication of *The Cyclopedia* (1862), a widely acclaimed reference book that he coedited.

Ripley, Tom \'täm-'rip-lē\   Fictional hero-villain of a series of psychologically acute crime novels by Patricia HIGHSMITH. An engagingly suave psychopathic murderer, Ripley evokes conflicting feelings of fear and trust in other characters as well as in the reader.

The series began with *The Talented Mr. Ripley* (1955). Other books about the character include *Ripley Under Ground* (1970), *Ripley's Game* (1974), and *The Boy Who Followed Ripley* (1980).

Rip Van Winkle \'rip-van-'wiŋ-kəl\   Short story by Washington IRVING, published in THE SKETCH BOOK in 1819–20. Though set in the Dutch culture of pre-Revolutionary War New York state, the story of Rip Van Winkle is based on a German folktale.

Rip Van Winkle is an amiable farmer who wanders into the Catskill Mountains, where he comes upon a group of dwarfs playing ninepins. Rip accepts their offer of a drink of liquor and promptly falls asleep. When he awakens, 20 years later, he is an old man with a long, white beard; the dwarfs are nowhere in sight. Rip goes into town and finds that everything is changed: his wife is dead, his children are grown, and George Washington's portrait hangs in place of King George III's. The old man entertains the townspeople with tales of the old days and of his encounter with the little men in the Catskill mountains.

Rise of Silas Lapham, The \'sī-ləs-'lap-əm\   The best-known novel of William Dean HOWELLS, published in 1885.

The novel recounts the moral dilemma of Colonel Silas Lapham, a newly wealthy, self-made businessman who has climbed over his former partner on the ladder to success. After Lapham moves from Vermont to Boston, his family befriends the Coreys, a Brahmin family in financial difficulties. Tom Corey, the son, appears to return the romantic interest of the Laphams' daughter Irene, but he really loves her older sister Penelope. Lapham and his wife move awkwardly in Boston's highly stratified society, and he gets drunk at a party and reveals his common origins. Meanwhile, business reversals cause him to entertain an offer to sell a worthless property to an English syndicate. The resulting money would enable him to continue to rise in society, but after struggling with his conscience, Silas at last refuses to sell and bankruptcy results. Though Silas has fallen socially, he has risen morally. Penelope elopes to Mexico with Tom, thus escaping Boston's tedious social strictures.

rising action   In drama and other literature, the events leading up to the climax of the plot. It is in contrast to *falling action*, the events that follow the climax and lead to the denouement.

rising rhythm   *also called* ascending rhythm.   In prosody, a rhythm in which the stresses regularly fall on the last syllable of each foot (as in iambic or anapestic lines). Its opposite is falling, or descending, rhythm. *See also* CADENCE.

rispetto \rē-'spet-tō\ *plural* rispetti \-tē\ [Italian, literally, respect]   A Tuscan folk verse form, a version of STRAMBOTTO. The rispetto lyric is generally composed of eight hendecasyllabic (11-syllable) lines. In its earliest form the rhyme scheme was usually *abababcc*; later, the scheme *ababccdd* became more prominent, and other variations can also be found.

The form reached its pinnacle of both artistic achievement and popularity in the 14th and 15th centuries, particularly in the work of Politian, to whom some 200 rispetti are ascribed.

Ritschl \'rich-əl\, F.W., *in full* Friedrich Wilhelm (b. April 6, 1806, Grossvargula, near Erfurt, Prussia [now in Germany]—d. Nov. 9, 1876, Leipzig)   German classical scholar remembered for his work on Plautus (the largest body of early Latin literature) and as the founder of the Bonn school of classical scholarship. Influenced by the textual criticism of the English and German classicists Richard Bentley and Gottfried Hermann, he made exhaustive studies that laid the scholarly foundations for research in archaic Latin.

Following his education at Leipzig and Halle universities, Ritschl was professor at Halle, Breslau, and Bonn. He conceived of a critical edition of Plautus based on new manuscript evidence, first editing nine of his comedies, *Plauti Comoedia*, 4 vol. (1848–54; incomplete), and an important interpretive discussion, *Prolegomena de Rationibus Criticis Grammaticis Emendationis Plautinoe* (1848; "Critical Grammatical Reasons for Correcting Plautus"). The complete text of Plautus' comedies was published in 1871–74, but it contains only one translation by Ritschl, the *Trinummus*, the rest having been prepared by his pupils and collaborators.

At Bonn, Ritschl published, with Theodor Mommsen, the *Priscae Latinitatis Monumenta Epigraphica* (1862; "Epigraphical Records of Ancient Latin"), an edition of Latin inscriptions from the earliest times to the end of the Roman Republic; this work established Ritschl as one of the founders of modern epigraphy. His studies include papers on early Latin grammar and meter and on the manuscript tradition of Plautus.

Ritsos \'rēt-sōs\, Yannis (b. May 1, 1909, Monemvasia, Greece—d. Nov. 11, 1990, Athens)   Greek poet whose work was periodically banned for its political content.

Ritsos was born into a wealthy but unfortunate family. His father died insane, and his mother and a brother died of tuber-culosis when Ritsos was an adolescent. Reared by relatives, Ritsos briefly attended Athens Law School (1925), was confined to a tuberculosis sanitarium (1927–31), and in the 1930s was an actor and dancer. He joined the Greek Communist Party in 1934, the year his first collection of poems, *Trakter* ("Tractors"), appeared. Both it and *Pyramides* (1935) mixed socialist philosophy with vivid images of his personal suffering.

His next collection, *O Epitaphios* (1936; "Funeral Procession"), was symbolically burned by the fascist government at the foot of the Acropolis, and for nearly a decade he could not publish freely. During the Nazi occupation of Greece (1944) and the subsequent civil war, Ritsos fought with the Communist guerrillas; after their defeat (1949) he was arrested and spent four years in prison camps. In the 1950s *O Epitaphios*, set to music by Mikis Theodorakis, became the anthem of the Greek left. In 1967 Ritsos was arrested and exiled, and he was prohibited from publishing until 1972. Despite the turbulence of his life he wrote 117 books, including plays and essays.

Rivals, The   Comedy in five acts by Richard Brinsley SHERIDAN, produced and published in 1775.

The Rivals concerns the romantic difficulties of Lydia Languish, who is determined to marry for love and into poverty. Realizing this, the aristocratic Captain Jack Absolute woos her while claiming to be Ensign Beverley. But her aunt, Mrs. Malaprop, will not permit her to wed a mere ensign, and Lydia will lose half her fortune if she marries without her aunt's permission. Among the play's many plot complications is the appearance of Sir Anthony (Jack's father). In the end, Lydia abandons her sentimental notions and agrees to marry Jack. The situations and characters of the play were not entirely new, but Sheridan's rich wit and remarkable sense of theatrical effect gave them freshness. Mrs. Malaprop proved one of the most popular caricatures in English drama.

Rivarol \rē-vä-'rôl\, Antoine Rivaroli, Count (comte) de (b. June 26, 1753, Bagnols-sur-Cèze, Fr.—d. April 11, 1801, Berlin [Germany])   French publicist, journalist, and epigrammatist and a would-be nobleman whose works supported monarchy and traditionalism in the era of the French Revolution.

He assumed the title of Count de Rivarol, claiming to come of a noble Italian family, but he is said to have been an innkeeper's son. His first important work was a treatise, *De l'universalité de la langue française* (1784), whose sweeping title, "On the Universality of the French Language," is almost justified by the prestige won by French culture throughout Europe in the 18th century. Rivarol's satirical gift is displayed to the full in his *Le Petit Almanach de nos grands-hommes* (1788; "The Little Almanac of Our Great Men"), in which he lampoons all the authors of the day. On the outbreak of the revolution, Rivarol enlisted his journalistic talents in the Royalist cause.

Rive \'rēv\, Richard Moore (b. March 1, 1931, Cape Town, S.Af.—d. June 4, 1989, Cape Town)   South African writer, literary critic, and teacher whose short stories, which were dominated by the ironics and oppression of apartheid and by the degradation of slum life, have been extensively anthologized and translated into more than a dozen languages. They are characterized by great imaginative and technical power, a skillful use of leitmotivs (dominant recurring themes), and realistic dialogue.

Rive attended the University of Cape Town and taught at Hewat Training College and at a large Cape Town high school.

His early works included *Quartet: New Voices from South Africa* (1963), a selection of 16 short stories by four writers, including Rive; *African Songs* (1963), Rive's own short stories; *Modern African Prose* (1964), an anthology edited by Rive and designed for use by students; and *Emergency* (1964), a novel about the events of the Sharpeville massacre and state of emergency in 1960. Rive attended Columbia University in New York City and Magdalen College, Oxford. His *Selected Writings*, a collection of essays, short stories, and plays, was published in 1977. In 1981 he published *Writing Black: An Author's Notebook*. His novel *Buckingham Palace, District Six* (1986) presents slices of life in a Cape Town district. *Emergency Continued* (1990), published posthumously, a sequel to *Emergency*, is set 30 years later.

Rivera \rē-'b̄a-rä\, José Eustasio (b. Feb. 19, 1889, Neiva, Colom.—d. Feb. 19, 1928, New York, N.Y., U.S.) Colombian poet and novelist whose novel of the South American tropical jungle, *La vorágine* (1924; *The Vortex*), a powerful denunciation of the exploitation of the rubber gatherers in the upper Amazon jungle, is considered by many critics to be the best of many Latin-American novels with jungle settings.

Rivera established his literary reputation with *Tierra de promisión* (1921; "The Promised Land"), a collection of sonnets portraying the untamed beauty of the Colombian tropics. He traveled through the Amazon region and along the Orinoco River, living for a time among the Indians. He contracted beriberi in the jungle and during his convalescence wrote *La vorágine*, which succeeds as a novel of both adventure and social protest. It was his only novel.

river-god Any deity who is believed to preside over a river as its tutelary divinity.

Rivière \rē-'vyer\, Jacques (b. July 15, 1886, Bordeaux, Fr.—d. Feb. 14, 1925, Paris) Writer, critic, and editor who was a major force in the intellectual life of France in the period immediately following World War I. His most important works were his thoughtful and finely written essays on the arts. In 1912 a collection of these essays was published as *Études*; a second such collection, entitled *Nouvelles études* ("New Essays"), was published posthumously in 1947.

From 1914 to 1918 Rivière was a prisoner of war in Germany; his book *L'Allemand* (1918; "The German") was based on that experience. He was a cofounder and, from 1919 to 1925, editor of the *Nouvelle Revue Française*, a leading magazine of the arts. He was influential in winning public acceptance of Marcel Proust as an important writer. Rivière wrote two psychological novels, *Aimée* (1922) and the unfinished *Florence* (1935). His personal anxiety, aspirations, and religious doubts are best reflected in his letters to his brother-in-law, Alain-Fournier; in his correspondence with the poet and playwright Paul Claudel; and in his book *À la trace de Dieu* (1925; "On the Track of God").

Roa Bastos \,rō-ä-'b̄äs-tōs\, Augusto (Antonio) (b. June 13, 1917, Iturbe, Paraguay) Paraguayan novelist and short-story writer, one of the leading Latin-American authors of the 20th century. He received Spain's prestigious Cervantes Prize in 1989.

Roa Bastos' first book of poetry, *El ruiseñor de la Aurora* (1942; "The Nightingale of the Dawn"), which he later renounced, is an imitation of the Spanish masters. The novel *Fulgencio Miranda* (written 1941) and a number of plays successfully performed during the 1940s were never published. Some of the poetry he wrote during the 1940s was collected in *El naranjal ardiente: Nocturno paraguayo: 1947–1949* (1960; "The Burning Orange Grove: Paraguayan Nocturne").

In 1947 Roa Bastos went into exile in Buenos Aires, where he lived until 1970. His first collection of short stories, *El trueno entre las hojas* (1953; "Thunder Among the Leaves"), describes the Paraguayan experience, with emphasis on violence and social injustice. With this volume Roa Bastos began to experiment with magic realism, the narrative technique that

incorporates fantastic or mythical elements into otherwise realistic fiction.

His novel *Hijo de hombre* (1960; *Son of Man*) was a critical and popular success. It re-creates Paraguay's history from the dictatorship of José Gaspar Rodríguez de Francia (known as "El Supremo") early in the 19th century through the Chaco War. By alternating narrative voices, Roa Bastos creates a tension that signals the moral and political stagnation of Paraguay. Stories collected in *El baldío* (1966; "The Wasteland") and *Moriencia* (1969; "Slaughter") treat the problems of Paraguayan exiles. The story collections *Los pies sobre el agua* (1967; "The Feet on the Water") and *Madera quemada* (1967; "Burnt Wood") rework earlier themes. His masterpiece, the novel *Yo, el Supremo* (1974; *I, the Supreme*), is based on the life of Francia and covers more than a hundred years of Paraguayan history.

In 1970 Roa Bastos returned to Paraguay, where he taught Latin-American literature. He settled in France in 1976, but after several visits to Paraguay, he was expelled from his homeland for life in 1982. After the fall of the dictatorship of Alfredo Stroessner in 1989, however, Roa Bastos returned to Paraguay.

Road Not Taken, The Poem by Robert FROST, published in *Atlantic Monthly* in August 1915, and used as the opening poem of his collection *Mountain Interval* (1916). Written in iambic tetrameter, it employs an *abaab* rhyme scheme in each of its four stanzas. The poem presents a narrator recalling a journey through a woods, when he had to choose which of two diverging roads to travel. The work's meaning has long been disputed by readers; Frost himself claimed that it was a parody of the Georgian poet Edward Thomas.

Roark, Howard \'haū-ərd-'rörk\ Fictional character, hero of THE FOUNTAINHEAD, the first best-selling novel by Ayn Rand.

Robbe-Grillet \ròb-grē-'yä\, Alain (b. Aug. 18, 1922, Brest, Fr.) A representative writer and leading theoretician of the NOUVEAU ROMAN ("new novel"), the French antinovel that emerged in the 1950s. He also became a screenwriter and film director.

Trained as a statistician and agronomist, Robbe-Grillet claimed to write novels for his time, especially attentive "to the ties that exist between objects, gestures, and situations, avoiding all psychological and ideological 'commentary' on the actions of the characters" (*Pour un nouveau roman*, 1963; *Towards a New Novel*). Robbe-Grillet's is a world of objects, hard, polished surfaces, with only the measurable characteristics of pounds, inches, and wavelengths of reflected light. His narratives lack conventional elements such as plot and character and are composed largely of recurring images.

Jerry Bauer

If Robbe-Grillet's fiction, with its timetables, careful inventories of things, and reports on arrivals and departures, owes anything to a traditional form of the novel, it is to the detective story. His first work, *Les Gommes* (1953; *The Erasers*), deals with a murder committed by the man who has come to investigate it. *Le Voyeur* (1955; *The Voyeur*) also deals with a murder, that of a young girl by a passing stranger. *La Jalousie* (1957; *Jealousy*) is concerned with the actions of a wife and her suspected lover as they are viewed by a jealous husband through a louvre shutter (the French word for which is also jalousie). Among his later novels are *Dans le labyrinthe* (1959; *In the Labyrinth*), *Instantanés* (1962; *Snapshots*), *Topologie d'une cité fantôme* (1976; *Topology of a Phantom City*), *Un Régicide* (1978; "A Regicide"), *Djinn* (1981), and two autobiographical works, *Le Miroir qui revient* (1984; *Ghosts in the Mirror*) and *Angélique, ou, L'Enchantement* (1987).

Robbe-Grillet's techniques were dramatized in his films, especially in *L'Année dernière à Marienbad* (1961; *Last Year at Marienbad*). Ultimately, his work raises questions about objectivity and subjectivity.

Robbers, The Drama in five acts by Friedrich von SCHILLER, published in 1781 and produced in 1782 as *Die Räuber*. Set in 16th-century Germany, *The Robbers* concerns the rivalry between the brothers Karl and Franz, both of whom operate outside conventional morality. A protest against official corruption, the play condemned a society in which men of high purpose could be driven to live outside the law when justice was denied them.

Franz, the younger brother, turns their father against Karl, who then collects a band of outlaws and lives in the forest. Franz imprisons and mistreats their father, who dies when he learns that Karl is a brigand. Amalia, Karl's faithful beloved, knows that Karl will never break his vow of allegiance to his robber comrades; she convinces Karl to kill her because she cannot live without him. Karl does so and then surrenders to the authorities, having decided that terrorism and criminal behavior are not acceptable solutions to human injustice.

Robbins \ˈräb-inz\, Tom, *in full* Thomas Eugene Robbins (b. July 22, 1936, Blowing Rock, N.C., U.S.) American countercultural novelist noted for his eccentric characters, playful optimism, and self-conscious wordplay.

Robbins served in the U.S. Air Force, hitchhiked across the United States, and worked as a journalist and art critic. His first two novels became popular only when they were released in paperback editions. *Another Roadside Attraction* (1971) is about a native of rural Washington who steals the mummy of Jesus Christ. *Even Cowgirls Get the Blues* (1976; film, 1994) is the story of a female hitchhiker with an enormous thumb who visits a woman's spa in South Dakota. Robbins' later novels include *Still Life with Woodpecker* (1980), *Jitterbug Perfume* (1984), and *Skinny Legs and All* (1990).

Robert \ˈräb-ərt\, Shaaban (b. January 1909, Tanga, German East Africa [now in Tanzania]—d. June 20, 1962, Dar es Salaam, Tanz.) Popular Swahili writer who was influenced by both Christian and Islāmic cultures, before himself becoming a Muslim. His work ranges from poetry to essay and didactic tale and reflects the stylistic influence of the Oriental tradition. Many of his poems follow the form of *utendi* verse (used for narration and didactic themes), but, like his famous predecessor, Muyaka bin Haji al-Ghassaniy, he used other traditional and experimental forms. His prose style is clear, concrete, and strongly individual.

Robert also produced an autobiography, *Maisha yangu* (1949; "My Life"), and a biography, *Maisha ya Siti Binti Saad, mwimbaji wa Unguja* (1958; "Life of Siti Binti Saad, Poetess of Zanzibar"). His essays on many subjects were collected in *Insha ya mashairi* (1959; "Essays and Poems"). He lectured on poetry and its relation to Swahili culture and supported the movement to preserve African verse traditions. The first volume of his complete works, *Diwani ya Shaaban*, appeared in

1966. An edition of selected poems translated into English was published in 1982.

Robert de Boron \rō-ˈber-də-bō-ˈrōⁿ\, Boron *also spelled* Borron (fl. late 12th–early 13th century) French poet who was known for his poems *Joseph d'Arimathie, ou le roman de l'estoire dou Graal; Merlin;* and *Perceval.* Together they constitute a trilogy that narrates the early history of the Grail and unites this independent legend more firmly with Arthurian legend, using the figure of Merlin, with his knowledge of past and future, as the connecting link.

Robert \ˈräb-ərt\ of Gloucester \ˈgläs-tər, ˈglȯs-\ (fl. 1260–1300) Early Middle English chronicler known only through his connection with the work called "The Chronicle of Robert of Gloucester"—a vernacular history of England from its legendary founding by Brut (Brutus), great-grandson of Aeneas, to the year 1270. It was written, probably around 1300, in rhymed couplets. Two versions exist, and it is now believed that only one part, dealing with recent or contemporary events—the last 3,000 lines of the longer version—was written by Robert. This section supplies interesting details of the civil strife during the reign of Henry III and a vivid description of the Battle of Evesham that has the value of contemporary authority.

Roberts \ˈräb-ərts\, Charles G.D., *in full* Sir Charles George Douglas Roberts (b. Jan. 10, 1860, Douglas, New Brunswick [Canada]—d. Nov. 26, 1943, Toronto, Ont.) Poet who was the first to express the new national feeling aroused by the Canadian confederation of 1867.

Roberts taught school, edited the influential Toronto magazine *The Week*, and for 10 years was a professor of English at King's College in Windsor, N.S. In 1897 he moved to New York City, where he worked as a journalist, and in 1911 he established residence in London. Returning to Canada 14 years later, Roberts embarked on a cross-Canada lecture tour and later settled in Toronto.

Roberts published some 12 volumes of verse beginning with *Orion, and Other Poems* (1880). He wrote of nature, love, and nationalism, but his best-remembered poems are simple descriptive lyrics about the scenery and rural life of New Brunswick and Nova Scotia. Outstanding among his poetic works are *In Divers Tones* (1887), *Songs of the Common Day* (1893), *The Vagrant of Time* (1927), and *The Iceberg, and Other Poems* (1934).

Roberts' most famous prose works are short stories in which his intimate knowledge of the woods and their animal inhabitants is displayed—*e.g., Earth's Enigmas* (1896), *The Kindred of the Wild* (1902), *Red Fox* (1905), and *Neighbours Unknown* (1911). His other prose includes the pioneer *History of Canada* (1897) and several novels dealing with the Maritime Provinces.

Roberts \ˈräb-ərts\, Elizabeth Madox (b. Oct. 30, 1886, Perryville, Ky., U.S.—d. March 13, 1941, Orlando, Fla.) American novelist, poet, and short-story writer noted especially for her vivid, impressionistic depiction of her protagonists' inner life and for her accurate portrayal of life in Kentucky.

Roberts' first novel, *The Time of Man* (1926), concerns a poor white woman living in Kentucky. Its rich texture, which contrasts inner growth with outward hardship, and its account of life in Kentucky brought her international acclaim. *The Great Meadow* (1930), her best-known novel, describes a woman's spiritual return to the wilderness. Her subsequent books generally dealt with similar themes and settings, but her fame declined in the 1930s. In addition to a number of lesser-known novels, Roberts wrote two books of short stories, *The Haunted Mirror* (1932) and *Not By Strange Gods* (1941), and two books of poetry, *Under the Tree* (1922; enlarged 1930) and *Song in the Meadow* (1940).

Roberts \'räb-ərts\, Kate (b. Feb. 13, 1891, Rhosgadfan, Caernarvonshire, Wales—d. April 4, 1985, Denbigh, Clwyd) One of the outstanding Welsh-language short-story writers of the mid-20th century. She was also a novelist and playwright.

Roberts was educated at the University College of North Wales, Bangor. She taught Welsh in Glamorganshire for 13 years and married in 1928. From 1935 to 1946 she and her husband edited a Welsh-language newspaper; she continued this work alone for a decade after his death in 1946. After a hiatus of 12 years, Roberts returned to fiction writing in 1949.

Roberts' works are set in the slate-quarrying districts of North Wales or in the mining villages of South Wales, where poverty is usually the harsh determinant of her characters' hopes and fates. Her works include *O Gors y Bryniau* (1925; "From the Swamp of the Hills"), *Rhigolau Bywyd* (1929; "The Grooves of Life"), *Traed mewn Cyffion* (1936; *Feet in Chains*), *Stryd y Glep* (1949; "Gossip Street"), *Y Byw Sy'n Cysgu* (1956; *The Living Sleep*), *Tywyll Heno* (1962; "Dark Tonight"), and *Tegwch y Bore* (1967; "Fair Weather in the Morning"). She also wrote stories for children. Some of her early short stories were translated and published in *A Summer Day and Other Stories* (1946). *The World of Kate Roberts: Selected Stories, 1925–1981* was published in 1991.

Roberts \'räb-ərts\, Kenneth (Lewis) (b. Dec. 8, 1885, Kennebunk, Maine, U.S.—d. July 21, 1957, Kennebunkport) American journalist and novelist who wrote fictional reconstructions of the American Revolution.

Roberts was staff correspondent of *The Saturday Evening Post* from 1919 until 1928, when he devoted himself to writing fiction. Believing that the past is only poorly understood through historical accounts, he wrote *Arundel* (1930), a fictional treatment of the Revolutionary War. He is best known for *Northwest Passage* (1937), dealing with the career of the American frontier soldier Major Robert Rogers, and *Rabble in Arms* (1933), a celebration of Revolutionary War heroes who fought the British under conditions of great hardship. *Oliver Wiswell* (1940), another novel of the American Revolution, was written from the Loyalist point of view. Other works include *The Lively Lady* (1931), *Lydia Bailey* (1947), and *Boon Island* (1956). Roberts researched his books carefully and was devoted to arguing over minute points of American history. He considered his home state a last outpost of rugged individualism, and several of his books are set there.

Robertson \'räb-ərt-sən\, Thomas William (b. Jan. 9, 1829, Newark-on-Trent, Nottinghamshire, Eng.—d. Feb. 3, 1871, London) British playwright whose realistic social comedies and pioneering work as a producer-director helped establish the late 19th-century revival of drama in England.

Robertson moved to London in 1848 to become an actor. In 1854 he was engaged as prompter at the Lyceum Theatre by Mme Vestris, its enterprising and influential manager. It was her work in refining the staging of comedy that he was eventually to perfect. After his marriage in 1856, Robertson gradually abandoned acting for writing. Some of his adaptations and translations had already been produced, and in 1861 a one-act farce called *The Cantab*, his first original play, was staged. From 1865 to 1870 a number of plays made Robertson famous: *Society*, *Ours*, *Caste*, *Play*, *School*, and *The M.P.* The plays give a convincing picture of the social scene, marred only by a strain of sentimentality.

Generally speaking, Robertson's characters are recognizable as individuals, his plots are skillfully manipulated, and his characters' dialogue is easy and conversational. As a director, Robertson stressed the performance as a whole, insisting upon adequate rehearsal, attention to detail, and ensemble playing. It

was his staging methods rather than his plays that proved most influential in the development of English theater.

Robert the Devil \'räb-ərt\ or **Robert le Diable** \rō-ber-lə-'dyäbl\ Legendary son of a duke of Normandy, born in answer to prayers addressed to the Devil. The earliest version of the legend is given in *Robert le Diable*, a late 12th-century romance. Robert is able to use his immense strength only for crime. Directed by the pope to consult a certain holy hermit, he is delivered from his curse by maintaining absolute silence, feigning madness, taking his food from the mouth of a dog, and provoking ill-treatment from the common people without retaliating. He later serves as the Holy Roman emperor's court fool but, at the bidding of an angel, three times rides out disguised as an unknown knight to deliver Rome from Saracen attacks. His disguise is pierced by the emperor's daughter. He refuses her hand in marriage, however, and withdraws to a hermitage. Other versions of the legend are told in two 14th-century poems.

Robin, Christopher \'kris-tə-fər-'räb-in\ Fictional character, an English boy whose adventures with Winnie-the-Pooh, Piglet, and other animals were the basis of the stories in the classic children's books WINNIE-THE-POOH and *The House at*

Illustration by the author for the original edition of *Winnie-the-Pooh*

Pooh Corner by A.A. Milne. The character was based on the author's young son. In the stories, Christopher Robin was usually the voice of reason and the character who could be relied on to get the animals out of the predicaments they got themselves into. He was also a character in the verse collections *When We Were Very Young* and *Now We Are Six*.

Robin Goodfellow \'räb-in-'gud-,fel-ō\ In medieval English folklore, a mischievous fairy also called PUCK.

Robin Hood \'räb-in-'hud\ Legendary hero of a series of English ballads, some of which date from at least the 14th cen-

"Robin Shooteth His Last Shaft," drawing by Howard Pyle for *The Merry Adventures of Robin Hood*, 1883
Copyright British Museum

tury. He was a rebel, and many of the most striking episodes in the tales about him show him and his companions robbing and killing representatives of authority and giving the gains to the poor. Their most frequent enemy was the Sheriff of Nottingham, a local agent of the central government (though internal evidence from the early ballads makes it clear that the action took place chiefly in south Yorkshire, not in Nottinghamshire). Other enemies included wealthy ecclesiastical landowners. Robin treated women, the poor, and people of humble status with courtesy. A good deal of the impetus against authority stems from restriction of hunting rights. The early ballads, especially, reveal the cruelty that was an inescapable part of medieval life.

Numerous attempts have been made to prove that there was a historical Robin Hood, though references to the legend by medieval writers make it clear that to them the ballads were the only evidence for his existence. A popular modern belief that he was of the time of Richard I probably stems from a "pedigree" fabricated by an 18th-century antiquary, Richard Stukely. A more serious view has been advanced that he was one of the disinherited followers of Simon de Montfort, after the latter's defeat in 1265.

The authentic Robin Hood ballads were the poetic expression of popular aspirations in the north of England during a turbulent era of baronial rebellions and agrarian discontent that culminated in the Peasants' Revolt of 1381. Robin Hood was a people's hero as King Arthur was a noble's hero.

Although many of the best-known Robin Hood ballads are postmedieval, there is a core that can be confidently attributed to the medieval period. These are *Robin Hood and the Monk*, *Robin Hood and Guy of Gisborne*, *Robin Hood and the Potter*, and the *Lytyll Geste of Robin Hode*. During the 16th century and later, the essential character of the legend was distorted by a suggestion that Robin was a fallen nobleman. Playwrights, eagerly adopting this new element, increased the romantic appeal of the stories but deprived them of their social bite. Postmedieval ballads (which gave Robin a companion, Maid Marian) also lost most of their vitality and poetic value, doubtless as a result of losing the original social impulse that brought the Robin Hood legend into existence.

Robinson \'räb-in-sən\, Edwin Arlington (b. Dec. 22, 1869, Head Tide, Maine, U.S.—d. April 6, 1935, New York, N.Y.) American poet who is best known for his short dramatic poems concerning the people in a small New England village.

After his family suffered financial reverses, Robinson cut short his attendance at Harvard and went to live in New York City, where he worked as a timekeeper on subway construction. From *The Children of the Night* (1897) to *The Man Against the Sky* (1916), his best poetic form was the dramatic lyric, as exemplified in the title poem of *The Man Against the Sky*. Among his best poems of this period are RICHARD CORY, MINIVER CHEEVY, "For a Dead Lady," "Flammonde," and "Eros Turannos." Robinson's work attracted the attention of President Theodore Roosevelt, who gave him a sinecure at the U.S. Customs House in New York (held from 1905 to 1909).

Merlin (1917) was the first of his long blank-verse narrative poems based on the King Arthur legends, followed by *Lancelot* (1920) and *Tristram* (1927). Robinson's *Collected Poems* appeared in 1921. *The Man Who Died Twice* (1924) and *Amaranth* (1934) are perhaps the most often acclaimed of his later narrative poems; later short poems include MR. FLOOD'S PARTY, "Many Are Called," and "The Sheaves."

Robinson \'räb-in-sən\, Henry Crabb (b. May 13, 1775, Bury St. Edmunds, Suffolk, Eng.—d. Feb. 5, 1867, London) English man of letters whose voluminous diaries provide valuable information on life in the early Romantic period and give lively portraits of a host of its literary personalities.

Living in London from 1796, Robinson practiced law as a barrister on the Norfolk circuit (1813–28). He also served as foreign correspondent for *The Times* of London (1807–09) and became involved in the antislavery campaign and in the founding of the University of London. Thus, he was well placed to record affairs in his age. He befriended the pre-Romantic visionary poet William Blake, of whose last years Robinson's diaries give the only firsthand account. He also knew Charles Lamb, Dorothy and William Wordsworth, and Samuel Taylor Coleridge. In Germany (1800–05) he met the leading poets and thinkers of his day, including J.W. von Goethe, Friedrich von Schiller, and J.G. von Herder; on his return to England, he was influential in making German literature and philosophy more widely known. A famous conversationalist, he was noted for his Sunday morning breakfast parties attended by men of affairs and letters.

Robinson's diaries were first published in 1869. Collections of his correspondence with the Wordsworth circle (1927), about Germany (1929), and about books and writers (1938) were edited by E.J. Morley.

Robinson \'räb-in-sən\, Lennox, *in full* Esmé Stuart Lennox Robinson (b. Oct. 4, 1886, Douglas, County Cork, Ire.—d. Oct. 14, 1958, Dublin) Irish playwright and theatrical producer associated with the Abbey Theatre; a leading figure in the later stages of the Irish literary renaissance.

When still young Robinson became devoted to the cause of Irish nationalism through seeing performances of the Abbey

Theatre Company in Cork, and his country's troubles were to be a frequent theme of his plays. His first work, *The Clancy Name*, was performed at the Abbey Theatre, Dublin, in 1908. He went on to write numerous plays—notably *Patriots* (first performed 1912), *The Whiteheaded Boy* (1916), and *The Lost Leader* (1918)—remarkable for their stagecraft and lively dialogue. During 1910–14 and 1919–23 Robinson was manager of the Abbey Theatre; in 1923 he became a director. Among his later plays were *Drama at Inish* (1933), *Church Street* (1934), and *Killycreggs in Twilight* (1937). Although not in the first rank of Irish playwrights, Robinson nevertheless made an invaluable contribution to the Irish theater. He was the author of several books, edited an anthology, *The Golden Treasury of Irish Verse* (1925), and wrote an autobiography, *Curtain Up* (1942).

Robinsonade \\,räb-in-sə-'näd, ,rō-bin-zō-'näd-ə\\ *plural* Robinsonades \\-'nädz\\ *or* Robinsonaden \\-'näd-ən\\   A fictitious narrative of often fantastic adventures in real or imaginary distant places; especially, a story of the adventures of a person marooned on a desert island. The word, originally coined in German, is derived from the fictional prose narrative *Robinson Crusoe* by Daniel Defoe.

Robinson Crusoe \\'räb-in-sən-'krü-,sō\\ (*in full* The Life and Strange Surprizing Adventures of Robinson Crusoe, of York, Mariner: Who Lived Eight and Twenty Years, All Alone in an Un-inhabited Island on the Coast of America, Near the Mouth of the Great River of Oroonoque; Having Been Cast on Shore by Shipwreck, Wherein All the Men Perished but Himself. With an Account how he was at last as Strangely Deliver'd by Pyrates. Written by Himself.)   Novel by Daniel DEFOE, published in 1719. The book is a unique fictional blending of the traditions of Puritan spiritual autobiography with an insistent scrutiny of the nature of men and women as social creatures, and it reveals an extraordinary ability to invent a sustaining modern myth.

The title character leaves his comfortable middle-class home in England to go to sea. Surviving shipwreck, he lives on an island for 28 years, alone for most of the time until he saves the life of a savage, whom he names Friday. The two men eventually leave the island for England. Defoe probably based part of Crusoe's tale on the real-life experiences of Alexander Selkirk, a Scottish sailor who at his own request was put ashore on an uninhabited island in 1704 after a quarrel with his captain. He stayed there until 1709.

The book was an immediate success in England and on the European continent, and Defoe wrote a sequel (*The Farther Adventures of Robinson Crusoe*) that was also published in 1719.

Many stage and film adaptations have been made of Robinson Crusoe's life, and the book has spawned many imitations, including Johann Wyss's *Swiss Family Robinson*.

Roblès \\rō-'blä\\, Emmanuel (b. May 4, 1914, Oran, Alg.)   Algerian-French novelist and playwright whose works emerged from the war and political strife that he witnessed in Europe and North Africa.

During World War II Roblès served in the French air force and as a Spanish translator and war correspondent for the Supreme Allied Command of the Mediterranean operations. He worked with Albert Camus, whom he had met in 1937, as a reporter for the liberal daily *Alger-Républicain*. He then became cofounder of and frequent contributor to the daily *Espoir-Algérie*. In 1958 the escalation of the Algerian war forced him into exile in Paris, where he worked to discover and publish new African talent.

Roblès published his first novel, *L'Action*, in 1938. Wider recognition came with his fourth novel, *Les Hauteurs de la ville* (1948; "City Heights"), in which a young Arab worker commits

a lonely act of revenge against the fascists responsible for the deportation and death of Algerians during World War II. Roblès achieved international success with *Cela s'appelle l'aurore* (1952; *Dawn on Our Darkness*), a novel set in Sardinia concerning a man caught between love and duty. *Le Vésuve* (1961; *Vesuvius*) and *Un Printemps d'Italie* (1970; "Italian Spring") are love stories set in wartime Italy. His later novels include *Venise en hiver* (1981; "Venice in Winter"), set against a background of political terrorism, and *L'Herbe des ruines* (1992).

Montserrat (1948), Roblès's most popular drama, is the story of a young Spanish officer who chooses to die for the liberation of Venezuela rather than reveal the hiding place of Simón Bolívar. Other plays include *La Vérité est morte* (1952; "Truth Is Dead"), about the Spanish Civil War, and *Plaidoyer pour un rebelle* (1965; *Case for a Rebel*), concerning terrorism.

Rob Roy \\'räb-'roi\\   Historical novel by Sir Walter SCOTT, published in three volumes in 1817. Full of intrigue with political overtones, it is set in northern England just before the Jacobite rebellion of 1715, and it is considered one of the author's masterpieces.

Francis Obaldistone, the novel's hero, contends with his jealous, unscrupulous cousin Rashleigh for the hand of the beautiful Diana Vernon. Aided by the Scottish outlaw Rob Roy (based on a historical Jacobite outlaw), Francis succeeds in exposing Rashleigh's villainy.

roc \\'räk\\ *or* **rukh** \\'rūk\\ [Arabic *rukhkh*]   A legendary bird of great size and strength said to carry off elephants and other large beasts for food and believed to inhabit the Indian Ocean area. *Aepyornis*, a genus of gigantic, usually flightless birds known only from remains found in Madagascar, is believed to have survived into historic times and to have been the source of legends about the roc. *Compare* SIMURGH.

The roc is mentioned in the famous collection of Arabic tales *The Thousand and One Nights* and by the Venetian traveler Marco Polo, who referred to it in describing Madagascar and other islands off the coast of eastern Africa.

Rochester \\'rä-chəs-tər, -,ches-\\, John Wilmot, 2nd Earl of (b. April 10, 1647, Ditchley Manor House, Oxfordshire, Eng.— d. July 26, 1680, Woodstock, Eng.)   Court wit and poet who helped establish English satiric poetry.

As a leader of the court wits, Rochester became known as one of the wildest debauchees at the Restoration court, the hero of numerous escapades, and the lover of various mistresses. In 1667 he married Elizabeth Malet and was appointed a gentleman of the bedchamber to King Charles II.

Rochester is generally considered to be the most considerable poet and the most learned among the Restoration wits. A few of his love songs have passionate intensity. He is also one of the most original and powerful of English satirists. His "History of Insipids" (1676) is a devastating attack on the government of Charles II, and his "Maim'd Debauchee" has been described as "a masterpiece of heroic irony." *A Satyr Against Mankind* (1675) anticipates Jonathan Swift in its scathing denunciation of rationalism and optimism and in the contrast it draws between human perfidy and folly and the instinctive wisdom of the animal world.

In 1675 Rochester was appointed ranger of Woodstock Forest, where much of his later poetry was written. In 1680 he became seriously ill and experienced a religious conversion, followed by a recantation of his past; he ordered "all his profane and lewd writings" burned.

His single dramatic work, the posthumous *Valentinian* (1685), an attempt to rework a tragedy of John Fletcher, contains two of his finest lyrics. Rochester's letters show an admirable mastery of easy, colloquial prose.

Rochester, Mr. Edward \'rä-chəs-tər, -ˌches-\ Fictional character in Charlotte Brontë's novel JANE EYRE, the brooding and tormented master of Thornfield Hall, who falls in love with and is loved by Jane Eyre.

Rococo \rə-'kō-kō, ˌrō-kō-'kō\ [French, irregular derivative of *rocaille*, 18th-century style of ornament characterized by sinuous foliate forms] Of or relating to an artistic style widespread in 18th-century Europe that was characterized by fanciful, curved asymmetrical forms and elaborate ornamentation. In literature, the term describes a style marked by lightheartedness, grace, and often wit. Examples include Alexander Pope's *The Rape of the Lock* and Voltaire's *Candide*.

Rod \'rȯd\, Édouard (b. March 29, 1857, Nyon, Switz.—d. Jan. 29, 1910, Grasse, Fr.) French-Swiss writer of psychological novels and a pioneer of comparative criticism.

Rod's first novels were written in the style of Émile Zola; the best of these was *Palmyre Veulard* (1881). He soon evolved his own highly sensitive, introverted psychological art in such novels as *La Course à la mort* (1885), *Le Sens de la vie* (1889), *La Vie privée de Michel Teissier* (1893; *The Private Life of an Eminent Politician*), and *Le Silence* (1894). Although often subject to pessimism and despondency, Rod insisted more and more on duty, conscience, and renunciation as decisive elements of life. As a critic he was a forerunner of modern comparative literary study, his chief works being *De la littérature comparée* (1886) and *Reflets d'Amérique* (1905).

Rodenbach \'rō-dən-ˌbäk\, Albrecht (b. Oct. 27, 1856, Roeselare, Belg.—d. June 23, 1880) One of the leaders of the revival in Flemish literature that developed in the late 1870s as a direct challenge to the growth of French influence in Belgian cultural life.

While he attended the university at Louvain, Rodenbach began to collaborate with another young poet, Pol de Monte, to promote a distinctly Flemish artistic revival. A volume of Rodenbach's verse, *Eerste Gedichten* (1878; "First Poems"), was published before his early death. He also wrote a grandiose verse play, *Gudrun*, which did not appear during his lifetime. On Rodenbach's death, Pol de Monte became the leader of the Flemish movement, which thereafter tended to look more to Germany for its inspiration.

Rodenbach \rō-deⁿ-'bȧk\, Georges(-Raymond-Constantin) (b. July 16, 1855, Tournai, Belg.—d. Dec. 25, 1898, Paris, Fr.) Symbolist poet and novelist whose writing was inspired by scenes of his native Belgium.

Rodenbach studied law in Ghent and Paris. He later renounced the profession to devote himself to the Belgian literary renaissance movement known as La Jeune Belgique.

Rodenbach's first collection of verse, *Le Foyer et les champs* ("The Hearth and the Fields"), was published in 1877. His early works were known mainly in Belgium, but with the publication of *La Jeunesse blanche* ("The White Youthfulness") in 1886 he also won recognition in France. His finest works include *Bruges-la-Morte* (1892; "Bruges, the Dead City"), a nostalgic novel evoking the landscape of Flanders, and *Les Vies encloses* (1896; "The Enclosed Lives"), moody, ruminative poems evoking the interior landscape of a self-absorbed mind.

Roderick Hudson \'räd-ər-ik-'həd-sən\ First novel by Henry JAMES, serialized in *The Atlantic Monthly* in 1875 and published in book form in 1876. It was revised by the author in 1879 for publication in England. *Roderick Hudson* is the story of the conflict between art and the passions; the title character is an American sculptor in Italy. Faltering in both his artistic ambitions and his personal relationships, he travels to Switzerland and dies there.

Roderick Random \'räd-ə-rik-'ran-dəm\ (*in full* The Adventures of Roderick Random) Picaresque novel by Tobias SMOLLETT, published in 1748. Modeled after Alain-René Lesage's *Gil Blas*, the novel consists of a series of episodes that give an account of the life and times of the Scottish rogue Roderick Random. At various times rich and then poor, the hero goes to sea, has romantic entanglements, travels the world, discovers his long-lost father, and marries his true love.

Rodolph *see* OUOLOGUEM.

rodomontade \ˌräd-ō-ˌmän-'tād, -'täd\ 1. A bragging speech. 2. Vain boasting or bluster. The word, originally coined in French, derives from the name of the character Rodomonte in Matteo Boiardo's *Orlando innamorato* and is used in literature in reference to boasting speech or behavior by a character such as William Shakespeare's Falstaff.

Rodrigues Lobo \rō-'drē-gesh-'lō-bu̇\, Francisco (b. 1580, Leiria, Port.—d. November 1621, Portugal) Pastoral poet known as the Portuguese Theocritus, after the classic Greek originator of the pastoral poetic genre.

Rodrigues Lobo's first book of poems, *Romances* (1596), written in the Baroque manner of the Spanish poet Luis de Góngora, reveals a refined sensibility and skill in describing the moods of nature. Most of the 61 poems are in Spanish, a second language for Portuguese writers until the end of the 17th century.

His best works are the eclogues interpolated in his trilogy of pastoral novels, *Primavera* (1601; "Spring"), *O pastor peregrino* (1608; "The Wandering Shepherd"), and *O desencantado* (1614; "The Disenchanted"). These poems combine pleasing descriptions of the countryside of his native region with witty dialogues between shepherds and shepherdesses on the wiles of love. His most masterful works in prose are the lively and elegant dialogues *Côrte na aldeia* (1619; "Village Court"), in which a young noble, a student, a wealthy gentleman, and a man of letters discuss manners, philosophy, social questions, and especially literary style.

Roethke \'ret-kē, 'reth-\, Theodore (b. May 25, 1908, Saginaw, Mich., U.S.—d. Aug. 1, 1963, Bainbridge Island, Wash.) American poet whose verse is characterized by introspection and intense lyricism.

Roethke was educated at the University of Michigan and Harvard University. He taught at several colleges and universities, notably the University of Washington. His later career was interrupted by hospitalizations for manic depression.

His first book of poetry, *Open House*, which W.H. Auden called "completely successful," was published in 1941. It was followed by *The Lost Son and Other Poems* (1948) and *Praise to the End!* (1951). *The Waking: Poems 1933–1953* (1953), was awarded a Pulitzer Prize; *Words for the Wind* (1957) won a Bollingen Prize and a National Book Award. Roethke won a second National Book Award for *The Far Field* (1964). His *Collected Poems* were published in 1966. His essays and lectures are collected in his *On the Poet and His Craft* (1965).

Roger Malvin's Burial \'räj-ər-'mal-vin\ Short story by Nathaniel HAWTHORNE, first published in 1832 in the periodical *The Token* and collected in *Mosses from an Old Manse* (1846). Based on an actual occurrence, the story is less concerned with historical narrative than with real or obsessive guilt, a theme to which Hawthorne returned in much of his fiction.

Roger Malvin and Reuben Bourne make their way home after participating in a skirmish with Indians. Badly wounded, Roger urges Reuben to leave him and return home alone. Reuben agrees to go on, swearing that he will either send help or will return himself to give Roger a decent burial. Reuben never fulfills his oath, and for years he lives as if under a curse. His guilt is finally expiated through a tragic sacrifice. *See also* MOSSES FROM AN OLD MANSE.

Rogers \'răj-ərz\, Samuel (b. July 30, 1763, Stoke Newington, near London, Eng.—d. Dec. 18, 1855, London)   English poet best remembered as a witty conversationalist and as a friend of greater poets.

Rogers attained eminence with the publication of his discursive poem *The Pleasures of Memory* (1792). On his father's death (1793) he inherited a banking firm, and for the next half century he maintained an influential position in London society. His acquisition of paintings and objets d'art made his home a center for anyone ambitious to be thought a person of taste. The amusing, though often unkind, conversations held at his breakfast and dinner parties were recorded by Alexander Dyce and published as *Recollections of the Table-Talk of Samuel Rogers* (1856). In spite of his sharp tongue, he performed many kind offices for his friends. He aided Richard Sheridan in his dying days and obtained a position for William Wordsworth as distributor of stamps for Westmorland. On Wordsworth's death in 1850, Rogers refused the offer of the laureateship.

Roget \'rō-zhā, rō-'zhā\, Peter Mark (b. Jan. 18, 1779, London, Eng.—d. Sept. 12, 1869, West Malvern, Worcestershire)   English physician and philologist remembered for his *Thesaurus of English Words and Phrases* (1852), a comprehensive classification of synonyms or verbal equivalents that is still popular in modern editions. The first edition of the *Thesaurus,* which was begun in Roget's 61st year and finished in his 73rd, was based on a system of verbal classification he had begun in 1805.

Rohmer \'rō-mər\, Sax, *pseudonym of* Arthur Sarsfield Wade \'wād\ *or* Ward \'wôrd\ (b. 1883?, Birmingham, Warwickshire, Eng.—d. June 1, 1959, London)   Internationally popular British writer who created the sinister Chinese criminal genius FU MANCHU.

Rohmer was interested from childhood in ancient Egypt, the Middle East, and the occult. After working briefly in the financial district of London and as a journalist there, his growing interest in the Far East led him into fiction writing. He published *Dr. Fu Manchu,* the first of the series, in 1913. The inscrutable and aristocratic Fu immediately caught the public's fancy, and Rohmer wrote several more novels over the next 45 years, gradually transforming him from an entirely self-serving villain into a dedicated anticommunist. The character also appeared in motion pictures, radio, and television.

Rojas \'rō-kăs\, Fernando de (b. *c.* 1465, La Puebla de Montalbán, Castile [Spain]—d. April 1541, Talavera de la Reina)   Spanish author whose single work is LA CELESTINA, an extended prose drama in dialogue that marked an important stage in the development of prose fiction in Spain and in Europe.

Little is known about Rojas except that his parents were Jews who had been forced to convert to Christianity. Rojas himself experienced discrimination while attending the University of Salamanca, and he later moved to Talavera, where he married, practiced law, and served briefly as lord mayor.

The first version of *La Celestina* appeared anonymously under the title *Comedia de Calisto y Melibea* (1499). One of the first works to present romance in everyday life, it combines a tragic love story with bawdy and picaresque scenes enacted by a cast of secondary characters. Some critics have interpreted *La Celestina,* in the light of Rojas' experiences, as a condemnation of anti-Semitism in Spanish society.

Rojas \'rō-kăs, -käh\, Manuel (Sepúlveda) (b. Jan. 8, 1896, Buenos Aires, Arg.—d. March 11, 1973, Santiago, Chile)   Chilean novelist and short-story writer.

As a youth, Rojas traveled along the Argentine and Chilean border while working as an unskilled laborer. Many of the situations and characters he encountered there later became part of his fictional world.

Rojas began as a poet (*Poeticus,* 1921) and then turned to writing short stories. His collections of short stories, *Hombres del sur* (1926; "Men of the South") and *El delincuente* (1929; "The Delinquent"), showed the influence of Ernest Hemingway and William Faulkner. Among his later volumes of short stories are *El vaso de leche y sus mejores cuentos* (1959; "The Glass of Milk and His Best Stories") and *El hombre de la rosa* (1963; "The Man of the Rose").

His first novel, *Lanchas en la bahía* (1932; "Launches in the Bay"), is a satirical presentation of some of the social ills afflicting Chile. Rojas' most acclaimed work is *Hijo de ladrón* (1951; "Son of a Thief"; *Born Guilty*), an autobiographical novel with existential preoccupations. The use of interior monologue, flashbacks, and stream of consciousness foreshadowed some of the techniques later employed in the Latin-American new novel. *Hijo de ladrón* was translated into the major European languages and established Rojas as an international writer. Other novels include *Mejor que el vino* (1958; "Better Than Wine"), *Punta de rieles* (1960; "Shining Tip"), and *Sombras contra el muro* (1964; "Shadows Against the Wall"), in which many of the characters of *Hijo de ladrón* reappear.

Rojas Villandrando \'rō-kăs-ˌbēl-yän-'drän-dō\, Agustín de (b. August 1572, Madrid, Spain—d. 1618, Paredes de Nava)   Spanish actor and author whose most important work, *El viaje entretenido* ("The Pleasant Voyage"), a picaresque novel in dialogue form, provides a valuable account of the Spanish theater in the 16th century and of the life of the actors. He is also considered the cleverest writer of *loas* (laudatory dramatic prologues) of his era.

Rojas Zorrilla \'rō-kăs-thôr-'rēl-yä\, Francisco de (b. Oct. 4, 1607, Toledo, Spain—d. Jan. 23, 1648, Madrid)   Spanish dramatist of the school of his more eminent contemporary, Pedro Calderón de la Barca. Rojas Zorrilla was noted for tragedies and a new type of play, the *comedia de figurón,* in which an eccentric is the chief figure. At their best, his plays have a sense of life and animation that is lacking in other drama influenced by Calderón.

The few good plays among the 70 that Rojas Zorrilla wrote have a sense of reality that partly overcomes the artificiality of the theatrical conventions. They also possess a naturalness in their plots that is particularly marked in his best-known play, *Del rey abajo, ninguno* ("Below the King, No One").

Roland   *see* ORLANDO.

Roland, Childe \'chīld-'rō-lənd\   Fictional character, the son of King Arthur in an old Scottish ballad. In the poem, Roland rescues his sister, who had been carried off by fairies. William Shakespeare and Robert Browning both refer to the character in works of their own.

Roland Holst-van der Schalk \'rō-länt-'hôlst-vän-dər-'skälk\, Henriëtte Goverdina Anna (b. Dec. 24, 1869, Noordwijk aan Zee, Neth.—d. Nov. 21, 1952, Amsterdam)   Dutch poet and active socialist whose work deals with the humanitarian concerns that informed her politics.

In 1896 she married the painter Richard Nicolaas Roland Holst, himself a talented prose writer. Influenced by the English poet and reformer William Morris, she became a socialist. Her volumes of poetry *De nieuwe geboort* (1902; "The New Birth") and *Opwaartsche wegen* (1907; "Upward Ways") reflect her political ideals. In her drama *Thomas More* (published 1912), dedicated to the German Marxist leader Karl Kautsky, Roland

Holst-van der Schalk depicted the last days of the great humanist, whom she regarded as having anticipated her own ideals.

She soon became internationally famous in left-wing circles. Roland Holst-van der Schalk at first eulogized the Russian Revolution of 1917, but after visiting Russia in 1925, she expressed her disappointment in Soviet communism in her poems in *Heldensage* (1927; "Heroic Saga"). She withdrew from active politics but in her later work remained loyal to her ideals, and her pacifist and anticolonial sentiment attracted much attention. She also wrote biographies of such figures as Jean-Jacques Rousseau (1912), Leo Tolstoy (1930), Romain Rolland (1946), and Mahatma Gandhi (1947).

Rolfe \'rälf\, Frederick William, *pseudonym* Baron Corvo \'kȯr-vō\ (b. July 22, 1860, London, Eng.—d. Oct. 25, 1913, Venice, Italy)   English author and eccentric who is best known for his autobiographical fantasy *Hadrian the Seventh* (1904). He provides the curious example of an artist rescued from obscurity by his biographer: many years after Rolfe's death A.J.A. Symons wrote a colorful biographical fantasy, *The Quest for Corvo* (1934), the publication of which marked the beginning of Rolfe's fame.

Rolfe left school at age 14 and became a schoolmaster. Reared as a Protestant, he had from boyhood been drawn to religion, and in 1886 he became a Roman Catholic. There followed two unsuccessful attempts to become a priest, but his independence and reputation as a pederast led to his dismissal from the Scots College in Rome.

For eight years he wandered, turning his hand to painting, photography, tutoring, inventing, and journalism. In 1898 he became a professional writer with the publication of retellings of the legends of Roman Catholic saints under the title *Stories Toto Told Me*, which made a name for him at the time. During the next decade his publications included a collection of short stories, *In His Own Image* (1901); a historical work, *Chronicles of the House of Borgia* (1901); and two novels, *Hadrian the Seventh* and *Don Tarquinio* (1905). Some of his works appeared after his death, notably *The Desire and Pursuit of the Whole* (1934). Rolfe was also a prolific letter writer, engaging in long and violent correspondence with his enemies.

Rolland \rȯ-'lä⁼\, Romain (b. Jan. 29, 1866, Clamecy, Fr.—d. Dec. 30, 1944, Vézelay)   Novelist, dramatist, essayist, and one of the great mystics of 20th-century French literature.

At age 14 Rolland went to Paris to study and found a society in spiritual disarray. He studied history and received a doctorate in art (1895), after which he went to Italy for two years. At first Rolland wrote the plays that were later collected in two cycles: *Les Tragédies de la foi* (1913; "The Tragedies of Faith"), which contains *Aërt* (1898); and *Le Théâtre de la révolution* (1904), which includes a presentation of the Dreyfus Affair, *Les Loups* (1898; *The Wolves*), and *Danton* (1900).

In 1912, after a brief career in teaching art and musicology, he resigned to devote his time to writing. He collaborated with Charles Péguy in the journal *Les Cahiers de la Quinzaine*, where he first published his best-known novel, JEAN-CHRISTOPHE, 10 vol. (1904–12). For this and for his pamphlet *Au-dessus de la mêlée* (1915; *Above the Battle*), a call for France and Germany to respect truth and humanity throughout their struggle in World War I, he was awarded the Nobel Prize for Literature in 1915.

After a burlesque fantasy, *Colas Breugnon* (1919), Rolland published a second novel cycle, *L'Âme-enchantée*, 7 vol. (1922–33; "The Enchanted Soul"), in which he exposed the cruel effects of political sectarianism. In the 1920s he turned to Asia, especially India, seeking to interpret its mystical philosophy to the West in such works as *Mahatma Gandhi* (1924). Rolland's *Mémoires* were published posthumously in 1956.

Rolli \'rȯl-lē\, Paolo Antonio (b. June 13, 1687, Rome, Papal States [Italy]—d. March 20, 1765, Todi)   Librettist, poet, and translator who helped to Italianize 18th-century English taste.

Rolli studied with the major Italian literary critic of the day, Gian Vincenzo Gravina. In 1715 he went to England and became the Italian teacher in the family of the Prince of Wales (later George II). He served the royal family for nearly 30 years, and during that time he had considerable influence on English taste, partially as a writer of operatic librettos (for George Frideric Handel, Giovanni Bononcini, Alessandro Scarlatti, and others), partially through his own smooth and charming, classically inspired lyric poetry, and partially through extensive translation of Italian classics. In addition, he translated *Paradise Lost* into Italian blank verse, and his rendition of Hamlet's "To be or not to be" soliloquy was the first Italian translation of William Shakespeare. He returned to Italy in 1744.

Rolli's Italian poetry is probably his finest personal achievement, consisting of easy and delightful lyrics in many forms—odes, *endecasillibi* (poems written in lines of 11 syllables), and *canzonette* (songs) based on the classical models of Horace, Catullus, and Anacreon but endowed with a musical charm all their own.

Rølvaag \'rœl-ˌvȯg, *Angl* 'rōl-ˌväg\, O.E., *in full* Ole Edvart (b. April 22, 1876, Dönna Island, Helgeland, Nor.—d. Nov. 5, 1931, Northfield, Minn., U.S.)   Norwegian-American novelist and educator noted for his realistic portrayals of Norwegian settlers on the Dakota prairies and of the clash between transplanted and native cultures in the United States.

Rølvaag immigrated to the United States in 1896 and was naturalized in 1908. Educated at St. Olaf College, Northfield, Minn., and the University of Oslo, Norway, he spent most of his life at St. Olaf as a teacher of Norwegian language and literature and the history of Norwegian immigration. He wrote in Norwegian, the language in which his works were originally published, and worked closely with the translators of the English versions.

Rølvaag gave epic sweep to his picture of pioneering but also deplored its cost in human values. Two novels, *I de dage* ("In Those Days," 1924) and *Riket grundlæges* ("The Kingdom Is Founded," 1925), were translated as GIANTS IN THE EARTH (1927). It was his best work, representing the positive aspects of pioneering in the character Per Hansa, the negative aspects in his wife Beret. *Peder Victorious* (1929) and *Their Fathers' God* (1931) continued the story to the second generation.

Romains \rȯ-'ma⁼\, Jules, *pseudonym of* Louis-Henri-Jean Farigoule \fä-rē-'gül\ (b. Aug. 26, 1885, Saint-Julien-Chapteuil, Fr.—d. Aug. 14, 1972, Paris)   French novelist, dramatist, poet, and a founder of the literary movement known as Unanimisme. In 1946 he was elected to the Académie Française.

Before World War I, Romains was known primarily as a poet and as founder, with the poet Georges Chennevière, of Unanimisme, a movement that combined belief in universal brotherhood with the psychological concept of group consciousness. His first notable book of poems was *La Vie unanime* (1908), and his first plays were Unanimiste verse dramas.

Romains's most popular work was the comedy *Knock, ou le triomphe de la médecine* (1923; *Knock*), a satire in the tradition of Molière on the power of doctors to impose upon human credulity. In his first important collective novel, *Mort de quelqu'un* (1911; *The Death of a Nobody*), Romains described the reactions of a group of people to the death of an insignificant member of society. *Les Copains* (1913; *The Boys in the Back Room*), a farcical tale told with Rabelaisian truculence, evokes the bonds that unite seven friends determined to carry out shocking practical jokes. Romains's masterpiece, the vast cyclic epic *Les Hommes de bonne volonté* (MEN OF GOOD WILL), was published in 27 volumes between 1932 and 1946.

roman à clef \rō-män-ä-'klä\ *plural* romans à clef \rō-mänz\ [French, literally, novel with a key] A novel that has the extraliterary interest of portraying identifiable, sometimes real people more or less thinly disguised as fictional characters.

The tradition dates to 17th-century France, when fashionable members of the aristocratic literary coteries, such as Mlle de Scudéry, enlivened their historical romances by including in them fictional representations of well-known figures in the court of Louis XIV. In the 20th century, W. Somerset Maugham's *Cakes and Ale* is widely held to contain portraits of the novelists Thomas Hardy and Hugh Walpole. A more common type of roman à clef is Simone de Beauvoir's *Les Mandarins*, in which the disguised characters are immediately recognizable only to a small circle of insiders.

In a general sense, every work of literary art offers a key or clue to the artist's preoccupations (for example, the jail in Charles Dickens or the mysterious tyrants in Franz Kafka, each leading back to the author's own father), but the true roman à clef is more specific in its disguised references. Jonathan Swift's *A Tale of a Tub*, John Dryden's *Absalom and Achitophel*, and George Orwell's *Animal Farm* make complete sense only when their disguised historical content is disclosed. These examples illustrate that the literary purpose is not primarily aesthetic. In understanding D.H. Lawrence's *Aaron's Rod* it helps to have a knowledge of the author's personal enmities, and to understand Aldous Huxley's *Point Counter Point* fully one should know, for instance, that the character of Mark Rampion represents D.H. Lawrence himself and that of Denis Burlap represents the critic John Middleton Murry. Marcel Proust's *À la recherche du temps perdu* becomes a richer literary experience when the author's social milieu is explored, and James Joyce's *Finnegans Wake* has so many personal references that it may be called the most massive roman à clef ever written. The more important the key becomes to full understanding, the closer the work comes to being didactic. That is, when it is dangerous to expose the truth directly, the novel or narrative poem may present it obliquely. Nonetheless, the ultimate vitality of the work depends on those elements in it that require no key.

romance \rō-'mans, 'rō-,mans\ [Old French *romans, romanz* French, something composed in French, tale in verse, from Medieval Latin *Romanice* in a vernacular language (as opposed to Latin), a derivative of Late Latin *Romanus* Gallo-Romance (as opposed to Frankish), from Latin, of Rome, Roman] **1.** A medieval tale based on legend, chivalric love and adventure, or the supernatural. *Compare* EPIC. **2.** A prose narrative treating imaginary characters involved in events remote in time or space and usually heroic, adventurous, or mysterious. *Compare* FANTASY; HISTORICAL NOVEL. **3.** A love story. **4.** A class or division of literature comprising romance or romantic fiction.

The romance literary form came into being in France in the mid-12th century. It had antecedents in many prose works from classical antiquity (the so-called Greek romances), but as a distinctive genre it was developed in the context of the aristocratic courts of such patrons as Eleanor of Aquitaine.

The romance had its heyday in France and Germany between the mid-12th and mid-13th century in the works of such masters as Chrétien de Troyes, Benoît de Sainte-Maure, and Gottfried von Strassburg. By the time it reached England (about 1250), it was already beginning to show signs of a decline from its original form.

The staple subject matter of romance is chivalric adventure. Love stories and religious allegories can often be found interwoven with this material, but they are not essential to it. The majority of romances drew their plots from three basic areas: classical history and legend, the adventures of King Arthur and the knights of the Round Table (certainly the most significant group), and the doings of Charlemagne and his knights. To these must be added a number of romances concerned specifically with the deeds of English heroes, such as Havelock the Dane and Richard Coeur de Lion (Richard the Lion-hearted), and a number of other romances, such as *Sir Orfeo* and *Floire et Blancheflor*, that belong to no particular cycle.

Among the earlier romances were those that took their subjects from classical antiquity. These include the *Roman de Thèbes* and the *Roman d'Enéas,* both adapted from the work of Latin poets. Benoît de Sainte-Maure's *Roman de Troie*, which tells the story of Troy, is notable in this group for containing the first literary treatment of the narrative of Troilus and Cressida, later developed by Giovanni Boccaccio, Geoffrey Chaucer, and William Shakespeare. Also popular were stories based on the life of Alexander the Great, among them the *Roman d'Alexandre* and the later *King Alisaunder*.

As the etymology of the word *romance* indicates, the romance was written in the vernacular rather than in Latin. There are examples of the genre in both verse and prose, though in general prose romances tend to belong to the later period. From the start, these works share a taste for the exotic, the remote, and the miraculous. Descriptive detail is lavish, and love stories on the whole end happily—*Tristan und Isolde*, written by Gottfried von Strassburg in the early 13th century, being a notable exception. Overall, it can be said that by comparison with the epic form of the chanson de geste ("song of deeds"), which it superseded, the romance shows a general sophistication of narrative method and psychological insight.

In later centuries the romance underwent various transformations. The continued popularity of one form of it, the prose romance of 15th- and 16th-century Spain, is attested by Miguel de Cervantes' satire of the romance in *Don Quixote*. Although the chivalric ideal of the perfect knight was essentially medieval, lingering echoes of romance can be found in the changing connotations of the word itself. Thus, at the end of the 18th century the Romantic movements beginning in England and Germany were in some respects an attempt to turn back to the spirit of medieval romance in reaction against the prevailing philosophies of the time. Even today, in the popular romantic novel, there can be detected within the formulaic plots a debased survival of some of the original values.

See also ALEXANDER ROMANCE; ARTHURIAN LEGEND; CHANSON DE GESTE.

Romance of 'Antar \'än-tär, *Arabic* "än-\, *Arabic* Sīrat 'Antar. Tales of chivalry centered on the black Arab desert poet and warrior 'Antarah ibn Shaddād, one of the poets of the celebrated pre-Islāmic collection the *Mu'allaqāt*. The work was composed anonymously between the 8th and the 12th century. Written in rhymed prose (*saj'*) interspersed with 10,000 poetic verses, it is commonly divided into 32 books, each leaving the conclusion of a tale in suspense.

The *Romance* tells of the fabulous childhood of 'Antar, son of an Arab king by a black slave girl, hence regarded as a bastard by his people, and the adventures he undertakes to attain the hand of his cousin 'Ablah in marriage. These take him beyond Arabia and his own time to Iraq, Iran, Syria, Spain, North Africa, Egypt, Constantinople, Rome, and the Sudan.

The *Romance of 'Antar* evolved out of a Bedouin tradition that stressed nobility of character and desert chivalry, of which 'Antar was made the epitome. With the advent of Islām, the stories assumed a new outlook that reinterpreted 'Antar as a precursor of the new religion. A strong Persian hand in the later authorship of the *Romance*—demonstrated by detailed knowledge of Persian history and court life—then shows 'Antar in Iran. A later influence is reflected in knowledge of Christianity and the crusades, an understanding of the West far greater than Western understanding of Islām.

Romance of the Three Kingdoms   Classic historical novel, published as *Sanguozhi yanyi*, about ancient China during the fall of the Han dynasty and the era of the Three Kingdoms (220–280 AD). Its provenance is ancient. As folktales and stage dramas were passed down through the centuries, it grew by accretion; the earliest extant version, published about 1522, has a preface dated to 1494. In the 17th century editorcritic Mao Zonggang compiled what became the standard version of the work.

Romance of the Three Kingdoms supports the claim of the Shu Han dynasty to be the legitimate successor to the Han dynasty, dismissing that of the Wei. The story's principal characters, all based on historical figures, became archetypes in popular Chinese fiction and theater. They include General Cao Cao, founder of Wei, portrayed as one of the most cunning and dastardly villains in all of literature; his heroic opponents, the loyal Brothers of the Peach Orchard; the benevolent leader Liu Bei, founder of Shu Han; the huge, great-hearted, fearless Guan Yu, who was deified as Guan Di in the 16th century; and the younger, courageous, impulsive Zhang Fei. The wise scholar and military strategist Zhuge Liang plays a crucial role in the novel's battles.

romancero \\,rō-män-'thä-rō\\ [Spanish *el Romancero,* from *romancero* collection of ballads, a derivative of *romance* ballad] Collective body of Spanish folk ballads (*romances*) constituting a unique tradition of European balladry. They resemble epic poetry in their heroic, aristocratic tone, their themes of battle and honor, and their pretense to historicity; but they are, nevertheless, ballads, compressed dramatic narratives sung to a tune.

Once thought to be the source of such 12th-century Spanish epics as *Cantar de mio Cid* ("Song of My Cid"), the genre is now believed to be a development of the epic tradition. The earliest known *romances* date from the late 14th and early 15th centuries.

Some ballads are brief dramatizations of episodes from known epics. They frequently deal with the conflicts between or the amours of Spaniards and Moors. Other popular subjects are the Arthurian and Charlemagne legends. Traditional ballads were collected in the Antwerp *Cancionero de romances* ("Ballad Songbook") and in the *Silva de varios romances* ("Miscellany of Various Ballads"), both first published about 1550 and thereafter repeatedly. The form (octosyllabic, alternate lines having a single assonance throughout) was soon exploited for lyrical purposes by the most famous poets of the age. Unlike the folk poetry of England, Scandinavia, or Germany, which followed a tradition independent of the national literatures, the ballads formed a continuous link in the chain of tradition from the earliest Spanish vernacular literature to the literature of the 20th century. As the sourcebook of history and of the character of Spaniards of all classes, they lie at the heart of the national consciousness. They inspired many of the poems, dramas, and novels by the masters of Spanish literature and remain the chosen medium for popular narrative verse.

romance stanza   *also called* romance-six.   A six-line verse stanza common in metrical romances in which lines 1, 2, 4, and 5 have four accents each and lines 3 and 6 have three accents each and in which the rhyme scheme is *aabaab.* It is a type of tail rhyme.

Roman de Fauvel \\rō-män-də-fō-'vel\\ ("Romance of Fauvel")   French poem by Gervais du Bus that, in addition to its literary value, is a crucial document for the history of music.

The poem, a lengthy allegory, condemns abuses in contemporary political and religious life. Fauvel, the story's protagonist, bears the name associated in French lore with the fawn-colored stallion, the symbol of cunning and duplicity.

A lavishly illuminated manuscript of the poem dated 1316 and preserved in Paris at the Bibliothèque Nationale has 130 musical works interspersed in the narrative, representing a remarkably rich anthology stretching over 150 years. Some are in their original form, some were adapted to fit the new context, and some, containing topical references, were presumably written specifically for the *Roman.*

Roman de la Rose \\rō-män-də-lä-'rōz\\ ("Romance of the Rose")   One of the most popular French poems of the late medieval period of European history.

Modeled on Ovid's *Ars amatoria* (*c.* 1 BC; *Art of Love*) and rooted in André le Chapelain's treatise on courtly love, the poem is composed of more than 21,000 lines of octosyllabic couplets and survives in more than 300 manuscripts. Nothing is known of the author of the first 4,058 lines except his name, GUILLAUME de Lorris. This section, which was written about 1230, is a charming dream allegory of the wooing of a maiden, symbolized by a rosebud, within the bounds of a garden, representing courtly society. It is one of the finer examples of allegorical literature, rising above the requisite didacticism of the genre.

No satisfactory conclusion was written until about 1280, when JEAN de Meun seized upon the original plot as a means of conveying a vast mass of encyclopedic information and opinions on a great variety of contemporary topics. At various times he relates the history of classical heroes, attacks the hoarding of money, and theorizes about astronomy. The original theme is frequently obscured for thousands of lines while the characters discourse at length. It was these digressions that secured the poem its fame and success, for Jean de Meun was writing from a bourgeois point of view that gradually superseded the aristocratic code of Guillaume de Lorris.

A Middle English version, of which the first 1,705 lines are translated by Geoffrey Chaucer, covers all of Guillaume de Lorris's section and 3,000 lines of Jean de Meun's. The original *Roman* was the single most important literary influence on Chaucer's writings.

Roman Elegies   Cycle of 20 lyric poems by J.W. von GOETHE, published in German in 1795 as "Römische Elegien" in Friedrich Schiller's literary periodical *Die Horen.* The cycle received considerable hostile public criticism. One of the poems, "Elegy 13," had been published in *Die deutsche Monatsschrift* in 1791.

Written in 1788–89, the poems were inspired by Goethe's first visit to Italy in 1786–88. Called elegies because of their form (elegiac couplets) rather than their subject matter, the poems are works of unabashed sensuality. They are at once highly civilized and pagan, reflecting Goethe's reveling in an intense physical, emotional, and aesthetic response to his surroundings. His love of the artistic heritage of Italy was combined with a newly awakened physical passion for Christiane Vulpius, his mistress and later his wife.

roman-fleuve \\rō-män-'flœv\\ *plural* romans-fleuves *same*\\ [French, literally, river novel]   A novel having the form of a long, multivolume, and usually loosely structured chronicle of persons comprising a family, community, or other social group.

Inspired by Honoré de Balzac's *Comédie humaine* and Émile Zola's Rougon-Macquart cycle, the *roman-fleuve* was a popular literary genre in France during the first half of the 20th century. Examples include *Jean-Christophe* (1904–12) by Romain Rolland, *À la recherche du temps perdu* (1913–27; *Remembrance of Things Past*) by Marcel Proust, *Les Thibault* (1922–40) by Roger Martin du Gard, and *Les Hommes de bonne volonté*, (1932–46; *Men of Good Will*) by Jules Romains. Proust's work is usually considered to be the masterpiece of the genre.

Romano \rō-'mȧn-ü\, Luís, *byname of* Luis Romano Madeira de Melo \mȧ-'dȧ-rȧ-dȧ-'mel-ü\ (b. June 10, 1922, Santo Antão, Cape Verde Islands)   Cape Verdean poet, novelist, and folklorist who wrote in both Portuguese and Crioulo (Cape Verdean Creole).

Romano's writings include *Famintos* (1962; "The Famished"), a novel influenced structurally and thematically by fiction from the Brazilian northeast. It is a realistic novel, portraying in detail the hardships of life in the Cape Verde Islands. A collection of his poetry, *Clima* (1963; "Climate"), criticizes Portuguese exploitation. *Renascença de uma civilização no Atlântico médio* (1967; "Renaissance of a Civilization in the Middle of the Atlantic") is a collection of poems and short stories based primarily on folklore. His poetry demonstrates understanding and advocates racial harmony, but according to some critics, it also presents misleading stereotypes of Africans. Romano wrote a bilingual text of poems and stories (in Portuguese and Cape Verdean Creole) entitled *Negrume/Lzimparin* (1973; "Dusk"), one of the first works to be written completely in the Cape Verdean language. Romano also collaborated on several journals.

Romanticism \rō-'man-tə-ˌsiz-əm\   A literary, artistic, and philosophical movement originating in Europe in the 18th century and lasting roughly until the mid-19th century. Romanticism is characterized chiefly by a reaction against the Enlightenment and Neoclassicism with their stress on reason, order, balance, harmony, rationality, and intellect. Romanticism emphasized the individual, the subjective, the irrational, the imaginative, the personal, the spontaneous, the emotional, the visionary, and the transcendental. *Compare* CLASSICISM.

Among the characteristic attitudes of Romanticism were a deepened appreciation of the beauties of nature; a general exaltation of emotion over reason and of the senses over intellect; a turning in upon the self and a heightened examination of human personality; a preoccupation with the genius, the hero, and the exceptional figure; a new view of the artist as a supremely individual creator, whose creative spirit is more important than strict adherence to formal rules and traditional procedures; an emphasis upon imagination as a gateway to transcendent experience and spiritual truth; a consuming interest in folk culture, national and ethnic cultural origins, and the medieval era; and a predilection for the exotic, the remote, the mysterious, the weird, the occult, the monstrous, the diseased, and even the satanic.

In literature, Romanticism proper was preceded by several related developments from the mid-18th century on that can be termed pre-Romanticism. Among such trends was a new appreciation of the medieval romance, from which the Romantic movement derives its name. The romance, with its emphasis on individual heroism and on the exotic and the mysterious, was in clear contrast to the elegant formality and artificiality of prevailing classical forms of literature, such as the French Neoclassical tragedy or the English heroic couplet in poetry. This new interest in relatively unsophisticated but overtly emotional literary expressions of the past was to be a dominant note in Romanticism.

Romanticism in English literature began in the late 1790s with the publication of *Lyrical Ballads* of William Wordsworth and Samuel Taylor Coleridge. Wordsworth's "Preface" to the second edition (1800) of *Lyrical Ballads*, in which he described poetry as "the spontaneous overflow of powerful feelings,"

became the manifesto of the English Romantic movement in poetry. William Blake was the third principal poet of the movement's early phase in England. The first phase of the Romantic movement in Germany—an outgrowth of the *Sturm und Drang* period—was marked by innovations in both content and literary style and by a preoccupation with the mystical, the subconscious, and the supernatural. A number of writers, including Friedrich Hölderlin, the early J.W. von Goethe, Jean Paul, Novalis, Ludwig Tieck, A.W. and Friedrich von Schlegel, Wilhelm Heinrich Wackenroder, and Friedrich Schelling belonged to this first phase. In Revolutionary France, the Viscount de Chateaubriand and Mme de Staël were the chief initiators of Romanticism by virtue of their influential historical and theoretical writings.

The second phase of Romanticism, comprising the period from about 1805 to the 1830s, was marked by a quickening of cultural nationalism and a new attention to national origins, as attested by the collection and imitation of native folklore, folk ballads and poetry, folk dance and music, and previously ignored medieval and Renaissance works. This revived appreciation of history was translated into imaginative writing by Sir Walter Scott, often considered the inventor of the historical novel. About the same time English Romantic poetry reached its zenith in the works of John Keats, Lord Byron, and Percy Bysshe Shelley.

A notable by-product of the Romantic interest in the emotional were works dealing with the supernatural, the weird, and the horrible, as in Mary Shelley's *Frankenstein* and works by C.R. Maturin, the Marquis de Sade, and E.T.A. Hoffmann. The second phase of Romanticism in Germany was dominated by Achim von Arnim, Clemens Brentano, J.J. von Görres, and Joseph von Eichendorff.

By the 1820s Romanticism had broadened to embrace the literatures of almost all of Europe. In this later phase, the movement also examined the passions and struggles of exceptional individuals. Romantic or Romantic-influenced writers across the European continent included Thomas De Quincey, William Hazlitt, and the Brontë sisters in England; Victor Hugo, Alfred de Vigny, Alphonse de Lamartine, Alfred de Musset, Stendhal, Prosper Mérimée, Alexandre Dumas (*père*), and Théophile Gautier in France; Alessandro Manzoni and Giacomo Leopardi in Italy; Aleksandr Pushkin and Mikhail Lermontov in Russia; José de Espronceda and Ángel de Saavedra in Spain; and Adam Mickiewicz in Poland. Almost all of the important writers in pre-Civil War America were influenced by Romanticism. *See also* TRANSCENDENTALISM.

Romeo and Juliet \'rō-mē-ō ... 'jü-lē-ət, jü-lē-'et\   Play by William SHAKESPEARE performed about 1594–95 and published in a "bad" quarto in 1597. The characters of Romeo and Juliet have been depicted in literature, music, dance, and theater. The appeal of the young hero and heroine—whose families, the Montagues and Capulets, respectively, are implacable enemies—is such that they have become, in the popular imagination, the representative type of star-crossed lovers.

Shakespeare's principal source for the plot was *The Tragicall Historye of Romeus and Juliet* (1562), a long narrative poem by the English poet Arthur Broke or Brooke (d. 1563). Broke had based his poem on a French translation of a tale by an Italian writer, Matteo Bandello (1485–1561).

Shakespeare set the scene in Verona, Italy, during July. Juliet, a Capulet, and Romeo, a Montague, fall in love at a masked ball of the Capulets and profess their love when Romeo later visits her at her private balcony in her family's home. Because the two noble families are enemies, the couple is married secretly by Friar Laurence. When Tybalt, a Capulet, kills Romeo's friend Mercutio in a quarrel, Romeo kills Tybalt and is banished to

Mantua. Juliet's father insists on her marrying Count Paris, and Juliet goes to consult the friar. He gives her a potion that makes a person appear to be dead. He proposes that she take it and that Romeo rescue her; she complies. Unaware of the friar's scheme, Romeo returns to Verona on hearing of Juliet's apparent death. He encounters Paris, kills him, and finds Juliet in the burial vault. He gives her a last kiss and kills himself with poison. Juliet awakens, sees the dead Romeo, and kills herself. The families learn what has happened and end their feud.

Romero \rō-'mā-rō\, José Rubén (b. Sept. 25, 1890, Cotija de la Paz, Mex.—d. July 4, 1952, Mexico City) Mexican novelist and short-story writer whose vivid depiction of the people and customs of his native state of Michoacán brought him critical acclaim as an outstanding modern *costumbrista* writer, or novelist of manners, and whose character Pito Pérez, a lovable rascal, won the hearts of a wide audience.

Romero began his literary career as a poet with *Fantasías* (1908; "Fantasies") and *La musa heroica* (1912; "The Heroic Muse"). He soon turned almost exclusively to prose. With broad humor that often masked an underlying bitterness, Romero depicted the postrevolutionary milieu in such novels as *Desbandada* (1934; "Disbandment") and *Anticipación a la muerte* (1939; "Anticipation of Death"). He achieved his greatest popularity, however, with *La vida inútil de Pito Pérez* (1938; "The Useless Life of Pito Pérez"), a picaresque novel chronicling the comic adventures of Pito Pérez, who reappeared in *Algunas cosillas de Pito Pérez* (1945; "Some Little Things About Pito Pérez").

Romola \'räm-ō-lə\ Novel by George ELIOT, first published in 1862–63 in *Cornhill Magazine*. The book was published in three volumes in 1863. Set in Florence at the end of the 15th century and scrupulously researched, the novel weaves into its plot the career of the reformer Girolamo Savonarola and the downfall of the ruling Medicis.

In the narrative, Tito, a handsome opportunist, marries Romola, the daughter of a scholar. He deceives Romola, is unscrupulous in his political dealings, and is finally killed by his adoptive father. Romola finds strength in helping to care for Tito's other wife and the children of that union. The novel suggests that the highest moral imperative and the reason for living, when all has been lost, is human sympathy.

romp \'rämp\ A high-spirited, carefree, and boisterous play. Also something suggestive of such a play, as a light, fast-paced narrative, dramatic, or musical work, usually in a comic mood.

Romulus and Remus \'räm-yù-ləs . . . .'rē-məs\ The legendary founders of Rome. Traditionally, they were the sons of Rhea Silvia, daughter of Numitor, king of Alba Longa.

Numitor had been deposed by his younger brother Amulius, who forced Rhea to become a vestal virgin to prevent her from giving birth to potential claimants to the throne. Nevertheless, Rhea bore the war god Mars the twins Romulus and Remus. Amulius ordered the infants drowned in the Tiber, but the trough in which they were placed floated down the river and came to rest at the site of the future Rome, near the *ficus ruminalis*, a sacred fig tree of historical times. There a she-wolf and a woodpecker—both sacred to Mars—suckled and fed them until they were found by the herdsman Faustulus.

The twins became leaders of a band of adventurous youths, eventually killing Amulius and restoring their grandfather to the throne. They subsequently founded a town on the site where they had been saved. When Romulus built a city wall, Remus jumped over it and was killed by his brother.

Romulus consolidated his power, and the city was named for him. He increased its population by offering asylum to fugitives and exiles. He invited the neighboring Sabines to a festival and abducted their women. The women married their captors and intervened to prevent the Sabines from seizing the city. In accordance with a treaty drawn up between the two peoples, Romulus accepted the Sabine king Titus Tatius as his coruler. Titus Tatius' early death left Romulus sole king again, and after a long rule he mysteriously disappeared in a storm. Believing that he had been changed into a god, the Romans worshiped him as the deity Quirinus.

The legend of Romulus and Remus probably originated in the 4th century BC and was set down in coherent form at the end of the 3rd century BC. It contains a mixture of Greek and Roman elements.

rondeau \'rän-dō, *French* rôⁿ-'dō\ *plural* rondeaux \'rän-dōz, *French* rôⁿ-'dō\ [French, from Old French *rondel* rondel] One of several fixed forms in French lyric poetry and song of the 14th and 15th centuries. The rondeau has only two rhymes (allowing no repetition of rhyme words) and consists of 13 or 15 lines of 8 or 10 syllables divided into three stanzas. The beginning of the first line of the first stanza serves as the refrain of the second and third stanzas. (This form is sometimes called rondel. *Compare* RONDEL.)

The full form of a rondeau consists of three stanzas of five, four, and six lines. If *c* stands for the refrain, the rhyme scheme of a rondeau is *aabba aabc aabbac*.

The earliest rondeaux had stanzas of two or three lines; later, especially in the 15th century, stanzas of four, five, or even six lines were common. Because of the unwieldy length of the refrains in such cases, the literary rondeau, which in the 15th century began to be distinct from the sung rondeau, often curtailed the refrains in the second and fourth stanzas, leaving only a *rentrement* ("reentry") of the opening words. This proved to be a pleasing development, because it often produced unexpected changes of meaning as a result of the new context.

rondeau redoublé \rôⁿ-'dō-rə-dü-'blā, 'rän-dō\ *plural* rondeaux redoublés *same*\ [French, literally, double rondeau] A fixed form of verse, a variant of the rondeau, that runs on two rhymes. The rondeau redoublé usually consists of five quatrains and one quintet. The lines of the first quatrain are used consecutively to end each of the remaining four quatrains; the quintet, which follows the rhyme scheme established in the five quatrains, terminates with the opening words of the poem.

rondel \'rän-,del, -dəl, *French* rôⁿ-'del\ or **rondelle** \rän-'del, *French* rôⁿ-'del\ [Old French *rondel*, a derivative of *ruunt, reont* round] A fixed form of verse, a variant of the rondeau, that runs on two rhymes. Also, a poem in this form.

The rondel often consists of 14 lines of 8 or 10 syllables divided into three stanzas (two quatrains and a sextet), with the first two lines of the first stanza serving as the refrain of the second and third stanzas. In some instances rondels are 13 lines long, with only the first line of the poem repeated at the end. The designation rondel is sometimes used interchangeably with rondeau. The form, which originated in 13th-century France, was later used by such poets as Edmund Gosse, Robert Louis Stevenson, and W.E. Henley. *Compare* RONDEAU.

rondelet \,rän-də-'let, *French* rôⁿd-'lā\ [Middle French, a diminutive of *rondel* rondel] A modified rondeau running on two rhymes and consisting usually of one stanza of seven lines in which the first line of four syllables is repeated as the third line and as the final line (or refrain). The remaining lines are made up of eight syllables each.

Ronsard \rôⁿ-'sâr\, Pierre de (b. Sept. 11, 1524, La Possonnière, near Couture, Fr.—d. Dec. 27, 1585, Saint-Cosme, near Tours) Poet, chief among the French Renaissance group of poets known as LA PLÉIADE.

Ronsard was a younger son of a noble family of the county of Vendôme. During a period of enthusiastic study of the classics he learned Greek from the brilliant tutor Jean Dorat, read all the Greek and Latin poetry then known, and gained some familiarity with Italian poetry. With a group of fellow students he formed the literary school that came to be called La Pléiade, in emulation of the seven ancient Greek poets of Alexandria.

The title of his first collection of poems, *Odes* (4 books, 1550), shows that he was attempting a French counterpart to the odes of the ancient Latin poet Horace. In *Les Amours* (1552) he also proved his skill as an exponent of the Italian *canzoniere*. Always responsive to new literary influences, he found fresh inspiration in the recently discovered verse of the Greek poet Anacreon. The more playful touch encouraged by this model is seen in *Bocage* ("Grove") of 1554 and in *Melanges* ("Miscellany") of that same year, which contain some of his most exquisite nature poems, and in the *Continuation des amours* and *Nouvelle Continuation des amours* (1555–56), addressed to a country girl, Marie. In 1555 he began to write a series of long poems, including the "Hymne du ciel" ("Hymn of the Sky"), that celebrate natural phenomena, abstract ideas like death or justice, or gods and heroes of antiquity; these poems were published as *Hymnes* (following the 3rd-century-BC Greek poet Callimachus, who had inspired them). Reminiscences of his boyhood inspired other poems, such as his "Complainte contre fortune," published in the second book of *Melanges* (1559). This poem is also notable for a celebrated denunciation of the colonization of the New World, whose people he imagined to be noble savages living in an unspoiled state of nature comparable to his idealized memories of childhood.

The outbreak of the religious wars found him committed to an extreme Royalist and Roman Catholic position, and he drew upon himself the hostility of the Protestants. To this period belong the *Discours des misères de ce temps* (1562; "Discourse on the Miseries of These Times") and other writings attacking his opponents. He also wrote much court poetry during this time, encouraged by the young king, Charles IX. If he was by now in some sense the poet laureate of France, he made slow progress with *La Franciade*, which he intended to be the national epic; this imitation of Virgil's great Latin epic, the *Aeneid*, was abandoned after the death of Charles IX, the four completed books being published in 1572. The collected edition of Ronsard's works published in 1578 included some remarkable new works, among them the "Invectives contre les bûcherons de la forêt de Gastine" ("Elegy Against the Woodcutters of Gâtine"), lamenting the destruction of the woods near his old home, a sequel to *Les Amours de Marie*, and the *Sonnets pour Hélène*. In the latter, which is now perhaps the most famous of his collections, the poet demonstrates his power to revivify the stylized patterns of courtly love poetry. Even in his last illness, Ronsard wrote verse that is sophisticated in form and rich with classical allusions. His posthumous collection, *Les Derniers Vers*, poignantly expresses the anguish of the incurable invalid in nights spent alone in pain, longing for sleep, watching for the dawn, and praying for death.

Portrait after an engraving by
L. Gaultier, 1557
Copyright British Museum

Ronsard perfected the 12-syllable, or alexandrine, line of French verse, hitherto despised as too long and pedestrian, and established it as the classic medium for scathing satire, elegiac tenderness, and tragic passion. In his lifetime Ronsard was recognized as the prince of poets, as well as a figure of national significance. This prominence faded into relative neglect in the 17th and 18th centuries, but his reputation was reinstated by the Romantic critic C.-A. Sainte-Beuve and has remained secure.

Room of One's Own, A Essay by Virginia WOOLF, published in 1929. The work was based on two lectures given by the author in 1928 at Newnham College and Girton College, Cambridge.

Woolf addressed the status of women, and women artists in particular, in this famous essay which asserts that a woman must have money and a room of her own if she is to write.

Woolf celebrates the work of women writers, including Jane Austen, George Eliot, and the Brontës. In the final section Woolf suggests that great minds are androgynous. She argues that intellectual freedom requires financial freedom, and she entreats her audience to write not only fiction but poetry, criticism, and scholarly works as well. The essay, written in lively, graceful prose, displays the same impressive descriptive powers evident in Woolf's novels and reflects her compelling conversational style.

Room with a View, A Novel by E.M. FORSTER, published in 1908. Forster's keen observation of character informed the work, which reflected the author's criticism of restrictive conventional British society.

While on vacation in Italy, affluent young Lucy Honeychurch becomes attracted to passionate, vital George Emerson. Once they are back in England, however, Lucy becomes engaged to the dilettante Cecil Vyse, an emblem of bloodless English society. When the Emersons move to town, Lucy, still attracted to George, realizes that she does not love Cecil. Encouraged by George's father, and despite opposition from her own family, she marries George, and they spend their honeymoon in Italy, which represents freedom and passion.

Rootabaga Stories \\'rü-tə-,bä-gə, 'rut-ə-\\ Collection of children's stories by Carl SANDBURG, published in 1922. These fanciful tales reflect Sandburg's interest in folk ballads and nonsense verse. He modeled his expansive fictional land on the American Midwest. The lighthearted stories, referred to as moral tales by Sandburg, feature such silly characters as Hot Dog the Tiger, Gimme the Ax, White Horse Girl, Blue Wind Boy, and Jason Squiff the Cistern Cleaner. Succeeding books in the same vein include *Rootabaga Pigeons* (1923), *Rootabaga Country* (1929), and *Potato Face* (1930).

Roots (*in full* Roots: The Saga of an American Family) Book combining history and fiction, by Alex HALEY, published in 1976 and awarded a special Pulitzer Prize.

Beginning with stories recounted by his grandmother in Henning, Tenn., Haley spent 12 years tracing the saga of seven generations of his family, beginning with Kunta Kinte, his ancestor from Gambia who had been enslaved and brought to America in 1767. Through oral tradition, the descendants of Kunta Kinte kept alive the tales of their forebears.

Roots was a runaway best-seller. It was adapted for television in 1977, and the eight installments were some of television's most widely viewed programs. The success of *Roots* precipitated a nationwide resurgence of interest in all phases of genealogical research. African-Americans who had felt cut off from their origins and whose heritage seemed untraceable were inspired to attempt to fill in the gaps in their family history. However, later investigations of Haley's methods and attempts to duplicate his research cast serious doubts on the accuracy of his story. A pivotal character—the griot, or African oral historian, who knew the name Kunta Kinte—proved to be a fraud. Despite its faults, the book retains its emotional impact and its significance for African-American literature.

Rosalind \\'röz-ə-lind, 'räz-\\ Fictional character, daughter of the deposed Duke of the court in William Shakespeare's AS YOU LIKE IT. One of Shakespeare's most notable female characters, Rosalind is banished to the Forest of Arden by the Duke's usurping brother Frederick after she falls in love with Orlando, the son of one of Frederick's enemies. Orlando, who has fallen in love with Rosalind, is also banished from the court. Witty and intelligent, Rosalind disguises herself as a young man named Ganymede who ironically pretends to heal Orlando's love-struck heart. Rosalind eventually reveals herself and orchestrates four weddings, including her own marriage to Orlando.

Rosegger \\'rō-ˌzeg-ər, rō-'zeg-ər\\, Peter (b. July 31, 1843, Alpl, Austria—d. June 26, 1918, Krieglach) Austrian writer known for his novels describing provincial life.

Rosegger's first published work (1869) was a collection of poems in dialect, but he soon began to write mildly didactic stories and novels about the people, customs, and landscape of his native Styria. His most famous novels are *Waldheimat* (1877; *The Forest Farm*) and *Die Schriften des Waldschulmeisters* (1875; *The Forest Schoolmaster*). Always concerned with social reform, he especially favored the spread of rural education. His autobiographical and religious writings were widely read and include *Der Gottsucher* (1883; *The God-Seeker*) and *Mein Weltleben* (1898). His *Gesammelte Werke*, 40 vol. ("Collected Works"), appeared in 1914–16.

Rosenberg \\'rō-zən-bərg\\, Isaac (b. Nov. 25, 1890, Bristol, Gloucestershire, Eng.—d. April 1918, France) British poet and painter killed in World War I.

Rosenberg trained to be a painter at the Slade School of Art, London. He enlisted in the British army in 1915 and is best known for his "trench poems," written between 1916 and 1918, which showed great imaginative power and originality in imagery. His *Collected Works*, with a foreword by Siegfried Sassoon, first appeared in 1937; an edition by Ian Parsons, including poetry, prose, letters, paintings, and drawings, was published in 1979.

Rosencrantz and Guildenstern \\'rō-zən-ˌkrants . . . 'gil-dən-ˌstərn\\ Minor fictional characters, former schoolmates of Hamlet in William Shakespeare's HAMLET. King Claudius commissions Rosencrantz and Guildenstern to spy on Hamlet and sends all three to England, with Rosencrantz and Guildenstern bearing a warrant for Hamlet's death. Hamlet returns safely to Denmark after altering the orders so that Rosencrantz and Guildenstern are put to death in his place.

The pair are the central characters in Tom Stoppard's play *Rosencrantz and Guildenstern Are Dead* (produced 1966), in which they play games, tell jokes, and have philosophical discussions in the intervals of time between the scenes in which they figure in Shakespeare's play. *Rosencrantz and Guildenstern Are Dead* addresses such issues as free will, death, and personal identity, as the characters, though more fully developed than in the earlier play, are still often mistaken for one another. Though they are bewildered by their lives, they try to live them with dignity, and they ultimately accept their fate willingly.

Rosinante \\rō-sē-'nän-tā, *Angl* ˌräz-ə-'nan-tē\\ Fictional character, the spavined, half-starved horse that Don Quixote designates his noble steed in the classic novel DON QUIXOTE by Miguel de Cervantes.

Rosmersholm \\'ròs-mərs-ˌhòlm\\ Four-act play written by Henrik IBSEN, published in 1886 and performed in 1887.

The play's plot revolves around ex-parson Johannes Rosmer, a representative of high ethical standards, and his housekeeper, the adventuress Rebecca West. Both are haunted by the spirit of Rosmer's late wife, who committed suicide under the subtle influence, the reader learns, of Rebecca West and because of her husband's high-minded indifference to sex. At issue for the future is a choice between bold, unrestricted freedom and the ancient, conservative traditions of Rosmer's house. Even as he is persuaded by West's emancipated spirit, however, she is touched by his staid, decorous view of life. Each is contaminated by the other, and for differing but complementary reasons, they tempt one another toward the fatal millpond in which the wife drowned herself. The play ends with a double suicide. It is from this play that novelist Rebecca West (Cicily Fairfield) chose her pseudonym.

Ross \\'ròs\\, Martin. Pseudonym of Violet Florence Martin, one half of the team of SOMERVILLE AND ROSS.

Rossetti \\rō-'zet-ē, -'set-\\, Christina (Georgina), *pseudonym* Ellen Alleyne \\'al-in\\ (b. Dec. 5, 1830, London, Eng.— d. Dec. 29, 1894, London) One of the most important of English women poets in both range and the quality of her opus. She excelled in works of fantasy, poems for children, and religious poetry.

Detail of a chalk drawing by Dante Gabriel Rossetti, 1866

Harold Rossetti; photograph, N.J. Cotterell

Christina was the youngest child of Gabriele Rossetti and Lavinia Polidori and the sister of the painter-poet Dante Gabriel Rossetti. Her first book of poetry was printed privately in 1847. In 1850, under the pseudonym Ellen Alleyne, she contributed seven poems to the Pre-Raphaelite journal *The Germ*. In 1853, when the family was in financial trouble, Rossetti helped her mother keep a school at Frome, Somerset, but it was not a success, and in 1854 they returned to London, where Rossetti's father died. In straitened circumstances, she then entered on her life work of companionship to her mother, devotion to her religion, and the writing of poetry. She was a firm High Church Anglican, and in 1859 she broke her engagement to the artist James Collinson, an original member of the Pre-Raphaelite Brotherhood, because he had become a Roman Catholic. For similar reasons she rejected Charles Bagot Cayley in 1864, though they maintained a warm friendship.

In 1862 Rossetti published *Goblin Market and Other Poems* and in 1866 *The Prince's Progress and Other Poems*, both illustrated by her brother Dante Gabriel. These two collections contain most of her finest work—notably the poem GOBLIN MARKET—and they established her among the poets of her day. The stories in her first prose work, *Commonplace and Other Short Stories* (1870), are of no great merit, but *Sing-Song: a Nursery Rhyme Book* (1872; enlarged 1893) takes a high place among children's books of the 19th century.

In 1871 Rossetti was stricken by Graves' disease, a thyroid disorder that marred her looks and left her life in danger. She continued to publish, issuing one collection of poems in 1875 and *A Pageant and Other Poems* in 1881. After the onset of her illness, however, she wrote mostly devotional prose. *Time Flies* (1885), a reading diary of mixed verse and prose, is the most personal of these works. Rossetti was considered a possible successor to Alfred, Lord Tennyson as poet laureate, but she developed a fatal cancer in 1891. *New Poems* (1896), published by her brother after her death, contained unprinted and previously uncollected poems.

Part of Rossetti's success as a poet arises from her ability to unite the devotional and the passionate sides of her nature. Her weaker verse is sometimes sentimental and didactic, but at its best her poetry is strong, personal, and unforced, with a metrical cadence that is unmistakably her own. The transience of material things is a theme that recurs throughout her poetry, and the resigned but passionate sadness of unhappy love is often a dominant note.

Rossetti \rō-'zet-ē, -'set-\, Dante Gabriel \'dan-tē-'gā-brē-əl\, *original name* Gabriel Charles Dante Rossetti (b. May 12, 1828, London, Eng.—d. April 9, 1882, Birchington-on-Sea, Kent) English painter and poet who helped found the Pre-Raphaelite Brotherhood.

By the time he was 20, Rossetti had already completed a number of translations of Italian poets and had composed original verse in English. He was also an art student and for a short time was a pupil of the painter Ford Madox Brown. He acquired from Brown an admiration for the German "Pre-Raphaelites," who had sought to bring back into German art a pre-Renaissance purity of style and aim. Rossetti initiated a similar reform in England when, largely through his efforts, the English Pre-Raphaelite Brotherhood was formed in 1848. Two years later his "The Blessed Damozel," with six sonnets and four lyrics, was published in *The Germ*, the Pre-Raphaelite periodical (1850).

In his paintings Rossetti progressed from traditional religious themes to scenes from William Shakespeare, Robert Browning, and Dante, which allowed more freedom of imaginative treatment. After 1856 he was led by Sir Thomas Malory's *Le Morte Darthur* and Alfred, Lord Tennyson's *Idylls of the King* to evoke an imaginary Arthurian epoch.

Although the Pre-Raphaelite movement was on the wane by the mid-1850s, two new disciples, Edward Burne-Jones and William Morris, initiated a second phase. This fresh departure brought a romantic enthusiasm for a legendary past and the ambition of reforming the applied arts of design. A new era of book decoration was foreshadowed by Rossetti's illustration for the Moxon edition of Tennyson's *Poems* (1857).

Rossetti enjoyed a modest success in 1861 with his published translations, *The Early Italian Poets*. When his wife of two years, the beautiful model Elizabeth Siddal, died of an overdose of laudanum in 1862, Rossetti buried the only complete manuscript of his poems with her. The manuscript was later recovered and was published in 1870. His later writings include *Ballads and Sonnets* (1881), containing the sonnet sequence "The House of Life," and a revised edition of *Poems* (1881).

Rossetti \rō-'zet-ē, -'set-\, Gabriele (Pasquale Giuseppe) (b. Feb. 28, 1783, Vasto, Kingdom of Naples [Italy]—d. April 24, 1854, London, Eng.) Italian poet, revolutionary, and scholar, remembered for his esoteric interpretation of Dante but best known as the father of several talented children.

Rossetti studied at the University of Naples and in 1807 was librettist at the San Carlo opera house in Naples. He was later appointed curator of a Naples museum.

He frequently improvised spirited verses on contemporary politics; one indignant outburst directed against Ferdinand II

(the tyrant king of Naples who had revoked the constitution in 1821), added to Rossetti's membership in the revolutionary society Carbonari, prompted a sentence of death. After a time in hiding, he escaped to England via Malta in 1824. There he supported himself by giving Italian lessons, and in 1831 he was appointed professor of Italian at King's College, London, a post he held until 1847.

When Rossetti became professor, he received fellow exiles, busied himself with propaganda for a liberally governed and united Italy, and elaborated a theory of the Italian poet Dante's profound symbolic meaning (*La Beatrice di Dante*, 1842). His love of Italian poetry and in particular his reverence for Dante's *La vita nuova* and *La divina commedia* were transmitted to his sons and daughters.

In 1826 he had married Frances Mary Lavinia Polidori, daughter of another Italian teacher and man of letters, Gaetano Polidori. There were four Rossetti children: Maria Francesca (b. Feb. 17, 1827—d. Nov. 24, 1876); Gabriel Charles Dante, who later called himself Dante Gabriel; William Michael; and Christina Georgina. The Rossetti family was a remarkable group. All of its members were endowed with unusual intelligence and creative gifts, were equally at home with the languages and literary traditions of both England and Italy, and were united among themselves by close ties of affection and mutual understanding.

Rossetti \rō-'zet-ē, -'set-\, William Michael (b. Sept. 25, 1829, London, Eng.—d. Feb. 5, 1919, London) English art critic, literary editor, and man of letters, brother of Dante Gabriel and Christina Rossetti.

Rossetti was in many ways a contrast to his more flamboyant brother—in his calm and rational outlook, financial prudence, and lack of egotism, for example. At the age of 16 he became a clerk in the Excise (later Inland Revenue) Office at £80 a year and a mainstay of the entire Rossetti family. His appointment as art critic to *The Spectator* magazine in 1850 and subsequent modest advancement in the civil service enabled him, in 1854, to establish his father, mother, and two sisters in a more comfortable home. In 1874 he married Emma Lucy, the daughter of the painter Ford Madox Brown. He retired from the Inland Revenue Office in 1894.

William Michael had literary interests almost as varied as those of the more talented Dante Gabriel. He was an early member of the Pre-Raphaelite Brotherhood and served as editor of its journal, *The Germ*. He edited the collected works of Christina (1904) and Dante Gabriel (1911) and wrote *D. G. Rossetti: a Memoir with Family Letters* (1895). He dealt conscientiously with a vast amount of family correspondence and material related to Pre-Raphaelism and his brother's place in the movement, proving himself an indispensable chronicler in such publications as *Preraphaelite Letters and Diaries* (1900) and *Ruskin, Rossetti, Preraphaelitism: Papers 1854–62* (1899). Rossetti was also an astute and independent-minded critic; he hailed Walt Whitman's controversial *Leaves of Grass* (1855) as a work of genius and introduced the poet to British readers with a selection of his poems in 1868. He was also an early admirer of William Blake, producing an edition of his *Poetical Works* in 1874, and he published studies of Dante and other medieval poets, both Italian and English.

Rostand \rȯ-'stäⁿ\, Edmond(-Eugène) (b. April 1, 1868, Marseille, Fr.—d. Dec. 2, 1918, Paris) French dramatist best known for his play CYRANO DE BERGERAC (1898), which represents a final, belated example of Romantic drama in France.

Rostand published poems and essays and wrote plays for puppet theater before his first play, a one-act farce entitled *Le Gant rouge* (*The Red Glove*), was performed in 1888. He continued to write poetry and drama, and in 1894 his first successful play, *Les Romanesques* (*The Romancers* or *The Fantasticks*), was produced. His most popular and enduring work was the heroic comedy *Cyrano de Bergerac*. (The connection between the Cyrano of the play and the 17th-century writer of the same name is purely nominal.) The plot revolves around the gallant Cyrano, who, despite his many gifts, feels that no woman can ever love him because of his enormous nose. First performed in Paris in 1897, *Cyrano* made a great impression in France and throughout Europe and the United States.

Rostand wrote a good deal for the theater, but the only other play of his that is still much remembered is *L'Aiglon* (1900; "The Eaglet"). This highly emotional patriotic tragedy in six acts centers on Napoleon's son, the Duke of Reichstadt, who never ruled and died of tuberculosis as a virtual prisoner in Austria. Sarah Bernhardt played the title role during its first run in 1900. Rostand was elected to the Académie Française in 1901. After *L'Aiglon*, Rostand wrote only two more plays, *Chantecler* (1910) and *La Dernière Nuit de Don Juan* (*The Last Night of Don Juan*), published posthumously in 1921.

Rosten \'ròs-tən\, Leo (Calvin), *pseudonym* Leonard Q. Ross \'ròs\ (b. April 11, 1908, Łódź [Poland])   Polish-born American author and social scientist best known for his popular books on Yiddish and for his comic novels concerning the immigrant night-school student Hyman Kaplan.

At age three Rosten immigrated with his parents to Chicago. After working as a screenwriter and having a series of wartime government-information jobs, he joined the staff of *Look* magazine in New York in 1949, where he worked until 1971; he also lectured at Columbia University.

In 1937 Rosten (as Leonard Q. Ross) published *The Education of H*Y*M*A*N K*A*P*L*A*N*; the book, based on the author's experiences teaching English to immigrants, is full of puns and malapropisms based on the fractured English of the cherubic, naive Kaplan, for whom the plural of "sandwich" is "delicatessen." It was acclaimed for its high spirits and its comic mastery of Yiddish-inflected English. Two sequels, *The Return of H*Y*M*A*N K*A*P*L*A*N* (1959) and *O K*A*P*L*A*N! My K*A*P*L*A*N!* (1976), were not as well received.

While at *Look*, Rosten edited a series of articles that formed the basis of *A Guide to the Religions of America* (1955), noted for its readability and scholarly accuracy. *The Story Behind the Painting* (1962), a respected popular art-history book, also grew from a magazine assignment. Rosten enjoyed instant success with *The Joys of Yiddish* (1968), a comic dictionary of Yiddish words and their many nuances, which he expanded in *The Joys of Yinglish* (1989).

Rostov family \,rə-'stòf\   Fictional characters, members of one of the central families in the epic novel WAR AND PEACE by Leo Tolstoy.

The Rostov family is headed by the Count, a well-meaning but ineffectual nobleman who manages his business affairs poorly. The Countess, who arranges advantageous marriages for her children, is pretentious and shallow. The eldest daughter, Vera, is rigid and formal. By contrast, her sister Natasha is a beautiful young woman of great personal charm. The older son, Nikolay, is a handsome and principled man who loves his impoverished cousin Sonya but accedes to pressure to find a wealthy, titled bride. The romantic younger son, Petya, is swept away by patriotic fervor and dies a pointless death in an unnecessary military encounter.

Roswitha   *see* HROSVITHA.

Roth \'ròth\, Henry (b. Feb. 8, 1906, Tysmenica, Galicia, Austria-Hungary [now Tismenitsya, Ukraine])   American teacher and author whose novel CALL IT SLEEP (1934) is consid-

ered one of the neglected masterpieces of American literature of the 1930s.

Roth graduated from the City College of New York. *Call It Sleep* appeared in 1934 to laudatory reviews and sold 4,000 copies before it went out of print and was apparently forgotten. In the late 1950s and '60s, however, Alfred Kazin, Irving Howe, and other American literary figures revived public interest in the book, which came to be recognized as a classic of Jewish-American literature and as an important proletarian novel of the 1930s. Although he attempted to write a second novel shortly after finishing the first and several of his short stories were printed in *The New Yorker*, Roth published no more novels until 1994. He began writing again in the late 1960s, and *Shifting Landscape: A Composite, 1925–87*, a collection of short stories and essays, appeared in 1987. His novels *Mercy of a Rude Stream* (1994) and *A Diving Rock on the Hudson* (1995) were the initial offerings of a projected six-volume work that returned to the themes of *Call it Sleep*.

Roth \'ròt\, Joseph (b. Sept. 2, 1894, Brody, Galicia, Austria-Hungary [now in Ukraine]—d. May 27, 1939, Paris, Fr.)   Journalist and regional novelist who mourned the passing of an age of stability he saw represented by the last pre-World War I years of the Habsburg empire of Austria-Hungary.

Details about Roth's early years and personal life are little known; Roth himself made a practice of concealing or transforming such biographical information. It is known that he studied at Lemberg (now Lviv, Ukraine) and Vienna and then served in the Austrian army from 1916 to 1918. After the war he worked as a journalist in Vienna and Berlin and was a regular contributor to the *Frankfurter Zeitung*. During this period he wrote several novels, including *Radetzkymarsch* (1932; *Radetzky March*), considered his best novel, an excellent portrait of the latter days of the Habsburg monarchy. Roth was concerned with the dilemma of individual moral heroes in a time of decadence and moribund traditions. Many of his plots treat the difficulties of the father-son relationship. In his final years he viewed the past with increasing nostalgia, a sentiment evident in the six novels written during a period of exile. *Die Kapuzinergruft* (1938; "The Capuchin Tomb") is an example. *Der stumme Prophet* (1966; *The Silent Prophet*), the story of a failed revolutionary, was written in 1929.

Roth \'ròth\, Philip (Milton) (b. March 19, 1933, Newark, N.J., U.S.)   American novelist and short-story writer whose works are characterized by an acute ear for dialogue, a concern with Jewish middle-class life, and the painful entanglements of sexual and familial love.

Roth attended the University of Chicago. He first achieved fame with *Goodbye Columbus* (1959), whose title story candidly depicts the boorish materialism of a Jewish middle-class suburban family. Roth's first novel, *Letting Go* (1962), was followed in 1967 by *When She Was Good*, but he did not recapture the success of his first book until PORTNOY'S COMPLAINT (1969). Several minor works, including *The Breast* (1972) and *The Professor of Desire* (1977), were followed by one of Roth's most important novels, *The Ghost Writer* (1979), centering on an aspiring young writer named Nathan Zuckerman. Roth's two subsequent novels, *Zuckerman Unbound* (1981) and *The Anatomy Lesson* (1983), trace his writer-protagonist's subsequent life and career. The three novels were republished together with the novella *The Prague Orgy* under the title *Zuckerman Bound* (1985). A fourth novel in the series, *The Counterlife*, was published in 1986. In 1993 Roth published *Operation Shylock*, a book in which a narrator named Philip Roth has several adventures, including meeting his double (who also calls himself Philip Roth) in Jerusalem.

Rotimi \rō-'tē-mē\, Ola, *byname of* Emmanuel Gladstone Olawale Rotimi (b. April 13, 1938, Sapele, Nigeria)   Nigerian scholar, playwright, and director.

Rotimi was educated in Port Harcourt and Lagos in Nigeria before going to the United States to study at Boston and Yale universities. Upon returning to Nigeria, he taught at the universities of Ife and Port Harcourt.

His first plays—*To Stir the God of Iron* (produced 1963) and *Our Husband Has Gone Mad Again* (produced 1966)—were staged at the drama schools of Boston University and Yale, respectively. His later dramas include *The Gods Are Not To Blame* (produced 1968), a retelling of the Oedipus myth in imagistic blank verse; *Kurunmi* and *The Prodigal* (produced 1969), written for the second Ife Festival of Arts; *Ovonramwen Nogbaisi* (produced 1971), about the last ruler of the Benin empire; and *Holding Talks* (produced 1979). Later plays, such as *If* (1983) and *Hopes of the Living Dead* (1988), premiered at the University of Port Harcourt. The radio play *Everyone His/Her Own Problem* was broadcast in 1987.

Rotrou \rō-'trü\, Jean de (baptized Aug. 21, 1609, Dreux, Fr.—d. June 28, 1650, Dreux)   One of the major French Neoclassical playwrights of the first half of the 17th century. He shares with Pierre Corneille the credit for the increased prestige and respectability that the theater gradually came to enjoy in Paris at the time.

Rotrou wrote his first play, the comedy *L'Hypocondriaque* ("The Hypochondriac"), before he was 20. He soon won Cardinal de Richelieu's support and became house dramatist at the Hôtel de Bourgogne, the most important theater in Paris. Rotrou's best plays owe much of their vigor and exuberance to the tradition of the tragicomedy, the favorite dramatic form in the 1630s. For his tragedies, Rotrou favored stories about characters who must resolve moral conflicts within themselves. These works are marked by closely knit plots and powerful rhetoric. Rotrou also showed an interest in illusion and surprisingly violent change, characteristics typical of Baroque drama, in such works as *Le Véritable Saint-Genest* (1647). Rotrou's best-known tragedies are *Venceslas* (1648) and *Cosroès* (1649).

Rouge et le noir, Le \lə-rūzh-ā-lə-'nwȧr\   *see* THE RED AND THE BLACK.

Roughing It   Semiautobiographical novel by Mark TWAIN, published in 1872. This humorous travel book, based on Twain's stagecoach journey through the American West and his adventures in the Pacific islands, is full of colorful caricatures of outlandish locals and detailed sketches of frontier life.

Roughing It describes how the narrator, a polite greenhorn from the East, is initiated into the rough-and-tumble society of the frontier. He works his way through Nevada, California, and the Pacific islands as a prospector, journalist, and lecturer, and along the way he meets a number of colorful characters.

Rougon-Macquart cycle \rü-ˌgȯⁿ-mȧ-'kär\   Sequence of 20 novels by Émile ZOLA, published between 1871 and 1893. The cycle is described in a subtitle as *The Natural and Social History of a Family Under the Second Empire*; it is a documentary of French life as seen through the lives of the violent Rougon family and the passive Macquarts, who are related to each other through the character of Tante Dide.

The series began with *La Fortune des Rougon* (1871; *The Rougon Family*; also translated as *The Fortune of the Rougons*), which introduces the Rougons (the legitimate branch) and the Macquarts (the illegitimate and lower-class branch). Zola examines the impact of environment by varying the social, economic, and professional milieu in which each novel takes place. *La Curée* (1872; *The Kill*), for example, explores the land speculation and financial dealings that accompanied the renovation

of Paris during the Second Empire. *Le Ventre de Paris* (1873; *Savage Paris*; also translated as *The Fat and the Thin*) examines the structure of the Halles, the vast central marketplace of Paris. *Son Excellence Eugène Rougon* (1876; *His Excellency Eugène Rougon*) traces the machinations and maneuverings of cabinet officials in Napoleon III's government.

L'Assommoir (1877; *Drunkard*), which is among the most successful and enduringly popular of Zola's novels, shows the effects of alcoholism in a working-class neighborhood by focusing on a laundress, Gervaise Macquart. NANA (1880) follows the life of Gervaise's daughter as her economic circumstances and hereditary penchants lead her to a career as an actress, then a courtesan. *Au Bonheur des dames* (1883; *Ladies' Delight*) depicts the mechanisms of a new economic entity, the department store, and its impact on smaller merchants.

Germinal (1885), which is generally acknowledged to be Zola's masterpiece, depicts life in a mining community by highlighting relations between the bourgeoisie and the working class. A quite different work, *L'Oeuvre* (1886; *The Masterpiece*), explores the milieu of the art world and the relationships among the arts through an examination of the friendship between an Impressionist painter, Claude Lantier, and a naturalist novelist, Pierre Sandoz.

In *La Terre* (1887; *Earth*) Zola shows what he considered to be the sordid lust for land among the French peasantry. In *La Bête humaine* (1890; *The Human Beast*) he analyzes the hereditary urge to kill that haunts the Lantier branch of the family. *La Débâcle* (1892; *The Debacle*) traces both the defeat of the French army by the Germans at the Battle of Sedan in 1870 and the anarchist uprising of the Paris Commune. Finally, in *Le Docteur Pascal* (1893; *Doctor Pascal*) he uses the main character, the doctor Pascal Rougon, to expound the theories of heredity underlying the entire series.

The other novels of the series are *La Conquête de Plassans* (1874; *The Conquest of Plassans*), *La Faute de L'abbé Mouret* (1875; *The Sin of Father Mouret*), *Une Page d'amour* (1878; *A Love Affair*), *Pot-Bouille* (1882; "Steaming Cauldron"; translated under a number of titles, including *Restless House*), *La Joie de vivre* (1884; *Zest for Life*), *Le Rêve* (1888; *The Dream*), and *L'Argent* (1891; *Money*).

Roumanille \rü-mȧ-'nē\, Joseph (b. Aug. 8, 1818, Saint-Remy-de-Provence, Fr.—d. May 24, 1891, Avignon)   Provençal poet and teacher, a founder and leader of the FÉLIBRIGE, a movement dedicated to the restoration and maintenance of Provençal language, literature, and customs; it stimulated the renaissance of the language and customs of the whole of southern France.

Roumanille was both a writer and a scholar of Provençal. His standardization of the orthography of the Provençal language, which he set forth in the introduction to his play *La Part dou bon Dieu* (1853), was considered the first attempt to regularize spelling and usage in the language. Working with Frédéric Mistral, Roumanille then began standardizing Provençal grammar. In 1854 the two, together with five other Provençal poets, founded Félibrige. The following year they established the annual *Armana Prouvençau* ("Provençal Almanac"). Roumanille also wrote many works of poetry and prose in Provençal, including the poems of *Li Margarideto* (1847; "The Daisies") and *Li Flour de Sauvi* (1859; "The Sage Flowers").

round character   *see* FLAT AND ROUND CHARACTERS.

rounded \'raůn-dəd\   Conceived, drawn, or presented in full form or in all aspects; shown perceptively or penetratingly; or comprehensively realized.

roundel or **roundle** \'raůn-dəl\ [Old French *rondel* rondel] An English modified rondeau, an 11-line poem in three stanzas.

The 4th and 11th lines constitute a refrain taken from the first part of the first line of the poem.

Used by its earliest practitioners as a synonym for rondel or rondeau, the term was appropriated by Algernon Swinburne, who in 1883 published a work entitled *A Century of Roundels*.

roundelay \'raún-də-,lā, 'rän-\ [modification of Middle French *rondelet* rondelet] A poem with a refrain that recurs frequently or at fixed intervals, as in a rondel. The term is also loosely used to refer to any of the fixed forms of poetry (such as the rondeau, the rondel, and the roundel) that use refrains extensively.

Round Table In Arthurian legend, the table of Arthur, Britain's legendary king, first mentioned in Wace of Jersey's *Roman de Brut* (1155). Wace reported that King Arthur had a round table made so that none of his barons, when seated at it, could claim precedence over the others.

The literary importance of the Round Table, especially in romances of the 13th century and afterward, lies in the fact that it served to provide the knights of Arthur's court with a name and a collective personality. The fellowship of the Round Table, in fact, became comparable to, and in many respects the prototype of, the many great orders of chivalry that were founded in Europe during the late Middle Ages.

In Robert de Boron's poem *Joseph d'Arimathie* (c. 1200), the Grail, which had been sought by the hero Perceval, was identified as the vessel used by Christ at the Last Supper. Joseph was commanded to make a table in commemoration of the Last Supper and to leave one place vacant. The vacant place symbolized the seat of Judas, who had betrayed Christ. This empty place, called the Siege Perilous, could not be occupied without peril except by the destined Grail hero. During the 13th century, when the Grail theme was fully integrated with Arthurian legend in the group of prose romances known as the Vulgate cycle and post-Vulgate romances, writers established that the Round Table—modeled on the Grail Table and, likewise, with an empty place—had been made by the enchanter and wise man Merlin for Uther Pendragon, Arthur's father. The table came into the possession of King Leodegrance of Carmeliardd, who gave it to Arthur as part of the dowry of his daughter Guinevere when she married Arthur. Admission to the fellowship of the Round Table was reserved to the most valiant, while the Siege Perilous was left waiting for the coming of Galahad, the pure knight who achieved the quest of the Grail and helped to bring the marvels of Arthur's kingdom to a close.

Rousseau \rü-'sō\, Jean-Baptiste (b. April 6, 1671, Paris, Fr.—d. March 17, 1741, Brussels, Belg.) French dramatist and poet who enjoyed great popularity in the witty Parisian society of his day.

Rousseau as a young man showed a talent for satiric verse. He later attempted to produce several of his comedies, *Le Café* (1694), *Le Flatteur* (1696; "The Flatterer"), and *Le Capricieux* (1700). His *Cantates* (1703; "Cantatas"), lyrics meant to be sung, comprised a type of chamber opera. His *Odes sacrées* (1702; "Sacred Odes") were better regarded. In 1710 he became embroiled in "the affair of the couplets" and was convicted of defamation for a satirical verse that he claimed (probably truthfully) he had never written, and he was exiled for life. He eventually died in extreme poverty in Brussels after 29 years in exile.

Rousseau \rü-'sō\, Jean-Jacques (b. June 28, 1712, Geneva, Switz.—d. July 2, 1778, Ermenonville, Fr.) French philosopher, writer, and political theorist whose treatises and novels inspired the leaders of the French Revolution and the Romantic generation.

After a Calvinist childhood, Rousseau immigrated to Turin, Italy, and became a Roman Catholic. In the late 1740s and early 1750s Rousseau devoted much of his energy to music. His opera *Le Devin du village* (1752; *The Cunning-Man*) was performed to great acclaim at Fontainebleau. Rousseau soon met Denis Diderot, who was to have a profound influence on him. Indeed, it was Diderot who encouraged Rousseau to write the essay *Discours sur les sciences et les arts* (1750; *Discourse on the Sciences and the Arts*), which won him fame. The essay was a bold attack on the arts as instruments of propaganda and sources of wealth in the hands of the rich. He followed this work with *Discours sur l'origine de l'inegalité* (1755; *Discourse on the Origin of Inequality*), in which he gave a hypothetical description of man's natural state, proposing that, although unequally gifted by nature in individual endowments, men at one time were in fact equal, but they remained so only when they lived apart from one another; inequality arose when men began to form societies and to compete with one another.

Rousseau visited his native Geneva in 1754, reverted to Protestantism, and renewed his citizenship rights. In 1756 he moved from Paris to Montmorency, where he began work on the novel *Julie; ou, la nouvelle Héloïse* (1761; *Julie; or, The New Eloise*), which became enormously popular. His four-volume novel *Émile; ou, De l'éducation* (1762; *Emile; or, On Education*) and the essay *Du Contrat social* (1762; *The Social Contract*), in which he discussed the idea of the *volonté général*, or general will, were both condemned by the Parlement of Paris. Rousseau was forced to seek asylum in Switzerland, which provoked Voltaire to write *Le Sentiment des citoyens* (1764; "The Feeling of the Citizens"). After renouncing his citizenship, Rousseau moved to England for a year but quarrelled with his benefactor David Hume and returned to France incognito in 1767. To justify himself he began writing his autobiography, *Confessions*, which was published posthumously in 1782–89.

rove-over \'rōv-,ō-vər\ Having an extrametrical syllable at the end of one line that forms a foot with the first syllable of the next line. The term is used of a type of verse in sprung rhythm, Gerard Manley Hopkins' method of counting only the stressed syllables of a line. Thus, the meter of a verse is determined by feet of varying length but always having the accent on the first syllable. The third and fourth lines of Hopkins' "Spring and Fall" (here shown for the sake of clarity without Hopkins' own accent marks) are an example of rove-over:

> Leaves, like the things of man, you
> With your fresh thoughts care for, can you?

Rover, The (*in full* The Rover; or, The Banish't Cavaliers) Comedy by Aphra BEHN, produced and published in two parts in 1677 and 1681. Set in Madrid and Naples during the exile of England's King Charles II, the play depicts the adventures of a small group of English Cavaliers. The protagonist, the charming but irresponsible Willmore, may have been modeled on John Wilmot Rochester, a poet in the inner circle of Charles II; the hero's real-life counterpart may also have been John Hoyle, who was a lover of the playwright.

row \'rō\ *obsolete* A written line, especially a metrical written line.

Rowe \'rō\, Nicholas (b. June 20, 1674, Little Barford, Bedfordshire, Eng.—d. Dec. 6, 1718, London) English writer who was the first to attempt a critical edition of the works of William Shakespeare. He succeeded Nahum Tate as poet laureate in 1715 and was also the foremost 18th-century English tragic dramatist, doing much to assist the rise of domestic tragedy (in which the protagonists were middle class rather than aristocratic).

Rowe's early plays, *The Ambitious Step-Mother* (1700) and *Tamerlane* (1702), are reminiscent of John Dryden's heroic drama in their pomp and bluster, but they contain elements that point the way to the spirit of sentiment that characterizes *The Fair Penitent* (1703) and later works. This latter play is of some literary significance; its hero, Lothario, was apparently the prototype of Lovelace, the hero of Samuel Richardson's novel *Clarissa*. Rowe composed *The Tragedy of Jane Shore* (1714) and *The Tragedy of the Lady Jane Grey* (1715) in imitation of Shakespeare's style. His only comedy, *The Biter* (1704), was a failure.

In *The Works of Mr. William Shakespear; Revis'd and Corrected*, 6 vol. (1709; 9 vol., including poems, 1714), Rowe mainly followed the fourth folio edition of 1685. He did, however, restore some passages in *Hamlet, Romeo and Juliet, Henry V*, and *King Lear* from early texts. He abandoned the clumsy folio format (a 9 × 12-inch page size), gave lists of characters in the plays, attempted act and scene divisions, and supplied a life of Shakespeare. Rowe's own poetic output included occasional odes and some translations. His version of Lucan's *Pharsalia*, in heroic couplets, published posthumously in 1718, was greatly admired throughout the 18th century.

Rowley \'rō-lē\, Samuel (fl. 1597–*c.* 1633?)   English dramatist apparently employed by the theatrical manager Philip Henslowe. Sometimes he is described as William Rowley's brother, but they seem not to have been related.

After 1601 Rowley acted with and wrote plays for the Admiral's Men and other companies. Several plays on which he is thought to have collaborated are lost. His *When You See Me, You Know Me, or The famous Chronicle Historie of King Henrie the Eight* (probably performed 1604; published 1605) resembles William Shakespeare's *Henry VIII* (which may have been influenced by it) in owing something to popular tradition. His only other extant play, *The Noble Souldier. Or, A Contract Broken, Justly Reveng'd*, a tragedy (1634), was probably written largely by Thomas Dekker. Rowley has also been credited with the prose scenes in some of Shakespeare's plays, and he is thought to have made some additions to Christopher Marlowe's *Doctor Faustus*.

Rowley \'rō-lē\, William (b. 1585?, London, Eng.—d. 1642?) English dramatist and actor who collaborated with several Jacobean dramatists, notably Thomas Middleton.

Rowley became an actor before 1610. He met Middleton about 1614, though he had been writing plays for his company for at least a year. Of some 50 plays known to have been written by Rowley alone or in collaboration, comparatively few are extant. The most important of those by Rowley alone is *All's Lost by Lust* (performed 1619; published 1633), a romantic tragedy with a strong strain of dramatic morality, written in harsh but powerful verse. His other extant plays are comedies and include *A New Wonder, A Woman Never Vext* (*c.* 1610; published 1632), *A Match at Mid-Night* (*c.* 1607; published 1633), and *A Shoo-maker a Gentleman* (*c.* 1608; published 1638). Plays written with Middleton include *The Old Law* (1618?; published 1656), on which Philip Massinger also collaborated; *A Faire Quarrell* (*c.* 1616; published 1617) and *The Changeling* (1622; published 1653), in both of which Rowley wrote the subplot and helped with the plan of the whole; *Wit at Several Weapons* (*c.* 1616), incorrectly attributed to John Fletcher; and *The World Tost at Tennis* (1620).

Other plays in which Rowley collaborated are *Fortune by Land and Sea* (*c.* 1609) with Thomas Heywood; *The Witch of Edmonton* (1621) with Thomas Dekker and John Ford; *The Maid in the Mill* (1623) with Fletcher; and *The Birth of Merlin, or: The Child Hath Found His Father* (1662), the title page of which wrongly attributes part authorship to William Shakespeare.

Rowse \'raús\, A.L. *in full* Alfred Leslie (b. Dec. 4, 1903, St. Austell, Cornwall, Eng.)   English historian and writer who became one of the 20th century's foremost authorities on Elizabethan England.

Rowse attended Christ Church College, Oxford. In 1925 he was elected a fellow of All Souls College, Oxford, where he lived and worked for the next 49 years as a teacher and historian.

Rowse's first book to attract attention, *Sir Richard Grenville of the Revenge* (1937), was a biography of an English naval commander during the time of Queen Elizabeth I. This was followed by *Tudor Cornwall* (1941), a vivid and highly detailed portrait of Cornish society in the 16th century. Rowse's most important work is the historical trilogy *The Elizabethan Age*, comprising *The England of Elizabeth* (1950), *The Expansion of Elizabethan England* (1955), and *The Elizabethan Renaissance* (1971–72). These volumes treat the social structure, overseas exploration, and cultural attitudes and achievements of England during Elizabeth's reign.

Rowse became a controversial Shakespearean scholar with his biography *Shakespeare the Man* (1973) and an annotated edition of the playwright's complete works (1978). He wrote several other biographies, many volumes of poetry, and a multivolume autobiography.

Rowson \'raú-sən\, Susanna, *original surname* Haswell \'haz-wel\ (b. *c.* 1762, Portsmouth, Hampshire, Eng.—d. March 2, 1824, Boston, Mass., U.S.)   English-born American actress, educator, and author of the first American best-seller, *Charlotte Temple*. The novel, a conventional, sentimental story of seduction and remorse, was immensely popular after its publication in 1791 and went through more than 200 editions.

In 1792 she went on the stage with her husband, William Rowson. They performed in Scotland and in Philadelphia, Baltimore, and Boston. Rowson also wrote numerous plays and musicals, promoting the development of the performing arts in the United States.

Among her other works are novels, including *Rebecca, or the Fille de Chambre* (1792); theatrical works, such as *Slaves in Algiers* (1794); and textbooks, such as *A Spelling Dictionary* (1807) and *Biblical Dialogues Between a Father and His Family* (1822).

Roxana \räk-'san-ə, -'sän-\   Novel by Daniel DEFOE, published in 1724 as *The Fortunate Mistress*. It was Defoe's last major work of fiction. Because of its realism, it is considered one of the prototypes of the modern novel.

The protagonist and narrator Mlle Beleau is an ambitious courtesan who later assumes the name Roxana. When her husband deserts her after squandering their money, she becomes her landlord's mistress. Both she and her devoted maid Amy have a child by him. After the landlord is murdered, she takes a series of lovers and then marries a Dutch merchant, in the process gaining and losing a fortune.

Roxane \rŏk-'sän, *Angl* räk-'san\   Fictional character, the beautiful, much-admired woman in CYRANO DE BERGERAC by Edmond Rostand.

Roy \'rwá\, Camille, *in full* Joseph Camille Roy (b. Oct. 22, 1870, Berthier-en-Bas, Que., Can.—d. June 24, 1943, Quebec) Critic and literary historian, noted as an authority on the development of French-Canadian literature.

Ordained a Roman Catholic priest in 1894, Roy received a doctorate from Catholic University in Paris. He taught French literature at Laval University in Quebec and then became a professor of Canadian literature. His many significant studies were based on the premise that the purpose of Canadian literature is to preserve the Christian heritage of 18th-century France while remaining untouched by contemporary French influence. These works include *Nos origines littéraires* (1909; "Our Literary Origins") and the standard text *Manuel d'histoire de la littérature canadienne-française* (1918; 10th edition, 1945; "Handbook of the History of French-Canadian Literature").

Roy \'rwȧ\, Gabrielle, *married name* Charbotte \shȧr-'bȯt\ (b. March 22, 1909, St. Boniface, Man., Can.—d. July 13, 1983, Quebec, Que.)   French-Canadian novelist praised for her skill in depicting the hopes and frustrations of the poor.

Roy taught school for a time, studied drama in Europe (1937–39), then returned to Canada and began her writing career. Her studies of poverty-stricken working-class people in cities include *Bonheur d'occasion* (1945; *The Tin Flute*) and *Alexandre Chenevert* (1954; *The Cashier*). Some of her novels, such as *La Petite Poule d'eau* (1950; *Where Nests the Water-Hen*) and *Rue Deschambault* (1955; *Street of Riches*), deal with isolated rural life in Manitoba. She also wrote a book of semiautobiographical stories, *La Route d'Altamont* (1966; *The Road Past Altamont*), and a novel based on her experiences as a schoolteacher, *Ces enfants de ma vie* (1977; *Children of My Heart*).

Royal Shakespeare Company *former name* (until 1961) Shakespeare Memorial Company.   Important English theatrical company, established in 1879 and currently based in Stratford-upon-Avon and in London. The repertoire of the original Stratford-based part of the company consists of works by William Shakespeare and other Elizabethan and Jacobean playwrights, while the newer London-based unit performs modern plays and non-Shakespearean classics.

Rozanov \'rō-zə-nəf\, Vasily Vasilyevich (b. April 20 [May 2, New Style], 1856, Vetluga, Russia—d. Feb. 5, 1919, Moscow) Russian writer known for his unorthodox religious ideas and for the exceptional originality and individuality of his prose works.

Rozanov studied at the University of Moscow, and for a while he taught. About 1880 he married Apollinaria Suslova, former mistress of the novelist Fyodor Dostoyevsky. He attracted attention in 1890 with a critical analysis of the "Legend of the Grand Inquisitor" chapter in *The Brothers Karamazov*, the first study in depth of Dostoyevsky's work.

During the 1880s Rozanov lived in St. Petersburg and wrote many works on religious issues, attacking Christianity for its asceticism and its emphasis on sorrow and renunciation. He advocated a naturalistic religion of sex and procreation. As a Slavophile, however, he was not accepted by the modernist literary groups, and his writings are frequently marred by an egregious anti-Semitism.

In 1899 Rozanov began writing for the conservative paper *Novoye vremya* ("New Time"); it was as a permanent contributor to this publication that he developed his characteristic fragmentary style. The Revolution of 1905 won his enthusiastic support, and for a time he wrote radical articles for the progressive publication *Russkoye slovo* ("Russian Word") under the pseudonym V. Vavarin while continuing to publish conservative articles in *Novoye vremya* under his real name. In 1912 he published the work most representative of his mature genius, *Uyedinyonnoye* ("Solitary Thoughts"; *Solitaria*). Described as a collection of maxims and short essays, it is more than that, for it evokes the intonations of a living voice, eloquent, rhythmic, and original. Shortly after the start of the Revolution of 1917, Rozanov settled in a monastery near Moscow, where he died in poverty but reconciled with the Orthodox church.

Różewicz \rū-'zhe-vᵊech\, Tadeusz (b. Oct. 9, 1921, Radomsko, Pol.)   Polish poet and playwright whose work combines elements of the Polish avant-garde and the Theater of the Absurd.

Różewicz made use of his wartime experiences in his first two volumes of poems, *Niepokój* (1947; "Anxiety") and *Czerwona rękawiczka* (1948; "The Red Glove"). These works were notable for their lack of traditional poetic devices such as meter, stanza, and rhyme. In the 1960s he began writing plays, including *Kartoteka* (1961; *The Card Index*), *Świadkowie albo nasza mała stabilizacja* (1962; "The Witnesses, or Our Little Stabilization"; *The Witnesses and Other Plays*), and *Stara kobieta wysiaduje* (produced 1968; *The Old Woman Broods* in *The Witnesses and Other Plays*).

Translations of his later plays include *Mariage Blanc and The Hunger Artist Departs* (1983). Among his poetry collections are *Poezje* (1987) and *Płaskorzeźba* (1991). In addition to his plays and poetry, Różewicz wrote novels, short stories, and works of nonfiction.

ruba'i \rü-'bä-ˌē, 'rü-ˌbī, 'rü-bä-ˌē\, *plural* rubaiyat \'rü-bī-ˌyät, -ˌbē-; rü-ˌbä-ē-'yät\ *or* rubais, *Persian* robā'ī, *Persian plural* robāīyāt [Persian *robā'ī* quatrain, from Arabic *rubā'ī*]   In Persian literature, a genre of poetry; specifically, a quatrain with a rhyme scheme *aaba*. With the *maṣnawī* (the rhymed couplet), it is a purely Persian poetic genre and not a borrowing from the Arabic, as were the formal ode (qasida) and the love lyric (ghazel). It was adopted and used in other countries under Persian influence.

The most famous example of the genre known in the Western world is the rubaiyat of 'Omar Khayyām, in the version *The Rubáiyát of Omar Khayyám* (1859), translated by Edward FitzGerald.

Rubáiyát of Omar Khayyám, The \'rü-bē-ˌät, -ˌbī-, -ˌat . . . 'ō-mär-kī-'yäm, -'yam\   Collection of the poetry of the 12th-century Persian poet 'Omar Khayyām as compiled and translated by Edward FITZGERALD, published in 1859. Working from two manuscripts, one from the 15th century and one of relatively modern origin, FitzGerald, who was a poet rather than a scholar, "distilled" and conflated some 600 quatrains (*rubaiyat*). Contemporary scholars now question the attribution of many of the poems in the collection, including some of the best-known verses. The conception of the poems presented as a continuous elegy in a unified work was also strictly FitzGerald's work, for the Persian quatrain stands alone, in the way the Japanese haiku does.

Since FitzGerald's time, many more manuscripts purporting to contain 'Omar Khayyām's *rubaiyat* have been examined, the earliest from the beginning of the 13th century. In quatrains known to have been written by him, mysticism, complexity and floweriness are completely lacking. His work is characterized instead by conciseness and pithiness, simplicity of language, lack of metaphor, and reference to the subjects in which he was accomplished (astronomy, metaphysics, and science). Though few would deny FitzGerald's ingenious and felicitous paraphrasing, his version was a product of the conscious Orientalism of 19th-century England. By modern lights Fitzgerald's work stands as a charming and personal reading that reveals more about 19th-century Western thought than it does about the scant poetry of 'Omar Khayyām. *See also* 'OMAR KHAYYĀM.

Rubaiyat stanza \'rü-bē-ˌät, -bī-, -ˌat\, *also called* Omar stanza \'ō-mär\   From *The Rubáiyát of Omar Khayyám*, an iambic pentameter quatrain (*ruba'i*) with a rhyme scheme *aaba*. *See* RUBA'I.

Rückert \'rᵫ-kərt\, Friedrich, *pseudonym* Freimund Raimar \'rī-mär\ (b. May 16, 1788, Schweinfurt, Saxe-Coburg-Gotha [Germany]—d. Jan. 31, 1866, Neuses, near Coburg)   Prolific German poet known for his facility with many different verse forms.

Rückert introduced his German readers to Arabic, Persian, Indian, and Chinese mythology and verse. He taught Oriental philology at Erlangen and Berlin universities before moving to Neuses to devote his life to scholarship and writing. He published several epic poems and historical plays but achieved greater success and repute with his lyric verse, particularly *Liebesfrühling* (1844; "Dawn of Love"), poems written during his courtship of Luise Wiethaus, whom he married in 1821. One of his best-known works, "Geharnischte Sonette" ("Armored Sonnets"), was first published in *Deutsche Gedichte* (1814; "German Poems"). The poem is a stirring exhortation to Prussians to join in the wars of liberation (1813–15) from Napoleonic domination. *Kindertotenlieder* ("Children's Death Songs") was written in 1834 on the death of his two children and published posthumously in 1872.

Rūdakī \'rü-dä-ˌkē\, *original name* Abū 'Abdi'llāh Ja'far ebn Moḥammad (b. *c.* 859, Rudak, Khorāsān [Iran]—d. 940/941, Rudak?) The first poet of note to compose poems in the "New Persian," written in Arabic alphabet, and widely regarded as the father of Persian poetry.

A talented singer and instrumentalist, Rūdakī served as a court poet to the Sāmānid ruler Naṣr II (914–943) in Bukhara until he fell out of favor in 937. He ended his life in wretched poverty. Approximately 100,000 couplets are attributed to Rūdakī, but of that enormous output, fewer than 1,000 have survived, and these are scattered among many anthologies and biographical works. His poems are written in a simple style, characterized by optimism and charm and, toward the end of his life, by a touching melancholy. In addition to parts of his divan (collection of poems), one of his most important contributions to literature is his translation from Arabic to New Persian of *Kalīlah wa Dimnah* (known in English as *The Fables of Bidpai*), a collection of fables of Indian origin.

Rudd \'rəd\, Steele, *pseudonym of* Arthur Hoey Davis \'dä-vis\ (b. Nov. 14, 1868, Drayton, Queensland [Australia]—d. Oct. 11, 1935, Brisbane, Queen.) Novelist, playwright, and short-story writer whose comic characters are a well-known part of Australia's literary heritage.

Rudd worked as a horse breaker, stockman, and drover before going to Brisbane, where he became a clerk and began to write poems and sketches for local journals. His first book was the largely autobiographical *On Our Selection* (1899), followed by a similar volume, *Sandy's Selection* (1904). In more than 20 volumes Rudd depicted farm life in the Darling Downs area of southern Queensland. Though his early work was often realistic and tragic, he later found popular success in creating caricatures of rustic types. In 1904 he founded *Steele Rudd's Magazine*, a popular periodical that appeared at irregular intervals over the next 25 years. He published the work of many unknown Australian writers who later achieved fame.

Rudge, Barnaby \'bär-nə-bē-ˌrəj\ Fictional character, the mentally retarded protagonist of Charles Dickens' historical novel BARNABY RUDGE.

Rudin \'rü-dʸin\ Novel by Ivan TURGENEV, published as a serial in the journal *Sovremennik* and as a book in 1856.

The novel tells of an eloquent intellectual, Dmitry Rudin, a character modeled partly on the revolutionary agitator Mikhail Bakunin, whom Turgenev had known in Moscow in the 1830s. Rudin's power of oratory and passionate belief in the need for progress so affect the younger members of a provincial salon that the heroine, Natalya, falls in love with him. But when she challenges him to live up to his words, he fails her.

Rudnicki \rūd-'nět-skʸē\, Adolf (b. Feb. 19, 1912, Warsaw, Poland, Russian Empire—d. Nov. 14, 1990, Warsaw) Polish novelist and essayist noted for his depictions of Jewish life and its destruction under the Nazis during World War II.

The first of Rudnicki's works to appear were novels on social problems. In *Szczury* (1932; "Rats") he depicted the drabness of everyday life in the sort of small provincial town where many Polish Jews lived. His novel *Żołnierze* (1933; "Soldiers") is a somber, naturalistic picture of life in an army barracks. *Niekochana* (1936; "Unloved") and the story *Lato* (1938; "Summer") encouraged critics to classify him as a psychological novelist.

Mobilized into the Polish army in 1939, Rudnicki fought in the September campaign and was taken prisoner by the Germans. He escaped and crossed to Lwów (now Lviv, Ukraine), in the Soviet-occupied zone of Poland, where he contributed to *Nowe widnokręgi* ("New Horizons"), a communist periodical. When the Germans occupied that city in 1941, Rudnicki returned to Warsaw. He worked in the Resistance movement and took part in the Warsaw uprising of 1944. After the war he settled in Łódź, joining the Marxist literary group *Kuźnica* ("The Forge"). He undertook to write a huge volume under the title *Żywe i martwe morze* (1952; *The Dead and the Living Sea*), a moving testament to the "nation of Polish Jews" and how they died. After 1953 Rudnicki began publishing weekly notes in literary periodicals, which were later collected into several volumes entitled *Niebieskie kartki* ("Blue Pages").

Rudolf von Ems \'rü-ˌdȯlf-fȯn-'ems\ (b. *c.* 1200, Hohenems, Swabia [now in Austria]—d. *c.* 1254, Italy) Prolific and versatile Middle High German poet. Between about 1220 and 1254 he wrote five epic poems, totaling more than 93,000 lines.

Though the influence of earlier masters of the courtly epic is evident in his work—his style is modeled on that of Gottfried von Strassburg, while his moral outlook derives from Hartmann von Aue—Rudolf's poems show considerable originality in subject matter. His earliest preserved poem, *Der guote Gerhart* ("Gerhard the Good"), is the story of a Cologne merchant who, despite his unaristocratic calling, has all the courtly qualities of an Arthurian knight. The charm and realism of this poem were not equaled in Rudolf's other works: *Barlaam und Josaphat*, a Christian version of the legend of Buddha; and the three historical epics, *Alexander*, *Willehalm von Orlens*, and *Weltchronik*, an ambitious, uncompleted world chronicle that ends with the death of Solomon.

Rueda \'rwä-thä\, Lope de (b. *c.* 1510, Seville [Spain]—d. 1565, Córdoba) Outstanding figure of the early Spanish theater who did much to popularize it and prepared the way for Lope de Vega.

Rueda was probably attracted to the stage by touring Italian actors. He organized a traveling theater company and as its *autor*, or author-manager, took his troupe throughout Spain. He became popular and played before all kinds of audiences, from Philip II to crowds of rural townsfolk. His work was seen by Miguel de Cervantes, who praised him both as an actor and as a writer of verse. His most important contributions to early Spanish drama are the *paso*s, comic representations drawn from the events of daily life and intended to be used as humorous relief between the acts of longer works or even incorporated into them as amusing interludes. Written in prose, they brought to the stage a natural language spoken by conventional figures such as the simpleton and the master. His longer works—the comedies *Medora*, *Armelina*, *Eufemia*, and *Los engañados* and the dialogues *Camila*, *Tymbria*, and *Prendas de amor*—derive directly from Italian comedy.

Ruggiero \rüd-'jä-rō\ Fictional character, a heroic Saracen knight beloved by Bradamante, a female Christian knight in Ludovico Ariosto's ORLANDO FURIOSO.

Ruggles, Marmaduke \'mär-mə-ˌdük-'rəg-əlz, -ˌdyük\ Fictional character, the protagonist of the humorous novel *Ruggles of Red Gap* (1915) by American author Harry Leon Wilson.

Ruggles is the quintessential gentleman's gentleman to an English earl. In Paris, the earl loses Ruggles in a poker game to Egbert Floud, a rough-edged but kindly American tourist from the frontier town of Red Gap, Wash. Although initially highly class-conscious, Ruggles gradually adjusts to the democratic, egalitarian life of Red Gap.

Ruiz \rü-'ēth\, Juan, *also called* Archpriest of Hita \'ē-tä\ *or* El Arcipreste de Hita \el-ˌär-thē-'präs-tā-ˌtha-'ē-tä\ (b. *c.* 1283, Alcalá, Spain—d. *c.* 1350) Spanish poet and cleric whose masterpiece, the *Libro de buen amor* (1330; expanded in 1343; *The Book of Good Love*), is perhaps the most important long poem in the literature of medieval Spain.

Almost nothing is known of Ruiz's life apart from the information he gives in the *Libro*: he was educated at Toledo and by 1330 had finished writing the *Libro* while serving as archpriest in the village of Hita, near Alcalá. He also apparently earned a measure of fame from the popular songs he composed.

The *Libro de buen amor* is a long poem composed mainly in the form known as *cuaderna vía*. The *Libro* contains 12 narrative poems, each describing a different love affair. The work's title refers to the distinction the author makes between *buen amor* (*i.e.*, love of God) and *loco amor* (*i.e.*, carnal love). While the author frequently indulges in sententious passages praising spiritual love, his narratives describe in great detail a male hero's wooings and unsuccessful seductions of various women. Besides its realistic and high-spirited descriptions of attempted amorous conquests, the book is remarkable for its satirical glimpses of Spanish medieval life. It contains vigorous descriptions of basic character types from the lower classes, including one of the first major comic personages in Spanish literature, the old panderess Trotaconventos. The author shows a mastery of popular speech and offers folk sayings and proverbs along with bits of obscure but impressive learning.

Ruiz derived his material from a wide range of literary and other sources, including the Bible, Spanish ecclesiastical treatises, Ovid and other ancient authors, the medieval goliard poets, fabliaux, various Arabic writings, and popular poetry and songs, impressing upon all these the cheerful cast of mind of a worldly, ribald, curiously learned priest.

Ruiz de Alarcón \rü-'ēs-ˌtha-ˌäl-är-'kòn, rü-'ēth\, Juan, *surname in full* Ruiz de Alarcón y Mendoza \ē-men-'dō-sä, -thä\ (b. *c.* 1581, Taxco, Mex.—d. Aug. 4, 1639, Madrid, Spain) Mexican-born Spanish dramatist of the colonial era who was the principal dramatist of early 17th-century Spain after Lope de Vega and Tirso de Molina.

Ruiz de Alarcón went to Spain in 1600 to study at the University of Salamanca, from which he graduated in about 1602. He settled permanently in Spain and wrote plays for his own enjoyment rather than for financial reward.

Less prolific than his contemporaries, Ruiz de Alarcón wrote some 25 plays, most of which were published in two separate volumes in 1628 and 1634. His plays are notable for their superb plot construction, psychological subtlety, and ethical teachings. Most of his comedies of life in Madrid center on a defect in a person's character: *La verdad sospechosa* ("The Suspicious Truth") is a study of inveterate lying; *Las paredes oyen* ("The Walls Have Ears") concerns slander; *La prueba de las promesas* ("The Proof of Promises") is an attack on ingratitude; and *Mudarse por mejorarse* ("To Change Oneself to Improve Oneself") inveighs against the fickleness of lovers.

Rukeyser \'rük-ī-zər, 'rük-\, Muriel (b. Dec. 15, 1913, New York, N.Y., U.S.—d. Feb. 12, 1980, New York City) American poet and activist best known for her poems concerning social and political issues.

While at college, Rukeyser contributed poems of a personal nature to *Poetry* magazine. Her *Theory of Flight* (1935) won the Yale Series of Younger Poets award. She broadened her experience by active involvement in the issues of the day. She attended the Scottsboro trials (a major civil-rights case) and witnessed the opening events of the Spanish Civil War, and the scope of her poetry widened accordingly. *U.S. 1* (1938) describes the oppressed poor along the industrial Atlantic seaboard. The work includes "The Book of the Dead," which tells of miners dying of silicosis in West Virginia, a piece considered one of Rukeyser's best works. Her use of fragmented, emotional imagery is sometimes thought lavish, but her poetry is praised for its power and acuity. *The Collected Poems of Muriel Rukeyser* was published in 1978. *Out of Silence* (1992) is a selection of Rukeyser's poetry edited by Kate Daniels.

Rukeyser wrote 14 volumes of poetry. In addition to her verse, she wrote a well-received biography of the mathematician and physicist Willard Gibbs, books for juveniles, and criticism. She also translated the poetry of Octavio Paz, Gunnar Ekelöf, and others.

Rule \'rül\, Jane (b. March 28, 1931, Plainfield, N.J., U.S.) Novelist, essayist, and short-story writer known for her exploration of lesbian themes.

Upon graduation from Mills College, Oakland, Calif., Rule studied briefly at University College, London, and Stanford University. She taught in Massachusetts before moving to Vancouver, where she joined the staff of the University of British Columbia. She began to write full-time in 1974.

Rule's characters are usually rewarded for following their hearts and punished for emotional cowardice. *Desert of the Heart* (1964; filmed as *Desert Hearts*, 1984), Rule's first, best-known novel, is considered a classic of lesbian literature; it traces the lives of two women, separated by age and background, who meet at a boardinghouse and fall in love. In contrast, *This Is Not for You* (1970) is written as an (unmailed) letter to the narrator's best friend, whose love she denies at the cost of her own happiness. *Against the Season* (1971) explores the interwoven lives of several people in a small town. Other novels include *The Young in One Another's Arms* (1977), *Contract with the World* (1980), *Memory Board* (1987), and *After the Fire* (1989).

Rule published three volumes of short stories: *Theme for Diverse Instruments* (1975); *Outlander* (1981), which includes essays; and *Inland Passage and Other Stories* (1985).

In *Lesbian Images* (1975) Rule discussed her own sexuality and the history of lesbianism; the bulk of the book addresses the work of 12 women writers, including Colette, Willa Cather, and Elizabeth Bowen, and the ways in which they projected lesbian experience in their work. Other essays are collected in *A Hot-Eyed Moderate* (1985).

Rulfo \'rül-fò\, Juan (Perez) (b. May 16, 1918, Sayula, Mex.—d. Jan. 7, 1986, Mexico City) Mexican writer who was important in the development of the magic realism school of Latin-American fiction.

As a child growing up in the rural countryside, Rulfo witnessed the horrors of the later Cristero uprisings of 1926–29. In these upheavals his family of prosperous landowners lost a considerable fortune. From 1933 Rulfo lived in Mexico City. Many of the short stories that were later published in *El llano en llamas* (1953; *The Burning Plain*) first appeared in the review *Pan*; they depict the violence of the rural environment and the moral stagnation of its people. In them Rulfo introduced narrative techniques that later would be incorporated into the Latin-American new novel, such as the use of interior monologue, stream of consciousness, flashbacks, and shifting points of view. *Pedro Páramo* (1955) examines the physical and moral disintegration of a laconic *cacique* ("boss") and is set in a mythical hell on earth inhabited by dead individuals who are constantly haunted by their past transgressions.

Rumaker \\'rü-,mä-kər\\, Michael (b. March 5, 1932, Philadelphia, Pa., U.S.)   American author whose early fiction reflected the disaffection of the Beat generation.

Rumaker graduated from Black Mountain College in North Carolina. In an unfinished memoir, "Robert Duncan in San Francisco," he described the new vitality the Beat movement brought to all the arts. In 1958 he suffered an emotional breakdown, for which he was hospitalized until 1960. He later attended Columbia University.

From the late 1950s Rumaker's short stories, such as "The Desert" (1957), were frequently anthologized. His semiautobiographical novel *The Butterfly* (1962) tells of a young man's struggles to gain control of his life following an emotional breakdown. *Exit 3, and Other Stories* (1966; U.S. title, *Gringos and Other Stories*) contains short fictions rife with marginal characters and random violence. *A Day and a Night at the Baths* (1979) and *My First Satyrnalia* (1981) are semiautobiographical accounts of initiation into New York's homosexual community. His later works include *3 × 3* (1989) and *To Kill a Cardinal* (1992).

Rūmī \\'rü-,mē\\, Jalāl ad-Dīn ar-, *also called by the honorific* Mawlānā \\'maù-lä-,nä\\ (b. *c.* Sept. 30, 1207, Balkh, Ghūrid empire [now in Afghanistan]—d. Dec. 17, 1273)   The greatest Ṣūfī mystic and poet in the Persian language, famous for his lyrics and for his didactic epic *Masnavī-ye Ma'navī* ("Spiritual Couplets"), which widely influenced Muslim mystical thought and literature. Rūmī's influence on Turkish cultural life can scarcely be overstated. After his death, his disciples were organized as the Mawlawīyah order, called in the West the whirling dervishes.

Rūmī was a theologian and teacher in Konya in Anatolia. The decisive moment in his life occurred on Nov. 30, 1244, when he met the wandering dervish—holy man—Shams ad-Dīn of Tabriz. Shams revealed to Rūmī the mysteries of divine majesty and beauty. For months the two mystics lived closely together, and Rūmī so neglected his disciples and family that his scandalized entourage forced Shams to leave the town and ultimately had him murdered. This experience of love, longing, and loss turned Rūmī into a poet. His mystical poems—some 30,000 verses and a large number of rubaiyat ("quatrains")—reflect the different stages of his love. He appended his lover's name as author of the verses, collected in The *Divan-e Shams* (*The Collected Poetry of Shams*). It is believed that the poetry was composed while Rūmī was in a state of ecstasy, induced by the music of the flute or the drum, the hammering of goldsmiths, or the sound of a water mill. He often accompanied his verses by a whirling dance.

A few years after Shams's death, Rūmī experienced a similar rapture in his acquaintance with an illiterate goldsmith, Ṣalāḥ ad-Dīn Zarkūb. After Ṣalāḥ's death, Ḥusām ad-Dīn Chelebi became his spiritual love and deputy. Rūmī's main work, the nearly 26,000 couplets of the *Masnavī-ye Ma'navī*, was composed under the latter's influence.

Rumpelstiltskin \\,rəm-pəl-'stilts-kin, *German* 'rùm-pəl-,shtilts-kin\\   German fairy tale collected by the Brothers Grimm for their GRIMM'S FAIRY TALES. Other variations occur in European folklore; in some British versions the title character is named "Terrytop," "Tom Tit Tot," or "Whuppity Stoorie."

The title character is a mysterious, gnomelike man who spins straw into gold for the benefit of a beautiful miller's daughter, in exchange for her future firstborn child. The little man reappears to demand his payment when the young woman, now the queen, bears her first child. After she begs him to release her from her thoughtless vow, he allows her three days in which to discover his name. If she cannot, he will take the child. All seems lost until someone overhears his premature celebration of his good fortune and gives the queen the information she needs to keep her child.

Rumpole, Horace \\'hôr-əs-'rəm-,pōl\\   Fictional character, a barrister featured in many television scripts and novels of John MORTIMER.

Rumpled, disreputable, curmudgeonly barrister Horace Rumpole often wins cases despite the disdain of his more aristocratic colleagues. Fond of cheap wine ("Château Thames Embankment") and Keats's poetry, he refers to his wife as "She Who Must Be Obeyed" (an allusion to the title character of H. Rider Haggard's *She*). First introduced in a 1975 BBC television drama, Rumpole reappeared many times in a series in the 1970s and 1980s. Mortimer based several books on the character, beginning with the story collection *Rumpole of the Bailey* (1978). Leo McKern played Rumpole in the series.

run \\'rən\\ [translation of Scottish Gaelic *ruith* or Irish *rith*]   A stereotyped passage of narrative or description introduced into Gaelic popular tales.

rune \\'rün\\ [Finnish *runo* poem, canto, of Germanic origin; akin to Old Norse *rūn* secret, character of the runic alphabet, writing]   A Finnish poem of folkloric origin, such as the *Kalevala* or one of its divisions. The word has also been applied in a technically incorrect way to medieval Scandinavian poems.

rune \\'rün\\ [Old Norse and Old English *rūn* mystery, runic character, writing]   Any of the characters of several scripts used by the Germanic peoples from about the 3rd to the 13th century.

Runeberg \\'rü-nə-,berʸ\\, Johan Ludvig (b. Feb. 5, 1804, Jakobstad, Swedish Finland [now Pietarsaari, Fin.]—d. May 6, 1877, Borgå, Russian Finland [now Porvoo, Fin.])   Finnish-Swedish poet, generally considered that country's greatest, whose works expressed Finnish patriotic spirit and, because they were written in Swedish, also exercised great influence on Swedish literature.

At Åbo (Turku) University, Runeberg came to know and love Finland's landscape and people and heard firsthand some of the stories of Finland's heroic past that were to be the themes of his best work. He returned to the university and became a lecturer in Latin language and literature. In the same year, he received a gold medal from the Swedish academy for his verse romance of Finnish life, *Grafven i Perho* ("The Grave at Perho"). He then moved to Borgå, where he was lecturer in classics and rector of the college. For the last 13 years of his life he was partly paralyzed and unable to write.

Runeberg's first book of poems (1830) showed freshness, vigor, and sympathy with the Finnish peasant. His two epic poems, *Elgskyttarne* (1832; "The Moose Hunters") and *Hanna* (1836), won him a place in Swedish literature second only to Esaias Tegnér. In 1844 he published *Kung Fjalar*, a cycle of unrhymed verse romances derived from old Scandinavian legends. "Vårt land" ("Our Country"), the first of his patriotic poems in *Fänrik Ståls sägner*, 2 vol. (1848 and 1860; *Tales of Ensign Stål*), became the Finnish national anthem.

Runeberg's work shows the influence of classical literature and of J.W. von Goethe in its high-mindedness and purity of form. His originality consists in his power to combine this classicism with Romantic feeling and in the realism that distinguishes his understanding of peasant life and character.

runic writing \'rū-nik\, *also called* futhark \'fū-,thärk\ Writing system of uncertain origin used by Germanic peoples of northern Europe, Britain, Scandinavia, and Iceland from roughly the 3rd century to the 16th or 17th century AD.

There are at least three main varieties of runic script: Early, or Common Germanic (Teutonic), used in northern Europe before about 800 AD; Anglo-Saxon, or Anglian, used in Britain from the 5th or 6th century to about the 12th century AD; and Nordic, or Scandinavian, used from the 8th to about the 12th or 13th century AD in Scandinavia and Iceland. The Common Germanic script had 24 letters, divided into three groups, called *ættir*, of 8 letters each. The sounds of the first six letters were *f, u, th, a, r,* and *k* (thus, futhark). The Anglo-Saxon script added letters to the futhark to represent sounds of Old English that did not occur in the languages that had used the Common Teutonic script. Anglo-Saxon had 28 letters, and after about 900 AD it had 33. There were also slight differences in letter shape. The Scandinavian languages were even richer in sounds than Old English; instead of adding letters to the futhark to represent the new sounds, however, the users of the Nordic script compounded the letter values, using the same letter to stand for more than one sound—*e.g.,* one letter for *k* and *g,* one letter for *a, æ,* and *o.* This compounding eventually resulted in the reduction of the futhark to 16 letters.

Other varieties of runes included the Hälsinge Runes, the Manx Runes, and the *stungnar runir,* or "dotted runes," all of which were variants of the Nordic script. More than 4,000 runic inscriptions and several runic manuscripts are extant. Approximately 2,500 of these come from Sweden, the remainder being from Norway, Denmark and Schleswig, Britain, Iceland, various islands off the coast of Britain and Scandinavia, and other countries of Europe.

run-on \'rən-,än, -,ón\   *see* ENJAMBMENT.

run-on couplet   *see* OPEN COUPLET.

Runyon \'rən-yən\, Damon, *in full* Alfred Damon Runyon (b. Oct. 4, 1884, Manhattan, Kan., U.S.—d. Dec. 10, 1946, New York, N.Y.)   American journalist and short-story writer, best known for his book *Guys and Dolls,* written in the regional slang that became his trademark.

At age 14 Runyon enlisted in the U.S. Army and was sent to the Philippines in the Spanish-American War (1898). After the war he wrote for western newspapers for 10 years. Although Runyon gained a reputation as a political and feature reporter, his passion for sports was paramount. In 1911 he moved to New York City, where he became a reporter for the *New York American.* He covered the New York baseball clubs for many years, as well as various other sports topics, and along the way he developed his style of focusing on human interest rather than strictly reporting facts. He began writing stories about a racy section of Broadway, and these were collected in *Guys and Dolls* (1931). The book is representative of Runyon's style in its use of an exaggerated version of local idiom to portray a particular class of characters—gamblers, promoters, fight managers, racetrack bookies, and other habitués of the street. The stories were the basis for a successful stage play.

In the 1930s Runyon began writing columns, and his popular feature "As I See It" was syndicated in the Hearst newspapers across the country.

R.U.R. (*in full* R.U.R.: Rossum's Universal Robots)   Drama in three acts by Karel ČAPEK, published in 1920 and performed in 1921. This cautionary play, for which Čapek invented the word "robot" (derived from the Czech word for forced labor),

involves a scientist named Rossum who discovers the secret of creating humanlike machines. He establishes a factory to produce and distribute these mechanisms worldwide. Another scientist decides to make the robots more human, which he does by gradually adding such traits as the capacity to feel pain. Years later, the robots, who were created to serve humans, have come to dominate them completely.

Ruritania \,rür-ə-'tā-nē-ə\   Fictional Central European kingdom that is the setting for THE PRISONER OF ZENDA and its sequel, *Rupert of Hentzau,* by Anthony Hope.

The notion of Ruritania evokes a late 19th-century milieu suffused with heightened romance, acts of chivalry, and political intrigue. *Compare* GRAUSTARK.

Rushdie \'rush-dē, *commonly* 'rəsh-\, Salman, *in full* Ahmed Salman Rushdie (b. June 19, 1947, Bombay, India)   Anglo-Indian novelist who was condemned to death by leading Iranian Muslim clerics in 1989 for allegedly having blasphemed Islām in his novel *The Satanic Verses* (1988). His case became the focus of an international controversy.

Rushdie was educated in England at Rugby School and Cambridge. Throughout most of the 1970s he worked in London as an advertising copywriter, and his first novel, *Grimus,* appeared in 1975. His next novel, MIDNIGHT'S CHILDREN (1981), an allegory about modern India, was an unexpected critical and popular success that won him international recognition.

The novel *Shame* (1983), based on contemporary politics in Pakistan, was also popular, but Rushdie's *The Satanic Verses* encountered a different reception. Some of the bizarre adventures in the book depict a character modeled on the Prophet Muḥammad and portray both him and his transcription of the Qur'ān in a dubious light. *The Satanic Verses* was angrily denounced as blasphemous by outraged Muslim leaders. On Feb. 14, 1989, the spiritual leader of revolutionary Iran, Ayatollah Ruhollah Khomeini, publicly condemned the book and called on his fellow Muslims worldwide to "execute" its author. Despite protests from the international literary community, Rushdie was compelled to remain in hiding, since Iran's religious leaders refused to lift their death sentence on him, thus rendering him liable to assassination at any time.

Rushdie continued to write. In 1990 he published a children's book, *Haroun and the Sea of Stories,* and *Imaginary Homelands: Essays and Criticism* was published in 1991.

Ruskin \'rəs-kin\, John (b. Feb. 8, 1819, London, Eng.—d. Jan. 20, 1900, Coniston, Lancashire)   English writer, critic, and artist who championed the Gothic Revival movement in architecture and the decorative arts and had a strong influence upon public taste in art in Victorian England.

As a youth Ruskin was overprotected, precocious, and unstable, early displaying a love of art and talents in writing and drawing. In 1836 he matriculated at Christ Church, Oxford, where he won the Newdigate prize for poetry in 1839.

A trip to Europe for his health confirmed a powerful response to the beauties of nature, the basis for his appreciation of art. Ruskin returned to Oxford and graduated in the spring of 1842. He began to plan a book in defense of J.M.W. Turner, whose late style of painting had been laughed at by the critics. In the first volume of *Modern Painters* he set out to examine the "truth to Nature" of the accepted masters of landscape painting, always with the glorification of Turner in mind. The book was published in 1843, and it had a considerable success. A second volume was published in 1846.

In April 1848 Ruskin married Euphemia (Effie) Gray; the marriage was ill-advised and never consummated. In August the couple visited northern France, for Ruskin had it in mind to write a book on Gothic architecture. By April 1849 THE

SEVEN LAMPS OF ARCHITECTURE was finished. In the autumn the Ruskins went to Venice for the winter. Ruskin wished to apply the general principles of *The Seven Lamps of Architecture*

Detail of an oil painting by Sir John Everett Millais; in a private collection

Royal Academy of Arts, London

to Venetian architecture and to relate its rise and fall to the working of spiritual forces. The first volume of THE STONES OF VENICE duly appeared in 1851.

In the course of that year Ruskin was induced to champion the Pre-Raphaelite Brotherhood, a group of young English artists founded in reaction against contemporary academic painting, less because he admired them than because he thought the critics unfair to them. He cultivated the company of John Everett Millais, with the result that the artist and Effie fell in love. In July 1854 Effie secured an annulment, and a few months later she married Millais.

The third and fourth volumes of *Modern Painters* were written on an increasingly authoritarian note. The fifth volume is extremely disconnected, and, indeed, Ruskin's mind was gradually declining. Having lost interest in art criticism, he turned to social and economic reform, but his essays on the nature of wealth, *Unto This Last* (1862), aroused much opposition. Near a breakdown, he retired for a time to Mornex, near Geneva.

In 1869 Ruskin was elected the first Slade professor of fine art at Oxford, and he enjoyed great personal success as a lecturer. Early in 1879 he resigned his professorship, giving as his excuse that the painter James McNeill Whistler had won a libel action against him for his intemperate criticism of one of the latter's "Nocturnes." He suffered from increasingly difficult episodes of mental illness. His last significant work was a charming autobiography, *Praeterita* (1885–89).

Ruslan and Lyudmila \rŭs-'làn . . . lʸŭd-'mʸi-lə\ Romantic narrative poem by Aleksandr PUSHKIN, published in Russian in 1820 as *Ruslan i Lyudmila*. The mock-heroic folk epic was influenced by the style of Ludovico Ariosto and Voltaire.

The hero of the poem, Ruslan, is modeled on the traditional Russian epic hero. He faces many trials before rescuing his bride, Lyudmila, daughter of Grand Prince Vladimir of Kiev, who, on her wedding night, is kidnapped by the evil magician Chernomor. The poem flouted accepted rules and genres and

was violently attacked by both of the established Russian literary schools of the day, classicism and sentimentalism. It nevertheless brought Pushkin fame, and the older poet and translator Vasily Zhukovsky presented his portrait to Pushkin with the inscription "To the victorious pupil from the defeated master."

Russell, George William   *see* Æ.

Rustaveli \rūs-'tä-,vä-lē\, Shota (b. *c.* 1172—d. *c.* 1216)   Major Georgian poet, author of the Georgian national epic, *Vepxistgaosani* ("one who wears a tiger's [panther's] skin"), usually known in English as *The Knight in the Panther's Skin*.

Little is known for certain of Rustaveli's early life. According to Georgian legend, he was orphaned as a child and was brought up by an uncle who was a monk. Such a background may be reflected in the poet's religious and philosophical preoccupations. Rustaveli later composed a series of odes to Queen Tamara (1184–1213), who reigned during the high point of Georgian power and cultural attainment. As a reward for his poetic praise, the queen appointed him treasurer of the court. Tradition has it that Rustaveli fell in love with her.

On the basis of his *Vepxistgaosani*, some scholars credit Rustaveli with the creation of the Georgian literary language. Reflected in his poetry are Chinese, Persian, and ancient Greek philosophy, including direct quotations from Plato.

Rutebeuf or **Rutebuef** \rūēd-'bœf\ or **Rustebeuf** \rūes-tə-bœf\ (fl. 1245–85)   French poet and jongleur whose pungent commentaries on the orders of society are considered the first expression of popular opinion in French literature.

The lack of any contemporary reference to someone of this name has led scholars to suppose that he wrote under a pseudonym. Autobiographical information is found in a number of his poems; for example, in *Le Mariage Rutebeuf* he records that he married an ugly old woman who had neither charm nor a dowry. Rutebeuf does not appear, however, to have lacked patrons. It was probably in response to commissions that he composed elegies on the deaths of some of the greatest personages of his time: Eude, count of Nevers; Thibaut V, king of Navarre; and Alphonse, count of Poitiers, brother of King Louis IX of France. He also wrote several poems urging commoners and princes to take part in the Crusades.

Rutebeuf's real strength as a poet, however, lay not in solemn official poems but in lively and biting satire and in amusing verse stories (fabliaux). The chief targets of his satire were the friars. Some of Rutebeuf's most successful works are in a far more popular vein—*e.g.*, *Le Dit de l'herberie*, a comic monologue supposed to be spoken by a sharp-tongued seller of quack medicines. Rutebeuf wrote one of the earliest miracle plays in French to have survived, *Le Miracle de Théophile*, on the traditional theme of a priest who sells his soul to the devil and is saved by the Virgin.

Ruth \'rüth\   Biblical character, a woman who after being widowed remains with her husband's mother. The story is told in the Old Testament Book of Ruth, part of the biblical canon called Ketuvim, or Writings. Ruth's story is celebrated during the Jewish festival of Shavuot, the Feast of Weeks, 50 days after Passover.

The Book of Ruth relates that Ruth and Orpah, two women of Moab, had married two sons of Elimelech and Naomi, Judeans who had settled in Moab to escape a famine in Judah. The husbands of all three women die; Naomi plans to return to her native Bethlehem, urging her daughters-in-law to return to their families. Orpah does so, but Ruth refuses to leave Naomi. Ruth accompanies Naomi to Bethlehem and later marries Boaz, a distant relative of her late father-in-law. She is a symbol of abiding loyalty and devotion.

Rutherford \\'rəth-ər-fərd\\, Mark, *pseudonym of* William Hale White \\'hwīt, 'wīt\\ (b. Dec. 22, 1831, Bedford, Bedfordshire, Eng.—d. March 14, 1913, Groombridge, Sussex) British writer distinguished as a novelist, critic, and religious thinker.

Trained for the Congregational ministry (but expelled from college for his heretical views on the inspiration of the Scriptures), White practiced journalism, then spent the rest of his life in the civil service at the Admiralty. The story of his inner life, however, is largely told in his novels and other writings, published under the name of Mark Rutherford. They include *The Autobiography of Mark Rutherford* (1881), *Mark Rutherford's Deliverance* (1885), *Miriam's Schooling and Other Papers* (1890), and *Clara Hopgood* (1896).

White wrote with a quiet intensity. All of his books deal with religious problems or with ordeals of the heart, the intellect, or the conscience.

Rutilius \\rū-'til-ē-əs\\ Claudius Namatianus (fl. *c.* AD 417) Roman poet who was the author of an elegiac poem, *De reditu suo*, describing a journey from Rome to his native Gaul in the autumn of AD 417.

The occasion of the journey described in his poem was his return to his Gaulish estates, which had been raided by Franks, Burgundians, and Visigoths in 412–414. He sailed up the Italian coast by short stages and reached Luna (on the Gulf of La Spezia). There the poem breaks off. The narrative is smooth and relaxed, full of personal observations and giving the impression of a diary. Much of the poem is taken up by digressions occasioned by places or events of the journey, and it is in these that the attitudes and values of the poet and his circle find their clearest expression. The poem is chiefly interesting for the light it throws on the ideology of the pagan landowning aristocracy of the rapidly disintegrating Western Roman Empire.

Rutilius wrote Latin of unusual purity for his age, and his elegant and correct elegiac couplets bear witness to his close familiarity with the Augustan elegiac poets, particularly Ovid.

Rybakov \\rə-,bə-'kóf\\, Anatoly Naumovich (b. Jan. 1 [Jan. 14, New Style], 1911, Chernigov, Russia [now Chernihiv, Ukraine]) Russian author noted for his novels of life in the Soviet Union under Joseph Stalin's dictatorship.

Rybakov spent three years in exile in Siberia for making "subversive" statements, but he cleared his record by serving as a tank commander in the Russian army during World War II. After the war he turned to writing, producing first a popular children's novel, *Kortik* (1948; *The Dirk*), then the adult novel *Voditeli* (1950; "The Drivers").

Rybakov wrote of the plight of Russian Jews confronting Nazi invaders during World War II in *Tyazholy pesok* (1979; *Heavy Sand*). With the official institution of glasnost, he was allowed to publish *Deti Arbata* (1987; *Children of the Arbat*), much of which had been suppressed for over two decades. The novel offered a horrifying view of Stalin's brutal rule in the early 1930s. *Strakh* (1990; "Fear"), a sequel, presents the techniques of interrogation and torture used by the Soviet secret police.

Rydberg \\'rūēd-,ber'\\, Viktor, *in full* Abraham Viktor Rydberg (b. Dec. 18, 1828, Jönköping, Swed.—d. Sept. 21, 1895, Djursholm) Author of the Romantic school who, with his broad range of achievements, greatly influenced Swedish cultural life.

In 1855 Rydberg began to work for the liberal newspaper *Göteborgs Handels- och Sjöfartstidning*, in which *Den siste Atenaren* (*The Last Athenian*), the novel that made his name, appeared serially in 1859. Its description of the clash between paganism and Christianity in ancient Athens revealed his opposition to clerical intolerance and orthodoxy and had a direct bearing on conditions in Sweden. He had previously published

Singoalla (1857; revised 1865), a romantic lyrical tale of the Middle Ages in Sweden.

In the 1870s Rydberg entered the Swedish Parliament for a short time. He advocated linguistic reform, particularly to reduce the number of words borrowed from German. In 1874 he visited Rome and on his return wrote *Romerska dagar* (1877; "Roman Days"), in which his interest in classical antiquity found its most mature expression. In 1876 he completed his translation of part one of J.W. von Goethe's *Faust*, which had occupied him for many years. He also displayed outstanding talent as a poet; his collection *Dikter* (1882; "Poems") established him as Sweden's foremost lyrical poet since Esaias Tegnér and Erik Stagnelius.

Rydberg gradually gained official recognition. He was given an honorary doctorate by Uppsala University in 1877, elected to the Swedish Academy in 1878, and became a professor at the University of Stockholm in 1884.

In the 1880s he was chiefly concerned with research into mythology, the results of which were published in *Undersökningar i germanisk mythologi*, 2 vol. (1886–89; *Teutonic Mythology*). In 1891 he published two literary works: *Vapensmeden* ("The Armorer"), a novel describing life at the time of the Reformation in Sweden, and a new collection of poems.

Ryder, Charles \\'rī-dər\\ Fictional character, a British officer who provides the narrative voice in Evelyn Waugh's novel BRIDESHEAD REVISITED.

Ryleyev or **Ryleev** \\rə-'lʸā-yif\\, Kondraty Fyodorovich (b. Sept. 18 [Sept. 29, New Style], 1795, Batovo, Russia—d. July 13 [July 25], 1826, St. Petersburg) Russian poet and revolutionary, a leader in the Decembrist uprising of 1825.

Ryleyev served in the army, spending time in Germany, Switzerland, and France. Upon his father's death he went to St. Petersburg and began a literary career. Some of his poems are historical and patriotic; perhaps his best verse, however, is that inspired by his revolutionary spirit.

Ryleyev was recruited into the Northern Society (a secret, patriotic society) in 1823 and soon came to head its radical wing. He assumed the leadership of the Decembrist conspiracy in St. Petersburg and tried unsuccessfully to gather support for the dissident troops in that city on December 14. The revolt was quickly suppressed, and Ryleyev was arrested and imprisoned that same night. He was hanged in Peter and Paul Fortress in 1826. Ryleyev continued to write up to the last few days before the Decembrist revolt, producing eloquent revolutionary verses.

Rymer \\'rī-mər\\, Thomas (b. 1643?, near Northallerton, Yorkshire, Eng.—d. Dec. 14, 1713, London) English literary critic who introduced into England the principles of French formalist Neoclassical criticism. As historiographer royal, he also compiled a collection of treaties of considerable value to the medievalist.

Rymer studied law at Gray's Inn, London. Although called to the bar in 1673, he almost immediately turned his attention to literary criticism. He translated René Rapin's *Réflexions sur la poétique d'Aristote* as *Reflections on Aristotle's Treatise of Poesie* in 1674. Rymer required that dramatic action be probable and reasonable, that it instruct by moral precept and example (it was Rymer who coined the expression "poetic justice"), and that characters behave either as idealized types or as average representatives of their class. In 1678 he wrote *The Tragedies of the Last Age*, in which he criticized plays by the Jacobean dramatists Francis Beaumont and John Fletcher for not adhering to the principles of classical tragedy. In 1693 he published *A Short View of Tragedy*, in which his Neoclassicism was at its narrowest. In *A Short View*, Rymer rejected all modern drama and advocated a return to the Greek tragedy of Aeschylus. Rymer's influence was considerable during the 18th century, but he was ridiculed in the 19th century.

In 1692 Rymer was appointed historiographer royal, and, when William III's government decided to publish for the first time copies of all past treaties entered into by England, Rymer was appointed editor of the project. Despite its deficiencies, the work, whose short title is *Foedera* ("Treaties"), is a considerable and valuable achievement.

Ryōkan \\'ryō-ˌkän\\, *original name* Yamamoto Eizō \\'yä-mä-ˌmō-tō-'ä-ˌzō\\ (b. 1758, Izumozaki, Japan—d. Feb. 18, 1831, Echigo province) Zen Buddhist priest of the late Tokugawa period (1603–1867) who was renowned as a poet and calligrapher.

The eldest son of a village headman and Shintō priest, he gave up his right of succession and became a Buddhist priest at age 17 under the religious name of Taigu Ryōkan. When he was 21 he met an itinerant monk, Kokusen, and followed him to his temple, Entsūji, at Tamashima, Bitchū province. He followed a life of monastic discipline there for 12 years. After Kokusen's death he traveled throughout western Japan as a mendicant priest. In old age he returned to his native Echigo province, where he studied the *Man'yōshū* and ancient calligraphy. He developed a strong master-pupil relationship with a young nun, Teishin-ni, who after his death compiled *Hachisu no tsuyu* (1835; "Dew on the Lotus"), a collection of his Japanese poems written mostly in tanka form. He also wrote hundreds of Chinese poems.

S

Sa'adāwī   *see* EL SAADAWI.

Saavedra \\ˌsä-ä-'b̤a̤th-rä\\, Ángel de, *in full* Ángel de Saavedra Ramírez de Baquendano \\tha̤-ˌsä-ä-'b̤a̤th-rä-rä-'mē-räth-tha̤-ˌbä-ken-'dä-nō\\, Duke de Rivas \\tha̤-'rē-b̤äs\\ (b. March 10, 1791, Córdoba, Spain—d. June 22, 1865, Madrid) Spanish poet, dramatist, and politician, whose fame rests principally on his play *Don Álvaro, o la fuerza del sino* ("Don Álvaro, or the Power of Fate"), which marked the triumph of Romantic drama in Spain.

After entering politics Saavedra was condemned to death in 1823 for his extreme liberal views. He fled the country, and during his exile he came under the Romantic influence that was already visible in *El moro expósito* (1834; "The Foundling Moor") and was to triumph in his *Romances históricos* (1841; "Historical Romances").

Returning to Spain after the amnesty of 1833, he staged *Don Álvaro* in 1835. Saavedra's later dramas are undistinguished. He remained active in politics and died while serving as president of the Spanish Royal Academy.

Saavedra Fajardo \\ˌsä-ä-'b̤a̤th-rä-fä-'k̤är-tho̤\\, Diego de (b. May 6, 1584, Algezares, Spain—d. Aug. 24, 1648, Madrid) Spanish diplomat and man of letters, best known for his anti-Machiavellian emblem book, the *Idea de un príncipe político cristiano* (1640; *The Royal Politician*), which urged a return to traditional virtues as the remedy for national decadence.

After studying law at the University of Salamanca, Saavedra went to Rome, where he served under the Spanish ambassador to the Vatican and rose steadily in the diplomatic ranks. Distressed by Spain's declining political strength and prestige, he wrote his *Idea* to counsel the Spanish ruler. It is a Christian answer to Niccoló Machiavelli in the form of a commentary on 100 emblems. Saavedra is also remembered for *La república literaria* (1655; "The Republic of Letters"), a witty survey of Spanish literature, and for his *Corona gótica* (1646; "The Gothic Kingdom"), a history of Spain under the Goths.

Saba \\'sä-bä\\, Umberto, *original surname* Poli \\'pō-lē\\ (b. March 9, 1883, Trieste, Austria-Hungary [now in Italy]—d. Aug. 25, 1957, Gorizia, Italy) Italian poet noted for his simple, lyrical autobiographical poems.

From age 17 Saba developed his interest in poetry while working as a clerk and a cabin boy and serving as a soldier in World War I. He established his reputation as a poet with the publication of *Il canzoniere* (1921; "The Songbook"), which was revised and enlarged in 1945, 1948, and 1961. It was followed by *Storia e cronistoria del canzoniere* (1948; "History and Chronicle of the Songbook"). Saba's formative poetry, written in the first two decades of the century, was influenced by Petrarch, Gabriele D'Annunzio, Giacomo Leopardi, and Giosuè Carducci. His notable poems from his early period include "A mia moglie" ("To My Wife"), "La Capra" ("The Goat"), and "Trieste." In the middle phase of his career, throughout the 1920s, he wrote in a Freudian vein on such topics as desire and childhood memories. The poetry of his final phase was largely reflective.

Sábato \\'sä-b̤ä-tō\\, Ernesto (b. June 24, 1911, Rojas, Arg.) Argentine writer who in 1984 received the Cervantes Prize, Hispanic literature's most prestigious award.

Sábato earned a doctorate in physics from the National University of La Plata and later studied at the Curie Laboratory in Paris and the Massachusetts Institute of Technology. From 1940 to 1945 he taught at the National University of La Plata and contributed articles to the literary section of *La Nación*, one of Argentina's leading newspapers. He was removed from his teaching post in 1945 for his opposition to the government.

Uno y el universo (1945; "One and the Universe"), a series of aphorisms, statements, and personal observations by Sábato on diverse philosophical, social, and political matters, was his first literary success. The novel *El túnel* (1948; "The Tunnel"; *The Outsider*) won Sábato national and international fame.

His second novel, *Sobre héroes y tumbas* (1961; *On Heroes and Tombs*), is a penetrating psychological study of man, interwoven with philosophical ideas and observations previously treated in his essays. *Tres aproximaciones a la literatura de nuestro tiempo* (1968; "Three Approximations to the Literature of Our Times") includes critical literary essays that deal specifically with the works of Alain Robbe-Grillet, Jorge Luis Borges, and Jean-Paul Sartre. The novel *Abaddón el exterminador* (1974; corrected and revised, 1978; *Angel of Darkness*) contains the ironic statements on literature, art, and philosophy and the excesses of rationalism that characterize Sábato's work.

Sá-Carneiro \\'sä-kâr-'nä-rü\\, Mário de (b. May 19, 1890, Lisbon, Port.—d. April 26, 1916, Paris, Fr.) Poet and novelist, one of the most original and complex figures of the Portuguese modernist movement.

Sá-Carneiro studied in Paris at the Sorbonne. His first poems, *Dispersão* ("Dispersion"), were written in Paris and published in 1914. In the same year he published a novel, *A confissão de Lúcio* ("The Confession of Lúcio"). Back in Portugal he launched the revue *Orpheu* in 1915 in collaboration with Fernando Pessoa, the greatest literary figure of the generation and a longtime friend and mentor. Returning to Paris, Sá-Carneiro suffered a moral and financial crisis and eventually committed suicide. Before his death, he sent his unpublished poems to Pessoa, and these appeared in 1937 under the title *Indicios de oiro* ("Traces of Gold").

Sacchetti \\säk-'kät-tē\\, Franco (b. 1330–35, Florence [Italy] or Ragusa [now Dubrovnik, Croatia]—d. Aug. 15?, 1400, San Miniato, near Florence) Italian poet and storyteller whose work is typical of late 14th-century Florentine literature. Sacchetti was born of a noble Florentine family and traveled widely. In his letters, in some of his verses, and in the *Sposizioni di Vangeli* ("Expositions on the Gospels") he expressed his political and moral views. Some of his poems are among the best of 14th-century minor poetry. He also wrote some 300 stories, of which 223 are known; they consist mainly of anecdotes and jokes derived from oral tradition and the author's direct observation of life. Their artistic value is to be found in the colorful and vivid descriptions of people and places, and their best passages depict scenes from everyday life.

Sachs \\'zäks, *Angl* 'saks\\, Hans (b. Nov. 5, 1494, Nürnberg, Ger.—d. Jan. 19, 1576, Nürnberg) German burgher, a popular meistersinger and poet, who was known for his huge output and for his aesthetic and religious influence. He is idealized in Richard Wagner's opera *Die Meistersinger von Nürnberg*.

Sachs became a master cobbler in about 1519. Many guild workmen and tradesmen of the day practiced a type of singing based on elaborate rules; to become meistersingers ("master singers"), they had to prove themselves in a contest. Sachs became a master in the Nürnberg Singschule in about 1520, conducted a school of meistersingers at Munich, and headed the Nürnberg group in 1554.

Sachs wrote some 4,000 *meisterlieder* ("master songs"). An early champion of Martin Luther's cause, he wrote a verse allegory, *Die Wittembergisch Nachtigall* (1523; "The Nightingale of Wittenberg"), that immediately became famous and advanced the Reformation in Nürnberg. His 2,000 other poetic works include 200 verse dramas, 85 of which are *Fastnachtsspiele*, or homely comedies written to entertain carnival crowds.

Virtually forgotten after his death, Sachs was rediscovered two centuries later by J.W. von Goethe. Some of Sachs's plays, such as *Der fahrend Schüler im Paradeis* (1550; *The Wandering Scholar*), are performed today, and renewed interest in Renaissance music has resulted in a revival of his songs.

Sachs \\'zäks, *Angl* 'saks\\, Nelly (Leonie) (b. Dec. 10, 1891, Berlin, Ger.—d. May 12, 1970, Stockholm, Swed.) German poet and dramatist who was transformed by the Nazi experience into a poignant spokesperson for her fellow Jews. In 1966 she shared the Nobel Prize for Literature with S.Y. Agnon.

Sachs grew up in Berlin and began writing verse at age 17. In 1940 she escaped from Nazism to Sweden with the help of the Swedish novelist Selma Lagerlöf. Sachs lived with her mother in a one-room apartment, learned Swedish, and translated German poetry into Swedish.

Her lyrics in those years combine lean simplicity with imagery variously tender, searing, or mystical. Her famous "O die Schornsteine" ("O the Chimneys"), in which Israel's body drifts upward as smoke from the Nazi death camps, was the title poem for a 1967 collection of her work in English translation. Her best-known play is *Eli: Ein Mysterienspiel vom Leiden Israels* (1951; *Eli: A Mystery Play of the Sufferings of Israel*, included in the *O the Chimneys* collection).

Sackville \\'sak-vil\\, Thomas, 1st Earl of Dorset \\'dòr-sət\\, *also called* (1567–1604) Baron Buckhurst of Buckhurst \\'bək-hərst, -ərst\\ (b. 1536, Buckhurst, Sussex, Eng.—d. April 19, 1608, London) English statesman, poet, and dramatist, remembered largely for his share in two achievements of significance in the development of Elizabethan poetry and drama: the collection *A Myrrour for Magistrates* (1563) and GORBODUC (1561).

Sackville became a member of the Privy Council, served on several diplomatic missions to The Hague, became chancellor of the University of Oxford, and was appointed lord high treasurer. He was created Earl of Dorset in 1604.

Sackville's "Induction," the most famous part of the *Myrrour*, describes the poet's visit to the infernal regions. Written with Thomas Norton, *Gorboduc* is the earliest English drama in blank verse.

Sackville-West \\'sak-vil-'west\\, V., *also called* Vita \\'vē-tə\\, *in full* Victoria Mary Sackville-West, *married name* Nicolson \\'nik-əl-sən\\ (b. March 9, 1892, Knole, Kent, Eng.—d. June 2, 1962, Sissinghurst Castle, Kent) English novelist and poet who wrote chiefly about the Kentish countryside.

Sackville-West was the daughter of the 3rd Baron Sackville and a granddaughter of Pepita, a Spanish dancer, whose story she told in *Pepita* (1937). In 1913 she married Harold Nicolson, a diplomat and author. Her poetic gift for evoking the beauty of the English countryside was recognized in her long poem *The Land* (1926). Her best-known novels are *The Edwardians* (1930) and *All Passion Spent* (1931), and she also wrote biographies and gardening books. *Dearest Andrew: Letters from V. Sackville-West to Andrew Reiber, 1959–1962* (1979) reveals her life in letters to a gardening friend. She was the chief model for the character Orlando in the novel of that title written by Virginia Woolf.

Portrait of a Marriage (1973) by her son Nigel Nicolson is based on his mother's journal detailing her by then sexless but loving friendship with her husband and her intense love affair with another woman.

sacra rappresentazione \\'säk-rä-,räp-prä-,zen-tä-'tsyō-nä\\ [Italian, literally, sacred performance] In theater, 15th-century Italian ecclesiastical drama similar to the mystery play of France and England and the *auto sacramental* of Spain. Originating and flourishing in Florence, these religious dramas represented scenes from the Old and New Testaments, from pious legends, and from the lives of the saints. The plays were didactic, using dialogues drawn from the sacred Scriptures to instruct the audience in lessons of good conduct by dramatizing the punishment of vice and the reward of virtue.

Sacred Wood, The Book of critical essays by T.S. ELIOT, published in 1920. In it, Eliot discusses several of the issues of modernist writings of the period.

The best-known essay of the collection, "Tradition and the Individual Talent," puts forth Eliot's theory of a literary tradition that comprises the whole of European literature from Homer to the present and of the relationship of the individual poet to that tradition. Another notable essay is "Hamlet and His Problems," in which Eliot expresses his theory of the OBJECTIVE CORRELATIVE, a phrase he adapted from either George Santayana or Washington Allston.

Sade \də-'sâd, *Angl* 'säd, 'sâd\, Marquis de, *byname of* Donatien-Alphonse-François, Count (comte) de Sade (b. June 2, 1740, Paris, Fr.—d. Dec. 2, 1814, Charenton, near Paris) Author of erotic writings that gave rise to the term *sadism*.

In the very first months of his marriage to the daughter of a high-ranking bourgeois family, de Sade began an affair with an actress. He also invited prostitutes to his house and subjected them to various sexual abuses. For this he was imprisoned for several weeks, after which he resumed his life of debauchery. After another imprisonment on a similar charge, he retired to his château of La Coste, but one incident followed another in an atmosphere of continual scandal, and, on his return to Paris, de Sade was arrested and sent to the dungeon of Vincennes on Feb. 13, 1777.

De Sade overcame his boredom and anger in prison by writing sexually graphic novels and plays. In July 1782 he finished his *Dialogue entre un prêtre et un moribond* (*Dialogue Between a Priest and a Dying Man*), in which he declared himself an atheist. On Feb. 27, 1784, he was transferred to the Bastille in Paris. There he wrote *Les 120 Journées de Sodome* (THE 120 DAYS OF SODOM), in which he graphically describes numerous varieties of sexual perversion. In 1787 he wrote *Les Infortunes de la vertu* ("The Adversities of Virtue") and in 1788, the novellas, tales, and short stories later published in the volume entitled *Les Crimes de l'amour* (*Crimes of Passion*). He was later transferred to the insane asylum at Charenton, where he remained until April 1790.

On his release, de Sade wrote his novels JUSTINE (1791) and *Juliette* (1798). In 1801 he was arrested at his publisher's, where copies of *Justine* and *Juliette* were found with notes in his hand and several handwritten manuscripts. Again he was sent to Charenton, where he caused new scandals. He began work on an ambitious 10-volume novel, at least two volumes of which were written: *Les Journées de Florbelle ou la nature dévoilée* ("The Days of Florbelle or Nature Unveiled"). After his death his elder son burned these and other manuscripts.

Sá de Miranda \'sä-dĕ-mĕ-'räⁿn-də\, Francisco de (b. Aug. 28, 1481?, Coimbra, Port.—d. May? 1558, Tapada) The first of the Portuguese Renaissance poets.

Sá de Miranda studied at the university, which was then in Lisbon, and traveled in Italy, where he became familiar with Italian verse forms and meters. He did not, however, abandon the Portuguese short meter, which he perfected in his *Cartas*, or epistles in verse.

His play *Os estrangeiros* ("The Foreigners"), written about 1527, was the first Portuguese prose comedy in the classical manner. His *Cleópatra* (written about 1550), of which only a dozen lines are extant, was probably the first Portuguese classical tragedy. About 1528 Sá de Miranda wrote a canzone entitled *Fábula do Mondego* ("Fable of the Mondego"). His best works were the eclogue *Basto*, the *Cartas*, and the satires, in which he shows himself a stern critic of contemporary society.

Sa'dī \'sä-,dĕ, *Persian* 'sä´-\, *byname of* Mosharref al-Dīn ebn Mosleh al-Dīn \'mōs-leḥ-al-'dēn\, *also called* Mosleḥ al-Dīn (b. *c.* 1213, Shīrāz, Persia [Iran]—d. Dec. 9, 1292, Shīrāz) Persian poet, one of the greatest figures in classical Persian literature.

Sa'dī studied in Baghdad at the renowned Nezāmīyeh College. The unsettled conditions following the Mongol invasion of Persia led him to wander abroad. He returned to his native Shīrāz in his old age and apparently spent the rest of his life there.

Sa'dī's best-known works are the *Būstān* (1257; *The Orchard*) and the *Golestān* (1258; *The Rose Garden*). The *Būstān* is entirely in verse (epic meter) and consists of stories illustrating the standard virtues recommended to Muslims as well as reflections on the practices of dervishes. The *Golestān* is mainly in prose and contains stories and personal anecdotes; the text is interspersed with a variety of short poems, containing aphorisms, advice, and humorous reflections.

For Western students the *Būstān* and *Golestān* have a special attraction, but Sa'dī is also remembered as the author of a number of masterly qasidas (odes) portraying human experience; among those particular odes best known is his lament on the fall of Baghdad after the Mongol invasion in 1258. His superb ghazels (lyrics) are responsible for the development of the ghazel as a major form. His odes can be found in *Qaṣā'id* ("Odes") and the ghazels in *Ghazalīyāt* ("Lyrics"). He is also known for a number of works in Arabic. He was much read by European writers of the Enlightenment period.

Sadji \'sä-jē\, Abdoulaye (b. 1910, Rufisque, Senegal, French West Africa—d. Dec. 25, 1961, Dakar) Senegalese writer who was one of the founders of African prose fiction in French.

Sadji graduated from teacher-training college and also earned a bachelor's degree. His early writings appeared locally in the 1940s. The story "Tounka," which deals with the migrations that had brought Sadji's people to the sea, later appeared in *Tounka, nouvelle africaine* (1965; "Tounka, African Stories"). A determination to preserve traditional oral lore led to *La Belle Histoire de Leuk-le-Lièvre* (1953; "The Splendid History of Leuk-the-Hare"), which he cowrote with Léopold Senghor. Sadji's two novels—*Maïmouna: petite fille noire* (1953; "Maimouna: Little Black Girl") and *Nini, mulâtresse du Sénégal* (1954; "Nini, Mulatress of Senegal")—focus on heroines who become victims of urban society.

Sadji's last piece of fiction, which many also regard as his best, is the story "Modou-Fatim" (1960), about a peasant who has to leave his land to work in Dakar.

saga \'säg-ə\ [Old Norse, story, legend, history, saga] A literary genre consisting of a prose narrative sometimes of legendary content but typically dealing with prominent figures and events of the heroic age in Norway and Iceland, especially as recorded in Icelandic manuscripts of the late 12th and 13th centuries.

Modern scholars recognize several subdivisions of the genre, including the kings' sagas, recounting the lives of Scandinavian rulers; the legendary sagas, treating themes from myth and legend; and the Icelanders' sagas, sometimes called family sagas. The last group, the best known and most important in terms of literary merit, are fictionalized accounts of life in Iceland during the so-called saga age (about 930 to 1030) and were written down during the 13th century.

In Icelandic, *saga* (related to *segja*, "to say") has the etymological sense "what is said, or told," a derivation that indicates the importance of oral tradition in the development of the form. Indeed, it used to be thought that the sagas of Icelanders were little more than collections of oral traditions, concerning real individuals, that had finally been given written form after generations of circulation among the people. This view has now been largely discredited, and contemporary scholars are increasingly inclined to regard these works as much closer to the modern conception of a historical novel, in which characters and situations may be real or imaginary but in which artistic rather than historical considerations are paramount. Although this view tends to decrease their value as historical record, it does not undermine the importance of the Icelanders' sagas in helping modern readers to understand the ethos of a past civilization.

Human tragedy is dominant in the Icelanders' sagas. Ideals of heroism and loyalty are important, and revenge—in particular, the blood feud—often plays a significant part in the unfolding of the narrative. Action is preferred to reflection, with the result that the inner motivation of the protagonists and the point of view of the author intrude far less than in most modern novels. Characterizations of surprising depth and subtlety are often achieved by this technique, and parallels have been drawn between this feature of saga writing and the works of some modern writers.

The kings' sagas tell of the kings of Norway and reflect the continued interest of Icelanders in their old homeland. The earliest collections of these sagas, the anonymous *Morkinskinna* and *Fagrskinna* and the monumental *Heimskringla* ("Orb of the World") by Snorri Sturluson, appeared in the period from 1200 to 1235.

As the 13th century progressed, legendary sagas became increasingly popular. These latter works make no pretentions to historical truth and express a delight in the bizarre and the supernatural. They are concerned with the Scandinavian and Germanic past, before the settlement of Iceland, and their heroes are usually legendary or semilegendary figures. They are of considerable antiquarian interest. A well-known example of this type of work is *Vǫlsunga saga* (c. 1270), a retelling of the legends of the German epic NIBELUNGENLIED. *See also* ICELANDERS' SAGAS.

The term *saga* is also used to refer to any of various historical or fictional narratives, such as a modern retelling usually in verse or highly stylized prose of the events of the Icelanders' sagas or of similar subjects; an episodic story centering on a usually heroic figure of earlier ages with factual or fictional details drawn from various sources; a series of legends that embodies in detail the oral history of a people; or a long, detailed narrative usually without psychological or historical depth (for example, of a particular occupation, area, historical event, period, or person).

sagaman \'säg-ə-,man\ *plural* sagamen \-,men\ [translation of Old Norse *sǫgumathr*]   A narrator of a saga.

Sagan \sà-'gäⁿ\, Françoise, *pseudonym of* Françoise Quoirez \kwä-'rä\ (b. June 21, 1935, Carjac, France)   French novelist and dramatist who wrote her first and best-known novel, the international best-seller BONJOUR TRISTESSE (1954), when she was 19. Sagan attended the Sorbonne. Among the novels that followed *Bonjour Tristesse* were *Un Certain Sourire* (1956; *A Certain Smile*), *Aimez-vous Brahms?* (1959), *Les Merveilleux Nuages* (1961; *Wonderful Clouds*), *Un Profil perdu* (1974; *Lost Profile*), and *Un Sang d'aquarelle* (1987; *Painting in Blood*). Most of Sagan's novels feature aimless people who are involved in tangled, often amoral relationships. Her plays, which resemble her novels in content, include *Château en Suède* (1960; *Castle in Sweden*) and *L'Excès contraire* (1987; *Opposite Extremes*). She also wrote film scripts, short stories, and nonfiction.

saga novel   A long, multivolume, and usually easygoing chronicle of persons comprising a family, community, or other social group. *See* ROMAN-FLEUVE.

sage-king \'sāj-'kiŋ\   In Confucianism, an exemplary mythological ruler of prehistoric China.

Sahgal \'sä-gəl\, Nayantara (Pandit) (b. May 10, 1927, Allahābād, India)   Indian journalist and novelist whose fiction presented the personal crises of India's elite amid settings of political upheaval.

Sahgal was educated in the United States at Wellesley College. Her uncle was Jawaharlal Nehru, India's first prime minister, and her cousin, Indira Gandhi, was a later Indian prime minister. *Prison and Chocolate Cake* (1954) was Sahgal's first book, an autobiographical memoir about her youth amid the Nehru family. She then turned to novel writing, often setting her stories of personal conflict amid Indian political crises, as in

her fourth novel, *The Day in Shadow* (1971), about a divorcée struggling in India's male-dominated society.

The contrast between the idealism at the beginning of India's independence and the moral decline of post-Nehru India that is particularly evident in *A Situation in New Delhi* (1977) recurs in such Sahgal novels as *Rich Like Us* (1985). Sahgal also wrote nonfiction that analyzed Indira Gandhi's isolated youth and subsequent harsh rule. The later Sahgal novels *Plans for Departure* (1985) and *Mistaken Identity* (1988) are set in preindependence India.

Ṣā'ib \'sä-ēb\, *in full* Mīrzā Muḥammad 'Alī Ṣā'ib, *also called* Ṣā'ib of Tabriz \tä-'brēz\ *or* Ṣā'ib of Eṣfahān \is-fä-'hän\ (b. 1601/02, Tabrīz, Iran—d. c. 1677)   Persian poet, one of the greatest masters of the ghazel, a form of classical Arabic and Persian lyric poetry characterized by rhymed couplets.

Ṣā'ib was educated in Eṣfahān (Isfahan), and about 1626/27 he traveled to India, where he was received into the court of Shāh Jahān. He stayed for a time in Kabul and in Kashmir, returning home after several years abroad. After his return Shāh 'Abbas II bestowed upon him the title King of Poets.

Ṣā'ib's reputation is based primarily on some 300,000 couplets, including his epic poem *Qandahār-nāma* ("The Campaign Against Qandahar"). His "Indian style" verses reveal an elegant wit, a gift for the aphorism and the proverb, and a keen appreciation of philosophical and intellectual exercise. In addition to his remarkable output of Persian verse, Ṣā'ib wrote poetry in Turkish.

Sa'īd \sä-'ēd, *Angl* -'ēd\, 'Alī Aḥmad, *pseudonym* Adonis \ə-'dän-is, -'dōn-\ *or* Adūnīs \ä-,dü-'nēs\ (b. 1930, Qassabin, near Latakia, Syria)   Lebanese poet and literary critic who was a leader of the modernist movement in Arabic poetry.

Sa'īd studied at the University of Damascus and at St. Joseph University in Beirut, Lebanon, and he served in the Syrian military. In 1957 he helped Yūsuf al-Khāl found the avant-garde poetry review *Shi'r*, and in 1968 he launched the more radical journal *Mawāqif*. His early volumes of poetry included *Dalīlia* (1950), *Qaṣā'id ūlā* (1956; "First Poems"), and *Awrāq fī al-rīh* (1958; "Leaves in the Wind").

In the 1960s Sa'īd helped create a new form of Arabic poetry, characterized by elevated diction and complex surrealism, with the publication of such works as *Aghānī Mihyār al-Dimashqī* (1961; "Songs of Mihyār of Damascus") and *Al-Masraḥ wa 'l-marāyā* (1968; "The Stage and the Mirrors"). He also wrote innovative prose poems, collected in such books as *Qabr min ajl New York* (1971; "A Tomb for New York"). His critical essays were collected in *Zaman al Shi'r* (1972; "The Time for Poetry") and *Al-Thābit wa 'l-mutaḥawwil* (1974; "Stability and Change"). English translations of selected poems appear in *The Blood of Adonis* (1971) and *The Transformation of the Lover* (1983).

Said \sä-'ēd\, Edward W., *in full* William (b. Nov. 1, 1935, Jerusalem)   Palestinian-American literary critic who studied literature in light of social and cultural politics and was an outspoken proponent of Arab issues.

Said attended Princeton University and Harvard University before joining the faculty of Columbia University in 1963. His first book, *Joseph Conrad and the Fiction of Autobiography* (1966), was an expansion of his doctoral thesis. In *Orientalism* (1978), perhaps his best-known work, Said examines Western stereotypes about the Islāmic world and argues that Orientalist scholarship is based on Western imperialism. His books about the Middle East include *The Question of Palestine* (1979), *Blaming the Victims: Spurious Scholarship and the Palestinian Question* (1988; coedited with Christopher Hitchens), and *The Politics of Dispossession* (1994). Among his other books are *Be-*

ginnings: *Intention and Method* (1975), *The World, the Text, and the Critic* (1983), *Nationalism, Colonialism, and Literature: Yeats and Decolonization* (1988), *Musical Elaborations* (1991), and *Culture and Imperialism* (1993).

Saigyō \'sī-gyō\, *also called* Sato Norikiyo \'sä-tō-'nō-rē-kē-yō\ (b. 1118, Japan—d. March 23, 1190, Ōsaka) Japanese Buddhist priest-poet, one of the greatest masters of the tanka (a traditional Japanese poetic form), whose life and works became the subject matter of many narratives, plays, and puppet dramas.

At the age of 23 Saigyō became a priest. His life was spent in travel throughout Japan, punctuated by periodic returns to the capital at Kyōto to participate in imperial ceremonies. Saigyō's poetry is largely concerned with a love of nature and devotion to Buddhism. Among his many works are the anthology *Sankashū* and the *Mimosusogawa utaawase* ("Poetry Contest at Mimosusu River")—a poetic masterpiece in which he pitted his own poems against one another. Many of his poems are included in the imperial anthology *Shin kokinshū*. Saigyō's influence was reflected in poets of later ages, particularly the haiku master Matsuo Bashō.

Saikaku *see* IHARA Saikaku.

Sailing to Byzantium \bi-'zan-tē-əm, -'zan-shəm\ Poem by W.B. YEATS, published in his collection *October Blast* in 1927 and considered one of his masterpieces. For Yeats, ancient Byzantium was the purest embodiment of transfiguration into the timelessness of art. Written when Yeats was in his 60s, the poem repudiates the sensual world in favor of "the artifice of eternity." It is known for its remarkable lyricism.

Saint, The *byname of* Simon Templar \'sī-mən-'tem-plər\ Fictional English gentleman-adventurer who was the protagonist of short stories and mystery novels by Leslie CHARTERIS.

Simon Templar is a good-natured, gallant figure who defies social convention; he lives outside the law and yet emerges untarnished from his shadowy adventures.

Meet the Tiger (1928; also published as *The Saint Meets the Tiger*) was the first Saint novel. Among many story collections and novels are *Knight Templar* (1930), *The Saint in New York* (1935), *The Saint Returns* (1969), and *The Saint in Pursuit* (1971). Until 1940, the stories were set in Britain; after World War II, they took place in the United States.

Saint-Amant \saⁿ-tä-'mäⁿ\, Antoine Girard, Sieur (Lord) de, *original name* Marc-Antoine Girard \zhē-'rár\ (b. *c.* Sept. 30, 1594, Rouen, Fr.—d. Dec. 29, 1661, Paris) One of the most original and interesting of early 17th-century French poets and one of the first members of the Académie Française.

The early poems of Saint-Amant are realistic and hilarious descriptions of the pleasures of the table and the tavern. A reflection of the long journeys abroad that he undertook with his patron, the Count d'Harcourt, is seen, for example, in *Albion* (1643). This mock-heroic poem contains a disenchanted account of a visit to England and includes an informative description of the London theaters. His *Rome ridicule* (1649) started the fashion for burlesque poems that was to be developed later by Paul Scarron. His biblical epic, *Moïse sauvé* (1653; "Moses Rescued"), though uneven, contains passages of great force and vividness.

Sainte-Beuve \saⁿt-'bœ̄v\, Charles-Augustin (b. Dec. 23, 1804, Boulogne, Fr.—d. Oct. 13, 1869, Paris) French literary historian and critic, noted for applying historical frames of reference to contemporary writing.

Sainte-Beuve attended the University of Paris and in 1825 was drawn into journalism by a former teacher, Paul Dubois, editor of a new liberal periodical, *Le Globe*, in whose pages he

Mary Evans Picture Library

published his first essays. He also contributed articles to the *Revue des deux mondes*. The success of these articles prompted him to collect them as *Critiques et portraits littéraires*, 5 vol. (1832–39). In these "portraits" of contemporaries, he developed a form of critique, new and much applauded at the time, based on the study of a well-known living writer in the round that entered into considerable biographical research to understand the mental attitudes of his subject.

In addition to his critical works, Sainte-Beuve anonymously published an autobiographical novel, *Volupté* (1834), which almost ruined his friendship with Victor Hugo. In the book, the hero Amaury's hopeless love for the saintly and unapproachable Madame de Couaën reflects the author's passion for Hugo's wife Adèle. Meanwhile Sainte-Beuve continued to produce intellectual portraits of his literary contemporaries, as further collected in *Portraits contemporains* (1846).

A suggestion about 1836 by François Guizot, then minister of education, that Sainte-Beuve demonstrate his eminence as a scholar by producing a major work led to PORT-ROYAL, his single most famous piece of writing.

In 1840 Sainte-Beuve was appointed to a post in the French Institute's Mazarine Library, a position he held until 1848. In 1849 he was asked by Louis Véron, editor of the newspaper *Le Constitutionnel*, to write a weekly article or essay on current literary topics, to appear every Monday. This was the start of the famous collection of studies that Sainte-Beuve named CAUSERIES DU LUNDI ("Monday Chats"). Except for two brief teaching jobs, one of which led to his *Étude sur Virgile* (1857), a full-length study of Virgil, his whole later career was based on freelance essay writing.

It was with Sainte-Beuve that French literary criticism first became fully independent and freed itself from personal prejudice and partisan passions. That he was able to revolutionize critical methods was partly a result of the rise of the newspaper and the critical review, which gave prestige and wide circulation to criticism and guaranteed its independence.

Saint-Évremond \saⁿ-tā-vrə-'mòⁿ\, Charles de Marguetel de Saint-Denis, Seigneur de (b. 1613/14, Saint-Denis-le-Gast, Fr.—d. Sept. 20, 1703, London, Eng.) French man of letters and amateur moralist who stands as a transitional figure between Michel de Montaigne (died 1592) and the 18th-century philosophes of the Enlightenment.

Saint-Évremond wrote for his friends, not for publication, but a few of his pieces were leaked to the press in his lifetime. His poems, mainly occasional pieces, are negligible; but *Les Académiciens* (1643), a comedy in verse, is still amusing, as is his prose comedy "in the English style," *Sir Politick Would-Be* (*c.* 1664).

Saint-Évremond's prose consists of letters and discourses ranging from hilarious satire (*Retraite de M. le duc de Longueville*, 1649; *Conversation du Maréchal d'Hoquincourt avec le Père Canaye*, *c.* 1663) to commonsense literary criticism on the various genres. It also includes a series of ethical writings that plead for a prudently moderated hedonism and for religious toleration.

Saint-Exupéry \saⁿ-tåg-zǖe-på-'rē\, Antoine de, *in full* Antoine-Marie-Roger de Saint-Exupéry (b. June 29, 1900, Lyon, Fr.—d. July 31, 1944, in flight over the Mediterranean) French aviator and writer whose works are the unique testimony of a pilot and a warrior who looked at adventure and danger with a poet's eyes.

Saint-Exupéry came from an impoverished aristocratic family. He obtained his pilot's license in 1922. In 1926 he joined the Compagnie Latécoère (an airline company) in Toulouse and helped establish several international airmail routes. In the 1930s he worked as a test pilot, a publicity attaché for Air France, and a reporter for *Paris-Soir*. In 1939 he became a military reconnaissance pilot; after the fall of France (1940) in World War II he escaped to the United States. In 1943 he rejoined the French air force in North Africa and the next year was shot down on a reconnaissance mission.

Saint-Exupéry's works exalt perilous adventures. In his first book, *Courrier-sud* (1929; *Southern Mail*), his protagonist, airmail pilot Jacques Bernis, dies in the desert of Río de Oro. His second novel, *Vol de nuit* (1931; *Night Flight*), was dedicated to the glory of the first airline pilots and their mystical exaltation in the face of great danger. His own flying adventures are lyrically recorded in *Terre des hommes* (1939; WIND, SAND AND STARS). *Pilote de Guerre* (1942; *Flight to Arras*) is a personal reminiscence of a reconnaissance sortie in May 1940. While in the United States he wrote *Lettre à un otage* (1943; *Letter to a Hostage*), a call to unity among Frenchmen, and *Le Petit Prince* (1943; THE LITTLE PRINCE), a child's fable for adults.

Growing sadness and pessimism is evident in *Citadelle* (1948; *The Wisdom of the Sands*), a posthumous volume of reflections which show his belief that the only lasting reason for living is to serve as a repository of the values of civilization.

Saint Joan \'jōn\ Chronicle play in six scenes and an epilogue by George Bernard SHAW, performed in 1923 and published in 1924. It was inspired by the canonization of Joan of Arc in 1920, nearly five centuries after her death in 1431.

Shaw attributes Joan's visions to her intuition and understanding of her historical mission. Joan leads France to victory over the English by dint of her innate intelligence and leadership and not through supernatural guidance. She is captured by the English, convicted of heresy, and burned at the stake. Joan is the personification of the tragic heroine; her martyrdom embodies the paradox that humans fear—and often kill—their saints and heroes.

The play's epilogue concerns the overturning of the church's verdict of heresy in 1456 and her canonization.

Saint-John Perse \saⁿd-zhòn-'pers\, *pseudonym of* Marie-René-Auguste-Aléxis Saint-Léger Léger \lä-'zher\ (b. May 31, 1887, Saint-Léger-les-Feuilles, Guadeloupe—d. Sept. 20, 1975, Presqu'île-de-Giens, Fr.) French poet and diplomat who was awarded the Nobel Prize for Literature in 1960 "for the soaring flight and evocative imagery of his poetry."

In 1914 Léger entered the diplomatic service. He went to China and was successively consul at Shanghai and secretary at Beijing. He was later secretary (1921–32) to the French statesman Aristide Briand, and in 1933 he was appointed secretary-general at the Foreign Ministry, with the rank of ambassador. Dismissed from office in 1940 and deprived of French citizenship by the collaborationist Vichy government, he went to the United States. He returned to France in 1957.

His early poetry includes *Éloges* (1911; *Éloges, and Other Poems*), which shows the influence of Symbolism; he later developed a more personal style. The language of his poetry, admired especially by poets for its precision and purity, is difficult, and he made little appeal to the general public. The best-known

early work is *Anabase* (1924; *Anabasis*, translated by T.S. Eliot). In the poems written in exile—*Exile* (1942; *Exile, and Other Poems*) *Vents* (1946; *Winds*), *Amers* (1957; *Seamarks*), *Chronique* (1960), and *Oiseaux* (1962; *Birds*)—he achieved a deeply personal note. For some, Saint-John Perse is the embodiment of the French national spirit—intellectual yet passionate, deeply conscious of the tragedy of life, a man of affairs with an artist's feeling for perfection and symmetry.

Saintsbury \'sānts-bər-ē, -,ber-\, George (Edward Bateman) (b. Oct. 23, 1845, Southampton, Hampshire, Eng.—d. Jan. 28, 1933, Bath, Somerset) The most influential English literary historian and critic of the early 20th century. His lively style and wide knowledge helped make his works both popular and authoritative.

Disappointed at not getting a fellowship at Merton College, Oxford (M.A., 1868), Saintsbury spent almost a decade as a schoolmaster. He began a lifelong study of French literature and started writing reviews for the *Academy*. His essay on Baudelaire in the *Fortnightly Review* in 1875 caught the attention of the literary world. He was an unorthodox critic of French literature, but his *Primer of French Literature* (1880), *A Short History of French Literature* (1882), and *Specimens of French Literature from Villon to Hugo* (1883) all had great success. His 1881 study of John Dryden ("English Men of Letters Series") was the first of his extensive writings on English literature. *Specimens of English Prose Style from Malory to Macaulay* (1885) and *A History of Elizabethan Literature* (1887) followed.

Saintsbury held the Regius chair of rhetoric and English literature at the University of Edinburgh from 1895 to 1915. At Edinburgh he produced, among other works, *A Short History of English Literature* (1898) and *A History of Criticism and Literary Taste in Europe from the Earliest Texts to the Present Day*, 3 vol. (1900–04), one of the first surveys of critical literary theory and practice. He also wrote *A History of English Prosody from the Twelfth Century to the Present Day*, 3 vol. (1906–10), the supplementary *Historical Manual of English Prosody* (1910), and the complementary *History of English Prose Rhythm* (1912).

Saintsbury wrote a book on 18th-century literature (1916) and a book on wine, *Notes on a Cellar-Book* (1920), which led to the foundation of the Saintsbury Club. Saintsbury's *Minor Poets of the Caroline Period*, 3 vol. (1905–1921), helped revive interest in 17th-century poetry, as did his editions of Dryden and Thomas Shadwell for Restoration drama.

Saint-Simon \saⁿ-sē-'mòⁿ\, Louis de Rouvroy, Duke (duc) de (b. Jan. 15, 1675, Paris, Fr.—d. March 2, 1755, Paris) French soldier and writer, one of the great memoirists of France. His *Mémoires* are an important historical document of his time.

From 1729 to 1738 Saint-Simon annotated the *Journal* of Philippe de Courcillon, Marquis de Dangeau, a work that provided a framework for his own memoirs, begun about 10 years later. Saint-Simon produced a composite narrative of court life based upon his own memory and papers, oral and written testimony from his fellow courtiers, and other sources. Saint-Simon's life at court limited his perspective, however, and consequently his memoirs overemphasized personalities and petty intrigue. Nonetheless, he presents an unforgettable picture of the last years of Louis XIV and the regency period.

The definitive edition of the *Mémoires* was produced in 41 volumes of text and 2 volumes of tables (1879–1928). A seven-volume Pléiade edition was published in 1947–61.

Saki \'säk-ē\, *pseudonym of* H.H. Munro \mən-'rō\ (b. Dec. 18, 1870, Akyab, Burma [now Myanmar]—d. Nov. 14, 1916, near Beaumont-Hamel, Fr.) Scottish writer whose stories depict the Edwardian social scene with a flippant wit and power of fantastic invention used both to satirize social pretension, unkindness, and stupidity and to create an atmosphere of horror.

Born the son of an officer in the Burma police, Munro was sent at the age of two to live with his aunts near Barnstaple in England. He later took revenge on their strictness and lack of understanding by portraying many tyrannical aunts. In 1893 Munro joined the Burma police but was invalided out. Turning to journalism, he wrote political satires for the *Westminster Gazette* and in 1900 published *The Rise of the Russian Empire*, a serious historical work.

After acting as foreign correspondent for *The Morning Post* in the Balkans, Russia, and Paris, in 1908 he settled in London. His short stories and sketches were published in the collections *Reginald* (1904), *Reginald in Russia* (1910), *The Chronicles of Clovis* (1911), and *Beasts and Super-Beasts* (1914). Written in a style studded with epigrams and with well-contrived plots often turning on practical jokes or surprise endings, his stories reveal a vein of cruelty and a self-identification with the enfant terrible. Among his most frequently anthologized works are TOBERMORY, THE OPEN WINDOW, "Sredni Vashtar," "Laura," and "The Schartz-Metterklume Method." His novel *The Unbearable Bassington* (1912) anticipates the early work of Evelyn Waugh. Munro was killed in action in World War I.

Śākti or **Shakti** \'shək-tē\   In Hindu religion and mythology, the paramount goddess or the consort of a male deity, generally Śiva. Broadly, cosmic energy as conceived in Hindu thought.

In popular worship the goddess Śākti is known by many names; she may be referred to simply as Devī (goddess). In her beneficent aspect she is known variously as Umā, Pārvatī, and Ambikā. In her fierce, destructive aspect she is represented as the black Kālī, the demon-destroying Durgā, and the goddess of smallpox, Śītalā. The goddess is also worshiped as the gracious Lakṣmī, who is the consort of Vishnu.

Śakuntalā \shä-'kūn-tə-,lä\   Fictional character, heroine of the Sanskrit drama *Abhijñānaśakuntala* ("The Recognition of Śakuntalā") by the 5th-century North Indian poet KĀLIDĀSA.

Sakurada Jisuke I \'sä-kū-,rä-dä-'jēs-ȯ-kä-'ēs-,sä\, *pseudonym* Sato \'sä-tō\ (b. 1734, Edo [now Tokyo], Japan—d. 1806, Edo)   Kabuki dramatist who composed more than 120 plays and at least 100 dance dramas.

After completing his studies with Horikoshi Nisōji in 1762, Sakurada moved to Kyōto to write plays for a theater there. On his return to Edo three years later he became chief playwright at the Morita Theater. His play *Edo no hana wakayagi soga*, a success at the Ichimura Theater in 1769, made his reputation, and for the next 40 years he was a leading playwright at Edo, becoming the chief writer for three renowned kabuki actors. Among his most popular plays were *Oshiegusa Yoshiwara suzume* (1768; "The Lesson of the Yoshiwara Sparrow") and *Modorikago iro ni aikata* (1788; "A Returning Palanquin").

Saladin \'sal-ə-din\   *Arabic in full* Ṣalāḥ ad-Dīn Yūsuf ibn Ayyūb \ṣȧ-'läḥ-ȧd-'dēn-'yü-süf-,ib-ən-ī-'yüb\, *also called* Al-Malik an-Nāṣir Ṣalāḥ ad-Dīn Yūsuf I (b. 1137/38, Tikrīt, Mesopotamia—d. March 4, 1193, Damascus)   Muslim sultan of Egypt, Syria, Yemen, and Palestine, founder of the Ayyūbid dynasty, and the most famous of Muslim heroes. In wars against the Christian crusaders, he achieved final success with the disciplined capture of Jerusalem (Oct. 2, 1187), ending its 88-year occupation by the Franks. The great Christian counterattack of the Third Crusade was then stalemated by Saladin's military genius. He was a learned and generous ruler, chivalrous and gallant toward his enemies and courteous and civilized toward the inhabitants of Jerusalem during the capture of that city. He appears as a model of these traits in several works, including Sir Walter Scott's novel *The Talisman* (1825).

salamander \'sal-ə-,man-dər\   [Greek *salamándra* any of several species of lizardlike amphibians thought to have magical powers]   **1.** A mythical and not clearly defined animal having the power to endure fire without harm.   **2.** According to a theory of the medieval physician Paracelsus, an elemental being inhabiting fire. *Compare* GNOME; SYLPH; UNDINE.

Salammbô \sȧ-län-'bō, -läm-\   Historical novel by Gustave FLAUBERT, published in 1862.

Set after the First Punic War (264–241 BC), *Salammbô* is the story of the siege of Carthage in 240–237 BC by mercenaries who had not been paid for their help in fighting the Romans. It is also the story of the love of Mathô, one of the mercenaries, for Salammbô, the daughter of Hamilcar, chief magistrate of Carthage, and priestess of the city's moon goddess. The novel is a historically accurate but highly romanticized portrait of the period.

Salih \'sä-lē\, Tayeb, *also spelled* aṭ-Ṭayyib Ṣāliḥ \ȧt-'tī-yeb\ (b. 1929, ash-Shamalīyah province, Sudan)   Arabic-language novelist and short-story writer whose stories and novels are set in the northern Sudanese village of Wād Ḥāmid.

Salih attended universities in the Sudan (in Khartoum) and in London and devoted much of his professional life to radio broadcasting, for many years as head of drama for the BBC Arabic Service. He attempted in his work to harmonize the traditions of the past with the worldliness of the "traveled man," the African who has returned from schooling abroad. His early novel *Mawsim al-hijrah ilā' l-shamāl* (1966; *Season of Migration to the North*) is a haunting prose poem that reflects the conflicts of modern Africa: traditions and common sense versus education, rural culture versus urban culture, and men versus women.

Salih also wrote *'Urs al-Zayn* (1966; *The Wedding of Zein*), a collection of tales that evoke the warmth, compassion, humor, and sadness of traditional Sudanese Arabic life, and the two-volume *Bandershah*, consisting of *Ḍaw' al-Bayt* (1971) and *Maryūd* (1977).

Salinas \sä-'lē-näs\, Pedro, *surname in full* Salinas y Serrano \-ē-ser-'rän-ō\ (b. Nov. 27, 1891, Madrid, Spain—d. Dec. 4, 1951, Boston, Mass., U.S.)   Spanish poet, scholar, dramatist, and essayist who was one of the outstanding writers of the Generation of 1927.

Salinas studied and lectured at the Sorbonne for three years and then returned to Spain to teach at the University of Seville. He later taught at the University of Cambridge, and, after the outbreak of the Spanish Civil War in 1936, he taught in the United States.

Salinas' first poems were published in the literary magazine *Prometeo*. His volumes of poetry include *Presagios* (1923; "Omens"), *Víspera del gozo* (1926; *Prelude to Pleasure*), *Seguro azar* (1929; "Certain Disaster"), *La voz a ti debida* (1933; *My Voice Because of You*), and *Todo más claro y otros poemas* (1949; "Everything Clearer and Other Poems"). *To Live in Pronouns* (1974) is an English translation of his love poems, and *Truth of Two* (1940) a bilingual collection. Salinas was also a respected scholar, known for studies on the 15th-century Spanish poet Jorge Manrique and the Nicaraguan poet Rubén Darío and for a modern verse rendition of the *Cantar de Mio Cid*.

Salinger \'sal-in-jər\, J.D., *in full* Jerome David (b. Jan. 1, 1919, New York, N.Y., U.S.)   American writer whose novel THE CATCHER IN THE RYE (1951) won critical acclaim and devoted admirers, especially among the post-World War II generation of college students. His entire corpus of published works consists of one novel and 13 short stories.

Salinger's stories began to appear in periodicals in 1940. He served in the army from 1942 to 1946. Salinger's name and writing style became increasingly associated with *The New Yorker* magazine, which published almost all of his later stories. Some of the best of these made use of his wartime experiences: "For Esmé—With Love and Squalor" (1950) describes a U.S. soldier's poignant encounter with two British children; "A Perfect Day for Bananafish" (1948) concerns the suicide of the sensitive, despairing veteran Seymour Glass.

Major critical and popular recognition came with the publication of *The Catcher in the Rye.* Its humor and colorful language place it in the tradition of Mark Twain's *The Adventures of Huckleberry Finn* and the stories of Ring Lardner, but its hero, like most of Salinger's child characters, views his life with an added dimension of precocious self-consciousness. *Nine Stories* (1953), a selection of Salinger's best work, added to his reputation.

The reclusive habits of Salinger in his later years made his personal life a matter of speculation among devotees, while his small literary output was a subject of controversy among critics. FRANNY AND ZOOEY (1961) brought together two earlier *New Yorker* stories; both deal with the Glass family, as do the two stories in *Raise High the Roof Beam, Carpenters; and Seymour: An Introduction* (1963).

Salis \'zä-lis\, Johann Gaudenz, Baron (Freiherr) von Salis-Seewis (b. Dec. 26, 1762, Malans, Switz.—d. Jan. 29, 1834, Malans) Swiss poet whose work is a tender and sometimes elegiac celebration of friendship, humanity, and the serenity of nature.

Some of Salis' poems, such as "Lied eines Landmanns in der Fremde" ("Song of a Countryman Abroad"), became anthology pieces. In 1779 he became an officer in the Swiss guards in Paris, but he supported the ideals of the French Revolution and voluntarily remained in Paris until 1793. In 1799 he became chief of staff of the Swiss militia, taking part in the Battle of Zürich, and later filled several public offices.

Salkey \'sȯk-ē, 'sȯl-kē\, Andrew, *in full* Felix Andrew Alexander Salkey (b. Jan. 30, 1928, Colón, Panama) Caribbean author, anthologist, and editor whose work reflects a commitment to Caribbean, particularly Jamaican, culture.

Salkey was reared and educated in Jamaica. He attended the University of London and became part of the London community of emerging West Indian writers. He taught for two years before becoming a freelance writer and journalist, and he regularly contributed to the BBC as a radio interviewer, critic, and author of radio plays and features. From 1976 he was a professor of writing at Hampshire College, Amherst, Mass.

His first novel, *A Quality of Violence* (1959), is set in a remote area of Jamaica around 1900, when a prolonged drought leads Christians to turn toward the older, "darker" ways of voodoo and *obeah.* The novel is narrated in the distinctive island patois, rich with folk-speech rhythms. After a second novel, *Escape to an Autumn Pavement* (1960), Salkey spent several years writing stories for children, including *Hurricane* (1964), *Earthquake* (1965), *Drought* (1966), and *Riot* (1967), all of which concern events in Jamaica. The short-story collection *Anancy's Score* (1973) introduced the trickster Anancy, a character to whom Salkey returned in the story collection *Anancy, Traveller* (1992). Collections of his poetry include *Jamaica* (1973), *In the Hills Where Her Dreams Live: Poems for Chile 1973–1978* (1979), and *Away* (1980). In addition to his own writing, Salkey edited such volumes as *West Indian Stories* (1960), *Caribbean Prose* (1967), *Island Voices* (1970), *Writing in Cuba Since the Revolution* (1975), and *Caribbean Folk Tales and Legends* (1980).

Sallust \'sal-əst\, *Latin in full* Gaius Sallustius Crispus (b. *c.* 86 BC, Amiternum, Samnium [now San Vittorino, near L'Aquila, Italy]—d. 35/34 BC) Roman historian and one of the great Latin literary stylists, noted for his narrative writings dealing with political personalities, corruption, and party rivalry.

Nothing is known of Sallust's early career, but he probably acquired military experience before taking political office. His experience gained during the political strife of the early 50s provided a major theme for his writings. His political career ended soon after 45 or early 44 BC.

Sallust may have begun to write before 43. Because he had been born in a time of civil war and had matured during a time of foreign war and political strife, it is not surprising that his writings are preoccupied with violence. His first monograph, *Bellum Catilinae* (43–42; *Catiline's War*), deals with corruption in Roman politics by tracing the conspiracy of Catiline, a ruthlessly ambitious patrician who had attempted to seize power in 63. Sallust describes the course of the conspiracy and the measures taken by the Senate and Cicero, who was then consul. He brings his narrative to a climax in a senatorial debate concerning the fate of the conspirators.

In Sallust's second monograph, *Bellum Jugurthinum* (41–40; *The Jugurthine War*), he explores in greater detail the origins of party struggles that arose in Rome when war broke out against Jugurtha, the king of Numidia, who rebelled against Rome at the close of the 2nd century. Sallust considered Rome's initial mismanagement of the war the fault of the "powerful few" who sacrificed the common interest to their own avarice and exclusiveness. Sallust's *Histories*, of which only fragments remain, describes the history of Rome from 78 to 67.

Sallust's influence pervades later Roman historiography, whether men reacted against him, as did Livy (59/64 BC–AD 17), or exploited and refined his manner and views, as did Tacitus (*c.* 56–*c.* 120). Sallust's narratives were enlivened with speeches, character sketches, and digressions, and, by skillfully blending archaism and innovation, he created a style of classic status.

Salmagundi \ˌsal-mə-'gən-dē\ (*in full* Salmagundi; or, The Whim-Whams and Opinions of Launcelot Langstaff, Esq., and Others) Popular American periodical consisting of pamphlets containing humorous and satiric essays and poems, published from 1807 to 1808 and from 1819 to 1820.

Salmagundi was originally published by William Irving, James Kirke Paulding, and Washington Irving, all writing under such pseudonyms as Anthony Evergreen, Jeremy Cockloft the Younger, Will Wizard, Pindar Cockloft, Esq., and Mustapha Rub-a-Dub Keli Khan (a Tripolitan prisoner of war observing American society from his cell in New York). The 20 pamphlets (Jan. 24, 1807, to Jan. 25, 1808) were collected and published in book form in 1808. The periodical consisted of light verse and droll commentary, and caricatures of New York City tastemakers and society were included, along with essays on such topics as "the conduct of the world," politics, public mores and women's fashions, music, and theater. The best of the satirical magazines yet published in the United States, *Salmagundi* was an immediate success.

Paulding published a second series (May 1819 to September 1820) by himself, but it did not contain the heterogeneous mixture that constitutes an authentic salmagundi, and it was unsuccessful.

salon \sə-'län, 'sal-ˌän, sa-'lōⁿ\ A social gathering place for nobles and intellectuals, including writers and artists. Salons were held in private homes and were especially popular in France in the 17th and 18th centuries. One of the first to be established was that of Madame de Rambouillet in about 1610 as a reaction against the coarseness of the French court at the time. Other well-known salons were those of Mme de Staël, Mme de Récamier, and Madeleine de Scudéry.

Salten \ˈzäl-tən\, Felix, *original name* Siegmund Salzmann \ˈzälts-mən\ (b. Sept. 6, 1869, Buda or Pest, Hungary—d. Oct. 8, 1945, Zürich, Switz.) Austrian novelist and journalist, author of the allegory BAMBI, a sensitively told, subjective story of the life of a wild deer.

As a self-taught young writer Salten was befriended by Hugo von Hofmannsthal, Arthur Schnitzler, and Hermann Bahr. A journalist at 18, he became an influential theater critic. He lived in Vienna until, as a Jew, he was forced to flee in 1939; he then settled in Switzerland.

The publication of *Bambi* brought Salten international fame. In 1933 he published another popular children's book, *Florian: Das Pferd des Kaisers (Florian, the Emperor's Stallion)*, the tale of a proud Lipizzaner horse who is reduced to pulling a cab after World War I.

Salterton trilogy \ˈsȯl-tər-tən\ Series of novels by Robertson DAVIES, consisting of *Tempest-Tost* (1951), *Leaven of Malice* (1954), and *A Mixture of Frailties* (1958).

The books are comedies of manners that are loosely connected by the fact that they are all set in Salterton, a provincial Canadian university town, and they feature recurring characters. *Tempest-Tost* concerns the efforts of a local theater company to put on a production of William Shakespeare's *The Tempest*. *Leaven of Malice* opens with the placement of a false notice of engagement in the local paper and examines the effects of the practical joke on those involved as they try to discover who placed the announcement. In *A Mixture of Frailties* a woman's will provides for the education in the arts of a young woman of the town. The book traces the young woman's experiences as she trains to be a singer.

Saltus \ˈsȯl-təs\, Edgar Evertson (b. Oct. 8, 1855, New York, N.Y., U.S.—d. July 31, 1921, New York City) One of the few American novelists who adopted the sophisticated cynicism, art-for-art's-sake credo, and mannerisms of the European school of Decadents. In his time his novels were popular for their wit and for their shocking, erotic incidents.

Educated at Yale and abroad, Saltus received a law degree at Columbia College in 1880 but never practiced. He wrote popularized histories of the Roman emperors and of the Russian czars, titled, respectively, *Imperial Purple* (1893) and *Imperial Orgy* (1920). In addition, he published books on Honoré de Balzac and the German philosopher Arthur Schopenhauer and wrote *The Anatomy of Negation* (1886), a study of antitheistic philosophies from earliest times.

Saltykov \səl-ti-ˈkȯf\, Mikhail Yevgrafovich, Count (Graf), *also called* Saltykov-Shchedrin, *pseudonym* N. Shchedrin \chi-ˈdrʸēn\ (b. Jan. 15 [Jan. 27, New Style], 1826, Spas-Ugol, Russia—d. April 28 [May 10], 1889, St. Petersburg) Writer of radical sympathies and one of the greatest of all Russian satirists.

As a boy, Saltykov was deeply shocked by his mother's cruel treatment of peasants, which he later described in one of his most important works, *Poshekhonskaya starina* (1887–89; "Old Times in Poshekhona"). In 1838 he was sent to the Imperial Lycée at Tsarskoye Selo (now Pushkin), Russia's training ground for high officers of state. He reacted violently against its bureaucratic regime and joined the revolutionary circles in St. Petersburg.

In 1847 Saltykov began his literary career as a reviewer in the radical periodicals *Sovremennik* and *Otechestvennyye zapiski*. As a result of the sympathy he expressed for French utopian socialists in his story *Zaputannoye delo* (1848; "A Complicated Affair"), he was exiled to Vyatka (now Kirov), where he worked in the provincial governor's office. After he returned to St. Petersburg in 1855, he published his first successful book, *Gubernskiye ocherki* (1856–57; selections in English translation,

Tchinovnicks: Sketches of Provincial Life), in which he satirized Vyatka officials.

In 1862 Saltykov retired from government service and devoted himself to literature. He was editor of *Sovremennik* and then joined the radical poet Nikolay Nekrasov as coeditor of *Otechestvennyye zapiski*, becoming editor after Nekrasov's death in 1878. A major work of this period is *Istoriya odnogo goroda* (written 1869–70; *The History of a Town*), a biting satire on the highest Russian officials. His last works include the novel *Gospoda Golovlyovy* (1876; *The Golovlyov Family*) and *Skazki* (1880–85; *Fables*).

Samaniego \sä-mä-ˈnyä-gō\, Félix María (b. Oct. 12, 1745, Laguardia, Spain—d. Aug. 11, 1801, Laguardia) Poet whose books of fables for schoolchildren have a grace and simplicity that has won them a place as the first poems that Spanish children learn to recite in school.

Born into an aristocratic Basque family, Samaniego came under the influence of the French philosophes during his early travels in France. Returning to his native country, he devoted the rest of his life to the welfare of his fellow Basques. He joined the Basque Society and taught at its seminary, composing the *Fábulas morales* (1781; "Moral Fables") for its students. They were an immediate success and were quickly established as part of the Spanish curriculum. The next year, Samaniego became involved in a literary dispute with his former friend and fellow fabulist Tomás de Iriarte, and, because of an anonymous attack on Iriarte that contained criticisms of the church, Samaniego was imprisoned in a monastery in 1793.

samizdat \ˈsä-mēz-ˌdät\ In the Soviet Union, the system by which government-suppressed literature was clandestinely written, printed, and distributed. The word was also applied to the literature itself.

Samizdat began appearing in the 1950s, largely as a revolt against official restrictions on artistic freedom of expression. After the ouster of Nikita Khrushchev in 1964, samizdat publications expanded their focus beyond freedom of expression to a critique of many aspects of official Soviet policies and activities. The Russian word *samizdat*, coined from *sam-* ("self") and *izdat*, short for *izdatelstvo* ("publishing house"), humorously imitated the compound names of state publishing monopolies, such as Goslitizdat. Because of the government's strict monopoly on presses, photocopiers, and other such devices, samizdat publications typically took the form of carbon copies of typewritten sheets that were passed by hand from reader to reader. The major genres of samizdat included reports of dissident activities and other news suppressed by official media, protests addressed to the regime, transcripts of political trials, analyses of socioeconomic and cultural themes, and even pornography.

In its earliest days, samizdat was largely a product of the intelligentsia of Moscow and Leningrad. Similar underground literatures later spread throughout the constituent republics of the Soviet Union and among its many ethnic minorities.

From its inception, the samizdat movement and its contributors were subjected to surveillance and harassment by the KGB (the secret police). The suppression worsened in the early 1970s at the height of samizdat activity. Culminating in a show trial of Pyotr Yakir and Viktor Krasin in August 1973, the government's assault wounded the movement. It survived, nonetheless, though reduced in numbers and deprived of many of its leaders.

Samizdat began to flourish again in the mid-1980s, but it had almost disappeared by the early 1990s following the emergence of publishing and other media outlets that were independent of government control.

Samsa, Gregor \'greg-ər-'sam-zə\ Fictional character, an overworked salesman whose transformation is the subject of Franz Kafka's symbolic novella THE METAMORPHOSIS.

Samson \'sam-sən\, *Hebrew* Shimshon. Israelite hero portrayed in an epic narrative in the Old Testament (Judges 13–16). He was a Nazirite (*i.e.*, one set aside for God by a vow to abstain from strong drink, from shaving or cutting the hair, and from contact with a dead body) and a legendary warrior whose incredible exploits hint at the weight of Philistine pressure on Israel during much of the early, tribal period in Canaan (1200–1000 BC).

Samson possessed extraordinary physical strength, and the moral of his saga connects the disastrous loss of his power with the violation of his Nazirite vow. Credited with remarkable exploits—*e.g.*, the slaying of a lion and moving the gates of Gaza—he first broke his religious promises by feasting with a Philistine woman. Other remarkable deeds follow—*e.g.*, his decimating the Philistines in a private war. On another occasion he repulsed their assault on him at Gaza. He finally fell victim to his foes through the love of Delilah, a Philistine woman of the valley of Sorek, who had been bribed by her people to discover the secret of his strength. When he eventually revealed that his long hair was the source of his strength, Delilah had his hair cut while he slept. He was captured, blinded, and enslaved by the Philistines, but in the end he was granted his revenge; through the return of his old strength, he demolished the great Philistine temple of the god Dagon at Gaza, destroying his captors and himself (Judges 16:4–30).

The character of Samson has been portrayed several times in literature, most notably in John Milton's epic poem *Samson Agonistes* (1671). The 18th-century French writer Voltaire wrote a libretto for an opera entitled *Samson* by Jean-Philippe Rameau.

Samson Agonistes \'sam-sən-,ag-ə-'nis-tēz\ ("Samson the Athlete" or "Samson the Wrestler") Tragedy by John MILTON, published in the same volume as his epic *Paradise Regained* in 1671. It is considered the greatest English drama based on the Greek model and is known as a closet tragedy (one more suited for reading than performance).

The work deals with the final phase of Samson's life and recounts the story as told in the Old Testament Book of Judges. Himself blind when he wrote *Samson Agonistes*, Milton depicts Samson, the once mighty warrior, as blinded and a prisoner of the Philistines ("eyeless in Gaza at the mill with slaves"). Samson conquers self-pity and despair, however, and is granted a return of his old strength. He pulls down the pillars that support the temple of the Philistine god Dagon, crushing himself along with his captors.

Samuel \'sam-yü-wəl\, *Hebrew* Shmu'el (fl. *c.* 11th century BC, Israel) Religious hero in the history of Israel, represented in Hebrew scriptures in every role of leadership open to a Jewish man of his day—seer, priest, judge, prophet, and military leader. His greatest distinction was his role in the establishment of the monarchy in Israel.

Samuel's initial resistance to the notion of kingship became a standard reference in the 17th- and 18th-century debates over kingship and constitution by such writers as John Milton and Thomas Paine. Samuel also plays a secondary role in works by Abraham Cowley and others and is the main character in a book by Laurence Housman.

Sanā'ī \sä-'nä-,ē\, *pseudonym of* Abū al-Majd \,äl-'mäzhd\ (*or* Abū'l-Majd) Majdūd Sanā'ī (d. 1131?, Ghazna [now Ghaznī, Afg.]) Persian poet, author of the first great mystical poem in the Persian language. He expanded the subject matter of the ghazel and made it the chosen form for lyrical expression.

Little is known of Sanā'ī's early life. He was a resident of Ghazna and served for a time as poet at the court of the sultans of the Turkish Ghaznavid dynasty (977–1186), composing panegyrics in praise of his patrons. At some point he underwent a spiritual conversion and, abandoning the court, went to Merv (near modern Mary, Turkmenistan), where he pursued a life of spiritual perfection. He returned to Ghazna years later but lived in retirement, resisting the blandishments of his Ghaznavid patron Bahrām Shāh.

Sanā'ī's best-known work is the *Ḥadīqat al-ḥaqīqah wa sharī'at aṭ-ṭarīqah* ("The Garden of Truth and the Law of the Path"). Dedicated to Bahrām Shāh, this great work, expressing the poet's ideas on God, love, philosophy, and reason, is composed of 10,000 couplets in 10 separate sections. The first section was translated into English as *The Enclosed Garden of Truth* (1910). Among his other works, a shorter poem, *Sayr al-'ibād ilā al-ma'ād* ("Journey of the Servants of God to the Place of Return"), is notable.

Sanā'ī's work is of major importance in Persian-Islāmic literature, for he was the first to use such verse forms as the qasida (ode), the ghazel (lyric), and the *maśnawī* (rhymed couplet) to express the philosophical, mystical, and ethical ideas of Ṣūfism (Islāmic mysticism). His divan, or collected poetry, contains some 30,000 verses.

Sanchez \'san-chez\, Sonia (Benita), *original name* Wilsonia Driver \'drī-vər\ (b. Sept. 9, 1934, Birmingham, Ala., U.S.) African-American poet, playwright, and educator noted for her activism.

Sanchez graduated from Hunter College in Manhattan and briefly studied poetry writing at New York University. From 1966 she taught in a succession of universities, including Temple University in Philadelphia.

In the 1960s Sanchez published poetry in such journals as *Liberator*, *Journal of Black Poetry*, *Black Dialogue*, and *Negro Digest*. Her first book, *Homecoming* (1969), contained much invective against "white America" and "white violence"; thereafter she continued to write on what she called "neoslavery," the social and psychological enslavement of blacks. Much of her verse is written in American black speech patterns, eschewing traditional English grammar and pronunciations. Some of her later works are *I've Been a Woman: New and Selected Poems* (1978), *Homegirls & Handgrenades* (1984), and *Under a Soprano Sky* (1986).

Sanctuary Novel by William FAULKNER, published in 1931. The book's depictions of degraded sexuality generated both controversy and spectacular sales, making it the author's only popular success during his lifetime.

A vision of a decayed South, the novel pitted idealistic lawyer Horace Benbow against a cast of amoral fiends. The book's seething violence and despair were characteristic of Faulkner, although elsewhere less brutally displayed.

Faulkner's publisher balked at releasing this study of human evil, set in the author's fictional Yoknapatawpha County, Miss., and asked him to rewrite it in proof. Faulkner did so, refining its art without softening its horror.

Sand \'sänd, *Angl* 'sand\, George, *pseudonym of* Amandine-Aurore-Lucile (Lucie) Dudevant \dūd-'vän\, *original surname* Dupin \dū-'pan\ (b. July 1, 1804, Paris, Fr.—d. June 8, 1876, Nohant) French Romantic writer, noted both for her so-called rustic novels and her numerous love affairs.

Aurore was brought up at the country home of her grandmother. There she gained the profound love and understanding of the countryside that were to inform most of her works. In 1822 she married Casimir Dudevant, but she soon tired of her somewhat insensitive husband and sought consolation in a passionate liaison with a neighbor. In January 1831 she moved to Paris, where she and her lover Jules Sandeau

wrote a novel and several articles under the pseudonym Jules Sand. In 1832 she adopted a new pseudonym, George Sand, for *Indiana*, a novel in which Sandeau had had no part. The novel, which brought her immediate fame, is a passionate protest against the social conventions that bind a wife to her husband against her will and an apologia for a heroine who abandons an unhappy marriage and finds love.

Musée Carnavalet, Paris

In *Valentine* (1832) and LÉLIA (1833) the ideal of free association is extended to the wider sphere of social and class relationships.

Meanwhile, the list of her lovers was growing; it eventually included, among others, Prosper Mérimée, Alfred de Musset, and Frédéric Chopin. Most of her early works, including *Mauprat* (1837), *Spiridion* (1839), and *Les Sept Cordes de la lyre* (1840; *A Woman's Version of the Faust Legend: The Seven Strings of the Lyre*), show the influence of one or another of the men with whom she associated.

She eventually found her true form in her rustic novels, which drew their chief inspiration from her lifelong love of the countryside and her sympathy for the poor. In *La Mare au diable* (1846; *The Devil's Pool*), *François le Champi* (1848; *The Country Waif*), and *La Petite Fadette* (1849; *Little Fadette*), the familiar theme of Sand's work—love transcending the obstacles of convention and class—is once more evident. In later life she produced a series of novels and plays of impeccable morality and conservatism. She also published her autobiography, *Histoire de ma vie* (1854–55; *Story of My Life*), and *Contes d'une grand'mère* (1873; *The Castle of Pictures and Other Stories: A Grandmother's Tales*), a collection of stories she wrote for her grandchildren.

Sandbox, The One-act play by Edward ALBEE, published in 1959 (with *The Death of Bessie Smith*) and produced in 1960. It is a trenchant satire on false values and the lack of love and empathy in the American family. For his expanded one-act play *The American Dream* (1961), Albee used the characters he created for *The Sandbox*—Mommy, Daddy, and Grandma— as well as some of the play's dramatic material.

Sandburg \'sand-,bərg\, Carl (b. Jan. 6, 1878, Galesburg, Ill., U.S.—d. July 22, 1967, Flat Rock, N.C.) American poet, historian, novelist, and folklorist.

When the Spanish-American War broke out in 1898, Sandburg enlisted in the 6th Illinois Infantry. These early years he later described in his autobiography, *Always the Young Strangers* (1953).

From 1910 to 1912 he acted as an organizer for the Social Democratic Party and secretary to the mayor of Milwaukee. Moving to Chicago in 1913, he became an editor of *System*, a business magazine, and later joined the staff of the *Chicago Daily News*.

In 1914 a group of his poems, including the well-known CHICAGO, appeared in *Poetry* magazine (they were issued as

Chicago Poems in 1916). Sandburg's poetry made an instant and favorable impression. In Whitmanesque free verse, he eulogized American workers: "Pittsburgh, Youngstown, Gary, they make their steel with men" (*Smoke and Steel*, 1920).

In *Good Morning, America* (1928) Sandburg seemed to have lost some of his faith in democracy, but from the depths of the Great Depression he wrote *The People, Yes* (1936), a poetic testament to the power of the people to go forward. The folk songs he sang before delighted audiences were issued in two collections, *The American Songbag* (1927) and *New American Songbag* (1950). He also wrote the popular biography *Abraham Lincoln: The Prairie Years*, 2 vol. (1926). Its sequel, ABRAHAM LINCOLN: THE WAR YEARS, 4 vol. (1939), won the Pulitzer Prize in history in 1940.

Another biography, *Steichen, the Photographer*, the life of his famous brother-in-law, Edward Steichen, appeared in 1929. In 1948 Sandburg published a long novel, REMEMBRANCE ROCK, that recapitulates the American experience from Plymouth Rock to World War II. *Complete Poems* appeared in 1950. He wrote four books for children—ROOTABAGA STORIES (1922), *Rootabaga Pigeons* (1923), *Rootabaga Country* (1929), and *Potato Face* (1930).

Sandeau \sän-'dō\, Jules, *in full* Léonard-Sylvain-Julien Sandeau (b. Feb. 19, 1811, Aubusson, Fr.—d. April 24, 1883, Paris) Prolific French novelist who is best remembered for his collaborations with more famous writers.

As a young man, Sandeau became the lover of Amandine-Aurore-Lucie Dudevant (later known as George Sand) and worked with her on the novel *Rose et Blanche* (1831; "Red and White"), which was published under the pseudonym Jules Sand. At the end of 1832, she broke off the affair and adopted the pen name George Sand. Sandeau's most successful novel was *Mademoiselle de la Seiglière* (1848), a tale about the conflict between love and class consciousness written in a mannered style, now read mainly for its portrayal of society during the reign of Louis-Philippe (1830–48). He also wrote a good deal for the theater. He met with considerable success with dramatizations of a number of his novels, and he collaborated with Émile Augier on several plays, including the famous *Le Gendre de Monsieur Poirier* (1854; "Son-in-Law of Monsieur Poirier"), which advocated the fusion of the new, prosperous middle class and the dispossessed nobility.

Sandemose \'sän-də-,mō-sə\, Aksel (b. March 19, 1899, Nykøbing, Mors Island, Den.—d. Aug. 6, 1965, Copenhagen) Danish-born Norwegian experimental novelist whose works frequently elucidate the theme that the repressions of society lead to violence.

Sandemose went to sea in his teens, jumped ship in Newfoundland, and worked in a lumber camp before returning to Denmark to write stories influenced by Jack London and Joseph Conrad. He later settled in Norway and during the 1930s published a series of partly autobiographical novels bitterly castigating the convention-ridden, small-town society of his Danish childhood and drawing on violent episodes from his later wanderings. Included among these works are *En sjømann går iland* (1931; "A Sailor Disembarks"), *En flyktning krysser sitt spor* (1933; *A Fugitive Crosses His Tracks*), and *Der stod en benk i haven* (1937; "A Bench Stood in the Garden"). Later novels include *Der svundne er en drøm* (1946; "The Past Is a Dream"), *Varulven* (1958; *The Werewolf*), and its continuation, *Felicias Bryllup* (1961; "Felicia's Wedding"). Like his early works, these later novels record an anguished man seeking to escape the repression and provincialism of small-town society.

Sandoz \'san-dōz\, Mari Susette (b. 1901, Sheridan county, Neb., U.S.—d. March 10, 1966, New York, N.Y.) American biographer and novelist known for her scrupulously researched books portraying the early American West.

Sandoz' life as a student and teacher in rural Nebraska—a rigorous life that left her blind in one eye at age 13—prepared her to depict pioneer and Indian life realistically. She wrote almost 80 stories while in college, but her first success came when she was in her mid-30s, with *Old Jules* (1935), a story of her father's hard farm life.

Sandoz' books include *Crazy Horse* (1942), a biography of the Sioux chief; *Cheyenne Autumn* (1953), which concerns Native Americans leaving a reservation to return home; *The Buffalo Hunters* (1954), which tells of the white settlers' slaughter of bison and its social impact on the West; and *The Battle of the Little Bighorn* (1966).

Sandys \'sandz\, George (b. March 2, 1578, near York, Yorkshire, Eng.—d. March 1664, Boxley Abbey, Kent)   English traveler, poet, colonist, and foreign-service career officer who played an important part in the development of English verse, especially of the heroic couplet. A journal of his travels in the Middle East, *Relation of a Journey* (1615), went through nine editions in the 17th century.

Sandys, who studied at Oxford, was treasurer and director of industry and agriculture in the colony of Virginia from 1621 to 1625. He published a translation of Ovid's *Metamorphoses* (1621–26), and his reputation largely rests on a revised edition of the work that he published in 1632. This revision also included philosophical commentaries translated from various ancient authors and a translation of Book I of Virgil's *Aeneid*. John Dryden called him "the best versifier of the former age" and commended his ability to give his verse the same turn as the original, and many later poet-critics also attested to the value of his translations. He prepared the way for the heroic couplets of Dryden and Alexander Pope.

śaṅgam literature   *see* CAṄKAM LITERATURE.

Sannazzaro \sän-näd-'dzä-rō\, Jacopo (b. July 28, 1456, Naples [Italy]—d. April 24, 1530, Naples)   Neapolitan poet whose *Arcadia* (1504) was the first pastoral romance and, until the rise of the Romantic movement, one of the most influential and popular works of Italian literature.

Sannazzaro became court poet of the house of Aragon at the age of 20. In 1501, when the last Aragonese king of Naples lost his throne, Sannazzaro accompanied him into exile in France. During this period he brought to light several lost Latin works, including Ovid's *Halieutica* and Nemesianus' *Cynegetica*. In 1504 Sannazzaro returned to Naples, where he spent the rest of his life.

Sannazzaro wrote in both Italian and Latin. *Arcadia*, which is partly autobiographical and partly allegorical, consists of short poems, in dialogue or soliloquy form, linked by prose narrative. In addition to *Arcadia*, his Italian works include lyric poems in Petrarchan style.

Sansom \'san-səm\, William (b. Jan. 18, 1912, London, Eng.—d. April 20, 1976, London)   Writer of short stories, novels, and travel books who is considered particularly acute in his dissections of London life and scenes.

Sansom worked in banking and advertising until World War II. After writing film scripts following the war, he became a full-time writer. His most important novels are *The Body* (1949), *A Bed of Roses* (1954), *The Loving Eye* (1956), and *Goodbye* (1966). His short stories have been collected in *Fireman Flower* (1944), *Something Terrible, Something Lovely* (1948), *A Touch of the Sun* (1952), *Blue Skies, Brown Studies* (1960), and *The Marmalade Bird* (1973), containing "Down at the Hydro," one of his best stories. He also wrote travel books about his European trips and a biography of Marcel Proust.

Santa Claus \'san-tə-,klȯs\, *also called* Father Christmas.   A legendary figure who is the traditional patron of Christmas in the United States and other countries. His popular image is based on traditions associated with the 4th-century Christian Saint Nicholas.

Nicholas' existence is not attested by any historical document, and nothing certain is known of his life except that he was probably bishop of Myra in the 4th century. During the 11th century his alleged remains were stolen from Myra by Italian sailors or merchants and taken to Bari [Italy]; this removal greatly increased the saint's popularity in Europe.

Nicholas' reputation for generosity and kindness gave rise to legends of miracles performed for the poor and unhappy. His miracles were a favorite subject for medieval artists and liturgical plays.

After the Reformation, Nicholas' cult disappeared in all the Protestant countries of Europe except Holland, where his legend persisted as Sinterklaas (a Dutch variant of the name Saint Nicholas). In the 17th century Dutch colonists took this tradition with them to New Amsterdam (now New York City) in the American colonies. Sinterklaas was adopted by the country's English-speaking majority under the name Santa Claus, and the legend of a kindly old man was united with Nordic folktales of a magician who punished naughty children and rewarded good children with presents. The resulting image of Santa Claus in the United States crystallized in the 19th century (particularly in the poem "A Visit from St. Nicholas" by Clement Clarke Moore), and he has ever since remained the patron of the gift-giving festival of Christmas.

Under various guises Saint Nicholas was transformed into a similar benevolent, gift-giving figure in The Netherlands, Belgium, and other northern European countries. In the United Kingdom, Santa Claus is known as Father Christmas.

Santareno \sän-tə-'reⁿn-ü\, Bernardo, *pseudonym of* António Martinho do Rosário \rō-'sär-yü\ (b. Nov. 19, 1924, Santarém, Port.—d. Aug. 30, 1980, Lisbon)   Portuguese poet and dramatist who is considered one of Portugal's leading 20th-century playwrights.

Santareno completed his university studies at Coimbra in medicine, and subsequently he pursued a dual career in Lisbon as a psychiatrist and writer.

Santareno typically examines the lives of Portuguese fishermen and offers a fusion of popular themes and superstitions and existential concerns. He seeks to identify the national "soul" or prototype of the Portuguese, and his characters oscillate between the sacred and the profane, the physical and the metaphysical. His dramas exhibit a tragic, morose quality that is frequently combined with the erotic. Among his more than a dozen well-known plays are *O lugre* (1959; "The Lugger"), *O crime de Aldeia Velha* (1959; "The Crime of Old Town"), *António Marinheiro* (1960), *O pecado de João Agonia* (1961; "The Sin of John Agony"), *Irmã Natividade* (1961; "Sister Nativity"), and *O inferno* (1967; "Hell").

Santayana \,sän-tä-'yä-nä, *commonly* ,san-tə-'yan-ə\, George, *original name* Jorge Augustín Nicolás Ruiz de Santayana (b. Dec. 16, 1863, Madrid, Spain—d. Sept. 26, 1952, Rome, Italy)   Spanish-American philosopher, poet, and humanist who made important contributions to aesthetics, speculative philosophy, and literary criticism.

Santayana was born of Spanish parents. He never relinquished his Spanish citizenship, and, although he was to write in English with subtlety and poise, he did not begin to learn the language until taken to join his mother in Boston in 1872. He graduated from Harvard College and studied at the University of Berlin before returning to Harvard. He joined the faculty of philosophy in 1889, forming with William James and the idealist Josiah Royce a brilliant triumvirate of philosophers.

At Harvard Santayana began to write. His *The Sense of Beauty* (1896), an important work on aesthetics, is concerned with the nature and elements of aesthetic feelings. The vital affinity between aesthetic and moral faculties is illustrated in Santayana's next book, *Interpretations of Poetry and Religion* (1900), particularly in the discussion of the poetry of Robert Browning. His five-volume *The Life of Reason* (1905–06) is a major theoretical work. A number of his essays are gathered into two volumes: *Three Philosophical Poets: Lucretius, Dante, and Goethe* (1910) and *Winds of Doctrine* (1913), in which the poetry of Percy Bysshe Shelley and the philosophies of Henri Bergson, a French evolutionary philosopher, and of Bertrand Russell are trenchantly discussed.

Santayana was in Europe when his mother died in 1912; he retired from teaching and never returned to America. He continued to write, and in 1924 he settled permanently in Rome. There he produced additional works that consolidated his reputation as a humanist critic and man of letters, an aspect of his writing that was brought to perfect expression in a novel, *The Last Puritan* (1935).

The bulk of Santayana's energies in his later years went into speculative philosophy. He also wrote a three-volume autobiography, *Persons and Places* (1944, 1945, 1953), and he was at work on a translation of Lorenzo de' Medici's love poem "Ambra" when he died.

Santillana \,sän-tēl-'yä-nä\, Iñigo López de Mendoza \'lō-päth-thä-men-'dō-thä\, Marqués de (b. Aug. 19, 1398, Carrión de los Condes, Castile and León [Spain]—d. March 25, 1458, Guadalajara, Castile)   Spanish poet and humanist who was one of the great literary and political figures of his time. He collected a magnificent library (now in the National Library in Madrid), patronized the arts, and wrote poetry of high quality.

An exceptionally well educated man, Santillana was instrumental in having Homer, Virgil, and Seneca translated into Spanish. Fluent in French, Italian, Galician, and Catalan and less so in Latin, he wrote the first sonnets in Spanish. They are admired but are highly imitative of Petrarch. He also collected proverbs and wrote traditional didactic and allegorical poetry, but he is primarily remembered for his 10 *serranillas* ("pastoral songs") and for the preface to his collected works.

The *serranillas*, which describe the encounters between a knight and a shepherdess, transformed popular lyrics into elegant, refined poetry. The *Proemio e carta al condestable de Portugal* (1449; "Preface and Letter to the Constable of Portugal") is the first example in Spanish of formal literary history and criticism. It distinguishes three literary styles: high, for classical writing in Greek and Latin; middle, for formal works in the vernacular; and low, for ballads and songs without formal order.

Sapper \'sap-ər\, *pseudonym of* Herman Cyril McNeile \mək-'nēl\ (b. Sept. 28, 1888, Bodmin, Cornwall, Eng.—d. Aug. 14, 1937, West Chiltington, Sussex)   British soldier and novelist who won immediate fame with his thriller *Bull-Dog Drummond* (1920), subtitled "The Adventures of a Demobilized Officer Who Found Peace Dull." Sapper published numerous popular sequels, but none had the impact and merit of the original. *See also* Hugh "Bulldog" DRUMMOND.

sapphic \'saf-ik\   Of, relating to, or consisting of an aeolic meter associated with the Greek lyric poet Sappho that scans as — ∪ — ⊻ | — ∪ ∪ — | ∪ — — (a sapphic hendecasyllable) or a four-line strophe that is characteristic of her verse. The first three lines of the strophe are sapphic hendecasyllables, and the fourth is an adonean (scanned as — ∪ ∪ — —). The strophe therefore scanned as follows:

— ∪ — ⊻ | — ∪ ∪ — | ∪ — —
— ∪ — ⊻ | — ∪ ∪ — | ∪ — —
— ∪ — ⊻ | — ∪ ∪ — | ∪ — —
— ∪ ∪ | — —

In Latin, Catullus first adapted the sapphic stanza or strophe, and Horace used it extensively in his *Odes*. In Horace's sapphics, the fourth syllable is always long, not variable, and there is always a caesura after the fifth or sixth syllable: — ∪ — — | ∪ | ∪ — ∪ — .

Sapphira and the Slave Girl \sə-'fīr-ə\   Novel by Willa CATHER, published in 1940. The novel is set in Virginia in the mid-1800s on the estate of a declining slaveholding family.

Sapphira and the Slave Girl centers on the family's matriarch, Sapphira Colbert, and her attempt to sell Nancy Till, a mixed-race slave girl. Sapphira's plot is foiled by her husband Henry and their widowed daughter Rachel Blake. A confident, strong-willed invalid, Sapphira has earned the respect of many of her slaves despite her subtle cruelty toward Nancy. Henry is a pious miller whose simple upbringing and passivity contrast with the aristocratic and manipulative nature of his wife. Henry's nephew Martin, a suave but lecherous ex-soldier, tries to seduce Nancy. Rachel, who helps Nancy flee to Canada, remains at odds with Sapphira over the issue of slavery until the death of Rachel's daughter reconciles the pair. Cather appears in the epilogue as a child who notes Nancy's triumphant return 25 years later.

Sappho or **Psappho** \'saf-ō\ (fl. *c.* 610–*c.* 580 BC, Lesbos, Asia Minor)   Celebrated lyric poet greatly admired in all ages for the beauty of her writing. Her vocabulary, like her dialect, is for the most part vernacular, not literary. Her phrasing is concise, direct, and picturesque. She had the power of standing aloof and critically judging her own ecstasies and pains, but her emotions lost nothing of their force by being recollected in comparative tranquillity.

It was the fashion in Lesbos during Sappho's lifetime for women of good family to assemble in informal societies and spend their days in idle, graceful pleasures, especially in the composition and recitation of poetry. Sappho was the leading spirit of one of these associations. The principal themes of her poetry are the loves and jealousies and hates that flourished in that atmosphere. Rival associations are fiercely or contemptuously attacked. For other women, usually nameless, Sappho expresses her feelings in terms that range from gentle affection to passionate love. Her works include epithalamiums (wedding songs) and poems of friendship and homoerotic desire.

It is not known how her poems were published and circulated in her own lifetime and for the following three or four centuries. In the era of Alexandrian scholarship (especially the 3rd and 2nd centuries BC), what remained of her work was collected and republished in a standard edition of nine books of lyrical verse and one of elegiac. This edition did not survive the early Middle Ages. By the 8th or 9th century AD Sappho was represented only by quotations in other authors. Only one poem, 28 lines long, was complete; the next longest was 16 lines. Since 1898 these fragments have been greatly increased by papyrus finds, though no complete poem has been recovered.

Sarashina nikki \'sä-rä-,shē-nä-'nēk-kē\ ("Sarashina Diary")   A classic of Japanese literature of the Heian period (794–1185), written about 1059 by a woman known only as Sugawara Takasue no Musume ("Daughter of Sugawara Takasue"). The work was translated into English as *As I Crossed a Bridge of Dreams*.

One of four major court diaries, *Sarashina nikki* is unique in the scope of its chronology: it begins when the author is 12 and ends when she is in her 50s. It is largely a record in both prose and poetry of the author's struggle with a strong tendency toward romanticism. Written simply and poignantly, the diary reveals daily events—her travels, service in the court, marriage, and the deaths of many of those closest to her—as well as the nocturnal dreams that influence her understanding of life.

Sarasin or **Sarrazin** or **Sarrasin** \så-rå-'saⁿ\, Jean-François (b. 1614, Caen, Fr.—d. Dec. 5, 1654, Pézenas)   French author of elegant verse who is best known for the mock epic *Dulot vaincu* ("Dulot Defeated"), the epic fragments *Rollon conquér-ant* ("Roland in Conquest") and *La Guerre espagnole* ("The Spanish War"), and *La Pompe funèbre de Voiture* ("Voiture's Funeral Pomp").

In his youth Sarasin undertook classical studies, and in 1648 he entered the household of Armand I de Bourbon, Prince de Conti, in whose service he remained until his death. His position permitted him to enter Paris high society and to move in the circles of the famous. He wrote witty, satiric poems, historical works (*Histoire du siège de Dunkerque*, 1649; "History of the Siege of Dunkirk"), and the unfinished work *La Con-spiration de Wallenstein* ("The Wallenstein Conspiracy"), an excellent model of historical narrative. He was responsible for introducing the Italian burlesque genre into France.

Sardou \sår-'dü\, Victorien (b. Sept. 5, 1831, Paris, Fr.—d. Nov. 8, 1908, Paris)   Playwright who, with Émile Augier and Alexandre Dumas *fils*, dominated the French stage in the late 19th century and is still remembered as a craftsman of bourgeois drama of a type belittled by George Bernard Shaw as "Sardoodledom." Sardou's work *Les Pattes de mouche* (1860; *A Scrap of Paper*) is a model of the well-made play. He relied heavily on theatrical devices to create an illusion of life, and this largely accounts for his rapid decline in popularity. *Madame Sans-Gêne*, his last success, is still performed, although his other successful plays are rarely done. He owed his initial popularity to the actress Virginie Déjazet, for whom he wrote several of his 70 works; others were written for Sarah Bernhardt. In 1877 he was elected to the Académie Française.

Sargeson \'sär-jə-sən\, Frank, *pseudonym of* Norris Frank Davey \'dā-vē\ (b. March 23, 1903, Hamilton, Waikato, N.Z.—d. March 1, 1982, Auckland)   Novelist and writer of short stories whose ironic, stylistically diverse works made him the most widely known New Zealand literary figure of his day.

Sargeson studied law and won admission as a solicitor before taking up writing in the late 1920s. His early work consisted principally of short stories, a number of which were first published in the United States, although Sargeson remained a lifelong resident of New Zealand. Collections include *Conversations with My Uncle* (1936), *A Man and His Wife* (1940), and *That Summer* (1946).

In his novels, from the early *I Saw in My Dream* (1949) to the later *Joy of the Worm* (1969) and *Sunset Village* (1976), he treated themes of social corruption and personal freedom in a variety of styles. The *Collected Stories* (1964) and *The Stories of Frank Sargeson* (1973) broadened his international readership.

Sarmiento \sär-'myen-tō\, Domingo Faustino (b. Feb. 14, 1811, San Juan, Viceroyalty of the Río de la Plata [now in Argentina]—d. Sept. 11, 1888, Asunción, Paraguay)   Writer, educator, and statesman who rose from rural schoolmaster to become Argentina's first civilian president (1868–74).

Largely self-taught, Sarmiento began his career as a rural schoolteacher at the age of 15 and soon entered public life as a provincial legislator. In 1840 he was exiled to Chile, where he was active in politics and education. During this period Sarmiento wrote *Civilización y barbarie: vida de Juan Facundo Quiroga, y aspecto físico, costumbres, y hábitos de la Repúbli-ca Argentina* (1845; *Life in the Argentine Republic in the Days of the Tyrants; or, Civilization and Barbarism*), the first seri-

ous prose written about the gaucho (South American cowboy) and an impassioned denunciation of the dictator Juan Manuel de Rosas. A quasi-biography of Juan Facundo Quiroga, Rosas' tyrannical gaucho lieutenant, the novel is considered to be the work that gave rise to the indigenous genre known as GAUCHO LITERATURE. Although criticized for its erratic style and over-simplifications, the book has also been called the single most important book produced in Latin America.

In 1845 the Chilean government sent Sarmiento abroad to study educational methods in Europe and the United States. After three years he returned, determined to follow the American model. In 1852 Sarmiento returned to Argentina to help overthrow Rosas, and he was elected president of Argentina in 1868. He brought primary and secondary schools, normal schools, and schools for professional and technical training, as well as libraries and museums, to the largely illiterate country. When his term ended in 1874, Sarmiento continued to be active in public life. Most of the 52 volumes of his published work are devoted to educational themes.

Saroyan \sə-'rȯi-ən\, William (b. Aug. 31, 1908, Fresno, Calif., U.S.—d. May 18, 1981, Fresno)   American writer who made his initial impact during the Great Depression with a deluge of brash, original, and irreverent stories celebrating the joy of living in spite of poverty, hunger, and insecurity.

The son of an Armenian immigrant, Saroyan left school at 15 and continued his education by reading and writing on his own. His first collection of stories, *The Daring Young Man on the Flying Trapeze* (1934), was soon followed by another collection, *Inhale and Exhale* (1936). His first play, *My Heart's in the Highlands*, was produced by the Group Theatre in 1939. In 1940 Saroyan refused the Pulitzer Prize for his play THE TIME OF YOUR LIFE (performed 1939) because he felt that it was no better than anything else he had written.

Saroyan was concerned with the basic goodness of all people, especially the obscure and naive, and with the value of life. His mastery of the vernacular makes his characters vibrantly alive. Most of his stories are based on his childhood and family, notably the collection MY NAME IS ARAM (1940) and the novel THE HUMAN COMEDY (1943). Novels such as *Rock Wa-gram* (1951) and *The Laughing Matter* (1953) were inspired by his own marriage, fatherhood, and divorce.

Although the autobiographical element was strong in all his fiction, some of his later memoirs—including *Here Comes, There Goes You Know Who* (1961), *Not Dying* (1963), *Days of Life and Death and Escape to the Moon* (1971), and *Places Where I've Done Time* (1975)—have their own enduring value.

Sarraute \så-'rōt\, Nathalie, *original name* Nathalie Ilyano-va Tcherniak \chir-'nʸåk\ (b. July 18, 1900, Ivanova, Russia)   French novelist and essayist, one of the earliest practitioners and a leading theorist of the NOUVEAU ROMAN.

Reared primarily in France and educated at the universities of Paris, Oxford, and Berlin, Sarraute practiced law until about 1940, when she became a full-time writer.

Sarraute's first book was *Tropismes* (1939; second edition, 1957), a collection of sketches in which she introduced the concept of tropisms (the term is borrowed from the natural sciences, where it denotes an involuntary response to a stimulus such as light or heat). She described tropisms as the "things that are not said and the movements that cross our consciousness very rapidly; they are the basis of most of our life and our relations with others—everything that happens within us which is not spoken by the interior monologue and which is transmitted by sensations." In subsequent novels, including *Portrait d'un inconnu* (1948; *Portrait of a Man Unknown*), *Martereau* (1953), *Le Planétarium* (1959), and *Les Fruits d'or* (1963; *The*

Golden Fruits), she continued to explore the psychological realities underlying human existence. To this end, she discarded conventional ideas about plot, chronology, characterization, and narrative point of view.

In *L'Ère du soupçon* (1956; *The Age of Suspicion*), a collection of essays, Sarraute analyzes the work of other novelists and discusses the theoretical bases and creative goals of her own work. During the 1960s she began writing plays; these include *Le Silence* (produced 1967) and *Le Mensonge* (produced 1967; *The Lie*). Like her novels, the plays focus on the unspoken "subconversations" that underlie human interactions. Sarraute also published an autobiographical work, *Enfance* (1983; *Childhood*).

Sarrazin or **Sarrasin**   *see* SARASIN.

Sarton \'särt-ən\, May, *original name* Eleanore Marie Sarton (b. May 3, 1912, Wondelgem, Belg.)   American poet, novelist, and essayist whose works were informed by themes of love, mind-body conflict, creativity, lesbianism, and the trials of age and illness.

Sarton began to write full-time after 1945. Her writing often earned greater acclaim from the public than from critics. Her novels increasingly reflected the concerns of her own life. Her early fiction, such as *The Single Hound* (1938) and *A Shower of Summer Days* (1952), was set in Europe and showed the merest glimpse of autobiography. *Mrs. Stevens Hears the Mermaids Singing* (1965), considered by many to be her most important novel, addressed issues of artistic expression. Her other novels include *As We Are Now* (1973), *A Reckoning* (1978), *The Magnificent Spinster* (1985), and *The Education of Harriet Hatfield* (1989).

Sarton preferred the writing of poetry to prose. Of her many volumes of poetry, *The Land of Silence* (1953), *In Time Like Air* (1958), and *A Private Mythology* (1966) are cited as among her best, the last for its varied forms and invocation of Japanese, Indian, and Greek cultures. Her *Collected Poems, 1930–1993* (1993) demonstrated her range of subjects and styles. Sarton's late autobiographical writings, such as *After the Stroke: A Journal* (1989) and *Encore: A Journal of the Eightieth Year* (1993), offered meditations on illness and aging.

Sartoris \sär-'tȯr-is\   Novel by William FAULKNER, published in 1929 as a shortened version of a novel that was eventually published in its entirety in 1973 under the original title *Flags in the Dust.*

Disproportioned and sometimes emotionally overwrought, Faulkner's third novel was the last of his apprentice works but also the first set in his imagined community of Yoknapatawpha County, Miss. The novel concerns the Sartoris family, which revels in a mythical history of clan heroism and nobility that is belied by their current desperation and recklessness. The work addresses many of the themes Faulkner developed at length in his later novels: innate brutality, racial tension, the contrast between a romanticized Southern past and a tawdry present. It also introduces characters who featured prominently in his other Yoknapatawpha novels, including the crass Snopes family and lawyer Horace Benbow. The early history of the Sartoris family is told in *The Unvanquished* (1938).

Sartor Resartus \'sär-,tȯr-rē-'sär-təs\   ("The Tailor Retailored")   Humorous essay by Thomas CARLYLE, ostensibly a learned treatise on the philosophy, symbolism, and influence of clothes, published serially in *Fraser's Magazine* (November 1833–August 1834). Subtitled *The Life and Opinions of Herr Teufelsdröckh* ("Mr. Devil's Dung"), *Sartor Resartus* was published in book form in 1836 in the United States, with a preface by Ralph Waldo Emerson. The main theme is that the intellectual forms in which the deepest human convictions have

been cast are dead and that new ones must be found to fit the time, but that the intellectual content of this new religious system is elusive.

Sartre \'sȧrtr, *Angl* 'särt, 'sär-trə\, Jean-Paul (b. June 21, 1905, Paris, Fr.—d. April 15, 1980, Paris)   French novelist, playwright, and exponent of existentialism, a philosophy acclaiming the freedom of the individual. He was awarded the Nobel Prize for Literature in 1964, but he declined the award.

Sartre graduated from the prestigious École Normale Supérieure in 1929. While still a student he formed with Simone de BEAUVOIR a romantic and an intellectual union that remained a partnership for life. From 1931 to 1945 Sartre taught in the lycées of Le Havre, Laon, and, finally, Paris. Twice this career was interrupted, once by a year of study in Berlin and the second time when Sartre was drafted in 1939 to serve in World War II. He was imprisoned in 1940 and released a year later.

In 1938 Sartre's first novel, *La Nausée* (NAUSEA), was published. He adopted the phenomenological method (which proposes careful, unprejudiced description rather than deduction) from the German philosopher Edmund Husserl and used it in three successive works: *L'Imagination* (1936; *Imagination: A Psychological Critique*), *Esquisse d'une théorie des émotions* (1939; *Sketch for a Theory of the Emotions*), and *L'Imaginaire: Psychologie phénoménologique de l'imagination* (1940; *The Psychology of Imagination*). It was in *L'Être et le néant* (1943; *Being and Nothingness*), however, that Sartre gave the fullest explication of his philosophical system. Sartre places human consciousness, or no-thingness (*néant*), in opposition to being, or thingness (*être*). Consciousness, as not-matter, escapes determinism and thus is the source of freedom. With freedom comes the responsibility for giving meaning to human endeavor, which otherwise remains futile.

From this basis Sartre examined the concept of social responsibility. Freedom itself became a tool for human struggle in his short work *L'Existentialisme est un humanisme* (1946; *Existentialism and Humanism*), in which he concluded that freedom implies social responsibility. In his novels and plays Sartre began to place his ethical message before the world at large. He began a four-volume novel in 1945 under the title *Les Chemins de la liberté*, of which three volumes were eventually written: *L'Âge de raison* (1945; *The Age of Reason*), *Le Sursis* (1945; *The Reprieve*), and *La Mort dans l'âme* (1949; *Iron in the Soul*; U.S. title, *Troubled Sleep*). After the publication of the third volume, Sartre rejected the validity of the novel form.

Believing that drama might be a more suitable medium, Sartre once again began writing plays. His dramatic works include *Les Mouches* (1943; *The Flies*), *Huis clos* (1945; *In Camera*; U.S. title, NO EXIT), *Les Mains sales* (1948; *Crime passionnel*; U.S. title, *Dirty Hands*), *Le Diable et le bon Dieu* (1951; *Lucifer and the Lord*), *Nekrassov* (1956), and *Les Séquestrés d'Altona* (1959; *Loser Wins*; U.S. title, *The Condemned of Altona*). Other publications of the same period include his book *Baudelaire* (1947); a study on the French writer and poet Jean Genet, entitled *Saint Genet, comédien et martyr* (1952; *Saint Genet, Actor and Martyr*); and innumerable articles for *Les Temps modernes*, the monthly review that Sartre and de Beauvoir founded and edited. These articles were later collected in several volumes under the title *Situations*. In *Critique de la raison dialectique* (1960; *Search for a Method*) Sartre set out to examine critically the Marxist dialectic. In 1964 the autobiographical *Les Mots* (*The Words*) was published.

From 1960 until 1971 most of Sartre's attention went into the writing of a planned four-volume study called *L'Idiot de la famille* (*The Family Idiot*). Two volumes with a total of some 2,130 pages appeared in the spring of 1971. This huge enterprise aimed at presenting the reader with a "total biography" of

Gustave Flaubert, using both Freudian and Marxist interpretations. The third volume of the study was published in 1972, and Sartre's enormous productivity ended with this book. Near the end of his life Sartre became blind and his health deteriorated.

Sassoon \sə-'sün, sa-\, Siegfried (Lorraine) (b. Sept. 8, 1886, Brenchley, Kent, Eng.—d. Sept. 1, 1967, Heytesbury, Wiltshire)   English poet and novelist who is known chiefly for his antiwar poetry. His fictionalized autobiographies were noteworthy for their evocation of English country life.

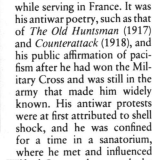

Sassoon enlisted in World War I and was twice wounded while serving in France. It was his antiwar poetry, such as that of *The Old Huntsman* (1917) and *Counterattack* (1918), and his public affirmation of pacifism after he had won the Military Cross and was still in the army that made him widely known. His antiwar protests were at first attributed to shell shock, and he was confined for a time in a sanatorium, where he met and influenced

Library of Congress

another pacifist soldier-poet, Wilfred Owen, whose works he published after Owen was killed at the front. Sassoon's autobiographical works include *The Memoirs of George Sherston*, 3 vol. (1928–36), and *Siegfried's Journey*, 3 vol. (1945), and more of his verse was published in *Collected Poems* (1947) and *The Path to Peace* (1960). His later poetry was increasingly devotional.

Sasuntzi Davith \,sä-sünt-'sē-,dä-'vēt\   Armenian folk epic dealing with the adventures of the Christian king David of Sasun in his defense against infidel invaders from Egypt and Persia. The epic was based on oral tradition that presumably dates from the 8th to the 10th century; it was widely known from the 16th through the 19th century and was finally written down in 1873. It is composed in poetic lines of irregular length arranged into rhyme groups. The appeal of the epic is enhanced by the devils and spirits that figure prominently in the numerous incidents and situations involving David and his son Mher the Younger.

Satanic school   Pejorative designation for the poets John Keats, Percy Bysshe Shelley, Leigh Hunt, and Lord Byron, used of them by Robert Southey in the preface to his *A Vision of Judgement* (1821). The term expressed Southey's disapproval of the unorthodox views and lifestyles of the poets.

Satin Slipper, The (*in full* The Satin Slipper; or, The Worst Is Not Always Certain)   Philosophical play in four "days" or sections by Paul CLAUDEL, published in 1929 in French as *Le Soulier de satin; ou, Le Pire n'est pas toujours sûr*. Designed to be read rather than performed (an abridged version was staged in 1943), it is often considered Claudel's masterpiece.

An ambiguous and convoluted epic work that celebrates Roman Catholic doctrine, it is set on four continents during the late 16th and early 17th centuries and concerns the love of Rodrigue, a Spanish conquistador, for Prouhèze, a married woman. The two are separated for many years while he is on a mission to the Americas to colonize for the Spanish crown and she is sent to North Africa. When Rodrigue and Prouhèze finally meet again, they do not consummate their great passion. They sacrifice their happiness in exchange for God's ultimate grace.

satire \'sa-,tīr\ [Latin *satura, satira,* perhaps from (*lanx*) *satura* dish of mixed ingredients]   A usually topical literary composition holding up human or individual vices, folly, abuses, or shortcomings to censure by means of ridicule, derision, burlesque, irony, or other methods, sometimes with an intent to bring about improvement.

Though there are examples of satire in Greek literature, notably the works of Aristophanes, the great Roman poets Horace and Juvenal established the genre known as the formal verse satire and, in so doing, exerted pervasive, if often indirect, influence on all subsequent literary satire. The two Romans approached the form from radically different perspectives. The character of the satirist as projected by Horace is that of an urbane man of the world, concerned about folly, which he sees everywhere, but moved to laughter rather than rage. Juvenal, more than a century later, conceives the satirist's role differently. His most characteristic posture is that of the upright man who looks with horror on the corruptions of his time, his heart consumed with anger and frustration. Satiric writing after Horace and Juvenal traditionally followed the example of one of the two writers. This resulted in the formation of two subgenres identified by John Dryden as comic satire and tragic satire. These denominations have come to mark the boundaries of the satiric spectrum, whether reference is to poetry or prose or to some form of satiric expression in another medium.

Satire is found embodied in an indefinite number of literary forms. Its targets range from one of Alexander Pope's dunces to the entire race of man, as in *Satyr Against Mankind* (1679) by John Wilmot, the Earl of Rochester, and from Erasmus' attack on corruptions in the church to Jonathan Swift's excoriation of all civilized institutions in *Gulliver's Travels*. Its forms are as varied as its victims: from an anonymous medieval invective against social injustice to the superb wit of Geoffrey Chaucer and the laughter of Rabelais; from the burlesque of Luigi Pulci to the scurrilities of Pietro Aretino and the "black humor" of Lenny Bruce; from the flailings of John Marston and the mordancies of Francisco Gómez de Quevedo to the bite of Jean de La Fontaine and the great dramatic structures of Ben Jonson and Molière; from an epigram of Martial to the fictions of Nikolay Gogol and of Günter Grass and the satirical utopias of Yevgeny Zamyatin, Aldous Huxley, and George Orwell.

Satires   Collection of 16 satiric poems published at intervals in five separate books by JUVENAL. Book One, containing Satires 1–5, was issued *c.* AD 100–110; Book Two, with Satire 6, *c.* 115; Book Three, which comprises Satires 7–9, contains what must be a reference to Hadrian, who ruled from 117 to 138; Book Four, made up of Satires 10–12, contains no datable allusion; and Book Five, containing Satires 13–16, has two references to the year 127.

The Satires address two main themes: the corruption of society in the city of Rome and human brutality and folly. In the first Satire, Juvenal declares that vice, crime, and the misuse of wealth have reached such a peak that it is impossible *not* to write satire, but that, since it is dangerous to attack powerful men in their lifetime, he will take his examples from the dead. In the second and ninth Satires he derides male homosexuals. The third and fifth Satires deal with aspects of a life of dependency on patronage. The fourth Satire illustrates the Roman emperor Domitian's pettiness. The sixth Satire, some 600 lines long, denounces Roman women. The poverty of Roman intellectuals is the subject of the seventh Satire, and the eighth attacks the cult of hereditary nobility. The 10th Satire examines human ambitions and recommends instead seeking "a sound mind in a sound body, and a brave heart." Satire 11 points up the foolish extravagance of the wealthy. The 12th Satire distinguishes between true and mercenary friendship; the 13th is a variation on the same theme. In the 14th Juvenal denounces parents who teach their children avarice. The 15th Satire reports an appalling incident of human savagery. Satire 16, which introduces the subject of the privileges of professional soldiers, is a fragment.

Sato   *see* SAKURADA.

Satō   Haruo \sä-'tō-'hä-rü-ō\ (b. April 9, 1892, Shingū, Wakayama prefecture, Japan—d. May 6, 1964, Tokyo) Japanese poet, novelist, and critic whose fiction is noted for its poetic vision and romantic imagination.

Satō came from a family of physicians with scholarly and literary interests. He entered Keiō University in Tokyo to study with the novelist Nagai Kafū in 1910, but he had already joined the Myōjō group of poets centering around Yosano Akiko and her husband Tekkan and left Keiō without graduating.

Satō began to attract attention with the short story "Supeinu ken-no-ie" (1916; "The House of a Spanish Dog"), a piece of fantasy with a dreamlike tone. The prose poems *Den'en no yūutsu* (1919; "Rural Melancholy") and *Tokai no yūutsu* (1922; "Urban Melancholy") established his style of lyrical world-weary self-reflection. Satō met the novelist Tanizaki Jun'ichirō in 1916, beginning a friendship that ended several years later when he became involved with Tanizaki's wife. His first independent volume of poetry, *Junjō shishū* (1921; "Poems of Mourning"), was inspired by his sorrow at parting from her; in 1930, however, they were married. He turned to criticism in later years; outstanding is *Akiko mandara* (1955; "A Mandala for Akiko"), a memorial to Yosano Akiko.

Sato   Norikiyo   *see* SAIGYŌ.

Saturday Club   *also called* Magazine Club *or* Atlantic Club. American social club of New England literati that was founded in 1855 and that met monthly at the Parker House, a Boston hotel. Notable members included Oliver Wendell Holmes, Ralph Waldo Emerson, Henry Wadsworth Longfellow, James Russell Lowell, Richard Henry Dana, John Greenleaf Whittier, William Dean Howells, Nathaniel Hawthorne, Henry James, and Charles Sumner.

Saturday Review, The   *also called* (until 1952) The Saturday Review of Literature.   Literary periodical founded in New York by Henry Seidel Canby in 1924. It was originally devoted to the work of new writers, including many foreign writers in translation, as well as to that of earlier writers such as Walt Whitman and Ralph Waldo Emerson. Among the early contributors to the periodical were Mary Austin, Edgar Lee Masters, and G.K. Chesterton. The scope of the review was expanded by Norman Cousins, who edited the magazine for more than 30 years, and for a time the magazine was published as four separate reviews of the arts, society, education, and the sciences. It folded in 1986.

Saturn   \'sat-ərn\ *or* **Saturnus**   \sa-'tər-nəs\   In Roman mythology, the god of sowing or seed. The Romans equated him with the Greek agricultural deity CRONUS.

Saturnian verse   *or* **Saturnian meter**   \sa-'tər-nē-ən\ [Latin *Saturnius* of Saturnian meter, literally, of Saturn]   The ancient Latin verse used mainly by Livius Andronicus and Gnaeus Naevius before the adoption of Greek verse forms by later Latin writers. Little is known about its origins or whether its rhythm was accentual or quantitative.

satyr   \'sāt-ər, 'sat-\ [Greek *sátyros*]   A type of ancient Greek sylvan deity having a fondness for Dionysian revelry. The Italian counterparts of the satyrs were the fauns. Satyrs were at first represented as uncouth men, with a horse's tail and ears and an erect phallus; later they came to be represented as men having

a goat's legs and tail. In the Great Dionysia festival at Athens three tragedies were followed by a satyr play in which the chorus was dressed to represent satyrs. In literature the Dionysian character of satyrs was reflected in the tone of the *Satyricon* (or *Satyricon liber*, "Book of Satyrlike Adventures"), an ancient Latin comic novel that depicts the adventures of a disreputable group of people. *See also* SILENUS.

Satyricon   *or* **Satyricon liber**   \sə-'tir-ə-,kän-'līb-er, 'lib-\ ("Book of Satyrlike Adventures")   A 1st-century-AD comic picaresque novel attributed to Gaius PETRONIUS ARBITER. In style it ranges between the highly realistic and the self-consciously literary. The work tells of the wanderings and escapades of a disreputable trio of adventurers, the narrator Encolpius ("Embracer"), his friend Ascyltos ("Scot-free"), and the boy Giton ("Neighbor"). The surviving portions of the *Satyricon* (parts of Books XV and XVI) probably represent about one-tenth of the complete work, which was evidently very long. The loose narrative framework encloses a number of independent tales, a classic instance being the famous "Widow of Ephesus" (*Satyricon*, chapters 111–112).

The longest and the best episode in the surviving portions of the *Satyricon* is the *Cena Trimalchionis*, or "Banquet of Trimalchio" (chapters 26–78). It is a description of a dinner party given by Trimalchio, an immensely rich and vulgar freedman (former slave), to a group of friends and hangers-on. The episode is notable for its extraordinary realism and the acute observation of the figure of Trimalchio, who, with his vast wealth, his tasteless ostentation, his affectation of culture, his superstition, and his maudlin lapses into natural vulgarity, is one of the great comic figures of literature.

The aim of the work as a whole was evidently to entertain by portraying certain aspects of contemporary society, and when considered as such, the book is of immense value: superficial details of the speech, behavior, appearance, and surroundings of the characters are exactly observed and vividly communicated.

satyr play   Burlesque comedy performed as comic relief after a classical Greek tragic trilogy. Satyr plays are believed to have developed from the dithyramb, a hymn to Dionysus, concurrently with tragedy. They were evidently introduced at the Great Dionysia drama festival at Athens in the late 6th century BC. Written by the competing authors of the three tragedies, these plays featured a legendary hero, frequently the protagonist of the preceding trilogy. This character was joined by a cowardly, lecherous, and wine-loving chorus of 11 satyrs led by Silenus, the foster father of Dionysus, in a farcical plot or a parody of a myth. Euripides' *Cyclops* is the only complete satyr play extant.

saudade   \saů-'däj-ē\ [Portuguese, literally, longing, yearning]   Overtone of melancholy and brooding loneliness and an almost mystical reverence for nature that permeates Portuguese and Brazilian lyric poetry. *Saudade* was a characteristic of the earliest Portuguese folk poetry and has been cultivated by sophisticated writers of later generations. In the late 19th century António Nobre and Teixeira de Pascoais were the foremost of a growing cult of *saudosismo*, a combination of *saudade* and pantheism that was a reflection of a type of mystical nationalism. Especially in the poems collected in *Só* (1892), Nobre was intensely Portuguese in his themes, his mood (an all-pervading *saudade*), and his rhythms, whereas Teixeira de Pascoais typified the pantheist tendencies of Portuguese poetry. They inspired the movement known as the Renascença Portuguesa (*c.* 1910), centered on Porto.

Saussure   \də-sō-'sūₑr\, Ferdinand de (b. Nov. 26, 1857, Geneva, Switz.—d. Feb. 22, 1913, Geneva)   Swiss linguist whose ideas on structure in language laid the foundation for much of the approach to and progress of the linguistic and related sciences in the 20th century.

While still a student, Saussure established his reputation with a brilliant contribution to comparative linguistics, *Mémoire sur le système primitif des voyelles dans les langues indo-européennes* (1879; "Memoir on the Original System of Vowels in the Indo-European Languages"). In it he explained how the knottiest of vowel alternations in Indo-European, those of *a*, take place. Though he wrote no other book, he was enormously influential as a teacher, serving as instructor at the School of Advanced Studies in Paris from 1881 to 1891 and as professor of Indo-European linguistics and Sanskrit (1901–13) and of general linguistics (1907–13) at the University of Geneva. His name is affixed to the *Cours de linguistique générale* (1916; *Course in General Linguistics*), a reconstruction of his lecture notes and other materials by two of his students, Charles Bally and Albert Séchehaye. The publication of this work is frequently considered the starting point of 20th-century linguistics.

Saussure contended that language must be considered as a social phenomenon, a structured system that can be viewed synchronically (as it exists at any particular time) and diachronically (as it changes in the course of time). He thus formalized the basic approaches to language study and asserted that the principles and methodology of each approach are distinct and mutually exclusive. He also introduced two terms that have become common currency in linguistics—*parole*, or the speech of the individual person, and *langue*, or a systematic, structured language, such as English, existing at a given time within a given society. His distinctions proved to be mainsprings to productive linguistic research and can be regarded as the starting points of structuralism.

Savage \'sav-ij\, Richard (b. *c.* 1697, England—d. Aug. 1, 1743, Bristol) English poet and satirist and subject of one of the best short biographies in English, Samuel Johnson's *Account of the Life of Mr Richard Savage* (1744).

By his own account in the preface to the second edition of his *Miscellaneous Poems* (1728; 1st edition, 1726), Savage was the illegitimate son of Anne, Countess of Macclesfield, and Richard Savage, the 4th Earl of Rivers. In 1717 he published *The Convocation*, a poem about a religious dispute known as the Bangorian controversy, and in 1718 *Love in a Veil* (1719), a comedy he adapted from the Spanish of Pedro Calderón de la Barca, was produced at Drury Lane. There, in 1723, Savage's Neoclassical tragedy *Sir Thomas Overbury* was also produced. His most considerable poem, *The Wanderer*, appeared in 1729, as did his prose satire on Grub Street, *An Author to Be Let*. In 1737–38 he met Johnson, then newly arrived in London, and to Johnson's perceptive and compassionate biography Savage owes his continuing fame. He was a quarrelsome and an impecunious man, and his friends, Alexander Pope prominent among them, eventually provided him money to convey him out of London. After a year in Wales, he died miserably in debtor's prison.

Savard \så-'vår\, Félix-Antoine (b. Aug. 31, 1896, Quebec, Que., Can.—d. Aug. 24, 1982, Quebec) French-Canadian priest, poet, novelist, and folklorist whose works show a strong French-nationalist bias and a love of the Canadian landscape.

Savard was ordained a Roman Catholic priest in 1922. He began to lecture in the faculty of arts at Laval University in Quebec in 1943 and was dean of arts there from 1950 to 1957. His works, which have been called both prose poems and novels, display a firsthand knowledge of Canadian logging and pioneering—*e.g., Menaud, maître-draveur* (1937; *The Boss of the River*), for which Savard received the literature prize both from the

Académie Française in 1945 and from the Grand Jury of Letters in 1961; *L'Abatis* (1943; "The Slaughter"); and *La Minuit* (1948; "Midnight"). He also wrote *Martin et le pauvre* (1959; "Martin and the Beggar"), the story of St. Martin of Tours, and *La Folle* (1960; "The Madwoman"), a drama in free verse. Among Savard's later works are *La Roche Ursule* (1972; "The Ursula Stone"), a volume of poems entitled *Aux marges du silence* (1975; "At the Borders of Silence"), and *Discours* (1975; "Speeches").

Sawa, Jan. Pseudonym of Maria KONOPNICKA.

Sawyer, Tom \'täm-'sȯi-ər, 'sȯ-yər\ Fictional character, the young protagonist of the novel TOM SAWYER by Mark Twain. Considered the epitome of the all-American boy, Tom Sawyer is full of mischief but basically pure-hearted. He is probably best remembered for the incident in which he gets a number of other boys to whitewash his Aunt Polly's fence—an unpleasant task in his eyes—by making the work seem to be extremely absorbing.

Twain wrote two sequels to his original story, *Tom Sawyer Abroad* (1894) and *Tom Sawyer, Detective* (1896), and Tom is also a character in Twain's *Huckleberry Finn* (1884).

Saxo Grammaticus \'sak-sō-grə-'mat-i-kəs\ (fl. mid-12th century–early 13th century) Historian whose GESTA DANORUM ("Story of the Danes") is the first important work on the history of Denmark and the first Danish contribution to world literature.

Little is known of Saxo's life except that he was a Zealander belonging to a family of warriors and was probably a clerk in the service of Absalon, archbishop of Lund from 1178 to 1201. Saxo is first mentioned in Svend Aggesen's *Historia Regum Danicae compendiosa* (1185; "Short History of the Danish Kings") as writing the history of Svend Estridsen (d. 1076).

The 16-volume *Gesta Danorum* is written in a brilliant, ornate Latin. It was his Latin eloquence that early in the 14th century caused Saxo to be called "Grammaticus." By presenting a 2,000-year-long panorama of Danish history, he aimed to show his country's antiquity and traditions. Saxo's work was a source of inspiration to many of the 19th-century Danish Romantic poets.

Sayat-Nova \,sä-yät-'nō-və\, *pseudonym of* Aruthin Sayadian \sä-'yäd-ē-ən\ (b. 1712, Tiflis [now Tbilisi], Georgia—d. 1795, Tiflis) Armenian troubadour known for his love songs.

Sayat-Nova worked first as a weaver and later (1750–65) became the court minstrel of Irakli II of Georgia. In 1770 he entered a monastery in Haghbat, and he was martyred by the Persian invaders of Georgia. Most of his extant songs are in Azeri Turkish; the rest are in Armenian and Georgian.

Sayers \'serz, 'sā-ərz\, Dorothy L., *in full* Leigh (b. June 13, 1893, Oxford, Eng.—d. Dec. 17, 1957, Witham, Essex) Scholar and writer best known for her mystery stories featuring the witty and charming Lord Peter WIMSEY.

Sayers received a degree in medieval literature from the Somerville College, University of Oxford, in 1915; she was one of the first women to graduate from the university. Her first major published work was *Whose Body?* (1923), a fairly standard detective novel but for her creation of Lord Peter, the dashing young gentleman-scholar whose erudition and native curiosity set him apart from the ordinary detective. Within the next 15 years, Sayers published one or two mysteries a year—including such well-known volumes as *The Unpleasantness at the Bellona Club* (1928); *Strong Poison* (1930), in which she introduced Lord Peter's future wife, Harriet Vane; *Have His Carcase* (1932); *Murder Must Advertise* (1933); *The Nine Tailors* (1934); *Gaudy Night* (1935); and *Busman's Honeymoon* (1937).

Both Lord Peter and another of Sayers' creations, Montague Egg, are featured in short stories.

With G.K. Chesterton and others, Sayers founded the Detection Club, a group composed of mystery writers, and they published a parody of the detective story in a novel entitled *The Floating Admiral* (1931). Sayers also published a three-volume anthology of detective stories entitled *Great Short Stories of Detection, Mystery and Horror* (1928, 1931, 1934; U.S. title, *The Omnibus of Crime*).

After the late 1930s, Sayers wrote no more detective fiction, concentrating rather on theological dramas, radio plays, and verse. She made several scholarly translations, including Anglo-Norman poet Thomas' *Tristan in Britanny* (1929) and *The Song of Roland* (1957). Her impressive and witty terza rima translation of Dante's *Divine Comedy*, which she published as *The Comedy of Dante Alighieri, the Florentine*, was issued in three volumes—*Hell*, *Purgatory*, and *Paradise*.

Scamandrius *see* ASTYANAX.

scan \'skan\ [Middle English *scanden, scannen,* from Late Latin *scandere,* from Latin, to climb] To read or mark so as to show metrical structure.

scansion \'skan-shən\ [Late Latin *scansio,* from Latin, act of climbing, a derivative of *scandere* to climb] The analysis of a rhythmic structure (such as a verse) so as to show its meter. Also, the product or result of scansion, such as a description or visual representation of a given metrical structure.

Scansion in English prosody employs a system of symbols to reveal the mechanics of a poem—*i.e.*, the predominant type of foot (the smallest metrical unit of stressed and unstressed syllables); the number of feet per line; and the rhyme scheme. The purpose of scansion is to enhance the reader's sensitivity to the ways in which rhythmic elements in a poem convey meaning.

English has three major types of scansion: the graphic, the musical, and the acoustic. The primary symbols used in graphic scansion, the most common type of scansion, are ($'$) to represent a syllable that is stressed in context; ($\cup$) to represent a syllable that is unstressed in context; a vertical line ($|$) to indicate a division between feet; and a double vertical line ($\|$) to show a caesura, a pause within a line of verse. Using these symbols, graphic scansion begins by marking the accented, then the unaccented, syllables according to the natural rhythm of speech. Following are the last two lines from Alfred, Lord Tennyson's "Ulysses," which are written in iambic pentameter, with the lines scanned in the graphic method:

Made weak | by time | and fate, | but strong | in will

To strive, | to seek, | to find, | and not | to yield.

Both musical and acoustic scansion, which are highly complex systems, afford greater sensitivity than graphic scansion to the tonal and accentual variety of speech. Musical symbols (*e.g.*, eighth notes for unstressed syllables, quarter or half notes for stressed syllables, and musical rests for pauses) record accentual differences. Machines such as the oscillograph are used by modern acoustic linguists to catch even slightly varying degrees of stress.

Modern scansion was adapted from the classical method of analyzing ancient Greek and Roman quantitative verse. The symbols used for classical prosody are ($-$) for long syllables, ($\cup$) for short syllables, and ($\cup$) for syllables of indeterminate length. Further distinctions include the symbol $\overline{\cup\cup}$, termed contraction, which indicates that two short syllables may be contracted into a single long syllable, and $\underset{\smile}{\smile}$, termed resolution, which indicates that one long syllable may be resolved into two short syllables.

scapigliatura \,skä-pēl-yä-'tū-rä\ [Italian, literally, a disheveled state, dissoluteness, loose living, a derivative of *scapigliare* to dishevel] A mid-19th-century Italian avant-garde movement centered in Milan. Influenced by Charles Baudelaire, the French Symbolist poets, Edgar Allan Poe, and German Romantic writers, it sought to replace the classical, Arcadian, and moralistic traditions of Italian literature with works that featured bizarre and pathological elements and direct, realistic narrative description. One of the founding members, Cletto Arrighi (pseudonym for Carlo Righetti), coined the name for the group in his novel *Scapigliatura e il 6 febbraio* (1862; "Scapigliatura and February 6").

Although some members of the group produced important literary work, they were more important as catalysts, inspiring the major writers of verismo ("realism"), the Futurists, and the Hermetic poets.

Scapin \skä-'paⁿ\ or **Scapino** \skä-'pē-nō\ Stock character of the Italian COMMEDIA DELL'ARTE; one of the comic servants, or zanni, who was especially noted for his cowardice. His name, derived from the Italian (*scappare*, "to flee"), was

Scapino.   *Cap: Zerbino*

Scapino and Zerbino conversing, engraving by Jacques Callot
Copyright British Museum

an accurate assessment of his character; he always took flight at the first sign of a conflict. Usually cast as an unreliable valet and general handyman, Scapin, wearing a bearded mask with a large hooked nose, was costumed in a loose-fitting green-and-white-striped tunic, pantaloons, and a rakish hat with two long feathers; he carried a wooden sword. Molière's *Les Fourberies de Scapin* (1671; *The Cheats of Scapin*) introduced this character into French comedy.

Scaramouche \skä-rä-'mūsh\ or **Scaramuccia** \,skä-rä-'mūt-chə\ Stock character of the Italian theatrical form known as the COMMEDIA DELL'ARTE, an unscrupulous and unreliable servant. His affinity for intrigue often placed him in difficult situations, yet he always managed to extricate himself, usually leaving an innocent bystander as his victim.

Scarlet Letter, The Novel by Nathaniel HAWTHORNE, published in 1850. It is considered a masterpiece of American literature and a classic moral study.

The novel is set in a village in Puritan New England. The main character is Hester Prynne, a young woman who has borne an illegitimate child. Hester believes herself a widow, but her husband, Roger Chillingworth, returns to New England very much alive and conceals his identity. He finds his wife forced to wear the scarlet letter *A* on her dress as punishment for her adultery. Chillingworth becomes obsessed with finding the identity of his wife's former lover. When he learns that the father of Hester's child is Arthur Dimmesdale, a saintly young minister who is the leader of those exhorting her to name the child's father, Chillingworth proceeds to torment the guilt-stricken young man.

In the end Chillingworth is morally degraded by his mono-maniacal pursuit of revenge; Dimmesdale is broken by his own sense of guilt, and he publicly confesses his adultery before dying in Hester's arms. Only Hester can face the future bravely, as she plans to take her daughter Pearl to Europe to begin a new life.

Scarlet Pimpernel, The   Romantic novel by Baroness Emmuska ORCZY, produced as a play in 1903 and published in book form in 1905.

The novel's protagonist, Sir Percy Blakeney, ostensibly a foppish English aristocrat, is secretly the Scarlet Pimpernel, a swashbuckling hero and elusive master of disguise who rescues French aristocrats and smuggles them out of France to safety during the French Revolution. His nemesis is Citizen Chauvelin, a ruthless agent of Robespierre.

The author chronicled further adventures of the hero in such sequels as *The Elusive Pimpernel* (1908) and *The Way of the Scarlet Pimpernel* (1933).

Scarron \skâ-'rōⁿ\, Paul (baptized July 4, 1610, Paris, Fr.—d. Oct. 7, 1660, Paris)   French writer who contributed significantly to the development of the drama, the burlesque epic, and the novel. He is remembered today for a single work, *Le Roman comique*, 3 vol. (1651–57; "The Comic Novel").

Scarron's first works were burlesques. The poet Antoine Girard Saint-Amant had already started the vogue for parodies of the classics, but Scarron is mainly responsible for making the burlesque one of the characteristic literary forms of the mid-17th century. His seven-volume *Virgile travesty* (1648–53), a parody of the *Aeneid*, had a tremendous success.

Scarron was also a considerable figure in the theatrical life of Paris in the years preceding Molière's arrival, and he often wrote with particular actors in mind. His plots are usually based upon Spanish originals, and even his most successful comedy, *Dom Japhet d'Arménie* (produced 1647), owes a good deal to a play by Alonso de Castillo Solórzano. *Le Roman comique*, 3 vol. (1651–57), composed in the style of a Spanish picaresque romance, recounts with gusto the comical adventures of a company of strolling players. The novel's realism makes it an invaluable source of information about conditions in the French provinces in the 17th century.

scazon \'skāz-ən\ [Greek *skázōn,* literally, one that limps, from present participle of *skázein* to limp], *also called* choliamb.   In classical poetry, a verse with a limping or halting movement; an iambic or trochaic verse in which the last foot consists of a spondee.

scél \'shkāl\ *plural* scéla \'shkā-lə\ [Old Irish, news, narration, tale]   In the Gaelic literature of Ireland, early prose and verse legends of gods and folk heroes, most of which originated during or before the 11th century. The primary types were classified according to the actions they celebrated: destructions, cattle raids, navigations, elopements, violent deaths, conflagrations, and other events. In modern times these tales have been grouped into cycles compromising (1) the mythological cycle, dealing with immortal beings; (2) the Ulster (Ulaid) cycle, dealing with the Ulster heroes during the reign of the semihistorical King Conor (Conchobar mac Nessa) in the 1st century BC; and (3) the Fenian cycle, dealing mainly with the deeds of Finn Mac-Cumhaill's war band during the reign of Cormac mac Art in the 3rd century AD. *See also* FENIAN CYCLE; ULSTER CYCLE.

scenario \sə-'nar-ē-ō, -'när-\ [French, from Italian, callboy's list of actors' entrances, stage scenery, flats, a derivative of *scena* stage, scene, from Latin *scena, scaena*]   An outline or synopsis of a play; specifically, a plot outline used by actors of the commedia dell'arte.

scene \'sēn\ [Middle French, stage, division of an act, from Latin *scena, scaena* stage, scene, ultimately from Greek *skēnē* booth, tent, structure serving as backdrop for plays, stage] **1.** One of the subdivisions of a play, such as a division of an act presenting continuous action in one place or a single situation or unit of dialogue.   **2.** The place in which represented action (as in a play or story) occurs.

Scenes from Private Life   Collection of six lengthy short stories by Honoré de BALZAC, published in 1830 as *Scènes de la vie privée*. They are for the most part detailed psychological studies of girls in conflict with parental authority.

Scenes of Clerical Life   The first novel by George ELIOT, comprising three tales that had originally appeared serially in *Blackwood's Magazine* in 1857 and were published together in two volumes in 1858. The stories, noted for their dialogue and characterization, drew upon Eliot's early experiences with religion in a provincial setting.

The title character of "The Sad Fortunes of the Reverend Amos Barton" is an awkward, unpopular clergyman of Shepperton whose hardworking, gentle wife, Milly, dies of exhaustion. "Mr. Gilfil's Love Story" concerns Barton's predecessor at Shepperton, whose long-suffering love for Tina is briefly satisfied when she, after being spurned by a previous lover, finally consents to marry Gilfil, only to die a few months later. In "Janet's Repentance," the Reverend Edgar Tryan is a sympathetic clergyman who helps to cure Janet Dempster of alcoholism after she flees her abusive husband, Robert.

Scève \'sev\, Maurice (b. *c.* 1501, Lyon, Fr.—d. 1560/64?, Lyon)   French poet who was noted chiefly for his verse cycle *Délie.*

Scève has often been described as the leader of the Lyonese school of writers (including Pernette du Guillet and Louise Labé), although there is no evidence that they formed an organized school. Scève first achieved fame in 1533 by his "discovery" of the tomb of Petrarch's Laura at Avignon, and he caught the public's attention again in 1536 with his *Blason du sourcil* ("Description of an Eyebrow"). The poem was later published in the anthology *Les Blasons du corps féminin* ("Descriptions of the Feminine Body"), often reprinted between 1537 and 1550.

His *Délie, objet de plus haute vertu* (1544; "Délie, Object of Highest Virtue") is a poetic cycle of 449 highly organized decasyllabic 10-line stanzas (*dizains*) that is rich in imagery and Platonic and Petrarchan in theme and style. "Délie" (an anagram of "L'Idée" ["The Idea"]), long thought to be an imaginary ideal, may have been Pernette du Guillet, whose death seems to have partly inspired *Saulsaye, églogue de la vie solitaire* (1547; "Willow Row, an Eclogue on the Solitary Life"), which Scève wrote while in retirement in the country.

Schaffner \'shäf-nər\, Jakob (b. Nov. 14, 1875, Basel, Switz.—d. Sept. 23, 1944, Strassburg, Ger. [now Strasbourg, Fr.])   Swiss writer who lived in Germany from 1913. He belonged to a new generation of Swiss writers who rejected the traditions of middle-class society and believed in life as a boundless adventure.

Schaffner described his life in four autobiographical novels: *Johannes* (1922), *Die Jünglingszeit des Johannes Schattenhold* (1930; "The Youth of Johann Schattenhold"), *Eine deutsche Wanderschaft* (1931; "A German Journey"), and *Kampf und Reife* (1939; "Struggle and Resolution"). These works depict his experiences as an orphan, a charity schoolboy, a shoemaker, and a self-taught writer. Schaffner's writing is colorful, spirited, and imaginative; his convictions, which were those of the philosopher Friedrich Nietzsche and, to some extent, of Fyodor Dostoyevsky, finally led him to follow the lure of Nazism. His other works include the novels *Konrad Pilater* (1910), *Der Dechant von Gottesbüren* (1917; "The Dean of Gottesbüren"), and *Die Glücksfischer* (1925; "The Fisher for Happiness") and a volume of poetry entitled *Bekenntnis* (1940; "Confessions"). He also wrote the essays *Die Predigt der Marienburg* (1931; "The Sermon of Marienburg") and *Berge, Ströme und Städte, eine schweizerische Heimatschau* (1938; "Mountains, Streams and Towns, a View of My Swiss Homeland").

Schauspiel \'shaủ-,shpēl\ [German, from *Schau* show, sight + *Spiel* play]   Any spectacle or public performance. In late 18th-century German literature the word took on the more specific meaning of a play that has characteristics of both a tragedy and a comedy in that it is a serious play with a happy ending.

Scheffel \'shef-əl\, Joseph Victor von (b. Feb. 16, 1826, Karlsruhe, Baden [Germany]—d. April 9, 1886, Karlsruhe) Poet and novelist whose immensely popular humorous epic poem *Der Trompeter von Säckingen* (1854; "The Trumpeter of Säckingen") and historical novel *Ekkehard* (1855) made him one of the most widely read German authors of his time.

A civil servant from 1848 to 1853, Scheffel served as librarian to Prince Fürstenberg at Donaueschingen from 1857 to 1859. In 1865 he was given the title of privy councillor, and in 1876 he was given a patent of nobility.

Scheffel's popularity was based on genuine poetic talent as well as on his romantic nationalism, an outlook that rejected contemporary realism for a rosy view of Germany's ancient glories. His meticulously researched book *Ekkehard* was set at the 10th-century monastery of St. Gall. His other works include *Hugideo* (1884), a historical novel set in the 5th century; *Frau Aventiure* (1863; "Lady Adventure"), a book of verse; and *Gaudeamus!* (1868), a collection of student songs. Scheffel's writings were later viewed as cloying and trivial.

Scheherazade \shə-,her-ə-'zäd, -'zä-də\ or **Shahrazad** \,shä-rə-'zäd\ Fictional character, ingenious storyteller in THE THOUSAND AND ONE NIGHTS.

scheme \'skēm\   In prosody, a diagram or table showing metrical structure or rhyme arrangement (such as of a stanza).

Schendel \vän-'sken-dəl\, Arthur van, *in full* Arthur-François-Émile van Schendel (b. March 5, 1874, Batavia, Java, Dutch East Indies [now Jakarta, Indon.]—d. Sept. 11, 1946, Amsterdam, Neth.)   Dutch novelist and short-story writer whose Romantic temperament, combined with a restrained style, produced some of the greatest novels of his period.

Schendel's first important novels, *Een zwerver verliefd* (1904; "A Wanderer in Love") and *Een zwerver verdwaald* (1907; "A Lost Wanderer"), are set in medieval Italy and concern the inner life and imagination of the hero, Tamalone. The theme of humanity's inevitable succumbing to fate is prevalent in these and all his later works, in which he turns to a more realistic style. Notable examples are *Het fregatschip Johanna Maria* (1930; *The Johanna Maria*), the history of one of the vanishing sailing ships and its sail maker, and his popular *Een Hollandsch drama* (1935; *The House in Haarlem*). His Romanticism reasserted itself in his last works, among which *De wereld een dansfeest* (1938; "The World of Dance") and *De grauwe vogels* (1937; *Grey Birds*) are perhaps the best known.

Schickele \'shik-ə-lə\, René (b. Aug. 4, 1883, Oberehnheim, Alsace, Ger. [now in France]—d. Jan. 31, 1940, Vence, Fr.) German journalist, poet, novelist, and dramatist whose personal experience of conflict between nations made his work an intense plea for peace and understanding.

Schickele was active as a foreign correspondent and editor, and from 1915 to 1919 he was publisher of the *Weissen Blätter* ("The White Papers"), which he transferred from Berlin to Zürich and which he made the most effective mouthpiece of European antiwar sentiment during World War I.

As an Alsatian, Schickele felt keenly the cultural and political conflicts between France and Germany. His own divided loyalties were manifest in the theme and style of his first collection of poetry, *Der Ritt ins Leben* (1905; "The Ride into Life"), and in his first novel, *Der Fremde* (1907; "The Stranger"). This conflict was powerfully dramatized in *Hans im Schnakenloch* (1916; "Hans in the Gnat Hole"), in which the protagonist, Hans, is forced to choose between Germany and France in time of war. His best-known work, the novel trilogy *Das Erbe am Rhein* ("The Inheritance on the Rhine")—comprising *Maria Capponi* (1925), *Blick auf die Vogesen* (1927; *Heart of Alsace*), and *Der Wolf in der Hürde* (1931; "The Wolf in the Pen")—also deals with the fusion of French and German cultures. Schickele fled Germany in 1933 and became a French citizen.

Schiller \'shil-ər\, Friedrich von, *in full* Friedrich Johann Christoph von Schiller (b. Nov. 10, 1759, Marbach, Württemberg [Germany]—d. May 9, 1805, Weimar, Saxe-Weimar) Leading German dramatist, poet, and literary theorist whose mature plays examine the inward freedom of the soul that enables the individual to rise above physical frailties and the pressure of material conditions.

Chalk drawing by
F.G. Weitsch, 1804
Staatliche Museen, Berlin

At the direction of Duke Karl Eugen of Württemberg, Schiller was sent at age 13 to the Military Academy (the Karlsschule). Schiller's resentment found expression in some of his early poems and especially in his first play, *Die Räuber* (1781; THE ROBBERS), a stirring protest against stifling convention and corruption in high places. Forbidden by the duke to write any more plays, Schiller fled. He found a temporary home in Thuringia, where he wrote the tragedy *Kabale und Liebe* (1784; *Cabal and Love*). His first major poetic drama, *Don Carlos* (1787), helped establish blank verse as the recognized medium of German poetic drama.

Schiller gave jubilant expression to his new mood of contentment in the hymn "An die Freude" ("Ode to Joy"), which Ludwig van Beethoven was to use for the choral movement of his *Ninth Symphony*. A chance meeting between Schiller and J.W. von Goethe in 1794 and the ensuing exchange of letters mark the beginning of their friendship, a union of opposites that forms an inspiring chapter in the history of German letters.

Schiller was appointed to a professorship of history at the University of Jena in 1789, having presented the requisite credentials in his *Geschichte des Abfalls der vereinigten Niederlande von der spanischen Regierung* (1788; "History of the Revolt of the United Netherlands Against the Spanish Government"). His *Geschichte des dreissigjährigen Krieges* (1791–93; "History of the Thirty Years' War") further enhanced his reputation as a historian; it also provided him with the material for his greatest drama, WALLENSTEIN (1800).

Schiller began to formulate his views on the character of aesthetic activity, its function in society, and its relation to moral experience. His ideas were set forth in his essays on moral grace and dignity, "Über Anmut und Würde," and on the sublime, "Über das Erhabene," as well as in the celebrated essay on the distinction between two types of poetic creativity, "Über naive und sentimentalische Dichtung."

This period of critical stocktaking also produced exquisite reflective poems: "Das Ideal und das Leben" ("Life and the Ideal"), "Der Spaziergang" ("The Walk"), "Die Macht des Gesanges" ("The Power of Song"). The ballads written in 1797—including "Der Handschuh" ("The Glove"), "Der Taucher" ("The Diver"), and "Die Kraniche des Ibykus" ("The Cranes of Ibycus")—are among his most popular works.

Schiller produced four more plays: *Maria Stuart* (first performed in 1800), a psychological drama concerned with the moral rebirth of Mary, Queen of Scots; *Die Jungfrau von Orleans* (1801; *The Maid of Orleans*), a "romantic tragedy" on the subject of Joan of Arc; *Die Braut von Messina* (1803; *The Bride of Messina*), written in emulation of Greek drama; and *Wilhelm Tell* (1804; WILLIAM TELL), which depicts the revolt of the Swiss forest cantons against Habsburg rule.

Schlegel \'shlä-gəl\, August Wilhelm von (b. Sept. 8, 1767, Hannover, Hanover [Germany]—d. May 12, 1845, Bonn) German scholar and critic, one of the most influential disseminators of the ideas of the German Romantic movement and the finest German translator of William Shakespeare. He was also an orientalist and a poet.

Schlegel studied at the University of Göttingen. From 1791 he was a private tutor in Amsterdam, but he moved to Jena in 1796 to write for Friedrich Schiller's short-lived periodical *Die Horen*. Thereafter, Schlegel, with his philosopher-critic brother Friedrich, started the periodical *Athenäum* (1798–1800), which became the organ of German Romanticism.

In 1798 Schlegel became extraordinary professor at the University of Jena, where he became a member of the Jena Romantics. At Jena, along with others, he also began his long-planned translation of the works of Shakespeare (1797–1810). He himself translated 17 plays. Schlegel's German translations of Shakespeare became the standard editions and are among the finest of all German literary translations. His incomplete translations of five plays by Pedro Calderón de la Barca (*Spanisches Theater*, 2 vol., 1803–09) likewise show his gift for language, as do his many other translations.

In 1801 Schlegel went to Berlin, where he lectured on the history of European literature and thought, casting scorn on classicism and the Enlightenment and exalting the timeless spirituality of the European Middle Ages. These lectures were later published as *Vorlesungen über schöne Literatur und Kunst* (1884; "Lectures on Literature and Fine Art"). He gave another series of important lectures while in Vienna in 1808, published as *Über dramatische Kunst und Literatur* (1809–11; *Lectures on Dramatic Art and Literature*). This volume was translated into many languages and helped spread fundamental Romantic ideas throughout Europe.

In 1818 Schlegel became a professor at the University of Bonn, where he published the scholarly journal *Indische Bibliothek*, 3 vol. (1820–30), and set up a Sanskrit printing press, with which he printed editions of the *Bhagavadgītā* (1823) and *Rāmāyaṇa* (1829). He founded Sanskrit studies in Germany.

Critics concede of Schlegel's poetry (*Gedichte*, 1800; *Ion*, 1803; *Poetische Werke*, 1811) that it shows mastery of form but amounts to only cultivated verse.

Schlegel \'shlä-gəl\, Friedrich von (b. March 10, 1772, Hannover, Hanover [Germany]—d. Jan. 12, 1829, Dresden, Sax-

ony) German writer, critic, and originator of many of the philosophical ideas that inspired the early German Romantic movement. His conception of a universal, historical, and comparative literary scholarship has had profound influence.

After studying at Göttingen and Leipzig, Schlegel became closely associated with his elder brother August William at Jena in the quarterly *Athenäum*. One of the Jena Romantics, he believed that Greek philosophy and culture were essential to complete education. Influenced also by J.G. Fichte's transcendental philosophy, he developed a theory that poetry should be at once philosophical and mythological, ironic and religious. His own imaginative works, a semiautobiographical novel fragment (*Lucinde*, 1799) and a tragedy (*Alarcos*, 1802), were indifferent.

After writing *Über die Sprache und Weisheit der Indier* (1808; "Concerning the Language and Wisdom of India"), a pioneering attempt at comparative Indo-European linguistics and the starting point of the study of Indo-Aryan languages and comparative philology, he became the ideological spokesman of the anti-Napoleonic movement for German liberation. He edited *Europa* and *Das Deutsche Museum*, periodicals on the arts, and in 1820 he became editor of the right-wing Roman Catholic paper *Concordia*.

Two series of lectures Schlegel gave in Vienna between 1810 and 1812—*Über die neuere Geschichte* (1811; *A Course of Lectures on Modern History*) and *Geschichte der alten und neueren Literatur* (1815; *Lectures on the History of Literature*)—developed his concept of a "new Middle Ages."

Schlegel \'shlä-gəl\, Johann Elias (b. Jan. 17, 1719, Meissen, Saxony [Germany]—d. Aug. 13, 1749, Sorø, Den.) German playwright and critic (uncle of August Wilhelm and Friedrich von Schlegel) whose works helped to shape German theater.

Schlegel was educated at the famous classical-humanist boarding school Schulpforte in Hesse, and from 1748 he taught at the Sorø Academy.

At a time when William Shakespeare was virtually unknown to the German public, Schlegel published *Vergleichung Shakespears und Andreas Gryphs* (1741), a discussion of the relative merits of Shakespeare and the leading 17th-century German dramatist and poet. Schlegel developed a theory of literary appreciation that anticipated later developments in the field of aesthetics, and he insisted that art aims at providing pleasure rather than instruction. His comedies are *Die stumme Schönheit* (1747; "The Silent Beauty") and *Der Triumph der guten Frauen* (1748; "The Triumph of Good Women").

Schlüsselroman \'shlües-əl-rō-,män\ [German, literally, key novel] A novel in which real people or actual events figure though they are portrayed as fictional. This type of novel is more commonly known by the French phrase ROMAN À CLEF.

Schmidt \'shmit\, Arno (Otto) (b. Jan. 18, 1914, Hamburg, Ger.—d. June 3, 1979, Celle, W.Ger.) German writer whose novels and short stories were highly experimental, employing complex structure, idiosyncratic orthography, and near-pornography.

In 1949 Schmidt published *Leviathan*, a collection of short stories in which God is malignant and society evil. This work would join with two others in a savagely pessimistic trilogy entitled *Nobodaddys Kinder* (1963; "Nobodaddy's Children"). Other early works were *Das steinerne Herz* (1956; "Heart of Stone") and *Die Gelehrtenrepublik* (1957; *The Egghead Republic*).

His most monumental work was *Zettels Traum* (1970; "Zettel's Dream"), which was Joycean in its language and complexity and occupied 1,330 pages of triple columns, each column rendering a different narrative of thought processes in a 24-hour period. Structural experimentation continued in such novels as *Schule der Atheisten* (1972; "School for Atheists") and *Abend mit Goldrand* (1975; *Evening Edged in Gold*). Schmidt also wrote critical essays and translations of the works of various English-language authors, including James Joyce and William Faulkner.

Schnitzler \'shnits-lǝr\, Arthur (b. May 15, 1862, Vienna, Austria—d. Oct. 21, 1931, Vienna) Austrian playwright and novelist known for his psychological dramas that dissect turn-of-the-century Viennese bourgeois life.

Brown Brothers

Schnitzler made his name as a writer with *Anatol* (1893), a series of seven one-act plays lightly depicting the casual amours of a wealthy young Viennese man-about-town. Although these plays were much less probing than his later works, they revealed a gift for characterization, a power to evoke moods, and a detached, often melancholic humor.

Schnitzler's *Reigen* (1897; *Merry-Go-Round*), a cycle of 10 dramatic dialogues, depicts the heartlessness of men and women in the grip of lust. When it was first performed in 1920, it was considered scandalous. He depicted the hollowness of the Austrian military code of honor in the plays *Liebelei* (1896; *Playing with Love*) and *Freiwild* (1896; "Free Game"). His most successful novel, *Leutnant Gustl* (1901; *None but the Brave*), dealing with a similar theme, was the first European masterpiece written as an interior monologue. In *Flucht in die Finsternis* (1931; *Flight into Darkness*), he showed the onset of madness, stage by stage. The play *Professor Bernhardi* (1912) and the novel *Der Weg ins Freie* (1908; *The Road to the Open*) concern the position of Jews in Austria.

Scholar Gipsy, The Lyric poem by Matthew ARNOLD, published in *Poems* (1853). It is a masterly handling of the 10-line stanza that John Keats used in many of his odes. The poem's subject is a legendary Oxford scholar who gives up his academic life to roam the world with a band of Gypsies, absorbing their customs and seeking the source of their wisdom. The poem is filled with vivid descriptions of the countryside around Oxford.

Schönherr \'shœn-ˌher\, Karl (b. Feb. 24, 1867, Axams, Austria—d. March 15, 1943, Vienna) Austrian writer known for his simple, robust plays dealing with the political and religious problems of peasant life.

Schönherr's first published works (1895) were unassuming dialect poems and short stories, but in 1897 he wrote a play, *Der Judas von Tirol* (rewritten 1927; "The Judas of the Tirol"), in which the Judas of a rural passion play becomes a real-life betrayer. *Glaube und Heimat* (1910; "Faith and Homeland"), often considered his best play, concerns peasant resistance to the Counter-Reformation of the Roman Catholic church.

Acknowledging Norwegian dramatist Henrik Ibsen as his master, Schönherr stood midway between realism and symbolism. Using few characters, his dramas have the directness of fate, as events inexorably push his characters through successions of crises. Other important works with peasant themes

include *Die Bildschnitzer* (1900; "The Woodcarvers"), *Erde* (1907; "Earth"), and *Volk in Not* (1915; "A People in Distress"). Schönherr also wrote several plays about the problems of the medical profession and of the middle class; the best include *Vivat academia* (1922), *Es* (1923; "It"), and *Die Hungerblockade* (1925; "The Hunger Blockade). His works were collected in *Gesammelte Werke* (1927).

school \'skül\ A group of writers or other artists under a common influence or that have certain common ideas or assumptions about their work.

school drama Any play performed by students in schools and colleges throughout Europe during the Renaissance. At first these plays were written by scholars in Latin as educational works, especially in Jesuit schools, but they later were viewed as entertainment as well and were performed in the vernacular. The first known English comedy, *Ralph Roister Doister*, was a school drama written by Nicholas Udall, a playwright and schoolmaster, to be performed at Westminster school.

School for Scandal, The Comedy in five acts by Richard Brinsley SHERIDAN, performed in 1777 and published in 1780. With its spirited ridicule of affectation and pretentiousness, it is one of the greatest comedy of manners in English.

Charles Surface is an extravagant but good-hearted young man. His brother Joseph, supposedly more respectable, is shown to be a conniving schemer who courts Lady Teazle, the young wife of a wealthy old nobleman. Sir Oliver Surface, their uncle, disguises himself to discover which of his nephews shall be his heir. Joseph is exposed as a hypocrite, and Charles triumphs, winning both fortune and true love.

School for Wives, The, Comedy in five acts by MOLIÈRE, performed in 1662 and published in 1663 as *L'Ecole des femmes.*

The School for Wives presents a pedant, Arnolphe, so frightened of femininity that he decides to marry his ward Agnès, a girl entirely unacquainted with the ways of the world. The delicate portrayal in Agnès of an awakening temperament, all the stronger for its absence of convention, is a marvel of comedy, as are Arnolphe's clumsy attempts at lover's talk. Meanwhile, a young man, Horace, falls in love with Agnès at first sight. Much of the play's comedy results from Horace's confiding in his new acquaintance Monsieur de la Souche, not realizing that de la Souche is actually his rival Arnolphe.

Schreiner \'shrī-nǝr\, Olive (Emilie Albertina), *pseudonym* Ralph Iron \'ī-ǝrn\ (b. March 24, 1855, Wittebergen, Cape Colony [South Africa]—d. Dec. 11, 1920, Cape Town) Writer of the first great South African novel, THE STORY OF AN AFRICAN FARM (1883). She had a powerful intellect and militantly feminist and liberal views on politics and society.

Schreiner wrote two semiautobiographical novels, *Undine* (published 1928) and *The Story of an African Farm*, and began *From Man to Man* (1926), which she worked on intermittently for 40 years but never finished. *The Story of an African Farm* concerns a girl, living on an isolated farm in the veld, who struggles to attain her independence in the face of rigid Boer social conventions.

Notable among Schreiner's other works are an attack on the activities of empire builder Cecil Rhodes and his associates, *Trooper Peter Halkett of Mashonaland* (1897), and a widely acclaimed bible of the women's movement, *Woman and Labour* (1911).

Schröder \'shrœ-dǝr\, Friedrich Ludwig (b. Nov. 3, 1744, Schwerin, Mecklenburg [Germany]—d. Sept. 3, 1816, Rellingen) German actor, manager, and playwright, the first to bring the plays of William Shakespeare to the German stage.

Schröder began his career as a child actor. In 1771 he became the manager of the Hamburg National Theater, where he remained for nine years. In addition to Shakespearean productions, he also presented the early dramas of J.W. von Goethe—*Götz von Berlichingen*, *Clavigo*, and *Stella*—and the plays of other Shakespeare-inspired Sturm und Drang dramatists.

Schröder left Hamburg in 1780 and spent four years at the Vienna Burgtheater, where he created the bases of the ensemble performing for which that company later became known. From 1785 to 1798 he was again director of the Hamburg theater. His own dramatic works were mostly adaptations and translations of other works, though he did produce some original plays, including *Der Fähndrich* (1786; *The Ensign*).

Schubart \\'shū-ˌbärt\\, Christian Friedrich Daniel (b. March 24, 1739, Obersontheim, Swabia [Germany]—d. Oct. 10, 1791, Stuttgart, Württemberg) German poet of the Sturm und Drang period, known for his pietistic and nationalistic leanings.

Schubart's parodies and satires caused him to be expelled from several cities, and he was arrested in 1777 and imprisoned without trial for 10 years in the fortress of Hohenasperg. There he studied mystical works and composed poetry. His *Sämtliche Gedichte* (1785–86; "Collected Poems") are characterized partly by the bombast of the Sturm und Drang period, partly by intense religious feelings of a pietistic nature, and partly by patriotic fervor. He was set at liberty in 1787 and was then appointed musical director and manager of the theater at Stuttgart, where he expanded his *Deutsche Chronik* ("German Chronicle"), first published in 1774–78. He also began his autobiography, *Schubarts Leben und Gesinnungen* (1791–93; "Schubart's Life and Mind"), but he died before its completion.

Schulberg \\'shūl-bərg\\, Budd (Wilson) (b. March 27, 1914, New York, N.Y., U.S.) American novelist, screenwriter, and journalist.

The son of a Hollywood motion-picture producer, Schulberg grew up in Hollywood and became a reader and then a screenwriter. His first novel, *What Makes Sammy Run* (1941), about an unprincipled motion-picture studio mogul, was a great success.

During and after World War II, Schulberg served in the military and was commended for collecting visual evidence of Nazi war crimes for the Nürnberg trials. In 1947 he published his second novel, *The Harder They Fall*, a fictional exposé of corrupt practices in professional boxing. In 1950 his novel *The Disenchanted* won an American Library Award for fiction. In 1954 his screenplay for the widely acclaimed *On the Waterfront* won an Academy Award for best story and screenplay. In the 1960s Schulberg helped establish the Douglass House Watts Writers Workshop in the Watts district of Los Angeles after riots there, and in 1971 he founded the Frederick Douglass Creative Arts Center in New York City. In *Moving Pictures: Memories of a Hollywood Prince* (1981), Schulberg described his childhood spent in the center of the American motion-picture industry; *Love, Action, Laughter, and Other Sad Tales* was published in 1989.

Schüttelreim \\'shŭet-əl-ˌrīm\\ [German, from *schütteln* to shake, jolt, churn + *Reim* rhyme] German equivalent of a spoonerism, in which the intial letters or syllables of two or more words are transposed. *See also* SPOONERISM.

Schuyler \\'skī-lər\\, James (Marcus) (b. Nov. 9, 1923, Chicago, Ill., U.S.—d. April 12, 1991, New York, N.Y.) American poet, playwright, and novelist, often associated with the New York school of poets, which included Frank O'Hara, John Ashbery, and Kenneth Koch. An acute observer of natural landscapes, Schuyler described common experiences with familiar images in compact lines of varied rhythm.

Schuyler settled in New York City and began writing for the magazine *Art News*, where he met other poets of the New York school. His best-known volumes of poetry are *Freely Espousing* (1969), *The Crystal Lithium* (1972), and *Hymn to Life* (1974). The title poem of *The Crystal Lithium* examines the variability of experience while describing a beach in winter.

Among his other verse collections are *Salute* (1960), *May 24th or So* (1966), *A Sun Cab* (1972), *Song* (1976), *The Fireproof Floors of Witley Court* (1976), *The Home Book* (1977), *The Morning of the Poem* (1980), *A Few Days* (1985), *Selected Poems* (1988), and *Collected Poems* (1993). He also wrote plays and novels.

Schwartz \\'shwȯrts\\, Delmore (b. Dec. 8, 1913, Brooklyn, N.Y., U.S.—d. July 11, 1966, New York City) American poet, short-story writer, and literary critic noted for his lyrical descriptions of cultural alienation and the search for identity.

Educated at the University of Wisconsin, New York University, and Harvard University, Schwartz later taught at Harvard and other schools. His first book, *In Dreams Begin Responsibilities* (1939), which brought him immediate fame, included the short story of the title and a group of lyrical and imaginative poems. Subsequent publications included *Shenandoah* (1941), a verse play; *Genesis, Book I* (1943), a long introspective poem; and *The World Is a Wedding* (1948) and *Successful Love, and Other Stories* (1961), short stories dealing primarily with middle-class Jewish family life.

Schwartz's lucid literary criticism was published in various periodicals. *New and Selected Poems, 1938–1958* appeared in 1959. Schwartz served as an editor for *Partisan Review* (1943–55) and *The New Republic* (1955–57). The brilliant but mentally unstable Schwartz was the model for the title character in Saul Bellow's novel *Humboldt's Gift* (1975).

Schwarz-Bart \\shfȧrts-'bȧr\\, André (b. 1928, Metz, Fr.) French novelist, author of what is regarded as one of the great literary works of the post-World War II period: *Le Dernier des justes* (1959; *The Last of the Just*).

By the time Schwarz-Bart was 13, his Polish-Jewish parents had been deported and killed by the Nazis. Young Schwarz-Bart was active in the Resistance movement and later taught himself to read and write French. *Le Dernier des justes* probes the conscience of Europe during centuries of the persecution and genocide of the Jewish people. It retraces the martyrdom of one of the traditional Jewish Lamed Waw Tzaddiqim ("The 36 Just Men"), Ernie Lévy, who, caught in the madness of Nazism, suffers every possible horror.

In 1967 Schwarz-Bart, with his West Indian wife, Simone, published *Un Plat de porc aux bananes vertes* ("A Plate of Pork with Green Bananas"). It was the first of a cycle of novels in which the authors approached the problem of racism, tracing the historical misfortunes of blacks. Schwarz-Bart also wrote *La Mulâtresse Solitude* (1972; *A Woman Named Solitude*). His wife wrote *Pluie et vent sur Télumée Miracle* (1972; "Rain and Wind on Télumée Miracle"; *The Bridge of Beyond*) and *Ti Jean L'horizon* (1979; *Between Two Worlds*).

sciapod \\'sī-ə-ˌpäd\\ or **skiapod** \\'skī-ə-ˌpäd\\ [Greek *Skiápodes* (plural), from *skiá* shadow + *pod-*, *poús* foot] One of a mythical people who have feet big enough for use as sunshades. In Aristophanes, the elder Pliny, and late Latin authors, the sciapods are represented as inhabiting the Libyan desert.

Sciascia \\'shä-shä\\, Leonardo (b. Jan. 8, 1921, Racalmuto, near Agrigento, Sicily, Italy—d. Nov. 20, 1989, Palermo, Sicily) Italian writer noted for his metaphysical examinations of political corruption and arbitrary power.

Sciascia held either clerical or teaching positions for much of his career, retiring to write full-time in 1968. His political career began in 1976, when he became a Communist Party member in the Palermo city council. In 1979 he was elected to the European Parliament.

Sciascia's first published work was *Favole della dittatura* (1950; "Fables of the Dictatorship"), a satire on fascism. His first significant work, *Le parrocchie di Regalpetra* (1956; *Salt in the Wound*), chronicles the social and political history of a small Sicilian town. He further examined what he termed *sicilitudine* ("Sicilian-ness") in the four stories of *Gli zii di Sicilia* (1958; *Sicilian Uncles*). Sciascia did not discover his favorite vehicle, the mystery novel, until the publication in 1961 of *Il giorno della civetta* ("The Day of the Owl"; first Eng. trans., *Mafia Vendetta*), a study of the Mafia. That novel was followed by many more mystery novels, among them *A ciascuno il suo* (1966; *A Man's Blessing*), *Il contesto* (1971; *Equal Danger*), and *Todo modo* (1974; *One Way or Another*). In addition to mysteries, Sciascia wrote historical analyses, plays, poems, short stories, and essays on Sicily and other subjects, and he edited a series of rare and unpublished works by Sicilian writers for the Sellario publishing house.

science fiction Fiction dealing principally with the impact of actual or imagined science upon society or individuals, or more generally, literary fantasy including a scientific factor as an essential orienting component.

Such literature may consist of a careful and informed extrapolation of scientific facts and principles, or it may range into far-fetched areas flatly contradictory of such facts and principles. In either case, plausibility based on science is a requisite, so that such a precursor of the genre as Mary Shelley's gothic novel *Frankenstein* (1818) is science fiction, whereas Bram Stoker's *Dracula* (1897), based as it is purely on the supernatural, is not. Science fiction proper began, however, toward the end of the 19th century with the scientific romances of Jules Verne, whose science was rather on the level of invention, as well as the science-oriented novels of social criticism by H.G. Wells.

The development of science fiction as a self-conscious genre dates from 1926 when Hugo Gernsback, who coined the portmanteau word scientifiction, founded *Amazing Stories* magazine, which was devoted exclusively to science-fiction stories that initially were viewed as sensationalist. With John W. Campbell's editorship (from 1937) of *Astounding Science Fiction* and with the publication of stories and novels by such writers as Isaac Asimov, Arthur C. Clarke, and Robert A. Heinlein, science fiction emerged as a mode of serious fiction. Ventures into the genre by writers not devoted exclusively to science fiction, such as Aldous Huxley, C.S. Lewis, and Kurt Vonnegut, also added respectability.

A great boom in the popularity of science fiction followed World War II. Science-fiction writers of notable merit in the postwar period included A.E. Van Vogt, J.G. Ballard, Ray Bradbury, Frank Herbert, Harlan Ellison, Poul Anderson, Samuel R. Delany, Ursula K. Le Guin, Frederik Pohl, Octavia E. Butler, and Brian Aldiss. These writers' approaches included predictions of future societies on Earth, analyses of the consequences of interstellar travel, and imaginative explorations of forms of intelligent life and their societies in other worlds.

Scoop Novel by Evelyn WAUGH, published in 1938. Sometimes published with the subtitle *A Novel about Journalists*, this savage satire of London journalism is based on Waugh's experiences as a reporter for the *Daily Mail* during the Italian invasion of Ethiopia in the mid-1930s.

The book tells of the circulation battles of two rival newspapers, *The Beast* and *The Brute*, during a war in the fictional African country of Ishmaelia. William Boot, a timid nature writer, is mistakenly dispatched to Ishmaelia as a foreign correspondent for *The Beast*. With comic innocence, he survives the ruthless absurdities of competitive journalism.

scop \'skäp, 'skōp\ [Old English] An Anglo-Saxon minstrel, usually attached to a particular royal court, although scops also traveled to various courts to recite their poetry. In addition to being an entertainer the scop served as a kind of historian and preserver of the oral tradition of the Germanic peoples. The Old English poem "Widsith," a fictional biography of a scop, gives an idea of the status and role of the scop in society. *Compare* MINSTREL.

Scorza \'skȯr-sä\, Manuel (b. 1928, Lima, Peru—d. Nov. 27, 1983, Madrid, Spain) Peruvian novelist, poet, and political activist who interwove mythic and fantastic elements with social realism in his depictions of the Indians' struggles against oppression and exploitation.

In 1949 Scorza joined a group that resisted the dictatorship of General Manuel Odría. That same year, his first book of poems, *Actas de la remota lejanía* ("Proceedings of a Remote Distance"), was published and was confiscated by the local police. He was forced into exile and lived in many countries. *Las imprecaciones* (1955; "Imprecations"), a collection of poems, won Scorza literary honors in Peru in 1956. That year he also joined the Communal Movement, became its secretary, and wrote its political manifestos.

Scorza's series of novels chronicling the Indians' revolt of 1955–62 includes *Redoble por Rancas* (1970; *Drums for Rancas*), *Historia de Garabombo, el invisible* (1972; "Story of Garabombo the Invisible"), *El jinete insomne* (1978; "The Insomniac Horseman"), *Cantar de Agapito Robles* (1978; "Song of Agapito Robles"), and *La tumba del relámpago* (1979; "The Tomb of the Lightning"). A basic theme of the series is the animistic vision of life shared by the Indians as they struggle against powerful feudal landowners and the forces of modern capitalism.

Scott \'skät\, Alexander (b. *c.* 1525—d. *c.* 1585) Scottish lyricist who is regarded as one of the last and most skillful of the makaris (courtly poets) of the 16th century.

Scott's 35 extant poems are contained in the *Bannatyne Manuscript* (1568). His reputation as a genuine minor lyric poet rests upon his love lyrics; these show a striking range of mood, from the tender to the coarse, and an admirable metrical suppleness and variety. He also left an amusing burlesque, "The Justing and Debait up at the Drum betuix William Adamsone and Johine Sym," and a ceremonial alliterative poem, "Ane New Yeir Gift to Quene Mary . . . ," which gives an interesting reflection of early Reformation Scotland.

Scott \'skät\, Duncan Campbell (b. Aug. 2, 1862, Ottawa, Canada West [Ontario, Can.]—d. Dec. 19, 1947, Ottawa) Canadian regionalist poet who wrote of the untamed aspects of nature in the northern wilderness and of Indian life.

An administrator for more than 50 years in the Department of Indian Affairs (1879–1932), Scott had a conscientious and sincere concern for Indians. His poetry was influenced by that of his close friend, the Ottawa poet Archibald Lampman, whose work he edited on Lampman's death (1899). Scott produced several volumes of verse of uneven quality from 1893 (*The Magic House, and Other Poems*) to 1947 (*The Circle of Affection*). He also published two volumes of stories, *In the Village of Viger* (1896) and *The Witching of Elspie* (1923).

Scott \'skät\, Francis Reginald, *byname* Frank *or* F.R. (b. Aug. 1, 1899, Quebec, Que., Can.—d. Jan. 31, 1985, Montreal) Member of the Montreal group of poets in the 1920s and an influential promoter of the cause of Canadian poetry.

Scott helped found various literary magazines and also edited poetry anthologies. As a poet, he is at his best as a satirist and social critic. His *Overture* (1945), *Events and Signals* (1954), and *The Eye of the Needle* (1957) are written in a colloquial, conversational style. His *Selected Poems* appeared in 1966 and *The Dance Is One* in 1973. He also wrote nonfiction concerning socialism and constitutional law and served as a UN representative in Burma (now Myanmar).

Scott \'skät\, Paul (Mark) (b. March 25, 1920, Palmers Green, Eng.—d. March 1, 1978, London) Novelist known for his chronicling of the decline of the British occupation of India, most fully realized in his series of novels known as THE RAJ QUARTET.

Scott entered military service in India in the 1940s and later became a director of a London literary agency; he resigned in 1960 to write full-time. A trip to India in 1964, underwritten by his publishers, helped inspire *The Raj Quartet—The Jewel in the Crown* (1966), *The Day of the Scorpion* (1968), *The Towers of Silence* (1971), and *A Division of the Spoils* (1975)—as well as *Staying On* (1977), which won the Booker Prize. While exploring the manifold consequences of the rape of an Englishwoman, the books illustrate in profuse detail the final years of the British occupation of India from the points of view of English, Hindu, and Muslim characters.

All of Scott's works employ Indian themes or characters, even those set outside India. His early novels, such as *Johnnie Sahib* (1952), *The Mark of the Warrior* (1958), and *The Chinese Love Pavilion* (1960; U.S. title, *The Love Pavilion*), address moral conflicts of British army officers in the East. *The Birds of Paradise* (1962) is also set in Asia.

Scott \'skät\, Sir Walter, 1st Baronet (b. Aug. 15, 1771, Edinburgh, Scot.—d. Sept. 21, 1832, Abbotsford, Roxburgh) Scottish writer who is often considered both the inventor and the greatest practitioner of the historical novel.

From his earliest years Scott was fond of listening to elderly relatives' accounts and stories of the Border region, and as a boy he became a voracious reader of poetry, history, drama, and fairy tales and romances. In 1786 he was apprenticed to his father, a lawyer. In 1799 he was appointed sheriff depute of the county of Selkirk, and in 1806 he became clerk to the Court of Session in Edinburgh.

Scott's first published work, *The Chase, and William and Helen* (1796), was a translation of two ballads by the German Romantic author G.A. Bürger. A poor translation of J.W. von Goethe's *Götz von Berlichingen* followed in 1799. Scott's interest in border ballads finally bore fruit in his collection entitled *Minstrelsy of the Scottish Border*, 3 vol. (1802–03). His attempts to "restore" the orally corrupted versions to their original compositions sometimes resulted in powerful poems that show a sophisticated Romantic flavor. The work made Scott's name known to a wide public, and he followed with a full-length narrative poem, THE LAY OF THE LAST MINSTREL (1805), which ran into many editions; *Marmion* (1808); THE LADY OF THE LAKE (1810), which was the most successful of these pieces; *Rokeby* (1813); and *The Lord of the Isles*

Detail of an oil painting by Sir Edwin Landseer, 1824

National Portrait Gallery, London

(1815). In 1808 his 18-volume edition of the works of John Dryden appeared, followed by his 19-volume edition of Jonathan Swift (1814).

Scott's involvement with a financially troubled printing firm, together with the cost of building and furnishing his country house at Abbotsford, nearly ruined him, and from 1813 everything he wrote was done partly in order to make money and pay off the lasting debts he had incurred. In the early summer of 1814 he completed his novel *Waverley*, a story of the Jacobite rebellion of 1745; it was published anonymously (as were all of the many novels he wrote to 1827, when his authorship was made public) and was immediately successful.

Scott followed *Waverley* with a series of historical novels set in Scotland that are now known as THE WAVERLEY NOVELS, including *Guy Mannering* (1815); *The Antiquary* (1816); *The Black Dwarf* (1816); the three masterpieces OLD MORTALITY (1816), ROB ROY (1817), and THE HEART OF MIDLOTHIAN (1818); *The Bride of Lammermoor* (1819); and *A Legend of Montrose* (1819). Many of these were originally published in a four-part series entitled *Tales of My Landlord*. Scott then turned to English history and other themes for IVANHOE (1819), *The Monastery* (1820), *The Abbot* (1820), KENILWORTH (1821), *The Pirate* (1822), *The Fortunes of Nigel* (1822), and QUENTIN DURWARD (1823). The best of his later novels were *Redgauntlet* (1824) and *The Talisman* (1825).

Scott was a born storyteller and a master of dialogue who had a deep knowledge of Scottish history and society. The attention he gave to ordinary people was a marked departure from previous historical novels' concentration on royalty. Scott was also the master of a rich and ornate literary style that blended energy with decorum, lyric beauty with clarity of description.

Scottish Enlightenment An intellectual movement that began in Glasgow, Scot., in the early 18th century and later was largely centered in the Old Town district of Edinburgh. Its leading figures included the philosophers Adam Ferguson, Francis Hutcheson, Adam Smith, John Millar, Dugald Stewart, Thomas Reid, and David Hume and the historian William Robertson. Perhaps the best-known publication to emerge from the Scottish Enlightenment was the *Encyclopædia Britannica*, first published in 1768–71. The movement qualified Edinburgh as one of the world's great cultural capitals.

Scottish Renaissance A movement in 20th-century Scottish literature, particularly vital between World Wars I and II. Its members sought to preserve regional dialects in their writings, and the poets among them modeled their verse on Scottish poetry of four and five centuries past. Politically they were inclined to Scottish nationalism, and they aimed to generate a Scottish national literature and to revive Lowland Scots (Lallans) as a literary language. The leading figure of the Scottish Renaissance was poet-critic Hugh MacDiarmid, who founded several small literary periodicals.

The book of essays *Scottish Literature, Character & Influence* (1919) by G. Gregory Smith was an important influence on the movement, as was the quarterly *Saltire Review*, published by the Saltire Society (1936–60) to stimulate research and writing in Scottish Gaelic. Other prominent Scottish Renaissance figures included poets Sorley Maclean and William Soutar and novelist Lewis Grassic Gibbon.

scrapiana \,skrap-ē-'an-ə\ Miscellaneous literary scraps.

screed \'skrēd\ **1.** A lengthy discourse. **2.** An informal piece of writing.

screeve \'skrēv\ *chiefly British* A piece of writing; especially, a begging letter. *Screeve* was originally an argot word that probably ultimately derives from Italian *scrivere* ("to write").

Screwtape Letters, The \'skrü-ˌtāp\ Epistolary novel by C.S. LEWIS, published serially in 1941 in *Guardian*, a weekly religious newspaper. The episodes were collected in book form in 1942 and revised as *The Screwtape Letters and Screwtape Proposes a Toast* in 1961.

Written in defense of Christian faith, this popular satire consists of a series of 31 letters in which Screwtape, an experienced devil, instructs his young charge, Wormwood, in the art of temptation. Confounded by church doctrines and a faithful Christian woman, their efforts are defeated when their subject—a World War II pilot—dies in a bombing raid with his soul at peace. Through his satiric use of the demonic narrative persona, Lewis examines the opposing sides in the battle between good and evil.

scribe \'skrīb\ [Latin *scriba* official in charge of public records, a derivative of *scribere* to mark, write, put down in writing, make a record of] **1.** A copier of manuscripts. **2.** A writer; specifically, a journalist.

Scribe \'skrēb\, Eugène, *in full* Augustin-Eugène Scribe (b. Dec. 24, 1791, Paris, Fr.—d. Feb. 20, 1861, Paris) French dramatist, master of the neatly plotted "well-made play."

Scribe is now celebrated chiefly for his prodigious output and his popular success. He wrote dramas of every kind, often in collaboration. His comedies express the values and predilections of bourgeois society and praise the virtues of commerce and family life. He is also remembered for his historical plays, *Le Verre d'eau* (1840; "The Glass of Water"), which derives great historical events from a trivial incident, and *Bertrand et Raton* (1833; *The School for Politicians*). His *Adrienne Lecouvreur* (1849), a melodrama about an actress who loves a nobleman though unaware of his high rank and true identity, was favored as a vehicle by such notable actresses of the day as Sarah Bernhardt and Helena Modjeska.

Scriblerus Club \skri-'blē-rəs\ Eighteenth-century British literary club whose founding members were the brilliant Tory wits Alexander POPE, Jonathan SWIFT, John GAY, Thomas PARNELL, and John ARBUTHNOT. Its purpose was to ridicule pretentious erudition and scholarly jargon through the person of a fictitious literary hack, Martinus Scriblerus (whose surname was a pseudo-Latin coinage signifying "a writer"). The collaboration of the five writers on the *Memoirs of Martinus Scriblerus* began as early as 1713 and led to frequent, spirited meetings when they were in London; when they were separated, they pursued their project through correspondence.

Of the five, only Pope and Swift lived to see the publication of the *Memoirs* in 1741, although miscellaneous minor pieces written in collaboration or individually had appeared earlier under the Scriblerus name. Although Pope is credited with originating the character of Scriblerus, most of the ideas were Arbuthnot's, and he was the most industrious of the collaborators. The stimulation the members derived from one another had far-reaching effects. Gay's *The Beggar's Opera* grew out of a suggestion made by Swift to the club, and the imprint of Scriblerus on *Gulliver's Travels*, especially Book III, describing the voyage to Laputa, is unmistakable.

Scribner \'skrib-nər\, Charles, *original surname* Scrivener \'skriv-ə-nər\ (b. Feb. 21, 1821, New York, N.Y., U.S.—d. Aug. 26, 1871, Luzern, Switz.) American publisher whose firm, founded in 1846 and named Charles Scribner's Sons from 1878, issued books by a diversity of authors and also produced several periodicals.

Scribner established the firm in partnership with Isaac D. Baker (who died in 1850) in New York City. The Baker and Scribner list initially constited of philosophical and theological (mainly Presbyterian) books. Near the end of Scribner's life

the firm began to publish reprints and translations of British and continental European literary works. After his death the company was headed successively by his three sons: John Blair, Charles, and Arthur Hawley Scribner. During the long presidency (1879–1928) of the second Charles Scribner, the firm published such authors as Henry James, George Washington Cable, Theodore Roosevelt, George Santayana, Edith Wharton, Ring Lardner, Ernest Hemingway, George Meredith, Robert Louis Stevenson, Rudyard Kipling, J.M. Barrie, and John Galsworthy.

scriptory \'skrip-tə-rē\ [Latin *scriptorius,* a derivative of *scribere* to mark, write] Of, relating to, expressed in, or used in writing.

scripture \'skrip-chər, -shər\ [Late Latin *scripturae* the Bible (translation of Greek *hai graphaí*), from Latin, plural of *scriptura* act of writing, text] **1.** *usually capitalized* The sacred writings of a religion; specifically, the books of the Bible—often used in the plural. **2.** A body of writings considered sacred or authoritative—often used in the plural. **3.** Something written.

scrivener \'skriv-ən-ər\ [Middle English *scriveiner,* an extension of *scrivein* copyist, scribe, from Old French *escrivein*] **1.** *also called* scribe. A professional or public copyist or writer. One of the most anthologized stories by Herman Melville, "Bartleby the Scrivener," concerns a man of this profession. **2.** A usually minor author.

Scrooge, Ebenezer \ˌeb-ə-'nē-zər-'skrüj\ Fictional character, the miserly protagonist of Charles Dickens' A CHRISTMAS CAROL.

Despite his transformation at the end of the story, the character is remembered as the embittered miser and not as the reformed sinner, and "Scrooge" has entered the English language as a synonym for a miser.

Scudéry \də-skǖ-dā-'rē\, Madeleine de (b. 1607, Le Havre, Fr.—d. June 2, 1701, Paris) French novelist and social figure whose romans à clef were immensely popular in the 17th century.

De Scudéry made her mark on the literary circle of the Hôtel de Rambouillet; by the late 1640s, she had replaced Mme de Rambouillet as the leading literary hostess in Paris and had established her own salon, known as the Société du Samedi ("Saturday Club").

De Scudéry's first novel, *Ibrahim ou l'illustre bassa* (1642; *Ibrahim or the Illustrious Bassa*), was published in four volumes. Her later works were even longer; both *Artamène ou le grand Cyrus* (1649–53; *Artamenes or the Grand Cyrus*) and *Clélie, histoire romaine* (1654–60; *Clelia*) were published in 10 volumes. Contemporary readers, accustomed to such long novels, appreciated de Scudéry's works both for their bulk and for the glimpses they provided into the lives of important society figures of the day, who were thinly disguised as Persian, Greek, and Roman warriors and maidens.

Her other works include *Almahide, ou l'esclave reine* (1660–63; "Almahide, or the Slave Queen"), *Mathilde d'Aguilar, histoire espagnole* (1667; "Mathilda of Aguilar, a Spanish Tale"), and *La Promenade de Versailles, ou l'histoire de Célanire* (1669; "The Versailles Promenade, or the Tale of Célanire"). Most of the novels were published anonymously or under the name of her brother Georges, a dramatist. They included long passages devoted to conversations on such topics as the education of women that were excerpted and published separately.

Scylla and Charybdis \'sil-ə . . . kə-'rib-dis\ In Greek mythology, two immortal monsters who beset the narrow waters traversed by the hero Odysseus in his wanderings (later localized in the Strait of Messina). Scylla was a supernatural creature, with 12 feet and 6 heads on long, snaky necks, each head having a triple row of sharklike teeth, while her loins were girt with the heads of baying dogs. From her lair in a cave she devoured whatever ventured within reach. Scylla was often rationalized in antiquity as a rock or reef. Charybdis, who lurked under a fig tree a bow shot away on the opposite shore, drank down and spewed forth the waters thrice a day and was fatal to shipping. Her character was most likely the personification of a whirlpool.

sdrucciola \\'strŭt-chŏ-lä\\ [Italian (*rima*) *sdrucciola,* literally, slippery rhyme]   In poetry, a triple rhyme in which the accent falls on the first syllable (as in *femina, semina*).

Seagull, The   Drama in four acts by Anton CHEKHOV, performed in 1896 and published in Russian the following year as *Chayka*. The play deals with lost opportunities and the clash between generations.

The main characters, all artists, are guests at a country estate. They are Mme Arkadina, a middle-aged actress; her lover, Trigonin, a successful writer; her son Konstantin, a writer; and Nina, a young, aspiring actress whom Konstantin loves. Mme Arkadina, jealous of Nina's youth and promising career, acts cruelly and hatefully toward Konstantin, withholding the approval he desperately seeks from her. Nina, impressed by Trigonin's fame, ignores Konstantin, who kills a seagull and shows it to her, perhaps symbolically referring to his broken dreams. All four go their separate ways, but two years later they are reunited at the same estate. When Nina again rejects Konstantin, he destroys his writings and shoots himself, while his mother, unaware, plays cards in another room.

Seami   *see* ZEAMI.

sea monster   *also called* sea serpent.   A fabulous monster of the sea often represented as an enormous snake that devours humans. The belief in huge creatures that inhabited the deep was widespread throughout the ancient world. In the Old Testament there are several allusions to a primordial combat between God and a monstrous adversary variously named Leviathan or Rahab. Although the references to Leviathan usually indicate a dragonlike sea creature, the name has also been used to denote a sea monster in general. Analogies to this combat are found throughout the ancient Middle East and also in Indo-European myth. In modern literature there are many references in poetry and prose to the Leviathan as a huge creature of the sea, including works by John Milton, Matthew Arnold, and Herman Melville.

Sea of Fertility, The   Four-part epic novel by MISHIMA Yukio, published in Japanese in 1965–70 as *Hōjō no umi* and widely regarded as his most lasting achievement. The four novels, *Haru no yuki* (*Spring Snow*), *Homma* (*Runaway Horses*), *Akatsuki no tera* (*The Temple of Dawn*), and *Tennin gosui* (*The Decay of the Angel*), are set in Japan from about 1912 to the 1960s. Each of them depicts a different reincarnation of the same being: as a young aristocrat in 1912, as a political fanatic in the 1930s, as a Thai princess before and after World War II, and as an evil young orphan in the 1960s. Taken together the novels are a clear indication of Mishima's increasing obsession with blood, death, and suicide, his interest in self-destructive personalities, and his rejection of the sterility of modern life.

Sea of Grass, The   Novel by Conrad RICHTER, published in 1936, presenting in epic scope the conflicts in the settling of the American Southwest.

Set in New Mexico in the late 19th century, the novel concerns the often violent clashes between the pioneering ranchers, whose cattle range freely through the vast sea of grass, and

the farmers, or "nesters," who build fences and turn the sod. Against this background is set the triangle of rancher Colonel Jim Brewton, his unstable Eastern wife Lutie, and the ambitious Brice Chamberlain. Richter casts the story in Homeric terms, with the children caught up in the conflicts of their parents.

Seascape   Drama in two acts by Edward ALBEE, produced and published in 1975; it won the Pulitzer Prize for drama.

The play presents Nancy and Charlie, a married couple. Picnicking by the ocean one day, they meet Leslie and Sarah, middle-aged giant lizards from beneath the sea who want to evolve. The witty dialogue between the couples affords the playwright an opportunity to examine humans as a species.

Season in Hell, A   Collection of prose and poetry pieces by French Symbolist poet Arthur RIMBAUD, published in 1873, when Rimbaud was 19, as *Une Saison en enfer.*

The collection is a form of spiritual autobiography in which the author comes to a new self-awareness through an examination of his life and his career as a poet. The collection, especially the last section, called "Adieu," is seen by some critics as Rimbaud's farewell to poetry. He gave up writing shortly after *A Season in Hell* was published.

Sea-Wolf, The   Novel by Jack LONDON, published in 1904. This highly popular novel combines elements of naturalism and romantic adventure.

The story concerns Humphrey Van Weyden, a refined castaway who is put to work on the motley schooner *Ghost*. The ship is run by brutal Wolf Larsen, who, despite his intelligence and strength, is antisocial and self-destructive. Hardened by his arduous experiences at sea, Humphrey develops strength of both body and will, protecting another castaway, Maud Brewster, and facing down the increasingly deranged Larsen.

Second Coming, The   Poem by William Butler YEATS, first printed in *The Dial* (November 1920) and published in his collection of verse entitled *Michael Robartes and the Dancer* (1921). Yeats believed that history was cyclical, and "The Second Coming," with its imagery of swirling chaos and terror, prophesies the cataclysmic end of an era. Critics associated the poem with various contemporary calamities, such as the Easter Rising of 1916, the Russian Revolution of 1917, the rise of fascism, and the political decay of eastern Europe.

Second Nun's Tale, The   One of the 24 stories in THE CANTERBURY TALES by Geoffrey Chaucer.

Taken from the 13th-century *Legenda aurea* (*Golden Legend*) of Jacobus de Voragine, "The Second Nun's Tale" relates the story of St. Cecilia. On her wedding night she tells her husband Valerian that an angel has instructed her to remain celibate. Valerian converts to Christianity and has a vision of the angel; awestruck, he persuades his brother to convert. The three perform miracles and convert others until they are tried and executed by Roman authorities.

Second Tree from the Corner, The   Collection of literary miscellanea by E.B. WHITE, published in 1954. Most of these essays, poems, and stories originally appeared in *The New Yorker* magazine over a period of two decades. White treats modernity and progress with skepticism and nostalgia.

Secret Agent, The (*in full* The Secret Agent: A Simple Tale)   Novel by Joseph CONRAD, first published serially in the New York weekly *Ridgeway's* in 1906–07 and in book form in 1907. This absurdist story is noted for its adept characterizations, melodramatic irony, and psychological intrigue.

Adolf Verloc is a languid eastern European secret agent posing as a London shop owner with anarchist leanings who is ordered to dynamite Greenwich Observatory. The plot fails when Verloc's mentally retarded brother-in-law is accidently killed by the explosives. Verloc's wife Winnie murders Verloc in a fit of rage. She commits suicide after she is betrayed by Ossipon, one of her husband's anarchist associates.

Secret Garden, The Novel for children by Frances Hodgson BURNETT, published in 1911. The book, considered Burnett's best, has become a classic of children's literature.

The novel's protagonist, Mary Lennox, a sickly and unpleasant orphan, is sent to England to live with a reclusive uncle she has never met. Her guardian's housekeeper takes charge of Mary, turning her into a healthy, delightful child. While exploring the estate, Mary discovers a secret garden that had been abandoned 10 years earlier, after the death of her uncle's wife. Mary brings the garden back to life and works a similar transformation on her guardian's spoiled, semi-invalid son.

Sedaine \sə-'den\, Michel-Jean (b. June 2, 1719, Paris, Fr.—d. May 17, 1797, Paris)   French dramatist who is best known as the author of a fine domestic comedy, *Le Philosophe sans le savoir* (1765; "A Philosopher Without Knowing It").

The son of a master builder, Sedaine began his career as a stonemason. In 1752 he published a volume of poetry, and his theatrical career began in 1756, when he wrote librettos for some light operas. He was made destitute by the French Revolution and in 1795 was deprived of his membership in the Académie Française, to which he had been elected in 1786.

Although Sedaine had a number of successes during his career, *Le Philosophe sans le savoir* is the only one of his plays to have endured. It is a textbook example of the new *drame bourgeois* ("bourgeois drama") called for by the philosopher Denis Diderot; mixing tragic and comic situations, it presents a charming, sentimental, and idealized picture of life in the family of a wealthy merchant. Sedaine defends middle-class values by criticising aristocratic prejudice and illustrating the virtues of commerce and of a rational concept of honor.

Sedley \'sed-lē\, Sir Charles, 4th Baronet (b. March 1639, Aylesford, Kent, Eng.—d. Aug. 20, 1701, Hampstead, London) English Restoration poet, dramatist, wit, and courtier.

Sedley attended the University of Oxford but left without taking a degree. After the restoration of the monarchy (1660) he was a prominent member of the group of court wits, and the dramatists John Dryden and Thomas Shadwell were among his friends. Dryden introduced him into his essay *Of Dramatick Poesie* under the name of Lisideius.

Notable among Sedley's plays is *Bellamira* (1687), a racy, amusing rehandling of the theme of *Eunuchus* (*The Eunuch*) of the Roman playwright Terence. Sedley's literary reputation, however, rests on his lyrics and verse translations. His best lyrics, such as the well-known "Phillis Is My Only Joy," have grace and charm. His verse translations of the eighth ode of Book II of Horace and the fourth *Georgic* of Virgil have been highly praised. The first collected edition of his works was published in 1702; a later one was published in 1928 with a study of the author.

Sedley, Amelia \ə-'mēl-yə-'sed-lē\ Fictional character whose effete sentimentality is contrasted with the lively ambition of her lifelong friend Becky Sharp in the novel VANITY FAIR by William Makepeace Thackeray.

Seeberg \'sā-,ber *with* r *labialized*\, Peter (b. June 22, 1925, Skrydstrup, Den.)   Danish modernist writer who was influenced by existentialism and nihilism.

Seeberg's first book, *Bipersonerne* ("Secondary Characters"), a novel about a collective of foreign workers in Berlin toward the end of World War II, appeared in 1956. The workers inhabit an unreal world—a film studio—at an unreal time, and their alienation gradually becomes symbolic of the human con-

dition in general. A similar theme runs through *Fugls føde* (1957; "Bird Pickings"; *The Imposter*), but in this novel reality is perceived exclusively through the consciousness of the main character, a nihilistic writer who vainly attempts to create something "real" with his literature. Loss of identity afflicts the depersonalized figures in Seeberg's collection of short stories, *Eftersøgningen* (1962; "The Search"). His later works are somewhat more optimistic.

Seers \'ser\, Eugène, *pseudonym* Louis Dantin \dä\n-'ta\n\ (b. 1865, Beauharnois, Que. [Canada]—d. Jan. 17, 1945, Boston, Mass., U.S.)   French-Canadian poet and critic who is regarded as the first major literary critic of Quebec.

While a member of the religious order Congrégation de Très Saint-Sacrement, Seers wrote religious poetry, short stories, and critical articles, especially on the poetry of the French-Canadian Émile Nelligan. He left the order in 1903. His criticism, at first in the form of correspondence with French-Canadian authors, achieved recognition in Montreal in the 1920s. In his *Poètes de l'Amérique française* (2 series, 1928 and 1934; "Poets of French America") and *Gloses critiques* (2 series, 1931 and 1935; "Critical Comments"), Seers stated his views that a work of art should exist for the sake of art alone and not for the promotion of any cause. He was also the author of *Le Coffret de Crusoé* (1932; "Crusoe's Chest"), a volume of poems dealing with his loss of faith, and *Les Enfances de Fanny* (1951), a semi-autobiographical novel.

Seferis \se-'fer-ēs\, George, *original name* Giórgios Stylianou Seferiadēs \,sef-er-'yä-thēs\, *also spelled* Yeoryios Stilianou Sepheriades (b. March 13, 1900, Smyrna, Anatolia, Ottoman Empire [now İzmir, Tur.]—d. Sept. 20, 1971, Athens, Greece) Greek poet, essayist, and diplomat who won the Nobel Prize for Literature in 1963.

After studying law in Paris, Seferis joined the Greek diplomatic service and served in London and Albania. Following World War II he held posts in Lebanon, Syria, Jordan, and Iraq and served as Greek ambassador in London (1957–62).

Seferis was at once acclaimed as "the poet of the future" on the publication of *I strofí* (1931; "The Turning Point"), his first collection of poems. It was followed by *I stérna* (1932; "The Cistern"), *Mithistórima* (1935; "Myth-History"), *Imerolóyion katastrómatos I* (1940; "Log Book I"), *Tetrádhio yimnasmáton* (1940; "Exercise Book"), *Poiímata* (1940; "Poems"), *Imerolóyion katastrómatos II* (1945), the long poem *Kíkhli* (1947; "Thrush"), *Poiímata 1924–46* (1950), and *Imerolóyion katastrómatos III* (1955). Selections of his poetry have been widely translated, the fullest English version being *George Seferis: Collected Poems 1924–1955* (1969). Seferis was honored by the Academy of Athens in 1947 and is considered to be the most distinguished Greek poet of "the generation of the '30s," which introduced Symbolism to modern Greek literature. His work is permeated by a deep feeling for the human predicament.

Sefrioui \sə-'frē-wē\, Ahmed (b. 1915, Fès, Mor.)   Moroccan novelist and short-story writer whose works record the everyday lives of the common people in Fès.

The son of a Berber miller, Sefrioui was educated in Fès and ultimately became director of the Bureau of Tourism there. He was one of the few French-speaking Maghribian writers to give sympathetic treatment to traditional Muslim life and values.

His first volume, *Le Chapelet d'ambre* (1949; "The Amber Beads"), consists of 14 short pieces dealing with the lives of people unassimilated into French colonial culture. In his first novel, *La Boîte à merveilles* (1954; "The Box of Wonders"), Sefrioui recalls his youth in this older, picturesque culture. *La Maison de servitude* (1973; "The House of Servitude") deals with the conflict raised by the demands of the Islāmic faith and those of poetry, love, and revolution. A collection of stories, *Le Jardin des sortilèges, ou Le Parfum des légendes* ("The Garden of Spells, or the Perfume of Legends"), was published in 1989.

seguidilla \‚sä-gĕ-'thĕl-yä, -'thē-yä\ [Spanish, probably a derivative of *seguida,* a name for the criminal underworld about 1600] In Spanish poetry, a stanza of seven short lines divided into two sections of alternating lines of five and seven syllables (arranged as 7,5,7,5; 5,7,5). There is a pause in thought between lines 4 and 5, and there is one assonance, or a kind of rhyme, in lines 2 and 4 and another in lines 5 and 7. The seguidilla form probably began as a dance song about the 17th century and gradually evolved from a four-line strophe of alternating long and short lines into its present form, which is sometimes used as a concluding section for another piece.

seicento \sā-'chen-tō\ [Italian, literally, six hundred, short for *mille seicento* the year 1600] The 17th century; specifically, the 17th-century period in Italian literature and art.

Seifert \'sā-fert\, Jaroslav (b. Sept. 23, 1901, Prague, Bohemia, Austria-Hungary [now in Czech Republic]—d. Jan. 10, 1986, Prague, Czech.) Czech poet and journalist who in 1984 became the first Czech to win the Nobel Prize for Literature.

Seifert made a living as a journalist until 1950, but his first book of poetry, *Město v slzách* ("City in Tears"), was published in 1920. His early poetry reflects his youthful expectations for the future of communism in the Soviet Union. In *Na vlnách T.S.F.* (1925; *Over the Waves of TSF*) and *Slavík zpívá špatně* (1926; *The Nightingale Sings Out of Tune*), more lyrical elements of so-called pure poetry were evident. In 1929 Seifert broke with the Communist Party.

The history and current events of Czechoslovakia were the most common subjects of his poetry: in *Zhasněte světla* (1938; "Switch Off the Lights") he wrote about the Munich agreement by which part of Czechoslovakia was annexed to Germany, Prague was the subject of *Světlena oděná* (1940; *Dressed in Light*), and the Prague uprising of 1945 provided the focus of *Přilba hlíny* (1945; "The Helmet of Clay"). In addition to writing some 30 volumes of poetry, Seifert contributed to several journals and wrote children's literature. His memoirs were published in 1981. In the 1980s and '90s many of his works were translated, including *Svatební cesta* (1938; *Honeymoon Ride*), *Vějíř Boženy Němcové* (1940; *Božena Němcová's Fan*), and *Halleyova kometa* (1967; *Halley's Comet*).

Sei Shōnagon \'sā-'shō-nä-gōn\ (b. 966/67—d. 1013?) Japanese diarist and poet, a witty, learned lady of the court, whose *Makura no sōshi* (PILLOW BOOK), apart from its brilliant and original Japanese prose style, is the best source on Japanese court life in the Heian period (794–1185).

Sei Shōnagon was the daughter of the poet Kiyohara Motosuke and was in the service of the empress Sadako from about 991 to 1000. *Makura no sōshi,* which covers the period of her life at court, consists in part of vividly recounted memoirs of her impressions and observations and in part of categories such as "Annoying Things" or "Things Which Distract in Moments of Boredom." The work is notable for Sei Shōnagon's sensitive descriptions of nature and everyday life and for its mingling of appreciative sentiments and the detached, even caustic, value judgments typical of a sophisticated court lady. Her ability to catch allusions or to compose in an instant a verse exactly suited to each occasion is evident in the bedside jottings that are contained in *Makura no sōshi.*

Seize the Day Novella by American author Saul BELLOW, published in 1956. This short novel examines one day in the unhappy life of Tommy Wilhelm, who has fallen from marginal middle-management respectability to unemployment, divorce, and despair. Like many of Bellow's other novels, *Seize the Day* exhibits an ambivalent attitude toward worldly success, and it follows its sensitive, gullible protagonist's quest for meaning in a chaotic and hostile world.

Sejarah Melayu \sä-'jä-rä-mä-'lä-yü\ ("Malay Annals") One of the finest literary and historical works in the Malay language. Concerning the Malaccan sultanate, it was composed sometime in the 15th or 16th century. The original text, written prior to 1536, underwent changes in 1612, ordered by Sultan Abdullah Maayah Shah. Only manuscripts of this modified version survive.

The *Sejarah Melayu* consists of a collection of stories, not historically connected, focusing on the activities of the Malaccan sultans, their courts, and government officials. In addition, foreign rulers were also described, as were Malacca's foreign relations and its importance as a regional trading center. A noteworthy omission was the absence of any mention of peasant life. The *Sejarah Melayu* is an important historical source about Malacca and the Malay world prior to Malacca's defeat by the Portuguese in 1511.

Selene \sə-'lē-nē\, *Latin* Luna \'lü-nə\ ("Moon") In Greek mythology, the personification of the moon as a goddess. She was worshiped at the new and full moons. Her parents were the Titans Hyperion and Theia; her brother was Helios, the sun god (sometimes called her father); her sister was Eos (Dawn); her husband was Zeus; her daughter was Pandia; and her lover was ENDYMION.

self-referential Referring to itself; especially, concerned with the mental attitudes and creative processes that brought it into existence.

self-reflexive novel *see* REFLEXIVE NOVEL.

Self-Reliance Essay by Ralph Waldo EMERSON, published in the first volume of his collected *Essays* (1841). Developed from his journals and from a series of lectures he gave in the winter of 1836–37, it exhorts the reader to consistently obey "the aboriginal self," or inner law, regardless of institutional rules, popular opinion, tradition, or other social regulators. Emerson's doctrine of self-sufficiency and self-reliance naturally arose from his view that the individual need only look inward for the spiritual guidance that was previously the province of the established churches.

Selormey \sä-lòr-'mä\, Francis (b. April 15, 1927, Dzelukofe, Gold Coast [now in Ghana]) Ghanaian writer and teacher whose sole novel, *The Narrow Path: An African Childhood* (1966), was a distinguished addition to African literature.

Selormey's first published work was "The Witch," a story published in *Okyeame* in 1965. His semiautobiographical *The Narrow Path,* written with freshness, simplicity, and disarming honesty, tells of a young man caught between his love for an overly strict father who insists on Christian, Western ways and his own appreciation for other, traditional influences. The novel has been praised for its humor and pathos and its study of the parent-child relationship.

Selvon \'sel-‚vän\, Sam, *in full* Samuel Dickson Selvon (b. May 20, 1923, Trinidad—d. April 16, 1994, Port of Spain) Trinidad-born Canadian novelist and short-story writer known for his vivid evocation of the life of East Indian immigrants in the West Indies.

Selvon's first novel, *A Brighter Sun* (1952), describes Trinidadians and Creoles in Trinidad, their prejudices and mutual distrusts, and the effect of this animosity on a young man. Its sequel, *Turn Again Tiger* (1958), follows the protagonist on a journey to his ancestral home. Perhaps the best of his novels,

The Lonely Londoners (1956) describes apparently naive immigrants living by their wits in a hostile city. In this novel Selvon, who drew heavily on oral tradition, made extensive and striking use of dialect.

His later works include a collection of short stories, *Ways of Sunlight* (1958); a collection of one-act plays, *Eldorado West One* (1988); and the novels *I Hear Thunder* (1963), *The Plains of Caroni* (1970), and *Moses Ascending* (1975) and *Moses Migrating* (1983), both sequels to *The Lonely Londoners*.

Sembène \sem-'ben\, Ousmane (b. Jan. 1, 1923, Ziguinchor-Casamance, Senegal, French West Africa)   Senegalese writer and film director known for his historical-political themes.

Sembène was drafted into the French army in 1939. In 1942 he joined the Free French Forces and landed in France for the first time in 1944. After the war he remained in France, working as a docker in Marseille.

Sembène taught himself to read and write in French and in 1956 published his first novel, *Le Docker noir* (*The Black Docker*), based on his experiences in Marseille. Among the works that followed were *O pays, mon beau peuple!* (1957; "O My Country, My Good People") and *Les Bouts de bois de dieu* (1960; *God's Bits of Wood*), which depicts an African workers' railroad strike and the attempts to combat colonialism; two volumes of short stories entitled *Voltaïques* (1962) and *L'Harmattan* (1964; "The Wind"); *Xala* (1974), which also provided the subject of one of his best films; and *Niiwam and Taaw* (1987), two novellas.

About 1960 Sembène developed an interest in motion pictures. After studying at the Moscow Film School, he returned to Africa and made three short-subject films, all reflecting a strong social commitment, and in 1966 a feature film, *La Noire de . . .* (*Black Girl*), the first ever produced by an African filmmaker.

With *Mandabi* ("The Money Order"), a comedy of daily life and corruption in Dakar, Sembène in 1968 made the revolutionary decision to film in the Wolof language. His later films include the brilliant *Ceddo* (1977; "Outsiders"), in Wolof, and *Camp de Thiaroye* (1988; "The Camp at Thiaroye").

Semele \'sem-ə-lē\, *also called* Thyone \'thī-ō-nē\   In Greek mythology, a daughter of Cadmus and Harmonia and mother of Dionysus (Bacchus) by Zeus. Semele's liaison with Zeus enraged Zeus's wife, Hera, who, disguised as an old nurse, coaxed Semele into asking Zeus to visit her in the same splendor in which he would appear before Hera. Zeus had already promised to grant Semele her every wish and thus was forced to grant a wish that would kill her: the splendor of his fire bolts, as god of thunder, destroyed Semele. Zeus saved their unborn child, Dionysus, from the womb.

semiotics \ˌsēm-ē-'ä-tiks, ˌsem-, -ī-'ä-\, *also called* semiology \-'äl-ə-jē\   The study of signs and sign-using behavior; both words are ultimately based on the Greek *sēmeion* ("sign"). Semiology was defined by one of its founders, the Swiss linguist Ferdinand de Saussure, as the study of "the life of signs within society." The idea of semiotics as an interdisciplinary mode for examining phenomena in different fields emerged in the late 19th and early 20th centuries with the independent work of Saussure and of the American philosopher Charles Sanders Peirce.

Peirce defined a sign as "something which stands to somebody for something," and one of his major contributions to semiotics was the categorization of signs into three main types: (1) an icon, which resembles its referent (such as a road sign for falling rocks); (2) an index, which is associated with its referent (as smoke is a sign of fire); and (3) a symbol, which is related to its referent only by convention (as with words or traffic signals).

Peirce also demonstrated that a sign can never have a definite meaning, because the meaning must be continuously qualified.

Saussure's work in linguistics supplied the concepts and methods that semioticians apply to sign systems other than language. One such basic semiotic concept is Saussure's distinction between the two inseparable components of a sign: the signifier, which in language is a set of speech sounds or marks on a page, and the signified, which is the concept or idea behind the sign. Saussure also distinguished *parole*, or actual individual utterances, from *langue*, the underlying system of conventions that makes such utterances understandable. Interest in the structure behind the use of particular signs links semiotics with the methods of STRUCTURALISM. Indeed, Saussure's theories are considered fundamental to structuralism (especially structural linguistics) and to POSTSTRUCTURALISM.

Modern semioticians have applied Peirce's and Saussure's principles to a variety of fields, including aesthetics, anthropology, communications, psychology, and semantics. Among the most influential of these thinkers are the Claude Lévi-Strauss, Jacques Lacan, Michel Foucault, Jacques Derrida, Roland Barthes, and Julia Kristeva.

Sempill \'sem-pil\, Robert (b. *c.* 1595—d. *c.* 1665)   Scottish poet who first used the meter that became the standard form for the Scottish humorous elegy.

The son of the poet Sir James Sempill of Beltrees, Robert wrote the elegy "The Life and Death of Habbie Simson, the Piper of Kilbarchan" (1640). This humorous poem in Scots was included by James Watson in his *Choice Collection* (1706), and its fame was assured when the poet Allan Ramsay called its meter "Standart Habbie" and used it himself in several poems. "Standart Habbie" was later known as the "Burns stanza" or "Burns meter," after its greatest exponent, Robert Burns.

Sempill \'sem-pil\ of Beltrees \'bel-trēz\, Sir James (b. 1566—d. February 1626, Paisley, Renfrewshire, Scot.)   Scottish poet remembered for his satirical poem *A Picktooth for the Pope; or, the Packman's Paternoster* (1630?), an antipapal dialogue between a peddler and a priest written in rhyming couplets. Born into a family of Scottish poets, Sempill was reared with the young King James VI. He became Scottish ambassador to England (1599) and to France (1601). He was knighted in 1600.

Şemseddin   *see* FRASHËRI.

Sénac \sā-'nåk\, Jean (b. Dec. 29, 1926, Beni Saf, Alg.—d. 1973, Algiers)   French-language poet active in the cause of national literature in Algeria.

Sénac's early poetry, as in the volume *Poèmes* (1954), is bitter and regretful in its treatment of his childhood but optimistic with regard to the future. With the outbreak of the Algerian War of Independence in 1954, however, he turned to themes of combat and of more militant national pride in *Le Soleil sous les armes* (1957; "The Sun Under Arms"), *Matinale de mon peuple* (1961; "Matinal of My People"), and later collections.

Sénac threw in his fortunes with Algeria in its struggle against French colonial rule. In 1962 he joined the Ministry of National Education and from 1963 until 1966 served as secretary-general of the Union of Algerian Writers. He edited *Anthologie de la nouvelle poésie algérienne* (1971; "Anthology of New Algerian Poetry"), in which he brought before the public the work of nine young Algerian poets.

Senancour \sā-naⁿ-'kür\, Étienne Pivert de (b. Nov. 16, 1770, Paris, Fr.—d. Jan. 10, 1846, Saint-Cloud)   French author of *Oberman* (1804), one of several early 19th-century novels that describe the sufferings of a sensitive and tormented hero. Rediscovered some 30 years after it first appeared, the book had great appeal to the later Romantics.

Senancour's father wanted him to enter the priesthood, but he fled to Switzerland in 1789 and made an unhappy marriage. He returned after the French Revolution and lived more or less as a recluse, writing for newspapers and reviews. In 1827 his *Résumé de l'histoire des traditions morales et religieuses* (1825; "Summary of the History of Moral and Religious Traditions") was judged blasphemous, and he was sentenced to a fine and imprisonment, though the sentence was reversed on appeal.

Oberman shows the influence of the French philosopher Jean-Jacques Rousseau, who felt that human nature had been perverted by the progress of civilization. The book's hero, a recluse living in the Swiss mountains, is tormented by melancholy and a sense of ineffectuality.

Sendak \'sen-dak\, Maurice (Bernard) (b. June 10, 1928, New York, N.Y., U.S.)   American artist and author of children's books.

Sendak was the son of Polish immigrants and received his formal art training at the Art Students' League in New York City. The first children's books he illustrated were Marcel Aymé's *The Wonderful Farm* (1951) and Ruth Krauss's *A Hole Is To Dig* (1952). Both were successful, and Sendak went on to illustrate more than 80 children's books by a number of writers, including Meindert De Jong, Else Holmelund Minarik, and Randall Jarrell. With *Kenny's Window* (1956), he began both writing and illustrating stories. These include the miniature four-volume *Nutshell Library* (1962) and his innovative trilogy composed of *Where the Wild Things Are* (1963; winner of the 1964 Caldecott Medal), *In the Night Kitchen* (1970), and *Outside Over There* (1981).

In 1975 Sendak wrote and directed *Really Rosie*, an animated television special based on some of the children in his stories. It was expanded into a musical play in 1978. In addition to creating opera versions of some of his own stories—including *Where the Wild Things Are*—Sendak designed a number of other works for the stage, notably a production of W.A. Mozart's *The Magic Flute* in 1980.

Sender \sen-'der\, Ramón José (b. Feb. 3, 1902, Alcolea de Cinca, Spain—d. Jan. 15, 1982, near San Diego, Calif., U.S.)   Spanish novelist whose works deal with Spanish history and social issues.

After studying at the University of Madrid, Sender became a lifelong Republican and was at one time imprisoned for political activities. In the early 1920s he served with the Spanish army in Morocco, and he later worked on the staff of *El Sol* in Madrid.

Imán (1929; *Pro Patria*), his first novel, was sharply critical of the war in Morocco. In the novels *O.P. (Orden público)* (1931; "Public Order"), on police brutality, and *Siete domingos rojos* (1932; *Seven Red Sundays*), on labor unrest, he addressed social injustice. His literary reputation was secured by the award of the National Prize for Literature for *Mr. Witt en el cantón* (1935; *Mr. Witt Among the Rebels*), which was based on an uprising in Cartagena in 1873.

Sender served as an officer in the Spanish Republican army during the Spanish Civil War (1936–39), in which his wife was killed by Nationalists. *Contra-ataque* (1938; *Counterattack*) was based on his war experiences. After the Nationalist victory, Sender went into exile, becoming a U.S. citizen in 1946.

Mosén Millán (1953; *Requiem for a Spanish Peasant*), on peasant life and the realities of war, was first published in Mexico because his work had been banned in Spain. From the mid-1960s Sender's work could once more be published in Spain. *Crónica del alba* (*Chronicle of Dawn*), a series of nine novels published over more than two decades, explores the relationship between social and individual needs. In *Las criaturas sa-*

turnianas (1968; "The Saturnian Creatures") and other works, Sender explores mythological and mystical subjects.

Seneca \'sen-i-kə\, Lucius Annaeus (b. *c.* 55 BC, Corduba [now Córdoba, Spain]—d. *c.* AD 39, Corduba?)   Author of a Latin work on declamation, a form of rhetorical exercise. Only about half of his book, *Oratorum sententiae divisiones colores*, survives; a 4th-century epitome preserves some of the rest, including two more prefaces, giving lively sketches of the persons he quotes and amusing observations on the literary life of the early empire. He also preserved various accounts, such as Livy's, of the death of Cicero.

Seneca disapproved of the artificial cleverness, often degenerating into absurdity, of many declaimers. He preferred the firmly disciplined style of Cicero.

Seneca \'sen-i-kə\, Lucius Annaeus, *byname* Seneca the Younger (b. *c.* 4 BC, Corduba [now Córdoba, Spain]—d. AD 65, Rome [Italy])   Roman philosopher, statesman, orator, and tragedian. He was Rome's leading intellectual figure in the mid-1st century AD and, with his friends, was virtual ruler of the Roman world between 54 and 62.

Marble bust, 3rd century, after an original bust of the 1st century
Staatliche Museen, Berlin

Taken to Rome as a boy, Seneca was trained as an orator and educated in philosophy. About the year 31, he began a career in politics and law. In 41 the emperor Claudius banished Seneca to Corsica on a charge of adultery with the emperor's niece. While there he studied natural science and philosophy and wrote the three treatises entitled *Consolationes*. After he was recalled to Rome in 49, he built up a powerful group of friends and became tutor to the future emperor Nero.

The murder of Claudius in 54 pushed Seneca and Sextus Afranius Burrus to the top as favorites of the new emperor, Nero. They introduced fiscal and judicial reforms and fostered a more humane attitude toward slaves, but they had powerful enemies. When Burrus died in 62, Seneca received permission to retire, and in his remaining years he wrote some of his best philosophical works. In 65 Seneca's enemies denounced him as having been a party to the conspiracy of Piso, and he was ordered to commit suicide.

The *Apocolocyntosis divi Claudii* (*The Pumpkinification of the Divine Claudius*), a witty and unscrupulous political skit, stands apart from the rest of Seneca's surviving works. The rest consist of philosophical works and tragedies. Seneca's major philosophical works include the three *Consolationes*; the *De ira*, which deals at length with the passion of anger, its consequences, and control; the *De clementia*, an exhortatory address to Nero, commending mercy as the sovereign quality for a Roman emperor; *De tranquillitate animi* ("On Tranquility of the Soul") and *De otio* ("On Leisure"), which consider various aspects of the life and qualities of the Stoic wise man; and *De beneficiis*, a diffuse treatment of benefits as seen by giver and recipient. Best written and most compelling are the *Epistulae morales*, 124 brilliant essays that treat a range of moral problems.

The "Senecan" tragedies handle familiar Greek tragic themes with some originality of detail. The principal representatives of classical tragedy known to the Renaissance world, these plays, particularly THYESTES, had a great influence, notably in England in the works of William Shakespeare, John Webster, and Cyril Tourneur.

Senecan tragedy \'sen-i-kən\ Body of nine closet dramas (plays intended to be read rather than performed) written in blank verse by the Roman Stoic philosopher Seneca in the 1st century AD. Rediscovered by Italian humanists in the mid-16th century, they became the models for the revival of tragedy on the Renaissance stage. The two great, but very different, dramatic traditions of the age—French Neoclassical tragedy and Elizabethan tragedy—both drew inspiration from Seneca.

Seneca's plays were reworkings chiefly of Euripides' dramas and also of works of Aeschylus and Sophocles. Probably meant to be recited at elite gatherings, they differ from their originals in their long declamatory, narrative accounts of action, their obtrusive moralizing, and their bombastic rhetoric. They dwell on detailed accounts of horrible deeds and contain long reflective soliloquies. Though the gods rarely appear in these plays, ghosts and witches abound. In an age when the Greek originals were scarcely known, Seneca's plays were mistaken for high classical drama.

The Elizabethan dramatists found Seneca's themes of bloodthirsty revenge more congenial to English taste than they did his form. The first English Senecan tragedy, *Gorboduc* (1561), by Thomas Sackville and Thomas Norton, is a chain of slaughter and revenge written in direct imitation of Seneca. Senecan tragedy is also evident in William Shakespeare's *Hamlet*.

Senghor \seⁿ-'gȯr, sän-\, Léopold (Sédar) (b. Oct. 9, 1906, Joal, Senegal, French West Africa) Poet and statesman who was a cofounder of the NEGRITUDE movement in African art and literature.

In 1928 Senghor went to Paris on a partial scholarship and continued his formal studies at the Lycée Louis-le-Grand and at the Sorbonne. He later taught in the French school system for several years. During these years Senghor discovered the unmistakable imprint of African art on modern painting, sculpture, and music, which confirmed his belief in Africa's contribution to modern culture.

Drafted in 1939 at the beginning of World War II, he was captured in 1940 and spent two years in Nazi concentration camps, where he wrote some of his finest poems. On his release, he joined the French Resistance. After the war Senghor became involved in politics. He helped found the Senegalese Progressive Union (after 1976, the Socialist Party), long the governing party of Senegal. In 1960, when Senegal gained its independence and became a republic, Senghor was unanimously elected president. He survived one coup attempt and retired from office on Dec. 31, 1980, midway through his fifth term.

Along with Aimé Césaire of Martinique and Léon Damas of French Guiana, Senghor was one of the originators in the 1930s and '40s of the concept of Negritude, which may be defined as the literary and artistic expression of the black African experience. Senghor became Negritude's foremost spokesman, and in 1948 he edited an anthology of French-language poetry by black Africans that became a seminal text of the Negritude movement. He was also a distinguished poet, whose own books include *Chants d'ombre* (1945; "Songs of Shadow"), *Hosties noires* (1948; "Black Offerings"), *Ethiopiques* (1956), *Nocturnes* (1961), and *Elegies majeures* (1979; "Major Elegies"). His poetry was collected in *Oeuvre poétique* (1990; "Poetical Work"). In 1984 Senghor was inducted into the Académie Française, becoming the first black member in that body's history.

Šenoa \she-'nō-ä\, August (b. Nov. 14, 1838, Zagreb, Croatia, Austrian Empire—d. Dec. 13, 1881, Zagreb) Croatian novelist, critic, editor, poet, and dramatist who urged the modernization and improvement of Croatian literature and led its transition from Romanticism to realism.

Introducing the historical novel to Croatian literature, Šenoa contributed to the growing sense of national identity among the Croatian people. He also wrote on contemporary social themes, claiming that literature should educate the public. He edited (after 1869) and contributed to the critical journal *Vijenac* ("The Wreath"), publishing many short stories, poems, and essays. His novels include *Seljačka buna* (1877; "Peasants' Revolt") and *Diogenes* (1878).

senryū \'sen-ˌryū\ *plural* senryū [Japanese] A three-line unrhymed Japanese poem structurally similar to haiku but treating human nature usually in an ironic or satiric vein. It is also unlike haiku in that it usually does not have any references to the seasons. Senryū developed from haiku and became especially popular among the common people about the 18th century. It was named for Karai Hachiemon (pen name Senryū), one of the most popular practitioners of the form.

Sense and Sensibility Novel by Jane AUSTEN, published anonymously in three volumes in 1811. The book, which Austen initially titled "Elinor and Marianne," tells the story of the impoverished Dashwood sisters. The open and enthusiastic Marianne becomes infatuated with John Willoughby, who seems to be a romantic lover but is in reality an unscrupulous fortune hunter. He deserts her for an heiress, and she eventually makes a sensible marriage with Colonel Brandon, a staid and settled bachelor. Marianne's older sister, the prudent and discreet Elinor, is constant toward her lover, Edward Ferrars, and, after some distressing vicissitudes, marries him.

sensibility \ˌsen-sə-'bil-ə-tē\ 1. A capacity of emotion or feeling as distinguished from intellect and will. Also, an acuteness of feeling. 2. Refined sensitiveness in emotion and taste with especial responsiveness to the pathetic. These qualities were especially admired and reflected in the literature of the 18th century as a reaction against the stoicism and emphasis on self-interest of the 17th century.

sentiment \'sen-tə-mənt\ [French, feeling] 1. Refined feeling; keen or delicate sensibility especially as expressed in a work of art or evinced in conduct. 2. An emotional idea as set forth in literature or art. 3. The emotional significance of a passage or expression as distinguished from its verbal context.

sentimental comedy A dramatic genre of 18th-century England, denoting plays in which middle-class protagonists triumphantly overcome a series of moral trials. The genre was similar to the French *comédie larmoyante*. Such comedy aimed at producing tears rather than laughter. Sentimental comedies reflected contemporary philosophical conceptions of humans as inherently good but capable of being led astray through bad example; by an appeal to their noble sentiments, men and women could be reformed and set back on the path of virtue. Although the plays contain characters whose natures seem overly virtuous and whose trials are too easily resolved, they were nonetheless accepted by audiences as truthful representations of the human predicament.

Writers of sentimental comedy included Colley Cibber and George Farquhar, with their respective plays *Love's Last Shift* (1696) and *The Constant Couple* (1699). The best-known sentimental comedy is Sir Richard Steele's *The Conscious Lovers* (1723), which deals with the trials and tribulations of its penniless heroine, Indiana.

Sentimental Education, A Novel by Gustave FLAUBERT, published in French in 1869 as *L'Éducation sentimentale: Histoire d'un jeune homme*. The protagonist, Frédéric Moreau, and his beloved, Mme Arnoux, are based on Flaubert's youthful infatuation with an older married woman.

Frédéric's puppy love for Mme Arnoux is at first steadfast and idealistic, and she remains faithful to her rather frivolous husband. Frédéric's love ends in disillusionment, as do the subsequent passions of his life. His youthful ambitions lead to failure and boredom, and his idealistic views of social progress are disappointed by reality. Among the novel's most remarkable qualities is Flaubert's vivid and faithful presentation of its social and political setting, including the Revolution of 1848, the republic that followed, and the mood of the French people amid the era's many changes.

Sentimental Journey Through France and Italy, A \\'frans . . . 'it-ə-lē\\   Comic novel by Laurence STERNE, published in two volumes in 1768. The book, a combination of autobiography, fiction, and observations made by Sterne on his own travels, chronicles the journey through France of a charming and sensitive young man named Yorick and his servant La Fleur. (Though the title mentions Italy, the book ends before they reach that country.)

The novel defies conventional expectations of what a travel book might be. An apparently random collection of scattered experiences, it mingles affecting vignettes with episodes in a heartier, comic mode, but coherence of imagination is secured by the delicate insistence with which Sterne ponders how the impulses of sentimental and erotic feeling are psychologically interdependent.

sentimental novel   Broadly, any novel that exploits the reader's capacity for tenderness, compassion, or sympathy to a disproportionate degree by presenting a beclouded or unrealistic view of its subject. In a restricted sense the term refers to a widespread European novelistic development that reflected the trend toward sensibility in the 18th century, which arose partly in reaction to the austerity and rationalism of the Neoclassical period. The sentimental novel exalted feeling above reason and raised the analysis of emotion to a fine art.

The assumptions underlying the sentimental novel were Jean-Jacques Rousseau's doctrine of the natural goodness of humans and his belief that moral development was fostered by experiencing powerful sympathies. In England, Samuel Richardson's sentimental novel *Pamela* was recommended by clergymen as a means of educating the heart. In the 1760s the sentimental novel developed into the "novel of sensibility," which presented characters possessing a pronounced susceptibility to delicate sensation. Such characters also reacted emotionally to the beauty inherent in natural settings and in works of art and music. The literature of Romanticism adopted many elements of the novel of sensibility, but it did not assimilate the novel of sensibility's characteristic optimism.

Separate Peace, A   Novel by John KNOWLES, published in 1959. It recalls with psychological insight the maturing of a 16-year-old student at a preparatory school during World War II.

Looking back to his youth, the adult Gene Forrester reflects on his life as a student at Devon School in New Hampshire in 1942. Although he is an excellent student, he envies the athleticism and vitality of his friend Phineas, or Finny. Unable to cope with this insecurity, Forrester causes Finny to break his leg, sabotaging his athletic career. When the incident is later examined in a mock trial, Finny runs away, reinjures himself, and dies during consequent surgery.

Sęp Szarzyński \\'semp-shà-'zhěⁿ-skʸē\\, Mikołaj (b. *c.* 1550, Zimna Woda, near Lwów, Pol. [now Lviv, Ukraine]—d. 1581, Wolica, near Przemyśl)   Polish poet and metaphysician.

A member of a noble Protestant family, Sęp Szarzyński studied in Wittenberg and Leipzig, moving later to the University of Padua. He returned to Poland in 1567 as a fervent Roman Catholic. He died young but left a collection of patriotic odes, sonnets, and psalms that were published by his brother under the title *Rytmy abo wiersze polskie* (1601; "Rhythms or Polish Verses"). His sonnets are considered some of the best of early Polish poetry. Sęp Szarzyński has been compared to the English Metaphysical poets for his deliberate obscurity, his tone of spiritual nostalgia, and his interest in mysticism.

September 1, 1939   Poem by W.H. AUDEN, published in the collection *Another Time* (1940). The poem conveys the poet's emotional response to the outbreak of World War II. The title of the work refers to the date of the German invasion of Poland, which precipitated the war.

Even though "September 1, 1939" became one of his best-known poems, Auden later criticized the poem for its "incurable dishonesty," and he revised it several times. He removed the final stanza in 1945 before repudiating the poem entirely by leaving it out of his *Collected Shorter Poems* (1966).

septenarius \\,sep-tə-'nar-ē-əs\\ *plural* **septenarii** \\-'nar-ē-,ī, -,ē\\ [Latin, from *septenarius* (adjective) consisting of seven (of something), a derivative of *septeni* seven each, a derivative of *septem* seven]   In classical Latin prosody, iambic or trochaic lines of seven feet (equal to Greek tetrameter catalectic verse). The septenarius was commonly used for dialogue in comedies.

septenary \\'sep-tə-,nar-ē; sep-'ten-ə-rē, -'tēn-\\   *see* FOURTEENER.

septet or **septette** \\sep-'tet\\   A stanza or poem having seven lines, such as a RHYME ROYAL.

septisyllable \\,sep-ti-'sil-ə-bəl\\   A word or line of verse having seven syllables.

Septuagint \\sep-'tū-ə-jint, -'tyū-; 'sep-tū-ə-jint\\, *abbreviation* LXX.   The earliest extant Greek translation of the Old Testament from the original Hebrew, presumably made for the use of the Jewish community in Egypt when Greek was the lingua franca throughout the region. Analysis of the language has established that the Torah, or Pentateuch (the first five books of the Old Testament), was translated near the middle of the 3rd century BC and that the rest of the Old Testament was translated in the 2nd century BC.

The name Septuagint (from Latin *septuaginta*, "70") was derived later from the legend that there were 72 translators, 6 from each of the 12 tribes of Israel, who worked in separate cells, translating the whole, and in the end that all their versions were identical. In fact, there are large differences in style and usage between the Septuagint's translation of the Torah and its translations of the later books in the Old Testament.

It was in the Septuagint text that many early Christians located the prophecies they claimed were fulfilled by Christ. Jews considered this a misuse of Holy Scripture, and they stopped using the Septuagint. Its subsequent history lies within the Christian church.

The Septuagint was the main basis for most later translations, and it has never ceased to be the standard version of the Old Testament in the Greek church.

sequel \\'sē-kwəl\\   The next installment (as of a speech or story); especially, a literary or cinematic work continuing the course of a story begun in a preceding work.

sequence \\'sē-kwəns, -,kwens\\   A group of similar or related elements; specifically, an extended series of poems united by a single theme. Examples include many sonnet sequences, such as Elizabeth Barrett Browning's *Sonnets from the Portuguese.*

Serao \\sä-'rä-ō\\, Matilde (b. March 7, 1856, Patras [now Pátrai], Greece—d. July 25, 1927, Naples, Italy)   Novelist and journalist who was founder and editor of the Neapolitan daily *Il Giorno*.

Born in Greece of a Neapolitan father and a Greek mother, Serao returned to Naples with her family; she studied there and worked in a telegraph office and then on the staff of Naples' *Corriere del mattino*. In 1882 she moved to Rome and two years later married Eduardo Scarfoglio, with whom she was to found *Corriere di Roma* and two other periodicals. Returning to Naples, she separated from her husband and in 1904 founded the influential *Il Giorno*, which she edited until her death.

While pursuing her journalistic career, Serao wrote some 40 very popular novels and a number of short stories dealing with lower middle-class Neapolitan life. Her best novel was probably *Il paese di cuccagna* (1890; *The Land of Cockayne*), a lively story of the Neapolitans' passion for the lottery. Other notable novels are *Il romanzo della fanciulla* (1886; "A Girl's Romance") and *Suor Giovanna della Croce* (1901).

Serapion Brothers \sə-'rä-pē-ən, -'rä- \, *Russian* Serapionovy Bratya \sʸi-rə-pʸi-'ŏn-ə-vȯ-'brăt-yə \ Group of young Russian writers formed in 1921. Though they had no specific program, they were united in their belief that a work of art must stand on its own intrinsic merits, that all aspects of life or fantasy were suitable subjects, and that experiments in a variety of styles were desirable. The writers were admirers of E.T.A. Hoffmann, the German Romantic storyteller who wrote a series of exotic tales that were supposedly exchanged by a group gathered around a hermit, Serapion. Though they retained social themes in their work, the Serapion Brothers introduced a fresh use of intricate plots, surprise endings, and techniques of mystery and suspense.

The Serapion Brothers met in the House of Arts, a cultural institute established in Petrograd (*i.e.,* St. Petersburg) by Maksim Gorky. They learned their craft from the innovative elder writer Yevgeny Zamyatin. The members, most of whom were in their early 20s, included Mikhail Zoshchenko, Vsevolod Ivanov, Veniamin Kaverin, Konstantin Fedin, Lev Lunts, Nikolay Nikitin, Nikolay Tikhonov, Vladimir Pozner, Mikhail Slonimsky, and Viktor Shklovsky.

Sereni \sā-'rā-nē \, Vittorio (b. July 27, 1913, Luino, Italy—d. Feb. 10, 1983, Milan) Italian poet, author, editor, and translator who was known for his lyric verse and for his translations into Italian of works by Pierre Corneille, Guillaume Apollinaire, Paul Valéry, René Char, Albert Camus, Ezra Pound, and William Carlos Williams.

Sereni was active in Milan's avant-garde literary circles and published his first poems in 1937 in the periodical *Il frontespizio*. He served as an infantry officer in the Italian army during World War II, was captured by the Allies, and was held in a prisoner-of-war camp from 1943 to 1945; he wrote of his experiences in *Diario d'Algeria* (1947; *Algerian Diary*). After the war, he returned to Milan. He was literary editor at the Mondadori publishing house, editor of the newspaper *La rassegna d'Italia*, and literary critic for *Milano-sera*.

In the 1930s, Sereni's poetry placed him among the Hermetic school. Influenced by the poets Guido Gozzano and Eugenio Montale, his work evolved, particularly after World War II, from a private, interior orientation to a more concrete exploration of life. Sereni's early work was influenced by Crepuscolarismo; an important theme is the concept of death as total and final. His poetry collections include *Frontiera* (1941; "The Border"); *Gli strumenti umani* (1965; "The Human Instruments"), and *Stella variabile* (1981; "Variable Star").

serial \'sir-ē-əl \ A novel or other work appearing (as in a magazine) in parts at intervals. It was a common way of publishing novels in the 19th century. Many works by Charles

Dickens, George Eliot, William Makepeace Thackeray, Anthony Trollope, and others first appeared serially in such magazines as Dickens's *Household Words* and Thackeray's *The Cornhill Magazine*.

series \'sir-ēz \ *plural* series 1. A group of works featuring the same characters or set in the same locations, such as Anthony Powell's 12-volume series *A Dance to the Music of Time*. Trilogies and quartets are specific kinds of series. 2. A succession of volumes or issues published with related subjects or authors, similar format and price, or continuous numbering.

serpentine verse In poetry, a line of verse beginning and ending with the same word, as in the following line from Matthew Arnold's "Dover Beach":

> Begin, and cease, and then again begin,

The phrase likens such verses to depictions of serpents with their tails in their mouths.

Service \'sər-vis \, Robert William (b. Jan. 16, 1874, Preston, Lancashire, Eng.—d. Sept. 11, 1958, Lancieux, Fr.) Popular verse writer called "the Canadian Kipling" for rollicking ballads of the "frozen North," notably "The Shooting of Dan McGrew" and THE CREMATION OF SAM MCGEE.

Service immigrated to Canada in 1894 and lived for eight years in the Yukon. He was a correspondent for the Toronto *Star* during the Balkan Wars of 1912–13 and an ambulance driver and correspondent during World War I.

Service's first verse collections, *Songs of a Sourdough* (1907) and *Ballads of a Cheechako* (1909), describing life in the Canadian north, were enormously popular. Among his later volumes of verse are *Rhymes of a Red Cross Man* (1916) and *Bar Room Ballads* (1940). *The Trail of '98* (1910) is a vivid novel of men and conditions in the Alaskan Klondike. Service also wrote two autobiographical works, *Ploughman of the Moon* (1945) and *Harper of Heaven* (1948).

servile \'sər-vəl, -ˌvīl \ Slavishly imitative of a model, especially in literature or art, or more generally, lacking independence or originality.

Servius \'sər-vē-əs \, *in full* Marius *or* Maurus Servius Honoratus (fl. 4th century AD, Rome [Italy]) Latin grammarian, commentator, and teacher, author of a valuable commentary on Virgil.

Servius' commentary on Virgil is extant in a longer and a shorter version. The longer version, first printed in 1600, consists of Servius' own work, in which he sought to meet the needs of schools and paid special attention to grammatical and stylistic points. With it are incorporated several valuable additions, largely from a more learned work—perhaps parts of an earlier commentary by Aelius Donatus—which mostly concern Virgil's rhetoric, mythology, and subject matter. The additions are a precious source of knowledge about Roman antiquities.

sestet \ses-'tet \ A stanza or poem of six lines; specifically, the last six lines of a Petrarchan sonnet. *Compare* OCTAVE.

sestina \ses-'tē-nə \ [Italian, a derivative of *sesto* sixth] *or* **sextain** \'seks-tān \ An elaborate lyrical verse form developed before 1200 by Provençal troubadours and employed by medieval Provençal and Italian, and occasional modern, poets. It consists, in its pure medieval form, of six stanzas of blank verse, each of six lines, followed by a three-line stanza. The final words of each line of the first stanza appear in varied order in the next five stanzas, the order used by the Provençals being *abcdef, faebdc, cfdabe, ecbfad, deacfb,* and *bdfeca.* In the final three-line stanza, the six key words are repeated in the middle and at the end of the lines, summarizing the poem or dedicating it to someone.

The sestina was invented by the Provençal troubadour Arnaut Daniel and was used in Italy by Dante and Petrarch. It was revived by the 16th-century French group of poets known as La Pléiade, particularly Pontus de Tyard. In the 19th century, Ferdinand, Count de Gramont, wrote a large number of sestinas, and Algernon Charles Swinburne's "Complaint of Lisa" is an astonishing tour de force—a double sestina of 12 stanzas of 12 lines each. In the 20th century Ezra Pound, T.S. Eliot, and W.H. Auden wrote noteworthy sestinas.

Seth \'set, 'sät\, *also called* Setekh \'set-ek\, Setesh \'set-esh\, *or* Set \'set, 'sät\   Ancient Egyptian god, originally a sky god, lord of the desert and master of storms, disorder, and warfare—in general, a trickster.

The Ramesside pharaohs (1292–*c.* 1075 BC), originating in the northeastern delta, ranked him among the great gods of Egypt and used his name in their personal names (Seti I and II, Setnakht). Seth also joined Amon, Re, and Ptah as the fourth principal god of the cosmos.

In myths, Seth was the brother of Osiris. His character was troublesome, for he was depicted as bursting out of the womb of his mother, Nut, and murdering Osiris. After Osiris' murder, Horus was conceived miraculously by Isis, the wife and sister of Osiris. Horus struggled with Seth, who sought to dispossess him of his father's throne. The struggle forms the theme of the Ramesside text *The Contending of Horus and Seth*, which borders on satire, and the later, much more somber version recorded by Plutarch, in which Seth is the embodiment of the Greek demon Typhon. As the cult of Osiris grew in prominence, Seth was gradually ousted from the Egyptian pantheon.

Seth \'sät\, Vikram (b. June 20, 1952, Calcutta, India)   Poet, novelist, and travel writer best known for his verse novel *The Golden Gate* (1986).

Seth was raised in London and India. He attended exclusive Indian schools and graduated from Corpus Christi College, Oxford. He received a master's degree from Stanford University and later studied at Nanjing University. In 1987 he returned to India to live with his family in New Delhi.

Seth's first volume of poetry, entitled *Mappings*, was published in 1980. He first attracted critical attention with his humorous travelogue *From Heaven Lake* (1983), the story of his journey hitchhiking from Nanjing to New Delhi via Tibet. The poetic craft of *The Humble Administrator's Garden* (1985) foreshadowed the polish of *The Golden Gate* (1986), a novel of the popular culture of California's Silicon Valley, written entirely in metered, rhyming 14-line stanzas. In the work Seth successfully harnessed contemporary situations to a demanding 19th-century form. He continued to use controlled poetic form in his 1990 collection *All You Who Sleep Tonight*, and he also wrote the 10 stories of *Beastly Tales from Here and There* (1992) in tetrameter couplets. He turned to prose, however, for his epic novel *A Suitable Boy* (1993), which depicts relations among four Indian families.

Seton \'set-ən\, Anya, *original name* Ann Seton (b. 1904?, New York, N.Y., U.S.—d. Nov. 8, 1990, Old Greenwich, Conn.)   American author of best-selling, exhaustively researched, romantic historical and biographical novels.

Seton was the daughter of Ernest Thompson Seton, the English naturalist, writer, and cofounder of the Boy Scouts of America, and Grace Gallatin, an American travel writer. She traveled extensively with her parents and used these and later travels as inspirations for her books. In 1941 she published her first book, *My Theodosia*, a novel about the daughter of Aaron Burr.

Seton's gothic romance *Dragonwyck* (1944) and her novel *Foxfire* (1950) were adapted for motion pictures. Among her many other novels are *The Turquoise* (1946), *The Hearth and Eagle* (1948), *The Winthrop Woman* (1958), and a number of dark romances with English settings, including *Devil Water* (1962), *Avalon* (1965), and *Green Darkness* (1972).

Seton \'set-ən\, Ernest Thompson, *original name* Ernest Evan Thompson \'tämp-sən\, *also called* Ernest Seton-Thompson (b. Aug. 14, 1860, South Shields, Durham, Eng.—d. Oct. 23, 1946, Seton Village, Santa Fe, N.M., U.S.)   Naturalist and writer best known for his animal stories.

Seton was raised in North America, his family having immigrated to Canada in 1866. He gained experience as a naturalist by trailing and hunting in the prairie country of Manitoba, using this knowledge as the basis for his animal stories. His most popular book, *Wild Animals I Have Known* (1898), is a collection of those stories.

Deeply concerned with the future of the prairie, Seton fought to establish reservations for Native Americans and parks for animals threatened by extinction. To provide children with the opportunities for nature study, he founded the Woodcraft Indians organization in 1902 and later was chairman of the committee that established the Boy Scouts of America.

set piece   In literature, a composition executed in a fixed or ideal form, often with studied artistry and brilliant effect. Or, a scene, depiction, speech, or event that is obviously designed to have an imposing effect.

settecento \,set-tā-'chen-tō\   The 18th century; specifically, the 18th-century period in Italian literature and art.

setting \'set-iŋ\   The location and time frame in which the action of a narrative takes place.

The makeup and behavior of fictional characters often depend on their environment quite as much as on their personal characteristics. Setting is of great importance for Émile Zola, for example, because he believed that environment determined character. In some cases the entire action of a novel is determined by the locale in which it is set. Gustave Flaubert's *Madame Bovary* could hardly have been placed in Paris, because the tragic life and death of the heroine have a great deal to do with the circumscriptions of her provincial milieu. It sometimes happens that the main locale of a novel assumes an importance in the reader's imagination comparable to that of the characters and yet somehow separable from them. Wessex is a giant, brooding presence in Thomas Hardy's novels. The popularity of Sir Walter Scott's "Waverley" novels is due in part to their evocation of a romanticized Scotland.

Setting Sun, The   Novel by DAZAI Osamu, published in 1947 as *Shayō*. It is a tragic, vividly painted story of life in postwar Japan.

The narrator is Kazuko, a young woman born to gentility but now impoverished. Though she wears Western clothes, her outlook is Japanese; her life is static, and she recognizes that she is spiritually empty. In the course of the novel she survives the deaths of her aristocratic mother and her sensitive, drug-addicted brother Naoji, an intellectual ravaged by his own and by society's spiritual failures. She also spends a sad, sordid night with the dissipated writer Uehara, and she conceives a child in the hope that it will be the first step in a moral revolution.

Seuss, Dr.   *see* Theodor Seuss GEISEL.

seven \'sev-ən\   Something having as an essential feature seven units or members; especially, an English trochaic meter with seven syllables to the line and typically four lines to the stanza—usually used in the plural.

Seven Against Thebes \'thēbz\ (*Greek* Hepta epi Thēbais)   Third and only surviving play of a connected trilogy by AESCHYLUS, presented in 467 BC. The play concerns the impious transgressions of Laius and the doom subsequently brought down upon his descendants.

The first play seems to have shown that Laius, king of Thebes, had fathered a son despite the prohibition of the oracle of Apollo. In the second play it appears that the son, Oedipus, killed his father and brought a curse on his own two sons, Eteocles and Polyneices. In *Seven Against Thebes* Eteocles is shown leading the defense of the city of Thebes against an invading army led by his brother Polyneices and six chieftains from the south of Greece who are bent on placing Polyneices on the Theban throne. The brothers kill each other, and the Theban royal family is thus extinguished.

seven deadly sins *also called* cardinal sins.   Any of the sins originally identified during the early history of Christian monasticism and grouped together as early as the 6th century by St. Gregory the Great. The traditional catalog of the seven deadly sins is: (1) vainglory, or pride; (2) covetousness; (3) lust, understood as inordinate or illicit sexual desire; (4) envy; (5) gluttony, which usually included drunkenness; (6) anger; and (7) sloth. The classical discussion of the subject is in the *Summa theologiae*, by the 13th-century theologian St. Thomas Aquinas. The seven deadly sins were a popular theme in the sermons, morality plays, and art of the European Middle Ages.

Seven Gothic Tales   Volume of short stories by Danish writer Isak DINESEN, published in English in 1934 and then translated by her into Danish as *Syv fantastiske fortællinger*. The stories, set in the 19th century and concerned with aristocracy, breeding and legitimacy, and self-delusion, combine romantic and supernatural elements with subtle narrative irony.

Seven Lamps of Architecture, The   Book-length essay on architecture by John RUSKIN, published in 1849. According to Ruskin, the leading principles of architecture are the "lamps" of Sacrifice, Truth, Power, Beauty, Life, Memory, and Obedience. The noblest style of architecture was Gothic, but in time medieval architecture had lost the power to resist innovation. This loss of vitality was the result of the spiritual decline of Christianity during the materialistic Renaissance. The essay took the studies of a generation of medievalists and provided them with a general framework and a moral flavor.

Seven Sages of the Bamboo Grove *also called* Seven Worthies of the Bamboo Grove, *Chinese* Zhulin qi xian \'jü-'lin-'shē-'shyan\   Group of Chinese scholars and poets of the mid-3rd century AD who banded together to escape from the hypocrisy and danger of the official world to a life of drinking wine and writing verse in the country. Their poems and essays frequently center on the impossibility of palace life for the scholar (with criticisms of the court sometimes necessarily veiled in allegory) and on the pleasures and hardships of country life.

Most prominent among the Seven Sages was the freethinking, eccentric, and highly skilled poet Yuan Ji. Xiang Xiu wrote a famous commentary, the *Zhuangzi zhu*, with Guo Xiang, a neo-Daoist contemporary, on the works of the early Daoist philosopher Zhuangzi (died *c.* 300 BC). Other members of the group included the musician Yuan Xian, the devout Daoist Shan Tao, the poet Liu Ling, and Wang Rong.

The gifted writer and amateur smith Xi Kang, whose independent thinking and scorn for court custom led to his execution by the state, was host of the group at his country home in Shanyang, in present-day Shandong province.

Seventeen   Humorous novel by Booth TARKINGTON, published in 1916. The novel recalls the events of one summer in the life of William Sylvanus Baxter, his family, and his friends in a Midwestern town in the early 20th century. Seventeen-year-old Willie develops a crush on Lola Pratt, a baby-talking, flirtatious visitor. The novel presents an accurate picture of the emotional ups and downs of a self-absorbed, love-struck teenager.

Seven Types of Ambiguity (*in full* Seven Types of Ambiguity: A Study of Its Effects on English Verse)   Critical work by Sir William EMPSON, published in 1930 and revised in 1947 and 1953. The book was one of the foundations of the school of literary theory known as New Criticism.

In *Seven Types of Ambiguity* Empson sought to enhance the reader's understanding of a poem by isolating the linguistic properties of the text. He suggested that words or references in poems are often ambiguous and, if presented coherently, carry multiple meanings that can enrich the reader's appreciation of the work. Some of his analyses of specific works came to be regarded by the New Critics as the standard readings of those texts.

77 Dream Songs   Volume of verse by American poet John BERRYMAN, published in 1964. It was awarded a Pulitzer Prize in 1965 and was later published together with its sequel, *His Toy, His Dream, His Rest* (1968), as *The Dream Songs* (1969). The entire sequence of 385 verses, consisting of three six-line stanzas each, is the self-narrated, confessional story of the antihero Henry, Berryman's poetic persona.

Seven Wise Masters *also called* The Seven Viziers, The Story of the Seven Sages, *or* Sinbadnameh \'sin-bad-,nä-mə, -,nȯ-\ ("The Book of Sindbad")   A cycle of stories, presumably Indian in origin, that made its way through Middle Persian and Arabic into Western lore. In the frame story, an Oriental king entrusted the education of his son to a wise tutor named Sindbad (not to be confused with the sailor of *The Thousand and One Nights*). During a week when the prince was ordered by Sindbad to maintain silence, his stepmother tried to seduce him. Having failed, she tried to accuse the prince before the king and sought to bring about his death by telling seven stories. Each of her narratives, however, was confuted by seven sages, who in turn told tales of the craft of women. The prince's lips were at last unsealed and the truth made known. The oldest surviving text of the story is in classical Arabic and is included in *The Thousand and One Nights*.

Sévigné \sā-vēn-'yā\, Marie de Rabutin-Chantal, Marquise de (b. Feb. 5, 1626, Paris, Fr.—d. April 17, 1696, Grignan)   French writer noted for some 1,700 letters written to her daughter. The natural, spontaneous tone of the letters broke established rules for the genre and served as a new model.

Of old Burgundian nobility, she was introduced into court society in Paris after her marriage in 1644 to Henri de Sévigné, a Breton gentleman of nobility who squandered most of her money before being killed in a duel in 1651. Mme de Sévigné was left with two children, Françoise Marguerite (b. 1646) and Charles (b. 1648). For some years she continued to frequent the fashionable social circles of Paris while also devoting herself to her children.

In 1669 her daughter married Count de Grignan and then moved to Provence with him. The separation from her daughter provoked acute loneliness in Sévigné; it also prompted her to write the letters on which her reputation is based. Most of the letters, written without literary intention or ambition, were composed in the first seven years after their separation in 1671. The letters recount current news and events in fashionable society, describe prominent persons, comment on contemporary topics, and provide details of her life from day to day— her household, her acquaintances, her visits, and her taste in reading. Sévigné's conversational manner makes her stories of current events and gossip unforgettable.

Sewanee Review, The \sə-'wȯn-ē, 'swȯn-\ Quarterly periodical of general culture with an emphasis on literature, founded at the University of the South in Sewanee, Tennessee, in 1892. In the early 1940s the review began publishing fiction, and the emphasis on criticism was also increased. *The Sewanee Review* became associated in particular with the New Criticism, though it published other views as well. Contributors included Cleanth Brooks, Robert Lowell, Wallace Stevens, Robert Penn Warren, Malcolm Cowley, W.H. Auden, Dylan Thomas, Louise Bogan, and George Woodcock.

Sewell \'syü-əl, 'sü-\, Anna (b. March 30, 1820, Yarmouth, Norfolk, Eng.—d. April 25, 1878, Old Catton, Norfolk) British author of the children's classic BLACK BEAUTY (1877).

Sewell's concern for the humane treatment of horses began early in life. She was introduced to writing when she helped to edit the works of her mother, a popular author of juvenile bestsellers. Sewell spent the last seven or eight years of her life—confined to her house as an invalid—writing *Black Beauty*. The book, a fictional autobiography of a gentle, highbred horse, had a strong moral purpose and is said to have been instrumental in abolishing the cruel practice of using the checkrein.

sextain \'seks-tān\ [modification (influenced by quat*r*ain) of French *sextine* sestina] *see* SESTINA.

sextet or **sextette** \seks-'tet\ A six-line stanza or poem, sometimes used as a synonym for SESTET.

Sexton \'seks-tən\, Anne, *original surname* Harvey \'här-vē\ (b. Nov. 9, 1928, Newton, Mass., U.S.—d. Oct. 4, 1974, Weston, Mass.) American poet whose work is noted for its confessional intensity.

A lifelong resident of New England, Sexton studied poetry under Robert Lowell at Boston University and also worked as a model and as a librarian. She taught briefly at a high school and also at several universities.

Her first book of poetry, *To Bedlam and Part Way Back* (1960), is an intense examination of her mental breakdowns and subsequent recoveries. In both *All My Pretty Ones* (1962) and *Live or Die* (1966) Sexton continues this probing treatment of her personal life, especially of her continuing emotional illness. The poet's later volumes include *Love Poems* (1969), *Transformations* (1971), and *The Book of Folly* (1972). Her last poems were published posthumously in *The Awful Rowing Toward God* (1975), *45 Mercy Street* (1976), and *Uncollected Poems with Three Stories* (1978). *No Evil Star: Selected Essays, Interviews, and Prose* was published in 1985. Sexton died a suicide.

Seyfeddin or **Seyfettin** \sā-fet-'tin, *Angl* sā-fi-'dēn\, Omer (b. 1884, Göhen, Bandirma, Ottoman Empire [now in Turkey]—d. March 6, 1920, Constantinople [now Istanbul]) Short-story writer who is considered to be one of the greatest modern Turkish authors.

Seyfeddin studied in the military schools of Edirne and Constantinople and then entered the army, eventually taking part in the Balkan Wars (1912–13). Seyfeddin wrote in a unique style and drew his stories from his personal experience, from history, and from popular traditions. His use of colloquial language gave his stories a vivid and charming quality. Seyfeddin's works cover a wide range of themes and include satires and polemical dramas featuring comical situations and social commentary. *Bahar ve Kelebekler* (1927; "Spring and the Butterflies") examines the conflicts between a grandmother and her granddaughter, who imitates Western ways and knows nothing of her own culture. *Bomba* (1935; "The Bomb"), the story of the cruel and grisly murder of a young Bulgarian socialist who refuses to cooperate with a group of his revolutionary compatriots, is considered Seyfeddin's masterpiece.

Şeyhî \she-'hē\ or **Sheykih** \shä-'kē\, Sinan, *in full* Yusef Sinaneddin Şeyhî (d. 1428, Kütahya, Ottoman Empire [now in Turkey]) Poet who was one of the most important figures in early Ottoman literature.

Besides being a poet, Şeyhî seems to have been a man of great learning and a disciple of the famous Turkish mystic and saint Haci (Hajji) Bayram Veli of Ankara, founder of the Bayrami order of dervishes. A prolific poet, he is best known for his rendition of a popular love story, *Hüsrev ü Şirin* ("Khosrow and Shirin"). Inspired by the work of the same name by the great Persian poet Nezāmī (d. 1209), Şeyhî's poem is written in *maš-nawī*s (rhymed couplets), and although left incomplete at his death, it is considered a masterpiece of eloquent and graceful verse. Şeyhî is considered to have introduced the classical Persian-style *mašnawī* into Ottoman literature. Other works include the lyric poems in his *Dīvān* ("Collected Poems") and a satirical narrative, *Harname* ("The Book of the Ass").

Shadbolt \'shad-,bōlt\, Maurice (Francis Richard) (b. June 4, 1932, Auckland, N.Z.) New Zealander author of novels and short stories set in his native land, which he has called "a last frontier for the human race, and a paradise lost."

As a young man, Shadbolt worked as a documentary-film scriptwriter and a director and then turned to journalism. He became a full-time freelance writer in 1957. His first two collections of stories were *The New Zealanders* (1959) and *Summer Fires and Winter Country* (1963). A recurring theme of these stories is the cultural clash between New Zealand's urban, modern society and its rural, traditional people.

Shadbolt's first novel, *Among the Cinders* (1965), was noted for his satiric views of New Zealand's social and intellectual life and for his invention of the character Grandfather Hubert, who travels the country with his grandson. Shadbolt's later novels include *This Summer's Dolphin* (1969), *An Ear of the Dragon* (1971), *Strangers and Journeys* (1972), *Danger Zone* (1975), *Season of the Jew* (1986), and *Monday's Warriors* (1990).

Shadow of a Gunman, The Drama in two acts by Sean O'CASEY, performed at the Abbey Theatre in Dublin in 1923 and published in 1925. Originally titled "On the Run," it was the fifth play O'Casey wrote but the first to be produced. The comic-tragic play is set in the tenement slums of Dublin in 1920 amidst guerrilla fighting between the Irish Republican Army (IRA) and the Black and Tans of the British police.

The plot concerns the poet Donal Davoren, whose neighbors think he is an IRA hero. He shares an apartment with the peddler Seumas Shields. One day Mr. Maguire, another peddler and a real IRA gunman, leaves a briefcase containing explosives with them. When the Black and Tans raid the apartment, the pair are saved by Minnie Powell, an admirer of Davoren, who removes the case but is captured. Ironically, she is killed when the IRA ambushes the police vehicle that is transporting her to prison.

shadow play Type of theatrical entertainment performed with puppets, probably originating in China and on the Indonesian islands of Java and Bali, where the form is called wayang. Flat images are manipulated by the puppeteers between a bright light and a translucent screen, on the other side of which sits the audience. Shadow plays are also performed in Turkey and Greece. In the 18th and 19th centuries, European versions of shadow plays, called *ombres chinoises* ("Chinese shadows"), achieved a limited degree of popularity, especially in France. *See also* KARAGÖZ.

Shadows on the Rock Novel by Willa CATHER, published in 1931. The novel is a detailed study of the lives of French colonists in the late 1600s on the "rock" that is Quebec city, Que., Can. Like many of Cather's novels, *Shadows on the Rock* evokes the pioneer spirit and emphasizes the importance of religious tradition.

Euclide Auclair is a widowed apothecary who initially desires to return to France but later accepts his frontier surroundings. Much of the story is presented from the perspective of Auclair's daughter, Cécile, who eventually marries the woodsman and fur trader Pierre Charron.

Shadwell \'shad-wəl, -,wel\, Thomas (b. 1642?, Norfolk, Eng.—d. Nov. 19, 1692, London)   English dramatist and poet laureate, known for his broad comedies of manners and as the butt of John Dryden's satire *MacFlecknoe*.

Shadwell became one of the court wits after the Restoration (1660). He became acquainted with Sir Robert Howard and his brother, Edward, both of whom he satirized in *The Sullen Lovers* (1668).

Shadwell wrote 18 plays, including *The Royal Shepherdess* (1669; a pastoral), *The Tempest* (1674; an opera), *Psyche* (1674–75; a tragedy), and *The Libertine* (1675; a blank-verse tragedy). He translated Juvenal's *The Tenth Satyr* (1687) and composed bitter attacks upon Dryden. He also instituted the New Year and birthday odes when he became poet laureate.

His friendship with Dryden had ended with the political crisis of 1678–79, when Shadwell espoused the Whig cause; he produced *The Lancashire Witches*, which caused offense with its antipapist propaganda and attacks upon the Anglican clergy. In the course of 1682, each of the men produced three satires. Of these, the two best known are Dryden's mock-heroic verse satire, *MacFlecknoe*, and his *Absalom and Achitophel*. The issue that divided Shadwell and Dryden was partly political, partly a difference of opinion over dramatic technique; Dryden scorned Ben Jonson's wit and Shadwell revered Jonson.

When Dryden was removed from the laureateship and the position of historiographer royal during the Revolution of 1688, Shadwell succeeded him. Shadwell continued Jonson's style of the comedy of humors in many of his plays. They form a link between Jonson's art and the realistic fiction that followed. *The Humourists* (1670) was a failure because Shadwell satirized the vices and follies of an age that did not care for generalized satire. *The Miser* (1671–72), was a rhymed adaptation of Molière that showed his gradual shift toward the wit of the comedy of manners. *Epsom-Wells* (1672) became his greatest success, being played for nearly half a century. *Bury-Fair* (1689) showed the influence of popular farce, which was to put his fame in eclipse in his later years. His last play, *The Scowrers* (1690), was a precursor of sentimental comedy.

Shaffer \'shaf-ər\, Peter Levin (b. May 15, 1926, London, Eng.)   British playwright of considerable range who moved easily from farce to the portrayal of human anguish.

Shaffer's first play, *Five-Finger Exercise* (1960), was a tautly constructed domestic drama that almost overnight established his reputation as a playwright. He followed it with a double bill, *The Private Ear* and *The Public Eye* (1962), before confirming his success with *The Royal Hunt of the Sun* (1964), a portrayal of the conflict between the Spanish and the Inca—"hope and hopelessness, faithlessness and faith." In 1965 Shaffer's *Black Comedy* was performed. It is an adroit farce, much of the comedy stemming from the central device of setting the actors in a supposedly pitch-black room that is flooded with light. EQUUS (1973; film, 1977), dealing with a mentally disturbed stable-boy's obsession with horses, was a success with both the public and the critics. *Amadeus*, produced at the National Theatre in 1979 and later filmed, is about the rivalry between Mozart and his fellow composer Antonio Salieri. After initial critical disagreement it won several dramatic awards. Shaffer also wrote *Yonadab* (1985) and *Lettice and Lovage* (1988).

Shāh-nāmeh \'shä-'nä-mə, 'shȯ-'nȯ-\ ("Book of Kings")   Celebrated work completed in 1010 by the Persian epic poet FERDOWSĪ. It is the composition in which the Persian national epic found its final and enduring form.

Ferdowsī's work was based mainly on the Pahlavi (Middle Persian) *Khvatay-nāmak*, a history of the kings of Persia. The first to undertake the versification of this chronicle was Daqīqī, a court poet who was killed after he had completed only 1,000 verses. Daqīqī's verses, which deal with the rise of the prophet Zoroaster, were afterward incorporated by Ferdowsī, with due acknowledgments, into his own poem. Dedicating his work to Sultan Maḥmūd of Ghazna, Ferdowsī updated the story to the time of the downfall of the Sāsānid empire (mid-7th century). Comprising nearly 60,000 short rhyming couplets, the *Shāh-nāmeh* has remained one of the most popular works in the Persian-speaking world. Its episodes have inspired miniaturists from the 14th century down to the present, and numerous attempts have been made to emulate it in Iran, India, and Turkey.

The work deals with Persian history from its mythical beginnings to historical events, including the acceptance of the Zoroastrian faith, Alexander's invasion, and the conquest of the country by the Arabs. A large part of the work centers on tales of the hero Rostam. The struggle between Persia and Tūrān (the central Asian steppes from which new waves of nomadic conquerors distributed Persian urban culture) forms the central theme, and the importance of the legitimate succession of kings, who are endowed with royal charisma, is reflected throughout the composition.

shāʿir \'shä-ēr, *Arabic* -'ēr\ [Arabic, poet]   In pre-Islāmic Arabic literature, a poet and tribal dignitary whose poetic utterances were deemed supernaturally inspired by such spirits as jinn and shaitans. As such, his word was believed to be necessary to insure the success of certain tribal activities, particularly war, grazing, and the invocation of the gods. In times of intertribal strife, the satire (*hijāʾ*) was the *shāʿir*'s most potent form of magic and equivalent to warfare itself.

In later times, when the supernatural association diminished, the *shāʿir* became the poetic spokesman for his tribe, praising its accomplishments and abusing its enemies. His art was highly respected, and the more famous poets were surrounded by *rāwīs* (reciters) who memorized their verses.

shaitan or **sheitan** \shä-'tän\ [Arabic *shayṭān*]   In Islāmic myth, an unbelieving class of jinn ("spirits"); it is also the name of Iblīs, the devil, when he is performing demonic acts.

In the system of evil jinn outlined by the Arab writer al-Jāḥiz, the shaitans are identified simply as unbelieving jinn. Folklore, however, describes them as exceptionally ugly creatures, either male or female, capable of assuming human form—though their feet always remain hooved. Indian and Syrian shaitans are described as the strongest of their class.

In the Qurʾān they assume the role of devil, an obvious borrowing from Judaic tradition. While they are not necessarily evil, they belong to the hordes commanded by Iblīs, who is also called *ash-Shayṭān* in Arabic. He and the shaitans whisper evil suggestions into people's ears but have no real power over humans. *See also* JINNI.

Shakespeare \'shāk-,spir\, William, Shakespeare *also spelled* Shakspere, *byname* Bard of Avon *or* Swan of Avon (baptized April 26, 1564, Stratford-upon-Avon, Warwickshire, Eng.—d. April 23, 1616, Stratford-upon-Avon)   English poet, dramatist, and actor, often called the English national poet and considered by many to be the greatest dramatist of all time.

Shakespeare's early life was spent in Stratford-upon-Avon, where he almost certainly attended the local grammar school. At 18 he married a local girl, Anne Hathaway. By

National Portrait Gallery, London

1584 he had emerged as a rising playwright in London. From then on he enjoyed fame and prosperity as a member of London's leading theater company, the Lord Chamberlain's Company (afterward known as the King's Men). About 1610 he retired to his birthplace and lived as a country gentleman.

The exact order in which Shakespeare's plays were written or first produced is not known with certainty. (Dates following titles in this article are performance dates.) His earliest plays date from the 1590s and include such comedies as THE COMEDY OF ERRORS (1592–93), THE TAMING OF THE SHREW (c. 1593), LOVE'S LABOUR'S LOST (1594–95), and A MIDSUMMER NIGHT'S DREAM (1595–96); history plays based on the lives of the English kings, including *Henry VI*, Part 1 (1589–92; *see* HENRY VI), RICHARD III (1592–93), and RICHARD II (1595–96); and the early tragedy ROMEO AND JULIET (1594–95). These early works are influenced by prevailing contemporary dramatic conventions and artifices but are also marked by vivid characterizations and an unprecedentedly rich and inventive use of the English language.

Shakespeare's plays written just before the turn of the century comprise mostly comedies, including THE MERCHANT OF VENICE (1596–97) and MUCH ADO ABOUT NOTHING (1598–99), and histories such as *Henry IV*, Part 1 (1597–98; *see* HENRY IV) and JULIUS CAESAR (1599–1600), which was the first of several plays based on the lives of figures from ancient Rome. The comedies take the mishaps of romantic courtship as their characteristic theme. The history plays center on struggles between individuals for supreme power in the state and interweave the presentation of real historical events with Shakespeare's own increasingly subtle and complex dramatic characters.

In the early 17th century Shakespeare produced his great tragedies, which mark both the summit of his art and one of the high points in the history of Western literature. The four principal tragedies are HAMLET (1600–01), OTHELLO (1604–05), KING LEAR (1605–06), and MACBETH (1605–06). These plays examine with great psychological subtlety how personality flaws in the main characters lead almost inevitably to the tragic destruction of themselves and others around them. However, these faults serve also as vehicles for profound explorations of human character, morality, and spirit.

Shakespeare's last plays combine elements of romance, comedy, and tragedy. THE WINTER'S TALE (1610–11) and THE TEMPEST (c. 1611) are clearly experimental in their lighthearted and fanciful but basically tragic form. The plays differ from Shakespeare's earlier works in their resolution of the dramatic conflict through penitence and forgiveness and in their emphasis on hope through mutual reconciliation. The first collected edition of Shakespeare's plays, known as the FIRST FOLIO, was printed in 1623 and contained all but one of his extant plays.

Shakespeare's sonnets were published in 1609. The dates of their composition are not known. The 154 sonnets refer cryptically to the author's relations with various persons—particularly a handsome young man, a dark woman, and a rival poet—whose identities remain the object of speculation and who may not even have been real people. The sonnets are characterized by the expression of strong feeling within an exquisitely controlled artistic form. Shakespeare also wrote two heroic narrative poems, *Venus and Adonis* (1593) and *Lucrece* (1594). *See also* ALL'S WELL THAT ENDS WELL; ANTONY AND CLEOPATRA; AS YOU LIKE IT; CORIOLANUS; CYMBELINE; HENRY V; HENRY VIII; KING JOHN; MEASURE FOR MEASURE; THE MERRY WIVES OF WINDSOR; PERICLES; TIMON OF ATHENS; TITUS ANDRONICUS; TROILUS AND CRESSIDA; TWELFTH NIGHT; THE TWO GENTLEMEN OF VERONA.

Shakespeare and Company A bookstore on the Left Bank in Paris, established in 1919 by Sylvia BEACH and operated by her until it was closed in 1941. In addition to offering the usual

James Joyce and Sylvia Beach at the Shakespeare and Company bookstore
Bettmann Archive

bookselling services, Beach's shop functioned as a literary center during the 1920s and '30s, providing a lending library and a congenial meeting place for American expatriates and the larger artistic community.

Shakespearean sonnet \shăk-'spir-ē-ən\ or **English sonnet** Poem of 14 lines grouped into three quatrains and a couplet with the rhyme scheme *abab cdcd efef gg*. It was developed in England by Sir Thomas Wyatt in the 16th century as an adaptation of the Petrarchan sonnet that had been imported from Italy, and it reached its maturest expression in the sonnets of William Shakespeare. *See also* PETRARCHAN SONNET; SONNET.

Shakti *see* ŚAKTI.

Shalamov \,shə-'lä-məf\, Varlam (Tikhonovich) (b. June 18 [July 1, New Style], 1907, Vologda, Russia—d. Jan. 17, 1982, Moscow) Russian writer best known for his short stories about imprisonment in Soviet labor camps.

Accused of counterrevolutionary activities while a law student at Moscow State University, Shalamov served two years at hard labor in the Urals. He returned to Moscow in 1932 and became a published writer, journalist, and critic. Rearrested in 1937, Shalamov spent the next 17 years in the extremely harsh labor camps of the Kolyma River basin in the Soviet Far East. He was released in the 1950s and was allowed to publish some of his poetry, including the collections *Ognivo* (1961; "Flint"), *Doroga i sudba* (1967; "Journey and Destiny"), and *Moskovskiye oblaka* (1972; "Moscow Clouds"). Among the collections of his poetry that were posthumously published are *Stikhotvoreniya* (1988) and *Kolymskiye tetradi* (1994; "The Kolyma Notebooks").

The *Kolymskiye rasskazy* (1978; "Kolyma Stories") is a unified collection of 103 brief sketches, vignettes, and short stories that chronicle the degradation and dehumanization of prison-camp life. Publication was banned in the Soviet Union until 1988, and the work was circulated through samizdat copies, some of which reached the West. Following the collapse of the Soviet Union, complete editions were released in Moscow in 1992. Selected tales from the collection were published in English in two volumes, *Kolyma Tales* (1980) and *Graphite* (1981).

Shamela \'sham-ə-lə\ (*in full* An Apology for the Life of Mrs. Shamela Andrews) Novel by Henry FIELDING, published under the pseudonym Conny Keyber in 1741. In this parody of Samuel Richardson's epistolary novel *Pamela*, Fielding transforms Richardson's virtuous servant girl into a predatory fortune hunter who lures her lustful, wealthy master into matrimony. It was the first of several books to burlesque the sentimental prudery of the immensely popular *Pamela*.

Shandy, Tristram \'tris-trəm-'shan-dē\ Fictional character, the protagonist of Laurence Sterne's TRISTRAM SHANDY.

Shange \'shäŋ-gä\, Ntozake, *original name* Paulette Williams \'wil-yəmz\ (b. Oct. 18, 1948, Trenton, N.J., U.S.) African-American author of plays, poetry, and fiction noted for their feminist themes and racial and sexual anger.

Shange taught at California colleges from 1972 to 1975. Her 1975 theater piece *For Colored Girls Who Have Considered Suicide/When the Rainbow Is Enuf* quickly brought her fame. *For Colored Girls* is a group of 20 poems for seven actors on the power of black women to survive in the face of despair and pain. It ran for seven months Off-Broadway in New York, then moved to Broadway and was subsequently produced throughout the United States and on television.

Shange created a number of other theater works that employed poetry, dance, and music while abandoning conventions of plot and character development. The most popular of these was her 1980 adaptation of Bertolt Brecht's *Mother Courage*, featuring a black family in the time of the American Civil War.

Shange's poetry collections include *Nappy Edges* (1978) and *Ridin' the Moon in Texas* (1987). She later published the novel *Sassafrass, Cypress & Indigo* (1982) and the autobiographical novel *Betsey Brown* (1985).

Shangri-la \ˌshaŋ-gri-'lä\ A remote and beautiful imaginary place where life approaches perfection in the novel *Lost Horizon* (1933) by James Hilton. It is used as a synonym for utopia.

shaped verse *see* PATTERN POETRY.

shape-shifter \'shāp-ˌshif-tər\ An individual (such as a werewolf) able or held to be able to change form, especially one who can do so at will. The Greek god Proteus was such a character.

Shapiro \shə-'pir-ō\, Karl Jay (b. Nov. 10, 1913, Baltimore, Md., U.S.) American poet and critic whose verse ranges from passionately physical love lyrics to sharp social satire.

Shapiro came to critical attention in 1942 with the collection *Person, Place and Thing*. He served in the U.S. Army during World War II, and his *V-Letter and Other Poems* (1944) won the Pulitzer Prize for Poetry in 1945. His later works include other volumes of poetry—notably *Poems of a Jew* (1958), *White-Haired Lover* (1968), and *Adult Bookstore* (1976)—and works of literary criticism such as *Beyond Criticism* (1953), *In Defense of Ignorance* (1960), and *The Poetry Wreck* (1975). Shapiro was consultant in poetry to the Library of Congress (1946–47) and editor of *Poetry* magazine (1950–56). From 1956 he taught at the universities of Nebraska, Illinois, and California. *Collected Poems, 1948–1978* was published in 1978 and *New & Selected Poems, 1940–86* in 1987. *Poet: An Autobiography in Three Parts* appeared in 1988.

Sharp, Becky \'bek-ē-'shärp\ Fictional character, an amoral adventuress in William Makepeace Thackeray's VANITY FAIR, a novel of the Regency period in England. She is one of the most vivid characters in English literature.

Shauqi *see* SHAWQI.

Shaw \'shȯ\, George Bernard (b. July 26, 1856, Dublin, Ire.—d. Nov. 2, 1950, Ayot St. Lawrence, Hertfordshire, Eng.)

Karsh—Rapho/Photo Researchers, Inc.

Irish comic dramatist, literary critic, and socialist propagandist, winner of the Nobel Prize for Literature in 1925.

While unsuccessfully attempting to establish a literary career in London in the 1880s, Shaw became a vegetarian, a socialist, a spellbinding orator, a polemicist, and tentatively a playwright. He became the force behind the newly founded (1884) Fabian Society, a middle-class socialist group.

In 1885 Shaw began writing book reviews and art and music criticism. He truly began to make his mark when he was recruited by *The Saturday Review* as theater critic (1895–98); in that position he used all his wit and polemical powers in a campaign to displace the artificialities of the Victorian stage with a theater of vital ideas. From his first play, *Widowers' Houses* (1893), he emphasized social and economic issues rather than romance and adopted an ironic comedic tone. These traits were also evident in MRS. WARREN'S PROFESSION (1898).

Shaw called his first plays "unpleasant," because "their dramatic power is used to force the spectator to face unpleasant facts." He followed them with four "pleasant" plays: ARMS AND THE MAN (1898), CANDIDA (1898), *The Man of Destiny* (1898), and *You Never Can Tell* (1898).

Shaw's next collection of plays, *Three Plays for Puritans* (1901), continued what became the traditional Shavian preface—an introductory essay in an electric prose style dealing as much with the themes suggested by the plays as with the plays themselves. *The Devil's Disciple* (1901) is set in New Hampshire during the American Revolution and is an inversion of traditional melodrama. The second work, CAESAR AND CLEOPATRA (1901) is Shaw's first great play. The third play, *Captain Brassbound's Conversion* (1901), is a sermon against various kinds of folly masquerading as duty and justice. In MAN AND SUPERMAN (1903) Shaw expounded his philosophy that humanity is the latest stage in an endless "creative evolution" of higher life-forms.

Shaw had already become established as a major playwright on the Continent, but it was only with the production of *John Bull's Other Island* (1907) in London that his stage reputation was belatedly made in England. He continued, through high comedy, to explore religious consciousness and to point out society's complicity in its own evils in MAJOR BARBARA (1907); THE DOCTOR'S DILEMMA (1911); PYGMALION (1914), Shaw's comedic masterpiece and certainly his funniest and most popular play; and ANDROCLES AND THE LION (1916).

World War I was a watershed for Shaw. His antiwar speeches and his pamphet "Common Sense About the War" made him the target of much criticism. In HEARTBREAK HOUSE (1919), Shaw exposed, in a country-house setting on the eve of war, the spiritual bankruptcy of the generation responsible for the war's bloodshed.

The five linked plays under the collective title *Back to Methuselah* (1921) expound his philosophy of creative evolution in an extended dramatic parable. The canonization of Joan of Arc in 1920 reawakened within Shaw ideas for a chronicle play about her. SAINT JOAN (1924) led to the 1925 Nobel Prize for Literature (Shaw accepted the honor but refused the money).

Shaw followed the encyclopedic political tract "The Intelligent Woman's Guide to Socialism and Capitalism" (1928) with *The Apple Cart* (1930), a futuristic high comedy. His later plays were minor works, with only flashes of the earlier Shaw.

Shaw \\'shȯ\\, Irwin, *original name* Irwin Gilbert Shamforoff \\'shäm-fə-rȯf\\ (b. Feb. 27, 1913, New York, N.Y., U.S.—d. May 16, 1984, Davos, Switz.)   Prolific playwright, screenwriter, and author of critically acclaimed short stories and best-selling novels.

Shaw began his career at age 21 by writing scripts for radio shows. He wrote his antiwar one-act play *Bury the Dead* for a 1935 contest; though it lost, it was produced the next year. He wrote his first screenplay, *The Big Game*, in 1936. His stories, which appeared in such magazines as *The New Yorker* and *Esquire* beginning in the late 1930s, were praised for their plotting, naturalness of narration, and characterization.

Shaw's experiences in the U.S. Army in Europe during World War II led to his writing *The Young Lions* (1948), a novel about three young soldiers in wartime; it became a best-seller, and thereafter Shaw devoted most of the rest of his career to writing novels. Among the best-known of his 12 novels are *Two Weeks in Another Town* (1960), *Evening in Byzantium* (1973), and *Beggarman, Thief* (1977). Probably his most popular novel, though it was derided by critics, was *Rich Man, Poor Man* (1970).

Shawqī or **Shauqi** \\shau̇-'kē, shȯ-\\, Aḥmad (b. 1868, Cairo, Egypt—d. Oct. 13, 1932, Cairo)   Egyptian poet and dramatist, the *amīr ash-shuʿarāʾ* ("prince of poets") of modern Arabic poetry and pioneer of the Arabic poetical drama.

Shawqī was sent by the khedive (viceroy) to France to study at Montpellier and Paris universities. On his return he was readily promoted, and by 1914 he was the leading literary figure in Egypt. He spent 1914–19 in exile in Spain but on his

return continued to dominate the Egyptian literary scene. In 1927 he was proclaimed *amīr ash-shuʿarāʾ*.

Shawqī was a prolific poet with a fine command of rhyme and diction, his verse forms ranging from conventional eulogy to poetic plays following such Western models as the plays of William Shakespeare, Pierre Corneille, and Jean Racine. While his efforts at imitating the ancient Arabic poets were unsuccessful, he adapted traditional poetic meters to dramatic dialogue in several of his plays, such as *Masraʿ Kulyubatarah* ("The Fall of Cleopatra").

Shchedrin   *see* SALTYKOV.

She (*in full* She: A History of Adventure)   Romantic novel by H. Rider HAGGARD, published in 1887, about two adventurers who search for a supernatural white queen, Ayesha, or "She-Who-Must-Be-Obeyed," ruler of a lost African city called Kôr. Ayesha has waited for 2,000 years for the reincarnation of her lover, whom she killed out of jealousy. Beautiful and powerful, she finds her reincarnated ideal in Leo Vincey, who is her lover's descendant. He falls under her spell, and she attempts to make him immortal; she tries to convince him to pass through a magic fire, but in doing so herself, she ages and crumbles into dust.

Shedal   *see* Samuel David LUZZATTO.

Sheed \\'shēd\\, Wilfrid (John Joseph) (b. Dec. 27, 1930, London, Eng.)   American author of essays, biographies, and other nonfiction works and of satirical fiction that contrasts transient modern values with steadfast traditional values.

Sheed's parents, authors themselves, founded Sheed & Ward, a leading Roman Catholic publishing firm. The family immigrated to the United States in 1940, and Sheed returned to England to study at Oxford University. In 1959 he began writing film, drama, and book criticism for magazines and newspapers in New York City.

The lives of individuals working in mass media are the subjects of most of his comic novels. Journalists battle over the editorial pecking order in *Office Politics* (1966), while compulsive analysis and perfectionism destroy the life of a critic in *Max Jamison* (1970). A reporter views the moral hypocrisy of a candidate in *People Will Always Be Kind* (1973).

Sheed's other novels include *The Hack* (1963), *Transatlantic Blues* (1978), and *The Boys of Winter* (1987). Among his nonfiction books are *Frank and Maisie: A Memoir with Parents* (1985), the biographies *Muhammad Ali* (1975) and *Clare Boothe Luce* (1982), the essay collections *The Good Word & Other Words* (1978) and *Essays in Disguise* (1990), and *Baseball and Lesser Sports* (1991).

Sheffield \\'shef-ēld\\, John, *in full* John Sheffield, 1st Duke of Buckingham and Normanby, 3rd Earl of Mulgrave (b. April 7, 1648, London, Eng.—d. Feb. 24, 1721, London)   English statesman, patron of the poet John Dryden, and author of poetic essays in heroic couplets.

As a poet Sheffield is chiefly remembered for *An Essay Upon Poetry* (1682) and *An Essay on Satire* (circulated in manuscript in 1679 but not published until later). *An Essay Upon Poetry*, written in couplets, aims to delineate the chief characteristics of such literary forms as the ode, the elegy, and the epic. *An Essay on Satire* begins as a critical treatise but develops into a satire, attacking Charles II, the Earl of Rochester, and many distinguished courtiers. The work was frequently attributed to Dryden (it appears in most editions of his work and he may have touched it up a bit), but it is generally acknowledged to be Sheffield's.

Shelley \\'shel-ē\\, Mary Wollstonecraft, *original surname* Godwin \\'gȯd-win\\ (b. Aug. 30, 1797, London, Eng.—d. Feb.

1, 1851, London)   English Romantic novelist best known as the author of FRANKENSTEIN (1818).

The only daughter of social philosopher William Godwin and feminist Mary Wollstonecraft, Mary Godwin met the young poet Percy Bysshe Shelley in the spring of 1814 and eloped with him to France in July of that year. The couple were married in 1816, after Shelley's first wife had committed suicide. Mary apparently came as near as any woman could to meeting Shelley's requirements for his life's partner: "one who can feel poetry and understand philosophy." After her husband's death in 1822, she returned to England and devoted herself to publicizing Shelley's writings and to educating their only surviving child, Percy Florence Shelley. She published her late husband's *Posthumous Poems* (1824), and she also edited his *Poetical Works* (1839), with long and invaluable notes, and his prose works. Her *Journal* and letters are a rich source of biographical information.

Detail of an oil painting by Richard Rothwell, first exhibited 1840

National Portrait Gallery, London

Mary Shelley's best-known novel is *Frankenstein; or, The Modern Prometheus*, in which she narrates the dreadful consequences that arise after a scientist has artificially created a human being. The novel belongs to the contemporary gothic school, which used horror as its primary device. It offered fertile ground for such typically Romantic themes as the relationship of science to humanity and the embodied alter ego.

Mary Shelley wrote several other novels, including *Valperga* (1823), *The Fortunes of Perkin Warbeck* (1830), *Lodore* (1835), and *Falkner* (1837), but *The Last Man* (1826), an account of the future destruction of the human race by a plague, is still ranked as her best work. Her travel book *History of a Six Weeks' Tour* (1817) recounts the continental tour she and Shelley took in 1814 following their elopement and then describes their summer near Geneva in 1816.

Shelley \\'shel-ē\\, Percy Bysshe (b. Aug. 4, 1792, Field Place, near Horsham, Sussex, Eng.—d. July 8, 1822, at sea off Livorno, Tuscany [Italy])   English Romantic poet whose passionate search for personal love and social justice was gradually channeled from overt actions into poems that are among the greatest in the English language.

Shelley was the heir to rich estates acquired by his grandfather. In the fall of 1810 he entered University College, Oxford, but in March 1811 he was expelled for refusing to admit authorship of *The Necessity of Atheism*. Late in August 1811, he eloped with Harriet Westbrook, the younger daughter of a London tavern owner. In 1813 he issued QUEEN MAB, his first major poem. A year later Shelley fell in love with Mary Wollstonecraft Godwin, and the two eloped to France, taking with them Mary's stepsister Jane (later Claire) Clairmont. After their return to London, Shelley came into an annual income under his grandfather's will.

In mid-May 1816, Shelley, Mary, and Claire Clairmont went to Geneva to join Lord Byron, with whom Clairmont had begun an affair. During this memorable summer, Shelley composed HYMN TO INTELLECTUAL BEAUTY and MONT

Detail of an oil painting by Amelia Curran, 1819

National Portrait Gallery, London

BLANC, and Mary began her novel *Frankenstein*. Shelley's party returned to England in September, settling in Bath. Late in the year, Harriet Shelley drowned herself in London, and on December 30, 1816, Shelley and Mary were married.

Because Shelley's health suffered from the climate and his financial obligations outran his resources, in 1818 the Shelleys and Clairmont went to Italy, where Byron was residing. That summer Shelley translated Plato's *Symposium* and wrote his own essay "On Love." Thus far, Shelley's literary career had been politically oriented; but in Italy, far from the daily irritations of British politics, Shelley deepened his understanding of art and literature and concentrated on embodying his ideals within his poems. He began *Julian and Maddalo*—in which Byron ("Maddalo") and Shelley debate human nature and destiny—and drafted Act I of PROMETHEUS UNBOUND, which was eventually published in 1820 with some of the poet's finest and most hopeful shorter poems, including "Ode to Liberty," ODE TO THE WEST WIND, "The Cloud," and TO A SKYLARK.

Settling early in 1819 at Rome, Shelley outlined THE CENCI (1819), a tragedy on the Elizabethan model based on a case of incestuous rape and patricide in 16th-century Rome.

After moving to Pisa in 1820, he reasserted his uncompromising idealism in EPIPSYCHIDION, a Dantesque fable of how human desire can be fulfilled through art. ADONAIS (1821) commemorates the death of John Keats. The verse drama *Hellas* (1822) celebrates the Greek revolution against Turkish rule. In Lerici, he began *The Triumph of Life*, a dark fragment on which he was at work until he sailed to Leghorn to welcome his friend Leigh Hunt, who had arrived to edit a periodical called *The Liberal*. During the stormy return voyage, the boat sank and Shelley drowned.

Sheltering Sky, The   First novel by Paul BOWLES, published in 1948. Considered a model of existential fiction, it sold well and was a critical success. The novel was described by the author as "an adventure story in which the adventures take place on two planes simultaneously: in the actual desert, and in the inner desert of the spirit."

Bowles's cool, detached prose contrasts with the increasingly violent and irrational events of the novel. Port and Kit Moresby, an American couple of independent means, have been traveling aimlessly for 12 years. By the time they reach Morocco they have become disaffected and alienated. They take up with a series of unreliable, rootless wanderers. On a trip to the interior Port contracts typhoid fever—out of apathy he has neglected to be vaccinated—and dies. Kit has an affair with an Arab and joins his household, but their relationship soon falls apart. Kit is found and returned to Oran. She is teetering on the brink of insanity and finds an opportunity to disappear into the crowded bazaar.

Shen Congwen or **Shen Ts'ung-wen** \\'shən-'tsûṇ-'wən\\, *original name* Shen Yuehuan \\'yūē-'hwǎn\\ (b. Nov. 29, 1902, Fenghuang, Hunan province, China—d. May 10, 1988, Beijing)   Chinese author of more than 35 volumes of fiction dealing with the struggles and triumphs of ordinary people in rural Hunan.

Trained for a military career, Shen Congwen joined a regiment in Yuanling, where he spent the next few years observing the culture of the local Miao peoples, who were featured in many of his earliest successful short stories. He began writing fiction in 1922, after arriving in Beijing, and from then until 1949 he rarely stopped writing, producing a tremendous number of novels and short stories of varying quality. He revised extensively, an unusual practice for a modern Chinese author.

During the Sino-Japanese War (1937–45), Shen Congwen taught at a number of universities. After the communists triumphed in 1949, the basically apolitical writer came under attack and suffered a breakdown under the pressure of "thought reform." He had recovered by 1955 and joined the staff of the Palace Museum in Beijing; after 1949, however, he produced no new fiction.

Shen Congwen was greatly influenced by the Western authors he had read in translation; the influence was apparent in his loose, vernacular style. Of his longer fiction, *Chang he* (1945; "The Long River"), written during the Sino-Japanese War, is generally considered his best. *Chundeng ji* (1943; "Lamp of Spring") and *Heifeng ji* (1943; "Black Phoenix") are his most important collections of short stories. English translations of some of his stories were collected in *The Chinese Earth* (1947) and *The Border Town and Other Stories* (1981).

Shenstone \'shen-₁stōn, -stən \, William (b. Nov. 18, 1714, Leasowes, Halesowen, Shropshire, Eng.—d. Feb. 11, 1763, Leasowes) Eighteenth-century English "man of taste" who, as a poet, amateur landscape gardener, and collector, influenced the trend away from Neoclassical formality in the direction of greater naturalness and simplicity.

From 1745, in response to the vogue for the *ferme ornée* ("ornamental farm"; *i.e.,* a farm that was as picturesque as it was profitable), Shenstone devoted his chief energies to beautifying his estate, the Leasowes, by "landscape gardening," a term he was the first to use. His theories, outlined in "Unconnected Thoughts on Gardening" (1764), involved the creation of winding waterways and walks and a series of picturesque views.

In his poetry Shenstone celebrated rustic virtue and simplicity, foreshadowing the sentiments of the early Romantics. His best-known poem, "The School-Mistress," commemorates Sarah Lloyd, his first teacher at the village school, in Spenserian stanzas. He was influential in reviving the ballad and advised and assisted Bishop Thomas Percy in the compilation and editing of Percy's *Reliques of Ancient English Poetry* (1765), the book that conferred literary status on the ballad.

Shepard \'shep-ərd \, Sam, *in full* Samuel Shepard Rogers \'räj-ərz\ (b. Nov. 5, 1943, Fort Sheridan, Ill., U.S.) American playwright and actor whose plays adroitly blend images of the American West, pop motifs, science fiction, and other elements of popular and youth culture.

After a year of college, Shephard joined a touring company of actors and, in 1963, moved to New York City to pursue his theatrical interests. His earliest attempts at playwriting, a rapid succession of one-act dramas, found a receptive audience in Off-Off Broadway productions. In the 1965–66 season, Shepard won Obie awards (presented by New York's *Village Voice* newspaper) for his plays *Chicago, Icarus's Mother,* and *Red Cross.*

Shepard lived in England from 1971 to 1974, and two notable plays of this period—*The Tooth of Crime* (1972) and *Geography of a Horse Dreamer* (1974)—premiered in London. In late 1974, he became playwright-in-residence at the Magic Theatre in San Francisco, where most of his subsequent plays were first produced.

Shepard's works of the mid-1970s showed a heightening of earlier techniques and themes. In *Killer's Head* (1975), for example, the rambling monologue—a Shepard stock-in-trade—blends horror and banality in a murderer's last thoughts before electrocution. *Angel City* (1976) depicts the destructive machinery of the Hollywood entertainment industry, and *Suicide in B-Flat* (1976) exploits the potentials of music as an expression of character.

In the late 1970s, Shepard wrote *Curse of the Starving Class* (1976), the Pulitzer Prize-winning BURIED CHILD (1979), and TRUE WEST (1981), plays linked thematically in their examination of troubled and tempestuous blood relationships in a fragmented society. His other plays include *La Turista* (1966), *Operation Sidewinder* (1970), *The Unseen Hand* (1970), *Seduced* (1979), FOOL FOR LOVE (1983; film, 1985), *Paris, Texas* (1984; film, 1984), and *A Lie of the Mind* (1985). Shepard also wrote several screenplays and acted in a number of motion pictures.

Shepheardes Calender, The \'shep-ərdz \ Series of poems by Edmund SPENSER, published in 1579 and considered to mark the beginning of the English Renaissance in literature.

Following the example of Virgil and others, Spenser began his career with a group of eclogues (short poems usually cast as pastoral dialogues), in which various characters, in the guise of innocent and simple shepherds, discuss life and love, formulating weighty—and often satirical—opinions on questions of the day. The *Calender* consists of 12 eclogues, one for each month, employing a variety of meters and including archaic vocabulary Spenser borrowed from earlier poetry (particularly that of Geoffrey Chaucer). The first and last of the eclogues, each presenting a "complaint" by the shepherd boy Colin Clout (Spenser), frame the remaining 10 rustic dialogues. The latter deploy the full complement of pastoral poetic conventions, including the singing contest, the encomium (a panegyric to Elisa [Elizabeth I]), the hymn to Pan, and the dirge.

Sheridan \'sher-i-dən \, Richard Brinsley (Butler) (baptized Nov. 4, 1751, Dublin, Ire.—d. July 7, 1816, London, Eng.) Irish-born playwright, impresario, orator, and Whig politician, whose plays are noted as a link between the comedy of manners as it existed at the end of the 17th century and as it was used by Oscar Wilde in the 19th century.

Sheridan's father wanted him to enter the legal profession, but in 1773, after just a week at the Middle Temple, Sheridan broke with his father and turned to the theater for a livelihood. His comedy THE RIVALS was produced and published in 1775. He followed it with *St. Patrick's Day; or, The Scheming Lieutenant* (1788; produced 1775) and *The Duenna* (1776; produced 1775). In less than a year Sheridan had brought himself to the forefront of contemporary dramatists. In 1776 Sheridan, his father-in-law Thomas Linley, and physician James Ford became partners in a half-share of Drury Lane Theatre. Two years later they bought the other half from Willoughby Lacy, Garrick's partner. There followed a revival of the plays of William Congreve at Drury Lane. In 1777 Sheridan brought out his adaptation of Sir John Vanbrugh's *The Relapse* as *A Trip to Scarborough,*

Mary Evans Picture Library

again showing his talent for revision. What Sheridan learned from the Restoration dramatists can be seen in THE SCHOOL FOR SCANDAL (1780), produced in 1777. Although resembling Congreve in having satirical wit so brilliant and general that it does not always distinguish one character from another, *The School for Scandal* does contain two subtle portraits, Joseph Surface and Lady Teazle. Sheridan's flair for stage effect was again demonstrated in a delightful prose and verse satire on stage conventions, THE CRITIC (1781; produced 1779). Sheridan's later works include the entertainments *The Glorious First of June* (1794) and *Cape St. Vincent* (1797) and the five-act tragedy *Pizarro* (1799), an adaptation of August von Kotzebue's *Die Spanier in Peru.*

Sheridan had become a member of Parliament for Stafford in 1780, and, except for a few years in governmental roles, he spent the rest of his 32 years in Parliament as a member of the minority Whig party in opposition to the governing Tories. He was recognized as one of the most persuasive orators of his time, but he never achieved great political influence in Parliament because he was thought to be an unreliable intriguer. Sheridan's last years were beset by financial difficulties that were exacerbated by the loss of his parliamentary seat and by the destruction by fire of Drury Lane Theatre in 1809.

Sherlock Holmes *see* Sherlock HOLMES.

Sherriff \'sher-if\, R.C., *in full* Robert Cedric (b. June 6, 1896, Hampton Wick, Surrey, Eng.—d. Nov. 13, 1975, London) English playwright and screenwriter who is remembered for his *Journey's End*, a World War I play that won wide critical acclaim.

Sherriff entered the army in World War I, serving as a captain in the East Surrey Regiment. He drew on his war experiences in the writing of *Journey's End* (1929). A moving account of life in a dugout on the Western Front in 1918, the play met with instant success in London and ran for 595 performances, later duplicating this success throughout the world. A London revival in 1972 testified to its continuing appeal. The rest of his plays suffered by comparison with his masterpiece, though *Home at Seven* (1950) is still sometimes performed.

Sherriff also wrote a number of successful film scripts. His autobiography, *No Leading Lady*, was published in 1968.

Sherwood \'shər-,wŭd\, Robert Emmet (b. April 4, 1896, New Rochelle, N.Y., U.S.—d. Nov. 14, 1955, New York City) American playwright whose works reflect involvement in human problems, both social and political.

Sherwood served as drama editor of *Vanity Fair* (1919–20) and was a member of the Algonquin Round Table, the center of a New York literary coterie. He then worked as associate editor (1920–24) and editor (1924–28) of the humor magazine *Life*. His first play, *The Road to Rome* (1927), criticizes the pointlessness of war, a recurring theme in his work. The heroes of THE PETRIFIED FOREST (1935) and *Idiot's Delight* (1936) begin as detached cynics but recognize their own moral bankruptcy and sacrifice themselves for their fellowmen. In ABE LINCOLN IN ILLINOIS (1939) and *There Shall Be No Night* (1941), in which his pacifist heroes decide to fight, Sherwood suggests that a person can make his own life significant only by losing it for others. In 1938 Sherwood formed, with Maxwell Anderson, Sidney Howard, Elmer Rice, and S.N. Behrman, the Playwrights' Company, which became a major producing company.

The Lincoln play led to Sherwood's introduction to Eleanor Roosevelt and ultimately to his working for President Franklin D. Roosevelt as speechwriter and adviser. From his association with Roosevelt came much of the material for *Roosevelt and Hopkins: An Intimate History* (1948). Sherwood wrote

the Academy Award-winning screenplay for the film *The Best Years of Our Lives* (1946), but otherwise his theatrical work after World War II was negligible.

She Stoops to Conquer Comedy in five acts by Oliver GOLDSMITH, produced and published in 1773. This comic masterpiece mocked the simple morality of sentimental comedies. Subtitled *The Mistakes of a Night*, the play is a lighthearted farce that derives its charm from the misunderstandings which entangle the well-drawn characters.

Mr. Hardcastle plans to marry his forthright daughter Kate to bashful Marlow, the son of his friend Sir Charles Marlow. Mrs. Hardcastle wants her recalcitrant son Tony Lumpkin to marry her ward Constance Neville, who is in love with Marlow's friend Hastings. Humorous mishaps occur when Tony dupes Marlow and Hastings into believing that Mr. Hardcastle's home is an inn. By posing as a servant, Kate wins the heart of Marlow, who is uncomfortable in the company of wellborn women but is flirtatious with barmaids. Through various deceptions, Tony releases himself from his mother's clutches and unites Constance with Hastings.

Shevchenko \sheŭ-'cheŋ-kō, *Russian* shȯf-'chen-kə\, Taras Hryhorovych, *patronymic also spelled* Grigoryevich (b. Feb. 25 [March 9, New Style], 1814, Morintsy, Ukraine, Russian Empire—d. Feb. 26 [March 10], 1861, St. Petersburg, Russia) Foremost Ukrainian poet of the 19th century and a major figure of the Ukrainian national revival.

Born a serf, Shevchenko was freed in 1838 while a student at the St. Petersburg Academy of Art. His first collection of poems, *Kobzar* (1840; "The Bard"), expressed the historicism and the folkloristic interests of the Ukrainian Romantics, but his poetry soon moved away from nostalgia for Cossack life to a more somber portrayal of Ukrainian history, particularly in the long poem *Haydamaky* (1841; "The Haydamaks"). When the secret Brotherhood of Saints Cyril and Methodius (a Ukrainian nationalist group to which Shevchenko belonged) was suppressed in 1847, he was punished by exile and compulsory military service. His particular offense was that he had written the poems *Son* ("The Dream"), *Kavkaz* ("The Caucasus"), and *Poslaniye* ("The Epistle"), which satirized the oppression of Ukraine by Russia and prophesied a revolution.

Though forbidden to write or paint, Shevchenko clandestinely wrote a few lyrical poems during the first years of his exile. He experienced a renewal of his creative powers after his release in 1857; his later poetry treats historical and moral issues.

Shiels \'shēlz\, Robert (b. before 1700, Roxburghshire, Scot.—d. Dec. 27, 1753, London, Eng.) Scottish poet and editor.

Shiels was employed by Samuel Johnson as an amanuensis (secretary) on the *Dictionary of the English Language*. When this work was completed, Shiels, with others, began the compilation of a five-volume *The Lives of the Poets of Great Britain and Ireland, to the Time of Dean Swift* (1753), published shortly before his death. Although this work bore the name of Theophilus Cibber, playwright and actor, it was actually Shiels who did most of the research for whatever original writing appeared in the work. Shiels also wrote a poem, "Marriage," in blank verse; "Musidorus," an elegy on the Scottish poet James Thomson; and several other pieces.

Shiga \'shē-gä\ Naoya (b. Feb. 20, 1883, Ishinomaki, Japan—d. Oct. 21, 1971, Tokyo) Japanese fiction writer, a master stylist whose intuitive delicacy and conciseness have been epitomized as the "Shiga style."

Born into an aristocratic samurai family, Shiga was taken by his parents to live with his paternal grandparents in Tokyo in

1885. After graduating from the Peers School in 1906, he entered the department of English literature at Tokyo Imperial University but left after two years without graduating. In 1910 he joined Mushanokōji Saneatsu, Arishima Takeo, Satomi Ton, and other friends of his Peers School days in founding the journal *Shirakaba* ("White Birch"), which gave rise to an important Japanese literary movement emphasizing individualism and Tolstoyan humanitarianism. The movement lasted until the early 1920s, but when Shiga found its idealism incompatible with his more realistic approach to literature, he distanced himself from the group. Through the years he refined his objective style, perceptively delineating the most sensitive reactions of his characters with subtle simplicity. He engaged in little abstract speculation, concentrating instead on a concrete, unsentimental depiction. Spurts of literary activity, which brought him a reputation as a fine short-story writer, were separated by long periods of inactivity, and he never earned a living from his writing.

Much of Shiga's fiction is concerned with difficult family relationships, and his concern with the psychological involvements of his first-person heroes places some of his stories in the category of *shishōsetsu* ("I novel," autobiographical fiction). Both the story *Wakai* (1917; "Reconciliation") and his masterpiece, the long novel *An'ya kōro* (written in two parts between 1921 and 1937; *A Dark Night's Passing*), describe the hero's search for peace of mind in the face of family and personal conflict. The short story "Kinosaki nite" (1917; "At Kinosaki") is a fine example of his sensitive, unsentimental treatment of his own state of mind. His writing career virtually ended with the completion of *An'ya kōro*.

Shiji or **Shih-chi** \\'shə-'jə\\ ("Historical Records") Early history of China written about 85 BC by SIMA QIAN. A two-volume English translation, *Records of the Grand Historian of China*, was published in 1961. A masterpiece that took 18 years to produce, it deals with major events and personalities of about 2,000 years (down to the author's time), comprising 130 chapters and totaling more than 520,000 words. The *Shiji* not only was the first general history of its kind attempted in China, but it also set a pattern in organization for dynastic histories of subsequent ages. An artist as well as a historian, Sima Qian succeeded in making events and personalities of the past into living realities for his readers; his biographies subsequently became models for authors of both fiction and history.

Sima Qian organized the events of the past into a new five-part plan. The "Basic Annals" gives a dated chronological outline centered on events at the court considered to have been the paramount power at the time. The succeeding section consists of chronological tables that elucidate the history of the various independent feudal kingdoms and enable the reader to see at a glance what was happening in each of the states at any given time. The detailed accounts of each state are given in chapters entitled "The Hereditary Houses." A number of monographs deal with various crucial aspects of government. The work ends with a collection of "Biographies" of famous individuals selected as exemplars of various types of conduct and also discusses the affairs of the various foreign peoples, whose existence was becoming increasingly important during the reign of the emperor Wu-ti.

Shi jing \\'shə-'jiŋ\\ ("Classic of Poetry") The first anthology of Chinese poetry. It was compiled by the ancient sage Confucius (551–479 BC) and cited by him as a model of literary expression, for, despite its numerous themes, the subject matter was always "expressive of pleasure without being licentious, and of grief without being hurtfully excessive" (*Lunyu*). The book, one of the Five Classics (*Wu jing*), contains 305 poems

(and six poem titles) that are classified either as popular songs or ballads (*feng*, "wind"), courtly songs (*ya*, "elegant"), or eulogies (*song*).

Four versions of the *Shi jing* came into existence after the Qin dynasty ruler Shi Huangdi ordered the famous burning of literary books in 213 BC. The only surviving version contains introductory remarks by Mao Chang, who flourished in the 2nd century BC.

shilling shocker 1. A novel of crime or violence especially popular in late Victorian England and originally costing one shilling. *Compare* DIME NOVEL; PENNY DREADFUL. 2. A usually short novel that is characterized by sensational incidents and lurid writing.

Shimazaki \\'shē-mä-ˌzä-kē\\ Tōson \\'tō-sōn\\, *pseudonym of* Shimazaki Haruki \\'hä-rū-kē\\ (b. March 25, 1872, Magome, Nagano prefecture, Japan—d. Aug. 22, 1943, Ōiso, Kanagawa prefecture) Japanese poet and novelist whose fiction illuminated the clash of old and new values in a Japan feverishly modernizing itself during the Meiji period (1868–1912).

Tōson was educated in Tokyo. In the early 1890s he began to write poetry and joined the short-lived Romantic movement of young poets and writers, which he later described in his novel *Haru* (1908; "Spring"). The first of his major novels, *Hakai* (1906; *The Broken Commandment*), the story of a young outcast schoolteacher's struggle for self-realization, has been called representative of the naturalistic school, then the vogue in Japan, although it more clearly reflects the influence of Jean-Jacques Rousseau than of Émile Zola. *Ie* (1910–11; *The Family*) depicts the stresses that Japan's modernization brought to his own family. *Shinsei* (1918–19; "New Life") narrates the unsavory affair of a writer with his niece in a manner that carries the confessional principle to extreme.

Tōson began research in 1928 for *Yoake mae* (1935; BEFORE THE DAWN), his greatest work and one of the masterpieces of modern Japanese literature. The work is a story of the struggle for the Meiji Restoration in the 1860s as mirrored in a rural community. A final novel, *Tōhō no Mon* ("Gate to the East"), incomplete at his death, seems to invoke the Buddhist wisdom of medieval Japan as a way out of the impasse of the present.

Shimerda, Ántonia \\'än-tō-ˌnē-ə-'shi-mər-ˌdə, 'shē-\\ Fictional character, the protagonist of Willa Cather's novel MY ÁNTONIA.

Shipman's Tale, The One of the 24 stories in THE CANTERBURY TALES by Geoffrey Chaucer. It is based on an old French fabliau and resembles a story found in Giovanni Boccaccio's *Decameron*.

In the tale told by Chaucer's Shipman, the wife of a rich merchant convinces a young monk that her husband refuses to pay for her clothes and asks him to lend her 100 francs. Smitten, he agrees. The monk then asks the husband to lend him 100 francs to buy cattle, and the monk gives the sum to the wife, who thanks him by taking him to bed. When the merchant later returns from a journey, the monk says that he has repaid the debt by returning the money to the wife. The wife admits that this is so, but says that she thought it was a gift and that she used it to outfit herself as becomes the wife of a successful merchant. She then offers to repay her husband with her "jolly body." Chaucer indulges in a bawdy pun about repayment by "taille" (meaning either tally or tail).

Ship of Fools, A Novel by Katherine Anne PORTER, published in 1962. Porter used as a framework *Das Narrenschiff* (1494; *The Ship of Fools*), by Sebastian Brant, a satire in which the world is likened to a ship whose passengers, fools and deranged people all, are sailing toward eternity.

Porter's novel is set in 1931 aboard a German passenger ship returning to Bremerhaven, Germany, from Veracruz, Mexico. The ship carries a microcosm of peoples, including Germans, Americans, Spaniards, Gypsies, and Mexicans. Jews, anti-Semites, political reactionaries, revolutionaries, and neutrals coexist aboard ship, at the same time that jealousy, cruelty, and duplicity pervade their lives.

Shirer \\'shīr-ər\\, William Lawrence (b. Feb. 23, 1904, Chicago, Ill., U.S.—d. Dec. 28, 1993, Boston, Mass.) American journalist, historian, and novelist who is best known for his massive study *The Rise and Fall of the Third Reich: A History of Nazi Germany* (1960).

In the 1920s, '30s, and '40s, Shirer was stationed in Europe and in India as a foreign correspondent for the *Chicago Tribune* and the Universal News Service. In addition, he served from 1937 to 1941 as radio broadcaster for CBS, relaying to North America news of the European crises leading to World War II. His impassioned statements alerting Americans to the Nazi danger earned him several journalistic awards.

Shirer collected his impressions of European political events in *Berlin Diary: The Journal of a Foreign Correspondent, 1934–1941* (1941), which gained an international audience for its simple documentation of survival amidst horror. In the 1950s he began his research for *The Rise and Fall of the Third Reich*, which won a National Book Award in 1961. The book is a comprehensive and readable study of the Nazis' rise to power under Adolf Hitler, their rule, and their eventual demise. Shirer's other major historical work is *The Collapse of the Third Republic: An Inquiry into the Fall of France in 1940* (1960). The book is considered by some to be the best one-volume study of France during the period between the world wars. In 1980 Shirer published *Gandhi: A Memoir*, in which he recalled a series of interviews he had conducted with Mahatma Gandhi during the early 1930s. Shirer's three-volume set of memoirs is collectively entitled *Twentieth-Century Journey* (1976, 1984, 1990). He also wrote *Love and Hatred: The Troubled Marriage of Leo and Sonya Tolstoy*, published posthumously in 1994.

Shirley \\'shər-lē\\ Novel by Charlotte BRONTË, published in 1849. The novel is set at the end of the Napoleonic Wars and during the period of the Luddite riots, when England's mill workers viewed the recent introduction of machinery as a threat to their livelihood and when the textile industry suffered almost total cessation of exports. *Shirley* chiefly concerns Caroline Helstone, the young niece and ward of a provincial rector. The novel portrays her relationship with her neighbors, particularly the strong-minded heiress Shirley Keeldar and Robert Moore, a mill owner whose irate employees try to destroy the mill and kill him when he installs laborsaving machinery.

Shirley \\'shər-lē\\, James (b. September 1596, London, Eng.—buried Oct. 29, 1666, London) English poet and dramatist who was one of the leading playwrights in the decade before the closing of the theaters by Parliament in 1642.

About 1624 Shirley moved to London and began to write for the stage. His first play, *The Schoole of Complement*, was performed in 1625 at the Phoenix, Drury Lane. When the theaters closed in 1636 as a precaution against the plague, he became dramatist for St. Werburgh's Theatre in Dublin. He returned to London in 1640, succeeding Philip Massinger as dramatist for the King's Men at the Blackfriars Theatre. After the English Civil Wars (1642–51) he published two Latin grammars and nondramatic verse and masques.

Of his works, 31 plays, 5 masques, and a moral allegory are extant. His elaborate masque *The Triumph of Peace* (1634) was performed at the Inns of Court, with scenery by Inigo Jones and music by William Lawes.

Shirley wrote plays in most of the current modes. Among the best are his mildly satirical comedies of fashionable London life. *The Wittie Faire One* and *The Lady Of Pleasure*, his most polished comedies of manners, were performed between 1626 and 1635. His best tragedies, both on dark, Italianate themes, are *The Traytor* (1631) and *The Cardinal* (1641).

Shirley, Anne \\'an-'shər-lē\\ Fictional character, the heroine of *Anne of Green Gables* (1908) and subsequent novels for children by Lucy Maud MONTGOMERY.

Anne, a red-haired Canadian orphan, is an imaginative, high-spirited girl who speaks her mind. She wants, above all, to find a home with people who will love her. She goes to live with an elderly brother and sister in a house with green gables on a farm on Prince Edward Island. Impulsive and sometimes mischievous, Anne has many misadventures, but she matures in the course of the book and in the end wins a scholarship to college.

The character also appeared in *Anne of Avonlea* (1909), *Anne of the Island* (1915), *Anne's House of Dreams* (1917), and *Anne of Windy Poplars* (1936).

Shiva *see* ŚIVA.

Shizhe Pseudonym of XU ZHIMO.

Shklovsky \\'shklôf-skʸē\\, Viktor Borisovich (b. Jan. 12 [Jan. 24, New Style], 1893, St. Petersburg, Russia—d. Dec. 8, 1984, Moscow) Russian literary critic and novelist. He was a major voice of Formalism, a critical school that had great influence in Russian literature in the 1920s.

Shklovsky helped found OPOYAZ (an acronym for the Russian words meaning "Society for the Study of Poetic Language") in 1914. He was also connected with the Serapion Brothers, a collection of writers that began meeting in Petrograd (St. Petersburg) in 1921. Both groups felt that literature's importance lay primarily not in its social content but rather in its independent creation of language. In *O teorii prozy* (1925; "On the Theory of Prose") and *Metod pisatelskogo masterstva* (1928; "The Technique of the Writer's Craft"), Shklovsky argued that literature is a collection of stylistic and formal devices that force the reader to view the world afresh by presenting old ideas or mundane experiences in new, unusual ways. His concept of *ostranenie*, or "making it strange," was his chief contribution to Russian Formalist theory.

Shklovsky also wrote autobiographical novels, chiefly *Sentimentalnoye puteshestviye, vospominaniya* (*A Sentimental Journey: Memoirs, 1917–1922*), a widely acclaimed memoir of life during the early years of Bolshevik rule, and *Zoo; Pisma ne o lyubvi, ili Tretya Eloiza* (*Zoo, or Letters Not About Love, or the Third Héloise*). Both of these books were published in 1923, during a period (1922–23) when he lived in Berlin. He returned permanently to the Soviet Union in 1923, at which time the Soviet authorities dissolved OPOYAZ, obliging Shklovsky to join other state-sanctioned literary organs. With his essay "Monument to a Scholarly Error" (1930), he finally bowed to the Stalinist authorities' displeasure with Formalism. Thereafter, he tried to write within the constraints of Socialist Realism. He continued to write voluminously, publishing historical novels, film criticism, and highly praised studies of Leo Tolstoy, Fyodor Dostoyevsky, and Vladimir Mayakovsky.

Shlonsky or **Shlonski** \\'shlôn-skē\\, Abraham or Avraham (b. March 6, 1900, Poltava province, Russia [now in Ukraine]—d. May 18, 1973, Tel Aviv-Yafo, Israel) Israeli poet who founded Israel's Symbolist school and was an innovator in using colloquial speech in Hebrew verse.

In the early 1920s Shlonsky immigrated to Palestine, becoming literary editor of various periodicals. He translated into Hebrew works by authors such as Bertolt Brecht, Nikolay Gogol,

Aleksandr Pushkin, William Shakespeare, and George Bernard Shaw. Much of Shlonsky's poetry concerns the Israeli pioneer's rejection of Western values and the emergence of Israel as a modern country. His verse collections include *Shire ha-mapo-let ve-ha-piyus* (1938; "Songs of Defeat and Conciliation") and *'Al mile't* (1947; "On Filling In").

shocker \'shäk-ər\   A work of fiction or drama designed to shock the moral sensibilities, especially by the use of sordid detail, or to hold interest by the use of a high proportion of suspense, intrigue, or sensational matter (as crime or violence). Compare DREADFUL.

Shōhaku \'shō-,hä-kù\, *also called* Muan \mū-'än\ (b. 1443, Japan—d. May 4, 1527, Japan)   Japanese scholar and author of the late Muromachi period (1338–1573) who is noted for his *waka* and *renga* (linked-verse) poetry. Along with two other *renga* masters, he composed *Minase sangin hyakuin* (1488; *Minase Sangin Hyakuin: A Poem of One Hundred Links Composed by Three Poets at Minase*).

Little is known of Shōhaku's early life, but at some time he became a student of the Buddhist monk and poet Sōgi. In early 1488 Shōhaku, Sōgi, and another student, Sōchō, met at Minase, a village between Kyōto and Ōsaka, and wrote *Minase sangin*. The poem, which was written when the *renga* form was at its peak of popularity, is considered to be one of the best examples of the genre.

Shōhaku assisted Sōgi in editing *Shinsen tsukubashu* (1495; "Newly Selected Tsukuba Collection"), an anthology of *renga* that included revised rules for linked-verse composition. His own works include *Ise monogatari shōbunshō*, a commentary on the *Tale of Ise*, and *Shōhaku kōden*, a scholarly treatise on *renga*.

Sholem Aleichem or **Sholem Aleykhem** \'shòl-əm-ə-'lä-kəm, 'shōl-, -kəm\, *pseudonym of* Sholem Yakov Rabinowitz \rə-'bin-ō-,wits\, Sholem *also spelled* Sha-lom *or* Sholom, Rabinowitz *also spelled* Rabinovitsh (b. Feb. 18, 1859, Pereyaslav, Ukraine, Russian Empire [now Pereyaslav-Khmelnytskyy, Ukraine]—d. May 13, 1916, New York, N.Y., U.S.)   Popular Yiddish classical author.

Drawn to writing as a youth, Rabinowitz became a private tutor of Russian at the age of 17 and later served as a government rabbi in Lubny. His first writing had been in Russian and Hebrew, but between 1883, when his first story in Yiddish appeared, and his death he published more than 40 volumes of novels, stories, and plays in Yiddish. A wealthy man through marriage, he used part of his fortune to encourage Yiddish writers and to edit the annual *Di yidishe folks-biblyotek* (1888–89; "The Yiddish Folk Library"). He lost the rest of his wealth in business.

The works of Sholem Aleichem were widely translated, and he became known in the United States as the "Jewish Mark Twain." He began a period of wandering in 1906, established his family in Switzerland, and lectured in Europe and the United States. English translations from his *Verk* (14 vol., 1908–14) include *Jewish Children, The Old Country, Tevye, the Dairyman,* and *Adventures of Mottel, the Cantor's Son*. Adaptations of Sholem Aleichem's work were important in the founding of the Yiddish Art Theatre in New York. His best-known character, Tevye the dairyman, was the subject of a volume of short stories—*Tevye der milkhiker*—that was subsequently adapted for the Yiddish stage and cinema and was eventually the basis for the musical comedy *The Fiddler on the Roof* (1964).

Sholokhov \'shòl-ə-kəf\, Mikhail Aleksandrovich (b. May 11 [May 24, New Style], 1905, Veshenskaya, Russia—d. Feb. 21, 1984, Veshenskaya, U.S.S.R.)   Russian novelist who won the 1965 Nobel Prize in Literature for his "artistic strength and

honesty when depicting a historical epoch in the life of the Russian people."

Sholokhov began writing at 17; his first published book was *Donskie rasskazy* (1926; *Tales of the Don*), a collection of short stories. In 1925 he began his novel *Tikhy Don* ("The Quiet Don"). Sholokhov's work evolved slowly; it took 12 years to publish *Tikhy Don*, 4 vol. (1928–40; translated in two parts as AND QUIET FLOWS THE DON, 1934, and *The Don Flows Home to the Sea*, 1940) and 28 years to complete another major novel, *Podnyataya tselina* (1932–60; translated in two parts as *Virgin Soil Upturned* [U.S. title, *Seeds of Tomorrow*], 1935, and *Harvest on the Don*, 1960). *Oni srazhalis za rodinu* (1942; *They Fought for Their Country*) is an epic tale of the Soviet people's bravery during the German invasion of World War II.

Tikhy Don, Sholokhov's most controversial work, is notable for the objectivity of its portrayal of the heroic and tragic struggle of the Don Cossacks for independence from the Bolsheviks. It became the most widely read novel in the Soviet Union and was heralded as a powerful example of Socialist Realism, winning the Stalin Prize in 1941.

It has been alleged by Soviet émigrés Aleksandr Solzhenitsyn and Zhores Medvedev, among others, that much of *Tikhy Don* was plagiarized from the Cossack writer Fyodor Kryukov, who died in 1920. Proponents of this theory cite Sholokhov's youth and inexperience at the time of the publication of the first volume and his failure to produce another work of comparable literary quality. In 1979 Sholokhov's *Collected Works* was published.

short \'shòrt\   *of a syllable in prosody*   **1.** Of relatively brief duration (in Greek and Latin prosody).   **2.** Unstressed (in English verse).

Short Happy Life of Francis Macomber, The \'fran-sis-mə-'käm-bər, mə-'kō-mər\   Short story by Ernest HEMINGWAY, first published in *Cosmopolitan* in 1936, collected in *The Fifth Column and the First Forty-Nine Stories* (1938). Set on an African safari, the story contains some of the author's recurrent themes—"grace under pressure" and adherence to a manly code of behavior. It is also known for its ambiguous depiction of emotions and motivations.

The character Francis Macomber, a wealthy American, and his wife, Margot, are on safari with their English guide, Robert Wilson. Macomber wounds a lion and runs away in fear. The guide is horrified at his bad sportsmanship; his wife ridicules him for his cowardice. Margot seduces Wilson, taking care that Macomber is not unaware of her infidelity and contempt. The next day, Macomber redeems himself by killing a buffalo cleanly and bravely. He achieves a feeling of happiness he has never known before; standing his ground, unafraid, he faces another buffalo, a charging, badly wounded bull. From the car where she has been watching, Margot takes aim and shoots at the charging buffalo, apparently to save her husband's life. Her shot strikes her husband, killing him at his moment of triumph.

Shorthouse \'shòrt-,haùs\, Joseph Henry (b. Sept. 9, 1834, Birmingham, Warwickshire, Eng.—d. March 4, 1903, Edgbaston, near Birmingham)   Novelist whose philosophical romance *John Inglesant* constitutes one of the few examples of the novel of ideas in English literature. Set in England and Italy during the 17th century, the work is concerned with conflicts between church and state, the Church of England and the Roman Catholic church, ritualism and simplicity, and different views of the sacraments, as well as other subjects. The novel takes the form of long dialogues, incorporating unacknowledged quotations from various 17th-century writers.

Shorthouse was brought up a Quaker, but, influenced by John Ruskin and the Pre-Raphaelites and attracted by Anglicanism, he became a convert to the Church of England. The contrast between the author's upbringing and his adopted religion gives a particular coloring to *John Inglesant*, which Shorthouse began writing in 1866. The narrative remained in manuscript until 1880, when 100 copies were privately printed. It was published in 1881 and sold 9,000 copies within the year, and it has continued to attract readers. Shorthouse's other novels (including *Sir Percival*, 1886) were less successful.

short meter *also called* short measure, *abbreviation* S.M. **1.** A quatrain of which the first, second, and fourth lines are in iambic trimeter and the third in iambic tetrameter. **2.** A poulter's measure (alternating lines of 12 and 14 syllables) written as a quatrain.

short-short \'shȯrt-,shȯrt\   An extremely brief short story usually seeking an effect of shock or surprise.

short story   Brief fictional prose narrative to be distinguished from longer, more expansive narrative forms such as the novel, epic, saga, and romance. The short story is usually concerned with a single effect conveyed in a single significant episode or scene and involving a limited number of characters, sometimes only one. The form encourages economy of setting and concise narration; character is disclosed in action and dramatic encounter but seldom fully developed. A short story may concentrate on the creation of mood rather than the telling of a story.

Despite the precedent of ancient Greek fables and brief romances, the tales of *The Thousand and One Nights*, and the earthy fabliaux that found their way into the collections of Geoffrey Chaucer and Giovanni Boccaccio or were inserted within longer narratives in novels, the short story did not emerge as a distinct literary genre until the 19th century. It was prompted at least in part by literary romanticism, which stimulated interest in the strange and fantastic and in abnormal sensation and heightened experience that was most intensely explored within the compass of a brief prose narrative. Edgar Allan Poe's *Tales of the Grotesque and Arabesque* are of this order and were very influential not only in the United States but also in Europe, particularly in France. In Germany the tales of Heinrich von Kleist and E.T.A. Hoffmann made use of the fabulous as a means of exploring psychological and metaphysical issues. Simultaneously with these developments, realistic fiction was aspiring to the function of investigative journalism, reporting on unfamiliar, unattractive, or neglected aspects of the contemporary situation with scrupulous fidelity. Prosper Mérimée can be regarded as a pioneer of the short story of detached, dispassionate observation, a technique perfected in the tales of Guy de Maupassant, whose special skill was to capture a particularly illuminating and revealing moment in the unremarkable, perhaps dreary or sordid lives of ordinary citizens.

Other notable writers of short narratives include Nathaniel Hawthorne, Herman Melville, Henry James, Mark Twain, Ernest Hemingway, Anton Chekhov, Nikolay Gogol, Fyodor Dostoyevsky, O. Henry, Saki, Jorge Luis Borges, Katherine Anne Porter, Eudora Welty, William Trevor, and Alice Munro.

short title   An abbreviated form of entry for a book in a list or catalog that usually gives only the author's name, the title in brief, the date and place of publication, and the publisher's or printer's name.

Showalter \'shō-,wȯl-tər\, Elaine (b. Jan. 21, 1941, Boston, Mass., U.S.)   American literary critic and teacher, founder of gynocritics, a school of feminist criticism that is concerned with "woman as writer ... with the history, themes, genres, and structures of literature by women."

Showalter studied English at Bryn Mawr College, Brandeis University, and the University of California at Davis (Ph.D.,

1970). She joined the faculty of Douglass College, the women's division of Rutgers University, in 1969, where she developed women's studies courses and began editing and contributing articles to books and periodicals about women's literature.

Showalter developed her doctoral thesis into her first book, *A Literature of Their Own: British Women Novelists from Brontë to Lessing* (1977), a pioneering study in which she created a critical framework for analyzing literature by women. As a result of the book, gynocritics became the leaders of feminist criticism in the United States. Her next book, *The Female Malady: Women, Madness, and English Culture, 1830–1980* (1985), was a historical examination of women and the practice of psychiatry. She also wrote *Sexual Anarchy: Gender and Culture at the Fin de Siècle* (1990) and *Sister's Choice: Tradition and Change in American Women's Writing* (1991) and edited several volumes, including *The New Feminist Criticism* (1985) and *Daughters of Decadence: Women Writers of the Fin de Siècle* (1993).

Show Boat   Popular sentimental novel by Edna FERBER, published in 1926. The book chronicles three generations of a theatrical family who perform and live on a Mississippi River steamboat. It was the basis of a successful Broadway musical and has been produced several times for film and television.

Shropshire Lad, A \'shräp-shər\   A collection of 63 poems by A.E. HOUSMAN, published in 1896. Housman's lyrics express a Romantic pessimism in a clear, direct style. The poems of Heinrich Heine, the songs of William Shakespeare, and Scottish border ballads were Housman's models, from which he learned to express emotion yet keep it at a certain distance. He assumed in his lyrics the persona of a farm laborer, and he set the poems in Shropshire, a west England county he had not yet visited when he began writing the poems. Among the most familiar of the poems are TO AN ATHLETE DYING YOUNG, WITH RUE MY HEART IS LADEN, and WHEN I WAS ONE AND TWENTY.

Shu jing or **Shu ching** \'shü-'jiŋ\ ("Classic of History"), *also called* Shang shu \'shäŋ-'shü\ ("Official History")   One of the Five Classics (*Wu jing*) of Chinese antiquity. The *Shu jing* is a compilation of documentary records related to events in China's ancient history. Though it has been demonstrated that certain chapters are forgeries, the authentic parts constitute the oldest Chinese writing of its kind.

The *Shu jing* consists of 58 chapters. Of these, 33 (originally 29, but some chapters have been divided), called the "modern script" text, are considered by most scholars to be authentic works of the 4th century BC or earlier. The first five chapters purport to preserve the sayings and recall the deeds of such illustrious emperors as Yao and Shun, who reigned during China's legendary golden age. Chapters six to nine are devoted to the quasi-legendary Xia dynasty. The next 17 chapters deal with the Shang dynasty and its collapse. The final 32 chapters cover the Western Zhou dynasty that ruled China until 771 BC.

Shu Sheyou   Pseudonym of LAO SHE.

Shute \'shüt\, Nevil, *original name* Nevil Shute Norway \'nȯr-wā\ (b. Jan. 17, 1899, Ealing, Middlesex, Eng.—d. Jan. 12, 1960, Melbourne, Vic., Australia)   English-born Australian novelist. His most famous work, *On the Beach* (1957; film, 1959), reflected his pessimism regarding the atomic age.

Marazan (1926) was the first of 25 books Shute wrote in a career that spanned 30 years. His major works include *So Disdained* (1928) and *What Happened to the Corbetts* (1939), a foretaste of the bombing of civilians in World War II. His later novels—all set in Australia—reflected a growing feeling of despair about the future of humanity. *A Town Like Alice* (1950) dealt with the East Asian theater of World War II. In *On The*

Beach Shute describes the effect of an atomic war and vividly pictures the annihilation of the human race.

Shylock \'shī-,läk\ Fictional character in William Shakespeare's comedy THE MERCHANT OF VENICE.

Shylock is a grasping but proud and tragic Jewish moneylender. He is portrayed as a vengeful villain for insisting on his payment of a pound of flesh from Antonio when Antonio is unable to repay a loan, but at the same time it is clear that Antonio and the other Christians have often mistreated him. In Act III, Shylock delivers his famous impassioned plea for understanding: "Hath not a Jew eyes? . . . If you prick us, do we not bleed? If you tickle us, do we not laugh? If you poison us, do we not die? and if you wrong us, shall we not revenge?"

sibyl or **sybil** \'sib-əl\, *also called* Sibylla \si-'bil-ə\ [Greek *Sibylla*] In Greek mythology, a prophetess. Tradition represented her as a woman of prodigious old age uttering predictions in ecstatic frenzy. She was always a figure of the mythical past, and her prophecies, in Greek hexameters, were handed down in writing. In the 5th and early 4th centuries BC, she was always referred to in the singular; Sibylla was treated as her proper name. From the late 4th century the number of sibyls was multiplied; they were traditionally located at all the famous oracle centers and elsewhere, particularly in association with Apollo, and were distinguished by individual names, "sibyl" being treated as a title.

Sibylline Oracles \'sib-ə-,līn, -,lēn\ Collection of oracular prophecies in which Jewish or Christian doctrines were allegedly confirmed by a sibyl (legendary Greek prophetess); the prophecies were actually the work of certain Jewish and Christian writers from about 150 BC to about AD 180 and are not to be confused with the Sibylline Books, a much earlier collection of sibylline prophecies.

Sicilian octave An Italian stanza or poem having eight lines of 11 syllables (hendecasyllables) rhyming *ababab*. The form may have originated in Tuscany about the 13th century, though little is known about its origins. The Sicilian octave was in use until the 16th century, when the madrigal overtook it in popularity.

Sicilian school A group of Sicilian, southern Italian, and Tuscan poets centered in the courts of Emperor Frederick II (reigned 1197–1250) and his son Manfred (d. 1266); they established the vernacular, as opposed to Provençal, as the standard language for Italian love poetry, and they are also credited with the invention of the canzone and the sonnet, two major Italian poetic forms that show the influence of Provençal, northern French, and possibly Arabic poetic traditions. Among the outstanding poets of the Sicilian school were GIACOMO da Lentini, Guido delle Colonne, Giacomino Pugliese, and Rinaldo d'Aquino.

The brilliant Frederick II, a writer himself and a generous patron of arts, attracted some of the finest minds and talents of his time to his court. His circle included perhaps 30 men, most of them Sicilians, with added groups of Tuscans and southern Italians. Dante's term for the group, "Sicilian," in *De vulgari eloquentia* (*Concerning Vernacular Eloquence*) is not entirely accurate; some of the poets were mainlanders, the court was not always located in Palermo, and their dialect was influenced by Provençal and southern Italian dialects. Acquainted with the poetry of the Provençal troubadours and the northern French and German minstrels, Frederick's poets produced many poems, of which some 125 are extant, all in Sicilian dialect. About 85 of these are canzone (adapted from a Provençal form called the canso), and most of the rest are sonnets, the invention of which is usually attributed to Giacomo, the author of most of them. The canzone became a standard form for Italian poets for centuries. The Sicilian-school sonnet became, with variations, the dominant poetic form in Renaissance Italy and in Elizabethan England, where it was modified to form the distinctive English, or Shakespearean, sonnet.

sic passim \'sik-'pas-əm, 'sēk-'päs-im\ Literally, in Latin, "so throughout," a phrase used especially to indicate that something (such as a word or idea) is to be found at various places throughout a book or writer's work.

Siddhartha \si-'där-tə\ Novel by Hermann HESSE, based on the early life of Buddha, published in German in 1922. It reflected a visit by the author to India before World War I.

The theme of the novel is the search for self-realization by a young Brahman, Siddhartha. Realizing the contradictions between reality and what he has been taught, he abandons his comfortable life to wander. His goal is to find the serenity that will enable him to defeat fear and to experience with equanimity the contrasts of life, including joy and sorrow, life and death. Asceticism, including fasting, does not prove satisfying, nor do wealth, sensuality, and the attentions of a lovely courtesan. Despairing of finding fulfillment, he goes to the river and there learns simply to listen. He discovers within himself a spirit of love and learns to accept human separateness. In the end Siddhartha grasps the wholeness of life and achieves a state of bliss and highest wisdom.

sídh \'shē\ or **síthe** \'shē\ [Irish, from Middle Irish *síd, síth*] In Irish folklore, a hill or mound under which fairies live. The phrase *aos sídhe* or the plural *sídhe* on its own (sometimes anglicized as *shee*) can denote fairy folk collectively. *See also* BANSHEE.

Sidney \'sid-nē\, Sir Philip (b. Nov. 30, 1554, Penshurst, Kent, Eng.—d. Oct. 17, 1586, Arnhem, Neth.) Elizabethan courtier, statesman, soldier, poet, and patron of scholars and poets, considered the ideal gentleman of his day.

Sidney was born into an aristocratic family and from an early age trained for a career as a statesman and soldier. He attended Christ Church, Oxford, afterward traveling in Europe for several years, where he gained firsthand knowledge of European politics and became acquainted with many of Europe's leading statesmen.

His first court appointment came in the spring of 1576, when he succeeded his father as cupbearer to the queen, a ceremonial position. He held a number of other minor official positions and busied himself in the politics and diplomacy of his country in an unofficial capacity. In 1579 he wrote privately to the queen advising her against a proposal that she enter into a marriage with the Duke of Anjou, the Roman Catholic heir to the French throne. Sidney, moreover, was a member of Parliament for Kent in 1581 and 1584–85.

Because the queen would not give him an important post, he

Detail of an oil painting, 1576; in the Warwick Castle Collection

turned to literature as an outlet for his energies. By 1580 he had completed a version of the heroic prose romance *Arcadia*, an intricately plotted narrative of 180,000 words.

Early in 1581 his aunt, the countess of Huntington, had brought to court her ward, Penelope Devereux, who later that year married the young Lord Rich. Some time afterward Sidney fell in love with her, and during the summer of 1582 he composed a sonnet sequence, ASTROPHEL AND STELLA, recounting the first stirrings of his passion, his struggles against it, and his final abandonment of his suit to give himself instead to the "great cause" of public service. About the same time he wrote THE DEFENCE OF POESIE, which introduced the critical ideas of Renaissance theorists to England. In 1584 he began a radical revision of his *Arcadia*, transforming its linear dramatic plot into a many-stranded, interlaced narrative. Although he left *Arcadia* half finished, it remains the most important work of prose fiction in English of the 16th century. None of his works was published in his lifetime. Wounded in action while soldiering in the Netherlands, he died from the resulting infection.

Siegfried \ˈsig-ˌfrēd, ˈsēg-, *German* ˈzēg-ˌfrēt\ or **Sigurd** \ˈsig-ùrd, -ərd, -ùrth\ Figure from the heroic literature of the ancient Germanic people. He appears in both German and Old Norse literature, although the versions of his stories told by these two branches of the Germanic tradition do not always agree. A feature common to all is his outstanding strength and courage.

Siegfried plays a major part in the NIBELUNGENLIED. He also appears in the Norse *Poetic Edda* and *Das Lied vom hürnen Seyfrid* ("Song of the Invincible Siegfried"). Scholars still dispute whether the figure of Siegfried is mythical or historical (if historical, he is thought to have lived during Merovingian times, 476–750). *See also* EDDA; GUDRUN; KRIEMHILD.

Sienkiewicz \shᵛen-ˈkᵛe-vᵛěch\, Henryk (Adam Alexander Pius), *pseudonym* Litwos \ˈlēt-vōs\ (b. May 5, 1846, Wola Okrzejska, Pol.—d. Nov. 15, 1916, Vevey, Switz.) Polish novelist and winner of the Nobel Prize for Literature in 1905.

Sienkiewicz had begun to publish critical articles in 1869 showing the influence of positivism, a system of philosophy emphasizing in particular the achievements of science. His first novel, *Na marne* (*In Vain*), appeared in 1872, and his first short story, "Stary sługa" ("An Old Retainer"), in 1875. He traveled in the United States (1876–78) as special correspondent of the *Gazeta polska* ("Polish Gazette") and, after his return to Poland, via Italy and France, published a number of successful short stories, among them "Janko Muzykant" (1879; "Yanko the Musician"), "Latarnik" (1882; "The Lighthouse-Keeper"), and "Bartek Zwycięzca" (1882; "Bartek the Conqueror"). From 1882 to 1887 he was coeditor of the daily *Słowo*. During World War I he promoted the cause of Polish independence and organized relief for Polish war victims.

Sienkiewicz's great trilogy of historical novels began to appear in *Słowo* in 1883. It is composed of *Ogniem i mieczem* (1884; *With Fire and Sword*), *Potop* (1886; *The Deluge*), and *Pan Wołodyjowski* (1887–88; *Pan Michael*). Set in the late 17th century, the trilogy describes Poland's struggles against Cossacks, Tatars, Swedes, and Turks, stressing Polish heroism in a vivid style of epic clarity and simplicity. The finest of the three works, *Ogniem i mieczem*, describes the Poles' attempts to halt the rebellion of the Zaporozhian Cossacks led by Bohdan Khmelnitsky. Sienkiewicz's other novels include the widely translated QUO VADIS? (1896), a historical novel set in Rome under Nero, which established Sienkiewicz's international reputation. Although Sienkiewicz's novels have been criticized for their theatricality and lack of historical accuracy, they display great narrative power and contain vivid characterizations.

sigmatism \ˈsig-mə-ˌtiz-əm\ [*sigma* Greek letter representing a dental or alveolar sibilant] In poetry, the deliberate concentration of sibilant speech sounds, as in the line "Softer be they than slippered sleep" from E.E. Cummings' poem "All in green went my love riding."

signature \ˈsig-nə-ˌchur, -chər\ 1. A letter or figure placed usually at the bottom of the first page on each sheet of printed pages (as of a book) as a direction to the binder in arranging and gathering the sheets. 2. A printer's sheet that is folded into four or more pages to form one unit of a book. A book is a collection of signatures that are bound together.

Sign in Sidney Brustein's Window, The \ˈsid-nē-ˈbrü-ˌstīn, -ˌstēn\ Drama in three acts by Lorraine HANSBERRY, produced in 1964 and published the following year. The play concerns the nature of personal commitment to an ideal.

The character Sidney Brustein is a disillusioned white intellectual. Alton Scales, a black activist who loves Sidney's sister-in-law, Gloria, persuades Sidney to support the candidacy of Wally O'Hara, a local reform politician. Sidney does so but eventually learns of O'Hara's corruption. Sidney's wife, Iris, is an aspiring actress who leaves him to act in television commercials. When Alton learns that Gloria is a prostitute and not a model, as she had claimed, he leaves her; Gloria kills herself. Her suicide effects a reconciliation between Sidney and Iris.

Sigourney \ˈsig-ər-nē\, L.H., *in full* Lydia Howard, *original surname* Huntley \ˈhənt-lē\ (b. Sept. 1, 1791, Norwich, Conn., U.S.—d. June 10, 1865, Hartford, Conn.) Popular writer, educator, and one of few American women of her time to succeed at a literary career. She was sometimes known as "the sweet singer of Hartford."

Huntley's first work, *Moral Pieces in Prose and Verse*, was published in 1815. She wrote more than 60 books and more than a thousand articles during her career. Her writing relied on sentimental conventions of moral and religious themes; death and piety were her most popular subjects. Her best-known prose work was *Letters to Young Ladies* (1833). Although she remained popular until the end of her life, she was not respected by contemporary American writers.

Sigurd *see* SIEGFRIED.

Sigurjónsson \ˈsē- ḡur-ˌyōn-sȯn\, Jóhann (b. June 19, 1880, Laxamýri, Ice.—d. Aug. 31, 1919, Copenhagen, Den.) Icelandic playwright who became internationally famous for one play, *Fjalla-Eyvindur* (1911; *Eyvind of the Hills*).

Sigurjónsson attended the University of Copenhagen, where he joined a group of young intellectuals who looked to the Danish critic Georg Brandes and the philosophy of Friedrich Nietzsche for guidance. He began to write his plays in Danish as well as Icelandic.

After two unsuccessful plays came *Fjalla-Eyvindur*, which took Copenhagen by storm. It is a dramatization of a popular Icelandic folktale of a wealthy young woman who gives up everything to join her outlaw lover, a sheep thief, in the hills. *Galdra-Loftur* (1915; "Loftur the Sorcerer"), also based on a folktale, is about a student at the Cathedral School at Hólar who sells his soul to the devil.

sijo \ˈshē-jō\ [Korean] A Korean verse form appearing in Korean in three lines of 14 to 16 syllables. In English translation the verse form is divided into six shorter lines.

Sikelianós \ˌsē-kel-yä-ˈnōs\, Angelos (b. March 28, 1884, Leucas island, Greece—d. June 19, 1951, Athens) One of the leading 20th-century Greek lyrical poets.

Sikelianós' first important work, the poem *O alaphroískiotos* (1909; "The Light-Shadowed"), revealed his lyrical powers. It was followed by collections of outstanding lyrics. His next period was introduced by the philosophic poem *Prólogos stí zoí* (1917; "Prologue to Life") and includes the long works *Mítir Theoú* ("Mother of God") and *Tó Páskha tón Ellínon* ("The Easter of the Greeks"), culminating in the *Delphikós Lógos* (1927; "Delphic Utterance"). In the last, Greek tradition and the national historic and religious symbols are given a mystic turn and a universal significance.

In the 1930s and '40s Sikelianós published a second group of lyrics. They express in rich and incisive language and with forceful imagery the poet's belief in the beauty and harmony of the world. Sikelianós' tragedies—*I Sívylla* ("The Sibyl"), *O Daídalos stín Kríti* ("Daedalus in Crete"), *O Khristós stí Rómi* ("Christ in Rome"), *O thánatos toú Digení* ("The Death of Digenis"), and *Asklipiós* ("Asclepius")—and the long dramatic poem *O Dithýrambos toú Rhodou* (*The Dithyramb of the Rose*) are more notable for their lyric than their dramatic qualities. In his mature works Sikelianós tried to express in poetry the aspirations of the Demotic movement of the 1880s, which sought to combine Greek tradition with Western thought, and to introduce as a consciously literary language the idiom of the people.

Sikes, Bill \\'bil-'sīks\\ Fictional character, a violent, brutish thief and burglar in the novel OLIVER TWIST by Charles Dickens.

Silas Marner \\'sī-ləs-'mär-nər\\ (*in full* Silas Marner: The Weaver of Raveloe) Novel by George ELIOT, published in 1861. The story's title character is a friendless weaver who cares only for his cache of gold. He is ultimately redeemed through his love for Eppie, an abandoned golden-haired baby girl, whom he discovers shortly after he is robbed and rears as his own child.

Silence Novel by ENDŌ Shūsaku, published in Japanese in 1966 as *Chimmoku*. The story is based on events in early 17th-century Japan, when Japanese Christians and Christian missionaries were brutally persecuted. In the novel, Sebastian Rodrigues, a Portuguese seminarian, journeys to Japan to investigate why his former teacher, a missionary to Japan, has chosen apostasy over martyrdom. Pervading the novel is the belief that Christianity is incompatible with Japanese culture. In the end, seeing the selfishness of martyrdom, Rodrigues also chooses apostasy.

Silent Cry, The Highly praised novel by ŌE Kenzaburō, published in Japanese in 1967 as *Man'en gannen no futtōbōru* (literally, "Football in the First Year of Man'en") and awarded the Tanizaki Prize. *The Silent Cry* is a nonlinear and difficult work whose subject matter bears little relationship to the events described therein. Most important are questions about personal identity, self-knowledge, and the ability to relate the complete truth.

Set in the 1960s, the primary story is about the relationship between two brothers. The elder, Mitsu, is a reclusive scholar; the younger, Takashi, is drawn to political activism. They return to their ancestral village, where Takashi attempts to stage a protest against the nouveau riche Korean who is taking over the village. As the last descendant of an old and honorable family, he considers this a significant gesture. Takashi becomes increasingly violent and eventually murders a young woman. In disgrace he reveals the guilt of his past to Mitsu and commits suicide.

silenus \\sī-'lē-nəs\\ *plural* sileni \\-,nī\\ [Greek *Silēnós*] A type of minor woodland deity of ancient Greek mythology usually having human form but with a horse's ears and tail and occasionally with the legs of a horse or goat. Sileni are companions of Dionysus and are usually distinguished from satyrs by being always old, frequently bald, and always bearded.

From the 5th century BC the name Silenus was applied specifically to Dionysus' foster father, which thus aided the gradual absorption of the satyrs and sileni into the Dionysiac cult. He was often portrayed as a jovial, drunken old man riding a donkey. *See also* MIDAS; SATYR.

Silius Italicus \\'sil-ē-əs-i-'tal-i-kəs\\, *in full* Tiberius Catius Asconius Silius Italicus (b. AD 25/26, Patavium [Italy]—d. 101) Latin poet noted for his epic 12,000-line *Punica* on the Second Punic War (218–201 BC).

Silius drew heavily on the historian Livy for his material. He recounts all six battles of the Second Punic War, imitating Virgil's *Aeneid* in form and mythology. Although the epic has been harshly judged by critics and scarcely has been edited since the 18th century, it contains at least a half dozen magnificent pieces of verse, mostly in dramatic scenes of war.

Silko \\'sil-kō\\, Leslie Marmon (b. 1948, Albuquerque, N.M., U.S.) Native American poet and novelist.

While growing up on the Laguna Pueblo reservation in New Mexico, Silko learned Laguna traditions and myths from senior family members. After attending Bureau of Indian Affairs schools and the University of New Mexico (B.A., 1969), she published several short stories and the 1974 poetry collection *Laguna Woman*. Her novel *Ceremony* (1977) was the first novel by a Native American woman to be published. It follows half-Laguna, half-white protagonist Tayo home to his reservation after his service in World War II; his future bleak, he learns Laguna folklore and ceremonies that restore him. Apart from Silko's close observation of human nature, *Ceremony* was also noted for its nonchronological narrative method.

Storyteller (1981) is a collection of poetry, tribal stories, fiction, and photographs, and *The Delicacy and Strength of Lace* (1986) is a collection of letters between Silko and writer James A. Wright. In her second novel, *Almanac of the Dead* (1991), Native Americans whose lives and values are in tune with nature retake America from the environmentally destructive, personally perverse, and brutal whites.

Sillanpää \\'sēl-län-,pa\\, Frans Eemil (b. Sept. 16, 1888, Hämeenkyrö, Finland, Russian Empire—d. June 3, 1964, Helsinki) Novelist who was the first Finnish writer to win the Nobel Prize for Literature (1939).

Sillanpää's first short stories were published in journals in 1915. His first novel, *Elämä ja aurinko* (1916; "Life and the Sun"), the story of a young man who returns home in midsummer and falls in love, reflects his conviction that people are essentially part of nature and that instinct rules human actions.

Shocked by the Finnish civil war of 1918, Sillanpää wrote his most substantial novel, *Hurskas kurjuus* (1919; *Meek Heritage*), describing how a humble cottager becomes involved with the Red Guards without clearly realizing the ideological implications. After several collections of short stories in the late 1920s, Sillanpää published his best-known, though not necessarily his best, work, *Nuorena nukkunut* (1931; U.K. title, *Fallen Asleep While Young*; U.S. title, *The Maid Silja*), a story of an old peasant family. Later novels include *Miehen tie* (1932; *Way of a Man*) and *Ihmiset suviyössä* (1934; *People in the Summer Night*), which is stylistically his most finished and poetic novel.

Sillitoe \\'sil-i-tō\\, Alan (b. March 4, 1928, Nottingham, Nottinghamshire, Eng.) Writer whose brash and angry accounts of working-class life injected new vigor into post-World War II British fiction.

Encouraged by Robert Graves, Sillitoe began work on the novel *Saturday Night and Sunday Morning* (1958; film, 1960). An immediate success, it tells the story of a rude and amoral young laborer for whom drink and debauchery on Saturday night provide the only relief from the drudgery of the working life. Other novels, such as *The Death of William Posters* (1965) and *The Widower's Son* (1976), deal with more intellectual working-class characters. Perhaps his best-known work is the title story in the short-story collection *The Loneliness of the Long-Distance Runner* (1959; film, 1962). Sillitoe's later novels include *The Storyteller* (1979), *Her Victory* (1982), *Life Goes On* (1985), *The Open Door* (1989), and *Last Loves* (1990). Notable short-story collections are *The Ragman's Daughter* (1963; film, 1974), *Men, Women, and Children* (1973), and *The Second Chance* (1981). Sillitoe also wrote children's books, poetry, and plays.

sillographer \si-'läg-rə-fər\ [Greek *sillógraphos,* from *síllos* invective, satirical poem in hexameters + *gráphein* to write]   A writer of satires.

Silone \sē-'lō-nä\, Ignazio, *pseudonym of* Secondo Tranquilli \trän-'kwē-lē\ (b. May 1, 1900, Pescina dei Marsi, Italy—d. Aug. 22, 1978, Geneva, Switz.)   Italian novelist, short-story writer, and political leader who during World War II was internationally known for his powerful antifascist novels.

In 1917 Silone began to work with socialist groups, becoming a leader of the antiwar movement. In 1921 he helped found the Italian Communist Party and in 1922 became the editor of the party's paper in Trieste. He was driven into exile by the fascists, and in 1930 he settled in Switzerland. He became disillusioned with communism, and he began to write, using a pseudonym to protect his family from fascist persecution.

Silone's first novel, *Fontamara* (1930), is a realistic and compassionate story of the exploitation of a village of southern Italian peasants. Later novels include *Pane e vino* (1937; revised as *Vino e pane,* 1955; *Bread and Wine*) and *Il seme sotto la neve* (1940; *The Seed Beneath the Snow*). Silone also wrote a powerful antifascist satire, *La scuola dei dittatori* (1938; *The School for Dictators*).

After World War II Silone returned to Italy, becoming active in Italian political life. In 1950 he retired to devote himself to writing, producing *Una manciata di more* (1952; *A Handful of Blackberries*), *Il segreto di Luca* (1956; *The Secret of Luca*), and *Uscita di sicurezza* (1965; *Emergency Exit*).

Silva \'sil-və\, Antônio José da, *byname* O Judeu \ü-zhü-'deü\ ("The Jew") (b. May 8, 1705, Rio de Janeiro, Braz.—d. Oct. 18, 1739, Lisbon, Port.)   Portuguese writer whose comedies, farces, and operettas briefly revitalized the Portuguese theater in a period of dramatic decadence.

As the son of Jewish parents, Silva suffered religious persecution in Portugal by the Inquisition. During a brief period (1729–37) in which he was free of harassment from authorities, Silva wrote eight plays, all for the *ópera dos bonecos* (puppet theater), performed at the Bairro Alto Theater in Lisbon. Prose dialogue in the plays is interspersed with arias, minuets, and *modinhas* (popular, light songs). His best plays are generally considered to be *A vida do grande D. Quixote de la Mancha* (1733; "The Life of the Great Don Quixote of La Mancha") and *As guerras do Alecrim e da Mangerona* (1737; "The Wars of the Rosemary and the Marjoram"). Together they constitute a skilled and witty satire against the pretensions of a society based on caste and privilege. In 1739 Silva was charged by the Inquisition with the heresy of Judaizing and was garroted and burned at the stake.

Silva \'sēl-bä\, José Asunción (b. Nov. 27, 1865, Bogotá, Colom.—d. May 23, 1896, Bogotá)   Colombian poet whose metrical experimentation and romantic reminiscences introduced a melancholy lyricism new to Latin-American poetry. His highly personal poetry was widely imitated and greatly influenced modernist poetry in Latin America.

Silva had a brief but brilliant poetic career; at the age of 30 he committed suicide. His complete works, including *Crepúscu-*

los ("Twilights") and the *Nocturnos* ("Nocturnes"), for which he is best known, are collected in *Obra completa de José Asunción Silva* (1956).

Silvanus \sil-'vā-nəs\   In Roman mythology, the god of the countryside, similar in character to the rural deity Faunus, with whom he is often identified. In Latin literature his character tended to merge with that of the Greek god Silenus, a minor woodland deity, or Pan, a god of forests, pastures, and shepherds, and to be assimilated into the Greco-Roman mythological tradition.

Silver, Long John \'jän-'sil-vər\   Fictional character, resourceful pirate in Robert Louis Stevenson's novel TREASURE ISLAND.

Silver Age   In Latin literature, the period from approximately AD 18 to AD 133 that is a time of marked literary achievement second only to the previous Golden Age (70 BC–AD 18). By the 1st century AD political patronage of the arts begun in the Augustan Age (43 BC–AD 18) and a stifling reverence for the literature of the Golden Age, particularly for the poetry of Virgil, had led to a general decline in original literary output. Under such tyrants as Caligula and Nero, speech making was a dangerous art and rhetoricians turned to literature, influencing the development of the elaborate and poetical style characteristic of Silver Age prose. An increased provincial influence in Rome, while leading to an adulteration of the pure classical forms, contributed to the cosmopolitan outlook that was reflected in the psychologically perceptive and humanist tone of much of the best works of the period.

A great variety of literary forms is evident during the Silver Age. Of these, satire is the most vigorous, as exemplified by Juvenal in virulent satires of rich and powerful figures; by Martial in elegant epigrams on contemporary society; by Petronius in the picaresque novel *The Satyricon* (1st century AD); and by Persius in poetic satires supporting the stoic philosophy. History was the particular realm of Tacitus and Suetonius; Pliny the Elder and Pliny the Younger wrote letters on biography, science, natural history, grammar, history, and contemporary affairs. Quintilian excelled in literary criticism, Lucan in the epic form, Statius in poetry, Lucius Annaeus Seneca in rhetoric, and his son of the same name in tragedy.

Sima Qian or **Ssu-ma Ch'ien** \'si-'mä-'chyen\ (b. c. 145 BC, Longmen, China—d. c. 85 BC)   Astronomer, calendar expert, and the first great Chinese historian, noted for his authorship of the SHIJI ("Historical Records"), which is considered to be one of the most important histories of China.

Sima Qian was the son and successor of Sima Tan, the grand historian (sometimes translated as "astronomer royal") at the Han court during the period 140–110 BC. In 105 Siam Qian was among those responsible for a complete reform of the Chinese calendar. At about the same time, he began to undertake a definitive history of the Chinese past.

The *Shiji* is his great claim to fame. Its major achievement was the reduction to an orderly narrative of the complex events of the past, which were recorded in often contradictory sources deriving from the many independent states, each of which employed its own chronology. Sima Qian's work belongs unmistakably to the didactic Chinese tradition of history. He makes moral judgments on his characters and attempts to characterize them by type, recording an individual's exemplary deeds in one chapter and his misdeeds elsewhere. He is most notable for the critical attention he devotes to his sources. His acute critical comments are appended at the end of each chapter.

Sima Qian's history is composed in racy, flexible prose. He exerted a potent influence on later writers, particularly upon the early writers of narrative prose and fiction.

Sima Xiangru or **Ssu-ma Hsiang-ju** \'si-'mä-'shyäŋ-'zhü\ (b. 179 BC, Chengdu [now in Sichuan province], China—d. 117 BC, Maoling, Nan Yue)   Famous Chinese writer of *fu*, a form of descriptive poetry.

Self-trained in literature and fencing, Sima Xiangru was appointed as Imperial bodyguard to the Han emperor Jingdi, but he soon took a new position at the court of Prince Xiao of Liang and began to compose his famous poem "Zi xu fu" ("Master Nil"), in which three imaginary characters describe the delights of the hunt.

After the death of Prince Xiao, Sima Xiangru returned to Chengdu, where he met, seduced, and eloped with Zhuo Wenjun, the recently widowed daughter of a wealthy man. Although her father at first opposed the marriage, he later relented and gave the penniless couple money and slaves as the result of Sima's appointment at the emperor's court. The poet had entrusted his "Zi xu fu" to a friend who had shown it to the emperor. Immediately charmed by the poem, the emperor asked Sima Xiangru to write a *fu* on the Imperial hunt. He extended his original work into a highly imaginative and successful *fu* entitled "Shanglin fu" ("Supreme Park") and was rewarded with the court post. Endowed with his wife's share of the immense family fortune, the poet lived in comfort while he continued to write. Only 29 of his *fu* and four prose selections survive.

Simenon \sē-me-'nōⁿ\, Georges (Joseph Chrétien) (b. Feb. 13, 1903, Liège, Belg.—d. Sept. 4, 1989, Lausanne, Switz.)   Belgian-French novelist whose Inspector Jules MAIGRET is one of the best-known characters in detective fiction. Simenon was one of the most widely published authors of the 20th century.

Jerry Bauer

Simenon began working on a local newspaper at age 16, and at 19 he went to Paris determined to be successful. Between 1923 and 1933 he wrote more than 200 books of pulp fiction under many different pseudonyms. The first novel to appear under his own name was *Pietr-le-Letton* (1931; *The Case of Peter the Lett*), in which he introduced to fiction the imperturbable, pipe-smoking Parisian police official Inspector Maigret. Simenon went on to write some 80 more detective novels featuring Maigret, as well as short-story collections, autobiographical works, and about 130 psychological novels.

Simenon's central theme is the isolated existence of the neurotic, abnormal individual. Employing a style of rigorous simplicity, he evokes a prevailing atmosphere of neurotic tensions with sharp economy.

Simic \'sim-ik, *originally* 'sē-mēch \, Charles (b. May 9, 1938, Belgrade, Yugos. [now in Serbia])   Poet who evoked his eastern European heritage and his childhood experiences to comment on the dearth of spirituality in contemporary life.

When he was 15, Simic and his mother moved to Paris, and after a year they immigrated to the United States, where they were reunited with Simic's father. After graduating from New York University, he translated the works of Yugoslavian poets into English. From 1974 he taught at the University of New Hampshire.

Simic's first volume of poetry, *What the Grass Says* (1967), was well received; critics commented on the poems' imagery, which was rural and European, rather than urban and American. Among Simic's many subsequent poetry collections were *Somewhere Among Us a Stone Is Taking Notes* (1969), *Dismantling the Silence* (1971), *School for Dark Thoughts* (1978), *Unending Blues* (1986), *The Book of Gods and Devils* (1990), and *Hotel Insomnia* (1993). He received a Pulitzer Prize for poetry for *The World Doesn't End* (1989). His *Dime-store Alchemy* (1992) was a collection of miscellaneous prose pieces written as a tribute to the artist Joseph Cornell.

simile \'sim-ə-lē\ [Latin, comparison, from neuter of *similis* like, similar]   Figure of speech involving a comparison between two unlike entities. In the simile, unlike the metaphor, the resemblance is explicitly indicated by the words "like" or "as." *Compare* METAPHOR.

A simile in literature may be specific and direct or more lengthy and complex, as in the following speech by Othello from William Shakespeare's *Othello*:

> Never, Iago. Like to the Pontic Sea,
> Whose icy current and compulsive course
> Ne'er feels retiring ebb, but keeps due on
> To the Propontic and the Hellespont;
> Even so my bloody thoughts, with violent pace,
> Shall ne'er look back . . .

The simile does more than merely assert that Othello's urge for vengeance cannot now be turned aside; it also suggests huge natural forces. *See also* EPIC SIMILE.

Simms \'simz\, William Gilmore (b. April 17, 1806, Charleston, S.C., U.S.—d. June 11, 1870, Charleston)   Outstanding Southern man of letters known especially for his historical novels.

Simms, who was a child prodigy, began publishing poetry in Charleston newspapers at age 16. He edited a magazine and published a volume of poetry at 19. As state legislator and magazine and newspaper editor, he became embroiled in political and literary quarrels, but he was admired in both the South and the North.

Simms was at his best in employing a racy and masculine English prose style and in dealing humorously with rowdy frontier characters. His gift as a teller of tales in the oral tradition and the care he took in preparing historical materials are evident in his works. Notable among them are *Pelayo* (1838), with its 8th-century setting; *Vasconselos* (1853), set in the 16th century; *The Yemassee* (1835), set in colonial times and his most popular work; and the series set during the Revolution that includes *The Partisan* (1835), *The Kinsmen* (1841), *Katherine Walton* (1851), *Woodcraft* (1854), *Eutaw* (1856), and *Joscelyn* (1867). He also wrote two noteworthy romances about frontier life in the South, *Richard Hurdis* (1838) and *Border Beagles* (1840); a short-story collection, *The Wigwam and the Cabin* (1845); and the *History of South Carolina* (1840). Of 19 volumes of poetry, the collected *Poems* (1853) deserves mention. Most popular of his biographies were *The Life of Francis Marion* (1844) and *The Life of Chevalier Bayard* (1847). His literary criticism is represented in *Views and Reviews of American Literature* (1845).

Simon \sē-'mōⁿ\, Claude(-Eugène-Henri) (b. Oct. 10, 1913, Tananarive, Madagascar)   Writer whose works are among the most authentic representatives of the French *nouveau roman* ("new novel") that emerged in the 1950s. He was awarded the Nobel Prize for Literature in 1985.

During World War II Simon was captured by the Germans in May 1940, escaped, and joined the French Resistance, managing to complete his first novel, *Le Tricheur* (1945; "The Trickster") during the war years.

In *Le Vent* (1957; *The Wind*) Simon defined his goal as being to challenge the fragmentation of his time and to rediscover the permanence of objects and people as evident by their survival through the upheavals of contemporary history. He treated the turmoil of the Spanish Civil War in *La Corde raide* (1947; "The Taut Rope") and *Le Sacre du printemps* (1954; "The Crowning of Spring") and the 1940 collapse of France in *Le Tricheur*. Four novels—*L'Herbe* (1958; *The Grass*), *La Route des Flandres* (1960; *The Flanders Road*), *La Palace* (1962; *The Palace*), and *Histoire* (1967)—constitute a cycle containing recurring characters and events. Many critics consider these novels, especially *La Route des Flandres*, to be his most important work. Later novels include *La Bataille de Pharsale* (1969; *The Battle of Pharsalus*), *Triptyque* (1973; *Triptych*), and *L'Acacia* (1989; *The Acacia*).

Simon's style is a mixture of narration and stream of consciousness. His prose frequently lacks punctuation and is densely constructed, with 1,000-word sentences, through which he attempts to capture the very progression of life. Despite such features, his novels remain accessible.

Simon \'sī-mən\, Kate, *original name* Kaila Grobsmith \'grōb-smit\ (b. Dec. 5, 1912, Warsaw, Pol.—d. Feb. 4, 1990, New York, N.Y., U.S.)   Memoirist and travel writer whose work was noted for its readability and its wit.

Simon's family immigrated to the United States in 1917 and settled in New York. She held various editorial positions, including jobs at *Publisher's Weekly* and *The New Republic*. Her first guidebook, *New York Places and Pleasures*, was published in 1959 and was well received. She won praise for similar guides to Italy, London, Mexico, and Paris, which combined carefully researched, up-to-date information with little-known facts and were written with elegance and verve.

Simon's three memoirs, BRONX PRIMITIVE: PORTRAITS IN A CHILDHOOD (1982), *A Wider World: Portraits in an Adolescence* (1986), and *Etchings in an Hourglass* (1990), won acclaim for their unsentimental evocation of her working-class immigrant Jewish family life.

Simon \'sī-mən\, Neil, *in full* Marvin Neil Simon (b. July 4, 1927, New York, N.Y., U.S.)   Playwright, screenwriter, television writer, and librettist who was one of the most popular playwrights in the history of theater.

Simon studied at New York University before working as a comedy writer for various television shows in the late 1940s and throughout the 1950s, an experience he later portrayed in the play *Laughter on the 23rd Floor* (1994). His autobiographical play *Come Blow Your Horn* was a great success on Broadway and ran for two years after opening in 1961. The plays that followed proved extremely popular with audiences and usually had very long runs on Broadway. They include *Barefoot in the Park* (1963), *The Odd Couple* (1965), *The Star-Spangled Girl* (1966), *Plaza Suite* (1968), *Last of the Red Hot Lovers* (1969), *The Prisoner of Second Avenue* (1971), *The Sunshine Boys* (1972), *California Suite* (1976), *Chapter Two* (1977), *I Ought to Be in Pictures* (1980), a trilogy of autobiographical plays consisting of *Brighton Beach Memoirs* (1983), *Biloxi Blues* (1985), and *Broadway Bound* (1986), and *Lost in Yonkers* (1991). Simon wrote the screenplays for motion-picture adaptations of many of his plays as well as screenplays for a number of original motion pictures. He also wrote the books for the musicals *Little Me* (1962), *Sweet Charity* (1966), *Promises, Promises* (1968), and *They're Playing Our Song* (1979).

Simon's plays deal with the everyday lives and domestic problems of ordinary middle-class people. He examines his characters' marital and other dilemmas and, for comic effect, plays up the incongruity of their situations.

Simonides \sī-'män-ə-ˌdēz\ (b. *c.* 556 BC, Ioulis, Ceos [now Kéa, Greece]—d. *c.* 468? BC, Syracuse, Sicily)   Greek lyric poet and epigrammatist who appears to have originated the epinicion ode in honor of victors in the Olympic Games, his epinicion of 520 BC being the earliest recorded.

His lines on the Spartan rear guard that held the pass of Thermopylae against the Persians in 480 BC are a memorable epitaph, and such was his fame that many epigrams were later wrongfully ascribed to him. Simonides was also the first Greek poet known to have written on commission for fees. The fragments of his dithyrambic (impassioned, chanted) poetry, which are known to have been successful in many Athenian competitions, the remains of his choral lyrics, and his epigrams indicate that he was well suited to express the Panhellenic ideals of the new age that developed after the Greek victories over Persia.

Simonin \sē-mō-'naⁿ\, Albert-Charles (b. April 18, 1905, Paris, Fr.—d. Feb. 15, 1980, Paris)   French writer who brilliantly exploited the language of the Parisian underworld in tough, fast-talking thrillers that rivaled those of the leading American practitioners in the genre.

Simonin's first book, *Voilà Taxi* (1935; "Taxi!"), was written in the slang that was to become his hallmark. He took up journalism and wrote popular fiction under various pseudonyms before achieving popular and critical success in 1953 with *Touchez pas au grisbi!* ("Don't Touch the Grisbi"). It received the Prix des Deux-Magots (for recognition of an avant-garde book by a young writer). Its sequel, *Le Cave se rebiffe* (1954; "The Angry Cave"), was equally successful and was followed by a dictionary of Parisian argot, *Le Petit Simonin illustré par l'exemple* (1957; "The Little Simonin Illustrated by Example"). Simonin also wrote film scripts and in 1977 published the first volume of his autobiography, *Confessions d'un enfant de La Chapelle* ("Confessions of a Child of La Chapelle").

Simplicissimus \ˌzim-plē-'tsis-ē-ˌmu̇s\   Novel by Hans Jacob Christoph von GRIMMELSHAUSEN, the first part of which was published in 1669 as *Der Abentheurliche Simplicissimus* ("The Adventurous Simplicissimus"). Considered one of the most significant works of German literature, it contains a satirical and partially autobiographical picture of the Thirty Years' War (1618–48).

Modeled on the 16th-century Spanish picaresque novel, *Simplicissimus* tells the story of an innocent child brought into contact with life through his experiences of the Thirty Years' War. The book traces the development of a human soul against the background of a depraved Germany riven by war, depopulation, cruelty, and fear. *Simplicissimus* gives full rein to Grimmelshausen's power of narration, eye for realistic detail, coarse humor, and social criticism.

Continuations of the novel include *Die Landstörtzerin Courasche* (1670; *Courage, the Adventuress*), which was the inspiration for Bertolt Brecht's play *Mutter Courage und ihre Kinder* (1941; *Mother Courage and Her Children*), and *Das wunderbarliche Vogel-Nest* (1672; "The Magical Bird's Nest"). One section of the latter, translated as *The False Messiah* (1964), is a satire on gullibility and greed.

Simpson \'simp-sən\, Louis (Aston Marantz) (b. March 27, 1923, Jamaica)   Jamaican-born American poet and critic, notable for his marked development in poetic style. In 1964 he won the Pulitzer Prize in poetry for his volume *At The End of the Open Road, Poems* (1963).

Simpson moved from Jamaica to New York City at age 17. He graduated from Columbia University. During the 1950s he worked as a book editor and taught at Columbia and at the University of California at Berkeley. From 1967 he taught at the State University of New York at Stony Brook.

Simpson's conventional early poetry—that of *The Arrivistes: Poems 1940–1949* (1949) and *Good News of Death and Other Poems* (1955)—gave way to experimental free verse in *A Dream of Governors* (1959). Simpson came to believe that poetry springs from the inner life of the poet and that its expression should be original and natural. By the publication of his next book of poetry, *At the End of the Open Road* (1963), he had abandoned the use of poetic conventions. Simpson's later collections of poetry include *Adventures of the Letter I* (1971), *Searching for the Ox* (1976), *Caviare at the Funeral* (1980), *The Best Hour of the Night* (1983), and *In the Room We Share* (1990). In addition to writing poetry, Simpson produced several critical studies of other poets and an autobiography, *North of Jamaica* (1972; U.K. title, *Air with Armed Men*).

Simpson \'simp-sən \, N.F., *in full* Norman Frederick (b. Jan. 29, 1919, London, Eng.)   British playwright who was noted for his absurdity and humor achieved chiefly by cunning manipulation of phrasing and by frequent use of double entendres and, especially, of non sequiturs.

Simpson's first play, *A Resounding Tinkle* (1958; performed 1956; shortened to one act, 1957), won a prize given by the London *Observer*. His most successful and probably most significant work is *One Way Pendulum* (1960; performed 1959). It revolves around a man who builds a model in his living room of London's famous criminal court, the Old Bailey, and finds himself in its dock. Simpson's other work includes *The Hole* (1958; performed 1964), *The Cresta Run* (1966), and *Was He Anyone?* (1973). He also wrote for television.

Simrock \'zim-ˌrȯk \, Karl Joseph (b. Aug. 28, 1802, Bonn, Ger.—d. July 18, 1876, Bonn)   German literary scholar and poet who preserved and made accessible much early German literature, either by translation into modern German (as with *Nibelungenlied*, 1827), by rewriting and paraphrasing (as with *Das Amelungenlied*, 1843–49), or by editing (as with *Die deutsche Volksbücher*, 18 vol., 1839–67).

Simrock studied law at Bonn and Berlin. He was removed from his judicial post in 1830 for a poem he had written praising the July Revolution of that year. Shortly afterward, he retired to Bonn and devoted himself to the study of literature.

simurgh or **simurg** or **simorg** or **simorgh** \sē-'mu̇rg, -'mȯrg \ [Persian *sīmurgh*]   A huge ancient bird of Persian legend credited with possessing great wisdom. *See also* ROC.

Şinasi \shē-nä-'sē \, İbrahim (b. 1826, Constantinople, Ottoman Empire [now Istanbul, Tur.]—d. Sept. 13, 1871, Constantinople)   Writer who founded and led a Western movement in 19th-century Turkish literature.

Şinasi spent five years in France (1849–53), meeting leading French intellectuals and poets. On his return he held a number of government posts but turned to journalism and poetry. His *Divan-i Şinasi* ("The Collected Poems of Şinasi") appeared in 1853, and, about the same time, he published an anthology of poems translated from the French. In 1860 he worked for a newspaper, and in 1862 he started his own paper, the *Tasvir-i efkâr* ("Picture of Ideas"), which soon became a vehicle for the expression of new political and literary ideas. Şinasi also wrote for the *Ceride-i askeriyye* ("The Military Gazette"). In 1865 he fled to Paris for five years, probably for political reasons, and spent most of his time there studying and working on a massive Turkish dictionary, a task he never completed.

Şinasi is considered the founder of the modern school of Ottoman literature. He directed literary expression to the masses through the reform of Turkish verse forms (based largely on imitation of French models, which he carefully studied and observed) and the adoption of a pure Turkish devoid of Arabic and Persian vocabulary and grammatical constructions.

Sinclair \sin-'klar \, Sir Keith (b. Dec. 5, 1922, Auckland, N.Z.—d. June 20, 1993, Quebec, Can.)   Historian, educator, and poet, noted for his histories of New Zealand.

Sinclair was educated at Auckland University College (until 1957 a college of the University of New Zealand; thereafter, the University of Auckland), where he taught from 1947 to 1987. He was knighted in 1985.

Sinclair wrote four volumes of verse—*Songs for a Summer and Other Poems* (1952), *Strangers or Beasts* (1954), *A Time to Embrace* (1963), and *The Firewheel Tree* (1973)—but he is best known for *A History of New Zealand* (1959; revised and enlarged 1980) and *The Origins of the Maori Wars* (1957; 2nd edition, 1961). He also wrote other historical works, including *A Destiny Apart: New Zealand's Search For National Identity* (1986), and an autobiography entitled *Halfway Round the Harbour* (1993).

Sinclair \sin-'klar \, Upton (Beall) (b. Sept. 20, 1878, Baltimore, Md., U.S.—d. Nov. 25, 1968, Bound Brook, N.J.)   American novelist and polemicist for socialism and other causes; his THE JUNGLE (1906) is a landmark among naturalistic, proletarian novels.

Sinclair supported himself by journalistic writing. It was a newspaper assignment that led him to write *The Jungle*, his sixth novel and first popular success. Published at Sinclair's own expense after several publishers rejected it, it became a best-seller, and Sinclair used the proceeds to open Helicon Hall, the site of a cooperative-living venture in Englewood, N.J. The building was destroyed by fire in 1907 and the project abandoned.

A long series of other topical novels—among them *Oil!* (1927), based on the Teapot Dome Scandal of the early 1920s, and *Boston* (1928), based on the controversial trial of the anarchists Sacco and Vanzetti—followed, but none achieved the popularity of *The Jungle*. Sinclair again reached a wide audience with the Lanny Budd series, 11 contemporary historical novels beginning with *World's End* (1940) that are constructed around an implausible antifascist hero.

During the economic crisis of the 1930s, Sinclair organized the EPIC (End Poverty in California) socialist reform movement; in 1934 he was defeated as Democratic candidate for governor. His autobiographical *American Outpost: A Book of Reminiscences* (1932; U.K. title, *Candid Reminiscences: My First Thirty Years*) was reworked and extended in *The Autobiography of Upton Sinclair* (1962).

Sindbad the Sailor \'sin-ˌbad \   One of the heroes in THE THOUSAND AND ONE NIGHTS who recounts his adventures on seven voyages. He is not to be confused with Sindbad the Wise, hero of the frame story of the Seven Wise Masters. In the frame story Sindbad is marooned, or shipwrecked, after he sets sail from Basra (Iraq) with merchandise. He is able to survive the terrible dangers he encounters by a combination of resourcefulness and luck, and he returns home with a fortune.

Sindbad's travails were based on the experiences of Basra merchants trading under great risk with the East Indies and China, probably in the early 'Abbāsid period (750–c. 850).

Singer \'siŋ-ər \, I.J., *in full* Israel Joshua (b. Nov. 30, 1893, Biłgoraj, Poland, Russian Empire—d. Feb. 10, 1944, New York, N.Y., U.S.)   Polish-born writer in Yiddish, noted for his realistic historical novels.

Singer was the son of a Ḥasidic rabbi and was the older brother of the writer Isaac Bashevis Singer. He began writing tales of Ḥasidic life in 1915 and then worked as a journalist in Warsaw during the 1920s and early 1930s. Several collections of his short stories were published during this time, including the short story "Perl" ("The Pearl"), which was his first international success. His novel *Yoshe Kalb*, a description of Ḥasidic life in Galicia, appeared in 1932, and the next year he immigrated to the United States. His subsequent writings appeared in serialized form in *Forverts* in New York City.

Like his brother, Singer wrote multigenerational family novels, but, unlike his brother, he firmly linked his vivid characters with a larger historical and socioeconomic setting. *Di Brider Ashkenazi* (1936; *The Brothers Ashkenazi*), which is considered to be Singer's masterpiece, examines the rivalry of two very different brothers whose fortunes parallel that of their birthplace, the Polish industrial city of Łódź. *Di Mishpokhe Karnovski* (1943; *The Family Carnovsky*) traces an assimilated German-Jewish family for several decades until its members must immigrate to the United States after the Nazi takeover. Singer also wrote short stories and plays.

Singer \\'siŋ-ər\\, Isaac Bashevis, *Yiddish* Yitskhok Bashevis Zinger \\'ziŋ-ər\\ (b. July 14?, 1904, Radzymin, Poland, Russian Empire—d. July 24, 1991, Miami, Fla., U.S.) Polish-born American writer of novels, short stories, and essays in Yiddish. He was the recipient in 1978 of the Nobel Prize for Literature. His fiction, depicting Jewish life in Poland and the United States, is remarkable for its rich blending of irony, wit, and wisdom, flavored distinctively with the occult and the grotesque.

Coming from a family of Ḥasidic rabbis, Singer received a traditional Jewish education at the Warsaw Rabbinical Seminary. His first novel, *Der Sotn in Goray* (*Satan in Goray*), was published in installments in Poland shortly before he immigrated to the United States in 1935. Settling in New York City, he initially worked for the Yiddish-language daily newspaper *Forverts*, and as a journalist he signed his articles with the pseudonym Varshavski. In 1943 he became a U.S. citizen.

Although Singer's works became most widely known in their English versions, he continued to write almost exclusively in Yiddish, personally supervising the trans-

Library of Congress/Jerry Bauer

lations. Among his most important novels are THE FAMILY MOSKAT (1950), THE MAGICIAN OF LUBLIN (1960), *The Slave* (1962), *The Manor* (1967), *The Estate* (1969), *Enemies, a Love Story* (1972), *Shosha* (1978), and *The Penitent* (1983). His short stories, including the well-known GIMPEL THE FOOL and THE SPINOZA OF MARKET STREET, were also popular. Titles of the collections include *Gimpel the Fool* (1957), *The Spinoza of Market Street* (1961), *Short Friday* (1964), *The Seance* (1968), *A Crown of Feathers* (1973; National Book Award), *Old Love* (1979), and *The Image and Other Stories* (1985). *The Collected Stories of Isaac Bashevis Singer* was published in 1982.

Singer's two most ambitious narratives, *The Family Moskat* and the continuous story spun out in *The Manor* and *The Estate*, chronicle the changes in and the eventual breakup of large Jewish families during the late 19th and early 20th centuries as their members are differently affected by the secularism and assimilationist opportunities of the modern era. Singer's shorter novels examine characters who are tempted by evil in various forms. His short stories are saturated with Jewish folklore, legends, and mysticism and display his incisive understanding of the weaknesses inherent in human nature.

Sinyavsky or **Siniavski** \\sʸi-'nʸȧf-skʸē\\, Andrey Donatovich, *pseudonym* Abram Terts or Tertz \\ə-'brȧm-'tʸerts\\ (b. Oct. 8, 1925, Moscow, Russia, U.S.S.R.) Russian critic and fiction writer who was convicted of subversion by the Soviet government in 1966.

Sinyavsky graduated from Moscow University and later joined the faculty of the Gorky Institute of World Literature. His works of fiction, none of which were published in the Soviet Union, were smuggled to the West and published under his pseudonym.

Sinyavsky's novel *Sud idyot* (1959; *The Trial Begins*) deals with the Doctors' Plot of 1953, during which nine Soviet doctors were unjustly accused of treason. It was not published in the Soviet Union until 1989. English translations of Sinyavsky's other fiction include an anthology of short stories, *Fantastic Stories* (1963); the novel *The Makepeace Experiment* (1965); and the essay *On Socialist Realism* (1960), which called for a new inventiveness in Soviet literature.

Sinyavsky and another writer, Yuly Daniel, were convicted of producing anti-Soviet propaganda through their writings. Daniel was sentenced to five years of hard labor and Sinyavsky to seven. The trial, a record of which was published in *On Trial* (1966), prompted domestic and international protest. Sinyavsky was released from prison in 1971 and two years later moved to Paris, where he taught Russian literature at the Sorbonne. Sinyavsky's later works include *Golos iz khora* (1973; *A Voice from the Chorus*) and *Spokoynoy nochi* (1984; *Goodnight!*).

Siôn Cent \\'shôn-'kent\\, *also called* Siôn Gwent, Siôn y Cent, Siôn Kemp, *or* Siôn Kempt (b. *c.* 1367—d. *c.* 1430) Welsh poet who opposed the bards who celebrated the heroic deeds of the nobles in an elevated tone. According to Siôn Cent, the traditional praise of the nobles was hollow flattery and lies. His writings (poems in cywydd meter) reflect the influence of the moralists of the European Middle Ages, treating religious or moral subjects and dwelling upon the uncertainty of life and the inevitability of death.

siren \\'sī-rən\\ [Latin *Siren,* from Greek *Seirēn*] In Greek mythology, one of a group of creatures having the heads and sometimes the breasts and arms of women but otherwise the forms of birds that were believed to lure mariners to destruction by their sweet singing. Sirens appear in many works of literature, including Homer's *Odyssey*, Dante's *The Divine Comedy*, and the *Argonautica* of Apollonius of Rhodes. *Compare* HARPY; LORELEI; MERMAID.

Sir Gawayne and the Grene Knight *also spelled* Sir Gawain and the Green Knight \\gə-'wān, 'gä-,wān, 'gaü-ən\\ Middle English alliterative poem written about 1375 and of unknown authorship. It is a chivalric romance that tells a tale of enchantment in an Arthurian setting. Its hero, Sir Gawayne, is presented as a devout but humanly imperfect Christian who wins a test of arms, resists temptation by a lord's wife, but succumbs to an offer of invulnerability.

The poem is technically brilliant. Its alliterative lines (some 2,500) are broken up into irregular stanzas by short rhyming passages; they are tautly constructed, and the vocabulary is astonishingly rich—influenced by French in the scenes at court but strengthened by many dialect words, often of Scandinavian origin, that belonged to northwestern England. The blend of sophisticated atmosphere, psychological depth, and vivid language produces an effect superior to that found in any other work of the time.

Preserved in the same manuscript with *Sir Gawayne* were three other poems, now generally accepted as the work of the same author. These are two alliterative, homiletic poems, *Patience* and *Purity*, and an intricate elegiac poem, *Pearl*. The author of *Sir Gawayne* and the other poems is frequently referred to as "the Pearl Poet." *See also* GAWAIN.

Si shu or **Ssu shu** \'si-'shü\ ("Four Books") Four ancient Confucian texts that were used as official subject matter for civil-service examinations in China from 1313 to 1905 and usually serve to introduce Chinese students to Confucian literature. Students later turn to the more extensive and, generally speaking, more difficult *Wu jing* ("Five Classics").

The publication of these four texts as a unit in 1190 with commentaries by Zhu Xi, a great Neo-Confucian philosopher, helped to revitalize Confucianism in China. From 1415 onward knowledge of Zhu's (and like-minded) commentaries was as indispensable to success in civil-service examinations as the texts themselves.

Even with its commentaries, the *Si shu* is a modest volume, the four parts of which have no consistent order. The first, DA XUE, is a short ethical and political treatise linking humane government with the personal integrity of rulers. The second, ZHONG YONG, is somewhat longer than *Da xue* and more abstract than the other three books. It speaks of such things as the Way of Heaven, motion, spiritual beings, and religious sacrifices. For each of these two books (both direct excerpts from *Li ji*, one of the Five Classics), Zhu Xi wrote an individual preface. The third book, LUN YU, reputedly contains direct quotations from the ancient sage Confucius (551–479 BC) as recorded by his disciples. It is considered the most reliable source of the Master's teachings. MENCIUS, the fourth and longest of the *Si shu*, contains the teachings of Mencius (372–289 BC), the most revered of all Confucian scholars.

Sister Carrie \'kar-ē\ First novel by Theodore DREISER, published in 1900, but suppressed until 1912.

Sister Carrie tells the story of a rudderless but pretty small-town girl who comes to the big city filled with vague ambitions. She is used by men and uses them in turn to become a successful Broadway actress, while George Hurstwood, the married man who has run away with her, loses his grip on life and descends into beggary and suicide. *Sister Carrie* was the first masterpiece of the American naturalistic movement in its grittily factual presentation of the vagaries of urban life and in its ingenuous heroine, who goes unpunished for her transgressions against conventional sexual morality. The book's strengths include a brooding but compassionate view of humanity, a memorable cast of characters, and a compelling narrative line. The emotional disintegration of Hurstwood is a much-praised triumph of psychological analysis. *Sister Carrie* is a work of pivotal importance in American literature, and it became a model for subsequent American writers of realism.

Sisyphus \'sis-ə-fəs\ In Greek mythology, the cunning king of Corinth who, as related in the *Odyssey*, was punished in the underworld by having repeatedly to roll a huge stone up a hill only to have it roll down again as soon as he had brought it to the summit.

Sisyphus angered Zeus, who sent Thanatos (Death) to kill him. Upon Thanatos' arrival, however, Sisyphus chained him up so that no one died until Ares came to Thanatos' aid. In the meantime, Sisyphus had told his wife, Merope, not to perform the usual sacrifices after his death and to leave his body unburied. Thus, when he reached the underworld, he was permitted to return to punish her for the omission. Once back home, he continued to live to a ripe old age before dying a second time. For having cheated Death, Sisyphus was punished in the manner described above.

Sisyphus was, like Autolycus and Prometheus, a widely popular figure of folklore—the trickster, or master thief. The origin of the particular punishment assigned him—the fruitless,

eternal rolling of the stone up the hill—is unknown. Albert Camus's *The Myth of Sisyphus* is a philosophical examination of contemporary nihilism and the need to confront absurdity as a condition of life.

Sittewald *see* MOSCHEROSCH.

situation \,sich-ú-'wā-shən\ A particular or striking complex of affairs at a stage in the action of a narrative or drama. *Compare* CRISIS; CLIMAX.

Sitwell \'sit-wəl\, Dame Edith (b. Sept. 7, 1887, Scarborough, Yorkshire, Eng.—d. Dec. 9, 1964, London) English poet who first gained fame for her stylistic artifices but who emerged during World War II as a poet of emotional depth and profoundly human concerns. She was equally famed for her formidable personality, Elizabethan dress, and eccentric opinions.

A member of a distinguished literary family, Sitwell was the daughter of Sir George Sitwell and the sister of Osbert and Sacheverell Sitwell. Her first book, *The Mother and Other Poems*, was published in 1915. The following year she attracted attention by editing an anthology, *Wheels*, in which she and her brothers led a spirited revolt against the prevailing Georgian poetry. The notoriety sought by the Sitwells in their artistic battles may, at the time, have obscured the originality of her talent. The visual sensibility and verbal music of her early poetry, *Clowns' Houses* (1918), *Bucolic Comedies* (1923), and *The Sleeping Beauty* (1924), in which she created her own world of beautiful objects, nursery symbols, and unfamiliar images, revealed the influence of William Butler Yeats and T.S. Eliot. Her emphasis on the value of sound in poetry was shown especially in *Façade* (1923), for which William Walton wrote a musical accompaniment. *Gold Coast Customs* (1929), with its harsher and more agonized imagery, marked the end of a period of experiment. In 1930 her *Collected Poems* appeared.

In her later work, especially *Street Songs* (1942), *Green Song* (1944), and *Song of the Cold* (1945), written during World War II, a greater mastery of technique and a deeper sense of suffering and spirituality are apparent. The religious symbolism that informs Sitwell's war poetry was further emphasized in *Gardeners and Astronomers* (1953) and *The Outcasts* (1962), works that brought her wide recognition as a poet of tragic grandeur and intensity.

Her wide reading and scholarship and her predilection for the splendors of a lost aristocratic age are revealed in the prose works *Alexander Pope* (1930), *Bath* (1932), *The English Eccentrics* (1933), *I Live Under a Black Sun* (1937), *A Poet's Notebook* (1943), and *A Notebook on William Shakespeare* (1948). She made visits to the United States, where, in 1953 in Hollywood, she completed the film script of her book on the girlhood of Elizabeth I, *A Fanfare for Elizabeth* (first published 1946). She was created Dame of the British Empire in 1954.

Sitwell \'sit-wəl\, Sir Osbert, 5th Baronet, *in full* Francis Osbert Sacheverell Sitwell (b. Dec. 6, 1892, London, Eng.—d. May 4, 1969, near Florence, Italy) English man of letters who became famous, with his sister Edith and brother Sacheverell, as a tilter at establishment windmills in literature and the arts. His best-known books are his prose memoirs.

Sitwell wrote poetry, novels, short stories, and criticism. His best novel is *Before the Bombardment* (1926), a satirical portrayal of the last phase of Victorian society. His reputation rests, however, on his autobiographical series *Left Hand! Right Hand!* (1944), *The Scarlet Tree* (1946), *Great Morning!* (1947), *Laughter in the Next Room* (1948), and *Noble Essences* (1950). In these he created with conscious nostalgia the portrait of a vanished age. *Queen Mary and Others* (1974) was a collection of essays published posthumously.

Sitwell \'sit-wəl\, Sir Sacheverell \sə-'shev-ə-rəl\, 6th Baronet (b. Nov. 15, 1897, Scarborough, Yorkshire, Eng.—d. Oct. 1, 1988, Weston Hall, near Towcester, Northamptonshire) English poet and critic, the younger brother of the poets and essayists Edith and Osbert Sitwell. He is best known for his books on art, architecture, and travel.

Sitwell's poetry—*The People's Palace* (1918), *The Thirteenth Caesar* (1924), *The Rio Grande* (performed 1929, with music by Constant Lambert), *Selected Poems* (1948), and other volumes—is written predominantly in traditional meters and reveals in its mannered style the effect of his interest in the arts and music. More original are his imaginative and interpretative books, of which the first, *Southern Baroque Art* (1924), was the forerunner of much academic research. His poetic prose is seen at its best in the "autobiographical fantasia" *All Summer in a Day* (1926) and the gloomily meditative *Splendours and Miseries* (1943). Disappointed in the lukewarm critical response to his poetry, Sitwell turned from poetry after the late 1930s; in 1972 he began publishing small books privately. *For Want of the Golden City* (1973) is a series of essays on life and art containing a considerable amount of autobiographical material.

Śiva \'shēv-ə, 'shiv-, 'sēv-, 'siv-\ or **Shiva** \'shēv-ə, 'shiv-\, *also spelled* Śiwa (Sanskrit: "Auspicious One") One of the main deities of Hinduism, worshiped as the paramount lord by the Śaiva (Shaivite) sects of India. Śiva is one of the most complex gods of India, embodying seemingly contradictory qualities. He is both the destroyer and the restorer, the great ascetic and the symbol of sensuality, the benevolent herdsman of souls and the wrathful avenger.

Śiva's female consort is known in various manifestations, including those of Pārvatī, Durgā, and Kālī, and Śiva is also sometimes paired with the supreme goddess, Śakti. The divine couple, together with their sons—the six-headed Skanda and the elephant-headed Gaṇeśa—are said to dwell on Mount Kailāsa in the Himalayas.

Śiva is usually depicted as white or ash-colored, with a blue neck, his hair arranged in a coil of matted locks and adorned with the crescent moon and the Ganges. He has three eyes, the third eye bestowing inward vision but capable of burning destruction when focused outward. He wears a garland of skulls and a serpent around his neck and carries a deerskin, a trident, a small hand drum, or a club with a skull at the end.

The great poet of classical Sanskrit, Kālidāsa, used part of the Śiva epic in *Kumārasaṃbhava* ("Birth of the War God"), written in the style known as *mahākāvya* ("great poem"; a form akin to the epyllion, or "miniature epic"). The *Kumārasaṃbhava* describes the courting of the ascetic Śiva, who is meditating in the mountains, by Pārvatī, the daughter of the Himalayas; the destruction of the god of love (after his arrow has struck Śiva) by the fire from Śiva's third eye; and the wedding and lovemaking of Śiva and Pārvatī, which results in the conception of Skanda, the war god.

Siwertz \'sē-,verts\, Sigfrid, *in full* Per Sigfrid Siwertz (b. Jan. 24, 1882, Stockholm, Swed.—d. Nov. 26, 1970, Stockholm) Swedish writer best known for his novel *Selambs* (1920; *Downstream*) and for several collections of short stories.

Siwertz studied at the University of Uppsala and the Collège de France in Paris. His early works largely display the decadence and pessimism that were typical of turn-of-the-century Swedish literature. Siwertz's best novel, *Selambs*, is a relentless exposé of the capitalistic mentality of wartime profiteers. In addition to publishing several collections of graceful short stories, Siwertz wrote a notable autobiography, *Att vara ung* (1949; "On Being Young"). He was elected to the Swedish Academy in 1932.

Six Characters in Search of an Author Play in three acts by Luigi PIRANDELLO, produced and published in Italian in 1921 as *Sei personaggi in cerca d'autore*. Introducing Pirandello's device of the "theater within the theater," the play explores various levels of illusion and reality. It had a great impact on later playwrights, particularly such practitioners of the Theater of the Absurd as Samuel Beckett, Eugène Ionesco, and Jean Genet, as well as Jean Anouilh and Jean-Paul Sartre.

Sjöberg \'shœ̄-berʸ, *Angl* 'shō-bərg\, Birger (b. Dec. 6, 1885, Vänersborg, Swed.—d. April 30, 1929, Växjö) Songwriter and poet known for his development of a strikingly original form in modern Swedish poetry.

After very little formal education and a number of occupations, Sjöberg became a journalist. In his spare time he wrote the lyrics and music of songs, which he sang occasionally to entertain friends. His first published collection of songs, *Fridas bok* (1922; "Frida's Book"), was highly successful and brought him much acclaim. He was hailed a modern troubadour, and he soon found himself on a series of concert tours with his songs. He recoiled from this attention, however, and withdrew in disgust, apparently preferring that his reputation be based on more significant work. His only novel, *Kvartetten som sprängdes* (1924; "The Quartet Which Was Broken Up"), also became highly popular. He unleashed his full fury in *Kriser och Kransar* (1926; "Crises and Laurel Wreaths"), a relentless and explosive confrontation with post–World War I life and an artistic breakthrough to new forms and highly modern poetic devices.

After his death, two further volumes of Sjöberg's work appeared, a second series of Frida songs (1929) and a selection from some 3,000 poems and fragments published under the title *Minnen från jorden* (1940; "Memories from Earth").

Sjöwall \'shœ̄-,väl\, Maj and **Wahlöö** \'vä-,lœ̄\, Per (respectively b. Sept. 25, 1935, Stockholm, Swed.; b. Aug. 5, 1926, Göteborg, Swed.—d. June 22, 1975, Malmö) Swedish journalists and innovative writers of detective fiction.

The husband-and-wife team Per Wahlöö and Maj Sjöwall wrote a series of detective stories in which Martin Beck and his colleagues at the Central Bureau of Investigation in Stockholm were the main characters. From *Roseanna* (1965) to *Terroristerna* (1975; *The Terrorists*), the series consists of 10 novels, all of which use the detective story as a vehicle for social criticism. Both the police force and the criminals mirror the shifting social forces within the Swedish welfare state. The authors strongly criticized abuses of power and the systematic use of propaganda in society. Many of these motifs were also examined in Wahlöö's novels of the late 1950s and early 1960s.

Skadi or **Skade** \'skäth̲-ē\, *Old Norse* Skathi. In Norse mythology, the giant wife of the sea god Njǫrd. In order to avenge the death of her father, the giant Thjazi (Thjassi), Skadi took up arms and went to Asgard to attack the Æsir (the rival tribe of the gods) in their dwelling place. The Æsir, wanting to appease Skadi's anger, offered her the choice of one of their number for a husband, with the stipulation that she choose a god by his legs (or feet) alone. She chose Njǫrd (one of the Vanir who was among the Æsir as a hostage), thinking that he was the fair god Balder; their marriage failed because Njǫrd preferred to live by the sea and Skadi was happier in Thrymheim, her father's home in the mountains.

skald or **scald** \'skôld, 'skäld\ [Old Norse *skald*] One of the ancient Scandinavian poets who developed skaldic poetry. One of the greatest skalds was EGIL SKALLAGRÍMSSON, whose life and works are preserved in *Egils saga*.

skaldic poetry or **scaldic poetry** \'skôl-dik, 'skäl-\ Oral court poetry originating in Norway but developed chiefly by

Icelandic poets (skalds) from the 9th to the 13th century. Skaldic poetry was contemporary with Eddic poetry but differed from it in meter, diction, and style. Eddic poetry is anonymous, simple, and terse, often taking the form of an objective dramatic dialogue. Skalds, on the other hand, were identified by name. Their poems were descriptive, occasional, and subjective, their meters strictly syllabic instead of free and variable, and their language ornamented with *heiti* and kennings. (*Heiti* ["names"] are uncompounded poetic nouns, fanciful art words rather than everyday terms—*e.g.*, "brand" for "sword." Kennings are metaphorical circumlocutions such as "wave-horse" for "ship.")

Of the 100 skaldic verse forms, the drótt-kvaett (court meter), which uses a syllable count and a regular pattern of alliteration, internal rhyme, and assonance, was most popular. The formal subjects of the skalds were shield poems (descriptions of the mythological engravings on shields), praise of kings, epitaphs, and genealogies. There were also less formal occasional poems, dream songs, magic curses, lampoons, flytings (poems of abuse), and (although forbidden by law) many love songs.

Skallagrímsson, Egill　　*see* EGILL SKALLAGRÍMSSON.

Skamander \skȧ-'mȧn-der\　Group of young Polish poets who were united in their desire to forge a new poetic language that would accurately reflect the experience of modern life.

Founded in Warsaw about 1918, the group had antecedents in the Young Poland movement. Its monthly publication (first published in January 1920) was named *Skamander*, and the group soon became known by that name. Skamander was co-founded by Jarosław Iwaszkiewicz, known primarily for his novels and short stories, and Julian Tuwim, a lyrical poet. Also associated with the group were Kazimierz Wierzyński, Jan Lechoń (pseudonym of Leszek Serafinowicz), Maria Pawlikowska-Jasnorzewska, Antoni Słonimski, and Władysław Broniewski.

Skanda \'skän-də\, *also called* Kārttikeya \ˌkärt-'tē-kä-yə\, Kumāra \kü-'mär-ə\, *or* Subrahmaṇya \'süb-rə-ˌmən-yə\　Hindu god of war and the firstborn son of Śiva. The many legends giving the circumstances of his birth are often at variance with one another. One account is given by Kālidāsa in his epic poem *Kumārasaṃbhava* ("The Birth of the War God"). The versions all generally agree that the gods wished for Skanda to be born in order to destroy the demon Tāraka, who could only be killed by a son of Śiva.

One tradition has it that Skanda was reared by, or even the son of, the six Kṛttikās, hence the name Kārttikeya ("Son of Kṛttikās"). He developed his six faces to drink the milk of his six nurses. His relationship with Pārvatī (one of the manifestations of Śiva's consort) is also acknowledged, and he is often depicted in painting and sculpture as a six-headed child held by his mother, Pārvatī, and accompanied by his brother Gaṇeśa. He is Kumāra ("adolescent, boy") because he is generally considered never to have married, and in Yoga he represents the power of chastity. He has enormous strength and leads the army of the gods. When he plants his spear in the earth, none can budge it save the god Vishnu, and then mountains and rivers shake.

In South India, where the god originated as Murugaṉ before merging with the North Indian Skanda, he has a large following under the name Subrahmaṇya ("Dear to the Brāhmaṇas"). *See also* ŚIVA.

skaz \'skȧs, *Angl* 'skäz\ [Russian, literally, tale, a derivative of *skazat'* to say]　In Russian literature, a device in which the author creates a persona through which he can present a first-person narrative using dialect, slang, and the peculiar idiom of that persona. Among the well-known writers who have used

this device are Nikolay Leskov, Aleksey Remizov, Mikhail Zoshchenko, and Yevgeny Zamyatin.

skeleton dance　A ceremonial dance in which dancers are costumed to represent skeletons or death; also, the DANCE OF DEATH in European folklore.

Skelton \'skelt-ən\, John (b. *c.* 1460—d. June 21, 1529, London, Eng.)　Tudor poet and satirist of both political and religious subjects whose individual poetic style of short rhyming lines, based on natural speech rhythms, has been given the name of Skeltonics.

Skelton was educated at the University of Cambridge and later achieved the status of "poet laureate" (a degree in rhetoric) at Oxford, Louvain (now in Belgium), and Cambridge. This success and also his skill at translating ancient Greek and Roman authors led to his appointment in 1489 as court poet to Henry VII and later, in addition, as "scolemaster" to the Duke of York (later Henry VIII). In 1498 Skelton took holy orders, and in 1502, when Henry became heir to the throne, he was appointed rector of Diss, in Norfolk. About 1512 Henry VIII granted him the title of orator regius, and in this capacity Skelton became an adviser to the king.

Skelton's most notable poem from the period of his tenure under Henry VII is *Bowge of Courte*, a satire of the disheartening experience of life at court; it was not until his years at Diss that he attempted to write the poetry for which he is now best known. Two major poems from this period are *Phyllyp Sparowe*, ostensibly a lament for the death of a young lady's pet but also a lampoon of the liturgical office for the dead, and *Ware the Hawke*, an angry attack on an irreverent hunting priest who had flown his hawk into Skelton's church. In 1516 he wrote the first secular morality play in English, *Magnyfycence*, a political satire. It was followed by *The Tunnyng of Elynour Rummynge*, a brilliant portrayal of a drunken woman in an alehouse. His three major political and clerical satires, *Speke, Parrot* (written 1521), *Collyn Clout* (1522), and *Why Come Ye Nat to Courte?* (1522), were all directed against the mounting power of Cardinal Thomas Wolsey, both in church and in state, and the dangers—as Skelton saw them—of the new learning of the humanists. Wolsey proved too strong an opponent to attack further, and Skelton turned to lyrical and allegorical themes in his last poems, dedicating them all to the cardinal himself. Skelton's reputation declined rapidly in the 16th century and was not reestablished until the 20th.

Skeltonics \skel-'tän-iks\　Short verses of an irregular meter much used by John Skelton. The verses have two or three stresses arranged sometimes in falling and sometimes in rising rhythm. They rely on such devises as alliteration, parallelism, and multiple rhymes and are related to doggerel. Skelton wrote his verses as works of satire and protest, and thus the form was considered deliberately unconventional and provocative.

sketch \'skech\　A short literary composition somewhat resembling the short story and the essay but intentionally slight in treatment, discursive in style, and familiar in tone. *See also* LITERARY SKETCH.

Sketch Book, The (*in full* The Sketch Book of Geoffrey Crayon, Gent. \'jef-rē-'krā-ən\）　Short-story collection by Washington IRVING, first published in 1819–20 in seven separate parts. Most of the book's 30-odd pieces concern Irving's impressions of England, but six chapters deal with American subjects. Of these, the tales THE LEGEND OF SLEEPY HOLLOW and RIP VAN WINKLE have been called the first American short stories, although both are actually Americanized versions of German folktales. In addition to the stories based on folklore, the collection contains travel sketches, literary essays, and miscellany. *The Sketch Book* was the first American work to gain international literary success and popularity. Its unprecedented success allowed Irving to devote himself to a career as a professional author.

Sketches by "Boz" \'bäz\   Title of two series of collected sketches and short tales by Charles DICKENS, writing under the pseudonym BOZ. First published in book form in 1836, *Sketches* contains some 60 pieces that had originally been published in the *Monthly Magazine* and the *Morning Chronicle* and other periodicals. Subtitled "Illustrative of Every-Day Life and Every-Day People," *Sketches* contains Dickens' impressions and graphically described observations of the teeming street life of Victorian London.

The critical and commercial success achieved by *Sketches* was partly a result of the clever illustrations by George Cruikshank, who also illustrated other novels by Dickens.

Skinner \'skin-ər\, Cornelia Otis (b. May 30, 1901, Chicago, Ill., U.S.—d. July 9, 1979, New York, N.Y.)   American actress and author who, with satirical wit, wrote light verse, monologues, anecdotes, sketches, and monodramas in which she displayed her versatile and distinctive acting skills.

Skinner made her first professional stage appearance with her father, the tragedian Otis Skinner, in *Blood and Sand* (1921), and she collaborated with him in writing her first play, *Captain Fury* (1925). During the 1930s she wrote and staged her own monodramas, including *The Loves of Charles II*, *The Empress Eugénie*, *The Mansions on the Hudson*, and *The Wives of Henry VIII*. In 1939, performing in *Candida*, Skinner established a reputation as a fine actress, and she confirmed her excellence as a dramatic actress in *Theatre* (1941). Other performances that won critical acclaim included her roles in *Lady Windermere's Fan* (1946), *Paris '90* (1952), and *The Pleasure of His Company* (1958), which she wrote with Samuel Taylor.

Skinner's diverse writing ability was evident in her 1942 bestseller *Our Hearts Were Young and Gay*, written with Emily Kimbrough, and in the moving *Madame Sarah* (1966), which chronicled the life of the French actress Sarah Bernhardt.

Skin of Our Teeth, The   Comedy in three acts by Thornton WILDER, performed and published in 1942. Known for its experimental representation of all of human history, it won Wilder one of his three Pulitzer Prizes.

With a cast of characters that includes a dinosaur and drum majorettes, *The Skin of Our Teeth* employs bizarre anachronisms and audience-involvement techniques to argue that human experience is much the same whatever the time or place. From their living room in New Jersey, George and Maggie Antrobus (from the Greek *anthropos*, "human"), their promiscuous daughter Gladys, hostile and destructive son Henry (who represents the biblical Cain), and maid Sabina (who represents Lilith, the eternal temptress) face the trials of humanity through the ages, from icy destruction to flood and war.

Skram \'skråm\, Amalie, *original surname* Alver \'ȧl-vər\ (b. Aug. 22, 1846/47, Bergen, Nor.—d. March 15, 1905, Copenhagen, Den.)   Norwegian novelist, one of the foremost naturalistic writers of her time.

Skram, who was married and divorced twice, decried the double standard brought to bear on women and deplored the sexual ignorance of most women before marriage. The novels in which she examines the inequalities of marriage include *Constance Ring* (1885); *Lucie* (1888) and *Fru Inés* (1891), both part of her classic naturalistic tetralogy, *Hellemyrsfolket* (1887–98); "People of Hellemyr"); and *Forraadt* (1892; *Betrayed*). Skram also wrote literary criticism, short stories, and two plays (with her second husband, Erik Skram).

Skunk Hour   Poem by Robert Lowell, published in LIFE STUDIES (1959). It is modeled on "The Armadillo," a poem by Elizabeth Bishop; both poets dedicated their respective poems to each other. Composed of eight six-line stanzas, "Skunk Hour" is one in a series of confessional poems that characterized Lowell's verse from the 1950s.

In the first four stanzas the narrator describes several residents of his coastal resort town in Maine. In the final four stanzas the narrator isolates himself from the other townspeople, focusing on his inner turmoil. His anguished reverie gives way to a concluding description of other inhabitants of the town, a bold family of hungry skunks in a single-minded and confident search for food.

slack \'slak\, *also called* unstress \'ən-,stres, ,ən-'stres\   In the prosodic theory of Gerard Manley Hopkins, the weak or stressless element in a rhythmic unit or foot.

slant rhyme   *see* HALF RHYME.

Slauerhoff \'slaù-ər-,hȯf\, Jan Jacob (b. Sept. 14, 1898, Leeuwarden, Neth.—d. Oct. 5, 1936, Hilversum)   Dutch poet whose romanticism led him to go to sea as a ship's doctor and whose pessimistic poetry reflects his subsequent disillusionment.

Slauerhoff's restlessness and his contempt for The Netherlands are prominent themes throughout his work, from the first volume, *Archipel* (1923; "Archipelago"), to the last, *Een eerlijk zeemansgraf* (1936; "An Honorable Sailor's Grave"). Other negative elements are also apparent, such as the revenge wish and a preoccupation with violent death and the destructive course of history. The image of his soul is the ship's prow, borne along by the sea of fate.

Slaughterhouse-Five (*in full* Slaughterhouse-Five; or, The Children's Crusade: A Duty-Dance with Death)   Novel by Kurt VONNEGUT, Jr., published in 1969. The book blends science fiction with historical facts, notably Vonnegut's own experience as a prisoner of war in Dresden, Ger., during the Allied firebombing of that city in early 1945.

While serving in the army during World War II Billy Pilgrim becomes "unstuck in time," and from that point on he lives concurrently on Earth and on the distant planet Tralfamadore. On Earth Billy preaches the fatalistic philosophy of the Tralfamadorians, who know the future of all things, including the inevitable demise of the universe. They are resigned to fate, unfailingly responding to events with their catchphrase "So it goes."

Slave, The   One-act play by Amiri BARAKA, performed and published in 1964. An examination of tension between blacks and whites in contemporary America, *The Slave* is the story of a visit by African-American Walker Vessles to the home of Grace, his white ex-wife, and Easley, her white husband. Baraka points up the black man's low status in American society but also stresses that he is victimized and enslaved by his own hatred and is thus unable to effect social change.

slave narrative   American literary genre consisting of slave memoirs of daily plantation life, including the sufferings and humiliations borne and the eventual escape to freedom. The narratives contain humorous anecdotes of the deception and pretenses that the slave was forced to practice, expressions of religious fervor and superstition, and, above all, a pervasive longing for freedom, dignity, and self-respect.

A Narrative of the Uncommon Sufferings and Surprising Deliverance of Briton Hammon, a Negro Man, which is often considered the first slave narrative, was published in Boston in 1760. (Some scholars cite *Adam Negro's Tryall* [1703] as the first slave narrative, but it is about Adam, not by him.) Other early examples, such as *A Narrative of the Lord's Wonderful Dealings with J. Murrant, a Black, Taken Down from His Own Relation* (1784) and *The Interesting Narrative of Olaudah Equiano, or Gustavus Vassa, the African* (1789), followed.

The major period of slave narratives was 1830–60. Their publication was encouraged by abolitionists, and during this period the narratives, many of them based on oral accounts, multiplied. Although some, such as *Scenes in the Life of Harriet Tubman* (1869), are factual autobiographies, many others were influenced or sensationalized by the writer's desire to arouse sympathy for the abolitionist cause. The reworkings and interpolations in such works are usually obvious. In some cases, such as *The Autobiography of a Female Slave* (1856) by Mattie Griffith and Richard Hildreth's *The Slave, or Memoirs of Archy Moore*, the accounts were entirely fictitious. The slave-narrative genre reached its height with Frederick Douglass' classic autobiography *Narrative of the Life of Frederick Douglass, an American Slave* (1845; revised 1882).

In the first half of the 20th century a number of folklorists and anthropologists compiled documentary narratives based on recorded interviews with former black slaves. Notable compilations of such narratives include the brief accounts in Charles S. Johnson's *Shadow of the Plantation* (1934) and the fuller narratives found in B.A. Botkin's *Lay My Burden Down* (1945), which was an extract from 17 volumes of slave narratives collected by black and white interviewers for the WPA Federal Writers' Project. In the second half of the 20th century the growth of black cultural consciousness stimulated a renewed interest in slave narratives.

Slaveykov \slə-'vei-kúf\, Pencho Petkov (b. April 27?, 1866, Tryavna, Bulgaria, Ottoman Empire—d. May 28, 1912, Brunate, Italy) Bulgarian poet and critic who attempted to modernize his country's poetry by introducing contemporary ideas from other European countries.

Slaveykov was the son of the poet Petko Slaveykov. The younger man's formal education was interrupted by an illness that made him an invalid for the rest of his life. He continued to read and study on his own and later attended the University of Leipzig, where he was exposed to German philosophy and literature. He was inspired especially by J.W. von Goethe, Heinrich Heine, and Friedrich Nietzsche, and his poems reflect this influence as well as that of the simple eloquence and realism of Bulgarian folk songs. These interests were combined in the poems of the collections *Epicheski pesni* (1907; "Epic Songs"), a revision of two earlier collections, and *Sŭn za shtastie* (1907; "Dream of Happiness").

After he returned to Bulgaria, Slaveykov spent most of the rest of his life working for the National Library. He was dismissed from the library, however, by a political opponent who had been named minister of education. Slaveykov protested the injustice by leaving the country. He died the next year in Italy.

Slaveykov's ideas were expressed in his essays and in his autobiographical anthology of "apocryphal" verse by fictitious poets, *Na ostrova na blazhenite* (1910; "On the Isle of the Blessed"). His greatest, though unfinished, work, *Kŭrvava pesen* (1913; "Song of Blood"), is an epic poem that describes the sacrifices of the Bulgarian people in their struggle for independence. He was also an outstanding essayist and translator of German and Russian literature.

Slaveykov \slə-'vei-kúf\, Petko Rachev (b. Nov. 17, 1827, Turnovo, Bulgaria, Ottoman Empire—d. July 1, 1895, Sofia) Bulgarian poet, journalist, and politician who helped to enrich Bulgarian literature by establishing a modern literary language. His commitment to social justice and democratic principles was reflected in his works as well as in his political activism.

Slaveykov became an itinerant schoolteacher at age 17. The poems in his early collection—*Smesena Kitka* ("Mixed Bouquet") and *Pesnopoyka* ("Songbook"), both published in 1852—were lyrical and patriotic. By establishing the vernacular as a medium for literature (the language of his translation of the Bible in 1862 was based on Bulgarian dialects), he prepared for the flowering of native poetry. As a patriot and politician he helped to shape resurgent Bulgaria, producing political pamphlets notorious for their outspokenness against Turkish oppression and against the spiritual domination of the Greek patriarchate. In 1863 he moved to Constantinople (Istanbul), where he contributed to Bulgarian émigré reviews and edited satirical and political periodicals. After his country's liberation (1878), he became an active politician, serving both as president of the constituent assembly and as cofounder of the Democratic Party. After the 1881 coup d'état he went to Plovdiv, then still under Turkish rule, and there he edited a series of periodicals, including *Nezavisimost* ("Independence"). Slaveykov's son Pencho also became a writer.

Sleepwalkers, The Trilogy of novels by Hermann BROCH, published in German in three volumes as *Die Schlafwandler* in 1931–32. The multilayered novels chronicle the dissolution of the fabric of European society from 1888 to the end of World War I and the consequent victory of the realist over the romantic and the anarchist. The trilogy was composed of *Pasenow oder die Romantik 1888* (1931; *The Romantic*), *Esch oder die Anarchie 1903* (1931; *The Anarchist*), and *Huguenau oder die Sachlichkeit 1918* (1932; *The Realist*).

In *The Romantic*, Joachim von Pasenow, an officer of noble birth, tries without success to give meaning to his life by defying convention. He leaves the military and has an affair with a dancer, but he ultimately marries the daughter of a baron. In *The Anarchist*, Pasenow's friend Eduard von Bertrand commits suicide after he is denounced to the police as a homosexual by anarchist August Esch. Wild and aggressive, Esch has lost his job and sees in the industrialist Bertrand the personification of society's ills. *The Realist* concerns Wilhelm Huguenau, who deserts from the army and becomes a partner in a newspaper Esch owns. Supremely selfish and egotistical, Huguenau kills Esch and rapes his widow. His crimes go unpunished, and he makes a conventional marriage and becomes very wealthy. The events of World War I precipitate Pasenow's descent into insanity. Huguenau's ascendency over Pasenow and Esch points up the disintegration of morality in the postwar world.

Sleipnir \'slãp-nir\ In Norse mythology, the god Odin's magical horse. *See* ODIN.

Slessor \'sles-ər\, Kenneth (b. March 27, 1901, Orange, N.S.W., Australia—d. July 30, 1971, Sydney) Australian poet and journalist best known for his poem "Beach Burial," a moving tribute to Australian troops who fought in World War II.

Slessor became a reporter for the *Sydney Sun* at the age of 19. He was editor of the journal *Smith's Weekly* for a time and then was a World War II correspondent (1940–44). He continued as an editor and literary critic after the war.

His earliest poetry, collected in *Earth Visitors* (1926), is characterized by gaiety and technical experimentation. The influence of the poets T.S. Eliot and Ezra Pound is evident in the sophisticated *Cuckooz Country* (1932). *Five Bells: XX Poems* (1939) and *Poems* (1957) demonstrate the poet's mature mastery of technique.

slice of life In literature, a straightforward, realistic portrayal of life. The phrase is a translation of the French *tranche de vie*, which was used in reference to the works of naturalistic French writers such as Émile Zola.

śloka \'shlō-kə\ [Sanskrit *ślokah* sound, song of praise, praise, stanza] Chief verse form of the Sanskrit epics. A fluid meter that lends itself well to improvisation, the *śloka* consists of two verse lines (a distich) of 16 syllables each or of four half lines (hemistichs) of eight syllables each.

Słonimski \swō-'nʸēm-skʸē\, Antoni (b. Nov. 15, 1895, Warsaw, Poland, Russian Empire—d. July 4, 1976, Warsaw) Polish poet, translator, and newspaper columnist known for his devotion to pacifism and social justice.

Słonimski published his first poetry in 1913. He was a member of the Skamander poets, a group of young Warsaw intellectuals who published their own literary journal, *Skamander*. After traveling to Palestine and Brazil he published the collection *Droga na wschód* (1924; "Road to the East"). In the early 1930s his poems reflected a world heading toward disaster, beset with economic and social problems, the rise of fascism, and the coming of war. His play *Rodzina* (1933; "Family") was a comedy about two brothers, one a communist and the other a Nazi. His satiric, prescient novel *Dwa końce świata* (1937; "Two Ends of the World") showed Warsaw totally destroyed by bombings ordered by a dictator named Retlich.

Słonimski converted from Judaism to Roman Catholicism. He spent the war years in exile, first in France, then in England. In 1951 he returned to Poland and became an outspoken anti-Stalinist. In addition to thousands of poems, Słonimski published several plays and novels and well-regarded translations of some of William Shakespeare's works.

Slothrop, Tyrone \'tī-,rōn-'slóth-rəp, tī-'rōn\ Fictional character, a naive American lieutenant working for Allied Intelligence in London in GRAVITY'S RAINBOW by Thomas Pynchon.

Slovenly Peter *see* STRUWWELPETER.

Słowacki \swō-'vàt-skʸē\, Juliusz (b. Aug. 23 [Sept. 4, New Style], 1809, Krzemieniec, Volhynia, Russian Empire [now Kremenets, Ukraine]—d. April 3, 1849, Paris, Fr.) Poet and playwright who, with Adam Mickiewicz and Zygmunt Krasiński, dominated the Romantic movement in Polish literature. His technical virtuosity, rich and inventive vocabulary, and evocative imagery foreshadowed the work of the Symbolists.

In 1829 Słowacki joined the Department of the Treasury in Warsaw. During the Polish uprising of 1830, he appears to have been made an envoy of the insurrectionary government. He resigned from the Treasury in 1831 and traveled to Dresden (Germany), Paris, and London, presumably carrying dispatches. In 1833–35 he was in Switzerland, and a year later he was in Italy, where he wrote his love idyll *W Szwajcarii* (1839; "In Switzerland"). His travels to the Middle East in 1837–38 are described in *Podróż do ziemi świętej* (published posthumously, 1866; "Voyage to the Holy Land"), a narrative poem. He spent many years in Paris, which was the center for the large number of Polish émigrés. His letters to his mother from Paris are classics of Polish prose.

Słowacki's other works include the prose poem *Anhelli* (1838), the poem *Król-Duch* ("The Spirit King"), published partially in 1847 and in full in 1925, and many narrative and historical poems. He wrote a variety of plays, largely inspired by William Shakespeare, classical Greek and Roman drama, and Pedro Calderón de la Barca. Most of these works, such as *Lilla Weneda* (1840), *Sen srebrny Salomei* (1844; "The Silver Dream of Salomea"), and the anti-Romantic comedy *Fantazy* (1843), were published posthumously in 1866. These dramas had a powerful influence and are still frequently staged in Poland.

Small House at Allington, The \'al-iŋ-tən\ Novel by Anthony TROLLOPE, published serially from September 1862 to April 1864 and in two volumes in 1864, the fifth of his six BARSETSHIRE NOVELS.

Smart \'smärt\, Christopher (b. April 11, 1722, Shipbourne, Kent, Eng.—d. May 21, 1771, London) English religious poet notable for flashes of childlike penetration and vivid imagination. Best known for *A Song to David* (1763), in praise of the author of the Psalms, Smart produced verse that in some respects anticipated the poetry of William Blake and John Clare.

After his education at the University of Cambridge, Smart was elected a fellow of Pembroke Hall (1745), but at about the age of 27 he became a hack writer in London. Three times confined for madness (a mild religious mania), his strange yet engaging personality won him the friendship of such people as Samuel Johnson, actor-manager David Garrick, playwright Oliver Goldsmith, and both Charles Burney, the musicologist, and his daughter, Fanny, the novelist. Smart died in a debtor's prison.

Smart Set, The American literary magazine founded by William D'Alton Mann and published monthly in New York City from 1900 to 1930. Most notable among its editors were S.S. Van Dine and the team of H.L. Mencken and George Jean Nathan. It was a consciously fashionable magazine that featured novelettes, short stories in English and in French, essays, poems, plays, criticisms, and humorous sketches.

Among the American writers whose early work was published in *The Smart Set* were Eugene O'Neill, F. Scott Fitzgerald, and O. Henry; it also introduced the nation to the writings of James Joyce, D.H. Lawrence, Ford Madox Ford, and Gabriele D'Annunzio. Other notable contributors included W. Somerset Maugham, Frank Norris, Sinclair Lewis, Theodore Dreiser, Willa Cather, Sherwood Anderson, Ezra Pound, and James Branch Cabell.

Smike \'smīk\ Fictional character, a feebleminded and frail boy in the novel NICHOLAS NICKLEBY by Charles Dickens.

Smiles \'smīlz\, Samuel (b. Dec. 23, 1812, Haddington, Berwickshire, Scot.—d. April 16, 1904, London, Eng.) Scottish author best known for his didactic work *Self-Help* (1859), which, with its successors, *Character* (1871), *Thrift* (1875), and *Duty* (1880), enshrined the basic Victorian values associated with the "gospel of work."

Smiles qualified in medicine at Edinburgh in 1832. He soon abandoned medical practice for journalism, and from 1838 to 1842 he edited the progressive and reformist *Leeds Times*. From 1845 to 1866 he was engaged in railway administration. Under the influence of the Utilitarian philosophers Jeremy Bentham and James Mill, Smiles gave a series of lectures on self-improvement to the young men of Leeds; these lectures were compiled and published as *Self-Help, with Illustrations of Character and Conduct*. The book was widely translated; it was one of the first nonliterary books to be translated into Japanese after the Meiji Restoration, and it became a bible for young Japanese men eager to emulate Western ways.

Smiley, George \'jòrj-'smī-lē\ Fictional character, a British secret service agent who appears in many of the espionage novels of John LE CARRÉ, beginning with *Call for the Dead* (1961).

Smiley is an unobtrusive secret agent who leads an unglamorous life. A deceptively bland middle-aged man, he is trusted and respected by his subordinates and colleagues. He occasionally clashes with the intelligence bureaucracy and sometimes feels that professional duty compromises his personal honor. His most formidable adversary is a Soviet master spy, Karla.

In the detective story *A Murder of Quality* (1962), Smiley, having resigned from the secret service, investigates the murder of a schoolmaster's wife. Having returned to the secret service, Smiley plays a minor role in *The Spy Who Came In from the Cold* (1963) and in *The Looking-Glass War* (1965). He is a central character in *Tinker, Tailor, Soldier, Spy* (1974), *The Honourable Schoolboy* (1977), *Smiley's People* (1980), and *The Secret Pilgrim* (1991).

Smith \\'smith\\, A.J.M., *in full* Arthur James Marshall (b. Nov. 8, 1902, Montreal, Ont., Can.—d. Nov. 21, 1980, East Lansing, Mich., U.S.) Canadian poet, anthologist, and critic who was a member of the Montreal group, which precipitated a revival of Canadian poetry in the 1920s.

As an undergraduate at McGill University in Montreal, Smith founded and edited the *McGill Fortnightly Review* (1925–27), a literary magazine dedicated to freeing Canadian literature from its narrow provincialism. He encouraged other young Canadian writers to broaden their outlook and to set high literary standards. After receiving his Ph.D. from the University of Edinburgh in 1932, he taught in the United States.

In a series of anthologies beginning with *The Book of Canadian Poetry* (1943), Smith approached Canadian literature in a scholarly manner that set the tone for modern Canadian criticism. His later anthologies include *The Blasted Pine* (1957), a collection of Canadian satiric and invective verse, *Modern Canadian Verse in English and French* (1967), and *The Colonial Century: English-Canadian Writing Before Confederation* (1973). In his own poetry, collected in such volumes as *News of the Phoenix* (1943), *Collected Poems* (1962), and *Poems: New and Collected* (1967), Smith displayed careful craftsmanship.

Smith \\'smith\\, Charlotte, *original surname* Turner \\'tər-nər\\ (b. May 4, 1749, London, Eng.—d. Oct. 28, 1806, Tilford, near Farnham, Surrey) English novelist and poet whose work typifies the art of other women novelists of her day. Smith's work is exceptional, however, for its celebration of nature, its radical attitudes toward conventional morality (the novel *Desmond* tells of the innocent love of a man for a married woman), and its political ideas of class equality.

In 1787 Smith left her husband and began writing to support her 12 children. *Elegiac Sonnets and Other Essays*, which she had published in 1784, had been well received, but because novels promised greater financial rewards, she wrote—after some free translations of French novels—*Emmeline; or, The Orphan of the Castle* (1788) and *Ethelinde; or, The Recluse of the Lake* (1789). *Desmond* appeared in 1792 and was followed by her best work, *The Old Manor-House* (1793). Toward the end of her life, she turned to writing instructive books for children, the best being *Conversations Introducing Poetry for the Use of Children* (1804).

Smith \\'smith\\, James and Horace (respectively b. Feb. 10, 1775, London, Eng.—d. Dec. 24, 1839, London; b. Dec. 31, 1779, London—d. July 12, 1849, Tunbridge Wells, Kent) Brothers who were coauthors of *Rejected Addresses* (1812), a collection of parodies of early 19th-century British writers.

James made his primary career as a solicitor in government service; Horace became a successful stockbroker. The occasion of their famous volume was the rebuilding of Drury Lane Theatre in 1812, after a fire. The managers had offered a monetary prize for an address to be recited at the reopening in October. The Smith brothers had the idea of making the most popular poets of the time figure as competitors and of issuing a volume of unsuccessful addresses in parody of their various styles. They divided the task between them. James took William Wordsworth, Robert Southey, Samuel Taylor Coleridge, and George Crabbe, while Horace took Thomas Moore, Sir Walter Scott, and William Lisle Bowles. Both had a hand in parodying Lord Byron. Seven editions of *Rejected Addresses; or, The New Theatrum Poetarum* were called for within three months. *Re-*

jected Addresses is a classic in the literature of parody. The only other undertaking of the two brothers was *Horace in London* (1813), an imitation of Horatian odes. James Smith also wrote a series of comic skits.

After making a fortune in his business, Horace Smith wrote some 20 historical novels—including *Brambletye House* (1826), *Reuben Apsley* (1827), *Zillah* (1828), *The New Forest* (1829), and *Walter Colyton* (1830)—but he was more of an essayist than a storyteller. His three-volume *Gaieties and Gravities* (1826) contained many witty essays in both prose and verse.

Smith \\'smith\\, Lee (b. Nov. 1, 1944, Grundy, Va., U.S.) American author of fiction about her native southeastern United States.

Smith's first novel, *The Last Day the Dogbushes Bloomed* (1968), was written while she was in college. Her stories are set in the contemporary South and, eschewing the gothic and grotesque, are filled with the details of everyday life. Her widely admired fourth novel, *Black Mountain Breakdown*, and her short-story collection *Cakewalk* were both published in 1980. Critics noted her powerful characterizations of rural Southerners in the novel *Oral History* (1983), a history of a family over the course of 100 years. Her later books include *Family Linens* (1985), *Fair and Tender Ladies* (1988), *Me and My Baby View the Eclipse* (1990), and *The Devil's Dream* (1992).

Smith \\'smith\\, Seba (b. Sept. 14, 1792, Buckfield, Maine, U.S.—d. July 28, 1868, Patchogue, N.Y.) American editor and humorist, creator of the fictional Major Jack Downing.

Smith founded (1829) the *Portland Courier*, in which the major's fictional letters first appeared in January 1830, continuing later in the *National Intelligencer* until July 1853. Major Jack was a common man magnified as oracle, a Yankee full of horse sense and wise saws, and a threadbare office seeker exposing follies in a "mobocracy." Shameless pirating of Smith's invention led to the author's collection of the letters in book form, the last volume being published in 1859 under the title *My Thirty Years Out of the Senate*. He further portrays New England character in *Way Down East* (1854).

Smith \\'smith\\, Stevie, *byname of* Florence Margaret Smith (b. Sept. 20, 1902, Hull, Yorkshire, Eng.—d. March 7, 1971, London) British poet who expressed an original and visionary personality in her work, combining the ludicrous and the pathetic with an absence of sentimentality.

For most of her life Smith lived with an aunt in Palmers Green, a northern London suburb. After attending school there, she worked, until the early 1950s, as a secretary in the London offices of a magazine publisher. She then lived and worked at home, caring for her elderly aunt. Palmers Green and the people there are subjects for some of her poetry.

In the 1960s Smith's poetry readings became popular, and she made radio broadcasts and recordings. In addition to her verse, for which she is chiefly remembered, Smith wrote short stories, literary reviews, essays, and three novels, the first of which, *Novel on Yellow Paper* (1936), is best known.

The Collected Poems of Stevie Smith (1975) was illustrated with her Thurber-like sketches; it includes her first book of poems, *A Good Time Was Had by All* (1937), and *Not Waving but Drowning* (1957), the title poem of which appears in many anthologies. The lines of Smith's verse are often short and telling. They slip in and out of meter and rest on assonance and broken rhyme in ways that arrest attention. She addresses serious themes with a clarity critics often call childlike. The theme of death recurs.

Me Again: Uncollected Writings of Stevie Smith, Illustrated by Herself (1981) is a posthumous compilation of her prose writings, letters, and previously uncollected poetry.

Smith \'smith\, Sydney (b. June 3, 1771, Woodford, Essex, Eng.—d. Feb. 22, 1845, London) One of the foremost English preachers of his day, a champion of parliamentary reform, and a notable wit. Through his writings he perhaps did more than anyone else to change public opinion regarding Roman Catholic emancipation. He also helped to found (1802) *The Edinburgh Review*, contributing trenchant articles to it for 25 years.

Smith \'smith\, William Jay (b. April 22, 1918, Winnfield, La., U.S.) American lyric poet who wrote for both adults and children.

The son of an army officer, Smith spent much of his early life on a U.S. Army post, a period he recalled in *Army Brat: A Memoir* (1980). Educated at Washington University, St. Louis, Mo. (B.A., 1939; M.A., 1941), he served in the U.S. Navy from 1941 to 1945, then attended Columbia University and the universities of Oxford and Florence. He taught at several colleges and universities, served in the Vermont House of Representatives from 1960 to 1962, and in 1968–70 was consultant in poetry to the U.S. Library of Congress.

Smith's first collections of poems, *Poems* (1947) and *Celebration at Dark* (1950), revealed the breadth of his narrative range, and with *The Tin Can and Other Poems* (1966) he began to experiment with free verse. His *Collected Poems: 1939–1989* was published in 1990.

Smith began collecting his whimsical and nonsense poems for children in *Laughing Time* (1955) and *Boy Blue's Book of Beasts* (1957); his later children's poetry included *Typewriter Town* (1960), *Ho for a Hat!* (1964; rev. ed., 1989), and *Laughing Time: Collected Nonsense* (1990). He also edited several volumes of children's poetry. He made a reputation as a translator with versions of *Poems of a Multimillionaire* by Valéry Larbaud (1955) and *Selected Writings of Jules Laforgue* (1956), and he edited and translated other poetry from several languages. He also wrote *The Spectra House* (1961), a study of well-known literary hoaxes and lampoons.

Smith, Winston \'wins-tən-'smith\ Fictional character, the protagonist of George Orwell's cautionary novel NINETEEN EIGHTY-FOUR. A minor bureaucrat in the civil service, Winston Smith lives a drab, conforming existence but wants to experience a meaningful life as an individual.

Smoke Novel by Ivan TURGENEV, published in Russian in 1867 as *Dym*. Set in Baden-Baden, Ger., it combines a sensitive love story with political satire.

While waiting in fashionable Baden to meet Tanya Shestoff, his fiancée, Grigory Litvinov, the young heir to a declining Russian estate, encounters his former love, the beautiful and covetous Irina. The working out of Grigory's choices in love provides the principal plot of *Smoke*. The political questions of the day are a secondary focus in the novel as Grigory also meets various members of both the left and the right wings of the intelligentsia and is equally appalled by all but Potugin, a Russian who voices the author's own views about life and politics.

Smollett \'smäl-ət\, Tobias (George) (baptized March 19, 1721, Cardross, Dumbartonshire, Scot.—d. Sept. 17, 1771, near Livorno, Tuscany [Italy]) English satirical novelist, best known for his picaresque novels.

Smollett apprenticed as a surgeon, and throughout his life he combined the roles of medical man and writer. In 1740 he was commissioned surgeon's second mate in the Royal Navy and in 1750 he obtained the degree of M.D. In 1746, after the defeat of the Jacobite rebels at Culloden, he wrote his most famous poem, "The Tears of Scotland." He next produced *Advice* (1746) and *Reproof* (1747), verse satires in the manner of the Roman poet Juvenal.

In 1748 Smollett published his novel RODERICK RANDOM, a graphic account of British naval life at the time, and he also translated from the French the great picaresque romance *Gil Blas*. PEREGRINE PICKLE was published in 1751, and *The Adventures of Ferdinand, Count Fathom* (now, with *The History and Adventures of an Atom*, the least regarded of his novels) appeared in 1753. Smollett was forced into hack writing by poor book sales, extravagant living, and generous lending. He translated *Don Quixote* from the Spanish (1755), and in 1756 he became editor of *The Critical Review*, a Tory and church paper, at the same time writing his four-volume *Complete History of England* (1757–58). A

Detail of an oil painting by an unknown artist, about 1770
National Portrait Gallery, London

year later, his farce *The Reprisal: or, The Tars of Old England* was produced at Drury Lane. In 1758 he became what today might be called general editor of *Universal History*, a compilation of 58 volumes; Smollett himself wrote on France, Italy, and Germany. In 1759 he was convicted for libel on Admiral Sir Charles Knowles in *The Critical Review*, fined, and sentenced to three months' imprisonment in the King's Bench Prison. He drew on his experiences there for his two-volume novel *The Adventures of Sir Launcelot Greaves* (1762).

In 1760 Smollett became editor of *The British Magazine*. Two years later he became editor of *The Briton*, a weekly. He was also writing an eight-volume work titled *The Present State of All Nations*, and he had begun a translation, in 36 volumes, of the varied works of Voltaire. Seriously ill with tuberculosis, Smollett retired to France. In 1766 he published TRAVELS THROUGH FRANCE AND ITALY, his one nonfiction work that is still read. His finest work, HUMPHRY CLINKER (1771), recounts the adventures of a family traveling through Britain.

Smollett is unrivaled for the pace and vigor that sustain his comedy. He is especially brilliant in the rendering of comic characters in their externals, anticipating the manner of Charles Dickens.

snallygaster \'snal-ē-,gas-tər, 'snäl-ē-,gäs-tər\ A mythical nocturnal creature that is reported chiefly from rural Maryland, is reputed to be part reptile and part bird, and is said to prey on poultry and children. It has been claimed that the word is altered from a Pennsylvania German form of German *schnella Geister* ("quick spirits") and that the creature can be traced to German folk beliefs. However, neither the phrase nor the creature appear to have been recorded in Pennsylvania's German-speaking areas.

Snark \'snärk\ Mysterious fictional creature who is the object of a massive search in Lewis Carroll's poem THE HUNTING OF THE SNARK.

Snodgrass \'snäd-gras\, W.D., *in full* William De Witt, *pseudonym* S.S. Gardons \'gär-dənz\ (b. Jan. 5, 1926, Wilkinsburg, Pa., U.S.) American poet whose powerful early work is described as formalist and confessional.

Snodgrass's first collection, *Heart's Needle* (1959), which won the Pulitzer Prize, is marked by careful formal control and a sensitive and solemn delineation of his experience of losing his daughter through divorce. The collection *After Experience* (1968) continues these formal and thematic concerns. His later work—including *Remains* (1970), *If Birds Build with Your Hair* (1979), *D.D. Byrde Calling Jennie Wrenn* (1984), and *The Death of Cock Robin* (1989)—employs free verse. Other writing by Snodgrass includes several volumes of translations of European ballads and *In Radical Pursuit* (1975), a volume of criticism.

Snoilsky \'snȯil-skē\, Carl Johan Gustaf, Count (greve) (b. Sept. 8, 1841, Stockholm, Swed.—d. May 19, 1903, Stockholm) Swedish poet who was the most notable of a group of early realist poets.

While a student at the University of Uppsala, Snoilsky first gained a reputation for his poetic talent. His *Dikter* (1869; "Poems"), written during an extended tour of the European continent and including his *Italian Pictures* (1865), enchanted the Swedish public with its carefree and sensuous celebrations of the Mediterranean landscape. After its publication Snoilsky joined the diplomatic corps, married advantageously, stopped writing, and lived the life of a Swedish aristocrat. In 1879, however, he ran away from that life, remarried, settled on the continent, and started writing poetry again. Three volumes of his verse appeared, respectively, in 1881, 1883, and 1887. He returned to Stockholm in 1890 and remained there until his death.

Snoilsky felt the need to write poetry reflecting the social problems he saw, and his later verse expresses his humane liberalism and his sympathy for the underprivileged. His poetry is clear, elegant, and polished, with a strong note of realism in spite of its rather traditional form.

Snopes family \'snōps\ Recurring characters in the Yoknapatawpha novels and stories of William FAULKNER, notably *The Hamlet* (1940), *The Town* (1957), and *The Mansion* (1959). Snopes family members also appear in *Sartoris* (1929), *As I Lay Dying* (1930), and *The Unvanquished* (1938).

Faulkner contrasted the verminlike rapacity of most of the Snopes family with the failing old order of the Sartoris clan. Through treachery and corruption Flem Snopes gathers power in Frenchman's Bend, Miss. His cousins are emblems of depravity, including murderous Mink, pedophile Wesley, bigamist I.O., idiot Ike who lusts after a cow, and Launcelot ("Lump"), who sells tickets to view Ike's perverted scenes. The next generation includes a pornographer, a venal politician, a thief, and the uniquely honest Wallstreet Panic Snopes.

Snorri Sturluson \'snȯr-rē-'stu̇r-lu̇e-sȯn\ (b. 1179, Iceland—d. Sept. 22, 1241, Reykjaholt) Icelandic poet, historian, and chieftain, author of the *Prose Edda* and the *Heimskringla*.

A descendant of the great poet and hero of the *Egils saga*, Egill Skallagrímsson, Snorri was brought up at Oddi from the age of three in the home of Jón Loptsson, the most influential chieftain in Iceland. From him Snorri acquired both a deep knowledge of Icelandic tradition and a European breadth of outlook. In 1199 Snorri married an heiress and began to acquire lands and power. In 1206 he settled at Reykjaholt, where most of his works were written between 1223 and 1235. During 1215–18 and 1222–32 he was "lawspeaker," or president, of the Icelandic high court. In 1218 he was invited to Norway by King Haakon IV. Snorri became involved in politics while visiting the Norwegians. He persuaded Haakon that he could become king of Iceland, and he became Haakon's vassal. Snorri returned to Iceland in 1220, but in the ensuing years his relations with Haakon deteriorated and in 1241, by Haakon's order, he was assassinated.

Snorri's writings are remarkable both for their scope and for their formal assurance. The *Prose Edda* is both a handbook on poetics and a recounting of the legends of Norse mythology. Snorri also wrote a biography of St. Olaf of Norway, which he included in *Heimskringla*, a history of the Norwegian kings. Snorri based the *Heimskringla* on earlier histories, but he gathered much fresh material of his own. His genius lay in his power to present all that he perceived critically as a historian with the immediacy of drama.

The qualities of intelligence, warmth, and scholarly industry in Snorri's writings contrast sharply with the weak, shifty character that emerges in the account of his life by his nephew in the *Sturlunga saga. See also* EDDA; HEIMSKRINGLA.

Snow \'snō\, C.P., *in full* Charles Percy Snow, Baron Snow of the City of Leicester \'les-tər\ (b. Oct. 15, 1905, Leicester, Leicestershire, Eng.—d. July 1, 1980, London) British novelist, scientist, and government administrator.

Snow was graduated from Leicester University and earned a doctorate in physics at the University of Cambridge, where, at the age of 25, he became a fellow of Christ's College. After working at Cambridge in molecular physics for some 20 years, he became a university administrator, and, with the outbreak of World War II, a scientific adviser to the British government. In 1950 he married the British novelist Pamela Hansford Johnson. He was knighted in 1957 and made a life peer in 1964.

In the 1930s Snow began the 11-volume novel sequence collectively called *Strangers and Brothers* (published 1940–70), about the academic, public, and private life of an Englishman named Lewis Eliot. The novels are a quiet and meticulous (though not dull) analysis of bureaucratic man and the corrupting influence of power. Several of Snow's novels were adapted for the stage. Later novels include *In Their Wisdom* (1974) and *Coat of Varnish* (1979).

As both a literary man and a scientist, Snow was particularly well equipped to write a book about science and literature; *The Two Cultures and the Scientific Revolution* (1959) and its sequel, *Second Look* (1964), constitute Snow's most widely known—and widely attacked—position. He argued that practitioners of either of the two disciplines know little, if anything, about the other and that communication between them is difficult, if not impossible. He acknowledged the emergence of a third "culture" as well, the social sciences and arts, concerned with "how human beings are living or have lived." Many of Snow's writings on science and culture are found in *Public Affairs* (1971). *Trollope: His Life and Art* (1975) exemplifies Snow's powers in literary criticism, as does *The Realists: Eight Portraits* (1979).

Snowball \'snō-ˌbȯl\ Fictional character, a pig who is one of the leaders of the revolt in ANIMAL FARM, George Orwell's allegorical tale about the early history of Soviet Russia. Most critics agree that Snowball represents Leon Trotsky.

Snow-Bound Poem by John Greenleaf WHITTIER, published in 1866. Subtitled "A Winter Idyll," this nostalgic pastoral poem recalls the New England rural home and family of the poet's youth, where, despite the pummeling of the winter winds and snow, he remained secure and comfortable inside the house.

Snow Country Short novel by KAWABATA Yasunari, published in Japanese in 1948 as *Yukiguni*. The work was begun in 1935 and completed in 1937, with a final version completed in 1947. It deals with psychological, social, and erotic interaction between an aesthetic man and a beautiful geisha and is set against the natural beauty and imagery of a remote area of Japan.

Snowe, Lucy \'lü-sē-'snō\ Fictional character, a shy, plain British teacher in Belgium who is the protagonist of Charlotte Brontë's semiautobiographical novel VILLETTE.

Snows of Kilimanjaro, The \,kil-i-mən-'jär-ō\ Short story by Ernest HEMINGWAY, first published in *Esquire* magazine in 1936 and later collected in *The Fifth Column and the First Forty-Nine Stories* (1938). The stream-of-consciousness narrative relates the feelings of Harry, a novelist dying of gangrene poisoning while on an African safari. Hemingway considered *The Snows of Kilimanjaro* his finest story.

Snyder \'snī-dər\, Gary (Sherman) (b. May 8, 1930, San Francisco, Calif., U.S.) American poet early identified with the Beat movement and, from the late 1960s, an important spokesman for the concerns of communal living and ecological activism. Snyder received the Pulitzer Prize for poetry in 1975.

Snyder's poetry is rooted in ancient, natural, and mythic experience. His style exhibits a variety of influences, from Walt Whitman to Ezra Pound to Japanese haiku. Prominent in his first two books of poems, *Riprap* (1959) and *Myths and Texts* (1960), are images and experiences drawn from his work as a logger and ranger in the Pacific Northwest. In *Six Sections from Mountains and Rivers Without End, Plus One* (excerpts from an ongoing cycle of poems, 1965), *The Back Country* (1967), and *Regarding Wave* (1969), the fusion of religion into everyday life reflects the author's increasing interest in Eastern philosophies. Later volumes include *Turtle Island* (1974), for which Snyder won the Pulitzer, and *Axe Handles* (1983). His alternatives to routine city life are presented in *Earth House Hold* (1969), a book of journal fragments and essays, and *The Real Work: Interviews and Talks 1964–1979* (1980).

Snyder's later publications include *The Old Ways* (1977), a selection of essays on aspects of tribal life; *He Who Hunted Birds in His Father's Village* (1979), an examination of Haida Indian myth; *Passage Through India* (1984), an account of an Asian pilgrimage; the essays found in *The Practice of the Wild* (1990); and *No Nature: New and Selected Poems* (1992).

So Big Novel by Edna FERBER, published in 1924 and awarded the Pulitzer Prize for fiction in 1925. The book tells the story of Selina Peake DeJong, a gambler's daughter with a love of life and a nurturing spirit.

Socé \sò-'sä\, Ousmane (Diop) (b. Oct. 31, 1911, Rufisque, Senegal, French West Africa—d. May 1974, Dakar) Senegalese writer and politician who was one of the first novelists of his country.

After attending Qur'ānic school, Socé entered the colonial school system and became one of the first African students to obtain a scholarship to study at a French university. While studying veterinary medicine he wrote two novels—*Karim* (1935) and *Mirages de Paris* (1937)—that were published in Paris. *Karim* was the first of Socé's books to express concern over the problems that young Africans face when moving from rural to urban areas.

Socé recorded a number of animal tales and historical legends from the oral tradition of Senegal in *Contes et légendes d'Afrique noire* (1942; "Stories and Legends of Black Africa"), edited *Le Phare du Sénégal* (1952–57), and in 1953 founded the magazine *Bingo*. He also produced a volume of poetry, *Rythmes du Khalam* (1956). He was Senegal's ambassador to the United States and delegate to the United Nations until 1968.

Sōchō \'sō-,chō\, *also called* Sōkan \'sō-,kän\ *or* Saiokuken \'sī-ō-,kü-ken\ (b. 1448, Japan—d. April 11, 1532, Japan) Japanese *renga* (linked-verse) poet and chronicler of the late Muromachi period (1338–1573) who, along with two other *renga* poets, wrote *Minase sangin hyakuin* (1488; *Minase Sangin Hyakuin: A Poem of One Hundred Links Composed by Three Poets at Minase*).

Little is known of Sōchō's early years, but he spent much of his adult life as a disciple of the Buddhist monk and *renga*

master Sōgi. In early 1488 Sōchō, Sōgi, and another student, Shōhaku, met at the village of Minase, between Kyōto and Ōsaka, and composed *Minase sangin*. The poem is considered to be one of the best examples of linked-verse poetry, which was at its peak during that time.

After the death of Sōgi in 1502, Sōchō wrote the narrative *Sōgi shūen ki* ("An Account of the Last Moments of Sōgi") to commemorate his master. Later works include *Sōchō shuki* (1522–27; "Memoirs of Sōchō"), in which he used *renga* and haikai (comic *renga*) to describe his travels during that period, and *Sōchō nikki* (1530–31; "Sōchō Diary").

Socialist Realism The officially sanctioned theory and method of artistic, including literary, composition prevalent in the Soviet Union from 1932 to the mid-1980s. For that period of history Socialist Realism, which called for the didactic use of art to develop social consciousness in an evolving socialist state, was the sole criterion for measuring artistic works. Defined and reinterpreted over half a century of polemical criticism, it remained a vague term.

In literature Socialist Realism followed the great tradition of 19th-century Russian realism in that it purported to serve as a faithful and objective mirror of life. It differed from the earlier tradition, however, in several important respects. The realism of Leo Tolstoy and Anton Chekhov inevitably conveyed a critical picture of the society it portrayed (hence the term *critical realism*). On the other hand, the primary theme of Socialist Realism was the struggle to build socialism and a classless society. In portraying this struggle, the writer could note imperfections but was expected to take a positive and optimistic view of socialist society and to keep in mind its larger historical relevance.

One requisite of Socialist Realism was *narodnost*, a doctrine of social responsibility both in portraying the aspirations of the proletariat and in making the work accessible to all. Another requisite was the hero who perseveres against all odds or handicaps. Socialist Realism thus looked back to Romanticism in that it encouraged a certain heightening and idealizing of characters and events to mold the consciousness of the masses. Hundreds of protagonists—usually engineers, inventors, or scientists—created to this specification were strikingly alike in their lack of credibility. In rare cases, when the writer's deeply felt experiences coincided with the official doctrine, the works were successful, as with the Soviet classic *Kak zakalyalas stal* (1932–34; *How the Steel Was Tempered*) by Nikolay Ostrovsky.

Socialist Realism remained the official aesthetic of the Soviet Union (and of its eastern European satellites) until the late 1980s, when changes in Soviet society led to the general decline of state socialism and of the rigid commitment to Marxism in the region.

sock \'säk\ [Latin *soccus*] A shoe worn by actors in Greek and Roman comedy. *Compare* BUSKIN.

Söderberg \'sœ-dər-,berʸ\, Hjalmar Erik Fredrik (b. June/July 2, 1869, Stockholm, Swed.—d. Oct. 14, 1941, Copenhagen, Den.) Swedish novelist, critic, and short-story writer noted for his elegant style and his ironic treatments of life's disappointments and inherent limitations.

Söderberg began his career as a civil servant but soon turned to writing, starting as a critic. His first novel, *Förvillelser* (1895), displays his characteristic irony, disillusionment with life, and a subdued compassion. His second novel, *Martin Bircks ungdom* (1901; *Martin Birck's Youth*), has much of the fin-de-siècle melancholy of the 1890s but is also one of the finest descriptions of childhood in Swedish literature. In this book Söderberg captured Stockholm's sights and sounds with an evocative language. His novel *Doktor Glas* (1905; *Doctor Glas*) caused a sensation because of its apparent justification of a deliberate ethical murder. His play *Gertrud* (1906) and his novel *Den all-varsamma leken* (1912; "The Serious Game") are tragicomic treatments of the illusions of romantic love.

Söderberg was also a skillful short-story writer, the best known of his four collections being *Historietter* (1898). In these brief sketches, he mocks human complacency and self-deception in a terse, probing, witty style. After 1910 Söderberg lived mainly in Copenhagen, later writing articles warning of the approaching threat of fascism and Nazism.

Södergran \\'sœ̄-dər-ˌgrän\\, Edith (Irene) (b. April 4, 1892, St. Petersburg, Russia—d. June 24, 1923, Raivola, Fin.)   Swedish-Finnish poet whose Expressionistic work influenced a generation of Finnish and Swedish writers.

Södergran's first book, *Dikter* (1916; "Poems"), expressed shifting moods of melancholy and joy in a free form that was indebted to the Symbolist poets. This collection inaugurated the Swedish-Finnish modernist movement, which looked to German Expressionism and Russian Futurism for inspiration. Her five later volumes—*Septemberlyran* (1918; "The September Lyre"), *Rosenaltaret* (1919; "The Rose Altar"), *Brokiga iakttagelser* (1919; "Gaudy Observations"), *Framtidens skugga* (1920; "The Shadow of Future"), and the posthumously published *Landet som icke är* (1925; "The Country That Is Not")—are intense and visionary, reflecting her reading of Friedrich Nietzsche. Initially appreciated by only one critic (Hagar Olsson) in a generally hostile critical climate, Södergran eventually became a much-loved figure. Olsson edited Södergran's last volume of poetry and in 1955 published their correspondence.

Sodom and Gomorrah \\'säd-əm . . . gə-'môr-ə\\   Notoriously sinful cities described in the Old Testament book of Genesis. They are now possibly covered by the shallow waters south of al-Lisān, a peninsula near the southern end of the Dead Sea in Israel. Sodom and Gomorrah constituted, along with the cities of Admah, Zeboiim, and Zoar (Bela), the five biblical "cities of the plain." Destroyed by "brimstone and fire" because of their wickedness (Genesis 19:24), Sodom and Gomorrah presumably were devastated about 1900 BC by an earthquake in the Dead Sea area of the Great Rift Valley, a large rift extending from the Jordan River valley in Israel to the Zambezi River system in East Africa.

Archaeological evidence indicates that the area was fertile in the Middle Bronze Age (c. 2000–1500 BC), with fresh water flowing into the Dead Sea in sufficient amounts to sustain agriculture. Because of the fertile land, the biblical Lot, the nephew of the Hebrew patriarch Abraham, selected the area of the cities of the Valley of Siddim (the Salt Sea, or the Dead Sea) to graze his flocks. When the catastrophic destruction occurred, the petroleum and gases existing in the area probably contributed to the imagery of "brimstone and fire" that accompanied the geological upheaval which destroyed the cities.

An inspiration to writers, artists, and psychologists, Sodom and Gomorrah and their legendary wickedness have been the subject of numerous dramas, including the medieval mystery play *History of Lot and Abraham* and modern plays by Jean Giraudoux and Níkos Kazantzákis. In art the subjects involved in the biblical accounts of Sodom and Gomorrah have been portrayed in numerous medieval psalters, Renaissance frescoes, and paintings down to the present. Sexual acts attributed to the Sodomites gave the city's name to the contemporary term *sodomy*.

soft-boiled   Of or relating to literary expression that is regarded satirically as given to wholesome sentiment and moralism. The term is used in opposition to *hard-boiled*, a tough, unsentimental style made popular in detective fiction. *See also* HARD-BOILED FICTION.

Soga \\'sō-gä\\, Tiyo (b. 1829, Tyume, Cape Colony [South Africa]—d. Aug. 12, 1871, Tutura Mission, near Butterworth)   Xhosa journalist, minister, translator, composer of hymns, and collector of black South African fables, legends, proverbs, history, praise songs, and customs. Soga's translation of John Bunyan's *The Pilgrim's Progress* (*U-Hambo lom-Hambi*, 1866) had almost as great an influence upon the Xhosa language as the King James Version of the Bible had upon English.

Soga was a part of the first literate generation of Xhosa speakers. The first African minister ordained in Great Britain, he contributed during the 1860s to *Indaba* ("The News"), published in Lovedale, S.Af. In this work he addressed himself primarily to a Christian audience on such topics as "Amakholwa nama-Qaba" ("The Believers and the Pagans"), "U-Tywala" ("Beer"), and "Amakristu Neenkosi" ("The Christians and the Chiefs"), reflecting social changes of the time and the widening gulf between Christians and traditionalists.

The many hymns Soga composed were very popular in the 19th century and are still sung in South African churches today. His literary influence upon the subsequent generation of Xhosa writers was notable.

Sōgi \\'sō-gē\\, *byname of* Iio Sōgi (b. 1421, Japan—d. Sept. 1, 1502, Hakone, Japan)   Buddhist monk and greatest master of *renga* (linked verse) who was the supreme Japanese poet of his age.

Sōgi was born of humble stock, and nothing is known of his career before 1457. His later writings suggest that, after serving as a Zen monk in Kyōto, he became, in his 30s, a professional *renga* poet. His teachers included not only provincial *renga* masters but also court nobles, and though his training undoubtedly benefited his poetry, it also exerted an inhibiting influence. Sōgi's own selection of his best work shows him at his most ingenious in the aristocratic tradition, but his modern reputation is based on the deeply moving vein found in his simpler and more personal poems.

Sōgi is known as a traveler-poet. His life for 40 years was divided between the capital and the provinces. From 1466 to 1472, a period when warfare ravaged Kyōto, he lived mainly in eastern Japan. His return to Kyōto in 1473 ushered in his most fruitful period. His residence became the center of literary activity in the city, and he compiled several collections of his poetry. In 1480 he made a journey to Kyushu (recorded in his *Tsukushi no michi no ki*; "A Record of the Road to Tsukushi"), not in the traditional manner as a wandering priest but as a celebrity, feted everywhere by his admirers.

Sōgi's reputation derives mainly from two *renga* sequences, *Minase sangin hyakuin* (1488; *Minase Sangin Hyakuin: A Poem of One Hundred Links Composed by Three Poets at Minase*) and *Yuyama sangin hyakuin* (1491; "One Hundred Poems Composed by Three Poets at Yuyama"); in each of these, three poets led by Sōgi took turns at composing short stanzas (links) to form a single poem with many shifts of mood and direction. Sōgi left more than 90 works, including *renga* anthologies, diaries, poetic criticism, and manuals.

Sohrab and Rustum \\'sō-ˌräb . . . 'rüs-ˌtəm\\   Epic poem in blank verse by Matthew ARNOLD, published in 1853 in his collection *Poems*. Among Arnold's sources for this heroic romance set in ancient Persia were translations of an epic by the Persian poet Ferdowsī and Sir John Malcolm's *History of Persia* (1815).

The poem is an account of Sohrab's search for his father, who disappeared years earlier. A warrior for the Tartars, Sohrab engages in battle with Persian forces. Not realizing that Rustum, the Persian chieftain, is his father, Sohrab challenges the older man in single combat. Only when the young warrior lies mortally wounded from Rustum's spear does he talk of his birth. It is then that father and son realize their relationship. Grief-stricken, Rustum promises to give Sohrab's body a royal burial.

solar myth **1.** A myth that concerns a sun god. **2.** *also called* solarism \'sō-lə-,riz-əm\ A traditional story (such as a folktale or legend) that is interpreted as a primitive explanation of the course, motion, or influence of the sun.

Soldier, The Sonnet by Rupert BROOKE, published in 1915 in the collection *1914*. Perhaps his most famous poem, it reflects British sorrow over and pride in the young men who died in World War I.

Narrated in the first person by an English soldier, the poem is sentimental, patriotic, and epitaphic. In the closing sestet, the poem's speaker suggests that his soul is eternally linked with England. The poem's familiar opening lines acquired even greater poignancy as a result of Brooke's own wartime death:

> If I should die, think only this of me:
> That there's some corner of a foreign field
> That is for ever England.

Soldier's Play, A Drama in two acts by Charles FULLER, produced and published in 1981 and awarded the Pulitzer Prize for drama in 1982.

Set on an army base in Louisiana during World War II, the play deals with the open and covert conflicts between whites and blacks that limit the possibility of personal growth and social progress. The work concerns an investigation into the murder of a black sergeant of an all-black company. By interviewing witnesses, the investigator discovers that the sergeant had been a tyrannical, sadistic man who had hated everyone, black and white. He eventually discovers that the murder was not committed by white soldiers, town bigots, or members of the Ku Klux Klan, but by a young black soldier whom the sergeant had goaded unmercifully.

soliloquy \sə-'lil-ə-kwē\ [Late Latin *soliloquium* monologue, from Latin *solus* alone + *loqui* to speak] In drama, a monologue that gives the illusion of being a series of unspoken reflections. The actor directly addresses the audience or speaks thoughts aloud, either alone upon the stage or with the other actors keeping silent.

The device was long an accepted dramatic convention, especially in the theater of the 16th, 17th, and 18th centuries. Long, ranting monologues were popular in the revenge tragedies of Elizabethan times, such as Thomas Kyd's *The Spanish Tragedy*, and in the works of Christopher Marlowe, who usually substituted the outpouring of one character's thoughts for normal dramatic writing. William Shakespeare used the device more artfully, as a true indicator of the mind of his characters, as in the famous "To be or not to be" soliloquy in *Hamlet*. Among the French playwrights, Pierre Corneille made use of the lyrical quality of the form, often producing soliloquies that are actually odes or cantatas, whereas Jean Racine, like Shakespeare, used the soliloquy more for dramatic effect. The soliloquy fell into disfavor after much exaggeration and overuse in the plays of the late 17th-century English Restoration, but it remains useful for revealing the inner life of characters.

Twentieth-century playwrights have experimented with various substitutes for the set speech of the soliloquy. Eugene O'Neill in *The Great God Brown* (1926) had the characters wear masks when they were presenting themselves to the world, but they were maskless when expressing what they actually felt or thought in soliloquy. In O'Neill's *Strange Interlude* (1928), the characters spoke a double dialogue—one to each other, concealing the truth, and one to the audience, revealing it. In

Samuel Beckett's *Krapp's Last Tape* (1958), interior monologue was presented through the device of having an old man replay tape recordings he made in his youth. *Compare* DRAMATIC MONOLOGUE.

Solitary Reaper, The Poem by William WORDSWORTH, published in 1807 in the collection *Poems, in Two Volumes*. It is a pastoral snapshot of a young woman working alone in a field in the Highlands of Scotland, singing a plaintive song in Gaelic.

The Solitary Reaper is made up of four octaves, primarily written in iambic tetrameter and generally following the rhyme scheme of *ababccdd*. The narrator is transfixed by the sight and sound of the titular figure, whose arresting voice fills the empty valley. Although he does not understand the language in which she sings, the narrarator imagines that her song describes ancient tragedies or personal sorrows.

Solness, Halvard \'häl-vərd-'sȯl-nəs\ Title character of Henrik Ibsen's THE MASTER BUILDER, whose past behavior haunts him.

Solomós \sō-lō-'mȯs\, Dhionísios, Count (komis) (b. April 8, 1798, Zante, Ionion Islands—d. Nov. 21, 1857, Corfu) One of the greatest of modern Greek poets, first to demonstrate the power and suppleness of Demotic Greek when it is inspired by wide culture and a first-rate lyrical fancy.

Solomós' earliest poems were written in Italian, but in 1822 he determined to write in the spoken tongue of Greece. His *Ímnos is tín elevtherían* ("Hymn to Liberty") was composed in 1823, and his poem on the death of Lord Byron in 1824–25. The unfinished *Lambros*, a Romantic poem of the revolutionary times, was begun in 1826. During the period from 1823 to 1828, Solomós also composed some shorter lyrical pieces and satires, of which the most notable is *I ginaíka tís Zakínthou* ("The Woman of Zante").

The poet's lyrical exuberance was curbed by a growing preoccupation with German theories of dramatic form and by an inhibiting dissatisfaction with the meager resources of his chosen linguistic medium. These impediments, together with a disastrous family quarrel, explain why Solomós' major poems of this period remain fragmentary. Nonetheless, *O kritikós* (1833; "The Cretan"), the second and third sketches of *Oi elévtheroi poliorkiménoi* (1827–49; "The Free Besieged")—which deals with the siege of Missolonghi during the war for Greek independence—and *O pórfiras* (1849; "The Shark"), despite their fragmentary nature, exhibit a sense of rhythm and a melody of cadence not found in his juvenilia.

Solon \'sō-,län, -lən\ (b. *c.* 630 BC—d. *c.* 560) Athenian statesman, known as one of the Seven Wise Men of Greece. He ended exclusive aristocratic control of the government, substituted a system of control by the wealthy, and introduced a new and more humane law code. He was also a noted poet, though only a few hundred lines of his poetry survive in quotation.

Solon was of noble descent but moderate means. As the tradition states and his travels and economic measures suggest, he may have been a merchant. He first became prominent about 600 BC, when the Athenians were disheartened by the outcome of a war with their neighbors of Megara for possession of the island of Salamis. By publicly reciting a poem that made the issue a matter of national honor and that called on the Athenians to "arise and come to Salamis, to win that fair island and undo our shame," Solon induced them to resume the war, which they eventually won. As the medium through which he warned, challenged, counseled the people, and urged them to action, his poetry was the instrument of his statesmanship.

Solstad \'sȯl-,stä\, Dag (b. July 16, 1941, Sandefjord, Nor.) Norwegian novelist, short-story writer, and dramatist, one of the most significant Norwegian writers to emerge during the 1960s.

Solstad began his career as a writer of short experimental works that investigated the themes of identity and alienation: *Spiraler* (1965; "Spirals") and *Svingstol* (1967; "Swing Chair"). His novel *Irr! Grønt!* (1969; "Patina! Green!") described the efforts of a peasant student to escape his limited background. Solstad's fiction took a more directly political turn with the novel *Arild Asnes, 1970* (1971), which traced the development of a young man to the point at which he perceived that political revolution was necessary and must be brought about by conflict. In *25 September Plassen* (1974; "September 25th Square") he showed the growing political awareness on the part of factory workers in the period following World War II. *Svik. Førkrigsår* (1977; "Betrayal: Prewar Years"), *Krig. 1940* (1978; "War: 1940"), and *Brod og våpen* (1980; "Bread and Weapons") were a series of novels that gave a minutely documented account of Norway in World War II.

Solzhenitsyn \səl-zhə-'nʸēt-sən, *Angl* ˌsōl-zhə-'nēt-sin, ˌsȯl-, -'nit-\, Aleksandr (Isayevich) (b. Dec. 11, 1918, Kislovodsk, Russia)   Russian novelist and historian who was awarded the 1970 Nobel Prize for Literature and was exiled from the Soviet Union in 1974.

Gilbert Uzan—Gamma Liaison

Solzhenitsyn attended the University of Rostov-na-Donu, graduating in mathematics, and took correspondence courses in literature at Moscow State University. He fought in World War II, achieving the rank of captain of artillery. In 1945, however, he was arrested for writing a letter in which he criticized Joseph Stalin, and he spent eight years in prisons and labor camps and three more years in enforced exile. Rehabilitated in 1956, he was allowed to settle in Ryazan, in central Russia, where he taught and began to write fiction.

He became an instant celebrity in 1962 with the publication of his short novel *Odin den Ivana Denisovicha* (ONE DAY IN THE LIFE OF IVAN DENISOVICH). His period of official favor proved to be short-lived, however, for he emerged as an eloquent opponent of repressive government policies. After the publication of a collection of his short stories in 1963, Solzhenitsyn was denied further official publication of his works, and he resorted to circulating them clandestinely as well as publishing them abroad.

The foreign publication of several ambitious novels—including *V kruge pervom* (1968; THE FIRST CIRCLE), *Rakovy korpus* (1968; CANCER WARD), and *Avgust 1914* (1971; AUGUST 1914)—secured Solzhenitsyn's international literary reputation. In 1970 he was awarded the Nobel Prize for Literature, but he declined to go to Stockholm to receive the prize for fear that he would not be readmitted to the Soviet Union upon his return. When the first parts of *Arkhipelag GULag* (THE GULAG ARCHIPELAGO) were published in Paris in December 1973, Solzhenitsyn was attacked in the Soviet press and arrested; he was charged with treason two months later. He was exiled from the Soviet Union in February 1974.

Solzhenitsyn settled in Cavendish, Vt., U.S., where he continued to write, concentrating on a series of books collectively called *Krasnoye koleso* (*The Red Wheel*), an epic history of the events that led to the Russian Revolution of 1917. In 1983 a greatly expanded and revised version of *August 1914* appeared in Russian as a part of that series. Other volumes (or *uzly* ["knots"]) in the series were *Oktyabr '16* (1984; "October 1916"), *Mart '17* (1986; "March 1917") and *Aprel '17* (1991; "April 1917").

In the late 1980s Solzhenitsyn's work received renewed attention in the Soviet Union, and in 1989 the Soviet literary magazine *Novy Mir* published the first officially approved excerpts from *The GULag Archipelago*. Other works were also published, and Solzhenitsyn's Soviet citizenship was officially restored in 1990. In 1994 he moved back to Russia.

Somadeva \'sō-mə-ˌdā-və\ (fl. 1070)   Kashmiri Brahman of the Śaiva (Shaiva) sect (cult of Shiva or Śiva worship) and Sanskrit writer who preserved much of India's ancient folklore in the form of a series of tales in verse.

The court poet to King Ananta of Kashmir, Somadeva apparently was commissioned to compose a cycle of stories to amuse and calm the queen, Sūryamati, during a political crisis. He borrowed from an earlier work, now lost, the *Bṛhat-katha* ("Great Tale") by the Sanskrit writer Guṇāḍhya, who probably had used Buddhist sources of an even earlier period. Somadeva's work *Kathā-saritsāgara* ("Ocean of Rivers of Stories") bears a strong resemblance to medieval European fairy tales: magic, demons, bloody orgies, vampires, love, and high adventure abound in the 124 sections, or chapters, known as *taranga* ("waves"). An English translation by Charles H. Tawney, titled *The Ocean of Story*, was published in 1924–28. Somadeva wrote his monumental work during the two periods of Ananta's interrupted rule, which ended in 1077.

Some Prefer Nettles   Autobiographical novel by TANIZAKI Jun'ichirō, published in Japanese in 1928–29 as *Tade kuu mushi*. It originally appeared as a newspaper serial and is generally considered one of the author's finest works.

Anticipating a common theme of post-World War II Japanese novels, *Some Prefer Nettles* examines the conflict between traditional and modern (*i.e.*, Westernized) culture in Japan. The protagonist, Kaname, considers himself to be a modern man in a modern marriage. The novel's other characters, including his wife, mistress, and father-in-law, and even the cities in which they live, each symbolize either modernity or ancient ways of life. In time Kaname, by degrees, resumes traditional attitudes and tastes. Eventually he makes love to his father-in-law's old-fashioned mistress and abandons the modern world entirely. Tanizaki's characteristic irony and eroticism are notable elements of the novel.

Somerville or **Somervile** \'səm-ər-ˌvil\, William (b. Sept. 2, 1675, Colwich, Staffordshire, Eng.—d. July 17, 1742, Henley-in-Arden, Warwickshire)   British writer who, after studies directed toward a career at law, lived the life of a country gentleman, indulging in the field sports that were to make up the subject matter of his best-known poems, especially *The Chace* (1735). That poem traces the history of hunting up to the time of the Norman Conquest of England (1066) and gives incidental information on kennel design, hare hunting, stag hunting, otter hunting, the breeding and training of dogs, and dog diseases and bites. Among the many digressions is one on Oriental hunting.

Somerville and Ross \'səm-ər-ˌvil . . . 'ròs\, *also called* E.Œ. Somerville and Martin Ross, *pseudonyms of* Edith Anna Oenone Somerville and Violet Florence Martin \'märt-ən\ (respectively b. May 2, 1858, Corfu, Greece—d. Oct. 8, 1949, Castlehaven, County Cork, Ire.; b. June 11, 1862, Ross House, County Galway, Ire.—d. Dec. 21, 1915, Cork, County Cork)

Irish cousins and writers who collaborated on a series of novels and short stories that wittily and sympathetically portrayed Irish society in the late 19th century. Edith Somerville continued to use their joint pseudonym after her cousin's death, claiming that she was still inspired by her.

The 27-year-old Somerville and the 23-year-old Martin first met on Jan. 17, 1886, and they began a literary partnership that resulted three years later in their first book, *An Irish Cousin* (1889). By the time Martin died in 1915 they had co-written 14 books, including a powerful novel called *The Real Charlotte* (1894) and a collection of short stories, *Some Experiences of an Irish R.M.* (1899); the latter, with its sequels, is their most popular work. After 1915 the Somerville and Ross name appeared on such Somerville works as *Irish Memories* (1917), *Mount Music* (1919), and *The Big House of Inver* (1925).

During their life together, the cousins resided at Ross House and Drishane House but traveled frequently, abroad and at home. Both were excellent riders to hounds, but Martin suffered a serious hunting accident in 1898, from which she never fully recovered. In later years Somerville often traveled, visiting Denmark and France and joining her friend the English composer, author, and feminist Dame Ethel Mary Smyth in trips to Italy and the United States.

Sommo \ˈsȯm-mō\, Judah Leone ben Isaac, *also called* Leone de Sommi Portaleone \ˌpȯr-tä-lä-ˈō-nä\, *original name* Yehuda Sommo (b. 1527, Mantua [Italy]—d. 1592, Mantua) Italian author whose writings are a primary source of information about 16th-century theatrical production in Italy.

Sommo wrote the first known Hebrew drama, *Tzaḥut bediḥuta de-qiddushin* (1550; "An Eloquent Comedy of a Marriage"), in which characters such as the pining lover, the comic servant, and the crafty lawyer reflect the influence of the Italian commedia dell'arte. Sommo's experience as a playwright and producer of dramas for various noble patrons was the basis for his *Dialoghi in materia di rappresentazioni sceniche* (c. 1565; *Dialogues on the Art of the Stage*), a summation of contemporary theater practice containing one of the earliest extant discussions of stage lighting.

Song *also called* Go and catch a falling star. Poem by John DONNE, written in the 1590s and published in 1633 in the first edition of *Songs and Sonnets*. Combining wry exaggeration with dark pessimism, it suggests that female virtue and honesty is rare, even impossible.

Song of Bernadette, The \ˌbər-nə-ˈdet, ˌber-\ Novel by Czech-born writer Franz WERFEL, published in 1941 in German as *Das Lied von Bernadette*. The book is based on the true story of a peasant girl of Lourdes, France, who had visions of the Virgin Mary. It was written to fulfill the vow Werfel had made in Lourdes in 1940, while trying to escape the Nazis: if he and his wife reached safety in the United States, he would write the story of Bernadette of Lourdes, who was canonized in 1933.

In the novel, Bernadette's visions begin in 1858, when a beautiful lady claiming to be the Virgin Mary appears to her at a grotto. News of the apparition and Bernadette's subsequent visitations invoke disbelief by the townspeople, harassment by civil officials, and skepticism by the clergy. After the Virgin causes roses to bloom in winter and reveals to Bernadette a previously unknown spring of water, both church and government accept the truth of Bernadette's revelations.

Song of Myself Poem of 52 sections and some 1,300 lines by Walt Whitman, first published untitled in the collection LEAVES OF GRASS in 1855. The expansive, exuberant poem was given its current title in 1881. Considered Whitman's most important work, and certainly his best-known, the poem revo-

lutionized American verse. It departed from traditional rhyme, meter, and form and introduced frank sexual imagery. Among its characteristic elements are repetition, exclamation, and an incantatory voice. Many sections, compelling in their unrelenting rhythm, are catalogs of individuals, locations, and actions that move the poet.

Song of Solomon \ˈsäl-ə-mən\, *also called* Canticle of Canticles *or* Song of Songs. An Old Testament book that belongs to the third section of the biblical canon, known as the Ketuvim, or "Writings." This book is the festal scroll read on Pesaḥ (Passover), which celebrates the Exodus of the Israelites from Egypt. The book in its present form postdates the Babylonian Exile (5th century BC onward), but the poems it preserves date from about the 10th century BC, the period of the Davidic monarchy.

The book, whose author is unknown (Solomon's name is a later addition), is a collection of love poems spoken alternately by a man and a woman. A number of the poems systematically describe the beauty and excellence of the beloved. The Song of Solomon has received various interpretations, the most common being allegorical, dramatic, cultic, or literal. Among Jews, the allegorical interpretation regards the book as a representation of God's love for the Israelites, with whom he has made a sacred covenant. Among Christians, the book is interpreted as describing the covenantal love of Christ for his church. In medieval mysticism, the Song of Solomon was construed to apply to the love between Christ and the human soul.

The fourth interpretation, and the one that has perhaps gained the most credence among modern scholars, is simply that the Song of Solomon is a collection of secular love poems without any religious implications. According to this interpretation, the songs celebrate the joy and goodness of human love between the sexes and the sense of inner fulfillment and harmony with creation that arises from such love.

Song of the Lark Novel by Willa CATHER, published in 1915. The heroine, Thea Kronborg, overcomes many hardships to become a leading Wagnerian soprano at the Metropolitan Opera. The *Song of the Lark* is one of several works in which Cather displayed her lyrical powers and in which she presented a protagonist who, by virtue of talent and determination, is able to rise above small-town provincialism.

Song of the Open Road Poem by Walt Whitman, first published in the second edition of LEAVES OF GRASS in 1856. The 15-stanza poem is an optimistic paean to wanderlust.

Whitman exalts the carefree pleasures of traveling, encouraging others to break free from their stifling domestic attachments to join him. Inspired by the expansive American landscape, he exhorts the reader to become his fellow traveler. Written in free verse, the poem is noted for its use of apostrophe, repetition, and exclamation.

Songs of Innocence and of Experience Masterpieces of English lyric poetry, written and illustrated by William BLAKE.

Songs of Innocence, published in 1789, was Blake's first great demonstration of "illuminated printing," his unique technique of publishing both text and hand-colored illustration together. The rhythmic subtlety and delicate beauty of both his lyrics and his designs created rare harmony on his pages. The poems transformed his era's street ballads and rhymes for children into some of the purest lyrics in the English language.

In 1794 Blake published *Songs of Innocence and of Experience: Shewing the Two Contrary States of the Human Soul*. It contained a slightly rearranged version of *Songs of Innocence* with the addition of *Songs of Experience*. The poems reflect Blake's views that experience brings the individual into conflict with rules, moralism, and repression; as a result, the songs of experience are bitter, ironic replies to those of the earlier volume. The Lamb is the key symbol of *Innocence*; in *Experience* its rival image is the Tyger, the embodiment of energy, strength, lust, and aggression. *See also* THE TYGER.

sonnet \'sän-ət\ [Italian *sonetto,* from Old Provençal *sonet* song, air, a derivative of *son* tune, sound] A fixed verse form of Italian origin consisting of 14 lines that are typically five-foot iambics rhyming according to a prescribed scheme; also, a poem in this pattern. *Compare* CURTAL SONNET; PETRARCHAN SONNET; SHAKESPEAREAN SONNET; SPENSERIAN SONNET; TAILED SONNET.

The sonnet is unique among poetic forms in Western literature in that it has retained its appeal for major poets for five centuries. The form seems to have originated in the 13th century among the Sicilian school of court poets. From there it spread to Tuscany, where it reached its highest expression in the 14th century in the poems of Petrarch. His *Canzoniere,* a sequence of poems that includes 317 sonnets, established the Petrarchan (or Italian) sonnet, which remains one of the two principal sonnet forms, as well as the one most widely used. The other major form is the Shakespearean (or English) sonnet.

The Petrarchan sonnet characteristically treats its theme in two parts. The first eight lines, the octave, state a problem, ask a question, or express an emotional tension. The last six lines, the sestet, resolve the problem, answer the question, or relieve the tension. The octave is rhymed *abbaabba*. The rhyme scheme of the sestet varies; it may be *cdecde, cdccdc,* or *cdedce*.

The sonnet was introduced to England, along with other Italian verse forms, by Sir Thomas Wyatt and Henry Howard, Earl of Surrey, in the 16th century. The new forms precipitated the great flowering of Elizabethan lyric poetry, and the period marks the peak of the sonnet's English popularity. In the course of adapting the Italian form to English, the Elizabethans gradually arrived at the distinctive English sonnet, composed of three quatrains, each having an independent rhyme scheme, and is ended with a rhymed couplet.

The Elizabethan sonnet typically appeared in a sequence of love poems in the manner of Petrarch. Although each sonnet was an independent poem, the sequence had the added interest of a narrative development. Among the notable Elizabethan sequences are Sir Philip Sidney's *Astrophel and Stella* (1591), Samuel Daniel's *Delia* (1592), Michael Drayton's *Ideas Mirrour* (1594), and Edmund Spenser's *Amoretti* (1595).

By the time John Donne wrote his religious sonnets (*c.* 1610) and John Milton wrote sonnets on political and religious subjects or on personal themes such as his blindness (*i.e.,* "When I consider how my light is spent"), the sonnet had been extended to embrace nearly all the subjects of poetry.

In the later 19th century the love sonnet sequence was revived by Elizabeth Barrett Browning in *Sonnets from the Portuguese* (1850) and by Dante Gabriel Rossetti in "The House of Life" (1870 and 1881). The most distinguished 20th-century work of the kind is Rainer Maria Rilke's *Sonette an Orpheus* (1923; *Sonnets to Orpheus*).

Use of the word *sonnet* to mean any short, usually lyric and amatory poem or piece of verse is now rare or obsolete.

sonnet sequence A series of sonnets often having a unifying theme.

Sonnets from the Portuguese Collection of love sonnets by Elizabeth Barrett BROWNING, published in 1850. The poet's reputation rests largely upon these sonnets, which constitute one of the best-known series of English love poems.

Elizabeth Barrett Browning presented this volume of 44 sonnets to her husband Robert Browning in 1847, a year after they eloped to Italy. The poems record the early days of their courtship, when the invalid author was reluctant to marry, her yielding to his love despite her father's objections, and their final happiness together. The 43rd sonnet contains the famous line "How do I love thee? Let me count the ways." The volume's title played on her husband's nickname for her, "the Portuguese," based on an earlier work of hers that he admired ("Catarina to Camoens") and that portrayed a Portuguese woman's love for a poet.

Sonnets to Orpheus \'òr-,fyüs, -fē-əs\ Series of 55 poems in two linked cycles by Rainer Maria RILKE, published in German in 1923 as *Die Sonette an Orpheus*. The *Sonnets to Orpheus* brought Rilke international fame.

The *Sonnets to Orpheus* are concerned with the relationship of art and poetry to life. In them Rilke sought to show poetry's power to transmute problems of existence and to justify reality. Some of the sonnets deal with aspects of the life and art of Orpheus, the legendary musician of ancient Greece.

Sons and Lovers Semiautobiographical novel by D.H. LAWRENCE, published in 1913. His first mature novel, it is a psychological study of the familial and love relationships of a working-class English family.

The novel revolves around Paul Morel, a sensitive young artist whose love for his mother, Gertrude, overshadows his romances with two women: Miriam Leivers, his repressed, religious girlfriend, and Clara Dawes, an experienced, independent married woman. Unable to watch his mother die slowly of cancer, Paul kills her with morphine. Despite losing her and rejecting both Miriam and Clara, Paul harbors hope for the future.

Sons of Ben *see* TRIBE OF BEN.

Sontag \'sän-,tag\, Susan (b. Jan. 16, 1933, New York, N.Y., U.S.) American intellectual and writer best known for her essays on modern culture.

Sontag attended the University of California at Berkeley and the University of Chicago, from which she graduated in 1951. She studied English literature and philosophy at Harvard University, teaching philosophy at several colleges and universities before the publication of her first novel, *The Benefactor* (1963). During the early 1960s she also wrote a number of essays and reviews, most of which were published in such periodicals as *The New York Review of Books, Commentary,* and *Partisan Review*. Some of these short pieces were collected in *Against Interpretation and Other Essays* (1968). Her second novel, *Death Kit* (1967), was followed by another collection of essays, *Styles of Radical Will* (1969). Her later critical works include *On Photography* (1977), *Illness as Metaphor* (1977), *Under the Sign of Saturn* (1980), and *AIDS and Its Metaphors* (1988). In 1992 her historical romance *The Volcano Lover* was published.

Sontag's essays are characterized by a serious philosophical approach to various aspects and personalities of modern culture. She first came to national attention in 1964 with an essay entitled "Notes on 'Camp'." In addition to criticism and fiction, she wrote screenplays and edited selected writings of Roland Barthes and Antonin Artaud.

sooterkin \'sůt-ər-kin, 'süt-\ Something that is imperfect or unsuccessful; in this sense the term is used especially to indicate an imperfect literary composition.

Sophie's Choice \'sō-fē\ Novel by William STYRON, published in 1979, that examines the historical, moral, and psychological ramifications of the Holocaust through the tragic life of a Roman Catholic survivor of Auschwitz.

Set in the late 1940s, the novel is narrated by Stingo, a young Southern writer who is the author's thinly veiled alter ego. In a boardinghouse in Brooklyn, N.Y., Stingo becomes friends with a pair of tormented lovers: Nathan Landau, a brilliant but unstable Jew, and Sophie Zawistowska, a beautiful and guilt-ridden Polish refugee. On a journey to the South, accompanied by Sophie, Stingo learns that while at Auschwitz, Sophie was forced to choose which of her two children would survive and which would die. Sophie leaves unexpectedly and Stingo trails her to the boardinghouse, where he discovers that Nathan and Sophie have committed suicide.

Sophocles \\'säf-ə-,klēz\\ (b. *c.* 496 BC, Colonus, near Athens [Greece]—d. 406, Athens) With Aeschylus and Euripides, one of classical Athens' three great tragic playwrights. The best

Roman copy of a Greek original, *c.* 340 BC
Vatican Library

known of his many dramas is *Oedipus the King (Oedipus Rex)*.

It is not known when Sophocles first competed in dramatic festivals; he gained his first victory in 468 BC, defeating Aeschylus. This began a career of unparalleled success and productivity. He wrote 123 dramas for the major dramatic competition, won perhaps as many as 24 victories, and never received less than second place at the competitions he entered.

Sophocles also distinguished himself in the public life of Athens. In 442 he was one of the treasurers responsible for receiving and managing the tribute from Athens' subject-allies in the Delian League. In 440 he was elected one of 10 strategoi (military and naval commanders); his senior colleague was Pericles. In 413, then aged about 83, Sophocles was one of 10 advisory commissioners who were entrusted with organizing Athens' financial and domestic recovery after its defeat at Syracuse. All the ancient biographical sources depict Sophocles as a gracious and well-loved public figure who participated actively in his community and exercised outstanding artistic talents. Outliving Euripides by a few months, he died just before the end of the Peloponnesian War.

Only seven of Sophocles' tragedies—AJAX, ANTIGONE, TRACHINIAN WOMEN, OEDIPUS THE KING, ELECTRA, PHILOCTETES, and *Oedipus at Colonus*—survive in their entirety, along with a fragment of TRACKERS, a satyr play, numerous fragments of other plays now lost, and 90 titles. All seven of the complete plays are works of his maturity, but only two of them, *Philoctetes* and *Oedipus at Colonus*, have fairly certain dates. Sophocles is credited with several dramatic innovations. They include an increase in the number of members in the chorus and the addition of a third actor onstage. He also is noted for his supple language and superb artistry. His plays portray the collision of defective personal judgment with an unkind fate that leads to human loss and disaster. The formal perfection and vivid characterizations in his plays make them the epitome of classical Greek drama.

Sophron \\'sō-,frän\\ of Syracuse \\'sir-ə-,kyūs\\ (fl. *c.* 430 BC) Author of rhythmic prose mimes in the Doric dialect. Although his mimes survive mostly in fragments of only a few words, it can be seen from their titles—*e.g., The Tunny-fisher, The Semp-*

stress—that they depicted scenes from daily life. One longer fragment deals with a magical ceremony. Plato thought highly of Sophron, who influenced both Theocritus and Herodas.

Sordello \\sȯr-'del-lō\\ (b. *c.* 1200, Gioto, near Mantua [Italy]—d. before 1269) Most renowned Provençal troubadour of Italian birth, whose *planh*, or lament, on the death of his patron Blacatz (Blacas), in which he invites all Christian princes to feed on the heart of the hero so that they might absorb his virtues, is one of the masterpieces of Provençal poetry.

Sordello became famous when, in 1224, at the court of Richard of Bonifacio at Verona, he abducted his master's wife at the instigation of her brother. He traveled as a troubadour throughout Spain and southern France and settled at the court of Raymond Berengar IV of Provence about 1237. He later became a companion of Charles of Anjou, with whom he returned to Italy in 1265.

Sordello wrote 1,325 lines of a didactic poem and 42 lyrical pieces, mostly love songs and satires. Representing the epitome of patriotic pride in Dante's *Purgatorio*, he is also the subject of a poem by Robert Browning.

Sordello \\sȯr-'del-ō\\ Poem by Robert BROWNING, published in 1840. The much-revised work is densely written, with multilayered meanings and many literary and historical allusions. On publication, the work was considered obscure and was a critical failure.

Sordello is a study in the psychology of genius and the development of a soul. A highborn poet and troubadour, Sordello lives in Italy in the early 13th century. He is torn between the demands of his poetic imagination and involvement in the power and glory of politics, but he dies before he can reconcile the practical and the sublime.

Sorel, Julien \\zhūēl-'yaⁿ-sȯ-'rel\\ Fictional character, the ambitious young protagonist of Stendhal's novel *Le Rouge et le noir* (THE RED AND THE BLACK).

Sørensen \\'sœ-ren-sən\\, Villy (b. Jan. 13, 1929, Copenhagen, Den.) Influential writer of modernist short stories and also a leading literary critic in Denmark after World War II.

Sørensen's first collection of short stories, *Sære historier* (1953; U.K. title, *Strange Stories*; U.S. title, *Tiger in the Kitchen and Other Strange Stories*), was followed two years later by *Ufarlige historier* (*Harmless Tales*) and in 1964 by the important collection *Formynderfortællinger* (*Tutelary Tales*). His short stories were experimental and often drew their material from the Bible, legends, ballads, and world history in general. Sørensen often treated the themes of the divided self and the loneliness of the individual in society. In 1982 his *Ragnarok* (*The Downfall of the Gods*) was published.

His stories and books exemplify in artistic form the theories of his philosophical writings, *Digtere og daemoner* (1959; "Poets and Demons"), *Hverken-eller* (1961; "Neither-Nor"), and *Jesus og Kristus* (1992; "Jesus and Christ"). Sørensen was strongly influenced in his thinking by German existentialism, in particular the writings of Martin Heidegger. Sørensen served as an editor of *Vindrosen* (1959–63).

Soromenho \\sō-rō-'meⁿn-yū\\, Fernando Monteiro de Castro (b. Jan. 31, 1910, Chinde, Mozambique—d. June 18, 1968, São Paulo, Braz.) White Angolan novelist writing in Portuguese who depicted African life in the interior of the country and condemned the Portuguese colonial administration there. He is known as the "father of the Angolan novel."

Soromenho's first job, as a recruiter of African contract labor for a mining company in northeastern Angola, gave him a chance to know and respect traditional African life. He then became a journalist, first in Luanda and later in Lisbon, where in 1937 he edited the weekly *Humanidade*. In 1943 he started his own publishing house, Sociedade de Intercâmbio Luso-Brasileiro.

Soromenho published five novels, four volumes of stories, and several sociological studies and travel books. *Nhárí: o drama da gente negra* (1938; "Nhari: The Drama of Black People"), his first work, contains stories dealing with traditional African societies. It is in later works, however, such as the novel *Terra morta* (1949; "Dead Land"), that he concentrated on the effects of colonialism in Luanda province. Published in Brazil, *Terra morta* was banned by Portuguese authorities. The government subsequently prevented the distribution of his other books. In 1960, to escape arrest in Portugal, he fled abroad and lived in France, the United States, and Brazil.

Soromenho's other novels include *Noite de angústia* (1939; "Night of Anguish"), *Homens sem caminho* (1941; "Men Without Direction"), *A viragem* (1957; "Turnabout"), and *A chaga* (1970; "The Wound").

Sorrel, Hetty \'het-ē-'sȯr-əl\ Fictional character, a naive dairy maid who is seduced and abandoned by Captain Arthur Donnithorne in the novel ADAM BEDE by George Eliot.

Sorrentino \ˌsȯr-en-'tē-nō\, Gilbert (b. April 27, 1929, Brooklyn, N.Y., U.S.) American poet and experimental novelist whose use of devices such as nonchronological structure illustrated his dictum that "form not only determines content but form *invents* content."

From 1956 to 1960 Sorrentino was editor and publisher of *Neon*, a magazine that featured works by Beat writers; he was also book editor (1961–65) for *Kulchur*. His poetry collections include *The Darkness Surrounds Us* (1960), *The Perfect Fiction* (1968), and *The Orangery* (1978).

Among his avant-garde novels are *The Sky Changes* (1966), each chapter of which is named for a town the protagonists visit; *Imaginative Qualities of Actual Things* (1971), a plotless, digressive satire of the New York art scene of the 1960s; *Splendide-Hôtel* (1973), a novelistic defense of poetry arranged in 26 alphabetical sections; *Mulligan Stew* (1979), considered by some critics to be the apotheosis of avant-garde fiction, a multilevel mélange of Joycean proportions that satirizes creativity; *Odd Number* (1985), which deals with unanswered questions; *Rose Theatre* (1987), each chapter of which is written in a different narrative style; *Misterioso* (1989), an exhaustive, alphabetical catalog of everything discussed in *Odd Number* and *Rose Theatre*; and *Under the Shadow* (1991), a series of 59 vignettes with recurring characters and images.

Sorrows of Young Werther, The \'ver-tər\ Novel by J.W. von GOETHE, published in German as *Die Leiden des jungen Werthers* in 1774. It was the first novel of the Sturm und Drang movement.

The novel is the story of a sensitive, artistic young man who demonstrates the fatal effects of a predilection for absolutes—whether those of love, art, society, or thought. Unable to reconcile his inner, poetic fantasies and ideas with the demands of the everyday world, Werther goes to the country in an attempt to restore his well-being. There, he falls in love with Charlotte (Lotte), the uncomplicated fiancée of a friend. Torn by unrequited passion and his perception of the emptiness of life, he commits suicide.

An exceptionally popular book, *The Sorrows of Young Werther* gave expression to what Thomas Carlyle called "the nameless unrest and longing discontent which was then agitating every bosom." The mind that conceived its symmetry, wove its intricate linguistic patterns, and handled the subtle differentiation of hero and narrator was moved by a formal as well as a personal passion. The translated title (which uses "Sorrows" instead of "Sufferings") obscures the allusion to the Passion of Christ and individualizes what Goethe himself thought of as a "general confession," in a tradition going back to St. Augustine.

sotadean verse \ˌsōt-ə-'dē-ən, ˌsät-\ A truncated four-measure line (catalectic tetrameter) of major ionics (two long and two short syllables) having the normal form $-\;-\;\cup\;\cup\;|\;-\;-\;\cup\;\cup\;|\;-\;-\;\cup\;\cup\;|\;-\;\underset{\smile}{}$. The meter was allegedly invented by Sotades, a Greek satirist of the 3rd century BC, and it was associated primarily with scurrilous or salacious verse.

sotie or **sottie** \sȯ-'tē\ [French *sotie, sottie,* from Middle French *sottie,* a derivative of *sot* fool] Short topical and farcical play popular in France in the 15th and early 16th centuries, in which a company of *sots* ("fools") exchanged badinage on contemporary persons and events. The *sots,* wearing the traditional short jacket, tights, bells, and dunce cap of the fool, also introduced acrobatics and farcical humor into the sketches. At first used as introductory pieces to mystery and morality plays, soties developed into an independent form. Pierre Gringore became the preeminent sotie dramatist. The sotie was proscribed in the 16th century and replaced by more general forms of satire.

Sot-Weed Factor, The \'sät-ˌwēd\ Picaresque novel by John BARTH, originally published in 1960 and revised in 1967. A parody of the historical novel, it is based on and takes its title from a satirical poem published in 1708 by Ebenezer Cooke, who is the protagonist of Barth's work. The novel's black humor is derived from its purposeful misuse of conventional literary devices.

soubrette \sü-'bret\ [French, lady's maid, from Provençal *soubreto,* feminine of *soubret* affected, coy] In theater, a comic female character usually in the role of a chambermaid. The soubrette first appears in French comedy, one of the earliest examples being Suzanne in Pierre-Augustin de Beaumarchais' *Le Mariage de Figaro* (1784). Still earlier, Molière's plays *Le Tartuffe* (1664) and *Le Bourgeois Gentilhomme* (1670) contained versions of the character in the roles of Dorine and Nicole.

Most often of an independent nature, the soubrette demonstrates a nonconformist attitude coupled with a down-to-earth approach and native humor. Quick-witted and subtle, as in the character Lisette in Pierre Marivaux's *Le Jeu de l'amour et du hasard* (1730; *The Game of Love and Chance*), the soubrette became fixed as a type in the early 18th century.

Sound and the Fury, The The first major novel by William FAULKNER, published in 1929.

The novel is set in Faulkner's fictional Yoknapatawpha County, Miss., in the early 20th century. It describes the decay and fall of the aristocratic Compson family, and, implicitly, of an entire social order, from four different points of view. The first three sections are presented from the perspectives of the three Compson sons: Benjy, an "idiot"; Quentin, a suicidal Harvard freshman; and Jason, the eldest. Each section is focused primarily on a sister who has married and left home. The fourth section comments on the other three as the Compsons' black servants, whose chief virtue is their endurance, reveal the family's moral decline. With *The Sound and the Fury*, Faulkner for the first time incorporated several challenging and sophisticated stylistic techniques, including interior monologues and stream-of-consciousness narrative.

Soupault \sü-'pō\, Philippe (b. Aug. 2, 1897, Chaville, Fr.—d. March 12, 1990, Paris) French poet, novelist, and critic who was instrumental in founding the Surrealist movement.

Soupault's earliest verse collection, *Aquarium* (1917), was published with the help of Guillaume Apollinaire. In 1919 Soupault, André Breton, and Louis Aragon cofounded the review *Littérature*. Originally drawn to the antirationalism of the Dada movement, Soupault soon rejected its nihilism, and he and Breton experimented with other revolutionary techniques. One result was the "automatic writing" of the jointly authored *Les Champs magnétiques* (1920; *The Magnetic Fields*), known as the first major Surrealist work. Soupault soon abandoned automatic writing to produce carefully crafted verses such as those in *Westwego* (1922) and *Georgia* (1926). As the Surrealist movement became increasingly dogmatic and political, Soupault grew dissatisfied with it and eventually broke with it and with Breton.

After the mid-1920s Soupault devoted himself primarily to writing novels and essays and to journalism. His novels—which include *Les Frères Durandeau* (1924; "The Durandeau Brothers"), *Le Nègre* (1927; "The Negro"), *Les Dernières Nuits de Paris* (1928; *Last Nights of Paris*), and *Les Moribonds* (1934; "The Dying")—examine the concepts of freedom and revolt. He wrote two memoirs, *Le Temps des assassins* (1945; *Age of Assassins*) and *Mémoires de l'oubli* (1981; "Memoirs of Oblivion"). He also wrote a number of biographies, plays, and critical essays. He was awarded the Grand Prix de Poésie of the Académie Française in 1972.

Sousa \'sō-zə\, Luís de, *original name* Mandel de Sousa Coutinho \kō-'tēⁿn-yū\ (b. 1555, Santarém, Port.—d. May 5, 1632, Benfica, near Lisbon)   Monastic historian whose prose style in his chronicle of the Dominican order earned him an important position in the history of Portuguese literature.

Sousa may have studied law at the University of Coimbra. About 1576 he became a novice in the Knights of Malta but did not continue his religious affiliation at that time. Between 1584 and 1586 he married Madalena de Vilhena, widow of a Portuguese military hero. In 1613, however, Sousa and Madalena decided to take religious vows and thereby separate for the rest of their lives. Sousa entered the Dominican monastery at Benfica, changing his name to Frei (Friar) Luís de Sousa and taking vows in 1614.

Sousa soon took over the order's chronicle begun by Friar Luís Cácegas, the *História de São Domingos*, 3 vol. (1623, 1662, 1678). Its publication brought him immediate recognition as a master stylist of Portuguese prose. In addition, he completed the *Vida do Arcebispo D. Frei Bartolomeu dos Mártires* (1619; "Life of Archbishop D[ominican] Friar Bartolomeu dos Mártires"), a biography of a 16th-century friar who became archbishop of the see of Braga, Port. The biography is considered a literary masterpiece, as well as a valuable historical record.

Nevertheless, Sousa might have remained known only to scholars had his own life not been dramatized and popularized by the 19th-century Portuguese writer João Baptista de Almeida Garrett. Garrett's romantic play *Frei Luís de Sousa* (1843), emphasizing the personal struggles of the man, made Sousa a legendary and heroic figure in Portuguese history.

Soutar \'sūt-ər\, William (b. April 28, 1898, Perth, Perthshire, Scot.—d. Oct. 15, 1943, Perth)   Scottish poet of the Scottish literary renaissance.

Soutar contracted osteoarthritis while serving in the navy, and from October 1923 he was a semi-invalid. After the failure of an operation in 1930 he was bedridden. He was saved from despair by his delight in the variety of nature and his devotion to the craft of letters. His "bairn-rhymes" in Scots, *Seeds in the Wind* (1933), are beast fables that express a mature insight into the life of things viewed with the "innocent eye" of childhood. In *Poems in Scots* (1935) he developed the bal-

lad style toward the objective expression of individual lyricism. During his last 10 years his principal output in Scots consisted of "whigmaleeries," humorous poems full of comic exaggeration, interweaving the fantastic and the familiar. He was fond of miniatures, publishing *Riddles in Scots* (1937), while as a poet in English he was at his best in the pointed epigrams of *Brief Words* (1935) and the short nature lyrics of *The Expectant Silence* (1944).

Southampton \saûth-'hamp-tən, saû-'thamp-\, Henry Wriothesley, 3rd Earl of, Baron Wriothesley \'rī-əth-slē, 'rōts-lē, 'rōt-is-lē, 'rith-lē, 'riz-lē\ of Titchfield \'tich-,fēld\ (b. Oct. 6, 1573, Cowdray, Sussex, Eng.—d. Nov. 10, 1624, Bergen op Zoom, Neth.)   English nobleman and William Shakespeare's patron.

Wriothesley succeeded to his father's earldom in 1581. Educated at the University of Cambridge and at Gray's Inn, London, he was 17 when he was presented at court, where he was favored by Queen Elizabeth I and befriended by Robert Devereux, 2nd Earl of Essex. He henceforth was active in the politics and intrigues of the court. Southampton became a munificent patron of writers, including Barnabe Barnes and Thomas Nashe. He is best known, however, as the patron of Shakespeare, who dedicated *Venus and Adonis* (1593) and *The Rape of Lucrece* (1594) to him.

Southern \'səth-ərn\, Terry (b. May 1, 1924, Alvarado, Texas, U.S.)   American writer of satirical novels and screenplays.

Southern was educated at Southern Methodist University, the University of Chicago, Northwestern University, and the Sorbonne. His first novel, *Flash and Filigree* (1958), satirizes the institutions of medicine and law. *Candy* (1958), written with Mason Hoffenberg under the pseudonym Maxwell Kenton, tells the tale of a libidinous young woman in a parody of pornography. His other novels include *The Magic Christian* (1959), *Blue Movie* (1970), and *Texas Summer* (1991). His *Red-Dirt Marijuana, and Other Tastes* (1967) is a collection of short stories and essays.

Southern also collaborated on screenplays for several popular movies of the 1960s.

Southerne \'səth-ərn\, Thomas (b. 1660, Oxmantown, Dublin, Ire.—d. May 26, 1746, London, Eng.)   Irish dramatist, long famous for two sentimental tragedies that were acted until well into the 19th century—*The Fatal Marriage* (performed 1694; adapted 1757 by the actor-manager David Garrick as *Isabella, or the Fatal Marriage*) and *Oroonoko* (performed 1695).

Southerne spent his life after about 1680 in London. His first play, *The Loyal Brother*, was produced at London's Drury Lane Theatre in 1682. From 1685 to 1688 he was soldiering, but he also wrote several other plays and contributed prologues and epilogues to John Dryden's plays during that period.

Both of Southerne's principal works were based on novels by Aphra Behn, a popular 17th-century novelist and poet. *The Fatal Marriage* anticipated 18th-century domestic tragedy, and *Oroonoko* showed affiliations with the earlier heroic plays of Dryden. The character of Oroonoko, an African prince enslaved in the English colony of Surinam, marked one of the first literary appearances of the "noble savage," and the play was a notably early English condemnation of the slave trade. As well as writing several other plays—lively comedies of manners and frigid tragedies in Roman settings—Southerne also revised and finished Dryden's tragedy *Cleomenes* (1692).

Southern gothic   A style of writing practiced by many writers of the American South whose stories set in that region are characterized by grotesque, macabre, or fantastic incidents. Flannery O'Connor, Tennessee Williams, Truman Capote,

William Faulkner, and Carson McCullers are among the best-known writers of Southern gothic. *See also* GOTHIC.

Southey \'saủ-<u>the</u>, 'sǝth-ē\, Robert (b. Aug. 12, 1774, Bristol, Gloucestershire, Eng.—d. March 21, 1843, Keswick, Cumberland) English poet and writer of miscellaneous prose who is chiefly remembered for his association with Samuel Taylor Coleridge and William Wordsworth.

Southey began to write while attending Westminster School in London, from which he was expelled for criticizing the practice of excessive whipping in a school magazine. His expulsion roused the rebellious side of his nature and confirmed his enthusiasm for the ideals of the French Revolution. When he entered Balliol College, Oxford, in 1792, Southey expressed his ardent sympathy for the revolution in the long poem *Joan of Arc* (1796). He first met Coleridge, who shared his views, in 1794, and together they wrote a verse drama, *The Fall of Robespierre* (1794). He later left Oxford without a degree.

In 1795 he secretly married Edith Fricker, whose sister, Sara, Southey encouraged Coleridge to marry. Late in 1795 he went to Portugal, and while there he wrote the letters published as *Letters Written During a Short Residence in Spain and Portugal* (1797), studied the literature of those two countries, and gradually became more conservative in his political views.

After 1799 Southey became a regular contributor to newspapers and reviews. He also made translations, edited the works of Thomas Chatterton, worked on his epic poem *Madoc* (1805), and completed the epic *Thalaba the Destroyer* (1801). He later was forced by circumstances to produce a vast amount of writing—poetry, criticism, history, biography, journalism, translations, and editions of earlier writers—in order to provide for his own family as well as that of Coleridge, who had left his family. In 1813 Southey was appointed poet laureate through the influence of Sir Walter Scott, and he eventually gained financial security through a government pension.

Except for a few lyrics, ballads, and comic-grotesque poems Southey's poetry is little read, but his prose style has been long regarded as masterly in its ease and clarity. These qualities are best seen in his *Life of Nelson* (1813); in the *Life of Wesley; and the Rise and Progress of Methodism* (1820); in the lively *Letters from England: By Don Manuel Alvarez Espriella* (1807), the observations of a fictitious Spaniard; and in the anonymously published seven-volume *The Doctor* (1834–47), a fantastic, rambling miscellany packed with comments, quotations, and anecdotes.

Southwell \'saủth-wǝl, -,wel\, Robert (b. 1561, Horsham St. Faith, Norfolk, Eng.—d. March 4, 1595, London) English poet and martyr remembered for his saintly life as a Jesuit priest and missionary during a time of Protestant persecution and for his religious poetry.

Southwell was educated at Jesuit colleges in France and in Rome. In 1585 he was ordained a priest. He returned to England as a missionary in 1586, when he became chaplain to Anne Howard and spiritual adviser to her husband, the 1st Earl of Arundel, a recusant imprisoned in the Tower of London. Southwell lived in concealment at Arundel House, writing letters of consolation to persecuted Roman Catholics and making pastoral journeys. His *An Epistle of Comfort* was printed secretly in 1587; other letters circulated in manuscript. Southwell was arrested in 1592 while celebrating mass. In 1595 he was tried for treason under the anti-Catholic penal laws of 1585 and was executed.

Southwell's best works achieve an unusual directness and simplicity, and his use of paradox and striking imagery is akin to that of the later Metaphysical poets. He is the foremost representative of Roman Catholic letters in Elizabethan England.

Southworth \'saủth-wǝrth\, Emma, *original name in full* Emma Dorothy Eliza Nevitte \'nev-it\, *also called* Mrs. E.D.E.N. Southworth (b. Dec. 26, 1819, Washington, D.C., U.S.—d. June 30, 1899, Georgetown, Washington, D.C.) One of the most popular of the 19th-century American sentimental novelists. For more than 50 years her domestic novels reached a wide audience in the United States and Europe.

After teaching school for five years, Nevitte married Frederick Southworth, an itinerant inventor. When the couple separated in 1844, she turned to writing to support her family. Her first novel, *Retribution* (1849), sold 200,000 copies. Southworth went on to write 66 more novels, many of them first published serially in such magazines as the *The Saturday Evening Post* and the *New York Ledger*. Her stories contributed two new character types to American fiction: the self-made man and the independent woman. Her works also relied on sentimental plots of the gothic genre that reflected prevailing values of piety and domesticity.

Southworth's *Ishmael* and *Self-Raised* (both 1876) were huge successes. Among her other successful novels were *The Curse of Clifton* (1852), *The Hidden Hand* (1859), and *The Fatal Marriage* (1863).

Soútsos \'sủt-sōs\, Aléxandros (b. 1803, Constantinople, Ottoman Empire [now Istanbul, Tur.]—d. 1863) Greek poet, one of the founders of the Greek Romantic school of poetry.

Soútsos studied in Chios (Khíos) and later in Paris, where he was influenced by the French Romantics and by liberal political opinion. His verse satires are his liveliest writings and inspired the early development of modern political liberalism in Greece. His dramas and one long prose work were considered cold and artificial, but his numerous lyrics were admired by his contemporaries in spite of their lack of originality and their rhetorical exuberance. Perhaps his most interesting work is *Panórama tis Helládos* (1833; "Panorama of Greece"). His collected works were published in 1916.

Soyinka \shô-'yeŋ-kä\, Wole, *in full* Akinwande Oluwole Soyinka (b. July 13, 1934, Abeokuta, Nigeria) Nigerian playwright, poet, novelist, and critic who received the Nobel Prize for Literature for 1986. He wrote of modern West Africa in a satirical style and with a tragic sense of the obstacles to human progress.

A member of the Yoruba people, Soyinka took a degree from the University of Leeds in England. Upon his return to Nigeria he wrote his first important play, *A Dance of the Forests* (produced 1960, published 1963), for the Nigerian independence celebrations. The play satirizes the fledgling nation by stripping it of romantic legend and by showing that the present is no more a golden age than was the past.

In plays of a lighter vein he made fun of pompous, Westernized schoolteachers, as in *The Lion and the Jewel* (1963), and he mocked the clever preachers of upstart churches who grow fat on the credulity of their parishioners, as in *The Trials of Brother Jero* (1960) and *Jero's Metamorphosis* (1972). But his more serious plays, such as *The Strong Breed* (1963), *Kongi's Harvest* (1965), *The Road* (1965), and *From Zia, with Love* (1992), reveal his disillusionment with African authoritarian leadership and with Nigerian society as a whole. Other notable plays include *Madmen and Specialists* (1971; later retitled *Madmen and Scientists*) and *Death and the King's Horseman* (1975).

From 1960 to 1964 Soyinka was coeditor of *Black Orpheus*, an important literary journal. He taught literature and drama and headed theater groups at various Nigerian universities from 1960.

Soyinka's novels are *The Interpreters* (1965), in which a group of young intellectuals function as artists in their talks with one another as they try to place themselves in the context of the world about them, and *Season of Anomy*, which appeared in 1973.

Soyinka's volumes of poetry include *Idanre and Other Poems* (1967), *Poems from Prison* (1969; republished as *A Shuttle in the Crypt*, 1972), and *Mandela's Earth and Other Poems* (1988). He wrote much of *Poems from Prison* while jailed in 1967–69 for allegedly conspiring to aid the attempted secession of Biafra from Nigeria; *The Man Died* (1972) is his prose account of his arrest and imprisonment. Soyinka's principal critical work is *Myth, Literature, and the African World* (1976), a collection of essays in which he examines the role of the artist in the light of Yoruba mythology and symbolism.

Soyinka was the first black African to be awarded the Nobel Prize for Literature. His autobiography, *Aké: The Years of Childhood*, was published in 1981 and a companion piece, *Isara: A Voyage Around Essay*, in 1989.

space opera   Futuristic melodramatic fantasy involving space travelers and extraterrestrial beings.

Spade, Sam \'sam-'spād\   Fictional character, the quintessential hard-boiled private detective, the protagonist of a novel (*The Maltese Falcon*) and several short stories by Dashiell HAMMETT. *See also* THE MALTESE FALCON.

Spanish Rogue, The   *see* GUZMÁN DE ALFARACHE.

Spark \'spärk\, Muriel (Sarah), *original surname* Camberg \'kam-bərg\ (b. Feb. 1, 1918, Edinburgh, Scot.)   British

Camera Press/Pictorial Parade

writer best known for the satire and wit with which the serious themes of her novels are presented.

Spark spent several years in Central Africa before she returned to Great Britain. She served as general secretary of the Poetry Society and editor of *The Poetry Review* (1947–49) and later published a series of critical biographies of literary figures and editions of 19th-century letters, including *Child of Light: A Reassessment of Mary Shelley* (1951; rev. ed., *Mary Shelley*, 1988), *John Masefield* (1953), and *The Brontë Letters* (1954). She converted to Roman Catholicism in 1954, and much of her work concerns questions of good and evil.

Until 1957 Spark published only criticism and poetry. With the publication of *The Comforters* (1957), however, her talent as a novelist—an ability to create disturbing, compelling characters and a disquieting sense of moral ambiguity—was immediately evident. Her third novel, MEMENTO MORI (1959), was adapted for the stage in 1964 and for television in 1992. Her best-known novel is probably THE PRIME OF MISS JEAN BRODIE (1961), which also became popular in its stage (1966) and film (1969) versions.

Some critics found Spark's earlier novels minor; some of these works, such as *The Ballad of Peckham Rye* (1960) and THE GIRLS OF SLENDER MEANS (1963), are characterized by mildly humorous fantasy. *The Mandelbaum Gate* (1965), however, marked a departure toward weightier themes, and later novels—*The Driver's Seat* (1970; film, 1974), *Not to Disturb* (1971), and *Loitering with Intent* (1981)—have a distinctly sinister tone. Her later novels include *The Abbess of Crewe* (1974),

Territorial Rights (1979), and *A Far Cry from Kensington* (1988). Spark also wrote poetry. An autobiography, *Curriculum Vitae* (1992), covers her life up to 1957.

Spasmodic school   Group of poets that included P.J. Bailey, Sydney Dobell, J.S. Bigg, and Alexander Smith, who were known for the erratic nature of their verse with its formlessness, chaotic imagery, and exaggerations of passion. The descriptive name was first applied to the group by Charles Kingsley in 1853 and was established by the Scottish poet and humorist W.E. Aytoun in his satirical light verse *Firmilian, or The Student of Badajoz: A Spasmodic Tragedy by 'T. Percy Jones'* (1854).

Speak, Memory   Autobiographical memoir of his early life and European years by Vladimir NABOKOV. Fifteen chapters were published individually (1948–50), mainly in *The New Yorker*. The book was originally published as *Conclusive Evidence: A Memoir* (1951); it was also published the same year as *Speak, Memory: A Memoir*. Nabokov translated into Russian and revised the original work as *Drugiye berega* ("Other Shores") in 1954; in 1966, he published a further revised and expanded English-language edition entitled *Speak, Memory: An Autobiography Revisited*, which contains family photographs and incorporates recollections and revisions by his sisters and cousins.

The memoir describes in the first 12 chapters Nabokov's happy childhood in an aristocratic family in St. Petersburg, Russia. The remaining three chapters cover his years as a university student at Cambridge and as an intellectual and fledgling writer in the Russian émigré communities of Berlin and Paris.

Spectator, The   Periodical published in London by the essayists Richard Steele and Joseph Addison from March 1, 1711, to Dec. 6, 1712 (appearing daily), and subsequently revived by Addison in 1714 (for 80 issues). It succeeded *The Tatler*, which Steele had launched in 1709. In its aim to "enliven morality with wit, and to temper wit with morality," *The Spectator* adopted a fictional method of presentation through a "Spectator Club," whose imaginary members expressed the authors' own ideas about society. These "members" included representatives of commerce, the army, the town (respectively, Sir Andrew Freeport, Captain Sentry, and Will Honeycomb), and the country gentry (Sir Roger de Coverley). The papers were ostensibly written by Mr. Spectator, an "observer" of the London scene.

Because of its fictional framework, *The Spectator* is sometimes said to have heralded the rise of the English novel in the 18th century. This is perhaps an overstatement, since the fictional framework, once adopted, ceased to be of primary importance and served instead as a social microcosm within which a tone at once grave, good-humored, and flexible could be sounded. The real authors of the essays were free to consider whatever topics they pleased, with reference to the fictional framework (as in Steele's account of Sir Roger's views on marriage, which appeared in issue no. 113) or without it (as in Addison's critical papers on *Paradise Lost*, John Milton's epic poem, which appeared in issues no. 267, 273, and others).

In addition to Addison and Steele themselves, contributors included Alexander Pope, Thomas Tickell, and Ambrose Philips. Addison's reputation as an essayist has surpassed that of Steele, but Steele's friendly tone was a perfect balance and support for the more dispassionate style of Addison. Their joint achievement was to make serious discussion a normal pastime of the leisured class. Together they set the pattern and established the vogue for the periodical throughout the rest of the century and helped to create a receptive public for novelists.

See also Joseph ADDISON; Richard STEELE.

speech, figure of *see* FIGURE OF SPEECH.

Spell, The Allegorical novel by Hermann BROCH, published posthumously in 1953 as *Der Versucher*. It was the only completed volume of a projected trilogy to have been called *Bergroman* ("Mountain Novel"). The author wrote it in the mid-1930s, then, dissatisfied, completely rewrote it twice more; by his death in 1951, he was halfway through a third revision. Versions of the novel have also been published as *Demeter* (1967) and *Die Verzauberung* (1976).

An allegory about the beginnings of Nazi rule in Germany, the novel tells of a case of mass hysteria brought about by a stranger's growing domination of a remote mountain village. Ratti, a demagogue, preaches antimodern attitudes, a return to "pure" living, and hatred of those who look different; he even persuades his frenzied listeners to commit ritual murder. Contrasted with Ratti is the aged, wise Mother Gisson, a Demeter figure who is in tune with the natural order.

Spelvin, George \\'jȯrj-'spel-vin\\ Name used by American theatrical convention in the credits commonly to conceal dual roles or for a corpse or anthropomorphic props. Spelvin first "appeared" on Broadway in the cast list of Charles A. Gardiner's *Karl the Peddler* in 1886. Winchell Smith employed the character in many of his plays, beginning with *Brewster's Millions* in 1906. Spelvin appeared with Maude Adams in *Joan of Arc* (1908), as a Betting Man in *High Button Shoes* (1947), and as Colonel Dent in *Jane Eyre* (1958).

When a female character is needed, the player is listed as Georgiana, or Georgette, Spelvin. Spelvin's British counterparts are Walter Plinge, Mr. F. Anney, and Mr. Bart.

Spender \\'spen-dər\\, Sir Stephen (Harold) (b. Feb. 28, 1909, London, Eng.) English poet and critic, who made his reputation in the 1930s with poems expressing the politically conscience-stricken, leftist "new writing" of that period. He was later known less for his poetry than for his perceptive criticism and for his editorial association with the influential reviews *Horizon* (1940–41) and *Encounter* (1953–67).

Spender was educated at University College School, London, and at University College, Oxford. While an undergraduate he met the poets W.H. Auden and C. Day-Lewis, and during 1930–33 he spent many months in Germany with the writer Christopher Isherwood. Among important influences shown in his early volumes—*Poems* (1933); *Vienna* (1934); *Trial of a Judge*, a verse play (1938); and *The Still Centre* (1939)—were the poetry of the German Rainer Maria Rilke and of the Spaniard Federico García Lorca. Above all, his poems express a self-critical, compassionate personality. His reputation for humanism and honesty is fully vindicated in subsequent volumes—*Ruins and Visions* (1942), *Poems of Dedication* (1947), *The Edge of Being* (1949), *Collected Poems* (1955), *Selected Poems* (1965), and *The Generous Days* (1971).

Spender's prose works include short stories (*The Burning Cactus*, 1936), a novel (*The Backward Son*, 1940), literary criticism (*The Destructive Element*, 1935; *The Creative Element*, 1953; *The Making of a Poem*, 1955; *The Struggle of the Modern*, 1963), an autobiography (*World Within World*, 1951), and uncollected essays with new commentary (*The Thirties and After*, 1978). His account of a trip to China, *Chinese Journal*, was published in 1982.

Spenlow, Dora \\'dȯr-ə-'spen-ˌlō\\ Fictional character, the childlike first wife of David Copperfield in the novel DAVID COPPERFIELD by Charles Dickens.

Spenser \\'spen-sər\\, Edmund (b. 1552/53, London, Eng.—d. Jan. 13, 1599, London) English poet best known for the long allegorical poem THE FAERIE QUEENE (first folio edition,

1609), an imaginative vindication of Protestantism and Puritanism and a glorification of England and Queen Elizabeth I.

In 1569 Spenser entered Pembroke Hall (now Pembroke College) of the University of Cambridge. At Cambridge he acquired a wide knowledge not only of the Latin and some of the Greek classics but also of Italian, French, and English literature of his own and earlier times. In 1569 Spenser's English versions of poems by the 16th-century French poet Joachim du Bellay and his translation of a French version of a poem by the Italian poet Petrarch were published with another work.

Master and Fellows, Pembroke College, Cambridge, England

Subsequently little is known about Spenser's activities until appointment in 1578 as secretary to Bishop John Young of Rochester, formerly master of Pembroke at Cambridge. His first important publication, THE SHEPHEARDES CALENDER (1579), can be called the first work of the English literary Renaissance.

By 1580 Spenser appears to have been serving the Earl of Leicester and to have become a member of the literary circle led by Sir Philip Sidney, Leicester's nephew, to whom the *Calender* was dedicated and who praised it in his important critical work *The Defence of Poesie* (1595). At the same time Spenser had also started work on *The Faerie Queene* and in 1579 had apparently married one Machabyas Chylde. In 1580 he was made secretary to the new lord deputy of Ireland, Arthur Lord Grey.

For four or five years beginning about 1584, Spenser served as clerk of the lords president (governors) of Munster, the southernmost Irish province. In 1588 or 1589 Spenser took over the 3,000-acre plantation of Kilcolman, near Cork.

Originally planned as 12 books, *The Faerie Queene* consists of six books and a fragment (known as the MUTABILITIE CANTOS). The poem was published with the help of Sir Walter Raleigh. Spenser implies that he was persuaded by Raleigh to accompany him back to England to present the completed portion of *The Faerie Queene* to Queen Elizabeth herself. Arriving thus in London with the support of the queen's favorite, Spenser was well received—not least by Elizabeth. The first three books of *The Faerie Queene* were duly published in 1590. Spenser saw the volume through the press and shortly thereafter supervised the printing of certain other of his poems in a collection called *Complaints* (1591), which suggests by its miscellaneous and uneven character that Spenser was hastily bringing to the light of day nearly every last shred he had to offer. In 1591 the queen gave Spenser a small pension for life.

Back in Ireland, Spenser pressed on with his writing, in spite of the burdens of his estate. In early 1595 he published *Amoretti*, a sonnet sequence, and EPITHALAMION, a marriage ode.

In the Irish uprising of 1598, Kilcolman was burned. Spenser, probably in despair despite the Privy Council's having just recommended his appointment to the important post of sheriff of Cork, carried official letters about the desperate state of affairs from Cork to London, where he died.

Spenserian sonnet \spen-'sir-ē-ən\   A sonnet in which the lines are grouped into three interlocked quatrains (four-line units) and a couplet, with the rhyme scheme *abab bcbc cdcd ee*. The Spenserian sonnet is a hybrid form, using a linked rhyme scheme, as does the Petrarchan, or Italian, sonnet, but merging that element with the Shakespearean (or English) quatrain and couplet scheme.

Spenserian stanza \spen-'sir-ē-ən\   A stanza that consists of eight lines of iambic pentameter (five feet) followed by a ninth line of iambic hexameter (six feet), known as an alexandrine; the rhyme scheme is *ababbcbcc*. The first eight lines produce an effect of formal unity, while the hexameter completes the thought of the stanza. Invented by Edmund Spenser for his poem *The Faerie Queene* (1590–1609), the Spenserian stanza was a revolutionary innovation in its day. It was revived in the 19th century by the Romantic poets—*e.g.*, by Lord Byron in *Childe Harold's Pilgrimage*, by John Keats in "The Eve of St. Agnes," and by Percy Bysshe Shelley in *Adonais*.

Sphinx \'sfiŋks\ [Greek *Sphínx, Sphíx, Phíx*]   In Greek mythology, a winged female monster having a woman's head and a lion's body. The most famous of the sphinxes of legend, the Sphinx was said to have terrorized the people of Thebes by demanding the answer to a riddle taught her by the Muses—what is it that has one voice and yet becomes four-footed and two-footed and three-footed?—and devouring a man each time the riddle was answered incorrectly. Eventually Oedipus gave the proper answer: man, who crawls on all fours in infancy, walks on two feet when grown, and leans on a staff in old age. The Sphinx thereupon killed herself. From this tale apparently grew the legend that the Sphinx was omniscient, and even today the wisdom of the Sphinx is proverbial.

Spieghel or **Spiegel** \'spē-gəl\, Henrick *or* Hendrik Laurenszoon (b. March 11, 1549, Amsterdam [Neth.]—d. Jan. 4, 1612, Alkmaar)   Poet of the northern Dutch Renaissance whose highly individual spiritual beliefs set him apart from his contemporaries.

In Spieghel's greatest work, *Hertspiegel* (1614; "Mirror of the Heart"), a long, often allegorical poem written in hexameters, he set out his philosophic vision in simple, direct style. His strong religious faith is based on an amalgam of Christian and Platonic ideas, together with an underlying pantheism. Spieghel was also active in the movement toward the purification and wider use of the Dutch language, principles that he advocated in his *Twe-spraack vande Nederduitsche letterkunst* (1584; "Dialogue on Dutch Literature").

Spielhagen \'shpēl-ˌhä-gən\, Friedrich von (b. Feb. 24, 1829, Magdeburg, Prussian Saxony [Germany]—d. Feb. 25, 1911, Berlin)   Popular writer whose works are considered representative of the social novel in Germany.

Spielhagen's third novel, *Problematische Naturen*, 4 vol. (1861; *Problematic Characters*), was a remarkable success and considered one of the best works of its time. The hero is pulled in opposite directions by the democratic ideals of society and state and by the distractions of social life. This was followed by *Durch Nacht zum Licht*, 4 vol. (1862; *Through Night to Light*), *Hammer und Amboss*, 5 vol. (1869; *Hammer and Anvil*), and *Sturmflut*, 3 vol. (1877; *The Breaking of the Storm*). The last is a powerful romance, using the grandiose symbolism of a tempest that flooded the Baltic coast in 1872 for the economic storm that burst on Berlin in the same year. From 1878 to 1884 Spielhagen was editor of *Westermanns Monatshefte*; he was also an actor and an active partisan in democratic movements.

Spielhagen's dramas include *Liebe für Liebe* (1875; "Love for Love") and *Hans und Grete* (1868).

Spielmann \'shpēl-män\ [German, from Old High German *spilman,* from *spil* play, diversion + *man* man, person] *plural* Spielleute   Wandering entertainer who performed at fairs, markets, and castles in medieval Europe. The *Spielleute* included singers, mimics, and sword-swallowers. Also among them were the storytellers credited with keeping alive the native Germanic vernacular legends at a time when nearly all written literature was religious and when the court poets were concerned chiefly with love lyrics and Arthurian legends.

Spillane \spi-'lān\, Mickey, *original name* Frank Morrison Spillane (b. March 9, 1918, Brooklyn, N.Y., U.S.)   American writer of pulp detective fiction, whose popular work is characterized by violence and sexual licentiousness.

Spillane began his career by writing for pulp magazines and comic books in order to pay for his schooling. His first novel— *I, The Jury* (1947)—introduced detective Mike HAMMER, who appeared in other works, such as *My Gun Is Quick* (1950), *The Big Kill* (1951), and *Kiss Me Deadly* (1952). In the early 1950s Spillane retired from writing. Ten years later he resumed his career with *The Deep* (1961). Spillane wrote the script and played the role of Hammer for the 1963 film version of *The Girl Hunters* (1962). *Day of the Guns* (1964) initiated another series, with the international agent Tiger Mann. Among Spillane's later books were *The Erection Set* (1972), *The Last Cop Out* (1973), and *The Killing Man* (1989). He also wrote two books for children and a book of short stories.

Spinoza of Market Street, The \spi-'nō-zə\   Title story of a short-story collection by Isaac Bashevis SINGER, published in Yiddish in 1944 as "Der Spinozist." The collection was published in English in 1961.

The story is set in Warsaw on the brink of World War I. There Dr. Nahum Fischelson lives a meager, isolated existence alone in an attic room overlooking teeming Market Street. He devotes his energies to explicating the philosophical works of the 17th-century Dutch-Jewish philosopher Benedict de Spinoza, descending to the street only once a week to buy food. Black Dobbe, an illiterate, ugly woman who lives in the attic room next to his, goes to the philosopher's room to have him read a letter she has received. When she discovers Fischelson unconscious and ill, she nurses him back to health. To the amusement of their neighbors, Fischelson and Black Dobbe are married. Fischelson discovers that he has the ardor and vigor of a young man. As he gazes at the stars, he silently asks Spinoza to forgive him his happiness and his acceptance of the world of passion and joy.

Spitteler \'shpit-ə-lər\, Carl (b. April 24, 1845, Liestal, Switz.—d. Dec. 29, 1924, Lucerne)   Swiss poet of visionary imagination and author of pessimistic yet heroic verse, winner of the 1919 Nobel Prize for Literature.

Spitteler's first great poetic work was the mythical epic *Prometheus und Epimetheus* (1881). His second great work was the poetic epic *Der olympische Frühling* (1900–05; revised 1910; "The Olympic Spring"), in which he found full scope for bold invention and vividly expressive power. He spent the last years of his life rewriting his first work. Tighter in composition than the early version and, like *Der olympische Frühling*, written in rhyming couplets, it appeared in 1924 under the title *Prometheus der Dulder* ("Prometheus the Long-suffering").

Widely varied peripheral works belong to Spitteler's middle period. He produced, in verse, *Extramundana* (1883), seven cosmic myths of his own invention; *Balladen* (1896); *Literarische Gleichnisse* (1892; "Literary Parables"); and two cycles of lyrics, *Schmetterlinge* (1889; "Butterflies") and *Gras- und Glockenlieder* (1906; "Grass and Bell Songs"). He also wrote two masterly stories—*Die Mädchenfeinde* (1907; *Two Little*

Misogynists), a childhood idyll derived from his own experience, and *Conrad der Leutnant* (1898), a dramatically finished novel in which he approached the naturalism he otherwise hated. His novel *Imago* (1906) so sharply reflected his inner conflict between a visionary creative gift and middle-class values that it was influential in the development of psychoanalysis. He published a volume of stimulating essays, *Lachende Wahrheiten* (1898; *Laughing Truths*), as well as biographical works of charm, including *Meine frühesten Erlebnisse* (1914; "My Earliest Experiences"). In 1914 he published a politically influential tract, "Unser Schweizer Standpunkt," directed against a one-sided pro-German view of World War I.

Spivak \ˈspē-ˌvak\, Gayatri \ˈgī-ə-trē\ (Chakravorty) (b. Feb. 24, 1942, Calcutta, India)   Indian literary theorist, feminist critic, and professor of comparative literature noted for her personal brand of deconstructive criticism, which she called "interventionist."

Educated in Calcutta and at the University of Cambridge and Cornell University, she taught at the universities of Iowa, Texas, and Pittsburgh.

In 1976 Spivak's English translation of French deconstructionist philosopher Jacques Derrida's *Of Grammatology* was published. In a series of later essays Spivak urged women to become involved in, and to intervene in, the evolution of deconstruction theory. She also urged her colleagues to focus on women's historicity. Critical of "phallogocentric" (imperialist as well as Marxist) historical interpretation, Spivak blamed bourgeois Western feminists for complicity with international capitalism in oppressing and exploiting women of the Third World.

Her critical writings include *In Other Worlds: Essays in Cultural Politics* (1987), *The Post-Colonial Critic* (1990), *Thinking Academic Freedom in Gendered Post-Coloniality* (1992), and *Outside in the Teaching Machine* (1993). She also published *Imaginary Maps* (1994), translations of Indian short stories.

Spoils of Poynton, The \ˈpȯin-tən\   Short novel by Henry JAMES, first published as a serial titled *The Old Things* in *The Atlantic Monthly* in 1896. Retitled *The Spoils of Poynton*, it was published as a book in 1897.

Poynton Park is the home of old Mrs. Gereth, an antique collector with impeccable taste who has filled her lodgings with splendid art objects and furniture. The possessive Mrs. Gereth wants her weak-willed son to marry a pleasant young woman who shares her refined tastes. Instead he becomes engaged to a vulgar, greedy woman, and the treasures of Poynton become the prize over which mother and fiancée battle. In the end Poynton and its spoils, which have destroyed all of the novel's relationships, are immolated in a fire of undetermined origin.

spondee \ˈspän-ˌdē\ [Greek *spondeîos* (short for *spondeîos poús* spondaic foot), from *spondeîos* of a libation, a derivative of *spondē* libation]   Metrical foot consisting of two long or stressed syllables occurring together. Verses consisting entirely of spondees were sung or chanted by the ancient Greeks during performance of a libation, and from such hymns the foot took its meaning.

Spondaic meter occurred occasionally in classical verse as two long syllables. It does not, however, form the basis for any English verse, as there are virtually no English words in which syllables receive equal stress. In English verse, the spondaic foot is usually composed of two monosyllables. It is frequently used as an introductory variation in a line of iambic meter, such as the following line from Robert Burns:

Green grow | the rush | es, O

spoonerism \ˈspü-nər-ˌiz-əm\   Reversal of the initial letters or syllables of two or more words, such as "I have a half-warmed fish in my mind" (for "half-formed wish") and "a blushing crow" (for "a crushing blow"). The word is derived from the name of William Archibald Spooner (1844–1930), a distinguished Anglican clergyman and warden of New College, Oxford, who was a nervous man who committed many "spoonerisms." Such transpositions are sometimes made intentionally for their comic effect.

Spoon River Anthology   Poetry collection, the major work of Edgar Lee MASTERS, published in 1915. It was inspired by the epigrams in the *Greek Anthology*.

The *Spoon River Anthology* is a collection of 245 free-verse epitaphs in the form of monologues. They are spoken from beyond the grave by former residents of a dreary, confining small town like the ones Masters himself had known during his Illinois boyhood. The speakers tell of their hopes and ambitions, and of their bitter, unrealized lives. The realistic poems contradicted the popular view of small towns as repositories of moral virtue and respectability. A theatrical version of *Spoon River Anthology* appeared on Broadway in 1963.

Sportsman's Sketches, A   Collection of short stories by Ivan TURGENEV published in Russian as *Zapiski okhotnika* in 1852; additional stories were included in the 1870s. The collection has also been translated as *Sketches from a Hunter's Album* and *A Sportsman's Notebook*.

The stories concern life in rural Russia, in particular the relationship between landowners and their serfs. Some sketches focus on the landowners or on episodes, drawn from Turgenev's experience, of the manorial, serf-owning Russian gentry. Far more significant are the sketches that tell of Turgenev's encounters with peasants during his hunting trips. His portraits suggest that, though the peasants may be "children of nature" who seek the freedom offered by the beauty of their surroundings, they are always circumscribed by their serfdom.

Sprat \ˈsprat\, Thomas (b. 1635, Beaminster, Dorset, Eng.—d. May 20, 1713, Bromley, Kent)   English man of letters, bishop of Rochester, and dean of Westminster.

A prose stylist, wit, and founding member and historian of the Royal Society, Sprat is chiefly remembered for his influence on language reform and for his biography of the poet Abraham Cowley. Sprat was Cowley's literary executor, and his *An Account of the Life of Mr. Abraham Cowley* (1668) was the first biography of a writer that attempted to show the relation between the poet's life and personality and his works.

Spring \ˈspriŋ\, Howard (b. Feb. 10, 1889, Cardiff, Wales—d. May 3, 1965, Falmouth, Cornwall, Eng.)   Welsh-born British novelist whose chief strength lay in his understanding of provincial life and ambition. Most of his books trace the rise of a character from poverty to affluence, often melodramatically.

The son of a gardener, Spring left school at the age of 11 but continued his education in the evenings, eventually becoming a newspaper reporter and book critic. His first novel, *Shabby Tiger* (1934), had a sequel, the partly autobiographical *Rachel Rosing* (1935). With his best-selling novel *O Absalom!* (1938)—afterward reissued as *My Son, My Son* (film, 1940)—Spring won worldwide fame. He settled in Cornwall, the setting for books that followed, such as *Fame Is the Spur* (1940), *Hard Facts* (1944), and *The Houses in Between* (1951).

Spring and All   Volume of poems and prose pieces by William Carlos WILLIAMS, published in 1923 in Paris in an edition of 300 copies. It contains Williams' attempts to articulate his beliefs about the role and form of art in a modern context. Included are some of Williams' best-known poems.

The prose portions of *Spring and All* were, according to the author, "a mixture of philosophy and nonsense" in a format that parodied contemporary experimentation with typography. The poetry, on the other hand, is straightforward and concerned with the matter of daily life. In "By the Road to the Contagious Hospital," the poet observes fragile signs of spring emerging from a blighted landscape, and the subject of awakening life recurs in many of the remaining 26 poems. Despite the harsh social criticism of "The Crowd at the Ball Game" and "The Pure Products of America," the dominant mood is hopeful, and the images, such as the often reprinted "The Red Wheelbarrow," are vivid and sensuous.

Spring and Fall (*in full* Spring and Fall: To a Young Child) Poem by Gerard Manley HOPKINS, written in 1880 and published posthumously in 1918 in *Poems of Gerard Manley Hopkins*. The poet likens a little girl's sorrow at the waning of summer to the larger, tragic nature of human life. Set in rhymed couplets, the melancholy poem is a notable example of SPRUNG RHYTHM, the irregular system of prosody that Hopkins developed.

sprite \'sprīt\ A tiny mythical being of folklore and romance. The word originally meant more broadly "spirit" and is a borrowing from Old French *esprit*. *See also* ELF; FAIRY.

sprung rhythm A poetic rhythm designed to approximate the natural rhythm of speech and characterized by the frequent juxtaposition of single accented syllables and the occurrence of mixed types of feet (such as the accentual trochee, dactyl, and first paeon) whose sequence is broken or interrupted by outrides (unstressed syllables that are not counted in the scansion).

This system of prosody was developed by the 19th-century English poet Gerard Manley Hopkins. In sprung rhythm, a foot may be composed of from one to four syllables. (In regular English meters, a foot consists of two or three syllables.) Because stressed syllables often occur sequentially in this patterning rather than in alternation with unstressed syllables, the rhythm is said to be "sprung." Hopkins claimed to be only the theoretician, not the inventor, of sprung rhythm. He saw it as the rhythm of common English speech and the basis of such early English poems as William Langland's *Piers Plowman* and of nursery rhymes such as the following:

Ding, dong, bell;

Pussy's in the well.

Sprung rhythm is a bridge between regular meter and free verse. The first two lines of Hopkins' "Spring and Fall: To a Young Child" are an example:

Margaret are you grieving

Over Goldengrove unleaving?

Spyri \'shpē-rē\, Johanna, *original surname* Heusser \'hòi-sər\ (b. June 12, 1829, Hirzel, Switz.—d. July 7, 1901, Zürich) Swiss writer whose story for children, HEIDI, 2 vol. (1880–81), is a classic of children's literature. Her understanding, her humor, and her ability to enter into childish joys and sorrows make her books attractive and enduring.

Spyri imbued both her life and her work with her love of homeland, feeling for nature, unobtrusive piety, and cheerful wisdom. Many of her later books also were translated into several languages, but none achieved the popularity of her story of Heidi.

spy story A tale of international intrigue and adventure. Among the best examples of the genre are works written by John Buchan, Len Deighton, Sapper (H. Cyril McNeile), and many others. Two directions taken by the modern spy story were typified by Ian Fleming's enormously popular James Bond

thrillers, which emphasized technological marvels much in the manner of science-fiction fantasy, and John Le Carré's bleakly realistic stories such as *The Spy Who Came in from the Cold*.

Squeers, Wackford \'wak-fərd-'skwirz\ Fictional character, the cruel headmaster of Dotheboys Hall in the novel NICHOLAS NICKLEBY by Charles Dickens.

squib \'skwib\ A short humorous, satiric, or lampooning piece of writing or speech.

Squire \'skwīr\, J.C., *in full* Sir John Collings Squire (b. April 2, 1882, Plymouth, Devon, Eng.—d. Dec. 20, 1958, Rushlake Green, Sussex) English journalist, playwright, and leading poet of the Georgian school, and an influential critic and editor.

Squire was appointed literary editor of the *New Statesman* in 1913 and acting editor in 1917. From 1919 to 1934 he was editor of *The London Mercury*, which was to become the unofficial organ of the Georgian poets. Squire's poetry appeared in *Collected Parodies* (1921), *Poems in One Volume* (1926), *Selected Poems* (1948), and *Collected Poems* (1959), volumes that demonstrate his technical competence as well as a delightful sense of parody. He also collaborated with J.L. Balderston on the hit play *Berkeley Square* (performed 1926), an adaptation of Henry James's *The Sense of the Past*. He was knighted in 1933.

Squire's Tale, The One of the 24 stories in THE CANTERBURY TALES by Geoffrey Chaucer.

The Squire relates an incomplete tale of the Tartar king Cambyuskan (Cambuscan), who receives four magical gifts: a brass horse that can fly anywhere safely but at astonishing speed, a sword that can penetrate armor and heal wounds, a mirror that tells of future dangers, and a ring that enables its wearer to understand the speech of birds and to know the medicinal properties of every plant.

Śrī *see* LAKṢMĪ.

Śrīharṣa \,shrē-'här-sə\ (fl. 12th century AD) Sanskrit author and epic poet whose *Naiṣadhaçarita* (also called *Naiṣadhīyacarita* or *Naiṣadha*) is one of the classical Sanskrit poems known as the *mahākāvya*s.

The details of Śrīharṣa's life are uncertain. Reportedly, when his father, a poet in King Vijayaçandra's court in Kannauj, was disgraced in a poetry contest, he retired and asked Śrīharṣa to avenge him. In time Vijayaçandra became Śrīharṣa's patron, and it was at the king's request that the poet composed *Naiṣadhaçarita*. Among his other writings are treatises on elements of Buddhist and Vedanta beliefs and eulogies on late kings.

The *Naiṣadhaçarita* is a 22-canto retelling of the tale of Nala, king of Niṣadha, and Damayantī, princess of Vidharbha, from the *Mahābhārata*. It is a story of love overcoming obstacles, ending happily in marriage. The poem is especially notable for its descriptive embellishments and skillful presentation of emotion.

Ssu-ma Ch'ien *see* SIMA QIAN.

Ssu-ma Hsiang-ju *see* SIMA XIANGRU.

Ssu shu *see* SI SHU.

Staël \də-'stäl\, Germaine de, *in full* Anne-Louise-Germaine Necker, Baroness (baronne) de Staël-Holstein \'hòl-,shtīn\, *byname* Madame de Staël (b. April 22, 1766, Paris, Fr.—d. July 14, 1817, Paris) French-Swiss writer, woman of letters, political propagandist, and conversationalist, who bridged the history of ideas from Neoclassicism to Romanticism and gained fame by maintaining a salon for leading intellectuals.

The young Germaine Necker early gained a reputation for lively wit. She was married in 1786 to the Swedish ambassador in Paris, Baron Erik de Staël-Holstein. It was a marriage of convenience and ended in 1797 in formal separation. Before she was 21, Mme de Staël had written a romantic drama and a tragedy, but it was her *Lettres sur les ouvrages et le caractère de J.-J. Rousseau* (1788; *Letters on the Works and the Character of J.-J. Rousseau*), which contained an unusual and irreconcilable mixture of Jean-Jacques Rousseau's enthusiasm and Montesquieu's rationalism, that made her known. Favoring the French Revolution, she acquired a reputation for Jacobinism.

Detail of a portrait by Jean-Baptiste Isabey, 1810; in the Louvre, Paris
Giraudon/Art Resource

Protected by her husband's diplomatic status, she was in no danger in Paris until 1793, when she retreated to Coppet, Switz., the family residence near Geneva. There she gained fame by establishing a meeting place for some of western Europe's leading intellectuals. After a brief stay in England, she returned to France, via Coppet, at the end of the Reign of Terror in 1794.

The most brilliant period of her career then began: her salon flourished, and she published several political and literary essays, notably *De l'influence des passions sur le bonheur des individus et des nations* (1796; *A Treatise on the Influence of the Passions upon the Happiness of Individuals and of Nations*), which became one of the important documents of European Romanticism. Under the influence of her new lover, Benjamin Constant, she began to study the latest ideas coming out of Germany, reading the work of brothers August Wilhelm and Friedrich von Schlegel, among others. Her *De la littérature considérée dans ses rapports avec les institutions sociales* (1800; *A Treatise of Ancient and Modern Literature* and *The Influence of Literature upon Society*) is a complex work, rich in new ideas and new perspectives—new, at least to France. Its fundamental theory, which was to be restated and developed in the positivism of Hippolyte Taine, is that a work must express the moral and historical reality (the zeitgeist) of the nation in which it is conceived. She also maintained that the Nordic and classical ideals were basically opposed, and she supported the Nordic, although her personal taste remained strongly classical. Her two novels, *Delphine* (1802) and *Corinne* (1807), to some extent illustrate her literary theories.

Mme de Staël was also an important political figure and was generally regarded as the personal enemy of Napoleon. With Constant and his friends she formed the nucleus of a liberal resistance which so embarrassed Napoleon that in 1803 he had her banished from Paris. Thenceforward, Coppet was her headquarters, and in 1804 she began what she called (in a work published posthumously in 1821) her *Dix Années d'exil* (*Ten Years' Exile*).

Probably her most important work is *De l'Allemagne* (1810; *Germany*), a serious study of German manners, literature and art, philosophy and morals, and religion that Napoleon took for an anti-French work; the French edition of 1810 (10,000 copies) was seized and destroyed. It was published in England in 1813. Meanwhile, Mme de Staël, persecuted by the police, fled from Napoleon's Europe. On the Bourbon restoration in 1814, she returned to Paris but was deeply disillusioned.

Staff \\'stȧf\\, Leopold (b. Sept. 14, 1878, Lwów, Galicia, Austria-Hungary [now Lviv, Ukraine]—d. May 31, 1957, Skarżysko-Kamienna, Pol.) Influential poet associated with the Neoromantic Young Poland movement at the end of the 19th century.

In 1901 his *Sny o potędze* ("Dreams of Power"), the first of his more than 30 volumes of verse, was published; two years later *Dzień duszy* (1903; "The Day of the Soul") appeared. From the very beginning Staff showed a talent for handling poetic form; he would create new forms if the old seemed insufficient. A later collection, *Ucho igielne* (1927; "The Needle's Eye"), was dominated by religious feeling, expressed in concise and direct verse. His last collection of poems appeared in 1954. Staff also made translations and wrote dramas.

Stafford \\'staf-ərd\\, Jean (b. July 1, 1915, Covina, Calif., U.S.—d. March 26, 1979, White Plains, N.Y.) American short-story writer and novelist noted for her deft development of fictional characters.

Stafford's first novel, *Boston Adventure* (1944), became a best-seller, reaching 400,000 copies. Its publication launched her career and guaranteed her a position of prominence in literary circles. She later wrote two more novels, *The Mountain Lion* (1947) and *The Catherine Wheel* (1952), as well as children's books. *The Collected Stories of Jean Stafford* (1969) won a Pulitzer Prize, and she contributed frequently to such journals as *The New Yorker*, *Kenyon Review*, *Partisan Review*, and *Harper's Bazaar*.

Stafford's personal life was marked by bouts of alcoholism and illnesses and by three troubled marriages (to the writers Robert Lowell, Oliver Jensen, and A.J. Liebling).

Stage Manager Fictional character who acts as the narrator of Thornton Wilder's play OUR TOWN. The Stage Manager both participates in and comments on the action of the play.

Stagnelius \\stȧg-'nä-lĕ-ûs\\, Erik Johan (b. Oct. 14, 1793, island of Öland, Sweden—d. April 3, 1823, Stockholm) One of the strangest and most romantic of the Swedish Romantic poets. His works reflect a conflict between strong erotic impulses and a radically ascetic religious position.

During the last few years of his short life, Stagnelius published two dramas, *Martyrerna* (1821; "The Martyrs") and *Backanterna* (1822; "The Bacchantes"), as well as a collection of religious lyrics, *Liljor i Saron* (1821; "Lilies in Sharon"). His *Samlade skrifter* (1824–26; "Collected Works"), containing his vast unpublished material, appeared shortly after his death.

Stahr, Monroe \\mən-'rō-'stär\\ Fictional character, prodigious protagonist of THE LAST TYCOON by F. Scott Fitzgerald.

Stanley \\'stan-lĕ\\, Thomas (b. 1625, Cumberlow, Hertfordshire, Eng.—d. April 12, 1678, London) English poet, translator, and the first English historian of philosophy.

Stanley studied at Pembroke Hall (later College), Cambridge, and at the University of Oxford. Stanley was the friend of many poets and himself a prolific translator and writer of verse. His first volume of poems appeared in 1647. Subsequent volumes included translations from Anacreon, Bion, Decimus Magnus Ausonius, Battista Guarini, Giambattista Marino, Petrarch, Pierre de Ronsard, and others. His classic renderings of the odes of Anacreon were published in 1651, and the same collection contains his version of Giovanni Pico della Mirandola's *A Platonick Discourse upon Love*. Stanley's *The History of Philosophy*, which long remained a standard work, was published in 1655–62, and his edition of Aeschylus with Latin translation and commentary in 1663.

stanza \\'stan-zə\\ [Italian, act or place of staying, abode, room, stanza] A division of a poem consisting of two or more lines arranged together as a unit. More specifically, a stanza usually is a group of lines arranged together in a recurring pattern of metrical lengths and a sequence of rhymes.

The structure of a stanza is determined by the number of lines, the dominant meter, and the rhyme scheme. Thus, a stanza of four lines of iambic pentameter, rhyming *abab*, would be described as a quatrain.

Some of the most common stanzaic forms are designated by the number of lines in each unit—*e.g.*, tercet or terza rima (three lines) and ottava rima (eight lines). Other stanzaic forms are named for poets who used them or poems that exemplify them—*e.g.*, the Spenserian stanza or the *In Memoriam* stanza, popularized by Alfred, Lord Tennyson in the poem by that title. The term *strophe* is often used interchangeably with stanza, although strophe is sometimes used specifically to refer to a unit of a poem that does not have a regular meter and rhyme pattern or to a unit of a Pindaric ode.

Stapledon \\'stä-pəl-dən\\, Olaf, *in full* William Olaf Stapledon (b. May 10, 1886, Wirral Peninsula, near Liverpool, Merseyside, Eng.—d. Sept. 6, 1950, Cheshire)   English novelist and philosopher whose "histories of the future" were a major influence on contemporary science fiction.

A pacifist, Stapledon served with a Friends' ambulance unit in World War I and was awarded the Croix de Guerre. He was educated at the University of Liverpool. In 1929 he published *A Modern Theory of Ethics* and seemed destined for an academic career, but after the success of his novel *Last and First Men* (1930), he began to write fiction.

Last and First Men traces the history of humanity from the First Men (present-day) to the Eighteenth Men, one of whom serves as narrator. The tale illustrates Stapledon's belief that to emphasize the physical (the flying Seventh Men of Venus) to the exclusion of the intellectual (the giant-brained Fourth Men), or vice versa, spells certain disaster. He emphasized the ideals of community, necessary for individual fulfillment and embodied by the Eighteenth Men, and of spirit, which gives purpose to human existence.

Stapledon also wrote for technical and scholarly reviews on ethics and philosophy. His other works include *The Last Men in London* (1932), *Odd John* (1935), *Philosophy and Living* (1938), *Star Maker* (1937), and *Sirius* (1944).

Starbuck \\'stär-,bək\\   Fictional character, the scrupulous and steadfast first mate of the *Pequod* in the novel MOBY-DICK by Herman Melville.

Stark \\'stärk\\, Freya, *in full* Dame Freya Madeline Stark (b. Jan. 31, 1893, Paris, Fr.—d. May 9, 1993, Asolo, Italy)   British travel writer who is noted for two dozen highly personal books in which she describes local history and culture as well as everyday life. Many of her trips were to remote areas in Turkey and the Middle East where few Europeans, particularly women, had traveled before.

In her first major book, *The Valleys of the Assassins* (1934), Stark established her style, combining practical travel tips with an entertaining commentary on the people, places, customs, and history of Persia (now Iran). Thereafter, she traveled extensively in the Middle East, Turkey, Greece, and Italy, where she made her home. During World War II she worked for the British Ministry of Information in Aden, Baghdad, and Cairo, where she founded the anti-Nazi Brotherhood of Freedom. She later visited Asia, notably Afghanistan and Nepal. Stark's other books include *The Southern Gates of Arabia* (1936), *Letters from Syria* (1942), *Alexander's Path* (1958), *The Minaret of Djam* (1970), several volumes of collected letters, and four volumes of memoirs. She was made Dame Commander of the Order of the British Empire in 1972.

Stark, Willie \\'wil-ē-'stärk\\   Fictional character, a central figure in the novel ALL THE KING'S MEN (1946) by Robert Penn Warren. The life and career of Willie Stark, a flamboyant governor of a Southern U.S. state, were based on those of Huey Long, governor of Louisiana from 1928 to 1931. Like Long, Stark is ultimately assassinated.

Statius \\'stā-shəs, -shē-əs\\, *in full* Publius Papinius Statius (b. *c.* AD 45, Neapolis, Campania [now Naples, Italy]—d. 96, probably Neapolis?)   One of the principal Roman epic and lyric poets of the Silver Age of Latin literature (AD 18–133). His occasional poems, collected under the title *Silvae* ("Forests"), apart from their literary merit, are valuable for their description of the lifestyle of a wealthy and fashionable class—the *liberti*, or freedmen—during the reign of the emperor Domitian.

Statius lived at Rome and was a court poet under Domitian, who awarded him a prize in 89 or 90. He was, however, unsuccessful in the Capitoline competition at Rome, probably on its third celebration in 94, and shortly afterward returned to Neapolis.

Statius is at his best in the five books of the *Silvae*. Of the 32 poems, five are devoted to flattery of the emperor and his favorites. Another group gives picturesque descriptions of the villas and gardens of his friends, members of an ostentatious class who patronized the poet in return for his versified praises. Also estimable are poems dealing with family affection and personal loss and one poem to sleep.

Statius completed one epic, the 12-book *Thebaid*, but only two books of another, the *Achilleid*. The *Thebaid*, a more ambitious work, describes the struggle of the brothers Polyneices and Eteocles for the throne of the ancient Greek city of Thebes. The work begins and ends with passages that convey an atmosphere of dramatic tension and considerable tragic power. The *Achilleid* gives a charming account of the early education of Achilles, but at the point at which he is taken off to Troy by Odysseus, the poem was evidently interrupted by the poet's death.

Stead \\'sted\\, Christina (Ellen) (b. July 17, 1902, Rockdale, Sydney, Australia—d. March 31, 1983, Sydney)   Australian novelist known for her political insights and firmly controlled but highly individual style.

Stead traveled widely and at various times lived in the United States, Paris, and London. In the early 1940s she worked briefly as a screenwriter.

Stead's first published work was a collection of short stories, *The Salzburg Tales* (1934). *Seven Poor Men of Sydney*, published later the same year, deals with a band of young revolutionaries and provides a fascinating portrayal of Sydney's waterfront. Her best-known and perhaps most highly praised novel is THE MAN WHO LOVED CHILDREN (1940; rev. ed., 1965), the story of a disintegrating family. Stead is sometimes regarded as a feminist writer, a label she adamantly rejected.

Stead's other works include *The Beauties and Furies* (1936), *House of All Nations* (1938), *For Love Alone* (1944), *A Little Tea, a Little Chat* (1948), *The People with the Dogs* (1952), *Dark Places of the Heart* (1966; U.K. title, *Cotters' England*), *The Little Hotel* (1973), and *Miss Herbert* (1976).

Stead \\'sted\\, C.K., *in full* Christian Karlson (b. Oct. 17, 1932, Auckland, New Zealand)   Poet and novelist who also gained an international reputation as a critic with *The New Poetic: Yeats to Eliot* (1964), which became a standard work on modernist poetry.

Stead studied at the University of Auckland and the University of Bristol. From 1959 to 1986 he taught at the University of Auckland. His first book of poetry, *Whether the Will Is Free: Poems 1954–62*, was published in 1964. In his second collection, *Crossing the Bar* (1972), he was moved by the Vietnam War to protest against the inhumanity and irresponsibility of people in power. His later poetry collections include *Quesada: Poems 1972–1974* (1975), *Paris* (1984), *Between* (1988), and *Voices* (1990).

Stead's first novel, *Smith's Dream* (1971), is a disturbing fantasy set in a fascist New Zealand of the future. His later novels include *All Visitors Ashore* (1984), *The Death of the Body* (1986), *Sister Hollywood* (1989), and *The End of the Century at the End of the World* (1992). Stead's critical works include *The New Poetic* (1964), *In the Glass Case: Essays on New Zealand Literature* (1981), and *Answering to the Language* (1989), essays on modern writers.

Stebnitsky   *see* LESKOV.

Stedman \'sted-mən\, Edmund Clarence (b. Oct. 8, 1833, Hartford, Conn., U.S.—d. Jan. 18, 1908, New York, N.Y.) Poet, critic, and editor whose writing was popular in the United States during the late 19th century.

As a critic Stedman wrote of contemporary authors in *Victorian Poets* (1875) and *Poets of America* (1885); he also edited the works of Edgar Allan Poe and Walter Savage Landor and was an important figure in the New York literary world. His *Poetical Works* appeared in 1875, *Hawthorne and Other Poems* in 1877, *Lyrics and Idylls, with Other Poems* in 1879, and *Mater Coronata* in 1900.

Steele \'stēl\, Richard, *in full* Sir Richard Steele, *pseudonym* Isaac Bickerstaff \'bik-ər-,staf\ (b. 1672, Dublin, Ire.—

Detail of an oil painting by Sir Godfrey Kneller, 1711

National Portrait Gallery, London

d. Sept. 1, 1729, Carmarthen, Carmarthenshire, Wales) English journalist, dramatist, essayist, and politician, best known as the principal author (with Joseph ADDISON) of the periodicals THE TATLER and THE SPECTATOR.

Steele was sent to study in England at Charterhouse school in 1684 (where he met Addison) and to Christ Church, Oxford, in 1689. In 1701 Steele wrote his first comedy, *The Funeral*. This

play made his reputation and helped to bring him to the notice of King William and the Whig leaders. Late in 1703 he followed this with his only stage failure, *The Lying Lover*, which is nevertheless of historical importance as one of the first sentimental comedies.

On April 12, 1709, he secured his place in literary history by launching the thrice-weekly essay periodical *The Tatler*. Writing under his pseudonym, Steele created the mixture of entertainment and instruction in manners and morals that was to be perfected in the enormously successful *The Spectator*.

First appearing on March 1, 1711, *The Spectator* was a joint venture; Steele's was probably the more original journalistic flair, and he evolved many of the most celebrated ideas and characters (such as Sir Roger de Coverley). Steele's attractive, often casual style formed a perfect foil for Addison's more measured, polished, and erudite writing.

Of Steele's many later ventures into periodical journalism, some, such as *The Englishman*, were mainly politically par-

tisan. *The Guardian* (to which Addison contributed substantially) contains some of his most distinguished work, and *The Lover* comprises 40 of his most attractive essays. Steele was appointed to the post of governor of Drury Lane Theatre in 1714, where he produced his last and most successful comedy, *The Conscious Lovers* (1723)—one of the most popular plays of the century and perhaps the best example of English sentimental comedy.

Steerforth, James \'jāmz-'stir-,fôrth\   Fictional character, a handsome, selfish aristocrat in the novel DAVID COPPERFIELD by Charles Dickens.

Stefánsson \'stā-,fän-sòn\, Davíth (b. Jan. 21, 1895, Fagriskógur, Eyjafjörthur, Ice.—d. March 1, 1964, Akureyri) One of the most popular poets of 20th-century Iceland.

Stefánsson lived most of his life in the little town of Akureyri, where he was a librarian (1925–51). His early poetry, including most of his folk themes and love lyrics, appeared in *Svartar fjathrir* (1919, "Black Feathers"), *Kvæthi* (1922, "Poems"), *Kvethjur* (1924; "Greetings"), and *Ný kvæthi* (1929; "New Poems"), which were combined and published as a collected volume in 1930. He wrote with a light touch, using simple language and metrical flexibility. His love lyrics are as gentle as a cradle song, yet his heroic verse is as virile as epic poetry.

Stefánsson's later poetry—darkening in social satire, reformatory zeal against capitalism and organized religion, and despair over the war—was published as *Í byggthum* (1933; "Among Human Habitations"), *Ath northan* (1936; "From the North"), *Ný kvæthabók* (1947; "A New Book of Poems"), and the posthumous *Sídustu ljóth* (1966; "Last Poems"). His prose works include a powerful sociological novel, *Sólon Íslandus* (1940), based on folk legend, and four plays, one of which (*Gullna hlithith*, 1941; "The Golden Gate") remains a popular play in Iceland.

Steffen \'shtef-ən\, Albert (b. Dec. 10, 1884, Murgenthal, Switz.—d. July 13, 1963, Dornach)   Swiss novelist and dramatist, one of the leading writers of the anthroposophical movement (founded by Rudolf Steiner and based on the premise that the human intellect has the ability to contact spiritual worlds).

Steffen's early works were compassionate messages of alarm at the disastrous effects of modern technological civilization and secularized thought on human relations. Moved by these problems, he joined the anthroposophical movement in 1907, settling at its center in Dornach, near Basel. (Steffen was later president of the Anthroposophical Society, and he was editor of its review, *Das Goetheanum*, from 1921 to 1950.) From that time his numerous writings became visions of a world permeated by metaphysical powers of good and evil, as revealed in old and esoteric European and Asian traditions. His novels include *Die Erneuerung des Bundes* (1913) and *Aus Georg Archibalds Lebenslauf* (1950); his plays include *Hieram und Salomo* (1927), *Das Todeserlebnis des Manes* (1934), and *Barrabas* (1949; *Christ or Barrabas?*). *Der Künstler zwischen Westen und Osten* (1925; *The Artist Between West and East*) is a book of essays, and *Buch der Rückschau* (1939) is autobiographical.

Steffens \'stef-ənz\, Lincoln, *in full* Joseph Lincoln Steffens (b. April 6, 1866, San Francisco, Calif., U.S.—d. Aug. 9, 1936, Carmel, Calif.)   American journalist, lecturer, and political philosopher, a leading figure among the writers whom Theodore Roosevelt called muckrakers.

During nine years of New York City newspaper work ending in 1901, Steffens discovered abundant evidence of the corruption of politicians by businessmen seeking special privileges. In 1901, after he became managing editor of *McClure's Magazine*, he began to publish the influential articles later collected as *The Shame of the Cities* (1906).

His many nationwide lecture tours won him recognition. Using comic irony, he jolted his audience into awareness of the ethical paradox of private interest in public affairs. He revealed the shortcomings of the popular dogmas that connected economic success with moral worth and national progress with individual self-interest.

Political events in Mexico and Russia turned Steffens' attention from reform to revolution. After a trip to Petrograd (St. Petersburg) in 1919 he wrote a friend, "I have seen the future; and it works." His unorthodoxy lost him his American audience during the 1920s, but he continued to study revolutionary politics in Europe and became something of a legendary character for the younger expatriates. His *Autobiography* (1931) was a great success.

Stegner \'steg-nər\, Wallace (Earle) (b. Feb. 18, 1909, Lake Mills, Iowa, U.S.—d. April 13, 1993, Santa Fe, N.M.) American author of fiction and historical nonfiction set mainly in the western United States. All of his writings are informed by a deep sense of the American experience and the potential, which he termed "the geography of promise," that the West symbolizes.

Stegner graduated from the University of Utah and the University of Iowa. He taught at several universities, notably Stanford University, where from 1945 to 1971 he directed the creative-writing program. His first novel, *Remembering Laughter* (1937), like his next three novels, was a relatively short work. His fifth novel, *The Big Rock Candy Mountain* (1943), the story of an American family moving from place to place in the West, seeking their fortune, was his first critical and popular success. Among his later novels are *The Preacher and the Slave* (1950; later titled *Joe Hill: A Biographical Novel*), the best-selling *A Shooting Star* (1961), the Pulitzer Prize-winning *Angle of Repose* (1971), and *The Spectator Bird* (1976), which won a National Book Award.

Stegner's nonfiction includes two histories of the Mormon settlement of Utah, *Mormon Country* (1942) and *The Gathering of Zion: The Story of the Mormon Trail* (1964), and a biography of Western explorer-naturalist John Wesley Powell, *Beyond the Hundredth Meridian: John Wesley Powell and the Second Opening of the West* (1954). A book of essays, *Where the Bluebird Sings to the Lemonade Springs: Living and Writing in the West*, was published in 1992.

Stein \'shtīn\, Charlotte von, *original surname* von Schardt \fŏn-'shärt\ (b. Dec. 25, 1742, Eisenach, Saxe-Weimar [Germany]—d. Jan. 6, 1827, Weimar) German writer who was an intimate friend of and important influence on J.W. von Goethe; she was the inspiration for his female figures Iphigenie in *Iphigenie auf Tauris* and Natalie in *Wilhelm Meister*.

Stein was the wife of Friedrich, Freiherr von Stein, equerry to Duke Karl August of Saxe-Weimar. On Goethe's arrival in Weimar (1775) an intimate friendship began, and the ensuing *Seelenbund* ("union of souls") was of considerable influence on Goethe's life and work; Goethe's letters and poems to Frau von Stein demonstrate their close attachment. After Goethe's return from Italy (1788), his relations with Christiane Vulpius, whom he later married, resulted in a complete break in the friendship.

Stein's own works include *Rino* (1776), a small, humorous piece on Goethe and various ladies of the court, and a prose tragedy *Dido* (1792; published 1867), a work containing many allusions to her break with him.

Stein \'stīn\, Gertrude (b. Feb. 3, 1874, Allegheny, Pa., U.S.—d. July 27, 1946, Neuilly-sur-Seine, Fr.) Avant-garde American writer, eccentric, and self-styled genius, whose Paris home was a salon for the leading artists and writers of the period between World Wars I and II.

Stein spent her infancy in Vienna and Passy, Fr., and her girlhood in Oakland, Calif. After studying at Radcliffe College in Cambridge, Mass., and at Johns Hopkins medical school, she went to Paris. From 1903 to 1909 she lived solely with her brother Leo, who became an accomplished art critic. In 1909 Alice B. Toklas, whom she had met in 1907, moved in with Gertrude and Leo, and Leo moved out in 1914.

Culver Pictures

Stein and her brother were among the first collectors of works by the Cubists and other experimental painters of the period, including Pablo Picasso (who painted her portrait), Henri Matisse, and Georges Braque, several of whom became her friends. At her salon they mingled with expatriate American writers, such as Sherwood Anderson and Ernest Hemingway, and other visitors drawn by her literary reputation (and Toklas' cooking). Stein's literary and artistic judgments were revered, and her chance remarks could make or destroy reputations. In her own work, she attempted to parallel the theories of Cubism, specifically in her concentration on the illumination of the present moment and her use of slightly varied repetitions and extreme simplification and fragmentation. The best explanation of her theory of writing is found in the essay *Composition as Explanation*, which was based on lectures that she gave at Oxford and Cambridge and was issued as a book in 1926. TENDER BUTTONS (1914) is a Cubist-inspired work that carries fragmentation and abstraction to an extreme.

Stein's first published book, *Three Lives* (1909), the stories of three working-class women, has been called a minor masterpiece. THE MAKING OF AMERICANS, a long composition written in 1906–11 but not published until 1925, was too convoluted and obscure for general readers, for whom she remained essentially the author of such lines as "Rose is a rose is a rose is a rose." Her only book to reach a wide public was THE AUTOBIOGRAPHY OF ALICE B. TOKLAS (1933), actually Stein's own autobiography. The performance in the United States of her FOUR SAINTS IN THREE ACTS (1934), which the composer Virgil Thomson had made into an opera, led to a triumphal American lecture tour in 1934–35. Thomson also wrote the music for her second opera, THE MOTHER OF US ALL (1947), based on the life of feminist Susan B. Anthony. One of Stein's early short stories, Q.E.D., was first published in *Things as They Are* (1950).

Stein became a legend in Paris, especially after surviving the German occupation of France and befriending the many young American servicemen who visited her. She wrote about these soldiers in *Brewsie and Willie* (1946).

Steinbeck \'stīn-,bek\, John Ernst (b. Feb. 27, 1902, Salinas, Calif., U.S.—d. Dec. 20, 1968, New York, N.Y.) American novelist, best known for THE GRAPES OF WRATH (1939), one of several naturalistic novels with proletarian themes that he wrote in the 1930s. These works, with their rich symbolic structures, effectively convey the mythopoetic and symbolic qualities of his characters. He received the Nobel Prize for Literature in 1962.

Steinbeck attended Stanford University intermittently between 1920 and 1926 but did not earn a degree. He worked as a manual laborer while writing, and his experiences lent authenticity to his depictions of the lives of the workers in his stories. He spent much of his life in Monterey county, Calif.

Steinbeck's first three novels—*Cup of Gold* (1929), *The Pastures of Heaven* (1932), and *To a God Unknown* (1933)—were unsuccessful. He first achieved popularity with TORTILLA FLAT (1935), an affectionately told story of Mexican-Americans. His next novel, *In Dubious Battle* (1936), is a classic account of a strike by farm workers. The novella OF MICE AND MEN (1937) is a tragic story about the strange, complex bond between two migrant laborers. A Pulitzer Prize and a National Book Award were granted to Steinbeck for his next work, *The Grapes of Wrath*. The novel is about the migration of a dispossessed family from the Oklahoma Dust Bowl to California and describes their subsequent exploitation by a ruthless system of agricultural economics. Another notable achievement of this period was THE RED PONY (1937), which contains four stories of initiation.

During World War II Steinbeck wrote several effective pieces of government propaganda, among them *The Moon Is Down* (1942), a novel of Norwegians under the Nazis, and he also served as a war correspondent. His immediate postwar work— CANNERY ROW (1945), THE PEARL (1947), *The Wayward Bus* (1947)—contained the familiar elements of his social criticism but were more relaxed in approach and sentimental in tone.

Steinbeck's later writings were comparatively slight works of entertainment and journalism interspersed with three attempts to reassert his stature as a major novelist: *Burning Bright* (1950), EAST OF EDEN (1952), and *The Winter of Our Discontent* (1961). In critical opinion, none equaled his earlier achievement. Steinbeck also wrote the scripts for the film versions of *The Pearl* and *The Red Pony*. Outstanding among the scripts he wrote directly for motion pictures were *Forgotten Village* (1941) and *Viva Zapata!* (1952).

Steiner \'stī-nər\, George, *in full* Francis George Steiner (b. April 23, 1929, Paris, France)   Influential European-born American literary critic who studied the relationship between literature and society, particularly in light of modern history. His writings on language and the Holocaust reached a wide, nonacademic audience.

Steiner was born in Paris of émigré Austrian parents and educated at the Sorbonne, the University of Chicago, Harvard University, and Oxford University. He became an American citizen in 1944 but spent much of his time in Europe. He was a member of the editorial staff of the *Economist* (1952–56) and worked at the Institute for Advanced Study at Princeton University (1956–58) before teaching at Churchill College, Cambridge University, and the University of Geneva, Switzerland.

His first book, *Tolstoy or Dostoevsky* (1959), compares the two authors on the basis of historical, biographical, and philosophical data. *Language and Silence* (1967) is a collection of essays that examines the dehumanizing effect that World War II and the Holocaust had on literature. Steiner explores the intersection of culture and linguistics that underlies translation and multilingualism in *Extraterritorial* (1971) and *After Babel: Aspects of Language and Translation* (1975).

Among his other critical works are *The Death of Tragedy* (1961), *In Bluebeard's Castle: Some Notes Towards the Redefinition of Culture* (1971), *On Difficulty and Other Essays* (1978), *Martin Heidegger* (1979), *Antigones* (1984), and *Real Presences* (1989). His fiction includes *Anno Domini* (1964), *The Portage to San Cristóbal of A.H.* (1981), and *Proofs and Three Parables* (1992).

stemma \'stem-ə\ *plural* **stemmata** \-ə-tə\ *or* **stemmas**.   A tree showing the relationships of the manuscripts of a literary work.

Stendhal \stan-'däl, *Angl* sten-'däl, stan-\, *pseudonym of* Marie-Henri Beyle \'bel\ (b. Jan. 23, 1783, Grenoble, Fr.—d. March 23, 1842, Paris)   One of the most original and complex French writers of the first half of the 19th century, chiefly known for the masterpieces *Le Rouge et le noir* (1830; THE RED AND THE BLACK) and *La Chartreuse de Parme* (1839; THE CHARTERHOUSE OF PARMA).

By 1802, Beyle had begun keeping a diary (posthumously published as his *Journal*) and writing other texts dealing with his intimate thoughts. His administrative career in the French army gave him direct experience of the Napoleonic regime and of Europe at war. In 1814, when the French empire fell, he decided to settle in Italy. His travel book *Rome, Naples et Florence en 1817* (1817) was the first publication for which he used the pseudonym Stendhal. As a result of romantic and political disappointments, he left Milan for Paris in 1821.

From 1821 to 1830 Stendhal made a name for himself in the Paris salons. His wit and unconventional views were much appreciated, and he had notable friendships and love affairs. In 1822 he published *De l'amour* (ON LOVE). In *Racine et Shakespeare* (1823, 1825), one of the first Romantic manifestos to appear in France, he developed the central idea that each historical period has been "romantic" in its own time, that Romanticism is a vital aspect of every cultural period. He contributed regularly to English journals and published *Vie de Rossini* (1823; *Life of Rossini*), his first novel, *Armance* (1827), and the travel book *Promenades dans Rome* (1829). During this period he also wrote *Le Rouge et le noir*.

Stendhal was appointed French consul in the small and isolated port of Civitavecchia in the Papal States. Lonely, aware of his age and failing health, he felt increasingly drawn to autobiography and wrote *Souvenirs d'égotisme* (1892; MEMOIRS OF AN EGOTIST) and *Vie de Henry Brulard* (1890; THE LIFE OF HENRY BRULARD), as well as a new and largely autobiographical novel entitled LUCIEN LEUWEN (1894). All these works remained unfinished, though they were published posthumously.

During a prolonged leave in Paris from 1836 to 1839, Stendhal again could concentrate on literary work. During this period he composed *Mémoires d'un touriste* and his second masterpiece, the novel *La Chartreuse de Parme*. He died in 1842, after suffering a stroke while again on leave in Paris.

Stephansson \'stä-,fän-sòn, *Angl* 'stef-ən-sən\, Stephan Gudmundarson (b. Oct. 3, 1853, Kirkjuhóll, Skagafjördur, Ice.—d. Aug. 10, 1927, Markerville, Alta., Can.)   Icelandic-Canadian poet who mastered both traditional Icelandic style and contemporary forms of poetry. He is considered to be one of the greatest Icelandic poets since Snorri Sturluson.

Stephansson immigrated to the United States at the age of 20 and lived in Icelandic settlements in Wisconsin and North Dakota. He set up a small farm in Alberta when he was 36.

Stephansson was the literary leader of the emigrant Icelanders. He lived a hard life as a pioneer farmer with a large family, and most of his poems were written after a long day's work—thus the title of his major collection, *Andvökur*, 6 vol. (1909–38; "Sleepless Nights"). Stephansson fought regimentation of many kinds: social, economic, and clerical. He wrote nostalgically about Iceland but with equal fervor about his new country. Though virtually all of his poetry was written while he lived in North America, he continued to write exclusively for an Icelandic-speaking public.

Stephen \'stē-vən\, Sir Leslie (b. Nov. 28, 1832, London, Eng.—d. Feb. 22, 1904, London)   English critic, man of letters, and first editor of the *Dictionary of National Biography*.

He was the father of the writer Virginia Woolf and the painter Vanessa Bell.

Stephen was educated at Eton, at King's College, London, and at Trinity Hall (later College), Cambridge. Stephen gained entry to the literary world and contributed to many periodicals. In 1871 he accepted the editorship of *The Cornhill Magazine*, for which he wrote literary criticism later republished in the three series of *Hours in a Library* (1874–79). After 11 years he resigned from the editorship of *Cornhill*, but he continued to write for periodicals.

Stephen's greatest learned work was his *History of English Thought in the Eighteenth Century* (1876). His most enduring legacy, however, is the *Dictionary of National Biography*, which he edited from 1882 to 1891. He edited the first 26 volumes and contributed 378 biographies to the important reference work. Stephen's *English Literature and Society in the Eighteenth Century* (1904) was a pioneer work in the sociological study of literature.

Stephens \'stē-vənz\, Alfred George (b. Aug. 28, 1865, Toowoomba, Queen., Australia—d. April 15, 1933, Sydney, N.S.W.)   Australian literary critic and journalist whose writings in newspapers and periodicals set standards for Australian literature. He is considered Australia's pioneer man of letters.

Joining the staff of *Boomerang*, a radical Brisbane weekly, Stephens wrote a column that surveyed American and British journals. After another brief stint as an editor, he traveled abroad, publishing *A Queenslander's Travel Notes* (1894) upon his return. In 1894 he joined the staff of the Sydney *Bulletin* and in 1896 developed his "Red Page" literary section, which included book reviews and other editorial notices. This famous feature appeared in the *Bulletin* until 1961 and came to play a key part in promoting the work of young Australian writers. He published a volume of poetry, *Oblation* (1902), and a selection of his Red Page reviews in *The Red Pagan* (1904).

In 1906 Stephens left the *Bulletin* and from 1907 to 1909 lived in New Zealand. He returned to Sydney, reviving a magazine (*Bookfellow*) that he had earlier attempted to establish and writing criticism on a freelance basis. The magazine was published monthly, except for a hiatus of three and a half years, until 1925. His later works include another volume of verse, a novel, two plays, and various other collections of critical writings.

Stephens \'stē-vənz\, James (b. Feb. 9, 1880?, Dublin, Ire.—d. Dec. 26, 1950, London, Eng.)   Irish poet and storyteller whose pantheistic philosophy is revealed in his fairy tales set in the Dublin slums of his childhood and in his compassionate poems about animals.

Stephens was working as a solicitor's clerk and educating himself when he met the Irish poet Æ (George William Russell), who encouraged him and helped him publish *Insurrections*, his first book of poetry, in 1909. His first novel, *The Charwoman's Daughter*, appeared in 1911 in *The Irish Review*, which he had helped found that year. It was his next book, *The Crock of Gold* (1912), with its rich Celtic theme, that established his fame.

Stephens' astringent use of irony suggests affinities with his friend James Joyce. He wrote *The Demi-Gods* (1914) in this vein, but *Deirdre* (1923) was constructed in a more formal, rhythmic prose. Short stories and lyric poems constitute the remainder of his work.

Steppenwolf \'shtep-ən-ˌvȯlf, *Angl* 'step-ən-ˌwu̇lf\   Novel by Hermann HESSE, published as *Der Steppenwolf* in 1927. The title refers to a style adopted by Harry Haller, Hesse's protagonist. Haller is a writer, a loner and an outsider who thinks of himself as a wolf of the steppes. Distrusting Western values and despising middle-class society, he despairs of connecting with

another human being. Eventually he learns that by conquering his sexual and emotional inhibitions, he can relate to others and still keep his ideals.

Sterling \'stər-liŋ\, Bruce (b. April 14, 1954, Brownsville, Tex., U.S.)   American author of science fiction who in the mid-1980s emerged as a proponent of the subgenre known as cyberpunk, notably as the editor of *Mirrorshades: The Cyberpunk Anthology* (1986).

In 1976 Sterling graduated from the University of Texas at Austin and published his first story, "Man-Made Self," in the anthology *Lone Star Universe*. His first novel, *Involution Ocean* (1977), describes a dystopian planet where inhabitants escape their confusing lives through drug abuse. The characters in *The Artificial Kid* (1980) struggle to gain stability in a world of fast-paced change.

Sterling's novel *Schismatrix* (1985) and the short-story collection *Crystal Express* (1989) examine the contrasting philosophies of the Shapers, who alter themselves genetically, and the Mechanists, who alter themselves with prosthetic devices. In *Islands in the Net* (1988) heroine Laura Webster is drawn into the geopolitics of a vast information network. In *The Difference Engine* (1990; written with William Gibson), Sterling imagined the ascent of the computer age during the 19th century. In 1992 he published *Globalhead*, a volume of short fiction, and *The Hacker Crackdown: Law and Disorder on the Electronic Frontier*, an exposé of computer crime.

Stern, Daniel.   Pseudonym of Marie de Flavigny, Countess d'AGOULT.

Stern \'stərn\, Richard G., *in full* Gustave (b. Feb. 25, 1928, New York, N.Y., U.S.)   American author and teacher whose literate fiction examines the intricacies of marital difficulties and family relationships.

Stern was educated at the University of North Carolina, Harvard University, and the University of Iowa. From 1955 he taught at the University of Chicago.

His novels include *Golk* (1960), a humorous examination of the television industry; *Europe: or, Up and Down with Schreiber and Baggish* (1961), concerning two middle-aged American men in postwar Germany; *Stitch* (1965), about an expatriate American sculptor, modeled after Ezra Pound; *Other Men's Daughters* (1973), an autobiographical account of a middle-aged professor in love with a young female student; *Natural Shocks* (1978), in which a journalist must deal with the deaths of those close to him; and *A Father's Words* (1986), about a divorced father and his relationship with his grown children. *Teeth, Dying, and Other Matters* (1964) is a collection of short fiction, a play, and an essay. *The Books in Fred Hampton's Apartment* (1973) contains essays and miscellaneous pieces. Stern's other compilations include *Noble Rot: Stories 1949–1988* (1989), *Shares and Other Fictions* (1992), and *One Person and Another: On Writers and Writing* (1993).

Sterne \'stərn\, Laurence (b. Nov. 24, 1713, Clonmel, County Tipperary, Ire.—d. March 18, 1768, London, Eng.)   Irish-born English novelist and humorist, author of the novel TRISTRAM SHANDY (1759–67), in which the story is subordinate to the free associations and digressions of its narrator.

Sterne attended Jesus College, Cambridge, where he was introduced to the philosophy of John Locke, which came to permeate his thought. After graduating he took holy orders and became vicar of Sutton-on-the-Forest, north of York, his home for two decades. He soon became a prebendary (or canon) of York and acquired the vicarage of Stillington.

As a clergyman Sterne worked hard but erratically. In 1759, to support his dean in a church squabble, Sterne wrote *A Political Romance* (later called *The History of a Good Warm Watch-*

Coat), a Swiftian satire on dignitaries of the spiritual courts. At the demands of embarrassed churchmen, the book was burned. Thus, Sterne lost his chances for clerical advancement but dis-

Detail of an oil painting by Sir Joshua Reynolds, 1760; in the National Portrait Gallery, London

covered his real talents. Turning over his parishes to a curate, he began *Tristram Shandy*. When the first two (of nine) volumes were published in 1759, they enjoyed great success. Sterne was then able to settle at his new home at Shandy Hall in the parish of Coxwold. The Dodsley firm brought out two more volumes of *Tristram Shandy*; thereafter, Sterne was his own publisher. In 1762 he fled the damp air of England into France, a journey he described as Tristram's flight from death. This and a later trip abroad gave him much material for the later novel A SENTIMENTAL JOURNEY THROUGH FRANCE AND ITALY (1768).

Sternheim \\'shtern-ˌhīm\\, Carl, *in full* William Adolf Carl Sternheim (b. April 1, 1878, Leipzig, Ger.—d. Nov. 3, 1942, Brussels, Belg.)   German dramatist best known for his plainly written satiric comedies about middle-class values and aspirations.

Sternheim was the son of a Jewish banker. He studied at the universities of Munich, Göttingen, Leipzig, and Berlin and performed his military service in a cavalry regiment. Family wealth and the wealth of his first two wives left him free to write and to travel.

Sternheim, who began writing plays at the age of 15, produced his best plays from 1911 through 1916. They were collectively titled *Aus dem bürgerlichen Heldenleben* ("From the Lives of Bourgeois Heroes"). The first play, *Die Hose* (1911; U.S. title, *The Underpants*; U.K. title, *The Knickers*), was originally produced under the title *Der Riese* ("The Giant"). Its principal character, Theobald Maske, and other members of the Maske family also appear in *Der Snob* (1914), *1913* (1915), and *Das Fossil* (1925). The four plays form the Maske-Tetralogie and portray the family as self-indulgent social climbers masked by bourgeois propriety.

Sternheim's later plays were less successful. The telegram-like language of his early plays forms a bridge between the work of Frank Wedekind and that of Bertolt Brecht. Sternheim is frequently named among the Expressionist dramatists, but he steadfastly maintained that he was a realist.

The avant-garde style of his short and long fiction precluded popular success. His autobiography, *Vorkriegseuropa im Gleichnis meines Lebens* ("Prewar Europe in the Image of My Life"), appeared in 1936. English translations of five of his plays (*Die Hose, Der Snob, 1913, Das Fossil,* and *Bürger Schippel* [1913; *Paul Schippel, Esq.*]) appeared in *Scenes from the Heroic Life of the Middle Classes* (1970).

Stesichorus or **Stesichoros** \\stə-'sik-ə-rəs\\ (b. 632/629 BC, Mataurus [Italy]—d. 556/553 BC)   Greek lyric poet who is credited with originating bucolic (pastoral) poetry in his *Daphnis*. He is also acknowledged as the forerunner of Hellenistic romantic poetry with such works as *Calyce* and *Rhadine.*

Stesichorus' works were mainly narrative poems dealing with myths, and he wrote in the Doric dialect. The Latin writers Horace and Quintilian spoke of him as a serious poet, but only about 100 lines of his work have survived; it is not even certain that he used the triadic stanza (divided into strophe, antistrophe, and epode) that is supposed to be his invention. Stesichorus was active mainly at Himera in Sicily.

Stevens \\'stē-vənz\\, Wallace (b. Oct. 2, 1879, Reading, Pa., U.S.—d. Aug. 2, 1955, Hartford, Conn.)   American poet whose work explores the interaction of reality and the human interpretation of reality.

Stevens attended Harvard University, worked briefly for the New York *Herald Tribune*, and then earned a degree (1904) at the New York Law School and practiced law in New York City. His first published poems, aside from college verse, appeared in *Poetry* in 1914, and thereafter he was a frequent contributor to literary magazines. In 1916 he joined an insurance firm in Hartford, rising in 1934 to vice president, a position he held until his death.

Harmonium (1923), his first book, sold fewer than 100 copies but received favorable critical notices; it was reissued in 1931 and in 1947. In the work, he introduced the imagination-reality theme that occupied his creative lifetime, making his work so unified that three decades later he considered calling his collected poems "The Whole of Harmonium."

Stevens displayed his most dazzling verbal brilliance in his first book; he later tended to relinquish surface luster for philosophical rigor. *Harmonium* contained such poems as "Le Monocle de Mon Oncle," "Sunday Morning," "Peter Quince at the Clavier," and Stevens' own favorites, "Domination of Black" and "The Emperor of Ice-Cream"; all were frequently republished in anthologies. *Harmonium* also contained "Sea Surface Full of Clouds"—in which waves are described in terms of such unlikely equivalents as umbrellas, French phrases, and varieties of chocolate—and "The Comedian as the Letter C," in which he examines the relation of the poet, or person of imagination, to society.

In the 1930s and early 1940s, this theme was to reappear, although not to the exclusion of others, in Stevens' *Ideas of Order* (1935), *The Man with the Blue Guitar* (1937), and *Parts of a World* (1942). *Transport to Summer* (1947) incorporated two long sequences that had appeared earlier: "Notes Towards a Supreme Fiction" and "Esthétique du Mal" ("Aesthetic of Evil"), in which he argued that beauty is inextricably linked with evil. *The Auroras of Autumn* (1950) was followed by his *Collected Poems* (1954), which earned him the Pulitzer Prize for poetry. It was not until late in life that Stevens was widely read at all or recognized as a major poet by more than a few. A volume of his critical essays, *The Necessary Angel*, appeared in 1951.

Stevenson \\'stē-vən-sən\\, Robert Louis (Balfour) (b. Nov. 13, 1850, Edinburgh, Scot.—d. Dec. 3, 1894, Vailima, Samoa)   Scottish essayist, poet, and author of fiction and travel books, known especially for his novels of adventure.

Stevenson studied law at Edinburgh University and in July 1875 was called to the Scottish bar, but he never practiced.

He first made a name for himself as a writer with the essays he wrote for several different periodicals. He also wrote accounts of his frequent travels; two of his journeys produced *An Inland Voyage* (1878) and TRAVELS WITH A DONKEY IN THE CÉVENNES (1879).

Brown Brothers

In 1876 Stevenson met Fanny Vandegrift Osbourne, an American woman separated from her husband, and the two fell in love. When she returned to California, he decided to join her in August 1879. The record of his arduous journey appeared later in *The Amateur Emigrant* (1895) and *Across the Plains* (1892). He married Fanny Osbourne (who was by then divorced from her first husband) early in 1880, and they soon returned to Scotland.

Stevenson was afflicted with tuberculosis, and he, his wife, and his stepson moved often in search of better climates. His first collection of essays, VIRGINIBUS PUERISQUE, was published in 1881, and TREASURE ISLAND appeared in 1883. There followed A CHILD'S GARDEN OF VERSES (first published 1885) and *The Black Arrow: A Tale of the Two Roses* (1888), a historical adventure tale deliberately written in anachronistic language. While living in England, Stevenson revised *A Child's Garden* and wrote KIDNAPPED (1886) and DR. JEKYLL AND MR. HYDE (1886).

After spending almost a year in America, during which time he wrote essays for *Scribner's* and began THE MASTER OF BALLANTRAE (1889), Stevenson, accompanied by his family, spent the rest of his life in the South Seas. He spent months wandering around South Sea islands and recorded his observations in *In the South Seas* (1896) and *A Footnote to History* (1892). The fiction he wrote during those years was moving toward a new maturity, seen to some degree in THE BEACH OF FALESÁ (1892) and culminating in WEIR OF HERMISTON (1896), his unfinished masterpiece.

Stewart \'stü-ərt, 'styü-\, Donald Ogden (b. Nov. 30, 1894, Columbus, Ohio, U.S.—d. Aug. 2, 1980, London, Eng.) American humorist, actor, playwright, and screenwriter who won a 1940 Academy Award for his screenplay adaptation of *The Philadelphia Story.*

After graduation from Yale University (1916), Stewart served in the U.S. Naval Reserve Force during World War I and worked briefly in private business before taking up humorous writing in 1921. His *A Parody Outline of History* (1921) was an instant success, and he quickly was received into the literary circle known as the Algonquin Round Table, famous for the witty repartee of members Dorothy Parker, Robert Benchley, and others. In 1928 Stewart made his New York City acting debut as Nick Potter in *Holiday* and subsequently wrote his first play, *Rebound,* in which he also appeared (1930).

It was, however, as a screenwriter, usually of adaptations of plays or novels, that Stewart achieved his most enduring success; his screenplays were notable for witty dialogue and for their fidelity to the original work. He fell victim to the anticommunist mania of the 1950s and was one of many Hollywood figures to be blacklisted. Thereafter, he retired to England. His autobiography, *By a Stroke of Luck,* was published in 1975.

Stewart \'stü-ərt, 'styü-\, Douglas (Alexander) (b. May 6, 1913, Eltham, N.Z.—d. Feb. 14, 1985, Sydney, Australia) Poet, playwright, and critic who helped establish an Australian national tradition through mythical re-creation of the past in his plays.

Stewart studied at Victoria University College but left to take up journalism. He traveled to Australia in search of work but returned to New Zealand in 1937 and financed publication of *Green Lions,* his first book of poems. Returning to Australia in 1938, he worked on the "Red Page" literary section in the *Bulletin,* Sydney's influential newspaper, serving as editor of the section from 1940 to 1961. Thereafter he worked as a literary adviser to Angus and Robertson publishers of Sydney.

His greatest literary success was the radio play *The Fire on the Snow* (1944, broadcast 1941), which described Robert Falcon Scott's expedition to Antarctica in 1912. This was followed by *The Golden Lover* (1944; published with *The Fire on the Snow*), the retelling of a Maori legend. *Ned Kelly* (1943), *Shipwreck* (1947), and *Fisher's Ghost* (1960) were three historical dramas for the stage.

Collected Poems, 1936–1967 was published in 1967, and another volume, *Poems: A Selection,* in 1972. *A Girl with Red Hair and Other Stories* (1944) is the only collection of Stewart's fiction. Critical works by Stewart include *The Flesh and the Spirit: An Outlook on Literature* (1948) and *The Broad Stream: Aspects of Australian Literature* (1975). He also anthologized bush ballads and other types of Australian poetry and wrote a volume of essays, *The Seven Rivers* (1960). He recalled the first 25 years of his life in *Springtime in Taranaki* (1983).

Stewart \'stü-ərt, 'styü-\, J.I.M., *in full* John Innes Mackintosh, *pseudonym* Michael Innes \'in-is\ (b. Sept. 30, 1906, Edinburgh, Scot.) Scots novelist and literary critic.

Educated at the Edinburgh Academy and at Oriel College, Oxford, Stewart taught for several years, publishing his first mystery story, *Hamlet, Revenge!* in 1937. In 1949 he became a fellow of Christ Church, Oxford. Stewart's works of literary criticism include *Character and Motive in Shakespeare* (1949), *Eight Modern Writers* (1963), *Rudyard Kipling* (1966), *Joseph Conrad* (1968), and *Thomas Hardy* (1971). He also wrote a number of novels and collections of short stories under his own name. He is probably best known popularly for the detective stories and broadcast scripts he wrote under his pseudonym. Most of these feature police detective (later chief police commissioner) John Appleby. His style in these mysteries was characterized as Victorian, donnish, and witty.

stich \'stik\ [Greek *stíchos* row, line, verse] A measured part (such as a line) of something written, especially in verse.

stichic \'stik-ik\ Of, relating to, or consisting of lines of verse, or lines that are rhythmic units; also, arranged or divided by lines rather than by stanzas.

stichomythia \‚stik-ə-'mith-ē-ə\ or **stichomythy** \sti-'käm-ə-thē\ *plural* stichomythias *or* stichomythies [Greek *stichomythía,* from *stíchos* row, line, verse + *mŷthos* thing said, speech, tale] Dialogue especially of altercation or dispute delivered in alternating lines (as in classical Greek drama).

This device, which is found in such plays as Aeschylus' *Agamemnon* and Sophocles' *Oedipus the King,* is frequently used as a means to show characters in vigorous contention or to heighten the emotional intensity of a scene. Characters may take turns voicing antithetical positions, or they may take up one another's words, suggesting other meanings or punning upon them.

Repartee in the form of polished aphorisms was a stylistic feature of the Roman tragedies of Seneca, which were intended for private readings rather than public performance. Through the influence of Seneca, stichomythia was adapted to the drama of Elizabethan England, most notably by William Shakespeare in comedies such as *Love's Labour's Lost* and in the memorable exchange between Richard and Queen Elizabeth in *Richard III* (Act IV, scene iv). A similar type of "cut-and-thrust" or "cut-and-parry" dialogue figures in the clipped, epigrammatic speech of the prose plays of the 1920s, such as those of Noël Coward.

Stiernhielm \'shern-,yelm\, Georg, *original name* Jöran Olofsson \'ö-lôf-,sôn\, *also called* Georgius Olai \'ö-,lī\ *or* Göran Lilia \'lē-lē-ə\ (b. Aug. 7, 1598, Vika, Swed.—d. April 22, 1672, Stockholm) Poet and scholar who is often called "the father of Swedish poetry."

Stiernhielm studied at Uppsala and spent several years at the German universities of Greifswald, Wittenberg, and Helmstedt. He returned to Sweden in 1626, and in 1631 he was raised to the nobility. Beginning about 1640 he was occasionally in Stockholm as poet in attendance at the court of Queen Christina, although his home was in Estonia until 1656, when he fled before the Russian invaders. Thereafter he lived in Stockholm in straitened circumstances.

Stiernhielm's first poetic works in Swedish appeared during the 1640s. They included verses in celebration of the queen and three court masques adapted from the French. His most important work is the allegorical, didactic epic *Hercules* (1658), a fine example of late Renaissance classicism. It is a sermon on virtue and honor and is imbued with the spirit of humanism. The theme is developed with power and originality; the imagery is exuberant; the construction, faultless. The work greatly influenced the development of Swedish poetry. Stiernhielm's poems were collected in *Musae suethizantes* (1668; "Swedish Muses").

Stifter \'shtif-tər\, Adalbert (b. Oct. 23, 1805, Oberplan, Austria—d. Jan. 28, 1868, Linz) Austrian writer whose novels of almost classical purity exalt the humble, solid virtues of a simple life.

Stifter enrolled as a law student in Vienna, but he took no degree. In 1840, after many years of precarious living as a tutor, artist, and writer, Stifter began to publish. His early story collections included *Der Condor* (1840), *Feldblumen* (1841; "Wildflowers"), and *Die Mappe meines Urgrossvaters* (1841–42; "My Great Grandfather's Portfolio"). In *Brigitta* (1844) the basic element of his major work began to emerge: an inner unity of landscape and character that would shape his stories. Collections of revised stories, *Studien*, 6 vol. (1844–50; "Studies"), and *Bunte Steine* (1853; "Colorful Stones"), brought him fame. In the important preface to the latter book, he expounded his doctrine of the "law of gentleness" as an enduring principle.

His greatest work, the novel *Der Nachsommer* (1857; "Indian Summer"), depicts a young man's development in the rural landscape so dear to Stifter. In his three-volume epic *Witiko* (1865–67), Stifter used medieval Bohemian history as a symbol for the human struggle for a just and peaceful order. He fell ill and died before completing his project of expanding *Die Mappe meines Urgrossvaters* into a novel; only the first volume was completed.

Still Life One-act play by Noël COWARD, produced and published in 1936, about a pair of middle-aged lovers doomed to part. *Still Life* was one of a group of one-act plays by Coward that were performed in various combinations, making up three shows entitled *Tonight at 8:30* (1936).

Laura and Alec become acquainted in the refreshment room of a railway station. Although both are quite content in their marriages, they fall in love and embark on a brief, passionate affair. Riddled with guilt, they know they must stop seeing each other. Their final parting, at the railway station where they met, is marred by the intrusiveness of a talkative acquaintance.

The play was adapted by Coward for the film *Brief Encounter* (1946).

Stilo Praeconinus \'stī-lō-,prē-kə-'nī-nəs\, Lucius Aelius, *also called* Aelius Stilo \'ē-lē-əs\ (b. *c.* 154 BC, Lanuvium, near Rome [Italy]—d. 74 BC, Rome?) First systematic student, critic, and teacher of Latin philology and literature and of the antiquities of Rome and Italy.

A member of a distinguished family, Stilo taught Varro and Cicero. Only a few fragments of Stilo's works remain. He wrote commentaries on the hymns of the Salii (minor priests who sang their Carmen Saliare at public meeting places at the beginning and end of the growing season); he probably wrote commentaries on the Twelve Tables, the earliest collected body of Roman law; and he produced a general work treating literary, historical, and antiquarian questions. His most important work was his investigation into the authenticity of the comedies of Plautus, of which he determined that 25 were genuine.

stock character A character in a drama or fiction that represents a type and that is recognizable as belonging to a certain genre. Most of the characters in the commedia dell'arte are stock characters. In Roman and Renaissance comedy there is the miles gloriosus, or braggart soldier; in Elizabethan drama there is usually a fool; in fairy tales a prince charming; and in melodrama a scheming villain.

Stockton \'stäk-tən\, Frank R., *in full* Francis Richard Stockton, *pseudonyms* Paul Fort, John Lewees (b. April 5, 1834, Philadelphia, Pa., U.S.—d. April 20, 1902, Washington, D.C.) American popular novelist and short-story writer of mainly humorous fiction, best known as the author of the title story of a collection called *The Lady, or the Tiger?* (1884).

Stockton contributed to and was on the staff of *Hearth and Home* and in 1873 became assistant editor of the *St. Nicholas Magazine*. His earliest fiction was written for children. Among his most popular children's stories were those collected in *Ting-a-Ling Tales* (1870) and *The Floating Prince, and Other Fairy Tales* (1881). "The Griffin and the Minor Canon" and the title story of the collection *The Bee-Man of Orn, and Other Fanciful Tales* (1887) were both republished in the 1960s with illustrations by Maurice Sendak.

His adult novel *Rudder Grange* (1879), originally serialized in *Scribner's Monthly*, recounted the whimsically fantastic and amusing adventures of a family living on a canal boat. Its success encouraged two sequels, *Rudder Grangers Abroad* (1891) and *Pomona's Travels* (1894). *The Casting Away of Mrs. Lecks and Mrs. Aleshine* (1886) tells of two middle-aged women on a sea voyage to Japan who become castaways on a deserted island. A sequel appeared in 1888 as *The Dussantes*. After 1887 Stockton wrote mostly for adults.

Stoddard \'städ-ərd\, Richard Henry (b. July 2, 1825, Hingham, Mass., U.S.—d. May 12, 1903, New York, N.Y.) American poet, critic, and editor, more important as a late 19th-century literary figure than as a poet.

In 1849 Stoddard gave up his trade and began writing for a living. He served as a literary reviewer and editor for a number of New York newspapers and magazines. His house was a leading gathering place for writers and artists in the last 30 years of the 19th century. Some of Stoddard's work—*Abraham Lincoln, An Horatian Ode* (1865) and parts of *Songs of Summer* (1857) and *The Book of the East* (1867)—can still be read with interest. Stoddard's autobiography, *Recollections Personal and Literary,* was published in 1903.

Stoker \'stō-kər\, Bram, *byname of* Abraham Stoker (b. 1847, Dublin, Ire.—d. April 20, 1912, London, Eng.) Author of the popular horror tale DRACULA (1897).

Stoker was a bedridden invalid until he was seven. He attended Trinity College (University of Dublin), where, having outgrown his youthful weakness, he became an outstanding athlete. After spending 10 years in the civil service at Dublin Castle, during which time he also served as an unpaid drama critic for the Dublin *Mail*, he made the acquaintance of his idol, the actor Sir Henry Irving; from 1878 until Irving's death 27 years later, Stoker acted as his manager, writing as many as 50 letters a day for him and accompanying him on his American tours. During this period Stoker began to write short stories. His first horror story was published in 1875. *The Snake's Pass*, his first novel, was published in 1890, and in 1897 his masterpiece, *Dracula*, appeared. The immensely popular novel enjoyed equal success in several versions as a play and as a motion picture.

Stoker wrote several other novels—among them *The Mystery of the Sea* (1902), *The Jewel of Seven Stars* (1904), *The Lady of the Shroud* (1909), and *The Lair of the White Worm* (1911)— but none of them approached the popularity, or, indeed, the quality, of *Dracula*.

Stolberg-Stolberg \'shtôl-,berk-'shtôl-,berk\, Christian, Count (Graf) zu and Friedrich Leopold, Count zu (respectively b. Oct. 15, 1748, Hamburg [Germany]—d. Jan. 18, 1821, Schloss Windebye, near Eckernförde; b. Nov. 7, 1750, Bramstedt, Holstein [Germany]—d. Dec. 5, 1819, Schloss Sondermühlen, near Osnabrück, Hanover) Brothers who were German lyric poets of the antirational Sturm und Drang and early Romantic periods.

Christian and Friedrich, noblemen who were actually Danish subjects, studied law at Halle and at Göttingen, where in 1772 both became members of the Göttinger Hain, a group that met to discuss their poems and to further the ideals of friendship, virtue, freedom, love of fatherland, and interest in Germanic history. In 1775 they toured Switzerland, part of the time with J.W. von Goethe. The brothers later collaborated on two books of poems, *Gedichte* (1779; "Poems") and *Vaterländische Gedichte* (1815; "Poems of the Fatherland").

In 1777 Christian became magistrate at a city in Holstein while Friedrich entered the diplomatic service and lived in Copenhagen and Berlin. Friedrich converted to Roman Catholicism in 1800 and became active in a group of Westphalian Catholics working to develop Romanticism. At the same time he continued to write poetry. Of the two brothers, Friedrich had more success as a writer than did Christian.

In addition to poetry, Friedrich wrote travel books and theoretical literary essays and translated Homer's *Iliad* (1778) and tragedies by Aeschylus (1802). His final work was the immense *Geschichte der Religion Jesu Christi*, 15 vol. (1806–18; "History of the Religion of Jesus Christ"), which traced the development of Christianity up until the year 430. Christian also produced a number of translations, including a two-volume version of *Sofokles* (1787).

Stone \'stōn\, Irving, *original surname* Tennenbaum \'ten-ən-,bôm, -,baùm\ (b. July 14, 1903, San Francisco, Calif., U.S.—d. Aug. 26, 1989, Los Angeles, Calif.) American writer of popular historical biographies. Stone first came to prominence with the publication of *Lust for Life* (1934), a fictionalized biography of the painter Vincent van Gogh.

Stone termed his work "bio-history." Through meticulous and exhaustive research, he verified and expanded his preconception of a selected historical character. Then, by immersing himself in the subject's native environment and reading all available original documents, from letters and diaries to research notes and household accounts, he acquired the basis for imaginary or reconstructed dialogue.

In addition to *Lust for Life*, Stone's many popular works include *Clarence Darrow for the Defense* (1941); *They Also Ran* (1943), biographies of 19 defeated presidential candidates; *President's Lady* (1951), based on the life of Rachel Jackson, wife of the seventh U.S. president; *Love Is Eternal* (1954), a fictionalized account of the marriage of Mary Todd and Abraham Lincoln; *The Agony and the Ecstasy* (1961), a life of the Renaissance artist Michelangelo; *The Passions of the Mind* (1971), about Sigmund Freud; and *The Origin* (1980), a life of Charles Darwin centered on the voyage of the *Beagle* and its aftermath.

Stone \'stōn\, Robert (Anthony) (b. Aug. 21, 1937, New York, N.Y., U.S.) American author of fiction about individuals in conflict with the decaying, late 20th-century Western societies in which they live.

Stone served in the U.S. Navy before attending New York and Stanford universities. *A Hall of Mirrors* (1967), his first novel, was set in New Orleans and revolved around a right-wing radio station and its chaotic "Patriotic Revival"; Stone adapted his novel for the screenplay of the film *WUSA* (1970). His second novel, *Dog Soldiers* (1974), brought the corruption of the Vietnam War home to the United States. The novel won the 1975 National Book Award, and Stone cowrote the screenplay for the film based on it, *Who'll Stop the Rain?* (1978).

In the late 1970s Stone visited Central America, the setting of his novel *A Flag for Sunrise* (1981), about four individuals in a corrupt, poverty-stricken country ripe for revolution. His novel *Children of Light* (1986) features a debauched screenwriter and a schizophrenic actress, both in decline. Stone's fifth novel, *Outerbridge Reach* (1992), was a well-received story of a foundering marriage and an around-the-world sailboat race.

Stone Guest, The Blank verse drama by Aleksandr PUSHKIN, published posthumously in 1839 as *Kamenny gost*. The work is one of four acclaimed "little tragedies" completed by Pushkin in the fall of 1830.

A highly intelligent poet and chronic seducer who thinks himself superior to almost everyone, Don Juan is alienated from society by his flawed character. He feels no guilt over seducing and abandoning countless women or over killing his rivals in duels. Don Juan is finally defeated by the stone statue of a knight commander whom he had killed in a duel. The statue comes to life when Don Juan seduces his widow.

Stones of Venice, The \'ven-is\ Treatise on architecture by John RUSKIN. It was published in three volumes in 1851–53.

Ruskin wrote the work in order to apply to the architecture of Venice the general principles enunciated in his *The Seven Lamps of Architecture*. Volume I, *The Foundations*, discusses architecture and its functional and ornamental aspects and presents a brief history of Venice. In Volume II, *The Sea Stories*, Ruskin discusses the Byzantine period and the climactic development of Venetian life, its Gothic period. In Volume III, *The Fall*, Ruskin puts forth his thesis that the onset of the Renaissance caused the city's architectural decline. Ruskin contended that Gothic architecture expressed "a state of pure national faith, and . . . domestic virtue" while Renaissance architecture expressed "concealed national infidelity, and . . . domestic corruption."

stop \'stäp\ A pause or break in a verse that marks the end of a grammatical unit.

Stoppard \'stäp-,ärd\, Tom, *original name* Tomas Straussler \'straús-lər\ (b. July 3, 1937, Zlín, Czech. [now in Czech Republic]) Czech-born British playwright whose work is marked by verbal brilliance, ingenious action, and structural dexterity.

Stoppard's father, a company physician, was killed in Singapore, where he had been posted with his family. The rest of the family escaped in 1942 to India, where in 1946 Stoppard's mother married a British officer, Kenneth Stoppard, whose surname Tom later assumed. The family went to live in England. Stoppard started his career as a journalist in Bristol in 1954 and began to write plays in 1960 after moving to London.

His first play, *A Walk on the Water* (1960), was revised as *Enter a Free Man* (produced 1968). His highly successful *Rosencrantz and Guildenstern Are Dead* was produced in 1966. The irony and brilliance of this work derive from Stoppard's placing two minor characters of *Hamlet* at the center of dramatic action, driving home his theme that humans are only minor characters in the greater scheme of things and are controlled by incomprehensible forces.

His later plays include the one-act *The Real Inspector Hound* (1968); *Jumpers* (1972), a witty view of academia in crisis; *Every Good Boy Deserves Favour* (produced 1977), with music by André Previn; *Night and Day* (1978); and *Undiscovered Country* (1980), an adaptation of a play by Arthur Schnitzler. *The Real Thing* (1982), Stoppard's first romantic comedy, deals with art and reality and features a playwright as protagonist. In addition to works for the stage, Stoppard wrote a number of acclaimed radio plays and screenplays. He directed and wrote the screenplay for the film version of *Rosencrantz and Guildenstern Are Dead* (1991). He also translated Václav Havel's *Largo desolato*.

Stopping by Woods on a Snowy Evening   Poem by Robert FROST, published in the collection *New Hampshire* (1923). One of his most frequently explicated works, it describes a solitary traveler in a carriage who is both driven by the business at hand and transfixed by a wintry woodland scene. The poem is composed of four iambic tetrameter quatrains, and the meditative lyric derives its incantatory tone from an interlocking rhyme scheme of *aaba bbcb ccdc dddd*.

Storey \'stôr-ē\, David (Malcolm) (b. July 13, 1933, Wakefield, Yorkshire, Eng.)   English novelist and playwright noted for his simple, powerful prose that won him early recognition as an accomplished storyteller and dramatist.

Storey, who had been a rugby player, had written and laid aside seven novels before his eighth, *This Sporting Life* (1960; film, 1966), was published. It is the story of a professional rugby player and his affair with his widowed landlady. Storey's *Flight into Camden* (1960) concerns an independent young woman who defies her mining family by going off to live with her married lover in London. *Radcliffe* (1963) is about the struggle for power in a homosexual relationship. His book *Pasmore* (1972) concerns a man's spiritual regeneration, and *Saville* (1976), which was awarded the Booker Prize, is an autobiographical account of the breaking away of a coal miner's son from village life. Storey's other novels include *A Prodigal Child* (1982) and *Present Times* (1984).

Storey also wrote plays, including *The Restoration of Arnold Middleton* (performed 1966), *In Celebration* (performed 1969; film, 1974), *The Contractor* (performed 1969), *Home* (1970), *The Changing Room* (1971), and *Life Class* (1974). Later plays include *Mother's Day* (1976), *Sisters* (1978), *Early Days* (1980), *The March on Russia* (1989), and *Phoenix* (1993).

storiette \,stôr-ē-'et\   A brief story or tale.

storify \'stôr-ə-,fī\   To narrate or describe in a story.

Storm \'shtôrm\, Theodor Woldsen, *in full* Hans Theodor Woldsen Storm (b. Sept. 14, 1817, Husum, Schleswig [Germany]—d. July 4, 1888, Hademarschen)   Poet and novelist who is an outstanding representative of German poetic realism.

Storm practiced law in Husum until 1853, when his opposition to Danish authority in Schleswig forced him to move to Potsdam. He returned to Schleswig in 1864. Storm's early

lyrics (*Gedichte*, 1852; "Poems") have as their main themes love, nature, and an intense love of homeland. They are songlike and characterized by simplicity and beauty of form. His best lyrics—those in the cycle *Tiefe Schatten* (1865; "Deep Shadows")—were written in sorrow over his wife's death.

One of his most important early novellas is *Immensee* (1850), a moving story of the vanished happiness of childhood, which, like so many of his works, is colored by a haunting nostalgia. As his writing matured Storm displayed subtler psychological insight, greater realism, and a wider scope of themes—including class tensions, social problems, and religious bigotry—expressing his recurrent concern with isolation and the struggle with fate. His last and greatest novella, *Der Schimmelreiter* (1888; *The Rider on the White Horse*), with its forceful hero and terse, objective style, shows vivid imagination and great narrative force. Among his other major works are the charming story *Pole Poppenspäler* (1874), the historical novella *Aquis submersus* (1875), and the novella *Im Schloss* (1861; "In the Castle").

Storni \'stôr-nē, 'shtôr-\, Alfonsina (b. May 29, 1892, Sala Capriasca, Switz.—d. Oct. 25, 1938, Mar del Plata, Arg.)   One of the foremost poets of Argentina and a pioneer feminist poet.

When Storni was four, her family immigrated to Argentina. In 1907 she joined a theatrical troupe and later taught school in the rural areas of Argentina. She was forced by the birth of her illegitimate child to move to Buenos Aires in 1912. There she held a variety of jobs and began to participate in the literary life of the city. Her first book, *La inquietud del rosal* (1916; "The Restless Rose Garden"), brought her some recognition, but it was her volume *El dulce daño* (1918; "Sweet Injury") that won her popular success. *Irremediablemente* (1919; "Without Remedy") and *Languidez* (1920; "Languor"), the books that rounded off her early phase, depict male sexual aggression as a necessary evil. The poetry of this period also expresses a strong need for love, and she was able to express the tension and passion of these ambivalent feelings in poetry both simple and deeply sensual. Her more mature style, seen in *Ocre* (1925; "Ocher"), *El mundo de siete pozos* (1934; "The World of Seven Wells"), and *Mascarilla y trébol* (1938; "Mask and Trefoil"), reveals a wider vision and less introspection. Her later poetry is more intellectual and more highly stylized. Many of her later poems seem to prefigure her suicide in 1938.

Storni also wrote two feminist plays, a book of prose poems, and some undistinguished plays for children.

story \'stôr-ē\ [Old French *storie, istorie, hystoire,* narrative, especially, of the remote past, from Latin *historia* record of research, history, narrative, from Greek *istoría*]   **1.** An account of incidents or events.   **2.** A fictional narrative shorter than a novel; specifically, a SHORT STORY.   **3.** The intrigue or plot of a narrative or dramatic work.

story line   The plot of a story or drama.

Story of a Bad Boy, The   Classic children's novel by Thomas Bailey ALDRICH, published serially in *Our Young Folks* (1869) and in book form in 1870. An autobiographical book about a happy boyhood, it was the first full-length work in which the protagonist was a realistic boy instead of a priggish paragon.

Story of an African Farm, The   Novel published in 1883, with its authorship credited to the pseudonymous Ralph Iron. The author was later revealed to be Olive SCHREINER. It was a best-seller, both praised and condemned for its powerfully feminist, unconventional, and anti-Christian views on religion and marriage.

The novel draws on Schreiner's memories of growing up on the isolated South African veld. Its protagonist, Lyndall, lives on an ostrich farm, and her choices are constrained by the strict conventions of Boer life. She struggles to achieve the freedom to make her own choices, rejecting marriage but deciding to have a child; she dies in childbirth. Her inner journey is paralleled by that of her suitor Waldo, who longs for spiritual and intellectual freedom.

Stout \'staùt\, Rex (Todhunter) (b. Dec. 1, 1886, Noblesville, Ind., U.S.—d. Oct. 27, 1975, Danbury, Conn.)   American author who wrote genteel mystery stories (both novelettes and novels), many of which revolve around the elegantly eccentric and reclusive detective Nero WOLFE and his wisecracking aide, Archie Goodwin.

Stout worked odd jobs until 1912, when he began to write sporadically for magazines. After writing four moderately successful novels, he turned to the form of the detective story. From 1927 Stout earned his living exclusively by writing. In *Fer-de-Lance* (1934) he introduced Nero Wolfe, the obese, brilliant aesthete who solves crimes without leaving his New York City apartment. Stout had a passion for gourmet foods and was obsessed with the growing of orchids, both of which characteristics he gave his detective. The Nero Wolfe mysteries are narrated by Archie Goodwin, a private detective and Wolfe's link to the outside world. Stout wrote 46 Wolfe mysteries, all of which were very popular.

Stow \'stō\, Randolph, *in full* Julian Randolph Stow (b. Nov. 28, 1935, Geraldton, W.Aus., Australia)   Australian novelist and poet noted for his economical style and great powers of description.

Stow's first novel, *A Haunted Land* (1956), a wild, almost gothic tale, appeared in the same year he graduated from the University of Western Australia. In 1957 he began to teach English at the University of Adelaide and brought out his second novel, *The Bystander*, a further treatment of the themes of *A Haunted Land. Tourmaline*, another strange, powerful, and terrifying novel, appeared in 1963, and in 1965 *The Merry-Go-Round in the Sea* was published. In the latter novel the heritage of a land built on its contrasting traditions of convict settlement and South Pacific paradise clashes with the values of a new Australia emerging from the impact of World War II. Other novels include *To the Islands* (1958; rev. ed., 1981); *Visitants* (1979), a study of the impact of tribal life on Australians; *The Girl Green as Elderflower* (1980); and *The Suburbs of Hell* (1984).

Among Stow's books of poetry are *Act One* (1957), *Outrider* (1962), and *A Counterfeit Silence* (1969). He also published *Poetry from Australia* (1969) with Judith Wright and William Hart-Smith. Stow also wrote a book for children entitled *Midnite* (1967) and two musicals, *Eight Songs for a Mad King* (1969) and *Miss Donnithorne's Maggot* (1977).

Stowe \'stō\, Harriet Beecher, *original name* Harriet Elizabeth Beecher \'bē-chər\ (b. June 14, 1811, Litchfield, Conn., U.S.—d. July 1, 1896, Hartford, Conn.)   American writer and philanthropist best known as the author of the powerful antislavery novel UNCLE TOM'S CABIN (1852).

Stowe was the daughter of a famous Congregationalist minister, Lyman Beecher. After 1832 she taught in Cincinnati, where she took an active part in literary and school life, contributing stories and sketches to local journals and compiling a school geography. She continued to write after the school closed in 1836 and after her marriage that year to Calvin Ellis Stowe. In 1843 she published *The Mayflower; or, Sketches of Scenes and Characters Among the Descendants of the Pilgrims.*

In Cincinnati, Stowe was separated only by the Ohio River from a slaveholding community; she came in contact with fugitive slaves and learned about life in the South from friends and

Library of Congress

from her own visits there. These experiences prompted her to write *Uncle Tom's Cabin*, which was published serially in the *National Era*, an antislavery paper of Washington, D.C. Stowe reinforced her story with *The Key to Uncle Tom's Cabin* (1853), in which she accumulated a large number of documents and testimonies against slavery.

In 1853, when Stowe made a journey to Europe, she was lionized in England. Later, however, British public opinion turned against her with publication in 1869 of the magazine article "The True Story of Lord Byron's Life," detailing her charge that the poet had had an incestuous love for his half sister. In 1856 she published *Dred: A Tale of the Great Dismal Swamp*, in which she depicted the deterioration of a society resting on a slave basis. When *The Atlantic Monthly* was established the following year, she found a ready vehicle for her writings; she also found outlets in the *Independent* of New York and later the *Christian Union*, of which papers her brother, Henry Ward Beecher, was editor.

Stowe thereafter led the life of a woman of letters, writing novels, of which *The Minister's Wooing* (1859) is best known, and many studies of social life in both fiction and essay. She also published a small volume of religious poems.

Strachey \'strā-chē\, Lytton, *in full* Giles Lytton Strachey (b. March 1, 1880, London, Eng.—d. Jan. 21, 1932, Ham Spray House, near Hungerford, Berkshire)   English biographer and critic who opened a new era of biographical writing at the close of World War I. Adopting an irreverent attitude to the past and especially to the monumental life-and-letters volumes of Victorian biography, Strachey proposed to write lives with "a brevity which excludes everything that is redundant and nothing that is significant." He is best known for EMINENT VICTORIANS (1918)—short sketches of the Victorian idols Cardinal Manning, Florence Nightingale, Thomas Arnold, and General Charles "Chinese" Gordon.

After studying at Cambridge, Strachey lived in London, where he became a leader in the artistic, intellectual, and literary Bloomsbury group. A self-identified homosexual, he was engaged for a time to Virginia Woolf. He published critical writings, especially on French literature, but his greatest achievement was in biography. After *Eminent Victorians* and *Queen Victoria* (1921), he wrote ELIZABETH AND ESSEX (1928) and *Portraits in Miniature* (1931). He was fascinated by personality and motive and treated his subjects from a highly idiosyncratic point of view. He delighted in pricking the pretensions of the great and reducing them to somewhat less than life-size. His methods occasionally led to caricature and sometimes, through tendentious selection of material, to inaccuracy, but he introduced a sense of form to the genre and demonstrated the value of a biographer's critical acumen.

Strachey saw politics largely as intrigue, religion as a ludicrous anachronism, and personal relations as life's supremely important facet. Though bitterly attacked during his lifetime and after, Strachey remains a phenomenon in English letters and a preeminent humorist and wit.

Strachwitz \\'shträk̲-vits\\, Moritz (Karl Wilhelm Anton), Count (Graf) von (b. March 13, 1822, Peterwitz, Silesia [Germany]—d. Dec. 11, 1847, Vienna, Austrian Empire) German poet who is remembered for his *Neue Gedichte* (1848; "New Poems"), which included such distinctive verses as "Der Himmel ist blau" ("The Sky Is Blue") and the patriotic song "Germania."

After studying in Breslau and Berlin, Strachwitz settled on his estate in Moravia, where he did his writing. He was involved with a Berlin literary club, Tunnel über der Spree, and competed with the novelist Theodor Fontane in writing ballads. Strachwitz was the most promising of the younger lyric poets of his time. His *Lieder eines Erwachenden* (1842; "Songs of an Awakening") especially showed his lyric genius and went through several editions. *Neue Gedichte* reveals a Romantic strain but also exhibits the influence of the Neoclassical German poet and dramatist August Platen. Strachwitz' political lyrics have aristocratic leanings lacking in those of his contemporaries. His collected works, *Sämtliche Lieder und Balladen* ("Collected Songs and Ballads"), appeared in 1912.

stracittà \\,strä-chĕt-'tä\\ An Italian literary movement that developed after World War I. Massimo Bontempelli was the leader of the movement, which was connected with his idea of *novecentismo.* Bontempelli called for a break from traditional styles of writing, and his own writings reflected his interest in such modern forms as Surrealism and magic realism. The name *stracittà,* a type of back-formation from the word *stracittadino* ("ultra-urban"), was meant to emphasize the movement's adherence to general trends in European literature, in opposition to *strapaese* (from *strapaesano* ["ultra-local"]), collectively, those authors who followed nationalist and regionalist trends.

strain \\'strān\\ A portion of a poem. Also, a passage of verbal or musical expression.

Strait Is the Gate Tale by André GIDE, published in 1909 as *La Porte étroite.* It is one of the first of his works to treat the problems of human relationships. The work contrasts the yearning toward asceticism and self-sacrifice with the need for sensual exploration as a young woman struggles with conflicting feelings about the man who wants to marry her. Gide designated *Strait Is the Gate* as a *récit,* which he defined as a consciously stark but basically ironic tale narrated by, and told from the viewpoint of, a single character.

strambotto \\sträm-'bòt-tō\\ *plural* strambotti \\-'bòt-tē\\ One of the oldest of Italian verse forms, composed of a single stanza of either six or eight hendecasyllabic (11-syllable) lines. *Strambotti* were particularly popular in Renaissance Sicily and Tuscany, and the origin of the form in either of the two regions is still uncertain. Variations of the eight-line *strambotto* include the Sicilian octave (*ottava siciliana*), with the rhyme scheme *abababab;* the OTTAVA RIMA, with the typical rhyme scheme *abababcc;* and the RISPETTO, a Tuscan form usually with the rhyme scheme *ababccdd* or with ottava rima. Six-line variants usually rhyme *ababab, ababcc,* or *aabbcc.* The subject of the *strambotto* was generally love (sometimes satire).

The Italian word *strambotto,* first attested in a Genoese document of the 13th century, is obscurely related to a group of words in other Romance dialects designating medieval poetic compositions, such as Old Provençal *estribot,* Old French *estrabot,* and Spanish *estribote* (later *estrambote*); their ultimate origin is uncertain.

Strand \\'strand\\, Mark (b. April 11, 1934, Summerside, P.E.I., Can.) Poet, writer of short fiction, and translator whose poetry, noted for its surreal quality, explores the boundaries of the self and the external world.

Educated at Antioch College, Yale University, and the University of Iowa, Strand later taught at several American universities. He was named American poet laureate in 1990.

Strand was influenced stylistically by Latin-American surrealism and European writers such as Franz Kafka, and his poetry, especially his earliest works, was known for its symbolic imagery and its minimalist sensibility. Collections of Strand's poetry include *Sleeping with One Eye Open* (1964), *Reasons for Moving* (1968), *Darker* (1970), *The Story of Our Lives* (1973), *The Late Hour* (1978), *Selected Poems* (1980), *The Continuous Life* (1990), and *Dark Harbor* (1993), the latter a book-length poem. A collection of prose pieces, *Mr. and Mrs. Baby and Other Stories,* was published in 1985. Among his translations of poetry by South American writers are *18 Poems from the Quechua* (1971) and Rafael Alberti's *The Owl's Insomnia* (1973). Strand edited *The Contemporary American Poets* (1969), *New Poetry of Mexico* (1970), and, with Charles Simic, *Another Republic: 17 European and South American Writers* (1976). He also wrote several children's books and works of art criticism.

Strange Interlude Pulitzer Prize-winning drama in two parts and nine acts by Eugene O'NEILL. It was produced in 1928 in New York City and was published the same year. The work's complicated plot is the story of a woman in her roles as daughter, wife, mistress, mother, and friend. Its length was an innovation, for in its original production it began in the late afternoon, paused for a dinner intermission, and resumed at the hour when most plays begin. It also employed innovative (at least in 20th-century drama) stage techniques, such as stream-of-consciousness soliloquies and asides.

Stranger, The Enigmatic first novel by Albert CAMUS, published in French as *L'Étranger* in 1942. It was published in England as *The Outsider.*

The title character of *The Stranger* is Meursault, who is sentenced to death ostensibly for shooting a man whom he had never met but perhaps more so, it is suggested, for his inability to dissemble, to experience conventional modes of feeling, or to conform to society's requirements. Meursault appears listless, emotionally detached from his heretofore uneventful life; his anomie is caught in the novel's famous opening lines: "Mother died today, or maybe it was yesterday." The shooting, which occurs midway through the novel, is an experience that opens Meursault to gradual self-awareness.

Straparòla \\,strä-pä-'rō-lä\\, Gianfrancesco (b. *c.* 1480, Caravaggio, duchy of Milan [Italy]—d. after 1557) Italian author of one of the earliest and most important collections of traditional tales.

Little is known of Straparòla's life. He is best known as the author of *Le piacevoli notti* (vol. 1, 1550; vol. 2, 1553; *The Nights of Straparola*). The work contains 75 novellas, or short prose tales—among them 20 folktales new to Europe, including "Beauty and the Beast" and "Puss in Boots"—set within a frame story. Straparòla's stories are told on successive nights during the last 13 days of Venetian carnival by a group of men and women gathered on Murano, an island off Venice. The collection, drawn from several sources, soon became famous throughout Europe. Many of the tales were later used as source material by William Shakespeare, Molière, and others.

Stratemeyer \\'strat-ə-,mī-ər\\, Edward (b. Oct. 4, 1862, Elizabeth, N.J., U.S.—d. May 10, 1930, Newark, N.J.) American writer of popular juvenile fiction, whose Stratemeyer Literary Syndicate (1906–84) produced such books as the *Rover Boys* series, the *Hardy Boys* series, the *Tom Swift* series, the *Bobbsey Twins* series, and the *Nancy Drew* series.

Stratemeyer began writing stories in imitation of those of Horatio Alger, Jr., and other popular adventure writers. He sold his first magazine story in 1888. In 1893 he became editor of *Good News*, for which he wrote boys' stories, and in 1896 he added the editorship of *Bright Days*. His first book, *Richard Dare's Venture*, appeared in 1894, the first in a series, and about 1896 he began writing concurrently several series, such as the *Rover Boys' Series for Young Americans*, beginning in 1899, and the *Boy Hunters Series*, beginning in 1906. Over the years he wrote hundreds of books and stories.

In 1906 he founded the Stratemeyer Literary Syndicate, which published various juvenile series, written by himself and others. (Any one series might have had several authors, all using the same pseudonym.) After his death in 1930, his company was largely directed by his daughter, Harriet Stratemeyer Adams (1893?–1982), who under pseudonyms wrote many of the novels in the *Nancy Drew, Dana Girls, Hardy Boys,* and *Bobbsey Twins* series. In 1984 the publisher Simon & Schuster acquired all rights to the Stratemeyer Literary Syndicate. *See also* BOBBSEY TWINS; Nancy DREW; HARDY BOYS; Tom SWIFT.

Stratfordian \strat-'fȯr-dē-ən\ [*Stratford*-upon-Avon, Shakespeare's birthplace] One who believes that William Shakespeare was the author of the dramatic works usually attributed to him. *Compare* OXFORDIAN.

Strayed Reveller, The Unrhymed lyric poem written in irregular meter by Matthew ARNOLD, originally published in his first volume of verse, *The Strayed Reveller, and Other Poems. By A.* (1849). An investigation of the creative process, the poem is notable for its vivid descriptive passages.

stream of consciousness Narrative technique in nondramatic fiction intended to render the flow of myriad impressions—visual, auditory, physical, associative, and subliminal—that together with rational thought impinge on the consciousness of an individual. The term was first used by the psychologist William James in *The Principles of Psychology* (1890). As the psychological novel developed in the 20th century, some writers attempted to capture the total flow of their characters' consciousness, rather than limit themselves to rational thoughts. To represent the full richness, speed, and subtlety of the mind at work, the writer may incorporate snatches of incoherent thought, ungrammatical constructions, and free association of ideas and images.

The stream-of-consciousness novel commonly uses the narrative techniques of INTERIOR MONOLOGUE. Probably the most famous example is James Joyce's *Ulysses* (1922). Other notable examples include *Leutnant Gustl* (1901) by Arthur Schnitzler, an early use of stream of consciousness to re-create the atmosphere of pre-World War I Vienna, and William Faulkner's *The Sound and the Fury* (1929). Another master of stream of consciousness is Virginia Woolf (especially in *The Waves* [1931]). An often overlooked English-language pioneer in the technique is Dorothy M. Richardson, whose multivolume *Pilgrimage* was published from 1915 to 1938.

Street, The Naturalistic novel by Ann PETRY, published in 1946, that was one of the first novels by an African-American woman to receive widespread critical acclaim. Set in Long Island, New York, in suburban Connecticut, and in Harlem, *The Street* is the story of intelligent, ambitious Lutie Johnson, who strives to make a better life for herself and her son despite a constant struggle with sexual brutality and racism.

Streetcar Named Desire, A Play in three acts by Tennessee WILLIAMS, first produced and published in 1947 and winner of the Pulitzer Prize for drama for that year. One of the most admired plays of its time, it concerns the mental and moral disintegration and ultimate ruin of Blanche DuBois, a former Southern belle. Her neurotic, genteel pretensions are no

match for the harsh realities symbolized by her brutish brother-in-law, Stanley Kowalski.

Street Scene Play in three acts by Elmer RICE, produced and published in 1929. The play is set in a New York City slum and offers a realistic portrayal of life in a tenement building. The story focuses particularly on the tragedy of one family, the Maurrants, which is destroyed when the husband shoots and kills his wife and her lover. *Street Scene* won a Pulitzer Prize and was adapted into a musical in 1947 with lyrics by Langston Hughes and music by Kurt Weill.

Strega Prize \'strā-gä\ Italian literary award established in 1947 by writers Goffredo and Maria Bellonci and the manufacturer of Strega liquor, Guido Alberti. It carries an award of one million lire, presented to the author of the outstanding Italian narrative (fiction or nonfiction) published the preceding year. Such writers as Cesare Pavese, Alberto Moravia, Elsa Morante, Carlo Cassola, Natalia Ginzburg, and Primo Levi have been recipients of the award.

stress \'stres\ In prosody, the relative force or prominence of a syllable in a verse. Though stress is often equated with accent, some prosodists make the distinction that accent refers to normal language usage while stress is used in metrics to fit a syllable to a particular metrical pattern. Stress is also sometimes considered one of the constituents of accent along with such things as tone and pitch. In modern accentual or accentual-syllabic prosody, the meter of a verse is determined by the pattern of stressed and unstressed syllables in the verse. In scansion, or analysis of the meter, a stressed syllable is marked with the symbol ´ and an unstressed syllable with the symbol ∪. *Compare* ACCENT.

Strether, Lambert \'lam-bərt-'streth-ər, 'streth-\ Fictional character, a sensitive middle-aged man from New England who is the central figure of the novel THE AMBASSADORS by Henry James.

Streuvels \'strœ-vəls\, Stijn, *pseudonym of* Frank Lateur \lä-'tœr\ (b. Oct. 3, 1871, Heule, near Courtrai, Belg.—d. Aug. 15, 1969, Ingooigem, near Courtrai) Belgian novelist and short-story writer whose works are among the masterpieces of Flemish prose.

Streuvels discovered his literary gifts while at school at Avelgem. Employed as a master baker in Avelgem for 15 years, he found time to learn German, English, Danish, and some Russian and, after 1892, to write his first stories. He contributed to the periodical *Van Nu en Straks* ("Today and Tomorrow") and in 1899 achieved fame with his first collection, *Lenteleven* (1915; *The Path of Life*).

Streuvels found his subjects in the village life of southwestern Flanders—an isolated and agrarian Flanders that no longer exists. His keen observation was enriched by his imaginative power, his feeling for atmosphere, and his rich resources of language. He created a world in which nature is an ever-present force, and he described it with a visionary power resembling that of the painter Vincent van Gogh. At his best he was a master of characterization, especially in his presentation of farmers and farm workers who struggle against the land and against destiny, as in *Langs de wegen* (1902; *The Long Road*) and in his masterpiece, *De vlaschaard* (1907; *The Flaxfield*). His epic but lyrical prose style, perfectly suited to his subject, is among the best of its period.

Strindberg \'strēn-,berʸ, *Angl* 'strind-,bȯrg, -,ber-ē\, August, *in full* Johan August Strindberg (b. Jan. 22, 1849, Stockholm, Swed.—d. May 14, 1912, Stockholm) Swedish playwright, novelist, and short-story writer, who combined psychology and naturalism in what evolved into Expressionist drama.

Strindberg's father was a bankrupt aristocrat, and his mother was a former waitress. His childhood was marred by emotional insecurity, poverty, religious fanaticism, and neglect, as he relates in his remarkable autobiography, *Tjänstekvinnans*

Brown Brothers

son (1886–87; *The Son of a Servant*). He worked as a freelance journalist in Stockholm as well as at other jobs that he almost invariably lost. Meanwhile, he struggled to complete his first important work, *Mäster Olof* (1872), a historical drama on the theme of the Swedish Reformation. The Royal Theater's rejection of *Mäster Olof* deepened his pessimism and sharpened his contempt for official institutions and traditions. For several years he continued revising the play—later recognized as the first modern Swedish drama—and it was finally produced in 1890.

In 1874 Strindberg became a librarian at the Royal Library, and in 1875 he met Siri von Essen, whom he married two years later. Their intense but ultimately disastrous relationship ended in divorce in 1891. At first, however, marriage stimulated his writing, and in 1879 he published his first novel, *Röda rummet* (*The Red Room*), a satirical account of abuses and frauds in Stockholm society. The book made its author nationally famous.

He also wrote more plays, of which *Lycko-Pers resa* (1881; *Lucky Peter's Travels*) contains the most biting social criticism. *Kamraterna* (1888; *Comrades*) followed. In 1883, the year after he published *Det nya riket* ("The New Kingdom"), a withering satire on contemporary Sweden, Strindberg left Stockholm with his family and for six years moved restlessly about Europe. The publication of the first volume of his collected stories, *Giftas* (1884–85; *Married*), led to a prosecution for blasphemy. He was acquitted, but the case affected his mind and he imagined himself persecuted.

Strindberg returned to drama with new intensity, and the conflict between the sexes inspired some of the outstanding works written at this time, such as *Fadren* (1887; THE FATHER), *Fröken Julie* (1888; MISS JULIE), and *Creditörer* (1890; THE CREDITORS). In these bold and concentrated works, he combined the techniques of dramatic naturalism—including unaffected dialogue, stark rather than luxurious scenery, and the use of stage props as symbols—with his own conception of psychology, thereby inaugurating a new movement in European drama. The novels *Hemsöborna* (1887; *The People of Hemsö*), about the Stockholm skerries (rocky islands), and *I havsbandet* (1890; *By the Open Sea*) were also produced during this intensively creative phase.

Even though Strindberg was a famous writer and was the acknowledged voice of modern Sweden, he was by this time an alcoholic unable to find steady employment. In 1892 he went abroad again, to Berlin. His second marriage lasted only from 1893 to 1895.

A period of stress and mental instability culminated in a religious conversion, the crisis he described in *Inferno* (1898). His experiments in alchemy and study of theosophy were reflected in a drama in three parts, *Till Damascus* (1898, 1904;

To Damascus), in which he depicts himself as "the Stranger," a wanderer seeking spiritual peace and finding it with another character, "the Lady."

By this time Strindberg had again returned to Sweden. His view that life is ruled by the "Powers," punitive but righteous, was reflected in a series of historical plays he began in 1889 with *Paria* (*Pariah*), followed by *Folkungasagan* (1899; *The Saga of the Folkungs*). Of these, *Gustav Vasa* (1899) is the best, masterly in its firmness of construction, characterization, and vigorous dialogue. In 1901 he married an actress, but in 1904 they parted.

His last marriage inspired, among other works, the plays *Dödsdansen* (1901; *The Dance of Death*) and *Ett drömspel* (1902; A DREAM PLAY), as well as the charming autobiography *Ensam* (1903; "Alone") and a number of lyrical poems. He also published collections of stories titled *Fagervik och skamsund* (1902; *Fair Haven and Foul Strand*) and *Sagor* (1903; *Tales*). Renewed bitterness after parting from his last wife provoked the grotesquely satirical novel *Svarta Fanor* (1907; "Black Banners"). *Kammarspel* ("Chamber Plays"), written for the Intima Theater, which Strindberg ran for a time with a young producer, August Falck, embody further developments of his dramatic technique: of these, *Spöksonaten* (1907; THE GHOST SONATA) is the most fantastic, anticipating trends in later European drama. His last play, *Stora landsvägen* (1909; *The Great Highway*), was a symbolic presentation of his own life.

strophe \\'strō-fē\\ [Greek *strophē* act of turning, turning of the chorus, strophe] In poetry, a group of verses that form a distinct unit within a poem. The term is sometimes used as a synonym for *stanza*, usually in reference to a Pindaric ode or to a poem that does not have a regular meter and rhyme pattern, such as free verse. In ancient Greek drama the strophe was the first part of a choral ode that was performed by the chorus while moving from one side of the stage to the other. The strophe was followed by an antistrophe of the same metrical structure (performed while the chorus reversed its movement) and then by an epode of different structure that was chanted as the chorus stood still. *Compare* STANZA.

structuralism \\'strək-chə-rə-ˌliz-əm\\ European critical movement of the mid-20th century. It was based on the linguistic theories of Ferdinand de Saussure, which held that language is a self-contained system of signs, and the cultural theories of Claude Lévi-Strauss, which held that cultures, like languages, could be viewed as systems of signs and could be analyzed in terms of the structural relations among their elements. Literary structuralism views literary texts as systems of interlocking signs and seeks to make explicit in a semiscientific way the "grammar" (the rules and codes or system of organization) that governs the form and content of all literature. Michel Foucault, Roman Jakobson, and Roland Barthes are among the more prominent structuralists. Areas of study that have adopted and developed structuralist premises and procedures are SEMIOTICS and NARRATOLOGY. *Compare* DECONSTRUCTION; POSTSTRUCTURALISM.

Struwwelpeter, Der \\der-'shtrův-əl-ˌpā-tər\\, *also called* Slovenly Peter \\'pē-tər\\ Illustrated collection of cautionary tales for young children, published in 1845 in German as *Lustige Geschichten und drollige Bilder mit fünfzehn schön kolorierten Tafeln für Kinder von 3–6 Jahren* ("Cheerful Stories and Funny Pictures with 15 Beautiful Color Plates for Children from Ages 3 to 6"). Its author, Heinrich HOFFMANN, was a physician and writer who used the pseudonym Reimerich Kinderlieb. The name Struwwelpeter (one of the characters in the book) was not part of the original title; it was added for the third German edition of the book.

The stories feature such characters as the title character, a boy whose untamed appearance is matched by his naughty behavior; a child who plays with matches and is burned to ashes; and a tailor who cuts off the thumbs of children who suck them. The tales in the collection are by some lights amusing and harmless and by others excessively gruesome and frightening.

Stuart Little \\'stü-ərt-'lit-əl, 'styü-\ Children's book by E.B. WHITE, published in 1945. The episodic story of the title character, a two-inch-tall boy who resembles a mouse, is noted for its understated humor, graceful wit, and ironic juxtaposition of fantasy and possibility.

Despite his diminutive stature—his family is of normal size—Stuart is a dashing, picaresque hero who is confident and courageous. His daring escapades include racing a toy boat in a Central Park pond, retrieving his mother's ring from a drain, and crawling inside a piano to fix the keys for his brother. He embarks on a quest to find his beloved Margalo, a little bird who is frightened away by the ferocious family cat, Snowbell.

Stubbs or **Stubbes** \\'stəbz\, Philip (b. *c.* 1555—d. *c.* 1610, London, Eng.) Vigorous Puritan pamphleteer and propagandist for a purer life and straiter devotion.

The Anatomie of Abuses (1583), Stubbs's most popular work, consists of an attack on English habits in dress, food, drink, games, theatergoing and, especially, sex. He also denounced usury, astrology, bearbaiting, and the state of prisons. At first Stubbs condemned only excessive concentration on worldly pastimes, but in later works he removed a preface that softened his position. His *A Christal Glasse for Christian Women* (1591) is a biography of and tribute to his wife, whom he depicts as an even narrower Puritan than he was himself. On her deathbed she declared her affection for a puppy to have been sinful vanity.

His style and conventional subject matter make it doubtful that, as some scholars have alleged, Stubbs had a part in writing the Marprelate tracts, articles published during the most famous Elizabethan pamphlet war.

Studies in Classic American Literature Collection of literary criticism by English writer D.H. LAWRENCE, published in 1923. In this series of essays about great American authors, Lawrence characterized American culture as unsteady and set adrift from the stable moorings of European culture.

Lawrence treated his American subjects with a mixture of awe and critical suspicion. He characterized Benjamin Franklin as a staunch, petty rationalist and Michel-Guillaume-Saint-Jean de Crèvecoeur as an emotional figure hiding behind the guise of false idealism; he viewed Edgar Allan Poe with condescension. Lawrence's assessment of the work of Herman Melville helped establish that author's reputation in the 1920s. He also examined James Fenimore Cooper, Nathaniel Hawthorne, Walt Whitman, and Richard Henry Dana.

Studs Lonigan \\'stədz-'län-i-gən\ Trilogy of novels by James T. FARRELL about life among lower-middle-class Irish Roman Catholics in Chicago during the first third of the 20th century. The trilogy consists of *Young Lonigan: A Boyhood in Chicago Streets* (1932), *The Young Manhood of Studs Lonigan* (1934), and *Judgment Day* (1935).

As a boy, William Lonigan (always referred to as "Studs") makes a slight effort to rise above his squalid urban environment. However, the combination of his own personality, unwholesome neighborhood friends, a small-minded family, and his schooling and religious training all condemn him to the life of futility and dissipation that are his inheritance.

study \\'stəd-ē\ A literary or artistic production intended as a preliminary outline, an experimental interpretation, or an exploratory analysis of specific features (such as those of character or motivation) or characteristics.

Sturgeon \\'stər-jən\, Theodore, *original name* Edward Hamilton Waldo \wäl-dō\, *pseudonyms* Frederick R. Ewing \\'yü-iŋ\, E. Waldo Hunter \\'hən-tər\, and E. Hunter Waldo (b. Feb. 26, 1918, Staten Island, N.Y., U.S.—d. May 8, 1985, Eugene, Ore.) American science-fiction writer who emphasized romantic and sexual themes in his stories.

Sturgeon sold his first short story in 1937 and began to publish in science-fiction magazines under several pseudonyms. He was especially prolific in the period between 1946 and 1958. His most noted work is *More Than Human* (1953), about six outcast children with extrasensory powers. In *Venus Plus X* (1960), he envisioned a utopia achieved by the elimination of all sexual differences. Sturgeon's other science-fiction and fantasy novels include *The Dreaming Jewels* (1950; also published as *The Synthetic Man*), *The Cosmic Rape* (1958), and *Some of Your Blood* (1961). He also wrote western, historical, and mystery novels.

Sturgeon was unusual among his peers in writing about loneliness, love, and sex. His stories were considered daring for featuring the problems of hermaphrodites, exiled lovers, and homosexuals.

Sturluson, Snorri *see* SNORRI STURLUSON.

Sturm und Drang \\'shtůrm-,ůnt-'dräŋ\ [German, storm and stress] A German literary movement of the latter half of the 18th century characterized by a revolt against the strictures imposed by the Enlightenment cult of rationalism and the sterile imitation of French literature. It exalted nature, intuition, impulse, instinct, emotion, fancy, and inborn genius as the wellsprings of literature.

Works of the Sturm und Drang movement typically are loosely constructed, written in direct language, and marked by rousing action and high emotionalism. They frequently deal with the individual in revolt against the injustices of society. J.W. von Goethe and Friedrich Schiller began their careers as prominent members of the movement.

The exponents of Sturm und Drang were profoundly influenced by the philosophy of Jean-Jacques Rousseau and Johann Georg Hamann, who held that the basic verities of existence were to be apprehended through faith and the experience of the senses. The young writers also found inspiration in the works of the English poet Edward Young, the pseudo-epic poetry of James Macpherson's "Ossian," and the works of William Shakespeare (which had just been translated into German).

While a student at Strasbourg, Goethe made the acquaintance of Johann Gottfried von Herder, a former pupil of Hamann, who interested him in Gothic architecture, German folk songs, and Shakespeare. Energized by Herder's ideas, Goethe embarked upon a period of extraordinary creativity. In 1773 he published the play *Götz von Berlichingen*, based upon the life of that 16th-century German knight, and he collaborated with Herder and others on the pamphlet "Von deutscher Art und Kunst," which served as a manifesto for the movement. Goethe's novel *Die Leiden des jungen Werthers* (1774; *The Sorrows of Young Werther*), which epitomized the spirit of the movement, made him world famous and inspired a host of imitators.

Dramatic literature was the most characteristic product of Sturm und Drang. Indeed, the very name of the movement was borrowed from the title of a play by Friedrich von Klinger. Inspired by the desire to present on the stage figures of Shakespearean grandeur, Klinger subordinated structural considerations to character and rejected the conventions of French Neoclassicism. With the production of *Die Räuber* (1781; *The*

Robbers) by Schiller, the drama of Sturm und Drang entered a new phase.

Self-discipline was not a tenet of Sturm und Drang, and the movement soon exhausted itself. Its two most gifted representatives, Goethe and Schiller, went on to produce great works that formed the body and soul of classical German literature.

style \'stīl\ [Latin *stilus* spike, stem, stylus (for writing on wax tablets), style of writing]   In literature, a distinctive manner of expression.

stylist \'stī-list\   A writer or speaker who is eminent in matters of style.

stylistics \stī-'lis-tiks\   An aspect of literary study that emphasizes the analysis of various elements of style (such as metaphor and diction).

The ancients saw style as the proper adornment of thought. In this view, which prevailed throughout the Renaissance, devices of style can be catalogued. The essayist or orator was expected to frame ideas with the help of model sentences and prescribed types of figures suited to the mode of discourse.

The traditional idea of style as something properly added to thoughts contrasts with the ideas that derive from Charles Bally (1865–1947), the Swiss philologist. According to followers of Bally, style in language arises from the possibility of choice among alternative forms of expression, as, for example, among the synonymous words "children," "kids," "youngsters," and "youths," each of which has a different evocative value. This theory emphasizes the relationship of style to linguistics, as does the theory of Edward Sapir, who talked about literature that is form-based (such as that of Algernon Charles Swinburne, Paul Verlaine, Horace, Catullus, and Virgil, and much of Latin literature) and literature that is content-based (such as that of Homer, Plato, Dante, and William Shakespeare) and the near untranslatability of the former. A linguist, for example, might note the effective placing of dental and palatal spirants in these famous lines from Verlaine:

> Les *s*anglots longs des violons de l'automne
> Ble*ss*ent mon coeur d'une langueur monotone,
> Tout *s*uffocant et blême quand *s*onne l'heure,
> *J*e me *s*ouviens des *j*ours anciens, et *j*e pleure.

The impressionistic "slow, dragging" effect of Edgar Allan Poe's

> On desperate seas long wont to roam

can be made more objective by the linguist's knowledge of the stress contour, or intonation.

stylometry \stī-'lăm-ə-trē\ [*style* + *-metry* (as in *craniometry*)]   The statistical study—based especially on analysis of the recurrence of particular turns of expression or trends of thought—of the literary style of an author or work.

Styron \'stī-rən\, William (b. June 11, 1925, Newport News, Va., U.S.)   American novelist noted for his treatment of tragic themes and his use of a rich, classical prose style.

Styron's first novel, *Lie Down in Darkness* (1951), set in his native tidewater Virginia, tells of a disturbed young woman from a loveless middle-class family who fights unsuccessfully for her sanity before committing suicide. His next work, the novella *The Long March* (1956), chronicles a brutal forced march undertaken by the recruits in a Marine training camp. The novel *Set This House on Fire* appeared in 1960. Styron's fourth novel, THE CONFESSIONS OF NAT TURNER (1967), is a tour de force of complex psychological presentation and a vivid evocation of slavery in the United States. It was awarded a Pulitzer Prize in 1968.

Styron's subsequent works include a play, *In the Clap Shack* (1972); the novel SOPHIE'S CHOICE (1979; film, 1982); *This*

Quiet Dust (1982), a collection of essays that treat the dominant themes of Styron's fiction; *Darkness Visible* (1990), a nonfiction account of Styron's struggle against depression; and *A Tidewater Morning* (1993), a collection of three previously published stories.

Styx \'stiks\   In Greek mythology, one of the rivers of the underworld. The word *styx* literally means "icy cold." In the Homeric epics, the gods swore by the water of the Styx as their most binding oath; those who violated the oath were rendered insensible for a year and then banished from the divine society for nine years.

suasoria \swä-'sȯr-ē-ə\ *plural* suasoriae \-ē-,ē, -,ī\ [Latin, from feminine of *suasorius* persuasive, from *suasus* + *-orius* -ory]   An ancient Roman form of oration dealing with a problem of conscience. The writer Seneca (the Elder) was a notable writer of suasoriae.

Suassuna \swä-'sü-nə\, Ariano Vilar (b. June 16, 1927, João Pessoa, Braz.)   Brazilian dramatist, fiction writer, and poet. He was the prime mover in an intellectual and folkloric group devoted to the discovery and re-creation of the historic roots of Luso-Brazilian culture.

A professor of aesthetics and theory of the theater, Suassuna taught playwriting and helped administer theatrical groups. He rehabilitated the medieval Iberian *auto* (morality or miracle play) as a theatrical form for use on the 20th-century stage in such works as *Auto da Compadecida* (1957; "Play of Our Lady of Mercy"; *The Rogues' Trial*) and *Auto de João da Cruz* (performed 1950; "Play of John of the Cross"). He drew on the tradition established by Gil Vicente in 16th-century Portugal for many of his plays, including *Uma mulher vestida de sol* (performed 1947; "A Woman Clothed in Sunshine") and *Farsa da boa preguiça* (performed 1960; "Farce of Happy Indolence"). He borrowed from puppet theater in plays such as *A pena e a lei* (performed 1959; "Punishment and the Law") and drew on northeastern Brazil's popular poetry and musical forms in the creation of a type of "circus theater."

Suassuna published two novels, following tenets of the Movimento Armorial. *Romance d'a Pedra do Reino e o Príncipe do sangue do Vai-e-Volta* (1971; "Romance of the Kingdom's Stone and the Prince of Come-and-Go Blood") incorporates elements of the traditions, still extant in northeastern Brazil, surrounding the belief that King Sebastian of Portugal (reigned 1557–78) would return to save his country from Spanish rule. His second novel, *História d'o rei degolado nas caatingas do Sertão* (1977; "Story of the Decapitated King in the Backwoods"), was a sequel to the first. Soon after publication of this work, Suassuna gave up prose writing.

sublime \sə-'blīm\   In literary criticism, grandeur of thought, emotion, and spirit that characterizes great literature. It is the topic of ON THE SUBLIME, an incomplete treatise attributed to Longinus.

The author of *On the Sublime* defines sublimity as "excellence in language," the "expression of a great spirit," and the power to provoke "ecstasy." Departing from traditional classical criticism, which sought to attribute the success of literary works to their balance of certain technical elements—diction, thought, metaphor, music, etc.—he saw the source of the sublime in the moral, emotional, and imaginative depth of the writer and its expression in the flare-up of genius that rules alone could not produce.

The concept had little influence on modern criticism until the late 17th and 18th centuries, when it had its greatest impact in England. Its vogue there coincided with renewed interest in the plays of William Shakespeare, and it served as an important critical basis for Romanticism.

subliterature \ˌsəb-'lit-ə-rə-ˌchûr, - chər, -ˌtyûr\ Popular writing (such as mystery or adventure stories) considered inferior to standard literature.

subplot \'səb-ˌplät\ In fiction or drama, a story line or plot that is subordinate to the main plot.

substitution \ˌsəb-stə-'tü-shən, -'tyü-\ **1.** In Greek or Latin prosody, the replacement of a prosodic element that is required or expected at a given place in a given meter by another which is more or less equivalent in temporal quantity. **2.** In modern prosody, the use within a metrical series of a foot other than the prevailing foot of the series. A silence may also replace expected sound and occupy the time of a foot or syllable. The early American poet Anne Bradstreet used substitution to great effect in the following lines from "The Author to Her Book":

> I stretched thy joints to make thee even feet,
> Yet still thou run'st more hobbling than is meet;

Compare INVERSION; IONIC DISPLACEMENT.

subtext \'səb-ˌtekst\ [probably translation of Russian *podtekst*] Of a literary text, the implicit or metaphorical meaning.

subtitle \'səb-ˌtīt-əl\ A secondary or explanatory title. Such titles can explain the form of the work, as in Samuel Taylor Coleridge's *Remorse: A Tragedy, in Five Acts*; they can give an idea of the theme or contents of the book, as in George Eliot's *Middlemarch: A Study of Provincial Life*; or they can be an alternate title, which may or may not be a comment on the work, such as *Pamela; or, Virtue Rewarded* by Samuel Richardson and Mary Shelley's *Frankenstein; or, the Modern Prometheus.*

succubus \'sək-yə-bəs\ *plural* succubi \-ˌbī\ [Medieval Latin, alteration (influenced by *incubus* incubus) of Latin *succuba* paramour, a derivative of *succubare* to lie underneath] A demon that assumes female human form to have sexual intercourse with men in their sleep. *Compare* INCUBUS.

Suckling \'sək-liŋ\, Sir John (b. February 1609, Whitton, Middlesex, Eng.—d. 1642, Paris, Fr.) English Cavalier poet, dramatist, and courtier, best known for his lyrics.

Suckling was educated at Cambridge, and he inherited his father's considerable estates at the age of 18. He entered Gray's Inn in 1627, was knighted in 1630, and became a prominent figure at court. In 1641 Suckling took an active part in the plot to rescue the Earl of Strafford from the Tower of London. When the plot was discovered, he fled to France and is believed to have committed suicide.

Suckling was the author of four plays, the most ambitious of which is the tragedy *Aglaura*, staged in 1637 and printed at the author's expense in 1638; the best of his work is the lively comedy *The Goblins* (1638).

Suckling's reputation as a poet rests on his lyrics, the best of which are easy and natural. He inherited from John Donne the tradition of the "anti-Platonic" deflation of high-flown love sentiment and used it with insouciance:

> Out upon it! I have loved
> Three whole days together;
> And am like to love three more,
> If it prove fair weather.

The skit *A Session of the Poets* (published posthumously in 1646) is the prototype of a long line of similar works in the 17th and 18th centuries. Suckling's masterpiece is undoubtedly "A Ballad Upon a Wedding," written in the style and meter of the contemporary street ballad. His extant letters are in lively, colloquial prose that anticipates that of the Restoration wits.

Suddenly Last Summer Drama in two acts by Tennessee WILLIAMS, published in 1958 and produced the same year under the title *Garden District*. The play concerns the voracious-

ness of violence; lobotomy, pederasty, and cannibalism are some of the subject matter. In the play, a self-involved, sadistic homosexual with an overprotective mother is eventually murdered on an island and eaten by cannibals.

Sudermann \'züd-ər-ˌmän\, Hermann (b. Sept. 30, 1857, Matziken, East Prussia [now Macikai, Lithuania]—d. Nov. 21, 1928, Berlin, Ger.) One of the leading writers of the German naturalist movement.

Sudermann worked as a journalist, then turned to writing novels. *Frau Sorge* (1887; *Dame Care*), dealing with the maturing of a sensitive youth, and *Der Katzensteg* (1889; *Regina*) are the best known of his early novels. He won renown, however, with his plays. *Die Ehre* ("Honor"; *What Money Cannot Buy*), first performed in 1889, was a milestone in the naturalist movement. *Heimat* (performed 1893; "Home"; *Magda*) portrays the conflicts of a celebrated opera singer who returns to confront her past in the provincial hometown she left in disgrace.

Sudermann's subsequent problem plays, notably *Glück im Winkel* (1895; *The Vale of Content*), *Morituri* (1896; "They Who Are About to Die"), *Es lebe das Leben!* (1902; *The Joy of Living*), and *Der gute Ruf* (1913; *A Good Reputation*), were usually successful on the stage of his time, but, because his work is often sentimental and his criticism of contemporary society—a recurrent motif—is generally considered to be superficial, his plays are seldom staged today.

Among Sudermann's other works, the novel *Das hohe Lied* (1908; *The Song of Songs*) and *Litauische Geschichten* (1917; *The Excursion to Tilsit*), a collection of stories, are notable. *Das Bilderbuch meiner Jugend* (1922; *The Book of My Youth*) is a vivid account of his early years in East Prussia.

Su Dongpo or **Su Tung-p'o** \'sü-'düŋ-'pō\, *pen name of* Su Shi \'sü-'shi\ (b. Dec. 19, 1036, Meishan [now in Sichuan province], China—d. July 28, 1101, Changzhou, Zhexia [now Jiangsu province]) One of China's greatest poets and essayists who was also an accomplished painter and a public official.

A member of a literary family, the young Su performed brilliantly in his official examinations and was rewarded with the first of the many official positions he occupied during his long and distinguished career. While Su was popular with the people of the various provinces in which he served, he sometimes encountered criticism from the frequently changing heads of state. Wang Anshi, prime minister under the Song emperor Shenzong and an accomplished poet himself, banished Su to Huangzhou, Hubei, in 1079 because of Su's opposition to some of Wang's radical reform measures. Yet, despite his five-year banishment, Su remained friendly to Wang, later exchanging poems with him. He demonstrated this same optimism and lack of bitterness when he was banished by other forces in 1094 to southern Guangdong. He was allowed to return from exile and was restored to favor and office shortly before his death.

Su was a leader of Song-dynasty poets in trying to loosen poetic conventions on form and content, especially in the song form known as *ci*. The optimism he demonstrated in his private and political life can be seen also in his verse.

Sue \'sü\, Eugène, *pseudonym of* Marie-Joseph Sue (b. Jan. 26, 1804, Paris, Fr.—d. Aug. 3, 1857, Annecy, Savoy) French author of sensational novels of the seamy side of urban life and a leading exponent of the *roman-feuilleton* ("newspaper serial"). His works, although faulted for their melodramatics, were the first to deal with many of the social ills that accompanied the Industrial Revolution in France.

Sue's early experiences as a naval surgeon prompted his first books, several highly colored sea stories (*e.g.*, *Plik et Plok*, 1831). He also wrote a number of historical novels and worked as a journalist. Having inherited a fortune from his father, Sue became a well-known dandy. He depicted contemporary "high life" in *Arthur* (1838) and *Mathilde* (1841). The latter showed socialist tendencies, and Sue turned in this direction in *Les Mystères de Paris* (1842–43; *The Mysteries of Paris*)—which influenced Victor Hugo's *Les Misérables*—and in *Le Juif errant* (1844–45; *The Wandering Jew*). Published in installments, these long but exciting novels vastly increased the circulation of the newspapers in which they appeared. Both books display Sue's fertile imagination and strong dramatic sense, which compensate somewhat for his unrealistic plots and flat characters. His later works were less successful.

Suetonius \swē-'tō-nē-əs, ,sü-ə-'tō-\, *in full* Gaius Suetonius Tranquillus (b. *c.* AD 69, probably Rome [Italy]—d. after 122) Roman biographer and antiquarian whose writings include *De viris illustribus* ("Concerning Illustrious Men"), a collection of short biographies of celebrated Roman literary figures, and *De vita Caesarum* (*Lives of the Caesars*). The latter book, seasoned with bits of gossip and scandal related to the lives of the first 11 emperors, secured him lasting fame.

Most of Suetonius' writings were antiquarian, dealing with such subjects as Greek pastimes, the history of Roman spectacles and shows, oaths and imprecations and their origins, terminology of clothing, well-known courtesans, and the growth of the civil service. An encyclopedia called *Prata* ("Meadows"), a work like the *Natural History* of Pliny the Elder, was attributed to him and often quoted in late antiquity.

Suetonis' *De viris illustribus* was divided into short books on Roman poets, orators, historians, grammarians and rhetoricians, and perhaps philosophers. Very nearly all that is known about the lives of Rome's eminent authors stems ultimately from this work, which survives only in the whole of one section and in the preface and five lives from another section. The lives of Horace, Lucan, Terence, and Virgil, for example, are known from writers who derived their facts from Suetonius.

De vita Caesarum, which treats Julius Caesar and the emperors up to Domitian, is largely responsible for the vivid picture of Roman society and its morally and politically decadent leaders that dominated historical thought until modified in modern times by the discovery of nonliterary evidence. The biographies are organized not chronologically but by topics: family background, career before accession, public actions, private life, appearance, personality, and death. Though free with scandalous gossip, they are largely silent on the growth, administration, and defense of the empire. Suetonius is free from the bias of the senatorial class that distorts much Roman historical writing. His sketches of the habits and appearance of the emperors are invaluable, but, like Plutarch, he used "characteristic anecdote" without exhaustive inquiry into its authenticity.

Sula \'sü-lə\   Novel by Toni MORRISON, published in 1973. It is the story of two black women friends and of their community of Medallion, Ohio. The community has been stunted and turned inward by the racism of the larger society. The rage and disordered lives of the townspeople are seen as a reaction to their stifled hopes. The novel follows the lives of Sula and Nel from childhood to maturity to death.

Süleyman Çelebi \sü-lā-'män-chä-lä-'bē\, *also called* Süleyman of Bursa \bür-'sä\ (b. *c.* 1351, Bursa, Ottoman Empire [now in Turkey]—d. *c.* 1422, Bursa)   One of the most famous early poets of Anatolia.

Süleyman's most famous and only surviving work is the great religious poem *Mevlûd-i Nebi*, or *Mevlûd-i Peygamberi* ("Hymn on the Prophet's Nativity"). The *Mevlûd*, as it is more commonly called, tells the story of the Prophet Muḥammad's birth, life, and death, his miracles, and his journey to heaven. Written in a simple 15th-century Ottoman Turkish style, it is a work inspired with religious fervor and is often recited at religious ceremonies, particularly funerals in present-day Turkey.

Sully Prudhomme \sü-lē-prǖ-'dóm\, *pseudonym of* René-François-Armand Prudhomme (b. March 16, 1839, Paris, Fr.—d. Sept. 7, 1907, Châtenay)   French poet who was a leading member of the Parnassian movement, which sought to restore elegance, balance, and aesthetic standards to poetry. He was elected to the Académie Française in 1881 and was awarded the first Nobel Prize for Literature in 1901.

Inspired by an unhappy love affair, Sully Prudhomme began to publish fluent and melancholic verse in 1865. *Stances et poemes* (1865) contains his best-known poem, "Le Vase brisé" ("The Broken Vase"). *Les Épreuves* (1866; "Trials") and *Les Solitudes* (1869; "Solitude") are also written in his early, sentimental style. He later renounced personal lyricism for the more objective approach of the Parnassians and wrote poems attempting to represent philosophical concepts in verse. Two of his best-known works in this vein are *La Justice* (1878; "Justice") and *Le Bonheur* (1888; "Happiness"), the latter an exploration of the Faustian search for love and knowledge. Sully Prudhomme's later work is sometimes obscure and naive.

Sumarokov \sü-,mə-'rò-kəf\, Aleksandr Petrovich (b. Nov. 14 [Nov. 25, New Style], 1717, St. Petersburg, Russia—d. Oct. 1 [Oct. 12], 1777, Moscow)   Russian Neoclassical poet and dramatist, director of the first permanent theater in St. Petersburg (1756–61) and author of several comedies and tragedies, including an adaptation of *Hamlet* (1748).

Influenced by French Neoclassical drama, Sumarokov transplanted the conventions of the French theater to dramas dealing with Russian history. This earned him the epithet "Racine of the North." His tragedies, which usually do not have tragic endings, portray conflicts between love and duty; his comedies are satires on ignorance and provincialism. His lyric poetry is still read, although his plays are not.

Summerson, Esther \'es-tər-'səm-ər-sən\   Fictional character, the strong, motherly heroine of the novel BLEAK HOUSE by Charles Dickens.

Summoner's Tale, The   One of the 24 stories in THE CANTERBURY TALES by Geoffrey Chaucer.

Told in retaliation for the Friar's unflattering portrait of a summoner, this earthy tale describes a hypocritical friar's attempt to wheedle a gift from an ailing benefactor. The angry man offers the friar a gift on the condition that he divide it equally among his fellows. The friar agrees and is instructed to reach under his patron's buttocks, whereupon he is rewarded with a fart. The friar is aghast—and perplexed as to how best to divide the gift among his 12 colleagues. A squire wins a coat from him by suggesting that the friars assemble around a wheel, with the benefactor at the hub, so that all could share equally in the flatulent offering.

Like "The Friar's Tale," "The Summoner's Tale" is based on a medieval French fabliau.

Sun Also Rises, The   Novel by Ernest HEMINGWAY, published in 1926. In England the book's title is *Fiesta*. Set in the 1920s, the novel deals with a group of aimless expatriates in France and Spain. They are members of the cynical and disillusioned post-World War I Lost Generation, many of whom suffer psychological and physical wounds as a result of the war. Two of the novel's main characters, Lady Brett Ashley and Jake Barnes, typify this generation. Lady Brett drifts through a series of affairs despite her love for Jake, who has been rendered impotent by a war wound. Friendship, stoicism, and natural grace under pressure are offered as the values that matter in an otherwise amoral and often senseless world.

Sundman \'sœnd-,mån\, Per Olof (b. Sept. 4, 1922, Vaxholm, Swed.)   Swedish novelist and poet whose belief in behaviorism was underscored by a simple, spare style and objective analysis of surface reality.

Sundman spent much of his life in the northern province of Jämtland. He used that isolated area as a locale for his first book, *Jägarna* (1957; "The Hunters"), a collection of short stories, and for many of his later works. In *Undersökningen* (1958; "The Investigation"), Sundman tells the story of the investigation of the head of a power station in a poverty-stricken and depopulated area in northern Sweden. Sundman's most successful novel, *Ingenjör Andrées luftfärd* (1967; *The Flight of the Eagle*; film, 1970), is supposedly pieced together from the remaining documents of an ill-fated attempt to reach the North Pole by balloon. *Berättlesen om Sâm* (1977; "The Story of Sam") examines the ancient Icelandic saga of Hrafnkel.

supercommentary \,sü-pər-'käm-ən-,tar-ē\   A commentary upon a commentary.

superfluous man [translation of Russian *lishniĭ chelovek*] Character type whose frequent recurrence in 19th-century Russian literature is sufficiently striking to make him a national archetype. He is usually an aristocrat, intelligent, well-educated, and informed by idealism and goodwill but incapable of engaging in effective action. Although he is aware of the stupidity and injustice surrounding him, he remains a bystander.

The term gained wide currency with the publication of Ivan Turgenev's story "The Diary of a Superfluous Man" (1850). Although most of Turgenev's heroes fall into this category, he was not the first to create the type. Aleksandr Pushkin introduced the type in *Eugene Onegin* (1833), the story of a Byronic youth who wastes his life, allows the girl who loves him to marry another, and lets himself be drawn into a duel in which he kills his best friend. The most extreme example of this character is the hero of Ivan Goncharov's *Oblomov* (1859). An idle, daydreaming noble who lives on the income of an estate he never visits, Oblomov spends all his time lying in bed thinking about what he will do when (and if) he gets up.

The radical critic Nikolay A. Dobrolyubov analyzed the superfluous man as an affliction peculiar to Russia and the by-product of serfdom. Throughout the 19th and early 20th century, the type dominated Russian novels and plays. Despite their inability to act, these men include some of the most attractive and sympathetic characters in literature: Pierre Bezukhov (in Leo Tolstoy's *War and Peace*, 1865–69), Prince Myshkin (in Fyodor Dostoyevsky's *The Idiot*, 1868–69), and several protagonists in the works of Anton Chekhov.

superhero \'sü-pər-,hir-ō, -,hē-rō\   A fictional hero (as in a comic book) having extraordinary or supernatural powers.

Supervielle \sǖ-per-'vyel\, Jules (b. Jan. 16, 1884, Montevideo, Uruguay—d. May 17, 1960, Paris, Fr.)   Poet, dramatist, and short-story writer of Basque descent who wrote in the French language but in the Spanish tradition. His themes are the love of a lonely but fraternal man for the Pampas and for the open spaces of his South American childhood and his nostalgia for a cosmic brotherhood.

Supervielle's early poetry was in imitation of the Parnassians. His later collections (*Gravitations*, 1925; *Les Amis inconnus*, 1934 ["The Unknown Friends"]; *La Fable du monde*, 1938 ["Fable of the World"]) are sensitive, sometimes humorous, sometimes precious. His novels *L'Homme de la pampa* (1923; "The Man from the Pampas"), *Le Voleur d'enfants* (1926; "The Kidnappers"; *The Colonel's Children*), and *Le Survivant* (1928; "The Survivor") were experimental. He also wrote short stories, plays, and a volume of autobiography.

Suppliants (*Greek* Hiketides, *Latin* Supplices)   The first and only surviving play of a trilogy by AESCHYLUS, believed to have been performed in 468.

As the play opens, the Danaïds (born in Egypt though of Greek descent) have fled with their father to Argos in Greece in order to avoid forced marriage with their cousins, the sons of Aegyptus. Pelasgus, the king of Argos, is torn between charity to the Danaïds and anxiety to appease Aegyptus but nobly agrees in the end to grant them asylum. The trilogy as a whole seems to have favorably stressed the saving power of domestic love as contrasted with both the willfulness of the Danaïds and the unfeeling, violent lust of their cousins.

Suppliants (*Greek* Hiketides, *Latin* Supplices)   Drama by EURIPIDES, performed about 423 BC. The title is also translated as *The Suppliant Women*. The individuals referred to in the title are the mothers and widows of the Argive leaders who have been killed while attacking Thebes under the leadership of Polyneices. The bodies of the warriors have been left unburied by the Thebans, and the women attempt to reclaim them.

Surface, Charles and Joseph \'chärlz-'sər-fəs . . . 'jō-səf, -zəf\   Fictional characters, the contrasting brothers whose entanglements provide one of the two plots of THE SCHOOL FOR SCANDAL by Richard Brinsley Sheridan.

Surrealism \sər-'rē-ə-,liz-əm\ [French *surréalisme*, from *sur*- above, over + *réalisme* realism]   The principles, ideals, or practice of producing fantastic or incongruous imagery in art or literature by means of unnatural juxtapositions and combinations. A movement in visual art and literature based on these principles flourished in Europe between World Wars I and II. Although Surrealism grew principally out of the earlier Dada movement, which before World War I produced works of anti-art that deliberately defied reason, Surrealism's emphasis was not on negation but on positive expression. The movement represented a reaction against what its members saw as the destruction wrought by the "rationalism" that had guided European culture and politics in the past and that had culminated in the horrors of World War I. According to the major spokesman of the movement, the poet and critic André Breton, who published "The Surrealist Manifesto" in 1924, Surrealism was a means of reuniting conscious and unconscious realms of experience so completely that the world of dream and fantasy would be joined to the everyday rational world in "an absolute reality, a surreality."

In the poetry of Breton, Paul Éluard, Pierre Reverdy, Louis Aragon, and others, Surrealism manifested itself in a juxtaposition of words that was startling because it was determined not by logical but by psychological—that is, unconscious—thought processes. Automatic writing was a technique favored by Surrealist writers because of its reliance on the power of the subconscious. The influence of Surrealism can be seen in the works of such later authors as Samuel Beckett, Jean Genet, and other writers of the Theater of the Absurd, the French writers of the *nouveau roman* of the 1950s and '60s, and the various practitioners of the stream-of-consciousness technique.

Surrey \'sər-ē\, Henry Howard, Earl of (b. 1517, Hunsdon?, Hertfordshire, Eng.—d. Jan. 13, 1547, London)   Poet who, with Sir Thomas Wyatt (1503–42), introduced into England the styles and meters of the Italian humanist poets and so laid the foundation of a great age of English poetry.

Because of his aristocratic birth and connections, Surrey was involved (though usually peripherally) in the jockeying for place that accompanied Henry VIII's policies. He served in campaigns in Scotland in 1542 and in France and Flanders from 1543 to 1546. He acted as field marshal in 1544 and won royal approval. Returning to England in 1546, Surrey found the king dying. His rivals intrigued against him, and his sister admitted that he was still a firm Roman Catholic. He defended himself unavailingly and at the age of 30 was executed on Tower Hill.

Most of Surrey's poetry was first published in 1557, 10 years after his death. He acknowledged Wyatt as a master and followed him in adapting Italian forms to English verse. For instance, Surrey's translation of Books II and IV of the *Aeneid* marked the first use in English of blank verse. He also translated a number of Petrarch's sonnets already translated by Wyatt. Surrey achieved a greater smoothness and firmness, qualities that were to be important in the evolution of the English sonnet. He was the first to develop the sonnet form used by William Shakespeare.

In his other short poems he wrote not only on the usual early Tudor themes of love and death but also of life in London, of friendship, and of youth. The love poems have little force except when, in two "Complaint[s] of the absence of her lover being upon the sea," he wrote, unusually for his period, from the woman's point of view.

His short poems were printed by Richard Tottel in his *Songes and Sonettes, Written by the Ryght Honorable Lorde Henry Howard Late Earle of Surrey and Other* (1557; usually known as *Tottel's Miscellany*). "Other" included Wyatt, and critics from George Puttenham onward have coupled their names.

Surtees \'sər-ˌtēz\, Robert Smith (b. May 17, 1803, The Riding, Northumberland, Eng.—d. March 16, 1864, Brighton, Sussex)   Novelist of English provincial life and the creator of Mr. Jorrocks, one of the great comic characters of English literature, a blunt Cockney grocer who is entirely given over to fox hunting.

Riding to hounds was a passion with Surtees, and nearly all his writing involved horses and riding. Surtees' earliest works were published in *The Sporting Magazine*, and in 1831, with Rudolph Ackermann as publisher, he launched the *New Sporting Magazine* (*N.S.M.*), editing it until 1836. His novels appeared as serials in the *N.S.M.* or elsewhere or in monthly parts before final publication in book form. JORROCKS'S JAUNTS AND JOLLITIES (1838), a collection of tales that was the prototype for Charles Dickens' *Pickwick Papers*; *Handley Cross* (1843; expanded 1854); and *Hillingdon Hall* (1845) all feature Mr. Jorrocks. There followed *Hawbuck Grange* (1847), *Mr. Sponge's Sporting Tour* (1853), *Ask Mamma* (1858), *Plain or Ringlets?* (1860), and *Mr. Facey Romford's Hounds* (posthumous, 1865).

Surtees was a mordant satirist. His portrayal of provincial England just entering the railway era exposes its boredom, ill manners, discomfort, and coarse food, and the matter-of-factness of his writing makes admirable social history. Nonetheless, it is the descriptions of fast runs with hounds over open country that leave the most lasting impression.

Sūrya \'sūr-yə\   In Hindu mythology and religion, the sun and the sun god. Although in the Vedic period several other deities also possessed solar characteristics, most of these were merged into a single god in later Hinduism. Sūrya once ranked together with Vishnu, Śiva, Śakti, and Gaṇeśa. In modern Hinduism he is worshiped as the supreme deity by only a small following, the Saura sect, though he is invoked by all Hindus, and the *Gāyatrī* mantra, uttered daily at dawn by orthodox Hindus, is addressed to the sun.

The *Purāṇa*s record that the weapons of the gods were forged from pieces trimmed from Sūrya, whose full emanation was too bright to bear. His power was conceived of as dispelling darkness, curing disease, and heating and illuminating the world. His wife Uṣas—in some accounts, his mother or mistress—is the personification of dawn.

Susanna \sū-'zan-ə\   Biblical character who appears in an apocryphal addition to the Old Testament Book of Daniel, in both the Septuagint (Greek) and Vulgate (Latin) versions. A beautiful woman, Susanna is spied upon by two elders while she is bathing. When she refuses their sexual advances, the men falsely accuse her of adultery. She is ultimately vindicated.

Susanoo \ˌsū-sä-'nō-wō\, *in full* Susanoo no Mikoto \nō-mē-'kō-tō\, *also spelled* Susanowo ("Impetuous Male")   In Japanese mythology, the storm god, younger brother of the sun goddess AMATERASU. He was driven out of heaven because of his outrageous behavior at the court of his sister Amaterasu.

Susanoo descended into the land of Izumo in western Japan and killed an eight-headed dragon that had been terrorizing the countryside. From the tail of the dragon he recovered the marvelous sword KUSANAGI, which he presented to his sister and which later came to form part of the Imperial Treasures of Japan.

Susanoo is the principal character of the Izumo Cycle, one of the two main traditions of Japanese mythology recorded in *Kojiki* and *Nikon shoki*.

Sutherland \'səth-ər-lənd\, Efua (Theodora), *original surname* Morgue \'mȯrg\ (b. June 27, 1924, Cape Coast, Gold Coast [now in Ghana])   Ghanaian playwright, poet, and children's author who founded the Drama Studio in Accra (now the Writers' Workshop in the Institute of African Studies, University of Ghana, Legon).

After completing her studies at the Teacher Training College in Ghana, Sutherland studied at Homerton College, Cambridge, and at the University of London's School of Oriental and African Studies. Upon her return to Accra, she helped establish the literary magazine *Okyeame*. At this time she founded the Experimental Theatre, which became the Ghana Drama Studio. A number of her plays were produced in 1962, including the well-known *Edufa* (1967), based on *Alcestis* by Euripides, and *Foriwa* (1967), a play that stresses the alliance of new ways and old traditions. *The Marriage of Anansewa: A Storytelling Drama* (1975) is considered Sutherland's most valuable work.

Sutherland established the Drama Studio as a workshop for writers of children's literature. The studio soon became a training ground for Ghanaian playwrights. Sutherland herself wrote several works for children, including two animated rhythm plays, *Vulture! Vulture!* and *Tahinta* (1968), and two pictorial essays, *The Roadmakers* (1961) and *Playtime in Africa* (1960). Many of her short stories can be described as rhythmic prose poems. One of her later plays, *Nyamekye*, a version of *Alice in Wonderland*, shows the influence of the folk-opera tradition. Her book of fairy tales and folklore of Ghana, *The Voice in the Forest*, was published in 1983.

Sutpen family \'sət-pen, -pin\   Fictional family whose rise and fall is told in several novels by William FAULKNER, chiefly *Absalom, Absalom!* (1936). One of the families of Faulkner's fictional Yoknapatawpha County, Miss., its line is traced back to Thomas Sutpen, a plantation owner who has risen from his poor-white origins in West Virginia. He marries Ellen Coldfield on the road to respectability with the dream of founding a dynasty. His white, legitimate offspring are Judith and Henry. Charles Bon is his son by a Haitian woman, and Clytemnestra (Clytie) is his daughter by a slave.

sutra \'sū-trə\, *Pali* sutta [Sanskrit *sūtram*, literally, thread]   In Hinduism, a brief, aphoristic composition summarizing a Vedic precept, or a collection of such compositions.

The early Indian philosophers did not work with written texts and later often disdained the use of them, and the sutras filled the need for explanatory works of the utmost brevity that could be committed to memory. The earliest sutras were expositions of ritual procedures, but their use spread. Pāṇini's grammatical sutras (5th–6th century BC) became in many respects a model for later compositions. All of the Indian philosophical systems (except the Saṃkhyā, which had its *kārikā*s, or doctrinal verses) had their own sutras, most of them preserved in writing early in the Christian era.

In Buddhism, the word *sutra* refers to a more extended exposition, the basic form of the scriptures of both the Theravāda ("Way of Elders") and Mahāyāna ("Greater Vehicle") traditions. Buddhist sutras are doctrinal works, sometimes of considerable length.

Su Tung-p'o *see* SU DONGPO.

Sutzkever \'sŭts-kə-vər\, Abraham, *also spelled* Avrom Sutskever (b. July 15, 1913, Smorgon, Russian Empire [now Smarhon, Belarus]) Yiddish-language poet whose works chronicle his childhood in Siberia, his life in the Vilna [Vilnius] ghetto during World War II, and his escape to join the Jewish partisans.

In 1915 Sutzkever and his family fled their home in eastern Europe to Siberia to escape World War I; they returned to the region in 1920 and lived near Vilna, where he later studied at the University of Vilna. Influenced by intellectual thought at the Yiddish Scientific Institute (YIVO), he became associated with "Yung Vilne" ("Young Vilna"), a group of aspiring Yiddish writers, and contributed to the modernist poetry journal *In zikh* ("In Oneself"). His first published collection, *Lider* (1937; "Songs"), received critical acclaim. His collection *Valdiks* (1940; "Sylvan") celebrates nature. *Di festung* (1945; "The Fortress") reflects his experiences as a member of the ghetto resistance movement in Belorussia and his service with the partisans during World War II. Sutzkever returned to Poland in 1946, then lived briefly in France and Holland before settling in Palestine [later Israel], where from 1949 he edited the Yiddish literary and political journal *Di goldene keyt* ("The Golden Chain").

The prose volume *Fun Vilner geto* (1946; "From the Vilna Ghetto") and the poetry collections *Lider fun geto* (1946; "Songs from the Ghetto"), *Geheymshtot* (1948; "Secret City"), and *Yidishe gas* (1948; "Jewish Street") are based on his experiences during World War II. *Sibir* (1953; *Siberia*) recalls his early childhood.

Svadilfari \'svä-thil-ˌfär-ē\ In Norse mythology, an unusually swift and intelligent horse belonging to a giant who offered to build a great wall around Asgard (the kingdom of the gods) to keep invaders away. The gods agreed that if the builder completed the wall in one winter's time, his reward would be the goddess Freyja and possession of the sun and the moon. Svadilfari gave his owner such assistance that the wall was almost completed a few days before the end of winter. The gods, however, were able to prevent the giant from winning his payment by the aid of the trickster god Loki, who changed himself into a mare and attracted Svadilfari away from his work. From their union Loki bore Odin's magical horse, Sleipnir.

Svengali \sven-'gäl-ē, sfen-\ Fictional character, the villain of the romantic novel TRILBY by George du Maurier.

The name Svengali became synonymous with an authority figure or mentor who exerts undue, usually evil influence over another person.

Svevo \'zvä-vō\, Italo, *pseudonym of* Ettore Schmitz \'shmēts\ (b. Dec. 19, 1861, Trieste, Austrian Empire [now in Italy]—d. Sept. 13, 1928, Motta di Livenza, Italy) Italian novelist and short-story writer, a pioneer of the psychological novel in Italy.

Svevo's first novel, *Una vita* (1892; *A Life*), was revolutionary in its analytical, introspective treatment of the agonies of an ineffectual hero (a pattern Svevo repeated in subsequent works). A powerful but rambling work, the book was ignored upon its publication, as was its successor, *Senilità* (1898; *As a Man Grows Older*). With *Senilità*'s failure, Svevo formally gave up writing and entered his father-in-law's firm.

Ironically, business frequently required Svevo to visit England in the years that followed, and he engaged a young man, James Joyce, in 1907 as his English tutor in Trieste. They became close friends and exchanged their works. Joyce's tremendous admiration for Svevo's two early novels was one of the factors that encouraged Svevo to return to writing. He wrote what became his most famous novel, *La coscienza di Zeno* (1923; *Confessions of Zeno*), a brilliant work in the form of a patient's statement written for his psychiatrist.

While working on a sequel to *Zeno*, Svevo was killed in an automobile accident. Among his posthumously published works are two short-story collections, *La novella del buon vecchio e della bella fanciulla, e altre prose inedite e postume* (1930; *The Nice Old Man and the Pretty Girl*) and *Corto viaggio sentimentale e altri racconti inedite* (1949; *Short Sentimental Journey and Other Stories*); as well as *Saggi e pagine sparse* (1954; "Essays and Scattered Pages"); *Commedie* (1960), a collection of dramatic works; and *Further Confessions of Zeno* (1969), an English translation of his incomplete novel. Svevo's correspondence with the Italian poet Eugenio Montale was published as *Lettere* (1966).

swan maiden *German* Schwanenjungfrau. A maiden of Germanic mythology who was able to transform herself into a swan by the use of a magical object (such as a ring or a cloak of swan feathers).

Swann, Charles \shärl-'swän, *Angl* 'chärlz-'swän\ Fictional character, the leading figure in Marcel Proust's extended novel REMEMBRANCE OF THINGS PAST.

swashbuckler \'swäsh-ˌbək-lər, 'swȯsh-\ A novel or drama dealing with the adventures of a swashbuckling hero and usually having a setting in a romantic past era or exotic locale. The protagonist is typically a daredevil, a boasting, violent soldier, an adventurer, or a ruffian.

Sweeney Agonistes \'swē-nē-ˌag-ə-'nis-tēz\ Poetic drama in two scenes by T.S. ELIOT, published in two parts in the *New Criterion* as "Fragment of a Prologue" (October 1926) and "Fragment of an Agon" (January 1927), and together in book form as *Sweeney Agonistes: Fragments of an Aristophanic Melodrama* (1932). Cast in a music-hall format with scenes interspersed with songs, *Sweeney Agonistes* comments on the meaninglessness of contemporary life and the pettiness and sinfulness of humanity.

Sweet Bird of Youth Drama in three acts by Tennessee WILLIAMS, published and produced in 1959 as an expanded version of Williams' one-act play *The Enemy: Time* (1959). An aging movie star, Princess Kosmonopolis, and her kept lover, Chance Wayne, return to Chance's Southern hometown to avoid what the princess assumes will be a negative reception of her latest movie. Chance is also a failure, having wasted his youth in the pursuit of fame. When the actress learns that her movie is in fact a success, she makes plans to leave and asks Chance to go with her. Chance has learned, however, that on a previous visit home he infected a local politician's daughter with a venereal disease. He decides to stay and face his punishment, which he knows will be castration.

sweetness and light Phrase used by Matthew Arnold in his book CULTURE AND ANARCHY to describe the elements of perfection. He equates sweetness with beauty and light with intelligence and says that the objective of culture is to bring all people together harmoniously, living in an atmosphere of sweetness and light. Arnold borrowed the phrase from Jonathan Swift, who, in the "Battle of the Books" section of his *A Tale of a Tub*, compared ancient and modern methods of scholarship and praised the ancients for their search for "The two noblest of things, which are Sweetness and Light."

Sweet Singer of Michigan \'mish-i-gən\ Byname of versifier Julia A. Moore, whose maudlin, often unintentionally hilarious poetry was parodied by Mark Twain in *Huckleberry Finn. See* Emmeline GRANGERFORD.

Swenson \'swen-sən\, May (b. May 28, 1919, Logan, Utah, U.S.—d. Dec. 4, 1989, Ocean View, Del.) American poet whose work was noted for its engaging imagery, intricate wordplay, and eccentric use of typography.

Swenson was educated at Utah State University. She later moved to New York City and worked for New Directions press. She was writer-in-residence at several North American universities.

Her first published volume of poetry, *Another Animal* (1954), also appeared in *Poets of Today* in 1954. Swenson's other verse collections include *A Cage of Spines* (1958), *To Mix with Time* (1963), *Poems to Solve* (1966), *Iconographs* (1970), *More Poems to Solve* (1971), *New & Selected Things Taking Place* (1978), and *In Other Words* (1987). *Half Sun, Half Sleep* (1967) contained new work and her translations of poetry by six Swedish authors. With Leif Sjoberg, Swenson translated from the Swedish *Windows and Stones, Selected Poems of Tomas Transtromer* (1972). Her own poetry was widely anthologized, and a collection entitled *Nature: Poems Old and New* (1994) was published posthumously.

Swift \'swift\, Graham Colin (b. May 4, 1949, London, Eng.) English novelist and short-story writer whose subtly sophisticated psychological fiction explored the effects of history, especially family history, on contemporary domestic life.

Swift's first novel, *The Sweet-Shop Owner* (1980), juxtaposes the final day of a shopkeeper's life with memories of his life as a whole. *Shuttlecock* (1981) concerns a police archivist whose work uncovers conflicting information about his father's mental illness and involvement in World War II.

After the publication of *Learning to Swim, and Other Stories* (1982), Swift released his most highly regarded novel, *Waterland* (1983). The story centers on a history teacher who is obsessed with local history and his family's past. Swift's other novels include *Out of This World* (1988), a metaphysical family saga, and *Ever After* (1992), a story of a man preoccupied with the life of a 19th-century scholar.

Swift \'swift\, Jonathan, *pseudonym* Isaac Bickerstaff \'bik-ər-,staf\ (b. Nov. 30, 1667, Dublin, Ire.—d. Oct. 19, 1745, Dublin) Irish author and dean of St. Patrick's Cathedral, Dublin (from 1713), the foremost prose satirist in the English language. Besides the celebrated GULLIVER'S TRAVELS (1726), he wrote such noted satires as A TALE OF A TUB (1704) and A MODEST PROPOSAL (1729).

Swift was a student at Trinity College in Dublin when the anti-Catholic Revolution of 1688 occurred in England. Irish Catholic reaction to the events in England led Swift, an Anglican, to seek security in England. He became a member of the household of Sir William Temple at Moor Park, Surrey, where he was to remain off and on until Temple's death in January 1699. During a visit to Ireland in 1695, Swift was ordained a priest.

It may be said that Swift came to intellectual maturity at Moor Park, with Temple's rich library at his disposal. Here,

too, he met Esther Johnson, the young daughter of Temple's widowed housekeeper. In later years there was much speculation about their relationship, but almost nothing is known with certainty.

After Temple's death in 1699, Swift returned to Ireland as chaplain and secretary to the Earl of Berkeley, a lord justice. He made several trips to London after that, however, and he became increasingly well known there through his religious and political essays; *A Tale of a Tub*, published anonymously but generally attributed to him; certain impish works, including the well-known "Bickerstaff" pamphlets of 1708–09; and several amusing pieces in a minor key, such as the short poem "A Description of the Morning," printed by Richard Steele in *The Tatler* in 1709.

In 1710 Swift returned to London and became the chief political writer for the new Tory ministry of Robert Harley (later Earl of Oxford); a lifelong Whig, Swift reluctantly changed his party because of the Tories' support of the established church against Dissenters. Swift's reactions to such a rapidly changing world are vividly recorded in his famous JOURNAL TO STELLA, a series of letters written between 1710 and 1713 and addressed to Esther Johnson and her companion, Rebecca Dingley. By the end of October 1710, Swift had taken over the Tory journal *The Examiner*, which he continued to edit until June 14, 1711. He then began preparing a pamphlet in support of the Tory drive for peace with France. His reward was the deanery of St. Patrick's Cathedral in Dublin.

With the death of Queen Anne in August 1714 and the accession of George I, the Tories were a ruined party and Swift's career in England was at an end. He withdrew to Ireland, where, except for two later visits to England, he was to pass the remainder of his life. Of Swift's writings on Irish issues, the "Drapier's Letters" (1724–25) and "A Modest Proposal" are the best known; they express Swift's indictment of English wrongheadedness.

Swift's greatest satire was *Gulliver's Travels*, a work designed, he said, "to vex the world rather than divert it." Its success was immediate. Until his death Swift was known as Dublin's foremost citizen and Ireland's great patriot dean.

Swift, Tom \'täm-'swift\ Fictional character, a boy inventor featured in a series of 40 adventure books for boys authored by Victor Appleton (a collective pseudonym, used by Edward Stratemeyer and, among others, by his daughter Harriet S. Adams). The series began with *Tom Swift and His Motor Cycle* (1910) and ended with *Tom Swift and His Magnetic Silencer* (1941).

In his private laboratory, Tom Swift combines scientific ingenuity and youthful daring to invent many mechanical and electrical contraptions and products. Recurring characters include his father, retired inventor Barton Swift, his friend and accountant Ned Newton, his girlfriend Mary Nestor, and his odd friend Wakefield Damon. Eradicate Sampson is his hired hand and Koku his huge servant. All of the Tom Swift stories are adventure tales with science used as a background. Tom overcomes all obstacles and outsmarts all villains.

A later series of books published from 1954 to 1971 featured Tom Swift, Jr.; the authors were designated Victor Appleton II. A third series was published from 1981 to 1984, and another revised version of Tom Swift, with the action set in southern California, was begun in 1991.

Swimmer, The Short story by John CHEEVER, published in *The New Yorker* (July 18, 1964) and collected in *The Brigadier and the Golf Widow* (1964). A masterful blend of fantasy and reality, it chronicles a middle-aged man's gradual acceptance of the truth that he has avoided facing—that his life is in ruins.

Swinburne \\'swin-bərn\\, Algernon Charles (b. April 5, 1837, London, Eng.—d. April 10, 1909, Putney, London)   English poet and critic who introduced prosodic innovations and who

Watercolor by Dante Gabriel Rossetti, 1862

Fitzwilliam Museum, Cambridge, England

became noteworthy as the symbol of mid-Victorian poetic revolt.

Swinburne attended Eton and Balliol College, Oxford, which he left in 1860 without earning a degree. In 1861 he met Richard Monckton Milnes (later Lord Houghton), who encouraged his writing and fostered his reputation. Literary success came with the verse drama *Atalanta in Calydon* (1865), in which he attempted to re-create in English the spirit and form of Greek tragedy;

his lyric powers are at their finest in this work. *Atalanta* was followed in 1866 by the first series of *Poems and Ballads*, which clearly display Swinburne's preoccupation with masochism, flagellation, and paganism. This volume contains some of his finest poems, among them "Dolores" and "The Garden of Proserpine." In 1867 Swinburne met his idol, the Italian patriot Giuseppe Mazzini, and his poetry collection *Songs Before Sunrise* (1871) reflects Mazzini's influence. The second series of *Poems and Ballads* appeared in 1878.

During this time Swinburne's health was being undermined by alcoholism and other excesses. In 1879 he collapsed completely and was rescued and restored to health by his friend the critic Theodore Watts-Dunton. The last 30 years of Swinburne's life were spent at The Pines, Putney, under the guardianship of Watts-Dunton, who maintained a strict regimen and encouraged Swinburne to devote himself to writing. Swinburne eventually became a figure of respectability and adopted reactionary views. He published 23 volumes of poetry, prose, and drama during these years, but apart from the long poem *Tristram of Lyonesse* (1882) and the verse tragedy *Marino Faliero* (1885), his most important poetry belongs to the first half of his life.

Swinburne was also an important and prolific literary critic of the later 19th century. Among his best critical writings are *Essays and Studies* (1875) and his monographs on William Shakespeare (1880), Victor Hugo (1886), and Ben Jonson (1889). His devotion to Shakespeare and his unrivaled knowledge of Elizabethan and Jacobean drama are reflected in his early play *Chastelard* (1865). Swinburne also wrote on William Blake, Percy Bysshe Shelley, and Charles Baudelaire, and his elegy on the latter, *Ave Atque Vale* (published 1868), is among his finest works.

Swiss Family Robinson, The \\'räb-in-sən\\   Novel for children completed and edited by Johann Rudolf WYSS, published in German as *Der schweizerische Robinson* (1812–27). The original manuscript of the novel had been written by Wyss's father, Johann David, a clergyman, for and with the aid of his four sons. After the initial publication of an incomplete version, which was translated into French (with additions) and English (also slightly altered), Johann Rudolf published a four-volume final version in 1827. *The Swiss Family Robinson* achieved worldwide popularity.

In the novel a minister, his wife, and their four sons are shipwrecked and become castaways on an island in the East Indies. Although they have lost almost everything in the shipwreck, they are so resourceful at constructing a life for themselves on the island that, when rescue comes, they decline to leave their refuge and their happy life.

Sword of Honour   Trilogy of novels by Evelyn WAUGH, published originally as *Men at Arms* (1952), *Officers and Gentlemen* (1955), and *Unconditional Surrender* (1961; U.S. title, *The End of the Battle*). Waugh reworked the novels and published them collectively in one volume as *Sword of Honour* in 1965.

The trilogy takes place during World War II and is the story of Guy Crouchback, an Englishman from an old, established Roman Catholic family who feels isolated from the rest of the world. He volunteers for service in the war because he believes that it is a noble effort, but he soon becomes disillusioned when he witnesses only chaos and ignoble actions. Despite this disillusionment, however, he gradually changes from a loner to a man of compassion as he decides to do what he can for those around him.

Sycorax \\'sik-ə-raks\\   Fictional character, a witch and the mother of Caliban in William Shakespeare's THE TEMPEST.

syllabic verse   In prosody, a metrical system based solely on the number of syllables in a line of verse. Syllabic verse is used mainly in Romance languages and in Japanese, although such English poets as Dylan Thomas, W.H. Auden, and Marianne Moore have experimented with the form. *See also* METER.

syllepsis \\si-'lep-sis\\ *plural* syllepses \\-,sēz\\ [Greek *sýllēpsis*, literally, taking together, inclusion, a derivative of *syllambánein* to take together, comprehend]   **1.** The use of a word to modify or govern syntactically two or sometimes more words with only one of which it formally agrees in gender, number, or case, as in "the pineapple was eaten and the apples neglected." **2.** The use of a word in the same grammatical relation to two adjacent words but with a different meaning for each, as in the sentence "The tank fired, and the bridge and many hopes sank." *See also* ZEUGMA.

sylph \\'silf\\ [New Latin *sylphes* (plural), *sylphus*]   An imaginary or elemental being that inhabits the air and is mortal but soulless. The existence of such beings was first postulated by the medieval physician Paracelsus, who associated a different being with each of the four elements (earth, air, fire, and water). *Compare* GNOME; SALAMANDER; UNDINE.

sylvan or **silvan** \\'sil-vən\\ [Latin *Silvanus, Sylvanus,* a god of woodlands, a derivative of *silva, sylva* forest]   A deity or spirit that frequents groves or woods.

Sylvester \\sil-'ves-tər\\, Josuah *or* Joshuah (b. 1563, Kent, Eng.—d. Sept. 28, 1618, Middelburg, Neth.)   English poet and translator, best known as the translator of a popular biblical epic, the *Devine Weekes and Workes*. Translated from a work by the French Protestant poet Guillaume du Bartas (1544–90), it appeared in sections beginning in 1592 and complete in 1605. This epic on the Creation, the Fall of Man, and other early parts of the book of Genesis was extremely popular in England through the first half of the 17th century.

Sylvie and Bruno \\'sil-vē . . . 'brü-nō\\   Novel for children by Lewis CARROLL published in 1889. The work evolved from his short story "Bruno's Revenge," published in 1867 in *Aunt Judy's Magazine*. With its sequel, *Sylvie and Bruno Concluded* (1893), it was his final work for children.

The novel attained some popularity, but was considered puzzling and disjointed. Containing more banter between the titular siblings than plot, the convoluted story operates on two parallel levels, one realistic and didactic, and the other dream-like and fantastic. It includes elements of fairy tales (Sylvie and Bruno are fairy children bent on doing good works and saving a throne), sentimental moralizing, and edifying episodes espousing social reform.

symbol \\'sim-bəl\\ [Greek *sýmbolon* token of identity verified by comparing its other half, sign, symptom, a derivative of *symbállein* to throw together, compare]　Something that stands for or suggests something else by reason of relationship, association, convention, or accidental resemblance; especially, a visible sign of something invisible (for example, the lion is a symbol of courage and the cross is a symbol of Christianity). In this sense all words can be called symbols, but the examples given—the lion and the cross—are really metaphors: that is, symbols that represent a complex of other symbols, and which are generally negotiable in a given society (just as money is a symbol for goods or labor). These are considered public symbols in that they are universally recognized. The symbols used in literature are often of a different sort: they are private or personal in that their significance is only evident in the context of the work in which they appear. For instance, the optician's trade sign of a huge pair of spectacles in F. Scott Fitzgerald's *Great Gatsby* (1925) is acceptable as a piece of scenic detail, but it can also be taken as a symbol of divine myopia.

Symbol is distinguished from allegory in that the allegorical figure has no meaning apart from the idea it is meant to idicate within the structure of the allegory, whereas a symbol has a meaning independent of the rest of the narrative in which it appears. A symbol can also have more than one meaning while the meaning of an allegorical figure is clear and specific to the rest of the allegory. *Compare* ALLEGORY.

Symbolist movement \\'sim-bə-list\\　Literary and artistic movement that originated with a group of French poets in the late 19th century, spread to painting and the theater, and influenced Russian, European, and American literature of the 20th century to varying degrees. Symbolist artists sought to express individual emotional experience through the subtle and suggestive use of highly metaphorical language. Because of their interest in the bizarre and the artificial and in themes of decay and ruin, many of the Symbolist poets were identified with the Decadent movement of the same period.

The principal Symbolist poets included Stéphane Mallarmé, Paul Verlaine, Arthur Rimbaud, Jules Laforgue, Henri de Régnier, Gustave Kahn, Émile Verhaeren, Georges Rodenbach, Jean Moréas, and Francis Viélé-Griffin. Rémy de Gourmont was the principal Symbolist critic. Symbolist criteria were applied most successfully to the novel by Joris-Karl Huysmans and to the theater by Maurice Maeterlinck.

Symbolism originated in the revolt of certain French poets against the rigid conventions governing traditional French poetry, as seen in the precise description of Parnassian poetry. The Symbolists wished to liberate poetry from its expository functions and its formalized oratory in order to evoke the fleeting, immediate sensations of human experience and the inner life. They sought to communicate the underlying mystery of existence through a free and highly personal use of metaphors and images that, though lacking in precise meaning, would nevertheless convey the state of the poet's mind and hint at the "dark and confused unity" of an inexpressible reality.

Such works as Verlaine's *Romances sans paroles* (1874; "Songs Without Words") and Mallarmé's *L'Après-midi d'un faune* (1876; "The Afternoon of a Faun") sparked a growing interest in the nascent innovations of progressive French poets. The Symbolist manifesto itself was published by Moréas in *Le Figaro* on Sept. 18, 1886; in it he attacked the descriptive tendencies of realist theater, naturalistic novels, and Parnassian poetry. He also proposed replacing the term *décadent*, which was used to describe Baudelaire and others, with the terms *symboliste* and *symbolisme*. Mallarmé became the leader of the Symbolists, and his *Divagations* (1897) remains the most valuable statement of the movement's aesthetics. In their efforts to escape rigid metrical patterns and to achieve freer poetic rhythms, many Symbolist poets resorted to the composition of prose poems and the use of vers libre ("free verse"), which has now become a fundamental form of contemporary poetry.

The Symbolist movement also spread to Russia, where Valery Bryusov published an anthology of Russian and French Symbolist poems in 1894–95. The revival of poetry in Russia stemming from this movement had as its leader Vladimir Sergeyevich Solovyov. His poetry expressed a belief that the world was a system of symbols expressing metaphysical realities. The greatest poet of the movement was Aleksandr Blok, who in *Dvenadtsat* (1918; *The Twelve*) united the Russian Revolution and God in an apocalyptic vision in which 12 Red Army men became apostles of the New World, headed by Christ. Other Russian Symbolist poets were Vyacheslav Ivanovich Ivanov, Fyodor Sologub, Andrey Bely, and Nikolay Gumilyov.

The movement reached its peak among French poets around 1890 and began to enter a precipitous decline in popularity around 1900. The atmospheric, unfocused imagery of Symbolist poetry eventually came to be seen as overrefined and affected, and the term *décadent*, which the Symbolists had once flaunted, became with others a term of derision denoting mere fin-de-siècle preciosity. Symbolist works nonetheless had a strong and lasting influence on much British and American literature in the 20th century. Their experimental techniques enriched the technical repertoire of modern poetry, and Symbolist theories bore fruit both in the poetry of William Butler Yeats and T.S. Eliot and in the modern novel as represented by James Joyce and Virginia Woolf, in which word harmonies and patterns of images often are more important than the narrative. *Compare* AESTHETICISM; DECADENT.

Symonds \\'sim-əndz\\, John Addington (b. Oct. 5, 1840, Bristol, Gloucestershire, Eng.—d. April 19, 1893, Rome, Italy) English essayist, poet, and biographer best known for his cultural history of the Italian Renaissance.

Symonds traveled extensively for his health. His chief work, *Renaissance in Italy*, 7 vol. (1875–86), is a series of extended essays. Fluent and picturesque, it was deeply indebted to such continental interpreters of the Renaissance as Jacob Burckhardt. With the diverse range of interests of the Victorian person of letters, Symonds diffused his literary energies over English literature, Greek poetry, travel sketches, translations, and studies of such literary and artistic personalities as Percy Bysshe Shelley (1878), Ben Jonson (1886), Sir Philip Sidney (1886), Michelangelo (1893), and Walt Whitman (1893), of whom he was one of the first European admirers. His translations of *The Sonnets of Michael Angelo Buonarroti and Tommaso Campanella* (1878; the first English translation of the poetry of Michelangelo) and of Benvenuto Cellini's autobiography, 2 vol. (1888), also were notable. Symonds' own personally revealing poetry received little critical attention; it served primarily as a release from his difficult emotional life. His *A Problem in Greek Ethics* (written, 1871; privately printed, 1883) and *A Problem in Modern Ethics* (privately printed, 1881) were two of the first serious works on the subject of homosexuality.

Symons \\'sim-ənz\\, A.J.A., *in full* Alphonse James Albert (b. 1900, London, Eng.—d. Aug. 26, 1941)　British author and biographer best known for his brilliant and unconventional biography *The Quest for Corvo* (1934).

Symons' formal education was private and scanty. He was employed as secretary and later director of the First Edition Club of London, and he became a skilled bibliographer.

His well-received biography *H.M. Stanley* (1933) was followed by his magnum opus, *The Quest for Corvo*, a biography of the English author and eccentric Frederick Rolfe (1860–1913), the self-styled Baron Corvo. Rolfe's life had fascinated Symons for years—an earlier work, *Frederick Baron Corvo*, had been printed privately in 1927—and his approach to the subject in *The Quest for Corvo*, subtitled "An Experiment in Biography," was novel in its anecdotal, fragmentary reconstruction of a life about which little factual evidence existed. The book won critical acclaim and came to be regarded as a masterpiece of modern biography.

Symons' other works include *Emin, Governor of Equatoria* (1928); the *Anthology of 'Nineties Verse* (1928), compiled and edited by Symons; and an uncompleted biography of Oscar Wilde. *A.J.A. Symons, His Life and Speculations*, a biography by his brother Julian, was published in 1950.

Symons \'sim-ənz\, Arthur (William) (b. Feb. 28, 1865, Milford Haven, Pembrokeshire, Eng.—d. Jan. 22, 1945, Wittersham, Kent) Poet and critic, the first English champion of the French Symbolist poets, who sought to convey impressions by suggestion rather than direct statement. Symons joined the Rhymers' Club (a group of poets including William Butler Yeats and Ernest Dowson) and contributed to *The Yellow Book*, an avant-garde journal. He also became editor of a new magazine, *The Savoy* (1896), and made Aubrey Beardsley art editor. Symons was versed in European literature, and his popularizing *Symbolist Movement in Literature* (1899) summed up a decade of interpretation and influenced both Yeats and T.S. Eliot. His criticism constitutes an ambitious attempt to create a general "aesthetic" from the unsystematized opus of the critic Walter Pater.

Symons' poetry is mainly fin de siècle (*i.e.,* disillusioned) in feeling. *Silhouettes* (1892) and *London Nights* (1895) contain admirable impressionist lyrics, and at his best he is sensitive to the complex moods of urban life. His translations from the French poet Paul Verlaine are notable, and he wrote elegant travel pieces. In 1908 he suffered a severe mental breakdown, and, apart from *Confessions* (1930), a moving account of his illness, his career was virtually over.

synaesthesis \,sin-is-'thē-sis\ [Greek *synaísthēsis* joint perception, awareness, a derivative of *synaisthánesthai* to perceive simultaneously, share in perception, from *syn-* together + *aisthánesthai* to perceive] Harmony of different or opposing impulses produced by a work of art. For example, one is said to experience synaesthesis of thought and feeling in philosophical poetry or the synaesthesis of anxiety and calmness in a tragedy. *See also* SYNESTHESIA.

synaloepha or **synalepha** \,sin-ə-'lē-fə\ [Greek *synaloiphḗ,* a derivative of *synaleíphein* to clog up, coalesce, unite two syllables into one, from *syn-* together + *aleíphein* to anoint] The reduction to one syllable of two vowels of adjacent syllables (as in *th' army* for *the army*). *Compare* ELISION.

synaphea \,sin-ə-'fē-ə\ [Greek *synápheia,* literally, connection, union] In classical prosody, metrical continuity between lines, in which the quantity of the last syllable of a line is determined by the beginning of the next line.

syncope \'siŋ-kə-,pē, 'sin-\ [Greek *synkopḗ,* literally, the act of cutting up or cutting short] The omission of one or more sounds or letters within a word in the pronunciation of the word (as in *fo'c'sle* for *forecastle*); also, a form resulting from such a loss of sounds or letters. Syncope is a form of elision,

and like elision it is a device that is often used in poetry to fit a word to a particular metrical pattern.

In classical prosody, syncope is a suppression or omission of a short syllable within a metrical foot or measure, usually with compensating protraction of an adjacent long. *See also* ELISION.

synecdoche \si-'nek-də-,kē\ [Greek *synekdochḗ,* from *syn-* together + *ekdochḗ* understanding in a certain way, interpretation, a derivative of *ekdéchesthai* to receive, understand] Figure of speech in which a part represents the whole, as in the expression "hired hands" for workmen or, less commonly, the whole represents a part, as in the use of the word "society" to mean high society. Closely related to metonymy—the replacement of a word by one closely related in meaning to the original—synecdoche is an important poetic device for creating vivid imagery. An example is Samuel Taylor Coleridge's line in "The Rime of the Ancient Mariner," "The western wave was all aflame," in which "wave" substitutes for "sea." *See also* METONYMY.

syneresis or **synaeresis** [Greek *synaíresis,* literally, drawing together, contraction] *see* SYNIZESIS.

synesthesia or **synaesthesia** \,sin-əs-'thē-zhə, -zhē-ə; ,sin-ēs-'thē-zē-ə\ [*syn-* together + -*esthesia* (as in *anesthesia*)] The evocation or transposition of one sense (such as sound) by another (such as vision). The device is much used in both poetry and common speech. In one of the poems from *Façade,* for example, Edith Sitwell refers to "The enormous and gold-rayed rustling sun." In stanza one of Rudyard Kipling's "Mandalay" is the phrase "An' the dawn comes up like thunder."

Synge \'siŋ\, John Millington (b. April 16, 1871, Rathfarnham, near Dublin, Ire.—d. March 24, 1909, Dublin) Poetic dramatist of great power who was a leading figure in the Irish Literary Renaissance. He portrayed the primitive life of the Aran Islands and the western Irish seaboard with sophisticated craftsmanship.

After studying languages at Trinity College, Dublin, Synge decided to become a musician, pursuing his studies from 1893 to 1897 in Germany, Italy, and France. By 1899, when he met William Butler Yeats in Paris, he had turned to writing literary criticism. Yeats inspired him with enthusiasm for the Irish renaissance and advised him to abandon scholarly pursuits to go to the Aran Islands and draw material from life. Synge lived in the islands during part of each year (1899–1902), observing the people and learning their language; he recorded his impressions in *The Aran Islands* (1907) and based his one-act plays *The Shadow of the Glen* (performed 1903) and RIDERS TO THE SEA (performed 1904) on islanders' stories. In 1905 his first three-act play, *The Well of the Saints,* was produced.

Travels in the congested districts of the Irish west coast inspired his most famous play, THE PLAYBOY OF THE WESTERN WORLD (1907). It was an unsentimental study of Irish character and as such was not initially popular with Irish or Irish-American audiences. Synge remained associated with the Abbey Theatre, where his plays gradually won acceptance, until his death. His unfinished *Deirdre of the Sorrows,* which dramatized one of Celtic mythology's greatest love stories, was performed there in 1910. *See also* IRISH LITERARY RENAISSANCE.

synizesis \,sin-i-'zē-sis\ [Greek *synízēsis,* literally, collapse], *also called* syneresis or synaeresis \si-'ner-ə-sis, -'nē-rə-\ The contraction of two syllables into one by uniting in pronunciation two adjacent vowels (as when the *ee* of *eleemosynary* is pronounced as one syllable).

Syrinx \'sir-iŋks\ In Greek mythology, a nymph who was loved and pursued by Pan. She took refuge in the river Ladon and was changed into a reed just as Pan was about to catch her. When Pan heard the sound produced by the wind blowing through the reeds he joined several reeds of varying length together and produced the musical instrument known as a syrinx or panpipe. The vocal organ of birds, which enables them to produce song, is also called the syrinx.

system \'sis-təm\   In classical prosody, a series with fixed limits, such as a group of two or more periods (*i.e.*, rhythmical units of two or more cola) or a group of verses in the same measure.

systole \'sis-tə-lē\ [Greek *systolḗ*, literally, contraction, a derivative of *systéllein* to draw together, contract, reduce]   In prosody, the shortening of a syllable that is by pronunciation or by position long. Systole is most often used to achieve metrical regularity. It is the opposite of DIASTOLE.

syzygy \'siz-i-jē\ [Greek *syzygía*, literally, the state of being yoked together, a derivative of *sýzygos* yoked together, united] In Greek or Latin prosody, a group of two coupled feet. Syzygy may be a combination of two differing feet or a foot of four syllables (such as the ionic foot).

Taban lo Liyong \tä-'bän-lō-'lyóŋ\ (b. 1938, Gulu, Acholi, Uganda)   Prolific Ugandan author whose experimental works and provocative opinions stimulated literary controversy in East Africa.

Taban attended National Teachers College in Kampala, Uganda, before attending Knoxville College in Tennessee, Howard University in Washington, D.C., and the University of Iowa. After returning to Uganda in 1968 he worked at the University of Nairobi in Kenya for several years. From 1975 to 1977 he served as chairman of the literature department at the University of Papua New Guinea, after which he returned to East Africa as a senior public relations officer at the University of Juba in The Sudan.

Taban's work includes highly imaginative short narratives (*Fixions*, 1969; and *The Uninformed Man*, 1971), unorthodox free verse (*Franz Fanon's Uneven Ribs*, 1971; *Another Nigger Dead*, 1972; and *Ballads of Underdevelopment*, 1976), and argumentative and amusing personal essays (*Meditations in Limbo*, 1970; and *The Meditations of Taban lo Liyong*, 1978). He also wrote bold literary criticism (*The Last Word*, 1969) and half-serious quasi-political commentary (*Thirteen Offensives Against Our Enemies*, 1973). He edited collections of oral lore (*Eating Chiefs*, 1970; and *Popular Culture of East Africa*, 1973) and an English translation of Ham Mukasa's *Sir Apolo Kagwa Discovers Britain* (1973). Taban lo Liyong's aim seems to be to startle the reader out of complacency by presenting challenging new ideas in an original manner. His *Another Last Word* was published in 1990 and his *Culture Is Rutan* in 1991.

table talk   Informal conversation at or as if at a dining table; especially, the social talk of a celebrity recorded for publication. Collections of such conversations exist from as early as the 3rd century AD, and the term has been in use in English since about the 16th century. The practice of recording conversations and sayings of the famous became especially popular in the 17th century. Such material is especially useful for biographers and can be a form of literary biography in itself. One of the best-known examples of this is James Boswell's biography of Samuel Johnson, which consists mostly of Johnson's own words reproduced by Boswell.

Tabulatur \,täb-ū-lä-'tūr\ [German (16th century) *Tablatur, Tabulatur* tablature, set of prescriptive rules, probably from Middle French *tabulature* tablature, Latinization of Italian *intavolatura*, a derivative of *intavolare* to tabulate, systematize]

The system of rules for poetic and musical composition that were established by the meistersingers, members of 15th- and 16th-century German guilds of poets and singers.

Tacitus \'tas-i-təs\, *in full* Publius, *or* Gaius, Cornelius Tacitus (b. *c.* AD 56, probably Gallia Narbonensis [now southeastern France]—d. *c.* 120)   Roman orator and public official, probably the greatest historian and one of the greatest prose stylists who wrote in the Latin language.

Tacitus studied rhetoric, which provided a general literary education that included the practice of prose composition. Beginning his career with a minor magistracy, in 88 he gained a praetorship (a post with legal jurisdiction) and became a member of the priestly college that kept the Sibylline Books of prophecy and supervised foreign-cult practice.

In 98 Tacitus wrote two works, *De vita Julii Agricolae* and *De origine et situ Germanorum* (the *Germania*), both reflecting his personal interests. The first is a biographical account of his father-in-law, Julius Agricola, with special reference to his governorship of Britain (78–84) and the later years under Domitian. The *Germania* describes the people of the Roman frontier on the Rhine. Tacitus emphasizes the simple virtues as well as the primitive vices of the Germanic tribes, in contrast to the moral laxity of contemporary Rome, and the threat that these tribes, if they acted together, could present to Roman Gaul. The decline of oratory seemed to provide the setting for his *Dialogus de oratoribus* (*c.* 98–102). In it Tacitus compares oratory with poetry as a way of literary life, marking the decline of oratory in public affairs: the Roman Republic had given scope for true eloquence; the empire limited its inspiration. The work reflects his mood at the time he turned from oratory to history.

In taking up history Tacitus joined the line of succession of those who described and interpreted their own period, and he covered the story from the political situation that followed Nero's death to the close of the Flavian dynasty. The *Historiae* (*Histories*) began on Jan. 1, 69, with Galba in power and proceeded to the death of Domitian, in 96. The work contained 12 or 14 books, of which only 5 books are extant. The narrative as it now exists, with its magnificent introduction, is a powerfully sustained piece of writing.

The *Annals* (*ab excessu divi Augusti*), following the form of a yearly narrative with literary elaborations, covered the period of the Julio-Claudian dynasty from the death of Augustus and the accession of Tiberius, in 14, to the end of Nero's reign, in 68. The work contained 18 or 16 books, but only Books I–IV, part of Book V, most of Book VI (treating the years 14–29 and 31–37 under Tiberius), and Books XI–XVI, incomplete (on Claudius from 47 to 51 and Nero from 51 to 66), are extant.

In effect, the *Annals* represents a diagnosis in narrative form of the decline of Roman political freedom, written to explain the condition of the empire Tacitus had already described in the *Histories*. In opening the *Annals*, he accepted the necessity of strong, periodic power in Roman government, providing it allowed the rise of fresh talent to take control. To secure the continuity of personal authority by dynastic convention, regardless of the qualifications for rule, was to subvert the Roman tradition and corrupt public morality. His criticism of dynastic power also stressed the effect of personality: Tiberius was false, Claudius was weak, Nero was not only unstable but evil, and the imperial wives were dangerous.

Because Tacitus was a conscious literary stylist, both his thought and his manner of expression gave life to his work. He wrote in the grand style, helped by the solemn and poetic usage of the Roman tradition, and he exploited the Latin qualities of strength, rhythm, and color.

tag \'tag\   **1.** A brief quotation used for rhetorical emphasis or sententious effect.   **2.** A rhyming end of a line of verse.

Tagelied \'täg-ə-ˌlēt\ *plural* **Tagelieder** \-ˌlē-dər\ [German, from Middle High German *tageliet*, literally, day song]   A medieval German dawn song, or song of lament by lovers parting at dawn. The *Tagelied* is similar to the Provençal *alba* and may have been derived from it. The most notable composer of *Tagelieder* was the 13th-century poet Wolfram von Eschenbach.

Tagore \tə-'gòr\, Rabindranath \rə-'bin-drə-ˌnät\, *also spelled* Rabīndranāth Ṭhākur \'tä-ˌkür\ (b. May 7, 1861, Calcutta [India]—d. Aug. 7, 1941, Calcutta)   Bengali poet and mystic who won the Nobel Prize for Literature in 1913.

The son of the Great Sage (Maharishi) Devendranath Tagore, he began early to write verses and, after several books of songs in the 1880s, wrote MĀNASĪ (1890), a collection that marks the maturing of his genius. It contains some of his best-known poems, including many in verse forms new to Bengali, among them the ode. It also contains his first social and political poems.

In 1891 Tagore went to manage his father's estates in Shilaidah and Saiyadpur. He lived there in close contact with villagers, and his sympathy for their poverty and backwardness was the keynote of much later writing. Stories "on humble lives and their small miseries" were collected in *Galpaguccha* (1912; "A Bunch of Stories"). During these years he published several collections—*Sonār Tari* (1893; "The Golden Boat"), *Citrā* (1896), *Caitāli* (1896; "Late Harvest"), *Kalpanā* (1900; "Dreams"), *Kṣaṇikā* (1900), and *Naibedya* (1901; "Sacrifice")—and two lyrical plays, *Chitrāṅgadā* (1892; *Chitra*) and *Mālinī* (1895).

Years of sadness (his wife and a son and daughter died between 1902 and 1907) inspired some of Tagore's best poetry. The English version of his well-known collection GĪTĀÑJALI (1910; "Song Offering") helped win him the Nobel Prize. He was awarded a knighthood in 1915, but he surrendered it in 1919 as a protest against the Massacre of Amritsar.

Despite the variety of his activities, Tagore was a prolific writer; his written works, still not completely collected, fill 26 substantial volumes. His novels, although less outstanding than his poems and short stories, are worthy of attention; the best known is *Gorā* (1907–10). Tagore was also a gifted composer, setting hundreds of poems to music; his song "Our Golden Bengal" became the national anthem of Bangladesh. He was also among India's foremost painters.

Taha Hussein or **Ṭāhā Ḥusayn** \tä-'hä-hùs-'sän\ (b. Nov. 14, 1889, Maghāghah, Egypt—d. Oct. 28, 1973, Cairo)   Out-

standing figure of the modernist movement in Egyptian literature. His writings, in Arabic, include novels, stories, criticism, and social and political essays. Outside his own country he is best known through his autobiography, *Al-Ayyam* (2 parts, 1929–32). The first modern Arab literary work to be acclaimed in the West, it appeared in English as *An Egyptian Childhood* (1932) and *The Stream of Days* (1943).

Taha Hussein was blinded by an illness at the age of two. In 1902 he was sent to al-Azhar seminary in Cairo, the leading orthodox center of higher Islāmic education, but he was soon at odds with its conservative authorities. In 1908 he entered the newly opened secular University of Cairo, and in 1914 he was the first to obtain a doctorate there. Further study at the Sorbonne familiarized him with the culture of the West.

Taha Hussein returned to Egypt from France to become a professor of Arabic literature at the University of Cairo; his career there was often stormy, for his bold views enraged religious conservatives. His application of modern critical methods in *Fi'l-shi'iv al-Jahili* (1926; "On Pre-Islāmic Poetry") embroiled him in fierce polemics. In this book he contended that much poetry reputed to be pre-Islāmic had been forged by Muslims of a later date for various reasons, one being to give credence to Qur'ānic myths. For this he was declared an apostate. Another book, *Mustaqbal al-thaqāfah fī Miṣr* (1938; *The Future of Culture in Egypt*), expounds his belief that Egypt belongs by heritage to the same wider Mediterranean civilization that embraces Greece, Italy, and France and advocates the assimilation of modern European culture.

In his later literary work Taha Hussein showed increasing concern for the plight of the poor and interest in governmental reforms. A further book of memoirs was published in 1967.

Ta hsüeh   *see* DA XUE.

tailed sonnet   A sonnet augmented by additional lines that are arranged systematically and are often shorter than the basic line of the sonnet proper.

tail rhyme or **tailed rhyme**   A verse form in which rhymed lines such as couplets or triplets are followed by a tail—a line of different (usually shorter) length that does not rhyme with the couplet or triplet. In a tail-rhyme stanza (also called a tail-rhymed stanza), the tails rhyme with each other.

Tairov \tə-'ĕ-rəf\, Aleksandr Yakovlevich, *original surname* Kornblit \'kòrn-bl'it\ (b. June 24, 1885, Romny, Russia—d. Sept. 25, 1950, Moscow)   Founder and producer-director (1914–49) of the Kamerny (Chamber) Theater in Moscow, which, during the era of the Russian Revolution, rivaled the Moscow Art Theater.

Tairov worked in several companies, including that of the Mobile Theater of P.P. Gaydeburov. In 1913–14 he managed the short-lived Free Theater Moscow before founding the Kamerny.

Tairov brought to Moscow audiences the work of the American playwright Eugene O'Neill, notably *The Hairy Ape, All God's Chillun Got Wings*, and *Desire Under the Elms*. Tairov's style was avant-garde, particularly with respect to staging. His approach to theater was stylized and antirealistic and was diametrically opposed to that of the followers of actor-director Konstantin Stanislavsky. His 1934 production of Vsevolod V. Vishnevsky's *An Optimistic Tragedy* was regarded as a high point of Socialist Realist theater. Under pressure from Stalinist authorities, however, Tairov was eventually compelled to work under the guidance of a state theater committee.

Taiyō \'tī-ˌyō\ ("The Sun")   Japanese magazine published from 1895 to 1928 known for its literary criticism, contemporary fiction, and translations of Western authors.

Although *Taiyō* treated various practical, intellectual, and aesthetic subjects, its literary editors Takayama Chogyū (1871–1902) and Hasegawa Tenkei (1876–1940) were especially instrumental in popularizing the literature of late Romanticism and naturalism, both from abroad and at home (in such fiction writers as the naturalists Tokuda Shūsei, Tayama Katai, and Shimazaki Tōson). When naturalism faded, the magazine also faded in importance.

Takahama Kyoshi \'tä-kä-ˌhä-mä-'kyō-shē\, *original name* Takahama Kiyoshi \'kē-yō-shē\ (b. Feb. 22, 1874, Matsuyama, Japan—d. April 8, 1959, Kamakura) Poet who made major contributions to the development of modern haiku literature.

Through his friend Kawahigashi Hekigotō, Kyoshi became a disciple of the renowned poet Masaoka Shiki and began to write haiku poems. In 1898 Kyoshi became the editor of *Hototogisu*, a magazine of haiku that was started by Masaoka. He and Kawahigashi became pitted against each other after Masaoka's death. Kawahigashi became the leader of a new style of haiku that disregarded the traditional pattern. Writing in *Hototogisu*, Kyoshi opposed Kawahigashi's new movement and advocated realism in haiku, stressing that haiku poets should contemplate nature as it is. He published these beliefs in *Susumubeki haiku no michi* (1918; "The Proper Direction for Haiku"). His many collections of poetry have been compiled into the two-volume anthology *Takahama Kyoshi zenhaiku shū* (1980; "The Complete Haiku Poems of Takahama Kyoshi"). He also wrote several novels, including *Haikaishi* (1909; "Haiku Master").

Takizawa Bakin \'tä-kē-ˌzä-wä-'bä-kēn\ (b. July 4, 1767, Edo [Tokyo], Japan—d. Dec. 1, 1848, Edo) The dominant Japanese writer of the early 19th century, known for his lengthy, didactic historical novels.

With his more than 30 long novels—known as *yomihon* ("reading books")—Bakin created the historical romance in Japan. He took his material from court romances, military chronicles, Nō plays, popular dramas, legends, and Chinese vernacular fiction. Loyalty, filial piety, and the restoration of once-great families were his main themes. His attention to Chinese civilization, Buddhist philosophy, and national history was tempered by a concern for language and style, compassion for others, and a belief in human dignity. Still, the samurai tradition and his own innate stubbornness led him to support the established order and gave a strong note of didacticism to his writing. Bakin's finest work is *Nansō Satomi hakkenden* (1814–42; "Satomi and the Eight Dogs"), on the theme of restoring a family's fortunes; it is acclaimed as a classic of Japanese literature.

talaria \tə-'lar-ē-ə\ [Latin, from neuter plural of *talaris* attached to the ankles, a derivative of *talus* ankle] Winged shoes fastened to the ankles and chiefly used as an attribute of the god Hermes or Mercury of classical mythology.

Tale of a Tub, A Prose satire by Jonathan SWIFT, written between 1696 and 1699, published anonymously in 1704, and expanded in 1710. Regarded as his first major work, it comprises three related sketches: the "Tale" itself, an energetic defense of literature and religion against zealous pedantry; "The Battle of the Books," a witty addition to the scholarly debate about the relative merits of ancient versus modern literature and culture; and "A Discourse Concerning the Mechanical Operation of the Spirit," a satire of religious fanaticism. In the preface Swift explains the title: sailors toss a tub overboard to distract a whale that might attack their ship; in the same way Swift's work may act as a decoy to deflect destructive criticism from the state and established religion.

The 11-part "A Tale of a Tub" is the most impressive of the three compositions for its wit and command of stylistic effects, notably parody. The sections of the "Tale" alternate between the main allegory about Christian history and ironic digressions on modern scholarship.

Tale of Gamelyn, The *see* The Tale of GAMELYN.

Tale of Genji, The \'gen-jē\ Masterpiece of Japanese literature written by Lady MURASAKI Shikibu toward the beginning of the 11th century; it was originally published as *Genji monogatari*. It is one of the world's earliest and greatest novels. *The Tale of Genji* depicts a unique society of ultrarefined and elegant aristocrats whose indispensable accomplishments were skill in poetry, music, calligraphy, and courtship. Much of the book is concerned with the loves of Prince Genji and the different women in his life. The novel is permeated with a sensitivity to human emotions and the beauties of nature hardly paralleled elsewhere. The tone of the novel darkens as it progresses, indicating perhaps a deepening of Murasaki's Buddhist conviction of the vanity of the world. Some, however, believe that its last 14 chapters were written by another author. The translation (1925–33) of *The Tale of Genji* by Arthur Waley is a classic of English literature. A new translation by Edward G. Seidensticker was published in 1976.

Tale of Melibeus, The \ˌmel-i-'bē-əs, -'bā-\, Melibeus *also called* Melibee \-'bā\ One of the 24 stories in THE CANTERBURY TALES by Geoffrey Chaucer.

Reproved by the Host of the inn for his tedious narrative of "The Tale of Sir Thopas," Chaucer in his own persona offers this prose allegory, a close translation of a French adaptation of a 13th-century Italian story. The long, dull tale is essentially a moral debate between Prudence and her husband Melibeus on the subject of vengeance. Prudence urges her husband to forgive the enemies who have assaulted and wounded their daughter. Her advice is couched largely in proverbs, and both sides quote liberally from various moral authorities. Melibeus eventually agrees to make peace with his enemies, but only after he has rebuked them.

Tale of Peter Rabbit, The \'pē-tər\ The best-selling children's book of all time, written and illustrated by Beatrix POT-

Illustration from *The Tale of Peter Rabbit*

TER, printed privately and published in 1902. Potter created the character of Peter Rabbit in 1893 in a letter she wrote to amuse a sick child. She devised adventures for Peter and gave him a mother and three siblings, Flopsy, Mopsy, and Cottontail, in *The Tale of Peter Rabbit and Mr. McGregor's Garden*, with 42 black-and-white illustrations and a colored frontispiece. This classic book was widely translated, went through countless editions, and had more than 20 sequels featuring animal protagonists. The simple text was greatly enhanced by Potter's delicate drawings of animals that were recognizably realistic woodland creatures despite their humanlike clothing and homes.

Tale of Sir Thopas, The \'tō-pəs\   One of the 24 stories in THE CANTERBURY TALES by Geoffrey Chaucer.

Chaucer himself narrates this tale, a witty parody of the worst poetic romances. In insipid language, obvious rhyme, and plodding rhythm, the poet tells of Sir Thopas' search for the Elf Queen and of his encounter with the giant Sir Olifaunt. Before Chaucer can finish the story, however, the Host of the Tabard Inn interrupts, begging him to stop the wretched doggerel.

Tale of Two Cities, A   Novel by Charles DICKENS, published both serially and in book form in 1859. The story is set in the late 18th century against the background of the French Revolution.

Although Dickens borrowed from Thomas Carlyle's history, *The French Revolution*, for his sprawling tale of London and revolutionary Paris, the novel offers more drama than accuracy. The scenes of large-scale mob violence are especially vivid, if superficial in historical understanding. The complex plot involves Sydney Carton's sacrifice of his own life on behalf of his friends Charles Darnay and Lucie Manette. While political events drive the story, Dickens takes a decidedly antipolitical tone, lambasting both aristocratic tyranny and revolutionary excess—the latter memorably caricatured in Madame Defarge, who knits beside the guillotine. The book is perhaps best known for its opening lines, "It was the best of times, it was the worst of times," and for Carton's last speech, in which he says of his replacing Darnay in a prison cell, "It is a far, far better thing that I do, than I have ever done; it is a far, far better rest that I go to, than I have ever known."

Tales of the Jazz Age   Second collection of short works by F. Scott FITZGERALD, published in 1922. Although the title of the collection alludes to the 1920s and the flapper era, all but two pieces were written before 1920.

The best-known of the tales is the critically acclaimed short story THE DIAMOND AS BIG AS THE RITZ. Also included are the novella "May Day," several sketches Fitzgerald had written in college, and two minor short plays. The collection was published to coincide with release, also in 1922, of Fitzgerald's novel *The Beautiful and Damned*.

Taliesin \tăl-'yes-in, *Angl* ,tal-ē-'es-\ (fl. 6th century AD)   One of five poets renowned among the Welsh in the latter part of the 6th century, according to the *Historia Brittonum* attributed to Nennius. The oldest surviving copy of his works, known as *The Book of Taliesin*, is dated to about 700 years after his time. It contains a variety of poems, some on religious themes, some arcane religious verses that belong to Celtic mythological traditions, and some that refer to known historical figures. Among the last, the poet praises Urien, king of the ancient Welsh territory of Rheged, and laments the loss of Owain, son of Urien. A eulogy to Cynan Garwyn ap Brochfael, king of Powys, attributed to Taliesin, suggests that the poet may have been a native of Powys, Wales.

Tallemant des Réaux \tăl-män-dă-rä-'ō\, Gédéon (b. Oct. 2, 1619, La Rochelle, Fr.—d. Nov. 10, 1692, Paris)   French writer of entertaining and informative *Historiettes*, or short biographies.

The son of a Huguenot banker, Tallemant took degrees in civil and canonical law at Paris, but he abandoned his government position and began to frequent literary circles. He gained entrée into the elegant society of the Hôtel de Rambouillet, run by the Marquise de Rambouillet, where he made the acquaintance of many of the leading literary figures whose lives are described in his work.

The *Historiettes*, completed in about 1659, were published in 1834–35. They contain a mass of information about leading men in Parisian society and French public life from the beginning of the 17th century. Several stories, such as the accounts of the reigns of Henry IV and Louis XIII that were originally told to him by the Marquise de Rambouillet, have real historical value. A good listener and an acute if somewhat malicious observer, he also sought out well-informed authorities with the aim of recording anything of interest that was not in printed histories. The new, sometimes disturbing information about prominent people was at first decried, but research has done much to establish its reliability. Much of Tallemant's material, recorded so near to the actual events, can be considered a firsthand source and has been useful as a corrective to later interpretations.

tall tale   Narrative that depicts the extravagantly exaggerated wild adventures of North American folk heroes.

The tall tale is essentially an oral form of entertainment; the audience appreciates the imaginative invention rather than the literal meaning of the tales. Associated with the lore of the American frontier, tall tales often explain the origins of lakes, mountains, and canyons; they are spun around such legendary heroes as Paul Bunyan, the giant lumberjack of the Pacific Northwest; Mike Fink, the rowdy Mississippi River keelboatman; and Davy Crockett, the backwoods Tennessee marksman. Other tall tales recount the superhuman exploits of Western cowboy heroes such as William F. Cody and Annie Oakley. Native to the New England region are the tales of Captain Stormalong, whose ship was driven by a hurricane across the Isthmus of Panama, digging the Panama Canal, and Johnny Appleseed, who planted apple orchards from the East Coast to the Western frontier. Washington Irving, in the *History of New York* (1809), and later Mark Twain, in *Life on the Mississippi* (1883), made literary use of the tall tale.

One of the few examples of the tall tale not native to the United States is found in the German collection *Baron Munchausen's Narratives of His Marvellous Travels and Campaigns in Russia* (1785) by the German scholar and adventurer R.E. Raspe.

Talmud \'tăl-,mủd, 'tal-məd\ (Hebrew: Study, or Learning), *also called* Gemara \gə-'mär-ə, -'môr-\   In Judaism, scholarly interpretations and annotations on the Mishna—the first authoritative codification of Jewish oral laws, which was given its final form early in the 3rd century CE (Common Era) by Judah ha-Nasi—and on other collections of oral laws, including the Tosefta.

Each of two groups of Jewish scholars (*amoraim*), one in Palestine and the other in Babylonia, independently produced a Talmud. The *amoraim* of Palestine labored for about two centuries, completing their work about 400 CE, approximately one century earlier than their counterparts in Babylonia. The Babylonian Talmud (Talmud Bavli) is consequently more extensive than the Palestinian Talmud (Talmud Yerushalmi) and, for that reason, more highly esteemed. Neither of the Talmuds covers every section of the Mishna; some commentaries were never written, and, presumably, others have been lost.

tamāshā \tə-'mä-ˌshä\ [Hindi or Marathi, spectacle, entertainment, from Persian, literally, a recreational walk, from Arabic *tamāshī*] Erotic form of Indian folk drama begun in the early 18th century in Mahārāshtra. In all other forms of Indian folk theater, men are cast in the major roles. The leading female role in *tamāshā*, however, is played by a woman. *Tamāshā* plays, which are known to be bawdy, originated as entertainments for encamped armies. In the 20th century they became commercially successful.

Tamayo y Baus \tä-'mä-yō-ē-'baùs\, Manuel (b. Sept. 15, 1829, Madrid, Spain—d. June 20, 1898, Madrid) Spanish dramatist who, with Adelardo López de Ayala y Herrera, dominated the Spanish stage in the mid-19th century. He was a key figure in the transition from Romanticism to realism in Spanish literature.

Tamayo y Baus was the son of a well-known actor and actress. He began writing plays at a very early age, and one of his dramas received its first production when he was 11 years old. A prolific and versatile playwright who wrote in every style and genre, he had an extremely successful career in the theater. In 1870, however, he stopped writing to become director of the National Library and secretary to the Spanish Academy.

His career falls into two phases. First, under the influence of the German dramatist Friedrich von Schiller, he produced Romantic historical dramas such as *La ricahembra* (1854; "The Lady") and *Locura de amor* (1855; "The Madness of Love"). In his second phase he wrote realistic, or problem, thesis plays that denounced the evils of contemporary Spanish society—materialism (*Lo positivo*, 1862; "The Real"), dueling (*Lances de honor*, 1863; "Quarrels of Honor"), and tolerance of corruption (*Los hombres de bien*, 1870; "Reputable Men"). His masterpiece, which brought him international fame, is *Un drama nuevo* (1867; *A New Drama*), a skillful and moving tragedy.

Tamburlaine *see* TIMUR.

Tamburlaine the Great \'tam-bər-ˌlān\ First play by Christopher MARLOWE, produced about 1587 and published in 1590. The play was written in two parts, each of which has five acts, and was based on the earlier *Silva de varia lección* (1540; *The Foreste; or, Collection of Histories*) by the early 16th-century Spanish scholar and humanist Pedro Mexía.

Marlowe's "mighty line," as Ben Jonson called it, established blank verse as the standard for later Elizabethan and Jacobean dramatic writing. The play recounts the brutal rise to power and the mysterious end of the bloody 14th-century Mongol conqueror Timur, or Tamburlaine. Marlowe's gifts are displayed not only in his supple poetry but also in his ability to view his tragic hero from several angles, revealing both the brutality and the grandeur of the character.

Tamerlane \'tam-ər-ˌlān\ Dramatic monologue by Edgar Allan POE, published in *Tamerlane and Other Poems* (1827) and revised in later editions of the book. Like much of Poe's early verse, "Tamerlane" shows the influence of the Romantic poets, in particular Lord Byron, with its themes of youthful loss, idealistic longing, and universal truths; it also contains an underlying sense of melancholy.

The narrator of the poem is a dying Turkic conqueror who makes his confession to a friar. He tells of his return to his native village and his dismay upon discovering that his beautiful childhood sweetheart is now dead.

Taming of the Shrew, The Comedy in five acts by William SHAKESPEARE, produced about 1593 and printed in the Folio of 1623.

Considered one of Shakespeare's bawdier works, the play describes the volatile courtship between the shrewish Katha-

rina and the canny Petruchio, who is determined to subdue Katharina's legendary temper and win her dowry. The main story is offered as a play within a play; the frame story consists of an initial two-scene "induction": a lord offers the love story as an entertainment for tinker Christopher Sly, recovering from a drunken binge at an alehouse.

Although Katharina repeatedly insults Petruchio, he woos, wins, and tames her by insisting that she is actually the soul of gentleness and patience. After their marriage, he makes her forgo food, sleep, and fancy clothing, and he outdoes her mean tongue by abusing the servants. In the final scene, Petruchio wins a bet that his wife is the most obedient after Katharina gives a speech extolling the virtues of wifely subservience.

Tan \'tan\, Amy (b. Feb. 19, 1952, Oakland, Calif., U.S.) American author of novels about Chinese-American women that contrast the hardships the immigrant women experienced in China with the very different lives of their American daughters. She is best known for her two semiautobiographical novels, *The Joy Luck Club* (1989; film, 1993) and *The Kitchen God's Wife* (1991). Tan also wrote two children's stories, *The Moon Lady* (1992) and *The Chinese Siamese Cat* (1994).

Tanakh \tä-'näk\ An acronym derived from the names of the three divisions of the Hebrew Bible: Torah (Instruction, or Law, also called the Pentateuch), Nevi'im (Prophets), and Ketuvim (Writings).

The Torah contains five books: Genesis, Exodus, Leviticus, Numbers, and Deuteronomy. The Nevi'im comprise eight books subdivided into the Former Prophets, containing the four historical works, Joshua, Judges, Samuel, and Kings, and the Latter Prophets, the oracular discourses of Isaiah, Jeremiah, Ezekiel, and the Twelve (Minor—*i.e.*, smaller) Prophets—Hosea, Joel, Amos, Obadiah, Jonah, Micah, Nahum, Habakkuk, Zephaniah, Haggai, Zechariah, and Malachi. The Twelve were all formerly written on a single scroll and thus reckoned as one book. The Ketuvim consist of religious poetry and wisdom literature—Psalms, Proverbs, and Job, a collection known as the "Five Megillot" ("scrolls"; *i.e.*, Song of Songs, Ruth, Lamentations, Ecclesiastes, and Esther, which have been grouped together according to the annual cycle of their public reading in the synagogue)—and the books of Daniel, Ezra and Nehemiah, and Chronicles.

Tanglewood Tales for Girls and Boys \'taŋ-gəl-ˌwùd\ Collection of children's stories by Nathaniel HAWTHORNE, published in 1853. The book comprises six Greek myths that Hawthorne bowdlerized.

Written as a sequel to *A Wonder-Book for Girls and Boys* (1851), *Tanglewood Tales* is more serious than its lighthearted predecessor. The tales are "The Minotaur," "The Pygmies," "The Dragon's Teeth," "Circe's Palace," "The Pomegranate Seeds," and "The Golden Fleece." Because Hawthorne considered the original myths to be impure and inappropriate for his readership, he altered such stories as the seduction of Ariadne by Theseus and the abduction of Proserpine by Pluto.

Tanizaki Jun'ichirō \ˌtä-nē-'zä-kē-'jūn-ē-ˌchē-rō\ (b. July 24, 1886, Tokyo, Japan—d. July 30, 1965, Yugawara) Major modern Japanese novelist whose writing is characterized by eroticism and ironic wit.

Tanizaki's earliest short stories, of which "Shisei" (1910; "The Tattooer") is an example, have affinities with Edgar Allan Poe and the French Decadents. After moving from Tokyo to the more conservative Ōsaka area in 1923, however, he seemed to turn toward the exploration of more traditional Japanese ideals of beauty. One of his first transitional novels was *Manji* (1928–30; *Quicksand*). Another of these, *Tade kuu mushi* (1928–29; SOME PREFER NETTLES), is one of his finest novels. Like *Manji* it reflects the change in his own system of values and tells of marital unhappiness that is in fact a conflict between the new and the old, with the implication that the old will win. In 1932 Tanizaki began to render into modern Japanese one of the monuments of classical Japanese literature, *Genji monogatari* (*The Tale of Genji*) of Murasaki Shikibu. This work undoubtedly had a deep influence on his style, for during the 1930s he produced a number of discursive lyrical works that echo the prose of the Heian period (794–1185), in which *Genji monogatari* is set. Another of his major novels, *Sasameyuki* (1943–48; THE MAKIOKA SISTERS), describes—in the leisurely style of classical Japanese literature—the inroads of the harsh modern world on traditional society. His postwar writings, including *Shōshō Shigemoto no Haha* (1949–50; in *The Cutter and Captain Shigemoto's Mother*), *Kagi* (1956; *The Key*), and *Fūten rōjin nikki* (1961–62; *Diary of a Mad Old Man*), show an eroticism that suggests a return to his youth. His *Bunshō tokuhon* (1934; "A Style Reader") is a minor masterpiece of criticism.

Tanizaki Prize \ˌtä-nē-ˈzä-kĕ\ Japanese literary award given annually to a Japanese writer in recognition of an exemplary literary work. The prize consists of a trophy and one million yen. It was established in honor of Japanese novelist Tanizaki Jun'ichirō in 1965, the year of his death. Winners have included Endō Shūsaku for the novel *Chimmoku* (1966; *Silence*) and Ōe Kenzaburō for *Man'en gannen no futtōbōru* (1967; *The Silent Cry*).

tanka \ˈtäŋ-kä\ [Japanese] A Japanese fixed form of verse of five lines, the first and third of which have five syllables and the others seven. It has historically been the basic form of Japanese poetry, and as such the term tanka is synonymous with the term WAKA, which more broadly denotes all traditional Japanese poetry in classical forms.

Tannhäuser \ˈtän-ˌhȯi-zər, *Angl* ˈtan-\ (b. *c.* 1200—d. *c.* 1270) German lyric poet who became the hero of a popular legend.

As a professional minnesinger, Tannhäuser served a number of noble patrons; his career spanned the period roughly from 1230 to 1270. Not much is known of his life, except that he traveled widely and almost certainly took part in the Crusade of 1228–29. There are six extant *Leiche* (lyric lays) by Tannhäuser, a few dance songs and love songs (the latter in a parodistic vein), and a group of *Sprüche* (gnomic poems).

The Tannhäuser legend is preserved in a popular ballad, *Danhauser*, traceable to 1515; the origins of the legend itself probably lie in the 13th century. Enticed to the court of Venus, Tannhäuser lives a life of earthly pleasure, but soon, torn by remorse, he makes a pilgrimage to Rome to seek remission of his sins. The pope tells him that, as his pilgrim's staff will never put on leaf again, so his sins can never be forgiven. In despair Tannhäuser returns to the court of Venus. Shortly afterward his discarded staff begins to put forth green leaves. The pope sends messengers to search for Tannhäuser, but he is never seen again.

The legend acquired great popularity among 19th-century Romantic writers. Its most famous presentation is in Richard Wagner's music drama *Tannhäuser* (produced 1845).

Tantalus or **Tantalos** \ˈtan-tə-ləs\ In Greek legend, the king of Sipylus in Lydia (or of Phrygia) and the intimate friend of the gods, to whose table he was admitted. Tantalus was punished for one of several possible offenses against the gods. According to various ancient authors he abused divine favor by revealing to mortals the secrets he had learned in heaven, offended the gods by killing his son Pelops and serving him to them, in order to test their powers of observation, or stole nectar and ambrosia from heaven and gave them to mortals.

The punishment took place in Hades, where Tantalus stood up to his neck in water, which flowed from him when he tried to drink it; over his head hung fruits that the wind wafted away whenever he tried to grasp them (hence the word tantalize).

Tantra \ˈtən-trə, ˈtän-, ˈtan-\ One of the later Hindu or Buddhist scriptures dealing especially with techniques and rituals, including meditative and sexual practices. In the orthodox classification of Hindu religious literature, *Tantra* refers to a class of post-Vedic Sanskrit treatises similar to the *Purāṇas* (medieval encyclopedic collections of myths, legends, and other topics). In this usage *Tantra*s theoretically deal with theology, yoga, construction of temples and images, and religious practices; in reality, they tend to deal with such aspects of popular Hinduism as spells, rituals, and symbols.

Tao Qian or **T'ao Ch'ien** \ˈtaȯ-ˈchyen\, *also called* Tao Yuanming \ˈywän-ˈmiŋ\ (b. 365, Xinyang district, now in Jiangsi province, China—d. 427, Jiangsi) One of China's greatest poets and a noted recluse.

Tao Qian took a minor official post in his 20s in order to support his aged parents. After about 10 years at the post and a brief term as county magistrate, he resigned from official life, repelled by its excessive formality and widespread corruption. With his wife and children he retired to a farming village south of the Yangtze River. Despite the hardships of the farmer's life and frequent food shortages, Tao Qian was content writing poetry, cultivating the chrysanthemums that became inseparably associated with his poetry, and drinking wine, also a common subject of his verse.

Because the taste of Tao Qian's contemporaries was for an elaborate and artificial style and his poetry is simple and straightforward, he was not fully appreciated until the Tang dynasty (618–907). A master of the five-word line, Tao Qian has been described as the first great poet of *tianyuan* ("fields and gardens").

Taos \ˈtaȯs\, Marguerite *see* Marguerite Taos AMROUCHE.

Tao-te ching *see* DAODE JING.

Ṭarafah \ˈtȧ-rȧ-fȧ\, *in full* Ṭarafah 'Amr ibn al-'Abd ibn Sufyān ibn Mālik ibn Ḍubay'ah al-Bakrī ibn Wā'il (fl. 6th century) Arab poet, author of the longest of the seven odes in the celebrated collection of pre-Islāmic poetry *Al-Mu'allaqāt*. Some critics judge him to be the greatest Arab poet.

Ṭarafah is traditionally acknowledged to have been an extraordinarily precocious poet, writing verses as a boy. After a wild youth spent in Bahrain, he went with his uncle Mutalammis, who was also a poet, to the court of 'Amr ibn Hind, the Lakhmid king of Al-Ḥīrah, and there became companion to the king's brother; Ṭarafah's association with the court of Al-Ḥirah (554–568) is the only certainly known fact of his life. Tradition relates that, after having ridiculed the king in some verses, he was sent with a letter to the ruler of Bahrain and, in accordance with the instructions contained in the letter, was buried alive.

Ṭarafah is one of the few pre-Islāmic poets whose works—collected poems and the *Mu'allaqāt* ode—are still extant. His poetry is passionate and eloquent, defending sensual pleasure and the pursuit of glory as the only proper goals of life.

Taras Bulba \ˌtȧ-tə-ˈrȧs-ˈbüly-bə\ Story by Nikolay GOGOL, published in Russian in 1835 in the book *Mirgorod*. "Taras Bulba," set on the Ukrainian steppe, is a tale in epic style of the lives of Cossack warriors.

The narrative follows the exploits of an aging Cossack, Taras Bulba, and his two sons. The younger, Andriy, falls in love with a Polish noblewoman and, after joining the garrison of a Polish town besieged by the Cossacks, is caught and shot by his father. Taras himself is eventually captured by the Poles and burnt alive on a commanding height, while undaunted he urges the retreating Cossacks to escape across the Dniester.

Gogol published a revised and expanded version of the story in 1842, introducing a curious note of Great Russian nationalism and removing any suggestion that Ukraine was a country distinct from Russia. Both versions are remarkable for their anti-Polish sentiment and virulent anti-Semitism.

Tar-Baby \'tär-,bā-bē\   Folk figure, a sticky tar doll, perhaps best known as the central character in African-American folk-

Brer Rabbit and the Tar-Baby, drawing by E.W. Kemble from "The Tar-Baby" by Joel Chandler Harris

tales popularized in written literature by Joel Chandler Harris. Harris' "Tar-Baby" (1879), one of the animal tales told by the character Uncle Remus, is but one example of numerous African-derived tales featuring the use of a wax, gum, or rubber figure to trap a rascal. The sticky-figure motif is also common in American Indian tales.

In Harris' version, the doll is made by Brer Fox and placed in the roadside to even a score with his archenemy Brer Rabbit. Brer Rabbit speaks to the Tar-Baby, gets angry when it does not answer him, strikes it, and gets stuck. The more he strikes and kicks the figure, the more hopelessly he becomes attached.

Tarbell \'tär-bəl\, Ida M., *in full* Minerva (b. Nov. 5, 1857, Erie county, Pa., U.S.—d. Jan. 6, 1944, Bridgeport, Conn.) Investigative journalist, lecturer, and chronicler of American industry, best known for her classic *The History of the Standard Oil Company* (1904). Tarbell was one of the journalists characterized by President Theodore Roosevelt as a muckraker.

The History of the Standard Oil Company, originally a serial in *McClure's*, is one of the most thorough accounts of the rise of a business monopoly and its use of unfair practices. Tarbell's association with *McClure's* lasted until 1906. She also wrote for *American Magazine*, which she also co-owned and coedited for several years. In addition, she penned several popular biographies, including eight books on Abraham Lincoln. Her autobiography, *All in the Day's Work*, was published in 1939.

Tarhan \tär-'hän\, Abdülhak Hamid (b. Feb. 2, 1852, Constantinople, Ottoman Empire [now Istanbul, Tur.]—d. April 12, 1937, Istanbul)   Poet and playwright considered one of the greatest Turkish Romantic writers. He was instrumental in introducing Western influences into Turkish literature.

Born into a family of famous scholars, Tarhan was educated in Istanbul, Paris, and Tehrān. Following in his father's foot-

steps, he became a diplomat. In 1908 he became a member of the Turkish Senate and, after World War I and following a stay in Vienna, he returned to Turkey.

Tarhan was a follower of the Tanzimat school of literature (based on a 19th-century political reform movement) and was influenced by his patriotic predecessor, the Young Turk writer Namık Kemal. His best dramas (notably *Tarik* and *Ibn-i Musa*) feature personages in Muslim history, although *Finten* (1887) deals with London society. Deeply moved by the death of his wife, he dedicated many poems to her, such as his famous "Makber" ("The Tomb"), written in 1885.

Tarkington \'tär-kiŋ-tən\, Booth, *in full* Newton Booth Tarkington (b. July 29, 1869, Indianapolis, Ind., U.S.—d. May 19, 1946, Indianapolis)   American novelist and dramatist, best known for his satirical and sometimes romanticized pictures of American Midwesterners.

Tarkington studied at Purdue University, Ind., and at Princeton but took no degree. He won early recognition with the melodramatic novel *The Gentleman from Indiana* (1899), reflecting his disillusionment with the corruption in the lawmaking process. His humorous portrayals of boyhood and adolescence, PENROD (1914), *Penrod and Sam* (1916), SEVENTEEN (1916), and *Gentle Julia* (1922), became young-people's classics. He was equally successful with his portrayals of Midwestern life and character: *The Turmoil* (1915), THE MAGNIFICENT AMBERSONS (1918; film, 1942), and *The Midlander* (1923), combined as the trilogy *Growth* (1927), and *The Plutocrat* (1927). ALICE ADAMS (1921), a searching character study, is perhaps his most finished novel. He continued his delineations of female character in *Claire Ambler* (1928), *Mirthful Haven* (1930), and *Presenting Lily Mars* (1933) and wrote several domestic novels in his later years. He also wrote many plays, including an adaptation of his immensely popular romance *Monsieur Beaucaire* (1901).

Tarlton \'tärl-tən\, Richard (b. Condover, Shropshire, Eng.—d. Sept. 3, 1588, London)   English actor, ballad writer, and the most popular comedian of his age.

Tarlton takes his place in theatrical history as creator of the stage yokel; his performance is thought to have influenced William Shakespeare's creation of the character Bottom in *A Midsummer Night's Dream*, and Tarlton is said to have been the model for the court jester Yorick described in *Hamlet*.

Tarlton was first mentioned in 1570 for his didactic ballad on the "late great floods." The Stationers' Register of 1576 credits him with "a newe booke in Englishe verse intituled Tarltons Toyes." By 1579 he was a well-known actor and Queen Elizabeth I's favorite jester. His plays, which were praised by contemporaries, are all lost. Of later jestbooks that were published as Tarlton's, including *Tarltons Newes out of Purgatorie* (c. 1590) and *Tarlton's Jests* (1611), most are of dubious authenticity, but, like inn signboards that depicted him as late as 1798, they attested to the long survival of his fame.

Tarrant, Verena \və-'rē-nə-'tar-ənt\   Fictional character, a beautiful, gifted, and naive young woman in the novel THE BOSTONIANS by Henry James.

Tartarus \'tär-tə-rəs\   The infernal regions of ancient Greek mythology. The name was originally used for the deepest region of the world, the lower of the two parts of the underworld, where the gods locked up their enemies. The name gradually became associated more generally with the entire underworld. As such it was the opposite of Elysium, where happy souls lived after death. In some accounts Tartarus was one of the personified elements of the world, along with Gaea (Earth) and others. *Compare* ELYSIUM; HADES.

Tartuffe \tär-ˈtü̈ef\   Comedy in five acts by MOLIÈRE, produced in 1664 and published in French in 1669 as *Le Tartuffe, ou l'imposteur* ("Tartuffe; or, The Imposter"). It was also published in English as *The Imposter*.

Tartuffe is a sanctimonious scoundrel who, professing extreme piety, is taken into the household of Orgon, a wealthy man. Under the guise of ministering to the family's spiritual and moral needs, he almost destroys Orgon's family. Elmire, Orgon's wife, sees through Tartuffe's wicked hypocrisy and exposes him.

Tarzan \ˈtär-ˌzan, -zən\   Fictional character, the hero of jungle adventures in a series of novels by Edgar Rice BURROUGHS. Tarzan first appeared in a magazine story in 1912. His popularity led to the publication of a novel, *Tarzan of the Apes* (1914), and to a series of phenomenally successful sequels.

Tasso \ˈtäs-sō\, Torquato (b. March 11, 1544, Sorrento, Kingdom of Naples [Italy]—d. April 25, 1595, Rome)   The greatest Italian poet of the late Renaissance, celebrated for his masterpiece of epic poetry, GERUSALEMME LIBERATA (1581; *Jerusalem Delivered*).

Detail of an oil painting by Federico Zuccari, 1594

L. Locatelli-Milesi-Tombini, Bergamo, Italy

The son of a poet and courtier, in 1565 Tasso entered the service of Luigi, cardinal d'Este. He frequented the court of Duke Alfonso II d'Este at Ferrara, where he enjoyed the patronage of the duke's sisters, for whom he wrote some of his finest lyrical poems. In 1571 he became one of the duke's courtiers, and devoting himself to intense poetic activity, he produced the pastoral drama *L'Aminta* (1581; performed 1573), which transcends the convention of artificial rusticity with its sensuous, lyrical picture of Arcadia.

In 1575 Tasso completed his epic poem on the First Crusade, a subject that had long fascinated him. In composing *Gerusalemme liberata*, he blended historical events with imaginary romantic and idyllic episodes that contribute much of the lyrical charm which the poem possesses. Aware of his epic's poetic novelty, Tasso went to Rome in order to arrange its revision by a group of critics, but back in Ferrara in 1576, he started revising his work in a contradictory mood. He developed a persecution mania, and the following years were characterized by sudden departures from Ferrara and by violent crises, the latter culminating in his incarceration in the hospital of Santa Anna (1579–86) by order of the duke of Ferrara. During his confinement Tasso wrote a number of philosophical and moral dialogues that, together with his numerous letters, are among the best examples of 16th-century Italian prose. In 1581 the first editions of the *Gerusalemme liberata* and portions of the *Rime e prose* were published.

In 1586 Tasso was released from Santa Anna, but after a brief period of creativity in which he completed his tragedy *Galealto*, retitled *Re Torrismondo* (1587), he relapsed into his usual inquietude. He managed to compose two religious poems, *Monte Oliveto* (1605; "Mount of Olives") and *Le sette giornate del mondo creato* (1607; "The Seven Days of Creation"), and was received in Rome. After producing an unfortunate revision of his epic entitled *Gerusalemme conquistata* (1593) and writing two more religious poems, he could write little more.

It was not long before *Gerusalemme liberata* was translated and imitated in many European languages, and legends about its restless, half-mad, and misunderstood author lived on for centuries.

Tassoni \täs-ˈsō-nē\, Alessandro (b. Sept. 28, 1565, Modena, duchy of Modena [Italy]—d. April 25, 1635, Modena)   Italian political writer, literary critic, and poet, remembered for his mock-heroic satiric poem *La secchia rapita* (1622; *The Rape of the Bucket*), the earliest and, according to most critics, the best of many Italian works in the genre.

Educated at the universities of Bologna, Pisa, and Ferrara, Tassoni joined the linguistically conservative Crusca Academy in 1589. Among his numerous prose works, the most interesting are an attack on Petrarch and his followers, *Considerazioni sopra le rime del Petrarca* (1609; "Observations on Petrarch's Poems"), together with a collection of philosophical, literary, scientific, and political thoughts, *Dieci libri di pensieri diversi di Alessandro Tassoni* (1620; "Ten Books of Diverse Thoughts of Alessandro Tassoni").

Tassoni's best-known work, *La secchia rapita*, is based on the early 14th-century warfare between the Italian cities of Bologna and Modena, during which the Modenese captured the bucket from Bologna's town well as a trophy. In Tassoni's poem the Bolognese offer entire towns and groups of hostages for their bucket, and every episode, beginning seriously, ends in some hilarious absurdity.

Tate \ˈtāt\, Allen, *in full* John Orley Allen Tate (b. Nov. 19, 1899, Winchester, Ky., U.S.—d. Feb. 9, 1979, Nashville, Tenn.)   American poet, teacher, and novelist, and a leading exponent of the New Criticism. In both his criticism and his poetry, he emphasized the writer's need for a tradition to adhere to; he found his own tradition in the culture of the conservative, agrarian South and, later, in Roman Catholicism, to which he was converted in 1950.

Tate entered Vanderbilt University, Nashville, Tenn., in 1918, where he helped found *The Fugitive* (1922–25), a poetry magazine. Along with several other Fugitive poets, Tate contributed to the symposium *I'll Take My Stand* (1930), a manifesto defending the traditional agrarian society of the South.

From 1934 Tate taught at several schools, including Princeton University and the University of Minnesota. He also edited *The Sewanee Review* in the mid-1940s, during which time it acquired wide importance as a literary magazine.

In his best-known poem, "Ode to the Confederate Dead" (1926; revised 1930), the dead symbolize the emotions he is no longer able to feel. The poems written from about 1930 to 1939 broaden the theme of disjointedness by showing its effect on society, as in the sadly ironical "The Mediterranean" (1932). In his later poems Tate suggested that only through the subjective wholeness of the individual can society itself be whole. The view emerged tentatively in "Seasons of the Soul" (1943) and confidently in "The Buried Lake" (1953), both devotional poems.

Tate's only novel, *The Fathers* (1938), refashions the Jason-Medea myth to promulgate agrarian beliefs. His *Collected Poems* was issued in 1977; *Essays of Four Decades* appeared in 1969. *See also* FUGITIVE.

Tate \ˈtāt\, Nahum (b. 1652, Dublin, Ire.—d. July 30, 1715, London, Eng.)   Poet laureate of England and playwright, adapter of plays, and collaborator with Nicholas Brady in *A New Version of the Psalms of David* (1696).

Tate graduated from Trinity College, Dublin, afterwards moving to London. Although he wrote some plays of his own, he is best known for his adaptations of the Elizabethan playwrights. His version of William Shakespeare's *King Lear*, to which he gave a happy ending, held the stage well into the 19th century. Tate also wrote the libretto for Henry Purcell's *Dido and Aeneas* (c. 1689). Some of his hymns found a lasting place in Protestant worship, notably "While shepherds watched" and "Through all the changing scenes of life."

Tate was commissioned by the poet John Dryden to write the second part of *Absalom and Achitophel* (1682), although Dryden added the finishing touches himself. The best of Tate's own poems is "Panacea: A Poem upon Tea" (1700). He succeeded Thomas Shadwell as poet laureate in 1692.

Tatler, The \ˈtat-lər\ Periodical launched in London by the essayist Richard Steele on April 12, 1709, appearing three times weekly until January 2, 1711. At first its avowed intention was to present poetry, foreign and domestic news, and accounts of gallantry, pleasure, and entertainment. In time *The Tatler* began to investigate manners and society, establishing its principles of ideal behavior, its concepts of a perfect gentleman and gentlewoman, and its standards of good taste.

Two months after *The Tatler* ceased publication, Joseph Addison and Steele launched the brilliant periodical *The Spectator*. *See also* Joseph ADDISON; Richard STEELE.

Tattycoram \ˌtat-ē-ˈkȯr-əm\ Fictional character, the Meagles family maid in the novel LITTLE DORRIT by Charles Dickens. "Tattycoram" is the nickname given to Harriet Beadle by the Meagles' daughter. Acutely irritated by the Meagles' patronizing ways, she runs away.

Tavares \tä-ˈvä-resh\ Eugénio (de Paulo) (b. May 11, 1867, Brava Island, Cape Verde Islands—d. Jan. 6, 1930, Brava Island) Cape Verdean poet who was one of the first Cape Verdeans to be published in the islands' vernacular, Crioulo, a creolized Portuguese with African-language influences.

Tavares' writing was heavily influenced by the islands' folklore, and he wrote poetry both in classical Portuguese and in Crioulo. His first books—*Amor que salva* ("The Love That Saves") and *Mal de amor: coroa de espinhos* ("Love's Sickness: The Crown of Thorns")—were published in 1916. His most important book, however, was *Mornas: cantigas crioulas* ("Mornas: Creole Songs"), which was published posthumously in 1932.

The *morna* is a uniquely Cape Verdean art form of song and dance, likened by some to the Brazilian samba or the Caribbean beguine. Tavares' *morna*s, the most serious poems to be written in Crioulo, deal with the power of true love, the sorrow of separation, and the sad, sweet longings for and memories of home.

Tavora, Orlando. Pseudonym of António JACINTO.

Tawdry, Suky \ˈsü-kē-ˈtȯ-drē\ Fictional character, one of several prostitutes who associate with the gangster Macheath, in THE THREEPENNY OPERA by Bertolt Brecht and Kurt Weill.

Tayama Katai \ˈtä-yä-mä-kä-ˈtī\, *also called* Tayama Rokuya \ˈrō-kü-yä\ (b. Dec. 13, 1871, Tatebayashi, Japan—d. May 13, 1930, Tokyo) Novelist who figured prominently in the development of the Japanese naturalist school of writing.

Tayama's early work was highly romantic, but with the essay "Rokotsu naru byōsha" (1904; "Bold Delineation") he pointed the way toward the more realistic path he was to follow under French influence. The injunction to observe strict objectivity and to describe things as they are, deriving from the early French naturalists Guy de Maupassant and the brothers Edmond and Jules Goncourt, inspired the development of a major genre in Japanese literature—the *watakushi shōsetsu*, or auto-

biographical "I novel." Tayama's *Futon* (1908; "The Bed"), an early exemplar of this genre, made his reputation. It describes in embarrassing detail the attraction of a middle-aged writer (the author) to a young female student. A trilogy of autobiographical novels, *Sei* (1908; "Life"), *Tsuma* (1908–09; "Wives"), and *En* (1910; "Ties") fixed the distinguishing form of Japanese naturalism. *Inaka kyōshi* (1909; "Country Teacher") shows the influence of the Goncourts and of Gustave Flaubert's *Madame Bovary*. An essay on Tayama's own literary theories, "Katai bunwa" (1911; "Katai's Literary Discourses"), introduced into the critical language the term *heimen byōsha* ("plain delineation"), with which he is identified. In later years, with the decline in the influence of naturalism, the novelist entered a period of personal confusion, from which he emerged with the calm, almost religious attitude that is reflected in *Zansetsu* (1917–18; "Remaining Snow").

Taylor \ˈtā-lər\, Bayard, *in full* James Bayard Taylor (b. Jan. 11, 1825, Kennett Square, Pa., U.S.—d. Dec. 19, 1878, Berlin, Ger.) American author known primarily for his lively travel narratives and for his translation of J.W. von Goethe's *Faust*.

In 1844 Taylor's first volume of verse, *Ximena*, was published. He then arranged with *The Saturday Evening Post* and the *United States Gazette* to finance a trip abroad in return for publication rights to travel letters, which were compiled in the extremely popular *Views Afoot* (1846). In 1847 he began a career in journalism in New York. He continued his trips — to the Orient, Africa, and Russia—and became renowned as something of a modern Marco Polo. In 1862 he became secretary of the U.S. legation at St. Petersburg, Russia, and in 1878, U.S. minister to Germany. Of his works in this later period, the translation of *Faust* (1870–71) remains his best known. His *Poems of the Orient* appeared in 1855.

Taylor \ˈtā-lər\, Edward (b. 1645?, in or near Coventry, Warwickshire, Eng.—d. June 24, 1729, Westfield, Mass. [U.S.]) One of the foremost poets in colonial British North America.

Unwilling to subscribe to a required oath of conformity because of his staunch adherence to Congregational principles, Taylor gave up schoolteaching in England, immigrated to New England, and entered Harvard College (later University). After his graduation in 1671, he became minister in the frontier village of Westfield, Mass., where he remained until his death.

Taylor's manuscript, *Poetical Works*, came into the possession of Yale in 1883 by the gift of a descendant, but it was not until 1939 that any of his poetry was published. The important poems fall into two broad divisions. "God's Determinations Touching His Elect" is an extended verse sequence setting forth the grace and majesty of God as a drama of sin and redemption. The "Sacramental Meditations," about 200 in number, were described by Taylor as "Preparatory Meditations Before My Approach to the Lord's Supper."

Taylor \ˈtā-lər\, Elizabeth, *original surname* Coles \ˈkōlz\ (b. July 3, 1912, Reading, Berkshire, Eng.—d. Nov. 19, 1975, Penn, Buckinghamshire) British novelist noted for her precise use of language and scrupulously understated style.

Her first novel, *At Mrs Lippincote's*, was published in 1945; like most of her work, it has a largely uneventful plot but portrays with unerring accuracy the behavior of women in contemporary society. Among her other works are *A Wreath of Roses* (1950), *A Game of Hide and Seek* (1951), *The Sleeping Beauty* (1953), and *The Wedding Group* (1968). Volumes of short stories include *A Dedicated Man* (1965) and *The Devastating Boys* (1972).

Taylor \ˈtā-lər\, John (b. Aug. 24, 1580, Gloucester, Gloucestershire, Eng.—d. December 1653, London) British pamphleteer and journalist, who called himself "the water-poet."

In his youth Taylor was apprenticed to a Thames boatman. He served in the navy and saw action at Cádiz (1596) and Flores (1597). Returning to London, he worked as a waterman transporting passengers up and down and across the River Thames. He increased his income by dedicating verses to noble patrons and won fame by making a series of whimsical journeys, which he described in lively, rollicking verse and prose published in oddly titled pamphlets. He journeyed, for example, from London to Queenborough, Kent, in a paper boat with two stockfish tied to canes for oars, and he nearly drowned in the attempt. He made other water journeys between London, York, and Salisbury, and *The Pennyles Pilgrimage; or, The Money-Lesse Perambulation of John Taylor from London to Edenborough* (1618) describes a journey he made on foot from London to Edinburgh without money. In 1620 he journeyed to Prague, where he was entertained by the Queen of Bohemia. When the English Civil War began in 1642 Taylor moved to Oxford, where he wrote Royalist pamphlets. After the city surrendered (1645), he returned to London and kept a public house, "The Crown" (later "The Poet's Head"), until his death.

Taylor \'tā-lər\, Peter (Hillsman) (b. Jan. 8, 1917, Trenton, Tenn., U.S.—d. Nov. 2, 1994, Charlottesville, Va.) American short-story writer, novelist, and playwright known for his portraits of Tennessee gentry caught in a changing society.

From 1936 to 1937 Taylor attended Vanderbilt University, Nashville, Tenn., then the center of a Southern literary renaissance led by poets Allen Tate, Robert Penn Warren, and John Crowe Ransom. He transferred to Southwestern College in Memphis to study with Tate in 1937, then completed his B.A. in 1940 under Ransom at Kenyon College, Ohio. Taylor taught at a number of schools until 1967, when he joined the faculty of the University of Virginia in Charlottesville.

Taylor was best known for his short stories, which are usually set in his contemporary Tennessee and which reveal conflicts between old rural society and the rough, industrialized "New South." His first collection, *A Long Fourth, and Other Stories* (1948), was praised for its subtle depictions of family disintegration. In his 1950 novella *A Woman of Means*, regarded by many as his finest work, a young narrator recalls his wealthy stepmother's nervous collapse and reveals the tension between her city ways and his father's rural values.

The Widows of Thornton (1954), *Happy Families Are All Alike* (1959), and *Miss Leonora When Last Seen and Fifteen Other Stories* (1963) secured the author's reputation as a master of short fiction. Later works include *In the Miro District and Other Stories* (1977); THE OLD FOREST, published in *The Old Forest and Other Stories* (1985); the Pulitzer Prize-winning novel *A Summons to Memphis* (1986); and *The Oracle at Stoneleigh Court* (1993), a collection of several short stories and three plays.

Tchernichowsky or **Chernikhovsky** \chir-n'i-'kôf-sk'ē\, Saul (Gutmanovich) (b. Aug. 20, 1875, Mikhaylovka [now Mikhaylivka], Ukraine, Russian Empire—d. Oct. 13, 1943, Jerusalem) Prolific Hebrew poet whose poetry, in strongly biblical language, deals with Russia, Germany, and Palestine and with the themes of love and beauty.

In 1922 Tchernichowsky left Ukraine, and, after several years of wandering, he settled in Palestine in 1931. His production of written material (chiefly poetry) was immense. It included sonnet cycles, short stories, idylls of Jewish village life in Russia, and translations of the *Epic of Gilgamesh*, Homer, William Shakespeare, Molière, and Henry Wadsworth Longfellow.

Tchernichowsky's poetry is deeply romantic and suffused with a love of Greek culture; the conflict between this and Judaism gave rise to what some consider to be his finest work.

Tchicaya U Tam'si \chē-kä-'yä-ū-täm-'sē\, *pseudonym of* Gérald Félix Tchicaya (b. Aug. 25, 1931, Mpili, near Brazzaville, French Equatorial Africa [now in the Congo]—d. April 21 or 22, 1988, Bazancourt, Oise, Fr.) Congolese French-language writer and poet whose work explores the relationships between victor and victim.

As the son of the Congolese first deputy to the French National Assembly, Tchicaya finished his secondary school in Orléans and Paris. From 1960 he worked with UNESCO in Paris.

Tchicaya's poetry—much influenced by Surrealism and Negritude—includes *Le Mauvais Sang* (1955; "Bad Blood"), *Feu de brousse* (1957; *Brush Fire*), *À Triche-coeur* (1960; "A Game of Cheat-Heart"), *Épitomé* (1962), *Le Ventre* (1964; "The Belly"), *L'Arc musical* (1969; "The Bow Harp"), *Selected Poems* (1970), and *La Veste d'intérieur* (1977; "The Inner Failure"). He also published *Légendes africaines* (1968; "African Stories"), a collection of folktales. His later works include a book of short stories, a novel, and three plays.

His poetry relates, through rich and varied imagery, the broken heritage of the African present and the roles of the Roman Catholic church, French colonialism, and education. Through fierce and startling symbols repetitively used like devices in oral African literature, Tchicaya expanded his verse to make large statements about life.

Teahouse of the August Moon Comedy in three acts by American playwright John Patrick, produced in 1953. Patrick satirized American good intentions in this lighthearted examination of an attempt by the military forces to Americanize a foreign culture. It was his most famous play and was based on a novel of the same name by Vern Sneider. The play was awarded the Pulitzer Prize for drama in 1954.

In the play, Colonel Purdy sends Captain Fisby to indoctrinate Okinawans in the virtues of American democracy. Fisby "goes native"; soon the islanders, inspired by American entrepreneurial techniques, are selling huge quantities of potato brandy, their only marketable product. They build a teahouse instead of the Americans' proposed schoolhouse. The U.S. government hails Fisby's work as a stellar example of American capitalism.

Teasdale \'tēz-ˌdāl\, Sara (b. Aug. 8, 1884, St. Louis, Mo., U.S.—d. Jan. 29, 1933, New York, N.Y.) American poet whose short, personal lyrics were noted for their classical simplicity and quiet intensity.

Teasdale made frequent trips to Chicago, where she eventually became part of Harriet Monroe's *Poetry* magazine circle. After rejecting the poet Vachel Lindsay as a suitor, she married a St. Louis businessman, Ernst Filsinger, in 1914. In 1929 she divorced him and moved to New York City, where she lived in virtual retirement until her suicide.

Her first book, *Sonnets to Duse and Other Poems*, was printed privately in 1907. From the beginning, her work was well received. With *Rivers to the Sea* (1915) she was established as a popular poet; she won the Pulitzer Prize in poetry in 1918 for *Love Songs* (1917). Her familiar "Let It Be Forgotten" is included in *Flame and Shadow* (1920). Gradually, as her technical competence increased, her poetry became simpler and more austere—e.g., the haunting "An End" (in *Dark of the Moon*, 1926). In her last book, *Strange Victory* (1933), many of the poems foreshadow her own death.

Teazle, Lady \'tē-zəl\ Fictional character, the young, flirtatious, naive wife of an old London man in Richard Brinsley Sheridan's comedy THE SCHOOL FOR SCANDAL.

Tegnér \teg-'när\, Esaias (b. Nov. 13, 1782, Kyrkerud, Swed.—d. Nov. 2, 1846, Östrabo) Swedish teacher, bishop, and his country's most popular poet of the period.

Tegnér graduated from the University of Lund in 1802 and was appointed professor of Greek there 10 years later. He continued to lecture at Lund until 1824, when he became bishop of Växjö, a position he retained for the rest of his life.

Originally associated with the Romantic movement, he eventually rejected its emotional and mystic aspects. His ideal of poetry became increasingly more classical but assimilated certain Romantic ingredients. His greatest poetic achievements were the much-translated *Frithiofs saga* (1825), a cycle based on an Old Icelandic saga, and two narrative poems, the sensitive religious idyll *Children of the Lord's Supper* (1820; translated by Henry Wadsworth Longfellow) and *Axel* (1822).

Teika   see FUJIWARA SADAIE.

Teirlinck \'ter-,liŋk\, Herman (Louis-Cesar) (b. Feb. 24, 1879, St.-Jans-Molenbeek, Belg.—d. Feb. 4, 1967, Beersel) Flemish novelist, poet, short-story writer, essayist, and playwright whose dramas influenced post-World War I European theater.

Teirlinck's first book, *Verzen* (1900), was a volume of poetry, but he soon demonstrated in fiction the virtuosity and thematic variety that would characterize his entire career. *De wonderbare wereld* (1902; "The Wondrous World") was a collection of fantastic tales set in rural Flanders, and *'t Bedrijf van den kwade* (1904; "The Demon in Action") and *Het ivoren aapje* (1909; "The Ivory Monkey") took place in Brussels. The highlight of Teirlinck's early career was the publication in 1908 of *Mijnheer J. B. Serjanszoon*, a witty and cynical novel whose elegant manner contrasted sharply with the conventions of Dutch fiction.

In the years after World War I, Expressionism was the dominant movement in Flemish literature. Flemish popular theater developed into one of the most original in Europe. Teirlinck introduced the concept of "total theater," combining dance, mime, music, cinematic effects, and echoes of medieval miracle plays. Some of his best-known plays are *De vertraagde film* (1922; "The Slow Motion Picture"), *Ik dien* (1924; "I Serve"), and *De man zonder lijf* (1925; "The Man Without a Body"). During World War II Teirlinck returned to writing fiction. *Zelfportret of het galgemaal* (1955; *The Man in the Mirror*) is considered the best work of his post-World War II career.

Telegonus \tə-'leg-ə-nəs\ In Greek mythology, especially the *Telegonia* of Eugamon of Cyrene, the son of the hero Odysseus by the sorceress Circe. Telegonus went to Ithaca in search of his father, whom he killed unwittingly. His spear had been tipped with the spine of a stingray, thus fulfilling the prophecy that death would come to Odysseus "from the sea." Telegonus then married Penelope, Odysseus' widow.

Telemachus \ti-'lem-ə-kəs\ In Greek mythology, son of Odysseus and his wife, Penelope. When Telemachus reached manhood, he visited Pylos and Sparta in search of his father, who had not returned from the Trojan War. He discovered, upon his return home, that Odysseus had returned. Then father and son together slayed the suitors who had gathered around Penelope. His story is told in Homer's *Odyssey*.

Telesilla \,tel-ə-'sil-ə\ (fl. 5th century BC, Argos) Greek poet noted for saving the city of Argos from attack by Cleomenes and his Spartan troops after their defeat of the Argive men. She wrote lyric poetry dedicated to Apollo and Artemis, of which only one brief fragment remains.

telestich \tə-'les-tik, 'tel-ə-,stik\ [Greek *têle* far off, at a distance (probably confused with *télos* end) + *stíchos* line] A poem in which the consecutive final letters of the lines spell a word or words. *Compare* ACROSTIC.

Tell, William \'wil-yəm-'tel\, *German* Wilhelm Tell \'vil-,helm-'tel\ Legendary Swiss hero who symbolizes the struggle for political and individual freedom.

The historical existence of Tell is disputed. According to popular legend, he was a peasant from Bürglen in the canton of Uri in the 13th and early 14th centuries who defied Austrian authority, was forced to shoot an apple from his son's head, was arrested for threatening the governor's life, saved the same governor's life en route to prison, escaped, and ultimately killed the governor in an ambush. These events, together with others, supposedly roused the people to rise in rebellion against Austrian rule.

The classic form of the legend appears in the *Chronicon Helveticum* (1734–36) by Gilg Tschudi. There is no evidence for the existence of Tell, but the story of the marksman's test is widely distributed in folklore. In the early Romantic era of nationalist revolutions, the Tell legend attained worldwide renown through the stirring play *Wilhelm Tell* (1804; WILLIAM TELL) by the German dramatist Friedrich von Schiller.

Tell-Tale Heart, The Short gothic horror story by Edgar Allan POE, published in *The Pioneer* in 1843.

Poe's tale of murder and terror, told by a nameless homicidal madman, influenced later stream-of-consciousness fiction and helped secure the author's reputation as master of the macabre. The narrator relates with relish his murder and dismemberment of an old man. Poe's revelation of the narrator's dementia is a classic study in psychopathology. Before killing the old man, the narrator is maddened by what he believes to be his victim's loud heartbeats. After he commits the murder the police arrive, having been summoned by a neighbor who heard a scream. While he is talking to the police, the narrator believes he can hear the corpse's heart still beating, and he hysterically confesses his crime.

Tel Quel \,tel-'kel\ French avant-garde literary review published from 1960 to 1982 by Éditions du Seuil. Founded by Philippe Sollers and other young writers, this eclectic magazine published works by such practitioners of the *nouveau roman* ("new novel") as Alain Robbe-Grillet and Nathalie Sarraute, as well as works by these writers' acknowledged predecessors, *e.g.*, James Joyce and Francis Ponge.

Much influenced by surrealism, *Tel Quel* had as a goal the evaluation of 20th-century literature; it printed previously unpublished works by Antonin Artaud, Georges Bataille, and Ezra Pound. The review promoted the renewal of French philosophy and literary criticism through contributions by Michel Foucault, Jacques Derrida, Julia Kristeva, Roland Barthes, and Jacques Lacan. From 1966 to 1970 *Tel Quel* represented a Maoist view of Marxism.

From 1974 the review relinquished political involvement, becoming a supporter of such intellectuals as Bernard-Henri Lévy and André Glucksmann and others in the "new philosophers" movement. The critical orientation of *Tel Quel* shifted toward the classical Greco-Hebrew tradition, including discussion of biblical and theological questions. Its new stance included unequivocal support of human rights and an appreciation of modern culture, particularly that of the United States.

Tempest, The Drama in five acts by William SHAKESPEARE, first performed about 1611 and published in the First Folio of 1623. Like many of Shakespeare's other late plays, *The Tempest* tells of reconciliation after strife.

The play opens with a storm raised by Prospero, who years earlier, as the rightful Duke of Milan, had been set adrift with his daughter Miranda by his usurping brother Antonio. Shipwrecked on an enchanted island, Prospero mastered the art of magic and liberated several good spirits who had been tormented by the sorceress Sycorax, including Ariel, who became his servant. The atavistic Caliban, Sycorax's son, became Prospero's slave. Prospero raises the tempest to overtake Antonio and his courtiers, casting them on the shores of his island at the beginning of the play.

With the arrival of the outsiders the process of reconciliation begins. The party is brought to shore by Ariel, but Ferdinand, son of Alonso, the King of Naples, is separated from the others, including his father, and is believed drowned. Ariel helps foil plots against Prospero by Caliban and against Alonso by Antonio. Alonso, believing Ferdinand dead, is convinced that his death was punishment for Alonso's crime and has a change of heart. Prospero reconciles all and prepares to return to Milan to reclaim his throne.

The Tempest inspired many other works, including John Milton's *Comus*, Percy Bysshe Shelley's "Ariel to Miranda," Robert Browning's "Caliban upon Setebos," and W.H. Auden's *The Sea and the Mirror*.

Tempest-Tost \'tem-pəst-'tòst, -'tăst\   Novel by Robertson Davies, the first in his series of books known as the SALTERTON TRILOGY.

Temple of the Golden Pavilion, The   Novel by MISHIMA Yukio, first published in Japanese as *Kinkakuji* in 1956. The novel is considered one of the author's masterpieces.

A fictionalized account of the actual torching of a Kyōto temple by a disturbed Buddhist acolyte in 1950, the novel reflects Mishima's preoccupations with beauty and death. The narrator, Mizoguchi, a young Zen acolyte, is alienated from the world around him; born physically unattractive and frail and into bleak poverty, he stutters badly and holds himself aloof from others. His obsessive feelings for the Golden Temple vary from disappointment to reverence to identification with the structure. Mizoguchi resembles other tormented Mishima heroes who become obsessed with unattainable ideals: realizing the profound lack of beauty in his own life, he decides he must destroy the temple.

temporal \'tem-pə-rəl\   In classical prosody, of or relating to the quantity of syllables, or the length of time it takes to pronounce them.

temporalist \'tem-pə-rə-list\   In prosody, one who emphasizes the temporal element in analyzing the rhythmic structures of verse.

Temptation of Saint Anthony, The \'anth-ə-nē\   Novel by Gustave FLAUBERT, published in 1874 as *La Tentation de Saint Antoine*. It was also translated as *The First Temptation of Saint Anthony*. Flaubert called the subject of the narrative his "old infatuation," which he had begun developing in 1839 as an attempt to create a *Faust* in the French language. The work is notable for its imagery and its depiction of spiritual torment.

The work takes as its subject the 4th-century Christian anchorite Saint Anthony, who lived in the Egyptian desert. It reflects on his life, his decision to become a hermit, and the temptations of sexuality and sensuality he undergoes. Enfeebled from fasting and beset with sinful feelings and remorse, he experiences hallucinations in which he is drawn to gustatory and sensual excesses and in which he is tormented by philosophical doubt. But he emerges from his agony after he awakens and sees on the sun the image of Christ's face.

Tenant of Wildfell Hall, The \'wīld-,fel\   Novel by Anne BRONTË (writing under the pseudonym Acton Bell), first published in three volumes in 1848. This epistolary novel presents a portrait of debauchery that is remarkable in light of the author's sheltered life. It is the story of young Helen Graham's disastrous marriage to the dashing drunkard Arthur Huntingdon—said to be modeled on the author's wayward brother Branwell—and her flight from him to the seclusion of Wildfell Hall. Pursued by Gilbert Markham, who is in love with her,

Graham refuses him and, by way of explanation, gives him her journal. There he reads of her wretched married life. Eventually, after Huntingdon's death, they marry.

Tench \'tench\, Watkin (b. *c*. 1758, England?—d. May 7, 1833, Devonport, Devonshire, Eng.)   British army officer who wrote two classic books about early Australia.

Tench shipped out for Australia in 1787 as a captain lieutenant of marines, arriving in Botany Bay on Jan. 20, 1788. A year later he published in London *A Narrative of the Expedition to Botany Bay*, in which he described his voyage and life in the settlement; it was an immediate popular success. He sailed for Europe in 1791, and his *Complete Account of the Settlement at Port Jackson* appeared in 1793. Made a prisoner of war by the French in 1794, two years later he published an account of his captivity, *Letters Written in France to a Friend in London*.

tendenz \ten-'dents\ *plural* **tendenzen** \-'dent-sən\ [German *Tendenz* intention, trend, tendency]   A dominating point of view or purpose influencing the structure and content of a literary work.

Tender Buttons   Book of poems by Gertrude STEIN, first published in 1914 as *Tender Buttons: Objects, Food, Rooms*.

Heavily influenced by Cubism, the poetry in this work was considered by some critics to have taken abstraction and fragmentation past the limits of comprehensibility. The poems are dense and obscure and are devoid of conventional logic, syntax, or grammar. Rather than using conventional ways of conveying meaning and impressions, Stein juggles the sequence of the sounds of words to make verbal still-lifes.

Tender Is the Night   Semiautobiographical novel by F. Scott FITZGERALD, published in 1934. It is the story of a psychiatrist who marries one of his patients; as she slowly recovers, she exhausts his vitality until he is, in Fitzgerald's words, *un homme épuisé* ("a used-up man").

At first a charming success, Dick Diver disintegrates into drunkenness, failure, and anonymity as his wife Nicole recovers her strength and independence. Fitzgerald's portrayal of the Divers' life of lassitude was a reflection of his years spent among the American expatriate community in France; his insight into Nicole's madness came from his observations of his wife Zelda's nervous breakdowns. Diver is said to be based on the author's friend Gerald Murphy, but the character reflects much of Fitzgerald as well.

A revised version, which appeared in 1948, abandons the original edition's flashbacks and relates the story in chronological order.

Tennant \'ten-ənt\, Kylie, *original name* Kathleen Tennant, *married name* Rodd \'räd\ (b. March 12, 1912, Manly, N.S.W., Australia—d. Feb. 28, 1988, Sydney)   Australian novelist and playwright famed for her realistic yet affirmative depictions of the lives of the underprivileged in Australia.

Tennant's first book, *Tiburon* (1935), set in a New South Wales country town, accurately and sensitively describes life among the unemployed during the Great Depression. For her novels set in the slums of Sydney—*Foveaux* (1939), *Ride On, Stranger* (1943), and *The Joyful Condemned* (1953; later expanded as *Tell Morning This*)—Tennant lived in poor areas of the city and took jobs ranging from social worker to barmaid. In preparation for *The Battlers* (1941), about migrant workers, Tennant dressed as a man and traveled for months with the unemployed along the roads of Australia. Later she lived in a fishing village for a while and worked as a boat builder before publishing *Lost Haven* (1946), a story of wartime shipbuilders. Her best-known play, *Tether a Dragon* (1952), about the early Australian prime minister Alfred Deakin, was conceived while she was in the process of researching her first nonfiction piece, *Australia: Her Story: Notes on a Nation* (1953; rev. ed., 1964, 1971). After spending time with the Aborigines of Australia and Papua New Guinea, Tennant wrote her first volume of children's stories, *All the Proud Tribesmen* (1959).

From 1959 to 1969 Tennant worked as a journalist, a publisher's reader, and a literary adviser and editor. In 1969 she resumed writing full-time, and her later works included more histories and biographies, children's plays, short stories, poems, travel books, critical essays, and an autobiography (*The Missing Heir*, 1986).

Tennyson \'ten-i-sən\, Alfred, *in full* Alfred Tennyson, 1st Baron Tennyson of Aldworth and Freshwater, *byname* Alfred, Lord Tennyson (b. Aug. 6, 1809, Somersby, Lincolnshire, Eng.—d. Oct. 6, 1892, Aldworth, Surrey)   English poet often regarded as the chief representative of the Victorian Age in poetry.

Detail of an oil painting by Samuel Laurence, *c.* 1840

National Portrait Gallery, London

Tennyson began writing at an early age; he collaborated with his brothers Frederick and Charles in *Poems by Two Brothers* (1826; dated 1827). In 1827 Tennyson entered Trinity College, Cambridge, where he became acquainted with Arthur Hallam, the gifted son of the historian Henry Hallam. This was the deepest friendship of his life. Tennyson's reputation as a poet increased at Cambridge, and in 1830 POEMS, CHIEFLY LYRICAL, which included the poem MARIANA, was published. The following year Tennyson's father died, and the young poet left Cambridge without taking a degree. In 1832 Tennyson published another volume of his poems (dated 1833), including THE LOTOS-EATERS and THE LADY OF SHALOTT.

In September 1833 Hallam died suddenly. The shock to Tennyson was severe, but it prompted him to write a series of poems that eventually became part of one of his most well-known works, IN MEMORIAM. To this period also belong some of the lyrics that were later worked into Tennyson's favorite poem, the brooding MAUD. In 1842 Tennyson published *Poems,* in two volumes, one containing a revised selection from the volumes of 1830 and 1832, the other, new poems. The new poems included ULYSSES, "Morte d'Arthur," "The Two Voices," LOCKSLEY HALL, and "The Vision of Sin" and other poems that reveal a strange naiveté. In 1847 he published his first long poem, THE PRINCESS, a singular antifeminist fantasia.

In 1850 Tennyson was appointed poet laureate by Queen Victoria. His position as the national poet was confirmed by his famous poem THE CHARGE OF THE LIGHT BRIGADE, published in 1855 in *Maud and Other Poems.* A project that Tennyson had long considered at last issued in IDYLLS OF THE KING (1859; later revised and enlarged), which enjoyed immediate success. The poem ENOCH ARDEN appeared in 1864 in a popular volume of the same name.

After trying his hand at drama for a decade, Tennyson in 1886 published a new volume of poetry, containing "Locksley Hall Sixty Years After" and consisting mainly of imprecations against modern decadence and liberalism and a retraction of the earlier poem's belief in inevitable human progress. In 1889 he wrote the famous short poem CROSSING THE BAR during a crossing to the Isle of Wight. In the same year, he published *Demeter and Other Poems.* His last volume, *The Death of Oenone, Akbar's Dream, and Other Poems*, appeared in 1892.

tenor and vehicle \'ten-ər ... 'vē-i-kəl, 'vē-ˌhi-\   The components of a metaphor, with the tenor referring to the concept, object, or person meant, and the vehicle being the image that carries the weight of the comparison. The words were first used in this sense by the critic I.A. Richards. In the first stanza of Abraham Cowley's poem "The Wish," the tenor is the city and the vehicle is a beehive:

> Well then; I now do plainly see,
> This busy world and I shall ne'er agree;
> The very honey of all earthly joy
>   Does of all meats the soonest cloy;
>   And they, methinks, deserve my pity
> Who for it can endure the stings,
> The crowd, and buzz, and murmurings
>   Of this great hive, the city.

Tenreiro \ten-'rā-rō\, Francisco José (de Vasques) (b. Jan. 20, 1921, São Tomé [now in São Tomé and Príncipe]—d. Dec. 31, 1963, Lisbon, Port.)   African poet whose verse, written in Portuguese, expresses the sufferings caused by colonialist exploitation of the indentured laborers of the island of São Tomé.

The son of a Portuguese administrator and an African woman, Tenreiro spent a good deal of his life in Portugal, where he earned a doctorate from the University of Lisbon. He subsequently taught and served as a deputy representing São Tomé and Príncipe in the Portuguese National Assembly.

Tenreiro's two volumes of poems, *Ilha do nome santo* (1942; "Island of a Holy Name") and the posthumous *Coração em Africa* (1964; "Courage in Africa"), record a love of Africa as well as a fraternal bond with oppressed blacks throughout the world. Tenreiro's *Panorama de literatura norte-americana* (1945) was inspired by reading black American poets of the Harlem Renaissance. In 1958 he coedited, with Mário Pinto de Andrade, a major anthology of Lusophone African poetry, *Antologia de poesia negra de expressão portuguesa.*

tension \'ten-chən, -shən\   A balance maintained in an artistic work (such as a poem) between opposing forces or elements; a controlled dramatic or dynamic quality.

In literature the term has been variously used and defined. The poet and critic Allen Tate used it to refer to the elements that are necessary for a work to be considered whole or complete. This sense of tension was derived by Tate from two terms used in logic—extension (literal meaning) and intension (metaphorical meaning)—from which he dropped the prefixes, and it refers to a mutually dependent relationship between these different forms of meaning. The term can also refer to a balance between other conflicting structures, such as the rhythm and meter of a poem.

tenson \'ten-sȯn\ or **tenso** \-sō\ or **tenzon** \-zȯn\ [*tenson* from French, from Middle French, from Old Provençal, literally, dispute, quarrel; *tenzon* from Italian *tenzone,* from Old

Provençal *tenson; tenso* from Provençal, from Old Provençal *tenson*] A lyric poem of dispute or personal abuse composed by Provençal troubadours in which two opponents speak alternate stanzas, lines, or groups of lines usually identical in structure. In some cases these debates were imaginary and both sides were composed by the same person. The tenson was a specific form of débat, a kind of medieval poetic contest. The form later spread to Italy, where it became popular among the poets of the *dolce stil nuovo*, including Dante. *Compare* DÉBAT; PARTIMEN.

teratology \ˌter-ə-ˈtäl-ə-jē\ [Greek *teratología*, from *téras* marvel, monster + *lógos* word, speech, account] **1.** Fantastic mythmaking or storytelling in which unusual events and monsters play a large part. **2.** A collection of such stories.

tercet \ˈtər-sət\ or **tiercet** \ˈtir-sət\ [French *tercet*, from Middle French *tiercet*, from Italian *terzetto*, a derivative of *terzo* third] A unit or group of three lines of verse, usually containing rhyme, as in William Shakespeare's "The Phoenix and the Turtle":

> Death is now the phoenix' nest;
> And the turtle's loyal breast
> To eternity doth rest, . . .

The term is often used specifically in reference to the three-line stanzas of the terza rima verse form or to one of the two groups of three lines that form the sestet in a Petrarchan sonnet.

Terence \ˈter-əns\, *Latin in full* Publius Terentius Afer (b. *c.* 195 BC, Carthage, North Africa [now in Tunisia]—d. 159? BC, in Greece or at sea) One of the greatest Roman comic dramatists, whose verse plays form the basis of the modern comedy of manners.

Terence was taken to Rome as a slave. He received a liberal education and, subsequently, was given his freedom. Other details about his life are more sketchy. Most reliable information about Terence relates to his career as a dramatist. During his short life he produced six plays: *Andria* (166 BC; THE WOMAN OF ANDROS), *Hecyra* (165 BC; *The Mother-in-Law*), *Heauton timoroumenos* (163 BC; *The Self-Tormentor*), *Eunuchus* (161 BC; *The Eunuch*), *Phormio* (161 BC), and *Adelphi* or *Adelphoe* (160 BC; *The Brothers*).

Terence had a number of jealous rivals, particularly one older playwright, Luscius Lanuvinus, who launched a series of accusations against him. The main source of contention was Terence's dramatic method. Although Terence was apparently fairly faithful to his Greek models, Luscius alleged that Terence was guilty of "contamination"—*i.e.*, that he had incorporated material from secondary Greek sources into his plots, to their detriment. He further charged that Terence's plays were composed with the help of unnamed nobles.

Recent critical opinion seems to accept that, in the main, Terence was faithful to the plots, ethos, and characterization of his Greek originals: thus, his humanity, his individualized characters, and his sensitive approach to relationships and personal problems all may be traced to his Greek model, Menander, and his obsessive attention to detail in the plots of *Hecyra* and *Phormio* derives from the Greek models of those plays by Apollodorus of Carystus of the 3rd century BC. Nevertheless, Terence shows both originality and skill in the incorporation of material from secondary models. He also cut the prologues of his Greek models, leaving his audiences in the same ignorance as his characters. This omission increases the element of suspense.

Striving for a refined but conventional realism, Terence eliminated or reduced such unrealistic devices as the actor's direct address to the audience. His language is a pure version of contemporary colloquial Latin, at times shaded subtly to emphasize a character's individual speech patterns. Because they are more realistic, most of his characters lack the vitality and panache of Plautus' adaptations, but they are often developed in depth and with subtle psychology. Individual scenes retain their power today, especially those presenting brilliant narratives.

Tereus \ˈtir-yüs, ˈtir-ē-əs\ In Greek legend, king of Thrace who married Procne, daughter of Pandion, king of Athens. Later Tereus seduced her sister Philomela, pretending that Procne was dead. To hide his guilt, he cut out Philomela's tongue. But she revealed the crime to her sister by working the details into an embroidered tapestry. Procne sought revenge by serving up her son Itys (or Itylus) for Tereus' supper. On learning what Procne had done, Tereus pursued the two sisters with an ax. But the gods took pity on the sisters and changed them all into birds: Tereus into a hoopoe (or a hawk), Procne into a nightingale (or a swallow), and Philomela into a swallow (or a nightingale). Algernon Charles Swinburne's poem "Itylus" refers to this legend.

Terhune \tər-ˈhyün\, Albert Payson (b. Dec. 21, 1872, Newark, N.J., U.S.—d. Feb. 18, 1942, near Pompton Lakes, N.J.) American novelist and short-story writer who became famous for his popular stories about dogs.

Terhune graduated from Columbia University (N.Y.), traveled in Egypt and Syria, and in 1894 joined the staff of the *New York Evening World*. His first book was *Syria from the Saddle* (1896); his first novel, *Dr. Dale* (1900), was written in collaboration with his mother. He published more than 12 books before he left the *Evening World* in 1916.

In 1919 appeared the first of his popular dog stories, *Lad, a Dog*. He wrote more than 25 books after 1919, nearly all of them novels in which dogs played conspicuous parts, including *Bruce* (1920), *The Heart of a Dog* (1924), *Lad of Sunnybank* (1928), and *A Book of Famous Dogs* (1937). He also wrote two autobiographical books, *Now That I'm Fifty* (1925) and *To the Best of My Memory* (1930).

terminal rhyme A rhyme that occurs at the end of two or more successive lines of verse. This is the most common form of rhyme in English poetry.

Terpander \tər-ˈpan-dər\ (fl. *c.* 647 BC, Lesbos, Asia Minor) Greek choral poet and musician of the Aegean island of Lesbos.

Almost nothing is known of Terpander's life, except that he is said to have won a prize for music at the 26th Olympiad held in Sparta, where he may have formed a school for music. He was proverbially famous as a singer to the accompaniment of the kithara, a seven-stringed instrument resembling a lyre, which he was said to have invented. His poetry, of which some fragments of doubtful authenticity survive, consisted mainly of *nomes* (settings of epic poetry), preludes to epics, and *scolia* (drinking songs).

Terpsichore \tərp-ˈsik-ə-rē\ In Greek mythology, one of the nine Muses, patron of dancing and choral song (in some versions, lyric poetry). She is perhaps the most widely known of the Muses, her name having entered general English in the adjective *terpsichorean*, "pertaining to dancing."

Terry \ˈter-ē\, Ellen, *in full* Dame Alice Ellen Terry (b. Feb. 27, 1847, Coventry, Warwickshire, Eng.—d. July 21, 1928, Small Hythe, Kent) English actress who became one of the most popular stage performers in both Great Britain and North America. In the 1890s she began a famous "paper courtship" with George Bernard Shaw that became one of the most brilliant correspondences in the history of English letter writing.

Terry was the second surviving daughter in a large family of which several members were to become well known on the stage. Trained by her parents, she rapidly developed into a celebrated child actress. She made her debut at the age of nine and from then on devoted most of her life to the stage. Her partnership with Sir Henry Irving was particularly notable, as she was his leading lady for 24 years (1878–1902).

In comedy and in plays of tender sentiment, as well as in Shakespearean drama, Terry's talent shone. She left Irving to appear in 1902 with Sir Herbert Beerbohm Tree in *The Merry Wives of Windsor*, and Shaw eventually persuaded her to appear in 1906 as Lady Cicely Waynflete in *Captain Brassbound's Conversion*, one of several parts he wrote with her in mind.

Terry continued to act until 1925, the year in which she was made a Dame of the Royal Empire. She also played in films and gave lecture-recitals on William Shakespeare. *Ellen Terry and Bernard Shaw: A Correspondence* was published in 1931.

Terry \'ter-ē\, Lucy, *married name* Prince \'prins\, *also called* Bijah's (Abijah's) Luce *or* Luce (Lucy) Abijah \'lü-sē-ə-'bī-jə\ (b. 1730, West Africa—d. 1821, Vermont, U.S.) American poet, storyteller, and activist of the colonial and postcolonial period. Her only surviving work, the poem "Bars Fight" (1746), is the earliest existing poem by an African-American; it was transmitted orally for over 100 years, first appearing in print in 1855. The poem commemorates white settlers who were killed in an encounter with Indians in 1746.

Born in Africa, Terry was taken by slave traders to Rhode Island at a very young age. She was baptized a Christian at age five, with the approval of her owner, Ebenezer Wells of Deerfield, Mass. She remained a slave in the Wells household until 1756, when she married Abijah Prince, a free black. In 1764 the Princes settled in Guilford, Vermont, where all six of their children were born.

Terry was considered a born storyteller and poet. She was also a persuasive orator, successfully negotiating a land case before the Supreme Court of Vermont. She delivered a three-hour address to the board of trustees of Williams College in a vain attempt to gain admittance for one of her sons.

Terts or **Tertz**　*see* SINYAVSKY.

tertulia \ter-'tü-lē-ä\ A type of Spanish literary salon that was popular in Spain from at least the 17th century and that eventually replaced the more formal academies. Some well-known *tertulias* were described in novels and memoirs of the participants, including *La fontana de oro* (1870) by Benito Pérez Galdós and *Pombo* (1918) by Ramón Gómez de la Serna. The popularity of *tertulias* continued well into the 20th century.

The Spanish word *tertulia*, originally referring to a section of a theater, may be a back formation from *tertuliante* or *tertuliano*, a name for a person frequenting this section. Both words appear to allude to the church father Tertullian (Spanish: *Tertuliano*), but the origin of the allusion is uncertain.

terza rima \'tert-sə-'rē-mə\ [Italian, stanza of three lines, literally, third stanza] A verse form consisting of tercets, or three-line stanzas, in which the second line of each rhymes with the first and third lines of the next. The series ends with a separate line that rhymes with the second line of the last stanza, so that the rhyme scheme is *aba, bcb, cdc, . . . , yzy, z*. In English poems of this form, the meter is often iambic pentameter.

The Italian poet Dante, in his *The Divine Comedy* (c. 1310–14), was the first to use terza rima for a long poem. Terza rima was favored in 14th-century Italy, especially for allegorical and didactic poetry, by Petrarch and Giovanni Boccaccio, and in the 16th century for satire and burlesque, notably by Ludovico Ariosto. A demanding form, terza rima has not been widely adopted in languages less rich in rhymes than Italian. It was introduced in England by Sir Thomas Wyatt in the 16th century. In the 19th century, Percy Bysshe Shelley, Lord Byron, Robert and Elizabeth Barrett Browning, and Henry

Wadsworth Longfellow experimented with it. In the 20th century, W.H. Auden used terza rima in *The Sea and the Mirror*, and Archibald MacLeish in *Conquistador*, but with deviations from the strict form.

Tess of the d'Urbervilles \'tes . . . 'dər-bər-vilz\ Novel by Thomas HARDY, first published serially in bowdlerized form in the *Graphic* (July–December 1891) and in its entirety in book form (three volumes) the same year. It was subtitled *A Pure Woman Faithfully Presented* because Hardy felt that its heroine was a virtuous victim of a rigid Victorian moral code. Now considered Hardy's masterwork, it departed from conventional Victorian fiction in its focus on the rural lower class and in its open treatment of sexuality and religion.

After her impoverished family learns of its noble lineage, naive Tess Durbeyfield is sent to make an appeal to a nearby wealthy family who bear the ancestral name d'Urberville. Tess is seduced by dissolute Alec d'Urberville and secretly bears a child, Sorrow, who dies in infancy. Later working as a dairymaid she meets and marries Angel Clare, an idealistic gentleman who rejects Tess after learning of her past on their wedding night. Emotionally bereft and financially impoverished, Tess is trapped by necessity into giving in once again to d'Urberville, but she murders him when Angel returns. After a few days with Angel, Tess is arrested and executed.

testament \'tes-tə-mənt\ In literature, a tribute or an expression of conviction, as in Thomas Usk's prose allegory *The Testament of Love* (c. 1384) and Robert Bridges' poem *The Testament of Beauty* (1929). A literary testament can also be a kind of last will and testament, a form that was popular in France and England during the 15th century. The mock legacies *Le Petit Testament* and *Le Grand Testament* of François Villon are well-known examples, as is Robert Henryson's *The Testament of Cresseid*, which completes the story of Geoffrey Chaucer's *Troilus and Criseyde*.

Testament, Le *also known as* Le Grand Testament \lə-'grän-tes-tȧ-'mäⁿ\ Long poem by François VILLON, written in 1461 and published in 1489. It consists of 2,023 octosyllabic lines arranged in 185 *huitains* (eight-line stanzas). These *huitains* are interspersed with a number of fixed-form poems, chiefly ballades and chansons, including the well-known "Ballade des dames du temps jadis" ("Ballad of the Ladies of Bygone Times"). While it is full of cruel humor, it is less overtly comic and much more complex than his earlier *Le Petit Testament*.

In *Le Testament* Villon bitterly reviews his life and expresses his horror of prison (the poem itself was written after he was released from prison), sickness, and old age, and his fear of death. It is notable for the poignant note of regret for his wasted youth and squandered talent. As in *Le Petit Testament*, he makes bequests to those he is leaving behind, but his tone in this work is much more scathing than that in his earlier work, and he writes with greater ironic detachment.

Tethys \'tē-this\ In Greek mythology, one of the Titans, wife of Oceanus and mother of the Oceanids. According to one legend, Tethys and Oceanus are said to have reared Zeus's wife, Hera, who had been entrusted to them by her mother, Rhea.

Tetmajer \tet-'mȧ-yer\, Kazimierz, *surname in full* Tetmajer Przerwa \'psher-vȧ\ (b. Feb. 11, 1865, Ludźmierz, Galicia, Austrian Empire [now in Poland]—d. Jan. 18, 1940, Warsaw) Poet and short-story writer who was a member of the Young Poland movement.

Much of Tetmajer's lyric poetry received publication in the Kraków periodical *Życie* ("Life"). His nostalgic and pessimistic *Poezje* ("Poetry"), published in eight series between 1891 and 1924, shows the influence of the Romantic poet and playwright Juliusz Słowacki and of French and Belgian verse. His five volumes of sketches and tales, *Na skalnym Podhalu* (1903–10; *Tales of the Tatras*), are considered his best work. Based in part on ancient legends of the area of the Tatras mountains, these colorful stories describe the mountaineers, their violent lives, and their intense love of freedom.

tetrabrach \'tet-rə-ˌbrak\ [Greek *tetrábrachys*, from *tetra-* four + *brachýs* short]   In classical prosody, a metrical foot of four short syllables.

tetracolon \ˌtet-rə-'kō-lən\ [Greek *tetrákōlon*, neuter of *tetrákōlos* having four members]   In classical prosody, a period made up of four colons, or a unit of four metrical sequences that each constitute a single metrical phrase of not more than about 12 syllables. A tetracolon recurs as a unit within a composition.

tetralogy \te-'tral-ə-jē\ [Greek *tetralogía*, from *tetra-* four + *lógos* word, speech, account]   **1.** In ancient Greek theater, a group of four dramatic pieces including three tragedies and one satyr play or sometimes four tragedies represented consecutively on the Attic stage at the Dionysiac festival.   **2.** A series of four connected works, such as Paul Scott's novel series *Raj Quartet*.

tetrameter \te-'tram-ə-tər\   In prosody, a line of four metrical units, either four metra (as in classical verse) or four feet (as in modern English verse).

In English versification, the feet are usually iambs, an unstressed syllable followed by a stressed one, as in the word

be|cause,

trochees, a stressed syllable followed by an unstressed one, as in the word

ti|ger,

or a combination of the two. Iambic tetrameter is, next to iambic pentameter, the most common meter in English poetry; it is used in the English and Scottish traditional ballads, which are usually composed of four-line stanzas of alternating iambic tetrameter and trimeter.

tetrapody \te-'träp-ə-dē\ [Greek *tetrapodía*, a derivative of *tetrápous* four-footed, from *tetra-* four + *pod-, poús* foot]   In classical prosody, a unit of four metrical feet, or two dimeters.

tetrasemic \ˌtet-rə-'sē-mik\ or **tetraseme** \'tet-rə-ˌsēm\ [Greek *tetrásēmos* having four time units (in music), from *tetra-* four + *sêma* mark, sign]   In classical prosody, consisting of or of the length of four morae, or of the equivalent of four short syllables or two long syllables.

tetrastich \'tet-rə-ˌstik\ [Greek *tetrástichos* of four lines, from *tetra-* four + *stíchos* row, line, verse]   In prosody, a unit or stanza of four lines.

Tevfik Fikret \tä-'fēk-fē-'kret\, *pseudonym of* Mehmed Tevfik, *also called* Tevfik Nazmi \näz-'mē\ (b. Dec. 26, 1867, Constantinople, Ottoman Empire [now Istanbul, Tur.]—d. Aug. 19, 1915, Constantinople)   Poet who is considered the founder of the modern school of Turkish poetry.

Tevfik Fikret was educated at Galatasaray Lycée, where he later became principal. In 1896 he became editor of the avantgarde periodical *Servet-i Fünun* ("The Wealth of Knowledge"). Together with a group of the most talented young authors of the day, he published Turkish works and translations of European (particularly French) poems and stories until the publication was censored by the government in 1901.

In attempting to define a new literature, Tevfik Fikret and his contemporaries often wrote in an obscure style and in language containing many Arabic and Persian words not easily accessible to the average reader. Greatly influenced by the French Symbolist poets, he sought to adapt Turkish poetry to Western themes and verse forms. Among his most important works are two collections of poems, *Rübab-ı Şikeste* (1900; "The Broken Lute") and *Halûk'un Defteri* (1911; "Halûk's Notebook").

text \'tekst\ [Medieval Latin *textus*, from Latin, interlacing, makeup, structure, a derivative of *texere* to weave, construct]   **1.** The original words and form of a written or printed work or an edited or emended copy of an original work.   **2.** The main body of printed or written matter on a page, or the principal part of a book exclusive of front and back matter.   **3.** A verse or passage of scripture chosen especially as the subject of a sermon or for authoritative support, or a passage from an authoritative source providing an introduction or basis (as for a speech).   **4.** The word of something (such as a poem) set to music.   **5.** Something written or spoken considered as an object to be examined, explicated, or deconstructed, or something likened to a text.

textual criticism   The study of a literary work for the purpose of establishing the original form or a single definitive form of its text. *Text* refers to any literary forms preserved in autograph or in transmitted form. Transmitted texts are those whose preserved forms were not written out by the author in any manner. When there is mixture, the transmitted and autograph parts are to be distinguished.

Textual criticism encompasses modern as well as historical works. Sometimes the author's intention may be difficult to discern. William Faulkner's novel *Absalom, Absalom!*, for example, is notorious for the many printing errors caused by the author's reliance on complex typography to represent narrative levels. Occasionally a text is studied to undo deliberate correction or censorship, as in the case of novels by Stephen Crane and Theodore Dreiser.

Variation occurs any time a text is transmitted, whether in print, in manuscript, or orally. Early printed books exhibit variation because printers did not emphasize textual accuracy. The problems with the study of manuscript transmission lie in establishing the genealogy of what may be a large number of handwritten versions, each of which is textually unique. When a text was originally transmitted orally—as were Homeric texts or the Provençal poets—critics often cannot reconstruct an "original" but must assume a common source.

The term textual criticism is also used to denote a critical study of literature emphasizing a close reading and analysis of the text. *See also* DECONSTRUCTION; NEW CRITICISM.

texture \'teks-chər\   The concrete, physical elements of prose or poetry that are separate from the structure or argument of the work. Such elements include metaphor, imagery, meter, and rhyme. The distinction between structure and texture is associated particularly with the New Critics, especially John Crowe Ransom.

textus receptus \ˌteks-təs-ri-'sep-təs\ [New Latin, literally, received text]   The generally accepted text of a literary work (such as the Greek New Testament).

Tey \'tā\, Josephine, *pseudonym of* Elizabeth Mackintosh \'mak-ən-ˌtäsh\ (b. 1897, Inverness, Inverness-shire, Scot.—d. Feb. 13, 1952, London, Eng.)   Scottish playwright and author of popular detective novels praised for their warm and readable style.

Tey became a full-time writer with the successful publication of her first book, *The Man in the Queue* (1929). She wrote some novels and the majority of her plays—including the successfully staged *Richard of Bordeaux* (produced 1933)—under the pseudonym Gordon Daviot.

Her detective fiction, which includes *Miss Pym Disposes* (1947), *The Franchise Affair* (1949), *The Daughter of Time* (1951), which reappraises Richard III's involvement in the murder of his two young nephews, and *The Singing Sands* (1952), was written under the pen name Josephine Tey. It frequently featured a fictional investigator named Inspector Grant.

Thackeray \'thak-ə-rē\, William Makepeace (b. July 18, 1811, Calcutta, India—d. Dec. 24, 1863, London, Eng.) English novelist whose reputation rests chiefly on VANITY FAIR (1847–48), a novel of the Napoleonic period in England, and HENRY ESMOND, 3 vol. (1852), set in the early 18th century.

Detail of an oil painting by Samuel Laurence

National Portrait Gallery, London

Thackeray attended Trinity College, Cambridge, but left in 1830 without taking a degree. During 1831–33 he studied law at the Middle Temple, London. He then considered painting as a profession; his artistic gifts are seen in many of his early writings, which are amusingly and energetically illustrated. In 1836, while studying art in Paris, he married Isabella Shawe, a penniless Irish girl. The following year they returned to London, where he became a hardworking and prolific professional journalist.

His work was unsigned or written under such pen names as Mr. Michael Angelo Titmarsh, Fitz-Boodle, The Fat Contributor, or Ikey Solomons. He collected the best of these early writings in *Miscellanies*, 4 vol. (1855–57), which included the historical novel BARRY LYNDON (1844). He also published *The Book of Snobs* (1848), a collection of articles that had appeared successfully in *Punch* as "The Snobs of England, by One of Themselves" in 1846–47.

The serial publication of his novel *Vanity Fair* brought Thackeray both fame and prosperity, and from then on he was an established author on the English scene. He followed with PENDENNIS (1848–50), a partly fictionalized autobiography, and then turned to the historical novel and the reign of Queen Anne for his *Henry Esmond*.

After a lecture tour of the United States in 1852, Thackeray returned to the novel with THE NEWCOMES (1853–55), a detailed study of prosperous middle-class society, and THE VIRGINIANS (1857–59), set partly in America and partly in England in the latter half of the 18th century. In addition to his literary activity, he stood unsuccessfully for Parliament in 1857, quarreled with Charles Dickens, formerly a friendly rival, in the so-called "Garrick Club Affair" (1858), and in 1860 founded *The Cornhill Magazine*, becoming its editor. After he died in 1863, a commemorative bust of him was placed in Westminster Abbey.

Thalia \thə-'lī-ə\ In Greek mythology, one of the nine Muses, patron of comedy. She is the mother of the Corybants, celebrants of the Great Mother of the Gods (Cybele); their father was Apollo, a god of music and dance. Thalia is also, according to the Greek poet Hesiod, the name of one of the Graces (a group of goddesses of fertility). *See also* GRACES; MUSE.

Thamyris \'tham-i-ris\ or **Thamyras** \-rəs\ In Greek mythology, a Thracian poet who loved the beautiful youth Hyacinthus. Thamyris' attentions, however, were rivaled by those of the god Apollo, who jealously reported to the Muses the boast by Thamyris that he could surpass them in song. The Muses immediately blinded Thamyris and robbed him of his talent.

Thanatopsis \,than-ə-'täp-sis\ Poem by William Cullen BRYANT, published in the *North American Review* in 1817 and then revised for the author's *Poems* (1821). The poem, written when Bryant was 17, was his best-known work.

In its musings on a magnificent, omnipresent Nature, the poem, whose Greek title means "view of death," shows the influence of deism, and it in turn influenced the Transcendentalist ideas of Ralph Waldo Emerson and Henry David Thoreau. The poem brought Bryant early fame and established him as a major nature poet. Bryant's colloquial voice and celebration of nature were considered poetic innovations.

Thanatos \'than-ə-täs\ In Greek mythology, the personification of death and the brother of Hypnos (Sleep). Thanatos was the son of Nyx (Night) and Erebus (Darkness).

Tharaud \tä-'rō\, Jérôme and Jean (respectively b. May 18, 1874, Saint-Junien, Fr.—d. Jan. 28, 1953, Varengeville-sur-Mer; b. May 9, 1877, Saint-Junien—d. April 9, 1952, Paris) French brothers noted for the extent and diversity of their literary production spanning 50 years of collaboration. Many of their early works were published in the periodical *Cahiers de la quinzaine*. The novel *Dingley* (1902), earned them the esteemed Prix Goncourt in 1906.

Precise observers, the brothers Tharaud were among the first and greatest of French reporters, recording their travels in such works as *La Fête arabe* (1912; "The Arab Festival") and *Rabat; ou, Les Heures marocaines* (1918; "Rabat; or, Moroccan Hours"). They also were concerned with the dynamics of current political events, as seen in *Quand Israël est roi* (1921; "When Israel Is King") and *L'An prochain à Jérusalem* (1924; "Next Year in Jerusalem"). They wrote numerous novels and reminiscences, including *La Randonné de Samba Diouf* (1922; *The Long Walk of Samba Diouf*) and *Notre cher Péguy* (1926; "Our Dear Péguy"). They were both elected to the Académie Française—Jérôme in 1938, Jean in 1946.

Thatcher, Becky \'bek-ē-'thach-ər\ Fictional character in the novel TOM SAWYER by Mark Twain. A stereotypical nice girl, Becky is the daughter of upright Judge Thatcher but is nonetheless Tom Sawyer's sweetheart, portrayed as pretty, sweet, and dependent.

That Hideous Strength Third novel in a science-fiction trilogy by C.S. LEWIS, published in 1945. The book, which was also published in the United States as *The Tortured Planet*, followed *Out of the Silent Planet* (1938) and *Perelandra* (1943).

Thea *see* THEIA.

Theater of Cruelty Project for an experimental theater that was proposed by the French poet, actor, and theorist Antonin ARTAUD and that became a major influence on avant-garde 20th-century theater. Artaud formulated a theory for what he called a Theater of Cruelty in a series of essays published in *La Nouvelle Revue Française* and collected in 1938 as *Le Théâtre et son double* (*The Theatre and Its Double*).

Artaud believed that civilization had turned people into sick and repressed creatures and that the true function of the theater was to rid them of these repressions and liberate their instinctual energy. He proposed removing the barrier of the stage between performers and audience and producing mythic spectacles that would include verbal incantations, groans and screams, pulsating lighting effects, and oversized stage puppets and props. Although only one of Artaud's plays, *Les Cenci* (1935), based on works by Percy Bysshe Shelley and Stendhal, was ever produced to illustrate these theories, his ideas influenced the productions of Jean-Louis Barrault, Jerzy Grotowski, Jean Vilar, and The Living Theatre as well as the work of such playwrights as Arthur Adamov, Jean Genet, and Jacques Audiberti.

Theater of Fact *also called* documentary theater, *German* Dokumentartheater *or* dokumentarisches Theater. German dramatic movement that arose during the early 1960s, associated primarily with Rolf Hochhuth, Peter Weiss, and Heinar Kipphardt. Their political plays examined recent historical events, often through official documents and court records. Their concern that the West was forgetting the horrors of the Nazi era led them to explore themes of guilt and responsibility. Hochhuth's *Der Stellvertreter* (1963; U.K. title, *The Representative*; U.S. title, *The Deputy*) indicts Pope Pius XII for not taking a public stand against the Nazi extermination of the Jews; Weiss's *Die Ermittlung* (1965; *The Investigation*) presents extracts from official hearings on the Auschwitz concentration camp; and Kipphardt's *In der Sache J. Robert Oppenheimer* (1964; *In the Matter of J. Robert Oppenheimer*) re-creates the American inquiry into Oppenheimer's loyalty because of his opposition to the development of the hydrogen bomb.

Theater of Fact playwrights sought to cut through official versions of recent history by using the techniques of advocacy journalism and by a reliance on edited documentary sources. Their work stimulated political drama in Europe and North America.

Theater of the Absurd The collection of dramatic works of certain European and American dramatists of the 1950s and early '60s who embraced Albert Camus's assessment, in his essay *Le Mythe de Sisyphe* (1942; *The Myth of Sisyphus*), that the human situation is essentially absurd, devoid of purpose. The term is also loosely applied to those dramatists and the production of those works. Dramatists as diverse as Samuel Beckett, Eugène Ionesco, Jean Genet, Arthur Adamov, Harold Pinter, and a few others shared a vision of a hopeless, bewildered, and anxious humanity struggling vainly to find a purpose and to control its fate.

The ideas that informed the plays also dictated their structure. Absurdist playwrights ignored most of the logical structures of traditional theater. Dramatic action as such is negligible; what action occurs only serves to underscore the absence of meaning in the characters' existence. In Beckett's *En attendant Godot* (*Waiting for Godot*), first performed 1953, plot is eliminated, and a timeless, circular quality emerges as two lost creatures spend their days waiting—but without any certainty of whom they are waiting for or of whether that person will ever come. The characters in Ionesco's *La Cantatrice chauve* (*The Bald Soprano*), first performed in 1950, sit and talk, repeating the obvious until it sounds like nonsense, thus revealing the inadequacies of verbal communication. The combination of purposeless behavior and ridiculous conversation gives the plays a sometimes dazzling comic surface, but there is an underlying message of metaphysical distress.

Initially shocking in its flouting of theatrical convention while popular for its apt expression of the preoccupations of the mid-20th century, the Theater of the Absurd had lost some of its shock value by the mid-1960s. Many of its innovations were absorbed into mainstream theater; other elements inspired a new avant-garde to further experimentation.

Théâtre de l'Oeuvre \tä-'ätr-də-'lœ̄vr, *Angl* tä-'ät-rə-də-'lər-vrə\ French Symbolist theater founded in Paris in 1893 by Aurélien-François-Marie Lugné-Poe and directed by him until 1929. Assisted by the poet and critic Camille Mauclair and the painter Édouard Vuillard, Lugné-Poe dedicated the Théâtre de l'Oeuvre to presenting the work of the young French Symbolist playwrights and introducing major foreign dramas. He produced works by Maurice Maeterlinck, Oscar Wilde, Gerhart Hauptmann, and Gabriele D'Annunzio and was instrumental in introducing Henrik Ibsen's plays to France. Alfred Jarry's nihilistic farce *Ubu roi* premiered there in 1896.

Lugné-Poe sought to create a unified nonrealistic theater of poetry and dreams through atmospheric staging and stylized acting. He closed the Théâtre de l'Oeuvre in 1899 but revived it in 1912 and again after World War I. He continued to produce the works of new French playwrights, such as Paul Claudel, and those of Dadaist and Surrealist writers.

Théâtre de Vieux-Colombier \tä-'ätr-də-,vyœ̄-kō-lôⁿ-'byä\ French experimental theater founded in Paris in 1913 by writer and critic Jacques Copeau to present alternatives to both the realistic "well-made" plays of the time and the star system of actor-celebrities. Copeau sought to renovate French theater by focusing attention on the actor, whom he viewed as the essential element in translating the dramatic text into the "poetry of the theater."

Theatre Guild A theatrical society founded in New York City in 1918 for the production of high-quality, noncommercial American and foreign plays. The guild, founded by Lawrence Langner, departed from the usual theater practice in that its board of directors shared the responsibility for choice of plays, management, and production. The first two seasons included plays by Jacinto Benavente y Martínez, Saint John Ervine, John Masefield, and August Strindberg.

Following the world premiere of George Bernard Shaw's *Heartbreak House* in 1920, the guild became Shaw's American agent, producing 15 of his plays, including world premieres of *Back to Methuselah* and *Saint Joan*. Eugene O'Neill's long association with the guild began with its production of *Marco Millions* in 1928. Other American authors whose works were produced by the guild included Sidney Howard, William Saroyan, Maxwell Anderson, and Robert Sherwood—all Pulitzer Prize winners. The Theatre Guild contributed to American musical theater by producing George Gershwin, Ira Gershwin, and DuBose Heyward's *Porgy and Bess* and by bringing Richard Rodgers and Oscar Hammerstein II together for such collaborations as *Oklahoma!* The "Theatre Guild of the Air" (1945–63) successfully produced plays for radio and television.

theatricalism \thē-'at-ri-kə-,liz-əm\ In 20th-century Western theater, the general movement away from the dominant 19th-century techniques of naturalism in acting, staging, and playwriting; it was especially directed against the illusion of reality that was the highest achievement of the naturalist theater.

Stylized acting, a projecting stage, and frank scenic artifices and conventions were the hallmarks of theatricalism. Even after the extreme stylization of acting and staging found in the Expressionist, Dadaist, and Surrealist drama of the early part of the century had subsided, theatricalism's frank acceptance of dramatic artifices remained a permanent part of the modern theater.

Theia \'thē-ə, 'thī-\ or **Thea** \'thē-ə\ In Greek mythology, a Titan, the daughter of Uranus (Heaven) and Gaea (Earth). She was the goddess of light and was the mother, by Hyperion, of Helios (Sun), Selene (Moon), and Eos (Dawn) and, by Oceanus, of the twin dwarfs known as the Cercopes.

Their Eyes Were Watching God Novel by Zora Neale HURSTON, published in 1937. It is considered her finest book.

In lyrical prose influenced by folk tales that the author heard while assembling her anthology of African-American folklore *Mules and Men* (1935), Janie Crawford tells of her three marriages, her growth to self-reliance, and her identity as a black woman. Much of the dialogue conveys psychological insight through plain speech written in dialect.

While her first two husbands are domineering, Janie's third husband is easy-going and reluctantly willing to accept Janie as an equal. Hurston manages to characterize these three very different men without resorting to caricature in the first two instances or idealization in the third. Janie is one of few fictional heroines of the period who is not punished for her sensual nature.

them   Novel by Joyce Carol OATES, published in 1969 and granted a National Book Award in 1970. Violent and explosive in both incident and tone, the work is set in urban Detroit from 1937 to 1967 and chronicles the efforts of the Wendell family to break away from their destructive, crime-ridden background. Critics praised the novel for its detailed social observation and its bitter indictment of American society.

Themba \'tem-bä\ Can, *byname of* Daniel Canadoise Dorsay Themba, *also called* Can von Themba (b. 1924, Pretoria, Transvaal, S.Af.—d. 1969, Manzini, Swaziland)   South African journalist and short-story writer associated with a brilliant group of young South African writers of the 1950s that included Moses Motsisi, Arthur Maimane, Es'kia Mphahlele, and Lewis Nkosi.

After graduating from the University of Fort Hare, S.Af., Themba worked as a reporter and later editor on the magazine *Drum* and the weekly *Golden City Post* in Johannesburg. His stories won several prizes, including the 1953 Drum Award. Themba's journalistic viewpoint conditioned all his writing. His short stories are anecdotes and vignettes depicting the harsh and depressing conditions of African life in the Johannesburg townships. They have a lively and perceptive wit, but their jaunty tone cannot conceal the self-lacerating cynicism that was required in order to survive under the existing social conditions. Some critics saw his apparent flippancy as evidence of a lack of commitment. Nevertheless, Themba's work has a lively force that illuminates the milieu in which he lived.

Themba left Johannesburg in the early 1960s to become a schoolteacher in Swaziland, where he died. His best pieces were collected posthumously in *The Will to Die* (1972).

theme \'thēm\   The dominant idea of a work of literature.

Themis \'thē-mis\   In Greek mythology, personification of justice, goddess of wisdom and good counsel, and the interpreter of the gods' will. According to some sources, she was the daughter of Uranus (Heaven) and Gaea (Earth). She was Zeus's second consort and by him the mother of the Horae, the Fates (the Moirai), and, in some traditions, the Hesperides. On Olympus, Themis maintained order and supervised the ceremonial. She was a giver of oracles, and one legend relates that she once owned the oracle at Delphi but later gave it to Apollo.

Theobald I \'thē-ə-,bōld, -,bäld; 'tib-əld\, *also called* Theobald the Troubadour *or* the Posthumous, *French* Thibaud (Thibaut) le Chansonnier *or* le Posthume, *Spanish* Teobaldo el Trovador *or* el Póstumo (b. May 30?, 1201, Troyes, Fr.—d. July 7?, 1253, Pamplona, Navarre [now in Spain])   Count of Troyes and of Champagne (from 1201), as Theobald IV, and king of Navarre (from 1234), the most famous of the aristocratic trouvères.

He was the son of Blanche of Navarre and Theobald III of Champagne, who died before his son was born. Theobald I lived for four years at the court of King Philip II of France, and after Philip died Theobald briefly supported Philip's son Louis VIII but deserted him in 1226. On the death of Louis a

few months later, Theobald joined a dissident league of barons who opposed Louis's widow and regent of France, Blanche of Castile. He soon abandoned the league and became reconciled with Blanche. It was rumored that he was her lover and had poisoned her husband, and many of his poems are believed to have been addressed to her.

Theobald left about 60 lyrics, mainly love songs and debates in verse, with two pastourelles (love songs between knight and shepherdess) and nine religious poems. He excelled at the composition of the *jeu-parti* (courtly love debate) in which he discusses with a crony whether it is better to embrace one's love in the dark or to see her without embracing her.

Theobald \'thē-ə-,bōld, -,bäld; 'tib-əld\, Lewis (baptized April 2, 1688, Sittingbourne, Kent, Eng.—d. Sept. 18, 1744, London)   The first editor of the works of William Shakespeare to approach the plays with something of the respect and attention then normally reserved for classical texts.

Theobald is best known for his work as an editor, which he began after Alexander Pope published a version of Shakespeare's works in 1725. When Theobald brought out his *Shakespeare Restored; or, A Specimen of the Many Errors As Well Committed As Unamended by Mr. Pope, in His Late Edition of This Poet* (1726), Pope was enraged and made Theobald the chief target of his satirical poem *The Dunciad* (1728). In 1734 Theobald produced his own edition of Shakespeare in seven volumes, often using Elizabethan parallels as a guide to some brilliant emendations.

Theocritus \thē-'äk-rə-təs\ (b. *c.* 310 BC, Syracuse, Sicily [Italy]—d. 250 BC)   Greek poet, the creator of pastoral poetry.

There is very little information about Theocritus' life. It is known that he lived in Sicily and at various times in Cos and Alexandria and perhaps in Rhodes. The surviving poems by Theocritus that are generally held to be authentic consist of bucolics and mimes, the scenes of which are laid in the country, and epics, lyrics, and epigrams, which are set in towns.

The bucolics are the most characteristic and influential of Theocritus' works. They introduced the pastoral setting in which shepherds wooed nymphs and shepherdesses and held singing contests with their rivals. They were the sources of Virgil's *Eclogues* and much of the poetry and drama of the Renaissance and were the ancestors of the famous English pastoral elegies, John Milton's "Lycidas," Percy Bysshe Shelley's *Adonais*, and Matthew Arnold's "Thyrsis." Among the best known of Theocritus' idylls are his first, *Thyrsis*, a lament for Daphnis, the original shepherd poet, who died of unrequited love, and his seventh, *Thalysia* ("Harvest Festival,"), describing a festival on the island of Cos. In this the poet introduces contemporary friends and rivals in the guise of rustics.

Theocritus' idylls have none of the artificial prettiness of the pastoral poetry of a later age. They have sometimes been criticized as attributing to peasants sentiments and language beyond their capacity, but comparison with modern Greek folk songs (which owe little to literary influences) reveals many striking resemblances between them. *See also* PASTORAL.

Theognis \thē-'äg-nis\ (fl. late 6th–early 5th century BC, Megara, near Athens [Greece])   Elegiac poet, many of whose poems were addressed to his beloved, Cyrnus. Theognis' poems are important for their portrayal of aristocratic society in a changing world. He allegedly wrote a poem on an unidentifiable episode in the history of Syracuse and 2,800 lines of admonitory verse, together with (or perhaps including) a collection of maxims for Cyrnus. Fewer than 1,400 lines survive. The poems ascribed to Theognis, many of them doubtfully, provide more than half the surviving corpus of classical Greek elegiac poetry.

Theogony \thē-'äg-ə-nē\ Work by HESIOD, produced about 700 BC, that constitutes a genealogy of the Greek gods and the source of the principal Greek cosmological myths. In it, following the Muses' instructions, Hesiod recounts the history of the gods, beginning with the emergence of Chaos (Space), Gaea (Earth), Tartarus (the Abyss), and Eros (Desire). Gaea gives birth to Uranus (Heaven), the Mountains, and Pontus (the Sea); and later, after uniting herself to Uranus, she bears many other deities. One of them is the Titan Cronus, who rebels against Uranus, emasculates him, and afterward rules until he in turn is overpowered by Zeus.

This story of crime and revolt, which is the central subject of the *Theogony*, is interrupted by many additional pedigrees of gods. The supreme and irresistible power of Zeus is most majestically displayed in the Titanomachia, the battle between the Olympian gods, led by Zeus, and the Titans, who support Cronus.

Theophilus North \thē-'äf-i-ləs-'nòrth\ Novel by Thornton WILDER, published in 1973. The last work published during Wilder's lifetime, it has striking parallels to his own life experiences and may be considered a fictionalized memoir of Wilder's idealized artistic and philosophical life.

A first-person reminiscence of life among the rich at Newport, R.I., during the summer of 1926, the novel is narrated by the elderly North from a distance of 50 years.

Theopompus \,thē-ō-'päm-pəs\ of Chios \'kī-,äs\ (b. *c.* 380 BC, Chios, Ionia [Greece]) Greek historian and rhetorician whose *Philippica*, though lost in original, has survived through the work of later writers to form one element in the tradition concerning the reign of Philip II of Macedon. Twice exiled, Theopompus spent time in Athens and Egypt.

Theopompus' works, which were chiefly historical, also included the *Hellenica*, which treated the history of Greece, in 12 books, from 411 (where Thucydides breaks off) to 394—the date of the Battle of Cnidus. Of this work only a few fragments survive. A far more elaborate work was the *Philippica*, a history in 58 books of Philip's reign (359–336). In spite of some extravagance both of style and of judgment, it seems likely that Theopompus was the most interesting and considerable of all the Greek historians whose writings are lost.

Theotokás \,thā-ō-tō-'käs\, Yórgos *or* Geórgios (b. Aug. 27, 1906, Constantinople [now Istanbul, Tur.]—d. Oct. 30, 1966, Athens, Greece) Greek novelist known for his clarity of expression and sophisticated style.

Theotokás studied in Athens and later in Paris and London. His first literary venture was an essay entitled "Eléfthero pnévma" (1929; "Free Spirit"). He published three novels before World War II: *Argó* (1936), probably the best known; *To dhemónio* (1938; "The Demon"); and *Leonís* (1940), perhaps his best, set in the Constantinople of his childhood.

After the war Theotokás turned his attention to the theater, writing plays and working as director of the National Theater and later as president of the administrative committee of the State Theater of Northern Greece. Of his plays, the best known, and perhaps his best, is *To paighnídhi tis tréllas ka: tis phronimádhas* (1961; "The Game of Madness and Prudence"), set in Byzantine times. His last works were books of travel, including *Taxídhi sti Mési Anatolí kai sto Ághion Oros* (1961; "Travel in the Middle East and the Holy Mountain").

Theotókis \,thā-ō-'tō-kēs\, Konstantínos (b. May 1872, Corfu, Greece—d. July 1, 1923, Corfu) Greek novelist of the realist school, whose clear and pure Demotic Greek was flavored by Corfiote idioms.

Theotókis was at first much under the influence of Friedrich Nietzsche. Later, in Germany, he became interested in social-ism, an interest that proved to be abiding and that colored all his works, such as *I timí kai to khríma* (1914; "Honor and Money"), a novel with a distinctly social focus. His long novel *Oi sklávoi sta dhesmá tous* (1922; "Slaves in Their Chains"), which is set in Corfu during a period of social change, reveals the old aristocracy trying to keep up a way of life that is long past, the bourgeoisie on the decline, and the newly rich trying to use their wealth to buy social status. Two long stories, *O katádhikos* (1919; "The Convict") and *I Zoí kai o thánatos tou Karavéla* (1920; "The Life and Death of Karavelas") are also notable.

Thérèse Raquin \tā-res-rà-'kaⁿ\ Novel by Émile ZOLA, first published serially as *Un Mariage d'Amour* in 1867 and published in book form with the present title in the same year.

Believing that an author must simply establish his characters in their particular environment and then observe and record their actions as if conducting an experiment, Zola nonetheless adopted a highly moral, unscientific tone in this grisly novel, the first to put his "analytical method" into practice. The sensual Thérèse and her lover Laurent murder her weak husband Camille. After marrying, they are haunted by Camille's ghost, and their passion for each other turns to hatred. They eventually kill themselves.

Conservative readers accused Zola of prurience; the novel, however, illustrates the author's belief that sexual pleasure leads only to brutality and destruction.

Thériault \tār-'yō\, Yves (b. Nov. 28, 1916, Quebec City, Que., Can.—d. Oct. 20, 1983, Montreal?, Que.) One of the most prolific writers in Canada, with some 1,300 radio and television scripts and some 50 books to his credit. He was hailed as a literary genius after the publication of *Agaguk* (1958), a poignant tale about an Inuit family faced with a European-based code of law.

Thériault, who dropped out of school at the age of 15, held a variety of jobs before becoming a professional writer. His other works include *Aaron* (1954), which explores the problems faced by a Jewish family in a Gentile world; *Ashini* (1960), a lyrical tale of the last chief of the Montagnais to live by ancestral customs; and *N'Tsuk* (1968), the life story of a 100-year-old native woman. Thériault's works were widely translated.

Theroux \thə-'rü\, Paul (Edward) (b. April 10, 1941, Medford, Mass., U.S.) American novelist and travel writer known for the exotic settings of his works, in which he often describes a clash between two cultures.

Theroux graduated from the University of Massachusetts. He then taught English in Malawi, Uganda, and Singapore; thereafter, he lived in England and devoted all his time to writing. Several of his early novels—including *Girls at Play* (1969) and *Saint Jack* (1973)—focus on the social and cultural dislocation of Westerners in postcolonial Africa and Southeast Asia. His later novels include *The Family Arsenal* (1976), *The Mosquito Coast* (1981), and *Millroy the Magician* (1993).

Theroux first achieved commercial success with a best-selling travel book, *The Great Railway Bazaar* (1975), describing his four-month train journey through Asia. He wrote several more travel books, including *The Old Patagonian Express* (1979) and *The Happy Isles of Oceania* (1992).

Theseus \'thēs-,yüs, 'thē-sē-əs\ Great hero of Attic legend, son of Aegeus (king of Athens) and Aethra (daughter of Pittheus, king of Troezen in Argolis) or of Poseidon and Aethra. Legend relates that when Theseus reached adulthood, Aethra sent him to Athens. On the journey he encountered many adventures. At the Isthmus of Corinth he killed Sinis, called the Pine Bender because he killed his victims by tearing them apart between two pine trees. Next Theseus dispatched the Crommyonian sow (or boar). Then from a cliff he flung the wicked Sciron, who had kicked his guests into the sea while they were washing his feet. Later he slew Procrustes, who fitted all comers to his iron bed by hacking or racking them to the right length.

On his arrival in Athens, Theseus found his father married to the sorceress Medea. Aegeus recognized Theseus and declared him heir to the throne. After several other heroic deeds came the adventure of the Cretan MINOTAUR, half man and half bull, shut up in the legendary Cretan Labyrinth. *See also* ARIADNE.

Theseus had promised Aegeus that if he returned successful from Crete, he would hoist a white sail in place of the black sail with which the fatal ship bearing the sacrificial victims to the Minotaur always put to sea. But he forgot his promise; and when Aegeus saw the black sail, he flung himself from the Acropolis and died.

Theseus then united the various Attic communities into a single state and extended the territory of Attica to the Isthmus of Corinth. Alone or with the Greek hero Heracles he attacked the Amazons; as a result the Amazons attacked Athens. By an Amazon queen (either Antiope or Hippolyte), he had a son, Hippolytus, beloved of Theseus' wife, Phaedra.

The famous friendship between Theseus and Pirithous, one of the Lapiths, originated when Pirithous drove away some of Theseus' cows. Theseus pursued, but when he caught up with him the two heroes were so filled with admiration for each other that they swore brotherhood.

When Theseus returned to Athens, he faced an uprising led by Menestheus, a descendant of Erechtheus, one of the old kings of Athens. Failing to quell the outbreak, Theseus sent his children to Euboea, and after solemnly cursing the Athenians he sailed away to the island of Scyros. But Lycomedes, king of Scyros, killed Theseus by casting him into the sea from the top of a cliff.

thesis \'thē-sis\ *plural* theses \-,sēz\ [Greek *thésis* act of placing or laying down, lowering of the foot in keeping time]   In prosody, the unaccented or shorter part of a poetic foot. Originally, in Greek poetry, the thesis was the accented part of the foot, but in Latin prosody it came to mean the unaccented part and this meaning has been retained in modern usage. *Compare* ARSIS.

thesis novel   *see* PROPAGANDA NOVEL.

thesis play   *see* PROBLEM PLAY.

Thespis \'thes-pis\ (fl. 6th century BC, Athens [Greece])   Attic Greek poet from the deme (district) of Icaria who reputedly originated the actor's role in drama. He was often considered the "inventor of tragedy" because he is the first recorded winner of a prize for tragedy at the Great Dionysia of about 534 BC. The significance scholars have attached to this claim depends on their interpretation of the scanty evidence which has survived about Thespis and their views of the development of Greek drama. Aristotle, according to the rhetorician Themistius, said that tragedy in its earliest stage was entirely choral until the prologue and speeches were first introduced by Thespis. Thespis, according to Themistius' account, was the first "actor," and tragic dialogue began when he exchanged words with the leader of the chorus.

Thetis \'thē-tis\   In Greek mythology, a Nereid (Homer calls her "silver-footed") loved by Zeus and Poseidon. When Themis (goddess of Justice), however, revealed that Thetis was destined to bear a son who would be mightier than his father, the two gods gave her to Peleus, king of the Myrmidons of Thessaly. Unwilling to wed a mortal, Thetis resisted Peleus' advances by changing herself into various shapes. But Peleus finally captured her with the help of the centaur Chiron.

All the gods brought gifts to their wedding. One of the children of their union was the warrior Achilles. According to some authorities, Thetis bore seven children, all of whom she attempted to render immortal by immersion in fire. Achilles alone survived the ordeal when his father interrupted Thetis in the middle of the ritual.

Thibault, Les \lä-tē-'bō\   Eight-part novel cycle by Roger MARTIN DU GARD, first published in 1922–40. The individual novels that make up the series are *Le Cahier gris* (1922; *The Gray Notebook*), *Le Pénitencier* (1922; *The Penitentiary* or *The Reformatory*), *La Belle Saison* (1923; *The Springtime of Life* or *High Summer*), *La Consultation* (1928; *The Consulting Day*), *La Sorellina* (1928), *La Mort du père* (1929; "The Death of the Father"), *L'Été 1914* (1936; *Summer 1914*), and *Épilogue* (1940). The series was published in two volumes in English as *The Thibaults* and *Summer 1914*.

This record of the Thibault family's development chronicles the social and moral issues confronting the French bourgeoisie from the beginning of the 20th century to World War I. The outstanding features of *Les Thibault* are the wide range of human relationships patiently explored, the graphic realism of the sickbed and death scenes, and, in the seventh volume, the dramatic description of European nations being swept into war.

Things Fall Apart   First novel by Chinua ACHEBE, written in English and published in 1958. The novel chronicles the life of Okonkwo, the leader of an Igbo (Ibo) community, from the events leading up to his banishment from the community for accidentally killing a clansman, through the seven years of his exile, to his return.

The novel addresses the problem of the intrusion in the 1890s of white missionaries and colonial government into tribal Igbo society. It describes the simultaneous disintegration of its protagonist Okonkwo and of his village. The novel was praised for its intelligent and realistic treatment of tribal beliefs and of psychological disintegration coincident with social unraveling. *Things Fall Apart* helped create the Nigerian literary renaissance of the 1960s.

Thin Man, The   Novel by Dashiell HAMMETT, published in 1934. Hammett's portrayal of sophisticated New York cafe society during Prohibition and his witty protagonists Nick and Nora Charles made this the most popular of his works, if not the most successful critically.

Nick Charles is a detective who has given up his profession to manage his wife Nora's fortune, which allows the couple to lead an easy life of nonstop parties and cocktails. Yet when the secretary of a former client is murdered, Nick is drawn in, urged on by Nora, who loves a mystery. The couple's playful banter, rather than the crime, forms the actual center of the book.

third person   *see* POINT OF VIEW.

Thirkell \'thər-kəl\, Angela (Margaret) (b. Jan. 30, 1890, London, Eng.—d. Jan. 29, 1961, Bramley, Surrey)   Author of more than 30 lighthearted novels about English middle- and upper-class life in Barsetshire, featuring the descendants of characters in Anthony Trollope's novels that are set in the same fictional locale.

Thirkell's novels, usually peopled with genteel, snobbish characters, are noted for their gentle irony, absurdity of tone, and understated sophistication. Some of her better-known works included *Coronation Summer* (1937), *The Brandons* (1939), *Northbridge Rectory* (1941), *Headmistress* (1945), and *The Duke's Daughter* (1951).

Thiruvalluvar   *see* TIRUVALLUVAR.

Thisbe   *see* PYRAMUS AND THISBE.

This Side of Paradise   First novel by F. Scott FITZGERALD, published in 1920. Immature though it seems today, the work when it was published was considered a revelation of the new morality of the young in the early Jazz Age; and it made Fitzgerald famous. The novel's hero, Amory Blaine, is a handsome, spoiled young man who attends Princeton, becomes involved in literary activities, and has several ill-fated romances. A portrait of the Lost Generation, the novel addresses Fitzgerald's later theme of love distorted by social climbing and greed.

Thomas \ˈtäm-əs\, Audrey (Grace), *original surname* Callahan \ˈkal-ə-hən, -ˌhan\ (b. Nov. 17, 1935, Binghamton, N.Y., U.S.) American-born Canadian author known for her autobiographical novels, short stories, and radio plays.

Thomas graduated from Smith College and settled in Canada. After receiving an M.A. from the University of British Columbia, she lived in Ghana from 1964 to 1966 and then returned to British Columbia.

Thomas wrote about domestic life, women's search for independence, and conflicts between men and women. She often threw her characters' inner conflicts into relief by transplanting them to foreign lands. Thomas' experimental style involved incorporating into her works word play and fragments of popular culture.

The stories of *Ten Green Bottles* (1967) are told by an unhappy female narrator of varying circumstances but consistent character. Thomas' alter ego Isobel Cleary narrates the novels *Mrs. Blood* (1970); *Songs My Mother Taught Me* (1973), based on Thomas's childhood memories; and *Blown Figures* (1974), set in Ghana and using Africa as a metaphor for the unconscious. Her later works include the story collections *Goodbye Harold, Good Luck* (1986) and *The Wild Blue Yonder* (1990) and the novel *Graven Images* (1993).

Thomas \ˈtäm-əs\, D.M., *in full* Donald Michael (b. Jan. 27, 1935, Redruth, Cornwall, Eng.) English poet and novelist best known for his novel *The White Hotel* (1981), in which fantasy and psychological insight are mingled.

Thomas made his initial reputation as a poet whose subjects ranged from eroticism to science fiction to his native Cornwall; later collections, including *The Shaft* (1973), *Love and Other Deaths* (1975), and *The Honeymoon Voyage* (1978), won praise for their examinations of death, loss, and aspects of sexuality.

His translations of Russian poet Anna Akhmatova, first collected in 1976, influenced his later fiction as well as his poetry. Akhmatova was the model for the title character of *The Flute-Player* (1979). Like that work, his second novel, *Birthstone* (1980), was a fantasy. *The White Hotel* concerns Lisa Erdman, an early patient of Sigmund Freud; it explores her sexual hysteria and her premonitions of the 1941 Baby Yar massacre in which she eventually dies. Thomas returned to fantasy in most of his later novels, including *Ararat* (1983), *Summit* (1987), *Lying Together* (1990), and *Flying into Love* (1992).

Thomas \ˈtäm-əs\, Dylan (Marlais) (b. Oct. 27, 1914, Swansea, Glamorgan, Wales—d. Nov. 9, 1953, New York, N.Y., U.S.) Welsh poet and prose writer whose work is known for comic exuberance, rhapsodic lilt, and pathos.

Thomas grew up in southwestern Wales. He performed poorly at school but through his own efforts gained a vast knowledge of English poetry. At age 16 he left school to work as a reporter on the *South Wales Evening Post*. His first book, *18 Poems* (1934), announced a strikingly new and individual voice in English poetry.

At age 21 Thomas moved to London, and in 1937 he married Caitlin Macnamara. During these years he developed his highly original verse style, producing *Twenty-Five Poems* in 1936 and *The Map of Love* in 1939. These poems provided a great contrast to the then-prevailing taste in English literature; they were primitive and had an overtly emotional impact. Thomas' concern with sound and rhythm and his mingling of sexual imagery and biblical phrasing made his work a sensation.

By the end of the 1930s, Thomas was famous in literary circles. Debt and heavy drinking began to take their toll on him. In 1947 he suffered a sort of mental breakdown but refused psychiatric assistance. Although the Thomases moved to Oxford, he continued to work in London, adding exhaustion to his difficulties. In 1949 Thomas returned to Wales, and in the following year he took his first American tour. There were four tours—one in 1950, one in 1952, and two in 1953; while on tour he collapsed and died.

Among his best-known works are the poems collected in DEATHS AND ENTRANCES (1946). More accessible than his earlier verse, these poems confirm Thomas as a religious poet; in them he often adopts a bardic tone and claims a priestlike function for the poet. In such poems as FERN HILL, Thomas exhibits complex technical discipline and verbal harmonies that are unique in English poetry. In 1952 Thomas published *In Country Sleep* (containing, among other notable poems, his DO NOT GO GENTLE INTO THAT GOOD NIGHT) and his *Collected Poems*. The latter volume was an immediate success in England and the United States.

Thomas' prose is linked with his development as a poet, and his first stories, included in *The Map of Love* and *A Prospect of the Sea* (1955), are a by-product of the early poetry. But in *Portrait of the Artist as a Young Dog* (1940), the half-mythical Welsh landscapes of the early stories have been replaced by realistically and humorously observed scenes. The poet's growing consciousness of himself and of the world around him is presented with the characteristic blend of humor and pathos which is later given such lively expression in his play UNDER MILK WOOD (1954). Quite possibly his best-known prose is that found in his reminiscence A CHILD'S CHRISTMAS IN WALES (1955), a celebration of the characters, events, and presents that form a child's experience of holiday.

Thomas \ˈtäm-əs\, Ebenezer, *also called* Eben *or* Eben Fardd \ˈeb-en-ˈvärth\ (b. August 1802, Llanarmon, Caernarvonshire, Wales—d. Feb. 17, 1863) Welsh-language poet, the last of the 19th-century bards to contribute works of genuine poetic distinction to the eisteddfods (poetic competitions).

Eben's best-known poems include *Dinystr Jerusalem* ("Destruction of Jerusalem"), an ode that won the prize at the Welshpool eisteddfod of 1824; *Job*, which won at Liverpool in 1840; and *Maes Bosworth* ("Bosworth Field"), which won at Llangollen in 1858. In addition to his eisteddfodic compositions, he wrote many hymns, a collection of which was published in 1862. His complete works appeared under the title *Gweithiau Barddonol Eben Fardd* (1875; "Poetic Works of Eben Fardd"). From 1827 he conducted a school at Clynnog, Caernarvonshire.

Thomas \ˈtäm-əs\, Edward, *in full* Philip Edward Thomas (b. March 3, 1878, Lambeth, London, Eng.—d. April 9, 1917, Arras, Fr.) English writer who turned to poetry only after a long career spent producing nature studies and critical works on such 19th-century writers as Richard Jefferies, George Borrow, Algernon Charles Swinburne, and Walter Pater.

Educated at the University of Oxford, Thomas spent most of his life unhappily employed as an essayist and journalist. In 1913 he met the American poet Robert Frost, who encouraged him to write poetry. Two years later Thomas enlisted in the British Army; freed from routine literary work he was able to produce increasingly fluent poetry. The rhythms of his verse are quiet and unstressed; he was above all a poet of the country.

He was killed during World War I, and most of his poems were published posthumously, though a few were published under the name Edward Eastaway during his lifetime. Thomas' *Collected Poems* appeared in 1920.

Thomas \'täm-əs\, Gwyn (b. July 6, 1913, Perth, Glamorgan, Wales—d. April 14, 1981, Cardiff) Welsh novelist and playwright whose works, many on grim themes, were marked with gusto, much humor, and compassion.

Thomas began writing seriously in the 1930s. His first novel, *The Dark Philosophers* (1946), built on the conversations of four unemployed Welsh miners, reminded critics of such disparate authors as Geoffrey Chaucer, the 16th-century French humorist François Rabelais, and the 20th-century American writer Damon Runyon. Thomas' next important novel, *All Things Betray Thee* (1949), set in an ironworks in industrial Wales in 1885, is grim in style and tone but relieved by an ironic humor. *A Few Selected Exits* (1968) is "a sort of autobiography." Among his plays are *The Keep* (1962), *The Councillors* (performed 1971), and *The Breakers* (1976). Thomas also wrote for radio and television.

Thomas \'täm-əs\, Lewis (b. Nov. 25, 1913, Flushing, N.Y., U.S.—d. Dec. 3, 1993, New York, N.Y.) American physician, researcher, author, teacher, and administrator best known for his collections of essays, which are meditations and reflections on the larger truths invoked by the study of biology.

Thomas was the son of a physician and a nurse. He attended Princeton University and Harvard Medical School (M.D., 1937). He served in the U.S. Navy Medical Corps and taught at Johns Hopkins and Tulane universities and at the University of Minnesota Medical School. In 1954 he moved to New York University School of Medicine, which he left as dean to teach in the pathology department at Yale. In 1973 he took the presidency of the Memorial Sloan-Kettering Cancer Center, becoming president emeritus in 1984.

Thomas' first book, *The Lives of a Cell: Notes of a Biology Watcher* (1974), was a collection of 29 essays originally written for the *New England Journal of Medicine*. His later books include *The Medusa and the Snail* (1979), *Late Night Thoughts on Listening to Mahler's Ninth Symphony* (1983), and *The Fragile Species* (1992).

Thomas \'täm-əs\, Lowell (Jackson) (b. April 6, 1892, Woodington, Ohio, U.S.—d. Aug. 29, 1981, Pawling, N.Y.) Preeminent American radio commentator and an explorer, lecturer, author, and journalist. He is especially remembered for his association with T.E. Lawrence (Lawrence of Arabia).

Thomas attended Valparaiso University, the University of Denver, and Princeton University. During his early 20s he worked as a war correspondent in Europe and the Middle East, eventually following Lawrence into the Arabian Desert and filing the exclusive story and pictures that helped make Lawrence legendary. Thomas became renowned as a globetrotter and his films and written records of his expeditions established his reputation as an adventurer and a reporter. He wrote more than 50 books, including *With Lawrence in Arabia* (1924), *Kabluk of the Eskimo* (1932), *Back to Mandalay* (1951), and *The Seven Wonders of the World* (1956).

Probably best known for his radio work, Thomas made nightly news broadcasts for nearly two generations. Volume one of his autobiography was entitled *Good Evening, Everybody* (1976); his sign-off—"So long, until tomorrow!"—became the title of the second volume (1977).

Thomas \'täm-əs\, R.S., *in full* Ronald Stuart (b. March 29, 1913, Cardiff, Glamorgan [now South Glamorgan], Wales) Welsh clergyman and poet whose lucid, austere verse expresses an undeviating affirmation of the values of the common man.

Thomas was ordained in the Church of Wales, in which he held several appointments. He retired from the priesthood in 1978.

Thomas published his first volume of poetry in 1946 and gradually developed his unadorned style with each new collection. His early poems, most notably those found in *Stones of the Field* (1946) and *Song at the Year's Turning Point: Poems 1942–1954* (1955), contain a harshly critical but increasingly compassionate view of the Welsh people and their stark homeland. In Thomas' later volumes, starting with *Poetry for Supper* (1958), the subjects of his poetry remain the same, yet his questions became more specific, his irony more bitter, and his compassion deeper. In such later works as *The Way of It* (1977), *Frequencies* (1978), *Between Here and Now* (1981), and *Experimenting With an Amen* (1986), Thomas described with mournful derision, though not without hope, the cultural decay affecting his parishioners, his country, and the modern world. He further addressed the theme of a changing Wales in the prose work *Cymru or Wales?* (1992).

Thomas \'täm-əs\, William, *also called* Islwyn \'is-,lwin \ (b. April 3, 1832, Ynysddu, Monmouthshire [now in Gwent], Wales—d. Nov. 20, 1878, Mynyddislwyn, Monmouthshire) Clergyman and poet, considered the only successful practitioner of the long Welsh poem in the 19th century. His major work is the uncompleted philosophical poem *Y Storm* (1856; *The Storm*).

From his youth Thomas wrote poetry in Welsh, under the bardic name Islwyn. A master of strict Welsh meters, he was also highly accomplished at blank verse; he published a considerable body of work, largely characterized by a mystical and melancholy tone. Although he was relatively unknown in his time, some of his work later was judged to be among the finest 19th-century Welsh poetry.

Thomas, Bigger \'big-ər-'täm-əs\ Principal character in Richard Wright's novel NATIVE SON, a 20-year-old African-American living in a Chicago slum who accidentally kills his white employer's daughter, then kills his girlfriend to prevent her from telling the police.

Thomas Aquinas \'täm-əs-ə-'kwī-nəs\, *also called* Aquinas, *Italian* Tommaso d'Aquino \tòm-'mä-sō-dä-'kē-nō\, *byname* Doctor Angelicus \an-'jel-i-kəs\ ("Angelic Doctor") (b. 1224/25, Roccasecca, near Aquino, Terra di Lavoro, Kingdom of Sicily [Italy]—d. March 7, 1274, Fossanova, near Terracina, Latium, Papal States) Italian Dominican theologian and the foremost medieval Scholasticist, whose *Summa theologiae* and *Summa contra gentiles* form the classic systematization of Roman Catholic theology. He also is known as a poet who wrote some of the most gravely beautiful eucharistic hymns in the church's liturgy.

Thomas \'täm-əs\ the Rhymer, *also called* Thomas Learmont \'ler-mənt, -,mänt\ *or* Thomas of Erceldoune \'ər-səl-,dün\ (fl. 1220–97) Scottish poet and prophet who was likely the author of the metrical romance *Sir Tristrem*, a version of the widely diffused Tristram (Tristan) legend. The romance was first printed in 1804 by Sir Walter Scott from a manuscript dating to about 1300. Thomas is now probably best known through the ballad "Thomas the Rhymer," included by Scott in volume 2 of his three-volume *Minstrelsy of the Scottish Border* (1802–03). In popular lore Thomas was usually coupled with Merlin and other English seers. His prophecies first appear in literary form in the early 15th-century *Romance and Prophecies of Thomas of Erceldoune*.

Thompson \'tämp-sən\, Dorothy (b. July 9, 1894, Lancaster, N.Y., U.S.—d. Jan. 30, 1961, Lisbon, Port.) American newspaperwoman and writer, one of the most famous journalists of the 20th century.

The daughter of a Methodist minister, Thompson attended the Lewis Institute in Chicago and Syracuse (New York) University. After World War I she went to Europe as a freelance correspondent and became famous for an exclusive interview with Empress Zita of Austria after Emperor Charles' unsuccessful attempt in 1921 to regain the throne of Hungary. She was married to novelist Sinclair Lewis from 1928 to 1942 and for a time led a domestic life. She returned to Europe, however, and began reporting on the Nazi movement, for which she became the first American correspondent to be expelled from Germany. In 1936, for the *New York Herald Tribune*, she began her newspaper column "On the Record," which eventually was syndicated to as many as 170 daily papers.

Thompson wrote many books, including *New Russia* (1928), *I Saw Hitler!* (1932), *Refugees: Anarchy or Organization* (1938), *Let the Record Speak* (1939), and *The Courage to Be Happy* (1957).

Thompson \'tämp-sən\, Francis (b. Dec. 18, 1859, Preston, Lancashire, Eng.—d. Nov. 13, 1907, London) English poet of the Aesthetic movement of the 1890s, whose most famous poem, "The Hound of Heaven," describes the pursuit of the human soul by God.

Thompson was educated in the Roman Catholic faith at Ushaw College, a seminary in the north of England. He went to London to seek a livelihood, but poverty reduced him to selling matches and newspapers, and ill health drove him to opium. He wrote his first poems after finding light work with a shoemaker, and in 1888 the publication of two of his poems in Wilfrid Meynell's periodical *Merry England* aroused the admiration of Robert Browning. Meynell and his wife, the author Alice Meynell, befriended Thompson, induced him to enter a hospital, and nursed him through convalescence. In 1893 they arranged publication of a collection, *Poems*, which was highly praised.

From 1893 to 1897 Thompson lived near a Franciscan priory in north Wales, during which period he composed *Sister Songs* (1895) and *New Poems* (1897). He also wrote a number of prose works, mostly published posthumously, including the essay *Shelley* (1909). *The Works of Francis Thompson*, 3 vol. (1913), were published by Meynell.

Thompson \'tämp-sən\, Jim, *in full* James Myers Thompson (b. Sept. 27, 1906, Anadarko, Okla., U.S.—d. April 7, 1977, Los Angeles, Calif.) Novelist and screenwriter best known for his paperback pulp novels narrated by seemingly normal men who are revealed to be psychopathic.

Thompson worked in a number of odd jobs before becoming affiliated with the Federal Writers Project in the 1930s. He later worked as a journalist for the New York *Daily News* and the Los Angeles *Times Mirror*. Blacklisted for leftist politics during the anti-communist scare of the early 1950s, Thompson was later summoned to Hollywood by director Stanley Kubrick to co-write screenplays for *The Killing* (1956) and *Paths of Glory* (1957).

Thompson's reputation rested on his ability to enter the minds of the criminally insane. *The Killer Inside Me* (1952) was admired as a chilling depiction of a criminally warped mind; its narrator, like most Thompson narrators, speaks directly and colloquially to the reader. *After Dark, My Sweet* (1955), considered one of Thompson's best works, presented a mentally imbalanced narrator who becomes embroiled in a kidnapping scheme with his lover but kills himself rather than harm her.

The posthumous publication of two Thompson omnibuses—*Hardcore* (1986) and *More Hardcore* (1987)—and a short-story collection, *Fireworks: The Lost Writings of Jim Thompson* (1988) revived interest in his work as classic hardboiled crime fiction.

Thompson \'tämp-sən\, William Tappan (b. Aug. 31, 1812, Ravenna, Ohio, U.S.—d. March 24, 1882, Savannah, Ga.) American humorist remembered for his character sketches of Georgia-Florida backwoodsmen.

Thompson worked briefly on a Philadelphia newspaper. He moved to Georgia in the early 1830s, and in 1838 he founded the *Augusta Mirror*, the first of several literary magazines he developed. Discovering that the South would not support literary periodicals, in 1850 he founded the *Savannah* (Ga.) *Morning News* and continued as its editor until his death. Influenced by jurist and sometime humorist Augustus Baldwin Longstreet, Thompson wrote amusing dialect letters from a Georgia Cracker known as Major Jones; these were collected in 1843 as *Major Jones's Courtship*, which achieved nationwide popularity. Other volumes followed.

Thompson, Sadie \'sā-dē-'tämp-sən\ Fictional character, the protagonist of the short story "Rain" (1921) by W. Somerset MAUGHAM.

Thompson is a lighthearted American prostitute who plies her trade in the South Seas and causes the downfall of Reverend Mr. Davidson, a fanatical missionary.

Thomson \'täm-sən\, James (b. Sept. 11, 1700, Ednam, Roxburgh, Scot.—d. Aug. 27, 1748, Richmond, Eng.) Scottish poet whose best verse foreshadowed some of the attitudes of the Romantic movement. His poetry also gave expression to the achievements of Newtonian science and to an England reaching toward great political power based on commercial and maritime expansion.

Educated at the University of Edinburgh, Thomson went to London in 1725. While earning his living there as a tutor, he published his masterpiece, a long blank verse poem in four parts called *The Seasons—Winter* in 1726, *Summer* in 1727, *Spring* in 1728, and the whole poem, including *Autumn*, in 1730. It was set to music by Joseph Haydn in 1801.

The first sustained nature poem in English, *The Seasons* was a revolutionary departure in both subject matter and structure. What was most striking to Thomson's earliest readers was his audacity in unifying his poem without a "plot" or other narrative device, thereby defying the Aristotelian criteria revered by the Neoclassicist critics.

Thomson's belief that the scientist and poet must collaborate in the service of God, as revealed through nature, found its best expression in *To the Memory of Sir Isaac Newton* (1727). The poet also is remembered as the author of the famous ode "Rule, Britannia," from *Alfred, a Masque* (1740, with music by T.A. Arne); for his ambitious poem in five parts, *Liberty* (1735–36); and for *The Castle of Indolence* (1748).

Thomson \'täm-sən\, James, *pseudonym* Bysshe Vanolis \və-'nō-lis\ *or* B.V. (b. Nov. 23, 1834, Port Glasgow, Renfrew, Scot.—d. June 3, 1882, London, Eng.) Scottish Victorian poet who is best remembered for his somber, imaginative poem "The City of Dreadful Night," a symbolic expression of his horror of urban dehumanization.

Thomson entered the Royal Military Academy, Chelsea, became a regimental schoolmaster, and in 1851 was sent to Ireland. There he met the freethinker and radical Charles Bradlaugh, who was to be of great importance to his literary career.

In 1862 Thomson was discharged from the army and went to London, where he supported himself as a clerk while writing essays, poems, and stories, many of them published in Bradlaugh's *National Reformer*, a worker's weekly. "The City of Dreadful Night" first appeared in this periodical in 1874.

Thomson's chronic depressions and periods of alcoholism made either social or professional success difficult, and eventually he quarreled even with Bradlaugh. Nevertheless, the publication of a volume of Thomson's poetry entitled *The City of Dreadful Night and Other Poems* (1880) received favorable critical attention.

Thomson's poem "Insomnia" is autobiographical; and in "Mater Tenebrarum" and elsewhere among his writings, passages of self-revelation are frequent. Thomson did not temper his pessimism with any kind of social optimism. No other Victorian poet displays more bleakly the dark underside of an age of change and hope.

Thor \\'thôr\\ Deity of pagan Scandinavia, a great warrior represented as a red-bearded, middle-aged man of enormous strength, an implacable foe to the harmful race of giants but benevolent toward mortals. His figure was generally secondary to that of Odin, who in some traditions was his father; but in Iceland, and perhaps among all North Germanic peoples except the royal families, he was apparently worshiped more than any other god. There is evidence that a corresponding deity named Thunor, or Thonar, was worshiped by West Germanic peoples in England and continental Europe, but little is known about him.

Thor's name is an outcome of a common Germanic word for thunder, and the thunderbolt is represented by his hammer, the symbol most commonly associated with him. The hammer, Mjǫllnir, had many marvelous qualities, including that of returning to the thrower like a boomerang.

Among Thor's chief enemies was the world serpent Jǫrmungand (Jǫrmungandr), symbol of evil. According to tradition, Thor failed to smash the skull of Jǫrmungand, and the two are destined to kill each other in the Ragnarǫk ("Doom of the Gods").

Thorarensen \\'thôr-är-en-sen\\, Bjarni Vigfússon (b. Dec. 30, 1786, Brautarholt, near Reykjavík, Ice.—d. Aug. 24, 1841, Modhruvellir) First Romantic nationalist poet of Iceland.

Thorarensen completed law studies in Copenhagen, where he also attended the lectures of the German philosopher Henrik Steffens, who introduced Romanticism to Denmark. His stay abroad increased his nostalgic devotion to Iceland, which he regarded as the birthplace of heroism, in contrast to cosmopolitan Denmark. Thorarensen's enthusiasm for Iceland's primitive traditions and his reintroduction of the simple Eddic meters were instrumental in turning the Icelanders' literary attention away from Europe and to their own past. His songs, such as "Thú nafnkunna Landith" ("You Renowned Land"), in which he eulogizes Iceland's poverty and isolation for preserving its people from softness, made him revered as a poet.

Thorarensen \\'thôr-är-en-sen\\, Jakob (b. May 18, 1886, Húnavatnssýsla, Ice.—d. 1972, Iceland) Icelandic poet whose interest was in the daily heroism of the worker.

Born in the barren country of the north, a kinsman of the Romantic nationalist poet Bjarni Thorarensen, Jakob worked on the farm and in fishing boats. He had only a simple elementary education, but he read widely and built up a library of books in Icelandic and the Scandinavian languages.

His first collection of verse, *Snæljós* (1914; "Snowblink"), interpreted the strength and self-sufficiency of the farmers and fishermen of Iceland. His short stories, published from 1929 to 1939, were in the same vein as his poetry and limned sharply drawn characters against a simple background.

Thoreau \\'thô-rō, 'thər-ō, *commonly* thə-'rō, thō-\\, Henry David (b. July 12, 1817, Concord, Mass., U.S.—d. May 6, 1862, Concord) American essayist, poet, and practical philosopher who is best known for having lived the doctrines of Tran-

scendentalism, recording his experience in his masterwork, WALDEN (1854).

Thoreau graduated from Harvard University and taught for a few years in a school he started with his brother John.

A canoe trip along the Concord and Merrimack rivers in 1839 confirmed him in the opinion that he ought to be not a schoolmaster but a poet of nature. By chance he met the essayist and poet Ralph Waldo Emerson, who had settled in Concord. With his magnetism Emerson attracted others to Concord. Out of their heady speculations and affirmatives came New England Transcendentalism, one of the most significant literary movements of 19th-century America. Late in 1837, at Emerson's suggestion, Thoreau began keeping a journal that would eventually cover thousands of pages. The Transcendentalist magazine *The Dial* published many of Thoreau's writings on the outdoors.

Portrait by Samuel Worcester Rowse, 1854
Concord Free Public Library

Thoreau grew restless, and in 1842 he tried unsuccessfully to cultivate the New York literary market. Confirmed in his distaste for city life and disappointed by his failure, he returned home to Concord in late 1843.

Early in the spring of 1845, Thoreau, then 27 years old, began to build a home on the shores of Walden Pond, a lake two miles south of Concord on land Emerson owned. From the outset the move gave him profound satisfaction. When not busy weeding his bean rows and trying to protect them from hungry woodchucks or occupied with fishing, swimming, or rowing, he spent long hours observing and recording the local flora and fauna, reading, writing A WEEK ON THE CONCORD AND MERRIMACK RIVERS (1849), and making entries in his journals, which later he would polish and include in *Walden*, a series of 18 essays describing his experiment in basic living. Thoreau stayed for two years at Walden Pond.

Midway in his Walden sojourn Thoreau had spent a night in jail, an event that he reflected on in his most famous essay, CIVIL DISOBEDIENCE (1849). When Thoreau left Walden, his life lost much of its illumination. Slowly his Transcendentalism drained away as he turned to a variety of tasks to support himself. In this period he made excursions, producing three magazine articles collected posthumously in THE MAINE WOODS (1864). He became a dedicated abolitionist and, as much as anyone in Concord, he helped to speed fleeing slaves north on the Underground Railroad. He lectured and wrote against slavery, with "Slavery in Massachusetts," a lecture delivered in 1854, his harshest indictment.

Thorild \\'tü-rild\\, Thomas, *original surname* Thorén \\,tü-'rän\\ (b. April 18, 1759, Svarteborg, Swed.—d. Oct. 1, 1808, Greifswald, Swedish Pomerania [Germany]) Poet and critic who opposed the influence of French classicism on Swedish culture.

Thorild studied at Lund and worked as a tutor in Stockholm. *Passionerna* (1781; "The Passions"), his first poem, a philosophic expression of a pantheistic feeling for nature, greatly startled literary Stockholm. Although Thorild became increasingly involved in political writing during his later years, he also wrote some of the best Swedish poetry of the time, including the *Götamannasånger* ("Gothic Men's Songs"), written in aphoristic formulations reminiscent of the ancient Swedish legal style. He pleaded for positive literary evaluation in his *En critik öfver critiker* (1791–92; "A Critique of Critics"). Thorild was banished for political libel after the assassination (March 1792) of Gustav III.

Thoroddsen \'thōr-ȯd-sen\, Jón (Thortharson) (b. Oct. 5, 1818, Reykhólar, Bardastrandarsýsla, Ice.—d. March 8, 1868, Leirá) Writer commonly known as the father of the Icelandic novel.

Born of yeoman stock, Thoroddsen studied law in Copenhagen, but an unhappy love affair—which is reflected in his novels—led him to seek solace in literature. Sir Walter Scott caught his imagination and undoubtedly influenced him.

His *Piltur og stúlka* (1850; *Lad and Lass*), is an unpretensious love story that reveals his gift for concise satirical sketches of people and places. It was the first full-scale Icelandic novel. His second novel, *Mathur og kona* (1876; "Man and Woman"), was unfinished when he died. His two works make up a picture of the Icelandic society of his day that has not since been surpassed.

Thorpe or **Thorp** \'thȯrp\, Thomas Bangs (b. March 1, 1815, Westfield, Mass., U.S.—d. Sept. 20, 1878, New York, N.Y.) American humorist and one of the most effective portrayers of American frontier life before Mark Twain.

Thorpe studied painting and at age 18 exhibited his "Ichabod Crane" at the American Academy of Fine Arts, New York City. In 1836 he moved to Louisiana, where he published a succession of newspapers. Thorpe's "The Big Bear of Arkansas" (published in 1841 in the New York City magazine *Spirit of the Times*), was so outstanding a tall tale that some historians have named certain southwestern contemporaries of Thorpe the Big Bear school of humorists.

Following a political defeat, Thorpe moved in 1854 to New York City and published his finest sketches as *The Hive of the Bee Hunter*. During the U.S. Civil War he saw service in New Orleans; afterward he returned to New York City and spent his remaining years painting, working at the customhouse, and writing for *Harper's*, *Appleton's*, and other magazines.

Thorsteinsson \'thȯr-ˌsten-sȯn\, Steingrímur (Bjarnason) (b. May 19, 1831, Snaefellsnes, Ice.—d. Aug. 21, 1913, Reykjavík) Icelandic patriotic poet and lyricist best remembered as a translator of many important works into Icelandic.

Thorsteinsson studied classical philology at the University of Copenhagen but, more important, read widely in the European literature of his day. After 20 years in Copenhagen, he went back to Iceland in 1872.

In Copenhagen Thorsteinsson had joined the group of young Icelandic nationalists who were campaigning for Iceland's independence from Denmark. Much of his poetry at that time was patriotic, and as an expatriate he wrote nostalgic lyrics in praise of Iceland's natural beauty. He also began to translate with the deliberate aim of widening the cultural horizons of Icelanders.

Thorsteinsson's poetry was of a uniformly high standard, and some of his lyrics were gems of delicacy, but he showed his highest level of skill in his translations. As well as a vast number of lyrics from a variety of languages, he translated *The Arabian Nights*, William Shakespeare's *King Lear*, Daniel Defoe's *Robinson Crusoe*, and Hans Christian Andersen's fairy tales.

Thoth \'thōth, 'tōt\, *also called* Djhuty \'dyü-tē\ (Djhowtey) In Egyptian mythology, a god of the moon, of reckoning, of learning, and of writing. He was held to be the inventor of writing, the creator of languages, the scribe, interpreter, and adviser

of the gods, and the representative of the sun god, Re. His responsibility for writing was shared with the goddess Seshat.

In the myth of Osiris, Thoth protected Isis (Osiris' wife) during her pregnancy and healed the injured eye of her son Horus. Thoth weighed the hearts of the deceased at their judgment and reported the result to the presiding god, Osiris, and his fellow judges. Thoth's sacred animals were the ibis and the baboon. Thoth was usually represented in human form with an ibis's head. The Greeks identified Thoth with their god Hermes, and they called him "Thoth, the thrice great" (Hermes Trismegistos).

Thousand and One Nights, The *also called* The Arabian Nights' Entertainment, *Arabic* Alf laylah wa laylah. Collection of Oriental stories of uncertain date and authorship whose tales of Aladdin, Ali Baba, and Sindbad the Sailor also captured the imagination of readers of Western folklore.

As in much medieval European literature, the stories—fairy tales, romances, legends, fables, parables, anecdotes, and exotic or realistic adventures—are set within a frame story. Its scene is Central Asia or "the islands or peninsulae of India and China," where King Shahryar, discovering his wife's unfaithfulness, kills her and her lovers. Then, loathing all womankind, he marries and kills a new wife each day. His vizier has two daughters, Scheherazade (Shahrazad) and Dunyazad; and the elder, Scheherazade, having devised a scheme to save herself and others, insists that her father give her in marriage to the king. Each evening she tells the king a story, leaving it incomplete and promising to finish it the following night. The stories are so entertaining and the king so eager to hear the end that he puts off her execution from day to day and finally abandons his cruel plan.

Though the names of its chief characters are Iranian, the frame story is probably Indian, and the largest proportion of names is Arabic. The tales' variety and geographic range of origin—India, Iran, Iraq, Egypt, Turkey, and possibly Greece—make single authorship unlikely. By the 20th century, Western scholars agreed that the *Nights* is a composite work consisting of popular stories originally transmitted orally and developed over a period of several centuries. The first European translation of the *Nights*, which also became the first published edition, was made in the early 18th century by Antoine Galland. His main text was a four-volume Syrian manuscript, but the later volumes contain many stories from oral and other sources. The Arabic text was first published in full at Calcutta, 4 vol. (1839–42). The source for most later translations, however, was the so-called Vulgate text, an Egyptian recension published at Bulaq, Cairo, in 1835, and several times reprinted.

John Payne's little-known full English translation, 13 vol. (9 vol., 1882–84; 3 supplementary vol., 1884; vol. xiii, 1889), was used by Sir Richard Burton for *The Book of the Thousand Nights and a Night*, 16 vol. (10 vol., 1885; 6 supplementary vol., 1886–88), with notes and commentary based on his own experience of the seamy side of Eastern life. Burton's version has become the best-known English translation.

Thousand Cranes Novel by KAWABATA Yasunari, published serially in several newspapers beginning in 1949 and published as *Sembazuru* with the novel *Yama no Oto* (*The Sound of the Mountain*) in 1952. One of Kawabata's finest works, *Thousand Cranes* was written in part as a sequel to *Yukiguni* (1948; *Snow Country*). This melancholy tale uses the classical tea ceremony as a background for the story of a young man's relationships to two women, his father's former mistress and her daughter. Although it has been praised for the beauty of its spare and elegant style, the novel has also been criticized for its coldness and its suggestion of nihilism.

Thrale *see* PIOZZI.

thread of life The course of individual existence especially as fabled in ancient times to be spun and cut by the Fates.

Three Musketeers, The Novel by Alexandre DUMAS *père*, published in French as *Les Trois Mousquetaires* in 1844. A historical romance, it relates the adventures of four fictional swashbuckling heroes who lived during the reigns of the French kings Louis XIII and Louis XIV.

At the beginning of the story D'Artagnan arrives in Paris from Gascony and becomes embroiled in three duels with the three musketeers Athos, Porthos, and Aramis. The four become such close friends that when D'Artagnan serves an apprenticeship as a cadet, which he must do before he can become a musketeer, each of his friends takes turns sharing guard duty with him. The daring escapades of the four comrades are played out against a background of court intrigue involving the powerful Cardinal Richelieu.

Dumas wrote two sequels that concerned D'Artagnan and the three musketeers: *Vingt Ans après* (1845; *Twenty Years After*) and *Le Vicomte de Bragelonne ou dix ans plus tard* (1848–50; *The Vicomte de Bragelonne; or, Ten Years Later*).

Threepenny Opera, The Musical drama in three acts written by Bertolt BRECHT in collaboration with composer Kurt Weill, produced in German as *Die Dreigroschenoper* in 1928 and published the following year. The play was adapted from John Gay's *The Beggar's Opera* (1728).

Antihero gangster Macheath ("Mackie") marries Polly Peachum, daughter of a leader of a ring of London beggars. Mr. Peachum contrives to have Macheath arrested; Macheath escapes but is betrayed to the police by a prostitute, Suky Tawdry. Condemned to the gallows, Macheath is saved by a last-minute pardon on Queen Victoria's coronation day.

Three Sisters Russian drama in four acts by Anton CHEKHOV, first performed in Moscow in 1901 and published as *Tri sestry* in the same year.

The Prozorov sisters (Olga, Masha, and Irina) yearn for the excitement of Moscow; their dreary provincial life is enlivened only by the arrival of the Imperial Army. The sisters' dreams of a new life are crushed when their brother marries a woman they consider ill-bred and mortgages the house; the army is withdrawn, and Irina's fiancé is killed in a duel.

The characters of *Three Sisters* are outstanding examples of Chekhovian boredom, longing, and listlessness. The playwright portrays the sisters' social aspirations with sensitivity and irony, using them as emblems of Russian middle-class pretensions and despair.

threnody \'thren-ə-dē\ [Greek *threnōidía*, from *thrênos* lamentation, dirge + *ōidé* song] A song, poem, composition, or speech of lamentation especially for the dead, similar to a DIRGE or ELEGY.

thriller \'thril-ər\ One that produces thrills; especially a work of fiction or drama designed to hold the interest by the use of a high degree of intrigue, adventure, or suspense.

Through the Looking-Glass (*in full* Through the Looking-Glass and What Alice Found There) Book by Lewis CARROLL, dated 1872, but actually published in December 1871.

Written as a sequel to ALICE'S ADVENTURES IN WONDERLAND, *Through the Looking-Glass* describes Alice's further adventures as she moves through a mirror into another unreal world of illogical behavior, this one dominated by chessboards and chess pieces. Like its predecessor, it contains a vast number of quotable remarks and poems that have been used by many authors since Carroll's time.

Thrymskvitha \'thrœms-,kvē-thə, 'thrims-\ ("Lay of Thrym") One of several individual poems of Eddic literature preserved in the Codex Regius.

It describes how the giant Thrym steals Mjǫllnir, the hammer of Thor, and demands marriage to the goddess Freyja if he returns the hammer. Freyja wants nothing to do with Thrym, so Thor disguises himself as the bride and presents himself to Thrym. The story's humor derives largely from the bride's behavior at the wedding feast, where "she" eats an entire ox and eight salmon and drinks three vessels of mead.

Thubron \'thyü-brən, 'thü-\, Colin (b. June 14, 1939, London, Eng.) Travel writer and novelist whose works, often set in foreign locales, explore the loss of faith, love, and memory as well as the differences between the ideal and the real.

Thubron's books about the Middle East, including *Mirror to Damascus* (1967) and *Journey into Cyprus* (1975), established him as a travel writer of original sensibility. Another travel book, *Among the Russians* (1983; U.S. title, *Where Nights Are Longest*), chronicles a 10,000-mile journey by car across what was then the Soviet Union and was praised for its richly textured descriptions of Russian life.

Thubron's gift for capturing the character of the countries he observed translated well into fiction. The setting of his third novel, *A Cruel Madness* (1984), is an insane asylum, where the narrator, a patient, searches for a woman with whom he once had an affair. *Falling* (1989) involves a paralyzed trapeze artist who begs her lover to kill her. The allegorical 1991 novel *Turning Back the Sun* has been compared to the novels of Graham Greene.

Thucydides \thü-'sid-ə-,dēz, thyü-\ (b. *c.* 454, Athens—d. *c.* 399 BC?) Greatest of ancient Greek historians and author of the *History of the Peloponnesian War*, which recounts the struggle between Athens and Sparta in the 5th century BC.

All that is certainly known of Thucydides' life is what he reveals about himself in the course of his narrative. He was given command of the fleet in the Thraceward region, based at Thasos. He failed to prevent the capture of the important city of Amphipolis by the Spartan general Brasidas; he was recalled, tried, and sentenced to exile. This, he says later, gave him greater opportunity for undistracted study for his *History* and for travel and wider contacts, especially on the Peloponnesian side—Sparta and its allies.

He lived through the war, and his exile of 20 years ended only with the fall of Athens and the peace of 404. The time and manner of his death are uncertain, but that he died some time soon after 399 is probable, and that he died by violence in the troubled times following the peace may well be true, for the *History* stops abruptly, long before its appointed end.

His work was the first recorded political and moral analysis of a nation's war policies. Thucydides was writing what few others have attempted—a strictly contemporary history of events that he lived through. He endeavored to do more than merely record events, in some of which he took an active part and in all of which he was a direct or indirect spectator.

thunderbird \'thən-dər-,bərd\ A mythical bird believed by Native Americans and some Asian peoples to cause lightning (by opening and closing its eyes) and thunder (by flapping its wings). It is frequently portrayed as a supernatural eagle and is conceived as the spirit or god of thunder and rain.

Thurber \'thər-bər\, James (Grover) (b. Dec. 8, 1894, Columbus, Ohio, U.S.—d. Nov. 2, 1961, New York, N.Y.) American writer and cartoonist noted for his vision of the urban man as one who escapes into fantasy because he is befuddled and beset by a world that he neither created nor understands. Thurber's best-known portrait of this character is probably

Walter MITTY. Thurber's stock characters—the snarling wife, her timid, hapless husband, and a roster of serene, silently observing animals—have become classics of urban mythology.

Thurber held several newspaper jobs before going in 1926 to New York City, where he was a reporter for the *Evening Post*. In 1927 he joined Harold Ross's newly established magazine, *The New Yorker*, as managing editor and staff writer, making a substantial contribution to its urbane tone. He was later to write an account of his associates there in *The Years with Ross* (1959).

Thurber, who considered himself primarily a writer, first published a drawing in *The New Yorker* in 1931, though his drawings had been used earlier—at the behest of his colleague E.B. White—to illustrate their jointly written *Is Sex Necessary?* (1929).

Copyright 1966 Helen Thurber; copyright 1994 Rosemary A. Thurber. Self-portrait from *Thurber & Company*, published by Harper and Row

After Thurber left *The New Yorker* staff in 1933, he remained a leading contributor. In 1940 failing eyesight forced him to curtail his drawing, and by 1952 he had to give it up altogether as his blindness became nearly total.

His collections of stories include *My Life and Hard Times* (1933), a whimsical group of autobiographical pieces; *Fables for Our Time* (1940), a stylistically simple and charming, yet unflinchingly clear-sighted appraisal of human foibles; a play, *The Male Animal* (1941; with Elliott Nugent), a serious but humorously written plea for academic freedom; and *The Thurber Album* (1952), a second collection of family sketches. His fantasies for children, *The 13 Clocks* (1950) and *The Wonderful O* (1957), are among the most successful modern fairy tales.

Thurman \\'thər-mən\\, Wallace Henry (b. Aug. 16, 1902, Salt Lake City, Utah, U.S.—d. Dec. 22, 1934, New York, N.Y.) African-American editor, critic, novelist, and playwright associated with the Harlem Renaissance of the 1920s.

Thurman moved to Harlem in 1925, and by the time he became managing editor of the black periodical *Messenger* in 1926 he had immersed himself in the Harlem literary scene and encouraged such writers as Langston Hughes and Zora Neale Hurston to contribute to his publication. That summer, Hughes asked Thurman to edit *Fire!!*, a literary magazine conceived as a forum for young black writers and artists. Despite outstanding contributors, who included Hughes, Hurston, and Gwendolyn Bennett, the publication folded after one issue. Two years later Thurman published *Harlem*, again with work by the younger writers of the Harlem Renaissance, but it too survived only one issue.

In 1929 Thurman's play *Harlem*, written with William Rapp, opened to mixed reviews, although its bawdy treatment of Harlem life made it a popular success. His first novel, *The Blacker the Berry: A Novel of Negro Life*, also appeared that year. Like his unfinished play *Black Cinderella*, it dealt with color prejudice within the black community. Thurman is perhaps best known for his novel *Infants of the Spring* (1932), a satire of what he believed were the overrated creative figures of the Harlem scene. Some reviewers welcomed Thurman's bold insight, while others vilified him as a racial traitor. Thurman never again wrote on African-American subjects.

Thus Spake Zarathustra \\,zar-ə-'thüs-trə\\, *also translated as* Thus Spoke Zarathustra. Treatise by Friedrich NIETZSCHE, written in four parts and published in German between 1883 and 1885 as *Also sprach Zarathustra*. The work is incomplete,

but it is the first thorough statement of Nietzsche's mature philosophy and the masterpiece of his career. It received little attention during his lifetime but its influence since his death has been considerable, in the arts as well as philosophy.

Written in the form of a prose narrative, *Thus Spake Zarathustra* offers the philosophy of its author through the voice of Zarathustra (based on the Persian prophet Zoroaster) who, after years of meditation, has come down from a mountain to offer his wisdom to the world. It is this work in which Nietzsche made his famous (and much misconstrued) statement that "God is dead" and in which he presented some of the most influential and well-known (and likewise misunderstood) ideas of his philosophy, including those of the *Übermensch* ("overman" or "superman") and the "will to power."

Though this is essentially a work of philosophy, it is also a masterpiece of literature. The book is a combination of prose and poetry, including epigrams, dithyrambs, and parodies as well as sections of pure poetry.

Thyestes \\thī-'es-tēz\\   Tragedy in five acts by Lucius Annaeus SENECA, written about AD 60. *Thyestes* is considered the ancient forerunner of the Elizabethan revenge tragedy.

The play is an account of the revenge exacted by Atreus, king of Argos, against his brother Thyestes, who years earlier had seduced and abducted Atreus' wife. Though Thyestes was subsequently banished from the kingdom, Atreus is not satisfied and plots further revenge. He invites Thyestes and his three sons to return from exile. He murders the sons and at a banquet serves their flesh to Thyestes. Unable to drink a cup of blood and wine served him by his brother, Thyestes demands to see his sons. Atreus produces their heads on a platter. Thyestes declares a curse on the House of Atreus. The play thus accounts for the origins of the eventual ruin of the House of Atreus that is a major theme of classical Greek literature.

Thyiad \\'thī-,yad, -əd\\ *plural* Thyiads *or* Thyiades \\'thī-ə-,dēz, thī-'ī-ə-\\ [Greek *thyiad-, thyiás*, a derivative of *thýein* to rage, seethe]   A member of a group of women in ancient Greece devoted to the orgiastic worship of Dionysus especially as practiced on Mount Parnassus. *See also* BACCHANTE.

Thyrsis \\'thər-sis\\   Elegiac poem by Matthew ARNOLD, first published in *Macmillan's Magazine* in 1866. It was included in Arnold's *New Poems* in 1867.

In *Thyrsis* Arnold mastered an intricate 10-line stanza form. The 24-stanza poem eulogizes his friend, poet Arthur Hugh Clough, who had died in 1861. In rich pastoral imagery Arnold recalls the Oxford countryside the two explored as students in the 1840s and reviews the fate of their youthful ideals after they left the university. *Thyrsis* is considered one of Arnold's finest poems.

thyrsus \\'thər-səs\\ *plural* thyrsi \\-,sī\\ [Greek *thýrsos*]   In Greek mythology, staff carried by Dionysus, the wine god, and his votaries (the Bacchae or Maenads). In early Greek art the Bacchae were usually depicted as holding branches of vine or ivy, but after 530 BC the staff to which the name thyrsus properly applied began to be shown as a stalk of giant fennel (*narthēx*) segmented like bamboo, sometimes with ivy leaves inserted in the hollow end. Bacchae were depicted and described using them as weapons.

Tian Han *or* **T'ien Han** \\'tyen-'hän\\, *pseudonym of* Tian Shouchang \\'shō-'jäŋ\\ (b. March 12, 1898, Changsha, Hunan province, China—d. Dec. 10, 1968, Beijing)   Chinese playwright and poet known for his expressive and powerful one-act plays.

Tian wrote librettos for traditional Chinese opera when he was a teenager. He studied for several years in Japan, where he developed a lasting interest in modern drama. Upon his return to China, he and Guo Moruo founded the Chuangzao she (Creation Society), promoting romanticism in creative writing. He also founded the Nanguo Society to experiment in and popularize modern vernacular drama and initiated the *Nanguo Fortnightly* as the organ of the society. His earliest plays of the period include *Kafeidian zhi yi ye* (1924; "A Night in a Café") and *Huo hu zhi ye* (1924; "The Night the Tiger Was Caught"). Among his published plays of this period are *Hushang de beiju* (1928; "Tragedy on the Lakeshore"), *Ming you zhi si* (1929; "Death of a Famous Actor"), *Suzhou yehua* (1929; "An Evening Talk in Suzhou"), and *Nan gui* (1929; "Return to the South"). In 1930 he joined the Left-wing Dramatists' League. His plays of the 1930s included *Meiyu* (1931; "The Rainy Season"), *Baofengyu zhong de qige nüxing* (1932; "Seven Women in Stormy Weather"), and *Yueguangqu* (1932; "The Moonlight Sonata").

During the Sino-Japanese War (1937–45), while serving in various capacities for wartime mobilization, he composed some 12 librettos for traditional Chinese opera. The play *Liren xing* (1947; "The Charming Ladies") is one of his major postwar dramatic works.

After 1949 Tian wrote and adapted a number of plays and librettos. *Guan Hanqing* (1958), *Baishe zhuan* (1958; "The Story of the White Snake"), *Wencheng gongzhu* (1960; "Princess Wencheng"), and *Xie Yaohuan* (1961) were remarkable successes on the stage and in print. Tian was also a talented writer of Chinese traditional verse. He was persecuted during the Cultural Revolution.

Tibetan Book of the Dead, The *Tibetan* Bardo Thödol. Sacred Tibetan Buddhist text recited by lamas in Tibet, Mongolia, and China to a dying person or a corpse as part of a religious death ritual. The work dates from the 8th century and authorship is attributed to Padmasambhava, the legendary mystic who introduced Tantric Buddhism to Tibet.

The Book of the Dead describes in detail the frightening apparitions the deceased encounters while in the 49-day interval between death and rebirth. The major phases of the ritual include the moment of death, the experience of spiritual realities, and the search for reincarnation. It is read to the dying person to prepare the mind for the moment of death, because, according to Buddhism, the thoughts held by a person at the moment of death are of essential significance. It is also read to the newly dead, since the conscious principle is thought to remain in the body for about three days following death.

Tibullus \ti-'bəl-əs, -'búl-\, Albius (b. *c.* 55 BC—d. *c.* 19 BC) Roman poet, one of the leading Latin elegiac poets.

As a young man Tibullus won the friendship and patronage of Marcus Valerius Messalla Corvinus, the statesman, soldier, and man of letters, and became a prominent member of Messalla's literary circle. Tibullus' first important love affair, with a woman he calls Delia, is the main subject of Book I of his poems. Book II of his poems recounts his difficulties with a woman he calls Nemesis.

For idyllic simplicity, grace, tenderness, and exquisiteness of feeling and expression, Tibullus stands alone among the Roman elegists. In many of his poems, moreover, a symmetry of composition can be discerned, though they are never forced into any fixed scheme. His clear, polished, and unaffected style made him a great favorite among Roman readers.

The works of Tibullus, as they have survived, form part of what is generally known as the *Corpus Tibullianum*, a collection of poetry that seems to have been deliberately put together to represent the work of Messalla's circle. The first two of the four books in the *Corpus* are undoubtedly by Tibullus. In its

entirety the collection forms a unique and charming documentation of the literary life of Augustan Rome.

Tieck \'tēk\, Ludwig, *in full* Johann Ludwig Tieck (b. May 31, 1773, Berlin, Prussia [Germany]—d. April 28, 1853, Berlin) Writer and critic of the early Romantic movement in Germany. He was a born storyteller, and his best work has the quality of a *Märchen* (fairy tale) that appeals to the emotions rather than the intellect.

Tieck was educated at the universities of Halle, Göttingen, and Erlangen. Characteristic of early German Romanticism are Tieck's *Die Geschichte des Herrn William Lovell*, 3 vol. (1795–96; "The Story of Mr. William Lovell"), a novel in letter form that describes the moral self-destruction of a sensitive young intellectual; *Karl von Berneck* (1797), a five-act tragedy set in the Middle Ages; and *Franz Sternbalds Wanderungen*, 2 vol. (1798; "Franz Sternbald's Travels"), a novel of artistic life in the late Middle Ages. Under the pseudonym Peter Leberecht, Tieck published a collection of fairy tales entitled *Volksmärchen*. This collection included a series of plays based on fairy tales—including *Ritter Blaubart* ("Bluebeard") and *Der gestiefelte Kater* ("Puss in Boots")—that parodied the rationalism of the 18th-century Enlightenment, as well as one of Tieck's best short novels, *Der blonde Eckbert* ("Fair Eckbert"), the fantastic story of an obsessive fear.

In 1799 Tieck published a translation of William Shakespeare's *The Tempest*. His early work culminated in the grotesque, lyrical plays *Leben und Tod der heiligen Genoveva* (1800; "Life and Death of St. Genevieve") and *Kaiser Octavianus* (1804; "Emperor Octavian"). *Phantasus*, 3 vol. (1812–16), a heterogeneous collection of works in a narrative framework, indicated a movement toward realism. After 1802 Tieck produced little original work.

In 1825 Tieck was appointed adviser and critic at the theater in Dresden, a post he held until 1842. During those years he became one of the greatest living literary authorities in Germany. His creative energies were renewed; he turned away from the fantasy of his earlier work and found his material in contemporary middle-class society or in history. The 40 short novels he wrote during this period contain polemics against both the younger Romantics and the contemporary Young Germany movement that was attempting to establish a national German theater based on democratic ideals.

T'ien Han *see* TIAN HAN.

Tietgens, Christopher \'kris-tə-fər-'tēt-gənz\ Fictional character, the idealistic protagonist of the tetralogy PARADE'S END by Ford Madox Ford.

Tikhonov \'tyē-kə-nəf\, Nikolay Semyonovich (b. Nov. 22 [Dec. 4, New Style], 1896, St. Petersburg, Russia—d. Feb. 8, 1979, Moscow, U.S.S.R.) Soviet poet and prose writer, notable for his heroic war ballads and for his originality and poetic experimentation.

Tikhonov fought in a hussar regiment during World War I, later joining the Red Army and participating in the Russian Revolution of 1917 and the Russian Civil War. During the early 1920s he settled in Leningrad and became a member of the literary group known as the Serapion Brothers. In his first two collections of poetry, *Orda* (1922; "The Horde") and *Braga* (1922; "Mead"), Tikhonov sought to express the sensations of his years of war and adventure. These and other early poems show the influence of Acmeism in their use of concrete images, pictorial detail, and semantic precision.

In the mid-1920s, under the influence of the poets Velimir Khlebnikov and Boris Pasternak, Tikhonov experimented in his poetry. His travels to the East and to Central Asia supplied new material for his verse.

In the early 1930s Tikhonov began to write poetry increasingly concerned with broad social issues. His prose works, however, continued to be romantic in style and in spirit, as in his short stories depicting socialist construction projects in Central Asia. A staunch supporter of the Soviet regime and an ardent patriot, he stressed in his World War II-era writings the same ideals of duty and courage that he had emphasized in earlier works.

Tikhonov served as chairman of the Union of Soviet Writers from 1944 to 1946. During the late 1950s he alienated many other Soviet writers because of his participation in a campaign of criticism and denunciation directed against Pasternak.

Tiller \'til-ər\, Rogers, *in full* Terence Rogers Tiller (b. Sept. 19, 1916, Truro, Cornwall, Eng.) English playwright, translator, and metaphysical poet whose best verse is noted for its perfect form and intense emotional content.

Until the outbreak of World War II, Tiller was research scholar and eventually lecturer in medieval European history at the University of Cambridge. From 1939 to 1947 he lectured in English history and literature at Fu'ād I University, Cairo; he then was employed by the BBC as a radio writer and producer. From 1976 Tiller worked as both a freelance writer and broadcaster.

Of his major poetry collections, *The Inward Animal* (1943) and *Unarm, Eros* (1947) are his most highly acclaimed. In these works, strong formal pattern, heraldic imagery, and striking sensuousness are combined to produce a masterly and genuinely witty effect. His later volumes, *Reading a Medal and Other Poems* (1957), *Notes for a Myth and Other Poems* (1968), and *That Singing Mesh and Other Poems* (1979), on the whole lack the tension and concreteness that give *The Inward Animal* and especially *Unarm, Eros* their immediacy.

In addition to his poetry and numerous plays and feature broadcasts for the BBC, Tiller wrote several prose pieces and edited and translated a number of books, including such classic works as Dante's *Inferno* (1966) and William Langland's *The Vision of Piers Plowman* (1981).

Time Machine, The First novel by H.G. WELLS, published in book form in 1895. The novel is considered one of the earliest works of science fiction and the progenitor of the "time travel" subgenre.

Wells advanced his social and political ideas in this narrative of a nameless Time Traveller who is hurtled into the year 802,701 by his elaborate ivory, crystal, and brass contraption. The world he finds is peopled by two races: the decadent Eloi, fluttery and useless, are dependent for food, clothing, and shelter on the simian subterranean Morlocks, who prey on them. The two races—whose names are borrowed from the Biblical Eli and Moloch—symbolize Wells's vision of the eventual result of unchecked capitalism: a neurasthenic upper class that would eventually be devoured by a proletariat driven to the depths.

Time of the Hero, The Novel by Mario VARGAS LLOSA, published in 1963 as *La ciudad y los perros* ("The City and the Dogs"). The novel describes adolescents in a Peruvian military school striving to survive in a hostile and violent environment. The corruption of the military school suggests a larger malaise afflicting Peru. The novel has a complex structure, with a nonlinear chronolgy and multiple narrative voices.

The story concerns the theft of an examination paper by the cadet Cava, under orders from Jaguar, the brutal top cadet. The theft is reported by a lowly cadet whom Jaguar consequently murders during military maneuvers. Concerned for the school's reputation, the administrators choose to ignore further evidence of Jaguar's guilt.

time-shift A narrative method that shifts back and forth in time from past to present instead of proceeding in strict chronological sequence.

Times Literary Supplement *abbreviation* TLS. Weekly literary journal long famous for its coverage of all aspects of literature and widely considered one of the finest literary reviews in the English language. Founded in 1902 as a supplement to *The Sunday Times* of London, TLS sets the tone and standards of excellence in the field of literary criticism. It presents reviews of major books of fiction and nonfiction published in every language, and its essays are written with sophistication and scholarly authority and in a lively style. It is also noted for its bibliographic thoroughness, for its topical essays by the world's leading scholars, and for the erudition of its readers' published letters to the editor.

Timmermans \'tim-ər-mäns\, Felix (b. July 5, 1886, Lier, Belg.—d. Jan. 24, 1947, Lier) Flemish writer who was an outstanding representative of the idyllic regionalism that enjoys recurrent popularity in Belgium.

Timmermans established his reputation with the novel *Pallieter* (1916), an "ode to life" written after a moral and physical crisis. In this book, Timmermans depicts his native province of Brabant as a paradise and creates a character, Pallieter, who has found a place in literature as the embodiment of a typically Flemish enjoyment of living—at once sensual and mystical.

Timmermans was also a painter and illustrator, finding inspiration in old prints and the works of Pieter Bruegel the Elder. For his fictional characters he drew on the people of his native town. His kindly, humorous point of view, warm coloring, wealth of anecdote, sympathetically caricatured characters, and pictorial skill mask his lack of depth. Besides many novels and short stories, he wrote romanticized biographies of Bruegel (1928) and St. Francis (1932), travel tales, autobiographical works, and plays. In 1935 he published *Boerenpsalm* ("Peasant Psalm"), a novel revealing deep knowledge of suffering, in which praise of nature gives way to praise of humanity.

Timon of Athens \'tī-mən, -,män . . . 'ath-ənz\ Unfinished tragedy in five acts by William SHAKESPEARE, probably first performed 1607–08 and published in the First Folio of 1623. It belongs to Shakespeare's late experimental period, when he explored a new kind of tragic form. Unlike the plots of his great tragedies, the story of *Timon of Athens* is simple and lacks development. It demonstrates events in the life of Timon, a man known for his great and universal generosity, who spends his fortune and then is spurned when he requires help. He puts on a feast, invites his fair-weather friends, serves them warm water, and throws it in their faces. With his servant Flavius, he leaves Athens and, filled with hatred, goes to live in a cave. While digging for roots to eat, Timon uncovers gold, most of which he gives to the soldier Alcibiades for his war against Athens. Word of his fortune reaches Athens, and as a variety of Athenians importune Timon again, he curses them and dies.

The first half of the play shows Timon's thoroughly unrealistic assessment of the people and events around him and makes it clear that he lives in a dream world. Into that world—as the audience watches, with some pain—reality intrudes. The second half of the play is a simple series of interviews between Timon and his Athenian visitors that seem arranged solely to allow Timon to vent his rage. Of the various explanations put forward for the uneven quality of the writing in this play, much the most probable is that this is Shakespeare's rough draft of a play.

Timrod \'tim-,räd\, Henry (b. Dec. 8, 1828, Charleston, S.C., U.S.—d. Oct. 6, 1867, Columbia, S.C.) American poet who was called "the laureate of the Confederacy."

The son of a bookbinder, Timrod attended Franklin College (later the University of Georgia), Athens, and for a short time read law in Charleston. In 1860 a collection of his poems was published. In his best-known essay, "Literature in the South" (1859), he criticized the lack of respect accorded Southern writers in both the North and the South. During the American Civil War he enlisted in the Confederate army but was soon discharged for reasons of health. Later he was an editor and part owner of the *South Carolinian* in Columbia. After the city was burned by Union forces, however, he suffered from poverty and chronic ill health. He died of tuberculosis.

In 1873 the Southern poet Paul Hamilton Hayne, who was Timrod's lifelong friend, edited *The Poems of Henry Timrod*. Among Timrod's poems supporting the South are "Ode Sung at the Occasion of Decorating the Graves of the Confederate Dead," "The Cotton Boll," and "Ethnogenesis." *Katie*, a lyric poem to his wife, was published in 1884 and *Complete Poems* in 1899.

Timur \'tim-u̇r\, *also spelled* Timour, *byname* Timur Lenk \'leŋk\ *or* Timurlenk ("Timur the Lame"), *English* Tamerlane \'tam-ər-ˌlān\ *or* Tamburlaine \'tam-bər-ˌlān\ (b. 1336, Kesh, near Samarkand, Transoxania [now in Uzbekistan]—d. Feb. 19, 1405, Otrar, near Chimkent [now in Kazakhstan]) Islāmic Turkic conqueror who is chiefly remembered for the barbarity of his conquests from India and Russia to the Mediterranean Sea and for the cultural achievements of his dynasty. He was portrayed in literature by such writers as Christopher Marlowe (*Tamburlaine the Great*, 1590), Nicholas Rowe (*Tamerlane*, 1702), and Edgar Allan Poe (*Tamerlane*, 1827).

Tin Drum, The Picaresque novel by Günter GRASS, a purported autobiography of a dwarf who lives through the birth and death of Nazi Germany, published in 1959 as *Die Blechtrommel*.

The work's protagonist, Oskar Matzerath, narrates the novel from an asylum for the insane. He claims to have consciously stopped growing at the age of three in protest against adulthood; although intellectually normal, he has the stunted body of a dwarf. Oskar's voice is shrill enough to shatter glass, and his passion is banging on his tin drum, which has properties by which he draws forth memories from the past and complains about shortcomings in the present. Detached from people and events, he comments on the horrors, injustices, and eccentricities he observes. Found guilty of a murder he did not commit, Oskar is incarcerated.

This exuberant novel, written in a variety of styles, imaginatively distorts and exaggerates Grass's personal experiences—the Polish-German dualism of Danzig, the creeping Nazification of average families, the attrition of the war years, the coming of the Russians, and the complacent atmosphere of West Germany's postwar "economic miracle."

Ting Ling *see* DING LING.

Tinker Bell \'tiŋ-kər-ˌbel\ Fictional character, the fairy companion of Peter Pan. *See* PETER PAN.

Tintern Abbey \'tin-tərn\ (*in full* Lines Composed a Few Miles above Tintern Abbey on Revisiting the Banks of the Wye during a Tour, July 13, 1798) Blank-verse poem by William WORDSWORTH that first appeared in *Lyrical Ballads*, a collaboration between Wordsworth and Samuel Taylor Coleridge published in 1798.

A celebration of the restorative power of nature, "Tintern Abbey" is one of the finest articulations of the Romantic sensibility. Wordsworth had visited the 12th-century abbey in 1793, then returned five years later with his beloved sister Dorothy, to whom the poem is addressed. The poet sees in his sister's

"wild eyes" a harmony with the primitive he himself enjoyed in earlier years.

Tiny Tim \'tim\ Fictional character, the crippled young son of Bob Cratchit, clerk to the miserly Ebenezer Scrooge, in Charles Dickens' A CHRISTMAS CAROL.

Tiresias \tī-'rē-sē-əs, -zē-\ In Greek mythology, a blind Theban seer. In the *Odyssey* he retained his prophetic gifts even in the underworld, where the hero Odysseus was sent to consult him. At Thebes he played an active part in the tragic events concerning Laius, the king of Thebes, and his son Oedipus. Later legend told that he lived for seven (or nine) generations, dying after the expedition of the Seven Against Thebes, and that he had once been turned into a woman as the result of killing the female of two coupling snakes (on killing the male he regained his own sex). His blindness was variously explained. In one version it was a punishment for revealing the secrets of the gods.

The figure of Tiresias recurs in European literature, both as prophet and as man-woman, as in Guillaume Apollinaire's surrealist play *Les Mamelles de Tirésias* (first performed 1917; "The Breasts of Tiresias") and T.S. Eliot's *The Waste Land* (1922).

Tirso de Molina \'tēr-sō-ˌthä-mō-'lē-nä\, *pseudonym of* Gabriel Téllez \'tel-leth\ (b. March 9?, 1584, Madrid, Spain—d. March 12, 1648, Soria) Spanish dramatist who followed the lead of Lope de Vega.

Tirso studied at the University of Alcalá and in 1601 was professed in the Mercedarian Order. As the order's official historian he wrote *Historia general de la orden de la Merced* in 1637. He was also a theologian of repute. Inspired by the achievements of Lope de Vega, creator of the Spanish *comedia*, Tirso wrote to the "free-and-easy" prescriptions that Vega had propounded for dramatic construction.

Three of his dramas appeared in his *Cigarrales de Toledo* (1621; "Weekend Retreats of Toledo"), a set of verses, tales, plays, and critical observations that, arranged within a frame story, affect to provide a series of summer recreations for a group of friends. Otherwise his extant output of about 80 dramas—a fragment of the whole—was published chiefly in five *Partes* between 1627 and 1636. The second part presents apparently insoluble problems of authenticity, and the authorship of certain other of his plays outside this part has also been disputed.

The most powerful dramas associated with his name are two tragedies, *El burlador de Sevilla* (1630; "The Seducer of Seville") and *El condenado por desconfiado* (1635; *The Doubted Damned*). The first introduced into literature the hero-villain DON JUAN, derived from popular legends but re-created with originality.

Tirso was at his best when portraying the psychological conflicts and contradictions of his characters. *Antona García* (1635) is notable for its objective analysis of mob emotion; *La prudencia en la mujer* (1634; "Prudence in Woman") offers insights into ancient regional strife; and the biblical *La venganza de Tamar* (1634; "The Vengeance of Tamar") presents violently realistic scenes. At his greatest, Tirso rivaled his peers in comedy and he towered above all in tragedy.

Tirukkuṟaḷ \'tir-u̇k-ku̇-'räl\ ("Sacred Couplets") Most celebrated of the *Patiṟeṇ-kīrkkaṇakku* ("Eighteen Ethical Works") in Tamil literature and immensely influential on Tamil culture and life. The work is usually ascribed to the poet TIRUVALLUVAR, who is thought to have lived in India in the 4th or 5th century AD.

The *Tirukkuṟaḷ* is an all-inclusive moral guide whose foremost moral imperatives are to not kill and to tell the truth. It also emphasizes compassion for all, regardless of caste or creed. Its 133 sections of 10 couplets each are divided in three books:

aṛam (virtue), *porul* (government and society), and *kāmam* or *inbam* (love or pleasure). The *aṛam* section opens with praise of God, Rain, Renunciation, and Virtue. It then summarizes a world-affirming vision, the wisdom of human sympathy, expanding from wife, children, and friends to clan, village, and country. The *porul* section projects a vision of an ideal state, and relates good citizenship to virtuous private life. The *kāmam* section addresses both "secret love" and married love; the section on married love is written as a dialogue between husband and wife.

Tiruvalluvar \'tir-ū-ˌwǎl-ū-'wǎr\, *also spelled* Thiruvalluvar (fl. 4th or 5th century AD, in India) Tamil poet-saint known as the author of the TIRUKKUṚAL ("Sacred Couplets"), considered a masterpiece of human thought, compared in India and abroad to the Bible, John Milton's *Paradise Lost*, and the works of Plato.

Tiruvalluvar is believed to have lived in Mylapore, India, no later than the fourth century. He most likely was a Jain ascetic of humble origins who worked as a weaver. Both Buddhists and Saivites, however, claim him as their own, and he is especially revered by those of low caste.

Tiruvalluvar's couplets in the *Tirukkuṛal* are highly aphoristic: "Adversity is nothing sinful, but/laziness is a disgrace"; "Wine cheers only when it is quaffed, but love/intoxicates at mere sight." Despite his reasonable tone, many of Tiruvalluvar's ideas were revolutionary. He dismissed the caste system: "One is not great because of one's birth in a noble family; one is not low because of one's low birth." The poet maintained that goodness is its own reward, and it should not be regarded as a mere means to a comfortable afterlife.

'Tis Pity She's a Whore Five-act tragedy by John FORD, performed sometime between 1629 and 1633 and published in 1633. The story concerns the incestuous love of Giovanni and his sister Annabella. When she is found to be pregnant, she agrees to marry her suitor Soranzo; the lovers' secret is discovered, but Soranzo's plan for revenge is outpaced by Giovanni's murder of Annabella and then Soranzo, and Giovanni himself is murdered by Soranzo's hired killers. The play exhibits an eloquent and glowing sympathy for the lovers, despite the unlawful nature of their union.

Titan \'tīt-ən\ In Greek mythology, one of a family or race of earth giants whose power was destroyed by the Olympian gods and who are usually held to have been characterized by gigantic size, immense brute strength, and primitive force and appetite rather than intelligence or morality.

The Titans were the children of Uranus (Heaven) and Gaea (Earth). According to Hesiod's *Theogony*, there were 12 original Titans: the brothers Oceanus, Coeus, Crius, Hyperion, Iapetus, and Cronus and the sisters Theia, Rhea, Themis, Mnemosyne, Phoebe, and Tethys. At the instigation of Gaea the Titans rebelled against their father, who had shut them up in the underworld (Tartarus). Under the leadership of Cronus they deposed Uranus and set up Cronus as their ruler. But one of Cronus' sons, Zeus, rebelled against his father, and a struggle ensued. Most of the Titans sided with Cronus. Zeus and his brothers and sisters finally defeated the Titans after 10 years of fierce battles (the Titanomachia). The Titans were then hurled down by Zeus and imprisoned in a cavity beneath Tartarus.

The Giants (Gigantes), another group of children of Uranus and Gaea, later tried to avenge the Titans by rebelling against Zeus and the other gods, but they were defeated.

Titania \ti-'tān-yə, tī-, -'tän-\ Fictional character, the queen of the fairies in the comedy A MIDSUMMER NIGHT'S DREAM by William Shakespeare.

Tithonus \tī-'thō-nəs\ In Greek legend, son of Laomedon, king of Troy, and of Strymo, daughter of the river Scamander. Eos (Aurora) fell in love with him and took him to Ethiopia, where she bore Emathion and Memnon. When Eos requested that Zeus grant Tithonus eternal life, the god consented. But Eos forgot to ask also for eternal youth, so her husband grew old and was transformed into a cicada. His plight was eloquently detailed in a poem by Alfred, Lord Tennyson.

title page A page of a book bearing the title and usually the names of the author, editor, or translator (if any) and the publisher and sometimes the place and date of publication. The title page may also carry the edition number if the book is a new edition of a previously published work.

Titmarsh, Michael Angelo \'mī-kəl-'an-jə-ˌlō-'tit-ˌmärsh\ Pseudonym used by William Makepeace THACKERAY for several of his early works. The name is a humorous reference to Thackeray's earlier desire to be an artist. Among the works written under the name of Titmarsh are *The Paris Sketch-Book* (1840); *The History of Samuel Titmarsh and the Great Hoggarty Diamond* (1841), in which the narrator was introduced as Michael Angelo's cousin Samuel; *The Irish Sketch-Book*, 2 vol. (1843); and *Rebecca and Rowena* (1850). These and other works written under such pseudonyms as Fitz-Boodle, The Fat Contributor, and Ikey Solomons, were published in the four-volume collection *Miscellanies* (1855–57).

Tituba \'tit-yū-bə\ Fictional character, a black slave who is accused of being a witch in THE CRUCIBLE by Arthur Miller.

Titus Andronicus \'tī-təs-an-'drän-i-kəs\ One of the earliest tragedies of William SHAKESPEARE, produced in 1593–94 and published in 1594. The play's crude, melodramatic style and its many savage incidents led many critics to believe it was not written by Shakespeare. Modern criticism, however, tends to regard the play as authentic. Although not ranked with Shakespeare's other great Roman plays, *Titus Andronicus* relates its story of revenge and political strife with a uniformity of tone and consistency of dramatic structure. Sources for the story include Euripides' *Hecuba*, Seneca's *Thyestes* and *Troades*, and parts of Ovid and Plutarch.

Titus Andronicus returns to Rome after defeating the Goths, bringing with him Queen Tamora, whose eldest son he has sacrificed. The late emperor's son Saturninus is supposed to marry Titus's daughter Lavinia; however, when his brother Bassianus runs away with her instead, Saturninus marries Tamora. Saturninus and Tamora then plot revenge against Titus. Beginning with the rape and mutilation of Lavinia, bloodshed and brutality run rampant, culminating in a cannibalistic banquet scene.

Tiutchev *see* TYUTCHEV.

Tiw *see* TYR.

tmesis \tə-'mē-sis, 'mē-sis\ [Late Latin, from Greek *tmêsis* act of cutting] Separation of parts of a compound word by the intervention of one or more words (as in *what place soever* for *whatsoever place*).

To An Athlete Dying Young Poem by A.E. Housman, published in the collection A SHROPSHIRE LAD. In seven melancholy stanzas, the poet reflects upon a young athlete brought home to be buried, musing that he was lucky to die at the peak of his glory since he will now never experience the fading of that glory. The poem reiterates the general themes of the collection: death is a release from the torment of existence, youth and life are brief, and human beings can count on neither earthly happiness nor immortality.

To a Skylark Lyric poem by Percy Bysshe SHELLEY, published in 1820 with *Prometheus Unbound*. Consisting of 21 five-line stanzas, "To a Skylark" is considered a work of metric virtuosity in its ability to convey the swift movement of the bird who swoops high above the earth, beyond mortal experience. The skylark is a symbol of the joyous spirit of the divine; it cannot be understood by ordinary, empirical methods. The poet, longing to be a skylark, muses that the bird has never experienced the disappointments and disillusionments of human life, including the diminishment of passion.

To Autumn Last major poem by John KEATS, published in *Lamia, Isabella, The Eve of St. Agnes, and Other Poems* (1820). "To Autumn" (often grouped with his other odes, although Keats did not refer to it as an ode) comprises three 11-line stanzas. Written shortly before the poet died, the poem is a celebration of autumn blended with an awareness of the passing of summer and of life's ephemeral quality. Less melancholy than Keats's earlier works, the poem treats autumn not as a time of decay but as a season of complete ripeness and fertility, a pause in time when everything has reached fruition and the question of transience is hardly raised. Although Keats's death was imminent, he did not include reference to his own condition in the metaphor of passing seasons.

To a Waterfowl Lyric poem by William Cullen BRYANT, published in 1818 and collected in *Poems* (1821). It is written in alternately rhymed quatrains. At the end of a difficult day filled with uncertainty and self-doubt, the poet is comforted by the sight of a solitary waterfowl on the horizon and realizes that everything in nature is guided by a protective divine providence.

Tobacco Road Novel by Erskine CALDWELL, published in 1932. A tale of violence and sex among rural poor in the American South, the novel was highly controversial in its time. It is the story of Georgia sharecropper Jeeter Lester and his family, who are trapped by the bleak economic conditions of the Depression as well as by their own limited intelligence and destructive sexuality. Its tragic ending is almost foreordained by the characters' inability to change their lives. Caldwell's skillful use of dialect and his plain style made the book one of the best examples of literary naturalism in contemporary American fiction. The novel was adapted as a successful play in 1933.

To Be a Pilgrim Second novel in a trilogy by Joyce CARY, published in 1942. The novel is told in the voice of Tom Wilcher, an old man who is out of touch with the values of his era. *Herself Surprised* (1941) and *The Horse's Mouth* (1944) are the first and third novels in the trilogy.

Tobermory \'tō-bər-,mȯr-ē\ Short story by SAKI, published in the 1911 collection *The Chronicles of Clovis*. This miniature masterpiece about a cool and malicious talking cat who threatens to reveal secrets he has heard at a country party satirizes the pretensions and hypocrisies of Edwardian society. Inventive and written in supple prose, this much-anthologized story reflects the witty, derisive, and slightly cruel style characteristic of the author.

To Be Young, Gifted, and Black Collection of writings, some previously unpublished, by playwright Lorraine HANSBERRY, produced in a stage adaptation Off-Broadway in 1969 and published in book form in 1970. Robert Nemiroff, Hansberry's literary executor and ex-husband, edited and published this collection after Hansberry's death in 1965. Subtitled *Lorraine Hansberry in Her Own Words*, the autobiographical work contains material from her letters, journals, essays, memoirs, and poetry, as well as scenes from her dramas.

To Build a Fire Short story by Jack LONDON, published in *Century Magazine* in 1908, later reprinted in the 1910 collection *Lost Face*. (An earlier draft had been published in 1902 in *Youth's Companion*.) London's widely anthologized master-

piece illustrates in graphic terms the futility of human efforts to conquer nature. Set in the Klondike in winter, the story concerns a man who ignores warnings and attempts to travel a great distance in the extreme cold. Although even his dog senses the folly of the journey, the man stubbornly continues to believe in his own infallibility. His doom is sealed when, after getting his feet wet, he is unable to build the crucial fire that might save his life. London's stark, unadorned prose is a powerful vehicle for his grim message.

Todd, Sweeney \'swē-nē-'täd\ Fictional character, a British barber who murders his customers and whose notorious career inspired a novel, many 19th-century melodramas, and a Broadway musical.

Sweeney Todd is a demented barber in London who slits the throats of his unsuspecting customers and has their bodies made into meat pies. In most adaptations of the tale, he has a female accomplice who prepares and later sells the meat pies.

A gruesomely comic character in British folklore, Sweeney Todd is believed to have been based on a legendary, unnamed 14th-century French murderer. The character named Sweeney Todd first appeared in a serialized novel, *The String of Pearls, or The Barber of Fleet Street* (c. 1840), by Thomas Peckett Prest. The work was adapted into a popular Victorian stage melodrama, *A String of Pearls, or the Fiend of Fleet Street* (1847), by George Dibdin Pitt; it was later retitled *Sweeney Todd, the Demon Barber of Fleet Street*. Numerous retellings of Sweeney Todd's exploits were staged throughout the 19th and 20th centuries.

To Have and Have Not Minor novel by Ernest HEMINGWAY, published in 1937. Set in and near Key West, Florida, the novel is about a cynical boat owner whose concern for his rum-soaked sidekick and love for a reckless woman lead him to risk everything to aid gunrunners in a noble cause.

To His Coy Mistress Poem of 46 lines by Andrew MARVELL, published in 1681. The poem treats the conventional theme of the conflict between love and time in a witty and ironic manner. The poet opens by telling his mistress that, given all the time in the world, he would spend hundreds of years praising each part of her body, while she could spend hundreds of years refusing his advances. But he reminds her that their mortal days are not so abundant and urges her to submit to his embraces before her beauty fades and they both die.

To Kill a Mockingbird Novel by Harper Lee, published in 1960. Winner of the Pulitzer Prize in 1961, the novel was praised for its sensitive treatment of a child's awakening to racism and prejudice in the American South. It takes place in a small Alabama town in the 1930s and is told from the point of view of six-year-old Jean Louise ("Scout") Finch. She is the daughter of Atticus Finch, a white lawyer hired to defend Tom Robinson, a black man accused of raping a white woman. By observing the townspeople's reactions to the trial, Scout becomes aware of the hypocrisy and prejudice that exist in the adult world.

Tokuda Shūsei \'tō-kü-dä-'shü-,sä\, *pseudonym of* Tokuda Sueo \'sü-a-ò\ (b. Dec. 23, 1871, Kanazawa, Japan—d. Nov. 18, 1943, Tokyo) Novelist who, with Masamune Hakuchō, Tayama Katai, and Shimazaki Tōson, is one of the "four pillars" of Japanese naturalism.

Shūsei left Kanazawa in 1894 to become a disciple of Ozaki Kōyō, then the leader of the literary world. Shūsei's talents were not suited to Kōyō's lush romantic style, and he was slow to gain recognition. But when, after the Russo-Japanese War (1904–05), the tide of literary taste began to turn toward realistic, objective description, Shūsei came into his own. His direct, terse style, drab by earlier standards, was the perfect vehicle for his sharp, unsentimental portrayal of people living economically and emotionally depressed lives. The first work to bring him public recognition was *Arajotai* (1907; "The New Household"), which recounts the life of the wife of a small businessman. *Ashiato* (1910; "Footprints"), about the passivity of his own wife's early life, and *Kabi* (1911; "Mold"), describing the circumstances of their marriage, continue the theme of inertia and general hopelessness, as does *Tadare* (1914; "Festering"). *Arakure* (1915; "The Tough One") presents a particularly fine portrait of a strong-willed woman. A more mellow tone characterizes *Kasō jimbutsu* (1935–38; "A Disguised Man"), the story of his love affair with a young would-be writer, and *Shukuzu* (1941–46; "Miniature"), concerning the life of an aging geisha as she recounts it to her patron.

Shūsei's sharp observation and firm character delineation produced some of the most memorable portraits in Japanese literature.

Tokutomi Rōka \\'tō-kū-,tō-mē-'rō-,kä\\, *pseudonym of* Tokutomi Kenjirō \\'ken-jē-,rō\\ (b. Dec. 9, 1868, Minamata, Japan—d. Sept. 18, 1927, Tokyo) Japanese novelist, the younger brother of the historian Tokutomi Sohō.

Tokutomi worked for years as a writer for his brother's publications, but he began going his own way in 1900 on the strength of the success of his novel *Hototogisu* (1898; "The Cuckoo"; Eng. trans. *Namiko*), a melodramatic tale of tragic parental interference in a young marriage. *Shizen to jinsei* (1900; "Nature and Man"), a series of nature sketches, and the semiautobiographical *Omoide no ki* (1901; *Footprints in the Snow*) confirmed his decision to pursue his own literary career. Through the ensuing years, Tokutomi turned toward an eccentric mysticism, which his wife came to share. As the result of a meeting with the novelist Leo Tolstoy, he retired to the country to live a Tolstoyan "peasant life," recorded in *Mimizu no tawagoto* (1913; "Gibberish of an Earthworm"). He died in the midst of writing four volumes of confessions, a monumental work later completed by his wife.

Tokutomi Sohō \\'tō-kū-,tō-mē-'sō-,hō\\, *pseudonym of* Tokutomi Ichirō \\'ē-chē-,rō\\ (b. March 14, 1863, Tsumori, near Minamata, Japan—d. Nov. 2, 1957, Atami) Influential Japanese historian, critic, journalist, and essayist and a leading nationalist writer before World War II.

In 1887 Tokutomi founded a publishing house, Min'yūsha ("Society of the People's Friends"). It launched a highly influential periodical, *Kokumin no tomo* ("Nation's Friend"), that was Japan's first general magazine. Tokutomi was particularly concerned with the modernization of Japan, and, in such influential early books as *Shōrai no Nihon* (1886; "The Future Japan"), he advocated that Western-style liberal and democratic reforms be undertaken in his country. In the following decades, however, he became a militant nationalist in favor of an imperialistic Japan, and during the 1920s and '30s he was one of the nation's most popular advocates for this ideal. Tokutomi was placed under house arrest by the American occupation authorities after World War II. His 100-volume *Kinsei Nihon kokumin shi* (1918–52; "A History of Early Modern Japan"), despite its ultranationalistic bias, is an exhaustive and invaluable compendium of events in Japan from 1534 until the late 19th century.

Tolentino de Almeida \\tō-len̄-'tē-nū-dē-àl-'mä-də\\, Nicolau (b. Sept. 10, 1740, Lisbon, Port.—d. June 23, 1811) Portugal's leading satirical poet of the 18th century.

At age 20 Tolentino entered the University of Coimbra to study law; he interrupted his studies three years later to become a teacher of rhetoric. In 1776 he was appointed to a post in Lis-

bon and the following year was named professor of rhetoric. About 1777, Tolentino grew tired of his teaching and aspired to public office. He dedicated numerous verses to members of the new political generation and, like other poets of the period, drew satirical sketches of the former minister, the Marquês de Pombal. He eventually was made an officer in the royal administration. In 1790 he was made a knight of the royal family, and in 1801 his works were published by the state.

Tolentino's literary importance is based on the wide range of social types depicted in his poetic vignettes and on the light he sheds on the writer's position in Portuguese society from Pombal's reign to the end of the century.

Tolkien \\'täl-,kēn, *commonly* 'tōl-, -,kin\\, J.R.R., *in full* John Ronald Reuel (b. Jan. 3, 1892, Bloemfontein, S.Af.—d. Sept. 2, 1973, Bournemouth, Hampshire, Eng.) English novelist and scholar who achieved fame with his richly inventive epic trilogy THE LORD OF THE RINGS (1954–56). By the mid-1960s this remarkable work had become a sociocultural phenomenon, especially in its appeal to young people.

Tolkien was educated at Oxford and served in World War I. He was a professor of Anglo-Saxon and of English language and literature at the University of Oxford. His scholarly works include an edition of *Sir Gawain and the Green Knight* (1925) with E.V. Gordon and *Beowulf: The Monsters and the Critics* (1936).

Tolkien began writing his trilogy as an undergraduate. While working on it, he wrote THE HOBBIT (1937), which served as an introduction to the series. Both *The Hobbit* and *The Lord of the Rings* are set in a mythical past; the latter work, which consists of *The Fellowship of the Ring*, *The Two Towers*, and *The Return of the King*, chronicles the struggle between various good and evil kingdoms for possession of a magic ring that can shift the balance of power in the world. The trilogy is remarkable for both its subtly delineated fantasy types (elves, dwarfs, hobbits) and its sustained imaginative storytelling. It is noteworthy as a rare, successful modern version of the heroic epic. A "prequel" of *The Lord of the Rings*, *The Silmarillion*, was published in 1977, as was an authorized biography by Humphrey Carpenter. *Unfinished Tales* was published in 1980.

Toller \\'tōl-ər\\, Ernst (b. Dec. 1, 1893, Samotschin, Ger. [now Szamocin, Poland]—d. May 22, 1939, New York, N.Y., U.S.) Dramatist, poet, and political activist who was a prominent exponent of Marxism and pacifism in Germany in the 1920s. His Expressionist plays embodied his spirit of social protest.

Toller was invalided (released for reasons of health) from the army after 13 months at the front during World War I. He then launched a peace movement in Heidelberg. To avoid arrest he fled to Munich, where he helped lead a strike of munitions workers and was finally arrested. In 1919 Toller, an Independent Socialist, was elected president of the Central Committee of the revolutionary Bavarian Soviet Republic. After its suppression he was sentenced to imprisonment for five years.

In confinement Toller wrote *Masse-Mensch* (1920; *Man and the Masses*), a play that brought him widespread fame. Books of lyrics added to his reputation. In 1933, immediately before the accession of Adolf Hitler, he immigrated to the United States. Also in that year he brought out his vivid autobiography, *Eine Jugend in Deutschland* (*I Was a German*).

In Hollywood Toller had a brief, unhappy stint as a scriptwriter. Impoverished, convinced that his plays were passé, and separated from his young wife, he hanged himself in his Manhattan hotel room.

Tolson \\'tōl-sən\\, Melvin (Beaunorus) (b. Feb 6, 1898, Moberly, Mo., U.S.—d. Aug. 29, 1966, Dallas, Tex.?) African-American poet who worked within the modernist tradition to explore African-American issues. His concern with poetic form and his abiding optimism set him apart from many of his contemporaries. Writing after the Harlem Renaissance but adhering to its ideals, Tolson was hopeful of a better political and economic future for African-Americans.

Tolson's first collection of poetry, *Rendezvous with America* (1944), includes one of his most popular works, "Dark Symphony," a poem in six "movements" that contrasts European-American history with African-American history. The success of this collection led to Tolson's appointment as poet laureate of Liberia in 1947. The last of his works to be published during his lifetime was *Harlem Gallery: Book I, The Curator* (1965), planned as the first of a projected five-volume history of African-Americans.

Tolson's most important work is the posthumous collection *A Gallery of Harlem Portraits* (1979). Modeled on Edgar Lee Masters' *Spoon River Anthology*, this collection is an epic portrait of a culturally and racially diverse community. The lives and emotions of its characters are portrayed in blues lyrics, dramatic monologues, and free verse.

Tolstoy \,təl-'stȯi, *Angl* ,tōl-'stȯi, 'tōl-,stȯi \, Aleksey Konstantinovich, Count (Graf) (b. Aug. 24 [Sept. 5, New Style], 1817, St. Petersburg, Russian Empire—d. Sept. 28 [Oct. 10], 1875, Krasny Rog, Russia)   Russian poet, novelist, and dramatist, an outstanding writer of humorous and satirical verse, serious poetry, and novels and dramas on historical themes.

A distant relative of Leo Tolstoy, Aleksey Konstantinovich held various honorary posts at court and spent much time in western Europe. In the 1850s, in collaboration with two cousins, Tolstoy began to publish comic verse under the joint pseudonym "Kozma Prutkov," who is portrayed as a clerk in the Ministry of Finance. Other satirical verses appeared under Tolstoy's own name. *Son statskogo sovetnika Popova* (1878; "The Dream of Councillor Popov") makes fun of Russian bureaucracy and political careerism.

Tolstoy had, together with his gift for humor, a deep interest in Russia's past, which he tended to contrast with the unsatisfactory and absurd present. Among his most popular historical works is *Knyaz Serebryany* (1862; *Prince Serebrenni*), a novel about 16th-century Russia inspired by the works of Sir Walter Scott and the German Romantics. Tolstoy's dramatic trilogy about the late 16th and early 17th centuries belongs to Russia's best historical dramatic writing. The three plays—*Smert Ioanna Groznogo* (1866; *The Death of Ivan the Terrible*); *Tsar Fyodor Ioannovich* (1868; *Czar Feodor Ioannovitch*); and *Tsar Boris* (1870)—are written in blank verse and inspired to some extent by William Shakespeare. *Tsar Fyodor*, the character study of a good man but a weak ruler, is probably his masterpiece. In the same historical vein he also wrote ballads based on Russian folk songs or idealized historical figures.

As a lyrical poet Tolstoy had a considerable range of style and feeling. In addition to many love and nature poems, he wrote a very effective paraphrase of St. John Damascene's prayer for the dead in *Ioann Damaskin* (1859). Much of his poetry was set to music by Peter Ilich Tchaikovsky, Modest Mussorgsky, Nicolay Rimsky-Korsakov, and others.

Tolstoy \,təl-'stȯi, *Angl* ,tōl-'stȯi, 'tōl-,stȯi \, Aleksey Nikolayevich, Count (Graf) (b. Dec. 29 [Jan. 10, 1882, New Style], 1883, Nikolayevsk, Russia—d. Feb. 23, 1945, Moscow, U.S.S.R.)   Novelist and short-story writer, a former nobleman and czarist Russian émigré who became a supporter of the Soviet regime and an honored artist of the Soviet Union.

Tolstoy studied engineering at St. Petersburg. His early novels *Chudaki* (1910; "The Eccentrics") and *Khromoy barin* (1912; "The Lame Squire") deal with gentry families in a spirit of comic realism reminiscent of Nikolay Gogol. After the Bolshevik Revolution Tolstoy supported the anti-Bolshevik White Army in the Russian Civil War and immigrated to western Europe, where he lived from 1919 to 1923. During this time he wrote one of his finest works, *Detstvo Nikity* (1921; *Nikita's Childhood*), a nostalgic, partly autobiographical study of a small boy's life.

In 1923 Tolstoy returned to Russia. He was a natural storyteller and many of his works are purely entertaining. He wrote science fiction (*Aelita*, 1922), children's stories, thrillers, stories of international intrigue, and more than 20 plays. His most extensive serious work is his trilogy of novels *Khozhdeniye po mukam*. Consisting of *Syostry* (1920–21; "Sisters"), *Vosemnadtsaty god* (1927–28; "The Year 1918"), and *Khmuroe utro* (1940–41; "A Gloomy Morning"), it is a study of the Russian intellectuals who converted to the Bolshevik cause during the Civil War. An English translation of the series appeared in 1946 under the title *The Road to Calvary*. For the trilogy and for his long unfinished historical novel *Pyotr I* (1929–45; *Peter the First*), he received Stalin prizes. During World War II Tolstoy was a prolific author of patriotic articles and also composed his two-part play *Ivan the Terrible* (1943), a dramatic apologia for the pathologically cruel czar. The play earned Tolstoy his third Stalin Prize.

Tolstoy or **Tolstoi** \,təl-'stȯi, *Angl* ,tōl-'stȯi, 'tōl-,stȯi \, Leo, *Russian in full* Lev Nikolayevich, Count (Graf) Tolstoy (b. Aug. 28 [Sept. 9, New Style], 1828, Yasnaya Polyana, Tula province, Russia—d. Nov. 7 [Nov. 20], 1910, Astapovo, Ryazan province)   Russian author, one of the world's greatest novelists.

Son of a noble family, Tolstoy was educated at Kazan University but, dissatisfied with the teaching, returned in 1847 to his estate at Yasnaya Polyana. Joining his brother Nikolay in the Caucasus in 1851, he entered the army a year later. He saw action in local engagements against hill tribesmen and at the siege of Sevastopol during the Crimean War. In 1857 he visited France, Switzerland, and Germany. On returning from his European travels he started a school for peasant children at Yasnaya. In 1862 he married Sonya (Sofya) Andreyevna Bers, a middle-class woman.

Tolstoy had already acquired a reputation as a brilliant short-story writer with his *Sevastopolskiye rasskazy* (1855–56; *Sevastopol Sketches*) and as a novelist with *Kazaki* (1863; *The Cossacks*). With the publication of *Voyna i mir* (1865–69; WAR AND PEACE) he was established as the preeminent Russian novelist. Set during the Napoleonic Wars, it examines the lives of a large cast of characters with the utmost objectivity. The structure of *War*

and Peace, with its flawless placement of complex characters in a turbulent historical setting, is regarded as one of the great technical achievements in the history of the Western novel.

Tolstoy's second major novel, ANNA KARENINA (1875–77), centers on a married woman whose life ends in tragedy and early death after she deserts her husband out of love for a younger man who has seduced her. It dwells upon the ultimate meaning and purpose of human existence.

In *Ispoved* (1884; *A Confession*) Tolstoy presents an account of the spiritual crisis he endured in his search for an answer to the meaning of life. He eventually turned to a form of Christian anarchism and devoted himself to social reform. In *Chto takoye iskusstvo* (1898; *What Is Art?*) Tolstoy developed an aesthetic system that gave art a religious and moral function. He wrote one more full-length novel, *Voskreseniye* (1899; *Resurrection*), and plays dealing with social problems, including *Vlast tmy* (performed 1888; *The Power of Darkness*). Torn between his urge to live as a wandering ascetic on the one hand and his responsibilities as a landed proprietor and successful artist on the other, Tolstoy left home one night and died a few days later at a remote railway junction.

Tomasi di Lampedusa \tō-'mä-sē-dē-läm-pä-'dü-sä\, Giuseppe (b. Dec. 23, 1896, Palermo, Sicily—d. July 23, 1957, Rome, Italy) Italian author, duke of Palma, and prince of Lampedusa, internationally renowned for his only novel, *Il gattopardo* (1958; THE LEOPARD).

Born into the Sicilian aristocracy, Lampedusa served as an artillery officer during World War I. After his capture and imprisonment in Hungary, he escaped and returned to Italy on foot. When a nervous breakdown precluded the diplomatic career to which he had aspired, he devoted himself to an intensely private life of intellectual activity, reading in several languages, discussing literature with a small group of friends, and writing for his own enjoyment.

In 1955 he began writing *Il gattopardo*, the novel that, although rejected by publishers during the author's lifetime, brought him world acclaim with its posthumous publication. The author's only other book, also published posthumously, is *Racconti* (1961; *Two Stories and a Memory*).

Tom Brown's School Days \'täm-'braún\ Novel by Thomas HUGHES, published in 1857. Tom Brown is an early, well-drawn character in what was to become a familiar genre in English fiction: a chronicle of life at an English boys' boarding school. In the novel, Tom, a student at Rugby School in the time of Thomas Arnold's headmastership, is harassed by the school bully, Flashman, but overcomes his trials. During his school career, Tom does very well academically and on the playing fields. A sequel, *Tom Brown at Oxford* (1861), was not as well received as its predecessor.

Tom Jones \'täm-'jōnz\ (*in full* The History of Tom Jones, a Foundling) Comic novel by Henry FIELDING, published in 1749.

Tom Jones, like its predecessor, *Joseph Andrews*, is constructed around a romance plot. Squire Allworthy suspects that the infant whom he adopts and names Tom Jones is the illegitimate child of his servant Jenny Jones. When Tom is a young man, he falls in love with Sophia Western, his beautiful and virtuous neighbor. In the end his true identity is revealed and he wins Sophia's hand, but numerous obstacles have to be overcome, and in the course of the action the various sets of characters pursue each other from one part of the country to another, giving Fielding an opportunity to paint an incomparably vivid picture of England in the mid-18th century.

Tomlinson \'täm-lin-sən\, Charles, *in full* Alfred Charles Tomlinson (b. Jan. 8, 1927, Stoke-upon-Trent, Staffordshire,

Eng.) English poet noted for his clear and sensitive perceptions of the world.

After graduating from the University of Cambridge, Tomlinson traveled extensively, especially in Italy and in the United States, where he was visiting professor at the University of New Mexico, Albuquerque, and professor in literature at Colgate University, Hamilton, N.Y. He later taught at the University of Bristol, Eng. Less concerned with people and emotions than with the physical world, his poetry has much in common with that of the American poets Wallace Stevens and Marianne Moore. His poems demonstrate great sensitivity to sound, and his writing expresses what he sees with rhythmic variety and subtlety. He often makes use of indirect quotation and intricate patterns of symbolism that can obscure his meaning.

Tomlinson's early published poetry includes *Relations and Contraries* (1951) and *The Necklace* (1955; rev. ed. 1966). He also wrote, among other volumes, *Seeing Is Believing* (1960) and *American Scenes* (1966), in which he captures the eeriness of ghost towns in the desert. Other collections include *The Poem as Initiation* (1968), *America West Southwest* (1969), and *Selected Poems 1951–1974* (1978). With Octavio Paz, Tomlinson wrote *Air Born/Hijos del aire* (1979), a bilingual English-Spanish volume for which each translated the other's poems. Later verse collections include *Collected Poems* (1985) and *Annunciations* (1989).

Tomlinson (in collaboration with Henry Gifford) made several verse translations of the poetry of César Vallejo. He also edited a number of critical works, and a series of lectures delivered at Cambridge was published as *Poetry and Metamorphosis*.

Tomlinson \'täm-lin-sən\, H.M., *in full* Henry Major (b. June 21, 1873, London, Eng.—d. Feb. 5, 1958, London) English novelist and essayist who wrote naturally and with feeling about London, the sea, the tropics, and the futility of war.

Tomlinson grew up in the East End docks and from early childhood developed a love for things connected with the sea. He became a journalist and fulfilled his ambition to travel. His first book, *The Sea and the Jungle* (1912), was written after he had made an expedition up the Amazon. Though ignored at the time, it remains his most representative book and is often reminiscent in style, as are his other works, of Henry David Thoreau and Ralph Waldo Emerson. Among his novels are *Gallions Reach* (1927), *All Our Yesterdays* (1930), and *Morning Light* (1946), but he is perhaps better known for his travel books: *London River* (1921), *The Turn of the Tide* (1945), and *Malay Waters* (1950).

Tom Sawyer \'täm-'sói-ər\ (*in full* The Adventures of Tom Sawyer) Novel by Mark TWAIN, published in 1876.

Tom Sawyer, an enduring narrative of youthful escapades, is perhaps Twain's best book for a juvenile audience. The setting is a small Mississippi River town in the 1830s, and the characters are the grownups and the children of the town. The book's nostalgic attitude and its wistful re-creation of pre-Civil War life are humorously spiced by its main character, Tom Sawyer. Rather than the preternaturally "model boy" of Sunday-school stories, Tom is mischievous and irresponsible but goodhearted.

Although Thomas Bailey Aldrich's *Story of a Bad Boy* was published seven years before it, *Tom Sawyer* and *Huckleberry Finn* changed the course of American writing and gave the first deeply felt vision of boyhood in juvenile literature.

To Nhu Pseudonym of NGUYEN DU.

Tonio Kröger \'tō-nē-ō-'krœg-ər\ Novella by Thomas MANN, originally published in German in 1903. The partially autobiographical work explores the problem of the artist who, in his devotion to his craft, confronts the antithesis of spirit and life.

From earliest childhood Tonio Kröger is aware of his separation from other people, in particular his two schoolmates Hans Hansen and Ingeborg Holm, who represent the bourgeois norm, symbolized by their blond good looks. Tonio longs to be accepted into their company, but his artistic nature will not permit him to fully join their ranks. As Tonio grows older his talent matures and he becomes a writer, but he still feels like a stranger and yearns to fit into the world. He continues to be preoccupied with the essential dichotomy between life and art, between personal happiness and the discipline that leads to great achievement. These themes are known to have obsessed Mann throughout his career, and Tonio Kröger is almost certainly a representation of the author's persona.

Tono-Bungay \'tō-nō-'bəŋ-gā\   Novel by H.G. WELLS, serialized in the *English Review* and published in book form in New York in 1908. Considered one of his most successful attempts at a social novel in the vein of Charles Dickens and William Makepeace Thackeray, Wells' tale is a panoramic view of an unravelling society. It is narrated by young George Ponderevo, who leaves college to help his Uncle Edward market Tono-Bungay, a worthless medicine. The medicine becomes a huge commercial success, causing George to reflect on the sickness at the heart of a society that lets itself be so easily duped. He begins to search for a new order to replace the old one, a quest that leads him to dangerous aeronautical experiments. At the end of the novel, George sails down the Thames to the open sea, toward the hopeful new world that awaits him.

Tonson \'tän-sən\, Jacob (b. 1656?—d. April 2, 1736, Ledbury, Eng.)   London bookseller and publisher.

Tonson set up as a bookseller and publisher in 1677. In 1679 he bought and published John Dryden's *Troilus and Cressida* and from that time was closely associated with Dryden, publishing most of his works. He also published William Congreve's *The Double-Dealer*, Sir John Vanbrugh's *The Faithful Friend* and *The Confederacy*, and the pastorals of Alexander Pope, thus justifying William Wycherley's description of him as "gentleman usher to the Muses." He bought also the valuable rights to John Milton's *Paradise Lost*, half in 1683 and half in 1690. This was his first profitable venture in poetry. In 1712 he became joint publisher with Samuel Buckley of Joseph Addison's and Richard Steele's *The Spectator* and in the following year published Addison's *Cato*. He was the original secretary and a prominent member of the Kit-Cat Club, a club of playgoers and dramatists.

Toomer \'tū-mər\, Jean (b. Dec. 26, 1894, Washington, D.C., U.S.—d. March 30, 1967)   African-American poet and novelist who was associated with the Harlem Renaissance.

After attending the University of Wisconsin and the City College of New York, Toomer taught briefly and then turned to lecturing and writing. CANE (1923; reprinted 1967), considered his best work, is an experimental novel, made up of poems, short stories, and a play, which depicts the experience of being black in America. Toomer also wrote extensively for *The Dial* and other little magazines and was the author of several experimental plays. In 1926 he attended the Gurdjieff Institute in France, dedicated to the expansion of consciousness and meditation, and upon his return led Gurdjieff groups in Harlem (N.Y.) and Chicago in the late 1920s and early 1930s. He began a similar institution in Portage, Wis., in 1931. Although he influenced other black writers, only after his death was he recognized as a writer of note, primarily for *Cane*.

Topelius \tö-'pā-lē-əs\, Zacharias (b. Jan. 14, 1818, Kuddnäs, Russian Finland—d. March 12, 1898, Helsinki)   The father of the Finnish historical novel. His works, written in Swedish, are classics of Finland's national literature.

Topelius published five collections of lyrics, but he is best known for *Fältskärns berättelser* (1853–67; *The King's Ring and the Surgeon's Stories*), a romanticized account of Swedish-Finnish history during the 17th and 18th centuries. In later years he wrote stories based on Finnish folktales and fairy tales for children. All his works have been translated into Finnish.

topographical poetry   Verse genre characterized by the description of a particular landscape. A subgenre, the prospect poem, details the view from a height. The form was established by John Denham in 1642 with the publication of his poem *Cooper's Hill*. Topographical poems were at their peak of popularity in the 17th and 18th centuries, though there are examples from the early 19th century, including several poems by George Crabbe, as well as by such modern writers as John Betjeman and Ted Hughes.

topos \'tō-,päs, 'tä-\ *plural* topoi \-,pöi \ [Greek *tópos,* short for *koinòs tópos,* literally, common place]   A conventional literary or rhetorical theme such as the quest or the family.

Topsy \'täp-sē\   Fictional character, a black slave child in UNCLE TOM'S CABIN by Harriet Beecher Stowe.

Torah \'tōr-ə, tö-'rä \   In Judaism, in the broadest sense the substance of divine revelation to the Jewish people: God's revealed teaching. The meaning of "Torah" is often restricted to signify the first five books of the Old Testament, also called the Law or the Pentateuch. These are the books traditionally ascribed to Moses, the recipient of the original revelation from God on Mt. Sinai. Jewish, Roman Catholic, Eastern Orthodox, and Protestant canons all agree on their order: Genesis, Exodus, Leviticus, Numbers, and Deuteronomy.

The written Torah, in the restricted sense of the Pentateuch, is preserved in all Jewish synagogues on handwritten parchment scrolls that reside inside the ark of the Law. They are handled with special reverence. Readings from the Torah (Pentateuch) form an important part of Jewish liturgical services.

The term Torah is also used to designate the entire Hebrew Bible. Since for some Jews the laws and customs passed down through oral traditions are part and parcel of God's revelation to Moses and constitute the "oral Torah," Torah is also understood to include both the Oral Law and the Written Law.

Rabbinic commentaries on and interpretations of both Oral and Written Law have been viewed by some as extensions of sacred oral tradition, thus broadening still further the meaning of Torah to designate the entire body of Jewish laws, customs, and ceremonies. *See also* TANAKH.

Torga \'tör-gä\, Miguel, *pseudonym of* Adolfo Correia da Rocha \kör-'rā-ə-dē-'rösh-ə\ (b. Aug. 12, 1907, São Martinho de Anta, Port.—d. Jan. 17, 1995, Coimbra)   Portuguese poet and diarist known for his forceful and highly individual literary style.

Torga began writing while a medical student at the University of Coimbra. After graduation he continued to write and publish while maintaining an active medical practice. In 1927 he helped found the literary magazine *Presença* ("Presence"), and his first volume of verse, *Ansiedade* ("Anxiety"), was published in 1928. Much of Torga's work—which includes novels, plays, and short stories as well as the poems and his *Diário*, 12 vol. (1941–77; "Diary"), for which he is best known—has as its subject the search for certainties in a changing world. His diary reveals a deeply religious man with a robust faith in the primitive virtues of humanity. Notable among his works of fiction are the autobiographical novel *A criação do mundo* (1935; "The Creation of the World") and stories in *Contos da montanha* (1941; *Tales from the Mountain*), and *Novos contos da montanha* (1944; "New Tales from the Mountain").

tornada \tȯr-'näd-ə\ [Old Provençal, from feminine of *tornat,* past participle of *tornar* to turn, return]   The refrain of a Provençal poem.

Torquemada \tȯr-kā-'mä-thä\ Fictional character, a miserly pawnbroker and usurer in a series of novels by Benito PÉREZ GALDÓS. The series includes *Torquemada en la hoguera* (1889; "Torquemada at the Stake"), *Torquemada en la cruz* (1893; "Torquemada on the Cross"), *Torquemada en el purgatorio* (1894; "Torquemada in Purgatory"), and *Torquemada y San Pedro* (1895; "Torquemada and Saint Peter"). These satirical novels, based on the tradition of *cuadros de costumbres* ("literary sketches on manners and society"), were part of Pérez Galdós' larger body of work, the *novelas españolas contemporáneas,* which offer a panoramic vision of 19th-century Spain.

The pawnbroker's ambitions bring him position and fortune but not happiness. Although his protagonist is generally portrayed as despicable, Pérez Galdós manages to convey sympathy for this man who has compromised his soul and, in spite of his deceitful nature, is still capable of suffering deeply. The depth of the author's psychological portrait of Torquemada has earned him comparisons to Flaubert and Balzac.

Torrents of Spring   Novella by Ivan TURGENEV, published in Russian as *Veshniye vody* in 1872. The book has also been translated as *Spring Torrents* and *Spring Freshets.*

Cast as a reminiscence, the work concerns the reflections of the middle-aged and world-weary Sanin on his youthful romance with Gemma, a young Italian woman. Although she willingly broke off her engagement with another man and declared her love for him, Sanin was unexpectedly seduced by an older Russian woman and became captivated by her. He disgracefully broke off relations with Gemma to follow the manipulative Madame Polozov, but now, as an older and wiser man, wonders what he has missed. Feeling he has wasted his life, he discovers that Gemma is happily married and living in America, and at the end he contemplates moving there himself.

Torres Bodet \'tȯr-rās-bō-'det\, Jaime (b. April 17, 1902, Mexico City, Mex.—d. May 13, 1974, Mexico City) Mexican poet, novelist, educator, and statesman.

Torres Bodet's first collection of verse, *Fervor* (1918), revealed Modernista tendencies. The theme of loneliness, his search for identity, and a longing for death expressed in these poems all foreshadowed the poet's later work. *El corazón delirante* (1922; "The Delirious Heart") and *Canciones* (1922; "Songs") include highly lyrical love poems. In *La casa* (1923; "The House"), Torres Bodet examined the constant renewal of life in poems that reflect the influence of the Spanish poet Juan Ramón Jiménez. *Los días* (1923; "The Days") stresses the poet's anguish at a dehumanized environment. He employed Japanese verse forms in *Biombo* (1925; "The Folding Screen"). In addition to these poetic efforts, Torres Bodet was the first editor (1928–31) of *Contemporáneos,* a cultural and literary magazine.

Destierro (1930; "Exile"), written shortly after he became secretary to the Mexican legation in Madrid, reflects the poet's attempt, often expressed in complex surrealist imagery, to rebel against a mechanized, hostile, and unfamiliar environment. *Cripta* (1937; "Crypt"), considered to include his most important poems, deals with basic human concerns and reveals in compact, powerful language a preoccupation with time, solitude, and the absurdity of life.

In *Fronteras* (1954; "Frontiers") and *Sin tregua* (1957; "Without Truce"), the mature poet dwelt on the isolation prevalent in modern society. Torres Bodet also wrote much prose, including highly acclaimed essays on Marcel Proust and Leo Tolstoy; in 1966 he was awarded the National Prize for Literature for a study of Rubén Darío. Of the six novels published

between 1927 and 1937, *Sombras* (1937; "Shadows") is considered his best. His poetry was collected in the two-volume *Obra poética* (1967; "Poetical Work"). *Selected Poems of Jaime Torres Bodet* (1964) is a bilingual edition.

Torres Naharro \'tȯr-rās-nä-'är-rō\, Bartolomé de (b. 1484?, La Torre de Miguel Sesmero, Spain—d. 1525?, Seville?) Playwright and theorist, the most important Spanish dramatist before Lope de Vega, and the first playwright to create realistic Spanish characters.

Torres Naharro's collected works, entitled *Propalladia* (1517; "The First Things of Pallas"), was prefaced with a discourse on dramatic art that distinguished between tragedy and comedy, a distinction that was lost in later Spanish drama. He classified his own plays as *comedias "a noticia,"* treating "things noted and seen in true reality," and *comedias "a fantasia,"* concerning those "fantastic or feigned, which though not true have the color of truth"; this classification implicitly grants equal validity to observation and imagination and thus represents a major advance in literary theory. His *Comedia tinellaria* ("Comedy of the Kitchen") is a brilliant satire on the corruption and intrigue in the palace of a Roman cardinal; the *Comedia Himenea,* based on the novel *La Celestina,* has been said to constitute the greatest single step toward the creation of the Golden Age comedia.

Torres Villarroel \'tȯr-rās-,bēl-yär-rō-'äl\, Diego de (b. *c.* 1693, Salamanca, Spain—d. June 19, 1770, Salamanca) Mathematician and writer, famous in his own time as the great maker of almanacs that delighted the Spanish public, now remembered for his *Vida* (1743; "Life"), picaresque memoirs that are among the best sources of information on life in 18th-century Spain.

Torres Villarroel ran away from home and school and began a remarkable career as a dancer, musician, bullfighter, poet, lockpicker, and seller of patent medicines. Returning home to Salamanca, he discovered a book on solid geometry and became a changed man. Mathematics was still viewed by some as related to magic, and for Torres Villarroel it had the power of a secret science. In 1721 he wrote his first almanac, and in 1726 he was made professor of mathematics at the University of Salamanca. He spent his final years in holy orders, spending his money on philanthropic enterprises.

The *Vida,* modeled on the work of the great Spanish poet Francisco Gómez de Quevedo, is written in the style of the 17th-century picaresque novels. The true adventures of a man imbued with enormous energy and panache, the book is full of fascinating details about Spanish life and customs. A fertile lyric poet as well, Torres Villarroel left 15 volumes of works.

Tortilla Flat   Novel by John STEINBECK, published in 1935. The first of his novels to be set in the Monterey peninsula of California, this episodic, humorous tale of the adventures of a group of pleasure-loving Mexican-Americans contains some of Steinbeck's most interesting characters. The men drink, steal, chase women, make music, and dance until they are eventually undone by a climactic fire.

Tosefta \tō-'sef-tə\ ("Supplement," or "Addition") A collection of oral traditions related to Jewish oral law. In form and content the Tosefta is quite similar to the Mishna, the first authoritative codification of such laws, which was given its final form early in the 3rd century AD by Judah ha-Nasi.

Though experts are not quite sure why two separate collections came into existence, it is probable that the Tosefta was meant to complement the Mishna by preserving certain traditions, proofs, examples, and explanations of oral law that came to light during the years that scholars spent researching the material.

To the Finland Station \'fin-lənd\ Critical and historical study of European writers and theorists of socialism who set the stage for the Russian Revolution of 1917, by Edmund WILSON. It was published in book form in 1940 although much of the material had previously appeared in *The New Republic*.

The work discusses European socialism, anarchism, and various theories of revolution from their origins to their implementation. It presents ideas and writings of political theorists representing all aspects of socialist, anarchist, and what would later be known as communist thought, among them Jules Michelet, Henri de Saint-Simon, Robert Owen, Mikhail Bakunin, Anatole France, Karl Marx, Friedrich Engels, Leon Trotsky, and Vladimir Ilich Lenin—who arrived at Petrograd's (St. Petersburg's) Finland Station in 1917 to lead the Bolshevik revolution.

To the Lighthouse Novel by Virginia WOOLF, published in 1927. The work is one of her most successful and accessible experiments in the stream-of-consciousness style.

The three sections of the book take place between 1910 and 1920 and revolve around various members of the Ramsay family during visits to their summer residence on the Isle of Skye in Scotland. A central motif of the novel is the conflict between the feminine and masculine principles at work in the universe.

With her emotional, poetical frame of mind, Mrs. Ramsay represents the female principle, while Mr. Ramsay, a self-centered philosopher, expresses the male principle in his rational point of view. Both are flawed by their limited perspectives. A painter and friend of the family, Lily Briscoe, is Woolf's vision of the androgynous artist who personifies the ideal blending of male and female qualities. Her successful completion of a painting that she has been working on since the beginning of the novel is symbolic of this unification.

Totius Pseudonym of Jakob Daniel DU TOIT.

Touchstone \'təch-,stōn\ Fictional character, a cynical court jester who comments on human foibles in William Shakespeare's play AS YOU LIKE IT.

toughie or **toughy** \'təf-ē\ *plural* toughies. A piece of writing characteristic of HARD-BOILED FICTION.

Tourneur \'tər-nər\, Cyril (b. *c.* 1575—d. Feb. 28, 1626, Kinsale, County Cork, Ire.) English dramatist whose reputation rests upon *The Atheist's Tragedie* and *The Revenger's Tragedie*, both in verse rich in macabre imagery.

Little is known about Tourneur's life except that his early years were devoted to literature and that after about 1613 he served the government in some capacity.

In addition to a satire, *The Transformed Metamorphosis* (1600), Tourneur is known for two dramas: *The Atheist's Tragedie: or, The Honest Man's Revenge* (1611) and *The Revenger's Tragedie*. The latter appeared anonymously in 1607; in 1656 the bookseller Edward Archer entered it as by Tourneur on his list. This attribution is not decisive, and internal evidence of authorship is conflicting; many attribute it to Thomas Middleton. The two plays differ in their attitude toward private revenge; and *The Revenger's Tragedie*, although earlier that *The Atheist's Tragedie*, is more mature in its structure and somber brilliance.

Tournier \tür-'nyā\, Michel (b. Dec. 19, 1924, Paris, Fr.) French novelist whose manipulation of mythology and old stories has often been called subversive insofar as it challenges the conventional assumptions of middle-class society.

Tournier's first novel, *Vendredi; ou, les limbes du Pacifique* (1967; *Friday; or, the Other Island*), is a revisionist *Robinson Crusoe*, with Crusoe as a colonialist who fails to coerce Friday into accepting his version of the world. Perhaps his most fa-

mous and controversial work, *Le Roi des aulnes* (1970; *The Erl-King*; U.S. title, *The Ogre*), is about a French prisoner in Germany who assists the Nazis during World War II by searching for boys for a Nazi military camp. *Les Météores* (1975; *Gemini*) involves the desperate measures one man takes to be reunited with his identical twin brother, who has broken away from their obsessive, singular world. Tournier's two subsequent novels recast ancient stories with a modern twist: *Gaspard, Melchior & Balthazar* (1980; *The Four Wise Men*) relates the story of the visit of the Magi to the infant Christ, and *Gilles & Jeanne* (1983) is about Joan of Arc's companion, a perverted murderer. Tournier's later novels include *La Goutte d'or* (1985; *The Golden Droplet*) and *Le Médianoche amoureux* (1989; *The Midnight Love Feast*).

Tower of Babel \'bāb-əl, 'bab-\ In biblical literature, structure built in the land of Shinar (Babylonia) some time after the Deluge. The story of its construction, given in Genesis 11:1–9, appears to be an attempt to explain the existence of diverse human languages. According to Genesis, the Babylonians wanted to make a name for themselves by building a mighty city and a tower "with its top in the heavens." God disrupted the work by so confusing the language of the workers that they could no longer understand one another. The city was never completed, and the people were dispersed over the face of the earth.

Town, The Novel by William FAULKNER, published in 1957. It is the second work in the Snopes family trilogy, which includes *The Hamlet* (1940) and *The Mansion* (1959). A dramatization of Faulkner's vision of the disintegration of the South after the Civil War, *The Town* relates through three narrators of varying reliability the story of Flem Snopes' rise to prominence in the fictional Yoknapatawpha County. Flem's coldly calculated vengeance on his wife, Eula, and her lover culminates in Eula's suicide and Flem's rise to power in Jefferson, the county seat. Because Flem longs for respect as well as money, he turns against the clan of shiftless Snopes cousins who have followed him to town and forces them to leave Jefferson. In his hunger for social validation, he denies his own origins, and the book ends with a hint that the cousins' revenge will follow.

Town, The Novel by Conrad RICHTER, published in 1950. The third book in a trilogy that includes *The Trees* and *The Fields*, *The Town* was awarded the Pulitzer Prize for fiction in 1951. The three books were published in a single volume as *The Awakening Land* in 1966.

The trilogy, which is set in the Ohio River valley in the late 18th- through mid-19th century, offers a realistic portrayal of frontier life as it chronicles the development of the area from wilderness. The changing landscape provides the background for the story of Sayward Luckett Wheeler, who embodies the strength and perseverance of the pioneer spirit. The books follow her life as she matures from a young girl to a wife and mother of many children to an old woman.

Toynbee \'tòin-bē\, Philip, *in full* Theodore Philip Toynbee (b. June 25, 1916, Oxford, Eng.—d. June 15, 1981, St. Briavels, near Lydney, Gloucestershire) English writer and editor best known for novels that experiment with time and symbolic elements.

Toynbee was the son of historian Arnold Joseph Toynbee and grandson of classical scholar Gilbert Murray. He was educated at Rugby School and the University of Oxford. In 1938-39 he edited a newspaper, the *Birmingham Town Crier*. After service in World War II he worked in publishing and from 1950 was on the editorial staff of the newspaper *The Observer*.

Of Toynbee's experimental, subjective novels, the best known are *The Savage Days* (1937), *The Barricades* (1943), and *Tea with Mrs. Goodman* (1947). Later he wrote novels in verse, notably the *Pantaloon* series: *Pantaloon or the Valediction* (1961), *Two Brothers* (1964), *A Learned City* (1966), and *Views from a Lake* (1968).

Trachinian Women \tra-'kin-ē-ən\ (*Greek* Trachiniai) Drama of domestic tragedy by SOPHOCLES, performed sometime after 458 BC. The play centers on the efforts of Deianeira to win back the wandering affections of her husband, Heracles, who—although he is away on one of his heroic missions—has sent back his latest concubine, Iole, to live with his wife at their home in Trachis. Deianeira uses a love charm on Heracles, learning too late that it is poisonous, and she kills herself when she learns of the agony she has caused her husband.

Trackers (*Greek* Ichneutai) Satyr play by SOPHOCLES. It is based on two stories about the miraculous early deeds of the god Hermes: that the infant, growing to maturity in a few days, stole cattle from Apollo, baffling discovery by reversing the animals' hoof marks, and that he invented the lyre by fitting strings to a tortoise shell. The title characters are the chorus of satyrs, who are looking for the cattle; they are amusingly dumbfounded at the sound of the new instrument Hermes has invented. Only four hundred lines of the play survive, enough to reveal that it is a genial, uncomplicated travesty of the tragic manner.

tract \'trakt\ [Middle English *tracte,* modification of Latin *tractatus* action of handling, treatment, discussion] A pamphlet or leaflet of political or religious propaganda.

tractarian \trak-'tar-ē-ən\ One who writes, prints, or distributes tracts.

Tractatus Coislinianus \trak-'tā-təs-,kȯis-,lin-ē-'ā-nəs\ Statement of a Greek theory of comedy found in a 10th-century manuscript (published 1839) in the collection of Henri Charles du Cambout de Coislin. The treatment of comedy displays marked Aristotelian influence, even to the point of paralleling the model offered in the *Poetics.* The *Tractatus* is assumed to be either a version of a lost Aristotelian original or a statement of the Aristotelian tradition. Accordingly, as Aristotle stated that tragedy should bring about a catharsis through the arousal of feelings of "terror and pity," comedy must bring about a catharsis through the use of laughter and pleasure. Comic plots include ludicrous mishaps, deception, unexpected developments, and clumsy dances. Characters include impostors, self-deprecators, and buffoons. While the language of comedy should be realistic, it may attain added comic force through the use of puns, dialect, and word malformations.

tradición \,trä-dē-'syȯn\ [Spanish, literally, tradition] In Latin-American literature, genre of light, short prose sketch in which a historical incident is related in an imaginative and literary style. An evocation of the South American past, the *tradición* may be set in the pre-colonial era, the age of discovery and conquest, the pre-revolutionary era of romance and political intrigue, or the time of the struggle for self-determination in the 19th century. Stimulated by the Romanticists' search for national roots, the Peruvian writer Ricardo Palma created the genre; his *Tradiciones peruanas* (first series, 1872), an entertaining six-volume collection of anecdotes from five centuries of South American history, contains some of the most representative examples of the form.

tradition \tra-'dish-ən\ A set of literary or artistic rules or conventions (as of theme, style, symbolism) that is handed down from generation to generation. A writer can be said to be working in a certain tradition, such as the Scottish ballad tradition. Similarly, a specific work or type of writing can belong to a tradition; heroic poetry, for example, is said to be part of the oral tradition. In a more general sense tradition can be seen as the whole of the inherited past or as a continuum into which every writer fits at some point.

tragedy \'traj-ə-dē\ [Greek *tragōidía,* a derivative of *tragōidós* singer in a tragic chorus, performer in tragedy, from *trágos* he-goat + *-ōidos,* a derivative of *aeídein* to sing] A drama of a serious and dignified character that typically describes the development of a conflict between the protagonist and a superior force (such as destiny, circumstance, or society) and reaches a sorrowful or disastrous conclusion. By extension the term may be applied to other literary forms, such as the novel. *Compare* COMEDY.

The origins of the tragic form are Greek, as are those of the term itself, meaning "goat-song" and possibly referring originally to the sacrifice of a goat in the vegetation and fertility rituals associated with the god Dionysus, in whose honor tragedies were performed. The materials of Greek tragedy were drawn from familiar myths of gods and mortals found in the works of Homer and elsewhere; this familiarity focused the dramatic interest on the presentation of the changing awareness and responses of those involved, rather than on plot. Major events tended to happen offstage and to be reported and commented on rather than presented directly, as in Sophocles' *Oedipus the King.* Prompted by will or circumstance, fatal ignorance, or binding obligation, the tragic protagonist is confronted in the end by an inexorable fate that ensures an unhappy outcome. In his *Poetics,* Aristotle stated that tragedy should imitate actions that arouse pity and fear and bring about the proper purgation (catharsis) of those emotions.

Roman adaptations of Greek tragedy, particularly by Seneca, tended toward violent sensation and declamatory rhetoric, qualities that were taken up in Elizabethan tragic drama. For Chaucer and the European Middle Ages, tragedy came to mean simply the edifying account of how a great man's fortunes altered from initial prosperity to final wretchedness. Elizabethan England produced a specific type known as the revenge tragedy. Christopher Marlowe's *Tamburlaine the Great* and *Doctor Faustus* introduced the overambitious hero, awe-inspiring in his ambition and magnificent even in his fall. Shakespearean tragedy incorporates elements of the drama of the time but goes further in presenting an imaginative vision of evil.

Seventeenth-century French classical tragedy, unlike Elizabethan tragedy, self-consciously returned both to the legendary subject matter and to the highly conventionalized unities of time, place, and action—as represented in the theater of Jean Racine and Pierre Corneille.

A new kind of tragedy emerged in the 19th century in the plays of Henrik Ibsen, August Strindberg, and Anton Chekhov. Written in prose rather than formal verse, they treated painful contemporary situations. Tragedy in its fullest dimensions is rarely conspicuous in 20th-century drama, though the American playwright Eugene O'Neill wrote many undeniably successful tragedies. Tragedy did assume prominence in the novel, particularly through such novelists as Fyodor Dostoyevsky, Thomas Hardy, Joseph Conrad, and William Faulkner. *See also* DOMESTIC TRAGEDY; REVENGE TRAGEDY; SENECAN TRAGEDY.

Tragic Death of the Sons of Usnech, The \'ush-nʸək\, *Irish* Oidheadh Chloinne Uisneach. In the Ulster cycle of Irish heroic myths, the love story of the ill-fated Deirdre and Noísi.

First composed in the 8th or 9th century, the story was revised and combined in the 15th century with *The Tragic Death of the Children of Tuireann* (*Oidheadh Chloinne Tuireann*) and *The Tragic Death of the Children of Lir* (*Oidheadh Chloinne Lir*) into *The Three Sorrows of Storytelling* (*Trí Truaighe na Scéalaigheachta*). The older version, preserved in *The Book of*

Leinster (c. 1160) as *Longes mac n-Uislenn* (*The Exile of the Sons of Uislin*), is more starkly tragic, less polished, and less romantic than the later version.

The story opens with a Druid's prediction at Deirdre's birth that many men will die on her account. Raised in seclusion, she grows to be a woman of astonishing beauty. King Conor (Conchobar mac Nessa) falls in love with her, but she falls in love with Noísi (Middle Irish: Noísiu), a son of Usnech. Deirdre and Noísi elope and flee to Scotland with Noísi's two brothers, where they live idyllically until they are lured back to Ireland by the treacherous Conor. The sons of Usnech are slain, causing revolt and bloodshed in Ulster. To avoid falling into Conor's hands, Deirdre takes her own life. The later version of the story omits the first half and expands the tragic ending, in which Deirdre lives for a year with Conor, never smiling, before killing herself.

The story was immensely popular in Ireland and Scotland and survived to the 20th century in Scottish oral tradition. Its literary influence continued into the early 20th century, when the Anglo-Irish writers, notably William Butler Yeats and John Millington Synge, dramatized the theme.

tragic flaw   A flaw that brings about the protagonist's downfall. *See* HAMARTIA.

Tragic Muse, The   Novel by Henry JAMES, published serially in *The Atlantic Monthly* from 1889 to 1890 and in book form in 1890. This study of the conflict between the demands of art and those of the "real world" is set in London and Paris in the 1880s. Nicholas Dormer, an Englishman, gives up a career in Parliament and marriage to a beautiful, wealthy woman to become a portrait painter. He is encouraged by his actress friend Miriam Rooth, the "tragic muse" of the title. Although by the end of the novel Nicholas has still not achieved his goal, James implies that he made the right decision in choosing to live at a higher level of consciousness, whether or not he achieves material success. Written when James himself was suffering setbacks in his career as a playwright, the novel reflects many of the author's concerns about personal sacrifice for the sake of art.

tragicomedy \ˌtraj-i-ˈkäm-ə-dē\   A literary genre consisting of dramas that combine tragic and comic elements with the tragic predominating. Also, a drama of this genre.

When coined by the Roman dramatist Plautus in the 2nd century BC, the Latin word *tragicocomoedia* denoted a play in which gods and mortals, masters and slaves reverse the roles traditionally assigned to them, gods and heroes acting in comic burlesque and slaves adopting tragic dignity. This startling innovation may be seen in Plautus' *Amphitruo*.

In the Renaissance, tragicomedy became a genre of play that mixed tragic elements into drama that was mainly comic. The Italian writer Battista Guarini defined tragicomedy as having most of tragedy's elements—*e.g.*, a certain gravity of diction, the depiction of important public events, and the arousal of compassion—but never carrying the action to tragedy's conclusion, and judiciously including such comic elements as low-born characters, laughter, and jests. Central to this kind of tragicomedy were danger, reversal, and a happy ending. John Fletcher provides a good example of the genre in *The Faithful Shepherdess* (1609?), itself a reworking of Guarini's *Il pastor fido*, first published in 1590. Nineteenth-century Romantic writers—such as Georg Büchner and Victor Hugo—espoused William Shakespeare's use of tragicomedy in the belief that his plays closely mirrored nature.

With the advent of realism later in the 19th century, the comic interludes of tragicomedy highlighted the ironic counterpoints inherent in a play, making the tragedy seem even more devastating. Such works as Henrik Ibsen's *Ghosts* (1881) and *The Wild Duck* (1884) reflect this technique. Modern tragicomedy is sometimes used synonymously with absurdist drama, which suggests that laughter is the only response left to people who are faced with the tragic emptiness and meaninglessness of existence. Examples of this modern type of tragicomedy are Samuel Beckett's *Endgame* (1958) and Harold Pinter's *The Dumb Waiter* (1960).

Traherne \trə-ˈhərn\, Thomas (b. 1637, Hereford, Eng.—d. 1674, Teddington)   Last of the mystical poets of the Anglican clergy, which included most notably George Herbert and Henry Vaughan.

Traherne was educated at the University of Oxford and ordained in 1660. The only work by Traherne published during his lifetime was *Roman Forgeries* (1673). His *Christian Ethicks* appeared posthumously in 1675, and his *Thanksgivings* in rhythmical prose were published anonymously as *A Serious and Patheticall Contemplation of the Mercies of God* in 1699. The greater part of Traherne's poetry and his prose meditations remained unknown until their recovery in modern times. The chance discovery in 1896 in a London street bookstall of the manuscripts of Traherne's *Poetical Works* (published 1903) and his *Centuries of Meditations* (published 1908) created a literary sensation. The manuscript of *Poems of Felicity* was subsequently found in the British Museum and published in 1910; other manuscripts were discovered later.

As a poet Traherne possessed originality of thought and intensity of feeling, but he lacked discipline in his use of meter and rhyme. Indeed, his poetry is overshadowed by the prose work *Centuries of Meditations*, in which he instructs an acquaintance in his personal philosophy of "felicity," an outlook based on Traherne's Christian training, his retention of vivid impressions of the wonder and joy of childhood, and his desire to regain that sense in a mature form.

Traill \ˈtrāl\, Catherine Parr, *original surname* Strickland \ˈstrik-lənd\ (b. Jan. 9, 1802, London, Eng.—d. Aug. 29, 1899, Lakefield, Ont., Can.)   Nature writer who, in richly detailed descriptions of frontier life, was one of the first to praise the beauties of the Canadian landscape.

A writer of children's books in England, Traill immigrated to the wilderness of Upper Canada (now Ontario) in 1832. *The Backwoods of Canada* (1836), which was based on a series of letters written to her mother in England, was the forerunner of the Canadian nature essay. This book was followed by *The Female Emigrant's Guide, and Hints on Canadian Housekeeping* (1854) and *The Canadian Settlers' Guide* (1860), entertaining and practical narratives of frontier life. Also a naturalist, Traill wrote *Canadian Wild Flowers* (1869), *Studies of Plant Life in Canada* (1885), and *Pearls and Pebbles* (1895), on birds and animals. She introduced the animal story for children into Canadian literature with the publication of *Afar in the Forest* (1869).

Trakl \ˈträk-əl\, Georg (b. Feb. 3, 1887, Salzburg, Austria—d. Nov. 3, 1914, Kraków, Galicia, Austria-Hungary [now in Poland])   Expressionist poet whose personal and wartime torments made him Austria's foremost elegist of decay and death. He influenced Germanic poets after both world wars.

Trakl trained as a pharmacist at the University of Vienna. The patronage of a periodical publisher and of the philosopher Ludwig Wittgenstein enabled Trakl to devote himself to poetry; he brought out his first volume in 1913. The following year he became a lieutenant in the army medical corps and, in Galicia, was placed in charge of 90 serious casualties whose agonies he, as a mere dispensing chemist, could hardly relieve. He became suicidal and was sent to a military hospital at Kraków for observation. There he died of an overdose of cocaine.

Throughout his intense lyrics, lamentation for the present is infused with longing for the golden spirit of a pastoral past and for rebirth, and in haunting imagery he sings of "the heart against a lonely sky."

Transcendentalism \,tran-sen-'den-tə-,liz-əm\ Movement of writers and philosophers in 19th-century New England who were loosely bound together by adherence to an idealistic system of thought based on a belief in the essential unity of all creation, the innate goodness of humankind, and the supremacy of insight over logic and experience for the revelation of the deepest truths. The writings of the Transcendentalists represent the first flowering of the American artistic genius and introduced the American Renaissance in literature.

Sources to which the New England Transcendentalists turned in their search for a liberating philosophy were German transcendentalism, especially as it was refracted by Samuel Taylor Coleridge and Thomas Carlyle; Platonism and Neoplatonism; the Indian and Chinese scriptures; and the writings of such mystics as Emanuel Swedenborg and Jakob Böhme. Part of the Romantic movement, New England Transcendentalism originated in the area around Concord, Mass., and from 1830 to 1855 represented a battle between the younger and older generations and the emergence of a new national culture based on native materials. It attracted such diverse and highly individualistic figures as Ralph Waldo Emerson, Henry David Thoreau, Margaret Fuller, Orestes Brownson, Elizabeth Palmer Peabody, and James Freeman Clarke, as well as George Ripley, Bronson Alcott, the younger W.E. Channing, and W.H. Channing. Emerson and Fuller founded *The Dial* (1840–44), the prototypal "little magazine" wherein some of the best writings by minor Transcendentalists appeared.

transformer \trans-'fôr-mər\ A mythical figure in the legends of preliterate cultures noted for bringing about the present order of the world by transforming its previous order.

transition \tran-'sish-ən, -'zish-\ English-language literary magazine founded in Paris in 1927 by Eugene and Maria JOLAS and Elliot Paul. The magazine, published monthly at first and later quarterly, was dedicated to the original, the revolutionary, and the experimental. Its editors were interested in exploring the role of the unconscious as a source of creation. They published works that used new forms of language to express the world of the imagination, including sections of James Joyce's *Finnegans Wake*. Other authors published in *transition* included Gertrude Stein, Archibald MacLeish, H.D. (Hilda Doolittle), Allen Tate, Samuel Beckett, William Carlos Williams, Ernest Hemingway, Hart Crane, Dylan Thomas, and Franz Kafka. The magazine was an immediate literary success and was published from 1927 to 1930 and 1932 to 1938.

transpose \tranz-'pōz, trans-\ To render into another language, style, or manner of expression, or to translate.

transprose \tranz-'prōz, trans-\ *archaic* To change from verse into prose.

Tranströmer \'trän-,strœm-ər\, Tomas (b. April 15, 1931, Stockholm, Swed.) Swedish lyrical poet noted for his resonant and strangely suggestive imagery.

Tranströmer earned a degree in psychology at the University of Stockholm. From the mid-1960s he divided his time between his writing and his work as a psychologist.

In his first published collection, *17 dikter* (1954; "Seventeen Poems"), Tranströmer displayed a bold, Surrealistic use of metaphor while also experimenting with free and blank verse and sapphic stanzas. The poetry in *Hemligheter på vägen* (1958; "Secrets on the Way") and *Klanger och spår* (1966; *Echoes and Traces*) is composed in a more personal style, with plainer dic-

tion and exceptionally strong rhythmic qualities evident in his free verse. His celebrations of the Baltic coast around Stockholm in such works as *Östersjöar* (1974; *Baltics*) rely on a deceptively plain imagery, which through daring leaps of association opens strange and uncanny perspectives. Later collections include *Sanningsbarriären* (1978; *The Truth Barrier*), *Det vilda torget* (1983; *The Wild Marketplace*), and *Collected Poems* (1987).

Tranströmer's direct language and powerful images made him the most widely translated Scandinavian poet in the English-speaking world in the later 20th century.

transumptive \tran-'zəmp-tiv, -'səmp-\ [Latin *transumptivus* (used by Quintilian to translate Greek *metálēpsis* use of one word for another), a derivative of *transumere* to take from one position to another] Of, relating to, or characterized by the transfer or substitution of terms. This is equivalent to a metaphorical use of a word, in which one word is used in place of another to suggest an analogy between the two.

transverse \tranz-'vərs, trans-\ To turn or render prose into verse.

travel literature Nonfiction prose form that depends largely on the wit, powers of observation, and character of the traveler for its success. In past centuries the traveler tended to be an adventurer or a connoisseur of art, landscapes, or strange customs who may also have been a writer of merit.

The roots of travel literature can be found in the works of ancient Greek geographers, such as Strabo and Pausanias of the 1st and 2nd centuries AD. These were followed by such literary accounts of foreign places as *I milione* (*Travels*) of Marco Polo and the *Riḥlah* (*Travels*) of the 14th-century Ibn Baṭṭūṭah.

The form was particularly suited to the Romantic age. Not only were the Romantics alive to picturesqueness and quaintness but also they were great appreciators of nature. Classics of the genre include *Pismo russkogo puteshestvennika* (1791–92; *Letters of a Russian Traveler, 1789–1790*) by Nikolay Karamzin, *Peterburg* (1913–14) by Andrey Bely, and *Das Reisetagebuch eines Philosophen* (1919; *Travel Diary of a Philosopher*) by Hermann Keyserling. An offshoot of the accounts of travelers has been a growing industry of such travel guidebooks as Michelin, Baedeker's, Fodor's, and the Blue Guide.

Travels (*Arabic Riḥlah, Arabic in full* Tuḥfat al-nuẓẓār fī gharā'ib al-amṣār wa-'ajā'ib al-asfār ["The Gift of the Beholders on the Peculiarities of the Regions and the Marvels of Journeys"]) Classic travel account by IBN BAṬṬŪṬAH of his journeys through virtually all Muslim countries and many adjacent lands. The narrative was dictated in 1353 to Ibn Juzayy, who embellished the simple prose of Ibn Baṭṭūṭah with an ornate style and fragments of poetry.

Travels is an important document shedding light on many aspects of the social, cultural, and political history of a great part of the Muslim world. A curious observer interested in the ways of life in various countries, Ibn Baṭṭūṭah describes his experiences with a human approach rarely encountered in official historiography. His accounts of his travels in Asia Minor, East and West Africa, the Maldives, and India form a major source for the histories of these areas, whereas the parts dealing with the Arab and Persian Middle East are valuable for their wealth of detail on aspects of social and cultural life.

Travels Through France and Italy \'frans, 'fräns . . . 'it-ə-lē\ Work by Tobias SMOLLETT, published in 1766.

The breakdown of Smollett's health and the death of his 15-year-old daughter in 1763 precipitated a year-long journey through France and Italy. The book takes the form of a series of letters in which he describes the social life, history, and physical setting of each city he encounters. Sick, irascible, severely prejudiced, and intolerant of pretense, Smollett argues with his hosts and fellow travelers and holds French and Italian art, politics, and Roman Catholic religion in contempt.

Travels With a Donkey in the Cévennes \sā-'ven\ Journal by Robert Louis STEVENSON, published in 1879. Recovering on the French Riviera from a respiratory ailment, Stevenson spent 12 days walking 120 miles from the town of Le Monastier to St. Jean du Gard in the Cévennes mountain range, accompanied only by his donkey, Modestine. A classic of travel literature, *Travels* gives a humorous account of Modestine's idiosyncrasies and the mutual adjustments of author and donkey. The account is enlivened by Stevenson's fresh, vivid descriptions of the landscape and its inhabitants, his detailed record of his travel preparations, and his depiction of his visit to a Trappist monastery.

Traven \'trāv-ən\, B., *also called* Berick Traven Torsvan \'tôrs-vän\ *or* Ret Marut \'mä-rût\ (b. March 5, 1890?, Chicago, Ill., U.S.?—d. March 27, 1969, Mexico City, Mex.) Novelist noted as a writer of adventure stories and as a chronicler of rural life in Mexico. A recluse, Traven refused personal data to publishers; hence many theories have arisen as to his parentage, his nationality, and his general identity. Most of his books were originally written in German and were first published in Germany.

In 1987 Karl S. Guthke published *B. Traven: Biographie eines Rätsels* (*B. Traven: The Life Behind the Legends*), based in part on Traven's personal papers and conversations with his widow, Rosa Elena Luján. Luján revealed that Traven had been the Bavarian revolutionary Ret Marut; Marut itself, however, was an assumed name. Guthke's conclusion was that Traven himself did not know who his parents were. Other scholars have argued that Traven was Otto Feige (b. 1882, East Prussia); still others believe he was the illegitimate son of Kaiser Wilhelm II.

Traven settled in Mexico in the 1920s; several years later his first book came out in Berlin. He published *Das Totenschiff* (1926; *The Death Ship*) and *Der Schatz der Sierra Madre* (1927; *The Treasure of the Sierra Madre*) before producing his most important work, a series of novels that trace the lives of impoverished Indians in southern Mexico just before the start of the Mexican Revolution. Among the books in this series are *Der Karren* (1931; *The Carreta*) and *Die Rebellion der Gehenkten* (1936; *The Rebellion of the Hanged*).

Traven's works are harsh and filled with depictions of danger and cruelty, but his lean, direct prose has a hypnotic immediacy and his narratives and themes are clear and compelling.

Travers \'trav-ərz\, P.L., *in full* Pamela Lyndon (b. Aug. 9, 1906, Queensland, Australia) Australian-born English writer known for her *Mary Poppins* books, which have been translated into more than 20 languages and were the basis for the successful motion picture *Mary Poppins* (1964).

Travers went to England at the age of 19 and became a dancer, an actress, and a journalist. The poet Æ (George William Russell) published some of her poems in *The Irish Statesman*. Her first book, *Mary Poppins* (1934), about a magical, good-hearted, and exceedingly efficient nanny, was an immediate success; many sequels followed. From 1965 to 1971 she served as writer-in-residence at several American colleges. Her later works include several travel books and a collection of essays, *What the Bee Knows: Reflections on Myth, Symbol and Story* (1989). *See also* Mary POPPINS.

travesty \'trav-əs-tē\ In literature, the treatment of a noble and dignified subject in an inappropriately light manner. Travesty is a crude form of burlesque in which the original subject matter is changed little but is transformed into something ridiculous through incongruous language and style. An early example of travesty is the humorous treatment of the Pyramus and Thisbe legend in William Shakespeare's play *A Midsummer Night's Dream*. After 1660, travesty became a popular literary device in England as seen in John Phillips' *Don Quixote*, a vulgar mockery of the original work, and Charles Cotton's travesty of Virgil, *Scarronides: or, Virgile Travestie*, an imitation of the French *Virgile travesty* by Paul Scarron. (The use of the word *travesti*—literally, "dressed in disguise"—in the title of Scarron's work gave rise to the English word, first as an adjective.) Later the French developed the *féeries folies*, a musical burlesque that travestied fairy tales. *Compare* BURLESQUE; PARODY.

Treasure Island Classic adventure novel by Robert Louis STEVENSON, serialized in the magazine *Young Folks* from October 1881 to January 1882 under the title "The Sea Cook, or Treasure Island" and published in book form in 1883.

Traditionally considered a boys' coming-of-age story, this book relates young Jim Hawkins' adventures with a group of pirates who are trying to locate an abandoned treasure trove. The leader of the pirates, Long John Silver, is initially hostile to Jim but eventually befriends him.

treatise \'trē-tis, -tiz\ [Middle English *tretis*, from Anglo-French *tretiz*, a derivative of Old French *traitier* to treat] A systematic exposition or argument in writing including a methodical discussion of the facts and principles involved and conclusions reached. The subjects of treatises are often religious, political, philosophical, or scientific. Examples include Geoffrey Chaucer's *Treatise on the Astrolabe*, John Milton's *A Treatise of Civil Power in Ecclesiastical Causes*, and David Hume's *A Treatise of Human Nature*.

treatment \'trēt-mənt\ The manner in which something, such as a subject, is handled in literature, especially in terms of style.

trecento \trā-'chen-tō\ [Italian, literally, three hundred, short for *mille trecento* the year 1300] The 14th century; specifically, the 14th-century period in Italian literature and art.

Trediakovsky \trʸi-dyi-'kôf-skʸē\, Vasily Kirillovich (b. Feb. 22 [March 5, New Style], 1703, Astrakhan, Russia—d. Aug. 6 [Aug. 17], 1768, St. Petersburg) Russian literary theoretician and poet whose writings contributed to the classical foundations of Russian literature.

Trediakovsky studied at the Sorbonne in Paris from 1727 to 1730. Soon after his return to Russia he became acting secretary of the Academy of Sciences and de facto court poet. In 1735 Trediakovsky published *Novy i kratky sposob k slozheniyu rossiyskikh stikhov* ("A New and Concise Method for the Composition of Russian Verses"), in an effort to reform Russian prosody. Trediakovsky advocated the use of accentual rather than syllabic versification, arguing that the syllabic system then in use was a Western form that had been imposed on Russian poetry and that it was unsuited for Slavic verse. He also wrote the first study of the phonetic structure of the Russian language, *Razgovor ob ortografii* (1748; "A Conversation on Orthography") and he continued his advocacy of poetic reform in *O drevnem, srednem i novom stikhotvorenii rossiyskom* (1752; "On Ancient, Middle, and New Russian Poetry"). Trediakovsky was a prolific translator of classical authors, medieval philosophers, and French literature. In 1759 he was dismissed from the Academy. His last major work was *Tilemakhida* (1766), a free rendering in Russian hexameters of François de Fénelon's *Les Aventures de Télémaque*.

Treece \'trēs\, Henry (b. 1911/12, Wednesbury, Staffordshire, Eng.—d. June 10, 1966, Barton-upon-Humber, Lincolnshire) English poet and historical novelist whose ability to bring the ancient world to life in fiction makes his work especially appealing to young readers. As a poet he—together with J.F. Hendry—was a founder of the New Apocalypse movement, a reaction against the politically oriented, machine-age literature and realist poetry of the 1930s.

Treece wrote drama, short stories, and radio scripts for the BBC, as well as poetry. His most important collections of verse are *The Black Seasons* (1945) and *The Exiles* (1952). His fiction consisted largely of historical novels both for adult and for juvenile readers. Those for adults include *Red Queen, White Queen* (1958) and *The Green Man* (1966). His best-known children's books include *Legions of the Eagle* (1954), *The Eagles Have Flown* (1954), *The Children's Crusade* (1958), and *The Bronze Sword* (1965).

tree nymph   In Greek mythology, a nymph who is associated with trees; specifically, a HAMADRYAD.

Trees, The   Novel by Conrad Richter, published in 1940. It was the first novel in a trilogy published collectively as *The Awakening Land*. The other novels in the trilogy are *The Fields* and THE TOWN.

Trelawny \tri-'lô-nē\, Edward John (b. Nov. 13, 1792, London, Eng.—d. Aug. 13, 1881, Sompting, Sussex)   English author and adventurer, a friend of Percy Bysshe Shelley and Lord Byron, whom he portrayed brilliantly in his books.

Trelawny was a handsome, dashing, and quixotic personality from an old and famous Cornish family. At the age of 13 he entered the Royal Navy, and he was discharged in 1812. He wrote of his experiences as a midshipman in *Adventures of a Younger Son* (1831).

In 1822 Trelawny met Shelley and Byron in Pisa, and in 1823 he accompanied Byron to Greece to aid in the struggle for Greek independence. Later Trelawny would vividly recount his friendships with the two great poets in his *Recollections of the Last Days of Shelley and Byron* (1858; revised as *Records of Shelley, Byron and the Author*, 1878). From 1833 to 1835 he traveled in the United States.

Tremain \tri-'mān\, Rose (b. Aug. 2, 1943, London, Eng.)   British novelist whose books often dramatize a moment of truth in the lives of lonely outsiders.

Tremain worked for the British Printing Corporation and wrote several nonfiction works about women's suffrage before publishing her first novel, *Sadler's Birthday* (1976). This book, presenting the reminiscences of a fictional elderly butler who lives alone in the house he has inherited from his former employers, established her reputation as a chronicler of despair and loneliness. In *Letter to Sister Benedicta* (1978), a middle-aged woman whose family life is unbearable writes to her former teacher, a nun, looking for solace. *The Cupboard* (1981) explores the relationship between an older, neglected writer and the journalist sent to interview her.

Tremain's subsequent books moved away from the intense focus on one or two characters and toward less restricted settings. Her novel *Restoration* (1989) offers a many-layered historical narrative about the interconnected lives of a group of characters during the reign of Charles II. *Sacred Country* (1992) relates the picaresque adventures of Mary Ward, who is convinced from the age of six that she is meant to be a boy and spends three decades trying to achieve this goal.

Trent, Nell   *see* LITTLE NELL.

Trevor \'trev-ər\, William, *original name* William Trevor Cox \'käks\ (b. May 24, 1928, Mitchelstown, County Cork, Ire.)   Irish writer who is noted for his wry and often macabre short stories and novels.

Trevor was educated at Trinity College, Dublin, and worked as a teacher, sculptor, and advertising copywriter before moving to Devon, England, to write full-time. His second novel, *The Old Boys* (1964), recounts the story of an "old boys" committee, whose rapidly aging members plot and plan against each other, driven by searing memories of the insults and rivalries of their school days. This was followed by the novels *The Boarding-House* (1965), *Mrs. Eckdorf in O'Neill's Hotel* (1969), *Elizabeth Alone* (1973), *The Children of Dynmouth* (1976), *Other People's Worlds* (1980), *Fools of Fortune* (1983), *The Silence in the Garden* (1988), and *Reading Turgenev* and *My House in Umbria*, published together as *Two Lives* (1991). He also wrote several highly acclaimed collections of short stories. *Stories of William Trevor* appeared in 1983 and *The Collected Stories* in 1992. Influenced by the writings of James Joyce and Charles Dickens, Trevor possessed a keen skill for characterization and irony. His works focus for the most part on the psychology of eccentrics and outcasts.

triad \'trī-,ad, -əd\   A union or group of three, especially of three closely related persons, beings, or things. In literature the term triad refers specifically to a gnomic literature in medieval Wales and Ireland consisting of short aphorisms grouped in threes. They are written in prose marked by rhythm and assonance and apply to various subjects (such as history, laws, or morals). The term also applies to the structure of a classical ode, which consists of a group of three strophes called the strophe, antistrophe, and epode.

Trial, The   Novel by Franz KAFKA, originally published posthumously in 1925 as *Der Prozess*. The chapters were organized and the book published by Kafka's friend and literary executor Max Brod despite Kafka's request that Brod destroy the manuscript. One of Kafka's major works, *The Trial*, is often considered to be an imaginative anticipation of totalitarianism.

In what may be Kafka's most pessimistic novel, the protagonist, Joseph K., a conscientious bank official, is awakened one morning by bailiffs who arrest him on charges that are never made clear. The complete ambiguity of the law, Joseph K.'s nagging sense of free-floating guilt, and his submission to the absurd stipulations and bureaucratic snares of the court all make for a compelling story. Resigned to his fate, though still questioning the situation, Joseph K. does not protest his execution at the end of the book.

Tribe of Ben \'ben\, *also called* Sons of Ben.   A group of young poets and dramatists of the 17th century who were admirers of Ben Jonson, especially his use of classical forms and style. It included many of the Cavalier poets, among them Robert Herrick, Thomas Carew, Sir John Suckling, Richard Lovelace, and Thomas Randolph.

tribrach \'trī-,brak\ [Greek *tríbrachys* having three short syllables, from *tri-* three + *brachýs* short]   In classical prosody, a metrical foot of three short syllables. This was usually a resolved iamb ($\cup$ —) or trochee (— $\cup$), in which the long syllable was broken down into two short ones. The accent was on the first two syllables if the foot was originally a trochee or on the last two if it was originally an iamb.

trickster \'trik-stər\   A mischievous supernatural being much given to capricious acts of sly deception, found in the folklore of various preliterate peoples, often functioning as a culture hero, or one that symbolizes the ideal of a people.

Oral traditions worldwide contain tales of deceit, magic, and violence perpetrated by tricksters. Usually grouped in cycles, these tales feature a trickster-hero who within a single society may be regarded as both creator god and innocent fool, evil destroyer and childlike prankster.

The characteristic trickster tale is in the form of a picaresque adventure: the trickster is "going along"; he encounters a situation to which he responds by knavery or stupidity; he meets a violent or ludicrous end; and then the next incident is told. Frequently, he is accompanied by an animal companion, who either serves as a stooge or tricks the trickster.

Until relatively recently the collection, examination, and comparison of trickster tales and trickster figures concentrated upon those of North American Indian groups. Coyote, the trickster of tales from California, the Southwest, and the plateau region, is perhaps the most widely known. In the Pacific Northwest, the trickster is the Raven, Mink, or Blue Jay, each of which is also viewed as a transformer figure, responsible for bringing the ordered world out of chaos, and a culture hero, credited with transmitting the skills of survival, such as fire making, from gods to mortals.

In East, Central, and Southern Africa and in the western Sudan, the trickster is the hare; in West Africa, the spider (in Ghana, Liberia, Sierra Leone) or the tortoise (among the Igbo and Yoruba people of Nigeria). Many African peoples also have tales about human tricksters (*e.g.*, the stories of Yo in Benin). In most African cycles the trickster is an underdog figure, smaller in stature and strength than his opponents (thus gaining the audience's sympathy) but much cleverer and always well in control of the situation. He is ruthless, greedy, and a glutton and often outwits his opponent through a calculating suaveness combined with sheer lack of scruples. African slaves brought trickster tales with them to the New World. In the United States the adventures of the trickster hare Brer Rabbit were first given literary form in the late 19th century by Joel Chandler Harris in a series of tales told by a wise old black character called Uncle Remus.

The existence of trickster figures appears to be universal. The Japanese trickster fox Kitsune is renowned for his mischievous metamorphic abilities. He is regarded in Shintō lore as the messenger who ensures that farmers pay their offerings to the rice god. Buddhist stories, however, cast the fox as an evil agent of possession. Numerous tales of Oceania recount the creative exploits of the trickster Maui, or Maui-tiki-tiki, such as his fishing out the land from the sea. Norse mythology recounts the deeds of the trickster Loki. The cunning and resourceful hero Odysseus also has elements of the trickster personality. *See also* COYOTE; RAVEN CYCLE.

Triclinius \trī-'klin-ē-əs\, Demetrius, *Italian* Demetrio Triclinio (fl. 14th century AD, Byzantium)   Byzantine scholar who edited the works of the ancient Greek poets, mainly the tragedians, with metrical and exegetical scholia (annotations).

Triclinius' editions incorporated notes by other scholars as well as scholia from earlier traditions. He was the first Byzantine scholar to examine closely the metrical structure of the lyrics of Attic plays; but, striving to apply the rules of the 2nd-century AD Greek scholar Hephaestion and misled by his own unsatisfactory views of Greek prosody, he often tampered with the text. His text of Aeschylus survives, probably in his own handwriting, as does his transcript of Hesiod; his text of Sophocles was not superseded until the 18th century. Triclinius also annotated works by Euripides, Pindar, Aristophanes, and Theocritus.

tricolon \trī-'kō-lən\ [Greek *tríkōlon,* neuter of *tríkōlos* having three members]   In classical prosody, a recurrent unit of verse composed of three cola, or a group of three metrical sequences that each constitute a single metrical phrase of not more than about 12 syllables.

tricorn \'trī-,kȯrn\ [Latin *tricornis* having three horns]   An imaginary three-horned beast.

trident \'trīd-ənt\ [Latin *trident-, tridens* three-pronged spear, from *tri-* three + *dent-, dens* tooth]   In classical mythology, a three-pronged scepter or spear that was one of the attributes or symbols of the sea god Poseidon (Neptune).

Trilby \'tril-bē\   Novel by George DU MAURIER, published in 1894. The novel tells the story of Trilby O'Ferrall, an artist's model in Paris, who falls under the spell of the compelling Svengali, a musician who trains her voice through hypnosis and turns her into a singing star. The pair travel throughout Europe on successful concert tours, Trilby as La Svengali, the famous singer, and Svengali as the accompanying orchestra conductor. When Svengali falls ill and dies, the spell is broken and Trilby loses her voice. The story of Trilby's total subjugation to Svengali has passed into the realm of popular mythology.

Trilling \'tril-iŋ\, Lionel (b. July 4, 1905, New York, N.Y., U.S.—d. Nov. 5, 1975, New York City)   American literary critic and teacher whose criticism was informed by psychological, sociological, and philosophical methods and insights.

Educated at Columbia University (Ph.D., 1938), Trilling taught briefly at the University of Wisconsin and at Hunter College in New York City before joining the faculty of Columbia in 1931.

Trilling's critical writings include studies of Matthew Arnold (1939) and E.M. Forster (1943), as well as collections of literary essays: *The Liberal Imagination* (1950), *Beyond Culture: Essays on Literature and Learning* (1965), and *Sincerity and Authenticity* and *Mind in the Modern World* (both 1972). He also wrote *Freud and the Crisis of Our Culture* (1955) and *The Life and Work of Sigmund Freud* (1962). His single novel, *The Middle of the Journey* (1947), concerns the moral and political developments of the liberal mind in America in the 1930s and '40s.

trilogy \'tril-ə-jē\ [Greek *trilogía,* from *tri-* three + *lógos* word, speech, account]   A series of three dramas or literary or musical compositions that, although each is in one sense complete, have a close mutual relation and form one theme or develop aspects of one basic concept. The term originally referred specifically to a group of three tragedies written by one author for competition. This trilogy constituted the traditional set of plays presented in Athens by a number of competitors at the 5th-century-BC drama festivals known as the Great Dionysia. One of the first authors to present such a trilogy was Aeschylus, whose ORESTEIA is the only surviving example from that time. Modern examples of trilogies include J.R.R. Tolkien's *The Lord of the Rings* and Robertson Davies' *Deptford Trilogy*.

trimeter \'trim-ə-tər\   In prosody, a line of three feet (as in modern English verse) or of three metra, or pairs of feet (as in classical iambic verse). A line of pure iambic trimeter is scanned ∪ — ∪ — ∪ — ∪ — ∪ — ∪ —.

Trindade Coelho \trin-'dä-jē-'kwel-yū\, José Francisco (b. June 18, 1861, Mogadouro, Trás-os-Montes e Alto Douro, Port.—d. June 9, 1908, Lisbon)   Portuguese writer who is best known for his regional short stories, most of which are set in remote, rural northern Portugal.

Trindade Coelho graduated in 1885 from the University of Coimbra and subsequently entered the government legal service. He was a magistrate in Lisbon from 1890 until his retirement in 1907. He committed suicide the following year. His fame rests upon a single volume of stories, *Os meus amores* (1891; "My Loves"). Though of unequal merit, these sketchily plotted vignettes of village life sympathetically explore a simple, primitive world in language so natural as to seem artless. Tragic elements are suggested with the stoical restraint of folklore, and realism is often tempered by lyrical descriptions of natural scenery and evocations of the author's childhood experiences.

triolet \'trī-ə-let, ,trē-ə-'lā\ [Middle French, literally, clover leaf, a derivative of *trefle* clover] A medieval French verse form of eight lines in which the first is repeated as the fourth and seventh and the second as the eighth and the rhyme scheme is *ABaAabAB* (the capital letters indicate the lines that are repeated). The name triolet is taken from the three repetitions of the first line. The great art of the triolet consists in using the refrain line with naturalness and ease and in each repetition slightly altering its meaning, or at least its relation to the rest of the poem. The triolet is preserved in many modern European literatures, especially for light and humorous verse.

Probably invented in the 13th century, the triolet was cultivated as a serious form by such medieval French poets as Adenet le Roi and Jean Froissart. Although its popularity declined in the 15th and 16th centuries, the triolet was revived in the 17th century by Jean de La Fontaine and in the 19th century by Alphonse Daudet and Théodore de Banville.

The earliest triolets in English are those of a devotional nature composed in 1651 by Patrick Cary, a Benedictine monk at Douai, France. Reintroduced into English by Robert Bridges in 1873, the triolet has since been cultivated widely in that language, most successfully by Austin Dobson.

In Germany, anthologies of triolets were published at Halberstadt in 1795 and at Braunschweig in 1796. Frederich Rassmann made collections in 1815 and 1817 in which he distinguished three species of triolet: the legitimate form; the loose triolet, which only approximately abides by the rules as to number of rhymes and lines; and single-strophe poems, which more or less accidentally approach the true triolet in character. The true form was employed particularly by German Romantic poets of the early 19th century.

triplet \'trip-lət\ A unit of three lines of verse. A triplet can be an independent stanza or a group of lines of the same pattern within a stanza of a different pattern, such as three lines that rhyme within a stanza of rhyming couplets. In the latter case, triplets are often set off by a marginal bracket, as in the following lines from John Dryden's *Absalom and Achitophel*:

> His eldest hope, with every grace adorned,
> By me (so Heaven will have it) always mourned,
> And always honored, snatched in manhood's prime
> by unequal fates, and Providence's crime:
> Yet not before the goal of honor won,
> All parts fulfilled of subject and of son;
> Swift was the race, but short the time to run.

Compare TERCET.

tripody \'trip-ə-dē\ [Greek *tripodía,* a derivative of *trípous* three-footed, from *tri-* three + *pod-, poús* foot] In classical prosody, a unit or group of three feet. It is used as a measure of trochaic or iambic verse. Trochaic tripody acatalectic is scanned $-\cup-\cup-\cup$, and iambic tripody acatalectic is scanned $\cup-\cup-\cup-$.

triseme \'trī-,sēm\ [Greek *trísēmos* having three time units (in music or prosody), from *tri-* three + *sêma* mark, sign] In classical prosody, a foot of three morae (the equivalent of three short syllables) found in answer to one long syllable. It may also be a two- or three-syllable foot ($-\cup\cup$ or $-\cup-$ or $--$) that appears associated with and equivalent to the iambic metron $\cup-\cup-$.

Trissino \trēs-'sē-nō\, Gian Giorgio (b. July 8, 1478, Vicenza, Republic of Venice [Italy]—d. Dec. 8, 1550, Rome) Literary theorist, philologist, dramatist, and poet who was an important innovator in Italian drama.

Trissino's most significant cultural contribution was the Hellenization of Italian drama, achieved almost solely through his masterpiece, the blank-verse tragedy *Sofonisba* (written 1514–15; published 1524; first performed 1562), based on a story about the Carthaginian wars by the Roman historian Livy and employing the dramatic techniques of Sophocles and Euripides. *Sofonisba*, though not an interesting drama in itself, incorporated profound innovations in content, structure, and form. The sources were Greek and were devoid of religious or educational purpose; choruses were used to indicate divisions in the action; the unities of time and action were studiously followed; and *versi sciolti* ("blank verse") was employed extensively for the first time in Italian drama. Trissino wrote a later verse comedy, *I simillimi* (1548), based on the Roman playwright Plautus' *Menaechmi.* He also composed the first Italian odes modeled on the irregular lyric verse of the Greek poet Pindar and the first Italian versions of the Horatian ode. His *La poetica* (1529) used Italian poetry to exemplify his theory.

Tristan \'tris-tən\ Novella by Thomas MANN, published in 1903 as one of six novellas in *Tristan: Sechs Novellen.*

The plot concerns three individuals, Anton Klöterjahn, a prosperous, unimaginative businessman from northern Germany, his tubercular wife, Gabriele, and Detlev Spinell, an effete, eccentric writer. Deposited by Anton at an Alpine sanatorium, Gabriele becomes the object of Detlev's exaggerated devotion. Claiming that Anton's attention to business is crushing Gabriele's artistic spirit, Detlev encourages her to tap her long-suppressed talent as a pianist. Gabriele performs for him a selection from the opera *Tristan und Isolde* by Richard Wagner that leaves them both in rapture. As a result of her reawakened emotions, Gabriele has a relapse.

An ironic reworking of the medieval legend of Tristan and Isolde, the novella presents Detlev, the Tristan figure, as both unheroic and overwrought. Anton, on the other hand, prevails (as his healthy infant son demonstrates) despite his burgherlike self-satisfaction.

Tristan L'Hermite \trēs-täⁿ-ler-'mēt\, *pseudonym of* François L'Hermite (b. *c.* 1601, La Marche, Fr.—d. Sept. 7, 1655, Paris) Dramatist and poet who was one of the creators of French classical drama. Long overshadowed by his contemporary Pierre Corneille, he was rediscovered in the late 19th century, and his work continues to excite scholarly and critical interest.

At the age of 11, Tristan was attached as page to the Marquise of Verneuil but was exiled to England after a duel. This incident and his vagabond life in the years that followed are described in his autobiographical novel *Le Page disgracié* (1643). Tristan remained in England until his pardon by Louis XIII in 1621. Like all French classical dramatists, he explored Greco-Roman or Oriental and biblical themes: *Marianne* (1637), his best-known tragedy, is the story of Herod's jealousy. His other major dramas were *La Mort de Sénèque* (1645; "The Death of Seneca"), *La Mort de Chrispe* (1645; "The Death of Chrispus"), and *Osman* (1656). Tristan was the first to write French tragedies in which love is central to the action.

Tristan and Isolde \'tris-tən . . . ē-'zōl-də, i-'sōld, i-'sōl-də\, Tristan *also called* Tristram *or* Tristrem \'tris-trəm\; Isolde *also called* Iseult \i-'sūlt, -'zūlt\, Isolt \i-'sōlt, -'zōlt\, *or* Yseult \i-'sūlt, -'zūlt\ Principal characters of a famous medieval love-romance, based on a Celtic legend (itself based on an actual Pictish king). Though the archetypal poem from which all extant forms of the legend are derived has not been preserved, a comparison of early versions yields an idea of its content.

The central plot of the archetype must have been roughly as follows: The young Tristan ventures to Ireland to ask the hand of the princess Isolde for his uncle, King Mark of Cornwall, and, having slain a dragon that is devastating the country, succeeds in his mission. On the homeward journey Tristan and

Isolde, by misadventure, drink the love potion prepared by the queen for her daughter and King Mark. Henceforward, the two are bound to each other by an imperishable love that dares all dangers and makes light of hardships but does not destroy their loyalty to the king.

They continue to meet in secret after they return, but eventually they are separated, in some versions because King Mark discovers them and Tristan is forced to flee, in others because the love potion wears off after several years and they separate voluntarily. In most versions of the story, Tristan then goes to Brittany, where he marries Isolde of the White Hands. Tristan's death is the last major event of the romance, though some versions do not mention it at all. In one, he is recalled to Cornwall, where Mark kills him, but in the most well-known adaptation, after Tristan is wounded by a poisoned weapon, he sends for the original Isolde, who alone can heal him. If she agrees to come, the returning ship is to have a white sail; if she refuses, a black. His jealous wife discovers this code, and, when she sees Isolde's ship approaching, she tells Tristan that she sees a black sail. Turning his face to the wall, Tristan dies, and Isolde, arriving too late to save her love, yields up her life in a final embrace.

The archetypal poem seems to have been a grim and violent work containing episodes of a coarse and even farcical character. Two adaptations made in the late 12th century, one by the Norman poet Béroul, preserved something of its barbarity. About 1170, however, the Anglo-Norman poet Thomas, who was probably associated with the court of Henry II of England, produced an adaptation in which the harshness of the archetype was considerably softened. A mellifluous German version of Thomas' adaptation by Gottfried von Strassburg is considered the jewel of medieval German poetry. Short episodic poems telling of Tristan's surreptitious visits to Isolde at King Mark's court appeared in the late 12th century. Of these, the most important are two versions of the *Folie Tristan*, in which Tristan is disguised as a fool, and the *Luite Tristan*, in which he appears as a minstrel. The popularity of prose versions of the Arthurian legend during the 13th century led to the Tristan story's also being embodied in a voluminous prose romance. In this, Tristan figured as the noblest of knights, and King Mark as a base villain, the whole being grafted onto Arthurian legend and bringing Tristan and King Arthur's knight Sir Lancelot into rivalry. This version, which recounts innumerable chivalric adventures of a conventional type, had superseded all other French versions by the end of the European Middle Ages, and it was in this form that Sir Thomas Malory knew the legend in the late 15th century, making it part of his *Le Morte Darthur*. A popular romance in English, *Sir Tristrem*, dates from about 1300 and is one of the first poems in the Middle English vernacular.

Renewed interest in the legend during the 19th century followed upon discovery of the old poems. Versions of the story can be found in works by Matthew Arnold, Alfred, Lord Tennyson, and Algernon Swinburne.

Tristram Shandy \'tris-trəm-'shan-dē\ (*in full* The Life and Opinions of Tristram Shandy, Gentleman) Experimental novel by Laurence STERNE, published in nine volumes from 1759 to 1767.

Narrated by Shandy, the story begins at the moment of his conception and diverts into endless digressions, interruptions, stories-within-stories, and other narrative devices. The focus shifts from the fortunes of the hero himself to the nature of his family, environment, and heredity, and the dealings within that family offer repeated images of human unrelatedness and disconnection. The narrator is isolated in his own privacy and doubts how much, if anything, he can know for certain even about himself. Sterne broke all the rules: events occur out of chronological order, anecdotes are often left unfinished, and

sometimes whole pages are filled with asterisks or dashes or are left entirely blank. Sterne is recognized as one of the most important forerunners of psychological fiction.

Sterne himself published volumes 1 and 2 at York late in 1759, but he sent half of the imprint to London to be sold. By March, when he went to London, *Tristram Shandy* was the rage, and he was famous. His London bookseller brought out a second edition and two more volumes of *Tristram Shandy*; thereafter, Sterne was his own publisher.

trithemimer \,trith-ə-'mim-ər\ [Greek *trítos* third + *-hēmimerēs* (as in *penthēmimerés* penthemimer)] In classical prosody, a group of three half-feet or a catalectic colon (a colon missing the final syllable) of a foot and a half. Iambic trithemimer scans ∪ – | ∪, trochaic trithemimer scans – ∪ | ∪, and dactylic trithemimer scans – ∪ ∪ | ⌣.

trithemimeral caesura \,trith-ə-'mim-ə-rəl\ *see* CAESURA.

Triton \'trīt-ən\ In Greek mythology, a merman, demigod of the sea; he was the son of the sea god, Poseidon, and his wife, Amphitrite. According to the Greek poet Hesiod, Triton dwelt with his parents in a golden palace in the depths of the sea. Sometimes he was not particularized but was one of many Tritons. He was represented as human down to his waist, with the tail of a fish. Triton's special attribute was a twisted seashell, on which he blew to calm or raise the waves.

trochaic \trō-'kā-ik\ In poetry, of, relating to, or consisting of trochees (feet consisting of a stressed followed by an unstressed syllable in modern poetry or a long followed by a short syllable in classical poetry).

trochee \'trō-kē\ [Greek *trochaîos,* short for *trochaîos poús,* literally, running foot] In prosody, a metrical foot consisting of one long syllable followed by one short syllable in classical verse. In English verse, a trochee is one stressed syllable followed by one unstressed syllable, as in the word

hap | py.

Trochaic meters were extensively used in ancient Greek and Latin tragedy and comedy in a form called trochaic catalectic tetrameter (seven and one half trochees), which was particularly favored by Plautus and Terence. Trochaic meters are not easily adapted to English verse. In long poems, such as Henry Wadsworth Longfellow's *The Song of Hiawatha*, their overall effect is monotonous. But they have been used with great effect in shorter poems, particularly by William Blake, as in his well-known poem "The Tyger":

Tyger! | Tyger! | burning | bright
In the | forests | of the | night

Trogus \'trō-gəs\, Pompeius (fl. late 1st century BC) Roman historian whose work is important for Hellenistic studies.

Trogus wrote a zoological work, *De animalibus*, quoted by the elder Pliny, and a history, *Historiae Philippicae*, in 44 books, so called because the Macedonian Empire founded by Philip II is its central theme. This work treated the ancient kingdoms from Assyria and Persia to Macedonia and the Hellenistic monarchies, followed by Parthia, Rome under the kings, and Gaul and Spain. Trogus probably took the bulk of his material from the *History of Kings* of Timagenes, his contemporary in Rome. In contrast to Livy's tradition, his perspective is cosmopolitan and Greek, not patriotic and Roman. The original work is lost, but its character is preserved in Justin's *Epitome*, the *prologi* (or summaries of books), and some fragments.

Troilus and Cressida \'tròi-ləs, 'trō-i-ləs . . . 'kres-i-də\ In Greek mythology, lovers whose story captured the imagination of artists through the ages. Troilus is the son of King Priam of Troy, and Cressida the daughter of Calchas, a Trojan seer who defected to the Greek side. Troilus and Cressida fall in love, but in an exchange of prisoners Cressida is sent to the Greek camp, and there she is loved by and eventually comes to love the Greek warrior Diomedes. In Homer's *Iliad* Troilus is killed before Greece's war with Troy begins; non-Homeric legend records that he was killed by the Greek hero Achilles.

In most medieval handlings of the Trojan story, Troilus is portrayed as the embodiment of an innocent young lover betrayed by a fickle girl. This story of Troilus' unhappy passion appears to have been invented by Benoît de Sainte-Maure in his 12th-century *Roman de Troie*. Benoît, who probably conflated the name of Chryseis (daughter of Chryses) with that of the Trojan Briseis, called the girl Briseida, a name later modified by other writers to Cressida. Two significant 14th-century treatments of the story are Giovanni Boccaccio's poem *Il filostrato* (derived from Benoît and from the *Historia destructionis Troiae* of Guido delle Colonne) and Geoffrey Chaucer's *Troilus and Criseyde* (based mainly on Boccaccio). The story was also the subject of William Shakespeare's *Troilus and Cressida* and many later writings.

Troilus and Cressida \ˈtròi-ləs, ˈtrō-i-ləs . . . ˈkres-i-də\ Drama in five acts by William SHAKESPEARE, performed about 1601–02 and printed in a quarto edition in 1609. Although this play is included among the tragedies in the First Folio, many critics prefer to classify it with the "problem plays" or the "darker comedies." Based on George Chapman's translation of the *Iliad* and on 15th-century accounts of the Trojan War by John Lydgate and William Caxton, *Troilus and Cressida* is an often cynical exploration of the betrayal of love, the absence of heroism, and the emptiness of honor. The play was also influenced by Geoffrey Chaucer's love poem *Troilus and Criseyde*, although Shakespeare's treatment of the lovers and his attitude toward their dilemma is in sharp contrast with Chaucer's.

Cressida, a Trojan woman whose father has defected to the Greeks, pledges her love to Troilus, one of King Priam's sons. However, when her father demands her presence in the Greek camp, she quickly switches her affections to Diomedes, the Greek soldier who is sent to escort her. The legendary Greek hero Achilles is depicted as petulant and self-centered, and Agamemnon is a foolish windbag. Thersites, a deformed Greek, comments wryly on the actions of the other characters, while Pandarus, the bawdy go-between of the lovers, enjoys watching their degradation. The drama ends on a note of complete moral and political disintegration, allowing none of the characters to rise above their foolish behavior.

Troilus and Criseyde \ˈtròi-ləs, ˈtrō-i-ləs . . . kri-ˈsā-də\ Tragic verse romance by Geoffrey CHAUCER, composed in the 1380s and considered by some critics to be his finest work. The plot of this 8,239-line poem was taken largely from Giovanni Boccaccio's *Il filostrato*. It recounts the love story of Troilus, son of the Trojan king Priam, and Criseyde, widowed daughter of the deserter priest Calchas.

The poem moves in leisurely fashion, with introspection and much of what would now be called psychological insight dominating many sections. Aided by Criseyde's uncle Pandarus, Troilus and Criseyde are united in love about halfway through the poem, but then she is sent to join her father in the Greek camp outside Troy. Despite her promise to return, she is loved by the Greek warrior Diomedes and comes to love him. Troilus, left in despair, is killed in the Trojan War. These events are interspersed with Boethian discussion of free will and determinism and the direct comments of the narrator. At the end of the poem, when Troilus' soul rises into the heavens, the folly

of complete immersion in sexual love is viewed in relation to the eternal love of God.

Trojan horse In Greek legend, a huge, hollow wooden horse constructed by the Greeks to gain entrance into Troy during the Trojan War. The horse was built by a master carpenter named Epeius. The Greeks, pretending to desert the war, sailed to the nearby island of Tenedos, leaving behind Sinon, who persuaded the Trojans that the horse was an offering to Athena that would make Troy impregnable. Despite the warnings of Laocoön and Cassandra, the horse was taken inside. That night warriors emerged from it and opened the city's gates to the returned Greek army. The story is told at length in Book II of the *Aeneid* and is touched upon in the *Odyssey*. The term Trojan horse has come to refer to subversion introduced from the outside. *See also* TROY.

Trojan Women (*Greek* Trōades) Drama by EURIPIDES, produced in 415 BC. The work, which is set during the period immediately after the taking of Troy, treats the sufferings of the wives and children of the city's defeated leaders, in particular the old Trojan queen Hecuba and the other royal women. Cassandra, Hecuba's daughter, is taken off to be the concubine of Agamemnon, and Andromache, one of Hecuba's daughters-in-law, is taken to serve Neoptolemus. Andromache's son Astyanax is taken from her and hurled to his death from the walls of Troy. Finally, as Troy goes up in flames, Hecuba and the other Trojan women are carried off to the ships to face slavery in Greece. The play is a famous and powerful indictment of the barbarous cruelties of war. It was first produced only months after the Athenians captured the city-state of Melos, and the mood of the drama may well have been influenced by Athenian atrocities.

troll \ˈtrōl\ [Norwegian *troll* and Danish *trold,* from Old Norse *troll* giant, fiend, demon] A supernatural being in Scandinavian folklore and mythology. In early Scandinavian folklore, trolls were giant beings that were hostile to humans, lived in castles, and haunted the surrounding districts after dark. In more recent tales trolls often are the size of humans or smaller. They live in mountains, sometimes steal human maidens, and can transform themselves and prophesy. In the Shetland and Orkney islands, areas of Scandinavian settlement, trolls are called trows and appear as small malignant creatures who dwell in mounds or near the sea. In the plays of the 19th-century Norwegian dramatist Henrik Ibsen, especially *Peer Gynt* and *The Master Builder*, trolls are used as symbols of destructive instincts. Trolls in modern tales for children often live under bridges, menacing travelers and exacting tasks or tolls.

Troll Garden, The First short-story collection by Willa CATHER, published in 1905. Publication of the collection, which contains some of her best-known work, led to Cather's appointment as managing editor of *McClure's Magazine*, a New York monthly.

The stories are linked thematically by their depiction of characters who seek the realm of beauty and imagination but are constantly assaulted by the vulgar and brutal outside world. The story "The Sculptor's Funeral," originally published in *McClure's* in 1905, concerns the reactions of the townspeople in a prairie village when the body of a famous sculptor is brought back to be buried there. The book's climactic story, now considered an American classic, is PAUL'S CASE.

Trollope \ˈträl-əp\, Anthony (b. April 24, 1815, London, Eng.—d. Dec. 6, 1882, London) English novelist whose popular success concealed until long after his death the nature and extent of his literary merit. A series of books set in the imaginary English county of Barsetshire remains his best-loved and most famous work, but he also wrote convincing novels of political life, as well as studies that show great psychological penetration. One of his greatest strengths was his ability to re-create in his fiction his own vision of the social structures of Victorian England.

Trollope grew up as the son of a sometime scholar, barrister, and failed gentleman farmer. He was unhappy at the great public schools of Winchester and Harrow and as a junior clerk in the General Post Office, but he was transferred as a postal surveyor to Ireland in 1841 and began to enjoy a social life. After marrying in 1844, he set up house at Clonmel and then embarked upon a literary career of immense energy and versatility.

The Warden (1855) was his first novel of distinction, a penetrating study of the warden of an old people's home who is attacked for making too much profit from a charitable sinecure. During the next 12 years Trollope produced five other books set, like *The Warden*, in Barsetshire: *Barchester Towers* (1857), *Doctor Thorne* (1858), *Framley Parsonage* (1861), *The Small House at Allington* (1864), and *The Last Chronicle of Barset* (1867). The BARSETSHIRE NOVELS abound in memorable characters and exude the atmosphere of the cathedral community and of the landed aristocracy.

In 1859 Trollope moved back to London, resigning from the civil service in 1867 and unsuccessfully standing as a Liberal parliamentary candidate in 1868. Before then, however, he had produced some 18 novels apart from the Barsetshire group. He wrote mainly before breakfast at a fixed rate of 1,000 words an hour. Outstanding among works of that period are ORLEY FARM (1862), which made use of the traditional plot of a disputed will, and *Can You Forgive Her?* (1864–65), which was the first of his political novels and introduced Plantagenet Palliser, later Duke of Omnium. In the political novels Trollope is less concerned with political ideas than with the practical working of the system—that is, with the mechanics of power.

About 1869 Trollope's last, and in some respects most interesting, period as a writer began. Traces of his new style are to be found in the slow-moving HE KNEW HE WAS RIGHT (1869), a subtle account of a rich man's jealous obsession with his innocent wife. Purely psychological studies include *Sir Harry Hotspur of Humblethwaite* (1871) and *Kept in the Dark* (1882). Some of the later works, including some of the remaining PALLISER NOVELS, were sharply satirical: *The Eustace Diamonds* (1872) is a study of money and its effects on human relationships; THE WAY WE LIVE NOW (1875) is remarkable for its villain-hero, the financier Melmotte; and *Mr. Scarborough's Family* (posthumously, 1883) shows what can happen when the rights of property are wielded by a man of nihilistic temperament intent upon his legal rights.

trope \ˈtrōp\ [Latin *tropus*, from Greek *trópos* figure of speech, manner, style, literally, turn]   The use of a word or expression in a figurative sense. *See* FIGURE OF SPEECH.

Tropic of Cancer   Autobiographical novel by Henry MILLER, published in France in 1934 and, because of censorship, not published in the United States until 1961. Written in the tradition of Walt Whitman and Henry David Thoreau, it is a monologue about Miller's picaresque life as an impoverished expatriate in France in the early 1930s. The book benefited from favorable early critical response and gained popular notoriety later as a result of obscenity trials.

Containing little plot or narrative, *Tropic of Cancer* is made up of anecdotes, philosophizing, and rambling celebrations of life. Despite his poverty, Miller extols his manner of living, unfettered as it is by moral and social conventions. He lives largely off the resources of his friends. In exuberant and sometimes preposterous passages of unusual sexual frankness, he

chronicles numerous encounters with women, including his mysterious wife Mona, as he pursues a fascination with female sexuality.

Tropic of Cancer was the first of an autobiographical trilogy, followed by *Black Spring* (1936) and *Tropic of Capricorn* (1939).

trot \ˈträt\, *also called* pony.   A literal translation of a foreign text.

Trotwood, Betsey \ˈbet-sē-ˈträt-ˌwu̇d\   Fictional character, the eccentric aunt of the protagonist of Charles Dickens' novel DAVID COPPERFIELD.

troubadour or **troubador** \ˈtrü-bə-ˌdȯr, -ˌdu̇r\ [Middle French *troubadour*, from Old Provençal *trobador*, a derivative of *trobar* to compose in verse, invent]   One of a class of lyric poets and poet-musicians, often of knightly rank, that flourished from the 11th to the end of the 13th century chiefly in Provence and other regions of southern France, northern Spain, and the north of Italy. They wrote in the *langue d'oc* of southern France and cultivated a lyric poetry intricate in meter and rhyme and usually of a romantic amatory strain. *Compare* TROUVÈRE.

The social influence of the troubadours was unprecedented in the history of medieval poetry. Favored at the courts, they had great freedom of speech, occasionally intervening even in the political arena, but their great achievement was to create around the ladies of the court an aura of cultivation and amenity. Troubadour poetry was to influence all later European lyrical poetry.

Much of the troubadours' work has survived, preserved in manuscripts known as chansonniers ("songbooks"), and the rules by which their art was governed are set out in a work called *Leys d'amors* (1340). The verse form they used most often was the canso, consisting of five or six stanzas with a shorter final stanza called an envoi. They also used the *dansa*, or *balada*, a dance song with a refrain; the pastourelle, telling the tale of the love request by a knight to a shepherdess; the *jeu parti*, or débat, a debate on love between two poets; and the alba, or morning song, in which lovers are warned by a night watchman that day approaches and that the jealous husband may at any time surprise them. Other forms included frameworks for a lyrical conversation between two or more persons discussing, as a rule, some point of amorous casuistry or matters of a religious, metaphysical, or satirical character. Troubadour poetry was often set to music, sometimes by the poets themselves.

trouvère \trü-ˈver\ [French, from Old French *troverre, troveor*, a derivative of *trover, trouver* to compose in verse, find]   One of a school of poets that flourished in northern France from the 11th to the 14th century. The trouvères were the counterparts in the language of northern France (the *langue d'oïl*) to the Provençal troubadour. The works of the trouvères, including the chansons de geste, are of a prevailingly narrative character. *Compare* TROUBADOUR.

The essence of trouvère rhetoric lies in the combination of traditional themes and the use of established forms in which to express them. The audience gained pleasure from familiarity with these clichés rather than from the poet's originality. It is thus perhaps the least characteristic trouvères who are most appreciated today.

The trouvères developed a lyric poetry distinct from that of the troubadours, and, unlike the latter, they did not prize obscurity of metaphor for its own sake. The poetry of the trouvères was sometimes satirical and sometimes concerned with the pleasures of the good life; but the basic subject of their work was courtly love, in which the poet describes his unrequited passion for an inaccessible lady.

Trouvère lyrics were intended to be sung, probably by the poet alone or with instrumental accompaniment provided by a hired musician. Although originally connected with feudal courts, the trouvères were popular outside aristocratic circles as well. Half the extant trouvère lyrics are the work of a guild of citizen poets of Arras. Many of the trouvères, such as Gace Brûlé (late 12th century), were of aristocratic birth; Thibaut de Champagne (1201–53) was king of Navarre. But others, including Rutebeuf (flourished 1245–85), were of humble origin.

The songs of the trouvères were monophonic (consisting solely of melodic line). The trouvères used a variety of musical forms, some for any of several of the various poetic categories and some linked to the type of the verse. Four broad categories can be discerned: musical forms based on multiple repetitions of a short phrase, as in a litany; dance songs with refrains; songs based on pairs of repeated lines; and through-composed songs, which used no repetition.

Troy \'troi\, *Greek* Troia, *also called* Ilios \'il-ē-əs\ *or* Ilion \-ən\, *Latin* Troia, Troja, *or* Ilium \'il-ē-əm\ Ancient city in northwestern Anatolia near the southern entrance of the Hellespont and north of the Scamander River on the plain of Troas (Troad). The legend of Troy forms the basis of the epics of Homer and was a popular theme of literature during the Middle Ages.

The legends of Troy developed continuously throughout Greek and Latin literature. In Homer's *Iliad* and *Odyssey*, the earliest literary evidence available, the chief stories have already taken shape. Individual themes were elaborated later, especially in Greek drama. The story of the Trojan origin, through Aeneas, of Rome helped to inspire Roman interest; Book 2 of Virgil's *Aeneid* contains the best-known account of the sack of Troy. Finally there are the pseudo-chronicles that go under the names of Dictys Cretensis and Dares Phrygius.

Priam, who was the only child of Laomedon left alive by Heracles and his companions, grew to be wealthy and powerful. His son Paris was invited to judge who of the goddesses Aphrodite, Hera, and Athena was the most beautiful. Paris named Aphrodite after she promised to procure for him the most beautiful woman in the world. With the goddess's help, he abducted Helen, wife of Menelaus of Sparta.

To recover Helen, the Greeks launched a great expedition under the overall command of Menelaus' brother, Agamemnon. The Trojans withstood the siege for 10 years. The *Iliad*, set in the 10th year, tells of the quarrel between Agamemnon and Achilles, the greatest Greek warrior, and the consequent deaths in battle of (among others) Achilles' friend Patroclus and Priam's eldest son, Hector.

After Hector's death the Trojans were joined by two exotic allies, Penthesilea, queen of the Amazons, and Memnon, king of the Ethiopians. Achilles killed both of them, but Paris killed him with an arrow. Before they could take Troy, the Greeks had to steal from the citadel the wooden image of Pallas Athena (the Palladium) and fetch Philoctetes from Lemnos and Achilles' son Neoptolemus (Pyrrhus) from Skyros; Odysseus and Diomedes performed these tasks. Finally, with Athena's help, Epeius built a huge wooden horse. Several Greek warriors hid inside it; the rest sailed away to Tenedos, a nearby island, pretending to abandon the siege. Despite the warnings of Priam's daughter Cassandra, the Trojans were persuaded to take the horse inside the walls of Troy as an offering to Athena. At night the Greek fleet returned, and the Greeks from the horse opened the gates of Troy. In the total sack that followed, Priam and his remaining sons were slaughtered. The adventurous and often disastrous homeward voyages of the Greek leaders were told in two epics, the *Returns* (*Nostoi*; lost) and the *Odyssey*.

Medieval writers, unacquainted with Homer at first hand, found in the Troy legend a rich source of heroic and romantic storytelling, a convenient framework into which to fit their own courtly and chivalric ideals, and an explanation of the origins of, notably, the French and British nations.

The key work in the medieval exploitation of the Trojan theme was the French *Roman de Troie* (1154–60) by Benoît de Sainte-Maure. An epic poem, it recounts the first destruction of Troy (by Jason and Hercules), its rebuilding (by Priam), the abduction of Helen (by Paris), Troy's siege, and the battles and their aftermath (including the wanderings of the hero Ulysses). Love stories, especially those of Helen and Paris, Achilles and Polyxena, and, above all, of Troilus and Briseida (Cressida), were given special emphasis.

Later medieval writers drew inspiration from a Latin prose account, the *Historia destructionis Troiae* ("History of the Destruction of Troy"), completed about 1287 by Guido delle Colonne (whose work was in fact an abridgment of the *Roman de Troie*, though it long enjoyed the prestige of originality).

The Trojan legend appears to have been particularly favored during the 15th century at the court of Burgundy, whose ducal library contained no fewer than 17 manuscripts relating to Troy. One of them, a version of Raoul Le Fèvre's *Recueil des histoires de Troye* (1464), based on Guido, was translated into English by William Caxton as *The Recuyell of the Historyes of Troye* (c. 1474) and became the first book to be printed in English. There were also Spanish, Italian, Danish, Dutch, Swedish, Icelandic, and Czech versions.

For some thousand years there persisted a literary—even a patriotic—tradition that the dispersed heroes of Troy had founded certain Western nations, notably the British and the French. The myth was still persistent enough in 16th-century France to inspire Jean Lemaire de Belges' *Illustrations de Gaule et singularitez de Troie* (c. 1510) and Pierre de Ronsard's national epic *La Franciade* (1572). In Britain the myth was used by Wace of Jersey in his *Roman de Brut* (1155), and it persisted until the time of William Shakespeare.

Troy, Sergeant Francis \'fran-sis-'troi\ Fictional character, a dashing but heartless cad who marries Bathsheba Everdene, the heroine of Thomas Hardy's novel FAR FROM THE MADDING CROWD.

True West Drama in two acts by Sam SHEPARD, produced in 1980 and published in 1981. The play concerns the struggle for power between two brothers—Lee, a drifter and petty thief, and Austin, a successful screenwriter—while they collaborate on a screenplay in their mother's southern California home. This savage and blackly humorous version of the Cain and Abel story also satirizes the modern West's exploitation of the romanticized cowboys-and-Indians West of American mythology.

Trumbull \'trəm-bəl\, John (b. April 24, 1750, Westbury, Conn. [U.S.]—d. May 11, 1831, Detroit, Michigan Territory) American poet and jurist, known for his political satire, who was a leader of the Hartford wits.

While a student at Yale College (now Yale University), Trumbull wrote two kinds of poetry: "correct" but undistinguished elegies of the Neoclassical school and brilliant comic verse that he circulated among friends. His burlesque "Epithalamium" (1769) combined wit and scholarship, and his essays in the style of Joseph Addison were published in *The Boston Chronicle* in 1770. While a tutor at Yale he wrote *The Progress of Dulness* (1772–73), an attack on educational methods. His major work was the comic epic *M'Fingal* (1776–82), which acquired an exaggerated reputation as anti-Tory (anti-royalist) propaganda. His literary importance declined after 1782, as he became increasingly interested in law and politics.

Trumpet of the Swan, The Novel by E.B. WHITE, published in 1970. The book is considered a classic of children's literature. White's version of the ugly duckling story involves a mute swan named Louis who becomes a famous jazz trumpet player to compensate for his lack of a natural voice. Aided by his father, who steals a trumpet for him, and by Sam Beaver, an 11-year-old human friend, Louis is able to attract a mate and eventually to return to the wilderness.

tsa-chü   *see* ZAJU.

Ts'ao Chan   *see* CAO ZHAN.

Ts'ao Chih   *see* CAO ZHI.

Ts'ao Yü   *see* CAO YU.

Tsegaye \tsä-'gä-yä\, Gabre-Medhin (b. Aug. 17, 1936, Ambo, Eth.)   Ethiopian playwright and poet who wrote in Amharic and English.

Tsegaye studied in Chicago and in England. When he returned to Ethiopia he became director of the Haile Selassie I Theatre (now the National Theatre). He wrote more than 20 plays, most of them in Amharic, and he translated a number of plays of William Shakespeare and Molière into that language. His dramas deal primarily with contemporary Ethiopia, especially with the plight of youth in urban settings and the need to respect traditional morality, as in *Crown of Thorns* (1959). *Oda Oak Oracle* (1965) is Tsegaye's best-known verse play written in English. Like his other English plays, it is based on Ethiopian history and focuses on religious conflict. *Collision of Altars* (1977) is an experimental play that includes mime, incantation, dance, and the use of masks.

Ts'en Shen   *see* CEN SHEN.

Tso chuan   *see* ZUO ZHUAN.

Tsubouchi Shōyō \tsȯ-'bō-chē-'shō-,yō\, *pseudonym of* Tsubouchi Yūzō \'yü-,zō\ (b. June 22, 1859, Ōta, near Nagoya, Japan—d. Feb. 28, 1935, Atami)   Playwright, novelist, critic, and translator who occupied a prominent position in Japanese letters for nearly half a century. He wrote the first major work of modern Japanese literary criticism, *Shōsetsu shinzui* (1885–86; "The Essence of the Novel"), translated the complete works of William Shakespeare, helped found the modern Japanese theater, and was the most famous lecturer at Waseda University in Tokyo.

Shōyō achieved fame in the 1880s as the translator of Sir Walter Scott, Edward Bulwer-Lytton, and Shakespeare and as the author of nine novels and many political allegories advocating parliamentarism.

In *Shōsetsu shinzui*, Shōyō attacked the loosely constructed plots and weak characterizations of contemporary Japanese novels and urged writers to concentrate on analyses of personality in realistic situations. His own best-known novel, however, *Tōsei shoseikatagi* (1885–86; "The Character of Present-Day Students"), depicting the foolish adventures of a group of contemporary university students, suffered from the same weaknesses that he decried.

In 1883 Shōyō began teaching social science at the school that later became Waseda University. In 1890 he helped organize its faculty of letters and then helped establish Waseda Middle School, which he later headed. He founded and began editing the literary journal *Waseda bungaku* in 1891. Shōyō was also one of the founders of the *shingeki* ("new drama") movement, which introduced the plays of Henrik Ibsen and George Bernard Shaw to Japan and provided an outlet for modern plays by Japanese authors. In 1915 he retired from Waseda University to devote his time to his translations of Shakespeare.

Tsuruya Namboku IV \'tsü-rü-yä-'näm-bō-,kü\, *original name* Ebiya Genzō \'eb-ē-yä-'gen-,zō\, *also called* Dai Namboku \'dī-'näm-bō-,kü\ (b. 1755, Edo [now Tokyo], Japan—d. Dec. 23, 1829, Edo)   Japanese kabuki playwright of the late Tokugawa period (1603–1867), known for his plays with supernatural themes and macabre and grotesque-looking characters.

In 1755 Ebiya became an apprentice of the dramatist Sakurada Jisuke I. About 1780 he married the daughter of Tsuruya Namboku III, a well-known kabuki actor. After a long apprenticeship he became the chief playwright for the Kawarazaki Theater in Edo in about 1801. He took the name Tsuruya Namboku IV in 1811.

His first major success was *Tenjiku Tokubei ikoku-banashi* (1804; "Tokubei of India: Tales of Strange Lands"), written for the leading actor of the day, Onoe Matsusuke I. Namboku wrote for the virtuoso performer, and his originality and stagecraft were immensely popular among the kabuki patrons of Edo. In all he wrote some 120 plays. His specialty was dark, macabre stories of the underworld, in which murderers are haunted by the ghosts of their victims. In these he vividly portrayed the lives of commoners, interweaving cruelty, humor, and pathos. His most popular works include *Osome Hisamatsu ukina no yomiuri* (1813; "Osome and Hisamatsu: a Scandal Sheet") and *Tōkaidō Yotsuya kaidan* (1825; "Ghost Story of Tōkaidō Yotsuya").

Tsvetayeva or **Tsvetaeva** \tsvˑyi-'tå-yə-və\, Marina Ivanovna, *married name* Marina Ivanovna Efron \i-'frȯn\ (b. Sept. 26 [Oct. 8, New Style], 1892, Moscow, Russia—d. Aug. 31, 1941, Yelabuga)   Russian poet whose verse is distinctive for its staccato rhythms, originality, and directness and who, though little known outside Russia, is considered one of the finest 20th-century poets in the Russian language.

Tsvetayeva spent most of her youth in Moscow, where her father was a university professor and her mother a talented pianist. The family traveled abroad extensively, and at the age of 16 she began studies at the Sorbonne in Paris. Her first collection of poetry, *Vecherny albom* ("Evening Album"), appeared in 1910. Many of her best and most typical poetic qualities are displayed in the long verse fairy tale *Tsar-devitsa* (1922; "Tsar-Maiden").

Tsvetayeva responded to the Russian Revolution with hostility (her husband, Sergei Efron, was an officer in the counterrevolutionary White Army), and many of her verses written at this time glorify the anti-Bolshevik resistance. Among these is the remarkable cycle *Lebediny stan* ("The Swans' Camp"), which was composed in 1917–21 but not published until 1957 in Munich, Ger. It is a moving lyrical chronicle of the Russian Civil War viewed through the eyes of the wife of a White Army officer.

Tsvetayeva left the Soviet Union in 1922, going to Berlin and Prague, and finally, in 1925, settling in Paris. During this period she corresponded with Boris Pasternak and, later, with Rainer Maria Rilke. While in Paris she published several volumes of poetry, including *Stikhi k Bloku* (1922; "Verses to Blok") and *Posle Rossii* (1928; "After Russia"), the last book of her poetry to be published during her lifetime. A bilingual version of the latter was published in 1992. She also composed two poetical tragedies on classical themes, *Ariadne* (1924) and *Phaedra* (1927); several essays on the creative process; and works of literary criticism, including the monograph *Moy Pushkin* (1937; "My Pushkin"). Her last cycle of poems, *Stikhi k Chekhi* (1938–39; "Verses to the Czech Land"), was an impassioned reaction to Nazi Germany's occupation of Czechoslovakia.

In the 1930s Tsvetayeva's poetry increasingly reflected alienation from her émigré existence and a deepening nostalgia for Russia, as in the poems "Toska po rodine" (1935; "Homesick for the Motherland") and "Rodina" (1936; "Motherland"). At the end of the '30s her husband—who had begun to cooperate with the communists—returned to the Soviet Union, taking their daughter with him (both were later victims of Joseph Stalin's terror). In 1939 Tsvetayeva followed them, settling in Moscow, where she worked on poetic translations. Upon the evacuation of Moscow during World War II, she was relocated to a remote town, where she committed suicide in 1941.

Tuchman \\'tək-mən\\, Barbara, *original surname* Wertheim (b. Jan. 30, 1912, New York, N.Y., U.S.—d. Feb. 6, 1989, Greenwich, Conn.) American writer whose popular histories are marked by masterful literary style and a clear and powerful understanding.

Educated at Radcliffe College, Tuchman worked as a research assistant for the Institute of Pacific Relations and then was a writer and correspondent for *The Nation* magazine and other publications. Although she had published two earlier books, she first gained notice with *The Zimmerman Telegram* (1958), a study of the World War I document in which Germany promised Mexico parts of the American Southwest in return for support of the German cause. *The Guns of August* (1962; also published as *August 1914*) was released to widespread critical and popular acclaim and was awarded a Pulitzer Prize in 1963. A detailed account of the first month of World War I, it describes the military errors and miscalculations that led to the stalemate of trench warfare.

Tuchman's next book, *The Proud Tower* (1966), was a survey of European and American society, culture, and politics in the 1890s. She was awarded a second Pulitzer Prize for *Stilwell and the American Experience in China, 1911–45* (1970), a study of the United States' relationship with 20th-century China as epitomized in the wartime experiences of General Joseph Stilwell. *A Distant Mirror: The Calamitous 14th Century* (1978), presents a vivid picture of the events, personalities, and texture of life in 14th-century France. Later works include *The March of Folly: From Troy to Vietnam* (1984) and *The First Salute* (1988).

Tucholsky \\tü-'ḳôl-skē\\, Kurt, *pseudonyms* Theobald Tiger, Peter Panter, Ignaz Wrobel, *and* Kaspar Hauser (b. Jan. 9, 1890, Berlin, Ger.—d. Dec. 21, 1935, Hindas, near Göteborg, Swed.) German satirical essayist, poet, and critic, best known for his cabaret songs.

Tucholsky left Germany in 1924 and lived first in Paris and after 1929 in Sweden. He contributed to *Rote Signale* (1931; "Red Signals"), a collection of communist poetry, and to *Schaubühne* (later *Die Weltbühne*), a journal published by the pacifist Carl von Ossietzky. In 1933 Tucholsky's works were denounced by the Nazi government and banned, and he was stripped of his German citizenship. He committed suicide in 1935.

Tucholsky's output includes aphorisms, book and drama reviews, light verse, short stories, and witty satirical essays in which he criticized German militarism and nationalism and the dehumanizing forces of the modern age. His poetry was set to music and performed widely in German cabarets.

Tu Fu *see* DU FU.

Tukārām \\tü-'kär-äm\\ (b. 1608, Dehu, near Pune, India—d. 1649) Marathi poet who is often considered to be the greatest writer in the language. His *abhaṅga*s, or "unbroken" hymns, are among the most famous Indian poems.

The son of a shopkeeper, Tukārām was orphaned in childhood. Failing in business and family life, he renounced the world and became an itinerant ascetic. It is believed that he threw himself into a river and drowned.

Tukārām is thought to have written more than 4,000 *abhaṅga*s, most of which were addressed to the god Viṭhoba of Pandharpur. An edition of his poems translated into English was published in 1909–15 and reprinted in 1981.

Tukulti-Ninurta epic \\tü-'ḳùl-tē-ni-'nùr-tə\\ The only extant Assyrian epic tale; it tells of the wars between Tukulti-Ninurta I of Assyria (reigned *c.* 1233–*c.* 1197 BC) and Kashtiliash IV of Babylonia (reigned *c.* 1232–*c.* 1225 BC). Written from the Assyrian point of view, the epic is a strongly biased, though poetic, narrative. It is a late example of the primary epic style that was used especially during the late 3rd and early 2nd millennia BC.

Tulliver family \\'təl-i-vər\\ Fictional family in George Eliot's novel THE MILL ON THE FLOSS. Mr. Tulliver is the stubborn and hot-tempered owner of Dorlcote Mill. Mrs. Tulliver is a dull-witted woman who cares more for her household goods than for her children. The central character of the novel is their daughter Maggie, an intelligent and sensitive woman who is stifled by the demands of her family and the community in which they live. Her arrogant, self-righteous brother Tom bans Maggie from the house after she is caught in a compromising situation, but the two are reconciled at the end.

Tully *see* Marcus Tullius CICERO.

Tulsīdās \\'tùl-sē-'däs\\ (b. 1543?, probably Rājāpur, India—d. 1623, Vārānasi) Indian sacred poet whose principal work, the RĀMCARITMĀNAS ("Sacred Lake of the Acts of Rāma"), is the greatest achievement of medieval Hindi literature and has exercised an abiding influence on the Hindu culture of northern India.

Tulsīdās lived most of his adult life at Vārānasi. The *Rāmcaritmānas* was written between 1574 and 1576 or 1577. A number of early manuscripts are extant—some fragmentary—and one is said to be an autograph. The oldest complete manuscript is dated 1647. The poem, written in Awadhi, a language of Uttar Pradesh, consists of seven cantos of unequal lengths. Although the ultimate source of the central narrative is the Sanskrit epic *Rāmāyaṇa*, Tulsīdās' principal immediate source was the *Adhyātma Rāmāyaṇa*, a late medieval recasting of the epic. The influence of the *Bhāgavata-Purāṇa*, the chief scripture of the Krishna cult, and of numerous minor sources, is also discernible.

Eleven other works are attributed with some certainty to Tulsīdās. These include *Kṛṣṇa gītāvalī*, a series of 61 songs in honor of Krishna; *Vinay pattrikā*, a series of 279 verse passages addressed to Hindu sacred places and deities (chiefly Rāma and Sītā); and *Kavitāvalī*, telling incidents from the story of Rāma.

Turberville or **Turbervile** \\'tər-bər-,vil\\, George (b. 1540?, Winterbourne Whitchurch, Dorset, Eng.—d. before 1597) First English poet to publish a book of verses to his lady, a genre that became popular in the Elizabethan Age.

Turberville went to Russia (1568–69) as secretary to Thomas Randolph, the first English ambassador there. He later settled at Shapwick, Dorset. In *Epitaphes, Epigrams, Songs and Sonets* (1567), Turberville followed models in Richard Tottel's *Miscellany* and the *Greek Anthology*, addressing poems to his lady, the Countess of Warwick. He was also notable for his translations of Ovid and Mantuanus (1567), which included some of the first attempts at blank verse in English.

Turgenev \\tùr-'gyä-nᵛif\\, Ivan (Sergeyevich) (b. Oct. 28 [Nov. 9, New Style], 1818, Oryol, Russia—d. Aug. 22 [Sept. 3], 1883, Bougival, near Paris, Fr.) Russian novelist, poet, and playwright known for his realistic, affectionate portrayals of the Russian peasantry and for his penetrating studies of the Russian intelligentsia who were attempting to move the country into a new age.

Although Turgenev was given an education of sorts at the universities of Moscow and St. Petersburg, he tended to regard his education as having taken place chiefly during his years at the University of Berlin. He returned home as a confirmed believer in the superiority of the West and in the need for Russia to follow a course of Westernization.

During the 1840s, Turgenev wrote long poems and criticism and began to publish short stories. The most famous of these was "Dnevnik lishnego cheloveka" (1850; "The Diary of a Superfluous Man"),

which supplied the epithet SUPERFLUOUS MAN for so many similar protagonists. At the same time, he tried his hand at writing plays. Although some were rather obviously imitative of the work of Nikolay Gogol, others of a more intimately penetrating character led to the detailed psychological studies in his dramatic masterpiece, *Mesyats v derevne* (1855; A MONTH IN THE COUNTRY). With the short-story cycle *Zapiski okhotnika* (1852; A SPORTSMAN'S SKETCHES), Turgenev

Culver Pictures

gained lasting fame, though its criticism of serfdom brought him a month of detention in St. Petersburg and 18 months of enforced house arrest.

His work began to evolve toward such extended character studies as *Yakov Pasynkov* (1855) and the subtle if pessimistic examinations of the contrariness of love found in "Faust" and "Perepiska" (1856; "A Correspondence"). The two novels that he published during the 1850s—RUDIN (1856) and *Dvoryanskoye gnezdo* (1859; *Home of the Gentry*), a delicate, elegaic study of unrequited love—are permeated by a spirit of ironic nostalgia for the weaknesses and futilities so manifest in his own generation.

Turgenev's interest in intergenerational differences was reflected in two novels of the early 1860s—*Nakanune* (1860; ON THE EVE) and *Ottsy i deti* (1862; FATHERS AND SONS). As a result of the hostile reaction to *Fathers and Sons*, Turgenev left Russia, living first in Baden-Baden in southern Germany and then in London and Paris. His only novel of this period, *Dym* (1867; SMOKE), set in Baden-Baden, is infused with a satirically embittered tone that caricatures both the left and the right wings of the intelligentsia.

The literary work of his final period combines nostalgia for the past—eloquently displayed in such beautiful pieces as *Stepnoy korol Lir* (1870; A LEAR OF THE STEPPES) and *Veshniye vody* (1872; TORRENTS OF SPRING)—with stories of a quasifantastic character. Turgenev's final novel was *Nov* (1877; VIRGIN SOIL).

Turner \ˈtər-nər\, Ethel (Sibyl), *married name* Mrs. Herbert Raine Curlewis \ˈkərl-wis\ (b. Jan. 24, 1872, Doncaster, Yorkshire, Eng.—d. April 8, 1958, Sydney, Australia) Australian novelist and writer for children, whose popular novel *Seven Little Australians* (1894) was filmed (1939), twice dramatized for television, once in Great Britain (1953) and once in Australia (1973), and made into a musical (1978).

Turner was educated and reared in Sydney. She and a sister published a monthly magazine, *The Parthenon*, from 1889 to 1892, and thereafter she was employed as a children's writer-editor for newspapers in Sydney. *Seven Little Australians*, her first book, was a quick success, being translated into several languages and eventually becoming an Australian children's classic. She wrote about 30 other novels and collections of short stories and verse, mostly about and for girls. Much of

her work is characterized by the sentimentality and melodrama prized during the late 19th and early 20th centuries.

Turn of the Screw, The Novella by Henry JAMES, published serially in *Collier's Weekly* in 1898 and published in book form later that year. One of the world's most famous ghost stories, the tale is told mostly through the journal of a governess and depicts her struggle to save her two young charges from the demonic influence of the eerie apparitions of two former servants in the household. The story inspired critical debate over the question of the "reality" of the ghosts and of James's intentions. James himself, in his preface to volume XII of *The Novels and Tales of Henry James*, called the tale a "fable" and said that he did not specify details of the ghosts' evil deeds because he wanted readers to supply their own vision of terror.

Turnus \ˈtər-nəs\ In Roman legend, king of the Rutuli (an ancient Italic tribe on the coast of Latium), and the accepted suitor of Lavinia, daughter of Latinus, king of the Latins. After Latinus betrothed Lavinia instead to the hero Aeneas, Turnus, joined by the Rutuli and the Latins, made war against Aeneas and the Trojans. Though Turnus was protected by the goddess Juno, Aeneas finally succeeded in pursuing and killing him. *See also* AENEID.

Turow \tü-ˈrō\, Scott (b. April 12, 1949, Chicago, Ill., U.S.) Best-selling American novelist, the creator of a genre of legal crime and suspense novels written by lawyers.

Turow, a practicing attorney, published a nonfiction work, *One L: What They Really Teach You at Harvard Law School* (1977), that is considered a classic for law students. His first novel, *Presumed Innocent* (1987; film, 1990), was written while he was an assistant U.S. attorney in Chicago. The story of Rusty Sabich, a deputy prosecutor assigned to investigate the murder of a female colleague with whom he has had an affair, is a well-crafted tale of suspense. *The Burden of Proof* (1990) and *Pleading Guilty* (1993) continue in the vein of legal drama.

Tutuola \ˌtü-tü-ˈwō-lä\, Amos (b. 1920, Abeokuta, Nigeria) Nigerian author of richly inventive fantasies. Tutuola wrote in English but incorporated Yoruba myths and legends into loosely constructed prose epics that improvise on traditional themes found in Yoruba folktales. Perhaps his best-known work is the novel THE PALM-WINE DRINKARD (1952).

My Life in the Bush of Ghosts (1954) reiterates the quest motif, introduced in *The Palm-Wine Drinkard*, through the experiences of a boy who, in trying to escape from slave traders, finds himself in the Bush of Ghosts. Another quest is found in *Simbi and the Satyr of the Dark Jungle* (1955), a more compact tale focusing upon a beautiful and rich young girl who leaves her home and experiences poverty and starvation. In this and other tales—*The Brave African Huntress* (1958), *The Feather Woman of the Jungle* (1962), *Ajaiyi and His Inherited Poverty* (1967), and *The Witch-Herbalist of the Remote Town* (1981)—Tutuola's rich vision imposes unity upon a series of relatively random events.

Tutuola was influenced by D.O. Fagunwa, a Nigerian author who wrote similar folk fantasies earlier in Yoruba, and he was also familiar with *The Thousand and One Nights*, *Pilgrim's Progress*, and other episodic adventure stories used as textbooks at the Salvation Army primary school that he attended. Some of these influences can be seen most clearly in one of his earliest narratives, a hunter's tale recounting visits to several extraterrestrial residences of ghosts, including heaven and hell.

Tutuola's vivid presentation of Yoruba mythology and religion and his grasp of literary form made him a success among a wide British, African, and American audience. His later works include *Yoruba Folktales* (1986), *Pauper, Brawler, and Slanderer* (1987), and *The Village Witch Doctor and Other Stories* (1990).

Tuwim \'tü-vēm\, Julian (b. Sept. 13, 1894, Łódź, Pol.—d. Dec. 27, 1953, Zakopane) Lyric poet who was leader of the 20th-century group of Polish poets called Skamander.

Tuwim began his career in 1915 with the publication of a flamboyant Futurist manifesto that created a scandal and presented a position that he soon abandoned. Tuwim's poetry is marked by explosive energy and great emotional tension. Among his works published in the years before World War II are *Czyhanie na Boga* (1918; "Lying in Wait for God"), *Sokrates tańczący* (1920; "The Dancing Socrates"), and his most important collection, *Słowa we krwi* (1926; "Words in Blood"). During his exile he wrote a long, discursive autobiographical poem, *Kwiaty polskie* (1949; "Polish Flowers"), and also produced a volume of children's songs.

Twain \'twān\, Mark, *pseudonym of* Samuel Langhorne Clemens \'klem-ənz\ (b. Nov. 30, 1835, Florida, Mo., U.S.—

E.B. Inc.

d. April 21, 1910, Redding, Conn.) American humorist, writer, and lecturer who won a worldwide audience for his stories of youthful adventures, especially TOM SAWYER (1876), LIFE ON THE MISSISSIPPI (1883), and HUCKLEBERRY FINN (1884).

Clemens grew up in Hannibal, Mo., on the west bank of the Mississippi. At the age of 13 he became a full-time apprentice to a local printer. When his older brother Orion established the *Hannibal Journal*, Samuel became a compositor for that paper. After working for a time as an itinerant printer, he rejoined Orion in Keokuk, Iowa, until the fall of 1856. He then began another period of wandering with a commission to write some comic travel letters for the Keokuk *Daily Post*. Only five letters appeared, for on the way down the Mississippi, Clemens signed on as an apprentice to a steamboat pilot. For almost four years he plied the Mississippi. After 1859 he was a licensed pilot in his own right, but two years later the Civil War put an end to the steamboat traffic.

In 1861 Clemens joined Orion in a trip to the Nevada Territory. Samuel became a writer for the Virginia City *Territorial Enterprise*, and there, on Feb. 3, 1863, "Mark Twain" was born when Clemens signed a humorous travel account with that pseudonym. The name was a riverman's term for water "two fathoms deep" and thus just barely safe for navigation. In 1864 Twain left Nevada for California. While at a mining camp Twain heard the story he would make famous as THE CELEBRATED JUMPING FROG OF CALAVERAS COUNTY, which was an immediate success.

In 1866 Twain visited Hawaii as a correspondent for *The Sacramento Union*, publishing letters on his trip and later giving popular lectures. He then set out on a world tour for California's largest paper, the *Alta California*. The letters that he wrote during the next five months for the *Alta California* and for Horace Greeley's *New York Tribune* caught the public fancy and, when revised for publication in 1869 as THE INNOCENTS ABROAD, established Twain as a popular favorite.

Twain married in 1870 and moved with his wife to Hartford, Conn., in 1871.

In 1872 he published ROUGHING IT, a chronicle of an overland stagecoach journey and of Twain's adventures in the Pacific islands. Meanwhile, he collaborated with his neighbor Charles Dudley Warner on *The Gilded Age* (1873), a satire on financial and political malfeasance that gave a name to the expansive post-Civil War era.

Twain continued to lecture with great success in the United States and, in 1872 and 1873, in England. In 1876 he published *Tom Sawyer*, a narrative of youthful escapades, followed in 1880 by *A Tramp Abroad*, in 1881 by THE PRINCE AND THE PAUPER, and in 1883 by the autobiographical *Life on the Mississippi*. Twain's next novel, *Huckleberry Finn*, is generally considered his finest and one of the masterpieces of American fiction. In 1889 he published A CONNECTICUT YANKEE IN KING ARTHUR'S COURT, in which a commonsensical Yankee is transported back in time to medieval Britain.

Various unsuccessful financial speculations, including his own publishing firm, left Twain bankrupt; however, the returns from PUDD'NHEAD WILSON (1894), *Personal Recollections of Joan of Arc* (1895), a lecture tour around the world, and *Following the Equator* (1897), in which he described the tour, made him solvent again. THE MAN THAT CORRUPTED HADLEYBURG was published with other stories and sketches in 1900.

In the fall of 1903 Twain and his family settled near Florence, Italy. His wife died six months later, and he expressed his grief, his loneliness, and his pessimism about the human character in several late works, including LETTERS FROM THE EARTH.

Twardowski \tfär-'dôf-sk'ē\, Samuel, *also called* Samuel Twardowski of Skrzpna (b. *c.* 1600, Lutynia, near Jarocin, Kingdom of Poland—d. 1661, Zalesie Wielkie, near Krotoszyn) Polish poet, diarist, and essayist who was noted for his popular verse narrative on the civil war.

An impoverished Polish nobleman, Twardowski was a hanger-on at various magnates' courts. While traveling as secretary with one of his patrons to Turkey on a diplomatic mission, he wrote a diary of the journey in verse: *Przeważna legacja J.O. Książęcia Krzysztofa Zbaraskiego* (1633; "The Important Mission of His Grace Duke Krzysztof Zbaraski"). He later wrote about many historical events, as in *Wojna domowa z Kozaki i Tatary* (1681; "A Civil War with the Cossacks and Tatars"), an account of the Zaporozhian Cossacks' revolt, under the leadership of Bohdan Khmelnitsky, against Polish domination in the mid-17th century. Twardowski also wrote Baroque pastoral romances, including *Nadobna Paskwalina* (1655; "Fair Pasqualina") and *Dafnis drzewem bobkowym* (1638; "Daphne Into Laurel Tree").

Tweedledum and Tweedledee \ˌtwēd-əl-'dəm . . . ˌtwēd-əl-'dē\ Fictional characters in Lewis Carroll's THROUGH THE LOOKING-GLASS. In keeping with the mirror-image scheme of Carroll's book, Tweedledum and Tweedledee are two rotund little men who are identical except that they are left-right reversals of each other. In the 18th century, before Carroll created the characters, "tweedledum and tweedledee" was a term used to describe the sounds of low and high instruments. By the 19th century, the phrase had come to indicate people or situations that were virtually interchangeable.

Twelfth Night (*in full* Twelfth Night, or What You Will) Comedy in five acts by William SHAKESPEARE, performed in 1601–02 and printed in the First Folio of 1623 from a promptbook or a transcript of it. One of Shakespeare's finest comedies, *Twelfth Night* precedes the great tragedies and problem plays in order of composition. The original source was probably the 1531 Sienese comedy *Gl'Ingannati* ("The Deceived").

Twins Sebastian and Viola are separated during a shipwreck; each believes the other dead. Viola disguises herself as a boy named Cesario and enters the service of Duke Orsino, who is in love with the Lady Olivia. He sends Viola/Cesario to plead his cause to Olivia, who promptly falls in love with the messenger. Viola, meanwhile, is in love with the Duke, and when Sebastian is rediscovered, many comic situations of mistaken identity ensue. There is a humorous subplot involving the members of Lady Olivia's household, who play a cruel joke on the high-minded, pompous Malvolio. This character, one of the most complex of Shakespeare's gallery of moody outsiders, is often considered to be a portrayal of a typical Puritan, one of the sort who were threatening to close down the theaters. Malvolio is left alone at the end of the play in the midst of all the happy lovers, who have paired up.

The play pokes gentle fun at wooing and the folly of lovers. Duke Orsino, for example, is in love with the state of being in love, and Lady Olivia's initial vow of isolation to honor her dead brother is exposed as excessive and self-indulgent. The two positions are contrasted with the mature and sensible attitude of Viola.

Twenty Love Poems and a Song of Despair   Verse collection by Pablo NERUDA, published in 1924 as *Veinte poemas de amor y una canción desesperada*. The book immediately established the author's reputation and became one of the most widely read collections of poetry written in Spanish.

The 20 love poems of the title poignantly describe remembered affairs with two women: a girl from the poet's native town of Temuco and a classmate at the University of Santiago. The collection begins with intensity, describing sensual passion that slackens into melancholy and detachment in the later verses. The closing poem, "A Song of Despair," hopelessly dwells upon bitter emotions.

Twenty-Six Men and a Girl   Short story by Maksim GORKY, published in Russian in 1899 as "Dvadtsat shest i odna" ("Twenty-Six and One"). It is a psychological profile of a group of long-suffering bakers who idolize a local seamstress. Critics praised Gorky's sympathetic tone and rhythmic prose, particularly evident in the emotional folk songs of the bakers.

The story is narrated by one of 26 bakers, whose only respite from misery is the daily visit of Tanya, a local girl whom the bakers gradually begin to worship. When the men learn that she has been seduced by a young man who works nearby, they revile Tanya. Her initial surprise soon gives way to anger as she upbraids the bakers for intruding upon her affairs and for making her an object of their worship. Only when she permanently takes leave of them do they realize their loss.

Twenty Thousand Leagues Under the Sea   Novel by Jules VERNE, first published in French as *Vingt Mille Lieues sous les mers* in 1869–70. It is perhaps the most popular book of his science-fiction series *Voyages extraordinaires* (1863–1910).

Professor Pierre Aronnax, the narrator of the story, boards an American frigate commissioned to investigate a rash of attacks on international shipping by what is thought to be an amphibious monster. The supposed sea creature, which is actually the submarine *Nautilus*, sinks Aronnax's vessel and imprisons him along with his devoted servant Conseil and Ned Land, a temperamental harpooner. The survivors meet Captain Nemo, an enigmatic misanthrope who leads them on a worldwide, yearlong underwater adventure. The novel is noted for its exotic situations, the technological innovations it describes, and the tense interplay of the three captives and Nemo (who reappears in *The Mysterious Island*).

Twice-Told Tales   Collection of previously published short stories by Nathaniel HAWTHORNE, issued in 1837 and revised and expanded in 1842. The 1837 edition consisted of 18 stories; the 1842 enlargement brought the total to 39.

Stories such as "The Gray Champion," "The May-pole of Marymount," "The Gentle Boy," and "Endicott and the Red Cross" reflect Hawthorne's moral insight and his lifelong interest in the history of Puritan New England. Among other tales are the allegorical "The Ambitious Guest"; "The Minister's Black Veil" and "Wakefield," psychological explorations of sin and guilt; "Howe's Masquerade," a ghostly legend set in Boston just prior to the American Revolution; and "Dr. Heidegger's Experiment," an allegorical search for the Fountain of Youth.

Twist, Oliver \\'äl-i-vər-'twist\   Fictional character, a young orphan who is the hero of Charles Dickens' OLIVER TWIST, a novel that illustrates how poverty nurtures crime.

two-dimensional   In literature, lacking depth of characterization.

Two Gentlemen of Verona, The \və-'rō-nə\   An early play in five acts by William SHAKESPEARE, performed 1594–95 and published in the First Folio of 1623.

The story of the play was taken from a translation of a long Spanish prose romance entitled *Diana* by Jorge de Montemayor. Shakespeare added new characters—including Valentine, one of the "Two Gentlemen," whose "ideal" friendship with Proteus is so developed that the plot seems to glorify friendship over romantic love. The abrupt last scene suggests that something has gone wrong with the text, and certainly Shakespeare was never again to use such preposterous motivation for the behavior of his lovers. But it is also clear that Shakespeare was developing a new kind of high comedy that was later to find expression in *The Merchant of Venice* and *Twelfth Night*.

Two Women   Novel by Alberto MORAVIA, published in Italian in 1957 as *La ciociara*. Based partially on Moravia's own experiences during World War II, the novel tells the story of Cesira, a strong-willed widow who is forced to flee Rome in 1943 with her 18-year-old daughter Rosetta. The two women suffer hunger, fear, betrayal, the brutality of their fellow peasants, and, finally, rape at the hands of the "liberators." Cesira loses her faith, and although she and her daughter are survivors, she comes to the conclusion that human nature—including her own—holds many possibilities for evil.

Tyard \'tyär\, Pontus de (b. *c.* 1522, Bissy-sur-Fley, Burgundy, Fr.—d. Sept. 23, 1605, Bragny-sur-Saône)   Burgundian poet and member of the literary circle known as La Pléiade who was a forthright theorist and a popularizer of Renaissance learning for the elite.

In 1551 Tyard translated Leone Ebreo's *Dialoghi di amore* ("Dialogues of Love"), the breviary of 16th-century philosophic lovers. His poetry collection *Les Erreurs amoureuses* (1549; "Mistakes in Love"), which includes one of the first French sonnet sequences, also revived the sestina verse form in France. *Les Erreurs* was augmented in successive editions, as was his important prose work *Discours philosophiques* ("Philosophical Discourses"), a Neoplatonic encyclopedia finally completed in 1587. Its first treatise, the *Solitaire premier* (1552), complements Joachim du Bellay's *La Défense et illustration de la langue française* (1549), which expounded the theories of poetic diction and language reform of La Pléiade.

In his enthusiasm for enriching the French language and adapting classical imagery and genres, Tyard shared the contempt for the masses felt by his associates. In the *Solitaire premier* he praises those poets who decorate their verse so richly with the ornaments of antiquity that the average reader cannot comprehend them. He remarks that the purpose of the poet is not to be understood by nor to lower himself to accommodate a popular audience still fond of medieval genres.

Tybalt \ 'tib-əlt \ Fictional character, a nephew to Lady Capulet in William Shakespeare's ROMEO AND JULIET. He murders Romeo's friend Mercutio and is killed by Romeo.

Tyche \ 'tī-kē \ In Greek mythology, the goddess of chance, with whom the Roman Fortuna was later identified; a capricious dispenser of good and ill fortune. The Greek poet Hesiod called her the daughter of the Titan Oceanus and his consort Tethys; other writers named Zeus as her father. She was also associated with the more beneficent Agathos Daimon, a good spirit protective of individuals and families, and with Nemesis, who, as an abstraction, represented punishment of overprosperous mortals and so was believed to act as a moderating influence. Among Tyche's monuments was a temple at Argos, where the legendary Palamedes is said to have dedicated to her the first set of dice, which he is supposed to have invented.

Tyger, The \ 'tī-gər \ Poem by William Blake, published in his SONGS OF INNOCENCE AND OF EXPERIENCE at the peak of his lyrical achievement.

The Tyger is the key image in the *Songs of Experience*, the embodiment of an implacable primal power. Its representation

Illustration by the author
Copyright British Museum

of a physicality that both attracts and terrifies is expressed in the poem's first stanza:

> Tyger, tyger, burning bright
> In the forests of the night;
> What immortal hand or eye
> Could frame thy fearful symmetry?

The next four stanzas elaborate on the concept of a creator forging a savage, beautiful creature. Blake posed an age-old puzzle in the poem's question "Did he who made the Lamb make thee?"

Tyler \ 'tī-lər \, Anne (b. Oct. 25, 1941, Minneapolis, Minn., U.S.) American novelist and short-story writer whose comedies of manners are marked by compassionate wit and precise details of domestic life.

Tyler spent much of her youth in North Carolina and at age 16 entered Duke University (Raleigh, N.C.). She worked as a bibliographer at Duke and as a librarian at McGill University (Montreal, Que.) for several years before settling in Baltimore, Md., in 1967 and turning to writing full-time.

Tyler's first published novel, *If Morning Ever Comes* (1964), is typical of her work in its polished prose and its understated examination of personal isolation and the difficulties of communication between people. Her subsequent novels include *The Clock Winder* (1972), *Celestial Navigation* (1974), *Searching for Caleb* (1975), *Dinner at the Homesick Restaurant* (1982), *The Accidental Tourist* (1985), *Breathing Lessons* (1988), and *Saint Maybe* (1991). Several of Tyler's best novels focus on eccentric middle-class people living in chaotic, disunited families.

Tyler \ 'tī-lər \, Royall, *original name* William Clark Tyler (b. July 18, 1757, Boston, Mass. [U.S.]—d. Aug. 26, 1826, Brattleboro, Vt.) American lawyer, teacher, and dramatist and author of the first American comedy, *The Contrast* (1787).

With Joseph Dennie, Tyler formed a literary partnership; using the pseudonyms Colon and Spondee, they contributed satirical pieces to local newspapers.

A meeting with Thomas Wignell, the star comedian of New York City's American Company, led Tyler to write *The Contrast*, which premiered in New York in 1787. The play is a light comedy echoing the English playwrights Oliver Goldsmith and Richard Brinsley Sheridan (especially Sheridan's *The School for Scandal*). It contains a Yankee character, the predecessor of many such in years to follow, who was notable as a distinctly American type. His other plays, some no longer extant, did not equal *The Contrast*.

tylwyth teg \ 'til-əth-'teg \ [Welsh, literally, fair family] The fairies of Welsh folklore. They are fair-haired and covet fair-haired human children. Like other fairies they live underground or under the water.

Tynan \ 'tī-nən \, Katherine, *married surname* Hinkson \ 'hiŋk-sən \ (b. Jan. 23, 1861, Dublin, Ire.—d. April 2, 1931, Wimbledon, Surrey, Eng.) Irish poet and novelist whose works are dominated by the combined influences of Roman Catholicism and Irish patriotism.

Like the poet William Butler Yeats, Tynan developed a deep and abiding interest in Celtic mythology. A prodigious writer, she produced five autobiographical volumes: *Twenty-five Years* (1913), *The Middle Years* (1917), *The Years of the Shadow* (1919), *The Wandering Years* (1922), and *Memories* (1924). She also wrote more than 100 romantic novels, the best known of which is *The House in the Forest* (1928). Her *Collected Poems* was published in 1930.

Typee \ ,tī-'pē \ (*in full* Typee: A Peep at Polynesian Life) First novel by Herman MELVILLE, published in London in 1846 as *Narrative of a Four Months' Residence Among the Natives of a Valley of the Marquesas Islands*. Initially regarded as a travel narrative, the novel is based on Melville's month-long adventure as a guest-captive of the Typee people, natives of the Marquesas Islands in present-day French Polynesia, following his desertion from the whaler *Acushnet* along with shipmate Richard Tobias Greene in July 1842. Melville injured his leg in the escape from the *Acushnet*, and Greene was allowed to leave the Typees to find Melville a doctor, but he became sidetracked and never returned. Shortly thereafter, Melville was rescued by the Australian whaler *Lucy Ann*.

Typee is an anthropological study of an exotic and savage native culture that both impressed and frightened Melville (allegedly the Typees were cannibals). The protagonist of the novel, Tom (also known as Tommo), spends four months with his companion Toby in a Polynesian island paradise as prisoners of the Typees. Tom's opportunities for escape are limited by his disease-swollen leg and by his personal jailer-servant, the devoted Kory-Kory. He befriends several natives, notably the beautiful Fayaway. Tom is intrigued by the Typees' social and religious customs, but he is also disgusted by their indolence and cannibalism. Ultimately, he chooses civilization over idyllic island life.

type name or **ticket name**   In dramatic practice, name given to a character to ensure that the personality may be instantly ascertained.

In England the allegorical morality plays of the late Middle Ages presented characters personifying, for example, the seven deadly sins—being named Envy, Sloth, Lust, and so forth. Tudor and Elizabethan dramatists were greatly influenced by the moralities, and Ben Jonson in particular adopted the habit of christening his characters in such a way that whatever "humor" governed them was pointed up. In his play *The Alchemist* are characters named Subtle and Face (two confidence tricksters), Sir Epicure Mammon (a voluptuary), Abel Drugger (a naive tobacconist), and Dol Common (a strumpet). Type names were later a feature of Restoration comedy. In Sir John Vanbrugh's comedy *The Relapse*, there appear, among a gallery of familiar characters with type names, Lord Foppington and his brother Young Fashion. Type names continued to be a fixture of English literature in the latter part of the 18th century, as is evident in some of the characters invented by the dramatist Richard Brinsley Sheridan: Joseph Surface and the dramatist Sir Fretful Plagiary. The most prominent and inventive user of type names in 19th-century English literature was the novelist Charles Dickens, though his are imaginatively suggestive creations rather than explicit labels of a character's occupation, attitudes, or flaws: Josiah Bounderby, Thomas Gradgrind, Mrs. Sparsit, Tulkinghorn, Dr. Blimber, Mrs. Jellyby, and Captain Cuttle. Anthony Trollope and other Victorian novelists also sometimes used type names, especially for comic or flawed characters.

Type names can be found in most other national literatures, and their use has persisted at a diminished level, usually in comedic works or for comic effect.

Typhon \'tī-ˌfän\ or **Typhaon** \tī-'fā-än\ or **Typhoeus** \tī-'fō-yūs\   In Greek mythology, youngest son of Gaea (Earth) and Tartarus (of the nether world). He is described as a grisly monster with a hundred dragons' heads who was conquered and cast into the underworld by Zeus. In other accounts he was confined in the land of the Arimi in Cilicia or under Mount Etna or in other volcanic regions, where he was the cause of eruptions. Typhon was thus the personification of volcanic forces. Among his children by his wife, Echidna, were Cerberus, the three-headed hound of hell, the multiheaded Hydra, and the Chimera. He was also the father of dangerous winds (typhoons), and he was identified by later writers with the Egyptian god Seth.

Typhoon   Novella by Joseph CONRAD, published in 1902 and included in the collection *Typhoon and Other Stories* the following year. This story about a stolid English sea captain's successful navigation of his steamship through a typhoon off the coast of China is an example of Conrad's use of the maritime tale to investigate the mysteries of human nature. Although men of more imagination and insight are undone by the terrors of the storm, Captain MacWhirr, with his literal mind and stubborn insistence on duty, behaves heroically under the threat of death. The very qualities that make him seem mediocre have made him a successful leader. Critics have seen the story as Conrad's ironic homage to a particular type of English seaman.

Tyr \'tir, 'tūr, 'tūer\, *Old Norse* Týr, *Old English* Tiw *or* Tiu \'tē-ū\   One of the oldest gods of the Germanic peoples and a somewhat enigmatic figure. He was apparently the god concerned with the formalities of war—especially treaties—and also, appropriately, of justice. It is in his character as guarantor of contracts and guardian of oaths that the most famous myth about him may be understood. As a guarantee of good faith, he placed his hand between the jaws of the monstrous wolf Fenrir while the gods, pretending sport but intending a trap, bound the wolf; when Fenrir realized he had been tricked, he bit off Tyr's hand (hence Tyr's identification as the one-handed god). Tyr came to be identified by the Romans with their own Mars; hence *dies Marti* (Mars' Day) came to be rendered *Týsdagr* (Tuesday).

Tyrone family \tī-'rōn, 'tī-ˌrōn\   Doomed fictional family, the four protagonists of the starkly autobiographical drama LONG DAY'S JOURNEY INTO NIGHT by Eugene O'Neill. The play concerns a father (James), mother (Mary), and two sons (Jamie and Edmund), all based closely on O'Neill's own troubled family.

Tyrtaeus \tər-'tē-əs\ (fl. *c.* 650 BC, Sparta)   Greek elegiac poet, author of stirring poetry on military themes supposedly composed to help Sparta win the Second Messenian War.

Greek tradition after Tyrtaeus' time claimed that he was an Athenian or Milesian schoolmaster who was sent to Sparta in reluctant compliance with an oracle to strengthen Spartan morale. It is probable, however, that stories of his non-Laconian origin were invented after the 6th-century revolution at Sparta, when other Greeks could no longer imagine that Sparta had ever been able to produce its own poets.

Only fragments of Tyrtaeus' poems survive; they combine exhortations to courage and self-discipline with reminders of past victories and assurances of future successes.

Tyrwhitt \'tir-it\, Thomas (b. March 27, 1730, London, Eng.—d. Aug. 15, 1786, London)   English scholar especially notable for his work on the medieval English poet Geoffrey Chaucer. In classical and English scholarship alike, Tyrwhitt showed the same qualities of balance, wide knowledge, and critical acumen. (He alone was able, on linguistic grounds, to identify as a forgery the poems written by Thomas Chatterton but passed off as the work of "the 15th-century monk Thomas Rowley.")

Tyrwhitt was deputy secretary of war (1756), then clerk of the House of Commons (1762); he retired in 1768. He edited Aristotle's *Poetics* (1794), but his fame rests chiefly upon an edition of Chaucer's *The Canterbury Tales*, 5 vol. (1775–78). Chaucer's reputation had suffered because the principles on which his verse depends were no longer understood; it was Tyrwhitt who pointed out that final *e*'s (by his time mute) ought to be pronounced as separate syllables and that the accent of a word was often placed in the French manner (*e.g.*, virtúe, not vírtue). Tyrwhitt's scholarship is still held in great respect.

Tyutchev or **Tiutchev** \'t'ū-chʸəf\, Fyodor Ivanovich (b. Nov. 23 [Dec. 5, New Style], 1803, Ovstug, Russia—d. July 15 [July 27], 1873, St. Petersburg)   Russian writer who was remarkable both as a highly original philosophical poet and as a militant Slavophile; his whole literary output constitutes a struggle to fuse political passion with poetic imagination.

Tyutchev served his country as a diplomat in Munich, Ger., and Turin, Italy. In Germany he developed a friendship with the poet Heinrich Heine and met frequently with the idealist philosopher Friedrich W.J. von Schelling. His protracted expatriate life, however, only made Tyutchev more Russian at heart. Though the bare and poverty-stricken Russian countryside depressed him, he voiced a proud, intimate, and tragic vision of the motherland in his poetry. He also wrote political articles and political verses which reflect his reactionary nationalist and Pan-Slavic views, as well as his deep love of Russia. He once wrote, "I love poetry and my country above all else in the world."

Tyutchev's love poems, most of them inspired by his liaison with his daughter's governess, are among the most passionate and poignant in the Russian language. He is regarded as one of the three greatest Russian poets of the 19th century, along with Aleksandr Pushkin and Mikhail Lermontov.

Tzara \ˈtsä-rä\, Tristan (b. 1896, Moineşti, Rom.—d. December 1963, Paris, Fr.)   Romanian-born French poet and essayist known mainly as a founder of Dada, a nihilistic revolutionary movement in the arts.

The Dadaist movement originated in Zürich during World War I; Tzara wrote the first Dada texts—*La Première Aventure céleste de Monsieur Antipyrine* (1916; "The First Heavenly Adventure of Mr. Antipyrine") and *Vingt-cinq poèmes* (1918; "Twenty-Five Poems")—and the movement's manifestos, *Sept manifestes Dada* (1924; "Seven Dada Manifestos"). In Paris he engaged in tumultuous activities with André Breton, Philippe Soupault, and Louis Aragon to shock the public and to disintegrate the structures of language. About 1930, weary of nihilism and destruction, he joined his friends in the more constructive activities of Surrealism. He devoted much time to the reconciliation of Surrealism and Marxism and joined the Communist Party in 1936 and the French Resistance movement during World War II. These political commitments brought him closer to his fellow human beings, and he gradually matured into a lyrical poet. His poems revealed the anguish of his soul, caught between revolt and wonderment at the daily tragedy of the human condition. His mature works started with *L'Homme approximatif* (1931; "The Approximate Man") and continued with *Parler seul* (1950; "Speaking Alone") and *La Face intérieure* (1953; "The Inner Face"). In these, the anarchically scrambled words of Dada were replaced with a difficult but humanized language.

Tzetzes \ˈtset-ˌses, -ˌsēz\, John (fl. 12th century AD, Constantinople)   Byzantine didactic poet and scholar who preserved much valuable information from ancient Greek literature and scholarship, in which he was widely read.

Tzetzes' literary and scholarly output was enormous, although it contained many inaccuracies—mostly because he was quoting from memory, since he lacked books, which he said his poverty forced him to do without. Of his numerous and varied works the most important is the *Chiliades* ("Thousands," named for the arbitrary decision of the first editor to divide it into sections of 1,000 lines). Also known as the *Book of Histories*, the work is a long poem (more than 12,000 lines of 15 syllables) containing literary, historical, antiquarian, and mythological miscellanies, intended to serve as a commentary on Tzetzes' own letters, which are addressed to friends and famous contemporaries as well as to fictitious persons. The total number of authors quoted exceeds 400, and the work contains much information unavailable elsewhere. Among Tzetzes' other works were the *Allegoriai* (two long didactic poems containing interpretations of Homeric theology) and commentaries on a number of Greek authors.

tz'u   *see* CI.

ubi sunt \ˈü-bē-ˈsu̇nt\   Derived from the opening words of a number of medieval Latin poems, the term now refers to a verse form in which the poem or its stanzas begin with the Latin words *ubi sunt* ("where are . . .") or their equivalent in another language and which has as a principal theme the transitory nature of all things. A well-known example is François Villon's "Ballade des dames du temps jadis" ("Ballade of the Ladies of Bygone Times"), with its refrain "Mais où sont les neiges d'antan?" ("But where are the snows of yesteryear?").

Ubu roi \ǖe-bǖe-ˈrwä\   Play by Alfred JARRY, published and produced in 1896. The play was translated into English and published under a variety of titles. This grotesque farce about the monstrous Ubu, originally written as a parody of one of Jarry's teachers, swiftly turned into a satire of the French middle class.

The title character, Père Ubu, is a gluttonous, greedy, and cruel individual who slaughters the royal family of Poland in order to ascend to the throne. Ubu ultimately proves himself a coward when he is forced to do battle with the king of Poland's surviving son. The play's scatological references, pompous style, and bastardized French caused the audience to riot when it was first produced. It was later championed by the Surrealists and Dadaists in the 1920s, who recognized in *Ubu roi* the first absurdist drama.

Jarry wrote several sequels, including *Ubu enchaîné* (1900; "Ubu Bound") and *Ubu cocu* (1944; "Ubu Cuckolded"), which were translated and published with *Ubu roi* as *The Ubu Plays* (1968).

Uchimura Kanzō \ü-ˈchē-mü-rä-ˈkän-ˌzō\ (b. April 2, 1861, Edo [now Tokyo], Japan—d. March 28, 1930, Tokyo)   Japanese religious thinker and critic who exerted an important formative influence on many writers and intellectual leaders of modern Japan.

Uchimura came from a samurai (warrior) family and studied at the Sapporo Agricultural School, where he was baptized in 1871. He continued his studies in the United States (1884–88) and returned to Japan to teach in Tokyo. By 1882 he had founded his own independent Japanese Christian church, and he became the center of controversy in 1891 when he questioned the divinity of the emperor by refusing to bow when presented with the Imperial Rescript on Education. Among his writings are *Kirisuto-shintō no nagusame* (1893; "Consolations of a Christian"), *Kyūanroku* (1893; "Seeking Peace of Mind"), and *Yo wa ikanishite Kirisuto-shintō to narishi ya* (1895; "How I Became a Christian"). His religious freethinking drew around him groups of young men, among them the writers Masamune Hakuchō, Mushanokōji Saneatsu, and Arishima Takeo, who in 1910 founded the influential *Shirakaba* ("White Birch") journal as a vehicle for their humanitarian ideals.

Udall \\'yüd-əl, -ˌȯl, -ˌal; yü-'dal, -'dȯl\\, Nicholas (b. December 1505?, Southampton, Hampshire, Eng.—d. December 1556, Westminster)   English playwright, translator, and schoolmaster who wrote the first known English comedy, RALPH ROISTER DOISTER (performed *c.* 1553).

Udall was educated at the University of Oxford, where he became lecturer and fellow. He became a schoolmaster in 1529 and was teaching in London in 1533 when he wrote "ditties and interludes" for Anne Boleyn's coronation. In 1534 he published *Floures for Latine Spekynge Selected and Gathered out of Terence . . . Translated into Englysshe* (dated 1533). The same year he became headmaster of Eton College.

Udall worked as a translator; in 1542 he published a version of Erasmus' *Apophthegmes*. In 1549 Udall became tutor to the young Edward Courtenay. In 1551 he obtained a prebend (stipend) at Windsor, and in 1553 he was given a living on the Isle of Wight.

Although Udall is credited in John Bale's catalog of English writers with "many comedies," the only play extant that can certainly be assigned to him is *Ralph Roister Doister*. The play—about a braggart soldier-hero who is finally shown to be an arrant coward—marks the emergence of English comedy from the medieval morality plays, interludes, and farces.

Ueda Akinari \\'ü-ä-dä-ä-'kē-nä-rē\\, *pseudonym of* Ueda Senjiro \\'sen-jē-ˌrō\\ (b. July 25, 1734, Ōsaka, Japan—d. Aug. 8, 1809, Kyōto)   Preeminent writer and poet of late 18th-century Japan who is best known for his tales of the supernatural.

Ueda had started to write *ukiyo-zōshi* ("tales of the floating world"), the popular fiction of the day, when in 1771 the business he had managed since his stepfather's death 10 years earlier burned down. He then devoted himself to writing full time. In 1776, after eight years of work, he produced *Ugetsu monogatari* (*Tales of Moonlight and Rain*). These ghost tales showed a concern for literary style uncharacteristic of most popular fiction of the time, in which the text often served simply as an accompaniment for the illustrations that formed the main part of the books. Ueda's *Harusame monogatari* (1808; *Tales of the Spring Rain*) is another fine story collection. A student of history and philology, Ueda called for a revival of classical literature and for language reform.

Ugly American, The   Novel by William J. Lederer and Eugene Burdick, published in 1958.

A fictionalized account of Americans working in Southeast Asia, the book was notable chiefly for exposing many of the deficiencies in the United States' foreign aid policy and for causing a furor in government circles. Eventually the uproar led to a congressional review of foreign aid. Although some of the novel's characters are committed to the local people, many others are incompetent and out of touch with the Asians they are supposedly helping. The term "ugly American" has since passed into the language as an expression of the boorishness and insensitive parochialism of Americans abroad.

Uhland \\'ü-länt\\, Ludwig, *in full* Johann Ludwig Uhland (b. April 26, 1787, Tübingen, Württemberg [Germany]—d. Nov.

13, 1862, Tübingen)   German Romantic poet and important figure in the development of German medieval studies.

Uhland studied at the University of Tübingen. He wrote his first poems while in Tübingen, publishing *Vaterländische Gedichte* ("Fatherland Poems") in 1815. It was the first of some 50 editions of the work issued during his lifetime. The collection, which was inspired by the contemporary political situation in Germany, reflected both his serious study of folklore and his ability to create ballads in the folk style.

Uhland worked for the government, practiced law, and supported the struggle for parliamentary democracy in Württemberg. In 1829 he was appointed professor at Tübingen, but, when he was refused leave of absence by the university to sit as a liberal in the Landtag (provincial diet), he resigned the professorship in 1833. In 1848 he was a member of the German National Assembly in Frankfurt.

The spirit of German Romanticism and nationalism inspired much of Uhland's poetry, as did his political career and his researches into the literary heritage of Germany. His poetry utilizes the classical form developed by Johann Wolfgang von Goethe and Friedrich von Schiller, but his naive, precise, and graceful style is uniquely his own.

Ukemochi no Kami \\ü-'kä-mō-chē-nō-'kä-mē\\ ("Goddess Who Possesses Food")   In Japanese mythology, the Shintō goddess of food. She is also sometimes identified as Wakaukanome ("Young Woman with Food") and is associated with Toyuke (Toyouke) Ōkami, the god of food, clothing, and housing, who is enshrined in the Outer Shrine of Ise.

Ukigumo \\ü-'kē-gə-mō\\ ("The Drifting Clouds")   Novel by FUTABATEI Shimei, published in 1887–89. The novel was published in three parts, at first under the name of the author's more famous friend, Tsubouchi Shōyō.

Ukigumo was one of the first attempts to replace classical Japanese literary language and syntax with the modern colloquial idiom. Utsumi Bunzō, the novel's antihero protagonist, refuses to compromise the ancient code of behavior ingrained in him by his samurai background. Although he is likable and decent, he is no match for the ambitious Noboru, to whom he loses the love of Osei, a girl who loves Western culture and ideals. The book ends abruptly and some critics feel that it was left unfinished. It was published in English as *Japan's First Modern Novel: Ukigumo of Futabatei Shimei*.

Ukrainka \\ü-krȧ-'yēn-kȧ\\, Lesia *or* Lesya, *pseudonym of* Larysa Petrivna Kosach-Kvitka \\kō-'sȧch-'kvēt-kȧ\\ (b. Feb. 13 [Feb. 25, New Style], 1871, Novograd-Volynsky [now Novohrad-Volynskyy], Ukraine, Russian Empire—d. July 19 [Aug. 1], 1913, Surami, Georgia)   Poet and dramatist of the Ukrainian modernist movement who was the most important writer of her generation.

Ukrainka's early lyrical work, influenced by Taras Shevchenko and Ivan Franko, dealt with the poet's loneliness and social alienation and was informed by a love of freedom (especially national freedom). Her first collection, *Na krylakh pisen* ("On Wings of Song"), was published in 1893. Two years later her powerful poetic cycle *Nevilnychi pisni* ("The Songs of the Slaves") appeared. Ukrainka was active in the Ukrainian struggle against czarism and joined Ukrainian Marxist organizations, translating the *Communist Manifesto* into Ukrainian in 1902. In 1907 she was arrested and, following her release, was kept under observation by the czarist police. Her later works, which included both dramatic poems and plays, were inspired by various historical milieus—*e.g.*, the classical world, the early Christian era, and the medieval period. This series was crowned by the plays *Lisova pisnia* (1911; *Forest Song*) and *Kaminny hospodar* (1912; *The Stone Host*).

Ulaid cycle *see* ULSTER CYCLE.

Ulalume \ˌyü-lə-'lü-mē\ Poem by Edgar Allan POE, published in the magazine *American Review* in December 1847. It is about a man who wanders unconsciously to his lover's tomb, and it is noted for its gothic imagery and hypnotic rhythm.

In "Ulalume" the narrator, with the nighttime stars as his guide, wanders through an eerie woodland. His dreamy walk abruptly concludes at a tomb, which he recognizes with anguish as belonging to his lover, Ulalume. He had buried her there exactly one year before. Regarded by Poe as a ballad, this lyrical poem is written in anapestic trimeter with consistent end rhyme. It originally comprised 10 stanzas, but it often is printed without the final stanza.

Ull \'ůl\, *Old Norse* Ullr \'ůl-ər\ In Norse mythology, the god of snowshoes, hunting, the bow, and the shield; he was a handsome stepson of the thunder god Thor. Ull possessed warriorlike attributes and was called upon for aid in individual combat. He resided at Ydalir ("Yew Dales").

Although not much has been recorded about Ull, he must have been a very prominent deity in the Norse pantheon at one time because his name appears as part of many Swedish and Norwegian place-names. In the chronicles of the Danish historian Saxo Grammaticus, Ollerus is the equivalent of Ull.

Ulrich von Hutten \'ůl-rik̲-fön-'hůt-ən\ (b. April 21, 1488, near Fulda, Abbacy of Fulda [Germany]—d. Aug. 29?, 1523, near Zürich, Switz.) Franconian knight and humanist, famed as a German patriot, satirist, and supporter of Luther's cause during the turbulent Reformation period.

As a supporter of the ancient status of the knightly order (*Ritterstand*), Ulrich looked back to the Middle Ages; but as a writer he looked forward, employing the new literary forms of the humanists in biting Latin dialogues satirizing the pretensions of princes, the papacy, scholasticism, and obscurantism. He was the main contributor to the second volume of the *Epistolae obscurorum virorum* (1515–17; "Letters of Obscure Men"), a famous attack on monkish life and letters. As a patriot, he envisioned a united Germany and after 1520 wrote satires in German. His vigorous series of satiric pamphlets on Martin Luther's behalf, which first were published in Latin, were subsequently translated into German in his *Gesprächbüchlein* (1522; "Little Conversation Book").

Ulster cycle \'əl-stər\ or **Ulaid cycle** \'ü-lət̲h̲ʸ, -ləgʸ\ In early Irish literature, a group of legends and tales dealing with the heroic age of the Ulaid, a people of northeastern Ireland from whom the English name Ulster ultimately derives. The stories, set in the 1st century BC, were recorded from oral tradition between the 8th and 11th century and are preserved in the 12th-century manuscripts THE BOOK OF THE DUN COW and THE BOOK OF LEINSTER and also in later compilations, such as *The Yellow Book of Lecan* (14th century). They reflect the customs of a free pre-Christian aristocracy who fought from chariots, took heads as trophies, were subject to taboo (*geis*), and were influenced by druids. Mythological elements are freely intermingled with legendary elements that have an air of authenticity. Events center on the reign of the semi-historical King Conor (Conchobar mac Nessa) at Emain Macha (near modern Armagh) and his Knights of the Red Branch (*i.e.*, the palace building in which the heads and arms of vanquished enemies were stored). A rival court at Connaught is ruled by King Ailill and Queen Medb. The chief hero of the Red Branch is the Achilles-like Cú Chulainn, born of a mortal mother, Dechtire, the sister of King Conor, and a divine father, the god Lug (Lugh) of the Long Arm.

Most of the stories are short prose narratives, using verse for description and for scenes of heightened emotion. They fall into types such as destructions, cattle raids, or elopements. The longest tale and the closest approach to an epic is THE CATTLE RAID OF COOLEY, dealing with a conflict between the men of Ulster and of Connaught. Another tale, BRICRIU'S FEAST, contains a beheading game that is the first appearance in print of a story that was later used in *Sir Gawayne and the Grene Knight* and several other medieval narratives. The tale having the most profound influence on later Irish literature is THE TRAGIC DEATH OF THE SONS OF USNECH.

ultima Thule \'əl-ti-mə-'thü-lē, 'thyü-lē, 'thül, 'thyül\ The furthest possible place in the world, or a remote goal. Thule was the northernmost part of the habitable ancient world. References to ultima Thule in modern literature appear in works by Edgar Allen Poe, Henry Wadsworth Longfellow, and the Australian writer Henry Handel Richardson.

Ultraísmo \ˌül-trä-'ēz-mō\ or **Ultraism** \'əl-trə-ˌiz-əm\ [Spanish *ultraísmo*, a derivative of *ultra-* beyond] Movement in Spanish and Spanish-American poetry after World War I, characterized by a tendency to use free verse, complicated metrical innovations, and daring imagery and symbolism instead of traditional form and content. Influenced by the emphasis on form of the French Symbolists and Parnassians, a distinguished group of poets (*ultraístas*) produced verse that often defied objective analysis and gave the impression of a coldly intellectual experimentation. Launched in Madrid in 1919 by the poet Guillermo de Torre, who coined the name, Ultraísmo found an outlet in the two major avant-garde periodicals, *Grecia* (1919–20) and *Ultra* (1921–22).

Jorge Luis Borges introduced Ultraísmo to South America in 1921. There the movement attracted poets such as the Chileans Pablo Neruda and Vicente Huidobro and the Mexicans Jaime Torres Bodet and Carlos Pellicer. Although the movement had subsided by 1923, the sociopolitical overtones of the writing of the South American *ultraístas*, as seen in the verse of César Vallejo of Peru, flowered into the Marxist poetry of the following decade. Later the verbal techniques of the *ultraístas* were revived by post-World War II avant-garde writers.

Ulysses \yů-'lis-ēz\ In Greek mythology, the hero of Homer's *Odyssey*. *See* ODYSSEUS.

Ulysses \yů-'lis-ēz\ Novel by James JOYCE, first excerpted in *The Little Review* in 1918–20, at which time further publication of the book was banned. *Ulysses* was published in book form in 1922 by Sylvia Beach. There have since been other editions published, but scholars cannot agree on the authenticity of any one of them. An edition published in 1984 that supposedly corrected some 5,000 standing errors generated controversy because of the inclusion by its editors of passages not in the original text and because it allegedly introduced hundreds of new errors.

The novel is constructed as a modern parallel to Homer's Odyssey. All of the action of the novel takes place in Dublin on a single day (June 16, 1904). The three central characters—Stephen Dedalus (the hero of Joyce's earlier Portrait of the Artist as a Young Man), Leopold Bloom, a Jewish advertising canvasser, and his wife Molly Bloom—are intended to be modern counterparts of Telemachus, Ulysses, and Penelope, and the events of the novel parallel the major events in Odysseus' journey home.

The main strength of *Ulysses* lies in its depth of character portrayal and its breadth of humor. Yet the book is most famous for its use of a variant of the interior monologue known as the stream-of-consciousness technique.

Ulysses \yů-'lis-ēz\ Blank-verse poem by Alfred, Lord TENNYSON, written in 1833 and published in the two-volume collection *Poems* (1842). In a stirring dramatic monologue, the aged title character outlines his plans to abandon his dreary kingdom of Ithaca to reclaim lost glory in a final adventure on the seas. It was one of several poems that Tennyson composed in response to the death of his friend Arthur Henry Hallam.

Restless and bored with Ithaca, Ulysses turns his throne over to his prudent son Telemachus and rallies his men with inspiring words of heroism. The ironic distance of the narrative voice intensifies the ambiguity as to whether Ulysses is proving his noble courage or shirking his responsibilities in Ithaca for a journey that may prove to be futile, fatal, or both. Tennyson based his two-sided view of Ulysses on Book XI of Homer's *Odyssey* and Canto XXVI of Dante's *Inferno*.

'Umar ibn Abī Rabī'ah \'ō-mȧr-,ib-ən-ȧ-'bē-rȧ-'bē-ȧ, *Arabic* "ō-mȧr, rȧ-'bē-'ȧ\, *in full* 'Umar ibn 'Abd Allāh ibn Abī Rabī'ah al-Makhzūmī (b. November 644, Mecca [now in Saudi Arabia]—d. 712/719, Mecca)   One of the greatest poets in early Arabic literature.

The verse of 'Umar ibn Abī Rabī'ah gives a valuable picture of the social life of the Meccan and Medinan aristocracy of his time. His poetry centers on his own life and emotions, eschewing the traditional themes of journeys, battles, and tribal lore, and celebrates his love affairs with the noble Arab ladies who came to Mecca on pilgrimage. Although the genre of Arabic poetry known as ghazel had been sporadically practiced before his time, 'Umar ibn Abī Rabī'ah was the first to refine it by using a light meter and expressing an accurate perception of human feeling.

Una \'yü-nȯ\   Fictional female character who represents true religion or true belief in Book I of THE FAERIE QUEENE by Edmund Spenser. Una is separated from her champion, the Red Cross Knight. Until she and the Red Cross Knight are reunited and subsequently married, Una is protected by a lion, who symbolizes England.

Unamuno \,ü-nä-'mü-nō\, Miguel, *surname in full* de Unamuno y Jugo \ē-'hü-gō\ (b. Sept. 29, 1864, Bilbao, Spain—d. Dec. 31, 1936, Salamanca)   Educator, philosopher, and author whose essays had great influence in early 20th-century Spain.

Unamuno was educated at the University of Madrid. In 1890 he was named professor at the University of Salamanca, becoming rector in 1901. He was relieved of his duties in 1914 after publicly espousing the Allied cause in World War I and was forced into exile in 1924. He returned and was reelected rector of the university in 1931 but was removed once again when, in October 1936, he denounced Francisco Franco's Falangists.

Although he also wrote poetry and plays, Unamuno was most influential as an essayist and novelist. His mature philosophy found its fullest expression in *Del sentimiento trágico de la vida en los hombres y en los pueblos* (1913; *The Tragic Sense of Life in Men and Peoples*), in which he stressed the role spiritual anxiety plays in driving one to live the fullest possible life.

Unamuno's novels are intensely psychological depictions of agonized characters who illustrate and give voice to his own philosophical ideas. His most famous novel is *Abel Sánchez: una historia de pasión* (1917; *Abel Sánchez*), a modern re-creation of the biblical story of Cain and Abel, which centers on the painfully conflicting impulses of the Cain figure. Other novels include *Amor y pedagogía* (1902; "Love and Pedagogy"), *Niebla* (1914; *Mist*), and *San Manuel Bueno, mártir* (1933; "Saint Manuel the Good, Martyr"). Unamuno's *El Cristo de Velázquez* (1920; *The Christ of Velázquez*), a study of the painter in poetry, is regarded as a superb example of modern Spanish verse.

Unanimisme \ū̇-nä-'nēz-mə\ or **Unanimism** \yü-'nan-i-,miz-əm\   French literary movement based on the psychological concept of group consciousness and collective emotion

that posited the need for the poet to merge with this transcendent consciousness. Founded by Jules Romains about 1908, Unanimisme particularly influenced some members of the Abbaye group, a loose organization of young artists and writers who were interested in printing and publicizing new works. *Petit Traité de versification* (1923; "Small Treatise on Versification"), by Romains and Georges Chennevière, and *Notes sur la technique poétique* (1910; "Notes on Poetic Technique"), by Georges Duhamel and Charles Vildrac, outlined the Unanimiste theories of prosody, which resembled those of the American poet Walt Whitman in encouraging the use of strongly accented rhythms and the replacement of symbols and allegory by simple and unadorned diction.

The name *Unanimisme* was based on the title of a poem by Romains, *La Vie unanime* (1908; "Life of One Mind"), that expressed his philosophy.

Unbearable Lightness of Being, The   Novel by Milan KUNDERA, first published in 1984 in an English translation and in a French translation as *L'Insoutenable Légèreté de l'être*. In 1985 the work was published in the original Czech as *Nesnesitelná lehkost bytí*, but it was banned in Czechoslovakia until 1989.

Set against the background of Czechoslovakia in the 1960s, the novel concerns a young Czech physician who substitutes a series of erotic adventures over which he thinks he can maintain control for becoming involved in his country's politics, where he feels he can have no power or freedom. Inevitably, he is drawn into Czechoslovakia's political unrest. In a parallel vein, he is forced to choose among the women with whom he is involved.

Uncle Remus \'rē-məs\   Fictional character, a former slave who narrates a series of tales by Joel Chandler HARRIS. The stories, which were based on African-American folklore, were first collected in book form as *Uncle Remus: His Songs and His Sayings* in 1880. The animal characters in his stories, known as Brer Rabbit, Brer Fox, and Brer Bear, have human qualities, and the tales of their adventures are concluded with moral teachings.

Further collections of stories include *Nights with Uncle Remus* (1883), *Uncle Remus and His Friends* (1892), and *The Tar-Baby and Other Rhymes of Uncle Remus* (1904).

Uncle Tom's Cabin \'täm\ (*in full* Uncle Tom's Cabin; or, Life Among the Lowly)   Novel by Harriet Beecher STOWE, published in serialized form in 1851–52 and in book form in 1852. Dramatizing the plight of slaves, the novel had so great an impact that it is sometimes cited as one of the causes of the American Civil War.

While being transported by boat to a slave auction in New Orleans, the protagonist, a saintly, dignified slave named Uncle Tom, saves the life of Little Eva St. Clare, whose grateful father then purchases Tom. Little Eva and Tom soon become great friends. Always frail, Eva's health begins to decline rapidly, and on her deathbed she asks her father to free all his slaves. Mr. St. Clare makes plans to manumit his slaves but is killed before he can do so, and the brutal Simon Legree, Tom's new owner, has Tom whipped to death after he refuses to divulge the whereabouts of certain runaway slaves.

The dramatic adaptation of *Uncle Tom's Cabin* played to capacity audiences and was a staple of touring companies through the rest of the 19th century and into the 20th century.

Uncle Tom's Children \'täm\   Collection of four novellas by Richard WRIGHT, published in 1938. The collection, Wright's first published book, was awarded the 1938 *Story* magazine prize for the best book written by anyone involved in the WPA Federal Writers' Project.

Set in the American Deep South, each novella concerns an aspect of the lives of black people and explores their resistance to white racism and oppression. The stories are "Big Boy Leaves Home," "Down by the Riverside," "Long Black Song," and "Fire and Cloud." Thematically and stylistically they form a consistent whole.

In 1940 an enlarged edition of *Uncle Tom's Children* was published. Subtitled "Five Long Stories," it also contained a nonfiction essay, "The Ethics of Living Jim Crow," and a polemical short story, "Bright and Morning Star"; both additions were thought by critics to have damaged the literary integrity of the book.

Uncle Vanya \\'vän-yə\\   Drama in four acts by Anton CHEKHOV, published in 1897 as *Dyadya Vanya* and first produced in 1899 in Moscow. Considered one of Chekhov's theatrical masterpieces, the play is a study of aimlessness and hopelessness.

Ivan Voynitsky, called Uncle Vanya, is bitterly disappointed when he realizes that he has wasted his life managing the business affairs of his former brother-in-law, Serebryakov, who, Vanya discovers, will never be anything more than a second-rate academic. Sonya, Serebryakov's daughter and Vanya's assistant, silently endures her unrequited love for a local physician. Vanya attempts to shoot Serebryakov but misses, and little changes. Neither of them can give up the work, however meaningless, to which they have devoted their lives.

Unconditional Surrender   Novel by Evelyn Waugh, originally published in 1961. It is the third volume of the trilogy SWORD OF HONOUR, set during World War II.

Underhill \\'ən-dər-,hil\\, Evelyn, *married name* Moore \\'mùr, 'mòr\\ (b. Dec. 6, 1875, Wolverhampton, Staffordshire, Eng.—d. June 15, 1941, London)   English mystical poet and author of several works that helped establish mystical theology as a respectable discipline among contemporary intellectuals.

Underhill was a prolific writer in a wide variety of genres, including biography, the essay, philosophy, and fiction. She is best known for her writings on mysticism, particularly *Mysticism* (1911), *The Mystic Way* (1913), and *Worship* (1936).

A frequent lecturer at conferences and seminars, Underhill also conducted retreats and gained a reputation as a leading religious counselor. She was a contributor to numerous journals and was the theology editor of *The Spectator* from 1929 to 1932. Among her works of fiction were three novels and the poetry collections *The Bar-Lamb's Ballad Book* (1902), *Immanence* (1912), and *Theophanies* (1916).

Under Milk Wood   Play for voices by Dylan THOMAS, performed in 1953 and published in 1954. Originally written as a radio play, *Under Milk Wood* is sometimes presented as a staged drama. Richly imaginative in language and characterization, and fertile in comic invention, the play evokes a day in the lives of the inhabitants of a small Welsh town.

understate \\,ən-dər-'stāt\\   **1.** To represent as less than is the case.   **2.** To state or present with restraint, especially for effect.

Under the Volcano   Masterwork of Malcolm LOWRY, published in 1947 and reissued in 1962.

Set in Mexico in the late 1930s, *Under the Volcano* is the story of the last desperate day in the life of Geoffrey Firmin, a dispirited alcoholic and former British consul. His estranged wife, Yvonne, attempts to repair their marriage despite the presence of two of her former lovers: a film director, Jacques Laruelle, and Geoffrey's half-brother, Hugh.

The novel's extraordinary, almost expressionistic juxtaposition of realistic images with the perceptions of an increasingly irrational man took on an even greater symbolic power when seen as a vision of Europe on the verge of war. Critically praised when it was released, the novel did not receive popular recognition until after Lowry's death.

Underwood \\'ən-dər-,wùd\\, Francis Henry (b. Jan. 12, 1825, Enfield, Mass., U.S.—d. Aug. 7, 1894, Edinburgh, Scot.)   American author and lawyer who became a founder of *The Atlantic Monthly* (later *The Atlantic*) in order to further the antislavery cause.

Underwood attended Amherst (Mass.) College and the University of Kentucky. He joined the publishing house of Phillips, Sampson and Company as assistant editor in the early 1850s. The antislavery atmosphere of the Northeast and his close observation of slavery in Kentucky led him to the idea of publishing a literary magazine to oppose slavery. By 1857, after several years of editorial experience, he had gained the support of such liberal writers as Harriet Beecher Stowe, Oliver Wendell Holmes, Ralph Waldo Emerson, Henry David Thoreau, Henry Wadsworth Longfellow, and James Russell Lowell and persuaded his firm to publish a magazine. Edited by Lowell, with Underwood as assistant editor, *The Atlantic Monthly* began publication in November 1857. Underwood left the magazine in 1859 after it was purchased by another firm. He wrote biographies of Lowell, Longfellow, and John Greenleaf Whittier, as well as several short stories and novels. His best-known book is *Quabbin: The Story of a Small Town* (1893), an account of his boyhood in Enfield.

undine \\,ən-'dēn, 'ən-,dēn\\ [New Latin *undina*, a derivative of Latin *unda* wave, water], *also spelled* Ondine.   Mythological figure of European tradition, a water nymph who becomes human when she falls in love with a man but is doomed to die if he is unfaithful to her. Derived from the Greek Nereids, attendants of the sea god Poseidon, Ondine was first mentioned in the writings of the Swiss author Paracelsus, who put forth his theory that there are spirits called "undines" who inhabit the element of water. A version of the myth was adapted as the romance *Undine* by Motte-Fouque in 1811. Maurice Maeterlinck's play *Pelleas and Melisande* (1892) was in part based on this myth, as was *Ondine* (1939), a drama by Jean Giraudoux. *Compare* GNOME; SALAMANDER; SYLPH.

Undset \\'ùn-set\\, Sigrid (b. May 20, 1882, Kalundborg, Den.—d. June 10, 1949, Lillehammer, Nor.)   Norwegian novelist whose readership is international and who received the Nobel Prize for Literature in 1928.

Undset's father was an archaeologist, and her home life was steeped in legend, folklore, and the history of Norway. Both this influence and her own life story are constantly present in her works—from *Elleve aar* (1934; *Eleven Years*), in which she tells of her childhood, to the story of her flight from Nazi-occupied Norway, published originally in English as *Return to the Future* (1942; Norwegian, *Tillbake til fremtiden*).

Her early novels deal with the position of women in the contemporary unromantic world of the lower middle class. These include *Splinten av troldspeilet* (1917; *Images in a Mirror*) and *Jenny* (1911). She then turned to the distant past and created what is considered her masterpiece, the trilogy KRISTIN LAVRANSDATTER (1920–22). Although the medieval milieu is strikingly portrayed, its story of the spiritual growth of a strong women is timeless. Both in this and in the four-volume historical novel *Olav Audunsson* (1925–27; *The Master of Hestviken*), religious problems are prominent and reflect the author's preoccupation with such matters. Undset was converted to the Roman Catholic faith in 1924, and in her later novels, in which she returned to contemporary themes, her new religion plays an important role.

Ungaretti \ˌün-gä-'rät-tē\, Giuseppe (b. Feb. 10, 1888, Alexandria, Egypt—d. June 1, 1970, Milan, Italy) Italian poet and founder of the Hermetic movement, which brought about a reorientation in modern Italian poetry.

Ungaretti lived in Alexandria until he was 24; the desert regions of Egypt were to provide recurring images in his later work. He went to Paris in 1912 to study at the Sorbonne and became close friends with the poets Guillaume Apollinaire, Charles Péguy, and Paul Valéry. Contact with French Symbolist poetry, particularly that of Stéphane Mallarmé, was one of the most important influences of his life.

At the outbreak of World War I, Ungaretti enlisted in the Italian Army, and while on the battlefield he wrote his first collection of poetry. These poems, published in *Il porto sepolto* (1916; "The Buried Port"), used no rhyme, punctuation, or traditional form; this was Ungaretti's first attempt to strip ornament from words and to present them in their purest, most evocative form. Though reflecting the experimental attitude of the Futurists, Ungaretti's poetry developed in a coherent and original direction, as is apparent in *Allegria di naufragi* (1919; "Gay Shipwrecks"), which shows the influence of Giacomo Leopardi and includes revised poems from Ungaretti's first volume. Further change is evident in *Sentimento del tempo* (1933; "The Feeling of Time"), which, containing poems written between 1919 and 1932, used more obscure language and difficult symbolism. *See also* HERMETICISM.

From 1936 to 1942 Ungaretti taught Italian literature at the University of São Paulo, Brazil. His son died in Brazil, and Ungaretti's anguish over his loss as well as his sorrow over the atrocities of Nazism and World War II are expressed in the poems of *Il dolore* (1947; "Grief "). Ungaretti's later volumes include *La terra promessa* (1950; "The Promised Land"), *Un grido e paesaggi* (1952; "A Cry and Landscapes"), *Il taccuino del vecchio* (1960; "An Old Man's Notebook"), and *Morte delle stagioni* (1967; "Death of the Seasons").

Ungaretti also translated works of Jean Racine, William Shakespeare, Luis de Góngora, Mallarmé, and William Blake; all were later incorporated in *Traduzioni*, 2 vol. (1946–50).

unghosted \ən-'gōs-təd\ Not ghostwritten; written firsthand, by the person whose name is on the work.

unicorn \'yü-ni-ˌkȯrn\ [Late Latin *unicornis* (translation of Greek *monókerōs*), from Latin, having a single horn, from *unus* one + *cornu* horn] A fabulous animal possibly based on faulty old descriptions of the rhinoceros and generally depicted (as in heraldry) with the body and head of a horse, the hind legs of a stag, the tail of a lion, and in the middle of the forehead a single long straight horn held to be a sovereign remedy against poisoning.

The unicorn was referred to in the ancient myths of India and China. The earliest description in Greek literature of a single-horned animal was by the historian Ctesias (*c.* 400 BC).

Certain poetical passages of the biblical Old Testament refer to a strong and splendid horned animal called *re'em*. This word was translated "unicorn" or "rhinoceros" in many versions of the Bible, but many modern translations prefer "wild ox" (aurochs), which is the correct meaning of the Hebrew *re'em*. As a biblical animal, the unicorn was interpreted allegorically in the early Christian church. One of the earliest such interpretations appears in the ancient Greek bestiary known as the *Physiologus*, which states that the unicorn is a strong, fierce animal that can be caught only if a virgin maiden is thrown before it. The unicorn leaps into the virgin's lap, and she suckles it and leads it to the king's palace. Medieval writers thus likened the unicorn to Christ, who dwelt in the womb of the Virgin Mary and raised up a horn of salvation.

union \'yün-yən\ Of a literary language, artificially created by a selection of vocabulary and usages from related dialects or languages with the intent of serving all equally, such as Esperanto.

Union of Writers of the U.S.S.R. *also called* Union of Soviet Writers. Organization formed in 1932 by a decree of the Central Committee of the Communist Party of the Soviet Union that abolished existing literary organizations and absorbed all professional Soviet writers into one large union. The union supported Communist Party policies and was the defender and interpreter of the single Soviet literary method, SOCIALIST REALISM. The union held its First All-Union Congress in 1934 and thereafter met at irregular intervals. The main union actually encompassed several different local unions, including one for each of the constituent republics of the Soviet Union. After the breakup of the Soviet Union in 1991, the main union was split into several groups and ceased to exist as a single entity.

Uniti \ü-'nē-tē\ (*in full* Compagnia degli Uniti) Company of actors performing commedia dell'arte in Italy in the late 16th and early 17th centuries.

unity \'yü-nə-tē\ *plural* unities. A combination or ordering of parts in a literary or artistic production that constitutes a whole or promotes an undivided total effect; also, the resulting singleness of effect or symmetry and consistency of style and character. *See also* ORGANIC UNITY.

In drama the term refers more specifically to any of three principles derived by French classicists from Aristotle's *Poetics* and requiring a play to have a single action represented as occurring in one place and within one day. They were called respectively *unity of action*, *unity of place*, and *unity of time*.

These three unities were redefined in 1570 by the Italian humanist Lodovico Castelvetro in his interpretation of Aristotle's *Poetics* and are usually referred to as "Aristotelian rules" for dramatic structure. Actually, Aristotle's observations on tragedy are descriptive rather than prescriptive, and he emphasizes only one unity, that of plot, or action.

In the French classical tragedy, the unities were adhered to literally and became the source of endless critical polemics. Disputes arose over such problems as whether a single day meant 12 or 24 hours and whether a single place meant one room or one city. In spite of such severe restrictions, the prestige of the unities continued to dominate French drama until the Romantic era. In England, however, the unities were esteemed in theory but ignored in practice.

University wit Any of a notable group of pioneer English dramatists writing during the last 15 years of the 16th century. They transformed the native dramatic inheritance of interlude and chronicle play into a potentially great drama by writing plays of quality and diversity. In doing so they prepared the ground for the genius of William Shakespeare. Their forerunner was John Lyly, an Oxford man, and they included Christopher Marlowe and Thomas Nashe (graduates of Cambridge), Thomas Lodge and George Peele (both of Oxford), and Robert Greene (who took degrees from both universities). Another of the wits, though not university trained, was Thomas Kyd.

unmeasured \ən-'mezh-ərd, -'māzh-\ Not measured; specifically, not metrical.

Unnamable, The \ˌən-'nā-mə-bəl\ Novel by Samuel BECKETT, published in French as *L'Innommable* in 1953 and then translated by the author into English. It was the third in a trilogy of prose narratives that began with MOLLOY (1951) and *Malone meurt* (1951; MALONE DIES), published together in English as *Three Novels* (1959). Lacking any plot in the conventional sense, *The Unnamable* furthers the general focus of the trilogy—the search for the self within the tragic realm of human suffering.

The obsessive narrator, who opens the novel asking, "Where now? Who now? When now?" is a disembodied person, living in a large jar in a restaurant window in Paris. Essentially "unnameable," the narrator is referred to as Mahood, Worm, and Basil, in a series of tales. The final sentence in the novel is a long dramatic monologue. The narrator concludes with the desire to continue living despite an inescapable sense of anguish and entropy: "I can't go on, I'll go on."

unreliable narrator   *see* NARRATOR.

Unruh \'ûn-rū\, Fritz von (b. May 10, 1885, Koblenz, Ger.—d. Nov. 28, 1970, Diez, W.Ger.)   Dramatist, poet, and novelist, one of the most poetically gifted of the younger German Expressionist writers.

The son of a general, Unruh was an army officer on active service until 1912, when he resigned his commission to devote his time to writing. His critical reflections on the military establishment in his play *Offiziere* ("Officers"), staged by Max Reinhardt in 1911, and the antiwar sentiments he expressed in the dramatic poem *Vor der Entscheidung* (1914; "Before the Decision") are early variations on the two themes basic to his entire work: the nature of the social order into which the individual has to be integrated, and the necessity to ground this order not in authority but in the integrity and responsibility of the individual toward humanity. He explored these themes on a metaphysical plane in his narrative *Der Opfergang* (1919; *Way of Sacrifice*), which was written in 1916 while he was on active duty in the Battle of Verdun. The same subjects are examined on a mythical level in the tragedy *Ein Geschlecht* (1916; "A Family"). His growing antimilitaristic attitude led to such later works as *Heinrich von Andernach* (1925), a festival play and a great plea for love among all people.

Unruh foresaw the coming Nazi dictatorship in his drama *Bonaparte* (1927) and continued to press his warnings in *Berlin in Monte Carlo* (1931) and *Zero* (1932). He left Germany in 1932 and lived in France and the United States until he returned to Germany in 1962.

Upanishad or **Upanisad** \ū-'pän-i-,shäd; ū-'pan-i-,shad, yū-\ One of a class of Vedic treatises dealing with broad philosophic problems.

The name Upanishad (Sanskrit *upaniṣad,* from a verb meaning "to sit down near") implies, according to some traditions, sitting at the feet of the teacher. The Upanishads, of which approximately 108 are known, record the views of a succession of Hindu teachers and sages who were active as early as 1000 BC and who flourished about 600 BC. The texts form the basis of much of later Indian philosophy. They represent the final stage in the tradition of the Vedas, so the teaching based on them is known as the Vedānta ("conclusion of the Veda"). The older Upanishads may be part of the Brāhmaṇas (commentaries) of their respective Vedas but are distinguished from them both by increased philosophical and mystical questioning and by their diminished concern with Vedic deities and sacrificial rites.

The Upanishads exhibit a development toward the concept of a single supreme being, and knowledge is directed toward reunion with it. Of fundamental importance to all Hindu thought is the equation in some of the Upanishads of atman (the self) with Brahman (ultimate reality). The nature of eternal life is discussed, as are such themes as the transmigration of souls and causality in creation. *Compare* ĀRAṆYAKA; BRĀHMAṆA. *See also* VEDA.

Updike \'əp-,dīk\, John (Hoyer) (b. March 18, 1932, Shillington, Pa., U.S.)   American writer of novels, short stories, and poetry, known for his careful craftsmanship and realistic but subtle depiction of "American, Protestant, small-town, middleclass" life.

In 1955 Updike began an association with *The New Yorker* magazine, to which he contributed editorials, poetry, stories, and criticism throughout his prolific career. His poetry—intellectual, witty pieces on the absurdities of modern life—was gathered in his first book, *The Carpentered Hen and Other Tame Creatures* (1958), which was followed by his first novel, *The Poorhouse Fair* (1958). RABBIT, RUN (1960), which is considered to be one of his best novels, concerns a former star athlete, Harry "Rabbit" Angstrom, who is unable to recapture success when bound by marriage and small-town life. Three subsequent novels, *Rabbit Redux* (1971), *Rabbit Is Rich* (1981), and *Rabbit at Rest* (1990)—the latter two winning Pulitzer Prizes—follow the same character during later periods of his life. *The Centaur* (1963) and *Of the Farm* (1965) are notable among his novels set in his native Pennsylvania. Most of his later fiction is set in New England, where he lived (in Ipswich, Mass.) from the 1960s.

His later novels include *Couples* (1968), *Bech: A Book* (1970), *Marry Me* (1976), *The Coup* (1976), and *The Witches of Eastwick* (1984). His several collections of short stories include *The Same Door* (1959), PIGEON FEATHERS (1962), *Museums and Women* (1972), *Problems* (1979), and *Trust Me* (1987). His nonfiction was collected in *Assorted Prose* (1965), *Picked-Up Pieces* (1975), *Hugging the Shore* (1983), *Just Looking* (1989), and *Odd Jobs* (1991).

Upfield \'əp-,fēld\, Arthur William (b. Sept. 1, 1888, Gosport, Hampshire, Eng.—d. Feb. 13, 1964, Bowral, N.S.W., Australia)   English-born Australian popular novelist who wrote more than 30 novels featuring Detective Inspector Napoleon (Boney) Bonaparte, a half-Aboriginal Australian detective.

Upfield immigrated to Australia in 1911 and was a sheepherder, gold miner, cowhand, soldier, and fur trapper before turning to writing. While working in the Australian wilderness Upfield met a half-Aborigine who became the prototype of his detective hero. His novels, all interspersed with lengthy descriptions of the colorful Australian landscape, include *The Barrakee Mystery* (1929), in which Bonaparte first appeared; *Murder Down Under* (1943); and *The Body at Madman's Bend* (1963). Upfield also wrote short stories, as well as newspaper and magazine articles on Australian topography and history.

Uppdal \'ûp-däl\, Kristofer Oliver (b. Feb. 19, 1878, Beitstad, Nor.—d. Dec. 26, 1961, Olbu)   Proletarian Norwegian novelist whose major work is the 10-volume *Dansen gjenom skuggeheimen* (1911–24; "The Dance Through the World of Shadows"), which deals with the development of the Norwegian industrial working class from its peasant origin. Uppdal's own life recapitulates the history of Norway's labor movement in his rise from farm boy to skilled worker and eventually labor leader.

Urania \yủ-'rā-nē-ə\   In Greek mythology, one of the nine Muses, patron of astronomy. Urania was also occasionally used as a byname for Aphrodite.

Uranus \'yủr-ə-nəs, yủ-'rā-nəs\   In Greek mythology, the personification of heaven. According to Hesiod's *Theogony,* Gaea (Earth) produced Uranus, the Mountains, and the Sea. From Gaea's subsequent union with Uranus were born the Titans, the Cyclopes, and the Hecatoncheires (three creatures, each having 50 heads and 100 arms).

Uranus hated the Hecatoncheires and hid them in Gaea's body. Gaea appealed to her other children for vengeance, but Cronus (a Titan) alone responded. With the *harpē* (a sickle) he removed the testicles of Uranus as he approached Gaea. From the drops of Uranus' blood that fell upon her were born the Furies, the Giants, and the Meliai (the ash-tree nymphs). The severed genitals floated on the sea, producing a white foam from which sprang the goddess of love, Aphrodite. Cronus by his action had separated Heaven and Earth.

Urchard   *see* URQUHART.

Urfé \düer-'fä\, Honoré d' (b. Feb. 10/11, 1568, Marseille, Fr.—d. June 1, 1625, Villefranche-sur-Mer)   French author whose pastoral romance *L'Astrée* (1607–27; *Astrea*) was extremely popular in the 17th century and inspired many later writers.

D'Urfé's first work, *Epistres Morales* (1598; "Moral Letters"), reveals the influence of Stoicism and Renaissance Platonism. His magnum opus, *L'Astrée*, appeared in five parts from 1607 to 1627 and altogether consists of some 5,000 pages. Part 4 of the book was edited by the author's secretary, Balthazar Baro, who also added Part 5 based on notes left by d'Urfé. With its scene set on the banks of the Lignon River in 5th-century Gaul and its atmosphere of paradisiacal innocence, *L'Astrée* describes the life and adventures of shepherds and shepherdesses whose main preoccupation is love. The book derives its title from the pair Astrée and Céladon, who are unable to marry because of enmity between their families.

D'Urfé's models for his novel were various Spanish and Italian pastoral romances read in the French court, notably *Diana* (1559) by Jorge de Montemayor.

Uris \'yuṙ-is\, Leon (Marcus) (b. Aug. 3, 1924, Baltimore, Md., U.S.)   American novelist known for such panoramic, action-filled works as *Battle Cry* (1953), a story about a battalion of Marines during World War II, and *Exodus* (1958), which deals with the struggle to establish and defend the state of Israel.

Uris also wrote *The Angry Hills* (1955), an account of the Jewish brigade from Palestine that fought with the British army in Greece; *Mila 18* (1961), a novel about the Jewish uprising against the Nazis in the Warsaw ghetto in 1943; *QB VII* (1970), dealing with Nazi war crimes; *Trinity* (1976), a chronicle of a Northern Irish farm family from the 1840s to 1916; *The Haj* (1984), depicting the lives of Palestinian Arabs from World War I to the Suez war of 1956; and *Mitla Pass* (1988), an account of the Sinai campaign of 1956.

urisk \'uṙ-isk\ [Scottish Gaelic *ùruisg*]   In Scottish folklore, a brownie said to frequent sequestered places and waterfalls.

Urizen \'yü-ri-zen\   Character in the mythology of William BLAKE. A godlike figure, Urizen personifies reason and law, and Blake believed him to be the true deity worshiped by his contemporaries. Blake first told Urizen's story, the struggle against the chaos caused by the loss of a true human spirit, in the so-called "Prophetic Books," including *America, A Prophecy* (1793), *The Book of Urizen* (1794), and *The Song of Los* (1795), and then, more ambitiously, in the unfinished manuscript *Vala, or The Four Zoas*, written from approximately 1796 to 1807. In an engraving from *Europe, A Prophecy* (1794), Blake depicts Urizen as a grim scientist, creating the earth with a huge pair of compasses.

Urquhart \'ər-kərt, -kärt, -kərt\ or **Urchard** \'ər-kərd, -kärd, -kərd\, Sir Thomas (b. 1611, Cromarty, Scot.—d. 1660)   Author of one of the most original and vivid translations from any foreign language into English. His works are marked by eccentricity of both language and method.

Urquhart studied at King's College, Aberdeen, and in 1639 fought with the English against the Covenanters, 17th-century Scottish Presbyterians who were fighting to maintain their religious liberty after England's Charles I attempted to impose a new liturgy on them. Urquhart was knighted by Charles I in

1641. His strong Royalist convictions led him in 1651 to join the army of Charles II in the latter's effort to reclaim the English throne after his father, Charles I, was executed. Taken prisoner at the Battle of Worcester, Urquhart was incarcerated. He was eventually released and probably took refuge on the European continent with other Cavaliers (supporters of the king).

In the 1640s and early '50s Urquhart published several fantastic works that combined an obscure and unintelligible symbolism with sharply drawn autobiographical reminiscences. His translation of Rabelais, *Works of Mr. Francis Rabelais* (Books I–II, 1653; part of Book III, 1693), became the long-established English-language version. Peter Anthony Motteux completed Book III (1693–94) as well as Books IV and V (1708).

U.S.A. \,yü-,es-'ā\   Trilogy by John DOS PASSOS, comprising *The 42nd Parallel* (1930), covering the period from 1900 up to World War I; *1919* (1932), dealing with the war and the critical year of the Treaty of Versailles; and *The Big Money* (1936), which moves from the boom of the '20s to the bust of the '30s. Dos Passos reinforces the histories of his fictional characters with interpolated montages of newspaper headlines and popular songs. He also includes biographies that range from representative members of the establishment such as Henry Ford and Thomas Edison to such figures as labor organizer and socialist Eugene V. Debs and economist and social scientist Thorstein Veblen.

Uşaklıgil \ü-,shäk-li-'gēl\, Halit Ziya (b. 1867, Constantinople [now Istanbul, Tur.]—d. March 27, 1945, Istanbul)   Writer who is considered the first true exponent in Turkey of the novel in its contemporary European form.

Uşaklıgil was educated at a French school in İzmir, where he was exposed to the works of the 19th-century French novelists. A journey to France contributed further to his knowledge of European culture, which deeply affected him and his writing. Such early novels as *Bir Ölünün Defteri* (1890; "Journal of a Dead Man") and *Ferdi ve Şürekâsı* (1894; "Ferdi and Company") reveal this French influence.

In 1896 Uşaklıgil became involved with *Servet-i Fünun* ("The Wealth of Knowledge"), an avant-garde journal that he and the other writers of the "new literature" published to inform their readers about European—particularly French—cultural and intellectual movements. The hero of one of his greatest novels, *Mai ve Siyah* (1895; "The Blue and the Black"), is a spokesman for the "new literature" movement. After the Young Turk revolution in 1908, Uşaklıgil taught courses in European literature at Istanbul University. The novel *Aşk-ı Memnu* (1925; "The Forbidden Love") is often considered his masterpiece. He also wrote short stories, dramas, articles, and memoirs.

Uspensky \ü-'spy̆en-skʸē\, Gleb Ivanovich (b. Oct. 13 [Oct. 25, New Style], 1843, Tula province, Russia—d. March 24 [April 6], 1902, St. Petersburg)   Russian intellectual and writer whose realistic portrayals of peasant life did much to amend the prevalent romantic view of the Russian agricultural worker.

Uspensky's first important work, *Nravy Rasteryayevoy ulitsy* (1866; "The Manners of Rasteryayeva Street"), is a series of essays about poverty and drunkenness in the suburbs of the city of Tula. For a time he was a follower of the Narodniki (radical populists), but unlike them he refused to idealize the Russian peasant, whose primitive life became the main subject of his writing, as in *Vlast zemli* (1882; "The Power of the Soil").

Ustinov \'yüs-ti-,nȯf\, Peter, *in full* Sir Peter Alexander Ustinov (b. April 16, 1921, London, Eng.)   English actor, director, playwright, screenwriter, novelist, and raconteur.

Ustinov studied at the London Theatre Studio and spent the war years (1942–46) in the British army. He began writing for the theater in 1939, principally for revues. His first full play, *House of Regrets*, opened in 1940. Thereafter he wrote prolifically for the stage, his most noted works perhaps being *The Love of Four Colonels* (1951), *Romanoff and Juliet* (1957; film, 1961), *The Unknown Soldier and His Wife* (1966), and *Beethoven's Tenth* (1985). Ustinov acted in more than 50 films in addition to acting in, producing, or directing many of his plays. He also wrote several novels and short stories, as well as an autobiography, *Dear Me* (1977).

utopia \yü-'tō-pē-ə\ [New Latin *Utopia,* from Greek *ou* not, no + *tópos* place]   In literature, a romance or other work describing an ideal commonwealth whose inhabitants exist under seemingly perfect conditions.

The word *utopia* first occurred in Sir Thomas More's book of that name, published in Latin as *Libellus . . . de optimo reipublicae statu, deque nova insula Utopia* (1516; "Concerning the highest state of the republic and the new island Utopia"). In *Utopia* More describes a pagan and communist city-state in which institutions and policies are entirely governed by reason. The order and dignity of such a state was intended to provide a notable contrast with his description of the unreasonable state of the Europe of his time, which he saw being divided by self-interest and greed for power and riches.

Utopias are far older than their name. Plato's *Republic* served as a model for many writers, from More to H.G. Wells. An early practical utopia was the comprehensive *La città del sole* (written *c.* 1602) of Tommaso Campanella. Francis Bacon's *New Atlantis* (1627) was practical in its scientific program but speculative concerning philosophy and religion. Puritanism produced many literary utopias, both religious and secular. *The Common-Wealth of Oceana* (1656) by James Harrington argued for the distribution of land as the condition of popular independence.

G.A. Ellis' *New Britain* (1820) and Étienne Cabet's *Voyage en Icarie* (1840) were related to experimental communities in the United States that revealed the limitations of purely eco-nomic planning. Nathaniel Hawthorne's novel *The Blithedale Romance* (1852) was based partly on his experiences at another such experimental community, that of Brook Farm near Boston, Mass. Two influential utopias, however, had economic bases: *Looking Backward* (1888) by Edward Bellamy and *Freiland* (1890; *A Visit to Freeland*) by Theodor Herzka. Wells in *A Modern Utopia* (1905) returned to speculation.

Many utopias are satires that ridicule existent conditions rather than offering practical solutions for them. In this class are Jonathan Swift's *Gulliver's Travels* (1726) and Samuel Butler's *Erewhon* (1872). In the 20th century, a number of bitterly anti-utopian, or dystopian, novels appeared. Among these are *The Iron Heel* (1907) by Jack London, *My* (1924; *We*) by Yevgeny Zamyatin, *Brave New World* (1932) by Aldous Huxley, and *Nineteen Eighty-four* (1949) by George Orwell. A recent example is Margaret Atwood's *The Handmaid's Tale* (1985).

Utsubo monogatari \'üt-sü-ˌbō-'mō-nō-ˌgä-tä-rē\, Utsubo *also spelled* Utsuho ("Tale of the Hollow Tree")   The first full-length Japanese novel and one of the world's oldest extant novels. Written probably in the late 10th century by an unknown author, the work has been ascribed to Minamoto Shitagō, a distinguished courtier and scholar, but later sources deny his authorship. It is possible that Minamoto was one of several authors who worked on the book.

The story is told in 20 sections. The nobleman Kiyowara no Toshikage is shipwrecked while sailing to China and lands on the shores of a fantastic country. In the midst of his adventures there, he learns to play a magical instrument called a koto and is blessed by the Buddha; the music sent by heaven through Toshikage and succeeding generations of koto players—his daughter, her son Nakatada, and Nakatada's daughter Inumiya—provides a unifying theme for the novel. Most of the novel takes place in Japan and concerns Nakatada's love for his mother, his complicated quest for a wife in the Heian court, and power struggles at court.

V \'vē\   Novel by Thomas PYNCHON, published in 1963 and granted the Faulkner Foundation award for a first novel. The complex and frequently whimsical narrative recounts the search of Benny Profane and Herbert Stencil for the mysterious and elusive V, a woman who surfaces in various incarnations and guises at crucial moments in the history of late 19th- and early 20th-century Europe.

Văcărescu family \ˌvə-kə-'res-kü\   Romanian family of Phanariote (Greek) origin that produced the first poets in Romanian literature.

Ienăchiță (1740–99), after traveling and studying in St. Petersburg and Vienna, wrote poems inspired by Russian folk songs. He also wrote the first Romanian grammar book (*Gramatica românească*, 1787). His chief poems, *Amărîtă turturea* ("Sad Turtledove") and *Testamentul*, reveal a high artistic ability and a mastery of a rich Romanian language. Ienăchiță's sons, Alecu (1765–99) and Nicolae (1784–1825), also wrote poems inspired by folk songs and modern Greek anacreontics.

Iancu (1792–1863), son of Alecu, was the most important writer of the Văcărescu family. A poet who was several times exiled for his anti-Russian activity, he was the first Romanian playwright and was also an able translator into Romanian of plays by Jean Racine, Molière, and August von Kotzebue. His *Colecții de poezii* ("Collected Poems") appeared in 1848.

Elena (also spelled Hélène; 1866–1947), a niece of Iancu, was a poet and novelist who spent much of her life in Paris and wrote in French. She published many volumes of lyrical verse, including *Chants d'aurore* (1886; "Songs of Dawn"), for which she was awarded the prize of the Académie Française; *L'Âme sereine* (1896; "The Serene Soul"), and *Dans l'or du soir* (1928; "In the Gold of the Evening"), and a few novels.

Valdés \bäl-'däs\, Alfonso de (b. 1490?, Cuenca, Spain—d. Oct. 3?, 1532, Vienna [Austria])   Humanist satirist, one of the most influential and cultured thinkers in Spain of the early 16th century and twin brother of Juan de Valdés.

Valdés joined the court of the emperor Charles V as a secretary. He held important positions at the Diet of Worms, where he worked for reconciliation between Martin Luther and the church, and at the Diet of Regensburg. He was named to the post of archivist in Naples but died of the plague in Vienna before he could assume the position. Valdés' principal works are the *Diálogo de Mercurio y Carón* (1528; "Dialogue of Mercury and Charon") and the *Diálogo de las cosas ocurridas en Roma* (c. 1529; "The Dialogue of What Happened at Rome"), which express his loyalty to the emperor and his devotion to the humanist ideals of Erasmus. In both he justified imperial policy and criticized the foes of a purified religion.

Valdés \bäl-'däs\, Juan de (b. 1490?, Cuenca, Spain—d. May 1541, Naples [Italy]) Spanish humanist and member of an influential intellectual family that played a significant role in the religious, political, and literary life of Spain and its empire. He was the twin brother of Alfonso de Valdés.

Valdés studied under Spain's leading humanists and developed religious views that closely followed the ideas of Erasmus, with whom he and his brother maintained a correspondence. His work *Diálogo de la doctrina cristiana* (1529; "Dialogue on Christian Doctrine") was not well received by the Catholic church, and Valdés found it prudent to leave Spain. Accepting a post from the emperor Charles V, he spent the rest of his life in Italy. The *Diálogo de la lengua* (c. 1535; "Dialogue on the Language") treated of Spanish style and language with that blend of wit, grace, learning, and common sense that characterizes humanism at its best.

Valediction: Forbidding Mourning, A Poem by John DONNE, published in 1633 in the first edition of *Songs and Sonnets*. It is one of his finest love poems, notable for its grave beauty and Metaphysical wit.

The narrator of the poem hopes to avoid a tearful departure from his mistress and explains to her that their mature, spiritual love can withstand their temporary separation, unlike "dull sublunary lovers' love" which demands physical presence. In a famous passage, Donne describes their souls as being affixed together like a pair of compasses joined by a pivot:

> And though it in the center sit,
>   Yet when the other far doth roam,
> It leans and hearkens after it,
>   And grows erect, as that comes home.

Valencia \bä-'län-syä, -thyä\, Guillermo (b. Oct. 29, 1873, Popayán, Colom.—d. July 8, 1943, Popayán) Colombian poet and statesman noted for his technical command of verse and skill at translation.

Valencia's first volume of poetry, *Ritos* (1898, rev. ed., 1914; "Rites"), containing original poems and free translations from French, Italian, and Portuguese, established his literary reputation at home and abroad as a leader of the experimental Modernismo movement. He led an active career as a statesman and a diplomat and was twice a candidate for the presidency of Colombia, in 1918 and 1930.

Valencia was never a prolific poet; in later years, he abandoned original poetry almost entirely, concentrating on translations. One of these was *Catay* (1928; "Cathay"), which he translated from Franz Toussaint's *La Flute de jade* ("The Jade Flute"), itself a French translation of an anthology of Chinese poems. He translated *La balada de la cárcel de Reading* (1932; "The Ballad of Reading Gaol") from the English poem by Oscar Wilde. He wrote essays, many of which are collected in *Panegíricos, discursos y artículos* (1933; "Panegyrics, Speeches, and Articles").

Valente \bä-'len-tā\, José Ángel (b. April 25, 1929, Orense, Galicia, Spain) Major Spanish poet who published translations and criticism in addition to more than 20 books of his own verse. The themes of his often philosophical poems are exile, death, and poverty in modern Spain.

Valente's earliest work is characterized by simple verse devoid of artifice and by an objective representation of reality. *A modo de esperanza* (1955; "In the Manner of Hope") confronts the problems of death and loss while presenting many scenes from everyday life. *La memoria y los signos* (1966; "The Memory and the Signs") deals in part with the Spanish Civil War and contains many biographical and historical sections.

In his later works Valente began to experiment with more complex and allusive verse. *Presentación y memorial para un monumento* (1970; "Presentation and Memorial for a Monument"), for example, discusses the dogmatism of modern society and the agony of the individual. In *Material memoria* (1979) Valente meditated on life and art. The 54 prose poems in *No amanece el cantor* (1992; "The Singer Does not Awake") play with the concept of negatives and positives, such as dark and light, absence and presence, silence and speech.

valentine \'val-ən-ˌtīn\ A piece of writing or a literary work expressing praise or affection for something—usually used with *to*.

Valera \bä-'lā-rä\, Juan, *surname in full* Valera y Alcalá Galiano \ē-äl-kä-'lä-ġäl-'yä-nō\ (b. Oct. 18, 1824, Cabra, Spain—d. April 18, 1905, Madrid) Important 19th-century Spanish novelist and stylist, as well as emissary and politician, who traveled in Europe and America in the diplomatic corps and served as deputy, senator, and undersecretary of state in Madrid.

Valera's novels are characterized by deep psychological analysis of their characters, especially women. Valera was opposed to naturalistic narrative and held that the novel is a form of poetry. His best-known works are *Pepita Jiménez* (1874), notable for its terse, elegant style and masterful character development, *Doña Luz* (1879), and *Juanita la Larga* (1895). Other important novels are *Las ilusiones del doctor Faustino* (1875), *Morsamor* (1899) and *El comendador Mendoza* (1877; "Commander Mendoza"). Valera's prolific literary output includes some very fine translations, including parts of J.W. von Goethe's *Faust* and Longus' *Daphnis and Chloe* (1907); literary criticism of Miguel de Cervantes' *Don Quixote*, Goethe's *Faust*, and other works; short stories, including *El pájaro verde* (1887; "The Green Bird"); plays; and numerous essays on religion, philosophy, history and politics. His letters constitute a valuable record of his impressions on many topics of the era.

Valerius Flaccus \və-'lir-ē-əs-'flak-əs\, Gaius (fl. 1st century AD) Epic poet, author of *Argonautica*, an epic which, though indebted to other sources, offers its own vivid characterizations and descriptions in a style unmarred by the excesses of other Latin poetry of the Silver Age (AD 18–133).

The *Argonautica*, Valerius' only surviving work, is an epic poem in hexameter verse dedicated to the emperor Vespasian. It describes the famous voyage of the ship *Argo* in which Jason and other heroes sailed to Colchis to bring the Golden Fleece back to Thessaly.

Valerius clearly borrowed material from the *Argonautica* of the Alexandrian poet Apollonius of Rhodes (fl. c. 295 BC); for his style and treatment he was deeply indebted to Virgil, and his verse technique owes much to Ovid. But he possessed creative gifts of his own; his work is written in simple and direct language and the narrative reveals strong dramatic talent. Valerius' work is also free of some of the vices of contemporary Latin poetry, such as the showy display of erudition and exaggerated rhetoric.

The *Argonautica* was unknown until the first three books and part of a fourth were discovered by the Italian humanist G.F. Poggio at St. Gall in 1416. The first edition was published in 1474.

Valero \bǎ-'lä-rō\, Roberto (b. 1955, Matazas, Cuba)   Cuban poet noted for his poetry on tyranny in Fidel Castro's Cuba and on the human predicament in general.

Valero attended the University of Havana but left because of his anti-government beliefs. In 1980 he fled Cuba as a dissident and arrived in Miami, eventually moving to Washington D.C., where he received a Ph.D. from Georgetown University. Valero's first published volume, *Desde un oscuro ángulo* (1982; "From a Dark Angle"), contains poems about love, childhood memories, and the joys and sorrows of being an artist. It was followed by *En fin, la noche* (1984; "At Last, the Night") and *Dharma* (1985), a book of nostalgic poems about Cuba. *Venías* ("You Were Coming") was published in 1990 and *No estaré en tu camino* ("I Will Not Be in Your Way") in 1991. Valero's work has often been compared to that of Federico García Lorca.

Valéry \vȧ-lā-'rē\, Paul, *in full* Ambroise-Paul-Toussaint-Jules Valéry (b. Oct. 30, 1871, Sète, Fr.—d. July 20, 1945, Paris)   French poet, essayist, and critic noted for his sensuous writing style.

E.B. Inc.

Valéry was educated at Montpellier, where he studied law. Among his friends at this time were the writers Pierre Louÿs and André Gide. His early literary idols were Edgar Allan Poe, J.-K. Huysmans, and Stéphane Mallarmé, to whom he was introduced in 1891 and whose artistic circle he came to frequent.

Valéry wrote many poems between 1888 and 1891, a few of which were published in magazines of the Symbolist movement and favorably reviewed, but artistic frustration and despair over an unrequited love made him dedicate himself to the "Idol of the Intellect." He disposed of most of his books, and from 1894 until the end of his life he would rise at dawn each day, meditate, and record his thoughts and aphorisms in his notebooks, which were later to be published as the famous *Cahiers*. Valéry's new-found ideals were Leonardo da Vinci, his paradigm of the Universal Man, and his own creation, "Monsieur Teste," an almost disembodied intellect who knows but two values, the possible and the impossible. They were presented in two short prose works, "Introduction à la méthode de Léonard de Vinci" (1895) and "La Soirée avec Monsieur Teste" (1896; "An Evening with Monsieur Teste").

Pressed by Gide in 1912 to revise some of his early writings for publication, Valéry began work on what was intended to be a valedictory poem to the collection but which was instead published separately as LA JEUNE PARQUE (1917; "The Young Fate"). It brought him immediate fame. The collection appeared in 1920 as *Album de vers anciens, 1890–1900*. With *Charmes ou poèmes* (1922), a collection that includes "Le Cimetière marin" (THE GRAVEYARD BY THE SEA), it established his reputation as the outstanding French poet of the time.

After 1922, Valéry became a prominent public personage. He was elected to the Académie Française in 1925, was made administrative head of the Centre Universitaire Méditerranéen at Nice in 1933, and became professor of poetry, a chair created especially for him, at the Collège de France in 1937.

Valhalla \val-'hal-ə, väl-'häl-ə\, *Old Norse* Valhǫll \'väl-ˌhœl\   In Norse mythology, the hall of slain warriors, who live there blissfully under the leadership of Odin. Valhalla is depicted as a splendid palace, roofed with shields, where the warriors feast on the flesh of a boar slaughtered daily and made whole again each evening. They drink liquor that flows from the udders of a goat, and their sport is to fight one another every day.

Thus they will live until the Ragnarǫk ("Doom of the Gods"), when they will march out the 540 doors of the palace to fight at the side of Odin against the giants.

Valjean, Jean \'zhäⁿ-väl-'zhäⁿ\   Fictional character, the fugitive protagonist of Victor Hugo's sweeping novel LES MISÉRABLES.

Valkyrie \val-'kir-ē, -'kī-rē; 'val-kə-rē\ *or* **Walkyrie** \väl-'kir-ē, -'kī-rē; 'väl-kə-rē\   One of the maidens of Norse mythology who hover over the field of battle choosing those to be slain and conducting the worthy heroes to Valhalla. The Old Norse word *valkyrja* means literally "chooser of the slain."

These foreboders of war ride to the battlefield on horses, wearing helmets and shields; in some accounts, they fly through the air and sea. Some Valkyries have the power to cause the death of the warriors they do not favor; others, especially heroine Valkyries, guard the lives and ships of those dear to them. Old Norse literature makes references to purely supernatural Valkyries and also to human Valkyries with certain supernatural powers.

Valle-Inclán \ˌbäl-yä-ēŋ-'klän\, Ramón María del (b. Oct. 28, 1866, Villanueva de Arosa, Spain—d. Jan. 5, 1936, Santiago de Compostela)   Spanish novelist, dramatist, and poet who combined a sensuous use of language with bitter social satire.

Valle-Inclán was raised in rural Galicia. He early came under French Symbolist influence, and his first notable works, the four novelettes known as the *Sonatas* (1902–05), feature a beautifully evocative prose and a tone of refined and elegant decadence. They narrate the seductions and other doings of a Galician womanizer who is partly an autobiographical figure. In his subsequent works Valle-Inclán developed a style that is rich in both popular and literary appeal, as in several plays featuring the patriarchal Don Juan Manuel de Montenegro and his brood of wild sons.

Some of Valle-Inclán's later plays and novels are in the manner he called *esperpento* ("horrible, nauseating persons or things"). This intentionally absurd and cruelly satirical style is intended to express the tragic meaning of Spanish life—which he saw as a gross deformation of European civilization—through the systematic distortion of classic heroes. The best of his *esperpento* plays are *Luces de Bohemia* (1920; *Bohemian Lights*) and *Los cuernos de Don Friolera* (1921; "Don Friolera's Horns"). His major novels of the later period include *La corte de los milagros* (1927; "The Court of Miracles"), *Viva mi dueño* (1928; "Hurrah to the Hilt"), and the unfinished *Baza de espadas* (1958; "Intervention of Swords"), part of an unfinished nine-volume cycle of historical novels collectively entitled *El ruedo ibérico* (1927–28; "The Iberian Circle"). The cycle deals with the political corruption and social degradation of Spain in the late 19th century. Valle-Inclán's novel *Tirano Banderas* (1926) is a vivid portrayal of a Latin-American despot.

Vallejo \bä-'yä-ḵō\, César (Abraham) (b. March 16, 1892, Santiago de Chuco, Peru—d. April 15, 1938, Paris, Fr.)   Peruvian poet who became a major voice of social change in Latin-American literature.

Born the 11th child to a family of mixed Spanish and Indian origins, Vallejo as a child witnessed firsthand the hunger, poverty, and injustices suffered by the Indians. He attended the University of Trujillo (1913–17), where he studied literature and law.

Vallejo's first book of poems, *Los heraldos negros* (1918; *The Black Heralds*), shows him under the stylistic influence of Parnassianism and Modernismo. In 1920 Vallejo's involvement in political matters concerning Indians led to his imprisonment for nearly three months. *Escalas melografiadas* (1923; "Musical Scales"), a collection of short stories, and many of the more complex poems of *Trilce* (1922; bilingual edition, 1992) were conceived during his imprisonment. *Trilce* signaled a complete break with tradition by incorporating neologisms, colloquialisms, typographic innovations, and startling imagery.

After publishing *Fabula salvaje* (1923; "Savage Story"), a short psychological novel about the decline of a mentally disturbed Indian, Vallejo left for Paris, never to return to his native land. Though he felt himself an outsider in Paris because of his Indian heritage, he succeeded in establishing contacts with leading avant-garde artists. He kept in touch with Peru by publishing articles in *Amauta*, the journal established by his friend José Carlos Mariátegui, founder of the Peruvian Communist party.

Vallejo was expelled from Paris in 1930 as a political militant and went to Madrid. There he wrote the proletarian novel *El tungsteno* (1931; *Tungsten*). The Spanish Civil War (1936–39) inspired most of his last important volume of poetry, *Poemas humanos* (1939; *Human Poems*), which presents an apocalyptic vision of an industrial society in crisis.

Most of the poems of the 1930s were published only after Vallejo's death. His fiction is collected in *Novelas y cuentos completos* (1967; "Complete Novels and Stories") and his poetry in *Obra poética completa* (1968; "Complete Poetical Works"). *César Vallejo: The Complete Posthumous Poetry* (1978) is a bilingual edition.

Valmont *in full* Vicomte de Valmont \vē-kȯⁿt-də-vȧl-'mȯⁿ\ Fictional character, an amoral libertine who amuses himself by corrupting innocents, in DANGEROUS LIAISONS, by Pierre Choderlos de Laclos.

vampire \'vam-ˌpīr\ [German *Vampir,* from Serbo-Croatian *vampir,* alteration of earlier *upir*] In folklore, a revenant, or dead person who has been diabolically reanimated and leaves the grave at night to disturb the living. Belief in revenants, though widespread in folk cultures of Europe and Asia, is particularly well-developed among the Slavic peoples of southeastern Europe. The vampire of Slavic tradition may simply engage in pranks such as throwing stones at roofs, but more often it malignantly causes the deaths of former neighbors and their livestock, by strangulation, sucking blood, or leaving disease behind. He—vampires are much more often men than women—is a shapeshifter who may wander in the form of a wolf or bat and find his way through locked doors and windows. The victims of vampires are doomed themselves to become vampires, and the plague can only be stopped by impaling the revenants in their coffins with a stake.

In 1725 and 1732, Austrian officials in Serbia attended at the disinterment of several fluid-filled corpses whom the local villagers claimed were behind a plague of vampirism. Reports of the disinterments and the villagers' beliefs, which diffused quickly in German intellectual circles and were the subject of learned dissertations, spread both the image of the vampire and the word itself throughout western Europe. The bloodsucking aspect of the myth—not always prominent in Slavic folklore—particularly excited the popular imagination; it led to the typical literary representation of the vampire as a monster with protruding canines who draws blood from his victims' throats.

Among the various demons of folk tradition, the vampire has enjoyed the most conspicuous and continual literary success. Vampires have been especially prominent in Gothic tales and Romantic poetry, including works by J.W. von Goethe, Robert Southey, Richard Brinsley Sheridan, J.S. Le Fanu, and J.W. Polidori, the author of *The Vampyre* (1819), the first vampire story in English. In the 20th century the interest in vampire stories was largely the result of the popularity of the gothic novel *Dracula* (1897) by the British author Bram Stoker. Count Dracula, its "undead" villain from Transylvania, became the representative type of vampire. The novel, a play (1927), and a popular series of films made vampire lore common currency. Tod Browning's classic film *Dracula* (1931), starring Bela Lugosi, set the pattern for the dozens of vampire movies that followed in the mid- and late 20th century. In the 1980s and '90s a popular series of books by Anne Rice contributed to the fascination with vampires.

Vanbrugh \'van-ˌbrŭk, *commonly* 'van-brə, van-'brü \, Sir John (baptized Jan. 24, 1664, London, Eng.—d. March 26, 1726, London) Dramatist of the Restoration comedy of manners who was also a distinguished architect.

Vanbrugh's first comedy, *The Relapse: Or Virtue in Danger,* was written as a sequel to Colley Cibber's *Love's Last Shift.* It opened in 1696 and was highly successful. His next important piece, *The Provok'd Wife* (1697), was also a triumph. In 1698 the churchman Jeremy Collier published an attack on the immorality of the theater, aimed especially at Vanbrugh, whose plays were more robust than those of such contemporaries as William Congreve. Vanbrugh and others retaliated but to little effect, and he kept silent until 1700. Then came a sequence of free and lively adaptations from the French, more farce than comedy, including *The Country House* (performed 1703) and *The Confederacy* (1705).

In 1702 Vanbrugh entered another field; he designed Castle Howard, Yorkshire, for Lord Carlisle. Through Lord Carlisle, who was head of the Treasury, Vanbrugh in 1702 became comptroller of the queen's works. In 1703 he designed the Queen's Theatre, or Opera House, in the Haymarket. Though a magnificent building, it proved a failure, partly because of its poor acoustics, and he lost considerable money in the venture. Vanbrugh also designed Blenheim Palace and several other country homes. He was knighted in 1714.

Vance, Philo \'fī-lō-'vans\ Fictional amateur detective, the protagonist of 12 detective novels by American writer S.S. VAN DINE.

A wealthy American graduate of Oxford University, Vance is a cultivated but snobbish man of wide-ranging interests and talents. He is a meticulous gatherer of clues, some of which involve knowledge of chess, mathematical theories, 19th-century drama, and esoteric writings on criminology. Logical as well as erudite, Vance frequently solves a series of murders by drawing on his finely tuned psychological insight as well as on physical evidence.

Van Dine \van-'dīn\, S.S., *pseudonym of* Willard Huntington Wright \'rīt\ (b. Oct. 15, 1888, Charlottesville, Va., U.S.—d. April 11, 1939, New York, N.Y.) American critic, editor, and author of a series of best-selling detective novels featuring the brilliant but arrogant sleuth Philo VANCE.

Pursuing a career as a writer, Wright became literary editor of the *Los Angeles Times* in 1907 and in 1912 moved to New York to become editor of *Town Topics* and *The Smart Set,* where he remained until 1914. With H.L. Mencken and George Jean Nathan he published a book of travel essays called *Europe After 8:15* (1914). He also wrote the poetry collection *Songs of Youth* (1913), the novel *The Man of Promise* (1916), and several critical works on art and philosophy, including *Modern Painting* (1915) and *What Nietzsche Taught* (1915).

While convalescing from an illness, Wright studied thousands of detective stories. As S.S. Van Dine, he eventually wrote a dozen Vance novels in that genre. Among them were *The Benson Murder Case* (1926), *The Bishop Murder Case* (1929),

The Kennel Murder Case (1933), and *The Winter Murder Case* (1939). The successful series inspired numerous films and radio programs. Wright also edited the anthology *The Great Detective Stories* (1927) and wrote the essays "Twenty Rules for Writing Detective Stories," which appeared in *American Magazine* (1928), and *I Used to Be a Highbrow But Look at Me Now* (1929).

Van Doren \van-'dȯr-ən\, Carl (Clinton) (b. Sept. 10, 1885, Hope, Ill., U.S.—d. July 18, 1950, Torrington, Conn.)   American author and teacher whose writings range through surveys of literature to novels, biography, and criticism.

Educated at Columbia University (Ph.D., 1911), Van Doren taught there until 1930. In that period he was one of a group of academicians who helped to establish American literature and history as an integral part of university programs. He also served as managing editor of the *Cambridge History of American Literature* (1917–21) and literary editor of *The Nation* (1919–22) and *Century Magazine* (1922–25).

For his discerning biography *Benjamin Franklin* (1938), Van Doren won a Pulitzer Prize. His other works include *The American Novel* (1921; revised 1940); *Contemporary American Novelists* (1922); *American and British Literature Since 1890* (1925), in collaboration with his brother, Mark Van Doren, and revised in 1939; and *What Is American Literature?* (1935). His autobiography, *Three Worlds,* appeared in 1936.

Van Doren \van-'dȯr-ən\, Mark (b. June 13, 1894, Hope, Ill., U.S.—d. Dec. 10, 1972, Torrington, Conn.)   American poet, writer, and eminent teacher. He upheld the writing of verse in traditional forms throughout a lengthy period of experiment in poetry. As a teacher at Columbia University (N.Y.) for 39 years (1920–59), he exercised a profound influence on generations of students.

Like his older brother Carl, Van Doren attended Columbia University, from which he received a Ph.D. in 1920, and worked as literary editor (1924–28) and film critic (1935–38) of *The Nation* in New York City.

Van Doren's literary criticism includes *The Poetry of John Dryden* (1920; rev. ed., 1946); *Shakespeare* (1939); *Nathaniel Hawthorne* (1949); and *The Happy Critic* (1961), a book of essays. In *The Noble Voice* (1946; reprinted as *Mark Van Doren on Great Poems of Western Literature*, 1962) he considers 10 long poems by authors ranging from Homer and Virgil through William Wordsworth and Lord Byron. His *Introduction to Poetry* (1951; rev. ed., 1966) examines shorter classic poems of English and American literature.

The author of more than 20 volumes of verse, Van Doren published his first, *Spring Thunder,* in 1924. In 1940 he won the Pulitzer Prize for his *Collected Poems (1922–38)* (1939), a work that was later followed by *Collected and New Poems, 1924–1963* (1963). His poetry includes the verse play *The Last Days of Lincoln* (1959) and three book-length narrative poems, *Jonathan Gentry* (1931), *Winter Diary* (1935), and *The Mayfield Deer* (1941). Van Doren was the author of three novels—*The Transients* (1935), *Windless Cabins* (1940), and *Tilda* (1943)—and several volumes of short stories; he also edited a number of anthologies. In 1922 he married Dorothy Graffe, author of five novels and the memoir *The Professor and I*.

Van Duyn \van-'dīn\, Mona (Jane) (b. May 9, 1921, Waterloo, Iowa, U.S.)   American poet noted for her examination of the daily lives of ordinary people, for mixing the prosaic with the unusual, the simple with the sophisticated. She is frequently described as a "domestic poet" who celebrates married love.

Van Duyn attended Iowa State Teachers College (now the University of Northern Iowa) and the University of Iowa. In 1947, with her husband, Jarvis Thurston, she founded *Perspective: A Quarterly of Literature and the Arts,* which she coedited

until 1967. Her first volume of poetry, *Valentines to the Wide World,* was published in 1959. She won recognition following the publication of *To See, To Take* (1970), receiving the 1970 Bollingen Prize for achievement in American poetry and the 1971 National Book Award. Her other works include *A Time of Bees* (1964), *Merciful Disguises* (1973), and *Near Changes* (1990), for which she was awarded the 1991 Pulitzer Prize for poetry. *Firefall* and *If It Be Not I: Collected Poems 1959–1982* were published in 1993.

Van Duyn used wry humor, insight, irony, and technical skill to find meaning and possibility in a merciless world. She found in love and art the possibility of redemption—"but against that rage slowly may learn to pit/ love and art, which are compassionate."

Van Dyke \van-'dīk\, Henry (b. Nov. 10, 1852, Germantown, Pa., U.S.—d. April 10, 1933, Princeton, N.J.)   American short-story writer, poet, and essayist.

Educated at Princeton, Van Dyke graduated from its theological seminary in 1877 and became a Presbyterian minister. His early works, "The Story of the Other Wise Man" (1896) and "The First Christmas Tree" (1897), were first read aloud to his congregation in New York as sermons. These quickly brought him recognition. His other stories and anecdotal tales were gathered at regular intervals into volumes. Among these collections were *The Ruling Passion* (1901), *The Blue Flower* (1902), *The Unknown Quantity* (1912), *The Valley of Vision* (1919), and *The Golden Key* (1926). Van Dyke's popularity also extended to his verse, collected in *Poems* (1920).

Vane \'vān\, Sutton, *original name* Vane Sutton-Vane \'sət-ən-'vān\ (b. Nov. 9, 1888, England—d. June 15, 1963, Hastings, Sussex)   English playwright remembered for his unusual and highly successful play *Outward Bound* (1923), about a group of passengers who find themselves making an ocean voyage on a ship that seems to have no crew. Slowly they realize that they are dead and bound for the other world, which is both heaven and hell.

Vane, who started his career as an actor, suffered shell-shock early in World War I. Later in the war he returned to France to perform behind the lines. Back home in England, he began to write plays. Because he could find no one willing to produce *Outward Bound,* he hired a small London suburban house called the Everyman Theatre and mounted the production himself at a total cost of £120. The play was an instant success and was transferred to a leading London theater. That success later was duplicated in New York, and the play has been twice filmed.

Vanir \'vän-ir\   In Norse mythology, race of gods responsible for wealth, fertility, and commerce; they are subordinate to the warlike Æsir. As reparation for the torture of their goddess Gullveig, the Vanir demanded from the Æsir monetary satisfaction or equal status. Declaring war instead, the Æsir suffered numerous defeats before granting equality. The birth of the poet-god Kvasir resulted from the peace ritual in which the two races mingled their saliva in the same vessel. *Compare* ÆSIR.

Vanity Fair   Novel of early 19th-century English society by William Makepeace THACKERAY, published serially from 1847 to 1848 and in book form in 1848. The novel takes its title from the place designated as the center of human corruption in John Bunyan's 17th-century allegory *Pilgrim's Progress.* The book is a densely populated, multi-layered panorama of manners and human frailties; subtitled *A Novel Without a Hero, Vanity Fair* metaphorically represents the human condition.

The novel deals mainly with the interwoven fortunes of two women, the wellborn, passive Amelia Sedley and the ambitious, essentially amoral Becky Sharp, the latter perhaps the most memorable character Thackeray created. The adventuress Becky is the character around whom all the men play their parts. Amelia marries George Osborne, but George, just before

"Virtue Rewarded: A Booth in Vanity Fair," drawing by the author for *Vanity Fair*
The Newberry Library

he is killed at the Battle of Waterloo, is ready to desert his young wife for Becky, who has fought her way up through society to marriage with Rawdon Crawley, a young officer from an aristocratic family. Crawley, disillusioned, finally leaves Becky, and in the end virtue apparently triumphs when Amelia marries her lifelong admirer, Captain William Dobbin, and Becky settles down to genteel living and charitable works.

Van nu en straks circle \vän-'nǖ-en-'sträks\ Group of writers associated with an influential Flemish review, *Van nu en straks* ("Of Now and Later"; 1893–94 and 1896–1901). Though holding a variety of opinions, they strove for an art that should comprehend all human activity and give universal significance to individual feelings. Led by the critic August Vermeylen, they included Prosper van Langendonck, Emmanuel Karel de Bom, and Alfred Hegenscheidt. *Van nu en straks* gave Flemish literature a greater significance in Europe as a whole.

Van Vechten \van-'vek-tən\, Carl (b. June 17, 1880, Cedar Rapids, Iowa, U.S.—d. Dec. 21, 1964, New York, N.Y.) American novelist and music and drama critic, an influential figure in New York literary circles in the 1920s; he was an early enthusiast of American black culture.

Van Vechten worked as assistant music critic for *The New York Times* (1906–08) and later as that paper's Paris correspondent. His elegant, sophisticated novels, *Peter Whiffle, His Life and Works* (1922), *The Tattooed Countess* (1924), and *Nigger Heaven* (1926), were very popular. He also wrote extensively on music and published an autobiography, *Sacred and Profane Memories* (1932), following which he vowed to write no more and to devote his time to photography. His extensive collec-

tion of books on black Americana, the James Weldon Johnson Memorial Collection of Negro Arts and Letters, is now at Yale University. He also established the Carl Van Vechten Collection at the New York City Public Library and the George Gershwin Memorial Collection of Music and Musical Literature at Fisk University, Nashville, Tenn.

Van Vogt \van-'vōkt\, A.E., *in full* Alfred Elton (b. April 26, 1912, near Winnipeg, Man., Can.) Canadian author of science fiction who emerged as one of the leading writers of the genre in the mid-20th century.

Van Vogt published his first story, "Black Destroyer," in the July 1939 issue of *Astounding Science Fiction*. He became a regular contributor to the magazine, which serialized his first novel, *Slan* (1946), from September to December of 1940. A story of mutants with superhuman powers, *Slan* was followed by *The Weapon Makers* (1947), which was first serialized in 1943. Other works first serialized in the 1940s were *The World of Ā* (1948; later published as *The World of Null-A*), a mysterious story about a developing superhero, and *The Weapon Shops of Isher* (1951), a sequel to *The Weapon Makers*.

Van Vogt took a break from science-fiction writing in the 1950s to help develop Dianetics, a form of psychotherapy that was later incorporated into Scientology. He resumed his writing career in the 1960s, but was unable to achieve his earlier fame. His later novels included *The Silkie* (1969), *Renaissance* (1979), and *The Cosmic Encounter* (1980).

Van Winkle, Rip \'rip-van-'wiŋ-kəl\ Fictional colonial Dutch-American noted for having slept for 20 years; he is the protagonist of Washington Irving's short story RIP VAN WINKLE.

Varden, Dolly \'däl-ē-'värd-ən\ Fictional character, a gaily dressed coquette in the novel BARNABY RUDGE by Charles Dickens.

Dolly's memorable costumes led to the naming for her of a style of 19th-century woman's ensemble consisting of a wide-skirted, tight-bodied print dress worn with a white fichu (light triangular scarf) and a flowered hat with wide, drooping brim. She was also commemorated in the brightly colored Dolly Varden trout.

Vargas Llosa \'bär-gäs-'lʸō-sä\, Mario, *in full* Jorge Mario Pedro Vargas Llosa (b. March 28, 1936, Arequipa, Peru) Peruvian writer whose commitment to social change was evident in his novels, plays, and essays.

Vargas Llosa received his early education in Cochabamba, Bol., where his grandfather was the Peruvian consul. He later attended a series of schools in Peru before entering a military school, Leoncio Prado, in Lima in 1950.

After his first publication, *La huida del Inca* (1952; "The Escape of the Inca"), a three-act play, his stories began to appear in Peruvian literary reviews, and he coedited *Cuadernos de composición* (1956–57; "Composition Book") and *Literatura* (1958–59). In 1959 he moved to Paris, where he lived until 1966. He later lived in England, the United States, and Spain before returning to Peru in 1974.

Vargas Llosa's first novel, *La ciudad y los perros* (1963; "The City and the Dogs"; THE TIME OF THE HERO), was widely acclaimed. It describes adolescents striving for survival in the hostile and violent environment of a military school. The novel *La casa verde* (1966; *The Green House*), set in the Peruvian jungle, combines mythical, popular, and heroic elements.

The title story of *Los cachorros* (1967; *The Cubs, and Other Stories*) is a psychoanalytic portrayal of an adolescent who has been accidentally castrated. *Conversación en La Catedral* (1969; *Conversation in The Cathedral*) deals with military repression. The novel *Pantaleón y las visitadoras* (1973; *Captain*

Pantoja and the Special Service) is a satire of military and religious fanaticism. His semiautobiographical novel *La tía Julia y el escribidor* (1977; AUNT JULIA AND THE SCRIPTWRITER) combines two distinct narrative points of view to provide a contrapuntal effect.

Vargas Llosa also wrote several works of criticism, including *García Márquez: Historia de un deicidio* (1971; "García Márquez: Story of a God-Killer"), *La orgía perpetua: Flaubert y "Madame Bovary"* (1975; *The Perpetual Orgy: Flaubert and 'Madame Bovary'*), and *Entre Sartre y Camus* (1981; "Between Sartre and Camus").

A collection of his critical essays in English translation was published in 1978. *La guerra del fin del mundo* (1981; *The War of the End of the World*), an account of a 19th-century Brazilian apocalyptic religious movement, became a best-seller in Spanish-speaking countries. His later works include the plays *La Señorita de Tacna* (1981; "The Lady of Tacna") and *La Chunga* (1986; "The Jest"), and the novels *El hablador* (1987; *The Storyteller*) and *Elogio de la madrasta* (1988; *In Praise of the Stepmother*). In 1990 he was an unsuccessful candidate for president of Peru. He won the Cervantes Prize in 1994.

variorum or **variorum edition** \,var-ē-'ȯr-əm\   **1.** An edition or text, usually of the complete works of an author, with notes by different people including critics and previous editors of the works. Variorum is short for the Latin phrase *editio cum notis variorum* ("edition with the notes of various people"). **2.** An edition containing variant readings of a text.

Varner family \'vär-nər\   Fictional characters in the novel THE HAMLET by William Faulkner. The leading landholder in Frenchman's Bend, Yoknapatawpha County, Miss., Will Varner is an aging, temperate lawyer who transfers many of his business affairs to his 30-year-old son, Jody. Varner's vapid daughter Eula marries Flem Snopes, the novel's avaricious working-class central character.

Varnhagen von Ense \'färn-hä-gən-fȯn-'en-zə\, Karl August (b. Feb. 21, 1785, Düsseldorf, Pfalz-Neuburg [Germany]—d. Oct. 10, 1858, Berlin)   German writer, diplomat, biographer, and, with his wife, Rahel, a leading figure of a Berlin salon that became a center of intellectual debate. His numerous biographies are smoothly written and well organized but rely heavily on anecdote.

Varnhagen began his literary career by becoming joint editor of a poetry annual in 1804. Enlisting in the Austrian army (1809), he was wounded at the Battle of Wagram the same year and later accompanied his superior officer, Prince Bentheim, to Paris. His experiences in Hamburg and Paris as an adjutant are recorded in *Geschichte der Hamburger Ereignisse* (1813; "History of the Hamburg Events"), and his campaigns are described in *Geschichte der Kriegzüge des Generals von Tettenborn* (1814; "History of the Campaign of General von Tettenborn").

Entering the Prussian diplomatic service, Varnhagen was present at the Congress of Vienna (1814–15). In 1814 he married Rahel Levin, whose salon was a gathering place for the writers, diplomats, and intellectuals of the day. After being dismissed from the diplomatic service in 1819 because of his liberal politics, he became more involved in literature, although he was occasionally recalled for important political assignments.

Varnhagen's biographies include those of General von Seydlitz (1834), Sophia Charlotte, queen of Prussia (1837), and General Bülow von Dennewitz (1853).

Varnhagen von Ense \'färn-hä-gən-fȯn-'en-zə\, Rahel, *original surname* Levin \'lä-vin\ (b. May 19, 1771, Berlin [Germany]—d. March 7, 1833, Berlin)   German literary hostess of the early 19th century whose soirees were attended by many of the Romantics, notably Heinrich Heine.

Levin was born into a wealthy and literate Jewish family of Berlin. By the beginning of the 19th century, she presided over one of the literary salons that became the centers of social activity for writers and their followers in Germany. A sudden loss of fortune in 1806 interrupted her salon, but she was able to resume it after she met Karl August Varnhagen von Ense, a writer and diplomat, in 1808. They were married in 1814. Many of Rahel Varnhagen's letters were published in 1967. An edition of her writings originally collected by her husband, *Rahel: Ein Buch des Andenkens für ihre Freunde*, 3 vol. (1834, "Rahel: A Book of Memories for Her Friends"), was reprinted in 1971.

Varro \'var-ō\, Marcus Terentius (b. 116 BC, probably Reate, [Italy]—d. 27 BC)   Rome's greatest scholar and a renowned satirist, best known for his *Saturae Menippeae* ("Menippean Satires"). He was a prolific author. Inspired by a deep patriotism, he sought in his writings to inculcate moral virtues and to link Rome's future with its glorious past.

In 59 BC Varro wrote a political pamphlet entitled *Trikaranos* ("The Three-Headed") on the coalition of Pompey, Julius Caesar, and Crassus. He sided with Pompey in Spain (49) but was pardoned (47) and appointed librarian by Caesar, to whom he dedicated the second part of his *Antiquitates rerum humanarum et divinarum* ("Antiquities of Human and Divine Things").

Varro wrote about 74 works in more than 600 books on a wide range of subjects: jurisprudence, astronomy, geography, education, and literary history, as well as satires, poems, orations, and letters. The only complete work to survive is the *Res rustica* ("Farm Topics"), a three-section work of practical instruction in general agriculture and animal husbandry, written to foster a love of rural life.

Dedicated to Cicero, Varro's *De lingua Latina* ("On the Latin Language") is of interest not only as a linguistic work but also as a source of valuable incidental information on a variety of subjects. Of the original 25 books there remain, apart from brief fragments, only Books V to X, which contain considerable gaps.

Of Varro's 150 books of the *Saturae Menippeae*, some 90 titles and nearly 600 fragments remain. The satires are humorous medleys in mixed prose and verse in the manner of the 3rd-century-BC cynic philosopher Menippus of Gadara. The subjects range from eating and drinking to literature and philosophy. In these satires, Varro makes fun of the follies and absurdities of modern times. He preaches a simple life of old-fashioned Roman virtue and piety, opposes luxury and philosophic dogmatism, and shows considerable skill in handling several meters and poetic manners.

Varronian satire \və-'rō-nē-ən\   *see* MENIPPEAN SATIRE.

Varthema \dä-'vär-tā-mä\, Lodovico de, de Varthema *also spelled* di Barthema \dē-'bär-tā-mä\, *Latin* Vartomanus \,vär-tə-'mä-nəs\ *or* Vertomannus \,vər-tə-'man-əs\ (b. c. 1465–70, Bologna [Italy]—d. June 1517, Rome)   Intrepid Italian traveler and adventurer whose account of his Middle Eastern and Asiatic wanderings was a popular piece of travel literature that was widely circulated throughout Europe.

Varthema's travels included trips to the Arabian peninsula, where he visited Mecca (now in Saudi Arabia) and Aden and Ṣanʿāʾ (now in Yemen); to India, where he sailed the length of the western coast, making stops at Cambay, Goa, and Cannanore; to Myanmar (Burma); and to Malacca on the southern Malay peninsula. He returned to India in the summer of 1505. Eager to return to Europe, Varthema joined the Portuguese garrison at Cannanore, fought for Portugal, and was knighted for his services. In 1507 he returned to Europe by way of the Cape of Good Hope.

Varthema's account, *Itinerario de Ludovico de Varthema bolognese* (1510), first appeared in English translation in Richard Eden's *History of Travayle* (1576–77).

Vasconcelos \ˌbäs-kōn-ˈsā-lōs\, José (b. Feb. 28, 1882, Oaxaca, Mex.—d. June 30, 1959, Mexico City)   Mexican educator, politician, essayist, and philosopher, whose four-volume autobiography—consisting of *Ulises criollo* (1935; "Creole Ulysses"), *La tormenta* (1936; "The Torment"), *El desastre* (1938; "The Disaster"), and *El proconsulado* (1939; "The Proconsulship")—is one of the finest sociocultural studies of 20th-century Mexico. *A Mexican Ulysses* (1963) is an English-language abridgement.

Vasconcelos graduated from law school in 1907. After serving as rector of the University of Mexico, he was appointed minister of public education (1920–24), during which time he initiated major reforms in the school system. In 1929 he ran unsuccessfully for the presidency of Mexico. Because of his political activism, he was forced to spend several periods of his life in exile.

His philosophy, which he called "aesthetic monism," essentially an attempt to deal with the world as a cosmic unity, is set forth in *Todología* (1952; "About Everything"). His other principal works include *La raza cósmica* (1925; "The Cosmic Race"), *Indología* (1929), *Bolivarismo y Monroísmo* (1934; "Bolivarism and Monroism"), and the autobiographical *La flama* (1959; "The Flame").

Vathek \vȧ-ˈtek\   Gothic novel by William BECKFORD, published in 1786. Considered a masterpiece of bizarre invention and sustained fantasy, *Vathek* was written in French in 1782 and was translated into English by the author's friend Samuel Henley, who published it anonymously, claiming in the preface that the novel was translated from an Arabic original.

The caliph Vathek is a blasphemous voluptuary who constructs a tower so tall that from it he can survey all the kingdoms of the world. Vathek impiously defies Mohammed in the seventh heaven, thus condemning himself to eternal damnation and expulsion to the netherworld.

vatic \ˈvat-ik\   Of, relating to, or characteristic of a prophet. The Latin word *vates* ("prophet"), from which *vatic* is derived, was applied in classical times to certain poets who were believed to be divinely inspired and therefore prophetic. The Greek Sibyl was one example. Several modern poets, including William Blake, Walt Whitman, and Allen Ginsberg, have been called vatic poets because of the prophetic or oracular nature of their work.

Vaughan \ˈvȯn\, Henry (b. April 17, 1622, Llansantffraed, Breconshire, Wales—d. April 23, 1695, Llansantffraed)   Anglo-Welsh poet and mystic remarkable for the range and intensity of his spiritual intuitions.

Educated at Oxford, Vaughan was studying law in London when he was recalled home in 1642 at the beginning of the first Civil War (1642–46). He remained in Wales the rest of his life.

In 1646 his *Poems, with the Tenth Satyre of Juvenal Englished* appeared, followed by a second volume in 1647. Meanwhile Vaughan had been "converted" by reading the religious poet George Herbert and gave up "idle verse." His *Silex Scintillans* (1650; enlarged 1655; "The Glittering Flint") and the prose *Mount of Olives; or, Solitary Devotions* (1652) show the depth of his religious convictions and the authenticity of his poetic genius. Vaughan also translated short moral and religious works and two medical works in prose.

Though Vaughan borrowed phrases from Herbert and other writers and wrote poems with the same titles as Herbert's, he was one of the most original poets of his day. He is chiefly remembered for a gift of spiritual vision or imagination that en-

abled him to write freshly and convincingly. Equally gifted in writing about nature, he held the view that every flower enjoys the air it breathes and that even sticks and stones share in the expectation of resurrection.

Vauquelin de La Fresnaye \vȯk-ˈlaⁿ-də-lä-fre-ˈnä\, Jean, Sieur (Lord) des Yveteaux (b. 1536, La Fresnaye-au-Sauvage or Caen, Fr.—d. 1606/08, Caen)   French magistrate, poet, and moralist who was credited with introducing satire to France as a literary genre.

Vauquelin studied the humanities at Paris and law at Poitiers and Bourges, later practicing as a magistrate in Caen. His poetic theory, based on that of Pierre de Ronsard, preserved the tenets of the literary circle known as La Pléiade and attempted to promote a pure, classical style. Vauquelin's poetic works include *Les Deux Premiers Livres des foresteries* (1555; "The Two First Books of Forestry"); *Idillies et pastorales*, published with his verse *L'Art poétique* (1605); five books entitled *Satires* (1581–85); and some sonnets, epigrams, and epitaphs. *L'Art poétique*, commissioned by Henry III in 1574, reflects Vauquelin's lifelong effort to persuade his fellow writers to abide by the precepts of Aristotle and Horace. He urged them to avoid Italianate excesses and to cultivate a pure French style in works that were moral, didactic, and based upon logic.

Vaux \ˈvȯks\ of Harrowden \ˈhar-ō-dən\, Thomas Vaux, 2nd Baron (b. 1510—d. October 1556)   Early English Tudor poet, associated with Sir Thomas Wyatt and the Earl of Surrey.

Vaux accompanied the lord chancellor Thomas Cardinal Wolsey on his embassy to France in 1527 and attended King Henry VIII to Calais and Boulogne in 1532. Created a Knight of the Bath at the coronation of Anne Boleyn (1533), he was captain of the Isle of Jersey until 1536.

Vaux's two best-known poems, included in Richard Tottel's *Miscellany* (1557), are "The aged lover renounceth love" and "The assault of Cupide upon the fort where the lovers hart lay wounded, and how he was taken." The *Paradyse of Daynty Devises* (1576) contains 13 poems signed by him.

Vazov \ˈvȧ-zūf\, Ivan (Minchov) (b. June 27, 1850, Sopot, Bulg.—d. Sept. 22, 1921, Sofia)   Man of letters whose poems, short stories, novels, and plays were inspired by patriotism and love of the Bulgarian countryside.

Vazov's father sent him to study commerce in Romania, where contact with the émigré leaders of the Bulgarian revolutionary movement inspired him to devote his life to the national cause as well as to literature. After the liberation of Bulgaria from the Turks (1878), Vazov was a civil servant and a district judge. In 1880 he settled in Plovdiv, where he edited several newspapers and periodicals. During the anti-Russian regime of Stefan Stambolov, Vazov went into exile in Odessa (1886–89), where he began his greatest novel, *Pod igoto* (1889–90; *Under the Yoke*), a chronicle of the trials of the Bulgarians under Ottoman rule. After Stambolov's fall (1894), Vazov was elected to the assembly and during the years 1898–99 served as minister of education.

His other works include the epic cycle of poems *Epopeya na zabravenite* (1881–84; "Epic of the Forgotten"); the novella *Nemili-nedragi* (1883; "Unloved and Unwanted"); the novels *Nova zemya* (1896; "New Land") and *Kazalarskata tsaritsa* (1903; "The Empress of Kazalar"); and the plays *Khŭshove* (1894), *Borislav* (1909), and *Kŭm propast* (1910; "Toward the Abyss").

Veda \ˈvā-də\   Sacred hymn or verse composed in archaic Sanskrit and current among the Indo-European-speaking peoples who entered India from the Iranian regions. No definite date can be ascribed to the composition of the Vedas, but most scholars believe it to have occurred in the period of about 1500–1200 BC. The hymns form a liturgical body that in part

grew up around the cult of the soma ritual (the extraction and
ingestion of the juice of a plant) and the sacrifice. They extol the hereditary deities, who for the most part personified
various natural and cosmic phenomena, such as fire (Agni),
the Sun (Sūrya and Savitṛ), dawn (Uṣas), storms (the Rudras),
war and rain (Indra), honor (Mitra), divine authority (Varuṇa),
and creation (Indra, with some aid of Vishnu). Hymns were
composed to these deities, and many were recited or chanted
during rituals.

The foremost collection, or Saṃhitā, of such hymns, from
which the *hotṛ* (chief priest) drew the material for his recitations, is the Rigveda (Ṛgveda). Sacred formulas known as
mantras were recited by the priest responsible for the sacrificial
fire and the carrying out of the ceremony; these mantras and
verses in time were drawn into Saṃhitās known collectively
as Yajurveda. A third group of priests, headed by the *udgātṛ*
("chanter"), performed melodic recitations linked to verses
that, although drawn almost entirely from the Rigveda, came
to be arranged as a separate Saṃhitā, the Sāmaveda ("Veda
of the Chants"). To these three Vedas—Ṛg, Yajur, and Sāma,
known as the *trayī-vidyā* ("threefold knowledge")—was added
a fourth, the Atharvaveda, a collection of hymns, magic spells,
and incantations that represents a more folk level of religion
and remains partly outside the Vedic sacrifice.

The entire corpus of Vedic literature—the Saṃhitās and the
expositions that came to be attached to them, the Brāhmaṇas,
the Āraṇyakas, and the Upanishads—was considered Śruti,
the product of divine revelation. The whole of the literature
seems to have been preserved orally (although scholars suspect
that there were early manuscripts to assist memory). *See also*
ĀRAṆYAKA; BRĀHMAṆA; UPANISHAD.

Vedāṅga \vā-'dāṅ-gə\   Any one of six classes of concise,
technical, and usually aphoristic Sanskrit works written in the
sutra style and designed to teach how to recite, understand,
and apply Vedic texts. The word Vedāṅga means literally "limb
of the Veda," the Veda being thought of as the body which the
limbs support and preserve.

The six areas of study covered by the Vedāṅgas are:
(1) *śikṣā* (instruction), which explains the proper articula-
tion and pronunciation of the Vedic texts. Different *śākhās*
(branches) had different ways of pronouncing the texts, and
these variations were recorded in *prātiśākhyas* (literally, "Instructions for the *śākhās*"), four of which are extant; (2) *chan-
das* (meter), of which there remains only one late representative;
(3) *vyākaraṇa* (analysis and derivation), in which the language
is grammatically described—Pāṇini's famous grammar (*c.* 400
BC) and the *prātiśākhyas* are the oldest examples of this discipline; (4) *nirukta* (lexicon), which discusses and gives meanings
for difficult words, represented by the *Nirukta* of Yāska (*c.* 600
BC); (5) *jyotiṣa* (luminaries), a system of astronomy and astrology used to determine the right times for rituals; and (6) *kalpa*
(mode of performance), which studies the correct ways of performing the ritual.

Vedānta \vā-'dän-tə\   One of the six orthodox systems (dar-
shans) of Indian philosophy and the one that forms the basis of
most modern schools of Hinduism. The term Vedānta means
in Sanskrit the "conclusion" (*anta*) of the Vedas, the earliest
sacred literature of India; it applies to the Upanishads, which
were elaborations of the Vedas, and to the school that arose
out of the study (mimamsa) of the Upanishads. Thus Vedānta
is also referred to as Vedānta-Mīmāṃsā ("Reflection on
Vedānta"), Uttara-Mīmāṃsā ("Reflection on the Latter Part of
the Vedas"), and Brahma-Mīmāṃsā ("Reflection on Brahma").

The three fundamental Vedānta texts are: the Upanishads;
the *Brahma-sūtra*s (also called *Vedānta-sūtra*s), which are very

brief, even one-word interpretations of the doctrine of the Upanishads; and the *Bhagavadgītā* ("Song of the Lord").

Vedel \'vā-thel\, Anders Sørensen (b. Nov. 9, 1542, Vejle,
Den.—d. Feb. 13, 1616, Ribe)   Danish historian and ballad
collector who translated the *Gesta Danorum* of the medieval
historian Saxo Grammaticus from Latin into Danish (1575).

Vedel was a clergyman at the royal court. In 1591 he published his *Et hundrede udvalde danske viser*, a collection of 100
medieval Danish folk songs and ballads. Based on oral and
manuscript sources, it was the earliest printed collection and
remains a principal source of Danish ballads. It was enlarged
and republished in 1695 by Peder Syv.

Vega \'bā-ğä, *Angl* 'vā-gə\, Lope de, *in full* Lope Félix de Vega
Carpio, *byname* The Phoenix of Spain, *Spanish* El Fénix de

Mary Evans Picture Library

España \el-'fā-nĕks-ˌthä-es-
'pä-nyä\ (b. Nov. 25, 1562,
Madrid, Spain—d. Aug.
27, 1635, Madrid)   Out-
standing dramatist of the
Spanish Golden Age, au-
thor of as many as 1,800
plays and several hundred
shorter dramatic pieces, of
which 431 plays and 50
shorter pieces are extant.

Vega's life was as event-
ful as his dramas. By 1583
he had established himself
as a playwright in Madrid
and was living from his *comedias* (tragicomic social
dramas). He also had be-
gun to exercise an unde-
fined role as gentleman attendant or secretary to a series of
nobles, adapting his role as servant or panderer according to
the situation. By this time, also, the poet's life was already
launched on a course of tempestuous passion; his many love
affairs brought him both notoriety and recurring brushes with
the law, resulting in prison terms and exile.

Vega became identified as a playwright with the *comedia*,
a comprehensive term for the new drama of Spain's Golden
Age. His productivity for the stage, however exaggerated by
report, was phenomenal. Vega's themes vary greatly; he essentially wrote two types of drama, both Spanish in setting: the
heroic, historical play based on some national story or legend,
and the CLOAK-AND-SWORD drama of contemporary manners
and intrigue.

For his historical plays Vega ransacked the medieval chronicle, the *romancero*, and popular legend and song for heroic
themes. *Peribáñez y el comendador de Ocaña* (*Peribáñez and the
Commander of Ocaña*), *El mejor alcalde, el rey* (*The King, the
Greatest Alcalde*), and *Fuente Ovejuna* (*All Citizens Are Soldiers*)
are still memorable and highly dramatic vindications of the in-
alienable rights of the individual, as is *El caballero de Olmedo*
(*The Knight from Olmedo*) on a more exalted social plane. In
Fuente Ovejuna the entire village assumes responsibility before
the king for the slaying of its overlord and wins his exoneration. This experiment in mass psychology is the best-known
outside Spain of all his plays.

Vega's cloak-and-sword plays are all compounded of the
same ingredients and feature the same basic situations: gallants
and ladies falling endlessly in and out of love, the "point of
honor" being sometimes engaged, but very rarely the heart,
while servants imitate or parody the main action and one, the
gracioso, exercises his wit and common sense in comment-

ing on the follies of his social superiors. *El perro del hortelano* (*The Gardener's Dog*), *Por la puente Juana* ("Across the Bridge, Juana"), *La dama boba* (*The Lady Nit-Wit*), *La moza del cántaro* ("The Girl with the Jug"), and *El villano en su rincón* ("The King and the Farmer") are reckoned among the best in this minor if still-entertaining kind of play.

A collection of Vega's nondramatic works in verse and prose published from 1776 to 1779 filled 21 volumes. He wrote pastoral romances, verse histories of recent events, verse biographies of Spanish saints, long epic poems and burlesques upon such works, and prose tales. His lyric compositions—ballads, elegies, epistles, sonnets (there are 1,587 of these)—are myriad. Formally they rely much on the conceit, and in content they provide a running commentary on the poet's whole emotional life.

Among specific nondramatic works that deserve to be mentioned are the 7,000-line *Laurel de Apolo* (1630), depicting Apollo's crowning of the poets of Spain on Helicon, which remains of interest as a guide to the poets and poetasters of the day; *La Dorotea* (1632), a thinly veiled chapter of autobiography cast in dialogue form that is considered the most mature and reflective of his writings; and the *Arte nuevo de hacer comedias en este tiempo* (1609; *The New Art of Writing Plays*), which provides a bridge and key to his plays.

vehicle   *see* TENOR AND VEHICLE.

Vélez \\'bā-lāth\\, Luis, *surname in full* Vélez de Guevara \\thā-gā-'bā-rä\\ (b. July 1579, Ecija, Spain—d. Nov. 10, 1644, Madrid)   Spanish poet, playwright, and novelist who ranks high among the followers of Lope de Vega and displays a gift for creating character. His fantastic satirical novel, *El diablo cojuelo* (1641; "The Crippled Devil"), became well known from its adaptation by the French dramatist Alain-René Lesage as *Le Diable boiteux* (1707; *The Devil upon Two Sticks*).

Vélez held various posts in noble and royal households and became a favorite of Philip IV of Spain. He was a remarkably prolific writer, composing more than 400 plays, several of which were based on those of Lope de Vega. A careless but entertaining playwright, he was called Quitapesares ("Care Dispeller") by Miguel de Cervantes for the gaiety and animation of his work. Unfortunately his productivity brought him little reward and he eventually died in poverty.

vellum \\'vel-əm\\ [Middle English *velim*, from Middle French *velin, veelin*, from *velin, veelin* (adjective) of a calf, a derivative of *veel* calf]   An especially fine parchment made from the thinner, more delicate skins of calf or kid or from stillborn or newly born calf or lamb. The term is often used interchangeably with PARCHMENT.

Venn, Diggory \\'dig-ə-rē-'ven\\   Fictional character, a reddleman (someone who delivers the red dye that farmers use to mark their sheep) who figures in Thomas Hardy's novel THE RETURN OF THE NATIVE.

Vennberg \\'ven-ˌberʸ\\, Karl (Gunnar) (b. April 11, 1910, Blädinge, Swed.)   Poet who was the leading critic and analyst of Swedish poetry in the 1940s.

Vennberg was a teacher of Norwegian in a Stockholm folk high school. His influential reviews and critical essays broke the ground for the radical cause of the *40-talslyrik* (1947; "Poetry of the 1940s"), an anthology that he edited together with Erik Lindegren. His two volumes of verse, in which he exposes contemporary deception and self-deception, *Halmfackla* (1944; "Straw Torch") and *Tideräkning* (1945; "Reckoning of Time"), together with Lindegren's collections from these years, are considered the central works of the new Swedish poetry of the 1940s.

Vennberg continued to be published into the 1980s and '90s. His collections of poetry include *Gatukorsning* (1952; "Intersection"), *Synfält* (1954; "Points of View"), *Sju ord på tunnelbanan* (1971; "Seven Words in the Subway"), *Vägen till Spånga folkan* (1976; "The Road to Spånga Community Center"), and *Visa solen ditt ansikte* (1978; "Show Your Face to the Sun").

Venus \\'vē-nəs\\   Ancient Italic goddess associated with cultivated fields and gardens and later identified by the Romans with the Greek goddess of love, APHRODITE.

Jupiter and Venus came to be associated, as father and daughter, with the Greek deities Zeus and Aphrodite. She was, therefore, also considered to be the wife of Vulcan and the mother of Cupid as Aphrodite was the wife of Hephaestus and the mother of Eros, the Greek counterparts of Vulcan and Cupid. In myth and legend Venus was famous for her romantic intrigues and affairs with both gods and mortals, and she became associated with many aspects, both positive and negative, of femininity. As Venus Verticordia, for example, she was charged with the protection of chastity in women and girls.

Because of her association with love and with feminine beauty, Venus has been a favorite subject in art since ancient times; notable representations include the statue known as the "Venus de Milo" and the paintings "The Birth of Venus" by Sandro Botticelli and "Venus and Adonis" by Titian. The legend of Venus and Adonis is also the subject of a poem by William Shakespeare. Other literary representations include the legend of Tannhäuser and poems by Algernon Charles Swinburne and Victor Hugo. *See also* ADONIS.

Venus and Adonis stanza \\'vē-nəs . . . ə-'dän-is, -'dön-\\   A stanza consisting of an iambic pentameter quatrain and couplet with the rhyme scheme *ababcc*. The stanza was so called because it was used by William Shakespeare in his poem *Venus and Adonis* (1593).

verbal icon   *see* ICON.

Vercelli Book \\ver-'chel-lē\\ (*Latin* Codex Vercellensis)   Old English manuscript written in the late 10th century. It contains texts of the poem *Andreas*, two poems by Cynewulf, *The Dream of the Rood*, an "Address of the Saved Soul to the Body," and a fragment of a homiletic poem, as well as 23 prose homilies and a prose life of St. Guthlac, the *Vercelli Guthlac*. The book is so named because it was found in the cathedral library at Vercelli, northern Italy, in 1822.

Marginalia in the manuscript indicate that it was in English use in the 11th century. The book was probably taken to Italy by an Anglo-Saxon pilgrim on the way to Rome.

Verde \\'ver-dē\\, Cesário, *in full* José Joaquim Cesário Verde (b. Feb. 25, 1855, Lisbon, Port.—d. July 18, 1886, Lisbon)   Poet who revived Portuguese poetry by introducing colloquial language and by expanding its expressive capacity beyond the accepted means of exalted rhetoric. He dealt extensively with themes pertaining to the growth of urban life.

Verde studied at the University of Lisbon but left without a degree. Adopting a bohemian life-style, he nevertheless earned a living as a fruit farmer and for a time as a businessman, and he published poetry in newspapers and literary magazines sporadically until his early death from tuberculosis.

After his death, a friend, the literary critic António da Silva Pinto, collected and published his poems as *O livro de Cesário Verde 1873–1886* (1887; "The Book of Cesário Verde").

Vere, Captain \\'vir\\   Fictional character, the captain of the warship *Indomitable* in the novel BILLY BUDD, FORETOPMAN, by Herman Melville.

Verfremdungseffekt   *see* ALIENATION EFFECT.

Verga \'vär-gä\, Giovanni (b. Sept. 2, 1840, Catania, Sicily [Italy]—d. Jan. 27, 1922, Catania) Novelist, short-story writer, and playwright who is considered the most important of the Italian VERISMO (realist) school of novelists. His reputation was slow to develop, but modern critics have judged him one of the greatest of all Italian novelists. His influence was particularly marked on the post-World War II generation of Italian authors; a landmark film of the Neorealist cinema movement, Luchino Visconti's *La terra trema* (1948; *The Earth Trembles*), was based on Verga's novel *I Malavoglia*.

Born to a family of Sicilian landowners, Verga went to Florence in 1869 and later lived in Milan. In 1893 he returned to Catania. Starting with historical and patriotic narratives, Verga went on to write novels in which psychological observation was combined with romantic elements, as in *Eva* (1873), *Tigre reale* (1873; "Royal Tigress"), and *Eros* (1875). These sentimental works were later referred to by Verga as novels "of elegance and adultery." Within a few years he produced his masterpieces: the short stories of *Vita dei campi* (1880; "Life in the Fields") and *Novelle rusticane* (1883; *Little Novels of Sicily*), the great novels *I Malavoglia* (1881; THE HOUSE BY THE MEDLAR TREE) and MASTRO-DON GESUALDO (1889), and CAVALLERIA RUSTICANA (1884; "Rustic Chivalry"), a play rewritten from a short story, which became immensely popular as the basis for an opera (1890) by Pietro Mascagni.

Verga's terse accuracy and intensity of human feeling produce a distinctively lyrical realism. His realistic representations of the life of the poor peasants and fishermen of Sicily are particularly notable, and his strong feeling for locale gave impetus to a movement of regionalist writing in Italy. D.H. Lawrence translated several of his works into English, including *Cavalleria rusticana* and *Mastro-don Gesualdo*.

Vergil *see* VIRGIL.

Verhaeren \ver-'hä-ren, ver-ä-'ren\, Émile (b. May 21, 1855, Saint Amand lez-Puers, Belg.—d. Nov. 27, 1916, Rouen, Fr.) Foremost among the Belgian poets who wrote in French. His work, in its strength and range, has been compared to that of Victor Hugo and Walt Whitman.

Verhaeren was educated at Brussels and Ghent and during the years 1875–81 studied law at Louvain, where he became acquainted with Max Waller, the founder of the influential periodical *La Jeune Belgique* (1881). He became one of the group in Brussels who brought about the literary and artistic renaissance of the 1890s.

His first book, a collection of violently naturalistic poems (*Les Flamandes*, 1883), created a sensation. It was followed by short stories, but his reputation as a lyric poet was confirmed by a succession of works: *Les Moines* (1886; "The Monks"), *Les Débâcles* (1888), *Les Flambeaux noirs* (1890; "The Black Torches"), *Au bord de la route* (1891; "Along the Way"; later retitled *Les Bords de la route*), and *Les Campagnes hallucinées* (1893; "The Moonstruck Countrysides").

In 1895, Verhaeren's growing concern for social problems inspired *Les Villages illusoires* ("The Illusory Villages"). *Les Heures claires* (1896; *The Sunlit Hours*), an avowal of his love for his wife, was the first of his major works, among which the most outstanding are *Les Visages de la vie* (1899; "The Faces of Life"), *Les Forces tumultueuses* (1902; "The Tumultuous Forces"), *Les Tendresses premières* (1904; "First Loves," the first part of the five-part *Toute la Flandre* ["All of Flanders"]), *La Multiple Splendeur* (1906; "The Manifold Splendor"), *Les Heures du soir* (1911; *The Evening Hours*), *Les Blés mouvants* (1912; "Wheat in Motion"), and *La Belgique sanglante* (1915; *Belgium's Agony*). He also published books on art, two further collections of personal lyrics to his wife, and plays—*Les Aubes*

(1898; *The Dawn*), *Le Cloître* (1900; *The Cloister*), *Philippe II* (1901), and *Hélène de Sparte* (1912; *Helen of Sparta*).

The qualities most noted in Verhaeren's considerable poems are vigor and breadth of vision. It is perhaps in the poems celebrating domestic joys that he is most moving. More generally popular are those glorifying Flanders and those that exalt the triumph of human intelligence over matter and praise the epic beauty of the industrial age.

verisimilitude \,ver-i-si-'mil-i-,tüd, -,tyüd\ [Latin *verisimilitudo* plausibility] The semblance of reality in dramatic or nondramatic fiction. The concept implies that either the action represented must be acceptable or convincing according to the audience's own experience or knowledge or, as in the presentation of science fiction or tales of the supernatural, the audience must be enticed into willingly suspending disbelief and accepting improbable actions as true within the framework of the narrative.

Aristotle in his *Poetics* insisted that literature should reflect nature—that even highly idealized characters should possess recognizable qualities—and that what was probable took precedence over what was merely possible. Following Aristotle, the 16th-century Italian critic Lodovico Castelvetro pointed out that the nondramatic poet had only words with which to imitate words and things but the dramatic poet could use words to imitate words, things to imitate things, and people to imitate people. His influence on the French neoclassical dramatists of the 17th century is reflected in their preoccupation with *vraisemblance* and their contribution of many refinements to the theory in respect to appropriate diction and gesture.

The concept of verisimilitude was incorporated most fully in the realist writing of the late 19th century, in which well-developed characters closely imitate real people in their speech, mannerisms, dress, and material possessions.

verismo \vā-'rēz-mō\ [Italian, realism, a derivative of *vero* true, true to life] Literary realism as it developed in Italy in the late 19th and early 20th centuries. Its primary exponents were the Sicilian novelists Luigi Capuana and Giovanni Verga. The realist movement arose in Europe after the French Revolution, and the realist influence reached Capuana and Verga particularly through the writings of Honoré de Balzac and Émile Zola in France and of the *scapigliatura* group in Italy. Verismo's overriding aim was the objective presentation of life, usually that of the lower classes, using direct, unadorned language, explicit descriptive detail, and realistic dialogue.

Capuana initiated the movement with the short-story collection *Profili di donne* (1877; "Studies of Women") and the novel *Giacinta* (1879) and other psychologically oriented, clinically rendered works, which were objective almost to the point of excising human emotion. Works by his friend Verga, of which the best known are *I Malavoglia* (1881) and *Mastro-don Gesualdo* (1889), described with more emotional warmth the dismal conditions in early 19th-century Sicily.

The best of the writers of the movement were regionalists, including the Neapolitan novelist Matilde Serao, the Tuscan Renato Fucini, and Grazia Deledda, the novelist of southern Italy who received the Nobel Prize for Literature in 1926.

Verismo faded from the scene in the 1920s but emerged after World War II in a new and explosively vital form, *Neorealismo* (Neorealism).

Veríssimo \vā-'rēs-sē-mü\, Érico Lopes (b. Dec. 17, 1905, Cruz Alta, Braz.—d. Nov. 28, 1975, Pôrto Alegre) Novelist, literary historian, and critic whose writings in Portuguese and English on Brazilian literature introduced readers throughout the world both to the literary currents of modern Brazil and to his country's social order and cultural heritage.

Veríssimo's popular first novel, *Clarissa* (1933), was followed by a series of best-selling novels, including *Caminhos cruzados* (1935; *Crossroads*), *Olhai os Lírios do campo* (1938; *Consider the Lilies of the Field*), and *O resto é silêncio* (1943; *The Rest Is Silence*). These novels, experimental in technique and use of language, reveal Veríssimo's deep preoccupation with the individual in a changing social structure.

Fluent in English, Veríssimo taught in the United States for a time. The series of lectures he gave at the University of California at Berkeley, 1943–44, was published in English in *Brazilian Literature: An Outline* (1945). Veríssimo's best-known work, the trilogy *O tempo e o vento* (1949–62; partial Eng. trans., *Time and the Wind*), traces the history of a Brazilian family through several generations to the late 20th century.

Verlaine \ver-'len \, Paul(-Marie) (b. March 30, 1844, Metz, Fr.—d. Jan. 8, 1896, Paris)   French lyric poet first associated with the Parnassians and later a leader of the Symbolists. With Stéphane Mallarmé and Charles Baudelaire he formed the so-called Decadents.

Culver Pictures

The first series of *Le Parnasse contemporain* (1886), a collection of pieces by contemporary French poets, contained eight poems by Verlaine. The same year, his first volume of poetry appeared. In addition to virtuoso imitations of Baudelaire and Charles Leconte de Lisle, *Poèmes saturniens* included several poignant expressions of love and melancholy.

In August 1870 Verlaine married Mathilde Mauté; in the delicious poems written during their engagement (*La Bonne Chanson*, 1870), he sees her as his long-hoped-for savior from his erring ways. Their marriage, however, was soon shattered by Verlaine's infatuation with the poet Arthur Rimbaud, who came to stay with the Verlaines in September 1871. Verlaine abandoned his wife and infant son in July 1872 to wander with Rimbaud and write "impressionist" sketches for his next collection, *Romances sans paroles* (1874; "Songs Without Words"). The opening pages, especially, attain a pure musicality rarely surpassed in French literature and embody some of his most advanced prosodic experiments. At the time of publication the author was serving a two-year sentence at Mons for shooting Rimbaud during a quarrel in July 1873.

Leaving prison in January 1875, Verlaine tried a Trappist retreat, then hurried to Stuttgart to meet Rimbaud, who apparently repulsed him with violence. He took refuge in England and taught for more than a year before returning to France. From this period (1873–78) date most of the poems

in *Sagesse* ("Wisdom"), including outstanding poetical expressions of simple Roman Catholic faith as well as of his emotional odyssey. About this time he gained recognition, and in 1882 his famous "Art poétique" was adopted by the young Symbolists.

The death of his favorite pupil in 1883, as well as that of the poet's mother in 1886, and the failure of all attempts at reconciliation with his wife broke down whatever will to respectability remained, and he relapsed into drink and debauchery.

Jadis et naguère (1884; "Yesteryear and Yesterday") consists mostly of pieces written years before but not fitting into previous carefully grouped collections. Similarly, *Parallèlement* (1889) comprises bohemian and erotic pieces often contemporary with, and technically equal to, his "respectable" ones. Prose works such as *Les Poètes maudits* (1884; "The Accursed Poets"), short biographical studies of six poets, among them Mallarmé and Rimbaud; *Les Hommes d'aujourd'hui* (1885–93; "The Men of Today"), brief biographies of contemporary writers, most of which appeared in 1886; *Mes hôpitaux* (1892; dated 1891), accounts of Verlaine's stays in hospitals; *Mes Prisons*, accounts of his incarcerations; and *Confessions, notes autobiographiques* (1895; *Confessions of a Poet*) helped attract notice to ill-recognized contemporaries as well as to himself.

Verne \'vern, *Angl* 'vərn \, Jules (b. Feb. 8, 1828, Nantes, Fr.— d. March 24, 1905, Amiens)   French author whose writings shaped the development of modern science fiction.

In Paris Verne studied law but afterward chose to follow his interest in literature. In 1850 his play *Les Pailles rompues* ("The

E.B. Inc.

Broken Straws") was successfully produced at the Théâtre Historique. He served as secretary at the Théâtre Lyrique (1852–54) and later became a stockbroker, but he continued writing comedies, librettos, and stories.

In 1863 Verne published the first of his *Voyages extraordinaires—Cinq semaines en ballon* (1863; *Five Weeks in a Balloon*). The great success of the tale encouraged him to produce others in the same vein of romantic adventure, with increasingly deft depictions of fantastic but nonetheless carefully conceived imaginary scientific wonders. The *Voyages* continued with *Le Voyage au centre de la Terre* (1864; A JOURNEY TO THE CENTER OF THE EARTH), *De la Terre à la Lune* (1865; FROM THE EARTH TO THE MOON), *Vingt Mille Lieues sous les mers* (1869–70; TWENTY THOUSAND LEAGUES UNDER THE SEA), and *L'Île mystérieuse* (1874; THE MYSTERIOUS ISLAND), in which he foresaw a number of scientific devices and developments, including the submarine, the aqualung, television, and space travel.

Verne's novels were enormously popular throughout the world; one in particular, the grippingly realistic *Le Tour du monde en quatre-vingt jours* (1873; AROUND THE WORLD IN EIGHTY DAYS), generated great excitement during its serial publication in *Le Temps* and remained one of his most popular works.

Verri \'vär-rē \, Pietro (b. Dec. 12, 1728, Milan [Italy]—d. June 28, 1797, Milan)   Political economist, journalist, government official, and man of letters, leader of a Milanese academy and director of its influential periodical, and author of literary, historical, and economic works.

Verri became the moving spirit of the Società dei Pugni, a group of Milanese intellectuals influenced by the French Encyclopédistes. From 1764 to 1766 he directed the society's periodical, *Il Caffè* ("The Coffeehouse"), with the collaboration of his novelist brother, Alessandro (1741–1816). Pietro Verri contributed at least 38 articles on literary subjects to *Il Caffè*. For much of his life he held important posts in the Milanese government, working for administrative reform and a revitalization of commerce. Among his important economic treatises are *Riflessioni sulle leggi vincolanti* (1769; "Reflections on the Banking Laws") and *Meditazioni sull' economia politica* (1771). His correspondence with his brother provides a vibrant picture of Milanese life in their time.

Verrius Flaccus \'ver-e-əs-'flak-əs\, Marcus (fl. late 1st century BC)   Roman freedman who became a learned scholar and grammarian and the most famous teacher of his day. He introduced the principle of competition among his pupils and awarded old books, beautiful or rare, as prizes. Augustus entrusted the education of his two grandsons to him, and thenceforward his school was in the imperial house on the Palatine.

The works of Verrius Flaccus are lost, but he is known to have written *fasti* (calendars) that were set up at Praeneste, where, in fact, *fasti* have been found that have been accepted as his. A work of his that was much used was *De significatu verborum* ("On the Meaning of Words"), a large lexicon that was the first of its kind and that was, moreover, a storehouse of antiquarian learning.

vers de société \ˌver-də-sōs-yā-'tā\ [French, society verse]   Witty and typically ironic light verse written to amuse a sophisticated circle of readers.

Vers de société has flourished in cultured societies, particularly in court circles and literary salons, from the time of the Greek poet Anacreon (6th century BC). Its tone is flippant or mildly ironic. Trivial subjects are treated in an intimate, subjective manner, and even when social conditions form the theme, the light mood prevails.

The Roman poets Catullus, Martial, and Horace produced much witty vers de société and have often been translated or closely paraphrased; but much strikingly original verse of this kind has come from poets or other writers known for their serious works. Jean Froissart, the 14th-century historian of feudal chivalry, wrote some of the most charming examples of the late Middle Ages. The English Cavalier poets Robert Herrick, Thomas Carew, and Richard Lovelace wrote much fine vers de société along with their elegant lyrics.

The 18th century was rich in examples, both in French and in English. Among the best English practitioners were John Gay and Alexander Pope, whose poem *The Rape of the Lock* is a masterpiece of the genre. Voltaire produced exquisite gems of occasional verse, epistles, and light satires.

Vers de société bloomed again in 19th-century literature after the Romantic movement's decline, with the poetry of William Ernest Henley and the scholarly Austin Dobson.

In the 20th century, the American poet Ogden Nash created a new, sophisticated, and urbane vers de société with a theme of self-ironic adult helplessness. In England the tradition was kept alive by the neo-Victorian topical poems of Sir John Betjeman.

verse \'vərs\ [Latin *versus* row, line, verse]   **1.** A line of metrical writing.   **2.** A unit of metrical writing larger than a single line, such as a stanza.   **3.** The shortest division of chapters of the Bible.   **4.** Poetry.   **5.** Metrical writing that is distinguished from poetry especially by its lower level of intensity.

verse-speaking choir   A group organized for the choral speaking of poetry.

verset \'vər-sət, vər-'set\ [French, verse in sacred scripture (as the Bible or Koran), group of sentences that form a verselike subdivision in a poetic text, a diminutive of *vers* verse]   A short verse, especially from a sacred book, such as those found in the Song of Solomon and the Psalms. Also, a stanza form modeled on such biblical verse. The stanza form is characterized by long lines and powerful, surging rhythms and usually expresses fervent religious or patriotic sentiments. The verset is a flexible form approximating free verse and the prose poem and is open to a wide range of emotional expression. The verset appears mainly in the literature of European Christian countries where it was first used in medieval religious and mystical texts. Friedrich Hölderlin, Charles Péguy, and Paul Claudel have all written poems in this form.

versicle \'vər-si-kəl\ [Latin *versiculus* short line of verse, a diminutive of *versus* line, verse]   A little verse. Also, a short response that is spoken or sung during a liturgy.

version \'vər-zhən\ [New Latin *versio*, from Medieval Latin, change, conversion, action of turning, a derivative of Latin *vertere* to turn]   **1.** A translation from another language; especially, a translation of the Bible or a part of it.   **2.** An adaptation of a literary work.

vers libre \ver-'lēbr, *Angl* 'lē-brə\ *plural* vers libres *same or* 'lē-brəz\ [French, free verse]   Nineteenth-century poetic innovation that liberated French poetry from its traditional prosodic rules. In vers libre, the basic metrical unit is the phrase rather than a line of a fixed number of syllables, as was traditional in French versification since the Middle Ages. In vers libre, the lengths of lines may vary according to the sense of the poem, the complete sentence replaces the stanza as a unit of meaning, and rhyme is optional.

Vers libre appears to have been the independent invention of several different French poets in the late 1880s. Among its early advocates and theoreticians were Gustave Kahn, Jules Laforgue, Francis Viélé-Griffin, and Édouard Dujardin. The widespread adoption of vers libre at the end of the 19th century influenced poetic trends in other countries, so that verse patterned on irregular metrical designs has become common in the modern poetry of all Western nations. *See also* FREE VERSE.

verso \'vər-sō\ [New Latin *verso* (*folio*) the page being turned]   **1.** The side of a leaf (such as of a manuscript) that is to be read second.   **2.** A left-hand page. *Compare* RECTO.

Verwey \vər-'vei, -'vā\, Albert (b. May 15, 1865, Amsterdam, Neth.—d. March 8, 1937, Noordwijk aan Zee)   Poet, scholar, and literary historian who played an important role in Dutch literary life in the late 19th and early 20th centuries.

Verwey's first book of poems, *Persephone*, was published in 1883. He was a cofounder in 1885 of the periodical *De Nieuwe Gids* ("The New Guide"), one of the chief organs of the Dutch literary revival of the 1880s, to which he also contributed sonnets and other poems. His poetry manifested a unique form of mysticism that was influenced by the pantheism of Benedict de Spinoza. Verwey's early poetry, such as that in *Cor Cordium* (1886), was notable for its air of spontaneity and its melodious and evocative qualities. His later poetry is still marked by these qualities but is at the same time highly intellectual, representing his attempts to express the mystical ideas that he saw as underlying the world of appearances. The concept of constant renewal of the self, long essential to Verwey, is exquisitely expressed in the free-verse poem *Een dag in April* (1926; "A Day in April"), in which the author's mastery of rhythm and "image thinking" is supremely evident.

Verwey was editor of his own periodical, *De beweging* (1905–19; "The Movement"), in which many influential young Dutch writers made their debut. Subsequently he was professor of Dutch literature at the University of Leiden from 1925 to 1935. As a scholar and literary historian, he wrote in particular on the 17th-century Dutch poets Joost van den Vondel and Henrick Laurenszoon Spieghel.

Very \'vir-ē, 'ver-\, Jones (b. Aug. 28, 1813, Salem, Mass., U.S.—d. May 8, 1880, Salem) American Transcendentalist poet and Christian mystic.

Very was descended from a seafaring family. He was educated at Harvard College and Harvard Divinity School. At Harvard he became a Greek tutor, but his faculty colleagues ultimately forced his resignation after he began to relate his mystic beliefs and his "visions."

Very first came to notice for his critical essays. He began writing religious sonnets as early as 1837, insisting that they were all "communicated" to him. Contemporary authors, including Ralph Waldo Emerson, praised his work for its beauty and simplicity. His *Essays and Poems* was published in 1839. In 1843 Very was licensed to preach as a Unitarian minister.

Vesaas \'vā-sȯs\, Tarjei (b. Aug. 20, 1897, Vinje, Nor.—d. March 15, 1970, Vinje) Norwegian novelist and short-story writer whose symbolic and allegorical narratives won him much recognition in Norway and other European countries.

Vesaas first experienced significant success with his novels about life on a Norwegian farm, *Det store spelet* (1934; *The Great Cycle*) and *Kvinner ropar heim* (1935; "Women Call Home"). His growing political and social awareness mark his *Kimen* (1940; *The Seed*), which shows how hatred is stirred up by mass psychology, and *Huset i mørkret* (1945; "House in Darkness"), a symbolic vision of the Nazi occupation of Norway. *Fuglane* (1957; *The Birds*), considered his greatest work, pleads for tolerance toward the outsider. He also wrote a renowned collection of short stories entitled *Vindane* (1952; "The Winds").

Vesper *see* HESPERUS.

Vesta \'ves-tə\ Roman goddess of the hearth, identified with the Greek HESTIA. The lack of an easy source of fire in the early Roman community placed a special premium on the ever-burning hearth fire, both publicly and privately maintained; thus, from the earliest times Vesta was assured of a prominent place in both family and state worship.

Vestdijk \'vest-ˌdeik, *Angl*-ˌdīk\, Simon (b. Oct. 17, 1898, Harlingen, Neth.—d. March 23, 1971, Utrecht) Prolific Dutch writer whose early novels, with their unrelenting exposure of the barrenness of middle-class provincial life, shocked the bourgeois world of the 1930s.

The cerebral approach that characterizes Vestdijk's writing was already apparent in his poetry, with which he started his literary career. In his first published novel, *Meneer Vissers hellevaart* (1936; "Mr. Visser's Journey Through Hell"), the influence of James Joyce is evident—from the wealth of interior monologue to the author's preoccupation with distasteful everyday details. His novel *Terug tot Ina Damman* (1934; "Back to Ina Damman"), a love story, was considered equally shocking when it appeared, but, having a less bitter theme, it probably remains the most popular of his 38 novels. His other novels include two that were translated into English: *Rumeiland* (1940; *Rum Island*) and *De koperen tuin* (1950; *The Garden Where the Brass Band Played*).

Viau or **Viaud** \'vyō\, Théophile de (b. 1590, Clairac, near Agen, Fr.—d. Sept. 25, 1626, Paris) French poet and dramatist of the pre-Neoclassical period.

Born into a Huguenot family of the minor nobility, Viau went to Paris, where he soon won a reputation as the leader of the *libertins* ("freethinkers"). He was briefly house dramatist to the Hôtel de Bourgogne in Paris, writing one important tragedy, *Pyrame et Thisbé* (1623). This period of prosperity ended when he was charged with irreligious activities. He fled, was sentenced in absentia to death, was rearrested, and was finally released in 1625 under sentence of banishment. His health broken, he died soon afterward.

Viau wrote odes and other poems on a wide range of topics. His verse is marked by a strong feeling for nature, great musicality, a use of original and ingenious imagery, and an epicurean outlook that is tempered by apocalyptic visions and the thought of death. Viau defended spontaneity and inspiration against the set of literary rules laid down by the influential poet François de Malherbe.

Vicar of Wakefield, The \'wāk-ˌfēld\ Novel by Oliver GOLDSMITH, published in two volumes in 1766. The story, a portrait of village life, is narrated by Dr. Primrose, the title character, whose family endures many trials—including the loss of most of their money, the seduction of one daughter, the destruction of their home by fire, and the vicar's incarceration—before all is put right in the end. The novel's idealization of rural life, sentimental moralizing, and melodramatic incidents are countered by a sharp but good-natured irony.

Vicente \vē-'säᵕ-tə\, Gil (b. *c.* 1465, Portugal—d. 1536/37) Major dramatist of Portugal whose plays, written in both Portuguese and Spanish, reveal a genuine comic vein and a great gift for the lyric as well as the satiric.

The record of much of Vicente's life is vague, to the extent that his identity is still uncertain. His first known work—a short play entitled *Auto da vistaçam* ("Play of the Visitation")—was produced in 1502 on the occasion of the birth of the future John III.

For the next 34 years Vicente was a kind of poet laureate, staging his plays to celebrate great events and the solemn occasions of Christmas, Easter, and Holy Thursday. The departure of a Portuguese fleet on the expedition against Azamor in 1513 turned his attention to more national themes, and in the *Exhortaçao da guerra* (produced 1513; *Exhortation to War* in *Four Plays of Gil Vicente*) and *Auto de la fama* (produced 1515; "Play of Fame"), inspired by the victories of Afonso de Albuquerque in the East, he wrote fervent patriotic verse.

Vicente's other plays included *Cortes de Jupiter* ("Jupiter's Courts"), acted on the occasion of the departure by sea of King Manuel's daughter Beatriz to wed the duke of Savoy in 1521; *Fragoa de amor* (produced 1524; "The Forge of Love"), written for the betrothal of King John III to the sister of the Holy Roman emperor Charles V; the *Templo de Apolo* (produced 1526; "The Temple of Apollo"); the biblical play *Sumario da historia de Deos* ("Summary of the History of God"); *Nao de amores* ("The Ship of Love"); *Divisa da cidade de Coimbra* ("The Coat of Arms of the City of Coimbra"); and *Farsa dos almocreves* (*The Carriers* in *Four Plays of Gil Vicente*), the last four produced in 1527.

The brilliant scenes of two of his last plays, *Romagen de aggravados* (produced 1533; "The Pilgrimage of the Aggrieved") and *Floresta de enganos* (produced 1536; "Forest of Deceits"), are loosely put together, and may well be earlier work; but the lyrical power of *Triumfo do inverno* (produced 1529; "Triumph of Winter") and the long, compact *Amadís de Gaula* (produced *c.* 1523/1533; "Amadis of Gaul") show that he retained his creative powers in his last decade.

Vicente's 44 plays reflect the change and upheaval of his era in all its splendor and its squalor. Twelve are written exclusively in Spanish, 14 in Portuguese; the rest use both languages. His plays were often elaborately staged: a ship was rowed on the scene, or a tower opened to display some splendid allegory; in this he anticipated the later Spanish drama. The various plays of the years 1513–19, composed when he was about 50, show Vicente at the height of his genius.

Victorian literature   Body of works written in England during the reign of Victoria (1837–1901), a long period of magnificent achievement. Its leading lights include, in poetry, Robert Browning, Edward Lear, and Alfred, Lord Tennyson; in criticism, Matthew Arnold and John Ruskin; and, above all, in the novel, Charles Dickens, Emily Brontë, George Eliot, Thomas Hardy, William Makepeace Thackeray, and a host of only slightly lesser names.

As the 20th century approached, the romantic, evangelical, and humanitarian impulses that had characterized the era began to lose momentum: poets became aesthetes instead of moral legislators, and novelists began to turn inward for their subject matter rather than looking outward to society. Certain prevailing values of the period (gentility, insularity, materialism, and, especially, censoriousness) have lent to the popular usage of "Victorian" a pejorative connotation that is far too simplistic to characterize the literature of the period.

Vidal \'vē-ˌdäl, vē-'däl\, Gore, *original name* Eugene Luther Vidal (b. Oct. 3, 1925, West Point, N.Y., U.S.)   Prolific American novelist, playwright, and essayist, noted for his irreverent and intellectually adroit novels.

Vidal graduated from Philips Exeter Academy in New Hampshire in 1943 and served in the U.S. Army in World War II. Thereafter he resided in many parts of the world—the east and west coasts of the United States, Europe, North Africa, and Central America. His first novel, *Williwaw* (1946), which was based on his wartime experiences, was praised by the critics, and his third novel, *The City and the Pillar* (1948), shocked the public with its direct and unadorned examination of a homosexual main character. Vidal's next five novels, including *Messiah* (1954), were received coolly by critics and were commercial failures. Abandoning novels, he turned to writing plays for the stage, television, and motion pictures and was successful in all three media. His best-known dramatic works from the next decade were *Visit to a Small Planet* (produced for television, 1955; on Broadway, 1957; for film, 1960), and *The Best Man* (play, 1960; film, 1964).

Vidal returned to writing novels with *Julian* (1964), a sympathetic fictional portrait of Julian the Apostate, the 4th-century pagan Roman emperor who opposed Christianity. *Washington, D.C.* (1967), an ironic examination of political morality in the U.S. capital, was followed by several popular novels that vividly re-created prominent figures and events in American history—*Burr* (1974), *1876* (1976), and *Lincoln* (1984). *Lincoln* presents a compelling portrait of President Abraham Lincoln's complex personality as viewed through the eyes of some of his closest associates during the American Civil War. Another success was the comedy *Myra Breckenridge* (1968), in which Vidal lampooned both transsexuality and contemporary American culture. In *Rocking the Boat* (1962), *Reflections upon a Sinking Ship* (1969), *The Second American Revolution* (1982), *A View from the Diners Club* (1991), and other essay collections, he incisively analyzed contemporary American politics and government.

Vídalín, Arngrímur Jónsson   *see* Arngrímur JÓNSSON.

Vídalín \'vē-dä-lēn\, Jón Thorkelsson, *also called* Magister Jón \'mä-gē-ster-'yòn\ (b. 1666, Gardhur, near Reykjavík, Ice.—d. 1720, Iceland)   Lutheran bishop, best known for his *Húss-Postilla* (1718–20; "Sermons for the Home"), one of the finest works of Icelandic prose of the 18th century.

The son of a learned physician and a grandson of the scholar Arngrímur Jónsson the Learned, Vídalín was educated at Skálholt in Iceland and at the University of Copenhagen. He rose rapidly in the church, becoming bishop of Skálholt in 1697. The extreme poverty of the Icelanders and the misery that had been caused by a series of epidemics aroused his indignation against the secular authorities, and he carried on a lifelong feud with them. His Baroque style sprinkled with proverbs, his ironic portrayals of prevailing abuses, and his vivid pictures of hell made Vídalín's homilies the most popular devotional work in Iceland down to the 19th century.

Vieira \'vyä-ē-rə\, José Luandino, *pseudonym of* José Vieira Matéus da Graça \mä-'tä-ūs-dä-'grä-sə\ (b. May 4, 1935, Lagoa de Furadouro, Port.)   Portuguese-language writer of short fiction and novels who is considered to be a major influence on Angolan literature of the late 20th century.

Vieira immigrated with his parents to Angola about 1936, living in and around the *musseques* (African quarters) of Luanda. His first collection of stories was *A cidade e a infância* (1957; "The City and Childhood"). A white Angolan, Vieira committed himself early to the overthrow of the Portuguese colonial government. He was twice arrested for his political activities, the second time spending 11 years in prison, mostly at the brutal camp Tarrafal, Cape Verde Islands.

Vieira is best known for his early collection of short stories, *Luuanda* (1964; *Luuanda: Short Stories of Angola*). The book, which received a Portuguese writers' literary award in 1965, was banned until the overthrow of the colonial government in 1974. Although the stories are not overtly political, their realism makes clear the oppressiveness of Portuguese occupation. Many of Vieira's stories follow the traditional structure of African oral narrative. He was also an innovator in the use of creolized Kimbundu (the language of the Mbundu people) and Portuguese and refused on principle to provide a glossary. His political novella *A vida verdadeira de Domingos Xavier* (1974; *The Real Life of Domingos Xavier*) portrays the cruelty of white "justice" and the courage of African men and women in preindependent Angola. His other works—among them *Velhas estórias* (1974; "Old Stories"), *Nós os do Makulusu* (1975; "Our Gang from Makulusu"), *Vidas novas* (1975; "New Lives"), *Macandumba* (1978), and *João Vêncio: Os sues amores* (1979; "João Vêncio: Regarding His Loves")—include both novels and collections of stories.

Vieira da Cruz \'vyä-rə-dä-'krüs\, Tomaz (b. April 22, 1900, Constância, Port.—d. June 7, 1960, Lisbon)   Portuguese poet, musician, and journalist.

Reared and educated in Portugal, Vieira da Cruz moved to Angola in 1924. Between 1929 and 1931 he edited the journal *Mocidade* ("Youth"). His first collection of poetry, *Quissange, saúdade nêgra* ("Thumb Piano, Black Nostalgia"), was published in 1932. Vieira da Cruz's poetry is a songlike evocation of Angolan and African themes of beauty, drama, love, and misfortune.

Vieira da Cruz was a pioneer in the literary use of the complex Angolan language; he structured his poetry with African expressions, fusing them with Portuguese rhymes. His best poetry can be found in *Quissange* and two other collections, *Tatuagem* (1941; "Tattoo") and *Cazumbi* (1950; "Spirits of the Dead"). The collection *Poesia angolana de Tomaz Vieira da Cruz* was published posthumously in 1963.

Viélé-Griffin \vyä-lä-grē-'feⁿ\, Francis, *pseudonym of* Egbert Ludovicus Viele \'vyäl\ (b. May 26, 1864, Norfolk, Va., U.S.—d. Nov. 12, 1937, Bergerac, Fr.)   American-born French poet who became an important figure in the French Symbolist movement.

Viélé-Griffin was sent to France at the age of eight to attend school and remained there for the rest of his life. His first collection of verse, *Cueille d'avril* (1886; "April's Harvest"), showed the influence of the Decadent movement, and the next two, *Les Cygnes* (1887; "The Swans") and *Les Joies* (1889; "The Joys"), established his reputation as a preeminent Symbolist.

In 1890 Viélé-Griffin cofounded the review *Les Entretiens politiques et littéraires* ("Political and Literary Conversations"), in which appeared many of his essays calling for the liberation of verse from the strictures of traditional poetic form. He himself pioneered the use of vers libre ("free verse"). Viélé-Griffin's work is marked by a fundamental optimism that is grounded in his delight in nature and his belief in the spiritual dimension of human life. He lived much of the time in Touraine, and many of his works—such as *La Clarté de vie* (1897; "The Brightness of Life") and *Le Domaine royale* (1923; "The Royal Domain")—celebrate the countryside. Others—such as *La Chevauchée d'Yeldis* (1893; "The Ride of Yeldis"), *Phocas le jardinier* (1898; "Phocas the Gardener"), and *La Légende ailée de Wieland le Forgeron* (1900; "The Winged Legend of Wieland the Blacksmith")—draw on Christian themes and Greek and medieval legends.

vignette \vin-'yet, vēn-\ A short descriptive literary sketch.

Vigny \vē-'nyē\, Alfred-Victor, Count (comte) de (b. March 27, 1797, Loches, Fr.—d. Sept. 17, 1863, Paris) Poet, dramatist, and novelist, the most philosophical of the French Romantic writers.

Vigny embarked upon a military career but soon turned to poetry. His first poem, "Le Bal," appeared in 1820. Two years later his first collection of verse followed, and salons and reviews in Paris hailed the birth of a poet who combined grace with a strength and depth that was totally Romantic. His *Poèmes antiques et modernes* (1826) was also a success.

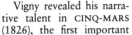

Bibliothèque Nationale, Paris

Vigny revealed his narrative talent in CINQ-MARS (1826), the first important historical novel in French. He also showed a typically Romantic interest in William Shakespeare, freely adapting *Othello* (*Le More de Venise*, performed 1829) as well as *The Merchant of Venice* (*Shylock*, 1829).

By 1830 Vigny had become disillusioned with the monarchy. He acknowledged his feelings as early as 1831 in "Paris," a poem of a new genre, which he called *élévations*. He felt all the more tormented, for he no longer could rely on the religious faith of his childhood. An unhappy love affair with an actress made his disillusion complete.

In *Stello* (1832) Vigny assembled a series of *consultations*, or dialogues, between two symbolic figures: Doctor Noir, who represents Vigny's own intellect; and Stello, who represents the poet's desire for an active part in the public arena. In seeking to preserve Stello from the dangers of his imprudent enthusiasm, Doctor Noir tells him three anecdotes in which a poet is harried to his death by a doctrinaire or uncaring politician. Vigny adapted one part of *Stello* into a prose drama in three acts, CHATTERTON (1835), in which he called the public to witness the misfortune of the poet in a materialist and pitiless society. The triumph of Vigny's career as a playwright, *Chatterton* remains one of the best Romantic dramas. Far superior to *La Maréchale d'Ancre* (performed 1831), it expresses the melan-

choly genius of Vigny more clearly and aptly than does his spiritual comedy *Quitte pour la peur* (performed 1833; "A Narrow Escape").

His severe and lofty pessimism was manifest again in *Servitude et grandeur militaires* (1835; *The Military Necessity*), also a *consultation*. The first and third stories in this volume are Vigny's masterpieces in prose. The book's three stories deal with the dignity and suffering of the soldier, who is obliged by his profession to kill yet who is condemned by it to passive obedience. Vigny began another *consultation* dealing with the religious prophet, but only one story, *Daphné* (1912), survives.

After 1838 Vigny again turned to poetry, slowly composing the 11 poems that were later collected under the title *Les Destinées* (1864).

In middle age Vigny gradually withdrew into a curious silence and retired, according to the famous expression of Charles Sainte-Beuve, to an "ivory tower." In 1841 he stood as a candidate to the Académie Française, but he was elected only in 1845. At his death Vigny left several unedited works whose posthumous publication enhanced his reputation: *Les Destinées*, *Le Journal d'un poète* (1867), *Daphné*, and *Mémoires inédits* (1958).

Vikramorvaśī \'vē-krə-'mōr-və-,shē\ ("Urvaśī Won by Valor") Drama by KĀLIDĀSA written in the 5th century AD. The subject of the play is the love of a mortal for a divine maiden. The play contains a well-known "mad scene" (Act IV) in which the king, grief-stricken, wanders through a lovely forest apostrophizing various flowers and trees as though they were his love.

vila \'vē-lə\ *plural* vilas *or* vily \'vē-lē\ [Slovene and Serbo-Croatian] A supernatural being of Slavic lands. Vilas are sometimes held to inhabit hills and woods and to appear in the form of a beautiful young woman.

Vilakazi \,vē-lä-'kä-zē\, Benedict Wallet (b. Jan. 6, 1906, near Stanger, Natal [now in South Africa]—d. Oct. 26, 1947, Johannesburg) Zulu poet, novelist, and educator who devoted his academic career to the teaching of Zulu and to the study of Bantu languages. He was awarded a master of arts degree for his work on the development of Zulu poetry and a doctor of literature degree for a study of oral and written literature in Nguni. In addition, he helped to compile a Zulu-English dictionary.

Vilakazi's literary output was large. He is best known for his poetry, which critics praise for the beauty and vitality resulting from his astute powers of observation and for his full use of the resources of the Zulu language. The first volume, *Inkondlo kaZulu* (1935; "Zulu National Songs"), was selected by Witwatersrand University in 1935 to be the lead volume of its Bantu Treasury Series, and *Amal' ezulu* (1945; "Zulu Treasures") became the eighth volume of the same series; they were both translated in *Zulu Horizons* (1962). Vilakazi also published a biography and three novels.

Vildrac \vēl-'drȧk\, Charles, *pseudonym of* Charles Messager \me-sȧ-'zhä\ (b. Nov. 22, 1882, Paris, Fr.—d. June 25, 1971, Saint-Tropez) French poet, playwright, and essayist whose idealistic commitment to humanitarianism characterized his artistic and personal life.

Vildrac, along with writer Georges Duhamel (later his brother-in-law) and others, founded the Abbaye, a community of young artists and writers; from 1906 to 1907 they lived together in the Paris suburb of Créteil. During World War II he was active in the French Resistance.

Some of his verse—including *Poèmes* (1905) and *Images et mirages* (1907)—celebrates brotherhood and proclaims a belief in the basic goodness of humanity, while *Chants du désespéré (1914–20)* (1920; "Songs of a Desperate Man") expresses anguish at the horrors of war. Vildrac's best-known play, *Le Paquebot Tenacity* (produced 1920; *S.S. Tenacity*), is a character study of two former soldiers about to immigrate to Canada. *Michel Auclair* (1921) concerns the loyalty of a man to a woman who has rejected him. *La Brouille* (1930; "The Misunderstanding") traces the quarrel of an idealist and a pragmatist. Other plays include *Madame Béliard* (1925), *Les Pères ennemis* (1946; "The Enemy Fathers"), and *Les Jouets du Père Noël* (1952; "The Toys of Father Christmas").

Vildrac also wrote travel memoirs and essays, such as *Notes sur la technique poétique* (1910; "Notes on Poetic Technique"), with Duhamel as coauthor. His works for children, including *L'Île rose* (1924; "The Pink Island"), have been praised as excellent examples of the genre.

Vile Bodies   Satiric novel by Evelyn WAUGH, published in 1930. Set in England between the wars, the novel examines the frenetic but empty lives of the Bright Young Things, young people who indulge in constant party-going, heavy drinking, and promiscuous sex. At the novel's end, the realities of the world intrude, with Adam Fenwick-Symes, the protagonist, serving on a battlefield at the onset of another world war.

villain \'vil-ən\   A character in a story or play who opposes the hero. A villain is also known as an ANTAGONIST.

villanelle \ˌvil-ə-'nel\ [French, from Italian *villanella* rustic song, a derivative of *villano* rustic, unrefined]   Rustic song in Italy, where the term originated; the term was used in France to designate a short poem of popular character favored by poets in the late 16th century. Joachim du Bellay's "Vanneur de Blé" and Philippe Desportes's "Rozette" are examples of this early type, unrestricted in form. Later poets patterned their villanelles on a highly popular example of the genre written by Jean Passerat. It established a rigorous and somewhat monotonous form: seven-syllable lines using two rhymes, distributed in (normally) five tercets (three-line stanzas) and a final quatrain with line repetitions.

The villanelle was revived in the 19th century by Philoxène Boyer and J. Boulmier. Charles Leconte de Lisle and later Maurice Rollinat also used the form. In England, the villanelle was cultivated by W.E. Henley, Austin Dobson, Andrew Lang, and Edmund Gosse. Examples in English include Henley's "A Dainty Thing's the Villanelle," which itself describes the form, and Dylan Thomas' "Do Not Go Gentle into That Good Night."

Villegas \bēl-'yā- găs\, Esteban Manuel de (b. 1589, Matute, near Nájera, Spain—d. Sept. 3, 1669, Matute)   Spanish lyric poet who achieved great popularity with an early book of poems, *Poesías eróticas y amatorias* (1617–18).

Villegas first studied classics at the University of Madrid, translating works of the 6th-century-BC Greek poet Anacreon at the age of 14, and later obtained a law degree from the University of Salamanca. Intending to devote his life to literature, he was forced to practice law to support his family. In 1659 he was jailed by the Inquisition because of satires he had published. Returning to Nájera, he spent his remaining years on a translation of *De consolatio philosophiae* (*Consolation of Philosophy*) by the Roman scholar Boethius (AD *c.* 470–542).

Villegas essentially exhausted his creativity in his youth. The *Poesías eróticas*, most of which were written in his teens, are a mixture of translations and imitations of Horace and Anacreon, satires, and idylls. Some critics regard these poems as possessing a grace and delicacy unequaled in Spanish literature.

Villette \vi-'let\   Novel by Charlotte BRONTË, published in three volumes in 1853. Based on Brontë's own experiences in Brussels (the "Villette" of the title), this tale of a poor young woman's emotional trial-by-fire while teaching in a girl's school in Belgium is one of the author's most complex books, a fine example of psychological realism laced with gothic romance. Depressed by the oppressive atmosphere of the school and unable to find an outlet for her turbulent emotions, Lucy Snowe suffers an inevitable nervous breakdown. The fiery Paul Emanuel, another teacher in the school, proves to be her savior when he recognizes her passionate nature in spite of the many barriers she has erected to hide it.

Villiers de L'Isle-Adam \vēl-yā-də-lēl-å-'dä^n\, Auguste, Count (comte) de, *in full* Jean-Marie-Mathias-Philippe-Auguste, Count de Villiers de L'Isle-Adam (b. Nov. 7, 1838, Saint-Brieuc, Fr.—d. Aug. 19, 1889, Paris)   French poet, dramatist, and short-story writer whose work reflects a revolt against naturalism and a combination of Romantic idealism and cruel sensuality. His hatred of the mediocrity of a materialistic age and his compelling personality made a considerable impression on later writers.

Villiers, the descendant of an aristocratic family, lived most of his life in poverty. He was a friend of the leading writers of his time but was not known to the general public until about five years before he died.

His most enduring works are the drama AXËL (1890) and the short stories in *Contes cruels* (1883; *Cruel Tales*). The latter, inspired by the works of Edgar Allan Poe, satirize bourgeois morality. Splendidly written, they often have an element of horror or even sadism that reveals both the desire to shock and some of Villiers's private obsessions. Villiers's *Correspondance* was published in 1962.

Villon \vē-'yô^n, -'lô^n\, François, *pseudonym of* François de Montcorbier *or* François des Loges (b. 1431, Paris—d. after 1463)   One of the greatest French lyric poets. His chief works

Woodcut from the first edition of Villon's works published by Pierre Levet, 1489
Bibliothèque Nationale, Paris

include LE PETIT TESTAMENT (1489), LE TESTAMENT (1489), and various ballades, chansons, and rondeaux.

The register of the faculty of arts of the University of Paris records that in March 1449 Villon received the degree of bachelor, and in May–August 1452, that of master. On June 5, 1455, a violent quarrel broke out between Villon, some drinking companions, and a priest, Philippe Sermoise, whom Villon killed with a sword thrust. He was banished from the city but, in January 1456, won a royal pardon. In December of the same year, however, he was implicated in a theft from the Collège de Navarre and was again obliged to leave Paris. A series of incarcerations climaxed in 1462 in a death sentence for brawling that was commuted to 10 years banishment. After 1463 nothing more is known of Villon.

The criminal history of Villon's life can all too easily obscure the scholar, trained in the rigorous intellectual disciplines of the medieval schools. While it is true that his poetry makes a direct unsentimental appeal to the emotions, it is also true that it displays a remarkable control of rhyme and reveals a disciplined composition that suggests a deep concern with form, and not just random inspiration. Perhaps the most deeply moving of French lyric poets, Villon ranges in his verse from themes of drunkenness and prostitution to the unsentimental humility of a ballade-prayer to "Our Lady" ("Pour prier Nostre-Dame"), written at the request of his mother. He speaks, with marvelous directness, of love and death, reveals a deep compassion for all suffering humanity, and tells unforgettably of regret for the wasted past.

Vincy, Rosamond \'räz-ə-mənd-'vin-sē\ Fictional character, the selfish, spoiled willful wife of Tertius Lydgate in the novel MIDDLEMARCH by George Eliot.

Vinje \'vin-yə\, Aasmund Olavsson (b. April 6, 1818, Vinje, Nor.—d. July 30, 1870, Gran) Poet and journalist who wrote some of the finest lyric poems in Norwegian literature.

Vinje took a law degree, then struggled to support himself by teaching, writing, and doing clerical work for the government. In 1851 he began writing for an Oslo newspaper, and in 1858 he started a newspaper of his own, *Dølen* ("The Dalesman"), in which he used the newly standardized rural variant of the Norwegian language known as New Norwegian, or Nynorsk. In his own newspaper Vinje wrote about everything from philosophy and literature to politics. It was not until he was 40 that Vinje started writing poetry, mostly lyrics about mountain scenes and other aspects of nature. His best-known work is his *Ferdaminni fraa sumaren 1860* (1861; "Travel Memoirs from the Summer of 1860"); this book combines essays and poems in a witty and amusing account of Vinje's journey on foot from Oslo to Trondheim to report on the coronation of the new Swedish-Norwegian king. His other more widely known works are the poetic cycle *Storegut* (1866) and his English-language account of his tour of England in *A Norseman's View of Britain and the British* (1863). Vinje's lyric poems are notable for their simplicity and directness and their deep appreciation of nature. His prose writings are marked by their abundant common sense and an amusing, sometimes caustic wit.

Viola \'vī-ə-lə, 'vē-\ Fictional character, a young woman who with her twin brother Sebastian is shipwrecked off the coast of Illyria in William Shakespeare's TWELFTH NIGHT. Viola, who stands at the center of the play, is Shakespeare's example of reason, intelligence, self-control, and mature love. For her moral stature and wit, Viola ranks with Portia and Rosalind, two other great female characters in Shakespeare's comedies.

Violent Bear It Away, The Southern gothic novel by Flannery O'CONNOR, published in 1960. It is the story of a young man's struggle to live with the burden of being a prophet and is

representative of the author's fierce, powerful, and original vision of Christianity.

Young Francis Marion Tarwater has been reared by his fanatical, tyrannical grand-uncle Mason to be a prophet; when Mason dies, however, Francis rejects his mission and consequently suffers tortures of doubt and indecision. Although for a time he weighs the value of humanistic rationalism (as exemplified by his uncle George Rayber), Tarwater unexpectedly experiences a vision and comes to accept his calling.

virelay or **virelai** \vēr-'lē\ [Middle French, alteration (influenced by *lai* lay) of *vireli* kind of dance, air accompanying a dance, probably a derivative of *virer* to turn, twist] One of several *formes fixes* ("fixed forms") in French lyric poetry and song of the 14th and 15th centuries.

It probably did not originate in France, and it takes on several different forms even within the French tradition. Similar forms can be found in most of the literatures of medieval and early Renaissance Europe: in the Galician *cantiga*, the Arabic *zajal* and *muwashshaḥ*, the Italian *lauda*, *ballata*, and *frottola*, the Spanish *villancico*, and the English carol. *Compare* BALLADE; RONDEAU.

The standard virelay form has three stanzas, each preceded and followed by a refrain. Each stanza is in three sections, the first two having the same rhyme scheme and the last having the rhyme scheme of the refrain. In a musical setting the third section of each stanza therefore takes the same music as the refrain, while the first two sections have different music.

The virelay fell out of favor in the first half of the 15th century but then returned in a curtailed form with just one stanza, and without the fixed musical and poetic style previously associated with it. These later virelays with only one stanza are often called *bergerettes*.

Virgil or **Vergil** \'vər-jil\, *Latin in full* Publius Vergilius Maro (b. Oct. 15, 70 BC, Andes, near Mantua [Italy]—d. Sept. 21, 19 BC, Brundisium) The greatest Roman poet, best known for his epic, the AENEID (written starting about 29 BC; unfinished at his death).

The son of a prosperous farmer in the Roman province of Cisalpine Gaul, Virgil received a thorough education. Although his life was quiet, his poetry reflects the general turbulence in Italy during an extended period of civil war and then the trend toward stability that followed the rise of Octavian (afterward the emperor Augustus) to undisputed power in 31–30

Roman mosaic of Virgil with the epic Muse (left) and the tragic Muse (right)
Musée Le Bardo, Tunis

BC. Virgil became a member of Augustus' court circle and was aided by the imperial minister Maecenas, one of the most famous patrons of the arts. He died of a fever contracted on a visit to Greece.

Virgil's first major work, the collection of 10 pastoral poems called the *Eclogues* (42–37 BC), may be read as a visionary prophecy of local tranquility and world peace—conditions that, in his last years, he saw imposed to a considerable degree by Augustus. His *Georgics* (37–30 BC) points toward a Golden Age in the form of immediate practical goals: the repopulation of rural Italy and the rehabilitation of agriculture by the government as soon as the civil wars shall have ended. Finally, the 12 completed books of the *Aeneid* celebrate the dual birth of Rome. The legendary founding of Rome by Aeneas of Troy and the Roman unification of the world by Augustus are viewed as extraordinary tasks, glorious achievements, and divinely ordained necessities.

Virginian, The (*in full* The Virginian: A Horseman of the Plains)   Western novel by Owen WISTER, published in 1902. Its great popularity contributed to enshrining the American cowboy as an icon of American popular culture and a folk ideal.

A chivalrous and courageous but mysterious cowboy known only as "the Virginian" works as foreman of a cattle ranch in the Wyoming territory during the late 1870s and 1880s. The gunplay and violence that are inherent in his frontier code of behavior threaten the Virginian's relationship with a pretty schoolteacher from the East. The novel's climactic gun duel is the first "showdown" in fiction. It also introduced the now-classic phrase that the Virginian utters when pushed to the limit by an adversary, "When you call me that, *smile!*"

Virginians, The (*in full* The Virginians: A Tale of the Last Century)   Novel by William Makepeace THACKERAY, first published serially in 24 parts in 1857–59 and as one volume in 1859.

A sequel to HENRY ESMOND, the novel is set, as is much of its precursor, chiefly in colonial Virginia. *The Virginians* follows the life of the family and descendants of Henry Esmond of Castlewood, Virginia. Although Esmond's grandsons take opposing positions during the American Revolutionary War, they reconcile after the war, Harry becoming owner of the family's Virginia estates and George of the land and property in England.

Virginibus Puerisque \vər-'jin-i-bəs-,pyü-ə-'ris-kwe\ ("Of Maidens and Youths")   Collection of essays by Robert Louis STEVENSON, published in 1881, most of which were first published in *The Cornhill Magazine*. These whimsical meditations on everyday life earned Stevenson a reputation as a popular philosopher. Modeling his essays on those of William Hazlitt and Charles Lamb among others, Stevenson tells personal anecdotes and derives generally applicable morals from them. The title essay analyzes marriage, "Ordered South" tells of the trips he made for his health, and "Crabbed Age and Youth" discusses the father-son bond.

Virgin Soil   Novel by Ivan TURGENEV, published in Russian as *Nov* in 1877. Its focus is the young populists who hoped to sow the seeds of revolution in the virgin soil of the Russian peasantry.

Turgenev presents realistic and somewhat sympathetic portraits of the many different types of characters who were involved in the revolutionary movement, from the ardent young Nezhdanov, whose speeches to peasants only confuse them, to his lover Marianna, who wears peasant clothes and affects peasant mannerisms in order to be an effective revolutionary worker, to the crude Markeloff, whose speeches advocating total armed revolution cause the peasants to turn him over to

the police. The novel's strongest character, and the one most representative of Turgenev's own views, is Solomin, a calm, efficient factory manager who despises the aristocracy and advocates gradual liberalization.

Vir Singh \,vir-'siŋ\, Bhai (b. Dec. 5, 1872, Amritsar, Punjab, India—d. June 1957, Punjab)   Sikh writer and theologian whose writings raised the Punjabi language to a literary level never before attained.

Vir Singh wrote at a time when Sikh religion and politics and the Punjabi language were under heavy attack by the English and Hindus. With his versatile pen he extolled Sikh courage, philosophy, and ideals, earning respect for the Punjabi language as a literary vehicle.

Vir Singh founded the weekly paper *Khalsa Samachar* ("News of the Khalsa") in Amritsar (1899), where it is still published. Among his novels are *Kalghi Dhar Chamatkar* (1925), a novel on the life of the 17th-century guru Gobind Singh, and *Guru Nanak Chamatkar*, 2 vol. (1928; "Stories of Guru Nanak"), a biography of the originator of the Sikh religion. Other novels on Sikh philosophy and martial excellence include *Sundri* (1898), *Bijai Singh* (1899), and *Baba Nandh Singh* (1922). He used poetical and literary forms never before known to Punjabi, such as short meter and blank verse. His poem "The Vigil" was published posthumously.

Vischer \'fish-ər\, Friedrich Theodor von (b. June 30, 1807, Ludwigsburg, Württemberg [now in Germany]—d. Sept. 14, 1887, Gmunden, Austria-Hungary)   German literary critic and aesthetician known for his efforts to create a theoretical basis for literary realism.

Vischer's theories of aesthetics, based on ideas of the philosopher G.W.F. Hegel, began to develop while he was teaching at Tübingen, where he had studied. He became a professor at the university in 1844 but was suspended for two years because of an outspokenly liberal inaugural address. His work was finally published in six volumes as *Ästhetik, oder Wissenschaft des Schönen* (1846–57; "Aesthetics, or the Science of Beauty"). In 1855 he became professor at Zürich, but he returned to Tübingen in 1866.

Vischer's other works include *Kritische Gänge*, 2 vol. (1844; "Critical Paths"), a collection of essays; and *Altes und Neues* (1881; "Old and New"). He also wrote a whimsical popular novel, *Auch Einer*, 2 vol. (1879; *The Humour of Germany*), and a collection of poems, *Lyrische Gänge* (1882; "Lyrical Paths").

Vishnu or **Viṣṇu** \'vish-nü\   One of the principal Hindu deities, worshiped as the protector and preserver of the world and restorer of dharma (moral order). Vishnu, like Śiva (the other major god of Hinduism), is a syncretic personality who combines many lesser cult figures and local heroes. He is known chiefly through his avatars (incarnations), particularly Rāma and Krishna.

Vishnu was not a major deity in the Vedic period. A few Rigvedic hymns (*c.* 1400–1000 BC) associate him with the sun and relate the always popular legend of his three strides across the universe (which later formed the basis of the mythology of his avatar Vāmana, the dwarf). Legends of other avatars are found in the early literature, and by the time of the *Mahābhārata* they begin to be identified with Vishnu. In theory, Vishnu manifests a portion of himself anytime he is needed to fight evil, and his appearances are innumerable.

Vishnu's mount is the bird Garuḍa; his heavenly abode is called Vaikuṇṭha. Among the 1,000 names of Vishnu (repeated as an act of devotion by his worshipers) are Vāsudeva, Nārāyaṇa, and Hari. *See also* BHAKTI POETRY.

vision \'vizh-ən\   A piece of writing (such as a poem) claiming to represent something beheld in a revelatory dream, trance, or ecstasy. These were especially popular in early Celtic literature. *See also* AISLING; DREAM VISION.

Vision of Adamnán, The \\'ad-əm-,nan, -nən\\, *Irish* Fís Adamnáin.   In the Gaelic literature of Ireland, one of the earliest and most outstanding of medieval Irish visions. This graceful prose work dates from the 10th century and is preserved in *The Book of the Dun Cow* (*c.* 1100). Patterned after pagan voyages (*immrama*) to the otherworld, *The Vision of Adamnán* vividly describes the journey of Adamnán's soul, guided by an angel, first through a delightful, fragrance-filled heaven; through the seven stages through which a sinful soul passes to reach perfection; and then through the monster-ridden Land of Torment. The work is often erroneously attributed to St. Adamnan (*c.* 625–704), the abbot of Iona.

Vision of Sir Launfal, The \\'lȯn-fəl\\   Long verse parable by James Russell LOWELL, published in 1848. Lowell, who was influenced by Alfred, Lord Tennyson and Thomas Malory, offers his version of the Grail story in this tale of a knight who decides not to take a journey in search of the Holy Grail after he learns, during the course of a long dream, that the real meaning of the Grail is charity. The poem is written in iambic tetrameter and is divided into two parts, each with a prelude. Although set in the medieval era, the poem contains moving descriptions of the American landscape.

Visit, The   Drama in three acts by Swiss playwright Friedrich DÜRRENMATT, performed and published in German in 1956 as *Der Besuch der alten Dame.*

The play's protagonist Claire, a multimillionaire, visits her hometown after an absence of many years and offers the residents great wealth if they will kill one of their leading citizens, Alfred, who had betrayed Claire shamefully many years before. In this morality play about vengeance and greed, the prospect of wealth is enough to corrupt the townspeople into agreeing to murder.

Visit from St. Nicholas, A \\'nik-ə-ləs\\, *also called* The Night Before Christmas.   Narrative poem by Clement Clarke MOORE, written for the enjoyment of Moore's own children for the Christmas of 1822 and first published anonymously in the *Troy* (N.Y.) *Sentinel* on Dec. 23, 1823. It was acknowledged as Moore's work when it was included in his collection entitled *Poems* (1844). The poem became an enduring part of Christmas tradition and because of its wide popularity, both Nicholas, the patron saint of Christmas, and the mythic American Santa Claus were permanently linked with the holiday.

Visscher \\'vis-ər\\, Anna (Roemersdochter) (b. Feb. 2?, 1583, Amsterdam, Neth.—d. Dec. 6, 1651, Alkmaar)   Dutch poet and daughter of the Renaissance man of letters Roemer Visscher. She was admired and praised in verse by such poets as Constantijn Huygens and Pieter Corneliszoon Hooft.

Visscher's poetry is rather stiff and impersonal; she wrote for the most part sonnets and *lofliederen*, cleverly devised odes to important personages. She spent 12 years (1602–14) translating *Cent emblèmes Christiens* ("A Hundred Christian Emblems") by Georgette Montenay (first published 1854), but her main contribution to Dutch literature was her publication of a revised and improved version of her father's *Sinnepoppen* ("Emblems") in 1640.

Visscher \\'vis-ər\\, Roemer (Pieterszoon) (b. 1547, Amsterdam, Spanish Habsburg domain [now in The Netherlands]—d. Feb. 19, 1620, Amsterdam)   Poet and moralist of the early Dutch Renaissance who was at the center of the cultural circle that included the young poets Pieter C. Hooft, Joost van den Vondel, and Gerbrand Bredero. A friend of Henrick L. Spieghel and Dirck Coornhert, he was foremost in the move-

ment for the purification and standardization of the Dutch language and the extension of its use in education.

Like most versatile Renaissance men of letters, Visscher did not take himself seriously as a poet. He called his only poetry volume *Brabbeling* ("Jabbering"), and it was first published in 1612 without his knowledge. Consisting for the most part of love poems, the work contains many allusions to Dutch social, political, and domestic life, presenting an authoritative picture of 17th-century Amsterdam. The style of the poems varies from fashionable wordplay to a simple, individual use of language that occasionally produces a poignancy rarely found in poetry of the time. Visscher's other main work, *Sinnepoppen* (1614; "Emblems"), is a collection of short moral pieces.

Vita nuova, La \\lä-'vē-tä-'nwō-vä\\ ("The New Life") Work written about 1293 by DANTE regarding his feelings for BEATRICE, who comes to represent for Dante the ideal woman. *La vita nuova* describes Dante's first sight of Beatrice when both are nine years of age, her salutation when they are 18, Dante's expedients to conceal his love for her, the crisis experienced when Beatrice withholds her greeting, Dante's anguish when he perceives that she is making light of him, his determination to rise above anguish and sing only of his lady's virtues, anticipations of her death and her actual death, Dante's mourning, the temptation of the sympathetic *donna gentile* (a young woman who temporarily replaces Beatrice), Beatrice's final triumph and apotheosis, and, in the last chapter, Dante's determination to write at some later time about her "that which has never been written of any woman."

The work contains 42 brief chapters with commentaries on 25 sonnets, one ballata, and four canzones; a fifth canzone is left dramatically interrupted by Beatrice's death. The prose commentary provides the frame story, which is not treated by the poems themselves.

Vitier \\vē-'tyär\\, Cintio *or* Cynthio (b. Sept. 25, 1921, Key West, Fla., U.S.)   Cuban poet, anthologist, critic, and scholar of Cuban poetry.

Vitier began as a writer of extremely difficult, hermetic poetry. His poetry until *Canto llano* (1956; "Plainsong") was primarily concerned with the nature of poetry, the function of memory, and the intricate role of language in the creative process. The essay "Poética" (1961) is a lucid exposition of his artistic credo. With the advent of the Castro revolution, Vitier radically changed his poetic style. His poems became direct, clear, and accessible to most readers. His poetry collections included *Vísperas* (1953; "Vespers"), *Testimonios* (1968), and *Poemas de mayo y junio: 1988* (1990; "Poems of May and June"). His concern for social justice and his belief in a socially conscious religion were reflected in a trilogy of novels: *De Peña Pobre: Memoria y novela* (1978; "Of Peña Pobre: Memory and Fiction"), *Los papeles de Jacinto Finalé* (1984; "The Papers of Jacinto Finalé"), and *Rajando la leña esta* (1986; "Splitting This Wood").

He compiled several anthologies of Cuban poetry, and his study *Lo cubano en la poesía* (1958; "The Cuban in Poetry") reveals the depth of his critical intuition. His literary essays, especially those on the works of José Martí, contributed to his reputation as one of the most important and influential scholars of Latin-American literature.

Vittorini \\,vēt-tō-'rē-nē\\, Elio (b. July 23, 1908, Syracuse, Sicily, Italy—d. Feb. 13, 1966, Milan)   Novelist, translator, and literary critic and the author of outstanding novels of Italian Neorealism that mirrored his country's experience of fascism and the social, political, and spiritual agonies of the 20th century. With Cesare Pavese he was also a pioneer in the translation into Italian of English and American writers.

Vittorini left school when he was 17 and became a road-construction worker in northern Italy. He then moved to Florence, learned English while working as a proofreader, and began to publish short stories in the journal *Solaria*. He made his living until 1941 by translating the works of such American and English writers as William Saroyan, D.H. Lawrence, Edgar Allan Poe, William Faulkner, Daniel Defoe, Ernest Hemingway, T.S. Eliot, W.H. Auden, and Louis MacNeice.

Vittorini's first major novel, *Il garofano rosso* (written 1933–35, published 1948; *The Red Carnation*), while overtly portraying the personal, scholastic, and sexual problems of an adolescent boy, also conveys the poisonous political atmosphere of fascism. In 1936 Vittorini began writing his most important novel, *Conversazione in Sicilia* (1941, rev. ed., 1965; U.K. title, *Conversation in Sicily*; U.S. title, *In Sicily*), the clearest expression of his antifascist feelings.

After the war Vittorini published the influential politico-cultural periodical *Il politecnico* (1945–47) and later edited the Milan literary quarterly *Il menabò* with Italo Calvino. He then worked for several major Italian publishing houses.

Among Vittorini's other important works were *Uomini e no* (1945; *Men and Not Men*), an account of his experiences as a member of the Resistance during the war; the allegorical Marxist novel *Il sempione strizza l'occhio al frejus* (1947; *The Twilight of the Elephant*); and another allegory, *Le donne di Messina* (1949; *Women on the Road*). Vittorini's critical writings were collected in *Diario in pubblico* (1957; "Public Diary") and the posthumously published *Le due tensione: appunti per una ideologia della letteratura* (1967; "The Two Tensions: Notes for an Ideology of Literature").

Vivien \vē-'vyeⁿ\, Renée, *pseudonym of* Pauline M. Tarn \'tärn\ (b. June 8, 1877, London, Eng.—d. Nov. 18, 1909, Paris, Fr.)   French poet whose poetry expresses ardent passion within rigid verse forms. She was an exacting writer, known for her mastery of the sonnet and of the rarely found 11-syllable line (hendecasyllable).

Of mixed Scottish and American ancestry, Vivien was educated in England, but she lived nearly all her life in Paris and wrote in French. Her poetry was influenced by that of John Keats, Algernon Charles Swinburne, and Charles Baudelaire; by Hellenic culture; by her extensive travels in Norway, Turkey, and Spain; and by her lesbianism, all of which imparted a certain exoticism to her writings. Gifted with beauty, fortune, talent, and fame, Vivien was nevertheless deeply unhappy, being unable to adjust to the crassness of the age. Her dark, candlelit apartment was decorated with objets d'art from past civilizations. Her major works are *Cendres et poussières* (1902; "Ashes and Dust"); *Les Kitharèdes* (1904; "The Women of Kithara"); translations from Sappho of Lesbos; and *Sillages* (1908; "Sea Wakes"). Vivien seems to have found peace shortly before her death with her conversion to Roman Catholicism, intimated in the new austerity of her last works, *Dans un coin de violettes* (1908; "In a Violet Garden") and *Le Vent des vaisseaux* (1909; "Ship Wind"). Her *Poésies complètes* were published in 12 volumes in 1901–10 and in 2 volumes in 1934.

Vogt \'fōkt\, Nils Collett (b. Sept. 24, 1864, Christiania [now Oslo], Nor.—d. Dec. 23, 1937, Oslo)   Norwegian novelist and poet who dealt with the conflict between the generations and the struggle for intellectual freedom.

Vogt was a rebel in a conservative family, and his first novel, *Familiens sorg* (1889; "A Grief to His Family"), is about youth in rebellion against a social order dominated by old men. He was greatly in sympathy with the workers' cause and composed songs for them. He wrote novels, plays, and short stories, but he is remembered mainly for his lyric poetry, published in many volumes, including *Det dyre brød* (1900; "The Precious Bread"), *Septemberbrand* (1907; "September Fire"), and his last poems, *Et liv i digt* (1937; "A Life in Poetry").

Voiture \vwȧ-'tūēr\, Vincent (b. Feb. 24, 1597, Amiens, Fr.—d. May 26, 1648, Paris)   French poet, letter writer, and animating spirit of the group that gathered at the salon of the Marquise de Rambouillet.

Voiture completed his education in Paris and early made the acquaintance of the aged poet François de Malherbe and of Jean-Louis Guez de Balzac, whose zeal for reforming the French language he shared. In 1634 Voiture was elected to the Académie Française.

Voiture excelled at writing occasional pieces of light verse, and his *Lettres* (posthumously, 1649) are full of witty and subtle allusions that were enjoyed by his narrow circle. His skillful use of stylistic conceits also appealed to the members of the Rambouillet salon. He was one of the two central figures in the "sonnets controversy," which briefly divided the Parisian literary world between the admirers of Isaac de Benserade's poem "Sonnet sur Job" and the admirers of Voiture's sonnet "L'Amour d'Uranie avec Philis." Voiture's admirers eventually won the argument, but the acrimony that developed, together with the outbreak of the civil wars of the Fronde (1648–53), put an end to the Rambouillet society.

Volpone \vȯl-'pō-nē\ (*in full* Volpone, or the Fox)   Comedy in five acts by Ben JONSON, performed about 1605/1606 and published in 1607.

Volpone ("Fox"), a wealthy Venetian without heirs, devises a scheme to become wealthier by playing on people's greed. With the complicity of his servant Mosca ("Fly"), Volpone pretends to be near death. He accepts valuable gifts from three fortune hunters, each of whom receives personal assurance from Mosca that he alone is to inherit all of Volpone's wealth. The three are Corvino ("Raven"), who offers Volpone his wife; Voltore ("Vulture"), an advocate; and Corbaccio ("Crow"), who disinherits his son in favor of Volpone. The plot is eventually revealed when Mosca attempts to take advantage of his master, and Volpone, Mosca, and the greedy trio are all punished according to their crimes and their social prominence.

Volsunga saga \'vœl-sùŋ-gǝ, 'vōl-\ ("Saga of the Volsungs") The best of the Icelandic sagas known as *fornaldarsǫgur* ("sagas of old times"). Dating from roughly 1270, it is the first of the *fornaldarsǫgur* to have been written down. It contains the Northern version of the story told in the Middle High German epic *Nibelungenlied*—that is, it relates the story of Sigurd (known in the *Nibelungenlied* as Siegfried), grandson of Vǫlsung, and the destruction of the Burgundians. The saga was based on the heroic poems in the *Poetic Edda* and is especially valuable because it has preserved in prose form some of the poems from the *Edda* that were lost.

volta \'vȯl-tǝ, 'väl-\ [Italian, turn, act of turning around]   The turn in thought in a sonnet that is often indicated by such initial words as "But," "Yet," or "And yet." The volta occurs between the octet and sestet in a Petrarchan sonnet and sometimes between the 8th and 9th or between the 12th and 13th lines of a Shakespearean sonnet, as in William Shakespeare's sonnet number 130:

> My mistress' eyes are nothing like the sun;
> Coral is far more red than her lips' red;
> If snow be white, why then her breasts are dun;
> If hairs be wires, black wires grow on her head.
> I have seen roses damask'd, red and white,
> But no such roses see I in her cheeks;
> And in some perfumes is there more delight
> Than in the breath that from my mistress reeks.

I love to hear her speak, yet well I know
That music hath a far more pleasing sound;
I grant I never saw a goddess go;
My mistress, when she walks, treads on the ground.
And yet, by heaven, I think my love as rare
As any she belied with false compare.

Voltaire \vôl-'ter, *Angl* vōl-'tar\, *pseudonym of* François-Marie Arouet (b. Nov. 21, 1694, Paris, Fr.—d. May 30, 1778, Paris) One of the greatest 18th-century European authors, remembered as a crusader against tyranny and bigotry and noted for his wit, satire, and critical capacity.

Portrait by an unknown artist after a portrait by Nicolas de Largillière, 1718; in the Château de Versailles
Cliché Musées Nationaux, Paris

Born of middle-class parents and educated by the Jesuits at the college of Louis-le-Grand in Paris, Voltaire studied law for a time but abandoned it to become a writer. He made his name with classical tragedies and continued to write for the theater all his life. Voltaire's epic poem *La Henriade* was well-received, but his lampoons of the Regency and his liberal religious opinions caused offense. He was imprisoned in the Bastille for nearly a year (1717) and in 1726 was driven into exile in England, where his philosophical interests deepened. Following his return to France, in 1728 or 1729, Voltaire continued to write plays, and his histories—*Charles XII* (1731) and *Le Siècle de Louis XIV* (1751)—marked new departures for him and for historiography. After publication in 1734 of the *Lettres philosophiques*, in which he spoke out against established religious and political systems, Voltaire fled from Paris and settled at Cirey in Champagne with Mme du Châtelet, who became his patroness and mistress. At Cirey, Voltaire turned to scientific research. He also began to work systematically on the study of religions and culture.

In 1750 Voltaire accepted an invitation from Frederick II of Prussia to go to Berlin. In 1754 he settled in Switzerland, where he spent the remainder of his life, apart from occasional trips and his final journey to Paris, where he died. In addition to his many works on philosophical and moral problems, Voltaire wrote several *contes* ("tales"), including *Micromégas* (1752), *Zadig* (1747), and CANDIDE (1759), a satire on philosophical optimism that became his best-known work. He kept up an immense correspondence and took an interest in any cases of injustice—especially those resulting from religious prejudice—that came to his notice.

Voluspá \'vœl-ūs-,pä, 'vōl-\ ("Sibyl's Prophecy") Poem consisting of about 65 short stanzas on Norse cosmogony, the history of the world of gods, men, and monsters from its beginning until the Ragnarǫk ("Doom of the Gods"). In spite of its clearly pagan theme, the poem reveals Christian influence in its imagery. The scenery described is that of Iceland, and it is commonly thought that it was composed in Iceland about the year 1000, when Icelanders perceived the fall of their ancient gods and the approach of Christianity.

The story is told by an age-old seeress who was reared by primeval giants. The cosmic cataclysm she narrates is essentially a symbolic reflection of the waning Germanic world, ineluctably moving to its destruction because of the outrages committed by its divine and human representatives.

Vondel \,vän-den-'vôn-dəl\, Joost van den (b. Nov. 17, 1587, Cologne [Germany]—d. Feb. 5, 1679, Amsterdam, Neth.) Dutch poet and dramatist who produced some of the greatest works of Dutch literature.

Van den Vondel studied French and Latin and eventually translated works by Virgil and Seneca. *Het Pascha* (1612; "The Passover"), a dramatization of the Exodus of the Jews from Egypt, was his most important early work, in which the power and splendor of his verse are already apparent. This play was an allegory for the Calvinists who had fled from Spanish tyranny in the southern Netherlands.

The execution in 1619 of Holland's lord advocate, Johan van Oldenbarnevelt, provoked van den Vondel to write a flood of spirited lampoons and satirical poems against the Dutch church and government. His play *Palamedes* (1625), which dramatized the political trial in a classical setting, led to his prosecution by the government. Around this time he also translated the great jurist Hugo Grotius' drama *Sophompaneas* into Dutch. Grotius influenced van den Vondel to turn from ancient Latin to ancient Greek drama as a model for his own works. Van den Vondel's *Gijsbrecht van Aemstel* (1637), written during this transitional period, provides a hero for the capital of the new Dutch republic who was modeled on Virgil's Aeneas. In 1639 van den Vondel completed his first translation of a Greek tragedy, Sophocles' *Electra*. His original play *Gebroeders* ("Brothers"), an Old Testament tragedy of the same year, is the first of his plays on the Greek model; others include *Jeptha* (1659) and his greatest achievement, the trilogy comprising *Lucifer* (1654), *Adam in ballingschap* (1664; *Adam in Exile*), and *Noah* (1667).

His dramatic tragedies, with their powerful and lyrical language and the grandeur of their conception, remain his most important literary achievement.

Vonnegut \'vän-ə-,gət\, Kurt, Jr. (b. Nov. 11, 1922, Indianapolis, Ind., U.S.) American novelist noted for his pessimistic and satirical novels that use fantasy and science fiction to highlight the horrors and ironies of 20th-century civilization.

Vonnegut's first novel, PLAYER PIANO (1952), visualizes a completely mechanized and automated society whose dehumanizing effects are unsuccessfully resisted by the scientists and workers in a New York factory town. *The Sirens of Titan* (1959) is a quasi-science-fiction novel in which the entire history of the human race is considered an accident attendant on an alien planet's search for a spare part for a spaceship. This he followed with CAT'S CRADLE (1963) and SLAUGHTER-HOUSE-FIVE (1969).

Vonnegut also wrote several plays, including *Happy Birthday, Wanda June* (1970); several works of nonfiction; and several collections of short stories, chief among which was *Welcome to the Monkey House* (1968). His other novels include *Mother Night* (1961), *God Bless You, Mr. Rosewater* (1965), *Breakfast of Champions* (1973), *Slapstick* (1976), *Jailbird* (1979), *Deadeye Dick* (1983), *Galápagos* (1985), *Bluebeard* (1987), and *Hocus Pocus* (1990).

Vörösmarty \'vœ-rœ-,shmôr-tē\, Mihály (b. Dec. 1, 1800, Nyék, Hung.—d. Nov. 19, 1855, Pest [Budapest]) Poet and dramatist who helped make the literature of Hungary's Reform Generation (1825–49) truly Hungarian.

Born into an impoverished noble family, Vörösmarty supported himself from an early age by private tutoring. In 1825 he published the epic poem *Zalán futása* ("The Flight of Zalán"), describing the conquest of Hungary by Árpád in the 9th century. Although it has great artistic merit, its resounding success was partly caused by the general patriotic upsurge of the period.

In 1828 Vörösmarty became the full-time editor of a well-known scholarly review, the *Tudományos Gyűjtemény*, and he was the first Hungarian man of letters to make a living from literature. In 1831 he completed his masterpiece, *Csongor és Tünde* ("Csongor and Tünde"), a symbolic fairy-tale play that is reminiscent of William Shakespeare's *A Midsummer Night's Dream*. He married late, in 1843, and his wife inspired many moving poems, among which "A merengőhöz" (1843; "To a Day-Dreamer") is outstanding. Vörösmarty was in a position to look forward to a contented old age when the Hungarian war of independence (1848–49) erupted, and his support of the losing side shattered his life.

Vorticism \'vȯr-ti-ˌsiz-əm\ [derivative of *vortex*] Literary and artistic movement that flourished in England from 1912 to 1915, on the brink of World War I. Founded by Wyndham LEWIS, Vorticism attempted to relate art to industrialization. It opposed the sentimentality held to be characteristic of the 19th century and extolled the energy of the machine and machine-made products, and it promoted something of a cult of sheer violence.

Artists involved in the movement included the poet Ezra Pound and the sculptor Jacob Epstein. In the visual arts, Vorticist compositions were abstract and sharp-planed, showing the influence of cubism and Futurism. The short-lived magazine *Blast: The Review of the Great English Vortex* (two editions, 1914 and 1915), edited by Lewis, was a typographically arresting, vigorous attempt to create a forum for English literary and plastic artists of the avant-garde.

Vortigern \'vȯr-ti-ˌgərn, -ˌgern\ or **Wyrtgeorn** \'wʉrt-ˌyern\ Legendary king of Britain who, in the 5th century AD, invited the Jutes into Britain to help him keep his throne and defeat the Picts. Legend relates that Vortigern married Rowena, the daughter of Hengist, leader of the Jutes. The Jutes then refused to leave Britain. Throughout his life, Vortigern alternately feuded and entered into alliances with the Jutes. He supposedly retired to Wales, where he was burnt alive in a tower.

Vortigern's story is related in the 9th-century *Historia Brittonum* and in Layamon's romance-chronicle, the *Brut*.

Vortigern and Rowena, a play purported to have been written by William Shakespeare but proved to have been penned by W. H. Ireland, was a notorious literary forgery of the late 18th century.

Voss \'fȯs\, Johann Heinrich (b. Feb. 20, 1751, Sommersdorf, Mecklenburg [Germany]—d. March 29, 1826, Heidelberg, Baden) German poet remembered chiefly for his translations of Homer.

In 1772 Voss went to Göttingen, where he became one of the leading spirits of the Göttinger Hain literary association. From 1778 to 1802 he was headmaster of schools, first at Otterndorf, Hanover, where he began to translate the *Odyssey*, then at Eutin; but he found the work uncongenial and became a private scholar in Jena. In 1805 he went to Heidelberg as professor of classical philology, devoting himself to his translations. An ardent rationalist, he waged an embittered struggle against the younger Romantics and became increasingly lonely before his death.

Voss published his collected poems in 1802. As a lyricist he wrote mainly songs, odes, elegies, and pastoral idylls in the style of the ancients and of the German lyric poet Friedrich Klopstock. Voss's fame, however, rests on his translations, particularly on his versions of the *Odyssey* (1781) and the *Iliad* (1793). Although he was regarded by many German poets as an authority on classical meters, his pedantic regard for the niceties

of form and language made his later translations seem strained. The classical authors he translated included Virgil (beginning in 1789), Ovid (1798), and Horace (1806). He also translated *The Thousand and One Nights* (1781–85) and, with his sons Heinrich and Abraham, William Shakespeare's plays (1818–29).

vowel rhyme *see* ASSONANCE.

Voyelles \vwȧ-'yel\ (*in full* Sonnet des voyelles; "Vowels") Sonnet by Arthur RIMBAUD published in Paul Verlaine's *Les Poètes maudits* (1884). Written in traditional alexandrine lines, the poem is far from traditional in its subject matter; it arbitrarily assigns to each of the vowels a different, specific color.

Suggestions as to the inspiration for the poem include a child's colored alphabet book, alchemy, or simple poetic obfuscation. The poem may also be a reference to Charles Baudelaire's theory of the role of synesthesia (the association of two different senses—in this case sight and sound) in poetry.

Voynovich \ˌvȯi-'nȯ-vᵛich\, Vladimir (Nikolayevich) (b. Sept. 26, 1932, Stalinabad, Tadzhik S.S.R., U.S.S.R. [now Dushanbe, Tajikistan]) Soviet dissident writer known for his irreverent and perceptive satire.

Voynovich's early fiction includes the short story "My zdes zhivyom" (1961; "We Live Here") and the novellas *Khochu byt chestnym* (1963; "I Want to Be Honest") and *Dva tovarishcha* (1964; "Two Comrades"), all of which concern pressures to conform to Soviet urban life. In 1974, after publishing a letter in defense of Aleksandr Solzhenitsyn, Voynovich was forbidden to work as a professional writer. In 1980 he settled in West Germany.

Voynovich's best-known work was the acclaimed underground novel *Zhizn i neobychaynyye priklyucheniya soldata Ivana Chonkina* (1975; *The Life and Extraordinary Adventures of Private Ivan Chonkin*), about a naive and unsophisticated man who battles the Soviet bureaucracy. The pseudo-epic, autobiographical *Ivankiada: ili rasskaz o vselenii pisatelya Voynovicha v novuyu kvartiru* (1976; *The Ivankiad: The Tale of the Writer Voynovich's Installation in His New Apartment*) details his personal battles with the Soviet bureaucracy to obtain a two-room apartment. He continued to write slyly humorous accounts of the vagaries of life under the Soviet system after he emigrated in works such as *Pretendent na prestol: novye priklyucheniya soldata Ivana Chonkina* (1979; *Pretender to the Throne: The Further Adventures of Private Ivan Chonkin*), *Anti Sovetsky Sovetsky Soyuz* (1985; *The Anti-Soviet Soviet Union*), *Moskva 2042* (1987; *Moscow 2042*), and *Shapka* (1988; *The Fur Hat*).

Voznesensky \vəz-nᵛi-'sᵛen-skᵛē\, Andrey Andreyevich (b. May 12, 1933, Moscow, Russian S.F.S.R., U.S.S.R.) Soviet poet who was one of the most prominent of the generation of writers that emerged after the Stalinist era.

While still a student, Voznesensky sent some of his own verses to the renowned author Boris Pasternak, who encouraged him and became his model and tutor for the next three years. Voznesensky's first published poems, which appeared in 1958, are experimental works marked by changing meters and rhythms, a distinctive use of assonance and sound associations, and a passionate but intellectually subtle moral fervor. His important early works include *Mastera* (1959; "The Masters"), *Mozaika* (1960; "Mosaic"), and *Parabola* (1960).

Voznesensky became a star attraction at the popular poetry readings that were held in the late 1950s and early 1960s in the Soviet Union. The readings came to a halt in 1963, however, when Soviet artists and writers working in "excessively experimental" styles were subjected to an official campaign of condemnation. Along with his fellow poets who rejected Socialist Realism, Voznesensky suffered seven months of official criticism; he was returned to partial favor only after writing an ironic recantation in the government newspaper *Pravda*. Despite his occasional outspoken criticisms of the Soviet government, Voznesensky's characteristic poems remained apolitical celebrations of art, freedom, and the unrestrained human spirit.

In what is perhaps his best-known poem, "Goya" (1960), the author uses a series of powerful metaphors to express the horrors of war. "Akhillesovo serdtse" ("Achilles Heart") and "Avtoportret" ("Self-Portrait") tell of his suffering and anger during the 1963 crackdown. His later works include the volumes *40 liricheskikh otstupleny iz poemy "Treugolnaya grusha"* (1962; "40 Lyric Digressions from the Poem 'Triangular Pear'"), *Antimiry* (1964; *Antiworlds*), *Vypusti ptitsu!* (1974; "Let the Bird Free!"), and *Soblazn* (1978; "Temptation"). Voznesensky's poetic production during the 1970s and '80s resulted in little that was new or distinctive. *An Arrow in the Wall: Selected Poetry and Prose* was published in a bilingual edition in 1987 and *On the Edge: Poems and Essays from Russia* in 1991.

Vronsky, Count Aleksey \'vrȯn-skʸē, *Angl* 'vrän-skē\   Fictional character, a handsome young army officer who seduces the title character of Leo Tolstoy's novel ANNA KARENINA.

Vulcan \'vəl-kən\   In Roman mythology, the god of fire, particularly in its destructive aspects as volcanoes or conflagrations. Poetically, he is given all the attributes of the Greek HEPHAESTUS. His worship was very ancient, and at Rome he had his own priest (*flamen*). Vulcan was invoked to avert fires, as his epithets Quietus and Mulciber ("Fire Allayer") suggest. Because he was a deity of destructive fire, his temples were properly located outside the city.

vulgate   A commonly accepted text or reading.

Vulgate \'vəl-ˌgāt\   A Latin version of the Bible made by Saint Jerome in the 4th century that is authorized and used by the Roman Catholic church.

Jerome started with the Gospels, using a Greek manuscript as his principal source. For the rest of the New Testament he stuck to the existing texts for the most part. Jerome then produced three revisions of the Psalms, all extant. The first, based on the Septuagint, is known as the Roman Psalter because it was incorporated into the liturgy at Rome. The second, produced in Palestine from the Hexaplaric Septuagint, tended to bring the Latin closer to the Hebrew. Its popularity in Gaul was such that it came to be known as the Gallican Psalter. This version was later adopted into the Vulgate. The third revision, actually a fresh translation, was made directly from the Hebrew, but it never enjoyed wide circulation. In the course of preparing the last, Jerome realized the futility of revising the Old Latin solely on the basis of the Greek, and by the end of 405 he had executed his own Latin translation of the entire Old Testament based on the "Hebrew truth" (*Hebraica veritas*).

Because of the canonical status of the Greek version within the church, Jerome's version was received at first with much suspicion, for it seemed to cast doubt on the authenticity of the Septuagint and exhibited divergences from the Old Latin. The innate superiority of Jerome's version assured its ultimate victory, and by the 8th century it had become the Latin Vulgate ("the common version") throughout the churches of Western Christendom, where it remained the chief Bible until the Reformation.

In the course of centuries of rival coexistence, the Old Latin and Jerome's Vulgate tended to react upon each other so that the Vulgate text became a composite. This problem was ultimately resolved by the production in 1592 of a fresh revision initiated by Pope Clement VIII. The *Nova Vulgata*, a new Latin biblical text that reflects current critical thinking and is considered suitable for liturgical use, was completed in 1977.

Vulgate cycle   Group of Arthurian romances in French prose, dating roughly to 1210–30. Traditionally attributed to Walter Map, a clerk for King Henry II, the cycle is now thought to have been written by a group of Cistercian monks. It comprises *L'Estoire del Saint Graal*, a *Merlin* based on Robert de Boron's version, and the Prose *Lancelot* (itself a compilation of three romances—the *Lancelot* proper, the *Queste del Saint Graal*, and *Mort Artu*).

vulgus \'vəl-gəs\   A short composition in Latin verse formerly common as an exercise in some English public schools. The word is probably a mock-Latin spelling of *vulgars* (plural of *vulgar*), formerly applied to English sentences to be translated into Latin.

Vulpius \'vu̇l-pē-u̇s\, Christian August (b. Jan. 23, 1762, Weimar, Saxe-Weimar [Germany]—d. June 26, 1827, Weimar)   Writer of popular historical novels and brother of Christiane Vulpius, Goethe's wife.

Vulpius began his writing career by translating Italian and French tales of chivalry into German, later publishing some unremarkable accounts of medieval German literature. Vulpius' most celebrated work is his three-volume *Rinaldo Rinaldini, der Rauberhauptmann* (1797–1800; "Rinaldo Rinaldini, the Robber Captain"), a work that served as a model for other historical novels. He wrote about 60 popular romantic narratives.

Vulpius also undertook researches in numismatics, heraldry, and history: his 10-volume *Kuriositöten der Physisch-littarisch, artistisch-historischen Vor und Mitwelt* (1810–23; "Physical-Literary and Artistic-Historical Curiosities of Past and Present") has some value as a collection of material. He published the periodical *Die Zeit* from 1817 to 1825.

Vyāsa \'vyä-sə\, *also called* Kṛishṇa Dvaipāyan \'krish-nə-'dvī-ˌpä-yən\ *or* Vedavyāsa \'vā-də-ˌvyä-sə\ (fl. 1500 BC?)   Legendary Indian sage who is traditionally credited with composing or compiling the MAHĀBHĀRATA, a collection of legendary and didactic poetry worked around a central heroic narrative (the name Vyāsa is Sanskrit for "arranger" or "compiler").

According to legend, Vyāsa was the son of the ascetic Parāśara and the Dāsa princess Satyavatī and grew up in forests living with hermits who taught him the Vedas (sacred hymns). Thereafter he lived in the forests near the banks of the river Sarasvatī, becoming a teacher and a priest, fathering a son and disciple, Śuka, and gathering a large group of disciples. Late in life, living in caves in the Himalayas, he is said to have divided the Vedas, composed Purāṇas (ancient legendary tales), and, in a period of two and one-half years, composed his great poetic work, the *Mahābhārata*, supposedly dictating it to his scribe, Gaṇeśa, the elephant god.

Vye, Eustacia \yū-'stā-shə-'vī\   Fictional character, a beautiful, sensual young woman who marries Clym Yeobright in the novel THE RETURN OF THE NATIVE by Thomas Hardy.

Wace \'wās, 'wäs\ (b. *c.* 1100, Jersey, Channel Islands—d. after 1174) Anglo-Norman author of two verse chronicles, the *Roman de Brut* (1155) and the *Roman de Rou* (1160–74), named respectively after the reputed founders of the Britons and Normans.

The *Rou* was commissioned by Henry II of England, who sometime before 1169 secured for Wace a canonry at Bayeux in northwestern France. The *Brut* may have been dedicated to Henry's queen, Eleanor of Aquitaine. Written in octosyllabic verse, it is a romanticized account of Geoffrey of Monmouth's *Historia regum Britanniae*, tracing the history of Britain from its founding by the legendary Brutus the Trojan. Its many fanciful additions (including the story of King Arthur's Round Table) helped increase the popularity of the Arthurian legends. The *Rou*, written in octosyllabic couplets and monorhyme stanzas of alexandrines, is a history of the Norman dukes from the time of Rollo the Viking (after 911) to that of Robert II Curthose (1106). In 1174, however, Henry II transferred his patronage to one Beneeit, who was writing a rival version, and Wace's work remained unfinished.

Wace's conscious literary artistry in the *Brut* exerted a stylistic influence on later verse romances (notably on a version of the Tristan story by Thomas the Rhymer, an Anglo-Norman writer), whereas the English poem *Brut* (*c.* 1200) by Layamon was the most notable of many direct imitations. Three devotional works by Wace also survive.

Wackenroder \'väk-ən-,rō-dər\, Wilhelm Heinrich (b. July 13, 1773, Berlin [Germany]—d. Feb. 13, 1798, Berlin) Writer and critic who was the originator, with his friend Ludwig Tieck, of some of the most important ideas of German Romanticism.

At school in Erlangen and Göttingen, Wackenroder formed a friendship with Tieck that was to be of great importance for the work of both men. Wackenroder returned to Berlin in 1794, being forced into the Prussian civil service by his father, but his preoccupations remained literary. He translated light English novels and wrote anecdotal accounts of the lives of the artists Albrecht Dürer, Leonardo da Vinci, Michelangelo, and Raphael. He also produced a "biography" of Joseph Berglinger, an imaginary musician and a spokesman for Wackenroder's views on art. In his stories he developed an enthusiastic emotional aesthetic, according to which the perfect work of art is created by a divine miracle and is a moral, aesthetic, and religious unity to be grasped only by the heart, not by the intellect. In 1797, on Tieck's advice, these writings were published under a title chosen by the publishers, *Herzensergiessungen eines kunstliebenden Klosterbruders* ("Outpourings of an Art-Loving Monk"); in 1799 Tieck published the continuation of *Herzensergiessungen* (with the addition of some of his own essays) as *Phantasien über die Kunst* ("Fantasies on Art").

Wahlöö, Per *see* Maj SJÖWALL and Per Wahlöö.

Wain \'wān\, John (Barrington) (b. March 14, 1925, Stoke-on-Trent, Staffordshire, Eng.—d. May 24, 1994, Oxford, Oxfordshire) English novelist and poet whose irreverent early works caused him to be identified as one of the "Angry Young Men" of the 1950s. He was also a critic and playwright.

Wain was educated at St. John's College, Oxford, of which he subsequently became a fellow. He was a lecturer in English literature at the University of Reading from 1949 to 1955 and from 1973 to 1978 was professor of poetry at Oxford.

Collections of his witty and hard-edged poetry include *Mixed Feelings* (1951), *A Word Carved on a Sill* (1956), *Weep Before God* (1961), *Wildtrack* (1965), *Letters to Five Artists* (1969), and *Feng* (1975). *Poems 1949–1979* was published in 1980. His poetry, witty and brittle, has been criticized for its occasionally contrived cleverness.

Hurry On Down (1953; U.S. title, *Born in Captivity*) was Wain's first novel and, with *Strike the Father Dead* (1962) and *A Winter in the Hills* (1970), one of his best. It follows the adventures of a university graduate valiantly trying to establish some sort of personal identity in the bewildering and rapidly changing society of postwar Britain. Wain's other novels include *The Contenders* (1958), *The Young Visitors* (1965), *The Smaller Sky* (1967), *The Pardoner's Tale* (1978), *Where the Rivers Meet* (1988), and *Comedies* (1990). He wrote several collections of short stories; a considerable body of literary criticism, including *Preliminary Essays* (1957), *Essays on Literature and Ideas* (1963), and *The Living World of Shakespeare* (1964; rev. ed., 1979); a biography of Samuel Johnson (1974; rev. ed., 1980); and an autobiography, *Sprightly Running* (1962).

Waiting for Godot \gə-'dō\ Tragicomedy in two acts by Samuel BECKETT, published in 1952 in French as *En attendant Godot* and first produced in 1953. *Waiting for Godot* was a true innovation in drama and the Theater of the Absurd's first theatrical success.

The play consists of conversations between Vladimir and Estragon, who are waiting for the arrival of the mysterious Godot, who continually sends word that he will appear but who never does. They encounter Lucky and Pozzo, they discuss their miseries and their lots in life, they consider hanging themselves, and yet they wait. Often perceived as being tramps, Vladimir and Estragon are a pair of human beings who do not know why they were put on earth; they make the tenuous assumption that there must be some point to their existence, and they look to Godot for enlightenment. Because they hold out hope for meaning and direction, they acquire a kind of nobility that enables them to rise above their futile existence.

Waiting for Lefty \'lef-tē\ One-act play by Clifford ODETS, published and produced in 1935. One of the first examples of proletarian drama, the play takes place during the Depression, in a meeting hall of the taxi drivers' union. The union members are waiting for their representative, Lefty, to arrive so that they can vote on a strike. In a series of six vignettes, various drivers make a plea to strike, relating the stories of their lives as justification for their decision. Odets placed actors representing members of the union in the audience to increase audience involvement in the play.

waka \'wä-kä\ [Japanese] Japanese poetry, specifically the court poetry of the 6th to the 14th century, including such forms as the *chōka* and *sedōka*, in contrast to such later forms as *renga*, haikai, and haiku. The term *waka* also is used, however, as a synonym for tanka, the short poem that is a basic Japanese form.

The *chōka*, or "long poem," is of indefinite length, formed of alternating lines of five and seven syllables ending with an extra seven-syllable line. Many *chōka* have been lost; the shortest of those extant are 7 lines long, while the longest have 150 lines. They may be followed by one or more *hanka* ("envoys"). The amplitude of the *chōka* permitted the poets to treat themes impossible within the compass of the tanka.

The *sedōka*, or "head-repeated poem," consists of two tercets of five, seven, and seven syllables each. An uncommon form, it was sometimes used for dialogues. Hitomaro's *sedōka* are noteworthy. *Chōka* and *sedōka* were seldom written after the 8th century.

The *tanka*, or "short poem," the basic form of Japanese poetry, has existed throughout the history of written verse, outlasting the *chōka* and preceding the haiku. It consists of 31 syllables in five lines of five, seven, five, seven, and seven syllables. The envoys to *chōka* were in tanka form. As a separate form, tanka also served as the progenitor of *renga* and haiku.

Japanese poetry has generally consisted of very small basic units, and its historical development has been one of gradual compression down to the three-line haiku, in which an instantaneous fragment of an emotion or perception takes the place of broader exposition. *See also* HAIKU; RENGA.

Wakefield plays \'wāk-,fēld\   A cycle of 32 scriptural (or mystery) plays written in the early 15th century that were performed regularly at Wakefield, a town in the north of England, as part of the summertime religious festival of Corpus Christi. The text of the plays has been preserved in the Towneley Manuscript (so called after a family that once owned it), now in the Huntington Library in California. The plays are sometimes referred to as the Towneley cycle.

The Wakefield cycle probably originated in the later 14th century, when the cycle of plays performed at York was transferred bodily to Wakefield and there established as a Corpus Christi cycle; six of the plays in each are virtually identical, and there are corresponding speeches here and there in others. On the whole, however, each cycle went its own way after the transfer. From a purely literary point of view, the Wakefield plays are considered superior to any other surviving cycle. In particular, the work of a talented reviser, known as the Wakefield Master, is easily recognizable for its brilliant handling of meter, language, and rhyme, and for its wit and satire.

It is not known how long the cycle, which begins with the fall of Lucifer and ends with the Last Judgment, took in performance: the Chester cycle, which is shorter, was given over three days; the York cycle, which is longer, was given in one. Two plays (about Jacob) are peculiar to the Wakefield cycle, which omits many narratives from the New Testament that are found in all the other surviving cycles. The cycle is unusual in that two shepherd's plays are given. *See also* MYSTERY PLAY.

Wakoski \wə-'käs-kē\, Diane (b. Aug. 3, 1937, Whittier, Calif., U.S.)   American poet known for her personal verses that examine loss, pain, and sexual desire and that frequently reproduce incidents and fantasies from her own turbulent life. Her poetry probes the difficulties that the individual encounters in relationships with others, with the natural world, and with the cultural and popular ideas by which personal lives are structured.

Wakoski studied at the University of California, Berkeley, where she published her first poetry. The collection *Coins & Coffins* (1962), the first of more than 60 published volumes, contains the poem "Justice Is Reason Enough," about the suicide of an imaginary twin brother. In *The George Washington Poems* (1967) Wakoski addresses Washington as an archetypal figure. *Waiting for the King of Spain* (1976) concerns an imaginary monarch. *The Collected Greed: Parts 1–13* (1984), in which "greed" is defined as "failing to choose," contains previously published as well as unpublished poetry. Later collections include *Emerald Ice: Selected Poems 1962–1987* (1988) and *Medea the Sorceress* (1991).

Walafrid Strabo \'väl-ə-,frēd-'sträb-ō\ (b. *c.* 808, Swabia [Germany]—d. Aug. 18, 849, Reichenau, Franconia)   Benedictine abbot, theologian, and poet whose Latin writings constitute the principal exemplar of German Carolingian culture (AD *c.* 750–*c.* 900).

At the abbey of Reichenau on Lake Constance, Walafrid received a liberal education. He later served the emperors Louis the Pious and Louis the German in various capacities.

Walafrid was esteemed by his contemporaries more for his theological writings than for his poetry, on which modern interest chiefly focuses. His best-known theological work, *Liber de exordiis et incrementis quarundam in observationibus ecclesiasticis rerum* (*c.* 841; "Book on the Origins and Development of Certain Matters in Church Practice"), is valuable for its data on Carolingian religious affairs and administration.

As a young monk at Reichenau about 826, Walafrid set to verse *Visio Wettini* ("The Vision of Wettin"), recording a mystical experience described by his first tutor. With poetic images of hell, purgatory, and paradise, *Visio Wettini* anticipated Dante's *The Divine Comedy*. Later Walafrid wrote his most important poem, *Liber de cultura hortorum*, sometimes called *Hortulus* ("Book on the Art of Gardening"), a lyrical piece describing 23 flowers and herbs, their mythological and Christian significances, and their healing properties. His other works include an important panegyric poem, *De imagine Tetrici* ("On the Statue of Theodoric"), and a revision of *Vita Karoli Magnus* ("Life of Charlemagne") by the Frankish historian Einhard.

Walcott \'wól-,kät\, Derek (Alton) (b. Jan. 23, 1930, Castries, Saint Lucia)   West Indian poet and playwright noted for works that explore the Caribbean cultural experience. He was awarded the Nobel Prize for Literature in 1992.

Walcott began writing poetry at an early age, taught at schools in Saint Lucia and Grenada, and contributed articles and reviews to periodicals in Trinidad and Jamaica. Production of his plays began in Saint Lucia in 1950, and he studied theater in New York City in 1958–59. He lived thereafter in Trinidad and the United States.

Walcott is best known for his poetry, beginning with *In a Green Night: Poems 1948–1960* (1962). The book is typical of his early poetry in its celebration of the Caribbean landscape's natural beauty. The verse in *Selected Poems* (1964), *The Castaway* (1965), and *The Gulf* (1969) is similarly lush in style and incantatory in mood as Walcott, caught between his European cultural orientation and the black folk cultures of his native Caribbean, expresses his feelings of personal isolation. *Another Life* (1973) is a book-length autobiographical poem. In *Sea Grapes* (1976) and *The Star-Apple Kingdom* (1979), Walcott uses a tenser, more economical style to examine the deep cultural divisions of language and race in the Caribbean. *The Fortunate Traveller* (1981) and *Midsummer* (1984) explore his own situation as a black writer in America who has become increasingly estranged from his Caribbean homeland. *Collected Poems 1948–1984* was published in 1986, and in 1990 Walcott won acclaim for his book-length poem *Omeros*, in which he linked the world of the Caribbean with that of Homer by recalling the dramas of Homer's *Iliad* and *Odyssey* in a Caribbean setting.

Of Walcott's approximately 30 plays, the best known are *Dream on Monkey Mountain* (produced 1967), *Ti-Jean and His Brothers* (1958), and *Pantomime* (1978). Many of his plays make use of themes from black folk culture in the Caribbean.

Waldeinsamkeit \'vält-,īn-zäm-,kīt\   In German Romantic literature, the longing for distant places or times or for a dream world as opposed to reality. The word, which means literally "forest solitude," was coined by Ludwig Tieck, who used it in his short novel *Der blonde Eckbert*. Clemens Brentano and J.W. von Goethe were among the other writers who expressed this idea in their works.

Walden \'wól-dən\ (*in full* Walden; or, Life in the Woods)   Series of 18 essays by Henry David THOREAU, published in 1854. An important contribution to New England Transcendentalism, the book was a record of Thoreau's experiment in simple living on the northern shore of Walden Pond in eastern Massachusetts (1845–47). *Walden* is viewed not only as a philosophical treatise on labor, leisure, self-reliance, and individualism, but also as an influential piece of nature writing. It is considered Thoreau's masterwork.

Relatively neglected during Thoreau's lifetime, *Walden* achieved tremendous popularity in the 20th century. The physical act of living day by day at Walden Pond is what gave the book authority, while Thoreau's command of a clear, straightforward, but elegant style helped raise it to the level of a literary classic.

Waley \'wā-lē\, Arthur David, *original surname* Schloss \'shlôs\ (b. Aug. 19, 1889, Tunbridge Wells, Kent, Eng.—d. June 27, 1966, London) Sinologist and translator from Chinese and Japanese whose outstanding renderings of Oriental classics into English had a profound effect on such modern poets as W.B. Yeats and Ezra Pound. (The family name was changed from Schloss to Waley, his mother's maiden name, at the outset of World War I.)

Among Waley's outstanding and most influential translations are *170 Chinese Poems* (1918), *Japanese Poems* (1919), and the six-volume translation of *The Tale of Genji* (1925–33), by Murasaki Shikibu, which is considered one of the oldest novels written. It faithfully depicts aristocratic life in 10th–11th-century Japan, as does a work by another court lady, which Waley translated as *The Pillow-Book of Sei Shōnagon* (1928). He also wrote on Oriental philosophy and translated and edited the *Analects* of Confucius (1938).

Other works include *The Nō Plays of Japan* (1921), *Introduction to the Study of Chinese Painting* (1923), *The Opium War through Chinese Eyes* (1958), and *The Ballads and Stories from Tun-huang* (1960).

Walker \'wôk-ər\, A'Lelia, *original name* Lelia McWilliams \mək-'wil-yəmz\ (b. June 6, 1885, Vicksburg, Miss., U.S.—d. Aug. 16, 1931, Long Branch, N.J.) American businesswoman associated with the Harlem Renaissance as a patron of the arts who provided an intellectual forum for the black literati of New York City during the 1920s.

Walker grew up in St. Louis, Mo., and attended Knoxville College in Tennessee before going to work for her mother, Madame C.J. Walker, who had made a fortune in the haircare business. When her mother died in 1919, Walker inherited the business and the lavish family estate, Villa Lewaro, in Irvington, N.Y. In the 1920s she entertained writers and artists at Villa Lewaro and at her apartment and her town house in New York City. Her regular guests at the townhouse—which she named The Dark Tower after Countee Cullen's column by that name—included Langston Hughes, Zora Neale Hurston, James Weldon Johnson, Jean Toomer, and other writers associated with the Harlem Renaissance.

Walker \'wôk-ər\, Alice (Malsenior) (b. Feb. 9, 1944, Eaton-ton, Ga., U.S.) American writer whose novels, short stories, and poems were noted for their insightful treatment of black American culture. Her novels focused particularly on women, most notably THE COLOR PURPLE (1982; film, 1985), which won a Pulitzer Prize in 1983.

After college Walker moved to Mississippi and became involved with the civil rights movement. She also began teaching and publishing short stories and essays and her first book of poetry, *Once* (1968). Her first novel, *The Third Life of Grange Copeland* (1970), traces a family's attempt to conquer a kind of emotional slavery that exists across three generations. In 1973 she published *In Love & Trouble: Stories of Black Women* and *Revolutionary Petunias & Other Poems*, before moving to New York to complete *Meridian* (1976), a novel about a young woman in the civil rights movement.

Walker later moved to California, where she wrote her most popular novel, *The Color Purple*. Written in epistolary form and in black English vernacular, the book depicts a black woman's struggle for racial and sexual equality. After releasing a collec-

tion of essays, *In Search of Our Mothers' Gardens* (1983), and a collection of poetry, *Horses Make a Landscape Look More Beautiful* (1984), she cofounded Wild Trees Press (1984–88). Her later novels include *The Temple of My Familiar* (1989) and *Possessing the Secret of Joy* (1992). Walker also wrote juvenile literature and critical essays on such women writers as Flannery O'Connor and Zora Neale Hurston.

Walker \'wôk-ər\, Kath, *original Anglo-Australian name in full* Kathleen Jean Mary Ruska \'rəs-kə\, *Aboriginal name* Oodgeroo Noonuccal \'ū-jə-,rū-'nū-nə-kəl\ (b. Nov. 3, 1920, Australia—d. Sept. 16, 1993, Brisbane) Australian writer and political activist, considered the first of the modern-day Aboriginal protest writers. Her first volume of poetry, *We Are Going* (1964), was the first book by an Aboriginal woman to be published.

Raised on Stradbroke Island, off Moreton Bay, Queensland, where many of the ancient Aboriginal customs were still practiced, Walker was a member of the Noonuccal (Noonuckle) tribe. Her formal education ended with primary school; at age 13 she entered domestic service in Brisbane. At age 16 she was rejected for nurse's training because of her Aboriginal descent. Walker became an activist for Aboriginal rights. She campaigned successfully for the 1967 abolition of discriminatory, anti-Aboriginal sections of the Australian constitution. Although she was a vocal critic of Australian government policies, she was awarded the M.B.E. (Member of the Order of the British Empire) in 1970; she returned the award in 1988.

Walker's writings include *The Dawn Is at Hand* (1966); *My People: A Kath Walker Collection* (1970), containing poetry, fiction, essays, and speeches; *Stradbroke Dreamtime* (1972), including stories of her childhood, traditional Aboriginal folktales, and new tales cast in traditional form; a children's book, *Father Sky and Mother Earth* (1981); and a treatment of Aboriginal creation myth in *The Rainbow Serpent* (1988).

Walker \'wôk-ər\, Margaret (Abigail), *married name* Alexander \,al-ig-'zan-dər\ (b. July 7, 1915, Birmingham, Ala., U.S.) American novelist and poet, one of the leading black woman writers of the mid-20th century.

After graduating from Northwestern University in Evanston, Ill., Walker joined the Federal Writers' Project in Chicago, where she began a brief literary relationship with novelist Richard Wright. She attended the University of Iowa and wrote *For My People* (1942), a critically acclaimed volume of poetry that celebrates black American culture. In the title poem, originally published in *Poetry* magazine in 1937, she recounts black American history and calls for a racial awakening.

Walker began teaching in the 1940s and joined the faculty at Jackson State College (now Jackson State University) at Jackson, Miss., in 1949. She completed her first novel, *Jubilee* (1966), as her doctoral dissertation for the University of Iowa. Based on the life of Walker's maternal great-grandmother, *Jubilee* chronicles the progress of a slave family from the mid to late 19th century. In *How I Wrote Jubilee* (1972), Walker traced her development of the story from her grandmother's oral family history through her extensive historical research. Her second volume of poetry, *Prophets for a New Day* (1970), makes comparisons between the prophets of the Bible and the black leaders of the civil rights movement. *October Journey* (1973) consists mostly of poems commemorating her personal heroes, such as Harriet Tubman, Gwendolyn Brooks, and her father. After she retired from teaching in 1979, Walker published *Richard Wright: Daemonic Genius* (1988) and a volume of poetry entitled *This Is My Century* (1989).

Walk on the Wild Side, A Novel by Nelson ALGREN, published in 1956. The book is a reworking of his earlier novel

Somebody in Boots (1935). Dove Linkhorn (Cass McKay from the earlier book), a drifter in Depression-era New Orleans, gets involved with prostitutes, pimps, and con men and eventually ends up isolated and hopeless after he has been blinded by a man whose girl he tried to steal. Written with black humor in Algren's characteristic tough-guy style, the novel has been called an erotic epic of bohemianism.

Walkyrie *see* VALKYRIE.

Wall, The Novel by John HERSEY, published in 1950. Based on historical fact but using fictional characters and fictional diary entries, the work presents the background of the valiant but doomed uprising of Jews in the Warsaw ghetto against the Nazis.

The Wall is a powerful presentation, in human terms, of the tragedy of the annihilation of European Jews. The novel relates the lives and actions of many different characters against the background of the Holocaust.

Wallace \'wäl-əs\, Edgar, *in full* Richard Horatio Edgar Wallace (b. April 1, 1875, Greenwich, London, Eng.—d. Feb.10, 1932, Hollywood, Calif., U.S.) British novelist, playwright, and journalist who produced enormously popular detective and suspense stories.

FPG International

Wallace left school at the age of 12 and held a variety of odd jobs until he joined the army at 18; he served in South Africa until 1899, when he became a reporter. He returned to England and produced his first success, *The Four Just Men* (1905).

Wallace practically invented the modern "thriller"; his works in this genre have complex but clearly developed plots and are known for their exciting climaxes. His literary output—175 books, 15 plays, and countless articles and review sketches—was prodigious, and his rate of production so great as to be the subject of humor. His literary reputation suffered after his death. His works include *Sanders of the River* (1911), *The Crimson Circle* (1922), *The Flying Squad* (1928), and *The Terror* (1930).

Wallace \'wäl-əs\, Lewis, *byname* Lew Wallace (b. April 10, 1827, Brookville, Ind., U.S.—d. Feb. 15, 1905, Crawfordsville, Ind.) American soldier, lawyer, diplomat, and author, principally known for his historical novel BEN-HUR (1880).

Son of an Indiana governor, Wallace left school at 16 and became a copyist in the county clerk's office, reading in his leisure time. He began his study of law in his father's office but left to recruit volunteers for the Mexican War, in which he served from 1846 to 1847. In 1849, already a practicing attorney in Indianapolis, he was admitted to the bar. In the American Civil War he served with the Union forces and attained the rank of major general of volunteers. In 1865 Wallace resigned from the army and returned to law practice. He later held two diplomatic positions by presidential appointment.

Though he also wrote poetry and a play, Wallace's literary reputation rests upon three historical novels: *The Fair God* (1873), a story of the Spanish conquest of Mexico; *The Prince of India* (1893), dealing with the Byzantine Empire; and above

all *Ben-Hur*, a romantic tale set in the Roman Empire during the time of Christ. *Lew Wallace: An Autobiography* was published in 1906.

Wallenstein \'väl-ən-,shtīn\ Three-part historical drama by Friedrich von SCHILLER, performed in 1798–99 and published in 1800. The three parts consist of a one-act prelude entitled *Wallensteins Lager* ("Wallenstein's Camp") and two five-act tragedies, *Die Piccolomini* and *Wallensteins Tod* ("Wallenstein's Death") written in blank verse. In addition there is a prefatory poem.

Schiller's epic masterpiece penetrates the psychology of Albrecht von Wallenstein, the general of the armies of the Holy Roman Empire during the Thirty Years' War. The prelude relates Wallenstein's rise to power and has many comic scenes of military life. *Die Piccolomini* reveals Wallenstein's treasonous plot to defect to the enemy and thereby gain power, and *Wallensteins Tod* chronicles Wallenstein's tragic end, the desertion of his troops, and his assassination. Schiller portrays Wallenstein as a complex man who is so carried away by the lust for power that he believes himself to be above the ordinary definitions of good and evil; at the same time he is a man of great courage and dignity.

Waller \'wäl-ər\, Edmund (b. March 3, 1606, Coleshill, Hertfordshire, Eng.—d. Oct. 21, 1687, Beaconsfield, Buckinghamshire) English poet whose adoption of smooth, regular versification prepared the way for the heroic couplet's emergence by the end of the 17th century as the dominant form of English poetic expression.

Waller entered Parliament while still a young man. During the political turmoil of the 1640s, he was arrested for his involvement in a conspiracy (sometimes known as Waller's plot) to establish London as a stronghold of the king. By wholesale betrayal of his colleagues, and by lavish bribes, he managed to avoid the death sentence, but he was banished and heavily fined. He then lived abroad until 1651, when he made his peace with his distant cousin Oliver Cromwell, later lord protector of the Commonwealth.

Several of Waller's poems, including "Go, lovely Rose!"—one of the most famous lyric poems in English literature—had circulated for some 20 years before the appearance of his *Poems* in 1645. The first edition claiming full authorization, however, was that of 1664. In 1655 his "Panegyrick to my Lord Protector" (*i.e.*, Cromwell) appeared, but in 1660 he also celebrated "To the King, upon his Majesties happy return." His later works include *Divine Poems* (1685). *The Second Part of Mr. Waller's Poems* was published in 1690.

Waller's poetry was held in high esteem throughout the 18th century, but his reputation waned in the 19th century along with that of Augustan poetry in general. Rejecting the dense verse of the Metaphysical poets, Waller substituted generalizing statement, easy associative development, and urbane social comment. Apart from this, Waller deserves to be remembered for the distinction of his poems on public themes and for his elegance, lyrical grace, and formal polish.

Waller \'wäl-ər\, Max, *pseudonym of* Léopold-Nicolas-Maurice-Édouard Warlomont \vär-lȯ-'mȯⁿ\ (b. Feb. 24, 1860, Brussels, Belg.—d. March 6, 1889, Saint-Gilles, near Brussels) Belgian writer best known as the founder of the review *La Jeune Belgique* ("Young Belgium"; 1881–97).

Waller studied at the Catholic University of Louvain, where he worked on the student paper. As a lyric poet, he was sympathetic to the ideals of careful craftsmanship characteristic of the French Parnassian poets. He died young and left just one important collection of verse, *La Flûte à Siebel* (1891; "Siebel's Flute"), made up of deft and clever poems in the Parnassian style. He also wrote novels, short stories, and plays, as well as works of criticism.

Walpole \'wȯl-ˌpōl\, Horace, 4th Earl of Orford, *original name* Horatio Walpole (b. Sept. 24, 1717, London, Eng.—d. March 2, 1797, London)   English writer, connoisseur, and collector who was famous in his day for his medieval horror tale THE CASTLE OF OTRANTO (1765), which initiated the vogue for gothic romances. He is remembered today as perhaps the most assiduous letter writer in the English language.

The youngest son of the prime minister Sir Robert Walpole, he was educated at Eton and at King's College, Cambridge. In 1741, Walpole entered Parliament, where his career was undistinguished.

The most absorbing interests of his life were his friendships and a small villa that he acquired at Twickenham in 1747 and transformed into a pseudo-Gothic showplace known as Strawberry Hill. Over the years he added cloisters, turrets, and battlements, filled the interior with pictures and curios, and amassed a valuable library. He established a private press on the grounds, where he printed his own works and those of his friends, notably the *Odes* (1757) of his Eton schoolmate Thomas Gray.

Walpole's literary output was extremely varied. In *The Castle of Otranto* he furnished the machinery for a genre of fiction wherein the wildest fancies found refuge. He also wrote *The Mysterious Mother* (1768), a tragedy with the theme of incest; amateur historical speculations such as *Historic Doubts on the Life and Reign of King Richard the Third* (1768); and a genuine contribution to art history, *Anecdotes of Painting in England*, 4 vol. (1762–71).

His most important works were intended for posthumous publication. His private correspondence of more than 3,000 letters constitutes a survey of the history, manners, and taste of his age. Most of his letters are addressed to Horace Mann, a British diplomat with whom he maintained a correspondence that lasted for 45 years. Walpole's correspondence, edited by W.S. Lewis and others, was published in 42 volumes (1937–80).

Walpole \'wȯl-ˌpōl\, Sir Hugh (Seymour) (b. March 13, 1884, Auckland, N.Z.—d. June 1, 1941, near Keswick, Cumberland, Eng.)   British novelist, critic, and dramatist, a natural storyteller with a fine flow of words and romantic invention.

Walpole was educated at King's School, Canterbury, then at Durham, and finally at Emmanuel College, Cambridge. After unsuccessful attempts at teaching and lay reading in the Anglican church, he devoted himself to writing and to reviewing books. He was knighted in 1937.

Walpole's first important works were the novels *Mr. Perrin and Mr. Traill* (1911), about two schoolmasters; *The Dark Forest* (1916), based on his experiences in Russia during World War I; and the semiautobiographical series that includes *Jeremy* (1919), *Jeremy and Hamlet* (1923), and *Jeremy at Crale* (1927). *The Cathedral* (1922) reflects his affection for the 19th-century English novelist Anthony Trollope. The four-volume "Herries Chronicle"—comprising *Rogue Herries* (1930), *Judith Paris* (1931), *The Fortress* (1932), and *Vanessa* (1933)—deals with an English country family. Walpole also wrote critical works on Trollope, Sir Walter Scott, and Joseph Conrad.

Walpurgisnacht \väl-'pu̇r-gis-ˌnäḵt\   Traditional nocturnal gathering of witches on April 30 (the eve of May Day), which is the feast day of Saint Walburga as well as a traditional Druid festival, in the Harz mountains of central Germany.

A colorful and intriguing part of the lore surrounding witches in Christian European tradition, *Walpurgisnacht* scenes appear in literary works such as *Faust* by J.W. von Goethe and *The Magic Mountain* by Thomas Mann.

The tradition seems to have originated about AD 1400, when the Inquisition began investigating witchcraft seriously, although revels and feasts mentioned by such classical authors as the Romans Apuleius and Petronius Arbiter may have served as inspiration.

Walrond \'wȯl-rənd\, Eric (Derwent) (b. 1898, Georgetown, British Guiana [now Guyana]—d. 1966, London, Eng.)   Caribbean writer who was associated with the Harlem Renaissance literary movement in New York City.

Walrond grew up in Guiana, Barbados, and Panama. From 1916 to 1918 he worked in the Panama Canal Zone as a clerk for the government and as a reporter for the Panama *Star-Herald*. In 1918 he immigrated to New York City, where he attended City College of New York and Columbia University.

Walrond was an editor and writer with the *Brooklyn and Long Island Informer* (1921–23), *Weekly Review* (1921–23), *Negro World* (1923–25), and *Opportunity* (1925–27). His articles and short fiction presented realistic examinations of racism in the United States, notably in the stories "On Being Black" (1922), "Cynthia Goes to the Prom" (1923), and "The Voodoo's Revenge" (1925), and in the article "The New Negro Faces America" (1923). His only book, *Tropic Death* (1926), a collection of short stories set against a lush Caribbean backdrop, juxtaposed impressionistic images of natural beauty with terse descriptions of misery and death in such stories as "The Yellow One," "The Palm Porch," and "Subjection." Walrond left the United States in 1927 and traveled throughout Europe before his death.

Waltari \'väl-tä-rē\, Mika (Toimi) (b. Sept. 19, 1908, Helsinki [Finland]—d. Aug. 26, 1979, Helsinki)   Finnish author whose historical novels were international best-sellers.

Waltari's early novels were concerned with the crises of the generation that came of age between the world wars. He gained international recognition with the appearance of *Sinuhe, egyptiläinen* (1945; THE EGYPTIAN), a story of life in Egypt 1,000 years before the birth of Christ. Other works include *Mikael Hakim* (1949; *The Wanderer*), *Johannes Angelos* (1952; *The Dark Angel*), *Turms, kuolematon* (1955; *The Etruscan*), *Valtakunnan salaisus* (1959; *The Secret of the Kingdom*), and *Ihmiskunnan viholliget* (1964; *The Roman*).

Waltharius \väl-'tär-ē-u̇s, wȯl-'thar-ē-əs\   A Latin heroic poem of the 9th or 10th century dealing with Germanic hero legend. Its author was once thought to be the Swiss monk Ekkehard I the Elder (d. 973), but research since 1941 has determined that the author was probably a Bavarian, one Geraldus (or Gerald), who was certainly the author of the metrical prologue.

The action of the 1,456-line poem is set in the time of the migrations of the peoples. Threatened by the Huns under Attila, the kings of the Franks, of the Burgundians, and of Aquitaine decide to pay tribute and give hostages: Gibicho gives his noble follower Hagano; Heriricus, his daughter Hiltgunt; and Alphere, his son Waltharius. The three children are educated by the Huns in a manner suited to their station.

Hagano escapes when it is learned that Gibicho has died and his son Guntharius does not intend to continue the tribute. In order to bind Waltharius to him, Attila proposes that he should marry a princess of the Hun realm; but he and Hiltgunt have been betrothed as children, and they plan an escape. Their presence in his realm is revealed to Guntharius as they cross the Rhine River, and he insists on pursuing them to take their treasure. The rest (and by far the larger part) of the poem is devoted to his attempts to do so.

When Waltharius sees the danger, he takes up his position in a narrow ravine in the Vosges, where only one adversary can approach at a time, and there follows a series of single combats (skillfully varied by the poet) of Waltharius with the 11 warriors of Guntharius, all of whom Waltharius kills. After resting for the night, he and Hiltgunt continue their journey and are attacked in open country by Guntharius and Hagano. Guntharius, Hagano, and Waltharius are all seriously wounded, but none is killed; and Waltharius and Hiltgunt continue on their way.

The story became well known in Germany, and there is an account, albeit with considerable differences, in the Norse *Thithriks saga*. Two short fragments of *Waldere* in Anglo-Saxon alliterative verse are clearly related, in spite of differences; they are not believed to predate *Waltharius*. It is possible that both *Waldere* and *Waltharius* are derived from a lost Germanic heroic lay; three of the principal characters, Attila, Gunther, and Hagen, are known from other poems of the heroic age. The part of the poem containing the single combats draws heavily on Latin literature, however.

Walther von der Vogelweide \ˈväl-tər-fȯn-dər-ˈfō-gəl-ˌvī-də\ (b. *c.* 1170—d. *c.* 1230, Würzburg? [Germany])   Greatest German lyric poet of the Middle Ages, whose poetry emphasizes the virtues of a balanced life, in the social as in the personal sphere.

The place of Walther's birth has never been satisfactorily identified, though the title *hêr*, which he is given by other poets, indicates that he was of knightly birth. It is clear from his poetry that he received a formal education at a monastery school. He gained the patronage of the Hohenstaufen king Philip of Swabia by writing in support of the Hohenstaufen cause against the Welf faction during the struggle that followed the death of the emperor Henry VI in 1197.

Disappointed with Philip's treatment of him, however, Walther then served several masters, both Welf and Hohenstaufen. From Frederick II he received a small fief, and it is likely that he spent the rest of his life there.

Walther's poetry went far beyond the artificial conventions followed by other minnesingers by introducing an element of realism. Rather more than half of the 200 or so of his extant poems are political, moral, or religious; the rest are love poems. In his religious poems he preaches the need to actively meet the claims of the Creator by, for instance, going on a pilgrimage or a crusade. In his moral-didactic poems he praises such human virtues as faithfulness, sincerity, charity, and self-discipline—virtues that were not especially prominent in his own life. As a love poet he developed a fresh and original treatment of the situations of courtly love and, ultimately, in such poems as the popular "Unter den Linden," achieves a free, uninhibited style in which the poses of court society give way before the natural affections of village folk.

Walton \ˈwȯl-tən\, Izaak (b. Aug. 9, 1593, Stafford, Staffordshire, Eng.—d. Dec. 15, 1683, Winchester, Hampshire)   English biographer and author of THE COMPLEAT ANGLER (1653), a classic idyll on the joys and stratagems of fishing.

After a few years of schooling, Walton was apprenticed to a London ironmonger, acquired a small shop of his own, and began to prosper. Despite his modest education Walton read widely, developed scholarly tastes, and associated with men of learning, including a number of churchmen. He lived and worked near St. Dunstan's Church, and he became active in parish affairs (later a vestryman) and a friend and fishing companion of the vicar, John Donne. For the posthumous publication of Donne's poetry in 1633, Walton composed "An Elegie." In 1640 he wrote *The Life and Death of Dr. Donne* to accompany a collection of Donne's sermons. The *Life* was revised and enlarged in 1658.

The second of Walton's biographies, *The Life of Sir Henry Wotton* (provost of Eton), appeared in 1651. Two years later *The Compleat Angler* was published. Walton also wrote *The Life of Mr. Richard Hooker* (1665). In 1670 *The Life of Mr. George Herbert* (a priest and poet who also had been a fishing companion) was published, and in the same year he brought out an edition containing all four lives.

Wandering Jew   In Christian legend, character doomed to live until the end of the world because he taunted Jesus on the way to the Crucifixion. A reference in John 18:20–22 to an officer who struck Jesus at his arraignment before Annas is sometimes cited as the basis for the legend. The medieval English chronicler Roger of Wendover describes in his *Flores historiarum* how an archbishop from Greater Armenia, visiting England in 1228, reported that there was in Armenia a man formerly called Cartaphilus who claimed he had been Pontius Pilate's doorkeeper and had struck Jesus on his way to Calvary, urging him to go faster. Jesus replied, "I go, and you will wait till I return." Cartaphilus was later baptized Joseph and lived piously among Christian clergy, hoping in the end to be saved.

The legend was revived in 1602 in a German pamphlet, "Kurze Beschreibung und Erzählung von einem Juden mit namen Ahasverus" ("A Brief Description and Narration Regarding a Jew Named Ahasuerus"). This version, in which the name Ahasuerus is first given to the wanderer, who was not baptized, describes how at Hamburg in 1542 Paulus von Eitzen, a Lutheran bishop of Schleswig, met an aged Jew who claimed to have taunted Jesus on the way to the Crucifixion. The popularity of the pamphlet may have been the result of the anti-Jewish feeling aroused by the belief that the Antichrist would appear in 1600 and be aided by the Jews. The pamphlet was rapidly translated into other languages. Appearances of the Wandering Jew were frequently reported in various European cities. As late as 1868 he was reported in Salt Lake City, Utah.

The Wandering Jew has been the subject of many plays, poems, novels, and works of visual art. One of the best-known literary treatments is Eugène Sue's Romantic novel *Le Juif errant*, 10 vol. (1844–45; *The Wandering Jew*), but this anti-Jesuit melodrama has little to do with the original legend.

Wang Anshi or **Wang An-shih** \ˈwäŋ-ˈän-ˈshə\ (b. 1021, Jiangsi province, China—d. 1086)   Chinese poet and prose writer, best known as a governmental reformer who implemented his unconventional idealism through the "New Laws," or "New Policies," of 1069–76. The academic controversy sparked by his reforms continued for centuries.

Wang emerged from a rising new group of southern bureaucrats with a strong utilitarian bent, who challenged their more conservative, large-landholding colleagues from the north. At the age of 21 Wang earned his *jinshi* ("doctorate") degree in the civil service examinations, and for nearly two decades he served ably as a local administrator in various posts in the south, finally achieving a powerful rank in 1067/68. He retired in 1076 and lived a simple, withdrawn life, continuing his literary endeavors and his scholarly pursuits, mostly in etymological study.

Desiring to emphasize the practical application of the Confucian Classics, Wang wrote original interpretations of several ancient works and instituted these as standard texts for the state examinations—moves that caused great consternation among conservatives. Friend and foe alike, however, acknowledged Wang's skill with the pen. The elegance and depth of his prose earned him fame as one of the "Eight Great Masters of the Tang and Song Dynasties." The facile genius of his verses, especially those composed later in his life, also earned high critical acclaim.

Wang Shifu or **Wang Shih-fu** \\'wäŋ-'shə-'fü\\, *also called* Wang Dexin \\'də-'shin\\ (b. *c.* 1250, Dadu [now Beijing, China]—d. 1337?, China) Leading dramatist of the Yuan dynasty (1206–1368), which saw the flowering of Chinese drama.

Of 14 plays attributed to Wang, only three survive, of which *Xi xiang ji* (*Romance of the Western Chamber*) is widely regarded as the best northern play of the period and is still popular. The work is an amplified *zaju* containing several of Wang's innovations—particularly that of giving singing parts to all, instead of only one, of the important characters. Despite the rigid conventions of the stock actor, Wang also succeeded in creating a convincing character in the maid, Hong Niang; the dialogue is also excellent. In five acts, the *Xi xiang ji* is several times the length of a regular *zaju*, foreshadowing the development of the *chuanqi*, the dominant dramatic form of the Ming (1368–1644) and Qing (1664–1911/12) dynasties.

Wapshot Chronicle, The \\'wap-,shät\\ Novel by John CHEEVER, published in 1957 and granted a National Book Award in 1958. Based in part on Cheever's adolescence in New England, the novel takes place in a small Massachusetts fishing village and relates the breakdown of both the Wapshot family and the town. Part One focuses on Leander, a gentle ferryboat operator harried by his tyrannical wife and his eccentric sister; he eventually swims out to sea and never returns. Part Two chronicles the disastrous lives of Leander's sons, Coverly and Moses. Told in a comic rather than a tragic vein, the novel uses experimental prose techniques to convey a nostalgic vision of a lost world. A sequel, *The Wapshot Scandal*, was published in 1964.

War and Peace Epic historical novel by Leo TOLSTOY, originally published as *Voyna i mir* in 1865–69. This panoramic study of early 19th-century Russian society, noted for its mastery of realistic detail and variety of psychological analysis, is generally regarded as one of the world's greatest novels.

War and Peace is primarily concerned with the histories of five aristocratic families—particularly the Bezukhovs, the Bolkonskys, and the Rostovs—the members of which are portrayed against a vivid background of Russian social life during the war against Napoleon (1805–14). The theme of war, however, is subordinate to the story of family existence, which involves Tolstoy's optimistic belief in the life-asserting pattern of human existence. The heroine, Natasha Rostova, for example, reaches her greatest fulfillment through her marriage to Pierre Bezukhov and her motherhood. The novel also sets forth a theory of history, concluding that there is a minimum of free choice; all is ruled by an inexorable historical determinism.

Ward \\'wȯrd\\, Artemus, *pseudonym of* Charles Farrar Browne \\'braŭn\\ (b. April 26, 1834, Waterford, Maine, U.S.—d. March 6, 1867, Southampton, Hampshire, Eng.) One of the most popular 19th-century American humorists, whose lecture techniques exercised much influence on such humorists as Mark Twain.

Starting as a printer's apprentice, Browne went to Boston to work as a compositor for *The Carpet-Bag*, a humor magazine. In 1860, after several years as local editor for the Toledo (Ohio) *Commercial* and the Cleveland *Plain Dealer*, he became staff writer for *Vanity Fair* in New York.

While working on the *Plain Dealer*, Browne created the character Artemus Ward, the manager of an itinerant sideshow who "commented" on a variety of subjects in letters to the *Plain Dealer*, *Punch*, and *Vanity Fair*. The most obvious features of his humor are puns and gross misspellings. In 1861 Browne turned to lecturing under the pseudonym Artemus Ward. Though his books were popular, it was his lecturing, delivered with deadpan expression, that brought him fame. His works include *Artemus Ward: His Book* (1862), *Artemus Ward: His Travels* (1865), and *Artemus Ward in London* (1867).

Ward \\'wȯrd\\, Elizabeth Stuart Phelps, *original name* Mary Gray Phelps \\'felps\\ (b. Aug. 31, 1844, Boston, Mass., U.S.—d. Jan. 28, 1911, Newton, Mass.) Popular 19th-century American author and feminist.

Mary Phelps assumed her mother's name, Elizabeth Stuart Phelps, after the latter's death in 1852. From the age of 13 she wrote juvenile fiction. In 1868 *The Gates Ajar*, her greatest success, was published. It is the story of a girl's struggle to renew her faith despite the death of a beloved brother. The novel was immediately popular, selling 80,000 copies in the United States and 100,000 in England; it was translated into at least four languages.

Phelps subsequently wrote 56 more books, in addition to poetry, pamphlets, and short articles. Her later work was often concerned with the domestic status of women. *The Story of Avis* (1877) and *Doctor Zay* (1882), for example, focus on the problems of women facing the demands of both career and marriage. Phelps also advocated the causes of labor, temperance, and antivivisection in her novels. Her autobiography, *Chapters From a Life*, was published in 1896.

Ward \\'wȯrd\\, Mrs. Humphry, *original name* Mary Augusta Arnold \\'är-nəld\\ (b. June 11, 1851, Tasmania, Australia—d. March 24, 1920, London, Eng.) English novelist whose best-known work, *Robert Elsmere*, created a sensation in its day by advocating a Christianity based on social concern rather than theology.

A niece of the poet and critic Matthew Arnold, Mary Augusta Arnold grew up in an atmosphere of religious searching. Her father resigned his position as a school official in Australia to become a Roman Catholic but later returned temporarily to the Anglican church and settled the family at Oxford. There she matured in stimulating scholarly surroundings. In 1872 she married Humphry Ward, a fellow at Brasenose College, Oxford. In 1881 they moved to London, where she wrote for the *Pall Mall Gazette* and other periodicals.

Ward's rejection of a supernaturally oriented Christianity in favor of a strong social commitment found eloquent expression in her novel *Robert Elsmere* (1888), the story of a young Anglican clergyman's conversion to the belief that "Religion consists alone in the service of the people." The popularity of this controversial work was only increased by William Gladstone's polemical reply, "Robert Elsmere and the Battle of Belief " (1888). Ward followed its success with more than 20 other didactic novels.

Warden, The   Novel by Anthony TROLLOPE, published in 1855. Trollope's first literary success, *The Warden* was also the initial work in a series of six books set in the fictional county of Barsetshire and known as the BARSETSHIRE NOVELS.

The Reverend Septimus Harding, the conscientious warden of a charitable retirement home for men, resigns after being accused of making too much profit from the sinecure. Trollope continued Harding's story in *Barchester Towers* (1857).

Ward Number Six   Short story by Anton CHEKHOV, published in Russian in 1892 as "Palata No. 6." The story is set in a provincial mental asylum and explores the philosophical conflict between Ivan Gromov, a patient, and Dr. Andrey Ragin, the director of the asylum. Gromov denounces the injustice he sees everywhere, while Dr. Ragin insists on ignoring injustice and other evils; partially as a result of this way of thinking, he neglects to remedy the shoddy conditions of the mental ward. When Dr. Ragin is himself committed, he realizes the fallacy of his philosophy and, too late, understands that evil must be confronted. The story made an enormous impression when it was first published. The mental ward was taken as a symbol for Russia itself and the madness of the upper classes who, instead of dealing with Russia's problems, chose to view them from a distance.

Warner \\'wôr-nər\\, Rex (Ernest) (b. March 9, 1905, Birmingham, Warwickshire, Eng.—d. June 24, 1986, Wallingford, Oxfordshire)   British novelist, Greek scholar, poet, translator, and critic who in his fictional work warned—in nightmarish allegory—against the evils of a capitalist society.

After graduating from Wadham College, Oxford, Warner was a schoolteacher in England and Egypt. In the 1940s he served as director of the British Institute in Athens. He moved to the United States in 1961 and was professor of English at the University of Connecticut from 1964 to 1974.

Warner wrote only one book of poetry, *Poems* (1937). His translations from the Greek—particularly Aeschylus' *Prometheus Bound* (1947), Xenophon's *Anabasis* (1949), and Euripides' *Hippolytus* (1950) and *Helen* (1951)—are elegant, clear, and direct. Most notable of Warner's novels are *The Professor* (1938) and *The Aerodrome* (1941). Warner also wrote two fictionalized "autobiographies" of Julius Caesar: *The Young Caesar* (1958) and *Imperial Caesar* (1960). Other works of historical fiction include *Pericles the Athenian* (1963) and *The Converts* (1967). *Men of Athens* (1972) is a series of essays on the great Athenians of the 5th century BC.

Warner \\'wôr-nər\\, Sylvia Townsend (b. Dec. 6, 1893, Harrow, Middlesex, Eng.—d. May 1, 1978, Maiden Newton, Dorset)   Writer who began her self-proclaimed "accidental career" as a poet after she was given paper with a "particularly tempting surface" and who wrote her first novel, *Lolly Willowes; or, The Loving Huntsman* (1926), because she "happened to find very agreeable thin lined paper in a job lot."

Educated privately, Warner originally intended to follow a career as a musicologist. One of the editors of the 10-volume *Tudor Church Music* (c. 1923–29), she was also a contributor to *Grove's Dictionary of Music.*

Her fiction was acclaimed for its wit and whimsical charm and for its elegant language. Many of her stories were peopled with eccentric characters. *Lolly Willowes* was the first selection of the Book of the Month Club. In addition to her short stories, 144 of which appeared in *The New Yorker* magazine, Warner also published many collections of short fiction, novels, volumes of poetry, and works of nonfiction including *Jane Austen: 1775–1817* (1951) and the semi-autobiographical, posthumously published *Scenes of Childhood* (1981). Her novels, some of which are based on historical events, include *Mr.*

Fortune's Maggot (1927), *The True Heart* (1929), and *The Flint Anchor* (1954). Her final story collections were *Kingdoms of Elfin* (1977) and the posthumously published *One Thing Leading to Another* (1984). Warner also translated two books from French, Marcel Proust's *By Way of Saint-Beuve* (1958) and Jean René Huguenin's *A Place of Shipwreck* (1963).

war of the theaters   In English literary history, conflict involving the English playwrights Ben Jonson, John Marston, and Thomas Dekker. It extended from 1599 to roughly 1603, a period when Jonson was writing for one children's company of players and Marston for a rival group. In 1599 Marston presented a mildly satiric portrait of Jonson in his *Histrio-mastix*. In the same year Jonson replied in *Every Man Out of His Humour*, ridiculing Marston's style as "fustian." Also that same year, Marston's *Jack Drum's Entertainment* presented Jonson, thinly disguised, as a cuckold. The quarrel reached its height about 1600: Jonson wrote *Cynthia's Revels* (performed c. 1600), satirizing Marston and Dekker; Marston satirized Jonson in *What You Will*; Jonson, anticipating Marston's attack, wrote *Poetaster* (produced 1601), representing Marston as an inferior poet and a plagiarist and Dekker as a playdresser and plagiarist; Dekker and Marston then lampooned Jonson as the laborious poet (Dekker in the play *Satiro-mastix* [produced 1601]). The quarrel was patched up by 1604, when Marston dedicated *The Malcontent* to Jonson.

Some scholars have seen the quarrel as based on a difference of opinion about the nature of drama; it was certainly sharpened by the intense competition that existed between children's companies at the time.

War of the Worlds, The   Science-fiction novel by H.G. WELLS, published in 1898. The story, which details twelve days in which invaders from Mars attack the planet Earth, captured popular imagination with its fast-paced narrative and images of Martians and interplanetary travel. The humans in *The War of the Worlds* initially treat the invasion with complacency but soon are provoked into a defensive state of war.

The novel helped launch the career of Orson Welles when he presented an adaptation of it on his radio program, "The Mercury Theatre on the Air," on Oct. 30, 1938. The simulated news broadcast of a Martian landing in New Jersey, complete with regularly updated news bulletins, caused a widespread panic among listeners. Later radio adaptations also produced mass hysteria, including an incident in Ecuador that resulted in several deaths.

Warren \\'wôr-ən\\, Robert Penn (b. April 24, 1905, Guthrie, Ky., U.S.—d. Sept. 15, 1989, Stratton, Vt.)   American novelist, poet, critic, and teacher, best known for his treatment of moral dilemmas in a South beset by the erosion of its traditional rural values. He won the Pulitzer Prize for fiction in 1947 and for poetry in 1958 and 1979, and he became the first poet laureate of the United States in 1986.

In 1921 Warren entered Vanderbilt University, Nashville, Tenn., where he joined a group of poets who called themselves the Fugitives. Warren was among several of the Fugitives who joined with other Southerners to publish the anthology of essays *I'll Take My Stand* (1930), a plea for the agrarian way of life in the South. After graduation from Vanderbilt, he studied at the University of California, Berkeley, and at Yale. He later served on the faculties of several colleges and universities—including Vanderbilt, the University of Minnesota, and Yale. With Cleanth Brooks and Charles W. Pipkin he founded and edited *The Southern Review* (1935–42), one of the most influential American literary magazines of the time.

Warren's first novel, *Night Rider* (1939), is based on the tobacco war (1905–08) between the independent growers in Kentucky and the large tobacco companies. It anticipates much of his later fiction in the way it treats a historical event with tragic irony, emphasizes violence, and portrays individuals caught in moral quandaries. His best-known novel is ALL THE KING'S MEN (1946), based on the career of the Louisiana demagogue Huey Long. Warren's other novels include *At Heaven's Gate* (1943), *World Enough and Time* (1950), *Band of Angels* (1956), and *The Cave* (1959). His long narrative poem *Brother to Dragons* (1953), dealing with the brutal murder of a slave by two nephews of Thomas Jefferson, is essentially a versified novel, and his poetry generally exhibits many of the concerns of his fiction. His other volumes of poetry include *Promises: Poems, 1954–1956* (1957); *You, Emperors, and Others* (1960); *Audubon: A Vision* (1969); *Now and Then: Poems, 1976–1978* (1978); *Rumor Verified* (1981); *Chief Joseph* (1983); and *New and Selected Poems, 1923–1985* (1985). *The Circus in the Attic* (1948), which included "Blackberry Winter," considered by some critics to be one of Warren's supreme achievements, is a volume of short stories, and *Selected Essays* (1958) is a collection of some of his critical writings.

Warton \'wȯrt-ən\, Joseph (baptized April 22, 1722, Dunsfold, Surrey, Eng.—d. Feb. 23, 1800, Wickham, Hampshire) English critic and classical scholar who anticipated some of the critical tenets of Romanticism. His brother Thomas was poet laureate from 1785 to 1790.

Warton was impatient with some aspects of Neoclassical poetry, as is shown by his poem *The Enthusiast; or the Lover of Nature* (1744). His *Odes on Various Subjects* (1746) was an attempt to emphasize the role of imagination in verse. This was followed in 1756 by the first part of the *Essay on the Writings and Genius of Pope*. The complete work is an essay of considerable scholarship. It contains valuable systematic accounts of Alexander Pope's work, with numerous general critical dicta. Its most striking feature is its insistence on the sublime and pathetic as the highest kinds of poetry and on the importance of originality and freedom from rules. Ethical, didactic, or satiric poetry, such as that of Pope, is considered in the work to be of a second and inferior order.

Warton \'wȯrt-ən\, Thomas, the Younger (b. Jan. 9, 1728, Basingstoke, Hampshire, Eng.—d. May 21, 1790, Oxford) Poet laureate from 1785 and author of the first history of English poetry.

Brother of the poet and critic Joseph Warton, Thomas Warton gained an early reputation as a poet. In his meditative, blank-verse poem *The Pleasures of Melancholy*, published anonymously in 1747, he displayed the love of medieval and "romantic" themes that colored much of his later work as a critic. Most of his best verse was written before he was 23.

Warton is now most highly regarded as a scholar and as a pioneer of literary history. His *Observations on the Faerie Queene of Spenser* (1754; 2nd enlarged edition, 1762) contains a section that briefly surveys English literature from the time of Geoffrey Chaucer to the Restoration. It prefigures the work that was to occupy Warton for the rest of his life: *The History of English Poetry from the Close of the Eleventh to the Commencement of the Eighteenth Century*, 3 vol. (1774–81). He did not live to complete the history, which advances only up to the end of Queen Elizabeth's reign early in the 17th century.

Washington Square \'wȯsh-iŋ-tən\ Short novel by Henry JAMES, published in 1880 and praised for its depiction of the complicated relationship between a stubborn father and his daughter.

The novel's main character, Catherine Sloper, lives with her widowed aunt and her physician father in New York City's fashionable Washington Square district. A plain, rather stolid young woman, Catherine is a disappointment to her father. She is courted by Morris Townsend, who is interested only in her potential inheritance. When her father threatens to disinherit her if she marries the fortune hunter, Townsend abandons her. Many years later, after her father's death, Townsend reappears and attempts to renew his suit. Catherine rejects him and lives on as a confirmed spinster in her Washington Square house.

Wasps (*Greek* Sphēkes) Comedy by ARISTOPHANES, produced in 422 BC. *Wasps* satirizes the litigiousness of the Athenians, who are represented by the mean and waspish old man Philocleon ("Love-Cleon"), who has a passion for serving on juries. In the play, Philocleon's son, Bdelycleon ("Loathe-Cleon"), arranges for his father to hold a "court" at home; but, because the first "case" to be heard is absurd—that of the house dog accused of the theft of a cheese—Philocleon is cured of his passion for the law courts. He becomes a boastful and uproarious drunkard. The play's main target is the politician Cleon's exploitation of the Athenian system of large subsidized juries.

Jean Racine's only comedy, the three-act *Les Plaideurs* (1668; *The Litigants*), is a slight but witty adaptation of *Wasps*.

Wassermann \'väs-ər-ˌmän, *Angl* 'wäs-ər-mən\, Jakob (b. March 10, 1873, Fürth, Bavaria [Germany]—d. Jan. 1, 1934, Altaussee, Austria) German novelist who is frequently compared to Fyodor Dostoyevsky in both his moral fervor and his tendency to sensationalism; his popularity was greatest in the 1920s and '30s.

Wassermann achieved success with his second published novel, *Die Juden von Zirndorf* (1897; *The Jews of Zirndorf*; republished as *The Dark Pilgrimage*), a study of Jews longing for the Messiah. He established his reputation with *Caspar Hauser* (1908), based on the true story of a strange boy found in Nürnberg in 1828 who was apparently unfamiliar with the ordinary world and whose identity and subsequent murder or suicide remained a mystery. Wassermann used the story to castigate bourgeois numbness of heart and lack of imagination in dealing with anything out of the ordinary. In *Christian Wahnschaffe* (1919; *The World's Illusion*), one of his most popular works, a millionaire's son, after experiencing all that high life, love, travel, and art have to offer, dedicates himself to the service of humanity.

Perhaps Wassermann's most enduring work is *Der Fall Maurizius* (1928; *The Maurizius Case*), which treats the theme of justice with the carefully plotted suspense of a detective story. It introduced the character Etzel Andergast, whose questioning of the judgment of his cold-hearted jurist father and whose own detective work eventually prove the innocence of a man his father had condemned. Andergast became a symbol for post-World War I German youth by rejecting the authority of the past and finding his own truth by trial-and-error, doggedly following elusive clues. This work was extended into a trilogy including *Etzel Andergast* (1931) and *Joseph Kerkhovens dritte Existenz* (1934; *Kerkhoven's Third Existence*). Wassermann's autobiography is entitled *Mein Weg als Deutscher und Jude* (1921; *My Life as German and Jew*).

Wasserstein \'wäs-ər-ˌstīn\, Wendy (b. Oct. 18, 1950, Brooklyn, N.Y., U.S.) Playwright whose work probes, with humor and sensibility, the situation of college-educated women and their responses to their own aspirations and to the feminism of the late 1960s. Her drama *The Heidi Chronicles* (1989) was awarded both a Pulitzer Prize and an Antoinette Perry award in 1989.

Wasserstein was educated at Mount Holyoke College, City College of the City University of New York, and Yale University. Her first play, *Any Woman Can't* (1973), is a cutting farce on one of her major themes—a woman's attempts to succeed in an environment traditionally dominated by men. Two other early works were *Uncommon Women and Others* (1978) and *Isn't It Romantic* (1984), which explore women's attitudes toward marriage and society's expectations of women. In *The Heidi Chronicles*, a successful art historian discovers that her independent life choices have alienated her from men as well as women. *The Sisters Rosensweig* (1993) continues the theme into middle age.

Other works include an adaptation for television of the John Cheever short story "The Sorrows of Gin" (1979); the play "When Dinah Shore Ruled the Earth" (produced 1975; with Christopher Durang); "The Man in Case," an adaptation of Anton Chekhov's short story, published in the anthology *Orchards* (1986); and a musical, "Miami" (produced in 1986).

Wast \'wäst\, Hugo, *pseudonym of* Gustavo Martínez Zuviría \,sü-vē-'rē-ä\ (b. Oct. 23, 1883, Córdoba, Arg.—d. March 28, 1962, Buenos Aires)   Argentine novelist and short-story writer who was one of his country's most popular and most widely translated authors.

A lawyer by profession, Wast served in various official posts throughout his career, including director of the National Library in Buenos Aires (1931–54). His career also included newspaper editing and university teaching. Wast continued to write while in public office, and thus his literary career spanned more than half a century. His most characteristic and most popular novels—such as *Flor de durazno* (1911; *Peach Blossom*), which established his literary reputation, and *Desierto de piedra* (1925; *A Stone Desert*), which won the Argentinian national prize for literature—portray rural people in their struggle against nature and adversity and their ability to endure personal hardship. In such novels as *La casa de los cuervos* (1916; *The House of Ravens*), he told tales of adventure set against historical backgrounds. At times he portrayed the modern urban environment, as in *Ciudad turbulenta, ciudad alegre* (1919; "Turbulent City, Lively City").

Wast's novels were translated into several languages; a four-volume English translation published in 1977 includes *Black Valley*, earlier titled *A Stone Desert*; *Peach Blossom*; and *The Strength of Lovers*. His reputation declined after his death.

Waste Land, The   Long poem by T.S. ELIOT, published in 1922, first in London in *The Criterion* (October), next in New York City in *The Dial* (November), and finally in book form, with footnotes by Eliot. The 433-line, five-part poem was dedicated to fellow poet Ezra Pound, who helped condense the original manuscript to nearly half its size. It was one of the most influential works of the 20th century.

The Waste Land expresses with great power the disillusionment and disgust of the period after World War I. In a series of fragmentary vignettes, loosely linked by the legend of the search for the Grail, it portrays a sterile world of panicky fears and barren lusts, and of human beings waiting for some sign or promise of redemption. The depiction of spiritual emptiness in the secularized city—the decay of *urbs aeterna* (the "eternal city")—is not a simple contrast of the heroic past with the degraded present; it is rather a timeless, simultaneous awareness of moral grandeur and moral evil.

The poem initially met with controversy as its complex and erudite style was alternately denounced for its obscurity and praised for its modernism.

Watch on the Rhine \'rīn\   Drama in three acts by Lillian HELLMAN, published and produced in 1941. Performed just eight months before the United States entered World War II, Hellman's play exposed the dangers of fascism in America, asserting that tyranny can also be battled on the home front.

The play is set in 1940 in the Washington, D.C., home of the wealthy widow Fanny Farrelly, who is expecting the arrival of her daughter Sara, Sara's German husband Kurt, and their three children. A leader in the anti-Nazi resistance movement, Kurt has been forced to flee Europe. Count Teck de Brancovis, a Romanian houseguest in the Farrelly home and a Nazi supporter, discovers Kurt's identity and threatens to expose him to the German embassy. From a comedy of manners the play gradually evolves into a tense thriller.

water horse   A fabulous water spirit resembling a horse. Specific forms of water horse include the hippocampus and the kelpie.

Waterhouse \'wȯt-ər-,haůs\, Keith (Spencer) (b. Feb. 6, 1929, Hunslet, Leeds, Yorkshire, Eng.)   English novelist, playwright, and screenwriter noted for his ability to create comedy and satire out of depressing human predicaments.

Waterhouse left school at the age of 15 and worked at various odd jobs before becoming a newspaperman, first in Yorkshire and then in London; he remained a columnist (for the *Daily Mirror* and *Punch*) for most of his life. His first novel, *There Is a Happy Land* (1957), was followed by the best-selling *Billy Liar* (1959). The public easily identified with its hero, a young man who compensates for his mundane, tawdry existence by a series of fantastic daydreams. *Billy Liar* was turned into a successful play in 1960, a film in 1963, and a musical in 1974. Together with Willis Hall, Waterhouse wrote several plays and revues, among them *Celebration* (performed 1961), *All Things Bright and Beautiful* (1962), *They Called the Bastard Stephen* (1964), *Whoops-a-Daisy* (1968), *Who's Who* (1971), *Lost Empires* (1985; adapted from the novel by J.B. Priestley), and *Budgie: The Musical* (1988). His other novels include *The Bucket Shop* (1968; U.S. title, *Everything Must Go*), *Billy Liar on the Moon* (1975), *Office Life* (1978), *Maggie Muggins* (1981), *In the Mood* (1983), *Our Song* (1987), and *Bimbo* (1990).

Water Margin   Ancient Chinese vernacular novel known from several widely varying manuscripts under the name *Shuihu zhuan*. Its variations are so extreme as to make the work the most textually complex in Chinese literature; the text cannot be dated with accuracy and its authors cannot be identified.

Based in part on ancient legends and oral tradition, *Water Margin* is generally divided into simpler text and fuller text versions, the earliest of which date from the early 16th century. Each manuscript within these series contains some combination of six episodic adventure tales about 108 bandit-heroes and their various campaigns.

A recent English translation (complete version of the first 70 chapters and an abridged version of the last 30) was published as *Outlaws of the Marsh* (1981).

water nymph   A goddess (such as one of the Naiads, Nereids, or Oceanids) of classical mythology associated with a body of water.

water sprite   A sprite, or tiny mythical being, held to inhabit or haunt the water. A female water sprite is sometimes known as a *water nixie*.

Watkins \'wät-kinz\, Vernon Phillips (b. June 27, 1906, Maesteg, Glamorgan, Wales—d. Oct. 8, 1967, near Swansea, Glamorgan)   English-language Welsh poet who drew from Welsh material and legend.

Watkins steeped himself in the study of French and German and developed a deep understanding of the poetry of both those countries while he was a student at Cambridge University. After graduation he became a bank clerk and wrote poetry. Watkins' work includes *Ballad of Mari Lwyd* (1941), *The Lamp and the Veil* (1945), *The Lady with the Unicorn* (1948),

The Death Bell (1954), *Cypress and Acacia* (1959), and *Affinities* (1962). *Selected Poems* was published in 1967. Also of considerable interest is his edition of *Letters to Vernon Watkins by Dylan Thomas* (1957).

Watson \'wät-sən\, William, *in full* Sir John William Watson (b. Aug. 2, 1858, Burley in Wharfedale, Yorkshire, Eng.— d. Aug. 11, 1935, Ditchling, Sussex)   English author of lyrical and political verse.

Watson's first collection, *The Prince's Quest,* appeared in 1880; from that time he wrote prolifically. He had a gift for occasional verse, and *Wordsworth's Grave* (1890), *Lachrymae Musarum* (1892), on the death of the poet laureate Alfred, Lord Tennyson, and his coronation ode for King Edward VII contributed to his reputation. His political views were strong, and he attacked the government on a number of issues. He was knighted in 1917. Watson's work was influenced by that of Tennyson and of Matthew Arnold. His later poetry, appearing in an edition of 1936, remained firmly Victorian in idea and idiom.

Watson, Dr. \'wät-sən\, *in full* Dr. John H. Watson.   Fictional English physician who is Sherlock Holmes's devoted friend and associate in a series of detective stories and novels by Sir Arthur Conan DOYLE.

Born in 1852, Watson has served as an army surgeon in India, where he was wounded during the second Afghan War, and has returned to England in impaired health. He and Holmes meet in London; they share rooms at 221B Baker Street. The medical practice Watson establishes does not prevent him from accompanying Holmes on his crime-fighting cases, which he later records and publishes.

The character of Watson, as written by Conan Doyle, is modest and intelligent. He is a patient and sensitive observer, but his detecting capabilities are no match for the lightning-swift deductive reasoning of Holmes.

Watt \'wät\   Absurdist novel by Samuel BECKETT, published in 1953. It was written in 1942–44 while Beckett, an early member of the French Resistance, was hiding in southern France from German occupying forces.

There is no conventional plot to *Watt*, nor are there always readily assignable meanings to the characters and events. Moreover, as in Beckett's earlier fiction, the milieu of *Watt* remains recognizably Irish, but most of the action takes place in a highly abstract, unreal world. The protagonist Watt, who seeks the meanings ("What?") of the people and objects he encounters, never succeeds in meeting his employer Mr. Knott, who does "not" appear in the novel.

While the search for meaning preoccupies Watt, grotesque characters and events provide comic relief. Beckett also treats the difficulty of communication, as Watt tells his story in increasingly convoluted anagrams to the narrator.

Watts \'wäts\, Isaac (b. July 17, 1674, Southampton, Hampshire, Eng.—d. Nov. 25, 1748, Stoke Newington, London) English Nonconformist (non-Church of England) minister, regarded as the father of English hymnody.

Watts was appointed assistant to the minister of Mark Lane Independent (*i.e.,* Congregational) Chapel, London, in 1699 and in March 1702 became full pastor. Because of a breakdown in health (1712) he went to stay with Sir Thomas Abney in Hertfordshire, where he remained for the rest of his life.

The hymns for which Watts is known were written during his Mark Lane ministry. His first collection of hymns and sacred lyrics was *Horae Lyricae* (1706), quickly followed by *Hymns and Spiritual Songs* (1707), which included "When I Survey the Wondrous Cross," "There is a Land of Pure Delight," and others that have become known throughout Protestant Chris-

tendom. The most famous of all his hymns, "Our God, Our Help in Ages Past" (from his paraphrase of Psalm 90), and "Jesus Shall Reign" (part of his version of Psalm 72), almost equally well known, were published in *The Psalms of David* (1719).

During the latter part of his life, Watts devoted much time to writing and eventually published a work that had occupied him for many years, *Logic, or the Right Use of Reason in the Enquiry After Truth* (1725), which was for several generations a standard textbook.

Watts-Dunton \'wäts-'dənt-ən\, Theodore, *in full* Walter Theodore Watts-Dunton (b. Oct. 12, 1832, St. Ives, Huntingdonshire, Eng.—d. June 6, 1914, London)   English critic and man of letters who was the friend and self-appointed protector of the poet Algernon Charles Swinburne.

Watts-Dunton studied law and practiced for some time in London, but his real interest was literature, and he eventually became an important literary critic. He contributed regularly to the *Examiner* and the *Athenaeum* and wrote the article on poetry for the 9th edition of *Encyclopædia Britannica* (1885).

With considerable persistence he formed the friendships that are the real basis of his reputation—particularly with notable writers of the period, such as Dante Gabriel Rossetti and Swinburne. The latter, who had been in poor health, collapsed completely in 1879 but recovered under Watts-Dunton's devoted care. For the next 30 years the strict regimen and enthusiastic encouragement of Watts-Dunton made possible Swinburne's enormous productivity.

Watts-Dunton's published works include two novels, *Alwin* (1898) and *Vesprie Towers* (1916), and a book of poems, *The Coming of Love* (1897). A book of his memoirs, *Old Familiar Faces*, was published in 1916.

Waugh \'wȯ\, Alec, *byname of* Alexander Raban Waugh (b. July 8, 1898, Hampstead, London, Eng.—d. Sept. 3, 1981, Tampa, Fla., U.S.)   English popular novelist and travel writer, older brother of the writer Evelyn Waugh.

Waugh was educated at Sherborne, from which he was expelled, and the Royal Military Academy at Sandhurst. While only 17 he wrote *The Loom of Youth* (1917), a novel about public school life that created a considerable stir. During World War I he served in France and was taken prisoner. After the war he worked as a publisher's reader until 1926, when he went to Tahiti. His love for tropical countries left its stamp on many of his novels. *Island in the Sun* (1956) explores the emotional and political problems between blacks and whites on a West Indian island. *The Mule on the Minaret* (1965) was based on the activities of British counterintelligence in the Middle East. *My Brother Evelyn and Other Profiles* (1967) is largely autobiographical. Waugh's later novels include *A Spy in the Family* (1970), *The Fatal Gift* (1973), and *A Year to Remember* (1975).

Waugh \'wȯ\, Evelyn (Arthur St. John) (b. Oct. 28, 1903, London, Eng.—d. April 10, 1966, Combe Florey, near Taunton, Somerset)   English writer regarded by many as the most brilliant satirical novelist of his day.

Waugh was educated at Lancing College, Sussex, and at Hertford College, Oxford. After short periods as an art student and schoolmaster, he devoted himself to solitary observant travel and to the writing of novels, soon earning a wide reputation for sardonic wit and technical brilliance. During World War II he served in the Royal Marines and the Royal Horse Guards; in 1944 he joined the British military mission to the Yugoslav Partisans. After the war he led a retired life in the west of England.

Waugh's novels, although always derived from firsthand experience, are unusually highly wrought and precisely written. The most noteworthy of his early, most satirical novels are as an effort to understand his youthful quarrel with his own father. Rich in psychological characterizations, with masterful dialogue and a beautiful prose style, the novel is often called Stevenson's masterpiece.

Weiss \'vīs\, Peter (Ulrich) (b. Nov. 8, 1916, Nowawes, near Potsdam, Ger.—d. May 10, 1982, Stockholm, Swed.) German dramatist and novelist whose plays achieved widespread success in both Europe and the United States in the 1960s. He is often associated with the "Theater of Fact" movement.

The son of a textile manufacturer who was Jewish by origin but Christian by conversion, Weiss was brought up a Lutheran. In 1934 he and his family were forced into exile by Nazi persecution. He lived in England, Switzerland, and Czechoslovakia before settling, in 1939, in Sweden. He painted and made films (which showed the influence of the Surrealists) and also illustrated a Swedish edition of *The Thousand and One Nights*. Later he turned to fiction and drama. He wrote his earliest works in Swedish, but he soon began publishing in German. His initial literary influence was Franz Kafka, whose dreamlike world of subtle menace and frustration impressed Weiss. An important later influence was the American writer Henry Miller.

Weiss's MARAT/SADE (1964) pits the ideals of individualism and of revolution against each other in a setting in which madness and reason seem inseparable. *Die Ermittlung* (1965; *The Investigation*) is a documentary drama re-creating the Frankfurt trials of the men who carried out mass murders at Auschwitz; at the same time, it attacks later German hypocrisy over the existence of concentration camps and investigates the root causes of aggression.

Weiss's other plays include documentary dramas attacking Portuguese imperialism in Angola, *Gesang vom lusitanischen Popanz* (1967; *Song of the Lusitanian Bogey*), and the destructiveness of American policy in the Vietnam War, *Viet Nam Diskurs* (1968; *Discourse on Vietnam*). Weiss wrote three semi-autobiographical novels, *Der Schatten des Körpers des Kutschers* (1960; *The Shadow of the Coachman's Body*), *Abschied von den Eltern* (1961; *The Leavetaking*), and *Fluchtpunkt* (1962; in *Exile*). The latter did much to establish him in Germany, especially when it won a literary prize in 1963.

Weissnichtwo \'vīs-,nikt-,vō\ An indefinite, unknown, or imaginary place. The word is derived from the name of the imaginary city in Thomas Carlyle's satirical work SARTOR RESARTUS. In German it means "(I) know not where."

Welch \'welch, 'welsh\, Denton (b. March 27, 1915, Shanghai, China—d. Dec. 30, 1948, Middle Orchard, near Borough Green, Kent, Eng.) English painter and novelist chiefly remembered for two imaginative novels of adolescence, *Maiden Voyage* (1943) and *In Youth Is Pleasure* (1944).

Welch was educated at Repton School in Derbyshire. After a visit to China he studied painting at the Goldsmith School of Art. In 1935, while still at school, he was severely injured in a cycling accident that left him an invalid for the rest of his life; but he continued painting, exhibiting frequently at the Leicester galleries, and began his career as a writer.

Only two of his novels and a volume of short stories, *Brave and Cruel* (1946), were published during his lifetime. Those published posthumously include *A Voice Through a Cloud* (1950), considered by many his best novel; *Journals* (1952); *I Left My Grandfather's House* (1958), which is only a rough draft; and *Denton Welch—Selections from His Published Works* (1963), which contains a notable introduction by Jocelyn Brooke.

Weldon \'wel-dən\, Fay, *original name* Franklin Birkinshaw \'bər-kən-,shȯ\ (b. Sept. 22, 1931?, Alvechurch, Worcestershire, Eng.) British novelist, playwright, and scriptwriter known for her thoughtful and witty stories of contemporary women.

Weldon grew up in New Zealand, attended St. Andrew's University in Scotland, and became an advertising copywriter in London. In the mid-1960s she began writing plays. Her first novel, *The Fat Woman's Joke* (1967; U.S. title, *. . . And the Wife Ran Away*), grew out of her 1966 television play *The Fat Woman's Tale*. The novels *Down Among the Women* (1971), *Female Friends* (1974), and *Remember Me* (1976) focus on various women's reactions to male-and-female relationships. *Praxis* (1978) was noted for the development of its heroine, who endures in the face of repeated disasters. *Puffball* (1980), a novel about motherhood, combines supernatural elements with technical information about pregnancy. *The Life and Loves of a She-Devil* (1983) is critical of the roles both men and women play in supporting the ideal image of feminine beauty.

Weldon successfully adapted several books, including her own, into television programs. Some of her other works include the radio plays *Spider* (1973) and *Polaris* (1978) and the stage plays *Words of Advice* (1974) and *Action Replay* (1979). Among her other novels are *The President's Child* (1982), *The Cloning of Joanna May* (1989), *Darcy's Utopia* (1990), *Growing Rich* (1992), and *Affliction* (1993; U.S. title, *Trouble*).

Welhaven \'vel-,hä-vən\, Johan Sebastian Cammermeyer (b. Dec. 22, 1807, Bergen, Nor.—d. Oct. 21, 1873, Christiania [now Oslo]) Norwegian poet and critic who attacked the crudity and extreme nationalism of many of his contemporaries, particularly the nationalist poet Henrik Wergeland, who advocated Norway's complete cultural independence from Denmark; their feud is the most famous in Norwegian literature.

Welhaven began but later abandoned the study of theology. He earned a meager living by tutoring and drawing to support his writing. He was above all a lyric poet and is remembered for his *Norges dæmering* (1834; "The Dawn of Norway"), a sonnet cycle attacking his contemporaries, and "Digtets aand" ("The Spirit of Poetry"), a short verse treatise. He later became professor of philosophy at King Frederick's University (now the University of Oslo). Welhaven sought to promote national progress by means of education and artistic refinement. He insisted that culture is indivisible and urged that whatever is valuable in Danish tradition be retained. His concepts of form and unity in art were very conservative. He was thus unable to recognize in Wergeland's poetry the breadth of spirit beneath its apparent surface crudity and was outraged by Wergeland's inclusion of words from Norwegian dialects in an otherwise Danish text.

Weller, Sam \'sam-'wel-ər\ Fictional character, a humorous Cockney bootblack who becomes Mr. Pickwick's devoted companion and servant in THE PICKWICK PAPERS by Charles Dickens.

Wellerism \'wel-ər-,iz-əm\ An expression of comparison comprising a usually well-known quotation followed by a facetious sequel (such as "every one to his own taste," said the old woman as she kissed the cow). The term is derived from the sayings of Sam Weller, a character in Charles Dickens' novel *The Pickwick Papers*.

well-made play *French* pièce bien faite \,pyes-byeⁿ-'fet\ A play constructed according to certain strict technical principles and aiming at neatness of plot and theatrical effectiveness. The form dominated the stages of Europe and the United States for most of the 19th century.

The technical formula of the well-made play, developed about 1825 by the French playwright Eugène Scribe, called for complex and highly artificial plotting, a build-up of suspense, a climactic scene in which all problems are resolved, and

DECLINE AND FALL (1928), VILE BODIES (1930), BLACK MISCHIEF (1932), A HANDFUL OF DUST (1934), and SCOOP (1938). A later work in that vein is THE LOVED ONE (1948), a satire on the morticians' industry in California.

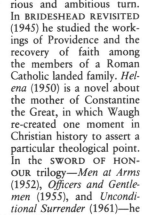

Culver Pictures

During the war Waugh's writing took a more serious and ambitious turn. In BRIDESHEAD REVISITED (1945) he studied the workings of Providence and the recovery of faith among the members of a Roman Catholic landed family. *Helena* (1950) is a novel about the mother of Constantine the Great, in which Waugh re-created one moment in Christian history to assert a particular theological point. In the SWORD OF HONOUR trilogy—*Men at Arms* (1952), *Officers and Gentlemen* (1955), and *Unconditional Surrender* (1961)—he analyzed the character of World War II, in particular its relationship with the eternal struggle between good and evil and the temporal struggle between civilization and barbarism.

Waugh also wrote travel books, as well as lives of Dante Gabriel Rossetti (1928), the martyred Jesuit Edmund Campion (1935), and theologian Ronald Knox (1959), and the first part of an autobiography, *A Little Learning* (1964). Waugh's letters were published in 1980.

Waverley Novels, The \'wā-vər-lē\ A series of more than two dozen historical novels published by Sir Walter SCOTT between 1814 and 1832. Although the novels were extremely popular and strongly promoted at the time, he did not publicly reveal his authorship of them until 1827. Notable works in the series include *Waverley* (1814), *Guy Mannering* (1815), ROB ROY (1817), THE HEART OF MIDLOTHIAN (1818), IVANHOE (1819), KENILWORTH (1821), QUENTIN DURWARD (1823), and *Redgauntlet* (1824). Some of the novels were originally published in a four-part series entitled *Tales of My Landlord*. All the stories were published together in a 48-volume series called *Waverley Novels* (1829–33), containing Scott's prefaces and final revisions but completed after his death. The series influenced generations of writers and earned Scott his reputation as the founder of the historical novel.

Scott's early Waverley books deal with several different phases of Scottish history and were noted for their characterizations of ordinary people and their use of regional Scottish dialect. These novels often concern the clash between heroic traditions of the past and practical visions of the future. *Waverley*, for example, treats the tensions between the Jacobites and the Hanoverians in the mid-18th century, while *The Heart of Midlothian* addresses the social conflict following the Porteous Riots of 1736 over the execution of a smuggler. Scott set his other novels in historical periods dating to the Middle Ages in locales such as England, France, Palestine, and the Orkney Islands.

Waves, The Experimental novel by Virginia WOOLF, published in 1931. *The Waves* was one of her most inventive and complex books. It reflects Woolf's greater concern with capturing the poetic rhythm of life than with maintaining a traditional focus on character and plot. Composed of dramatic (and sometimes narrative) monologues, the novel traces six friends through seven stages of their lives, from childhood to old age, by making parallels to the changing position of the sun and the tides.

Waxman \'väks-mən, 'waks-\, Meyer (b. 1887, Slutsk, Russia [now in Belarus]—d. March 7, 1969, Miami Beach, Fla., U.S.) Jewish literary historian, rabbi, educator, and scholar.

Trained in Ḥasidic seminaries in Mir and Slutsk, Waxman continued his studies, after immigrating to the United States in 1905, at New York University, Columbia University, and at the Jewish Theological Seminary, where he was ordained in 1913. In 1917 he founded the Teachers Institute of Mizrachi, later affiliated with Yeshiva College (renamed Yeshiva University), New York City. In 1925 he was appointed professor of Hebrew literature and philosophy at Hebrew Theological College, Skokie, Ill., where he remained until 1955, when he retired to New York City to continue his scholarly work.

Waxman's principal work is the monumental *History of Jewish Literature*, 4 vol. (1930–41), in which he summarizes and evaluates the various fields of Jewish literature from the end of biblical times to the mid-20th century. His religious studies include the *Handbook of Judaism* (1947) and *Judaism—Religion and Ethics* (1958), which were regarded as standard works. Many of his hundreds of articles in English, Hebrew, and Yiddish on the history of Jewish thought and the history of Jewish literature are in *Ketavim nivḥarim*, 2 vol. (1943–44; "Special Masterpieces"), *Galut ve-ge'ulah* (1952; "Diaspora and Return"), and *Moreh ha-dorot* (1963; "Teacher of the Generations"). Among his early works are *Philosophy of Don Hasdai Crescas* (1920) and a translation of Moses Hess's *Rome and Jerusalem* (1918).

Wayland or **Weland** \'wā-lənd, -,land; 'vā-,länt\ the Smith. In Scandinavian, German, and Anglo-Saxon legend, a smith of outstanding skill. He was, according to some legends, a lord of the elves. His story is told in the *Völundarkvitha*, one of the poems in the 13th-century Icelandic *Elder Edda* (*Poetic Edda*), and, with variations, in the mid-13th-century Icelandic prose *Thithriks saga*. He is also mentioned in *Beowulf*, in the Anglo-Saxon poems "Waldere" and "Deor," and in a note inserted by Alfred the Great into his 9th-century translation of Boethius.

Wayland was captured by the Swedish king Nídud (Nithad, or Níduth), lamed to prevent his escape, and forced to work in the king's smithy. In revenge, he killed the king's two young sons and made drinking bowls from their skulls, which he sent to their father. He also raped their sister, Bödvild, when she brought a gold ring to be mended, and then he escaped by magical flight through the air.

Way of All Flesh, The Autobiographical novel by Samuel BUTLER, published posthumously in 1903 though written almost two decades earlier.

Beginning with the life of John Pontifex, a carpenter, the novel traces four generations of the Pontifex family, each of which perpetuates the frustration and unhappiness of its predecessor largely as a result of parental repression. Only Ernest Pontifex, the great-grandson of John, is able to break the cycle. After being ordained a minister, serving a prison term because of a naive misunderstanding, and unwittingly entering into a bigamous marriage with the family's sluttish servant girl, Ernest providentially inherits enough money from a favorite aunt to change his life and become a writer.

Way of the World, The Comedy of manners in five acts by William CONGREVE, performed and published in 1700. The play, which is considered Congreve's masterpiece, ridicules the assumptions that governed the society of his time, especially those concerning love and marriage. The plot concerns the efforts of the lovers Millamant and Mirabell to obtain the permission of Millamant's aunt for their marriage. Despite a scheme that goes awry and after several misunderstandings are cleared up, the two finally obtain her consent.

Way We Live Now, The Novel by Anthony TROLLOPE, published serially in 1874–75 and in book form in 1875. This satire of Victorian society was one of Trollope's later and more highly regarded works.

The novel chronicles the fleeting fame of Augustus Melmotte, a villainous financier of obscure origins who briefly captivates the aristocratic society of London with his image as a man of wealth and prestige. Lady Matilda Carbury, mother of the incompetent Felix, is a novelist who prefers popularity to critical acclaim. Marie Melmotte, Hetta Carbury, and Georgiana Longstaffe struggle to negotiate the mutable marketplace of marriage. Some critics view the virtuous and nostalgic Roger Carbury as Trollope's mouthpiece, voicing concern over the selfishness of other characters.

Ważyk \'vá-zhik\, Adam (b. Nov. 17, 1905, Warsaw, Pol.—d. Aug. 13, 1982, Warsaw) Polish poet and novelist who began his career as a propagandist for but ended as a fierce opponent of Stalinism.

Ważyk's earliest volumes of poetry, *Semafory* (1924; "Semaphores") and *Oczy i usta* (1926; "Eyes and Lips"), were written between the ages of 17 and 20 and reflect the instability of life after World War I and the pervasive sense of loss left in its wake. Ważyk became a social activist during the 1930s and was jailed for his beliefs from 1932 to 1939. Exiled to the Soviet Union during World War II, he became a confirmed Marxist. After his return to Poland, Ważyk devoted himself to the communist cause. Named the "poet laureate of the 'People's Poland'," he was also the editor from 1946 to 1950 of *Kuźnica* ("The Anvil") and from 1950 to 1954 of the literary journal *Twórczość*.

In the mid-1950s Ważyk was sent to Kraków to write an article about a nearby industrial town. His observations there led him to become a fierce opponent of Stalin, and these feelings were expressed in "Poemat dla dorosłych" ("A Poem for Adults"), published in the journal *Nowa kultura* in 1955. This poem in 15 parts makes a plea for freedom and in one of many powerful images refers to people being forced to swallow brine they are told is lemonade. The poem had a huge political impact; although the government tried to suppress it, copies were passed from hand to hand in Poland and Hungary, students rioted, and Ważyk became a hero.

Weavers, The Naturalistic drama in five acts by Gerhart HAUPTMANN, published in 1892 and performed in 1893 as *Die Weber*. The play is based on the revolt of the Silesian weavers of 1844 and portrays in a starkly realistic manner the human cost of the Industrial Revolution.

The work reveals how, reduced to destitution because of the introduction of power looms, the weavers are driven to revolt. They march on the home of Dreissiger, their arrogant, exploitive employer, sack his house, and achieve a temporary victory over a company of armed soldiers.

Web and the Rock, The Novel by Thomas WOLFE, published posthumously in 1939 after being reworked by editor Edward Aswell from a larger manuscript. Like Wolfe's other novels, *The Web and the Rock* is an autobiographical account of a successful young writer from North Carolina living in New York City in the early 20th century.

The main character, George Webber, bears many similarities to Eugene Gant, the soul-searching protagonist of Wolfe's earlier novels *Look Homeward, Angel* (1929) and *Of Time and The River* (1935). Esther Jack, who first appeared in *Of Time and the River*, is an urban sophisticate who becomes Webber's lover and muse. *The Web and the Rock* has been criticized for its inconsistent style but praised for its poetry and passion. Its sequel is *You Can't Go Home Again* (1940).

Webb \'web\, Mary (Gladys), *original surname* Meredith \'mer-ə-dith\ (b. March 25, 1881, Leighton-under-the-Wrekin, Shropshire, Eng.—d. Oct. 8, 1927, St. Leonards, Sussex) English novelist who is best known for PRECIOUS BANE (1924). Webb's lyrical style conveys a rich and intense impression of her native Shropshire countryside and its people. Her love of nature and the sense of impending doom within her novels invite comparison with those same qualities in the works of Thomas Hardy.

Mary Meredith was educated in Southport. In 1912 she married Henry Webb, a schoolteacher, and except for her last six years (which were spent in London), the Webbs lived in Shropshire. Her other works include *The Golden Arrow* (1916), *Gone to Earth* (1917), *The House in Dormer Forest* (1920), *Seven for a Secret* (1922), and the unfinished historical novel *Armour Wherein He Trusted* (1929). Her *Fifty-One Poems* appeared posthumously in 1946.

Webster \'web-stər\, John (b. *c.* 1580—d. *c.* 1625) English dramatist whose THE WHITE DEVIL (1612) and THE DUCHESS OF MALFI (1623) are generally regarded as the paramount 17th-century English tragedies apart from those of William Shakespeare.

Little is known of Webster's life. His preface to *Monuments of Honor*, his Lord Mayor's Show for 1624, says he was born a freeman of the Merchant Taylors Company. Possibly he was an actor who became a playwright later in life. He may be the John Webster mentioned among the English comedians under Robert Browne in the service (1595) of the German Landgrave Maurice of Hesse-Kassel, or the John Webster who was admitted to the Middle Temple in 1598. He was probably dead by 1634. Apart from his two major plays and *Appius and Virginia* (*c.* 1608; published 1654) and *The Devils Law Case* (*c.* 1620; published 1623), his dramatic work consists of collaborations (not all extant) with leading writers, including Thomas Dekker (chiefly), Thomas Middleton, Michael Drayton, John Ford, and perhaps Philip Massinger. Eight extant plays and some nondramatic verse and prose are wholly or partly his; the most standard edition is *The Complete Works of John Webster*, 4 vol. (1927).

Wedekind \'vā-də-ˌkint\, Frank, *in full* Benjamin Franklin Wedekind (b. July 24, 1864, Hannover, Hanover [Germany]—d. March 9, 1918, Munich, Ger.) Actor and dramatist, an intense force in the German artistic world on the eve of World War I. A direct forebear of the modern Theater of the Absurd, Wedekind used episodic scenes, fragmented dialogue, distortion, and caricature in his dramas, which formed the transition from the realism of his age to the Expressionism of the next generation.

Bavaria-Verlag

Wedekind lived in Switzerland from 1872 to 1884, when he moved to Munich, his home until his death. He was successively an advertising manager, a secretary of a circus, a journalist for the satirical weekly *Simplicissimus*, a cabaret performer, and the producer of his own plays. The electric quality of his personality has been attested by his contemporaries.

The characteristic theme in Wedekind's dramas was the antagonism between the elemental force of sex and the philistinism of society. In 1891 the publication of his tragedy *Frühlings Erwachen* (*The Awakening of Spring*) created a scandal. Successfully produced by Max Reinhardt in 1905, the play is a series of brief scenes, some poetic and tender, others harsh and frank, dealing with the awakening of sexuality in three adolescents. In the *Lulu* cycle, *Erdgeist* (1895; EARTH SPIRIT) and *Die Büchse der Pandora* (1904; PANDORA'S BOX), he extended the theme of sex to the underworld of society and introduced the eternal, amoral femme fatale Lulu, who is destroyed in the tragic conflict of sexual freedom with hypocritical bourgeois morality.

Wedekind's other plays include *Der Kammersänger* (1899; *The Court Singer*), *Marquis von Keith* (1901); *The Marquis of Keith*), *So ist das Leben* (1902; *Such Is Life*), *Hidalla* (1904), and *Franziska* (1912). He also wrote poetry, novels, songs, and essays. His diary was posthumously published as *Die Tagebücher: ein erotisches Leben* (1986; *Diary of an Erotic Life*).

wedge verse *see* RHOPALIC.

wee folk Collective nickname for fairies. *See* FAIRY.

Week on the Concord and Merrimack Rivers, A \'käŋ-kərd, 'käŋ-, -ˌkȯrd . . . 'mer-i-ˌmak\ Autobiographical narrative by Henry David THOREAU, published in 1849. This Transcendental work is a philosophical treatise couched as a travel adventure.

Written mainly during the two years he lived in a cabin on the shores of Walden Pond in Massachusetts (1845–47), *A Week on the Concord and Merrimack Rivers* chronicles a boating trip Thoreau took with his brother John to the White Mountains in New Hampshire in 1839. Comprising both prose and poetry, the book includes romantic descriptions of the natural environment and thoughtful digressions on philosophy, literature, and history. Like *Walden* (1854), Thoreau's masterwork, *A Week on the Concord and Merrimack Rivers* achieved fame only after the author's death.

weight \'wāt\ In prosody, stress value or quantity of individual sounds, syllables, and units of rhythmic structure in verse.

Weil \'vei, *Angl* 'vā\, Simone (b. Feb. 3, 1909, Paris, Fr.—d. Aug. 24, 1943, Ashford, Kent, Eng.) French mystic, social philosopher, and activist in the French Resistance during World War II, whose posthumously published works had particular influence on French and English social thought.

Intellectually precocious, Weil also expressed social awareness at an early age. She studied philosophy, classical philology, and science and taught philosophy at a number of schools; she often clashed with school boards over her social activism.

To learn the psychological effects of heavy industrial labor, she took a job in a factory in 1934–35. Her experience caused her to renounce all hope for social revolution. In 1936 she joined an anarchist unit in the Spanish Civil War.

Soon thereafter Weil had the first of several mystical experiences. She subsequently came to view her social concerns as "ersatz Divinity." Though born of Jewish parents, she was considered by some critics to be almost anti-Semitic in her religious writings, which abound in paradox. She tended toward the existential Christianity prefigured by Søren Kierkegaard.

After the German occupation of Paris during World War II, Weil moved to Marseille, where she wrote for *Cahiers du Sud* and other journals related to the French Resistance. She accompanied her parents to the United States in 1942 but then went to England to work with the Resistance. Weil's death, officially a suicide, was the result of voluntary starvation undertaken to identify herself with her French compatriots under German occupation.

The Iliad; or, The Poem of Force, translated by Mary McCarthy and published by *Politics* magazine in 1945, was the first of Weil's works to be read in English translation. *La Pesanteur et la grâce* (1947; *Gravity and Grace*), is her major work. Among her other books are *L'Enracinement* (1949; *The Need for Roots*), about her factory experiences; *Attente de Dieu* (1950; *Waiting for God*), a spiritual autobiography; *Cahiers* (1951; *Notebooks*); and *Intuitions pré-chrétiennes* (1951; *Intimations of Christianity Among the Ancient Greeks*).

Weinheber \'vīn-ˌhā-bər\, Josef (b. March 9, 1892, Vienna [Austria]—d. April 9, 1945, Vienna) Austrian poet noted for his technical mastery.

Weinheber's early books—*Von beiden Ufern* (1923; "From Both Shores"), the autobiographical *Das Weisenhaus* (1924; "The Orphanage"), and *Boot in der Bucht* (1926, "Boat in the Bay")—had little success, but he achieved fame with *Adel und Untergang* (1932, enlarged 1934; "Nobleness and Extinction"), a sonnet sequence using the repeated, interlocking lines of terza rima. *Späte Krone* (1936; "Belated Crown") indicated his feelings about his late success; in it he used his key imagery of night and dark forces.

Weinheber had great range, composing verse forms as varied as Viennese popular songs, metaphysical poems, sonnet cycles, odes, and elegies. His own style developed synthetically, borrowing elements of classical and modern forms. His belief that poetic language embodies the essence of the *Volk* ("people") rather than of the individual made him a favorite poet of the Nazis. Weinheber's other important works include *Wien wörtlich* (1935; "Vienna Revealed in Words"), which cast the poet in the role of peoples' singer; *O Mensch, gib acht* (1937; "Hearken, Ye Men"), vignettes and songs using folk tunes; *Kammermusik* (1939; "Chamber Music"); *Zwischen Göttern und Dämonen* (1938; "Between Gods and Demons"), four odes on the poet's vision of reality; and *Hier ist das Wort* (posthumously published 1947; "Here Is the Word"). He committed suicide as the Soviet Red Army approached Vienna in 1945. For a time after World War II his books were proscribed by the Austrian government, but his complete works appeared in five volumes in 1953–56.

weird \'wird\ Fate or destiny, a now archaic word that originated and survived longest in Scots and northern English dialects.

Weird Sister A compound used by Scots writers as a sobriquet for the Fates of Greek and Roman myth. Through its appearance in Raphael Holinshed's *Chronicles*, the expression passed to William Shakespeare, who used it in *Macbeth* for the three witches who prophesy the destinies of the main characters. *See also* FATE; NORN.

Weir of Hermiston \'wir . . . 'hər-mis-tən\ (*in full* Weir of Hermiston: An Unfinished Romance) Fragment of an uncompleted novel by Robert Louis STEVENSON, published posthumously in 1896.

The novel relates the story of Adam Weir, a strict Scottish judge who banishes his rebellious son Archie to their moorland estate of Hermiston for publicly disagreeing with one of his father's sentences. Stevenson's story breaks off after Kirstie Elliott severs her love affair with Archie because she has heard vicious tales of his life. Based on notes that Stevenson left, the novel would have continued with Archie killing the friend who betrayed him to Kirstie and being sentenced by his own father to die for this crime. Stevenson used the novel in part

a happy ending. Conventional romantic conflicts were a staple subject of such plays (for example, the problem of a pretty girl who must choose between a wealthy, unscrupulous suitor and a poor but honest young man). Suspense was created by misunderstandings between characters, mistaken identities, secret information (the poor young man is really of noble birth), lost or stolen documents, and similar contrivances. Later critics, such as Émile Zola and George Bernard Shaw, denounced Scribe's work and that of his successor, Victorien Sardou, for exalting the mechanics of playmaking at the expense of honest characterizations and serious content, but both men's plays were enormously popular in their day. Scribe, with the aid of hack assistants, wrote literally hundreds of plays that were translated, adapted, and imitated all over Europe. In England the well-made play was taken up by such practitioners as Wilkie Collins, who summed up the formula succinctly: "Make 'em laugh; make 'em weep; make 'em wait." Henry Arthur Jones and Arthur Pinero used the technique successfully, with somewhat improved characterizations and emotional tension, and Pinero actually brought it to the level of art with *The Second Mrs. Tanqueray* in 1893. The polished techniques of the well-made play were also turned to serious purposes in the plays of Émile Augier and Alexandre Dumas *fils*, which dealt with social conditions such as prostitution and the emancipation of women and are regarded as the precursors of the PROBLEM PLAY.

Wells \'welz\, Charles Jeremiah (b. 1800?, London, Eng.—d. Feb. 17, 1879, Marseille, Fr.)   English writer, author of *Joseph and His Brethren* (1823), a long dramatic poem in the style of the Elizabethan dramatists. It enjoyed an immense vogue among the Pre-Raphaelites and their followers after it was praised first by Dante Gabriel Rossetti and then, in 1875, by Algernon Charles Swinburne.

As a young man, Wells was a member of the poet John Keats's circle of literary friends. He abandoned a legal career from boredom and ill health, leaving England in 1840 for France. He lectured in English in Brittany and finally settled in Marseille.

Wells \'welz\, H.G., *in full* Herbert George (b. Sept. 21, 1866, Bromley, Kent, Eng.—d. Aug. 13, 1946, London)   English novelist, journalist, sociologist, and historian, best known for his science-fiction novels.

Wells received a scholarship to the Normal School of Science in London, where he formulated a romantic conception of science that would inspire many of his novels. His first attempt at fiction writing was merely imitative, but he eventually set himself up as a freelance writer. Almost immediately he became a successful journalist and short-story writer, the possessor of a lively and humorous style and the exponent in fiction of the relatively new subject of science. The hugely popular THE TIME MACHINE (1895) was followed by a succession of striking scientific fantasies, including THE INVISIBLE MAN (1897) and THE WAR OF THE WORLDS (1898). Soon he was able to retire to the country to become a full-time novelist.

Beneath Wells's inventiveness lay a passionate concern for humanity and society. This was reflected in his successful nonfiction work on social progress, *Anticipations* (1901), which in turn led to his joining the socialist Fabian Society in London. Wells eventually quarreled with the society's leaders, George Bernard Shaw and Sidney and Beatrice Webb. Thinly disguised, these experiences are the source for *Ann Veronica* (1909), a novel that depicts his own passionate love for Amber Reeves, a gifted younger Fabian. The story is retold in *The New Machiavelli* (1911), in which the Webbs are parodied as the Baileys. This period also saw Wells abandon science fiction for sym-

pathetic comic novels of lower-middle-class life, including *The History of Mr. Polly* (1910), and the social novel, notably TONO-BUNGAY (1908).

At the outbreak of war in 1914, Wells was involved in a love affair with the young English author Rebecca West. By his own admission, this experience was a major influence on his work and life.

Karsh—Rapho/Photo Researchers

In 1915 he published *Boon*, which included a wickedly spiteful parody of Henry James that brought Wells into deep disgrace with the literary establishment.

Wells threw himself into a number of nonfiction works, including the popular *The Outline of History* (1920; rev. ed., 1931), *The Science of Life* (1929–30), and *The Work, Wealth and Happiness of Mankind* (1931), the latter two written with collaborators. *Experiment in Autobiography*, a masterpiece of self-revelation, appeared in 1934. With occasional exceptions, however, his outlook and his works grew steadily less optimistic and even bitter.

Other works include the fictional *Tales of Space and Time* (1899), *The Food of the Gods* (1904), and *Mr. Britling Sees It Through* (1916) and the nonfictional *Mind at the End of Its Tether* (1945).

Welsh literary renaissance   Literary activity in Wales and England in the mid-18th century that attempted to stimulate interest in the Welsh language and in the classical bardic verse forms of Wales. The movement centered on Lewis, Richard, and William Morris, a family of Welsh scholars who preserved ancient texts and encouraged contemporary poets to use the strict meters of the ancient Welsh bards. Other scholars also collected and copied bardic manuscripts, laying the groundwork for later research. A new classical school of poetry was led by Goronwy Owen, a poet who wrote verse modeled on that of the medieval bards. The Cymmrodorion Society, established by the Welsh community in London as a center for Welsh literary studies, combined with other such scholarly groups to encourage the reestablishment of local eisteddfods (poetic assemblies or contests). As a result, the National Eisteddfod was revived in the early 19th century.

A great number of publications, popular as well as scholarly, resulted from the revival, which also produced religious verse in free meters, lyrical hymns, popular ballads employing cynghanedd (a complex system of accentuation, alliteration, and internal rhyme), and verse dramas based on historical tales, incidents from the Bible, and Welsh mythology and legend.

By the 19th century the arts in Wales had become almost totally dominated by English culture, and the revival subsided. A second revival, based on the scholarly groundwork of the first, occurred at the end of the 19th century, centered in the newly established University of Wales. It brought careful scholarship to bear on the study of ancient texts.

weltschmerz \'velt-ˌshmerts\ [German, from *Welt* world + *Schmerz* pain, grief]   A feeling of melancholy and pessimism or of vague yearning and discontent caused by comparison of the actual state of the world with an ideal state. The term has been used in reference to individuals as well as to the prevailing mood of a whole generation or specific group of people. It is particularly associated with the poets of the Romantic era who refused or were unable to adjust to those realities of the world that they saw as destructive of their right to personal freedom—a phenomenon thought to typify Romanticism. The word was coined by Jean Paul in his pessimistic novel *Selina* (1827) to describe Lord Byron's discontent (especially as shown in *Manfred* and *Childe Harold's Pilgrimage*). In France, where it was called the *mal du siècle*, weltschmerz was expressed during this period by the Viscount de Chateaubriand, Alfred de Vigny, and Alfred de Musset; in Russia by Aleksandr Pushkin and Mikhail Lermontov; in Poland by Juliusz Słowacki; and in America by Nathaniel Hawthorne.

Welty \'wel-tē\, Eudora (b. April 13, 1909, Jackson, Miss., U.S.) American short-story writer and novelist whose work is focused with great precision on the regional manners of people inhabiting a small Mississippi town that resembles her own birthplace and the Delta country.

Welty was educated at the Mississippi State College for Women in Columbus, the University of Wisconsin, and the Columbia University School of Advertising in New York City. During the Great Depression she worked as a photographer on the Works Progress Administration's guide to Mississippi, and photography remained a lifelong interest. She also worked as a writer for a Jackson radio station and newspaper before her fiction won critical acclaim. Her readership grew steadily after the publication of *A Curtain of Green* (1941; enlarged 1979), a volume of short stories that contained two of her most anthologized stories—"Petrified Man" and WHY I LIVE AT THE P.O. Her novels include *The Robber Bridegroom* (1942), DELTA WEDDING (1946), THE PONDER HEART (1954), *Losing Battles* (1970), and THE OPTIMIST'S DAUGHTER (1972), which won a Pulitzer Prize. THE WIDE NET (1943), THE GOLDEN APPLES (1949), and THE BRIDE OF THE INNISFALLEN (1955) are collections of short stories, and *The Eye of the Story* (1978) is a volume of essays. *The Collected Stories of Eudora Welty* was published in 1980.

Welty's main subject is the intricacies of human relationships, particularly as revealed through her characters' interactions in intimate social encounters. Among her themes are the subjectivity and ambiguity of people's perception of character and the presence of virtue hidden beneath an obscuring surface of convention, insensitivity, and social prejudice. Welty's outlook is hopeful, and love is viewed as a redeeming presence in the midst of isolation and indifference. Her works combine humor and psychological acuity with a sharp ear for regional speech patterns.

One Writer's Beginnings, an autobiographical work, was published in 1984. Originating in a series of three lectures given at Harvard, it beautifully evoked what Welty styled her "sheltered life" in Jackson, Miss., and how her early fiction grew out of it.

Wendt \'went\, Albert (b. Oct. 27, 1939, Apia, Western Samoa) Samoan novelist and poet who wrote about present-day Samoan life and, in contemporizing Samoan myths, discovered how the old ways illuminate the present. Perhaps the best-known writer in the South Pacific, Wendt sought to redress the frequently romanticized, often racist literature about Polynesians that had been written by outsiders.

Wendt was educated at Victoria University, New Zealand. He edited several collections of modern poetry, including *Lali, A Pacific Anthology* (1980), and promoted the culture and arts of the Pacific Islands. In 1977 Wendt established in Western Samoa a branch of the University of the South Pacific. He

taught at colleges and universities in Western Samoa, Fiji, and New Zealand.

Wendt synthesized the history, myths, and other oral traditions with contemporary written fiction, unifying them with his unique vision. His fiction portrayed the traditions and mores of the *papalagi* (people descended from Europeans) and depicted their effect on Samoan culture. An early example of this theme appears in *Sons for the Return Home* (1973), his first novel. Other novels include *Pouliuli* (1977), which is a Polynesian version of *King Lear*, and a Samoan family saga, *Leaves of the Banyan Tree* (1979). Short-story collections include *Flying-Fox in a Freedom Tree* (1974) and *The Birth and Death of the Miracle Man* (1986). Wendt's poetry was collected in *Inside Us the Dead: Poems 1961 to 1974* (1976) and *Shaman of Visions* (1984).

Wen Tingyun or **Wen T'ing-yün** \'wən-'tiŋ-'yūen\, *original name* Wen Qi \'shē\ (b. 812, Taiyuan [now in Shanxi province], China—d. c. 870, China) Chinese lyric poet of the late Tang dynasty who helped to establish a new style of versification associated with the *ci* form, which flourished in the subsequent Song dynasty. His courtesy name (*zi*) was Feiqing.

Wen was born into an aristocratic family. This circumstance allowed him a life of leisure, and he frequented the urban amusement quarters to collect the ballads sung by professional female singers (called "flowers") in the wineshops and brothels of the day. These he used as models for his own love lyrics. Admired for the delicate sensuality of his verse and his skill at evoking feminine sensibility, Wen was chosen as the lead poet in the first major anthology of *ci* poetry, the *Hua jian ji* ("Among the Flowers"), compiled by Zhao Congzu in 940 to popularize the new genre.

Wentworth, Frederick \'fred-ə-rik-'went-wərth\ Fictional character, a young naval officer who is the hero of Jane Austen's novel PERSUASION.

wenyan [Chinese *wényán*, from *wén* character, writing + *yán* speech] *see* GUWEN.

Weöres \'vœr-əsh\, Sándor (b. June 22, 1913, Szombathely, Hung.—d. Jan. 22, 1989, Budapest) Hungarian poet who wrote imaginative lyrical verse that encompassed a wide range of techniques and metric forms.

Weöres, who published his first poem at the age of 15, graduated from the University of Pécs and worked as a librarian and as a freelance writer. He rejected officially sanctioned Socialist Realism to explore such subjects as Eastern philosophy, Polynesian myths, and children's nursery rhymes. From 1949 to 1964 his poetry was suppressed by the communist government of Hungary, with a few exceptions, such as *A hallgatás tornya* ("The Tower of Silence"), which was published during a brief period of relative freedom prior to the revolution of 1956. After the publication of *Tűzkút* (1964; "The Well of Fire") in Paris, his poetry again was officially tolerated in Hungary. Weöres's later works include *Psyché* (1972), a fictitious collection of 19th-century letters and poems; the poetry collection *Ének a határtalanról* (1980; "Song of the Limitless"); and several verse dramas, which were collected in the volume *Színjátékok* (1983; "Plays"). He also edited *Három veréb hat szemmel* (1977; "Three Sparrows with Six Eyes"), an influential anthology of Hungarian poetry. In 1970 Weöres received the Kossuth Prize, the nation's highest award.

werewolf \'wir-,wu̇lf, 'wer-, 'wər-\ [Old English *werwulf*, from *wer* man + *wulf* wolf] In European folklore, a man who turns into a wolf at night and devours animals, people, or corpses but returns to human form by day. Some werewolves change shape at will; others, in whom the condition is hereditary or acquired by having been bitten by a werewolf, change shape involuntarily under the influence of a full moon. If a werewolf is wounded in wolf form, the wounds will show in his human form and may lead to his detection. The legend of the werewolf was developed from stories of the berserker, a warrior in Norse and Germanic folklore who was particularly savage in battle and who wore animal skins.

In countries in which wolves are not common, the monster may assume the form of another dangerous animal, such as the bear, tiger, or hyena. In French folklore the werewolf is called *loup-garou*. France was particularly afflicted with reports of such creatures in the 16th century, and there were many notable convictions and executions of *loups-garous*.

Werfel \'ver-fəl\, Franz (b. Sept. 10, 1890, Prague, Bohemia, Austro-Hungarian Empire [now in Czech Republic]—d. Aug. 26, 1945, Hollywood, Calif., U.S.) German writer who attained prominence as an Expressionist poet, playwright, and novelist. As a consequence of his experiences with Nazism, he espoused human brotherhood, heroism, and religious faith.

Werfel's first publication was a book of lyric poems. After fighting on the Italian and Galician fronts in World War I, he became antimilitary, took to reciting pacifistic poems in cafés, and was arrested. His playwriting career began in 1916 with an adaptation of Euripides' *Trojan Women*, which had a successful run in Berlin. He turned to fiction in 1924 with *Verdi, Roman der Oper* (*Verdi, A Novel of the Opera*). International fame came with *Die vierzig Tage des Musa Dagh* (1933; *The Forty Days of Musa Dagh*), an epic novel in which Armenian villagers resist savage Turks until rescued by the French.

Keeping ahead of a spreading Nazism, Werfel, a Jew, settled in an old mill in southern France. With the fall of France in 1940 (reflected in his play *Jakobowsky und der Oberst*, written in 1944 and successfully produced in New York City that year as *Jakobowsky and the Colonel*), he decided to flee to the United States. In the course of his journey he found solace in the pilgrimage town of Lourdes, Fr., where St. Bernadette had had visions of the Virgin. He vowed to write about the saint if he ever reached America and kept the vow with *Das Lied von Bernadette* (1941; THE SONG OF BERNADETTE).

Wergeland \'ver-gə-län\, Henrik Arnold (b. June 17, 1808, Kristiansand, Nor.—d. July 12, 1845, Christiania [now Oslo]) Norway's great national poet, symbol of Norway's independence, whose humanitarian activity, revolutionary ideas, and love of freedom made him a legendary figure. In the Norwegian literary world the clash between his faction (the "patriots") and the pro-Danish "intelligentsia" led by Johan Welhaven marked the beginning of an ideological conflict that persisted throughout the century.

Wergeland graduated from the University of Christiania with a degree in theology in 1829. In the 1830s he became involved in the battle for social equality. He gave lectures, distributed books, and established lending libraries. He founded two journals, *For Almuen* ("For the Common People") and *For Arbeiderklassen* ("For the Working Class"), which he edited from 1830 to 1839 and 1839 to 1845, respectively. He also edited a third, *Statsborgeren* ("The Citizen").

Of Wergeland's enormous and varied output, his poetry has stood the test of time. Some of the best-known titles are *Digte, første ring* (1829; "Poems, First Cycle"), *Skabelsen, mennesket og messias* (1830; "Creation, Humanity, and Messiah"), *Spaniolen* (1833; "The Spaniard"), and *Jøden* (1842; "The Jew"). His narrative poems *Jan van Huysums blomsterstykke* (1840; "Jan van Huysum's Flowerpiece") and *Den engelske lods* (1844; "The English Pilot") are often cited as his finest works. Selections from various cycles were translated into English and published in *Poems* (1929, reprinted 1970).

Werther \'ver-tər\ Fictional character, a German Romantic poet who is the melancholy young hero of the novel *Die Leiden des jungen Werthers* (1774; THE SORROWS OF YOUNG WERTHER), by Johann Wolfgang von Goethe.

Wessel \'ves-əl\, Johan Herman (b. Oct. 6, 1742, Jonsrud, near Vestby, Nor.—d. Dec. 29, 1785, Copenhagen, Den.) Norwegian-born Danish writer and wit, known for his epigrams and light verse and for a famous parody of Neoclassical tragedy.

From 1761, when he entered the University of Copenhagen, until his death at 43, Wessel lived the bohemian life of a debt-ridden perpetual student. He was one of the founders (1772) and the outstanding talent of the Norske Selskab ("Norwegian Society"), an influential literary and convivial club of Norwegian students at Copenhagen. Reacting against the early signs of literary Romanticism coming from Germany, the Norwegian students opted for rationalism and chose as their motto "*Vos exemplaria Graeca*" ("Let the Greeks be your models"). Wessel contributed epigrams, verse, and impromptus to the anthologies that the club began to publish in 1775. He aimed his satiric wit at the excesses of both Neoclassicism and Romanticism. His only important long work, *Kierlighed uden strømper* (1772; "Love Without Stockings"), is a "tragedy" in five acts dealing with the theft of an apprentice's stockings on his wedding day. It is written in alexandrines and observes the classical unities to the letter; at the end all the characters die, on the same day and in the same place.

Wessex \'wes-iks\ A fictional region of southwestern England that is the setting of most of the novels of Thomas HARDY, beginning with *Far from the Madding Crowd*. Wessex was largely based on the county of Dorset and its principal town, Dorchester, which Hardy renamed Casterbridge in his stories. Hardy also set several short stories there, including those in *Wessex Tales: Strange, Lively and Commonplace* (1888), and his first collection of poetry was entitled *Wessex Poems and Other Verses* (1898).

West \'west\, Morris Langlo (b. April 26, 1916, Melbourne, Vic., Australia) Australian novelist noted for such best-sellers as *The Devil's Advocate* (1959) and *The Shoes of the Fisherman* (1963).

Educated at the University of Melbourne, West taught as a member of the Christian Brothers Order in New South Wales and Tasmania from 1933 until he joined the army in 1939, having left the order before taking his final vows. In 1943 he was released from the army and shortly thereafter began working for the radio network of *The Herald* in Melbourne. He later became a partner in Australasian Radio Productions, but after 10 years he suffered a breakdown, sold his share of the business, and settled near Sydney as a writer. In 1955 he established himself permanently in Sorrento, Italy. Though West had previously written several novels, his first popular success was *Children of the Sun* (1957), a nonfiction account of the slum children of Naples. It was followed by such novels as *The Devil's Advocate*, *Daughter of Silence* (1961), *The Shoes of the Fisherman*, *The Ambassador* (1965), *The Tower of Babel* (1968), *Summer of the Red Wolf* (1971), *The Navigator* (1976), *Proteus* (1979), *The Clowns of God* (1981), *The World is Made of Glass* (1983), *Cassidy* (1986), and *Lazarus* (1990). West worked with themes of international interest; his best-known books combine religion and intrigue in what have been called "religious thrillers."

West \'west\, Nathanael, *original name* Nathan Weinstein \'wīn-,stīn, -,stēn\ (b. Oct. 17, 1903, New York, N.Y., U.S.—d. Dec. 22, 1940, near El Centro, Calif.) American writer best known for satiric novels of the 1930s.

Of middle-class Jewish immigrant parentage, West graduated from Brown University, Providence, R.I. During a 15-month stay in Paris he completed his first novel, *The Dream Life of Balso Snell*, which tells the story of an odd assortment of grotesque characters inside the Trojan horse. It was published in 1931 in an edition of only 500 copies. After his return to New York, West supported himself by working as a hotel manager, giving free or low-rent rooms to such struggling fellow writers as Dashiell Hammett, James T. Farrell, and Erskine Caldwell. His second novel, MISS LONELYHEARTS (1933), deals with an advice columnist whose manipulative attempts to solace his correspondents end in ironic defeat.

In *A Cool Million* (1934), West effectively mocks the American success dream popularized by Horatio Alger by portraying a hero who slides from bad to worse while doing what he supposes to be the right thing. In his last years West worked as a screenwriter in Hollywood. THE DAY OF THE LOCUST (1939) is, in the opinion of many, the best novel written about Hollywood. It dramatizes the false world and people on the fringes of the movie industry.

West was killed in an automobile accident with his wife, Eileen McKenney, who was the subject of Ruth McKenney's popular book *My Sister Eileen* (1938). Never widely read during his lifetime, West attracted attention after World War II, at first in France, where a successful translation of *Miss Lonelyhearts* appeared in 1946. Publication in 1957 of *The Complete Works of Nathanael West* sparked new interest in West's work in the United States.

West \\'west\\, Rebecca, *in full* Dame Rebecca West, *pseudonym of* Cicily Isabel Andrews \\'an-,drüz\\, *original surname* Fairfield \\'far-,fēld\\ (b. Dec. 21, 1892, London, Eng.—d. March 15, 1983, London)   British journalist, novelist, and critic, perhaps best known for her reports on the Nürnberg trials of war criminals (1945–46).

West was the daughter of an army officer and was educated in Edinburgh after her father's death in 1902. She later trained in London as an actress (taking her pseudonym from a role that she had played in Henrik Ibsen's *Rosmersholm*).

From 1911 she became involved in journalism, contributing frequently to the left-wing press and making a name for herself as a fighter for woman suffrage. In 1916 she published a critical biography of Henry James that revealed something of her lively intellectual curiosity, and she then embarked on her career as a novelist. Among her novels are *The Judge* (1922), *Harriet Hume* (1929), *The Thinking Reed* (1936), *The Fountain Overflows* (1956), and *The Birds Fall Down* (1966). They have attracted much less attention than have her social and cultural writings. In 1937 she visited Yugoslavia and later wrote *Black Lamb and Grey Falcon*, 2 vol. (1942),

E.B. Inc.

an examination of Balkan politics, culture, and history. In 1946 she reported on the trial for treason of Nazi propagandist William Joyce ("Lord Haw-Haw") for *The New Yorker* magazine. Published as *The Meaning of Treason* (1949; rev. ed., 1965), it examined not only the traitor's role in modern society but also that of the intellectual and of the scientist. Later she published a similar collection, *The New Meaning of*

Treason (1964). Her brilliant reports on the Nürnberg trials were collected in *A Train of Powder* (1955). She was created Dame of the British Empire in 1959.

Rebecca West: A Celebration, a selection of her works, was published in 1977, and her personal reflections on the turn of the century, *1900*, was published in 1982. The critic and author Anthony West is the son of Dame Rebecca and the English novelist H.G. Wells.

Westcott \\'west-kət\\, Edward Noyes (b. Sept. 27, 1846, Syracuse, N.Y., U.S.—d. March 31, 1898, Syracuse)   American novelist and banker whose posthumously published novel *David Harum: A Story of American Life* (1898) proved to be immensely popular.

Westcott attended schools in Syracuse until age 16, when he became a junior clerk in a local bank. He devoted the next 30 years of his life to the banking business. In the summer of 1895 Westcott began to write *David Harum* while recuperating in the Adirondacks from tuberculosis. He continued writing the book in Italy and finished it in late 1896 after returning to the United States.

Westcott died six months before the publication of *David Harum*, which became a best-seller. More than 1,000,000 copies of the book were sold in the next four decades. *David Harum* is the story of a shrewd, crusty small-town banker in upstate New York who has an abundant fund of humor, an obvious talent for horse trading, and a strong streak of Yankee decency.

western \\'wes-tərn\\   A genre of novels and short stories that are set in the American West, usually in the period from the 1850s to 1900 when the area was fully opened to white settlers. Though basically an American creation, the western has its counterparts in the gaucho literature of Argentina and even in tales of the settlement of the Australian outback.

The western has as its setting the immense plains, rugged tablelands, and mountain ranges of that portion of the United States lying west of the Mississippi River, in particular the Great Plains and the Southwest. The conflict between white pioneers and Indians and between cattle ranchers and fence-building farmers form two basic themes. Cowboys, the town sheriff, and the U.S. marshal are staple figures. Actual historical persons in the American West have figured prominently: Wild Bill Hickok, Wyatt Earp, and other lawmen, notorious outlaws such as Billy the Kid and Jesse James, and Indian leaders such as Sitting Bull and Geronimo.

In literature, the western story had its beginnings in the first adventure narratives, accounts of the western plainsmen, scouts, buffalo hunters, and trappers. Perhaps the earliest and finest work in this genre was James Fenimore Cooper's *The Prairie* (1827). E.Z.C. Judson (Ned Buntline) wrote dozens of western stories and was responsible for transforming Buffalo Bill into an archetype. Owen Wister wrote the first western that won critical praise, *The Virginian* (1902). By far the best-known and one of the most prolific writers of westerns was Zane Grey, an Ohio dentist who became famous with the classic *Riders of the Purple Sage* in 1912. Another prolific author of westerns was Louis L'Amour.

Notable among the authors of western short stories are A.H. Lewis, Stephen Crane, and Conrad Richter. Many western novels and short stories first appeared in pulp magazines, such as *Ace-High Western Stories* and *Double Action Western*.

Other western classics are Walter van Tilburg Clark's *The Ox-Bow Incident* (1940) and A.B. Guthrie, Jr.'s *The Big Sky* (1947) and *The Way West* (1949). Larry McMurtry's *Lonesome Dove* (1985) was a Pulitzer-Prize winning paean to the bygone cowboy.

Western, Sophia \sō-'fē-ə-'wes-tərn\ Fictional character, the beloved and, eventually, the wife of Tom Jones, hero of Henry Fielding's picaresque novel TOM JONES.

W.H., Mr. Person known only by his initials, to whom the first edition, published in 1609, of William Shakespeare's sonnets was dedicated. The mystery of his identity has tantalized generations of biographers and critics, who have generally argued either that W.H. was also the "Fair Youth" to whom many of the sonnets are addressed or that he was a friend or patron who earned the gratitude of one or both parties by procuring Shakespeare's manuscript for the printer, Thomas Thorpe. Among the names offered for consideration are those of Henry Wriothesley, 3rd Earl of Southampton, and William Herbert, 3rd Earl of Pembroke, with both of whom Shakespeare is believed to have had some connection, albeit slight. Also suggested are William Hatcliffe, who was "lord of misrule" during the celebrations at Gray's Inn (1587–88), and William Hall (a printer) and Sir William Harvey, both of whom could well have conveyed the manuscript to Thorpe.

Whalen \'hwā-lən, 'wā-\, Philip (Glenn) (b. Oct. 20, 1923, Portland, Ore., U.S.) American poet who emerged from the Beat movement of the mid-20th century, known for his wry and innovative poetry.

Whalen served in the U.S. Army from 1943 to 1946 and attended Reed College, Portland, before joining the West Coast's nascent Beat movement. Like other Beats, he was contemptuous of structured, academic writing and was interested in Asian religions, personal freedom, and literary experimentation. Unlike the Beats, however, his poetry was often apolitical, whimsical, and steeped in the quotidian. In 1960 he published *Like I Say* and *Memoirs of an Interglacial Age*, both candid reflections of his "beatnik" life of the late 1950s. His poetry of the 1960s culminated in *Every Day* (1965) and *On Bear's Head* (1969), both of which include thoughtful observations of everyday life. He became an ordained Zen Buddhist priest in 1973, serving at centers in San Francisco and New Mexico. His later collections of poetry include *Decompressions* (1978), *Enough Said* (1980), and *Heavy Breathing* (1983). He also wrote the novels *You Didn't Even Try* (1967) and *Imaginary Speeches for a Brazen Head* (1972).

whangdoodle \hwaŋ-'düd-əl, waŋ-\ [of echoic origin] An imaginary creature of undefined character that figures in tall tales of the American Southwest.

Wharton \'hwȯrt-ən, 'wȯrt-\, Edith (Newbold), *original surname* Jones \'jōnz\ (b. Jan. 24, 1862, New York, N.Y., U.S.—d. Aug. 11, 1937, St.-Brice-sous-Forêt, Fr.) American author best known for her stories and novels about the upper-class society into which she was born.

Wharton was educated privately at home and in Europe. In 1885 she married Edward Wharton, a Boston banker, and a few years later resumed the literary career she had begun tentatively as a young girl. Her major literary model was Henry James, whom she knew, and her work reveals James's concern for form and ethical issues.

The best of her early tales were collected in *The Greater Inclination* (1899). Her novel *The Valley of Decision* was published in 1902, followed in 1905 by the critical and popular success of her novel THE HOUSE OF MIRTH, which established her as a leading writer. After 1907 Wharton lived in France, visiting the United States only at rare intervals. In 1913 she was divorced from her husband.

In the two decades following the publication of *The House of Mirth*—before the quality of her work began to decline under the demands of writing for women's magazines—she wrote such novels as *The Reef* (1912), THE CUSTOM OF THE COUN-

TRY (1913), *Summer* (1917), and the Pulitzer Prize-winning AGE OF INNOCENCE (1920).

Her best-known work, however, was the long tale ETHAN FROME (1911), exploiting the grimmer possibilities of the New England farm life she had observed from her home in Lenox, Mass. She also wrote many short stories and poems, several books of travel reflecting her interest in architecture and landscape gardening, and a manual, *The Writing of Fiction* (1925). Her novel *Twilight Sleep* was a best-seller in 1927.

Bettmann Archive

The most ambitious project of her later years was the novel *Hudson River Bracketed* (1929) and its sequel, *The Gods Arrive* (1932), books comparing the cultures of Europe and the sections of the United States she knew. Her best writing of that period was in the posthumous *The Buccaneers* (1938). Her autobiography, *A Backward Glance*, appeared in 1934.

Wharton \'hwȯrt-ən, 'wȯrt-\, William (b. Philadelphia, Pa.) Pseudonymous novelist best known for his innovative first novel *Birdy* (1979; film, 1984), a critical and popular success.

Wharton wrote under that pseudonym to protect his privacy. Trained as a painter at the University of California at Los Angeles, he worked as an artist for almost 25 years before *Birdy*'s publication. During that time he and his family settled permanently in France.

Autobiographical elements and fantastic characters blend in Wharton's novels. *Birdy* tells of a man with a lifelong obsession with birds. Hospitalized as a result of his service in World War II, Birdy seems to want only to become a bird. Al, another scarred veteran and childhood friend, tries to help him. Wharton's second novel, *Dad* (1981), is about a middle-aged painter living in France who returns to the United States to care for his ailing parents. Further novels include the World War II story *A Midnight Clear* (1982; film, 1992); *Scumbler* (1984), about an American artist in Paris; *Pride* (1985), a story of the Depression; *Tidings* (1987); and *Last Loves* (1991). Wharton also illustrated his seventh novel, *Franky Furbo* (1989).

What Maisie Knew \'mā-zē\ Novel by Henry JAMES, published in 1897.

Set mostly in England, the novel is related from the perspective of Maisie, a preadolescent whose parents were divorced when she was six years old and who spends six months of the year with each parent. The only emotional constant in Maisie's life is Mrs. Wix, a motherly old governess. Maisie's parents marry other partners, but neither marriage succeeds. Her new stepparents are attracted to each other, divorce Maisie's parents, and marry. Maisie knows intuitively that she cannot depend on the adults in her life, and she chooses to live with Mrs. Wix, on whose unconditional love she can depend.

What's Bred in the Bone   Novel by Robertson DAVIES, published in 1985 as the second volume of his so-called Cornish trilogy. The other books in the trilogy are *The Rebel Angels* (1981) and *The Lyre of Orpheus* (1988). Two angels narrate this story about the mysterious life of a famous art collector named Francis Cornish.

Wheatley \ˈhwēt-lē, ˈwēt-\, Phillis (b. *c.* 1753, Senegal?—d. Dec. 5, 1784, Boston, Mass., U.S.)   The first black woman poet and, after Anne Bradstreet, the second woman poet of note in the United States.

Wheatley, who is believed to have been of Fulani origin, is assumed to have been born in or near what is now Senegal or The Gambia. Transported on the slaver *Phillis*, she was sold in 1761 (at the age of about seven) to John Wheatley, a Boston merchant. The Wheatleys soon recognized her talents and gave her privileges unusual for a slave, including teaching her to read and write not only English but Latin as well. She read poetry and at the age of about 14 began to write it, taking Pope and other Neoclassical writers as models. Her elegy on the death of the famous Church of England evangelist George Whitefield, published in 1770, attracted much attention. To a surprising degree, she was accepted in Boston society. In 1773 her *Poems on Various Subjects, Religious and Moral*, consisting of 39 poems, was published in England under the sponsorship of the Countess of Huntingdon, and Wheatley's reputation spread in Europe as well as in America; the volume was issued more than a decade later in the United States. Upon her return from a trip to England in 1773 she was manumitted.

Mrs. Wheatley died in 1774 (her illness had prompted the poet's return from England), but Phillis remained with the family until the death of John Wheatley in 1778. In April of that year she married John Peters, a free black man who later failed in business and was sent to debtors' prison. At the end of her life Wheatley was working as a servant, and she died in poverty.

Wheatley's poetry, largely of the occasional type, was written in Neoclassical style. It reflected her own Christian concerns with morality and piety, and in that sense it was conventional. Until the later part of the 20th century many critics contended that her significance stemmed from the attention that she drew to her successful education, but later critical reevaluations were less patronizing and brought attention to bear on her mastery of style and suggested evidence of African influences on her work.

Wheeler, Simon \ˈsī-mən-ˈhwē-lər, ˈwē-\   Fictional character, the garrulous, folksy storyteller in THE CELEBRATED JUMPING FROG OF CALAVERAS COUNTY and "Jim Wolfe and the Tom-cats," both short stories by Mark Twain.

When I Was One-And-Twenty   Poem in the collection A SHROPSHIRE LAD by A.E. Housman. Noted for its sprightly cadence of alternating seven- and six-syllable lines, the two-stanza poem addresses the theme of unrequited love. It was likely written as a memoir of a critical time in Housman's life, when his love for a fellow student at Oxford University was rejected.

> When I was one-and-twenty
>   I heard a wise man say,
> "Give crowns and pounds and guineas
>   But not your heart away."

When Lilacs Last in the Dooryard Bloom'd   Elegy in free verse by Walt WHITMAN mourning the death of President Abraham Lincoln. First published in Whitman's collection *Sequel to Drum-Taps* (1865) and later included in the 1867 edition of *Leaves of Grass*, the poem expresses revulsion at the assassination of the country's first "great martyr chief." Implicitly, it also condemns the brutality and waste of war. This elegy is notable for its use of pathetic fallacy in attributing grief to nature. Also included in the 1867 edition of *Leaves of Grass* was a second elegy Whitman wrote for Lincoln, "O Captain! My Captain!"

When We Dead Awaken   Play in three acts by Henrik IBSEN, published in Norwegian in 1899 as *Naar vi døde vaagner* and produced in 1900. Ibsen's last play, his most confessional work, is an examination of the problem that had obsessed him throughout his career: the struggle between art and life. Arnold Rubek, a famous sculptor, is vacationing at a mountain resort. There he meets Irene von Satow, a former model of his, whose love he rejected years ago because of his plan to consecrate his life to his art. Rubek confesses that his art has been a poor substitute for love and tries to renew his old relationship with Irene. But she rejects him, saying that the dead cannot come back to life. On a climb up the mountain the artist and his muse are both buried in an apocalyptic avalanche.

Whitbread Literary Award \ˈhwit-ˌbred, ˈwit-\   Any of a series of annual awards given to the authors of the most distinguished books first published in the United Kingdom or Ireland within the previous year. Although the rules have varied slightly over the years, the most consistent requirement has been that the authors must have resided in these countries for a specified period of time, at least the previous three years. Since the award was established by the Whitbread Breweries in 1971, the categories have expanded to include the novel, first novel, children's novel, poetry, and biography or autobiography. The Whitbread Book of the Year is chosen from these five category winners. The award is determined by a panel of judges and is presented every winter by the Booksellers Association of Great Britain and Ireland.

White \ˈhwīt, ˈwīt\, E.B., *in full* Elwyn Brooks (b. July 11, 1899, Mount Vernon, N.Y., U.S.—d. Oct. 1, 1985, North Brooklin, Maine)   Leading American essayist and literary stylist of his time.

White, who graduated from Cornell University, Ithaca, N.Y., in 1921, was a reporter and free-lance writer before joining *The New Yorker* magazine as a writer and contributing editor in 1927. He married Katherine Sergeant Angell, *The New Yorker*'s first fiction editor, in 1929 (he remained with the weekly magazine for the rest of his career). White collaborated with James Thurber on *Is Sex Necessary?* (1929), a spoof of the then-current sex manuals. From 1938 to 1943 he also contributed a monthly column to *Harper's* magazine. In 1959 White revised and published *The Elements of Style*, a manual originally written by William Strunk, Jr., whose student White had been; the book became a standard style manual for writing in the English language. In 1941 he edited with his wife *A Subtreasury of American Humor*. His three books for children—STUART LITTLE (1945), CHARLOTTE'S WEB (1952), and THE TRUMPET OF THE SWAN (1970)—are considered classics. His other works include *The Second Tree from the Corner* (1954) and *Points of My Compass* (1962). *Letters of E.B. White*, edited by D.L. Guth, appeared in 1976, his collected essays in 1977, and *Poems and Sketches of E.B. White* in 1981. He was awarded a Pulitzer Prize special citation in 1978.

White \ˈhwīt, ˈwīt\, Edmund (Valentine) (b. Jan. 13, 1940, Cincinnati, Ohio, U.S.)   Writer of novels, short fiction, and nonfiction whose critically acclaimed work focuses on male homosexual society in America. His studies of evolving attitudes toward homosexuality and of the impact of AIDS on homosexual communities in the United States were significant contributions to contemporary sociological and social history.

Educated at the University of Michigan, White taught writing seminars and creative writing at Columbia, Yale, New York, and George Mason universities. He was a frequent contributor of articles, reviews, and commentary to periodicals such as *New York Times Book Review*, *Mother Jones*, and *Architectural Digest*.

White's nonfiction includes *The Joy of Gay Sex* (1977; with Charles Silverstein), *States of Desire: Travels in Gay America* (1980), and a biography of Jean Genet (1993). Among White's novels are *Forgetting Elena* (1973), *Nocturnes for the King of Naples* (1978), *A Boy's Own Story* (1982), *Caracole* (1985), and *The Beautiful Room Is Empty* (1988). His play *Blue Boy in Black* was produced in 1963.

White \\'hwīt, 'wīt\\, Patrick (Victor Martindale) (b. May 28, 1912, London, Eng.—d. Sept. 30, 1990, Sydney, N.S.W., Australia) The most influential of a group of mid-20th-century writers in Australia, winner of the Nobel Prize for Literature in 1973.

White was born in London while his parents were there on a visit, and he returned to England (after 12 years in Australia) for schooling. He then worked for a time at his father's sheep ranch in Australia before returning to study modern languages at King's College, Cambridge. By the time he entered the Royal Air Force during World War II he had already published some early work, traveled extensively, and been involved with the theater. After 1945 he returned to Australia, but he also lived intermittently in England and in the United States.

White's first novel, *Happy Valley* (1939), was set in New South Wales and showed the influence of D.H. Lawrence and Thomas Hardy. The material of White's later novels is distinctly Australian, but his treatment of it has a largeness of vision not limited to any one country or period. White saw Australia as a country in a highly volatile process of growth and self-definition, and his novels explore the possibilities of savagery to be found within such a context. His conception of Australia reflected in *The Tree of Man* (1955), *Voss* (1957), *Riders in the Chariot* (1961), *The Solid Mandala* (1966), *The Eye of the Storm* (1973), *The Twyborn Affair* (1979), and *Memoirs of Many in One* (1986) is the product of an individual, critical, poetic imagination. His style is dense with myth, symbol, and allegory. His deepest concern is for the human sense of isolation and the search for meaning.

White wrote plays, including *The Season at Sarsaparilla* (produced 1962; published in *Four Plays*, 1965), *Night on Bald Mountain* (produced 1964), and *Signal Driver* (1982); short stories; the autobiographical *Flaws in the Glass* (1981); a screenplay; a book of poems; and many essays, articles, and speeches, which were collected in *Patrick White Speaks* (1989).

White \\'hwīt, 'wīt\\, T.H., *in full* Terence Hanbury (b. May 29, 1906, Bombay, India—d. Jan. 17, 1964, Piraeus, Greece) English novelist, social historian, and satirist who was best known for his brilliant adaptation of Sir Thomas Malory's 15th-century romance *Le Morte Darthur* into a quartet of novels called THE ONCE AND FUTURE KING (1958).

White was educated at Cheltenham College and at Cambridge. He taught at Stowe School (1930–36), and while there he attained his first real critical success with an autobiographical volume, *England Have My Bones* (1936). He afterward devoted himself exclusively to writing and to studying such recondite subjects as the Arthurian legends, which were to pro-

vide the material for his books. White was by nature a recluse, for long periods isolating himself from human society and spending his time hunting, fishing, and looking after his strange collection of pets.

In addition to *The Once and Future King*, White's works include *The Goshawk* (1951), a study of falconry, and two works of social history, *The Age of Scandal* (1950) and *The Scandalmonger* (1951).

White \\'hwīt, 'wīt\\, Theodore Harold (b. May 6, 1915, Boston, Mass., U.S.—d. May 15, 1986, New York, N.Y.) American journalist, historian, and novelist, best known for his astute, suspenseful accounts of the 1960 and 1964 presidential elections.

After graduating from Harvard in 1938, White served as one of *Time* magazine's first foreign correspondents, being stationed in East Asia from 1939 to 1945. He then served as European correspondent for the Overseas News Agency (1948–50) and for *The Reporter* (1950–53). With this extensive background in analyzing other cultures, White was well equipped to tackle the American scene in *The Making of the President, 1960* (1961) and *The Making of the President, 1964* (1965). Accepted as standard histories of presidential campaigns, these books present their subjects by intelligently juxtaposing events and treating politicians as personalities rather than as symbols. White's approach elevated this type of history to an art form and won him the 1962 Pulitzer Prize for general nonfiction for *The Making of the President, 1960*. He went on to analyze the elections of 1968 and 1972 in similar books.

White was the coauthor (with Annalee Jacoby) of *Thunder Out of China* (1946) and also wrote *Fire in the Ashes* (1953), *The Mountain Road* (1958), *Breach of Faith: The Fall of Richard Nixon* (1975), the autobiographical *In Search of History: A Personal Adventure* (1978), and *America in Search of Itself: The Making of the President, 1956–1980* (1982). His books convey a genuine excitement about American institutions and politics.

White Devil, The Tragedy in five acts by John WEBSTER, performed and published as *The White Divel* in 1612. Based on historical events that occurred in Italy during the 1580s, this dark Jacobean drama is considered one of the finest of the period.

The White Devil centers on the love affair between the Duke of Brachiano and Vittoria Corombona, two of the play's many unscrupulous characters. Despite her role as a vicious heroine, Vittoria elicits sympathy in her attempt to endure a deeply corrupt society. In *The White Devil* both evil and good characters are drawn into schemes involving political intrigue, adulterous desire, and bloody revenge. Criticized for its plot construction, the play is noted for its characterizations and use of dramatic tension and physical horror.

White Fang Novel by Jack LONDON, published in 1906. The novel was intended as a companion piece to *The Call of the Wild* (1903), in which a domesticated dog reverts to a wild state. *White Fang* is the story of a wolf dog that is rescued from its brutal owner and gradually becomes domesticated through the patience and kindness of its new owner, Weedon Scott. White Fang eventually defends Scott's father from attack by an escaped convict.

White Goddess, The (*in full* The White Goddess: A Historical Grammar of Poetic Myth) Scholarly work by Robert GRAVES, published in 1948 and revised in 1952 and 1961. Graves's controversial and unorthodox theories of mythology, part invention and part based on his research into pre-classical religions, shocked many because of their basic feminist premise. According to Graves, the White Goddess combines the powers of love, destructiveness, and poetic inspiration. She ruled during a matriarchal period in the distant past before she was deposed by the patriarchal gods, who represent cold reason and logic. It was at this point, Graves claimed, that "Apollonian" or academic poetry began to dominate. Graves further argued that the White Goddess was again in evidence during the Romantic era. The best poets—the only ones really capable of writing poetry, according to Graves—continue to worship her and are honored with her gifts of poetic insight.

Whitehead \'hwīt-,hed, 'wīt-\, William (b. Feb. 12, 1715, Cambridge, Cambridgeshire, Eng.—d. April 14, 1785, London) British poet laureate from 1757 to 1785.

Whitehead was educated at Winchester College and Clare Hall, Cambridge, becoming a fellow in 1740. At Cambridge he published a number of poems, including a heroic epistle *Ann Boleyn to Henry the Eighth* (1743), and in 1745 he became tutor to Viscount Villiers, son of the Earl of Jersey, taking up residence in London. In 1757, upon the death of Colley Cibber, he was appointed poet laureate and proceeded to write annual effusions in the royal honor. That he was not altogether happy in his position appears from "A Pathetic Apology for All Laureates, Past, Present and to Come," privately circulated among his friends.

After the success of his best play, *The School for Lovers* (1762), he read plays for the producer David Garrick. His collected *Plays and Poems* appeared in 1774.

White-Jacket \'hwīt-jak-ət, 'wīt-\ Novel by Herman MELVILLE, published in 1850. Based on the author's experiences in 1834–44 as an ordinary seaman aboard the U.S. frigate *United States*, the critically acclaimed novel won political support for its stand against the use of flogging as corporal punishment aboard naval vessels. It is not known if *White-Jacket* was directly responsible for the cessation of flogging; however, members of Congress received copies of the novel during the Congressional debate over the issue, and flogging in the U.S. Navy was abolished that year.

Subtitled *The World in a Man-of-War*, the novel depicts life aboard a typical frigate, the *Neversink*, and describes the tyrannies to which ship's officers subject ordinary seamen and the appalling conditions under which the seamen live.

White Rabbit Character in ALICE'S ADVENTURES IN WONDERLAND, the children's classic by Lewis Carroll.

The White Rabbit—who reappears several times in the story—wears a waistcoat, carries a pocket watch, and is always in a great hurry, fearing the fury of the Duchess at his tardiness. Curiosity about the White Rabbit leads to Alice's fateful fall down the rabbit hole.

Whitman \'hwit-mən, 'wit-\, Walt, *in full* Walter Whitman (b. May 31, 1819, West Hills, Long Island, N.Y., U.S.—d. March 26, 1892, Camden, N.J.) American journalist, essayist, and poet whose style of writing in such works as LEAVES OF GRASS (first edition, 1855) revolutionized American literature. Such poems as I SING THE BODY ELECTRIC and SONG OF MYSELF asserted the beauty of the human body, physical health, and sexuality.

Whitman started work as a journeyman printer in 1835. A year later he began teaching and thereafter he held a great variety of jobs while writing and editing for several periodicals. He spent a great deal of his time walking and observing in New York City and Long Island; he visited the theater frequently; he developed a strong love of music, especially opera, and he read widely.

No publisher's or author's name appeared on the first edition of *Leaves of Grass* in 1855. But the cover had a portrait of Walt Whitman, "broad shouldered, rouge fleshed, Bacchus-browed, bearded like a satyr." The poems in *Leaves of Grass*

addressed the citizens of the United States, urging them to be large and generous in spirit, a new race of races nurtured in political liberty. Whitman had been practicing his own

Library of Congress

style of writing in his private notebooks, and in 1856, after much rewriting, the second edition of *Leaves of Grass* appeared. This collection contained revisions of the poems of the first edition and several new ones, including the "Sundown Poem" (later to become CROSSING BROOKLYN FERRY). All his later volumes of new poems were to be incorporated into successive editions of *Leaves of Grass*.

From 1857 to 1859 Whitman edited the *Brooklyn Times*, and his way of life became bohemian. This period up to 1860, when the third edition of *Leaves of Grass* was published, was that of the "I" who was "turbulent, fleshy, sensual, eating, drinking and breeding." Notable in the 1860 volume were the "Calamus" poems, which record a personal crisis of some intensity in his life, apparently a homosexual love affair; "Premonition" (later entitled "Starting from Paumanok"), which records the violent emotions that often drained the poet's strength; and "A Word Out of the Sea" (later entitled OUT OF THE CRADLE ENDLESSLY ROCKING).

When his brother was wounded at Fredericksburg, Whitman went there in 1862 to care for him. For the rest of the Civil War he spent much time cheering and caring for both Union and Confederate soldiers. In May 1865 DRUM-TAPS showed Whitman's readers a new kind of poetry, ranging from his early oratorical excitement to his later awareness of the horrors of war. The *Sequel to Drum-Taps*, published in the autumn of 1865, contained his great elegy on Lincoln, WHEN LILACS LAST IN THE DOORYARD BLOOM'D. The war had had its effect on Whitman's larger views, some of which emerged in the prose of DEMOCRATIC VISTAS (1871). His last works, aside from the ninth (authorized) edition of *Leaves of Grass* (1891–92), were the prose *Specimen Days & Collect* (1882–83) and a collection of 62 new poems entitled *November Boughs* (1888).

Whittemore \'hwit-ə-,mòr, 'wit-\, Reed, *in full* Edward Reed Whittemore II (b. Sept. 11, 1919, New Haven, Conn., U.S.) American teacher and poet noted for his free-flowing ironic verse.

Whittemore cofounded the literary magazine *Furioso* while he was a student at Yale University. He served in the U.S. Army Air Forces during World War II and afterwards revived and edited *Furioso* and its successor, *The Carleton Miscellany*, while a professor of English at Carleton College in Northfield, Minn. From 1968 to 1984 he taught at the University of Maryland, and he revived the magazine *Delos* in Maryland in 1988. Characters and quotes from literature inspired many of the whimsical poems in his first collection, *Heroes & Heroines* (1946). Daily life, the seasons, nature, and modern culture are the subjects of his verses in *An American Takes a Walk* (1956) and *The Self-Made Man* (1959).

In the 1960s, while his humorous tone remained, a note of sadness also began to make itself felt in such collections as *The Boy from Iowa* (1962) and *Poems, New and Selected* (1967);

in *Fifty Poems Fifty* (1970) and *The Mother's Breast and the Father's House* (1974) the poet's bitterness emerges also. Whittemore's later collections include *The Past, the Future, the Present: Poems Selected and New* (1990). Among his prose writings are the biography *William Carlos Williams: Poet from Jersey* (1975) and a group portrait entitled *Six Literary Lives* (1993).

Whittier \'hwit-ē-ər, 'wit-\, John Greenleaf (b. Dec. 17, 1807, near Haverhill, Mass., U.S.—d. Sept. 7, 1892, Hampton Falls, Mass.) American author and Abolitionist noted for his vivid and deeply truthful portrayals of rural New England life.

Born on a farm, of Puritan and Quaker ancestry, Whittier had limited formal education, but he became acquainted with poetry at an early age. William Wordsworth, Samuel Taylor Coleridge, and Charles Lamb were lasting favorites, but his deepest admiration was for John Milton, whose role as apostle of freedom and goad to righteous living he sought to imitate.

Encouraged by the Abolitionist William Lloyd Garrison, Whittier wrote copiously and enthusiastically. When his father convinced him of the impracticality of poetry as a vocation, he turned to journalism. He edited newspapers in Boston and Haverhill and by 1830 had become editor of the *New England Weekly Review* in Hartford, Conn., the most important Whig journal in New England. During this period Whittier was also writing verse, sketches, and tales of New England, and he published his first volume of poems, *Legends of New England* (1831).

By 1843 Whittier had broken with Garrison, but he continued actively to support humanitarian causes. He also became more active in literature. In the next two decades he published eight additional volumes of poems, which included "Songs of Labor" (1850), "Maud Muller" (1854), "The Barefoot Boy" (1855), and "Barbara Frietchie" (1863). Most of his literary prose, including his one novel, *Leaves from Margaret Smith's Journal* (1849), was also published during this period.

The American Civil War encompassed the deaths of several friends as well as his beloved younger sister Elizabeth, who with their mother had influenced him greatly. But national and personal grief furthered his literary maturity. The publication in 1866 of his best-known poem, SNOW-BOUND, in a collection of the same name, was followed by other triumphs in *The Tent on the Beach* (1867), *Among the Hills* (1868), and *The Pennsylvania Pilgrim* (1872).

whodunit or **whodunnit** \hū-'dən-it\ A detective story or a mystery story.

Who's Afraid of Virginia Woolf? \vər-'jin-yə-'wùlf\ Play in three acts by Edward ALBEE, published and produced in 1962. The action takes place in the living room of a middle-aged couple, George and Martha, who have come home from a faculty party drunk and quarrelsome. When Nick, a young biology professor, and his strange wife Honey stop by for a nightcap, they are enlisted as fellow fighters, and the battle begins. A long night of malicious games, insults, humiliations, betrayals, painful confrontations, and savage witticisms ensues. The secrets of both couples are laid bare and illusions are viciously exposed. When, in a climactic moment, George decides to "kill" the son they have invented to compensate for their childlessness, George and Martha finally face the truth and, in a quiet ending to a noisy play, stand together against the world, sharing their sorrow.

Why I Live at the P.O. Short story by Eudora WELTY, first published in the *Atlantic Monthly* in 1941 and collected in *A Curtain of Green* (1941).

This comic monologue by Sister, a young woman in a small Mississippi town who has set up housekeeping in the post office to escape from her eccentric family, is a prime example of

Southern gothic writing. As Sister's story of betrayal and injustice unfolds, the reader gradually becomes aware that Sister's view of the world is as strange as that of the various members of her family. The narrow-minded and hostile characters are portrayed as cartoonish grotesques; at the same time, however, Welty's accurate depiction of small town Southern life lends an air of uncomfortable realism, and her perfectly nuanced dramatic monologue gives the story a wickedly funny air that has made it a classic of American literature.

Wickfield, Agnes \'ag-nəs-'wik-,fēld\ Fictional character, David's second wife in Charles Dickens's novel DAVID COPPERFIELD.

Wideman \'wīd-mən\, John Edgar (b. June 14, 1941, Washington, D.C., U.S.) American writer regarded for his intricate literary style in novels about the experiences of black men in contemporary urban America.

Until the age of 10, Wideman lived in Homewood, a black section of Pittsburgh, Pa., which later became the setting of many of his novels. An outstanding scholar and athlete at the University of Pennsylvania, he became the second black American to receive a Rhodes scholarship to Oxford University. He joined the faculty of the University of Pennsylvania in 1966, and the following year he published his first novel, *A Glance Away*, about a day in the lives of a reformed drug addict and a homosexual English professor. His second novel, *Hurry Home* (1970), is the story of an intellectual alienated from his black ancestry and the black community. *The Lynchers* (1973) was his first novel to focus on interracial issues.

Wideman left Pennsylvania to become a professor at the University of Wyoming (1975–85). The so-called *Homewood Trilogy*, an historical exploration of family and community, comprised two novels, *Hiding Place* (1981) and *Sent for You Yesterday* (1983), and a collection of short stories, *Damballah* (1981). In *Brothers and Keepers* (1984), his first nonfiction book, he contemplated the role of the black intellectual by studying his relationship with his brother, who was serving a life sentence in prison. After joining the faculty at the University of Massachusetts in 1985, Wideman published the short-story collection *Fever* (1989) and the novel *Philadelphia Fire* (1990). *The Stories of John Edgar Wideman* was published in 1992.

Wide Net, The Short-story collection by Eudora WELTY, published in 1943. In the title story, a man quarrels with his pregnant wife, leaves the house, and descends into a mysterious underwater kingdom where he meets "The King of the Snakes" who forces him to confront the darker mysteries of nature. He returns to his wife better capable of living a meaningful, fulfilling life. This blend of domestic realism with mythology and ancient fertility tales is characteristic of the entire collection.

Wide Sargasso Sea \sär-'gas-ō\ Novel by Jean RHYS, published in 1966. A well-received work of fiction, it takes its theme from the novel *Jane Eyre* by Charlotte Brontë.

The book details the life of Antoinette Mason (known in *Jane Eyre* as Bertha), a West Indian who marries an unnamed man in Jamaica and returns with him to his home in England. Locked in a loveless marriage and settled in an inhospitable climate, Antoinette goes mad and is frequently violent. Her husband confines her to the attic of his house at Thornfield. Only he and Grace Poole, the attendant he has hired to care for her, know of Antoinette's existence. The reader gradually learns that Antoinette's unnamed husband is Mr. Rochester, later to become the beloved of Jane Eyre.

Much of the action of the novel takes place in the West Indies. The first and third sections are narrated by Antoinette, the middle section by her husband.

Widmann \'vēt-‚män\, Joseph Viktor (b. Feb. 20, 1842, Nennowitz, Moravia, Austrian Empire [now in Brno, Czech Republic]—d. Nov. 6, 1911, Bern, Switz.) Swiss writer, editor, and critic who encouraged many gifted writers and wrote poetry, drama, and travel books.

As literary editor of the Bern daily *Der Bund* from 1880 to 1910, Widmann occupied an authoritative position in Swiss letters and promoted many talents. He was himself an accomplished though not a strikingly original writer, and he handled such classic forms as the short epic ("Buddha," 1869), the idyll ("Mose und Zipora," 1874), and iambic drama (*Oenone*, 1880) with charming ease. His travel books, notably *Spaziergänge in den Alpen* (1885; "Walks in the Alps"), belong to the best of their kind; his plays include *Maikäferkomödie* (1897; "Cockchafer [Beetle] Comedy"), a pleasant and humorous allegory, and *Der Heilige und die Tiere* (1905; "The Holy and the Animals"), his most profound poetic utterance.

Widsith \'wid-‚sith\ ("Far Traveler") Old English poem, probably from the 7th century, preserved in the Exeter Book, a 10th-century collection of Old English poetry. "Widsith" is an idealized self-portrait of a scop (minstrel) of the Germanic heroic age who wanders widely and is welcomed in many mead halls. It is an ingenious compendium of the important figures in Germanic hero legend and a remarkable record of the scop's role in early Germanic society. *See also* EXETER BOOK.

Wied \'vith\, Gustav (Johannes) (b. March 6, 1858, Holmegaard, near Nakskov, Den.—d. Oct. 24, 1914, Roskilde) Danish dramatist, poet, novelist, and rational satirist chiefly remembered for a series of what he called satyr-dramas.

Although the satyr-dramas were meant to be read rather than performed, one, *Skærmydsler* (1901; "Skirmishes"), became one of the great successes of the Royal Theater. The play *Ranke Viljer og 2 × 2 = 5* (1906; *2 × 2 = 5*), and two collections of short stories, *Menneskenes Børn* (1894; *Children of Men*) and *En "Bohéme"* (1894; *A Bohemian*), attained great popularity abroad.

Wieland \'vē-länt\ (*in full* Wieland, or The Transformation) Gothic novel by Charles Brockden BROWN, published in 1798. The story concerns Theodore Wieland, whose father has died by spontaneous combustion apparently for violating a vow to God. The younger Wieland, also a religious enthusiast, misguidedly assumes that a ventriloquist's utterances are supernatural in origin; driven insane, he acts upon the prompting of this "inner voice" and murders his wife and children. He is eventually driven to kill himself.

Wieland \'vē-‚länt\, Christoph Martin (b. Sept. 5, 1733, Oberholzheim, near the Imperial City of Biberach [now in Germany]—d. Jan. 20, 1813, Weimar, Saxe-Weimar) German poet and man of letters of the early 18th-century German Rococo period whose work spans the major trends of his age, from rationalism and the Enlightenment to classicism and pre-Romanticism.

Wieland was the son of a Pietist parson, and his early writings from the 1750s were strongly devotional. During the 1760s, however, he discovered another, more sensual aspect of his nature and moved toward a worldly, rationalistic philosophy. *Geschichte des Agathon*, 2 vol. (1766–67; *History of Agathon*), which describes the process, is considered the first bildungsroman, or novel of psychological development.

Between 1762 and 1766 Wieland published the first German translations of 22 of William Shakespeare's plays, which were to be influential models for dramatists of the Sturm und Drang literary movement. In 1773 he established *Der teutsche Merkur* ("The German Mercury"), which was a leading literary periodical for 37 years. Late in life, Wieland considered himself

a classicist and devoted most of his time to translating Greek and Latin authors. His allegorical verse epic *Oberon* (1780) foreshadows many aspects of Romanticism. This is ironic because Wieland was highly critical of the tenets of Romanticism, and the movement's foremost writers were largely contemptuous of his work.

Wierzyński \vᵛe-'zhәnᵞ-skᵞē\, Kazimierz (b. Aug. 27, 1894, Drohobycz, Galicia, Austria-Hungary [now Drohobych, Ukraine]—d. Feb. 13, 1969, London, Eng.) Polish poet noted as a leader of the Skamander group of poets.

Wierzyński moved to Warsaw after the restoration of Poland's independence at the close of World War I and joined the Skamander group. His poetical debut was *Wiosna i wino* (1919; "Spring and Wine"), followed by *Wróble na dachu* (1921; "Sparrows on the Roof") and *Wielka niedźwiedzica* (1923; "The Great She-Bear")—all inspired by carefree juvenile optimism. Out of his interest in sports, he published in 1927 a collection of poems, *Laur Olimpijski* ("The Olympic Laurel Wreath"), for which he was awarded a special gold medal at the 1928 Olympic Games in Amsterdam. When World War II began he left Poland to live in exile, settling in London. From the 1930s his poetry dealt increasingly with patriotic and religious themes. Among his collections from this period are *Wolność tragiczna* (1936; "Tragic Freedom") and *Krzyże i miecze* (1946; "Crosses and Swords"). In his later poems, published in *Cygańskim wozem* (1966; "With a Gypsy Cart"), *Czarny polonez* (1968; "The Black Polonaise"), and other collections, Wierzyński abandoned traditional meter and rhyme for more modern poetic devices.

Wiesel \vē-'zel\, Elie, *in full* Elizer (b. Sept. 30, 1928, Sighet, Romania) Romanian-born American novelist whose works provide a sober yet passionate testament of the destruction of European Jewry during World War II. He was awarded the Nobel Prize for Peace in 1986.

Wiesel's early life, spent in a small Ḥasidic community in the town of Sighet, was a rather hermetic existence of prayer and contemplation and was barely touched by the war. In 1944, however, all the Jews of the town (annexed by Hungary in 1940), including Wiesel and the other members of his family, were deported to Auschwitz, where his mother and younger sister were killed. He was then sent as a slave laborer to Buchenwald, where his father was killed. After the war he settled in France, studied at the Sorbonne, and wrote for French and Israeli newspapers. He moved to the United States in 1956 and was naturalized in 1963. Wiesel taught at City College of New York and at Boston University.

While living in France, he was urged by the novelist François Mauriac to bear witness to what he had experienced in the concentration camps. The outcome was Wiesel's first book, his only work in Yiddish, *Un di velt hot geshvign* (1956; "And the World Remained Silent"), abridged as *La Nuit* (1958; *Night*). It is a semiautobiographical account of a young boy's spiritual reaction to Auschwitz and is one of the most powerful literary expressions of the Holocaust. All of Wiesel's works concern, in some manner, his wartime experiences and his reflections on their broader significance. They include *La Ville de la chance* (1962; *The Town Beyond the Wall*), a novel examining human apathy; *Le Mendiant de Jérusalem* (1968; *A Beggar in Jerusalem*), which ponders why people kill; *Célébration hassidique* (1972; *Souls on Fire*), a critically acclaimed collection of Ḥasidic tales; *Le Testament d'un poète juif assassiné* (1980; *The Testament*); *Le Cinquième fils* (1983; *The Fifth Son*); *Le Crépuscule, au loin* (1987; *Twilight*); and *L'Oublié* (1989; *The Forgotten*), in which a Holocaust survivor develops Alzheimer's disease and begins to lose his memories.

Wife of Bath's Tale, The \\'băth, 'bath\\ One of the 24 stories in THE CANTERBURY TALES by Geoffrey Chaucer. Before the Wife of Bath tells her tale, she offers in a long prologue a condemnation of celibacy and a lusty account of her five marriages. It is for this prologue that her tale is perhaps best known.

The tale concerns a knight accused of rape, whose life shall be spared if in one year he discovers what women most desire. He eventually turns to an ugly, old witch who promises him the answer that will save his life if he will do the first thing she asks of him. The answer—that it is "maistrie," or sovereignty over men, that women desire—is accepted in court, and the witch then demands that he marry her. In bed, she asks him if he would wish her ugly yet faithful, or beautiful and faithless. He insists the choice must be hers. This concession of her mastery restores her youth and beauty, and they live happily ever after.

The story is a version of the Arthurian romance *The Wedding of Sir Gawain and Dame Ragnell* and it is similar to one of the tales in the 14th-century *Confessio amantis* by John Gower.

Wigglesworth \\'wig-əlz-,wərth\\, Michael (b. Oct. 18, 1631, Yorkshire?, Eng.—d. June 10, 1705, Malden, Mass. [U.S.]) British-American clergyman, physician, and author of rhymed treatises expounding Puritan doctrines.

Wigglesworth immigrated to America in 1638 with his family and settled in New Haven, Conn. In 1651 he graduated from Harvard College [later University], where he was a tutor and a fellow. He preached at Charlestown, Mass., in 1653–54 and was pastor at Malden from 1656 until his death. In addition to his clerical duties, Wigglesworth practiced medicine and wrote numerous poems, including "A Short Discourse on Eternity," "Vanity of Vanities," and *God's Controversy with New England* (published 1871). The first two were appended to *The Day of Doom: or a Poetical Description of the Great and Last Judgment* (1662), a long poem in ballad measure using horrific imagery to describe the Last Judgment. Once the most widely read poet of early New England, Wigglesworth declined in popularity together with Puritanism and has since been considered a writer of doggerel verse. A modern edition of *The Day of Doom* prepared by Kenneth B. Murdock was published in 1929.

wight \\'wīt\\ [Old English *wiht* creature, being, thing] *archaic* A preternatural being (such as a fairy or a witch).

Wilamowitz-Moellendorff \\,vē-lä-'mō-,vits-'mœl-ən-,dörf\\, Ulrich von, *in full* Emmo Friedrich Richard Ulrich von Wilamowitz-Moellendorff (b. Dec. 22, 1848, Markowitz, Prussia— d. Sept. 25, 1931, Berlin, Ger.) German classical scholar and teacher whose studies advanced knowledge in the historical sciences of metrics, epigraphy, papyrology, topography, and textual criticism.

Educated at the universities of Bonn and Berlin, Wilamowitz-Moellendorff taught successively at the universities of Berlin, Greifswald, and Göttingen before accepting the chair of Greek studies at Berlin in 1897.

Among Wilamowitz-Moellendorff's many books were studies and texts of the Greek tragedians, Homer and the *Iliad*, Hesiod, Pindar, Plato, and Aristotle. His *Griechisches Lesebuch* (1902; "Greek Reader"), which became a standard text, was influential in its emphasis on Hellenistic and later Greek writers, including the Church Fathers, as well as classical authors. In 1902 he became editorial director of the *Inscriptiones Graecae*, a multivolume collection of Greek inscriptions. He also was editor of the series *Philologische Untersuchungen* (1880–1925; "Philological Investigations"). His last book was *Der Glaube der Hellenen* (1931–32; "The Religious Belief of the Greeks").

Wilbur \\'wil-bər\\, Richard (Purdy) (b. March 1, 1921, New York, N.Y., U.S.) American poet, critic, editor, and translator noted for his urbane and well-crafted verse.

Wilbur was educated at Amherst College and Harvard University. With *The Beautiful Changes and Other Poems* (1947) and *Ceremony and Other Poems* (1950), he established himself as an important young writer. These early poems are technically exquisite and formal in their adherence to the convention of rhyme and other devices.

Wilbur next tried translating and in 1955 produced a version of Molière's play *Le Misanthrope*, later followed by Molière's *Tartuffe* (1963), *The School for Wives* (1971), *The Learned Ladies* (1977), and *The School for Husbands; and Sganarelle, or, the Imaginary Cuckold* (1994). He also translated Racine's *Andromache* (1982). In 1957 he won a Pulitzer Prize for poetry for *Things of This World: Poems* (1956). Wilbur wrote within the poetic tradition established by T.S. Eliot, using irony and intellect to create tension in his poems. His other collections include *Advice to a Prophet and Other Poems* (1961), *Walking to Sleep* (1969), and *The Mind Reader: New Poems* (1976). He also wrote the lyrics for Leonard Bernstein's musical comedy version of Voltaire's *Candide* (1957), children's books such as *Loudmouse* (1963) and *Opposites* (1973), and criticism, collected as *Responses: Prose Pieces 1953–1976* (1976). He was poet laureate of the United States in 1987–88, and in 1988 he published *New and Collected Poems*.

Wilcher, Tom \\'täm-'wil-chər\\ Fictional character, protagonist and narrator of the novel TO BE A PILGRIM by Joyce Cary.

Wild Ass's Skin, The Novel by Honoré de BALZAC, published in two volumes in 1831 as *La Peau de chagrin* and later included as part of the *Études philosophiques* section of *La Comédie humaine* (THE HUMAN COMEDY). A poor young writer, Raphael de Valentin, is given a magical ass's skin that will grant his wishes—for a price. With each wish granted, the skin shrinks and the owner's life is shortened. Ironically, although he had previously been hard at work on a book about the powers of the human will, Valentin himself soon loses all control over his own life and slips into debauchery. He eventually uses up the skin, bringing on his death.

Wild Duck, The Drama in five acts by Henrik IBSEN, published in 1884 as *Vildanden* and produced the following year. In the play, an idealistic outsider's gratuitous truth-telling destroys a family.

Gregers Werle, who has a compulsion to tell the truth at all costs, reveals to the Ekdal family certain unasked-for information about each family member's past. The knowledge destroys their illusions and their family life. As the final destructive act Hedvig, the Ekdals' adolescent daughter, kills herself after Werle informs the family that she may be the illegitimate daughter of a man other than her beloved father.

Wilde \\'wīld\\, Oscar (Fingal O'Flahertie Wills) (b. Oct. 16, 1854, Dublin, Ire.—d. Nov. 30, 1900, Paris, Fr.) Irish wit, poet, and dramatist whose reputation rests on his comic masterpieces LADY WINDERMERE'S FAN (1893) and THE IMPORTANCE OF BEING EARNEST (1899). He was a spokesman for Aestheticism, the late 19th-century movement in England that advocated art for art's sake.

Wilde attended Trinity College, Dublin, and Magdalen College, Oxford. In the early 1880s he established himself in social and artistic circles by his wit and flamboyance. In 1881 Wilde published his highly derivative *Poems*. He agreed to lecture in the United States and Canada in 1882. Despite widespread hostility in the press to his languid poses and dandified costume, for 12 months Wilde exhorted eager audiences of Americans to love beauty and art.

In 1884 Wilde married Constance Lloyd, daughter of a prominent Irish barrister; they had two children. Meanwhile, Wilde wrote reviews for the *Pall Mall Gazette* and then became editor of *Woman's World* (1887–89). *The Happy Prince and Other Tales* (1888) reveals his gift for romantic allegory in the form of the fairy tale.

In his only novel, THE PICTURE OF DORIAN GRAY (1891), Wilde combined the supernatural elements of the gothic novel with the depravity typical of French Decadent fiction. In the same year he published a book of essays and two volumes of stories and fairy tales, testifying to his extraordinary creative inventiveness.

But Wilde's greatest successes were his society comedies. He employed his paradoxical, epigrammatic wit to create a form of comedy new to the 19th-century English theater. His first success, *Lady Windermere's Fan*, demonstrated that this wit could revitalize the rusty machinery of the French well-made play. In 1892 rehearsals of his macabre play *Salomé*, designed, as he said, to make his audience shudder by its depiction of unnatural passion, were halted by the censor. It was published in 1893, and an English translation appeared in 1894 with Aubrey Beardsley's celebrated illustrations. A second society comedy, *A Woman of No Importance* (produced 1893), confirmed his reputation. In rapid succession, Wilde's final plays, *An Ideal Husband* and *The Importance of Being Earnest*, were produced early in 1895. In the latter, his greatest achievement, the conventional elements of farce are transformed into satirical epigrams—seemingly trivial but mercilessly exposing Victorian hypocrisies.

Wilde's relationship with Lord Alfred Douglas, whom he had met in 1891, infuriated the Marquess of Queensberry, Douglas' father. Accused, finally, by the marquess of being a sodomite, Wilde sued for criminal libel. Wilde's case collapsed, however, when the evidence went against him, and he dropped the suit. He was then arrested and ordered to stand trial for the crime of sodomy. Found guilty and sentenced to two years at hard labor, he served most of his sentence at Reading Gaol, where he wrote a long, recriminatory letter to Douglas (published in 1905 as DE PROFUNDIS).

In May 1897 Wilde was released, a bankrupt, and he immediately went to France. His only remaining work was THE BALLAD OF READING GAOL (1898), revealing his concern for inhumane prison conditions.

Wildenvey \\'vil-dən-ˌvā\\, Herman, *pseudonym of* Herman Theodor Portaas \\'pȯr-täs\\ (b. July 20, 1886, Eikar, Nor.—d. Sept. 27, 1959, Larvik)   Norwegian poet whose sunny songs of simple sensual pleasure are unusual in the somber history of Norwegian verse.

Wildenvey's first collection of verse was *Nyinger* (1907; "Bonfires"). He developed a technique of constructing his verse so as to give it a lightness matching its mood, as in such collections as *Kjærtegn* (1916; "Caresses"), *Høstens lyre* (1931; "The Lyre of Autumn"), and many others. He was able to extract fresh effects from language. In 1935 *Owls to Athens*, a selection of his poems in English translation, was published.

Wilder \\'wīl-dər\\, Laura Ingalls (b. Feb. 7, 1867, Lake Pepin, Wis., U.S.—d. Feb. 10, 1957, Mansfield, Mo.)   American author of children's fiction based on her own youth as a pioneer in the American Midwest.

Wilder spent 12 years editing the *Missouri Ruralist* before she began to write fiction. Her stories centered on the unrest of the men and patience of the women who were pioneers in the mid-1800s. She celebrated their peculiarly American spirit and independence. Her novels included *Little House in the Big Woods* (1932), *Farmer Boy* (1933), *Little House on the Prairie* (1935), *On the Banks of Plum Creek* (1937), *By the Shores of Silver Lake* (1939), *The Long Winter* (1940), *Little Town on the Prairie* (1941), and *These Happy Golden Years* (1943).

Wilder \\'wīl-dər\\, Thornton (Niven) (b. April 17, 1897, Madison, Wis., U.S.—d. Dec. 7, 1975, Hamden, Conn.)   American writer known for his innovative novels and plays.

After graduating from Yale University, Wilder studied archaeology in Rome. His first novel, *The Cabala* (1926), while set in 20th-century Rome, is essentially a fantasy about the death of the pagan gods. His most popular novel, THE BRIDGE OF SAN LUIS REY (1927), examines the lives of five persons who died in the collapse of a bridge in Peru in the 18th century. *The Woman of Andros* (1930) is an interpretation of Terence's *Andria*. *Heaven's My Destination* (1934) is about a quixotically good hero in a contemporary setting. His later novels are *The Ides of March* (1948), *The Eighth Day* (1967), and THEOPHILUS NORTH (1973).

Wilder's plays, which are much better known than his novels, engage the audience in make-believe by having the actors address the spectators directly, by discarding props and scenery, and by treating time in an unrealistic manner through such devices as having the same characters appear in different historical periods and using deliberate anachronisms. Notable among them are OUR TOWN (1938), THE SKIN OF OUR TEETH (1942), and THE MATCHMAKER (1954). Wilder won Pulitzer Prizes for *The Bridge of San Luis Rey*, *Our Town*, and *The Skin of Our Teeth*.

Wildeve, Damon \\'dā-mən-'wīld-ˌēv\\   Fictional character, an innkeeper who is secretly involved in a passionate affair with Eustacia Vye though engaged to (and later married to) Thomasin Yeobright, in the novel THE RETURN OF THE NATIVE by Thomas Hardy.

Wildgans \\'vilt-gäns\\, Anton (b. April 17, 1881, Vienna, Austria—d. May 3, 1932, Mödling, near Vienna)   Austrian dramatist and poet known for his mystical dramas charged with the symbolic messages typical of German Expressionism.

His early poems, among which was the collection *Herbstfrühling* (1909; "Autumn-Spring"), sold well; they recall the themes of idealism and reality in the late romantic works of Hugo von Hofmannsthal. Wildgans' plays, such as the trilogy *Armut* (1914; "Poverty"), *Liebe* (1916; "Love"), and *Dies irae* (1918; "Day of Wrath"), begin in a realistic world that becomes less and less comprehensible and culminates in a mystical sensing of the truth. As a counterpart to this trilogy of Viennese middle-class family life, he planned another of a mythological or religious character; only the first part, *Kain* (1920; "Cain"), was published. Wildgans directed the celebrated Vienna Burgtheater in 1921–22 and 1930–31. He also translated Italian and French poets into German. His own collected poems were published in 1929.

Wild Swans at Coole, The \\'kül\\   Poem by William Butler YEATS, printed in *The Little Review* (June 1917) and published in a collection entitled *The Wild Swans at Coole* (1917; enlarged, 1919). Comprising five six-line stanzas, this mature, reflective work addresses the onslaught of old age.

In "The Wild Swans at Coole," Yeats compares two visits that he made to Coole Park in County Galway, one in 1897 and the second in 1916. Observing swans at a pond, the narrator laments that "All's changed" since the previous visit. The time of day, an autumn evening, reflects the narrator's advancing age.

Wilhelm Meister's Apprenticeship \\'vil-ˌhelm-'mīs-tər\\   Classic bildungsroman by Johann Wolfgang von GOETHE, published in German in four volumes in 1795–96 as *Wilhelm Meisters Lehrjahre*. *Wilhelm Meisters Wanderjahre* (1821; published in final form, 1829; *Wilhelm Meister's Travels*), Goethe's final novel, can be considered a sequel in which Wilhelm moves deeper into life after completing his apprenticeship.

The *Apprenticeship* sets forth the 18th-century humanistic ideal of self-education and the development of intellect. The *Travels* reflects Goethe's commitment to 19th-century social and technological progress. In the *Apprenticeship*, Wilhelm Meister is a young man who, after being disillusioned by his first love, sets out to travel. Following a series of incidents—including his rescue of a mistreated young girl from a group of traveling acrobats and his joining an acting troupe—he learns that life itself is an apprenticeship. In the *Travels*, Wilhelm and his son Felix wander. Their adventures are less important than Goethe's interpolated social philosophy, including his discourses on the individual's role in society.

Wilhelm Tell   *see* WILLIAM TELL.

Willems \'vil-əms\, Jan Frans (b. March 11, 1793, Boechout, Brabant, Austrian Netherlands [now in Belgium]—d. June 24, 1846, Ghent)   Flemish poet, playwright, essayist, polemicist, and the most important philologist of the Dutch language of his time.

Willems wrote plays, poems, and essays in the style of the *rederijkers* ("rhetoricians"). His two-volume *Verhandeling over de nederduytsche tael- en letter-kunde* (1819, 1820–24) is a milestone in the history of literary studies in the Low Countries. He published a modern Flemish translation of the 13th-century *Van den vos Reinaerde* ("Of Reynard the Fox"), with an epoch-making introduction, in 1834, followed by a scholarly edition (1836), which won him fame abroad. In 1835 he moved to Ghent, where he became active as a scholar and leader of the Flemish national and Romantic revival. Among other activities, he founded the periodical *Belgisch museum* (1837–46), a repository of information on medieval Flanders.

William IX \'wil-yəm\ (b. Oct. 22, 1071—d. Feb. 10, 1127, Poitiers, Fr.)   Medieval troubadour, count of Poitiers and duke of Aquitaine and of Gascony (1086–1127), son of William VIII and grandfather of the famous Eleanor of Aquitaine.

William IX spent most of his life in warfare. He led an unsuccessful Crusade to the Holy Land (1101–02) and battled the Moors near Cordova (1120–23). His fame rests chiefly, however, on his being the first poet in the Provençal language whose works are extant. His chansons are boisterous, amorous, and humorous, and are usually delicate but sometimes coarsely obscene.

Williams \'wil-yəmz\, C.K., *in full* Charles Kenneth (b. Nov. 4, 1936, Newark, N.J., U.S.)   American poet whose early work is characterized by short lines and an acid tone, but who later altered both the form and content of his poetry.

Educated at Bucknell University (Lewisburg, Pa.) and the University of Pennsylvania, Williams was a contributing editor for *American Poetry Review* from 1972. His first collection of verse, *Lies* (1969), contains lyrical yet vituperative poems railing against human callousness and dishonesty. *I Am the Bitter Name* (1972), an overtly political collection, inveighs against the American military-industrial complex and the complacency of governments. A stylistic and thematic departure is evident in *With Ignorance* (1977). It is an exploration of the American psyche rather than a diatribe, and its long-lined, conversational poems have a dramatic and investigative quality. His later works include *Tar* (1983), *Flesh and Blood* (1987), and *A Dream of Mind* (1992).

Williams \'wil-yəmz\, Emlyn, *in full* George Emlyn Williams (b. Nov. 26, 1905, Mostyn, Flintshire, Wales—d. Sept. 25, 1987, London, Eng.)   Welsh actor and playwright, author of some highly effective, often macabre plays.

Williams was educated in Geneva and at Christ Church, Oxford. In the 1930s and '40s he wrote some immensely suc-

cessful plays, which contained starring parts for himself. The best-known of these was *Night Must Fall* (performed 1935). Williams' other plays include *A Murder Has Been Arranged* (1930), *The Corn Is Green* (1938; film, 1945), and *The Druid's Rest* (1944). He acted in many films and was also renowned for his public readings from the works of Charles Dickens, Dylan Thomas, and Saki. He wrote two volumes of autobiography, *George* (1961) and *Emlyn* (1973). His *Beyond Belief* (1967) concerns a couple living in the Pennine Moors, Eng., who were convicted of the murders of children, and *Headlong* (1980) is an adventure novel. Williams also composed a fictional diary of a murderer, *Dr. Crippen's Diary* (1987).

Williams \'wil-yəmz\, Tennessee, *original name* Thomas Lanier Williams (b. March 26, 1911, Columbus, Miss., U.S.—d. Feb. 25, 1983, New York, N.Y.)   American dramatist whose plays reveal a world of human frustration in which sex and violence often underlie a pervasive atmosphere of romantic gentility.

E.B. Inc.

Williams became interested in playwriting while at the University of Missouri at Columbia and Washington University, St. Louis, Mo. Little theater groups produced some of his work, encouraging him to study dramatic writing at the University of Iowa. His first recognition came when *American Blues* (1939), a group of one-act plays, won a Group Theatre award.

Success came with THE GLASS MENAGERIE (1945), which portrays a declassed Southern family living in a tenement. Williams' next major play, A STREETCAR NAMED DESIRE (1947), is the story of the ruin of one member of a once-genteel Southern family. The play won a Pulitzer Prize. In 1953 *Camino Real*, a complex and bizarre work set in a mythical, microcosmic town whose inhabitants include Lord Byron and Don Quixote, was a commercial failure, but CAT ON A HOT TIN ROOF (1955) was awarded a Pulitzer Prize and was successfully filmed, as was THE NIGHT OF THE IGUANA (1961). In SUDDENLY LAST SUMMER (1958) Williams deals with lobotomy, pederasty, and cannibalism, and in SWEET BIRD OF YOUTH (1959) the gigolo hero is castrated for having infected a Southern politician's daughter with venereal disease.

Williams was in ill health frequently during the 1960s, culminating in a severe mental and physical breakdown in 1969. His later plays were unsuccessful. They include *Vieux Carré* (1977), *A Lovely Sunday for Crève Coeur* (1978–79), and *Clothes for a Summer Hotel* (1980). Williams also wrote two novels, *The Roman Spring of Mrs. Stone* (1950) and *Moise and the World of Reason* (1975), essays, poetry, film scripts, short stories, and an autobiography, *Memoirs* (1975). His works won four Drama Critics' awards and were widely translated and performed around the world.

Williams \'wil-yəmz\, William Carlos (b. Sept. 17, 1883, Rutherford, N.J., U.S.—d. March 4, 1963, Rutherford)   American poet who succeeded in making the ordinary appear extraordinary through the clarity and discreteness of his imagery. Williams, trained as a pediatrician, devoted himself to a lifetime of poetry writing and medical practice in his hometown. In *Al Que Quiere!* (1917), roughly translated "To Him Who Wants It," his style is distinctly his own. Characteristic poems that express Williams' fresh, direct impression of the sensuous world are the frequently anthologized "Lighthearted William" and "By the Road to the Contagious Hospital" and "The Red Wheelbarrow," both of the latter published in SPRING AND ALL (1923).

In the 1930s, during the Depression, his images became less a celebration of the world and more a catalog of its wrongs. Such poems as "Proletarian Portrait" and "The Yachts" reveal his skill in conveying attitudes by presentation rather than explanation. The five-volume PATERSON (1946–58) is based on an examination of the industrial city in New Jersey and evokes a complex vision of America and modern life.

A prolific writer of prose, Williams analyzed the American character and culture through essays on historical figures in *In the American Grain* (1925). He also wrote a trilogy of novels about a family—*White Mule* (1937), *In the Money* (1940), and *The Build-Up* (1952). Among his notable short stories are "Jean Beicke," "A Face of Stone," and "The Farmers' Daughters." He also published the play *A Dream of Love* (1948) and his *Autobiography* (1951). In 1963 he was posthumously awarded the Pulitzer Prize in poetry for his PICTURES FROM BRUEGHEL (1962).

Williamson \'wil-yəm-sən\, David (Keith) (b. Feb. 24, 1942, Melbourne, Victoria, Australia) Australian dramatist and screenwriter known for topical satiric comedies that display his flair for naturalism and local vernacular. He explored the psychology of social interaction, focusing on the social and cultural attitudes of the Australian middle class.

Williamson worked as a design engineer and taught mechanical engineering and psychology before becoming a full-time writer. His *Three Plays* (1974) includes *The Coming of Stork*, his farcical first play; *Jugglers Three*, a black comedy about marital tensions; and *What If You Died Tomorrow*, an autobiographical work about a novelist dealing with success.

Williamson first earned acclaim with *The Removalists* (1972; film, 1974), an absurdist look at authority, violence, and sexuality; and *Don's Party* (1973; film, 1976), about a group of frustrated former radicals. He examines the social dynamics of bureaucracies in *The Department* (1975) and *The Club* (1978; film, 1980). *The Perfectionist* (1983) and *Emerald City* (1987) are both comedies of manners. His other plays include *A Handful of Friends* (1976), *Travelling North* (1980), *Sons of Cain* (1985), *Top Silk* (1989), *Siren* (1991), and *Money & Friends* (1992).

Williamson \'wil-yəm-sən\, Henry (b. Dec. 1, 1895, Bedfordshire, Eng.—d. Aug. 13, 1977, Berkshire) English novelist who is known for his sensitive but unsentimental handling of nature themes.

Williamson first came to notice as a writer with four novels written between 1921 and 1928 and published under the title of *The Flax of Dream* (1936). *Tarka the Otter* (1927), however, was the book that established his reputation. Its nonhuman hero was presented without any of the mawkish sentiment that mars many "animal" stories. Williamson later produced another ambitious series of novels under the general title of *A Chronicle of Ancient Sunlight* (1951–69).

William Tell \'wil-yəm-'tel\ Verse drama in five acts by German dramatist Friedrich von SCHILLER, published and produced in 1804 as *Wilhelm Tell*.

During the 15th century, in the Swiss canton of Uri, the legendary hero Wilhelm Tell leads the people of the forest cantons in rebellion against tyrannical Austrian rule. Tell himself assassinates the corrupt Austrian governor. The play's underlying theme is the justifiability of violence in political action. The most recognizable incident in the play is the dramatic moment when, at the governor's orders, Tell must shoot an arrow from a distance of 70 paces through an apple placed on the head of his son Walter.

Wilson \'wil-sən\, A.N., *in full* Andrew Norman (b. Oct. 27, 1950, Stone, Staffordshire, Eng.) English essayist, journalist, and author of satirical novels of British society and of scholarly biographies of literary figures. His characters are typically eccentric, sexually ambiguous, and aimless.

Wilson attended New College, Oxford, began a teaching career, and spent a year training for the priesthood before deciding to concentrate on writing. His first novel, *The Sweets of Pimlico* (1977), centers upon an introverted woman who is drawn into the mysterious world of an elderly, aristocratic man. His next two novels, *Unguarded Hours* (1978) and *Kindly Light* (1979), chronicle the misadventures of a man who begins a career in organized religion.

Wilson's satiric writing ranged from the sometimes outrageous comedy of *Who Was Oswald Fish?* (1981) and *Scandal* (1983) to the black comedy of *The Healing Art* (1980) and *Wise Virgin* (1982). His other novels include works set in the past, *Gentleman in England* (1985) and *Love Unknown* (1986), and a trilogy about a well-known biographer, *Incline Our Hearts* (1988), *A Bottle in the Smoke* (1990), and *Daughters of Albion* (1991). An esteemed biographer himself, Wilson wrote books on Sir Walter Scott, John Milton, Hilaire Belloc, Leo Tolstoy, C.S. Lewis, and Jesus Christ. He also composed essays on religion and contributed regularly to several London newspapers.

Wilson \'wil-sən\, Angus, *in full* Sir Angus Frank Johnstone Wilson (b. Aug. 11, 1913, Bexhill, East Sussex, Eng.—d. May 31, 1991, Bury St. Edmunds, Suffolk) British writer whose fiction—sometimes serious, sometimes richly satirical—portrays conflicts in contemporary English social and intellectual life.

Wilson was born to an upper-middle-class family who lived a shabby-genteel existence in small hotels and boarding houses, chiefly in London. This unsettled world on the fringe of society is featured in many of his short stories, and he describes it in his autobiographical *Wild Garden* (1963). He was educated at Westminster School, London, and Merton College, Oxford, and then worked as a cataloger at the British Museum Reading Room. He was professor of English literature at the University of East Anglia (1966–78), becoming emeritus thereafter.

Death Dance: 25 Stories (1969) is a collection of early stories. His first novel, *Hemlock and After* (1952), is regarded by some critics as his best. Before that he had already been noticed by the reading public through the stories collected as *The Wrong Set* (1949) and *Such Darling Dodos* (1950). *Anglo-Saxon Attitudes* (1956) and *The Old Men at the Zoo* (1961) offer acute pictures of a wide array of characters, chiefly learned or propertied, in British life. *The Middle Age of Mrs. Eliot* (1958) is a psychological portrait. Later novels include *Late Call* (1964), *As If By Magic* (1973), and *Setting the World on Fire* (1980). *The World of Charles Dickens* (1970) and *The Strange Ride of Rudyard Kipling* (1977) are notable biographies. *The Collected Stories of Angus Wilson* was published in 1987. Wilson was knighted in 1980.

Wilson \'wil-sən\, August (b. April 27, 1945, Pittsburgh, Pa., U.S.) American playwright, author of a cycle of plays, each set in a different decade of the 20th century, about black American life. He won Pulitzer Prizes for FENCES (1986) and for THE PIANO LESSON (1990).

Largely self-educated, Wilson grew up in poverty and quit school at age 15. He joined the black aesthetic movement in the late 1960s, became the cofounder and director of Black Horizons Theatre in Pittsburgh (1968), and published poetry in such journals as *Black World* (1971) and *Black Lines* (1972). In the early 1980s he wrote several unpublished plays, including *Jitney* and *Fullerton Street*.

Wilson's first major play, MA RAINEY'S BLACK BOTTOM (1985), opened on Broadway in 1984. Set in Chicago in 1927, the play centers upon a verbally abusive blues singer, her fellow black musicians, and their white manager. *Fences*, first produced in 1985, is about a conflict between a father and son in the 1950s. Wilson's chronicle of the black American experience continued with JOE TURNER'S COME AND GONE (1988), a play about neighbors in a Pittsburgh boardinghouse in 1911; *The Piano Lesson*, set in the 1930s and concerning a family's ambivalence about selling an heirloom; and *Two Trains Running* (1992), whose action takes place in a Pittsburgh coffeehouse in the 1960s. His next play, *Seven Guitars*, was produced in 1995.

Wilson \'wil-sən\, Colin (Henry) (b. June 26, 1931, Leicester, Leicestershire, Eng.)   English novelist and writer on philosophy, sociology, music, literature, and the occult.

Wilson's first book, *The Outsider* (1956), is a study of alienation as glimpsed through the lives and writings of some of the principal intellectual figures of the 20th century. Initial critical response catapulted him to fame at the age of 24, in the process making *The Outsider* a best-seller. Wilson's *Religion and the Rebel* (1957), however, was dismissed as unoriginal and superficial. This negative criticism dogged him until his first novel, *Ritual in the Dark* (1960), was published. When his second novel, *Adrift in Soho*, appeared in 1961, he was well on his way to repairing his tarnished reputation.

Many of Wilson's books deal with the psychology of crime, the occult, human sexuality, or his own original form of existential philosophy. An extremely prolific author, he wrote more than 70 books by the early 1990s. Among his novels are *Necessary Doubt* (1964), *The Mind Parasites* (1967), *The God of the Labyrinth* (1970; also published as *The Hedonists*), *The Personality Surgeon* (1985), and *The Magician from Siberia* (1988).

Wilson \'wil-sən\, Dover, *in full* John Dover Wilson (b. July 13, 1881, London, Eng.—d. Jan. 15, 1969, Balerno, Midlothian, Scot.)   British Shakespearean scholar and educator.

Educated at the University of Cambridge, Wilson taught at King's College, London (1924–35), and at the University of Edinburgh (1935–45). Besides serving as chief editor of the New Cambridge edition of William Shakespeare's plays (from 1921), he was a trustee of Shakespeare's birthplace and also of the National Library of Scotland. Wilson made important if controversial contributions to Shakespearean scholarship by a bold elucidation of textual obscurities and original, stimulating interpretations of the plays. His critical judgments have been variously labeled extreme, faulty, or inspired. His intensive study of Elizabethan handwriting proved helpful in reconstructing Shakespeare's text. His most famous book, *What Happens in Hamlet* (1959), was an original reading of that play, and *The Fortunes of Falstaff* (1943) presented a picture of Falstaff as a force of evil ultimately rejected by the king. His other works include *Life in Shakespeare's England: A Book of Elizabethan Prose* (1911), *The Essential Shakespeare: A Biographical Adventure* (1932), *Shakespeare's Happy Comedies* (1962), and *Shakespeare's Sonnets* (1963).

Wilson \'wil-sən\, Edmund (b. May 8, 1895, Red Bank, N.J., U.S.—d. June 12, 1972, Talcottville, N.Y.)   American critic and essayist recognized as the leading critic of his time.

Educated at Princeton, Wilson worked first as a newspaper reporter in New York before becoming managing editor of *Vanity Fair* (1920–21) and associate editor of *The New Republic* (1926–31). His first critical work, AXEL'S CASTLE (1931), was an important international survey of the Symbolist poets. During this period Wilson was married to writer Mary McCarthy. His next major book, TO THE FINLAND STATION (1940), was a historical study of the thinkers who laid the groundwork for the Russian Revolution. Until late in 1940 he was a contributor to *The New Republic*, and much of his work for it was collected in *Travels in Two Democracies* (1936), *The Triple Thinkers* (1938), and THE WOUND AND THE BOW (1941).

After World War II Wilson wrote *The Scrolls from the Dead Sea* (1955), for which he learned to read Hebrew; *Red, Black, Blond and Olive: Studies in Four Civilizations: Zuni, Haiti, Soviet Russia, Israel* (1956); *Apologies to the Iroquois* (1960); PATRIOTIC GORE (1962), an analysis of American Civil War literature; and *O Canada: An American's Notes on Canadian Culture* (1965).

In other works Wilson gave evidence of his crotchety character: *A Piece of My Mind: Reflections at Sixty* (1956), *The Cold War and the Income Tax* (1963), and *The Fruits of the MLA* (1968), a lengthy attack on the Modern Language Association's editions of American authors, which he felt buried their subjects in pedantry. His plays are in part collected in *Five Plays* (1954) and in *The Duke of Palermo and Other Plays with an Open Letter to Mike Nichols* (1969). His poems appear in *Notebooks of Night* (1942) and in *Night Thoughts* (1961); an early collection, *Poets, Farewell*, appeared in 1929. MEMOIRS OF HECATE COUNTY (1946) is a collection of short stories that encountered censorship problems when it first appeared. Wilson edited the posthumous papers and notebooks of his friend F. Scott Fitzgerald, published as *The Crack-Up* (1945), and also edited the novel *The Last Tycoon* (1941), which Fitzgerald had left uncompleted at his death. Wilson wrote one novel himself, *I Thought of Daisy* (1929). Wilson's journals were published posthumously in five volumes, each of which covers a decade.

Wilson \'wil-sən\, Harriet E., *original surname* Adams \'ad-əmz\ (b. 1828?, Milford, New Hampshire?, U.S.—d. 1863?, Boston, Mass?)   Probably the first African-American to publish a novel in English in the United States. Her work, entitled *Our Nig; or, Sketches from the Life of a Free Black, in a Two-Story White House, North. Showing that Slavery's Shadows Fall Even There. By "Our Nig."* (1859), treated racism in the pre-Civil War North.

Almost nothing is known of Wilson's personal history until 1850. She may have been an indentured servant living with a family in Milford before she left to work as a domestic in Massachusetts, marrying Thomas Wilson, a fugitive slave, in 1851. He ran off to sea before the birth of their son, George. The abandoned wife eventually left the baby in a white foster home in New Hampshire so that she could find work. In the preface to *Our Nig*, Wilson states that she wrote the novel to make money to reclaim her son. Unfortunately, George died of a fever in 1860. After 1863 Wilson disappeared from official public records.

Our Nig is largely autobiographical. Its protagonist, Frado, is of mixed race. Abandoned by her white mother, she is mistreated by the bigoted white family who employ her as an indentured servant. She eventually marries but is deserted by her husband.

Wilson \'wil-sən\, Lanford (Eugene) (b. April 13, 1937, Lebanon, Mo., U.S.)   American playwright, a pioneer of the Off-Off Broadway and regional theater movements. His plays are known for experimental staging, simultaneous dialogue, and deferred character exposition. He won a 1980 Pulitzer Prize for TALLEY'S FOLLY (1979).

From 1963 his plays were produced regularly at Off-Off-Broadway theaters. *Home Free!*, and *The Madness of Lady Bright* (published together in 1968) are two one-act plays first performed in 1964; the former involves a pair of incestuous siblings, and the latter features an aging transvestite. *Balm in Gilead* (1965), Wilson's first full-length play, is set in a crowded world of hustlers and junkies. *The Rimers of Eldritch* (1967) examines life in a small town.

In 1969, along with long-time associate Marshall W. Mason and others, he founded the Circle Theatre (later Circle Repertory Company), a regional theater in New York City. Wilson achieved commercial success with *The Great Nebula in Orion* (1971), *The Hot l Baltimore* (1973), and *The Mound Builders* (1975). He also wrote a cycle of plays about the effects of war on a family from Missouri; these included *The 5th of July* (1978), *Talley's Folly, A Tale Told* (1981), and *Talley and Son* (1985). His other plays include *The Gingham Dog* (1969), *Lemon Sky* (1970), *Burn This* (1987), and *Redwood Curtain* (1993).

Wilson, Pudd'nhead \'pŭd-ən-ˌhed-'wil-sən\ Fictional character, the protagonist of Mark Twain's satiric novel PUDD'NHEAD WILSON.

Wimsey, Lord Peter \'pē-tər-'wim-zē\ Fictional character, a monocled aristocratic dilettante turned professional detective, created by Dorothy L. SAYERS in *Whose Body?* (1923).

After his graduation from the University of Oxford, Wimsey, who is the second son of the Duke of Denver, finds that he has a gift for crime detection. His social role is as a dapper young bachelor of wit and charm, a gentleman-scholar, and a lover of rare books. Supported by his private income and by the companionship and service of his loyal manservant Bunter, Wimsey often works closely with Inspector Parker of Scotland Yard (who marries Wimsey's sister). He eventually marries Harriet Vane, a writer of mystery books, whom he meets in *Strong Poison* (1930) and clears of a murder charge.

The Wimsey novels and short-story collections include *Clouds of Witness* (1926), *Unnatural Death* (1927), *Lord Peter Views the Body* (1928), *The Five Red Herrings* (1931), *Have His Carcase* (1932), *Murder Must Advertise* (1933), *The Nine Tailors* (1934), *Gaudy Night* (1935), and *Busman's Honeymoon* (1937).

Winchilsea \'win-chəl-ˌsē\, Anne Finch, Countess of, *original surname* Kingsmill \'kiŋz-mil\ (b. April 1661, Sydmonton, near Newbury, Berkshire, Eng.—d. Aug. 5, 1720, Eastwell Park, Kent) English poet who was one of the outstanding female poets of the era. In 1684 she married Colonel Heneage Finch, who in 1712, on the death of his nephew Charles, became the 4th Earl of Winchilsea.

Finch wrote satiric works on manners, lyric nature poems, and works of devotion to her husband, to fallen royalty, and to friends; the latter featured themes of morality, piety, and ardent sentiment. She was well-known in literary circles and counted Alexander Pope and Jonathan Swift among her friends. Much of her poetry was published in her lifetime, notably "The Spleen," published anonymously in Charles Gildon's *A New Miscellany of Original Poems on Several Occasions* (1701). Some of her work, including her Arcadian tragedy, *Aristomenes*, was issued in *Miscellany Poems on Several Occasions, Written by a Lady* (1713; acknowledged as Finch's work in the second issue, 1714). William Wordsworth gave her poems foremost place in a manuscript anthology made for Lady Mary Lowther (1819; published 1905).

Windhover, The Sonnet by Gerard Manley HOPKINS, completed in May 1877 and collected posthumously in 1918 in *Poems of Gerard Manley Hopkins*. Written shortly before Hopkins' ordination as a Jesuit priest, the poem is dedicated "To Christ our Lord." It concerns Hopkins' philosophy of INSCAPE, the essential nature of a person or thing.

Wind in the Willows, The A linked series of animal tales by Kenneth GRAHAME, considered a classic of English children's literature. The book was begun as a series of bedtime stories for Grahame's son and was published in 1908. The tales relate the adventures of four animal friends and neighbors in the English countryside—Mole, Rat, Toad (of Toad Hall), and Badger. Although the animals converse and behave like humans, each creature also retains its distinctive animal habits.

Wind, Sand and Stars Lyrical and humanistic chronicle of the adventures of Antoine de SAINT-EXUPÉRY, published as *Terre des hommes* in 1939. He used the memoir as a platform to extol cooperation, individual responsibility, and dedication to universal human values.

Wind, Sand and Stars is a collection of philosophical musings, meditations, anecdotes, and reminiscences about flying, the universe, politics, the Spanish Civil War, the North African desert, Tierra del Fuego, and the heroism and nobility of both ordinary people and fellow pilots.

Wingfield family \'wiŋ-ˌfēld\ Fictional family, the main characters in Tennessee Williams' drama THE GLASS MENAGERIE. Amanda, the head of the family, attempts to manage the lives of Tom and Laura, her two adult children. Pathetically unrealistic in her view of the world, Amanda shatters her daughter's fragile sensibility and drives her son away.

Wings of the Dove, The Novel by Henry JAMES, published in 1902. It explores one of James's favorite themes: the cultural clash between naive Americans and sophisticated, often decadent Europeans.

The story is set in London and Venice. Kate Croy is a Londoner who encourages her secret fiancé, Merton Densher, to woo and marry Milly Theale, a wealthy young American who is dying of a mysterious malady. Thus, Kate reasons, although Milly will die soon, she will at least be happily in love, Merton will inherit her fortune, and Kate and Merton can marry and be rich. Shortly after Milly learns of Merton's and Kate's motives, she dies, leaving Merton a legacy that he is too guilt-ridden to accept. Kate is unwilling to forgo the inheritance, and she and Merton part forever, their relationship destroyed by Milly's unwittingly prescient gift.

Winnie-the-Pooh \'win-ē-thə-'pü\ A story collection for children by A.A. MILNE, published in 1926. Milne wrote the episodic stories of *Winnie-the-Pooh* and its sequel, *The House at Pooh Corner* (1928), for his young son Christopher Robin, whose toy animals were the basis for the characters and whose name was used for the young boy who appears in the tales as the benign master of the animals.

The main character, Winnie-the-Pooh (sometimes called simply Pooh or Edward Bear), is a good-natured, honey-loving bear who lives in the Forest surrounding the Hundred Acre Wood. His companions are Eeyore, a gloomy gray donkey; Tigger, a frisky tiger; Piglet, a timid pig; Owl, a pontificating bird; the meddlesome Rabbit; and Kanga, an energetic kangaroo whose inquisitive baby, Roo, lives in her pouch.

Winters \'win-tərz\, Yvor, *in full* Arthur Yvor Winters (b. Oct. 17, 1900, Chicago, Ill., U.S.—d. Jan. 25, 1968, Palo Alto, Calif.) American poet, critic, and teacher who held that literature should be evaluated for its moral and intellectual content as well as its aesthetic appeal.

Educated at the University of Chicago, University of Colorado, and Stanford University, Winters taught at the University of Idaho from 1925 to 1927 and at Stanford from 1928 to 1966. He wrote one book of short stories and several books of poetry. His *Collected Poems* were published in 1952 (rev. ed., 1960).

Winters is probably best known for his literary criticism. His attacks on such contemporary literary idols as T.S. Eliot and Henry James aroused much controversy. His major critical works, including *Primitivism and Decadence: A Study of American Experimental Poetry* (1937), *Maule's Curse: Seven Studies in the History of American Obscurantism* (1938), and *The Anatomy of Nonsense* (1943), were collected as *In Defense of Reason* (1947; rev. ed., 1960). *Forms of Discovery: Critical and Historical Essays on the Forms of the Short Poem in English* appeared in 1967.

Winterson \'win-tər-sən\, Jeanette (b. Aug. 27, 1959, Manchester, Eng.)   Novelist noted for her quirky, unconventional, and often comic novels.

Winterson's first novel, *Oranges Are Not the Only Fruit* (1985), won a Whitbread award as that year's best first novel. It concerns the relationship between a young lesbian and her adoptive mother, a religious fanatic. *The Passion* (1987), her second work, is a picaresque historical novel that chronicles the adventures of Villanelle, an enslaved Venetian woman who is rescued by Henri, a cook from Napoleon's army. Winterson's other works include the novels *Sexing the Cherry* (1989), *Written on the Body* (1992), and *Art and Lies* (1994), and screenplays for television.

Winter's Tale, The   Play in five acts by William SHAKESPEARE, produced in 1610–11 and published in the First Folio of 1623. One of Shakespeare's final plays, *The Winter's Tale* is a romantic comedy with elements of tragedy and is noted for its use of realism.

The plot is based on the play *Pandosto* (1588) by Robert Greene. Leontes, the king of Sicilia, jealously believes that his faithful wife Hermione has committed adultery with his old friend Polixenes, the king of Bohemia. After various mishaps, all three are ultimately reconciled after the wedding of Florizel (son of Polixenes) and Perdita (daughter of Leontes and Hermione).

Winter's Tales   Collection of short stories by Isak DINESEN, originally published in Danish as *Vinter-eventyr* in 1942 and then translated by the author into English in the same year. Mostly set against the backdrop of historic Denmark, the 11 stories trace the symbolic destinies of simple characters caught up in expansive, romantic situations.

Based on a Danish folktale, "Sorrow Acre" is one of the author's best-known works. A feudal lord offers to release the imprisoned son of a peasant woman if she mows a field of rye by herself in one day; she fulfills the bargain and falls dead. "The Young Man with the Carnation" and "A Consolatory Tale" both concern Charlie Despard, a writer who grows to understand his dependence on his audience and his ability to interpret the world at the cost of experiencing it. Replete with images of the sea, "Peter and Rosa" is about two young lovers who tragically fulfill their dreams. The other fables are "The Sailor-Boy's Tale," "The Dreaming Child," "The Fish," "Alkmene," "The Pearls," "The Invincible Slave-Owners," and "The Heroine."

wisdom literature   Type of literature that flourished throughout the ancient Middle East, with Egyptian examples dating to before the middle of the 3rd millennium BCE. It revolved around the professional sages and scribes in the service of the court and consisted primarily of maxims about the practical, intelligent way to conduct one's life and of speculations about the worth and meaning of human life. The most common form of these wise sayings, which were intended for oral instruction, was the *mashal* (Hebrew: "comparison" or "parable," although frequently translated "proverb").

Wise Blood   First novel by Flannery O'CONNOR, published in 1952. This darkly comic and disturbing novel about religious beliefs was noted for its witty characterizations, ironic symbolism, and use of Southern dialect.

Wise Blood centers on Hazel Motes, a discharged serviceman who abandons his fundamentalist faith to become a preacher of anti-religion in a Tennessee city, establishing the "Church Without Christ." Motes is a ludicrous and tragic hero who meets a collection of equally grotesque characters. One of his young followers, Enoch Emery, worships a museum mummy. Hoover Shoats is a competing evangelist who creates the "Holy Church of Christ Without Christ." Asa Hawks is an itinerant preacher who pretends to have blinded himself to show his faith in redemption.

Wispelaere \də-'vis-pə-ˌlär\, Paul de (b. July 4, 1928, Assebroek, near Bruges, Belg.)   Flemish novelist, essayist, and critic whose avant-garde works examine the individual's search for identity and the relationship between literature and life.

De Wispelaere began his career as an editor for several literary periodicals. From 1972 he was professor of modern literature of the Netherlands at the University of Antwerp, and he was editor-in-chief of the *Nieuw Vlaams Tijdschrift* ("New Flemish Review") from 1981. In his writing and his literary criticism, de Wispelaere resisted the prevalent influence of structuralism and deliberately created an ambivalence about the process of writing and his own insights.

The novels *Een eiland worden* (1963; "To Become an Island") and *Mijn levende schaduw* (1965; "My Living Shadow") deal with the writer as "I" and explore the polarity of author and observer. In *Paul-tegenpaul, 1969–1970* (1970; "Paul Against Paul") and *Een dag op het land* (1976; "A Day on the Ground"), the central theme is the duality of the writer's personality. Other novels were *Tussen tuin en wereld* (1979; "Between Garden and World"), *Mijn huis is nergens meer* (1982; "I Have No Home Now"), and *Brieven uit nergenshuizen* (1986; "Letters from Nowhere").

Some of Wispelaere's works combine narrative with autobiographical notes, diary entries, polemics, and literary criticism. His collections of critical essays include *Het Perzische tapijt* (1966; "The Persian Rug"), *Met kritisch oog* (1967; "With a Critical Eye"), and *De broek van Sartre en andere essays* (1987; "Sartre's Trousers and Other Essays").

Wister \'wis-tər\, Owen (b. July 14, 1860, Philadelphia, Pa., U.S.—d. July 21, 1938, North Kingstown, R.I.)   Novelist whose THE VIRGINIAN (1902) helped establish the cowboy as an American folk hero and stock fictional character.

Wister graduated from Harvard Law School in 1888 and practiced for two years in Philadelphia. He spent his summers in the West, and in 1891, after the enthusiastic acceptance by *Harper's* of two of his Western sketches, he devoted himself to a literary career.

The Virginian is the story of a cowboy ranch foreman and was a great popular success.

Library of Congress

Wister's other major work was *Roosevelt: The Story of a Friendship, 1880–1919* (1930), detailing his long acquaintance with Theodore Roosevelt, a Harvard classmate. He also wrote a number of books for children. Wister's collected writings were published in 11 volumes in 1928. His journals and letters from 1885 to 1895 were published in *Owen Wister Out West* (1958), edited by his daughter, Fanny Kemble Wister.

Witch of Endor \'en-ˌdȯr\ Female sorcerer mentioned in Chapter 28 of the First Book of Samuel in the Old Testament. Saul, the first king of Israel, asks her to conjure up the spirit of the prophet Samuel to tell his fortune. The spirit informs Saul that he and his three sons will die in battle the next day and that Israel will fall to the Philistines.

The story of the Witch of Endor has excited literary imagination through the ages and inspired further embellishment of her character and practices. Geoffrey Chaucer, for example, in "The Friar's Tale" of *The Canterbury Tales*, speaks of her as a "pithonesse," and the 16th-century writer Guillaume du Bartas suggests in his poem *La Semaine* that in her necromantic art she used a "flambeau" made from the fat of her own son.

Wither \'with-ər\ or **Withers** \'with-ərz\, George (b. June 11, 1588, Bentworth, Hampshire, Eng.—d. May 2, 1667, London) English poet and Puritan pamphleteer.

Wither's *Abuses Stript and Whipt* (1613)—with its satiric treatment of lust, avarice, and pride—apparently gave offense, and he was imprisoned for some months. In prison he wrote *The Shepherd's Hunting* (1615), whose five eclogues are among his finest verse. *Fidelia* (1617), an elegiac epistle lamenting a lover's inconstancy, contains in later editions the famous lyric "Shall I, wasting in despair." For *Wither's Motto: Nec Habeo, nec Careo, nec Curo* (1621; "I Don't Have, I Don't Lack, I Don't Care"), an assertion of his own virtue and a lively denunciation of others' vices, he was again imprisoned.

The eulogy *Faire-Virtue, The Mistresse of Phil'Arete* and the collection of love and pastoral poems *Juvenilia* appeared in 1622. After their publication Wither became a convinced Puritan and wrote only about religious and political matters. *The Hymnes and Songs of the Church* (1623) is the first hymnbook in English not based entirely on the Psalms; it contains passages of rugged, simple prose. Wither was in London during the plague of 1625 and published *Britain's Remembrancer* (1628), a voluminous poem on the subject, interspersed with invective and prophecy. His religious poems and hymns were published in 1641 in *Haleluiah or, Britans Second Remembrancer*. He was imprisoned from 1660 to 1663 for an unpublished poem criticizing the new House of Commons.

With Rue My Heart Is Laden Short, epigrammatic poem in the collection A SHROPSHIRE LAD by A.E. Housman. A blend of Romantic lyricism and elegant classicism, it typifies the elegiac tone of the collection. The poem comprises two stanzas of alternating seven- and six-syllable lines.

Witkiewicz \vit-'kʸev-ēch\, Stanisław Ignacy, byname **Witkacy** \vit-'kát-si\ (b. Feb. 24, 1885, Warsaw [Poland]—d. Sept. 18, 1939, Jeziory, near Dombrovitsa, Pol. [now Dubrovytsya, Ukraine]) Polish painter, novelist, and playwright noted for developing many of the ideas of the literary Awangarda movement. He was the main exponent of the Polish literary movement known as "catastrophism," a precursor of the Theater of the Absurd.

Witkiewicz's plays anticipated those of Eugène Ionesco and Samuel Beckett in their deliberately contorted characters and plots and their use of grotesque parody. Rapid tempos, warped time juxtapositions, and catastrophic incidents are combined with an original and symbolic use of language in such plays as *Kurka wodna* (1921; "The Water Hen") and *Wariat i zakon-*

nica (1925; *The Madman and the Nun*). His novels *Pożegnanie jesieni* (1927; "Farewell to Autumn") and *Nienasycenie* (1930; "Insatiability") express the same philosophy. His dramas began to be revived in Poland and the West in the 1950s and are now a permanent feature of Polish theatrical repertoires.

Wittig \vē-'tēg\, Monique (b. 1935, Dannemarie, Haut-Rhin, Alsace, Fr.) French avant-garde novelist and radical feminist whose works include unconventional narratives about utopian nonhierarchical worlds, often devoid of men.

Wittig attended the Sorbonne, and in 1976 she immigrated to the United States. Her first novel, *L'Opoponax* (1964; *The Opoponax*), is viewed through the consciousness of a rebellious young girl in a convent school. Its unorthodox, minimally punctuated, and nonchronological narrative established Wittig's course as a writer. She sought to avoid traditional forms and accepted devices, the use of which, she asserted, gave unspoken assent to the male-oriented power structure that had established them. Her second novel, *Les Guérillères* (1969; *The Guérillères*), is a two-part series of prose poems about women warriors in a female-oriented culture. Wittig's other works include *Le Corps lesbien* (1973; *The Lesbian Body*), a collection of fierce prose poems extolling lesbian love and the female body; the novel *Virgile, non* (1985; *Across the Acheron*), a feminist parody of Dante's *Divine Comedy*; and (with Sande Zeig) the play *Le Voyage sans fin* (1985; *The Constant Journey*), a feminist send-up of *Don Quixote*. She also collaborated with Zeig to produce a feminist dictionary entitled *Brouillon pour un dictionnaire des amantes* (1976; *Lesbian Peoples: Material for a Dictionary*). A collection *The Straight Mind and Other Essays* (1992) was published in English.

Wittlin \'vēt-lēn\, Józef (b. Aug. 17, 1896, Dmytrów, Galicia, Austria-Hungary [now Dmytriv, Ukraine]—d. Feb. 29, 1976, New York, N.Y., U.S.) Polish novelist, essayist, and poet, a master of the Polish language.

Having receieved a classical education in Lwów (now Lviv, Ukraine), he studied at the University of Vienna and served for two years in the Austro-Hungarian army. In his early poetry collection *Hymny* (1920; "Hymns"), he voiced a humanistic protest against the debasement of individuals as the victims of powerful states and social systems. In 1924 Wittlin's translation into Polish of *The Odyssey* was published.

The work that ensured him a place in Polish literature is *Sól ziemi* (1936; *Salt of the Earth*), a novel about an illiterate Polish peasant who is unwillingly drafted into the Austrian army to fight a war he doesn't understand. Wittlin left Poland a few weeks before World War II began, eventually settling in New York City, where he wrote a warm book of yearning for his native city, *Mój Lwów* (1946; "My Lwów"). He became a U.S. citizen in 1949.

Wivallius \vē-'väl-yůs\, Lars (b. 1605, Wivalla, Swed.—d. April 6, 1669, Stockholm) Swedish poet and adventurer whose lyrics show a feeling for the beauties of nature new to Swedish poetry in his time.

Wivallius studied at Uppsala and in 1625 left Sweden to travel. Frequently posing as a nobleman, he swindled his way across Europe and was imprisoned for a time in Nürnberg [Ger.]. Back in Sweden (1629), he succeeded in marrying the daughter of a nobleman by false pretenses but was found out and again imprisoned. In 1634 he was deported to Kajaneborg, northern Finland, where he spent seven years of severe hardship. Subsequently he became an advocate in Stockholm.

Though unscrupulous and antisocial, Wivallius was full of gaiety in his youth. Of his many ballads, written mainly in prison, the best are those inspired by longing for freedom (for example, "Ack libertas," an ode to liberty) and love of nature.

Wives and Daughters Novel by Elizabeth GASKELL, first published serially in the *Cornhill Magazine* (August 1864–January 1866) and then in book form in 1866; it was unfinished at the time of her death in November 1865. Known as her last, longest, and perhaps finest work, it concerns the interlocking fortunes of several families in the country town of Hollingford.

Wives and Daughters chronicles the maturation of Molly Gibson, a sincere young woman whose widowed father, the town doctor, marries Hyacinth Kirkpatrick, a charming but petty widow and former governess in the household of Lord Cumnor. Although Molly resents her stepmother, she befriends her stepsister Cynthia, who is secretly engaged to Lord Cumnor's land agent, Mr. Preston. Molly is warmly received at the home of Squire Hamley and his disabled wife. The Hamleys' two sons are Osborne, a clever but shallow man who marries unwisely and dies young, and Roger, an honest scientist who eventually marries Molly after being engaged to Cynthia, who ultimately weds a London barrister.

Wodan *see* ODIN.

Wodehouse \\'wůd-‚haůs\\, P.G., *in full* Sir Pelham Grenville Wodehouse (b. Oct. 15, 1881, Guildford, Surrey, Eng.—d. Feb. 14, 1975, Southampton, Long Island, N.Y., U.S.) English-born comic novelist, short-story writer, lyricist, and playwright, best known as the creator of JEEVES, the supreme "gentleman's gentleman." He was the author of more than 90 books, collaborated on more than 30 plays and musical comedies, and wrote more than 20 film scripts.

Wodehouse was educated at Dulwich College, London, and took a job as a humorous columnist on the London *Globe* (1902) and wrote freelance for many other publications. After 1909 he lived and worked for long periods in the United States and in France. He was captured in France by the Germans in 1940 and spent much of the war interned in Berlin. In 1941 he made five radio broadcasts from there to the United States in which he humorously described his experiences as a prisoner and subtly ridiculed his captors. His use of enemy broadcasting facilities evoked deep and lasting resentment in Britain, however. After the war Wodehouse settled in the United States, becoming a citizen in 1955.

It was not until 1913 (in *Something New*; published in England as *Something Fresh,* 1915) that Wodehouse turned to the farce, which became his special strength. His plots are highly complicated and set in the English social atmosphere of the early 20th century. The young bachelor Bertie WOOSTER and his effortlessly superior manservant Jeeves were still together, their ages unadvanced, in *Much Obliged, Jeeves* (1971), though they first appeared together in a story in "Extricating Young Gussie" (1915). Among his other notable characters are Lord EMSWORTH and the EMPRESS OF BLANDINGS.

Wodehouse's plays include adaptations of his novels and of the work of continental playwrights such as Ferenc Molnár and Siegfried Geyer. He wrote books and lyrics for Jerome Kern, Victor Herbert, Rudolf Friml, Sigmund Romberg, and George Gershwin. *Leave It to Jane* (1917), written with Kern and Guy Bolton, was an innovative musical comedy that was successfully revived in 1971.

Woden *see* ODIN.

Woestijne \\vů-'stein-ə, *Angl* -'stän-\\, Karel van de (b. March 10, 1878, Ghent, Belg.—d. Aug. 23, 1929, Zwijnaarde) Flemish poet whose work constitutes a symbolic autobiography of a typical turn-of-the-century personality—the sophisticated, world-weary sensualist striving after spiritual detachment.

Woestijne studied German philology and worked as a journalist and government official in Brussels (1907–20) and a professor of literature at Ghent from 1920 until his death. His early, subjective poetry includes *Het vaderhuis* (1903; "The Father House"), about his childhood; *De boomgaard der vogelen en der vruchten* (1905; "The Orchard of Birds and Fruit"), on his youth and courtship; and *De gulden schaduw* (1910; "The Golden Shadow"), on his marriage and fatherhood. The tormented awareness of the conflict between sense and spirit, inherent in all his works, reaches a bitter climax in *De modderen man* (1920; "The Man of Mud"). His body of verse constitutes one of the highest achievements of European Symbolism.

Woiwode \\'wī-wůd-ē\\, Larry (Alfred) (b. Oct. 30, 1941, Carrington, North Dakota, U.S.) American writer whose fiction reflects his early childhood in a tiny town on the western North Dakota plains where five generations of his family had lived.

Woiwode first published fiction while at the University of Illinois, which he attended from 1959 to 1964. His short stories and poetry later appeared in such magazines as *Harper's, Partisan Review, The Atlantic,* and *The New Yorker.* Woiwode taught and led writing workshops at Dartmouth College and various universities, including the State University of New York at Binghamton.

Woiwode's critically acclaimed first novel, *What I'm Going to Do, I Think* (1969), is a study of a newly married couple. *Beyond the Bedroom Wall: A Family Album* (1975) is a multigenerational saga of a North Dakota family; *Born Brothers* (1988) continues the story of Charles and Jerome Neumiller, characters from *Beyond the Bedroom Wall,* who also appear in *The Neumiller Stories* (1989). *Poppa John* (1981) concerns an out-of-work television actor. *Indian Affairs* (1992) is a sequel to *What I'm Going to Do.* In 1977 Woiwode's collected poems were published under the title *Even Tide,* and a volume of short stories, *Silent Passengers,* appeared in 1993.

Wolf \\'wůlf\\, Christa, *original surname* Ihlenfeld \\'ē-lən-‚felt\\ (b. March 18, 1929, Landsberg an der Warthe, Ger. [now Gorzów Wielkopolski, Pol.]) German novelist, essayist, and screenwriter whose work reflects her experiences in Germany during World War II under the Nazi regime and her postwar life in communist East Germany.

Wolf was reared in a middle-class, pro-Nazi family. With the defeat of Germany in 1945, she moved with her family to East Germany. After studying at the universities of Jena and Leipzig, she worked as editor of the East German Writers' Union magazine and was also a reader for book publishers. From 1959 to 1962 she worked in a factory, and from 1962 she was a full-time writer.

Wolf's first novel was *Moskauer Novelle* (1961; "Moscow Novella"). Her second novel, *Der geteilte Himmel* (1963; *Divided Heaven*), established her reputation. This work explores the political and romantic conflicts of Rita and Manfred. He defects to West Berlin for greater personal and professional freedom; she, after a brief stay with him, rejects the West and returns to East Berlin. The novel brought Wolf political favor; she was elected an alternate member of the central committee of the Socialist Unity Party, a post she later resigned.

Nachdenken über Christa T. (1968; *The Quest for Christa T.*) concerns an ordinary woman who questions her socialist beliefs and life in a socialist state, and who dies prematurely of leukemia. Though well received by Western critics, the novel was severely attacked by the East German Writers' Congress as a depressing and pessimistic work, and its sale was forbidden in East Germany.

Wolf's other works include *Kindheitsmuster* (1976; *A Model Childhood*), a semiautobiographical account of growing up in the Third Reich; *Till Eulenspiegel* (1972), which interprets the legend from a Marxist point of view; and *Kassandra* (1983; *Cassandra*), an inner monologue that associates nuclear power with patriarchal power. *Was bleibt* (*What Remains*), written in 1979 but not published until 1990, is an account of the methods of surveillance practiced by the East German government, in which Wolf implicated herself.

Wolfdietrich \\‚vȯlf-'dē-triḱ\ Germanic hero of romance who appears in the Middle High German poems *Ortnit* and *Wolfdietrich* in *Das Heldenbuch* as the son of Hugdietrich, emperor of Constantinople. Repudiated by his father, who mistakenly believes him illegitimate, he is brought up by the emperor's faithful retainer Berchtung von Meran. Berchtung and his 16 sons support Wolfdietrich, who, after his father's death, is driven from his inheritance by his own brothers. After a long exile in Lombardy at the court of King Ortnit, the hero returns to liberate Berchtung's imprisoned sons and regain his kingdom. Among the exploits of Wolfdietrich is his killing of the dragon that had slain Ortnit.

The story of Wolfdietrich attached itself to the family of Clovis, king of the Franks. Some critics believe Hugdietrich to be the epic counterpart of Theodoric (Dietrich); the name might be a Latinized form of Hugo Theodericus, eldest son of Clovis. Wolfdietrich would thus represent Theodoric's son Theodebert (died *c.* 548), whose succession was disputed by his uncles. But father and son are merged by a process of epic fusion, so that Wolfdietrich appears to be the counterpart sometimes of Theodoric and sometimes of Theodebert.

The story of how Hugdietrich won his bride Hildburg, daughter of the king of Salonika, forms in one manuscript version a separate introduction to the Wolfdietrich romance.

Wolfe \'wu̇lf\, Charles (b. Dec. 14, 1791, Dublin, Ire.—d. Feb. 21, 1823, Queenstown, County Cork) Irish poet and clergyman whose "The Burial of Sir John Moore" (1817), commemorating the commander of the British forces at the Battle of Corunna (La Coruña, Spain) during the Peninsular War (1808–14), is one of the best-known funeral elegies in English. Wolfe attended Trinity College, Dublin, was ordained in 1817, and held curacies in County Tyrone.

Wolfe \'wu̇lf\, Thomas (Clayton) (b. Oct. 3, 1900, Asheville, N.C., U.S.—d. Sept. 15, 1938, Baltimore, Md.) American writer best known for his first novel, LOOK HOMEWARD, ANGEL (1929).

Educated privately, Wolfe entered the University of North Carolina in 1916, where he wrote and acted in several one-act plays. In 1920 he enrolled in George Pierce Baker's 47 Workshop at Harvard, intending to become a dramatist. Several of his works were produced at Harvard, including *Welcome to Our City* (1923), in which the town of Altamont (Asheville) first appeared. There, too, he began the play *Mannerhouse* (published 1948; never produced during his lifetime).

In 1923 Wolfe left Harvard for New York City where, except for trips to Europe and elsewhere, he resided most of his life. Some of his stories, notably "Only the Dead Know Brooklyn," contain observations of city life. Still intending to be a playwright, he taught at the Washington Square College of New York University, described in several of his novels. In 1926, while abroad, he began work on what eventually became *Look Homeward, Angel*, in which he recounted the growth of an autobiographical protagonist, Eugene Gant, in the mountain town of Altamont.

After publication of *Look Homeward, Angel*, Wolfe quit teaching to write full time. OF TIME AND THE RIVER (1935) is perhaps the most turbulent of his books. In his memoir *The Story of a Novel* (1936) he describes his close working relation with the editor Maxwell PERKINS to bring the enormous manuscripts of these two works into manageable novelistic proportions.

Wolfe did not publish another novel during his lifetime, though at his death he left a prodigious quantity of manuscript, from which the editor Edward Aswell extracted two more novels, THE WEB AND THE ROCK (1939) and YOU CAN'T GO HOME AGAIN (1940), and a collection of shorter pieces and chapters of an uncompleted novel, *The Hills Beyond* (1941). Wolfe's *Letters to His Mother* (1943) were also published, as well as his *Selected Letters* (1956).

Wolfe \'wu̇lf\, Tom, *in full* Thomas Kennerly Wolfe, Jr. (b. March 2, 1930, Richmond, Va., U.S.) American novelist, journalist, and social commentator who is known as a leading critic of contemporary life and as a proponent of New Journalism (the application of fiction-writing techniques to journalism).

After studying at Washington and Lee University and Yale University, Wolfe wrote for several newspapers, including the *Springfield Union* in Massachusetts and the *Washington Post*. He later worked as an editor on such magazines as *New York* and *Esquire* (from 1977) and as an artist for *Harper's*.

His first book, *The Kandy-Kolored Tangerine-Flake Streamline Baby* (1964), is a collection of essays satirizing American trends and celebrities of the 1960s. *The Electric Kool-Aid Acid Test* (1968) chronicles the psychedelic drug culture of the 1960s. His other works include *The Pump House Gang* (1968), *Radical Chic & Mau-Mauing the Flak Catchers* (1970), *The Painted Word* (1975), *Mauve Gloves & Madmen, Clutter & Vine* (1976), and *From Bauhaus to Our House* (1981). *The Right Stuff* (1979), which examines aspects of the first U.S. astronaut program, and *The Bonfire of the Vanities* (1987), a novel of urban greed and corruption, were best-sellers.

Wolfe, Nero \'nir-ō-'wu̇lf\ Fictional American private detective, the eccentric protagonist of 46 mystery stories by Rex STOUT. Wolfe was introduced in *Fer-de-Lance* (1934).

A man of expansive appetites and sophisticated tastes, Wolfe is corpulent and moody. Detesting mechanized vehicles and disdaining most humans, he is averse to leaving his home for business reasons; he assigns the physical investigations of murders to his associate and friend, Archie Goodwin, and manages to solve his mysteries without leaving his own confines. Another of Wolfe's associates is his private chef, Fritz Brenner, who also works as Wolfe's butler and handyman. Wolfe's interest in food is equaled only by his passion for orchids: with the aid of Theodore Horstman, he nurtures some 10,000 orchid plants in his rooftop garden.

The many novels featuring Nero Wolfe include *The League of Frightened Men* (1935), *Too Many Cooks* (1938), *The Golden Spiders* (1953), *Champagne for One* (1958), *Gambit* (1962), and *A Family Affair* (1975).

Wolff \'vȯlf\, Betje, *in full* Elizabeth Wolff-Bekker \'vȯlf-'bek-ər\ (b. July 24, 1738, Vlissingen, Neth.—d. Nov. 5, 1804, The Hague) Dutch writer and collaborator with Aagje DEKEN on the first Dutch novel, *De historie van mejuffrouw Sara Burgerhart*, 2 vol. (1782; "The History of Miss Sara Burgerhart").

Wolff, the daughter of a prosperous family, ran away with a naval officer at the age of 17, only to return home in a few days, deeply hurt by the experience. In 1759 she married Adriaan Wolff, a minister more than 30 years her senior.

The first writing she did was classical poetry in imitation of Alexander Pope; she also wrote lyrical poetry and satire. She directed most of her satire at her conservative, provincial neighbors. From 1767 to 1769 Wolff contributed to the periodical *Gryzaard*. By the time she met Deken in 1776, she was a well-known and widely discussed writer. After the death of her husband, Wolff set up house with Deken. Five years later

Sara Burgerhart, an epistolary novel inspired by Samuel Richardson's *Pamela*, was published. It was a realistic, subtly developed character study and included circumstances drawn from the lives of both women—particularly from Wolff's youthful adventure with the ensign.

After the success of *Sara Burgerhart*, the two women continued to work together, producing among other works three more epistolary novels. The nature and extent of their literary collaboration remains in dispute. Some critics, reflecting on Deken's mediocre output prior to *Sara Burgerhart*, maintain that Wolff was the principal author of the joint works. Wolff in fact had a far greater canon and reputation.

Wolff \'wu̇lf\, Tobias (Jonathan Ansell) (b. June 19, 1945, Birmingham, Ala., U.S.)　Writer primarily known for his short stories, in which many voices and a wide range of emotions are skillfully depicted.

Wolff's parents divorced when he was a child; from age 10 until he joined the U.S. Army, he traveled with his mother, who relocated frequently and finally settled in Seattle, Wash., where she remarried. Wolff wrote about his childhood in the 1950s, including his relationship with his abusive stepfather, in *This Boy's Life: A Memoir* (1989; film, 1993). His older brother, the novelist Geoffrey Wolff, was brought up by their father and wrote about his childhood in *The Duke of Deception: Memories of My Father* (1979). The brothers were reunited when Tobias was a young teenager.

Wolff served in Vietnam, after which he was educated at Oxford University and Stanford University. His first published collection of short stories was *In the Garden of the North American Martyrs* (1981; U.K. title, *Hunters in the Snow*). He also wrote a novella, *The Barracks Thief* (1984), and *Back in the World* (1985), a collection of short stories.

Wolfram von Eschenbach \'vȯl-främ-fȯn-'esh-ən-ˌbäk\ (b. c. 1170—d. c. 1220)　German poet whose epic PARZIVAL, distinguished alike by its moral elevation and its imaginative power, is one of the most profound literary works of the Middle Ages.

An impoverished Bavarian knight, Wolfram apparently served a succession of Franconian lords: Abensberg, Wildenberg, and Wertheim are among the places he names in his work. He also knew the court of the Landgrave Hermann I of Thuringia, where he met the great medieval lyric poet Walther von der Vogelweide.

Wolfram's surviving literary works, all bearing the stamp of his original personality, consist of eight lyric poems, chiefly *Tagelieder* ("Dawn Songs," describing the parting of lovers at morning); the epic *Parzival*; the unfinished epic *Willehalm*, telling the history of the crusader William of Orange; and short fragments of a further epic, the so-called *Titurel*, which elaborates the tragic love story of Sigune from Book 3 of *Parzival*. Wolfram's influence on later poets was profound, and he is a member, with Hartmann von Aue and Gottfried von Strassburg, of the great triumvirate of Middle High German epic poets.

Wollstonecraft \'wu̇l-stən-ˌkräft\, Mary, *married name* Godwin \'gȯd-win\ (b. April 27, 1759, London, Eng.—d. Sept. 10, 1797, London)　English writer, noted as a passionate advocate of educational and social equality for women. Her early *Thoughts on the Education of Daughters* (1787) foreshadowed her mature work on the place of women in society, *A Vindication of the Rights of Woman* (1792); the core of the *Vindication* is a plea for equality of education for men and women.

After teaching school and working as a governess, Wollstonecraft went to work for the London publisher James Johnson, who had published several of her works, including the novel *Mary: A Fiction* (1788). In 1792 she left England to observe the French Revolution in Paris, where she lived with an American, Captain Gilbert Imlay. In the spring of 1794 she gave birth to a daughter, Fanny. The following year, distraught over the breakdown of her relationship with Imlay, she attempted suicide.

She returned to London to work again for Johnson and became one of the influential radical group that centered upon his home and that included William Godwin, Thomas Paine, Thomas Holcroft, William Blake, and, after 1793, William Wordsworth. In 1796 she began a liaison with Godwin, and on March 29, 1797, because Mary was pregnant, they were married. The marriage was happy but brief; Wollstonecraft died 11 days after the birth of her second daughter, Mary. *See* Mary Wollstonecraft SHELLEY.

The life of Mary Wollstonecraft has been the subject of several biographies, beginning with one by her husband. Those written in the 19th century tended to emphasize the scandalous aspects of her life at the expense of the intellectual. With the renewed interest in women's rights in the later 20th century, she again became the subject of a number of books.

Woman in the Dunes, The　Novel by ABE Kōbō, published in Japanese as *Suna no onna* in 1962. This avant-garde allegory is esteemed as one of the finest Japanese novels of the postwar period; it was the first of Abe's novels to be translated into English.

The protagonist of *The Woman in the Dunes* is Niki Jumpei, an amateur entomologist who, on a weekend trip from the city, discovers a bizarre village in the dunes where residents live in deep sand pits. Imprisoned with a widow in one of the pits, he must shovel the omnipresent sand that threatens to bury the community. The novel relates Niki's attempts to escape the pit, his relationship with the woman, and his gradual acceptance of a new identity. Showing more similarities to the works of Franz Kafka than to those of Japanese contemporaries, *The Woman in the Dunes* is noted for its unusual plot, its detailed descriptions of the sand, and its existential examination of the human condition.

Woman in White, The　Novel by Wilkie COLLINS, published serially in *All the Year Round* (November 1859–July 1860) and in book form in 1860. Noted for its suspenseful plot and unique characterization, the successful novel brought Collins great fame; he adapted it into a play in 1871.

This dramatic tale, inspired by an actual criminal case, is told through multiple narrators. Frederick Fairlie, a wealthy hypochondriac, hires virtuous Walter Hartright to tutor his beautiful niece and heiress, Laura, and her homely, courageous half-sister, Marian Halcombe. Although Hartright and Laura fall in love, she honors her late father's wish that she marry Sir Percival Glyde, a villain who plans to steal her inheritance. Glyde is assisted by sinister Count Fosco, a cultured, corpulent Italian who became the archetype of subsequent villains in crime novels. Their plot is threatened by Anne Catherick, a mysterious fugitive from a mental asylum who dresses in white, resembles Laura, and knows the secret of Glyde's illegitimate birth. Through the perseverance of Hartright and Marian, Glyde and Fosco are defeated and killed, allowing Hartright to marry Laura.

Woman of Andros, The \'an-ˌdräs\　Play by TERENCE, produced in 166 BC as *Andria*. It has also been translated as *The Andrian Girl*. Terence adapted it from the Greek play *Andria* by Menander and added material from Menander's *Perinthia* (*The Perinthian Girl*).

The relationship of a father, Simo, and his son, Pamphilus, is central to *The Woman of Andros*, in which Simo engages

Pamphilus in an arranged marriage although Pamphilus wants to marry his sweetheart from Andros, the mother of his child. Simo's schemes and self-delusion set up the play's comic situations. Dialogues, rather than the conventional monologues used by other playwrights of the time, enhance the play's dramatic movement. Also unusual in a Roman comedy is the fact that Terence's characters are not comic caricatures but fully realized people. Terence's *The Woman of Andros* was the basis of several later works, including the play *The Conscious Lovers* by Sir Richard Steele (1723) and the novel *The Woman of Andros* by Thornton Wilder (1930).

woman of letters 1. A woman who is a scholar. 2. A woman who is an author.

Women at the Ecclesia \i-'klē-zhē-ə, e-, -zē-\ (*Greek* Ekklēsiazousai) Drama by ARISTOPHANES, performed about 392 BC. One of Aristophanes' less appealing plays, it treats the takeover by the women of Athens of the Ecclesia, the Athenian democratic assembly. They carry out this mission dressed as men, and once they have achieved their goal, they introduce a communistic system of wealth, sex, and property.

Women at the Thesmophoria \,thes-mō-'fôr-ē-ə, ,thez-\ (*Greek* Thesmophoriazousai) Play by ARISTOPHANES, performed in 411 BC. The play develops from Euripides' discovery that the women of Athens, angered by his constant attacks upon them in his tragedies, mean to discuss during their coming festival (the Thesmophoria) the question of contriving his death. Euripides tries to persuade the effeminate Agathon, a tragic poet, to plead his cause. Agathon refuses, and Euripides persuades his brother-in-law Mnesilochus to undertake the assignment. Mnesilochus is disguised with great thoroughness as a woman and sent on his mission, but his true sex is discovered and he is at once seized by the women. There follow three scenes in which he tries unsuccessfully to escape; all three involve brilliant parodies of Euripides' tragedies. Finally, Euripides himself arrives and succeeds in rescuing his advocate by promising never again to revile women.

Women in Love Novel by D.H. LAWRENCE, privately printed in 1920 and published commercially in 1921. Following the characters Lawrence had created for *The Rainbow* (1915), *Women in Love* examines the ill effects of industrialization on the human psyche, resolving that individual and collective rebirth is possible only through human intensity and passion.

Women in Love contrasts the love affair of Rupert Birkin and Ursula Brangwen with that of Gudrun, Ursula's artistic sister, and Gerald Crich, a domineering industrialist. Birkin, an introspective misanthrope, struggles to reconcile his metaphysical drive for self-fulfillment with Ursula's practical view of sentimental passion. Their love affair and eventual marriage are set as a positive antithesis to the destructive relationship of Gudrun and Crich. The novel also explores the relationship between Birkin and Crich. According to critics, Birkin is a self-portrait of Lawrence, and Ursula represents Lawrence's wife, Frieda.

Women of Brewster Place, The \'brüs-tər\ Novel by Gloria NAYLOR, published in 1982. It chronicles the communal strength of seven diverse black women who live in decaying rented houses on a walled-off street of an urban neighborhood.

As the middle-aged matriarch of the group, Mattie Michael is a source of comfort and strength. She recalls her past tragedies in flashbacks. Her close friend, Etta Mae Johnson, is a restless free spirit who repeatedly attaches herself to disappointing men. Embracing racial pride, idealistic Kiswana Browne initially disparages her mother's middle-class values but later accepts them. Mattie saves the long-suffering Ciel Turner from self-destruction after she barely endures a series of personal disasters. Kiswana helps Cora Lee, a young unmarried mother, realize that her many children should not be treated like dolls. Lorraine seeks social acceptance, unlike her outspoken lesbian lover, Theresa. When she is gang-raped, Lorraine is deranged by the attack and murders one of her only supporters, Ben, the kind janitor of Brewster Place. At the novel's end the women angrily demolish the wall that separates them from the rest of the city.

Wonderful One-Hoss Shay, The \'wən-'hós\ (*in full* The Deacon's Masterpiece, or The Wonderful "One-Hoss Shay") Poem by Oliver Wendell HOLMES, published in his "Breakfast-Table" column in *The Atlantic Monthly* (September 1858).

Often interpreted as a satire on the breakdown of Calvinism in America, the poem concerns a "one-hoss shay" (*i.e.*, one-horse chaise) constructed logically and with all parts of equal strength by a New England deacon. Though it is meant to last forever, the vehicle spontaneously falls apart 100 years after it was built.

Wood \'wùd\, Mrs. Henry, *original name* Ellen Price \'prīs\ (b. Jan. 17, 1814, Worcester, Worcestershire, Eng.—d. Feb. 10, 1887, London) English novelist who wrote the sensational and extremely popular *East Lynne* (1861), a melodramatic and moralizing tale of the fall of virtue. Translated into many languages, it was dramatized with great success, and its plot has been frequently imitated in popular fiction.

Other highly successful novels followed, and in some of them (notably *The Channings*, 1862) Wood showed great ability in storytelling and in creating natural middle-class characters and relationships. In 1867 she became proprietor and editor of *Argosy* magazine.

Woodcock \'wùd-,käk\, George (b. May 8, 1912, Winnipeg, Man., Can.—d. Jan. 28, 1995, Vancouver, B.C.) Canadian poet, critic, historian, travel writer, playwright, scriptwriter, and editor whose work, particularly his poetry, reflects his belief that revolutionary changes would take place in society.

Woodcock published dozens of books. His poetry, particularly that published before World War II, expresses his anarchistic, rather than communistic, expectation of revolutionary changes in society. His poetry includes *The White Island* (1940), *The Centre Cannot Hold* (1943), *Imagine the South* (1947), *Selected Poems* (1967), *Notes on Visitations: Poems 1936–1975* (1975), *The Mountain Road* (1980), and *Collected Poems* (1983). Among his other works are travel books, including *To the City of the Dead* (1956) and *Incas and Other Men* (1959); collections of essays, such as *The Rejection of Politics* (1972); and biographies of Mordecai Richler (1970) and Sir Herbert Read (1972). *Letter to the Past*, an autobiography, appeared in 1982.

Woodhouse, Emma \'em-ə-'wùd-,haùs\ Fictional character, the attractive and intelligent but meddlesome heroine of Jane Austen's EMMA.

Woodlanders, The Novel by Thomas HARDY, published serially in *Macmillan's Magazine* from 1886 to 1887 and in book form in 1887.

The story begins as Grace Melbury, daughter of a timber merchant in a Dorset village, returns from finishing school and rejects her simple but understanding fiance, the apple grower Giles Winterbourne. Grace accedes to the urgings of her father and marries Edred Fitzpiers, a young doctor of great charm but questionable moral character. Grace soon turns to Giles for comfort after Edred goes off with Mrs. Felice Charmond, a local upper-class woman. Giles, who is seriously ill, relinquishes his cottage to Grace and moves into a rude hut, where he soon dies of exposure. Although Grace mourns his loss, she eventually reconciles with Edred.

wood nymph *also called* dryad.   In Greek mythology, a nymph that lives in woods and forests.

Woolf \\'wu̇lf\\, Douglas (b. March 23, 1922, New York, N.Y., U.S.—d. Jan. 18, 1992, Urbana, Ill.)   American author of gently comic fiction about people unassimilated into materialistic, technological society.

Woolf's short stories were published in literary periodicals beginning in the 1940s, and his first novel, *The Hypocritic Days*, was published in 1955. Most of Woolf's longer works concern cross-country journeys. In his most popular novel, *Fade Out* (1959), an elderly man rejected by his offspring makes a comic odyssey to an Arizona ghost town. *Wall to Wall* (1962), the story of a car salesman's son traveling from Los Angeles to New England, is often considered Woolf's finest work. The travels of the protagonist in *On Us* (1977) are interrupted by a meeting with a movie producer, and *The Timing Chain* (1985) relates events that occur on a car trip from the Rocky Mountains to Boston. Woolf's short novels *Ya!* and *John-Juan* were published together in 1971, and some of his short fiction was published in *Hypocritic Days & Other Tales* (1993).

Woolf \\'wu̇lf\\, Leonard (Sidney) (b. Nov. 25, 1880, London, Eng.—d. Aug. 14, 1969, Rodmell, Sussex)   British man of letters, publisher, political worker, journalist, and internationalist who influenced literary and political life and thought more by his personality than by any one achievement.

Woolf's most enduring accomplishment was probably his autobiography, an expression of the toughness of moral fiber and quality of mind and spirit that made him one of the outstanding men of his time. Its first three volumes, *Sowing* (1960), *Growing* (1961), and *Beginning Again* (1964), re-create the world of liberal Jewry into which he was born, the intellectual excitement of life at the University of Cambridge in the early years of the 20th century, his experience as a civil servant in Ceylon (now Sri Lanka) in 1904–11 that made him an anti-imperialist, and the atmosphere of the Bloomsbury group of artists and writers, in which he and his wife, novelist Virginia Woolf, played a formative part. In 1917 they founded their own publishing house, the Hogarth Press, and their discerning understanding encouraged such writers as T.S. Eliot and E.M. Forster.

The last volumes of the autobiography (*Downhill All the Way*, 1967; *The Journey Not the Arrival Matters*, 1969) span the years 1919 to 1969, a period during which Woolf exercised a certain amount of political influence through editorial activity on left-wing and internationalist journals and through his writings.

Woolf \\'wu̇lf\\, Virginia, *in full* Adeline Virginia Woolf, *original surname* Stephen \\'stē-vən\\ (b. Jan. 25, 1882, London, Eng.—d. March 28, 1941, near Rodmell, Sussex)   British author who made an original contribution to the form of the novel and was one of the most distinguished critics of her time.

She was educated at home by her father, Sir Leslie Stephen, and, after his death in 1904, lived in Gordon Square, London, which became the center of the Bloomsbury group. In 1912 she married Leonard Woolf, and in 1917 they founded the Hogarth Press, which published her books.

After her novels *The Voyage Out* (1915) and *Night and Day* (1919) appeared, she began to experiment. She wanted to stress the continuous flow of experience and the indefinability of character and external circumstances as they impinge on consciousness. She was also interested in the way time is experienced both as a sequence of disparate moments and as the flow of years and of centuries. From JACOB'S ROOM (1922) onward, she tried to convey the impression of time present and of time passing in individual experience and also of the characters' awareness of historic time.

In MRS. DALLOWAY (1925) and TO THE LIGHTHOUSE (1927) she extended her technical mastery; above all, she gave to

Gisèle Freund

both of these novels a tightly organized form, partly by using poetic devices such as recurrent images and partly by restricting the time of the action. ORLANDO (1928) is a historical fantasy with evocations of England, and especially literary England, from the mid-16th century to 1928. In her long essay A ROOM OF ONE'S OWN (1929) she described the status of women and the difficulties encountered by women writers in a man's world. She returned to this theme in *Three Guineas* (1938).

Returning to the novel, in THE WAVES (1931) she confined herself to recording the stream of consciousness. The reader lives within the minds of one or another of six characters from their childhood to their old age. Human experience of the "seven ages of man," rather than character or event, is paramount. *The Years* (1937) is more expansive and traditional. In *Between the Acts* (1941) the action, as in *Mrs. Dalloway*, occurs on a single day, but extended time is suggested by the staging of a village pageant recording English history, while the reader is also kept aware of impending war. In a recurrence of mental illness, after finishing *Between the Acts*, Woolf drowned herself near her Sussex home.

Woolf wrote two biographies: one is fanciful, a fragment of the life of the Brownings through the imagined memories of Elizabeth Barrett Browning's dog (*Flush*, 1933); the other is a full-length biography of the art critic Roger Fry (1940). Her best critical studies are in THE COMMON READER (first series, 1925; second series, 1932), *The Death of the Moth* (1942), and *Granite and Rainbow* (1958).

Woolf's diaries and correspondence have been collected and published in several editions, including *The Diary of Virginia Woolf*, 5 vol. (1977–84).

Woollcott \\'wu̇l-kət\\, Alexander (Humphreys) (b. Jan. 19, 1887, Phalanx, N.J., U.S.—d. Jan. 23, 1943, New York, N.Y.)   American author, critic, and actor known for his acerbic wit. He was the self-appointed leader of the Algonquin Round Table, an informal luncheon club at New York City's Algonquin Hotel in the 1920s and '30s.

After graduating from Hamilton College, Clinton, N.Y., in 1909, Woollcott joined the staff of *The New York Times* as cub reporter and succeeded to the post of drama critic in 1914. After a brief stint in the U.S. Army, reporting for *The Stars and Stripes*, he returned to the *Times* and subsequently worked for the *New York Herald* and the *New York World*. He also wrote for *The New Yorker*, and beginning in 1929 he appeared on radio, establishing a nationwide reputation as raconteur, gossip, conversationalist, wit, and man-about-town. As a literary critic Woollcott wielded great influence. He was the author of *Mrs. Fiske, Her Views on Actors, Acting, and the Problems of Production* (1917), *Two Gentlemen and a Lady* (1928), and *While Rome Burns* (1934) and the publisher of two anthologies, *The Woollcott Reader* (1935) and *Woollcott's Second Reader* (1937).

Wooster, Bertie \\'bər-tē-'wu̇s-tər\\   Fictional character, an inane English gentleman in several comic stories and novels set in the early 20th century, written by P.G. WODEHOUSE. Wooster is the employer of Jeeves, a valet who is the ultimate "gentleman's gentleman." They first appeared together in the story "Extricating Young Gussie" in 1915.

A simple-minded but good-hearted bachelor who fears his aunts and the prospect of marriage, Wooster is rescued from innumerable complicated situations by the resourceful and innately superior Jeeves.

Worde \də-'wôrd\, Wynkyn de, *original name* Jan van Wynkyn \văn-'viŋ-kin\ (d. 1534/35) Alsatian-born printer in London, an astute businessman who published a large number of books (at least 600 titles from 1501). He was also the first printer in England to use italic type (1524).

De Worde was employed at William Caxton's press, Westminster (the first printing enterprise in England), from its foundation in 1476 until Caxton's death in 1491, when he assumed control of the business. In 1500/01 he moved his press from Westminster to Fleet Street, London. Whereas Caxton and numerous continental European contemporaries were also editors and translators, Wynkyn was purely a commercial printer.

wordsmanship \'wərdz-mən-,ship\ [*word + -smanship* (as in *craftsmanship*)]   The art or craft of writing.

Wordsworth \'wərdz-wərth\, Dorothy (b. Dec. 25, 1771, Cockermouth, Cumberland, Eng.—d. Jan. 25, 1855, Rydal, Cumberland)   English prose writer whose *Alfoxden Journal 1798* and *Grasmere Journals 1800–03*, published posthumously in 1897, are appreciated as much for the imaginative power of their description of nature, their perfection of style, and their revelation of a personality of unusual quality as they are for the light they throw on her brother William.

Their mother's death in 1778 separated Dorothy from her brothers, and from 1783 they were without a family home. When in 1795 William was lent a house in Dorset, she made a home for him there. From this time on she also acted as his secretary. At Alfoxden, Somerset, in 1796–98, she enjoyed with Wordsworth and Samuel Taylor Coleridge a companionship of "three persons with one soul." She went with them to Germany (1798–99), and in December 1799 she and William settled for the first time in a home of their own, Dove Cottage, Grasmere, in the Lake District, remaining there after his marriage (1802) until 1808, when she moved with the family to Rydal.

In 1829 she was dangerously ill and henceforward was obliged to lead the life of an invalid. Her ill-health apparently affected her intellect, and during the last 20 years of her life her mind was clouded.

Her prose is spontaneous, transparent, and completely natural. As a record of her brother's life and the dates and circumstances of writing of almost all his poems in the years of his greatest poetic achievement, the *Grasmere Journals* is invaluable. The *Alfoxden Journal* is a record of William's friendship with Coleridge that resulted in their *Lyrical Ballads* (1798), with which the Romantic movement began; and the *Grasmere Journals* provides a picture of early 19th-century cottage life in a remote part of England.

Wordsworth \'wərdz-wərth\, William (b. April 7, 1770, Cockermouth, Cumberland, Eng.—d. April 23, 1850, Rydal Mount, Westmorland)   Major English Romantic poet. His LYRICAL BALLADS (1798), written with Samuel Taylor Coleridge, helped launch the English Romantic movement.

Wordsworth was born in the Lake District of northern England, the second of five children. He attended St. John's College, Cambridge. During a summer vacation in 1790 he took a long walking tour through revolutionary France. There he was caught up in the passionate enthusiasm that followed the fall of the Bastille and became an ardent republican sympathizer. After a second journey to France, he spent three or four of the darkest years of his life. Unprepared for any profession, rootless, virtually penniless, bitterly hostile to his own country's opposition to the French, he knocked about London. Even-

tually, in 1795, a friend's legacy made possible Wordsworth's reunion with his beloved sister Dorothy; the two were never again to live apart.

Portrait by Henry Eldridge, 1804

About this time Wordsworth became friends with Coleridge, and they formed a partnership that would alter the course of English poetry. Stimulated by Coleridge and under the healing influences of nature and his sister, Wordsworth began in 1797–98 to compose the short lyrical and dramatic poems for which he is best remembered. Many were written to a daringly original program aimed at breaking the decorum of Neoclassical verse. These poems appeared in 1798 in a slim, anonymously authored volume entitled *Lyrical Ballads*, which opened with Coleridge's long poem "The Rime of the Ancient Mariner" and closed with Wordsworth's TINTERN ABBEY.

About 1798 Wordsworth began writing the autobiographical poem that would absorb him intermittently for the next 40 years, and which was eventually published in 1850 under the title THE PRELUDE. In the company of Dorothy, Wordsworth spent the winter of 1798–99 in Germany, where he wrote some of his most moving poetry, including the "Lucy" and "Matthew" elegies. Upon his return to England, Wordsworth incorporated several new poems in the second edition of *Lyrical Ballads* (1800), notably two tragic pastorals of country life, "The Brothers" and "Michael." These poems, together with the brilliant lyrics that were assembled in Wordsworth's second verse collection, *Poems, in Two Volumes* (1807), help to make up what is now recognized as his great decade, stretching from his meeting with Coleridge in 1797 until 1808.

In 1805 the drowning of Wordsworth's brother John gave Wordsworth a deep shock and brought about a new sobriety, a new restraint, and a lofty, almost Miltonic elevation of tone and diction, as can be seen in ODE: INTIMATIONS OF IMMORTALITY; but little of Wordsworth's later verse matches the best of his earlier years.

The most memorable poems of Wordsworth's middle and late years were often cast in elegaic mode. Only in 1820, with the publication of *The River Duddon*, was Wordsworth appreciated by the critics. In 1843 he succeeded Robert Southey as poet laureate.

word value   The effectiveness of a word to express the exact shade of meaning desired and to fit into the rhythmic structure of a phrase or sentence.

Works and Days   Epic poem by the 8th-century BC Greek writer HESIOD that is part almanac, part agricultural treatise, and part homily. It is addressed to his brother Perses, who by guile and bribery has already secured for himself an excessive share of their inheritance and is seeking to gain another advantage in a similar manner. Trying to dissuade him from such practices, Hesiod recounts in the first part of the poem two myths illustrating the necessity for honest, hard work in life. One takes up and continues the story of Pandora, who out of curiosity opens a jar, loosing multifarious evils on humanity; the other traces human decline since the Golden Age. Against the brutality and injustice of his contemporaries Hesiod affirms his unshakable belief in the power of justice.

The part of Hesiod's message that exalts justice and deprecates hubris is addressed to the leaders of his community, who seem inclined to abet Perses. Hesiod also speaks to Perses directly, urging him to abandon his schemes and thenceforth to gain his livelihood through strenuous and persistent work. Hard work is for Hesiod the only way to prosperity and distinction. The concept of life that Hesiod develops is in conscious opposition to the more glorious ideals of the heroic epic of Homer.

In the second half of the poem, Hesiod describes with much practical detail the kind of work appropriate to each part of the calendar and explains how to set about it. The description of the rural year is enlivened by a vivid feeling for the rhythm of human life and the forces of nature, from the overpowering winter storm, which keeps one homebound, to the parching heat of summer, during which one must have respite from labor.

The poem ends with a series of primitive taboos and superstitions, followed by a section explaining which parts of the month are auspicious for sowing, threshing, shearing, and the begetting of children. It is difficult to believe that either of these sections could have been composed by Hesiod.

World Is Too Much with Us, The Sonnet by William WORDSWORTH, published in 1807 in *Poems, in Two Volumes*. True to the tenets of English Romanticism, the poem decries the narrowness of modern daily life, especially its disconnection from and ignorance of the beauty of nature:

> The world is too much with us; late and soon
> Getting and spending, we lay waste our powers;
> Little we see in Nature that is ours;
> We have given our hearts away, a sordid boon!

The poet concludes with praise for ancient mythology, which, despite its paganism, recognized the intrinsic power of nature, as personified by such sea deities as Proteus and Triton.

World of Wonders Third of a series of novels by Robertson Davies known collectively as THE DEPTFORD TRILOGY.

Wotton \'wŭt-ən, 'wŏt-\, Sir Henry (b. March 30, 1568, Boughton Malherbe, Kent, Eng.—d. December 1639, Eton, Buckinghamshire) English poet, diplomat, and art connoisseur who was a friend of John Donne and John Milton.

Of his few surviving poems, "You Meaner Beauties of the Night," written to Elizabeth of Bohemia, is the most famous. Izaak Walton's *The Life of Sir Henry Wotton* was prefixed to the *Reliquiae Wottonianae* (1651), the volume in which most of Wotton's writings first appeared.

Wotton was knighted in 1604, served as ambassador to Venice intermittently from 1604 to 1623, and was a member of Parliament in 1614 and 1625. In 1624 he became provost of Eton and in 1627 he took holy orders. Long residence in Venice developed in Wotton a taste for architecture and painting far more sophisticated than that of his contemporaries. In *The Elements of Architecture* (1624) he expresses his views clearly and briefly.

Wouk \'wōk\, Herman (b. May 27, 1915, New York, N.Y., U.S.) American novelist best known for his epic war novels.

During World War II Wouk served in the Pacific aboard the destroyer-minesweeper *Zane*. One of his best-known novels, THE CAINE MUTINY (1951), was based on that experience. This drama of naval tradition presented the unforgettable character Captain Queeg and won the Pulitzer Prize for fiction in 1952.

Wouk's novels are all meticulously researched, and they provide an accurate and in-depth portrait of a particular slice of the world. They are built on a belief in the goodness of man or, in the case of MARJORIE MORNINGSTAR (1955), the purity of women, and revolve around moral dilemmas. Wouk wrote with little technical innovation, but his novels have been tremendously popular. Most have been made into screenplays. Popular television mini-series were based on his expansive two-volume historical novel set in World War II: *The Winds of War* (1971) and *War and Remembrance* (1978). A later novel was *Inside, Outside* (1985).

Wound and the Bow, The Book of literary criticism by Edmund WILSON, published in 1941. Employing psychological and historical analysis, Wilson examines the childhood psychological traumas experienced by such writers as Charles Dickens, Ernest Hemingway, James Joyce, Rudyard Kipling, and Edith Wharton and the effects of those experiences on their writing.

The title of the book comes from a myth retold by Wilson in which an injured, foul-smelling Greek warrior who has been banished because of his odor is sought out by his fellow Greeks because they need his prowess with the magic bow given to him by Apollo in order to win the Trojan War.

Woyzeck \'vòit-sek\ Dramatic fragment by Georg BÜCHNER, written between 1835 and 1837; it was discovered and published posthumously in 1879 as *Wozzek* and first performed in 1913. Best known as the libretto for Alban Berg's opera *Wozzeck* (performed 1925), the work was published in a revised version in 1922, under its original title, *Woyzeck*. Both naturalist and expressionist elements added to the work's continued interest for audiences in the late 20th century.

The title character is a religious man preoccupied with sin and guilt. An army barber, he endures psychological humiliation by his captain and painful physical experimentation by his doctor to make extra money for Marie, his common-law wife, and their child. Woyzeck is jealous of Marie's affair with a drum major. Filled with rage, he explodes into violence.

Büchner based *Woyzeck* on an account of an actual murder case in which a soldier killed his mistress in a jealous frenzy and was subsequently the object of medical controversy regarding his sanity. Büchner did not organize the work into acts, and there is no definitive text of the play. The events, rather than appearing in definite chronological sequence, are presented as a series of related occurrences.

WPA Federal Theatre Project National theater project sponsored and funded by the U.S. government as part of the Works Progress Administration (WPA). Its purpose was to create jobs for unemployed theatrical people in the Great Depression years of 1935–39.

While the project was in operation, some 10,000 professionals were employed in all facets of the theater. The four-year effort involved about 1,000 productions in 40 states; performances were often free to the public. These productions included classical and modern drama, children's plays, puppet shows, musical comedies, and documentary theater known as Living Newspaper. Other projects included the production of plays by young, unknown American playwrights, the promotion of black American theater, and the presentation of radio broadcasts of dramatic works. Following a series of controversial investigations by the House Committee on Un-American Activities and Subcommittee on Appropriations into leftist commentary on social and economic issues, the Federal Theatre Project was terminated in 1939 by congressional action.

WPA Federal Writers' Project A program established in 1935 by the Works Progress Administration (WPA) as part of the New Deal struggle against the Great Depression. It provided jobs for unemployed writers, editors, and research workers. Directed by Henry G. Alsberg, it operated in all states and at one time employed 6,600 individuals. The American

Guide series, the project's most important achievement, included guidebooks to every state and territory (except Hawaii), as well as to Washington, D.C., New York City, Los Angeles, San Francisco, New Orleans, and Philadelphia; to several major highways (U.S. 1, Ocean Highway, Oregon Trail); and to scores of towns, villages, and counties. The project also produced ethnic studies, folklore collections, local histories, and nature studies—totaling more than 1,000 books and pamphlets.

In accordance with WPA regulations, most of the project's personnel came from the relief rolls. They included such already prominent authors as Conrad Aiken, Maxwell Bodenheim, and Claude McKay and such future luminaries as Richard Wright, Ralph Ellison, Nelson Algren, Frank Yerby, Saul Bellow, Loren Eiseley, and Weldon Kees. (Eudora Welty was a photographer for the Mississippi guide.) Congress ended federal sponsorship of the project in 1939 but allowed it to continue under state sponsorship until 1943.

Wreck of the Deutschland, The \\'dȯich-ˌlänt\\ Ode by Gerard Manley HOPKINS, written in the mid-1870s and published posthumously in 1918 in *Poems of Gerard Manley Hopkins*. One of Hopkins' longest poems, comprising 35 eight-line stanzas, it commemorates the death of five Franciscan nuns, exiled from Germany, who drowned when their ship the *Deutschland* ran aground near Kent, Eng., on Dec. 6–7, 1875. It was the first poem Hopkins wrote in seven years, having abstained from verse writing upon his decision to become a Jesuit priest.

Following a general invocation at the beginning of the work, the bulk of the poem describes the shipwreck, focusing on one particular nun whose final agony is compared to the Passion of Jesus Christ. The ode concludes with a prayer for the religious conversion of England.

wrenched accent \\'rencht\\ In prosody, an accent that is forced for the sake of the meter of a verse or that is counter to the regular accent that a given syllable would have in normal speech.

Wright \\'rīt\\, James (Arlington) (b. Dec. 13, 1927, Martin's Ferry, Ohio, U.S.—d. March 25, 1980, New York, N.Y.) American poet of the postmodern era who wrote about sorrow, salvation, and self-revelation, often drawing on his native Ohio River valley for images of nature and industry. In 1972 he won the Pulitzer Prize for *Collected Poems* (1971).

Wright studied under John Crowe Ransom at Kenyon College (Gambier, Ohio), attended the University of Vienna, and continued his studies under Theodore Roethke at the University of Washington. Wright taught at the University of Minnesota, Macalester College, St. Paul, Minn., and Hunter College, New York City. His first two books, *The Green Wall* (1957) and *Saint Judas* (1959), were influenced by the poetry of Edwin Arlington Robinson, Georg Trakl, and Robert Frost.

The Branch Will Not Break (1963), the watershed of Wright's career, is characterized by free verse, simple diction, and a casual mix of objective and subjective imagery, as illustrated by the poem "Lying in a Hammock at William Duffy's Farm in Pine Island, Minnesota." The successful *Collected Poems* was followed by *Two Citizens* (1973), *Shall We Gather at the River* (1968), *To a Blossoming Pear Tree* (1977), and *This Journey* (1982). Wright also translated the works of Trakl, César Vallejo, Hermann Hesse, and Pablo Neruda, often in collaboration with Robert Bly.

Wright \\'rīt\\, Judith (Arundell) (b. May 31, 1915, Armidale, N.S.W., Australia) Australian poet whose verse, thoroughly modern in idiom, is noted for skillful technique.

After completing her education at the University of Sydney, Wright worked in an advertising agency, for the University of Sydney as a secretary, as a clerk in Brisbane, and later as a statis-tician. From 1949 she lectured part-time at various Australian universities, becoming honors tutor in English at the University of Queensland, Brisbane, from 1967. She was also active as a literary editor.

Among her volumes of poetry are *The Moving Image* (1946), *Woman to Man* (1949), *The Gateway* (1953), *The Two Fires* (1955), *City Sunrise* (1964), *Fourth Quarter* (1976), *The Double Tree: Selected Poems 1942–1976* (1978), *Phantom Dwelling* (1985), and *A Human Pattern* (1990). A volume of short stories, *The Nature of Love*, was published in 1966. Wright's many nonfiction works include a biography of the Australian poet Charles Harpur and a book on the Australian short-story writer Henry Lawson. She also wrote several books for children.

Wright \\'rīt\\, Richard (b. Sept. 4, 1908, near Natchez, Miss., U.S.—d. Nov. 28, 1960, Paris, Fr.) Novelist and short-story writer who was among the first American black writers to protest white treatment of blacks, notably in his novel NATIVE SON (1940).

Library of Congress

Wright's grandparents had been slaves. His father left home when he was five, and the boy, who grew up in poverty, was often shifted from one relative to another. He worked at a number of jobs before joining the northward migration, first to Memphis, Tenn., and then to Chicago. There, after working in unskilled jobs, he was given an opportunity to write through the Federal Writers' Project. In 1932 he became a member of the Communist Party and was executive secretary of the local John Reed Club of leftist writers and artists of Chicago. In 1937 he went to New York City, where he became Harlem editor of the communist *Daily Worker* and, later, vice president of the League for American Writers.

Wright first came to the general public's attention with a volume of novellas, UNCLE TOM'S CHILDREN (1938). His fictional scene shifted to Chicago in *Native Son*. It presents the story of Bigger Thomas, whose accidental killing of a white girl makes clear and immediate his hitherto vague awareness of antagonism from a white world.

Early versions of Wright's best novella, "The Man Who Lived Underground" (collected in its final version in a posthumous volume of stories, *Eight Men*, 1961), appeared in 1942 and 1944. The absurd, isolated subterranean life of its black hero foreshadows the existentialism that guided Wright's later works.

In 1944 Wright left the Communist Party because of political and personal differences. The autobiographical BLACK BOY, a moving account of his childhood and young manhood, appeared in 1945. Soon thereafter he settled in Paris as a permanent expatriate. *The Outsider* (1953), acclaimed as the first American existential novel, warned that blacks had awakened in a disintegrating society not ready to include them. Three later novels were not well-received. Among his polemical writings of that period was *White Man, Listen!* (1957), which was originally a series of lectures given in Europe. The autobiographical *American Hunger* was published posthumously in 1977.

Wrinkle in Time, A   Juvenile novel by Madeleine L'ENGLE, published in 1962. It won a Newbery Medal in 1963.

Combining theology, fantasy, and science, it is the story of travel through space and time to battle a cosmic evil. With their neighbor Calvin O'Keefe, young Meg Murry and her brother Charles Wallace embark on a cosmic journey to find their lost father, a scientist studying time travel. Assisted by three eccentric women—Mrs. Whatsit, Mrs. Who, and Mrs. Which—the children travel to the planet Camazotz where they encounter a repressed society controlled by IT, a disembodied brain that represents evil. Among the themes of the work are the dangers of unthinking conformity and scientific irresponsibility and the saving power of love. The sequels are *A Wind in the Door* (1973), *A Swiftly Tilting Planet* (1978), and *Many Waters* (1986).

writerly \\'rī-tər-lē\   **1.** Of, relating to, or typical of a writer. **2.** Of or relating to a text that demands some effort on the part of the reader, as opposed to a readerly text. The critic Roland Barthes used the terms *lisible* ("readerly") and *scriptible* ("writerly") to distinguish between texts that are straightforward and those whose meaning is not immediately evident. Writerly texts, such as James Joyce's *Ulysses* and William Faulkner's *The Sound and the Fury*, are self-consciously literary works characterized by an emphasis on the mechanics of writing, specifically in their elaborate use of language. *Compare* READERLY.

Wu Chengen or **Wu Ch'eng-en** \\'wū-'chəŋ-'ən\ (b. *c.* 1500, Shanyang, Huaian [now in Jiangsu province], China—d. *c.* 1582, Jiangsu)   Novelist and poet of the Ming dynasty (1368–1644), generally acknowledged as the author of the Chinese folk novel XIYOU JI (1592; *Journey to the West*, also partially translated as *Monkey*).

Wu received a traditional Confucian education and became known for his cleverness in the composition of poetry and prose in the classical style. Throughout his life he displayed a marked interest in bizarre stories, such as the set of oral and written folktales that formed the basis of *Xiyou ji*. Like all novels of its time, *Xiyou ji* was written in the vernacular and published anonymously to protect the author's reputation. As a result, the identity of the novelist was long unknown outside Wu's native district. Only two volumes of Wu's other writings have survived.

Wu jing or **Wu ching** \\'wū-'jiŋ\ ("Five Classics")   Five ancient Chinese books whose prestige is so great that in the fourfold classification of Chinese writings the *jing* ("classics") are placed before *shi* ("history"), *zi* ("philosophy"), and *ji* ("literature"). For 2,000 years these classics, all associated in some way with the name of the sage Confucius (551–479 BC), were invoked as norms for Chinese society, law, government, education, literature, and religion. As such, their influence is without parallel in the long history of China. Chinese students, however, do not generally attempt the *Wu jing* without having first studied the shorter—and generally speaking less complicated—Confucian texts called *Si shu* ("Four Books").

In 136 BC the Han dynasty ruler Wudi declared Confucianism to be the state ideology of China. Doctoral chairs (*bo shi*) were thereupon established for the teaching of the *Wu jing* and continued to exist into the 20th century. In 124 BC the *Wu jing* were accepted by the national university as its core curriculum. Proficiency in interpreting and expounding the texts of the *Wu jing* became a requirement for all scholars who wanted to obtain posts in the government bureaucracy.

The *Wu jing* collection consists of the *Yi jing* ("Classic of Changes"; often rendered *I ching*), *Shu jing* ("Classic of History"), *Shi jing* ("Classic of Poetry"), *Li ji* ("Collection of Rituals"), and *Chunqiu* ("Spring and Autumn" [Annals]).

Wu Jingzi or **Wu Ching-tzu** \\'wū-'jiŋ-'dzi\ (b. 1701, Quanjiao, Anhui province, China—d. Dec. 12, 1754, Yangzhou, Jiangsu province)   Author of the first Chinese satirical novel, *Rulin waishi* (*c.* 1750; *The Scholars*).

Wu Jingzi was a member of a scholarly and well-to-do family. He succeeded neither academically nor financially, however, and he was unable or unwilling to pass the higher official examinations. He mismanaged his inheritance and at the age of 32 was forced by poverty to move to Nanjing, where he led a life of drinking and carousing.

Probably around 1740, Wu Jingzi began work on the semi-autobiographical *Rulin waishi*, completing it about 10 years later. In this picaresque romance, he used sharp satire to attack the corrupt official practices and personalities that he had observed.

Wuthering Heights   Novel by Emily BRONTË, published in 1847 under the pseudonym Ellis Bell. This intense, solidly imagined novel is distinguished from other novels of the period by its dramatic and poetic presentation, its abstention from authorial intrusion, and its unusual structure.

The story is recounted by Lockwood, a disinterested party, whose narrative serves as the frame for a series of retrospective shorter narratives by Ellen Dean, a housekeeper. All concern the impact of the foundling Heathcliff on the two families of Earnshaw and Linton in a remote Yorkshire district at the end of the 18th century. Embittered by abuse and by the marriage of Cathy Earnshaw—who shares his stormy nature and whom he loves—to Edgar Linton, Heathcliff plans a revenge on both families, extending into the second generation. Cathy's death in childbirth fails to set him free from his obsession with her, which persists until his death; the marriage of the surviving heirs of Earnshaw and Linton restores peace.

Wyatt or **Wyat** \\'wī-ət\, Sir Thomas (b. 1503, Allington, near Maidstone, Kent, Eng.—d. Oct. 6, 1542, Sherborne, Dorset)   Poet who introduced the Italian sonnet and terza rima verse form and the French rondeau into English literature.

Wyatt was a member of the court circle of Henry VIII, where he seems to have been admired for his skill in music, languages, and arms. During his career he served a number of diplomatic missions and was knighted in 1537, but his fame rests on his poetic achievements, particularly his songs. His poems are unusual for their time in carrying a strong sense of individuality. They consist of *Certayne Psalmes . . . drawen into Englyshe meter* (1549); three satires; and songs identified in manuscript, published in 19th- and 20th-century editions. He also contributed to the Earl of Surrey's *Songes and Sonettes*, published in *Tottel's Miscellany* (1557).

Wycherley \\'wich-ər-lē\, William (b. 1640, Clive, near Shrewsbury, Shropshire, Eng.—d. Jan. 1, 1716, London)   English dramatist noted for his comedies of manners in which he attempted to reconcile a personal conflict between deep-seated puritanism and an ardent physical nature. He perhaps succeeded best in THE COUNTRY-WIFE (1675), in which satirical comment on excessive jealousy and complacency was blended with a richly comic presentation, the characters unconsciously revealing themselves in laughter-provoking colloquies.

Wycherley was sent to be educated in France at the age of 15. There he became a Roman Catholic, but, on returning to England to study at the University of Oxford in 1660, he reverted to Protestantism. Leaving Oxford without a degree, he began to study law, although he seems to have preferred a life of pleasure that included study of the theater. He had earlier drafted a first play, *Love in a Wood; or, St. James's Park*, and in the autumn of 1671 it was presented in London, bringing its author instant acclaim. Wycherley was taken up by Barbara

Villiers, Duchess of Cleveland, whose favors he shared with King Charles II, and he was admitted to the circle of wits at court. His next play, *The Gentleman Dancing-Master*, was presented in 1672 but proved unsuccessful. These early plays—both of which have some good farcical moments—followed tradition in "curing excess" by presenting a satirical portrait of variously pretentious characters—fops, rakes, would-be wits, and the solemn of every kind. *The Plain-Dealer*, presented in 1676, satirizes rapacious greed. The satire is crude and brutal, but pointed and effective. In *The Country-Wife*, acted a year earlier, the criticism of manners and society is also severe, but in this case there is no sense of the author hating his characters.

Wycherley eventually lost favor at court. At about the same time his wife died and left him a fortune, but the will was contested and Wycherley ruined himself fighting the case. Cast into a debtor's prison, he was rescued seven years later by King James II, who paid off most of his debts and allowed him a small pension.

Wylie \\'wī-lē\\, Elinor, *original name* Elinor Morton Hoyt \\'hóit\\ (b. Sept. 7, 1885, Somerville, N.J., U.S.—d. Dec. 16, 1928, New York, N.Y.) American poet and novelist whose work, written from an aristocratic and traditionalist point of view, reflected changing American attitudes in the aftermath of World War I.

Wylie came from a prominent Philadelphia family. Her work included four volumes of poetry and four novels. Her poetry, carefully structured and sensuous in mood, shows the influence of 16th- and 17th-century English verse. Her novels combine gentle fantasy and classical formality with thoroughly researched historical settings. *The Orphan Angel* (1926) imagines the life of the English poet Percy Bysshe Shelley if he had been rescued from drowning and taken to America. Her third husband, William Rose Benét, edited Wylie's *Collected Poems* (1932), *Collected Prose* (1933), and *Last Poems* (1943).

Wyndham \\'win-dəm\\, John, *pseudonym of* John Wyndham Parkes Lucas Beynon Harris \\'har-is\\ (b. 1903, Birmingham, Warwickshire, Eng.—d. March 11, 1969, London) English science-fiction writer who examined the human struggle for survival when catastrophic natural phenomena unexpectedly invade a comfortable English setting.

Educated in Derbyshire, Wyndham tried his hand at various jobs, from farming to advertising. During the mid-1920s he wrote short stories for various American pulp magazines, but not until after World War II did he publish his first novel, *The Day of the Triffids* (1951). The book's depiction of lethal, mobile plants that menace the human race established Wyndham as a science-fiction writer.

His work includes *The Kraken Wakes* (1953), *The Chrysalids* (1955), *The Midwich Cuckoos* (1957; filmed as *The Village of the Damned*, 1960), and *The Trouble with Lichen* (1960). His short stories are collected in *Consider Her Ways* (1961) and *The Seeds of Time* (1969).

Wynne \\'win\\, Ellis, *in full* Ellis Wynne o Lasynys \\ō-'läs-i-nis\\ (b. March 7, 1671, Y Lasynys, Meirionnydd, Wales—d. July 13, 1734, Llanfair, Meirionnydd) Clergyman and author whose *Gweledigaetheu y Bardd Cwsc* (1703; *The Visions of the Sleeping Bard*) is generally considered the greatest Welsh prose classic. Educated at the University of Oxford, Wynne practiced law before becoming a rector. Wynne's masterpiece, *Gweledigaetheu y Bardd Cwsc*, was an adaptation of Sir Roger L'Estrange's translation of the Spanish satirist Francisco Gómez de Quevedo's *Sueños* (1627; *Dreams*). Wynne closely followed the spirit of the original, which painted savage pictures of contemporary evils. Wynne, however, used colloquial language and transmuted the characters and the scenery of the

Spanish work into Welsh characters and scenery of the late 17th century. More than 30 Welsh editions and several English translations of the text exist.

Wynne also translated into Welsh Jeremy Taylor's *The Rule and Exercises of Holy Living* and wrote several hymns and carols.

Wyntoun, Andrew of \\'an-drü . . . 'win-tən\\ (b. *c.* 1350—d. *c.* 1423) Scottish chronicler whose *Orygynale Cronykil* is a prime historical source for the later 14th and early 15th centuries and is one of the few extensive examples of early Scots writing.

Wyntoun was a canon of St. Andrews, and, from approximately 1393 until his retirement in 1421, he served as prior of St. Serf's, Loch Leven (Kinross, Scotland). Wyntoun's chronicle is a prosaic vernacular account, in octosyllabic couplets, of human history, especially in Scotland, from the creation up to 1420. Wyntoun drew freely on ancient monastic records, Latin chronicles, standard ecclesiastical authorities, and other Scottish chronicles. The *Orygynale Cronykil* is the original source for the encounter between Macbeth and the weird sisters that appears in William Shakespeare's *Macbeth*. It is valuable for its account of the death of the Scottish hero Robert the Bruce.

Wyspiański \\vəs-'pyäny-skyē\\, Stanisław (b. Jan. 15, 1869, Kraków, Pol.—d. Nov. 28, 1907, Kraków) Dramatist and painter of the Young Poland movement, considered the creator of modern Polish drama. In his plays, themes from Greek mythology and Polish history are blended to produce a new and highly original form of drama.

Wyspiański's early education included classical literature and fine arts. In 1890 he received a grant enabling him to travel to Italy, Germany, and France. His first published work, *Legenda* ("A Legend"), a dramatic fantasy, appeared in 1897. It was followed by two tragedies after the Greek pattern, *Klątwa* (1899; "The Malediction") and *Sędziowie* (1900; "The Judges"), and *Kazimierz Wielki* (1900; "Casimir the Great"), a poem on patriotic themes. *Wesele* (*The Wedding*), his greatest and most popular play, premiered in 1901. Its story was suggested by the actual marriage of the poet Lucjan Rydel to a beautiful peasant girl in a village near Kraków. The marriage is used symbolically to present a sweeping panorama of Poland's past, present, and future. The great emotional and political impact of *Wesele* shook Kraków at its first performance; the drama was later staged throughout Poland. A later play, *Wyzwolenie* ("Liberation"), published two years later, contained ideological commentary on *Wesele*.

Wyss \\'vēs\\, Johann Rudolf (b. March 4, 1782, Bern, Switz.—d. March 21, 1830, Bern) Folklorist, editor, and writer, remembered for his collections of Swiss folklore and for his completion and editing of his father's novel THE SWISS FAMILY ROBINSON.

Wyss became professor of philosophy at the academy at Bern in 1805 and later chief librarian of the municipal library. He was a collector of Swiss tales and folklore, published in *Idyllen, Volkssagen, Legenden und Erzählungen aus der Schweiz* (1815; "Idylls, Folksayings, Legends, and Tales from Switzerland"). He also edited the *Alpenrosen* almanac (1811–30), with the collaboration of the best Swiss writers of his time. One of his most important contributions was the completion and editing of *Der schweizerische Robinson* (1812–27), a manuscript originally written by his father, Johann David Wyss, a pastor attached to the ministry in Bern. Translated into English as *The Swiss Family Robinson* in 1814 and into many other languages, the book became one of the most widely popular novels ever written. Wyss was also the author of the Swiss national anthem, "Rufst du mein Vaterland" (1811).

Xanadu \'zan-ə-ˌdü, ˌzan-ə-'dü\ Fictional place in the laudanum-induced vision that Samuel Taylor Coleridge recorded in the poetic fragment KUBLA KHAN. Xanadu is the site of the "stately pleasure dome" that Kubla Khan decreed.

Xanthus or **Xanthos** \'zan-thəs\ Horse mentioned in Homer's *Iliad*. Not only could he fly as fast as the wind, but he could speak. Xanthus foretold the death of Achilles.

Xenophanes \zē-'näf-ə-ˌnēz\ (b. probably *c.* 560 BC, Colophon, Ionia—d. probably *c.* 478) Greek poet and rhapsode (reciter of epic poetry), religious thinker, and reputed precursor of the Eleatic school of philosophy, which stressed unity rather than diversity and viewed the separate existences of material things as apparent rather than real.

Xenophanes was probably exiled from Greece by the Persians who conquered Colophon about 546. After living in Sicily for a time and wandering elsewhere in the Mediterranean, he evidently settled at Elea in southern Italy.

Xenophanes' philosophy found expression primarily in the poetry that he recited in the course of his travels. Fragments of his epics reflect his contempt for contemporary anthropomorphism and for popular acceptance of Homeric mythology. Most celebrated are his trenchant attacks on the immorality of the Olympian gods and goddesses. In his elegiac fragments he ridicules the doctrine of the transmigration of souls, condemns the luxuries introduced from the nearby colony of Lydia into Colophon, and advocates wisdom and the reasonable enjoyment of social pleasure in the face of prevalent excess.

Xenophon \'zen-ə-ˌfän, 'gzen-, -fən\ (b. 431 BC, Attica, Greece—d. shortly before 350, Attica) Greek historian, author of the ANABASIS. Its prose was highly regarded by literary critics in antiquity and exerted a strong influence on Latin literature.

Xenophon grew up during the great war between Athens and Sparta (431–404 BC) and served in the elite force of Athenian cavalry. When democracy was reestablished in Athens in 401, Xenophon chose to go abroad. His dislike of extreme democracy was deepened by the execution of Socrates in 399; a few years later he was himself exiled as a traitor.

The great experience of his life was his service with the Greek mercenaries of the Persian prince Cyrus, on which he based his work *Anabasis*. It made his name and his fortune at a young age. Service followed under a prince in Thrace and then in Asia Minor under the Spartan king Agesilaus II, who at the Battle of Coronea defeated a coalition of Greek states, including Athens. It was probably at this time that he was banished by Athens. When Athens and Sparta became allies against Thebes, his banishment was revoked, and he went home about 365.

Xenophon's other works include *Peri hippikēs* (*On Horsemanship*); *Hipparchikos* (*Cavalry Officer*); *Kynēgetikos* (*On Hunting*); *Cyropaedia*, a historical novel about Cyrus, founder of the Persian Empire; *Hieron*, a fictitious dialogue on kingship between a king and a poet; a treatise on estate management, *Oeconomicus*; *Lakedaimoniōn politeia* (*The Constitution of Sparta*); *Agesilaus*; and his completion of a work of Thucydides, a history of the period 411–403 BC, which later formed books I and II of the *Hellenica*, a history of Greek affairs from 411 to 362.

Xiaojing or **Hsiao-ching** \'shyaù-'jiŋ\ ("Classic of Filial Piety") Chinese text consisting of a conversation between Confucius and a disciple of his concerning the idea of filial piety, or the reverence for parents. The work is thought to have existed since at least the last years of the Zhou dynasty (traditionally 1122–256/255 BC).

Xia Yan or **Hsia Yen** \'shyä-'yen\, *pseudonym of* Shen Duanxian \'shən-'dwän-'shyen\ (b. Oct. 30, 1900, Hangzhou, Zhejiang province, China) Chinese writer, journalist, and playwright.

Xia studied in Japan, and after his return to China in 1927 he joined the Chinese Communist Party. He founded the Art Theater in 1929, was the first to call for a "drama of the proletariat," and became one of the leaders of the League of Leftwing Writers when it was formed in 1930. In the same year he helped found the League of Left-wing Dramatists and translated Maksim Gorky's novel *Mat* ("Mother") into Chinese. After 1932 he wrote and adapted several screenplays. In the mid-1930s he wrote several plays, including *Sai Jinhua* (1936), the story of a prostitute, and *Shanghai wuyan xia* (1937; *Under Shanghai Eaves*), one of his most successful works. After the outbreak of the Sino-Japanese War, Xia worked as a journalist, meanwhile continuing his creative writing. In 1944 he published *Faxisi xijun* ("The Fascist Bacillus"). He held several official positions after the war. His subsequent works include a stage play and two screenplays. In 1965 he was removed from the office of Vice-Minister of Culture. He spent more than eight years in prison during the Cultural Revolution (1966–76) and was rehabilitated in 1978.

Xie Lingyun or **Hsieh Ling-yün** \'shye-'liŋ-'yŵen\, *also called* Xie Kangluo \'käŋ-'lwŏ\ (b. 385, Yangxia, China—d. 433, Canton) Prominent Chinese writer of the Six Dynasties era, known chiefly as a nature poet.

Xie was an official under the Eastern Jin (317–420) and Liu-Song (420–479) dynasties. Factional intrigues later disrupted his career, leading to his frequent dismissal and eventual execution in exile.

A devout Buddhist who supported the famed Mount Lu Monastery (in modern Jiangxi province), Xie both translated and wrote religious works. His literary reputation, however, derives from his poetry, particularly his evocation of a spiritual presence in the wild southern landscape. His erudite, imagistic verse set the fashion for his age, prompting early critics to prize his *shan-shui*, or "mountain and stream," landscapes above the more pastoral *tian-yuan*, or "field and garden," scenes depicted by Tao Qian, his countryman and contemporary. Indeed, Xie's poems outnumber those of other Six Dynasties poets in the *Wen xuan* ("Literary Anthology"), the 6th-century canon that defined medieval Chinese literary tastes.

Xin Qiji or **Hsin Ch'i-chi** \'shin-'chē-'jē\ (b. 1140, Shandong province, China—d. 1207, Shangrao, Jiangxi province) Chinese poet and master soldier whose *ci*, poems written to existing musical patterns, are considered by many critics to be the best of the Southern Song dynasty (1127–1279).

Xin Qiji was a soldier by upbringing and a brilliant tactician by the age of 20. He retired in 1194 and built a retreat in beautiful Shangrao county, where he spent his time reading and creating the *ci* that were to bring him lasting fame. His 623 carefully crafted poems are important for their controlled experimentation with, and expansion of, the existing *ci* form, adding to it an emotional depth until that time untapped and afterward widely imitated.

Xiong Foxi or **Hsiung Fo-hsi** \'shyùŋ-'fŏ-'shi, 'shē\, Foxi *also spelled* Fuxi (b. Dec. 12, 1900, Fengcheng, Jiangxi province, China—d. Oct. 26, 1965, Shanghai) Chinese playwright who helped to create popular drama intended to entertain and educate the peasantry.

While at Yanjing University, Xiong Foxi helped to establish the Minzhong xiju she (People's Dramatic Society). After graduate work at Columbia University in New York City he returned to China as a professor of dramatic arts and as the editor of a drama magazine. The high point of Xiong Foxi's career came in 1932, when he was appointed director of experimental rural theater in Dingxian, Hebei province. His works from this period include *Chutou jian'er* (1932; "Young Man with a Hoe"), *Tuhu* (1933; "The Butcher"), and *Guodu* (1936; "River Crossing"). His productions, which often used Western dramatic techniques and emphasized the importance of staging, won him wide renown; he describes his experiences with the theater in the book *Xiju dazhonghua zhi shiyan* (1936; "Experiments in Popularizing Drama").

During the Sino-Japanese War (1937–45), Xiong Foxi served the Nationalist government as a theater director, president of a dramatic arts college, and founder of two literary magazines. He also produced two novels and numerous short stories. After the Communist government was established in 1949, he was a member of many of its cultural and educational committees.

Xirgu \ˈsher-gü\, Margarita, *in full* Margarita Xirgu i Subirà \ē-ˌsü-ḇē-ˈrä\ (b. June 18, 1888, Molíns de Rey, Spain—d. April 25, 1969, Montevideo, Uruguay)   Catalan actress and producer whose greatest contribution was her advancement of the plays of Federico García Lorca.

Xirgu made her professional debut in Barcelona in 1906 and five years later joined the Teatro Principal. She made her first appearance in Madrid in 1914, performing exclusively in the Catalan language. Xirgu became director of the Teatro Español in Barcelona, where she produced and starred in the premiere performances of many of García Lorca's plays, notably *Mariana Pineda* (1927) and *Yerma* (1934). She was on tour in Latin America when the Spanish Civil War broke out in 1936, and she spent the remainder of her life in voluntary exile in Argentina (where she staged the world premiere of García Lorca's *La casa de Bernarda Alba* in 1945) and in Uruguay (where she headed the Montevideo drama school).

Xiyou ji or **Hsi-yu chi** \ˈshē-ˈyō-ˈjē\ ("Record of a Journey to the West")   Foremost Chinese comic novel, written about 1500–82 by the long-anonymous WU CHENGEN. The novel is based on the actual 7th-century pilgrimage of the Buddhist monk Xuanzang (602–664) to India in search of sacred texts. The story itself had long been a part of Chinese folk and literary tradition when Wu Chengen formed it into his long and richly humorous novel.

Composed of 100 chapters, the novel can be divided into three major sections. The first seven chapters deal with the birth of a monkey from a stone egg and his acquisition of magic powers. Five chapters relate the story of Xuanzang, known as Tripitaka, and the origin of his mission to the Western Paradise. The bulk of the novel recounts the 81 adventures that befall Tripitaka and his entourage of three animal spirits—the magically gifted Monkey, the slow-witted and clumsy Pigsy, and the fish spirit Sandy—on their journey to India, culminating in their attainment of the sacred scrolls.

In addition to the novel's comedy and adventure, *Xiyou ji* has been enjoyed for its biting satire of society and Chinese bureaucracy and for its allegorical presentation of humanity's striving and perseverance. *Monkey*, an English translation by Arthur Waley, was published in 1942 (reissued 1989).

Xu Zhimo or **Hsü Chih-mo** \ˈshᵫ-ˈjə-ˈmō\, *original name* Xu Yousen \ˈyō-ˈsən\, *pseudonyms* Nanhu \ˈnän-ˈhü\ *and* Shizhe \ˈshi-ˈjə\ (b. 1896, Xiashi, Zhejiang province, China—d. Nov. 19, 1931, Jinan, Shandong province)   Free-thinking Chinese poet who strove to loosen Chinese poetry from its traditional forms and to reshape it under the influences of Western poetry and the vernacular Chinese language.

After receiving a classical Chinese education at Beijing University, Xu Zhimo went to the United States in 1918 to study economics and political science. Finding life there intolerable, he went to England in 1920 to study at Cambridge University, where he became fascinated with English Romantic poetry and decided upon a literary career.

Returning to China in 1922, Xu Zhimo began writing poems and essays in the vernacular style. He fell under the influence of the Indian poet Rabindranath Tagore while he was serving as interpreter for him during a lecture tour of China. All the foreign literature to which Xu Zhimo had been exposed served to shape his own poetry and establish him as a leader in the modern poetry movement in China. He served as an editor of the literary supplement of the *Chen bao* ("Morning Post") and as a professor at various universities. In 1928 he helped organize the Xinyue shudian (Crescent Moon Book Company), which published a literary journal featuring Western literature. In addition to four collections of verse, Xu Zhimo produced several volumes of translations from many languages.

Yacine Kateb   *see* KATEB.

Yahoo \ˈyā-ˌhü, yā-ˈhü\   Any member of a fictional race of subhuman brutes encountered by Lemuel Gulliver in his fourth and final voyage, in Jonathan Swift's satire GULLIVER'S TRAVELS. "Yahoo" entered the English language as a synonym for a boorish, crass, or stupid person.

Yale school \ˈyāl\   A group of literary critics, specifically several English professors at Yale University, who became known in the 1970s and '80s for their deconstructionist theories. The Yale school's skeptical, relativistic brand of deconstruction expanded upon the groundwork of French

philosopher Jacques Derrida and helped to popularize the deconstruction movement.

The most prominent members of the Yale school were Paul de Man and J. Hillis Miller. They contributed essays to the collection *Deconstructionism and Criticism* (1979), which analyzed the poem *The Triumph of Life* by P.B. Shelley. De Man, the most influential member, was closely allied to Derrida and based his theories on a system of rhetorical figures. The writings of Geoffrey H. Hartman and Harold Bloom (both of whom were also at Yale) were frequently critical of the Yale school, while Miller, whose work focused on textual opposites and differences, often defended charges that the Yale school was nihilistic. Other American deconstructionists included Barbara Johnson and Jonathan Culler. *See also* DECONSTRUCTION.

Yamanoue Okura \'yä-mä-ˌnō-wä-'ō-kū-rä\ (b. *c.* 660—d. *c.* 733) One of the most individualistic, even eccentric, of Japan's classical poets, who lived and wrote in an age of bold experimentation when native Japanese poetry was developing rapidly under the stimulus of Chinese literature. His poems are characterized by a Confucian-inspired moral emphasis unique in Japanese poetry. The stern logic of Confucian morality, however, is often tempered with a Buddhist resignation more in keeping with the typical Japanese view of the world.

From 726 to 732 Okura was governor of the province of Chikuzen, in Kyushu. There he was responsible to the governor-general of the island, Ōtomo Tabito, himself a major poet and patron of letters, and the two formed a close literary relationship that both influenced and encouraged Okura. All of Okura's extant work is contained in the 8th-century anthology *Man'yōshū.* The most famous of his poems is the "Hinkyū mondō" ("Dialogue on Poverty"), which treats the sufferings of poverty in the form of an exchange between a poor man and a destitute man. Also outstanding are poems expressing love for his children and laments on the death of his son, on the instability of human life, and on his own sickness and old age.

Yamazaki Sōkan \'yä-mä-ˌzä-kē-'sō-ˌkän\ (b. *c.* 1465, Ōmi province, Japan—d. *c.* 1552, Shikoku?) Japanese *renga* (linked-verse) poet of the late Muromachi period (1338–1573) who is best known as the compiler of *Inu tsukuba shū* (*c.* 1615; "Mongrel Renga Collection"), the first published anthology of haikai (comic *renga*).

According to tradition Sōkan served as a retainer to the shogun Ashikaga Yoshihisa and became a monk after his death in 1489. Other legendary tales usually characterize him as being destitute and mad, but historical evidence indicates that he earned a comfortable income from teaching poetry and from his calligraphy.

The *Inu tsukuba shū*, containing haikai by Sōkan and others, was probably written over a period of several years but was not published until some 100 years after its completion, possibly because of the coarse and profane nature of many of its poems. Despite their earthiness, the poems contain a wit and freshness that appealed to the aspiring haikai poets of the 17th century, especially those of the Danrin school, who often tried to imitate their style.

Yáñez \'yä-nyäs\, Agustín (b. May 4, 1904, Guadalajara, Mex.—d. Jan. 17, 1980, Mexico City) Mexican novelist and short-story writer who held several government posts.

Yáñez was a member of the Generation of 1924 group of writers, a literary circle associated with the journal *Banderas de Provincias* ("The Provincial Banner"). A lawyer by profession, he began to publish novels in the 1940s.

The novel *Al filo del agua* (1947; "To the Edge of the Water"; *The Edge of the Storm*), his masterpiece, presents life in a typical Mexican village just before the Mexican Revolution of 1910–20. Its use of stream of consciousness, interior monologue, and complex structure anticipates many traits of the Latin-American new novel of the 1950s and '60s. *La creación* (1959; "The Creation") is an attempt to define the new cultural climate that resulted from the revolution. *La tierra pródiga* ("The Lavish Land") appeared in 1960. *Las tierras flacas* (1962; *The Lean Lands*) shows the effect of industrialization on a peasant society.

Yáñez also wrote short stories, including those published in *Tres cuentos* (1964; "Three Stories") and *Los sentidos del aire* (1964; "The Ways the Wind Blows"). His *Obras escogidas* ("Selected Works") were published in 1968.

Most of Yáñez' works are set in his native state, Jalisco. *Genio y figuras de Guadalajara* (1941; "The Character and Person-

ages of Guadalajara") recalls the men who developed that city. The essay collections *Mitos indígenas* (1942; "Native Myths"), *El clima espiritual de Jalisco* (1945; "The Spiritual Climate of Jalisco"), and *Don Justo Sierra* (1950) reveal a critical and sensitive mind.

yangbanxi \'yäŋ-'bän-'shē\ [Chinese *yàngbǎnxì*, from *yàngbǎn* model + *xì* play, drama] Form of Chinese drama that flourished during the Cultural Revolution (1966–76). The plays were a mixture of Peking opera and modern, Western features, and they dealt with contemporary topics.

Yang Guifei or **Yang Kuei-fei** \'yäŋ-'gwē-'fä\ (d. 756, Mawei, China) Notorious beauty and concubine of the great Tang emperor Xuanzong (reigned 712–756). Because of her the emperor is said to have neglected his duties, and the Tang dynasty (618–907) was greatly weakened by a rebellion that ensued. Yang's story has been the subject of many outstanding Chinese poems and dramas. The daughter of a high official, she was one of the few obese women in Chinese history to have been considered beautiful. She became a concubine to Xuanzong's son, but the 60-year-old emperor found the girl so desirable that he forced his son to divorce her. Soon her two sisters were admitted into the Imperial harem, and her brother Yang Guozhong became the first minister of the empire.

Through Yang's influence, An Lushan, a cunning young general of Turkish origin, rose to great prominence. Yang adopted him as her legal son and is said to have made him her lover. With such powerful patronage, An Lushan came to control an army of 200,000. Jealous of the power of Yang's brother, An Lushan soon turned against the emperor and led a great rebellion against him. When the capital was captured in 756, Xuanzong and his court were forced to flee to the south. On the road the Imperial soldiers became enraged with members of the Yang family, whom they thought responsible for the debacle, and executed both Yang and her brother.

Yang Xiong or **Yang Hsiung** \'yäŋ-'shyùŋ\ (b. *c.* 53 BC, near Chengdu [now in Sichuan province], China—d. AD 18, Changan [now Sian, Shensi province]) Chinese poet and philosopher best known for his poetry written in the form known as *fu.*

A quiet and studious young man, Yang Xiong came to admire and practice the *fu* form. When he was over 40 he went to live in the Imperial capital, Changan, where his reputation as a poet won him a position at court. In AD 9, when Wang Mang usurped the Imperial throne and executed or imprisoned many prominent persons, Yang Xiong, about to be arrested and fearful that he could not clear himself, threw himself from the high window of a pavilion and was badly injured. The emperor, finding that Yang had no interest in politics, ordered that his case be dropped.

In later life Yang Xiong turned from poetry to philosophy, in which he was influenced by both Confucianism and Daoism. The doctrine for which he is remembered reflects the perennial Chinese interest in human nature, which Yang regarded as a mixture of good and evil, avoiding the extreme positions taken by Mencius (original goodness) and Xunzi (original evil). His chief works in philosophy were the *Fayan* ("Model Sayings") and the *Taixuan jing* ("Classic of the Supremely Profound Principle"), 15 essays imitating *Yi jing* in form.

Ya'qūbī \äl-yä-'kū-ˌbē, *Arabic* yä'-\, al-, *in full* Aḥmad ibn Abū Ya'qūb ibn Ja'far ibn Wahb ibn Wāḍiḥ al-Ya'qūbī (d. 897, Egypt) Arab historian and geographer, author of a history of the world, *Ta'rīkh ibn Wāḍiḥ* ("Chronicle of Ibn Wāḍiḥ"), and a general geography, *Kitāb al-buldān* ("Book of the Countries").

Until 873 al-Ya'qūbī lived in Armenia and Khorāsān, under the patronage of the Iranian Ṭāhirid dynasty (821–873), and wrote his history there. After the fall of the Ṭāhirids he traveled to India and the Maghreb (North Africa) and died in Egypt.

The *Ta'rīkh ibn Wāḍiḥ* is divided into two parts. The first is a comprehensive account of pre-Islāmic and non-Islāmic peoples, especially of their religion and literature; it includes extracts from the Greek philosophers and accounts from stories and fables. The second part covers Islāmic history up to 872. The author's Shī'ite bias pervades the work.

In the *Kitāb al-buldān*, a large part of which is lost, al-Ya'qūbī analyzes statistics, topography, and taxation in describing the larger cities of Iraq, Iran, Arabia, Syria, Egypt, the Maghreb, India, China, and the Byzantine Empire.

Yavorov \'yä-vü-rüf\, Peyo, *pseudonym of* Peyo Kracholov \krə-'chō-lüf\ (b. May 6, 1877, Chirpan, Bulgaria, Ottoman Empire—d. Jan. 20, 1914, Sofia)   Bulgarian poet and dramatist, the founder of the Symbolist movement in Bulgarian poetry.

Yavorov took part in the preparation for the ill-fated Macedonian uprising against Ottoman hegemony in August 1903, edited revolutionary papers, and crossed twice into Macedonia with partisan bands. He committed suicide at age 36.

Until 1900 Yavorov mainly wrote poetry of a social-political character, inspired by compassion for the peasantry, for the struggles of the Macedonians, and for the suffering of the Armenian exiles. Disillusionment with radicalism led him then to abandon realism for introspection and Symbolism. Besides several collections of poems, including *Stikhotvoreniya* (1901; "Poems") and *Bezsŭnitsi* (1907; "Insomnia"), Yavorov wrote the plays *V polite na Vitosha* (1911; "In the Foothills of Vitosha") and *Kogato grum udari* (1912; "When Thunder Rolls"); a biography of the Macedonian leader Gotse Delchev; and a book of reminiscences of his fighting days with partisan bands, *Khaydushki kopneniya* (1908; "Rebel Yearnings").

Yāzijī \'yä-zē-,zhē\, Nāṣif (b. March 25, 1800, Kafr Shīmā, Lebanon—d. Feb. 8, 1871, Beirut)   Lebanese scholar who played a significant role in the revitalization of Arabic literary traditions.

Until 1840 Yāzijī was employed in the service of Bashīr Shihāb II, the emir of Lebanon. He then moved to Beirut, where he continued his literary work. He was a Christian, and for a while he helped some American missionaries prepare Arabic textbooks for use in local mission schools. He had a deep love for the Arabic language and a deep appreciation for the beauty of classical Arabic literature. He was also a purist in that he sought to eliminate "corruptions" that through the centuries had been absorbed into the language and to return to the practices of the classical scholars. The writings of Yāzijī and of other Christian Arabs helped to revive classical literature as an active element in contemporary Arabic culture.

Yearling, The   Novel by Marjorie Kinnan RAWLINGS, published in 1938 and awarded the Pulitzer Prize in 1939.

Set in the backwoods of northern Florida, the story concerns the relationship between 12-year-old Jody Baxter and Flag, the fawn he adopts. When the fawn cannot be stopped from eating the family's crops, Jody's father forces Jody to shoot Flag. This tragedy propels Jody into greater maturity and a better understanding of his parents' hardscrabble life.

Yeats \'yāts\, William Butler (b. June 13, 1865, Sandymount, Dublin, Ire.—d. Jan. 28, 1939, Roquebrune-Cap-Martin, Fr.)   Irish poet, dramatist, and prose writer who was one of the greatest English-language poets of the 20th century. He received the Nobel Prize for Literature in 1923.

Yeats was born into an Anglo-Irish Protestant family in Dublin but at the age of two moved with his family to London. In 1880 Yeats's family returned to Dublin, and in 1883

he attended the Metropolitan School of Art in Dublin. Yeats's first publication, two brief lyrics, appeared in the *Dublin University Review* in 1885. When the family returned to London in 1887, Yeats took up the life of a professional writer. Himself a visionary, he began a study of the prophetic books of William Blake, and this enterprise brought him into contact with other visionary traditions, such as the Platonic, the Neoplatonic, the Swedenborgian, and the alchemical.

Brown Brothers

Yeats's early poems, collected in *The Wanderings of Oisin and Other Poems* (1889), are often beautiful but always rarefied. He quickly became involved in the literary life of London. In 1889 he met and fell in love with Maud Gonne, an ardent and brilliant Irish beauty, but his feelings were not reciprocated. A few years later he produced *The Celtic Twilight* (1893). His life changed greatly when in 1898 he met Isabella Augusta, Lady Gregory, who was already collecting the lore of the west of Ireland. Yeats found that this lore chimed with his feeling for ancient ritual, for pagan beliefs never entirely destroyed by Christianity. From 1898 Yeats spent his summers at Lady Gregory's home, Coole Park, County Galway, and he eventually purchased a ruined Norman castle nearby. Under the name of the Tower, this structure would become a dominant symbol in many of his latest and best poems.

Together with Lady Gregory and others, Yeats founded the Irish Literary Theatre, which gave its first performance in Dublin in 1899 with Yeats's play THE COUNTESS CATHLEEN. To the end of his life Yeats remained a director of this theater, which became the Abbey Theatre in 1904. In the crucial period from 1899 to 1907 he managed the theater's affairs, encouraged its playwrights (notably John Millington Synge), and contributed many of his own plays, among them *The Land of Heart's Desire* (1894), *The Hour Glass* (1903), *The King's Threshold* (1904), *On Baile's Strand* (1905), and *Deirdre* (1907).

The years from 1909 to 1914 marked a decisive change in his poetry. The otherworldly, ecstatic atmosphere of the early lyrics cleared, his verse line tightened, his imagery became more sparse and resonant, and he began to confront reality with a new directness. This maturity is evident in both *Responsibilities: Poems and a Play* (1914) and THE WILD SWANS AT COOLE (1917). From that point onward he reached and maintained the height of his achievement—a renewal of inspiration and a perfecting of technique which are almost without parallel in the history of English poetry. Notable among the poems of this period are SAILING TO BYZANTIUM, THE SECOND COMING, and EASTER 1916. *The Tower* (1928) is the work of a fully accomplished artist; in it, the experience of a lifetime is brought to perfection of form. Still, some of Yeats's greatest verse was written subsequently, appearing in *The Winding Stair* (1929). Under the influence of Nō drama, Yeats produced *Four Plays for Dancers* (1921), *At the Hawk's Well* (performed 1916), and several others. He completed *The Herne's Egg*, his most raucous work, in 1938. Yeats's last two verse collections, *New Poems* and *Last Poems and Two Plays*, appeared in 1938 and 1939 respectively.

Yellow Book, The   Short-lived but influential illustrated quarterly magazine devoted to aesthetics, literature, and art, published in London from 1894 to 1897.

"The Reflected Faun," drawing by Laurence Housman for *The Yellow Book*

From its initial visually arresting issue, for which Aubrey Beardsley was art editor and for which Max Beerbohm wrote an essay, "In Defense of Cosmetics," *The Yellow Book* attained immediate notoriety. Published by John Lane and edited by Henry Harland, *The Yellow Book* attracted many outstanding writers and artists of the era, such as Arnold Bennett, Charlotte Mew, Henry James, Edmund Gosse, Richard Le Gallienne, and Walter Sickert.

Yellow Wallpaper, The   Short story by Charlotte Perkins GILMAN, published in *New England Magazine* in May 1892 and in book form in 1899.

The Yellow Wallpaper, initially interpreted as a gothic horror tale, was an autobiographical account fictionalized in the first person. It describes the gradual emotional and intellectual deterioration of a young wife and mother who, apparently suffering from postpartum depression, undergoes a "rest cure," involving strict bed rest and a complete absence of mental stimulation, under the care of her male neurologist.

Yeobright, Clym \'klim-'yō-,brīt\   Fictional character, an idealistic young man who returns from a stay in Paris to his home on England's Egdon Heath, in Thomas Hardy's novel THE RETURN OF THE NATIVE.

Yerby \'yər-bē\, Frank (Garvin) (b. Sept. 5, 1916, Augusta, Ga., U.S.—d. Nov. 29, 1991, Madrid, Spain)   African-American author of popular historical fiction.

Yerby's story "Health Card" won the O. Henry award for best first published short story in 1944. In 1946 his first novel, *The Foxes of Harrow*, was an immediate success. His novels are action-packed, usually featuring a strong hero in an earlier period. The stories unfold in colorful language and include characters of all ethnic backgrounds, enmeshed in complex story lines laced with romantic intrigue and violence. His best work may be his novel *The Dahomean* (1971).

Yerma \'yer-mä\   Tragedy in three acts by Federico GARCÍA LORCA, produced in 1934 and published in 1937. It is the second play in a trilogy that also includes *Blood Wedding* and *The House of Bernarda Alba*. The drama's frustrated title character cannot accept her childlessness, and she is driven to increasingly irrational behavior, finally strangling her husband.

Yesenin or **Esenin** \yi-'sʸenʸ-in\, Sergey Aleksandrovich (b. Sept. 21 [Oct. 3, New Style], 1895, Konstantinovo, Ryazan province, Russia—d. Dec. 27, 1925, Leningrad [now St. Petersburg])   The self-styled "last poet of wooden Russia," whose dual image—that of a devout and simple peasant singer and that of a rowdy and blasphemous exhibitionist—reflects his tragic maladjustment to the changing world of the revolutionary era.

The son of a peasant family of Old Believers (Russian religious dissidents), he left his village at age 17. In the cities he became acquainted with Aleksandr Blok, the peasant poet Nikolay Klyuyev, and revolutionary politics. In 1916 he published his first book, *Radunitsa*. It celebrates in church book imagery the "wooden Russia" of his childhood.

Yesenin welcomed the Revolution of 1917 as the social and spiritual transformation that would lead to the peasant millennium he envisioned in his next book, *Inoniya* (1918; "Otherland"). His roseate utopian view of Otherland was still informed by a simple ethos—the defense of "wooden things" against urban industrialization. In 1920–21 he composed his long poetic drama *Pugachyov*, glorifying the 18th-century rebel who led a mass peasant revolt. In 1919 he signed the literary manifesto of the Imaginists (or Imagists, a group of Russian poets unrelated to the Anglo-American movement of this name). He was soon the leading exponent of the school.

For some time Yesenin had been writing the consciously cynical, swaggering tavern poetry that appeared in *Ispoved khuligana* (1921; *Confessions of a Hooligan*) and *Moskva kabatskaya* (1924; "Moscow of the Taverns"). His verse barely concealed the sense of self-depreciation that was overwhelming him. In 1924 he tried to go home again but found the village peasants quoting Soviet slogans. Tormented by guilt that he had been unable to fulfill the messianic role of poet of the people, he tried to get in step with the national trend. In the poem "Neuyutnaya zhidkaya lunnost" (1925; "Desolate and Pale Moonlight"), he went so far as to praise stone and steel as the secret of Russia's coming strength. But another poem, "The Stern October Has Deceived Me," bluntly voiced his alienation from Bolshevik Russia. His last major work, the confessional poem "Chyorny chelovek" ("The Black Man"), is a ruthless self-castigation for his failures. In 1925 he was briefly hospitalized for a nervous breakdown. Soon after, he hanged himself in a Leningrad hotel, having written his last lines in his own blood.

Ye Shengtao or **Yeh Sheng-t'ao** \'yə-'shəŋ-'taù\, *pseudonym of* Ye Shaojun \'shaù-'jün\ (b. Oct. 28, 1894, Suzhou, Jiangsu province, China—d. Feb. 16, 1988, Beijing)   Chinese writer and teacher.

Ye taught at primary schools after his graduation from middle school and in 1914 began writing short stories in classical Chinese for several periodicals. Influenced by the May 4th Movement of 1919, he turned to writing in the vernacular and was one of the founders of the Literary Research Association in 1921, which called for a reality-oriented literature. He worked as a teacher and editor and, with Zhu Ziqing, founded the monthly *Poetry* in 1922. In the 1920s Ye wrote a considerable number of short stories collected in *Gemo* (1922; "Estrangement"), *Huozai* (1923; "Conflagration"), *Xianxia* (1925; "Below the Horizon"), *Chengzhong* (1926; "In the City"), *Weiyan ji* (1928; "Unsatisfied"), and *Sisen ji* (1936; "At Forty-three"), all portraying the life and characters of intellectuals and townspeople. The short story "Mr. Pan in Distress" is a small masterpiece. In 1928 he published the novel *Ni Huanzhi* (*Schoolmaster Ni Huan-chih*), which chronicles the life and times of an intellectual from the time of the Chinese Revolution of 1911–12 to 1927. The novel was recognized as one of the landmarks of the new vernacular literature.

His sketches, notes, and other miscellanea, remarkable for their simplicity and fluidity, were collected in *Jiaobu ji* (1931; "Footsteps") and *Weiyan ju xizuo* (1935; "Études of Mine"). His *Daocaoren* (1923; *The Scarecrow*) and *Gudai yingxiongde shixiang* (1931; *The Stone Statue of an Ancient Hero*) are both notable works in Chinese children's literature. A selection of Ye's short stories was translated into English and published as *How Mr. Pan Weathered the Storm* (1987).

Yet Do I Marvel　Sonnet by Countee CULLEN, published in the collection *Color* in 1925. Reminiscent of the Romantic sonnets of William Wordsworth and William Blake, the poem is concerned with racial identity and injustice.

The poet ponders the nature of God, stating "I do not doubt God is good, well-meaning, kind." While he accepts God's wisdom in most puzzling matters of life and death, he is confounded by the contradiction of his own plight in a racist society: "Yet do I marvel at this curious thing:/ To make a poet black, and bid him sing!"

Yevgeny Onegin　*see* EUGENE ONEGIN.

Yevtushenko \yif-tû-'shen-kə\, Yevgeny (Aleksandrovich), *also spelled* Evgenii Evtushenko (b. July 18, 1933, Zima, Russian S.F.S.R., U.S.S.R.)　Poet and spokesman for the post-Stalin generation of Russian poets. His internationally publicized demands for greater artistic freedom and for a literature based on aesthetic rather than political standards signaled an easing of Soviet control over artists in the late 1950s and '60s.

Yevtushenko, a fourth-generation descendant of Ukrainians exiled to Siberia, grew up in Moscow and in the small town on the Trans-Siberian Railway line that is the setting of his first important narrative poem, *Stantsiya Zima* (1956; "Zima Junction"). He was invited to study at the Gorky Institute of World Literature in Moscow. Yevtushenko's gifts as an orator and publicist, his magnetic personality, and his fearless fight for a return to artistic honesty soon made him a leader of Soviet youth. He revived the brash, slangy, unpoetic language of the early Revolutionary poets Vladimir Mayakovsky and Sergey Yesenin and reintroduced such traditions as love lyrics and personal lyrics, frowned upon under Stalinism. His poem *Baby Yar* (1961), mourning the Nazi massacre of an estimated 34,000 Ukrainian Jews, was an attack on lingering Soviet anti-Semitism. His travels and poetry readings in the United States and Europe established cultural links with the West, but he fell into disfavor at home when he published his *A Precocious Autobiography* in English in 1963. He was recalled and his privileges were withdrawn, but he was restored to favor when he published his most ambitious cycle of poems, *Bratskaya GES* (1965; *The Bratsk Station*), in which he contrasts the symbol of a Siberian power plant bringing light to Russia with the symbol of Siberia as a prison throughout Russian history. Later works include his first novel *Yagodnyye mesta* (1981; *Wild Berries*) and the novella *Ardabiola* (1981). *The Collected Poems, 1952–1990* appeared in 1991.

Yggdrasil or **Yggdrasill** \'ig-drə-,sil\, *also called* Mímameithr \'mē-mə-,ma̱th-ər\　In Norse mythology, the world tree, a giant ash supporting the universe. One of its roots extended into Niflheim, the underworld; another into Jǫtunheim, land of the giants; and the third into Asgard, home of the gods. After Rag-

narǫk ("Doom of the Gods"), the world tree, though it would be badly shaken, was to be the source of new life.

Yiddish drama　The literature, productions, and acting style of the professional Yiddish theater, which developed in Europe beginning in the mid-19th century.

European Jewish drama had its origin in the Middle Ages, when dancers, mimics, and professional jesters entertained at weddings and Purim celebrations with songs and monologues. Purim, the holiday celebrating the downfall of Haman, a persecutor of the Jews in the Bible, became the occasion for increasingly elaborate plays, some of which continue to the present day. By the 16th century these plays, with their interpolated songs and free use of improvisation, were being performed in Yiddish, the language of the majority of central and eastern European Jews.

The beginning of professional Yiddish theater is usually dated to 1876, when Abraham Goldfaden, a former schoolteacher and journalist, joined forces with two traveling musicians to present his own two-act musical sketch in a tavern in Romania. Goldfaden went on to organize a full-time professional troupe, for which he eventually wrote full-length plays.

Goldfaden and newer Yiddish dramatists, such as Joseph Judah Lerner, became well established in Russia, but the anti-Semitic laws promulgated in 1883 expressly forbade Yiddish plays, and the playwrights and many of their actors immigrated to England and the United States. New York, with its vast immigrant population, became the center of Yiddish drama at the turn of the century.

In the early 1880s Boris Tomashevsky and others went to New York from London and presented the first Yiddish play in the United States. Jacob Gordin is credited with bringing new material and new life into the American Yiddish theater with free adaptations of the works of major European dramatists, such as his *The Jewish King Lear* (1892). Other notable authors are Sholem-Asch, Sholem Aleichem, and H. Leivick (pseudonym of Leivick Halpern).

In 1918 Maurice Schwartz founded the Yiddish Art Theatre, in which he served as director and leading actor. World War II and the Nazi concentration camps destroyed most of the Yiddish culture of Germany and eastern Europe, and the language is rapidly dying out elsewhere, as the children of immigrants are assimilated into new cultures. All of these factors combined have had a devastating impact on the Yiddish theater. In the second half of the 20th century only a few Yiddish theaters of uncertain future survived in New York City, London, Bucharest, Buenos Aires, and Warsaw.

Yi jing or **I ching** or **Yi ching** \'ē-'jiŋ\ ("Classic of Changes," or "Book of Changes")　Ancient Chinese text, one of the Five Classics (*Wu jing*) of Confucianism. The main body of the work, traditionally attributed to Wen Wang (fl. 12th century BC), contains a discussion of the divinatory system used by the Zhou dynasty wizards. A supplementary section of "commentaries" is believed to be the work of authors of the Warring States period (475–221 BC) and, as a philosophical exposition, represents an attempt to explain the world and its ethical principles, applying a largely dialectic method. For this the work came to have great importance in the history of Chinese philosophy. Modern scholars, nevertheless, have been troubled by the inclusion of the *Yi jing* among the Confucian classics, for Confucius (551–479 BC) seems to have deliberately avoided speaking of anything that suggested esoteric doctrines. The answer seems to be that Han dynasty Confucianists (*c.* 2nd century BC), influenced by the Daoist quest for immortality, justified their use of *Yi jing* by attributing certain of its commentaries to Confucius.

Though the book was originally used for divination, its influence on Chinese minds and its universal popularity are due to a system of cosmology that involves humans and nature in a single system. The uniqueness of the *Yi jing* consists in its presentation of 64 symbolic hexagrams that, if properly understood and interpreted, are said to contain profound meanings applicable to daily life.

Yi li or **I li** \'ē-'lē\ ("Ceremonies and Rituals") Collection of Chinese rituals probably compiled during Western Han times (206 BC–AD 8) and listed, along with two other ritual texts, the *Li ji* ("Collection of Rituals") and *Zhou li* ("Rites of Zhou"), among the Nine, Twelve, and Thirteen Classics of Confucianism. Its subject matter is somewhat different from the other ritual classics in that it gives special emphasis to such events as weddings, funerals, religious sacrifices, festivals, and official audiences.

Ymir *see* AURGELMIR.

Yoknapatawpha County \,yäk-nə-pə-'tȯf-ə\ Fictional county in the state of Mississippi, U.S., created by William Faulkner as the setting for 14 of his novels and for much of his short fiction. Yoknapatawpha County was based largely on the region in which Faulkner lived for most of his life, and its fictional county seat, Jefferson, was based largely on Oxford, Miss., where Faulkner's home, Rowan Oak, was located.

Yokomitsu Riichi \yō-kō-'mē-tsū-'rē-ē-chē\, *also called* Yokomitsu Toshikazu \tō-shə-'kä-zū\ (b. March 17, 1898, Higashiyama Hot Springs, Fukushima prefecture, Japan—d. Dec. 30, 1947, Tokyo) Japanese writer who, with Kawabata Yasunari, was one of the mainstays of the New Sensationalist school (Shinkankaku-ha) of Japanese writers, influenced by the avant-garde trends in European literature of the 1920s.

Yokomitsu began writing while attending Waseda University in Tokyo; he later joined the playwright Kikuchi Kan's journal *Bungei shunjū*. In 1924 he joined Kawabata in publishing the journal *Bungei jidai* ("Literary Age"). Critics hailed Yokomitsu's story *Atama narabi ni hara* (1924; "Heads and Bellies") as a new kind of writing. In opposition to the autobiographical legacy of naturalism and the social pleading of proletarian literature, Yokomitsu developed an aesthetic of sensual impressions presented in fresh, startling ways. His subsequent works include *Haru wa basha ni notte* (1926; *Spring Came on a Horse-Drawn Cart*), a lyrical, sensitive story dealing with his wife's fatal illness, and *Kikai* (1930; *Machine*), which shows his growing obsession with the idea of a mechanistic principle governing human behavior. Concerned always with the theory of writing, Yokomitsu put forth his ideas in *Junsui shōsetsu ron* (1935; "On the Pure Novel").

yomihon \'yō-mē-,hȯn, -,hȯŋ\ [Japanese, storybook, literally, book for reading (as opposed to a picture book)] A subgenre of *gesaku*, a type of popular Japanese literature of the Edo, or Tokugawa, period (1603–1867). *Yomihon* were notable for their extended plots culled from Chinese and Japanese historical sources. These novels were openly moralistic romances, and their highly schematized characters often included witches, fairy princesses, and impeccably noble gentlemen. Where *yomihon* succeeded, as in a few works by Takizawa Bakin, they are absorbing as examples of storytelling rather than as moral lessons.

Yonge \'yəŋ\, Charlotte Mary (b. Aug. 11, 1823, Otterbourne, Hampshire, Eng.—d. March 24, 1901, Otterbourne) English novelist who dedicated her talents as a writer to the service of the church. Her books helped to spread the influence of the Oxford Movement in the Church of England, which favored a return to liturgical, ceremonial, and traditional elements.

Her first success came with *The Heir of Redclyffe* (1853), whose hero made goodness attractive and romantic. Her other novels include *Heartsease* (1854); *The Daisy Chain* (1856), which depicts the moral conflict of sheltered lives; and *The Young Stepmother* (1861). She also edited a magazine for girls, *The Monthly Packet*, for which she wrote historical cameos and religious tracts.

York plays \'yȯrk\ A cycle of 48 plays, dating from the 14th century, of unknown authorship, which were performed during the European Middle Ages by craft guilds in the city of York, in the north of England, on the summer feast day of Corpus Christi. Some of the York plays are almost identical with corresponding plays in the Wakefield cycle.

The plays were given in York on one day, in chronological order, on pageant wagons proceeding from one selected place to another. The cycle covers the story of the Fall of Man and his redemption, from the creation of the angels to the Final Judgment. *See also* MYSTERY PLAY.

In the last revision of the York plays, about 14 plays (mainly those concerning Christ's Passion) were redacted into alliterative verse. These powerful adaptations were the work of a dramatic genius, often referred to as the York Realist.

Yosa Buson *see* BUSON.

Yosano Akiko \'yō-,sä-nō-'ä-kē-kō\, *also called* Ho Sho \'hō-'shō\ (b. Dec. 7, 1878, near Ōsaka, Japan—d. May 29, 1942, Tokyo) Japanese poet whose new style caused a sensation in contemporary literary circles.

Akiko was interested in poetry from her school days, and with a group of friends she published a private poetry magazine. In 1900 she joined the Shinshisha ("New Poetry Association") of Yosano Tekkan and began to contribute to his magazine *Myōjō* ("Morning Star"). She met Tekkan that year and the next year left her family and went to Tokyo, where she married him. The freshness and unconventionality of her poetry had already attracted attention; *Midaregami* (1901; *Tangled Hair*) brought her fame. *Yume no hana* (1906; "Dream Flowers") revealed her developing art.

In 1912 Akiko followed her husband to France and spent a year there; *Natsu yori aki e* (1914; "From Summer to Autumn") is a collection of poetry resulting from that period. Upon her return from France she embarked on a project of translating into modern Japanese the 11th-century classic *Genji monogatari* (*The Tale of Genji*) of Murasaki Shikibu. A posthumous collection of poetry, *Hakuōshū* (1942; "White Cherry"), expressed her feelings in the years following the death of her husband in 1935.

Yoshida Kenkō \'yō-shē-dä-'keŋ-,kō\, *original name* Urabe Kaneyoshi \'ū-rä-bä-,kä-nä-'yō-shē\ (b. *c.* 1283, Kyōto, Japan?—d. *c.* 1350/52, near Kyōto?) Japanese poet and essayist who was the outstanding literary figure of his time. His collection of essays *Tsurezuregusa* (*c.* 1330; ESSAYS IN IDLENESS) became, especially after the 17th century, a basic part of the Japanese educational canon.

Kenkō early served at court and took Buddhist orders after the death of the emperor Go-Uda in 1324, but becoming a priest did not cause him to withdraw from society. On the contrary, he continued to take an active interest in all forms of worldly activities, as his essays indicate. While his poetry is conventional, the essays of *Tsurezuregusa* display a perceptiveness and wit that have delighted readers since the 14th century. The work has also been acclaimed for its treatment of aesthetic matters. Some of the essays express Kenkō's view that beauty implies impermanence; that the shorter-lived a moment or object of beauty, the more precious it must be considered. In a similarly elegiac vein, *Tsurezuregusa*'s lamentations over the passing of old customs express the author's conviction that life had sadly deteriorated from its former glory.

Yoshikawa Eiji \'yō-shē-kä-wä-'ä-jē\, *pseudonym of* Yoshikawa Hidetsugu \ˌhē-de-'tsü-gù\ (b. Aug. 11, 1892, Kanagawa prefecture, Japan—d. Sept. 7, 1962, Tokyo) Japanese novelist who was esteemed among the first rank of 20th-century writers both for his popularized versions of classical Japanese literary works and for his own original novels.

In 1925 Yoshikawa published *Kennan jonan* ("Troubles with Swords and Women"), and his position as a writer was established with *Naruto hichō* (1926–27; "A Secret Record of Naruto"). Later he wrote some light novels in the romantic tradition, but gradually he turned to a more serious exploration of the human character; he achieved a kind of perfection with the historical novel *Miyamoto Musashi* (1935–39; *Musashi*), dealing with the life of a famous samurai. Later he tried to penetrate more deeply into the lives of Japanese historical figures in *Shin Heike monogatari* (1950–57; *The Heike Story*) and *Shihon taihei-ki* (1958–61; "A Private Book of War History"). Yoshikawa's exquisite style, psychological insight, and knowledge of history brought him a broad range of readers.

Yossarian, Captain John \'jän-yō-'sar-ē-ən\ Fictional character, an American bombardier of the 256th Squadron who is stationed on a Mediterranean island during World War II, in Joseph Heller's novel CATCH-22.

You Can't Go Home Again Novel by Thomas WOLFE, published posthumously in 1940 after heavy editing by Edward Aswell. This novel, like Wolfe's other works, is largely autobiographical, reflecting details of his life in the 1930s.

As the sequel to *The Web and the Rock* (1939), *You Can't Go Home Again* continues the story of George Webber, a thoughtful author in search of meaning in his personal life and in American society. Leaving New York City, he is dismayed at the social decay he finds on his travels to England, Germany, and his small hometown in the Carolinas. Nonetheless, he is optimistic about the future of the United States.

Young \'yəŋ\, Arthur (b. Sept. 11, 1741, London, Eng.—d. April 20, 1820, London) Prolific English writer on agriculture, politics, and economics. Besides his books on agricultural subjects, he was the author of the famous *Travels in France* (or *Travels During the Years 1787, 1788 and 1789, Undertaken More Particularly with a View of Ascertaining the Cultivation, Resources, and National Prosperity, of the Kingdom of France*; 1792). The book is especially valued for its vivid descriptions of the French Revolution.

When he was only 17 years old Young published the pamphlet *On the War in North America*, and in 1761 he went to London to start a periodical, *The Universal Museum*. He also wrote four novels during this period. In the 1760s he began a series of journeys through England and Wales, and he gave an account of his observations in several books that appeared from 1768 to 1770, including *A Six Weeks Tour Through the Southern Counties of England and Wales*.

Young's first visit to France was made in 1787. Traversing that country just before and during the first movements of the Revolution, he gave valuable accounts of the condition of the people and the conduct of public affairs at that critical juncture. The *Travels in France* appeared in two volumes in 1792. On his return home he was appointed secretary of the British government's newly created Board of Agriculture.

Young \'yəŋ\, Edward (baptized July 3, 1683, Upham, Hampshire, Eng.—d. April 5, 1765, Welwyn, Hertfordshire) English poet, dramatist, and literary critic, author of *The Complaint: or, Night-Thoughts on Life, Death and Immortality*

(1742–45), a long, didactic poem on death. It was inspired by the successive deaths of his stepdaughter in 1736, her husband in 1740, and Young's wife in 1741. The poem, a blank-verse dramatic monologue of nearly 10,000 lines divided into nine parts, or "Nights," was an enormously popular example of the graveyard school of poetry.

As a dramatist, Young lacked a theatrical sense, and his plays are rarely performed. Of them, *The Revenge* (performed 1721) is generally thought to be the best. Young's fame in Europe, particularly in Germany, was augmented by a prose work, the *Conjectures on Original Composition* (1759), addressed to his friend Samuel Richardson. It sums up succinctly and forcefully many strains of thought later regarded as Romantic.

Young \'yəŋ\, Francis Brett (b. June 29, 1884, Halesowen, Worcestershire, Eng.—d. March 28, 1954, Cape Town, S.Af.) English doctor, novelist, and poet who, although at times sentimental and long-winded, achieved wide popularity for his considerable skill as a storyteller.

Among Young's best-known novels, many of which are set in his native Worcestershire, are *The Dark Tower* (1914), *Portrait of Claire* (1927), *My Brother Jonathan* (1928), *They Seek a Country* (1937), and *A Man About the House* (1942). *The Island* (1944) is a verse history of England written in a chronological progression of verse forms appropriate to each period.

Young \'yəŋ\, Marguerite (Vivian) (b. 1909, Indianapolis, Ind., U.S.) Writer best known for *Miss MacIntosh, My Darling* (1965), a mammoth, many-layered novel of illusion and reality.

Young's first published works were two books of poetry, *Prismatic Ground* (1937) and *Moderate Fable* (1944). *Angel in the Forest: A Fairy Tale of Two Utopias* (1945) examines the foundation of two utopian communities of New Harmony, Ind. *Miss MacIntosh, My Darling*, the project that occupied virtually the next two decades of Young's life, is an exploration of myth and the mythmaking impulse. The book's protagonist, Vera Cartwheel, rejects her mother's opium-induced vagueness and searches for her long-lost nursemaid, Miss MacIntosh, who represents common sense and reality. Cartwheel's journey ends in disillusionment.

The author's later works include a collection of short stories entitled *Below the City* (1975) and *Inviting the Muses: Stories, Essays, Reviews* (1994).

Young Germany \'jər-mə-nē\, *also called* Junges Deutschland \'yùŋ-əs-'dòich-ˌlänt\ A social reform and literary movement in 19th-century Germany (about 1830–50), influenced by French revolutionary ideas, which was opposed to the extreme forms of Romanticism and nationalism then current. The name was first used in Ludolf Wienbarg's *Ästhetische Feldzüge* (1834; "Aesthetic Campaigns"). Members of Young Germany, in spite of their intellectual and literary gifts and penetrating political awareness, failed to command the enthusiasm of their compatriots and, indeed, excited widespread animosity. This was partly due to their lack of social standing and higher education. The Jewish origins of some of the members was also a hindrance. The movement leaders were Wienbarg, Karl Gutzkow, and Theodor Mundt. Heinrich Laube, Georg Herwegh, Ludwig Börne, and Heinrich Heine were also associated with the movement. A resolution of the Diet of the German Confederation passed on Dec. 10, 1835, demanded the suppression of their writings by strict censorship in all the German states. In addition to their interest in social reform, Young Germany also aimed for a vital democratic and national theater and, in what was their most direct influence on literature, prepared the way for dramatic realism in Germany. The revolutionary movements of 1848–49 led to the decline of Young Germany.

Young Goodman Brown \'gu̇d-mən-'brau̇n\   Allegorical short story by Nathaniel Hawthorne, published in 1835 in *New England Magazine* and collected in MOSSES FROM AN OLD MANSE (1846). Considered an outstanding tale of witchcraft, it concerns a young Puritan who ventures into the forest to meet with a stranger. It soon becomes clear that he is approaching a witches' Sabbath; he views with horror prominent members of his community participating in the ceremonies. Ultimately Brown is led to a flaming altar where he sees his wife, Faith. He cries out to her to "resist" and suddenly finds himself alone among the trees. He returns home but loses forever his faith in goodness or piety.

Young Poland movement \'pō-lənd\, *Polish* Młoda Polska   Diverse group of late 19th-century and early 20th-century Neoromantic writers brought together in reaction against naturalism and positivism to revive the unfettered expression of feeling and imagination in Polish literature and to extend this reawakening to all the Polish arts. They looked back to the Polish Romantic writers and also to contemporary western European trends, such as Symbolism, for inspiration. Centered in Kraków, the movement was pioneered by the poet Antoni Lange and the editor and critic Zenon Przesmycki ("Miriam").

The most prominent figure of the Young Poland movement was the painter and dramatist Stanisław Wyspiański. Other writers included the peasant poet Jan Kasprowicz, who established a tonic poetic meter that became the characteristic rhythm of modern Polish poetry, and the novelists Stefan Żeromski, Władysław Stanisław Reymont, and Karol Irzykowski.

Yourcenar \yu̇r-sə-'när\, Marguerite, *original name* Marguerite de Crayencour \krä-yaⁿ-'kür\ (b. June 8, 1903, Brussels, Belg.—d. Dec. 17, 1987, Northeast Harbor, Maine, U.S.)   Novelist, essayist, and short-story writer who became the first woman to be elected to the Académie Française.

Crayencour began writing as a teenager and continued to do so after her father's death left her independently wealthy. She led a nomadic life until the outbreak of World War II, at which time she settled permanently in the United States.

Gisèle Freund

Yourcenar's literary works are notable for their rigorously classical style, their erudition, and their psychological subtlety. In her most important books she re-creates past eras and personages, meditating thereby on human destiny, morality, and power. Her masterpiece is *Mémoires d'Hadrien* (1951; MEMOIRS OF HADRIAN), a historical novel constituting the fictionalized memoirs of that 2nd-century Roman emperor. Another historical novel is *L'Oeuvre au noir* (1968; *The Abyss*), a biography of a fictitious 16th-century alchemist and scholar. Among Yourcenar's other works are the short stories collected in *Nouvelles orientales* (1938; *Oriental Tales*), the prose poem *Feux* (1936; *Fires*), and the short novel *Le Coup de grâce* (1939). She wrote numerous essays and also translated Negro spirituals and various English and American novels into French.

Youth and the Bright Medusa \mə-'dü-sə, -'dyü-, -zə\   Collection of eight short stories about artists and the arts by Willa CATHER, published in 1920. Four of the stories were reprinted from Cather's first collection, *The Troll Garden* (1905).

The stories include "Flavia and Her Artists," in which an artist exploits a benefactor; "The Garden Lodge," about a woman who suppresses her artistic impulses in exchange for a well-ordered life; "A Wagner Matinée," in which a nephew witnesses his aunt's communion with music; and PAUL'S CASE, Cather's most famous short story. The remaining four stories—"Coming, Aphrodite!," "The Diamond Mine," "A Gold Slipper," and "Scandal"—all concern opera singers.

Yovkov \'yȯf-kȯf\, Yordan Stefanovich (b. Nov. 9, 1880, Zheravna, Bulg.—d. Oct. 15, 1937, Sofia)   Bulgarian short-story writer, novelist, and dramatist whose stories of Balkan peasant life and military experiences show a fine mastery of prose.

Yovkov grew up in the Dobruja region and, after studying in Sofia, returned there to teach. He later worked in the Bulgarian legation in Bucharest, Romania. He drew upon Balkan folktales for *Staroplaninski legendi* (1927; "Balkan Legends"). His novel *Chiflikŭt kray granitsata* (1933; "The Farm by the Frontier") deals with village life in the Dobruja region. His plays included *Albena* (1930), *Boryana* (1932), and a comedy, *Milionerŭt* (1930; "The Millionaire").

Ysopet or **Isopet** \ē-zō-'pā\   In French literature, a medieval collection of fables, often versions of Aesop's *Fables*. The word was first applied to a collection of tales written by Marie de France in the late 12th century; they were said to be based directly on an English version of Aesop's *Fables* attributed to King Alfred the Great of Wessex and no longer extant. Another source, better-documented, is the medieval *Romulus* (falsely credited to Romulus, son of Tiberius), which includes fables by the Latin writers Phaedrus and Avienus.

Yuan Ji or **Yüan Chi** \'ywän-'jē\ (b. 210, Kaifeng, Henan province, China—d. 263, China)   Eccentric Chinese poet and most prominent member of the Seven Sages of the Bamboo Grove, a group of 3rd-century poets and philosophers who sought refuge from worldly pressures in a life of drinking and verse making.

Born into a prominent family, Yuan Ji was faced with the choice of silent acceptance of the corrupt political maneuverings of the Wei dynasty court (220–265/266) or severe punishment. He found a solution that enabled him to escape both hypocrisy and harm. In a successful effort to avoid commitment to a marriage alliance that he considered dangerous and distasteful, the poet purposely remained drunk for 60 days. When he felt the need to speak out against the ruling class, he did so through poems and essays heavily veiled in allegory. Finally he retired to a life of pleasure and poetry in the countryside, far from the pressures of the palace.

Despite Yuan Ji's clever tricks at court and his hedonistic outlook on life, his poetry is melancholy and pessimistic and has been praised for its profound view of a troubled time. His best-known collection is *Yong huai shi* ("Singing of Thoughts").

Yuan Zhen or **Yüan Chen** \'ywän-'jən\ (b. 779, Luoyang, China—d. 831, Wuchang)   A key literary figure of the middle Tang dynasty of China who was influential in the *guwen* ("ancient literature") revival.

Yuan, whose courtesy name was Weizhi, entered state service through the examination system and briefly held ministerial rank. While in office he joined a famous literary circle under the poet-official Bo Juyi. Deeming literature an instrument of ethical and social improvement, the group rejected the courtly trends of the time and called for a revival of the moral themes and the straightforward style of ancient literature. Yuan thus joined Bo Juyi in reviving an old ballad tradition associated with social protest. Though famed for these *xin yuefu*, or "new music bureau" ballads, as well as for his more conventional poetry, Yuan was best known for his short fiction. Using contemporary settings, figures, and themes, he adapted the traditional *chuan qi*, or "marvel tale," to serious moral and social purposes. Works such as his semiautobiographical *Yingying zhuan* ("Story of Ying-ying") thus set a new standard for the genre of the tale in Chinese literature.

Yu Dafu or **Yü Ta-fu** \\'yǖ-'dä-'fü\ (b. 1896, Fuyang, Zhejiang province, China—d. September 1945, Sumatra, Dutch East Indies [now part of Indonesia]) Popular short-story writer and one of the founding members of the literary Creation Society.

Yu Dafu received his higher education in Japan, where he met other young Chinese writers with whom he founded the Creation Society in 1921. His first collection of short stories, *Chenlun* (1921; "Sinking"), was written in vernacular Chinese, as advocated by the new writers. *Chenlun* became a popular success in China because of its frank treatment of sex; when Yu returned to his country in 1922 he found himself a literary celebrity.

Yu continued his work with the Creation Society and edited or contributed to literary journals. In 1923, however, his concerns changed abruptly, and in 1926 he was forced to resign from the Creation Society.

Yu's first novel appeared in 1928 and was only moderately successful; his second followed four years later. In 1935 his last major work of fiction, *Chuben* ("Flight"), was published. During the Sino-Japanese War, Yu wrote anti-Japanese propaganda from Hangzhou and Singapore. When Singapore fell to the Japanese in 1942, he fled to Sumatra, only to be executed by Japanese military police there shortly before the end of the war.

Of Yu's many works the most popular was *Riji jiuzhong* (1927; "Nine Diaries"), an account of his affair with the young left-wing writer Wang Yingxia; the book broke all previous sales records in China. The critics' favorite is probably *Guoqu* (1927; "The Past"), praised for its psychological depth.

yuefu or **yüeh-fu** \\'ywe-'fü\ [Chinese *yuèfǔ*] Form of Chinese poetry derived from the folk-ballad tradition. The *yuefu* takes its name from the Yue Fu ("Music Bureau") created in 120 BC by Emperor Wu for the purpose of collecting songs and their musical scores for ceremonial occasions at court. The music for these songs was later lost, but the words remained, forming a collection of Han dynasty (206 BC–AD 220) folk poetry that served as the basis of the *yuefu* form. These poems were significant because they consisted of lines of varying lengths, some having a regular form of five syllables per line rather than the then-standard four-syllable line. The *yuefu* thus broke ground for the later classic *gushi* ("ancient-style poetry"), with its broader use of rhyme and fewer metrical restrictions. Many later writers, including the great Li Bo (701–762) and Bo Juyi (772–846), continued to create poems derived from the *yuefu* tradition.

Yunus Emre \yü-'nüs-em-'re\ (b. mid-13th century, Anatolia [Turkey]—d. *c.* 1321, Anatolia) Poet and mystic who exercised a powerful influence on Turkish literature.

Yunus Emre is known to have been a Ṣūfī (Islāmic mystic). He sat for 40 years at the feet of his master, Tapduk Emre. Yunus Emre was well versed in mystical philosophy, especially that of the 13th-century poet and mystic Jalāl ad-Dīn ar-Rūmī. Like Jalāl ad-Dīn, he became a leading representative of mysticism in Anatolia, but on a more popular level; he was venerated as a saint after his death.

His poems, mainly on the themes of divine love and human destiny, are characterized by deep feeling. He wrote in a straightforward, almost austere style and mainly in the traditional syllabic meter of Anatolian folk poetry. His verse had a decisive influence on later Turkish mystics and inspired the poets of the renaissance of Turkish national poetry after 1910.

Ż

Żagary group \zä-'gä-ri\ Group of students in Wilno, Poland (now Vilnius, Lithuania) who were associated with the short-lived literary review *Żagary* ("Burning Twigs"; 1931–32), which first appeared as a supplement to the conservative daily *Słowo* ("Word"). The group was representative of the trend known as "catastrophism," the European obsession with cultural cataclysm in the period between the two world wars.

Founded by Teodor Bujnicki, Jerzy Zagórski, and Czesław Miłosz, the group also included Jerzy Putrament and Aleksander Rymkiewicz. Although these writers did not have a clear agenda, they declared their independence from previous literary groups and were sympathetic to Marxism.

Zagreus \'zä-grē-əs\ In Greek myth, a divine child who was the son of Zeus (as a snake) and his daughter Persephone. Zeus intended to make Zagreus his heir and bestow on him unlimited power, but Hera out of jealousy urged the Titans to attack the child. The Titans, who were opposed to Zeus's power, tore Zagreus to pieces and consumed him except for his heart. Athena managed to save the child's heart and brought it to Zeus, who swallowed it. Zeus punished the Titans for their crime by blasting them into soot with his thunderbolts. The remains of the Titans became humans, partly wicked and partly divine (because the Titans had eaten Zagreus). Zeus then begot a son by Semele, and this child, made from the heart of Zagreus, was called Dionysus.

Zahn \'tsän\, Ernst (b. Jan. 24, 1867, Zürich, Switz.—d. Feb. 12, 1952, Zürich) Swiss writer, one of the contributors to the *Heimatkunst* (local color or regionalist movement which attempted to reproduce the life and atmosphere of the provinces). Zahn's realistic prose, though conventional, shows insight into the daily life of the alpine people.

Zahn was at first president of the Diet (parliament) of the canton of Uri. After 1917, literary success enabled him to devote his life solely to writing, and he moved to Meggen, near Lucerne. His more popular works include collections of short stories *Bergvolk* (1896; "Mountain Folk") and *Helden des Alltags* (1906; "Weekday Heroes") and the novels *Albin Indergand* (1901), *Herrgottsfäden* (1901; *Golden Threads*), *Frau Sixta* (1926), and *Die grosse Lehre* (1943; "The Large Lesson").

zaju or **tsa-chü** \'dzä-'jūē\ [Chinese *zájù,* from *zá* mixed, sundry + *jù* drama, play]   One of the major forms of Chinese drama. The style originated as a short variety play in North China during the Northern Song dynasty (960–1127) and during the Yuan dynasty (1206–1368) developed into a mature four-act dramatic form, in which songs alternate with dialogue. The *zaju,* or northern drama, was distinguished from the *nanxi,* or southern drama (and later the *chuanqi*), by a more rigid form. In the *zaju,* singing was restricted to a single character in each play and each act had a single and distinct rhyme and musical mode. Of the thousands of romances, religious plays, histories, and domestic, bandit, and lawsuit plays that were composed, only about 200 *zaju* plays survive. One of these, *Huilan ji* (*The Chalk Circle*), demonstrating the cleverness of a famous judge, Pao, was adapted in 1948 by Bertolt Brecht in *The Caucasian Chalk Circle.*

Zamyatin or **Zamiatin** \ˌzə-'mʸa-tʸin\, Yevgeny Ivanovich (b. Jan. 20 [Feb. 1, New Style], 1884, Lebedyan, Tambov province, Russia—d. March 10, 1937, Paris, Fr.)   Russian novelist, playwright, and satirist, one of the most brilliant and cultured minds of the postrevolutionary period, and creator of the antiutopian novel.

Zamyatin's early works were *Uyezdnoye* (1913; "A Provincial Tale"), a satire of provincial life, and *Na kulichkakh* (1914; "At the World's End"), an attack on military life. The latter was condemned by czarist censors, and Zamyatin was brought to trial; although acquitted, he stopped writing for some time. While in England during World War I he wrote *Ostrovityane* (1918; "The Islanders"), satirizing the meanness and emotional repression of English life. He returned to Russia in 1917.

A chronic dissenter, Zamyatin was a Bolshevik before the Russian Revolution of 1917 but disassociated himself from the party afterward. His ironic criticism of literary politics kept him out of official favor, but he was influential as the mentor of the Serapion Brothers, a brilliant younger generation of writers whose artistic creed was to have no creeds. During the 1920s Zamyatin wrote some of his best short stories. His most ambitious work, the novel *My* (1924; *We*), circulated in manuscript in the Soviet Union. (It was not published there until 1989.) It portrays life in the "Single State," where workers live in glass houses, have numbers rather than names, wear identical uniforms, eat chemical foods, and enjoy rationed sex. *My* is a literary ancestor of Aldous Huxley's *Brave New World* and George Orwell's *Nineteen Eighty-four.*

The publication of *We* abroad and his continuous ridicule of artistic orthodoxy made him the victim of a press persecution that resulted in the banning of his works. In 1931 he left the Soviet Union and spent the remainder of his life in Paris.

Zangwill \'zaŋ-gwil\, Israel (b. Feb. 14, 1864, London, Eng.—d. Aug. 1, 1926, Midhurst, West Sussex)   Novelist, playwright, and Zionist leader, one of the earliest English interpreters of Jewish immigrant life.

The son of eastern European immigrants, Zangwill grew up in London's East End and was educated at the Jews' Free School and at the University of London. His early writings were on popular subjects of his day, but with *Children of the Ghetto: A Study of a Peculiar People* (1892) he drew on his intimate knowledge of ghetto life to present a gallery of Dickensian portraits of Whitechapel immigrant Jews struggling to survive in a new environment. The novelty of the subject, enhanced by Zangwill's emphasis on the Jews' exotic traits and by his simulation in English of Yiddish sentence structure, aroused great interest. Other works of Jewish content include a picaresque novel, *The King of Schnorrers* (1894), concerning an 18th-century rogue, and *Dreamers of the Ghetto* (1898), essays on

such famous Jews as the philosopher Benedict de Spinoza and the poet Heinrich Heine. The metaphor of America as a crucible wherein the European nationalities would be transformed into a new race owes its origin to the title and theme of Zangwill's play *The Melting Pot* (1908).

zanni \'tsän-nē\ *plural* zanni *or* zannis.   Stock servant character in the Italian COMMEDIA DELL'ARTE. Zanni were valet buffoons, clowns, and knavish jacks-of-all-trades. All possessed common sense, intelligence, pride, and a love of practical jokes and intrigue; they were, however, often quarrelsome, cowardly, envious, spiteful, vindictive, and treacherous. The name is traditionally explained as a dialectal diminutive form of Giovanni common to Bergamo, in Lombardy, where the zanni character originated, and it refers to male servants. *Dei zanni* ("the zanni") was a generic term for the commedia dell'arte itself.

Zanni initiated the action of the play and produced comic impact based on repeated comic actions (lazzi), topical jokes, and practical jokes (burle), often directed against the smug, the proud, and the pretentious. Zanni were also notable for their feats of acrobatics.

In some performances there was only one zanni; in others there might be two to four. The principal character among them was often called simply Zanni, while his companion(s) had such names as Panzanino, Buratino, Pedrolino (or Pierrot), Scapin, Scaramouche, Fritellino, Trappolino, Brighella, and most notably Arlecchino (Harlequin) and Pulcinella (related to the English Punchinello, or Punch). Pulcinella, like Capitano, "outgrew" his mask and became a character in his own right. Columbina, a maidservant, was often paired in love matches with Arlecchino, Pedrolino, or the Capitano. Frequently two zanni played contrasting roles, the first clever and adept at confounding, the second a dull-witted foil.

Zapata \sä-'pä-tä\, Luis (b. 1951)   Mexican novelist who rose to popularity in the 1970s with books about the youth subculture of Mexico City. His novels examine the connection between daily life and the popular culture of radio, television, and film.

Zapata chronicled the lives of urban homosexuals in *Las aventuras, desaventuras y sueños de Adonis García, el vampiro de la colonia Roma* (1979; *Adonis García: A Picaresque Novel*). His other works include *Hasta en las mejores familias* (1975; "Even in the Best Families"), *De pétalos perennes* (1981; "Of Perennial Petals"), *De amor es mi negra pena* (1983; "Of Love That Is My Hell"), *En jirones* (1985; "In Pieces"), *Ese amor que hasta ayer nos quemaba* (1989; "That Love That Until Yesterday in Us Burned"), *La hermana secreta de Angélica María* (1989; "The Secret Sister of Angélica María"), *De cuerpo entero* (1990; "At Full-Length"), and *Por qué mejor no nos vamos?* (1992; "Why Don't We Leave?").

Zapolska \zä-'pōl-skä\, Gabriela, *pseudonym of* Maria Gabriela Korwin-Piotrowska \'kōr-vēn-pʸō-'trōf-skä\ (b. March 30, 1857, Podhajce, Galicia, Austria [now Pidhaytsi, Ukraine]—d. Dec. 17, 1921, Lwów, Pol. [now Lviv, Ukraine])   Polish novelist and playwright of the naturalist school.

Having tried unsuccessfully to pursue an acting career in Paris, Zapolska started writing cheap, sensationalist novels, full of bitterness toward middle-class values, morality, and hypocrisy. Of her several novels written over a period of 20 years, only two continue to be read: *Zaszumi las* (1899; "The Forest Will Murmur"), a roman à clef about Polish revolutionaries in Paris, and *Sezonowa miłość* (1905; "Love in the Season"), a novel about fashionable life among the middle class in the resort town of Zapotane. Zapolska also wrote plays, mostly melodramas, which had the same ephemeral quality as most of her novels, but one is still remembered: *Moralność pani Dul-*

skiej (1906; "Mrs. Dulska's Morality"), a comedy-farce about the dominating matriarch of a bourgeois family.

zarzuela \thär-'thwä-lä, *Angl* zär-'zwä-lə\ [Spanish] Spanish musical play consisting of spoken passages, songs, choruses, and dances. It originated in the 17th century as an aristocratic entertainment dealing with mythological or heroic subject matter. The first performances were at the royal residence of La Zarzuela, near Madrid. Writers of zarzuelas included the playwrights Lope de Vega and Pedro Calderón de la Barca. The form declined in the late 17th and the 18th centuries as Italian opera rose in popularity. In the mid-19th century the zarzuela was revived as a popular musical play, an expanded version of the similar 18th-century *tonadilla*. Witty and satirical, it dealt with characters from everyday life and included folk music, dance, and improvisation. Two definite varieties evolved: the *género chico*, a one-act comic zarzuela, and the *género grande*, a serious musical play in two to four acts.

Zayas \'thä-yäs\, María de, *surname in full* Zayas y Sotomayor \ē-,sō-tō-mä-'yōr\ (b. Sept. 12, 1590, Madrid [Spain]—d. *c.* 1661) The most important of the minor 17th-century Spanish novelists and one of the first women to publish prose fiction in the Castilian dialect.

Zaya's novels about love and intrigue, which used melodramatic and frequently horrific elements, were widely read and very popular. *Novelas amorosas y ejemplares* (1637; *The Enchantments of Love*) presents an evening's exchange between men and women about the romantic complications of married life. The stories are mostly about women who are mistreated by husbands or seducers. *Novelas y saraos* (1647; "Novels and Soirees") and *Parte segunda del sarao y entretenimientos honestos* (1649; "Soiree Part Two and Decorous Amusements") are sequels.

Zeami \zä-'äm-ē\ or **Seami** \sä-'äm-ē\, *also called* Kanze Motokiyo \'kän-zä-mō-tō-'kē-yō\ (b. 1363/64, Japan—d. Sept. 1, 1443, Kyōto?) The greatest playwright and theorist of the Japanese Nō theater. He and his father Kan'ami were the creators of the Nō drama in its present form.

Under the patronage of the shogun Ashikaga Yoshimitsu, whose favor Zeami enjoyed after performing before him in 1374, the Nō was able to shake off the crudities of its past and to develop as a complex and aristocratic theater. After his father's death, Zeami became the chief figure in the Nō. He directed the Kanze school that his father had established and that had profound and lasting influence. Zeami not only continued to perform brilliantly but also wrote and revised plays prolifically. He is credited with about 90 (and most of the greatest) of the approximately 230 plays in the present repertoire. In 1422 he became a Zen monk, and his son Motomasa succeeded him. But Ashikaga Yoshinori, who became shogun in 1429, favored On'ami (Zeami's nephew) and refused to allow the son to perform before him. Motomasa died in 1432, and Yoshinori exiled Zeami to the island of Sado in 1434. After the shogun died in 1441, Zeami returned to Kyōto.

In his treatises written as manuals for his pupils, of which the most important is the collection *Fūshi kaden* (1400–18; "The Transmission of the Flower of Acting Style"), Zeami set forth the principles of Nō drama that were followed for centuries. According to Zeami the most important element was *yūgen*, by which the drama should suggest a kind of ethereal and profound beauty that lies beneath the surface of things and cannot be explicitly expressed. Such plays as *Matsukaze* ("Wind in the Pines"), written by Kan'ami and adapted by Zeami, have a mysterious stillness that seems to envelop the visible or audible parts of the work. In other of Zeami's dramas there is less *yūgen* and more action and occasionally even realism.

Zenodotus \zə-'näd-ə-təs\ of Ephesus \'ef-ə-səs\ (fl. late 3rd century BC) Greek grammarian and first superintendent (from *c.* 284 BC) of the library at Alexandria, noted for editions of Greek poets and especially for producing the first critical edition of Homer.

While serving as librarian at Alexandria, Zenodotus directed the work of editing the Greek epic and perhaps the lyric poets. After comparing different manuscripts of Homer, he deleted doubtful lines, transposed others, made emendations, and divided the *Iliad* and the *Odyssey* into 24 books each.

Zenodotus' edition—knowledge of which is derived almost entirely from later scholia on Homer—was severely attacked for its subjectivity by later scholars, notably one of his successors at the library, Aristarchus of Samothrace (*c.* 217–*c.* 145 BC) who modified Zenodotus' work.

Zenodotus also compiled a Homeric glossary, edited the *Theogony* of Hesiod, and published studies of Pindar and Anacreon, traces of which survive in a papyrus from Oxyrhyncus. He is also said to have written epic poetry.

Zephyrus \'zef-ə-rəs\ or **Zephyr** \'zef-ər\ In Greek mythology, the god of the west wind. In one version of the story of Hyacinthus' death, both Zephyrus and the god Apollo loved the handsome young man. Jealous of Hyacinthus' apparent preference for Apollo, Zephyrus blew at a discus that Apollo threw, causing it to change its course and to strike and kill Hyacinthus.

Żeromski \zhe-'róm-sk'ē\, Stefan (b. Nov. 1, 1864, Strawczyn, Poland, Russian Empire—d. Nov. 20, 1925, Warsaw) Polish novelist admired for his naturalistic and lyrical style.

After attending the veterinary college in Warsaw, Żeromski worked at first as a resident tutor in country houses and then as an assistant librarian in Switzerland and at the Zamoyski Library in Warsaw (1897–1903). From 1905, while living at Nałęczów, he furthered the cause of education for the masses and was arrested by the Russian authorities in 1908 for these activities. He subsequently lived in Paris (1909–12) and in Warsaw. Żeromski's first short stories were published in 1889. His first novel, *Syzyfowe prace* ("Sisyphean Labors"), appeared in 1897. *Popioły*, 3 vol. (1904; *The Ashes*) finally established his reputation. His last novel, *Przedwiośnie* (1925; "Before the Spring"), is about the first fruits of Polish national independence.

Zetes *see* CALAIS AND ZETES.

Zethus *see* AMPHION AND ZETHUS.

zeugma \'züg-mə\ [Greek *zeûgma*, literally, juncture, joining] The use of a word to modify or govern two or more words usually in such a manner that it applies to each in a different sense (as in "She opened the door and her heart to the homeless boy.") or makes sense with only one (as in "Kill the boys and the luggage!").

Zeus \'züs, 'zyüs\ In ancient Greek mythology, chief deity of the pantheon, a sky and weather god who was later identified with the Roman god JUPITER. Zeus was regarded as the sender of thunder and lightning, rain, and winds, and his traditional weapon was the thunderbolt. He was called the father (*i.e.*, the ruler and protector) of both gods and humans.

According to a Cretan myth that was later adopted by the Greeks, Cronus, king of the Titans, upon learning that one of his children was fated to dethrone him, swallowed his children as soon as they were born. But Rhea, his wife, saved the infant Zeus by substituting a stone wrapped in swaddling clothes for Cronus to swallow and hiding Zeus in a cave on Crete. There he was nursed by the nymph (or female goat) Amalthaea and guarded by the Curetes (young warriors). After Zeus grew to manhood he led a revolt against the Titans and succeeded in dethroning Cronus, with the assistance of his brothers Hades and Poseidon, with whom he then divided dominion over the world.

As ruler of heaven Zeus led the gods to victory against the Giants (offspring of Gaea) and successfully crushed several revolts against him by his fellow gods. From his exalted position atop Mount Olympus Zeus was thought to observe the affairs of humans, seeing everything, governing all, and rewarding good conduct and punishing evil. Besides dispensing justice, Zeus protected cities, the home, property, strangers, guests, and supplicants.

Zeus was well-known for his amorousness—a source of perpetual discord with his wife, Hera—and he had many love affairs with both mortal women and goddesses. In order to achieve his amorous designs, Zeus frequently assumed animal forms, such as that of a cuckoo when he ravished Hera, a swan when he raped Leda, or a bull when he carried off Europa. Notable among his offspring were the twins Apollo and Artemis, by the Titaness Leto; Helen, by Leda of Sparta; Persephone, by the goddess Demeter; Athena, born from his head after he had swallowed the Titaness Metis; Hephaestus, Hebe, Ares, and Eileithyia, by his wife, Hera; Dionysus, by Semele; and many others. *See also* HERA.

Zhang Guangren   *see* HU FENG.

Zhang Junxiang or **Chang Chün-hsiang** \ˈjäŋ-ˈjūͤn-ˈshyäŋ\ (b. Dec. 17, 1910, Zhenjiang, Jiangsu province, China)   One of the leading playwrights and motion-picture directors in China.

Zhang was educated at Qinghua University, Beijing, and at Yale University and then studied film technique in Hollywood. Returning to China during the Sino-Japanese War of 1937–45, he directed several successful plays in Chongqing and rose to preeminence in the Chinese film industry. After the establishment of the communist regime in 1949, Zhang became a director of the governmental Central Motion Picture Company. His film *Cuigang hongqi* (1952; *Red Banner on the Emerald Ridge*) won acclaim throughout China.

Zhang's first published play, *Xiaocheng gushi* (1941; "Tale of a Small Town"), is a comedy about the psychological conflicts of a woman in love; *Wanshi shibiao* (1945; "Model Teacher of Myriad Generations"), considered his best play, follows the fortunes of a group of Chinese intellectuals from 1919 to 1937.

Zhang Tianyi or **Chang T'ien-i** \ˈjäŋ-ˈtyan-ˈē\ (b. 1907, Jiangning [now Nanjing], Jiangsu province, China)   Chinese writer whose brilliant, socially realistic short stories achieved considerable renown in the 1930s.

Zhang Tianyi was born into a scholarly family. In 1924 he moved to Beijing and, stimulated by the intellectual activity there, began to write. His first short story, "Sanriban zhi meng" (1928; "A Dream of Three-and-a-Half Days"), was written in a realistic and direct manner. Collections of his stories include *Xiao Bide* (1931; "Little Bide"), *Tuanyuan* (1935; "Family Reunion"), and *Suxie sanpian* (1943; "Three Sketches"). He also wrote several satirical novels, including *Guitu riji* (1931; "Ghostland Diary") and *Yangjingbang* (1936; "The Strange Knight-errant of the Shanghai Concessions").

Zhang Tianyi's career as a writer was curtailed in 1943, when tuberculosis forced him to retire. After recuperating, he was assigned to a trusted position in the new communist regime as a writer of children's plays. He also served as editor in chief of the magazine *Renmin wenxue* ("People's Literature").

Zhang Ziping or **Chang Tzu-p'ing** \ˈjäŋ-ˈdzŭ-ˈpiŋ\ (b. 1893, Meixian, Guangdong province, China—d. 1947?)   Chinese author of popular romantic fiction and a founder of the Creation Society, a literary association devoted to the propagation of Romanticism.

After receiving a classical Chinese education and attending an American Baptist mission school for three years, Zhang Ziping went to Japan to continue his studies. He took a degree in geology in 1922 but chose to pursue a literary career. While in Japan he met Guo Moruo and other Chinese writers, with whom he founded the Creation Society and edited the group's magazine. At this time the novel *Chongjiqi huashi* (1922; "Fossils in Alluvial Deposits"), the first of his many novels and short stories, was published. After a brief flirtation with political themes in support of the Chinese republic, he returned to his original literary philosophy. During the Sino-Japanese War (1937–45), he worked with the Japanese and, after their defeat, was tried in 1947 by the Chinese on charges of collaboration. Nothing further is known of his fate.

Zhao Shuli or **Chao Shu-li** \ˈjaŭ-ˈshū-ˈlē\ (b. Sept. 24, 1906, Qinshui, Shanxi province, China—d. Sept. 23, 1970, Taiyuan, Shanxi)   Chinese novelist and short-story writer.

Zhao's familiarity with rural life in North China and his fascination for folk literature and art determined the substance and style of his later writings. After attending a teachers' college, he taught in primary schools. To supplement his earnings he began writing short stories for local newspapers. A zealous promoter of folk literature and art, he wrote a considerable number of rhythmic talks, mini-tales, and sketches. He made his name by his short stories "Xiao Erhei jie hun" (1943; "Little Blacky's Wedding") and "Li Youcai banhua" (1943; "The Rhymes of Li Youcai"). They were followed in 1946 by the novel *Lijiazhuang de bianqian* ("The Changes in Li Village") and the stories "Fugui" ("Lucky"), "Diban" ("Land"), and "Cuiliangchai" ("The Tax Collector"). His works were read and his native humor and grace appreciated by even the barely literate. After 1949 he continued to write prose and edited two magazines. His novel *Sanliwan* was published in 1955. During the Cultural Revolution (1966–76) he was persecuted.

Zhdanovshchina \ˈzhdȧ-nəf-shchi-nə\ or **Zhdanovism** \ˈzhdan-ə-ˌviz-əm\   Cultural policy of the Soviet Union during the Cold War period following World War II that called for stricter government control of art and promoted an extreme anti-Western bias. Originally applied to literature, it soon spread to other arts and gradually affected all spheres of intellectual activity in the Soviet Union, including philosophy, biology, medicine, and other sciences. It was initiated by a resolution (1946) of the Central Committee of the Communist Party of the Soviet Union that was formulated by the party secretary and cultural advisor Andrey Aleksandrovich Zhdanov. It was directed against two literary magazines, *Zvezda* and *Leningrad*, which had published supposedly apolitical, bourgeois, individualistic works of the satirist Mikhail Zoshchenko and the poet Anna Akhmatova, who were expelled from the Union of Soviet Writers.

As the campaign accelerated, all vestiges of Westernism, or cosmopolitanism, in Soviet life were ferreted out. Earlier critics and literary historians were denounced for suggesting that Russian classics had been influenced by Jean-Jacques Rousseau, Molière, Lord Byron, or Charles Dickens. Western inventions and scientific theories were claimed to be of Russian origin. Although Zhdanov died in 1948, the campaign against "cosmopolites" continued until the death of Joseph Stalin in 1953, acquiring increasingly anti-Semitic overtones. This period (1946–53) is generally regarded as the lowest ebb of Soviet literature.

Zheng Zhenduo or **Cheng Chen-to** \ˈjəŋ-ˈjən-ˈdwȯ\ (b. 1898, Fuzhou, Fujian province, China—d. Oct. 17, 1958, en route from China to Afghanistan) Literary historian of Chinese vernacular literature who was instrumental in promoting the "new literature" of 20th-century China.

After studying in his native Fujian, where he began writing short stories and verse as a youth, Zheng Zhenduo went to Shanghai and then to Beijing to further his education. In Beijing he became involved in the movement for literary reform and began what was to become his life-long study of vernacular Chinese literature.

With other young writers Zheng Zhenduo helped to change the staid and established *Xiaoshuo yuebao* ("Fiction Monthly") into a stimulating journal of the new literature, including poetry, essays, and translations, as well as short stories, the most popular literary genre in China in the 1920s. The magazine served as the organ of the Literary Research Society, committed to realism in literature, to the introduction of foreign literature into China, and to the creation of a new Chinese literature. Zheng Zhenduo was made Beijing editor of the magazine upon its reorganization in 1920 and became chief editor in 1926, also contributing essays and translations.

In 1927 he traveled to Europe, spending most of his time in the libraries of Paris and London. On his return to China he continued editing and writing and published in 1932 his first major work on the history of Chinese vernacular literature, followed by three volumes of general and critical essays and an outline of Russian literature.

During the Sino-Japanese War (1937–45), Zheng Zhenduo roamed the streets of Shanghai in search of the many literary treasures that private owners were forced to sell. After the war he headed institutes in the Ministry of Culture.

Zhong yong or **Chung yung** \\'jůŋ-'yůŋ\\ One of four Confucian texts that, when published together in 1190 by Zhu Xi, a great Neo-Confucian philosopher, became the famous SI SHU ("Four Books"). *Zhong yong* was chosen by Zhu Xi for its metaphysical interest, which had already attracted the attention of Buddhists and earlier Neo-Confucianists. In his preface, Zhu Xi attributed authorship of the treatise (which was actually a chapter from *Li ji*, one of the Five Classics of antiquity) to Zi Si (also called Kong Ji; 483–402 BC), a grandson of Confucius.

Zi Si presented *Zhong yong* as the central theme of Confucian thought. The two Chinese characters *zhong yong* (often translated "doctrine of the mean") express a Confucian ideal that is so broad and so all-embracing as to encompass virtually every relationship and every activity of human life. In practice, *zhong yong* means countless things: moderation, rectitude, objectivity, sincerity, honesty, truthfulness, propriety, equilibrium, and lack of prejudice. Ideally, one must adhere unswervingly to the mean, or center course, at all times and in every situation. Such behavior conforms to the laws of nature, is the distinctive mark of the superior individual, and is the essence of true orthodoxy.

Zhou li or **Chou li** \\'jō-'lē\\ ("Rites of Zhou"), *also called* Zhou guan ("Offices of Zhou") Any one of three ancient ritual texts listed among the Nine, Twelve, and Thirteen Classics of Confucianism. Though tradition ascribes the text to Zhougung (12th century BC), the work is considered by modern scholars to have been an anonymous utopian "constitution" written perhaps about 300 BC. For many centuries *Zhou li* was joined to *Li ji* ("Collection of Rituals") and thus constituted one of the Six Classics (*Liu Jing*) of Chinese literature.

Influenced by Legalist as well as Confucian ideas, *Zhou li* discusses government in general under "Offices of Heaven," education under "Offices of Earth," social and religious institutions under "Offices of Spring," the army under "Offices of Summer," justice under "Office of Autumn," and population, territory, and agriculture under "Office of Winter."

Zhou Yang or **Chou Yang** \\'jō-'yäŋ\\, *pseudonym of* Zhou Qiying \\'shē-'yäŋ\\ (b. Nov. 7, 1908, Yiyang, Hunan province, China—d. July 31, 1989, Beijing) Chinese critic.

Zhou joined the Chinese Communist Party soon after the failure of the revolution in 1927. A graduate of the Daxia University in Shanghai in 1928, he went to Japan for advanced study in 1929 and returned to China in 1931 and became one of the leaders of the League of Left-wing Writers. In 1932 he edited the League's organ *Wenxue yuebao* ("Literature Monthly"). He went to Yan'an in 1937 and served in several official posts. During the Cultural Revolution (1966–76) he was repudiated at mass meetings and ruthlessly persecuted. He was rehabilitated in 1978.

Zhou Yang's lifelong interest was in literary theory and criticism. In the 1930s he had introduced to China Marxist concepts and theories of literature and the aesthetic theory of the Russian revolutionary democrat, Nikolay Chernyshevsky. In 1933 he introduced to China the socialist realism that was then being fostered in the Soviet Union. While in Yan'an he compiled *Makesizhuyi yu wenyi* (1944; "Marxism and Literature"), a systematic presentation of what the outstanding Marxists had to say about literature, and he translated Leo Tolstoy's *Anna Karenina*. His essays and dissertations were later collected in many volumes.

Zhou Zuoren or **Chou Tso-jen** \\'jō-'dzwô-'ren\\ (b. Jan. 16, 1885, Shaoxing, Zhejiang province, China—d. November 1966, Beijing?) Essayist and literary scholar who translated fiction from many languages into vernacular Chinese.

Zhou Zuoren and his elder brother, the writer and literary critic known as Lu Xun, received a classical education. Although Zhou Zuoren passed the examinations to qualify for an official career, he chose to devote himself to scholarship, learning English and studying Western intellectual history. In 1905 his first translation, of Edgar Allan Poe's "The Gold Bug," was published. The following year he and his brother went to Japan, where Zhou Zuoren studied Japanese language and literature, classical Greek literature, and English literature. He continued his translating and published a collection of European fiction, selecting works to stimulate the people of China with the examples of others who had rebelled under oppressive rule.

In 1912 Zhou Zuoren and his Japanese wife returned to China, where he taught at Beijing University and began writing the essays that won him renown. One of his favorite topics was the need for language reform and the use of the vernacular; he also pleaded for what he termed a "humane" literature and praised the realism of Western writers. His collections of translations—from Greek, Latin, Russian, and Japanese literature—continued to be published as his popularity as an authority on foreign literature increased.

During the 1920s he was active in several socially and politically oriented literary societies, which led to his being blacklisted in 1926 for radical activities. This, combined with increasingly frequent attacks from leftists on his stand against propagandist literary doctrines, forced Zhou Zuoren out of public literary life in China, but he resumed his studies privately in Beijing.

Because he remained in his home in northern China during the Sino-Japanese War (1937–45) and worked for a Japanese-sponsored bureau of education, he was tried as a collaborator by the National Government after the war ended and was condemned to death. His sentence was commuted to imprisonment, and he received a full pardon in 1949.

Zhukovsky \\zhů-'kôf-sk^yē\\, Vasily Andreyevich (b. Jan. 29 [Feb. 9, New Style], 1783, Tula province, Russia—d. April 12 [April 24], 1852, Baden-Baden, Baden [Germany]) Russian poet and translator, one of Aleksandr Pushkin's most important precursors in forming Russian verse style and language. Zhukovsky was educated in Moscow. He served in the Napoleonic War of 1812 and in 1815 became a member of the czar's entourage, being appointed tutor to the heir to the throne in 1826. In 1841 he retired to Germany.

Zhukovsky was a follower of Nikolay Karamzin, the leader of a Romantic literary movement that countered the classical emphasis on reason with the belief that poetry should be an expression of feeling. Zhukovsky was one of the founders of the Arzamas Society, a semihumorous, pro-Karamzin literary group established to oppose the classicists. Like Pushkin, Zhukovsky was interested especially in personal experience, Romantic conceptions of landscape, and folk ballads. His first publication was a translation of Thomas Gray's *An Elegy Written in a Country Church Yard* (1802), and the bulk of his work consists of translations. He introduced into Russia the works of such German and English contemporaries as Gottfried Bürger, Friedrich von Schiller, J.W. von Goethe, Sir Walter Scott, Lord Byron, and Robert Southey. His collected works were published in four volumes in 1959–60.

Zhulin qi xian   *see* SEVEN SAGES OF THE BAMBOO GROVE.

Zhu Yizun or **Chu Yi-tsun** \'jü-ē-'dzwŭn\, Yi-tsun *also spelled* Chu I-tsun, *also called* Zhu Zhucha \'jü-'chä\ (b. Oct. 7, 1629, Xiushui, Zhejiang province, China—d. Nov. 14, 1709, Xiushui)   Eminent Chinese scholar and poet of the early Qing dynasty (1644–1911/12).

Though his family had been prominent under the Ming dynasty, Zhu was forced to spend much of his life as a private tutor and personal secretary to various local officials and men of letters. His considerable intellectual accomplishments, however, earned him a summons to a special Qing examination in 1678. Eventually he won an appointment to the prestigious Hanlin Academy at the court in Beijing, where he became an editor on the official Ming history project. While at the capital he wrote a number of other histories, including a noted history of Beijing and its environs (1688), and produced his *Jingyi kao* (1701; expanded ed. 1755; "General Bibliography of the Classics"), a massive descriptive catalog of both lost and extant works in the Confucian canon.

Preserving a lively interest in poetry throughout his career, Zhu edited a collection of Ming verse and a definitive anthology of lyric *ci* poetry. Indeed, he is regarded as one of the best of the early Qing poets. He was a prolific composer of *ci* poetry, his work in that genre being traditional in form, though somewhat obscure and allegorical in approach. His courtesy name is Xichang.

Zimorowic \zi-mō-'rō-vēts\ or **Zimorowicz** \-vēch\, Józef Bartłomiej, *original name* Józef Bartłomiej Ozimek \ō-'zĕ-mek\ (b. Aug. 20, 1597, Lwów, Pol. [now Lviv, Ukraine]—d. Oct. 14, 1677, Lwów)   Polish writer who was a prolific author of satirical and erotic epigrams.

When well-advanced in years, Zimorowic published a series of verse descriptions of Ukrainian peasant life, *Sielanki nowe ruskie* (1663; "New Ruthenian Idylls"), under the name of his more gifted younger brother Szymon (1608–29). This collection also included two versified narratives of the Cossack rebellion in 1648–49 against Polish rule in Ukraine, *Kozaczyzna* ("The Cossacks") and *Burda Ruska* ("The Ruthenian Skirmish").

Zindel \zin-'del\, Paul (b. May 15, 1936, Staten Island, N.Y., U.S.)   American playwright and novelist whose largely autobiographical work features poignant, alienated characters who deal with life's difficulties in pragmatic and straightforward ways.

Zindel attended Wagner College, Staten Island, N.Y., and taught high school chemistry for several years before becoming a full-time writer in 1972. In most of Zindel's dramas the main tension is between a nonconformist, domineering mother and an impressionable, bewildered young person. His plays include the Pulitzer Prize-winning THE EFFECT OF GAMMA RAYS ON MAN-IN-THE-MOON MARIGOLDS (1971), *And Miss Reardon Drinks a Little* (1971), *The Secret Affairs of Mildred Wild* (1973), *Let Me Hear You Whisper* (1970), *The Ladies Should Be in Bed* (1973), *A Destiny with Half Moon Street* (produced 1983; published 1992), and *Amulets Against the Dragon Forces* (1989; based partly on his novel *Confessions of a Teenage Baboon*). Among his novels for young adults are *The Pigman* (1968), *My Darling, My Hamburger* (1969), *Harry and Hortense at Hormone High* (1984), and *A Begonia for Miss Applebaum* (1989).

Zola \zō-'lä, *Angl* 'zō-lə, -,lä\, Émile(-Édouard-Charles-Antoine) (b. April 2, 1840, Paris, Fr.—d. Sept. 28, 1902, Paris)   French novelist and critic, the founder of the naturalist movement in literature.

Detail of an oil painting by Édouard Manet, 1868; in the Louvre, Paris
Cliché Musées Nationaux, Paris

Zola grew up in straitened circumstances. After failing his *baccalauréat* examination, he spent two years in a vain search for employment. He eventually secured a clerical post in a shipping firm, which he loathed, and in 1862 moved to the sales department of the publishing house of Louis-Christophe-François Hachette. Hachette encouraged him in his writing. Zola's first book, published in 1864, was a collection of short stories called *Contes à Ninon*. It was followed in 1865 by a sordid autobiographical novel, *La Confession de Claude*, which attracted the attention of the police and led to Zola's departure from Hachette.

THÉRÈSE RAQUIN, a gruesome novel in which he put his "scientific" theories into practice for the first time, appeared in 1867. *Madeleine Férat* (*Shame*), another experiment in scientific fiction, followed in 1868. In 1870 he wrote the first two novels of an ambitious project, later called the ROUGON-MACQUART CYCLE (1871–93), originally intended to include 10 novels but expanded to 20. The opening volume of the cycle, *La Fortune des Rougon*, was published in book form in 1871, and five more volumes followed in the next five years. The appearance in 1877 of *L'Assommoir* (*Drunkard*), a study of alcoholism, made Zola the best-known writer in France. The remaining 13 novels—including such well-known works as *Nana* (1880), *Germinal* (1885), *L'Oeuvre* (1886), and *La Bête humaine* (1890)—occupied him for another 16 years. The Rougon-Macquart cycle was followed by two short cycles, *Les Trois Villes* ("The Three Cities") and *Les Quatre Évangiles* ("The Four Gospels").

As a writer, Zola was both inspired and limited by his credulous faith in science and his uncritical acceptance of scientific determinism. He maintained that naturalism was indigenous to French life and believed that human nature was completely determined by heredity.

Zola's career is also notable for his involvement in the Dreyfus affair, especially for his open letter, J'ACCUSE, denouncing the French army general staff. Zola died under mysterious circumstances, overcome by carbon monoxide fumes in his sleep.

Although nominated 19 times for inclusion in the Académie Française, he was never elected.

Zollinger \'tsô-liŋ-ər\, Albin (b. Jan. 24, 1895, Zürich, Switz.—d. Nov. 7, 1941, Zürich) Poet and novelist, the leading figure in the revival of Swiss poetry between World Wars I and II.

Zollinger wrote most of his work in the 10 years before his death. Following Impressionist trends, he became a master of landscape description, inspired by a refined sensuous delight. He also aspired to transcend the narrow limits of human nature. Encouraged by the examples of Friedrich Hölderlin, Rainer Maria Rilke, and Thomas Wolfe, he created an effusive lyrical imagery. His volumes of verse include *Gedichte* (1933; "Poems"), *Sternfrühe* (1936; "Starlit Early Morning"), *Stille des Herbstes* (1939; "Autumn Tranquility"), and *Haus des Lebens* (1939; "House of Life"). His novels *Der halbe Mensch* (1929; "Half a Human," *Die grosse Unruhe* (1939; "The Great Restlessness"), and *Pfannenstiel* (1940; "Panhandle") and his novella *Das Gewitter* (1943; "The Thunderstorm") are confrontations with the great movements of his epoch. While Zollinger's plots suffer from looseness, his language is rich and evocative.

Zoo Story, The One-act play by Edward ALBEE, produced and published in 1959, about an isolated young man desperate to interact with other people.

As the play opens, Peter (a publishing executive who is reading in New York City's Central Park) is approached by a stranger named Jerry. Announcing "I've been to the zoo!" Jerry proceeds to probe deep into Peter's life. He relates details from his own life—his stay in a rooming house with a bizarre landlady and her repulsive dog and his unsuccessful attempt to poison the dog. Peter grows increasingly agitated by this encounter. Jerry becomes abusive, tosses Peter a knife, provokes him into a fight, and impales himself on the knife.

Zorba the Greek \'zôr-bə, *Greek* zôr-'bä\ Novel by Nikos KAZANTZÁKIS, published in Greek in 1946 as *Víos kai politía tou Aléxi Zormpá*.

The unnamed narrator is a scholarly, introspective writer who opens a coal mine on the fertile island of Crete. He is gradually drawn out of his ascetic shell by an elderly employee named Zorba, an ebullient man who revels in the social pleasures of eating, drinking, and dancing. The narrator's reentry into a life of experience is completed when his newfound lover, the village widow, is ritually murdered by a jealous mob.

Zorrilla \thôr-'rēl-yä\, José, *surname in full* Zorrilla y Moral \ē-mô-'räl\ (b. Feb. 21, 1817, Valladolid, Spain—d. Jan. 23, 1893, Madrid) Poet and dramatist, the major figure of the nationalist wing of the Spanish Romantic movement. His work was enormously popular and is now regarded as quintessentially Spanish in style and tone.

After studying law at Toledo and Valladolid, Zorrilla devoted himself to literature. In 1837 he became an overnight success with his recitation of an elegy at the funeral of the satirist Mariano José de Larra. He ran away from his wife and financial distress and was abroad from 1855 to 1866, during which time he wrote prolifically but remained insolvent. In 1889 he was crowned as the national poet and was granted a government pension.

Zorrilla wrote effortlessly; he was an improviser who made his name with his *leyendas* ("legends"), which told of remote times and places. His first collection of verse *leyendas, Cantos del trovador* (1841; "Songs of the Troubadour"), however, suffered—like much of his other poetry—from carelessness and verbosity.

Zorrilla's greatest success was achieved with his version of the Don Juan story, the play DON JUAN TENORIO (1844). Writ-

ten while he was in his 20s and later despised by him as a failure, it was the most popular play of 19th-century Spain and is still frequently performed. Like his other works, it exhibits those typically Spanish qualities that have made Zorrilla a uniquely national author: picturesque characters, intrigues and coincidences in its plot, lyrical flights, and great Romantic coloring.

Zorrilla de San Martín \sôr-'rē-yä-t͟hä-,sän-mär-'tēn\, Juan (b. Dec. 28, 1855, Montevideo, Uru.—d. Nov. 3, 1931, Montevideo) Uruguayan poet famous for a long historical verse epic, *Tabaré* (1886; final edition after several revisions, 1926). A poem in six cantos, it was based upon a legend of the love between a Spanish girl and an Indian boy.

Zorrilla de San Martín was educated in various Jesuit schools throughout South America. His first work, *Notas de un himno* (1876; "Notes for a Hymn"), dealing with themes of sadness and patriotism, clearly reflects the influence of the famous Spanish Romantic poet Gustavo Adolfo Bécquer and set the tone for all his poetic work that followed. In 1878 he founded the Catholic periodical *El bien público* and the next year achieved renown for his patriotic ode *La leyenda patria* ("The Fatherland Legend"). Throughout his life he held various government posts, including Uruguayan minister to France, Portugal, Spain, and the Vatican.

Zoshchenko \'zôsh-chin-kə\, Mikhail Mikhaylovich (b. July 29 [Aug. 10, New Style], 1895, Poltava, Ukraine, Russian Empire—d. July 22, 1958, Leningrad, Russian S.F.S.R., U.S.S.R. [now St. Petersburg, Russia]) Soviet satirist whose short stories and sketches are among the best comic literature of the Soviet period.

Zoshchenko studied law and then in 1915 joined the army. Between 1917 and 1920 he lived in many different cities and worked at a variety of odd jobs and trades. In 1921 he joined the Serapion Brothers literary group. Zoshchenko's tales are primarily satires on contemporary Soviet life. One of his main targets was bureaucratic red tape and corruption, which he attacked with tongue-in-cheek wit, using artificial language and malapropisms that make his works virtually untranslatable.

Beginning in the 1930s, Zoshchenko was subjected to increasingly severe criticism from officialdom. He tried to conform to the requirements of Socialist Realism—notably in *Istoriya odnoy zhizhni* (1935; "The Story of One Life"), dealing with the construction, by forced labor, of the White Sea–Baltic Waterway—but with little success.

In 1946 Zoshchenko published the short story "Priklyucheniya obezyany" ("The Adventures of a Monkey") in the literary magazine *Zvezda*. The work was condemned by Communist critics as malicious and insulting to the Soviet people. He was expelled from the Union of Soviet Writers, which meant the virtual end of his literary career.

After his death the Soviet press tended to ignore him; but some of his works were reissued, and their prompt sale indicated his continuing popularity.

Zrínyi \'zrē-nyē\, Miklós (b. Jan. 5, 1620, Csákvár, Hung.—d. Nov. 18, 1664, Csáktornya [now Čakovec, Croatia]) Statesman, military leader, and author of the first epic poem in Hungarian literature.

Born into an extremely wealthy aristocratic family, Zrínyi was educated by the Jesuits and became viceroy of Croatia in 1647. At the time, the Ottoman Turks occupied much of Hungary, and Zrínyi's chief concern was driving them out of the country. He spent his entire life fighting the conquerors, becoming the outstanding Hungarian military leader of his century. In 1664 he started an organization to oppose the Habsburgs, who ruled the unoccupied part of the country, but he was killed that same year by a wild boar.

Zrínyi's finest literary work, and one of the major works of Hungarian literature, is his epic *Szigeti veszedelem* (1651; published as "The Peril of Sziget"), which deals with the heroic defense of the fortress of Szigetvár in 1566 against the armies of the sultan Süleyman I. The commander of the fortress, the central figure of the epic, was the poet's great-grandfather, who fell during the siege.

Zuckmayer \\'tsŭk-ˌmī-ər\\, Carl (b. Dec. 27, 1896, Nackenheim, Ger.—d. Jan. 18, 1977, Visp, Switz.) German playwright whose works deal critically with many of the contemporary problems engendered by two world wars.

Zuckmayer's first notable dramatic success was the earthy comedy *Der fröhliche Weinberg* (1925; "The Happy Vineyard"). *Der Hauptmann von Köpenick* (1931; *The Captain of Köpenick*), one of his most highly regarded works, is a satire on Prussian militarism. In 1933 political pressure forced him to immigrate to Austria, where he wrote *Der Schelm von Bergen* (1934; "The Villain of Bergen").

Zuckmayer fled to the United States in 1939 and became a U.S. citizen. There he wrote one of his best-known dramas, *Des Teufels General* (1946; *The Devil's General*). With this play, which dramatizes the plight of men torn between loyalty to country and the demands of conscience, Zuckmayer's dramatic career entered a new phase. The zestful, life-affirming spirit of his earlier works was thereafter tempered with critical moral evaluation. In this spirit he wrote *Barbara Blomberg* (1949), *Der Gesang im Feuerofen* (1950; "The Song in the Fiery Furnace"), and *Das kalte Licht* (1955; "The Cold Light"), based on the treason case of the atomic scientist Klaus Fuchs.

Among his other works are essays, dramatic adaptations, motion-picture scenarios, novels (*Salwàre; oder, die Magdalena von Bozen*, 1936; *The Moons Ride Over*, 1937), and two autobiographical works, *Second Wind* (1940; only an English version was published) and *Als wär's ein Stück von mir* (1966; abridged English version, *A Part of Myself*).

Zuhayr \\zŭ-'hīr\\, *in full* Zuhayr ibn Abī Sulmā Rabī'ah ibn Rīyāḥ al-Muzanī (b. *c.* 520—d. *c.* 609, Najd region, Arabia [now in Saudi Arabia]) One of the greatest of the Arab poets of pre-Islāmic times, best known for his long ode in the *Al-Mu'allaqāt* collection.

Zuhayr was of the Muzaynah tribe but lived among the Ghaṭafān. His father was a poet, his first wife the sister of a poet, and two of his sons were poets. Zuhayr's poem in *Al-Mu'allaqāt* praises the men who brought peace between the clans of 'Abs and Dhubyān. In the poem, war is compared to a millstone that grinds those who set it moving, and the poet speaks as one who has learned from a long life about the human need for morality. Zuhayr's extant poetry, available in several Arabic editions, includes other poems of praise and satires.

Zukofsky \\zŭ-'kôf-skē\\, Louis (b. Jan. 23, 1904, New York, N.Y., U.S.—d. May 12, 1978, Port Jefferson, N.Y.) American poet, the founder of Objectivist poetry and author of the massive poem *"A"*.

The son of Jewish immigrants from Russia, Zukofsky grew up in New York, attended Columbia University, and taught for several years at Polytechnic Institute of Brooklyn. By the 1930s he had begun the ill-defined Objectivist movement, and poets as radically different as William Carlos Williams, T.S. Eliot, and Ezra Pound contributed to the special Objectivist issue of *Poetry* magazine (1931) and to An *"Objectivist" Anthology* (1932), which Zukofsky edited.

Meanwhile, in 1928 he had embarked upon *"A"*, the great work of his life, which treats subjects as diverse as history, politics, aesthetics, science, and life in general. The poem was organized in a mosaic structure and planned in 24 parts. The complete poem, 826 pages long, beginning with the word "A" and ending with "Zion," was published in 1978. Zukofsky described himself as a comic poet, and punning is the characteristic medium of his and his wife Celia's *Catullus Fragmenta* (1969), a translation of the Roman poet Catullus' works into an obscure English that attempts to reproduce the sounds of the original Latin. His several volumes of prose include the critical study *Bottom: On Shakespeare* (1963) and *Little: A Fragment For Careenagers* (1967), which is a short novel about a youthful violin prodigy. *All: The Collected Short Poems, 1923–1964* was published in 1971.

Zunz \\'tsûnts\\, Leopold, *also called* Yom-Tob Lippmann \\'lip-ˌmän\\ (b. Aug. 10, 1794, Detmold, Lippe [now in Germany]—d. March 18, 1886, Berlin, Ger.) German historian of Jewish literature who is often considered the greatest Jewish scholar of the 19th century. In 1819 he started the movement called Wissenschaft des Judentums ("Science of Judaism"), which stressed the analysis of Jewish literature and culture with the tools of modern scholarship.

Zunz studied classics and history at Berlin University, taking his doctorate at the University of Halle. He served as a lay preacher for a congregation and worked from 1824 to 1831 as a newspaper editor and from 1840 to 1850 as a teacher and principal at the Jewish teachers' seminary in Berlin.

The Science of Judaism was initiated with his seminal work, *Etwas über die rabbinische Litteratur* (1818; "On Rabbinic Literature"), which revealed to the interested public for the first time the scope and beauty of postbiblical Jewish literature. In 1819 Zunz cofounded the Verein für Kultur und Wissenschaft der Juden ("Society for Jewish Culture and Science"). From 1822 to 1823, Zunz edited the society's periodical, *Zeitschrift*, to which he contributed a classic biography of Rashi, the great medieval commentator on biblical and rabbinical texts. After the society disbanded in 1824 he continued its work alone.

Zunz's *Die Gottesdienstlichen Vorträge der Juden, historisch entwickelt* (1832; "The Sermons of the Jews, Historically Developed") is a historical analysis of Jewish homiletic literature and its evolutionary development up to the modern-day sermon. *Zur Geschichte und Literatur* (1845; "On History and Literature") is a wide-ranging work that places Jewish literary activity in the context of European literature and politics. Zunz wrote three important works on the liturgies of Judaism and served as editor in chief of a translation of the Bible (1838), for which he translated the Books of Chronicles. In his last years he wrote a series of essays on the Bible, collected in *Gesammelte Schriften*, 3 vol. (1875–76; "Collected Writings").

Zunzunegui \\ˌthün-thü-'nä-ḡē\\, Juan Antonio de, *surname in full* Zunzunegui y Loredo \\ē-lō-'rä-t͟hō\\ (b. Dec. 21, 1901, Portugalete, Spain—d. May 31, 1982, Madrid) Spanish novelist and short-story writer who wrote in a traditional 19th-century manner about society in Bilbao and Madrid. A member of the Spanish Academy from 1957, Zunzunegui received the National Prize for Literature for *El premio* (1961; "The Prize"), itself a satire on literary prizes in Spain.

The novels Zunzunegui produced between 1926 and 1950 generally center on contemporary life in Bilbao—for example, *Chiripi* (1931) and *El chiplichandle* (1939; "The Ship-Chandler"), criticizing Spain's immoral social climate; *¡Ay . . . estos hijos!* (1943; "Oh, These Children!"), on family life in Bilbao; two novels on Bilbao bankers collectively entitled *La quiebra* (1947; "The Bankruptcy"); and *La úlcera* (1949; "The Ulcer"), a naturalistic novel featuring characters who are grotesquely deformed.

Beginning with *El supremo bien* (1951; "The Highest Good"), the setting of Zunzunegui's narratives was Madrid. *La vida como es* (1954; "Life As It Is"), often considered his best work, depicts Madrid's underworld and captures its argot and local color. Zunzunegui's other works include *Las ratas del barco* (1950; "The Ship Rats"), *Una mujer sobre la tierra* (1959; "A Woman on Earth"), *El mundo sigue* (1960; "The World Continues"), *Una ricahembra* (1970; "A Noblewoman"), *La hija malograda* (1973; "The Unfortunate Daughter"), and *De la vida y de la muerte* (1979; "Of Life and Death").

Zuo zhuan or **Tso chuan** \'dzwô-'jwän\ ("Zuo's Commentary")   Ancient commentary on the CHUNQIU and the first sustained narrative work in Chinese literature. The *Chunqiu*, which records events during the Spring and Autumn period (770–476 BC) of China's history, is the first Chinese chronological history. The *Zuo zhuan* is a detailed commentary on this work and provides extensive narrative accounts and ample background materials. The commentary also occupies a seminal place in the history of Chinese literature because of its narrative style; it presents historical events and personages directly through action and speech, and the book's third-person narrative is notable for its orderly structure and clear and laconic presentation.

The *Zuo zhuan* was once believed to have been written by Zuo, an ancient historian about whom virtually nothing is known. It is now thought to have been compiled by an anonymous author during the early part of the Warring States period (475–221 BC).

Zweig \'tsvīk\, Arnold (b. Nov. 10, 1887, Glogau, Silesia, Ger. [now Głogów, Poland]—d. Nov. 26, 1968, East Berlin, E. Ger.) German-Jewish writer best known for his novel *Der Streit um den Sergeanten Grischa* (1927; *The Case of Sergeant Grischa*). The novel depicts the social organism of the German army during World War I through the story of the Russian prisoner Grischa's tragic encounter with the vast machine of Prussian military bureaucracy.

Deprived of German nationality by the Nazis, Zweig lived as an émigré in Palestine from 1933 to 1948 and in East Germany from 1948. His other works include *Junge Frau von 1914* (1931; *Young Woman of 1914*), *De Vriendt kehrt Heim* (1932; *De Vriendt Goes Home*), *Erziehung vor Verdun* (1935; *Education Before Verdun*), and *Einsetzung eines Königs* (1937; *The Crowning of a King*), each of which pursues the fortunes of characters introduced in *Sergeant Grischa*.

Zweig \'tsvīk\, Stefan (b. Nov. 28, 1881, Vienna, Austro-Hungarian Empire [now in Austria]—d. Feb. 22, 1942, Petrópolis, Braz.)   German writer who achieved distinction in several genres—poetry, essays, short stories, and dramas—most notably in his interpretations of imaginary and historical characters.

Zweig studied in Austria, France, and Germany before settling in Salzburg in 1913. In 1934 he was driven into exile by the Nazis and immigrated to England and in 1940 to Brazil. Finding only growing loneliness and disillusionment in their new surroundings, he and his second wife committed suicide.

Zweig's interest in psychology and the teachings of Sigmund Freud is reflected in his subtle portrayal of character. Zweig's essays include studies of Honoré de Balzac, Charles Dickens, and Fyodor Dostoyevsky (*Drei Meister*, 1920; *Three Masters*) and of Friedrich Hölderlin, Heinrich von Kleist, and Friedrich Nietzsche (*Der Kampf mit dem Dämon*, 1925; *Master Builders*). He achieved popularity with *Sternstunden der Menschheit* (1928; *The Tide of Fortune*), five historical portraits in miniature. He wrote full-scale, intuitive rather than objective biographies of the French statesman Joseph Fouché (1929), Mary Stuart (1935), and others. His stories include those in *Verwirrung der Gefühle* (1925; *Conflicts*). He also wrote a psychological novel, *Ungeduld des Herzens* (1938; *Beware of Pity*), and translated works of Charles Baudelaire, Paul Verlaine, and Émile Verhaeren. *The Royal Game and Other Stories* (1981) is a translation of a collection of his short stories.